WORKERS' COMPENSATION LAWS OF CALIFORNIA QUICK GUIDE

AFFIRMATIVE DEFENSES: LC 3600
APP-BASED WORKERS: B&P 7448-7467
APPEAL: LC 5902, 5910, CCR 10840 (*10940)
APPORTIONMENT: LC 4663, 4664
ARBITRATION: LC 5270-5277, CCR 10995-10999 (*10900, 10995, [illegible])
ATTORNEY'S FEES: LC 4903, 5814.5, CCR 10774-10779 (*10844, 10840, 10842, [illegible])
AVERAGE WEEKLY WAGE: LC 4453, 4659
BURDEN OF PROOF: LC 3202, 3202.5
C & R AGREEMENTS: LC 5000, 5001, CCR 10870-10888 (*10700, 10702, 10705)
CALIFORNIA CONSTITUTION: ART. XIV, SECTION 4
CARVE-OUTS: LC 3201.5, 3201.7
CIGA, "COVERED CLAIMS": INS CODE 1063-1063.145, 1063.1(c)(9)
COLA INCREASES TO LIFE PENSION & 100% AWARDS: LC 4659
CONTRIBUTION: LC 5500.5
COVID-19 PANDEMIC: LC 77.8, 3212.86, 3212.87, 3212.88, 6409.6, 6325, 6432
CT INJURIES: LC 5412, 5500.5
DEATH BENEFITS: LC 3501-3503, 4700-4725, 4856, CCR 9900-9918
DEPOSITIONS: LC 5710, CCR 35.5(f) (QME)
DISCOVERY CUT-OFF: LC 5502(e)(3)
DISCRIMINATION: LC 132a, CCR 10447 (*10528)
DOR: LC 5502, CCR 10414, 10416 (*10742, 10744)
EMPLOYEE & EMPLOYER, DEFINED: LC 3351-53, 3357, 2750.5; LC 3300-01; LC 2775-2787
EN BANC DECISIONS BINDING: CCR 10341 (*10325)
EXCLUSIVE REMEDY DOCTRINE: LC 3601
FEE SCHEDULES: LC 4600, 5307.7, 5307.9, 5811
HEARINGS: CCR 10541-10593 (*10360, 10390, 10396, 10398, 10421, 10550, 10672, 10748, 10750-52, 10755, 10757-58, 10761, 10782, 10785, 10787-88, 10790, 10833, 10888)
IBR: LC 4603.2, 4603.3, 4603.4, 4603.6, CCR 9792.5.1-9792.5.15, 9793-9795
IMR (UR): LC 4062, 4610.5, CCR 9792.6-9792.15
IMR (MPN): LC 4616.3, 4616.4, CCR 9767.7, 9768.1-9768.17
INSURANCE COVERAGE: LC 3700, 3602(d); INS CODE 11650-11653, 11663
JUDICIAL ETHICS: CCR 9720.1-9723
LIEN CLAIMS: LC 4603.3-.4, .6, 4615, 4903-4903.08, 4620-21, 139.21, CCR 10770-72, 10888 (*10862-63, 10865, 10872, 10875, 10877, 10880, 10888, 10890, 10892, 10899)
MEDICAL EVALUATIONS: LC4061.5, 4062.1 (UNREP), 4062.2 (REPPED); CCR 9785
MEDICAL TREATMENT: LC 4600, 4601, 4603.5, 4616, CCR 9785
MEDICAL TREATMENT UTILIZATION SCHEDULE: LC 4604.5, CCR 9792.20-9792.26
MPN: LC 4616, CCR 9767.1-9767.19
OMFS: LC 5307.1, 5307.12, CCR 9789.10-9789.111, 9790
PD: LC 4650, 4660, 4660.1, 4658 (15% bump up or down)
PENALTIES: LC 5814, 5814.5
PETITIONS, GENERALLY: CCR 10450 (*10510)
PRESUMPTION OF COMPENSABILITY: LC 5402
PRESUMPTION, EMPLOYMENT: LC 3357
PRESUMPTION, INJURIES; CERTAIN OCCUPATIONS: LC 3212-3213.2; See COVID-19, above.
PRESUMPTION, TOTAL PD: LC 4662
PSYCHIATRIC INJURIES: LC 3208.3, CCR 43, 9726; but see LC 4660.1
PTP, RIGHT TO SELECT: LC 4603.5, CCR 9780, 9780.1
QME, QME PANEL, QME DEPO: CCR 1-159; LC 4060-4062.2, CCR 30-36, CCR 35.5(f)
RECONSIDERATION, PETITIONS FOR: LC 5903, CCR 10840, 10842 (*10940, 10945)
REMOVAL, PETITIONS FOR: LC 5310, CCR 10840-10843, 10845-10850, 10860 (*10940, 10945, 10955, 10962)
REOPEN, PETITIONS TO: LC 5803-5805, CCR 10455, 10458 (*10534, 10536)
RETURN TO WORK FUND: LC 139.48, CCR 17300-17310
SAFETY OFFICERS: LC 4850
SERIOUS AND WILFUL: LC 4551-4553, 5407, 6400-6423, CCR 10440, 10445 (*10525)
SERVICE OF PROCESS: CCR 10500 (*10628, 10629)
SUPPLEMENTAL JOB DISPLACEMENT BENEFITS: LC 4658.5-4658.7
STATUTE OF LIMITATIONS: LC 5401-5410 (GENERALLY), LC 5406 (DEATH BENEFITS)
SUBROGATION: LC 3852-3864
SUBSEQUENT INJURIES: LC 4751
TD: LC 4653, 4655, 4656
TPD: LC 4654, 4657
UNINSURED EMPLOYERS: LC 3710-3716
UTILIZATION REVIEW: LC 4610, 4610.5-4610.6, CCR 9792.6-9792.15
VENUE: LC 5501.5
WRIT OF REVIEW, PETITIONS FOR: LC 5950

PUBLICATION UPDATE

Route to: ☐ ____ ☐ ____ ☐ ____ ☐ ____
☐ ____ ☐ ____ ☐ ____ ☐ ____

Workers' Compensation Laws of California

Publication 840 2021 Edition December 2020

HIGHLIGHTS

2020 State Legislation and Proposition 22

- 90 statutory changes

Administrative Regulations

- 358 changes made through Register 2020, No. 42

Sign Up for Free eNewsletter Calif. Workers' Comp

- Go to www.lexisnexis.com/wcnews
- Articles, noteworthy decisions & much more

CALIFORNIA LEGISLATION AND PROPOSITION 22. The following are selected highlights of recent workers' compensation statutory changes. For a complete list of workers' compensation-related statutes that were amended, adopted, or repealed, see the table at the beginning of this 2021 Edition of *Workers' Compensation Laws of California*.

Presumption of Industrial Causation; COVID-19. In urgency legislation effective September 17, 2020, the legislature has added Labor Code §§ 3212.86, 3212.87, and 3212.88, defining "injury" to include illness or death resulting from COVID-19 under specified circumstances, until January 1, 2023, and creating a rebuttable presumption that a COVID-19-related injury is industrial and compensable for specified dates of injury. The new provisions require employees to exhaust their paid sick leave benefits and meet specified certification requirements before receiving any temporary disability benefits or, for police officers, firefighters, and other specified employees, to exhaust their leave of absence benefits. Additionally, the new provisions make claims related to COVID-19 illnesses presumptively compensable beginning 30 days or 45 days, rather than 90 days, after a claim is filed if the claim is not rejected. Until January 1, 2023, the new presumption of industrial injury related to COVID-19 applies to all employees whose co-employees experience specified levels of positive testing, and whose employer has five or more employees.

Employer Notice Requirements; COVID-19. The legislature has added Labor Code § 6409.6 to provide that employers who receive notice of potential exposure to COVID-19 must notify employees who were on the premises within the infectious period that they may have been exposed, and provide information regarding COVD-19-related benefits to which the employees may be entitled, including workers' compensation benefits.

Study of COVID-19 Impacts on Workers' Compensation. In urgency legislation effective September 17, 2020, the legislature has added Labor Code § 77.8, to order the Commission on Health and Safety and Workers' Compensation to conduct a study of COVID-19's impact on workers' compensation claims and the workers' compensation system, including overall impacts on indemnity benefits, medical benefits, and death benefits, with consideration of differences in the impacts across differing occupational groups, and including the effect of the new Labor Code §§ 3212.87 and 3212.88.

Employment Relationships; Employees vs. Independent Contractors. In urgency legislation effective September 4, 2020, the legislature has repealed Labor Code § 2750.3, the statute codifying the

California Supreme Court's holding in *Dynamex Operations West, Inc. v. Superior Court*, enacted in 2019, and revised and recast the statute's provisions in Labor Code §§ 2775–2786 in a new Article 1.5, Chapter 2, Division 3, of the Labor Code. Under Labor Code § 2775, a person providing labor or services for remuneration on or after January 1, 2020, is considered an employee rather than an independent contractor unless the hiring entity demonstrates that all of certain specified conditions are satisfied. The statutory framework provides extensive exceptions to the general rule, and exempts specified occupations and professions, including newspaper distributors and carriers, as set forth in Labor Code §§ 2776–2784.

App-based Workers. Proposition 22, which passed on election day, adds a new Chapter 10.5 to the Business and Professions Code (Sections 7448–7467) to shield digital app-based transportation services, such as Uber and Lyft, and other similar app-based services from being forced to classify their workers as employees under these recent Labor Code changes (see paragraph above).

Employment Relationships; Newspaper Carriers. The legislature amended Labor Code § 2783 to expand the exemption from *Dynamex* applicable to newspaper carriers by deleting the condition that a newspaper carrier work under contract either with a newspaper publisher or newspaper distributor. The exemption period is extended to January 1, 2022.

California Insurance Guarantee Association; Covered Claims. The legislature has amended Insurance Code § 1063.1 to expand "covered claims" to include: (1) benefits under the workers' compensation law of state's other than California if the injured worker is a California resident and not otherwise entitled to coverage from another organization similar to CIGA; (2) obligations for medical services provided by a medical facility owned by a state or federal agency; and (3) claims arising under a policy that has been statutorily allocated or assumed by a company that later becomes insolvent, if the claim would have been covered had the original company been liquidated.

Insurance Coverage; Policy Renewal. The legislature has amended Insurance Code § 678 to require an offer of renewal stating a reduction of limits or elimination of coverage to identify the specific limits being reduced or the coverage being eliminated by the offer of renewal.

CALIFORNIA REGULATIONS. The 2021 Edition of *Workers' Compensation Laws of California* contains rule amendments, additions, repeals, etc., through Register 2020, No. 42 (10/16/2020). For information regarding specific changes to a regulation, the reader is referred to the "History" notes following the text of each regulation. For a complete list of changes, see the table at the beginning of this book. The following are selected highlights of recent regulatory changes.

WCAB Rules of Practice and Procedure. This edition incorporates the WCAB rule changes effective January 1, 2020. For a complete list of WCAB rule changes, see the Table of Amendments at the beginning of this publication. Some notable changes include:

Cal. Code Regs., tit. 8, § 10301 (definitions)

Cal. Code Regs., tit. 8, § 10302 (rule-making notices)

Cal. Code Regs., tit. 8, § 10305 (definitions)

Cal. Code Regs., tit. 8, § 10320 (WCAB decisions/orders)

Cal. Code Regs., tit. 8, § 10322 (inspection of WCAB records)

Cal. Code Regs., tit. 8, § 10325 (WCAB en bancs)

Cal. Code Regs., tit. 8, § 10330 (authority of WCJ)

Cal. Code Regs., tit. 8, § 10338 (authority of WCAB commissioners)

Cal. Code Regs., tit. 8, § 10340 (WCAB decisions/orders)

Cal. Code Regs., tit. 8, § 10341 (WCAB en bancs)

Cal. Code Regs., tit. 8, § 10342 (authority of WCAB commissioners)

Cal. Code Regs., tit. 8, § 10346 (authority of PWCJ to transfer/assign cases)

Cal. Code Regs., tit. 8, § 10348 (authority of WCJ)

Cal. Code Regs., tit. 8, § 10440 (contempt)

Cal. Code Regs., tit. 8, §§ 10350–10352 (appointment/authority of pro tem WCJs)

Cal. Code Regs., tit. 8, § 10353 (mandatory settlement conferences)

Cal. Code Regs., tit. 8, § 10355 (appointment/authority of pro tem WCJs)

Cal. Code Regs., tit. 8, § 10360 (testimony of judicial/quasi-judicial officers)

Cal. Code Regs., tit. 8, § 10382 (joinder of parties)

Cal. Code Regs., tit. 8, § 10400 (applications for adjudication)

Cal. Code Regs., tit. 8, § 10401 (applications for adjudication)

Cal. Code Regs., tit. 8, § 10402 (applications for adjudication) (substitution/dismissal of attorneys)

Cal. Code Regs., tit. 8, § 10404 (change of venue)

Cal. Code Regs., tit. 8, § 10409 (venue)

Cal. Code Regs., tit. 8, § 10421 (sanctions)

Cal. Code Regs., tit. 8, § 10440 (S&W misconduct)

Cal. Code Regs., tit. 8, § 10445 (S&W misconduct) (disbarred attorneys)

Cal. Code Regs., tit. 8, § 10447 (LC 132a)

Cal. Code Regs., tit. 8, § 10450 (petitions/answers)

Cal. Code Regs., tit. 8, § 10451.1 (med-legal expenses)

Cal. Code Regs., tit. 8, § 10452 (disqualification of WCJ)

Cal. Code Regs., tit. 8, § 10453 (reassignment of WCJ)

Cal. Code Regs., tit. 8, § 10455 (applications for adjudication) (petitions to reopen)

Cal. Code Regs., tit. 8, § 10458 (new and further disability)

Cal. Code Regs., tit. 8, § 10462 (petition to terminate liability) (SIBTF applications)

Cal. Code Regs., tit. 8, § 10464 (petition to terminate liability)

Cal. Code Regs., tit. 8, § 10465 (Answers)

Cal. Code Regs., tit. 8, § 10466 (petition to terminate liability)

Cal. Code Regs., tit. 8, § 10480 (venue) (answers)

Cal. Code Regs., tit. 8, § 10484 (answers-procedural requirements)

Cal. Code Regs., tit. 8, § 10490 (change of venue)

Cal. Code Regs., tit. 8, § 10497 (stipulations)

Cal. Code Regs., tit. 8, § 10507 (time to act)

Cal. Code Regs., tit. 8, § 10510 (petitions/answers) (service)

Cal. Code Regs., tit. 8, § 10525 (S&W misconduct)

Cal. Code Regs., tit. 8, § 10528 (LC 132a)

Cal. Code Regs., tit. 8, § 10530 (subpoenas)

Cal. Code Regs., tit. 8, § 10534 (petitions to reopen)

Cal. Code Regs., tit. 8, § 10540 (petition to terminate liability)

Cal. Code Regs., tit. 8, § 10560 (trials)

Cal. Code Regs., tit. 8, § 10561 (sanctions)

Cal. Code Regs., tit. 8, § 10562 (failure to appear)

Cal. Code Regs., tit. 8, § 10564 (interpreters)

Cal. Code Regs., tit. 8, § 10565 (petitions appealing denial of return to work supplement)

Cal. Code Regs., tit. 8, § 10580 (evidence taken without notice)

Cal. Code Regs., tit. 8, § 10590 (penalty assessment appeal)

Cal. Code Regs., tit. 8, § 10602 (formal PD ratings)

Cal. Code Regs., tit. 8, § 10605 (time to act)

Cal. Code Regs., tit. 8, § 10606 (physician's reports)

Cal. Code Regs., tit. 8, § 10607 (service of benefit printouts)

Cal. Code Regs., tit. 8, § 10608 (service of documents)

Cal. Code Regs., tit. 8, § 10615 (service of documents)

Cal. Code Regs., tit. 8, §§ 10610–10637 (filing and service of docs)

Cal. Code Regs., tit. 8, § 10622 (failure to comply)

Cal. Code Regs., tit. 8, § 10625 (service)

Cal. Code Regs., tit. 8, § 10629 (filing of exhibits)

Cal. Code Regs., tit. 8, § 10632 (service of SIBTF applications)

Cal. Code Regs., tit. 8, § 10635 (service of documents)

Cal. Code Regs., tit. 8, § 10637 (service of documents)

Cal. Code Regs., tit. 8, §§ 10640–10660 (subpoenas)

Cal. Code Regs., tit. 8, § 10670 (documentary evidence)

Cal. Code Regs., tit. 8, § 10672 (evidence taken without notice)

Cal. Code Regs., tit. 8, § 10675 (formal PD ratings)

Cal. Code Regs., tit. 8, §§ 10700–10705 (approval of C&R)

Cal. Code Regs., tit. 8, § 10759 (MSCs)

Cal. Code Regs., tit. 8, § 10682 (physician's reports)

Cal. Code Regs., tit. 8, § 10750 (record of proceedings)

Cal. Code Regs., tit. 8, § 10755 (failure to appear)

Cal. Code Regs., tit. 8, § 10759 (mandatory settlement conferences)

Cal. Code Regs., tit. 8, § 10774 (substitution/dismissal of attorneys)

Cal. Code Regs., tit. 8, §§ 10775–10778 (attorney's fees)

Cal. Code Regs., tit. 8, § 10779 (disbarred attorneys)

Cal. Code Regs., tit. 8, § 10786 (med-legal expenses)

Cal. Code Regs., tit. 8, § 10787 (trials)

Cal. Code Regs., tit. 8, § 10788 (reassignment of WCJ)

Cal. Code Regs., tit. 8, § 10790 (interpreters)

Cal. Code Regs., tit. 8, § 10803 (record of proceedings)

Cal. Code Regs., tit. 8, § 10835 (stipulations)

Cal. Code Regs., tit. 8, §§ 10840–10844 (attorney's fees)

Cal. Code Regs., tit. 8, § 10856 (newly discovered evidence)

Cal. Code Regs., tit. 8, § 10870 (approval of C&R)

Cal. Code Regs., tit. 8, §§ 10940–10946 (SIBTF applications)

Cal. Code Regs., tit. 8, § 10953 (penalty assessment appeal)

Cal. Code Regs., tit. 8, § 10960 (disqualification of WCJ)

Cal. Code Regs., tit. 8, § 10974 (newly discovered evidence)

Medical Treatment Utilization Schedule. The DWC Administrative Director ordered evidence-based updates to the MTUS contained in Cal. Code Regs., tit. 8, §§ 9792.23.6, 9792.23.8, 9792.23.11 and 9792.23.12, to be effective on September 21, 2020. Those MTUS updates addressed treatment guidelines for interstitial lung disease, knee disorders, depressive disorders, and occupational asthma.

Telehealth. Emergency regulations adopted effective May 14, 2020 set forth a protocol for telehealth QME evaluations. See Cal. Code Regs., tit. 8, §§ 36.7 and 46.2.

TABLES AND SCHEDULES. The following tables were revised: Table 14 and Table 17.

TRACK NATIONAL WORKERS' COMP TRENDS. LexisNexis announces a new resource for workers' compensation professionals to track national and state trends. *Workers' Compensation Emerging Issues Analysis*, 2020 Edition, contains a state survey of workers' compensation trends with commentary, a survey of interesting workers' compensation cases nationwide, and analysis of key topics. To order Publication #1874, contact Customer Service at 1-800-223-1940 or order online at the LexisNexis Store: www.lexisnexis.com/store.

FREE LEXISNEXIS eNEWSLETTER CALIFORNIA WORKERS' COMPENSATION. Receive weekly news and articles as well as special alerts when an en banc or significant panel decision issues. Find solutions and strategies to help your law firm practice or business. Find out why workers' compensation professionals and judges rely on our free eNewsletter service. Sign up at www.lexisnexis.com/wcnews today.

www.lexis.com

Publication 840, 2021 Edition, December 2020

THE
WORKERS' COMPENSATION LAWS
OF CALIFORNIA

Compiled from
THE LABOR CODE, INSURANCE CODE,
UNEMPLOYMENT INSURANCE CODE, AND
OTHER SOURCES

2021 Edition

QUESTIONS ABOUT THIS PUBLICATION?

For questions about the **Editorial Content** appearing in these volumes or reprint permission, please call:

Robin Kobayashi at .... (415) 908-3352
Email: .... robin.e.kobayashi@lexisnexis.com
Katie Komer at .... (925) 284-0168
Email: .... katie.komer@lexisnexis.com
or e-mail at .... CalCodes@lexisnexis.com

For assistance with replacement pages, shipments, billing or other customer service matters, please call:

Customer Services Department at .... (800) 833-9844

Outside the United States and Canada, please call .... (518) 487-3000

Fax number .... (518) 487-3584

Customer Service Website .... http://www.lexisnexis.com/custserv/

For information on other Matthew Bender publications, please call:

Your account manager .... (800) 223-1940

Outside the United States and Canada, please call .... (518) 487-3000

ISBN 978-1-66330-597-8

Editorial Offices
230 Park Ave., 7th Floor, New York, NY 10169 (800) 543-6862
555 Middle Creek Parkway, Colorado Springs, CO 80921 (800) 833-9844
www.lexisnexis.com
Printed in Canada

Publisher's Editorial Staff

Jill M. Melchoir, J.D.
Director, Content Development

Shelly McCaleb
Director, Content Operations

Michael Dougherty
Kathleen Hoover
Katie Komer
Content Editors

Mark Dempsey, J.D.
Index Analyst

Cheryl Kirby
Index Editor

BOARD OF EDITORIAL CONSULTANTS

PREFACE

California Statutes

This publication contains selected provisions relating to workers' compensation law from the Insurance, Labor, and Unemployment Insurance Codes. Following these provisions are miscellaneous related statutes from the California Constitution and the following Codes: Business & Professions, Civil, Code of Civil Procedure, Education, Evidence, Government, Harbors & Navigation, Health & Safety, Military & Veterans, Penal, Vehicle, and Welfare & Institutions. Legislative histories ("Leg.H.") beginning with 1991 are given for each statute.

This 2021 Edition of the Workers' Compensation Laws of California incorporates all changes required by legislative enactments up to and including ch. 372 of the second year of the 2019–2020 Regular Session and all propositions approved by the electorate at the November 3, 2020, General Election. Amendments made in 2020 are highlighted by printing in boldface type all matter added to a section and indicating by a figure within brackets, such as [1], each point of deletion. The deleted matter is then shown by bracketed footnotes keyed to the corresponding figures. Where changes are extensive, the former section may be reprinted in full. Some sections contain bracketed notes indicating material is not reproduced; this indicates that portions of the section having no workers' compensation applications have not been reproduced.

The following reproduction of Section 4600.4 of the Labor Code clearly illustrates the "stressed amendment" feature:

> **§4600.4. Availability during normal business day.**
> (a) A workers' compensation insurer, third-party administrator, or other entity that requires, or pursuant to regulation requires, a treating physician to obtain either utilization review or prior authorization in order to diagnose or treat injuries or diseases compensable under this article, shall ensure the availability of those services from 9 a.m. to 5:30 p.m. Pacific [1] **standard** time of each normal business day.
> (b) For purposes of this [2] **article,** "normal business day" [3] **does not include Saturday, Sunday, or any day that is declared by the Governor to be an official state holiday or a holiday listed on the Department of Human Resources internet website**. **Leg.H.** 1999 ch. 124, 2019 ch. 647 (SB 537) §4.
> **§4600.4. 2019 Deletes. [1]** coast **[2]** section **[3]** means a business day as defined in Section 9 of the Civil Code

To read Section 4600.4 as amended, you read the section as printed, omitting the bracketed figures "[1]" through "[3]":

> (a) A workers' compensation insurer, third-party administrator, or other entity that requires, or pursuant to regulation requires, a treating physician to obtain either utilization review or prior authorization in order to diagnose or treat injuries or diseases compensable under this article, shall ensure the availability of those services from 9 a.m. to 5:30 p.m. Pacific **standard** time of each normal business day.
> (b) For purposes of this **article,** "normal business day" **does not include Saturday, Sunday, or any day that is declared by the Governor to be an official state holiday or a holiday listed on the Department of Human Resources internet website**.

To reconstruct the section as it read before being amended, you read the section as printed, omitting the words in boldface type and inserting the words appearing in the footnote under Section 4600.4 and referred to by the bracketed figures [1] through [3] in the section:

(a) A workers' compensation insurer, third-party administrator, or other entity that requires, or pursuant to regulation requires, a treating physician to obtain either utilization review or prior authorization in order to diagnose or treat injuries or diseases compensable under this article, shall ensure the availability of those services from 9 a.m. to 5:30 p.m. Pacific coast time of each normal business day.

(b) For purposes of this section "normal business day" means a business day as defined in Section 9 of the Civil Code.

California Code of Regulations

This publication contains selected Title 2, Title 8, Title 10, and Title 16 regulations relating to workers' compensation. This 2021 Edition of the Workers' Compensation Laws of California incorporates all changes made to the regulations through Register 2020, Number 42 (October 16, 2020).

United States Code

This publication contains selected provisions relating to workers' compensation law from Titles 5, 26, 28, 33, 40, 42, 43, 45, and 46 of the United States Code. These code provisions are current through Public Law 116-182 (October 21, 2020).

Cross-References

Where applicable, statutes and regulations in this publication are followed by cross-reference lines ("Ref.") containing citations to related sections of the following:

"C.C.R." — California Code of Regulations;

"Hanna" — *California Law of Employee Injuries and Workers' Compensation*, a three-volume treatise (Matthew Bender);

"Herlick Handbook" — *California Workers' Compensation Handbook* (Matthew Bender);

"Lawyer's Guide to AMA *Guides* and Calif. Workers' Comp." — *The Lawyer's Guide to the AMA* Guides *and California Workers' Compensation* (Matthew Bender);

To order the Matthew Bender products listed above, please contact our Customer Service Department at 1-800-833-9844.

In presenting this Edition of the Workers' Compensation Laws of California, we wish to acknowledge with gratitude the many helpful suggestions received from users, and to express the hope that this Edition will serve effectively the needs of the workers' compensation community.

THE PUBLISHER

TABLE OF CONTENTS

REFERENCE DIRECTORY . . . xi

TABLE OF 2020 LEGISLATIVE ACTION . . . xv

TABLE OF 2019–2020 REGULATORY ACTION . . . xvii

CALIFORNIA STATUTES AND CONSTITUTION

- Insurance Code Synopsis . . . 1
- Provisions of the Insurance Code . . . 7
- Labor Code Synopsis . . . 73
- Provisions of the Labor Code . . . 95
- Unemployment Insurance Code Synopsis . . . 445
- Provisions of the Unemployment Insurance Code . . . 447
- Miscellaneous Provisions
  - Synopsis . . . 465
  - California Constitution . . . 479
  - Business and Professions Code . . . 481
  - Civil Code . . . 493
  - Code of Civil Procedure . . . 509
  - Education Code . . . 543
  - Evidence Code . . . 551
  - Government Code . . . 569
  - Harbors and Navigation Code . . . 603
  - Health and Safety Code . . . 605
  - Military and Veterans Code . . . 607
  - Penal Code . . . 611
  - Vehicle Code . . . 623
  - Welfare and Institutions Code . . . 625

CALIFORNIA CODE OF REGULATIONS

- Synopsis . . . 629
- Provisions of Title 2 pertaining to workers' compensation . . . 647
- Provisions of Title 8 pertaining to workers' compensation . . . 649
- Provisions of Title 10 pertaining to workers' compensation . . . 1317
- Provisions of Title 16 pertaining to workers' compensation . . . 1329

TABLES AND SCHEDULES . . . 1337

UNITED STATES CODE

- Synopsis . . . 1505

Provisions of miscellaneous titles pertaining to workers' compensation . . . 1509

INDEX . . . I-1

REFERENCE DIRECTORY

FOR ASSISTANCE ON HOW TO READ AND USE THIS EDITION:

See the Preface on pages vii-viii

Contact Robin Kobayashi, J.D., Practice Area Editor at Matthew Bender, 415-908-3352, robin.e.kobayashi@lexisnexis.com with questions about:

- Location of statutes and regulations covered in this and prior editions
- Coverage of recent workers' comp legislation
- Index entries

Contact Katie Komer, Content Editor at Matthew Bender, 925-284-0168, katie.komer@lexisnexis.com with questions about:

- Tables and schedules
- Permission to reprint parts of this edition

FOR FREE eNEWSLETTER ON CALIFORNIA WORKERS' COMPENSATION:

Sign up at http://www.lexisnexis.com/wcnews

FOR QUESTIONS REGARDING WORKERS' COMPENSATION RULES AND PROCEDURES, CONTACT:

Workers' Compensation Appeals Board Information and Assistance (I&A) at the field office near you:

Toll Free:	(800) 736-7401
Anaheim:	(714) 414-1801
Bakersfield:	(661) 395-2514
Eureka:	(707) 441-5723
Fresno:	(559) 445-5355
Long Beach:	(562) 590-5240
Los Angeles:	(213) 576-7389
Marina del Rey:	(310) 482-3820
Oakland:	(510) 622-2861
Oxnard:	(805) 485-3528
Pomona:	(909) 623-8568
Redding:	(530) 225-2047
Riverside:	(951) 782-4347
Sacramento:	(916) 928-3158
Salinas:	(831) 443-3058
San Bernardino:	(909) 383-4522
San Diego:	(619) 767-2082
San Francisco:	(415) 703-5020
San Jose:	(408) 277-1292
San Luis Obispo:	(805) 596-4159
Santa Ana:	(714) 942-7576
Santa Barbara:	(805) 568-1295
Santa Rosa:	(707) 576-2452
Stockton:	(209) 948-7980
Van Nuys:	(818) 901-5367

OTHER RESOURCES:

LexisNexis: Print, eBooks and Electronic Products toll-free ordering (800-223-1940) *www.lexisnexis.com/store*

- *California Compensation Cases* (monthly advance sheets and yearly hardbound volumes covering workers' comp cases)
- *California WCAB Noteworthy Panel Decisions Reporter*
- *LexisNexis Automated California Workers' Compensation Forms* (forms software)
- Hanna, *California Law of Employee Injuries and Workers' Compensation* (3-volume treatise)
- Rassp & Herlick, *California Workers' Compensation Law* (2-volume treatise)
- Herlick, *California Workers' Compensation Handbook*
- *The Lawyer's Guide to the AMA Guides and California Workers' Compensation*
- *Workers' Compensation Index: A Topical Guide to California Workers' Compensation Law*
- *The Complete Guide to Medicare Secondary Payer Compliance* (2-volume treatise)
- *Occupational Injuries and Illnesses* (3-volume treatise)
- *Judicial Council of California Civil Jury Instructions (Matthew Bender, Official Publisher)*
- *Larson's Workers' Compensation Law* (17-volume treatise)
- *Larson's Workers' Compensation, Desk Edition* (3-volume treatise)
- *Workers' Compensation Emerging Issues Analysis* (50 state legislative survey, interesting cases, expert analysis)
- *Matthew Bender® Practice Guide: California Civil Discovery*
- *Matthew Bender® Practice Guide: California E-Discovery and Evidence*
- *Matthew Bender® Practice Guide: California Pretrial Civil Procedure*
- *Matthew Bender® Practice Guide: California Trial and Post-Trial Civil Procedure*
- NOSSCR, *Social Security Practice Guide* (5-volume treatise)
- *Attorneys' Textbook of Medicine* (23-volume treatise)
- *Attorneys' Dictionary of Medicine*
- *Proving Medical Diagnosis and Prognosis* (14-volume treatise)
- *Common Diagnostic Procedures* (1-volume treatise)
- *Health Care Reform: Law and Practice* (2-volume treatise)

Other Publications

- *The Ultimate Guide to Mastering Workers Compensation Cost Containment* (Amaxx Risk Solutions, Inc. *www.WCManual.com*)
- *California Workers' Comp: How to Take Charge When You're Injured on the Job* (Nolo Press, *www.nolo.com*)
- *Official Medical Fee Schedule (OMFS),* (see 8 CCR §9791.1 for information on ordering a copy of the fee schedule or obtain an order form at *http://www.dir.ca.gov/dwc/OMFS9904.htm*)

Websites Education, and Informational Resources

- Dept. of Industrial Relations: *http://www.dir.ca.gov*
- State Compensation Insurance Fund: *http://www.statefundca.com*
- California Applicants' Attorneys Association: *http://www.caaa.org*
- California Manufacturers & Technology Association: *http://www.cmta.net*
- California Self-Insurers Association: *http://www.caself-insurers.com*
- California Society of Industrial Medicine and Surgery: *http://www.csims.org*
- California Workers' Compensation Institute: *http://www.cwci.org*
- California Coalition on Workers' Compensation: *http://www.ccwcworkcomp.org*
- Workers Compensation Resource Center: *www.ReduceYourWorkersComp.com*

- Insurance Educational Association: *http://www.ieatraining.com*
- Combined Claims Conference: *http://www.combinedclaims.com*
- San Francisco Industrial Claims Association: *http://sfica.tripod.com*
- Mid Valley Claims Association: *http://www.midvalleyclaims.org*
- Sacramento Claims Association: *http://www.sacramentoclaims.org*
- Professionals in Workers' Comp: *http://www.piwcfresno.com*

2020 LEGISLATIVE ACTION

Effective January 1, 2021, unless otherwise noted at end of section.

BUSINESS AND PROFESSIONS CODE

Section	Effect	Chap.
Ch. 10.5 (comm. w/§7448)	Added	Prop. 22*
Art. 1 (comm. w/§7448)	Added	Prop. 22*
7448–7450	Added	Prop. 22*
Art. 2 (comm. w/§7451)	Added	Prop. 22*
7451–7452.5	Added	Prop. 22*
Art. 3 (comm. w/§7453)	Added	Prop. 22*
7453	Added	Prop. 22*
Art. 4 (comm. w/§7454)	Added	Prop. 22*
7454	Added	Prop. 22*
7455	Added	Prop. 22*
Art. 5 (comm. w/§7456)	Added	Prop. 22*
7456–7462	Added	Prop. 22*
Art. 6 (comm. w/§7463)	Added	Prop. 22*
7463	Added	Prop. 22*
Art. 7 (comm. w/§7464)	Added	Prop. 22*
7464	Added	Prop. 22*
Art. 8 (comm. w/§7464.5)	Added	Prop. 22*
7464.5	Added	Prop. 22*
Art. 9 (comm. w/§7465)	Added	Prop. 22*
7465	Added	Prop. 22*
Art. 10 (comm. w/§7466)	Added	Prop. 22*
7466	Added	Prop. 22*
Art. 11 (comm. w/§7467)	Added	Prop. 22*
7467	Added	Prop. 22*

CODE OF CIVIL PROCEDURE

Section	Effect	Chap.
2025.310	Amended	112

EVIDENCE CODE

Section	Effect	Chap.
1010.5	Amended	370

GOVERNMENT CODE

Section	Effect	Chap.
8610	Amended	254
12926	Amended	36, 370
12940	Amended	36

INSURANCE CODE

Section	Effect	Chap.
678	Amended	258, 263
1063.1	Amended	258
1063.5	Amended	258
1063.14	Amended	258
11873	Amended	16

LABOR CODE

Section	Effect	Chap.
77.8	Added	85
96.1	Added	14
246	Amended	11
248	Added	45
248.1	Added	45
248.5	Amended	45
2750.3	Repealed	38
	Amended	341, 370
Art. 1.5 (comm. w/§2775)	Added	38
2775–2782	Added	38
2783	Added	38
	Amended	341
2784–2787	Added	38
2802.1	Added	351
3212.86–3212.88	Added	85
6310	Amended	288
6311	Amended	288
6311.5	Added	288
6325	Amended & Added	84
6403.1	Added	301
6403.3	Added	313
6409.6	Added	84
6432	Amended & Added	84
6709	Amended	370
6725	Added	212

MILITARY AND VETERANS CODE

Section	Effect	Chap.
562	Amended	97

PENAL CODE

Section	Effect	Chap.
803	Amended	244
1524	Amended	219

UNEMPLOYMENT INSURANCE CODE

Section	Effect	Chap.
3302	Amended	348
3307	Amended	348

*Proposition 22, approved by the electorate at the November 3, 2020, General Election

2019–2020 REGULATORY ACTION

Effective on the dates shown below.

California Code of Regulations
TITLE 8

Regulation	Effect	Eff. Date
31.5	Amended	4-6-20
36.7	Added	5-14-20
	Amended	5-14-20
46.2	Added	5-14-20
	Amended	5-14-20
9713	Amended	5-7-20
9714	Amended	5-7-20
9714.5	Amended	5-7-20
9767.2	Amended	5-7-20
9767.8	Amended	5-7-20
9789.25	Amended	11-1-19
9789.39	Amended	3-1-20
9792.23.6	Amended	9-21-20
9792.23.8	Amended	9-21-20
9792.23.10	Amended	10-7-19
9792.23.11	Amended	9-21-20
9792.23.12	Amended	9-21-20
Subch. 1.7 (comm. w/§10175)	Repealed	11-6-19
10175–10181	Repealed	11-6-19
10300	Repealed / Added	1-1-20
10301	Renumbered to 10305	1-1-20
10302	Repealed / Added	1-1-20
10304	Repealed	1-1-20
10305	Amended & Renumbered from 10301	1-1-20
Art. 2 (comm. w/§10320)	Added	1-1-20
10320	Amended & Renumbered from 10340	1-1-20
10322	Repealed	1-1-20
10324	Renumbered to 10410	1-1-20
10325	Amended & Renumbered from 10341	1-1-20
10330	Amended & Renumbered from 10348	1-1-20
10338	Amended & Renumbered from 10342	1-1-20
Art. 2 (comm. w/§10340)	Repealed	1-1-20
10340	Renumbered to 10320	1-1-20
10341	Renumbered to 10325	1-1-20
10342	Renumbered to 10338	1-1-20
10344	Amended	1-1-20
10346	Amended	1-1-20
10348	Renumbered to 10330	1-1-20
10349	Repealed	1-1-20
10350	Repealed	1-1-20
10351	Repealed	1-1-20
10352	Repealed	1-1-20
10353	Repealed	1-1-20
10355	Added	1-1-20
Art. 3 (comm. w/§10360)	Repealed	1-1-20
10360	Renumbered to 10380 / Amended & Renumbered from 10593	1-1-20
10364	Repealed	1-1-20
10370	Added	1-1-20
Art. 3 (comm. w/§10380)	Added	1-1-20
10380	Repealed / Amended & Renumbered from 10360	1-1-20
10382	Added	1-1-20
Art. 4 (comm. w/§10390)	Repealed	1-1-20
10390	Repealed / Amended & Renumbered from 10550	1-1-20
10391	Repealed	1-1-20
10392	Repealed	1-1-20
10393	Repealed	1-1-20
10396	Amended & Renumbered from 10589	1-1-20
10397	Renumbered to 10617	1-1-20
10398	Amended & Renumbered from 10592	1-1-20
Art. 4 (comm. w/§10400)	Added	1-1-20
Art. 5 (comm. w/§10400)	Repealed	1-1-20
10400	Repealed & Added	1-1-20
10401	Repealed & Added	1-1-20
10402	Repealed / Amended & Renumbered from 10774	1-1-20
10403	Repealed / Added	1-1-20
10404	Renumbered to 10470 / Added	1-1-20
10405	Renumbered to 10460	1-1-20
10408	Renumbered to 10500	1-1-20
10409	Renumbered to 10480	1-1-20
10410	Renumbered to 10488 / Amended &	

Section	Action	Effective
	Renumbered from 10324	1-1-20
10411	Renumbered to 10490	1-1-20
10412	Repealed	1-1-20
10414	Renumbered to 10742	1-1-20
10416	Renumbered to 10744	1-1-20
10417	Renumbered to 10789	1-1-20
10420	Renumbered to 10745	1-1-20
10421	Amended & Renumbered from 10561	1-1-20
10430	Repealed / Amended & Renumbered from 10782	1-1-20
10440	Repealed & Added	1-1-20
10445	Repealed / Amended & Renumbered from 10779	1-1-20
10447	Renumbered to 10528	1-1-20
Art. 5 (comm. w/§10450)	Added	1-1-20
10450	Renumbered to 10510 / Added	1-1-20
10451.1	Repealed	1-1-20
10451.2	Repealed	1-1-20
10451.3	Renumbered to 10545	1-1-20
10451.4	Renumbered to 10570	1-1-20
10452	Renumbered to 10960	1-1-20
10453	Renumbered to 10788	1-1-20
10454	Repealed	1-1-20
10455	Renumbered to 10534 / Added	1-1-20
10458	Renumbered to 10534	1-1-20
10460	Amended & Renumbered from 10405	1-1-20
10462	Repealed / Added	1-1-20
10464	Repealed	1-1-20
10465	Added	1-1-20
10466	Repealed	1-1-20
10470	Renumbered to 10530 / Amended & Renumbered from 10404	1-1-20
Art. 6 (comm. w/§10480)	Added	1-1-20
10480	Repealed / Amended & Renumbered from 10409	1-1-20
10482	Added	1-1-20
10484	Repealed	1-1-20
10488	Amended & Renumbered from 10410	1-1-20
10490	Renumbered to 10515 / Amended & Renumbered from 10411	1-1-20
10492	Renumbered to 10517	1-1-20
10496	Repealed	1-1-20
10497	Repealed	1-1-20
10498	Renumbered to 10520	1-1-20
Art. 6 (comm. w/§10500)	Repealed	1-1-20
Art. 7 (comm. w/§10500)	Added	1-1-20
10500	Repealed / Amended & Renumbered from 10408	1-1-20
10501	Repealed	1-1-20
10505	Repealed	1-1-20
10506	Repealed	1-1-20
10507	Renumbered to 10605	1-1-20
10508	Renumbered to 10600	1-1-20
10510	Repealed / Amended & Renumbered from 10450	1-1-20
10515	Amended & Renumbered from 10490	1-1-20
10517	Amended & Renumbered from 10492	1-1-20
10520	Amended & Renumbered from 10498	1-1-20
10525	Added	1-1-20
10528	Amended & Renumbered from 10447	1-1-20
Art. 7 (comm. w/§10530)	Repealed	1-1-20
10530	Renumbered to 10640 / Amended & Renumbered from 10470	1-1-20
10532	Renumbered to 10642	1-1-20
10534	Renumbered to 10644 / Renumbered from 10455	1-1-20
10536	Renumbered to 10647 / Amended & Renumbered from 10458	1-1-20
10537	Renumbered to 10650	1-1-20
10538	Renumbered to 10655	1-1-20
10540	Added	1-1-20
Art. 8 (comm. w/§10541)	Repealed	1-1-20
10541	Renumbered to 10761	1-1-20
10544	Renumbered to 10750	1-1-20
10545	Amended & Renumbered from 10451.3	1-1-20
10547	Added	1-1-20
10548	Renumbered to 10748	1-1-20
10549	Renumbered to 10757	1-1-20
10550	Renumbered to 10390 / Amended & Renumbered from 10582	1-1-20
10552	Renumbered to 10782	1-1-20
10555	Renumbered to 10785 / Added	1-1-20
Art. 8 (comm. w/§10560)	Added	1-1-20
10560	Repealed / Added	1-1-20
10561	Renumbered to 10421	1-1-20
10562	Repealed	1-1-20
10563	Repealed	1-1-20
10563.1	Repealed	1-1-20
10564	Renumbered to 10790	1-1-20
10565	Added	1-1-20
10566	Repealed	1-1-20

10567	Amended & Renumbered from 10957	1-1-20
10570	Renumbered to 10833 / Amended & Renumbered from 10451.4	1-1-20
10575	Amended & Renumbered from 10957.1	1-1-20
10578	Repealed	1-1-20
10580	Renumbered to 10672 / Amended & Renumbered from 10959	1-1-20
10582	Renumbered to 10550	1-1-20
10582.5	Repealed	1-1-20
10583	Repealed	1-1-20
10589	Renumbered to 10396	1-1-20
10590	Amended & Renumbered from 10953	1-1-20
10592	Renumbered to 10398	1-1-20
10593	Renumbered to 10360	1-1-20
Art. 9 (comm. w/§10600)	Amended	1-1-20
10600	Repealed / Amended & Renumbered from 10508	1-1-20
10601	Repealed	1-1-20
10602	Renumbered to 10675	1-1-20
10603	Renumbered to 10677	1-1-20
10604	Repealed	1-1-20
10605	Renumbered to 10680 / Amended & Renumbered from 10507	1-1-20
10606	Renumbered to 10682	1-1-20
10606.5	Renumbered to 10685	1-1-20
10607	Repealed	1-1-20
10608	Repealed	1-1-20
10608.5	Repealed	1-1-20
10610	Added	1-1-20
10615	Repealed / Added	1-1-20
10616	Repealed	1-1-20
10617	Amended & Renumbered from 10397	1-1-20
10618	Renumbered to 10660	1-1-20
10620	Added	1-1-20
10622	Repealed	1-1-20
10625	Added	1-1-20
10626	Repealed	1-1-20
10628	Added	1-1-20
10629	Repealed / Added	1-1-20
10631	Renumbered to 10683	1-1-20
10632	Repealed / Added	1-1-20
10633	Repealed	1-1-20
10634	Repealed	1-1-20
10635	Added	1-1-20
10637	Added	1-1-20
Art. 10 (comm. w/§10640)	Added	1-1-20
10640	Amended & Renumbered from 10953	1-1-20
10642	Renumbered from 10532 & Note Amended	1-1-20
10644	Amended & Renumbered from 10534	1-1-20
10647	Renumbered from 10536 & Note Amended	1-1-20
10650	Amended & Renumbered from 10537	1-1-20
10655	Amended & Renumbered from 10538	1-1-20
10660	Amended & Renumbered from 10618	1-1-20
Art. 11 (comm. w/§10670)	Added	1-1-20
10670	Added	1-1-20
10672	Renumbered from 10580	1-1-20
10675	Amended & Renumbered from 10602	1-1-20
10677	Amended & Renumbered from 10603	1-1-20
10680	Amended & Renumbered from 10605	1-1-20
10682	Amended & Renumbered from 10606	1-1-20
10683	Amended & Renumbered from 10631	1-1-20
10685	Amended & Renumbered from 10606.5	1-1-20
Art. 10 (comm. w/§10700)	Repealed	1-1-20
Art. 12 (comm. w/§10700)	Added	1-1-20
10700	Added	1-1-20
10702	Amended & Renumbered from 10886	1-1-20
10705	Amended & Renumbered from 10875	1-1-20
Art. 11 (comm. w/§10740)	Repealed	1-1-20
10740	Renumbered to 10800	1-1-20
Art. 13 (comm. w/§10742)	Added	1-1-20
10742	Amended & Renumbered from 10414	1-1-20
10744	Amended & Renumbered from 10416	1-1-20
10745	Amended & Renumbered from 10420	1-1-20
10748	Amended & Renumbered from 10548	1-1-20
Art. 12 (comm. w/§10750)	Repealed	1-1-20
10750	Repealed / Amended & Renumbered from 10544	1-1-20
10751	Repealed / Added	1-1-20
10752	Added	1-1-20
10753	Repealed	1-1-20
10754	Renumbered to 10813	1-1-20
10755	Renumbered to 10811 / Added	1-1-20
10756	Added	1-1-20
10757	Amended & Renumbered from 10549	1-1-20
10758	Added	1-1-20

Section	Effect	Date
10759	Added	1-1-20
10760	Renumbered to 10818	1-1-20
10761	Amended & Renumbered from 10541	1-1-20
Art. 13 (comm. w/§10770)	Repealed	1-1-20
10770	Repealed	1-1-20
10770.1	Repealed	1-1-20
10770.5	Renumbered to 10863	1-1-20
10770.6	Renumbered to 10874	1-1-20
10770.7	Repealed	1-1-20
10772	Repealed	1-1-20
10773	Repealed	1-1-20
Art. 14 (comm. w/§10774)	Repealed	1-1-20
10774	Renumbered to 10402	1-1-20
10774.5	Repealed	1-1-20
10775	Renumbered to 10844	1-1-20
10776	Renumbered to 10840	1-1-20
10778	Renumbered to 10842	1-1-20
10779	Renumbered to 10445	1-1-20
Art. 15 (comm. w/§10780)	Repealed	1-1-20
10780	Renumbered to 10850	1-1-20
10782	Renumbered to 10430 / Amended & Renumbered from 10552	1-1-20
10785	Repealed / Amended & Renumbered from 10555	1-1-20
10786	Added	1-1-20
10787	Added	1-1-20
10788	Amended & Renumbered from 10453	1-1-20
10789	Amended & Renumbered from 10417	1-1-20
10790	Amended & Renumbered from 10564	1-1-20
Art. 14 (comm. w/§10800)	Added	1-1-20
10800	Amended & Renumbered from 10740	1-1-20
10803	Added	1-1-20
10807	Added	1-1-20
10811	Amended & Renumbered from 10755	1-1-20
10813	Amended & Renumbered from 10754	1-1-20
10818	Amended & Renumbered from 10760	1-1-20
Art. 16 (comm. w/§10820)	Repealed	1-1-20
10820	Amended	1-1-20
10825	Amended	1-1-20
10828	Repealed	1-1-20
Art. 15 (comm. w/§10832)	Added	1-1-20
10832	Added	1-1-20
10833	Amended & Renumbered from 10570	1-1-20
10835	Added	1-1-20
Art. 17 (comm. w/§10840)	Repealed	1-1-20
10840	Repealed / Amended & Renumbered from 10776	1-1-20
10842	Renumbered to 10945 / Amended & Renumbered from 10778	1-1-20
10843	Renumbered to 10955	1-1-20
10844	Repealed / Amended & Renumbered from 10775	1-1-20
10845	Repealed	1-1-20
10846	Renumbered to 10972	1-1-20
10848	Renumbered to 10964	1-1-20
10850	Repealed / Amended & Renumbered from 10780	1-1-20
10852	Repealed	1-1-20
10856	Renumbered to 10974	1-1-20
10858	Renumbered to 10966	1-1-20
10859	Renumbered to 10961	1-1-20
10860	Renumbered to 10962	1-1-20
Art. 16 (comm. w/§10862)	Added	1-1-20
10862	Renumbered to 10984 / Added	1-1-20
10863	Amended & Renumbered from 10770.5	1-1-20
10864	Renumbered to 10986	1-1-20
10865	Renumbered to 10990	1-1-20
10866	Renumbered to 10995	1-1-20
10868	Added	1-1-20
Art. 18 (comm. w/§10870)	Repealed	1-1-20
10870	Repealed	1-1-20
10872	Added	1-1-20
10873	Added	1-1-20
10874	Repealed / Amended & Renumbered from 10770.6	1-1-20
10875	Renumbered to 10705 / Added	1-1-20
10876	Added	1-1-20
10878	Repealed / Added	1-1-20
10880	Added	1-1-20
10882	Repealed	1-1-20
10886	Renumbered to 10702	1-1-20
10888	Repealed / Added	1-1-20
10899	Amended & Renumbered from 10772	1-1-20
Art. 17 (comm. w/§10900)	Added	1-1-20
10900	Added	1-1-20
10905	Added	1-1-20
10910	Added	1-1-20
10912	Amended & Renumbered from 10998	1-1-20
10914	Added	1-1-20
10920	Amended & Renumbered from 10999	1-1-20
Art. 18 (comm. w/§10940)	Added	1-1-20

Section	Action	Date
Art. 19 (comm. w/§10940)	Repealed	1-1-20
10940	Repealed / Added	1-1-20
10942	Repealed	1-1-20
10945	Amended & Renumbered from 10842	1-1-20
10946	Repealed	1-1-20
Art. 20 (comm. w/§10950)	Repealed	1-1-20
10950	Repealed	1-1-20
10953	Renumbered to 10590	1-1-20
10955	Amended & Renumbered from 10843	1-1-20
10957	Renumbered to 10567	1-1-20
10957.1	Renumbered to 10575	1-1-20
10959	Renumbered to 10580	1-1-20
Art. 21 (comm. w/§10960)	Repealed	1-1-20
10960	Amended & Renumbered from 10452	1-1-20
10961	Amended & Renumbered from 10859	1-1-20
10962	Amended & Renumbered from 10860	1-1-20
10964	Amended & Renumbered from 10848	1-1-20
10966	Renumbered from 10858 & Note Amended	1-1-20
10972	Renumbered from 10846 & Note Amended	1-1-20
10974	Amended & Renumbered from 10856	1-1-20
10984	Amended & Renumbered from 10862	1-1-20
10986	Amended & Renumbered from 10864	1-1-20
10990	Amended & Renumbered from 10865	1-1-20
Art. 22 (comm. w/§10995)	Repealed	1-1-20
10995	Repealed / Amended & Renumbered from 10866	1-1-20
10996	Repealed	1-1-20
10997	Repealed	1-1-20
10998	Renumbered to 10912	1-1-20
10999	Renumbered to 10920	1-1-20
14300.35	Certificate of Compliance & Note Amended	12-11-19
14300.41	Certificate of Compliance & Amended	12-11-19
14300.48	Certificate of Compliance & Amended	12-11-19
15203.2	Amended	7-1-20
15203.11	Adopted	7-1-20
15251	Amended	7-1-20
15430	Amended	7-1-20
17304	Amended	5-7-20
17309	Amended	5-7-20

WCAB RULES CONCORDANCE
Reprinted with permission

Number	Old Title	New Title/Repeal	New Number
10300	Adoption, Amendment or Rescission of Rules.	Construction of Rules.	10300
		Rulemaking Notices.	10302
10301	Definitions.	Definitions.	10305
10302	Working Titles of Workers' Compensation Judges.	Definitions.	10305
10304	Article and Section Headings.	Construction of Rules.	10300
10322	Workers' Compensation Appeals Board Records Not Subject to Subpoena.	Inspection of Workers' Compensation Appeals Board Records.	10807
10324	Ex Parte Communications.	Ex Parte Communications.	10410
10340	Appeals Board Decisions and Orders.	Appeals Board Decisions and Orders.	10320
10341	En Banc Decisions.	En Banc and Significant Panel Decisions.	10325
10342	Appeals Board Member Orders.	Authority of Commissioners of the Appeals Board.	10338
10344	Appeals Board, Commissioner, Deputy Commissioner and Presiding Workers' Compensation Judges Orders.	Authority of Commissioners, Deputy Commissioners and Presiding Workers' Compensation Judges.	10344
10346	Assignment or Transfer of Cases.	Authority of Presiding Workers' Compensation Judge to Assign or Transfer Cases.	10346

10348	Authority of Workers' Compensation Judges.	Authority of Workers' Compensation Judges.	10330
10349	Order Equivalent to Notices of Intention.	Notices of Intention and Orders after Notices of Intention.	10832
10350	Trials: Appointment and Authority of Pro Tempore Workers' Compensation Judges.	Appointment and Authority of Pro Tempore Workers' Compensation Judges.	10355
10351	Conference Hearings: Appointment and Authority of Pro Tempore Workers' Compensation Judges.	Appointment and Authority of Pro Tempore Workers' Compensation Judges.	10355
10352	Reconsideration of Pro Tempore Workers' Compensation Judge's Orders, Decisions, or Awards.	Appointment and Authority of Pro Tempore Workers' Compensation Judges.	10355
10353	Settlement Conference Authority.	Mandatory Settlement Conferences.	10759
New Rule		Extensions of Time During Public Emergencies.	10370
10360	Necessary Parties.	Necessary Parties.	10380
10364	Parties Applicant.	Joinder of Parties.	10382
10380	Joinder of Parties.	Joinder of Parties.	10382
10390	Place of Filing Documents After Initial Application or Case Opening Document.	Filing of Documents.	10615
10391	Filing of Documentary Evidence.	Filing of Documents.	10615
10392	Time of Filing Documents.	Filing of Documents.	10615

10393	Filing of Medical Reports, Medical Legal Reports, and Various Records.	Filing Proposed Exhibits.	10620
		Documentary Evidence.	10670
		Approval of Settlements	10700
		Mandatory Settlement Conferences	10759
10397	Restrictions on the Rejection for Filing of Documents Subject to a Statute of Limitations or a Jurisdictional Time Limitation.	Restrictions on the Rejection for Filing of Documents Subject to a Statute of Limitations or a Jurisdictional Time Limitation.	10617
10400	Filing and Service of Applications.	Invoking the Jurisdiction of the Workers' Compensation Appeals Board.	10450
		Applications.	10455
10401	Separate Application for Each Injury.	Applications.	10455
10402	Minors and Incompetents as Applicants.	Applications.	10455
10403	Application Required Before Jurisdiction Invoked and Before Compelled Discovery May Be Commenced.	Invoking the Jurisdiction of the Workers' Compensation Appeals Board.	10450
10404	Labor Code Section 4906(g) Statement.	Labor Code Section 4906(h) Statement.	10470
10405	Request for Findings of Fact.	Request for Findings of Fact.	10460

10408	Application for Adjudication of Claim Form and Other Forms.	Form Pleadings.	10500
10409	Venue.	Venue.	10480 10482
10410	Objection to Venue Under Labor Code Section 5501.5(c).	Objection to Venue Based on an Attorney's Principal Place of Business.	10488
10411	Petition for Change of Venue Under Labor Code Section 5501.6.	Petition for Change of Venue for Good Cause.	10490
10412	Proceedings and Decision After Venue Change.	**Repeal.**	**Repeal.**
10414	Declaration of Readiness to Proceed.	Declaration of Readiness to Proceed.	10742
10416	Objection to Declaration of Readiness to Proceed.	Objection to Declaration of Readiness to Proceed.	10744
10417	Walk-Through Documents.	Walk-Through Documents.	10789
10420	Setting the Case.	Setting the Case.	10745.
10430	Letters of Appointment for Medical Examiners.	**Repeal.**	**Repeal.**
10440	Pleadings–Serious and Willful Misconduct.	Petition for Increased or Decreased Compensation – Serious and Willful Misconduct.	10525
10445	Allegations.	Petition for Increased or Decreased Compensation – Serious and Willful Misconduct.	10525

10447	Pleadings –Discrimination.	Petition for Increased Compensation–Discrimination under Labor Code section 132a.	10528
10450	Petitions and Answers.	Petitions and Answers to Petitions.	10510
10451.1	Determination of Medical-Legal Expense Disputes.	Determination of Medical-Legal Expense Dispute.	10786
10451.2	Determination of Medical Treatment Disputes.	**Repeal.**	**Repeal.**
10451.3	Petition for Costs.	Petition for Costs.	10545
New Rule		Petition for Labor Code Section 5710 Attorney's Fees.	10547
10451.4	Petition to Enforce Independent Bill Review Determination.	Petition to Enforce an Administrative Director Determination.	10570
10452	Petition for Disqualification of Judge.	Petition for Disqualification of Judge.	10960.
10453	Petition for Automatic Reassignment of Trial or Expedited Hearing to Another Workers' Compensation Judge.	Petition for Automatic Reassignment of Trial or Expedited Hearing to Another Workers' Compensation Judge.	10788
10454	Automatic Reassignment After Reversal.	**Repeal.**	**Repeal.**
10455	Petition to Reopen.	Petition to Reopen.	10534

10458	Petition for New and Further Disability	Petition for New and Further Disability.	10536
10462	Petition to Terminate Liability; Filing.	Petition to Terminate Liability for Continuing Temporary Disability.	10540
10464	Contents of Petition to Terminate Liability.	Petition to Terminate Liability for Continuing Temporary Disability.	10540
10466	Objections to Petition, Hearing, Interim Order	Petition to Terminate Liability for Continuing Temporary Disability.	10540
10470	Emergency Petition for Stay.	Emergency Petition for Stay.	10530
10480	Answers.	Answers.	10465
10484	Procedural Requirement.	Answers.	10465
10490	Demurrer, Judgement on the Pleadings, and Summary Judgment Not Permitted; Unintelligible Pleadings.	Demurrer, Judgement on the Pleadings, and Summary Judgment Not Permitted.	10515
10492	When Pleadings Deemed Amended.	When Pleadings Deemed Amended.	10517
New Rule		Petition for Credit.	10555
10496	Awards and Orders Without Hearing.	Effect of Stipulations.	10835
10497	Rejection of Stipulations.	Effect of Stipulations.	10835

10498	Special Requirements for Pleadings Filed or Served by Attorneys or by Non-Attorney Employees of an Attorney or Law Firm.	Special Requirements for Pleadings Filed or Served by Representatives.	10520
10500	Service by the Workers' Compensation Appeals Board.	Service by the Workers' Compensation Appeals Board.	10628
New Rule		Designated Service	10629
10501	Service in Death Cases.	Service on the Division of Workers' Compensation and the Director of Industrial Relations.	10632
10505	Service by Parties or Lien Claimants.	Service.	10625
10506	Service: Mail Box.	Service by the Workers' Compensation Appeals Board.	10628
10507	Time Within Which to Act When a Document is Served by Mail, Fax, or E-Mail.	Time Within Which to Act When a Document is Served by Mail, Fax or E-Mail.	10605
10508	Extension of Time for Weekends and Holidays.	Time for Actions.	10600
10510	Service on Represented Employees or Dependents and on Attorneys or Agents.	Service.	10625
New Rule		**Filing and Service of Documents.**	10610
10530	Subpoenas.	Subpoenas.	10640

10532	Notice to Appear or Produce.	Notice to Appear or Produce.	10642
10534	Microfilm.	Subpoenas of Electronic Records.	10644
10536	Witness Fees and Subpoenas.	Witness Fees and Subpoenas.	10647
10537	Subpoena for Med Witness.	Subpoena for Medical Witness.	10650
10538	Subpoenas for Medical Information by Non-Physician Lien Claimants.	Subpoenas for Medical Information by Non-Physician Lien Claimants.	10655
10541	Submission at Conference.	Submission at Conference.	10761
10544	Notice of Hearing.	Notice of Hearing.	10750
10548	Continuances.	Continuances.	10748
10549	Appearances in Settled Cases.	Appearances in Settled Cases.	10757
10550	Proper Identification of the Parties and Lien Claimants.	Proper Identification of Parties.	10390
10552	Expedited Hearing Calendar.	Expedited Hearing.	10782
10555	Priority Conference Calendar.	Priority Conference.	10785
10560	Submission at Single Trial.	Trials.	10787
10561	Sanctions.	Sanctions.	10421
10562	Failure to Appear.	Failure to Appear at Mandatory Settlement Conference or Trial.	10755
		Dismissal of Lien Claims.	10888

New Rule		Appearances by Representatives Not Identified on Notice of Representation	10751
10563	Appearances Required of Parties to Case-in-Chief.	Appearances Required.	10752
10563.1	Other Appearances Required.	Appearances Required.	10752
New Rule		Status Conferences.	10758
10564	Interpreters.	Interpreters.	10790
10566	Minutes of Hearing and Summary of Evidence.	Trials.	10787
10570	Minute Orders.	Minute Orders.	10833
10578	Waiver of Summary of Evidence.	Trials.	10787
10580	Evidence Taken Without Notice.	Evidence Taken Without Notice.	10672
10582	Inactive Cases.	Petition to Dismiss Inactive Case.	10550
10582.5	Dismissal of Inactive Lien Claimants for Lack of Prosecution.	Dismissal of Lien Claims.	10888
10583	Dismissal of Claim Form–Labor Code Section 5404.5.	**Repeal.**	**Repeal.**
10589	Consolidation of Cases.	Consolidation of Cases.	10396
10592	Assignment of Consolidated Cases.	Assignment of Consolidated Cases.	10398
10593	Testimony of Judicial or Quasi-Judicial Officers.	Testimony of Judicial or Quasi-Judicial Officers.	10360
10600	Evidence and Reports.	Documentary Evidence.	10670

10601	Copies of Reports and Records.	Duty to Serve Documents.	10635
10602	Formal Permanent Disability Rating Determinations.	Formal Permanent Disability Rating Determinations.	10675
10603	Oversized Exhibits, Diagnostic Imaging, Physical Exhibits, and Exhibits on Media.	Oversized Exhibits, Diagnostic Imaging, Physical Exhibits and Exhibits on Media.	10677
10604	Certified Copies.	Documentary Evidence.	10670
10605	Reproductions of Documents.	Reproductions of Documents.	10680
10606	Physicians' Reports as Evidence.	Physicians' Reports as Evidence.	10682
10606.5	Vocational Experts' Reports as Evidence.	Vocational Experts' Reports as Evidence.	10685
10607	Computer Printouts of Benefits Paid.	Duty to Serve Documents.	10635
10608	Service of Medical Reports, Medical-Legal Reports, and Other Medical Information.	Duty to Serve Documents.	10635
		Service of Medical Reports, Medical-Legal Reports, and Other Medical Information on a Non-Physician Lien Claimant.	10637
10608.5	Service by Parties and Lien Claimants of Reports and Records on Other Parties and Lien Claimants.	Service.	10625
10615	Continuing Duty to Serve.	Duty to Serve Documents.	10635

10616	Employer-Maintained Medical Records.	Duty to Serve Documents.	10635
10618	X-Rays.	X-Rays.	10660
10622	Failure to Comply.	Documentary Evidence.	10670
10626	Examining and Copying Hospital and Physicians' Records.	**Repeal.**	**Repeal.**
10629	Filing and Listing of Exhibits.	Mandatory Settlement Conferences.	10759
10631	Specific Finding of Fact—Labor Code section 139.2(d)(2).	Specific Finding of Fact—Labor Code section 139.2(d)(2).	10683
10632	Labor Code Section 4065–Evidence.	**Repeal.**	**Repeal.**
10633	Proposed Rating–Labor Code Section 4065.	**Repeal.**	**Repeal.**
10634	Labor Code Section 4628(k) Requests.	Documentary Evidence.	10670
10740	Transcripts.	Transcripts.	10800
10750	Record of Proceedings.	Record of Proceedings Maintained in Adjudication File.	10803
10751	Adjudication File.	Record of Proceedings Maintained in Adjudication File.	10803
10753	Inspection of Files.	Inspection of Workers' Compensation Appeals Board Records.	10807
10754	Sealing Documents.	Sealed Documents.	10813
10755	Destruction of Records.	Destruction of Records.	10811

10760	Recording of Trial Level Proceedings.	Recording of Proceedings.	10818
10770	Filing and Service of Lien Claims.	Filing and Service of Lien Claims and Supporting Documents.	10862
		Notification of Resolution or Withdrawal of Lien Claims.	10872
10770.1	Lien Conferences and Lien Trials.	Lien Conferences and Lien Trials.	10875
		Fees Required at Lien Conference.	10877
		Submission at Lien Conferences.	10880
		Dismissal of Lien Claims.	10888
10770.5	Verification to Filing of Lien Claim or Application by Lien Claimant.	Verification of Compliance with Labor Code section 4906.3 on Filing o Lien Claim or Application by Lien Claimant.	10890
10770.6	Verification to Filing Declaration of Readiness By or on Behalf of Lien Claimant.	Verification to Filing Declaration of Readiness to Proceed by or on Behalf of Lien Claimant.	10874
10770.7	Requirement for Liens Filed Before January 1, 2017.	Requirement for Liens Filed Before January 1, 2017.	10863

10772	Unemployment Compensation Disability Liens.	Unemployment Compensation Disability Liens.	10899
10773	Law Firm Employees.	Non-Attorney Representatives.	10400
10774	Substitution or Dismissal of Attorneys	Substitution or Dismissal of Attorneys and Non-Attorney Representatives.	10405
10774.5	Notices of Representation, Change of Representation, and Non-Representation for Lien Claimants.	Notices of Representation, Change of Representation and Non-Representation for Lien Claimants.	10868
10775	Reasonable Attorney's Fee.	Reasonable Attorney's Fee.	10844
10776	Approval of Attorney's Fee.	Approval of Attorney's Fee by Workers' Compensation Appeals Board Required.	10840
10778	Request for Increase of Attorney's Fee.	Request for increase of Attorney's Fee.	10842
10779	Disbarred and Suspended Attorneys.	Non-Attorney Representatives.	10440
		Disbarred and Suspended Attorneys.	10445
10780	Dismissal Orders.	Order Dismissing Application.	10850
10782	Vexatious Litigants.	Vexatious Litigants.	10430

New Rule		Contempt.	10440
10785	Electronically filed decisions	**Repeal**	**Repeal**
10820	When Certified Copies Will Issue.	When Certified Copies Will Issue.	10820
10825	Withholding Certified Copies.	Withholding Certified Copies.	10825
10828	Necessity for Bond.	**Repeal.**	**Repeal.**
10840	Filing Petitions for Reconsideration, Removal, and Disqualification and Answers.	Filing and Service of Petitions for Reconsideration, Removal, Disqualification and Answers.	10940
10842	Contents of Petitions for Reconsideration, Removal, and Disqualification and Answers.	Required Content of Petitions for Reconsideration, Removal, and Disqualification and Answers.	10945
10843	Petitions for Removal and Answers.	Petitions for Removal and Answers.	10955
10844	Petitions for Disqualification and Answers.	Filing and Service of Petitions for Reconsideration, Removal, Disqualification and Answers.	10940

10845	General Requirements for Petitions for Reconsideration, Removal, and Disqualification, and for Answers and Other Documents.	Filing and Service of Petitions for Reconsideration, Removal, Disqualification and Answers.	10940
10846	Skeletal Petitions.	Skeletal Petitions.	10972
10848	Supplemental Petitions.	Supplemental Petitions.	10964
10850	Proof of Service.	Filing and Service of Petitions for Reconsideration, Removal, Disqualification and Answers.	10940
10852	Insufficiency of Evidence.	**Repeal.**	**Repeal.**
10856	Allegations of Newly Discovered Evidence and Fraud.	Allegations of Newly Discovered Evidence and Fraud.	10974
10858	Correction of Errors.	Correction of Errors.	10966
10859	Orders After Filing of Petition for Reconsideration.	Actions by Workers' Compensation Judge After Petition for Reconsideration is Filed.	10961
10860	Report of Workers' Compensation Judge.	Report of Workers' Compensation Judge.	10962
10862	Hearing After Reconsideration is Granted.	Hearing After Reconsideration is Granted.	10984

10864	Authority of Workers' Compensation Judge After Decision After Reconsideration.	Authority of Workers' Compensation Judge After Decision After Reconsideration.	10986
10865	Reconsideration of Arbitration Decisions Made Pursuant To–Labor Code Sections 3201.5 and 3201.7.	Reconsideration of Arbitration Decisions Made Pursuant To–Labor Code Sections 3201.5 and 3201.7.	10990
10866	Reconsideration of Arbitrator's Decisions or Awards Made Pursuant to the Mandatory or Voluntary Arbitration Provisions of Labor Code Sections 5270 through 5275.	Reconsideration of Arbitrator's Decisions or Awards Made Pursuant to the Mandatory or Voluntary Arbitration Provisions of Labor Code Sections 5270 through 5275.	10995
10870	Approval of Compromise and Release.	Approval of Settlements.	10700
10874	Form.	**Repeal.**	**Repeal.**
10875	Procedures–Labor Code section 3761.	Procedures–Labor Code section 3761.	10705
10878	Settlement Document as an Application.	**Repeal.**	**Repeal.**
10882	Action on Settlement Agreement.	Approval of Settlements.	10700
10886	Service on Lien Claimants.	Service of Settlements on Lien Claimants.	10702
10888	Resolution of Liens.	**Repeal.**	**Repeal.**

10940	Application.	Subsequent Injuries Benefits Trust Fund Application.	10462
10942	Service.	Service on the Division of Workers' Compensation and the Director of Industrial Relations.	10632
10946	Medical Reports in Subsequent Injuries Benefits Trust Fund Cases.	Subsequent Injuries Benefits Trust Fund Application.	10462
10950	Petitions Appealing Orders Issued by the Administrative Directors.	Petitions Related to Orders Issued by the Division of Workers' Compensation Administrative Director or the Director of Industrial Relations.	10560
10953	Petition Appealing Audit Penalty Assessment–Labor Code Section 129.5(g).	Petition Appealing Audit Penalty Assessment–Labor Code Section 129.5(g).	10590
10957	Petition Appealing Independent Bill Review determination of the Administrative Director.	Petition Appealing Independent Bill Review Determination.	10567
10957.1	Petition Appealing Independent Medical Review Determination of the Administrative Director.	Petition Appealing Independent Medical Review Determination.	10575
New Rule		**Petition Appealing Denial of Return-to-Work Supplement.**	10565

10959	Petition Appealing Medical Provider Network Determination of the Administrative Director.	Petition Appealing Medical Provider Network Determination of the Administrative Director.	10580
10995	Mandatory Arbitration.	Mandatory Arbitration.	10900
		Selection of Arbitrator.	10910
10996	Voluntary Arbitration.	Voluntary Arbitration.	10905
		Selection of Arbitrator.	10910
10997	Request for Arbitration.	**Repeal.**	**Repeal.**
10998	Disqualification of Arbitrator.	Disqualification of Arbitrator.	10912
10999	Arbitrator Fee and Cost Disputes.	Arbitrator Fee and Cost Disputes.	10920
New Rule		Complaints Regarding Violations of Labor Code Section 4907	10401
New Rule		Complaints Regarding Violations of Labor Code Section 4907	10402

INSURANCE CODE
[Selected Provisions]

SYNOPSIS

GENERAL PROVISIONS
[Selected Provisions]

§20.5. Terms referring to Division of Industrial Accidents.
§42. Use of "group" in designating insurance coverage; application of section.
§46. "Workmen's compensation" to become "workers' compensation."

DIVISION 1
GENERAL RULES GOVERNING INSURANCE

PART 1
The Contract

CHAPTER 1
CLASSES OF INSURANCE
[Selected Provisions]

§100. Classes of insurance.
§108. Liability insurance.
§108.1. Liability insurers as workers' compensation insurers.
§109. "Workers' compensation insurance."
§110. "Common carrier liability insurance."

CHAPTER 11
CANCELLATION AND FAILURE TO RENEW CERTAIN PROPERTY INSURANCE
[Selected Provisions]

§676. Grounds for cancellation.
§676.1. Arbitrary cancellation or refusal to renew homeowners' policy due to operation of family day care business; coverage to be by separate endorsement.
§676.2. Grounds for cancellation of commercial insurance policies.
§676.3. Remedial underwriting on medical malpractice insurance for dentists, physicians and surgeons.
§676.4. Changes in rate on which premium based or conditions of coverage of policies insuring health care facilities.
§676.5. Length of term for commercial insurance policies.
§676.6. Commercial umbrella liability, commercial excess liability, and commercial excess property insurance policies; notice of cancellation or nonrenewal.
§676.7. Applicant or policyholder engaged in foster home activities.
§676.75. Prohibited acts related to foster home activities; coverage against public policy.
§676.8. Workers' compensation insurance policies.
§676.9. Discrimination against domestic violence victims; nature and use of information about domestic violence victims.
§676.10. Applicability of section; cancellation or nonrenewal due to hate crime or anti-reproductive-rights crime losses; "hate crime" and "anti-reproductive-rights crime"; reporting procedures; violation.
§677. Notice of cancellation.
§677.2. Notice of cancellation for commercial insurance policies.
§677.4. Notice of cancellation for certain property insurance policies.
§678. Notice of nonrenewal.

PART 2
The Business of Insurance

CHAPTER 1
GENERAL REGULATIONS

ARTICLE 3
Certificate of Authority
[Selected Provisions]

§703.5. Advertising of qualifications to advise employers—Penalty.

ARTICLE 4
Examination by Commissioner
[Selected Provisions]

§738. Authority of commissioner to examine State Compensation Insurance Fund.

ARTICLE 5.1
Unlawful Practices
[Selected Provisions]

§756. Misrepresentation of payroll; penalty.
§757. Insurer's acceptance of false payroll information.

ARTICLE 10
Financial Statements of Insurers
[Selected Provisions]

§923.5. Required reserves.
§923.6. Submission of statement of actuarial opinion; duties of property and casualty insurer; confidentiality of documents; exceptions.

ARTICLE 14.2
California Insurance Guarantee Association
[Selected Provisions]

§1063. California Insurance Guarantee Association.

§1063.1. Definitions.
§1063.2. Association's duties; authority; exceptions to "covered claims."
§1063.3. Reports and recommendations pertaining to regulation for solvency.
§1063.5. Collection and allocation of premium payments from member insurers; applicability.
§1063.14. Surcharge on premiums; applicability.
§1063.15. Association's time limits.
§1063.17. Public meeting; scope; notice; certain closed meeting or session permitted; requirements.
§1063.18. Claims against insolvent insurers; denial of nonworkers' compensation claim.

ARTICLE 14.26
Workers' Compensation Bond Fund

§1063.70. Issuance of bonds for payment of covered claims against insolvent insurers.
§1063.71. Definitions.
§1063.72. Workers' Comp Bond Fund.
§1063.73. CIGA's request for issuance of bonds—Copy to commissioner; commissioner may modify, cancel, or delay requested issuance.
§1063.74. Funding workers' compensation claims—Special bond assessments, current funds, premium assessments, and advances or dividends.
§1063.75. Terms and conditions of bonds.
§1063.76. Collateral—Permitted use; subject to first priority statutory lien; exempt from specified claims.
§1063.77. Contracts or agreements with banks, insurers, or other financial institutions or parties; optional terms in contracts or agreements.

CHAPTER 12
THE INSURANCE FRAUDS PREVENTION ACT

ARTICLE 1
False and Fraudulent Claims
[Selected Provisions]

§1871. Insurance fraud—Generally.
§1871.1. Access to records required to be open for inspection in fraud claims.
§1871.2. Notice of penalties on claim forms; exception.
§1871.4. Penalties for making false or fraudulent written or oral statements.
§1871.5. Ineligibility to receive or retain compensation.
§1871.6. Provisions of Penal Code §781 applicable to prosecutions for violations of §1871.4.
§1871.7. Employing persons to procure clients or patients to perform or obtain benefits unlawful; penalties; bringing action.
§1871.8. Notice to injured worker regarding penalties and prosecution for fraudulent receipt of temporary disability benefits.
§1871.9. Posting information on Web site of person convicted of violation of article.

ARTICLE 2
Bureau of Fraudulent Claims
[Selected Provisions]

§1872.84. Information to be forwarded to appropriate disciplinary body.
§1872.95. Medical and chiropractic boards and State Bar; investigation of workers' compensation, motor vehicle, or disability insurance fraud by licensees.

ARTICLE 4
Motor Vehicle Theft and Motor Vehicle Insurance Fraud Reporting
[Selected Provisions]

§1874.1. Definitions.

ARTICLE 7
Workers' Compensation Insurance Fraud Reporting

§1877. Title.
§1877.1. Definitions.
§1877.2. Authorized governmental agency.
§1877.3. Insurer's or licensed rating organization's release of requested information to governmental agency; requirement to notify when fraud committed.
§1877.35. Public Employees' Retirement System—Request for information from insurer relating to investigation of eligibility, unlawful application, or receipt of benefits.
§1877.4. Confidentiality of information acquired; exception to privilege.
§1877.5. Immunity from civil liability when acting in good faith.

DIVISION 2
CLASSES OF INSURANCE

PART 3
Liability, Workers' Compensation, and Common Carrier Liability Insurance

CHAPTER 1
GENERAL REGULATIONS

ARTICLE 2
Actions on Policies Containing Liability Provisions
[Selected Provisions]

§11580.1. Required provisions for automobile liability insurance.
§11580.2. Uninsured vehicle coverage; limitations.

ARTICLE 2.5
Personal Liability Insurance Providing Workers' Compensation Coverage for Household Employees

§11590. Personal liability insurance policies to contain coverage for workers' compensation; inapplicability.
§11591. Exception to §11590.
§11592. Law governing rates, rating systems, and classifications for workers' compensation insurance.
§11593. Premium charge for workers' compensation insurance not to be separately stated.

CHAPTER 2
WORKERS' COMPENSATION POLICIES

ARTICLE 1
Definitions

§11630. "Compensation."

§11631. "Insurer."

ARTICLE 2
Policy Provisions
[Selected Provisions]

§11650. Conclusive presumption of compliance with this article.
§11651. Contract/policy statement of insurer's liability.
§11652. Employer knowledge of injury as imputed to insurer.
§11653. Employer's and insurer's jurisdiction.
§11654. Insurer bound by findings against employer; insurance contract to govern liability.
§11655. Effect of employer's insolvency or bankruptcy on insurer's liability.
§11656. Employee's lien.
§11658.5. Insurer disclosures for dispute resolution or arbitration; default; applicability.
§11661. Insurance for employer's serious and willful misconduct.
§11661.5. Injuries to illegally employed minors.
§11661.6. Insuring compensation for increased indemnity prohibited.
§11662. Insurer's subrogation to employer's rights.
§11663. Liability of general and special employers.
§11663.5. Insurer provides premium and loss history report.
§11664. Notice of nonrenewal.
§11665. Payroll audits for roofing contractors; annual report.

CHAPTER 3
REGULATION OF BUSINESS OF WORKERS' COMPENSATION INSURANCE

ARTICLE 1
Deposits by Workers' Compensation Insurers

§11690. Definitions.
§11691. Deposit required by insurer desiring admission to transact workers' compensation insurance, or reinsurance, or desiring to reinsure the injury, disablement, or death portions of policies; notice to commissioner; trust agreement; fee.
§11691.1. Fee for filing schedule of securities.
§11691.2. Deposit as security for payment of obligations on workers' compensation insurance transacted in state.
§11691.3. List of authorized insurers and reinsurers.
§11692. Issuance of certificate of authority.
§11692.5. Late filing fee.
§11693. Annual adjustment of deposit.
§11694. Computation of deposit from figures in annual report.
§11694.5. Deposit reports.
§11695. Fixing deposit for insurer who voluntarily ceases to do business in state.
§11696. Use of deposit when insurer fails to pay compensation claim.
§11697. Payment of claim by commissioner as satisfaction of claim.
§11698. Circumstances authorizing commissioner to take control or possession of deposit.
§11698.01. Options of commissioner upon taking control or possession of deposit.
§11698.02. Use of proceeds from deposit.
§11698.1. Accounting of funds.
§11698.2. Provisions of reinsurance and assumption agreement.
§11698.21. Reimbursement agreement to provide for transfer of securities in the deposit.
§11698.22. Circumstances where commissioner prohibited from entering into reinsurance agreement.
§11698.3. Association member subject to liquidation order.
§11699. Repayment of deposit to insurer upon satisfaction of liabilities.
§11700. Deposit used for unpaid compensable claims.
§11701. Revocation of certificate of authority.
§11702. Article not to apply to certain employees.
§11703. Occupational safety and health loss control consultation services required.

ARTICLE 2
State Rate Supervision

§11730. Definitions.
§11731. Application of article.
§11732. Limitations on rates; presumption of monopoly.
§11732.5. Criteria for determination of discriminatory rates.
§11733. Criteria for determination of rates.
§11734. Adherence to uniform experience rating plan; assistance by rating organization with statistics and classification system; manual rules developed by rating organization; adherence to manual rules; weekly premium developed by rating organization.
§11735. Filing of rates and supplementary rate information; filings open to public inspection; using rates in excess of those stated in filing, disallowance of rating systems violating Unruh Act; filing requirements for plans with deductibles; reporting losses subject to deductibles.
§11736. Requirements of experience rating plan.
§11736.5. Collateral or security for deductible amount on policy; reserves and recognition of receivables.
§11737. Disapproval of rate by commissioner; notice of disapproval; request for review of rating system of insurer or rating organization by aggrieved party; appeal to commissioner after request; hearing; issuance of order by commissioner upon disapproval; specification of interim rates; rate increase for policies with inception dates before January 1, 2003.
§11738. Factors not considered in classification.
§11739. Dividend payments to policyholders—Restrictions and filing requirement.
§11740. Effective dates for rates and supplementary rate information pursuant to this article.
§11742. Workers' compensation insurance online rate comparison guide.

ARTICLE 3
Rating and Other Organizations

§11750. Purpose of this article.
§11750.1. Definitions.
§11750.2. Scope of article.
§11750.3. Permissible purposes of rating organization.
§11751. License; fee; required information.
§11751.1. License requirements.
§11751.2. Investigation of rating organizations; findings

of commissioner; denial of application; duration of license.
§11751.25. License fee due annually.
§11751.3. Rules of rating organizations; State Fund's committee membership.
§11751.35. Public members of managing committee.
§11751.4. Insurer as rating organization member.
§11751.5. Provision of statistics to commissioner.
§11751.55. Filing fee if public hearing is required.
§11751.7. Statistical agent information request.
§11751.8. Reporting loss corrections or revisions to rating organization; when insurer must report.
§11751.82. Reporting workers' compensation losses and payroll information by insurer under wrap-up insurance policy.
§11751.9. Revision of experience rating upon closure and reporting of claims.
§11752. Examination of rating organizations; acceptable substitutes.
§11752.1. Examination of personnel and records.
§11752.2. Cost of commissioner's examination.
§11752.5. Release of policy information to governmental agencies.
§11752.6. Release of policy information to employer.
§11752.7. Availability of experience rating information.
§11752.75. Licensed rating organization to establish and maintain Internet Web site to assist person in determining whether employer is insured for workers' compensation.
§11752.8. Notice of workers' compensation rating laws to be provided to policyholder.
§11752.9. Written notification of change in classification assignment to be provided to policyholder.
§11753. Information required of advisory organizations; notification of all changes; prohibition on unfair practices.
§11753.1. Appeal of decision, action, or omission of rating organization by aggrieved party; hearing by commissioner; notice to employer of change in classification assignment; request for reconsideration by employer.
§11753.2. Effective date of classification change resulting in a decreased premium.
§11753.3. Workers' compensation insurance rating organization's exemption and authority.
§11754. Noncompliance.
§11754.1. Wilful or uncorrected noncompliance.
§11754.2. Ordering compliance; suspension or revocation of license.
§11754.3. Suspension or revocation for noncompliance within time limits.
§11754.4. Procedures for denial, suspension, or revocation of license.
§11754.5. Court review of commissioner's rulings.
§11755. False or misleading information; refusal to allow examination.
§11756. Penalties for noncompliance with final order.
§11757. Dividends, savings, or unabsorbed premium deposits.
§11758. Violation of other state laws.
§11758.1. Exemption for household employees.
§11759. Rating organizations' and personnel's exemption from liability.
§11759.1. Rating organizations must make available report of prior year's losses and expenses.
§11759.2. Report on underreported workers' compensation exposure in taxicab industry.

ARTICLE 4
Penalties for Misrepresentation

§11760. Penalties for misrepresentation to obtain reduced rate.
§11760.1. Audit of employer; failure to provide access to records; costs.

ARTICLE 5
Standards Applicable to Claims Adjusters

§11761. Workers' compensation claims adjusters—Minimum standards of training, experience, and skill; certification to commissioner by specified entities that employees meet minimum standards.

CHAPTER 4
THE STATE COMPENSATION INSURANCE FUND

ARTICLE 1
Organization and Powers

§11770. State Compensation Insurance Fund; board of directors.
§11771. State's limited liability.
§11771.5. Advertising disclaimer.
§11772. Directors' and personnel's limited liability.
§11773. Organization as public enterprise fund.
§11774. Use of fund assets.
§11775. Competitiveness with other insurers.
§11776. Annual accountings; possible dividends and credits.
§11777. Amount of dividends or credits.
§11778. Ability to transact workers' compensation insurance.
§11779. Ability to insure under federal or maritime laws.
§11780. Ability to insure under state law.
§11780.5. Ability to insure employees temporarily out of California.
§11781. Board of directors' powers.
§11781.5. Authority to acquire property in Los Angeles.
§11782. Business name.
§11783. Powers of fund.
§11784. Powers of fund president.
§11785. Appointment of officers to fund; applicability of Government Code and Public Contract Code provisions.
§11785.5. Former members of fund's board of directors and former fund officers prohibited from lobbying for fund for two years after leaving fund; consulting for fund by specified persons to be approved by fund's board.
§11786. President's bond and oath.
§11787. Board's delegation of authority to president.
§11788. State Treasurer as custodian of fund's securities.
§11790. Delivery of securities to State Treasurer.
§11793. Exemption for fund's expenditures.
§11797. Investment of moneys; purchase of bonds and other evidence of indebtedness; report [First of Two; Repealed January 1, 2025].
§11797. Investment of moneys; purchase of bonds and other evidence of indebtedness [Second of Two; Operative January 1, 2025].
§11800. Deposit of excess moneys.
§11800.1. Fund account in State Treasury.
§11800.2. Special ledger account by State Controller.

§11801. Prohibition on use of certain assets to satisfy federal claims.
§11802. Separate accounts for funds acquired for federal claims.
§11803. Federal claims and costs to be paid from separate account.
§11804. Charges for insurance classes' use of facilities, supplies, or equipment.
§11805. Annual report to Legislature.

ARTICLE 2
Rates

§11820. Rates.
§11821. Factors considered in setting rates.
§11822. Percentage basis of rates.

ARTICLE 3
Policies

§11840. Insurance contracts and policies.
§11841. Chapter's limitations on temporary coverage and policy surrender.
§11843. Policies for employers and families.
§11844. Same compensation and rates for employers and employees.
§11845. Estimates of employers' wage values.
§11846. Policies for self-employed persons and casual employees.

ARTICLE 4
Reports and Statements

§11860. Quarterly report to Governor; annual audit publication; reports to commissioner.

ARTICLE 5
Coverage of Public Employers

§11870. Potential insurers; premiums.
§11871. Master agreement with Department of Human Resources.
§11872. Annual agreements with state agencies.
§11873. Laws applicable to fund.
§11874. Treasurer's payment of warrant.

ARTICLE 6
Penalties

§11880. Willful misrepresentation to obtain reduced rate—Punishment; enhancement for prior conviction.
§11881. Other names for Board of Directors.

ARTICLE 7
Transfer of Ownership

§11885. Sale of portion of State Compensation Insurance Fund's assets and liabilities.
§11885.3. Participation by board of directors; acting in good faith.
§11885.5. Approvals not required.
§11885.7. Deposit of proceeds.
§11885.9. Advisers.
§11886. Selection of firms providing advisory services.
§11886.2. Notification by Director of Finance.

SELECTED PROVISIONS Of The INSURANCE CODE

GENERAL PROVISIONS [Selected Provisions]

§20.5. Terms referring to Division of Industrial Accidents.

Whenever in this code the terms "State Industrial Accident Commission" or "Industrial Accident Commission" or "commission," relating to the said "State Industrial Accident Commission" or the said "Industrial Accident Commission," appear, said terms shall mean "Division of Industrial Accidents," including "administrative director" of said division or "appeals board," or both, as the context may require.

§42. Use of "group" in designating insurance coverage; application of section.

The designation of insurance coverage as "group" in any code or law of this state other than this code does not authorize its representation as a group coverage or as a group policy, certificate, or contract by any person licensed or certificated by the commissioner unless the policy providing the coverage is defined as group insurance by a specific provision of this code or of the laws of the state in which the policy, certificate, or contract is issued. This section shall apply only to life, disability, and workers' compensation insurance. **Leg.H.** 1961 ch. 398 §1, 2018 ch. 231 (AB 2045) §1.

§46. "Workmen's compensation" to become "workers' compensation."

The Legislature hereby declares its intent that the term "workmen's compensation" shall hereafter also be known as "workers' compensation." In furtherance of this policy it is the desire of the Legislature that references to the term "workmen's compensation" in this code be changed to "workers' compensation" when such code sections are being amended for any purpose. This act is declaratory and not amendatory of existing law.

DIVISION 1
GENERAL RULES GOVERNING INSURANCE

PART 1
The Contract

CHAPTER 1
CLASSES OF INSURANCE
[Selected Provisions]

§100. Classes of insurance.

Insurance in this state is divided into the following classes:

(1) Life.

(2) Fire.

(3) Marine.

(4) Title.

(5) Surety.

(6) Disability.

(7) Plate glass.

(8) Liability.

(9) Workers' compensation.

(10) Common carrier liability.

(11) Boiler and machinery.

(12) Burglary.

(13) Credit.

(14) Sprinkler.

(15) Team and vehicle.

(16) Automobile.

(17) [Reserved]

(18) Aircraft.

(19) Mortgage guaranty.

(19.5) Insolvency.

(19.6) Legal insurance.

(20) Miscellaneous. **Leg.H.** 1935 ch. 145, 1939 ch. 936 §1, 1961 ch. 719 §2, 1969 ch. 1347 §1, effective September 2, 1969, 1974 ch. 1161 §1, 2012 ch. 786 (AB 2303) §3.

Ref.: Hanna § 1.22.

§108. Liability insurance.

Liability insurance includes:

(a) Insurance against loss resulting from liability for injury, fatal or nonfatal, suffered by any natural person, or resulting from liability for damage to property, or property interests of others but does not include workers' compensation, common carrier liability, boiler and machinery, or team and vehicle insurance.

[Subsections (b)–(e) Not Reproduced]

§108.1. Liability insurers as workers' compensation insurers.

Insurers admitted to transact liability insurance are also deemed to be admitted to transact workers' compensation insurance for the purpose of covering those persons defined as employees by subdivision (d) of Section 3351 of the Labor Code.

§109. "Workers' compensation insurance."

Workers' compensation insurance includes insurance against loss from liability imposed by law upon employers to compensate employees and their dependents for injury sustained by the employees arising out of and in the course of the employment, irrespective of negligence or of the fault of either party. **Leg.H.** 1935 ch. 145, 2018 ch. 231 (AB 2045) §2.

Ref.: Hanna §§ 1.22, 2.10[2].

§110. "Common carrier liability insurance."

Common carrier liability insurance includes insurance against loss resulting from liability of a common carrier for accident or injury, fatal or nonfatal, to any person but does not include liability or workers' compensation insurance. **Leg.H.** 1935 ch. 145, 2018 ch. 231 (AB 2045) §3.

CHAPTER 11
CANCELLATION AND FAILURE TO RENEW CERTAIN PROPERTY INSURANCE
[Selected Provisions]

§676. Grounds for cancellation.

After a policy specified in Section 675 has been in effect for 60 days, or, if the policy is a renewal, effective immediately, no notice of cancellation shall be effective unless it is based on the occurrence, after the effective date of the policy, of one or more of the following:

(a) Nonpayment of premium, including nonpayment of any additional premiums, calculated in accordance with the current rating manual of the insurer, justified by a physical change in the insured property or a change in its occupancy or use.

(b) Conviction of the named insured of a crime having as one of its necessary elements an act increasing any hazard insured against.

(c) Discovery of fraud or material misrepresentation by either of the following:

(1) The insured or his or her representative in obtaining the insurance.

(2) The named insured or his or her representative in pursuing a claim under the policy.

(d) Discovery of grossly negligent acts or omissions by the insured or his or her representative substantially increasing any of the hazards insured against.

(e) Physical changes in the insured property which result in the property becoming uninsurable. **Leg.H.** 1970 ch. 313 §1, 1986 ch. 1321 §2.

§676.1. Arbitrary cancellation or refusal to renew homeowners' policy due to operation of family day care business; coverage to be by separate endorsement.

(a) The arbitrary cancellation of a policy of homeowners' insurance solely on the basis that the policyholder has a license to operate a family day care home at the insured location shall subject the insurer to administrative sanctions authorized by this code unless, there has been a material misrepresentation of fact, the risk has changed substantially since the policy was issued, there has been a nonpayment of premium, or the insurer no longer writes homeowners policies.

(b) The arbitrary refusal to renew a policy of homeowners' insurance solely on the basis that the policyholder has a license to operate a family day care home at the insured location shall subject the insurer to administrative sanctions authorized by this code unless, there has been a material misrepresentation of fact, the risk has changed substantially since the policy was issued, there has been a nonpayment of premium, or the insurer no longer writes homeowners' policies. For purposes of this subdivision, an insured's purchase of a policy of homeowner's insurance to cover a new, primary residence from the same insurer which insured his or her previous primary residence, provided that the insurer then underwrites homeowners' insurance in the geographic area containing the new residence, shall be deemed a renewal of the policy on the previous, primary residence.

(c) It shall be against public policy for a residential property insurance policy to provide coverage for liability for losses arising out of, or in connection with, the operation of a family day care home. This coverage shall only be provided by a separate endorsement or insurance policy for which premiums have been assessed and collected. **Leg.H.** 1985 ch. 1362 §2, effective October 1, 1985, 1991 ch. 784 (AB 676) §1.

§676.2. Grounds for cancellation of commercial insurance policies.

(a) This section applies only to policies of commercial insurance that are subject to Section 675.5.

(b) After a policy has been in effect for more than 60 days, or if the policy is a renewal, effective immediately, no notice of cancellation shall be effective unless it complies with Section 677.2 and it is based on the occurrence, after the effective date of the policy, of one or more of the following:

(1) Nonpayment of premium, including payment due on a prior policy issued by the insurer and due during the current policy term covering the same risks.

(2) A judgment by a court or an administrative tribunal that the named insured has violated any law of this state or of the United States having as one of its necessary elements an act that materially increases any of the risks insured against.

(3) Discovery of fraud or material misrepresentation by either of the following:

(A) The insured or his or her representative in obtaining the insurance.

(B) The named insured or his or her representative in pursuing a claim under the policy.

(4) Discovery of willful or grossly negligent acts or omissions, or of any violations of state laws or regulations establishing safety standards, by the named insured or his or her representative, which materially increase any of the risks insured against.

(5) Failure by the named insured or his or her representative to implement reasonable loss control requirements that were agreed to by the insured as a condition of policy issuance or that were conditions precedent to the use by the insurer of a particular rate or rating plan, if the failure materially increases any of the risks insured against.

(6) A determination by the commissioner that the loss of, or changes in, an insurer's reinsurance covering all or part of the risk would threaten the financial integrity or solvency of the insurer. A certification made under penalty of perjury to the commissioner by an officer of the insurer of the loss of, or change in, reinsurance and that the loss or change will threaten the financial integrity or solvency of the insurer if the cancellation of the policy is not permitted shall constitute this determination unless disapproved by the commissioner within 30 days of the filing. There shall be no extensions to this 30-day period.

(7) A determination by the commissioner that a continuation of the policy coverage would place the insurer in violation of the laws of this state or the state of its domicile or that the continuation of coverage would threaten the solvency of the insurer.

(8) A change by the named insured or his or her representative in the activities or property of the commercial or industrial enterprise that results in a material added risk, a materially increased risk, or a materially changed risk, unless the added, increased, or changed risk is included in the policy.

(c)(1) After a policy has been in effect for more than 60 days, or if the policy is a renewal, effective immediately upon renewal, no increase in the rate upon which the premium is based, reduction in limits, or change in the conditions of coverage shall be effective during the policy period unless a written notice is mailed or delivered to the named insured and the producer of record at the mailing address shown on the policy, at least 30 days prior to the effective date of the increase, reduction, or change. Subdivision (a) of Section 1013 of the Code of Civil Procedure is applicable if the notice is mailed. The notice shall state the effective date of, and the reasons for, the increase, reduction, or change.

(2) The increase, reduction, or change shall not be effective unless it is based upon one of the following reasons:

(A) Discovery of willful or grossly negligent acts or omissions, or of any violations of state laws or regulations establishing safety standards by the named insured that materially increase any of the risks or hazards insured against.

(B) Failure by the named insured to implement reasonable loss control requirements that were agreed to by the insured as a condition of policy issuance or that were conditions precedent to the use by the insurer of a particular rate or rating plan, if the failure materially increases any of the risks insured against.

(C) A determination by the commissioner that loss of or changes in an insurer's reinsurance covering all or part of the risk covered by the policy would threaten the financial integrity or solvency of the insurer unless the change in the terms or conditions or rate upon which the premium is based is permitted.

(D) A change by the named insured in the activities or property of the commercial or industrial enterprise that results in a materially added risk, a materially increased risk, or a materially changed risk, unless the added, increased, or changed risk is included in the policy.

(E) With respect to a change in the rate of a policy of professional liability insurance for a health care provider, the insurer's offer of renewal notifies the policyholder that the insurer has an application filed pursuant to Section 1861.05 pending with the commissioner for approval of a change in the rate upon which the premium is based, and the commissioner subsequently approves the rate change, or some different amount for the policy period. The change shall not be retroactive.

(d) The Administrative Procedure Act (Chapter 3.5 (commencing with Section 11340), Chapter 4 (commencing with Section 11370), and Chapter 5 (commencing with Section 11500) of Title 2 of Division 3 of the Government Code) shall not apply to a determination pursuant to paragraph (6) or (7) of subdivision (b) or subparagraph (C) of paragraph (2) of subdivision (c). The commissioner shall charge an insurer who requests a determination pursuant to paragraph (6) or (7) of subdivision (b) a fee sufficient to recover the costs of making the determination. If the commissioner does not act upon a request by an insurer to cancel or change a policy pursuant to those provisions within 30 days, the request shall be deemed to be approved.

(e) This section shall not prohibit an insurer from increasing a premium during the policy period if the increase is calculated in accordance with the current rating manual of the insurer and is justified by a physical change in the insured property or by a change in the activities of the commercial or industrial enterprise that materially increases any of the risks insured against.

(f) This section shall not apply to a transfer of a policy without a change in its terms or conditions or the rate upon which the premium is based between insurers that are members of the same insurance group. **Leg.H.** 1986 ch. 1321 §3, 1990 ch. 216 (SB 2510) §84, 1993 ch. 1198 (SB 581) §1, 2006 ch. 538 (SB 1852) §451.

§676.3. Remedial underwriting on medical malpractice insurance for dentists, physicians and surgeons.

Nothing in Section 676.2 shall preclude the imposition of remedial underwriting action upon coverage insuring dentists or physicians and surgeons against legal liability arising from the rendering of professional services by an insured licensed pursuant to Chapter 4 (commencing with Section 1600) or Chapter 5 (commencing with Section 2000) of Division 2 of the Business and Professions Code, respectively, if remedial underwriting action is imposed pursuant to the recommendation of an underwriting committee advising the insurer; provided that a majority of the members of that committee are licensed pursuant to the chapter of Division 2 of the Business and Professions Code that is applicable to that particular insured, and written notification of the proposed remedial underwriting action is first given to the insured, and the insured is afforded not less than 30 days to present opposition or argument to the underwriting committee as to why the remedial underwriting action should be modified or withheld, prior to any imposition thereof. Remedial underwriting action includes all actions described in subdivision (c) of Section 676.2. Remedial underwriting action imposed pursuant to this section shall not be subject to Article 7 (commencing with Section 1858) of Chapter 9 of Part 2, but nothing in this section shall deny the right of the commissioner to investigate, pursue enforcement action, and seek other remedies as authorized by Article 1 (commencing with Section 12919) of Chapter 2 of Division 3.

It is the intent of the Legislature to encourage peer review by insurers providing coverage to persons engaged in the provision of health services and the adoption of conditions of coverage which are intended to protect the public. **Leg.H.** 1988 ch. 1618 §1, 1995 ch. 600 (AB 852) §1.

§676.4. Changes in rate on which premium based or conditions of coverage of policies insuring health care facilities.

Nothing in Section 676.2 shall preclude, while the policies are in force, changes in the rate upon which the premium is based or the conditions of coverage, or both, of policies insuring health care facilities licensed pursuant to Chapter 2 (commencing with Section 1250) of Division 2 of the Health and Safety Code, if the change is imposed pursuant to the recommendation of a health care facility professional liability advisory committee advising the insurer; provided that a majority of the members of the committee are duly authorized representatives of health care facilities licensed pursuant to that Chapter 2 (commencing with Section 1250) of Division 2 of the Health and Safety Code, and written notification of the change is given to all affected insureds at least 30 days prior to any such change. **Leg.H.** 1988 ch. 1618 §2.

§676.5. Length of term for commercial insurance policies.

(a) This section applies only to policies of commercial insurance which are subject to Section 675.5.

(b) Except as provided in subdivision (c), for purposes of this chapter only, a policy with no fixed expiration, or with a term of less than one year, shall be considered to be a policy for a term of one year, and a policy written for a term of more than one year shall be considered as if written for successive terms of one year.

(c) For purposes of this chapter, a policy shall be considered to be for a term of less than one year if the policy is issued for a specific risk which does not continue beyond the period of the policy, or if the insured requests a policy for a term of less than one year. **Leg.H.** 1986 ch. 1321 §4.

§676.6. Commercial umbrella liability, commercial excess liability, and commercial excess property insurance policies; notice of cancellation or nonrenewal.

(a) This section applies to commercial umbrella liability insurance policies, commercial excess liability insurance policies, and commercial excess property insurance policies.

(b) As used in this section:

(1) "Umbrella liability insurance policy" means an insurance policy providing liability coverage per person or per occurrence or per claim, when written over one or more underlying liability policies or over a specified amount of self-insured retention.

(2) "Excess liability insurance policy" means an insurance policy providing liability covrage per person or per occurrence or per claim when written over one or more underlying liability policies. Excess liability policies shall include policies written over umbrella liability policies.

(3) "Excess property insurance policy" means a policy providing property coverage per occurrence or per location when written over one or more underlying property insurance policies or a specified amount of self-insured retention.

(c) After a policy defined in subdivision (b) of this section has been in effect for more than 60 days, or if the policy is a renewal, effective immediately, no notice of cancellation shall be effective unless it complies with Section 677.2, is based on one or more of the grounds set forth in subdivision (b) of Section 676.2, or is based on one or more of the following:

(1) A material change in limits, type or scope of coverage, or exclusions in one or more of the underlying policies.

(2) Cancellation or nonrenewal of one or more of the underlying policies where such policies are not replaced without lapse.

(3) A reduction in financial rating or grade of one or more insurers, insuring one or more underlying policies based on an evaluation obtained from a recognized financial rating organization.

(d) A notice of nonrenewal shall not be required in any of the following situations:

(1) The transfer of, or renewal of, a policy without a change in its terms or conditions or the rate on which the premium is based between insurers which are members of the same insurance group.

(2) The policy has been extended for 90 days or less, if the notice required in subdivision (c) has been given prior to the extension.

(3) The named insured has obtained replacement coverage or has agreed, in writing, within 60 days of the termination of the policy, to obtain that coverage.

(4) The policy is for a period of no more than 60 days and the insured is notified at the time of issuance that it may not be renewed.

(5) The named insured requests a change in the terms or conditions or risks covered by the policy within 60 days prior to the end of the policy period.

(6) The insurer has made a written offer to the insured, within the time period specified in subdivision (c), to renew the policy under changed terms or conditions or at a changed premium rate. As used herein, "terms or conditions" includes, but is not limited to, a reduction in limits, elimination of coverages, or an increase in deductibles. **Leg.H.** 1988 ch. 1618 §3.

§676.7. Applicant or policyholder engaged in foster home activities.

(a) No admitted insurer, licensed to issue and issuing homeowner's or tenant's policies, as described in Section 122, shall (1) fail or refuse to accept an application for that insurance or to issue that insurance to an applicant or (2) cancel that insurance, solely on the basis that the applicant or policyholder is engaged in foster home activities in a licensed foster family home or licensed small family home, as defined in Section 1502 of the Health and Safety Code, or an approved resource family, as defined in Section 16519.5 of the Welfare and Institutions Code.

(b) Coverage under policies described in subdivision (a) with respect to a foster child shall be the same as that provided for a natural child. However, unless specifically provided in the policy, there shall be no coverage expressly provided in the policy for any bodily injury arising out of the operation or use of any motor vehicle, aircraft, or watercraft owned or operated by, or rented or loaned to, any foster parent.

(c) It is against public policy for a policy of homeowner's or tenant's insurance subject to this section to provide liability coverage for any of the following losses:

(1) Claims of a foster child, or a parent, guardian, or guardian ad litem thereof, of a type payable by the Foster Family Home and Small Family Home Insurance Fund established by Section 1527.1 of the Health and Safety Code, regardless of whether the claim is within the limits of coverage specified in Section 1527.4 of the Health and Safety Code.

(2) An insurer shall not be liable, under a policy of insurance subject to this section, to any governmental agency for damage arising from occurrences peculiar to the foster-care relationship and the provision of foster-care services.

(3) Alienation of affection of a foster child.

(4) Any loss arising out of licentious, immoral, or sexual behavior on the part of a foster parent intended to lead to, or culminating in, any sexual act.

(5) Any loss arising out of a dishonest, fraudulent, criminal, or intentional act.

(d) There shall be no penalty for violations of this section prior to January 1, 1987.

(e) Insurers may provide a special endorsement to a homeowners' or tenants' policy covering claims related to foster care that are not excluded by subdivision (c).

(f) Insurers may provide by a separate policy for some or all of the claims related to foster care that are excluded by subdivision (c). **Leg.H.** 1986 ch. 1330 §4, effective September 29, 1986, as §676.2, 1988 ch. 195 §3, effective June 16, 1988, 1990 ch. 216 §85 (renumbered), 2016 ch. 612 (AB 1997) §56.

2016 Note: (a) The State Department of Social Services and the State Department of Health Care Services shall adopt regulations as required to implement this act and Chapter 773 of the Statutes of 2015.

(b) Notwithstanding the rulemaking provisions of the Administrative Procedure Act (Chapter 3.5 (commencing with Section 11340) of Part 1 of Division 3 of Title 2 of the Government Code), the State Department of Social Services and the State Department of Health Care Services may implement and administer the changes made by this act through all-county letters or similar written instructions until regulations are adopted. Stats. 2016 ch. 612 (AB 1997) §131.

§676.75. Prohibited acts related to foster home activities; coverage against public policy.

(a) No admitted insurer, licensed to issue and issuing homeowner's or tenant's policies, as described in Section 122, shall (1) fail or refuse to accept an application for that insurance or to issue that insurance to an applicant or (2) cancel that insurance, solely on the basis that the applicant or policyholder is engaged in foster home activities in a certified family home, as defined in Section 1506 of the Health and Safety Code.

(b) Coverage under policies described in subdivision (a) with respect to a foster child shall be the same as that provided for a natural child. However, unless specifically provided in the policy, there shall be no coverage expressly provided in the policy for any bodily injury arising out of the operation or use of any motor vehicle, aircraft, or watercraft owned or operated by, or rented or loaned to, any foster parent.

(c) It is against public policy for a policy of homeowner's or tenant's insurance subject to this section to provide liability coverage for any of the following losses:

(1) An insurer shall not be liable, under a policy of insurance subject to this section, to any governmental agency for damage arising from occurrences peculiar to the foster care relationship and the provision of foster care services.

(2) Alienation of affection of a foster child.

(3) Any loss arising out of licentious, immoral, or sexual behavior on the part of a foster parent intended to lead to, or culminating in, any sexual act.

(4) Any loss arising out of a dishonest, fraudulent, criminal, or intentional act.

(d) There shall be no penalty for violations of this section prior to January 1, 2013.

(e) Insurers may provide a special endorsement to a homeowner's or tenant's policy covering claims related to foster care that are not excluded by subdivision (c).

(f) Insurers may provide by a separate policy for some or all of the claims related to foster care that are excluded by subdivision (c). **Leg.H.** 2012 ch. 642 (AB 2019) §3, 2013 ch. 76 (AB 383) §133.

§676.8. Workers' compensation insurance policies.

(a) This section applies only to policies of workers' compensation insurance.

(b) After a policy is in effect, no notice of cancellation shall be effective unless it complies with the notice requirements of this section and is based upon the occurrence, after the effective date of the policy, of one or more of the following:

(1) The policyholder's failure to make any workers' compensation insurance premium payment when due.

(2) The policyholder's failure to report payroll, to permit the insurer to audit payroll as required by the terms of the policy or of a previous policy issued by the insurer, or to pay any additional premium as a result of a audit of payroll as required by the terms of the policy or of a previous policy.

(3) The policyholder's material failure to comply with federal or state safety orders or written recommendations of the insurer's designated loss control representative.

(4) A material change in ownership or any change in the policyholder's business or operations that materially increases the hazard for frequency or severity of loss, requires additional or different classifications for premium calculations, or contemplates an activity excluded by the insurer's reinsurance treaties.

(5) Material misrepresentation by the policyholder or its agent.

(6) Failure to cooperate with the insurer in the insurer's investigation of a claim.

(c) A policy shall not be canceled for the conditions specified in paragraph (1), (2), (5), or (6) of subdivision (b) except upon 10 days' written notice to the policyholder by the insurer. A policy shall not be canceled for the conditions specified in paragraph (3) or (4) of subdivision (b) except upon 30 days' written notice to the policyholder by the insurer, provided that no notice is required if an insured and insurer consent to the cancellation and reissuance of a policy effective upon a material change in ownership or operations of the insured. If the policyholder remedies the condition to the insurer's satisfaction within the specified time period, the policy shall not be canceled by the insurer.

(d) Nothing in this section shall preclude, while policies are in force, changes in the premium rate required or authorized by law, regulation, or order of the commissioner, or otherwise agreed to between the policyholder and insurer.

(e) Any policy written for a term longer than one year, or any policy with no fixed expiration date, shall be considered as if written for successive policy periods of one year. **Leg.H.** 1993 ch. 121 (AB 110) §2, effective July 16, 1993, 1993 ch. 1242 (SB 223) §1.

Ref.: Hanna § 2.61[2]; Herlick Handbook § 3.15.

§676.9. Discrimination against domestic violence victims; nature and use of information about domestic violence victims.

(a) This section applies to policies covered by Sections 675 and 675.5.

(b) No insurer issuing policies subject to this section shall deny or refuse to accept an application, refuse to insure, refuse to renew, cancel, restrict, or otherwise terminate, or charge a different rate for the same coverage, on the basis that the applicant or insured person is, has been, or may be, a victim of domestic violence.

(c) Nothing in this section shall prevent an insurer subject to this section from taking any of the actions set forth in subdivision (b) on the basis of criteria not otherwise made invalid by this section or any other act, regulation, or rule of law. If discrimination by an insurer is not in violation of this section but is based on any other criteria that are allowable by law, the fact that the applicant or insured is, has been, or may be the subject of domestic violence shall be irrelevant.

(d) For purposes of this section, information that indicates that a person is, has been, or may be a victim of domestic violence is personal information within the meaning of Article 6.6 (commencing with Section 791) of Chapter 1 of Part 2.

(e) No insurer that issues policies subject to this section, and no person employed by or under contract with an insurer that issues policies subject to this section, shall request any information the insurer or person knows or reasonably should know relates to acts of domestic violence or an applicant's or insured's status as a victim of domestic violence, or make use of this information however obtained, except for the limited purpose of complying with legal obligations, verifying a person's claim to be a subject of domestic violence, or cooperating with a victim of domestic violence in seeking protection from domestic violence or facilitating the treatment of a domestic violence-related medical condition. This subdivision does not prohibit an insurer from asking an applicant or insured about a property and casualty claim, even if the claim is related to domestic violence, or from using information thereby obtained in evaluating and carrying out its rights and duties under the policy, to the extent otherwise permitted by this section and other applicable law.

(f) As used in this section, "domestic violence" means domestic violence as defined in Section 6211 of the Family Code. **Leg.H.** 1997 ch. 845 (AB 588) §1.

§676.10. Applicability of section; cancellation or nonrenewal due to hate crime or anti-reproductive-rights crime losses; "hate crime" and "anti-reproductive-rights crime"; reporting procedures; violation.

(a) This section applies to policies covered by Section 675, 675.5, or 676.5 if the insured is a religious organization described in clause (i) of subparagraph (A) of paragraph (1) of subsection (b) of Section 170 of Title 26 of the United States Code, an educational organization described in clause (ii) of subparagraph (A) of paragraph (1) of subsection (b) of Section 170 of Title 26 of the United States Code, or other nonprofit organization described in clause (vi) of subparagraph (A) of paragraph (1) of subsection (b) of Section 170 of Title 26 of the United States Code that is organized and operated for religious, charitable, or educational purposes, or a reproductive health services facility, as defined in subdivision (h) of Section 423.1 of the Penal Code, or its administrative offices.

(b) No insurer issuing policies subject to this section shall cancel or refuse to renew the policy, nor shall any premium be excessive or unfairly discriminatory solely on the basis that one or more claims has been made against the policy during the preceding 60 months for a loss that is the result of a hate crime committed against the person or property of the insured, or an antireproductive rights crime.

(c) As it relates to this section, if determined by a law enforcement agency, a "hate crime" may include any of the following:

(1) By force or threat of force, willfully injure, intimidate, interfere with, oppress, or threaten any other person in the free exercise or enjoyment of any right or privilege secured to him or her by the Constitution or laws of this state or by the Constitution or laws of the United States because of the other person's race, color, religion, ancestry, national origin, disability, gender, gender identity, gender expression, or sexual orientation, or because he or she perceives that the other person has one or more of those characteristics. However, the foregoing offense does not include speech alone, except upon a showing that the speech itself threatened violence against a specific person or group of persons and that the defendant had the apparent ability to carry out the threat.

(2) Knowingly deface, damage, or destroy the real or personal property of any other person for the purpose of intimidating or interfering with the free exercise or enjoyment of any right or privilege secured to the other person by the Constitution or laws of this state or by the Constitution or laws of the United States, because of the other person's race, color, religion, ancestry, national origin, disability, gender, gender identity, gender expression, or sexual orientation, or because he or she perceives that the other person has one or more of those characteristics.

(d) As it relates to this section, if determined by a law enforcement agency, "anti-reproductive-rights crime" shall have the meaning set forth in subdivision (a) of Section 13776 of the Penal Code, and shall also include a violation of subdivision (e) of Section 423.2 of the Penal Code, if the crime results in a covered loss under a policy subject to this section.

(e) Upon cancellation of or refusal to renew a policy subject to this section after an insured has submitted a claim to the insurer that is the result of a hate crime committed against the person or property of the insured, or an anti-reproductive-rights crime, the insurer shall report the cancellation or nonrenewal to the commissioner.

(f) A violation of this section shall be an unfair practice subject to Article 6.5 (commencing with Section 790) of Chapter 1 of Division 2.

(g) Nothing in this section shall prevent an insurer subject to this section from taking any of the actions set forth in subdivision (b) on the basis of criteria not otherwise made invalid by this section or any other act, regulation, or law. **Leg.H.** 2001 ch. 253 (AB 1193) §1, 2003 ch. 647 (AB 996), 2011 ch. 719 (AB 887) §25.

2011 Note: In subdivision (b), "antireproductive rights crime" appears as enacted. It is the Publisher's belief that the Legislature intended the phrase to read "anti-reproductive-rights crime."

§677. Notice of cancellation.

(a) All notices of cancellation shall be in writing, mailed to the named insured at the address shown in the policy, or to the insured's last known address, and shall state, with respect to policies in effect after the time limits specified in Section 676, all of the following:

(1) Which of the grounds set forth in Section 676 is relied upon.

(2) In accordance with the requirements of subdivisions (a) and (e) of Section 791.10, the specific information supporting the cancellation, the specific items of personal and privileged information that support those reasons, if applicable, and corresponding summary of rights.

(3) On or after July 1, 2020, a notification that if the policyholder believes the policy has been wrongfully canceled, the policyholder may have the matter reviewed by the department. The notification shall include the department's internet website, www.insurance.ca.gov, the department's telephone number, 1-800-927-HELP (4357), and the mailing address of the department's Consumer Services Division, 300 South Spring Street, Los Angeles, CA 90013.

(b) For purposes of this section, a lienholder's copy of those notices shall be deemed mailed if, with the lienholder's consent, it is delivered by electronic transmittal, facsimile, or personal delivery. **Leg.H.** 1970 ch. 313 §1, 1972 ch. 237 §1, 1987 ch. 800 §2, 2004 chs. 939 (AB 1979), 940 (AB 2693), 2006 ch. 740 (AB 2125) §3, 2019 ch. 201 (AB 1813) §1.

§677.2. Notice of cancellation for commercial insurance policies.

(a) This section applies only to policies covered by Section 675.5.

(b) A notice of cancellation shall be in writing and shall be delivered or mailed to the producer of record, provided that the producer of record is not an employee of the insurer, and to the named insured at the mailing address shown on the policy. Subdivision (a) of Section 1013 of the Code of Civil Procedure is applicable if the notice is mailed.

The notice of cancellation shall include the effective date of the cancellation and the reasons for the cancellation.

(c) The notice of cancellation shall be given at least 30 days prior to the effective date of the cancellation, except that in the case of cancellation for nonpayment of premiums or for fraud the notice shall be given no less than 10 days prior to the effective date of the cancellation. Notice of a proposed cancellation pursuant to subdivision (d) of Section 676.2 given prior to a finding of the commissioner shall satisfy the requirements of this section if it is given no less than 30 days prior to the effective date of the cancellation and if it states that cancellation will be effective only upon the approval of the commissioner.

(d) This section applies only to cancellations pursuant to Section 676.2. **Leg.H.** 1986 ch. 1321 §5.

§677.4. Notice of cancellation for certain property insurance policies.

A notice of cancellation with respect to a policy covered under Section 675 shall be delivered at least 20 calendar days prior to the effective date of the cancellation, except that in the case of a cancellation for nonpayment of premiums, or for fraud, the notice shall be given at least 10 calendar days prior to the effective date of the cancellation. Subdivision (a) of Section 1013 of the Code of Civil Procedure is applicable if the notice is mailed. **Leg.H.** 2003 ch. 148 (AB 1727).

§678. Notice of nonrenewal.

(a) At least 45 days before **the** policy expiration, an insurer shall deliver to the named insured or mail to the named insured at the address shown in the policy, either of the following:

(1) An offer of renewal of the policy contingent upon payment of premium as stated in the offer, stating each of the following:

(A) Any reduction of limits or elimination of coverage. **That reduction of limits or elimination of coverage shall identify the specific limits being reduced or coverage being eliminated by the offer of renewal. The elimination of coverage for the previously covered peril of fire shall be subject to subdivision (b) of Section 10103.6.**

(B) The telephone number of the insurer's representatives who handle consumer inquiries or complaints. The telephone number shall be displayed prominently in a font size consistent with the other text of the renewal offer.

(2) A notice of nonrenewal of the policy. That notice shall contain all of the following:

(A) The **specific** reason or reasons for the nonrenewal.

(B) The telephone number of the insurer's representatives who handle consumer inquiries or complaints. The telephone number shall be displayed prominently in a font size consistent with the other text of the notice of nonrenewal.

(C) Until July 1, 2020, a brief statement indicating that if the consumer has contacted the insurer to discuss the nonrenewal and remains unsatisfied, the consumer may have the matter reviewed by the department. The statement shall include the telephone number of the unit within the department that responds to consumer inquiries and complaints.

(D) On or after July 1, 2020, a statement that if the consumer has contacted the insurer to discuss the nonrenewal and remains unsatisfied, the consumer may have the matter reviewed by the department. The statement shall include the department's internet website, www.insurance.ca.gov, the department's telephone number, (800) 927-HELP (4357), and the mailing address of the department's Consumer Services Division, 300 S. Spring Street, Los Angeles, CA 90013.

(b) If an insurer fails to give the named insured either an offer of renewal or notice of nonrenewal as required by this section, the existing policy, with no change in its terms and conditions, shall remain in effect for 45 days from the date that either the offer to renew or the notice of nonrenewal is delivered or mailed to the named insured. A notice to this effect shall be provided by the insurer to the named insured with the policy or the notice of renewal or nonrenewal.

(c) Notwithstanding subdivisions (a) and (b), with respect to a notice of nonrenewal for a policy that expires on or after July 1, 2020, the following timelines apply:

(1) At least 75 days [1] **before** the policy expiration, the insurer shall deliver the notice of nonrenewal to the named insured or mail the notice of nonrenewal to the named insured at the address shown in the policy. The notice shall include the information contained in paragraph (2) of subdivision (a).

(2) If an insurer fails to give the named insured a notice of nonrenewal at least 75 days [2] **before** the policy expiration, as required by paragraph (1), the existing policy, with no change in its terms and conditions, shall remain in effect for 75 days from the date that the notice of nonrenewal is delivered or mailed to the named insured. A notice to this effect shall be provided by the insurer to the named insured with the notice of nonrenewal.

(d) A policy written for a term of less than one year shall be considered as if written for a term of one year. A policy written for a term longer than one year, or a policy with no fixed expiration date, shall be considered as if written for successive policy periods or terms of one year.

(e) **A notice of nonrenewal for a residential property insurance policy expiring on or after July 1, 2021, shall be accompanied by the following notice:**

The California Department of Insurance has developed the California Home Insurance Finder, an online tool that can assist you in obtaining insurance for your home. The Finder contains names, addresses, telephone numbers, and internet website links of licensed insurance agents, brokers, and insurance companies that may be able to sell insurance to you. The Finder is organized by ZIP Code and the languages in which the agent, broker, or insurance company sells insurance.

The California FAIR Plan (FAIR Plan) provides basic property insurance as the "insurer of last resort" if you cannot find insurance coverage for your property in the normal (voluntary) insurance market. The FAIR Plan provides basic property insurance coverage for residential structures, as well as personal property coverage for residential and business occupancies. However, FAIR Plan policies may not cover liability, theft, or water damage, among other things. There are also optional coverages available for both residential properties. Applications can be made directly with the FAIR Plan (cfpnet.com), although the FAIR Plan strongly encourages use of a licensed agent or broker for assistance in preparing and obtaining a quote. There is no additional cost for using an agent or broker for purchasing a FAIR Plan policy.

California law requires an agent or broker to assist a person seeking a FAIR Plan policy by (1) submitting a coverage application to the FAIR Plan on behalf of the consumer, (2) providing the consumer the FAIR Plan's internet website address and toll-free telephone number, or (3) obtaining a policy for the consumer through an admitted or nonadmitted insurer.

To supplement a FAIR Plan policy, a Difference in Conditions (DIC) policy should be considered. A DIC policy is sold by some private insurers, and provides coverage for things not covered by the basic property insurance policy provided by the FAIR Plan. A consumer who wants broader coverage than that provided by the FAIR Plan policy should contact an agent, broker, or insurance company that offers a DIC policy to obtain this additional coverage. The Department of Insurance maintains a list of insurance companies that sell DIC policies on its internet website (insurance.ca.gov). Additional assistance may be obtained by contacting an agent or broker listed with the department's online agent locator.

(f) An insurer may use a notice substantially similar to the notice set forth in subdivision (e) to the extent that the notice provides additional or more detailed information.

(g) This section applies only to policies of insurance specified in Section 675. **Leg.H.** 2013 ch. 369 (SB 251) §9, 2019 chs. 201 (AB 1813) §2, 833 (AB 1816) §1, effective October 12, 2019, 2020 chs. 258 (AB 3012) §1, 263 (AB 2756) §1.5.

§678. 2020 Deletes. [1] prior to **[2]** prior to

Ref.: Hanna § 2.61[2].

PART 2
The Business of Insurance

CHAPTER 1
GENERAL REGULATIONS

ARTICLE 3
Certificate of Authority
[Selected Provisions]

§703.5. Advertising of qualifications to advise employers—Penalty.

Any person, including, but not limited to, persons licensed or certificated under this code or exempted from regulation under this code, who as a part of any business advertises as, or holds himself or herself out as, qualified to advise the public concerning insurance or qualified to administer workers' compensation for employers and who in connection with or as part of that business also, with or without consideration, (a) suggests or recommends to an employer, or advises an employer, that the employer purchase aggregate excess or aggregate stop-loss workers' compensation insurance, or (b) names or suggests to an employer, or advises an employer of, a nonadmitted insurer from whom aggregate excess or aggregate stop-loss workers' compensation insurance might be purchased, is guilty of a misdemeanor. This section does not apply if the employer is a self-insured public entity, including any agency, board, or commission provided for by a joint exercise of powers agreement, or those who have been issued a certificate by the Director of the Department of Industrial Relations to self-insure. **Leg.H.** 1992 ch. 378.

Ref.: Herlick Handbook §§ 3.16, 3.22.

ARTICLE 4
Examination by Commissioner
[Selected Provisions]

§738. Authority of commissioner to examine State Compensation Insurance Fund.

The commissioner shall have the same powers and authority to examine the State Compensation Insurance Fund as are conferred upon him by law relative to the examination of other insurers except where the fund is specifically exempted by reference. **Leg.H.** 2006 ch. 740 (AB 2125) §3.3.

ARTICLE 5.1
Unlawful Practices
[Selected Provisions]

§756. Misrepresentation of payroll; penalty.

When the premium on a policy insuring an employer is based upon the amount or segregation of the employer's payroll, and the employer, personally or knowingly through his or her employee, procures a lower premium by willfully misrepresenting the amount or segregation, that misrepresentation is an unlawful act as to the employer.

In addition to any penalty provided by law, the employer in that case is liable to the state in an amount 10 times the difference between the lower premium paid and the premium properly payable. The commissioner shall collect the amount so payable and may bring a civil action in his or her name as commissioner to enforce collection unless the misrepresentation is made to, and the lower premium procured from the State Compensation Insurance Fund. In the latter case the liability to the state under this section shall be enforced in a civil action in the name of the State Compensation Insurance Fund and any amount so collected shall become a part of that fund.

Ref.: Herlick Handbook §§ 3.2, 3.15.

§757. Insurer's acceptance of false payroll information.

When a statement of the amount or segregation of a payroll is materially false, and an insurer, through a person employed by it in a managerial capacity, accepts the statement as the basis for the premium on a policy, the acceptance is an unlawful act if the accepting employee knows of the falsity.

ARTICLE 10
Financial Statements of Insurers
[Selected Provisions]

§923.5. Required reserves.

Each insurer transacting business in this state shall at all times maintain reserves in an amount estimated in the aggregate to provide for the payment of all losses and claims for which the insurer may be liable, and to provide for the expense of adjustment or settlement of losses and claims.

The reserves shall be computed in accordance with regulations made from time to time by the commissioner. The promulgation of the regulations by the commissioner, or any changes thereto or amendments thereof, shall be in accordance with the procedure provided in Chapter 3.5 (commencing with Section 11340) of Part 1 of Division 3 of Title 2 of the Government Code. The commissioner shall make the regulations upon reasonable consideration of the ascertained experience and the character of such kinds of business for the purpose of adequately protecting the insured and securing the solvency of the insurer.

The commissioner may prescribe the manner and form of reporting pertinent information concerning the reserves provided for in this section.

This section shall not apply to life insurance, title insurance, disability insurance, mortgage insurance, or mortgage guaranty insurance. **Leg.H.** 2007 ch. 431 (SB 316) §1, 2010 ch. 61 (AB 2002) §1.

Ref.: Herlick Handbook §§ 3.2, 3.12, 12.13.

§923.6. Submission of statement of actuarial opinion; duties of property and casualty insurer; confidentiality of documents; exceptions.

(a) Every admitted property and casualty insurer, unless otherwise exempted by the domiciliary commissioner, shall annually submit the opinion of an Appointed Actuary entitled "Statement of Actuarial Opinion." This opinion shall be filed in accordance with the appropriate Property and Casualty Annual Statement Instructions of the National Association of Insurance Commissioners (NAIC).

(1) For purposes of this section, the term, "property and casualty insurer" means any admitted insurer writing insurance as described in Section 102, 103, 105, 107, 108, 109, 110, 111, 112, 113, 114, 115, 116, 118, 119, 119.6, 120, 124, or 124.5.

(2) For purposes of this section, the following terms have the same meaning as used in the Property and Casualty Annual Statement Instructions of the NAIC:

(A) Actuarial Opinion.

(B) Actuarial Opinion Summary.

(C) Actuarial Report.

(D) Appointed Actuary.

(E) Statement of Actuarial Opinion.

(F) Property and Casualty Annual Statement Instructions.

(3) The commissioner may adopt regulations related to the terms and conditions required by the Property and Casualty Annual Statement Instructions of the NAIC.

(b) Every property and casualty insurer domiciled in this state that is required to submit a Statement of Actuarial Opinion shall annually submit an Actuarial Opinion Summary, written by the insurer's Appointed Actuary. This Actuarial Opinion Summary shall be filed in accordance with the appropriate Property and Casualty Annual Statement Instructions of the NAIC and shall be considered as a document supporting the Actuarial Opinion required in subdivision (a).

(c) An admitted insurer not domiciled in this state shall provide the Actuarial Opinion Summary upon request of the commissioner.

(d) An Actuarial Report and underlying workpapers as required by the appropriate Property and Casualty Annual Statement Instructions of the NAIC shall be prepared to support each Actuarial Opinion. If an insurer fails to provide either a supporting Actuarial Report or workpapers at the request of the commissioner, or if the commissioner determines that the supporting Actuarial Report or workpapers provided by the insurer are otherwise unacceptable to the commissioner, the commissioner may engage a qualified actuary at the expense of the insurer to review the opinion and the basis for the opinion and prepare the supporting Actuarial Report or workpapers.

(e) Notwithstanding subdivision (d) of Section 6254 of the Government Code, subdivision (f), or any other provision of law, the Statement of Actuarial Opinion required by subdivision (a) shall be a public record and open to inspection.

(f)(1) Documents, materials, or other information in the possession or control of the commissioner that are considered an Actuarial Report, workpapers, or Actuarial Opinion Summary provided in support of the Statement of Actuarial Opinion, and any other material provided by the insurer to the commissioner in connection with the Actuarial Report, workpapers, or Actuarial Opinion Summary shall be confidential by law and privileged, shall not be made public by the commissioner or any other person and are exempt from the California Public Records Act (Chapter 3.5 (commencing with Section 6250) of Division 7 of Title 1 of the Government Code), shall not be subject to subpoena, and shall not be subject to discovery or admissible in evidence in any civil action brought by a private party.

(2) This subdivision shall not limit the commissioner's authority to release the documents, materials, and other information described in paragraph (1) to the American Academy of Actuaries' Actuarial Board for Counseling and Discipline (ABCD), or its successor, so long as those documents, materials, and other information are required for the purpose of professional disciplinary proceedings, and the ABCD establishes procedures satisfactory to the commissioner for preserving the confidentiality of the documents, nor shall this subdivision limit the commissioner's authority to use those documents, materials, or other information in furtherance of any regulatory or legal action brought as part of the commissioner's official duties.

(3) The commissioner may also exercise, with respect to the documents, materials, or other information described in paragraph (1), all the authority specified in subdivision (b) of Section 735.5, or any successor provision. **Leg.H.** 2011 ch. 426 (SB 712) §2, 2012 ch. 786 (AB 2303) §7.

2011 Note: The Legislature finds and declares that Section 2 of this act imposes a limitation on the public's right of access to the writings of public officials and agencies within the meaning of Section 3 of Article I of the California Constitution. Pursuant to that constitutional provision, the Legislature makes the following findings to demonstrate the interest protected by this limitation and the need for protecting that interest:

In order to protect proprietary information, it is necessary to enact legislation that the actuarial supporting documents provided pursuant to this act are kept confidential. Stats. 2011 ch. 426 (SB 712) §14.

ARTICLE 14.2
California Insurance Guarantee Association [Selected Provisions]

§1063. California Insurance Guarantee Association.

(a) Within 60 days after the original effective date of this article, all insurers, including reciprocal insurers, admitted to transact insurance in this state of any or all of the following classes only in accordance with the provisions of Chapter 1 (commencing with Section 100) of Part 1 of this division: fire (see Section 102), marine (see Section 103), plate glass (see Section 107), liability (see Section 108), workers' compensation (see Section 109), common carrier liability (see Section 110), boiler and machinery (see Section 111), burglary (see Section 112), sprinkler (see Section 114), team and vehicle (see Section 115), automobile (see Section 116), aircraft (see Section 118), and miscellaneous (see Section 120), shall establish the California Insurance Guarantee Association (the association); provided, however, this article shall not apply to the following classes or kinds of insurance: life and annuity (see Section 101), title (see Section 104), fidelity or surety including fidelity or surety bonds, or any other bonding obligations (see Section 105), disability or health (see Section 106), credit (see Section 113), mortgage guaranty, insolvency or legal (see Section 119), financial guaranty or other forms of insurance offering protection against investment risks (see Section 124), the ocean marine portion of any marine insurance or ocean marine coverage under any insurance policy including the following: the Jones Act (46 U.S.C. Sec. 688), the Longshore and Harbor Workers' Compensation Act (33 U.S.C. Sec. 901 et seq.), or any other similar federal statutory enactment, or any endorsement or policy affording protection and indemnity coverage, or reinsurance as defined in Section 620, or fraternal fire insurance written by associations organized and operating under Sections 9080 to 9103, inclusive. Any insurer admitted to transact only those classes or kinds of insurance excluded from this article shall not be a member insurer of the association. Each insurer admitted to transact a class of insurance included in this article, including the State Compensation Insurance Fund, as a condition of its authority to transact insurance in this state, shall participate in the association whether established voluntarily or by order of the commissioner after the elapse of 60 days following the original effective date of this article in accordance with rules to be established as provided in this article. It shall be the purpose of the association to provide for each member insurer insolvency insurance as defined in Section 119.5.

[Subsections (b)–(j) Not Reproduced]

Leg.H. 1994 ch. 6, effective February 10, 1994, 1996 ch. 252, 2001 ch. 296, effective September 12, 2001, 2002 ch. 431 (AB 2007), 2003 ch. 635 (AB 227), 2012 ch. 786 (AB 2303) §16.

Ref.: Hanna § 2.84; Herlick Handbook §§ 3.13, 8.23.

§1063.1. Definitions.

As used in this article:

(a) "Member insurer" means an insurer required to be a member of the association in accordance with subdivision (a) of Section 1063, except and to the extent that the insurer is participating in an insolvency program adopted by the United States government.

(b) "Insolvent insurer" means an insurer that was a member insurer of the association, consistent with paragraph (11) of subdivision (c), either at the time the policy was issued or when the insured event occurred, and against which an order of liquidation with a finding of insolvency has been entered by a court of competent jurisdiction, or, in the case of the State Compensation Insurance Fund, if a finding of insolvency is made by a duly enacted legislative measure.

(c)(1) "Covered claims" means the obligations of an insolvent insurer, including the obligation for unearned premiums, that satisfy all of the following requirements:

(A) Imposed by law and within the coverage of an insurance policy of the insolvent insurer.

(B) Which were unpaid by the insolvent insurer.

(C) Which are presented as a claim to the liquidator in the state of domicile of the insolvent insurer or to the association on or before the last date fixed for the filing of claims in the domiciliary liquidating proceedings.

(D) Which were incurred before the date coverage under the policy terminated and before, on, or within 30 days after the date the liquidator was appointed.

(E) For which the assets of the insolvent insurer are insufficient to discharge in full.

(F) In the case of a policy of workers' compensation insurance, to provide workers' compensation benefits under the workers' compensation law of this state **or under the workers' compensation law of any state if the injured worker is a resident of this state and not otherwise entitled to coverage from an organization similar to the association in any other state**.

(G) In the case of other classes of insurance if the claimant or insured is a resident of this state at the time of the insured occurrence, or the property from which the claim arises is permanently located in this state.

(2) "Covered claims" also includes the obligations assumed by an assuming insurer from a ceding insurer when the assuming insurer subsequently becomes an insolvent insurer if, at the time of the insolvency of the assuming insurer, the ceding insurer is no longer admitted to transact business in this state. Both the assuming insurer and the ceding insurer shall have been member insurers at the time the assumption was made. "Covered claims" under this paragraph shall satisfy the requirements of subparagraphs (A) to (G), inclusive, of paragraph (1), except for the requirement that the claims be against policies of the insolvent insurer. The association has a right to recover a deposit, bond, or other assets that may have been required to be posted by the ceding company to the extent of covered claim payments and shall be subrogated to any rights the policyholders may have against the ceding insurer.

(3) "Covered claims" does not include obligations arising from the following:

(A) Life, annuity, health, or disability insurance.

(B) Mortgage guaranty, financial guaranty, or other forms of insurance offering protection against investment risks.

(C) Fidelity or surety insurance including fidelity or surety bonds, or any other bonding obligations.

(D) Credit insurance.

(E) Title insurance.

(F) Ocean marine insurance or ocean marine coverage under an insurance policy, including claims arising from the following: the Jones Act (46 U.S.C. Secs. 30104 and 30105), the Longshore and Harbor Workers' Compensation Act (33 U.S.C. Sec. 901 et seq.), or any other similar federal statutory enactment, or an endorsement or policy affording protection and indemnity coverage.

(G) A claims servicing agreement or insurance policy providing retroactive insurance of a known loss or losses, except a special excess workers' compensation policy issued pursuant to subdivision (c) of Section 3702.8 of the Labor Code that covers all or any part of workers' compensation liabilities of an employer that is issued, or was previously issued, a certificate of consent to self-insure pursuant to subdivision (b) of Section 3700 of the Labor Code.

(4) "Covered claims" does not include an obligation of the insolvent insurer arising out of a reinsurance contract, an obligation incurred after the expiration date of the insurance policy or after the insurance policy has been replaced by the insured, canceled at the insured's request, or canceled by the liquidator, or an obligation to a state or to the federal government. **If the individual has a covered claim that includes medical services provided by a medical facility owned in whole or in part by a state or federal agency, the association may pay that claim directly to the facility, as long as the services provided otherwise qualify as a covered claim and the claim is owned by the medical facility asserting the claim.**

(5)(A) "Covered claims" does not include an obligation to insurers, insurance pools, or underwriting associations, nor their claims for contribution, indemnity, or subrogation, equitable or otherwise, except as otherwise provided in this chapter.

(B) An insurer, insurance pool, or underwriting association may not maintain, in its own name or in the name of its insured, a claim or legal action against the insured of the insolvent insurer for contribution, indemnity, or by way of subrogation, except insofar as, and to the extent only, that the claim exceeds the policy limits of the insolvent insurer's policy. In those claims or legal actions, the insured of the insolvent insurer is entitled to a credit or setoff in the amount of the policy limits of the insolvent insurer's policy, or in the amount of the limits remaining, when those limits have been diminished by the payment of other claims.

(6) "Covered claims," except in cases involving a claim for workers' compensation benefits or for unearned premiums, does not include a claim in an amount of one hundred dollars ($100) or less or the portion of a claim that is in excess of the applicable limits provided in the insurance policy issued by the insolvent insurer.

(7)(A) "Covered claims" does not include that portion of a claim, other than a claim for workers' compensation benefits, that is in excess of five hundred thousand dollars ($500,000).

(B) For purposes of subparagraph (A), with respect to a policy of residential property insurance, each claim for a loss under a different coverage category shall be considered a separate covered claim.

(C) Notwithstanding subparagraph (A), a claim for damage to, or loss of, a dwelling structure under a policy of residential property insurance shall not exceed one million dollars ($1,000,000) or the amount recoverable under the policy, whichever is less.

(8) "Covered claims" does not include an amount awarded as punitive or exemplary damages, or an amount awarded by the Workers' Compensation Appeals Board pursuant to Section 5814 or 5814.5 of the Labor Code because payment of compensation was unreasonably delayed or refused by the insolvent insurer.

(9) "Covered claims" does not include either of the following:

(A) A claim to the extent it is covered by any other insurance of a class covered by this article available to the claimant or insured.

(B) A claim by a person other than the original claimant under the insurance policy in the claimant's own name, the claimant's assignee as the person entitled thereto under a premium finance agreement as defined in Section 673 and entered into before insolvency, or the claimant's executor, administrator, guardian, or other personal representative or trustee in bankruptcy, and does not include a claim asserted by an assignee or one claiming by right of subrogation, except as otherwise provided in this chapter.

(10) "Covered claims" does not include an obligation arising out of the issuance of an insurance policy written by the separate division of the State Compensation Insurance Fund pursuant to Sections 11802 and 11803.

(11) "Covered claims" does not include an obligation of the insolvent insurer arising from a policy or contract of insurance issued or renewed before the insolvent insurer's admission to transact insurance in the State of California.

(12) "Covered claims" does not include surplus deposits of subscribers as defined in Section 1374.1.

(13) "Covered claims" shall also include an obligation arising under an insurance policy written to indemnify a permissibly self-insured employer pursuant to subdivision (b) or (c) of Section 3700 of the Labor Code for its liability to pay workers' compensation benefits in excess of a specific or aggregate retention. However, for purposes of this article, those claims shall not be considered workers' compensation claims and therefore are subject to the per-claim limit in paragraph (7), and any payments and expenses related thereto shall be allocated to category (c) for claims other than workers' compensation, [1] **homeowners'**, and automobile, as provided in Section 1063.5.

These provisions shall apply to obligations arising under a policy as described herein issued to a permissibly self-insured employer or group of self-insured employers pursuant to Section 3700 of the Labor Code and notwithstanding any other provision of this code, those obligations shall be governed by this provision in the event that the Self-Insurers' Security Fund is ordered to assume the liabilities of a permissibly self-insured employer or group of self-insured employers pursuant to Section 3701.5 of the Labor Code. This paragraph applies only to insurance policies written to indemnify a permissibly self-insured employer or group of self-insured employers under subdivision (b) or (c) of Section 3700 of the Labor Code, for its liability to pay workers' compensation benefits in excess of a specific or aggregate retention, and this paragraph does not apply to special excess workers' compensation insurance policies unless issued pursuant to authority granted in subdivision (c) of Section 3702.8 of the Labor Code, and as provided for in subparagraph (G) of paragraph (3). In addition, this paragraph does not apply to a claims servicing agreement or insurance policy providing retroactive insurance of a known loss or losses as are excluded in subparagraph (G) of paragraph (3).

A permissibly self-insured employer or group of self-insured employers, or the Self-Insurers' Security Fund, shall, to the extent required by the Labor Code, be responsible for paying, adjusting, and defending each claim arising under policies of insurance covered under this section, unless the benefits paid on a claim exceed the specific or aggregate retention, in which case:

(A) If the benefits paid on the claim exceed the specific or aggregate retention, and the policy requires the insurer to defend and adjust the claim, the [2] **association** shall be solely responsible for adjusting and defending the claim, and shall make all payments due under the claim, subject to the limitations and exclusions of this article with regard to covered claims. As to each claim subject to this paragraph, notwithstanding any other provisions of this code or the Labor Code, and regardless of whether the amount paid by CIGA is adequate to discharge a claim obligation, neither the self-insured employer, group of self-insured employers, nor the Self-Insurers' Security Fund shall have an obligation to pay benefits over and above the specific or aggregate retention, except as provided in this subdivision.

(B) If the benefits paid on the claim exceed the specific or aggregate retention, and the policy does not require the insurer to defend and adjust the claim, the permissibly self-insured employer or group of self-insured employers, or the Self-Insurers' Security Fund, shall not have any further payment obligations with respect to the claim, but shall continue defending and adjusting the claim, and shall have the right, but not the obligation, in a proceeding to assert all applicable statutory limitations and exclusions as contained in this article with regard to the covered claim. CIGA shall have the right, but not the obligation, to intervene in a proceeding in which the self-insured employer, group of self-insured employers, or the Self-Insurers' Security Fund is defending a claim and shall be permitted to raise the appropriate statutory limitations and exclusions as contained in this article with respect to covered claims. Regardless of whether the self-insured employer or group of self-insured employers, or the Self-Insurers' Security Fund, asserts the applicable statutory limitations and exclusions, or whether CIGA intervenes in a proceeding, CIGA shall be solely responsible for paying all benefits due on the claim, subject to the exclusions and limitations of this article with respect to covered claims. As to each claim subject to this paragraph, notwithstanding any other provision of this code or the Labor Code and regardless of whether the amount paid by CIGA is adequate to discharge a claim obligation, neither the self-insured employer, group of self-insured employers, nor the Self-Insurers' Security Fund, shall have an obligation to pay benefits over and above the specific or aggregate retention, except as provided in this subdivision.

(C) In the event that the benefits paid on the covered claim exceed the per-claim limit in paragraph (7), the responsibility for paying, adjusting, and defending the claim shall be returned to the permissibly self-insured employer or group of employers, or the Self-Insurers' Security Fund.

These provisions shall apply to all pending and future insolvencies. For purposes of this paragraph, a pending insolvency is one involving a company that is currently receiving benefits from the guarantee association.

(14) Notwithstanding any other provision in this section or Section 1063, if an insurance policy has been allocated to or assumed by a company that did not issue the policy pursuant to a state statute that provides for the division of an insurance company or the statutory assumption of designated policies by a new company, that statute provides a novation has been deemed to have occurred with respect to those policies, and that company is placed in liquidation, then to the extent a claim arising under that allocated or transferred policy would have been a covered claim had the original company been placed in liquidation before the statutory allocation or assumption, any claim arising under that same policy shall be a covered claim regardless of whether the company that allocated or assumed the policy was or was not a member at the time the policy was issued or when the insured event occurred.

(d) "Admitted to transact insurance in this state" means an insurer possessing a valid certificate of authority issued by the department.

(e) "Affiliate" means a person who directly or indirectly, through one or more intermediaries, controls, is controlled by, or is under common control with an insolvent insurer on December 31 of the year next preceding the date the insurer becomes an insolvent insurer.

(f) "Control" means the possession, direct or indirect, of the power to direct or cause the direction of the management and policies of a person, whether through the ownership of voting securities, by contract other than a commercial contract for goods or nonmanagement services, or otherwise, unless the power is the result of an official position with or corporate office held by the person. Control is presumed to exist if a person, directly or indirectly, owns, controls, holds with the power to vote, or holds proxies representing, 10 percent or more of the voting securities of any other person. This presumption may be rebutted by showing that control does not in fact exist.

(g) "Claimant" means an insured making a first party claim or a person instituting a liability claim. However, no person who is an affiliate of the insolvent insurer may be a claimant.

(h) **"Net direct written premiums" means the amount of direct written premiums in the annual financial statement on file with the commissioner, adjusted for any premiums written for any lines of insurance or types of coverages not covered by this article, plus premiums written in this state for coverage under a special excess workers' compensation policy.**

(i) "Ocean marine insurance" includes marine insurance as defined in Section 103, except for inland marine insurance, as well as any other form of insurance, regardless of the name, label, or marketing designation of the insurance policy, that insures against maritime perils or risks and other related perils or risks, that are usually insured against by traditional marine insurance such as hull and machinery, marine builders' risks, and marine protection and indemnity. Those perils and risks insured against include, without limitation, loss, damage, or expense or legal liability of the insured arising out of or incident to ownership, operation, chartering, maintenance, use, repair, or construction of a vessel, craft, or instrumentality in use in ocean or inland waterways, including liability of the insured for personal injury, illness, or death for loss or damage to the property of the insured or another person.

[3] **(j)** "Unearned premium" means that portion of a premium as calculated by the liquidator that had not been earned because of the cancellation of the insolvent insurer's policy and is that premium remaining for the unexpired term of the insolvent insurer's policy. "Unearned premium" does not include an amount sought as return of a premium under a policy providing retroactive insurance of a known loss or return of a premium under a retrospectively rated

policy or a policy subject to a contingent surcharge or a policy in which the final determination of the premium cost is computed after expiration of the policy and is calculated on the basis of actual loss experienced during the policy period. **Leg.H.** 1991 ch. 537, 1992 ch. 227, 1994 ch. 6, effective February 10, 1994, 1997 ch. 372 §1, ch. 497 §2.5, 1999 ch. 721, 2003 ch. 635 (AB 227), 2005 ch. 395 (AB 817) §1, 2006 ch. 740 (AB 2125) §4, 2007 ch. 100 (SB 1038) §2, 2008 chs. 80 (AB 3055) §1, 179 (SB 1498) §166 (ch. 80 prevails; ch. 179 not effective), 2009 ch. 140 (AB 1164) §127, 2010 chs. 140 (AB 2781) §1, 328 (SB 1330) §142 (ch. 140 prevails; ch. 328 not effective), 2012 ch. 57 (AB 2301) §1, 2013 ch. 76 (AB 383) §135, 2019 ch. 833 (AB 1816) §2, effective October 12, 2019, 2020 ch. 258 (AB 3012) §2.

§1063.1. 2020 Deletes. [1] homeowners **[2]** California Insurance Guarantee Association (CIGA) **[3]** (i)

Ref.: Hanna § 2.84; Herlick Handbook § 3.13.

§1063.2. Association's duties; authority; exceptions to "covered claims."

(a) The association shall pay and discharge covered claims and, in connection therewith, pay for or furnish loss adjustment services and defenses of claimants when required by policy provisions. It may do so either directly by itself or through a servicing facility or through a contract for reinsurance and assumption of liabilities by one or more member insurers or through a contract with the liquidator, upon terms satisfactory to the association and to the liquidator, under which payments on covered claims would be made by the liquidator using funds provided by the association. Alternatively, the association may, with the express approval of the commissioner, reinsure with, or transfer liabilities to, a California admitted and authorized reinsurer or other reinsurer approved by the commissioner to limit or eliminate adverse development, to stabilize or limit the need for assessments, or to reduce its potential ultimate liability for covered claims, provided the association retains the ultimate responsibility to the policyholder or beneficiary for payment of claims covered by the reinsurance agreement. A reinsurance agreement or transfer of liabilities shall be paid for using the association's available funds from one of its accounts and shall not be charged to administrative expense or allocated to any liquidation estate. The payment and discharge of covered claims shall be undertaken by the association, either directly or through an authorized third-party administrator. Recoveries from a reinsurance agreement or transfer of liabilities shall solely be the property of the association, shall not inure to the benefit of any liquidation estate, and shall be paid to the association account from which the payment for the reinsurance or transfer of liabilities was made.

(b)(1) The association shall be a party in interest in all proceedings involving a covered claim, and shall have the same rights as the insolvent insurer would have had if not in liquidation, including, but not limited to, the right to all of the following:

(A) Appear, defend, and appeal a claim in a court of competent jurisdiction.

(B) Receive notice of, investigate, adjust, compromise, settle, and pay a covered claim.

(C) Investigate, handle, and deny a noncovered claim.

(2) The association shall have no cause of action against the insureds of the insolvent insurer for any sums it has paid out, except as provided by this article.

(3) Paragraph (2) does not limit the association's right to pursue unpaid reimbursements owed by an employer pursuant to a workers' compensation insurance policy with a deductible if the employer was obligated to reimburse the insurer for benefits payments and related expenses paid by the insurer or the association from a special deposit or from other association funds pursuant to the terms of the policy and related agreements.

(c)(1) If damages against uninsured motorists are recoverable by the claimant from his or her own insurer, the applicable limits of the uninsured motorist coverage shall be a credit against a covered claim payable under this article. A person having a claim that may be recovered under more than one insurance guaranty association or its equivalent shall seek recovery first from the association of the place of residence of the insured, except that if it is a first-party claim for damage to property with a permanent location, he or she shall seek recovery first from the association of the permanent location of the property, and if it is a workers' compensation claim, he or she shall seek recovery first from the association of the residence of the claimant. A recovery under this article shall be reduced by the amount of recovery from any other insurance guaranty association or its equivalent. A member insurer may recover in subrogation from the association only one-half of any amount paid by that insurer under uninsured motorist coverage for bodily injury or wrongful death (and nothing for a payment for anything else), in those cases where the injured person insured by such an insurer has proceeded under his or her uninsured motorist coverage on the ground that the tortfeasor is uninsured as a result of the insolvency of his or her liability insurer (an insolvent insurer as defined in this article), provided that the member insurer shall waive all rights of subrogation against the tortfeasor. An amount paid a claimant in excess of the amount authorized by this section may be recovered by action, or other proceeding, brought by the association.

(2) A claimant having collision coverage on a loss that is covered by the insolvent company's liability policy shall first proceed against his or her collision carrier. That claimant or the collision carrier, if it is a member of the association, does not have the right to sue or continue a suit against the insured of the insolvent insurance company for that collision damage.

(d) The association shall have the right to recover from any person who is an affiliate of the insolvent insurer and whose liability obligations to other persons are satisfied in whole or in part by payments made under this article the amount of any covered claim and allocated claims expense paid on behalf of that person pursuant to this article.

(e) A person having a claim or legal right of recovery under any governmental insurance or guaranty program that is also a covered claim, shall be required to first exhaust his or her right under the program. An amount payable on a covered claim shall be reduced by the amount of any recovery under the program.

(f) "Covered claims" for unearned premium by lenders under insurance premium finance agreements as defined in

Section 673 shall be computed as of the earliest cancellation date of the policy pursuant to Section 673.

(g) "Covered claims" shall not include any judgments against or obligations or liabilities of the insolvent insurer or the commissioner, as liquidator, or otherwise resulting from alleged or proven torts, nor shall any default judgment or stipulated judgment against the insolvent insurer, or against the insured of the insolvent insurer, be binding against the association.

(h) "Covered claims" shall not include any loss adjustment expenses, including adjustment fees and expenses, attorney's fees and expenses, court costs, interest, and bond premiums, incurred before the appointment of a liquidator. **Leg.H.** 1991 ch. 537, 1992 chs. 227, 427 (ch. 227 prevails; ch. 427 not effective), 1994 ch. 6, effective February 10, 1994, 2008 ch. 80 (AB 3055) §2, 2009 ch. 140 (AB 1164) §128, 2010 ch. 328 (SB 1330) §143, 2016 ch. 137 (AB 2710) §1, 2017 ch. 268 (SB 430) §1, 2018 ch. 92 (SB 1289) §154.

Ref.: Hanna § 2.84[1]; Herlick Handbook § 3.13.

§1063.3. Reports and recommendations pertaining to regulation for solvency.

To aid in the detection and prevention of member insurer insolvencies:

(a) The board may, upon majority vote, make recommendations to the commissioner on matters pertaining to regulation for solvency.

(b) The board may prepare a report on the history and causes of any member insurer insolvency in which the association was obligated to pay covered claims, based on the information available to the association, and submit that report along with any recommendations resulting therefrom to the commissioner.

(c) The board may request the Self-Insurers' Security Fund to prepare, and the Self-Insurers' Security Fund may provide to the board, a report identifying the aggregate amount of liability, including the estimated exposure for every insurance carrier admitted to transact workers' compensation insurance in this state, under all specific excess workers' compensation policies in existence for a given period in this state as reported by the private self-insured employers to the Director of Industrial Relations in the annual reports submitted pursuant to Section 3702.2 of the Labor Code. **Leg.H.** 1994 ch. 6 (AB 1667) §5, effective February 10, 1994, 2005 ch. 395 (AB 817) §2.

§1063.45. Enacted 1992. Repealed operative January 1, 2020, by its own provisions. 2016 ch. 137 (AB 2710) §2 (amended & renumbered from §1063.5).

§1063.5. Collection and allocation of premium payments from member insurers; applicability.

(a)(1) To the extent necessary to secure funds for the association for payment of the administrative expenses of the association, covered claims of insolvent insurers, and for payment of reasonable costs of adjusting the claims, the association shall collect premium payments from its member insurers sufficient to discharge its obligations.

(2) The association shall allocate its claim payments and costs, incurred or estimated to be incurred, to one or more of the following categories:

(A) Workers' compensation claims.

(B) Homeowners' claims and automobile claims, including all of the following:

(i) Automobile material damage.

(ii) Automobile liability (both personal injury and death and property damage).

(iii) Medical payments.

(iv) Uninsured motorist claims.

(C) Claims other than workers' compensation, homeowners', and automobile, as defined above.

(3) Separate premium payments shall be required for each category.

(4) The premium payments for each category shall be used to pay the claims and costs allocated to that category.

(b)(1) The rate of premium charged shall be a uniform percentage of net direct written premium in the preceding calendar year applicable to that category.

(2) The rate of premium charges to each member insurer in the appropriate categories shall be based on the net direct written premium of each member insurer as shown in the latest year's annual financial statement on file with the commissioner.

[1] **(3)** In cases of a dispute as to the amount of the net direct written premium between the association and one of its member insurers, the written decision of the commissioner shall be final.

(c) Within 90 days after the filing of an annual statement, each member insurer shall file a report to the association indicating the amount of premiums not subject to the association's premium charge and the amount of special excess workers' compensation premiums for the preceding calendar year. The report is not required in any year in which a premium charge is not made by the association.

(d) In charging premiums to member insurers, the association shall adjust, if necessary, the net direct written premiums shown on a member insurer's annual statement by excluding any premiums written for any lines of insurance or types of coverage not covered by this article under paragraph (3) of subdivision (c) of Section 1063.1.

(e)(1) The premium charged to any member insurer for any of the three categories or a category established by the association shall not be more than 2 percent of the net direct written premium unless there are bonds outstanding that were issued pursuant to Article 14.25 (commencing with Section 1063.50) or Article 14.26 (commencing with Section 1063.70).

(2) If bonds issued pursuant to either article are outstanding, the premium charged to a member insurer for the category for which the bond proceeds are being used to pay claims and expenses shall not be more than 1 percent of the net direct written premium for that category.

(f)(1) The association may exempt or defer, in whole or in part, the premium charge of any member insurer, if the premium charge would cause the member insurer's financial statement to reflect an amount of capital or surplus less than the minimum amounts required for a certificate of authority by any jurisdiction in which the member insurer is authorized to transact insurance. However, during the period of deferment, no dividends shall be paid to shareholders or policyholders by the company whose premium charge was deferred.

(2) Deferred premium charges shall be paid when the payment will not reduce capital or surplus below required minimums.

(g) After all covered claims of insolvent insurers and expenses of administration have been paid, any unused premiums and any reimbursements or claims dividends from liquidators remaining in any category shall be retained by the association and applied to reduce future premium charges in the appropriate category.

(h) The commissioner may suspend or revoke the certificate of authority to transact business in this state of a member insurer that fails to pay a premium when due and after demand has been made.

(i) Interest at a rate equal to the current federal reserve discount rate plus 2½ percent per annum shall be added to the premium of any member insurer that fails to submit the premium requested by the association within 30 days after the mailing request. However, in no event shall the interest rate exceed the legal maximum.

(j) This section shall apply only to premium charges paid on or after January 1, 2017. **Leg.H.** 2016 ch. 137 (AB 2710) §3, 2020 ch. 258 (AB 3012) §3.

§1063.5. 2020 Deletes. [1] (c) (1) For purposes of this section, "net direct written premiums" means the amount of gross premiums, less return premiums, received in that calendar year upon business done in this state, other than premiums received for reinsurance. (2)

§1063.135. Enacted 1992. Repealed operative January 1, 2020, by its own provisions. 2017 ch. 561 (AB 1516) §138.

§1063.14. Surcharge on premiums; applicability.

(a)(1) The plan of operation adopted pursuant to subdivision (c) of Section 1063 shall contain provisions whereby each member insurer is required to recoup, in the year following the premium charge, a sum calculated to recoup the premium charge paid by the member insurer under this article by way of a surcharge on premiums charged for insurance policies to which this article applies.

(2) Amounts recouped shall not be considered premiums for any other purpose, including the computation of gross premium tax or agents' commission.

(b)(1) The amount of any surcharge shall be separately stated on either a billing or policy declaration sent to an insured. The association shall determine the rate of the surcharge and the collection period for each category, and these shall be mandatory for all member insurers of the association who write business in those categories.

(2) Each member insurer shall file a report in accordance with the provisions of the plan of operation indicating the amount of surcharges it has collected.

(A) Member insurers who collect surcharges in excess of premium charges paid in the preceding year pursuant to Section 1063.5 shall remit the excess to the association as an additional premium within 30 days after the association has determined the amount of the excess recoupment and given notice to the member insurer of that amount. The excess shall be applied to reduce future premium charges in the appropriate category.

(B) Member insurers who report surcharge collections that are less than what they paid in the preceding year's premium charge shall receive reimbursement from the association for the shortfall in surcharge collection.

(C) Member insurers may amend their reports indicating the amount of surcharges collected for the prior five years if they discover there was an error in the original reports filed with the association.

(c) [1] The plan of operation may permit a member insurer to omit collection of the surcharge from **any of** its insureds [2] **only if** the expense of collecting the surcharge would exceed the amount of the surcharge [3]**, provided, however, that** a member insurer [4] **is not** entitled to [5] reimbursement from the association pursuant to **subparagraph (B) of paragraph (2) of** subdivision (b) **of any amount omitted from collection pursuant to this subdivision.**

[6]

(d) This section applies only to premium charges paid on or after January 1, 2017. **Leg.H.** 2016 ch. 137 (AB 2710) §5, 2017 ch. 561 (AB 1516) §139, 2020 ch. 258 (AB 3012) §4.

§1063.14. 2020 Deletes. [1] (1) **[2]** when **[3]** . (2) **[4]** electing to omit collecting surcharges from any of its insureds shall not be **[5]** any **[6]** (3) However, this section does not relieve the member insurer of its obligation to recoup the amount of surcharge otherwise collectible.

§1063.15. Association's time limits.

In any workers' compensation matter the association shall have the same period of time within which to act or to exercise a right as is accorded to the insurer by the Labor Code, and those time periods shall be tolled against the association until 45 days after the appointment of a domiciliary or receiver. **Leg.H.** 1991 ch. 537.

Ref.: Hanna § 2.84; Herlick Handbook § 3.13.

§1063.17. Public meeting; scope; notice; certain closed meeting or session permitted; requirements.

(a) All meetings of the board of governors of the association and its investment and audit committees shall be open and public, and all persons shall be permitted to attend any meeting of the association except as otherwise provided in subdivision (g). This shall apply to meetings conducted in person and via teleconference. Attendance at telephonically conducted meetings by members of the public shall be made available by the publication by the association in its meeting notices as set forth below of a call-in number and passcode that members of the public may use to participate in the meeting.

(b) As used in this section, "meeting" includes any congregation of a majority of the members of the board of governors or the investment and audit committee, as applicable, at the same time to hear, discuss, or deliberate upon any item that is within the responsibility of the association as set forth in this article or in the association's plan of operations. Notwithstanding the foregoing, a meeting shall not include any of the following:

(1) Individual contacts or conversations between a member of the board of governors and any other person, including, but not limited to, any employee or official of the association, that do not violate subdivision (c).

(2) The attendance of a majority of the members of the board of governors or a committee at an industry conference or other gathering organized by a person or organization other than the association, provided that a majority of the members do not discuss among themselves any item that is within the responsibility of the association as set forth in this article or in the association's plan of operations.

(3) The attendance of a majority of the members, the board of governors, or a committee at a purely social or ceremonial occasion, provided that a majority of the members do not discuss among themselves any item that is within the responsibility of the association as set forth in this article or in the association's plan of operations.

(c)(1) A majority of the members of the board of governors shall not, outside a meeting authorized by this article, use a series of communications of any kind, directly or through intermediaries, to discuss, deliberate, or take action on any item of business that is within the responsibility of the association as set forth in this article or in the association's plan of operations.

(2) Paragraph (1) shall not be construed as preventing any employee or officer of the association from engaging in separate conversations or communications outside of a meeting authorized by this article with members of the board of governors in order to answer questions or provide information regarding matters within the responsibility of the association, if that person does not communicate to members of the board of governors the comments or position of any other member or members of the board.

(d) All meetings of the association authorized under this article shall comply with the protections and prohibitions contained in Section 202 of the Americans with Disabilities Act of 1990 (42 U.S.C. Sec. 12132), and the federal rules and regulations adopted in implementation of that act.

(e) The association shall provide notice of its meetings that are open and public pursuant to subdivision (a). This notice and an agenda of items to be discussed shall be provided at least 10 days in advance of the meeting via the association's Internet Web site, and the notice shall be published in a newspaper of general circulation in the State of California. In addition, members of the public may request notice by regular mail or by e-mail by making a written request to the association for notice of meetings that are open and public pursuant to subdivision (a). Notice may be waived, or the 10-day period modified with respect to any particular meeting by the board of governors of the association upon request submitted to the commissioner stating the need for a modified notice and exigent circumstances requiring waiver of the notice requirement at least 24 hours in advance of the meeting time set. The approval of the commissioner shall be deemed granted if a written denial of the request for waiver or modification of the notice period is not received at least four hours prior to the commencement of the meeting to be conducted under the modified notice. Notice of a meeting that does not meet the 10-day notice requirement under this subdivision shall be posted on the association's Internet Web site and provided by e-mail to members of the public who have made a written request for e-mail notice to the association of meetings that are open and public pursuant to subdivision (a). A summary agenda shall be included in each such notice, but members of the board of governors may bring additional items of business to any such meeting.

(f) At any meeting where notice is required pursuant to this section, the association shall reserve time for public comment on the issues addressed at the meeting.

(g) Nothing in this section shall be construed to prohibit the board of governors of the association or its investment and audit committees from holding a closed meeting or a closed session of an open and public meeting to discuss any of the following subjects:

(1) Bond issuances or other matters relating to borrowings of the association.

(2) Matters regarding the detection and prevention of insolvency of members of the association as contemplated by this article.

(3) Nonpublic information received from liquidators, receivers, and regulators regarding members of the association.

(4) Nonpublic information received from the California Liquidation Office.

(5) Proprietary information regarding third-party administrators, vendors that provide products and services in connection with claims administration, or investments made by the association. Proprietary information also includes information which the association and its corresponding out-of-state associations only have access to pursuant to binding contractual confidentiality provisions.

(6) Nonpublic financial information regarding members of the association, including information in support of requests for assessment deferrals.

(7) Statutory interpretations and other advice received from legal counsel to the association, whether in connection with litigation or otherwise.

(8) Appointment, employment, evaluation of performance, or dismissal of any employee or vendor that provides products and services in connection with claims administration of the association.

(9) Deliberations concerning the purchase, sale, exchange, or lease of real or personal property, including investment property.

(10) Matters posing a threat of criminal or terrorist activity against the association, its personnel, or its property.

(11) Covered claims and purported covered claims against the association.

(12) Disputes and purported disputes with or involving members of the association.

(13) Any other matters as permitted by the commissioner under the association's approved plan, provided such matters may be heard in a closed meeting or a closed session consistent with Section 11126 of the Government Code.

(h) With respect to any closed meeting or session held as permitted by subdivision (g), the association shall do both of the following:

(1) Disclose, prior to the closed meeting or the closed session, the general nature of the item or items to be discussed in the closed session. The disclosure may take

the form of a reference to the item or items as they are listed by number or letter on the agenda. In the closed session, the board of governors may consider only those matters covered in its disclosure. After any closed session, the board of governors shall reconvene in open session prior to adjournment and shall make any reports, provide any documentation, or make any other disclosures that may be required consistent with this article. The announcements required to be made in open session pursuant to this subdivision may be made at the location announced in the agenda for the closed session, as long as the public is allowed to be present at that location for the purpose of hearing the announcement.

(2) Provide periodic reports to the commissioner identifying the matters covered in each such closed meeting or session and the provision of subdivision (g) pursuant to which the subject was discussed.

(i) Nothing in this section shall require or authorize the disclosure of names or other information that would constitute an invasion of privacy or otherwise unnecessarily divulge the particular facts concerning the closed session or the disclosure of which is prohibited by state or federal law.

(j) The commissioner or his or her designated representative shall be permitted to attend all meetings of the board of governors and its investment and audit committees, specifically including closed meetings and sessions. Any information discussed in closed meetings or sessions shall be treated by the commissioner and his or her designated representatives as confidential pursuant to the provisions of Section 12919. **Leg.H.** 2008 ch. 407 (SB 1467) §1.

§1063.18. Claims against insolvent insurers; denial of nonworkers' compensation claim.

(a) Nothing in this article requires a final determination of a claim in an insolvent insurer's liquidation proceeding before a covered claim may be submitted to the California Insurance Guarantee Association (CIGA). Nothing in this article requires a claim to first be determined and approved by the liquidator before CIGA pays and discharges a covered claim. If a claim is presented to the association and all requirements under paragraph (1) of subdivision (c) of Section 1063.1 for processing a covered claim are satisfied, the association shall proceed to process the claim for payment under this article.

(b) If the association provides a written denial of a nonworkers' compensation claim, the person asserting the claim against the association shall have one year to bring an action challenging the denial, including an action for declaratory relief. If the written denial is based on a failure to exhaust other insurance available to pay the claim, a claim shall be reasserted against the association within six months after all other insurance has been exhausted. **Leg.H.** 2015 ch. 85 (AB 822) §1.

Ref.: Hanna § 2.84[2].

ARTICLE 14.26
Workers' Compensation Bond Fund

§1063.70. Issuance of bonds for payment of covered claims against insolvent insurers.

The California Insurance Guarantee Association is authorized to pay and discharge certain claims of insolvent insurers as defined in Section 1063.1 through the collection of premiums from its members, which amounts are limited by law and take time to assess and collect. This article provides for the ability of CIGA to request the issuance of bonds by the California Infrastructure and Economic Development Bank pursuant to Article 8 (commencing with Section 63049.6) of Chapter 2 of Division 1 of Title 6.7 of the Government Code to more expeditiously and effectively provide for the payment of covered claims that arise as a result of the insolvencies of insurance companies providing workers' compensation insurance. The bonds are to be paid from the special bond assessments assessed by CIGA for those purposes and the other funds provided pursuant to Section 1063.74. Special bond assessments to repay bonds issued for payment of workers compensation benefits shall be assessed, to the extent necessary, for the claims category. It is a public purpose and in the best interest of the public health, safety, and general welfare of the residents of this state to provide for the issuance of bonds to pay claimants and policyholders having covered claims against insolvent insurers operating in this state. **Leg.H.** 2003 ch. 635 (AB 227).

Ref.: Herlick Handbook § 3.13.

§1063.71. Definitions.

(a) The terms "member insurer," "insolvent insurer," and "covered claims" have the meanings assigned those terms in Section 1063.1.

(b) The terms "CIGA," "commissioner," "board," and "department" have the meanings assigned those terms in Section 1063.51.

(c) "Bank" means the California Infrastructure and Economic Development Bank created pursuant to Article 1 (commencing with Section 63020) of Chapter 2, Division 1 of Title 6.7 of the Government Code.

(d) "Bonds" means bonds issued by the Bank pursuant to Article 8 (commencing with Section 63049.6) of Chapter 2 of Division 1 of Title 6.7 of the Government Code to provide funds for the payment of the covered claims and the adjusting and defense expenses relating to those claims that are issued at the request of the board pursuant to Section 1063.73.

(e) "Collateral" means the special bond assessments, the right of CIGA to be paid the special bond assessments, all revenues therefrom, the separate account of the Workers' Comp Bond Fund into which special bond assessments are deposited, and the proceeds thereof.

(f) "Special bond assessment" means the premiums collected by CIGA pursuant to Section 1063.74.

(g) "Workers' Comp Bond Fund" means the fund created pursuant to Section 1063.72. **Leg.H.** 2003 ch. 635 (AB 227).

Ref.: Herlick Handbook § 3.13.

§1063.72. Workers' Comp Bond Fund.

The Workers' Comp Bond Fund is hereby created. Proceeds from the sale of bonds shall be deposited in a separate account in the Workers' Comp Bond Fund. Only CIGA, and with respect to payment of the bonds, the trustee for the bonds, shall have the ability to authorize disbursements from the separate account. Special bond assessments shall be deposited in a separate account in the

Workers' Comp Bond Fund and shall not be commingled with any other moneys. Only the trustee for the bonds shall have the ability to authorize disbursements from this separate account, and CIGA shall have no right or authority to authorize disbursements from this separate account. The Workers' Comp Bond Fund shall be maintained with the trustee for the bonds. Following payment or provision for payment of the bonds, amounts in the Workers' Comp Bond Fund shall be transferred to the fund that is designated in the indenture. All money in the Workers' Comp Bond Fund and all special bond assessments shall be used by CIGA for the exclusive purpose of carrying out the purposes of this part, and, notwithstanding any other provisions of law, the Workers' Comp Bond Fund shall not be a state fund, shall not be subject to the rules or procedures of any fund in the State Treasury, and application of the fund shall not be subject to the supervision or budgetary approval of any officer or division of state government. CIGA and the trustee for the bonds may as necessary or convenient to the accomplishment of any other purpose under this article, divide the fund into separate accounts. **Leg.H.** 2003 ch. 635 (AB 227).

Ref.: Herlick Handbook § 3.13.

§1063.73. CIGA's request for issuance of bonds—Copy to commissioner; commissioner may modify, cancel, or delay requested issuance.

In the event CIGA determines that the insolvency of one or more member insurers providing workers' compensation insurance will result in covered claim obligations for workers' compensation claims in excess of CIGA's capacity to pay from current funds, the board, in its sole discretion, may by resolution request the Bank to issue bonds pursuant to Article 8 (commencing with Section 63049.6) of Chapter 2 of Division 1 of Title 6.7 of the Government Code to provide funds for the payment of the covered claims and the adjusting and defense expenses relating to those claims. Notwithstanding any other provision of law, CIGA is hereby authorized to borrow proceeds of the bonds to provide for those purposes. CIGA may request the Bank to issue bonds pursuant to Article 8 (commencing with Section 63049.6) of Chapter 2 of Division 1 of Title 6.7 of the Government Code. CIGA shall provide the commissioner with a copy of the request and the commissioner may, within 30 days of receipt of the request, modify, cancel, or require a delay in the requested issuance. The proceeds of bonds issued for workers' compensation benefits may be used by CIGA to reimburse funds advanced or temporarily loaned from other categories to fund workers' compensation claims. **Leg.H.** 2003 ch. 635 (AB 227).

Ref.: Herlick Handbook § 3.13.

§1063.74. Funding workers' compensation claims—Special bond assessments, current funds, premium assessments, and advances or dividends.

(a) Notwithstanding any other limits on assessments, CIGA shall have the authority to levy upon member insurers special bond assessments in the amount necessary to pay the principal of and interest on the bonds, and to meet other requirements established by agreements relating to the bonds. The assessments shall be collected only from the member insurers providing workers' compensation insurance, in the same manner as separate premium payments are used to pay the claims and costs allocated to that category pursuant to Section 1063.5. Special bond assessments made pursuant to this section shall also be subject to the surcharge provisions in Sections 1063.14 and 1063.145.

(b) Notwithstanding any other law, after all bonds issued pursuant to this article have been redeemed, no further initial special bond assessments shall be levied or made. Any premium adjustments called for and described in Section 1063.5, as applied to special bond assessments initially charged, shall continue to be made and determined. Any credits or charges that result from the premium adjustments on the special bond assessments shall be credited or charged to the assessments called for and described in Section 1063.5.

(c) In addition to the special bond assessments provided for in this section, the board in its discretion and subject to other obligations of the association, may utilize current funds of CIGA, premium assessments made under Section 1063.5, and advances or dividends received from the liquidators of insolvent insurers to pay the principal and interest on any bonds issued at the board's request and shall utilize, to the extent feasible, the recoveries from the liquidators of the estates of insolvent workers' compensation carriers to pay bonds issued at the board's request to fund workers' compensation claims. **Leg.H.** 2003 ch. 635 (AB 227), 2014 ch. 76 (AB 2230) §2.

Ref.: Herlick Handbook § 3.13.

§1063.75. Terms and conditions of bonds.

Any bonds issued to provide funds for covered claim obligations for workers' compensation claims shall be issued prior to January 1, 2023, in an aggregate principal amount outstanding at any one time not to exceed one billion five hundred million dollars ($1,500,000,000), and any bonds issued or issued to refund bonds shall not have a final maturity exceeding 20 years from the date of issuance. The bonds shall be issued at the request of CIGA, shall be in the form, shall bear the date or dates, and shall mature at the time or times as the indenture authorized by the request may provide. The bonds may be issued in one or more series, as serial bonds or as term bonds, or as a combination thereof, and, notwithstanding any other provision of law, the amount of principal of, or interest on, bonds maturing at each date of maturity need not be equal. The bonds shall bear interest at the rate or rates, variable or fixed or a combination thereof, be in the denominations, be in the form, either coupon or registered, carry the registration privileges, be executed in the manner, be payable in the medium of payment at the place or places within or without the state, be subject to the terms of redemption, contain the terms and conditions, and be secured by the covenants as the indenture may provide. The indenture may provide for the proceeds of the bonds and funds securing the bonds to be invested in any securities and investments, including investment agreements, as specified therein. CIGA may enter into or authorize any ancillary obligations or derivative agreements as it determines necessary or desirable to manage interest rate risk or security features related to the bonds. The bonds shall be sold at public or private sale by the Treasurer at, above, or below the principal amount thereof, on the terms and conditions and for the consideration in the medium of payment that the Treasurer shall determine prior to the sale. **Leg.H.** 2003 ch. 635 (AB 227), 2006 ch. 112 (AB 3072) §1, 2008 ch. 80 (AB 3055) §3, 2010 ch. 140 (AB 2781) §2, 2011 chs. 296 (AB 1023) §183, 426 (SB 712) §3.

Ref.: Herlick Handbook § 3.13.

§1063.76. Collateral—Permitted use; subject to first priority statutory lien; exempt from specified claims.

(a) The collateral shall be used solely for the purpose of paying the principal and redemption price of, and interest on, the bonds and any amounts owing by CIGA under contracts entered into pursuant to Section 1063.77, and shall not be used for any other purpose. Member insurers shall pay the special bond assessments directly to the trustee for the bonds. Any collateral in the possession of CIGA shall be held by CIGA in trust for the benefit of the trustee for the bonds.

(b) Upon the issuance of the first bond, the collateral shall be subject to a first priority statutory lien in favor of the trustee for the bonds, for the benefit of the holders of the bonds and the parties to the contracts entered into pursuant to Section 1063.77, to secure the payment of the principal and redemption price of, and interest on, the bonds and any amounts owing by CIGA under contracts entered into pursuant to Section 1063.77. This lien shall arise by operation of law automatically without any action on the part of CIGA, the bank, or any other person. This lien is a continuous lien on all collateral effective from the time the first bond is issued, whether or not a particular item of collateral exists at the time of the issuance. From the time the first bond is issued, this lien shall be valid, effective, prior, perfected, binding, and enforceable against CIGA, its successors, purchasers of the collateral, creditors, and all others asserting rights in the collateral, irrespective of whether those parties have notice of the lien and without the need for any physical delivery, recordation, filing, or further act. Upon default in the payment of the principal or redemption price of, or interest on, the bonds, or any amounts owing by CIGA under contracts entered into pursuant to Section 1063.77, the trustee for the bonds shall be entitled to foreclose or otherwise enforce this lien on the collateral.

(c) No person acting under any provision of law or principle of equity shall be permitted in any way to impede or in any manner interfere with (1) the full and timely payment of the principal and redemption price of, and interest on, the bonds and any amounts owing by CIGA under contracts entered into pursuant to Section 1063.77, or (2) the statutory lien created by this section and the full and timely application of the collateral to the payment of the principal and redemption price of, and interest on, the bonds and any amounts owing by CIGA under contracts entered into pursuant to Section 1063.77.

(d) None of the collateral shall be subject to garnishment, levy, execution, attachment, or other process, writ (including writ of mandate), or remedy in connection with the assertion or enforcement of any debt, claim, settlement, or judgment against the state, the department, the commissioner, the bank, CIGA, or the board, nor shall any of the collateral be subject to the claims of any creditor of the state, the department, the commissioner, the bank, CIGA, or the board. This paragraph shall not limit the rights or remedies of the trustee for the bonds, the holders of the bonds, or the parties to contracts entered into pursuant to Section 1063.77.

(e) As long as any bond is outstanding, CIGA shall not be subject to Article 14 (commencing with Section 1010) or Article 14.3 (commencing with Section 1064.1) of Chapter 1 of Part 2 of Division 1 of the Insurance Code. **Leg.H.** 2003 ch. 635 (AB 227).

Ref.: Herlick Handbook § 3.13.

§1063.77. Contracts or agreements with banks, insurers, or other financial institutions or parties; optional terms in contracts or agreements.

CIGA is authorized to enter into those contracts or agreements with those banks, insurers, or other financial institutions or parties that it determines are necessary or desirable to improve the security and marketability of, or to manage interest rates or other risks associated with, the bonds issued pursuant to Article 8 (commencing with Section 63049.6) of Chapter 2 of Division 1 of Title 6.7 of the Government Code. Those contracts or agreements may contain an obligation to reimburse, with interest, any of those banks, insurers, or other financial institutions or parties for advances used to pay the purchase price of, or principal or interest on, the bonds or other obligations. **Leg.H.** 2003 ch. 635 (AB 227).

Ref.: Herlick Handbook § 3.13.

CHAPTER 12 THE INSURANCE FRAUDS PREVENTION ACT

ARTICLE 1 False and Fraudulent Claims [Selected Provisions]

§1871. Insurance fraud—Generally.

The Legislature finds and declares as follows:

(a) The business of insurance involves many transactions that have the potential for abuse and illegal activities. There are numerous law enforcement agencies on the state and local levels charged with the responsibility for investigating and prosecuting fraudulent activity. This chapter is intended to permit the full utilization of the expertise of the commissioner and the department so that they may more effectively investigate and discover insurance frauds, halt fraudulent activities, and assist and receive assistance from federal, state, local, and administrative law enforcement agencies in the prosecution of persons who are parties in insurance frauds.

(b) Insurance fraud is a particular problem for automobile policyholders; fraudulent activities account for 15 to 20 percent of all auto insurance payments. Automobile insurance fraud is the biggest and fastest growing segment of insurance fraud and contributes substantially to the high cost of automobile insurance with particular significance in urban areas.

(c) Prevention of automobile insurance fraud will significantly reduce the incidence of severity and automobile insurance claim payments and will therefore produce a commensurate reduction in automobile insurance premiums.

(d) Workers' compensation fraud harms employers by contributing to the increasingly high cost of workers' compensation insurance and self-insurance and harms employees by undermining the perceived legitimacy of all workers' compensation claims.

(e) Prevention of workers' compensation insurance fraud may reduce the number of workers' compensation claims and claim payments thereby producing a commensurate reduction in workers' compensation costs. Prevention of workers' compensation insurance fraud will assist in restoring confidence and faith in the workers' compensation system, and will facilitate expedient and full compensation for employees injured at the workplace.

(f) The actions of employers who fraudulently underreport payroll or fail to report payroll for all employees to their insurance company in order to pay a lower workers' compensation premium result in significant additional premium costs and an unfair burden to honest employers and their employees.

(g) The actions of employers who fraudulently fail to secure the payment of workers' compensation as required by Section 3700 of the Labor Code harm employees, cause unfair competition for honest employers, and increase costs to taxpayers.

(h) Health insurance fraud is a particular problem for health insurance policyholders. Although there are no precise figures, it is believed that fraudulent activities account for billions of dollars annually in added health care costs nationally. Health care fraud causes losses in premium dollars and increases health care costs unnecessarily. **Leg.H.** 1991 chs. 116, 1008, 1995 ch. 885, 2001 ch. 159, 2002 ch. 6 (AB 749).

Ref.: Hanna § 2.03[1]; Herlick Handbook § 9.18.

§1871.1. Access to records required to be open for inspection in fraud claims.

Insurers and their agents, while they are investigating suspected fraud claims, shall have access to all relevant public records that are required to be open for inspection under Chapter 3.5 (commencing with Section 6250) of Division 7 of Title 1 of the Government Code, and any regulations thereunder. This section restates existing law, and the Legislature does not intend to grant insurers or their agents access to public records other than to those public records available to them under existing law. **Leg.H.** 1993 ch. 323.

Ref.: 8 C.C.R. §2695.7; Hanna § 2.03[2], [5]; Herlick Handbook § 9.18.

§1871.2. Notice of penalties on claim forms; exception.

(a) Any insurer who, in connection with any insurance contract or provision of contract described in Section 108, prints, reproduces, or furnishes a form to any person upon which that person gives notice to the insurer or makes claim against it by reason of accident, injury, death, or other noticed or claimed loss, or on a rider attached thereto, shall cause to be printed or displayed in comparative prominence with other content the statement: "Any person who knowingly presents false or fraudulent claim for the payment of a loss is guilty of a crime and may be subject to fines and confinement in state prison." This statement shall be preceded by the words: "For your protection California law requires the following to appear on this form" or other explanatory words of similar meaning.

(b) This section is not applicable to a contract of reinsurance as defined in Section 620. **Leg.H.** 1989 ch. 1119, 2000 ch. 470.

Ref.: Hanna § 25.20[2]; Herlick Handbook § 9.18.

§1871.4. Penalties for making false or fraudulent written or oral statements.

(a) It is unlawful to do any of the following:

(1) Make or cause to be made a knowingly false or fraudulent material statement or material representation for the purpose of obtaining or denying any compensation, as defined in Section 3207 of the Labor Code.

(2) Present or cause to be presented a knowingly false or fraudulent written or oral material statement in support of, or in opposition to, a claim for compensation for the purpose of obtaining or denying any compensation, as defined in Section 3207 of the Labor Code.

(3) Knowingly assist, abet, conspire with, or solicit a person in an unlawful act under this section.

(4) Make or cause to be made a knowingly false or fraudulent statement with regard to entitlement to benefits with the intent to discourage an injured worker from claiming benefits or pursuing a claim.

For the purposes of this subdivision, "statement" includes, but is not limited to, a notice, proof of injury, bill for services, payment for services, hospital or doctor records, X-ray, test results, medical-legal expense as defined in Section 4620 of the Labor Code, other evidence of loss, injury, or expense, or payment.

(5) Make or cause to be made a knowingly false or fraudulent material statement or material representation for the purpose of obtaining or denying any of the benefits or reimbursement provided in the Return-to-Work Program established under Section 139.48 of the Labor Code.

(6) Make or cause to be made a knowingly false or fraudulent material statement or material representation for the purpose of discouraging an employer from claiming any of the benefits or reimbursement provided in the Return-to-Work Program established under Section 139.48 of the Labor Code.

(b) Every person who violates subdivision (a) shall be punished by imprisonment in a county jail for one year, or pursuant to subdivision (h) of Section 1170 of the Penal Code, for two, three, or five years, or by a fine not exceeding one hundred fifty thousand dollars ($150,000) or double the value of the fraud, whichever is greater, or by both that imprisonment and fine. Restitution shall be ordered, including restitution for any medical evaluation or treatment services obtained or provided. The court shall determine the amount of restitution and the person or persons to whom the restitution shall be paid. A person convicted under this section may be charged the costs of investigation at the discretion of the court.

(c) A person who violates subdivision (a) and who has a prior felony conviction of that subdivision, of former Section 556, of former Section 1871.1, or of Section 548 or 550 of the Penal Code, shall receive a two-year enhancement for each prior conviction in addition to the sentence provided in subdivision (b).

The existence of any fact that would subject a person to a penalty enhancement shall be alleged in the information or indictment and either admitted by the defendant in open court, or found to be true by the jury trying the issue of guilt or by the court where guilt is established by plea of guilty or nolo contendere or by trial by the court sitting without a jury.

(d) This section may not be construed to preclude the applicability of any other provision of criminal law that applies or may apply to a transaction. **Leg.H.** 1991 chs. 116, 934, 1992 chs. 675, 1352 §2, effective September 30, 1992, §2.5, operative January 1, 1993, 1993 ch. 120, effective July 16, 1993, 1995 ch. 574, 2002 ch. 6 (AB 749), 2003 ch. 635 (AB 227), 2004 ch. 2 (SB 2 Fourth Extra. Sess.), effective March 6, 2005, 2011 ch. 15 (AB 109) §212, effective April 4, 2011, operative October 1, 2011.

2011 Notes: This act is titled and may be cited as the 2011 Realignment Legislation addressing public safety. Stats. 2011 ch. 15 (AB 109) §1.

This act will become operative no earlier than October 1, 2011, and only upon creation of a community corrections grant program to assist in implementing this act and upon an appropriation to fund the grant program. Stats. 2011 ch. 15 (AB 109) §636; Stats. 2011 ch. 39 (AB 117) §68.

The Community Corrections Grant Program referred to in Stats. 2011 ch. 15 §636, as amended by Stats. 2011 ch. 39 §68, was created by Stats. 2011 ch. 40 §3, operative October 1, 2011.

Ref.: Hanna §§ 2.03[1]–[3], [5], 5.06, 20.07, 22.16, 28.02; Herlick Handbook §§ 9.18, 14.18.

§1871.5. Ineligibility to receive or retain compensation.

Any person convicted of workers' compensation fraud pursuant to Section 1871.4 or Section 550 of the Penal Code shall be ineligible to receive or retain any compensation, as defined in Section 3207 of the Labor Code, where that compensation was owed or received as a result of a violation of Section 1871.4 or Section 550 of the Penal Code for which the recipient of the compensation was convicted. **Leg.H.** 1993 ch. 120, effective July 16, 1993.

Ref.: Hanna § 2.03[2]; Herlick Handbook §§ 1.01[1], 9.18, 14.18.

§1871.6. Provisions of Penal Code §781 applicable to prosecutions for violations of §1871.4.

The provisions of Section 781 of the Penal Code are applicable to any prosecutions for violations of Section 1871.4. This section is declaratory of existing law and shall not be interpreted to limit the applicability of Section 781 of the Penal Code to any other criminal provisions. **Leg.H.** 1993 ch. 120, effective July 16, 1993.

Ref.: Herlick Handbook § 9.18.

§1871.7. Employing persons to procure clients or patients to perform or obtain benefits unlawful; penalties; bringing action.

(a) It is unlawful to knowingly employ runners, cappers, steerers, or other persons to procure clients or patients to perform or obtain services or benefits pursuant to Division 4 (commencing with Section 3200) of the Labor Code or to procure clients or patients to perform or obtain services or benefits under a contract of insurance or that will be the basis for a claim against an insured individual or his or her insurer.

(b) Every person who violates any provision of this section or Section 549, 550, or 551 of the Penal Code shall be subject, in addition to any other penalties that may be prescribed by law, to a civil penalty of not less than five thousand dollars ($5,000) nor more than ten thousand dollars ($10,000), plus an assessment of not more than three times the amount of each claim for compensation, as defined in Section 3207 of the Labor Code or pursuant to a contract of insurance. The court shall have the power to grant other equitable relief, including temporary injunctive relief, as is necessary to prevent the transfer, concealment, or dissipation of illegal proceeds, or to protect the public. The penalty prescribed in this paragraph shall be assessed for each fraudulent claim presented to an insurance company by a defendant and not for each violation.

(c) The penalties set forth in subdivision (b) are intended to be remedial rather than punitive, and shall not preclude, nor be precluded by, a criminal prosecution for the same conduct. If the court finds, after considering the goals of disgorging unlawful profit, restitution, compensating the state for the costs of investigation and prosecution, and alleviating the social costs of increased insurance rates due to fraud, that such a penalty would be punitive and would preclude, or be precluded by, a criminal prosecution, the court shall reduce that penalty appropriately.

(d) The district attorney or commissioner may bring a civil action under this section. Before the commissioner may bring that action, the commissioner shall be required to present the evidence obtained to the appropriate local district attorney for possible criminal or civil filing. If the district attorney elects not to pursue the matter due to insufficient resources, then the commissioner may proceed with the action.

(e)(1) Any interested persons, including an insurer, may bring a civil action for a violation of this section for the person and for the State of California. The action shall be brought in the name of the state. The action may be dismissed only if the court and the district attorney or the commissioner, whichever is participating, give written consent to the dismissal and their reasons for consenting.

(2) A copy of the complaint and written disclosure of substantially all material evidence and information the person possesses shall be served on the district attorney and commissioner. The complaint shall be filed in camera, shall remain under seal for at least 60 days, and shall not be served on the defendant until the court so orders. The local district attorney or commissioner may elect to intervene and proceed with the action within 60 days after he or she receives both the complaint and the material evidence and information. If more than one governmental entity elects to intervene, the district attorney shall have precedence.

(3) The district attorney or commissioner may, for good cause shown, move the court for extensions of the time during which the complaint remains under seal under paragraph (2). The motions may be supported by affidavits or other submissions in camera. The defendant shall not be required to respond to any complaint filed under this section until 20 days after the complaint is unsealed and served upon the defendant.

(4) Before the expiration of the 60-day period or any extensions obtained under paragraph (3), the district attorney or commissioner shall either:

(A) Proceed with the action, in which case the action shall be conducted by the district attorney or commissioner.

(B) Notify the court that it declines to take over the action, in which case the person bringing the action shall have the right to conduct the action.

(5) When a person or governmental agency brings an action under this section, no person other than the district attorney or commissioner may intervene or bring a related action based on the facts underlying the pending action unless that action is authorized by another statute or common law.

(f)(1) If the district attorney or commissioner proceeds with the action, he or she shall have the primary responsibility for prosecuting the action, and shall not be bound by an act of the person bringing the action. That person shall have the right to continue as a party to the action, subject to the limitations set forth in paragraph (2).

(2)(A) The district attorney or commissioner may dismiss the action notwithstanding the objections of the person initiating the action if the person has been notified by the district attorney or commissioner of the filing of the motion, and the court has provided the person with an opportunity for a hearing on the motion.

(B) The district attorney or commissioner may settle the action with the defendant notwithstanding the objections of the person initiating the action if the court determines, after a hearing, that the proposed settlement is fair, adequate, and reasonable under all the circumstances. Upon a showing of good cause, the hearing may be held in camera.

(C) Upon a showing by the district attorney or commissioner that unrestricted participation during the course of the litigation by the person initiating the action would interfere with or unduly delay the district attorney's or commissioner's prosecution of the case, or would be repetitious, irrelevant, or for purposes of harassment, the court may, in its discretion, impose limitations on the person's participation, including, but not limited to, the following:

(i) Limiting the number of witnesses the person may call.

(ii) Limiting the length of the testimony of those witnesses.

(iii) Limiting the person's cross-examination of witnesses.

(iv) Otherwise limiting the participation by the person in the litigation.

(D) Upon a showing by the defendant that unrestricted participation during the course of the litigation by the person initiating the action would be for purposes of harassment or would cause the defendant undue burden or unnecessary expense, the court may limit the participation by the person in the litigation.

(3) If the district attorney or commissioner elects not to proceed with the action, the person who initiated the action shall have the right to conduct the action. If the district attorney or commissioner so requests, he or she shall be served with copies of all pleadings filed in the action and shall be supplied with copies of all deposition transcripts, at the district attorney's or commissioner's expense. When a person proceeds with the action, the court, without limiting the status and rights of the person initiating the action, may nevertheless permit the district attorney or commissioner to intervene at a later date upon a showing of good cause.

(4) If at any time both a civil action for penalties and equitable relief pursuant to this section and a criminal action are pending against a defendant for substantially the same conduct, whether brought by the government or a private party, the civil action shall be stayed until the criminal action has been concluded at the trial court level. The stay shall not preclude the court from granting or enforcing temporary equitable relief during the pendency of the actions. Whether or not the district attorney or commissioner proceeds with the action, upon a showing by the district attorney or commissioner that certain actions of discovery by the person initiating the action would interfere with a law enforcement or governmental agency investigation or prosecution of a criminal or civil matter arising out of the same facts, the court may stay discovery for a period of not more than 180 days. A hearing on a request for the stay shall be conducted in camera. The court may extend the 180-day period upon a further showing in camera that the agency has pursued the criminal or civil investigation or proceedings with reasonable diligence and any proposed discovery in the civil action will interfere with the ongoing criminal or civil investigation or proceedings.

(5) Notwithstanding subdivision (e), the district attorney or commissioner may elect to pursue its claim through any alternate remedy available to the district attorney or commissioner.

(g)(1)(A)(i) If the district attorney proceeds with an action brought by a person under subdivision (e), that person shall, subject to subparagraph (B), receive at least 30 percent but not more than 40 percent of the proceeds of the action or settlement of the claim, depending upon the extent to which the person substantially contributed to the prosecution of the action.

(ii) If the commissioner has brought an action or has proceeded with an action brought by another person under this section on or after January 1, 2006, the commissioner shall be entitled to attorney's fees and costs in addition to any judgment, regardless of the date that judgment is entered. The court shall determine and award the commissioner the amount of reasonable attorney's fees, including, but not limited to, reasonable fees for time expended by attorneys employed by the department and for costs incurred. Any attorney's fees or costs awarded to the commissioner and collected shall be deposited in the Insurance Fund. In cases in which the commissioner has intervened, the commissioner and the person bringing the claim may stipulate to an allocation. The court may allocate the funds pursuant to the stipulation if, after the court's ruling on objection by the district attorney, if any, the court finds it is in the interests of justice to follow the stipulation.

(iii) If the commissioner has proceeded with an action, if there is no stipulation regarding allocation, and if a judgment has been obtained or a settlement has been reached with the defendants, the court shall determine the allocation, upon motion of the commissioner or the person bringing the action, according to the following priority:

(I) The person bringing the action, regardless of whether that person paid money to the defendants as part of the acts alleged in the complaint, shall first receive the amount the court determines is reasonable for attorney's fees, costs, and expenses that the court determines to have been necessarily incurred.

(II) The commissioner shall receive the amount the court determines for reasonable attorney's fees and costs.

(III) If the person bringing the suit has paid moneys to the defendants as part of the acts alleged in the complaint, that person shall receive the amount paid to the defendants.

(IV) At least 30 percent, but not more than 40 percent, of the remaining assets or moneys, shall be allocated to the person bringing the action, depending upon the extent to which the person substantially contributed to the prosecution of the action.

(iv) Those portions of a judgment or settlement not distributed pursuant to this subdivision shall be paid to the General Fund of the state and, upon appropriation by the Legislature, shall be apportioned between the Department of Justice and the Department of Insurance for enhanced fraud investigation and prevention efforts.

(B) Where the action is one that the court finds to be based primarily on disclosures of specific information, other than information provided by the person bringing the action, relating to allegations or transactions in a criminal, civil, or administrative hearing, in a legislative or administrative report, hearing, audit, or investigation, or from the news media, the court may award those sums that it considers appropriate, but in no case more than 10 percent of the proceeds, taking into account the significance of the information and the role of the person bringing the action in advancing the case to litigation.

(C) Any payment to a person under subparagraph (A) or under subparagraph (B) shall be made from the proceeds. The person shall also receive an amount for reasonable expenses that the court finds to have been necessarily incurred, plus reasonable attorney's fees and costs. All of those expenses, fees, and costs shall be awarded against the defendant.

(2)(A) If the district attorney or commissioner does not proceed with an action under this section, the person bringing the action or settling the claim shall receive an amount that the court decides is reasonable for collecting the civil penalty and damages. Except as provided in subparagraph (B), the amount shall not be less than 40 percent and not more than 50 percent of the proceeds of the action or settlement and shall be paid out of the proceeds. That person shall also receive an amount for reasonable expenses that the court finds to have been necessarily incurred, plus reasonable attorney's fees and costs. All of those attorney's fees and costs shall be imposed against the defendant. The parties shall serve the commissioner and the local district attorney with complete copies of any and all settlement agreements, and terms and conditions, for actions brought under this article at least 10 days prior to filing any motion for allocation with the court under this paragraph. The court may allocate the funds pursuant to the settlement agreement if, after the court's ruling on objection by the commissioner or the local district attorney, if any, the court finds it is in the interests of justice to follow the settlement agreement.

(B) If the person bringing the action, as a result of a violation of this section has paid money to the defendant or to an attorney acting on behalf of the defendant in the underlying claim, then he or she shall be entitled to up to double the amount paid to the defendant or the attorney if that amount is greater than 50 percent of the proceeds. That person shall also receive an amount for reasonable expenses that the court finds to have been necessarily incurred, plus reasonable attorney's fees and costs. All of those expenses, fees, and costs shall be awarded against the defendant.

(3) If a local district attorney has proceeded with an action under this section, one-half of the penalties not awarded to a private party, as well as any costs awarded shall go to the treasurer of the appropriate county. Those funds shall be used to investigate and prosecute fraud, augmenting existing budgets rather than replacing them. All remaining funds shall go to the state and be deposited in the General Fund and, when appropriated by the Legislature, shall be apportioned between the Department of Justice and the Department of Insurance for enhanced fraud investigation and prevention efforts.

(4) Whether or not the district attorney or commissioner proceeds with the action, if the court finds that the action was brought by a person who planned and initiated the violation of this section, that person shall be dismissed from the civil action and shall not receive any share of the proceeds of the action. The dismissal shall not prejudice the right of the district attorney or commissioner to continue the action on behalf of the state.

(5) If the district attorney or commissioner does not proceed with the action, and the person bringing the action conducts the action, the court may award to the defendant its reasonable attorney's fees and expenses if the defendant prevails in the action and the court finds that the claim of the person bringing the action was clearly frivolous, clearly vexatious, or brought primarily for purposes of harassment.

(h)(1) In no event may a person bring an action under subdivision (e) that is based upon allegations or transactions that are the subject of a civil suit or an administrative civil money penalty proceeding in which the Attorney General, district attorney, or commissioner is already a party.

(2)(A) No court shall have jurisdiction over an action under this section based upon the public disclosure of allegations or transactions in a criminal, civil, or administrative hearing in a legislative or administrative report, hearing, audit, or investigation, or from the news media, unless the action is brought by the Attorney General or the person bringing the action is an original source of the information.

(B) For purposes of this paragraph, "original source" means an individual who has direct and independent knowledge of the information on which the allegations are based and has voluntarily provided the information to the district attorney or commissioner before filing an action under this section that is based on the information.

(i) Except as provided in subdivision (j), the district attorney or commissioner is not liable for expenses that a person incurs in bringing an action under this section.

(j) In civil actions brought under this section in which the commissioner or a district attorney is a party, the court shall retain discretion to impose sanctions otherwise allowed by law, including the ability to order a party to pay expenses as provided in Sections 128.5 and 1028.5 of the Code of Civil Procedure.

(k) Any employee who is discharged, demoted, suspended, threatened, harassed, or in any other manner discriminated against in the terms and conditions of employment by his or her employer because of lawful acts done by the employee on behalf of the employee or others in furtherance of an action under this section, including investigation for, initiation of, testimony for, or assistance in, an action filed or to be filed under this section, shall be entitled to all relief necessary to make the employee whole. That relief shall include reinstatement with the same seniority status the employee would have had but for the discrimination, two times the amount of backpay, interest on the backpay, and compensation for any special damages sustained as a result of the discrimination, including litigation costs and reasonable attorney's fees. An employee may bring an action in the appropriate superior court for the relief provided in this subdivision. The remedies under this section are in addition to any other remedies provided by existing law.

(*l*)(1) An action pursuant to this section may not be filed more than three years after the discovery of the facts constituting the grounds for commencing the action.

(2) Notwithstanding paragraph (1) no action may be filed pursuant to this section more than eight years after the commission of the act constituting a violation of this section or a violation of Section 549, 550, or 551 of the Penal Code. **Leg.H.** 1993 ch. 120, effective July 16, 1993, 1994 ch. 1247, 1995 ch. 574, 1999 ch. 885, 2005 ch. 380 (SB 706) §1, 2010 ch. 400 (AB 2782) §26.

Ref.: Hanna §§ 20.01[1][e], 22.15; Herlick Handbook § 9.18.

§1871.8. Notice to injured worker regarding penalties and prosecution for fraudulent receipt of temporary disability benefits.

An insurer or self-insured employer shall provide the following notice, in both English and Spanish, to an injured worker on or with a check for temporary disability benefits:

WARNING: You are required to report to your employer or the insurance company any money that you earned for work during the time covered by this check, and before cashing this check. If you do not follow these rules, you may be in violation of the law and the penalty may be jail or prison, a fine, and loss of benefits.

ADVERTENCIA: Es necesario que usted le avise a su patrón o a su compañía de seguro todo dinero que usted ha ganado por trabajar, durante el tiempo cubierto por éste cheque, y antes de cambiar éste cheque. Si usted no sigue estos reglamentos, Usted puede estar en violación de la ley y el castigo podría ser cárcel o prisión, una multa, y pérdida de beneficios.

Leg.H. 1996 ch. 1005, 2004 ch. 2 (SB 2 Fourth Extra. Sess.), effective March 6, 2005, operative January 1, 2005.

2004 Note: The changes to Section 1871.8 of the Insurance Code made by Section 2 of this act shall become operative on January 1, 2005. Stats. 2004 ch. 2 (SB 2 (Fourth Extra. Sess.)) §9.

Ref.: Hanna § 7.03[1]; Herlick Handbook § 9.18.

§1871.9. Posting information on Web site of person convicted of violation of article.

The department shall post all of the following information on its Internet Web site for each person, as defined in Section 19, convicted of a violation of this article, Section 11760 or 11880, Section 3700.5 of the Labor Code, or Section 487 or 550 of the Penal Code, if the violation involved workers' compensation insurance, services, or benefits:

(a) The name, case number, county or court, and other identifying information with respect to the case.

(b) The full name of the defendant.

(c) The city and county of the defendant's last known residence or business address.

(d) The date of conviction.

(e) A description of the offense.

(f) The amount of money alleged to have been defrauded.

(g) A description of the punishment imposed, including the length of any sentence of imprisonment and the amount of any fine imposed.

The information required to be posted under this section shall be maintained on the department's Web site for a period of five years from the date of conviction or until the department is notified in writing by the person that the conviction has been reversed or expunged. **Leg.H.** 2004 ch. 281 (AB 2866).

Ref.: Hanna § 2.03[3]; Herlick Handbook § 9.18.

ARTICLE 2
Bureau of Fraudulent Claims
[Selected Provisions]

§1872.84. Information to be forwarded to appropriate disciplinary body.

The commissioner shall ensure that the Fraud Division forwards to the appropriate disciplinary body, in addition to the names and supporting evidence of individuals described in subdivision (a) of Section 1872.83, the names, along with all supporting evidence, of any individuals licensed under the Chiropractic Initiative Act who are suspected of actively engaging in fraudulent activity. **Leg.H.** 2005 ch. 415 (AB 1760) §2.

§1872.95. Medical and chiropractic boards and State Bar; investigation of workers' compensation, motor vehicle, or disability insurance fraud by licensees.

(a) Within existing resources, the Medical Board of California, the Board of Chiropractic Examiners, and the State Bar shall each designate employees to investigate and report on possible fraudulent activities relating to workers' compensation, motor vehicle insurance, or disability insurance by licensees of the board or the bar. Those employees shall actively cooperate with the Fraud Division in the investigation of those activities.

(b) The Medical Board of California and the Board of Chiropractic Examiners shall each report annually, on or before March 1, to the committees of the Senate and Assembly having jurisdiction over insurance on their activities established pursuant to subdivision (a) for the previous year. The State Bar shall include this report in its Annual Discipline Report on or before April 30. That report shall specify, at a minimum, the number of cases investigated, the number of cases forwarded to the Fraud Division or other law enforcement agencies, the outcome of all cases listed in the report, and any other relevant information concerning those cases or general activities conducted under subdivision (a) for the previous year. The report shall include information regarding activities conducted in connection with cases of suspected automobile insurance fraud. **Leg.H.** 1995 ch. 167, 1999 ch. 885, 2005 ch. 717 (AB 1183) §11, 2018 ch. 659 (AB 3249) §149.

Ref.: Hanna § 2.03[3].

ARTICLE 4
Motor Vehicle Theft and Motor Vehicle Insurance Fraud Reporting [Selected Provisions]

§1874.1. Definitions.

The following definitions govern the construction of this article, unless the context requires otherwise:

(a) "Authorized governmental agency" means the Department of the California Highway Patrol, the Department of Insurance, the Department of Justice, the Department of Motor Vehicles, the police department of a city, or a city and county, the sheriff's office or department of a county, a law enforcement agency of the federal government, the district attorney of any county, or city and county, and any licensing agency governed by the Business and Professions Code or the Chiropractic Initiative Act.

(b) "Relevant" means having a tendency to make the existence of any fact that is of consequence to the investigation or determination of an issue more probable or less probable than it would be without the information.

(c) Information shall be deemed important if, within the sole discretion of the authorized governmental agency, that information is requested by that authorized governmental agency.

(d) "Insurer" means the automobile assigned risk plan established pursuant to Section 11620 of the Insurance Code, as well as any insurer writing insurance for motor vehicles or otherwise liable for any loss due to motor vehicle theft or motor vehicle insurance fraud.

(e) "Motor vehicle" means motor vehicle as defined in Section 415 of the Vehicle Code. **Leg.H.** 1989 ch. 1119, 2005 ch. 415 (AB 1760) §3.

ARTICLE 7
Workers' Compensation Insurance Fraud Reporting

§1877. Title.

This article shall be known and may be cited as the Workers' Compensation Insurance Fraud Reporting Act. **Leg.H.** 1991 ch. 116.

Ref.: Hanna § 2.03[3]; Herlick Handbook § 9.18.

§1877.1. Definitions.

The following definitions govern the construction of this article, unless the context requires otherwise:

(a) "Authorized governmental agency" means the district attorney of any county, any city attorney whose duties include criminal prosecutions, any law enforcement agency investigating workers' compensation fraud, the office of the Attorney General, the Department of Insurance, the Department of Industrial Relations, the Employment Development Department, the Department of Corrections and Rehabilitation, the Public Employees' Retirement System, and any licensing agency governed by the Business and Professions Code.

(b) "Relevant" means having a tendency to make the existence of any fact that is of consequence to the investigation or determination of an issue more probable or less probable than it would be without the information.

(c) "Insurer" means an insurer admitted to transact workers' compensation insurance in this state, the State Compensation Insurance Fund, an employer that has secured a certificate of consent to self-insure pursuant to subdivision (b) or (c) of Section 3700 of the Labor Code, or a third-party administrator that has secured a certificate pursuant to Section 3702.1 of the Labor Code.

(d) "Licensed rating organization" means a rating organization licensed by the Insurance Commissioner pursuant to Section 11750.1.

(e) Information shall be deemed important if, within the sole discretion of the authorized governmental agency, that information is requested by that authorized governmental agency. **Leg.H.** 1991 chs. 116, 934, 2003 ch. 636 (AB 1099), 2004 chs. 490 (SB 1344), 1 (AB 13 Fourth Extra. Sess.), effective March 6, 2005 (ch. 490 prevails; ch. 1 (Fourth Extra. Sess.) not effective), 2008 ch. 369 (AB 1844) §6.

Ref.: Hanna § 2.03[2], [3]; Herlick Handbook § 9.18.

§1877.2. Authorized governmental agency.

For the purposes of this article, "authorized governmental agency" includes, in addition to the entities listed in subdivision (a) of Section 1877.1, any licensing agency governed by the Chiropractic Initiative Act. **Leg.H.** 2005 ch. 415 (AB 1760) §4.

§1877.3. Insurer's or licensed rating organization's release of requested information to governmental agency; requirement to notify when fraud committed.

(a) Upon written request to an insurer or a licensed rating organization by an authorized governmental agency, an insurer, an agent authorized by that insurer, or a licensed rating organization to act on behalf of the insurer, shall release to the requesting authorized governmental agency any or all relevant information deemed important to the authorized governmental agency that the insurer or licensed rating organization may possess relating to any specific workers' compensation insurance fraud investigation.

(b)(1) When an insurer or licensed rating organization knows or reasonably believes it knows the identity of a person or entity whom it has reason to believe committed a fraudulent act relating to a workers' compensation insurance claim or a workers' compensation insurance policy, including any policy application, or has knowledge of such a fraudulent act that is reasonably believed not to have been reported to an authorized governmental agency, then, for the purpose of notification and investigation, the insurer, or agent authorized by an insurer to act on its behalf, or licensed rating organization shall notify the local district attorney's office and the Fraud Division of the Department of Insurance, and may notify any other authorized governmental agency of that suspected fraud and provide any additional information in accordance with subdivision (a). The insurer or licensed rating organization shall state in its notice the basis of the suspected fraud.

(2) Insurers shall use a form prescribed by the department for the purposes of reporting suspected fraudulent workers' compensation acts pursuant to this subdivision.

(3) This section does not abrogate or impair the rights or powers created under subdivision (a).

(c) The authorized governmental agency provided with information pursuant to subdivision (a), (b), or (e) shall, upon request, unless it would violate federal law or otherwise compromise an investigation, release or provide that information in a confidential manner to any other authorized governmental agency for purposes of investigation, prosecution, or prevention of insurance fraud or workers' compensation fraud.

(d) An insurer or licensed rating organization providing information to an authorized governmental agency pursuant to this section shall provide the information within a reasonable time, but not exceeding 60 days from the day on which the duty arose.

(e) Upon written request by an authorized governmental agency, as specified in subdivision (o) of Section 1095 of the Unemployment Insurance Code, the Employment Development Department shall release to the requesting agency any or all relevant information that the Employment Development Department may possess relating to any specific workers' compensation insurance fraud investigation. If an authorized governmental agency seeks to disclose this information to any other governmental agency that is not authorized to receive that information pursuant to subdivision (o) of Section 1095 of the Unemployment Insurance Code or subdivision (c) of Section 603.9 of Title 20 of the Code of Federal Regulations, that agency shall submit a request to the Employment Development Department for approval prior to disclosure. Relevant information may include, but is not limited to, all of the following:

(1) Copies of unemployment and disability insurance application and claim forms and copies of any supporting medical records, documentation, and records pertaining thereto.

(2) Copies of returns filed by an employer pursuant to Section 1088 of the Unemployment Insurance Code and copies of supporting documentation.

(3) Copies of benefit payment checks issued to claimants.

(4) Copies of any documentation that specifically identifies the claimant by social security number, residence address, or telephone number. **Leg.H.** 1991 chs. 116, 934, 1992 ch. 1352, effective September 30, 1992, 1995 ch. 885, 2003 ch. 636 (AB 1099), 2005 ch. 717 (AB 1183) §16, 2018 ch. 709 (AB 2046) §2.

Ref.: Hanna § 2.03[3]; Herlick Handbook § 9.18.

§1877.35. Public Employees' Retirement System—Request for information from insurer relating to investigation of eligibility, unlawful application, or receipt of benefits.

(a) The Public Employees' Retirement System may request information from an insurer for any specific investigation of eligibility for, and unlawful application or receipt of, benefits provided under Part 3 (commencing with Section 20000) of Division 5 of Title 2 of the Government Code.

(b) Information received by the Public Employees' Retirement System pursuant to this article may be used for purposes of determining eligibility for, and unlawful application or receipt of, benefits provided under Part 3 (commencing with Section 20000) of Division 5 of Title 2 of the Government Code. **Leg.H.** 2008 ch. 369 (AB 1844) §7.

§1877.4. Confidentiality of information acquired; exception to privilege.

(a) Any information acquired pursuant to this article shall not be a part of the public record. Except as otherwise provided by law, any authorized governmental agency, an insurer, or an agent authorized to act on its behalf, which receives any information furnished pursuant to this article shall not release that information to any person not authorized to receive the information under this article. Any person who violates the prohibition of this subdivision is guilty of a misdemeanor.

(b) The evidence or information described in this section shall be privileged and shall not be subject to subpoena or subpoena duces tecum in a civil or criminal proceeding, unless, after reasonable notice to any insurer, an agent authorized by an insurer to act on its behalf, licensed rating organization, or authorized governmental agency which has an interest in the information, and a hearing, the court determines that the public interest and any ongoing investigation by the authorized governmental agency, insurer, or an agent authorized by the insurer to act on its behalf, or licensed rating organization will not be jeopardized by its disclosure, or by the issuance of and compliance with a subpoena or subpoena duces tecum. **Leg.H.** 1991 ch. 116, 2003 ch. 636 (AB 1099).

Ref.: Hanna §§ 2.03[3], 2.35; Herlick Handbook § 9.18.

§1877.5. Immunity from civil liability when acting in good faith.

No insurer, agent authorized by an insurer to act on its behalf, or licensed rating organization who furnishes information, written or oral, pursuant to this article, and no authorized governmental agency or its employees who (a) furnishes or receives information, written or oral, pursuant to this article, or (b) assists in any investigation of a suspected violation of Section 1871.1, 1871.4, 11760, or 11880, or of Section 549 of the Penal Code, or of Section 3215 or 3219 of the Labor Code conducted by an authorized governmental agency, shall be subject to any civil liability in a cause or action of any kind where the insurer, authorized agent, licensed rating organization, or authorized governmental agency acts in good faith, without malice, and reasonably believes that the action taken was warranted by the then known facts, obtained by reasonable efforts. Nothing in this chapter is intended to, nor does in any way or manner, abrogate or lessen the existing common law or statutory privileges and immunities of an insurer, agent authorized by that insurer to act on its behalf, licensed rating organization, or any authorized governmental agency or its employees. **Leg.H.** 1991 chs. 116, 934, 1993 ch. 120, effective July 16, 1993, 2003 ch. 636 (AB 1099).

Ref.: Hanna § 2.03[3]; Herlick Handbook §§ 9.18, 12.13.

DIVISION 2
CLASSES OF INSURANCE

PART 3
Liability, Workers' Compensation, and Common Carrier Liability Insurance

CHAPTER 1
GENERAL REGULATIONS

ARTICLE 2
Actions on Policies Containing Liability Provisions
[Selected Provisions]

§11580.1. Required provisions for automobile liability insurance.

(a) No policy of automobile liability insurance described in Section 16054 of the Vehicle Code covering liability arising out of the ownership, maintenance, or use of any motor vehicle shall be issued or delivered in this state on or after the effective date of this section unless it contains the provisions set forth in subdivision (b). However, none of the requirements of subdivision (b) shall apply to the insurance afforded under the policy (1) to the extent that the insurance exceeds the limits specified in subdivision (a) of Section 16056 of the Vehicle Code, or (2) if the policy contains an underlying insurance requirement, or provides for a retained limit of self-insurance, equal to or greater than the limits specified in subdivision (a) of Section 16056 of the Vehicle Code.

(b) Every policy of automobile liability insurance to which subdivision (a) applies shall contain all of the following provisions:

[Subsections (b)(1)–(3) Not Reproduced]

(4) Provision affording insurance to the named insured with respect to any owned or leased motor vehicle covered by the policy, and to the same extent that insurance is afforded to the named insured, to any other person using the motor vehicle, provided the use is by the named insured or with his or her permission, express or implied, and within the scope of that permission, except that: (A) … (B) the insurance afforded to any person other than the named insured need not apply to: (i) any employee with respect to bodily injury sustained by a fellow employee injured in the scope and course of his or her employment, or (ii) ….

(c) In addition to any exclusion provided in paragraph (3) of subdivision (b), the insurance afforded by any policy of automobile liability insurance to which subdivision (a) applies, including the insurer's obligation to defend, may, by appropriate policy provision, be made inapplicable to any or all of the following:

[Subsections (c)(1) and (2) Not Reproduced]

(3) Liability imposed upon or assumed by the insured under any workers' compensation law.

(4) Liability for bodily injury to any employee of the insured arising out of and in the course of his or her employment.

[Subsections (c)(5)–(h) Not Reproduced]

Leg.H. 1993 ch. 408, 1999 ch. 313, 2006 ch. 538 (SB 1852) §471, 2016 ch. 31 (SB 836) §176, effective June 27, 2016.

Ref.: Hanna § 7.04[9][b]; Herlick Handbook § 12.15.

§11580.2. Uninsured vehicle coverage; limitations.

[Subsections (a) and (b) Not Reproduced]

(c) The insurance coverage provided for in this section does not apply either as primary or as excess coverage:

[Subsections (c)(1)–(3) Not Reproduced]

(4) In any instance where it would inure directly or indirectly to the benefit of any workers' compensation carrier or to any person qualified as a self-insurer under any workers' compensation law, or directly to the benefit of the United States, or any state or any political subdivision thereof.

[Subsections (c)(5)–(e) Not Reproduced]

(f) The policy or an endorsement added thereto shall provide that the determination as to whether the insured shall be legally entitled to recover damages, and if so entitled, the amount thereof, shall be made by agreement between the insured and the insurer or, in the event of disagreement, by arbitration. The arbitration shall be conducted by a single neutral arbitrator. An award or a judgment confirming an award shall not be conclusive on any party in any action or proceeding between (i) the insured, his or her insurer, his or her legal representative, or his or her heirs and (ii) the uninsured motorist to recover damages arising out of the accident upon which the award is based. If the insured has or may have rights to benefits, other than nonoccupational disability benefits, under any workers' compensation law, the arbitrator shall not proceed with the arbitration until the insured's physical condition is stationary and ratable. In those cases in which the insured claims a permanent disability, the claims shall, unless good cause be shown, be adjudicated by award or settled by compromise and release before the arbitration may proceed. Any demand or petition for arbitration shall contain a declaration, under penalty of perjury, stating whether (i) the insured has a workers' compensation claim; (ii) the claim has proceeded to findings and award or settlement on all issues reasonably contemplated to be determined in that claim; and (iii) if not, what reasons amounting to good cause are grounds for the arbitration to proceed immediately. The arbitration shall be deemed to be a proceeding and the hearing before the arbitrator shall be deemed to be the trial of an issue therein for purposes of issuance of a subpoena by an attorney of a party to the arbitration under Section 1985 of the Code of Civil Procedure. Title 4 (commencing with Section 2016.010) of Part 4 of the Code of Civil Procedure shall be applicable to these determinations, and all rights, remedies, obligations, liabilities and procedures set forth in Title 4 (commencing with Section 2016.010) of Part 4 of the Code of Civil Procedure shall be available to both the insured and the insurer at any time after the accident, both before and after the commencement of arbitration, if any, with the following limitations:

[Subsections (f)(1)–(g) Not Reproduced]

(h) An insured entitled to recovery under the uninsured motorist endorsement or coverage shall be reimbursed within the conditions stated herein without being required to sign any release or waiver of rights to which he or she may be entitled under any other insurance coverage applicable; nor shall payment under this section to the insured be delayed or made contingent upon the decisions as to liability or distribution of loss costs under other bodily injury liability insurance or any bond applicable to the accident. Any loss payable under the terms of the uninsured motorist endorsement or coverage to or for any person may be reduced:

(1) By the amount paid and the present value of all amounts payable to him or her, his or her executor, administrator, heirs, or legal representative under any workers' compensation law, exclusive of nonoccupational disability benefits.

[Subsections (h)(2)–(q) Not Reproduced]

Leg.H. 1995 ch. 738, 2001 ch. 95, 2003 ch. 56 (SB 333), 2005 ch. 294 (AB 333) §23.

Ref.: Hanna § 2.85; Herlick Handbook § 12.15.

ARTICLE 2.5
Personal Liability Insurance Providing Workers' Compensation Coverage for Household Employees

§11590. Personal liability insurance policies to contain coverage for workers' compensation; inapplicability.

Except as provided in Section 11591, no policy providing comprehensive personal liability insurance may be issued or renewed in this state on or after January 1, 1977, unless it contains a provision for coverage against liability for the payment of compensation, as defined in Section 3207 of the Labor Code, to any person defined as an employee by subdivision (d) of Section 3351 of the Labor Code. Any such policy in effect on or after January 1, 1977, whether or not actually containing such provisions, shall be construed as if such provisions were embodied therein. However, such coverage shall not apply if any other existing, valid and collectible, workers' compensation insurance for such liability is applicable to the injury or death of such employee.

Ref.: Hanna §§ 2.82, 3.80; Herlick Handbook §§ 2.4, 2.5, 3.17.

§11591. Exception to §11590.

The requirements of Section 11590 shall be inapplicable to any such policy of insurance or endorsement where the services of such employee are in connection with the trade, business, profession, or occupation, as such terms are defined in Sections 3355 and 3356 of the Labor Code, of the insured.

Ref.: Hanna § 2.82; Herlick Handbook §§ 2.5, 3.17.

§11592. Law governing rates, rating systems, and classifications for workers' compensation insurance.

Notwithstanding the provisions of subdivision (f) of Section 1851, the rates, classifications, and rating systems for the workers' compensation insurance covering those persons defined as employees by subdivision (d) of Section 3351 of the Labor Code, and the insurers issuing such insurance coverage, shall be subject to the provisions of Chapter 9 (commencing with Section 1850) of Part 2 of Division 1.

Ref.: Herlick Handbook § 3.17.

§11593. Premium charge for workers' compensation insurance not to be separately stated.

The premium charge for the coverage required by Section 11590 shall not be separately stated from that charged for other coverage under the policy in the insured's copy of the following: premium notice, policy, endorsement or memorandum of insurance.

Ref.: Herlick Handbook § 3.17.

CHAPTER 2
WORKERS' COMPENSATION POLICIES

ARTICLE 1
Definitions

§11630. "Compensation."

As used in this chapter, the term "compensation" means the benefits insured by workers' compensation insurance.

§11631. "Insurer."

As used in this chapter, the term "insurer" includes the State Compensation Insurance Fund.

ARTICLE 2
Policy Provisions
[Selected Provisions]

§11650. Conclusive presumption of compliance with this article.

Every contract insuring against liability for compensation and every compensation policy is conclusively presumed to contain all of the provisions required by this article.

Ref.: Hanna §§ 2.50[1][a], [b], 26.06[9][b]; Herlick Handbook § 3.1.

§11651. Contract/policy statement of insurer's liability.

Every such contract or policy shall contain a clause to the effect that the insurer will be directly and primarily liable to any proper claimant for payment of any compensation for which the employer is liable, subject to the provisions, conditions and limitations of the policy.

Ref.: 8 C.C.R. §9811; Hanna §§ 2.50[1][a], [b], 5.04[4]; Herlick Handbook § 3.1.

§11652. Employer knowledge of injury as imputed to insurer.

Every such contract or policy shall contain a clause to the effect that, as between the employee and the insurer, notice to or knowledge of the occurrence of the injury on the part of the employer will be deemed notice or knowledge, as the case may be, on the part of the insurer.

Ref.: 8 C.C.R. §9811; Hanna §§ 2.50[1][a], [b], 5.04[4]; Herlick Handbook § 3.1.

§11653. Employer's and insurer's jurisdiction.

Every such contract or policy shall contain a clause to the effect that jurisdiction of the employer will, for the purpose of the law imposing liability for compensation, be jurisdiction of the insurer.

Ref.: Hanna §§ 2.50[1][a], [b], 5.04[4], 21.03[5]; Herlick Handbook § 3.1.

§11654. Insurer bound by findings against employer; insurance contract to govern liability.

Every such contract or policy shall contain a clause to the effect that the insurer will in all things be bound by and subject to the orders, findings, decisions or awards rendered against the employer under the provisions of the law imposing liability for compensation, subject to the provisions, conditions and limitations of the policy. The insurance contract shall govern as between the employer and insurer as to payments by either in discharge of the employer's liability for compensation.

Ref.: Hanna §§ 2.50[1][a], [b], 5.04[4].

§11655. Effect of employer's insolvency or bankruptcy on insurer's liability.

Such policy shall not contain any provisions relieving the insurer from payment when the employer becomes insolvent or obtains a discharge in bankruptcy, or otherwise, during the period that the policy is in operation or the compensation remains owing. **Leg.H.** 1935 ch. 145, effective September 15, 1935, 2009 ch. 500 (AB 1059) §56.

Ref.: Hanna §§ 2.50[1][a], [b], 5.04[4], 27.04.

§11656. Employee's lien.

Such policy shall also provide that the employee has a first lien upon any amount which becomes owing to the employer from the insurer on account of the policy, and that in case of the legal incapacity or inability of the employer to receive the money and pay it to the claimant, the insurer will pay it directly to the claimant. To the extent of such payment, the obligations of the employer to the claimant are thereby discharged.

Ref.: Hanna §§ 2.50[1][a], [b], 5.04[4].

§11658.5. Insurer disclosures for dispute resolution or arbitration; default; applicability.

(a)(1) An insurer that intends to use a dispute resolution or arbitration agreement to resolve disputes arising in California out of a workers' compensation insurance policy or endorsement issued to a California employer shall disclose to the employer, contemporaneously with any written quote that offers to provide insurance coverage, that choice of law and choice of venue or forum may be a jurisdiction other than California and that these terms are negotiable between the insurer and the employer. The disclosure shall be signed by the employer as evidence of receipt where the employer accepts the offer of coverage from that insurer.

(2) After compliance with paragraph (1), a dispute resolution or arbitration agreement may be negotiated by the insurer and the employer before any dispute arises.

(b) Nothing in this section is intended to interfere with any authority granted to the Insurance Commissioner under current law.

(c) Failure by the insurer to observe the requirements of subdivision (a) shall result in a default to California as the choice of law and forum for resolution of disputes arising in California.

(d) For purposes of this section, a "California employer" means an employer whose principal place of business is in California and whose California payroll constitutes the majority of the employer's payroll for purposes of determining premium under the policy.

(e) This section shall apply to workers' compensation policies issued or renewed on or after July 1, 2012. **Leg.H.** 2011 ch. 566 (SB 684) §2.

Ref.: Hanna § 2.70[2].

§11661. Insurance for employer's serious and willful misconduct.

An insurer shall not insure against the liability of the employer for the additional compensation recoverable for serious and willful misconduct of the employer or his agent. An insurer may, however, provide insurance against the expense of defending any suit for serious and willful misconduct against an employer or his agent.

Ref.: Hanna §§ 2.50[4][b], 2.62[2][b], 10.01[2], 25.10[7]; Herlick Handbook §§ 3.8, 9.6.

§11661.5. Injuries to illegally employed minors.

An insurer shall not insure an employer against his liability for additional compensation arising out of injuries to illegally employed persons under 16 years of age, as provided for by Part 4 (commencing with Section 1171) of Division 2 of the Labor Code.

Note: See Labor Code §4557.

Ref.: Hanna §§ 2.50[3], [4][b], 2.62[2][c], 2.63[3][c], 10.10; Herlick Handbook § 3.8.

§11661.6. Insuring compensation for increased indemnity prohibited.

(a) An insurer shall not insure an employer against his or her obligation to reimburse the insurer for the amount of increase in indemnity payment as provided for by subdivision (e) of Section 4650 of the Labor Code. Every contract insuring against liability for compensation and every compensation policy shall provide that the insured employer is obligated to reimburse the insurer for the amount of increase in indemnity payment required by Section 4650 of the Labor Code, if the late indemnity payment which gives rise to the increase in the amount of payment is due less than seven days after the insurer receives the completed claim form from the employer.

(b) An insurer shall not report the amount of any increase in indemnity required by Section 4650 of the Labor Code as incurred indemnity to the Insurance Commissioner's designated statistical agent.

Ref.: Hanna §§ 2.62[2][f], 2.72[2]; Herlick Handbook §§ 5.15, 9.5.

§11662. Insurer's subrogation to employer's rights.

Whenever any employer is insured against liability for compensation with any insurer, such insurer is subrogated to the rights of the employer to recover losses arising out of any of the following acts by the insurer:

(a) Assuming the liability of the employer for compensation in the manner provided by the law relating thereto.

(b) Payment of any compensation for which the employer is liable.

Such insurer may enforce any such subrogated rights in its own name.

Ref.: Hanna §§ 2.71, 5.05[4], [11], 11.40[1], 11.41; Herlick Handbook §§ 3.7, 12.2.

§11663. Liability of general and special employers.

As between insurers of general and special employers, one which insures the liability of the general employer is liable for the entire cost of compensation payable on account of injury occurring in the course of and arising out of general and special employments unless the special employer had the employee on his or her payroll at the time of injury, in which case the insurer of the special employer is solely liable. For the purposes of this section, a self-insured or lawfully uninsured employer is deemed and treated as an insurer of his or her workers' compensation liability.

Ref.: Hanna §§ 2.60[3], 3.142[5]; Herlick Handbook § 3.9.

§11663.5. Insurer provides premium and loss history report.

(a) Upon receiving a written request from an insured or the agent or broker of record where authorized by the insured, an insurer shall provide a premium and loss history report to the requesting party for the account's tenure or the three-year period ending with the inception of the current policy period, whichever is shorter, plus loss experience during the current policy period that is in force if any of the following occur.

(1) The policy is canceled or nonrenewed.

(2) The policyholder requests the information within 60 days prior to the renewal date of an existing policy.

(3) The policyholder's current insurer's rating is downrated by a nationally recognized insurance rating service to a financial rating below secure or good or to a rating that would negatively impact the ability of the policyholder to conduct its business operations.

(4) The policyholder's current insurer is conserved by the department under Section 1011, or is ordered to cease writing business under Sections 1065.1 and 1065.2.

The premium and loss history report, and the loss experience information for the current policy period, shall be provided within 10 business days of receiving the request.

(b) This section applies only to workers' compensation insurance.

(c) This section shall not apply to a policyholder who, through automated or other means, is provided direct, ongoing access to claims information by the insurer.

(d) For purposes of this section, a loss history report includes, but is not limited to, a list of individual claims detailed by date of claim and total incurred and paid losses. **Leg.H.** 2001 ch. 102.

§11664. Notice of nonrenewal.

(a) This section applies only to policies of workers' compensation insurance.

(b) A notice of nonrenewal shall be in writing and shall be delivered or mailed to the producer of record and to the named insured at the mailing address shown on the policy. Subdivision (a) of Section 1013 of the Code of Civil Procedure shall be applicable if the notice is mailed.

(c) An insurer, at least 30 days, but not more than 120 days, in advance of the end of the policy period, shall give notice of nonrenewal, and the reasons for the nonrenewal, if the insurer intends not to renew the policy.

(d) If an insurer fails to give timely notice required by subdivision (c), the policy of insurance shall be continued, with no change in its premium rate, for a period of 60 days after the insurer gives the notice.

(e) A notice of nonrenewal shall not be required in any of the following situations.

(1) The transfer of, or renewal of, a policy without a change in its terms or conditions or the rate on which the premium is based between insurers that are members of the same insurance group.

(2) The policy has been extended for 90 days or less, if the notice required in subdivision (c) has been given prior to the extension.

(3) The named insured has obtained replacement coverage or has agreed, in writing, within 60 days of the termination of the policy, to obtain that coverage.

(4) The policy is for a period of no more than 60 days and the insured is notified at the time of issuance that it may not be renewed.

(5) The named insured requests a change in the terms or conditions or risks covered by the policy within 60 days prior to the end of the policy period.

(6) The insurer has made a written offer to the insured to renew the policy at a premium rate increase of less than 25 percent.

(A) If the premium rate in the governing classification for the insured is to be increased 25 percent or greater and the insurer intends to renew the policy, the insurer shall provide a written notice of a renewal offer not less than 30 days prior to the policy renewal date. The governing classification shall be determined by the rules and regulations established in accordance with subdivision (c) of Section 11750.3.

(B) For purposes of this section, "premium rate" means the cost of insurance per unit of exposure prior to the application of individual risk variations based on loss or expense considerations such as scheduled rating and experience rating. **Leg.H.** 1994 ch. 398, effective September 1, 1994, operative November 30, 1994, 1995 ch. 375, 1997 ch. 385, 2000 ch. 884, effective September 29, 2000, 2001 ch. 102.

Ref.: Herlick Handbook §§ 3.2, 3.15.

§11665. Payroll audits for roofing contractors; annual report.

(a) An insurer who issues a workers' compensation insurance policy to a roofing contractor holding a C-39 license from the Contractors' State License Board shall perform an annual payroll audit for the contractor. This audit shall include an in-person visit to the place of business of the roofing contractor to verify whether the number of employees reported by the contractor is accurate. The insurer may impose a surcharge on each policyholder audited under this subdivision in an amount necessary to recoup the reasonable costs of conducting the annual payroll audits.

(b) The commissioner shall direct the rating organization designated as his or her statistical agent to compile pertinent statistical data on those holding C-39 licenses, as reported by the appropriate state entity, on an annual basis and provide a report to him or her each year. The data shall track the total annual payroll and loss data reported on those holding C-39 licenses in accordance with the standard workers' compensation insurance classifications applicable to roofing operations. The data shall include the number of employers, total payroll, total losses, and the losses per one hundred dollars ($100) of payroll by the employers' annual payroll intervals as follows:

1 to	4,999
5,000 to	9,999
10,000 to	14,999
15,000 to	19,999
20,000 to	24,999
25,000 to	29,999
30,000 to	39,999
40,000 to	49,999
50,000 to	74,999
75,000 to	99,999
100,000 to	199,999
200,000 to	299,999
300,000 to	399,999
400,000 to	499,999
500,000 to	599,999
600,000 to	699,999
700,000 to	799,999
800,000 to	899,999
900,000 to	999,999
1,000,000 to	1,099,999
1,100,000 to	1,199,999
1,200,000 to	1,299,999
1,300,000 to	1,399,999
1,400,000 to	1,499,999
1,500,000 or more	

The report shall also be provided to the Legislature by the commissioner, in compliance with Section 9795 of the Government Code. **Leg.H.** 2006 ch. 38 (AB 881) §3, 2010 ch. 423 (AB 2305) §3, 2012 ch. 389 (AB 2219) §3, 2013 ch. 76 (AB 383) §140.

Ref.: Hanna § 3.134; Herlick Handbook § 3.23.

CHAPTER 3 REGULATION OF BUSINESS OF WORKERS' COMPENSATION INSURANCE

ARTICLE 1 Deposits by Workers' Compensation Insurers

§11690. Definitions.

For purposes of this article:

(a) "Compensable workers' compensation claim" means a claim where the claimant is entitled to benefits under the workers' compensation law of the state.

(b) "Delinquency proceeding" means any proceeding commenced against an insurer for the purpose of liquidating, rehabilitating, reorganizing, or conserving that insurer, where there has not been a court order finding the insurer insolvent.

(c) "Receiver" means liquidator, rehabilitator, or conservator, as appropriate. **Leg.H.** 2002 ch. 899 (SB 2093) §2.

Ref.: Hanna § 2.30[2]–[5]; Herlick Handbook §§ 3.12, 3.13, 3.15.

§11691. Deposit required by insurer desiring admission to transact workers' compensation insurance, or reinsurance, or desiring to reinsure the injury, disablement, or death portions of policies; notice to commissioner; trust agreement; fee.

(a)(1) In order to provide protection to the workers of this state in the event that the insurers issuing workers' compensation insurance to employers fail to pay compensable workers' compensation claims when due, except in the case of the State Compensation Insurance Fund, every insurer desiring admission to transact workers' compensation insurance, or workers' compensation reinsurance business, or desiring to reinsure the injury, disablement, or death portions of policies of workers' compensation insurance under the class of disability insurance shall, as a prerequisite to admission, or ability to reinsure the injury, disablement, or death portion of policies of workers' compensation insurance under the class of disability insurance, deposit cash instruments or approved interest-bearing securities or approved stocks readily convertible into cash, investment certificates, or share accounts issued by a savings and loan association doing business in this state and insured by the Federal Deposit Insurance Corporation, certificates of deposit, or savings deposits in a bank licensed to do business in this state, or approved letters of credit that perform in material respects as any other security allowable as a form of deposit for purposes of a workers' compensation deposit and that meet the standard set forth in Section 922.5, or approved securities registered with a qualified depository located in a reciprocal state as defined in Section 1104.9, with that deposit to be in an amount and subject to any exceptions as set forth in this article. The deposit shall be made from time to time as demanded by the commissioner and may be made with the Treasurer, or a bank or savings and loan association authorized to engage in the trust business pursuant to Division 1 (commencing with Section 99) or Division 2 (commencing with Section 5000) of the Financial Code, or a trust company. A deposit of securities registered with a qualified depository located in a reciprocal state as defined in Section 1104.9 may only be made in a bank or savings and loan association authorized to engage in the trust business pursuant to Division 1 (commencing with Section 99) or Division 2 (commencing with Section 5000) of the Financial Code, or a trust company, licensed to do business and located in this state that is either domiciled in and has a principal place of business in this state, or is a national bank association with a trust office located in this state, that is a qualified custodian as defined in paragraph (1) of subdivision (a) of Section 1104.9, and that maintains deposits of at least seven hundred fifty million dollars ($750,000,000). The deposit shall be made subject to the approval of the commissioner under those rules and regulations that he or she shall promulgate. The deposit shall be maintained at a deposit value specified by the commissioner, but in any event no less than one hundred thousand dollars ($100,000), nor less than the reserves required of the insurer to be maintained under any of the provisions of Article 1 (commencing with Section 11550) of Chapter 1, relating to loss reserves on workers' compensation business of the insurer in this state, nor less than the sum of the amounts specified in subdivision (a) of Section 11693, whichever is greater. The deposit shall be for the purpose of paying compensable workers' compensation claims under policies issued by the insurer or reinsured by the admitted reinsurer and expenses as provided in Section 11698.02, in the event the insurer or reinsurer fails to pay those claims when they come due. If the insurer providing the deposit is domiciled in a state where a state statute, regulation, or court decision provides that, with respect to covered claims within the deductible amount that are paid by a guarantee association after the entry of an order of liquidation under large deductible workers' compensation policies, any part of the reimbursement proceeds, other than the reasonable expenses of the receiver related to treatment of deductible policy arrangements of insurance companies in liquidation, owed by insureds on those deductible amounts, whether paid directly or through a draw of collateral, are general assets of the estate, then the amount of the insurer's deposit pursuant to this article shall be calculated based on the gross amount of that insurer's liabilities for loss and loss adjustment expenses under those policies without regard to the deductible, and those reserves shall not be reduced by any collateral or reimbursement obligations insureds were required to provide under those policies.

(2) This section does not require that the deposit be calculated based on gross amounts of liabilities described above if the domiciliary state does not have an existing statute, regulation, or court decision providing that the reimbursement proceeds described above are general assets of the estate.

(b) Each insurer or reinsurer desiring to have the ability to reinsure the injury, disablement, or death portions of policies of workers' compensation under the class of disability insurance shall provide prior notice to the commissioner, in the manner and form prescribed by the commissioner of its intent to reinsure that insurance. In the event of late notice, a late filing fee shall be imposed on the reinsurer pursuant to Section 924 for failure to notify the commissioner of its intent to reinsure workers' compensation insurance.

(c) If the deposit required by this section is not made with the Treasurer, then the depositor shall execute a trust agreement in a form approved by the commissioner between the insurer, the institution in which the deposit is made or, where applicable, the qualified custodian of the deposit, and the commissioner, that grants to the commissioner the authority to withdraw the deposit as set forth in Sections 11691.2, 11696, 11698, and 11698.3. The insurer shall also execute and deliver in duplicate to the commissioner a power of attorney in favor of the commissioner for the purposes specified herein, supported by a resolution of the depositor's board of directors. The power of attorney and director's resolution shall be on forms approved by the commissioner, shall provide that the power of attorney cannot be revoked or withdrawn without the consent of the commissioner, and shall be acknowledged as required by law.

(d)(1) The commissioner shall require payment, in advance, of a fee of two hundred eighty-three dollars ($283) for the initial filing of a trust agreement with a bank, savings and loan association, or trust company on deposits made pursuant to subdivision (a); for each amendment, supplement, or other change to the deposit agreement; for receiving and processing deposit schedules pursuant to this section; and for each withdrawal, substitution, or any other change in the deposit.

(2) The commissioner shall require payment, in advance, of a fee of four hundred twenty-four dollars ($424) for the initial filing of each letter of credit utilized pursuant to subdivision (a). In addition, the commissioner shall require payment, in advance, of a fee of two hundred eighty-three dollars ($283) annually for each amendment of a letter of credit.

(e) Any workers' compensation insurer that deposits cash or cash equivalents pursuant to this section shall be entitled to a prompt refund of those deposits in excess of the amount determined by the commissioner pursuant to subdivision (a). The commissioner shall cause to be refunded any deposits determined by the commissioner to be in excess of the amount required by subdivision (a) within 30 days of that determination. In the alternative, an insurer may use any excess deposit funds to offset a demand by the commissioner to increase its deposit due to the failure of a reinsurer to make a deposit pursuant to this section.

(f)(1) An admitted insurer reinsuring business covered in this article (hereafter referred to as reinsurer) shall identify to the commissioner, in a form prescribed by the commissioner, amounts deposited for credit in the name of each ceding insurer.

(2) All reinsurance agreements covering claims and obligations under business covered by this article, and allowable for purposes of granting a ceding carrier a deposit credit, shall include a provision granting the commissioner, in the event of a delinquency proceeding, receivership, or insolvency of a ceding insurer, any sums from a reinsurer's deposit that are necessary for the commissioner to pay those reinsured claims and obligations, or to ensure their payment by the California Insurance Guarantee Association, deemed by the commissioner due under the reinsurance agreement, upon failure of the reinsurer for any reason to make payments under the policy of reinsurance. The commissioner shall give 30 days' notice prior to drawing upon these funds of an intent to do so. Notwithstanding the commissioner's right to draw on these funds, the reinsurer shall otherwise retain its right to determine the validity of those claims and obligations and to contest their payment under the reinsurance agreement. Prior to a reinsurer's deposit being drawn upon, in whole or in part, by the department, the department shall provide a reinsurer with an explanation of procedures that a reinsurer may use to explain to the department why the use of the reinsurer's deposit may not be appropriate under the reinsurance agreement.

(3) A reinsurer entering into a contract identified in paragraph (2), beginning on or after January 1, 2005, may not cede claims or obligations assumed from a ceding insurer unless the deposit securing the ceded claims or obligations is governed by paragraph (2) or, upon approval of the commissioner, would secure the ceded claims or obligations in all material respects and in the same manner as a deposit identified in paragraph (2) above.

(4) All sums received from the reinsurer by the commissioner for those claims paid by the California Insurance Guarantee Association shall be held separate and apart from and not included in the general assets of the insolvent insurer, and shall be transferred to the California Insurance Guarantee Association upon receipt by the commissioner. In the event of a final judgment or settlement adverse to the drawing of funds by the commissioner pursuant to paragraph (2) or (3), the California Insurance Guarantee Association shall repay funds it obtained to pay covered claims and shall, if necessary, either levy a surcharge as needed or seek legislative approval to levy the surcharge if the California Insurance Guarantee Association is already levying the maximum surcharge permissible under law.

(g) If a reinsurer has not maintained deposits as required by subdivision (a) in amounts equal to the amounts of deposit credits claimed by its ceding insurers, the commissioner, after notifying the reinsurer and its ceding insurers of the deposit shortfall and allowing 15 days from the date of the notice for the deposit shortfall to be corrected, may disallow all or a portion of the reserve credits claimed by the ceding insurers. A ceding insurer disallowed a reserve credit pursuant to this provision shall immediately make the deposit required by this section.

(h) For interest-bearing securities that are debt securities and include principal payment features prior to maturity that are utilized pursuant to subdivision (a), all principal payments received shall be retained as part of the deposit.

(i) Withdrawal of any amount of the deposit required under subdivision (a) that results in a reduction of the required amount of the deposit may only occur with the prior written consent of the commissioner. **Leg.H.** 2002 ch. 899 (SB 2093) §2, 2005 ch. 415 (AB 1760) §6, 2007 ch. 117 (AB 1364) §1, 2011 ch. 411 (AB 1416) §56, 2016 ch. 304 (AB 2884) §19, 2017 ch. 534 (AB 1699) §70.

Ref.: Hanna § 2.30[2]–[5]; Herlick Handbook §§ 3.12, 3.13, 3.15.

§11691.1. Fee for filing schedule of securities.

The fees for filing a schedule of securities with the Treasurer, and making a deposit of the same, and for each withdrawal, substitution, or any other change in the securities comprising this deposit with the Treasurer, shall be paid to the commissioner for the costs of review and approval of deposits, and shall be the same as are prescribed by Article 11 (commencing with Section 939) of Chapter 1 of Part 2 of Division 1.

All other reasonable charges made by the Treasurer for servicing securities deposited with him or her shall be paid to the Treasurer by the insurer that has deposited the security, and shall not be charged to the commissioner. **Leg.H.** 2002 ch. 899 (SB 2093) §2.

Ref.: Hanna § 2.30[2]–[5]; Herlick Handbook §§ 3.12, 3.13, 3.15.

§11691.2. Deposit as security for payment of obligations on workers' compensation insurance transacted in state.

The deposit required pursuant to Section 11691 shall be security for the payment of the insurer's obligations on worker's compensation insurance transacted in this state. The deposit shall not be withdrawn except upon the written order of the commissioner to use the proceeds thereof in payment of compensable worker's compensation claims and expenses as provided in Section 11698.02, or as otherwise provided in this article, but shall be forthwith payable to the commissioner or at the direction of the commissioner by the Treasurer or the bank, savings and loan association, or trust company approved by the commissioner upon that order. No deposit so placed with a bank, savings and loan association, or trust company shall be subject to any lien or claim asserted by it or be subject to any disposition obligation, demand, liability, cause of action, judgment, or other claim, or cost or expense attendant thereon, other than as is permitted by the commissioner. Notwithstanding any other provisions of this code, the deposit shall be retained by the Treasurer or the bank, savings and loan association, or trust company approved by the commissioner and only released in accordance with the provisions of this article or pursuant to regulations or a written order of the commissioner. **Leg.H.** 2002 ch. 899 (SB 2093) §2.

Ref.: Hanna § 2.30[2]–[5]; Herlick Handbook §§ 3.12, 3.13, 3.15.

§11691.3. List of authorized insurers and reinsurers.

The commissioner shall establish a list of all insurers or reinsurers authorized to reinsure the injury, disablement, or death portions of policies of workers' compensation insurance under the class of disability insurance. An insurer or reinsurer shall be authorized to reinsure the injury, disablement, or death portions of policies of workers' compensation insurance under the class of disability insurance if it has complied with Section 11691. The commissioner shall publish a master list of those insurers or reinsurers at least semiannually. Any insurer or reinsurer providing the notification and deposit required by Section 11691, shall be added by addendum to the list at the time of approval, and shall be incorporated into the master list at the next date of publication. The list and addenda required by this section shall be published so that they are readily accessible to insurers and producers. The list and addenda required by this section shall also contain a notice that if an insurer enters into a contract of reinsurance with an insurer or reinsurer reinsuring the injury, disablement, or death portions of policies of workers' compensation insurance under the class of disability insurance that is not authorized pursuant to this section, the ceding insurer may not be able to claim that reinsurance for reserve credit. **Leg.H.** 2002 ch. 899 (SB 2093) §2.

Ref.: Hanna § 2.30[2]–[5]; Herlick Handbook §§ 3.12, 3.13, 3.15.

§11692. Issuance of certificate of authority.

A certificate of authority to transact workers' compensation insurance in this state shall not be issued nor renewed to any insurer until the deposit required pursuant to Section 11691 is approved by the commissioner. **Leg.H.** 2002 ch. 899 (SB 2093) §2, 2005 ch. 415 (AB 1760) §7.

Ref.: Hanna § 2.30[2]–[5]; Herlick Handbook §§ 3.12, 3.13, 3.15.

§11692.5. Late filing fee.

On and after the effective date of this article, the commissioner shall collect a late filing fee from any admitted insurer or reinsurer that fails to deposit the securities when required by this code in the following amount:

(a) If the deposit shortfall is outstanding for less than 31 days, 0.5 percent of the deposit shortfall, but in no event not less than six hundred dollars ($600).

(b) If the deposit shortfall is outstanding for more than 30 days but less than 61 days, an additional late filing fee in the amount of 1 percent of the deposit shortfall, but in no event not less than one thousand two hundred dollars ($1,200) shall be due.

(c) If the deposit shortfall is outstanding for 61 days or greater, an additional late filing fee of 1.5 percent of the deposit shortfall for every 30-day period thereafter, or fraction thereof, but in no event shall this portion of the late filing fee for each additional 30-day period or fraction thereof be less than three thousand dollars ($3,000). The late filing fees provided herein are in addition to all other rights and remedies granted the commissioner by this article. **Leg.H.** 2002 ch. 899 (SB 2093) §2, 2005 ch. 415 (AB 1760) §8.

Ref.: Hanna § 2.30[2]–[5]; Herlick Handbook §§ 3.12, 3.13, 3.15.

§11693. Annual adjustment of deposit.

The deposit required pursuant to Section 11691 shall be adjusted on or prior to March 31 of each year in an amount as follows:

(a) Not less than the sum of the following amounts computed, less credits and deductions allowable with respect to reinsurance in admitted insurers, as provided under Section 11691, as of the close of the last preceding December 31 or as of any calendar quarter end as directed by the commissioner pursuant to Section 11694 in respect to workers' compensation insurance written subject to the workers' compensation laws of this state:

(1) The aggregate of the present values at 6 percent interest, or at the rate of the company's investment yield as determined by the NAIC Insurance Regulatory Information System Ratio Number 5 for Property and Casualty Companies, whichever is lower, of the determined and estimated future payments upon compensation claims not included in paragraph (2), including in those claims both benefits and loss expenses.

(2) The aggregate of the amounts computed as follows: For each of the preceding three years, 65 percent of the earned compensation premiums for that year less all loss and loss expense payments made upon claims incurred in the corresponding year from that 65 percent; except that the amount for each year shall not be less than the present value at 6 percent interest of the determined and the estimated unpaid claims incurred in that year, including both benefits and loss expenses.

(b) Not less than one hundred thousand dollars ($100,000).

(c) If the aggregate amount computed under subdivision (a) exceeds fifty thousand dollars ($50,000), not more than double the aggregate amount.

(d) The commissioner may utilize securities valuation software programs or services to validate the value of securities held in workers' compensation deposits of insurers authorized to transact workers' compensation insurance in California as direct writers or reinsurers, or reinsurers of workers' compensation under the class of disability. **Leg.H.** 2002 ch. 899 (SB 2093) §2, 2005 ch. 415 (AB 1760) §9.

Ref.: Hanna § 2.30[2]–[5]; Herlick Handbook §§ 3.12, 3.13, 3.15.

§11694. Computation of deposit from figures in annual report.

After the first annual statement to the commissioner covering business of the insurer for a full year in this state, the deposit required pursuant to Section 11691 shall be computed from the figures shown in the last preceding report of business as of December 31, filed with the commissioner, and shall be reported to the commissioner on or before March 1 of each year in a form and manner prescribed by the commissioner. Notwithstanding anything to the contrary in this article, should the commissioner determine that there has been a material change in the insurer's ultimate liability for future payments upon compensable workers' compensation claims in this state, at the commissioner's discretion, the amount of the deposit shall then be fixed by the commissioner at the amount that he or she deems sufficient to secure the payment of the insurer's ultimate obligations on its workers' compensation insurance transacted in this state, and upon notification from the commissioner the insurer shall immediately, but in no event less than 30 days after notification, increase the deposit as directed. **Leg.H.** 2002 ch. 899 (SB 2093) §2, 2005 ch. 415 (AB 1760) §10.

Ref.: Hanna § 2.30[2]–[5]; Herlick Handbook §§ 3.12, 3.13, 3.15.

§11694.5. Deposit reports.

On or before March 1 and May 15 of each year, the insurers or reinsurers subject to Section 11694 shall file a report in the form and manner prescribed by the commissioner that valuates and details the deposit as of December 31 of the preceding year and March 31 of the current year. The commissioner may require additional reporting by any insurer or reinsurer when it is deemed necessary. **Leg.H.** 2005 ch. 415 (AB 1760) §11.

§11695. Fixing deposit for insurer who voluntarily ceases to do business in state.

Where an admitted insurer has voluntarily ceased to do in this state the business for which a deposit is required pursuant to Section 11691, the deposit shall be fixed by the commissioner at the amount that he or she deems sufficient for the protection of the beneficiaries of the policies of that insurer. **Leg.H.** 2002 ch. 899 (SB 2093) §2.

Ref.: Hanna § 2.30[2]–[5]; Herlick Handbook §§ 3.12, 3.13, 3.15.

§11696. Use of deposit when insurer fails to pay compensation claim.

In the event an insurer not in a delinquency proceeding fails to pay any compensable workers' compensation claim against it, or fails to pay, to the extent of its liability as a reinsurer, any compensable workers' compensation claim covered by a policy wholly or partly reinsured by it, the commissioner shall use the proceeds of the deposit required pursuant to Section 11691 to pay all those compensable workers' compensation claims and related expenses as described in Section 11698.02. **Leg.H.** 2002 ch. 899 (SB 2093) §2.

Ref.: Hanna § 2.30[2]–[5]; Herlick Handbook §§ 3.12, 3.13, 3.15.

§11697. Payment of claim by commissioner as satisfaction of claim.

The payment of a workers' compensation claim by the commissioner shall constitute a satisfaction of the claim to the extent of the payment made. In the event any judgment is entered on the claim, the commissioner shall file a proportionate satisfaction thereof in the office of the clerk of the court wherein the judgment is entered. **Leg.H.** 2002 ch. 899 (SB 2093) §2.

Ref.: Hanna § 2.30[2]–[5]; Herlick Handbook §§ 3.12, 3.13, 3.15.

§11698. Circumstances authorizing commissioner to take control or possession of deposit.

(a) In the event any one of the eventualities described in paragraph (1), (2), (3), or (4), transpires, the commissioner shall immediately take control or possession of the deposit required pursuant to Section 11691 and may use the deposit to pay or procure the payment of those compensable workers' compensation claims against the insurer, and those expenses described in Section 11698.02. The proceeds of the deposit shall in that event inure to the commissioner as a trust to be held separate and apart from all other assets of the insurer held by the commissioner. They shall be used only for the purposes set forth and in accordance with the procedures established in this article. Once it is determined that there are no remaining undischarged liabilities for compensable workers' compensation claims or it is actuarially demonstrated that the deposit exceeds those liabilities, the commissioner shall transfer the remaining amount of the deposit to the general assets of the estate.

(1) If the commissioner is named conservator of that insurer pursuant to Article 14 (commencing with Section 1011) of Chapter 1 of Part 2 of Division 1.

(2) The proper court has appointed the commissioner ancillary receiver of the insurer or reinsurer.

(3) A delinquency proceeding has been instituted by the proper court against the insurer or reinsurer.

(4) If it appears to the commissioner that any of the conditions set forth in Section 1011 exist or that irreparable loss and injury to the property and business of the insurer or reinsurer has occurred or may occur unless the commissioner acts immediately without notice and before applying to the court for any order.

(b) If the commissioner has proceeded under subdivision (a) or Section 11696 or 11698.3 and a deposit of securities registered with a qualified depository located in a reciprocal state and in the custody of a qualified custodian pursuant to Section 1104.9 cannot be released to the commissioner according to the terms of the agreement entered into pursuant to Section 11691 or the requirements of Section 11691.2 because of a delinquency proceeding initiated in the reciprocal state in which the qualified depository is located, or, if the deposit of securities registered with a qualified depository has been executed upon at any time by any creditor of an insurer and that execution has been affirmed by a written opinion of a court of competent federal appellate jurisdiction, the commissioner may, after a public hearing and upon a finding that deposits of securities registered with that depository do not allow the commissioner to discharge his or her responsibilities as set forth in this chapter, require workers' compensation insurers authorized to transact insurance in this state to cease and desist making any further deposits authorized by Section 11691 in approved securities registered with that depository. For the purposes of this subdivision, the term "delinquency proceeding" shall have the same meaning as contained in subdivision (b) of Section 1064.1. **Leg.H.** 2002 ch. 899 (SB 2093) §2.

Ref.: Hanna § 2.30[2]–[5]; Herlick Handbook §§ 3.12, 3.13, 3.15.

§11698.01. Options of commissioner upon taking control or possession of deposit.

When the commissioner is authorized to proceed under Section 11698 he or she may do either of the following:

(a) Subject to Sections 11698.2, 11698.21, and 11698.22, enter into reinsurance and assumption agreements with one or more admitted solvent workers' compensation insurers by the terms of which liability for all those obligations is reinsured and assumed by such insurer.

(b) Use the deposit required pursuant to Section 11691 to pay or procure payment of the insurer's compensable workers' compensation claims and those expenses authorized in Section 11698.02. **Leg.H.** 2002 ch. 899 (SB 2093) §2.

Ref.: Hanna § 2.30[2]–[5]; Herlick Handbook §§ 3.12, 3.13, 3.15.

§11698.02. Use of proceeds from deposit.

The proceeds of the deposit required pursuant to Section 11691 shall be used solely to pay compensable workers' compensation claims under the insured or reinsured policies, allocated claims expense necessary to pay those claims, and the expenses connected with all proceedings or actions permitted or required by this article in furtherance of the payment of those claims, or should the commissioner pursuant to subdivision (a) of Section 11698.01 enter into reinsurance and assumption agreements with one or more reinsurers, the proceeds of the deposit shall be used to reimburse those reinsurers. **Leg.H.** 2002 ch. 899 (SB 2093) §2.

Ref.: Hanna § 2.30[2]–[5]; Herlick Handbook §§ 3.12, 3.13, 3.15.

§11698.1. Accounting of funds.

From time to time and in any event at or prior to the time of the filing of his or her petition for discharge as receiver, the commissioner shall do the following:

(a) File with the Workers' Compensation Appeals Board an accounting of all trust funds received and used from the proceeds of the deposit required pursuant to Section 11691.

(b) File with the court an accounting of all funds received and used as expenses from the general funds of the insurer. **Leg.H.** 2002 ch. 899 (SB 2093) §2.

Ref.: Hanna § 2.30[2]–[5]; Herlick Handbook §§ 3.12, 3.13, 3.15.

§11698.2. Provisions of reinsurance and assumption agreement.

If the commissioner enters into a reinsurance and assumption agreement as provided in subdivision (a) of Section 11698.01, that agreement shall provide for all of the following:

(a) The reinsurance and assumption of all those obligations by the reinsuring and assuming insurers.

(b) If there is more than one reinsurer the proportion of all those obligations assumed by each reinsurer and a method for the actual processing and payment of those obligations by the reinsurers or their representatives.

(c) The reimbursement of the reinsuring and assuming insurers from the deposit of the insurer in the delinquency proceeding. The provision shall conform with Section 11698.21 and shall not be effective unless approved by the Workers' Compensation Appeals Board.

(d) The amounts, if any, to be paid the reinsurers from the general funds of the insurer. If the agreement provides that amounts from the general funds of the insurer are to be paid to the reinsurers, those payments shall be approved by the court where the delinquency proceedings are pending.

(e) Any other matters as are necessary and proper to achieve the purposes of the reinsurance and assumption agreement. **Leg.H.** 2002 ch. 899 (SB 2093) §2.

Ref.: Hanna § 2.30[2]–[5]; Herlick Handbook §§ 3.12, 3.13, 3.15.

§11698.21. Reimbursement agreement to provide for transfer of securities in the deposit.

(a) The reimbursement provision referred to in subdivision (c) of Section 11698.2 shall provide for the transfer of the securities in the deposit to the deposits of the reinsurers. Thereafter, except as provided in subdivision (b), the deposit of the reinsuring and assuming insurers shall be security for the payment of all of those obligations assumed by the agreement as well as those obligations on workers' compensation insurance transacted in this state by the reinsurer, provided, however, that in determining the amount which shall remain on deposit as security for those obligations that are reinsured and assumed, the method prescribed by paragraph (1) of subdivision (a) of Section 11693 shall be used without any limitation as to time. In providing for the transfer of the securities the agreement may provide for their direct transfer to the deposit account of the reinsurers, or, if the securities deposited are in denominations or units as to make the equitable transfer to more than one reinsurer impossible, it may provide either for a formula under which the transfers may be made and differences in value reconciled by payments or credits among the reinsurers or for the sale of those securities by the commissioner and the reinvestment of the proceeds in other securities in amounts that can be so equitably transferred.

(b) The agreement shall provide that if it appears that the market value of the securities on deposit will exceed the obligations assumed by the reinsurers, the commissioner may withhold the transfer of a portion of the deposit and may after a two-year period enter into a final settlement with the reinsurers with respect thereto at which time any excess in that deposit shall be transferred to the general assets of the insurer in the delinquency proceeding. **Leg.H.** 2002 ch. 899 (SB 2093) §2.

Ref.: Hanna § 2.30[2]–[5]; Herlick Handbook §§ 3.12, 3.13, 3.15.

§11698.22. Circumstances where commissioner prohibited from entering into reinsurance agreement.

The commissioner shall not enter into an agreement with an insurer if its reinsurance and assumption of liability will impair its solvency or render its further transaction of business hazardous under subdivision (d) of Section 1011. **Leg.H.** 2002 ch. 899 (SB 2093) §2.

Ref.: Hanna § 2.30[2]–[5]; Herlick Handbook §§ 3.12, 3.13, 3.15.

§11698.3. Association member subject to liquidation order.

(a) If the insurer is a member insurer of the California Insurance Guarantee Association (the association) and has been the subject of an order of liquidation or receivership with a finding of insolvency which has been entered by a court of competent jurisdiction the association then becomes obligated to pay compensable workers' compensation claims arising under the insurer's policies, which are otherwise "covered claims" as defined in Article 14.2 (commencing with Section 1063) of Chapter 1 of Part 2 of Division 2. The commissioner shall immediately take control or possession of the deposit required pursuant to Section 11691 and shall transfer the deposit to the association.

(b) The association shall use the proceeds of the deposit and any interest earned thereon, for the payment of compensable workers' compensation claims arising under the insolvent insurer's policies and which are otherwise covered claims, as defined in Article 14.2 (commencing with Section 1063) of Chapter 1 of Part 2 of Division 2, and all expenses related thereto.

(c) The association shall make a full report and accounting of the disposition of the deposit on or in the form and at the times as the commissioner shall request, including a report of all interest income earned on the deposit.

(d) At the time all of the insolvent insurer's California workers' compensation claims liabilities are discharged, or at the time it is actuarially determined that the remaining proceeds, and any interest earned thereon, exceed those liabilities, the association shall return the surplus to the insolvent insurer's estate. **Leg.H.** 2002 ch. 899 (SB 2093) §2.

Ref.: Hanna § 2.30[2]–[5]; Herlick Handbook §§ 3.12, 3.13, 3.15.

§11699. Repayment of deposit to insurer upon satisfaction of liabilities.

Unless the deposit required pursuant to Section 11691 is withdrawn by the commissioner pursuant to the authority granted him or her by this article, it, or any remainder thereof, may be repaid to the insurer either upon satisfactory showing to the commissioner that every liability to pay compensable workers' compensation claims has been assumed and reinsured with a solvent admitted insurer or fully paid and discharged. In the event the insurer remains admitted for workers' compensation insurance, or desires to reinsure the injury, disablement, or death portions of policies of workers' compensation under the class of disability insurance, then it must maintain at least the minimum deposit required by Section 11691. **Leg.H.** 2002 ch. 899 (SB 2093) §2.

Ref.: Hanna § 2.30[2]–[5]; Herlick Handbook §§ 3.12, 3.13, 3.15.

§11700. Deposit used for unpaid compensable claims.

The deposit required pursuant to Section 11691, unless withdrawn by the commissioner, shall be used only for the payment of compensable workers' compensation claims and expenses as provided in Section 11698.02 as long as there remains unpaid any claim or any part thereof. **Leg.H.** 2002 ch. 899 (SB 2093) §2.

Ref.: Hanna § 2.30[2]–[5]; Herlick Handbook §§ 3.12, 3.13, 3.15.

§11701. Revocation of certificate of authority.

The commissioner may revoke the certificate of authority to transact workers' compensation insurance or to reinsure the injury, disablement, or death portions of policies of workers' compensation under the class of disability insurance in this state of any insurer failing to comply with the requirements of this article. The power vested in the commissioner by this section is additional to any and all other powers and remedies vested in the commissioner by law. Failure to make the deposit required by this article within the required time shall be deemed to constitute a condition of hazard as set forth in Section 1011. **Leg.H.** 2002 ch. 899 (SB 2093) §2.

Ref.: Hanna § 2.30[2]–[5]; Herlick Handbook §§ 3.12, 3.13, 3.15.

§11702. Article not to apply to certain employees.

The provisions of this article shall not apply to workers' compensation insurance covering those persons defined as employees by subdivision (d) of Section 3351 of the Labor Code. **Leg.H.** 2002 ch. 899 (SB 2093) §2.

Ref.: Hanna § 2.30[2]–[5]; Herlick Handbook §§ 3.12, 3.13, 3.15.

§11703. Occupational safety and health loss control consultation services required.

An insurer desiring to write workers' compensation insurance shall maintain or provide occupational safety and health loss control consultation services pursuant to Section 6354.5 of the Labor Code. **Leg.H.** 2002 ch. 899 (SB 2093) §2, 2003 ch. 13 (SB 581), effective May 28, 2003.

Ref.: Hanna § 2.30[2]–[5]; Herlick Handbook §§ 3.12, 3.13, 3.15.

ARTICLE 2
State Rate Supervision

§11730. Definitions.

The following definitions govern the construction and meaning of the terms used in this article:

(a) "Classification system" or "classification" means a plan, system, or arrangement for recognizing differences in exposure to hazards among industries, occupations, or operations of insurance policyholders.

(b) "Expenses" means that portion of any rate attributable to acquisition, field supervision, collection expenses, general expenses, taxes, licenses, and fees.

(c) "Experience rating" means a rating procedure utilizing past insurance experience of the individual policyholder to forecast future losses by measuring the policyholder's loss experience against the loss experience of policyholders in the same classification to produce a prospective premium credit, debit, or unity modification.

(d) "Loss trending" means any procedure for projecting developed losses to the average date of loss for the period during which the policies are to be effective.

(e) "Market" means the interaction between buyers and sellers of workers' compensation insurance within this state pursuant to the provisions of this article.

(f) "Pure premium rate" means that portion of the rate which represents the loss cost per unit of exposure, including loss adjustment expense.

(g) "Rate" means the cost of insurance per exposure base unit, prior to any application of individual risk variations based on loss or expenses considerations and does not include minimum premiums.

(h) "Rating organization" means an entity licensed by the commissioner pursuant to Section 11751.1.

(i) "Statistical plan" means the plan, system, or arrangement used in collecting data.

(j) "Supplementary rate information" means any manual or plan of rates, classification system, rating schedule, minimum premium, policy fee, rating rule, rating plan, and any other similar information needed to determine the applicable premium for an insured.

(k) "Supporting information" means the experience and judgment of the filer and the experience or data of other insurers or organizations relied on by the filer, the interpretation of any statistical data relied on by the filer, descriptions of methods used in making the rates, and any other similar information required to be filed by the commissioner. **Leg.H.** 1993 chs. 228 §2, 1242, operative January 1, 1995.

Ref.: Hanna §§ 2.02[1][b], 2.33, 2.40[1]; Herlick Handbook § 3.2.

§11731. Application of article.

This article applies to workers' compensation insurance and employers' liability insurance written in connection therewith. **Leg.H.** 1993 ch. 228 §2, operative January 1, 1995.

Ref.: Hanna § 2.33; Herlick Handbook § 3.2.

§11732. Limitations on rates; presumption of monopoly.

Rates shall be adequate to cover an insurer's losses and expenses. Rates shall not tend to create a monopoly in the market. For the purpose of this section, the rates of any individual insurer, other than the State Compensation Insurance Fund, are presumed to create a monopoly in the market if the insurer has a market share, based on a percentage of statewide workers' compensation premium, equivalent to 20 percent or more of the premium written by all insurers other than the State Compensation Insurance Fund. **Leg.H.** 1993 chs. 228 §2, 1242, operative January 1, 1995, 2002 ch. 873 (AB 1985).

Ref.: Hanna § 2.33; Herlick Handbook § 3.2.

§11732.5. Criteria for determination of discriminatory rates.

Rates shall not be unfairly discriminatory. Rates are unfairly discriminatory if, after allowing for practical limitations, price differentials fail to reflect equitably the difference in expected losses and expenses. A rate of an insurer shall not be deemed unfairly discriminatory because different premiums result for policyholders with like loss exposures but different expenses, or like expenses but different loss exposures, as long as the rate reflects the differences with reasonable accuracy. **Leg.H.** 1994 ch. 732.

Ref.: Hanna § 2.40[1]; Herlick Handbook § 3.2.

§11733. Criteria for determination of rates.

In determining whether rates comply with Section 11732, the following criteria shall apply:

(a) Due consideration may be given to past and prospective loss and expenses experience within this state, to catastrophe hazards and contingencies, to events or trends within this state, to loadings for leveling premium rates over time or for dividends or savings to be allowed or returned by insurers to their policyholders, members or subscribers, and to all other relevant factors, including judgment.

(b) The expense provisions included in the rates to be used by an insurer shall reflect the operating methods of the insurer and, so far as is credible, its own actual and anticipated expense experience.

(c) The rates may contain a provision for contingencies and an allowance permitting a reasonable profit. In determining the reasonableness of profit, consideration shall be given to all investment income attributable to premiums and the reserves associated with those premiums. **Leg.H.** 1993 chs. 228 §2, 1242, operative January 1, 1995, 2002 ch. 873 (AB 1985).

Ref.: Hanna § 2.33; Herlick Handbook § 3.2.

§11734. Adherence to uniform experience rating plan; assistance by rating organization with statistics and classification system; manual rules developed by rating organization; adherence to manual rules; weekly premium developed by rating organization.

(a) Every workers' compensation insurer shall adhere to a uniform experience rating plan filed with the commissioner by a rating organization designated by the commissioner and subject to his or her disapproval.

(b) The commissioner shall designate a rating organization to assist him or her in gathering, compiling, and reporting relevant statistical information, and to develop a classification system. An insurer may develop its own classification system upon which a rate may be made or adopt the classification system developed by the designated rating organization; provided, however, that any classification system developed by an insurer must be filed with the commissioner 30 days prior to its use. The commissioner shall disapprove a classification system filed by an insurer pursuant to this section if the insurer fails to demonstrate that the data thereby produced can be reported consistent with the uniform statistical plan or the classification system developed by the rating organization. Every workers' compensation insurer shall record and report its workers' compensation experience to the designated rating organization as set forth in the uniform statistical plan approved by the commissioner.

(c) The designated rating organization shall develop and file manual rules, subject to the approval of the commissioner, reasonably related to the recording and reporting of data pursuant to the uniform statistical plan, uniform experience rating plan, and any classification systems that may be in effect. Every workers' compensation insurer shall adhere to the approved manual rules and experience rating plan in writing and reporting its business. No insurer shall agree with any other insurer or with a rating organization to adhere to manual rules that are not reasonably related to the recording and reporting of data pursuant to the uniform statistical plan or classification system developed by the rating organization.

(d) The designated rating organization shall also develop and file with the commissioner a weekly premium per employee for each classification used or proposed for use by that organization. The weekly premium shall be developed by applying the proposed rate for each classification to the state average weekly wage. For the purpose of this section, "state average weekly wage" means the average weekly wage paid by employers to employees covered by unemployment insurance as reported by the United States Department of Labor for California for the 12 months ending March 31 of the calendar year preceding the year in which the injury occurred. **Leg.H.** 1993 ch. 228 §2, operative January 1, 1995, ch. 1242, 2002 ch. 6 (AB 749).

Ref.: Hanna §§ 2.01, 2.02[2], 2.40[1]; Herlick Handbook § 3.2.

§11735. Filing of rates and supplementary rate information; filings open to public inspection; using rates in excess of those stated in filing; disallowance of rating systems violating Unruh Act; filing requirements for plans with deductibles; reporting losses subject to deductibles.

(a) Every insurer shall file with the commissioner all rates and supplementary rate information that are to be used in this state. The rates and supplementary rate information shall be filed not later than 30 days prior to the effective date. Upon application by the filer, the commissioner may authorize an earlier effective date. To the extent possible, rates and supplementary rate information shall be based upon supporting information derived from the experience or data of the insurer, rating organization, advisory organization, or other insurers. For the purposes of this subdivision, "rating organization" shall have the same meaning as set forth in subdivision (b) of Section 11750.1, and "advisory organization" shall have the same meaning as set forth in subdivision (e) of that section.

(b) Rates filed pursuant to this section shall be filed in the form and manner prescribed by the commissioner. All rates, supplementary rate information, and any supporting information for rates filed under this article, as soon as filed, shall be open to public inspection at any reasonable time. Copies may be obtained by any person upon request and the payment of a reasonable charge.

(c) Upon the written application of the insurer and insured, stating its reasons therefor, filed with the commissioner, a rate in excess of that provided by a filing otherwise applicable may be used on any specific risk.

(d) Notwithstanding Section 679.70, no rating organization may issue, nor may any insurer use, any classification system or rate, as applied or used, that violates Section 679.71 or 679.72 or that violates the Unruh Civil Rights Act.

(e) Notwithstanding Sections 11657 to 11660, inclusive, supplementary rate information filed with the commissioner for purposes of offering deductibles to policyholders for all or part of benefits payable under the policy shall be deemed complete if the filing contains all of the following:

(1) A copy of the deductible endorsement that is to be attached to the policy to effectuate deductible coverage.

(2) Endorsement language that protects the rights of injured workers and ensures that benefits are paid by the insurer without regard to any deductible. The endorsement shall specify that the nonpayment of deductible amounts by the policyholder shall not relieve the insurer from the payment of compensation for injuries sustained by the employee during the period of time the endorsed policy was in effect. The endorsement shall provide that deductible policies for workers' compensation insurance coverage shall not be terminated retroactively for the nonpayment of deductible amounts.

(3) The endorsement shall provide that notwithstanding the deductible, the insurer shall pay all of the obligations of the employer for workers' compensation benefits for injuries occurring during the policy period. Payment by the insurer of any amounts within the deductible shall be treated as an advancement of funds by the insurer to the employer and shall create a legal obligation for reimbursements, and may be secured by appropriate security.

(4) The endorsement shall specify whether loss adjustment expenses are to be treated as advancements within the deductible to be reimbursed by the employer.

(5) An explanation of premium reductions reflecting the type and level of the deductible shall be clearly set forth for the policyholder.

(6) The filing shall provide that premium reductions for deductibles are determined before application of any experience modification, premium surcharge, or premium discount, and the premium reductions reflect the type and level of deductible consistent with accepted actuarial standards.

(7) The filing shall provide that the nonpayment of deductible amounts by the insured employer to its insurer, or the failure to comply with any security-related terms of the policy, shall be treated under the policy in the same manner as the payment or nonpayment of the premium pursuant to paragraph (1) of subdivision (b) of Section 676.8.

(f) The insurer shall report and record losses subject to the deductible as losses for purposes of ratemaking and application of an experience rating plan on the same basis as losses under policies providing first dollar coverage. **Leg.H.** 1993 ch. 228 §2, operative January 1, 1995, 1994 chs. 732, 1097, 1131 §1.5, 1997 ch. 748, 2002 ch. 873 (AB 1985).

Ref.: Hanna § 2.40[1]; Herlick Handbook §§ 3.2, 3.14.

§11736. Requirements of experience rating plan.

An experience rating plan shall contain reasonable eligibility standards, provide adequate incentives for loss prevention, and shall provide for sufficient premium differentials so as to encourage safety. **Leg.H.** 1993 ch. 228 §2, operative January 1, 1995, 1997 ch. 748.

Ref.: Hanna § 2.40[1]; Herlick Handbook § 3.2.

§11736.5. Collateral or security for deductible amount on policy; reserves and recognition of receivables.

(a) The commissioner shall establish, by regulation, those forms of collateral or security that an insurer may designate to secure the deductible amount of any policy of workers' compensation insurance and the establishment of reserves and recognition of receivables for insurers writing workers' compensation deductible policies.

The commissioner, by order, exempt from the requirements of the Administrative Procedure Act, shall establish those forms of security or collateral that the insurer may designate to secure the deductible amount of any policy of workers' compensation insurance that provides for a deductible and the establishment of reserves and recognition of receivables for insurers writing workers' compensation deductible policies. This authority shall expire if regulations required by subdivision (a) are not drafted and filed with the Office of Administrative Law by December 31, 1995; if the regulations are filed with the Office of Administrative Law by December 31, 1995, this authority shall expire December 31, 1996, or upon filing of the regulations with the Secretary of State, whichever is earlier. **Leg.H.** 1994 ch. 1131.

1994 Note: The Legislature inadvertently added a subsection (a) designation without any additional subsection designations.

Ref.: Herlick Handbook § 3.2.

§11737. Disapproval of rate by commissioner; notice of disapproval; request for review of rating system of insurer or rating organization by aggrieved party; appeal to commissioner after request; hearing; issuance of order by commissioner upon disapproval; specification of interim rates; rate increase for policies with inception dates before January 1, 2003.

(a) The commissioner may disapprove a rate if the insurer fails to comply with the filing requirements under Section 11735.

(b) The commissioner may disapprove rates if the commissioner determines that premiums charged, in the aggregate, resulting from the use of the rates or the rates as modified by any supplementary rate information, would be inadequate to cover an insurer's losses and expenses, unfairly discriminatory, or tend to create a monopoly in the market pursuant to Section 11732, 11732.5, or 11733.

(c) The commissioner shall disapprove rates if the commissioner determines that premiums charged, in the aggregate, resulting from the use of the rates or the rates as modified by any supplementary rate information would, if continued in use, tend to impair or threaten the solvency of an insurer. In determining whether the premium charged in the aggregate would, if continued in use, tend to impair or threaten the solvency of the insurer, the commissioner shall consider the insurer's experience in other states.

(d) If the commissioner intends to disapprove rates pursuant to subdivision (a) or (b), the commissioner shall serve notice on the insurer of the intent to disapprove and shall schedule a hearing to commence within 60 days of the date of the notice.

(e) If the commissioner disapproves rates pursuant to subdivision (c), the commissioner shall immediately serve notice on the insurer of the disapproval. An insurer whose rates have been disapproved pursuant to that subdivision may, within 20 days of the date of the notice of disapproval, request a hearing, and the commissioner shall hold a hearing within 60 days of the date of the notice of disapproval.

(f) Every insurer or rating organization shall provide within this state reasonable means whereby any person aggrieved by the application of its filings may be heard by the insurer or rating organization on written request to review the manner in which the rating system has been applied in connection with the insurance afforded or offered. If the insurer or rating organization fails to grant or reject the request within 30 days, the applicant may proceed in the same manner as if the application had been rejected. Any party affected by the action of the insurer or rating organization on the request may appeal, within 30 days after written notice of the action, to the commissioner who, after a hearing held within 60 days from the date on which the party requests the appeal, or longer upon agreement of the parties and not less than 10 days' written notice to the appellant and to the insurer or rating organization, may affirm, modify, or reverse that action. If the commissioner has information on the subject from which the appeal is taken and believes that a reasonable basis for the appeal does not exist or that the appeal is not made in good faith, the commissioner may deny the appeal without a hearing. The denial shall be in writing, set forth the basis for the denial, and be served on all parties.

(g) If the commissioner disapproves a rate, the commissioner shall issue an order specifying in what respects the rate fails to meet the requirements of this article and stating when, within a reasonable period thereafter, that rate shall be discontinued for any policy issued or renewed after a date specified in the order. The order shall be issued within 20 days after the notice prescribed in subdivision (e) is served. If a hearing is held pursuant to subdivision (d) or (e), the order shall be issued, instead, within 30 days after the close of the hearing. The order may include a provision for premium adjustment for the period after the effective date of the order for policies in effect on that date.

(h) Whenever an insurer has no legally effective rates as a result of the commissioner's disapproval of rates or other act, the commissioner shall specify interim rates for the insurer that protect the interests of all parties and may order that a specified portion of the premiums be placed in an escrow account approved by the commissioner. When new rates become legally effective, the commissioner shall order the escrowed funds or any overcharge in the interim rates to be distributed appropriately, except that refunds of less than ten dollars ($10) per policyholder shall not be required. However, if the commissioner has disapproved rates pursuant to subdivision (c), the commissioner shall order the insurer in the interim to use, at a minimum, the approved advisory pure premium rates pursuant to subdivision (b) of Section 11750, as modified by the uniform experience rating plan established pursuant to subdivision (c) of Section 11734, without any deviations on account of any supplementary rate information and reflecting the actual expenses of the insurer, until the time that a final determination of rates is adjudicated and ordered through a hearing.

(i) Notwithstanding any other provision of law, an insurer may increase rates on policies with inception dates prior to January 1, 2003, in an amount no greater than the pure premium rate increase approved by the commissioner reflecting the cost of the change in benefit levels authorized by the act adding this subdivision. **Leg.H.** 1993 ch. 228 §2, operative January 1, 1995, ch. 1242, 1994 ch. 1097, 1997 ch. 517, 2002 chs. 6 (AB 749), 873 (AB 1985).

Ref.: Hanna § 2.40[1]; Herlick Handbook § 3.2.

§11738. Factors not considered in classification.

A classification shall take no account of any physical impairment of employees or the extent to which employees may have persons dependent upon them for support. **Leg.H.** 1993 ch. 228 §2, operative January 1, 1995.

Ref.: Hanna § 2.40[1]; Herlick Handbook § 3.2.

§11739. Dividend payments to policyholders—Restrictions and filing requirement.

(a) An insurer shall not use any plan for the payment of dividends to policyholders by reason of a participating provision in a workers' compensation insurance policy which is unfairly discriminatory.

(b) Every insurer issuing workers' compensation insurance policies under the laws of this state shall file annually with the rating organization designated by the commissioner information relating to dividend payments made to its policyholders. Information filed shall be in sufficient detail to permit the rating organization to prepare for the commissioner's review and approval, a report showing in the aggregate for all companies premiums earned, losses incurred, and dividends paid the preceding calendar year under policies containing a participating provision, separately by premium size and loss ratio categories, as may reasonably be prescribed by the commissioner.

(c) Information submitted by individual companies pursuant to this section shall be confidential and not subject to public disclosure under any law of this state. **Leg.H.** 1993 ch. 228 §2, operative January 1, 1995.

Ref.: Herlick Handbook § 3.2.

§11740. Effective dates for rates and supplementary rate information pursuant to this article.

Rates and supplementary rate information filed for use in this state pursuant to this article and Article 3 (commencing with Section 11750), as added and amended by Chapter 228 of the Statutes of 1993, shall not be effective prior to the first normal anniversary rating date of a policy on or after January 1, 1995. Rates, any rating plan or plans, and policy forms issued or approved prior to January 1, 1995, shall remain in effect only until the first normal anniversary rating date on or after January 1, 1995, as determined by a licensed rating organization pursuant to rules issued or approved by the commissioner in effect on July 16, 1993. Prior to January 1, 1995, no policy may be issued or renewed for a term of less than one year for the purpose of changing the normal anniversary date of the policy or the preceding policy. No policy may be canceled, amended, or rewritten for the purpose of avoiding this section.

Notwithstanding Section 7 of Chapter 228 of the Statutes of 1993, this section shall become operative January 1, 1994. **Leg.H.** 1993 ch. 1242.

Ref.: Hanna § 2.40[1].

§11742. Workers' compensation insurance online rate comparison guide.

(a) The Legislature finds and declares that the insolvencies of more than a dozen workers' compensation insurance carriers have seriously constricted the market and led to a dangerous increase in business at the State Compensation Insurance Fund. Yet more than 200 insurance companies are still licensed to offer workers' compensation insurance in California. Unfortunately, many employers do not know which carriers are offering coverage, and it is both difficult and time consuming to try to get information on rates and coverages from competing insurance companies. A central information source would help employers find the required coverage at the best competitive rate.

(b) On or before July 1, 2004, the commissioner shall establish and maintain, on the Internet Web site maintained by the department, an online rate comparison guide showing workers' compensation insurance rates for the 50 insurance companies writing the highest volume of business in this line during the two preceding years.

(c) The online comparison shall display rates for each class set forth in the classification system adopted by the commissioner pursuant to Section 11734, shall include the effective date of each rate, and shall list the rates for each class from the lowest to the highest rate.

(d) The rating organization designated by the commissioner as his or her statistical agent pursuant to Section 11751.5 shall determine the cost savings achieved in the 2003 workers' compensation reform legislation. Each insurer shall certify, in the form and manner determined by the commissioner, that its rates reflect those cost savings. The certifications shall be made available to the public on the Internet Web site maintained by the department. **Leg.H.** 2003 ch. 635 (AB 227).

Ref.: Hanna § 2.40[1]; Herlick Handbook §§ 3.2, 3.10.

ARTICLE 3
Rating and Other Organizations

§11750. Purpose of this article.

(a) The purpose of this article is to promote the public welfare by regulating concert of action between insurers in collecting and tabulating rating information and other data that may be helpful in the making of adequate pure premium rates for workers' compensation insurance and for employers liability insurance incidental thereto and written in connection therewith for all admitted insurers and in submitting them to the commissioner for approval; to authorize and regulate the existence and cooperation of qualified rating organizations to one of which each workers' compensation insurer shall belong; to authorize and regulate cooperation between insurers, rating organizations and advisory organizations in ratemaking and other related matters to the end that the purposes of this chapter may be complied with and carried into effect.

(b) Notwithstanding any other provision of law, within 60 days of receiving an advisory pure premium rate filing made pursuant to subdivision (b) of Section 11750.3, the Insurance Commissioner shall hold a public hearing, and within 30 days of the conclusion of the hearing, approve, disapprove, or modify the proposed rate. **Leg.H.** 1993 ch. 1242, 2000 ch. 884, effective September 29, 2000.

Ref.: Hanna §§ 2.01, 2.02[2], 2.16, 2.40[1], 2.50[1][a], 2.70[2]; Herlick Handbook § 3.10.

§11750.1. Definitions.

As used in this article, unless a different meaning is manifest, the term:

(a) "Insurer" means every insurer authorized to transact workers' compensation insurance and employer's liability insurance incidental thereto and written in connection therewith in this state, including the State Compensation Insurance Fund;

(b) "Rating organization" means any organization which has as its primary object or purpose the collecting of loss and expense statistics and other statistical information and data, the making of pure premium rates and those rating plans authorized by Section 11734 for workers' compensation insurance and employer's liability insurance incidental thereto and written in connection therewith and presenting them to the commissioner for approval;

(c) "Insurance" means workers' compensation insurance and employer's liability insurance incidental thereto and written in connection therewith;

(d) "Willful" or "willfully" in relation to an act or omission which constitutes a violation of this article means with actual knowledge or belief that such act or omission constitutes such violation and with specific intent to commit such violation.

(e) "Advisory organization" means every person, group or organization, other than an insurer, whether located within or without this state, which prepares policy forms or underwriting rules incidental to or in connection with workers' compensation insurance and employer's liability insurance incidental thereto and written in connection therewith or which collects and furnishes to admitted insurers or rating organizations loss statistics or other statistical information and data relating to workers' compensation insurance and employer's liability insurance incidental thereto and written in connection therewith and acts in an advisory capacity to such insurers or rating organizations as distinguished from a ratemaking capacity. No duly authorized attorney at law acting in the usual course of his profession shall be deemed to be an advisory organization.

(f) "Employer's liability insurance incidental thereto and written in connection therewith" means insurance of any liability of employers for injuries to, or death of, employees arising out of, and in the course of, employment when this insurance is incidental to, and written in connection with, the workers' compensation insurance issued to the same employer and covering the same employer interests. **Leg.H.** 1993 chs. 228, 1242.

Ref.: Hanna §§ 2.02[2], 2.16, 2.63[1]; Herlick Handbook § 3.10.

§11750.2. Scope of article.

The provisions of this article shall apply to all workers' compensation insurance and employer's liability insurance incidental thereto and written in connection therewith in this state, except reinsurance.

Ref.: Herlick Handbook § 3.10.

§11750.3. Permissible purposes of rating organization.

A rating organization may be organized pursuant to this article and maintained in this state for the following purposes:

(a) To provide reliable statistics and rating information with respect to workers' compensation insurance and employer's liability insurance incidental thereto and written in connection therewith.

(b) To collect and tabulate information and statistics for the purpose of developing pure premium rates to be submitted to the commissioner for issuance or approval.

(c) To formulate rules and regulations in connection with pure premium rates and the administration of classifications and rating systems.

(d) To inspect risks for classification or rate purposes and to furnish to the insurer and upon request of the employer and after notice to the insurer, to furnish to the employer full information concerning the rates applicable to the employer's insurance.

(e) To examine policies, daily reports, endorsements or other evidences of insurance for the purpose of ascertaining whether they comply with the provisions of law and to make reasonable rules governing their submission. A rating organization may develop loss data on behalf of its members to assist members in developing plans pursuant to subdivision (e) of Section 11735 and other loss sensitive plans.

(f) Within one year after expiration of any workers' compensation insurance policy, to initiate test audits of insured employer's payrolls and insurer's audits of those payrolls to check the accuracy and reliability thereof, and to examine all records relative thereto and premises of insured employers.

(g) To exchange information and experience data with rating organizations, advisory organizations, and insurers in this and other states, with respect to ratemaking.

(h) To become a member or subscriber of any lawfully authorized ratemaking or advisory organization whenever membership in the organization is necessary or helpful to the rating organization.

(i) To perform all acts necessary, incidental, or convenient to carry out the foregoing purposes or the provisions of this chapter relating to rating organizations. **Leg.H.** 1993 ch. 228, operative January 1, 1995, 1994 ch. 1131.

Ref.: Hanna §§ 2.02[2], 2.16, 2.50[1][a]; Herlick Handbook §§ 3.2, 3.10, 12.13.

§11751. License; fee; required information.

On and after January 1, 1952, a rating organization shall not conduct its operations in this state without first having filed with the commissioner a written application for and securing a license to act as a rating organization. Any rating organization may make application for and obtain a license as a rating organization if it meets the requirements for license set forth in this article. The fee for filing an application for a license as a rating organization is two hundred twenty-four dollars ($224) payable in advance to the commissioner. Every rating organization shall file with its application:

(a) A copy of its constitution, its articles of incorporation, agreement of association, and of its bylaws, rules and regulations governing the conduct of its business, all certified by the custodian of the originals thereof.

(b) A list of its members who shall not number less than five insurers authorized to write and writing workers' compensation insurance in this state and whose combined experience shall be determined by the commissioner to be reasonably adequate for ratemaking purposes.

(c) The name and address of a resident of this state upon whom notices of the commissioner or process affecting that rating organization may be served.

(d) A statement of its qualifications as a rating organization. **Leg.H.** 1951 ch. 1123 §1, 1969 ch. 559 §2, 1976 ch. 879 §35, 2017 ch. 534 (AB 1699) §71.

Ref.: Herlick Handbook § 3.10.

§11751.1. License requirements.

To obtain and retain a license, a rating organization shall provide satisfactory evidence to the commissioner that it shall do all of the following:

(a) Permit any insurer to become a member at a reasonable cost and without discrimination, or to withdraw therefrom.

(b) Neither have nor adopt any rule or exact any agreement, the effect of which would be to require any member as a condition of membership to adhere to any rates.

(c) Neither adopt any rule nor exact any agreement, the effect of which would be to prohibit or regulate the payment of dividends, savings, or unabsorbed premium deposits allowed or returned by insurers to their policyholders or members.

(d) Neither practice nor sanction any plan or act of boycott, coercion, or intimidation.

(e) Neither enter into nor sanction any contract or act by which any person is restrained from lawfully engaging in the insurance business.

(f) Notify the commissioner promptly of every change in its constitution or articles of incorporation, agreement of association, or in its bylaws, rules and regulations governing the conduct of its business; its list of members; and the name and address of the resident of this state designated by it upon whom notices or orders of the commissioner or process affecting the organization may be served.

(g) Agree that the commissioner or his or her representative may attend all meetings of the organization or any of its committees.

(h) Agree to permit four members of the public, two representing organized labor and two representing insured employers, to serve on the managing or governing committee of the organization as specified in Section 11751.35.

(i) Maintain reasonable records of the experience of its members and of the data, statistics or information collected or used in connection with the pure premium rates, classifications, manual rules, and policy and endorsement forms used by its members so that these records will be available at all reasonable times to enable the commissioner to determine whether the rating organization and its members comply with the provisions of this chapter applicable to them. These records shall be maintained in an office within this state. The commissioner may prescribe a uniform system for the keeping of the records which shall be reasonably adapted to the rating organization and its members' method of operation and which shall be applicable to all rating organizations licensed under this article and their members. **Leg.H.** 1993 ch. 228, operative January 1, 1995.

1989 Note: This section is applicable only to injuries occurring on or after January 1, 1990. Stats. 1989 ch. 893 §6.

Ref.: Herlick Handbook § 3.10.

§11751.2. Investigation of rating organizations; findings of commissioner; denial of application; duration of license.

The commissioner shall examine each application for license to act as a rating organization and the documents filed therewith and may make any further investigation of the applicant, its affairs and its proposed plan of business, as he deems desirable.

The commissioner shall issue the license applied for within 60 days of its filing with him if from such examination and investigation he is satisfied that:

(a) The business reputation of the applicant and its officers is good.

(b) The facilities of the applicant are adequate to enable it to furnish the services it proposes to furnish.

(c) The applicant and its proposed plan of operation conform to the requirements of this chapter.

Otherwise, but only after hearing upon notice, the commissioner shall in writing deny the application and notify the applicant of his decision and his reasons therefor.

Licenses issued pursuant to this section shall remain in effect until suspended or revoked.

Ref.: Herlick Handbook § 3.10.

§11751.25. License fee due annually.

Notwithstanding Section 11751, each rating organization possessing a license of indefinite term pursuant to this article shall owe and pay to the commissioner an annual fee of one hundred fifty dollars ($150), in advance, on account of that license until its final termination. That fee shall be for annual periods commencing on July 1 of each year and ending on June 30 of each year and shall be due and payable on each March 1 and shall be delinquent on and after each April 1. **Leg.H.** 1969 ch. 559 §3, effective July 21, 1969, 2017 ch. 534 (AB 1699) §72.

Ref.: Herlick Handbook § 3.10.

§11751.3. Rules of rating organizations; State Fund's committee membership.

(a) Subject to the approval of the commissioner, a rating organization licensed under this article may adopt any reasonable constitution, articles of incorporation, or agreement of association, and may make reasonable rules for the regulation of its members and the conduct of its business by bylaws or otherwise. In a rating organization of which the State Compensation Insurance Fund is a member, it shall be entitled without election to membership on the managing or governing committee and on the classification and rating committee thereof.

(b) In addition, after consultation with the California Labor Federation, AFL-CIO, other statewide organized labor organizations, and statewide associations representing business, the commissioner shall appoint two public members representing insured employers and two public members representing organized labor to serve on the managing or governing committee of a rating organization. The bylaws of a rating organization shall permit a public member from time to time to designate in his or her stead a representative from the same employer organization or an affiliated employee union, as the case may be, to attend and participate in any meeting of the governing committee of a rating organization.

1989 Note: This section is applicable only to injuries occurring on or after January 1, 1990. Stats. 1989 ch. 893 §6.

Ref.: Herlick Handbook § 3.10.

§11751.35. Public members of managing committee.

(a) Four members of the public, two representing organized labor and two representing insured employers, appointed pursuant to subdivision (b) of Section 11751.3, shall be entitled to serve on the managing or governing committee of a rating organization licensed under this article. A public member shall be entitled to vote on all issues involving pure premium rates, classifications, rating plans, rating systems, manual rules and policy, and endorsement forms which are properly brought before the committee. A public member shall be removed by the commissioner only for cause.

(b) In the event a public member is unable or unwilling to complete his or her term, after consultation with the California Labor Federation, AFL-CIO, other statewide organized labor organizations, and statewide organizations representing business, as the case may be, the commissioner shall appoint a successor from organized labor or an insured employer to complete the unexpired term.

(c) The public members who serve on the governing committee of a rating organization licensed under this article together may, by a majority vote, retain experts who shall include a fellow of the Casualty Actuarial Society, to advise them on any matter specified in subdivision (a). The actuary hired may participate in all proceedings of the actuarial committee of the rating organization. The reasonable expense of retaining these experts shall not exceed one hundred thousand dollars ($100,000) per year and shall be paid from the budget of the department. The commissioner shall increase this amount annually to reflect any needed cost-of-living adjustments. The public members may submit information obtained from these experts, as well as any other information they deem appropriate, to the commissioner for his or her consideration in approving a change of any matter specified in subdivision (a).

(d) In addition to the expenses authorized pursuant to subdivision (c), the public members who serve on the governing committee of a rating organization licensed under this article may expend up to an additional one hundred thousand dollars ($100,000) per year, which shall be paid by insurer members of the rating organization. Those funds shall be used to retain staff, who shall be hired by a majority vote of the public members. **Leg.H.** 1993 ch. 121, effective July 16, 1993, ch. 1242, 1995 ch. 375.

1989 Note: This section is applicable only to injuries occurring on or after January 1, 1990. Stats. 1989 ch. 893 §6.

Ref.: Herlick Handbook § 3.10.

§11751.4. Insurer as rating organization member.

From and after the taking effect of this act, it shall be the duty of every insurer to be a member of a rating organization. No insurer may at the same time belong to more than one rating organization licensed under this article.

Ref.: Hanna §§ 2.50[1][a], 2.16; Herlick Handbook § 3.10.

§11751.5. Provision of statistics to commissioner.

The commissioner, after notice and hearing, may promulgate reasonable rules and statistical plans, which may be modified from time to time and which shall be used thereafter in the recording and reporting by insurers of their loss and expense experience in order that the experiences of all insurers may be made available in such form and detail as may be necessary to aid the commissioner in administering the provisions of Article 2 (commencing with Section 11730). The commissioner shall designate a rating organization licensed under this article as his or her statistical agent to gather and compile such experience statistics and all licensed rating organizations shall report the experience of their members to such designated rating organization. Subject to reasonable rules approved by the commissioner, such designated rating organization shall make such experience statistics, when compiled, available to all licensed rating organizations and may make a reasonable charge to other rating organizations for the expense incurred by it in combining, tabulating and compiling the experience of all workers' compensation insurers. **Leg.H.** 1993 ch. 1242.

Ref.: Herlick Handbook § 3.10.

§11751.55. Filing fee if public hearing is required.

If an insurer, the State Compensation Insurance Fund, a rating organization, or an advisory organization requests an official action by the commissioner under Chapters 2 (commencing with Section 11630), 3 (commencing with Section 11690), or 4 (commencing with Section 11770) of this part which he can lawfully consummate only after a noticed public hearing required by law, the commissioner shall require the request to be in writing and require the payment of five hundred ninety dollars ($590), in advance, as a fee for filing such request. Such fee shall be earned even if the request is denied or is granted in an altered form.

Ref.: Herlick Handbook § 3.10.

§11751.7. Statistical agent information request.

(a) The rating organization designated the statistical agent pursuant to Section 11751.5 shall provide to the Director of Industrial Relations, upon request, any information in the possession of, or reasonably attainable by the rating organization, that would assist the Director of Industrial Relations to identify employers who fail to secure adequate insurance in violation of Section 3700 of the Labor Code. The information requested pursuant to this section shall be provided by the rating organization in a form and manner prescribed by the Director of Industrial Relations.

(b) The rating organization designated the statistical agent pursuant to Section 11751.5 shall provide to the Registrar of Contractors of the Contractor's State License Board, upon request, any information in the possession of, or reasonably attainable by, the rating organization that would assist in identifying licensed contractors who fail to secure adequate insurance in violation of Section 3700 of the Labor Code. The information requested pursuant to this section shall be provided by the rating organization in a form and manner prescribed by the Registrar of Contractors. **Leg.H.** 1992 ch. 1276, 2005 ch. 428 (AB 1027) §1.

Ref.: Herlick Handbook § 3.10.

§11751.8. Reporting loss corrections or revisions to rating organization; when insurer must report.

An insurer shall report to its rating organization as corrections or revisions of losses, pursuant to the unit statistical plan and uniform experience rating plans approved by the commissioner, if any of the following is applicable:

(a) A loss record detail was incorrectly reported through mistake other than error of judgment.

(b) One or more claims are declared noncompensable. A claim is declared noncompensable if any of the following applies:

(1) There is an official ruling specifically holding that a claimant is not entitled to benefits under the workers' compensation laws of the state, even though the claimant may have been awarded reimbursement for expenses incurred by the claimant in presenting the case.

(2) No claim was filed during the period of limitation provided by the workers' compensation laws for the filing of the claim, and the carrier, therefore, closes the claim.

(3) Where the carrier contends, prior to the valuation date, that a claimant is not entitled to benefits under the workers' compensation laws and the claim is officially closed because of the claimant's failure to prosecute the claim.

(c) The carrier has recovered in an action against a third party.

(d) A death claim has been compromised over the sole issue of the applicability of the workers' compensation laws of the state.

(e) The exposure has been reassigned to another classification through the revision of an audit, in which case the insurer shall file with the revision of exposure a revision of losses that will reassign all claims to the appropriate classification.

(f) A clerical error in either the classification assignment or the type of injury assignment of a given claim, or a group of claims, has been discovered by the insurer.

(g) A clerical error in either the classification assignment or the type of injury assignment of a given claim has been discovered by the rating organization. The insurer shall, when notified by the rating organization, file a revision of losses or make satisfactory explanation.

(h) A correction is made in a classification assignment of a given claim, or a group of claims, as a result of the organization test audit of an insured for which the experience has been submitted.

(i) The claim has been determined to be a joint coverage claim in accordance with the unit statistical plan approved by the commissioner. **Leg.H.** 1994 ch. 776, 1995 ch. 161, 1997 ch. 748.

Ref.: Hanna § 2.36; Herlick Handbook § 3.10.

§11751.82. Reporting workers' compensation losses and payroll information by insurer under wrap-up insurance policy.

(a) An insurer under a wrap-up insurance policy shall report workers' compensation losses and payroll information for each contractor and subcontractor to its rating organization on a timely basis and in accordance with the uniform statistical plan. Within 10 days, upon request, the insurer shall provide to each contractor and subcontractor copies of the report covering workers' compensation losses and payroll information for that contractor or subcontractor.

(b) For the purposes of this section, a "wrap-up insurance policy" is an insurance policy, or series of policies, written to cover risks associated with a work of improvement, as defined in Section 8050 of the Civil Code, and covering two or more of the contractors or subcontractors that work on that work of improvement. **Leg.H.** 2004 ch. 777 (AB 2147), 2010 ch. 697 (SB 189) §41, operative July 1, 2012.

§11751.9. Revision of experience rating upon closure and reporting of claims.

Whenever a claim or claims used in an experience rating are closed and reported pursuant to the unit statistical plan approved by the commissioner and are valued, in the aggregate, at an amount that is less than 60 percent of the highest reported aggregate value of all of these claims, then the experience rating shall be revised pursuant to the uniform experience rating plan approved by the commissioner based on the most current reported values for all claims used in the experience rating. **Leg.H.** 1997 ch. 748.

Ref.: Hanna § 2.36; Herlick Handbook § 3.10.

§11752. Examination of rating organizations; acceptable substitutes.

The commissioner may, as often as reasonable and necessary, make or cause to be made an examination of each rating or advisory organization to ascertain whether such organizations comply with the legal requirements applicable to it under this article.

In lieu of any such examination the commissioner may accept the report of an examination made by the insurance supervisory official of another state or the report of a representative designated by the National Association of Insurance Commissioners.

Ref.: Herlick Handbook § 3.10.

§11752.1. Examination of personnel and records.

The officers, managers, agents and employees of any such organization may be examined by the commissioner at any time under oath and shall exhibit all books, records, accounts, documents or agreements governing its method of operation together with all data, statistics and information of every kind and character collected or considered by such organization in the conduct of the operations to which the examination relates.

Ref.: Herlick Handbook § 3.10.

§11752.2. Cost of commissioner's examination.

The reasonable cost of any examination authorized by this article of any rating or advisory organization shall be paid by the organization examined.

Ref.: Herlick Handbook § 3.10.

§11752.5. Release of policy information to governmental agencies.

(a) Subject to subdivision (b), a licensed rating organization shall make available any policy information contained in its records to the following:

(1) The Department of Industrial Relations.

(2) Any other governmental agency if the Insurance Commissioner, after consultation with the licensed rating organization, approves the release of the policy information requested to the agency.

(b) The Department of Industrial Relations and any other governmental agency shall specify to the licensed rating organization, in writing, the information requested, that the information requested is to be used to facilitate the agency's performance of its constitutional or statutory duties, and that the information received will not be released to others, except in the discharge of a specific statutory or constitutional duty, or published without the prior written consent of the licensed rating organization. In addition, if the Insurance Commissioner's approval is required for the release of the policy information requested, a written copy of the approval shall be submitted to the licensed rating organization.

(c) As used in this section, "policy information" means information which is contained in a workers' compensation policy, including, but not limited to, the identity and address of the employer, the identity of the insurer, the policy number, and the policy period.

(d) Information obtained by a governmental agency pursuant to this section shall be confidential and not subject to public disclosure under any other law of this state.

(e) No licensed rating organization or member thereof, or member of a committee of a licensed rating organization when acting in its capacity as a member of the committee, or officer or employee of a licensed rating organization, when acting within the scope of his or her employment, shall be liable to any person for injury, personal or otherwise, or damages caused or alleged to have been caused, either directly or indirectly, by the disclosure of information to a governmental agency pursuant to this section, or for the accuracy or completeness of the information so disclosed.

(f) This section shall not be construed as implying the existence of liability in circumstances not defined in this section, nor as implying a legislative recognition that, except for enactment of this section, a liability has existed or would exist in the circumstances stated in this section.

(g) This section shall not be construed as limiting any authority of a licensed rating organization to disclose information contained in its records to others **Leg.H.** 1984 ch. 909 §1, 2006 ch. 452 (SB 1452) §5.

Ref.: Herlick Handbook § 3.10.

§11752.6. Release of policy information to employer.

(a) A licensed rating organization shall make available, in writing, to an employer insured under a workers' compensation policy, all policyholder information contained in its records upon request of the employer and after notice to the employer's insurer.

(b) As used in this section, "policyholder information" means all information relating to the employer's loss experience, claims, classification assignments, and policy contracts. Policyholder information also includes information relating to rating plans, rating systems, manual rules, and any other information that impacts the policyholder's pure premium rates.

(c) If a licensed rating organization rejects an employer's request for policyholder information, the rating organization shall notify the employer in writing of the reasons for the rejection. An employer whose request has been rejected in whole or in part may appeal to the commissioner in accordance with Section 11753.1. If the commissioner finds that the reasons for the rejection are not justified, he or she may order the rating organization to furnish that information to the employer.

(d) No licensed rating organization or member of the organization, or member of a committee of a licensed rating organization when acting in its capacity as a member of the committee, or officer or employee of a licensed rating organization, when acting within the scope of his or her employment, is liable to any person for injury, personal or otherwise, or damages caused or alleged to have been caused, either directly or indirectly, by the disclosure of information to an employer under this section or for the accuracy or completeness of the information disclosed.

(e) This section does not imply the existence of liability in circumstances not defined in this section, nor does it imply a legislative recognition that, except for enactment of this section, a liability has existed or would exist in the circumstances stated in this section.

(f) This section does not limit any authority of a licensed rating organization to disclose information contained in its records to others.

(g) There shall be established in all licensed rating organizations a policyholder ombudsman. The policyholder ombudsman shall be a person with sufficient knowledge of the workers' compensation ratemaking process to provide information and assistance to policyholders in obtaining and evaluating the information provided in Article 2 (commencing with Section 11730) and this article, and in Sections 3761 and 3762 of the Labor Code. Every rating organization licensed in this state shall provide compensation for the ombudsman and necessary staff and other necessary resources to allow the ombudsman to provide prompt and complete service to workers' compensation policyholders of this state. The policyholder ombudsman may advise the policyholder in any dispute with insurers or the rating organization that the ombudsman serves, or on appeal to the commissioner as provided in Section 11737.

(h) For all policies of insurance issued or renewed on or after January 1, 1994, the insurer shall advise the policyholder in writing of the following:

(1) The policyholder's right to request a written report containing the information set forth in this section from the licensed rating organization of which the insurer is a member, and the policyholder's right to contact the policyholder ombudsman to assist in obtaining and evaluating information relating to rates, together with the telephone number and address of the ombudsman, as well as the policyholder's right to contact the department to resolve a dispute with an insurer, as provided in this section and Section 11737.

(2) If a participating policy, that upon payment or nonpayment of a dividend the policyholder shall be provided a written explanation, in clear and understandable language, setting forth the basis of the calculation and expressing any dividend in both dollar amount and as a percentage of earned premium under the policy.

(3) The date when the insurer is required to file the first unit statistical report with the licensed rating organization designated by the commissioner. **Leg.H.** 1993 ch. 121, effective July 16, 1993, 1995 ch. 582.

Ref.: Herlick Handbook § 3.10.

§11752.7. Availability of experience rating information.

(a) A licensed rating organization may make available experience rating information contained in its records to any insurer admitted to transact workers' compensation insurance in this state or to any insurance agent or broker that is licensed to transact workers' compensation insurance in this state, if the insurer, agent, or broker submits a written request to the licensed rating organization stating all of the following:

(1) The requesting insurer is admitted to transact workers' compensation insurance in this state or that the requesting agent or broker is licensed to transact workers' compensation insurance in this state.

(2) The information requested.

(3) The information requested will be used to facilitate the transaction of workers' compensation insurance by the insurer, agent, or broker.

(4) The information received will not be released by the agent or broker to others, except to facilitate the transaction of workers' compensation insurance by the requesting agent or broker.

(b) The licensed rating organization may, but shall not be required to, verify that an insurer requesting information under this section is admitted to transact workers' compensation insurance in this state or that an insurance agent or broker requesting information under this section is licensed to transact workers' compensation insurance in this state.

(c) For purposes of this section:

(1) "Experience rating information" means information released on microfiche, at an Internet Web site or other electronic format, or in other forms or media by a licensed rating organization that identifies all experience-rated employers, and the experience ratings and classifications or experience modifications that apply or applied to those employers.

(2) "Transaction," as applied to workers' compensation insurance, includes any of the following:

(A) Solicitation.

(B) Negotiations preliminary to execution of a contract of insurance.

(C) Execution of a contract of insurance.

(D) Resolution of matters arising out of the contract and subsequent to its execution.

(d) Experience rating information made available pursuant to this section shall be confidential and shall not be used for any purpose other than to facilitate the transaction of workers' compensation insurance by the insurer, agent, or broker receiving the information pursuant to this section.

(e) Notwithstanding any other provision of law, including this section, a licensed rating organization may not enter into a contract or other agreement, including its constitution, articles of incorporation, or bylaws that prohibits information services companies in the business of publishing or providing experience rating information immediately prior to September 15, 1989, from continuing on or after September 15, 1989, to receive and provide to others experience rating information from whatever sources and in whatever forms or media.

(f) No licensed rating organization, member of a licensed rating organization, member of a committee of a licensed rating organization when acting in its capacity as a member of the committee, or officer or employee of a licensed rating organization when acting within the scope of his or her employment, shall be liable to any person for injury, personal or otherwise, or damages caused or alleged to have been caused, either directly or indirectly, by the disclosure of information pursuant to this section, or to the members of those organizations, or for the accuracy or completeness of the information disclosed.

(g) This section shall not be construed as implying the existence of liability in circumstances not defined in this section, nor as implying a legislative recognition that, except for the enactment of this section, a liability has existed or would exist in the circumstances stated in this section.

(h) This section shall not be construed as limiting any authority of a licensed rating organization to disclose information contained in its records to others. **Leg.H.** 1998 ch. 176, 2002 ch. 879 (AB 2192).

Ref.: Herlick Handbook § 3.10.

§11752.75. Licensed rating organization to establish and maintain Internet Web site to assist person in determining whether employer is insured for workers' compensation.

(a)(1) Notwithstanding any other provision of law, a licensed rating organization shall, pursuant to regulations adopted by the commissioner after notice and hearing, establish and maintain an Internet Web site for the purposes of assisting any person to determine whether an employer is insured for workers' compensation.

(2) An Internet Web site developed pursuant to this section shall not include any links to a commercial, for-profit Internet Web site, other than a link to the licensed rating organization's homepage, and shall not contain any advertising other than the name, logo, and contact information of the licensed rating organization.

(b) The Internet Web site shall:

(1) Permit a person to submit a query for coverage information concerning a specified employer on a specified date. The specified date shall be within five years of the date of query.

(2) Permit the query to specify an employer, using the name, address, or other identifying information of the employer, or combinations of identifying information, as may be provided by regulations adopted by the commissioner. Other identifying information may include, but need not be limited to, the employer's federal employer identification number.

(3) In response to the query, provide the name of the workers' compensation insurer or insurers for the employer on the date specified in the query according to the most recent information available to the rating organization, subject to paragraph (7), and provide a contact address for the insurer from information available to the rating organization, or by providing a hypertext link to insurer information available on the department's Internet Web site.

(4) Be accessible for inquiries without charge. However, the commissioner may, at his or her discretion, permit the rating organization to impose access restrictions as necessary to deter the use of the Internet Web site for purposes other than those for which it was intended.

(5) Contain a hypertext link to the Department of Industrial Relations' Internet Web site for the purpose of locating employers who may be self-insured.

(6) Include any disclaimers that the commissioner may prescribe.

(7) Be updated to reflect policy information as soon as is reasonably feasible following submission of that information by insurers to the rating organization, as the commissioner shall require.

(8) Include a disclaimer stating that the search results may not reflect recent changes in information.

(9) Include a disclaimer stating that the failure of an employer to appear in response to a query does not mean that the employer does not have insurance or is operating in violation of California law.

(10) Include the date that the Internet Web site was last updated.

(c) A rating organization shall not be required to disclose on the Internet Web site any policy numbers, inception or expiration dates, or confidential information, as defined by the commissioner.

(d) The Internet Web site specified in this section shall become operative no later than one year after the effective date of regulations adopted by the commissioner implementing this section.

(e) The commissioner shall adopt regulations to implement this section no later than January 1, 2011. These regulations shall specify a method by which an employer may dispute through the rating organization or the employer's insurance company the accuracy of the information displayed on the Internet Web site.

(f) No rating organization, member of a rating organization, or member of a committee of a rating organization when acting within his or her capacity as a member of the committee, or officer or employee of a rating organization when acting within the scope of his or her employment, shall be liable to any person for injury, personal or otherwise, or damages caused, or alleged to have been caused, either directly or indirectly, by the good faith disclosure of information pursuant to this section, or for the accuracy or completeness of any information disclosed in good faith.

(g) This section shall not be construed to create liability except as provided in this section, nor as a legislative recognition that, except for the enactment of this section, a liability would exist.

(h) Nothing in this section shall be construed as limiting the authority of a rating organization to disclose information contained in its records to others.

(i) The commissioner shall conduct a review and evaluation of the establishment and operation of the Internet Web site and an assessment of whether it is achieving its intended purpose and provide a written report on his or her findings no later than July 1, 2013. The report shall include, to the extent possible, statistics on usage, error rates, user complaints, and efforts undertaken by the commissioner to improve the operation of the Internet Web site. The commissioner shall present a copy of the report to the office of the President pro Tempore of the Senate, the Speaker of the Assembly, the Senate Committee on Banking, Finance and Insurance, the Assembly Committee on Insurance, the Department of Finance, and the Department of Industrial Relations and shall make it available on the Internet Web site of the Department of Insurance. **Leg.H.** 2009 ch. 241 (AB 483) §1.

Ref.: Hanna § 2.02[2]; Herlick Handbook § 3.10.

§11752.8. Notice of workers' compensation rating laws to be provided to policyholder.

(a) For all policies of insurance issued, or renewed for the first time on or after January 1, 1995, the insurer shall provide a notice, approved by the commissioner, to the policyholder, explaining in easily understandable language the workers' compensation rating laws. For policies issued or renewed between January 1, 1994, and January 1, 1995, inclusive, the insurer shall include a notice to the policyholder, in easily understandable language, containing a summary of the changes in the rating laws enacted during the 1993-94 Regular Session of the Legislature.

(b) The notice required by this section may be combined with the notice required by subdivision (h) of Section 11752.6. **Leg.H.** 1993 ch. 121, effective July 16, 1993, ch. 1242 §12.

Ref.: Hanna § 2.33; Herlick Handbook § 3.10.

§11752.9. Written notification of change in classification assignment to be provided to policyholder.

Notwithstanding subdivision (d) of Section 11750.3, a rating organization shall provide a policyholder with written notification if it imposes a change in the classification assignment of the policyholder. The written notification shall be provided to the policyholder at the same time that it is provided to the insurer. A rating organization may satisfy this requirement by furnishing the policyholder with a copy of the notice that it provides to the insurer regarding the change in classification assignment. **Leg.H.** 2003 ch. 121 (SB 176).

Ref.: Hanna § 2.02[2].

§11753. Information required of advisory organizations; notification of all changes; prohibition on unfair practices.

No advisory organization shall conduct its operations in this State unless and until it has filed with the commissioner:

(a) A copy of its constitution, articles of incorporation, agreement of association, and of its by-laws, rules and regulations governing its activities, all duly certified by the custodian of the originals thereof.

(b) A list of its members and subscribers.

(c) The name and address of a resident of this State upon whom notices or orders of the commissioner or process may be served.

Every such advisory organization shall notify the commissioner promptly of every change in its constitution, its articles of incorporation, agreement of association, and of its by-laws, rules and regulations governing the conduct of its business; its list of members and subscribers; and the name and address of the resident of this State designated by it upon whom notices or orders of the commissioner or process affecting such organizations may be served.

No such advisory organization shall engage in any unfair or unreasonable practice with respect to its activities.

Ref.: Herlick Handbook § 3.10.

§11753.1. Appeal of decision, action, or omission of rating organization by aggrieved party; hearing by commissioner; notice to employer of change in classification assignment; request for reconsideration by employer.

(a) Any person aggrieved by any decision, action, or omission to act of a rating organization may request that the rating organization reconsider the decision, action, or omission. If the request for reconsideration is rejected or is not acted upon within 30 days by the rating organization, the person requesting reconsideration may, within a reasonable time, appeal from the decision, action, or omission of the rating organization. The appeal shall be made to the commissioner by filing a written complaint and request for a hearing specifying the grounds relied upon. If the commissioner has information on the subject appealed from and believes that probable cause for the appeal does not exist or that the appeal is not made in good faith, the commissioner may deny the appeal without a hearing. The commissioner shall otherwise hold a hearing to consider and determine the matter presented by the appeal.

(b) Any insurer adopting a change in the classification assignment of an employer that results in an increased premium shall notify the employer in writing, or if the insurance was transacted through an insurance agent or broker, the insurer shall notify the agent or broker who shall notify the employer in writing of the change and the reasons for the change. Any employer receiving this notice shall have the right to request reconsideration and appeal the reclassification pursuant to this section. The notice required by this section shall inform the employer of his or her rights pursuant to this section. No notification shall be required when the change is a result of a regulation adopted by the Department of Insurance or other action by or under the authority of the commissioner.

An insurer shall provide written notification of the revised classification assignment to an employer within 30 days after adoption. **Leg.H.** 1994 ch. 501, 1995 ch. 91, 1997 ch. 517, 2002 ch. 873 (AB 1985).

Ref.: Hanna §§ 2.02[1][c], [2], 2.16; Herlick Handbook § 3.10.

§11753.2. Effective date of classification change resulting in a decreased premium.

(a) If a change in a classification assignment on a workers' compensation insurance policy is due to an erroneous classification and results in a decreased premium, the classification change shall become effective as of the inception date of a policy in effect on the date the revised classification assignment is published by an insurer or, if the classification is assigned by the designated rating organization, when the insurer and insured are notified in writing by the designated rating organization that the erroneous classification assignment is under review. The revised classification assignment shall be applied as of the inception date of a policy that expired no more than 12 months prior to the date the revised classification assignment was published or the insurer and insured were notified in writing by the designated rating organization that assigned the classification that the erroneous classification assignment was under review, provided that the erroneous classification assignment was applicable to that policy.

(b) If a change in a classification assignment on a workers' compensation insurance policy is due to an erroneous classification and results in an increased premium, the classification change shall become effective on the effective date of the erroneous classification assignment provided any of the following conditions occur:

(1) The revised classification assignment is published within three months of the effective date or publication date of the erroneous assignment.

(2) The insurer or, where applicable, the designated rating organization, was notified in writing within three months of the effective date or publication date of the erroneous classification assignment of a possible error.

(3) The designated rating organization notified the insurer in writing within three months of the effective date or publication date of the erroneous classification assignment that the erroneous classification assignment was under review.

If one or more of the conditions set forth in paragraphs (1), (2), and (3) do not occur, the revised classification assignment shall become effective as of the date it is published unless the publication date is less than three months prior to the expiration date of the outstanding policy, in which case the revised classification assignment shall become effective as of the inception date of the policy that replaced the outstanding policy.

(c) If a change in a classification assignment on a workers' compensation policy is due to an insured's change of operations, any resulting increase or decrease in premium shall become effective on the date of the change of operations.

(d) Any insurer that violates this section shall be subject to civil penalties in an amount of up to five thousand dollars ($5,000) per violation. **Leg.H.** 1994 ch. 501, 1995 ch. 375.

Ref.: Hanna §§ 2.02[1][c], 2.16; Herlick Handbook § 3.10.

§11753.3. Workers' compensation insurance rating organization's exemption and authority.

Notwithstanding Section 1851.1, a workers' compensation insurance rating organization licensed pursuant to the provisions of this article which does not make rates, rating plans or rating systems for insurance covering employers against their liability for compensation or damages under the United States Longshoremen's and Harbor Workers' Compensation Act (33 U.S.C. 901, et seq.) shall not be required to be licensed as a rating organization or registered as an advisory organization pursuant to the provisions of Chapter 9 (commencing with Section 1850) of Part 2 of Division 1, and shall have authority under its license as a workers' compensation insurance rating organization issued pursuant to this article to:

(a) Collect and tabulate loss and expense experience statistics and other information and data relating to insurance covering employers against their liability for compensation under the United States Longshoremen's and Harbor Workers' Compensation Act.

(b) Furnish or exchange such information and experience data to or with rating organizations, advisory organizations and insurers in this and other states.

(c) Adopt and enforce compliance by its insurer members with reasonable rules and statistical plans to be used in the recording and reporting by insurer members of their California longshoremen and harbor workers' insurance loss and expense experience in order that such experience of all of its insurer members shall be available in such form and detail as will be of aid to the commissioner in the enforcement of and to its insurer members in complying with the provisions of Chapter 9 (commencing with Section 1850) of Part 2 of Division 1.

(d) Engage in the same activities and carry out the same functions with respect to insurance covering the liability of employers for compensation or damages under the United States Longshoremen's and Harbor Workers' Compensation Act that it is authorized to engage in or carry out with respect to California workers' compensation insurance generally under the provisions of this article other than the making of rates, rating plans and rating systems.

Ref.: Herlick Handbook § 3.10.

§11754. Noncompliance.

If the commissioner has good cause to believe that a rating or advisory organization or an insurer does not comply with the requirements of this article applicable to it, he shall, unless he has good cause to believe that such noncompliance is wilful, give notice in writing to such organization or insurer, stating therein in what manner and to what extent such noncompliance is alleged to exist and specifying therein a reasonable time, not less than 10 days thereafter, in which such noncompliance may be corrected. Notices under this section shall be confidential as between the commissioner and the organization or insurer unless a hearing is held under Section 11754.1.

Ref.: Herlick Handbook § 3.10.

§11754.1. Wilful or uncorrected noncompliance.

If the commissioner has good cause to believe such noncompliance to be wilful, or if within the period prescribed by the commissioner in the notice required by Section 11754 the organization or insurer does not make such change as may be necessary to correct the noncompliance specified by the commissioner or establish to the satisfaction of the commissioner that such noncompliance does not exist, then the commissioner may hold a public hearing in connection therewith, provided that within a reasonable period of time, which shall not be less than 10 days before the date of such hearing, he shall mail written notice specifying the matters to be considered at such hearing to such organization or insurer. Such notice shall conform to the requirements for an accusation as prescribed by Section 11503 of the Government Code. If no notice has been given as provided in Section 11754 such notice shall state therein in what manner and to what extent noncompliance is alleged to exist. The hearing shall not include any additional subjects not specified in the notices required by Section 11754 or this section.

Ref.: Herlick Handbook § 3.10.

§11754.2. Ordering compliance; suspension or revocation of license.

If, after a hearing pursuant to Section 11754.1, the commissioner finds:

(a) That any rating or advisory organization or other organization authorized by this article or any insurer has violated the provisions of this article applicable to it, he may issue an order to such organization or insurer which has been the subject of the hearing, specifying in what respect such violation exists and stating when, within a reasonable period of time, the violation shall cease.

(b) That any conditions prerequisite to the granting of a license to a rating organization no longer exists, he may issue an order to such organization which has been the subject of the hearing specifying the condition which has ceased to exist and stating when within a reasonable time the condition shall be complied with. If the condition is not complied with within the time specified the commissioner may suspend or revoke the license of such organization, in addition to any other penalty provided in this article.

(c) That any rating organization has wilfully engaged in any fraudulent, dishonest act or practice, he may suspend or revoke the license of such organization, in addition to any other penalty provided for in this article.

Ref.: Herlick Handbook § 3.10.

§11754.3. Suspension or revocation for noncompliance within time limits.

In addition to other penalties provided in this code the commissioner may suspend or revoke the license of any rating organization or insurer which fails to comply within the time limited by such order or extension thereof which the commissioner may grant, with an order of the commissioner lawfully made by him pursuant to Section 11754.1 and effective pursuant to Section 11754.5.

Ref.: Herlick Handbook § 3.10.

§11754.4. Procedures for denial, suspension, or revocation of license.

Except as otherwise provided in this article, all proceedings in connection with the denial, suspension or revocation of a license of a rating organization or insurer under this article shall be conducted in accordance with the provisions of Chapter 5 of Part 1 of Division 3 of Title 2 of the Government Code and the commissioner shall have all the powers granted to him therein.

Ref.: Herlick Handbook § 3.10.

§11754.5. Court review of commissioner's rulings.

Any finding, determination, rule, ruling, or order made by the commissioner under this article or Article 2 (commencing with Section 11730) shall be subject to review by the courts of the state pursuant to Section 1094.5 of the Code of Civil Procedure. **Leg.H.** 1995 ch. 582.

Ref.: Hanna § 2.02[2]; Herlick Handbook § 3.10.

§11755. False or misleading information; refusal to allow examination.

No person, insurer, rating or advisory organization shall willfully withhold information from, or knowingly give false or misleading information to, the commissioner or to any rating organization, which will affect the rates, rating systems or premiums for workers' compensation insurance and employer's liability insurance incidental thereto and written in connection therewith.

In the event of the refusal by any insured employer to permit an audit or an examination provided for in subdivision (f) of Section 11750.3, the commissioner shall, upon the verified petition of the rating organization concerned, take such action as the commissioner may be authorized to take pursuant to and subject to the provisions of this code and of the Government Code.

Ref.: Hanna § 2.02[2]; Herlick Handbook § 3.10.

§11756. Penalties for noncompliance with final order.

(a) Any person, insurer, or organization, who fails to comply with a final order of the commissioner under this article shall be liable to the State in an amount not exceeding fifty dollars ($50), but if the failure is wilful, he, she, or it shall be liable to the state in an amount not exceeding five thousand dollars ($5,000) for the failure. The commissioner shall collect the amount so payable and may bring an action in the name of the people of the state of California to enforce collection. These penalties may be in addition to any other penalties provided by law.

(b) A willful violation of the provisions of this article by any person is a misdemeanor.

Ref.: Herlick Handbook § 3.10.

§11757. Dividends, savings, or unabsorbed premium deposits.

Nothing in this article shall be construed to prohibit or regulate the payment of dividends, savings or unabsorbed premium deposits allowed or returned by insurers to their policyholders, members or subscribers. A plan for the payment of dividends, savings or unabsorbed premium deposits allowed or returned by insurers to their policyholders, members or subscribers shall not be deemed a rating plan or system.

Ref.: Hanna § 2.43; Herlick Handbook § 3.10.

§11758. Violation of other state laws.

No act done, action taken or agreement made pursuant to the authority conferred by this article shall constitute a violation of or grounds for prosecution or civil proceedings under any other law of this State heretofore or hereafter enacted which does not specifically refer to insurance.

Ref.: Hanna § 2.70[2]; Herlick Handbook §§ 3.10, 12.13.

§11758.1. Exemption for household employees.

The provisions of this article shall not apply to the workers' compensation insurance covering those persons defined as employees by subdivision (d) of Section 3351 of the Labor Code.

Ref.: Herlick Handbook § 3.10.

§11759. Rating organizations' and personnel's exemption from liability.

The Legislature hereby finds and declares as follows: The Legislature pursuant to its plenary power over workers' compensation granted by Section 4 of Article XIV of the California Constitution has authorized classification of risks and premium rates and systems of merit rating for workers' compensation insurance. The selective and discretionary inspection of locations, plants and operations of employers for classification and rating purposes, the gathering and compiling of experience statistics and other data by rating organizations licensed by the Insurance Commissioner, and the application of standards predicated upon the reliability of such classifications and merit rating data are essential to the proper functioning of the classifications of risks and premium rates and systems of merit rating which are regulated by the Insurance Commissioner as authorized by the Legislature.

In order to implement and facilitate the proper and adequate administration of such classifications of risks and rates and systems of rating by such licensed rating organizations and the Insurance Commissioner, it is important and in the public interest that licensed rating organizations and their officers and employees shall not be liable for injury or death or other damage caused or alleged to have been caused by their failure to inspect, or negligent or incomplete inspection of, an employer's location, plant or operation for classification or rating purposes.

No licensed rating organization or member thereof in its character as a member, or officer or employee of such licensed rating organization when acting within the scope of his employment, shall be liable for injury or death or other damage proximately caused by a failure to inspect, or the manner or extent of inspection of, an employer's locations, plants or operations for classification or rating purposes, or by such person's comment, or failure to comment, on the subject matter or object of such inspection.

This section shall not be construed as implying the existence of liability in circumstances not defined in this section; nor as implying a legislative recognition that, except for the enactment of this section, a liability has existed or would exist in circumstances stated in this section.

Ref.: Herlick Handbook §§ 3.10, 12.13.

§11759.1. Rating organizations must make available report of prior year's losses and expenses.

A rating organization shall, no later than June 1 of each year, notify the Governor and the Legislature that a report containing an analysis of all losses and expenses for the prior year by all insurers who are members of the organization is available on request. The first report shall be due June 1, 1996. The report shall include, but not be limited to, the following:

(a) An analysis of all medical costs identifying separately the amounts paid for medical treatment to hospitals and physicians, and the amounts paid for medical-legal expenses. The amounts paid for medical treatment to physicians shall also identify the amounts paid for each specialty authorized to provide medical services pursuant to Sections 3209.3, 3209.5, and 3209.8 of the Labor Code. The amounts paid for medical-legal evaluations shall also be subcategorized by specialty and shall identify average costs paid per claim.

(b) An analysis of indemnity benefits paid for temporary disability, permanent total disability, permanent partial disability, life pensions, death benefits, and funeral expenses. The permanent partial disability benefits also shall be reported according to the degree of impairment in the following categories: .25 to 24.75 percent, 25 to 69.75 percent, and 70 to 99.75 percent.

(c) An analysis of amounts paid for vocational rehabilitation subcategorized by amounts paid for maintenance allowance, evaluation, education and training.

(d) An analysis of expenses of insurers categorized by loss adjustment, acquisition, general expenses, profit, and taxes. Amounts spent for defense attorneys' expense shall be separately identified.

(e) An analysis of attorney's fees paid to applicant attorneys.

(f) An analysis of workers' compensation costs by the type of injury or illness generally following the injury classification in the Annual Redesigned Occupational Safety and Health Statistical Program used by the Department of Industrial Relations in its annual report on California work injuries and illnesses. **Leg.H.** 1993 ch. 121, effective July 16, 1993, ch. 1242, 1995 ch. 556.

Ref.: Herlick Handbook § 3.10.

§11759.2. Report on underreported workers' compensation exposure in taxicab industry.

(a) A licensed rating organization designated as the Insurance Commissioner's statistical agent shall prepare a report to be submitted to the Insurance Commissioner by April 1, 2003, on the potential underreporting of workers' compensation exposure in the taxicab industry. The report shall include an analysis of workers' compensation exposure, loss, and premium in the taxicab industry. The licensed rating organization shall submit a report to the Governor, the Legislature, and the commissioner by May 1, 2003, that describes its findings.

(b) A licensed rating organization designated as the insurance commissioner's statistical agent may confer with state agencies, including, but not limited to, the Employment Development Department, in the preparation of the study. The state agencies shall provide all necessary statistical or other information requested by the licensed rating organization designated as the Insurance Commissioner's statistical agent. **Leg.H.** 2002 ch. 893 (SB 1407).

ARTICLE 4
Penalties for Misrepresentation

§11760. Penalties for misrepresentation to obtain reduced rate.

(a) It is unlawful to make or cause to be made any knowingly false or fraudulent statement, whether made orally or in writing, of any fact material to the determination of the premium, rate, or cost of any policy of workers' compensation insurance, for the purpose of reducing the premium, rate, or cost of the insurance. Any person convicted of violating this subdivision shall be punished by imprisonment in a county jail for one year, or pursuant to subdivision (h) of Section 1170 of the Penal Code for two, three, or five years, or by a fine not exceeding fifty thousand dollars ($50,000), or double the value of the fraud, whichever is greater, or by both that imprisonment and fine.

(b) Any person who violates subdivision (a) and who has a prior felony conviction of the offense set forth in that subdivision shall receive a two-year enhancement for each prior conviction in addition to the sentence provided in subdivision (a). The existence of any fact that would subject a person to a penalty enhancement shall be alleged in the information or indictment and either admitted by the defendant in open court, or found to be true by the jury trying the issue of guilt or by the court where guilt is established by plea of guilty or nolo contendere or by trial by the court sitting without a jury. **Leg.H.** 1991 chs. 116, 934, 1995 ch. 885, 2011 ch. 15 (AB 109) §217, effective April 4, 2011, operative October 1, 2011.

2011 Notes: This act is titled and may be cited as the 2011 Realignment Legislation addressing public safety. Stats. 2011 ch. 15 (AB 109) §1.

This act will become operative no earlier than October 1, 2011, and only upon creation of a community corrections grant program to assist in implementing this act and upon an appropriation to fund the grant program. Stats. 2011 ch. 15 (AB 109) §636; Stats. 2011 ch. 39 (AB 117) §68.

The Community Corrections Grant Program referred to in Stats. 2011 ch. 15 §636, as amended by Stats. 2011 ch. 39 §68, was created by Stats. 2011 ch. 40 §3, operative October 1, 2011.

Ref.: Hanna § 2.03[3], [4]; Herlick Handbook § 9.18.

§11760.1. Audit of employer; failure to provide access to records; costs.

(a) If an employer fails to provide for access by the insurer or its authorized representative to its records, to enable the insurer to perform an audit to determine the remuneration earned by the employer's employees and by any of its uninsured subcontractors and the employees of any of its uninsured subcontractors during the policy period, the employer shall be liable to pay to the insurer a total premium for the policy equal to three times the insurer's then-current estimate of the annual premium on the expiration date of the policy. The employer shall also be liable, in addition to the premium, for costs incurred by the insurer in its attempts to perform an audit, after the insured has failed upon the insurer's third request during at least a 90-day period to provide access, and the insured has provided no compelling business reason for the failure. This section shall only apply if the insurer elects to comply with the conditions set forth in subdivision (d).

(b) "Access" shall mean access at any time during regular business hours during the policy period and within three years after the policy period ends. "Access" may also include any other time mutually agreed upon by the employer and insurer.

(c) The insurer shall have and follow regular and reasonable rules and procedures to notify employers of their duty to provide for access to records, and to contact employers to make appointments during regular business hours for that purpose.

(d) Upon the employer's failure to provide access after the insurer's third request during at least a 90-day period, the insurer may notify the employer through its mailing of a certified, return-receipt, document of the increased premium and the total amount of the costs incurred by the insurer for its attempts to perform an audit as described under subdivision (a). Upon the expiration of 30 days after the delivery of the notice, collection by the insurer of the amount of premium and costs described under subdivision (a), less all premiums previously paid by the employer for the policy, shall be fully enforceable and executable.

(e) If the employer provides for access to its records after having received the notice described in subdivision (d), and if the insurer then succeeds in performing the audit to its satisfaction, the insurer shall revise the total premium and costs payable for the policy by the employer to reflect the results of its audit. **Leg.H.** 2007 ch. 615 (AB 812) §1.

ARTICLE 5
Standards Applicable to Claims Adjusters

§11761. Workers' compensation claims adjusters—Minimum standards of training, experience, and skill; certification to commissioner by specified entities that employees meet minimum standards.

(a) The commissioner shall adopt regulations setting forth the minimum standards of training, experience, and skill that workers' compensation claims adjusters must possess to perform their duties with regard to workers' compensation claims. The regulations adopted pursuant to this section shall, to the greatest extent possible, encourage the use of existing private and public education, training, and certification programs.

(b) Every insurer shall certify to the commissioner that the personnel employed by the insurer to adjust workers' compensation claims, or employed for that purpose by any medical billing entity with which the insurer contracts, meet the minimum standards adopted by the commissioner pursuant to subdivision (a).

(c) For the purposes of this section, "medical billing entity" means a third party that reviews or adjusts workers' compensation medical bills for insurers.

(d) For the purposes of this section, "insurer" means an insurer admitted to transact workers' compensation insurance in this state, the State Compensation Insurance Fund, an employer that has secured a certificate of consent to self-insure pursuant to subdivision (b) or (c) of Section 3700 of the Labor Code, or a third-party administrator that has secured a certificate of consent pursuant to Section 3702.1 of the Labor Code. **Leg.H.** 2003 ch. 637 (AB 1262).

Ref.: Hanna § 2.70[2]; Herlick Handbook § 3.15.

CHAPTER 4
THE STATE COMPENSATION INSURANCE FUND

ARTICLE 1
Organization and Powers

§11770. State Compensation Insurance Fund; board of directors.

(a) The State Compensation Insurance Fund is continued in existence, to be administered by its board of directors for the purpose of transacting workers' compensation insurance, and insurance against the expense of defending any suit for serious and willful misconduct, against an employer or his or her agent, and insurance to employees and other persons of the compensation fixed by the workers' compensation laws for employees and their dependents. Any appropriation made therefrom or thereto before the effective date of this code shall continue to be available for the purposes for which it was made.

(b)(1) The Board of Directors of the State Compensation Insurance Fund is composed of 11 members, nine of whom shall be appointed by the Governor. The Governor shall appoint the chairperson. One of the members appointed by the Governor shall be from organized labor. The members appointed by the Governor, other than the labor member, shall have substantial experience in positions involving workers' compensation, legal, investment, financial, corporate governance and management, accounting, or auditing responsibilities with entities of sufficient size as to make their qualifications relevant to an enterprise of the financial and operational size of the State Compensation Insurance Fund. At all times the board shall have a member with auditing background for the purposes of fulfilling the responsibility of the chair of the audit committee. A quorum is a majority of those appointed, provided that at no time shall a quorum be established with fewer than five members.

(2) The Speaker of the Assembly shall appoint one member who shall represent organized labor, and the Senate Committee on Rules shall appoint one member who shall have been a policyholder of the State Compensation Insurance Fund, or an officer or employee of a policyholder, for one year immediately preceding the appointment, and must continue in this status during the period of his or her membership.

(3) The Director of Industrial Relations shall be an ex officio, nonvoting member of the board, and shall not be counted as members of the board for quorum purposes or any other purpose.

(4) Notwithstanding subdivision (c), the initial term of the members of the board added in the 2008 portion of the 2007–08 Regular Session shall be as follows:

(A) One of the members appointed by the Governor shall serve an initial term of two years, one shall serve an initial term of four years, and two shall serve an initial term of five years.

(B) The member appointed by the Senate Committee on Rules shall serve an initial term of four years.

(C) The member appointed by the Speaker of the Assembly shall serve an initial term of three years.

(c) The term of office of the members of the board, other than that of the director, shall be five years and they shall hold office until the appointment and qualification of their successors.

(d)(1) Each member of the board shall receive his or her actual and necessary traveling expenses incurred in the performance of his or her duties as a member and, with the exception of the ex officio members, one hundred dollars ($100) for each day of his or her actual attendance at meetings of the board.

(2)(A) Each member of the board appointed pursuant to paragraphs (1) and (2) of subdivision (b) shall receive the compensation fixed pursuant to subparagraph (B).

(B) Each board member described in subparagraph (A) shall be paid an annual compensation of fifty thousand dollars ($50,000), to be automatically adjusted beginning January 1, 2010, by multiplying the compensation in effect the prior June 30 by the percentage of inflation that occurred during the previous year, adding this amount to the annual compensation from the previous year, and rounding off the result to the nearest dollar. "Percentage of inflation" means the percentage of inflation specified in the Consumer Price Index for All Urban Consumers, as published by the Department of Industrial Relations, or its successor index.

(e) Each member of the board of directors shall attend training approved by the board of directors that covers topics, including, but not limited to, the duties and obligations of members of a board of directors, corporate governance, ethics, board of director legal issues, insurance, finance and investment, and information technology. The training shall be conducted by persons or entities not affiliated with the State Compensation Insurance Fund.

(f) No person who has had a direct or indirect interest in any transaction with the State Compensation Insurance Fund since the beginning of the last fiscal year of the fund, or who has a direct or indirect material interest in any proposed transaction with the fund, where the amount involved in the transaction exceeds one hundred twenty thousand dollars ($120,000) shall be eligible for appointment as a member of the board of directors of the fund. Once appointed, no member of the board of directors shall have a financial conflict of interest, as defined in Chapter 7 of Title 9 (commencing with Section 87100) of the Government Code, and every member shall be subject to Article 4 (commencing with Section 1090) of Chapter 1 of Division 4 of Title 1 of the Government Code, provided that the existence of a contract of insurance between the State Compensation Insurance Fund and the policyholder member appointed by the Senate Committee on Rules shall not constitute a conflict of interest pursuant to this subdivision. For purposes of board actions affecting generally applicable rates, a member of the board of directors shall not be deemed to have a financial interest, as defined in Article 4 (commencing with Section 1090) of Chapter 1 of Division 4 of Title 1 of, or pursuant to Chapter 7 (commencing with Section 87100) of Title 9 of, the Government Code, in a contract of insurance between the State Compensation Insurance Fund and an organization of which any member of the board of directors is an owner, officer, or employee.

(g) The appointing authority of a member of the board may remove the member and make an appointment replacing the member for the duration of the term if the member ceases to discharge the duties of his or her office for the period of three consecutive board meetings.

(h) The board of the State Compensation Insurance Fund shall create, at a minimum, an audit committee, an investment committee, a corporate governance committee, and other committees as the board determines are necessary. **Leg.H.** 2002 ch. 6 (AB 749), 2008 ch. 322 (AB 1874) §3, 2009 ch. 136 (AB 1117) §2, effective August 6, 2009, 2012 ch. 46 (SB 1038) §76, effective June 27, 2012.

2009 Note: The Legislature finds and declares that the amendments made to Section 11770 of the Insurance Code by this act are technical in nature, do not change the law, and are intended to ensure that members of the board of directors of the State Compensation Insurance Fund are not incorrectly disqualified from participating in important decisions of the board that impact policyholders generally and no board member uniquely. Stats. 2009 ch. 136 (AB 1117) §1.

Ref.: Herlick Handbook § 1.07[1].

§11771. State's limited liability.

The State shall not be liable beyond the assets of the State Compensation Insurance Fund for any obligations in connection therewith.

Ref.: Hanna § 1.20[4]; Herlick Handbook § 1.07[3].

§11771.5. Advertising disclaimer.

Any advertising of the State Compensation Insurance Fund shall include the following disclaimer: "The State Compensation Insurance Fund is not a branch of the State of California." **Leg.H.** 2002 ch. 6 (AB 749).

§11772. Directors' and personnel's limited liability.

There shall not be any liability in a private capacity on the part of the board of directors or any member thereof, or any officer or employee of the fund for or on account of any act performed or obligation entered into in an official capacity, when done in good faith, without intent to defraud and in connection with the administration, management or conduct of the fund or affairs relating thereto.

Ref.: Hanna § 1.20[4].

§11773. Organization as public enterprise fund.

The fund shall be organized as a public enterprise fund.

Ref.: Hanna § 1.20[1]; Herlick Handbook § 1.07[1].

§11774. Use of fund assets.

The assets of the fund shall be applicable to the payment of losses sustained on account of insurance and to the payment of the salaries and other expenses charged against it in accordance with the provisions of this chapter.

Ref.: Hanna §§ 1.20[1], 2.30[1]; Herlick Handbook § 1.07[1].

§11775. Competitiveness with other insurers.

The fund shall, after a reasonable time during which it may establish a business, be fairly competitive with other insurers, and it is the intent of the Legislature that the fund shall ultimately become neither more nor less than self-supporting. For that purpose loss experience and expense shall be ascertained and dividends or credits may be made as provided in this article.

Ref.: Hanna §§ 1.20[1], 2.30[1]; Herlick Handbook § 1.07[1].

§11776. Annual accountings; possible dividends and credits.

The actual loss experience and expense of the fund shall be ascertained on or about the first of January in each year for the year preceding. If it is then shown that there exists an excess of assets over liabilities, necessary reserves, and a reasonable surplus for the catastrophe hazard, then a cash dividend may be declared to, or a credit allowed on the renewal premium of each employer who has been insured with the fund.

Ref.: Hanna §§ 1.20[5], 2.30[1]; Herlick Handbook § 3.2.

§11777. Amount of dividends or credits.

Such cash dividend or credit is to be an amount which the board of directors in its discretion considers to be the employer's proportion of divisible surplus.

Ref.: Hanna §§ 1.20[5], 2.30[1]; Herlick Handbook § 3.2.

§11778. Ability to transact workers' compensation insurance.

The fund may transact workers' compensation insurance required or authorized by law of this state to the same extent as any other insurer. The fund shall be subject to the powers and authority of the commissioner to the same extent as any other insurer transacting workers' compensation insurance, except where specifically exempted by reference. For purposes of Section 700, the fund shall be deemed admitted to transact this class of insurance. **Leg.H.** 1981 ch. 714 §305, 2006 ch. 740 (AB 2125) §13.1.

Ref.: Hanna §§ 1.20[1], [2], 2.30[1]; Herlick Handbook § 1.07[1], [2].

§11779. Ability to insure under federal or maritime laws.

The fund may insure California employers against their liability for compensation or damages for injury or death under the United States Longshoremen's and Harbor Workers' Compensation Act, or other federal or maritime laws, as fully as any private insurer.

Ref.: Hanna §§ 1.20[2], 2.30[1]; Herlick Handbook §§ 1.07[2], 13.2.

§11780. Ability to insure under state law.

The fund may also insure an employer against his or her liability for damages under the laws of the State of California arising out of bodily injury to or death of the employer's employees occurring within the State of California if the fund also issues workers' compensation insurance to the employer as to his or her employees.

Ref.: Hanna §§ 1.20[2], 2.30[1]; Herlick Handbook § 1.07[2].

§11780.5. Ability to insure employees temporarily out of California.

(a) The fund may also insure a California employer against his or her liability for workers' compensation benefits, under the law of any other state, for California employees temporarily working outside of California on a specific assignment if the fund insures the employer's other employees who work within California.

(b)(1) The fund is only authorized under this subdivision to insure an employer whose principal place of business is in California, provided the majority of the employer's operations and employees are located within California, against his or her liability for workers' compensation benefits, under the law of any other state, if the fund insures the employer's employees who work within California.

(2) The fund is only authorized pursuant to this subdivision to contract as a reinsurer with a ceding insurer that has responded to a request for proposal from the fund and is admitted to transact workers' compensation insurance in California and in the out-of-state jurisdiction where the non-California employees are located. The fund may only contract for purposes of this subdivision if the ceding insurer meets all of the following criteria:

(A) The insurer has an A minus (A-) rating or better from A.M. Best Company.

(B) The insurer has substantial prior experience in transacting workers' compensation business on another insurer's behalf.

(C) The insurer has a minimum surplus of one hundred million dollars ($100,000,000).

(c) The fund shall not initiate paid advertising or solicit sponsorship of advertising campaigns to market or promote to prospective insureds the ability to insure qualified employers under the law of any other state. **Leg.H.** 1978 ch. 647 §1, 2011 ch. 670 (AB 228) §1, 2012 ch. 162 (SB 1171) §115, 2016 ch. 206 (AB 2887) §1.

Ref.: Hanna §§ 1.20[2], 2.30[1]; Herlick Handbook §§ 1.07[2], 13.2.

§11781. Board of directors' powers.

The board of directors is hereby vested with full power, authority and jurisdiction over the State Compensation Insurance Fund. The board of directors may perform all acts necessary or convenient in the exercise of any power, authority or jurisdiction over the fund, either in the administration thereof or in connection with the insurance business to be carried on by it under the provisions of this chapter, as fully and completely as the governing body of a private insurance carrier. The principal office for the transaction of the business of the State Compensation Insurance Fund is located in the City and County of San Francisco.

Ref.: Hanna §§ 1.20[1], [3], 2.30[1].

§11781.5. Authority to acquire property in Los Angeles.

The State Compensation Insurance Fund may acquire and own real property for a branch office in the City of Los Angeles when so determined by the board of directors, and may, if necessary, construct suitable buildings thereon in accordance with law.

Ref.: Hanna § 2.30[1].

§11782. Business name.

All business and affairs of the fund shall be conducted in the name of the State Compensation Insurance Fund, and in that name, without any other name or title, the board of directors may perform the acts authorized by this chapter.

Ref.: Hanna § 2.30[1].

§11783. Powers of fund.

The State Compensation Insurance Fund may:

(a) Sue and be sued in all actions arising out of any act or omission in connection with its business or affairs.

(b) Enter into any contracts or obligations relating to the State Compensation Insurance Fund which are authorized or permitted by law.

(c) Invest and reinvest the moneys belonging to the fund as provided by this chapter.

(d) Conduct all business and affairs and perform all acts relating to the fund whether or not specifically designated in this chapter.

(e) Commission an independent study, with the assistance of an investment banking firm, to determine the feasibility of the State Compensation Insurance Fund issuing bonds or securities. The study may include, among other things, the purpose for issuing bonds and any potential adverse consequences that may arise from that issuance. **Leg.H.** 2002 ch. 6 (AB 749).

§11784. Powers of fund president.

In conducting the business and affairs of the fund, the president of the fund may do any of the following:

(a) Enter into contracts of workers' compensation insurance.

(b) Sell annuities covering compensation benefits.

(c) Decline to insure any risk in which the minimum requirements of the industrial accident prevention authorities with regard to construction, equipment, and operation are not complied with, or which is beyond the safe carrying of the fund. Otherwise, he or she shall not refuse to insure any workers' compensation risk under state law, tendered with the premium therefor.

(d) Reinsure any risk or any part thereof.

(e) Cause to be inspected and audited the payrolls of employers applying to the fund for insurance.

(f) Make rules for the settlement of claims against the fund and determine to whom and through whom the payments of compensation are to be made.

(g) Contract with physicians and surgeons, and hospitals, for medical and surgical treatment and the care and nursing of injured persons entitled to benefits from the fund. **Leg.H.** 2001 ch. 159, 2002 ch. 6 (AB 749).

§11785. Appointment of officers to fund; applicability of Government Code and Public Contract Code provisions.

(a) The board of directors shall appoint a president, a chief financial officer, a chief operating officer, a chief information technology officer, a chief investment officer, a chief risk officer, a general counsel, a chief medical officer, a chief actuarial officer, a chief claims operations officer, and a chief of internal affairs. The board may appoint a chief underwriting officer, a senior vice president of insurance services, an executive vice president of corporate claims, an executive vice president of strategic planning, and a pricing actuary. The board of directors shall set the salary for each position in amounts that are reasonably necessary to attract and retain individuals of superior qualifications. The board shall submit its salary-setting criteria, including salary surveys, to the Department of Human Resources. These positions shall not be subject to otherwise applicable provisions of the Government Code and the Public Contract Code, and for those purposes the fund shall not be considered a state agency or other public entity. The president shall manage and conduct the business and affairs of the fund under the general direction and subject to the approval of the board of directors, and shall perform other duties as the board of directors prescribes.

(b) Section 87406 of the Government Code, the Milton Marks Postgovernment Employment Restrictions Act of 1990, shall apply to the fund. Members of the board, a person who held a position designated in subdivision (a), and any other person designated by the fund shall be deemed to be designated employees for the purpose of that act.

(c) Both the Bagley-Keene Open Meeting Act (Article 9 (commencing with Section 11120) of Chapter 1 of Part 1 of Division 3 of Title 2 of the Government Code) and the California Public Records Act (Chapter 3.5 (commencing with Section 6250) of Division 7 of Title 1 of the Government Code) shall apply to the fund.

(d)(1) The board shall, by September 1, 2018, and subsequently on a biennial basis, make a report to the Legislature and to the committees of the Senate and Assembly having jurisdiction over insurance that provides any salary-setting criteria and salary surveys submitted to the Department of Human Resources pursuant to subdivision (a), and the salary and total compensation of each position appointed pursuant to subdivision (a), for the previous two fiscal years.

(2) A report submitted pursuant to this subdivision shall be submitted in compliance with Section 9795 of the Government Code. **Leg.H.** 2002 ch. 6 (AB 749), 2008 ch. 344 (SB 1145) §5, effective September 26, 2008, 2013 ch. 309 (AB 1394) §1, 2017 ch. 539 (SB 272) §1.

§11785.5. Former members of fund's board of directors and former fund officers prohibited from lobbying for fund for two years after leaving fund; consulting for fund by specified persons to be approved by fund's board.

(a) Notwithstanding any other provision of law to the contrary, the members of the Board of Directors of the State Compensation Insurance Fund and officers of the fund appointed by the board of directors, including, but not limited to, the president, chief financial officer, chief operating officer, chief information technology officer, chief investment officer, chief risk officer, and general counsel, are prohibited from lobbying the fund for two years after leaving employment with the fund.

(b) Notwithstanding any other provision of law to the contrary, any consulting for the fund by former members of the Board of Directors of the State Compensation Insurance Fund and former officers of the fund appointed by the board of directors, including, but not limited to, the president, chief financial officer, chief operating officer, chief information technology officer, chief investment officer, chief risk officer, and general counsel, shall be approved by the board of directors. **Leg.H.** 2011 ch. 53 (AB 1263) §2.

§11786. President's bond and oath.

Before entering on the duties of his or her office, the president shall qualify by giving an official bond approved by the board of directors in the sum of fifty thousand dollars ($50,000) and by taking and subscribing to an official oath. The approval of the board shall be by written endorsement on the bond. The bond shall be filed in the office of the Secretary of State. **Leg.H.** 2001 ch. 159, 2002 ch. 6 (AB 749).

§11787. Board's delegation of authority to president.

The board of directors may delegate to the president of the fund, under those rules and regulations and subject to those conditions as it from time to time prescribes, any power, function, or duty conferred by law on the board of directors in connection with the fund or in connection with the administration, management, and conduct of the business and affairs of the fund. The president may exercise those powers and functions and perform those duties with the same force and effect as the board of directors, but subject to its approval. **Leg.H.** 2001 ch. 159, 2002 ch. 6 (AB 749).

§11788. State Treasurer as custodian of fund's securities.

The State Treasurer shall be custodian of all securities belonging to the State Compensation Insurance Fund, except as otherwise provided in this chapter. He or she shall be liable on his or her official bond for the safe keeping thereof. **Leg.H.** 1935 ch. 145, effective September 15, 1935, 1979 ch. 738 §2, 2011 ch. 426 (SB 712) §9.

§11790. Delivery of securities to State Treasurer.

All securities belonging to the fund shall be delivered to the State Treasurer and held by him or her until otherwise disposed of as provided in this chapter. Upon delivery of those securities into the custody of the State Treasurer, the securities shall be credited by the State Treasurer to the fund. **Leg.H.** 1935 ch. 145, effective September 15, 1935, 1979 ch. 738 §4, 2011 ch. 426 (SB 712) §10.

§11793. Exemption for fund's expenditures.

Expenditures made by the State Compensation Insurance Fund are exempted from the provisions of Part 3 (commencing with Section 900) of Division 3.6 of Title I of the Government Code.

§11797. [First of Two; Repealed January 1, 2025] Investment of moneys; purchase of bonds and other evidence of indebtedness; report.

(a) The board of directors shall cause all moneys in the State Compensation Insurance Fund that are in excess of current requirements to be invested and reinvested, from time to time, in the same manner as provided for private insurance carriers pursuant to Article 3 (commencing with Section 1170) and Article 4 (commencing with Section 1190) of Chapter 2 of Part 2 of Division 1, but excluding Sections 1191, 1191.1, 1191.5, 1192.2, 1192.4, 1192.6, 1192.7, 1192.9, 1192.95, 1192.10, 1194.7, 1194.8, 1194.81, 1194.82, 1194.85, 1198, and 1199. Notwithstanding the foregoing, the State Compensation Insurance Fund may invest or reinvest an aggregated maximum of 20 percent of moneys that are in excess of the admitted assets over the liabilities and required reserves in the investments allowed pursuant to Sections 1191, 1192.4, 1192.6, 1192.10, 1194.7, and 1198.

(b)(1)(A) Notwithstanding any other law, the State Compensation Insurance Fund may purchase general obligation bonds or other evidence of indebtedness issued by the state, including, but not limited to, warrants issued pursuant to Part 4 (commencing with Section 17000) of Division 4 of Title 2 of the Government Code or notes issued pursuant to Part 5 (commencing with Section 17300) of Division 4 of Title 2 of the Government Code, in any amount and to enter into purchase contracts with the state for this purpose.

(B) Notwithstanding any other law, the State Compensation Insurance Fund may purchase Property Assessed Clean Energy (PACE) bonds, as defined in Section 26054 of the Public Resources Code.

(2) The bonds or other evidence of indebtedness specified in paragraph (1), upon delivery to the State Compensation Insurance Fund, shall, for all purposes, be valid and binding obligations of the issuer thereof, be validly issued and outstanding in accordance with their stated terms, and not be deemed to be owned by or on behalf of the issuer thereof.

(c) The Department of Insurance shall submit to the Legislature by January 31, 2019, a report that assesses the benefit and risk of the State Compensation Insurance Fund's equities investment history by measuring the volatility and total return of the State Compensation Insurance Fund's investment portfolio with and without equities. The report shall be submitted pursuant to Section 9795 of the Government Code.

(d) This section shall remain in effect only until January 1, 2025, and as of that date is repealed, unless a later enacted statute, that is enacted before January 1, 2025, deletes or extends that date. **Leg.H.** 1935 ch. 145, effective September 15, 1935, 1945 ch. 1431 §157, 1979 ch. 738 §10, 2009–10 ch. 24 (Fourth Extra. Sess.) (AB 25 (Fourth Extra. Sess.)) §3, effective July 29, 2009, 2010 chs. 583 (AB 1873) §5, 651 (SB 1407) §1.5, 2012 ch. 839 (SB 1513) §1, 2019 ch. 396 (AB 1513) §12.

§11797. [Second of Two; Operative January 1, 2025] Investment of moneys; purchase of bonds and other evidence of indebtedness.

(a) The board of directors shall cause all moneys in the State Compensation Insurance Fund that are in excess of current requirements to be invested and reinvested, from time to time, in the same manner as provided for private insurance carriers pursuant to Article 3 (commencing with Section 1170) and Article 4 (commencing with Section 1190) of Chapter 2 of Part 2 of Division 1, but excluding Sections 1191, 1191.1, 1191.5, 1192.2, 1192.4, 1192.6, 1192.7, 1192.9, 1192.95, 1192.10, 1194.7, 1194.8, 1194.81, 1194.82, 1194.85, 1198, and 1199.

(b)(1)(A) Notwithstanding any other law, the State Compensation Insurance Fund may purchase general obligation bonds or other evidence of indebtedness issued by the state, including, but not limited to, notes issued pursuant to Part 5 (commencing with Section 17300) of Division 4 of Title 2 of the Government Code or warrants issued pursuant to Part 4 (commencing with Section 17000) of Division 4 of Title 2 of the Government Code, in any amount and to enter into purchase contracts with the state for this purpose.

(B) Notwithstanding any other law, the State Compensation Insurance Fund may purchase Property Assessed Clean Energy (PACE) bonds, as defined in Section 26054 of the Public Resources Code.

(2) The bonds or other evidence of indebtedness specified in paragraph (1), upon delivery to the State Compensation Insurance Fund, shall, for all purposes, be valid and binding obligations of the issuer thereof, be validly issued and outstanding in accordance with their stated terms, and not be deemed to be owned by or on behalf of the issuer thereof.

(c) This section shall become operative on January 1, 2025. **Leg.H.** 2012 ch. 839 (SB 1513) §2, 2019 ch. 396 (AB 1513) §13.

§11800. Deposit of excess moneys.

All moneys in the State Compensation Insurance Fund, in excess of current requirements and not otherwise invested, may be deposited by the board of directors from time to time in financial institutions authorized by law to receive deposits of public moneys.

§11800.1. Fund account in State Treasury.

The board of directors may, with the approval of the State Treasurer, authorize the establishment of an account or fund in the State Treasury in the name of the State Compensation Insurance Fund, but such moneys deposited with the State Treasurer are not state moneys within the intent of Section 16305.2 of the Government Code.

§11800.2. Special ledger account by State Controller.

The State Controller shall keep a special ledger account pertaining to the State Compensation Insurance Fund. In the State Controller's general ledger this account may appear as a cash account, like other accounts of funds in the State Treasury, and only the actual cash credited or deposited to the credit of the State Compensation Insurance Fund shall be entered in the account.

§11801. Prohibition on use of certain assets to satisfy federal claims.

The assets, premiums, reserves, investment income, and any and all property of whatsoever kind derived or acquired by the fund from its transaction of its workers' compensation insurance business shall not be used, attached or levied upon in any manner whatsoever by any person to satisfy claims or any other obligations or liability incurred, arising out of, or related to, the fund's transaction of insurance pursuant to the United States Longshoremen's and Harbor Workers' Compensation Act.

Ref.: Hanna § 1.20[2].

§11802. Separate accounts for funds acquired for federal claims.

All premiums, reserves, investment income, and all property of whatsoever kind derived or acquired by the fund from its transaction of insurance pursuant to the United States Longshoremen's and Harbor Workers' Compensation Act shall be maintained and identified in separate accounts and records.

Ref.: Hanna § 1.20[2].

§11803. Federal claims and costs to be paid from separate account.

All claims, costs of doing business, liabilities, expenses, and obligations arising out of or related to the fund's transaction of insurance pursuant to the United States Longshoremen's and Harbor Workers' Compensation Act shall be paid and charged to the income of whatsoever nature derived from its United States Longshoremen's and Harbor Workers' Compensation Act insurance business only.

Ref.: Hanna § 1.20[2].

§11804. Charges for insurance classes' use of facilities, supplies, or equipment.

Joint or shared use of office building space, whether owned, leased or rented, and the joint use of all furniture, automobiles, office equipment, supplies and services shall be charged to each class of insurance business on an equitable and proportional basis.

§11805. Annual report to Legislature.

The State Compensation Insurance Fund shall report annually to the Legislature as soon after the close of the calendar year as is feasible, with respect to its experience handling United States longshoremen's and harbor workers' insurance pursuant to this chapter, including, but not limited to, a statement of resources and liabilities at the close of each annual period commencing December 31, 1979.

Ref.: Hanna § 1.20[2].

ARTICLE 2
Rates

§11820. Rates.

Subject to the provisions of Article 2 (commencing with Section 11730) of Chapter 3, the board of directors shall establish the rates to be charged by the State Compensation Insurance Fund for insurance issued by it. These rates shall be fixed with due regard to the physical hazards of each industry, occupation, or employment. **Leg.H.** 2002 ch. 6 (AB 749).

§11821. Factors considered in setting rates.

Within each class of business insured such rates shall be fixed, so far as practicable, in accordance with the following elements:

(a) Bodily risk or safety, or other hazard of the plant, premises or work of each insured employer.

(b) The manner in which the work is conducted.

(c) A reasonable regard for the accident experience and history of each such insured.

(d) A reasonable regard for the insured's means and methods of caring for injured persons.

Such rates shall take no account of the extent to which the employees in any particular establishment have or have not persons dependent upon them for support.

§11822. Percentage basis of rates.

The rates fixed by the board of directors shall be that percentage of the payroll of any employer which, in the long run and on the average, will produce a sufficient sum, when invested in a way as to realize the maximum return consistent with safe and prudent management practices:

(a) To carry all claims to maturity. The rates shall be based upon the "reserve" and not upon the "assessment" plan.

(b) To meet the reasonable expenses of conducting the business of the fund.

(c) To produce a reasonable surplus to cover the catastrophe hazard. **Leg.H.** 2002 ch. 6 (AB 749).

ARTICLE 3
Policies

§11840. Insurance contracts and policies.

The insurance contracts or policies of the State Compensation Insurance Fund may be either limited or unlimited. The insurance contracts or policies may be issued for like periods as are allowed by law to other workers' compensation insurers or, in the form of stamps or tickets or otherwise, for one month, for any number of months less than one year, for one day, for any number of days less than one month or during the performance of any particular work, job or contract. The rates charged shall be proportionately greater for a shorter than for a longer period and a minimum premium charge shall be fixed in accordance with a reasonable rate for insuring one person for one day.

§11841. Chapter's limitations on temporary coverage and policy surrender.

Nothing in this chapter shall prevent:

(a) Any applicant for insurance from being covered temporarily until the application is finally acted upon.

(b) An insured from surrendering any policy at any time and having returned to him the difference between the premium paid and the premium at the customary short term for the shorter period which such policy has already run.

§11843. Policies for employers and families.

The State Compensation Insurance Fund may issue policies including, with their employees, employers who perform labor incidental to their occupations, and including also members of the families of such employers engaged in the same occupation.

Ref.: Hanna § 1.20[2]; Herlick Handbook § 3.2.

§11844. Same compensation and rates for employers and employees.

Such policies covering employers shall insure to such employers and working members of their families the same compensations provided for their employees, and at the same rates.

Ref.: Hanna § 1.20[2]; Herlick Handbook § 3.2.

§11845. Estimates of employers' wage values.

The estimations of the wage values, respectively, of such insured employers and members of their families shall be reasonable and shall be separately stated in and added to the valuation of the pay rolls upon which their premium is computed.

Ref.: Herlick Handbook § 3.2.

§11846. Policies for self-employed persons and casual employees.

The policies may likewise be sold to self-employing persons and to casual employees. The insureds, for the purpose of the insurance, shall be deemed to be employees within the meaning of the workers' compensation laws.

Ref.: Hanna §§ 1.20[2], 2.10[4], 3.144; Herlick Handbook § 3.2.

ARTICLE 4
Reports and Statements

§11860. Quarterly report to Governor; annual audit publication; reports to commissioner.

Each quarter the president of the State Compensation Insurance Fund shall make a report to the Governor of the business done by the State Compensation Insurance Fund during the previous quarter and a statement of the fund's resources and liabilities at the close of that previous quarter. The State Compensation Insurance Fund shall, at its own expense, hire a recognized firm of certified public accountants to audit annually the books and records of the State Compensation Insurance Fund and cause an abstract summary thereof to be published one or more times in at least two newspapers of general circulation in the state. The president of the fund shall additionally provide the commissioner with all reports required by law to be made to him or her by other insurers. **Leg.H.** 2002 ch. 6 (AB 749).

ARTICLE 5
Coverage of Public Employers

§11870. Potential insurers; premiums.

The state, any agency, department, division, commission, board, bureau, officer or other authority thereof, and each county, city and county, city, school district, irrigation district, any other district established by law, or other public corporation or quasi public corporation within the state, including any public utility operated by a private corporation may insure against its liability for compensation with the State Compensation Insurance Fund. Where the state or any agency, department, division, commission, board, bureau, officer or authority thereof is the insured, the premium for that insurance shall be a proper charge against any moneys appropriated for the support of or expenditure by the insured, except that in the case of an insured supported by or authorized to expend moneys appropriated out of more than one fund, the insured, with the approval of the Director of Finance, may determine the proportion of the premium to be paid out of each fund. In that case the insured, with the approval of the Director of Finance, may pay the entire premium out of any of those funds and thereafter the funds used for payment shall be reimbursed in proper proportion out of the other funds. In case a county, city and county, city, school district, irrigation district, or other district established by law, or other public corporation or quasi public corporation within the state is the insured, the premium therefor shall be a proper charge against the general fund of the insured. **Leg.H.** 1994 ch. 373.

Ref.: Hanna §§ 2.10[4], 3.111; Herlick Handbook § 3.21.

§11871. Master agreement with Department of Human Resources.

The State Compensation Insurance Fund may enter into a master agreement with the Department of Human Resources to render services in the adjustment and disposition of claims for workers' compensation to any state agencies, including any officer, department, division, bureau, commission, board or authority, not insured with the fund.

The master agreement shall provide for rendition of services at a uniform rate to all agencies, except that the rate for the Department of the California Highway Patrol may be fixed independently of the uniform rate.

The fund may, in accordance with the agreement, adjust and dispose of claims for workers' compensation made by an officer or employee of any state agency not insured with the fund.

The fund may make all expenditures, including payment to claimants for medical care or for adjustment or settlement of claims, necessary to the adjustment and final disposition of claims. The agreement shall provide that the state agency whose officer or employee is a claimant shall reimburse the fund for the expenditures and for the actual cost of services rendered.

The fund may in its own name, or in the name of the state agency for which the services are performed, do any and all things necessary to recover on behalf of the state agency for which it renders service any and all amounts which an employer might recover from third persons under Chapter 5 (commencing with Section 3850) of Part 1 of Division 4 of the Labor Code, or which an insurer might recover pursuant to Section 11662 including the right to commence and prosecute actions, to file, pursuant to Chapter 5 (commencing with Section 3850) of Part 1 of Division 4 of the Labor Code, liens for whatever sums would be recoverable by suit against a third person, to intervene in other court proceedings, and to compromise claims and actions before or after commencement of suit or after entry of judgment when in the opinion of the fund full collection cannot be enforced. **Leg.H.** 1939 ch. 902 §1, 1943 ch. 667 §1, 1947 ch. 432 §1, 1965 ch. 371 §230, 1981 ch. 714 §310, 1989 ch. 492 §3, effective September 15, 1989, see this section as modified in Governor's Reorganization Plan No. 1 §193 of 2011, 2012 ch. 665 (SB 1308) §173.

2012 Note: Stats. 2012 ch. 665 (SB 1308) enacts the statutory changes necessary to reflect the changes made by the Governor's Reorganization Plan No. 1 of 2011.

2011 Note: 2011 Governor's Reorganization Plan No. 1 was submitted to the Legislature on June 9, 2011, and became effective September 9, 2011, pursuant to Gov C §12080.5, and substantively operative July 1, 2012.

Ref.: Hanna § 11.41; Herlick Handbook § 3.21.

§11872. Annual agreements with state agencies.

The fund may annually enter into agreements with state agencies for service to be rendered to the fund. These state agencies include, but shall not be limited to: the Department of Finance, Department of General Services, State Personnel Board, and the Public Employees' Retirement System. If these agencies and the fund cannot agree upon the cost of services provided by the agreements, the Department of General Services shall be requested to arrive at an equitable settlement. **Leg.H.** 1979 ch. 738 §14, 2006 ch. 538 (SB 1852) §472, 2016 ch. 31 (SB 836) §177, effective June 27, 2016.

Ref.: Herlick Handbook § 3.21.

§11873. Laws applicable to fund.

(a) Except as provided by subdivision (b), the fund shall not be subject to the provisions of the Government Code made applicable to state agencies generally or collectively, unless the section specifically names the fund as an agency to which the provision applies.

(b) The fund shall be subject to the provisions of Chapter 10.3 (commencing with Section 3512) of Division 4 of Title 1 of, Chapter 3.5 (commencing with Section 6250) of Division 7 of Title 1 of, Chapter 6.5 (commencing with Section 8543) of Division 1 of Title 2 of, Article 9 (commencing with Section 11120) of Chapter 1 of Part 1 of Division 3 of Title 2 of, the Government Code, and Division 5 (commencing with Section 18000) of Title 2 of the Government Code, with the exception of all of the following provisions of that division:

(1) Article 1 (commencing with Section 19820) and Article 2 (commencing with Section 19823) of Chapter 2 of Part 2.6 of Division 5.

(2) Sections 19849.2, 19849.3, 19849.4, and 19849.5.

(3) Chapter 4.5 (commencing with Section 19993.1) of Part 2.6 of Division 5.

(c) Except as provided in subdivisions (d) and (e) for the period from July 1, 2012, to June 30, 2013, inclusive, **and for the period from July 1, 2020, to June 30, 2021, inclusive,** and notwithstanding any provision of the Government Code or any other provision of law, the positions funded by the State Compensation Insurance Fund are exempt from any hiring freezes and staff cutbacks otherwise required by law. This subdivision is declaratory of existing law.

(d) Notwithstanding any other law, employees of the fund shall, without limitation, be subject to any and all reductions in state employee compensation imposed by the Legislature on other state employees for the period from July 1, 2012, to June 30, 2013, inclusive, **and for the period from July 1, 2020, to June 30, 2021, inclusive,** regardless of the means adopted to effect those reductions.

(e) With the exception of the reductions authorized in subdivision (d), if any provision of this section, or any practice or procedure adopted pursuant to this section, is in conflict with the provisions of a memorandum of understanding reached pursuant to Section 3517.5 of the Government Code, the memorandum of understanding shall be controlling without further legislative action, except that if the provisions of a memorandum of understanding require the expenditure of funds, the provisions shall not become effective unless approved by the Legislature in the annual Budget Act. **Leg.H.** 2003 ch. 635 (AB 227), 2006 ch. 452 (SB 1452) §6, 2008 ch. 344 (SB 1145) §6, effective September 26, 2008, 2012 ch. 32 (SB 1006) §26, effective June 27, 2012, 2020 ch. 16 (AB 84) §9, effective June 29, 2020.

Ref.: Hanna § 1.20[1], [4]; Herlick Handbook § 1.07[1], [3].

§11874. Treasurer's payment of warrant.

On the effective date of this act the Controller shall draw his or her warrant in favor of the State Compensation Insurance Fund for the total amount of the funds in the custody of the Treasurer belonging to the State Compensation Insurance Fund, and the Treasurer shall pay that warrant. **Leg.H.** 1979 ch. 738 §16, 2011 ch. 426 (SB 712) §11.

ARTICLE 6
Penalties

§11880. Willful misrepresentation to obtain reduced rate—Punishment; enhancement for prior conviction.

(a) It is unlawful to make or cause to be made any knowingly false or fraudulent statement, whether made orally or in writing, of any fact material to the determination of the premium, rate, or cost of any policy of workers' compensation insurance issued or administered by the State Compensation Insurance Fund for the purpose of reducing the premium, rate, or cost of the insurance. Any person convicted of violating this subdivision shall be punished by imprisonment in a county jail for one year, or pursuant to subdivision (h) of Section 1170 of the Penal Code for two, three, or five years, or by a fine not exceeding fifty thousand dollars ($50,000), or double the value of the fraud, whichever is greater, or by both that imprisonment and fine.

(b) Any person who violates subdivision (a) and who has a prior felony conviction of the offense set forth in that subdivision shall receive a two-year enhancement for each prior conviction in addition to the sentence provided in subdivision (a). The existence of any fact that would subject a person to a penalty enhancement shall be alleged in the information or indictment and either admitted by the defendant in open court, or found to be true by the jury trying the issue of guilt or by the court where guilt is established by plea of guilty or nolo contendere or by trial by the court sitting without a jury. **Leg.H.** 1991 chs. 116, 934, 1995 ch. 885, 2011 ch. 15 (AB 109) §218, effective April 4, 2011, operative October 1, 2011.

2011 Notes: This act is titled and may be cited as the 2011 Realignment Legislation addressing public safety. Stats. 2011 ch. 15 (AB 109) §1.

This act will become operative no earlier than October 1, 2011, and only upon creation of a community corrections grant program to assist in implementing this act and upon an appropriation to fund the grant program. Stats. 2011 ch. 15 (AB 109) §636; Stats. 2011 ch. 39 (AB 117) §68.

The Community Corrections Grant Program referred to in Stats. 2011 ch. 15 §636, as amended by Stats. 2011 ch. 39 §68, was created by Stats. 2011 ch. 40 §3, operative October 1, 2011.

Ref.: Hanna § 2.03[3], [4]; Herlick Handbook § 9.18.

§11881. Other names for Board of Directors.

Whenever in Chapter 4, Part 3, Division 2 of the Insurance Code the term "State Industrial Accident Commission" or "Industrial Accident Commission" or "commission" or "director" or similar designation occurs, it means the Board of Directors of the State Compensation Insurance Fund except when such meaning is inconsistent with the intent and context of said chapter.

ARTICLE 7
Transfer of Ownership

§11885. Sale of portion of State Compensation Insurance Fund's assets and liabilities.

(a) The Director of Finance is hereby authorized to act as agent for the state and, in that capacity, to sell a portion of, or otherwise obtain value for, the State Compensation Insurance Fund's assets and liabilities. That authorized sale or other disposition shall be transacted with an entity that the director, in consultation with the State Treasurer, determines will provide the best combination of each of the following:

(1) The highest price for the State Compensation Insurance Fund's workers' compensation insurance assets and liabilities or the best value to the General Fund, or both.

(2) The greatest security for the payment of the purchase price.

(3) Demonstrated competence and professional qualifications for the continued satisfactory performance of the workers' compensation insurance services offered for sale or other disposition.

(b) Prior to releasing any Notice of Request for Qualifications, a majority of the State Compensation Insurance Fund Board of Directors shall concur that the assets and liabilities that are identified by the Director of Finance, in consultation with the State Treasurer, in subdivision (a) are appropriate for sale or other disposition.

(c) Notwithstanding any other law, the process for sale or other disposition shall include the steps the director, in consultation with the State Treasurer, deems necessary or convenient to achieve the ends set forth in this section. The process shall include, but not necessarily be limited to, all of the following:

(1) The satisfaction of criteria established by the director, in consultation with the State Treasurer, consistent with achieving the best price or other value for those workers' compensation insurance assets and liabilities. These criteria shall include any pertinent requirements of the State Compensation Insurance Fund Board of Directors.

(2) A Notice of Request for Qualifications sent by the Director of Finance to each firm currently providing workers' compensation insurance coverage to California employers and any entity proposed by the State Compensation Insurance Fund Board of Directors. In addition, it shall be advertised in the State Contracts Register pursuant to Sections 14827.1 and 14827.2 of the Government Code. This notice shall include a description of the workers' compensation insurance program, a summary description of the workers' compensation insurance assets and liabilities offered for sale or other disposition, and a description of the due diligence review process to provide potential purchasers with further information regarding the workers' compensation insurance assets and liabilities offered for sale or other disposition, the selection criteria on which the transaction will be based, the submission requirements and deadlines, and a Department of Finance contact name and telephone number for more information. A copy of the Notice of Request for Qualifications shall be provided to the Joint Legislative Budget Committee within seven days of its release.

(3) The evaluation by the director, in consultation with the State Treasurer, of all statements timely submitted in response to the Notice of Request for Qualifications sent pursuant to paragraph (2), using the criteria contained in the notice, and, based on those statements, the establishment of a qualified participant list.

(4) For purposes of Section 11772, any action by the board of directors related to any transaction contemplated by this article, including, but not limited to, any approvals of such transactions, shall be deemed to be in good faith.

(5) The Director of Finance shall notify the Joint Legislative Budget Committee in writing within seven days of completing a sale pursuant to subdivision (a). **Leg.H.** 2009–10 ch. 12 (Fourth Extra. Sess.) (AB 12 (Fourth Extra. Sess.)) §21, effective July 28, 2009.

Ref.: Hanna § 1.20.

§11885.3. Participation by board of directors; acting in good faith.

In order to accomplish the purpose of this article, the State Compensation Insurance Fund and its board of directors shall participate fully in good faith with the Director of Finance, and the Director of Finance shall act in good faith in carrying out the duties prescribed by this article. **Leg.H.** 2009–10 ch. 12 (Fourth Extra. Sess.) (AB 12 (Fourth Extra. Sess.)) §21, effective July 28, 2009.

Ref.: Hanna § 1.20.

§11885.5. Approvals not required.

Notwithstanding any other law, the approval of neither the Attorney General, nor the Insurance Commissioner, nor the Director of General Services is required for execution and implementation of the sale or other disposition of the assets and liabilities of the State Compensation Insurance Fund or any other agreement authorized by this article. **Leg.H.** 2009–10 ch. 12 (Fourth Extra. Sess.) (AB 12 (Fourth Extra. Sess.)) §21, effective July 28, 2009.

Ref.: Hanna § 1.20.

§11885.7. Deposit of proceeds.

(a) The Director of Finance shall deposit all proceeds of any sale of, or any funds achieved through any other disposition of, the State Compensation Insurance Fund's workers' compensation insurance assets and liabilities under this article, less any costs related to that transaction, into the General Fund.

(b) The proceeds of any sale of, or any funds achieved through any other disposition of, the State Compensation Insurance Fund's workers' compensation insurance assets and liabilities are not "proceeds of taxes" as that term is used in subdivision (c) of Section 8 of Article XIII B of the

California Constitution. The disbursement of these proceeds is not subject to the limitations imposed by that article. **Leg.H.** 2009–10 ch. 12 (Fourth Extra. Sess.) (AB 12 (Fourth Extra. Sess.)) §21, effective July 28, 2009.

Ref.: Hanna § 1.20.

§11885.9. Advisers.

(a) Notwithstanding any other law, the Director of Finance is authorized to enter into agreements with firms or individuals to act as advisers to the state in the transactions contemplated by this article. Section 14838 of the Government Code and Article 4 (commencing with Section 10335) of Chapter 2 of Part 2 of Division 2 of the Public Contract Code do not apply to any agreement entered into by the director with advisers pursuant to this section.

(b) Notwithstanding any other law, the Director of Finance is also authorized to enter into legal services agreements to obtain specialized legal advice related to the transactions contemplated by this article. Section 11040 of the Government Code and Section 6072 of the Business and Professions Code shall not apply to the legal services agreements entered into by the director pursuant to this section. **Leg.H.** 2009–10 ch. 12 (Fourth Extra. Sess.) (AB 12 (Fourth Extra. Sess.)) §21, effective July 28, 2009.

Ref.: Hanna § 1.20.

§11886. Selection of firms providing advisory services.

(a) The Director of Finance, in consultation with the State Treasurer, shall select firms or individuals to provide advisory services based on demonstrated competence and professional qualifications necessary for the satisfactory performance of the services required and in the manner described in this section.

(b) The Director of Finance, in consultation with the State Treasurer, shall establish selection criteria for selecting advisers. The criteria may include, but are not necessarily limited to, factors such as professional excellence, demonstrated competence, specialized experience in performing similar services, education and experience of key personnel to be assigned, staff capability, ability to meet schedules, nature and quality of similar completed work of the firm or individual, reliability and continuity of the firm or individual, and other considerations deemed by the director, in consultation with the State Treasurer, to be relevant and necessary to the performance of advisory services.

(c) In order to select advisers, the director shall publish a Notice of Request for Qualifications in the State Contracts Register pursuant to Sections 14827.1 and 14827.2 of the Government Code. The notice shall include a description of the advisory services required, the selection criteria on which the contract award will be based, submission requirements and deadlines, and a Department of Finance contact name and telephone number for more information. A copy of the Notice of Request for Qualifications shall be provided to the Joint Legislative Budget Committee within seven days of publication in the State Contracts Register.

(d)(1) After the final response date stated in the Notice of Request for Qualifications, the Director of Finance, in consultation with the State Treasurer, shall review the responses submitted, and shall evaluate them using the criteria contained in the notice. The director shall rank, in order of preference based on the criteria contained in the notice, the firm or individuals determined to be qualified to perform the required services.

(2) The Director of Finance, in consultation with the State Treasurer, may interview any of the qualified firms or individuals regarding the experience and qualifications of those firms or individuals, as well as anticipated concepts and the benefits of alternative methods of furnishing the required services.

(e)(1) Following the interviews, if any, held pursuant to subdivision (d), the Director of Finance shall adjust the ranking of the qualified individuals or firms to reflect those firms or individuals deemed to be the most highly qualified to perform the required services.

(2) The Director of Finance, in consultation with the State Treasurer, shall enter into negotiations with the firm or individual most highly ranked pursuant to paragraph (1). If negotiations are concluded successfully, the director shall enter into a contract. If the director, in his or her sole discretion, concludes that the negotiations are unsuccessful, the director shall terminate the negotiations, and begin new negotiations, in consultation with the State Treasurer, with the other firms or individuals ranked pursuant to paragraph (1) in order of their ranking, and either contract with or terminate negotiations with each next most highly ranked firm or individual.

(3) If, after pursuing the negotiation process set forth in paragraph (2), the Director of Finance has been unable to negotiate a satisfactory contract at fair and reasonable compensation, the director may reinstate the selection process prescribed in this section, commencing with the issuance of a new Notice of Request for Qualifications.

(4) The Director of Finance shall notify the Joint Legislative Budget Committee in writing within seven days of entering into a contract with an individual or firm for advisory services.

(f) This section shall not apply to the selection of a legal services adviser. **Leg.H.** 2009–10 ch. 12 (Fourth Extra. Sess.) (AB 12 (Fourth Extra. Sess.)) §21, effective July 28, 2009.

Ref.: Hanna § 1.20.

§11886.2. Notification by Director of Finance.

(a) The Director of Finance shall notify the Joint Legislative Budget Committee in writing upon his or her determination that neither the sale nor any other transaction authorized by this article is anticipated to achieve the purposes of this article or upon the completion of a disposition of State Compensation Insurance Fund assets and liabilities pursuant to this article.

(b) The Director of Finance shall cease those activities he or she is authorized or directed to undertake pursuant to this article upon the earlier of either:

(1) The 30th day following written notice by the director to the Chairperson of the Joint Legislative Budget Committee pursuant to subdivision (a).

(2) January 10, 2012. **Leg.H.** 2009–10 ch. 12 (Fourth Extra. Sess.) (AB 12 (Fourth Extra. Sess.)) §21, effective July 28, 2009.

Ref.: Hanna § 1.20.

LABOR CODE
[Selected Provisions]

SYNOPSIS

GENERAL PROVISIONS
[Selected Provisions]

§1. Title.
§2. Construction of Labor Code.
§5. General provisions govern construction.
§6. Headings not to affect meaning or intent.
§7. Administrative powers.
§8. "Writing"; mailings by certified mail.
§9. References to code include amendments and additions.
§10. "Section."
§11. Tenses.
§12. Gender.
§12.1. References to "man" to be changed to "person."
§12.2. "Spouse" to include "registered domestic partner."
§13. Singulars and plurals.
§14. "County."
§15. "Shall"; "may."
§16. "Oath."
§17. "Signature" or "subscription" includes mark; acknowledgement of mark.
§18. "Person."
§18.5. "Agency."
§19. "Department."
§19.5. "Secretary."
§20. "Director."
§21. "Labor Commissioner."
§22. "Violation."
§23. Punishment for offenses.
§24. Invalid provisions.
§25. "Sheriff."
§26. Rehabilitated criminals.
§27. Use of term "workers' compensation judge" or "workers' compensation referee" means "workers' compensation administrative law judge."
§28. "Independent medical examiner" means "qualified medical evaluator."
§29. Definition of "medical director."

DIVISION 1
DEPARTMENT OF INDUSTRIAL RELATIONS

CHAPTER 1
GENERAL POWERS AND DUTIES
[Selected Provisions]

§50. Department of Industrial Relations.
§50.5. Functions of department.
§50.6. Enforcement of Fair Labor Standards Act of 1938.
§50.7. Administration and enforcement of OSHA standards.
§50.8. Occupational health and medicine programs; occupational health centers; reports.
§50.9. Director's comments.
§51. Appointment of director.
§52. Application of Government Code to state departments.
§53. Head of department.
§54. Duties of director.
§54.5. Legal services.
§55. Administrative organization.
§56. Departmental divisions.
§57. Division chiefs.
§57.1. Chief's salary; appointments; salaries.
§57.5. Board of Directors of State Compensation Insurance Fund.
§58. Title to departmental property.
§59. Departmental law enforcement.
§60. Administration and enforcement of code.
§60.5. Division of Occupational Safety and Health: duties and powers.
§61. Enforcement of chapter.
§62. Expenditures.
§62.5. Workers' Compensation Administration Revolving Fund; Uninsured Employers Benefits Trust Fund; Subsequent Injuries Benefits Trust Fund; Occupational Safety and Health Fund; Labor Enforcement and Compliance Fund; surcharges on employers.
§62.6. Assessments.
§62.8. Appropriation; loan; repayment.

CHAPTER 3
COMMISSION ON HEALTH AND SAFETY AND WORKERS' COMPENSATION

§75. Composition of Commission; selection of chair; terms; meetings.
§76. Commission personnel.
§77. Commission duties and powers.
§77.5. Medical treatment utilization standards—Survey and evaluation of standards of care; report to administrative director.
§77.7. Study; requirements; report [Repealed January 1, 2024].
§77.8. Commission on Health and Safety and Workers' Compensation to conduct study of impacts of COVID-19; report.
§78. Review of grant applications.

CHAPTER 4
DIVISION OF LABOR STANDARDS ENFORCEMENT
[Selected Provisions]

§90.3. Enforcement of payment for workers'

compensation coverage; targeted program; contact and inspection; annual report.
§90.5. Enforcement of minimum labor standards; establishment of field units; adoption of plan; report to Legislature.
§96. Assignment of claims.
§96.1. Report to Legislature; wage claims; alleged violations; amount of unpaid wages, penalties, and other compensation [Repealed January 1, 2031].
§96.3. Employees represented by collective bargaining agreements.
§96.5. Certification of claims.
§96.6. Industrial Relations Unpaid Wage Fund.
§96.7. Collection and disbursement of unpaid wages and benefits.
§96.8. Collection of outstanding amount of judgment entered in favor of Labor Commissioner or employee pursuant to Section 98.2(e); notice of levy; execution of levy on property.

CHAPTER 5
DIVISION OF WORKERS' COMPENSATION

§110. Definitions.
§111. Powers of appeals board and administrative director.
§112. Appointment and composition of appeals board.
§113. Appointment of chairperson.
§115. Appeals board decisions; reconsideration.
§116. Appeals board seal.
§117. Appointment of attorney.
§119. Duties of attorney.
§120. Appointment of secretaries.
§121. Acts by deputies; validity.
§122. Medical director and assistants; appointment; qualifications; salaries.
§123. Administrative personnel; salaries of workers' compensation administrative law judges.
§123.3. Official reporters.
§123.5. Workers' compensation administrative law judges.
§123.6. Workers' compensation administrative law judges to adhere to Code of Judicial Ethics; prior approval by administrative director for honoraria or travel payments.
§123.7. Certified workers' compensation specialists; pro tempore judges.
§124. Protection of interests of injured workers; forms and notices; availability in other languages; annual review.
§125. Blank forms.
§126. Records.
§127. Administrative director—Authority.
§127.1. Report to Legislature comparing potential payment alternatives for providers to official medical fee schedule.
§128. Enforcement of Longshoremen's and Harbor Workers' Compensation Act.
§129. Audits.
§129.5. Administrative and civil penalties; schedule of violations.
§130. Authority to administer oaths and issue subpoenas.
§131. Fees and mileage for witnesses.
§132. Refusal to obey subpoena; contempt.
§132a. Nondiscrimination policy.
§133. Division of Workers' Compensation—Power and jurisdiction.
§134. Contempt proceedings; process service.
§135. Destruction of files.
§138. Appointment of deputy in director's absence.
§138.1. Administrative director; appointment; salary.
§138.2. Division of Workers' Compensation headquarters; administrative offices; notice of public meetings.
§138.3. Notice to injured employee of right to benefits.
§138.4. Injuries involving lost time; claims administrator's duties and responsibilities; claim form and notice of potential eligibility of benefits; regulatory authority of administrative director.
§138.5. Enforcement of child support obligations; Workers' Compensation Notification Project.
§138.6. Development of workers' compensation information system.
§138.7. "Individually identifiable information"; restricted access.
§138.8. Utilization data for physicians who treated 10 or more injured workers.
§139.2. Appointment, qualification, suspension, termination of QMEs; timeframes, guidelines, procedures, and admissibility of medical evaluations.
§139.21. Suspension of physician, practitioner, or provider from participation in workers' compensation system for cause; notice and hearing; adjudication of liens.
§139.3. Referral to person with whom physician has financial interest unlawful.
§139.31. Exceptions to §139.3.
§139.32. Restrictions on interested parties with financial interests in any entity providing services; violation.
§139.4. Council review of advertising; disciplinary actions and proceedings; adoption of advertising regulations and report to Legislature.
§139.43. False or misleading advertising prohibited; adoption of regulations by administrative director; physicians and attorneys exempted.
§139.45. Care required in promulgating advertising regulations; description of false or misleading advertisements.
§139.47. Program established to educate employers about early and sustained return to work after employee's occupational injury or illness.
§139.48. Return-to-work program; funding; purpose.
§139.5. Independent review program; requirements; liability.
§139.6. Program to provide workers' compensation information.

CHAPTER 6
OCCUPATIONAL SAFETY AND HEALTH STANDARDS BOARD

§140. Occupational Safety and Health Standards Board.
§141. Term of office; compensation.
§142. Enforcement of occupational safety and health standards.
§142.1. Public meetings; notice.
§142.2. Proposals at meetings.
§142.3. Standards: vote required; state building standards; warnings of hazards to

employees; medical examinations provided by employer.
§142.4. Adoption of standards; emergency regulations.
§142.7. Standards for hazardous substance removal work.
§143. Permanent variances.
§143.1. Variance requests; hearings.
§143.2. Procedural rules for hearings.
§144. Enforcement of occupational safety and health standards; assistance of other agencies.
§144.5. Division of Occupational Safety and Health; duties.
§144.6. Toxic materials; standards.
§144.7. Needle safety standards.
§144.8. Standard for handling antineoplastic drugs in health care facilities.
§145. Employment of personnel.
§145.1. Powers of board.
§146. Permanent variances; hearings.
§147. Evaluation of standards and variances from other sources.
§147.1. Division of Occupational Safety and Health; duties; federal standards; proposed standards.
§147.2. Information repository on toxic materials; "Hazard Evaluation System and Information Service" or "HESIS."
§147.3. Contents of report; investigation; blood lead level.
§147.4. Establishment of advisory board to ensure compliance with standards promulgated by National Fire Protection Association.
§147.5. Advisory committee to evaluate need to develop industry-specific regulations related to medical cannabis facilities.
§147.6. Advisory committee to evaluate need to develop industry-specific regulations related to the cultivation, distribution, transport, storage, manufacturing, processing, and sale of nonmedical marijuana and marijuana products.

CHAPTER 6.5
OCCUPATIONAL SAFETY AND HEALTH APPEALS BOARD

§148. Occupational Safety and Health Appeals Board; designation of chairperson.
§148.1. Term of office.
§148.2. Employment of appeals board personnel; salaries of hearing officers.
§148.4. Orders and decisions to be in writing.
§148.5. Finality of decisions.
§148.6. Director's right to seek judicial review.
§148.7. Procedural rules for hearings; adoption.
§148.8. Powers of appeals board.
§148.9. Decisions by majority of board.
§149. Executive officer as acting deputy.
§149.5. Costs and attorney's fees.

DIVISION 2
EMPLOYMENT REGULATION AND SUPERVISION

PART 1
Compensation

CHAPTER 1
PAYMENT OF WAGES
[Selected Provisions]

ARTICLE 1
General Occupations

§226.2. Compensation on piece-rate basis.
§226.8. Unlawful activities; penalties; disciplinary action; information to be posted on Internet Web site; enforcement.

ARTICLE 1.5
Paid Sick Days

§245. Citation of article; provisions of article in addition to and independent of other rights.
§245.5. Definitions.
§246. Entitlement; accrual; use of accrued paid sick days; carryover; separation from employment; written notice of available paid sick leave; calculation of paid sick leave; workgroup and guidance for implementation for in-home supportive services providers.
§246.5. Purposes for which paid sick leave may be granted; unlawful retaliation.
§247. Poster; requirements.
§247.5. Recordkeeping requirement.
§248. Supplemental paid sick leave for food sector workers during COVID-19 pandemic; requirement; enforcement; expiration.
§248.1. Supplemental paid sick leave for covered workers during COVID-19 pandemic; requirement; enforcement; expiration.
§248.5. Enforcement of article; violation.
§249. Effect of article on privacy of health and domestic relations information; article establishes minimum requirements pertaining to paid sick days.

PART 4
Employees

CHAPTER 1
WAGES, HOURS AND WORKING CONDITIONS
[Selected Provisions]

§1171.5. Legislative findings and declarations regarding employment protections available regardless of immigration status.

PART 7
Public Works and Public Agencies

CHAPTER 1
PUBLIC WORKS
[Selected Provisions]

ARTICLE 2
WAGES

§1776. Payroll record of wages paid; inspection; forms; effect of noncompliance; penalties.

ARTICLE 5
Securing Workers' Compensation

§1860. Public works contracts; compensation clause required.
§1861. Public works contracts; certificate of insurance.

Labor

PART 9
Health

CHAPTER 1
SANITARY CONDITIONS
[Selected Provisions]

ARTICLE 5
General Health Provisions

§2440. Employers' compliance with medical services and first aid standards.

§2441. Provision of drinking water.

PART 13
The Labor Code Private Attorneys General Act of 2004

§2698. Citation of part.

§2699. Recovery of civil penalty for violation of Labor Code through civil action brought by aggrieved employee; amount of penalty; attorney's fees and costs; distribution of penalty proceeds; applicability of section.

§2699.3. Requirements for commencement of civil actions under Labor Code Section 2699 alleging specified violations; time limits [First of Two; Repealed July 1, 2021].

§2699.3. Requirements for commencement of civil actions under Labor Code Section 2699 alleging specified violations; time limits [Second of Two; Operative July 1, 2021].

§2699.5. Applicability of Labor Code Section 2699.3.

§2699.6. Applicability of part [Repealed January 1, 2028].

DIVISION 3
EMPLOYMENT RELATIONS

CHAPTER 1
SCOPE OF DIVISION

§2700. Scope.

CHAPTER 2
EMPLOYER AND EMPLOYEE

ARTICLE 1
The Contract of Employment
[Selected Provisions]

§2750. "Employment contract."

§2750.5. Rebuttable presumption that worker is employee; proof of independent contractor status.

§2750.6. Physician contracting with primary care clinic as independent contractor; rebuttable presumption.

§2750.8. Motor Carrier Employer Amnesty Program.

§2753. Liability of person who advises employer to treat individual as independent contractor to avoid employee status.

§2754. Cheerleader for California-based professional sports team.

ARTICLE 1.5
Worker Status: Employees

§2775. Employee versus independent contractor; applicable law.

§2776. Exception for bona fide business-to-business contracting relationship.

§2777. Exception for relationship between referral agency and service provider.

§2778. Exception for contract for "professional services."

§2779. Exception for relationship between individuals acting as sole proprietor or separate partnership, limited liability company, limited liability partnership, or corporation performing contract work for single-engagement event.

§2780. Exception for specified occupations related to creating, marketing, promoting, or distributing sound recordings or musical compositions.

§2781. Exception for relationship between contractor and individual performing work pursuant to subcontract in construction industry.

§2782. Exception for relationship between data aggregator and individual providing feedback to data aggregator.

§2783. Exceptions for other specific occupations.

§2784. Exception for relationship between motor club and individual performing services pursuant to contract between motor club and third party.

§2785. Declaratory nature of Section 2775; retroactive and prospective application of exceptions; when employment status governed by Borello.

§2786. Injunctive relief.

§2787. Severability of article.

ARTICLE 2
Obligations of Employer
[Selected Provisions]

§2800. Indemnification of employee; employer's want of care.

§2800.1. Safeguard of musical instruments.

§2800.2. Employer provided medical coverage; notice of conversion coverage; continuation coverage under COBRA and notification of conversion coverage.

§2800.3. Availability of coverage conversion.

§2801. Contributory negligence no bar to recovery; employer defenses limited.

§2802. Indemnification of employee for expenditures or losses in discharge of duties or obedience to directions; citation for violation of reimbursement obligations.

§2802.1. Applicability of indemnification to employer-required training.

§2803. Death of employee; survivor's rights.

§2803.4. Health benefits under ERISA; no reduction of benefits for Medi-Cal or medicaid coverage.

§2803.5. Compliance with provisions on health care coverage of children.

§2804. Waiver of benefits as null and void.

§2806. Employer discontinuing coverage; notice.

§2807. Notification to former employees of availability of continued medical coverage.

§2809. Employer-managed deferred compensation

plans—Risks; summary of financial condition.
§2810. Persons contracting for specified labor or services without providing sufficient funds for compliance with applicable laws or regulations subject to liability and civil penalties; rebuttable presumption; exceptions.
§2810.3. Definitions.
§2810.4. Port drayage motor carriers; unsatisfied court judgments; notification; joint and several liability; definitions.
§2810.5. Required written notice; notification of changes.
§2810.7. Notification of flexible spending accounts deadlines.

DIVISION 4 WORKERS' COMPENSATION AND INSURANCE

PART 1 Scope and Operation

CHAPTER 1 GENERAL PROVISIONS

§3200. "Workmen's compensation" to become "workers' compensation."
§3201. Purposes of Divisions 4 and 5 of Labor Code.
§3201.5. Validity of collective bargaining agreements—Prohibitions; applicability; premium rate; filing with director; confidentiality.
§3201.7. Labor-management agreements—Criteria; applicability; requirements.
§3201.81. Collective bargaining agreements for licensed jockeys.
§3201.9. Reports under collective bargaining agreements; required provisions.
§3202. Liberal construction of Divisions 4 and 5.
§3202.5. Preponderance of evidence standard.
§3203. Inapplicability of Divisions 4 and 5 to interstate commerce.
§3204. Chapter's definitions to govern construction.
§3205. "Division."
§3205.5. "Appeals board."
§3206. "Administrative director."
§3207. "Compensation."
§3208. "Injury."
§3208.05. Injury to health care worker from preventative care.
§3208.1. Specific and cumulative injuries.
§3208.2. Combined injuries; separate determinations.
§3208.3. Threshold of compensability for psychiatric injury.
§3208.4. Discovery requirements in proceedings involving injury arising from sexual conduct; nonadmissible evidence.
§3209. "Damages."
§3209.3. "Physician"; "psychologist"; "acupuncturist"; request for medical collaboration; acupuncturist unauthorized to determine disability.
§3209.4. Optometrists not physicians.
§3209.5. Medical, surgical, and hospital treatment.
§3209.6. Chiropractors not physicians.
§3209.7. Agreements on other healing practices.
§3209.8. Treatment by marriage and family therapists and clinical social workers.
§3209.9. Acupuncturists not physicians or surgeons.
§3209.10. Physician assistant or nurse practitioner may provide treatment for work-related injury under supervision; supervising physician deemed treating physician.
§3210. "Persons."
§3211. "Insurer."
§3211.5. "Firefighter," "firefighting member," or "member of a fire department."
§3211.9. "Disaster council."
§3211.91. "Accredited disaster council."
§3211.92. "Disaster service worker."
§3211.93. "Disaster service."
§3211.93a. Exception to "disaster service."
§3212. Hernia; heart trouble; pneumonia.
§3212.1. Cancer presumption; active firefighters and peace officers.
§3212.15. Applicability to certain state and local firefighting personnel and peace officers; "injury" includes post-traumatic stress; compensation for injury [Repealed January 1, 2025].
§3212.2. Employees of Department of Corrections, Department of Youth Authority, Atascadero State Hospital—Heart trouble.
§3212.3. California Highway Patrol—Heart trouble; pneumonia.
§3212.4. University of California fire department—Heart trouble; hernia; pneumonia.
§3212.5. Peace officers—Heart trouble; pneumonia.
§3212.6. Peace officers, prison guards, correctional officers, and firefighters—Tuberculosis; tuberculosis test for firefighter applicants.
§3212.7. Department of Justice—Heart trouble; hernia; pneumonia; tuberculosis.
§3212.8. "Injury" includes blood-borne infectious disease or methicillin-resistant Staphylococcus aureus skin infection.
§3212.85. "Injury" includes death or illness from exposure to biochemical substances.
§3212.86. Employees with COVID-19-related illness [Repealed January 1, 2023].
§3212.87. Applicability to active firefighting members and other specific employees; injury definition; COVID-19 definition [Repealed January 1, 2023].
§3212.88. Applicability to employees not described in Section 3212.87; injury definition; COVID-19 definition [Repealed January 1, 2023].
§3212.9. Peace officers, probation officers, district attorney investigators, and firefighters—Meningitis.
§3212.10. Heart trouble, pneumonia, tuberculosis, and meningitis as compensable for certain peace officers.
§3212.11. Skin cancer as "injury" for lifeguards arising out of and in course of employment.
§3212.12. Lyme disease as injury for specified peace officers and corpsmembers.
§3213. University of California police—Heart trouble; pneumonia.
§3213.2. "Injury" includes lower back impairment for certain law enforcement officers; "duty belt" defined.
§3214. Early intervention program.
§3215. Crime to offer or receive compensation for referring clients or patients.
§3217. Exceptions to prohibitions of §3215.
§3218. Penalties for violating §3215.

Labor

§3219. Felony to offer compensation to claims adjuster; felony for adjuster to accept compensation; contract for services obtained through false statements is void; allocation of recoverable fees.

CHAPTER 2
EMPLOYERS, EMPLOYEES, AND DEPENDENTS

ARTICLE 1
Employers

§3300. "Employer."
§3301. Specified sponsors not "employers."
§3302. Payment of workers' compensation premiums by temporary employment agency, employment referral service, labor contractor, or similar entity.

ARTICLE 2
Employees

§3350. Division's definitions to govern construction.
§3351. "Employee."
§3351.5. Employees included.
§3352. Persons excluded from definition of employee.
§3352.94. Exclusions for disaster service workers as "employees."
§3353. "Independent contractor."
§3354. Employers of household workers.
§3355. "Course of trade, business, profession, or occupation."
§3356. "Trade, business, profession, or occupation."
§3357. Presumption that one rendering service is employee.
§3358. Watchmen.
§3360. Partners for particular piece of work.
§3361. Volunteer firefighters.
§3361.5. Authorized volunteers of recreation and park districts.
§3362. Active police officers.
§3362.5. Reserve and auxiliary peace officers.
§3363. Registered members of reserve fish and game warden program.
§3363.5. Public agency volunteers.
§3363.6. Volunteers for private, nonprofit organizations.
§3364. Sheriff's reserve volunteers.
§3364.5. Volunteers for school districts and county superintendents of schools.
§3364.55. Juvenile court wards doing rehabilitative work.
§3364.6. Juvenile traffic offenders doing rehabilitative work.
§3364.7. Juvenile court wards committed to regional youth educational facility.
§3365. Persons engaged in suppressing fires.
§3366. Persons assisting in active law enforcement.
§3367. Technical assistants to fire or law enforcement officers.
§3368. Supervision of work experience education, cooperative vocational education, community classroom, or student apprenticeship program by school, school district, or county superintendent; school, school district, or county superintendent as "employer"; exceptions; "registered student apprentice"; regional and joint supervision of program.
§3369. Effect of coverage by this division.
§3370. State penal or correctional institution inmates.
§3370.1. State Department of State Hospitals facility patient.
§3371. Attorney referral for inmates.
§3371.1. Attorney referral for patient applicant.

ARTICLE 3
Dependents

§3501. Presumption; minor's or incapacitated adult's dependence on deceased parent.
§3502. Factual determination of dependency.
§3503. Qualifications for dependency.

ARTICLE 4
Employee Notice

§3550. Posting of notice; failure to post; applicability; form and content of notice.
§3551. Written notice to new employee; contents.
§3553. Employee who is victim of workplace crime; provision of written notice to employee concerning workers' compensation eligibility; when employer must provide notice.

CHAPTER 3
CONDITIONS OF COMPENSATION LIABILITY

§3600. Conditions of compensation for employer liability.
§3600.1 State firefighters not acting under employer's immediate direction.
§3600.2. Peace officers not acting under employer's immediate direction.
§3600.3. Scope of employment; off-duty peace officers.
§3600.4. Local firefighters not acting under employer's immediate direction.
§3600.5. Out-of-state injury of resident; exemption; certificate of insurance for out-of-state employer.
§3600.6. Disaster service workers.
§3600.8. Participation in alternative commute program not acting within course of employment—Definitions; exceptions.
§3601. Employee's liability to another employee.
§3602. Employer's personal liability.
§3603. Discharge of claims.
§3604. Unavailable defense for public employers.
§3605. Injured minors; compensation.

CHAPTER 4
COMPENSATION INSURANCE AND SECURITY

ARTICLE 1
Insurance and Security

§3700. Employer's possible means of securing payment.
§3700.1. Definitions.
§3700.5. Penalty for failure to secure payment; enhancement for subsequent conviction; recovery of investigative costs.
§3701. Private self-insuring employer; surety.
§3701.3. Return of overpayments to self-insured employers.
§3701.5. Private self-insured employer; payment of obligations.
§3701.7. Special conditions to be met after period of unlawful uninsurance.

§3701.8. Alternative security system for securing aggregate liabilities of private, self-insured employers through the Self-Insurers' Security Fund.
§3701.9. Restriction on issuance of certificate of consent to self-insure after January 1, 2013.
§3702. Certificate of consent to self-insure; revocation.
§3702.1. Third-party administrators; certificate of consent.
§3702.2. Self-insurer's annual report; director's annual aggregated summary.
§3702.3. Failure to submit reports or information; fines; handling of funds.
§3702.5. Costs of administration of self-insured programs; fines for late filing; handling of funds.
§3702.6. Audit cycle for private self-insured employers; special audit of public self-insured employers.
§3702.7. Revocation of certificate of consent; fine in lieu of.
§3702.8. Obligations of former self-insured employers.
§3702.9. Director's order for compliance, restitution, and civil penalty.
§3702.10. Authorization to adopt, amend, and repeal regulations.
§3703. Self-insurer's independent administration.
§3705. Surety's equal preference over other debts.
§3706. Employer's failure to secure payment.
§3706.5. Exceptions to penalty for failure to secure payment.
§3707. Attachment of employer's property.
§3708. Employer's negligence; presumption; defenses unavailable.
§3708.5. Employee's complaint; service; consolidation of actions.
§3709. Judgments.
§3709.5. Employer's and Uninsured Employers Fund's relief from obligation to pay more.

ARTICLE 2
Uninsured Employers Fund

§3710. Director of Industrial Relations; powers; "director."
§3710.1. Stop orders.
§3710.2. Penalties for failure to observe stop order.
§3710.3. Transmittal of stop orders issued to certain carriers.
§3711. Proof of insurance.
§3712. Purpose for compensation laws; court procedure.
§3714. Case hearing and filing procedures.
§3715. Employee's remedies.
§3716. Uninsured Employers Benefits Trust Fund.
§3716.1. Representation and investigation.
§3716.2. Extent of payments from Uninsured Employers Fund.
§3716.3. Enforcement of judgment by nonjudicial foreclosure.
§3716.4. Copy of judgment against carrier may be transmitted to Public Utilities Commission.
§3716.5. Director's responsibility to designate job classifications of payees.
§3717. Employer's liability to Uninsured Employers Fund; corporation's liability; definitions.
§3717.1. Substantial shareholders and parents joined in action against uninsured employer.
§3717.2. Board of appeals determination as to shareholder or parent status.
§3718. Joinder of actions against employers; recovered amount paid into State Treasury.
§3719. Suit against uninsured employers.
§3720. Certificate that employer is uninsured; effect; service.
§3720.1. Determination of person as prima facie parent or shareholder; appeal of determination.
§3721. Certificate of cancellation of lien.
§3722. Penalty assessments.
§3725. Penalty assessment order; contest procedure.
§3726. Penalty assessment order; uncontested procedure.
§3727. Certificate of penalty assessment; filing; recording certificate of cancellation.
§3727.1. Withdrawal of stop order or penalty assessment order.
§3728. Cash revolving fund.
§3730. Effect of weekend or holiday on last day for filing.
§3731. Personal service of stop orders or penalty assessment orders.
§3732. Payment from Uninsured Employers Fund: third party liability.
§3733. No prohibition on receipt of compensation solely because of citizenship or immigration status; legislative intent.

ARTICLE 2.5
Self-Insurers' Security Fund

§3740. Intent of Legislature.
§3741. Definitions.
§3742. Establishment of fund; governing board; bylaws; obligations; requirement of fund members.
§3743. Assumption of workers' compensation obligations.
§3744. Rights and obligations of fund.
§3745. Maintenance of assets; assessment of members.
§3746. Annual contract for audit; annual report.
§3747. How to refer to article.

ARTICLE 3
Insurance Rights and Privileges

§3750. Limitations on division.
§3751. Cost of compensation; no employee contribution; violation; no employee payments to medical provider while claim pending.
§3752. Effect of insurance or other benefits.
§3753. Effect of insurance.
§3754. Effect of amount paid on recovery.
§3755. Substitution of insurer.
§3756. Notice of insurer liability.
§3757. Substitution of insurer; employer's relief from liability.
§3758. Substitution of insurer; no abatement of proceeding.
§3759. Joinder of insurer; employer's relief from liability.
§3760. Employer notice to insurer.
§3761. Insurer must notify employer of indemnity claims; employer's notification of insurer regarding facts to disprove claim, report of reserve amount.
§3762. Employer's right to information and documents affecting premium—Exceptions; disclosure of employee's medical information prohibited—Exceptions.

ARTICLE 4
Construction Permit

§3800. Construction permits; verification of workers' compensation coverage.

ARTICLE 5
Workers' Compensation Misrepresentations

§3820. Workers' compensation fraud—Civil penalties; additional penalties for prior felony conviction; Worker's Compensation Fraud Account.
§3822. Annual fraud warning notices.
§3823. Medical billing and provider fraud—Protocols for reporting apparent fraudulent claims; immunity from civil liability for reporting apparent fraud.

CHAPTER 5
SUBROGATION OF EMPLOYER

§3850. "Employee"; "employer."
§3851. Death of employee; effect.
§3852. Claim for compensation; effect on third party action.
§3853. Service of complaint on employer or employee; consolidation of actions.
§3854. Action by employer alone; evidence of amounts paid.
§3855. Joint action; evidence of damages.
§3856. Suit against third party; costs and attorney's fees.
§3857. Subsequent compensation paid by employer; application for further lien.
§3858. Employer's release from further compensation.
§3859. Release or settlement; written agreement; claims against third parties.
§3860. Release or settlement; notice; employer's claim for reimbursement; settlement expenses.
§3861. Employee recovery credited to employer's liability.
§3862. Enforcement of judgment lien by employer against third party.
§3864. Action against third party; prior written agreement of employer to reimburse.
§3865. Duplication of payment under this chapter.

CHAPTER 7
MEDICAL EXAMINATIONS

ARTICLE 1
[In General]

§4050. Medical examinations; written request of employer; order of appeals board.
§4051. Time and place of examination.
§4052. Presence of employee's physician.
§4053. Failure or refusal to submit to examination at employer's request.
§4054. Failure or refusal to submit to examination on order of appeals board.
§4055. Physician's report.
§4055.2. Subpoena of records; copies.
§4056. Disability caused or aggravated by refusal to submit to medical treatment.

ARTICLE 2
Determination of Medical Issues

§4060. Comprehensive medical-legal evaluation.
§4061. Notice of permanent disability indemnity; evaluation.
§4061.5. Treating physician to render opinions on medical issues needed to determine eligibility for compensation.
§4062. Objections to medical determination; procedures when employer objects to treating physician's recommendations.
§4062.1. Unrepresented employee—Medical evaluation.
§4062.2. Comprehensive medical evaluation to resolve dispute over injuries on or after January 1, 2005, when employee is represented by attorney.
§4062.3. Information provided to qualified medical evaluator; service on opposing party; discovery; ex parte communications; contempt; evaluation and summary form; new medical issues.
§4062.5. Failure of QME to complete timely evaluation.
§4062.8. Educational materials for treating physicians and other providers.
§4063. Commencement of payment; declaration of readiness to proceed.
§4064. Employer liability for costs and attorney's fees.
§4067. Subsequent formal evaluations.
§4067.5. Operative date.
§4068. Determination that treating physician's reports are biased and unsupported; notification to appropriate licensing body.

CHAPTER 8
ELECTION TO BE SUBJECT TO COMPENSATION LIABILITY

§4150. Person not "employee"; joint election of employer and employee.
§4151. Methods of employer election.
§4152. Effect statement of acceptance.
§4153. Persons included in statement of acceptance.
§4154. Employer election.
§4155. Coverage of state institutions; presumption.
§4156. Liability for compensation; effective date of division.
§4157. Application of chapter to independent contractor vending periodicals.

CHAPTER 9
ECONOMIC OPPORTUNITY PROGRAMS

ARTICLE 1
General Provisions

§4201. Legislative intent; application of chapter.
§4202. "Economic Opportunity Program."
§4203. "Enrollee."
§4204. "Sponsoring agency."
§4205. "Participating agency."
§4206. Enrollee's right to compensation.
§4207. Conditions for compensation.
§4208. Compensation under chapter; exclusive remedy.
§4209. Application of division to enrollees.

ARTICLE 2
Benefits

§4211. Limitations on compensation.
§4212. Injury or death of enrollee.
§4213. Injury causing permanent disability; percentage of disability.
§4214. Fatal injury; enrollee's burial expenses.

ARTICLE 3
Adjustment of Claims

§4226. Effect of benefits provided under federal statute.
§4227. Effect of medical treatment provided by federal government.
§4228. Effect of medical treatment provided by federal government; reimbursement.
§4229. Right to recover benefits under federal statute supersedes rights under chapter.

CHAPTER 10
DISASTER SERVICE WORKERS

§4350. Office of Emergency Services to administer benefits for volunteer disaster service workers.
§4351. Exclusive remedy.
§4352. Liability for compensation dependent upon and limited to appropriated money; when funds are temporarily unavailable for disbursement; reserve fund.
§4353. Maximum benefits.
§4354. Determination of permanent disability percentage.
§4355. State benefits reduced by amount of federal benefits received.

CHAPTER 11
ASBESTOS WORKERS' ACCOUNT

ARTICLE 1
General Provisions

§4401. Asbestosis; state policy.
§4402. Definitions.
§4403. Asbestos Workers' Account.
§4404. Scope.
§4405. Asbestos workers' benefits; temporary remedy.
§4406. Conditions for receiving asbestos workers' benefits.

ARTICLE 2
Benefits

§4407. Payments as advances.
§4407.3. Death benefit.
§4407.5. No lump-sum payment.
§4408. Compensation procedures.
§4409. Investigations and claims adjustment.
§4409.5. Workers' compensation judges and support staff; appointment.
§4410. Information and assistance officers; duties.
§4411. Claims against Account; responsible employer; Account as party; termination of benefits.

ARTICLE 3
Collections

§4412. Benefits paid and costs incurred; recovery.
§4413. Statutes of limitation under division inapplicable against account.
§4414. Liens filed by account.
§4415. Legal representation for Director of Industrial Relations.
§4416. Responsible employer; notice of amount to satisfy lien; priority of lien.
§4417. Suit against third party.
§4418. Termination date of chapter; benefits under chapter.

PART 2
Computation of Compensation

CHAPTER 1
AVERAGE EARNINGS

§4451. "Average annual earnings."
§4452. Minimum and maximum limits.
§4452.5. "Permanent total disability"; "permanent partial disability."
§4453. Computing average weekly earnings.
§4453.5. Subsequent statutory changes in allowable indemnity.
§4454. Overtime and value of board and lodging; determination of average weekly earnings.
§4455. Injured employee under 18 years old; average weekly earnings.
§4456. Injured employee engaged in unemployment work relief program conducted by State.
§4457. Workers under partnership agreement; average weekly earnings.
§4458. Active firefighter; average weekly earnings.
§4458.2. Active police officer; average weekly earnings.
§4458.5. Injury after termination of active service; average weekly earnings.
§4459. Previous disability and compensation; determination of average weekly earnings.

CHAPTER 2
COMPENSATION SCHEDULES

ARTICLE 1
General Provisions

§4550. Payment of compensation by employer.
§4551. Willful misconduct of injured employee.
§4552. Reduction of compensation; determination by appeals board.
§4553. Willful misconduct of employer.
§4553.1. Serious and willful misconduct; appeals board findings.
§4554. Employer's willful failure to secure payment of compensation.
§4555. Employer's failure to secure payment of compensation; attorney's fees.
§4555.5. Denial of petition to reduce award.
§4556. Increases unaffected by maximums for computation of average earnings.
§4557. Injury to illegally employed person under 16.
§4558. Definitions; employee's action against employer; injury from absence of power press guard.

ARTICLE 2
Medical and Hospital Treatment

§4600. Medical treatment provided by employer; liability for reasonable expense; medical provider network; predesignation of personal physician; expenses incurred in submitting to examination; qualified interpreter.
§4600.05. Immediate support from nurse case manager for employees injured by act of domestic terrorism; applicability; regulations.
§4600.1. Dispensing generic drug equivalent.
§4600.2. Continuing availability of medicines and medical supplies to injured employees.
§4600.3. Employee to choose health care provider; health care organization contract—Standards; payment for services; option to switch health care provider.
§4600.35. Licensing requirements for entities seeking to reimburse health care providers.
§4600.4. Availability during normal business day.
§4600.5. Application for certification as health care organization; application fee; certification requirements for health care service plan, disability insurer, workers' compensation insurer, third-party administrator, workers' compensation health care provider and other entities; claimant's medical treatment records; health care service plan charges; limitations and allowances of act; grounds for refusal, revocation or suspension of certification; provision and regulation of chiropractic care, acupuncture treatment; individual patient information.
§4600.6. Rules and procedures for certification as health care organization; application requirements; disclosure requirements; contracts with prospective purchasers; restrictions on advertisements; name of organization; licensing requirements for facilities, personnel, and equipment; scope of workers' compensation health care; grievance system; cause of action against organization; delegation of responsibility to subcommittees; periodic on-site medical survey by administrative director.
§4600.7. Workers' Compensation Managed Care Fund.
§4601. Employee request to change physician.
§4602. Employee request for certification of competency of consulting physicians.
§4603. Employer request for change of physician.
§4603.2. Notice to employer of selected physician; reports to employer; payment by employer; penalties and liabilities for late payment; review of itemization.
§4603.3. Explanation of review upon payment, adjustment, or denial of itemization of medical services.
§4603.4. Regulatory authority for payment processing and confidentiality of medical information.
§4603.5. Adoption of rules; notice to employees of rights.
§4603.6. Request for independent review; procedure.
§4604. Jurisdiction of appeals board to settle disputes.
§4604.5. Medical treatment utilization schedule—Guidelines; limitations on chiropractic, occupational therapy, and physical therapy visits.
§4605. Consulting or attending physicians provided at employee's expense.
§4606. Public self-insured employer; 90-day limitation inapplicable.
§4607. Denial of petition to terminate benefits; attorney's fees.
§4608. Pharmacy benefits; form requirements.
§4609. Disclosure relating to health care provider's participation in network; disclosures by contracting agent conveying its list of contracted health care providers and reimbursement rates; election by provider to be excluded from list; demonstration by payor of entitlement to pay contracted rate.
§4610. Utilization review process to be established; administrative penalties for failure to meet certain requirements.
§4610.1. Increase in compensation under §5814—Inapplicable for unreasonable delay in medical treatment for periods of time necessary to complete utilization review process; exception.
§4610.3. Employer prohibited to rescind or modify authorization for medical treatment already provided.
§4610.5. Review of utilization review decision.
§4610.6. Independent medical review organization to conduct review of utilization review decision; procedure upon final determination of review.
§4611. Rights and obligations of health care provider contract governed by underlying contract between provider and contracting agent upon contracting agent's sale, lease, or transfer of contract to payor.
§4614. Payment for services.
§4614.1. Certified health care service plan permitted to accept payment from self-insured employers.
§4615. Lien on behalf of physician, practitioner, or provider of medical services; stay pending criminal charges for fraud against workers' compensation system, medical billing, insurance; posting of information on Internet Web site.

ARTICLE 2.3
Medical Provider Networks

§4616. Establishment of medical provider network; requirements; regulations.
§4616.1. Economic profiling; filing of policies and procedures; disclosure to public.
§4616.2. Continuity of care policy; filing and approval; revisions; notice; completion of treatment by terminated provider.
§4616.3. Initial medical evaluation; notice of right to change treating physician; second and third opinions; specialists.
§4616.4. Contract for medical provider network (MPN) independent medical reviews; duties; requirements; when employee may request MPN independent medical review; standard; applications; examination, determination, and report; deadlines; treatment.
§4616.5. "Employer" and "Entity that provides physician network services" defined.
§4616.6. Additional examinations and reports precluded.
§4616.7. Requirements for approval; health care

organization; health care service plan; group disability insurance policy; Taft-Hartley health and welfare fund.

ARTICLE 2.5
Medical-Legal Expenses

§4620. Definitions.
§4621. Reimbursement of medical-legal expenses.
§4622. Employer's liability for expenses; penalty.
§4625. Prompt payment of all reasonable charges for reports.
§4626. Billing of diagnostic tests in accordance with official medical fee schedule.
§4627. Appeals board and administrative director may promulgate rules and regulations.
§4628. Responsibilities of physician signing medical-legal report; information required in report; billable amounts; admissibility of report; civil penalty; contempt; declaration by physician; provision of physician's curriculum vitae.

ARTICLE 3
Disability Payments

§4650. Timing of payments; when employer obligated to reimburse insurer.
§4650.5. Time of first payment; civil service employees; employees of Regents of University of California; Board of Trustees of California State University.
§4651. Payment by written instrument; deposits; applicability of state and federal law; employer disability indemnity payment program [First of Two; Repealed January 1, 2023].
§4651. Disability indemnity payment [Second of Two; Operative January 1, 2023].
§4651.1. Petition alleging disability has decreased or terminated.
§4651.2. Limitations on filing petition alleging disability has decreased or terminated.
§4651.3. Denial of petition alleging disability has decreased or terminated; attorney's fees.
§4652. Disability suffered after employee leaves work because of injury.
§4653. Temporary total disability; amount.
§4654. Temporary partial disability; amount.
§4655. Temporary disability, both total and partial; amount.
§4656. Maximum period for temporary disability payments.
§4657. Temporary partial disability; lost wages.
§4658. Permanent disability; computation.
§4658.1. Meaning of "regular work," "modified work," and "alternative work"; equivalent wages and compensation; location.
§4658.5. Supplemental job displacement benefits—Eligibility; voucher; applicability.
§4658.6. When employer not liable for supplemental job displacement benefit.
§4658.7. Eligibility for supplemental job displacement for injuries occurring on or after January 1, 2013.
§4659. Permanent disability; average weekly earnings; life pensions or total permanent disability.
§4660. Percentage of permanent disability; schedule.
§4660.1. Percentages of permanent disability for injuries occurring on or after January 1, 2013; how determined; adjusted rating schedule; amendments and revisions to schedule.
§4661. Compensation for causing both temporary and permanent disability.
§4661.5. Temporary total disability; payment made two years after injury.
§4662. Permanent disability; presumption of total disability.
§4663. Apportionment of permanent disability; causation as basis; physician's report; apportionment determination; disclosure by employee.
§4664. Liability of employer for percentage of permanent disability directly caused by injury; conclusive presumption from prior award of permanent disability; accumulation of permanent disability awards.

ARTICLE 4
Death Benefits

§4700. Death of employee; employer's liability.
§4701. Fatal injury; burial expenses; death benefits.
§4702. Death benefits; computation; payable in installments; no deduction for disability indemnity.
§4703. Dependent's right to death benefits.
§4703.5. Payment of death benefits to dependent children.
§4703.6. Application of death benefit payments to totally dependent minor child of certain local safety members.
§4704. Control assignment of death benefits.
§4705. Trustee to application of death benefits to beneficiaries.
§4706. Death of dependent beneficiary.
§4706.5. Payment of death benefits where no surviving dependent.
§4707. Limitation on benefits for member of Public Employees' Retirement System.
§4708. Joinder of Public Employees' Retirement System.
§4709. Scholarships for dependents of specified employees; "dependent."

ARTICLE 4.5
Public Official Death Benefits

§4720. "Elected public official"; "assassination."
§4721. Special death benefits upon assassination of elected public official.
§4722. Persons entitled to special death benefits.
§4723. Types of special death benefits; election.
§4724. Filing claim for special death benefits.
§4725. State Compensation Insurance Fund as disbursing agent.
§4726. Joint adoption of rules to carry out article's provisions.
§4727. Assassin's ineligibility for benefits.
§4728. Scholarships for dependents of elected public officials intentionally killed in retaliation for or to prevent their performance of official duties.

ARTICLE 5
Subsequent Injuries Payments

§4751. Compensation for specified additions to permanent partial disabilities.

§4753. Reduction of additional compensation.
§4753.5. Legal representation of state.
§4754. Special additional compensation; awards, payment; reimbursement.
§4754.5. Compromises and release agreements.
§4755. Cash revolving funds.
§4756. No prohibition on receipt of compensation solely because of citizenship or immigration status; legislative intent.

ARTICLE 6
Special Payments to Certain Persons

§4800. Paid leave of absence for specified employees of Department of Justice and San Francisco Port Commission.
§4800.5. Paid leave of absence for specified employees of Department of the California Highway Patrol—Limitations; appeals board jurisdiction in determining disability; eligibility of other peace officers.
§4801. Disability occurring in course of duty.
§4802. Medical, surgical, and hospital benefits.
§4803. Disability continuing beyond one year.
§4804. Prohibition on temporary disability payments concurrent with salary payments.
§4804.1. Paid leave of absence for specified University of California fire department employees.
§4804.2. University of California firefighter's disability occurring in course of duty; determination.
§4804.3. Medical, surgical, and hospital benefits for University of California firefighters.
§4804.4. University of California firefighter's disability continuing beyond one year.
§4804.5. Prohibition on temporary disability payments concurrent with salary payments for University of California firefighters.
§4806. Paid leave of absence for active law enforcement officers of University of California Police Department.
§4807. Appeals board to determine relationship of disability to duty.
§4808. Medical, surgical, and hospital benefits for University of California police officers.
§4809. University of California police officer's disability continuing beyond one year.
§4810. Prohibition on temporary disability payments concurrent with salary payments for University of California police officers.
§4816. California State University Police Department collective bargaining agreement for enhanced industrial disability leave.
§4817. Appeals board to determine relationship of disability to duty.
§4819. California State University police officer's disability continuing beyond one year.
§4820. Prohibition on temporary disability payments concurrent with salary payments for California State University police officers.

ARTICLE 7
City Police and Firemen, Sheriffs, and Others

§4850. Paid leave of absence for specified public employees.
§4850.3. Advanced disability pension payments—Local safety officer.
§4850.4. Advanced disability pension payments.
§4850.5. Benefits for firefighters, sheriff's and probation office employees, and other specified employees of San Luis Obispo County.
§4850.7. Firefighters' entitlement to benefits.
§4851. Request to make disability determinations.
§4852. Article's effect on medical, surgical, and hospital benefits.
§4853. Disability continuing beyond one year.
§4854. Prohibition on temporary disability payments concurrent with salary payments.
§4855. Non-applicability to reserve public safety employees.
§4856. Continued provision of health benefits to surviving spouse and dependents of deceased firefighter or peace officer; limitations.

PART 3
Compensation Claims

CHAPTER 1
PAYMENT AND ASSIGNMENT

§4900. Claim for compensation; assignment.
§4901. Effect of debts on claims.
§4902. Payment of claim directly to attorney or agent.
§4903. Determination of liens against compensation payable.
§4903.05. Filing of written lien claim required; form; fee; required documents to accompany lien filing.
§4903.06. Fees for claims filed prior to January 1, 2013.
§4903.07. Conditions for entitlement to order or award for reimbursement of lien filing or activation fee.
§4903.1. Determination of reimbursement for benefits paid or services provided.
§4903.2. Attorney's fee allowed from lien claimant's recovery.
§4903.3. Compensation provided from fund.
§4903.4. Disputes over liens for expenses.
§4903.5. Limitations period for filing lien claim.
§4903.6. Lien claim or application for adjudication; requirements for filing; exemptions.
§4903.8. Person to whom payment of lien to be made; assignment of lien; multiple assignments; conditions under which lien may not be assigned; invalidity of lien.
§4904. Adjustment and disallowance of liens; liens on unemployment compensation benefits.
§4904.1. Lien does not affect payment of balance of award.
§4905. Determination when lien not duly requested.
§4906. Reasonableness of charges or claims; attorney fees; disclosures.
§4907. Removal of privilege to represent party.
§4908. Compensation claim's equal preference over other debts.
§4909. Effect of employer's payment of benefits before settlement.
§4909.1. State fund may administer benefits.

CHAPTER 2
COMPROMISE AND RELEASE

§5000. Limitations of this division.
§5001. "Compensation"; validity of compromise and release.
§5002. Appeals board's power to enter award once copy of compromise and release filed.

§5003. Required information for compromise and release.
§5004. Additional required information for compromise and release agreements in case of death.
§5005. Compromises and release agreements; occupational disease or cumulative injury.
§5006. Board's findings as having no collateral estoppel effect on subsequent criminal proceedings.

CHAPTER 3
LUMP SUM PAYMENTS

§5100. Lump sum payments; commutation.
§5100.5. When commutation not possible.
§5100.6. No commutation or settlement of rehabilitation benefits.
§5101. Determination of lump sum amount.
§5102. Method of payment of lump sums.
§5103. Trustee's payments from deposited lump sum.
§5104. Preference in trustee appointment.
§5105. Receipt and certificate for lump sum payment.
§5106. Present worth of uninsured employer's future payments.

PART 3.5
Arbitration

§5270. Representation.
§5270.5. List of eligible arbitrators.
§5271. Selection of arbitrator.
§5272. Arbitrators' duties and limits of power.
§5273. Payment of costs of proceedings.
§5275. Types of disputes submitted.
§5276. Date, time, and place of proceedings.
§5277. Findings and award.
§5278. Disclosure of settlement to arbitrator prior to award prohibited.

PART 4
Compensation Proceedings

CHAPTER 1
JURISDICTION

§5300. Proceedings to be handled by appeals board.
§5301. Appeals board power and jurisdiction.
§5302. Presumptions regarding all appeals board decisions.
§5303. Separate cause of action; joined claims.
§5304. Appeals board jurisdiction over medical, surgical, and hospital treatment.
§5305. Jurisdiction of resident's out-of-state injuries.
§5306. Employee's rights against employer's estate.
§5307. Appeals board powers; procedure for adopting, amending or rescinding regulations.
§5307.1. Official medical fee schedule.
§5307.11. Permissible contracts for reimbursement rates outside official fee schedule.
§5307.12. Written disclosure when contract for reimbursement is more than 20 percent below the official medical fee schedule [Operative July 1, 2021].
§5307.2. Study of access to medical treatment, quality health care or products, including prescription drugs and pharmacy services, for injured workers; authority of administrative director to adjust medical and facilities' fees.
§5307.27. Adoption of medical treatment utilization schedule; evidence-based updates; inclusion of drug formulary.
§5307.28. Consultation with stakeholders regarding establishment of drug formulary; interim reports.
§5307.29. Quarterly updates to drug formulary; issuance of order for changes; independent pharmacy and therapeutics committee.
§5307.3. Administrative director's powers; changing regulations.
§5307.4. Public hearings.
§5307.5. Appeals board or workers' compensation judge's powers.
§5307.6. Director to adopt fee schedule for medical-legal expenses.
§5307.7. Vocational expert fees.
§5307.8. Schedule of fees for services not covered by Medicare or by Section 5307.1.
§5307.9. Schedule of fees for copy and related services.
§5308. Appeals board jurisdiction over insurance controversies involving self-employed persons.
§5309. Appeals board power over workers' compensation judge.
§5310. Workers' compensation administrative law judges appointed by appeals board or administrative director.
§5311. Objections to particular workers' compensation judges.
§5311.5. Requirement that workers' compensation administrative law judges participate in continuing education.
§5312. Swearing in of workers' compensation judge.
§5313. Decisions of appeals board or workers' compensation judge.
§5315. Time limits for appeals board to act on decision of workers' compensation judge.
§5316. Method of service.
§5317. Service of public official.

CHAPTER 2
LIMITATIONS OF PROCEEDINGS

§5400. Time limits for notice of injury.
§5401. Claim form and notice of potential eligibility for benefits; form and content; when and where to file claim form.
§5401.7. Statement required on claim form; optional statements.
§5402. Employer's knowledge equivalent to notice; employer's notice to employee or employee's dependents.
§5403. Effect of failure to give notice or of defective notice.
§5404. Barring of untimely claims; further claims barred by timely filing.
§5404.5. Dismissal of claims with no activity for 180 days.
§5405. Time limits for benefits collection proceedings.
§5406. Time limits for commencement of benefits collection proceedings; generally.
§5406.5. Time limits for commencement of benefits collection proceedings; asbestosis.
§5406.6. Limitations period for claim for workers'

Labor

compensation benefits for death from HIV-related disease.
§5406.7. Limitations period for commencement of proceedings to collect dependency death benefits.
§5407. Time limits for commencement of compensation collection proceedings in case of misconduct.
§5407.5. Time limits for commencement of compensation reduction proceedings in case of employee misconduct.
§5408. Guardian/conservator to exercise minor's or incompetent's rights.
§5409. Statute of limitations is affirmative defense.
§5410. Time limits; proceedings for aggravated disabilities.
§5410.1. Attorney's fee for defendant in action to reduce permanent disability benefits.
§5411. Date of injury.
§5412. Date of injury for occupational diseases or cumulative injuries.
§5413. Board's findings as having no collateral estoppel effect on subsequent criminal proceedings.

CHAPTER 2.3
WORKERS' COMPENSATION—TRUTH IN ADVERTISING

§5430. Title.
§5431. Purpose.
§5432. Notice requirements.
§5433. Disclosure requirements.
§5434. Penalty for violation; "advertiser" defined.

CHAPTER 2.5
ADMINISTRATIVE ASSISTANCE

§5450. Assistance from Division of Workers' Compensation.
§5451. Duties of information and assistance officer.
§5453. Recommendation of information and assistance officer.
§5454. Statute of limitations tolled by submission to information and assistance officer.
§5455. Application for benefits; admissible evidence.

CHAPTER 3
APPLICATIONS AND ANSWERS

§5500. Required pleadings.
§5500.3. Uniformity among offices.
§5500.5. Employers liable for occupational disease or cumulative injury.
§5500.6. Employers liable for occupational disease or cumulative injury; household employee.
§5501. Filing of application; subsequent procedure.
§5501.5. Where application for adjudication of claim may be filed.
§5501.6. Petition for change of venue.
§5502. Time for hearing; priority calendar; mandatory settlement conference.
§5502.5. Hearing continuance—Good cause required.
§5503. "Applicant"; "defendant."
§5504. Service of notice of hearing.
§5505. Defendant's answer.
§5506. Defendant's failure to appear or answer.
§5507. Dismissal of application without hearing.

CHAPTER 4
ATTACHMENTS

§5600. Appeals board authority to order writs of attachment.
§5601. Procedure for attachment proceedings.
§5602. Issuance and discharge of attachment.
§5603. Preference when attachments levied.

CHAPTER 5
HEARINGS

§5700. Adjournment of hearing; parties permitted at hearing.
§5701. Appeals board authority to take testimony or direct examination.
§5702. Stipulations.
§5703. Specified additional evidence allowed.
§5703.5. Examination of injured employee by QME.
§5704. Transcripts of testimony.
§5705. Burden of proof; affirmative defenses.
§5706. Appeals board authority to order autopsy.
§5707. Appeals board limited authority to order autopsy when body not in coroner's custody.
§5708. Appeals board authority to conduct hearings by own rules.
§5709. Informality in proceedings; no effect on validity.
§5710. Deposition of witnesses.

CHAPTER 6
FINDINGS AND AWARDS

§5800. Interest on compensation or death benefit payments.
§5800.5. Clarification of §5313.
§5801. Appeals board determination of payment matters; attorney's fees.
§5802. Nominal disability indemnity.
§5803. Appeals board continuing jurisdiction.
§5803.5. Grounds for reconsideration of order, decision, or award.
§5804. Altering award after five years.
§5805. Effect of altered decision.
§5806. Certified copy of decision; filing.
§5807. Certified copy as judgment roll.
§5808. Stay of execution of appeals board decision.
§5809. Satisfaction of judgment in fact.
§5810. Court review.
§5811. Limited fees; appeals board allowance of costs; interpreter fees.
§5813. Sanctions for bad-faith actions or tactics.
§5814. Unreasonable delay or refusal of payment of compensation; increase; self-imposed penalty; conclusive presumption on approval of compromise and release, etc.; actions; applicability.
§5814.1. Employer's penalty paid to director.
§5814.5. Reasonable attorneys' fees awarded when payment of compensation delayed or refused.
§5814.6. Administrative penalties for knowing violation of §5814.
§5815. Statement of determination of issues raised.
§5816. No collateral estoppel effect on subsequent criminal proceedings.

CHAPTER 7
RECONSIDERATION AND JUDICIAL REVIEW

ARTICLE 1
Reconsideration

§5900. Reconsideration; petition.
§5901. Accrual of cause of action in court.
§5902. Requirements of petition for reconsideration.
§5903. Grounds for reconsideration.
§5904. Waiver of irregularities.
§5905. Petition for reconsideration; service; answer.
§5906. Petition for reconsideration; notice of hearings on reconsideration.
§5907. Decision without hearing.
§5908. Effect of order on reconsideration.
§5908.5. Decision on reconsideration.
§5909. Denial of reconsideration.
§5910. Filing petition for reconsideration.
§5911. Limitations on article.

ARTICLE 2
Judicial Review

§5950. Writ of review; time limit for filing.
§5951. Writ of review; based on record of appeals board.
§5952. Extent of review.
§5953. Appeals board's findings of fact are final; right to appear at hearing.
§5954. Code of Civil Procedure governs proceedings; service of pleadings.
§5955. Exclusive jurisdiction of Supreme Court or appellate courts.
§5956. Stay of appeals board decision not automatic.

ARTICLE 3
Undertaking on Stay Order

§6000. Limitations on authority of reviewing court to issue stay order.
§6001. Undertaking.
§6002. Filing of undertaking with appeals board.

DIVISION 4.5
WORKERS' COMPENSATION AND INSURANCE: STATE EMPLOYEES NOT OTHERWISE COVERED

CHAPTER 1
GENERAL PROVISIONS

§6100. Purpose of division.
§6101. Definitions.

CHAPTER 2
DIRECT PAYMENTS

§6110. Voluntary offering of benefits.
§6111. State Compensation Insurance Fund; master agreement to dispose of claims.
§6112. Master agreement; uniform rates for state agencies.
§6113. Authorization for fund to make expenditures.
§6114. Reimbursement of expenditures by claimant's agency.
§6115. Right of fund to recover from third parties.

CHAPTER 3
INSURANCE

§6130. Insurance from other insurer.
§6131. Payment of premium.

CHAPTER 4
BENEFITS AND PROCEDURE

§6140. Benefits employees entitled to.
§6141. Applicable procedure and limitations.
§6142. Exceptions.
§6143. Powers of appeals board.
§6144. Trial and determination of controversies.
§6145. Submission of controversies for arbitration.
§6146. Powers of appeals board as arbitrator.
§6147. Benefits received by state agency.
§6148. Payment of benefits by insurer.
§6149. Negotiation of agreement.

DIVISION 4.7
RETRAINING AND REHABILITATION

§6200. Rehabilitation procedures; purpose of division.
§6201. Availability of rehabilitation services; notice to employee.
§6202. Initiation of rehabilitation plan.
§6203. Subsistence allowance.
§6204. Rehabilitation plan; employee cooperation.
§6205. Rehabilitation plan without state approval.
§6206. Rehabilitative services; extent.
§6207. Rehabilitative benefits; nature.
§6208. Initiation and acceptance of rehabilitation program.

DIVISION 5
SAFETY IN EMPLOYMENT

PART 1
Occupational Safety and Health

CHAPTER 1
JURISDICTION AND DUTIES

§6300. Purpose.
§6301. Construction and interpretation.
§6302. Definitions.
§6303. "Place of employment" and "employment."
§6303.5. Unlimited jurisdiction of state where federal law authorizes concurrent jurisdiction.
§6304. "Employer."
§6304.1. "Employee."
§6304.2. State prisoners as employees; Department of Corrections as employer.
§6304.3. Correctional Industry Safety Committee; establishment and duties.
§6304.4. When prisoners are not "employees."
§6304.5. Applicability.
§6305. Definitions.
§6306. Definitions.
§6307. Scope of power and jurisdiction.
§6307.1. Role of State Department of Health Services.
§6308. Enforcement powers.
§6308.5. Hearings.
§6309. Investigation procedures.
§6310. Discrimination against employee for filing complaint or otherwise exercising rights; employer prohibited from retaliation.

Labor

§6311. Employee's refusal to work when health or safety threatened.
§6311.5. Willful and knowing direction of employee to remain in, or enter, an area closed due to public health or safety menace; exemption.
§6312. Employee's recourse for violation of §6310 or §6311.
§6313. Cases for investigation.
§6313.5. Transmission of contractor citations to State License Board.
§6314. Access to place of employment for investigative purposes.
§6314.1. High hazardous industries.
§6314.5. Scope of inspection.
§6315. Bureau of Investigations.
§6315.3. Submission of report of bureau activities.
§6315.5. Admissibility as evidence of division's standards, findings, etc.
§6316. Limitations on powers of other governing bodies.
§6317. Steps taken against employers violating regulations.
§6317.5. Employer's falsification of materials posted or distributed in workplace—Notice of violation; posting of citation.
§6317.7. Notice of no violations.
§6318. Posting of citations.
§6319. Procedures for citation or order issuance; appeal; setting of penalties.
§6319.3. Civil penalty assessed against new employer.
§6319.5. Employer's showing of good-faith compliance effort.
§6320. Reinspection.
§6321. Limitation on advance warning; penalties for violation.
§6322. Confidentiality of information obtained.
§6323. Injunctions.
§6324. Temporary restraining orders.
§6325. Prohibition of entry into dangerous place or use of dangerous equipment [First of Two; Repealed January 1, 2023].
§6325. Prohibition of entry into dangerous place or use of dangerous equipment [Second of Two; Operative January 1, 2023].
§6325.5. Order prohibiting use of workplace containing friable asbestos.
§6326. Penalties for violation of no-entry or no-use orders.
§6327. Contesting prohibition of use or entry.
§6327.5. Employee action if division fails to act.
§6328. Informational notices.
§6329. Payment of money collected from employers.
§6330. Annual report to Legislature.
§6331. Testing of self-contained breathing apparatus.
§6332. Employers to keep record of violence committed against community health care worker.

CHAPTER 2
EDUCATION AND RESEARCH
[Selected Provisions]

§6350. Educational and research program.
§6351. Preparation and distribution of health and safety information.
§6352. Safety training programs; priority of program development.
§6353. Continuing research.
§6354. Consulting services.
§6354.5. Insurer's provision of occupational safety and health loss control consultation services; standards; insurance loss control services coordinator.
§6354.7. Workers' Occupational Safety and Health Education Fund; development of worker safety and health training and education program.
§6355. Employer's immunity from prosecution or penalties.
§6356. Worker Safety Bilingual Investigative Support, Enforcement, and Training Account.
§6357. Adoption of standards for ergonomics in the workplace.

CHAPTER 2.5
HAZARDOUS SUBSTANCES INFORMATION AND TRAINING

ARTICLE 3
Hazardous Substances
[Selected Provisions]

§6380. List of hazardous substances.

ARTICLE 4
Duties

§6390. Preparation and provision of MSDS.
§6390.2. Manufacturers or importers of cosmetics or disinfectants with hazardous substances to post and maintain safety data sheet (SDS) on website accessible to public.
§6390.5. Labeling.
§6391. Information manufacturers must provide purchasers.
§6392. Proof of compliance—Federal MSDS.
§6393. Relief of obligation to provide MSDS.
§6394. Transmission of copy of MSDS to department.
§6395. MSDS for entire product mixture.
§6396. Protection from disclosure of trade secrets.
§6397. Provision of MSDS to direct purchaser at time of sale.
§6398. Employer's duties toward employees.
§6398.5. Availability of printable information on certain cleaning product ingredients and nonfunctional constituents.
§6399. Availability of MSDS to employees.
§6399.1. Compliance with Food and Agricultural Code §12981.
§6399.2. Operative date of article.

CHAPTER 3
RESPONSIBILITIES AND DUTIES OF EMPLOYERS AND EMPLOYEES

§6400. Employer to furnish safe and healthy workplace; employer categories that may be issued citations when employee exposed to hazard on multiemployer worksites.
§6401. Safe and healthy equipment and practices requirement.
§6401.5. Prohibition against salvaging materials during demolition.
§6401.7. Injury prevention programs.
§6401.8. Adoption of workplace violence prevention plan by certain licensed hospitals; duty of hospital to report violent incidents.

§6402. Allowing employee to work in unsafe conditions prohibited.
§6403. Requirements of employer.
§6403.1. Health care employer personal protective equipment inventory requirements.
§6403.3. Definitions; personal protective equipment stockpile requirements.
§6403.5. Adoption of patient protection and health care worker back and musculoskeletal injury prevention plan; safe patient handling policy; training; duties of coordinator of care; disciplinary action.
§6404. Prohibition against unsafe or unhealthy work sites.
§6404.5. Prohibition against smoking in the workplace.
§6405. Prohibition against construction of unhealthy or unsafe work sites.
§6406. Prohibition against interfering with or neglecting to provide safe or healthful equipment or practices.
§6407. Employer's and employee's obligation to comply with regulations.
§6408. Obligation to provide specified information to employees.
§6409. Requirements of physicians treating injured employees; "occupational illness."
§6409.1. Requirements of employers when employee is occupationally injured or ill; subsequent death of employee.
§6409.2. Notification when fire or police are called to serious or fatal accident.
§6409.3. Pesticide poisoning treatment.
§6409.5. Notification of Division of Occupational Safety and Health and Division of Labor Standards Enforcement regarding garment manufacturing hazards—Investigation by local public fire agency.
§6409.6. COVID-19 employer notice requirements.
§6410. Requirements for reports and records.
§6410.1. Legislative intent.
§6410.2. Track and implement changes consistent with Occupational Safety and Health Administration's Improve Tracking of Workplace Injuries and Illnesses rule.
§6410.5. Statement must accompany reports.
§6411. Requirement to fully and accurately complete forms.
§6412. Report's confidentiality and admissibility as evidence.
§6413. Requirements when state prisoner is injured.
§6413.2. Division's powers regarding Department of Corrections and Rehabilitation.
§6413.5. Penalties for violation of reporting requirements.

CHAPTER 4
PENALTIES

§6423. Violations as misdemeanors; penalties.
§6425. Penalties for willful violations causing death or serious bodily impairment; violations within 7 years of first conviction.
§6426. Penalties for knowingly falsifying reports or records.
§6427. Civil penalty for non-serious violations.
§6428. Civil penalty for serious violations.
§6428.5. Criteria for "operative" injury prevention program.
§6429. Civil penalties for willful or repetitious violations.
§6430. Civil penalties for failure to correct violations.
§6431. Civil penalty for violation of posting or recordkeeping requirements.
§6432. Rebuttable presumption of "serious violation"; considerations prior to issuance of violation; "serious physical harm" [First of Two; Repealed January 1, 2023].
§6432. Rebuttable presumption of "serious violation"; considerations prior to issuance of violation; "serious physical harm" [Second of Two; Operative January 1, 2023].
§6433. Civil penalties distinguished.
§6434. Civil or administrative penalties assessed against educational entities to be deposited with fund; application for refund upon abatement—Time limit.
§6434.5. Refund plan for civil and administrative penalties.
§6435. Civil penalty for violation of permit requirements.
§6436. Jurisdiction of actions involving asbestos-related complaints.

CHAPTER 5
TEMPORARY VARIANCES

§6450. Temporary order for variance from health and safety standards.
§6451. Information needed for temporary variance application.
§6452. Temporary variance to test new techniques.
§6454. Rules for temporary variances.
§6455. Time limits to appeal temporary variance.
§6456. Temporary variance decisions binding on parties.
§6457. Standards board decisions.

CHAPTER 6
PERMIT REQUIREMENTS

§6500. Permit requirement for dangerous employment or place of employment; application to certain construction, demolition, and underground activities and motion picture, television, and theater stages or sets on and after January 1, 2000.
§6501. Permit information required of employer.
§6501.5. Employer registration of asbestos-related work.
§6501.7. Definition of "asbestos."
§6501.8. "Asbestos-related work" and "asbestos containing construction material."
§6501.9. Employer or contractor shall determine if asbestos is present.
§6502. Division's issuance of permits.
§6503. Safety conferences.
§6503.5. Safety conference for all asbestos handling jobs.
§6504. Employers to post copies of permits.
§6505. Revocation of permits.
§6505.5. Penalties for failure to determine if asbestos is present.
§6506. Appeal of permit denial or revocation.
§6507. Permit and registration fees.
§6508. Entities exempt from permit requirements.
§6508.5. No exemption from registration.
§6509. Penalty for permit violations.
§6509.5. Asbestos consultant may not require contract for corrective work as condition to performing inspection.

§6510. Temporary restraining order for permit violation.

CHAPTER 7
APPEAL PROCEEDINGS

§6600. Time limit for appeal of citation or penalty.
§6600.5. Time limit for appeal of special order or action order.
§6601. Failure to act within time limit for appeal of citation or penalty.
§6601.5. Failure to act within time limit for appeal of special order or action order.
§6602. Appeal procedures.
§6603. Appeals board rules of practice and procedure.
§6604. Duties of hearing officer.
§6605. Powers of hearing officer.
§6606. Objection to hearing officer.
§6607. Hearing officer must be sworn.
§6608. Findings; decision.
§6609. Appeals board's action on decision.
§6610. Service of notice, order, decision.
§6611. Employer's failure to appear at appeal.
§6612. Informality of proceedings does not affect decision.
§6613. Use of depositions on appeal.
§6614. Time for reconsideration.
§6615. Accrual of cause of action; role of appeals board.
§6616. Information required in petition for reconsideration.
§6617. Grounds for reconsideration.
§6618. Waiver of objections not set forth in petition for reconsideration.
§6619. Service petition for reconsideration; answer.
§6620. Appeals board's power to reconsider; notice of hearing.
§6621. Decision based on record without further hearing.
§6622. Effect of appeals board's alteration of decision.
§6623. Procedure for decisions.
§6624. Denial of reconsideration; presumption.
§6625. Filing for reconsideration; effect on original decision.
§6626. Time for reconsideration of appeals board order.
§6627. Writ of mandate in superior court.
§6628. Procedure for superior court's consideration.
§6629. Scope of superior court review.
§6630. Appeals board's factual findings and conclusions as controlling.
§6631. Procedure for writ of mandate.
§6632. Courts having jurisdiction over appeals board decisions.
§6633. Court's power to postpone operation of appeals board decision.

CHAPTER 8
ENFORCEMENT OF CIVIL PENALTIES

§6650. Procedures for unpaid civil penalty.
§6651. Deadline to commence action to collect civil penalty.
§6652. Notice to Contractors' State License Board of civil penalty.

CHAPTER 9
MISCELLANEOUS SAFETY PROVISIONS

§6700. Gas pipelines; conclusive presumptions.
§6701. Internal combustion engines used within structures.
§6702. Exhaust purifier devices.
§6703. Exceptions to rules for internal combustion engines used within structures.
§6704. Boomstops for crawler and wheel cranes.
§6705. Restrictions on contracts involving trench excavations.
§6705.5. Application of shoring, bracing, and sloping regulations to swimming pool excavations found unsafe.
§6706. One permit per project; exceptions.
§6707. Bids for local government projects involving trenches or open excavations.
§6708. Adequate emergency first aid treatment; requirement.
§6709. Valley Fever; awareness training.
§6710. Explosives.
§6711. Examination of persons using explosives for snow avalanche blasting.
§6712. Occupational safety and health standard for field sanitation.
§6716. "Lead-related construction work."
§6717. Standard that protects employees engaged in lead-related construction.
§6717.5. Cal/OSHA to submit to Occupational Safety and Health Standards Board rulemaking proposal to revise lead standards for purposes of general industry safety orders and construction safety orders.
§6718. Restrictions on test procedures for vapor emission from vehicles transporting gasoline.
§6719. Concern over repetitive motion injuries.
§6720. Standard that minimizes heat-related illness and injury among indoor workers.
§6721. Maria Isabel Vasquez Jimenez heat illness standard.
§6725. Dissemination of best practices for COVID-19 infection prevention among agricultural employees.

PART 3
Safety on Buildings

CHAPTER 1
BUILDINGS UNDER CONSTRUCTION OR REPAIR

ARTICLE 1
Floors and Walls

§7100. "Building."
§7101. Protective flooring.
§7102. Protective flooring in concrete buildings.
§7103. Protective wooden flooring.
§7104. Supportive intermediate beams.
§7105. Replanking.
§7106. Building sections as "buildings."
§7107. Planked floors.
§7108. Safety belts and nets.
§7109. Working without required planking or nets.
§7110. Enforcement by Division.

ARTICLE 2
Scaffolding

§7150. "Scaffolding."
§7151. Suspended scaffolding.

§7152. Employers using scaffolding.
§7153. Scaffolding platforms or floors.
§7154.1. Prohibition of lean-to scaffolds.
§7155. Penalty for scaffolding requirement violations.
§7156. Employer violations and penalty.
§7157. Division's power regarding safety orders.
§7158. Enforcement by division.

ARTICLE 3
Construction Elevators

§7200. "Construction elevator" and "building."
§7201. Signals for construction elevators.
§7202. Employee to give signals.
§7203. Board's regulation of signals.
§7204. Inspection of construction elevators.
§7205. Penalties for violation.

ARTICLE 4
Structural Steel Framed Buildings

§7250. "Building."
§7251. Buildings affected.
§7252. Decking of derricks or working floors.
§7253. Temporary floor and safety belt protection.
§7254. Temporary floors.
§7255. Protection against temporary floor displacement.
§7256. Plank extension.
§7257. Covering openings by columns.
§7258. Metal decking instead of wood planking.
§7259. Replacement of floor planks.
§7260. Employee instruction before planking removed.
§7261. Removing temporary planking.
§7262. Protection while removing temporary planking.
§7263. Constantly maintaining structural frame's stability.
§7264. Section as "building."
§7265. Safety belts and nets.
§7266. Penalty for violation.
§7267. Enforcement by Division.

CHAPTER 2
ELEVATORS, ESCALATORS, PLATFORM AND STAIRWAY CHAIR LIFTS, DUMBWAITERS, MOVING WALKS, AUTOMATED PEOPLE MOVERS, AND OTHER CONVEYANCES

§7300. Standards to promote public safety awareness.
§7300.1. Definitions.
§7300.2. Equipment covered.
§7300.3. Equipment not covered.
§7300.4. Work exemptions.
§7301. Permit required for conveyance operation.
§7301.1. Requirements for permit.
§7301.5. Adoption of fire and emergency regulations for conveyance operation; emergency certification.
§7302. Conveyance operation without permit.
§7302.1. Conveyance authorization without permit.
§7302.2. Assessment of penalty.
§7303. Remedies for dangerous operation without permit.
§7304. Conveyance inspection and permit issuance.
§7305. Division's power over unsafe conveyances.
§7306. Challenging division orders.
§7307. Procedural choices of division; later review.
§7308. Temporary permits.
§7309. Inspectors.
§7309.1. Requirements for certification of inspectors.
§7310. Division's acceptance of other inspections.
§7311. Requirements for inspectors.
§7311.1. Certified qualified conveyance company—Application and certification.
§7311.2. Certified competent conveyance mechanic.
§7311.25. Exception to certified competent conveyance mechanic requirement for certain agricultural production, processing, and handling facilities.
§7311.3. Certificate—2-year term; renewal—Continuing education of certificate holders.
§7311.4. Certification fees.
§7311.5. Persons maintaining certain personnel elevators on marine terminal cranes; experiential requirements; proscriptions.
§7312. Revocation of conveyance operation permit.
§7313. Requirements for inspection reports.
§7314. Inspection fees.
§7315. Payment of inspection fees; temporary permit issuance; fees—Exceptions.
§7316. Disposition and reporting requirements for inspection fee funds.
§7317. Exempted conveyances.
§7318. Division's authority over safety orders.
§7319. Seat for elevator operator; penalty for violation.
§7320. Penalty for failure to display permit.
§7321. Penalty for operation of unsafe conveyance.
§7321.5. Enforcement of penalties; appeals.
§7322. Hearing on order prohibiting use of conveyance.
§7323. Regulations for equipment.
§7324. Compliance with State Fire Prevention and Building Code.
§7324.1. Responsibility and liability of persons, firms or corporations.
§7324.2. Requirements not retroactive.

CHAPTER 3
SAFETY DEVICES UPON BUILDINGS TO SAFEGUARD WINDOW CLEANERS

§7325. "Building."
§7326. Window sill or frame fixtures.
§7327. Approval of alternative fixtures.
§7328. Penalty for employer violation.
§7329. Obligation to install and maintain safety fixtures; penalty for violation.
§7330. Penalty for failure to provide safety devices.
§7331. Division's powers.
§7332. Enforcement by division.

CHAPTER 4
PASSENGER TRAMWAYS

§7340. "Passenger tramway" and "permit."
§7341. Permit requirement.
§7342. Violation by operation without permit.
§7343. Remedies for dangerous operation.
§7344. Inspection and permit issuance.
§7345. Division's powers when tramways are unsafe.
§7346. Procedure to challenge division orders.
§7347. Procedural choices of division; later review.
§7348. Temporary permits.
§7349. Inspectors; temporary permits.
§7350. Fees.
§7351. Payment of fees; temporary permit exception.
§7352. Disposition of fees.

§7353. Certification of construction and repair plans.
§7354. Certification.
§7354.5. Ski lift inspections.
§7355. Division's authority.
§7356. Report of tramway injury.
§7357. Qualification of tramway operators.

CHAPTER 5
CRANES

ARTICLE 1
Permits for Tower Cranes

§7370. Legislative declaration; priority of tower crane safety inspections.
§7371. Definitions.
§7372. Employment of safety inspectors; establishment of safety inspection program.
§7373. Issuance and validity of permits.
§7374. Suspension or revocation of permit.

ARTICLE 2
Certification
[Selected Provisions]

§7376. Suspension or revocation of license to certify crane safety.
§7377. Appeal of revocation of license.
§7378. Penalties for fraudulent certification.
§7379. Penalties for certifying without license.
§7380. Collection of fees.
§7381. Penalties for violation of safety standards if serious injury or death results; penalties for serious violations.
§7382. Presence of safety representative required while installing, dismantling, or "jumping" crane.

PART 6
Tanks and Boilers

CHAPTER 6
MISMANAGEMENT OF STEAM BOILERS

§7770. Penalty for undue quantity of steam endangering human life.
§7771. Imprisonment for causing death.

PART 7
Volatile Flammable Liquids
[Selected Provisions]

§7800. "Volatile flammable liquids."
§7803. Means of flame extinguishment.

PART 7.5
Refinery and Chemical Plants

CHAPTER 1
GENERAL

§7850. Title of part.
§7851. Legislative declaration.
§7852. Legislative intent.
§7853. "Process safety management" defined.

CHAPTER 2
PROCESS SAFETY MANAGEMENT STANDARDS

§7855. Purpose of chapter.
§7856. Process safety management standards—Adoption of federal standards; facilities not covered under federal rules.
§7857. Standards to include prescribed items.
§7858. Written safety information; employee participation; content and availability.
§7859. Hazard analysis; availability of risk management prevention program information.
§7860. Written operating procedures; availability; review.
§7861. Safety and health hazard training; refresher courses; employer duty to train; training certification and testing.
§7862. Contractor's employees working near potential hazard.
§7863. Prestartup safety review for new and modified facilities.
§7864. Inspection and testing procedures.
§7865. Permits for "hot work."
§7866. Procedure for managing changes.
§7867. Procedure for investigating incidents and potential incidents.
§7868. Emergency action plan.
§7870. Collection of fees.
§7872. Petroleum refinery turnaround—Definition; when required; review of records.
§7873. When petroleum refinery turnaround information is trade secret; protected information; conditions for release of information to public; court orders; notification.

PART 9
Tunnel and Mine Safety

CHAPTER 1
TUNNELS AND MINES

§7950. Citation of part.
§7951. Definitions.
§7952. Safety engineers unit.
§7953. Inspection of mines and tunnels.
§7954. Availability of additional personnel, facilities, and services.
§7955. Notification before operation or construction; prejob safety conferences; classification of tunnels and underground mines; reclassification.
§7956. Posting of classification and special regulations.
§7957. Emergency rescue plans.
§7958. Trained rescue crews.
§7959. Rescue crews: equipment familiarity, regular practices, placement.
§7960. Tests in potentially gassy tunnels and mines.
§7961. Investigation of specified gas readings.
§7962. Safety representatives.
§7963. Communication systems.
§7964. Fireproof access shafts.
§7964.5. Division's authority.

CHAPTER 2
GASSY AND EXTRAHAZARDOUS TUNNELS

§7965. Operational procedures for gassy tunnels and mines.
§7966. Gas tests and probe holes.
§7967. Division notification of specified gas levels.
§7968. Shutdown orders for gas or vapor testing.

§7969. Review of electric plans for gassy tunnels and mines.
§7970. Smoking and ignition sources prohibited in gassy mines; employer's responsibility.
§7971. Procedures when gas or vapor ignites.
§7972. Removal of workers at specified gas levels.
§7973. Employee notification and posting of special orders following inspection.
§7974. Ventilation in gassy tunnels.
§7975. "Kill" buttons for electrical equipment; procedures.
§7976. Fire extinguishers in gassy tunnels and mines.
§7977. Extrahazardous tunnels and mines.
§7978. Smoking or open flame in extrahazardous tunnel or mine; welding or cutting.
§7979. Air composition of extrahazardous tunnels and mines.
§7980. Equipment in extrahazardous tunnels and mines.
§7981. Escape chambers and routes; rescue equipment.
§7982. Employer's obligation to record air flow and air samples.
§7983. Main fan lines.
§7984. Testing for gases or vapors using mechanical excavation.
§7985. Testing device requirements; permissible levels.

CHAPTER 3
LICENSING AND PENALTIES
[Selected Provisions]

§7990. Limitation on explosive use.
§7991. License to use explosives.
§7996. Acceptable safety equipment.
§7997. General orders; review; update; suggested changes.

SELECTED PROVISIONS Of The LABOR CODE

GENERAL PROVISIONS [Selected Provisions]

§1. Title.

This Act shall be known as the Labor Code.

§2. Construction of Labor Code.

The provisions of this code, in so far as they are substantially the same as existing provisions relating to the same subject matter, shall be construed as restatements and continuations thereof and not as new enactments.

§5. General provisions govern construction.

Unless the context otherwise requires, the general provisions hereinafter set forth shall govern the construction of this code.

§6. Headings not to affect meaning or intent.

Division, part, chapter, article and section headings contained herein shall not be deemed to govern, limit, modify or in any manner affect the scope, meaning, or intent of the provisions of any division, part, chapter, article, or section hereof.

§7. Administrative powers.

Whenever, by the provisions of this code, an administrative power is granted to a public officer or duty imposed upon such an officer, the power may be exercised or the duty performed by a deputy of the officer or by a person authorized pursuant to law.

Ref.: 8 C.C.R. §§9820, 9821, 9822, 9823, 9824, 9825, 9826, 9827, 9828, 9829, 9830, 9831, 9832, 9833, 9834, 9835, 9836, 9837, 10100, 10100.1, 10100.2, 10106, 10106.1, 10113, 10114, 10114.1, 10114.2, 10114.3, 10114.4, 10115.2.

§8. "Writing"; mailings by certified mail.

Writing includes any form of recorded message capable of comprehension by ordinary visual means. Whenever any notice, report, statement or record is required by this code, it shall be made in writing.

Wherever any notice or other communication is required by this code to be mailed by registered mail by or to any person or corporation, the mailing of such notice or other communication by certified mail shall be deemed to be a sufficient compliance with the requirements of law.

§9. References to code include amendments and additions.

Whenever any reference is made to any portion of this code or of any other law of this State, such reference shall apply to all amendments and additions thereto now or hereafter made.

§10. "Section."

"Section" means a section of this code unless some other statute is specifically mentioned.

§11. Tenses.

The present tense includes the past and future tenses; and the future, the present.

§12. Gender.

The masculine gender includes the feminine and neuter.

§12.1. References to "man" to be changed to "person."

The Legislature hereby declares its intent that the terms "man" or "men" where appropriate shall be deemed "person" or "persons" and any references to the terms "man" or "men" in sections of this code be changed to "person" or "persons" when such code sections are being amended for any purpose. This section is declaratory and not amendatory of existing law.

§12.2. "Spouse" to include "registered domestic partner."

"Spouse" includes "registered domestic partner," as required by Section 297.5 of the Family Code. **Leg.H.** 2016 ch. 50 (SB 1005) §62.

2016 Note: It is the intent of the Legislature that the changes made by this act have only technical and nonsubstantive effect. Hence, no change made by this act shall create any new right, duty, or other obligation that did not exist immediately preceding the effective date of this act, or result in the limitation or termination of any right, duty, or other obligation that existed immediately preceding the effective date of this act. Stats. 2016 ch. 50 (SB 1005) §125.

§13. Singulars and plurals.

The singular number includes the plural, and the plural the singular.

§14. "County."

"County" includes "city and county."

§15. "Shall"; "may."

"Shall" is mandatory and "may" is permissive.

§16. "Oath."

"Oath" includes affirmation.

§17. "Signature" or "subscription" includes mark; acknowledgement of mark.

"Signature" or "subscription" includes mark when the signer or subscriber can not write, such signer's or subscriber's name being written near the mark by a witness who writes his own name near the signer's or subscriber's name; but a signature or subscription by mark can be acknowledged or can serve as a signature or subscription to a sworn statement only when two witnesses so sign their own names thereto.

§18. "Person."

"Person" means any person, association, organization, partnership, business trust, limited liability company, or corporation. **Leg.H.** 1994 ch. 1010.

§18.5. "Agency."

"Agency" means the Labor and Workforce Development Agency. **Leg.H.** 2002 ch. 859 (SB 1236).

§19. "Department."

"Department" means Department of Industrial Relations.

§19.5. "Secretary."

"Secretary" means the Secretary of Labor and Workforce Development. **Leg.H.** 2002 ch. 859 (SB 1236).

§20. "Director."

"Director" means Director of Industrial Relations.

§21. "Labor Commissioner."

"Labor Commissioner" means Chief of the Division of Labor Standards Enforcement.

§22. "Violation."

"Violation" includes a failure to comply with any requirement of the code.

§23. Punishment for offenses.

Except in cases where a different punishment is prescribed, every offense declared by this code to be a misdemeanor is punishable by imprisonment in a county jail, not exceeding six months, or by a fine not exceeding one thousand dollars ($1,000), or both.

Ref.: Hanna §§ 10.26, 10.52.

§24. Invalid provisions.

If any provision of this code, or the application thereof to any person or circumstances, is held invalid the remainder of the code, and the application of its provisions to other persons or circumstances, shall not be affected thereby.

§25. "Sheriff."

"Sheriff" includes "marshal." **Leg.H.** 1996 ch. 872.

§26. Rehabilitated criminals.

Notwithstanding any other provision of this code, no person who has not previously obtained a license regulated by this code shall be denied a license solely on the basis that he has been convicted of a crime if he has obtained a certificate of rehabilitation under Section 4852.01 and following of the Penal Code, and if his probation has been terminated and the information or accusation has been dismissed pursuant to Section 1203.4 of the Penal Code.

§27. Use of term "workers' compensation judge" or "workers' compensation referee" means "workers' compensation administrative law judge."

Whenever the term "workers' compensation judge" or "workers' compensation referee" is used in this code in connection with the workers' compensation law, the term shall mean "workers' compensation administrative law judge." **Leg.H.** 1993 ch. 121, effective July 16, 1993, 1998 ch. 448.

Ref.: Hanna § 1.11[3]; Herlick Handbook § 1.01[s].

§28. "Independent medical examiner" means "qualified medical evaluator."

For injuries occurring on and after January 1, 1991, whenever the term "independent medical examiner" is used in this code, the term shall mean "qualified medical evaluator."

Ref.: Hanna § 27.07[3].

§29. Definition of "medical director."

"Medical director" means the physician appointed by the administrative director pursuant to Section 122. **Leg.H.** 2003 ch. 639 (SB 228).

DIVISION 1
DEPARTMENT OF INDUSTRIAL RELATIONS

CHAPTER 1
GENERAL POWERS AND DUTIES
[Selected Provisions]

§50. Department of Industrial Relations.

There is in the Labor and Workforce Development Agency the Department of Industrial Relations. **Leg.H.** 2002 ch. 859 (SB 1236).

Ref.: Hanna § 1.10.

§50.5. Functions of department.

One of the functions of the Department of Industrial Relations is to foster, promote, and develop the welfare of the wage earners of California, to improve their working conditions, and to advance their opportunities for profitable employment.

§50.6. Enforcement of Fair Labor Standards Act of 1938.

The Department of Industrial Relations may assist and cooperate with the Wage and Hour Division, and the Children's Bureau, United States Department of Labor, in the enforcement within this State of the Fair Labor Standards Act of 1938, and, subject to the regulations of the Administrator of the Wage and Hour Division, or the Chief of the Children's Bureau, and subject to the laws of the State applicable to the receipt and expenditures of money, may be reimbursed by the division or the bureau for the reasonable cost of such assistance and cooperation.

§50.7. Administration and enforcement of OSHA standards.

(a) The Department of Industrial Relations is the state agency designated to be responsible for administering the state plan for the development and enforcement of occupational safety and health standards relating to issues covered by corresponding standards promulgated under the federal Occupational Safety and Health Act of 1970 (Public Law 91-596). The state plan shall be consistent with the provisions of state law governing occupational safety and health, including, but not limited to, Chapter 6 (commencing with Section 140) and Chapter 6.5 (commencing with Section 148) of Division 1, and Division 5 (commencing with Section 6300), of this code.

(b) The budget and budget bill submitted pursuant to Article IV, Section 12 of the California Constitution shall include in the item for the support of the Department of Industrial Relations amounts sufficient to fully carry out the purposes and provisions of the state plan and this code in a manner which assures that the risk of industrial injury, exposure to toxic substances, illness and death to employees will be minimized.

(c) Because Federal grants are available, maximum Federal funding shall be sought and, to the extent possible, the cost of administering the state plan shall be paid by funds obtained from federal grants.

(d) The Governor and the Department of Industrial Relations shall take all steps necessary to prevent withdrawal of approval for the state plan by the Federal government. If Federal approval of the state plan has been withdrawn before passage of this initiative, or if it is withdrawn at any time after passage of this initiative, the Governor shall submit a new state plan immediately so that California shall be approved and shall continue to have access to Federal funds. **Leg.H.** Amended November 8, 1988, by initiative Proposition 95.

Note: Sec. 4 of Prop. 95 provides for direct amendment by the Legislature.

Ref.: Herlick Handbook § 1.09.

§50.8. Occupational health and medicine programs; occupational health centers; reports.

The department shall develop a long range program for upgrading and expanding the resources of the State of California in the area of occupational health and medicine. The program shall include a contractual agreement with the University of California for the creation of occupational health centers affiliated with regional schools of medicine and public health. One such occupational health center shall be situated in the northern part of the state and one in the southern part. The primary function of these occupational health centers shall be the training of occupational physicians and nurses, toxicologists, epidemiologists, and industrial hygienists. In addition, the centers shall serve as referral centers for occupational illnesses and shall engage in research on the causes, diagnosis, and prevention of occupational illnesses.

The centers shall also inform the Division of Occupational Safety and Health Administration of the Department of Industrial Relations, State Department of Health Services, and the Department of Food and Agriculture of their clinical and research findings.

§50.9. Director's comments.

In furtherance of the provisions of Section 50.5, the director, or the Director of Employment Development, may comment on the impact of actions or projects proposed by public agencies on opportunities for profitable employment, and such agencies shall consider such comments in their decisions.

§51. Appointment of director.

The department shall be conducted under the control of an executive officer known as Director of Industrial Relations. The Director of Industrial Relations shall be appointed by the Governor with the advice and consent of the Senate and hold office at the pleasure of the Governor and shall receive an annual salary provided for by Chapter 6 (commencing with Section 11550) of Part 1 of Division 3 of Title 2 of the Government Code.

Ref.: 8 C.C.R. §15600.

§52. Application of Government Code to state departments.

Except as otherwise prescribed in this code, the provisions of the Government Code relating to departments of the State shall govern and apply to the conduct of the department.

§53. Head of department.

Whenever in Section 1001 or in Part 1 (commencing with Section 11000) of Division 3 of Title 2 of the Government Code "head of the department" or similar designation occurs, the same shall, for the purposes of this code, mean the director, except that in respect to matters which by the express provisions of this code are committed to or retained under the jurisdiction of the Division of Workers' Compensation, the State Compensation Insurance Fund, the Occupational Safety and Health Standards Board, the Occupational Safety and Health Appeals Board, or the Industrial Welfare Commission the designation shall mean the Division of Workers' Compensation, the Administrative Director of the Division of Workers' Compensation, the Workers' Compensation Appeals Board, the State Compensation Insurance Fund, the Occupational Safety and Health Standards Board, the Occupational Safety and Health Appeals Board, or the Industrial Welfare Commission, as the case may be. **Leg.H.** 1994 chs. 146, 1097.

Ref.: 8 C.C.R. §§10106, 10106.1; Hanna § 1.10.

§54. Duties of director.

The director shall perform all duties, exercise all powers and jurisdiction, assume and discharge all responsibilities, and carry out and effect all purposes vested by law in the department, except as otherwise expressly provided by this code.

Ref.: 8 C.C.R. §§15202, 15250.1, 15300, 15301, 15302, 15303, 15354, 15420, 15422, 15424, 15425, 15426, 15427, 15428.

§54.5. Legal services.

The director may appoint an attorney and assistants licensed to practice law in this state. In the absence of an appointment, the attorney for the Division of Workers' Compensation shall also perform legal services for the department as the Director of Industrial Relations may direct. **Leg.H.** 1994 chs. 146, 1097.

§55. Administrative organization.

For the purpose of administration the director shall organize the department subject to the approval of the Governor, in the manner he deems necessary properly to segregate and conduct the work of the department. Notwithstanding any provision in this code to the contrary, the director may require any division in the department to assist in the enforcement of any or all laws within the jurisdiction of the department. Except as provided in Section 18930 of the Health and Safety Code, the director may, in accordance with the provisions of Chapter 4.5 (commencing with Section 11371), Part 1, Division 3, Title 2 of the Government Code, make rules and regulations that are reasonably necessary to carry out the provisions of this chapter and to effectuate its purposes. The provisions of this section, however, shall not apply to the Division of Workers' Compensation or the State Compensation Insurance Fund, except as to any power or jurisdiction within those divisions as may have been specifically conferred upon the director by law. **Leg.H.** 1994 chs. 146, 1097.

Ref.: 8 C.C.R. §§15202, 15300, 15301, 15302, 15303, 15354, 15420, 15422, 15424, 15425, 15426, 15427, 15428.

§56. Departmental divisions.

The work of the department shall be divided into at least five divisions known as the Division of Workers' Compensation, the Division of Occupational Safety and Health, the Division of Labor Standards Enforcement, the Division of Apprenticeship Standards, and the State Compensation Insurance Fund. **Leg.H.** 1994 chs. 146, 1097, 2012 ch. 46 (SB 1038) §77, effective June 27, 2012.

Ref.: Hanna §§ 1.10, 1.16[1], 1.17.

§57. Division chiefs.

Each division shall be in charge of a chief who shall be appointed by the Governor and shall receive a salary fixed in accordance with law, and shall serve at the pleasure of the director.

§57.1. Chief's salary; appointments; salaries.

(a) The Chief of the Division of Occupational Safety and Health shall receive an annual salary as provided by Chapter 6 (commencing with Section 11550) of Part 1 of Division 3 of Title 2 of the Government Code.

(b) All officers or employees of the Division of Occupational Safety and Health employed after the operative date of this section shall be appointed by the director in accordance with the provisions of the State Civil Service Act. Notwithstanding the foregoing, two deputy chiefs of the Division of Occupational Safety and Health shall be appointed by the Governor, with the advice of the Director of Industrial Relations, to serve at the pleasure of the Director of Industrial Relations. The two deputy chiefs shall be exempt from civil service. The annual salaries of the two exempted deputy chiefs shall be fixed by the Director of Industrial Relations, subject to the approval of the Director of Finance.

§57.5. Board of Directors of State Compensation Insurance Fund.

All duties, powers, and jurisdiction relating to the administration of the State Compensation Insurance Fund shall be vested in the Board of Directors of the State Compensation Insurance Fund.

Ref.: Hanna § 1.20[3].

§58. Title to departmental property.

The department shall have possession and control of all records, books, papers, offices, equipment, supplies, moneys, funds, appropriations, land, and other property, real and personal, held for the benefit or use of all commissions, divisions, and offices of the department and the title to all such property held for the use and benefit of the State is hereby transferred to the State.

§59. Departmental law enforcement.

The department through its appropriate officers shall administer and enforce all laws imposing any duty, power, or function upon the offices or officers of the department.

Ref.: 8 C.C.R. §§10106.5, 15201, 15202, 15203.1, 15203.2, 15203.3, 15203.4, 15203.5, 15203.6, 15203.7, 15203.8, 15203.9, 15203.10, 15204, 15205, 15210, 15210.1, 15210.2, 15210.3, 15211.2, 15211.3, 15212, 15213, 15214, 15215, 15216, 15230, 15231, 15232, 15233, 15234, 15251, 15300, 15301, 15302, 15303, 15353, 15354, 15400, 15400.1, 15400.2, 15402, 15402.1, 15402.2, 15402.3, 15402.4, 15403, 15403.1, 15404, 15404.1, 15404.2, 15405, 15420, 15422, 15424, 15425, 15426, 15427, 15428, 15430, 15431, 15431.1, 15431.2, 15432, 15433, 15434, 15435, 15436, 15437, 15438, 15450, 15452, 15454, 15458, 15459, 15463, 15470.

§60. Administration and enforcement of code.

Except as otherwise provided, the provisions of Divisions 4 and 4.5 of this code shall be administered and enforced by the Division of Workers' Compensation. **Leg.H.** 1994 ch. 146.

Ref.: 8 C.C.R. §10106.5; Hanna § 1.10.

§60.5. Division of Occupational Safety and Health: duties and powers.

(a) The provisions of Part 1 of Division 5 of this code shall be administered and enforced by the department through the Division of Occupational Safety and Health, subject to the direction of the director pursuant to Section 50.7.

(b) The Division of Occupational Safety and Health succeeds to, and is vested with, all of the powers, duties, purposes, responsibilities, and jurisdiction of the Division of Industrial Safety, which is hereby abolished, and any other jurisdiction conferred by law.

(c) All powers, duties, and responsibilities of the Chief of the Division of Industrial Safety are hereby transferred to the Chief of the Division of Occupational Safety and Health.

(d) Any regulation or other action made, prescribed, issued, granted, or performed by the abolished Division of Industrial Safety in the administration of a function transferred pursuant to subdivision (b) shall remain in effect and shall be deemed to be a regulation or action of the Division of Occupational Safety and Health unless and until repealed, modified, or rescinded by such division.

(e) Whenever any reference is made in any law to the abolished Division of Industrial Safety, it shall be deemed to be a reference to, and to mean, the Division of Occupational Safety and Health.

Ref.: Hanna § 1.16[1]; Herlick Handbook § 1.09.

§61. Enforcement of chapter.

The provisions of Chapter 1 (commencing with Section 1171) of Part 4 of Division 2 shall be administered and enforced by the department through the Division of Labor Standards Enforcement.

§62. Expenditures.

The department may expend money appropriated for the administration of the provisions of the laws, the enforcement of which is committed to the department. The department may expend such money for the use, support, or maintenance of any commission or office of the department. Such expenditures by the department shall be made in accordance with law in carrying on the work for which such appropriations were made.

§62.5. Workers' Compensation Administration Revolving Fund; Uninsured Employers Benefits Trust Fund; Subsequent Injuries Benefits Trust Fund; Occupational Safety and Health Fund; Labor Enforcement and Compliance Fund; surcharges on employers.

(a)(1) The Workers' Compensation Administration Revolving Fund is hereby created as a special account in the State Treasury. Money in the fund may be expended by the department, upon appropriation by the Legislature, for all of the following purposes, and may not be used or borrowed for any other purpose:

(A) For the administration of the workers' compensation program set forth in this division and Division 4 (commencing with Section 3200), other than the activities financed pursuant to paragraph (2) of subdivision (a) of Section 3702.5.

(B) For the Return-to-Work Program set forth in Section 139.48.

(C) For the enforcement of the insurance coverage program established and maintained by the Labor Commissioner pursuant to Section 90.3.

(2) The fund shall consist of surcharges made pursuant to paragraph (1) of subdivision (f).

(b)(1) The Uninsured Employers Benefits Trust Fund is hereby created as a special trust fund account in the State Treasury, of which the director is trustee, and its sources of funds are as provided in paragraph (1) of subdivision (f). Notwithstanding Section 13340 of the Government Code, the fund is continuously appropriated for the payment of nonadministrative expenses of the workers' compensation program for workers injured while employed by uninsured employers in accordance with Article 2 (commencing with Section 3710) of Chapter 4 of Part 1 of Division 4, and shall not be used for any other purpose. All moneys collected shall be retained in the trust fund until paid as benefits to workers injured while employed by uninsured employers. Nonadministrative expenses include audits and reports of services prepared pursuant to subdivision (b) of Section 3716.1. The surcharge amount for this fund shall be stated separately.

(2) Notwithstanding any other provision of law, all references to the Uninsured Employers Fund shall mean the Uninsured Employers Benefits Trust Fund.

(3) Notwithstanding paragraph (1), in the event that budgetary restrictions or impasse prevent the timely payment of administrative expenses from the Workers' Compensation Administration Revolving Fund, those expenses shall be advanced from the Uninsured Employers Benefits Trust Fund. Expense advances made pursuant to this paragraph shall be reimbursed in full to the Uninsured Employers Benefits Trust Fund upon enactment of the annual Budget Act.

(4) Any moneys from penalties collected pursuant to Section 3722 as a result of the insurance coverage program established under Section 90.3 shall be deposited in the State Treasury to the credit of the Workers' Compensation

Labor

Administration Revolving Fund created under this section, to cover expenses incurred by the director under the insurance coverage program. The amount of any penalties in excess of payment of administrative expenses incurred by the director for the insurance coverage program established under Section 90.3 shall be deposited in the State Treasury to the credit of the Uninsured Employers Benefits Trust Fund for nonadministrative expenses, as prescribed in paragraph (1), and notwithstanding paragraph (1), shall only be available upon appropriation by the Legislature.

(c)(1) The Subsequent Injuries Benefits Trust Fund is hereby created as a special trust fund account in the State Treasury, of which the director is trustee, and its sources of funds are as provided in paragraph (1) of subdivision (f). Notwithstanding Section 13340 of the Government Code, the fund is continuously appropriated for the nonadministrative expenses of the workers' compensation program for workers who have suffered serious injury and who are suffering from previous and serious permanent disabilities or physical impairments, in accordance with Article 5 (commencing with Section 4751) of Chapter 2 of Part 2 of Division 4, and Section 4 of Article XIV of the California Constitution, and shall not be used for any other purpose. All moneys collected shall be retained in the trust fund until paid as benefits to workers who have suffered serious injury and who are suffering from previous and serious permanent disabilities or physical impairments. Nonadministrative expenses include audits and reports of services pursuant to subdivision (c) of Section 4755. The surcharge amount for this fund shall be stated separately.

(2) Notwithstanding any other law, all references to the Subsequent Injuries Fund shall mean the Subsequent Injuries Benefits Trust Fund.

(3) Notwithstanding paragraph (1), in the event that budgetary restrictions or impasse prevent the timely payment of administrative expenses from the Workers' Compensation Administration Revolving Fund, those expenses shall be advanced from the Subsequent Injuries Benefits Trust Fund. Expense advances made pursuant to this paragraph shall be reimbursed in full to the Subsequent Injuries Benefits Trust Fund upon enactment of the annual Budget Act.

(d)(1) The Occupational Safety and Health Fund is hereby created as a special account in the State Treasury. Moneys in the account may be expended by the department, upon appropriation by the Legislature, for support of the Division of Occupational Safety and Health, the Occupational Safety and Health Standards Board, and the Occupational Safety and Health Appeals Board, and the activities these entities perform as set forth in this division, and Division 5 (commencing with Section 6300).

(2) On and after the effective date of the act amending this section to add this paragraph in the 2013–14 Regular Session of the Legislature, any moneys in the Cal-OSHA Targeted Inspection and Consultation Fund and any assets, liabilities, revenues, expenditures, and encumbrances of that fund, less five million dollars ($5,000,000), shall be transferred to the Occupational Safety and Health Fund. On June 30, 2014, the remaining five million dollars ($5,000,000) in the Cal-OSHA Targeted Inspection and Consultation Fund, or any remaining balance in that fund, shall be transferred to, and become part of, the Occupational Safety and Health Fund.

(e) The Labor Enforcement and Compliance Fund is hereby created as a special account in the State Treasury. Moneys in the fund may be expended by the department, upon appropriation by the Legislature, for the support of the activities that the Division of Labor Standards Enforcement performs pursuant to this division and Division 2 (commencing with Section 200), Division 3 (commencing with Section 2700), and Division 4 (commencing with Section 3200). The fund shall consist of surcharges imposed pursuant to paragraph (3) of subdivision (f).

(f)(1) Separate surcharges shall be levied by the director upon all employers, as defined in Section 3300, for purposes of deposit in the Workers' Compensation Administration Revolving Fund, the Uninsured Employers Benefits Trust Fund, the Subsequent Injuries Benefits Trust Fund, and the Occupational Safety and Health Fund. The total amount of the surcharges shall be allocated between self-insured employers and insured employers in proportion to payroll respectively paid in the most recent year for which payroll information is available. The director shall adopt reasonable regulations governing the manner of collection of the surcharges. The regulations shall require the surcharges to be paid by self-insurers to be expressed as a percentage of indemnity paid during the most recent year for which information is available, and the surcharges to be paid by insured employers to be expressed as a percentage of premium. In no event shall the surcharges paid by insured employers be considered a premium for computation of a gross premium tax or agents' commission. In no event shall the total amount of the surcharges paid by insured and self-insured employers exceed the amounts reasonably necessary to carry out the purposes of this section.

(2) The surcharge levied by the director for the Occupational Safety and Health Fund, pursuant to paragraph (1), shall not generate revenues in excess of fifty-seven million dollars ($57,000,000) on and after the 2013–14 fiscal year, adjusted for each fiscal year as appropriate to fund any increases in the appropriation as approved by the Legislature, and to reconcile any over/under assessments from previous fiscal years pursuant to Sections 15606 and 15609 of Title 8 of the California Code of Regulations. For the 2013–14 fiscal year only, the revenue cap established in this paragraph shall be reduced by an amount equivalent to the balance transferred from the Cal-OSHA Targeted Inspection and Consultation Fund established in Section 62.7, less any amount of that balance loaned to the State Public Works Enforcement Fund, to the Occupational Safety and Health Fund pursuant to subdivision (d).

(3) A separate surcharge shall be levied by the director upon all employers, as defined in Section 3300, for purposes of deposit in the Labor Enforcement and Compliance Fund. The total amount of the surcharges shall be allocated between employers in proportion to payroll respectively paid in the most recent year for which payroll information is available. The director shall adopt reasonable regulations governing the manner of collection of the surcharges. In no event shall the total amount of the surcharges paid by employers exceed the amounts reasonably necessary to carry out the purposes of this section.

(4) The surcharge levied by the director for the Labor Enforcement and Compliance Fund shall not exceed forty-six million dollars ($46,000,000) in the 2013–14 fiscal

year, adjusted as appropriate to fund any increases in the appropriation as approved by the Legislature, and to reconcile any over/under assessments from previous fiscal years pursuant to Sections 15606 and 15609 of Title 8 of the California Code of Regulations.

(5) The regulations adopted pursuant to paragraph (1) to (4), inclusive, shall be exempt from the rulemaking provisions of the Administrative Procedure Act (Chapter 3.5 (commencing with Section 11340) of Part 1 of Division 3 of Title 2 of the Government Code). **Leg.H.** 2009 ch. 341 (SB 73) §12, 2012 ch. 363 (SB 863) §4, 2013 ch. 28 (SB 71) §33, effective June 27, 2013.

2012 Notes: The Legislature finds and declares all of the following:

(a) That Section 4 of Article XIV of the California Constitution authorizes the creation of a workers' compensation system that includes adequate provision for the comfort, health and safety, and general welfare of workers and their dependents to relieve them of the consequences of any work-related injury or death, irrespective of the fault of any party and requires the administration of the workers' compensation system to accomplish substantial justice in all cases expeditiously, inexpensively, and without encumbrance of any character, all of which matters are expressly declared to be the social public policy of this state.

(b) That the current system of determining permanent disability has become excessively litigious, time consuming, procedurally burdensome and unpredictable, and that the provisions of this act will produce the necessary uniformity, consistency, and objectivity of outcomes, in accordance with the constitutional mandate to accomplish substantial justice in all cases expeditiously, inexpensively, and without encumbrance of any character, and that in enacting subdivision (c) of Section 4660.1 of the Labor Code, the Legislature intends to eliminate questionable claims of disability when alleged to be caused by a disabling physical injury arising out of and in the course of employment while guaranteeing medical treatment as required by Division 4 (commencing with Section 3200) of the Labor Code.

(c) That in enacting this act, it is not the intent of the Legislature to overrule the holding in Milpitas Unified School District v. Workers Comp. Appeals Bd. (Guzman) (2010) 187 Cal.App.4th 808.

(d) That the current system of resolving disputes over the medical necessity of requested treatment is costly, time consuming, and does not uniformly result in the provision of treatment that adheres to the highest standards of evidence-based medicine, adversely affecting the health and safety of workers injured in the course of employment.

(e) That having medical professionals ultimately determine the necessity of requested treatment furthers the social policy of this state in reference to using evidence-based medicine to provide injured workers with the highest quality of medical care and that the provision of the act establishing independent medical review are necessary to implement that policy.

(f) That the performance of independent medical review is a service of such a special and unique nature that it must be contracted pursuant to paragraph (3) of subdivision (b) of Section 19130 of the Government Code, and that independent medical review is a new state function pursuant to paragraph (2) of subdivision (b) of Section 19130 of the Government Code that will be more expeditious, more economical, and more scientifically sound than the existing function of medical necessity determinations performed by qualified medical evaluators appointed pursuant to Section 139.2 of the Labor Code. The existing process of appointing qualified medical evaluators to examine patients and resolve treatment disputes is costly and time-consuming, and it prolongs disputes and causes delays in medical treatment for injured workers. Additionally, the process of selection of qualified medical evaluators can bias the outcomes. Timely and medically sound determinations of disputes over appropriate medical treatment require the independent and unbiased medical expertise of specialists that are not available through the civil service system.

(g) That the establishment of independent medical review and provision for limited appeal of decisions resulting from independent medical review are a necessary exercise of the Legislature's plenary power to provide for the settlement of any disputes arising under the workers' compensation laws of this state and to control the manner of review of such decisions.

(h) That the performance of independent bill review is a service of such a special and unique nature that it must be contracted pursuant to paragraph (3) of subdivision (b) of Section 19130 of the Government Code, and that independent bill review is a new state function pursuant to paragraph (2) of subdivision (b) of Section 19130 of the Government Code. Existing law provides no method of medical billing dispute resolution short of litigation. Existing law does not provide for medical billing and payment experts to resolve billing disputes, and billing issues are frequently submitted to workers' compensation judges without the benefit of independent and unbiased findings on these issues. Medical billing and payment systems are a field of technical and specialized expertise, requiring services that are not available through the civil service system. The need for independent and unbiased findings and determinations requires that this new function be contracted pursuant to subdivision (b) of Section 19130 of the Government Code. Stats. 2012 ch. 363 (SB 863) §1.

This act shall apply to all pending matters, regardless of date of injury, unless otherwise specified in this act, but shall not be a basis to rescind, alter, amend, or reopen any final award of workers' compensation benefits. Stats. 2012 ch. 363 (SB 863) §84.

Ref.: Herlick Handbook § 1.01[3][a].

§62.6. Assessments.

(a) The director shall levy and collect assessments from employers in accordance with subdivision (b), as necessary, to collect the aggregate amount determined by the Fraud Assessment Commission pursuant to Section 1872.83 of the Insurance Code. Revenues derived from the assessments shall be deposited in the Workers' Compensation Fraud Account in the Insurance Fund and shall only be expended, upon appropriation by the Legislature, for the investigation and prosecution of workers' compensation fraud and the willful failure to secure payment of workers' compensation, as prescribed by Section 1872.83 of the Insurance Code.

(b) Assessments shall be levied by the director upon all employers as defined in Section 3300. The total amount of the assessment shall be allocated between self-insured employers and insured employers in proportion to payroll respectively paid in the most recent year for which payroll information is available. The director shall promulgate reasonable rules and regulations governing the manner of collection of the assessment. The rules and regulations shall require the assessment to be paid by self-insurers to be expressed as a percentage of indemnity paid during the most recent year for which information is available, and the assessment to be paid by insured employers to be expressed as a percentage of premium. In no event shall the assessment paid by insured employers be considered a premium for computation of a gross premium tax or agents' commission. **Leg.H.** 1991 chs. 116, 934, 2002 ch. 6 (AB 749).

Ref.: 8 C.C.R. §§15600, 15601.5, 15602, 15603, 15605, 15606, 15607, 15608, 15609.

Labor

§62.8. Appropriation; loan; repayment.

Five million dollars ($5,000,000) is hereby appropriated for transfer by the State Controller upon order of the Director of Finance from the Cal-OSHA Targeted Inspection and Consultation Fund as a loan to the State Public Works Enforcement Fund. This loan shall be repaid to the Occupational Safety and Health Fund by June 30, 2015. This loan shall be repaid with interest calculated at the rate earned by the Pooled Money Investment Account at the time of the transfer. **Leg.H.** 2013 ch. 28 (SB 71) §35, effective June 27, 2013.

CHAPTER 3
COMMISSION ON HEALTH AND SAFETY AND WORKERS' COMPENSATION

§75. Composition of Commission; selection of chair; terms; meetings.

(a) There is in the department the Commission on Health and Safety and Workers' Compensation. The commission shall be composed of eight voting members. Four voting members shall represent organized labor, and four voting members shall represent employers. Not more than one employer member shall represent public agencies. Two of the employer and two of the labor members shall be appointed by the Governor. The Senate Committee on Rules and the Speaker of the Assembly shall each appoint one employer and one labor representative. The public employer representative shall be appointed by the Governor. No action of the commission shall be valid unless agreed to by a majority of the membership and by not less than two members representing organized labor and two members representing employers.

(b) The commission shall select one of the members representing organized labor to chair the commission during the 1994 calendar year, and thereafter the commission shall alternatively select an employer and organized labor representative to chair the commission for one-year terms.

(c) The initial terms of the members of the commission shall be four years, and they shall hold office until the appointment of a successor. However, the initial terms of one employer and one labor member appointed by the Governor shall expire on December 31, 1995; the initial terms of the members appointed by the Senate Committee on Rules shall expire December 31, 1996; the initial terms of the members appointed by the Speaker of the Assembly shall expire on December 31, 1997; and the initial term of one employer and one labor member appointed by the Governor shall expire on December 31, 1998. Any vacancy shall be filled by appointment to the unexpired term.

(d) The commission shall meet every other month and upon the call of the chair. Meetings shall be open to the public. Members of the commission shall receive one hundred dollars ($100) for each day of their actual attendance at meetings of the commission and other official business of the commission and shall also receive their actual and necessary traveling expenses incurred in the performance of their duty as a member. Payment of per diem and traveling expenses shall be made from the Workers' Compensation Administration Revolving Fund, when appropriated by the Legislature. **Leg.H.** 1993 ch. 227, 2002 ch. 6 (AB 749).

Ref.: Hanna §§ 1.10, 1.18; Herlick Handbook § 1.10.

§76. Commission personnel.

The commission may employ officers, assistants, experts, and other employees it deems necessary. All personnel of the commission shall be under the supervision of the chair or an executive officer to whom he or she delegates this responsibility. All personnel shall be appointed pursuant to the State Civil Service Act (Part 2 (commencing with Section 18500) of Division 5 of Title 2 of the Government Code), except for the one exemption allowed by subdivision (e) of Section 4 of Article VII of the California Constitution. **Leg.H.** 1993 ch. 227.

Ref.: Herlick Handbook § 1.10.

§77. Commission duties and powers.

(a) The commission shall conduct a continuing examination of the workers' compensation system, as defined in Section 4 of Article XIV of the California Constitution, and of the state's activities to prevent industrial injuries and occupational diseases. The commission may conduct or contract for studies it deems necessary to carry out its responsibilities. In carrying out its duties, the commission shall examine other states' workers' compensation programs and activities to prevent industrial injuries and occupational diseases. All state departments and agencies, and any rating organization licensed by the Insurance Commissioner pursuant to Article 3 (commencing with Section 11750) of Chapter 3 of Part 3 of Division 2 of the Insurance Code, shall cooperate with the commission and upon reasonable request provide information and data in their possession that the commission deems necessary for the purpose of carrying out its responsibilities. The commission shall issue an annual report on the state of the workers' compensation system, including recommendations for administrative or legislative modifications which would improve the operation of the system. The report shall be made available to the Governor, the Legislature, and the public on request.

(b) On or before July 1, 2003, and periodically thereafter as it deems necessary, the commission shall issue a report and recommendations on the improvement and simplification of the notices required to be provided by insurers and self-insured employers.

(c) The commission succeeds to, and is vested with, all of the powers, duties, purposes, responsibilities, and jurisdiction of the Health and Safety Commission which is hereby abolished, including the administration of grants to assist in establishing effective occupational injury and illness prevention programs. **Leg.H.** 1993 ch. 227, 2002 ch. 6 (AB 749).

Ref.: Hanna § 1.18; Herlick Handbook § 1.10.

§77.5. Medical treatment utilization standards—Survey and evaluation of standards of care; report to administrative director.

(a) On or before July 1, 2004, the commission shall conduct a survey and evaluation of evidence-based, peer-reviewed, nationally recognized standards of care, including existing medical treatment utilization standards, including independent medical review, as used in other states, at the national level, and in other medical benefit systems. The survey shall be updated periodically.

(b) On or before October 1, 2004, the commission shall issue a report of its findings and recommendations to the administrative director for purposes of the adoption of a medical treatment utilization schedule. **Leg.H.** 2003 ch. 639 (SB 228).

Ref.: Hanna § 1.18; Herlick Handbook § 1.10.

§77.7. [Repealed January 1, 2024] Study; requirements; report.

(a) On or before January 1, 2021, the commission shall, in partnership with the County of Los Angeles and relevant labor organizations, submit a study to the Legislature, the Occupational Safety and Health Standards Board, and the Los Angeles County Board of Supervisors on the risk of exposure to carcinogenic materials and incidence of occupational cancer in mechanics who repair and clean firefighting vehicles. At a minimum, the study shall include all of the following:

(1) Site visits at a representative sample of facilities, including, but not limited to, facilities in the County of Los Angeles, where firefighting equipment is cleaned and repaired.

(2) Interviews and surveys with current and former mechanics of firefighting equipment in a sample of facilities regarding the frequency of exposure to potential carcinogens, use and availability of safety equipment, and experience or knowledge of cancer incidence among current or former mechanics who cleaned or repaired firefighting equipment.

(3) A measurement of the current levels of carcinogenic material exposure to mechanics who repair and clean firefighting vehicles in the County of Los Angeles and other facilities included in the study, in order to develop a baseline of carcinogenic material exposure.

(b)(1) A report to be submitted pursuant to subdivision (a) shall be submitted in compliance with Section 9795 of the Government Code.

(2) Pursuant to Section 10231.5 of the Government Code, this section is repealed on January 1, 2024. **Leg.H.** 2019 ch. 717 (AB 1400) §1.

§77.8. Commission on Health and Safety and Workers' Compensation to conduct study of impacts of COVID-19; report.

The Commission on Health and Safety and Workers' Compensation shall conduct a study of the impacts claims of COVID-19 have had on the workers' compensation system, including overall impacts on indemnity benefits, medical benefits, and death benefits, including differences in the impacts across differing occupational groups, and including the effect of Sections 3212.87 and 3212.88. A preliminary report or a final report shall be delivered to the Legislature, pursuant to Section 9795 of the Government Code, and the Governor by December 31, 2021, and the final report shall be delivered to the Legislature, pursuant to Section 9795 of the Government Code, and the Governor no later than April 30, 2022. **Leg.H.** 2020 ch. 85 (SB 1159) §1, effective September 17, 2020.

§78. Review of grant applications.

(a) The commission shall review and approve applications from employers and employee organizations, as well as applications submitted jointly by an employer organization and an employee organization, for grants to assist in establishing effective occupational injury and illness prevention programs. The commission shall establish policies for the evaluation of these applications and shall give priority to applications proposing to target high-risk industries and occupations, including those with high injury or illness rates, and those in which employees are exposed to one or more hazardous substances or conditions or where there is a demonstrated need for research to determine effective strategies for the prevention of occupational illnesses or injuries.

(b) Civil and administrative penalties assessed and collected pursuant to Sections 129.5 and 4628 shall be deposited in the Workers' Compensation Administration Revolving Fund. Moneys in the fund, when appropriated by the Legislature to fund the grants under subdivision (a) and other activities and expenses of the commission set forth in this code, shall be expended by the department, upon approval by the commission. **Leg.H.** 1993 ch. 227, 2002 chs. 6 (AB 749), 866 (AB 486).

Ref.: Hanna § 1.18; Herlick Handbook § 1.10.

CHAPTER 4 DIVISION OF LABOR STANDARDS ENFORCEMENT [Selected Provisions]

§90.3. Enforcement of payment for workers' compensation coverage; targeted program; contact and inspection; annual report.

(a) It is the policy of this state to vigorously enforce the laws requiring employers to secure the payment of compensation as required by Section 3700 and to protect employers who comply with the law from those who attempt to gain a competitive advantage at the expense of their workers by failing to secure the payment of compensation.

(b) In order to ensure that the laws requiring employers to secure the payment of compensation are adequately enforced, the Labor Commissioner shall establish and maintain a program that systematically identifies unlawfully uninsured employers. The Labor Commissioner, in consultation with the Administrative Director of the Division of Workers' Compensation and the director, may prioritize targets for the program in consideration of available resources. The employers shall be identified from data from the Uninsured Employers' Fund, the Employment Development Department, the rating organizations licensed by the Insurance Commissioner pursuant to Article 3 (commencing with Section 11750) of Chapter 3 of Part 3 of Division 2 of the Insurance Code, and any other sources deemed likely to lead to the identification of unlawfully uninsured employers. All state departments and agencies and any rating organization licensed by the Insurance Commissioner pursuant to Article 3 (commencing with Section 11750) of Chapter 3 of Part 3 of Division 2 of the Insurance Code shall cooperate with the Labor Commissioner and on reasonable request provide information and data in their possession reasonably necessary to carry out the program.

(c) As part of the program, the Labor Commissioner shall establish procedures for ensuring that employers with payroll but with no record of workers' compensation coverage are contacted and, if no valid reason for the lack of record of coverage is shown, inspected on a priority basis.

(d) The Labor Commissioner shall annually, not later than March 1, prepare a report concerning the effectiveness of the program, publish it on the Labor Commissioner's Web site, as well as notify the Legislature, the Governor, the Insurance Commissioner, and the Administrative Director of the Division of Workers' Compensation of the report's availability. The report shall include, but not be limited to, all of the following:

(1) The number of employers identified from records of the Employment Development Department who were screened for matching records of insurance coverage or self-insurance.

(2) The number of employers identified from records of the Employment Development Department that were matched to records of insurance coverage or self-insurance.

(3) The number of employers identified from records of the Employment Development Department that were notified that there was no record of their insurance coverage.

(4) The number of employers responding to the notices, and the nature of the responses, including the number of employers who failed to provide satisfactory proof of workers' compensation coverage and including information about the reasons that employers who provided satisfactory proof of coverage were not appropriately recognized in the comparison performed under subdivision (b). The report may include recommendations to improve the accuracy and efficiency of the program in screening for unlawfully uninsured employers.

(5) The number of employers identified as unlawfully uninsured from records of the Uninsured Employers' Benefits Trust Fund or from records of the Division of Workers' Compensation, and the number of those employers that are also identifiable from the records of the Employment Development Department. These statistics shall be reported in a manner to permit analysis and estimation of the percentage of unlawfully uninsured employers that do not report wages to the Employment Development Department.

(6) The number of employers inspected.

(7) The number and amount of penalties assessed pursuant to Section 3722 as a result of the program.

(8) The number and amount of penalties collected pursuant to Section 3722 as a result of the program.

(e) The allocation of funds from the Workers' Compensation Administration Revolving Fund pursuant to subdivision (a) of Section 62.5 shall not increase the total amount of surcharges pursuant to subdivision (e) of Section 62.5. Startup costs for this program shall be allocated from the fiscal year 2007–08 surcharges collected. The total amount allocated for this program under subdivision (a) of Section 62.5 in subsequent years shall not exceed the amount of penalties collected pursuant to Section 3722 as a result of the program. **Leg.H.** 2002 ch. 6 (AB 749), 2007 ch. 662 (SB 869) §2.

§90.5. Enforcement of minimum labor standards; establishment of field units; adoption of plan; report to Legislature.

(a) It is the policy of this state to vigorously enforce minimum labor standards in order to ensure employees are not required or permitted to work under substandard unlawful conditions or for employers that have not secured the payment of compensation, and to protect employers who comply with the law from those who attempt to gain a competitive advantage at the expense of their workers by failing to comply with minimum labor standards.

(b) In order to ensure that minimum labor standards are adequately enforced, the Labor Commissioner shall establish and maintain a field enforcement unit, which shall be administratively and physically separate from offices of the division that accept and determine individual employee complaints. The unit shall have offices in Los Angeles, San Francisco, San Jose, San Diego, Sacramento, and any other locations that the Labor Commissioner deems appropriate. The unit shall have primary responsibility for administering and enforcing those statutes and regulations most effectively enforced through field investigations, including Sections 226, 1021, 1021.5, 1193.5, 1193.6, 1194.5, 1197, 1198, 1771, 1776, 1777.5, 2651, 2673, 2675, and 3700, in accordance with the plan adopted by the Labor Commissioner pursuant to subdivision (c). Nothing in this section shall be construed to limit the authority of this unit in enforcing any statute or regulation in the course of its investigations.

(c) The Labor Commissioner shall adopt an enforcement plan for the field enforcement unit. The plan shall identify priorities for investigations to be undertaken by the unit that ensure the available resources will be concentrated in industries, occupations, and areas in which employees are relatively low paid and unskilled, and those in which there has been a history of violations of the statutes cited in subdivision (b), and those with high rates of noncompliance with Section 3700.

(d) The Labor Commissioner shall annually report to the Legislature, not later than March 1, concerning the effectiveness of the field enforcement unit. The report shall include, but not be limited to, all of the following:

(1) The enforcement plan adopted by the Labor Commissioner pursuant to subdivision (c), and the rationale for the priorities identified in the plan.

(2) The number of establishments investigated by the unit, and the number of types of violations found.

(3) The amount of wages found to be unlawfully withheld from workers, and the amount of unpaid wages recovered for workers.

(4) The amount of penalties and unpaid wages transferred to the General Fund as a result of the efforts of the unit. **Leg.H.** 2002 ch. 6 (AB 749).

§96. Assignment of claims.

The Labor Commissioner and his or her deputies and representatives authorized by him or her in writing shall, upon the filing of a claim therefor by an employee, or an employee representative authorized in writing by an employee, with the Labor Commissioner, take assignments of:

(a) Wage claims and incidental expense accounts and advances.

(b) Mechanics' and other liens of employees.

(c) Claims based on "stop orders" for wages and on bonds for labor.

(d) Claims for damages for misrepresentations of conditions of employment.

(e) Claims for unreturned bond money of employees.

(f) Claims for penalties for nonpayment of wages.

(g) Claims for the return of workers' tools in the illegal possession of another person.

(h) Claims for vacation pay, severance pay, or other compensation supplemental to a wage agreement.

(i) Awards for workers' compensation benefits in which the Workers' Compensation Appeals Board has found that the employer has failed to secure payment of compensation and where the award remains unpaid more than 10 days after having become final.

(j) Claims for loss of wages as the result of discharge from employment for the garnishment of wages.

(k) Claims for loss of wages as the result of demotion, suspension, or discharge from employment for lawful conduct occurring during nonworking hours away from the employer's premises. **Leg.H.** 1999 ch. 692.

Ref.: Hanna §§ 27.05, 30.01.

§96.1. [Repealed January 1, 2031] Report to Legislature; wage claims; alleged violations; amount of unpaid wages, penalties, and other compensation.

(a) By March 1, 2022, and by that date annually thereafter, the division shall submit a report to the Department of Finance and the budget committees and relevant policy committees of the Legislature that includes the following information pertaining to the prior calendar year:

(1) The number of wage claims submitted.

(2) The number and type of alleged labor law violations in those claims.

(3) The average estimated prehearing amounts of unpaid wages, penalties, and other demands for compensation, including, but not limited to, liquidated damages.

(4) The total of unpaid wages, penalties, and other compensation, including, but not limited to, liquidated damages, agreed to in settlements enforceable by the Labor Commissioner.

(5) The total of unpaid wages, penalties, and other compensation, including, but not limited to, liquidated damages, payable to aggrieved employees under orders, decisions, and awards issued during the reporting year pursuant to Section 98.

(6) The total amount of wages, penalties, and other compensation, including, but not limited to, liquidated damages, arising from orders, decisions, and awards issued during the reporting year that remain unpaid.

(b) The information provided in subdivision (a) shall also be broken down by industry sectors.

(c) The division shall also include in each annual report a discussion of the major challenges to adjudicating wage claims, ongoing efforts to address those challenges, and options to improve the state's wage claim process.

(d) A report to be submitted pursuant to this section shall be submitted in compliance with Section 9795 of the Government Code.

(e) This section shall remain in effect only until January 1, 2031, and as of that date is repealed. **Leg.H.** 2020 ch. 14 (AB 82) §6, effective June 29, 2020.

§96.3. Employees represented by collective bargaining agreements.

In cases where employees are covered by a collective bargaining agreement, the collective bargaining representative by virtue of such agreement may be the assignee of all such covered employees for purposes of filing claims for wages with the Labor Commissioner, subject to the option of the employee to reject such representation and to represent himself or herself.

§96.5. Certification of claims.

The Labor Commissioner shall conduct such hearings as may be necessary for the purpose of Section 7071.11 of the Business and Professions Code. In any action to recover upon a cash deposit after a determination made under Section 7071.11, the Labor Commissioner shall certify in writing to the appropriate court that he has heard and determined the validity of claims and demands and that the sum specified therein is the amount found due and payable. The certificate of the commissioner shall be considered by the court but shall not, by itself, be sufficient evidence to support a judgment.

§96.6. Industrial Relations Unpaid Wage Fund.

The Industrial Relations Unpaid Wage Fund is hereby created as a special fund in the State Treasury, which is continuously appropriated for the purposes of subdivision (c) of Section 96.7.

§96.7. Collection and disbursement of unpaid wages and benefits.

The Labor Commissioner, after investigation and upon determination that wages or monetary benefits are due and unpaid to any worker in the State of California, may collect such wages or benefits on behalf of the worker without assignment of such wages or benefits to the commissioner.

(a) The Labor Commissioner shall act as trustee of all such collected unpaid wages or benefits, and shall deposit such collected moneys in the Industrial Relations Unpaid Wage Fund.

(b) The Labor Commissioner shall make a diligent search to locate any worker for whom the Labor Commissioner has collected unpaid wages or benefits.

(c) All wages or benefits collected under this section shall be remitted to the worker, his lawful representative, or to any trust or custodial fund established under a plan to provide health and welfare, pension, vacation, retirement, or similar benefits from the Industrial Relations Unpaid Wage Fund.

(d) Any unpaid wages or benefits collected by the Labor Commissioner pursuant to this section shall be retained in the Industrial Relations Unpaid Wage Fund until remitted pursuant to subdivision (c), or until deposited in the General Fund.

(e) The Controller shall, at the end of each fiscal year, transfer to the General Fund the unencumbered balance, less six months of expenditures as determined by the Director of Finance, in the Industrial Relations Unpaid Wage Fund.

(f) All wages or benefits collected under this section which cannot be remitted from the Industrial Relations Unpaid Wage Fund pursuant to subdivision (c) because money has been transmitted to the General Fund shall be paid out of the General Fund from funds appropriated for that purpose. **Leg.H.** 1975 ch. 714, 1981 ch. 562, effective September 19, 1981, 2005 ch. 74 (AB 139) §54, effective July 19, 2005.

§96.8. Collection of outstanding amount of judgment entered in favor of Labor Commissioner or employee pursuant to Section 98.2(e); notice of levy; execution of levy on property.

(a) Notwithstanding any other law, beginning 20 days after a judgment is entered by a court of competent jurisdiction in favor of the Labor Commissioner, or in favor of any employee pursuant to subdivision (e) of Section 98.2, the Labor Commissioner may, with the consent of any employee in whose favor the judgment is entered, collect any outstanding amount of the judgment by mailing a notice of levy upon all persons having in their possession, or who will have in their possession or under their control, any credits, money, or property belonging to the judgment debtor, or who owe any debt to the judgment debtor at the time they receive the notice of levy.

(b) Notwithstanding any other law, the Labor Commissioner may execute a levy on any property that may be levied under Section 700.140, 700.150, 700.160, or 700.170 of the Code of Civil Procedure by mailing a notice of levy to the person against whom the levy is directed and serving a copy on the judgment debtor. The notice of levy shall contain all of the information required to be included in a writ of execution under Section 699.520 of the Code of Civil Procedure and in a notice of levy under Section 699.540 of the Code of Civil Procedure.

(c) Any person, upon whom a levy has been noticed having in his or her possession or under his or her control any credits, money, or property belonging to the judgment debtor or owing any debts to the judgment debtor at the time of receipt of the levy or coming into his or her possession or under his or her control within one year of receipt of the notice of levy, shall surrender the credits, money, or property to the Labor Commissioner or pay to the Labor Commissioner the amount of any debt owed to the judgment debtor within 10 days of service of the levy, and shall surrender the credits or property, or the amount of any debt owing to the judgment debtor coming into his or her own possession or control within one year of receipt of the notice of levy within 10 days of the date of coming into possession or control of the credits or property or the amount of any debt owed to the judgment debtor.

(d) Any person who surrenders to the Labor Commissioner pursuant to this section any credits, money, or property, or pays the debts owed to the judgment debtor, shall be discharged from any obligation or liability to the judgment debtor to the extent of the amount paid to the Labor Commissioner as a result of the levy.

(e) If the levy is made on a deposit or credits, money, or property in the possession or under the control of a bank, savings and loan association, or other financial institution as defined by Section 669a(d)(1) of Title 42 of the United States Code, the notice of levy may be delivered or mailed to a centralized location designated by the bank, savings and loan association, or other financial institution pursuant to Section 690.050 of the Code of Civil Procedure.

(f) Any person who is noticed with a levy pursuant to this section and who fails or refuses to surrender any credits, money, or property or pay any debts owed to the judgment debtor shall be liable in his or her own person or estate to the Labor Commissioner in an amount equal to the value of the credits, money, or other property or in the amount of the levy, up to the amount specified in the levy.

(g) The fees, commissions, expenses, and the reasonable costs associated with the sale of property levied upon by warrant or levy pursuant to this section, including, but not limited to, appraisers' fees, auctioneers' fees, and advertising fees are an obligation of the judgment debtor and may be collected from the judgment debtor by virtue of the warrant or levy or in any other manner as though these items were part of the judgment or award outstanding.

(h) This section shall not apply to the judgment debtor's interest in real property.

(i) This section shall not apply if enforcement of the judgment has been stayed on appeal pursuant to Chapter 2 (commencing with Section 916) of Title 13 of Part 2 of the Code of Civil Procedure. **Leg.H.** 2015 ch. 803 (SB 588) §2.

CHAPTER 5
DIVISION OF WORKERS' COMPENSATION

§110. Definitions.

As used in this chapter:

(a) "Appeals board" means the Workers' Compensation Appeals Board. The title of a member of the board is "commissioner."

(b) "Administrative director" means the Administrative Director of the Division of Workers' Compensation.

(c) "Division" means the Division of Workers' Compensation.

(d) "Medical director" means the physician appointed by the administrative director pursuant to Section 122.

(e) "Qualified medical evaluator" means physicians appointed by the administrative director pursuant to Section 139.2. **Leg.H.** 1965 ch. 1513 §5, operative January 15, 1966, 1967 ch. 1462 §1, 1981 ch. 21 §2, effective April 18, 1981, 1989 ch. 892 §10, 1990 ch. 1550 (AB 2910) §8, 1993 ch. 121, effective July 16, 1993, 2002 ch. 6 (AB 749), 2003 ch. 639 (SB 228), 2011 ch. 559 (AB 1426) §2, effective October 7, 2011.

1989 Note: This section is applicable only to injuries occurring on or after January 1, 1990. Stats. 1989 ch. 893 §6.

Ref.: Hanna §§ 1.10, 1.12[2A]; Herlick Handbook § 1.01[3][a].

§111. Powers of appeals board and administrative director.

The Workers' Compensation Appeals Board, consisting of seven members, shall exercise all judicial powers vested in it under this code. In all other respects, the Division of Workers' Compensation is under the control of the administrative director and, except as to those duties, powers, jurisdiction, responsibilities, and purposes as are specifically vested in the appeals board, the administrative director shall exercise the powers of the head of a department within the meaning of Article 1 (commencing with Section 11150) of Chapter 2 of Part 1 of Division 3 of Title 2 of the Government Code with respect to the Division of Workers' Compensation which shall include supervision of, and responsibility for, personnel, and the coordination of the work of the division, except personnel of the appeals board. **Leg.H.** 1965 ch. 1513 §7, operative January 15, 1966, 1981 ch. 21 §3, effective April 18, 1981, 1989 ch. 892 §11, 2012 ch. 728 (SB 71) §117.

1989 Note: This section is applicable only to injuries occurring on or after January 1, 1990. Stats. 1989 ch. 893 §6.

Ref.: 8 C.C.R. §§9720.1, 9720.2, 9721.1, 9721.2, 9721.31, 9721.32, 9722, 9722.1, 9722.2, 9723, 10106, 10106.1, 10106.5, 10107, 10107.1, 10563, 10582, 10622, 10753; Hanna §§ 1.10, 1.11[1], [6], 1.12[2], 21.02[1]; Herlick Handbook §§ 1.01[3][a], 1.02[2], [3][b].

§112. Appointment and composition of appeals board.

The members of the appeals board shall be appointed by the Governor with the advice and consent of the Senate. The term of office of the members appointed prior to January 1, 1990, shall be four years, and the term of office of members appointed on or after January 1, 1990, shall be six years and they shall hold office until the appointment and qualification of their successors.

Five of the members of the appeals board shall be experienced attorneys at law admitted to practice in the State of California. The other two members need not be attorneys at law. All members shall be selected with due consideration of their judicial temperament and abilities. Each member shall receive the salary provided for by Chapter 6 (commencing with Section 11550) of Part 1 of Division 3 of Title 2 of the Government Code.

1990 Note: The amendments made by this act to Section 112 of the Labor Code are declaratory of existing law. Stats. 1990 ch. 1550 §66.

1989 Note: This section is applicable only to injuries occurring on or after January 1, 1990. Stats. 1989 ch. 893 §6.

Ref.: Hanna § 1.11[1]; Herlick Handbook § 1.01[2], [3][a].

§113. Appointment of chairperson.

The Governor shall designate the chairman of the appeals board from the membership of the appeals board. The person so designated shall hold the office of chairman at the pleasure of the Governor.

The chairman may designate in writing one of the other members of the appeals board to act as chairman during such time as he may be absent from the state on official business, on vacation, or absent due to illness.

Ref.: Hanna § 1.11[2]; Herlick Handbook § 1.01[2], [3][a].

§115. Appeals board decisions; reconsideration.

Actions of the appeals board shall be taken by decision of a majority of the appeals board except as otherwise expressly provided.

The chairman shall assign pending cases in which reconsideration is sought to any three members thereof for hearing, consideration and decision. Assignments by the chairman of members to such cases shall be rotated on a case-by-case basis with the composition of the members so assigned being varied and changed to assure that there shall never be a fixed and continued composition of members. Any such case assigned to any three members in which the finding, order, decision or award is made and filed by any two or more of such members shall be the action of the appeals board unless reconsideration is had in accordance with the provisions of Article 1 (commencing with Section 5900), Chapter 7, Part 4, Division 4 of this code. Any case assigned to three members shall be heard and decided only by them, unless the matter has been reassigned by the chairman on a majority vote of the appeals board to the appeals board as a whole in order to achieve uniformity of decision, or in cases presenting novel issues.

Ref.: 8 C.C.R. §§10340, 10341, 10342; Hanna §§ 1.11[2], 28.35[1]; Herlick Handbook § 1.01[2], [3][a].

§116. Appeals board seal.

The seal of the appeals board bearing the inscription "Workers' Compensation Appeals Board, Seal" shall be affixed to all writs and authentications of copies of records and to such other instruments as the appeals board directs.

Ref.: Herlick Handbook § 1.01[3][a].

§117. Appointment of attorney.

The administrative director may appoint an attorney licensed to practice law in the state as counsel to the division.

1989 Note: This section is applicable only to injuries occurring on or after January 1, 1990. Stats. 1989 ch. 893 §6.

Ref.: Hanna § 1.12[4]; Herlick Handbook § 1.01[3][a].

§119. Duties of attorney.

The attorney shall:

(a) Represent and appear for the state and the Division of Workers' Compensation and the appeals board in all actions and proceedings arising under any provision of this code administered by the division or under any order or act of the division or the appeals board and, if directed so to do, intervene, if possible, in any action or proceeding in which any such question is involved.

(b) Commence, prosecute, and expedite the final determination of all actions or proceedings, directed or authorized by the administrative director or the appeals board.

(c) Advise the administrative director and the appeals board and each member thereof, upon request, in regard to the jurisdiction, powers or duties of the administrative director, the appeals board and each member thereof.

(d) Generally perform the duties and services as attorney to the Division of Workers' Compensation and the appeals board which are required of him or her. **Leg.H.** 1994 chs. 146, 1097.

Ref.: Herlick Handbook § 1.01[3][a].

§120. Appointment of secretaries.

The administrative director and the chairman of the appeals board may each respectively appoint a secretary and assistant secretaries to perform such services as shall be prescribed.

Ref.: Herlick Handbook § 1.01[3][a].

§121. Acts by deputies; validity.

The chairman of the appeals board may authorize its secretary and any two assistant secretaries to act as deputy appeals board members and may delegate authority and duties to these deputies. Not more than three deputies may act as appeals board members at any one time. No act of any deputy shall be valid unless it is concurred in by at least one member of the appeals board.

Ref.: 8 C.C.R. §§10348, 10349, 10350, 10351, 10352; Herlick Handbook § 1.01[2], [3][a].

§122. Medical director and assistants; appointment; qualifications; salaries.

The administrative director shall appoint a medical director who shall possess a physician's and surgeon's certificate granted under Chapter 5 (commencing with Section 2000) of Division 2 of the Business and Professions Code. The medical director shall employ medical assistants who shall also possess physicians' and surgeons' certificates and other staff necessary to the performance of his or her duties. The salaries for the medical director and his or her assistants shall be fixed by the Department of Human Resources, commensurate with the salaries paid by private industry to medical directors and assistant medical directors. **Leg.H.** 2003 ch. 639 (SB 228), see this section as modified in Governor's Reorganization Plan No. 1 §196 of 2011, 2012 ch. 665 (SB 1308) §176.

2012 Note: Stats. 2012 ch. 665 (SB 1308) enacts the statutory changes necessary to reflect the changes made by the Governor's Reorganization Plan No. 1 of 2011.

2011 Note: 2011 Governor's Reorganization Plan No. 1 was submitted to the Legislature on June 9, 2011, and became effective September 9, 2011, pursuant to Gov C §12080.5, and substantively operative July 1, 2012.

1989 Note: This section is applicable only to injuries occurring on or after January 1, 1990. Stats. 1989 ch. 893 §6.

Ref.: Herlick Handbook § 1.01[3][a].

§123. Administrative personnel; salaries of workers' compensation administrative law judges.

The administrative director may employ necessary assistants, officers, experts, statisticians, actuaries, accountants, workers' compensation administrative law judges, stenographic shorthand reporters, legal secretaries, disability evaluation raters, program technicians, and other employees to implement new, efficient court management systems. The salaries of the workers' compensation administrative law judges shall be fixed by the Department of Human Resources for a class of positions which perform judicial functions. **Leg.H.** 2002 ch. 6 (AB 749), see this section as modified in Governor's Reorganization Plan No. 1 §197 of 2011, 2012 ch. 665 (SB 1308) §177.

2012 Note: Stats. 2012 ch. 665 (SB 1308) enacts the statutory changes necessary to reflect the changes made by the Governor's Reorganization Plan No. 1 of 2011.

2011 Note: 2011 Governor's Reorganization Plan No. 1 was submitted to the Legislature on June 9, 2011, and became effective September 9, 2011, pursuant to Gov C §12080.5, and substantively operative July 1, 2012.

Ref.: Herlick Handbook § 1.01[3][a].

§123.3. Official reporters.

Any official reporter employed by the administrative director shall render stenographic or clerical assistance as directed by the presiding workers' compensation administrative law judge of the office to which the reporter is assigned, when the presiding workers' compensation administrative law judge determines that the reporter is not engaged in the performance of any other duty imposed by law. **Leg.H.** 2002 ch. 6 (AB 749).

Ref.: Herlick Handbook § 1.01[3][a].

§123.5. Workers' compensation administrative law judges.

(a) Workers' compensation administrative law judges employed by the administrative director shall be taken from an eligible list of attorneys licensed to practice law in this state, who have the qualifications prescribed by the State Personnel Board. In establishing eligible lists for this purpose, state civil service examinations shall be conducted in accordance with the State Civil Service Act (Part 2 (commencing with Section 18500) of Division 5 of Title 2 of the Government Code). Every workers' compensation judge shall maintain membership in the State Bar of California during his or her tenure.

A workers' compensation administrative law judge may not receive his or her salary as a workers' compensation administrative law judge while any cause before the workers' compensation administrative law judge remains pending and undetermined for 90 days after it has been submitted for decision.

(b) All workers' compensation administrative law judges appointed on or after January 1, 2003, shall be attorneys licensed to practice law in California for five or more years prior to their appointment and shall have experience in workers' compensation law. **Leg.H.** 2002 chs. 6 (AB 749), 866 (AB 486), 2011 ch. 559 (AB 1426) §3, effective October 7, 2011.

1989 Note: This section is applicable only to injuries occurring on or after January 1, 1990. Stats. 1989 ch. 893 §6.

Ref.: 8 C.C.R. §§9710, 9711, 9712, 9713, 9714, 9714.5, 9715, 10302; Hanna §§ 1.11[3], 24.11[1]; Herlick Handbook § 1.01[2], [3][a].

§123.6. Workers' compensation administrative law judges to adhere to Code of Judicial Ethics; prior approval by administrative director for honoraria or travel payments.

(a) All workers' compensation administrative law judges employed by the administrative director shall subscribe to the Code of Judicial Ethics adopted by the Supreme Court pursuant to subdivision (m) of Section 18 of Article VI of the California Constitution for the conduct of judges and shall not otherwise, directly or indirectly, engage in conduct contrary to that code or to the commentary to the Code of Judicial Ethics.

In consultation with the Commission on Judicial Performance, the administrative director shall adopt regulations to enforce this section. To the extent possible, the rules shall be consistent with the procedures established by the Commission on Judicial Performance for regulating the activities of state judges, and, to the extent possible, with the gift, honoraria, and travel restrictions on legislators contained in the Political Reform Act of 1974 (Title 9 (commencing with Section 81000) of the Government Code).

(b) Honoraria or travel allowed by the administrative director, and not otherwise prohibited by this section in connection with any public or private conference, convention, meeting, social event, or like gathering, the cost of which is significantly paid for by attorneys who practice before the board, may not be accepted unless the administrative director has provided prior approval in writing to the workers' compensation administrative law judge allowing him or her to accept those payments. **Leg.H.** 1993 ch. 483, effective September 27, 1993, 1998 chs. 95, 448, 2002 chs. 6 (AB 749), 866 (AB 486), 2005 ch. 706 (AB 1742) §35, 2011 ch. 559 (AB 1426) §4, effective October 7, 2011.

Ref.: 8 C.C.R. §§9720.1, 9720.2, 9721.1, 9721.2, 9721.31, 9721.32, 9722, 9722.1, 9722.2, 9723, 10166; Hanna § 1.11[3][a]; Herlick Handbook § 1.01[2], [3][a].

§123.7. Certified workers' compensation specialists; pro tempore judges.

The appeals board may, by rule or regulation, establish procedures whereby attorneys who are either certified specialists in workers' compensation by the California State Bar, or are eligible for this certification, may be appointed by the presiding workers' compensation judge of each board office to serve as a pro tempore workers' compensation judge in a particular case, upon the stipulation of the employee or his or her representative, and the employer or the insurance carrier. Service in this capacity by an attorney shall be voluntary and without pay. It is the intent of the Legislature that the use of pro tempore workers' compensation judges pursuant to this section shall not result in a reduction of the number of permanent civil service employees or the number of authorized full-time equivalent positions.

Ref.: 8 C.C.R. §§10166, 10349, 10350, 10351, 10352; Hanna § 1.11[1]; Herlick Handbook § 1.01[2], [3][a].

§124. Protection of interests of injured workers; forms and notices; availability in other languages; annual review.

(a) In administering and enforcing this division and Division 4 (commencing with Section 3200), the division shall protect the interests of injured workers who are entitled to the timely provision of compensation.

(b) Forms and notices required to be given to employees by the division shall be in English and Spanish.

(c) In addition to the requirement in subdivision (b), no later than January 1, 2018, the department and the division shall make at least the following forms, notices, and materials available in Chinese, Korean, Tagalog, and Vietnamese:

(1) The workers' compensation claim form required pursuant to Section 5401.

(2) The application for the Return-to-Work Supplement Program authorized pursuant to Section 139.48.

(3) Supplemental Job Displacement Non-Transferable Voucher.

(4) Division of Workers' Compensation fact sheets distributed to injured workers, including, but not limited to, those addressing the following topics:

(A) Temporary disability.

(B) Permanent disability.

(C) Qualified medical evaluators.

(D) Uninsured Employers Benefits Trust Fund.

(E) Utilization review.

(F) Basic facts on workers' compensation.

(G) Glossary of terms in workers' compensation.

(d)(1) Commencing January 1, 2018, the Administrative Director shall annually review the forms, notices, and materials that are published and distributed by the division to injured workers and recommend to the division any other documents that should be translated into languages other than English pursuant to subdivisions (b) and (c).

(2) Commencing January 1, 2018, and annually thereafter, the department and the division shall submit the recommendations and any translated documents to the Legislature. **Leg.H.** 1993 ch. 1241, 2002 ch. 6 (AB 749), 2003 ch. 639 (SB 228), 2015 ch. 515 (AB 438) §1.

1989 Note: This section is applicable only to injuries occurring on or after January 1, 1990. Stats. 1989 ch. 893 §6.

Ref.: 8 C.C.R. §§10100, 10100.1, 10100.2, 10101, 10101.1, 10102, 10103, 10103.1, 10103.2, 10106, 10106.1, 10106.5, 10107, 10108, 10109, 10111, 10111.1, 10111.2, 10113, 10114, 10114.1, 10114.2, 10114.3, 10114.4, 10122, 10133.50, 10150, 10151, 10152, 10156, 10158, 10160, 10160.1, 10160.5, 10161, 10162, 10163, 10164, 10165, 10165.5, 10166, 10168; Hanna § 1.12[15]; Herlick Handbook §§ 1.01[3][a], 6.01[3].

§125. Blank forms.

The administrative director shall cause to be printed and furnished free of charge to any person blank forms that may facilitate or promote the efficient performance of the duties of the Division of Workers' Compensation. **Leg.H.** 1994 ch. 146.

Ref.: Hanna §§ 1.12[2], 23.12[1]; Herlick Handbook § 1.01[3][a].

§126. Records.

The Division of Workers' Compensation, including the administrative director and the appeals board, shall keep minutes of all their proceedings and other books or records requisite for proper and efficient administration. All records shall be kept in their respective offices. **Leg.H.** 1994 ch. 146.

Ref.: 8 C.C.R. §§10306, 10308, 10360, 10390, 10392, 10395, 10396, 10400, 10412, 10450, 10630, 10750, 10751, 10753, 10842; Hanna §§ 1.11[5], 1.12[5]; Herlick Handbook § 1.01[3][a].

§127. Administrative director—Authority.

The administrative director may do all of the following:

(a) Charge and collect fees for copies of papers and records, for certified copies of official documents and orders or of the evidence taken or proceedings had, for transcripts of testimony, and for inspection of case files not stored in the place where the inspection is requested. The administrative director shall fix those fees in an amount sufficient to recover the actual costs of furnishing the services. No fees for inspection of case files shall be charged to an injured employee or his or her representative.

(b) Publish and distribute from time to time, in addition to the reports to the Governor, further reports and pamphlets covering the operations, proceedings, and matters relative to the work of the division.

(c) Prepare, publish, and distribute an office manual, for which a reasonable fee may be charged, and to which additions, deletions, amendments, and other changes from time to time may be adopted, published, and distributed, for which a reasonable fee may be charged for the revision, or for which a reasonable fee may be fixed on an annual subscription basis.

(d) Fix and collect reasonable charges for publications issued. **Leg.H.** 2002 ch. 6 (AB 749), 2011 ch. 559 (AB 1426) §5, effective October 7, 2011.

Ref.: 8 C.C.R. §§9990, 9992, 9994, 10322, 10740; Hanna §§ 1.12[2], [5], 23.13[1]; Herlick Handbook § 1.01[3][a], [b].

§127.1. Report to Legislature comparing potential payment alternatives for providers to official medical fee schedule.

(a) The administrative director, with input from the Commission on Health and Safety and Workers' Compensation, shall issue a report to the Legislature, on or before January 1, 2023, comparing potential payment alternatives for providers to the official medical fee schedule, including, but not limited to, capitation, bundled payments, quality incentives, and value-based payment systems.

(b) The report shall address advantages and disadvantages of each alternative payment system to the official medical fee schedule and make recommendations to the Legislature on alternative payment pilot programs.

(c) The report shall be submitted in compliance with Section 9795 of the Government Code. The requirement for submitting a report imposed by this section shall be inoperative on January 1, 2024, pursuant to Section 10231.5 of the Government Code. **Leg.H.** 2019 ch. 647 (SB 537) §1.

Ref.: Hanna § 22.05[2].

§128. Enforcement of Longshoremen's and Harbor Workers' Compensation Act.

The appeals board may accept appointment as deputy commissioner under, or any delegation of authority to enforce, the United States Longshoremen's and Harbor Worker's Compensation Act. The appeals board may enter into arrangements with the United States, subject to the approval of the Department of Finance, for the payment of any expenses incurred in the performance of services under said act. In the performance of any duties under said act, appointment, or authority, the appeals board may, subject to the provisions thereof, exercise any authority conferred upon the appeals board by the laws of this state.

Ref.: Hanna § 21.01[5]; Herlick Handbook § 1.01[2], [3][a].

§129. Audits.

(a) To make certain that injured workers, and their dependents in the event of their death, receive promptly and accurately the full measure of compensation to which they are entitled, the administrative director shall audit insurers, self-insured employers, and third-party administrators to determine if they have met their obligations under this code. Each audit subject shall be audited at least once every five years. The audit subjects shall be selected and the audits conducted pursuant to subdivision (b). The results of audits of insurers shall be provided to the Insurance Commissioner, and the results of audits of self-insurers and third-party administrators shall be provided to the Director of Industrial Relations. Nothing in this section shall restrict the authority of the Director of Industrial Relations or the Insurance Commissioner to audit their licensees.

(b) The administrative director shall schedule and conduct audits as follows:

(1) A profile audit review of every audit subject shall be conducted once every five years and on additional occasions indicated by target audit criteria. The administrative director shall annually establish a profile audit review performance standard that will identify the poorest performing audit subjects.

(2) A full compliance audit shall be conducted of each profile audited subject failing to meet or exceed the profile audit review performance standard. The full compliance audit shall be a comprehensive and detailed evaluation of the audit subject's performance. The administrative director shall annually establish a full compliance audit performance standard that will identify the audit subjects that are performing satisfactorily. Any full compliance audit subject that fails to meet or exceed the full compliance audit performance standard shall be audited again within two years.

(3) A targeted profile audit review or a full compliance audit may be conducted at any time in accordance with target audit criteria adopted by the administrative director. The target audit criteria shall be based on information obtained from benefit notices, from information and assistance officers, and from other reliable sources providing factual information that indicates an insurer, self-insured employer, or third-party administrator is failing to meet its obligations under this division or Division 4 (commencing with Section 3200) or the regulations of the administrative director.

(c) If, as a result of a profile audit review or a full compliance audit, the administrative director determines that any compensation, interest, or penalty is due and unpaid to an employee or dependent, the administrative director shall issue and cause to be served upon the insurer, self-insured employer, or third-party administrator a notice of assessment detailing the amounts due and unpaid in each case, and shall order the amounts paid to the person entitled thereto. The notice of assessment shall be served personally or by registered mail in accordance with subdivision (c) of Section 11505 of the Government Code. A copy of the notice of assessment shall also be sent to the affected employee or dependent.

If the amounts are not paid within 30 days after service of the notice of assessment, the employer shall also be liable for reasonable attorney's fees necessarily incurred by the employee or dependent to obtain amounts due. The administrative director shall advise each employee or dependent still owed compensation after this 30-day period of his or her rights with respect to the commencement of proceedings to collect the compensation owed. Amounts unpaid because the person entitled thereto cannot be located shall be paid to the Workers' Compensation Administration Revolving Fund. The Director of Industrial Relations shall promulgate rules and regulations establishing standards and procedures for the payment of compensation from moneys deposited in the Workers' Compensation Administration Revolving Fund whenever the person entitled thereto applies for compensation.

(d) A determination by the administrative director that an amount is or is not due to an employee or dependent shall not in any manner limit the jurisdiction or authority of the appeals board to determine the issue.

(e) Annually, commencing on April 1, 1991, the administrative director shall publish a report detailing the results of audits conducted pursuant to this section during the preceding calendar year. The report shall include the name of each insurer, self-insured employer, and third-party administrator audited during that period. For each insurer, self-insured employer, and third-party administrator audited, the report shall specify the total number of files audited, the number of violations found by type and amount of compensation, interest and penalties payable, and the amount collected for each violation. The administrative director shall also publish and make available to the public on request a list ranking all insurers, self-insured employers, and third-party administrators audited during the period according to their performance measured by the profile audit review and full compliance audit performance standards.

These reports shall not identify the particular claim file that resulted in a particular violation or penalty. Except as required by this subdivision or other provisions of law, the contents of individual claim files and auditor's working papers shall be confidential. Disclosure of claim information to the administrative director pursuant to an audit shall not waive the provisions of the Evidence Code relating to privilege.

(f) A profile audit review of the adjustment of claims against the Uninsured Employers Fund by the claims and collections unit of the Division of Workers' Compensation shall be conducted at least every five years. The results of this profile audit review shall be included in the report required by subdivision (e). **Leg.H.** 1993 ch. 1241, 2001 ch. 159, 2002 ch. 6 (AB 749).

1989 Note: This section is applicable only to injuries occurring on or after January 1, 1990. Stats. 1989 ch. 893 §6.

Ref.: 8 C.C.R. §§9703, 10100, 10100.1, 10100.2, 10101, 10101.1, 10102, 10103, 10103.1, 10103.2, 10104, 10105, 10106, 10106.1. 10106.5, 10107, 10107.1, 10108, 10109, 10110, 10111, 10111.1, 10111.2, 10112, 10113, 10113.1, 10113.2, 10113.3, 10113.4, 10113.5, 10113.6, 10115, 10115.1, 10115.2, 10952, 15201, 15210.2, 15210.3, 15211, 15211.2, 15212, 15216, 15251, 15300, 15301, 15302, 15303, 15360, 15362, 15400, 15400.1, 15400.2, 15402, 15402.1, 15402.2, 15402.4, 15403, 15403.1, 15403.2, 15404, 15404.1, 15404.2, 15405, 15420, 15422, 15423, 15424, 15425, 15426, 15427, 15428, 15458, 15459; Hanna §§ 1.12[8]–[9], 2.02[1]; Herlick Handbook §§ 1.01[3][a], [b], 4.16[3], 10.09[5].

§129.5. Administrative and civil penalties; schedule of violations.

(a) The administrative director may assess an administrative penalty against an insurer, self-insured employer, or third-party administrator for any of the following:

(1) Failure to comply with the notice of assessment issued pursuant to subdivision (c) of Section 129 within 15 days of receipt.

(2) Failure to pay when due the undisputed portion of an indemnity payment, the reasonable cost of medical treatment of an injured worker, or a charge or cost implementing an approved vocational rehabilitation plan.

(3) Failure to comply with any rule or regulation of the administrative director.

(b) The administrative director shall promulgate regulations establishing a schedule of violations and the amount of the administrative penalty to be imposed for each type of violation. The schedule shall provide for imposition of a penalty of up to one hundred dollars ($100) for each violation of the less serious type and for imposition of penalties in progressively higher amounts for the most serious types of violations to be set at up to five thousand dollars ($5,000) per violation. The administrative director is authorized to impose penalties pursuant to rules and regulations which give due consideration to the appropriateness of the penalty with respect to the following factors;

(1) The gravity of the violation.

(2) The good faith of the insurer, self-insured employer, or third-party administrator.

(3) The history of previous violations, if any.

(4) The frequency of the violations.

(5) Whether the audit subject has met or exceeded the profile audit review performance standard.

(6) Whether a full compliance audit subject has met or exceeded the full compliance audit performance standard.

(7) The size of the audit subject location.

(c) The administrative director shall assess penalties as follows:

(1) If, after a profile audit review, the administrative director determines that the profile audit subject met or exceeded the profile audit review performance standard, no penalties shall be assessed under this section, but the audit subject shall be required to pay any compensation due and penalties due under subdivision (d) of Section 4650 as provided in subdivision (c) of Section 129.

(2) If, after a full compliance audit, the administrative director determines that the audit subject met or exceeded the full compliance audit performance standards, penalties for unpaid or late paid compensation, but no other penalties under this section, shall be assessed. The audit subject shall be required to pay any compensation due and penalties due under subdivision (d) of Section 4650 as provided in subdivision (c) of Section 129.

(3) If, after a full compliance audit, the administrative director determines that the audit subject failed to meet the full compliance audit performance standards, penalties shall be assessed as provided in a full compliance audit failure penalty schedule to be adopted by the administrative

director. The full compliance audit failure penalty schedule shall adjust penalty levels relative to the size of the audit location to mitigate inequality between total penalties assessed against small and large audit subjects. The penalty amounts provided in the full compliance audit failure penalty schedule for the most serious type of violations shall not be limited by subdivision (b), but in no event shall the penalty for a single violation exceed forty thousand dollars ($40,000).

(d) The notice of penalty assessment shall be served personally or by registered mail in accordance with subdivision (c) of Section 11505 of the Government Code. The notice shall be in writing and shall describe the nature of the violation, including reference to the statutory provision or rule or regulation alleged to have been violated. The notice shall become final and the assessment shall be paid unless contested within 15 days of receipt by the insurer, self-insured employer, or third-party administrator.

(e) In addition to the penalty assessments permitted by subdivisions (a), (b), and (c), the administrative director may assess a civil penalty, not to exceed one hundred thousand dollars ($100,000), upon finding, after hearing, that an employer, insurer, or third-party administrator for an employer has knowingly committed or performed with sufficient frequency so as to indicate a general business practice any of the following:

(1) Induced employees to accept less than compensation due, or made it necessary for employees to resort to proceedings against the employer to secure compensation.

(2) Refused to comply with known and legally indisputable compensation obligations.

(3) Discharged or administered compensation obligations in a dishonest manner.

(4) Discharged or administered compensation obligations in a manner as to cause injury to the public or those dealing with the employer or insurer.

Any employer, insurer, or third-party administrator that fails to meet the full compliance audit performance standards in two consecutive full compliance audits shall be rebuttably presumed to have engaged in a general business practice of discharging and administering its compensation obligations in a manner causing injury to those dealing with it.

Upon a second or subsequent finding, the administrative director shall refer the matter to the Insurance Commissioner or the Director of Industrial Relations and request that a hearing be conducted to determine whether the certificate of authority, certificate of consent to self-insure, or certificate of consent to administer claims of self-insured employers, as the case may be, shall be revoked.

(f) An insurer, self-insured employer, or third-party administrator may file a written request for a conference with the administrative director within seven days after receipt of a notice of penalty assessment issued pursuant to subdivision (a) or (c). Within 15 days of the conference, the administrative director shall issue a notice of findings and serve it upon the contesting party by registered or certified mail. Any amount found due by the administrative director shall become due and payable 30 days after receipt of the notice of findings. The 30-day period shall be tolled during any appeal. A writ of mandate may be taken from the findings to the appropriate superior court upon the execution by the contesting party of a bond to the state in the principal sum that is double the amount found due and ordered by the administrative director, on the condition that the contesting party shall pay any judgment and costs rendered against it for the amount.

(g) An insurer, self-insured employer, or third-party administrator may file a written request for a hearing before the Workers' Compensation Appeals Board within seven days after receipt of a notice of penalty assessment issued pursuant to subdivision (e). Within 30 days of the hearing, the appeals board shall issue findings and orders and serve them upon the contesting party in the manner provided in its rules. Any amount found due by the appeals board shall become due and payable 45 days after receipt of the notice of findings. Judicial review of the findings and order shall be had in the manner provided by Article 2 (commencing with Section 5950) of Chapter 7 of Part 4 of Division 4. The 45-day period shall be tolled during appellate proceedings upon execution by the contesting party of a bond to the state in a principal sum that is double the amount found due and ordered by the appeals board on the condition that the contesting party shall pay the amount ultimately determined to be due and any costs awarded by an appellate court.

(h) Nothing in this section shall create nor eliminate a civil cause of action for the employee and his or her dependents.

(i) All moneys collected under this section shall be deposited in the State Treasury and credited to the Workers' Compensation Administration Revolving Fund. **Leg.H.** 1993 ch. 1241, 2002 ch. 6 (AB 749).

1989 Note: This section is applicable only to injuries occurring on or after January 1, 1990. Stats. 1989 ch. 893 §6.

Ref.: 8 C.C.R. §§10100, 10100.1, 10100.2, 10101, 10101.1, 10102, 10103, 10103.1, 10103.2, 10104, 10105, 10106, 10106.1, 10106.5, 10107, 10107.1, 10108, 10111, 10111.1, 10111.2, 10112, 10113, 10113.1, 10113.2, 10113.3, 10113.4, 10113.5, 10113.6, 10114, 10114.1, 10114.2, 10114.3, 10114.4, 10115, 10115.1, 10115.2, 10953; Hanna § 10.51[2][a]; Herlick Handbook §§ 1.01[3][a], [b], 4.16[2]–[4], 9.5.

§130. Authority to administer oaths and issue subpoenas.

The appeals board and each of its members, its secretary, assistant secretaries, and workers' compensation judges, may administer oaths, certify to all official acts, and issue subpoenas for the attendance of witnesses and the production of papers, books, accounts, documents and testimony in any inquiry, investigation, hearing or proceeding in any part of the state.

Ref.: 8 C.C.R. §§10530, 10534, 10536, 10563, 10820, 10825, 10828; Hanna §§ 1.11[3], [6], 21.03[8], 25.29[3], 25.43; Herlick Handbook §§ 1.01[2], [3][a], 10.03[1].

§131. Fees and mileage for witnesses.

Each witness who appears by order of the appeals board or any of its members, or a workers' compensation judge, shall receive, if demanded, for his or her attendance the same fees and mileage allowed by law to a witness in civil cases, paid by the party at whose request the witness is subpoenaed, unless otherwise ordered by the appeals board. When any witness who has not been required to attend at the request of any party is subpoenaed by the appeals board, his or her fees and mileage may be paid from the funds appropriated for the use of the appeals board in the same manner as other expenses of the appeals board are paid. Any witness subpoenaed, except one whose fees and mileage are paid from the funds of the appeals board, may, at the time of service, demand the fee to which he or she is entitled for travel to and from the place at which he or she is required to appear, and one day's attendance. If a witness demands his or her fees at the time of service, and they are not at that time paid or tendered, he or she shall not be required to attend as directed in the subpoena. All fees and mileage to which any witness is entitled under this section may be collected by action therefor instituted by the person to whom the fees are payable.

Ref.: 8 C.C.R. §10536; Hanna §§ 21.03[8], 23.10[2], 23.13[2], 25.10[2]; Herlick Handbook § 1.01[3][a].

§132. Refusal to obey subpoena; contempt.

The superior court in and for the county in which any proceeding is held by the appeals board or a workers' compensation judge may compel the attendance of witnesses, the giving of testimony and the production of papers, including books, accounts, and documents, as required by any subpoena regularly issued hereunder. In case of the refusal of any witness to obey the subpoena the appeals board or the workers' compensation judge, before whom the testimony is to be given or produced, may report to the superior court in and for the county in which the proceeding is pending, by petition, setting forth that due notice has been given of the time and place of attendance of the witness, or the production of the papers, that the witness has been subpoenaed in the prescribed manner, and that the witness has failed and refused to obey the subpoena, or has refused to answer questions propounded to him or her in the course of the proceeding, and ask an order of the court, compelling the witness to attend and testify or produce the papers before the appeals board. The court shall thereupon enter an order directing the witness to appear before the court at a time and place fixed in the order, the time to be not more than 10 days from the date of the order, and then and there show cause why he or she had not attended and testified or produced the papers before the appeals board or the workers' compensation judge. A copy of the order shall be served upon the witness. If it appears to the court that the subpoena was regularly issued hereunder and that the witness was legally bound to comply therewith, the court shall thereupon enter an order that the witness appear before the appeals board or the workers' compensation judge at a time and place fixed in the order, and testify or produce the required papers, and upon failure to obey the order, the witness shall be dealt with as for contempt of court. The remedy provided in this section is cumulative, and shall not impair or interfere with the power of the appeals board or a member thereof to enforce the attendance of witnesses and the production of papers, and to punish for contempt in the same manner and to the same extent as courts of record.

Ref.: 8 C.C.R. §§10532, 10534, 10536, 10537; Hanna §§ 20.01[2], 21.09[1]–[3], 25.43; Herlick Handbook § 1.01[3][a].

§132a. Nondiscrimination policy.

It is the declared policy of this state that there should not be discrimination against workers who are injured in the course and scope of their employment.

(1) Any employer who discharges, or threatens to discharge, or in any manner discriminates against any employee because he or she has filed or made known his or her intention to file a claim for compensation with his or her employer or an application for adjudication, or because the employee has received a rating, award, or settlement, is guilty of a misdemeanor and the employee's compensation shall be increased by one-half, but in no event more than ten thousand dollars ($10,000), together with costs and expenses not in excess of two hundred fifty dollars ($250). Any such employee shall also be entitled to reinstatement and reimbursement for lost wages and work benefits caused by the acts of the employer.

(2) Any insurer that advises, directs, or threatens an insured under penalty of cancellation or a raise in premium or for any other reason, to discharge an employee because he or she has filed or made known his or her intention to file a claim for compensation with his or her employer or an application for adjudication, or because the employee has received a rating, award, or settlement, is guilty of a misdemeanor and subject to the increased compensation and costs provided by paragraph (1).

(3) Any employer who discharges, or threatens to discharge, or in any manner discriminates against any employee because the employee testified or made known his or her intentions to testify in another employee's case before the appeals board, is guilty of a misdemeanor, and the employee shall be entitled to reinstatement and reimbursement for lost wages and work benefits caused by the acts of the employer.

(4) Any insurer that advises, directs, or threatens an insured employer under penalty of cancellation or a raise in premium or for any other reason, to discharge or in any manner discriminate against an employee because the employee testified or made known his or her intention to testify in another employee's case before the appeals board, is guilty of a misdemeanor.

Proceedings for increased compensation as provided in paragraph (1), or for reinstatement and reimbursement for lost wages and work benefits, are to be instituted by filing an appropriate petition with the appeals board, but these proceedings may not be commenced more than one year from the discriminatory act or date of termination of the employee. The appeals board is vested with full power, authority, and jurisdiction to try and determine finally all matters specified in this section subject only to judicial review, except that the appeals board shall have no jurisdiction to try and determine a misdemeanor charge. The appeals board may refer and any worker may complain of suspected violations of the criminal misdemeanor provisions of this section to the Division of Labor Standards Enforcement, or directly to the office of the public prosecutor.

1989 Note: This section is applicable only to injuries occurring on or after January 1, 1990. Stats. 1989 ch. 893 §6.

Ref.: 8 C.C.R. §10447; Hanna §§ 10.11[1]–[4], 21.03[2][d], 21.07[7], 35.103[2], 35.104[2]; Herlick Handbook §§ 1.01[3][a], 9.12.

§133. Division of Workers' Compensation—Power and jurisdiction.

The Division of Workers' Compensation, including the administrative director and the appeals board, shall have power and jurisdiction to do all things necessary or convenient in the exercise of any power or jurisdiction conferred upon it under this code. **Leg.H.** 1994 chs. 146, 1097, 2002 ch. 6 (AB 749), 2011 ch. 559 (AB 1426) §7, effective October 7, 2011.

Ref.: 8 C.C.R. §§151, 9900, 10109, 10122.1, 10304, 10450, 10946; Herlick Handbook § 1.01[3][a].

§134. Contempt proceedings; process service.

The appeals board or any member thereof may issue writs or summons, warrants of attachment, warrants of commitment and all necessary process in proceedings for contempt, in like manner and to the same extent as courts of record. The process issued by the appeals board or any member thereof shall extend to all parts of the state and may be served by any person authorized to serve process of courts of record or by any person designated for that purpose by the appeals board or any member thereof. The person executing process shall receive compensation allowed by the appeals board, not to exceed the fees prescribed by law for similar services. Such fees shall be paid in the same manner as provided herein for the fees of witnesses.

Ref.: 8 C.C.R. §§10348, 10414, 10416, 10536, 10820, 10825, 10828; Hanna § 21.09[1]; Herlick Handbook §§ 1.01[2], [3][a], 10.03[2].

§135. Destruction of files.

In accordance with rules of practice and procedure that it may adopt, the appeals board may, with the approval of the Secretary of State, destroy or otherwise dispose of any file kept by it in connection with any proceeding under Division 4 (commencing with Section 3200) or Division 4.5 (commencing with Section 6100). **Leg.H.** 1995 ch. 556, 2014 ch. 28 (SB 854) §61, effective June 20, 2014.

Ref.: 8 C.C.R. §§10168, 10755, 10758; Herlick Handbook § 1.01[3][a].

§138. Appointment of deputy in director's absence.

The administrative director may appoint a deputy to act when he or she is absent from the state due to official business, vacation, or illness. **Leg.H.** 2002 ch. 6 (AB 749), 2011 ch. 559 (AB 1426) §8, effective October 7, 2011.

Ref.: Hanna § 1.12[1]; Herlick Handbook § 1.01[3][a].

§138.1. Administrative director; appointment; salary.

The administrative director shall be appointed by the Governor with the advice and consent of the Senate and shall hold office at the pleasure of the Governor. He or she shall receive the salary provided for by Chapter 6 (commencing with Section 11550) of Part 1 of Division 3 of Title 2 of the Government Code. **Leg.H.** 2002 ch. 6 (AB 749), 2003 ch. 639 (SB 228), 2011 ch. 559 (AB 1426) §9, effective October 7, 2011.

Ref.: Hanna § 1.12[1]; Herlick Handbook § 1.01[3][a], [b].

§138.2. Division of Workers' Compensation headquarters; administrative offices; notice of public meetings.

(a) The headquarters of the Division of Workers' Compensation shall be based at and operated from a centrally located city.

The administrative director shall have an office in that city with suitable rooms, necessary office furniture, stationery, and supplies, and may rent quarters in other places for the purpose of establishing branch or service offices, and for that purpose may provide those offices with necessary furniture, stationery, and supplies.

(b) The administrative director shall provide suitable rooms, with necessary office furniture, stationery, and supplies, for the appeals board at the centrally located city in which the board shall be based and from which it shall operate, and may rent quarters in other places for the purpose of establishing branch or service offices for the appeals board, and for that purpose may provide those offices with necessary furniture, stationery, and supplies.

(c) All meetings held by the administrative director shall be open and public. Notice thereof shall be published in papers of general circulation not more than 30 days and not less than 10 days prior to each meeting in Sacramento, San Francisco, Fresno, Los Angeles, and San Diego. Written notice of all meetings shall be given to all persons who request, in writing directed to the administrative director, that they be given notice. **Leg.H.** 1994 chs. 146, 1097, 2002 ch. 6 (AB 749), 2011 ch. 559 (AB 1426) §10, effective October 7, 2011.

Ref.: 8 C.C.R. §9900; Hanna §§ 1.11[1], 1.12[1], [5]; Herlick Handbook § 1.01[3][a].

§138.3. Notice to injured employee of right to benefits.

The administrative director shall, with respect to all injuries, prescribe, pursuant to Section 5402, reasonable rules and regulations requiring the employer to serve notice on the injured employee that he may be entitled to benefits under this division.

Ref.: 8 C.C.R. §§9900, 10101, 10101.1, 10102; Herlick Handbook §§ 1.01[3][a], 16.3.

§138.4. Injuries involving lost time; claims administrator's duties and responsibilities; claim form and notice of potential eligibility of benefits; regulatory authority of administrative director.

(a) For the purpose of this section, "claims administrator" means a self-administered workers' compensation insurer; or a self-administered self-insured employer; or a self-administered legally uninsured employer; or a self-administered joint powers authority; or a third-party claims administrator for an insurer, a self-insured employer, a legally uninsured employer, or a joint powers authority.

(b) With respect to injuries resulting in lost time beyond the employee's work shift at the time of injury or medical treatment beyond first aid:

(1) If the claims administrator obtains knowledge that the employer has not provided a claim form or a notice of potential eligibility for benefits to the employee, it shall

provide the form and notice to the employee within three working days of its knowledge that the form or notice was not provided.

(2) If the claims administrator cannot determine if the employer has provided a claim form and notice of potential eligibility for benefits to the employee, the claims administrator shall provide the form and notice to the employee within 30 days of the administrator's date of knowledge of the claim.

(c) The administrative director, in consultation with the Commission on Health and Safety and Workers' Compensation, shall prescribe reasonable rules and regulations, including notice of the right to consult with an attorney, where appropriate, for serving on the employee (or employee's dependents, in the case of death), the following:

(1) Notices dealing with the payment, nonpayment, or delay in payment of temporary disability, permanent disability, supplemental job displacement, and death benefits.

(2) Notices of any change in the amount or type of benefits being provided, the termination of benefits, the rejection of any liability for compensation, and an accounting of benefits paid.

(3) Notices of rights to select the primary treating physician, written continuity of care policies, requests for a comprehensive medical evaluation, and offers of regular, modified, or alternative work.

(d) The administrative director, in consultation with the Commission on Health and Safety and Workers' Compensation, shall develop, make fully accessible on the department's Internet Web site, and make available at district offices informational material written in plain language that describes the overall workers' compensation claims process, including the rights and obligations of employees and employers at every stage of a claim when a notice is required.

(e) Each notice prescribed by the administrative director shall be written in plain language, shall reference the informational material described in subdivision (d) to enable employees to understand the context of the notices, and shall clearly state the Internet Web site address and contact information that an employee may use to access the informational material.

(f) On or before January 1, 2018, the administrative director shall adopt regulations to provide employees with notice that they may access medical treatment outside of the workers' compensation system following the denial of their claim. **Leg.H.** 1999 ch. 83, 2002 ch. 6 (AB 749), 2011 ch. 544 (AB 335) §1, 2016 ch. 868 (SB 1160) §1.

2016 Note: The Legislature finds and declares the following:

(a) Section 4 of Article XIV of the California Constitution vests the Legislature with plenary power to create and to enforce a complete system of workers' compensation by appropriate legislation, and that plenary power includes, without limitation, the power and authority to make full provision for the manner and means by which any lien for compensation for those services may be filed or enforced within the workers' compensation system.

(b) Despite prior legislative action to reform the lien filing and recovery process within the workers' compensation system, including Senate Bill 863 in 2012, there continues to be abuse of the lien process within the workers' compensation system by some providers of medical treatment and other medical-legal services who have engaged in fraud or other criminal conduct within the workers' compensation system, or who have engaged in medical billing fraud, insurance fraud, or fraud against the federal Medicare or Medi-Cal systems.

(c) Notwithstanding fraudulent and criminal conduct by some providers of medical treatment or other medical-legal services, those providers have continued to file and to collect on liens within the workers' compensation system while criminal charges alleging fraud within the workers' compensation system, or medical billing or insurance fraud, or fraud within the federal Medicare or Medi-Cal systems, are pending against those providers.

(d) The ability of providers of medical treatment or other medical-legal services to continue to file and to collect on liens, while criminal charges are pending against the provider, including through the use of lien or collection assignments, has created excessive and unnecessary administrative burdens for the workers' compensation system, has resulted in pressure on employers and insurers to settle liens that may in fact have arisen from prior or ongoing criminal conduct, has threatened the health and safety of workers who may be referred for or receive medical treatment or other medical-legal services that not reasonable and necessary, has allowed continued funding of fraudulent practices through ongoing lien collections during the pendency of criminal proceedings, and has undermined public confidence in the workers' compensation system.

(e) Therefore, in order to ensure the efficient, just, and orderly administration of the workers' compensation system, and to accomplish substantial justice in all cases, the Legislature declares that it is necessary to enact legislation to provide that any lien filed by, or for recovery of compensation for services rendered by, any provider of medical treatment or other medical-legal services shall be automatically stayed upon the filing of criminal charges against that provider for an offense involving fraud against the workers' compensation system, medical billing fraud, insurance fraud, or fraud against the federal Medicare or Medi-Cal programs, and that the stay shall remain in effect until the resolution of the criminal proceedings. Stats. 2016 ch. 868 (SB 1160) §16.

Ref.: 8 C.C.R. §§9702, 9703, 9810, 9811, 9812, 9813, 9815, 10101, 10101.1, 10103, 10103.1, 10103.2; Hanna § 24.01[2]; Herlick Handbook §§ 1.01[3][a], 14.2, 16.3.

§138.5. Enforcement of child support obligations; Workers' Compensation Notification Project.

The Division of Workers' Compensation shall cooperate in the enforcement of child support obligations. At the request of the Department of Child Support Services, the administrative director shall assist in providing to the State Department of Child Support Services information concerning persons who are receiving permanent disability benefits or who have filed an application for adjudication of a claim which the Department of Child Support Services determines is necessary to carry out its responsibilities pursuant to Section 17510 of the Family Code.

The process of sharing information with regard to applicants for and recipients of permanent disability benefits required by this section shall be known as the Workers' Compensation Notification Project. **Leg.H.** 1994 chs. 146, 1097, 2000 ch. 808, effective September 28, 2000.

Ref.: Herlick Handbook §§ 1.01[3][a], 10.10[3].

§138.6. Development of workers' compensation information system.

(a) The administrative director, in consultation with the Insurance Commissioner and the Workers' Compensation Insurance Rating Bureau, shall develop a cost-efficient workers' compensation information system, which shall be administered by the division. The administrative director shall adopt regulations specifying the data elements to be collected by electronic data interchange.

(b) The information system shall do the following:

(1) Assist the department to manage the workers' compensation system in an effective and efficient manner.

(2) Facilitate the evaluation of the efficiency and effectiveness of the delivery system.

(3) Assist in measuring how adequately the system indemnifies injured workers and their dependents.

(4) Provide statistical data for research into specific aspects of the workers' compensation program.

(c) The data collected electronically shall be compatible with the Electronic Data Interchange System of the International Association of Industrial Accident Boards and Commissions. The administrative director may adopt regulations authorizing the use of other nationally recognized data transmission formats in addition to those set forth in the Electronic Data Interchange System for the transmission of data required pursuant to this section. The administrative director shall accept data transmissions in any authorized format. If the administrative director determines that any authorized data transmission format is not in general use by claims administrators, conflicts with the requirements of state or federal law, or is obsolete, the administrative director may adopt regulations eliminating that data transmission format from those authorized pursuant to this subdivision.

(d)(1) The administrative director shall assess an administrative penalty against a claims administrator for a violation of data reporting requirements adopted pursuant to this section. The administrative director shall promulgate a schedule of penalties providing for an assessment of no more than ten thousand dollars ($10,000) against a claims administrator in any single year, calculated as follows:

(A) No more than one hundred dollars ($100) multiplied by the number of violations in that year that resulted in a required data report not being submitted or not being accepted.

(B) No more than fifty dollars ($50) multiplied by the number of violations in that year that resulted in a required report being late or accepted with an error.

(C) Multiple errors in a single report shall be counted as a single violation.

(D) No penalty shall be assessed pursuant to Section 129.5 for any violation of data reporting requirements for which a penalty has been or may be assessed pursuant to this section.

(2) The schedule promulgated by the administrative director pursuant to paragraph (1) shall establish threshold rates of violations that shall be excluded from the calculation of the assessment, as follows:

(A) The threshold rate for reports that are not submitted or are submitted but not accepted shall not be less than 3 percent of the number of reports that are required to be filed by or on behalf of the claims administrator.

(B) The threshold rate for reports that are accepted with an error shall not be less than 3 percent of the number of reports that are accepted with an error.

(C) The administrative director shall set higher threshold rates as appropriate in recognition of the fact that the data necessary for timely and accurate reporting may not be always available to a claims administrator or the claims administrator's agents.

(D) The administrative director may establish higher thresholds for particular data elements that commonly are not reasonably available.

(3) The administrative director may estimate the number of required data reports that are not submitted by comparing a statistically valid sample of data available to the administrative director from other sources with the data reported pursuant to this section.

(4) All penalties assessed pursuant to this section shall be deposited in the Workers' Compensation Administration Revolving Fund.

(5) The administrative director shall publish an annual report disclosing the compliance rates of claims administrators and post the report and a list of claims administrators who are in violation of the data reporting requirements on the Internet Web site of the Division of Workers' Compensation. **Leg.H.** 1993 ch. 121, effective July 16, 1993, ch. 1242, 1997 ch. 729, 2000 ch. 318, 2011 ch. 568 (SB 826) §2, 2016 ch. 868 (SB 1160) §2.

2016 Note: For legislative findings and declarations, see the 2016 Note following Lab C §138.4.

Ref.: 8 C.C.R. §§9700, 9701, 9702, 9703, 9704; Hanna § 1.12[2]; Herlick Handbook § 1.01[3][a], [b].

§138.7. "Individually identifiable information"; restricted access.

(a) Except as expressly permitted in subdivision (b), a person or public or private entity not a party to a claim for workers' compensation benefits shall not obtain individually identifiable information obtained or maintained by the division regarding that claim. For purposes of this section, "individually identifiable information" means any data concerning an injury or claim that is linked to a uniquely identifiable employee, employer, claims administrator, or any other person or entity.

(b)(1)(A) The administrative director, or a statistical agent designated by the administrative director, may use individually identifiable information for purposes of creating and maintaining the workers' compensation information system as specified in Section 138.6.

(B) The administrative director may publish the identity of claims administrators in the annual report disclosing the compliance rates of claims administrators pursuant to subdivision (d) of Section 138.6.

(C) The administrative director shall use individually identifiable information for purposes of creating provider medical utilization data as specified in Section 138.8.

(2)(A) The State Department of Public Health may use individually identifiable information for purposes of establishing and maintaining a program on occupational health and occupational disease prevention as specified in Section 105175 of the Health and Safety Code.

(B)(i) The State Department of Health Care Services may use individually identifiable information for purposes of seeking recovery of Medi-Cal costs incurred by the state for treatment provided to injured workers that should have been incurred by employers and insurance carriers pursuant to Article 3.5 (commencing with Section 14124.70) of Chapter 7 of Part 3 of Division 9 of the Welfare and Institutions Code.

(ii) The Department of Industrial Relations shall furnish individually identifiable information to the State Department of Health Care Services, and the State Department of Health Care Services may furnish the information to its designated agent, provided that the individually identifiable information shall not be disclosed for use other than the purposes described in clause (i). The administrative director may adopt regulations solely for the purpose of governing access by the State Department of Health Care Services or its designated agents to the individually identifiable information as defined in subdivision (a).

(3)(A) Individually identifiable information may be used by the Division of Workers' Compensation and the Division of Occupational Safety and Health as necessary to carry out their duties. The administrative director shall adopt regulations governing the access to the information described in this subdivision by these divisions. Any regulations adopted pursuant to this subdivision shall set forth the specific uses for which this information may be obtained.

(B) Individually identifiable information maintained in the workers' compensation information system and the Division of Workers' Compensation may be used by researchers employed by or under contract to the Commission on Health and Safety and Workers' Compensation as necessary to carry out the commission's research. The administrative director shall adopt regulations governing the access to the information described in this subdivision by commission researchers. These regulations shall set forth the specific uses for which this information may be obtained and include provisions guaranteeing the confidentiality of individually identifiable information. Individually identifiable information obtained under this subdivision shall not be disclosed to commission members. Individually identifiable information obtained by researchers under contract to the commission pursuant to this subparagraph may not be disclosed to any other person or entity, public or private, for a use other than that research project for which the information was obtained. Within a reasonable period of time after the research for which the information was obtained has been completed, the data collected shall be modified in a manner so that the subjects cannot be identified, directly or through identifiers linked to the subjects.

(C) Individually identifiable information may be used by the Office of Self-Insurance Plans of the Department of Industrial Relations as necessary to carry out its duties, including evaluating the costs of administration, workers' compensation benefit expenditures, and solvency and performance of the public self-insured employers' workers' compensation programs.

(4) The administrative director shall adopt regulations allowing reasonable access to individually identifiable information by other persons or public or private entities for the purpose of bona fide statistical research. This research shall not divulge individually identifiable information concerning a particular employee, employer, claims administrator, or any other person or entity. The regulations adopted pursuant to this paragraph shall include provisions guaranteeing the confidentiality of individually identifiable information. Within a reasonable period of time after the research for which the information was obtained has been completed, the data collected shall be modified in a manner so that the subjects cannot be identified, directly or through identifiers linked to the subjects.

(5)(A) This section shall not operate to exempt from disclosure any information that is considered to be a public record pursuant to the California Public Records Act (Chapter 3.5 (commencing with Section 6250) of Division 7 of Title 1 of the Government Code) contained in an individual's file once an application for adjudication has been filed pursuant to Section 5501.5.

(B) Individually identifiable information shall not be provided to any person or public or private entity who is not a party to the claim unless that person self-identifies or that public or private entity identifies itself and states the reason for making the request. The administrative director may require the person or public or private entity making the request to produce information to verify that the name and address of the requester is valid and correct. If the purpose of the request is related to preemployment screening, the administrative director shall notify the person about whom the information is requested that the information was provided and shall include the following in 12-point type:

"IT MAY BE A VIOLATION OF FEDERAL AND STATE LAW TO DISCRIMINATE AGAINST A JOB APPLICANT BECAUSE THE APPLICANT HAS FILED A CLAIM FOR WORKERS' COMPENSATION BENEFITS."

(C) Any residence address is confidential and shall not be disclosed to any person or public or private entity except to a party to the claim, a law enforcement agency, an office of a district attorney, any person for a journalistic purpose, or other governmental agency.

(D) This paragraph does not prohibit the use of individually identifiable information for purposes of identifying bona fide lien claimants.

(c) Except as provided in subdivision (b), individually identifiable information obtained by the division is privileged and is not subject to subpoena in a civil proceeding unless, after reasonable notice to the division and a hearing, a court determines that the public interest and the intent of this section will not be jeopardized by disclosure of the information. This section shall not operate to restrict access to information by any law enforcement agency or district attorney's office or to limit admissibility of that information in a criminal proceeding.

(d) It is unlawful for any person who has received individually identifiable information from the division pursuant to this section to provide that information to any person who is not entitled to it under this section. **Leg.H.** 1997 ch. 674, 1998 ch. 624, 2001 ch. 792, 2010 ch. 611 (AB 2780) §1, effective September 30, 2010, 2011 ch. 568 (SB 826) §3, 2012 ch. 46 (SB 1038) §80, effective June 27, 2012, 2016 ch. 30 (SB 833) §18, effective June 27, 2016, 2018 ch. 538 (AB 2334) §2, 2019 chs. 497 (AB 991) §182, 647 (SB 537) §2.

Ref.: 8 C.C.R. §§9700, 9701, 9702, 9703, 9704, 9990; Hanna § 1.12[2]; Herlick Handbook § 1.01[3][a], [b].

§138.8. Utilization data for physicians who treated 10 or more injured workers.

(a) On or before January 1, 2024, and annually thereafter, the administrative director shall publish on the division's internet website provider utilization data, as reported to the Division of Workers' Compensation, for physicians who treated 10 or more injured workers during the 12 months before July 1 of the previous year. The provider utilization data shall include all of the following:

(1) The physician's first and last name.

(2) The physician's specialty.

(3) The physician's National Provider Identifier.

(4) The number of injured workers treated by the physician.

(5) The International Statistical Classification of Diseases and Related Health Problems, 10th revision (ICD-10) codes by both diagnosis and procedure.

(6) A short description of the ICD-10 codes used by the physician.

(7) The number of utilization review decisions that resulted in a modification or denial of a request for authorization of medical treatment based upon a determination of medical necessity.

(8) The number of independent medical review decisions issued in response to an appeal of a utilization review decision that resulted in a modification or denial based upon medical necessity and the number of independent medical review decisions that resulted in the utilization review modification or denial being overturned.

(9) Any additional data as determined by the administrative director.

(b) For purposes of this section, "physician" has the same meaning as set forth in Section 3209.3.

(c) The administrative director may withhold data contained in subdivision (a) if deemed necessary to protect patient privacy. **Leg.H.** 2019 ch. 647 (SB 537) §3.

§139.2. Appointment, qualification, suspension, termination of QMEs; timeframes, guidelines, procedures, and admissibility of medical evaluations.

(a) The administrative director shall appoint qualified medical evaluators in each of the respective specialties as required for the evaluation of medical-legal issues. The appointments shall be for two-year terms.

(b) The administrative director shall appoint or reappoint as a qualified medical evaluator a physician, as defined in Section 3209.3, who is licensed to practice in this state and who demonstrates that he or she meets the requirements in paragraphs (1), (2), (6), and (7), and, if the physician is a medical doctor, doctor of osteopathy, doctor of chiropractic, or a psychologist, that he or she also meets the applicable requirements in paragraph (3), (4), or (5).

(1) Prior to his or her appointment as a qualified medical evaluator, passes an examination written and administered by the administrative director for the purpose of demonstrating competence in evaluating medical-legal issues in the workers' compensation system. Physicians shall not be required to pass an additional examination as a condition of reappointment. A physician seeking appointment as a qualified medical evaluator on or after January 1, 2001, shall also complete prior to appointment, a course on disability evaluation report writing approved by the administrative director. The administrative director shall specify the curriculum to be covered by disability evaluation report writing courses, which shall include, but is not limited to, 12 or more hours of instruction.

(2) Devotes at least one-third of total practice time to providing direct medical treatment, or has served as an agreed medical evaluator on eight or more occasions in the 12 months prior to applying to be appointed as a qualified medical evaluator.

(3) Is a medical doctor or doctor of osteopathy and meets one of the following requirements:

(A) Is board certified in a specialty by a board recognized by the administrative director and either the Medical Board of California or the Osteopathic Medical Board of California.

(B) Has successfully completed a residency training program accredited by the Accreditation Council for Graduate Medical Education or the osteopathic equivalent.

(C) Was an active qualified medical evaluator on June 30, 2000.

(D) Has qualifications that the administrative director and either the Medical Board of California or the Osteopathic Medical Board of California, as appropriate, both deem to be equivalent to board certification in a specialty.

(4) Is a doctor of chiropractic and has been certified in California workers' compensation evaluation by a provider recognized by the administrative director. The certification program shall include instruction on disability evaluation report writing that meets the standards set forth in paragraph (1).

(5) Is a psychologist and meets one of the following requirements:

(A) Is board certified in clinical psychology by a board recognized by the administrative director.

(B) Holds a doctoral degree in psychology, or a doctoral degree deemed equivalent for licensure by the Board of Psychology pursuant to Section 2914 of the Business and Professions Code, from a university or professional school recognized by the administrative director and has not less than five years' postdoctoral experience in the diagnosis and treatment of emotional and mental disorders.

(C) Has not less than five years' postdoctoral experience in the diagnosis and treatment of emotional and mental disorders, and has served as an agreed medical evaluator on eight or more occasions prior to January 1, 1990.

(6) Does not have a conflict of interest as determined under the regulations adopted by the administrative director pursuant to subdivision (o).

(7) Meets any additional medical or professional standards adopted pursuant to paragraph (6) of subdivision (j).

(c) The administrative director shall adopt standards for appointment of physicians who are retired or who hold teaching positions who are exceptionally well qualified to serve as a qualified medical evaluator even though they do not otherwise qualify under paragraph (2) of subdivision (b). A physician whose full-time practice is limited to the forensic evaluation of disability shall not be appointed as a qualified medical evaluator under this subdivision.

(d) The qualified medical evaluator, upon request, shall be reappointed if he or she meets the qualifications of subdivision (b) and meets all of the following criteria:

(1) Is in compliance with all applicable regulations and evaluation guidelines adopted by the administrative director.

(2) Has not had more than five of his or her evaluations that were considered by a workers' compensation administrative law judge at a contested hearing rejected by the workers' compensation administrative law judge or the appeals board pursuant to this section during the most recent two-year period during which the physician served as a qualified medical evaluator. If the workers' compensation administrative law judge or the appeals board rejects the qualified medical evaluator's report on the basis that it fails to meet the minimum standards for those reports established by the administrative director or the appeals board, the workers' compensation administrative law judge or the appeals board, as the case may be, shall make a specific finding to that effect, and shall give notice to the medical evaluator and to the administrative director. Any rejection shall not be counted as one of the five qualifying rejections until the specific finding has become final and time for appeal has expired.

(3) Has completed within the previous 24 months at least 12 hours of continuing education in impairment evaluation or workers' compensation-related medical dispute evaluation approved by the administrative director.

(4) Has not been terminated, suspended, placed on probation, or otherwise disciplined by the administrative director during his or her most recent term as a qualified medical evaluator.

If the evaluator does not meet any one of these criteria, the administrative director may, in his or her discretion, reappoint or deny reappointment according to regulations adopted by the administrative director. A physician who does not currently meet the requirements for initial appointment or who has been terminated under subdivision (e) because his or her license has been revoked or terminated by the licensing authority shall not be reappointed.

(e) The administrative director may, in his or her discretion, suspend or terminate a qualified medical evaluator during his or her term of appointment without a hearing as provided under subdivision (k) or (*l*) whenever either of the following conditions occurs:

(1) The evaluator's license to practice in California has been suspended by the relevant licensing authority so as to preclude practice, or has been revoked or terminated by the licensing authority.

(2) The evaluator has failed to timely pay the fee required by the administrative director pursuant to subdivision (n).

(f) The administrative director shall furnish a physician, upon request, with a written statement of its reasons for termination of, or for denying appointment or reappointment as, a qualified medical evaluator. Upon receipt of a specific response to the statement of reasons, the administrative director shall review his or her decision not to appoint or reappoint the physician or to terminate the physician and shall notify the physician of its final decision within 60 days after receipt of the physician's response.

(g) The administrative director shall establish agreements with qualified medical evaluators to ensure the expeditious evaluation of cases assigned to them for comprehensive medical evaluations.

(h)(1) When requested by an employee or employer pursuant to Section 4062.1, the medical director appointed pursuant to Section 122 shall assign three-member panels of qualified medical evaluators within five working days after receiving a request for a panel. Preference in assigning panels shall be given to cases in which the employee is not represented. If a panel is not assigned within 20 working days, the employee shall have the right to obtain a medical evaluation from any qualified medical evaluator of his or her choice within a reasonable geographic area. The medical director shall use a random selection method for assigning panels of qualified medical evaluators. The medical director shall select evaluators who are specialists of the type requested by the employee. The medical director shall advise the employee that he or she should consult with his or her treating physician prior to deciding which type of specialist to request.

(2) The administrative director shall promulgate a form that shall notify the employee of the physicians selected for his or her panel after a request has been made pursuant to Section 4062.1 or 4062.2. The form shall include, for each physician on the panel, the physician's name, address, telephone number, specialty, number of years in practice, and a brief description of his or her education and training, and shall advise the employee that he or she is entitled to receive transportation expenses and temporary disability for each day necessary for the examination. The form shall also state in a clear and conspicuous location and type: "You have the right to consult with an information and assistance officer at no cost to you prior to selecting the doctor to prepare your evaluation, or you may consult with an attorney. If your claim eventually goes to court, the workers' compensation administrative law judge will consider the evaluation prepared by the doctor you select to decide your claim."

(3) When compiling the list of evaluators from which to select randomly, the medical director shall include all qualified medical evaluators who meet all of the following criteria:

(A) He or she does not have a conflict of interest in the case, as defined by regulations adopted pursuant to subdivision (o).

(B) He or she is certified by the administrative director to evaluate in an appropriate specialty and at locations within the general geographic area of the employee's residence. An evaluator shall not conduct qualified medical evaluations at more than 10 locations.

(C) He or she has not been suspended or terminated as a qualified medical evaluator for failure to pay the fee required by the administrative director pursuant to subdivision (n) or for any other reason.

(4) When the medical director determines that an employee has requested an evaluation by a type of specialist that is appropriate for the employee's injury, but there are not enough qualified medical evaluators of that type within the general geographic area of the employee's residence to establish a three-member panel, the medical director shall include sufficient qualified medical evaluators from other geographic areas and the employer shall pay all necessary travel costs incurred in the event the

employee selects an evaluator from another geographic area.

(i) The medical director appointed pursuant to Section 122 shall continuously review the quality of comprehensive medical evaluations and reports prepared by agreed and qualified medical evaluators and the timeliness with which evaluation reports are prepared and submitted. The review shall include, but not be limited to, a review of a random sample of reports submitted to the division, and a review of all reports alleged to be inaccurate or incomplete by a party to a case for which the evaluation was prepared. The medical director shall submit to the administrative director an annual report summarizing the results of the continuous review of medical evaluations and reports prepared by agreed and qualified medical evaluators and make recommendations for the improvement of the system of medical evaluations and determinations.

(j) After public hearing pursuant to Section 5307.3, the administrative director shall adopt regulations concerning the following issues:

(1)(A) Standards governing the timeframes within which medical evaluations shall be prepared and submitted by agreed and qualified medical evaluators. Except as provided in this subdivision, the timeframe for initial medical evaluations to be prepared and submitted shall be no more than 30 days after the evaluator has seen the employee or otherwise commenced the medical evaluation procedure. The administrative director shall develop regulations governing the provision of extensions of the 30-day period in both of the following cases:

(i) When the evaluator has not received test results or consulting physician's evaluations in time to meet the 30-day deadline.

(ii) To extend the 30-day period by not more than 15 days when the failure to meet the 30-day deadline was for good cause.

(B) For purposes of subparagraph (A), "good cause" means any of the following:

(i) Medical emergencies of the evaluator or evaluator's family.

(ii) Death in the evaluator's family.

(iii) Natural disasters or other community catastrophes that interrupt the operation of the evaluator's business.

(C) The administrative director shall develop timeframes governing availability of qualified medical evaluators for unrepresented employees under Section 4062.1. These timeframes shall give the employee the right to the addition of a new evaluator to his or her panel, selected at random, for each evaluator not available to see the employee within a specified period of time, but shall also permit the employee to waive this right for a specified period of time thereafter.

(2) Procedures to be followed by all physicians in evaluating the existence and extent of permanent impairment and limitations resulting from an injury in a manner consistent with Sections 4660 and 4660.1.

(3) Procedures governing the determination of any disputed medical treatment issues in a manner consistent with Section 5307.27.

(4) Procedures to be used in determining the compensability of psychiatric injury. The procedures shall be in accordance with Section 3208.3 and shall require that the diagnosis of a mental disorder be expressed using the terminology and criteria of the American Psychiatric Association's Diagnostic and Statistical Manual of Mental Disorders, Third Edition-Revised, or the terminology and diagnostic criteria of other psychiatric diagnostic manuals generally approved and accepted nationally by practitioners in the field of psychiatric medicine.

(5) Guidelines for the range of time normally required to perform the following:

(A) A medical-legal evaluation that has not been defined and valued pursuant to Section 5307.6. The guidelines shall establish minimum times for patient contact in the conduct of the evaluations, and shall be consistent with regulations adopted pursuant to Section 5307.6.

(B) Any treatment procedures that have not been defined and valued pursuant to Section 5307.1.

(C) Any other evaluation procedure requested by the Insurance Commissioner, or deemed appropriate by the administrative director.

(6) Any additional medical or professional standards that a medical evaluator shall meet as a condition of appointment, reappointment, or maintenance in the status of a medical evaluator.

(k) Except as provided in this subdivision, the administrative director may, in his or her discretion, suspend or terminate the privilege of a physician to serve as a qualified medical evaluator if the administrative director, after hearing pursuant to subdivision (*l*), determines, based on substantial evidence, that a qualified medical evaluator:

(1) Has violated any material statutory or administrative duty.

(2) Has failed to follow the medical procedures or qualifications established pursuant to paragraph (2), (3), (4), or (5) of subdivision (j).

(3) Has failed to comply with the timeframe standards established pursuant to subdivision (j).

(4) Has failed to meet the requirements of subdivision (b) or (c).

(5) Has prepared medical-legal evaluations that fail to meet the minimum standards for those reports established by the administrative director or the appeals board.

(6) Has made material misrepresentations or false statements in an application for appointment or reappointment as a qualified medical evaluator.

A hearing shall not be required prior to the suspension or termination of a physician's privilege to serve as a qualified medical evaluator when the physician has done either of the following:

(A) Failed to timely pay the fee required pursuant to subdivision (n).

(B) Had his or her license to practice in California suspended by the relevant licensing authority so as to preclude practice, or had the license revoked or terminated by the licensing authority.

(*l*) The administrative director shall cite the qualified medical evaluator for a violation listed in subdivision (k) and shall set a hearing on the alleged violation within 30 days of service of the citation on the qualified medical evaluator. In addition to the authority to terminate or suspend the qualified medical evaluator upon finding a violation listed in subdivision (k), the administrative director may, in his or her discretion, place a qualified medical evaluator on probation subject to appropriate conditions, including ordering continuing education or training. The administrative director shall report to the appropriate licensing board the name of any qualified medical evaluator who is disciplined pursuant to this subdivision.

(m) The administrative director shall terminate from the list of medical evaluators any physician where licensure has been terminated by the relevant licensing board, or who has been convicted of a misdemeanor or felony related to the conduct of his or her medical practice, or of a crime of moral turpitude. The administrative director shall suspend or terminate as a medical evaluator any physician who has been suspended or placed on probation by the relevant licensing board. If a physician is suspended or terminated as a qualified medical evaluator under this subdivision, a report prepared by the physician that is not complete, signed, and furnished to one or more of the parties prior to the date of conviction or action of the licensing board, whichever is earlier, shall not be admissible in any proceeding before the appeals board nor shall there be any liability for payment for the report and any expense incurred by the physician in connection with the report.

(n) A qualified medical evaluator shall pay a fee, as determined by the administrative director, for appointment or reappointment. These fees shall be based on a sliding scale as established by the administrative director. All revenues from fees paid under this subdivision shall be deposited into the Workers' Compensation Administration Revolving Fund and are available for expenditure upon appropriation by the Legislature, and shall not be used by any other department or agency or for any purpose other than administration of the programs of the Division of Workers' Compensation related to the provision of medical treatment to injured employees.

(o) An evaluator shall not request or accept any compensation or other thing of value from any source that does or could create a conflict with his or her duties as an evaluator under this code. The administrative director, after consultation with the Commission on Health and Safety and Workers' Compensation, shall adopt regulations to implement this subdivision. **Leg.H.** 1992 ch. 1352, effective September 30, 1992, 1993 ch. 4, effective April 3, 1993, ch. 121, effective July 16, 1993, ch. 1242, 1994 ch. 301, effective July 21, 1994, ch. 1118, 1995 ch. 319, 2000 ch. 54, 2003 chs. 228 (AB 1756), effective August 11, 2003, 639 (SB 228), 2004 ch. 34 (SB 899), effective April 19, 2004, 2012 ch. 363 (SB 863) §5, 2013 ch. 287 (SB 375) §2, 2014 ch. 71 (SB 1304) §106, 2016 ch. 86 (SB 1171) §214.

2012 Note: For legislative findings, declarations, and applicability of Stats. 2012 ch. 363, see the 2012 Notes following Lab C §62.5.

2004 Note: The amendment to §139.2 made by this act shall apply prospectively from the date of enactment of this act, regardless of the date of injury, unless otherwise specified, but shall not constitute good cause to reopen or rescind, alter, or amend any existing order, decision, or award of the Workers' Compensation Appeals Board. Stats. 2004 ch. 34 (SB 899) §47.

2003 Note: The regulations adopted by the Industrial Medical Council contained in Chapter 1 (commencing with Section 1) of Division 1 of Title 8 of the California Code of Regulations, except for those regulations repealed in Section 50 of this act, shall remain in effect and shall be deemed to be regulations adopted by the Administrative Director of the Division of Workers' Compensation. The terms of all qualified medical examiners appointed by the Industrial Medical Council shall be unaffected by the changes made by this act. All qualified medical examiners appointed by the Industrial Medical Council shall be deemed to be appointments made by the Administrative Director of the Division of Workers' Compensation. Any pending disciplinary actions against qualified medical examiners shall not be affected by the changes made by this act. Stats. 2003 ch. 639 (SB 228) §52.

1993 Note: Section 139.2, as amended by ch. 121, applies only to injuries occurring on or after January 1, 1994. Stats. 1993 ch. 121 §77.

Ref.: 8 C.C.R. §§1, 10, 10.2, 10.5, 11, 11.5, 12, 13, 14, 15, 16, 17, 18, 19, 30, 30.5, 31, 31.5, 32, 33, 35, 38, 39, 39.5, 40, 41, 43, 44, 45, 46, 47, 48, 49, 49.2, 49.4, 49.6, 49.8, 49.9, 50, 51, 52, 53, 54, 55, 56, 57, 60, 61, 62, 65, 74, 107, 108, 109, 110, 111, 112, 113, 114, 115, 116, 117, 150, 153, 154, 9795, 10631; Hanna §§ 22.11, 22.13; Herlick Handbook §§ 1.01[3][a], 1.02, 4.07[2], 6.04[5], 9.18, 10.09[1], 14.4, 14.21.

§139.21. Suspension of physician, practitioner, or provider from participation in workers' compensation system for cause; notice and hearing; adjudication of liens.

(a)(1) The administrative director shall promptly suspend, pursuant to subdivision (b), any physician, practitioner, or provider from participating in the workers' compensation system as a physician, practitioner, or provider if the individual or entity meets any of the following criteria:

(A) The individual or entity has been convicted of any felony or misdemeanor and that crime comes within any of the following descriptions:

(i) It involves fraud or abuse of the federal Medicare or Medicaid programs, the Medi-Cal program, or the workers' compensation system, or fraud or abuse of any patient.

(ii) It relates to the conduct of the individual's medical practice as it pertains to patient care.

(iii) It is a financial crime that relates to the federal Medicare or Medicaid programs, the Medi-Cal program, or the workers' compensation system.

(iv) It is otherwise substantially related to the qualifications, functions, or duties of a provider of services.

(B) The individual or entity has been suspended, due to fraud or abuse, from the federal Medicare or Medicaid programs or the Medi-Cal program.

(C) The individual's license, certificate, or approval to provide health care has been surrendered or revoked.

(D) The entity is controlled by an individual who has been convicted of a felony or misdemeanor described in subparagraph (A).

(E) The changes made to clauses (i) and (iii) of subparagraph (A) and subparagraph (B) during the 2017–18 Regular Session of the Legislature do not constitute a change in, but are declaratory of, the existing law.

(2) The administrative director shall exercise due diligence to identify physicians, practitioners, or providers who have been suspended pursuant to subparagraph (B) of paragraph (1) by accessing the quarterly updates to the list of suspended and ineligible providers maintained by the State Department of Health Care Services for the Medi-Cal program at https://files.medi-cal.ca.gov/pubsdoco/SandILanding.asp.

Labor

(3) For purposes of this section and Section 4615, an entity is controlled by an individual if the individual is an officer or a director of the entity, or a shareholder with a 10 percent or greater interest in the entity.

(4) For purposes of this section and Section 4615, an individual or entity is considered to have been convicted of a crime if any of the following applies:

(A) A judgment of conviction has been entered by a federal, state, or local court, regardless of whether there is an appeal pending or whether the judgment of conviction or other record relating to criminal conduct has been expunged.

(B) There has been a verdict or finding of guilt by a federal, state, or local court.

(C) A plea of guilty has been accepted by a federal, state, or local court.

(5) Notwithstanding the initiation or completion of a prior suspension pursuant to this section, the administrative director may amend an existing notice of suspension or commence a subsequent suspension proceeding based upon new or additional grounds for suspending the physician, practitioner, or provider pursuant to paragraph (1).

(6) The administrative director may adopt regulations specifying any exemptions that shall not serve as the basis for exclusion under paragraph (1).

(b)(1) The administrative director shall adopt regulations for suspending a physician, practitioner, or provider from participating in the workers' compensation system, subject to the notice and hearing requirements in paragraph (2).

(2) The administrative director shall furnish to the physician, practitioner, or provider written notice of the right to a hearing regarding the suspension and the procedure to follow to request a hearing. The notice shall state that the administrative director is required to suspend the physician, practitioner, or provider pursuant to subdivision (a) after 30 days from the date the notice is mailed unless the physician, practitioner, or provider requests a hearing and, in that hearing, the physician, practitioner, or provider provides proof that paragraph (1) of subdivision (a) is not applicable. The physician, practitioner, or provider may request a hearing within 10 days from the date the notice is sent by the administrative director. The request for the hearing shall stay the suspension. The hearing shall be held within 30 days of the receipt of the request. Upon the completion of the hearing, if the administrative director finds that paragraph (1) of subdivision (a) is applicable, the administrative director shall immediately suspend the physician, practitioner, or provider.

(3) The administrative director shall have power and jurisdiction to do all things necessary or convenient to conduct the hearings provided for in paragraph (2). The hearings and investigations may be conducted by any designated hearing officer appointed by the administrative director. Any authorized person conducting that hearing or investigation may administer oaths, subpoena and require the attendance of witnesses and the production of books or papers, and cause the depositions of witnesses residing within or without the state to be taken in the manner prescribed by law for like depositions in civil cases in the superior court of this state under Title 4 (commencing with Section 2016.010) of Part 4 of the Code of Civil Procedure.

(c) The administrative director shall promptly notify the physician's, practitioner's, or provider's state licensing, certifying, or registering authority of a suspension imposed pursuant to this section and shall update the division's qualified medical evaluator and medical provider network databases, as appropriate.

(d) Upon suspension of a physician, practitioner, or provider pursuant to this section, the administrative director shall give notice of the suspension to the chief judge of the division, and the chief judge or his or her designee shall promptly thereafter provide written notification of the suspension to district offices and all workers' compensation judges. The method of notification to all district offices and to all workers' compensation judges shall be in a manner determined by the chief judge in his or her discretion. The administrative director shall also post notification of the suspension on the department's Internet Web site.

(e) The following procedures apply for the adjudication of any liens of a physician, practitioner, or provider suspended pursuant to subparagraph (A) or (D) of paragraph (1) of subdivision (a), including any liens filed by or on behalf of the physician, practitioner, or provider or any entity controlled by the suspended physician, practitioner, or provider:

(1) If the disposition of the criminal proceeding provides for or requires, whether by plea agreement or by judgment, dismissal of liens and forfeiture of sums claimed therein, as specified in the criminal disposition, all of those liens shall be deemed dismissed with prejudice by operation of law as of the effective date of the final disposition in the criminal proceeding, and orders notifying of those dismissals shall be entered by workers' compensation judges.

(2) All liens that have not been dismissed in accordance with paragraph (1) and remain pending in any workers' compensation case in any district office within the state shall be consolidated and adjudicated in a special lien proceeding as described in subdivisions (f) to (i), inclusive.

(f) After notice of suspension, pursuant to subdivision (d), and if subdivision (e) applies, the administrative director shall appoint a special lien proceeding attorney, who shall be an attorney employed by the division or by the department. The special lien proceeding attorney shall, based on the information that is available, identify liens subject to disposition pursuant to subdivision (e), and workers' compensation cases in which those liens are pending, and shall notify the chief judge regarding those liens. Based on this information, the chief judge or his or her designee shall identify a district office for a consolidated special lien proceeding to adjudicate those liens, and shall appoint a workers' compensation judge to preside over that proceeding.

(g) It shall be a presumption affecting the burden of proof that all liens to be adjudicated in the special lien proceeding, and all underlying bills for service and claims for compensation asserted therein, arise from the conduct subjecting the physician, practitioner, or provider to suspension, and that payment is not due and should not be made on those liens because they arise from, or are connected to, criminal, fraudulent, or abusive conduct or activity. A lien claimant shall not have the right to payment unless he or she rebuts that presumption by a preponderance of the evidence.

(h) The special lien proceedings shall be governed by the same laws, regulations, and procedures that govern all other matters before the appeals board. The administrative director may adopt regulations for the implementation of this section.

(i) If it is determined in a special lien proceeding that a lien does not arise from the conduct subjecting a physician, practitioner, or provider to suspension, the workers' compensation judge shall have the discretion to adjudicate the lien or transfer the lien back to the district office having venue over the case in which the lien was filed.

(j) At any time following suspension, a physician, practitioner, or provider lien claimant may elect to withdraw or to dismiss his or her lien with prejudice, which shall constitute a final disposition of the claim for compensation asserted therein.

(k) The provisions of this section do not affect, amend, alter, or in any way apply to the provisions of Section 139.2. **Leg.H.** 2016 ch. 852 (AB 1244) §1, 2017 chs. 300 (AB 1422) §1, 561 (AB 1516) §141 (ch. 300 prevails; ch. 561 not effective).

Ref.: Hanna § 30.22[1]; Herlick Handbook § 1.02.

§139.3. Referral to person with whom physician has financial interest unlawful.

(a) Notwithstanding any other law, to the extent those services are paid pursuant to Division 4 (commencing with Section 3200), it is unlawful for a physician to refer a person for clinical laboratory, diagnostic nuclear medicine, radiation oncology, physical therapy, physical rehabilitation, psychometric testing, home infusion therapy, outpatient surgery, diagnostic imaging goods or services, or pharmacy goods, whether for treatment or medical-legal purposes, if the physician or his or her immediate family has a financial interest with the person or in the entity that receives the referral.

(b) For purposes of this section and Section 139.31, the following shall apply:

(1) "Diagnostic imaging" includes, but is not limited to, all X-ray, computed axial tomography magnetic resonance imaging, nuclear medicine, positron emission tomography, mammography, and ultrasound goods and services.

(2) "Immediate family" includes the spouse and children of the physician, the parents of the physician, and the spouses of the children of the physician.

(3) "Physician" means a physician as defined in Section 3209.3.

(4) A "financial interest" includes, but is not limited to, any type of ownership, interest, debt, loan, lease, compensation, remuneration, discount, rebate, refund, dividend, distribution, subsidy, or other form of direct or indirect payment, whether in money or otherwise, between a licensee and a person or entity to whom the physician refers a person for a good or service specified in subdivision (a). A financial interest also exists if there is an indirect relationship between a physician and the referral recipient, including, but not limited to, an arrangement whereby a physician has an ownership interest in any entity that leases property to the referral recipient. Any financial interest transferred by a physician to, or otherwise established in, any person or entity for the purpose of avoiding the prohibition of this section shall be deemed a financial interest of the physician.

(5) A "physician's office" is either of the following:

(A) An office of a physician in solo practice.

(B) An office in which the services or goods are personally provided by the physician or by employees in that office, or personally by independent contractors in that office, in accordance with other provisions of law. Employees and independent contractors shall be licensed or certified when that licensure or certification is required by law.

(6) The "office of a group practice" is an office or offices in which two or more physicians are legally organized as a partnership, professional corporation, or not-for-profit corporation licensed according to subdivision (a) of Section 1204 of the Health and Safety Code for which all of the following are applicable:

(A) Each physician who is a member of the group provides substantially the full range of services that the physician routinely provides, including medical care, consultation, diagnosis, or treatment, through the joint use of shared office space, facilities, equipment, and personnel.

(B) Substantially all of the services of the physicians who are members of the group are provided through the group and are billed in the name of the group and amounts so received are treated as receipts of the group, and except that in the case of multispecialty clinics, as defined in subdivision (*l*) of Section 1206 of the Health and Safety Code, physician services are billed in the name of the multispecialty clinic and amounts so received are treated as receipts of the multispecialty clinic.

(C) The overhead expenses of, and the income from, the practice are distributed in accordance with methods previously determined by members of the group.

(7) Outpatient surgery includes both of the following:

(A) Any procedure performed on an outpatient basis in the operating rooms, ambulatory surgery rooms, endoscopy units, cardiac catheterization laboratories, or other sections of a freestanding ambulatory surgery clinic, whether or not licensed under paragraph (1) of subdivision (b) of Section 1204 of the Health and Safety Code.

(B) The ambulatory surgery itself.

(8) "Pharmacy goods" means any dangerous drug or dangerous device as defined by Section 4022 of the Business and Professions Code, any medical food as defined by Section 109971 of the Health and Safety Code, and any over-the-counter drug as classified by the federal Food and Drug Administration, except over-the-counter drugs sold at commercially reasonable rates in physical retail outlets commonly accessed by the public.

(c)(1) It is unlawful for a licensee to enter into an arrangement or scheme, such as a cross-referral arrangement, that the licensee knows, or should know, has a principal purpose of ensuring referrals by the licensee to a particular entity that, if the licensee directly made referrals to that entity, would be in violation of this section.

(2) It shall be unlawful for a physician to offer, deliver, receive, or accept any rebate, refund, commission, preference, patronage dividend, discount, or other consideration, whether in the form of money or otherwise, as compensation or inducement for a referred evaluation or consultation.

Labor

(d) No claim for payment shall be presented by an entity to any individual, third-party payor, or other entity for any goods or services furnished pursuant to a referral prohibited under this section.

(e) A physician who refers to or seeks consultation from an organization in which the physician has a financial interest shall disclose this interest to the patient or if the patient is a minor, to the patient's parents or legal guardian in writing at the time of the referral.

(f) No insurer, self-insurer, or other payor shall pay a charge or lien for any goods or services resulting from a referral in violation of this section.

(g) A violation of subdivision (a) shall be a misdemeanor. The appropriate licensing board shall review the facts and circumstances of any conviction pursuant to subdivision (a) and take appropriate disciplinary action if the licensee has committed unprofessional conduct. Violations of this section may also be subject to civil penalties of up to five thousand dollars ($5,000) for each offense, which may be enforced by the Insurance Commissioner, Attorney General, or a district attorney. A violation of subdivision (c), (d), (e), or (f) is a public offense and is punishable upon conviction by a fine not exceeding fifteen thousand dollars ($15,000) for each violation and appropriate disciplinary action, including revocation of professional licensure, by the Medical Board of California or other appropriate governmental agency. **Leg.H.** 1993 ch. 121 §20, effective July 16, 1993, ch. 1242, 2003 ch. 639 (SB 228), 2011 ch. 545 (AB 378) §2.

1993 Note: Section 139.3, as added by ch. 121, applies only to injuries occurring on or after January 1, 1994. Stats. 1993 ch. 121 §77.

Ref.: 8 C.C.R. §9768.12; Hanna §§ 22.14, 25.06[3]; Herlick Handbook §§ 1.01[3][a], 9.18.

§139.31. Exceptions to §139.3.

The prohibition of Section 139.3 shall not apply to or restrict any of the following:

(a) A physician may refer a patient for a good or service otherwise prohibited by subdivision (a) of Section 139.3 if the physician's regular practice is where there is no alternative provider of the service within either 25 miles or 40 minutes traveling time, via the shortest route on a paved road. A physician who refers to, or seeks consultation from, an organization in which the physician has a financial interest under this subdivision shall disclose this interest to the patient or the patient's parents or legal guardian in writing at the time of referral.

(b) A physician who has one or more of the following arrangements with another physician, a person, or an entity, is not prohibited from referring a patient to the physician, person, or entity because of the arrangement:

(1) A loan between a physician and the recipient of the referral, if the loan has commercially reasonable terms, bears interest at the prime rate or a higher rate that does not constitute usury, is adequately secured, and the loan terms are not affected by either party's referral of any person or the volume of services provided by either party.

(2) A lease of space or equipment between a physician and the recipient of the referral, if the lease is written, has commercially reasonable terms, has a fixed periodic rent payment, has a term of one year or more, and the lease payments are not affected by either party's referral of any person or the volume of services provided by either party.

(3) A physician's ownership of corporate investment securities, including shares, bonds, or other debt instruments that were purchased on terms that are available to the general public through a licensed securities exchange or NASDAQ, do not base profit distributions or other transfers of value on the physician's referral of persons to the corporation, do not have a separate class or accounting for any persons or for any physicians who may refer persons to the corporation, and are in a corporation that had, at the end of the corporation's most recent fiscal year, total gross assets exceeding one hundred million dollars ($100,000,000).

(4) A personal services arrangement between a physician or an immediate family member of the physician and the recipient of the referral if the arrangement meets all of the following requirements:

(A) It is set out in writing and is signed by the parties.

(B) It specifies all of the services to be provided by the physician or an immediate family member of the physician.

(C) The aggregate services contracted for do not exceed those that are reasonable and necessary for the legitimate business purposes of the arrangement.

(D) A written notice disclosing the existence of the personal services arrangement and including information on where a person may go to file a complaint against the licensee or the immediate family member of the licensee, is provided to the following persons at the time any services pursuant to the arrangement are first provided:

(i) An injured worker who is referred by a licensee or an immediate family member of the licensee.

(ii) The injured worker's employer, if self-insured.

(iii) The injured worker's employer's insurer, if insured.

(iv) If the injured worker is known by the licensee or the recipient of the referral to be represented, the injured worker's attorney.

(E) The term of the arrangement is for at least one year.

(F) The compensation to be paid over the term of the arrangement is set in advance, does not exceed fair market value, and is not determined in a manner that takes into account the volume or value of any referrals or other business generated between the parties, except that if the services provided pursuant to the arrangement include medical services provided under Division 4, compensation paid for the services shall be subject to the official medical fee schedule promulgated pursuant to Section 5307.1 or subject to any contract authorized by Section 5307.11.

(G) The services to be performed under the arrangement do not involve the counseling or promotion of a business arrangement or other activity that violates any state or federal law.

(c)(1) A physician may refer a person to a health facility as defined in Section 1250 of the Health and Safety Code, to any facility owned or leased by a health facility, or to an outpatient surgical center, if the recipient of the referral does not compensate the physician for the patient referral, and any equipment lease arrangement between the physician and the referral recipient complies with the requirements of paragraph (2) of subdivision (b).

(2) Nothing shall preclude this subdivision from applying to a physician solely because the physician has an

ownership or leasehold interest in an entire health facility or an entity that owns or leases an entire health facility.

(3) A physician may refer a person to a health facility for any service classified as an emergency under subdivision (a) or (b) of Section 1317.1 of the Health and Safety Code. For nonemergency outpatient diagnostic imaging services performed with equipment for which, when new, has a commercial retail price of four hundred thousand dollars ($400,000) or more, the referring physician shall obtain a service preauthorization from the insurer, or self-insured employer. Any oral authorization shall be memorialized in writing within five business days.

(d) A physician compensated or employed by a university may refer a person to any facility owned or operated by the university, or for a physician service, to another physician employed by the university, provided that the facility or university does not compensate the referring physician for the patient referral. For nonemergency diagnostic imaging services performed with equipment that, when new, has a commercial retail price of four hundred thousand dollars ($400,000) or more, the referring physician shall obtain a service preauthorization from the insurer or self-insured employer. An oral authorization shall be memorialized in writing within five business days. In the case of a facility which is totally or partially owned by an entity other than the university, but which is staffed by university physicians, those physicians may not refer patients to the facility if the facility compensates the referring physician for those referrals.

(e) The prohibition of Section 139.3 shall not apply to any service for a specific patient that is performed within, or goods that are supplied by, a physician's office, or the office of a group practice. Further, the provisions of Section 139.3 shall not alter, limit, or expand a physician's ability to deliver, or to direct or supervise the delivery of, in-office goods or services according to the laws, rules, and regulations governing his or her scope of practice. With respect to diagnostic imaging services performed with equipment that, when new, had a commercial retail price of four hundred thousand dollars ($400,000) or more, or for physical therapy services, or for psychometric testing that exceeds the routine screening battery protocols, with a time limit of two to five hours, established by the administrative director, the referring physician obtains a service preauthorization from the insurer or self-insured employer. Any oral authorization shall be memorialized in writing within five business days.

(f) The prohibition of Section 139.3 shall not apply where the physician is in a group practice as defined in Section 139.3 and refers a person for services specified in Section 139.3 to a multispecialty clinic, as defined in subdivision (*l*) of Section 1206 of the Health and Safety Code. For diagnostic imaging services performed with equipment that, when new, had a commercial retail price of four hundred thousand dollars ($400,000) or more, or physical therapy services, or psychometric testing that exceeds the routine screening battery protocols, with a time limit of two to five hours, established by the administrative director, performed at the multispecialty facility, the referring physician shall obtain a service preauthorization from the insurer or self-insured employer. Any oral authorization shall be memorialized in writing within five business days.

(g) The requirement for preauthorization in Sections (c), (e), and (f) shall not apply to a patient for whom the physician or group accepts payment on a capitated risk basis.

(h) The prohibition of Section 139.3 shall not apply to any facility when used to provide health care services to an enrollee of a health care service plan licensed pursuant to the Knox-Keene Health Care Service Plan Act of 1975 (Chapter 2.2 (commencing with Section 1340) of Division 2 of the Health and Safety Code).

(i) The prohibition of Section 139.3 shall not apply to an outpatient surgical center, as defined in paragraph (7) of subdivision (b) of Section 139.3, where the referring physician obtains a service preauthorization from the insurer or self-insured employer after disclosure of the financial relationship.

(j) The prohibition of Section 139.3 shall not apply to a physician's financial interest in a retailer of prescription drugs sold by a physical retail outlet commonly accessed by the public or a mail-order pharmacy serving a broad national or regional market, provided that the majority of the physician's practice, with regard to income, time, and number of patients, does not relate to occupational medicine and the physician receives no remuneration from the retailer of prescription drugs to market or otherwise solicit occupational injury or occupational disease patients. **Leg.H.** 1993 ch. 121, effective July 16, 1993, ch. 1242, 2002 ch. 309 (SB 1907), 2003 ch. 639 (SB 228), 2011 ch. 545 (AB 378) §3.

1993 Note: Section 139.31, as added by ch. 121, applies only to injuries occurring on or after January 1, 1994. Stats. 1993 ch. 121 §77.

Ref.: Hanna § 22.14; Herlick Handbook §§ 1.01[3][a], 4.18[1], 9.18.

§139.32. Restrictions on interested parties with financial interests in any entity providing services; violation.

(a) For the purpose of this section, the following definitions apply:

(1) "Financial interest in another entity" means, subject to subdivision (h), either of the following:

(A) Any type of ownership, interest, debt, loan, lease, compensation, remuneration, discount, rebate, refund, dividend, distribution, subsidy, or other form of direct or indirect payment, whether in money or otherwise, between the interested party and the other entity to which the employee is referred for services.

(B) An agreement, debt instrument, or lease or rental agreement between the interested party and the other entity that provides compensation based upon, in whole or in part, the volume or value of the services provided as a result of referrals.

(2) "Interested party" means any of the following:

(A) An injured employee.

(B) The employer of an injured employee, and, if the employer is insured, its insurer.

(C) A claims administrator, which includes, but is not limited to, a self-administered workers' compensation insurer, a self-administered self-insured employer, a self-administered joint powers authority, a self-administered legally uninsured employer, a third-party claims administrator for an insurer, a self-insured employer, a joint powers authority, or a legally uninsured employer or a subsidiary of a claims administrator.

(D) An attorney-at-law or law firm that is representing or advising an employee regarding a claim for compensation under Division 4 (commencing with Section 3200).

(E) A representative or agent of an interested party, including either of the following:

(i) An employee of an interested party.

(ii) Any individual acting on behalf of an interested party, including the immediate family of the interested party or of an employee of the interested party. For purposes of this clause, immediate family includes spouses, children, parents, and spouses of children.

(F) A provider of any medical services or products.

(3) "Services" means, but is not limited to, any of the following:

(A) A determination regarding an employee's eligibility for compensation under Division 4 (commencing with Section 3200), that includes both of the following:

(i) A determination of a permanent disability rating under Section 4660.

(ii) An evaluation of an employee's future earnings capacity resulting from an occupational injury or illness.

(B) Services to review the itemization of medical services set forth on a medical bill submitted under Section 4603.2.

(C) Copy and document reproduction services.

(D) Interpreter services.

(E) Medical services, including the provision of any medical products such as surgical hardware or durable medical equipment.

(F) Transportation services.

(G) Services in connection with utilization review pursuant to Section 4610.

(b) All interested parties shall disclose any financial interest in any entity providing services.

(c) Except as otherwise permitted by law, it is unlawful for an interested party other than a claims administrator or a network service provider to refer a person for services provided by another entity, or to use services provided by another entity, if the other entity will be paid for those services pursuant to Division 4 (commencing with Section 3200) and the interested party has a financial interest in the other entity.

(d)(1) It is unlawful for an interested party to enter into an arrangement or scheme, such as a cross-referral arrangement, that the interested party knows, or should know, has a purpose of ensuring referrals by the interested party to a particular entity that, if the interested party directly made referrals to that other entity, would be in violation of this section.

(2) It is unlawful for an interested party to offer, deliver, receive, or accept any rebate, refund, commission, preference, patronage, dividend, discount, or other consideration, whether in the form of money or otherwise, as compensation or inducement to refer a person for services.

(e) A claim for payment shall not be presented by an entity to any interested party, individual, third-party payer, or other entity for any services furnished pursuant to a referral prohibited under this section.

(f) An insurer, self-insurer, or other payer shall not knowingly pay a charge or lien for any services resulting from a referral for services or use of services in violation of this section.

(g)(1) A violation of this section shall be misdemeanor. If an interested party is a corporation, any director or officer of the corporation who knowingly concurs in a violation of this section shall be guilty of a misdemeanor. The appropriate licensing authority for any person subject to this section shall review the facts and circumstances of any conviction pursuant to this section and take appropriate disciplinary action if the licensee has committed unprofessional conduct, provided that the appropriate licensing authority may act on its own discretion independent of the initiation or completion of a criminal prosecution. Violations of this section are also subject to civil penalties of up to fifteen thousand dollars ($15,000) for each offense, which may be enforced by the Insurance Commissioner, Attorney General, or a district attorney.

(2) For an interested party, a practice of violating this section shall constitute a general business practice that discharges or administers compensation obligations in a dishonest manner, which shall be subject to a civil penalty under subdivision (e) of Section 129.5.

(3) For an interested party who is an attorney, a violation of subdivision (b) or (c) shall be referred to the Board of Governors of the State Bar of California, which shall review the facts and circumstances of any violation pursuant to subdivision (b) or (c) and take appropriate disciplinary action if the licensee has committed unprofessional conduct.

(4) Any determination regarding an employee's eligibility for compensation shall be void if that service was provided in violation of this section.

(h) The following arrangements between an interested party and another entity do not constitute a "financial interest in another entity" for purposes of this section:

(1) A loan between an interested party and another entity, if the loan has commercially reasonable terms, bears interest at the prime rate or a higher rate that does not constitute usury, and is adequately secured, and the loan terms are not affected by either the interested party's referral of any employee or the volume of services provided by the entity that receives the referral.

(2) A lease of space or equipment between an interested party and another entity, if the lease is written, has commercially reasonable terms, has a fixed periodic rent payment, has a term of one year or more, and the lease payments are not affected by either the interested party's referral of any person or the volume of services provided by the entity that receives the referral.

(3) An interested party's ownership of the corporate investment securities of another entity, including shares, bonds, or other debt instruments that were purchased on terms that are available to the general public through a licensed securities exchange or NASDAQ.

(i) The prohibitions described in this section do not apply to any of the following:

(1) Services performed by, or determinations of compensation issues made by, employees of an interested party in the course of that employment.

(2) A referral for legal services if that referral is not prohibited by the Rules of Professional Conduct of the State Bar.

(3) A physician's referral that is exempted by Section 139.31 from the prohibitions prescribed by Section 139.3. **Leg.H.** 2012 ch. 363 (SB 863) §6.

2012 Note: For legislative findings, declarations, and applicability of Stats. 2012 ch. 363, see the 2012 Notes following Lab C §62.5.

Ref.: Hanna § 10.53; Herlick Handbook §§ 1.01[3][a], 9.21.

§139.4. Council review of advertising; disciplinary actions and proceedings; adoption of advertising regulations and report to Legislature.

(a) The administrative director may review advertising copy to ensure compliance with Section 651 of the Business and Professions Code and may require qualified medical evaluators to maintain a file of all advertising copy for a period of 90 days from the date of its use. Any file so required to be maintained shall be available to the administrative director upon the administrative director's request for review.

(b) No advertising copy shall be used after its use has been disapproved by the administrative director and the qualified medical evaluator has been notified in writing of the disapproval.

(c) A qualified medical evaluator who is found by the administrative director to have violated any provision of this section may be terminated, suspended, or placed on probation.

(d) Proceedings to determine whether a violation of this section has occurred shall be conducted pursuant to Chapter 4 (commencing with Section 11370) of Part 1 of Division 3 of Title 2 of the Government Code.

(e) The administrative director shall adopt regulations governing advertising by physicians with respect to industrial injuries or illnesses.

(f) Subdivision (a) shall not be construed to alter the application of Section 651 of the Business and Professions Code. **Leg.H.** 1991 ch. 116, 2003 ch. 639 (SB 228).

Ref.: 8 C.C.R. §§150, 151, 152, 153, 154, 155, 156, 157, 158, 159; Hanna § 1.12[2A]; Herlick Handbook § 1.01[3][a].

§139.43. False or misleading advertising prohibited; adoption of regulations by administrative director; physicians and attorneys exempted.

(a) No person or entity shall advertise, print, display, publish, distribute, or broadcast, or cause or permit to be advertised, printed, displayed, published, distributed, or broadcast in any manner, any statement concerning services or benefits to be provided to an injured worker, that is paid for directly or indirectly by that person or entity and is false, misleading, or deceptive, or that omits material information necessary to make the statement therein not false, misleading, or deceptive.

(b) As soon as reasonably possible, but not later than January 1, 1994, the administrative director shall adopt regulations governing advertising by persons or entities other than physicians and attorneys with respect to services or benefits for injured workers. In promulgating regulations pursuant to this subdivision, the administrative director shall review existing regulations, including those adopted by the State Bar, to identify those regulatory approaches that may serve as a model for regulations required by this subdivision.

(c) A violation of subdivision (a) is a misdemeanor, punishable by incarceration in the county jail for not more than one year, or by a fine not exceeding ten thousand dollars ($10,000), or both.

(d) This section shall not apply to physicians or attorneys. It is the intent of the Legislature to exempt physicians and attorneys from this section because the conduct regulated by this section, with respect to physicians and attorneys, is governed by other provisions of law. **Leg.H.** 1991 ch. 116, 1992 ch. 1352, effective September 30, 1992, 2004 ch. 193 (SB 111).

Ref.: 8 C.C.R. §§9820, 9821, 9822, 9823, 9824, 9825, 9826, 9827, 9828, 9829, 9830, 9831, 9832, 9833, 9834, 9835, 9836, 9837; Hanna § 1.23; Herlick Handbook § 1.01[3][a].

§139.45. Care required in promulgating advertising regulations; description of false or misleading advertisements.

(a) In promulgating regulations pursuant to Sections 139.4 and 139.43, the administrative director shall take particular care to preclude any advertisements with respect to industrial injuries or illnesses that are false or mislead the public with respect to workers' compensation. In promulgating rules with respect to advertising, the State Bar and physician licensing boards shall also take particular care to achieve the same goal.

(b) For purposes of subdivision (a), false or misleading advertisements shall include advertisements that do any of the following:

(1) Contain an untrue statement.

(2) Contain any matter, or present or arrange any matter in a manner or format that is false, deceptive, or that tends to confuse, deceive, or mislead.

(3) Omit any fact necessary to make the statement made, in the light of the circumstances under which the statement is made, not misleading.

(4) Are transmitted in any manner that involves coercion, duress, compulsion, intimidation, threats, or vexatious or harassing conduct.

(5) Entice a person to respond by the offering of any consideration, including a good or service but excluding free medical evaluations or treatment, that would be provided either at no charge or for less than market value. No free medical evaluation or treatment shall be offered for the purpose of defrauding any entity. **Leg.H.** 1991 ch. 116, 1992 ch. 1352, effective September 30, 1992, 2003 ch. 639 (SB 228).

Ref.: 8 C.C.R. §§150, 151, 152, 153, 154, 155, 156, 157, 158, 159, 9820, 9821, 9822, 9823, 9824, 9825, 9826, 9827, 9828, 9829, 9830, 9831, 9832, 9833, 9834, 9835, 9836, 9837; Hanna §§ 1.12[2A], 1.23; Herlick Handbook §§ 1.01[3][a], 9.18.

§139.47. Program established to educate employers about early and sustained return to work after employee's occupational injury or illness.

The Director of Industrial Relations shall establish and maintain a program to encourage, facilitate, and educate employers to provide early and sustained return to work after occupational injury or illness. The program shall do both of the following:

(a) Develop educational materials and guides, in easily understandable language in both print and electronic form, for employers, health care providers, employees, and labor unions. These materials shall address issues including, but not limited to, early return to work, assessment of functional abilities and limitations, development of appropriate work restrictions, job analysis, worksite modifications, assistive equipment and devices, and available resources.

(b) Conduct training for employee and employer organizations and health care providers concerning the accommodation of injured employees and the prevention of reinjury. **Leg.H.** 2002 ch. 6 (AB 749).

Ref.: Hanna §§ 7.02[3][d][i], [ii], 35.03[3A]; Herlick Handbook §§ 1.01[3][a], 5.20.

§139.48. Return-to-work program; funding; purpose.

(a) There is in the department a return-to-work program administered by the director, funded by one hundred twenty million dollars ($120,000,000) annually derived from non-General Funds of the Workers' Compensation Administration Revolving Fund, for the purpose of making supplemental payments to workers whose permanent disability benefits are disproportionately low in comparison to their earnings loss. Moneys shall remain available for use by the return-to-work program without respect to the fiscal year.

(b) Eligibility for payments and the amount of payments shall be determined by regulations adopted by the director, based on findings from studies conducted by the director in consultation with the Commission on Health and Safety and Workers' Compensation. Determinations of the director shall be subject to review at the trial level of the appeals board upon the same grounds as prescribed for petitions for reconsideration.

(c) This section shall apply only to injuries sustained on or after January 1, 2013. **Leg.H.** 2012 ch. 363 (SB 863) §6.5, 2013 ch. 28 (SB 71) §37, effective June 27, 2013.

2012 Note: For legislative findings, declarations, and applicability of Stats. 2012 ch. 363, see the 2012 Notes following Lab C §62.5.

Ref.: Hanna §§ 7.02[4][d][iii], 8.08[1], 32.01[3][e]; Herlick Handbook §§ 1.01[3][a], 5.2, 6.02[8].

§139.5. Independent review program; requirements; liability.

(a)(1) The administrative director shall contract with one or more independent medical review organizations and one or more independent bill review organizations to conduct reviews pursuant to Article 2 (commencing with Section 4600) of Chapter 2 of Part 2 of Division 4. The independent review organizations shall be independent of any workers' compensation insurer or workers' compensation claims administrator doing business in this state. The administrative director may establish additional requirements, including conflict-of-interest standards, consistent with the purposes of Article 2 (commencing with Section 4600) of Chapter 2 of Part 2 of Division 4, that an organization shall be required to meet in order to qualify as an independent review organization and to assist the division in carrying out its responsibilities.

(2) To enable the independent review program to go into effect for injuries occurring on or after January 1, 2013, and until the administrative director establishes contracts as otherwise specified by this section, independent review organizations under contract with the Department of Managed Health Care pursuant to Section 1374.32 of the Health and Safety Code may be designated by the administrative director to conduct reviews pursuant to Article 2 (commencing with Section 4600) of Chapter 2 of Part 2 of Division 4. The administrative director may use an interagency agreement to implement the independent review process beginning January 1, 2013. The administrative director may initially contract directly with the same organizations that are under contract with the Department of Managed Health Care on substantially the same terms without competitive bidding until January 1, 2015.

(b)(1) The independent medical review organizations and the medical professionals retained to conduct reviews shall be deemed to be consultants for purposes of this section.

(2) There shall be no monetary liability on the part of, and no cause of action shall arise against, any consultant on account of any communication by that consultant to the administrative director or any other officer, employee, agent, contractor, or consultant of the Division of Workers' Compensation, or on account of any communication by that consultant to any person when that communication is required by the terms of a contract with the administrative director pursuant to this section and the consultant does all of the following:

(A) Acts without malice.

(B) Makes a reasonable effort to determine the facts of the matter communicated.

(C) Acts with a reasonable belief that the communication is warranted by the facts actually known to the consultant after a reasonable effort to determine the facts.

(3) The immunities afforded by this section shall not affect the availability of any other privilege or immunity which may be afforded by law. This section shall not be construed to alter the laws regarding the confidentiality of medical records.

(c)(1) An organization contracted to perform independent medical review or independent bill review shall be required to employ a medical director who shall be responsible for advising the contractor on clinical issues. The medical director shall be a physician and surgeon licensed by the Medical Board of California or the Osteopathic Medical Board of California.

(2) The independent review organization, any experts it designates to conduct a review, or any officer, director, or employee of the independent review organization shall not have any material professional, familial, or financial affiliation, as determined by the administrative director, with any of the following:

(A) The employer, insurer or claims administrator, or utilization review organization.

(B) Any officer, director, employee of the employer, or insurer or claims administrator.

(C) A physician, the physician's medical group, the physician's independent practice association, or other provider involved in the medical treatment in dispute.

(D) The facility or institution at which either the proposed health care service, or the alternative service, if any, recommended by the employer, would be provided.

(E) The development or manufacture of the principal drug, device, procedure, or other therapy proposed by the employee whose treatment is under review, or the alternative therapy, if any, recommended by the employer.

(F) The employee or the employee's immediate family, or the employee's attorney.

(d) The independent review organizations shall meet all of the following requirements:

(1) The organization shall not be an affiliate or a subsidiary of, nor in any way be owned or controlled by, a workers' compensation insurer, claims administrator, or a trade association of workers' compensation insurers or claims administrators. A board member, director, officer, or employee of the independent review organization shall not serve as a board member, director, or employee of a workers' compensation insurer or claims administrator. A board member, director, or officer of a workers' compensation insurer or claims administrator or a trade association of workers' compensation insurers or claims administrators shall not serve as a board member, director, officer, or employee of an independent review organization.

(2) The organization shall submit to the division the following information upon initial application to contract under this section and, except as otherwise provided, annually thereafter upon any change to any of the following information:

(A) The names of all stockholders and owners of more than 5 percent of any stock or options, if a publicly held organization.

(B) The names of all holders of bonds or notes in excess of one hundred thousand dollars ($100,000), if any.

(C) The names of all corporations and organizations that the independent review organization controls or is affiliated with, and the nature and extent of any ownership or control, including the affiliated organization's type of business.

(D) The names and biographical sketches of all directors, officers, and executives of the independent review organization, as well as a statement regarding any past or present relationships the directors, officers, and executives may have with any employer, workers' compensation insurer, claims administrator, medical provider network, managed care organization, provider group, or board or committee of an employer, workers' compensation insurer, claims administrator, medical provider network, managed care organization, or provider group.

(E)(i) The percentage of revenue the independent review organization receives from expert reviews, including, but not limited to, external medical reviews, quality assurance reviews, utilization reviews, and bill reviews.

(ii) The names of any workers' compensation insurer, claims administrator, or provider group for which the independent review organization provides review services, including, but not limited to, utilization review, bill review, quality assurance review, and external medical review. Any change in this information shall be reported to the department within five business days of the change.

(F) A description of the review process, including, but not limited to, the method of selecting expert reviewers and matching the expert reviewers to specific cases.

(G) A description of the system the independent medical review organization uses to identify and recruit medical professionals to review treatment and treatment recommendation decisions, the number of medical professionals credentialed, and the types of cases and areas of expertise that the medical professionals are credentialed to review.

(H) A description of how the independent review organization ensures compliance with the conflict-of-interest requirements of this section.

(3) The organization shall demonstrate that it has a quality assurance mechanism in place that does all of the following:

(A) Ensures that any medical professionals retained are appropriately credentialed and privileged.

(B) Ensures that the reviews provided by the medical professionals or bill reviewers are timely, clear, and credible, and that reviews are monitored for quality on an ongoing basis.

(C) Ensures that the method of selecting medical professionals for individual cases achieves a fair and impartial panel of medical professionals who are qualified to render recommendations regarding the clinical conditions and the medical necessity of treatments or therapies in question.

(D) Ensures the confidentiality of medical records and the review materials, consistent with the requirements of this section and applicable state and federal law.

(E) Ensures the independence of the medical professionals or bill reviewers retained to perform the reviews through conflict-of-interest policies and prohibitions, and ensures adequate screening for conflicts of interest, pursuant to paragraph (5).

(4) Medical professionals selected by independent medical review organizations to review medical treatment decisions shall be licensed physicians, as defined by Section 3209.3, in good standing, who meet the following minimum requirements:

(A) The physician shall be a clinician knowledgeable in the treatment of the employee's medical condition, knowledgeable about the proposed treatment, and familiar with guidelines and protocols in the area of treatment under review.

(B) Notwithstanding any other law, the physician shall hold a nonrestricted license in any state of the United States, and for physicians and surgeons holding an M.D. or D.O. degree, a current certification by a recognized American medical specialty board in the area or areas appropriate to the condition or treatment under review. The independent medical review organization shall give preference to the use of a physician licensed in California as the reviewer.

(C) The physician shall have no history of disciplinary action or sanctions, including, but not limited to, loss of staff privileges or participation restrictions, taken or pending by any hospital, government, or regulatory body.

Labor

(D) Commencing January 1, 2014, the physician shall not hold an appointment as a qualified medical evaluator pursuant to Section 139.2.

(5) Neither the expert reviewer, nor the independent review organization, shall have any material professional, material familial, or material financial affiliation with any of the following:

(A) The employer, workers' compensation insurer or claims administrator, or a medical provider network of the insurer or claims administrator, except that an academic medical center under contract to the insurer or claims administrator to provide services to employees may qualify as an independent medical review organization provided it will not provide the service and provided the center is not the developer or manufacturer of the proposed treatment.

(B) Any officer, director, or management employee of the employer or workers' compensation insurer or claims administrator.

(C) The physician, the physician's medical group, or the independent practice association proposing the treatment.

(D) The institution at which the treatment would be provided.

(E) The development or manufacture of the treatment proposed for the employee whose condition is under review.

(F) The employee or the employee's immediate family.

(6) For purposes of this subdivision, the following terms shall have the following meanings:

(A) "Material familial affiliation" means any relationship as a spouse, child, parent, sibling, spouse's parent, or child's spouse.

(B) "Material financial affiliation" means any financial interest of more than 5 percent of total annual revenue or total annual income of an independent review organization or individual to which this subdivision applies. "Material financial affiliation" does not include payment by the employer to the independent review organization for the services required by the administrative director's contract with the independent review organization, nor does "material financial affiliation" include an expert's participation as a contracting medical provider where the expert is affiliated with an academic medical center or a National Cancer Institute-designated clinical cancer research center.

(C) "Material professional affiliation" means any physician-patient relationship, any partnership or employment relationship, a shareholder or similar ownership interest in a professional corporation, or any independent contractor arrangement that constitutes a material financial affiliation with any expert or any officer or director of the independent review organization. "Material professional affiliation" does not include affiliations that are limited to staff privileges at a health facility.

(e) The division shall provide, upon the request of any interested person, a copy of all nonproprietary information, as determined by the administrative director, filed with it by an independent review organization under contract pursuant to this section. The division may charge a fee to the interested person for copying the requested information.

(f) The Legislature finds and declares that the services described in this section are of such a special and unique nature that they must be contracted out pursuant to paragraph (3) of subdivision (b) of Section 19130 of the Government Code. The Legislature further finds and declares that the services described in this section are a new state function pursuant to paragraph (2) of subdivision (b) of Section 19130 of the Government Code. **Leg.H.** 2012 ch. 363 (SB 863) §7, 2013 ch. 287 (SB 375) §3, 2014 ch. 71 (SB 1304) §107.

2012 Note: For legislative findings, declarations, and applicability of Stats. 2012 ch. 363, see the 2012 Notes following Lab C §62.5.

Ref.: Hanna §§ 5.02[2][d], 5.07[10][d], 22.05[6][b][iv]; Herlick Handbook §§ 1.01[2], [3][a], 4.10[2], [3].

§139.6. Program to provide workers' compensation information.

(a) The administrative director shall establish and effect within the Division of Workers' Compensation a continuing program to provide information and assistance concerning the rights, benefits, and obligations of the workers' compensation law to employees and employers subject thereto. The program shall include, but not be limited to, the following:

(1) The preparation, publishing, and as necessary, updating, of guides to the California workers' compensation system for employees and employers. The guides shall detail, in easily understandable language, the rights and obligations of employees and employers, the procedures for obtaining benefits, and the means provided for resolving disputes. Separate guides may be prepared for employees and employers. The appropriate guide shall be provided to all labor and employer organizations known to the administrative director, and to any other person upon request.

(2) The preparation, publishing, and as necessary, updating, of a pamphlet advising injured workers of their basic rights under workers' compensation law, and informing them of rights under the Americans with Disabilities Act, and the provisions of the Fair Employment and Housing Act relating to individuals with a disability. The pamphlet shall be written in easily understandable language. The pamphlet shall be available in both English and Spanish, and shall include basic information concerning the circumstances under which injured employees are entitled to the various types of workers' compensation benefits, the protections against discrimination because of an injury, the procedures for resolving any disputes which arise, and the right to seek information and advice from an information and assistance officer or an attorney.

(b) In each district office of the division, the administrative director shall appoint an information and assistance officer, and any other deputy information and assistance officers as the work of the district office may require. The administrative director shall provide office facilities and clerical support appropriate to the functions of these information and assistance officers.

(c) Each information and assistance officer shall be responsible for the performance of the following duties:

(1) Providing continuing information concerning rights, benefits, and obligations under workers' compensation laws to injured workers, employers, lien claimants, and other interested parties.

(2) Upon request by the injured worker, assisting in the prompt resolution of misunderstanding, disputes, and controversies arising out of claims for compensation, without formal proceedings, in order that full and timely compensation benefits shall be furnished. In performing this duty, information and assistance officers shall not be responsible for reviewing applications for adjudication or declarations of readiness to proceed. This function shall be performed by workers' compensation judges. This function may also be performed by settlement conference referees upon delegation by the appeals board.

(3) Distributing any information pamphlets in English and Spanish as are prepared and approved by the administrative director to all inquiring injured workers and any other parties that may request copies of these pamphlets.

(4) Establishing and maintaining liaison with the persons located in the geographic area served by the district office, with other affected state agencies, and with organizations representing employees, employers, insurers, and the medical community. **Leg.H.** 1993 ch. 121, effective July 16, 1993.

Ref.: 8 C.C.R. §§9880, 9883, 9885, 9900, 9928.1; Hanna §§ 23.02, 23.03[1], [2]; Herlick Handbook §§ 1.01[3][a], 1.06, 14.11, 16.3.

CHAPTER 6
OCCUPATIONAL SAFETY AND HEALTH STANDARDS BOARD

§140. Occupational Safety and Health Standards Board.

(a) There is in the Department of Industrial Relations, the Occupational Safety and Health Standards Board which consists of seven members who shall be appointed by the Governor. Two members shall be from the field of management, two members shall be from the field of labor, one member shall be from the field of occupational health, one member shall be from the field of occupational safety and one member shall be from the general public. Members representing occupational safety and health fields and the public member shall be selected from other than the fields of management or labor.

(b) Terms of office for members of the Industrial Safety Board shall expire 60 days after the effective date of the amendment of this section enacted at the 1973–74 Regular Session. Newly appointed members of the Occupational Safety and Health Standards Board shall assume their duties upon that date.

(c) The Governor shall designate the chairman of the board from the membership of the board. The person so designated shall hold the office of chairman at the pleasure of the Governor. The chairman shall designate a member of the board to act as chairman in his absence.

(d) As used in this chapter, "board" means the Occupational Safety and Health Standards Board.

(e) All references in this or any other code to the Industrial Safety Board shall be deemed to mean the Occupational Safety and Health Standards Board.

Ref.: Herlick Handbook §§ 1.09, 9.10.

§141. Term of office; compensation.

(a) The terms of office of the members of the board shall be four years and they shall hold office until the appointment and qualification of a successor. The terms of the members of the board first appointed shall expire as follows: three members, one representative from management, one representative from labor, and one representative from occupational health, on June 1, 1974; three members, one representative from management, one representative from labor, and one representative from occupational safety, on June 1, 1975; one member June 1, 1976. The terms shall thereafter expire in the same relative order. Vacancies occurring shall be filled by appointment to the unexpired term.

(b) Each member of the board shall receive one hundred dollars ($100) for each day of his or her actual attendance at meetings of the board, and other official business of the board, and his or her actual and necessary traveling expenses incurred in the performance of his or her duty as a member. **Leg.H.** 2004 ch. 183 (AB 3082).

Ref.: Herlick Handbook §§ 1.09, 9.10.

§142. Enforcement of occupational safety and health standards.

The Division of Occupational Safety and Health shall enforce all occupational safety and health standards adopted pursuant to this chapter, and those heretofore adopted by the Industrial Accident Commission or the Industrial Safety Board. General safety orders heretofore adopted by the Industrial Accident Commission or the Industrial Safety Board shall continue to remain in effect, but they may be amended or repealed pursuant to this chapter. **Leg.H.** 2002 ch. 1124 (AB 3000), effective September 30, 2002.

Ref.: Hanna §§ 1.16[1], 25.10[7]; Herlick Handbook §§ 1.09, 9.10.

§142.1. Public meetings; notice.

The board shall meet at least monthly. The meetings shall be rotated throughout the state at locations designated by the chairman. All meetings held by the board shall be open and public. Written notice of all meetings and a proposed agenda shall be given to all persons who make request for the notice in writing to the board.

Ref.: Hanna § 1.16[2]; Herlick Handbook §§ 1.09, 9.10.

§142.2. Proposals at meetings.

At each of its meetings, the board shall make time available to interested persons to propose new or revised orders or standards appropriate for adoption pursuant to this chapter or other items concerning occupational safety and health. The board shall consider such proposed orders or standards and report its decision no later than six months following receipt of such proposals.

Ref.: Herlick Handbook §§ 1.09, 9.10.

§142.3. Standards: vote required; state building standards; warnings of hazards to employees; medical examinations provided by employer.

(a)(1) The board, by an affirmative vote of at least four members, may adopt, amend or repeal occupational safety and health standards and orders. The board shall be the only agency in the state authorized to adopt occupational safety and health standards.

(2) The board shall adopt standards at least as effective as the federal standards for all issues for which federal standards have been promulgated under Section 6 of the Occupational Safety and Health Act of 1970 (P.L. 91-596) within six months of the promulgation date of the federal standards and which, when applicable to products which are distributed or used in interstate commerce, are required by compelling local conditions and do not unduly burden interstate commerce.

(3) No standard or amendment to any standard adopted by the board that is substantially the same as a federal standard shall be subject to Article 5 (commencing with Section 11346) and Article 6 (commencing with Section 11349) of Chapter 3.5 of Part 1 of Division 3 of Title 2 of the Government Code. For purposes of this subdivision, "substantially the same" means identical to the federal standard with the exception of editorial and format differences needed to conform to other state laws and standards.

(4) If a federal standard is promulgated and no state standard that is at least as effective as the federal standard is adopted by the board within six months of the date of promulgation of the federal standard, the following provisions shall apply unless adoption of the state standard is imminent:

(A) If there is no existing state standard covering the same issues, the federal standard shall be deemed to be a standard adopted by the board and enforceable by the division pursuant to Section 6317. This standard shall not be subject to Article 5 (commencing with Section 11346) and Article 6 (commencing with Section 11349) of Chapter 3.5 of Part 1 of Division 3 of Title 2 of the Government Code.

(B) If a state standard is in effect at the time a federal standard is promulgated covering the same issue or issues, the board may adopt the federal standard, or a portion thereof, as a standard enforceable by the division pursuant to Section 6317; provided, however, if a federal standard or portion thereof is adopted which replaces an existing state standard or portion thereof, the federal standard shall be as effective as the state standard or portion thereof. No adoption of or amendment to any federal standard, or portion thereof shall be subject to Article 5 (commencing with Section 11346) and Article 6 (commencing with Section 11349) of Chapter 3.5 of Part 1 of Division 3 of Title 2 of the Government Code.

(C) Any state standard adopted pursuant to subparagraph (A) or (B) shall become effective at the time the standard is filed with the Secretary of State, unless otherwise provided, but shall not take effect before the effective date of the equivalent federal standard and shall remain in effect for six months unless readopted by the board for an additional six months or superseded by a standard adopted by the board pursuant to paragraph (2) of subdivision (a).

(D) Any standard adopted pursuant to subparagraph (A), (B), or (C), shall be published in Title 8 of the California Code of Regulations in a manner similar to any other standards adopted pursuant to paragraphs (1) and (2) of subdivision (a) of this section.

(b) The State Building Standards Commission shall codify and publish in a semiannual supplement to the California Building Standards Code, or in a more frequent supplement if required by federal law, all occupational safety and health standards that would otherwise meet the definition of a building standard described in Section 18909 of the Health and Safety Code adopted by the board in the State Building Standards Code without reimbursement from the board. These occupational safety and health standards may also be published by the Occupational Safety and Health Standards Board in other provisions in Title 8 of the California Code of Regulations prior to publication in the California Building Standards Code if that other publication includes an appropriate identification of occupational safety and health standards contained in the other publication.

(c) Any occupational safety or health standard or order promulgated under this section shall prescribe the use of labels or other appropriate forms of warning as are necessary to ensure that employees are apprised of all hazards to which they are exposed, relevant symptoms and appropriate emergency treatment, and proper conditions and precautions for safe use or exposure. Where appropriate, these standards or orders shall also prescribe suitable protective equipment and control or technological procedures to be used in connection with these hazards and shall provide for monitoring or measuring employee exposure at such locations and intervals and in a manner as may be necessary for the protection of employees. In addition, where appropriate, the occupational safety or health standard or order shall prescribe the type and frequency of medical examinations or other tests which shall be made available, by the employer or at his or her cost, to employees exposed to such hazards in order to most effectively determine whether the health of such employee is adversely affected by this exposure.

(d) The results of these examinations or tests shall be furnished only to the Division of Occupational Safety and Health, the State Department of Health Services, any other authorized state agency, the employer, the employee, and, at the request of the employee, to his or her physician. **Leg.H.** 1992 ch. 1214, 2002 ch. 1124 (AB 3000), effective September 30, 2002.

Ref.: Herlick Handbook §§ 1.09, 9.10.

§142.4. Adoption of standards; emergency regulations.

(a) Occupational safety and health standards and orders shall be adopted, amended, or repealed as provided in Chapter 3.5 (commencing with Section 11340) of Part 1 of Division 3 of Title 2 of the Government Code, except as modified by this chapter.

(b) If an emergency regulation is based upon an emergency temporary standard published in the Federal Register by the Secretary of Labor pursuant to Section 6(c)(1) of the Federal Occupational Safety and Health Act of 1970 (P.L. 91–596; 29 U.S.C. Sec. 655(c)(1)), the 120-day period specified in Section 11346.1 of the Government Code shall be deemed not to expire until 120 days after a permanent standard is promulgated by the Secretary of Labor pursuant to Section 6(c)(3) of the Federal Occupational Safety and Health Act of 1970 (29 U.S.C. Sec.

655(c)(3)). **Leg.H.** 1973 ch. 993 §17, effective October 1, 1973, 1982 ch. 454 §129, 2006 ch. 538 (SB 1852) §478.

Ref.: Herlick Handbook §§ 1.09, 9.10.

§142.7. Standards for hazardous substance removal work.

(a) On or before October 1, 1987, the board shall adopt an occupational safety and health standard concerning hazardous substance removal work, so as to protect most effectively the health and safety of employees. The standard shall include, but not be limited to, requirements for all of the following:

(1) Specific work practices.

(2) Certification of all employees engaged in hazardous substance removal-related work, except that no certification shall be required for an employee whose only activity is the transportation of hazardous substances which are subject to the requirement for a certificate under Section 12804.1 of the Vehicle Code.

(3) Certification of supervisors with sufficient experience and authority to be responsible for hazardous substance removal work.

(4) Designation of a qualified person who shall be responsible for scheduling any air sampling, laboratory calibration of sampling equipment, evaluation of soil or other contaminated materials sampling results, and for conducting any equipment testing and evaluating the results of the tests.

(5) Requiring that a safety and health conference be held for all hazardous substance removal jobs before the start of actual work. The conference shall include representatives of the owner or contracting agency, the contractor, the employer, employees, and employee representatives, and shall include a discussion of the employer's safety and health program and the means, methods, devices, processes, practices, conditions, or operations which the employer intends to use in providing a safe and healthy place of employment.

(b) For purposes of this section, "hazardous substance removal work" means cleanup work at any of the following:

(1) A site where removal or remedial action is taken pursuant to either of the following:

(A) Chapter 6.8 (commencing with Section 25300) of Division 20 of the Health and Safety Code, regardless of whether the site is listed pursuant to Section 25356 of the Health and Safety Code.

(B) The federal Comprehensive Environmental Response, Compensation, and Liability Act of 1980 (42 U.S.C. Sec. 9601 et seq.).

(2) A site where corrective action is taken pursuant to Section 25187 or 25200.10 of the Health and Safety Code or the federal Resource Conservation and Recovery Act of 1976 (42 U.S.C. Sec. 6901 et seq.).

(3) A site where cleanup of a discharge of a hazardous substance is required pursuant to Division 7 (commencing with Section 13000) of the Water Code.

(4) A site where removal or remedial action is taken because a hazardous substance has been discharged or released in an amount that is reportable pursuant to Section 13271 of the Water Code or the federal Comprehensive Environmental Response, Compensation, and Liability Act of 1980 (42 U.S.C. Sec. 9601 et seq.). "Hazardous substance removal work" does not include work related to a hazardous substance spill on a highway.

(c) Until the occupational safety and health standard required by subdivision (a) is adopted by the board and becomes effective, the occupational safety and health standard concerning hazardous substance removal work shall be the standard adopted by the federal government and codified in Section 1910.120 of Title 29 of the Code of Federal Regulations. In addition, before actual work is started on a hazardous substance removal job, a safety and health conference shall be held that shall include the participants and involve a discussion of the subjects described in paragraph (5) of subdivision (a).

Ref.: Herlick Handbook §§ 1.09, 9.10.

§143. Permanent variances.

(a) Any employer may apply to the board for a permanent variance from an occupational safety and health standard, order, special order, or portion thereof, upon a showing of an alternate program, method, practice, means, device, or process which will provide equal or superior safety for employees.

(b) The board shall issue such variance if it determines on the record, after opportunity for an investigation where appropriate and a hearing, that the proponent of the variance has demonstrated by a preponderance of the evidence that the conditions, practices, means, methods, operations, or processes used or proposed to be used by an employer will provide employment and places or employment to his employees which are as safe and healthful as those which would prevail if he complied with the standard. The variance so issued shall prescribe the conditions the employer must maintain, and the practices, means, methods, operations, and processes which he must adopt and utilize to the extent they differ from the standard in question.

(c) The board is authorized to grant a variance from any standard or portion thereof whenever it determines such variance is necessary to permit an employer to participate in an experiment approved by the director designed to demonstrate or validate new and improved techniques to safeguard the health or safety of workers.

(d) A permanent variance may be modified or revoked upon application by an employer, employees, or the division, or by the board on its own motion, in the manner prescribed for its issuance under this section at any time.

Ref.: Herlick Handbook §§ 1.09, 9.10.

§143.1. Variance requests; hearings.

The board shall conduct hearings on such requests for a permanent variance after employees or employee representatives are properly notified and given an opportunity to appear. All board decisions on permanent variance requests shall be final except for any rehearing or judicial review provided for by law.

Ref.: Herlick Handbook §§ 1.09, 9.10.

§143.2. Procedural rules for hearings.

The board, acting as a whole, may adopt, amend, or repeal rules of practice and procedure pertaining to hearings on applications for permanent variances, variance appeals, and other matters within its jurisdiction. All rules of practice and procedure amendments thereto, or repeal thereof, shall be made in accordance with the provisions of Chapter 3.5 (commencing with Section 11340) of Part 1 of Division 3 of Title 2 of the Government Code. **Leg.H.** 2004 ch. 183 (AB 3082).

Ref.: Herlick Handbook §§ 1.09, 9.10.

§144. Enforcement of occupational safety and health standards; assistance of other agencies.

(a) The authority of any agency, department, division, bureau or any other political subdivision other than the Division of Occupational Safety and Health to assist in the administration or enforcement of any occupational safety or health standard, order, or rule adopted pursuant to this chapter shall be contained in a written agreement with the Department of Industrial Relations or an agency authorized by the department to enter into such agreement.

(b) No such agreement shall deprive the Division of Occupational Safety and Health or other state agency to which authority has been delegated of any power or authority of the state agency.

(c) Such an agreement may provide for the right of access of an authorized representative of the designated agency to enter any place of employment which is under the jurisdiction of the Division of Occupational Safety and Health.

(d) If any representative of an agency operating under such an agreement becomes aware of an imminent hazard, he shall notify the employer and affected employees of the hazard and immediately notify the Division of Occupational Safety and Health.

(e) Nothing in this section shall affect or limit the authority of any state or local agency as to any matter other than the enforcement of occupational safety and health standards adopted by the board; however, nothing herein shall limit or reduce the authority of local agencies to adopt and enforce higher standards relating to occupational safety and health for their own employees.

Ref.: Herlick Handbook §§ 1.09, 9.10.

§144.5. Division of Occupational Safety and Health; duties.

(a) The Division of Occupational Safety and Health in connection with the enforcement of occupational safety and health standards adopted pursuant to this chapter shall do all of the following:

(1) Conduct inspections or investigations related to specific workplaces for the evaluation of occupational health problems or environmental conditions which may be harmful to the health of employees.

(2) Upon request of any employer or employee, or on its own initiative, conduct special investigations or studies of occupational health problems which are unrelated to a specific enforcement action to the extent the circumstances indicate and priorities permit.

(3) Provide a continuing program of training for safety engineers of the Division of Occupational Safety and Health in the recognition of health hazards, in dealing with such hazards that do not require specialized competence or equipment and in acquainting them with the skills available from the State Department of Health Services and local health agencies.

(b)(1) When requested by a local health department, the Division of Occupational Safety and Health shall enter into a written agreement with such local health department to conduct inspections and evaluations of occupational health problems, including environmental and sanitary conditions, in places of employment.

(2) Any such agreement shall be subject to the provisions of Section 144. It shall be entered into only after a finding that the local health department can meet the necessary standards of performance for inspections and evaluations to be conducted pursuant to the agreement.

(3) Such agreement shall not be binding upon either party unless and until it has been fully approved by the United States Department of Labor.

(4) Such agreements shall be completed by the Division of Occupational Safety and Health and submitted for approval to the United States Department of Labor not later than six months from the date of request by the local health department.

(5) Inspection services performed under the agreement shall be conducted pursuant to the occupational safety and health standards adopted pursuant to this chapter.

Ref.: Hanna § 1.16[1]; Herlick Handbook §§ 1.09, 9.10.

§144.6. Toxic materials; standards.

In promulgating standards dealing with toxic materials or harmful physical agents, the board shall adopt that standard which most adequately assures, to the extent feasible, that no employee will suffer material impairment of health or functional capacity even if such employee has regular exposure to a hazard regulated by such standard for the period of his working life. Development of standards under this section shall be based upon research, demonstrations, experiments, and such other information as may be appropriate. In addition to the attainment of the highest degree of health and safety protection for the employee, other considerations shall be the latest available scientific data in the field, the reasonableness of the standards, and experience gained under this and other health and safety laws. Whenever practicable, the standard promulgated shall be expressed in terms of objective criteria and of the performance desired.

Ref.: Herlick Handbook §§ 1.09, 9.10.

§144.7. Needle safety standards.

(a) The board shall, no later than January 15, 1999, adopt an emergency regulation revising the bloodborne pathogen standard currently set forth in Section 5193 of Title 8 of the California Code of Regulations in accordance with subdivision (b). Following adoption of the emergency regulation, the board shall complete the regulation adoption process and shall formally adopt a regulation embodying a bloodborne pathogen standard meeting the requirements of subdivision (b), which regulation shall become operative no later than August 1, 1999. Notwithstanding Section

11346.1 of the Government Code, the emergency regulation adopted pursuant to this subdivision shall remain in effect until the nonemergency regulation becomes operative or until August 1, 1999, whichever first occurs.

(b) The board shall adopt a standard, as described in subdivision (a), to be developed by the Division of Occupational Safety and Health. The standard shall include, but not be limited to, the following:

(1) A revised definition of "engineering controls" that includes sharps injury prevention technology including, but not limited to, needleless systems and needles with engineered sharps injury protection, which shall be defined in the standard.

(2) A requirement that sharps injury prevention technology specified in paragraph (1) be included as engineering or work practice controls, except in cases where the employer or other appropriate party can demonstrate circumstances in which the technology does not promote employee or patient safety or interferes with a medical procedure. Those circumstances shall be specified in the standard, and shall include, but not be limited to, circumstances where the technology is medically contraindicated or not more effective than alternative measures used by the employer to prevent exposure incidents.

(3) A requirement that written exposure control plans include an effective procedure for identifying and selecting existing sharps injury prevention technology of the type specified in paragraph (1).

(4) A requirement that written exposure control plans be updated when necessary to reflect progress in implementing the sharps injury prevention technology specified in paragraph (1).

(5) A requirement that information concerning exposure incidents be recorded in a sharps injury log, including, but not limited to, the type and brand of device involved in the incident.

(c) The Division of Occupational Safety and Health may consider and propose for adoption by the board additional revisions to the bloodborne pathogen standards to prevent sharps injuries or exposure incidents including, but not limited to, training requirements and measures to increase vaccinations.

(d) The Division of Occupational Safety and Health and the State Department of Health Services shall jointly compile and maintain a list of existing needleless systems and needles with engineered sharps injury protection, which shall be available to assist employers in complying with the requirements of the bloodborne pathogen standard adopted pursuant to this section. The list may be developed from existing sources of information, including, but not limited to, the federal Food and Drug Administration, the federal Centers for Disease Control, the National Institute of Occupational Safety and Health, and the United States Department of Veterans Affairs. **Leg.H.** 1998 ch. 999, 2001 ch. 370.

Ref.: Herlick Handbook §§ 1.09, 9.10.

§144.8. Standard for handling antineoplastic drugs in health care facilities.

(a) As used in this section the following definitions shall apply:

(1) "Antineoplastic drug" means a chemotherapeutic agent that controls or kills cancer cells.

(2) "NIOSH" means the National Institute for Occupational Safety and Health.

(b) The board shall adopt an occupational safety and health standard for the handling of antineoplastic drugs in health care facilities regardless of the setting. In developing the standard, the board shall consider input from hospitals, practicing physicians from impacted specialties, including oncology, organizations representing health care personnel, including registered nurses and pharmacists, and other stakeholders, and shall determine a reasonable time for facilities to implement new requirements imposed by the adopted standard. The standard, to the extent feasible, shall be consistent with and not exceed recommendations in the NIOSH 2004 alert entitled "Preventing Occupational Exposures to Antineoplastic and Other Hazardous Drugs in Health Care Settings," as updated in 2010. The standard may incorporate applicable updates and changes to NIOSH guidelines. **Leg.H.** 2013 ch. 678 (AB 1202) §2.

Ref.: Herlick Handbook § 1.09.

§145. Employment of personnel.

The board may employ necessary assistants, officers, experts, and such other employees as it deems necessary. All such personnel of the board shall be under the supervision of the chairman of the board or an executive officer to whom he delegates such responsibility. All such personnel shall be appointed pursuant to the State Civil Service Act (Part 1 (commencing with Section 18000) of Division 5 of Title 2 of the Government Code), except for the one exempt deputy or employee allowed by subdivision (e) of Section 4 of Article XXIV of the California Constitution.

Ref.: Herlick Handbook §§ 1.09, 9.10.

§145.1. Powers of board.

The board and its duly authorized representatives in the performance of its duties shall have the powers of a head of a department as set forth in Article 2 (commencing with Section 11180) of Chapter 2 of Part 1 of Division 3 of Title 2 of the Government Code.

Ref.: Herlick Handbook §§ 1.09, 9.10.

§146. Permanent variances; hearings.

In the conduct of hearings related to permanent variances, the board and its representatives are not bound by common law or statutory rules of evidence or by technical or formal rules of procedure but shall conduct the hearings in accordance with Article 8 (commencing with Section 11435.05) of Chapter 4.5 of Part 1 of Division 3 of Title 2 of, and Section 11513 of, the Government Code. A full and complete record shall be kept of all proceedings. **Leg.H.** 1995 ch. 938, operative July 1, 1997.

Ref.: Herlick Handbook §§ 1.09, 9.10.

§147. Evaluation of standards and variances from other sources.

The board shall refer to the Division of Occupational Safety and Health for evaluation any proposed occupational safety or health standard or variance from adopted standards received by the board from sources other than the division. The division shall submit a report on the proposed standard or variance within 60 days of receipt thereof.

Ref.: Herlick Handbook §§ 1.09 9.10.

§147.1. Division of Occupational Safety and Health; duties; federal standards; proposed standards.

In connection with the development and promulgation of occupational health standards the Division of Occupational Safety and Health shall perform all of the following functions:

(a) Analyze proposed and new federal occupational health standards, evaluate their impact on California, determine any necessity for their modification, and present proposed standards to the board in sufficient time for the board to conduct hearings and adopt standards within the time required.

(b) Maintain liaison with the National Institute of Occupational Safety and Health and the federal Occupational Safety and Health Administration in the development of recommended federal standards and when appropriate provide representation on federal advisory committees dealing with the development of occupational health standards.

(c) On occupational health issues not covered by federal standards maintain surveillance, determine the necessity for standards, develop and present proposed standards to the board.

(d) Evaluate any proposed occupational health standard or application for a variance of an occupational health standard received by the board, and submit a report to the board on the proposed standard or variance within 60 days of receipt thereof.

(e) Appear and testify at board hearings and other public proceedings involving occupational health matters.

Ref.: Herlick Handbook §§ 1.09 9.10.

§147.2. Information repository on toxic materials; "Hazard Evaluation System and Information Service" or "HESIS."

(a) As used in this section, "Hazard Evaluation System and Information Service" or "HESIS" means the repository established pursuant to subdivision (b).

(b) In accordance with Chapter 2 (commencing with Section 6350) of Part 1 of Division 5 of this code and Section 105175 of the Health and Safety Code, the Department of Industrial Relations, by interagency agreement with the State Department of Public Health, shall establish a repository of current data on toxic materials and harmful physical agents in use or potentially in use in places of employment in the state, known as the Hazard Evaluation System and Information Service, or HESIS.

(c) HESIS shall fulfill all of the following functions:

(1) Provide reliable information of practical use to employers, employees, representatives of employees, and other governmental agencies on the possible hazards to employees of exposure to toxic materials or harmful physical agents.

(2) Collect and evaluate toxicological and epidemiological data and any other information that may be pertinent to establishing harmful effects on health of exposure to toxic materials or harmful physical agents. Nothing in this subdivision shall be construed as authorizing HESIS to require employers, other than chemical manufacturers, formulators, suppliers, distributors, importers, and their agents, to report any information not otherwise required by law.

(3) When there is new scientific or medical information and the Chief of HESIS, in consultation with the Director of Industrial Relations and the Chief of the Division of Environmental and Occupational Disease Control in the State Department of Public Health, determines that a substance may be in use in a place of employment, may pose a hazard under a reasonable anticipated condition of use, and potentially poses a serious new or unrecognized health hazard to an employee, including, but not limited to, cancer, reproductive or developmental harm, organ system impairment, or death, chemical manufacturers, formulators, suppliers, distributors, importers, and their agents, as specified in subparagraph (A), shall provide to HESIS the names and addresses of their customers who have purchased certain chemicals, as specified by HESIS, or commercial products containing those chemicals and information related to those shipments, including the quantities and dates of shipments, and the proportion of a specified chemical within a mixture containing the specified chemical, upon written request by HESIS, for every product the final destination of which may be a place of employment in California. This paragraph shall not apply to a retail seller of the substance, whether sold individually or as part of a commercial product to the public. The following shall apply to this paragraph:

(A) On or after January 1, 2016, the information requested shall include current and past customers for not more than a one-year period prior to the date the request is issued. The information shall be provided within a reasonable timeframe, not to exceed 30 calendar days from the date the request is issued. The information shall be provided in a format specified by the State Department of Public Health but consistent with the responding entity's current data system.

(B) Unless, pursuant to other law or regulation the following persons, any other person, or any governmental entity is required to publicly disclose the following information, the names and addresses of customers, the quantities and dates of shipments, and the proportion of a specified chemical within a mixture provided by chemical manufacturers, formulators, suppliers, distributors, importers, and their agents pursuant to this paragraph shall be considered confidential and, except as specified in this subparagraph, exempt from public disclosure under the California Public Records Act (Chapter 3.5 (commencing with Section 6250) of Division 7 of Title 1 of the Government Code). HESIS may disclose that information to officers or employees of the State Department of Public Health, to officers or employees of the state who are responsible for carrying out the purposes of Division 5 (commencing with Section 6300), or to the state agencies of the state officers specified in paragraphs (5) and (6). Any officer, employee, or agency to which the information is disclosed shall be subject to this subparagraph.

(C) The State Department of Public Health shall be entitled to reimbursement of attorney's fees and costs incurred in seeking an injunction to enforce this paragraph.

(4) Recommend to the Chief of the Division of Occupational Safety and Health Administration that an occupational safety and health standard be developed whenever it has been determined that a substance in use or potentially in use in places of employment is potentially toxic at the concentrations or under the conditions used.

(5) Notify the Director of Pesticide Regulation of any information developed by HESIS that is relevant to carrying out his or her responsibilities under Chapters 2 (commencing with Section 12751) and 3 (commencing with Section 14001) of Division 7 of the Food and Agricultural Code.

(6) Notify the Secretary for Environmental Protection of any information developed by HESIS that is relevant to carrying out his or her responsibilities.

(d) The Director of Industrial Relations shall appoint an advisory committee to HESIS. The advisory committee shall consist of four representatives from labor, four representatives from management, four active practitioners in the occupational health field, and three persons knowledgeable in biomedical statistics or information storage and retrieval systems. The advisory committee shall meet on a regular basis at the request of the director. The committee shall be consulted by, and shall advise the director at each phase of the structuring and functioning of the repository and alert system with regard to, the procedures, methodology, validity, and practical utility of collecting, evaluating, and disseminating information concerning hazardous substances, consistent with the primary goals and objectives of the repository.

(e) Nothing in this section shall be construed to limit the ability of the State Department of Public Health to propose occupational safety and health standards to the Occupational Safety and Health Standards Board.

(f) Policies and procedures shall be developed to assure, to the extent possible, that HESIS uses and does not duplicate the resources of the federal government and other states.

(g) On or before December 31 of each year, the Department of Industrial Relations shall submit a report to the Legislature detailing the implementation and operation of HESIS including, but not limited to, the amount and source of funds allocated and spent on repository activities, the toxic materials and harmful physical agents investigated during the past year and recommendations made concerning them, actions taken to inform interested persons of the possible hazards of exposure to toxic materials and harmful physical agents, and any recommendations for legislative changes relating to the functions of HESIS. **Leg.H.** 1996 ch. 1023, effective September 29, 1996, 2014 ch. 830 (SB 193) §2.

Ref.: Herlick Handbook §§ 1.09 9.10.

§147.3. Contents of report; investigation; blood lead level.

(a) When the Division of Occupational Safety and Health receives a report from the State Department of Public Health pursuant to subdivision (c) of Section 105185 of the Health and Safety Code, the report shall constitute a complaint from a government agency representative charging a serious violation and shall subject the employer or place of employment to the requirements of subdivision (a) of Section 6309 for the Division of Occupational Safety and Health to initiate an investigation within three working days. Upon the completion of the investigation, any citations and fines imposed by the division shall be made publicly available on an annual basis pursuant to subdivision (d) of Section 6309.

(b) The blood lead level established in subdivision (c) of Section 105185 of the Health and Safety Code is not intended to supersede any lower blood lead level that may be actionable under the Division of Occupational Safety and Health's lead standards in its general industry safety order (Section 5198 of Title 8 of the California Code of Regulations) or construction safety order (Section 1532.1 of Title 8 of the California Code of Regulations). For purposes of this section, an actionable employee blood lead level means a level that triggers an employer obligation to reduce lead exposure in the workplace or an investigation by the division. **Leg.H.** 2019 ch. 710 (AB 35) §2.

§147.4. Establishment of advisory board to ensure compliance with standards promulgated by National Fire Protection Association.

(a) By January 1, 2016, the department shall convene an advisory committee to evaluate whether changes are needed to align the general industry safety orders in Sections 3403 to 3411, inclusive, of Article 10.1 (commencing with Section 3401) of Group 2 of Subchapter 7 of Chapter 4 of Article 8 of Division 1 of Title 8 of the California Code of Regulations with the applicable and most recently promulgated standards of the National Fire Protection Association. The committee shall be composed of parties in both management and labor, represent a cross section of the fire protection industry and community, and be competent and knowledgeable regarding personal protective clothing and equipment for firefighters and firefighting practices generally.

(b) By July 1, 2016, the advisory committee shall present its findings and recommendations for consideration by the board. No later than July 1, 2017, the board shall render a decision regarding the adoption of changes to the general industry safety orders in Sections 3403 to 3411, inclusive, of Article 10.1 (commencing with Section 3401) of Group 2 of Subchapter 7 of Chapter 4 of Article 8 of Division 1 of Title 8 of the California Code of Regulations, or other applicable standards and regulations, in order to maintain alignment with the applicable National Fire Protection Association standards.

(c) Beginning July 1, 2018, and every five years thereafter, the board, in consultation with the department, shall complete a comprehensive review of all revisions to National Fire Protection Association standards pertaining to personal protective equipment covered by the general industry safety orders in Sections 3403 to 3411, inclusive, of Article 10.1 (commencing with Section 3401) of Group 2 of Subchapter 7 of Chapter 4 of Article 8 of Division 1 of Title 8 of the California Code of Regulations. If the review finds that the revisions to applicable National Fire Protection Association standards provide a greater degree of personal protection than the safety orders, the board shall consider modifying existing safety orders and shall render a decision regarding the adoption of necessary changes to safety orders, or other applicable standards and regulations, no later than July 1 of the subsequent year, in order to maintain alignment of the safety orders with the applicable National Fire Protection Association standards. **Leg.H.** 2014 ch. 811 (AB 2146) §1.

§147.5. Advisory committee to evaluate need to develop industry-specific regulations related to medical cannabis facilities.

(a) By January 1, 2017, the Division of Occupational Safety and Health shall convene an advisory committee to evaluate whether there is a need to develop industry-specific regulations related to the activities of facilities issued a license pursuant to Chapter 3.5 (commencing with Section 19300) of Division 8 of the Business and Professions Code.

(b) By July 1, 2017, the advisory committee shall present to the board its findings and recommendations for consideration by the board. By July 1, 2017, the board shall render a decision regarding the adoption of industry-specific regulations pursuant to this section. **Leg.H.** 2015 ch. 689 (AB 266) §7.

§147.6. Advisory committee to evaluate need to develop industry-specific regulations related to the cultivation, distribution, transport, storage, manufacturing, processing, and sale of nonmedical marijuana and marijuana products.

(a) By March 1, 2018, the Division of Occupational Safety and Health shall convene an advisory committee to evaluate whether there is a need to develop industry-specific regulations related to the activities of licensees under Division 10 (commencing with Section 26000) of the Business and Professions Code, including but not limited to, whether specific requirements are needed to address exposure to second-hand marijuana smoke by employees at facilities where on-site consumption of marijuana is permitted under subdivision (d) of Section 26200 of the Business and Professions Code, and whether specific requirements are needed to address the potential risks of combustion, inhalation, armed robberies or repetitive strain injuries.

(b) By October 1, 2018, the advisory committee shall present to the board its findings and recommendations for consideration by the board. By October 1, 2018, the board shall render a decision regarding the adoption of industryspecific regulations pursuant to this section. **Leg.H.** Adopted by Initiative (Prop. 64 §6.2) at the November 8, 2016, General Election, effective November 9, 2016.

CHAPTER 6.5 OCCUPATIONAL SAFETY AND HEALTH APPEALS BOARD

§148. Occupational Safety and Health Appeals Board; designation of chairperson.

(a) There is in the Department of Industrial Relations the Occupational Safety and Health Appeals Board, consisting of three members appointed by the Governor, subject to the approval of the Senate. One member shall be from the field of management, one shall be from the field of labor and one member shall be from the general public. The public member shall be chosen from other than the fields of management and labor. Each member of the appeals board shall devote his full time to the performance of his duties.

(b) The chairman and each member of the appeals board shall receive the annual salary provided for by Chapter 6 (commencing with Section 11550) of Part 1 of Division 3 of Title 2 of the Government Code.

(c) The Governor shall designate the chairman of the appeals board from the membership of the appeals board. The person so designated shall hold the office of chairman at the pleasure of the Governor. The chairman shall designate a member of the appeals board to act as chairman in his absence.

Ref.: Hanna § 1.16[3]; Herlick Handbook § 9.10.

§148.1. Term of office.

Each member of the appeals board shall serve for a term of four years and until his successor is appointed and qualifies. The terms of the first three members appointed to the appeals board shall expire on the second, third, and fourth January 15th following the date of the appointment of the first appointed member. A vacancy shall be filled by the Governor, subject to the approval of the Senate by appointment for the unexpired term.

Ref.: Herlick Handbook § 9.10.

§148.2. Employment of appeals board personnel; salaries of hearing officers.

The appeals board may employ necessary assistants, officers, experts, hearing officers, and such other employees as it deems necessary. All such personnel of the appeals board shall be under the supervision of the chairman of the appeals board or an executive officer to whom the chairman delegates such responsibility. All such personnel shall be appointed pursuant to the State Civil Service Act (Part 2 (commencing with Section 18500) of Division 5 of Title 2 of the Government Code), except for the one exempt deputy or employee allowed by subdivision (e) of Section 4 of Article XXIV of the California Constitution. The salaries of the hearing officers shall be fixed by the State Personnel Board at a rate comparable to that of other referees or hearing officers in state service whose duties and responsibilities are comparable, without regard to whether such other positions have membership in the State Bar of California as a prerequisite to appointment.

Ref.: Herlick Handbook § 9.10.

§148.4. Orders and decisions to be in writing.

All decisions and orders of the appeals board shall be in writing.

Ref.: Herlick Handbook § 9.10.

§148.5. Finality of decisions.

A decision of the appeals board is final, except for any rehearing or judicial review as permitted by Chapter 4 (commencing with Section 6600) of Part 1 of Division 5.

Ref.: Herlick Handbook § 9.10.

§148.6. Director's right to seek judicial review.

A decision of the appeals board is binding on the director and the Division of Occupational Safety and Health with respect to the parties involved in the particular appeal. The director shall have the right to seek judicial review of an appeals board decision irrespective of whether or not he or she appeared or participated in the appeal to the appeals board or its hearing officer.

Ref.: Herlick Handbook § 9.10.

§148.7. Procedural rules for hearings; adoption.

The appeals board, acting as a whole, may adopt, amend, or repeal rules of practice and procedure pertaining to hearing appeals and other matters falling within its jurisdiction. All such rules, amendments thereto, or repeals thereof shall be made in accordance with the provisions of Chapter 3.5 (commencing with Section 11340) of Part 1 of Division 3 of Title 2 of the Government Code.

Ref.: Herlick Handbook § 9.10.

§148.8. Powers of appeals board.

The appeals board and its duly authorized representatives in the performance of its duties shall have the powers of a head of a department as set forth in Article 2 (commencing with Section 11180) of Chapter 2 of Part 1 of Division 3 of Title 2 of the Government Code, except for Section 11185 of the Government Code.

Ref.: Herlick Handbook § 9.10.

§148.9. Decisions by majority of board.

Decisions of the appeals board shall be made by a majority of the appeals board, except as otherwise expressly provided.

Ref.: Herlick Handbook § 9.10.

§149. Executive officer as acting deputy.

The chairman of the appeals board may authorize its executive officer to act as deputy appeals board member, and may delegate authority and duties to the executive officer in the event of the absence of a member of the appeals board.

Ref.: Herlick Handbook § 9.10.

§149.5. Costs and attorney's fees.

The appeals board may award reasonable costs, including attorney's fees, consultant's fees, and witness' fees, not to exceed five thousand dollars ($5,000) in the aggregate, to any employer who appeals a citation resulting from an inspection or investigation conducted on or after January 1, 1980, issued for violation of an occupational safety and health standard, rule, order, or regulation established pursuant to Chapter 6 (commencing with Section 140) of Division 1, if (1) either the employer prevails in the appeal, or the citation is withdrawn, and (2) the appeals board finds that the issuance of the citation was the result of arbitrary or capricious action or conduct by the division.

The appeals board shall adopt rules of practice and procedure to implement this section.

The payment of costs pursuant to this section shall be from funds in the regular operating budget of the division. The division shall show in its proposed budget for each fiscal year the following information with respect to the prior fiscal year:

(a) The total costs paid.

(b) The number of cases in which costs were paid.

Ref.: Herlick Handbook § 9.10.

DIVISION 2
EMPLOYMENT REGULATION AND SUPERVISION

PART 1
Compensation

CHAPTER 1
Payment of Wages
[Selected Provisions]

ARTICLE 1
General Occupations

§226.2. Compensation on piece-rate basis.

This section shall apply for employees who are compensated on a piece-rate basis for any work performed during a pay period. This section shall not be construed to limit or alter minimum wage or overtime compensation requirements, or the obligation to compensate employees for all hours worked under any other statute or local ordinance. For the purposes of this section, "applicable minimum wage" means the highest of the federal, state, or local minimum wage that is applicable to the employment, and "other nonproductive time" means time under the employer's control, exclusive of rest and recovery periods, that is not directly related to the activity being compensated on a piece-rate basis.

(a) For employees compensated on a piece-rate basis during a pay period, the following shall apply for that pay period:

(1) Employees shall be compensated for rest and recovery periods and other nonproductive time separate from any piece-rate compensation.

(2) The itemized statement required by subdivision (a) of Section 226 shall, in addition to the other items specified in that subdivision, separately state the following, to which the provisions of Section 226 shall also be applicable:

(A) The total hours of compensable rest and recovery periods, the rate of compensation, and the gross wages paid for those periods during the pay period.

(B) Except for employers paying compensation for other nonproductive time in accordance with paragraph (7), the total hours of other nonproductive time, as determined under paragraph (5), the rate of compensation, and the gross wages paid for that time during the pay period.

(3)(A) Employees shall be compensated for rest and recovery periods at a regular hourly rate that is no less than the higher of:

(i) An average hourly rate determined by dividing the total compensation for the workweek, exclusive of compensation for rest and recovery periods and any premium compensation for overtime, by the total hours worked during the workweek, exclusive of rest and recovery periods.

(ii) The applicable minimum wage.

(B) For employers who pay on a semimonthly basis, employees shall be compensated at least at the applicable minimum wage rate for the rest and recovery periods together with other wages for the payroll period during which the rest and recovery periods occurred. Any additional compensation required for those employees pursuant to clause (i) of subparagraph (A) is payable no later than the payday for the next regular payroll period.

(4) Employees shall be compensated for other nonproductive time at an hourly rate that is no less than the applicable minimum wage.

(5) The amount of other nonproductive time may be determined either through actual records or the employer's reasonable estimates, whether for a group of employees or for a particular employee, of other nonproductive time worked during the pay period.

(6) An employer who is found to have made a good faith error in determining the total or estimated amount of other nonproductive time worked during the pay period shall remain liable for the payment of compensation for all hours worked in other nonproductive time, but shall not be liable for statutory civil penalties, including, but not limited to, penalties under Section 226.3, or liquidated damages based solely on that error, provided that both of the following are true:

(A) The employer has provided the wage statement information required by subparagraph (B) of paragraph (2) and paid the compensation due for the amount of other nonproductive time determined by the employer in accordance with the requirements of paragraphs (4) and (5).

(B) The total compensation paid for any day in the pay period is no less than what is due under the applicable minimum wage and any required overtime compensation.

(7) An employer who, in addition to paying any piece-rate compensation, pays an hourly rate of at least the applicable minimum wage for all hours worked, shall be deemed in compliance with paragraph (4).

(b) This section shall become operative on January 1, 2021. **Leg.H.** 2015 ch. 754 (AB 1513) §5.

Former Sections: Former Lab C §226.2 was enacted in 2015 and repealed operative January 1, 2021, by its own provisions. 2015 ch. 754 (AB 1513) §4.

§226.8. Unlawful activities; penalties; disciplinary action; information to be posted on Internet Web site; enforcement.

(a) It is unlawful for any person or employer to engage in any of the following activities:

(1) Willful misclassification of an individual as an independent contractor.

(2) Charging an individual who has been willfully misclassified as an independent contractor a fee, or making any deductions from compensation, for any purpose, including for goods, materials, space rental, services, gov-

ernment licenses, repairs, equipment maintenance, or fines arising from the individual's employment where any of the acts described in this paragraph would have violated the law if the individual had not been misclassified.

(b) If the Labor and Workforce Development Agency or a court issues a determination that a person or employer has engaged in any of the enumerated violations of subdivision (a), the person or employer shall be subject to a civil penalty of not less than five thousand dollars ($5,000) and not more than fifteen thousand dollars ($15,000) for each violation, in addition to any other penalties or fines permitted by law.

(c) If the Labor and Workforce Development Agency or a court issues a determination that a person or employer has engaged in any of the enumerated violations of subdivision (a) and the person or employer has engaged in or is engaging in a pattern or practice of these violations, the person or employer shall be subject to a civil penalty of not less than ten thousand dollars ($10,000) and not more than twenty-five thousand dollars ($25,000) for each violation, in addition to any other penalties or fines permitted by law.

(d)(1) If the Labor and Workforce Development Agency or a court issues a determination that a person or employer that is a licensed contractor pursuant to the Contractors' State License Law has violated subdivision (a), the agency, in addition to any other remedy that has been ordered, shall transmit a certified copy of the order to the Contractors' State License Board.

(2) The registrar of the Contractors' State License Board shall initiate disciplinary action against a licensee within 30 days of receiving a certified copy of an agency or court order that resulted in disbarment pursuant to paragraph (1).

(e) If the Labor and Workforce Development Agency or a court issues a determination that a person or employer has violated subdivision (a), the agency or court, in addition to any other remedy that has been ordered, shall order the person or employer to display prominently on its Internet Web site, in an area which is accessible to all employees and the general public, or, if the person or employer does not have an Internet Web site, to display prominently in an area that is accessible to all employees and the general public at each location where a violation of subdivision (a) occurred, a notice that sets forth all of the following:

(1) That the Labor and Workforce Development Agency or a court, as applicable, has found that the person or employer has committed a serious violation of the law by engaging in the willful misclassification of employees.

(2) That the person or employer has changed its business practices in order to avoid committing further violations of this section.

(3) That any employee who believes that he or she is being misclassified as an independent contractor may contact the Labor and Workforce Development Agency. The notice shall include the mailing address, e-mail address, and telephone number of the agency.

(4) That the notice is being posted pursuant to a state order.

(f) In addition to including the information specified in subdivision (e), a person or employer also shall satisfy the following requirements in preparing the notice:

(1) An officer shall sign the notice.

(2) It shall post the notice for one year commencing with the date of the final decision and order.

(g)(1) In accordance with the procedures specified in Sections 98 to 98.2, inclusive, the Labor Commissioner may issue a determination that a person or employer has violated subdivision (a).

(2) If, upon inspection or investigation, the Labor Commissioner determines that a person or employer has violated subdivision (a), the Labor Commissioner may issue a citation to assess penalties set forth in subdivisions (b) and (c) in addition to any other penalties or damages that are otherwise available at law. The procedures for issuing, contesting, and enforcing judgments shall be the same as those set forth in Section 1197.1.

(3) The Labor Commissioner may enforce this section pursuant to Section 98 or in a civil suit.

(h) Any administrative or civil penalty pursuant to subdivision (b) or (c) or disciplinary action pursuant to subdivision (d) or (e) shall remain in effect against any successor corporation, owner, or business entity that satisfies both of the following:

(1) Has one or more of the same principals or officers as the person or employer subject to the penalty or action.

(2) Is engaged in the same or a similar business as the person or employer subject to the penalty or action.

(i) For purposes of this section, the following definitions apply:

(1) "Determination" means an order, decision, award, or citation issued by an agency or a court of competent jurisdiction for which the time to appeal has expired and for which no appeal is pending.

(2) "Labor and Workforce Development Agency" means the Labor and Workforce Development Agency or any of its departments, divisions, commissions, boards, or agencies.

(3) "Officer" means the chief executive officer, president, any vice president in charge of a principal business unit, division, or function, or any other officer of the corporation who performs a policymaking function. If the employer is a partnership, "officer" means a partner. If the employer is a sole proprietor, "officer" means the owner.

(4) "Willful misclassification" means avoiding employee status for an individual by voluntarily and knowingly misclassifying that individual as an independent contractor.

(j) Nothing in this section is intended to limit any rights or remedies otherwise available at law. **Leg.H.** 2011 ch. 706 (SB 459) §1, 2012 ch. 162 (SB 1171) §116.

Ref.: Hanna § 3.07[5].

ARTICLE 1.5
Paid Sick Days

§245. Citation of article; provisions of article in addition to and independent of other rights.

(a) This article shall be known and may be cited as the Healthy Workplaces, Healthy Families Act of 2014.

Labor

(b) The provisions of this article are in addition to and independent of any other rights, remedies, or procedures available under any other law and do not diminish, alter, or negate any other legal rights, remedies, or procedures available to an aggrieved person. **Leg.H.** 2014 ch. 317 (AB 1522) §3.

2014 Note: For legislative intent, see the 2014 Note following Lab C §249.

§245.5. Definitions.

As used in this article:

(a) "Employee" does not include the following:

(1) An employee covered by a valid collective bargaining agreement if the agreement expressly provides for the wages, hours of work, and working conditions of employees, and expressly provides for paid sick days or a paid leave or paid time off policy that permits the use of sick days for those employees, final and binding arbitration of disputes concerning the application of its paid sick days provisions, premium wage rates for all overtime hours worked, and regular hourly rate of pay of not less than 30 percent more than the state minimum wage rate.

(2) An employee in the construction industry covered by a valid collective bargaining agreement if the agreement expressly provides for the wages, hours of work, and working conditions of employees, premium wage rates for all overtime hours worked, and regular hourly pay of not less than 30 percent more than the state minimum wage rate, and the agreement either (A) was entered into before January 1, 2015, or (B) expressly waives the requirements of this article in clear and unambiguous terms. For purposes of this subparagraph, "employee in the construction industry" means an employee performing work associated with construction, including work involving alteration, demolition, building, excavation, renovation, remodeling, maintenance, improvement, repair work, and any other work as described by Chapter 9 (commencing with Section 7000) of Division 3 of the Business and Professions Code, and other similar or related occupations or trades.

(3) An individual employed by an air carrier as a flight deck or cabin crew member that is subject to the provisions of Title II of the federal Railway Labor Act (45 U.S.C. Sec. 151 et seq.), provided that the individual is provided with compensated time off equal to or exceeding the amount established in paragraph (1) of subdivision (b) of Section 246.

(4) An employee of the state, city, county, city and county, district, or any other public entity who is a recipient of a retirement allowance and employed without reinstatement into his or her respective retirement system pursuant to either Article 8 (commencing with Section 21220) of Chapter 12 of Part 3 of Division 5 of Title 2 of the Government Code, or Article 8 (commencing with Section 31680) of Chapter 3 of Part 3 of Division 4 of Title 3 of the Government Code.

(b) "Employer" means any person employing another under any appointment or contract of hire and includes the state, political subdivisions of the state, and municipalities.

(c) "Family member" means any of the following:

(1) A child, which for purposes of this article means a biological, adopted, or foster child, stepchild, legal ward, or a child to whom the employee stands in loco parentis. This definition of a child is applicable regardless of age or dependency status.

(2) A biological, adoptive, or foster parent, stepparent, or legal guardian of an employee or the employee's spouse or registered domestic partner, or a person who stood in loco parentis when the employee was a minor child.

(3) A spouse.

(4) A registered domestic partner.

(5) A grandparent.

(6) A grandchild.

(7) A sibling.

(d) "Health care provider" has the same meaning as defined in paragraph (6) of subdivision (c) of Section 12945.2 of the Government Code.

(e) "Paid sick days" means time that is compensated at the same wage as the employee normally earns during regular work hours and is provided by an employer to an employee for the purposes described in Section 246.5. **Leg.H.** 2014 ch. 317 (AB 1522) §3, 2015 ch. 67 (AB 304) §1, effective July 13, 2015, 2016 ch. 4 (SB 3) §1.

2014 Note: For legislative intent, see the 2014 Note following Lab C §249.

§246. Entitlement; accrual; use of accrued paid sick days; carryover; separation from employment; written notice of available paid sick leave; calculation of paid sick leave; workgroup and guidance for implementation for in-home supportive services providers.

(a)(1) An employee who, on or after July 1, 2015, works in California for the same employer for 30 or more days within a year from the commencement of employment is entitled to paid sick days as specified in this section. **For an individual provider of waiver personal care services under Section 14132.97 of the Welfare and Institutions Code who also provides in-home supportive services in an applicable month, eligibility shall be determined based on the aggregate number of monthly hours worked between in-home supportive services and waiver personal care services pursuant to subdivision (d) of Section 14132.971.**

(2) On and after July 1, 2018, a provider of in-home supportive services under Section 14132.95, 14132.952, or 14132.956 of, or Article 7 (commencing with Section 12300) of Chapter 3 of Part 3 of Division 9 of, the Welfare and Institutions Code, who works in California for 30 or more days within a year from the commencement of employment is entitled to paid sick days as specified in subdivision (e) and subject to the rate of accrual in paragraph (1) of subdivision (b). **For an individual provider of waiver personal care services under Section 14132.97 of the Welfare and Institutions Code, entitlement to paid sick days begins on July 1, 2019.**

(b)(1) An employee shall accrue paid sick days at the rate of not less than one hour per every 30 hours worked, beginning at the commencement of employment or the operative date of this article, whichever is later, subject to the use and accrual limitations set forth in this section.

(2) An employee who is exempt from overtime requirements as an administrative, executive, or professional employee under a wage order of the Industrial Welfare

Commission is deemed to work 40 hours per workweek for the purposes of this section, unless the employee's normal workweek is less than 40 hours, in which case the employee shall accrue paid sick days based upon that normal workweek.

(3) An employer may use a different accrual method, other than providing one hour per every 30 hours worked, provided that the accrual is on a regular basis so that an employee has no less than 24 hours of accrued sick leave or paid time off by the 120th calendar day of employment or each calendar year, or in each 12-month period.

(4) An employer may satisfy the accrual requirements of this section by providing not less than 24 hours or three days of paid sick leave that is available to the employee to use by the completion of [1] **the employee's** 120th calendar day of employment.

(c) An employee shall be entitled to use accrued paid sick days beginning on the 90th day of employment, after which day the employee may use paid sick days as they are accrued.

(d) Accrued paid sick days shall carry over to the following year of employment. However, an employer may limit an employee's use of accrued paid sick days to 24 hours or three days in each year of employment, calendar year, or 12-month period. This section shall be satisfied and no accrual or carryover is required if the full amount of leave is received at the beginning of each year of employment, calendar year, or 12-month period. The term "full amount of leave" means three days or 24 hours.

(e) For a provider of in-home supportive services under Section 14132.95, 14132.952, or 14132.956 of, or Article 7 (commencing with Section 12300) of Chapter 3 of Part 3 of Division 9 of, **and an individual provider of waiver personal care services under Section 14132.97 of,** the Welfare and Institutions Code, the term "full amount of leave" is defined as follows:

(1) Eight hours or one day in each year of employment, calendar year, or 12-month period beginning July 1, 2018.

(2) Sixteen hours or two days in each year of employment, calendar year, or 12-month period beginning when the minimum wage, as set forth in paragraph (1) of subdivision (b) of Section 1182.12 and accounting for any years postponed under subparagraph (D) of paragraph (3) of subdivision (d) of Section 1182.12, has reached thirteen dollars ($13) per hour.

(3) Twenty-four hours or three days in each year of employment, calendar year, or 12-month period beginning when the minimum wage, as set forth in paragraph (1) of subdivision (b) of Section 1182.12 and accounting for any years postponed under subparagraph (D) of paragraph (3) of subdivision (d) of Section 1182.12, has reached fifteen dollars ($15) per hour.

(f) An employer is not required to provide additional paid sick days pursuant to this section if the employer has a paid leave policy or paid time off policy, the employer makes available an amount of leave applicable to employees that may be used for the same purposes and under the same conditions as specified in this section, and the policy satisfies one of the following:

(1) Satisfies the accrual, carryover, and use requirements of this section.

(2) Provided paid sick leave or paid time off to a class of employees before January 1, 2015, pursuant to a sick leave policy or paid time off policy that used an accrual method different than providing one hour per 30 hours worked, provided that the accrual is on a regular basis so that an employee, including an employee hired into that class after January 1, 2015, has no less than one day or eight hours of accrued sick leave or paid time off within three months of employment of each calendar year, or each 12-month period, and the employee was eligible to earn at least three days or 24 hours of sick leave or paid time off within nine months of employment. If an employer modifies the accrual method used in the policy it had in place prior to January 1, 2015, the employer shall comply with any accrual method set forth in subdivision (b) or provide the full amount of leave at the beginning of each year of employment, calendar year, or 12-month period. This section does not prohibit the employer from increasing the accrual amount or rate for a class of employees covered by this subdivision.

(3) Notwithstanding any other law, sick leave benefits provided pursuant to the provisions of Sections 19859 to 19868.3, inclusive, of the Government Code, or annual leave benefits provided pursuant to the provisions of Sections 19858.3 to 19858.7, inclusive, of the Government Code, or by provisions of a memorandum of understanding reached pursuant to Section 3517.5 that incorporate or supersede provisions of Section 19859 to 19868.3, inclusive, or Sections 19858.3 to 19858.7, inclusive of the Government Code, meet the requirements of this section.

(g)(1) Except as specified in paragraph (2), an employer is not required to provide compensation to an employee for accrued, unused paid sick days upon termination, resignation, retirement, or other separation from employment.

(2) If an employee separates from an employer and is rehired by the employer within one year from the date of separation, previously accrued and unused paid sick days shall be reinstated. The employee shall be entitled to use those previously accrued and unused paid sick days and to accrue additional paid sick days upon rehiring, subject to the use and accrual limitations set forth in this section. An employer is not required to reinstate accrued paid time off to an employee that was paid out at the time of termination, resignation, or separation of employment.

(h) An employer may lend paid sick days to an employee in advance of accrual, at the employer's discretion and with proper documentation.

(i) An employer shall provide an employee with written notice that sets forth the amount of paid sick leave available, or paid time off leave an employer provides in lieu of sick leave, for use on either the employee's itemized wage statement described in Section 226 or in a separate writing provided on the designated pay date with the employee's payment of wages. If an employer provides unlimited paid sick leave or unlimited paid time off to an employee, the employer may satisfy this section by indicating on the notice or the employee's itemized wage statement "unlimited." The penalties described in this article for a violation of this subdivision shall be in lieu of the penalties for a violation of Section 226. This subdivision shall apply to employers covered by Wage Order 11 or

12 of the Industrial Welfare Commission only on and after January 21, 2016.

(j) An employer has no obligation under this section to allow an employee's total accrual of paid sick leave to exceed 48 hours or 6 days, provided that an employee's rights to accrue and use paid sick leave are not limited other than as allowed under this section.

(k) An employee may determine how much paid sick leave [2] **they need** to use, provided that an employer may set a reasonable minimum increment, not to exceed two hours, for the use of paid sick leave.

(*l*) For the purposes of this section, an employer shall calculate paid sick leave using any of the following calculations:

(1) Paid sick time for nonexempt employees shall be calculated in the same manner as the regular rate of pay for the workweek in which the employee uses paid sick time, whether or not the employee actually works overtime in that workweek.

(2) Paid sick time for nonexempt employees shall be calculated by dividing the employee's total wages, not including overtime premium pay, by the employee's total hours worked in the full pay periods of the prior 90 days of employment.

(3) Paid sick time for exempt employees shall be calculated in the same manner as the employer calculates wages for other forms of paid leave time.

(m) If the need for paid sick leave is foreseeable, the employee shall provide reasonable advance notification. If the need for paid sick leave is unforeseeable, the employee shall provide notice of the need for the leave as soon as practicable.

(n) An employer shall provide payment for sick leave taken by an employee no later than the payday for the next regular payroll period after the sick leave was taken.

(o) The State Department of Social Services, in consultation with stakeholders, shall convene a workgroup to implement paid sick leave for in-home supportive services providers as specified in this section. This workgroup shall finish its implementation work by November 1, 2017, and the State Department of Social Services shall issue guidance such as an all-county letter or similar instructions by December 1, 2017.

(p) No later than February 1, 2019, the State Department of Social Services, in consultation with the Department of Finance and stakeholders, shall reconvene the paid sick leave workgroup for in-home supportive services providers. The workgroup shall discuss how paid sick leave affects the provision of in-home supportive services. The workgroup shall consider the potential need for a process to cover an in-home supportive services recipient's authorized hours when a provider needs to utilize [3] **their** sick time. This workgroup shall finish its work by November 1, 2019.

(q) Notwithstanding the rulemaking provisions of the Administrative Procedure Act (Chapter 3.5 (commencing with Section 11340) of Part 1 of Division 3 of Title 2 of the Government Code), the State Department of Social Services may implement, interpret, or make specific this section by means of an all-county letter, or similar instructions, without taking any regulatory action. **Leg.H.** 2014 ch. 317 (AB 1522) §3, 2015 ch. 67 (AB 304) §2, effective July 13, 2015, 2016 ch. 4 (SB 3) §2, 2018 ch. 35 (AB 1811) §8, effective June 27, 2018, 2020 ch. 11 (AB 79) §13, effective June 29, 2020.

§246. 2020 Deletes. [1] his or her **[2]** he or she needs **[3]** his or her

2014 Note: For legislative intent, see the 2014 Note following Lab C §249.

§246.5. Purposes for which paid sick leave may be granted; unlawful retaliation.

(a) Upon the oral or written request of an employee, an employer shall provide paid sick days for the following purposes:

(1) Diagnosis, care, or treatment of an existing health condition of, or preventive care for, an employee or an employee's family member.

(2) For an employee who is a victim of domestic violence, sexual assault, or stalking, the purposes described in subdivision (c) of Section 230 and subdivision (a) of Section 230.1.

(b) An employer shall not require as a condition of using paid sick days that the employee search for or find a replacement worker to cover the days during which the employee uses paid sick days.

(c)(1) An employer shall not deny an employee the right to use accrued sick days, discharge, threaten to discharge, demote, suspend, or in any manner discriminate against an employee for using accrued sick days, attempting to exercise the right to use accrued sick days, filing a complaint with the department or alleging a violation of this article, cooperating in an investigation or prosecution of an alleged violation of this article, or opposing any policy or practice or act that is prohibited by this article.

(2) There shall be a rebuttable presumption of unlawful retaliation if an employer denies an employee the right to use accrued sick days, discharges, threatens to discharge, demotes, suspends, or in any manner discriminates against an employee within 30 days of any of the following:

(A) The filing of a complaint by the employee with the Labor Commissioner or alleging a violation of this article.

(B) The cooperation of an employee with an investigation or prosecution of an alleged violation of this article.

(C) Opposition by the employee to a policy, practice, or act that is prohibited by this article. **Leg.H.** 2014 ch. 317 (AB 1522) §3.

2014 Note: For legislative intent, see the 2014 Note following Lab C §249.

§247. Poster; requirements.

(a) In each workplace of the employer, the employer shall display a poster in a conspicuous place containing all the information specified in subdivision (b). The Labor Commissioner shall create a poster containing this information and make it available to employers.

(b) The poster shall state all of the following:

(1) An employee is entitled to accrue, request, and use paid sick days.

(2) The amount of sick days provided for by this article.

(3) The terms of use of paid sick days.

(4) That retaliation or discrimination against an employee who requests paid sick days or uses paid sick days, or both, is prohibited and that an employee has the right under this article to file a complaint with the Labor Commissioner against an employer who retaliates or discriminates against the employee.

(c) An employer who willfully violates the posting requirements of this section is subject to a civil penalty of not more than one hundred dollars ($100) per each offense. **Leg.H.** 2014 ch. 317 (AB 1522) §3.

2014 Note: For legislative intent, see the 2014 Note following Lab C §249.

§247.5. Recordkeeping requirement.

(a) An employer shall keep for at least three years records documenting the hours worked and paid sick days accrued and used by an employee, and shall allow the Labor Commissioner to access these records pursuant to the requirements set forth in Section 1174. An employer shall make these records available to an employee in the same manner as described in Section 226. If an employer does not maintain adequate records pursuant to this section, it shall be presumed that the employee is entitled to the maximum number of hours accruable under this article, unless the employer can show otherwise by clear and convincing evidence.

(b) Notwithstanding any other provision of this article, an employer is not obligated to inquire into or record the purposes for which an employee uses paid leave or paid time off. **Leg.H.** 2014 ch. 317 (AB 1522) §3, 2015 ch. 67 (AB 304) §3, effective July 13, 2015.

2014 Note: For legislative intent, see the 2014 Note following Lab C §249.

§248. Supplemental paid sick leave for food sector workers during COVID-19 pandemic; requirement; enforcement; expiration.

(a) As used in this section:

(1) "COVID-19 food sector supplemental paid sick leave" means supplemental paid sick leave provided pursuant to this section.

(2) "Food sector worker" means any person who satisfies all of the following criteria:

(A) The person satisfies one or more of the following criteria:

(i) The person works in an industry or occupation defined in paragraph (B) of Section 2 of IWC Wage Order 3-2001, paragraph (H) of Section 2 of IWC Wage Order 8-2001, paragraph (H) of Section 2 of IWC Wage Order 13-2001, or paragraph (D) of Section 2 of IWC Wage Order 14-2001.

(ii) The person works for a hiring entity that operates a food facility, as defined in Section 113789 of the Health and Safety Code.

(iii) The person delivers food from a food facility, as defined in Section 113789 of the Health and Safety Code, for or through a hiring entity.

(B) The person leaves the person's home or other place of residence to perform work for or through the person's hiring entity.

(3) "Hiring entity" means a private sole proprietorship or any kind of private entity whatsoever, including, but not limited to, any kind of corporation, partnership, limited liability company, limited liability partnership, or any other kind of business enterprise, and specifically including, but not limited to, any delivery network company, as defined in subdivision (b) of Section 6041.5 of the Revenue and Taxation Code, and any transportation network company, as defined in subdivision (c) of Section 5431 of the Public Utilities Code, that has 500 or more employees in the United States. For purposes of this paragraph, Section 826.40(a)(1) and (2) of Title 29 of the Code of Federal Regulations shall be used to determine the number of employees that the hiring entity employs.

(4) "IWC Wage Order" means a wage order of the Industrial Welfare Commission.

(b) A food sector worker shall be entitled to COVID-19 food sector supplemental paid sick leave as follows:

(1) A hiring entity shall provide COVID-19 food sector supplemental paid sick leave to each food sector worker who performs work for or through the hiring entity if that food sector worker is unable to work due to any of the following reasons:

(A) The food sector worker is subject to a federal, state, or local quarantine or isolation order related to COVID-19.

(B) The food sector worker is advised by a health care provider to self-quarantine or self-isolate due to concerns related to COVID-19.

(C) The food sector worker is prohibited from working by the food sector worker's hiring entity due to health concerns related to the potential transmission of COVID-19.

(2) A food sector worker shall be entitled to the following number of hours of COVID-19 food sector supplemental paid sick leave:

(A) A food sector worker is entitled to 80 hours of COVID-19 food sector supplemental paid sick leave, if the food sector worker satisfies either of the following criteria:

(i) The hiring entity considers the food sector worker to work "full time."

(ii) The food sector worker worked or was scheduled to work, on average, at least 40 hours per week for the hiring entity in the two weeks preceding the date the food sector worker took COVID-19 food sector supplemental paid sick leave.

(B) A food sector worker who does not satisfy either of the criteria in subparagraph (A) is entitled to an amount of COVID-19 food sector supplemental paid sick leave as follows:

(i) If the food sector worker has a normal weekly schedule, the total number of hours the food sector worker is normally scheduled to work for or through a hiring entity over two weeks.

(ii) If the food sector worker works a variable number of hours, 14 times the average number of hours the food sector worker worked each day for or through the hiring entity in the six months preceding the date the food sector worker took COVID-19 food sector supplemental paid sick leave. If the food sector worker has worked for the hiring entity fewer than six months, this calculation shall instead be made over the entire period the food sector worker has worked for the hiring entity.

Labor

(C) The total number of hours of COVID-19 food sector supplemental paid sick leave to which a food sector worker is entitled pursuant to subparagraph (A) or (B) shall be in addition to any paid sick leave that may be available to the food sector worker under Section 246, but shall not be in addition to the total number of hours of supplemental paid sick leave available to the worker under Executive Order N-51-20.

(D) A food sector worker may determine how many hours of COVID-19 food sector supplemental paid sick leave to use, up to the total number of hours to which the food sector worker is entitled pursuant to subparagraph (A) or (B). The hiring entity shall make COVID-19 food sector supplemental paid sick leave available for immediate use by the food sector worker, upon the oral or written request of the worker to the hiring entity.

(E) A hiring entity is not required to provide a food sector worker more than the total number of hours of COVID-19 food sector supplemental paid sick leave to which the food sector worker is entitled pursuant to subparagraph (A) or (B) above.

(3)(A) Each hour of COVID-19 food sector supplemental paid sick leave shall be compensated at a rate equal to the highest of the following:

(i) The food sector worker's regular rate of pay for the food sector worker's last pay period.

(ii) The state minimum wage.

(iii) The local minimum wage to which the food sector worker is entitled.

(B) Notwithstanding subparagraph (A), a hiring entity shall not be required to pay more than five hundred eleven dollars ($511) per day and five thousand one hundred ten dollars ($5,110) in the aggregate to a food sector worker for COVID-19 food sector supplemental paid sick leave taken by the worker.

(4) A hiring entity shall not require a food sector worker to use any other paid or unpaid leave, paid time off, or vacation time provided by the hiring entity to the food sector worker before the food sector worker uses COVID-19 food sector supplemental paid sick leave or in lieu of COVID-19 food sector supplemental paid sick leave.

(c) Notwithstanding subdivision (b), if a hiring entity already provides the relevant food sector worker with a supplemental benefit, such as supplemental paid leave, that is payable for the reasons listed in paragraph (1) of subdivision (b) and that would compensate the food sector worker in an amount equal to or greater than the amount of compensation for taking COVID-19 food sector supplemental paid sick leave to which the food sector worker would otherwise be entitled as set forth under paragraph (3) of subdivision (b), then the hiring entity may count the hours of the other paid benefit or leave towards the total number of hours of COVID-19 food sector supplemental paid sick leave that the hiring entity is required to provide to the food sector worker under paragraph (2) of subdivision (b). For purposes of the foregoing, the other supplemental paid benefit or leave that may be counted does not include paid sick leave to which the food sector worker is entitled under Section 246, but may include paid leave already provided by the hiring entity pursuant to Executive Order N-51-20 or supplemental paid leave provided pursuant to federal or local law for the same reasons set forth in paragraph (1) of subdivision (b).

(d)(1) In addition to other remedies as may be provided by the laws of this state or its subdivisions, including, but not limited to, the remedies available to redress any unlawful business practice under Chapter 5 (commencing with Section 17200) of Part 2 of Division 7 of the Business and Professions Code, the Labor Commissioner shall enforce this section. For purposes of such enforcement and to implement COVID-19 food sector supplemental paid sick leave, this section shall apply as follows:

(A) The Labor Commissioner shall enforce this section as if COVID-19 food sector supplemental paid sick leave constitutes "paid sick days," "paid sick leave," or "sick leave" under subdivision (n) of Section 246, subdivisions (b) and (c) of Section 246.5, Section 247, Section 247.5, and Section 248.5. Any claim by a covered worker that is enforceable by the Labor Commissioner for supplemental paid sick leave pursuant to Executive Order N-51-20 shall also be enforceable through this section.

(B) Section 249 applies to COVID-19 food sector supplemental paid sick leave.

(2) For purposes of sections of this code cited in subparagraphs (A) to (C), inclusive, of paragraph (1), in construing this section all food sector workers shall be considered employees and any hiring entity shall be considered an employer.

(e) The requirement to provide COVID-19 food sector supplemental paid sick leave as set forth in this section applies retroactively to April 16, 2020, and shall expire on December 31, 2020 or upon the expiration of any federal extension of the Emergency Paid Sick Leave Act established by the federal Families First Coronavirus Response Act (Public Law 116-127), whichever is later, except that a food sector worker taking COVID-19 food sector supplemental paid sick leave at the time of the expiration of this section shall be permitted to take the full amount of COVID-19 food sector supplemental paid sick leave to which that food sector worker otherwise would have been entitled under this section. **Leg.H.** 2020 ch. 45 (AB 1867) §3, effective September 9, 2020.

§248.1. Supplemental paid sick leave for covered workers during COVID-19 pandemic; requirement; enforcement; expiration.

(a) As used in this section:

(1) "COVID-19 supplemental paid sick leave" means supplemental paid sick leave provided pursuant to this section.

(2) "Covered worker" means any person who satisfies the following criteria:

(A) The person satisfies one or more of the following criteria:

(i) The person is employed by a hiring entity, as defined in subparagraph (A) of paragraph (3).

(ii) The person is employed as a health care provider or emergency responder, as defined under Section 826.30(c) of Title 29 of the Code of Federal Regulations, by a hiring entity as defined in subparagraph (B) of paragraph (3) that has elected to exclude such employees from emergency paid sick leave under the federal Families First Coronavirus Response Act (Public Law 116-127).

(B) The person satisfying one or more of the criteria in subparagraph (A) leaves the person's home or other place of residence to perform work for the person's hiring entity.

(C) Notwithstanding subparagraph (A), a "covered worker" shall not include any of the following:

(i) A person who works in an industry or occupation defined in paragraph (B) of Section 2 of IWC Wage Order 3-2001, paragraph (H) of Section 2 of IWC Wage Order 8-2001, paragraph (H) of Section 2 of IWC Wage Order 13-2001, or paragraph (D) of Section 2 of IWC Wage Order 14-2001.

(ii) A person who works for a hiring entity that operates a food facility, as defined in Section 113789 of the Health and Safety Code.

(iii) A person who delivers food from a food facility, as defined in Section 113789 of the Health and Safety Code, for or through a hiring entity.

(3) "Hiring entity" means either of the following:

(A) A private sole proprietorship or any kind of private entity whatsoever, including, but not limited to, any kind of corporation, partnership, limited liability company, limited liability partnership, or any other kind of business enterprise that has 500 or more employees in the United States. For purposes of this paragraph, Section 826.40(a)(1) and (2) of Title 29 of the Code of Federal Regulations shall be used to determine the number of employees that the hiring entity employs.

(B) An entity, including a public entity, that employs health care providers or emergency responders as defined under Section 826.30(c) of Title 29 of the Code of Federal Regulations, and that has elected to exclude such employees from emergency paid sick leave under the federal Families First Coronavirus Response Act (Public Law 116-127).

(4) "IWC Wage Order" means a wage order of the Industrial Welfare Commission.

(b) A covered worker shall be entitled to COVID-19 supplemental paid sick leave as follows:

(1) A hiring entity shall provide COVID-19 supplemental paid sick leave to each covered worker who performs work for the hiring entity if that covered worker is unable to work due to any of the following reasons:

(A) The covered worker is subject to a federal, state, or local quarantine or isolation order related to COVID-19.

(B) The covered worker is advised by a health care provider to self-quarantine or self-isolate due to concerns related to COVID-19.

(C) The covered worker is prohibited from working by the covered worker's hiring entity due to health concerns related to the potential transmission of COVID-19.

(2) A covered worker shall be entitled to the following number of hours of COVID-19 supplemental paid sick leave:

(A) A covered worker is entitled to 80 hours of COVID-19 supplemental paid sick leave, if the covered worker satisfies either of the following criteria:

(i) The hiring entity considers the covered worker to work "full time."

(ii) The covered worker worked or was scheduled to work, on average, at least 40 hours per week for the hiring entity in the two weeks preceding the date the covered worker took COVID-19 supplemental paid sick leave.

(B) Notwithstanding subparagraph (A), a covered worker who is an active firefighter who was scheduled to work more than 80 hours for the hiring entity in the two weeks preceding the date the covered worker took COVID-19 supplemental paid sick leave is entitled to an amount of COVID-19 supplemental paid sick leave equal to the total number of hours that the covered worker was scheduled to work for the hiring entity in those two preceding weeks. This subparagraph applies to an active firefighting member of any of the following:

(i) A fire department of a city, county, city and county, district, or other public or municipal corporation or political subdivision.

(ii) A fire department of the University of California and the California State University.

(iii) The Department of Forestry and Fire Protection.

(iv) A county forestry or firefighting department or unit.

(v) A fire department that serves a United States Department of Defense installation and whose firefighters are certified by the United States Department of Defense as meeting its standards for firefighters.

(vi) A fire department that serves a National Aeronautics and Space Administration installation and that adheres to training standards established in accordance with Article 4 (commencing with Section 13155) of Chapter 1 of Part 2 of Division 12 of the Health and Safety Code.

(vii) A fire department that provides fire protection to a commercial airport regulated by the Federal Aviation Administration (FAA) under Part 139 (commencing with Section 139.1) of Subchapter G of Chapter 1 of Title 14 of the Federal Code of Regulations whose firefighters are trained and certified by the State Fire Marshal as meeting the standards of Fire Control 5 and Section 139.319 of Title 14 of the Federal Code of Regulations.

(viii) Fire and rescue services coordinators who work for the Office of Emergency Services. For purposes of this clause, "fire and rescue services coordinators" means coordinators with any of the following job classifications: coordinator, senior coordinator, or chief coordinator.

(C) A covered worker who does not satisfy either of the criteria in subparagraph (A) or (B) is entitled to an amount of COVID-19 supplemental paid sick leave as follows:

(i) If the covered worker has a normal weekly schedule, the total number of hours the covered worker is normally scheduled to work for the hiring entity over two weeks.

(ii) If the covered worker works a variable number of hours, 14 times the average number of hours the covered worker worked each day for the hiring entity in the six months preceding the date the covered worker took COVID-19 supplemental paid sick leave. If the covered worker has worked for the hiring entity over a period of fewer than six months but more than 14 days, this calculation shall instead be made over the entire period the covered worker has worked for the hiring entity.

(iii) If the covered worker works a variable number of hours and has worked for the hiring entity over a period of 14 days or fewer, the total number of hours the covered worker has worked for that hiring entity.

(D) The total number of hours of COVID-19 supplemental paid sick leave to which a covered worker is entitled pursuant to subparagraph (A), (B), or (C) shall be

Labor

in addition to any paid sick leave that may be available to the covered worker under Section 246.

(E) A covered worker may determine how many hours of COVID-19 supplemental paid sick leave to use, up to the total number of hours to which the covered worker is entitled pursuant to subparagraph (A), (B), or (C). The hiring entity shall make COVID-19 supplemental paid sick leave available for immediate use by the covered worker, upon the oral or written request of the worker to the hiring entity.

(F) A hiring entity is not required to provide a covered worker more than the total number of hours of COVID-19 supplemental paid sick leave to which the covered worker is entitled pursuant to subparagraph (A), (B), or (C).

(3)(A) Each hour of COVID-19 supplemental paid sick leave shall be compensated at a rate equal to the highest of the following:

(i) The covered worker's regular rate of pay for the covered worker's last pay period, including pursuant to any collective bargaining agreement that applies.

(ii) The state minimum wage.

(iii) The local minimum wage to which the covered worker is entitled.

(B) Notwithstanding subparagraph (A), a covered worker who is entitled to an amount of COVID-19 supplemental paid sick leave under subparagraph (B) of paragraph (2), shall be compensated for each hour of COVID-19 supplemental paid sick leave at the regular rate of pay to which the worker would be entitled as if the worker had been scheduled to work those hours, pursuant to existing law or an applicable collective bargaining agreement.

(C) Notwithstanding subparagraph (A) or (B), a hiring entity shall not be required to pay more than five hundred eleven dollars ($511) per day and five thousand one hundred ten dollars ($5,110) in the aggregate to a covered worker for COVID-19 supplemental paid sick leave taken by the worker.

(4) A hiring entity shall not require a covered worker to use any other paid or unpaid leave, paid time off, or vacation time provided by the hiring entity to the covered worker before the covered worker uses COVID-19 supplemental paid sick leave or in lieu of COVID-19 supplemental paid sick leave.

(c) Notwithstanding subdivision (b), if a hiring entity already provides a covered worker with a supplemental benefit, such as supplemental paid leave, that is payable for the reasons listed in paragraph (1) of subdivision (b) and that would compensate the covered worker in an amount equal to or greater than the amount of compensation for COVID-19 supplemental paid sick leave to which the covered worker is entitled as set forth under paragraph (3) of subdivision (b), then the hiring entity may count the hours of the other paid benefit or leave towards the total number of hours of COVID-19 supplemental paid sick leave that the hiring entity is required to provide to the covered worker under paragraph (2) of subdivision (b). For purposes of the foregoing, the other supplemental paid benefit or leave that may be counted does not include paid sick leave to which the covered worker is entitled under Section 246, but may include paid leave already provided by the hiring entity pursuant to Executive Order N-51-20 or Section 248, or supplemental paid leave provided pursuant to federal or local law for the same reasons set forth in paragraph (1) of subdivision (b). Additionally, if a hiring entity already provided supplemental paid leave between March 4, 2020, and the effective date of this section for the reasons listed in paragraph (1) of subdivision (b) but did not compensate the covered worker in an amount equal to or greater than the amount of compensation for COVID-19 supplemental paid sick leave to which the covered worker is entitled as set forth under paragraph (3) of subdivision (b), the employer may retroactively provide supplemental pay to the covered worker to satisfy the compensation requirements under paragraph (3) of subdivision (b), in which case those hours may count towards the total number of hours of COVID-19 supplemental paid sick leave required under paragraph (2) of subdivision (b).

(d)(1) In addition to other remedies as may be provided by the laws of this state or its subdivisions, including, but not limited to, the remedies available to redress any unlawful business practice under Chapter 5 (commencing with Section 17200) of Part 2 of Division 7 of the Business and Professions Code, the Labor Commissioner shall enforce this section. For purposes of such enforcement and to implement COVID-19 supplemental paid sick leave, this section shall apply as follows:

(A) The Labor Commissioner shall enforce this section as if COVID-19 supplemental paid sick leave constitutes "paid sick days," "paid sick leave," or "sick leave" under subdivisions (i) and (n) of Section 246, subdivisions (b) and (c) of Section 246.5, Section 247, Section 247.5, and Section 248.5. However, the requirement in subdivision (i) of Section 246 is not enforceable until the next full pay period following the date of enactment of this section.

(B) Section 249 applies to COVID-19 supplemental paid sick leave.

(C) By seven days after the effective date of this section, the Labor Commissioner shall make publicly available a model notice for purposes of Section 247. Only for purposes of COVID-19 supplemental paid sick leave, if a hiring entity's covered workers do not frequent a workplace, the hiring entity may satisfy the notice requirement of subdivision (a) of Section 247 by disseminating notice through electronic means, such as by electronic mail.

(2) For purposes of sections of this code cited in subparagraphs (A) to (C), inclusive, of paragraph (1), in construing this section all covered workers shall be considered employees and any hiring entity shall be considered an employer.

(e) The requirement to provide COVID-19 supplemental paid sick leave as set forth in this section shall take effect not later than 10 days after the date of enactment of this section.

(f) The requirement to provide COVID-19 supplemental paid sick leave as set forth in this section shall expire on December 31, 2020, or upon the expiration of any federal extension of the Emergency Paid Sick Leave Act established by the federal Families First Coronavirus Response Act (Public Law 116-127), whichever is later, except that a covered worker taking COVID-19 supplemental paid sick leave at the time of the expiration of this section shall be permitted to take the full amount of COVID-19 supplemental paid sick leave to which that covered worker otherwise would have been entitled under this section.

Leg.H. 2020 ch. 45 (AB 1867) §4, effective September 9, 2020.

§248.5. Enforcement of article; violation.

(a) The Labor Commissioner shall enforce this article, including investigating an alleged violation, and ordering appropriate temporary relief to mitigate the violation or to maintain the status quo pending the completion of a full investigation or hearing **through the procedures set forth in Sections 98, 98.3, 98.7, 98.74, or 1197.1, including by issuance of a citation against an employer who violates this article, and by filing a civil action. If a citation is issued, the procedures for issuing, contesting, and enforcing judgments for citations and civil penalties issued by the Labor Commissioner shall be the same as those set out in Section 98.74 or 1197.1, as appropriate.**

(b)(1) If the Labor Commissioner, [1] **in any administrative proceeding under subdivision (a)**, determines that a violation of this article has occurred, [2] **they** may order any appropriate relief, including reinstatement, backpay, the payment of sick days unlawfully withheld, and the payment of an additional sum in the form of an administrative penalty to an employee or other person whose rights under this article were violated.

(2) If paid sick days were unlawfully withheld, the dollar amount of paid sick days withheld from the employee multiplied by three, or two hundred fifty dollars ($250), whichever amount is greater, but not to exceed an aggregate penalty of four thousand dollars ($4,000), shall be included in the administrative penalty.

(3) If a violation of this article results in other harm to the employee or person, such as discharge from employment, or otherwise results in a violation of the rights of the employee or person, the administrative penalty shall include a sum of fifty dollars ($50) for each day or portion thereof that the violation occurred or continued, not to exceed an aggregate penalty of four thousand dollars ($4,000).

(c) Where prompt compliance by an employer is not forthcoming, the Labor Commissioner may take any appropriate enforcement action to secure compliance, including the filing of a civil action. In compensation to the state for the costs of investigating and remedying the violation, the commissioner may order the violating employer to pay to the state a sum of not more than fifty dollars ($50) for each day or portion of a day a violation occurs or continues for each employee or other person whose rights under this article were violated.

(d) An employee or other person may report to the Labor Commissioner a suspected violation of this article. The commissioner shall encourage reporting pursuant to this subdivision by keeping confidential, to the maximum extent permitted by applicable law, the name and other identifying information of the employee or person reporting the violation. However, the commissioner may disclose that person's name and identifying information as necessary to enforce this article or for other appropriate purposes, upon the authorization of that person.

(e) The Labor Commissioner or the Attorney General may bring a civil action in a court of competent jurisdiction against the employer or other person violating this article and, upon prevailing, shall be entitled to collect legal or equitable relief on behalf of the aggrieved as may be appropriate to remedy the violation, including reinstatement, backpay, the payment of sick days unlawfully withheld, the payment of an additional sum, not to exceed an aggregate penalty of four thousand dollars ($4,000), as liquidated damages in the amount of fifty dollars ($50) to each employee or person whose rights under this article were violated for each day or portion thereof that the violation occurred or continued, plus, if the employer has unlawfully withheld paid sick days to an employee, the dollar amount of paid sick days withheld from the employee multiplied by three; or two hundred fifty dollars ($250), whichever amount is greater; and reinstatement in employment or injunctive relief; and further shall be awarded reasonable attorney's fees and costs, provided, however, that any person or entity enforcing this article on behalf of the public as provided for under applicable state law shall, upon prevailing, be entitled only to equitable, injunctive, or restitutionary relief, and reasonable attorney's fees and costs.

(f) In an administrative or civil action brought under this article, the Labor Commissioner or court, as the case may be, shall award interest on all amounts due and unpaid at the rate of interest specified in subdivision (b) of Section 3289 of the Civil Code.

(g) The remedies, penalties, and procedures provided under this article are cumulative.

(h) An employer shall not be assessed any penalty or liquidated damages under this article due to an isolated and unintentional payroll error or written notice error that is a clerical or an inadvertent mistake regarding the accrual or available use of paid sick leave. In reviewing for compliance with this section, the factfinder may consider as a relevant factor whether the employer, prior to an alleged violation, has adopted and is in compliance with a set of policies, procedures, and practices that fully comply with this section. **Leg.H.** 2014 ch. 317 (AB 1522) §3, 2020 ch. 45 (AB 1867) §5, effective September 9, 2020.

§248.5. 2020 Deletes. [1] after a hearing that contains adequate safeguards to ensure that the parties are afforded due process **[2]** he or she

2014 Note: For legislative intent, see the 2014 Note following Lab C §249.

§249. Effect of article on privacy of health and domestic relations information; article establishes minimum requirements pertaining to paid sick days.

(a) This article does not limit or affect any laws guaranteeing the privacy of health information, or information related to domestic violence or sexual assault, regarding an employee or employee's family member. That information shall be treated as confidential and shall not be disclosed to any person except to the affected employee, or as required by law.

(b) This article shall not be construed to discourage or prohibit an employer from the adoption or retention of a paid sick days policy more generous than the one required herein.

(c) This article does not lessen the obligation of an employer to comply with a contract, collective bargaining agreement, employment benefit plan, or other agreement providing more generous sick days to an employee than required herein.

(d) This article establishes minimum requirements pertaining to paid sick days and does not preempt, limit, or otherwise affect the applicability of any other law, regulation, requirement, policy, or standard that provides for greater accrual or use by employees of sick days, whether paid or unpaid, or that extends other protections to an employee. **Leg.H.** 2014 ch. 317 (AB 1522) §3.

2014 Note: In enacting this act, it is the intent of the Legislature to do the following:

(a) Ensure that workers in California can address their own health needs and the health needs of their families by requiring employers to provide a minimum level of paid sick days including time for family care.

(b) Decrease public and private health care costs in California by enabling workers to seek early and routine medical care for themselves and their family members and to address domestic violence or sexual assault.

(c) Protect employees in California from losing their jobs while they use sick days to care for themselves or their families.

(d) Provide economic security to employees in California who take time off from work for reasons related to domestic violence or sexual assault.

(e) Safeguard the welfare, health, safety, and prosperity of the people of and visitors to California. Stats. 2014 ch. 317 (AB 1522) §2.

PART 4
Employees

CHAPTER 1
WAGES, HOURS AND WORKING CONDITIONS
[Selected Provisions]

§1171.5. Legislative findings and declarations regarding employment protections available regardless of immigration status.

The Legislature finds and declares the following:

(a) All protections, rights, and remedies available under state law, except any reinstatement remedy prohibited by federal law, are available to all individuals regardless of immigration status who have applied for employment, or who are or who have been employed, in this state.

(b) For purposes of enforcing state labor, employment, civil rights, consumer protection, and housing laws, a person's immigration status is irrelevant to the issue of liability, and in proceedings or discovery undertaken to enforce those state laws no inquiry shall be permitted into a person's immigration status unless the person seeking to make this inquiry has shown by clear and convincing evidence that the inquiry is necessary in order to comply with federal immigration law.

(c) The provisions of this section are declaratory of existing law.

(d) The provisions of this section are severable. If any provision of this section or its application is held invalid, that invalidity shall not affect other provisions or applications that can be given effect without the invalid provision or application. **Leg.H.** 2002 ch. 1071 (SB 1818), 2017 ch. 160 (AB 1690) §4.

Ref.: Hanna §§ 3.31, 35.30[4]; Herlick Handbook § 2.3.

PART 7
Public Works and Public Agencies

CHAPTER 1
PUBLIC WORKS

ARTICLE 2
Wages

§1776. Payroll record of wages paid; inspection; forms; effect of noncompliance; penalties.

(a) Each contractor and subcontractor shall keep accurate payroll records, showing the name, address, social security number, work classification, straight time and overtime hours worked each day and week, and the actual per diem wages paid to each journeyman, apprentice, worker, or other employee employed by him or her in connection with the public work. Each payroll record shall contain or be verified by a written declaration that it is made under penalty of perjury, stating both of the following:

(1) The information contained in the payroll record is true and correct.

(2) The employer has complied with the requirements of Sections 1771, 1811, and 1815 for any work performed by his or her employees on the public works project.

(b) The payroll records enumerated under subdivision (a) shall be certified and shall be available for inspection at all reasonable hours at the principal office of the contractor on the following basis:

(1) A certified copy of an employee's payroll record shall be made available for inspection or furnished to the employee or his or her authorized representative on request.

(2) A certified copy of all payroll records enumerated in subdivision (a) shall be made available for inspection or furnished upon request to a representative of the body awarding the contract and the Division of Labor Standards Enforcement of the Department of Industrial Relations.

(3) A certified copy of all payroll records enumerated in subdivision (a) shall be made available upon request by the public for inspection or for copies thereof. However, a request by the public shall be made through either the body awarding the contract or the Division of Labor Standards Enforcement. If the requested payroll records have not been provided pursuant to paragraph (2), the requesting party shall, prior to being provided the records, reimburse the costs of preparation by the contractor, subcontractors, and the entity through which the request was made. The public may not be given access to the records at the principal office of the contractor.

(c) Unless required to be furnished directly to the Labor Commissioner in accordance with paragraph (3) of subdivision (a) of Section 1771.4, the certified payroll records shall be on forms provided by the Division of Labor Standards Enforcement or shall contain the same information as the forms provided by the division. The payroll records may consist of printouts of payroll data that are maintained as computer records, if the printouts contain the same information as the forms provided by the division and the printouts are verified in the manner specified in subdivision (a).

(d) A contractor or subcontractor shall file a certified copy of the records enumerated in subdivision (a) with the entity that requested the records within 10 days after receipt of a written request.

(e) Except as provided in subdivision (f), any copy of records made available for inspection as copies and furnished upon request to the public or any public agency by the awarding body or the Division of Labor Standards Enforcement shall be marked or obliterated to prevent disclosure of an individual's name, address, and social security number. The name and address of the contractor awarded the contract or the subcontractor performing the contract shall not be marked or obliterated. Any copy of records made available for inspection by, or furnished to, a multiemployer Taft-Hartley trust fund (29 U.S.C. Sec. 186(c)(5)) that requests the records for the purposes of allocating contributions to participants shall be marked or obliterated only to prevent disclosure of an individual's full social security number, but shall provide the last four digits of the social security number. Any copy of records made available for inspection by, or furnished to, a joint labor-management committee established pursuant to the federal Labor Management Cooperation Act of 1978 (29 U.S.C. Sec. 175a) shall be marked or obliterated only to prevent disclosure of an individual's social security number.

(f)(1) Notwithstanding any other provision of law, agencies that are included in the Joint Enforcement Strike Force on the Underground Economy established pursuant to Section 329 of the Unemployment Insurance Code and other law enforcement agencies investigating violations of law shall, upon request, be provided nonredacted copies of certified payroll records. Any copies of records or certified payroll made available for inspection and furnished upon request to the public by an agency included in the Joint Enforcement Strike Force on the Underground Economy or to a law enforcement agency investigating a violation of law shall be marked or redacted to prevent disclosure of an individual's name, address, and social security number.

(2) An employer shall not be liable for damages in a civil action for any reasonable act or omission taken in good faith in compliance with this subdivision.

(g) The contractor shall inform the body awarding the contract of the location of the records enumerated under subdivision (a), including the street address, city, and county, and shall, within five working days, provide a notice of a change of location and address.

(h) The contractor or subcontractor has 10 days in which to comply subsequent to receipt of a written notice requesting the records enumerated in subdivision (a). In the event that the contractor or subcontractor fails to comply within the 10-day period, he or she shall, as a penalty to the state or political subdivision on whose behalf the contract is made or awarded, forfeit one hundred dollars ($100) for each calendar day, or portion thereof, for each worker, until strict compliance is effectuated. Upon the request of the Division of Labor Standards Enforcement, these penalties shall be withheld from progress payments then due. A contractor is not subject to a penalty assessment pursuant to this section due to the failure of a subcontractor to comply with this section.

(i) The body awarding the contract shall cause to be inserted in the contract stipulations to effectuate this section.

(j) The director shall adopt rules consistent with the California Public Records Act (Chapter 3.5 (commencing with Section 6250) of Division 7 of Title 1 of the Government Code) and the Information Practices Act of 1977 (Title 1.8 (commencing with Section 1798) of Part 4 of Division 3 of the Civil Code) governing the release of these records, including the establishment of reasonable fees to be charged for reproducing copies of records required by this section. **Leg.H.** 1997 ch. 757 (SB 1328) §4, 2001 ch. 804 (SB 588) §2, 2002 chs. 28 (AB 1448) §1, 664 §161 (AB 3034) (ch. 28 prevails; ch. 664 not effective), 2003 ch. 62 (SB 600) §205, 2005 ch. 500 (SB 759) §1, 2011 chs. 481 (AB 766) §1, 677 (AB 551) §2.5, 2012 ch. 46 (SB 1038) §94, effective June 27, 2012, 2013 ch. 792 (AB 1336) §3, 2014 ch. 28 (SB 854) §71, effective June 20, 2014.

ARTICLE 5
Securing Workers' Compensation

§1860. Public works contracts; compensation clause required.

The awarding body shall cause to be inserted in every public works contract a clause providing that, in accordance with the provisions of Section 3700, every contractor will be required to secure the payment of compensation to his or her employees. **Leg.H.** 1965 ch. 1000 §2, 2017 ch. 28 (SB 96) §26, effective June 27, 2017.

§1861. Public works contracts; certificate of insurance.

Each contractor to whom a public works contract is awarded shall sign and file with the awarding body the following certification prior to performing the work of the contract: "I am aware of the provisions of Section 3700 of the Labor Code which require every employer to be insured against liability for workers' compensation or to undertake self-insurance in accordance with the provisions of that code, and I will comply with such provisions before commencing the performance of the work of this contract."

PART 9
Health

CHAPTER 1
SANITARY CONDITIONS

ARTICLE 5
General Health Provisions

§2440. Employers' compliance with medical services and first aid standards.

All employers shall comply with standards relating to the ready availability of medical services and first aid adopted by the Occupational Safety and Health Standards Board, pursuant to Chapter 6 (commencing with Section 140) of Division 1. **Leg.H.** 1994 ch. 486 §9.

Ref.: Hanna § 5.02[4]; Herlick Handbook § 4.04[1].

§2441. Provision of drinking water.

(a) Every employer of labor in this state shall, without making a charge therefor, provide fresh and pure drinking water to his or her employees during working hours. Access to the drinking water shall be permitted at reasonable and convenient times and places. Any violation of this section is punishable for each offense by a fine of not less than fifty dollars ($50), nor more than two hundred dollars ($200), or by imprisonment for not more than 30 days, or by both the fine and imprisonment.

(b) The State Department of Health Services and all health officers of counties, cities, and health districts shall enforce the provisions of this section pursuant to subdivision (b) of Section 118390 of the Health and Safety Code. The enforcement shall not be construed to abridge or limit in any manner the jurisdiction of the Division of Industrial Safety of the Department of Industrial Relations pursuant to Division 5 (commencing with Section 6300). **Leg.H.** 1996 ch. 1023, effective September 29, 1996.

Ref.: Herlick Handbook § 4.04[1].

PART 13
The Labor Code Private Attorneys General Act of 2004

§2698. Citation of part.

This part shall be known and may be cited as the Labor Code Private Attorneys General Act of 2004. **Leg.H.** 2003 ch. 906 (SB 796).

§2699. Recovery of civil penalty for violation of Labor Code through civil action brought by aggrieved employee; amount of penalty; attorney's fees and costs; distribution of penalty proceeds; applicability of section.

(a) Notwithstanding any other provision of law, any provision of this code that provides for a civil penalty to be assessed and collected by the Labor and Workforce Development Agency or any of its departments, divisions, commissions, boards, agencies, or employees, for a violation of this code, may, as an alternative, be recovered through a civil action brought by an aggrieved employee on behalf of himself or herself and other current or former employees pursuant to the procedures specified in Section 2699.3.

(b) For purposes of this part, "person" has the same meaning as defined in Section 18.

(c) For purposes of this part, "aggrieved employee" means any person who was employed by the alleged violator and against whom one or more of the alleged violations was committed.

(d) For purposes of this part, "cure" means that the employer abates each violation alleged by any aggrieved employee, the employer is in compliance with the underlying statutes as specified in the notice required by this part, and any aggrieved employee is made whole. A violation of paragraph (6) or (8) of subdivision (a) of Section 226 shall only be considered cured upon a showing that the employer has provided a fully compliant, itemized wage statement to each aggrieved employee for each pay period for the three-year period prior to the date of the written notice sent pursuant to paragraph (1) of subdivision (c) of Section 2699.3.

(e)(1) For purposes of this part, whenever the Labor and Workforce Development Agency, or any of its departments, divisions, commissions, boards, agencies, or employees, has discretion to assess a civil penalty, a court is authorized to exercise the same discretion, subject to the same limitations and conditions, to assess a civil penalty.

(2) In any action by an aggrieved employee seeking recovery of a civil penalty available under subdivision (a) or (f), a court may award a lesser amount than the maximum civil penalty amount specified by this part if, based on the facts and circumstances of the particular case, to do otherwise would result in an award that is unjust, arbitrary and oppressive, or confiscatory.

(f) For all provisions of this code except those for which a civil penalty is specifically provided, there is established a civil penalty for a violation of these provisions, as follows:

(1) If, at the time of the alleged violation, the person does not employ one or more employees, the civil penalty is five hundred dollars ($500).

(2) If, at the time of the alleged violation, the person employs one or more employees, the civil penalty is one hundred dollars ($100) for each aggrieved employee per pay period for the initial violation and two hundred dollars ($200) for each aggrieved employee per pay period for each subsequent violation.

(3) If the alleged violation is a failure to act by the Labor and Workplace Development Agency, or any of its departments, divisions, commissions, boards, agencies, or employees, there shall be no civil penalty.

(g)(1) Except as provided in paragraph (2), an aggrieved employee may recover the civil penalty described in subdivision (f) in a civil action pursuant to the procedures specified in Section 2699.3 filed on behalf of himself or herself and other current or former employees against whom one or more of the alleged violations was committed. Any employee who prevails in any action shall be entitled to an award of reasonable attorney's fees and costs, including any filing fee paid pursuant to subparagraph (B) of paragraph (1) of subdivision (a) or subparagraph (B) of paragraph (1) of subdivision (c) of Section 2699.3. Nothing in this part shall operate to limit an employee's right to pursue or recover other remedies available under state or federal law, either separately or concurrently with an action taken under this part.

(2) No action shall be brought under this part for any violation of a posting, notice, agency reporting, or filing requirement of this code, except where the filing or reporting requirement involves mandatory payroll or workplace injury reporting.

(h) No action may be brought under this section by an aggrieved employee if the agency or any of its departments, divisions, commissions, boards, agencies, or employees, on the same facts and theories, cites a person within the timeframes set forth in Section 2699.3 for a violation of the same section or sections of the Labor Code under which the aggrieved employee is attempting to recover a civil penalty on behalf of himself or herself or others or initiates a proceeding pursuant to Section 98.3.

(i) Except as provided in subdivision (j), civil penalties recovered by aggrieved employees shall be distributed as follows: 75 percent to the Labor and Workforce Development Agency for enforcement of labor laws, including the administration of this part, and for education of employers and employees about their rights and responsibilities under this code, to be continuously appropriated to supplement and not supplant the funding to the agency for those purposes; and 25 percent to the aggrieved employees.

(j) Civil penalties recovered under paragraph (1) of subdivision (f) shall be distributed to the Labor and Workforce Development Agency for enforcement of labor laws, including the administration of this part, and for education of employers and employees about their rights and responsibilities under this code, to be continuously appropriated to supplement and not supplant the funding to the agency for those purposes.

(k) Nothing contained in this part is intended to alter or otherwise affect the exclusive remedy provided by the workers' compensation provisions of this code for liability against an employer for the compensation for any injury to or death of an employee arising out of and in the course of employment.

(*l*)(1) For cases filed on or after July 1, 2016, the aggrieved employee or representative shall, within 10 days following commencement of a civil action pursuant to this part, provide the Labor and Workforce Development Agency with a file-stamped copy of the complaint that includes the case number assigned by the court.

(2) The superior court shall review and approve any settlement of any civil action filed pursuant to this part. The proposed settlement shall be submitted to the agency at the same time that it is submitted to the court.

(3) A copy of the superior court's judgment in any civil action filed pursuant to this part and any other order in that action that either provides for or denies an award of civil penalties under this code shall be submitted to the agency within 10 days after entry of the judgment or order.

(4) Items required to be submitted to the Labor and Workforce Development Agency under this subdivision or to the Division of Occupational Safety and Health pursuant to paragraph (4) of subdivision (b) of Section 2699.3, shall be transmitted online through the same system established for the filing of notices and requests under subdivisions (a) and (c) of Section 2699.3.

(m) This section shall not apply to the recovery of administrative and civil penalties in connection with the workers' compensation law as contained in Division 1 (commencing with Section 50) and Division 4 (commencing with Section 3200), including, but not limited to, Sections 129.5 and 132a.

(n) The agency or any of its departments, divisions, commissions, boards, or agencies may promulgate regulations to implement the provisions of this part. **Leg.H.** 2003 ch. 906 (SB 796), 2004 chs. 34 (SB 899), effective April 19, 2004, 221 (SB 1809), effective August 11, 2004, 2015 ch. 445 (AB 1506) §1, effective October 2, 2015, 2016 ch. 31 (SB 836) §189, effective June 27, 2016.

2016 Note: It is the intent of the Legislature that the Labor and Workforce Development Agency shall continue to assign the duties prescribed in the Labor Code Private Attorneys General Act of 2004 (Part 13 (commencing with Section 2698) of Division 2 of the Labor Code) to the departments, divisions, commissions, boards, or agencies where those duties are customarily performed. Stats. 2016 ch. 31 (SB 836) §188.

2004 Notes: The amendment, addition, or repeal of, any provision of law made by this act shall apply prospectively from the date of enactment of this act, regardless of the date of injury, unless otherwise specified, but shall not constitute good cause to reopen or rescind, alter, or amend any existing order, decision, or award of the Workers' Compensation Appeals Board. Stats. 2004 ch. 34 (SB 899) §34.

(a) The Legislature finds and declares that, as enunciated in long-standing judicial precedent, its inherent authority to create causes of action or remedies necessarily includes the authority to abolish them. Therefore, a plaintiff seeking recovery upon a legislatively created cause of action runs the risk that the Legislature may repeal or alter that cause during the pendency of the claim. Thus, the Legislature further finds and declares that the alteration of the right to recover civil penalties for violations of the Labor Code made by this act may be applied retroactively to any applicable pending proceeding without depriving any person of a substantive right without due process of law.

(b) (1) The provisions of paragraph (2) of subdivision (g) of Section 2699 of the Labor Code shall apply retroactively to January 1, 2004, the effective date of Chapter 906 of the Statutes of 2003, and shall affect all applicable pending proceedings.

(2) The provisions of subdivision (*l*) of Section 2699 of the Labor Code shall apply retroactively to January 1, 2004, the effective date of Chapter 906 of the Statutes of 2003, and shall affect all applicable pending proceedings. Stats. 2004 ch. 221 (SB 1809) §6.

Ref.: Hanna § 11.01[9]; Herlick Handbook § 9.1.

§2699.3. [First of Two; Repealed July 1, 2021] Requirements for commencement of civil actions under Labor Code Section 2699 alleging specified violations; time limits.

(a) A civil action by an aggrieved employee pursuant to subdivision (a) or (f) of Section 2699 alleging a violation of any provision listed in Section 2699.5 shall commence only after the following requirements have been met:

(1)(A) The aggrieved employee or representative shall give written notice by online filing with the Labor and Workforce Development Agency and by certified mail to the employer of the specific provisions of this code alleged to have been violated, including the facts and theories to support the alleged violation.

(B) A notice filed with the Labor and Workforce Development Agency pursuant to subparagraph (A) and any employer response to that notice shall be accompanied by a filing fee of seventy-five dollars ($75). The fees required by this subparagraph are subject to waiver in accordance with the requirements of Sections 68632 and 68633 of the Government Code.

(C) The fees paid pursuant to subparagraph (B) shall be paid into the Labor and Workforce Development Fund and used for the purposes specified in subdivision (j) of Section 2699.

(2)(A) The agency shall notify the employer and the aggrieved employee or representative by certified mail that it does not intend to investigate the alleged violation within 60 calendar days of the postmark date of the notice received pursuant to paragraph (1). Upon receipt of that notice or if no notice is provided within 65 calendar days of the postmark date of the notice given pursuant to paragraph (1), the aggrieved employee may commence a civil action pursuant to Section 2699.

(B) If the agency intends to investigate the alleged violation, it shall notify the employer and the aggrieved employee or representative by certified mail of its decision within 65 calendar days of the postmark date of the notice received pursuant to paragraph (1). Within 120 calendar days of that decision, the agency may investigate the alleged violation and issue any appropriate citation. If the agency, during the course of its investigation, determines that additional time is necessary to complete the investigation, it may extend the time by not more than 60 additional calendar days and shall issue a notice of the extension. If the agency determines that no citation will be issued, it shall notify the employer and aggrieved employee of that decision within five business days thereof by certified mail. Upon receipt of that notice or if no citation is issued by the agency within the time limits prescribed by subparagraph (A) and this subparagraph or if the agency fails to provide timely or any notification, the aggrieved employee may commence a civil action pursuant to Section 2699.

(C) Notwithstanding any other provision of law, a plaintiff may as a matter of right amend an existing complaint to add a cause of action arising under this part at any time within 60 days of the time periods specified in this part.

(D) The time limits prescribed by this paragraph shall only apply if the notice required by paragraph (1) is filed with the agency on or after July 1, 2016. For notices submitted prior to July 1, 2016, the time limits in effect on the postmark date of the notice shall apply.

(b) A civil action by an aggrieved employee pursuant to subdivision (a) or (f) of Section 2699 alleging a violation of any provision of Division 5 (commencing with Section 6300) other than those listed in Section 2699.5 shall commence only after the following requirements have been met:

(1) The aggrieved employee or representative shall give notice by online filing with the Division of Occupational Safety and Health and by certified mail to the employer, with a copy to the Labor and Workforce Development Agency, of the specific provisions of Division 5 (commencing with Section 6300) alleged to have been violated, including the facts and theories to support the alleged violation.

(2)(A) The division shall inspect or investigate the alleged violation pursuant to the procedures specified in Division 5 (commencing with Section 6300).

(i) If the division issues a citation, the employee may not commence an action pursuant to Section 2699. The division shall notify the aggrieved employee and employer in writing within 14 calendar days of certifying that the employer has corrected the violation.

(ii) If by the end of the period for inspection or investigation provided for in Section 6317, the division fails to issue a citation and the aggrieved employee disputes that decision, the employee may challenge that decision in the superior court. In such an action, the superior court shall follow precedents of the Occupational Safety and Health Appeals Board. If the court finds that the division should have issued a citation and orders the division to issue a citation, then the aggrieved employee may not commence a civil action pursuant to Section 2699.

(iii) A complaint in superior court alleging a violation of Division 5 (commencing with Section 6300) other than those listed in Section 2699.5 shall include therewith a copy of the notice of violation provided to the division and employer pursuant to paragraph (1).

(iv) The superior court shall not dismiss the action for nonmaterial differences in facts or theories between those contained in the notice of violation provided to the division and employer pursuant to paragraph (1) and the complaint filed with the court.

(B) If the division fails to inspect or investigate the alleged violation as provided by Section 6309, the provisions of subdivision (c) shall apply to the determination of the alleged violation.

(3)(A) Nothing in this subdivision shall be construed to alter the authority of the division to permit long-term abatement periods or to enter into memoranda of understanding or joint agreements with employers in the case of long-term abatement issues.

(B) Nothing in this subdivision shall be construed to authorize an employee to file a notice or to commence a civil action pursuant to Section 2699 during the period that an employer has voluntarily entered into consultation with the division to ameliorate a condition in that particular worksite.

(C) An employer who has been provided notice pursuant to this section may not then enter into consultation with the division in order to avoid an action under this section.

(4) The superior court shall review and approve any proposed settlement of alleged violations of the provisions of Division 5 (commencing with Section 6300) to ensure that the settlement provisions are at least as effective as the protections or remedies provided by state and federal law or regulation for the alleged violation. The provisions of the settlement relating to health and safety laws shall be submitted to the division at the same time that they are submitted to the court. This requirement shall be construed to authorize and permit the division to comment on those settlement provisions, and the court shall grant the division's commentary the appropriate weight.

(c) A civil action by an aggrieved employee pursuant to subdivision (a) or (f) of Section 2699 alleging a violation of any provision other than those listed in Section 2699.5 or Division 5 (commencing with Section 6300) shall commence only after the following requirements have been met:

(1)(A) The aggrieved employee or representative shall give written notice by online filing with the Labor and Workforce Development Agency and by certified mail to the employer of the specific provisions of this code alleged to have been violated, including the facts and theories to support the alleged violation.

(B) A notice filed with the Labor and Workforce Development Agency pursuant to subparagraph (A) and any employer response to that notice shall be accompanied by a filing fee of seventy-five dollars ($75). The fees required by this subparagraph are subject to waiver in accordance with the requirements of Sections 68632 and 68633 of the Government Code.

(C) The fees paid pursuant to subparagraph (B) shall be paid into the Labor and Workforce Development Fund and used for the purposes specified in subdivision (j) of Section 2699.

(2)(A) The employer may cure the alleged violation within 33 calendar days of the postmark date of the notice sent by the aggrieved employee or representative. The employer shall give written notice within that period of time by certified mail to the aggrieved employee or representative and by online filing with the agency if the alleged violation is cured, including a description of actions taken, and no civil action pursuant to Section 2699 may commence. If the alleged violation is not cured within the 33-day period, the employee may commence a civil action pursuant to Section 2699.

(B)(i) Subject to the limitation in clause (ii), no employer may avail himself or herself of the notice and cure provisions of this subdivision more than three times in a

Labor

12-month period for the same violation or violations contained in the notice, regardless of the location of the worksite.

(ii) No employer may avail himself or herself of the notice and cure provisions of this subdivision with respect to alleged violations of paragraph (6) or (8) of subdivision (a) of Section 226 more than once in a 12-month period for the same violation or violations contained in the notice, regardless of the location of the worksite.

(3) If the aggrieved employee disputes that the alleged violation has been cured, the aggrieved employee or representative shall provide written notice by online filing with the agency and by certified mail to the employer, including specified grounds to support that dispute, to the employer and the agency. Within 17 calendar days of the receipt of that notice, the agency shall review the actions taken by the employer to cure the alleged violation, and provide written notice of its decision by certified mail to the aggrieved employee and the employer. The agency may grant the employer three additional business days to cure the alleged violation. If the agency determines that the alleged violation has not been cured or if the agency fails to provide timely or any notification, the employee may proceed with the civil action pursuant to Section 2699. If the agency determines that the alleged violation has been cured, but the employee still disagrees, the employee may appeal that determination to the superior court.

(d) The periods specified in this section are not counted as part of the time limited for the commencement of the civil action to recover penalties under this part.

(e) This section shall remain in effect only until July 1, 2021, and as of that date is repealed, unless a later enacted statute, that is enacted before July 1, 2021, deletes or extends that date. **Leg.H.** 2004 ch. 221 (SB 1809), effective August 11, 2004, 2015 ch. 445 (AB 1506) §2, effective October 2, 2015, 2016 ch. 31 (SB 836) §190, effective June 27, 2016.

2016 Note: It is the intent of the Legislature that the Labor and Workforce Development Agency shall continue to assign the duties prescribed in the Labor Code Private Attorneys General Act of 2004 (Part 13 (commencing with Section 2698) of Division 2 of the Labor Code) to the departments, divisions, commissions, boards, or agencies where those duties are customarily performed. Stats. 2016 ch. 31 (SB 836) §188.

Ref.: Hanna § 11.01[9].

§2699.3. [Second of Two; Operative July 1, 2021] Requirements for commencement of civil actions under Labor Code Section 2699 alleging specified violations; time limits.

(a) A civil action by an aggrieved employee pursuant to subdivision (a) or (f) of Section 2699 alleging a violation of any provision listed in Section 2699.5 shall commence only after the following requirements have been met:

(1)(A) The aggrieved employee or representative shall give written notice by online filing with the Labor and Workforce Development Agency and by certified mail to the employer of the specific provisions of this code alleged to have been violated, including the facts and theories to support the alleged violation.

(B) A notice filed with the Labor and Workforce Development Agency pursuant to subparagraph (A) and any employer response to that notice shall be accompanied by a filing fee of seventy-five dollars ($75). The fees required by this subparagraph are subject to waiver in accordance with the requirements of Sections 68632 and 68633 of the Government Code.

(C) The fees paid pursuant to subparagraph (B) shall be paid into the Labor and Workforce Development Fund and used for the purposes specified in subdivision (j) of Section 2699.

(2)(A) The agency shall notify the employer and the aggrieved employee or representative by certified mail that it does not intend to investigate the alleged violation within 60 calendar days of the postmark date of the notice received pursuant to paragraph (1). Upon receipt of that notice or if no notice is provided within 65 calendar days of the postmark date of the notice given pursuant to paragraph (1), the aggrieved employee may commence a civil action pursuant to Section 2699.

(B) If the agency intends to investigate the alleged violation, it shall notify the employer and the aggrieved employee or representative by certified mail of its decision within 65 calendar days of the postmark date of the notice received pursuant to paragraph (1). Within 120 calendar days of that decision, the agency may investigate the alleged violation and issue any appropriate citation. If the agency determines that no citation will be issued, it shall notify the employer and aggrieved employee of that decision within five business days thereof by certified mail. Upon receipt of that notice or if no citation is issued by the agency within the time limits prescribed by subparagraph (A) and this subparagraph or if the agency fails to provide timely or any notification, the aggrieved employee may commence a civil action pursuant to Section 2699.

(C) Notwithstanding any other provision of law, a plaintiff may as a matter of right amend an existing complaint to add a cause of action arising under this part at any time within 60 days of the time periods specified in this part.

(b) A civil action by an aggrieved employee pursuant to subdivision (a) or (f) of Section 2699 alleging a violation of any provision of Division 5 (commencing with Section 6300) other than those listed in Section 2699.5 shall commence only after the following requirements have been met:

(1) The aggrieved employee or representative shall give notice by online filing with the Division of Occupational Safety and Health and by certified mail to the employer, with a copy to the Labor and Workforce Development Agency, of the specific provisions of Division 5 (commencing with Section 6300) alleged to have been violated, including the facts and theories to support the alleged violation.

(2)(A) The division shall inspect or investigate the alleged violation pursuant to the procedures specified in Division 5 (commencing with Section 6300).

(i) If the division issues a citation, the employee may not commence an action pursuant to Section 2699. The division shall notify the aggrieved employee and employer in writing within 14 calendar days of certifying that the employer has corrected the violation.

(ii) If by the end of the period for inspection or investigation provided for in Section 6317, the division fails to issue a citation and the aggrieved employee disputes that decision, the employee may challenge that decision in the superior court. In such an action, the superior court shall follow precedents of the Occupational Safety and Health Appeals Board. If the court finds that the division should have issued a citation and orders the division to issue a citation, then the aggrieved employee may not commence a civil action pursuant to Section 2699.

(iii) A complaint in superior court alleging a violation of Division 5 (commencing with Section 6300) other than those listed in Section 2699.5 shall include therewith a copy of the notice of violation provided to the division and employer pursuant to paragraph (1).

(iv) The superior court shall not dismiss the action for nonmaterial differences in facts or theories between those contained in the notice of violation provided to the division and employer pursuant to paragraph (1) and the complaint filed with the court.

(B) If the division fails to inspect or investigate the alleged violation as provided by Section 6309, the provisions of subdivision (c) shall apply to the determination of the alleged violation.

(3)(A) Nothing in this subdivision shall be construed to alter the authority of the division to permit long-term abatement periods or to enter into memoranda of understanding or joint agreements with employers in the case of long-term abatement issues.

(B) Nothing in this subdivision shall be construed to authorize an employee to file a notice or to commence a civil action pursuant to Section 2699 during the period that an employer has voluntarily entered into consultation with the division to ameliorate a condition in that particular worksite.

(C) An employer who has been provided notice pursuant to this section may not then enter into consultation with the division in order to avoid an action under this section.

(4) The superior court shall review and approve any proposed settlement of alleged violations of the provisions of Division 5 (commencing with Section 6300) to ensure that the settlement provisions are at least as effective as the protections or remedies provided by state and federal law or regulation for the alleged violation. The provisions of the settlement relating to health and safety laws shall be submitted to the division at the same time that they are submitted to the court. This requirement shall be construed to authorize and permit the division to comment on those settlement provisions, and the court shall grant the division's commentary the appropriate weight.

(c) A civil action by an aggrieved employee pursuant to subdivision (a) or (f) of Section 2699 alleging a violation of any provision other than those listed in Section 2699.5 or Division 5 (commencing with Section 6300) shall commence only after the following requirements have been met:

(1)(A) The aggrieved employee or representative shall give written notice by online filing with the Labor and Workforce Development Agency and by certified mail to the employer of the specific provisions of this code alleged to have been violated, including the facts and theories to support the alleged violation.

(B) A notice filed with the Labor and Workforce Development Agency pursuant to subparagraph (A) and any employer response to that notice shall be accompanied by a filing fee of seventy-five dollars ($75). The fees required by this subparagraph are subject to waiver in accordance with the requirements of Sections 68632 and 68633 of the Government Code.

(C) The fees paid pursuant to subparagraph (B) shall be paid into the Labor and Workforce Development Fund and used for the purposes specified in subdivision (j) of Section 2699.

(2)(A) The employer may cure the alleged violation within 33 calendar days of the postmark date of the notice sent by the aggrieved employee or representative. The employer shall give written notice within that period of time by certified mail to the aggrieved employee or representative and by online filing with the agency if the alleged violation is cured, including a description of actions taken, and no civil action pursuant to Section 2699 may commence. If the alleged violation is not cured within the 33-day period, the employee may commence a civil action pursuant to Section 2699.

(B)(i) Subject to the limitation in clause (ii), no employer may avail himself or herself of the notice and cure provisions of this subdivision more than three times in a 12-month period for the same violation or violations contained in the notice, regardless of the location of the worksite.

(ii) No employer may avail himself or herself of the notice and cure provisions of this subdivision with respect to alleged violations of paragraph (6) or (8) of subdivision (a) of Section 226 more than once in a 12-month period for the same violation or violations contained in the notice, regardless of the location of the worksite.

(3) If the aggrieved employee disputes that the alleged violation has been cured, the aggrieved employee or representative shall provide written notice by online filing with the agency and by certified mail to the employer, including specified grounds to support that dispute, to the employer and the agency. Within 17 calendar days of the receipt of that notice, the agency shall review the actions taken by the employer to cure the alleged violation, and provide written notice of its decision by certified mail to the aggrieved employee and the employer. The agency may grant the employer three additional business days to cure the alleged violation. If the agency determines that the alleged violation has not been cured or if the agency fails to provide timely or any notification, the employee may proceed with the civil action pursuant to Section 2699. If the agency determines that the alleged violation has been cured, but the employee still disagrees, the employee may appeal that determination to the superior court.

(d) The periods specified in this section are not counted as part of the time limited for the commencement of the civil action to recover penalties under this part.

(e) This section shall become operative on July 1, 2021. **Leg.H.** 2016 ch. 31 (SB 836) §191, effective June 27, 2016.

2016 Note: It is the intent of the Legislature that the Labor and Workforce Development Agency shall continue to assign the duties prescribed in the Labor Code Private Attorneys General Act of 2004 (Part 13 (commencing with Section 2698) of Division 2 of the Labor Code) to the departments, divisions, commissions,

Labor

boards, or agencies where those duties are customarily performed. Stats. 2016 ch. 31 (SB 836) §188.

Ref.: Hanna § 11.01[9].

§2699.5. Applicability of Labor Code Section 2699.3.

The provisions of subdivision (a) of Section 2699.3 apply to any alleged violation of the following provisions: subdivision (k) of Section 96, Sections 98.6, 201, 201.3, 201.5, 201.7, 202, 203, 203.1, 203.5, 204, 204a, 204b, 204.1, 204.2, 205, 205.5, 206, 206.5, 208, 209, and 212, subdivision (d) of Section 213, Sections 221, 222, 222.5, 223, and 224, paragraphs (1) to (5), inclusive, (7), and (9) of subdivision (a) of Section 226, Sections 226.7, 227, 227.3, 230, 230.1, 230.2, 230.3, 230.4, 230.7, 230.8, and 231, subdivision (c) of Section 232, subdivision (c) of Section 232.5, Sections 233, 234, 351, 353, and 403, subdivision (b) of Section 404, Sections 432.2, 432.5, 432.7, 435, 450, 510, 511, 512, 513, 551, 552, 601, 602, 603, 604, 750, 751.8, 800, 850, 851, 851.5, 852, 921, 922, 923, 970, 973, 976, 1021, 1021.5, 1025, 1026, 1101, 1102, 1102.5, and 1153, subdivisions (c) and (d) of Section 1174, Sections 1194, 1197, 1197.1, 1197.5, and 1198, subdivision (b) of Section 1198.3, Sections 1199, 1199.5, 1290, 1292, 1293, 1293.1, 1294, 1294.1, 1294.5, 1296, 1297, 1298, 1301, 1308, 1308.1, 1308.7, 1309, 1309.5, 1391, 1391.1, 1391.2, 1392, 1683, and 1695, subdivision (a) of Section 1695.5, Sections 1695.55, 1695.6, 1695.7, 1695.8, 1695.9, 1696, 1696.5, 1696.6, 1697.1, 1700.25, 1700.26, 1700.31, 1700.32, 1700.40, and 1700.47, Sections 1735, 1771, 1774, 1776, 1777.5, 1811, 1815, 2651, and 2673, subdivision (a) of Section 2673.1, Sections 2695.2, 2800, 2801, 2802, 2806, and 2810, subdivision (b) of Section 2929, and Sections 3073.6, 6310, 6311, and 6399.7. **Leg.H.** 2004 ch. 221 (SB 1809), effective August 11, 2004, 2005 ch. 22 (SB 1108) §141, 2008 ch. 169 (SB 940) §8, 2009 ch. 140 (AB 1164) §136, 2015 ch. 445 (AB 1506) §3, effective October 2, 2015, 2018 ch. 704 (AB 235) §18, effective September 22, 2018, 2019 ch. 497 (AB 991) §184.

2004 Note: Notwithstanding any other provision of law, the provisions of Section 2699.5 relating to the duties and functions of the Division of Occupational Safety and Health shall be subject to review by the Joint Committee on Boards, Commissions, and Consumer Protection pursuant to Chapter 2 (commencing with Section 474) of Division 1.2 of the Business and Professions Code in consultation with the Senate Committee on Labor and Industrial Relations and the Assembly Committee on Labor and Employment. The first review shall be completed no later than three years from the effective date of this act. Stats. 2004 ch. 221 (SB 1809) §8.

Ref.: Hanna § 11.01[9].

§2699.6. [Repealed January 1, 2028] Applicability of part.

(a) This part shall not apply to an employee in the construction industry with respect to work performed under a valid collective bargaining agreement in effect any time before January 1, 2025, that expressly provides for the wages, hours of work, and working conditions of employees, premium wage rates for all overtime hours worked, and for the employee to receive a regular hourly pay rate of not less than 30 percent more than the state minimum wage rate, and the agreement does all of the following:

(1) Prohibits all of the violations of this code that would be redressable pursuant to this part, and provides for a grievance and binding arbitration procedure to redress those violations.

(2) Expressly waives the requirements of this part in clear and unambiguous terms.

(3) Authorizes the arbitrator to award any and all remedies otherwise available under this code, provided that nothing in this section authorizes the award of penalties under this part that would be payable to the Labor and Workforce Development Agency.

(b) Except for a civil action under Section 2699, nothing in this section precludes an employee from pursuing any other civil action against an employer, including, but not limited to, an action for a violation of the California Fair Employment and Housing Act (Part 2.8 (commencing with Section 12900) of Division 3 of Title 2 of the Government Code), Title VII of the Civil Rights Act of 1964 (Public Law 88-352), or any other prohibition of discrimination or harassment.

(c) The exception provided by this section shall expire on the date the collective bargaining agreement expires or on January 1, 2028, whichever is earlier.

(d) For purposes of this section, "employee in the construction industry" means an employee performing work associated with construction, including work involving alteration, demolition, building, excavation, renovation, remodeling, maintenance, improvement, repair work, and any other work as described by Chapter 9 (commencing with Section 7000) of Division 3 of the Business and Professions Code, and other similar or related occupations or trades.

(e) This section shall remain in effect only until January 1, 2028, and as of that date is repealed. **Leg.H.** 2018 ch. 529 (AB 1654) §1.

Ref.: Hanna § 11.01[9].

DIVISION 3
EMPLOYMENT RELATIONS

CHAPTER 1
SCOPE OF DIVISION

§2700. Scope.

The provisions of this division shall not limit, change, or in any way qualify the provisions of Division 4 of this code, but shall be fully operative and effective in all cases where the provisions of Division 4 are not applicable.

Ref.: Hanna § 3.100[1].

CHAPTER 2
EMPLOYER AND EMPLOYEE

ARTICLE 1
The Contract of Employment
[Selected Provisions]

§2750. "Employment contract."

The contract of employment is a contract by which one, who is called the employer, engages another, who is called the employee, to do something for the benefit of the employer or a third person.

Ref.: Hanna § 3.21[1]; Herlick Handbook § 2.8.

§2750.3. Enacted 2019. Repealed 2020 ch. 38 (AB 2257) §1, effective September 4, 2020, ch. 370 (SB 1371) §224 (ch. 38 prevails; ch. 370 not effective).

§2750.5. Rebuttable presumption that worker is employee; proof of independent contractor status.

There is a rebuttable presumption affecting the burden of proof that a worker performing services for which a license is required pursuant to Chapter 9 (commencing with Section 7000) of Division 3 of the Business and Professions Code, or who is performing such services for a person who is required to obtain such a license is an employee rather than an independent contractor. Proof of independent contractor status includes satisfactory proof of these factors:

(a) That the individual has the right to control and discretion as to the manner of performance of the contract for services in that the result of the work and not the means by which it is accomplished is the primary factor bargained for.

(b) That the individual is customarily engaged in an independently established business.

(c) That the individual's independent contractor status is bona fide and not a subterfuge to avoid employee status. A bona fide independent contractor status is further evidenced by the presence of cumulative factors such as substantial investment other than personal services in the business, holding out to be in business for oneself, bargaining for a contract to complete a specific project for compensation by project rather than by time, control over the time and place the work is performed, supplying the tools or instrumentalities used in the work other than tools and instrumentalities normally and customarily provided by employees, hiring employees, performing work that is not ordinarily in the course of the principal's work, performing work that requires a particular skill, holding a license pursuant to the Business and Professions Code, the intent by the parties that the work relationship is of an independent contractor status, or that the relationship is not severable or terminable at will by the principal but gives rise to an action for breach of contract.

In addition to the factors contained in subdivisions (a), (b), and (c), any person performing any function or activity for which a license is required pursuant to Chapter 9 (commencing with Section 7000) of Division 3 of the Business and Professions Code shall hold a valid contractors' license as a condition of having independent contractor status.

For purposes of workers' compensation law, this presumption is a supplement to the existing statutory definitions of employee and independent contractor, and is not intended to lessen the coverage of employees under Division 4 and Division 5.

Ref.: Hanna §§ 3.49[1]–[5], 10.24[5]; Herlick Handbook §§ 2.8, 12.11.

§2750.6. Physician contracting with primary care clinic as independent contractor; rebuttable presumption.

There is a rebuttable presumption affecting the burden of proof that a physician and surgeon, licensed pursuant to Division 2 (commencing with Section 500) of the Business and Professions Code, who enters into a contract for the performance of health services on behalf of a licensed primary care clinic, as defined in paragraph (1) of subdivision (a) of Section 1204 of the Health and Safety Code, is an independent contractor rather than an employee. Nothing in this section shall authorize the employment of a physician and surgeon to provide professional services when the employment would violate any other provision of law.

Ref.: Herlick Handbook § 2.8.

§2750.8. Motor Carrier Employer Amnesty Program.

(a) The Labor Commissioner and the Employment Development Department shall administer the Motor Carrier Employer Amnesty Program pursuant to which, notwithstanding any law, an eligible motor carrier performing drayage services at any port shall be relieved of liability for statutory or civil penalties associated with the misclassification of commercial drivers as independent contractors, as provided by this program, if the eligible motor carrier executes a settlement agreement with the Labor Commissioner whereby the eligible motor carrier

Labor

agrees to, among other things, properly classify all of its commercial drivers as employees.

(b) As used in this section, the following terms shall have the following meanings:

(1) "Commercial driver" means a person who holds a valid commercial driver's license who is hired or contracted to provide port drayage services.

(2) "Department" means the Employment Development Department.

(3) "Eligible motor carrier" means a motor carrier that shall not have any of the following on the date it applies to participate in the program:

(A) A civil lawsuit that was filed on or before December 31, 2015, pending against it in a state or federal court that alleges or involves a misclassification of a commercial driver.

(B) A penalty assessed by the department pursuant to Section 1128 of the Unemployment Insurance Code that is final imposition of that penalty.

(4) "Motor carrier" means a registered owner, lessee, licensee, or bailee of a commercial motor vehicle, as set forth in subdivision (b) of Section 15210 of the Vehicle Code, that operates or directs the operation of a commercial motor vehicle on a for-hire or not-for-hire basis to perform port drayage services.

(5) "Port" means any sea or river port located in this state.

(6) "Program" means the Motor Carrier Employer Amnesty Program established by this section and as provided by Article 8.6 (commencing with Section 1160) of Chapter 4 of Part 1 of Division 1 of the Unemployment Insurance Code.

(c)(1) A motor carrier shall only apply to participate in the program by doing all of the following:

(A) Submit an application to the Labor Commissioner, on a form provided by the Labor Commissioner. The application shall, at a minimum, require the motor carrier to establish it qualifies as an eligible motor carrier.

(B) Report on the results of a self-audit in accordance with the guidelines provided by the Labor Commissioner.

(2) A motor carrier that voluntarily or as a result of a final disposition in a civil proceeding reclassified its commercial drivers as employees on or before January 1, 2016, shall, in addition to other information requested by the Labor Commissioner, also submit with its application all of the following:

(A) Documentation demonstrating that the motor carrier reclassified its commercial drivers as employees, including the commencement period applicable to the reclassification.

(B) The identification of each commercial driver reclassified in the documents provided in subparagraph (A), the amounts paid to each commercial driver to compensate for the previous misclassification, and the time period applicable to the amount paid to each commercial driver prior to reclassification.

(C) A report of a self-audit for all commercial drivers reclassified by the motor carrier identified in subparagraphs (A) and (B), and also include a separate self-audit report for any commercial driver who is subject to reclassification, but is not identified in subparagraph (B).

(3) A proceeding or action against a motor carrier pursuant to Sections 2698 to 2699.5, inclusive, shall not be initiated after the motor carrier has submitted an application for participation in the program, but may be initiated if the motor carrier's application is denied.

(4) If a motor carrier's application to participate in the program is denied by the Labor Commissioner, the application or its submission shall not be considered an acknowledgment or admission by the motor carrier that it misclassified its commercial drivers as independent contractors, and the application or its submission shall not be construed in any way to support an evidentiary inference that the motor carrier failed to properly classify its commercial drivers as employees.

(d) The Labor Commissioner shall analyze the information provided pursuant to paragraph (2) of subdivision (c) for the purpose of evaluating the scope of a prior reclassification of an eligible motor carrier's commercial drivers to employees and has discretionary authority to determine whether the scope was sufficient to afford relief to the misclassified commercial drivers.

(e) Before January 1, 2017, the Labor Commissioner, with the cooperation and consent of the department, may negotiate and execute a settlement agreement with an eligible motor carrier pursuant to the program that applied to participate in the program. The Labor Commissioner shall not execute a settlement agreement on or after January 1, 2017.

(f) Prior to the Labor Commissioner executing a settlement agreement, an eligible motor carrier shall file its contribution returns and report unreported wages and taxes for the time period it seeks relief under the settlement agreement.

(g) A settlement agreement executed by the Labor Commissioner and an eligible motor carrier pursuant to the program shall require an eligible motor carrier to do all of the following:

(1) Pay all wages, benefits, and taxes owed, if any, to or in relation to all of its commercial drivers reclassified from independent contractors to employees for the period of time from the first date of misclassification to the date the settlement agreement is executed, but not exceeding the applicable statute of limitations.

(2) Maintain any converted commercial driver positions as employee positions.

(3) Consent that any future commercial drivers hired to perform the same or similar duties as those employees converted pursuant to the settlement agreement shall be presumed to have employee status and that the eligible motor carrier shall have the burden to prove by clear and convincing evidence that they are not employees in any administrative or judicial proceeding in which their employment status is an issue.

(4) Immediately after the execution of the settlement agreement, secure the workers' compensation coverage that is legally required for the commercial drivers who were reclassified as employees, effective on or before the date the settlement agreement is executed.

(5) Provide the Labor Commissioner and the department with proof of workers' compensation insurance coverage in compliance with paragraph (4) within five days of securing the coverage.

(6) Pay the costs authorized by subdivision (h), if required.

(7) Perform any other requirements or provisions the Labor Commissioner and the department deem necessary to carry out the intent of this section, the program, or to enforce the settlement agreement.

(h) A settlement agreement may require an eligible motor carrier to pay the reasonable, actual costs of the Labor Commissioner and the department for their respective review, approval, and compliance monitoring of the settlement agreement. The costs shall be deposited into the Labor Enforcement and Compliance Fund. The portion of the costs attributable to the department shall be transferred to the department upon appropriation by the Legislature.

(i) The settlement agreement may include provisions for an eligible motor carrier to make installment payments of amounts due pursuant to paragraphs (1) and (6) of subdivision (g) in lieu of a full payment. An installment payment agreement shall be included within the settlement agreement and charge interest on the outstanding amounts due at the rate prescribed in Sections 1113 and 1129 of the Unemployment Insurance Code. Interest on amounts due shall be charged from the day after the date the settlement agreement is executed. The settlement agreement shall contain a provision that if a motor carrier fails, without good cause, to fully comply with terms of the settlement agreement authorizing installment payments, the settlement agreement shall be null and void and the total amount of tax, interest, and penalties for the time period covered by the settlement agreement shall be immediately due and payable.

(j) The Labor Commissioner and the department may share any information necessary to carry out the program. Sharing information pursuant to this subdivision shall not constitute a waiver of any applicable confidentiality requirements and the party receiving the information shall be subject to any existing confidentiality requirements for that information.

(k)(1) Notwithstanding any other law and pursuant to the program, an eligible motor carrier that executed and performed its obligations pursuant to a settlement agreement shall not be liable, and the Labor Commissioner or the department shall not enforce, any civil or statutory penalties, including, but not limited to, remedies available under subdivision (e) of Section 226, that might have become due and payable for the time period covered by the settlement agreement, except for the following penalties:

(A) A penalty charged under Section 1128 of the Unemployment Insurance Code that is final on the date of the settlement agreement is executed, unless the penalty is reversed by the California Unemployment Insurance Appeals Board.

(B) A penalty for an amount an eligible motor carrier admitted was based on fraud or made with the intent to evade the reporting requirements set forth in this division or authorized regulations.

(C) A penalty based on a violation of this division or Division 6 (commencing with Section 13000) of the Unemployment Insurance Code and either of the following:

(i) The eligible motor carrier was on notice of a criminal investigation due to a complaint having been filed or by written notice having been mailed to the eligible motor carrier informing the motor carrier that it is under criminal investigation.

(ii) A criminal court proceeding has already been initiated against the eligible motor carrier.

(2)(A) Notwithstanding any other law and pursuant to the program, an eligible motor carrier that executed and performed its obligations pursuant to a settlement agreement shall not be liable, and the Labor Commissioner or the department shall not enforce, any unpaid penalties, and interest owed on unpaid penalties, on or before the date the settlement agreement was executed, pursuant to Sections 1112.5, 1126, and 1127 of the Unemployment Insurance Code for the tax reporting periods for which the settlement agreement is applicable, that are owed as a result of the nonpayment of tax liabilities due to the misclassification of one or more commercial drivers as independent contractors and the reclassification of these commercial drivers as employees, except that penalties, and interest owed on penalties, established as a result of an assessment issued by the department before the date the settlement agreement was executed shall not be waived pursuant to the program.

(B) For purposes of paragraph (1), state personal income taxes required to be withheld by Section 13020 of the Unemployment Insurance Code and owed by the motor carrier pursuant to Section 13070 of the Unemployment Insurance Code shall not be collected, if the eligible motor carrier issued an information return pursuant to Section 6041A of the Internal Revenue Code reporting payment or if the commercial driver certifies that the state personal tax has been paid or that he or she has reported to the Franchise Tax Board the payment against which the state personal income tax would have been imposed.

(3) A refund or credit for any penalty or interest paid prior to the date an eligible motor carrier applied to participate in the program shall not be granted.

(4) Except for violations described in Section 2119 of the Unemployment Insurance Code, the department shall not bring a criminal action for failing to report tax liabilities against an eligible motor carrier that executed and performed its obligations pursuant to a settlement agreement for the tax reporting periods subject to the settlement agreement.

(*l*) The statute of limitations on any claim or liability that might have been asserted against a motor carrier based on the motor carrier having misclassified a commercial driver as an independent contractor shall be tolled from the date a motor carrier applies for participation in the program through the date the Labor Commissioner either denies the motor carrier participation in the program or the motor carrier, as an eligible motor carrier, has failed to perform an obligation under the settlement agreement, whichever is later.

(m) The recovery obtained by the Labor Commissioner on behalf of a reclassified commercial driver pursuant to a settlement agreement shall be tendered to the commercial driver on the condition that the commercial driver shall execute a release of all claims the commercial driver may have against the eligible motor carrier based on the eligible motor carrier's failure to classify the commercial driver as an employee. A commercial driver shall not be under any obligation to accept the terms of a settlement agreement. If a commercial driver declines to accept the terms of a settlement agreement, the commercial driver shall not be bound by the settlement agreement, except that the eligible motor carrier shall still reclassify the commercial driver as an employee and that commercial driver shall be precluded from pursuing a claim for civil penalties or statutory penalties covered by the period of time covered by the settlement agreement. If a commercial driver does not accept the terms of a settlement agreement, the motor carrier shall be excused from performing its requirement under the settlement agreement to pay the amount acknowledged in the settlement agreement to be due to that commercial driver.

(n)(1) If the Labor Commissioner determines an eligible motor carrier violated or failed to perform any of its obligations under a settlement agreement, the Labor Commissioner may file a civil action to enforce the settlement agreement.

(2)(A) If the Labor Commissioner files a civil action seeking only recovery of the amounts due to commercial drivers under the settlement agreement, the Labor Commissioner may obtain judicial enforcement by filing a petition for entry of judgment for the liabilities due and remaining pursuant to the settlement agreement.

(B) After filing a petition pursuant to subparagraph (A), the Labor Commissioner may file an application for an order to show cause and serve it on the eligible motor carrier. Within 60 days of the date the Labor Commissioner filed the order to show cause, the court shall hold a hearing and enter a judgment. The judgment shall be in amounts which are due and owing to commercial drivers pursuant to the settlement agreement with credits, if any, for applicable payments the eligible motor carrier made under the settlement agreement. A judgment entered pursuant to this paragraph shall not preclude subsequent action to recover civil penalties or statutory penalties by the Labor Commissioner, or by an employee pursuant to Sections 2698 to 2699.5, inclusive.

(3) If the court determines in any action filed by the Labor Commissioner that a motor carrier has violated or otherwise failed to perform any of its obligations under a settlement agreement, the court shall award the Labor Commissioner costs and reasonable attorney's fees. **Leg.H.** 2015 ch. 741 (AB 621) §1, 2016 ch. 86 (SB 1171) §216.

§2753. Liability of person who advises employer to treat individual as independent contractor to avoid employee status.

(a) A person who, for money or other valuable consideration, knowingly advises an employer to treat an individual as an independent contractor to avoid employee status for that individual shall be jointly and severally liable with the employer if the individual is found not to be an independent contractor.

(b) This section does not apply to the following persons:

(1) A person who provides advice to his or her employer.

(2) An attorney authorized to practice law in California or another United States jurisdiction who provides legal advice in the course of the practice of law. **Leg.H.** 2011 ch. 706 (SB 459) §2.

Ref.: Hanna § 3.07[5].

§2754. Cheerleader for California-based professional sports team.

(a) For the purposes of this section, the following definitions shall apply:

(1) "California-based team" means a team that plays a majority of its home games in California.

(2) "Cheerleader" means an individual who performs acrobatics, dance, or gymnastics exercises on a recurring basis. This term shall not include an individual who is not otherwise affiliated with a California-based professional sports team and is utilized during its exhibitions, events, or games no more than one time in a calendar year.

(3) "Professional sports team" means a team at either a minor or major league level in the sport of baseball, basketball, football, ice hockey, or soccer.

(b) Notwithstanding any other law, for purposes of all of the provisions of state law that govern employment, including this code, the Unemployment Insurance Code, and the California Fair Employment and Housing Act (Part 2.8 (commencing with Section 12900) of Division 3 of Title 2 of the Government Code), a cheerleader who is utilized by a California-based professional sports team directly or through a labor contractor during its exhibitions, events, or games, shall be deemed to be an employee.

(c) The professional sports team shall ensure that the cheerleader is classified as an employee. **Leg.H.** 2015 ch. 102 (AB 202) §1.

Ref.: Hanna § 3.03; Herlick Handbook § 2.5.

ARTICLE 1.5
Worker Status: Employees

§2775. Employee versus independent contractor; applicable law.

(a) As used in this article:

(1) "Dynamex" means Dynamex Operations W. Inc. v. Superior Court (2018) 4 Cal.5th 903.

(2) "Borello" means the California Supreme Court's decision in S. G. Borello & Sons, Inc. v. Department of Industrial Relations (1989) 48 Cal.3d 341.

(b)(1) For purposes of this code and the Unemployment Insurance Code, and for the purposes of wage orders of the Industrial Welfare Commission, a person providing labor or services for remuneration shall be considered an employee rather than an independent contractor unless the hiring entity demonstrates that all of the following conditions are satisfied:

(A) The person is free from the control and direction of the hiring entity in connection with the performance of the work, both under the contract for the performance of the work and in fact.

(B) The person performs work that is outside the usual course of the hiring entity's business.

(C) The person is customarily engaged in an independently established trade, occupation, or business of the same nature as that involved in the work performed.

(2) Notwithstanding paragraph (1), any exceptions to the terms "employee," "employer," "employ," or "independent contractor," and any extensions of employer status or liability, that are expressly made by a provision of this code, the Unemployment Insurance Code, or in an appli-

cable order of the Industrial Welfare Commission, including, but not limited to, the definition of "employee" in subdivision 2(E) of Wage Order No. 2, shall remain in effect for the purposes set forth therein.

(3) If a court of law rules that the three-part test in paragraph (1) cannot be applied to a particular context based on grounds other than an express exception to employment status as provided under paragraph (2), then the determination of employee or independent contractor status in that context shall instead be governed by the California Supreme Court's decision in S. G. Borello & Sons, Inc. v. Department of Industrial Relations (1989) 48 Cal.3d 341 (Borello). **Leg.H.** 2020 ch. 38 (AB 2257) §2, effective September 4, 2020.

Ref.: Herlick Handbook § 2.8.

§2776. Exception for bona fide business-to-business contracting relationship.

Section 2775 and the holding in Dynamex do not apply to a bona fide business-to-business contracting relationship, as defined below, under the following conditions:

(a) If an individual acting as a sole proprietor, or a business entity formed as a partnership, limited liability company, limited liability partnership, or corporation ("business service provider") contracts to provide services to another such business or to a public agency or quasi-public corporation ("contracting business"), the determination of employee or independent contractor status of the business services provider shall be governed by Borello, if the contracting business demonstrates that all of the following criteria are satisfied:

(1) The business service provider is free from the control and direction of the contracting business entity in connection with the performance of the work, both under the contract for the performance of the work and in fact.

(2) The business service provider is providing services directly to the contracting business rather than to customers of the contracting business. This subparagraph does not apply if the business service provider's employees are solely performing the services under the contract under the name of the business service provider and the business service provider regularly contracts with other businesses.

(3) The contract with the business service provider is in writing and specifies the payment amount, including any applicable rate of pay, for services to be performed, as well as the due date of payment for such services.

(4) If the work is performed in a jurisdiction that requires the business service provider to have a business license or business tax registration, the business service provider has the required business license or business tax registration.

(5) The business service provider maintains a business location, which may include the business service provider's residence, that is separate from the business or work location of the contracting business.

(6) The business service provider is customarily engaged in an independently established business of the same nature as that involved in the work performed.

(7) The business service provider can contract with other businesses to provide the same or similar services and maintain a clientele without restrictions from the hiring entity.

(8) The business service provider advertises and holds itself out to the public as available to provide the same or similar services.

(9) Consistent with the nature of the work, the business service provider provides its own tools, vehicles, and equipment to perform the services, not including any proprietary materials that may be necessary to perform the services under the contract.

(10) The business service provider can negotiate its own rates.

(11) Consistent with the nature of the work, the business service provider can set its own hours and location of work.

(12) The business service provider is not performing the type of work for which a license from the Contractors' State License Board is required, pursuant to Chapter 9 (commencing with Section 7000) of Division 3 of the Business and Professions Code.

(b) When two bona fide businesses are contracting with one another under the conditions set forth in subdivision (a), the determination of whether an individual worker who is not acting as a sole proprietor or formed as a business entity, is an employee or independent contractor of the business service provider or contracting business is governed by Section 2775.

(c) This section does not alter or supersede any existing rights under Section 2810.3. **Leg.H.** 2020 ch. 38 (AB 2257) §2, effective September 4, 2020.

Ref.: Herlick Handbook § 2.8

§2777. Exception for relationship between referral agency and service provider.

Section 2775 and the holding in Dynamex do not apply to the relationship between a referral agency and a service provider, as defined below, under the following conditions:

(a) If an individual acting as a sole proprietor, or a business entity formed as a partnership, limited liability company, limited liability partnership, or corporation ("service provider") provides services to clients through a referral agency, the determination of whether the service provider is an employee or independent contractor of the referral agency shall be governed by Borello, if the referral agency demonstrates that all of the following criteria are satisfied:

(1) The service provider is free from the control and direction of the referral agency in connection with the performance of the work for the client, both as a matter of contract and in fact.

(2) If the work for the client is performed in a jurisdiction that requires the service provider to have a business license or business tax registration in order to provide the services under the contract, the service provider shall certify to the referral agency that they have the required business license or business tax registration. The referral agency shall keep the certifications for a period of at least three years. As used in this paragraph:

(A) "Business license" includes a license, tax certificate, fee, or equivalent payment that is required or collected by a local jurisdiction annually, or on some other fixed cycle, as a condition of providing services in the local jurisdiction.

Labor

(B) "Local jurisdiction" means a city, county, or city and county, including charter cities.

(3) If the work for the client requires the service provider to hold a state contractor's license pursuant to Chapter 9 (commencing with Section 7000) of Division 3 of the Business and Professions Code, the service provider has the required contractor's license.

(4) If there is an applicable professional licensure, permit, certification, or registration administered or recognized by the state available for the type of work being performed for the client, the service provider shall certify to the referral agency that they have the appropriate professional licensure, permit, certification, or registration. The referral agency shall keep the certifications for a period of at least three years.

(5) The service provider delivers services to the client under the service provider's name, without being required to deliver the services under the name of the referral agency.

(6) The service provider provides its own tools and supplies to perform the services.

(7) The service provider is customarily engaged, or was previously engaged, in an independently established business or trade of the same nature as, or related to, the work performed for the client.

(8) The referral agency does not restrict the service provider from maintaining a clientele and the service provider is free to seek work elsewhere, including through a competing referral agency.

(9) The service provider sets their own hours and terms of work or negotiates their hours and terms of work directly with the client.

(10) Without deduction by the referral agency, the service provider sets their own rates, negotiates their rates with the client through the referral agency, negotiates rates directly with the client, or is free to accept or reject rates set by the client.

(11) The service provider is free to accept or reject clients and contracts, without being penalized in any form by the referral agency. This paragraph does not apply if the service provider accepts a client or contract and then fails to fulfill any of its contractual obligations.

(b) For purposes of this section, the following definitions apply:

(1) "Client" means:

(A) A person who utilizes a referral agency to contract for services from a service provider, or

(B) A business that utilizes a referral agency to contract for services from a service provider that are otherwise not provided on a regular basis by employees at the client's business location, or to contract for services that are outside of the client's usual course of business. Notwithstanding subdivision (a), it is the responsibility of a business that utilizes a referral agency to contract for services, to meet the conditions outlined in this subparagraph.

(2)(A) "Referral agency" is a business that provides clients with referrals for service providers to provide services under a contract, with the exception of services in subparagraph (C).

(B) Under this paragraph, referrals for services shall include, but are not limited to, graphic design, web design, photography, tutoring, consulting, youth sports coaching, caddying, wedding or event planning, services provided by wedding and event vendors, minor home repair, moving, errands, furniture assembly, animal services, dog walking, dog grooming, picture hanging, pool cleaning, yard cleanup, and interpreting services.

(C) Under this paragraph, referrals for services do not include services provided in an industry designated by the Division of Occupational Safety and Health or the Department of Industrial Relations as a high hazard industry pursuant to subparagraph (A) of paragraph (3) of subdivision (e) of Section 6401.7 of the Labor Code or referrals for businesses that provide janitorial, delivery, courier, transportation, trucking, agricultural labor, retail, logging, in-home care, or construction services other than minor home repair.

(3)(A) "Referral agency contract" is the agency's contract with clients and service providers governing the use of its intermediary services described in paragraph (2). The intermediary services provided to the service provider by the referral agency are limited to client referrals and other administrative services ancillary to the service provider's business operation.

(B) A referral agency's contract may include a fee or fees to be paid by the client for utilizing the referral agency. This fee shall not be deducted from the rate set or negotiated by the service provider as set forth in paragraph (10) of subdivision (a).

(4) "Service provider" means an individual acting as a sole proprietor or business entity that agrees to the referral agency's contract and uses the referral agency to connect with clients.

(5) "Tutor" means a person who develops and teaches their own curriculum, teaches curriculum that is proprietarily and privately developed, or provides private instruction or supplemental academic enrichment services by using their own teaching methodology or techniques. A "tutor" does not include an individual who contracts with a local education agency or private school through a referral agency for purposes of teaching students of a public or private school in a classroom setting.

(6)(A) "Youth sports coaching" means services provided by a youth sports coach who develops and implements their own curriculum, which may be subject to requirements of a youth sports league, for an athletic program in which youth who are 18 years of age or younger predominantly participate and that is organized for the purposes of training for and engaging in athletic activity and competition. "Youth sports coaching" does not mean services provided by an individual who contracts with a local education agency or private school through a referral agency for purposes of teaching students of a public or private school.

(7) "Interpreting services" means:

(A) Services provided by a certified or registered interpreter in a language with an available certification or registration through the Judicial Council of California, State Personnel Board, or any other agency or department in the State of California, or through a testing organization, agency, or educational institution approved or recognized by the state, or through the Registry of Interpreters for the Deaf, Certification Commission for Healthcare Interpreters, National Board of Certification for Medical Interpreters, International Association of Conference Interpreters, United States Department of State, or the Administrative Office of the United States Courts.

(B) Services provided by an interpreter in a language without an available certification through the entities listed in subparagraph (A).

(8) "Consulting" means providing substantive insight, information, advice, opinions, or analysis that requires the exercise of discretion and independent judgment and is based on an individual's knowledge or expertise of a particular subject matter or field of study.

(9) "Animal services" means services related to daytime and nighttime pet care including pet boarding under Section 122380 of the Health and Safety Code.

(c) The determination of whether an individual worker is an employee of a service provider or whether an individual worker is an employee of a client is governed by Section 2775. **Leg.H.** 2020 ch. 38 (AB 2257) §2, effective September 4, 2020.

2020 Note: There is no subparagraph (b)(6)(B).

Ref.: Herlick Handbook § 2.8.

§2778. Exception for contract for "professional services."

(a) Section 2775 and the holding in Dynamex do not apply to a contract for "professional services" as defined below, and instead the determination of whether the individual is an employee or independent contractor shall be governed by Borello if the hiring entity demonstrates that all of the following factors are satisfied:

(1) The individual maintains a business location, which may include the individual's residence, that is separate from the hiring entity. Nothing in this paragraph prohibits an individual from choosing to perform services at the location of the hiring entity.

(2) If work is performed more than six months after the effective date of this section and the work is performed in a jurisdiction that requires the individual to have a business license or business tax registration, the individual has the required business license or business tax registration in order to provide the services under the contract, in addition to any required professional licenses or permits for the individual to practice in their profession.

(3) The individual has the ability to set or negotiate their own rates for the services performed.

(4) Outside of project completion dates and reasonable business hours, the individual has the ability to set the individual's own hours.

(5) The individual is customarily engaged in the same type of work performed under contract with another hiring entity or holds themselves out to other potential customers as available to perform the same type of work.

(6) The individual customarily and regularly exercises discretion and independent judgment in the performance of the services.

(b) For purposes of this section:

(1) An "individual" includes an individual providing services as a sole proprietor or other business entity.

(2) "Professional services" means services that meet any of the following:

(A) Marketing, provided that the contracted work is original and creative in character and the result of which depends primarily on the invention, imagination, or talent of the individual or work that is an essential part of or necessarily incident to any of the contracted work.

(B) Administrator of human resources, provided that the contracted work is predominantly intellectual and varied in character and is of such character that the output produced or the result accomplished cannot be standardized in relation to a given period of time.

(C) Travel agent services provided by either of the following:

(i) A person regulated by the Attorney General under Article 2.6 (commencing with Section 17550) of Chapter 1 of Part 3 of Division 7 of the Business and Professions Code.

(ii) An individual who is a seller of travel within the meaning of subdivision (a) of Section 17550.1 of the Business and Professions Code and who is exempt from the registration under subdivision (g) of Section 17550.20 of the Business and Professions Code.

(D) Graphic design.

(E) Grant writer.

(F)(i) Fine artist.

(ii) For the purposes of this subparagraph, "fine artist" means an individual who creates works of art to be appreciated primarily or solely for their imaginative, aesthetic, or intellectual content, including drawings, paintings, sculptures, mosaics, works of calligraphy, works of graphic art, crafts, or mixed media.

(G) Services provided by an enrolled agent who is licensed by the United States Department of the Treasury to practice before the Internal Revenue Service pursuant to Part 10 of Subtitle A of Title 31 of the Code of Federal Regulations.

(H) Payment processing agent through an independent sales organization.

(I) Services provided by any of the following:

(i) By a still photographer, photojournalist, videographer, or photo editor who works under a written contract that specifies the rate of pay and obligation to pay by a defined time, as long as the individual providing the services is not directly replacing an employee who performed the same work at the same volume for the hiring entity; the individual does not primarily perform the work at the hiring entity's business location, notwithstanding paragraph (1) of subdivision (a); and the individual is not restricted from working for more than one hiring entity. This subclause is not applicable to a still photographer, photojournalist, videographer, or photo editor who works on motion pictures, which is inclusive of, but is not limited to, theatrical or commercial productions, broadcast news, television, and music videos. Nothing in this section restricts a still photographer, photojournalist, photo editor, or videographer from distributing, licensing, or selling their work product to another business, except as prohibited under copyright laws or workplace collective bargaining agreements.

(ii) To a digital content aggregator by a still photographer, photojournalist, videographer, or photo editor.

(iii) For the purposes of this subparagraph the following definitions apply:

(I) "Photo editor" means an individual who performs services ancillary to the creation of digital content, such as retouching, editing, and keywording.

(II) "Digital content aggregator" means a licensing intermediary that obtains a license or assignment of copyright from a still photographer, photojournalist, videographer, or photo editor for the purposes of distributing that copyright by way of sublicense or assignment, to the intermediary's third party end users.

(J) Services provided by a freelance writer, translator, editor, copy editor, illustrator, or newspaper cartoonist who works under a written contract that specifies the rate of pay, intellectual property rights, and obligation to pay by a defined time, as long as the individual providing the services is not directly replacing an employee who performed the same work at the same volume for the hiring entity; the individual does not primarily perform the work at the hiring entity's business location, notwithstanding paragraph (1) of subdivision (a); and the individual is not restricted from working for more than one hiring entity.

(K) Services provided by an individual as a content contributor, advisor, producer, narrator, or cartographer for a journal, book, periodical, evaluation, other publication or educational, academic, or instructional work in any format or media, who works under a written contract that specifies the rate of pay, intellectual property rights and obligation to pay by a defined time, as long as the individual providing the services is not directly replacing an employee who performed the same work at the same volume for the hiring entity, the individual does not primarily perform the work at the hiring entity's business location notwithstanding paragraph (1) of subdivision (a); and the individual is not restricted from working for more than one hiring entity.

(L) Services provided by a licensed esthetician, licensed electrologist, licensed manicurist, licensed barber, or licensed cosmetologist provided that the individual:

(i) Sets their own rates, processes their own payments, and is paid directly by clients.

(ii) Sets their own hours of work and has sole discretion to decide the number of clients and which clients for whom they will provide services.

(iii) Has their own book of business and schedules their own appointments.

(iv) Maintains their own business license for the services offered to clients.

(v) If the individual is performing services at the location of the hiring entity, then the individual issues a Form 1099 to the salon or business owner from which they rent their business space.

(vi) This subparagraph shall become inoperative, with respect to licensed manicurists, on January 1, 2022.

(M) A specialized performer hired by a performing arts company or organization to teach a master class for no more than one week. "Master class" means a specialized course for limited duration that is not regularly offered by the hiring entity and is taught by an expert in a recognized field of artistic endeavor who does not work for the hiring entity to teach on a regular basis.

(N) Services provided by an appraiser, as defined in Part 3 (commencing with Section 11300) of Division 4 of the Business and Professions Code.

(O) Registered professional foresters licensed pursuant to Article 3 (commencing with Section 750) of Chapter 2.5 of Division 1 of the Public Resources Code.

(b) Section 2775 and the holding in Dynamex do not apply to the following, which are subject to the Business and Professions Code:

(1) A real estate licensee licensed by the State of California pursuant to Division 4 (commencing with Section 10000) of the Business and Professions Code, for whom the determination of employee or independent contractor status shall be governed by subdivision (b) of Section 10032 of the Business and Professions Code. If that section is not applicable, then this determination shall be governed as follows:

(A) For purposes of unemployment insurance by Section 650 of the Unemployment Insurance Code.

(B) For purposes of workers' compensation by Section 3200 et seq.

(C) For all other purposes in the Labor Code by Borello. The statutorily imposed duties of a responsible broker under Section 10015.1 of the Business and Professions Code are not factors to be considered under the Borello test.

(2) A home inspector, as defined in Section 7195 of the Business and Professions Code, and subject to the provisions of Chapter 9.3 (commencing with Section 7195) of Division 3 of that code.

(3) A repossession agency licensed pursuant to Section 7500.2 of the Business and Professions Code, for whom the determination of employee or independent contractor status shall be governed by Section 7500.2 of the Business and Professions Code, if the repossession agency is free from the control and direction of the hiring person or entity in connection with the performance of the work, both under the contract for the performance of the work and in fact. **Leg.H.** 2020 ch. 38 (AB 2257) §2, effective September 4, 2020.

Ref.: Herlick Handbook § 2.8.

§2779. Exception for relationship between individuals acting as sole proprietor or separate partnership, limited liability company, limited liability partnership, or corporation performing contract work for single-engagement event.

(a) Section 2775 and the holding in Dynamex do not apply to the relationship between two individuals wherein each individual is acting as a sole proprietor or separate business entity formed as a partnership, limited liability company, limited liability partnership, or corporation performing work pursuant to a contract for purposes of providing services at the location of a single-engagement event, as defined below, under the following conditions:

(1) Neither individual is subject to control and direction by the other, in connection with the performance of the work, both under the contract for the performance of the work and in fact.

(2) Each individual has the ability to negotiate their rate of pay with the other individual.

(3) The written contract between both individuals specifies the total payment for services provided by both individuals at the single-engagement event, and the specific rate paid to each individual.

(4) Each individual maintains their own business location, which may include the individual's personal residence.

(5) Each individual provides their own tools, vehicles, and equipment to perform the services under the contract.

(6) If the work is performed in a jurisdiction that requires an individual to have a business license or business tax registration, then each individual has the required business license or business tax registration.

(7) Each individual is customarily engaged in the same or similar type of work performed under the contract or each individual separately holds themselves out to other potential customers as available to perform the same type of work.

(8) Each individual can contract with other businesses to provide the same or similar services and maintain their own clientele without restrictions.

(b) "Single-engagement event" means a stand-alone non-recurring event in a single location, or a series of events in the same location no more than once a week.

(c) "Services" under this section do not include services provided in an industry designated by the Division of Occupational Safety and Health or the Department of Industrial Relations as a high hazard industry pursuant to subparagraph (A) of paragraph (3) of subdivision (e) of Section 6401.7 or janitorial, delivery, courier, transportation, trucking, agricultural labor, retail, logging, in-home care, or construction services other than minor home repair. **Leg.H.** 2020 ch. 38 (AB 2257) §2, effective September 4, 2020.

Ref.: Herlick Handbook § 2.8.

§2780. Exception for specified occupations related to creating, marketing, promoting, or distributing sound recordings or musical compositions.

(a)(1) Section 2775 and the holding in Dynamex do not apply to the following occupations in connection with creating, marketing, promoting, or distributing sound recordings or musical compositions, and instead the holding in Borello shall apply to all of the following:

(A) Recording artists, subject to the below.

(B) Songwriters, lyricists, composers, and proofers.

(C) Managers of recording artists.

(D) Record producers and directors.

(E) Musical engineers and mixers engaged in the creation of sound recordings.

(F) Musicians engaged in the creation of sound recordings, subject to the below.

(G) Vocalists, subject to the below.

(H) Photographers working on recording photo shoots, album covers, and other press and publicity purposes.

(I) Independent radio promoters.

(J) Any other individual engaged to render any creative, production, marketing, or independent music publicist services related primarily to the creation, marketing, promotion, or distribution of sound recordings or musical compositions.

(2) This subdivision shall not apply to any of the following:

(A) Film and television unit production crews, as such term is commonly used in the film and television industries, working on live or recorded performances for audiovisual works, including still photographers and cinematographers.

(B) Publicists who are not independent music publicists.

(3) Notwithstanding Section 2775, paragraphs (1) and (2), and the holding in Dynamex, the terms and conditions of any current or future collective bargaining agreements or contractual agreements between the applicable labor unions and respective employers shall govern the determination of employment status in all events.

(4) The following shall apply to recording artists, musicians, and vocalists:

(A) Recording artists, musicians, and vocalists shall not be precluded from organizing under applicable provisions of labor law, or otherwise exercising rights granted to employees under the National Labor Relations Act (29 U.S.C. Sec. 151 et seq.).

(B)(i) Musicians and vocalists who are not royalty-based participants in the work created during any specific engagement shall be treated as employees solely for purposes of receiving minimum and overtime wages for hours worked during the engagement, as well as any damages and penalties due to the failure to receive minimum or overtime wages. Any such wages, damages, and penalties owed under this subparagraph shall be determined according to the applicable provisions of this code, wage orders of the Industrial Welfare Commission, or applicable local laws.

(ii) "Royalty-based participant" means an individual who has either negotiated for the collection or direct administration of royalties derived from the exploitation of a sound recording or musical composition, or is entitled to control, administer or collect royalties related to the exploitation of a sound recording or musical composition as a co-author or joint owner thereof.

(C) In all events, and notwithstanding subparagraph (B), the terms and conditions of any current or future collective bargaining agreements or contractual agreements between the applicable labor unions and respective employers shall govern the determination of employment status.

(b)(1) Section 2775 and the holding in Dynamex do not apply to a musician or musical group for the purpose of a single-engagement live performance event, and instead the determination of employee or independent contractor status shall be governed by Borello, unless one of the following conditions is met:

(A) The musical group is performing as a symphony orchestra, the musical group is performing at a theme park or amusement park, or a musician is performing in a musical theater production.

(B) The musical group is an event headliner for a performance taking place in a venue location with more than 1,500 attendees.

(C) The musical group is performing at a festival that sells more than 18,000 tickets per day.

(2) This subdivision is inclusive of rehearsals related to the single-engagement live performance event.

(3) As used in this subdivision:

(A) "Event headliner" means the musical group that appears most prominently in an event program, advertisement, or on a marquee.

(B) "Festival" means a single day or multiday event in a single venue location that occurs once a year, featuring performances by various musical groups.

(C) "Musical group" means a solo artist, band, or a group of musicians who perform under a distinct name.

(D) "Musical theater production" means a form of theatrical performance that combines songs, spoken dialogue, acting, and dance.

(E) "Musician" means an individual performing instrumental, electronic, or vocal music in a live setting.

(F) "Single-engagement live performance event" means a stand-alone musical performance in a single venue location, or a series of performances in the same venue location no more than once a week. This does not include performances that are part of a tour or series of live performances at various locations.

(G) "Venue location" means an indoor or outdoor location used primarily as a space to hold a concert or musical performance. "Venue location" includes, but is not limited to, a restaurant, bar, or brewery that regularly offers live musical entertainment.

(c) Section 2775 and the holding in Dynamex do not apply to the following, and instead, the determination of employee or independent contractor status shall be governed by Borello:

(1) An individual performance artist performing material that is their original work and creative in character and the result of which depends primarily on the individual's invention, imagination, or talent, given all of the following conditions are satisfied:

(A) The individual is free from the control and direction of the hiring entity in connection with the performance of the work, both as a matter of contract and in fact. This includes, and is not limited to, the right for the performer to exercise artistic control over all elements of the performance.

(B) The individual retains the rights to their intellectual property that was created in connection with the performance.

(C) Consistent with the nature of the work, the individual sets their terms of work and has the ability to set or negotiate their rates.

(D) The individual is free to accept or reject each individual performance engagement without being penalized in any form by the hiring entity.

(2) "Individual performance artist" shall include, but is not limited to, an individual performing comedy, improvisation, stage magic, illusion, mime, spoken word, storytelling, or puppetry.

(3) This subdivision does not apply to an individual participating in a theatrical production, or a musician or musical group as defined in subdivision (b).

(4) In all events, notwithstanding paragraph (1), the terms and conditions of any current or future collective bargaining agreements or contractual agreements between the applicable labor unions and respective employer shall govern the determination of employment status. **Leg.H.** 2020 ch. 38 (AB 2257) §2, effective September 4, 2020.

Ref.: Herlick Handbook § 2.8.

§2781. Exception for relationship between contractor and individual performing work pursuant to subcontract in construction industry.

Section 2775 and the holding in Dynamex do not apply to the relationship between a contractor and an individual performing work pursuant to a subcontract in the construction industry, and instead the determination of whether the individual is an employee of the contractor shall be governed by Section 2750.5 and by Borello, if the contractor demonstrates that all the following criteria are satisfied:

(a) The subcontract is in writing.

(b) The subcontractor is licensed by the Contractors' State License Board and the work is within the scope of that license.

(c) If the subcontractor is domiciled in a jurisdiction that requires the subcontractor to have a business license or business tax registration, the subcontractor has the required business license or business tax registration.

(d) The subcontractor maintains a business location that is separate from the business or work location of the contractor.

(e) The subcontractor has the authority to hire and to fire other persons to provide or to assist in providing the services.

(f) The subcontractor assumes financial responsibility for errors or omissions in labor or services as evidenced by insurance, legally authorized indemnity obligations, performance bonds, or warranties relating to the labor or services being provided.

(g) The subcontractor is customarily engaged in an independently established business of the same nature as that involved in the work performed.

(h)(1) Subdivision (b) shall not apply to a subcontractor providing construction trucking services for which a contractor's license is not required by Chapter 9 (commencing with Section 7000) of Division 3 of the Business and Professions Code, provided that all of the following criteria are satisfied:

(A) The subcontractor is a business entity formed as a sole proprietorship, partnership, limited liability company, limited liability partnership, or corporation.

(B) For work performed after January 1, 2020, the subcontractor is registered with the Department of Industrial Relations as a public works contractor pursuant to Section 1725.5, regardless of whether the subcontract involves public work.

(C) The subcontractor utilizes its own employees to perform the construction trucking services, unless the subcontractor is a sole proprietor who operates their own truck to perform the entire subcontract and holds a valid motor carrier permit issued by the Department of Motor Vehicles.

(D) The subcontractor negotiates and contracts with, and is compensated directly by, the licensed contractor.

(2) For work performed after January 1, 2020, any business entity that provides construction trucking services to a licensed contractor utilizing more than one truck shall be deemed the employer for all drivers of those trucks.

(3) For purposes of this subdivision, "construction trucking services" mean hauling and trucking services provided in the construction industry pursuant to a contract with a licensed contractor utilizing vehicles that require a commercial driver's license to operate or have a gross vehicle weight rating of 26,001 or more pounds.

(4) This subdivision shall only apply to work performed before January 1, 2022.

(5) Nothing in this subdivision prohibits an individual who owns their truck from working as an employee of a trucking company and utilizing that truck in the scope of that employment. An individual employee providing their own truck for use by an employer trucking company shall be reimbursed by the trucking company for the reasonable expense incurred for the use of the employee-owned truck. **Leg.H.** 2020 ch. 38 (AB 2257) §2, effective September 4, 2020.

Ref.: Herlick Handbook § 2.8.

§2782. Exception for relationship between data aggregator and individual providing feedback to data aggregator.

(a)(1) Section 2775 and the holding in Dynamex do not apply to the relationship between a data aggregator and an individual providing feedback to the data aggregator, and instead the holding in Borello shall apply, under the following conditions:

(A) The individual is free from control and direction from the data aggregator with respect to the substance and content of the feedback.

(B) Any consideration paid for the feedback provided, if prorated to an hourly basis, is an amount equivalent to or greater than the minimum wage.

(C) The nature of the feedback requested requires the individual providing feedback to the data aggregator to exercise independent judgment and discretion.

(D) The individual has the ability to reject feedback requests, without being penalized in any form by the data aggregator.

(2) As used in this section:

(A) "Data aggregator" is a business, research institution, or organization that requests and gathers feedback on user interface, products, services, people, concepts, ideas, offerings, or experiences from individuals willing to provide it.

(B) "Minimum wage" is local or state minimum wage, whichever is greater. **Leg.H.** 2020 ch. 38 (AB 2257) §2, effective September 4, 2020.

Ref.: Herlick Handbook § 2.8.

§2783. Exceptions for other specific occupations.

Section 2775 and the holding in Dynamex do not apply to the following occupations as defined in the paragraphs below, and instead, the determination of employee or independent contractor status for individuals in those occupations shall be governed by Borello:

(a) A person or organization who is licensed by the Department of Insurance pursuant to Chapter 5 (commencing with Section 1621), Chapter 6 (commencing with Section 1760), or Chapter 8 (commencing with Section 1831) of Part 2 of Division 1 of the Insurance Code or a person who provides underwriting inspections, premium audits, risk management, or loss control work for the insurance and financial service industries.

(b) A physician and surgeon, dentist, podiatrist, psychologist, or veterinarian licensed by the State of California pursuant to Division 2 (commencing with Section 500) of the Business and Professions Code, performing professional or medical services provided to or by a health care entity, including an entity organized as a sole proprietorship, partnership, or professional corporation as defined in Section 13401 of the Corporations Code. Nothing in this subdivision shall circumvent, undermine, or restrict the rights under federal law to organize and collectively bargain.

(c) An individual who holds an active license from the State of California and is practicing one of the following recognized professions: lawyer, architect, landscape architect, engineer, private investigator, or accountant.

(d) A securities broker-dealer or investment adviser or their agents and representatives that are either of the following:

(1) Registered with the Securities and Exchange Commission or the Financial Industry Regulatory Authority.

(2) Licensed by the State of California under Chapter 2 (commencing with Section 25210) or Chapter 3 (commencing with Section 25230) of Division 1 of Part 3 of Title 4 of the Corporations Code.

(e) A direct sales salesperson as described in Section 650 of the Unemployment Insurance Code, so long as the conditions for exclusion from employment under that section are met.

(f) A manufactured housing salesperson, subject to all obligations under Part 2 (commencing with Section 18000) of Division 13 of the Health and Safety Code, including all regulations promulgated by the Department of Housing and Community Development relating to manufactured home salespersons and all other obligations of manufactured housing salespersons to members of the public.

(g) A commercial fisher working on an American vessel.

(1) For the purposes of this subdivision:

(A) "American vessel" has the same meaning as defined in Section 125.5 of the Unemployment Insurance Code.

(B) "Commercial fisher" means a person who has a valid, unrevoked commercial fishing license issued pursuant to Article 3 (commencing with Section 7850) of Chapter 1 of Part 3 of Division 6 of the Fish and Game Code.

(C) "Working on an American vessel" means the taking or the attempt to take fish, shellfish, or other fishery resources of the state by any means, and includes each individual aboard an American vessel operated for fishing purposes who participates directly or indirectly in the taking of these raw fishery products, including maintaining the vessel or equipment used aboard the vessel. However, "working on an American vessel" does not apply to anyone aboard a licensed commercial fishing vessel as a visitor or guest who does not directly or indirectly participate in the taking.

(2) For the purposes of this subdivision, a commercial fisher working on an American vessel is eligible for unemployment insurance benefits if they meet the definition of "employment" in Section 609 of the Unemployment Insurance Code and are otherwise eligible for those benefits pursuant to the provisions of the Unemployment Insurance Code.

(3)**(A)** On or before March 1, 2021, and each March 1 thereafter, the Employment Development Department shall issue an annual report to the Legislature on the use of unemployment insurance in the commercial fishing industry. This report shall include, but not be limited to, **all of the following:**

(i) Reporting the number of commercial fishers who apply for unemployment insurance benefits [1].

(ii) The number of commercial fishers who have their claims disputed [2].

(iii) The number of commercial fishers who have their claims denied [3].

(iv) The number of commercial fishers who receive unemployment insurance benefits.

(B) The report required by this subparagraph shall be submitted in compliance with Section 9795 of the Government Code.

(4) This subdivision shall become inoperative on January 1, 2023, unless extended by the Legislature.

(h)**(1)** A newspaper distributor working under contract with a newspaper publisher, as defined in [4] **paragraph (2), or** a newspaper carrier [5].

(2) For purposes of this subdivision:

(A) "Newspaper" means a newspaper of general circulation, as defined in Section 6000 of the Government Code, and any other publication circulated to the community in general as an extension of or substitute for that newspaper's own publication, whether that publication be designated a "shoppers' guide," as a zoned edition, or otherwise.

(B) "Publisher" means the natural or corporate person that manages the newspaper's business operations, including circulation.

(C) "Newspaper distributor" means a person or entity that contracts with a publisher to distribute newspapers to the community.

(D) "Carrier" means a person who effects physical delivery of the newspaper to the customer or reader.

[6] **(3)** This subdivision shall become inoperative on January 1, [7] **2022**, unless extended by the Legislature.

(i) An individual who is engaged by an international exchange visitor program that has obtained and maintains full official designation by the United States Department of State under Part 62 (commencing with Section 62.1) of Title 22 of the Code of Federal Regulations for the purpose of conducting, instead of participating in, international and cultural exchange visitor programs and is in full compliance with Part 62 (commencing with Section 62.1) of Title 22 of the Code of Federal Regulations.

(j) A competition judge with a specialized skill set or expertise providing services that require the exercise of discretion and independent judgment to an organization for the purposes of determining the outcome or enforcing the rules of a competition. This includes, but is not limited to, an amateur umpire or referee. **Leg.H.** 2020 ch. 38 (AB 2257) §2, effective September 4, 2020, ch. 341 (AB 323) §2.5.

§2783. 2020 Deletes. [1] , **[2]** , **[3]** , and **[4]** subparagraph (A), and **[5]** working under contract either with a newspaper publisher or newspaper distributor. (1) **[6]** (2) **[7]** 2021

2020 Prior Urgency Law: Below is the version of §2783 as added by Stats. 2020 ch. 38 (AB 2257) §2, effective September 4, 2020, until January 1, 2021.

§2783. Exceptions for other specific occupations.

Section 2775 and the holding in Dynamex do not apply to the following occupations as defined in the paragraphs below, and instead, the determination of employee or independent contractor status for individuals in those occupations shall be governed by Borello:

(a) A person or organization who is licensed by the Department of Insurance pursuant to Chapter 5 (commencing with Section 1621), Chapter 6 (commencing with Section 1760), or Chapter 8 (commencing with Section 1831) of Part 2 of Division 1 of the Insurance Code or a person who provides underwriting inspections, premium audits, risk management, or loss control work for the insurance and financial service industries.

(b) A physician and surgeon, dentist, podiatrist, psychologist, or veterinarian licensed by the State of California pursuant to Division 2 (commencing with Section 500) of the Business and Professions Code, performing professional or medical services provided to or by a health care entity, including an entity organized as a sole proprietorship, partnership, or professional corporation as defined in Section 13401 of the Corporations Code. Nothing in this subdivision shall circumvent, undermine, or restrict the rights under federal law to organize and collectively bargain.

(c) An individual who holds an active license from the State of California and is practicing one of the following recognized professions: lawyer, architect, landscape architect, engineer, private investigator, or accountant.

(d) A securities broker-dealer or investment adviser or their agents and representatives that are either of the following:

(1) Registered with the Securities and Exchange Commission or the Financial Industry Regulatory Authority.

(2) Licensed by the State of California under Chapter 2 (commencing with Section 25210) or Chapter 3 (commencing with Section 25230) of Division 1 of Part 3 of Title 4 of the Corporations Code.

(e) A direct sales salesperson as described in Section 650 of the Unemployment Insurance Code, so long as the conditions for exclusion from employment under that section are met.

(f) A manufactured housing salesperson, subject to all obligations under Part 2 (commencing with Section 18000) of Division 13 of the Health and Safety Code, including all regulations promulgated by the Department of Housing and Community Development relating to manufactured home salespersons and all other obligations of manufactured housing salespersons to members of the public.

(g) A commercial fisher working on an American vessel.

(1) For the purposes of this subdivision:

(A) "American vessel" has the same meaning as defined in Section 125.5 of the Unemployment Insurance Code.

(B) "Commercial fisher" means a person who has a valid, unrevoked commercial fishing license issued pursuant to Article 3 (commencing with Section 7850) of Chapter 1 of Part 3 of Division 6 of the Fish and Game Code.

(C) "Working on an American vessel" means the taking or the attempt to take fish, shellfish, or other fishery resources of the state by any means, and includes each individual aboard an American vessel operated for fishing purposes who participates directly or

indirectly in the taking of these raw fishery products, including maintaining the vessel or equipment used aboard the vessel. However, "working on an American vessel" does not apply to anyone aboard a licensed commercial fishing vessel as a visitor or guest who does not directly or indirectly participate in the taking.

(2) For the purposes of this subdivision, a commercial fisher working on an American vessel is eligible for unemployment insurance benefits if they meet the definition of "employment" in Section 609 of the Unemployment Insurance Code and are otherwise eligible for those benefits pursuant to the provisions of the Unemployment Insurance Code.

(3) On or before March 1, 2021, and each March 1 thereafter, the Employment Development Department shall issue an annual report to the Legislature on the use of unemployment insurance in the commercial fishing industry. This report shall include, but not be limited to, the number of commercial fishers who apply for unemployment insurance benefits, the number of commercial fishers who have their claims disputed, the number of commercial fishers who have their claims denied, and the number of commercial fishers who receive unemployment insurance benefits. The report required by this subparagraph shall be submitted in compliance with Section 9795 of the Government Code.

(4) This subdivision shall become inoperative on January 1, 2023, unless extended by the Legislature.

(h) A newspaper distributor working under contract with a newspaper publisher, as defined in subparagraph (A), and a newspaper carrier working under contract either with a newspaper publisher or newspaper distributor.

(1) For purposes of this subdivision:

(A) "Newspaper" means a newspaper of general circulation, as defined in Section 6000 of the Government Code, and any other publication circulated to the community in general as an extension of or substitute for that newspaper's own publication, whether that publication be designated a "shoppers' guide," as a zoned edition, or otherwise.

(B) "Publisher" means the natural or corporate person that manages the newspaper's business operations, including circulation.

(C) "Newspaper distributor" means a person or entity that contracts with a publisher to distribute newspapers to the community.

(D) "Carrier" means a person who effects physical delivery of the newspaper to the customer or reader.

(2) This subdivision shall become inoperative on January 1, 2021, unless extended by the Legislature.

(i) An individual who is engaged by an international exchange visitor program that has obtained and maintains full official designation by the United States Department of State under Part 62 (commencing with Section 62.1) of Title 22 of the Code of Federal Regulations for the purpose of conducting, instead of participating in, international and cultural exchange visitor programs and is in full compliance with Part 62 (commencing with Section 62.1) of Title 22 of the Code of Federal Regulations.

(j) A competition judge with a specialized skill set or expertise providing services that require the exercise of discretion and independent judgment to an organization for the purposes of determining the outcome or enforcing the rules of a competition. This includes, but is not limited to, an amateur umpire or referee. ***Leg.H.*** *2020 ch. 38 (AB 2257) §2, effective September 4, 2020.*

Ref.: Herlick Handbook § 2.8.

§2784. Exception for relationship between motor club and individual performing services pursuant to contract between motor club and third party.

Section 2775 and the holding in Dynamex do not apply to the relationship between a motor club holding a certificate of authority issued pursuant to Chapter 2 (commencing with Section 12160) of Part 5 of Division 2 of the Insurance Code and an individual performing services pursuant to a contract between the motor club and a third party to provide motor club services utilizing the employees and vehicles of the third party and, instead, the determination of whether such an individual is an employee of the motor club shall be governed by Borello, if the motor club demonstrates that the third party is a separate and independent business from the motor club. **Leg.H.** 2020 ch. 38 (AB 2257) §2, effective September 4, 2020.

Ref.: Herlick Handbook § 2.8.

§2785. Declaratory nature of Section 2775; retroactive and prospective application of exceptions; when employment status governed by Borello.

(a) Section 2775 does not constitute a change in, but is declaratory of, existing law with regard to wage orders of the Industrial Welfare Commission and violations of this code relating to wage orders.

(b) Insofar as the application of Sections 2776 to Section 2784 would relieve an employer from liability, those sections shall apply retroactively to existing claims and actions to the maximum extent permitted by law.

(c) Except as provided in subdivisions (a) and (b) of this section, this article shall apply to work performed on or after January 1, 2020.

(d) If a hiring entity can demonstrate compliance with all of conditions set forth in any one of Sections 2776 to 2784, inclusive, then Section 2775 and the holding in Dynamex do not apply to that entity, and instead the determination of an individual's employment status as an employee or independent contractor shall be governed by Borello. **Leg.H.** 2020 ch. 38 (AB 2257) §2, effective September 4, 2020.

§2786. Injunctive relief.

In addition to any other remedies available, an action for injunctive relief to prevent the continued misclassification of employees as independent contractors may be prosecuted against the putative employer in a court of competent jurisdiction by the Attorney General, by a district attorney, or by a city attorney of a city having a population in excess of 750,000, or by a city attorney in a city and county or, with the consent of the district attorney, by a city prosecutor in a city having a full-time city prosecutor in the name of the people of the State of California upon their own complaint or upon the complaint of a board, officer, person, corporation, or association. **Leg.H.** 2020 ch. 38 (AB 2257) §2, effective September 4, 2020.

§2787. Severability of article.

The provisions of this Article are severable. If any provision of this Article or its application is held invalid, that invalidity shall not affect other provisions or applications that can be given effect without the invalid provision or application. **Leg.H.** 2020 ch. 38 (AB 2257) §2, effective September 4, 2020.

ARTICLE 2
Obligations of Employer
[Selected Provisions]

§2800. Indemnification of employee; employer's want of care.

An employer shall in all cases indemnify his employee for losses caused by the employer's want of ordinary care.

Ref.: Hanna § 11.02[4][m].

§2800.1. Safeguard of musical instruments.

An employer shall in all cases take reasonable and necessary precautions to safeguard musical instruments and equipment, belonging to an employed musician, located on premises under the employer's control. In the event such equipment is damaged or stolen as a result of the employer's failure or refusal to take such reasonable and necessary precautions, the employer shall be liable to the owner for repair or replacement thereof if the employed musician has taken reasonable and necessary precautions to safeguard the musical instruments and equipment.

For the purposes of this section: (a) "employer" includes a purchaser of services and the owner of premises upon which an employed musician is working; and (b) "employee" is any employed musician working on premises which are under an employer's control.

§2800.2. Employer provided medical coverage; notice of conversion coverage; continuation coverage under COBRA and notification of conversion coverage.

(a) Any employer, employee association, or other entity otherwise providing hospital, surgical, or major medical benefits to its employees or members is solely responsible for notification of its employees or members of the conversion coverage made available pursuant to Part 6.1 (commencing with Section 12670) of Division 2 of the Insurance Code or Section 1373.6 of the Health and Safety Code.

(b) Any employer, employee association, or other entity, whether private or public, that provides hospital, medical, or surgical expense coverage that a former employee may continue under Section 4980B of Title 26 of the United States Code, Section 1161 et seq. of Title 29 of the United States Code, or Section 300bb of Title 42 of the United States Code, as added by the Consolidated Omnibus Budget Reconciliation Act of 1985 (Public Law 99-272), and as may be later amended (hereafter "COBRA"), shall, in conjunction with the notification required by COBRA that COBRA continuation coverage will cease and conversion coverage is available, and as a part of the notification required by subdivision (a), also notify the former employee, spouse, or former spouse of the availability of the continuation coverage under Section 1373.621 of the Health and Safety Code, and Sections 10116.5 and 11512.03 of the Insurance Code.

(c) On or after July 1, 2006, notification provided to employees, members, former employees, spouses, or former spouses under subdivisions (a) and (b) shall also include the following notification:

"Please examine your options carefully before declining this coverage. You should be aware that companies selling individual health insurance typically require a review of your medical history that could result in a higher premium or you could be denied coverage entirely." **Leg.H.** 1995 ch. 489, 1996 ch. 1118, effective September 30, 1996, operative January 1, 1997, 2005 ch. 526 (AB 356) §8.

§2800.3. Availability of coverage conversion.

Any employer, other than a self-insurer, employee association or other entity otherwise providing hospital, surgical or major medical benefits to its employees or members shall also make available conversion coverage which complies with the provisions of Part 6.1 (commencing with Section 12670) of Division 2 of the Insurance Code and Section 1373.6 of the Health and Safety Code.

§2801. Contributory negligence no bar to recovery; employer defenses limited.

In any action to recover damages for a personal injury sustained within this State by an employee while engaged in the line of his duty or the course of his employment as such, or for death resulting from personal injury so sustained, in which recovery is sought upon the ground of want of ordinary or reasonable care of the employer, or of any officer, agent or servant of the employer, the fact that such employee has been guilty of contributory negligence shall not bar a recovery therein where his contributory negligence was slight and that of the employer was gross, in comparison, but the damages may be diminished by the jury in proportion to the amount of negligence attributable to such employee.

It shall be conclusively presumed that such employee was not guilty of contributory negligence in any case where the violation of any law enacted for the safety of employees contributed to such employee's injury.

It shall not be a defense that:

(a) The employee either expressly or impliedly assumed the risk of the hazard complained of.

(b) The injury or death was caused in whole or in part by the want of ordinary or reasonable care of a fellow servant.

No contract, or regulation, shall exempt the employer from any provisions of this section.

Ref.: Hanna §§ 1.01[3], 11.03[2]; Herlick Handbook §§ 1.01[1], 12.11.

§2802. Indemnification of employee for expenditures or losses in discharge of duties or obedience to directions; citation for violation of reimbursement obligations.

(a) An employer shall indemnify his or her employee for all necessary expenditures or losses incurred by the employee in direct consequence of the discharge of his or her duties, or of his or her obedience to the directions of the employer, even though unlawful, unless the employee, at the time of obeying the directions, believed them to be unlawful.

(b) All awards made by a court or by the Division of Labor Standards Enforcement for reimbursement of necessary expenditures under this section shall carry interest at the same rate as judgments in civil actions. Interest shall accrue from the date on which the employee incurred the necessary expenditure or loss.

(c) For purposes of this section, the term "necessary expenditures or losses" shall include all reasonable costs, including, but not limited to, attorney's fees incurred by the employee enforcing the rights granted by this section.

(d) In addition to recovery of penalties under this section in a court action or proceedings pursuant to Section 98, the commissioner may issue a citation against an employer or other person acting on behalf of the employer who violates reimbursement obligations for an amount determined to be due to an employee under this section. The procedures for issuing, contesting, and enforcing judgments for citations or civil penalties issued by the commissioner shall be the same as those set forth in Section 1197.1. Amounts recovered pursuant to this section shall be paid to the affected employee. **Leg.H.** 1937 ch. 90, 2000 ch. 990, 2015 ch. 783 (AB 970) §4.

2000 Note: Nothing in this act is intended to establish the right of the Division of Labor Standards Enforcement to be awarded costs and attorney's fees. Stats. 2000 ch. 990 §2.

Ref.: Hanna § 4.01[2].

§2802.1. Applicability of indemnification to employer-required training.

(a)(1) Section 2802 applies to any expense or cost of any employer-provided or employer-required educational program or training for an employee providing direct patient care or an applicant for direct patient care employment. Those expenses or costs shall constitute a necessary expenditure or loss incurred by the employee in direct consequence of the discharge of the employee's duties, as that phrase is used in Section 2802.

(2) For purposes of this section, "employer-provided or employer-required educational program or training" includes, but is not limited to, residencies, orientations, or competency validations necessary for direct patient care employment. "Employer-provided or employer-required educational program or training" does not include either of the following:

(A) Requirements for a license, registration, or certification necessary to legally practice in a specific employee classification to provide direct patient care.

(B) Education or training that is voluntarily undertaken by the employee or applicant solely at their discretion.

(b) An employer, or any person acting on behalf of the employer, shall not retaliate against an applicant for employment or employee for refusing to enter into a contract or agreement that violates subdivision (a).

(c) This section shall only apply to applicants for employment and employees providing direct patient care for an employer for a "general acute care hospital," as defined in subdivision (a) of Section 1250 of the Health and Safety Code.

(d) In addition to injunctive relief and any other remedies available, a court shall award, in any action brought pursuant to this section, a prevailing plaintiff reasonable attorney's fees and costs.

(e) This section is declaratory of and clarifies existing law with respect to employer-required training for employees. **Leg.H.** 2020 ch. 351 (AB 2588) §2.

§2803. Death of employee; survivor's rights.

When death, whether instantaneously or otherwise, results from an injury to an employee caused by the want of ordinary or reasonable care of an employer or of any officer, agent, a servant of the employer, the personal representative of such employee shall have a right of action therefor against such employer, and may recover damages in respect thereof, for and on behalf of the surviving spouse, children, dependent parents, and dependent brothers and sisters, in order of precedence as stated, but no more than one action shall be brought for such recovery.

§2803.4. Health benefits under ERISA; no reduction of benefits for Medi-Cal or medicaid coverage.

(a) Any employer providing health benefits under the Employee Retirement Income Security Act of 1974 (29 U.S.C. Sec. 1001, et seq.) shall not provide an exception for other coverage where the other coverage is entitlement to Medi-Cal benefits under Chapter 7 (commencing with Section 14000) or Chapter 8 (commencing with Section 14200) of Part 3 of Division 9 of the Welfare and Institutions Code, or medicaid benefits under Subchapter 19 (commencing with Section 1396) of Chapter 7 of Title 42 of the United States Code. Any employer providing health benefits under the Employee Retirement Income Security Act of 1974 shall not provide an exception for the Medi-Cal or medicaid benefits.

(b) Any employer providing health benefits under the Employee Retirement Income Security Act of 1974 shall not provide that the benefits payable are subject to reduction if the individual insured has entitlement to Medi-Cal or medicaid benefits.

(c) Any employer providing health benefits under the Employee Retirement Income Security Act of 1974 shall not provide an exception for enrollment for benefits because of an applicant's entitlement to Medi-Cal benefits under Chapter 7 (commencing with Section 14000) or Chapter 8 (commencing with Section 14200) of Part 3 of Division 9 of the Welfare and Institutions Code, or medicaid benefits under Subchapter 19 (commencing with Section 1396) of Chapter 7 of Title 42 of the United States Code.

(d) The State Department of Health Services shall consider health benefits available under the Employee Retirement Income Security Act of 1974 in determining legal liability of any third party for medical expenses incurred by a Medi-Cal or medicaid recipient under Section 14124.90 of the Welfare and Institutions Code and Subchapter 19 (commencing with Section 1396) of Chapter 7 of Title 42 of the United States Code. **Leg.H.** 1994 ch. 147, effective July 11, 1994.

§2803.5. Compliance with provisions on health care coverage of children.

Any employer who offers health care coverage, including employers and insurers, shall comply with the standards set forth in Chapter 7 (commencing with Section 3750) of Part 1 of Division 9 of the Family Code and Section 14124.94 of the Welfare and Institutions Code. **Leg.H.** 1994 ch. 147, effective July 11, 1994, 1996 ch. 1062.

§2804. Waiver of benefits as null and void.

Any contract or agreement, express or implied, made by any employee to waive the benefits of this article or any part thereof, is null and void and this article shall not deprive any employee or his personal representative of any right or remedy to which he is entitled under the laws of this State.

§2806. Employer discontinuing coverage; notice.

(a) No employer, whether private or public, shall discontinue coverage for medical, surgical, or hospital benefits for employees unless the employer has notified and advised all covered employees in writing of any discontinuation of coverage, inclusive of nonrenewal and cancellation, but not inclusive of employment termination or cases in which substitute coverage has been provided, at least 15 days in advance of such discontinuation.

(b) If coverage is provided by a third party, failure of the employer to give the necessary notice shall not require the third party to continue the coverage beyond the date it would otherwise terminate.

(c) This section shall not apply to any employee welfare benefit plan that is subject to the Employee Retirement Income Security Act of 1974. **Leg.H.** 1992 ch. 722, effective September 15, 1992.

§2807. Notification to former employees of availability of continued medical coverage.

(a) All employers, whether private or public, shall provide notification to former employees, along with the notification required by federal law pursuant to the Consolidated Omnibus Budget Reconciliation Act of 1985 (Public Law 99-272), of the availability of continued coverage for medical, surgical, or hospital benefits, a standardized written description of the Health Insurance Premium Program established by the State Department of Health Services pursuant to Section 120835 of the Health and Safety Code and Section 14124.91 of the Welfare and Institutions Code. The employer shall utilize the standardized written description prepared by the State Department of Health Services pursuant to subdivision (b).

(b) The State Department of Health Services shall prepare and make available, on request, a standardized written description of the Health Insurance Premium Program, at cost. **Leg.H.** 1992 ch. 722, effective September 15, 1992, 1996 ch. 1023, effective September 29, 1996.

§2809. Employer-managed deferred compensation plans—Risks; summary of financial condition.

(a) Any employer, whether private or public, that offers its employees an employer-managed deferred compensation plan shall provide to each employee, prior to the employee's enrollment in the plan, written notice of the reasonably foreseeable financial risks accompanying participation in the plan, historical information to date as to the performance of the investments or funds available under the plan, and an annual balance sheet, annual audit, or similar document that describes the employer's financial condition as of a date no earlier than the immediately preceding year.

(b) Within 30 days after the end of each quarter of the calendar year, the employer, who directly manages the investments of a deferred compensation plan, shall provide, to each employee enrolled in a deferred compensation plan offered by the employer, a written report summarizing the current financial condition of the employer, summarizing the financial performance during the preceding quarter of each investment or fund available under the plan, and describing the actual performance of the employee's funds that are invested in each investment or fund in the plan.

(c) The obligations described in subdivisions (a) and (b) may be performed by a plan manager designated by the employer, who may contract with an investment manager for that purpose.

(d) If an employee is enrolled in a deferred compensation plan that is self-directed through a financial institution, the requirements set forth in this section shall be deemed to have been met. **Leg.H.** 1996 ch. 1160.

§2810. Persons contracting for specified labor or services without providing sufficient funds for compliance with applicable laws or regulations subject to liability and civil penalties; rebuttable presumption; exceptions.

(a) A person or entity shall not enter into a contract or agreement for labor or services with a construction, farm labor, garment, janitorial, security guard, or warehouse contractor, where the person or entity knows or should know that the contract or agreement does not include funds sufficient to allow the contractor to comply with all applicable local, state, and federal laws or regulations governing the labor or services to be provided.

(b) There is a rebuttable presumption affecting the burden of proof that there has been no violation of subdivision (a) where the contract or agreement with a construction, farm labor, garment, janitorial, security guard, or warehouse contractor meets all of the requirements in subdivision (d).

(c) Subdivision (a) does not apply to a person or entity who executes a collective bargaining agreement covering the workers employed under the contract or agreement, or to a person who enters into a contract or agreement for labor or services to be performed on his or her home residences, provided that a family member resides in the residence or residences for which the labor or services are to be performed for at least a part of the year.

(d) To meet the requirements of subdivision (b), a contract or agreement with a construction, farm labor, garment, janitorial, security guard, or warehouse contractor for labor or services shall be in writing, in a single document, and contain all of the following provisions, in addition to any other provisions that may be required by regulations adopted by the Labor Commissioner from time to time:

(1) The name, address, and telephone number of the person or entity and the construction, farm labor, garment, janitorial, security guard, or warehouse contractor through whom the labor or services are to be provided.

(2) A description of the labor or services to be provided and a statement of when those services are to be commenced and completed.

(3) The employer identification number for state tax purposes of the construction, farm labor, garment, janitorial, security guard, or warehouse contractor.

(4) The workers' compensation insurance policy number and the name, address, and telephone number of the insurance carrier of the construction, farm labor, garment, janitorial, security guard, or warehouse contractor.

(5) The vehicle identification number of any vehicle that is owned by the construction, farm labor, garment, janitorial, security guard, or warehouse contractor and used for transportation in connection with any service provided pursuant to the contract or agreement, the number of the vehicle liability insurance policy that covers the vehicle, and the name, address, and telephone number of the insurance carrier.

(6) The address of any real property to be used to house workers in connection with the contract or agreement.

(7) The total number of workers to be employed under the contract or agreement, the total amount of all wages to be paid, and the date or dates when those wages are to be paid.

(8) The amount of the commission or other payment made to the construction, farm labor, garment, janitorial, security guard, or warehouse contractor for services under the contract or agreement.

(9) The total number of persons who will be utilized under the contract or agreement as independent contractors, along with a list of the current local, state, and federal contractor license identification numbers that the independent contractors are required to have under local, state, or federal laws or regulations.

(10) The signatures of all parties, and the date the contract or agreement was signed.

(e)(1) To qualify for the rebuttable presumption set forth in subdivision (b), a material change to the terms and conditions of a contract or agreement between a person or entity and a construction, farm labor, garment, janitorial, security guard, or warehouse contractor must be in writing, in a single document, and contain all of the provisions listed in subdivision (d) that are affected by the change.

(2) If a provision required to be contained in a contract or agreement pursuant to paragraph (7) or (9) of subdivision (d) is unknown at the time the contract or agreement is executed, the best estimate available at that time is sufficient to satisfy the requirements of subdivision (d). If an estimate is used in place of actual figures in accordance with this paragraph, the parties to the contract or agreement have a continuing duty to ascertain the information required pursuant to paragraph (7) or (9) of subdivision (d) and to reduce that information to writing in accordance with the requirements of paragraph (1) once that information becomes known.

(f) A person or entity who enters into a contract or agreement referred to in subdivisions (d) or (e) shall keep a copy of the written contract or agreement for a period of not less than four years following the termination of the contract or agreement. Upon the request of the Labor Commissioner, any person or entity who enters into the contract or agreement shall provide to the Labor Commissioner a copy of the provisions of the contract or agreement, and any other documentation, related to paragraphs (1) to (10), inclusive, of subdivision (d). Documents obtained pursuant to this section are exempt from disclosure under the California Public Records Act (Chapter 3.5 (commencing with Section 6250) of Division 7 of Title 1 of the Government Code).

(g)(1) An employee aggrieved by a violation of subdivision (a) may file an action for damages to recover the greater of all of his or her actual damages or two hundred fifty dollars ($250) per employee per violation for an initial violation and one thousand dollars ($1,000) per employee for each subsequent violation, and, upon prevailing in an action brought pursuant to this section, may recover costs and reasonable attorney's fees. An action under this section shall not be maintained unless it is pleaded and proved that an employee was injured as a result of a violation of a labor law or regulation in connection with the performance of the contract or agreement.

(2) An employee aggrieved by a violation of subdivision (a) may also bring an action for injunctive relief and, upon prevailing, may recover costs and reasonable attorney's fees.

(h) The phrase "construction, farm labor, garment, janitorial, security guard, or warehouse contractor" includes any person, as defined in this code, whether or not licensed, who is acting in the capacity of a construction, farm labor, garment, janitorial, security guard, or warehouse contractor.

(i)(1) The term "knows" includes the knowledge, arising from familiarity with the normal facts and circumstances of the business activity engaged in, that the contract or agreement does not include funds sufficient to allow the contractor to comply with applicable laws.

(2) The phrase "should know" includes the knowledge of any additional facts or information that would make a reasonably prudent person undertake to inquire whether, taken together, the contract or agreement contains sufficient funds to allow the contractor to comply with applicable laws.

(3) A failure by a person or entity to request or obtain any information from the contractor that is required by any applicable statute or by the contract or agreement between them, constitutes knowledge of that information for purposes of this section.

(j) For the purposes of this section, "warehouse" means a facility the primary operation of which is the storage or distribution of general merchandise, refrigerated goods, or other products. **Leg.H.** 2003 ch. 908 (SB 179), 2012 ch. 813 (AB 1855) §1.

Labor

§2810.3. Definitions.

(a) As used in this section:

(1)(A) "Client employer" means a business entity, regardless of its form, that obtains or is provided workers to perform labor within its usual course of business from a labor contractor.

(B) "Client employer" does not include any of the following:

(i) A business entity with a workforce of fewer than 25 workers, including those hired directly by the client employer and those obtained from, or provided by, any labor contractor.

(ii) A business entity with five or fewer workers supplied by a labor contractor or labor contractors to the client employer at any given time.

(iii) The state or any political subdivision of the state, including any city, county, city and county, or special district.

(2) "Labor" has the same meaning provided by Section 200.

(3) "Labor contractor" means an individual or entity that supplies, either with or without a contract, a client employer with workers to perform labor within the client employer's usual course of business. "Labor contractor" does not include any of the following:

(A) A bona fide nonprofit, community-based organization that provides services to workers.

(B) A bona fide labor organization or apprenticeship program or hiring hall operated pursuant to a collective bargaining agreement.

(C) A motion picture payroll services company, as defined in subparagraph (A) of paragraph (4) of subdivision (f) of Section 679 of the Unemployment Insurance Code.

(D) A third party who is a party to an employee leasing arrangement, as defined by Rule 4 of Section V of the California Workers' Compensation Experience Rating Plan-1995 (Section 2353.1 of Title 10 of the California Code of Regulations), as it read on January 1, 2014, except those arrangements described in subrule d of Rule 4 of Section V, if the employee leasing arrangement contractually obligates the client employer to assume all civil legal responsibility and civil liability under this act.

(4) "Wages" has the same meaning provided by Section 200 and all sums payable to an employee or the state based upon any failure to pay wages, as provided by law.

(5) "Worker" does not include an employee who is exempt from the payment of an overtime rate of compensation for executive, administrative, and professional employees pursuant to wage orders by the Industrial Welfare Commission described in Section 515.

(6) "Usual course of business" means the regular and customary work of a business, performed within or upon the premises or worksite of the client employer.

(b) A client employer shall share with a labor contractor all civil legal responsibility and civil liability for all workers supplied by that labor contractor for both of the following:

(1) The payment of wages.

(2) Failure to secure valid workers' compensation coverage as required by Section 3700.

(c) A client employer shall not shift to the labor contractor any legal duties or liabilities under Division 5 (commencing with Section 6300) with respect to workers supplied by the labor contractor.

(d) At least 30 days prior to filing a civil action against a client employer for violations covered by this section, a worker or the worker's representative shall notify the client employer of violations under subdivision (b).

(e) Neither the client employer nor the labor contractor may take any adverse action against any worker for providing notification of violations or filing a claim or civil action.

(f) The provisions of subdivisions (b) and (c) are in addition to, and shall be supplemental of, any other theories of liability or requirement established by statute or common law.

(g) This section does not prohibit a client employer from establishing, exercising, or enforcing by contract any otherwise lawful remedies against a labor contractor for liability created by acts of a labor contractor.

(h) This section does not prohibit a labor contractor from establishing, exercising, or enforcing by contract any otherwise lawful remedies against a client employer for liability created by acts of a client employer.

(i) Upon request by a state enforcement agency or department, a client employer or a labor contractor shall provide to the agency or department any information within its possession, custody, or control required to verify compliance with applicable state laws. Upon request, these records shall be made available promptly for inspection, and the state agency or department shall be permitted to copy them. This subdivision does not require the disclosure of information that is not otherwise required to be disclosed by employers upon request by a state enforcement agency or department.

(j) The Labor Commissioner may adopt regulations and rules of practice and procedure necessary to administer and enforce the provisions of subdivisions (b) and (i) that are under the Labor Commissioner's jurisdiction.

(k) The Division of Occupational Safety and Health may adopt regulations and rules of practice and procedure necessary to administer and enforce the provisions of subdivisions (c) and (i) that are under its jurisdiction.

(*l*) The Employment Development Department may adopt regulations and rules of practice and procedure necessary to administer and enforce the provisions of subdivisions (b) and (i) that are under its jurisdiction.

(m) A waiver of this section is contrary to public policy, and is void and unenforceable.

(n) This section does not impose individual liability on a homeowner for labor or services received at the home or the owner of a home-based business for labor or services received at the home.

(o) This section does not impose liability on a client employer for the use of an independent contractor other than a labor contractor or to change the definition of independent contractor.

(p) This section does not impose liability on the following:

(1) A client employer that is not a motor carrier of property based solely on the employer's use of a third-party

motor carrier of property with interstate or intrastate operating authority to ship or receive freight.

(2) A client employer that is a motor carrier of property subcontracting with, or otherwise engaging, another motor carrier of property to provide transportation services using its own employees and commercial motor vehicles, as defined in Section 34601 of the Vehicle Code.

(3) A client employer that is not a household mover based solely on the employer's use of a third-party household mover permitted by the Bureau of Household Goods and Services pursuant to Chapter 3.1 (commencing with Section 19225) of Division 8 of the Business and Professions Code to move household goods.

(4) A client employer that is a household mover permitted by the Bureau of Household Goods and Services pursuant to Chapter 3.1 (commencing with Section 19225) of Division 8 of the Business and Professions Code subcontracting with, or otherwise engaging, another permitted household mover to provide transportation of household goods using its own employees and motor vehicles, as defined in former Section 5108 of the Public Utilities Code.

(5) A client employer that is a cable operator, as defined by Section 5830 of the Public Utilities Code, a direct-to-home satellite service provider, or a telephone corporation, as defined by Section 234 of the Public Utilities Code, based upon its contracting with a company to build, install, maintain, or perform repair work utilizing the employees and vehicles of the contractor if the name of the contractor is visible on employee uniforms and vehicles.

(6) A motor club holding a certificate of authority issued pursuant to Chapter 2 (commencing with Section 12160) of Part 5 of Division 2 of the Insurance Code when it contracts with third parties to provide motor club services utilizing the employees and vehicles of the third-party contractor if the name of the contractor is visible on the contractor's vehicles. **Leg.H.** 2014 ch. 728 (AB 1897) §1, 2015 ch. 792 (AB 1509) §3, 2019 ch. 643 (SB 358) §1.

Ref.: Hanna § 3.145; Herlick Handbook § 3.9.

§2810.4. Port drayage motor carriers; unsatisfied court judgments; notification; joint and several liability; definitions.

(a) As used in this section:

(1) "Commercial driver" means a person who holds a valid commercial driver's license who is hired or contracted to provide port drayage services either as an independent contractor or an employee driver.

(2)(A) "Customer" means a business entity, regardless of its form, that engages or uses a port drayage motor carrier to perform port drayage services on the customer's behalf, whether the customer directly engages or uses a port drayage motor carrier or indirectly engages or uses a port drayage motor carrier through the use of an agent, including, but not limited to, a freight forwarder, motor transportation broker, ocean carrier, or other motor carrier.

(B) "Customer" does not include any of the following:

(i) A business entity with a workforce of fewer than 25 workers, including those hired directly by the customer or through a temporary employer or labor contractor.

(ii) The state or any political subdivision of the state, including any city, county, city and county, or special district.

(iii) A business entity, including, but not limited to, a marine terminal operator, who is not a customer, and who, incidental to the transportation of the freight for the customer, receives, makes available, or exchanges intermodal equipment, loaded or unloaded, or conducts any other transaction of equipment subject to an equipment interchange agreement with a motor carrier who is a signatory to an equipment interchange agreement.

(3) "Labor" has the same meaning provided by Section 200.

(4)(A) "Port drayage motor carrier" means an individual or entity that hires or engages commercial drivers in the port drayage industry.

(B) "Port drayage motor carrier" also means a registered owner, lessee, licensee, or bailee of a commercial motor vehicle, as defined in subdivision (b) of Section 15210 of the Vehicle Code, that operates or directs the operation of a commercial motor vehicle by a commercial driver on a for-hire or not-for-hire basis to perform port drayage services in the port drayage industry.

(C) "Port drayage motor carrier" also means an entity or individual who succeeds in the interest and operation of a predecessor port drayage motor carrier consistent with the provisions of Section 2684.

(5) "Port" means any sea or river port located in this state.

(6) "Port drayage services" means the movement within California of cargo or intermodal equipment by a commercial motor vehicle whose point-to-point movement has either its origin or destination at a port, including any interchange of power units, chassis, or intermodal containers, or the switching of port drayage drivers that occurs during the movement of that freight. It shall not include employees performing the intra-port or inter-port movement of cargo or cargo handling equipment under the control of their employers.

(7) "Wages" has the same meaning provided by Section 200 and all sums payable to an employee or the state based upon any failure to pay wages, as provided by law.

(b)(1) The Division of Labor Standards Enforcement shall post on its Internet Web site the names, addresses, and essential information for any port drayage motor carrier with any unsatisfied final court judgment, tax assessment, or tax lien that may be released to the public under federal and state disclosure laws, including any order, decision, or award obtained by a public or private person or entity pursuant to Section 98.1 finding that a port drayage motor carrier has engaged in illegal conduct including failure to pay wages, imposing unlawful expenses on employees, failure to remit payroll taxes, failure to provide workers' compensation insurance, or misclassification of employees as independent contractors with regard to a port drayage commercial driver. The Division of Labor Standards Enforcement shall update the Internet Web site monthly by the fifth day of each month. The Division of Labor Standards Enforcement shall not place the information on the Internet Web site until the period for all judicial appeals has expired. This posting shall be removed within 15 business days after the Division of Labor Standards Enforcement

Labor

determines there has been full payment of the unsatisfied judgment or that the port drayage motor carrier has entered into an approved settlement dispensing of the judgment.

(2) No less than 15 business days prior to posting on its Internet Web site the names, addresses, and essential information for any port drayage motor carrier pursuant to paragraph (1), the Division of Labor Standards Enforcement shall provide notification by certified mail to the port drayage motor carrier which, at a minimum, shall include all of the following:

(A) The name, email address, and telephone number of a contact person at the division.

(B) The alleged conduct and a copy of the unsatisfied court judgment, assessment, order, decision, or award.

(C) A copy of the regulations or rules of practice or procedure adopted pursuant to subdivision (k) or (*l*) for removal of the posting.

(3) A customer that, as part of its business, engages or uses a port drayage motor carrier that is on the list established pursuant to paragraph (1) to perform port drayage services shall share with the motor carrier or the motor carrier's successor all civil legal responsibility and civil liability owed to a port drayage driver for port drayage services obtained after the date the motor carrier appeared on the list, meaning joint and several liability with the motor carrier for the full amount of unpaid wages, unreimbursed expenses, damages and penalties, including applicable interest, which are found due for all of the following:

(A) Minimum, regular, or premium wages that are unpaid by the motor carrier, including any wages that are found due under Section 226.7, 227.3, or 246.

(B) Unlawful deductions by the motor carrier from wages pursuant to Section 2802.

(C) Out-of-pocket business expenses incurred by the commercial driver that are not reimbursed by the motor carrier as required pursuant to Section 2802.

(D) Civil penalties for the failure to secure valid workers' compensation coverage as required by Section 3700.

(E) Damages or penalties as provided for by law that are due to the commercial driver or the state based upon the failure of the motor carrier to pay wages owed, including those set forth under Sections 203, 226, 226.8, 248.5, 558, 1194.2, and 1197.1.

(F) Applicable interest due for any sum described above.

(4) Pursuant to paragraph (3), each and every customer that engages or uses a port drayage motor carrier to provide port drayage services in a given workweek shall be jointly and severally liable with the motor carrier for the full amount of all unpaid wages, unreimbursed expenses, damages, and penalties, including applicable interest, which are found owed by the motor carrier for that workweek. The customer shall be jointly and severally liable from the time the driver is dispatched to begin work on behalf of the customer until all tasks are completed incidental to that work, including the return of an unladen chassis or intermodal container to its point of origin, and the driver is ready to be dispatched to haul freight on behalf of another customer.

(c) A customer's liability under this section shall be determined by either one of the following:

(1) The Labor Commissioner, in an administrative proceeding pursuant to Section 98, de novo appeal under Section 98.2, or pursuant to the Labor Commissioner's citation authority under this code.

(2) By a court in a civil action brought by the Labor Commissioner, or by a commercial driver or his or her representative, where at least 30 business days prior to filing the civil action, the Labor Commissioner, or commercial driver or representative, notifies the customer of its potential joint and several liability for any of the wages, expenses, damages, or penalties listed in paragraph (3) of subdivision (b). No civil action for a violation or enforcement of this section shall be brought pursuant to Part 13 (commencing with Section 2698) of Division 2.

(d) The joint and several liability provided by this section shall not apply as follows:

(1) To customers who engage or use a port drayage motor carrier whose employees are covered by a bona fide collective bargaining agreement, if the agreement expressly provides for wages, hours of work, working conditions, a process to resolve disputes concerning nonpayment of wages, expenses, damages, and penalties listed in paragraph (3) of subdivision (b), including applicable interest, and a waiver of the joint and several liability provided by this section.

(2) Where the customer and port drayage motor carrier had an existing contract for port drayage services at the time a port drayage motor carrier is listed on the Internet Web site maintained by the Division of Labor Standards Enforcement and the customer wishes to terminate the agreement, joint and several liability shall not apply until the expiration of the existing contract or a period of 90 business days following the listing, whichever is shorter. This paragraph does not apply to contracts entered into, renegotiated, or extended after the date a port drayage motor carrier is listed on the Internet Web site.

(3) Where a port drayage motor carrier is not listed on the Division of Labor Standards Enforcement's Internet Web site pursuant to subdivision (b).

(4) Where a port drayage motor carrier satisfied the conditions for removal from the Internet Web site pursuant to paragraph (1) of subdivision (b) prior to the time period for which the joint and several liability is alleged.

(e) A port drayage motor carrier that provides port drayage services to a customer, prior to providing these services to the customer, shall furnish written notice to the customer of any unsatisfied final judgments against the motor carrier for unpaid wages, damages, unreimbursed expenses, and penalties, including applicable interest. The notice shall also provide the text of this section. The failure of the motor carrier to provide notice under this subdivision shall not be a defense to the joint and several liability provided by this section.

(f) A port drayage motor carrier that provides port drayage services to a customer shall provide, within 30 business days of entry of the judgment, written notice of any unsatisfied final judgments against the motor carrier for unpaid wages, damages, unreimbursed expenses, and penalties, including applicable interest, to any customer to which the motor carrier is presently providing port drayage services. The failure of the motor carrier to provide notice under this subdivision shall not be a defense to the joint and several liability provided by this section.

(g) A customer or port drayage motor carrier shall not take any adverse action against any commercial driver for providing notification of violations or filing a claim or civil action pertaining to unpaid wages, unreimbursed expenses, or the recovery of damages and penalties, including applicable interest.

(h) The remedies provided by this section are in addition to, and shall be supplemental of, any other theories of liability or requirement established by statute or common law.

(i) Two or more parties who are held jointly and severally liable under this section after a final judgment is rendered by the court shall not be prohibited from establishing, exercising, or enforcing by contract or otherwise, any lawful or equitable remedies, including, but not limited to, a right of contribution and indemnity against each other for liability created by acts of a port drayage motor carrier.

(j) Pursuant to the Labor Commissioner's citation authority, a customer or a port drayage motor carrier shall provide to the Labor Commissioner any information within its possession, custody, or control required to verify compliance with applicable state laws. Upon request, the records that contain this information shall be made available promptly for inspection, and the Labor Commissioner shall be permitted to copy them.

(k) The Labor Commissioner may adopt regulations and rules of practice and procedure necessary to administer and enforce the provisions of subdivisions (b) and (j) that are under his or her jurisdiction.

(*l*) The Employment Development Department may adopt regulations and rules of practice and procedure necessary to administer and enforce the provisions of subdivision (b) that are under its jurisdiction.

(m) A waiver of this section is contrary to public policy, and is void and unenforceable.

(n) The provisions of this section are severable. If any provision of this section or its application is held invalid, that invalidity shall not affect other provisions or applications that can be given effect without the invalid provision or application. **Leg.H.** 2018 ch. 702 (SB 1402) §2.

§2810.5. Required written notice; notification of changes.

(a)(1) At the time of hiring, an employer shall provide to each employee a written notice, in the language the employer normally uses to communicate employment-related information to the employee, containing the following information:

(A) The rate or rates of pay and basis thereof, whether paid by the hour, shift, day, week, salary, piece, commission, or otherwise, including any rates for overtime, as applicable.

(B) Allowances, if any, claimed as part of the minimum wage, including meal or lodging allowances.

(C) The regular payday designated by the employer in accordance with the requirements of this code.

(D) The name of the employer, including any "doing business as" names used by the employer.

(E) The physical address of the employer's main office or principal place of business, and a mailing address, if different.

(F) The telephone number of the employer.

(G) The name, address, and telephone number of the employer's workers' compensation insurance carrier.

(H) That an employee: may accrue and use sick leave; has a right to request and use accrued paid sick leave; may not be terminated or retaliated against for using or requesting the use of accrued paid sick leave; and has the right to file a complaint against an employer who retaliates.

(I) Any other information the Labor Commissioner deems material and necessary.

(2) The Labor Commissioner shall prepare a template that complies with the requirements of paragraph (1). The template shall be made available to employers in such manner as determined by the Labor Commissioner.

(3) If the employer is a temporary services employer, as defined in Section 201.3, the notice described in paragraph (1) must also include the name, the physical address of the main office, the mailing address if different from the physical address of the main office, and the telephone number of the legal entity for whom the employee will perform work, and any other information the Labor Commissioner deems material and necessary. The requirements of this paragraph do not apply to a security services company that is licensed by the Department of Consumer Affairs and that solely provides security services.

(b) An employer shall notify his or her employees in writing of any changes to the information set forth in the notice within seven calendar days after the time of the changes, unless one of the following applies:

(1) All changes are reflected on a timely wage statement furnished in accordance with Section 226.

(2) Notice of all changes is provided in another writing required by law within seven days of the changes.

(c) For purposes of this section, "employee" does not include any of the following:

(1) An employee directly employed by the state or any political subdivision thereof, including any city, county, city and county, or special district.

(2) An employee who is exempt from the payment of overtime wages by statute or the wage orders of the Industrial Welfare Commission.

(3) An employee who is covered by a valid collective bargaining agreement if the agreement expressly provides for the wages, hours of work, and working conditions of the employee, and if the agreement provides premium wage rates for all overtime hours worked and a regular hourly rate of pay for those employees of not less than 30 percent more than the state minimum wage. **Leg.H.** 2011 ch. 655 (AB 469) §12, 2012 ch. 844 (AB 1744) §3, 2014 ch. 317 (AB 1522) §4.

2014 Note: For legislative intent, see the 2014 Note following Lab C §249.

2011 Note: This act shall be known and may be cited as the Wage Theft Prevention Act of 2011. Stats. 2011 ch. 655 (AB 469) §1.

§2810.7. Notification of flexible spending accounts deadlines.

(a) An employer shall notify an employee who participates in a flexible spending account, including, but not limited to, a dependent care flexible spending account, a health flexible spending account, or adoption assistance flexible spending account, of any deadline to withdraw funds before the end of the plan year. Notice shall be by two different forms, one of which may be electronic.

(b) Notices made pursuant to subdivision (a) may include, but are not limited to the following:

(1) Electronic mail communication.

(2) Telephone communication.

(3) Text message notification.

(4) Postal mail notification.

(5) In-person notification. **Leg.H.** 2019 ch. 195 (AB 1554) §1.

DIVISION 4
WORKERS' COMPENSATION AND INSURANCE

PART 1
Scope and Operation

CHAPTER 1
GENERAL PROVISIONS

§3200. "Workmen's compensation" to become "workers' compensation."

The Legislature hereby declares its intent that the term "workmen's compensation" shall hereafter also be known as "workers' compensation." and that the "Workmen's Compensation Appeals Board" shall hereafter be known as the "Workers' Compensation Appeals Board." In furtherance of this policy it is the desire of the Legislature that references to the terms "workmen's compensation" and "Workmen's Compensation Appeals Board" in this code or elsewhere be changed to "workers' compensation" and "Workers' Compensation Appeals Board" when such laws are being amended for any purpose. This act is declaratory and not amendatory of existing law.

Ref.: Hanna § 4.06[1].

§3201. Purposes of Divisions 4 and 5 of Labor Code.

This division and Division 5 (commencing with Section 6300) are an expression of the police power and are intended to make effective and apply to a complete system of workers' compensation the provisions of Section 4 of Article XIV of the California Constitution.

Ref.: Hanna § 1.10; Herlick Handbook § 3.4.

§3201.5. Validity of collective bargaining agreements—Prohibitions; applicability; premium rate; filing with director; confidentiality.

(a) Except as provided in subdivisions (b) and (c), the Department of Industrial Relations and the courts of this state shall recognize as valid and binding any provision in a collective bargaining agreement between a private employer or groups of employers engaged in construction, construction maintenance, or activities limited to rock, sand, gravel, cement and asphalt operations, heavy-duty mechanics, surveying, and construction inspection and a union that is the recognized or certified exclusive bargaining representative that establishes any of the following:

(1) An alternative dispute resolution system governing disputes between employees and employers or their insurers that supplements or replaces all or part of those dispute resolution processes contained in this division, including, but not limited to, mediation and arbitration. Any system of arbitration shall provide that the decision of the arbiter or board of arbitration is subject to review by the appeals board in the same manner as provided for reconsideration of a final order, decision, or award made and filed by a workers' compensation administrative law judge pursuant to the procedures set forth in Article 1 (commencing with Section 5900) of Chapter 7 of Part 4 of Division 4, and the court of appeals pursuant to the procedures set forth in Article 2 (commencing with Section 5950) of Chapter 7 of Part 4 of Division 4, governing orders, decisions, or awards of the appeals board. The findings of fact, award, order, or decision of the arbitrator shall have the same force and effect as an award, order, or decision of a workers' compensation administrative law judge. Any provision for arbitration established pursuant to this section shall not be subject to Sections 5270, 5270.5, 5271, 5272, 5273, 5275, and 5277.

(2) The use of an agreed list of providers of medical treatment that may be the exclusive source of all medical treatment provided under this division.

(3) The use of an agreed, limited list of qualified medical evaluators and agreed medical evaluators that may be the exclusive source of qualified medical evaluators and agreed medical evaluators under this division.

(4) Joint labor management safety committees.

(5) A light-duty, modified job or return-to-work program.

(6) A vocational rehabilitation or retraining program utilizing an agreed list of providers of rehabilitation services that may be the exclusive source of providers of rehabilitation services under this division.

(b)(1) Nothing in this section shall allow a collective bargaining agreement that diminishes the entitlement of an employee to compensation payments for total or partial disability, temporary disability, vocational rehabilitation, or medical treatment fully paid by the employer as otherwise provided in this division. The portion of any agreement that violates this paragraph shall be declared null and void.

(2) The parties may negotiate any aspect of the delivery of medical benefits and the delivery of disability compensation to employees of the employer or group of employers that are eligible for group health benefits and nonoccupational disability benefits through their employer.

(c) Subdivision (a) shall apply only to the following:

(1) An employer developing or projecting an annual workers' compensation insurance premium, in California, of two hundred fifty thousand dollars ($250,000) or more, or any employer that paid an annual workers' compensation insurance premium, in California, of two hundred fifty thousand dollars ($250,000) in at least one of the previous three years.

(2) Groups of employers engaged in a workers' compensation safety group complying with Sections 11656.6 and 11656.7 of the Insurance Code, and established pursuant to a joint labor management safety committee or committees, that develops or projects annual workers'

Labor

compensation insurance premiums of two million dollars ($2,000,000) or more.

(3) Employers or groups of employers that are self-insured in compliance with Section 3700 that would have projected annual workers' compensation costs that meet the requirements of, and that meet the other requirements of, paragraph (1) in the case of employers, or paragraph (2) in the case of groups of employers.

(4) Employers covered by an owner or general contractor provided wrap-up insurance policy applicable to a single construction site that develops workers' compensation insurance premiums of two million dollars ($2,000,000) or more with respect to those employees covered by that wrap-up insurance policy.

(d) Employers and labor representatives who meet the eligibility requirements of this section shall be issued a letter by the administrative director advising each employer and labor representative that, based upon the review of all documents and materials submitted as required by the administrative director, each has met the eligibility requirements of this section.

(e) The premium rate for a policy of insurance issued pursuant to this section shall not be subject to the requirements of Section 11732 or 11732.5 of the Insurance Code.

(f) No employer may establish or continue a program established under this section until it has provided the administrative director with all of the following:

(1) Upon its original application and whenever it is renegotiated thereafter, a copy of the collective bargaining agreement and the approximate number of employees who will be covered thereby.

(2) Upon its original application and annually thereafter, a valid and active license where that license is required by law as a condition of doing business in the state within the industries set forth in subdivision (a) of Section 3201.5.

(3) Upon its original application and annually thereafter, a statement signed under penalty of perjury, that no action has been taken by any administrative agency or court of the United States to invalidate the collective bargaining agreement.

(4) The name, address, and telephone number of the contact person of the employer.

(5) Any other information that the administrative director deems necessary to further the purposes of this section.

(g) No collective bargaining representative may establish or continue to participate in a program established under this section unless all of the following requirements are met:

(1) Upon its original application and annually thereafter, it has provided to the administrative director a copy of its most recent LM-2 or LM-3 filing with the United States Department of Labor, along with a statement, signed under penalty of perjury, that the document is a true and correct copy.

(2) It has provided to the administrative director the name, address, and telephone number of the contact person or persons of the collective bargaining representative or representatives.

(h) Commencing July 1, 1995, and annually thereafter, the Division of Workers' Compensation shall report to the Director of Industrial Relations the number of collective bargaining agreements received and the number of employees covered by these agreements.

(i) The data obtained by the administrative director pursuant to this section shall be confidential and not subject to public disclosure under any law of this state. However, the Division of Workers' Compensation shall create derivative works pursuant to subdivision (h) based on the collective bargaining agreements and data. Those derivative works shall not be confidential, but shall be public. On a monthly basis the administrative director shall make available an updated list of employers and unions entering into collective bargaining agreements containing provisions authorized by this section. **Leg.H.** 1993 ch. 117, effective July 16, 1993, 1994 ch. 963, effective September 28, 1994, 1995 ch. 886, 2002 ch. 866 (AB 486), 2004 ch. 34 (SB 899), effective April 19, 2004, 2012 chs. 363 (SB 863) §8, 728 (SB 71) §118 (ch. 363 prevails; ch. 728 not effective).

2012 Note: For legislative findings, declarations, and applicability of Stats. 2012 ch. 363, see the 2012 Notes following Lab C §62.5.

2004 Note: The amendment to §3201.5 made by this act shall apply prospectively from the date of enactment of this act, regardless of the date of injury, unless otherwise specified, but shall not constitute good cause to reopen or rescind, alter, or amend any existing order, decision, or award of the Workers' Compensation Appeals Board. Stats. 2004 ch. 34 (SB 899) §47.

Ref.: 8 C.C.R. §§10200, 10201, 10202, 10203, 10203.1, 10203.2, 10204, 10865; Hanna §§ 1.04[1], [2], [4], 1.04A[2], 28.27; Herlick Handbook §§ 3.4, 14.4, 14.32.

§3201.7. Labor-management agreements—Criteria; applicability; requirements.

(a) Except as provided in subdivision (b), the Department of Industrial Relations and the courts of this state shall recognize as valid and binding any labor-management agreement that meets all of the following requirements:

(1) The labor-management agreement has been negotiated separate and apart from any collective bargaining agreement covering affected employees.

(2) The labor-management agreement is restricted to the establishment of the terms and conditions necessary to implement this section.

(3) The labor-management agreement has been negotiated in accordance with the authorization of the administrative director pursuant to subdivision (d), between an employer or groups of employers and a union that is the recognized or certified exclusive bargaining representative that establishes any of the following:

(A) An alternative dispute resolution system governing disputes between employees and employers or their insurers that supplements or replaces all or part of those dispute resolution processes contained in this division, including, but not limited to, mediation and arbitration. Any system of arbitration shall provide that the decision of the arbiter or board of arbitration is subject to review by the appeals board in the same manner as provided for reconsideration of a final order, decision, or award made and filed by a workers' compensation administrative law judge pursuant to the procedures set forth in Article 1 (commencing with Section 5900) of Chapter 7 of Part 4 of Division 4, and the court of appeals pursuant to the procedures set forth in Article 2 (commencing with Section 5950) of Chapter 7 of

Part 4 of Division 4, governing orders, decisions, or awards of the appeals board. The findings of fact, award, order, or decision of the arbitrator shall have the same force and effect as an award, order, or decision of a workers' compensation administrative law judge. Any provision for arbitration established pursuant to this section shall not be subject to Sections 5270, 5270.5, 5271, 5272, 5273, 5275, and 5277.

(B) The use of an agreed list of providers of medical treatment that may be the exclusive source of all medical treatment provided under this division.

(C) The use of an agreed, limited list of qualified medical evaluators and agreed medical evaluators that may be the exclusive source of qualified medical evaluators and agreed medical evaluators under this division.

(D) Joint labor management safety committees.

(E) A light-duty, modified job, or return-to-work program.

(F) A vocational rehabilitation or retraining program utilizing an agreed list of providers of rehabilitation services that may be the exclusive source of providers of rehabilitation services under this division.

(b)(1) Nothing in this section shall allow a labor-management agreement that diminishes the entitlement of an employee to compensation payments for total or partial disability, temporary disability, vocational rehabilitation, or medical treatment fully paid by the employer as otherwise provided in this division; nor shall any agreement authorized by this section deny to any employee the right to representation by counsel at all stages during the alternative dispute resolution process. The portion of any agreement that violates this paragraph shall be declared null and void.

(2) The parties may negotiate any aspect of the delivery of medical benefits and the delivery of disability compensation to employees of the employer or group of employers that are eligible for group health benefits and nonoccupational disability benefits through their employer.

(c) Subdivision (a) shall apply only to the following:

(1) An employer developing or projecting an annual workers' compensation insurance premium, in California, of fifty thousand dollars ($50,000) or more, and employing at least 50 employees, or any employer that paid an annual workers' compensation insurance premium, in California, of fifty thousand dollars ($50,000), and employing at least 50 employees in at least one of the previous three years.

(2) Groups of employers engaged in a workers' compensation safety group complying with Sections 11656.6 and 11656.7 of the Insurance Code, and established pursuant to a joint labor management safety committee or committees, that develops or projects annual workers' compensation insurance premiums of five hundred thousand dollars ($500,000) or more.

(3) Employers or groups of employers, including cities and counties, that are self-insured in compliance with Section 3700 that would have projected annual workers' compensation costs that meet the requirements of, and that meet the other requirements of, paragraph (1) in the case of employers, or paragraph (2) in the case of groups of employers.

(4) The State of California.

(d) Any recognized or certified exclusive bargaining representative in an industry not covered by Section 3201.5, may file a petition with the administrative director seeking permission to negotiate with an employer or group of employers to enter into a labor-management agreement pursuant to this section. The petition shall specify the bargaining unit or units to be included, the names of the employers or groups of employers, and shall be accompanied by proof of the labor union's status as the exclusive bargaining representative. The current collective bargaining agreement or agreements shall be attached to the petition. The petition shall be in the form designated by the administrative director. Upon receipt of the petition, the administrative director shall promptly verify the petitioner's status as the exclusive bargaining representative. If the petition satisfies the requirements set forth in this subdivision, the administrative director shall issue a letter advising each employer and labor representative of their eligibility to enter into negotiations, for a period not to exceed one year, for the purpose of reaching agreement on a labor-management agreement pursuant to this section. The parties may jointly request, and shall be granted, by the administrative director, an additional one-year period to negotiate an agreement.

(e) No employer may establish or continue a program established under this section until it has provided the administrative director with all of the following:

(1) Upon its original application and whenever it is renegotiated thereafter, a copy of the labor-management agreement and the approximate number of employees who will be covered thereby.

(2) Upon its original application and annually thereafter, a statement signed under penalty of perjury, that no action has been taken by any administrative agency or court of the United States to invalidate the labor-management agreement.

(3) The name, address, and telephone number of the contact person of the employer.

(4) Any other information that the administrative director deems necessary to further the purposes of this section.

(f) No collective bargaining representative may establish or continue to participate in a program established under this section unless all of the following requirements are met:

(1) Upon its original application and annually thereafter, it has provided to the administrative director a copy of its most recent LM-2 or LM-3 filing with the United States Department of Labor, where such filing is required by law, along with a statement, signed under penalty of perjury, that the document is a true and correct copy.

(2) It has provided to the administrative director the name, address, and telephone number of the contact person or persons of the collective bargaining representative or representatives.

(g) Commencing July 1, 2005, and annually thereafter, the Division of Workers' Compensation shall report to the Director of Industrial Relations the number of labor-management agreements received and the number of employees covered by these agreements.

(h) The data obtained by the administrative director pursuant to this section shall be confidential and not subject

Labor

to public disclosure under any law of this state. However, the Division of Workers' Compensation shall create derivative works pursuant to subdivision (g) based on the labor-management agreements and data. Those derivative works shall not be confidential, but shall be public. On a monthly basis, the administrative director shall make available an updated list of employers and unions entering into labor-management agreements authorized by this section. **Leg.H.** 2003 ch. 639 (SB 228) §14.7, 2004 ch. 34 (SB 899), effective April 19, 2004, 2012 chs. 363 (SB 863) §9, 728 (SB 71) §119 (ch. 363 prevails; ch. 728 not effective).

2012 Note: For legislative findings, declarations, and applicability of Stats. 2012 ch. 363, see the 2012 Notes following Lab C §62.5.

2004 Note: The amendment to §3201.7 made by this act shall apply prospectively from the date of enactment of this act, regardless of the date of injury, unless otherwise specified, but shall not constitute good cause to reopen or rescind, alter, or amend any existing order, decision, or award of the Workers' Compensation Appeals Board. Stats. 2004 ch. 34 (SB 899) §47.

Ref.: 8 C.C.R. §§10200, 10202, 10203, 10203.1, 10203.2, 10204, 10865; Hanna §§ 1.04[1], 1.04A; Herlick Handbook §§ 3.4, 14.4.

§3201.81. Collective bargaining agreements for licensed jockeys.

In the horse racing industry, the organization certified by the California Horse Racing Board to represent the majority of licensed jockeys pursuant to subdivision (b) of Section 19612.9 of the Business and Professions Code is the labor organization authorized to negotiate the collective bargaining agreement establishing an alternative dispute resolution system for licensed jockeys pursuant to Section 3201.7. **Leg.H.** 2003 ch. 884 (AB 1719), 2007 ch. 130 (AB 299) §184.

§3201.9. Reports under collective bargaining agreements; required provisions.

(a) On or before June 30, 2004, and biannually thereafter, the report required in subdivision (i) of Section 3201.5 and subdivision (h) of Section 3201.7 shall include updated loss experience for all employers and groups of employers participating in a program established under those sections. The report shall include updated data on each item set forth in subdivision (i) of Section 3201.5 and subdivision (h) of Section 3201.7 for the previous year for injuries in 2003 and beyond. Updates for each program shall be done for the original program year and for subsequent years. The insurers, the Department of Insurance, and the rating organization designated by the Insurance Commissioner pursuant to Article 3 (commencing with Section 11750) of Chapter 3 of Part 3 of Division 2 of the Insurance Code, shall provide the administrative director with any information that the administrative director determines is reasonably necessary to conduct the study.

(b) Commencing on and after June 30, 2004, the Insurance Commissioner, or the commissioner's designee, shall prepare for inclusion in the report required in subdivision (i) of Section 3201.5 and subdivision (h) of Section 3201.7 a review of both of the following:

(1) The adequacy of rates charged for these programs, including the impact of scheduled credits and debits.

(2) The comparative results for these programs with other programs not subject to Section 3201.5 or Section 3201.7.

(c) Upon completion of the report, the administrative director shall report the findings to the Legislature, the Department of Insurance, the designated rating organization, and the programs and insurers participating in the study.

(d) The data obtained by the administrative director pursuant to this section shall be confidential and not subject to public disclosure under any law of this state. **Leg.H.** 2002 ch. 6 (AB 749), 2004 ch. 34 (SB 899), effective April 19, 2004.

2004 Note: The amendment to §3201.9 made by this act shall apply prospectively from the date of enactment of this act, regardless of the date of injury, unless otherwise specified, but shall not constitute good cause to reopen or rescind, alter, or amend any existing order, decision, or award of the Workers' Compensation Appeals Board. Stats. 2004 ch. 34 (SB 899) §47.

Ref.: 8 C.C.R. §§10203, 10203.1, 10203.2, 10204.

§3202. Liberal construction of Divisions 4 and 5.

This division and Division 5 (commencing with Section 6300) shall be liberally construed by the courts with the purpose of extending their benefits for the protection of persons injured in the course of their employment.

Ref.: Hanna §§ 3.23, 4.05[1], 28.36[2][d]; Herlick Handbook §§ 1.01[1], 14.6.

§3202.5. Preponderance of evidence standard.

All parties and lien claimants shall meet the evidentiary burden of proof on all issues by a preponderance of the evidence in order that all parties are considered equal before the law. "Preponderance of the evidence" means that evidence that, when weighed with that opposed to it, has more convincing force and the greater probability of truth. When weighing the evidence, the test is not the relative number of witnesses, but the relative convincing force of the evidence. **Leg.H.** 1993 ch. 4, effective April 3, 1993, 2004 ch. 34 (SB 899), effective April 19, 2004.

2004 Note: The amendment to §3202.5 made by this act shall apply prospectively from the date of enactment of this act, regardless of the date of injury, unless otherwise specified, but shall not constitute good cause to reopen or rescind, alter, or amend any existing order, decision, or award of the Workers' Compensation Appeals Board. Stats. 2004 ch. 34 (SB 899) §47.

Ref.: Hanna §§ 3.05, 4.05[1], [2][a], 26.06[6]; Herlick Handbook §§ 10.03[2], 14.6.

§3203. Inapplicability of Divisions 4 and 5 to interstate commerce.

This division and Division 5 (commencing with Section 6300) do not apply to employers or employments which, according to law, are so engaged in interstate commerce as not to be subject to the legislative power of the state, nor to employees injured while they are so engaged, except in so far as these divisions are permitted to apply under the Constitution or laws of the United States.

Ref.: Hanna § 21.01[1], [3]; Herlick Handbook § 13.2.

§3204. Chapter's definitions to govern construction.

Unless the context otherwise requires, the definitions hereinafter set forth in this chapter shall govern the construction and meaning of the terms and phrases used in this division.

§3205. "Division."

"Division" means the Division of Workers' Compensation. **Leg.H.** 1994 chs. 146, 1097.

§3205.5. "Appeals board."

"Appeals board" means the Workers' Compensation Appeals Board of the Division of Workers' Compensation. **Leg.H.** 1994 chs. 146, 1097.

§3206. "Administrative director."

"Administrative director" means the Director of the Division of Workers' Compensation. **Leg.H.** 1994 chs. 146, 1097.

§3207. "Compensation."

"Compensation" means compensation under this division and includes every benefit or payment conferred by this division upon an injured employee, or in the event of his or her death, upon his or her dependents, without regard to negligence. **Leg.H.** 2004 ch. 34 (SB 899), effective April 19, 2004.

2004 Note: The amendment to §3207 made by this act shall apply prospectively from the date of enactment of this act, regardless of the date of injury, unless otherwise specified, but shall not constitute good cause to reopen or rescind, alter, or amend any existing order, decision, or award of the Workers' Compensation Appeals Board. Stats. 2004 ch. 34 (SB 899) §47.

Ref.: 8 C.C.R. §§10110, 10115; Hanna §§ 2.70[1], 10.01[1][b], 20.01[1][d], 22.02[6], 22.08[3][b], 35.03[1].

§3208. "Injury."

"Injury" includes any injury or disease arising out of the employment, including injuries to artificial members, dentures, hearing aids, eyeglasses and medical braces of all types; provided, however, that eyeglasses and hearing aids will not be replaced, repaired, or otherwise compensated for, unless injury to them is incident to an injury causing disability.

Ref.: 8 C.C.R. §§9767.1, 9811; Hanna § 4.01[2][a]; Herlick Handbook §§ 4.06[6], 8.19.

§3208.05. Injury to health care worker from preventative care.

(a) "Injury" includes a reaction to or a side effect arising from health care provided by an employer to a health care worker, which health care is intended to prevent the development or manifestation of any bloodborne disease, illness, syndrome, or condition recognized as occupationally incurred by Cal-OSHA, the federal Centers for Disease Control and Prevention, or other appropriate governmental entities. This section shall apply only to preventive health care that the employer provided to a health care worker under the following circumstances: (1) prior to an exposure because of risk of occupational exposure to such a disease, illness, syndrome, or condition, or (2) where the preventive care is provided as a consequence of a documented exposure to blood or bodily fluid containing blood that arose out of and in the course of employment. Such a disease, illness, syndrome, or condition includes, but is not limited to, hepatitis, and the human immunodeficiency virus. Such preventive health care, and any disability indemnity or other benefits required as a result of the preventive health care provided by the employer, shall be compensable under the workers' compensation system. The employer may require the health care worker to document that the employer provided the preventive health care and that the reaction or side effects arising from the preventive health care resulted in lost work time, health care costs, or other costs normally compensable under workers' compensation.

(b) The benefits of this section shall not be provided to a health care worker for a reaction to or side effect from health care intended to prevent the development of the human immunodeficiency virus if the worker claims a work-related exposure and if the worker tests positive within 48 hours of that exposure to a test to determine the presence of the human immunodeficiency virus.

(c) For purposes of this section, "health care worker" includes any person who is an employee of a provider of health care as defined in Section 56.05 of the Civil Code, and who is exposed to human blood or other bodily fluids contaminated with blood in the course of employment, including, but not limited to, a registered nurse, a licensed vocational nurse, a certified nurse aide, clinical laboratory technologist, dental hygienist, physician, janitor, and housekeeping worker. "Health care worker" does not include an employee who provides employee health services for an employer primarily engaged in a business other than providing health care. **Leg.H.** 1992 ch. 1085, 2013 ch. 444 (SB 138) §19.

Ref.: Hanna § 4.71; Herlick Handbook §§ 8.19, 8.22.

§3208.1. Specific and cumulative injuries.

An injury may be either: (a) "specific," occurring as the result of one incident or exposure which causes disability or need for medical treatment; or (b) "cumulative," occurring as repetitive mentally or physically traumatic activities extending over a period of time, the combined effect of which causes any disability or need for medical treatment. The date of a cumulative injury shall be the date determined under Section 5412.

Ref.: Hanna § 4.01[2][a]; Herlick Handbook § 8.23.

§3208.2. Combined injuries; separate determinations.

When disability, need for medical treatment, or death results from the combined effects of two or more injuries, either specific, cumulative, or both, all questions of fact and law shall be separately determined with respect to each such injury, including, but not limited to, the apportionment between such injuries of liability for disability benefits, the cost of medical treatment, and any death benefit.

Ref.: 8 C.C.R. §10401; Hanna §§ 8.02[3], 26.10[2]; Herlick Handbook § 8.23.

§3208.3. Threshold of compensability for psychiatric injury.

(a) A psychiatric injury shall be compensable if it is a mental disorder which causes disability or need for medical treatment, and it is diagnosed pursuant to procedures promulgated under paragraph (4) of subdivision (j) of Section 139.2 or, until these procedures are promulgated, it is diagnosed using the terminology and criteria of the American Psychiatric Association's Diagnostic and Statistical Manual of Mental Disorders, Third Edition-Revised, or the terminology and diagnostic criteria of other psychiatric diagnostic manuals generally approved and accepted nationally by practitioners in the field of psychiatric medicine.

(b)(1) In order to establish that a psychiatric injury is compensable, an employee shall demonstrate by a preponderance of the evidence that actual events of employment were predominant as to all causes combined of the psychiatric injury.

(2) Notwithstanding paragraph (1), in the case of employees whose injuries resulted from being a victim of a violent act or from direct exposure to a significant violent act, the employee shall be required to demonstrate by a preponderance of the evidence that actual events of employment were a substantial cause of the injury.

(3) For the purposes of this section, "substantial cause" means at least 35 to 40 percent of the causation from all sources combined.

(c) It is the intent of the Legislature in enacting this section to establish a new and higher threshold of compensability for psychiatric injury under this division.

(d) Notwithstanding any other provision of this division, no compensation shall be paid pursuant to this division for a psychiatric injury related to a claim against an employer unless the employee has been employed by that employer for at least six months. The six months of employment need not be continuous. This subdivision shall not apply if the psychiatric injury is caused by a sudden and extraordinary employment condition. Nothing in this subdivision shall be construed to authorize an employee, or the employee's dependents, to bring an action at law or equity for damages against the employer for a psychiatric injury, where those rights would not exist pursuant to the exclusive remedy doctrine set forth in Section 3602 in the absence of the amendment of this section by the act adding this subdivision.

(e) Where the claim for compensation is filed after notice of termination of employment or layoff, including voluntary layoff, and the claim is for an injury occurring prior to the time of notice of termination or layoff, no compensation shall be paid unless the employee demonstrates by a preponderance of the evidence that actual events of employment were predominant as to all causes combined of the psychiatric injury and one or more of the following conditions exist:

(1) Sudden and extraordinary events of employment were the cause of the injury.

(2) The employer has notice of the psychiatric injury under Chapter 2 (commencing with Section 5400) prior to the notice of termination or layoff.

(3) The employee's medical records existing prior to notice of termination or layoff contain evidence of treatment of the psychiatric injury.

(4) Upon a finding of sexual or racial harassment by any trier of fact, whether contractual, administrative, regulatory, or judicial.

(5) Evidence that the date of injury, as specified in Section 5411 or 5412, is subsequent to the date of the notice of termination or layoff, but prior to the effective date of the termination or layoff.

(f) For purposes of this section, an employee provided notice pursuant to Sections 44948.5, 44949, 44951, 44955, 44955.6, 72411, 87740, and 87743 of the Education Code shall be considered to have been provided a notice of termination or layoff only upon a district's final decision not to reemploy that person.

(g) A notice of termination or layoff that is not followed within 60 days by that termination or layoff shall not be subject to the provisions of this subdivision, and this subdivision shall not apply until receipt of a later notice of termination or layoff. The issuance of frequent notices of termination or layoff to an employee shall be considered a bad faith personnel action and shall make this subdivision inapplicable to the employee.

(h) No compensation under this division shall be paid by an employer for a psychiatric injury if the injury was substantially caused by a lawful, nondiscriminatory, good faith personnel action. The burden of proof shall rest with the party asserting the issue.

(i) When a psychiatric injury claim is filed against an employer, and an application for adjudication of claim is filed by an employer or employee, the division shall provide the employer with information concerning psychiatric injury prevention programs.

(j) An employee who is an inmate, as defined in subdivision (e) of Section 3351, or their family on behalf of an inmate, shall not be entitled to compensation for a psychiatric injury except as provided in subdivision (d) of Section 3370.

(k) An employee who is a patient, as defined in subdivision (h) of Section 3351, or their family on behalf of a patient, shall not be entitled to compensation for a psychiatric injury except as provided in subdivision (d) of Section 3370.1. **Leg.H.** 1991 ch. 115, effective July 16, 1991, 1993 ch. 118, effective July 16, 1993, ch. 1242, 1994 ch. 497, 2019 ch. 38 (SB 78) §32, effective June 27, 2019.

1989 Note: This section is applicable only to injuries occurring on or after January 1, 1990. Stats. 1989 ch. 893 §6.

Ref.: Hanna §§ 4.02[3][b]–[f], 4.65[1], 4.69[3][d]; Herlick Handbook §§ 6.02[3], [14], 8.19, 8.21; Lawyer's Guide to AMA *Guides* and Calif. Workers' Comp. §§ 2.06, 13.14.

§3208.4. Discovery requirements in proceedings involving injury arising from sexual conduct; nonadmissible evidence.

In any proceeding under this division involving an injury arising out of alleged conduct that constitutes sexual harassment, sexual assault, or sexual battery, any party seeking discovery concerning sexual conduct of the applicant with any person other than the defendant, whether consensual or nonconsensual or prior or subsequent to the alleged act complained of, shall establish specific facts showing good cause for that discovery on a noticed motion to the appeals board. The motion shall not be made or considered at an ex parte hearing.

The procedures set forth in Section 783 of the Evidence Code shall be followed if evidence of sexual conduct of the applicant is offered to attack his or her credibility. Opinion evidence, evidence of reputation, and evidence of specific instances of sexual conduct of the applicant with any person other than the defendant, or any of such evidence, is not admissible by the defendant to prove consent by or the absence of injury to the applicant, unless the injury alleged by the applicant is in the nature of loss of consortium. **Leg.H.** 1993 ch. 121, effective July 16, 1993.

1993 Note: Section 3208.4, as added by 1993 ch. 121, applies only to injuries occurring on or after January 1, 1994. Stats. 1993 ch. 121 §77.

Ref.: Herlick Handbook § 8.8.

§3209. "Damages."

"Damages" means the recovery allowed in an action at law as contrasted with compensation.

Ref.: Hanna § 2.70[1].

§3209.3. "Physician"; "psychologist"; "acupuncturist"; request for medical collaboration; acupuncturist unauthorized to determine disability

(a) "Physician" includes physicians and surgeons holding an M.D. or D.O. degree, psychologists, acupuncturists, optometrists, dentists, podiatrists, and chiropractic practitioners licensed by California state law and within the scope of their practice as defined by California state law.

(b) "Psychologist" means a licensed psychologist with a doctoral degree in psychology, or a doctoral degree deemed equivalent for licensure by the Board of Psychology pursuant to Section 2914 of the Business and Professions Code, and who either has at least two years of clinical experience in a recognized health setting or has met the standards of the National Register of the Health Service Providers in Psychology.

(c) When treatment or evaluation for an injury is provided by a psychologist, provision shall be made for appropriate medical collaboration when requested by the employer or the insurer.

(d) "Acupuncturist" means a person who holds an acupuncturist's certificate issued pursuant to Chapter 12 (commencing with Section 4925) of Division 2 of the Business and Professions Code.

(e) Nothing in this section shall be construed to authorize acupuncturists to determine disability for the purposes of Article 3 (commencing with Section 4650) of Chapter 2 of Part 2, or under Section 2708 of the Unemployment Insurance Code. **Leg.H.** 1992 ch. 824 §1, 1994 ch. 1118 §3, 1996 ch. 26 §1, 1997 ch. 98 §1.

Ref.: 8 C.C.R. §§9767.1, 9767.3, 9773, 9773.1, 9792.6; Hanna §§ 22.05[2], 22.09[5], 26.06[12]; Herlick Handbook §§ 1.02, 4.07[1], [3], 10.08[2]–[4].

§3209.4. Optometrists not physicians.

The inclusion of optometrists in Section 3209.3 does not imply any right or entitle any optometrist to represent, advertise, or hold himself out as a physician.

§3209.5. Medical, surgical, and hospital treatment.

Medical, surgical, and hospital treatment, including nursing, medicines, medical and surgical supplies, crutches, and apparatus, includes but is not limited to services and supplies by physical therapists, chiropractic practitioners, and acupuncturists, as licensed by California state law and within the scope of their practice as defined by law. **Leg.H.** 1998 ch. 440.

Ref.: 8 C.C.R. §9767.1; Herlick Handbook §§ 4.05[1], [3], 4.06[7], 4.07[1].

§3209.6. Chiropractors not physicians.

The inclusion of chiropractors in Sections 3209.3 and 3209.5 does not imply any right or entitle any chiropractor to represent, advertise, or hold himself out as a physician.

Labor

§3209.7. Agreements on other healing practices.

Treatment of injuries at the expense of the employer may also include, either in addition to or in place of medical, surgical, and hospital services, as specified in Section 3209.5, any other form of therapy, treatment, or healing practice agreed upon voluntarily in writing, between the employee and his employer. Such agreement may be entered into at any time after employment and shall be in a form approved by the Department of Industrial Relations, and shall include at least the following items:

(a) A description of the form of healing practice intended to be relied upon and designation of individuals and facilities qualified to administer it.

(b) The employee shall not by entering into such an agreement or by selecting such therapy, treatment or healing practice, waive any rights conferred upon him by law, or forfeit any benefits to which he might otherwise be entitled.

(c) The employer and the employee shall each reserve the right to terminate such agreement upon seven days written notice to the other party.

No liability shall be incurred by the employer under the provisions of this section, except as provided for in Chapter 3 (commencing with Section 3600), of this part.

Ref.: Herlick Handbook § 4.12.

§3209.8. Treatment by marriage and family therapists and clinical social workers.

Treatment reasonably required to cure or relieve from the effects of an injury shall include the services of marriage and family therapists, professional clinical counselors, and clinical social workers licensed by California state law and within the scope of their practice as defined by California state law if the injured person is referred to the marriage and family therapist, the professional clinical counselor, or the clinical social worker by a licensed physician and surgeon, with the approval of the employer, for treatment of a condition arising out of the injury. This section does not authorize marriage and family therapists, professional clinical counselors, or clinical social workers to determine disability for the purposes of Article 3 (commencing with Section 4650) of Chapter 2 of Part 2. The requirement of this section that the employer approve the referral by a licensed physician or surgeon shall not be construed to preclude reimbursement for self-procured treatment, found by the appeals board to be otherwise compensable pursuant to this division, if the employer has refused to authorize any treatment for the condition arising from the injury treated by the marriage and family therapist, professional clinical counselor, or clinical social worker. **Leg.H.** 1991 ch. 234, 2002 ch. 1013 (SB 2026), 2018 ch. 389 (AB 2296) §18.

Ref.: Herlick Handbook § 4.07[1], [3].

§3209.9. Acupuncturists not physicians or surgeons.

The inclusion of acupuncturists in Section 3209.3 does not imply any right or entitle any acupuncturist to represent, advertise, or hold himself or herself out as a physician or surgeon holding an M.D. or D.O. degree. **Leg.H.** 1997 ch. 98.

Ref.: Herlick Handbook § 4.07[1].

§3209.10. Physician assistant or nurse practitioner may provide treatment for work-related injury under supervision; supervising physician deemed treating physician.

(a) Medical treatment of a work-related injury required to cure or relieve the effects of the injury may be provided by a state licensed physician assistant or nurse practitioner, acting under the review or supervision of a physician and surgeon pursuant to standardized procedures or protocols within their lawfully authorized scope of practice. The reviewing or supervising physician and surgeon of the physician assistant or nurse practitioner shall be deemed to be the treating physician. For the purposes of this section, "medical treatment" includes the authority of the nurse practitioner or physician assistant to authorize the patient to receive time off from work for a period not to exceed three calendar days if that authority is included in a standardized procedure or protocol approved by the supervising physician. The nurse practitioner or physician assistant may cosign the Doctor's First Report of Occupational Injury or Illness. The treating physician shall make any determination of temporary disability and shall sign the report.

(b) The provision of subdivision (a) that requires the cosignature of the treating physician applies to this section only and it is not the intent of the Legislature that the requirement apply to any other section of law or to any other statute or regulation. Nothing in this section implies that a nurse practitioner or physician assistant is a physician as defined in Section 3209.3. **Leg.H.** 2001 ch. 229, 2004 ch. 100 (AB 2919).

2001 Notes: The addition of Section 3209.10 to the Labor Code made by this act does not constitute a change in, but is declaratory of, existing law and neither expands nor limits the scope of practice of nurse practitioners or physician assistants with regard to the delivery of care pursuant to Division 4 of the Labor Code. Stats. 2001 ch. 229 §2.

In enacting this act, the Legislature intends to abrogate the opinions expressed by the Administrative Director or the Division of Workers' Compensation as set forth in *Minnie Martin* v. *Los Angeles Unified School District,* AD No. 9786-4895, July 6, 1999, to the extent that it precluded a physician assistant from practicing within the scope of the protocol approved by the supervising physician and their lawful scope of practice. Stats. 2001 ch. 229 §3.

Ref.: Hanna § 5.02[2][a]; Herlick Handbook §§ 4.07[1], 4.08[2], 4.18[1].

§3210. "Persons."

"Persons" includes an individual, firm, voluntary association, or a public, or quasi public, or private corporation.

§3211. "Insurer."

"Insurer" includes the State Compensation Insurance Fund and any private company, corporation, mutual association, reciprocal or interinsurance exchange authorized under the laws of this State to insure employers against liability for compensation and any employer to whom a certificate of consent to self-insure has been issued.

§3211.5. "Firefighter," "firefighting member," or "member of a fire department."

For purposes of this division, whenever the term "firefighter," "firefighting member," and "member of a fire department" is used, the term shall include, but shall not be limited to, unless the context expressly provides otherwise, a person engaged in providing firefighting services who is an apprentice, volunteer, or employee on a partly paid or fully paid basis. **Leg.H.** 2002 ch. 870 (AB 1847).

Ref.: Herlick Handbook § 2.5.

§3211.9. "Disaster council."

"Disaster council" means a public agency established by ordinance which is empowered to register and direct the activities of disaster service workers within the area of the county, city, city and county, or any part thereof, and is thus, because of such registration and direction, acting as an instrumentality of the state in aid of the carrying out of the general governmental functions and policy of the state.

§3211.91. "Accredited disaster council."

"Accredited disaster council" means a disaster council that is certified by the Office of Emergency Services as conforming with the rules and regulations established by the office pursuant to Article 10 (commencing with Section 8610) of Chapter 7 of Division 1 of Title 2 of the Government Code. A disaster council remains accredited only while the certification of the Office of Emergency Services is in effect and is not revoked. **Leg.H.** 1971 ch. 438 §139, 2006 ch. 502 (AB 1889) §9, 2010 ch. 618 (AB 2791) §187, 2013 ch. 352 (AB 1317) §400, effective September 26, 2013, operative July 1, 2013.

Ref.: Hanna § 3.117[2][b].

§3211.92. "Disaster service worker."

(a) "Disaster service worker" means any natural person who is registered with an accredited disaster council or a state agency for the purpose of engaging in disaster service pursuant to the California Emergency Services Act without pay or other consideration.

(b) "Disaster service worker" includes public employees performing disaster work that is outside the course and scope of their regular employment without pay and also includes any unregistered person impressed into service during a state of war emergency, a state of emergency, or a local emergency by a person having authority to command the aid of citizens in the execution of his or her duties.

(c) Persons registered with a disaster council at the time that council becomes accredited need not reregister in order to be entitled to the benefits provided by Chapter 10 (commencing with Section 4351).

(d) "Disaster service worker" does not include any member registered as an active firefighting member of any regularly organized volunteer fire department, having official recognition, and full or partial support of the county, city, or district in which the fire department is located. **Leg.H.** 2000 ch. 506.

Ref.: Hanna §§ 3.117[1], 21.07[4].

§3211.93. "Disaster service."

"Disaster service" means all activities authorized by and carried on pursuant to the California Emergency Services Act, including training necessary or proper to engage in such activities.

§3211.93a. Exception to "disaster service."

"Disaster service" does not include any activities or functions performed by a person if the accredited disaster council with which that person is registered receives a fee or other compensation for the performance of those activities or functions by that person. **Leg.H.** 2000 ch. 506.

§3212. Hernia; heart trouble; pneumonia.

In the case of members of a sheriff's office or the California Highway Patrol, district attorney's staff of inspectors and investigators or of police or fire departments of cities, counties, cities and counties, districts or other public or municipal corporations or political subdivisions, whether those members are volunteer, partly paid, or fully paid, and in the case of active firefighting members of the Department of Forestry and Fire Protection whose duties require firefighting or of any county forestry or firefighting department or unit, whether voluntary, fully paid, or partly paid, and in the case of members of the warden service of the Wildlife Protection Branch of the Department of Fish and Game whose principal duties consist of active law enforcement service, excepting those whose principal duties are clerical or otherwise do not clearly fall within the scope of active law enforcement service such as stenographers, telephone operators, and other officeworkers, the term "injury" as used in this act includes hernia when any part of the hernia develops or manifests itself during a period while the member is in the service in the office, staff, division, department, or unit, and in the case of members of fire departments, except those whose principal duties are clerical, such as stenographers, telephone operators, and other officeworkers, and in the case of county forestry or firefighting departments, except those whose principal duties are clerical, such as stenographers, telephone operators, and other officeworkers, and in the case of active firefighting members of the Department of Forestry and Fire Protection whose duties require firefighting, and in the case of members of the warden service of the Wildlife Protection Branch of the Department of Fish and Game whose principal duties consist of active law enforcement service, excepting those whose principal duties are clerical or otherwise do not clearly fall within the scope of active law enforcement service such as stenographers, telephone operators, and other officeworkers, the term "injury" includes pneumonia and heart trouble that develops or manifests itself during a period while the member is in the service of the office, staff, department, or unit. In the case of regular salaried county or city and county peace officers, the term "injury" also includes any hernia that manifests itself or develops during a period while the officer is in the service. The compensation that is awarded for the hernia, heart trouble, or pneumonia shall include full hospital, surgical, medical treatment, disability indemnity, and death benefits, as provided by the workers' compensation laws of this state.

The hernia, heart trouble, or pneumonia so developing or manifesting itself in those cases shall be presumed to arise out of and in the course of the employment. This presumption is disputable and may be controverted by other evidence, but unless so controverted, the appeals board is bound to find in accordance with it. The presumption shall be extended to a member following termination of service for a period of three calendar months for each full year of the requisite service, but not to exceed 60 months in any circumstance, commencing with the last date actually worked in the specified capacity.

The hernia, heart trouble, or pneumonia so developing or manifesting itself in those cases shall in no case be attributed to any disease existing prior to that development or manifestation. **Leg.H.** 1992 ch. 427, 2001 ch. 833, 2002 ch. 664 (AB 3034).

Ref.: Hanna § 3.113[4]; Herlick Handbook §§ 5.3, 6.09, 8.27.

§3212.1. Cancer presumption; active firefighters and peace officers.

(a) This section applies to all of the following:

(1) Active firefighting members, whether volunteers, partly paid, or fully paid, of all of the following fire departments:

(A) A fire department of a city, county, city and county, district, or other public or municipal corporation or political subdivision.

(B) A fire department of the University of California and the California State University.

(C) The Department of Forestry and Fire Protection.

(D) A county forestry or firefighting department or unit.

(2) Active firefighting members of a fire department that serves a United States Department of Defense installation and who are certified by the Department of Defense as meeting its standards for firefighters.

(3) Active firefighting members of a fire department that serves a National Aeronautics and Space Administration installation and who adhere to training standards established in accordance with Article 4 (commencing with Section 13155) of Chapter 1 of Part 2 of Division 12 of the Health and Safety Code.

(4) Peace officers, as defined in Section 830.1, subdivision (a) of Section 830.2, and subdivisions (a) and (b) of Section 830.37, of the Penal Code, who are primarily engaged in active law enforcement activities.

(5)(A) Fire and rescue services coordinators who work for the Office of Emergency Services.

(B) For purposes of this paragraph, "fire and rescue services coordinators" means coordinators with any of the following job classifications: coordinator, senior coordinator, or chief coordinator.

(b) The term "injury," as used in this division, includes cancer, including leukemia, that develops or manifests itself during a period in which any member described in subdivision (a) is in the service of the department or unit, if the member demonstrates that he or she was exposed, while in the service of the department or unit, to a known carcinogen as defined by the International Agency for Research on Cancer, or as defined by the director.

(c) The compensation that is awarded for cancer shall include full hospital, surgical, medical treatment, disability indemnity, and death benefits, as provided by this division.

(d) The cancer so developing or manifesting itself in these cases shall be presumed to arise out of and in the course of the employment. This presumption is disputable and may be controverted by evidence that the primary site of the cancer has been established and that the carcinogen to which the member has demonstrated exposure is not reasonably linked to the disabling cancer. Unless so controverted, the appeals board is bound to find in accordance with the presumption. This presumption shall be extended to a member following termination of service for a period of three calendar months for each full year of the requisite service, but not to exceed 120 months in any circumstance, commencing with the last date actually worked in the specified capacity.

(e) The amendments to this section enacted during the 1999 portion of the 1999–2000 Regular Session shall be applied to claims for benefits filed or pending on or after January 1, 1997, including, but not limited to, claims for benefits filed on or after that date that have previously been denied, or that are being appealed following denial.

(f) This section shall be known, and may be cited, as the William Dallas Jones Cancer Presumption Act of 2010. **Leg.H.** 1999 ch. 595, 2000 ch. 887, 2008 ch. 747 (SB 1271) §1, 2010 ch. 672 (AB 2253) §1, 2011 ch. 550 (AB 585) §1.

Ref.: Hanna § 3.113[4][b]; Herlick Handbook §§ 6.09, 8.28.

§3212.15. [Repealed January 1, 2025] Applicability to certain state and local firefighting personnel and peace officers; "injury" includes post-traumatic stress; compensation for injury.

(a) This section applies to all of the following:

(1) Active firefighting members, whether volunteers, partly paid, or fully paid, of all of the following fire departments:

(A) A fire department of a city, county, city and county, district, or other public or municipal corporation or political subdivision.

(B) A fire department of the University of California and the California State University.

(C) The Department of Forestry and Fire Protection.

(D) A county forestry or firefighting department or unit.

(2) Active firefighting members of a fire department that serves a United States Department of Defense installation and who are certified by the Department of Defense as meeting its standards for firefighters.

(3) Active firefighting members of a fire department that serves a National Aeronautics and Space Administration installation and who adhere to training standards established in accordance with Article 4 (commencing with Section 13155) of Chapter 1 of Part 2 of Division 12 of the Health and Safety Code.

(4) Peace officers, as defined in Section 830.1, subdivisions (a), (b), and (c) of Section 830.2, Section 830.32, subdivisions (a) and (b) of Section 830.37, and Sections 830.5 and 830.55 of the Penal Code, who are primarily engaged in active law enforcement activities.

(5)(A) Fire and rescue services coordinators who work for the Office of Emergency Services.

(B) For purposes of this paragraph, "fire and rescue services coordinators" means coordinators with any of the following job classifications: coordinator, senior coordinator, or chief coordinator.

(b) In the case of a person described in subdivision (a), the term "injury," as used in this division, includes "post-traumatic stress disorder," as diagnosed according to the most recent edition of the Diagnostic and Statistical Manual of Mental Disorders published by the American Psychiatric Association and that develops or manifests itself during a period in which any member described in subdivision (a) is in the service of the department or unit.

(c) For an injury that is diagnosed as specified in subdivision (b):

(1) The compensation that is awarded shall include full hospital, surgical, medical treatment, disability indemnity, and death benefits, as provided by this division.

(2) The injury so developing or manifesting itself in these cases shall be presumed to arise out of and in the course of the employment. This presumption is disputable and may be controverted by other evidence, but unless so controverted, the appeals board is bound to find in accordance with the presumption. This presumption shall be extended to a member following termination of service for a period of 3 calendar months for each full year of the requisite service, but not to exceed 60 months in any circumstance, commencing with the last date actually worked in the specified capacity.

(d) Compensation shall not be paid pursuant to this section for a claim of injury unless the member has performed services for the department or unit for at least six months. The six months of employment need not be continuous. This subdivision does not apply if the injury is caused by a sudden and extraordinary employment condition.

(e) This section applies to injuries occurring on or after January 1, 2020.

(f) This section shall remain in effect only until January 1, 2025, and as of that date is repealed. **Leg.H.** 2019 ch. 390 (SB 542) §2.

Ref.: Hanna § 4.138[4][q]; Herlick Handbook § 8.29.

§3212.2. Employees of Department of Corrections, Department of Youth Authority, Atascadero State Hospital—Heart trouble.

In the case of officers and employees in the Department of Corrections having custodial duties, each officer and employee in the Department of Youth Authority having group supervisory duties, and each security officer employed at the Atascadero State Hospital, the term "injury" includes heart trouble which develops or manifests itself during a period while such officer or employee is in the service of such department or hospital.

The compensation which is awarded for such heart trouble shall include full hospital, surgical, medical treatment, disability indemnity, and death benefits, as provided by the workers' compensation laws of this state.

Such heart trouble so developing or manifesting itself in such cases shall be presumed to arise out of and in the course of the employment. This presumption is disputable and may be controverted by other evidence, but unless so controverted, the appeals board is bound to find in accordance with it. This presumption shall be extended to a member following termination of service for a period of three calendar months for each full year of the requisite service, but not to exceed 60 months in any circumstance, commencing with the last date actually worked in the specified capacity.

Ref.: Herlick Handbook §§ 6.09, 8.27.

§3212.3. California Highway Patrol—Heart trouble; pneumonia.

In the case of a peace officer who is designated under subdivision (a) of Section 2250.1 of the Vehicle Code and who has graduated from an academy certified by the Commission on Peace Officer Standards and Training, when that officer is employed upon a regular, full-time salary, the term "injury," as used in this division, includes heart trouble and pneumonia which develops or manifests itself during a period while that officer is in the service of the Department of the California Highway Patrol. The compensation which is awarded for the heart trouble or pneumonia shall include full hospital, surgical, medical treatment, disability indemnity, and death benefits as provided by this division.

The heart trouble or pneumonia so developing or manifesting itself shall be presumed to arise out of and in the course of the employment. However, a peace officer of the Department of the California Highway Patrol, as designated under subdivision (a) of Section 2250.1 of the Vehicle Code, shall have served five years or more in that capacity or as a peace officer with the former California State Police Division, or in both capacities, before the presumption shall arise as to the compensability of heart trouble so developing or manifesting itself. This presumption is disputable and may be controverted by other evidence, but unless so controverted, the appeals board is bound to find in accordance with it. This presumption shall be extended to a member following termination of service for a period of three calendar months for each full year of the requisite service, but not to exceed 60 months in any circumstance, commencing with the last date actually worked in the specified capacity.

The heart trouble or pneumonia so developing or manifesting itself in these cases shall in no case be attributed to any disease existing prior to that development or manifestation.

The term "peace officers" as used herein shall be limited to those employees of the Department of the California Highway Patrol who are designated as peace officers under subdivision (a) of Section 2250.1 of the Vehicle Code. **Leg.H.** 1995 Gov. Reorg. Plan 1, effective May 12, 1995, 1996 ch. 305 (codification of the 1995 Gov. Reorg. Plan).

§3212.4. University of California fire department—Heart trouble; hernia; pneumonia.

In the case of a member of a University of California fire department located at a campus or other facility administered by the Regents of University of California, when any such member is employed by such a department upon a regular, full-time salary, on a nonprobationary basis, the term "injury" as used in this division includes heart trouble, hernia, or pneumonia which develops or manifests itself during a period while such member is in the service of such a University of California fire department. The compensation which is awarded for such heart trouble, hernia, or pneumonia shall include full hospital, surgical, medical treatment disability indemnity, and death benefits as provided by the provisions of this division.

Such heart trouble, hernia, or pneumonia so developing or manifesting itself shall be presumed to arise out of and in the course of the employment. This presumption is disputable and may be controverted by other evidence, but unless so controverted, the appeals board is bound to find in accordance with it. This presumption shall be extended to a member following termination of service for a period of three calendar months for each full year of the requisite service, but not to exceed 60 months in any circumstance, commencing with the last date actually worked in the specified capacity.

Such heart trouble, hernia, or pneumonia so developing or manifesting itself in such cases shall in no case be attributed to any disease existing prior to such development or manifestation.

The term "member" as used herein shall exclude those employees of a University of California fire department whose principal duties are those of a telephone operator, clerk, stenographer, machinist, mechanic, or otherwise, and whose functions do not clearly fall within the scope of active firefighting and prevention service.

§3212.5. Peace officers—Heart trouble; pneumonia.

In the case of a member of a police department of a city or municipality, or a member of the State Highway Patrol, when any such member is employed upon a regular, full-time salary, and in the case of a sheriff or deputy sheriff, or an inspector or investigator in a district attorney's office of any county, employed upon a regular, full-time salary, the term "injury" as used in this division includes heart trouble and pneumonia which develops or manifests itself during a period while such member, sheriff, or deputy sheriff, inspector or investigator is in the service of the police department, the State Highway Patrol, the sheriff's office or the district attorney's office, as the case

Labor

may be. The compensation which is awarded for such heart trouble or pneumonia shall include full hospital, surgical, medical treatment, disability indemnity, and death benefits as provided by the provisions of this division.

Such heart trouble or pneumonia so developing or manifesting itself shall be presumed to arise out of and in the course of the employment; provided, however, that the member of the police department, State Highway Patrol, the sheriff or deputy sheriff, or an inspector or investigator in a district attorney's office of any county shall have served five years or more in such capacity before the presumption shall arise as to the compensability of heart trouble so developing or manifesting itself. This presumption is disputable and may be controverted by other evidence, but unless so controverted, the appeals board is bound to find in accordance with it. This presumption shall be extended to a member following termination of service for a period of three calendar months for each full year of the requisite service, but not to exceed 60 months in any circumstance, commencing with the last date actually worked in the specified capacity.

Such heart trouble or pneumonia so developing or manifesting itself in such cases shall in no case be attributed to any disease existing prior to such development or manifestation.

The term "members" as used herein shall be limited to those employees of police departments, the California Highway Patrol and sheriffs' departments and inspectors and investigators of a district attorney's office who are defined as peace officers in Section 830.1, 830.2, or 830.3 of the Penal Code.

Ref.: Hanna §§ 10.40[3][c], 33.02[4][d][i].

§3212.6. Peace officers, prison guards, correctional officers, and firefighters—Tuberculosis; tuberculosis test for firefighter applicants.

In the case of a member of a police department of a city or county, or a member of the sheriff's office of a county, or a member of the California Highway Patrol, or an inspector or investigator in a district attorney's office of any county whose principal duties consist of active law enforcement service, or a prison or jail guard or correctional officer who is employed by a public agency, when that person is employed upon a regular, full-time salary, or in the case of members of fire departments of any city, county, or district, or other public or municipal corporations or political subdivisions, when those members are employed on a regular fully paid basis, and in the case of active firefighting members of the Department of Forestry and Fire Protection whose duties require firefighting and first-aid response services, or of any county forestry or firefighting department or unit, where those members are employed on a regular fully paid basis, excepting those whose principal duties are clerical or otherwise do not clearly fall within the scope of active law enforcement, firefighting, or emergency first-aid response service such as stenographers, telephone operators, and other officeworkers, the term "injury" includes tuberculosis that develops or manifests itself during a period while that member is in the service of that department or office. The compensation that is awarded for the tuberculosis shall include full hospital, surgical, medical treatment, disability indemnity, and death benefits as provided by the provisions of this division.

The tuberculosis so developing or manifesting itself shall be presumed to arise out of and in the course of the employment. This presumption is disputable and may be controverted by other evidence, but unless so controverted, the appeals board is bound to find in accordance with it. This presumption shall be extended to a member following termination of service for a period of three calendar months for each full year of the requisite service, but not to exceed 60 months in any circumstance, commencing with the last date actually worked in the specified capacity.

A public entity may require applicants for employment in firefighting positions who would be entitled to the benefits granted by this section to be tested for infection for tuberculosis. **Leg.H.** 1995 ch. 683, 1996 ch. 802, 2001 ch. 833.

Ref.: Herlick Handbook § 8.27.

§3212.7. Department of Justice—Heart trouble; hernia; pneumonia; tuberculosis.

In the case of an employee in the Department of Justice falling within the "state safety" class, when any such individual is employed under civil service upon a regular, full-time salary, the term "injury", as used in this division, includes heart trouble or hernia or pneumonia or tuberculosis which develops or manifests itself during the period while such individual is in the service of the Department of Justice. The compensation which is awarded for any such injury shall include full hospital, surgical, medical treatment, disability indemnity, and death benefits as provided by the provisions of this division.

Such heart trouble, hernia, pneumonia, or tuberculosis so developing or manifesting itself shall be presumed to arise out of and in the course of the employment. This presumption is disputable and may be controverted by other evidence but unless so controverted, the appeals board is bound to find in accordance with it. This presumption shall be extended to a member following termination of service for a period of three calendar months for each full year of the requisite service, but not to exceed 60 months in any circumstance, commencing with the last date actually worked in the specified capacity.

Such heart trouble, hernia, pneumonia, or tuberculosis developing or manifesting itself in such cases shall in no case be attributed to any disease existing prior to such development or manifestation.

Ref.: Herlick Handbook §§ 5.3, 8.27.

§3212.8. "Injury" includes blood-borne infectious disease or methicillin-resistant Staphylococcus aureus skin infection.

(a) In the case of members of a sheriff's office, of police or fire departments of cities, counties, cities and counties, districts, or other public or municipal corporations or political subdivisions, or individuals described in Chapter 4.5 (commencing with Section 830) of Title 3 of Part 2 of the Penal Code, whether those persons are volunteer, partly paid, or fully paid, and in the case of active firefighting members of the Department of Forestry and Fire Protection, or of any county forestry or firefighting department or unit, whether voluntary, fully paid, or partly paid, excepting those whose principal duties are clerical or otherwise do not clearly fall within the scope of active law enforcement service or active firefighting services, such as stenographers, telephone operators, and other office workers, the term "injury" as used in this division, includes a blood-borne infectious disease or methicillin-resistant Staphylococcus aureus skin infection when any part of the blood-borne infectious disease or methicillin-resistant Staphylococcus aureus skin infection develops or manifests itself during a period while that person is in the service of that office, staff, division, department, or unit. The compensation that is awarded for a blood-borne infectious disease or methicillin-resistant Staphylococcus aureus skin infection shall include, but not be limited to, full hospital, surgical, medical treatment, disability indemnity, and death benefits, as provided by the workers' compensation laws of this state.

(b)(1) The blood-borne infectious disease or methicillin-resistant Staphylococcus aureus skin infection so developing or manifesting itself in those cases shall be presumed to arise out of and in the course of the employment or service. This presumption is disputable and may be controverted by other evidence, but unless so controverted, the appeals board is bound to find in accordance with it.

(2) The blood-borne infectious disease presumption shall be extended to a person covered by subdivision (a) following termination of service for a period of three calendar months for each full year of service, but not to exceed 60 months in any circumstance, commencing with the last date actually worked in the specified capacity.

(3) Notwithstanding paragraph (2), the methicillin-resistant Staphylococcus aureus skin infection presumption shall be extended to a person covered by subdivision (a) following termination of service for a period of 90 days, commencing with the last day actually worked in the specified capacity.

(c) The blood-borne infectious disease or methicillin-resistant Staphylococcus aureus skin infection so developing or manifesting itself in those cases shall in no case be attributed to any disease or skin infection existing prior to that development or manifestation.

(d) For the purposes of this section, "blood-borne infectious disease" means a disease caused by exposure to pathogenic microorganisms that are present in human blood that can cause disease in humans, including those pathogenic microorganisms defined as blood-borne pathogens by the Department of Industrial Relations. **Leg.H.** 2000 ch. 490, 2001 ch. 833, 2008 ch. 684 (AB 2754) §2.

Ref.: Herlick Handbook § 8.27.

§3212.85. "Injury" includes death or illness from exposure to biochemical substances.

(a) This section applies to peace officers described in Sections 830.1 to 830.5, inclusive, of the Penal Code, and members of a fire department.

(b) The term "injury," as used in this division, includes illness or resulting death due to exposure to a biochemical substance that develops or occurs during a period in which any member described in subdivision (a) is in the service of the department or unit.

(c) The compensation that is awarded for injury pursuant to this section shall include full hospital, surgical, medical treatment, disability indemnity, and death benefits, as provided by this division.

(d) The injury that develops or manifests itself in these cases shall be presumed to arise out of, and in the course of, the employment. This presumption is disputable and may be controverted by other evidence. Unless controverted, the appeals board is bound to find in accordance with the presumption. This presumption shall be extended to a member following termination of service for a period of three calendar months for each full year of the requisite service, but not to exceed 60 months in any circumstance, commencing with the last date actually worked in the specified capacity.

(e) For purposes of this section, the following definitions apply:

(1) "Biochemical substance" means any biological or chemical agent that may be used as a weapon of mass destruction, including, but not limited to, any chemical warfare agent, weaponized biological agent, or nuclear or radiological agent, as these terms are defined in Section 11417 of the Penal Code.

(2) "Members of a fire department" includes, but is not limited to, an apprentice, volunteer, partly paid, or fully paid member of any of the following:

(A) A fire department of a city, county, city and county, district, or other public or municipal corporation or political subdivision.

(B) A fire department of the University of California and the California State University.

(C) The Department of Forestry and Fire Protection.

(D) A county forestry or firefighting department or unit. **Leg.H.** 2002 ch. 870 (AB 1847).

Ref.: Herlick Handbook § 8.27.

§3212.86. [Repealed January 1, 2023] Employees with COVID-19-related illness.

(a) This section applies to any employee with a COVID-19-related illness.

(b) The term "injury," as used in this division, includes illness or death resulting from COVID-19 if both of the following circumstances apply:

(1) The employee has tested positive for or was diagnosed with COVID-19 within 14 days after a day that the employee performed labor or services at the employee's place of employment at the employer's direction.

(2) The day referenced in paragraph (1) on which the employee performed labor or services at the employee's place of employment at the employer's direction was on or after March 19, 2020, and on or before July 5, 2020. The date of injury shall be the last date the employee performed labor or services at the employee's place of employment at the employer's direction.

(3) If paragraph (1) is satisfied through a diagnosis of COVID-19, the diagnosis was done by a licensed physician and surgeon holding an M.D. or D.O. degree or state licensed physician assistant or nurse practitioner, acting under the review or supervision of a physician and surgeon pursuant to standardized procedures or protocols within their lawfully authorized scope of practice, and that diagnosis is confirmed by testing or by a COVID-19 serologic test within 30 days of the date of the diagnosis.

(c) The compensation that is awarded for injury pursuant to this section shall include full hospital, surgical, medical treatment, disability indemnity, and death benefits, as provided by this division.

(d)(1) If an employee has paid sick leave benefits specifically available in response to COVID-19, those benefits shall be used and exhausted before any temporary disability benefits or benefits under Section 4800, 4800.5, or 4850 are due and payable. If an employee does not have those sick leave benefits, the employee shall be provided temporary disability benefits or Section 4800, 4800.5, or 4850 benefits, if applicable, from the date of disability. There shall not be a waiting period for temporary disability benefits.

(2) To qualify for temporary disability or Section 4800, 4800.5, or 4850 benefits under this section, an employee shall satisfy either of the following:

(A) If the employee has tested positive or is diagnosed with COVID-19 on or after May 6, 2020, the employee shall be certified for temporary disability within the first 15 days after the initial diagnosis, and shall be recertified for temporary disability every 15 days thereafter, for the first 45 days following diagnosis.

(B) If the employee has tested positive or was diagnosed with COVID-19 before May 6, 2020, the employee shall have obtained a certification, no later than May 21, 2020, documenting the period for which the employee was temporarily disabled and unable to work, and shall be recertified for temporary disability every 15 days thereafter, for the first 45 days following diagnosis.

(3) An employee shall be certified for temporary disability by a physician holding a physician's and surgeon's license issued pursuant to Chapter 5 (commencing with Section 2000) of Division 2 of the Business and Professions Code. If the employee has a predesignated physician pursuant to subdivision (d) of Section 4600, is covered by a medical provider network pursuant to Article 2.3 (commencing with Section 4616) of Chapter 2 of Part 2, is covered by a workers' compensation health care organization pursuant to Article 2 (commencing with Section 4600) of Chapter 2 of Part 2, or is covered by a group health plan, the certifying physician shall be a physician and surgeon in that network, organization, or plan. Otherwise, the certifying physician may be a physician and surgeon of the employee's choosing.

(e) An injury described in subdivision (b) is presumed to arise out of and in the course of the employment. This presumption is disputable and may be controverted by other evidence. Unless controverted, the appeals board is bound to find in accordance with the presumption.

(f) Notwithstanding Section 5402, if liability for a claim of a COVID-19-related illness is not rejected within 30 days after the date the claim form is filed pursuant to Section 5401, the illness shall be presumed compensable. The presumption of this subdivision is rebuttable only by evidence discovered subsequent to the 30-day period.

(g) The Department of Industrial Relations shall waive the right to collect any death benefit payment due pursuant to Section 4706.5 arising out of claims covered by this section.

(h) This section applies to all pending matters except as otherwise specified, including, but not limited to, pending claims relying on Executive Order N-62-20. This section is not a basis to rescind, alter, amend, or reopen any final award of workers' compensation benefits.

(i) For purposes of this section:

(1) "COVID-19" means the 2019 novel coronavirus disease.

(2) "Place of employment" does not include an employee's residence.

(j) This section shall remain in effect only until January 1, 2023, and as of that date is repealed. **Leg.H.** 2020 ch. 85 (SB 1159) §2, effective September 17, 2020.

Ref.: Herlick Handbook § 8.30.

§3212.87. [Repealed January 1, 2023] Applicability to active firefighting members and other specific employees; injury definition; COVID-19 definition.

(a) This section applies to the following employees:

(1) Active firefighting members, whether volunteers, partly paid, or fully paid, of all of the following fire departments:

(A) A fire department of a city, county, city and county, district, or other public or municipal corporation or political subdivision.

(B) A fire department of the University of California and the California State University.

(C) The Department of Forestry and Fire Protection.

(D) A county forestry or firefighting department or unit.

(2) Active firefighting members of a fire department that serves a United States Department of Defense installation and who are certified by the United States Department of Defense as meeting its standards for firefighters.

(3) Active firefighting members of a fire department that serves a National Aeronautics and Space Administration installation and who adhere to training standards established in accordance with Article 4 (commencing with Section 13155) of Chapter 1 of Part 2 of Division 12 of the Health and Safety Code.

(4) Active firefighting members of a fire department that provides fire protection to a commercial airport regulated by the Federal Aviation Administration (FAA) under Part 139 (commencing with Section 139.5) of Subchapter G of Chapter 1 of Title 14 of the Federal Code of Regulations and are trained and certified by the State Fire Marshal as meeting the standards of Fire Control 5 and Section 139.319 of Title 14 of the Federal Code of Regulations

(5) Peace officers, as defined in Section 830.1 of the Penal Code, subdivisions (a), (b), (e), (f), and (h) of Section 830.2 of the Penal Code, subdivision (a) of Section 830.3 of the Penal Code, subdivisions (a) and (b) of Section 830.37 of the Penal Code, subdivisions (a) and (b) of Section 830.5 of the Penal Code, and subdivision (a) of Section 830.53 of the Penal Code, who are primarily engaged in active law enforcement activities.

(6)(A) Fire and rescue services coordinators who work for the Office of Emergency Services.

(B) For purposes of this paragraph, "fire and rescue services coordinators" means coordinators with any of the following job classifications: coordinator, senior coordinator, or chief coordinator.

(7) An employee who provides direct patient care, or a custodial employee in contact with COVID-19 patients, who works at a health facility. For the purposes of this subdivision, "health facility" means a health facility as defined in subdivision (a), (b), (c), (m), or (n) of Section 1250 of the Health and Safety Code.

(8) An authorized registered nurse, emergency medical technician-I, emergency medical technician-II, emergency medical technician-paramedic, as described in Chapter 2 (commencing with Section 1797.50) of Division 2.5 of the Health and Safety Code.

(9) An employee who provides direct patient care for a home health agency, as defined under Section 1727 of the Health and Safety Code.

(10) Employees of health facilities, other than those described in paragraph (7). For these employees, the presumption shall not apply if the employer can establish that the employee did not have contact with a health facility patient within the last 14 days who tested positive for COVID-19. If it is determined that the presumption does not apply, the claim shall be evaluated pursuant to Sections 3202.5 and 3600. For the purposes of this subdivision, "health facility" means a health facility, as defined in subdivision (a), (b), (c), (m), or (n) of Section 1250 of the Health and Safety Code.

(11) A provider of in-home supportive services under Article 7 (commencing with Section 12300) of Chapter 3 of Part 3 of Division 9 of, or Sections 14132.95, 14132.952, and 14132.956 of, the Welfare and Institutions Code, when they provide the in-home supportive services outside their own home or residence.

(b) The term "injury," as used in this division, includes illness or death resulting from COVID-19 if all of the following circumstances apply:

(1) The employee has tested positive for COVID-19 within 14 days after a day that the employee performed labor or services at the employee's place of employment at the employer's direction.

(2) The day referenced in paragraph (1), on which the employee performed labor or services at the employee's place of employment at the employer's direction, was on or after July 6, 2020. The date of injury shall be the last date the employee performed labor or services at the employee's place of employment at the employer's direction prior to the positive test.

(c) The compensation that is awarded for injury pursuant to this section shall include full hospital, surgical, medical treatment, disability indemnity, and death benefits, as provided by this division.

(d) If an employee has paid sick leave benefits specifically available in response to COVID-19, those benefits shall be used and exhausted before any temporary disability benefits or benefits under Section 4800, 4800.5, or 4850 are due and payable. If an employee does not have those sick leave benefits, the employee shall be provided temporary disability benefits or Section 4850 benefits, if applicable, from the date of disability. There shall not be a waiting period for temporary disability benefits.

(e) An injury described in subdivision (b) is presumed to arise out of and in the course of the employment, except as provided in this subdivision. This presumption is disputable and may be controverted by other evidence. Unless controverted, the appeals board is bound to find in accordance with the presumption. This presumption shall be extended to a person described in subdivision (a) following termination of service for a period of 14 days, commencing with the last date actually worked in the specified capacity at the employee's place of employment as described in subdivision (b).

(f) Notwithstanding Section 5402, if liability for a claim of a COVID-19-related illness is not rejected within 30 days after the date the claim form is filed pursuant to Section 5401, the illness shall be presumed compensable. The presumption of this subdivision is rebuttable only by evidence discovered subsequent to the 30-day period.

(g) The Department of Industrial Relations shall waive the right to collect any death benefit payment due pursuant to Section 4706.5 arising out of claims covered by this section.

(h) This section applies to all pending matters, unless otherwise specified in this section, but shall not be a basis to rescind, alter, amend, or reopen any final award of workers' compensation benefits.

(i) For purposes of this section:

(1) "COVID-19" means the 2019 novel coronavirus disease.

(2) Unless otherwise indicated, "test" or "testing" means a PCR (Polymerase Chain Reaction) test approved for use or approved for emergency use by the United States Food and Drug Administration to detect the presence of viral RNA. "Test" or "testing" does not include serologic testing, also known as antibody testing. "Test" or "testing" may include any other viral culture test approved for use or approved for emergency use by the United States Food and Drug Administration to detect the presence of viral RNA which has the same or higher sensitivity and specificity as the PCR Test.

(3) An "employee's place of employment" does not include an employee's home or residence.

(j) This section shall remain in effect only until January 1, 2023, and as of that date is repealed. **Leg.H.** 2020 ch. 85 (SB 1159) §3, effective September 17, 2020.

Ref.: Herlick Handbook § 8.30.

§3212.88. [Repealed January 1, 2023] Applicability to employees not described in Section 3212.87; injury definition; COVID-19 definition.

(a) This section applies to employees who are not described in Section 3212.87, who test positive during an outbreak at the employee's specific place of employment, and whose employer has five or more employees.

(b) The term "injury," as used in this division, includes illness or death resulting from COVID-19 if all of the following circumstances apply:

(1) The employee tests positive for COVID-19 within 14 days after a day that the employee performed labor or services at the employee's place of employment at the employer's direction.

(2) The day referenced in paragraph (1) on which the employee performed labor or services at the employee's

place of employment at the employer's direction was on or after July 6, 2020. The date of injury shall be the last date the employee performed labor or services at the employee's place of employment at the employer's direction prior to the positive test.

(3) The employee's positive test occurred during a period of an outbreak at the employee's specific place of employment.

(c) The compensation that is awarded for injury pursuant to this section shall include full hospital, surgical, medical treatment, disability indemnity, and death benefits, as provided by this division.

(d) If an employee has paid sick leave benefits specifically available in response to COVID-19, those benefits shall be used and exhausted before any temporary disability benefits, benefits under Section 4800, 4800.5, or 4850 or Section 44977, 44984, 45192, 45196, 87780, 87787, 88192, or 88196 of the Education Code are due and payable. If an employee does not have those sick leave benefits, the employee shall be provided temporary disability benefits or Section 4850 benefits, if applicable, from the date of disability. There shall not be a waiting period for temporary disability benefits.

(e)(1) An injury described in subdivision (b) is presumed to arise out of and in the course of the employment, except as provided in this subdivision. This presumption is disputable and may be controverted by other evidence. Unless controverted, the appeals board is bound to find in accordance with the presumption. This presumption shall be extended to a person described in subdivision (a) following termination of service for a period of 14 days, commencing with the last date actually worked in the specified capacity at the employee's place of employment. This section does not affect an employee's rights to compensation for an injury or illness under this division in accordance with a preponderance of evidence.

(2) Evidence relevant to controverting the presumption may include, but is not limited to, evidence of measures in place to reduce potential transmission of COVID-19 in the employee's place of employment and evidence of an employee's nonoccupational risks of COVID-19 infection.

(f) Notwithstanding Section 5402, if liability for a claim of a COVID-19-related illness is not rejected within 45 days after the date the claim form is filed pursuant to Section 5401, the illness shall be presumed compensable. The presumption of this subdivision is rebuttable only by evidence discovered subsequent to the 45-day period.

(g) The Department of Industrial Relations shall waive the right to collect any death benefit payment due pursuant to Section 4706.5 arising out of claims covered by this section.

(h) This section applies to all pending matters, unless otherwise specified in this section, but is not a basis to rescind, alter, amend, or reopen any final award of workers' compensation benefits.

(i) When the employer knows or reasonably should know that an employee has tested positive for COVID-19, the employer shall report to their claims administrator in writing via electronic mail or facsimile within three business days all of the following:

(1) An employee has tested positive. For purposes of this reporting, the employer shall not provide any personally identifiable information regarding the employee who tested positive for COVID-19 unless the employee asserts the infection is work related or has filed a claim form pursuant to Section 5401.

(2) The date that the employee tests positive, which is the date the specimen was collected for testing.

(3) The specific address or addresses of the employee's specific place of employment during the 14-day period preceding the date of the employee's positive test.

(4) The highest number of employees who reported to work at the employee's specific place of employment in the 45-day period preceding the last day the employee worked at each specific place of employment.

(j) An employer or other person acting on behalf of an employer who intentionally submits false or misleading information or fails to submit information when reporting pursuant to subdivision (i) is subject to a civil penalty in the amount of up to ten thousand dollars ($10,000) to be assessed by the Labor Commissioner.

(1) If, upon inspection or investigation, the Labor Commissioner determines that an employer or other person has intentionally submitted false or misleading information in violation of subdivision (i), the Labor Commissioner may issue a citation to the person in violation. The citation may be served personally, in the same manner as provided for service of a summons as described in Chapter 4 (commencing with Section 413.10) of Title 5 of Part 2 of the Code of Civil Procedure, by certified mail with return receipt requested, or by registered mail in accordance with subdivision (c) of Section 11505 of the Government Code. Each citation shall be in writing and shall describe the nature of the violation, including reference to the statutory provision alleged to have been violated.

(2) If a person desires to contest a citation or the proposed assessment of a civil penalty therefor, they shall, within 15 business days after service of the citation, notify the office of the Labor Commissioner which appears on the citation of their request for an informal hearing. The Labor Commissioner or their deputy or agent shall, within 30 days, hold a hearing at the conclusion of which the citation or proposed assessment of a civil penalty shall be affirmed, modified, or dismissed. The decision of the Labor Commissioner shall consist of a notice of findings, findings, and order which shall be served on all parties to the hearing within 15 days after the hearing by regular first-class mail at the last known address of the party on file with the Labor Commissioner. Service shall be completed pursuant to Section 1013 of the Code of Civil Procedure. Any amount found due by the Labor Commissioner as a result of a hearing shall become due and payable 45 days after notice of the findings and written findings and order have been mailed to the party assessed. A writ of mandate may be taken from this finding to the appropriate superior court, as long as the party agrees to pay any judgment and costs ultimately rendered by the court against the party for the assessment. The writ of mandate shall be taken within 45 days of service of the notice of findings, findings, and order thereon.

(3) An employer or person to which a citation has been issued shall, in lieu of contesting a citation pursuant to this section, transmit to the office of the Labor Commissioner designated on the citation the amount specified for the

violation within 15 business days after issuance of the citation.

(4) If the party filing a writ of mandate is unsuccessful in challenging the decision of the hearing officer, the Labor Commissioner shall recover costs and attorney fees.

(k)(1) The claims administrator shall use information reported pursuant to subdivision (i) to determine if an outbreak has occurred for the purpose of administering a claim pursuant to this section. To calculate the number of employees at a specific place of employment, the claims administrator shall utilize the data reported pursuant to subdivision (i) for the first employee who is part of the outbreak, or, for claims between July 6, 2020, and the effective date of this section, the number reported under paragraph (2).

(2) Any employer who is aware of an employee testing positive on or after July 6, 2020, and prior to the effective date of this section, shall report to their claims administrator, in writing via electronic mail or facsimile, within 30 business days of the effective date of this section, all of the data required in subdivision (i). For the data required by paragraph (4) of subdivision (i), the employer shall instead report the highest number of employees who reported to work at each of the employee's specific places of employment on any given work day between July 6, 2020, and the effective date of this section. The claims administrator shall use the information reported under this paragraph to determine if an outbreak has occurred from July 6, 2020, to the effective date of this section, for the purpose of applying the presumption under this section.

(*l*) A claim is not part of an outbreak if it occurs during a continuous 14-day period where the requisite number of positive tests under paragraph (4) of subdivision (m) have not been met. For purposes of applying the presumption in this section, the claims administrator shall continually evaluate each claim to determine whether the requisite number of positive tests have occurred during the surrounding 14-day periods.

(m) For purposes of this section:

(1) "COVID-19" means the 2019 novel coronavirus disease.

(2) Unless otherwise indicated, "test" or "testing" means a PCR (Polymerase Chain Reaction) test approved for use or approved for emergency use by the United States Food and Drug Administration to detect the presence of viral RNA. "Test" or "testing" does not include serologic testing, also known as antibody testing. "Test" or "testing" may include any other viral culture test approved for use or approved for emergency use by the United States Food and Drug Administration to detect the presence of viral RNA which has the same or higher sensitivity and specificity as the PCR Test.

(3)(A) "A specific place of employment" means the building, store, facility, or agricultural field where an employee performs work at the employer's direction. "A specific place of employment" does not include the employee's home or residence, unless the employee provides home health care services to another individual at the employee's home or residence.

(B) In the case of an employee who performs work at the employer's direction in multiple places of employment within 14 days of the employee's positive test, the employee's positive test shall be counted for the purpose of determining the existence of an outbreak at each of those places of employment, and if an outbreak exists at any one of those places of employment, that shall be the employee's "specific place of employment."

(4) An "outbreak" exists if within 14 calendar days one of the following occurs at a specific place of employment:

(A) If the employer has 100 employees or fewer at a specific place of employment, 4 employees test positive for COVID-19.

(B) If the employer has more than 100 employees at a specific place of employment, 4 percent of the number of employees who reported to the specific place of employment, test positive for COVID-19.

(C) A specific place of employment is ordered to close by a local public health department, the State Department of Public Health, the Division of Occupational Safety and Health, or a school superintendent due to a risk of infection with COVID-19.

(n) This section shall remain in effect only until January 1, 2023, and as of that date is repealed. **Leg.H.** 2020 ch. 85 (SB 1159) §4, effective September 17, 2020.

Ref.: Herlick Handbook § 8.30.

§3212.9. Peace officers, probation officers, district attorney investigators, and firefighters—Meningitis.

In the case of a member of a police department of a city, county, or city and county, or a member of the sheriff's office of a county, or a member of the California Highway Patrol, or a county probation officer, or an inspector or investigator in a district attorney's office of any county whose principal duties consist of active law enforcement service, when that person is employed on a regular, full-time salary, or in the case of a member of a fire department of any city, county, or district, or other public or municipal corporation or political subdivision, or any county forestry or firefighting department or unit, when those members are employed on a regular full-time salary, excepting those whose principal duties are clerical or otherwise do not clearly fall within the scope of active law enforcement or firefighting, such as stenographers, telephone operators, and other officeworkers, the term "injury" includes meningitis that develops or manifests itself during a period while that person is in the service of that department, office, or unit. The compensation that is awarded for the meningitis shall include full hospital, surgical, medical treatment, disability indemnity, and death benefits as provided by the provisions of this division.

The meningitis so developing or manifesting itself shall be presumed to arise out of and in the course of the employment. This presumption is disputable and may be controverted by other evidence, but unless so controverted, the appeals board is bound to find in accordance with it. This presumption shall be extended to a person following termination of service for a period of three calendar months for each full year of the requisite service, but not to exceed 60 months in any circumstance, commencing with the last date actually worked in the specified capacity. **Leg.H.** 2000 ch. 883, 2001 ch. 833.

§3212.10. Heart trouble, pneumonia, tuberculosis, and meningitis as compensable for certain peace officers.

In the case of a peace officer of the Department of Corrections who has custodial or supervisory duties of inmates or parolees, or a peace officer of the Department of the Youth Authority who has custodial or supervisory duties of wards or parolees, or a peace officer as defined in Section 830.5 of the Penal Code and employed by a local agency, the term "injury" as used in this division includes heart trouble, pneumonia, tuberculosis, and meningitis that develops or manifests itself during a period in which any peace officer covered under this section is in the service of the department or unit. The compensation that is awarded for that injury shall include full hospital, surgical, medical treatment, disability indemnity, and death benefits as provided by the provisions of this division.

The heart trouble, pneumonia, tuberculosis, and meningitis so developing or manifesting itself shall be presumed to arise out of and in the course of employment. This presumption is disputable and may be controverted by other evidence, but unless so controverted, the appeals board is bound to find in accordance with it. This presumption shall be extended to a member following termination of service for a period of three calendar months for each full year of requisite service, but not to exceed 60 months in any circumstance, commencing with the last date actually worked in the specified capacity. **Leg.H.** 2001 ch. 835, 2002 ch. 664 (AB 3034).

Ref.: Herlick Handbook §§ 3.113[4][m], 8.27.

§3212.11. Skin cancer as "injury" for lifeguards arising out of and in course of employment.

This section applies to both of the following: (a) active lifeguards employed by a city, county, city and county, district, or other public or municipal corporation or political subdivision, and (b) active state lifeguards employed by the Department of Parks and Recreation. The term "injury," as used in this division, includes skin cancer that develops or manifests itself during the period of the lifeguard's employment. The compensation awarded for that injury shall include full hospital, surgical, and medical treatment, disability indemnity, and death benefits, as provided by the provisions of this division.

Skin cancer so developing or manifesting itself shall be presumed to arise out of and in the course of the employment. This presumption is disputable and may be controverted by other evidence, but unless so controverted, the appeals board shall find in accordance with it. This presumption shall be extended to a lifeguard following termination of service for a period of three calendar months for each full year of the requisite service, but not to exceed 60 months in any circumstance, commencing with the last date actually worked in the specified capacity.

Skin cancer so developing or manifesting itself in these cases shall not be attributed to any disease existing prior to that development or manifestation.

This section shall only apply to lifeguards employed for more than three consecutive months in a calendar year. **Leg.H.** 2001 ch. 846.

Ref.: Herlick Handbook §§ 3.113[4][n], 8.27.

§3212.12. Lyme disease as injury for specified peace officers and corpsmembers.

(a) This section applies to peace officers, as defined in subdivision (b) of Section 830.1 of the Penal Code, subdivisions (e), (f), and (g) of Section 830.2 of the Penal Code, and corpsmembers, as defined by Section 14302 of the Public Resources Code, and other employees at the California Conservation Corps classified as any of the following:

Title	Class
Backcounty Trails Camp Supervisor, California Conservation Corps	1030
Conservationist I, California Conservation Corps	1029
Conservationist II, California Conservation Corps	1003
Conservationist II, Nursery California Conservation Corps	7370

(b) The term "injury," as used in this division, includes Lyme disease that develops or manifests itself during a period in which any person described in subdivision (a) is in the service of the department.

(c) The compensation that is awarded for Lyme disease shall include full hospital, surgical, medical treatment, disability indemnity, and death benefits, as provided by this division.

(d) Lyme disease so developing or manifesting itself in these cases shall be presumed to arise out of and in the course of the employment. This presumption is disputable and may be controverted by evidence that the Lyme disease is not reasonably linked to the work performance. Unless so controverted, the appeals board shall find in accordance with the presumption. This presumption shall be extended to a person described in subdivision (a) following termination of service for a period of three calendar months for each full year of the requisite service, but not to exceed 60 months in any circumstance, commencing with the last date actually worked in the specified capacity. **Leg.H.** 2002 ch. 876 (AB 2125).

Ref.: Hanna § 3.113[4][o]; Herlick Handbook § 8.27.

§3213. University of California police—Heart trouble; pneumonia.

In the case of a member of the University of California Police Department who has graduated from an academy certified by the Commission on Peace Officer Standards and Training, when he and all members of the campus department of which he is a member have graduated from such an academy, and when any such member is employed upon a regular, full-time salary, the term "injury" as used in this division includes heart trouble and pneumonia which develops or manifests itself during a period while such member is in the service of such campus department of the University of California Police Department. The compensation which is awarded for such heart trouble or pneumonia shall include full hospital, surgical, medical treatment, disability indemnity, and death benefits as provided by the provisions of this division.

Such heart trouble or pneumonia so developing or manifesting itself shall be presumed to arise out of and in the course of the employment; provided, however, that the member of the University of California Police Department shall have served five years or more in such capacity before the presumption shall arise as to the compensability of heart trouble so developing or manifesting itself. This presumption is disputable and may be controverted by other evidence, but unless so controverted, the appeals board is bound to find in accordance with it. This presumption shall be extended to a member following termination of service for a period of three calendar months for each full year of the requisite service, but not to exceed 60 months in any circumstance, commencing with the last date actually worked in the specified capacity.

Such heart trouble or pneumonia so developing or manifesting itself in such cases shall in no case be attributed to any disease existing prior to such development or manifestation.

As used in this section:

(a) "Members" shall be limited to those employees of the University of California Police Department who are defined as peace officers in Section 830.2 of the Penal Code.

(b) "Campus" shall include any campus or other installation maintained under the jurisdiction of the Regents of the University of California.

(c) "Campus department" means all members of the University of California Police Department who are assigned and serve on a particular campus.

Ref.: Herlick Handbook § 8.27.

§3213.2. "Injury" includes lower back impairment for certain law enforcement officers; "duty belt" defined.

(a) In the case of a member of a police department of a city, county, or city and county, or a member of the sheriff's office of a county, or a peace officer employed by the Department of the California Highway Patrol, or a peace officer employed by the University of California, who has been employed for at least five years as a peace officer on a regular, full-time salary and has been required to wear a duty belt as a condition of employment, the term "injury," as used in this division, includes lower back impairments. The compensation that is awarded for lower back impairments shall include full hospital, surgical, medical treatment, disability indemnity, and death benefits as provided by the provisions of this division.

(b) The lower back impairment so developing or manifesting itself in the peace officer shall be presumed to arise out of and in the course of the employment. This presumption is disputable and may be controverted by other evidence, but unless so controverted, the appeals board is bound to find in accordance with it. This presumption shall be extended to a person following termination of service for a period of three calendar months for each full year of the requisite service, but not to exceed 60 months in any circumstance, commencing with the last date actually worked in the specified capacity.

(c) For purposes of this section, "duty belt" means a belt used for the purpose of holding a gun, handcuffs, baton, and other items related to law enforcement. **Leg.H.** 2001 ch. 834.

Ref.: Hanna § 3.113[4][*l*]; Herlick Handbook § 8.27.

§3214. Early intervention program.

(a) The Department of Corrections and the Department of the Youth Authority shall, in conjunction with all recognized employee representative associations, develop policy and implement the workers' compensation early intervention program by December 31, 1989, for all department employees who sustain an injury. The program shall include, but not be limited to, counseling by an authorized independent early intervention counselor and the services of an agreed medical panel to assist in timely decisions regarding compensability. Costs of services through early intervention shall be borne by the departments.

(b) It is the intent of the Legislature to reduce all costs associated with the delivery of workers' compensation benefits, in balance with the need to ensure timely and adequate benefits to the injured worker. Toward this goal the workers' compensation early intervention program was established in the Department of Corrections and the Department of the Youth Authority. The fundamental concept of the program is to settle disputes rather than to litigate them. This is a worthwhile concept in terms of cost control for the employer and timely receipt of benefits for the worker. To ascertain the effectiveness of the program is crucial in helping guide policy in this arena. **Leg.H.** 1994 ch. 1034, effective September 29, 1994, 2001 ch. 745, effective October 12, 2001.

Ref.: Herlick Handbook § 2.5.

§3215. Crime to offer or receive compensation for referring clients or patients.

Except as otherwise permitted by law, any person acting individually or through his or her employees or agents, who offers, delivers, receives, or accepts any rebate, refund, commission, preference, patronage, dividend, discount or other consideration, whether in the form of money or otherwise, as compensation or inducement for referring clients or patients to perform or obtain services or benefits pursuant to this division, is guilty of a crime. **Leg.H.** 1991 ch. 116.

Ref.: Hanna §§ 20.01[1][d], 22.14; Herlick Handbook § 9.18.

§3217. Exceptions to prohibitions of §3215.

(a) Section 3215 shall not be construed to prevent the recommendation of professional employment where that recommendation is not prohibited by the Rules of Professional Conduct of the State Bar.

(b) Section 3215 shall not be construed to prohibit a public defender or assigned counsel from making known his or her availability as a criminal defense attorney to persons unable to afford legal counsel, whether or not those persons are in custody.

(c) Any person who commits an act that violates both Section 3215 and either Section 650 of the Business and Professions Code or Section 750 of the Insurance Code shall, upon conviction, have judgment and sentence imposed for only one violation for any act.

(d) Section 3215 shall not be construed to prohibit the payment or receipt of consideration or services that is lawful pursuant to Section 650 of the Business and Professions Code.

(e) Notwithstanding Sections 3215 and 3219, and Section 750 of the Insurance Code, nothing shall prevent an attorney at law or a law firm from providing any person or entity with legal advice, information, or legal services, including the providing of printed, copied, or written documents, either without charge or for an otherwise lawfully agreed upon attorney fee.

(f) Section 3215 shall not be construed to prohibit a workers' compensation insurer from offering, and an employer from accepting, a workers' compensation insurance policy with rates that reflect premium discounts based upon the employer securing coverage for occupational or nonoccupational illnesses or injuries from a health care service plan or disability insurer that is owned by, affiliated with, or has a contractual relationship with, the workers' compensation insurer. **Leg.H.** 1991 ch. 116, 1993 ch. 120, effective July 16, 1993, ch. 1242, 1995 ch. 886.

Ref.: Herlick Handbook §§ 3.2, 9.18.

§3218. Penalties for violating §3215.

A violation of Section 3215 is a public offense punishable upon a first conviction by incarceration in the county jail for not more than one year, or by incarceration in the state prison, or by a fine not exceeding ten thousand dollars ($10,000), or by both incarceration and fine. A second or subsequent conviction is punishable by incarceration in state prison. **Leg.H.** 1991 ch. 116.

Ref.: Herlick Handbook § 9.18.

§3219. Felony to offer compensation to claims adjuster; felony for adjuster to accept compensation; contract for services obtained through false statements is void; allocation of recoverable fees.

(a)(1) Except as otherwise permitted by law, any person acting individually or through his or her employees or agents, who offers or delivers any rebate, refund, commission, preference, patronage, dividend, discount, or other consideration to any adjuster of claims for compensation, as defined in Section 3207, as compensation, inducement, or reward for the referral or settlement of any claim, is guilty of a felony.

(2) Except as otherwise permitted by law, any adjuster of claims for compensation, as defined in Section 3207, who accepts or receives any rebate, refund, commission, preference, patronage, dividend, discount, or other consideration, as compensation, inducement, or reward for the referral or settlement of any claim, is guilty of a felony.

(b) Any contract for professional services secured by any medical clinic, laboratory, physician or other health care provider in this state in violation of Section 550 of the Penal Code, Section 1871.4 of the Insurance Code, Section 650 or 651 of the Business and Professions Code, or Section 3215 or subdivision (a) of Section 3219 of this code is void. In any action against any medical clinic, laboratory, physician, or other health care provider, or the owners or operators thereof, under Chapter 4 (commencing with Section 17000) or Chapter 5 (commencing with Section 17200) of Division 7 of the Business and Professions Code, any judgment shall include an order divesting the medical clinic, laboratory, physician, or other health care provider, and the owners and operators thereof, of any fees and other compensation received pursuant to any such void contract. Those fees and compensation shall be recoverable as additional civil penalties under Chapter 4 (commencing with Section 17000) or Chapter 5 (commencing with Section 17200) of Division 7 of the Business and Professions Code. The judgment may also include an order prohibiting the person from further participating in any manner in the entity in which that person directly or indirectly owned or operated for a time period that the court deems appropriate. For the purpose of this section, "operated" means participated in the management, direction, or control of the entity.

(c) Notwithstanding Section 17206 or any other provision of law, any fees recovered pursuant to subdivision (b) in an action involving professional services related to the provision of workers' compensation shall be allocated as follows: if the action is brought by the Attorney General, one-half of the penalty collected shall be paid to the State General Fund, and one-half of the penalty collected shall be paid to the Workers' Compensation Fraud Account in the Insurance Fund; if the action is brought by a district attorney, one-half of the penalty collected shall be paid to the treasurer of the county in which the judgment was entered, and one-half of the penalty collected shall be paid to the Workers' Compensation Fraud Account in the Insurance Fund; if the action is brought by a city attorney or city prosecutor, one-half of the penalty collected shall be paid to the treasurer of the city in which the judgment was entered, and one-half of the penalty collected shall be paid to the Workers' Compensation Fraud Account in the Insurance Fund. Moneys deposited into the Workers' Compensation Fraud Account pursuant to this subdivision shall be used in the investigation and prosecution of workers' compensation fraud, as appropriated by the Legislature. **Leg.H.** 1993 ch. 120, effective July 16, 1993.

Ref.: Herlick Handbook § 9.18.

CHAPTER 2 EMPLOYERS, EMPLOYEES, AND DEPENDENTS

ARTICLE 1 Employers

§3300. "Employer."

As used in this division, "employer" means:

(a) The State and every State agency.

(b) Each county, city, district, and all public and quasi public corporations and public agencies therein.

(c) Every person including any public service corporation, which has any natural person in service.

(d) The legal representative of any deceased employer.

Ref.: 8 C.C.R. §§9770, 9811, 15430.1; Herlick Handbook § 2.1.

§3301. Specified sponsors not "employers."

As used in this division, "employer" excludes the following:

(a) Any person while acting solely as the sponsor of a bowling team.

(b) Any private, nonprofit organization while acting solely as the sponsor of a person who, as a condition of sentencing by a superior or municipal court, is performing services for the organization.

The exclusions of this section do not exclude any person or organization from the application of this division which is otherwise an employer for the purposes of this division.

Ref.: Herlick Handbook §§ 2.1, 2.2, 2.4, 8.7.

§3302. Payment of workers' compensation premiums by temporary employment agency, employment referral service, labor contractor, or similar entity.

(a)(1) When a licensed contractor enters an agreement with a temporary employment agency, employment referral service, labor contractor, or other similar entity for the entity to supply the contractor with an individual to perform acts or contracts for which the contractor's license is required under Chapter 9 (commencing with Section 7000) of Division 3 of the Business and Professions Code and the licensed contractor is responsible for supervising the employee's work, the temporary employment agency, employment referral service, labor contractor, or other similar entity shall pay workers' compensation premiums based on the contractor's experience modification rating.

(2) The temporary employment agency, employment referral service, labor contractor, or other similar entity described in paragraph (1) shall report to the insurer both of the following:

(A) Its payroll on a monthly basis in sufficient detail to allow the insurer to determine the number of workers provided and the wages paid to these workers during the period the workers were supplied to the licensed contractor.

(B) The licensed contractor's name, address, and experience modification factor as reported by the licensed contractor.

(C) The workers' compensation classifications associated with the payroll reported pursuant to subparagraph (A). Classifications shall be assigned in accordance with the rules set forth in the California Workers' Compensation Uniform Statistical Reporting Plan published by the Workers' Compensation Insurance Rating Bureau.

(b) The temporary employment agency, employment referral service, labor contractor, or other similar entity supplying the individual under the conditions specified in subdivision (a) shall be solely responsible for the individual's workers' compensation, as specified in subdivision (a).

(c) Nothing in this section is intended to change existing law in effect on December 31, 2002, as it relates to the sole remedy provisions of this division and the special employer provisions of Section 11663 of the Insurance Code.

(d) A licensed contractor that is using a temporary worker supplied pursuant to subdivision (a) shall notify the temporary employment agency, employment referral service, labor contractor, or other similar entity that supplied that temporary worker when either of the following occurs:

(1) The temporary worker is being used on a public works project.

(2) The contractor reassigns a temporary worker to a position other than the classification to which the worker was originally assigned.

(e) A temporary employment agency, employment referral service, labor contractor, or other similar entity may pass through to a licensed contractor any additional costs incurred as a result of this section. **Leg.H.** 2002 ch. 1098 (AB 2816).

Ref.: Hanna § 3.134.

ARTICLE 2
Employees

§3350. Division's definitions to govern construction.

Unless the context otherwise requires, the definitions set forth in this article shall govern the construction and meaning of the terms and phrases used in this division.

§3351. "Employee."

"Employee" means every person in the service of an employer under any appointment or contract of hire or apprenticeship, express or implied, oral or written, whether lawfully or unlawfully employed, and includes:

(a) Aliens and minors.

(b) All elected and appointed paid public officers.

(c) All officers and members of boards of directors of quasi-public or private corporations while rendering actual service for the corporations for pay. An officer or member of a board of directors may elect to be excluded from coverage in accordance with paragraph (16), (18), or (19) of subdivision (a) of Section 3352.

(d) Except as provided in paragraph (8) of subdivision (a) of Section 3352, any person employed by the owner or occupant of a residential dwelling whose duties are incidental to the ownership, maintenance, or use of the dwelling, including the care and supervision of children, or whose duties are personal and not in the course of the trade, business, profession, or occupation of the owner or occupant.

(e) All persons incarcerated in a state penal or correctional institution while engaged in assigned work or employment as defined in paragraph (1) of subdivision (a) of Section 10021 of Title 8 of the California Code of Regulations, or engaged in work performed under contract.

(f) All working members of a partnership or limited liability company receiving wages irrespective of profits from the partnership or limited liability company. A general partner of a partnership or a managing member of a limited liability company may elect to be excluded from coverage in accordance with paragraph (17) of subdivision (a) of Section 3352.

(g) A person who holds the power to revoke a trust, with respect to shares of a private corporation held in trust or general partnership or limited liability company interests held in trust. To the extent that this person is deemed to be an employee described in subdivision (c) or (f), as applicable, the person may also elect to be excluded from coverage as described in subdivision (c) or (f), as applicable, if that person otherwise meets the criteria for exclusion, as described in Section 3352.

(h) A person committed to a state hospital facility under the State Department of State Hospitals, as defined in Section 4100 of the Welfare and Institutions Code, while engaged in and assigned work in a vocation rehabilitation program, including a sheltered workshop.

(i) Beginning on July 1, 2020, any individual who is an employee pursuant to Section 2750.3. This subdivision shall not apply retroactively. **Leg.H.** 2017 ch. 770 (SB 189) §2, 2019 ch. 38 (SB 78) §33, effective June 27, 2019, ch. 296 (AB 5) §3.

2019 Notes: The Legislature finds and declares all of the following:

(a) On April 30, 2018, the California Supreme Court issued a unanimous decision in *Dynamex Operations West, Inc. v. Superior Court of Los Angeles* (2018) 4 Cal.5th 903 (*Dynamex*).

(b) In its decision, the Court cited the harm to misclassified workers who lose significant workplace protections, the unfairness to employers who must compete with companies that misclassify, and the loss to the state of needed revenue from companies that use misclassification to avoid obligations such as payment of payroll taxes, payment of premiums for workers' compensation, Social Security, unemployment, and disability insurance.

(c) The misclassification of workers as independent contractors has been a significant factor in the erosion of the middle class and the rise in income inequality.

(d) It is the intent of the Legislature in enacting this act to include provisions that would codify the decision of the California Supreme Court in *Dynamex* and would clarify the decision's application in state law.

(e) It is also the intent of the Legislature in enacting this act to ensure workers who are currently exploited by being misclassified as independent contractors instead of recognized as employees have the basic rights and protections they deserve under the law, including a minimum wage, workers' compensation if they are injured on the job, unemployment insurance, paid sick leave, and paid family leave. By codifying the California Supreme Court's landmark, unanimous *Dynamex* decision, this act restores these important protections to potentially several million workers who have been denied these basic workplace rights that all employees are entitled to under the law.

(f) The *Dynamex* decision interpreted one of the three alternative definitions of "employ," the "suffer or permit" definition, from the wage orders of the Industrial Welfare Commission (IWC). Nothing in this act is intended to affect the application of alternative definitions from the IWC wage orders of the term "employ," which were not addressed by the holding of *Dynamex*.

(g) Nothing in this act is intended to diminish the flexibility of employees to work part-time or intermittent schedules or to work for multiple employers. Stats. 2019 ch. 296 (AB 5) §1.

No provision of this measure shall permit an employer to reclassify an individual who was an employee on January 1, 2019, to an independent contractor due to this measure's enactment. Stats. 2019 ch. 296 (AB 5) §6.

Ref.: 8 C.C.R. §§9811, 10133.4; Hanna §§ 2.50[4][f], 2.63[3][c], 2.82, 3.30, 3.34, 3.36[3], 3.89; Herlick Handbook §§ 2.3, 2.4, 8.21.

§3351.5. Employees included.

"Employee" includes:

(a) Any person whose employment training is arranged by the State Department of Rehabilitation with any employer. Such person shall be deemed an employee of such employer for workers' compensation purposes; provided that, the department shall bear the full amount of any additional workers' compensation insurance premium expense incurred by the employer due to the provisions of this section.

(b) Any person defined in subdivision (d) of Section 3351 who performs domestic service comprising in-home supportive services under Article 7 (commencing with Section 12300), Chapter 3, Part 3, Division 9 of the Welfare and Institutions Code. For purposes of Section 3352, such person shall be deemed an employee of the recipient of such services for workers' compensation purposes if the state or county makes or provides for direct payment to such person or to the recipient of in-home supportive services for the purchase of services, subject to the provisions of Section 12302.2 of the Welfare and Institutions Code.

(c) Any person while engaged by contract for the creation of a specially ordered or commissioned work of authorship in which the parties expressly agree in a written instrument signed by them that the work shall be considered a work made for hire, as defined in Section 101 of Title 17 of the United States Code, and the ordering or commissioning party obtains ownership of all the rights comprised in the copyright in the work.

Ref.: 8 C.C.R. §9811; Herlick Handbook § 2.5.

§3352. Persons excluded from definition of employee.

(a) "Employee," excludes the following:

(1) A person defined in subdivision (d) of Section 3351 who is employed by his or her parent, spouse, or child.

(2) A person performing services in return for aid or sustenance only, received from any religious, charitable, or relief organization.

(3) A person holding an appointment as deputy clerk or deputy sheriff appointed for his or her own convenience, and who does not receive compensation from the county or municipal corporation or from the citizens of that county or municipal corporation for his or her services as the deputy. This exclusion is operative only as to employment by the county or municipal corporation and does not deprive that person of recourse against a private person employing him or her for injury occurring in the course of, and arising out of, the employment.

(4) A person performing voluntary services at or for a recreational camp, hut, or lodge operated by a nonprofit organization, exempt from federal income tax under Section 501(c)(3) of the Internal Revenue Code, of which he or she or a member of his or her family is a member and who does not receive compensation for those services, other than meals, lodging, or transportation.

(5) A person performing voluntary service as a ski patrolman who does not receive compensation for those services, other than meals or lodging or the use of ski tow or ski lift facilities.

(6) A person employed by a ski lift operator to work at a snow ski area who is relieved of, and is not performing any, prescribed duties, while participating in recreational activities on his or her own initiative.

(7) A person, other than a regular employee, participating in sports or athletics who does not receive compensation for the participation other than the use of athletic equipment, uniforms, transportation, travel, meals, lodgings, or other expenses incidental thereto.

(8) A person described in subdivision (d) of Section 3351 whose employment by the employer to be held liable, during the 90 calendar days immediately preceding the date of injury, for injuries as described in Section 5411, or during the 90 calendar days immediately preceding the date of the last employment in an occupation exposing the employee to the hazards of the disease or injury, for diseases or injuries as described in Section 5412, comes within either of the following descriptions:

(A) The employment was, or was contracted to be, for less than 52 hours.

(B) The employment was, or was contracted to be, for wages of not more than one hundred dollars ($100).

(9) A person performing voluntary service for a public agency or a private, nonprofit organization who does not receive remuneration for the services, other than meals, transportation, lodging, or reimbursement for incidental expenses.

(10) A person, other than a regular employee, performing officiating services relating to amateur sporting events sponsored by a public agency or private, nonprofit organization, who does not receive remuneration for these services, other than a stipend for each day of service no greater than the amount established by the Department of Human Resources as a per diem expense for employees or officers of the state. The stipend shall be presumed to cover incidental expenses involved in officiating, including, but not limited to, meals, transportation, lodging, rule books and courses, uniforms, and appropriate equipment.

(11) A student participating as an athlete in amateur sporting events sponsored by a public agency or public or private nonprofit college, university, or school, who does not receive remuneration for the participation, other than the use of athletic equipment, uniforms, transportation, travel, meals, lodgings, scholarships, grants-in-aid, or other expenses incidental thereto.

(12) A law enforcement officer who is regularly employed by a local or state law enforcement agency in an adjoining state and who is deputized to work under the supervision of a California peace officer pursuant to paragraph (4) of subdivision (a) of Section 832.6 of the Penal Code.

(13) A law enforcement officer who is regularly employed by the Oregon State Police, the Nevada Department of Public Safety, or the Arizona Department of Public Safety and who is acting as a peace officer in this state pursuant to subdivision (a) of Section 830.39 of the Penal Code.

(14) A person, other than a regular employee, performing services as a sports official for an entity sponsoring an intercollegiate or interscholastic sports event, or any person performing services as a sports official for a public agency, public entity, or a private nonprofit organization, which public agency, public entity, or private nonprofit organization sponsors an amateur sports event. For purposes of this subdivision, "sports official" includes an umpire, referee, judge, scorekeeper, timekeeper, or other person who is a neutral participant in a sports event.

(15) A person who is an owner-builder, as defined in subdivision (a) of Section 50692 of the Health and Safety Code, who is participating in a mutual self-help housing program, as defined in Section 50087 of the Health and Safety Code, sponsored by a nonprofit corporation.

(16)(A)(i) An officer or member of the board of directors, as described in subdivision (c) of Section 3351, if he or she owns at least 10 percent of the issued and outstanding stock of the corporation, or at least 1 percent of the issued and outstanding stock of the corporation if that officer's or member's parent, grandparent, sibling, spouse, or child owns at least 10 percent of the issued and outstanding stock of the corporation and that officer or member is covered by a health insurance policy or a health care service plan, and executes a written waiver of his or her rights under this chapter stating under penalty of perjury that the person is a qualifying officer or director. The waiver shall be effective upon the date of receipt and acceptance by the corporation's insurance carrier. The insurance carrier, with the consent of the individual executing the waiver, may elect to backdate the acceptance of the waiver up to 15 days prior to the date of receipt of the waiver. The insurance carrier, insurance agent, or insurance broker is not required to investigate, verify, or confirm the accuracy of the facts contained in the waiver. There is a conclusive presumption that a person who executes a waiver pursuant to this subdivision is not covered by workers' compensation benefits.

(ii) A written waiver that is executed pursuant to this subparagraph, including, but not limited to, a written waiver that was executed prior to January 1, 2017, and is accepted by the insurance carrier on or before December 31, 2017, may be deemed to be accepted by the insurance carrier as of January 1, 2017. The written waiver shall remain in effect until the officer or member of the board of directors provides the corporation's insurance carrier with a written withdrawal of the waiver.

(B) Notwithstanding subparagraph (A), an officer or director of a private corporation who is the sole shareholder of the private corporation, unless the officer, director, or private corporation has elected to be subject to liability for workers' compensation pursuant to subdivision (a) of Section 4151.

(17)(A) An individual who is a general partner of a partnership or a managing member of a limited liability company who executes a written waiver of his or her rights under this chapter stating under penalty of perjury that the person is a qualifying general partner or managing member. The waiver shall be effective upon the date of receipt and acceptance by the partnership's or limited liability company's insurance carrier. The insurance carrier, with the consent of the individual executing the waiver, may elect to backdate the acceptance of the waiver up to 15 days prior to the date of receipt of the waiver. The insurance carrier, insurance agent, or insurance broker is not required to investigate, verify, or confirm the accuracy of the facts contained in the waiver. There is a conclusive presumption that a person who executes a waiver pursuant to this subdivision is not covered by workers' compensation benefits.

(B) A written waiver that is executed pursuant to this paragraph, including, but not limited to, a written waiver that was executed prior to January 1, 2017, and is accepted

Labor

by the insurance carrier on or before December 31, 2017, may be deemed to be accepted by the insurance carrier as of January 1, 2017. The written waiver shall remain in effect until the general partner provides the partnership's insurance carrier or the managing member provides the limited liability company's insurance carrier with a written withdrawal of the waiver.

(18)(A)(i) An owner of a professional corporation, as defined in Section 13401 of the Corporations Code, who is a practitioner rendering the professional services for which the professional corporation is organized and who executes a document, in writing and under penalty of perjury, both waiving his or her rights under this chapter and stating that he or she is covered by a health insurance policy or a health care service plan. The owner shall provide a copy of the waiver to all other owners of the professional corporation and the professional corporation shall keep a copy of the waiver on file. The waiver is effective upon the date of receipt and acceptance by the professional corporation's insurance carrier. The insurance carrier, with the consent of the individual executing the waiver, may elect to backdate the acceptance of the waiver up to 15 days prior to the date of receipt of the waiver. The insurance carrier, insurance agent, or insurance broker is not required to investigate, verify, or confirm the accuracy of the facts contained in the waiver. There is a conclusive presumption that a person who executes a waiver pursuant to this subdivision is not covered by workers' compensation benefits.

(ii) A written waiver that is executed pursuant to this subparagraph and is accepted by the insurance carrier on or before December 31, 2017, may be deemed to be accepted by the insurance carrier as of January 1, 2017. The written waiver shall remain in effect until the owner provides the professional corporation's insurance carrier with a written withdrawal of the waiver.

(B) Notwithstanding subparagraph (A), an owner of a private professional corporation who is the sole shareholder of the private professional corporation, unless the owner or private professional corporation has elected to be subject to liability for workers' compensation pursuant to subdivision (a) of Section 4151.

(19)(A)(i) An officer or member of the board of directors of a cooperative corporation organized pursuant to the Cooperative Corporation Law, as set forth in Part 2 (commencing with Section 12200) of Division 3 of Title 1 of the Corporations Code, who executes a document, in writing and under penalty of perjury, both waiving his or her rights under this chapter and stating that he or she is covered by both a health care service plan or health insurance policy, and a disability insurance policy that is comparable in scope and coverage, as determined by the Insurance Commissioner, to a workers' compensation policy. The officer or member of the board of directors shall provide a copy of the waiver to all other officers and members of the board of directors of the cooperative corporation, and the cooperative corporation shall keep a copy of the waiver on file. The waiver is effective upon the date of receipt and acceptance by the cooperative corporation's insurance carrier. The insurance carrier, with the consent of the individual executing the waiver, may elect to backdate the acceptance of the waiver up to 15 days prior to the date of receipt of the waiver. The insurance carrier, insurance agent, or insurance broker is not required to investigate, verify, or confirm the accuracy of the facts contained in the waiver. There is a conclusive presumption that a person who executes a waiver pursuant to this subdivision is not covered by workers' compensation benefits.

(ii) A written waiver that is executed pursuant to this subparagraph and is accepted by the insurance carrier on or before December 31, 2017, may be deemed to be accepted by the insurance carrier as of January 1, 2017. The written waiver shall remain in effect until the officer or member of the board provides the cooperative corporation's insurance carrier with a written withdrawal of the waiver.

(B) Notwithstanding subparagraph (A), an officer or director of a private cooperative corporation who is the sole shareholder of the private cooperative corporation, unless the officer, director, or private cooperative corporation has elected to be subject to liability for workers' compensation pursuant to subdivision (a) of Section 4151.

(b)(1) This section shall become operative on July 1, 2018.

(2) A policy or contract that is entered into or renewed in compliance with this section is subject to this section as it read on the date that the policy or contract was entered into or renewed. **Leg.H.** 2017 ch. 770 (SB 189) §4.

Ref.: Hanna §§ 3.36[1], [2][a], [b], [3], 3.40, 3.80, 3.89, 21.04[1][a]; Herlick Handbook §§ 2.1, 2.4, 2.5.

§3352.94. Exclusions for disaster service workers as "employees."

"Employee" excludes a disaster service worker while performing services as a disaster service worker except as provided in Chapter 10 of this part. "Employee" excludes any unregistered person performing like services as a disaster service worker without pay or other consideration, except as provided by Section 3211.92 of this code.

Ref.: Herlick Handbook § 2.4.

§3353. "Independent contractor."

"Independent contractor" means any person who renders service for a specified recompense for a specified result, under the control of his principal as to the result of his work only and not as to the means by which such result is accomplished.

Ref.: Herlick Handbook §§ 2.7, 2.8.

§3354. Employers of household workers.

Employers of employees defined by subdivision (d) of Section 3351 shall not be subject to the provisions of Sections 3710, 3710.1, 3710.2, 3711, 3712, and 3722, or any other penalty provided by law, for failure to secure the payment of compensation for such employees.

This section shall not apply to employers of employees specified in subdivision (b) of Section 3715, with respect to such employees.

Ref.: Hanna § 10.27; Herlick Handbook § 2.4.

§3355. "Course of trade, business, profession, or occupation."

As used in subdivision (d) of Section 3351, the term "course of trade, business, profession, or occupation" includes all services tending toward the preservation, maintenance, or operation of the business, business premises, or business property of the employer.

Ref.: Herlick Handbook § 2.5.

§3356. "Trade, business, profession, or occupation."

As used in subdivision (d) of Section 3351 and in Section 3355, the term "trade, business, profession, or occupation" includes any undertaking actually engaged in by the employer with some degree of regularity, irrespective of the trade name, articles of incorporation, or principal business of the employer.

Ref.: Herlick Handbook §§ 2.4, 2.5.

§3357. Presumption that one rendering service is employee.

Any person rendering service for another, other than as an independent contractor, or unless expressly excluded herein, is presumed to be an employee.

Ref.: Herlick Handbook §§ 2.3, 2.7, 2.8.

§3358. Watchmen.

Watchmen for nonindustrial establishments, paid by subscription by several persons, are not employees under this division. In other cases where watchmen, paid by subscription by several persons, have at the time of the injury sustained by them taken out and maintained in force insurance upon themselves as self-employing persons, conferring benefits equal to those conferred by this division, the employer is not liable under this division.

Ref.: Herlick Handbook § 2.4.

§3360. Partners for particular piece of work.

Workers associating themselves under a partnership agreement, the principal purpose of which is the performance of the labor on a particular piece of work are employees of the person having such work executed. In respect to injuries which occur while such workers maintain in force insurance in an insurer, insuring to themselves and all persons employed by them benefits identical with those conferred by this division the person for whom such work is to be done is not liable as an employer under this division.

Ref.: Herlick Handbook § 2.4.

§3361. Volunteer firefighters.

Each member registered as an active firefighting member of any regularly organized volunteer fire department, having official recognition, and full or partial support of the government of the county, city, town, or district in which the volunteer fire department is located, is an employee of that county, city, town, or district for the purposes of this division, and is entitled to receive compensation from the county, city, town, or district in accordance with the provisions thereof.

Ref.: Herlick Handbook § 2.5.

§3361.5. Authorized volunteers of recreation and park districts.

Notwithstanding Section 3351, a volunteer, unsalaried person authorized by the governing board of a recreation and park district to perform volunteer services for the district shall, upon the adoption of a resolution of the governing board of the district so declaring, be deemed an employee of the district for the purposes of this division and shall be entitled to the workers' compensation benefits provided by this division for any injury sustained by him or her while engaged in the performance of any service under the direction and control of the governing board of the recreation and park district.

§3362. Active police officers.

Each male or female member registered as an active policeman or policewoman of any regularly organized police department having official recognition and full or partial support of the government of the county, city, town, or district in which such police department is located, shall, upon the adoption of a resolution by the governing body of the county, city, town or district so declaring, be deemed an employee of such county, city, town or district for the purpose of this division and shall be entitled to receive compensation from such county, city, town or district in accordance with the provisions thereof.

Ref.: Hanna § 33.02[3][a]; Herlick Handbook § 2.5.

§3362.5. Reserve and auxiliary peace officers.

Whenever any qualified person is deputized or appointed by the proper authority as a reserve or auxiliary sheriff or city police officer, a deputy sheriff, or a reserve police officer of a regional park district or a transit district, and is assigned specific police functions by that authority, the person is an employee of the county, city, city and county, town, or district for the purposes of this division while performing duties as a peace officer if the person is not performing services as a disaster service worker for purposes of Chapter 10 (commencing with Section 4351).

1989 Note: This section is applicable only to injuries occurring on or after January 1, 1990. Stats. 1989 ch. 893 §6.

§3363. Registered members of reserve fish and game warden program.

Each member registered with the Department of Fish and Game as an active member of the reserve fish and game warden program of the department is an employee of the department for the purposes of this division and is entitled to receive compensation from the department in accordance with the provisions thereof.

Ref.: Herlick Handbook § 2.5.

§3363.5. Public agency volunteers.

(a) Notwithstanding Sections 3351, 3352, and 3357, a person who performs voluntary service without pay for a public agency, as designated and authorized by the governing body of the agency or its designee, shall, upon adoption of a resolution by the governing body of the agency so declaring, be deemed to be an employee of the agency for purposes of this division while performing such service.

(b) For purposes of this section, "voluntary service without pay" shall include services performed by any person, who receives no remuneration other than meals, transportation, lodging, or reimbursement for incidental expenses.

Ref.: Herlick Handbook § 2.5.

§3363.6. Volunteers for private, nonprofit organizations.

(a) Notwithstanding Sections 3351, 3352, and 3357, a person who performs voluntary service without pay for a private, nonprofit organization, as designated and authorized by the board of directors of the organization, shall, when the board of directors of the organization, in its sole discretion, so declares in writing and prior to the injury, be deemed an employee of the organization for purposes of this division while performing such service.

(b) For purposes of this section, "voluntary service without pay" shall include the performance of service by a parent, without remuneration in cash, when rendered to a cooperative parent participation nursery school if such service is required as a condition of participation in the organization.

(c) For purposes of this section, "voluntary service without pay" shall include the performance of services by a person who receives no remuneration other than meals, transportation, lodging, or reimbursement for incidental expenses.

Ref.: Herlick Handbook § 2.5.

§3364. Sheriff's reserve volunteers.

Notwithstanding paragraph (3) of subdivision (a) of Section 3352, a volunteer, unsalaried member of a sheriff's reserve in any county who is not deemed an employee of the county under Section 3362.5, shall, upon the adoption of a resolution of the board of supervisors declaring that the member is deemed an employee of the county for the purposes of this division, be entitled to the workers' compensation benefits provided by this division for any injury sustained by him or her while engaged in the performance of any active law enforcement service under the direction and control of the sheriff. **Leg.H.** 1961 ch. 901 §1, 1989 ch. 892 §26, 2006 ch. 538 (SB 1852) §488, 2017 ch. 770 (SB 189) §5.

1989 Note: This section is applicable only to injuries occurring on or after January 1, 1990. Stats. 1989 ch. 893 §6.

Ref.: Herlick Handbook §§ 2.4, 2.5.

§3364.5. Volunteers for school districts and county superintendents of schools.

Notwithstanding Section 3351 of the Labor Code, a volunteer, unsalaried person authorized by the governing board of a school district or the county superintendent of schools to perform volunteer services for the school district or the county superintendent shall, upon the adoption of a resolution of the governing board of the school district or the county board of education so declaring, be deemed an employee of the district or the county superintendent for the purposes of this division and shall be entitled to the workers' compensation benefits provided by this division for any injury sustained by him while engaged in the performance of any service under the direction and control of the governing board of the school district or the county superintendent.

Ref.: Herlick Handbook § 2.5.

§3364.55. Juvenile court wards doing rehabilitative work.

A ward of the juvenile court engaged in rehabilitative work without pay, under an assignment by order of the juvenile court to a work project on public property within the jurisdiction of any governmental entity, including the federal government, shall, upon the adoption of a resolution of the board of supervisors declaring that such ward is deemed an employee of the county for purposes of this division, be entitled to the workers' compensation benefits provided by this division for injury sustained while in the performance of such assigned work project, provided:

(a) That such ward shall not be entitled to any temporary disability indemnity benefits.

(b) That in determining permanent disability benefits, average weekly earnings shall be taken at the minimum provided therefor in Section 4453.

Ref.: Herlick Handbook § 2.5.

§3364.6. Juvenile traffic offenders doing rehabilitative work.

Notwithstanding Sections 3351 and 3352, juvenile traffic offenders pursuant to Section 564 of the Welfare and Institutions Code, or juvenile probationers pursuant to subdivision (a) of Section 725 of the Welfare and Institutions Code, engaged in rehabilitative work without pay, under an assignment by order of the juvenile court to a work project on public property within the jurisdiction of any governmental entity, including the federal government, shall, upon the adoption of a resolution of the board of supervisors declaring that such traffic offenders or probationers, or both such groups, shall be deemed employees of the county for purposes of this division, be entitled to the workers' compensation benefits provided by this division for injury sustained while in the performance of such assigned work project, provided:

(a) That such traffic offender or probationer shall not be entitled to any temporary disability indemnity benefits.

(b) That in determining permanent disability benefits, average weekly earnings shall be taken at the minimum provided therefor in Section 4453.

Ref.: Herlick Handbook §2.5.

§3364.7. Juvenile court wards committed to regional youth educational facility.

Notwithstanding Sections 3351 and 3352, a ward of the juvenile court committed to a regional youth educational facility pursuant to Article 24.5 (commencing with Section 894), engaged in rehabilitative work without pay on public property within the jurisdiction of any governmental entity, including the federal government, shall, upon the adoption of a resolution of the board of supervisors declaring that such wards shall be deemed employees of the county for purposes of this division, be entitled to the workers' compensation benefits provided by this division for injury sustained while in the performance of such public work project, provided:

(a) That the ward shall not be entitled to any disability indemnity benefits.

(b) That in determining permanent disability benefits, average weekly earnings shall be taken at the minimum provided therefor in Section 4453.

§3365. Persons engaged in suppressing fires.

For the purposes of this division:

(a) Except as provided in subdivisions (b) and (c), each person engaged in suppressing a fire pursuant to Section 4153 or 4436 of the Public Resources Code, and each person (other than an independent contractor or an employee of an independent contractor) engaged in suppressing a fire at the request of a public officer or employee charged with the duty of preventing or suppressing fires, is deemed, except when the entity is the United States or an agency thereof, to be an employee of the public entity that he is serving or assisting in the suppression of the fire, and is entitled to receive compensation from such public entity in accordance with the provisions of this division. When the entity being served is the United States or an agency thereof, the State Department of Corrections shall be deemed the employer and the cost of workers' compensation may be considered in fixing the reimbursement paid by the United States for the service of prisoners. A person is engaged in suppressing a fire only during the period he (1) is actually fighting the fire, (2) is being transported to or from the fire, or (3) is engaged in training exercises for fire suppression.

(b) A member of the armed forces of the United States while serving under military command in suppressing a fire is not an employee of a public entity.

(c) Neither a person who contracts to furnish aircraft with pilots to a public entity for fire prevention or suppression service, nor his employees, shall be deemed to be employees of the public entity; but a person who contracts to furnish aircraft to a public entity for fire prevention or suppression service and to pilot the aircraft himself shall be deemed to be an employee of the public entity.

Ref.: Hanna § 6.05[2]; Herlick Handbook § 2.5.

§3366. Persons assisting in active law enforcement.

(a) For the purposes of this division, each person engaged in the performance of active law enforcement service as part of the posse comitatus or power of the county, and each person (other than an independent contractor or an employee of an independent contractor) engaged in assisting any peace officer in active law enforcement service at the request of such peace officer, is deemed to be an employee of the public entity that he or she is serving or assisting in the enforcement of the law, and is entitled to receive compensation from the public entity in accordance with the provisions of this division.

(b) Nothing in this section shall be construed to provide workers' compensation benefits to a person who is any of the following:

(1) A law enforcement officer who is regularly employed by a local or state law enforcement agency in an adjoining state and who is deputized to work under the supervision of a California peace officer pursuant to paragraph (4) of subdivision (a) of Section 832.6 of the Penal Code.

(2) A law enforcement officer who is regularly employed by the Oregon State Police, the Nevada Department of Motor Vehicles and Public Safety, or the Arizona Department of Public Safety and who is acting as a peace officer in this state pursuant to subdivision (a) of Section 830.32 of the Penal Code.

Ref.: Herlick Handbook §§ 2.4, 2.5.

§3367. Technical assistants to fire or law enforcement officers.

(a) For purposes of this division any person voluntarily rendering technical assistance to a public entity to prevent a fire, explosion, or other hazardous occurrence, at the request of a duly authorized fire or law enforcement officer of that public entity is deemed an employee of the public entity to whom the technical assistance was rendered, and is entitled to receive compensation benefits in accordance with the provisions of this division. Rendering technical assistance shall include the time that person is traveling to, or returning from, the location of the potentially hazardous condition for which he or she has been requested to volunteer his or her assistance.

(b) Nothing in this section shall be construed to provide workers' compensation benefits to a person who is any of the following:

(1) A law enforcement officer who is regularly employed by a local or state law enforcement agency in an adjoining state and who is deputized to work under the supervision of a California peace officer pursuant to paragraph (4) of subdivision (a) of Section 832.6 of the Penal Code.

(2) A law enforcement officer who is regularly employed by the Oregon State Police, the Nevada Department of Motor Vehicles and Public Safety, or the Arizona Department of Public Safety and who is acting as a peace officer in this state pursuant to subdivision (a) of Section 830.32 of the Penal Code.

Ref.: Herlick Handbook §§ 2.4, 2.5.

§3368. Supervision of work experience education, cooperative vocational education, community classroom, or student apprenticeship program by school, school district, or county superintendent; school, school district, or county superintendent as "employer"; exceptions; "registered student apprentice"; regional and joint supervision of program.

Notwithstanding any provision of this code or the Education Code to the contrary, the school district, county superintendent of schools, or any school administered by the State Department of Education under whose supervision work experience education, cooperative vocational education, or community classrooms, as defined by regulations adopted by the Superintendent of Public Instruction, or student apprenticeship programs registered by the Division of Apprenticeship Standards for registered student apprentices, are provided, shall be considered the employer under Division 4 (commencing with Section 3200) of persons receiving this training unless the persons during the training are being paid a cash wage or salary by a private employer. However, in the case of students being paid a cash wage or salary by a private employer in supervised work experience education or cooperative vocational education, or in the case of registered student apprentices, the school district, county superintendent of schools, or any school administered by the State Department of Education may elect to provide workers' compensation coverage, unless the person or firm under whom the persons are receiving work experience or occupational training elects to provide workers' compensation coverage. If the school district or other educational agency elects to provide workers' compensation coverage for students being paid a cash wage or salary by a private employer in supervised work experience education or cooperative vocational education, it may only be for a transitional period not to exceed three months. A registered student apprentice is a registered apprentice who is (1) at least 16 years of age, (2) a full-time high school student in the 10th, 11th, or 12th grade, and (3) in an apprenticeship program for registered student apprentices registered with the Division of Apprenticeship Standards. An apprentice, while attending related and supplemental instruction classes, shall be considered to be in the employ of the apprentice's employer and not subject to this section, unless the apprentice is unemployed. Whenever this work experience education, cooperative vocational education, community classroom education, or student apprenticeship program registered by the Division of Apprenticeship Standards for registered student apprentices, is under the supervision of a regional occupational center or program operated by two or more school districts pursuant to Section 52301 of the Education Code, the district of residence of the persons receiving the training shall be deemed the employer for the purposes of this section. **Leg.H.** 1997 ch. 345, 1998 ch. 541.

Ref.: Herlick Handbook § 2.5.

§3369. Effect of coverage by this division.

The inclusion of any person or groups of persons within the coverage of this division shall not cause any such person or group of persons to be within the coverage of any other statute unless any other such statute expressly so provides.

Ref.: Herlick Handbook § 2.1.

§3370. State penal or correctional institution inmates.

(a) Each inmate of a state penal or correctional institution shall be entitled to the workers' compensation benefits provided by this division for injury arising out of and in the course of assigned employment and for the death of the inmate if the injury proximately causes death, subject to all of the following conditions:

(1) The inmate was not injured as the result of an assault in which the inmate was the initial aggressor, or as the result of the intentional act of the inmate injuring himself or herself.

(2) The inmate shall not be entitled to any temporary disability indemnity benefits while incarcerated in a state prison.

(3) No benefits shall be paid to an inmate while he or she is incarcerated. The period of benefit payment shall instead commence upon release from incarceration. If an inmate who has been released from incarceration, and has been receiving benefits under this section, is reincarcerated in a city or county jail, or state penal or correctional institution, the benefits shall cease immediately upon the inmate's reincarceration and shall not be paid for the duration of the reincarceration.

(4) This section shall not be construed to provide for the payment to an inmate, upon release from incarceration, of temporary disability benefits which were not paid due to the prohibition of paragraph (2).

(5) In determining temporary and permanent disability indemnity benefits for the inmate, the average weekly earnings shall be taken at not more than the minimum amount set forth in Section 4453.

(6) Where a dispute exists respecting an inmate's rights to the workers' compensation benefits provided herein, the inmate may file an application with the appeals board to resolve the dispute. The application may be filed at any time during the inmate's incarceration.

(7) After release or discharge from a correctional institution, the former inmate shall have one year in which to file an original application with the appeals board, unless the time of injury is such that it would allow more time under Section 5804 of the Labor Code.

(8) The percentage of disability to total disability shall be determined as for the occupation of a laborer of like age by applying the schedule for the determination of the percentages of permanent disabilities prepared and adopted by the administrative director.

(9) This division shall be the exclusive remedy against the state for injuries occurring while engaged in assigned work or work under contract. Nothing in this division shall affect any right or remedy of an injured inmate for injuries not compensated by this division.

(b) The Department of Corrections shall present to each inmate of a state penal or correctional institution, prior to his or her first assignment to work at the institution, a printed statement of his or her rights under this division, and a description of procedures to be followed in filing for benefits under this section. The statement shall be approved by the administrative director and be posted in a conspicuous place at each place where an inmate works.

(c) Not withstanding any other provision of this division, the Department of Corrections shall have medical control over treatment provided an injured inmate while incarcerated in a state prison, except, that in serious cases, the inmate is entitled, upon request, to the services of a consulting physician.

(d) Paragraphs (2), (3), and (4) of subdivision (a) shall also be applicable to an inmate of a state penal or correctional institution who would otherwise be entitled to receive workers' compensation benefits based on an injury sustained prior to his or her incarceration. However, temporary and permanent disability benefits which, except for this subdivision, would otherwise be payable to an inmate during incarceration based on an injury sustained prior to incarceration shall be paid to the dependents of the inmate. If the inmate has no dependents, the temporary disability benefits which, except for this subdivision, would otherwise be payable during the inmate's incarceration shall be paid to the State Treasury to the credit of the Uninsured Employers Fund, and the permanent disability benefits which would otherwise be payable during the inmate's incarceration shall be held in trust for the inmate by the Department of Corrections during the period of incarceration.

For purposes of this subdivision, "dependents" means the inmate's spouse or children, including an inmate's former spouse due to divorce and the inmate's children from that marriage.

(e) Notwithstanding any other provision of this division, an employee who is an inmate, as defined in subdivision (e) of Section 3351 who is eligible for vocational rehabilitation services as defined in Section 4635 shall only be eligible for direct placement services. **Leg.H.** 1994 ch. 497.

Ref.: 8 C.C.R. §10133.4; Hanna §§ 3.100[1], [2][b], 6.05[3]; Herlick Handbook § 2.4.

§3370.1. State Department of State Hospitals facility patient.

(a) Each patient in a State Department of State Hospital facility shall be entitled to the workers' compensation benefits provided by this division for injury arising out of and in the course of a vocational rehabilitation program work assignment, including a sheltered workshop work assignment, and for the death of the patient if the injury proximately causes death, subject to all of the following conditions:

(1) The patient was not injured as the result of an assault in which the patient was the initial aggressor, or as the result of the intentional act of the patient injuring themselves.

(2) The patient shall not be entitled to any temporary disability indemnity benefits while committed in a state hospital facility or reincarcerated in a city or county jail or state penal or correctional institution.

(3) Benefits shall not be paid to a patient while the patient is committed in a state hospital facility. The period of benefit payment shall instead commence upon release from a state hospital. If a patient who has been released from a state hospital facility, and has been receiving benefits under this section, is recommitted to a state hospital facility, a jail-based competency treatment program, an Admission, Evaluation, and Stabilization (AES) Center, or any other program considered to be a facility of the State Department of State Hospitals under Section 4100 of the Welfare and Institutions Code, or if the patient is reincarcerated in a city or county jail or state penal or correctional institution, the benefits shall cease immediately upon the patient's recommitment or reincarceration and shall not be paid for the duration of the recommitment or reincarceration.

(4) This section shall not be construed to provide for the payment to a patient, upon release from a state hospital facility, a jail-based competency treatment program, an Admission, Evaluation, and Stabilization (AES) Center, or any other program considered to be a facility of the State Department of State Hospitals under Section 4100 of the Welfare and Institutions Code, or upon release from incarceration, of temporary disability benefits that were not paid due to the prohibition of paragraph (2).

(5) In determining temporary and permanent disability indemnity benefits for the patient, the average weekly earnings shall be taken at not more than the minimum amount set forth in Section 4453.

(6) If a dispute exists respecting a patient's rights to the workers' compensation benefits provided herein, the patient may file an application with the workers' compensation appeals board to resolve the dispute. The application may be filed at any time during the patient's commitment at a state hospital facility.

(7) After release or discharge from a state hospital facility, the former patient shall have one year in which to file an original application with the workers' compensation appeals board, unless the time of injury is such that it would allow more time under Section 5804.

(8) The percentage of disability to total disability shall be determined as for the occupation of a laborer of like age by applying the schedule for the determination of the percentages of permanent disabilities prepared and adopted by the administrative director.

(9) This division shall be the exclusive remedy against the state for injuries occurring while engaged in a vocational rehabilitation program. Nothing in this division shall affect any other right or remedy of an injured patient resulting from injuries not compensated by this division.

(b) The State Department of State Hospitals shall present to each patient worker, prior to their first vocational rehabilitation assignment, a printed statement of their rights under this division, and a description of procedures to be followed in filing for benefits under this section. The statement shall be approved by the Director of State Hospitals or their designee and shall be posted in various conspicuous locations where patients work or reside.

(c) Notwithstanding any other provision of this division, the State Department of State Hospitals shall provide medical care for its patients, which may include medical services at an outside facility.

(d)(1) Paragraphs (2), (3), and (4) of subdivision (a) shall also be applicable to a patient who would otherwise be entitled to receive workers' compensation benefits based on an injury sustained prior to their commitment to a state hospital facility. However, temporary and permanent disability benefits which, except for this subdivision, would otherwise be payable to a patient based on an injury sustained prior to commitment to a state hospital facility, a jail-based competency treatment program, an Admission, Evaluation, and Stabilization (AES) Center, or any other program considered to be a facility of the State Department of State Hospitals under Section 4100 of the Welfare and Institutions Code, shall be paid to the dependents of the patient. If the patient has no dependents, the temporary disability benefits which, except for this subdivision, would otherwise be payable during the patient's commitment shall be paid to the State Treasury to the credit of the Uninsured Employers Benefits Trust Fund, and the permanent disability benefits that would otherwise be payable during the patient's commitment shall be held in trust for the patient by the State Department of State Hospitals during the period of commitment.

(2) For purposes of this subdivision, "dependents" means the patient's spouse or children, including a patient's former spouse due to divorce and the patient's children from that marriage.

(e) Notwithstanding any other provision of this division, a patient who is an employee, as defined in subdivision (h) of Section 3351, is eligible for supplemental job displacement benefits as defined in Section 4658.7. **Leg.H.** 2019 ch. 38 (SB 78) §34, effective June 27, 2019.

Ref.: Hanna § 4.69[1]; Herlick Handbook § 8.21.

§3371. Attorney referral for inmates.

If the issues are complex or if the inmate applicant requests, the Department of Corrections shall furnish a list of qualified workers' compensation attorneys to permit the inmate applicant to choose an attorney to represent him or her before the appeals board. **Leg.H.** 1994 ch. 497 §5.

§3371.1. Attorney referral for patient applicant.

If the issues are complex or if the patient applicant requests, the State Department of State Hospitals shall furnish a list of qualified workers' compensation attorneys to permit the patient applicant to choose an attorney to represent them before the workers' compensation appeals board. **Leg.H.** 2019 ch. 38 (SB 78) §35, effective June 27, 2019.

Ref.: Hanna § 4.69[1].

ARTICLE 3
Dependents

§3501. Presumption; minor's or incapacitated adult's dependence on deceased parent.

(a) A child under the age of 18 years, or a child of any age found by any trier of fact, whether contractual, administrative, regulatory, or judicial, to be physically or mentally incapacitated from earning, shall be conclusively presumed to be wholly dependent for support upon a deceased employee-parent with whom that child is living at the time of injury resulting in death of the parent or for whose maintenance the parent was legally liable at the time of injury resulting in death of the parent.

(b) A spouse to whom a deceased employee is married at the time of death shall be conclusively presumed to be wholly dependent for support upon the deceased employee if the surviving spouse earned thirty thousand dollars ($30,000) or less in the twelve months immediately preceding the death. **Leg.H.** 2002 chs. 6 (AB 749), 866 (AB 486), 2013 ch. 786 (AB 607) §1.

1989 Note: This section is applicable only to injuries occurring on or after January 1, 1990. Stats. 1989 ch. 893 §6.

Ref.: Hanna § 9.05[3][a]–[d], [4][a], [b]; Herlick Handbook §§ 7.1, 7.2, 7.6, 7.9, 7.10, 14.38.

§3502. Factual determination of dependency.

In all other cases, questions of entire or partial dependency and questions as to who are dependents and the extent of their dependency shall be determined in accordance with the facts as they exist at the time of the injury of the employee.

Ref.: Hanna §§ 9.05[2], [3][b], [c], [4][a], [b], 25.10[6]; Herlick Handbook §§ 7.2, 7.9.

§3503. Qualifications for dependency.

No person is a dependent of any deceased employee unless in good faith a member of the family or household of the employee, or unless the person bears to the employee the relation of spouse, child, posthumous child, adopted child or stepchild, grandchild, father or mother, father-in-law or mother-in-law, grandfather or grandmother, brother or sister, uncle or aunt, brother-in-law or sister-in-law, or nephew or niece. **Leg.H.** 1937, 1979 ch. 749 §3, 2016 chs. 50 (SB 1005) §63, 86 (SB 1171) §217 (ch. 50 prevails; ch. 86 not effective).

2016 Note: For legislative intent, see the 2016 Note following Lab C §12.2.

Ref.: Hanna § 9.05[2]; Herlick Handbook §§ 7.1, 7.9, 7.12, 14.38.

ARTICLE 4
Employee Notice

§3550. Posting of notice; failure to post; applicability; form and content of notice.

(a) Every employer subject to the compensation provisions of this division shall post and keep posted in a conspicuous location frequented by employees, and where the notice may be easily read by employees during the hours of the workday, a notice that states the name of the current compensation insurance carrier of the employer, or when such is the fact, that the employer is self-insured, and who is responsible for claims adjustment.

(b) Failure to keep any notice required by this section conspicuously posted shall constitute a misdemeanor, and shall be prima facie evidence of noninsurance.

(c) This section shall not apply with respect to the employment of employees as defined in subdivision (d) of Section 3351.

(d) The form and content of the notice required by this section shall be prescribed by the administrative director, after consultation with the Commission on Health and Safety and Workers' Compensation, and shall advise employees that all injuries should be reported to their employer. The notice shall be easily understandable. It shall be posted in both English and Spanish where there are Spanish-speaking employees. The notice shall include the following information:

(1) How to get emergency medical treatment, if needed.

(2) The kinds of events, injuries, and illnesses covered by workers' compensation.

(3) The injured employee's right to receive medical care.

(4) The rights of the employee to select and change the treating physician pursuant to the provisions of Section 4600.

(5) The rights of the employee to receive temporary disability indemnity, permanent disability indemnity, supplemental job displacement, and death benefits, as appropriate.

(6) To whom injuries should be reported.

(7) The existence of time limits for the employer to be notified of an occupational injury.

(8) The protections against discrimination provided pursuant to Section 132a.

(9) The Internet Web site address and contact information that employees may use to obtain further information about the workers' compensation claims process and an injured employee's rights and obligations, including the location and telephone number of the nearest information and assistance officer.

(e) Failure of an employer to provide the notice required by this section shall automatically permit the employee to be treated by his or her personal physician with respect to an injury occurring during that failure.

(f) The form and content of the notice required to be posted by this section shall be made available to self-insured employers and insurers by the administrative director. Insurers shall provide this notice to each of their policyholders, with advice concerning the requirements of this section and the penalties for a failure to post this notice. **Leg.H.** 2002 ch. 6 (AB 749), 2011 ch. 544 (AB 335) §2.

Ref.: 8 C.C.R. §§9880, 9881, 9883, 15203.1, 15203.7; Hanna §§ 2.10[1], 10.20, 10.26, 10.27, 22.01[2]–[3]; Herlick Handbook §§ 4.04[2], 9.3, 14.3.

§3551. Written notice to new employee; contents.

(a) Every employer subject to the compensation provisions of this code, except employers of employees defined in subdivision (d) of Section 3351, shall give every new employee, either at the time the employee is hired or by the end of the first pay period, written notice of the information contained in Section 3550. The content of the notice required by this section shall be prescribed by the administrative director after consultation with the Commission on Health and Safety and Workers' Compensation.

(b) The notice required by this section shall be easily understandable and available in both English and Spanish. In addition to the information contained in Section 3550, the content of the notice required by this section shall include:

(1) Generally, how to obtain appropriate medical care for a job injury.

(2) The role and function of the primary treating physician.

(3) A form that the employee may use as an optional method for notifying the employer of the name of the employee's "personal physician," as defined by Section 4600, or "personal chiropractor," as defined by Section 4601.

(c) The content of the notice required by this section shall be made available to employers and insurers by the administrative director. Insurers shall provide this notice to each of their policyholders, with advice concerning the requirements of this section and the penalties for a failure to provide this notice to all employees. **Leg.H.** 2002 ch. 6 (AB 749).

Ref.: 8 C.C.R. §§9880, 9883; Herlick Handbook §§ 4.04[2], 9.3, 14.3, 16.3.

§3553. Employee who is victim of workplace crime; provision of written notice to employee concerning workers' compensation eligibility; when employer must provide notice.

Every employer subject to the compensation provisions of this code shall give any employee who is a victim of a crime that occurred at the employee's place of employment written notice that the employee is eligible for workers' compensation for injuries, including psychiatric injuries, that may have resulted from the place of employment crime. The employer shall provide this notice, either personally or by first-class mail, within one working day of the place of employment crime, or within one working day of the date the employer reasonably should have known of the crime. **Leg.H.** 1997 ch. 527.

Ref.: Herlick Handbook §§ 3.23, 4.04[2], 8.9, 8.15, 14.3.

CHAPTER 3 CONDITIONS OF COMPENSATION LIABILITY

§3600. Conditions of compensation for employer liability.

(a) Liability for the compensation provided by this division, in lieu of any other liability whatsoever to any person except as otherwise specifically provided in Sections 3602, 3706, and 4558, shall, without regard to negligence, exist against an employer for any injury sustained by his or her employees arising out of and in the course of the employment and for the death of any employee if the injury proximately causes death, in those cases where the following conditions of compensation concur:

(1) Where, at the time of the injury, both the employer and the employee are subject to the compensation provisions of this division.

(2) Where, at the time of the injury, the employee is performing service growing out of and incidental to his or her employment and is acting within the course of his or her employment.

(3) Where the injury is proximately caused by the employment, either with or without negligence.

(4) Where the injury is not caused by the intoxication, by alcohol or the unlawful use of a controlled substance, of the injured employee. As used in this paragraph, "controlled substance" shall have the same meaning as prescribed in Section 11007 of the Health and Safety Code.

(5) Where the injury is not intentionally self-inflicted.

(6) Where the employee has not willfully and deliberately caused his or her own death.

(7) Where the injury does not arise out of an altercation in which the injured employee is the initial physical aggressor.

(8) Where the injury is not caused by the commission of a felony, or a crime which is punishable as specified in subdivision (b) of Section 17 of the Penal Code, by the injured employee, for which he or she has been convicted.

(9) Where the injury does not arise out of voluntary participation in any off-duty recreational, social, or athletic activity not constituting part of the employee's work-related duties, except where these activities are a reasonable expectancy of, or are expressly or impliedly required by, the employment. The administrative director shall promulgate reasonable rules and regulations requiring employers to post and keep posted in a conspicuous place or places a notice advising employees of the provisions of this subdivision. Failure of the employer to post the notice shall not constitute an expression of intent to waive the provisions of this subdivision.

(10) Except for psychiatric injuries governed by subdivision (e) of Section 3208.3, where the claim for compensation is filed after notice of termination or layoff, including voluntary layoff, and the claim is for an injury occurring prior to the time of notice of termination or layoff, no compensation shall be paid unless the employee demonstrates by a preponderance of the evidence that one or more of the following conditions apply:

(A) The employer has notice of the injury, as provided under Chapter 2 (commencing with Section 5400), prior to the notice of termination or layoff.

(B) The employee's medical records, existing prior to the notice of termination or layoff, contain evidence of the injury.

(C) The date of injury, as specified in Section 5411, is subsequent to the date of the notice of termination or layoff, but prior to the effective date of the termination or layoff.

(D) The date of injury, as specified in Section 5412, is subsequent to the date of the notice of termination or layoff.

For purposes of this paragraph, an employee provided notice pursuant to Sections 44948.5, 44949, 44951, 44955, 72411, 87740, and 87743 of the Education Code shall be considered to have been provided a notice of termination or layoff only upon a district's final decision not to reemploy that person.

A notice of termination or layoff that is not followed within 60 days by that termination or layoff shall not be subject to the provisions of this paragraph, and this paragraph shall not apply until receipt of a later notice of termination or layoff. The issuance of frequent notices of termination or layoff to an employee shall be considered a bad faith personnel action and shall make this paragraph inapplicable to the employee.

(b) Where an employee, or his or her dependents, receives the compensation provided by this division and secures a judgment for, or settlement of, civil damages pursuant to those specific exemptions to the employee's exclusive remedy set forth in subdivision (b) of Section 3602 and Section 4558, the compensation paid under this division shall be credited against the judgment or settlement, and the employer shall be relieved from the obligation to pay further compensation to, or on behalf of, the employee or his or her dependents up to the net amount of the judgment or settlement received by the employee or his or her heirs, or that portion of the judgment as has been satisfied.

(c) For purposes of determining whether to grant or deny a workers' compensation claim, if an employee is injured or killed by a third party in the course of the employee's employment, no personal relationship or personal connection shall be deemed to exist between the employee and the third party based only on a determination that the third party injured or killed the employee solely because of the third party's personal beliefs relating to his or her perception of the employee's race, religious creed, color, national origin, age, disability, sex, gender, gender identity, gender expression, or sexual orientation. **Leg.H.** 1993 ch. 118, effective July 16, 1993, ch. 1242, 2009 ch. 272 (AB 1093) §1, 2011 ch. 719 (AB 887) §29.

Ref.: 8 C.C.R. §§9880, 9881; Hanna §§ 4.53[1], [2], 11.01[1], [4][b], 11.02[3][a], 11.04[2], 21.03[1][b]; Herlick Handbook §§ 1.01[1], 4.02[2]; 8.1–8.7, 8.9, 8.17.

§3600.1. State firefighters not acting under employer's immediate direction.

(a) Whenever any firefighter of the state, as defined in Section 19886 of the Government Code, is injured, dies, or is disabled from performing his or her duties as a firefighter by reason of his or her proceeding to or engaging in a fire-suppression or rescue operation, or the protection or preservation of life or property, anywhere in this state, including the jurisdiction in which he or she is employed, but is not at the time acting under the immediate direction of his or her employer, he or she or his or her dependents, as the case may be, shall be accorded by his or her employer all of the same benefits of this division that he, she, or they would have received had that firefighter been acting under the immediate direction of his or her employer. Any injury, disability, or death incurred under the circumstances described in this section shall be deemed to have arisen out of, and been sustained in, the course of employment for purposes of workers' compensation and all other benefits.

(b) Nothing in this section shall be deemed to do either of the following:

(1) Require the extension of any benefits to a firefighter who, at the time of his or her injury, death, or disability, is acting for compensation from one other than the state.

(2) Require the extension of any benefits to a firefighter employed by the state where by departmental regulation, whether now in force or hereafter enacted or promulgated, the activity giving rise to the injury, disability, or death is expressly prohibited.

(c) If the provisions of this section are in conflict with the provisions of a memorandum of understanding reached pursuant to Section 3517.5 of the Government Code, the memorandum of understanding shall be controlling without further legislative action, except that if the provisions of a memorandum of understanding require the expenditure of funds, the provisions shall not become effective unless approved by the Legislature in the annual Budget Act. **Leg.H.** 2004 ch. 183 (AB 3082), 2005 ch. 22 (SB 1108) §143.

§3600.2. Peace officers not acting under employer's immediate direction.

(a) Whenever any peace officer, as defined in Section 50920 of the Government Code, is injured, dies, or is disabled from performing his or her duties as a peace officer by reason of engaging in the apprehension or attempted apprehension of law violators or suspected law violators, or protection or preservation of life or property, or the preservation of the peace, anywhere in this state, including the local jurisdiction in which he or she is employed, but is not at the time acting under the immediate direction of his or her employer, the peace officer or his or her dependents, as the case may be, shall be accorded by the peace officer's employer all of the same benefits, including the benefits of this division, that the peace officer or his or her dependents would have received had that peace officer been acting under the immediate direction of his or her employer. Any injury, disability, or death incurred under the circumstances described in this section shall be deemed to have arisen out of and been sustained in the course of employment for purposes of workers' compensation and all other benefits.

(b) Nothing in this section shall be deemed to:

(1) Require the extension of any benefits to a peace officer who at the time of his or her injury, death, or disability is acting for compensation from one other than the city, county, city and county, judicial district, or town of his or her primary employment.

(2) Require the extension of any benefits to a peace officer employed by a city, county, city and county, judicial district, or town which by charter, ordinance, or departmental regulation, whether now in force or hereafter enacted or promulgated, expressly prohibits the activity giving rise to the injury, disability, or death.

(3) Enlarge or extend the authority of any peace officer to make an arrest; provided, however, that illegality of the arrest shall not affect the extension of benefits by reason of this act if the peace officer reasonably believed that the arrest was not illegal.

(4) Preclude an employer, at its discretion or in accordance with written policies adopted by resolution of the employer's governing body, from accepting liability for compensation under this division for an injury sustained by a peace officer, as defined in Section 50920 of the Government Code, by reason of engaging in the apprehension or attempted apprehension of law violators or suspected law violators, or protection or preservation of life or property, or the preservation of the peace, outside the state of California, but who was not at the time acting under the immediate direction of his or her employer, including any claims for injuries sustained by peace officers during the October 1, 2017, mass shooting in Las Vegas, Nevada, if the employer determines that providing compensation serves the public purposes of the employer. For claims filed pursuant to this paragraph by peace officers for injuries sustained during the October 1, 2017, mass shooting in Las Vegas, Nevada, the date of injury for purposes of subdivision (a) of Section 5405 shall be deemed the operative date of the act adding this paragraph. Acceptance of liability under this subdivision shall not affect the determination of whether or not the peace officer acted within the scope of his or her employment for any other purpose. **Leg.H.** 1980 ch. 407 §2, 2018 ch. 707 (AB 1749) §1.

§3600.3. Scope of employment; off-duty peace officers.

(a) For the purposes of Section 3600, an off-duty peace officer, as defined in subdivision (b), who is performing, within the jurisdiction of his or her employing agency, a service he or she would, in the course of his or her employment, have been required to perform if he or she were on duty, is performing a service growing out of and incidental to his or her employment and is acting within the course of his or her employment if, as a condition of his or her employment, he or she is required to be on call within the jurisdiction during off-duty hours.

(b) As used in subdivision (a), "peace officer" means those employees of the Department of Forestry and Fire Protection named as peace officers for purposes of subdivision (b) of Section 830.37 of the Penal Code.

(c) This section does not apply to any off-duty peace officer while he or she is engaged, either as an employee or as an independent contractor, in any capacity other than as a peace officer. **Leg.H.** 1992 ch. 427.

Ref.: Hanna § 4.130[2].

§3600.4. Local firefighters not acting under employer's immediate direction.

(a) Whenever any firefighter of a city, county, city and county, district, or other public or municipal corporation or political subdivision, or any firefighter employed by a private entity, is injured, dies, or is disabled from performing his or her duties as a firefighter by reason of his or her proceeding to or engaging in a fire suppression or rescue operation, or the protection or preservation of life or property, anywhere in this state, including the local jurisdiction in which he or she is employed, but is not at the time acting under the immediate direction of his or her employer, he or she or his or her dependents, as the case may be, shall be accorded by his or her employer all of the same benefits of this division which he or she or they would have received had that firefighter been acting under the immediate direction of his or her employer. Any injury, disability, or death incurred under the circumstances described in this section shall be deemed to have arisen out of and been sustained in the course of employment for purposes of workers' compensation and all other benefits.

(b) Nothing in this section shall be deemed to:

(1) Require the extension of any benefits to a firefighter who at the time of his or her injury, death, or disability is acting for compensation from one other than the city, county, city and county, district, or other public or municipal corporation or political subdivision, or private entity, of his or her primary employment or enrollment.

(2) Require the extension of any benefits to a firefighter employed by a city, county, city and county, district, or other public or municipal corporation or political subdivision, or private entity, which by charter, ordinance, departmental regulation, or private employer policy, whether now in force or hereafter enacted or promulgated, expressly prohibits the activity giving rise to the injury, disability, or death. However, this paragraph shall not apply to relieve the employer from liability for benefits for any injury, disability, or death of a firefighter when the firefighter is acting pursuant to Section 1799.107 of the Health and Safety Code. **Leg.H.** 1998 ch. 617.

§3600.5. Out-of-state injury of resident; exemption; certificate of insurance for out-of-state employer.

(a) If an employee who has been hired or is regularly working in the state receives personal injury by accident

Labor

arising out of and in the course of employment outside of this state, he or she, or his or her dependents, in the case of his or her death, shall be entitled to compensation according to the law of this state.

(b) (1) An employee who has been hired outside of this state and his or her employer shall be exempted from the provisions of this division while the employee is temporarily within this state doing work for his or her employer if the employer has furnished workers' compensation insurance coverage under the workers' compensation insurance or similar laws of a state other than California, so as to cover the employee's work while in this state if both of the following apply:

(A) The extraterritorial provisions of this division are recognized in the other state.

(B) The employers and employees who are covered in this state are likewise exempted from the application of the workers' compensation insurance or similar laws of the other state.

(2) In any case in which paragraph (1) is satisfied, the benefits under the workers' compensation insurance or similar laws of the other state, and other remedies under those laws, shall be the exclusive remedy against the employer for any injury, whether resulting in death or not, received by the employee while working for the employer in this state.

(c)(1) With respect to an occupational disease or cumulative injury, a professional athlete who has been hired outside of this state and his or her employer shall be exempted from the provisions of this division while the professional athlete is temporarily within this state doing work for his or her employer if both of the following are satisfied:

(A) The employer has furnished workers' compensation insurance coverage or its equivalent under the laws of a state other than California.

(B) The employer's workers' compensation insurance or its equivalent covers the professional athlete's work while in this state.

(2) In any case in which paragraph (1) is satisfied, the benefits under the workers' compensation insurance or similar laws of the other state, and other remedies under those laws, shall be the exclusive remedy against the employer for any occupational disease or cumulative injury, whether resulting in death or not, received by the employee while working for the employer in this state.

(3) A professional athlete shall be deemed, for purposes of this subdivision, to be temporarily within this state doing work for his or her employer if, during the 365 consecutive days immediately preceding the professional athlete's last day of work for the employer within the state, the professional athlete performs less than 20 percent of his or her duty days in California during that 365-day period in California.

(d)(1) With respect to an occupational disease or cumulative injury, a professional athlete and his or her employer shall be exempt from this division when all of the professional athlete's employers in his or her last year of work as a professional athlete are exempt from this division pursuant to subdivision (c) or any other law, unless both of the following conditions are satisfied:

(A) The professional athlete has, over the course of his or her professional athletic career, worked for two or more seasons for a California-based team or teams, or the professional athlete has, over the course of his or her professional athletic career, worked 20 percent or more of his or her duty days either in California or for a California-based team. The percentage of a professional athletic career worked either within California or for a California-based team shall be determined solely by taking the number of duty days the professional athlete worked for a California-based team or teams, plus the number of duty days the professional athlete worked as a professional athlete in California for any team other than a California-based team, and dividing that number by the total number of duty days the professional athlete was employed anywhere as a professional athlete.

(B) The professional athlete has, over the course of his or her professional athletic career, worked for fewer than seven seasons for any team or teams other than a California-based team or teams as defined in this section.

(2) When subparagraphs (A) and (B) of paragraph (1) are both satisfied, liability for the professional athlete's occupational disease or cumulative injury shall be determined in accordance with Section 5500.5.

(e) An employer of professional athletes, other than a California-based team, shall be exempt from Article 4 (commencing with Section 3550) of Chapter 2, and subdivisions (a) to (c), inclusive, of Section 5401.

(f) For purposes of this section, a certificate from the duly authorized officer of the appeals board or similar department of another state certifying that the employer of the other state is insured in that state and has provided extraterritorial coverage insuring his or her employees while working within this state shall be prima facie evidence that the employer carries workers' compensation insurance.

(g) For purposes of this section, the following definitions apply:

(1) The term "professional athlete" means an athlete who is employed at either a minor or major league level in the sport of baseball, basketball, football, ice hockey, or soccer.

(2) The term "California-based team" means a team that plays a majority of its home games in California.

(3) The term "duty day" means a day in which any services are performed by a professional athlete under the direction and control of his or her employer pursuant to a player contract.

(4) The term "season" means the period from the date of the first preseason team activity for that contract year, through the date of the last game the professional athlete's team played during the same contract year.

(h) The amendments made to this section by the act adding this subdivision apply to all claims for benefits pursuant to this division filed on or after September 15, 2013. The amendments made to this section by the act adding this subdivision shall not constitute good cause to reopen any final decision, order, or award.

(i) If any provision of this section or the application thereof to any person or circumstances is held invalid, that invalidity shall not affect other provisions or applications of this section that can be given effect without the invalid provision or application, and to this end the provisions of this section are severable. **Leg.H.** 2013 ch. 653 (AB 1309) §1.

2013 Notes: It is the intent of the Legislature that the changes made to law by this act shall only affect specified professional athletes and employers of specified professional athletes. The changes made to law by this act shall not affect any other employer or employee in California. Stats. 2013 ch. 653 (AB 1309) §2; Stats. 2014 ch. 71 (SB 1304) §215.

It is the intent of the Legislature that the changes made to law by this act shall have no impact or alter in any way the decision of the court in Bowen v. Workers' Comp. Appeals Bd. (1999) 73 Cal.App.4th 15. Stats. 2013 ch. 653 (AB 1309) §3.

It is the intent of the Legislature that the decision of the Workers' Compensation Appeals Board in Wesley Carroll v. Cincinnati Bengals, et al. (2013) 78 Cal.Comp.Cases 655 (ADJ2295331) (WCAB En Banc) be limited to professional athletes, as defined in this act. Stats. 2013 ch. 653 (AB 1309) §4.

It is the intent of the Legislature that the changes made to law by this act have no impact or alter in any way the decision of the Workers' Compensation Appeals Board in Dennis McKinley v. Arizona Cardinals et al. (2013) 78 CCC 23 (ADJ7460656). Stats. 2013 ch. 653 (AB 1309) §5.

Ref.: Hanna §§ 21.06, 21.07[5].

§3600.6. Disaster service workers.

Disaster service workers registered by a disaster council while performing services under the general direction of the disaster council shall be entitled to all of the same benefits of this division as any other injured employee, except as provided by Chapter 10 (commencing with Section 4351) of Part 1. For purposes of this section, an unregistered person impressed into performing service as a disaster service worker during a state of war emergency, a state of emergency, or a local emergency by a person having authority to command the aid of citizens in the execution of his or her duties shall also be deemed a disaster service worker and shall be entitled to the same benefits of this division as any other disaster service worker.

§3600.8. Participation in alternative commute program not acting within course of employment—Definitions; exceptions.

(a) No employee who voluntarily participates in an alternative commute program that is sponsored or mandated by a governmental entity shall be considered to be acting within the course of his or her employment while utilizing that program to travel to or from his or her place of employment, unless he or she is paid a regular wage or salary in compensation for those periods of travel. An employee who is injured while acting outside the course of his or her employment, or his or her dependents in the event of the employee's death, shall not be barred from bringing an action at law for damages against his or her employer as a result of this section.

(b) Any alternative commute program provided, sponsored, or subsidized by an employee's employer in order to comply with any trip reduction mandates of an air quality management district or local government shall be considered a program mandated by a governmental entity. An employer's reimbursement of employee expenses or subsidization of costs related to an alternative commute program shall not be considered payment of a wage or salary in compensation for the period of travel. If an employer's salary is not based on the hours the employee works, payment of his or her salary shall not be considered to be in compensation for the period of travel unless there is a specific written agreement between the employer and the employee to that effect. If an employer elects to provide workers' compensation coverage for those employees who are passengers in a vehicle owned and operated by the employer or an agent thereof, those employees shall be considered to be within the course of their employment, provided the employer notifies employees in writing prior to participation of the employee or coverage becoming effective.

(c) As used in this section, "governmental entity" means a regional air district, air quality management district, congestion management agency, or other local jurisdiction having authority to enact air pollution or congestion management controls or impose them upon entities within its jurisdiction.

(d) Notwithstanding any other provision of law, vanpool programs may continue to provide workers' compensation benefits to employees who participate in an alternative commute program by riding in a vanpool, in the case in which the vanpool vehicle is owned or registered to the employer.

(e) Employees of the state who participate in an alternative commute program, while riding in a vanpool vehicle that is registered to or owned by the state, shall be deemed to be within the course and scope of employment for workers' compensation purposes only. **Leg.H.** 1994 ch. 622.

1994 Note: It is the intent of the Legislature in enacting this section only to declare existing law and to clarify, and not to expand, limit, or otherwise alter the ability under existing law of any employee, or his or her dependents, to bring an action at law for damages. Stats. 1994 ch. 622 §5.

Ref.: Hanna § 4.151[3].

§3601. Employee's liability to another employee.

(a) Where the conditions of compensation set forth in Section 3600 concur, the right to recover such compensation, pursuant to the provisions of this division is, except as specifically provided in this section, the exclusive remedy for injury or death of an employee against any other employee of the employer acting within the scope of his or her employment, except that an employee, or his or her dependents in the event of his or her death, shall, in addition to the right to compensation against the employer, have a right to bring an action at law for damages against the other employee, as if this division did not apply, in either of the following cases:

(1) When the injury or death is proximately caused by the willful and unprovoked physical act of aggression of the other employee.

(2) When the injury or death is proximately caused by the intoxication of the other employee.

(b) In no event, either by legal action or by agreement whether entered into by the other employee or on his or her behalf, shall the employer be held liable, directly or indirectly, for damages awarded against, or for a liability

Labor

incurred by the other employee under paragraph (1) or (2) of subdivision (a).

(c) No employee shall be held liable, directly or indirectly, to his or her employer, for injury or death of a coemployee except where the injured employee or his or her dependents obtain a recovery under subdivision (a).

Ref.: Hanna §§ 2.10[2], 3.142[2][a], 4.51[1], 11.21[2][a]; Herlick Handbook §§ 12.10, 12.11.

§3602. Employer's personal liability.

(a) Where the conditions of compensation set forth in Section 3600 concur, the right to recover compensation is, except as specifically provided in this section and Sections 3706 and 4558, the sole and exclusive remedy of the employee or his or her dependents against the employer. The fact that either the employee or the employer also occupied another or dual capacity prior to, or at the time of, the employee's industrial injury shall not permit the employee or his or her dependents to bring an action at law for damages against the employer.

(b) An employee, or his or her dependents in the event of his or her death, may bring an action at law for damages against the employer, as if this division did not apply, in the following instances:

(1) Where the employee's injury or death is proximately caused by a willful physical assault by the employer.

(2) Where the employee's injury is aggravated by the employer's fraudulent concealment of the existence of the injury and its connection with the employment, in which case the employer's liability shall be limited to those damages proximately caused by the aggravation. The burden of proof respecting apportionment of damages between the injury and any subsequent aggravation thereof is upon the employer.

(3) Where the employee's injury or death is proximately caused by a defective product manufactured by the employer and sold, leased, or otherwise transferred for valuable consideration to an independent third person, and that product is thereafter provided for the employee's use by a third person.

(c) In all cases where the conditions of compensation set forth in Section 3600 do not concur, the liability of the employer shall be the same as if this division had not been enacted.

(d)(1) For the purposes of this division, including Sections 3700 and 3706, an employer may secure the payment of compensation on employees provided to it by agreement by another employer by entering into a valid and enforceable agreement with that other employer under which the other employer agrees to obtain, and has, in fact, obtained workers' compensation coverage for those employees. In those cases, both employers shall be considered to have secured the payment of compensation within the meaning of this section and Sections 3700 and 3706 if there is a valid and enforceable agreement between the employers to obtain that coverage, and that coverage, as specified in subdivision (a) or (b) of Section 3700, has been in fact obtained, and the coverage remains in effect for the duration of the employment providing legally sufficient coverage to the employee or employees who form the subject matter of the coverage. That agreement shall not be made for the purpose of avoiding an employer's appropriate experience rating as defined in subdivision (c) of Section 11730 of the Insurance Code.

(2) Employers who have complied with this subdivision shall not be subject to civil, criminal, or other penalties for failure to provide workers' compensation coverage or tort liability in the event of employee injury, but may, in the absence of compliance, be subject to all three.

(e) As provided in paragraph (12) of subdivision (f) of Section 1202.4 of the Penal Code, in cases where an employer is convicted of a crime against an employee, a payment to the employee or the employee's dependent that is paid by the employer's workers' compensation insurance carrier shall not be used to offset the amount of the restitution order unless the court finds that the defendant substantially met the obligation to pay premiums for that insurance coverage. **Leg.H.** 1995 ch. 800, 2012 ch. 868 (SB 1177) §1.

Ref.: Hanna § 11.02[1], [6][a], [c], [7][a]–[c], [8]; Herlick Handbook §§ 1.01[1], 12.10, 12.11.

§3603. Discharge of claims.

Payment of compensation in accordance with the order and direction of the appeals board shall discharge the employer from all claims therefor.

§3604. Unavailable defense for public employers.

It is not a defense to the State, any county, city, district or institution thereof, or any public or quasi-public corporation, that a person injured while rendering service for it was not lawfully employed by reason of the violation of any civil service or other law or regulation respecting the hiring of employees.

Ref.: Hanna § 3.111.

§3605. Injured minors; compensation.

The compensation due an injured minor may be paid to him until his parent or guardian gives the employer or the latter's compensation insurance carrier written notice that he claims such compensation.

Compensation paid to such injured minor prior to receipt of such written notice is in full release of the employer and insurance carrier for the amount so paid. The minor cannot disaffirm such payment upon appointment of a guardian or coming of age.

CHAPTER 4 COMPENSATION INSURANCE AND SECURITY

ARTICLE 1 Insurance and Security

§3700. Employer's possible means of securing payment.

Every employer except the state shall secure the payment of compensation in one or more of the following ways:

(a) By being insured against liability to pay compensation by one or more insurers duly authorized to write compensation insurance in this state.

(b) By securing from the Director of Industrial Relations a certificate of consent to self-insure either as an individual employer, or as one employer in a group of employers, which may be given upon furnishing proof satisfactory to the Director of Industrial Relations of ability to self-insure and to pay any compensation that may become due to his or her employees.

(c) For any county, city, city and county, municipal corporation, public district, public agency, or any political subdivision of the state, including each member of a pooling arrangement under a joint exercise of powers agreement (but not the state itself), by securing from the Director of Industrial Relations a certificate of consent to self-insure against workers' compensation claims, which certificate may be given upon furnishing proof satisfactory to the director of ability to administer workers' compensation claims properly, and to pay workers' compensation claims that may become due to its employees. On or before March 31, 1979, a political subdivision of the state which, on December 31, 1978, was uninsured for its liability to pay compensation, shall file a properly completed and executed application for a certificate of consent to self-insure against workers' compensation claims. The certificate shall be issued and be subject to the provisions of Section 3702.

For purposes of this section, "state" shall include the superior courts of California. **Leg.H.** 1993 ch. 121, effective July 16, 1993, 2002 ch. 905 (SB 2011).

Ref.: 8 C.C.R. §§9767.1, 9767.4, 9767.8, 9811, 10100, 10100.1, 10100.2, 10181, 14000, 15201, 15203, 15203.1, 15203.2, 15203.3, 15203.4, 15203.6, 15203.7, 15203.8, 15203.10, 15204, 15205, 15210, 15210.1, 15210.2, 15210.3, 15211, 15211.2, 15212, 15213, 15214, 15215, 15230, 15231, 15232, 15233, 15234, 15251, 15300, 15301, 15302, 15303, 15353, 15354, 15360, 15400, 15400.1, 15400.2, 15402, 15402.1, 15402.2, 15402.3, 15402.4, 15403, 15405, 15420, 15422, 15423, 15424, 15425, 15426, 15427, 15428, 15430, 15430.1, 15431, 15431.1, 15431.2, 15432, 15433, 15434, 15435, 15436, 15437, 15438, 15450.1, 15458, 15459, 15470, 15471, 15472, 15473, 15474, 15475, 15476, 15477, 15478, 15479, 15480, 15481, 15550, 15551, 15552, 15553, 15554, 15555, 15556, 15557, 15558, 15559, 15560, 15561, 15562, 15563, 15564, 15565, 15566, 15567, 15568, 15569, 15570, 15571, 15571.5, 15572, 15573, 15574, 15575, 15576, 15578, 15579, 15580, 15581, 15582, 15583, 15584, 15585, 15586, 15587, 15588, 15589, 15590, 15591, 15592, 15593, 15594, 15595, 15596, 15600; Hanna §§ 1.03, 2.12, 21.05[1]; Herlick Handbook §§ 1.05, 3.1, 3.14, 3.19, 3.21.

§3700.1. Definitions.

As used in this article:

(a) "Director" means the Director of Industrial Relations.

(b) "Private self-insurer" means a private employer which has secured the payment of compensation pursuant to Section 3701.

(c) "Trustees" means the Board of Trustees of the Self-Insurers' Security Fund.

(d) "Member" means a private self-insurer which participates in the Self-Insurers' Security Fund.

(e) "Incurred liabilities for the payment of compensation" means the sum of an estimate of future compensation, as compensation is defined by Section 3207, plus an estimate of the amount necessary to provide for the administration of claims, including legal costs. **Leg.H.** 1986 ch. 1128 §2, effective September 25, 1986, 1987 ch. 169 (AB 1703) §1, effective July 23, 1987, 2012 ch. 363 (SB 863) §10.

2012 Note: For legislative findings, declarations, and applicability of Stats. 2012 ch. 363, see the 2012 Notes following Lab C §62.5.

Ref.: 8 C.C.R. §15475.

§3700.5. Penalty for failure to secure payment; enhancement for subsequent conviction; recovery of investigative costs.

(a) The failure to secure the payment of compensation as required by this article by one who knew, or because of his or her knowledge or experience should be reasonably expected to have known, of the obligation to secure the payment of compensation, is a misdemeanor punishable by imprisonment in the county jail for up to one year, or by a fine of up to double the amount of premium, as determined by the court, that would otherwise have been due to secure the payment of compensation during the time compensation was not secured, but not less than ten thousand dollars ($10,000), or by both that imprisonment and fine.

(b) A second or subsequent conviction shall be punished by imprisonment in the county jail for a period not to exceed one year, by a fine of triple the amount of premium, or by both that imprisonment and fine, as determined by the court, that would otherwise have been due to secure the payment of compensation during the time payment was not secured, but not less than fifty thousand dollars ($50,000).

(c) Upon a first conviction of a person under this section, the person may be charged the costs of investigation at the discretion of the court. Upon a subsequent conviction, the person shall be charged the costs of investigation in addition to any other penalties pursuant to subdivision (b). The costs of investigation shall be paid only after the payment of any benefits that may be owed to injured workers, any reimbursement that may be owed to the director for benefits provided to the injured worker pursuant to Section 3717, and any other penalty assessments that may be owed. **Leg.H.** 1999 ch. 553, 2004 ch. 2 (SB 2 Fourth Extra. Session), effective March 6, 2005.

Ref.: Hanna §§ 2.11[5], 2.17; Herlick Handbook § 3.19.

§3701. Private self-insuring employer; surety.

(a) Each year every private self-insuring employer shall secure incurred liabilities for the payment of compensation and the performance of the obligations of employers imposed under this chapter by renewing the prior year's security deposit or by making a new deposit of security. If a new deposit is made, it shall be posted within 60 days of the filing of the self-insured employer's annual report with the director, but in no event later than May 1.

(b) The solvency risk and security deposit amount for each private and group self-insurer shall be acceptable to the Self-Insurers' Security Fund.

(c) Unless otherwise permitted by regulation, the deposit shall be an amount equal to the self-insurer's projected losses, net of specific excess insurance coverage, if any, and inclusive of incurred but not reported (IBNR) liabilities, allocated loss adjustment expense, and unallocated loss adjustment expense, calculated as of December 31 of each year. The calculation of projected losses and expenses shall be reflected in a written actuarial report that projects ultimate liabilities of the private self-insured employer at the expected actuarial confidence level, to ensure that all claims and associated costs are recognized. The written actuarial report shall be prepared by an actuary meeting the qualifications prescribed by the director in regulation.

(d) In determining the amount of the deposit required to secure incurred liabilities for the payment of compensation and the performance of obligations of a self-insured employer imposed under this chapter, the director shall offset estimated future liabilities for the same claims covered by a self-insured plan under the federal Longshore and Harbor Workers' Compensation Act (33 U.S.C. Sec. 901 et seq.), but in no event shall the offset exceed the estimated future liabilities for the claims under this chapter.

(e) The director may only accept as security, and the employer shall deposit as security, cash, securities, surety bonds, or irrevocable letters of credit in any combination the director, in his or her discretion, deems adequate security. The current deposit shall include any amounts covered by terminated surety bonds or excess insurance policies, as shall be set forth in regulations adopted by the director pursuant to Section 3702.10.

(f) Surety bonds, irrevocable letters of credit, and documents showing issuance of any irrevocable letter of credit shall be deposited with, and be in a form approved by, the director, shall be exonerated only according to its terms and, in no event, by the posting of additional security.

(g) The director may accept as security a joint security deposit that secures an employer's obligation under this chapter and that also secures that employer's obligations under the federal Longshore and Harbor Workers' Compensation Act.

(h) The liability of the Self-Insurers' Security Fund, with respect to any claims brought under both this chapter and under the federal Longshore and Harbor Workers' Compensation Act, to pay for shortfalls in a security deposit shall be limited to the amount of claim liability owing the employee under this chapter offset by the amount of any claim liability owing under the federal Longshore and Harbor Workers' Compensation Act, but in no event shall the liability of the fund exceed the claim liability under this chapter. The employee shall be entitled to pursue recovery under either or both the state and federal programs.

(i) Securities shall be deposited on behalf of the director by the self-insured employer with the Treasurer. Securities shall be accepted by the Treasurer for deposit and shall be withdrawn only upon written order of the director.

(j) Cash shall be deposited in a financial institution approved by the director, and in the account assigned to the director. Cash shall be withdrawn only upon written order of the director.

(k) Upon the sending by the director of a request to renew, request to post, or request to increase or decrease a security deposit, a perfected security interest is created in the private self-insured's assets in favor of the director and the Self-Insurers' Security Fund to the extent of any then unsecured portion of the self-insured's incurred liabilities. That perfected security interest is transferred to any cash or securities thereafter posted by the private self-insured with the director and is released only upon either of the following:

(1) The acceptance by the director of a surety bond or irrevocable letter of credit for the full amount of the incurred liabilities for the payment of compensation.

(2) The return of cash or securities by the director.

The private self-insured employer loses all right, title, and interest in, and any right to control, all assets or obligations posted or left on deposit as security. The director may liquidate the deposit as provided in Section 3701.5 and apply it to the self-insured employer's incurred liabilities either directly or through the Self-Insurers' Security Fund. **Leg.H.** 1993 chs. 917, 1242, 1994 ch. 56, 2012 ch. 363 (SB 863) §11.

2012 Note: For legislative findings, declarations, and applicability of Stats. 2012 ch. 363, see the 2012 Notes following Lab C §62.5.

Ref.: 8 C.C.R. §§15201, 15203, 15203.1, 15203.2, 15203.3, 15203.5, 15203.7, 15203.8, 15203.9, 15203.10, 15210, 15210.1, 15210.2, 15210.3, 15211, 15211.1, 15211.2, 15211.3, 15212, 15213, 15214, 15215, 15216, 15220, 15220.4, 15302, 15303, 15360, 15400, 15420, 15422, 15423, 15424, 15425, 15426, 15427, 15428, 15430, 15430.1, 15431, 15431.1, 15431.2, 15432, 15433, 15434, 15435, 15436, 15437, 15438, 15450.1, 15458, 15459, 15470, 15471, 15472, 15475, 15476, 15477, 15478, 15479, 15480, 15481, 15600; Hanna § 27.10[1]; Herlick Handbook §§ 1.05, 3.20.

§3701.3. Return of overpayments to self-insured employers.

The director shall return to a private self-insured employer all individual security determined, with the consent of the Self-Insurers' Security Fund, to be in excess of that needed to ensure the administration of the employer's self insuring, including legal fees, and the payment of any future claims. This section shall not apply to any security posted as part of the composite deposit, or to any security turned over to the Self-Insurers' Security Fund following an order of default under Section 3701.5. **Leg.H.** 1986 ch. 1128 §5, effective September 25, 1986, 2012 ch. 363 (SB 863) §12.

2012 Note: For legislative findings, declarations, and applicability of Stats. 2012 ch. 363, see the 2012 Notes following Lab C §62.5.

§3701.5. Private self-insured employer; payment of obligations.

(a) If the director determines that a private self-insured employer has failed to pay workers' compensation as required by this division, the security deposit shall be utilized to administer and pay the employer's compensation obligations.

(b) If the director determines the security deposit has not been immediately made available for the payment of compensation, the director shall determine the method of payment and claims administration as appropriate, which may include, but is not limited to, payment by a surety that issued the bond, or payment by an issuer of an irrevocable letter of credit, and administration by a surety or by an adjusting agency, or through the Self-Insurers' Security Fund, or any combination thereof. If the director arranges for administration and payment by any person other than the Self-Insurers' Security Fund after a default is declared, the fund shall have no responsibility for claims administration or payment of the claims.

(c) If the director determines the payment of benefits and claims administration shall be made through the Self-Insurers' Security Fund, the fund shall commence payment of the private self-insured employer's obligations for which it is liable under Section 3743 within 30 days of notification. Payments shall be made to claimants whose entitlement to benefits can be ascertained by the fund, with or without proceedings before the appeals board. Upon the assumption of obligations by the fund pursuant to the director's determination, the fund shall have a right to immediate possession of any posted security and the custodian, surety, or issuer of any irrevocable letter of credit shall turn over the security to the fund together with the interest that has accrued since the date of the self-insured employer's default or insolvency.

(d) The payment of benefits by the Self-Insurers' Security Fund from security deposit proceeds shall release and discharge any custodian of the security deposit, surety, any issuer of a letter of credit, and the self-insured employer, from liability to fulfill obligations to provide those same benefits as compensation, but does not release any person from any liability to the fund for full reimbursement. Payment by a surety constitutes a full release of the surety's liability under the bond to the extent of that payment, and entitles the surety to full reimbursement by the principal or his or her estate. Full reimbursement includes necessary attorney fees and other costs and expenses, without prior claim or proceedings on the part of the injured employee or other beneficiaries. Any decision or determination made, or any settlement approved, by the director or by the appeals board under subdivision (f) shall conclusively be presumed valid and binding as to any and all known claims arising out of the underlying dispute, unless an appeal is made within the time limit specified in Section 5950.

(e) The director shall advise the Self-Insurers' Security Fund promptly after receipt of information indicating that a private self-insured employer may be unable to meet its compensation obligations. The director shall also advise the Self-Insurers' Security Fund of all determinations and directives made or issued pursuant to this section. All financial, actuarial, or claims information received by the director from any self-insurer may be shared by the director with the Self-Insurers' Security Fund.

(f) Disputes concerning the posting, renewal, termination, exoneration, or return of all or any portion of the security deposit, or any liability arising out of the posting or failure to post security, or adequacy of the security or reasonableness of administrative costs, including legal fees, and arising between or among a surety, the issuer of an agreement of assumption and guarantee of workers' compensation liabilities, the issuer of a letter of credit, any custodian of the security deposit, a self-insured employer, or the Self-Insurers' Security Fund shall be resolved by the director. An appeal from the director's decision or determination may be taken to the appropriate superior court by petition for writ of mandate. Payment of claims from the security deposit or by the Self-Insurers' Security Fund shall not be stayed pending the resolution of the disputes unless and until the superior court issues a determination staying a payment of claims decision or determination of the director. **Leg.H.** 1984 ch. 252 §2, effective June 27, 1984, 1986 ch. 1128 §6, effective September 25, 1986, 1989 ch. 1258 (AB 1302) §2, 2012 ch. 363 (SB 863) §13.

2012 Note: For legislative findings, declarations, and applicability of Stats. 2012 ch. 363, see the 2012 Notes following Lab C §62.5.

Ref.: 8 C.C.R. §§15201, 15203.1, 15203.5, 15203.8, 15203.9, 15210, 15210.1, 15210.2, 15210.3, 15211.2, 15211.3, 15212, 15213, 15214, 15215, 15216, 15251, 15301, 15302, 15303, 15420, 15422, 15424, 15425, 15426, 15427, 15428, 15430, 15430.1, 15431, 15431.1, 15431.2, 15432, 15433, 15434, 15435, 15436, 15437, 15438, 15450.1, 15470, 15472, 15475, 15477, 15478, 15479, 15480, 15481; Hanna § 2.11[1], [5].

§3701.7. Special conditions to be met after period of unlawful uninsurance.

Where any employer requesting coverage under a new or existing certificate of consent to self-insure has had a period of unlawful uninsurance, either for an applicant in its entirety or for a subsidiary or member of a joint powers authority legally responsible for its own workers' compensation obligations, the following special conditions shall apply before the director may determine if the requesting employer can operate under a certificate of consent to self-insure:

(a) The director may require a deposit of not less than 200 percent of the outstanding liabilities remaining unpaid at the time of application, which had been incurred during the uninsurance period.

(b) At the discretion of the director, where a public or private employer has been previously totally uninsured for workers' compensation pursuant to Section 3700, the director may require an additional deposit not to exceed 100 percent of the total outstanding liabilities for the uninsured period, or the sum of two hundred fifty thousand dollars ($250,000), whichever is greater.

(c) In addition to the deposits required by subdivisions (a) and (b), a penalty shall be paid to the Uninsured Employers Fund of 10 percent per year of the remaining unpaid liabilities, for every year liabilities remain outstanding. In addition, an additional application fee, not to exceed one thousand dollars ($1,000), plus assessments, pursuant to Section 3702.5 and subdivision (b) of Section 3745, may be imposed by the director and the Self-Insurers' Security Fund, respectively, against private self-insured employers.

(d) A certificate of consent to self-insure shall not be granted to an applicant that has had a period of unlawful uninsurance without the written approval of the Self-Insurers' Security Fund.

(e) An employer may retrospectively insure the outstanding liabilities arising out of the uninsured period, either before or after an application for self-insurance has been approved. Upon proof of insurance acceptable to the director, no deposit shall be required for the period of uninsurance.

The penalties to be paid to the Uninsured Employers Fund shall consist of a one-time payment of 20 percent of the outstanding liabilities for the period of uninsurance remaining unpaid at the time of application, in lieu of any other penalty for being unlawfully uninsured pursuant to this code.

(f) In the case of a subsidiary which meets all of the following conditions, a certificate shall issue without penalty:

(1) The subsidiary has never had a certificate revoked for reasons set forth in Section 3702.

(2) Employee injuries were reported to the Office of Self-Insurance Plans in annual reports.

(3) The security deposit of the certificate holder was calculated to include the entity's compensation liabilities.

(4) Application for a separate certificate or corrected certificate is made within 90 days and completed within 180 days of notice from the Office of Self-Insurance Plans. If the requirements of this subdivision are not met, all penalties pursuant to subdivision (b) of Section 3702.9 shall apply.

(g) The director may approve an application on the date the application is substantially completed, subject to completion requirements, and may make the certificate effective on an earlier date, covering a period of uninsurance, if the employer complies with the requirements of this section.

(h) Any decision by the director may be contested by an entity in the manner provided in Section 3701.5.

(i) Nothing in this section shall abrogate the right of an employee to bring an action against an uninsured employer pursuant to Section 3706.

(j) Nothing in this statute shall abrogate the right of a self-insured employer to insure against known or unknown claims arising out of the self-insurance period. **Leg.H.** 1989 ch. 507 (AB 2380) §1, 1990 ch. 704 (AB 3853) §1, 2012 ch. 363 (SB 863) §14.

2012 Note: For legislative findings, declarations, and applicability of Stats. 2012 ch. 363, see the 2012 Notes following Lab C §62.5.

Ref.: 8 C.C.R. §15210.1; Hanna § 2.11[1].

§3701.8. Alternative security system for securing aggregate liabilities of private, self-insured employers through the Self-Insurers' Security Fund.

(a) As an alternative to each private self-insuring employer securing its own incurred liabilities as provided in Section 3701, the director may provide by regulation for an alternative security system whereby all private self-insureds designated for full participation by the director shall collectively secure their aggregate incurred liabilities through the Self-Insurers' Security Fund. The regulations shall provide for the director to set a total security requirement for these participating self-insured employers based on a review of their annual reports and any other self-insurer information as may be specified by the director. The Self-Insurers' Security Fund shall propose to the director a combination of cash and securities, surety bonds, irrevocable letters of credit, insurance, or other financial instruments or guarantees satisfactory to the director sufficient to meet the security requirement set by the director. Upon approval by the director and posting by the Self-Insurers' Security Fund on or before the date set by the director, that combination shall be the composite deposit. The noncash elements of the composite deposit may be one-year or multiple-year instruments. If the Self-Insurers' Security Fund fails to post the required composite deposit by the date set by the director, then within 30 days after that date, each private self-insuring employer shall secure its incurred liabilities in the manner required by Section 3701. Self-insured employers not designated for full participation by the director shall meet all requirements as may be set by the director pursuant to subdivision (g).

(b) In order to provide for the composite deposit approved by the director, the Self-Insurers' Security Fund shall assess, in a manner approved by the director, each fully participating private self-insuring employer a deposit assessment payable within 30 days of assessment. The amount of the deposit assessment charged each fully participating self-insured employer shall be set by the Self-Insurers' Security Fund, based on its reasonable consideration of all the following factors:

(1) The total amount needed to provide the composite deposit.

(2) The self-insuring employer's paid or incurred liabilities as reflected in its annual report.

(3) The financial strength and creditworthiness of the self-insured.

(4) Any other reasonable factors as may be authorized by regulation.

(5) In order to make a composite deposit proposal to the director and set the deposit assessment to be charged each fully participating self-insured, the Self-Insurers' Security Fund shall have access to the annual reports and other information submitted by all self-insuring employers to the director, under terms and conditions as may be set by the director, to preserve the confidentiality of the self-insured's financial information.

(c) Upon payment of the deposit assessment and except as provided herein, the self-insuring employer loses all right, title, and interest in the deposit assessment. To the extent that in any one year the deposit assessment paid by self-insurers is not exhausted in the purchase of securities, surety bonds, irrevocable letters of credit, insurance, or other financial instruments to post with the director as part of the composite deposit, the surplus shall remain posted with the director, and the principal and interest earned on that surplus shall remain as part of the composite deposit in subsequent years. In the event that in any one year the Self-Insurers' Security Fund fails to post the required composite deposit by the date set the by the director, and the director requires each private self-insuring employer to secure its incurred liabilities in the manner required by Section 3701, then any deposit assessment paid in that year shall be refunded to the self-insuring employer that paid the deposit assessment.

(d) If any private self-insuring employer objects to the calculation, posting, or any other aspect of its deposit assessment, upon payment of the assessment in the time provided, the employer shall have the right to appeal the assessment to the director, who shall have exclusive jurisdiction over this dispute. If any private self-insuring employer fails to pay the deposit assessment in the time provided, the director shall order the self-insuring employer to pay a penalty of not less than 10 percent of its deposit assessment, plus interest on any unpaid amount at the prejudgment rate, and to post a separate security deposit in the manner provided by Section 3701. The penalty and interest shall be paid directly to the Self-Insurers' Security

Fund. The director may also revoke the certificate of consent to self-insure of any self-insuring employer who fails to pay the deposit assessment in the time provided.

(e) Upon the posting by the Self-Insurers' Security Fund of the composite deposit with the director, the deposit shall be held until the director determines that a private self-insured employer has failed to pay workers' compensation as required by this division, and the director orders the Self-Insurers' Security Fund to commence payment. Upon ordering the Self-Insurers' Security Fund to commence payment, the director shall make available to the fund that portion of the composite deposit necessary to pay the workers' compensation benefits of the defaulting self-insuring employer. In the event additional funds are needed in subsequent years to pay the workers' compensation benefits of any self-insuring employer who defaulted in earlier years, the director shall make available to the Self-Insurers' Security Fund any portions of the composite deposit as may be needed to pay those benefits. In making the deposit available to the Self-Insurers' Security Fund, the director shall also allow any amounts as may be reasonably necessary to pay for the administrative and other activities of the fund.

(f) The cash portion of the composite deposit shall be segregated from all other funds held by the director, and shall be invested by the director for the sole benefit of the Self-Insurers' Security Fund and the injured workers of private self-insured employers, and may not be used for any other purpose by the state. Alternatively, the director, in his discretion, may allow the Self-Insurers' Security Fund to hold, invest, and draw upon the cash portion of the composite deposit as prescribed by regulation.

(g) Notwithstanding any other provision of this section, the director shall, by regulation, set minimum credit, financial, or other conditions that a private self-insured must meet in order to be a fully participating self-insurer in the alternative security system. In the event any private self-insuring employer is unable to meet the conditions set by the director, or upon application of the Self-Insurers' Security Fund to exclude an employer for credit or financial reasons, the director shall exclude the self-insuring employer from full participation in the alternative security system. In the event a self-insuring employer is excluded from full participation, the nonfully participating private self-insuring employer shall post a separate security deposit in the manner provided by Section 3701 and pay a deposit assessment set by the director. Alternatively, the director may order that the nonfully participating private self-insuring employer post a separate security deposit to secure a portion of its incurred liabilities and pay a deposit assessment set by the director.

(h) An employer who self-insures through group self-insurance and an employer whose certificate to self-insure has been revoked may fully participate in the alternative security system if both the director and the Self-Insurers' Security Fund approve the participation of the self-insurer. If not approved for full participation, or if an employer is issued a certificate to self-insure after the composite deposit is posted, the employer shall satisfy the requirements of subdivision (g) for nonfully participating private self-insurers.

(i) At all times, a self-insured employer shall have secured its incurred workers' compensation liabilities either in the manner required by Section 3701 or through the alternative security system, and there shall not be any lapse in the security. **Leg.H.** 2002 ch. 866 (AB 486) §7, 2012 ch. 363 (SB 863) §15.

2012 Note: For legislative findings, declarations, and applicability of Stats. 2012 ch. 363, see the 2012 Notes following Lab C §62.5.

Ref.: 8 C.C.R. §§15201, 15210, 15210.1, 15210.2, 15216, 15220, 15220.1, 15220.2, 15220.3, 15220.4, 15220.5, 15220.6, 15220.7, 15220.8, 15430; Hanna § 2.11[5]; Herlick Handbook § 3.20.

§3701.9. Restriction on issuance of certificate of consent to self-insure after January 1, 2013.

(a) A certificate of consent to self-insure shall not be issued after January 1, 2013, to any of the following:

(1) A professional employer organization.

(2) A leasing employer, as defined in Section 606.5 of the Unemployment Insurance Code.

(3) A temporary services employer, as defined in Section 606.5 of the Unemployment Insurance Code.

(4) Any employer, regardless of name or form of organization, which the director determines to be in the business of providing employees to other employers.

(b) A certificate of consent to self-insure that has been issued to any employer described in subdivision (a) shall be revoked by the director not later than January 1, 2015. **Leg.H.** 2012 ch. 363 (SB 863) §16.

2012 Note: For legislative findings, declarations, and applicability of Stats. 2012 ch. 363, see the 2012 Notes following Lab C §62.5.

Ref.: Hanna § 2.11[1].

§3702. Certificate of consent to self-insure; revocation.

(a) A certificate of consent to self-insure may be revoked by the director at any time for good cause after a hearing. Good cause includes, among other things, a recommendation by the Self-Insurers' Security Fund to revoke the certificate of consent, the impairment of the solvency of the employer to the extent that there is a marked reduction of the employer's financial strength, failure to maintain a security deposit as required by Section 3701, failure to pay assessments of the Self-Insurers' Security Fund, frequent or flagrant violations of state safety and health orders, the failure or inability of the employer to fulfill his or her obligations, or any of the following practices by the employer or his or her agent in charge of the administration of obligations under this division:

(1) Habitually and as a matter of practice and custom inducing claimants for compensation to accept less than the compensation due or making it necessary for them to resort to proceedings against the employer to secure compensation due.

(2) Where liability for temporary disability indemnity is not in dispute, intentionally failing to pay temporary disability indemnity without good cause in order to influence the amount of permanent disability benefits due.

(3) Intentionally refusing to comply with known and legally indisputable compensation obligations.

Labor

(4) Discharging or administering his or her compensation obligations in a dishonest manner.

(5) Discharging or administering his or her compensation obligations in such a manner as to cause injury to the public or those dealing with the employer.

(b) Where revocation is in part based upon the director's finding of a marked reduction of the employer's financial strength or the failure or inability of the employer to fulfill his or her obligations, or a practice of discharging obligations in a dishonest manner, it is a condition precedent to the employer's challenge or appeal of the revocation that the employer have in effect insurance against liability to pay compensation.

(c) The director may hold a hearing to determine whether good cause exists to revoke an employer's certificate of consent to self-insure if the employer is cited for a willful, or repeat serious violation of the standard adopted pursuant to Section 6401.7 and the citation has become final. **Leg.H.** 1937, 1945 ch. 1431 §65, 1978 ch. 1379 §4, 1984 ch. 252 §3, effective June 27, 1984, ch. 1521 §1, operative July 1, 1985, 1989 ch. 1369 (SB 198) §2, effective October 2, 1989, 2012 ch. 363 (SB 863) §17.

2012 Note: For legislative findings, declarations, and applicability of Stats. 2012 ch. 363, see the 2012 Notes following Lab C §62.5.

Ref.: 8 C.C.R. §§9767.1, 15201, 15203, 15203.1, 15203.2, 15203.3, 15203.4, 15203.7, 15203.8, 15203.10, 15210, 15210.1, 15210.2, 15210.3, 15211, 15211.2, 15211.3, 15212, 15213, 15214, 15215, 15216, 15302, 15353, 15354, 15360, 15400, 15402.2, 15420, 15422, 15423, 15424, 15425, 15426, 15427, 15428, 15430, 15431, 15431.1, 15431.2, 15432, 15433, 15434, 15435, 15436, 15437, 15438, 15450, 15450.1, 15452, 15470, 15472, 15479, 15480; Hanna § 2.11[3]; Herlick Handbook §§ 1.05, 3.20.

§3702.1. Third-party administrators; certificate of consent.

(a) No person, firm, or corporation, other than an insurer admitted to transact workers' compensation insurance in this state, shall contract to administer claims of self-insured employers as a third-party administrator unless in possession of a certificate of consent to administer self-insured employers' workers' compensation claims.

(b) As a condition of receiving a certificate of consent, all persons given discretion by a third-party administrator to deny, accept, or negotiate a workers' compensation claim shall demonstrate their competency to the director by written examination, or other methods approved by the director.

(c) A separate certificate shall be required for each adjusting location operated by a third-party administrator. A third-party administrator holding a certificate of consent shall be subject to regulation only under this division with respect to the adjustment, administration, and management of workers' compensation claims for any self-insured employer.

(d) A third-party administrator retained by a self-insured employer to administer the employer's workers' compensation claims shall estimate the total accrued liability of the employer for the payment of compensation for the employer's annual report to the director and shall make the estimate both in good faith and with the exercise of a reasonable degree of care. The use of a third-party administrator shall not, however, discharge or alter the employer's responsibilities with respect to the report. **Leg.H.** 1984 ch. 1521 §2, operative July 1, 1985, 1986 ch. 1128 §7, effective September 25, 1986, 2009 ch. 140 (AB 1164) §137.

Ref.: 8 C.C.R. §§10100, 10100.1, 10100.2, 15400, 15400.1, 15400.2, 15402, 15402.1, 15402.2, 15402.4, 15430, 15430.1, 15431, 15431.1, 15431.2, 15432, 15433, 15434, 15435, 15436, 15437, 15438, 15450, 15450.1, 15452, 15454, 15458, 15459, 15463, 15471, 15474, 15475, 15479; Hanna §§ 2.11[2], [4], 20.01[1][d], 22.14; Herlick Handbook § 3.22.

§3702.2. Self-insurer's annual report; director's annual aggregated summary.

(a) All self-insured employers shall file a self-insurer's annual report in a form prescribed by the director. Public self-insured employers shall provide detailed information as the director determines necessary to evaluate the costs of administration, workers' compensation benefit expenditures, and solvency and performance of the public self-insured employer workers' compensation programs, on a schedule established by the director. The director may grant deferrals to public self-insured employers that are not yet capable of accurately reporting the information required, giving priority to bringing larger programs into compliance with the more detailed reporting.

(b) To enable the director to determine the amount of the security deposit required by subdivision (c) of Section 3701, the annual report of a self-insured employer who has self-insured both state and federal workers' compensation liability shall also set forth (1) the amount of all compensation liability incurred, paid-to-date, and estimated future liability under both this chapter and under the federal Longshore and Harbor Workers' Compensation Act (33 U.S.C. Sec. 901 et seq.), and (2) the identity and the amount of the security deposit securing the employer's liability under state and federal self-insured programs.

(c) The director shall annually prepare an aggregated summary of all self-insured employer liability to pay compensation reported on the self-insurers' employers annual reports, including a separate summary for public and private employer self-insurers. The summaries shall be in the same format as the individual self-insured employers are required to report that liability on the employer self-insurer's annual report forms prescribed by the director. The aggregated summaries shall be made available to the public on the self-insurance section of the department's Internet Web site. This subdivision does not authorize the director to release or make available information regarding private self-insured employers that is aggregated by industry or business type, that identifies individual self-insured filers, or that includes any individually identifiable claimant information. The director may publish information regarding the costs of administration, workers' compensation benefit expenditures, and solvency and performance of public self-insured employers' workers' compensation programs, including, but not limited to, information aggregated by industry or business type, and that may contain data identifying individual public self-insured filers, their third-party administrators, and their joint powers authorities, as long as the information does not include any individually identifiable claimant information. For purposes of this section, "individually identifiable claimant information" means any data concerning an injury or claim that is linked to a uniquely identifiable employee, employee's dependent, or a specific claim.

(d) The director may release a copy, or make available an electronic version, of the data contained in any public sector employer self-insurer's annual reports received from an individual public entity self-insurer or from a joint powers authority employer and its membership. However, the release of any annual report information by the director shall not include any portion of any listing of open indemnity claims that contains individually identifiable claimant information, or any portion of excess insurance coverage information that contains any individually identifiable claimant information. **Leg.H.** 1986 ch. 1128 §8, effective September 25, 1986, 1993 ch. 917, 2006 ch. 115 (AB 2087) §1, 2012 ch. 363 (SB 863) §18, 2018 ch. 538 (AB 2334) §3.

2012 Note: For legislative findings, declarations, and applicability of Stats. 2012 ch. 363, see the 2012 Notes following Lab C §62.5.

Ref.: 8 C.C.R. §§15251, 15402.1, 15402.2, 15450.1, 15470, 15472, 15474, 15475, 15479; Hanna §§ 1.19, 2.11[2]; Herlick Handbook § 1.05.

§3702.3. Failure to submit reports or information; fines; handling of funds.

Failure to submit reports or information as deemed necessary by the director to implement the purposes of Section 3701, 3702, or 3702.2 may result in the assessment of a civil penalty as set forth in subdivision (a) of Section 3702.9. Moneys collected shall be used for the administration of self-insurance plans. **Leg.H.** 1992 ch. 532.

Ref.: 8 C.C.R. §§15201, 15203.8, 15210, 15210.1, 15210.2, 15215, 15216, 15251, 15300, 15301, 15302, 15303, 15420, 15422, 15424, 15425, 15426, 15427, 15428, 15450.1, 15479; Hanna § 2.11[2].

§3702.5. Costs of administration of self-insured programs; fines for late filing; handling of funds.

(a)(1) The cost of administration of the public self-insured program by the Director of Industrial Relations shall be borne by the Workers' Compensation Administration Revolving Fund.

(2) The cost of administration of the private self-insured program by the Director of Industrial Relations shall be borne by the private self-insurers through payment of certificate fees which shall be established by the director in broad ranges based on the comparative numbers of employees insured by the private self-insurers and the number of adjusting locations. The director may assess other fees as necessary to cover the costs of special audits or services rendered to private self-insured employers. The director may assess a civil penalty for late filing as set forth in subdivision (a) of Section 3702.9.

(b) All revenues from fees and penalties paid by private self-insured employers shall be deposited into the Self-Insurance Plans Fund, which is hereby created for the administration of the private self-insurance program. Any unencumbered balance in subdivision (a) of Item 8350-001-001 of the Budget Act of 1983 shall be transferred to the Self-Insurance Plans Fund. The director shall annually eliminate any unused surplus in the Self-Insurance Plans Fund by reducing certificate fee assessments by an appropriate amount in the subsequent year. Moneys paid into the Self-Insurance Plans Fund for administration of the private self-insured program shall not be used by any other department or agency or for any purpose other than administration of the private self-insurance program. Detailed accountability shall be maintained by the director for any security deposit or other funds held in trust for the Self-Insurer's Security Fund in the Self-Insurance Plans Fund.

Moneys held by the director shall be invested in the Surplus Money Investment Fund. Interest shall be paid on all moneys transferred to the General Fund in accordance with Section 16310 of the Government Code. The Treasurer's and Controller's administrative costs may be charged to the interest earnings upon approval of the director. **Leg.H.** 1971 ch. 1758 §2, 1978 ch. 1379 §7, 1984 ch. 1734 §1, effective September 30, 1984, operative July 1, 1984, 1992 ch. 532 (AB 2771) §2, 2012 ch. 363 (SB 863) §20.

2012 Note: For legislative findings, declarations, and applicability of Stats. 2012 ch. 363, see the 2012 Notes following Lab C §62.5.

Ref.: 8 C.C.R. §§15201, 15203, 15204, 15205, 15211, 15211.2, 15212, 15230, 15231, 15233, 15234, 15360, 15400, 15402.3, 15420, 15422, 15423, 15430, 15432, 15433, 15434, 15435, 15436, 15437, 15438, 15454, 15470, 15479.

§3702.6. Audit cycle for private self-insured employers; special audit of public self-insured employers.

(a) The director shall establish an audit program addressing the adequacy of estimates of future liability of claims for all private self-insured employers, and shall ensure that all private self-insured employers are audited within a three-year cycle by the Office of Self Insurance Plans.

(b) Each public self-insurer shall advise its governing board within 90 days after submission of the self-insurer's annual report of the total liabilities reported and whether current funding of those workers' compensation liabilities is in compliance with the requirements of Government Accounting Standards Board Publication No. 10.

(c) The director shall, upon a showing of good cause, order a special audit of any public self-insured employer to determine the adequacy of estimates of future liability of claims.

(d) For purposes of this section, "good cause" means that there exists circumstances sufficient to raise concerns regarding the adequacy of estimates of future liability of claims to justify a special audit. **Leg.H.** 1992 ch. 532.

1989 Note: This section is applicable only to injuries occurring on or after January 1, 1990. Stats. 1989 ch. 893 §6.

Ref.: 8 C.C.R. §§15201, 15210, 15210.1, 15210.2, 15211, 15211.2, 15211.3, 15212, 15213, 15214, 15215, 15216, 15300, 15301, 15302, 15303, 15360, 15400, 15403, 15403.1, 15404, 15404.1, 15404.2, 15405, 15420, 15422, 15423, 15424, 15425, 15426, 15427, 15428, 15430, 15432, 15433, 15434, 15435, 15436, 15437, 15438; Hanna § 2.11[2]; Herlick Handbook §§ 1.05, 3.20.

§3702.7. Revocation of certificate of consent; fine in lieu of.

A certificate of consent to administer claims of self-insured employers may be revoked by the director at any time for good cause after a hearing. Good cause includes, but is not limited to, the violation of subsection (1), (2), (3), (4), or (5) of subdivision (a) of Section 3702. In lieu of revocation of a certificate of consent, the director may impose a fine of not less than fifty dollars ($50) nor more than five hundred dollars ($500) for each violation.

Ref.: 8 C.C.R. §§15402.2, 15430, 15430.1, 15431, 15431.1, 15431.2, 15432, 15433, 15434, 15435, 15436, 15437, 15438, 15463, 15479; Hanna § 2.11[4]; Herlick Handbook §§ 1.05, 3.22.

§3702.8. Obligations of former self-insured employers.

(a) Employers who have ceased to be self-insured employers shall discharge their continuing obligations to secure the payment of workers' compensation that accrued during the period of self-insurance, for purposes of Sections 3700, 3700.5, 3706, and 3715, and shall comply with all of the following obligations of current certificate holders:

(1) Filing annual reports as deemed necessary by the director to carry out the requirements of this chapter.

(2) In the case of a private employer, depositing and maintaining a security deposit for accrued liability for the payment of any workers' compensation that may become due, pursuant to subdivision (b) of Section 3700 and Section 3701, except as provided in subdivision (c).

(3) Paying within 30 days all assessments of which notice is sent, pursuant to subdivision (b) of Section 3745, within 36 months from the last day the employer's certificate of self-insurance was in effect. Assessments shall be based on the benefits paid by the employer during the last full calendar year of self-insurance on claims incurred during that year.

(b) In addition to proceedings to establish liabilities and penalties otherwise provided, a failure to comply may be the subject of a proceeding before the director. An appeal from the director's determination shall be taken to the appropriate superior court by petition for writ of mandate.

(c) Notwithstanding subdivision (a), any employer who is currently self-insured or who has ceased to be self-insured may purchase a special excess workers' compensation policy to discharge any or all of the employer's continuing obligations as a self-insurer to pay compensation or to secure the payment of compensation.

(1) The special excess workers' compensation insurance policy shall be issued by an insurer authorized to transact workers' compensation insurance in this state.

(2) Each carrier's special excess workers' compensation policy shall be approved as to form and substance by the Insurance Commissioner, and rates for special excess workers' compensation insurance shall be subject to the filing requirements set forth in Section 11735 of the Insurance Code.

(3) Each special excess workers' compensation insurance policy shall be submitted by the employer to the director. The director shall adopt and publish minimum insurer financial rating standards for companies issuing special excess workers' compensation policies.

(4) Upon acceptance by the director, a special excess workers' compensation policy shall provide coverage for all or any portion of the purchasing employer's claims for compensation arising out of injuries occurring during the period the employer was self-insured in accordance with Sections 3755, 3756, and 3757 of the Labor Code and Sections 11651 and 11654 of the Insurance Code. The director's acceptance shall discharge the Self-Insurer's Security Fund, without recourse or liability to the Self-Insurer's Security Fund, of any continuing liability for the claims covered by the special excess workers' compensation insurance policy.

(5) For public employers, no security deposit or financial guarantee bond or other security shall be required. The director shall set minimum financial rating standards for insurers issuing special excess workers' compensation policies for public employers.

(d)(1) In order for the special excess workers' compensation insurance policy to discharge the full obligations of a private employer to maintain a security deposit with the director for the payment of self-insured claims, applicable to the period to be covered by the policy, the special excess policy shall provide coverage for all claims for compensation arising out of that liability. The employer shall maintain the required deposit for the period covered by the policy with the director for a period of three years after the issuance date of the special excess policy.

(2) If the special workers' compensation insurance policy does not provide coverage for all of the continuing obligations for which the private self-insured employer is liable, to the extent the employer's obligations are not covered by the policy a private employer shall maintain the required deposit with the director. In addition, the employer shall maintain with the director the required deposit for the period covered by the policy for a period of three years after the issuance date of the special excess policy.

(e) The director shall adopt regulations pursuant to Section 3702.10 that are reasonably necessary to implement this section in order to reasonably protect injured workers, employers, the Self-Insurers' Security Fund, and the California Insurance Guarantee Association.

(f) The posting of a special excess workers' compensation insurance policy with the director shall discharge the obligation of the Self-Insurer's Security Fund pursuant to Section 3744 to pay claims in the event of an insolvency of a private employer to the extent of coverage of compensation liabilities under the special excess workers' compensation insurance policy. The California Insurance Guarantee Association and the Self-Insurers' Security Fund shall be advised by the director whenever a special excess workers' compensation insurance policy is posted. **Leg.H.** 1986 ch. 1128 §11, effective September 25, 1986, 1989 ch. 1258 (AB 1302) §3, 1990 ch. 704 (AB 3853) §2, 1999 ch. 721 (AB 1309) §7, 2012 ch. 363 (SB 863) §21.

2012 Note: For legislative findings, declarations, and applicability of Stats. 2012 ch. 363, see the 2012 Notes following Lab C §62.5.

Ref.: 8 C.C.R. §§10103, 10103.1, 10103.2, 15210.2, 15360, 15437; Hanna § 1.19; Herlick Handbook §§ 1.05, 3.20.

§3702.9. Director's order for compliance, restitution, and civil penalty.

(a) In addition to remedies and penalties otherwise provided for a failure to secure the payment of compensation, the director may, after a determination that an obligation created in this article has been violated, also enter an order against any self-insured employer, including employers who are no longer self-insured, but who are required to comply with Section 3702.8, directing compliance, restitution for any losses, and a civil penalty in an amount not to exceed the following:

(1) For a failure to file a complete or timely annual report, an amount up to 5 percent of the incurred liabilities in the last report or one thousand five hundred dollars ($1,500), whichever is less, for each 30 days or portion thereof during which there is a failure.

(2) For failure to deposit and maintain a security deposit, an amount up to 10 percent of the increase not timely filed or five thousand dollars ($5,000), whichever is less, for each 30 days or portion thereof during which there is a failure.

(3) For a failure to timely or completely pay an assessment, an amount up to the assessment or two thousand five hundred dollars ($2,500), whichever is less, for each 30 days or portion thereof during which there is a failure.

(4) Where the failure was by an employer which knew or reasonably should have know of the obligation, the director shall, in addition, award reimbursement for all expenditures and costs by the fund or any intervening party, including a reasonable attorney fee.

(5) Where the failure was malicious, fraudulent, in bad faith, or a repeated violation, the director may award, as an additional civil penalty, liquidated damages of up to double the amounts assessed under paragraphs (1) to (4), inclusive, for deposit in the General Fund.

(b) An employer may deposit and maintain a security deposit or pay an assessment, reserving its right to challenge the amount or liability therefor at a hearing. If the director or the appeals board or a court, upon appeal, concludes that the employer is not liable or the amounts are excessive, then the director may waive, release, compromise, refund, or otherwise remit amounts which had been paid or deposited by an employer. The director may condition the waiver, release, compromise, refund, or remittance upon the present and continued future compliance with the obligations of subdivision (a) of Section 3702.8 for a period up to two years.

(c) Notwithstanding subdivision (b), where a violation has occurred, the director may waive, release, compromise, or otherwise reduce any civil penalty otherwise due upon a showing that a violation occurred through the employer's mistake, inadvertence, surprise, or excusable neglect. Neglect is not excusable within the meaning of this subdivision where the employer knew, or reasonably should have known, of the obligations.

Ref.: 8 C.C.R. §§15232, 15251, 15430, 15431.1, 15431.2, 15432, 15433, 15434, 15435, 15436, 15437, 15438; Hanna § 2.11[1].

§3702.10. Authorization to adopt, amend, and repeal regulations.

The director, in accordance with Chapter 3.5 (commencing with Section 11340) of Part 1 of Division 3 of Title 2 of the Government Code, may adopt, amend, and repeal rules and regulations reasonably necessary to carry out the purposes of Section 129 and Article 1 (commencing with Section 3700), Article 2 (commencing with Section 3710), and Article 2.5 (commencing with Section 3740). This authorization includes, but is not limited to, the adoption of regulations to do all of the following:

(a) Specifying what constitutes ability to self-insure and to pay any compensation which may become due under Section 3700.

(b) Specifying what constitutes a marked reduction of an employer's financial strength.

(c) Specifying what constitutes a failure or inability to fulfill the employer's obligations under Section 3702.

(d) Interpreting and defining the terms used.

(e) Establishing procedures and standards for hearing and determinations, and providing for those determinations to be appealed to the appeals board.

(f) Specifying the standards, form, and content of agreements, forms, and reports between parties who have obligations pursuant to this chapter.

(g) Providing for the combinations and relative liabilities of security deposits, assumptions, and guarantees used pursuant to this chapter.

(h) Disclosing otherwise confidential financial information concerning self-insureds to courts or the Self-Insurers' Security Fund and specifying appropriate safeguards for that information.

(i) Requiring an amount to be added to each security deposit to secure the cost of administration of claims and to pay all legal costs.

(j) Regulating the workers' compensation self-insurance obligations of self-insurance groups and professional employer organizations, leasing employers as defined in Section 606.5 of the Unemployment Insurance Code, or temporary services employers, as defined in Section 606.5 of the Unemployment Insurance Code, holding certificates of consent to self-insure. **Leg.H.** 1986 ch. 1128 §13, effective September 25, 1986, 1993 ch. 121 (AB 110) §26, effective July 16, 1993, 2012 ch. 363 (SB 863) §22.

2012 Note: For legislative findings, declarations, and applicability of Stats. 2012 ch. 363, see the 2012 Notes following Lab C §62.5.

Ref.: 8 C.C.R. §§15201, 15202, 15203.1, 15203.2, 15203.3, 15203.4, 15203.5, 15203.6, 15203.7, 15203.8, 15203.9, 15203.10, 15204, 15205, 15210, 15210.1, 15211.2, 15211.3, 15212, 15213, 15214, 15215, 15220.1, 15220.2, 15220.4, 15230, 15231, 15232, 15233, 15234, 15250, 15250.1, 15251, 15300, 15301, 15302, 15353, 15354, 15400.1, 15400.2, 15402, 15402.1, 15402.2, 15402.3, 15402.4, 15403, 15403.1, 15404, 15404.1, 15404.2, 15405, 15420, 15424, 15425, 15426, 15427, 15428, 15431.1, 15431.2, 15432, 15433, 15434, 15435, 15436, 15437, 15438, 15452, 15454, 15458, 15459, 15461, 15463, 15470, 15472, 15473, 15474, 15475, 15476, 15477, 15478, 15479, 15480, 15481; Hanna § 2.10[5]; Herlick Handbook § 3.20.

§3703. Self-insurer's independent administration.

So long as the certificate has not been revoked, and the self-insurer maintains on deposit the requisite bond or securities, the self-insurer shall not be required or obliged to pay into the State Compensation Insurance Fund any sums covering liability for compensation excepting life pensions; and the self-insurer may fully administer any compensation benefits assessed against the self-insurer.

Ref.: 8 C.C.R. §§15201, 15203.8, 15211, 15211.2, 15211.3, 15212, 15213, 15214, 15216, 15300, 15303, 15360, 15400, 15420, 15422, 15423, 15424, 15425, 15426, 15427, 15428; Hanna § 2.11[1].

§3705. Surety's equal preference over other debts.

The Self-Insurers' Security Fund or the surety making payment of compensation hereunder shall have the same preference over the other debts of the principal or his or her estate as is given by law to the person directly entitled to the compensation.

Ref.: 8 C.C.R. §§15201, 15203.1, 15211, 15211.2, 15211.3, 15212, 15213, 15214, 15216, 15360, 15400, 15420, 15422, 15423, 15424, 15425, 15426, 15427, 15428, 15430, 15432, 15433, 15434, 15435, 15436, 15437, 15438.

§3706. Employer's failure to secure payment.

If any employer fails to secure the payment of compensation, any injured employee or his dependents may bring an action at law against such employer for damages, as if this division did not apply.

Ref.: Hanna §§ 10.25, 11.02[4], 11.03[2], 21.05[1], 27.12[1][c]; Herlick Handbook §§ 9.2, 12.11.

§3706.5. Exceptions to penalty for failure to secure payment.

The provisions of this article and Sections 4553, 4554, and 4555, and any other penalty provided by law for failure to secure the payment of compensation for employees, shall not apply to individual members of a board or governing body of a public agency or to members of a private, nonprofit organization, if the agency or organization performs officiating services relating to amateur sporting events and those members are excluded from the definition of "employee" pursuant to paragraph (10) of subdivision (a) of Section 3352. **Leg.H.** 1981 ch. 21 §9, effective April 18, 1981, 2017 ch. 770 (SB 189) §6.

Ref.: Hanna § 21.05[1].

§3707. Attachment of employer's property.

The injured employee or his dependents may in such action attach the property of the employer, at any time upon or after the institution of such action, in an amount fixed by the court, to secure the payment of any judgment which is ultimately obtained. The provisions of the Code of Civil Procedure, not inconsistent with this division, shall govern the issuance of, and proceedings upon such attachment.

§3708. Employer's negligence; presumption; defenses unavailable.

In such action it is presumed that the injury to the employee was a direct result and grew out of the negligence of the employer, and the burden of proof is upon the employer, to rebut the presumption of negligence. It is not a defense to the employer that the employee was guilty of contributory negligence, or assumed the risk of the hazard complained of, or that the injury was caused by the negligence of a fellow servant. No contract or regulation shall restore to the employer any of the foregoing defenses.

This section shall not apply to any employer of an employee, as defined in subdivision (d) of Section 3351, with respect to such employee, but shall apply to employers of employees described in subdivision (b) of Section 3715, with respect to such employees.

Ref.: Hanna §§ 2.17, 11.02[4][e], [f], 11.03[2]; Herlick Handbook §§ 2.5, 4.15[1].

§3708.5. Employee's complaint; service; consolidation of actions.

If an employee brings such an action for damages, the employee shall forthwith give a copy of the complaint to the Uninsured Employers Fund of the action by personal service or certified mail. Proof of such service shall be filed in such action. If a civil action has been initiated against the employer pursuant to Section 3717, the actions shall be consolidated.

§3709. Judgments.

If, as a result of such action for damages, a judgment is obtained against the employer, any compensation awarded, paid, or secured by the employer shall be credited against the judgment. The court shall allow as a first lien against such judgment the amount of compensation paid by the director from the Uninsured Employers Fund pursuant to Section 3716.

Such judgment shall include a reasonable attorney's fee fixed by the court. The director, as administrator of the Uninsured Employers Fund, shall have a first lien against any proceeds of settlement in such action, before or after judgment, in the amount of compensation paid by the director from the Uninsured Employers Fund pursuant to section 3716.

No satisfaction of a judgment in such action, in whole or in part, shall be valid as against the director without giving the director notice and a reasonable opportunity to perfect and satisfy his lien.

Ref.: Herlick Handbook § 12.11.

§3709.5. Employer's and Uninsured Employers Fund's relief from obligation to pay more.

After the payment of attorney's fees fixed by the court, the employer shall be relieved from the obligation to pay further compensation to or on behalf of the employee under this division up to the entire amount of the balance of the judgment, if satisfied, or such portion as has been satisfied.

After the satisfaction by the employer of the attorney's fees fixed by the court, the Uninsured Employers Fund shall be relieved from the obligation to pay further compensation to or on behalf of the employee pursuant to Section 3716, up to the entire amount of the balance of the judgment, if satisfied, or such portion as has been satisfied.

The appeals board shall allow as a credit to the employer and to the Uninsured Employers Fund, to be applied against the liability for compensation, the amount recovered by the employee in such action, either by settlement or after the judgment, as has not been applied to the expense of attorney's fees and costs.

ARTICLE 2
Uninsured Employers Fund

§3710. Director of Industrial Relations; powers; "director."

(a) The Director of Industrial Relations shall enforce the provisions of this article. He may employ necessary investigators, clerks, and other employees, and make use of the services of any employee of the department whom he may assign to assist him in the enforcement of this article. Prosecutions for criminal violations of this division may be conducted by the appropriate public official of the county in which the offense is committed, by the Attorney General, or by any attorney in the civil service of the Department of Industrial Relations designated by the director for such purpose.

(b) The director, in accordance with the provisions of Chapter 4 (commencing at Section 11370) of Part 1 of Division 3 of Title 2 of the Government Code, may adopt, amend and repeal such rules and regulations as are reasonably necessary for the purpose of enforcing and administering this article and as are not inconsistent with law.

(c) As used in this article, "director" means the Director of Industrial Relations or the director's designated agents.

Ref.: 8 C.C.R. §§15550, 15551, 15552, 15553, 15554, 15555, 15556, 15557, 15558, 15559, 15560, 15561, 15562, 15563, 15564, 15565, 15566, 15567, 15568, 15569, 15570, 15571, 15571.5, 15572, 15573, 15574, 15575, 15576, 15578, 15579, 15580, 15581, 15582, 15583, 15584, 15585, 15586, 15587, 15588, 15589, 15590, 15591, 15592, 15593, 15594, 15595, 15596; Herlick Handbook §§ 3.14, 3.19, 3.23.

§3710.1. Stop orders.

Where an employer has failed to secure the payment of compensation as required by Section 3700, the director shall issue and serve on such employer a stop order prohibiting the use of employee labor by such employer until the employer's compliance with the provisions of Section 3700. Such stop order shall become effective immediately upon service. Any employee so affected by such work stoppage shall be paid by the employer for such time lost, not exceeding 10 days, pending compliance by the employer. Such employer may protest the stop order by making and filing with the director a written request for a hearing within 20 days after service of such stop order. Such hearing shall be held within 5 days from the date of filing such request. The director shall notify the employer of the time and place of the hearing by mail. At the conclusion of the hearing, the stop order shall be immediately affirmed or dismissed, and within 24 hours thereafter the director shall issue and serve on all parties to the hearing by registered or certified mail a written notice of findings and findings. A writ of mandate may be taken from the findings to the appropriate superior court. Such writ must be taken within 45 days after the mailing of the notice of findings and findings.

Ref.: 8 C.C.R. §§15550, 15551, 15552, 15553, 15554, 15555, 15556, 15557, 15558, 15559, 15560, 15561, 15562, 15563, 15564, 15565, 15566, 15567, 15568, 15569, 15570, 15571, 15571.5, 15572, 15573, 15574, 15575, 15576, 15578, 15579, 15580, 15581, 15582, 15583, 15584, 15585, 15586, 15587, 15588, 15589, 15590, 15591, 15592, 15593, 15594, 15595, 15596.

§3710.2. Penalties for failure to observe stop order.

Failure of an employer, officer, or anyone having direction, management, or control of any place of employment or of employees to observe a stop order issued and served upon him or her pursuant to Section 3710.1 is a misdemeanor punishable by imprisonment in the county jail not exceeding 60 days or by a fine not exceeding ten thousand dollars ($10,000), or both. Fines shall be paid into the State Treasury to the credit of the Uninsured Employers Fund. The director may also obtain injunctive and other relief from the courts to carry out the purposes of Section 3710.1. The failure to obtain a policy of workers' compensation insurance or a certificate of consent to self-insure as required by Section 3700 is a misdemeanor in accordance with Section 3700.5. **Leg.H.** 1991 ch. 600.

Ref.: 8 C.C.R. §§15550, 15551, 15552, 15553, 15554, 15555, 15556, 15557, 15558, 15559, 15560, 15561, 15562, 15563, 15564, 15565, 15566, 15567, 15568, 15569, 15570, 15571, 15571.5, 15572, 15573, 15574, 15575, 15576, 15578, 15579, 15580, 15581, 15582, 15583, 15584, 15585, 15586, 15587, 15588, 15589, 15590, 15591, 15592, 15593, 15594, 15595, 15596.

§3710.3. Transmittal of stop orders issued to certain carriers.

Whenever a stop order has been issued pursuant to Section 3710.1 to a motor carrier of property subject to the jurisdiction and control of the Department of Motor Vehicles or to a household goods carrier, passenger stage corporation, or charter-party carrier of passengers subject to the jurisdiction and control of the Public Utilities Commission, the director shall transmit the stop order to the Public Utilities Commission or the Department of Motor Vehicles, whichever has jurisdiction over the affected carrier, within 30 days. **Leg.H.** 1991 ch. 1071, 1996 ch. 1042, effective September 29, 1996, 1998 ch. 485.

Ref.: Herlick Handbook § 3.23.

§3711. Proof of insurance.

The director, an investigator for the Department of Insurance Fraud Bureau or its successor, or a district attorney investigator assigned to investigate workers' compensation fraud may, at any time, require an employer to furnish a written statement showing the name of his or her insurer or the manner in which the employer has complied with Section 3700. Failure of the employer for a period of 10 days to furnish the written statement is prima facie evidence that he or she has failed or neglected in respect to the matters so required. The 10-day period may not be construed to allow an uninsured employer, so found by the director, any extension of time from the application of the provisions of Section 3710.1. An insured employer who fails to respond to an inquiry respecting his or her status as to his or her workers' compensation security shall be assessed and required to pay a penalty of five hundred dollars ($500) to the director for deposit in the State

Treasury to the credit of the Uninsured Employers Fund. In any prosecution under this article, the burden of proof is upon the defendant to show that he or she has secured the payment of compensation in one of the two ways set forth in Section 3700. **Leg.H.** 1991 ch. 600, 1992 ch. 1276, 1993 ch. 60, effective June 30, 1993, 2004 ch. 2 (SB 2 Fourth Extra. Sess.), effective March 6, 2005.

Ref.: 8 C.C.R. §§15550, 15551, 15552, 15553, 15554, 15555, 15556, 15557, 15558, 15559, 15560, 15561, 15562, 15563, 15564, 15565, 15566, 15567, 15568, 15569, 15570, 15571, 15571.5, 15572, 15573, 15574, 15575, 15576, 15578, 15579, 15580, 15581, 15582, 15583, 15584, 15585, 15586, 15587, 15588, 15589, 15590, 15591, 15592, 15593, 15594, 15595, 15596; Hanna §§ 2.14, 10.20; Herlick Handbook § 3.23.

§3712. Purpose for compensation laws; court procedure.

(a) The securing of the payment of compensation in a way provided in this division is essential to the functioning of the expressly declared social public policy of this state in the matter of workers' compensation. The conduct or operation of any business or undertaking without full compensation security, in continuing violation of social policy, shall be subject to imposition of business strictures and monetary penalties by the director, including, but not limited to, resort to the superior court of any county in which all or some part of the business is being thus unlawfully conducted or operated, for carrying out the intent of this article.

(b) In a proceeding before the superior court in matters concerned with this article, no filing fee shall be charged to the plaintiff; nor may any charge or cost be imposed for any act or service required of or done by any state or county officer or employee in connection with the proceeding. If the court or the judge before whom the order to show cause in the proceeding is made returnable, finds that the defendant is conducting or operating a business or undertaking without the full compensation security required, the court or judge shall forthwith, and without continuance, issue an order restraining the future or further conduct and operation of the business or undertaking so long as the violation of social public policy continues. The action shall be prosecuted by the Attorney General of California, the district attorney of the county in which suit is brought, the city attorney of any city in which such a business or undertaking is being operated or conducted without full compensation security, or any attorney possessing civil service status who is an employee of the Department of Industrial Relations who may be designated by the director for that purpose. No finding made in the course of any such action is binding on the appeals board in any subsequent proceeding before it for benefits under this division.

Ref.: 8 C.C.R. §§15550, 15551, 15552, 15553, 15554, 15555, 15556, 15557, 15558, 15559, 15560, 15561, 15562, 15563, 15564, 15565, 15566, 15567, 15568, 15569, 15570, 15571, 15571.5, 15572, 15573, 15574, 15575, 15576, 15578, 15579, 15580, 15581, 15582, 15583, 15584, 15585, 15586, 15587, 15588, 15589, 15590, 15591, 15592, 15593, 15594, 15595, 15596.

§3714. [See Subdivision (d) for Inoperative and Repeal Information] Case hearing and filing procedures.

(a) All cases involving the Uninsured Employers Fund or the Subsequent Injuries Fund as a party or involving death without dependents shall only be heard for conference, mandatory settlement conference pursuant to subdivision (d) of Section 5502, standby conference, or rating calendar at the district Workers' Compensation Appeals Board located in San Francisco, Los Angeles, Van Nuys, Anaheim, Sacramento, or San Diego, except for good cause shown and with the consent of the director. This subdivision shall not apply to trials or hearings pursuant to Section 5309 or to expedited hearings pursuant to subdivision (b) of Section 5502.

(b) For the cases specified in subdivision (a), the presiding judge of the Workers' Compensation Appeals Board located in San Francisco, Los Angeles, Van Nuys, Anaheim, Sacramento, or San Diego shall have the authority, either by standing order or on a case-by-case basis, to order a conference, mandatory settlement conference pursuant to subdivision (d) of Section 5502, standby conference, or rating calendar in which no testimony will be taken to be conducted by telephone conference call among the parties and their attorneys of record who do not reside in the county in which that appeals board is located. The cost of the scheduling of the conference call shall be charged against the appropriate fund of the department.

(c) Any filings of documents necessary for the proceedings specified in subdivisions (a) and (b) may be served on the appeals board and the parties by facsimile machine, but if so served, within five workings days service shall be made on the appeals board and the parties as required by regulation.

(d) This section shall remain in effect for two years commencing on the date that the administrative director certifies and publishes that the rearrangement of judicial resources required by this section, and conference call facilities required for this section are in place. The certification shall be published in the California Notice Register, but shall be required to have been posted in the office of each appeals board at least 30 days prior to that publication. Notwithstanding this section, with the permission of the presiding judge and under standards set by the administrative director, parties may be permitted to conclude existing cases where they were filed. This section shall cease to be operative at the end of that two-year period, and shall be repealed on January 1 following that date. **Leg.H.** 1992 ch. 611.

Ref.: 8 C.C.R. §§15550, 15551, 15552, 15553, 15554, 15555, 15556, 15557, 15558, 15559, 15560, 15561, 15562, 15563, 15564, 15565, 15566, 15567, 15568, 15569, 15570, 15571, 15571.5, 15572, 15573, 15574, 15575, 15576, 15578, 15579, 15580, 15581, 15582, 15583, 15584, 15585, 15586, 15587, 15588, 15589, 15590, 15591, 15592, 15593, 15594, 15595, 15596; Herlick Handbook § 14.15.

§3715. Employee's remedies.

(a) Any employee, except an employee as defined in subdivision (d) of Section 3351, whose employer has failed to secure the payment of compensation as required by this division, or his or her dependents in case death has ensued, may, in addition to proceeding against his or her employer by civil action in the courts as provided in Section 3706, file his or her application with the appeals board for compensation and the appeals board shall hear and determine the application for compensation in like manner as in other claims and shall make the award to the claimant as he or she would be entitled to receive if the employer had secured the payment of compensation as required, and the employer shall pay the award in the manner and amount fixed thereby or shall furnish to the appeals board a bond, in any amount and with any sureties as the appeals board requires, to pay the employee the award in the manner and amount fixed thereby.

(b) Notwithstanding this section or any other provision of this chapter except Section 3708, any person described in subdivision (d) of Section 3351 who is (1) engaged in household domestic service who is employed by one employer for over 52 hours per week, (2) engaged as a part-time gardener in connection with a private dwelling, if the number of hours devoted to the gardening work for any individual regularly exceeds 44 hours per month, or (3) engaged in casual employment where the work contemplated is to be completed in not less than 10 working days, without regard to the number of persons employed, and where the total labor cost of the work is not less than one hundred dollars ($100) (which amount shall not include charges other than for personal services), shall be entitled, in addition to proceeding against his or her employer by civil action in the courts as provided in Section 3706, to file his or her application with the appeals board for compensation. The appeals board shall hear and determine the application for compensation in like manner as in other claims, and shall make the award to the claimant as he or she would be entitled to receive if the person's employer had secured the payment of compensation as required, and the employer shall pay the award in the manner and amount fixed thereby, or shall furnish to the appeals board a bond, in any amount and with any sureties as the appeals board requires, to pay the employee the award in the manner and amount fixed thereby.

It is the intent of the Legislature that the amendments to this section by Chapter 17 of the Statutes of 1977, make no change in the law as it applied to those types of employees covered by this subdivision prior to the effective date of Chapter 1263 of the 1975 Regular Session.

(c) In any claim in which it is alleged that the employer has failed to secure the payment of compensation, the director, only for purposes of this section and Section 3720, shall determine, on the basis of the evidence available to him or her, whether the employer was prima facie illegally uninsured. A finding that the employer was prima facie illegally uninsured shall be made when the director determines that there is sufficient evidence to constitute a prima facie case that the employer employed an employee on the date of the alleged injury and had failed to secure the payment of compensation, and that the employee was injured arising out of, and occurring in the course of, the employment.

Failure of the employer to furnish within 10 days the written statement in response to a written demand for a written statement prescribed in Section 3711, addressed to the employer at its address as shown on the official address record of the appeals board, shall constitute in itself sufficient evidence for a prima facie case that the employer failed to secure the payment of compensation.

A written denial by the insurer named in the statement furnished by the employer as prescribed in Section 3711, that the employer was so insured as claimed, or the nonexistence of a valid certificate of consent to self-insure for the time of the claimed injury, if the statement furnished by the employer claims the employer was self-insured, shall constitute in itself sufficient evidence for a prima facie case that the employer had failed to secure the payment of compensation.

The nonexistence of a record of the employer's insurance with the Workers' Compensation Insurance Rating Bureau shall constitute in itself sufficient evidence for a prima facie case that the employer failed to secure the payment of compensation.

The unrebutted written declaration under penalty of perjury by the injured employee, or applicant other than the employee, that the employee was employed by the employer at the time of the injury, and that he or she was injured in the course of his or her employment, shall constitute, in itself, sufficient evidence for a prima facie case that the employer employed the employee at the time of the injury, and that the employee was injured arising out of, and occurring in the course of, the employment.

(d) When the director determines that an employer was prima facie illegally uninsured, the director shall mail a written notice of the determination to the employer at his or her address as shown on the official address record of the appeals board, and to any other more recent address the director may possess. The notice shall advise the employer of its right to appeal the finding, and that a lien may be placed against the employer's and any parent corporation's property, or the property of substantial shareholders of a corporate employer as defined by Section 3717.

Any employer aggrieved by a finding of the director that it was prima facie illegally uninsured may appeal the finding by filing a petition before the appeals board. The petition shall be filed within 20 days after the finding is issued. The appeals board shall hold a hearing on the petition within 20 days after the petition is filed with the appeals board. The appeals board shall have exclusive jurisdiction to determine appeals of the findings by the director, and no court of this state has jurisdiction to review, annul, or suspend the findings or the liens created thereunder, except as provided by Article 2 (commencing with Section 5950) of Chapter 7 of Part 4 of Division 4.

(e) Any claim brought against an employer under this section may be resolved by the director by compromise and release or stipulated findings and award as long as the appeals board has acquired jurisdiction over the employer and the employer has been given notice and an opportunity to object.

Notice may be given by service on the employer of an appeals board notice of intention to approve the compromise and release or stipulated findings and award. The employer shall have 20 days after service of the notice of intention to file an objection with the appeals board and show good cause therefor.

If the employer objects, the appeals board shall determine if there is good cause for the objection.

If the appeals board finds good cause for the objection, the director may proceed with the compromise and release or stipulated findings and award if doing so best serves the interest of the Uninsured Employers Fund, but shall have no cause of action against the employer under Section 3717 unless the appeals board case is tried to its conclusion and the employer is found liable.

If the appeals board does not find good cause for the objection, and the compromise and release or stipulated findings and award is approved, the Uninsured Employers Fund shall have a cause of action against the employer pursuant to Section 3717.

(f) The director may adopt regulations to implement and interpret the procedures provided for in this section.

Ref.: 8 C.C.R. §§15710, 15720, 15721, 15722, 15723, 15730, 15731; Hanna §§ 10.24[3], [4], 11.02[4][c]; Herlick Handbook §§ 2.5, 3.2.

§3716. Uninsured Employers Benefits Trust Fund.

(a) If the employer fails to pay the compensation required by Section 3715 to the person entitled thereto, or fails to furnish the bond required by Section 3715 within a period of 10 days after notification of the award, the award, upon application by the person entitled thereto, shall be paid by the director from the Uninsured Employers Benefits Trust Fund. The expenses of the director in administering these provisions, directly or by contract pursuant to Section 3716.1, shall be paid from the Workers' Compensation Administration Revolving Fund. Refunds may be paid from the Uninsured Employers Benefits Trust Fund for amounts remitted erroneously to the fund, or the director may authorize offsetting subsequent remittances to the fund.

(b) It is the intent of the Legislature that the Uninsured Employers Benefits Trust Fund is created to ensure that workers who happen to be employed by illegally uninsured employers are not deprived of workers' compensation benefits, and is not created as a source of contribution to insurance carriers, or self-insured, or legally insured employers. The Uninsured Employers Benefits Trust Fund has no liability for claims of occupational disease or cumulative injury unless no employer during the period of the occupational disease or cumulative injury during which liability is imposed under Section 5500.5 was insured for workers' compensation, was permissibly self-insured, or was legally uninsured. No employer has a right of contribution against the Uninsured Employers Benefits Trust Fund for the liability of an illegally uninsured employer under an award of benefits for occupational disease or cumulative injury, nor may an employee in a claim of occupational disease or cumulative injury elect to proceed against an illegally uninsured employer.

(c) The Uninsured Employers Benefits Trust Fund has no liability to pay for medical, surgical, chiropractic, hospital, or other treatment, the liability for which treatment is imposed upon the employer pursuant to Section 4600, and which treatment has been provided or paid for by the State Department of Health Services pursuant to the California Medical Assistance Program.

(d) The Uninsured Employers Benefits Trust Fund shall have no liability to pay compensation, nor shall it be joined in any appeals board proceeding, unless the employer alleged to be illegally uninsured shall first either have made a general appearance or have been served with the application specified in Section 3715 and with a special notice of lawsuit issued by the appeals board. The special notice of lawsuit shall be in a form to be prescribed by the appeals board, and it shall contain at least the information and warnings required by the Code of Civil Procedure to be contained in the summons issued in a civil action. The special notice of lawsuit shall also contain a notice that if the appeals board makes an award against the defendant that his or her house or other dwelling and other property may be taken to satisfy the award in a nonjudicial sale, with no exemptions from execution. The special notice of lawsuit shall, in addition, contain a notice that a lien may be imposed upon the defendant's property without further hearing and before the issuance of an award. The applicant shall identify a legal person or entity as the employer named in the special notice of lawsuit. The reasonable expense of serving the application and special notice of lawsuit, when incurred by the employee, shall be awarded as a cost. Proof of service of the special notice of lawsuit and application shall be filed with the appeals board.

(1) The application and special notice of lawsuit may be served, within or without this state, in the manner provided for service of summons in the Code of Civil Procedure. Thereafter, an employer, alleged to be illegally uninsured, shall notify the appeals board of the address at which it may be served with official notices and papers, and shall notify the appeals board of any changes in the address. No findings, order, decision, award, or other notice or paper need be served in this manner on an employer, alleged to be illegally uninsured, who has been served as provided in this section, and who has not filed an answer, otherwise made a general appearance, or furnished the appeals board with its address. The findings, orders, decisions, awards, or other notice or paper may be mailed to the employer as the board, by regulation, may provide.

(2) Notwithstanding paragraph (1), if the employer alleged to be illegally uninsured has not filed an answer, otherwise made a general appearance, or furnished the appeals board with its address, the appeals board shall serve any findings, order, decision, award, or other notice or paper on the employer by mail at the address the appeals board has for the employer. The failure of delivery at that address or the lack of personal service on an employer who has been served as provided in this section, of these findings, order, decision, award, or other notice or paper, shall not constitute grounds for reopening or invalidating any appeals board action pursuant to Section 5506, or for contesting the validity of any judgment obtained under Section 3716 or 5806, a lien under Section 3720, or a settlement under subdivision (e) of Section 3715.

(3) The board, by regulation, may provide for service procedures in cases where a request for new and further benefits is made after the issuance of any findings and award and a substantial period of time has passed since the first service or attempted service.

(4) The director, on behalf of the Uninsured Employers Benefits Trust Fund, shall furnish information as to the identities, legal capacities, and addresses of uninsured employers known to the director upon request of the board or upon a showing of good cause by the employee or the employee's representative. Good cause shall include a declaration by the employee's representative, filed under penalty of perjury, that the information is necessary to represent the employee in proceedings under this division. **Leg.H.** 1993 ch. 1241, 2003 ch. 228 (AB 1756), effective August 11, 2003.

Ref.: 8 C.C.R. §§15740, 15741; Herlick Handbook §§ 1.08, 2.5, 3.19, 14.11.

§3716.1. Representation and investigation.

(a) In any hearing, investigation, or proceeding, the Attorney General, or attorneys of the Department of Industrial Relations, shall represent the director and the state. Expenses incident to representation of the director and the state, before the appeals board and in civil court, by the Attorney General or Department of Industrial Relations attorneys, shall be reimbursed from the Workers' Compensation Administration Revolving Fund. Expenses incident to representation by the Attorney General or attorneys of the Department of Industrial Relations incurred in attempts to recover moneys pursuant to Section 3717 of the Labor Code shall not exceed the total amounts recovered by the director on behalf of the Uninsured Employers Benefits Trust Fund pursuant to this chapter.

(b) The director shall assign investigative and claims' adjustment services respecting matters concerning uninsured employers injury cases. The director or his or her representative may make these service assignments within the department, or he or she may contract for these services with the State Compensation Insurance Fund, except insofar as these matters might conflict with the interests of the State Compensation Insurance Fund. The administrative costs associated with these services shall be reimbursed from the Workers' Compensation Administration Revolving Fund and the nonadministrative costs from the Uninsured Employers Benefits Trust Fund, except when a budget impasse requires advances as described in subdivision (c) of Section 62.5. To the extent permitted by state law, the director may contract for audits or reports of services under this section. **Leg.H.** 2003 ch. 228 (AB 1756), effective August 11, 2003, 2012 ch. 728 (SB 71) §120.

Ref.: 8 C.C.R. §§15740, 15741.

§3716.2. Extent of payments from Uninsured Employers Fund.

Notwithstanding the precise elements of an award of compensation benefits, and notwithstanding the claim and demand for payment being made therefor to the director, the director, as administrator of the Uninsured Employers Fund, shall pay the claimant only such benefits allowed, recognizing proper liens thereon, that would have accrued against an employer properly insured for workers' compensation liability. The Uninsured Employers Fund shall not be liable for any penalties or for the payment of interest on any awards. However, in civil suits by the director to enforce payment of an award, including procedures pursuant to Section 3717, the total amount of the award, including interest, other penalties, and attorney's fees granted by the award, shall be sought. Recovery by the director, in a civil suit or by other means, of awarded benefits in excess of amounts paid to the claimant by the Uninsured Employers Fund shall be paid over to the injured employee or his representative, as the case may be. **Leg.H.** 1999 ch. 83.

Ref.: 8 C.C.R. §§15740, 15741; Hanna §§ 1.21, 2.13, 10.24[7], 27.10[6]; Herlick Handbook § 1.08.

§3716.3. Enforcement of judgment by nonjudicial foreclosure.

(a) Notwithstanding any other provision of law to the contrary, when the director obtains a judgment against an uninsured employer, the director may, in addition to any other remedies provided by law, enforce the judgment by nonjudicial foreclosure. This enforcement shall not be subject to Chapter 4 (commencing with Section 703.010) of Division 2 of Title 9 of Part 2 of the Code of Civil Procedure relating to claiming exemptions after levy.

(b) To enforce the judgment by nonjudicial foreclosure, the director shall record with the county recorder of any county in which real property of the parties against whom the judgment is taken is located, a certified copy of the judgment together with the director's notice of intent to foreclose. The notice of intent to foreclose shall set forth all of the following:

(1) The name, address, and telephone number of the trustee authorized by the director to enforce the lien by sale.

(2) The legal description of the real property to be foreclosed upon.

(3) Proof of service by registered or certified mail on the following:

(A) The parties against whom the foreclosure is sought at their last known address as shown on the official records of the appeals board and as shown on the latest recorded deed, deed of trust, or mortgage affecting the real property which is the subject of the foreclosure.

(B) All of the owners of the real property which is subject to the foreclosure at their last address as shown on the latest equalized assessment roll.

(c) Upon the expiration of 20 days following recording of the judgment and notice of intent to foreclose, the trustee may proceed to sell the real property. Any sale by the trustee shall be conducted in accordance with Article 1 (commencing with Section 2920) of Chapter 2 of Title 14 of Part 4 of Division 3 of the Civil Code applicable to the exercise of powers of sale of property under powers created by mortgages and deeds of trust.

(d) The director may authorize any person, including an attorney, corporation, or other business entity, to act as trustee pursuant to subdivision (b).

(e) Except as provided in subdivision (f), this section shall apply to all judgments which the director has obtained or may obtain pursuant to Section 3717, 3726, or 5806.

(f) This section shall not apply to the principal residence of an employer if the appeals board finds that the employer, on the date of injury, employed 10 or fewer employees. An employer seeking this exemption shall provide proof of payment of tax withholding required pursuant to Division 6 (commencing with Section 13000) of the Unemployment Insurance Code, to assist in determining the number of employees on the date of injury.

1990 Note: Section 3716.3 shall be retroactive in effect and shall apply to all obligations of illegally uninsured employers to the director, regardless of the date of injury to the employee. Stats. 1990 ch. 770 §4.

§3716.4. Copy of judgment against carrier may be transmitted to Public Utilities Commission.

Whenever a final judgment has been entered against a motor carrier of property subject to the jurisdiction and control of the Department of Motor Vehicles or a passenger stage corporation, charter-party carrier of passengers, or a household goods carrier subject to the jurisdiction and control of the Public Utilities Commission as a result of an award having been made pursuant to Section 3716.2, the director may transmit to the Public Utilities Commission or the Department of Motor Vehicles, whichever has jurisdiction over the affected carrier, a copy of the judgment along with the name and address of the regulated entity and any other persons, corporations, or entities named in the judgment which are jointly and severally liable for the debt to the State Treasury with a complaint requesting that the Public Utilities Commission or the Department of Motor Vehicles immediately revoke the carrier's Public Utilities Commission certificate of public convenience and necessity or Department of Motor Vehicles motor carrier permit. **Leg.H.** 1991 ch. 1071, 1996 ch. 1042, effective September 29, 1996.

§3716.5. Director's responsibility to designate job classifications of payees.

In the payment of workers' compensation benefits from the Uninsured Employers Fund, the director shall do the following:

(a) Designate the job classifications of employees who are paid compensation from the fund.

(b) Compile data on the job classifications of employees paid compensation from the fund and report this data to the Legislature by November 1, 1990, and annually thereafter.

§3717. Employer's liability to Uninsured Employers Fund; corporation's liability; definitions.

(a) A findings and award that is the subject of a demand on the Uninsured Employers Fund or an approved compromise and release or stipulated findings and award entered into by the director pursuant to subdivision (e) of Section 3715, or a decision and order of the rehabilitation unit of the Division of Workers' Compensation, that has become final, shall constitute a liquidated claim for damages against an employer in the amount so ascertained and fixed by the appeals board, and the appeals board shall certify the same to the director who may institute a civil action against the employer in the name of the director, as administrator of the Uninsured Employers Fund, for the collection of the award, or may obtain a judgment against the employer pursuant to Section 5806. In the event that the appeals board finds that a corporation is the employer of an injured employee, and that the corporation has not secured the payment of compensation as required by this chapter, the following persons shall be jointly and severally liable with the corporation to the director in the action:

(1) All persons who are a parent, as defined in Section 175 of the Corporations Code, of the corporation.

(2) All persons who are substantial shareholders, as defined in subdivision (b), of the corporation or its parent. In the action it shall be sufficient for plaintiff to set forth a copy of the findings and award of the appeals board relative to the claims as certified by the appeals board to the director and to state that there is due to plaintiff on account of the finding and award of the appeals board a specified sum which plaintiff claims with interest. The director shall be further entitled to costs and reasonable attorney fees, and to his or her investigation and litigation expenses for the appeals board proceedings, and a reasonable attorney fee for litigating the appeals board proceedings. A certified copy of the findings and award in the claim shall be attached to the complaint. The contents of the findings and award shall be deemed proved. The answer or demurrer to the complaint shall be filed within 10 days, the reply or demurrer to the answer within 20 days, and the demurrer to the reply within 30 days after the return day of the summons or service by publication. All motions and demurrers shall be submitted to the court within 10 days after they are filed. At the time the civil action filed pursuant to this section is at issue, it shall be placed at the head of the trial docket and shall be first in order for trial.

Nothing in this chapter shall be construed to preclude informal adjustment by the director of a claim for compensation benefits before the issuance of findings and award wherever it appears to the director that the employer is uninsured and that informal adjustment will facilitate the expeditious delivery of compensation benefits to the injured employee.

(b) As used in this section, "substantial shareholder" means a shareholder who owns at least 15 percent of the total value of all classes of stock, or, if no stock has been issued, who owns at least 15 percent of the beneficial interests in the corporation.

(c) For purposes of this section, in determining the ownership of stock or beneficial interest in the corporation, in the determination of whether a person is a substantial shareholder of the corporation, the rules of attribution of ownership of Section 17384 of the Revenue and Taxation Code shall be applied.

(d) For purposes of this section, "corporation" shall not include:

(1) Any corporation which is the issuer of any security which is exempted by Section 25101 of the Corporations Code from Section 25130 of the Corporations Code.

(2) Any corporation which is the issuer of any security exempted by subdivision (c), (d), or (i) of Section 25100 of the Corporations Code from Sections 25110, 25120, and 25130 of the Corporations Code.

(3) Any corporation which is the issuer of any security which has qualified either by coordination, as provided by Section 25111 of the Corporations Code, or by notification, as provided by Section 25112 of the Corporations Code. **Leg.H.** 1994 ch. 146.

Ref.: Hanna § 10.24[4], [7]; Herlick Handbook § 3.19.

§3717.1. Substantial shareholders and parents joined in action against uninsured employer.

In any claim in which an alleged uninsured employer is a corporation, the director may cause substantial shareholders and parents, as defined by Section 3717, to be joined as parties. Substantial shareholders may be served as provided in this division for service on adverse parties, or if they cannot be found with reasonable diligence, by serving the corporation. The corporation, upon this service, shall notify the shareholder of the service, and mail the served document to him or her at the shareholder's last address known to the corporation.

Ref.: Hanna § 10.24[7].

§3717.2. Board of appeals determination as to shareholder or parent status.

Upon request of the director, the appeals board shall make findings of whether persons are substantial shareholders or parents, as defined in Section 3717. The director may in his or her discretion proceed against substantial shareholders and parents pursuant to Section 3717 without those findings of the appeals board.

Ref.: 8 C.C.R. §§15710, 15720, 15721, 15722, 15723, 15730, 15731.

§3718. Joinder of actions against employers; recovered amount paid into State Treasury.

The cause of action provided in Section 3717 and any cause of action arising out of Section 3722 may be joined in one action against an employer. The amount recovered in such action from such employer shall be paid into the State Treasury to the credit of the Uninsured Employers Fund.

Ref.: 8 C.C.R. §§15550, 15551, 15552, 15553, 15554, 15555, 15556, 15557, 15558, 15559, 15560, 15561, 15562, 15563, 15564, 15565, 15566, 15567, 15568, 15569, 15570, 15571, 15571.5, 15572, 15573, 15574, 15575, 15576, 15578, 15579, 15580, 15581, 15582, 15583, 15584, 15585, 15586, 15587, 15588, 15589, 15590, 15591, 15592, 15593, 15594, 15595, 15596.

§3719. Suit against uninsured employers.

Any suit, action, proceeding, or award brought or made against any employer under Section 3717 may be compromised by the director, or such suit, action, or proceeding may be prosecuted to final judgment as in the discretion of the director may best subserve the interests of the Uninsured Employers Fund.

§3720. Certificate that employer is uninsured; effect; service.

(a) When the appeals board or the director determines under Section 3715 or 3716 that an employer has not secured the payment of compensation as required by this division or when the director has determined that the employer is prima facie illegally uninsured, the director may file for record in the office of the county recorder in the counties where the employer's property is possibly located, a certificate of lien showing the date that the employer was determined to be illegally uninsured or the date that the director has determined that the employer was prima facie illegally uninsured. The certificate shall show the name and address of the employer against whom it was filed, and the fact that the employer has not secured the payment of compensation as required by this division. Upon the recordation, the certificate shall constitute a valid lien in favor of the director, and shall have the same force, effect and priority as a judgment lien and shall continue for 10 years from the time of the recording of the certificate unless sooner released or otherwise discharged. A copy of the certificate shall be served upon the employer by mail, by the director. A facsimile signature of the director accompanied by the seal imprint of the department shall be sufficient for recording purposes of liens and releases or cancellations thereof considered herein. Certificates of liens may be filed in any or all counties of the state, depending upon the information the director obtains concerning the employer's assets.

(b) For purposes of this section, in the event the employer is a corporation, those persons whom either the appeals board finds are the parent or the substantial shareholders of the corporation or its parent, or whom the director finds pursuant to Section 3720.1 to be prima facie the parent or the substantial shareholders of the corporation or its parent, as defined in Section 3717, shall be deemed to be the employer, and the director may file the certificates against those persons.

(c) A person who claims to be aggrieved by the filing of a lien against the property of an uninsured employer because he or she has the same or a similar name, may apply to the director to have filed an amended certificate of lien which shows that the aggrieved applicant is not the uninsured employer which is the subject of the lien. If the director finds that the aggrieved applicant is not the same as the uninsured employer, the director shall file an amended certificate of lien with the county recorder of the county in which the aggrieved applicant has property, which shall show, by reasonably identifying information furnished by the aggrieved applicant, that the uninsured employer and the aggrieved applicant are not the same. If the director does not file the amended certificate of lien within 60 days of application therefor, the applicant may appeal the director's failure to so find by filing a petition with the appeals board, which shall make a finding as to whether the applicant and the uninsured employer are the same.

(d) Liens filed under this section have continued existence independent of, and may be foreclosed upon independently of, any right of action arising out of Section 3717 or 5806. **Leg.H.** 1992 ch. 1226.

Ref.: 8 C.C.R. §§15710, 15720, 15721, 15722, 15723, 15730, 15731; Hanna § 27.10[6][c][i]; Herlick Handbook § 3.19.

§3720.1. Determination of person as prima facie parent or shareholder; appeal of determination.

(a) In any claim in which the alleged uninsured employer is a corporation, for purposes of filing certificates of lien pursuant to Section 3720, the director may determine, according to the evidence available to him or her, whether a person is prima facie a parent or substantial shareholder, as defined in Section 3717. A finding that a person was prima facie a parent or substantial shareholder shall be made when the director determines that there is sufficient evidence to constitute a prima facie case that the person was a parent or substantial shareholder.

(b) Any person aggrieved by a finding of the director that he or she was prima facie a parent or substantial shareholder may request a hearing on the finding by filing a written request for hearing with the director. The director shall hold a hearing on the matter within 20 days of the receipt of the request for hearing, and shall mail a notice of time and place of hearing to the person requesting hearing at least 10 days prior to the hearing. The hearing officer shall hear and receive evidence, and within 10 days of the

Labor

hearing, file his or her findings on whether there is sufficient evidence to constitute a prima facie case that the person was a substantial shareholder or parent. The hearing officer shall serve with his or her findings a summary of evidence received and relied upon, and the reasons for the findings. A party may at his or her own expense require that the hearing proceedings be recorded and transcribed.

(c) A party aggrieved by the findings of the hearing officer may within 20 days apply for a writ of mandate to the superior court. Venue shall lie in the county in which is located the office of the director which issued the findings after the hearing.

Ref.: 8 C.C.R. §§15710, 15720, 15721, 15722, 15723, 15730, 15731; Hanna § 10.24[8][a], [b].

§3721. Certificate of cancellation of lien.

The director shall provide the employer with a certificate of cancellation of lien after the employer has paid to the claimant or to the Uninsured Employers Fund the amount of the compensation or benefits which has been ordered paid to the claimant, or when the application has finally been denied after the claimant has exhausted the remedies provided by law in those cases, or when the employer has filed a bond in the amount and with such surety as the appeals board approves conditioned on the payment of all sums ordered paid to the claimant, or when, after a finding that the employer was prima facie illegally uninsured, it is finally determined that the finding was in error. The recorder shall make no charge for filing the certificates of lien, for filing amended certificates of lien, or for cancellation when liens are filed in error. Cancellation of lien certificates provided to the employer may be filed for recordation by the employer at his or her expense.

Ref.: 8 C.C.R. §§15710, 15720, 15721, 15722, 15723, 15730, 15731; Hanna § 10.24[8][d].

§3722. Penalty assessments.

(a) At the time the stop order is issued and served pursuant to Section 3710.1, the director shall also issue and serve a penalty assessment order requiring the uninsured employer to pay to the director, for deposit in the State Treasury to the credit of the Uninsured Employers Fund, the sum of one thousand five hundred dollars ($1,500) per employee employed at the time the order is issued and served, as an additional penalty for being uninsured at that time or issue and serve a penalty assessment order pursuant to subdivision (b).

(b) At any time that the director determines that an employer has been uninsured for a period in excess of one week during the calendar year preceding the determination, the director shall issue and serve a penalty assessment order requiring the uninsured employer to pay to the director, for deposit in the State Treasury to the credit of the Uninsured Employers Fund, the greater of (1) twice the amount the employer would have paid in workers' compensation premiums during the period the employer was uninsured, determined according to subdivision (c), or (2) the sum of one thousand five hundred dollars ($1,500) per employee employed during the period the employer was uninsured. A penalty assessment issued and served by the director pursuant to this subdivision shall be in lieu of, and not in addition to, any other penalty issued and served by the director pursuant to subdivision (a).

(c) If the employer is currently insured, or becomes insured during the period during which the penalty under subdivision (b) is being determined, the amount an employer would have paid in workers' compensation premiums shall be calculated by prorating the current premium for the number of weeks the employer was uninsured within the three-year period immediately prior to the date the penalty assessment is issued. If the employer is uninsured at the time the penalty under subdivision (b) is being determined, the amount an employer would have paid in workers' compensation premiums shall be the product of the employer's payroll for all periods of time the employer was uninsured within the three-year period immediately prior to the date the penalty assessment is issued multiplied by a rate determined in accordance with regulations that may be adopted by the director or, if none has been adopted, the manual rate or rates of the State Compensation Insurance Fund for the employer's governing classification pursuant to the standard classification system approved by the Insurance Commissioner. The classification shall be determined by the director or the director's designee at the time the penalty assessment is issued on the basis of any information available to the director regarding the employer's operations. Unless the amount of the employer's payroll for all periods during which the employer was uninsured within the three-year period is otherwise proven by a preponderance of evidence, the employer's payroll for each week the employer was uninsured shall be presumed to be the state average weekly wage multiplied by the number of persons employed by the employer at the time the penalty assessment is issued. For purposes of this subdivision, "state average weekly wage" means the average weekly wage paid by employers to employees covered by unemployment insurance as reported by the United States Department of Labor for California for the 12-month period ending March 31 of the calendar year preceding the year in which the penalty assessment order is issued.

(d) If upon the filing of a claim for compensation under this division the Workers' Compensation Appeals Board finds that any employer has not secured the payment of compensation as required by this division and finds the claim either noncompensable or compensable, the appeals board shall mail a copy of their findings to the uninsured employer and the director, together with a direction to the uninsured employer to file a verified statement pursuant to subdivision (e).

After the time for any appeal has expired and the adjudication of the claim has become final, the uninsured employer shall be assessed and pay as a penalty either of the following:

(1) In noncompensable cases, two thousand dollars ($2,000) per each employee employed at the time of the claimed injury.

(2) In compensable cases, ten thousand dollars ($10,000) per each employee employed on the date of the injury.

(e) In order to establish the number of employees the uninsured employer had on the date of the claimed injury in noncompensable cases and on the date of injury in compensable cases, the employer shall submit to the director within 10 days after service of findings, awards, and orders of the Workers' Compensation Appeals Board a verified statement of the number of employees in his or her employ on the date of injury. If the employer fails to submit to the director this verified statement or if the director disputes the accuracy of the number of employees reported by the employer, the director shall use any information regarding the number of employees as the director may have or otherwise obtains.

(f) Except for penalties assessed under subdivision (b), the maximum amount of penalties which may be assessed pursuant to this section is one hundred thousand dollars ($100,000). Payment shall be transmitted to the director for deposit in the State Treasury to the credit of the Uninsured Employers Fund.

(g)(1) The Workers' Compensation Appeals Board may provide for a summary hearing on the sole issue of compensation coverage to effect the provisions of this section.

(2) In the event a claim is settled by the director pursuant to subdivision (e) of Section 3715 by means of a compromise and release or stipulations with request for award, the appeals board may also provide for a summary hearing on the issue of compensability. **Leg.H.** 1991 ch. 600, 2002 ch. 6 (AB 749), 2009 ch. 640 (SB 313) §1, effective January 1, 2011.

Ref.: 8 C.C.R. §§15550, 15551, 15552, 15553, 15554, 15555, 15556, 15557, 15558, 15559, 15560, 15561, 15562, 15563, 15564, 15565, 15566, 15567, 15568, 15569, 15570, 15571, 15571.5, 15572, 15573, 15574, 15575, 15576, 15578, 15579, 15580, 15581, 15582, 15583, 15584, 15585, 15586, 15587, 15588, 15589, 15590, 15591, 15592, 15593, 15594, 15595, 15596; Hanna Ch. 10, § 10.22[2]; Herlick Handbook §§ 1.08, 3.19, 9.2.

§3725. Penalty assessment order; contest procedure.

If an employer desires to contest a penalty assessment order, the employer shall file with the director a written request for a hearing within 15 days after service of the order. Upon receipt of the request, the director shall set the matter for a hearing within 30 days thereafter and shall notify the employer of the time and place of the hearing by mail at least 10 days prior to the date of the hearing. The decision of the director shall consist of a notice of findings and findings which shall be served on all parties to the hearing by registered or certified mail within 15 days after the hearing. Any amount found due by the director as a result of a hearing shall become due and payable 45 days after notice of the findings and written findings have been mailed by registered or certified mail to the party assessed. A writ of mandate may be taken from these findings to the appropriate superior court upon the execution by the party assessed of a bond to the state in double the amount found due and ordered paid by the director, as long as the party agrees to pay any judgment and costs rendered against the party for the assessment. The writ shall be taken within 45 days after mailing the notice of findings and findings.

Ref.: 8 C.C.R. §§15550, 15551, 15552, 15553, 15554, 15555, 15556, 15557, 15558, 15559, 15560, 15561, 15562, 15563, 15564, 15565, 15566, 15567, 15568, 15569, 15570, 15571, 15571.5, 15572, 15573, 15574, 15575, 15576, 15578, 15579, 15580, 15581, 15582, 15583, 15584, 15585, 15586, 15587, 15588, 15589, 15590, 15591, 15592, 15593, 15594, 15595, 15596; Hanna §§ 10.22[4], 22.08[2]; Herlick Handbook §§ 3.19, 14.2.

§3726. Penalty assessment order; uncontested procedure.

(a) When no petition objecting to a penalty assessment order is filed, a certified copy of the order may be filed by the director in the office of the clerk of the superior court in any country in which the employer has property or in which the employer has or had a place of business. The clerk, immediately upon such filing, shall enter judgment for the state against the employer in the amount shown on the penalty assessment order.

(b) When findings are made affirming or modifying a penalty assessment order after hearing, a certified copy of such order and a certified copy of such findings may be filed by the director in the office of the clerk of the superior court in any county in which the employer has property or in which the employer has or had a place of business. The clerk, immediately upon such filing, shall enter judgment for the state against the employer in the amount shown on the penalty assessment order or in the amount shown in the findings if the order has been modified.

(c) A judgment entered pursuant to the provisions of this section may be filed by the clerk in a looseleaf book entitled "Special Judgments for State Uninsured Employers Fund." Such judgment shall bear the same rate of interest and shall have the same effect as other judgments and be given the same preference allowed by law on other judgments rendered for claims for taxes. The clerk shall make no charge for the service provided by this section to be performed by him.

Ref.: 8 C.C.R. §§15550, 15551, 15552, 15553, 15554, 15555, 15556, 15557, 15558, 15559, 15560, 15561, 15562, 15563, 15564, 15565, 15566, 15567, 15568, 15569, 15570, 15571, 15571.5, 15572, 15573, 15574, 15575, 15576, 15578, 15579, 15580, 15581, 15582, 15583, 15584, 15585, 15586, 15587, 15588, 15589, 15590, 15591, 15592, 15593, 15594, 15595, 15596; Hanna § 10.22[5].

§3727. Certificate of penalty assessment; filing; recording certificate of cancellation.

If the director determines pursuant to Section 3722 that an employer has failed to secure the payment of compensation as required by this division, the director may file with the county recorder of any counties in which such employer's property may be located his certificate of the amount of penalty due from such employer and such amount shall be a lien in favor of the director from the date of such filing against the real property and personal property of the employer within the county in which such certificate is filed. The recorder shall accept and file such certificate and record the same as a mortgage on real estate and shall file the same as a security interest and he shall index the same as mortgage on real estate and as a security interest. Certificates of liens may be filed in any and all counties of the state, depending upon the information the director obtains concerning the employer's assets. The recorder shall make no charge for the services provided by this section to be performed by him. Upon payment of the penalty assessment, the director shall issue a certificate of cancellation of penalty assessment, which may be recorded by the employer at his expense.

Ref.: 8 C.C.R. §§15550, 15551, 15552, 15553, 15554, 15555, 15556, 15557, 15558, 15559, 15560, 15561, 15562, 15563, 15564, 15565, 15566, 15567, 15568, 15569, 15570, 15571, 15571.5, 15572, 15573, 15574, 15575, 15576, 15578, 15579, 15580, 15581,

15582, 15583, 15584, 15585, 15586, 15587, 15588, 15589, 15590, 15591, 15592, 15593, 15594, 15595, 15596; Hanna § 10.22[7].

§3727.1. Withdrawal of stop order or penalty assessment order.

The director may withdraw a stop order or a penalty assessment order where investigation reveals the employer had secured the payment of compensation as required by Section 3700 on the date and at the time of service of such order. The director also may withdraw a penalty assessment order where investigation discloses that the employer was insured on the date and at the time of an injury or claimed injury, or where an insured employer responded in writing to a request to furnish the status of his workers' compensation coverage within the time prescribed.

Ref.: Hanna §§ 10.21[4], 10.22[6].

§3728. Cash revolving fund.

(a) The director may draw from the State Treasury out of the Uninsured Employers Benefits Trust Fund for the purposes of Sections 3716 and 3716.1, without at the time presenting vouchers and itemized statements, a sum not to exceed in the aggregate the level provided for pursuant to Section 16400 of the Government Code, to be used as a cash revolving fund. The revolving fund shall be deposited in any banks and under any conditions as the Department of General Services determines. The Controller shall draw his or her warrants in favor of the Director of Industrial Relations for the amounts so withdrawn and the Treasurer shall pay these warrants.

(b) Expenditures made from the revolving fund in payment of claims for compensation due from the Uninsured Employers Benefits Trust Fund and from the Workers' Compensation Administration Revolving Fund for administrative and adjusting services rendered are exempted from the operation of Section 925.6 of the Government Code. Reimbursement of the revolving fund from the Uninsured Employers Benefits Trust Fund or the Workers' Compensation Administration Revolving Fund for expenditures shall be made upon presentation to the Controller of an abstract or statement of the expenditures. The abstract or statement shall be in any form as the Controller requires. **Leg.H.** 1992 ch. 100, effective June 26, 1992, 2003 ch. 228 (AB 1756), effective August 11, 2003.

§3730. Effect of weekend or holiday on last day for filing.

When the last day for filing any instrument or other document pursuant to this chapter falls upon a Saturday, Sunday, or other holiday, such act may be performed upon the next business day with the same effect as if it had been performed upon the day appointed.

§3731. Personal service of stop orders or penalty assessment orders.

Any stop order or penalty assessment order may be personally served upon the employer either by (1) manual delivery of the order to the employer personally or by (2) leaving signed copies of the order during usual office hours with the person who is apparently in charge of the office and by thereafter mailing copies of the order by first class mail, postage prepaid to the employer at the place where signed copies of the order were left.

Ref.: Hanna § 10.22[3].

§3732. Payment from Uninsured Employers Fund: third party liability.

(a) If compensation is paid or becomes payable from the Uninsured Employers Fund, whether as a result of a findings and award, award based upon stipulations, compromise and release executed on behalf of the director, or payments voluntarily furnished by the director pursuant to Section 4903.3, the director may recover damages from any person or entity, other than the employer, whose tortious act or omission proximately caused the injury or death of the employee. The damages shall include any compensation, including additional compensation by way of interest or penalty, paid or payable by the director, plus the expense incurred by the director in investigating and litigating the workers' compensation claim and a reasonable attorney fee for litigating the workers' compensation claim. The director may compromise, or settle and release any claim, and may waive any claim, including the lien allowed by this section, in whole or in part, for the convenience of the director.

(b) Except as otherwise provided in this section, Chapter 5 (commencing with Section 3850) of Part 1 of Division 4 shall be applicable to these actions, the director being treated as an employer within the meaning of Chapter 5 to the extent not inconsistent with this section.

(c) Actions brought under this section shall be commenced within one year after the later of either the time the director pays or the time the director becomes obligated to pay any compensation from the Uninsured Employers Fund.

(d) In the trial of these actions, any negligence attributable to the employer shall not be imputed to the director or to the Uninsured Employers Fund, and the damages recoverable by the director shall not be reduced by any percentage of fault or negligence attributable to the employer or to the employee.

(e) In determining the credit to the Uninsured Employers Fund provided by Section 3861, the appeals board shall not take into consideration any negligence of the employer, but shall allow a credit for the entire amount of the employee's recovery either by settlement or after judgment, as has not theretofore been applied to the payment of expenses or attorney's fees.

(f) When an action or claim is brought by an employee, his or her guardian, conservator, personal representative, estate, survivors, or heirs against a third party who may be liable for causing the injury or death of the employee, any settlement or judgment obtained is subject to the director's claim for damages recoverable by the director pursuant to subdivision (a), and the director shall have a lien against any settlement in the amount of the damages.

(g) No judgment or settlement in any action or claim by an employee, his or her guardian, conservator, personal representative, survivors, or heirs to recover damages for injuries, where the director has an interest, shall be satisfied without first giving the director notice and a reasonable opportunity to perfect and satisfy his or her lien. The director shall be mailed a copy of the complaint in the third-party action as soon as reasonable after it is filed with the court.

(h) When the director has perfected a lien upon a judgment or settlement in favor of an employee, his or her guardian, conservator, personal representative, survivors or heirs against any third party, the director shall be entitled to a writ of execution as a lien claimant to enforce payment of the lien against the third party with interest and other accruing costs as in the case of other executions. In the event the amount of the judgment or settlement so recovered has been paid to the employee, his or her guardian, conservator, personal representative, survivors, or heirs, the director shall be entitled to a writ of execution against the employee, his or her guardian, conservator, personal representative, survivors, or heirs to the extent of the director's lien, with interest and other accruing costs as in the cost of other executions.

(i) Except as otherwise provided in this section, notwithstanding any other provision of law, the entire amount of any settlement of the action or claim of the employee, his or her guardian, conservator, personal representative, survivors, or heirs, with or without suit, is subject to the director's lien claim for the damages recoverable by the director pursuant to subdivision (a).

(j) Where the action or claim is brought by the employee, his or her guardian, conservator, personal representative, estate, survivors, or heirs, and the director has not joined in the action, and the employee, his or her guardian, conservator, personal representative, estate, survivors, or heirs incur a personal liability to pay attorney's fees and costs of litigation, the director's claim for damages shall be limited to the amount of the director's claim for damages less that portion of the costs of litigation expenses determined by multiplying the total cost of litigation expenses by the ratio of the full amount of the director's claim for damages to the full amount of the judgment, award, or settlement, and less 25 percent of the balance after subtracting the director's share of litigation expenses, which represents the director's reasonable share of attorney's fees incurred.

(k) In the trial of the director's action for damages, and in the allowance of his or her lien in an action by the employee, guardian, executor, personal representative, survivors, or heirs, the compensation paid from the Uninsured Employers Fund pursuant to an award as provided in Section 3716 is conclusively presumed to be reasonable in amount and to be proximately caused by the event or events which caused the employee's injury or death.

(*l*) In the action for damages the director shall be entitled to recover, if he or she prevails, the entire amount of the damages recoverable by the director pursuant to subdivision (a), regardless of whether the damages recoverable by the employee, guardian, conservator, personal representative, survivors, or heirs are of lesser amount.

Ref.: Hanna §§ 11.42[3][b], 11.44[3], 27.10[6][c][ii].

§3733. No prohibition on receipt of compensation solely because of citizenship or immigration status; legislative intent.

(a) The Legislature finds and declares that it is in the best interest of the State of California to provide a person, regardless of his or her citizenship or immigration status, with the benefits provided pursuant to this article, and therefore enacts this section pursuant to Section 1621(d) of Title 8 of the United States Code.

(b) A person shall not be prohibited from receiving compensation paid or payable from the Uninsured Employers Benefits Trust Fund solely because of his or her citizenship or immigration status.

(c) It is the intent of the Legislature to override Section 15740 of Article 1 of Subchapter 2.1.1 of Chapter 8 of Division 1 of Title 8 of the California Code of Regulations.

(d) The provisions of this section are declaratory of existing law. **Leg.H.** 2015 ch. 290 (SB 623) §1.

Ref.: Hanna § 3.31; Herlick Handbook § 2.3.

ARTICLE 2.5
Self-Insurers' Security Fund

§3740. Intent of Legislature.

It is the intent of the Legislature in enacting this article and Article 1 (commencing with Section 3700) to provide for the continuation of workers' compensation benefits delayed due to the failure of a private self-insured employer to meet its compensation obligations when the employers' security deposit is either inadequate or not immediately accessible for the payment of benefits. With respect to the continued liability of a surety for claims that arose under a bond after termination of that bond and to a surety's liability for the cost of administration of claims, it is the intent of the Legislature to clarity existing law. The Legislature finds and declares that the establishment of the Self-Insurers' Security Fund is a necessary component of a complete system of workers' compensation, required by Section 4 of Article XIV of the California Constitution, to have adequate provisions for the comfort, health and safety, and general welfare of any and all workers and their dependents to the extent of relieving the consequences of any industrial injury or death, and full provision for securing the payment of compensation.

Ref.: 8 C.C.R. §§15201, 15210, 15210.1, 15210.2, 15210.3, 15211, 15211.2, 15211.3, 15212, 15213, 15214, 15215, 15216, 15300, 15301, 15302, 15303, 15360, 15420, 15422, 15424, 15425, 15426, 15427, 15428, 15430, 15430.1, 15431, 15431.1, 15431.2, 15432, 15433, 15434, 15435, 15436, 15437, 15438, 15478; Hanna § 2.11[5]; Herlick Handbook § 3.20.

§3741. Definitions.

As used in this article:

(a) "Director" means the Director of Industrial Relations.

(b) "Private self-insurer" means a private employer which has secured the payment of compensation pursuant to subdivision (b) of Section 3700.

(c) "Insolvent self-insurer" means a private self-insurer who has failed to pay compensation and whose security deposit has been called by the director pursuant to Section 3701.5.

(d) "Fund" means the Self-Insurers' Security Fund established pursuant to Section 3742.

(e) "Trustees" means the Board of Trustees of the Self-Insurers' Security Fund.

Labor

(f) "Member" means a private self-insurer which participates in the Self-Insurers' Security Fund.

Ref.: 8 C.C.R. §§15201, 15210, 15210.1, 15210.2, 15211, 15211.2, 15211.3, 15212, 15213, 15214, 15215, 15216, 15300, 15301, 15302, 15303, 15360, 15420, 15422, 15424, 15425, 15426, 15427, 15428, 15430, 15430.1, 15431, 15431.1, 15431.2, 15432, 15433, 15434, 15435, 15436, 15437, 15438, 15478.

§3742. Establishment of fund; governing board; bylaws; obligations; requirement of fund members.

(a) The Self-Insurers' Security Fund shall be established as a Nonprofit Mutual Benefit Corporation pursuant to Part 3 (commencing with Section 7110) of Division 2 of Title 1 of the Corporations Code and this article. If any provision of the Nonprofit Mutual Benefit Corporation Law conflicts with any provision of this article, the provisions of this article shall apply. Each private self-insurer shall participate as a member in the fund, unless its liabilities have been turned over to the fund pursuant to Section 3701.5, at which time its membership in the fund is relinquished.

(b) The fund shall be governed by a board of trustees with no more than eight members, as established by the bylaws of the Self-Insurers' Security Fund. The director shall hold ex officio status, with full powers equal to those of a trustee, except that the director shall not have a vote. The director, or a delegate authorized in writing to act as the director's representative on the board of trustees, shall carry out exclusively the responsibilities set forth in Division 1 (commencing with Section 50) through Division 4 (commencing with Section 3200) and shall not have the obligations of a trustee under the Nonprofit Mutual Benefit Corporation Law. The fund shall adopt bylaws to segregate the director from all matters that may involve fund litigation against the department or fund participation in legal proceedings before the director. Although not voting, the director or a delegate authorized in writing to represent the director, shall be counted toward a quorum of trustees. The remaining trustees shall be representatives of private self-insurers. The self-insurer trustees shall be elected by the members of the fund, each member having one vote. Trustees shall be elected to four-year terms, and shall serve until their successors are elected and assume office pursuant to the bylaws of the fund.

(c) The fund shall establish bylaws as are necessary to effectuate the purposes of this article and to carry out the responsibilities of the fund, including, but not limited to, any obligations imposed by the director pursuant to Section 3701.8. The fund may carry out its responsibilities directly or by contract, and may purchase services and insurance and borrow funds as it deems necessary for the protection of the members and their employees. The fund may receive confidential information concerning the financial condition of self-insured employers whose liabilities to pay compensation may devolve upon it and shall adopt bylaws to prevent dissemination of that information.

(d) The director may also require fund members to subscribe to financial instruments or guarantees to be posted with the director in order to satisfy the security requirements set by the director pursuant to Section 3701.8.

Leg.H. 1984 ch. 252 §5, effective June 27, 1984, 1986 ch. 1128 §16, effective September 25, 1986, 2002 ch. 866 (AB 486) §8, 2012 ch. 363 (SB 863) §23.

2012 Note: For legislative findings, declarations, and applicability of Stats. 2012 ch. 363, see the 2012 Notes following Lab C §62.5.

Ref.: 8 C.C.R. §§15201, 15210, 15210.1, 15210.2, 15211, 15211.2, 15211.3, 15212, 15213, 15214, 15215, 15216, 15300, 15301, 15302, 15303, 15360, 15420, 15422, 15424, 15425, 15426, 15427, 15428, 15430, 15430.1, 15431, 15431.1, 15431.2, 15432, 15433, 15434, 15435, 15436, 15437, 15438, 15478.

§3743. Assumption of workers' compensation obligations.

(a) Upon order of the director pursuant to Section 3701.5, the fund shall assume the workers' compensation obligations of an insolvent self-insurer.

(b) Notwithstanding subdivision (a), the fund shall not be liable for the payment of any penalties assessed for any act or omission on the part of any person other than the fund, including, but not limited to, the penalties provided in Section 132a, 3706, 4553, 4554, 4556, 4557, 4558, 4601.5, 5814, or 5814.1.

(c) The fund shall be a party in interest in all proceedings involving compensation claims against an insolvent self-insurer whose compensation obligations have been paid or assumed by the fund. The fund shall have the same rights and defenses as the insolvent self-insurer, including, but not limited to, all of the following:

(1) To appear, defend, and appeal claims.

(2) To receive notice of, investigate, adjust, compromise, settle, and pay claims.

(3) To investigate, handle, and deny claims.

Ref.: 8 C.C.R. §§9767.1, 9767.4, 9767.8, 15201, 15210, 15210.2, 15210.3, 15211, 15211.2, 15211.3, 15212, 15213, 15214, 15216, 15300, 15301, 15302, 15303, 15360, 15420, 15422, 15424, 15425, 15426, 15427, 15428, 15430, 15430.1, 15431, 15431.1, 15431.2, 15432, 15433, 15434, 15435, 15436, 15437, 15438, 15478; Hanna §§ 2.11[5], 11.41.

§3744. Rights and obligations of fund.

(a)(1) The fund shall have the right and obligation to obtain reimbursement from an insolvent self-insurer up to the amount of the self-insurer's workers' compensation obligations paid and assumed by the fund, including reasonable administrative and legal costs. This right includes, but is not limited to, a right to claim for wages and other necessities of life advanced to claimants as subrogee of the claimants in any action to collect against the self-insured as debtor. For purposes of this section, "insolvent self-insurer" includes the entity to which the certificate of consent to self-insure was issued, any guarantor of the entity's liabilities under the certificate, any member of a self-insurance group to which the certificate was issued, and any employer who obtained employees from a self-insured employer under subdivision (d) of Section 3602.

(2) The Legislature finds and declares that the amendments made to this subdivision by the act adding this paragraph are declaratory of existing law.

(b) The fund shall have the right and obligation to obtain from the security deposit of an insolvent self-insurer the amount of the self-insurer's compensation obligations, including reasonable administrative and legal costs, paid or assumed by the fund. Reimbursement of administrative costs, including legal costs, shall be subject to approval by a majority vote of the fund's trustees. The fund shall be a party in interest in any action to obtain the security deposit for the payment of compensation obligations of an insolvent self-insurer.

(c) The fund shall have the right to bring an action against any person to recover compensation paid and liability assumed by the fund, including, but not limited to, any excess insurance carrier of the self-insured employer, and any person whose negligence or breach of any obligation contributed to any underestimation of the self-insured employer's total accrued liability as reported to the director.

(d) The fund may be a party in interest in any action brought by any other person seeking damages resulting from the failure of an insolvent self-insurer to pay workers' compensation required pursuant to this division.

(e) At the election of the Self-Insurers' Security Fund, venue shall be in the Superior Court for the State of California, County of Sacramento, for any action under this section. All actions in which the Self-Insurers' Security Fund and two or more members or former members of one self-insurance group are parties shall be consolidated if requested by the Self-Insurers' Security Fund. **Leg.H.** 1984 ch. 252 §5, effective June 27, 1984, 1986 ch. 1128 §17, effective September 25, 1986, 2012 ch. 363 (SB 863) §24.

2012 Note: For legislative findings, declarations, and applicability of Stats. 2012 ch. 363, see the 2012 Notes following Lab C §62.5.

Ref.: 8 C.C.R. §§15201, 15210, 15210.2, 15210.3, 15211, 15211.2, 15211.3, 15212, 15213, 15214, 15216, 15300, 15301, 15302, 15303, 15360, 15420, 15422, 15424, 15425, 15426, 15427, 15428, 15430, 15430.1, 15431, 15431.1, 15431.2, 15432, 15433, 15434, 15435, 15436, 15437, 15438, 15478.

§3745. Maintenance of assets; assessment of members.

(a) The fund shall maintain cash, readily marketable securities, or other assets, or a line of credit, approved by the director, sufficient to immediately continue the payment of the compensation obligations of an insolvent self-insurer pending assessment of the members. The director may establish the minimum amount to be maintained by, or immediately available to, the fund for this purpose.

(b) The fund may assess each of its members a pro rata share of the funding necessary to carry out the purposes of this article.

(c) The trustees shall certify to the director the collection and receipt of all moneys from assessments, noting any delinquencies. The trustees shall take any action deemed appropriate to collect any delinquent assessments. **Leg.H.** 1984 ch. 252 §5, effective June 27, 1984, 1986 ch. 1128 §18, effective September 25, 1986, 2012 ch. 363 (SB 863) §25.

2012 Note: For legislative findings, declarations, and applicability of Stats. 2012 ch. 363, see the 2012 Notes following Lab C §62.5.

Ref.: 8 C.C.R. §§15201, 15210, 15210.2, 15211, 15211.3, 15213, 15214, 15216, 15220.4, 15300, 15301, 15302, 15303, 15360, 15420, 15422, 15424, 15425, 15426, 15427, 15428, 15430, 15430.1, 15431, 15431.1, 15431.2, 15432, 15433, 15434, 15435, 15436, 15437, 15438, 15478.

§3746. Annual contract for audit; annual report.

The fund shall annually contract for an independent certified audit of the financial activities of the fund. An annual report on the financial status of the fund as of June 30 shall be submitted to the director and to each member, or at the election of the fund, posted on the fund's Internet Web site. **Leg.H.** 1984 ch. 252 §5, effective June 27, 1984, 2012 ch. 363 (SB 863) §26.

2012 Note: For legislative findings, declarations, and applicability of Stats. 2012 ch. 363, see the 2012 Notes following Lab C §62.5.

Ref.: 8 C.C.R. §§15201, 15430, 15430.1, 15431, 15431.1, 15431.2, 15432, 15433, 15434, 15435, 15436, 15437, 15438, 15478.

§3747. How to refer to article.

This article shall be known and may be referred to as the "Young-La Follette Self-Insurers' Security Act."

Ref.: 8 C.C.R. §§15201, 15430, 15430.1, 15431, 15431.1, 15431.2, 15432, 15433, 15434, 15435, 15436, 15437, 15438, 15478.

ARTICLE 3
Insurance Rights and Privileges

§3750. Limitations on division.

Nothing in this division shall affect:

(a) The organization of any mutual or other insurer.

(b) Any existing contract for insurance.

(c) The right of the employer to insure in mutual or other insurers, in whole or in part, against liability for the compensation provided by this division.

(d) The right to provide by mutual or other insurance, or by arrangement with his employees, or otherwise, for the payment to such employees, their families, dependents or representatives, of sick, accident, or death benefits, in addition to the compensation provided for by this division.

(e) The right of the employer to waive the waiting period provided for herein by insurance coverage.

§3751. Cost of compensation; no employee contribution; violation; no employee payments to medical provider while claim pending.

(a) No employer shall exact or receive from any employee any contribution, or make or take any deduction from the earnings of any employee, either directly or indirectly, to cover the whole or any part of the cost of compensation under this division. Violation of this subdivision is a misdemeanor.

(b) If an employee has filed a claim form pursuant to Section 5401, a provider of medical services shall not, with actual knowledge that a claim is pending, collect money directly from the employee for services to cure or relieve the effects of the injury for which the claim form was filed, unless the medical provider has received written notice that liability for the injury has been rejected by the employer and the medical provider has provided a copy of this notice to the employee. Any medical provider who violates this subdivision shall be liable for three times the amount unlawfully collected, plus reasonable attorney's fees and costs.

Ref.: 8 C.C.R. §§10107, 10107.1; Hanna §§ 2.10[2], 11.02[4][b][i]; Herlick Handbook §§ 3.2, 4.01[2], 4.18[1], 9.5, 10.08[4].

§3752. Effect of insurance or other benefits.

Liability for compensation shall not be reduced or affected by any insurance, contribution or other benefit whatsoever due to or received by the person entitled to such compensation, except as otherwise provided by this division.

Ref.: 8 C.C.R. §§10107, 10107.1; Hanna §§ 2.10[2], 7.04[9][b]; Herlick Handbook § 12.15.

§3753. Effect of insurance.

The person entitled to compensation may, irrespective of any insurance or other contract, except as otherwise provided in this division, recover such compensation directly from the employer. In addition thereto, he may enforce in his own name, in the manner provided by this division the liability of any insurer either by making the insurer a party to the original application or by filing a separate application for any portion of such compensation.

Ref.: 8 C.C.R. §9811; Hanna § 2.71.

§3754. Effect of amount paid on recovery.

Except as provided in paragraph (12) of subdivision (f) of Section 1202.4 of the Penal Code, payment, in whole or in part, of compensation by either the employer or the insurer shall, to the extent thereof, be a bar to recovery against each of them of the amount so paid. **Leg.H.** 1937, 1955 ch. 1672 §2, 2012 ch. 868 (SB 1177) §2.

§3755. Substitution of insurer.

If the employer is insured against liability for compensation, and if after the suffering of any injury the insurer causes to be served upon any compensation claimant a notice that it has assumed and agreed to pay any compensation to the claimant for which the employer is liable, such employer shall be relieved from liability for compensation to such claimant upon the filing of a copy of such notice with the appeals board. The insurer shall, without further notice, be substituted in place of the employer in any proceeding theretofore or thereafter instituted by such claimant to recover such compensation, and the employer shall be dismissed therefrom.

Such proceedings shall not abate on account of such substitution but shall be continued against such insurer.

Ref.: Hanna § 25.28; Herlick Handbook §§ 14.7, 14.43.

§3756. Notice of insurer liability.

If at the time of the suffering of a compensable injury, the employer is insured against liability for the full amount of compensation payable, he may cause to be served upon the compensation claimant and upon the insurer a notice that the insurer has agreed to pay any compensation for which the employer is liable. The employer may also file a copy of such notice with the appeals board.

Ref.: Hanna § 25.28.

§3757. Substitution of insurer; employer's relief from liability.

If it thereafter appears to the satisfaction of the appeals board that the insurer has assumed the liability for compensation, the employer shall thereupon be relieved from liability for compensation to the claimant. The insurer shall, after notice, be substituted in place of the employer in any proceeding instituted by the claimant to recover compensation, and the employer shall be dismissed therefrom.

Ref.: Hanna § 25.28.

§3758. Substitution of insurer; no abatement of proceeding.

A proceeding to obtain compensation shall not abate on account of substitution of the insurer in place of the employer and on account of the dismissal of the employer, but shall be continued against such insurer.

Ref.: Hanna § 25.28.

§3759. Joinder of insurer; employer's relief from liability.

The appeals board may enter its order relieving the employer from liability where it appears from the pleadings, stipulations, or proof that an insurer joined as party to the proceeding is liable for the full compensation for which the employer in such proceeding is liable.

Ref.: Herlick Handbook §§ 3.6, 14.43.

§3760. Employer notice to insurer.

Every employer who is insured against any liability imposed by this division shall file with the insurer a complete report of every injury to each employee as specified in Section 6409.1. If not so filed, the insurer may petition the appeals board for an order, or the appeals board may of its own motion issue an order, directing the employer to submit a report of the injury within five days after service of the order. Failure of the employer to comply with the appeals board's order may be punished by the appeals board as a contempt.

Ref.: Hanna § 25.20[3]; Herlick Handbook § 14.2.

§3761. Insurer must notify employer of indemnity claims; employer's notification of insurer regarding facts to disprove claim, report of reserve amount.

(a) An insurer securing an employer's liability under this division shall notify the employer, within 15 days, of each claim for indemnity filed against the employer directly with the insurer if the employer has not timely provided to the insurer a report of occupational injury or occupational illness pursuant to Section 6409.1. The insurer shall furnish an employer who has not filed this report with an opportunity to provide to the insurer, prior to the expiration of the 90-day period specified in Section 5402, all relevant information available to the employer concerning the claim.

(b) An employer shall promptly notify its insurer in writing at any time during the pendency of a claim when the employer has actual knowledge of any facts which would tend to disprove any aspect of the employee's claim. When an employer notifies its insurer in writing that, in the employer's opinion, no compensation is payable to an employee, at the employer's written request, to the appeals board, the appeals board may approve a compromise and release agreement, or stipulation, that provides compensation to the employee only where there is proof of service upon the employer by the insurer, to the employer's last known address, not less than 15 days prior to the appeals board action, of notice of the time and place of the hearing at which the compromise and release agreement or stipulation is to be approved. The insurer shall file proof of this service with the appeals board.

Failure by the insurer to provide the required notice shall not prohibit the board from approving a compromise and release agreement, or stipulation; however, the board shall order the insurer to pay reasonable expenses as provided in Section 5813.

(c) In establishing a reserve pursuant to a claim that affects premiums against an employer, an insurer shall provide the employer, upon request, a written report of the reserve amount established. The written report shall include, at a minimum, the following:

(1) Estimated medical-legal costs.

(2) Estimated vocational rehabilitation costs, if any.

(3) Itemization of all other estimated expenses to be paid from the reserve.

(d) When an employer properly provides notification to its insurer pursuant to subdivision (b), and the appeals board thereafter determines that no compensation is payable under this division, the insurer shall reimburse the employer for any premium paid solely due to the inclusion of the successfully challenged payments in the calculation of the employer's experience modification. The employee shall not be required to refund the challenged payment. **Leg.H.** 1991 ch. 116, 1993 ch. 121, effective July 16, 1993, 1994 ch. 1118.

1993 Note: Section 3761, as amended by ch. 121, applies only to injuries occurring on or after January 1, 1994. Stats. 1993 ch. 121 §77.

Ref.: 8 C.C.R. §10875; Hanna §§ 2.34, 2.70[1], 29.04[7]; Herlick Handbook §§ 3.2, 11.01, 11.05, 14.2, 14.32.

§3762. Employer's right to information and documents affecting premium—Exceptions; disclosure of employee's medical information prohibited—Exceptions.

(a) Except as provided in subdivisions (b) and (c), the insurer shall discuss all elements of the claim file that affect the employer's premium with the employer, and shall supply copies of the documents that affect the premium at the employer's expense during reasonable business hours.

(b) The right provided by this section shall not extend to any document that the insurer is prohibited from disclosing to the employer under the attorney-client privilege, any other applicable privilege, or statutory prohibition upon disclosure, or under Section 1877.4 of the Insurance Code.

(c) An insurer, third-party administrator retained by a self-insured employer pursuant to Section 3702.1 to administer the employer's workers' compensation claims, and those employees and agents specified by a self-insured employer to administer the employer's workers' compensation claims, are prohibited from disclosing or causing to be disclosed to an employer, any medical information, as defined in Section 56.05 of the Civil Code, about an employee who has filed a workers' compensation claim, except as follows:

(1) Medical information limited to the diagnosis of the mental or physical condition for which workers' compensation is claimed and the treatment provided for this condition.

(2) Medical information regarding the injury for which workers' compensation is claimed that is necessary for the employer to have in order for the employer to modify the employee's work duties. **Leg.H.** 1993 ch. 121, effective July 16, 1993, ch. 1242, 1999 ch. 766, 2000 ch. 135, 2002 ch. 6 (AB 749), 2013 ch. 444 (SB 138) §20.

1993 Note: Section 3762, as added by ch. 121, applies only to injuries occurring on or after January 1, 1994. Stats. 1993 ch. 121 §77.

Ref.: Herlick Handbook §§ 3.2, 4.13.

ARTICLE 4
Construction Permit

§3800. Construction permits; verification of workers' compensation coverage.

(a) Every county or city which requires the issuance of a permit as a condition precedent to the construction, alteration, improvement, demolition, or repair of any building or structure shall require that each applicant for the permit sign a declaration under penalty of perjury verifying workers' compensation coverage or exemption from coverage, as required by Section 19825 of the Health and Safety Code.

(b) At the time of permit issuance, contractors shall show their valid workers' compensation insurance certificate, or the city or county may verify the workers' compensation coverage by electronic means. **Leg.H.** 1994 ch. 178, 1999 ch. 982.

Ref.: Hanna § 2.10[1]; Herlick Handbook § 3.23.

ARTICLE 5
Workers' Compensation Misrepresentations

§3820. Workers' compensation fraud—Civil penalties; additional penalties for prior felony conviction; Worker's Compensation Fraud Account.

(a) In enacting this section, the Legislature declares that there exists a compelling interest in eliminating fraud in the workers' compensation system. The Legislature recognizes that the conduct prohibited by this section is, for the most part, already subject to criminal penalties pursuant to other provisions of law. However, the Legislature finds and declares that the addition of civil money penalties will provide necessary enforcement flexibility. The Legislature, in exercising its plenary authority related to workers' compensation, declares that these sections are both necessary and carefully tailored to combat the fraud and abuse that is rampant in the workers' compensation system.

Labor

(b) It is unlawful to do any of the following:

(1) Willfully misrepresent any fact in order to obtain workers' compensation insurance at less than the proper rate.

(2) Present or cause to be presented any knowingly false or fraudulent written or oral material statement in support of, or in opposition to, any claim for compensation for the purpose of obtaining or denying any compensation, as defined in Section 3207.

(3) Knowingly solicit, receive, offer, pay, or accept any rebate, refund, commission, preference, patronage, dividend, discount, or other consideration, whether in the form of money or otherwise, as compensation or inducement for soliciting or referring clients or patients to obtain services or benefits pursuant to Division 4 (commencing with Section 3200) unless the payment or receipt of consideration for services other than the referral of clients or patients is lawful pursuant to Section 650 of the Business and Professions Code or expressly permitted by the Rules of Professional Conduct of the State Bar.

(4) Knowingly operate or participate in a service that, for profit, refers or recommends clients or patients to obtain medical or medical-legal services or benefits pursuant to Division 4 (commencing with Section 3200).

(5) Knowingly assist, abet, solicit, or conspire with any person who engages in an unlawful act under this section.

(c) For the purposes of this section, "statement" includes, but is not limited to, any notice, proof of injury, bill for services, payment for services, hospital or doctor records, X-ray, test results, medical-legal expenses as defined in Section 4620, or other evidence of loss, expense, or payment.

(d) Any person who violates any provision of this section shall be subject, in addition to any other penalties that may be prescribed by law, to a civil penalty of not less than four thousand dollars ($4,000) nor more than ten thousand dollars ($10,000), plus an assessment of not more than three times the amount of the medical treatment expenses paid pursuant to Article 2 (commencing with Section 4600) and medical-legal expenses paid pursuant to Article 2.5 (commencing with Section 4620) for each claim for compensation submitted in violation of this section.

(e) Any person who violates subdivision (b) and who has a prior felony conviction of an offense set forth in Section 1871.1 or 1871.4 of the Insurance Code, or in Section 549 of the Penal Code, shall be subject, in addition to the penalties set forth in subdivision (d), to a civil penalty of four thousand dollars ($4,000) for each item or service with respect to which a violation of subdivision (b) occurred.

(f) The penalties provided for in subdivisions (d) and (e) shall be assessed and recovered in a civil action brought in the name of the people of the State of California by any district attorney.

(g) In assessing the amount of the civil penalty the court shall consider any one or more of the relevant circumstances presented by any of the parties to the case, including, but not limited to, the following: the nature and seriousness of the misconduct, the number of violations, the persistence of the misconduct, the length of time over which the misconduct occurred, the willfulness of the defendant's misconduct, and the defendant's assets, liabilities, and net worth.

(h) All penalties collected pursuant to this section shall be paid to the Workers' Compensation Fraud Account in the Insurance Fund pursuant to Section 1872.83 of the Insurance Code. All costs incurred by district attorneys in carrying out this article shall be funded from the Workers' Compensation Fraud Account. It is the intent of the Legislature that the program instituted by this article be supported entirely from funds produced by moneys deposited into the Workers' Compensation Fraud Account from the imposition of civil money penalties for workers' compensation fraud collected pursuant to this section. All moneys claimed by district attorneys as costs of carrying out this article shall be paid pursuant to a determination by the Fraud Assessment Commission established by Section 1872.83 of the Insurance Code and on appropriation by the Legislature. **Leg.H.** 1993 ch. 120, effective July 16, 1993, ch. 1242, 2002 ch. 6 (AB 749).

Ref.: Hanna § 2.03[5]; Herlick Handbook § 9.18.

§3822. Annual fraud warning notices.

The administrative director shall, on an annual basis, provide to every employer, claims adjuster, third party administrator, physician, and attorney who participates in the workers' compensation system, a notice that warns the recipient against committing workers' compensation fraud. The notice shall specify the penalties that are applied for committing workers' compensation fraud. The Fraud Assessment Commission, established by Section 1872.83 of the Insurance Code, shall provide the administrative director with all funds necessary to carry out this section. **Leg.H.** 2002 ch. 6 (AB 749).

§3823. Medical billing and provider fraud—Protocols for reporting apparent fraudulent claims; immunity from civil liability for reporting apparent fraud.

(a) The administrative director shall, in coordination with the Bureau of Fraudulent Claims of the Department of Insurance, the Medi-Cal Fraud Task Force, and the Bureau of Medi-Cal Fraud and Elder Abuse of the Department of Justice, or their successor entities, adopt protocols, to the extent that these protocols are applicable to achieve the purpose of subdivision (b), similar to those adopted by the Department of Insurance concerning medical billing and provider fraud.

(b) Any insurer, self-insured employer, third-party administrator, workers' compensation administrative law judge, audit unit, attorney, or other person that believes that a fraudulent claim has been made by any person or entity providing medical care, as described in Section 4600, shall report the apparent fraudulent claim in the manner prescribed by subdivision (a).

(c) No insurer, self-insured employer, third-party administrator, workers' compensation administrative law judge, audit unit, attorney, or other person that reports any apparent fraudulent claim under this section shall be subject to any civil liability in a cause of action of any kind when the insurer, self-insured employer, third-party administrator, workers' compensation administrative law judge, audit unit, attorney, or other person acts in good faith, without malice, and reasonably believes that the action taken was warranted by the known facts, obtained by reasonable efforts. Nothing in this section is intended to, nor does in any manner, abrogate or lessen the existing common law or statutory privileges and immunities of any insurer, self-insured employer, third-party administrator, workers' compensation administrative law judge, audit unit, attorney, or other person. **Leg.H.** 2003 ch. 639 (SB 228), 2004 ch. 34 (SB 899), effective April 19, 2004.

2004 Note: The amendment to §3823 made by this act shall apply prospectively from the date of enactment of this act, regardless of the date of injury, unless otherwise specified, but shall not constitute good cause to reopen or rescind, alter, or amend any existing order, decision, or award of the Workers' Compensation Appeals Board. Stats. 2004 ch. 34 (SB 899) §47.

Ref.: Hanna § 2.03[3]; Herlick Handbook § 9.18.

CHAPTER 5 SUBROGATION OF EMPLOYER

§3850. "Employee"; "employer."

As used in this chapter:

(a) "Employee" includes the person injured and any other person to whom a claim accrues by reason of the injury or death of the former.

(b) "Employer" includes insurer as defined in this division.

(c) "Employer" also includes the Self-Insurers' Security Fund, where the employer's compensation obligations have been assumed pursuant to Section 3743.

Ref.: 8 C.C.R. §15201; Hanna §§ 11.06[1], 11.21[1], 11.40[1], 21.03[5]; Herlick Handbook § 12.2.

§3851. Death of employee; effect.

The death of the employee or of any other person, does not abate any right of action established by this chapter.

§3852. Claim for compensation; effect on third party action.

The claim of an employee, including, but not limited to, any peace officer or firefighter, for compensation does not affect his or her claim or right of action for all damages proximately resulting from the injury or death against any person other than the employer. Any employer who pays, or becomes obligated to pay compensation, or who pays, or becomes obligated to pay salary in lieu of compensation, or who pays or becomes obligated to pay an amount to the Department of Industrial Relations pursuant to Section 4706.5, may likewise make a claim or bring an action against the third person. In the latter event the employer may recover in the same suit, in addition to the total amount of compensation, damages for which he or she was liable including all salary, wage, pension, or other emolument paid to the employee or to his or her dependents. The respective rights against the third person of the heirs of an employee claiming under Section 377.60 of the Code of Civil Procedure, and an employer claiming pursuant to this section, shall be determined by the court. **Leg.H.** 1993 ch. 589.

Ref.: Hanna §§ 11.04[1], 11.06[2], 11.20[2], 11.24[1][a], 11.25[2]; Herlick Handbook §§ 12.2, 12.5–12.7, 12.10.

§3853. Service of complaint on employer or employee; consolidation of actions.

If either the employee or the employer brings an action against such third person, he shall forthwith give to the other a copy of the complaint by personal service or certified mail. Proof of such service shall be filed in such action. If the action is brought by either the employer or employee, the other may, at any time before trial on the facts, join as party plaintiff or shall consolidate his action, if brought independently.

Ref.: Hanna §§ 11.22[3], [4], 11.42[3][b]; Herlick Handbook §§ 12.2, 12.3, 12.7.

§3854. Action by employer alone; evidence of amounts paid.

If the action is prosecuted by the employer alone, evidence of any amount which the employer has paid or become obligated to pay by reason of the injury or death of the employee is admissible, and such expenditures or liability shall be considered as proximately resulting from such injury or death in addition to any other items of damage proximately resulting therefrom.

Ref.: Hanna §§ 11.42[2], [3][e], 11.43; Herlick Handbook §§ 12.6, 12.7.

§3855. Joint action; evidence of damages.

If the employee joins in or prosecutes such action, either the evidence of the amount of disability indemnity or death benefit paid or to be paid by the employer or the evidence of loss of earning capacity by the employee shall be admissible, but not both. Proof of all other items of damage to either the employer or employee proximately resulting from such injury or death is admissible and is part of the damages.

Ref.: Hanna §§ 11.22[6], 11.24[1][a]; Herlick Handbook §§ 12.3, 12.7.

§3856. Suit against third party; costs and attorney's fees.

In the event of suit against such third party:

(a) If the action is prosecuted by the employer alone, the court shall first order paid from any judgment for damages recovered the reasonable litigation expenses incurred in preparation and prosecution of such action, together with a reasonable attorney's fee which shall be based solely upon the services rendered by the employer's attorney in effecting recovery both for the benefit of the employer and the employee. After the payment of such expenses and attorney's fees, the court shall apply out of the amount of such judgment an amount sufficient to reimburse the employer for the amount of his expenditure for compensation together with any amounts to which he may be entitled as special damages under Section 3852 and shall order any excess paid to the injured employee or other person entitled thereto.

(b) If the action is prosecuted by the employee alone, the court shall first order paid from any judgment for damages recovered the reasonable litigation expenses incurred in preparation and prosecution of such action, together with a reasonable attorney's fee which shall be based solely upon the services rendered by the employee's attorney in effecting recovery both for the benefit of the employee and the employer. After the payment of such expenses and attorney's fee the court shall, on application of the employer, allow as a first lien against the amount of such judgment for damages, the amount of the employer's expenditure for compensation together with any amounts to which he may be entitled as special damages under Section 3852.

(c) If the action is prosecuted both by the employee and the employer, in a single action or in consolidated actions, and they are represented by the same agreed attorney or by separate attorneys, the court shall first order paid from any judgment for damages recovered, the reasonable litigation expenses incurred in preparation and prosecution of such action or actions, together with reasonable attorneys' fees based solely on the services rendered for the benefit of both parties where they are represented by the same attorney, and where they are represented by separate attorneys, based solely upon the service rendered in each instance by the attorney in effecting recovery for the benefit of the party represented. After the payment of such expenses and attorneys' fees the court shall apply out of the amount of such judgment for damages an amount sufficient to reimburse the employer for the amount of his expenditures for compensation together with any other amounts to which he may be entitled as special damages under Section 3852.

(d) The amount of reasonable litigation expenses and the amount of attorneys' fees under subdivisions (a), (b), and (c) of this section shall be fixed by the court. Where the employer and employee are represented by separate attorneys they may propose to the court, for its consideration and determination, the amount and division of such expenses and fees.

Ref.: Hanna §§ 11.24[2], 11.42[2][f], [3][a], 11.46, 11.47; Herlick Handbook §§ 10.16, 12.4, 12.7.

§3857. Subsequent compensation paid by employer; application for further lien.

The court shall, upon further application at any time before the judgment is satisfied, allow as a further lien the amount of any expenditures of the employer for compensation subsequent to the original order.

Ref.: Herlick Handbook §§ 10.16, 12.3, 12.7.

§3858. Employer's release from further compensation.

After payment of litigation expenses and attorneys' fees fixed by the court pursuant to Section 3856 and payment of the employer's lien, the employer shall be relieved from the obligation to pay further compensation to or on behalf of the employee under this division up to the entire amount of the balance of the judgment, if satisfied, without any deduction. No satisfaction of such judgment in whole or in part, shall be valid without giving the employer notice and a reasonable opportunity to perfect and satisfy his lien.

Ref.: Herlick Handbook §§ 9.12, 10.16, 12.3, 12.6, 12.7.

§3859. Release or settlement; written agreement; claims against third parties.

(a) No release or settlement of any claim under this chapter as to either the employee or the employer is valid without the written consent of both. Proof of service filed with the court is sufficient in any action or proceeding where such approval is required by law.

(b) Notwithstanding anything to the contrary contained in this chapter, an employee may settle and release any claim he may have against a third party without the consent of the employer. Such settlement or release shall be subject to the employer's right to proceed to recover compensation he has paid in accordance with Section 3852.

Ref.: Hanna §§ 11.25[2], 11.42[4][a]; Herlick Handbook §§ 11.07, 12.4–12.6.

§3860. Release or settlement; notice; employer's claim for reimbursement; settlement expenses.

(a) No release or settlement under this chapter, with or without suit, is valid or binding as to any party thereto without notice to both the employer and the employee, with opportunity to the employer to recover the amount of compensation he has paid or become obligated to pay and any special damages to which he may be entitled under Section 3852, and opportunity to the employee to recover all damages he has suffered and with provision for determination of expenses and attorney's fees as herein provided.

(b) Except as provided in Section 3859, the entire amount of such settlement, with or without suit, is subject to the employer's full claim for reimbursement for compensation he has paid or become obligated to pay and any special damages to which he may be entitled under Section 3852, together with expenses and attorney fees, if any, subject to the limitations in this section set forth.

(c) Where settlement is effected, with or without suit, solely through the efforts of the employee's attorney, then prior to the reimbursement of the employer, as provided in subdivision (b) hereof, there shall be deducted from the amount of the settlement the reasonable expenses incurred in effecting such settlement, including costs of suit, if any, together with a reasonable attorney's fee to be paid to the employee's attorney, for his services in securing and effecting settlement for the benefit of both the employer and the employee.

(d) Where settlement is effected, with or without suit, solely through the efforts of the employer's attorney, then, prior to the reimbursement of the employer as provided in subdivision (b) hereof, there shall be deducted from the amount of the settlement the reasonable expenses incurred in effecting such settlement, including costs of suit, if any, together with a reasonable attorney's fee to be paid to the employer's attorney, for his services in securing and effecting settlement for the benefit of both the employer and the employee.

(e) Where both the employer and the employee are represented by the same agreed attorney or by separate attorneys in effecting a settlement, with or without suit, prior to reimbursement of the employer, as provided in subdivision (b) hereof, there shall be deducted from the amount of the settlement the reasonable expenses incurred by both the employer and the employee or on behalf of either, including costs of suit, if any, together with reasonable attorneys' fees to be paid to the respective attorneys for the employer and the employee, based upon the respective services rendered in securing and effecting settlement for the benefit of the party represented. In the event both parties are represented by the same attorney, by agreement, the attorney's fee shall be based on the services rendered for the benefit of both.

(f) The amount of expenses and attorneys' fees referred to in this section shall, on settlement of suit, or on any settlement requiring court approval, be set by the court. In all other cases these amounts shall be set by the appeals board. Where the employer and the employee are represented by separate attorneys they may propose to the court or the appeals board, for consideration and determination, the amount and division of such expenses and fees.

Ref.: Hanna §§ 11.25[2], [3], 20.02[2][m]; Herlick Handbook §§ 12.3, 12.4, 12.6, 12.7.

§3861. Employee recovery credited to employer's liability.

The appeals board is empowered to and shall allow, as a credit to the employer to be applied against his liability for compensation, such amount of any recovery by the employee for his injury, either by settlement or after judgment, as has not theretofore been applied to the payment of expenses or attorneys' fees, pursuant to the provisions of Sections 3856, 3858, and 3860 of this code, or has not been applied to reimburse the employer.

Ref.: Hanna §§ 11.42[5][a]–[d], 31.14[2]; Herlick Handbook § 6.10[5].

§3862. Enforcement of judgment lien by employer against third party.

Any employer entitled to and who has been allowed and has perfected a lien upon the judgment or award in favor of an employee against any third party for damages occasioned to the same employer by payment of compensation, expenses of medical treatment, and any other charges under this act, may enforce payment of the lien against the third party, or, in case the damages recovered by the employee have been paid to the employee, against the employee to the extent of the lien, in the manner provided for enforcement of money judgments generally.

Ref.: Hanna § 11.42[2][f].

§3864. Action against third party; prior written agreement of employer to reimburse.

If an action as provided in this chapter prosecuted by the employee, the employer, or both jointly against the third person results in judgment against such third person, or settlement by such third person, the employer shall have no liability to reimburse or hold such third person harmless on such judgment or settlement in absence of a written agreement so to do executed prior to the injury.

Ref.: Hanna §§ 2.63[3][a], 11.48; Herlick Handbook §§ 12.8, 12.12.

§3865. Duplication of payment under this chapter.

Any judgment or settlement of an action as provided for in this chapter is, upon notice to the court, subject to the same lien claims of the Employment Development Department as are provided for in Chapter 1 (commencing with Section 4900) of Part 3, and shall be allowed by the court as it determines necessary to avoid a duplication of payment as compensation to the employee for lost earnings.

CHAPTER 7
MEDICAL EXAMINATIONS

ARTICLE 1
[In General]

§4050. Medical examinations; written request of employer; order of appeals board.

Whenever the right to compensation under this division exists in favor of an employee, he shall, upon the written request of his employer, submit at reasonable intervals to examination by a practicing physician, provided and paid for by the employer, and shall likewise submit to examination at reasonable intervals by any physician selected by the administrative director or appeals board or referee thereof.

Ref.: Hanna §§ 5.02[10][b], 22.07[2][a], 31.11[3]; Herlick Handbook §§ 14.21, 14.22.

§4051. Time and place of examination.

The request or order for the medical examination shall fix a time and place therefor, due consideration being given to the convenience of the employee and his physical condition and ability to attend at the time and place fixed.

Ref.: Hanna § 22.07[2][a]; Herlick Handbook § 4.06[1].

§4052. Presence of employee's physician.

The employee may employ at his own expense a physician, to be present at any examination required by his employer.

§4053. Failure or refusal to submit to examination at employer's request.

So long as the employee, after written request of the employer, fails or refuses to submit to such examination or in any way obstructs it, his right to begin or maintain any proceeding for the collection of compensation shall be suspended.

Ref.: 8 C.C.R. §10890; Hanna §§ 5.02[10][b], 22.07[2][b], 25.40[2], 31.11[3].

§4054. Failure or refusal to submit to examination on order of appeals board.

If the employee fails or refuses to submit to examination after direction by the appeals board, or a referee thereof, or in any way obstructs the examination, his right to the disability payments which accrue during the period of such failure, refusal or obstruction, shall be barred.

Labor

Ref.: 8 C.C.R. §10890; Hanna §§ 5.02[10][b], 22.07[2][b]; Herlick Handbook § 14.43.

§4055. Physician's report.

Any physician who makes or is present at any such examination may be required to report or testify as to the results thereof.

Ref.: Hanna § 22.08[3][c].

§4055.2. Subpoena of records; copies.

Any party who subpoenas records in any proceeding under this division shall concurrent with service of the subpoena upon the person who has possession of the records, send a copy of the subpoena to all parties of record in the proceeding. **Leg.H.** 1999 ch. 444.

Ref.: Hanna §§ 22.08[4][c], 25.29[3][a], 25.43; Herlick Handbook § 14.21.

§4056. Disability caused or aggravated by refusal to submit to medical treatment.

No compensation is payable in case of the death or disability of an employee when his death is caused, or when and so far as his disability is caused, continued, or aggravated, by an unreasonable refusal to submit to medical treatment, or to any surgical treatment, if the risk of the treatment is, in the opinion of the appeals board, based upon expert medical or surgical advice, inconsiderable in view of the seriousness of the injury.

Ref.: Hanna §§ 5.05[9][a]–[c], [10][e], 22.02[6]; Herlick Handbook §§ 4.03[3], 4.15[1], 14.22.

ARTICLE 2
Determination of Medical Issues

§4060. Comprehensive medical-legal evaluation.

(a) This section shall apply to disputes over the compensability of any injury. This section shall not apply where injury to any part or parts of the body is accepted as compensable by the employer.

(b) Neither the employer nor the employee shall be liable for any comprehensive medical-legal evaluation performed by other than the treating physician, except as provided in this section. However, reports of treating physicians shall be admissible.

(c) If a medical evaluation is required to determine compensability at any time after the filing of the claim form, and the employee is represented by an attorney, a medical evaluation to determine compensability shall be obtained only by the procedure provided in Section 4062.2.

(d) If a medical evaluation is required to determine compensability at any time after the claim form is filed, and the employee is not represented by an attorney, the employer shall provide the employee with notice either that the employer requests a comprehensive medical evaluation to determine compensability or that the employer has not accepted liability and the employee may request a comprehensive medical evaluation to determine compensability. Either party may request a comprehensive medical evaluation to determine compensability. The evaluation shall be obtained only by the procedure provided in Section 4062.1.

(e) The notice required by subdivision (d) shall be accompanied by the form prescribed by the administrative director for requesting the assignment of a panel of qualified medical evaluators. **Leg.H.** 1993 ch. 121, effective July 16, 1993, ch. 1242, 2004 ch. 34 (SB 899), effective April 19, 2004, 2011 ch. 544 (AB 335) §3.

2004 Note: The amendment to §4060 made by this act shall apply prospectively from the date of enactment of this act, regardless of the date of injury, unless otherwise specified, but shall not constitute good cause to reopen or rescind, alter, or amend any existing order, decision, or award of the Workers' Compensation Appeals Board. Stats. 2004 ch. 34 (SB 899) §47.

1993 Note: Section 4060, as added by ch. 121, applies only to injuries occurring on or after January 1, 1994. Stats. 1993 ch. 121 §77.

Ref.: 8 C.C.R. §§1, 10, 10.2, 11.5, 12, 13, 14, 15, 20, 30, 30.1, 35, 35.5, 36, 39, 39.5, 40, 41, 44, 45, 46, 46.1, 47, 50, 53, 55, 62, 112, 113, 114, 115, 116; Hanna § 22.06[8]; Herlick Handbook §§ 8.25, 14.1, 14.4, 14.11, 14.21.

§4061. Notice of permanent disability indemnity; evaluation.

This section shall not apply to the employee's dispute of a utilization review decision under Section 4610, nor to the employee's dispute of the medical provider network treating physician's diagnosis or treatment recommendations under Sections 4616.3 and 4616.4.

(a) Together with the last payment of temporary disability indemnity, the employer shall, in a form prescribed by the administrative director pursuant to Section 138.4, provide the employee one of the following:

(1) Notice either that no permanent disability indemnity will be paid because the employer alleges the employee has no permanent impairment or limitations resulting from the injury or notice of the amount of permanent disability indemnity determined by the employer to be payable. If the employer determines permanent disability indemnity is payable, the employer shall advise the employee of the amount determined payable and the basis on which the determination was made, whether there is need for future medical care, and whether an indemnity payment will be deferred pursuant to paragraph (2) of subdivision (b) of Section 4650.

(2) Notice that permanent disability indemnity may be or is payable, but that the amount cannot be determined because the employee's medical condition is not yet permanent and stationary. The notice shall advise the employee that his or her medical condition will be monitored until it is permanent and stationary, at which time the necessary evaluation will be performed to determine the existence and extent of permanent impairment and limitations for the purpose of rating permanent disability and to determine whether there will be the need for future medical care, or at which time the employer will advise the employee of the amount of permanent disability indemnity the employer has determined to be payable.

(b) If either the employee or employer objects to a medical determination made by the treating physician concerning the existence or extent of permanent impairment and limitations or the need for future medical care, and the employee is represented by an attorney, a medical evaluation to determine permanent disability shall be obtained as provided in Section 4062.2.

(c) If either the employee or employer objects to a medical determination made by the treating physician concerning the existence or extent of permanent impairment and limitations or the need for future medical care, and if the employee is not represented by an attorney, the employer shall immediately provide the employee with a form prescribed by the medical director with which to request assignment of a panel of three qualified medical evaluators. Either party may request a comprehensive medical evaluation to determine permanent disability or the need for future medical care, and the evaluation shall be obtained only by the procedure provided in Section 4062.1.

(d)(1) Within 30 days of receipt of a report from a qualified medical evaluator who has evaluated an unrepresented employee, the unrepresented employee or the employer may each request one supplemental report seeking correction of factual errors in the report. Any of these requests shall be made in writing. A request made by the employer shall be provided to the employee, and a request made by the employee shall be provided to the employer, insurance carrier, or claims administrator at the time the request is sent to the evaluator. A request for correction that is made by the employer shall also inform the employee of the availability of information and assistance officers to assist him or her in responding to the request, if necessary.

(2) The permanent disability rating procedure set forth in subdivision (e) shall not be invoked by the unrepresented employee or the employer when a request for correction pursuant to paragraph (1) is pending.

(e) The qualified medical evaluator who has evaluated an unrepresented employee shall serve the comprehensive medical evaluation and the summary form on the employee, employer, and the administrative director. The unrepresented employee or the employer may submit the treating physician's evaluation for the calculation of a permanent disability rating. Within 20 days of receipt of the comprehensive medical evaluation, the administrative director shall calculate the permanent disability rating according to Section 4660 or 4660.1, as applicable, and serve the rating on the employee and employer.

(f) Any comprehensive medical evaluation concerning an unrepresented employee which indicates that part or all of an employee's permanent impairment or limitations may be subject to apportionment pursuant to Sections 4663 and 4664 shall first be submitted by the administrative director to a workers' compensation judge who may refer the report back to the qualified medical evaluator for correction or clarification if the judge determines the proposed apportionment is inconsistent with the law.

(g) Within 30 days of receipt of the rating, if the employee is unrepresented, the employee or employer may request that the administrative director reconsider the recommended rating or obtain additional information from the treating physician or medical evaluator to address issues not addressed or not completely addressed in the original comprehensive medical evaluation or not prepared in accord with the procedures promulgated under paragraph (2) or (3) of subdivision (j) of Section 139.2. This request shall be in writing, shall specify the reasons the rating should be reconsidered, and shall be served on the other party. If the administrative director finds the comprehensive medical evaluation is not complete or not in compliance with the required procedures, the administrative director shall return the report to the treating physician or qualified medical evaluator for appropriate action as the administrative director instructs. Upon receipt of the treating physician's or qualified medical evaluator's final comprehensive medical evaluation and summary form, the administrative director shall recalculate the permanent disability rating according to Section 4660 or 4660.1, as applicable, and serve the rating, the comprehensive medical evaluation, and the summary form on the employee and employer.

(h)(1) If a comprehensive medical evaluation from the treating physician or an agreed medical evaluator or a qualified medical evaluator selected from a three-member panel resolves any issue so as to require an employer to provide compensation, the employer shall commence the payment of compensation, except as provided pursuant to paragraph (2) of subdivision (b) of Section 4650, or promptly commence proceedings before the appeals board to resolve the dispute.

(2) If the employee and employer agree to a stipulated findings and award as provided under Section 5702 or to compromise and release the claim under Chapter 2 (commencing with Section 5000) of Part 3, or if the employee wishes to commute the award under Chapter 3 (commencing with Section 5100) of Part 3, the appeals board shall first determine whether the agreement or commutation is in the best interests of the employee and whether the proper procedures have been followed in determining the permanent disability rating. The administrative director shall promulgate a form to notify the employee, at the time of service of any rating under this section, of the options specified in this subdivision, the potential advantages and disadvantages of each option, and the procedure for disputing the rating.

(i) No issue relating to a dispute over the existence or extent of permanent impairment and limitations resulting from the injury may be the subject of a declaration of readiness to proceed unless there has first been a medical evaluation by a treating physician and by either an agreed or qualified medical evaluator. With the exception of an evaluation or evaluations prepared by the treating physician or physicians, no evaluation of permanent impairment and limitations resulting from the injury shall be obtained, except in accordance with Section 4062.1 or 4062.2. Evaluations obtained in violation of this prohibition shall not be admissible in any proceeding before the appeals board. **Leg.H.** 1993 ch. 121, effective July 16, 1993, chs. 1241, 1242, 2002 ch. 6 (AB 749), 2003 ch. 639 (SB 228), 2004 ch. 34 (SB 899), effective April 19, 2004, 2011 ch. 544 (AB 335) §4, 2012 ch. 363 (SB 863) §27, 2013 ch. 287 (SB 375) §4.

2012 Note: For legislative findings, declarations, and applicability of Stats. 2012 ch. 363, see the 2012 Notes following Lab C §62.5.

2004 Note: The amendment to §4061 made by this act shall apply prospectively from the date of enactment of this act, regardless of the date of injury, unless otherwise specified, but shall not constitute good cause to reopen or rescind, alter, or amend any existing order, decision, or award of the Workers' Compensation Appeals Board. Stats. 2004 ch. 34 (SB 899) §47.

1993 Note: Section 4061, as amended by ch. 121, applies only to injuries occurring on or after January 1, 1994. Stats. 1993 ch. 121 §77.

Ref.: 8 C.C.R. §§1, 10, 10.2, 11.5, 12, 13, 14, 15, 20, 30, 30.5, 31, 31.5, 32, 32.5, 33, 34, 35, 36, 37, 38, 39, 39.5, 40, 41, 44, 45, 46, 46.1, 47, 50, 53, 55, 62, 108, 109, 110, 111, 112, 113, 114, 115, 116, 9785, 9793, 9795, 9810, 9812, 9813, 9815, 10101, 10101.1, 10102, 10109, 10111, 10111.1, 10111.2, 10150, 10152, 10156, 10158, 10160, 10160.1, 10160.5, 10161, 10162, 10163, 10164, 10165, 10165.5, 10168; Hanna §§ 22.06[1][a], [b], [e]–[g], 32.06[2][a], [b], [f], [g], [h]; Herlick Handbook §§ 4.08[1], 6.03[1], 6.04[5], 14.4; Lawyer's Guide to AMA *Guides* and Calif. Workers' Comp. §§ 2.02, 2.05, 2.06[2].

§4061.5. Treating physician to render opinions on medical issues needed to determine eligibility for compensation.

The treating physician primarily responsible for managing the care of the injured worker or the physician designated by that treating physician shall, in accordance with rules promulgated by the administrative director, render opinions on all medical issues necessary to determine eligibility for compensation. In the event that there is more than one treating physician, a single report shall be prepared by the physician primarily responsible for managing the injured worker's care that incorporates the findings of the various treating physicians. **Leg.H.** 1993 ch. 121, effective July 16, 1993.

1993 Note: Section 4061.5, as added by ch. 121, applies only to injuries occurring on or after January 1, 1994. Stats. 1993 ch. 121 §77.

Ref.: 8 C.C.R. §§1, 11.5, 31.5, 32.7, 37, 46.1, 50, 62, 108, 113, 9770, 9785, 9785.2, 9785.3, 9785.4, 9785.5, 9793, 9795, 10160.1; Hanna § 22.08[3][b]; Herlick Handbook §§ 4.08[3], 14.4.

§4062. Objections to medical determination; procedures when employer objects to treating physician's recommendations.

(a) If either the employee or employer objects to a medical determination made by the treating physician concerning any medical issues not covered by Section 4060 or 4061 and not subject to Section 4610, the objecting party shall notify the other party in writing of the objection within 20 days of receipt of the report if the employee is represented by an attorney or within 30 days of receipt of the report if the employee is not represented by an attorney. These time limits may be extended for good cause or by mutual agreement. If the employee is represented by an attorney, a medical evaluation to determine the disputed medical issue shall be obtained as provided in Section 4062.2, and no other medical evaluation shall be obtained. If the employee is not represented by an attorney, the employer shall immediately provide the employee with a form prescribed by the medical director with which to request assignment of a panel of three qualified medical evaluators, the evaluation shall be obtained as provided in Section 4062.1, and no other medical evaluation shall be obtained.

(b) If the employee objects to a decision made pursuant to Section 4610 to modify, delay, or deny a request for authorization of a medical treatment recommendation made by a treating physician, the objection shall be resolved only in accordance with the independent medical review process established in Section 4610.5.

(c) If the employee objects to the diagnosis or recommendation for medical treatment by a physician within the employer's medical provider network established pursuant to Section 4616, the objection shall be resolved only in accordance with the independent medical review process established in Sections 4616.3 and 4616.4. **Leg.H.** 2003 ch. 639 (SB 228) §17, 2004 ch. 34 (SB 899), effective April 19, 2004, 2012 ch. 363 (SB 863) §28.

2012 Note: For legislative findings, declarations, and applicability of Stats. 2012 ch. 363, see the 2012 Notes following Lab C §62.5.

2004 Note: The amendment to §4062 made by this act shall apply prospectively from the date of enactment of this act, regardless of the date of injury, unless otherwise specified, but shall not constitute good cause to reopen or rescind, alter, or amend any existing order, decision, or award of the Workers' Compensation Appeals Board. Stats. 2004 ch. 34 (SB 899) §47.

2003 Note: The Commission on Health and Safety and Workers' Compensation shall conduct a study of the spinal surgery second opinion procedure established in subdivision (b) of Section 4062 of the Labor Code. The study shall be completed by June 30, 2006. The commission shall issue a report concerning the findings of the study and recommendations for further legislation. Stats. 2003 ch. 639 (SB 228) §48.

Ref.: 8 C.C.R. §§1, 10, 10.2, 11.5, 12, 13, 14, 15, 20, 30, 30.5, 31, 31.5, 32, 33, 34, 35, 35.5, 36, 38, 39, 39.5, 40, 41, 44, 45, 46, 46.1, 47, 50, 62, 108, 109, 110, 112, 113, 114, 115, 116, 9785, 9788.01, 9788.1, 9788.11, 9788.2, 9788.3, 9788.31, 9788.32, 9788.4, 9788.45, 9788.5, 9788.6, 9788.7, 9788.8, 9788.9, 9788.91, 9792.6, 9792.7, 9792.8, 9792.9, 9792.10, 9793, 10152, 10160, 10160.1, 10160.5, 10163, 10165.5; Hanna §§ 22.05[6][c], 22.06[2], 32.06[3]; Herlick Handbook §§ 4.08[1], 4.09[3], [6], [7], 4.10[1], 14.4.

§4062.1. Unrepresented employee—Medical evaluation.

(a) If an employee is not represented by an attorney, the employer shall not seek agreement with the employee on an agreed medical evaluator, nor shall an agreed medical evaluator prepare the formal medical evaluation on any issues in dispute.

(b) If either party requests a medical evaluation pursuant to Section 4060, 4061, or 4062, either party may submit the form prescribed by the administrative director requesting the medical director to assign a panel of three qualified medical evaluators in accordance with Section 139.2. However, the employer may not submit the form unless the employee has not submitted the form within 10 days after the employer has furnished the form to the employee and requested the employee to submit the form. The party submitting the request form shall designate the specialty of the physicians that will be assigned to the panel.

(c) Within 10 days of the issuance of a panel of qualified medical evaluators, the employee shall select a physician from the panel to prepare a medical evaluation, the employee shall schedule the appointment, and the employee shall inform the employer of the selection and the appointment. If the employee does not inform the employer of the selection within 10 days of the assignment of a panel of qualified medical evaluators, then the employer may select the physician from the panel to prepare a medical evaluation. If the employee informs the employer of the selection within 10 days of the assignment of the panel but has not made the appointment, or if the employer selects the physician pursuant to this subdivision, then the employer shall arrange the appointment. Upon receipt of written notice of the appointment arrangements from the employee, or upon giving the employee notice of an appointment arranged by the employer, the employer shall furnish payment of estimated travel expense.

(d) The evaluator shall give the employee, at the appointment, a brief opportunity to ask questions concerning the evaluation process and the evaluator's background. The unrepresented employee shall then participate in the evaluation as requested by the evaluator unless the employee has good cause to discontinue the evaluation. For purposes of this subdivision, "good cause" shall include evidence that the evaluator is biased against the employee because of his or her race, sex, national origin, religion, or sexual preference or evidence that the evaluator has requested the employee to submit to an unnecessary medical examination or procedure. If the unrepresented employee declines to proceed with the evaluation, he or she shall have the right to a new panel of three qualified medical evaluators from which to select one to prepare a comprehensive medical evaluation. If the appeals board subsequently determines that the employee did not have good cause to not proceed with the evaluation, the cost of the evaluation shall be deducted from any award the employee obtains.

(e) If an employee has received a comprehensive medical-legal evaluation under this section, and he or she later becomes represented by an attorney, he or she shall not be entitled to an additional evaluation. **Leg.H.** 2004 ch. 34 (SB 899), effective April 19, 2004.

2004 Note: The amendment to §4062.1 made by this act shall apply prospectively from the date of enactment of this act, regardless of the date of injury, unless otherwise specified, but shall not constitute good cause to reopen or rescind, alter, or amend any existing order, decision, or award of the Workers' Compensation Appeals Board. Stats. 2004 ch. 34 (SB 899) §47.

Ref.: 8 C.C.R. §§10152, 10160, 10160.1, 10160.5, 10161, 10163, 10165.5; Hanna §§ 22.06[1][b], 32.06[2][b]; Herlick Handbook § 14.4.

§4062.2. Comprehensive medical evaluation to resolve dispute over injuries on or after January 1, 2005, when employee is represented by attorney.

(a) Whenever a comprehensive medical evaluation is required to resolve any dispute arising out of an injury or a claimed injury occurring on or after January 1, 2005, and the employee is represented by an attorney, the evaluation shall be obtained only as provided in this section.

(b) No earlier than the first working day that is at least 10 days after the date of mailing of a request for a medical evaluation pursuant to Section 4060 or the first working day that is at least 10 days after the date of mailing of an objection pursuant to Sections 4061 or 4062, either party may request the assignment of a three-member panel of qualified medical evaluators to conduct a comprehensive medical evaluation. The party submitting the request shall designate the specialty of the medical evaluator, the specialty of the medical evaluator requested by the other party if it has been made known to the party submitting the request, and the specialty of the treating physician. The party submitting the request form shall serve a copy of the request form on the other party.

(c) Within 10 days of assignment of the panel by the administrative director, each party may strike one name from the panel. The remaining qualified medical evaluator shall serve as the medical evaluator. If a party fails to exercise the right to strike a name from the panel within 10 days of assignment of the panel by the administrative director, the other party may select any physician who remains on the panel to serve as the medical evaluator. The administrative director may prescribe the form, the manner, or both, by which the parties shall conduct the selection process.

(d) The represented employee shall be responsible for arranging the appointment for the examination, but upon his or her failure to inform the employer of the appointment within 10 days after the medical evaluator has been selected, the employer may arrange the appointment and notify the employee of the arrangements. The employee shall not unreasonably refuse to participate in the evaluation.

(e) If an employee has received a comprehensive medical-legal evaluation under this section, and he or she later ceases to be represented, he or she shall not be entitled to an additional evaluation.

(f) The parties may agree to an agreed medical evaluator at any time, except as to issues subject to the independent medical review process established pursuant to Section 4610.5. A panel shall not be requested pursuant to subdivision (b) on any issue that has been agreed to be submitted to or has been submitted to an agreed medical evaluator unless the agreement has been canceled by mutual written consent. **Leg.H.** 2004 ch. 34 (SB 899) §18, effective April 19, 2004, 2012 ch. 363 (SB 863) §29.

2012 Note: For legislative findings, declarations, and applicability of Stats. 2012 ch. 363, see the 2012 Notes following Lab C §62.5.

2004 Note: The addition of §4062.2 made by this act shall apply prospectively from the date of enactment of this act, regardless of the date of injury, unless otherwise specified, but shall not constitute good cause to reopen or rescind, alter, or amend any existing order, decision, or award of the Workers' Compensation Appeals Board. Stats. 2004 ch. 34 (SB 899) §47.

Ref.: 8 C.C.R. §§41, 10160, 10160.1, 10160.5, 10161, 10163, 10165.5; Hanna §§ 22.06[1][a], 32.06[2][a]; Herlick Handbook §§ 4.08[3], 4.14[3], 14.4.

§4062.3. Information provided to qualified medical evaluator; service on opposing party; discovery; ex parte communications; contempt; evaluation and summary form; new medical issues.

(a) Any party may provide to the qualified medical evaluator selected from a panel any of the following information:

(1) Records prepared or maintained by the employee's treating physician or physicians.

(2) Medical and nonmedical records relevant to determination of the medical issue.

(b) Information that a party proposes to provide to the qualified medical evaluator selected from a panel shall be served on the opposing party 20 days before the information is provided to the evaluator. If the opposing party objects to consideration of nonmedical records within 10 days thereafter, the records shall not be provided to the evaluator. Either party may use discovery to establish the accuracy or authenticity of nonmedical records prior to the evaluation.

(c) If an agreed medical evaluator is selected, as part of their agreement on an evaluator, the parties shall agree on what information is to be provided to the agreed medical evaluator.

(d) In any formal medical evaluation, the agreed or qualified medical evaluator shall identify the following:

(1) All information received from the parties.

(2) All information reviewed in preparation of the report.

(3) All information relied upon in the formulation of his or her opinion.

(e) All communications with a qualified medical evaluator selected from a panel before a medical evaluation shall be in writing and shall be served on the opposing party 20 days in advance of the evaluation. Any subsequent communication with the medical evaluator shall be in writing and shall be served on the opposing party when sent to the medical evaluator.

(f) Communications with an agreed medical evaluator shall be in writing, and shall be served on the opposing party when sent to the agreed medical evaluator. Oral or written communications with physician staff or, as applicable, with the agreed medical evaluator, relative to nonsubstantial matters such as the scheduling of appointments, missed appointments, the furnishing of records and reports, and the availability of the report, do not constitute ex parte communication in violation of this section unless the appeals board has made a specific finding of an impermissible ex parte communication.

(g) Ex parte communication with an agreed medical evaluator or a qualified medical evaluator selected from a panel is prohibited. If a party communicates with the agreed medical evaluator or the qualified medical evaluator in violation of subdivision (e), the aggrieved party may elect to terminate the medical evaluation and seek a new evaluation from another qualified medical evaluator to be selected according to Section 4062.1 or 4062.2, as applicable, or proceed with the initial evaluation.

(h) The party making the communication prohibited by this section shall be subject to being charged with contempt before the appeals board and shall be liable for the costs incurred by the aggrieved party as a result of the prohibited communication, including the cost of the medical evaluation, additional discovery costs, and attorney's fees for related discovery.

(i) Subdivisions (e) and (g) shall not apply to oral or written communications by the employee or, if the employee is deceased, the employee's dependent, in the course of the examination or at the request of the evaluator in connection with the examination.

(j) Upon completing a determination of the disputed medical issue, the medical evaluator shall summarize the medical findings on a form prescribed by the administrative director and shall serve the formal medical evaluation and the summary form on the employee and the employer. The medical evaluation shall address all contested medical issues arising from all injuries reported on one or more claim forms prior to the date of the employee's initial appointment with the medical evaluator.

(k) If, after a medical evaluation is prepared, the employer or the employee subsequently objects to any new medical issue, the parties, to the extent possible, shall utilize the same medical evaluator who prepared the previous evaluation to resolve the medical dispute.

(*l*) No disputed medical issue specified in subdivision (a) may be the subject of declaration of readiness to proceed unless there has first been an evaluation by the treating physician or an agreed or qualified medical evaluator. **Leg.H.** 2004 ch. 34 (SB 899) §19, effective April 19, 2004, 2012 ch. 363 (SB 863) §30.

2012 Note: For legislative findings, declarations, and applicability of Stats. 2012 ch. 363, see the 2012 Notes following Lab C §62.5.

2004 Note: The addition of §4062.3 made by this act shall apply prospectively from the date of enactment of this act, regardless of the date of injury, unless otherwise specified, but shall not constitute good cause to reopen or rescind, alter, or amend any existing order, decision, or award of the Workers' Compensation Appeals Board. Stats. 2004 ch. 34 (SB 899) §47.

Ref.: Hanna §§ 22.06[1][d], [e], [4], 32.06[2][c], [f]; Herlick Handbook §§ 4.14[3], 14.4.

§4062.5. Failure of QME to complete timely evaluation.

If a qualified medical evaluator selected from a panel fails to complete the formal medical evaluation within the timeframes established by the administrative director pursuant to paragraph (1) of subdivision (j) of Section 139.2, a new evaluation may be obtained upon the request of either party, as provided in Sections 4062.1 or 4062.2. Neither the employee nor the employer shall have any liability for payment for the formal medical evaluation which was not completed within the required timeframes unless the employee or employer, on forms prescribed by the administrative director, each waive the right to a new evaluation and elects to accept the original evaluation even though it was not completed within the required timeframes. **Leg.H.** 2003 ch. 639 (SB 228), 2004 ch. 34 (SB 899), effective April 19, 2004.

2004 Note: The amendment to §4062.5 made by this act shall apply prospectively from the date of enactment of this act, regardless of the date of injury, unless otherwise specified, but shall not constitute good cause to reopen or rescind, alter, or amend any existing order, decision, or award of the Workers' Compensation Appeals Board. Stats. 2004 ch. 34 (SB 899) §47.

Ref.: 8 C.C.R. §§112, 113, 114, 115, 116, 10160, 10160.1, 10160.5, 10161, 10163, 10165.5; Hanna § 22.06[5]; Herlick Handbook § 14.4.

§4062.8. Educational materials for treating physicians and other providers.

The administrative director shall develop, not later than January 1, 2004, and periodically revise as necessary thereafter, educational materials to be used to provide treating physicians, as described in Section 3209.3, or other providers, as described in Section 3209.5, with information and training in basic concepts of workers' compensation, the role of the treating physician, the conduct of permanent and stationary evaluations, and report writing, as appropriate. **Leg.H.** 2004 ch. 34 (SB 899), effective April 19, 2004.

2004 Note: The addition of §4062.8 made by this act shall apply prospectively from the date of enactment of this act, regardless of the date of injury, unless otherwise specified, but shall not constitute good cause to reopen or rescind, alter, or amend any existing order, decision, or award of the Workers' Compensation Appeals Board. Stats. 2004 ch. 34 (SB 899) §47.

Ref.: Hanna § 1.12[2].

§4063. Commencement of payment; declaration of readiness to proceed.

If a formal medical evaluation from an agreed medical evaluator or a qualified medical evaluator selected from a three member panel resolves any issue so as to require an employer to provide compensation, the employer shall, except as provided pursuant to paragraph (2) of subdivision (b) of Section 4650, commence the payment of compensation or file a declaration of readiness to proceed. **Leg.H.** 1989 ch. 892 (AB 276) §28, 2012 ch. 363 (SB 863) §31.

2012 Note: For legislative findings, declarations, and applicability of Stats. 2012 ch. 363, see the 2012 Notes following Lab C §62.5.

Ref.: Herlick Handbook § 14.4.

§4064. Employer liability for costs and attorney's fees.

(a) The employer shall be liable for the cost of each reasonable and necessary comprehensive medical-legal evaluation obtained by the employee pursuant to Sections 4060, 4061, and 4062. Each comprehensive medical-legal evaluation shall address all contested medical issues arising from all injuries reported on one or more claim forms, except medical treatment recommendations, which are subject to utilization review as provided by Section 4610, and objections to utilization review determinations, which are subject to independent medical review as provided by Section 4610.5.

(b) For injuries occurring on or after January 1, 2003, if an unrepresented employee obtains an attorney after the evaluation pursuant to subdivision (d) of Section 4061 or subdivision (b) of Section 4062 has been completed, the employee shall be entitled to the same reports at employer expense as an employee who has been represented from the time the dispute arose and those reports shall be admissible in any proceeding before the appeals board.

(c) Subject to Section 4906, if an employer files a declaration of readiness to proceed and the employee is unrepresented at the time the declaration of readiness to proceed is filed, the employer shall be liable for any attorney's fees incurred by the employee in connection with the declaration of readiness to proceed.

(d) The employer shall not be liable for the cost of any comprehensive medical evaluations obtained by the employee other than those authorized pursuant to Sections 4060, 4061, and 4062. However, no party is prohibited from obtaining any medical evaluation or consultation at the party's own expense. In no event shall an employer or employee be liable for an evaluation obtained in violation of subdivision (b) of Section 4060. All comprehensive medical evaluations obtained by any party shall be admissible in any proceeding before the appeals board except as provided in Section 4060, 4061, 4062, 4062.1, or 4062.2. **Leg.H.** 1993 ch. 121, effective July 16, 1993, ch. 1242 §30, 1998 ch. 485, 2002 ch. 6 (AB 749), 2012 ch. 363 (SB 863) §32.

2012 Note: For legislative findings, declarations, and applicability of Stats. 2012 ch. 363, see the 2012 Notes following Lab C §62.5.

1993 Notes: The elimination of subdivision (d) of Section 4064 of the Labor Code made by this act shall not affect the applicability of Section 4064 of the Labor Code, as it existed prior to changes made during the 1993-94 Regular Session, to injuries arising prior to those changes. Stats. 1993 ch. 1242 §44.

Section 4064, as amended by ch. 121, applies only to injuries occurring on or after January 1, 1994. Stats. 1993 ch. 121 §77.

Ref.: 8 C.C.R. §§10160, 10160.1, 10160.5, 10161, 10163, 10165.5; Hanna § 22.06[1][b], [6], [7], [9]; Herlick Handbook §§ 4.07[5], 4.11[7], 10.09[5], 14.4, 14.21.

§4067. Subsequent formal evaluations.

If the jurisdiction of the appeals board is invoked pursuant to Section 5803 upon the grounds that the effects of the injury have recurred, increased, diminished, or terminated, a formal medical evaluation shall be obtained pursuant to this article.

When an agreed medical evaluator or a qualified medical evaluator selected by an unrepresented employee from a three-member panel has previously made a formal medical evaluation of the same or similar issues, the subsequent or additional formal medical evaluation shall be conducted by the same agreed medical evaluator or qualified medical evaluator, unless the workers' compensation judge has made a finding that he or she did not rely on the prior evaluator's formal medical evaluation, any party contested the original medical evaluation by filing an application for adjudication, the unrepresented employee hired an attorney and selected a qualified medical evaluator to conduct another evaluation pursuant to subdivision (b) of Section 4064, or the prior evaluator is no longer qualified or readily available to prepare a formal medical evaluation, in which case Sections 4061 or 4062, as the case may be, shall apply as if there had been no prior formal medical evaluation. **Leg.H.** 2002 ch. 6 (AB 749).

Ref.: 8 C.C.R. §§10160, 10160.1, 10160.5, 10161, 10163, 10165.5; Herlick Handbook §§ 14.4, 14.9, 14.21, 14.22.

§4067.5. Operative date.

This article shall become operative for injuries occurring on and after January 1, 1991.

Ref.: 8 C.C.R. §38; Hanna §§ 20.02[2][b], 32.04[1][a], 32.06[1].

§4068. Determination that treating physician's reports are biased and unsupported; notification to appropriate licensing body.

(a) Upon determining that a treating physician's report contains opinions that are the result of conjecture, are not supported by adequate evidence, or that indicate bias, the appeals board shall so notify the administrative director in writing in a manner he or she has specified.

(b) If the administrative director believes that any treating physician's reports show a pattern of unsupported opinions, he or she shall notify in writing the physician's applicable licensing body of his or her findings. **Leg.H.** 1993 ch. 121, effective July 16, 1993, 2003 ch. 639 (SB 228).

1993 Note: Section 4068, as added by ch. 121, applies only to injuries occurring on or after January 1, 1994. Stats. 1993 ch. 121 §77.

Ref.: Herlick Handbook § 14.4.

CHAPTER 8 ELECTION TO BE SUBJECT TO COMPENSATION LIABILITY

§4150. Person not "employee"; joint election of employer and employee.

When an employer has in his employment any person not included within the term "employee" as defined by Article 2 of Chapter 2 of Part 1 of this division or a person not entitled to compensation under this division, such employer and such person employed by him may, by their joint election, come under the compensation provisions of this division in the manner hereinafter provided.

Ref.: Hanna § 21.04[2][a]; Herlick Handbook §§ 2.5, 2.9.

§4151. Methods of employer election.

Election on the part of the employer shall be made in one of the following ways:

(a) By insuring against liability for compensation, in which case he is deemed, as to all persons employed by him and covered by insurance, to have so elected during the period such insurance remains in force.

(b) By filing with the administrative director a statement to the effect that he accepts the compensation provisions of this division.

Ref.: Hanna §§ 3.33, 3.34, 3.88, 11.03[1], 21.04[2][a]; Herlick Handbook §§ 2.3–2.5.

§4152. Effect statement of acceptance.

The statement, when filed, shall operate, within the meaning of Chapter 3 (commencing with Section 3600), to subject him or her to the compensation provisions thereof for the term of one year from the date of filing. Thereafter, without further act on his or her part, he or she shall be so subject for successive terms of one year each, unless at least 60 days prior to the expiration of such first or succeeding year, he or she files with the administrative director a notice that he or she withdraws his or her election.

§4153. Persons included in statement of acceptance.

Such statement of acceptance includes persons whose employment is both casual and not in the course of the trade, business, profession, or occupation of the employer, unless expressly excluded therefrom.

§4154. Employer election.

Where any employer has made an election in either of the modes above prescribed, any person in his service is deemed to have accepted the compensation provisions of this division if, at the time of the injury for which liability is claimed:

(a) Such employer is subject to the compensation provisions of this division and;

(b) Such person in his service has not, either upon entering into the employment, or within five days after the filing of an election by the employer, given to such employer notice in writing that he elects not to be subject to the compensation provisions of this division.

In case of such acceptance, the person employed becomes subject to the compensation provisions at the time of the filing of the election or entry in the employment.

Ref.: Hanna § 3.88.

§4155. Coverage of state institutions; presumption.

The State and each county, city, district, and public agency thereof and all State institutions are conclusively presumed to have elected to come within the provisions of this division as to all employments otherwise excluded from this division.

§4156. Liability for compensation; effective date of division.

Liability for compensation does not attach to any employer of a person excluded by paragraph (8) of subdivision (a) of Section 3352 from the definition of "employee" for an injury to or the death of a person so excluded which occurs on or after the effective date of this section if the employer elected to come under the compensation provisions of this division pursuant to subdivision (a) of Section 4151 prior to the effective date of this section by purchasing or renewing a policy providing comprehensive personal liability insurance containing a provision for coverage against liability for the payment of compensation, as defined in Section 3207 of the Labor Code, to any person defined as an employee by subdivision (d) of Section 3351 of the Labor Code, however, this section does not prohibit an employer from providing compensation pursuant to the provisions of this chapter. **Leg.H.** 1977 ch. 17 §25, effective March 25, 1977, 2017 ch. 770 (SB 189) §7.

Ref.: Herlick Handbook §§ 2.5, 2.9.

§4157. Application of chapter to independent contractor vending periodicals.

Where any employer has made an election pursuant to this chapter to include under the compensation provisions of this division an independent contractor engaged in vending, selling, offering for sale, or delivering directly to the public any newspaper, magazine, or periodical, the status of such person as an independent contractor for all other purposes shall not be affected by such election.

Ref.: Herlick Handbook §§ 2.5, 2.8.

CHAPTER 9 ECONOMIC OPPORTUNITY PROGRAMS

ARTICLE 1 General Provisions

§4201. Legislative intent; application of chapter.

It is the intent of this chapter to apply to all enrollees in economic opportunity programs, including, but not limited to, work training or work study authorized by or financed in whole or in part through provisions of Public Law 88–452 (Economic Opportunity Act of 1964).

§4202. "Economic Opportunity Program."

"Economic Opportunity Program" means any program adopted pursuant to Public Law 88–452, including, but not limited to, work training and work study.

§4203. "Enrollee."

"Enrollee" means any person enrolled in an economic opportunity program.

§4204. "Sponsoring agency."

"Sponsoring agency" means any agency, entity, or institution, public or private, receiving grants or financial assistance, either directly or as a subcontractor, pursuant to Public Law 88–452.

§4205. "Participating agency."

"Participating agency" means any agency, entity or institution, public or private, taking part in an economic opportunity program, other than a sponsoring agency.

§4206. Enrollee's right to compensation.

Except as provided in this chapter, an enrollee within a given economic opportunity program shall have no right to receive compensation from sponsoring or participating agencies, entities, and institutions, public or private.

Ref.: Herlick Handbook § 2.5.

§4207. Conditions for compensation.

Compensation shall be furnished an enrollee for injury or to dependents if injury causes death, suffered within or without the state occurring in the course of his duties for a sponsoring agency within an economic opportunity program if the following conditions occur:

(a) Where, at the time of injury, the enrollee is performing services and is acting within the scope of his duties as a recipient of aid within an economic opportunity program.

(b) Where injury is proximately caused by his service as an enrollee within an economic opportunity program either with or without negligence.

(c) Where injury is not caused by the intoxication of the injured enrollee.

(d) Where the injury is not intentionally self-inflicted.

§4208. Compensation under chapter; exclusive remedy.

Where the conditions of compensation exist, the right to recover such compensation pursuant to the provisions of this chapter is the exclusive remedy for injury or death of an enrollee against the sponsoring agency, or the participating agency.

§4209. Application of division to enrollees.

Insofar as not inconsistent with the provisions of this chapter, all of the provisions of this division shall pertain to enrollees and their dependents and the furnishing of compensation benefits thereto.

ARTICLE 2
Benefits

§4211. Limitations on compensation.

Where liability for compensation exists, such compensation shall be provided as limited by this chapter.

§4212. Injury or death of enrollee.

If an enrollee suffers injury or death in the performance of his duties under an economic opportunity program, then, irrespective of his remuneration from this or other employment, his average weekly earnings for the purpose of determining temporary and permanent disability indemnity shall be determined in accordance with Section 4453, provided that for the purpose of this chapter only, there shall be no statutory minimum average weekly earnings for temporary disability indemnity. If the injury sustained by an enrollee causes death, death benefits shall be determined in accordance with Sections 4701 and 4702 of this code.

§4213. Injury causing permanent disability; percentage of disability.

If the injury sustained by an enrollee causes permanent disability, the percentage of disability to total disability shall be determined for the occupation of a laborer of like age by applying the schedule for the determination of the percentage of permanent disabilities prepared and adopted by the appeals board.

§4214. Fatal injury; enrollee's burial expenses.

In addition to death benefit in the event of fatal injury, the reasonable expenses of the enrollee's burial shall be paid not to exceed six hundred dollars ($600).

ARTICLE 3
Adjustment of Claims

§4226. Effect of benefits provided under federal statute.

Should the United States government or any agent thereof, pursuant to federal statute, rule or regulations furnish benefits to enrollees or dependents of enrollees under an economic opportunity program, then the amount of indemnity which an enrollee or his dependents are entitled to receive under this chapter shall be reduced by the amount of monetary benefits the enrollee or his dependents have and will receive from the above source as a result of injury.

§4227. Effect of medical treatment provided by federal government.

If the United States government or any agent thereof furnishes medical treatment to an injured enrollee, the enrollee will have no right to receive the same or similar treatment under this chapter.

§4228. Effect of medical treatment provided by federal government; reimbursement.

If the furnishing of medical treatment by the United States government or its agent takes the form of reimbursement of the enrollee, he shall have no right to receive the same or similar treatment under this chapter.

§4229. Right to recover benefits under federal statute supersedes rights under chapter.

If the furnishing of compensation benefits to an enrollee or his dependents under this chapter prevents such enrollee or his dependents from receiving benefits under the provisions of federal statute, rule or regulations, then the enrollee or his dependents shall have not right and shall not receive compensation benefits under this chapter.

Ref.: Herlick Handbook § 2.5.

CHAPTER 10
DISASTER SERVICE WORKERS

§4350. Office of Emergency Services to administer benefits for volunteer disaster service workers.

The Office of Emergency Services shall administer this chapter as it relates to volunteer disaster service workers. **Leg.H.** 2003 ch. 228 (AB 1756), effective August 11, 2003, 2010 ch. 618 (AB 2791) §189, 2013 ch. 352 (AB 1317) §401, effective September 26, 2013, operative July 1, 2013.

Ref.: Hanna § 3.117[1], [4].

§4351. Exclusive remedy.

Compensation provided by this division is the exclusive remedy of a disaster service worker, or his or her dependents, for injury or death arising out of, and in the course of, his or her activities as a disaster service worker as against the state, the disaster council with which he or she is registered, and the county or city which has empowered the disaster council to register and direct his or her activities. Liability for compensation provided by this division is in lieu of any other liability whatsoever to a disaster service worker or his or her dependents or any other person on his or her behalf against the state, the disaster council with which the disaster service worker is registered, and the county or city which has empowered the disaster council to register and direct his or her activities, for any injury or death arising out of, and in the course of, his or her activities as a disaster service worker.

Ref.: Hanna § 3.117[1].

§4352. Liability for compensation dependent upon and limited to appropriated money; when funds are temporarily unavailable for disbursement; reserve fund.

(a) No compensation shall be paid or furnished to a disaster service worker or a dependent of a disaster service worker pursuant to this division absent an initial appropriation of funds for the purpose of furnishing compensation to a disaster service worker or a dependent of a disaster service worker. Liability for the initial payment or furnishing of compensation is dependent upon and limited to the availability of money so appropriated.

(b) Notwithstanding subdivision (a), when appropriated funds are temporarily unavailable for disbursement, the State Compensation Insurance Fund may provide compensation to an eligible claimant under this section whose injuries have previously either been accepted or found to be compensable by the Workers' Compensation Appeals Board.

(1) Compensation to, and benefits for, an eligible claimant provided for under this subdivision may include the issuance of checks by the State Compensation Insurance Fund.

(2) Within 30 days of the date funds that had been temporarily unavailable are appropriated, and therefore become available, the California Emergency Management Agency shall reimburse the State Compensation Insurance Fund for compensation paid to, or benefits paid for, a claimant pursuant to paragraph (1), in addition to any applicable interest, service fees, or charges.

(c) After all money appropriated as described in subdivision (a) is expended or set aside in bookkeeping reserves for the payment or furnishing of compensation and reimbursing the State Compensation Insurance Fund for its services, the payment or furnishing of compensation for an injury to a disaster service worker or his or her dependents is dependent upon there having been a reserve set up for the payment or furnishing of compensation to that disaster service worker or his or her dependents and for that injury, and liability is limited to the amount of the reserve. The excess in a reserve for the payment or furnishing of compensation or for reimbursing the State Compensation Insurance Fund for its compensation payments and services may be transferred to reserves of other disaster service workers for the payment or furnishing of compensation and reimbursing the State Compensation Insurance Fund, or may be used to set up reserves for other disaster service workers. **Leg.H.** 2009–10 ch. 12 (Fourth Extra. Sess.) (AB 12 (Fourth Extra. Sess.)) §25, effective July 28, 2009.

2009 Note: The Legislature finds and declares that Section 28 of Article I of the California Constitution imposes certain notification requirements on prosecutors. It is the intent of the Legislature that the changes made by Section 25 of this act conform the statutory notification requirements in paragraph (12) of subdivision (a) of Section 679.02 of the Penal Code to those in Section 28 of Article I of the California Constitution, as established by the Victims' Bill of Rights Act of 2008: Marsy's Law, and that any additional duties previously imposed on local governments by that paragraph shall no longer be mandated. Stats. 2009–10 ch. 12 (Fourth Extra. Sess.) (AB 12 (Fourth Extra. Sess.)) §37.

Ref.: Hanna § 3.117[1]; Herlick Handbook § 2.4.

§4353. Maximum benefits.

If a disaster service worker suffers injury or death while in the performance of duties as a disaster service worker, then, irrespective of his or her remuneration from this or other employment or from both, the average weekly earnings for the purposes of determining temporary and permanent disability indemnity shall be taken at the maximum fixed for each, respectively, in Section 4453.

Ref.: Hanna § 3.117[3].

§4354. Determination of permanent disability percentage.

If the injury sustained by a disaster service worker causes permanent disability, the percentage of disability to total disability shall be determined as for the occupation of a laborer of like age by applying the schedule for the determination of the percentages of permanent disabilities prepared and adopted by the administrative director. The amount of the weekly payment for permanent disability shall be the same as the weekly benefit which would be paid for temporary total disability pursuant to Section 4353.

Ref.: Hanna § 3.117[3]; Herlick Handbook § 2.4.

§4355. State benefits reduced by amount of federal benefits received.

(a) Should the United States Government or any agent thereof, in accordance with any federal statute, rule, or regulation, furnish monetary assistance, benefits, or other temporary or permanent relief to disaster service workers or to disaster service workers and their dependents for injuries arising out of and occurring in the course of their activities as disaster service workers, the amount of compensation that any disaster service worker or his or her dependents are otherwise entitled to receive from the State of California under this division for any injury shall be reduced by the amount of monetary assistance, benefits, or other temporary or permanent relief the disaster service worker or his or her dependents have received and will receive from the United States or any agent thereof as a result of the injury.

(b) If, in addition to monetary assistance, benefits, or other temporary or permanent relief, the United States Government or any agent thereof furnishes medical, surgical, or hospital treatment, or any combination thereof, to an injured disaster service worker, the disaster service worker has no right to receive similar medical, surgical, or hospital treatment under this division.

(c) If, in addition to monetary assistance, benefits, or other temporary or permanent relief, the United States Government or any agent thereof will reimburse a disaster service worker or his or her dependents for medical, surgical, or hospital treatment, or any combination thereof, furnished to the injured disaster service worker, the disaster service worker has no right to receive similar medical, surgical, or hospital treatment under this division.

(d) If the furnishing of compensation under this division to a disaster service worker or his or her dependents prevents the disaster service worker or his or her dependents from receiving assistance, benefits, or other temporary or permanent relief under a federal statute, rule, regulation, the disaster service worker and his or her dependents shall have no right to, and may not receive, any compensation from the State of California under this division for any injury for which the United States Government or any agent thereof will furnish assistance, benefits, or other temporary or permanent relief in the absence of the furnishing of compensation by the State of California. **Leg.H.** 2003 ch. 228 (AB 1756), effective August 11, 2003.

CHAPTER 11
ASBESTOS WORKERS' ACCOUNT

ARTICLE 1
General Provisions

§4401. Asbestosis; state policy.

It is the declared policy of the state that qualified injured workers with asbestosis which arises out of and occurs in the course of employment shall receive workers' compensation asbestos workers' benefits promptly and not be subjected to delays of litigation to determine the responsible employer.

Ref.: Herlick Handbook § 3.19.

§4402. Definitions.

(a) "Asbestosis" means any pathology, whether or not combined with preexisting pathology, which results in disability or need for medical treatment from inhalation of asbestos fibers.

(b) "Asbestos worker" means any person whose occupation subjected him or her to an exposure to asbestos fibers.

(c) "Asbestos workers' benefits" means temporary total disability benefits, permanent total disability benefits, death benefits, and medical benefits.

(d) "Dependents" means, and is limited to, a surviving spouse who at the time of injury was dependent on the deceased asbestos worker for half or more of his or her support, and minor children of the deceased asbestos worker.

§4403. Asbestos Workers' Account.

The Asbestos Workers' Account is hereby created in the Uninsured Employers Fund in the State Treasury, and shall be administered by the Director of Industrial Relations. The money in the Asbestos Workers' Account is hereby continuously appropriated for the purposes of this chapter, and to pay the expenses of the director in administering these provisions.

§4404. Scope.

Insofar as not inconsistent with the provisions of this chapter, all of the provisions of this division shall pertain to asbestos workers and their dependents for purposes of furnishing workers' compensation asbestos workers' benefits thereto.

§4405. Asbestos workers' benefits; temporary remedy.

Where the conditions of compensation exist under this division the right to recover workers' compensation asbestos workers' benefits pursuant to the provisions of this chapter is a temporary remedy for injury to an asbestos worker against the Asbestos Workers' Account, and such asbestos worker or his or her dependents shall make all reasonable effort to establish the identity of the employer responsible for securing the payment of compensation.

Labor

§4406. Conditions for receiving asbestos workers' benefits.

(a) Payments as advances on workers' compensation asbestos workers' benefits shall be furnished an asbestos worker for injury resulting in asbestosis, or the dependents of the asbestos worker in the case of his or her death due to asbestosis, subject to the provisions of this division, if all of the following conditions occur:

(1) The asbestos worker demonstrates to the account that at the time of exposure, the asbestos worker was performing services and was acting within the scope of his or her duties in an occupation that subjected the asbestos worker to the exposure to asbestos.

(2) The asbestos worker demonstrates to the account that he or she is suffering from asbestosis.

(3) The asbestos worker demonstrates to the account that he or she developed asbestosis from the employment.

(4) The asbestos worker is entitled to compensation for asbestosis as otherwise provided for in this division.

(b) The findings of the account with regard to the conditions in subdivision (a) shall not be evidence in any other proceeding.

(c) The account shall require the asbestos worker to submit to an independent medical examination unless the information and assistance officer, in consultation with the medical director or his or her designee, determines that there exists adequate medical evidence that the worker developed asbestosis from the employment.

ARTICLE 2
Benefits

§4407. Payments as advances.

When the account determines that the conditions in Section 4406 have occurred, payments as advances on workers' compensation asbestos workers' benefits shall be provided in accordance with this chapter, notwithstanding the right of the asbestos worker to secure compensation as otherwise provided for in this division.

§4407.3. Death benefit.

For purposes of this chapter, the death benefit shall be paid in installments in the same manner and amounts as temporary disability indemnity.

§4407.5. No lump-sum payment.

Benefits provided by this chapter shall not be commuted into a lump-sum payment.

§4408. Compensation procedures.

Prior to seeking compensation benefits under this chapter, the asbestos worker shall first make claim on the employer or its workers' compensation insurance carrier for payment of compensation under this division. If the asbestos worker is unable to locate the responsible employer or insurance carrier, or if the employer or insurance carrier fails to pay or denies liability for the compensation required by this division to the person entitled thereto, within a period of 30 days after the assertion of such a claim, the asbestos worker may seek payment of workers' compensation asbestos workers' benefits required by this division from the Asbestos Workers' Account.

§4409. Investigations and claims adjustment.

The Director of Industrial Relations, or his or her representative, shall assign investigative and claims adjustment services respecting matters concerning Asbestos Workers' Account cases. Those assignments may be made within the department, including the Division of Workers' Compensation, and excluding the State Compensation Insurance Fund. **Leg.H.** 1994 chs. 146, 1097.

§4409.5. Workers' compensation judges and support staff; appointment.

The administrative director shall appoint workers' compensation judges and support staff who shall give priority to the processing of the claims of asbestos workers.

Ref.: Hanna § 26.02[2].

§4410. Information and assistance officers; duties.

The administrative director shall appoint at least two information and assistance officers who shall give priority to assisting asbestos workers pursuant to the provisions of this chapter. The information and assistance officer shall assist to the fullest extent possible any asbestos worker seeking benefits under this chapter. In assisting the asbestos worker, the information and assistance officer shall conduct necessary investigation and procure those records, reports, and information which are necessary to the identification of responsible employers and insurance carriers, and to facilitate in the expediting of payments of benefits that may be due under this division.

Ref.: 8 C.C.R. §9928.1.

§4411. Claims against Account; responsible employer; Account as party; termination of benefits.

(a) When a claim is made against the Asbestos Workers' Account, the account shall secure appropriate information, adjust the claim, and pay benefits provided by this chapter in accordance with the provisions of this division.

(b) The asbestos worker shall, prior to the first payment of benefits by the Asbestos Workers' Account, file an application before the Workers' Compensation Appeals Board to determine the responsible employer for payment of compensation under this division.

(c) In every case before the Workers' Compensation Appeals Board in which a claim of injury from exposure to asbestos is alleged, the appeals board shall join the Asbestos Workers' Account as a party to the proceeding and serve the fund with copies of all decisions and orders including findings and awards, and order approving compromise and release.

(d) Once a decision establishing the responsible employer or insurance carrier is agreed upon between the parties, or is issued by the Workers' Compensation Appeals Board, and becomes final, the Asbestos Workers' Account shall terminate payment of compensation benefits, notify all interested parties accordingly, and seek collection as provided for under this chapter. Responsibility for payment of all future compensation benefits shall be in accordance with such agreement, order, or decision.

(e) The account shall terminate the payment of benefits to any employee who fails to cooperate fully in determining the responsible employer or insurance carrier.

(f) The Asbestos Workers' Account may, at any time, commence or join in proceedings before the Workers' Compensation Appeals Board by filing an application on its own behalf. In any case in which the Asbestos Workers' Account has been joined as a party or has filed an application on its own behalf, the Asbestos Workers' Account shall have all of the rights and privileges of a party applicant.

Ref.: Hanna § 30.10.

ARTICLE 3
Collections

§4412. Benefits paid and costs incurred; recovery.

The Asbestos Workers' Account shall take all reasonable and appropriate action to insure that recovery is made by the account for all moneys paid as compensation benefits and as costs.

In the event that the responsible employer is uninsured, the account shall not be entitled to reimbursement from the Uninsured Employers Fund.

§4413. Statutes of limitation under division inapplicable against account.

No limitation of time provided by this division shall run against the Asbestos Workers' Account to initiate proceedings before the Workers' Compensation Appeals Board when the account has made any payment of moneys, incurred any costs for services, or encumbered any liability of the account.

§4414. Liens filed by account.

Immediately following the receipt of knowledge of initiation of proceedings before the Workers' Compensation Appeals Board, or any other jurisdiction providing benefits for the same injury, the Asbestos Workers' Account shall file a lien and may invoke such other remedies as are available to recover moneys expended for compensation benefits.

§4415. Legal representation for Director of Industrial Relations.

In any hearing or proceeding, the Director of Industrial Relations may use attorneys from within the department, or the Attorney General, to represent the director and the state.

§4416. Responsible employer; notice of amount to satisfy lien; priority of lien.

Once an agreement as to the responsible employer is reached, or a decision is issued by the Workers' Compensation Appeals Board and becomes final, the Asbestos Workers' Account shall notify the responsible employer or insurance carrier of the amount of payment necessary to satisfy the lien in full. Full payment of the lien shall be made by the responsible employer or insurance carrier within 30 days of the issue of such notification. The account may grant a reasonable extension of time for payment of the lien beyond 30 days. This payment shall be for all moneys expended for compensation benefits, and for all recoverable costs including the cost of independent medical examination and all costs reasonably incidental thereto, including, but not limited to, costs of transportation, hospitalization, consultative evaluation, X-rays, laboratory tests, and other diagnostic procedures. The payment shall bear interest, as provided in Section 5800, from the date of the agreement or decision through the date of payment.

The lien of the Asbestos Workers' Account shall be allowed as a first lien against compensation, and shall have priority over all other liens. The lien of the Asbestos Workers' Account may not be reduced by the Workers' Compensation Appeals Board or by the parties unless express written consent to the proposed reduction of the lien is given by the Asbestos Workers' Account and is filed in the record of proceedings before the Workers' Compensation Appeals Board.

Ref.: Hanna § 30.10.

§4417. Suit against third party.

Nothing in this chapter shall be construed to preclude the filing by an asbestos worker of a claim or suit for damages or indemnity against any person other than his or her employer. The Asbestos Workers' Account shall be entitled to recover from, and shall have a first lien against any amount which is recoverable by the injured employee pursuant to civil judgment or settlement in relation to a claim for damages or indemnity for the effect of exposure to asbestos, for all compensation benefits paid to the injured employee by the Asbestos Workers' Account which have not previously been recovered from the responsible employer or employers by the Asbestos Workers' Account. Recovery by the Asbestos Workers' Account pursuant to the provisions of this section shall not have the effect of extinguishing or diminishing the liability of the responsible employer or employers to the injured employee for compensation payable under the provisions of this division.

Ref.: Herlick Handbook § 12.2.

§4418. Termination date of chapter; benefits under chapter.

The provisions of this chapter providing for the payment of workers' compensation asbestos workers' benefits from the Asbestos Workers' Account shall be operative only until January 1, 1989, and as of that date all payments from the fund shall be terminated, and the state shall have no further obligation to pay asbestos workers' benefits, unless a later enacted statute which is chaptered before January 1, 1989, deletes or extends that date. However, if no statute is enacted to delete or extend that date prior to January 1, 1989, the authority of the Asbestos Workers' Account under this chapter to recover the benefits and costs paid to asbestos workers prior to that date shall continue until the benefits and costs have been recovered.

Ref.: Hanna § 7.06; Herlick Handbook § 3.19.

PART 2
Computation of Compensation

CHAPTER 1
AVERAGE EARNINGS

§4451. "Average annual earnings."

Average annual earnings shall be taken as fifty-two times the average weekly earnings referred to in this chapter.

§4452. Minimum and maximum limits.

Four times the average annual earnings shall be taken at not less than four thousand eight hundred dollars and sixty-four cents ($4,800.64) nor more than fifteen thousand two hundred dollars and sixty-four cents ($15,200.64) in disability cases, and in death cases shall be taken at not less than the minimum nor more than the maximum limits as provided in section 4702 of this code.

§4452.5. "Permanent total disability"; "permanent partial disability."

As used in this division:

(a) "Permanent total disability" means a permanent disability with a rating of 100 percent permanent disability only.

(b) "Permanent partial disability" means a permanent disability with a rating of less than 100 percent permanent disability.

Ref.: Hanna § 6.01[2].

§4453. Computing average weekly earnings.

(a) In computing average annual earnings for the purposes of temporary disability indemnity and permanent total disability indemnity only, the average weekly earnings shall be taken at:

(1) Not less than one hundred twenty-six dollars ($126) nor more than two hundred ninety-four dollars ($294), for injuries occurring on or after January 1, 1983.

(2) Not less than one hundred sixty-eight dollars ($168) nor more than three hundred thirty-six dollars ($336), for injuries occurring on or after January 1, 1984.

(3) Not less than one hundred sixty-eight dollars ($168) for permanent total disability, and, for temporary disability, not less than the lesser of one hundred sixty-eight dollars ($168) or 1.5 times the employee's average weekly earnings from all employers, but in no event less than one hundred forty-seven dollars ($147), nor more than three hundred ninety-nine dollars ($399), for injuries occurring on or after January 1, 1990.

(4) Not less than one hundred sixty-eight dollars ($168) for permanent total disability, and for temporary disability, not less than the lesser of one hundred eighty-nine dollars ($189) or 1.5 times the employee's average weekly earnings from all employers, nor more than five hundred four dollars ($504), for injuries occurring on or after January 1, 1991.

(5) Not less than one hundred sixty-eight dollars ($168) for permanent total disability, and for temporary disability, not less than the lesser of one hundred eighty-nine dollars ($189) or 1.5 times the employee's average weekly earnings from all employers, nor more than six hundred nine dollars ($609), for injuries occurring on or after July 1, 1994.

(6) Not less than one hundred sixty-eight dollars ($168) for permanent total disability, and for temporary disability, not less than the lesser of one hundred eighty-nine dollars ($189) or 1.5 times the employee's average weekly earnings from all employers, nor more than six hundred seventy-two dollars ($672), for injuries occurring on or after July 1, 1995.

(7) Not less than one hundred sixty-eight dollars ($168) for permanent total disability, and for temporary disability, not less than the lesser of one hundred eighty-nine dollars ($189) or 1.5 times the employee's average weekly earnings from all employers, nor more than seven hundred thirty-five dollars ($735), for injuries occurring on or after July 1, 1996.

(8) Not less than one hundred eighty-nine dollars ($189), nor more than nine hundred three dollars ($903), for injuries occurring on or after January 1, 2003.

(9) Not less than one hundred eighty-nine dollars ($189), nor more than one thousand ninety-two dollars ($1,092), for injuries occurring on or after January 1, 2004.

(10) Not less than one hundred eighty-nine dollars ($189), nor more than one thousand two hundred sixty dollars ($1,260), for injuries occurring on or after January 1, 2005. For injuries occurring on or after January 1, 2006, average weekly earnings shall be taken at not less than one hundred eighty-nine dollars ($189), nor more than one thousand two hundred sixty dollars ($1,260) or 1.5 times the state average weekly wage, whichever is greater. Commencing on January 1, 2007, and each January 1 thereafter, the limits specified in this paragraph shall be increased by an amount equal to the percentage increase in the state average weekly wage as compared to the prior year. For purposes of this paragraph, "state average weekly wage" means the average weekly wage paid by employers to employees covered by unemployment insurance as reported by the United States Department of Labor for California for the 12 months ending March 31 of the calendar year preceding the year in which the injury occurred.

(b) In computing average annual earnings for purposes of permanent partial disability indemnity, except as provided in Section 4659, the average weekly earnings shall be taken at:

(1) Not less than seventy-five dollars ($75), nor more than one hundred ninety-five dollars ($195), for injuries occurring on or after January 1, 1983.

(2) Not less than one hundred five dollars ($105), nor more than two hundred ten dollars ($210), for injuries occurring on or after January 1, 1984.

(3) When the final adjusted permanent disability rating of the injured employee is 15 percent or greater, but not more than 24.75 percent: (A) not less than one hundred five dollars ($105), nor more than two hundred twenty-two dollars ($222), for injuries occurring on or after July 1,

1994; (B) not less than one hundred five dollars ($105), nor more than two hundred thirty-one dollars ($231), for injuries occurring on or after July 1, 1995; (C) not less than one hundred five dollars ($105), nor more than two hundred forty dollars ($240), for injuries occurring on or after July 1, 1996.

(4) When the final adjusted permanent disability rating of the injured employee is 25 percent or greater, not less than one hundred five dollars ($105), nor more than two hundred twenty-two dollars ($222), for injuries occurring on or after January 1, 1991.

(5) When the final adjusted permanent disability rating of the injured employee is 25 percent or greater but not more than 69.75 percent: (A) not less than one hundred five dollars ($105), nor more than two hundred thirty-seven dollars ($237), for injuries occurring on or after July 1, 1994; (B) not less than one hundred five dollars ($105), nor more than two hundred forty-six dollars ($246), for injuries occurring on or after July 1, 1995; and (C) not less than one hundred five dollars ($105), nor more than two hundred fifty-five dollars ($255), for injuries occurring on or after July 1, 1996.

(6) When the final adjusted permanent disability rating of the injured employee is less than 70 percent: (A) not less than one hundred fifty dollars ($150), nor more than two hundred seventy-seven dollars and fifty cents ($277.50), for injuries occurring on or after January 1, 2003; (B) not less than one hundred fifty-seven dollars and fifty cents ($157.50), nor more than three hundred dollars ($300), for injuries occurring on or after January 1, 2004; (C) not less than one hundred fifty-seven dollars and fifty cents ($157.50), nor more than three hundred thirty dollars ($330), for injuries occurring on or after January 1, 2005; and (D) not less than one hundred ninety-five dollars ($195), nor more than three hundred forty-five dollars ($345), for injuries occurring on or after January 1, 2006.

(7) When the final adjusted permanent disability rating of the injured employee is 70 percent or greater, but less than 100 percent: (A) not less than one hundred five dollars ($105), nor more than two hundred fifty-two dollars ($252), for injuries occurring on or after July 1, 1994; (B) not less than one hundred five dollars ($105), nor more than two hundred ninety-seven dollars ($297), for injuries occurring on or after July 1, 1995; (C) not less than one hundred five dollars ($105), nor more than three hundred forty-five dollars ($345), for injuries occurring on or after July 1, 1996; (D) not less than one hundred fifty dollars ($150), nor more than three hundred forty-five dollars ($345), for injuries occurring on or after January 1, 2003; (E) not less than one hundred fifty-seven dollars and fifty cents ($157.50), nor more than three hundred seventy-five dollars ($375), for injuries occurring on or after January 1, 2004; (F) not less than one hundred fifty-seven dollars and fifty cents ($157.50), nor more than four hundred five dollars ($405), for injuries occurring on or after January 1, 2005; and (G) not less than one hundred ninety-five dollars ($195), nor more than four hundred five dollars ($405), for injuries occurring on or after January 1, 2006.

(8) For injuries occurring on or after January 1, 2013:

(A) When the final adjusted permanent disability rating is less than 55 percent, not less than two hundred forty dollars ($240) nor more than three hundred forty-five dollars ($345).

(B) When the final adjusted permanent disability rating is 55 percent or greater but less than 70 percent, not less than two hundred forty dollars ($240) nor more than four hundred five dollars ($405).

(C) When the final adjusted permanent disability rating is 70 percent or greater but less than 100 percent, not less than two hundred forty dollars ($240) nor more than four hundred thirty-five dollars ($435).

(9) For injuries occurring on or after January 1, 2014, not less than two hundred forty dollars ($240) nor more than four hundred thirty-five dollars ($435).

(c) Between the limits specified in subdivisions (a) and (b), the average weekly earnings, except as provided in Sections 4456 to 4459, shall be arrived at as follows:

(1) Where the employment is for 30 or more hours a week and for five or more working days a week, the average weekly earnings shall be the number of working days a week times the daily earnings at the time of the injury.

(2) Where the employee is working for two or more employers at or about the time of the injury, the average weekly earnings shall be taken as the aggregate of these earnings from all employments computed in terms of one week; but the earnings from employments other than the employment in which the injury occurred shall not be taken at a higher rate than the hourly rate paid at the time of the injury.

(3) If the earnings are at an irregular rate, such as piecework, or on a commission basis, or are specified to be by week, month, or other period, then the average weekly earnings mentioned in subdivision (a) shall be taken as the actual weekly earnings averaged for this period of time, not exceeding one year, as may conveniently be taken to determine an average weekly rate of pay.

(4) Where the employment is for less than 30 hours per week, or where for any reason the foregoing methods of arriving at the average weekly earnings cannot reasonably and fairly be applied, the average weekly earnings shall be taken at 100 percent of the sum which reasonably represents the average weekly earning capacity of the injured employee at the time of his or her injury, due consideration being given to his or her actual earnings from all sources and employments.

(d) Every computation made pursuant to this section beginning January 1, 1990, shall be made only with reference to temporary disability or the permanent disability resulting from an original injury sustained after January 1, 1990. However, all rights existing under this section on January 1, 1990, shall be continued in force. Except as provided in Section 4661.5, disability indemnity benefits shall be calculated according to the limits in this section in effect on the date of injury and shall remain in effect for the duration of any disability resulting from the injury. **Leg.H.** 1993 ch. 121, effective July 16, 1993, 2002 chs. 6 (AB 749), 866 (AB 486), 2012 ch. 363 (SB 863) §34.

2012 Note: For legislative findings, declarations, and applicability of Stats. 2012 ch. 363, see the 2012 Notes following Lab C §62.5.

1993 Note: Section 4453, as amended by ch. 121, applies only to injuries occurring on or after January 1, 1994. Stats. 1993 ch. 121 §77.

Ref.: 8 C.C.R. §§10101, 10101.1, 10102, 10110, 10111, 10111.1, 10111.2; Hanna §§ 6.02[1], [2], 6.05[2], 7.04[1][a], [b], 8.08[4];

Herlick Handbook §§ 5.1–5.3, 5.5–5.8, 5.11, 6.10[4], 6.11[1], 6.12, 14.37.

§4453.5. Subsequent statutory changes in allowable indemnity.

Benefits payable on account of an injury shall not be affected by a subsequent statutory change in amounts of indemnity payable under this division, and shall be continued as authorized, and in the amounts provided for, by the law in effect at the time the injury giving rise to the right to such benefits occurred.

Ref.: Hanna § 32.04[1][b]; Herlick Handbook §§ 5.2, 5.8, 6.10[4].

§4454. Overtime and value of board and lodging; determination of average weekly earnings.

In determining average weekly earnings within the limits fixed in Section 4453, there shall be included overtime and the market value of board, lodging, fuel, and other advantages received by the injured employee as part of his remuneration, which can be estimated in money, but such average weekly earnings shall not include any sum which the employer pays to or for the injured employee to cover any special expenses entailed on the employee by the nature of his employment, nor shall there be included either the cost or the market value of any savings, wage continuation, wage replacement, or stock acquisition program or of any employee benefit programs for which the employer pays or contributes to persons other than the employee or his family.

Ref.: 8 C.C.R. §§10101, 10101.1, 10102, 10111, 10111.1, 10111.2; Hanna § 6.04[4]; Herlick Handbook § 5.3.

§4455. Injured employee under 18 years old; average weekly earnings.

If the injured employee is under 18 years of age, and his or her incapacity is permanent, his or her average weekly earnings shall be deemed, within the limits fixed in Section 4453, to be the weekly sum that under ordinary circumstances he or she would probably be able to earn at the age of 18 years, in the occupation in which he or she was employed at the time of the injury or in any occupation to which he or she would reasonably have been promoted if he or she had not been injured. If the probable earnings at the age of 18 years cannot reasonably be determined, his or her average weekly earnings shall be taken at the maximum limit established in Section 4453. **Leg.H.** 2001 ch. 159, 2002 ch. 6 (AB 749).

Ref.: Herlick Handbook § 5.7.

§4456. Injured employee engaged in unemployment work relief program conducted by State.

Where any employee is injured while engaged on any unemployment work relief program conducted by the State, or a political subdivision, or any State or governmental agency, the disability payments due under this division shall be determined solely on the monthly earnings or anticipated earnings of such person from such program, such payments to be within the minimum and maximum limits set forth in section 4453.

§4457. Workers under partnership agreement; average weekly earnings.

In the event the average weekly earnings of workers associating themselves under a partnership agreement, the principal purpose of which is the performance of labor on a particular piece of work, are not otherwise ascertainable, they shall be deemed to be forty dollars ($40).

Ref.: Hanna § 6.05[6]; Herlick Handbook § 5.3.

§4458. Active firefighter; average weekly earnings.

If a member registered as an active firefighting member of any regularly organized volunteer fire department as described in Section 3361 suffers injury or death while in the performance of his duty as a fireman, or if a person engaged in fire suppression as described in Section 3365 suffers injury or death while so engaged, then, irrespective of his remuneration from this or other employment or from both, his average weekly earnings for the purposes of determining temporary disability indemnity and permanent disability indemnity shall be taken at the maximum fixed for each, respectively, in Section 4453. Four times his average annual earnings in disability cases and in death cases shall be taken at the maximum limits provided in Sections 4452 and 4702 respectively.

Ref.: Herlick Handbook § 5.3.

§4458.2. Active police officer; average weekly earnings.

If an active peace officer of any department as described in Section 3362 suffers injury or death while in the performance of his or her duties as a peace officer, or if a person engaged in the performance of active law enforcement service as described in Section 3366 suffers injury or death while in the performance of that active law enforcement service, or if a person registered as a reserve peace officer of any regularly organized police or sheriff's department as described in Section 3362.5 suffers injury or death while in the performance of his or her duties as a peace officer, then, irrespective of his or her remuneration from this or other employment or from both, his or her average weekly earnings for the purposes of determining temporary disability indemnity and permanent disability indemnity shall be taken at the maximum fixed for each, respectively, in Section 4453. Four times his or her average annual earnings in disability cases and in death cases shall be taken at the maximum limits provided in Sections 4452 and 4702 respectively.

1989 Note: This section is applicable only to injuries occurring on or after January 1, 1990. Stats. 1989 ch. 893 §6.

§4458.5. Injury after termination of active service; average weekly earnings.

If a member suffers "an injury" following termination of active service, and within the time prescribed in Section 3212, 3212.2, 3212.3, 3212.4, 3212.5, 3212.6, 3212.7, or 3213, then, irrespective of his remuneration from any postactive service employment, his average weekly earnings for the purposes of determining temporary disability indemnity, permanent total disability indemnity, and permanent partial disability indemnity, shall be taken at the maximum fixed for each such disability, respectively, in Section 4453.

§4459. Previous disability and compensation; determination of average weekly earnings.

The fact that an employee has suffered a previous disability, or received compensation therefor, does not preclude him from compensation for a later injury, or his dependents from compensation for death resulting therefrom, but in determining compensation for the later injury, or death resulting therefrom, his average weekly earnings shall be fixed at the sum which reasonably represents his earning capacity at the time of the later injury.

CHAPTER 2
COMPENSATION SCHEDULES

ARTICLE 1
General Provisions

§4550. Payment of compensation by employer.

Where liability for compensation exists under this division, such compensation shall be furnished or paid by the employer and shall be as provided in this chapter.

Ref.: 8 C.C.R. §§10109, 10110, 10111, 10111.1, 10111.2, 10115, 10440, 10445.

§4551. Willful misconduct of injured employee.

Where the injury is caused by the serious and willful misconduct of the injured employee, the compensation otherwise recoverable therefor shall be reduced one-half, except:

(a) Where the injury results in death.

(b) Where the injury results in a permanent disability of 70 percent or over.

(c) Where the injury is caused by the failure of the employer to comply with any provision of law, or any safety order of the Division of Occupational Safety and Health, with reference to the safety of places of employment.

(d) Where the injured employee is under 16 years of age at the time of injury.

Ref.: 8 C.C.R. §§10440, 10445; Hanna §§ 10.02[2], 24.03[6][b]; Herlick Handbook §§ 9.6, 14.36.

§4552. Reduction of compensation; determination by appeals board.

The reduction of compensation because of the serious and willful misconduct of an employee is not enforceable, valid, or binding in any respect until the appeals board has so determined by its findings and award as provided in Chapter 6 of Part 4 of this division.

Ref.: 8 C.C.R. §§10440, 10445; Hanna § 31.20[3]; Herlick Handbook § 9.6.

§4553. Willful misconduct of employer.

The amount of compensation otherwise recoverable shall be increased one-half, together with costs and expenses not to exceed two hundred fifty dollars ($250), where the employee is injured by reason of the serious and willful misconduct of any of the following:

(a) The employer, or his managing representative.

(b) If the employer is a partnership, on the part of one of the partners or a managing representative or general superintendent thereof.

(c) If the employer is a corporation, on the part of an executive, managing officer, or general superintendent thereof.

Ref.: 8 C.C.R. §§10440, 10445; Hanna §§ 10.01[1][a], [b], [d], [e], [3], [4][b], 24.03[6][a]; Herlick Handbook §§ 9.6, 9.7, 12.10, 14.42.

§4553.1. Serious and willful misconduct; appeals board findings.

In order to support a holding of serious and willful misconduct by an employer based upon violation of a safety order, the appeals board must specifically find all of the following:

(1) The specific manner in which the order was violated.

(2) That the violation of the safety order did proximately cause the injury or death, and the specific manner in which the violation constituted the proximate cause.

(3) That the safety order, and the conditions making the safety order applicable, were known to, and violated by, a particular named person, either the employer, or a representative designated by Section 4553, or that the condition making the safety order applicable was obvious, created a probability of serious injury, and that the failure of the employer, or a representative designated by Section 4553, to correct the condition constituted a reckless disregard for the probable consequences.

Ref.: 8 C.C.R. §§10440, 10445; Hanna §§ 10.03, 25.05[4], 25.10[7]; Herlick Handbook §§ 9.7, 14.36.

§4554. Employer's willful failure to secure payment of compensation.

In case of the willful failure by an employer to secure the payment of compensation, the amount of compensation otherwise recoverable for injury or death as provided in this division shall be increased 10 percent. Failure of the employer to secure the payment of compensation as provided in Article 1 (commencing at Section 3700) of Chapter 4 of Part 1 of this division is prima facie evidence of willfulness on his part.

Ref.: Hanna §§ 2.17, 10.24[5], 10.25, 11.02[4][a].

§4555. Employer's failure to secure payment of compensation; attorney's fees.

In case of failure by an employer to secure the payment of compensation, the appeals board may award a reasonable attorney's fee in addition to the amount of compensation recoverable. When a fee is awarded under this section no further fee shall be allowed under Section 4903 but the provisions of Section 4903 shall be applicable to secure the payment of any fee awarded under this section.

Ref.: Hanna §§ 10.24[6], 20.02[2][f]; Herlick Handbook §§ 9.2, 10.09[5], 14.42.

§4555.5. Denial of petition to reduce award.

Whenever a petition to reduce an award, based upon a permanent disability rating which has become final, is denied, the appeals board may order the petitioner to pay to the injured employee all costs incident to the furnishing of X-rays, laboratory services, medical reports, and medical testimony incurred by such employee in connection with the proceeding on such petition.

Ref.: Herlick Handbook § 9.13.

§4556. Increases unaffected by maximums for computation of average earnings.

The increases provided for by this article shall not be limited by the provisions of Chapter 1 of this part relating to maximum amounts in the computation of average earnings.

§4557. Injury to illegally employed person under 16.

Where the injury is to an employee under 16 years of age and illegally employed at the time of injury, the entire compensation otherwise recoverable shall be increased fifty percent (50%), and such additional sum shall be paid by the employer at the same time and in the same manner as the normal compensation benefits.

An employer shall not be held liable for the additional compensation provided by this section if such an employee is hired pursuant to a birth certificate, automobile driver's license, or other reasonable evidence of the fact that the employee is over the age of 15 years, even though such evidence of the age were falsely obtained by the employee. The additional compensation provided by this section shall not exceed the maximum sum specified by Section 4553 for additional compensation payable for serious and willful misconduct on the part of an employer. This section shall not apply to the State or any of its political subdivisions or districts.

Note: See Insurance Code §11661.5.

§4558. Definitions; employee's action against employer; injury from absence of power press guard.

(a) As used in this section:

(1) "Employer" means a named identifiable person who is, prior to the time of the employee's injury or death, an owner or supervisor having managerial authority to direct and control the acts of employees.

(2) "Failure to install" means omitting to attach a point of operation guard either provided or required by the manufacturer, when the attachment is required by the manufacturer and made known by him or her to the employer at the time of acquisition, installation, or manufacturer-required modification of the power press.

(3) "Manufacturer" means the designer, fabricator, or assembler of a power press.

(4) "Power press" means any material-forming machine that utilizes a die which is designed for use in the manufacture of other products.

(5) "Removal" means physical removal of a point of operation guard which is either installed by the manufacturer or installed by the employer pursuant to the requirements or instructions of the manufacturer.

(6) "Specifically authorized" means an affirmative instruction issued by the employer prior to the time of the employee's physical injury or death, but shall not mean any subsequent acquiescence in, or ratification of, removal of a point of operation safety guard.

(b) An employee, or his or her dependents in the event of the employee's death, may bring an action at law for damages against the employer where the employee's injury or death is proximately caused by the employer's knowing removal of, or knowing failure to install, a point of operation guard on a power press, and this removal or failure to install is specifically authorized by the employer under conditions known by the employer to create a probability of serious injury or death.

(c) No liability shall arise under this section absent proof that the manufacturer designed, installed, required, or otherwise provided by specification for the attachment of the guards and conveyed knowledge of the same to the employer. Proof of conveyance of this information to the employer by the manufacturer may come from any source.

(d) No right of action for contribution or indemnity by any defendant shall exist against the employer; however, a defendant may seek contribution after the employee secures a judgment against the employer pursuant to the provisions of this section if the employer fails to discharge his or her comparative share of the judgment.

Ref.: Hanna §§ 11.02[5][a]–[c], [e], [f], 21.05[3][d]; Herlick Handbook §§ 12.8, 12.11, 13.3.

ARTICLE 2
Medical and Hospital Treatment

§4600. Medical treatment provided by employer; liability for reasonable expense; medical provider network; predesignation of personal physician; expenses incurred in submitting to examination; qualified interpreter.

(a) Medical, surgical, chiropractic, acupuncture, and hospital treatment, including nursing, medicines, medical and surgical supplies, crutches, and apparatuses, including orthotic and prosthetic devices and services, that is reasonably required to cure or relieve the injured worker from the effects of the worker's injury shall be provided by the employer. In the case of the employer's neglect or refusal reasonably to do so, the employer is liable for the reasonable expense incurred by or on behalf of the employee in providing treatment.

(b) As used in this division and notwithstanding any other law, medical treatment that is reasonably required to cure or relieve the injured worker from the effects of the worker's injury means treatment that is based upon the guidelines adopted by the administrative director pursuant to Section 5307.27.

(c) Unless the employer or the employer's insurer has established or contracted with a medical provider network as provided for in Section 4616, after 30 days from the date the injury is reported, the employee may be treated by a physician of the employee's own choice or at a facility of the employee's own choice within a reasonable geographic area. A chiropractor shall not be a treating physician after the employee has received the maximum number of chiropractic visits allowed by subdivision (c) of Section 4604.5.

(d)(1) If an employee has notified the employee's employer in writing prior to the date of injury that the employee has a personal physician, the employee shall have the right to be treated by that physician from the date of injury if the employee has health care coverage for nonoccupational injuries or illnesses on the date of injury in a plan, policy, or fund as described in subdivisions (b), (c), and (d) of Section 4616.7.

(2) For purposes of paragraph (1), a personal physician shall meet all of the following conditions:

(A) Be the employee's regular physician and surgeon, licensed pursuant to Chapter 5 (commencing with Section 2000) of Division 2 of the Business and Professions Code.

(B) Be the employee's primary care physician and has previously directed the medical treatment of the employee, and who retains the employee's medical records, including the employee's medical history. "Personal physician" includes a medical group, if the medical group is a single corporation or partnership composed of licensed doctors of medicine or osteopathy, which operates an integrated multispecialty medical group providing comprehensive medical services predominantly for nonoccupational illnesses and injuries.

(C) The physician agrees to be predesignated.

(3) If the employee has health care coverage for nonoccupational injuries or illnesses on the date of injury in a health care service plan licensed pursuant to Chapter 2.2 (commencing with Section 1340) of Division 2 of the Health and Safety Code, and the employer is notified pursuant to paragraph (1), all medical treatment, utilization review of medical treatment, access to medical treatment, and other medical treatment issues shall be governed by Chapter 2.2 (commencing with Section 1340) of Division 2 of the Health and Safety Code. Disputes regarding the provision of medical treatment shall be resolved pursuant to Article 5.55 (commencing with Section 1374.30) of Chapter 2.2 of Division 2 of the Health and Safety Code.

(4) If the employee has health care coverage for nonoccupational injuries or illnesses on the date of injury in a group health insurance policy as described in Section 4616.7, all medical treatment, utilization review of medical treatment, access to medical treatment, and other medical treatment issues shall be governed by the applicable provisions of the Insurance Code.

(5) The insurer may require prior authorization of any nonemergency treatment or diagnostic service and may conduct reasonably necessary utilization review pursuant to Section 4610.

(6) An employee is entitled to all medically appropriate referrals by the personal physician to other physicians or medical providers within the nonoccupational health care plan. An employee is entitled to treatment by physicians or other medical providers outside of the nonoccupational health care plan pursuant to standards established in Article 5 (commencing with Section 1367) of Chapter 2.2 of Division 2 of the Health and Safety Code.

(e)(1) When at the request of the employer, the employer's insurer, the administrative director, the appeals board, or a workers' compensation administrative law judge, the employee submits to examination by a physician, the employee is entitled to receive, in addition to all other benefits herein provided, all reasonable expenses of transportation, meals, and lodging incident to reporting for the examination, together with one day of temporary disability indemnity for each day of wages lost in submitting to the examination.

(2) Regardless of the date of injury, "reasonable expenses of transportation" includes mileage fees from the employee's home to the place of the examination and back at the rate of twenty-one cents ($0.21) a mile or the mileage rate adopted by the Director of Human Resources pursuant to Section 19820 of the Government Code, whichever is higher, plus any bridge tolls. The mileage and tolls shall be paid to the employee at the time the employee is given notification of the time and place of the examination.

(f) When at the request of the employer, the employer's insurer, the administrative director, the appeals board, or a workers' compensation administrative law judge, an employee submits to examination by a physician and the employee does not proficiently speak or understand the English language, the employee shall be entitled to the services of a qualified interpreter in accordance with conditions and a fee schedule prescribed by the administrative director. These services shall be provided by the employer. For purposes of this section, "qualified interpreter" means a language interpreter certified, or deemed certified, pursuant to Article 8 (commencing with Section 11435.05) of Chapter 4.5 of Part 1 of Division 3 of Title 2 of, or Section 68566 of, the Government Code.

(g) If the injured employee cannot effectively communicate with the employee's treating physician because the employee cannot proficiently speak or understand the English language, the injured employee is entitled to the services of a qualified interpreter during medical treatment appointments. To be a qualified interpreter for purposes of medical treatment appointments, an interpreter is not required to meet the requirements of subdivision (f), but shall meet any requirements established by rule by the administrative director that are substantially similar to the requirements set forth in Section 1367.04 of the Health and Safety Code. The administrative director shall adopt a fee schedule for qualified interpreter fees in accordance with this section. Upon request of the injured employee, the employer or insurance carrier shall pay for interpreter services. An employer shall not be required to pay for the services of an interpreter who is not certified or is provisionally certified by the person conducting the medical treatment or examination unless either the employer consents in advance to the selection of the individual who provides the interpreting service or the injured worker requires interpreting service in a language other than the languages designated pursuant to Section 11435.40 of the Government Code.

(h) Home health care services shall be provided as medical treatment only if reasonably required to cure or relieve the injured employee from the effects of the employee's injury and prescribed by a physician and surgeon licensed pursuant to Chapter 5 (commencing with Section 2000) of Division 2 of the Business and Professions Code, and subject to Section 5307.1 or 5307.8. The employer is not liable for home health care services that are provided more than 14 days prior to the date of the employer's receipt of the physician's prescription. **Leg.H.** 2009 ch. 565 (SB 186) §2, see this section as modified in Governor's Reorganization Plan No. 1 §199 of 2011, 2012 chs. 363 (SB 863) §35, 665 (SB 1308) §179 (ch. 363 prevails; ch. 665 not effective), 2013 ch. 793 (AB 1376) §1, effective October 13, 2013, 2014 chs. 71 (SB 1304) §111, 217 (AB 2732) §1, 2019 ch. 497 (AB 991) §188.

2012 Note: For legislative findings, declarations, and applicability of Stats. 2012 ch. 363, see the 2012 Notes following Lab C §62.5.

2011 Note: 2011 Governor's Reorganization Plan No. 1 was submitted to the Legislature on June 9, 2011, and became effective September 9, 2011, pursuant to Gov C §12080.5, and substantively operative July 1, 2012.

Ref.: 8 C.C.R. §§9771, 9773, 9773.1, 9774, 9775, 9777, 9778, 9779, 9779.1, 9779.2, 9779.3, 9779.4, 9779.45, 9779.5, 9779.8, 9779.9, 9785, 9785.2, 9785.3, 9785.4, 9786, 9786.1, 9787, 9788.01, 9788.1, 9788.11, 9788.2, 9788.3, 9788.31, 9788.32, 9788.4, 9788.45, 9788.5, 9788.6, 9788.7, 9788.8, 9788.9, 9788.91, 9789.10, 9789.11, 9789.20, 9789.21, 9789.22, 9789.24, 9789.30, 9789.31, 9789.32, 9789.33, 9789.34, 9789.35, 9789.36, 9789.37, 9789.38, 9789.40, 9789.50, 9789.60, 9789.70, 9789.110, 9789.111, 9790, 9790.1, 9791, 9791.1, 9792, 9792.1, 9792.6, 9792.7, 9792.8, 9792.9, 9792.10, 9795.1, 9795.2, 9795.3, 9795.4, 9880, 9881, 10101, 10101.1, 10102, 10108, 10109, 10110, 10111, 10111.1, 10111.2, 10115, 10118.1, 10564, 10606, 10608, 10616, 10618, 10626, 10727, 10950; Hanna §§ 5.02[1], [3], 5.03[4], 5.05[1], [6][b], [7][a], 22.02[1], 23.13[3]; Herlick Handbook §§ 4.01[3], [4], 4.03[1], 4.05[1], [3], 4.06[1], [3], [4], [5], [7], 4.07[2], 4.08[1], 4.14[1], 4.17[2], 10.01[2], 10.08[1], [3], 14.22, 14.26, 14.33, 15.6.

§4600.05. Immediate support from nurse case manager for employees injured by act of domestic terrorism; applicability; regulations.

(a) An employer, as defined in Section 3300, shall provide immediate support from a nurse case manager for employees injured by an act of domestic terrorism, as defined in Section 2331 of Title 18 of the United States Code, whose injuries arise out of and in the course of employment, to assist injured employees in obtaining medically necessary medical treatment, as defined by the medical treatment utilization schedule adopted pursuant to Section 5307.27, and to assist providers of medical services in seeking authorization of medical treatment.

(b)(1) This section shall apply only if the Governor has declared a state of emergency pursuant to subdivision (b) of Section 8558 of the Government Code in connection with the act of domestic terrorism.

(2) Upon the issuance of a declaration pursuant to paragraph (1), an employer that has been notified of a claim for compensation arising out of the acts that resulted in the declaration shall provide a notice within three days to the claimant advising the claimant of medically necessary services provided pursuant to subdivision (a). In the case of a claim for compensation subject to this section that is filed after the declaration, the employer shall provide the notice to the claimant within three days. The notice shall be in the form adopted by the administrative director pursuant to subdivision (d).

(c) This section shall not alter the conditions for compensability of an injury, as described in Sections 3208.3 and 3600.

(d) The administrative director shall adopt regulations to implement this section, including, but not limited to, the definition of a nurse case manager's qualifications, the scope and timing of immediate support from a nurse case manager, and the contents of the notice that employers shall provide to claimants. **Leg.H.** 2017 ch. 736 (AB 44) §2.

2017 Note: The Legislature finds and declares all of the following:

(a) Acts of domestic terrorism, such as the December 2, 2015, attack on the Inland Regional Center in San Bernardino, with the number and severity of the injuries inflicted upon people at work, can present unique issues for the workers' compensation system.

(b) Victims of acts of domestic terrorism, as defined by Section 2331 of Title 18 of the United States Code, whose injuries arise out of and in the course of employment, are entitled to the full benefits of the workers' compensation laws of this state, including medically necessary medical treatment, as defined by the medical treatment utilization schedule, for all accepted, diagnosed, physical and mental injuries, which may include counseling or other mental health services.

(c) Treatment provided to all injured workers, including mental health treatment and counseling services for psychological injuries and post-traumatic stress disorder, is provided by health care providers who are trained and qualified to treat those injuries, and providers who are not competent on the basis of training and experience to treat specific patients referred to the provider have a duty under existing law to refer the patient to a qualified provider.

(d) Because of the unique circumstances surrounding the number and severity of injuries that can be caused by a single act of domestic terrorism, and the extent to which the needs to provide this treatment quickly and comprehensively in potentially small service markets, it is appropriate to provide workers with injuries that result from an act of domestic terrorism with additional advocacy services, as provided by this bill. Stats. 2017 ch. 736 (AB 44) §1.

Ref.: Hanna § 5.04[6][a].

§4600.1. Dispensing generic drug equivalent.

(a) Subject to subdivision (b), any person or entity that dispenses medicines and medical supplies, as required by Section 4600, shall dispense the generic drug equivalent.

(b) A person or entity is not required to dispense a generic drug equivalent under either of the following circumstances:

(1) When a generic drug equivalent is unavailable.

(2) When the prescribing physician specifically provides in writing that a nongeneric drug must be dispensed.

(c) For purposes of this section, "dispense" has the same meaning as the definition contained in Section 4024 of the Business and Professions Code.

(d) Nothing in this section shall be construed to preclude a prescribing physician, who is also the dispensing physician, from dispensing a generic drug equivalent.

(e) This section shall only apply to medicines dispensed prior to the operative date of the drug formulary adopted pursuant to Section 5307.27. **Leg.H.** 2003 ch. 639 (SB 228) §24, 2015 ch. 525 (AB 1124) §2.

2015 Note: It is the intent of the Legislature that the Administrative Director of the Division of Workers' Compensation create an evidence-based drug formulary, with the maximum transparency possible, for use in the workers' compensation system, and that the formulary include the following in addition to the provisions of this act:

(a) Evidence-based guidelines for access to appropriate medications pursuant to pain management prescription drug therapies.

(b) Guidance regarding how an injured worker may access off-label use of prescription drugs, when evidenced-based and medically necessary.

(c) Use of generic or generic-equivalent drugs in the formulary pursuant to evidence-based practices, with consideration being given to use of brand name medication when its use is cost-effective, medically necessary, and evidence-based.

(d) The drug formulary shall not apply to care provided in an emergency department or inpatient setting.

(e) Guidance on the use of the formulary to further the goal of providing appropriate medications expeditiously while minimizing administrative burden and associated administrative costs. Stats. 2015 ch. 525 (AB 1124) §1.

Ref.: Hanna § 5.02[8]; Herlick Handbook §§ 4.06[4], 10.01[2].

§4600.2. Continuing availability of medicines and medical supplies to injured employees.

(a) Notwithstanding Section 4600, if a self-insured employer, group of self-insured employers, insurer of an employer, or group of insurers contracts with a pharmacy, group of pharmacies, or pharmacy benefit network to provide medicines and medical supplies required by this article to be provided to injured employees, those injured employees that are subject to the contract shall be provided medicines and medical supplies in the manner prescribed in the contract for as long as medicines or medical supplies are reasonably required to cure or relieve the injured employee from the effects of the injury. Medicines provided pursuant to the contract shall be subject to the drug formulary adopted by the administrative director pursuant to Section 5307.27, and such contracts may not limit the availability of medications otherwise prescribed pursuant to the formulary based on whether the pharmacy services are provided within or outside a medical provider network.

(b) Nothing in this section shall affect the ability of employee-selected physicians to continue to prescribe and have the employer provide medicines subject to the drug formulary and medical supplies that the physicians deem reasonably required to cure or relieve the injured employee from the effects of the injury.

(c) Each contract described in subdivision (a) shall comply with standards adopted by the administrative director. In adopting those standards, the administrative director shall seek to reduce pharmaceutical costs and may consult any relevant studies or practices in other states. The standards shall provide for access to a pharmacy within a reasonable geographic distance from an injured employee's residence. **Leg.H.** 2002 ch. 6 (AB 749), 2015 ch. 525 (AB 1124) §3.

2015 Note: For legislative intent, see the 2015 Note following Lab C §4600.1.

Ref.: Hanna § 5.02[8]; Herlick Handbook § 10.01[2].

§4600.3. Employee to choose health care provider; health care organization contract—Standards; payment for services; option to switch health care provider.

(a)(1) Notwithstanding Section 4600, when a self-insured employer, group of self-insured employers, or the insurer of an employer contracts with a health care organization certified pursuant to Section 4600.5 for health care services required by this article to be provided to injured employees, those employees who are subject to the contract shall receive medical services in the manner prescribed in the contract, providing that the employee may choose to be treated by a personal physician, personal chiropractor, or personal acupuncturist that he or she has designated prior to the injury, in which case the employee shall not be treated by the health care organization. Every employee shall be given an affirmative choice at the time of employment and at least annually thereafter to designate or change the designation of a health care organization or a personal physician, personal chiropractor, or personal acupuncturist. The choice shall be memorialized in writing and maintained in the employee's personnel records. The employee who has designated a personal physician, personal chiropractor, or personal acupuncturist may change their designated caregiver at any time prior to the injury. Any employee who fails to designate a personal physician, personal chiropractor, or personal acupuncturist shall be treated by the health care organization selected by the employer. If the health care organization offered by the employer is the workers' compensation insurer that covers the employee or is an entity that controls or is controlled by that insurer, as defined by Section 1215 of the Insurance Code, this information shall be included in the notice of contract with a health care organization.

(2) Each contract described in paragraph (1) shall comply with the certification standards provided in Section 4600.5, and shall provide all medical, surgical, chiropractic, acupuncture, and hospital treatment, including nursing, medicines, medical and surgical supplies, crutches, and apparatus, including artificial members, that is reasonably required to cure or relieve the effects of the injury, as required by this division, without any payment by the employee of deductibles, copayments, or any share of the premium. However, an employee may receive immediate emergency medical treatment that is compensable from a medical service or health care provider who is not a member of the health care organization.

(3) Insured employers, a group of self-insured employers, or self-insured employers who contract with a health care organization for medical services shall give notice to employees of eligible medical service providers and any other information regarding the contract and manner of receiving medical services as the administrative director may prescribe. Employees shall be duly notified that if they choose to receive care from the health care organization they must receive treatment for all occupational injuries and illnesses as prescribed by this section.

(b) Notwithstanding subdivision (a), no employer which is required to bargain with an exclusive or certified bargaining agent which represents employees of the employer in accordance with state or federal employer-employee relations law shall contract with a health care

Labor

organization for purposes of Section 4600.5 with regard to employees whom the bargaining agent is recognized or certified to represent for collective bargaining purposes pursuant to state or federal employer-employee relations law unless authorized to do so by mutual agreement between the bargaining agent and the employer. If the collective bargaining agreement is subject to the National Labor Relations Act, the employer may contract with a health care organization for purposes of Section 4600.5 at any time when the employer and bargaining agent have bargained to impasse to the extent required by federal law.

(c)(1) When an employee is not receiving or is not eligible to receive health care coverage for nonoccupational injuries or illnesses provided by the employer, if 90 days from the date the injury is reported the employee who has been receiving treatment from a health care organization or his or her physician, chiropractor, acupuncturist, or other agent notifies his or her employer in writing that he or she desires to stop treatment by the health care organization, he or she shall have the right to be treated by a physician, chiropractor, or acupuncturist or at a facility of his or her own choosing within a reasonable geographic area.

(2) When an employee is receiving or is eligible to receive health care coverage for nonoccupational injuries or illnesses provided by the employer, and has agreed to receive care for occupational injuries and illnesses from a health care organization provided by the employer, the employee may be treated for occupational injuries and diseases by a physician, chiropractor, or acupuncturist of his or her own choice or at a facility of his or her own choice within a reasonable geographic area if the employee or his or her physician, chiropractor, acupuncturist, or other agent notifies his or her employer in writing only after 180 days from the date the injury was reported, or upon the date of contract renewal or open enrollment of the health care organization, whichever occurs first, but in no case until 90 days from the date the injury was reported.

(3) For purposes of this subdivision, an employer shall be deemed to provide health care coverage for nonoccupational injuries and illnesses if the employer pays more than one-half the costs of the coverage, or if the plan is established pursuant to collective bargaining.

(d) An employee and employer may agree to other forms of therapy pursuant to Section 3209.7.

(e) An employee enrolled in a health care organization shall have the right to no less than one change of physician on request, and shall be given a choice of physicians affiliated with the health care organization. The health care organization shall provide the employee a choice of participating physicians within five days of receiving a request. In addition, the employee shall have the right to a second opinion from a participating physician on a matter pertaining to diagnosis or treatment from a participating physician.

(f) Nothing in this section or Section 4600.5 shall be construed to prohibit a self-insured employer, a group of self-insured employers, or insurer from engaging in any activities permitted by Section 4600.

(g) Notwithstanding subdivision (c), in the event that the employer, group of employers, or the employer's workers' compensation insurer no longer contracts with the health care organization that has been treating an injured employee, the employee may continue treatment provided or arranged by the health care organization. If the employee does not choose to continue treatment by the health care organization, the employer may control the employee's treatment for 30 days from the date the injury was reported. After that period, the employee may be treated by a physician of his or her own choice or at a facility of his or her own choice within a reasonable geographic area. **Leg.H.** 1993 ch. 121, effective July 16, 1993, ch. 1242, 1998 chs. 440, 485 (ch. 440 prevails; ch. 485 not effective), 2002 ch. 6 (AB 749).

1993 Note: Section 4600.3, as added by ch. 121, applies only to injuries occurring on or after January 1, 1994. Stats. 1993 ch. 121 §77.

Ref.: 8 C.C.R. §§9771.1, 9771.2, 9771.6, 9771.60, 9771.61, 9771.62, 9771.63, 9771.64, 9771.65, 9771.66, 9771.67, 9771.68, 9771.69, 9771.70, 9771.71, 9771.72, 9771.73, 9771.74, 9771.75, 9771.76, 9771.77, 9771.78, 9771.79, 9771.80, 9771.81, 9771.82, 9771.83, 9779.3, 9779.45, 9785; Hanna § 22.01[6]; Herlick Handbook §§ 4.08[1], 4.12, 10.01[2].

§4600.35. Licensing requirements for entities seeking to reimburse health care providers.

Any entity seeking to reimburse health care providers for health care services rendered to injured workers on a capitated, or per person per month basis, shall be licensed pursuant to the Knox-Keene Health Care Service Plan Act of 1975 (Chapter 2.2 (commencing with Section 1340) of Division 2 of the Health and Safety Code). **Leg.H.** 2002 ch. 6 (AB 749).

Ref.: Herlick Handbook § 10.01[2].

§4600.4. Availability during normal business day.

(a) A workers' compensation insurer, third-party administrator, or other entity that requires, or pursuant to regulation requires, a treating physician to obtain either utilization review or prior authorization in order to diagnose or treat injuries or diseases compensable under this article, shall ensure the availability of those services from 9 a.m. to 5:30 p.m. Pacific standard time of each normal business day.

(b) For purposes of this article, "normal business day" does not include Saturday, Sunday, or any day that is declared by the Governor to be an official state holiday or a holiday listed on the Department of Human Resources internet website. **Leg.H.** 1999 ch. 124, 2019 ch. 647 (SB 537) §4.

Ref.: 8 C.C.R. §§9792.6, 9792.7, 9792.8, 9792.9, 9792.10; Hanna § 22.05[6][c][iii]; Herlick Handbook § 10.01[2].

§4600.5. Application for certification as health care organization; application fee; certification requirements for health care service plan, disability insurer, workers' compensation insurer, third-party administrator, workers' compensation health care provider and other entities; claimant's medical treatment records; health care service plan charges; limitations and allowances of act; grounds for refusal, revocation or suspension of certification; provision and regulation of chiropractic care, acupuncture treatment; individual patient information.

(a) Any health care service plan licensed pursuant to the Knox-Keene Health Care Service Plan Act, a disability insurer licensed by the Department of Insurance, or any entity, including, but not limited to, workers' compensation insurers and third-party administrators authorized by the administrative director under subdivision (e), may make written application to the administrative director to become certified as a health care organization to provide health care to injured employees for injuries and diseases compensable under this article.

(b) Each application for certification shall be accompanied by a reasonable fee prescribed by the administrative director, sufficient to cover the actual cost of processing the application. A certificate is valid for the period that the director may prescribe unless sooner revoked or suspended.

(c) If the health care organization is a health care service plan licensed pursuant to the Knox-Keene Health Care Service Plan Act, and has provided the Managed Care Unit of the Division of Workers' Compensation with the necessary documentation to comply with this subdivision, that organization shall be deemed to be a health care organization able to provide health care pursuant to Section 4600.3, without further application duplicating the documentation already filed with the Department of Managed Health Care. These plans shall be required to remain in good standing with the Department of Managed Health Care, and shall meet the following additional requirements:

(1) Proposes to provide all medical and health care services that may be required by this article.

(2) Provides a program involving cooperative efforts by the employees, the employer, and the health plan to promote workplace health and safety, consultative and other services, and early return to work for injured employees.

(3) Proposes a timely and accurate method to meet the requirements set forth by the administrative director for all carriers of workers' compensation coverage to report necessary information regarding medical and health care service cost and utilization, rates of return to work, average time in medical treatment, and other measures as determined by the administrative director to enable the director to determine the effectiveness of the plan.

(4) Agrees to provide the administrative director with information, reports, and records prepared and submitted to the Department of Managed Health Care in compliance with the Knox-Keene Health Care Service Plan Act, relating to financial solvency, provider accessibility, peer review, utilization review, and quality assurance, upon request, if the administrative director determines the information is necessary to verify that the plan is providing medical treatment to injured employees in compliance with the requirements of this code.

Disclosure of peer review proceedings and records to the administrative director shall not alter the status of the proceedings or records as privileged and confidential communications pursuant to Sections 1370 and 1370.1 of the Health and Safety Code.

(5) Demonstrates the capability to provide occupational medicine and related disciplines.

(6) Complies with any other requirement the administrative director determines is necessary to provide medical services to injured employees consistent with the intent of this article, including, but not limited to, a written patient grievance policy.

(d) If the health care organization is a disability insurer licensed by the Department of Insurance, and is in compliance with subdivision (d) of Sections 10133 and 10133.5 of the Insurance Code, the administrative director shall certify the organization to provide health care pursuant to Section 4600.3 if the director finds that the plan is in good standing with the Department of Insurance and meets the following additional requirements:

(1) Proposes to provide all medical and health care services that may be required by this article.

(2) Provides a program involving cooperative efforts by the employees, the employer, and the health plan to promote workplace health and safety, consultative and other services, and early return to work for injured employees.

(3) Proposes a timely and accurate method to meet the requirements set forth by the administrative director for all carriers of workers' compensation coverage to report necessary information regarding medical and health care service cost and utilization, rates of return to work, average time in medical treatment, and other measures as determined by the administrative director to enable the director to determine the effectiveness of the plan.

(4) Agrees to provide the administrative director with information, reports, and records prepared and submitted to the Department of Insurance in compliance with the Insurance Code relating to financial solvency, provider accessibility, peer review, utilization review, and quality assurance, upon request, if the administrative director determines the information is necessary to verify that the plan is providing medical treatment to injured employees consistent with the intent of this article.

Disclosure of peer review proceedings and records to the administrative director shall not alter the status of the proceedings or records as privileged and confidential communications pursuant to subdivision (d) of Section 10133 of the Insurance Code.

(5) Demonstrates the capability to provide occupational medicine and related disciplines.

(6) Complies with any other requirement the administrative director determines is necessary to provide medical services to injured employees consistent with the intent of this article, including, but not limited to, a written patient grievance policy.

(e) If the health care organization is a workers' compensation insurer, third-party administrator, or any other entity that the administrative director determines meets the requirements of Section 4600.6, the administrative director shall certify the organization to provide health care pursuant to Section 4600.3 if the director finds that it meets the following additional requirements:

(1) Proposes to provide all medical and health care services that may be required by this article.

(2) Provides a program involving cooperative efforts by the employees, the employer, and the health plan to promote workplace health and safety, consultative and other services, and early return to work for injured employees.

(3) Proposes a timely and accurate method to meet the requirements set forth by the administrative director for all carriers of workers' compensation coverage to report necessary information regarding medical and health care

service cost and utilization, rates of return to work, average time in medical treatment, and other measures as determined by the administrative director to enable the director to determine the effectiveness of the plan.

(4) Agrees to provide the administrative director with information, reports, and records relating to provider accessibility, peer review, utilization review, quality assurance, advertising, disclosure, medical and financial audits, and grievance systems, upon request, if the administrative director determines the information is necessary to verify that the plan is providing medical treatment to injured employees consistent with the intent of this article.

Disclosure of peer review proceedings and records to the administrative director shall not alter the status of the proceedings or records as privileged and confidential communications pursuant to subdivision (d) of Section 10133 of the Insurance Code.

(5) Demonstrates the capability to provide occupational medicine and related disciplines.

(6) Complies with any other requirement the administrative director determines is necessary to provide medical services to injured employees consistent with the intent of this article, including, but not limited to, a written patient grievance policy.

(7) Complies with the following requirements:

(A) An organization certified by the administrative director under this subdivision may not provide or undertake to arrange for the provision of health care to employees, or to pay for or to reimburse any part of the cost of that health care in return for a prepaid or periodic charge paid by or on behalf of those employees.

(B) Every organization certified under this subdivision shall operate on a fee-for-service basis. As used in this section, fee for service refers to the situation where the amount of reimbursement paid by the employer to the organization or providers of health care is determined by the amount and type of health care rendered by the organization or provider of health care.

(C) An organization certified under this subdivision is prohibited from assuming risk.

(f)(1) A workers' compensation health care provider organization authorized by the Department of Business Oversight on December 31, 1997, shall be eligible for certification as a health care organization under subdivision (e).

(2) An entity that had, on December 31, 1997, submitted an application with the Commissioner of Business Oversight under Part 3.2 (commencing with Section 5150) shall be considered an applicant for certification under subdivision (e) and shall be entitled to priority in consideration of its application. The Commissioner of Business Oversight shall provide complete files for all pending applications to the administrative director on or before January 31, 1998.

(g) The provisions of this section shall not affect the confidentiality or admission in evidence of a claimant's medical treatment records.

(h) Charges for services arranged for or provided by health care service plans certified by this section and that are paid on a per-enrollee-periodic-charge basis shall not be subject to the schedules adopted by the administrative director pursuant to Section 5307.1.

(i) Nothing in this section shall be construed to expand or constrict any requirements imposed by law on a health care service plan or insurer when operating as other than a health care organization pursuant to this section.

(j) In consultation with interested parties, including the Department of Business Oversight and the Department of Insurance, the administrative director shall adopt rules necessary to carry out this section.

(k) The administrative director shall refuse to certify or may revoke or suspend the certification of any health care organization under this section if the director finds that:

(1) The plan for providing medical treatment fails to meet the requirements of this section.

(2) A health care service plan licensed by the Department of Managed Health Care, a workers' compensation health care provider organization authorized by the Department of Business Oversight, or a carrier licensed by the Department of Insurance is not in good standing with its licensing agency.

(3) Services under the plan are not being provided in accordance with the terms of a certified plan.

(*l*)(1) When an injured employee requests chiropractic treatment for work-related injuries, the health care organization shall provide the injured worker with access to the services of a chiropractor pursuant to guidelines for chiropractic care established by paragraph (2). Within five working days of the employee's request to see a chiropractor, the health care organization and any person or entity who directs the kind or manner of health care services for the plan shall refer an injured employee to an affiliated chiropractor for work-related injuries that are within the guidelines for chiropractic care established by paragraph (2). Chiropractic care rendered in accordance with guidelines for chiropractic care established pursuant to paragraph (2) shall be provided by duly licensed chiropractors affiliated with the plan.

(2) The health care organization shall establish guidelines for chiropractic care in consultation with affiliated chiropractors who are participants in the health care organization's utilization review process for chiropractic care, which may include qualified medical evaluators knowledgeable in the treatment of chiropractic conditions. The guidelines for chiropractic care shall, at a minimum, explicitly require the referral of any injured employee who so requests to an affiliated chiropractor for the evaluation or treatment, or both, of neuromusculoskeletal conditions.

(3) Whenever a dispute concerning the appropriateness or necessity of chiropractic care for work-related injuries arises, the dispute shall be resolved by the health care organization's utilization review process for chiropractic care in accordance with the health care organization's guidelines for chiropractic care established by paragraph (2).

Chiropractic utilization review for work-related injuries shall be conducted in accordance with the health care organization's approved quality assurance standards and utilization review process for chiropractic care. Chiropractors affiliated with the plan shall have access to the health care organization's provider appeals process and, in the case of chiropractic care for work-related injuries, the review shall include review by a chiropractor affiliated with the health care organization, as determined by the health care organization.

(4) The health care organization shall inform employees of the procedures for processing and resolving grievances, including those related to chiropractic care, including the location and telephone number where grievances may be submitted.

(5) All guidelines for chiropractic care and utilization review shall be consistent with the standards of this code that require care to cure or relieve the effects of the industrial injury.

(m) Individually identifiable medical information on patients submitted to the division shall not be subject to the California Public Records Act (Chapter 3.5 (commencing with Section 6250) of Division 7 of Title 1 of the Government Code).

(n)(1) When an injured employee requests acupuncture treatment for work-related injuries, the health care organization shall provide the injured worker with access to the services of an acupuncturist pursuant to guidelines for acupuncture care established by paragraph (2). Within five working days of the employee's request to see an acupuncturist, the health care organization and any person or entity who directs the kind or manner of health care services for the plan shall refer an injured employee to an affiliated acupuncturist for work-related injuries that are within the guidelines for acupuncture care established by paragraph (2). Acupuncture care rendered in accordance with guidelines for acupuncture care established pursuant to paragraph (2) shall be provided by duly licensed acupuncturists affiliated with the plan.

(2) The health care organization shall establish guidelines for acupuncture care in consultation with affiliated acupuncturists who are participants in the health care organization's utilization review process for acupuncture care, which may include qualified medical evaluators. The guidelines for acupuncture care shall, at a minimum, explicitly require the referral of any injured employee who so requests to an affiliated acupuncturist for the evaluation or treatment, or both, of neuromusculoskeletal conditions.

(3) Whenever a dispute concerning the appropriateness or necessity of acupuncture care for work-related injuries arises, the dispute shall be resolved by the health care organization's utilization review process for acupuncture care in accordance with the health care organization's guidelines for acupuncture care established by paragraph (2).

Acupuncture utilization review for work-related injuries shall be conducted in accordance with the health care organization's approved quality assurance standards and utilization review process for acupuncture care. Acupuncturists affiliated with the plan shall have access to the health care organization's provider appeals process and, in the case of acupuncture care for work-related injuries, the review shall include review by an acupuncturist affiliated with the health care organization, as determined by the health care organization.

(4) The health care organization shall inform employees of the procedures for processing and resolving grievances, including those related to acupuncture care, including the location and telephone number where grievances may be submitted.

(5) All guidelines for acupuncture care and utilization review shall be consistent with the standards of this code that require care to cure or relieve the effects of the industrial injury. **Leg.H.** 1993 ch. 121, effective July 16, 1993, ch. 1242, 1994 chs. 285, 1118, 1997 ch. 346, 1998 ch. 440, 1999 ch. 525, operative July 1, 2000, 2000 ch. 857, 2002 chs. 6, 866 (AB 486), 2015 ch. 190 (AB 1517) §70.

1993 Note: Section 4600.5, as added by ch. 121, applies only to injuries occurring on or after January 1, 1994. Stats. 1993 ch. 121 §77.

Ref.: 8 C.C.R. §§9770, 9771, 9771.1, 9771.2, 9771.6, 9771.60, 9771.61, 9771.62, 9771.63, 9771.64, 9771.65, 9771.66, 9771.67, 9771.68, 9771.69, 9771.70, 9771.71, 9771.72, 9771.73, 9771.74, 9771.75, 9771.76, 9771.77, 9771.78, 9771.79, 9771.80, 9771.81, 9771.82, 9771.83, 9772, 9773, 9773.1, 9774, 9775, 9777, 9778, 9779, 9779.1, 9779.2, 9779.3, 9779.4, 9779.45, 9779.5, 9779.8, 9779.9; Hanna § 1.24; Herlick Handbook §§ 4.11[2], 4.12, 10.01[2], 16.20.

§4600.6. Rules and procedures for certification as health care organization; application requirements; disclosure requirements; contracts with prospective purchasers; restrictions on advertisements; name of organization; licensing requirements for facilities, personnel, and equipment; scope of workers' compensation health care; grievance system; cause of action against organization; delegation of responsibility to subcommittees; periodic on-site medical survey by administrative director.

Any workers' compensation insurer, third-party administrator, or other entity seeking certification as a health care organization under subdivision (e) of Section 4600.5 shall be subject to the following rules and procedures:

(a) Each application for authorization as an organization under subdivision (e) of Section 4600.5 shall be verified by an authorized representative of the applicant and shall be in a form prescribed by the administrative director. The application shall be accompanied by the prescribed fee and shall set forth or be accompanied by each and all of the following:

(1) The basic organizational documents of the applicant, such as the articles of incorporation, articles of association, partnership agreement, trust agreement, or other applicable documents and all amendments thereto.

(2) A copy of the bylaws, rules, and regulations, or similar documents regulating the conduct of the internal affairs of the applicant.

(3) A list of the names, addresses, and official positions of the persons who are to be responsible for the conduct of the affairs of the applicant, which shall include, among others, all members of the board of directors, board of trustees, executive committee, or other governing board or committee, the principal officers, each shareholder with over 5 percent interest in the case of a corporation, and all partners or members in the case of a partnership or association, and each person who has loaned funds to the applicant for the operation of its business.

(4) A copy of any contract made, or to be made, between the applicant and any provider of health care, or persons listed in paragraph (3), or any other person or organization agreeing to perform an administrative function or service for the plan. The administrative director by rule may identify contracts excluded from this requirement

Labor

and make provision for the submission of form contracts. The payment rendered or to be rendered to the provider of health care services shall be deemed confidential information that shall not be divulged by the administrative director, except that the payment may be disclosed and become a public record in any legislative, administrative, or judicial proceeding or inquiry. The organization shall also submit the name and address of each provider employed by, or contracting with, the organization, together with his or her license number.

(5) A statement describing the organization, its method of providing for health services, and its physical facilities. If applicable, this statement shall include the health care delivery capabilities of the organization, including the number of full-time and part-time physicians under Section 3209.3, the numbers and types of licensed or state-certified health care support staff, the number of hospital beds contracted for, and the arrangements and the methods by which health care will be provided, as defined by the administrative director under Sections 4600.3 and 4600.5.

(6) A copy of the disclosure forms or materials that are to be issued to employees.

(7) A copy of the form of the contract that is to be issued to any employer, insurer of an employer, or a group of self-insured employers.

(8) Financial statements accompanied by a report, certificate, or opinion of an independent certified public accountant. However, the financial statements from public entities or political subdivisions of the state need not include a report, certificate, or opinion by an independent certified public accountant if the financial statement complies with any requirements that may be established by regulation of the administrative director.

(9) A description of the proposed method of marketing the organization and a copy of any contract made with any person to solicit on behalf of the organization or a copy of the form of agreement used and a list of the contracting parties.

(10) A statement describing the service area or areas to be served, including the service location for each provider rendering professional services on behalf of the organization and the location of any other organization facilities where required by the administrative director.

(11) A description of organization grievance procedures to be utilized as required by this part, and a copy of the form specified by paragraph (3) of subdivision (j).

(12) A description of the procedures and programs for internal review of the quality of health care pursuant to the requirements set forth in this part.

(13) Evidence of adequate insurance coverage or self-insurance to respond to claims for damages arising out of the furnishing of workers' compensation health care.

(14) Evidence of adequate insurance coverage or self-insurance to protect against losses of facilities where required by the administrative director.

(15) Evidence of adequate workers' compensation coverage to protect against claims arising out of work-related injuries that might be brought by the employees and staff of an organization against the organization.

(16) Evidence of fidelity bonds in such amount as the administrative director prescribes by regulation.

(17) Other information that the administrative director may reasonably require.

(b)(1) An organization, solicitor, solicitor firm, or representative may not use or permit the use of any advertising or solicitation that is untrue or misleading, or any form of disclosure that is deceptive. For purposes of this chapter:

(A) A written or printed statement or item of information shall be deemed untrue if it does not conform to fact in any respect that is or may be significant to an employer or employee, or potential employer or employee.

(B) A written or printed statement or item of information shall be deemed misleading whether or not it may be literally true, if, in the total context in which the statement is made or the item of information is communicated, the statement or item of information may be understood by a person not possessing special knowledge regarding health care coverage, as indicating any benefit or advantage, or the absence of any exclusion, limitation, or disadvantage of possible significance to an employer or employee, or potential employer or employee.

(C) A disclosure form shall be deemed to be deceptive if the disclosure form taken as a whole and with consideration given to typography and format, as well as language, shall be such as to cause a reasonable person, not possessing special knowledge of workers' compensation health care, and the disclosure form therefor, to expect benefits, service charges, or other advantages that the disclosure form does not provide or that the organization issuing that disclosure form does not regularly make available to employees.

(2) An organization, solicitor, or representative may not use or permit the use of any verbal statement that is untrue, misleading, or deceptive or make any representations about health care offered by the organization or its cost that does not conform to fact. All verbal statements are to be held to the same standards as those for printed matter provided in paragraph (1).

(c) It is unlawful for any person, including an organization, subject to this part, to represent or imply in any manner that the person or organization has been sponsored, recommended, or approved, or that the person's or organization's abilities or qualifications have in any respect been passed upon, by the administrative director.

(d)(1) An organization may not publish or distribute, or allow to be published or distributed on its behalf, any advertisement unless (A) a true copy thereof has first been filed with the administrative director, at least 30 days prior to any such use, or any shorter period as the administrative director by rule or order may allow, and (B) the administrative director by notice has not found the advertisement, wholly or in part, to be untrue, misleading, deceptive, or otherwise not in compliance with this part or the rules thereunder, and specified the deficiencies, within the 30 days or any shorter time as the administrative director by rule or order may allow.

(2) If the administrative director finds that any advertisement of an organization has materially failed to comply with this part or the rules thereunder, the administrative director may, by order, require the organization to publish in the same or similar medium, an approved correction or retraction of any untrue, misleading, or deceptive statement contained in the advertising.

(3) The administrative director by rule or order may classify organizations and advertisements and exempt certain classes, wholly or in part, either unconditionally or upon specified terms and conditions or for specified periods, from the application of subdivision (a).

(e)(1) The administrative director shall require the use by each organization of disclosure forms or materials containing any information regarding the health care and terms of the workers' compensation health care contract that the administrative director may require, so as to afford the public, employers, and employees with a full and fair disclosure of the provisions of the contract in readily understood language and in a clearly organized manner. The administrative director may require that the materials be presented in a reasonably uniform manner so as to facilitate comparisons between contracts of the same or other types of organizations. The disclosure form shall describe the health care that is required by the administrative director under Sections 4600.3 and 4600.5, and shall provide that all information be in concise and specific terms, relative to the contract, together with any additional information as may be required by the administrative director, in connection with the organization or contract.

(2) All organizations, solicitors, and representatives of a workers' compensation health care provider organization shall, when presenting any contract for examination or sale to a prospective employee, provide the employee with a properly completed disclosure form, as prescribed by the administrative director pursuant to this section for each contract so examined or sold.

(3) In addition to the other disclosures required by this section, every organization and any agent or employee of the organization shall, when representing an organization for examination or sale to any individual purchaser or the representative of a group consisting of 25 or fewer individuals, disclose in writing the ratio of premium cost to health care paid for contracts with individuals and with groups of the same or similar size for the organization's preceding fiscal year. An organization may report that information by geographic area, provided the organization identifies the geographic area and reports information applicable to that geographic area.

(4) Where the administrative director finds it necessary in the interest of full and fair disclosure, all advertising and other consumer information disseminated by an organization for the purpose of influencing persons to become members of an organization shall contain any supplemental disclosure information that the administrative director may require.

(f) When the administrative director finds it necessary in the interest of full and fair disclosure, all advertising and other consumer information disseminated by an organization for the purpose of influencing persons to become members of an organization shall contain any supplemental disclosure information that the administrative director may require.

(g)(1) An organization may not refuse to enter into any contract, or may not cancel or decline to renew or reinstate any contract, because of the age or any characteristic listed or defined in subdivision (b) or (e) of Section 51 of the Civil Code of any contracting party, prospective contracting party, or person reasonably expected to benefit from that contract as an employee or otherwise.

(2) The terms of any contract shall not be modified, and the benefits or coverage of any contract shall not be subject to any limitations, exceptions, exclusions, reductions, copayments, coinsurance, deductibles, reservations, or premium, price, or charge differentials, or other modifications because of the age or any characteristic listed or defined in subdivision (b) or (e) of Section 51 of the Civil Code of any contracting party, potential contracting party, or person reasonably expected to benefit from that contract as an employee or otherwise; except that premium, price, or charge differentials because of the sex or age of any individual when based on objective, valid, and up-to-date statistical and actuarial data are not prohibited. Nothing in this section shall be construed to permit an organization to charge different rates to individual employees within the same group solely on the basis of the employee's sex.

(3) It shall be deemed a violation of subdivision (a) for any organization to utilize marital status, living arrangements, occupation, gender, beneficiary designation, ZIP Codes or other territorial classification, or any combination thereof for the purpose of establishing sexual orientation. Nothing in this section shall be construed to alter in any manner the existing law prohibiting organizations from conducting tests for the presence of human immunodeficiency virus or evidence thereof.

(4) This section shall not be construed to limit the authority of the administrative director to adopt or enforce regulations prohibiting discrimination because of sex, marital status, or sexual orientation.

(h)(1) An organization may not use in its name any of the words "insurance," "casualty," "health care service plan," "health plan," "surety," "mutual," or any other words descriptive of the health plan, insurance, casualty, or surety business or use any name similar to the name or description of any health care service plan, insurance, or surety corporation doing business in this state unless that organization controls or is controlled by an entity licensed as a health care service plan or insurer pursuant to the Health and Safety Code or the Insurance Code and the organization employs a name related to that of the controlled or controlling entity.

(2) Section 2415 of the Business and Professions Code, pertaining to fictitious names, does not apply to organizations certified under this section.

(3) An organization or solicitor firm may not adopt a name style that is deceptive, or one that could cause the public to believe the organization is affiliated with or recommended by any governmental or private entity unless this affiliation or endorsement exists.

(i) Each organization shall meet the following requirements:

(1) All facilities located in this state, including, but not limited to, clinics, hospitals, and skilled nursing facilities, to be utilized by the organization shall be licensed by the State Department of Health Services, if that licensure is required by law. Facilities not located in this state shall conform to all licensing and other requirements of the jurisdiction in which they are located.

(2) All personnel employed by or under contract to the organization shall be licensed or certified by their respective board or agency, where that licensure or certification is required by law.

Labor

(3) All equipment required to be licensed or registered by law shall be so licensed or registered and the operating personnel for that equipment shall be licensed or certified as required by law.

(4) The organization shall furnish services in a manner providing continuity of care and ready referral of patients to other providers at any time as may be appropriate and consistent with good professional practice.

(5) All health care shall be readily available at reasonable times to all employees. To the extent feasible, the organization shall make all health care readily accessible to all employees.

(6) The organization shall employ and utilize allied health manpower for the furnishing of health care to the extent permitted by law and consistent with good health care practice.

(7) The organization shall have the organizational and administrative capacity to provide services to employees. The organization shall be able to demonstrate to the department that health care decisions are rendered by qualified providers, unhindered by fiscal and administrative management.

(8) All contracts with employers, insurers of employers, and self-insured employers and all contracts with providers, and other persons furnishing services, equipment, or facilities to or in connection with the workers' compensation health care organization, shall be fair, reasonable, and consistent with the objectives of this part.

(9) Each organization shall provide to employees all workers' compensation health care required by this code. The administrative director shall not determine the scope of workers' compensation health care to be offered by an organization.

(j)(1) Every organization shall establish and maintain a grievance system approved by the administrative director under which employees may submit their grievances to the organization. Each system shall provide reasonable procedures in accordance with regulations adopted by the administrative director that shall ensure adequate consideration of employee grievances and rectification when appropriate.

(2) Every organization shall inform employees upon enrollment and annually thereafter of the procedures for processing and resolving grievances. The information shall include the location and telephone number where grievances may be submitted.

(3) Every organization shall provide forms for complaints to be given to employees who wish to register written complaints. The forms used by organizations shall be approved by the administrative director in advance as to format.

(4) The organization shall keep in its files all copies of complaints, and the responses thereto, for a period of five years.

(k) Every organization shall establish procedures in accordance with regulations of the administrative director for continuously reviewing the quality of care, performance of medical personnel, utilization of services and facilities, and costs. Notwithstanding any other provision of law, there shall be no monetary liability on the part of, and no cause of action for damages shall arise against, any person who participates in quality of care or utilization reviews by peer review committees that are composed chiefly of physicians, as defined by Section 3209.3, for any act performed during the reviews if the person acts without malice, has made a reasonable effort to obtain the facts of the matter, and believes that the action taken is warranted by the facts, and neither the proceedings nor the records of the reviews shall be subject to discovery, nor shall any person in attendance at the reviews be required to testify as to what transpired thereat. Disclosure of the proceedings or records to the governing body of an organization or to any person or entity designated by the organization to review activities of the committees shall not alter the status of the records or of the proceedings as privileged communications.

The above prohibition relating to discovery or testimony does not apply to the statements made by any person in attendance at a review who is a party to an action or proceeding the subject matter of which was reviewed, or to any person requesting hospital staff privileges, or in any action against an insurance carrier alleging bad faith by the carrier in refusing to accept a settlement offer within the policy limits, or to the administrative director in conducting surveys pursuant to subdivision (o).

This section shall not be construed to confer immunity from liability on any workers' compensation health care organization. In any case in which, but for the enactment of the preceding provisions of this section, a cause of action would arise against an organization, the cause of action shall exist notwithstanding the provisions of this section.

(*l*) Nothing in this chapter shall be construed to prevent an organization from utilizing subcommittees to participate in peer review activities, nor to prevent an organization from delegating the responsibilities required by subdivision (i) as it determines to be appropriate, to subcommittees including subcommittees composed of a majority of nonphysician health care providers licensed pursuant to the Business and Professions Code, as long as the organization controls the scope of authority delegated and may revoke all or part of this authority at any time. Persons who participate in the subcommittees shall be entitled to the same immunity from monetary liability and actions for civil damages as persons who participate in organization or provider peer review committees pursuant to subdivision (i).

(m) Every organization shall have and shall demonstrate to the administrative director that it has all of the following:

(1) Adequate provision for continuity of care.

(2) A procedure for prompt payment and denial of provider claims.

(n) Every contract between an organization and an employer or insurer of an employer, and every contract between any organization and a provider of health care, shall be in writing.

(o)(1) The administrative director shall conduct periodically an onsite medical survey of the health care delivery system of each organization. The survey shall include a review of the procedures for obtaining health care, the procedures for regulating utilization, peer review mechanisms, internal procedures for assuring quality of care, and the overall performance of the organization in providing health care and meeting the health needs of employees.

(2) The survey shall be conducted by a panel of qualified health professionals experienced in evaluating the delivery of workers' compensation health care. The administrative director shall be authorized to contract with professional organizations or outside personnel to conduct medical surveys. These organizations or personnel shall have demonstrated the ability to objectively evaluate the delivery of this health care.

(3) Surveys performed pursuant to this section shall be conducted as often as deemed necessary by the administrative director to assure the protection of employees, but not less frequently than once every three years. Nothing in this section shall be construed to require the survey team to visit each clinic, hospital, office, or facility of the organization.

(4) Nothing in this section shall be construed to require the medical survey team to review peer review proceedings and records conducted and compiled under this section or in medical records. However, the administrative director shall be authorized to require onsite review of these peer review proceedings and records or medical records where necessary to determine that quality health care is being delivered to employees. Where medical record review is authorized, the survey team shall ensure that the confidentiality of the physician-patient relationship is safeguarded in accordance with existing law and neither the survey team nor the administrative director or the administrative director's staff may be compelled to disclose this information except in accordance with the physician-patient relationship. The administrative director shall ensure that the confidentiality of the peer review proceedings and records is maintained. The disclosure of the peer review proceedings and records to the administrative director or the medical survey team shall not alter the status of the proceedings or records as privileged and confidential communications.

(5) The procedures and standards utilized by the survey team shall be made available to the organizations prior to the conducting of medical surveys.

(6) During the survey, the members of the survey team shall offer such advice and assistance to the organization as deemed appropriate.

(7) The administrative director shall notify the organization of deficiencies found by the survey team. The administrative director shall give the organization a reasonable time to correct the deficiencies, and failure on the part of the organization to comply to the administrative director's satisfaction shall constitute cause for disciplinary action against the organization.

(8) Reports of all surveys, deficiencies, and correction plans shall be open to public inspection, except that no surveys, deficiencies or correction plans shall be made public unless the organization has had an opportunity to review the survey and file a statement of response within 30 days, to be attached to the report.

(p)(1) All records, books, and papers of an organization, management company, solicitor, solicitor firm, and any provider or subcontractor providing medical or other services to an organization, management company, solicitor, or solicitor firm shall be open to inspection during normal business hours by the administrative director.

(2) To the extent feasible, all the records, books, and papers described in paragraph (1) shall be located in this state. In examining those records outside this state, the administrative director shall consider the cost to the organization, consistent with the effectiveness of the administrative director's examination, and may upon reasonable notice require that these records, books, and papers, or a specified portion thereof, be made available for examination in this state, or that a true and accurate copy of these records, books, and papers, or a specified portion thereof, be furnished to the administrative director.

(q)(1) The administrative director shall conduct an examination of the administrative affairs of any organization, and each person with whom the organization has made arrangements for administrative, or management services, as often as deemed necessary to protect the interest of employees, but not less frequently than once every five years.

(2) The expense of conducting any additional or nonroutine examinations pursuant to this section, and the expense of conducting any additional or nonroutine medical surveys pursuant to subdivision (o) shall be charged against the organization being examined or surveyed. The amount shall include the actual salaries or compensation paid to the persons making the examination or survey, the expenses incurred in the course thereof, and overhead costs in connection therewith as fixed by the administrative director. In determining the cost of examinations or surveys, the administrative director may use the estimated average hourly cost for all persons performing examinations or surveys of workers' compensation health care organizations for the fiscal year. The amount charged shall be remitted by the organization to the administrative director.

(3) Reports of all examinations shall be open to public inspection, except that no examination shall be made public, unless the organization has had an opportunity to review the examination report and file a statement or response within 30 days, to be attached to the report. **Leg.H.** 1997 ch. 346, 2008 ch. 682 (AB 2654) §9.

Ref.: 8 C.C.R. §§9771.6, 9771.60, 9771.61, 9771.62, 9771.63, 9771.64, 9771.65, 9771.66, 9771.67, 9771.68, 9771.69, 9771.70, 9771.71, 9771.72, 9771.73, 9771.74, 9771.75, 9771.76, 9771.77, 9771.78, 9771.79, 9771.80, 9771.81, 9771.82, 9771.83; Herlick Handbook §§ 4.12, 10.01[2].

§4600.7. Workers' Compensation Managed Care Fund.

(a) The Workers' Compensation Managed Care Fund is hereby created in the State Treasury for the administration of Sections 4600.3 and 4600.5 by the Division of Workers' Compensation. The administrative director shall establish a schedule of fees and revenues to be charged to certified health care organizations and applicants for certification to fully fund the administration of these provisions and to repay amounts received as a loan from the General Fund. All fees and revenues shall be deposited in the Workers' Compensation Managed Care Fund and shall be used when appropriated by the Legislature solely for the purpose of carrying out the responsibilities of the Division of Workers' Compensation under Section 4600.3 or 4600.5.

(b) On and after July 1, 1998, no funds received as a loan from the General Fund shall be used to support the administration of Sections 4600.3 and 4600.5. The loan amount shall be repaid to the General Fund by assessing a surcharge on the enrollment fee for each of the next five fiscal years. In the event the surcharge does not produce sufficient revenue over this period, the surcharge shall be adjusted to fully repay the loan over the following three fiscal years, with the final assessment calculated by dividing the balance of the loan by the enrollees at the end of the final fiscal year. **Leg.H.** 1994 ch. 152, effective July 11, 1994, 1998 ch. 282.

Ref.: 8 C.C.R. §§9779, 9779.1; Herlick Handbook § 10.01[2].

§4601. Employee request to change physician.

(a) If the employee so requests, the employer shall tender the employee one change of physician. The employee at any time may request that the employer tender this one-time change of physician. Upon request of the employee for a change of physician, the maximum amount of time permitted by law for the employer or insurance carrier to provide the employee an alternative physician or, if requested by the employee, a chiropractor, or an acupuncturist shall be five working days from the date of the request. Notwithstanding the 30-day time period specified in Section 4600, a request for a change of physician pursuant to this section may be made at any time. The employee is entitled, in any serious case, upon request, to the services of a consulting physician, chiropractor, or acupuncturist of his or her choice at the expense of the employer. The treatment shall be at the expense of the employer.

(b) If an employee requesting a change of physician pursuant to subdivision (a) has notified his or her employer in writing prior to the date of injury that he or she has a personal chiropractor, the alternative physician tendered by the employer to the employee, if the employee so requests, shall be the employee's personal chiropractor. For the purpose of this article, "personal chiropractor" means the employee's regular chiropractor licensed pursuant to Chapter 2 (commencing with Section 1000) of Division 2 of the Business and Professions Code, who has previously directed treatment of the employee, and who retains the employee's chiropractic treatment records, including his or her chiropractic history.

(c) If an employee requesting a change of physician pursuant to subdivision (a) has notified his or her employer in writing prior to the date of injury that he or she has a personal acupuncturist, the alternative physician tendered by the employer to the employee, if the employee so requests, shall be the employee's personal acupuncturist. For the purpose of this article, "personal acupuncturist" means the employee's regular acupuncturist licensed pursuant to Chapter 12 (commencing with Section 4935) of Division 2 of the Business and Professions Code, who has previously directed treatment of the employee, and who retains the employee's acupuncture treatment records, including his or her acupuncture history. **Leg.H.** 1998 ch. 440.

Ref.: 8 C.C.R. §§9880, 9881; Hanna § 5.05[7][a]; Herlick Handbook § 10.01[2].

§4602. Employee request for certification of competency of consulting physicians.

If the employee so requests, the employer shall procure certification by either the administrative director or the appeals board as the case may be of the competency, for the particular case, of the consulting or additional physicians.

Ref.: Hanna § 22.04; Herlick Handbook § 10.01[2].

§4603. Employer request for change of physician.

If the employer desires a change of physicians or chiropractor, he may petition the administrative director who, upon a showing of good cause by the employer, may order the employer to provide a panel of five physicians, or if requested by the employee, four physicians and one chiropractor competent to treat the particular case, from which the employee must select one.

Ref.: 8 C.C.R. §§9786, 9786.1, 9787, 9880, 9881, 10950; Hanna §§ 5.05[7][b], 23.03[2]; Herlick Handbook § 10.01[2].

§4603.2. Notice to employer of selected physician; reports to employer; payment by employer; penalties and liabilities for late payment; review of itemization.

(a)(1) Upon selecting a physician pursuant to Section 4600, the employee or physician shall notify the employer of the name and address, including the name of the medical group, if applicable, of the physician. The physician shall submit a report to the employer within five working days from the date of the initial examination, as required by Section 6409, and shall submit periodic reports at intervals that may be prescribed by rules and regulations adopted by the administrative director.

(2) If the employer objects to the employee's selection of the physician on the grounds that the physician is not within the medical provider network used by the employer, and there is a final determination that the employee was entitled to select the physician pursuant to Section 4600, the employee shall be entitled to continue treatment with that physician at the employer's expense in accordance with this division, notwithstanding Section 4616.2. The employer shall be required to pay from the date of the initial examination if the physician's report was submitted within five working days of the initial examination. If the physician's report was submitted more than five working days after the initial examination, the employer and the employee shall not be required to pay for any services prior to the date the physician's report was submitted.

(3) If the employer objects to the employee's selection of the physician on the grounds that the physician is not within the medical provider network used by the employer, and there is a final determination that the employee was not entitled to select a physician outside of the medical provider network, the employer is not liable for treatment provided by or at the direction of that physician or for any consequences of the treatment obtained outside the network.

(b)(1)(A) A provider of services provided pursuant to Section 4600, including, but not limited to, physicians, hospitals, pharmacies, interpreters, copy services, transportation services, and home health care services, shall submit its request for payment with an itemization of services provided and the charge for each service, a copy of all reports showing the services performed, the prescription or referral from the primary treating physician if the services were performed by a person other than the primary treating physician, and any evidence of authorization for the services that may have been received. This section does not prohibit an employer, insurer, or third-party claims administrator from establishing, through written agreement, an alternative manual or electronic request for payment with providers for services provided pursuant to Section 4600.

(B) Effective for services provided on or after January 1, 2017, the request for payment with an itemization of services provided and the charge for each service shall be submitted to the employer within 12 months of the date of service or within 12 months of the date of discharge for inpatient facility services. The administrative director shall adopt rules to implement the 12-month limitation period. The rules shall define circumstances that constitute good cause for an exception to the 12-month period, including provisions to address the circumstances of a nonoccupational injury or illness later found to be a compensable injury or illness. The request for payment is barred unless timely submitted.

(C) The request for payment with an itemization of services provided and the charge for each service shall be submitted to the employer with the national provider identifier (NPI) number for the physician or provider who provided the service for which payment is sought in accordance with rules adopted by the administrative director pursuant to Section 4603.4. Failure to include the physician's or provider's NPI shall result in the request for payment being barred until the physician's or provider's NPI is submitted with the request for payment. This subparagraph does not preclude an employer, insurer, pharmacy benefit manager, or third-party claims administrator from requiring the physician's or provider's NPI at an earlier date. This subparagraph is declaratory of existing law.

(D) Notwithstanding the requirements of this paragraph, a copy of the prescription shall not be required with a request for payment for pharmacy services, unless the provider of services has entered into a written agreement, as provided in this paragraph, that requires a copy of a prescription for a pharmacy service.

(E) This section does not preclude an employer, insurer, pharmacy benefits manager, or third-party claims administrator from requesting a copy of the prescription during a review of any records of prescription drugs that were dispensed by a pharmacy.

(2) Except as provided in subdivision (d) of Section 4603.4, or under contracts authorized under Section 5307.11, payment for medical treatment provided or prescribed by the treating physician selected by the employee or designated by the employer shall be made at reasonable maximum amounts in the official medical fee schedule, pursuant to Section 5307.1, in effect on the date of service. Payments shall be made by the employer with an explanation of review pursuant to Section 4603.3 within 45 days after receipt of each separate itemization of medical services provided, together with any required reports and any written authorization for services that may have been received by the physician. If the itemization or a portion thereof is contested, denied, or considered incomplete, the physician shall be notified, in the explanation of review, that the itemization is contested, denied, or considered incomplete, within 30 days after receipt of the itemization by the employer. An explanation of review that states an itemization is incomplete shall also state all additional information required to make a decision. A properly documented list of services provided and not paid at the rates then in effect under Section 5307.1 within the 45-day period shall be paid at the rates then in effect and increased by 15 percent, together with interest at the same rate as judgments in civil actions retroactive to the date of receipt of the itemization, unless the employer does both of the following:

(A) Pays the provider at the rates in effect within the 45-day period.

(B) Advises, in an explanation of review pursuant to Section 4603.3, the physician, or another provider of the items being contested, the reasons for contesting these items, and the remedies available to the physician or the other provider if the physician or provider disagrees. In the case of an itemization that includes services provided by a hospital, outpatient surgery center, or independent diagnostic facility, advice that a request has been made for an audit of the itemization shall satisfy the requirements of this paragraph.

An employer's liability to a physician or another provider under this section for delayed payments shall not affect its liability to an employee under Section 5814 or any other provision of this division.

(3) Notwithstanding paragraph (1), if the employer is a governmental entity, payment for medical treatment provided or prescribed by the treating physician selected by the employee or designated by the employer shall be made within 60 days after receipt of each separate itemization, together with any required reports and any written authorization for services that may have been received by the physician.

(4) Duplicate submissions of medical services itemizations, for which an explanation of review was previously provided, shall require no further or additional notification or objection by the employer to the medical provider and shall not subject the employer to any additional penalties or interest pursuant to this section for failing to respond to the duplicate submission. This paragraph applies only to duplicate submissions and does not apply to any other penalties or interest that may be applicable to the original submission.

(5)(A) An employer may defer objecting to or paying any bill submitted by, or on behalf of, a provider whose liens are stayed pursuant to Section 4615, and the time limits for taking any action prescribed by paragraphs (2) and (3) shall not commence until the stay is lifted pursuant to Section 4615.

(B) An employer may object to any bill submitted by, or on behalf of, a provider who has been suspended pursuant to Section 139.21.

(c) Interest or an increase in compensation paid by an insurer pursuant to this section shall be treated in the same manner as an increase in compensation under subdivision (d) of Section 4650 for the purposes of any classification of risks and premium rates, and any system of merit rating approved or issued pursuant to Article 2 (commencing with Section 11730) of Chapter 3 of Part 3 of Division 2 of the Insurance Code.

(d)(1) Whenever an employer or insurer employs an individual or contracts with an entity to conduct a review of an itemization submitted by a physician or medical provider, the employer or insurer shall make available to that individual or entity all documentation submitted together with that itemization by the physician or medical provider. When an individual or entity conducting an itemization review determines that additional information or documentation is necessary to review the itemization, the individual or entity shall contact the claims administrator or insurer to obtain the necessary information or documentation that was submitted by the physician or medical provider pursuant to subdivision (b).

(2)(A) An individual or entity reviewing an itemization of service submitted by a physician or medical provider, including a medical provider network, an entity that provides ancillary services, as defined in Section 4616.5, or an entity providing services for or on behalf of the medical provider network or its providers, shall not alter the procedure codes listed or recommend reduction of the amount of the payment unless the documentation submitted by the physician or medical provider with the itemization of service has been reviewed by that individual or entity. If the reviewer does not recommend payment for services as itemized by the physician or medical provider, the explanation of review shall provide the physician or medical provider with a specific explanation as to why the reviewer altered the procedure code or changed other parts of the itemization and the specific deficiency in the itemization or documentation that caused the reviewer to conclude that the altered procedure code or amount recommended for payment more accurately represents the service performed.

(B) The amendments to subparagraph (A) made by the act adding this subparagraph are declaratory of existing law.

(e)(1) If the provider disputes the amount paid, the provider may request a second review within 90 days of service of the explanation of review or an order of the appeals board resolving the threshold issue as stated in the explanation of review pursuant to paragraph (5) of subdivision (a) of Section 4603.3. The request for a second review shall be submitted to the employer on a form prescribed by the administrative director and shall include all of the following:

(A) The date of the explanation of review and the claim number or other unique identifying number provided on the explanation of review.

(B) The item and amount in dispute.

(C) The additional payment requested and the reason therefor.

(D) The additional information provided in response to a request in the first explanation of review or any other additional information provided in support of the additional payment requested.

(2) If the only dispute is the amount of payment and the provider does not request a second review within 90 days, the bill shall be deemed satisfied and neither the employer nor the employee shall be liable for any further payment.

(3) Within 14 days of a request for second review, the employer shall respond with a final written determination on each of the items or amounts in dispute. Payment of any balance not in dispute shall be made within 21 days of receipt of the request for second review. This time limit may be extended by mutual written agreement.

(4) If the provider contests the amount paid, after receipt of the second review, the provider shall request an independent bill review as provided for in Section 4603.6.

(f) Except as provided in paragraph (4) of subdivision (e), the appeals board shall have jurisdiction over disputes arising out of this section pursuant to Section 5304. **Leg.H.** 1999 ch. 124, 2000 ch. 1069, 2001 ch. 240, 2003 ch. 639 (SB 228), 2004 ch. 34 (SB 899), effective April 19, 2004, 2006 ch. 69 (AB 1806) §24, effective July 12, 2006, 2012 ch. 363 (SB 863) §36, 2013 ch. 129 (SB 146) §1, effective August 19, 2013, 2016 ch. 214 (SB 1175) §1, 2017 chs. 300 (AB 1422) §2, 561 (AB 1516) §173 (ch. 300 prevails; ch. 561 not effective), 2019 ch. 647 (SB 537) §5.

2012 Note: For legislative findings, declarations, and applicability of Stats. 2012 ch. 363, see the 2012 Notes following Lab C §62.5.

2004 Note: The amendment to §4603.2 made by this act shall apply prospectively from the date of enactment of this act, regardless of the date of injury, unless otherwise specified, but shall not constitute good cause to reopen or rescind, alter, or amend any existing order, decision, or award of the Workers' Compensation Appeals Board. Stats. 2004 ch. 34 (SB 899) §47.

Ref.: 8 C.C.R. §§9785, 9785.2, 9785.3, 9785.4, 9786, 9786.1, 9787, 9789.10, 9789.11, 9789.20, 9789.21, 9789.22, 9789.24, 9789.30, 9789.31, 9789.32, 9789.33, 9789.34, 9789.35, 9789.36, 9789.37, 9789.38, 9789.40, 9789.50, 9789.60, 9789.70, 9789.110, 9789.111, 9790, 9790.1, 9791, 9791.1, 9792, 9792.1, 9792.5, 9900, 10101, 10101.1, 10102, 10111, 10111.1, 10111.2, 10606, 10950; Hanna §§ 5.05[6][b], [10][b], 5.06, 10.40[3][b], 22.02[2], [3], 22.05[1], [3], 30.22[1]; Herlick Handbook §§ 4.03[2], 4.06[1], [3], 4.09[6], 4.10[2], [3], 4.11[6], 4.18[1], 9.5, 10.01[2], 10.02[3], [4], 10.03[2], 10.05, 10.08[1], [3].

§4603.3. Explanation of review upon payment, adjustment, or denial of itemization of medical services.

(a) Upon payment, adjustment, or denial of a complete or incomplete itemization of medical services, an employer shall provide an explanation of review in the manner prescribed by the administrative director that shall include all of the following:

(1) A statement of the items or procedures billed and the amounts requested by the provider to be paid.

(2) The amount paid.

(3) The basis for any adjustment, change, or denial of the item or procedure billed.

(4) The additional information required to make a decision for an incomplete itemization.

(5) If a denial of payment is for some reason other than a fee dispute, the reason for the denial.

(6) Information on whom to contact on behalf of the employer if a dispute arises over the payment of the billing. The explanation of review shall inform the medical provider of the time limit to raise any objection regarding the items or procedures paid or disputed and how to obtain an

independent review of the medical bill pursuant to Section 4603.6.

(b) The administrative director may adopt regulations requiring the use of electronic explanations of review. **Leg.H.** 2012 ch. 363 (SB 863) §37.

2012 Note: For legislative findings, declarations, and applicability of Stats. 2012 ch. 363, see the 2012 Notes following Lab C §62.5.

Ref.: Hanna §§ 5.02[2][d], 22.05[3]; Herlick Handbook §§ 4.10[2], [3], 4.18[1], 10.01[2], 10.02[4].

§4603.4. Regulatory authority for payment processing and confidentiality of medical information.

(a) The administrative director shall adopt rules and regulations to do all of the following:

(1) Ensure that all health care providers and facilities submit medical bills for payment on standardized forms.

(2) Require acceptance by employers of electronic claims for payment of medical services.

(3) Ensure confidentiality of medical information submitted on electronic claims for payment of medical services.

(4) Require the timely submission of paper or electronic bills in conformity with subparagraph (B) of paragraph (1) of subdivision (b) of Section 4603.2.

(b) To the extent feasible, standards adopted pursuant to subdivision (a) shall be consistent with existing standards under the federal Health Insurance Portability and Accountability Act of 1996.

(c) Require all employers to accept electronic claims for payment of medical services.

(d) Payment for medical treatment provided or prescribed by the treating physician selected by the employee or designated by the employer shall be made with an explanation of review by the employer within 15 working days after electronic receipt of an itemized electronic billing for services at or below the maximum fees provided in the official medical fee schedule adopted pursuant to Section 5307.1. If the billing is contested, denied, or incomplete, payment shall be made with an explanation of review of any uncontested amounts within 15 working days after electronic receipt of the billing, and payment of the balance shall be made in accordance with Section 4603.2. **Leg.H.** 2002 ch. 6 (AB 749), 2003 ch. 639 (SB 228), 2012 ch. 363 (SB 863) §38, 2016 ch. 214 (SB 1175) §2.

2012 Note: For legislative findings, declarations, and applicability of Stats. 2012 ch. 363, see the 2012 Notes following Lab C §62.5.

Ref.: Hanna §§ 1.12[6], 5.05[6][b], 22.02[3], 22.05[1]; Herlick Handbook §§ 4.10[2], [3], 4.18[1], 10.01[2].

§4603.5. Adoption of rules; notice to employees of rights.

The administrative director shall adopt rules pertaining to the format and content of notices required by this article; define reasonable geographic areas for the purposes of Section 4600; specify time limits for all such notices, and responses thereto; and adopt any other rules necessary to make effective the requirements of this article.

Employers shall notify all employees of their rights under this section.

Ref.: 8 C.C.R. §§9900, 10950; Herlick Handbook §§ 4.04[2], 4.10[2], 10.01[2].

§4603.6. Request for independent review; procedure.

(a) If the only dispute is the amount of payment and the provider has received a second review that did not resolve the dispute, the provider may request an independent bill review within 30 calendar days of service of the second review pursuant to Section 4603.2 or 4622. If the provider fails to request an independent bill review within 30 days, the bill shall be deemed satisfied, and neither the employer nor the employee shall be liable for any further payment. If the employer has contested liability for any issue other than the reasonable amount payable for services, that issue shall be resolved prior to filing a request for independent bill review, and the time limit for requesting independent bill review shall not begin to run until the resolution of that issue becomes final, except as provided for in Section 4622.

(b) A request for independent review shall be made on a form prescribed by the administrative director, and shall include copies of the original billing itemization, any supporting documents that were furnished with the original billing, the explanation of review, the request for second review together with any supporting documentation submitted with that request, and the final explanation of the second review. The administrative director may require that requests for independent bill review be submitted electronically. A copy of the request, together with all required documents, shall be served on the employer. Only the request form and the proof of payment of the fee required by subdivision (c) shall be filed with the administrative director. Upon notice of assignment of the independent bill reviewer, the requesting party shall submit the documents listed in this subdivision to the independent bill reviewer within 10 days.

(c) The provider shall pay to the administrative director a fee determined by the administrative director to cover no more than the reasonable estimated cost of independent bill review and administration of the independent bill review program. The administrative director may prescribe different fees depending on the number of items in the bill or other criteria determined by regulation adopted by the administrative director. If any additional payment is found owing from the employer to the medical provider, the employer shall reimburse the provider for the fee in addition to the amount found owing.

(d) Upon receipt of a request for independent bill review and the required fee, the administrative director or the administrative director's designee shall assign the request to an independent bill reviewer within 30 days and notify the medical provider and employer of the independent reviewer assigned.

(e) The independent bill reviewer shall review the materials submitted by the parties and make a written determination of any additional amounts to be paid to the medical provider and state the reasons for the determination. If the independent bill reviewer deems necessary, the independent bill reviewer may request additional docu-

Labor

ments from the medical provider or employer. The employer shall have no obligation to serve medical reports on the provider unless the reports are requested by the independent bill reviewer. If additional documents are requested, the parties shall respond with the documents requested within 30 days and shall provide the other party with copies of any documents submitted to the independent reviewer, and the independent reviewer shall make a written determination of any additional amounts to be paid to the medical provider and state the reasons for the determination within 60 days of the receipt of the administrative director's assignment. The written determination of the independent bill reviewer shall be sent to the administrative director and provided to both the medical provider and the employer.

(f) The determination of the independent bill reviewer shall be deemed a determination and order of the administrative director. The determination is final and binding on all parties unless an aggrieved party files with the appeals board a verified appeal from the medical bill review determination of the administrative director within 20 days of the service of the determination. The medical bill review determination of the administrative director shall be presumed to be correct and shall be set aside only upon clear and convincing evidence of one or more of the following grounds for appeal:

(1) The administrative director acted without or in excess of his or her powers.

(2) The determination of the administrative director was procured by fraud.

(3) The independent bill reviewer was subject to a material conflict of interest that is in violation of Section 139.5.

(4) The determination was the result of bias on the basis of race, national origin, ethnic group identification, religion, age, sex, sexual orientation, color, or disability.

(5) The determination was the result of a plainly erroneous express or implied finding of fact, provided that the mistake of fact is a matter of ordinary knowledge based on the information submitted for review and not a matter that is subject to expert opinion.

(g) If the determination of the administrative director is reversed, the dispute shall be remanded to the administrative director to submit the dispute to independent bill review by a different independent review organization. In the event that a different independent bill review organization is not available after remand, the administrative director shall submit the dispute to the original bill review organization for review by a different reviewer within the organization. In no event shall the appeals board or any higher court make a determination of ultimate fact contrary to the determination of the bill review organization.

(h) Once the independent bill reviewer has made a determination regarding additional amounts to be paid to the medical provider, the employer shall pay the additional amounts per the timely payment requirements set forth in Sections 4603.2 and 4603.4. **Leg.H.** 2012 ch. 363 (SB 863) §39.

2012 Note: For legislative findings, declarations, and applicability of Stats. 2012 ch. 363, see the 2012 Notes following Lab C §62.5.

Ref.: Hanna §§ 5.02[2][d], 22.05[3]; Herlick Handbook §§ 4.10[2], [3], 10.01[2], 10.02[3], [4], 10.08[1].

§4604. Jurisdiction of appeals board to settle disputes.

Controversies between employer and employee arising under this chapter shall be determined by the appeals board, upon the request of either party, except as otherwise provided by Section 4610.5. **Leg.H.** 1937, 1965 ch. 1513 §88, operative January 15, 1966, 2012 ch. 363 (SB 863) §40.

2012 Note: For legislative findings, declarations, and applicability of Stats. 2012 ch. 363, see the 2012 Notes following Lab C §62.5.

Ref.: 8 C.C.R. §10950; Hanna §§ 5.05[10][d], 21.02[1], 22.10; Herlick Handbook §§ 4.18[1], 10.01[2].

§4604.5. Medical treatment utilization schedule—Guidelines; limitations on chiropractic, occupational therapy, and physical therapy visits.

(a) The recommended guidelines set forth in the medical treatment utilization schedule adopted by the administrative director pursuant to Section 5307.27 shall be presumptively correct on the issue of extent and scope of medical treatment. The presumption is rebuttable and may be controverted by a preponderance of the scientific medical evidence establishing that a variance from the guidelines reasonably is required to cure or relieve the injured worker from the effects of his or her injury. The presumption created is one affecting the burden of proof.

(b) The recommended guidelines set forth in the schedule adopted pursuant to subdivision (a) shall reflect practices that are evidence and scientifically based, nationally recognized, and peer reviewed. The guidelines shall be designed to assist providers by offering an analytical framework for the evaluation and treatment of injured workers, and shall constitute care in accordance with Section 4600 for all injured workers diagnosed with industrial conditions.

(c)(1) Notwithstanding the medical treatment utilization schedule, for injuries occurring on and after January 1, 2004, an employee shall be entitled to no more than 24 chiropractic, 24 occupational therapy, and 24 physical therapy visits per industrial injury.

(2)(A) Paragraph (1) shall not apply when an employer authorizes, in writing, additional visits to a health care practitioner for physical medicine services. Payment or authorization for treatment beyond the limits set forth in paragraph (1) shall not be deemed a waiver of the limits set forth by paragraph (1) with respect to future requests for authorization.

(B) The Legislature finds and declares that the amendments made to subparagraph (A) by the act adding this subparagraph are declaratory of existing law.

(3) Paragraph (1) shall not apply to visits for postsurgical physical medicine and postsurgical rehabilitation services provided in compliance with a postsurgical treatment utilization schedule established by the administrative director pursuant to Section 5307.27.

(d) For all injuries not covered by the official utilization schedule adopted pursuant to Section 5307.27, authorized treatment shall be in accordance with other evidence-based medical treatment guidelines that are recognized generally by the national medical community and scientifically based. **Leg.H.** 2003 ch. 639 (SB 228), 2004 ch. 34 (SB 899), effective April 19, 2004, 2007 ch. 621 (AB 1073) §1, 2008 ch. 179 (SB 1498) §175, 2012 ch. 363 (SB 863) §41.

2012 Note: For legislative findings, declarations, and applicability of Stats. 2012 ch. 363, see the 2012 Notes following Lab C §62.5.

2004 Note: The amendment to §4604.5 made by this act shall apply prospectively from the date of enactment of this act, regardless of the date of injury, unless otherwise specified, but shall not constitute good cause to reopen or rescind, alter, or amend any existing order, decision, or award of the Workers' Compensation Appeals Board. Stats. 2004 ch. 34 (SB 899) §47.

Ref.: 8 C.C.R. §§9767.6, 9792.6, 9792.7, 9792.8, 9792.9, 9792.10, 9881, 10118.1, 10950; Hanna §§ 5.02[3A], 22.05[6][b]; Herlick Handbook §§ 4.01[3], 4.05[3], 4.07[2], 10.01[2].

§4605. Consulting or attending physicians provided at employee's expense.

Nothing contained in this chapter shall limit the right of the employee to provide, at his or her own expense, a consulting physician or any attending physicians whom he or she desires. Any report prepared by consulting or attending physicians pursuant to this section shall not be the sole basis of an award of compensation. A qualified medical evaluator or authorized treating physician shall address any report procured pursuant to this section and shall indicate whether he or she agrees or disagrees with the findings or opinions stated in the report, and shall identify the bases for this opinion. **Leg.H.** 1937, 2012 ch. 363 (SB 863) §42.

2012 Note: For legislative findings, declarations, and applicability of Stats. 2012 ch. 363, see the 2012 Notes following Lab C §62.5.

Ref.: Herlick Handbook §§ 4.07[5], 4.11[7], 10.01[2].

§4606. Public self-insured employer; 90-day limitation inapplicable.

Any county, city and county, city, school district, or other public corporation within the state which was a self-insured employer under the "Workmen's Compensation, Insurance and Safety Act," enacted by Chapter 176 of the Statutes of 1913, may provide such medical, and hospital treatment, including nursing, medicines, medical and surgical supplies, crutches, and apparatus, including artificial members which is reasonably required to cure or relieve from the effects of an injury to a former employee who was covered under such act, without regard to the 90-day limitation of subdivision (a) of Section 15 of such act for medical treatment. The provisions of this section shall not be operative in any such county, city and county, city, school district, or other public corporation unless adopted by a resolution of the governing body of such public entity.

Ref.: Herlick Handbook § 10.01[2].

§4607. Denial of petition to terminate benefits; attorney's fees.

Where a party to a proceeding institutes proceedings to terminate an award made by the appeals board to an applicant for continuing medical treatment and is unsuccessful in such proceedings, the appeals board may determine the amount of attorney's fees reasonably incurred by the applicant in resisting the proceeding to terminate the medical treatment, and may assess such reasonable attorney's fees as a cost upon the party instituting the proceedings to terminate the award of the appeals board.

Ref.: Hanna § 20.02[2][h]; Herlick Handbook §§ 9.13, 10.01[2], 10.09[5], 14.42.

§4608. Pharmacy benefits; form requirements.

No workers' compensation insurer, self-insured employer, or agent of an insurer or self-insured employer, shall refuse to pay pharmacy benefits solely because the claim form utilized is reproduced by the person providing the pharmacy benefits, provided the reproduced form is an exact copy of that used by the insurer, self-insured employer, or agent.

Ref.: Herlick Handbook § 10.01[2].

§4609. Disclosure relating to health care provider's participation in network; disclosures by contracting agent conveying its list of contracted health care providers and reimbursement rates; election by provider to be excluded from list; demonstration by payor of entitlement to pay contracted rate.

(a) In order to prevent the improper selling, leasing, or transferring of a health care provider's contract, it is the intent of the Legislature that every arrangement that results in any payor paying a health care provider a reduced rate for health care services based on the health care provider's participation in a network or panel shall be disclosed by the contracting agent to the provider in advance and shall actively encourage employees to use the network, unless the health care provider agrees to provide discounts without that active encouragement.

(b) Beginning July 1, 2000, every contracting agent that sells, leases, assigns, transfers, or conveys its list of contracted health care providers and their contracted reimbursement rates to a payor, as defined in subparagraph (A) of paragraph (3) of subdivision (d), or another contracting agent shall, upon entering or renewing a provider contract, do all of the following:

(1) Disclose whether the list of contracted providers may be sold, leased, transferred, or conveyed to other payors or other contracting agents, and specify whether those payors or contracting agents include workers' compensation insurers or automobile insurers.

(2) Disclose what specific practices, if any, payors utilize to actively encourage employees to use the list of contracted providers when obtaining medical care that entitles a payor to claim a contracted rate. For purposes of this paragraph, a payor is deemed to have actively encouraged employees to use the list of contracted providers if the employer provides information directly to employees during the period the employer has medical control advising them of the existence of the list of contracted providers through the use of a variety of advertising or marketing approaches that supply the names, addresses, and telephone numbers of contracted providers to employees; or in

Labor

advance of a workplace injury, or upon notice of an injury or claim by an employee, the approaches may include, but are not limited to, the use of provider directories, the use of a list of all contracted providers in an area geographically accessible to the posting site, the use of wall cards that direct employees to a readily accessible listing of those providers at the same location as the wall cards, the use of wall cards that direct employees to a toll-free telephone number or Internet Web site address, or the use of toll-free telephone numbers or Internet Web site addresses supplied directly during the period the employer has medical control. However, Internet Web site addresses alone shall not be deemed to satisfy the requirements of this paragraph. Nothing in this paragraph shall prevent contracting agents or payors from providing only listings of providers located within a reasonable geographic range of an employee. A payor who otherwise meets the requirements of this paragraph is deemed to have met the requirements of this paragraph regardless of the employer's ability to control medical treatment pursuant to Sections 4600 and 4600.3.

(3) Disclose whether payors to which the list of contracted providers may be sold, leased, transferred, or conveyed may be permitted to pay a provider's contracted rate without actively encouraging the employees to use the list of contracted providers when obtaining medical care. Nothing in this subdivision shall be construed to require a payor to actively encourage the employees to use the list of contracted providers when obtaining medical care in the case of an emergency.

(4) Disclose, upon the initial signing of a contract, and within 15 business days of receipt of a written request from a provider or provider panel, a payor summary of all payors currently eligible to claim a provider's contracted rate due to the provider's and payor's respective written agreements with any contracting agent.

(5) Allow providers, upon the initial signing, renewal, or amendment of a provider contract, to decline to be included in any list of contracted providers that is sold, leased, transferred, or conveyed to payors that do not actively encourage the employees to use the list of contracted providers when obtaining medical care as described in paragraph (2). Each provider's election under this paragraph shall be binding on the contracting agent with which the provider has the contract and any other contracting agent that buys, leases, or otherwise obtains the list of contracted providers.

A provider shall not be excluded from any list of contracted providers that is sold, leased, transferred, or conveyed to payors that actively encourage the employees to use the list of contracted providers when obtaining medical care, based upon the provider's refusal to be included on any list of contracted providers that is sold, leased, transferred, or conveyed to payors that do not actively encourage the employees to use the list of contracted providers when obtaining medical care.

(6) If the payor's explanation of benefits or explanation of review does not identify the name of the network that has a written agreement signed by the provider whereby the payor is entitled, directly or indirectly, to pay a preferred rate for the services rendered, the contracting agent shall do the following:

(A) Maintain a Web site that is accessible to all contracted providers and updated at least quarterly and maintain a toll-free telephone number accessible to all contracted providers whereby providers may access payor summary information.

(B) Disclose through the use of an Internet Web site, a toll-free telephone number, or through a delivery or mail service to its contracted providers, within 30 days, any sale, lease assignment, transfer or conveyance of the contracted reimbursement rates to another contracting agent or payor.

(7) Nothing in this subdivision shall be construed to impose requirements or regulations upon payors, as defined in subparagraph (A) of paragraph (3) of subdivision (d).

(c) Beginning July 1, 2000, a payor, as defined in subparagraph (B) of paragraph (3) of subdivision(d), shall do all of the following:

(1) Provide an explanation of benefits or explanation of review that identifies the name of the network with which the payor has an agreement that entitles them to pay a preferred rate for the services rendered.

(2) Demonstrate that it is entitled to pay a contracted rate within 30 business days of receipt of a written request from a provider who has received a claim payment from the payor. The provider shall include in the request a statement explaining why the payment is not at the correct contracted rate for the services provided. The failure of the provider to include a statement shall relieve the payor from the responsibility of demonstrating that it is entitled to pay the disputed contracted rate. The failure of a payor to make the demonstration to a properly documented request of the provider within 30 business days shall render the payor responsible for the lesser of the provider's actual fee or, as applicable, any fee schedule pursuant to this division, which amount shall be due and payable within 10 days of receipt of written notice from the provider, and shall bar the payor from taking any future discounts from that provider without the provider's express written consent until the payor can demonstrate to the provider that it is entitled to pay a contracted rate as provided in this subdivision. A payor shall be deemed to have demonstrated that it is entitled to pay a contracted rate if it complies with either of the following:

(A) Describes the specific practices the payor utilizes to comply with paragraph (2) of subdivision (b), and demonstrates compliance with paragraph (1).

(B) Identifies the contracting agent with whom the payor has a written agreement whereby the payor is not required to actively encourage employees to use the list of contracted providers pursuant to paragraph (5) of subdivision (b).

(d) For the purposes of this section, the following terms have the following meanings:

(1) "Contracting agent" means an insurer licensed under the Insurance Code to provide workers' compensation insurance, a health care service plan, including a specialized health care service plan, a preferred provider organization, or a self-insured employer, while engaged, for monetary or other consideration, in the act of selling, leasing, transferring, assigning, or conveying a provider or provider panel to provide health care services to employees for work-related injuries.

(2) "Employee" means a person entitled to seek health care services for a work-related injury.

(3)(A) For the purposes of subdivision (b), "payor" means a health care service plan, including a specialized health care service plan, an insurer licensed under the Insurance Code to provide disability insurance that covers hospital, medical, or surgical benefits, automobile insurance, or workers' compensation insurance, or a self-insured employer that is responsible to pay for health care services provided to beneficiaries.

(B) For the purposes of subdivision (c), "payor" means an insurer licensed under the Insurance Code to provide workers' compensation insurance, a self-insured employer, a third-party administrator or trust, or any other third party that is responsible to pay health care services provided to employees for work-related injuries, or an agent of an entity included in this definition.

(4) "Payor summary" means a written summary that includes the payor's name and the type of plan, including, but not limited to, a group health plan, an automobile insurance plan, and a workers' compensation insurance plan.

(5) "Provider" means any of the following:

(A) Any person licensed or certified pursuant to Division 2 (commencing with Section 500) of the Business and Professions Code.

(B) Any person licensed pursuant to the Chiropractic Initiative Act or the Osteopathic Initiative Act.

(C) Any person licensed pursuant to Chapter 2.5 (commencing with Section 1440) of Division 2 of the Health and Safety Code.

(D) A clinic, health dispensary, or health facility licensed pursuant to Division 2 (commencing with Section 1200) of the Health and Safety Code.

(E) Any entity exempt from licensure pursuant to Section 1206 of the Health and Safety Code.

(e) This section shall become operative on July 1, 2000. **Leg.H.** 1999 ch. 545, 2000 ch. 1069, 2001 ch. 159.

2000 Note: The amendments made by this act to Section 4609 of the Labor Code do not apply retroactively, and shall become operative on January 1, 2001. Stats. 2000 ch. 1069 §6.

Ref.: 8 C.C.R. §§9767.3, 9767.15.

§4610. Utilization review process to be established; administrative penalties for failure to meet certain requirements.

(a) For purposes of this section, "utilization review" means utilization review or utilization management functions that prospectively, retrospectively, or concurrently review and approve, modify, or deny, based in whole or in part on medical necessity to cure and relieve, treatment recommendations by physicians, as defined in Section 3209.3, prior to, retrospectively, or concurrent with the provision of medical treatment services pursuant to Section 4600.

(b) For all dates of injury occurring on or after January 1, 2018, emergency treatment services and medical treatment rendered for a body part or condition that is accepted as compensable by the employer and is addressed by the medical treatment utilization schedule adopted pursuant to Section 5307.7, by a member of the medical provider network or health care organization, or by a physician predesignated pursuant to subdivision (d) of Section 4600, within the 30 days following the initial date of injury, shall be authorized without prospective utilization review, except as provided in subdivision (c). The services rendered under this subdivision shall be consistent with the medical treatment utilization schedule. In the event that the employee is not subject to treatment with a medical provider network, health care organization, or predesignated physician pursuant to subdivision (d) of Section 4600, the employee shall be eligible for treatment under this section within 30 days following the initial date of injury if the treatment is rendered by a physician or facility selected by the employer. For treatment rendered by a medical provider network physician, health care organization physician, a physician predesignated pursuant to subdivision (d) of Section 4600, or an employer-selected physician, the report required under Section 6409 and a complete request for authorization shall be submitted by the physician within five days following the employee's initial visit and evaluation.

(c) Unless authorized by the employer or rendered as emergency medical treatment, the following medical treatment services, as defined in rules adopted by the administrative director, that are rendered through a member of the medical provider network or health care organization, a predesignated physician, an employer-selected physician, or an employer-selected facility, within the 30 days following the initial date of injury, shall be subject to prospective utilization review under this section:

(1) Pharmaceuticals, to the extent they are neither expressly exempted from prospective review nor authorized by the drug formulary adopted pursuant to Section 5307.27.

(2) Nonemergency inpatient and outpatient surgery, including all presurgical and postsurgical services.

(3) Psychological treatment services.

(4) Home health care services.

(5) Imaging and radiology services, excluding X-rays.

(6) All durable medical equipment, whose combined total value exceeds two hundred fifty dollars ($250), as determined by the official medical fee schedule.

(7) Electrodiagnostic medicine, including, but not limited to, electromyography and nerve conduction studies.

(8) Any other service designated and defined through rules adopted by the administrative director.

(d)(1) Except for emergency treatment services, any request for payment for treatment provided under subdivision (b) shall comply with Section 4603.2 and be submitted to the employer, or its insurer or claims administrator, within 30 days of the date the service was provided.

(2)(A) In the case of emergency treatment services, any request for payment for treatment provided under subdivision (b) shall comply with Section 4603.2 and be submitted to the employer, or its insurer or claims administrator, within 180 days of the date the service was provided.

(B) For the purposes of this subdivision, "emergency treatment services" means treatment for an emergency medical condition defined in subdivision (b) of Section 1317.1 of the Health and Safety Code and provided in a licensed general acute care hospital, as defined in Section 1250 of the Health and Safety Code.

(e) If a physician fails to submit the report required under Section 6409 and a complete request for authoriza-

Labor

tion, as described in subdivision (b), an employer may remove the physician's ability under this subdivision to provide further medical treatment to the employee that is exempt from prospective utilization review.

(f) An employer may perform retrospective utilization review for any treatment provided pursuant to subdivision (b) solely for the purpose of determining if the physician is prescribing treatment consistent with the schedule for medical treatment utilization, including, but not limited to, the drug formulary adopted pursuant to Section 5307.27.

(1) If it is found after retrospective utilization reviews that there is a pattern and practice of the physician or provider failing to render treatment consistent with the schedule for medical treatment utilization, including the drug formulary, the employer may remove the ability of the predesignated physician, employer-selected physician, or the member of the medical provider network or health care organization under this subdivision to provide further medical treatment to any employee that is exempt from prospective utilization review. The employer shall notify the physician or provider of the results of the retrospective utilization review and the requirement for prospective utilization review for all subsequent medical treatment.

(2) The results of retrospective utilization review may constitute a showing of good cause for an employer's petition requesting a change of physician or provider pursuant to Section 4603 and may serve as grounds for termination of the physician or provider from the medical provider network or health care organization.

(g) Each employer shall establish a utilization review process in compliance with this section, either directly or through its insurer or an entity with which an employer or insurer contracts for these services.

(1) Each utilization review process that modifies or denies requests for authorization of medical treatment shall be governed by written policies and procedures. These policies and procedures shall ensure that decisions based on the medical necessity to cure and relieve of proposed medical treatment services are consistent with the schedule for medical treatment utilization, including the drug formulary, adopted pursuant to Section 5307.27.

(2)(A) Unless otherwise indicated in this section, a physician providing treatment under Section 4600 shall send any request for authorization for medical treatment, with supporting documentation, to the claims administrator for the employer, insurer, or other entity according to rules adopted by the administrative director. The employer, insurer, or other entity shall employ or designate a medical director who holds an unrestricted license to practice medicine in this state issued pursuant to Section 2050 or 2450 of the Business and Professions Code. The medical director shall ensure that the process by which the employer or other entity reviews and approves, modifies, or denies requests by physicians prior to, retrospectively, or concurrent with the provision of medical treatment services complies with the requirements of this section. This section does not limit the existing authority of the Medical Board of California.

(B) A request for authorization, including its supporting documentation, shall not be altered or amended by any entity other than the requesting physician or provider prior to the submission of the request to the claims administrator in accordance with subparagraph (A). This subparagraph is declaratory of existing law.

(3)(A) A person other than a licensed physician who is competent to evaluate the specific clinical issues involved in the medical treatment services, if these services are within the scope of the physician's practice, requested by the physician, shall not modify or deny requests for authorization of medical treatment for reasons of medical necessity to cure and relieve or due to incomplete or insufficient information under subdivisions (i) and (j).

(B)(i) The employer, or any entity conducting utilization review on behalf of the employer, shall neither offer nor provide any financial incentive or consideration to a physician based on the number of modifications or denials made by the physician under this section.

(ii) An insurer or third-party administrator shall not refer utilization review services conducted on behalf of an employer under this section to an entity in which the insurer or third-party administrator has a financial interest as defined under Section 139.32. This prohibition does not apply if the insurer or third-party administrator provides the employer and the administrative director with prior written disclosure of both of the following:

(I) The entity conducting the utilization review services.

(II) The insurer or third-party administrator's financial interest in the entity.

(C) The administrative director has authority pursuant to this section to review any compensation agreement, payment schedule, or contract between the employer, or any entity conducting utilization review on behalf of the employer, and the utilization review physician. Any information disclosed to the administrative director pursuant to this paragraph shall be considered confidential information and not subject to disclosure pursuant to the California Public Records Act (Chapter 3.5 (commencing with Section 6250) of Division 7 of Title 1 of the Government Code). Disclosure of the information to the administrative director pursuant to this subdivision shall not waive the provisions of the Evidence Code relating to privilege.

(4) A utilization review process that modifies or denies requests for authorization of medical treatment shall be accredited on or before July 1, 2018, and shall retain active accreditation while providing utilization review services, by an independent, nonprofit organization to certify that the utilization review process meets specified criteria, including, but not limited to, timeliness in issuing a utilization review decision, the scope of medical material used in issuing a utilization review decision, peer-to-peer consultation, internal appeal procedure, and requiring a policy preventing financial incentives to doctors and other providers based on the utilization review decision. The administrative director shall adopt rules to implement the selection of an independent, nonprofit organization for those accreditation purposes. Until those rules are adopted, the administrative director shall designate URAC as the accrediting organization. The administrative director may adopt rules to do any of the following:

(A) Require additional specific criteria for measuring the quality of a utilization review process for purposes of accreditation.

(B) Exempt nonprofit, public sector internal utilization review programs from the accreditation requirement pursuant to this section, if the administrative director has adopted minimum standards applicable to nonprofit, public sector internal utilization review programs that meet or exceed the accreditation standards developed pursuant to this section.

(5) On or before July 1, 2018, each employer, either directly or through its insurer or an entity with which an employer or insurer contracts for utilization review services, shall submit a description of the utilization review process that modifies or denies requests for authorization of medical treatment and the written policies and procedures to the administrative director for approval. Approved utilization review process descriptions and the accompanying written policies and procedures shall be disclosed by the employer to employees and physicians and made available to the public by posting on the employer's, claims administrator's, or utilization review organization's internet website.

(h) The criteria or guidelines used in the utilization review process to determine whether to approve, modify, or deny medical treatment services shall be all of the following:

(1) Developed with involvement from actively practicing physicians.

(2) Consistent with the schedule for medical treatment utilization, including the drug formulary, adopted pursuant to Section 5307.27.

(3) Evaluated at least annually, and updated if necessary.

(4) Disclosed to the physician and the employee, if used as the basis of a decision to modify or deny services in a specified case under review.

(5) Available to the public upon request. An employer shall only be required to disclose the criteria or guidelines for the specific procedures or conditions requested. An employer may charge members of the public reasonable copying and postage expenses related to disclosing criteria or guidelines pursuant to this paragraph. Criteria or guidelines may also be made available through electronic means. A charge shall not be required for an employee whose physician's request for medical treatment services is under review.

(i) In determining whether to approve, modify, or deny requests by physicians prior to, retrospectively, or concurrent with the provisions of medical treatment services to employees, all of the following requirements shall be met:

(1) Except for treatment requests made pursuant to the formulary, prospective or concurrent decisions shall be made in a timely fashion that is appropriate for the nature of the employee's condition, not to exceed five normal business days from the receipt of a request for authorization for medical treatment and supporting information reasonably necessary to make the determination, but in no event more than 14 days from the date of the medical treatment recommendation by the physician. Prospective decisions regarding requests for treatment covered by the formulary shall be made no more than five normal business days from the date of receipt of the medical treatment request. The request for authorization and supporting documentation may be submitted electronically under rules adopted by the administrative director.

(2) In cases where the review is retrospective, a decision resulting in denial of all or part of the medical treatment service shall be communicated to the individual who received services, or to the individual's designee, within 30 days of the receipt of the information that is reasonably necessary to make this determination. If payment for a medical treatment service is made within the time prescribed by Section 4603.2, a retrospective decision to approve the service need not otherwise be communicated.

(3) If the employee's condition is one in which the employee faces an imminent and serious threat to the employee's health, including, but not limited to, the potential loss of life, limb, or other major bodily function, or the normal timeframe for the decisionmaking process, as described in paragraph (1), would be detrimental to the employee's life or health or could jeopardize the employee's ability to regain maximum function, decisions to approve, modify, or deny requests by physicians prior to, or concurrent with, the provision of medical treatment services to employees shall be made in a timely fashion that is appropriate for the nature of the employee's condition, but not to exceed 72 hours after the receipt of the information reasonably necessary to make the determination.

(4)(A) Final decisions to approve, modify, or deny requests by physicians for authorization prior to, or concurrent with, the provision of medical treatment services to employees shall be communicated to the requesting physician within 24 hours of the decision by telephone, facsimile, or, if agreed to by the parties, secure email.

(B) Decisions resulting in modification or denial of all or part of the requested health care service shall be communicated in writing to the employee, and to the physician if the initial communication under subparagraph (A) was by telephone, within 24 hours for concurrent review, or within two normal business days of the decision for prospective review, as prescribed by the administrative director. If the request is modified or denied, disputes shall be resolved in accordance with Section 4610.5, if applicable, or otherwise in accordance with Section 4062.

(C) In the case of concurrent review, medical care shall not be discontinued until the employee's physician has been notified of the decision and a care plan has been agreed upon by the physician that is appropriate for the medical needs of the employee. Medical care provided during a concurrent review shall be care that is medically necessary to cure and relieve, and an insurer or self-insured employer shall only be liable for those services determined medically necessary to cure and relieve. If the insurer or self-insured employer disputes whether or not one or more services offered concurrently with a utilization review were medically necessary to cure and relieve, the dispute shall be resolved pursuant to Section 4610.5, if applicable, or otherwise pursuant to Section 4062. A compromise between the parties that an insurer or self-insured employer believes may result in payment for services that were not medically necessary to cure and relieve shall be reported by the insurer or the self-insured employer to the licensing board of the provider or providers who received the payments, in a manner set forth by the respective board and in a way that minimizes reporting costs both to the board and to the insurer or self-insured employer, for evaluation as to possible violations of the statutes governing appro-

Labor

priate professional practices. Fees shall not be levied upon insurers or self-insured employers making reports required by this section.

(5) Communications regarding decisions to approve requests by physicians shall specify the specific medical treatment service approved. Responses regarding decisions to modify or deny medical treatment services requcsted by physicians shall include a clear and concise explanation of the reasons for the employer's decision, a description of the criteria or guidelines used, and the clinical reasons for the decisions regarding medical necessity. If a utilization review decision to deny a medical service is due to incomplete or insufficient information, the decision shall specify all of the following:

(A) The reason for the decision.

(B) A specific description of the information that is needed.

(C) The date and time of attempts made to contact the physician to obtain the necessary information.

(D) A description of the manner in which the request was communicated.

(j)(1) Unless otherwise indicated in this section, a physician providing treatment under Section 4600 shall send any request for authorization for medical treatment, with supporting documentation, to the claims administrator for the employer, insurer, or other entity according to rules adopted by the administrative director. If an employer, insurer, or other entity subject to this section requests medical information from a physician in order to determine whether to approve, modify, or deny requests for authorization, that employer, insurer, or other entity shall request only the information reasonably necessary to make the determination.

(2) If the employer, insurer, or other entity cannot make a decision within the timeframes specified in paragraph (1), (2), or (3) of subdivision (i) because the employer or other entity is not in receipt of, or in possession of, all of the information reasonably necessary to make a determination, the employer shall immediately notify the physician and the employee, in writing, that the employer cannot make a decision within the required timeframe, and specify the information that must be provided by the physician for a determination to be made. Upon receipt of all information reasonably necessary and requested by the employer, the employer shall approve, modify, or deny the request for authorization within the timeframes specified in paragraph (1), (2), or (3) of subdivision (i).

(k) A utilization review decision to modify or deny a treatment recommendation shall remain effective for 12 months from the date of the decision without further action by the employer with regard to a further recommendation by the same physician, or another physician within the requesting physician's practice group, for the same treatment unless the further recommendation is supported by a documented change in the facts material to the basis of the utilization review decision.

(*l*) Utilization review of a treatment recommendation shall not be required while the employer is disputing liability for injury or treatment of the condition for which treatment is recommended pursuant to Section 4062.

(m) If utilization review is deferred pursuant to subdivision (*l*), and it is finally determined that the employer is liable for treatment of the condition for which treatment is recommended, the time for the employer to conduct retrospective utilization review in accordance with paragraph (2) of subdivision (i) shall begin on the date the determination of the employer's liability becomes final, and the time for the employer to conduct prospective utilization review shall commence from the date of the employer's receipt of a treatment recommendation after the determination of the employer's liability.

(n) Each employer, insurer, or other entity subject to this section shall maintain telephone access during California business hours for physicians to request authorization for health care services and to conduct peer-to-peer discussions regarding issues, including the appropriateness of a requested treatment, modification of a treatment request, or obtaining additional information needed to make a medical necessity decision.

(o) The administrative director shall develop a system for the mandatory electronic reporting of documents related to every utilization review performed by each employer, which shall be administered by the Division of Workers' Compensation. The administrative director shall adopt regulations specifying the documents to be submitted by the employer and the authorized transmission format and timeframe for their submission. For purposes of this subdivision, "employer" means the employer, the insurer of an insured employer, a claims administrator, or a utilization review organization, or other entity acting on behalf of any of them.

(p) If the administrative director determines that the employer, insurer, or other entity subject to this section has failed to meet any of the timeframes in this section, or has failed to meet any other requirement of this section, the administrative director may assess, by order, administrative penalties for each failure. A proceeding for the issuance of an order assessing administrative penalties shall be subject to appropriate notice to, and an opportunity for a hearing with regard to, the person affected. The administrative penalties shall not be deemed to be an exclusive remedy for the administrative director. These penalties shall be deposited in the Workers' Compensation Administration Revolving Fund.

(q) The administrative director shall contract with an outside, independent research organization on or after March 1, 2019, to evaluate the impact of the provision of medical treatment within the first 30 days after a claim is filed, for a claim filed on or after January 1, 2017, and before January 1, 2019. The report shall be provided to the administrative director, the Senate Committee on Labor and Industrial Relations, and the Assembly Committee on Insurance before January 1, 2020. **Leg.H.** 2016 ch. 868 (SB 1160) §4.5, 2017 ch. 240 (SB 489) §1, 2019 ch. 647 (SB 537) §6.

2016 Note: For legislative findings and declarations, see the 2016 Note following Lab C §138.4.

Ref.: Hanna § 5.06.

§4610.1. Increase in compensation under §5814—Inapplicable for unreasonable delay in medical treatment for periods of time necessary to complete utilization review process; exception.

An employee shall not be entitled to an increase in compensation under Section 5814 for unreasonable delay in the provision of medical treatment for periods of time necessary to complete the utilization review process in compliance with Section 4610. A determination by the appeals board or a final determination of the administrative director pursuant to independent medical review that medical treatment is appropriate shall not be conclusive evidence that medical treatment was unreasonably delayed or denied for purposes of penalties under Section 5814. In no case shall this section preclude an employee from entitlement to an increase in compensation under Section 5814 when an employer has unreasonably delayed or denied medical treatment due to an unreasonable delay in completion of the utilization review process set forth in Section 4610. **Leg.H.** 2003 ch. 638 (AB 1557), 2012 ch. 363 (SB 863) §44.

2012 Note: For legislative findings, declarations, and applicability of Stats. 2012 ch. 363, see the 2012 Notes following Lab C §62.5.

Ref.: Hanna § 22.05[6][c][v]; Herlick Handbook § 4.16[2], [5].

§4610.3. Employer prohibited to rescind or modify authorization for medical treatment already provided.

(a) Regardless of whether an employer has established a medical provider network pursuant to Section 4616 or entered into a contract with a health care organization pursuant to Section 4600.5, an employer that authorizes medical treatment shall not rescind or modify that authorization after the medical treatment has been provided based on that authorization for any reason, including, but not limited to, the employer's subsequent determination that the physician who treated the employee was not eligible to treat that injured employee. If the authorized medical treatment consists of a series of treatments or services, the employer may rescind or modify the authorization only for the treatments or services that have not already been provided.

(b) This section shall not be construed to expand or alter the benefits available under, or the terms and conditions of, any contract, including, but not limited to, existing medical provider network and health care organization contracts.

(c) This section shall not be construed to impact the ability of the employer to transfer treatment of an injured employee into a medical provider network or health care organization. This subdivision is declaratory of existing law.

(d) This section shall not be construed to establish that a provider of authorized medical treatment is the physician primarily responsible for managing the injured employee's care for purposes of rendering opinions on all medical issues necessary to determine eligibility for compensation. **Leg.H.** 2009 ch. 436 (AB 361) §1.

Ref.: Hanna § 22.05[6][b][i]; Herlick Handbook § 4.09[2].

§4610.5. Review of utilization review decision.

(a) This section applies to the following disputes:

(1) Any dispute over a utilization review decision regarding treatment for an injury occurring on or after January 1, 2013.

(2) Any dispute over a utilization review decision if the decision is communicated to the requesting physician on or after July 1, 2013, regardless of the date of injury.

(3) Any dispute occurring on or after January 1, 2018, over medication prescribed pursuant to the drug formulary adopted pursuant to Section 5307.27.

(b) A dispute described in subdivision (a) shall be resolved only in accordance with this section.

(c) For purposes of this section and Section 4610.6, the following definitions apply:

(1) "Disputed medical treatment" means medical treatment that has been modified or denied by a utilization review decision on the basis of medical necessity.

(2) "Medically necessary" and "medical necessity" mean medical treatment that is reasonably required to cure or relieve the injured employee of the effects of his or her injury and based on the following standards, which shall be applied as set forth in the medical treatment utilization schedule, including the drug formulary, adopted by the administrative director pursuant to Section 5307.27:

(A) The guidelines, including the drug formulary, adopted by the administrative director pursuant to Section 5307.27.

(B) Peer-reviewed scientific and medical evidence regarding the effectiveness of the disputed service.

(C) Nationally recognized professional standards.

(D) Expert opinion.

(E) Generally accepted standards of medical practice.

(F) Treatments that are likely to provide a benefit to a patient for conditions for which other treatments are not clinically efficacious.

(3) "Utilization review decision" means a decision pursuant to Section 4610 to modify or deny, based in whole or in part on medical necessity to cure or relieve, a treatment recommendation or recommendations by a physician prior to, retrospectively, or concurrent with, the provision of medical treatment services pursuant to Section 4600 or subdivision (c) of Section 5402. "Utilization review decision" may also mean a determination, occurring on or after January 1, 2018, by a physician regarding the medical necessity of medication prescribed pursuant to the drug formulary adopted pursuant to Section 5307.27.

(4) Unless otherwise indicated by context, "employer" means the employer, the insurer of an insured employer, a claims administrator, or a utilization review organization, or other entity acting on behalf of any of them.

(d) If a utilization review decision denies or modifies a treatment recommendation based on medical necessity, the employee may request an independent medical review as provided by this section.

(e) A utilization review decision may be reviewed or appealed only by independent medical review pursuant to this section. Neither the employee nor the employer shall have any liability for medical treatment furnished without

Labor

the authorization of the employer if the treatment is modified or denied by a utilization review decision, unless the utilization review decision is overturned by independent medical review in accordance with this section.

(f) As part of its notification to the employee regarding an initial utilization review decision based on medical necessity that denies or modifies a treatment recommendation, the employer shall provide the employee with a one-page form prescribed by the administrative director, and an addressed envelope, which the employee may return to the administrative director or the administrative director's designee to initiate an independent medical review. The employee may also request independent medical review electronically under rules adopted by the administrative director. The employer shall include on the form any information required by the administrative director to facilitate the completion of the independent medical review. The form shall also include all of the following:

(1) Notice that the utilization review decision is final unless the employee requests independent medical review.

(2) A statement indicating the employee's consent to obtain any necessary medical records from the employer or insurer and from any medical provider the employee may have consulted on the matter, to be signed by the employee.

(3) Notice of the employee's right to provide information or documentation, either directly or through the employee's physician, regarding the following:

(A) The treating physician's recommendation indicating that the disputed medical treatment is medically necessary for the employee's medical condition.

(B) Medical information or justification that a disputed medical treatment, on an urgent care or emergency basis, was medically necessary for the employee's medical condition.

(C) Reasonable information supporting the employee's position that the disputed medical treatment is or was medically necessary for the employee's medical condition, including all information provided to the employee by the employer or by the treating physician, still in the employee's possession, concerning the employer's or the physician's decision regarding the disputed medical treatment, as well as any additional material that the employee believes is relevant.

(g) The independent medical review process may be terminated at any time upon the employer's written authorization of the disputed medical treatment. Notice of the authorization, any settlement or award that may resolve the medical treatment dispute, or the requesting physician withdrawing the request for treatment, shall be communicated to the independent medical review organization by the employer within five days.

(h)(1) The employee may submit a request for independent medical review to the division. The request may be made electronically under rules adopted by the administrative director. The request shall be made no later than as follows:

(A) For formulary disputes, 10 days after the service of the utilization review decision to the employee.

(B) For all other medical treatment disputes, 30 days after the service of the utilization review decision to the employee.

(2) If at the time of a utilization review decision the employer is also disputing liability for the treatment for any reason besides medical necessity, the time for the employee to submit a request for independent medical review to the administrative director or administrative director's designee is extended to 30 days after service of a notice to the employee showing that the other dispute of liability has been resolved.

(3) If the employer fails to comply with subdivision (f) at the time of notification of its utilization review decision, the time limitations for the employee to submit a request for independent medical review shall not begin to run until the employer provides the required notice to the employee.

(4) A provider of emergency medical treatment when the employee faced an imminent and serious threat to his or her health, including, but not limited to, the potential loss of life, limb, or other major bodily function, may submit a request for independent medical review on its own behalf. A request submitted by a provider pursuant to this paragraph shall be submitted to the administrative director or administrative director's designee within the time limitations applicable for an employee to submit a request for independent medical review.

(i) An employer shall not engage in any conduct that has the effect of delaying the independent review process. Engaging in that conduct or failure of the employer to promptly comply with this section is a violation of this section and, in addition to any other fines, penalties, and other remedies available to the administrative director, the employer shall be subject to an administrative penalty in an amount determined pursuant to regulations to be adopted by the administrative director, not to exceed five thousand dollars ($5,000) for each day that proper notification to the employee is delayed. The administrative penalties shall be paid to the Workers' Compensation Administration Revolving Fund.

(j) For purposes of this section, an employee may designate a parent, guardian, conservator, relative, or other designee of the employee as an agent to act on his or her behalf. A designation of an agent executed prior to the utilization review decision shall not be valid. The requesting physician may join with or otherwise assist the employee in seeking an independent medical review, and may advocate on behalf of the employee.

(k) The administrative director or his or her designee shall expeditiously review requests and immediately notify the employee and the employer in writing as to whether the request for an independent medical review has been approved, in whole or in part, and, if not approved, the reasons therefor. If there appears to be any medical necessity issue, the dispute shall be resolved pursuant to an independent medical review, except that, unless the employer agrees that the case is eligible for independent medical review, a request for independent medical review shall be deferred if at the time of a utilization review decision the employer is also disputing liability for the treatment for any reason besides medical necessity.

(*l*) Upon notice from the administrative director that an independent review organization has been assigned, the employer shall electronically provide to the independent medical review organization under rules adopted by the administrative director a copy and list of all of the following documents within 10 days of notice of assignment:

(1) A copy of all of the employee's medical records in the possession of the employer or under the control of the employer relevant to each of the following:

(A) The employee's current medical condition.

(B) The medical treatment being provided by the employer.

(C) The request for authorization and utilization review decision.

(2) A copy of all information provided to the employee by the employer concerning employer and provider decisions regarding the disputed treatment.

(3) A copy of any materials the employee or the employee's provider submitted to the employer in support of the employee's request for the disputed treatment.

(4) A copy of any other relevant documents or information used by the employer or its utilization review organization in determining whether the disputed treatment should have been provided, and any statements by the employer or its utilization review organization explaining the reasons for the decision to deny or modify the recommended treatment on the basis of medical necessity. The employer shall concurrently provide a copy of the documents required by this paragraph to the employee and the requesting physician, except that documents previously provided to the employee or physician need not be provided again if a list of those documents is provided.

(m) Any newly developed or discovered relevant medical records in the possession of the employer after the initial documents are provided to the independent medical review organization shall be forwarded immediately to the independent medical review organization. The employer shall concurrently provide a copy of medical records required by this subdivision to the employee or the employee's treating physician, unless the offer of medical records is declined or otherwise prohibited by law. The confidentiality of medical records shall be maintained pursuant to applicable state and federal laws.

(n) If there is an imminent and serious threat to the health of the employee, as specified in subdivision (c) of Section 1374.33 of the Health and Safety Code, all necessary information and documents required by subdivision (*l*) shall be delivered to the independent medical review organization within 24 hours of approval of the request for review.

(o) The employer shall promptly issue a notification to the employee, after submitting all of the required material to the independent medical review organization, that lists documents submitted and includes copies of material not previously provided to the employee or the employee's designee.

(p) The claims administrator who issued the utilization review decision in dispute shall notify the independent medical review organization if there is a change in the claims administrator responsible for the claim. Notice shall be given to the independent medical review organization within five working days of the change in administrator taking effect. **Leg.H.** 2012 ch. 363 (SB 863) §45, 2013 ch. 287 (SB 375) §5, 2014 ch. 217 (AB 2732) §2, 2016 ch. 868 (SB 1160) §5.

2016 Note: For legislative findings and declarations, see the 2016 Note following Lab C §138.4.

2012 Note: For legislative findings, declarations, and applicability of Stats. 2012 ch. 363, see the 2012 Notes following Lab C §62.5.

Ref.: Hanna §§ 5.02[2][c], [d], 5.07[10][d], 22.05[6][b][iii], [iv]; Herlick Handbook §§ 4.04[5], 4.09[6], [7], 4.10[1], [2], 4.14[3], 4.16[2], 4.18[1], 10.02[3], [4], 10.08[1].

§4610.6. Independent medical review organization to conduct review of utilization review decision; procedure upon final determination of review.

(a) Upon receipt of a case pursuant to Section 4610.5, an independent medical review organization shall conduct the review in accordance with this article and any regulations or orders of the administrative director. The organization's review shall be limited to an examination of the medical necessity of the disputed medical treatment.

(b) Upon receipt of information and documents related to a case, the medical reviewer or reviewers selected to conduct the review by the independent medical review organization shall promptly review all pertinent medical records of the employee, provider reports, and any other information submitted to the organization or requested from any of the parties to the dispute by the reviewers. If the reviewers request information from any of the parties, a copy of the request and the response shall be provided to all of the parties. The reviewer or reviewers shall also review relevant information related to the criteria set forth in subdivision (c).

(c) Following its review, the reviewer or reviewers shall determine whether the disputed health care service was medically necessary based on the specific medical needs of the employee and the standards of medical necessity as defined in subdivision (c) of Section 4610.5.

(d)(1) The organization shall complete its review and make its determination in writing, and in layperson's terms to the maximum extent practicable, and the determination shall be issued, as follows:

(A) For a dispute over medication prescribed pursuant to the drug formulary submitted under subdivision (h) of Section 4610.5, within five working days from the date of receipt of the request for review and supporting documentation, or within less time as prescribed by the administrative director.

(B) For all other medical treatment disputes submitted for review under subdivision (h) of Section 4610.5, within 30 days of receipt of the request for review and supporting documentation, or within less time as prescribed by the administrative director.

(C) If the disputed medical treatment has not been provided and the employee's provider or the administrative director certifies in writing that an imminent and serious threat to the health of the employee may exist, including, but not limited to, serious pain, the potential loss of life, limb, or major bodily function, or the immediate and serious deterioration of the health of the employee, the analyses and determinations of the reviewers shall be expedited and rendered within three days of the receipt of the information.

(2) Subject to the approval of the administrative director, the deadlines for analyses and determinations involving both regular and expedited reviews may be extended for up to three days in extraordinary circumstances or for good cause.

(e) The medical professionals' analyses and determinations shall state whether the disputed health care service is medically necessary. Each analysis shall cite the employee's medical condition, the relevant documents in the record, and the relevant findings associated with the provisions of subdivision (c) to support the determination. If more than one medical professional reviews the case, the recommendation of the majority shall prevail. If the medical professionals reviewing the case are evenly split as to whether the disputed health care service should be provided, the decision shall be in favor of providing the service.

(f) The independent medical review organization shall provide the administrative director, the employer, the employee, and the employee's provider with the analyses and determinations of the medical professionals reviewing the case, and a description of the qualifications of the medical professionals. The independent medical review organization shall keep the names of the reviewers confidential in all communications with entities or individuals outside the independent medical review organization. If more than one medical professional reviewed the case and the result was differing determinations, the independent medical review organization shall provide each of the separate reviewer's analyses and determinations.

(g) The determination of the independent medical review organization shall be deemed to be the determination of the administrative director and shall be binding on all parties.

(h) A determination of the administrative director pursuant to this section may be reviewed only by a verified appeal from the medical review determination of the administrative director, filed with the appeals board for hearing pursuant to Chapter 3 (commencing with Section 5500) of Part 4 and served on all interested parties within 30 days of the date of mailing of the determination to the aggrieved employee or the aggrieved employer. The determination of the administrative director shall be presumed to be correct and shall be set aside only upon proof by clear and convincing evidence of one or more of the following grounds for appeal:

(1) The administrative director acted without or in excess of the administrative director's powers.

(2) The determination of the administrative director was procured by fraud.

(3) The independent medical reviewer was subject to a material conflict of interest that is in violation of Section 139.5.

(4) The determination was the result of bias on the basis of race, national origin, ethnic group identification, religion, age, sex, sexual orientation, color, or disability.

(5) The determination was the result of a plainly erroneous express or implied finding of fact, provided that the mistake of fact is a matter of ordinary knowledge based on the information submitted for review pursuant to Section 4610.5 and not a matter that is subject to expert opinion.

(i) If the determination of the administrative director is reversed, the dispute shall be remanded to the administrative director to submit the dispute to independent medical review by a different independent review organization. In the event that a different independent medical review organization is not available after remand, the administrative director shall submit the dispute to the original medical review organization for review by a different reviewer in the organization. In no event shall a workers' compensation administrative law judge, the appeals board, or any higher court make a determination of medical necessity contrary to the determination of the independent medical review organization.

(j) Upon receiving the determination of the administrative director that a disputed health care service is medically necessary, the employer shall promptly implement the decision as provided by this section unless the employer has also disputed liability for any reason besides medical necessity. In the case of reimbursement for services already rendered, the employer shall reimburse the provider or employee, whichever applies, within 20 days, subject to resolution of any remaining issue of the amount of payment pursuant to Sections 4603.2 to 4603.6, inclusive. In the case of services not yet rendered, the employer shall authorize the services within five working days of receipt of the written determination from the independent medical review organization, or sooner if appropriate for the nature of the employee's medical condition, and shall inform the employee and provider of the authorization.

(k) Failure to pay for services already provided or to authorize services not yet rendered within the time prescribed by subdivision (*l*) is a violation of this section and, in addition to any other fines, penalties, and other remedies available to the administrative director, the employer shall be subject to an administrative penalty in an amount determined pursuant to regulations to be adopted by the administrative director, not to exceed five thousand dollars ($5,000) for each day the decision is not implemented. The administrative penalties shall be paid to the Workers' Compensation Administration Revolving Fund.

(*l*) The costs of independent medical review and the administration of the independent medical review system shall be borne by employers through a fee system established by the administrative director. After considering any relevant information on program costs, the administrative director shall establish a reasonable, per-case reimbursement schedule to pay the costs of independent medical review organization reviews and the cost of administering the independent medical review system, which may vary depending on the type of medical condition under review and on other relevant factors.

(m) The administrative director may publish the results of independent medical review determinations after removing individually identifiable information.

(n) If any provision of this section, or the application thereof to any person or circumstances, is held invalid, the remainder of the section, and the application of its provisions to other persons or circumstances, shall not be affected thereby. **Leg.H.** 2012 ch. 363 (SB 863) §46, 2016 ch. 868 (SB 1160) §6.

2016 Note: For legislative findings and declarations, see the 2016 Note following Lab C §138.4.

2012 Note: For legislative findings, declarations, and applicability of Stats. 2012 ch. 363, see the 2012 Notes following Lab C §62.5.

Ref.: Hanna §§ 5.02[2][c], [d], 5.07[10][d], 22.05[6][b][iv]; Herlick Handbook §§ 4.10[2], 10.02[3], [4], 10.08[1].

§4611. Rights and obligations of health care provider contract governed by underlying contract between provider and contracting agent upon contracting agent's sale, lease, or transfer of contract to payor.

(a) When a contracting agent sells, leases, or transfers a health provider's contract to a payor, the rights and obligations of the provider shall be governed by the underlying contract between the health care provider and the contracting agent.

(b) For purposes of this section, the following terms have the following meanings:

(1) "Contracting agent" has the meaning set forth in paragraph (2) of subdivision (d) of Section 4609.

(2) "Payor" has the meaning set forth in paragraph (3) of subdivision (d) of Section 4609. **Leg.H.** 2003 ch. 203 (AB 175), 2004 ch. 183 (AB 3082) (amended & renumbered from §4610).

§4614. Payment for services.

(a)(1) Notwithstanding Section 5307.1, where the employee's individual or organizational provider of health care services rendered under this division and paid on a fee-for-service basis is also the provider of health care services under contract with the employee's health benefit program, and the service or treatment provided is included within the range of benefits of the employee's health benefit program, and paid on a fee-for-service basis, the amount of payment for services provided under this division, for a work-related occurrence or illness, shall be no more than the amount that would have been paid for the same services under the health benefit plan, for a non-work-related occurrence or illness.

(2) A health care service plan that arranges for health care services to be rendered to an employee under this division under a contract, and which is also the employee's organizational provider for nonoccupational injuries and illnesses, with the exception of a nonprofit health care service plan that exclusively contracts with a medical group to provide or arrange for medical services to its enrollees in a designated geographic area, shall be paid by the employer for services rendered under this division only on a capitated basis.

(b)(1) Where the employee's individual or organizational provider of health care services rendered under this division who is not providing services under a contract is not the provider of health care services under contract with the employee's health benefit program or where the services rendered under this division are not within the benefits provided under the employer-sponsored health benefit program, the provider shall receive payment that is no more than the average of the payment that would have been paid by five of the largest preferred provider organizations by geographic region. Physicians, as defined in Section 3209.3, shall be reimbursed at the same averaged rates, regardless of licensure, for the delivery of services under the same procedure code. This subdivision shall not apply to a health care service plan that provides its services on a capitated basis.

(2) The administrative director shall identify the regions and the five largest carriers in each region. The carriers shall provide the necessary information to the administrative director in the form and manner requested by the administrative director. The administrative director shall make this information available to the affected providers on an annual basis.

(c) Nothing in this section shall prohibit an individual or organizational health care provider from being paid fees different from those set forth in the official medical fee schedule by an employer, insurance carrier, third-party administrator on behalf of employers, or preferred provider organization representing an employer or insurance carrier provided that the administrative director has determined that the alternative negotiated rates between the organizational or individual provider and a payer, a third-party administrator on behalf of employers, or a preferred provider organization will produce greater savings in the aggregate than if each item on billings were to be charged at the scheduled rate.

(d) For the purposes of this section, "organizational provider" means an entity that arranges for health care services to be rendered directly by individual caregivers. An organizational provider may be a health care service plan, disability insurer, health care organization, preferred provider organization, or workers' compensation insurer arranging for care through a managed care network or on a fee-for-service basis. An individual provider is either an individual or institution that provides care directly to the injured worker. **Leg.H.** 1993 ch. 121, effective July 16, 1993, ch. 1242, 2002 ch. 866 (AB 486).

1993 Note: Section 4614, as added by ch. 121, applies only to injuries occurring on or after January 1, 1994. Stats. 1993 ch. 121 §77.

Ref.: Herlick Handbook § 4.17[1].

§4614.1. Certified health care service plan permitted to accept payment from self-insured employers.

Notwithstanding subdivision (f) of Section 1345 of the Health and Safety Code, a health care service plan licensed pursuant to the Knox-Keene Health Care Service Plan Act and certified by the administrative director pursuant to Section 4600.5 to provide health care pursuant to Section 4600.3 shall be permitted to accept payment from a self-insured employer, a group of self-insured employers, or the insurer of an employer on a fee-for-service basis for the provision of such health care as long as the health care service plan is not both the health care organization in which the employee is enrolled and the plan through which the employee receives regular health benefits. **Leg.H.** 1993 ch. 121, effective July 16, 1993, ch. 1242.

1993 Note: Section 4614.1, as added by ch. 121, applies only to injuries occurring on or after January 1, 1994. Stats. 1993 ch. 121 §77.

Ref.: Herlick Handbook § 4.17[1].

§4615. Lien on behalf of physician, practitioner, or provider of medical services; stay pending criminal charges for fraud against workers' compensation system, medical billing, insurance; posting of information on Internet Web site.

(a) Upon the filing of criminal charges against a physician, practitioner, or provider for any crime described in subparagraph (A) of paragraph (1) of subdivision (a) of Section 139.21, the following shall occur:

(1) Any lien filed by, or on behalf of, the physician, practitioner, or provider or any entity controlled, as defined in paragraph (3) of subdivision (a) of Section 139.21, by the physician, practitioner, or provider for medical treatment services under Section 4600 or medical-legal services under Section 4621, and any accrual of interest related to the lien, shall be automatically stayed.

(2) Except as provided in subdivisions (b) and (c), the stay shall be in effect from the time of the filing of the charges until the disposition of the criminal proceedings.

(b) Upon conviction, as defined in paragraph (4) of subdivision (a) of Section 139.21, of the physician, practitioner, or provider for any crime described in subparagraph (A) of paragraph (1) of subdivision (a) of Section 139.21, the automatic stay shall remain in effect for any liens not dismissed pursuant to paragraph (1) of subdivision (e) of Section 139.21 until the commencement of lien consolidation procedures under paragraph (2) of subdivision (e) of Section 139.21.

(c) The automatic stay required by this section shall not preclude a physician, practitioner, or provider from requesting the dismissal with prejudice and forfeiture of sums claimed therein of any liens subject to the stay. Upon the receipt of that request and for good cause shown, the chief judge of the Division of Workers Compensation or his or her designee may lift the stay as to one or more of those liens and order that they be dismissed with prejudice.

(d) The administrative director shall promptly post on the division's Internet Web site the names of any physician, practitioner, or provider of medical treatment services whose liens are stayed pursuant to this section.

(e) The automatic stay required by this section shall not preclude the appeals board from inquiring into and determining within a workers' compensation proceeding whether a lien is stayed pursuant to subdivision (a) or whether a lien claimant is controlled by a physician, practitioner, or provider.

(f) The administrative director may adopt rules for the implementation of this section.

(g) Notwithstanding this section, the filing of new or additional criminal charges against a physician, practitioner, or provider who has been suspended pursuant to subparagraph (A) of paragraph (1) of subdivision (a) of Section 139.21 shall not stay liens that are subject to consolidation and adjudication pursuant to subdivisions (e) to (i), inclusive, of Section 139.21, unless a determination has been made pursuant to subdivision (i) of Section 139.21 that a lien did not arise from the conduct that subjected the physician, practitioner, or provider to suspension. **Leg.H.** 2016 ch. 868 (SB 1160) §7, 2017 ch. 300 (AB 1422) §3.

2016 Note: For legislative findings and declarations, see the 2016 Note following Lab C §138.4.

Ref.: Hanna §§ 30.04[4][a], 30.22[1]; Herlick Handbook § 10.08[1].

ARTICLE 2.3
Medical Provider Networks

§4616. Establishment of medical provider network; requirements; regulations.

(a)(1) An insurer, employer, or entity that provides physician network services may establish or modify a medical provider network for the provision of medical treatment to injured employees. The network shall include physicians primarily engaged in the treatment of occupational injuries. The administrative director shall encourage the integration of occupational and nonoccupational providers. The number of physicians in the medical provider network shall be sufficient to enable treatment for injuries or conditions to be provided in a timely manner. The provider network shall include an adequate number and type of physicians, as described in Section 3209.3, or other providers, as described in Section 3209.5, to treat common injuries experienced by injured employees based on the type of occupation or industry in which the employee is engaged, and the geographic area where the employees are employed.

(2) Medical treatment for injuries shall be readily available at reasonable times to all employees. To the extent feasible, all medical treatment for injuries shall be readily accessible to all employees. With respect to availability and accessibility of treatment, the administrative director shall consider the needs of rural areas, specifically those in which health facilities are located at least 30 miles apart and areas in which there is a health care shortage.

(3) A treating physician shall be included in the network only if, at the time of entering into or renewing an agreement by which the physician would be in the network, the physician, or an authorized employee of the physician or the physician's office, provides a separate written acknowledgment in which the physician affirmatively elects to be a member of the network. Copies of the written acknowledgment shall be provided to the administrative director upon the administrative director's request. This paragraph shall not apply to a physician who is a shareholder, partner, or employee of a medical group that elects to be part of the network.

(4)(A)(i) Commencing July 1, 2021, every medical provider network shall post on its internet website a roster of all participating providers, which includes all physicians and ancillary service providers in the medical provider network, and shall update the roster at least quarterly. Every network shall provide to the administrative director the internet website address of the network and of its roster of participating providers. The roster of participating providers shall include, at a minimum, the name of each individual provider and their office address and office telephone number. If the ancillary service is provided by an entity rather than an individual, then that entity's name, address, and telephone number shall be listed.

(ii) The administrative director shall post, on the division's internet website, the internet website address of every approved medical provider network.

(B) Every medical provider network shall post on its internet website information about how to contact the medical provider network contact and medical access assistants, and information about how to obtain a copy of any notification regarding the medical provider network that is required to be given to an employee by regulations adopted by the administrative director.

(5) Every medical provider network shall provide one or more persons within the United States to serve as medical access assistants to help an injured employee find an available physician of the employee's choice, and subsequent physicians if necessary, under Section 4616.3. Medical access assistants shall have a toll-free telephone number that injured employees may use and shall be available at least from 7 a.m. to 8 p.m. Pacific standard time, Monday through Saturday, to respond to injured employees, contact physicians' offices during regular business hours, and schedule appointments. The administrative director shall promulgate regulations governing the provision of medical access assistants.

(b)(1) An insurer, employer, or entity that provides physician network services shall submit a plan for the medical provider network to the administrative director for approval. The administrative director shall approve the plan for a period of four years if the administrative director determines that the plan meets the requirements of this section. If the administrative director does not act on the plan within 60 days of submitting the plan, it shall be deemed approved. Commencing January 1, 2014, existing approved plans shall be deemed approved for a period of four years from the approval date of the most recent application or modification submitted prior to 2014. Plans for reapproval for medical provider networks shall be submitted at least six months before the expiration of the four-year approval period. Commencing January 1, 2016, a modification that updates an entire medical provider network plan to bring the plan into full compliance with all current statutes and regulations shall be deemed approved for a period of four years from the modification approval date. An approved modification that does not update an entire medical provider network plan to bring the plan into full compliance with all current statutes and regulations shall not alter the expiration of the medical provider network's four-year approval period. Upon a showing that the medical provider network was approved or deemed approved by the administrative director, there shall be a conclusive presumption on the part of the appeals board that the medical provider network was validly formed.

(2) Every medical provider network shall establish and follow procedures to continuously review the quality of care, performance of medical personnel, utilization of services and facilities, and costs.

(3) Every medical provider network shall submit geocoding of its network for reapproval to establish that the number and geographic location of physicians in the network meets the required access standards.

(4) Approval of a plan may be denied, revoked, or suspended if the medical provider network fails to meet the requirements of this article. Any person contending that a medical provider network is not validly constituted may petition the administrative director to suspend or revoke the approval of the medical provider network. The administrative director may adopt regulations establishing a schedule of administrative penalties not to exceed five thousand dollars ($5,000) per violation, or probation, or both, in lieu of revocation or suspension for less severe violations of the requirements of this article. Penalties, probation, suspension, or revocation shall be ordered by the administrative director only after notice and opportunity to be heard. Unless suspended or revoked by the administrative director, the administrative director's approval of a medical provider network shall be binding on all persons and all courts. A determination of the administrative director may be reviewed only by an appeal of the determination of the administrative director filed as an original proceeding before the reconsideration unit of the workers' compensation appeals board on the same grounds and within the same time limits after issuance of the determination as would be applicable to a petition for reconsideration of a decision of a workers' compensation administrative law judge.

(c) Physician compensation may not be structured in order to achieve the goal of reducing, delaying, or denying medical treatment or restricting access to medical treatment.

(d) If the employer or insurer meets the requirements of this section, the administrative director may not withhold approval or disapprove an employer's or insurer's medical provider network based solely on the selection of providers. In developing a medical provider network, an employer or insurer shall have the exclusive right to determine the members of their network.

(e) All treatment provided shall be provided in accordance with the medical treatment utilization schedule established pursuant to Section 5307.27.

(f) Only a licensed physician who is competent to evaluate the specific clinical issues involved in the medical treatment services, when these services are within the scope of the physician's practice, may modify, delay, or deny requests for authorization of medical treatment.

(g) Every contracting agent that sells, leases, assigns, transfers, or conveys its medical provider networks and their contracted reimbursement rates to an insurer, employer, entity that provides physician network services, or another contracting agent shall, upon entering or renewing a provider contract, disclose to the provider whether the medical provider network may be sold, leased, transferred, or conveyed to other insurers, employers, entities that provide physician network services, or another contracting agent, and specify whether those insurers, employers, entities that provide physician network services, or contracting agents include workers' compensation insurers.

(h) On or before November 1, 2004, the administrative director, in consultation with the Department of Managed Health Care, shall adopt regulations implementing this article. The administrative director shall develop regulations that establish procedures for purposes of making medical provider network modifications.

(i) The administrative director has the authority and discretion to investigate complaints, conduct random reviews, and take enforcement action against medical provider networks, an entity that provides ancillary services, or an entity providing services for or on behalf of the medical provider network or its providers regarding noncompliance with the requirements of this section or Section 4603.2 or 4610. **Leg.H.** 2004 ch. 34 (SB 899), effective April 19, 2004, 2012 ch. 363 (SB 863) §47, 2015 ch. 542 (SB 542) §1, 2019 ch. 647 (SB 537) §7.

2012 Note: For legislative findings, declarations, and applicability of Stats. 2012 ch. 363, see the 2012 Notes following Lab C §62.5.

2004 Note: The addition of §4616 made by this act shall apply prospectively from the date of enactment of this act, regardless of the date of injury, unless otherwise specified, but shall not constitute good cause to reopen or rescind, alter, or amend any existing order, decision, or award of the Workers' Compensation Appeals Board. Stats. 2004 ch. 34 (SB 899) §47.

Ref.: 8 C.C.R. §§9767.1, 9767.2, 9767.3, 9767.4, 9767.5, 9767.6, 9767.7, 9767.8, 9767.9, 9767.12, 9767.13, 9767.14, 9767.15, 9881, 10118.1; Hanna § 5.05[13][a]; Herlick Handbook §§ 4.01[4], 4.11[1], [2], [4], [7].

§4616.1. Economic profiling; filing of policies and procedures; disclosure to public.

(a) An insurer, employer, or entity that provides physician network services that offers a medical provider network under this division and that uses economic profiling shall file with the administrative director a description of any policies and procedures related to economic profiling utilized. The filing shall describe how these policies and procedures are used in utilization review, peer review, incentive and penalty programs, and in provider retention and termination decisions. The insurer, employer, or entity that provides physician network services shall provide a copy of the filing to an individual physician, provider, medical group, or individual practice association.

(b) The administrative director shall make each approved medical provider network economic profiling policy filing available to the public upon request. The administrative director may not publicly disclose any information submitted pursuant to this section that is determined by the administrative director to be confidential pursuant to state or federal law.

(c) For the purposes of this article, "economic profiling" shall mean any evaluation of a particular physician, provider, medical group, or individual practice association based in whole or in part on the economic costs or utilization of services associated with medical care provided or authorized by the physician, provider, medical group, or individual practice association. **Leg.H.** 2004 ch. 34 (SB 899), effective April 19, 2004, 2012 ch. 363 (SB 863) §48.

2012 Note: For legislative findings, declarations, and applicability of Stats. 2012 ch. 363, see the 2012 Notes following Lab C §62.5.

2004 Note: The addition of §4616.1 made by this act shall apply prospectively from the date of enactment of this act, regardless of the date of injury, unless otherwise specified, but shall not constitute good cause to reopen or rescind, alter, or amend any existing order, decision, or award of the Workers' Compensation Appeals Board. Stats. 2004 ch. 34 (SB 899) §47.

Ref.: 8 C.C.R. §§9767.1, 9767.3, 9767.11; Hanna § 5.05[13][b]; Herlick Handbook §§ 4.01[4], 4.11[5].

§4616.2. Continuity of care policy; filing and approval; revisions; notice; completion of treatment by terminated provider.

(a) A medical provider network shall file a written continuity of care policy with the administrative director.

(b) If approved by the administrative director, the provisions of the written continuity of care policy shall replace all prior continuity of care policies. A medical provider network shall file a revision of the continuity of care policy with the administrative director if it makes a material change to the policy.

(c) The medical provider network shall provide all employees entering the workers' compensation system notice of the medical provider network's written continuity of care policy and information regarding the process for an employee to request a review under the policy and, upon request, a copy of the medical provider network's written continuity of care policy.

(d)(1) At the request of an injured employee, completion of treatment shall be provided by a terminated provider as set forth in this section.

(2) The completion of treatment shall be provided by a terminated provider to an injured employee who, at the time of the contract's termination, was receiving services from that provider for one of the conditions described in paragraph (3).

(3) The employer or its claims administrator shall provide for the completion of treatment for the following conditions subject to coverage through the workers' compensation system:

(A) An acute condition. An acute condition is a medical condition that involves a sudden onset of symptoms due to an illness, injury, or other medical problem that requires prompt medical attention and that has a limited duration. Completion of treatment shall be provided for the duration of the acute condition.

(B) A serious chronic condition. A serious chronic condition is a medical condition due to a disease, illness, or other medical problem or medical disorder that is serious in nature and that persists without full cure or worsens over an extended period of time or requires ongoing treatment to maintain remission or prevent deterioration. Completion of treatment shall be provided for a period of time necessary to complete a course of treatment and to arrange for a safe transfer to another provider, as determined by the employer or its claims administrator in consultation with the injured employee and the terminated provider and consistent with good professional practice. Completion of treatment under this paragraph shall not exceed 12 months from the contract termination date.

(C) A terminal illness. A terminal illness is an incurable or irreversible condition that has a high probability of causing death within one year or less. Completion of treatment shall be provided for the duration of a terminal illness.

(D) Performance of a surgery or other procedure that is authorized by the employer or its claims administrator as part of a documented course of treatment and has been recommended and documented by the provider to occur within 180 days of the contract's termination date.

(4)(A) The employer or its claims administrator may require the terminated provider whose services are continued beyond the contract termination date pursuant to this section to agree in writing to be subject to the same contractual terms and conditions that were imposed upon the provider prior to termination. If the terminated provider does not agree to comply or does not comply with these contractual terms and conditions, the employer or its claims administrator is not required to continue the provider's services beyond the contract termination date.

(B) Unless otherwise agreed by the terminated provider and the employer or its claims administrator, the services rendered pursuant to this section shall be compensated at rates and methods of payment similar to those used by the medical provider network for currently contracting providers providing similar services who are practicing in the same or a similar geographic area as the terminated provider. The employer or its claims administrator is not required to continue the services of a terminated provider if the provider does not accept the payment rates provided for in this paragraph.

(5) An employer or its claims administrator shall ensure that the requirements of this section are met.

(6) This section shall not require an employer or its claims administrator to provide for completion of treatment by a provider whose contract with the medical provider network has been terminated or not renewed for reasons relating to a medical disciplinary cause or reason, as defined in paragraph (6) of subdivision (a) of Section 805 of the Business and Professions Code, or fraud or other criminal activity.

(7) Nothing in this section shall preclude an employer or its claims administrator from providing continuity of care beyond the requirements of this section. **Leg.H.** 2004 ch. 34 (SB 899), effective April 19, 2004, 2012 ch. 363 (SB 863) §49, 2015 ch. 542 (SB 542) §2.

2012 Note: For legislative findings, declarations, and applicability of Stats. 2012 ch. 363, see the 2012 Notes following Lab C §62.5.

2004 Note: The addition of §4616.2 made by this act shall apply prospectively from the date of enactment of this act, regardless of the date of injury, unless otherwise specified, but shall not constitute good cause to reopen or rescind, alter, or amend any existing order, decision, or award of the Workers' Compensation Appeals Board. Stats. 2004 ch. 34 (SB 899) §47.

Ref.: 8 C.C.R. §§9767.3, 9767.7, 9767.8, 9767.9, 9767.10, 9767.12, 9767.15; Hanna § 5.05[13][c]; Herlick Handbook §§ 4.01[4], 4.11[6].

§4616.3. Initial medical evaluation; notice of right to change treating physician; second and third opinions; specialists.

(a) If the injured employee notifies the employer of the injury or files a claim for workers' compensation with the employer, the employer shall arrange an initial medical evaluation and begin treatment as required by Section 4600.

(b) The employer shall notify the employee of the existence of the medical provider network established pursuant to this article, the employee's right to change treating physicians within the network after the first visit, and the method by which the list of participating providers may be accessed by the employee. The employer's failure to provide notice as required by this subdivision or failure to post the notice as required by Section 3550 shall not be a basis for the employee to treat outside the network unless it is shown that the failure to provide notice resulted in a denial of medical care.

(c) If an injured employee disputes either the diagnosis or the treatment prescribed by the treating physician, the employee may seek the opinion of another physician in the medical provider network. If the injured employee disputes the diagnosis or treatment prescribed by the second physician, the employee may seek the opinion of a third physician in the medical provider network.

(d)(1) Selection by the injured employee of a treating physician and any subsequent physicians shall be based on the physician's specialty or recognized expertise in treating the particular injury or condition in question.

(2) Treatment by a specialist who is not a member of the medical provider network may be permitted on a case-by-case basis if the medical provider network does not contain a physician who can provide the approved treatment and the treatment is approved by the employer or the insurer. **Leg.H.** 2004 ch. 34 (SB 899), effective April 19, 2004, 2012 ch. 363 (SB 863) §50.

2012 Note: For legislative findings, declarations, and applicability of Stats. 2012 ch. 363, see the 2012 Notes following Lab C §62.5.

2004 Note: The addition of §4616.3 made by this act shall apply prospectively from the date of enactment of this act, regardless of the date of injury, unless otherwise specified, but shall not constitute good cause to reopen or rescind, alter, or amend any existing order, decision, or award of the Workers' Compensation Appeals Board. Stats. 2004 ch. 34 (SB 899) §47.

Ref.: 8 C.C.R. §§9767.1, 9767.3, 9767.5, 9767.6, 9767.15, 9768.9, 9768.10; Hanna § 5.05[13][d]; Herlick Handbook §§ 4.01[4], 4.10[1], 4.11[7], 10.02[4].

§4616.4. Contract for medical provider network (MPN) independent medical reviews; duties; requirements; when employee may request MPN independent medical review; standard; applications; examination, determination, and report; deadlines; treatment.

(a)(1) The administrative director shall contract with individual physicians, as described in paragraph (2), or an independent medical review organization to perform medical provider network (MPN) independent medical reviews pursuant to this section.

(2) Only a physician licensed pursuant to Chapter 5 (commencing with Section 2000) of the Business and Professions Code may be an MPN independent medical reviewer.

(3) The administrative director shall ensure that an MPN independent medical reviewer or those within the review organization shall do all of the following:

(A) Be appropriately credentialed and privileged.

(B) Ensure that the reviews provided by the medical professionals are timely, clear, and credible, and that reviews are monitored for quality on an ongoing basis.

(C) Ensure that the method of selecting medical professionals for individual cases achieves a fair and impartial panel of medical professionals who are qualified to render recommendations regarding the clinical conditions consistent with the medical utilization schedule established pursuant to Section 5307.27.

(D) Ensure the confidentiality of medical records and the review materials, consistent with the requirements of this section and applicable state and federal law.

(E) Ensure the independence of the medical professionals retained to perform the reviews through conflict-of-interest policies and prohibitions, and ensure adequate screening for conflicts of interest.

(4) A medical professional selected by the administrative director or the independent medical review organization to review medical treatment decisions shall be a physician, as specified in paragraph (2) of subdivision (a), who meets the following minimum requirements:

(A) The medical professional shall be a clinician knowledgeable in the treatment of the employee's medical condition, knowledgeable about the proposed treatment, and familiar with guidelines and protocols in the area of treatment under review.

(B) Notwithstanding any other law, the medical professional shall hold a nonrestricted license in any state of the United States, and for a physician, a current certification by a recognized American medical specialty board in the area or areas appropriate to the condition or treatment under review.

(C) The medical professional shall have no history of disciplinary action or sanctions, including, but not limited to, loss of staff privileges or participation restrictions taken or pending by any hospital, government, or regulatory body.

(b) If, after the third physician's opinion, the treatment or diagnostic service remains disputed, the injured employee may request an MPN independent medical review regarding the disputed treatment or diagnostic service still in dispute after the third physician's opinion in accordance with Section 4616.3. The standard to be utilized for an MPN independent medical review is identical to that contained in the medical treatment utilization schedule established in Section 5307.27.

(c) An application for an MPN independent medical review shall be submitted to the administrative director on a one-page form provided by the administrative director entitled "MPN Independent Medical Review Application." The form shall contain a signed release from the injured employee, or a person authorized pursuant to law to act on behalf of the injured employee, authorizing the release of medical and treatment information. The injured employee may provide any relevant material or documentation with the application. The administrative director or the independent medical review organization shall assign the MPN independent medical reviewer.

(d) Following receipt of the application for an MPN independent medical review, the employer or insurer shall provide the MPN independent medical reviewer, assigned pursuant to subdivision (c), with all information that was considered in relation to the disputed treatment or diagnostic service, including both of the following:

(1) A copy of all correspondence from, and received by, any treating physician who provided a treatment or diagnostic service to the injured employee in connection with the injury.

(2) A complete and legible copy of all medical records and other information used by the physicians in making a decision regarding the disputed treatment or diagnostic service.

(e) Upon receipt of information and documents related to the application for an MPN independent medical review, the MPN independent medical reviewer shall conduct a physical examination of the injured employee at the employee's discretion. The MPN independent medical reviewer may order any diagnostic tests necessary to make his or her determination regarding medical treatment. Utilizing the medical treatment utilization schedule established pursuant to Section 5307.27, and taking into account any reports and information provided, the MPN independent medical reviewer shall determine whether the disputed health care service was consistent with Section 5307.27 based on the specific medical needs of the injured employee.

(f) The MPN independent medical reviewer shall issue a report to the administrative director, in writing, and in layperson's terms to the maximum extent practicable, containing his or her analysis and determination as to whether the disputed health care service was consistent with the medical treatment utilization schedule established pursuant to Section 5307.27, within 30 days of the examination of the injured employee, or within less time as prescribed by the administrative director. If the disputed health care service has not been provided and the MPN independent medical reviewer certifies in writing that an imminent and serious threat to the health of the injured employee may exist, including, but not limited to, serious pain, the potential loss of life, limb, or major bodily function, or the immediate and serious deterioration of the injured employee, the report shall be expedited and rendered within three days of the examination by the MPN independent medical reviewer. Subject to the approval of the administrative director, the deadlines for analyses and determinations involving both regular and expedited reviews may be extended by the administrative director for up to three days in extraordinary circumstances or for good cause.

(g) The MPN independent medical reviewer's analysis shall cite the injured employee's medical condition, the relevant documents in the record, and the relevant findings associated with the documents or any other information submitted to the MPN independent medical reviewer in order to support the determination.

(h) The administrative director shall immediately adopt the determination of the MPN independent medical reviewer, and shall promptly issue a written decision to the parties.

(i) If the determination of the MPN independent medical reviewer finds that the disputed treatment or diagnostic service is consistent with Section 5307.27, the injured employee may seek the disputed treatment or diagnostic service from a physician of his or her choice from within or outside the medical provider network. Treatment outside the medical provider network shall be provided consistent with Section 5307.27. The employer shall be liable for the cost of any approved medical treatment in accordance with Section 5307.1 or 5307.11. **Leg.H.** 2004 ch. 34 (SB 899), effective April 19, 2004, 2015 ch. 542 (SB 542) §3, 2016 ch. 84 (SB 914) §1, 2017 ch. 561 (AB 1516) §174.

2004 Note: The addition of §4616.4 made by this act shall apply prospectively from the date of enactment of this act, regardless of the date of injury, unless otherwise specified, but shall not constitute good cause to reopen or rescind, alter, or amend any existing order, decision, or award of the Workers' Compensation Appeals Board. Stats. 2004 ch. 34 (SB 899) §47.

Ref.: 8 C.C.R. §§9768.1, 9768.2, 9768.3, 9768.4, 9768.5, 9768.6, 9768.7, 9768.8, 9768.9, 9768.10, 9768.11, 9768.12, 9768.13, 9768.14, 9768.15, 9768.17; Hanna § 5.05[13][e]; Herlick Handbook §§ 4.01[4], 4.10[1], 4.11[8], 10.02[4].

§4616.5. "Employer" and "Entity that provides physician network services" defined.

(a) For purposes of this article, "employer" means a self-insured employer, joint powers authority, or the state.

(b) For purposes of this article, "entity that provides physician network services" means a medical network licensed by the Department of Insurance or Department of Managed Health Care, or a third-party claims adjusting organization licensed by the Department of Insurance or certified by the Office of Self-Insurance Plans, or a legal entity that offers medical management or physician network services within California.

(c) For purposes of this article, "entity that provides ancillary services" means an entity that provides medical services or goods, as authorized by Section 4600, by a nonphysician, including, but not limited to, interpreter services, physical therapy, and pharmaceutical services. **Leg.H.** 2004 ch. 34 (SB 899), effective April 19, 2004, 2015 ch. 542 (SB 542) §4, 2019 ch. 647 (SB 537) §8.

2004 Note: The addition of §4616.5 made by this act shall apply prospectively from the date of enactment of this act, regardless of the date of injury, unless otherwise specified, but shall not constitute good cause to reopen or rescind, alter, or amend any existing order, decision, or award of the Workers' Compensation Appeals Board. Stats. 2004 ch. 34 (SB 899) §47.

Ref.: 8 C.C.R. §§9767.1, 9767.3, 9767.4, 9767.8; Hanna § 5.05[13][a]; Herlick Handbook § 4.01[4].

§4616.6. Additional examinations and reports precluded.

No additional examinations shall be ordered by the appeals board and no other reports shall be admissable to resolve any controversy arising out of this article. **Leg.H.** 2004 ch. 34 (SB 899), effective April 19, 2004.

2004 Notes: The addition of §4616.6 made by this act shall apply prospectively from the date of enactment of this act, regardless of the date of injury, unless otherwise specified, but shall not constitute good cause to reopen or rescind, alter, or amend any existing order, decision, or award of the Workers' Compensation Appeals Board. Stats. 2004 ch. 34 (SB 899) §47.

It appears the Legislature inadvertently substituted "admissable" for "admissible".

Ref.: Hanna § 5.05[13][e]; Herlick Handbook §§ 4.01[4], 4.11[7], [8].

§4616.7. Requirements for approval; health care organization; health care service plan; group disability insurance policy; Taft-Hartley health and welfare fund.

(a) A health care organization certified pursuant to Section 4600.5 shall be deemed approved pursuant to this article if the requirements of this article are met, as determined by the administrative director.

(b) A health care service plan, licensed pursuant to Chapter 2.2 (commencing with Section 1340) of Division 2 of the Health and Safety Code, shall be deemed approved for purposes of this article if it has a reasonable number of physicians with competency in occupational medicine, as determined by the administrative director.

(c) A group disability insurance policy, as defined in subdivision (b) of Section 106 of the Insurance Code, that covers hospital, surgical, and medical care expenses shall be deemed approved for purposes of this article if it has a reasonable number of physicians with competency in occupational medicine, as determined by the administrative director. For the purposes of this section, a group disability insurance policy shall not include Medicare supplement, vision-only, dental-only, and Champus-supplement insurance. For purposes of this section, a group disability insurance policy shall not include hospital indemnity, accident-only, and specified disease insurance that pays benefits on a fixed benefit, cash-payment-only basis.

(d) Any Taft-Hartley health and welfare fund shall be deemed approved for purposes of this article if it has a reasonable number of physicians with competency in occupational medicine, as determined by the administrative director. **Leg.H.** 2004 ch. 34 (SB 899), effective April 19, 2004, 2012 ch. 363 (SB 863) §51.

2012 Note: For legislative findings, declarations, and applicability of Stats. 2012 ch. 363, see the 2012 Notes following Lab C §62.5.

2004 Note: The addition of §4616.7 made by this act shall apply prospectively from the date of enactment of this act, regardless of the date of injury, unless otherwise specified, but shall not constitute good cause to reopen or rescind, alter, or amend any existing order, decision, or award of the Workers' Compensation Appeals Board. Stats. 2004 ch. 34 (SB 899) §47.

Ref.: 8 C.C.R. §§9767.1, 9767.3, 9767.4; Hanna §§ 5.05[1], 22.02[1]; Herlick Handbook §§ 4.01[4], [5], 4.11[2].

ARTICLE 2.5
Medical-Legal Expenses

§4620. Definitions.

(a) For purposes of this article, a medical-legal expense means any costs and expenses incurred by or on behalf of any party, the administrative director, or the board, which expenses may include X-rays, laboratory fees, other diagnostic tests, medical reports, medical records, medical testimony, and, as needed, interpreter's fees by a certified interpreter pursuant to Article 8 (commencing with Section 11435.05) of Chapter 4.5 of Part 1 of Division 3 of Title 2 of, or Section 68566 of, the Government Code, for the purpose of proving or disproving a contested claim.

(b) A contested claim exists when the employer knows or reasonably should know that the employee is claiming entitlement to any benefit arising out of a claimed industrial injury and one of the following conditions exists:

(1) The employer rejects liability for a claimed benefit.

(2) The employer fails to accept liability for benefits after the expiration of a reasonable period of time within which to decide if it will contest the claim.

(3) The employer fails to respond to a demand for payment of benefits after the expiration of any time period fixed by statute for the payment of indemnity.

(c) Costs of medical evaluations, diagnostic tests, and interpreters incidental to the production of a medical report do not constitute medical-legal expenses unless the medical report is capable of proving or disproving a disputed medical fact, the determination of which is essential to an adjudication of the employee's claim for benefits. In determining whether a report meets the requirements of this subdivision, a judge shall give full consideration to the substance as well as the form of the report, as required by applicable statutes and regulations.

(d) If the injured employee cannot effectively communicate with an examining physician because he or she cannot proficiently speak or understand the English language, the injured employee is entitled to the services of a qualified interpreter during the medical examination. Upon request of the injured employee, the employer or insurance carrier shall pay the costs of the interpreter services, as set forth in the fee schedule adopted by the administrative director pursuant to Section 5811. An employer shall not be required to pay for the services of an interpreter who is provisionally certified unless either the employer consents in advance to the selection of the individual who provides the interpreting service or the injured worker requires interpreting service in a language other than the languages designated pursuant to Section 11435.40 of the Government Code. **Leg.H.** 1993 ch. 4, effective April 3, 1993, 2012 ch. 363 (SB 863) §52.

2012 Note: For legislative findings, declarations, and applicability of Stats. 2012 ch. 363, see the 2012 Notes following Lab C §62.5.

Ref.: 8 C.C.R. §§9793, 9794, 9795, 9795.1, 9795.2, 9795.3, 9795.4, 10564, 10771; Hanna §§ 5.04[2][a], [c], 22.09[1], [3], 23.13[3]; Herlick Handbook §§ 4.06[5], 4.17[1], [2], 14.33[1].

§4621. Reimbursement of medical-legal expenses.

(a) In accordance with the rules of practice and procedure of the appeals board, the employee, or the dependents of a deceased employee, shall be reimbursed for his or her medical-legal expenses and reasonably, actually, and necessarily incurred, except as provided in Section 4064. The reasonableness of, and necessity for, incurring these expenses shall be determined with respect to the time when the expenses were actually incurred. Costs for medical evaluations, diagnostic tests, and interpreters' services incidental to the production of a medical report shall not be incurred earlier than the date of receipt by the employer, the employer's insurance carrier, or, if represented, the attorney of record, of all reports and documents required by the administrative director incidental to the services. This subdivision is not applicable unless there has been compliance with Section 4620.

(b) Except as provided in subdivision (c) and Sections 4061 and 4062, no comprehensive medical-legal evaluations, except those at the request of an employer, shall be performed during the first 60 days after the notice of claim has been filed pursuant to Section 5401, and neither the employer nor the employee shall be liable for any expenses incurred for comprehensive medical-legal evaluations performed within the first 60 days after the notice of claim has been filed pursuant to Section 5401.

(c) Comprehensive medical-legal evaluations may be performed at any time after the claim form has been filed pursuant to Section 5401 if the employer has rejected the claim.

(d) Where, at the request of the employer, the employer's insurance carrier, the administrative director, the appeals board, or a referee, the employee submits to examination by a physician, he or she shall be entitled to receive, in addition to all other benefits herein provided, all reasonable expenses of transportation, meals, and lodging incident to reporting for the examination to the same extent and manner as provided for in Section 4600. **Leg.H.** 1993 ch. 4, effective April 3, 1993, ch. 121, effective July 16, 1993.

1993 Note: Section 4621, as amended by ch. 121, applies only to injuries occurring on or after January 1, 1994. Stats. 1993 ch. 121 §77.

Ref.: 8 C.C.R. §§9793, 9794, 9795, 9795.1, 9795.2, 9795.3, 9795.4, 10101, 10101.1, 10102, 10108, 10110, 10111, 10111.1, 10111.2, 10115, 10536, 10564, 10608, 10771; Herlick Handbook § 14.33.

§4622. Employer's liability for expenses; penalty.

All medical-legal expenses for which the employer is liable shall, upon receipt by the employer of all reports and documents required by the administrative director incident to the services, be paid to whom the funds and expenses are due, as follows:

(a)(1) Except as provided in subdivision (b), within 60 days after receipt by the employer of each separate, written billing and report, and if payment is not made within this period, that portion of the billed sum then unreasonably unpaid shall be increased by 10 percent, together with interest thereon at the rate of 7 percent per annum retroactive to the date of receipt of the bill and report by the employer. If the employer, within the 60-day period, contests the reasonableness and necessity for incurring the fees, services, and expenses using the explanation of review required by Section 4603.3, payment shall be made within 20 days of the service of an order of the appeals board or the administrative director pursuant to Section 4603.6 directing payment.

(2) The penalty provided for in paragraph (1) shall not apply if both of the following occur:

(A) The employer pays the provider that portion of his or her charges that do not exceed the amount deemed reasonable pursuant to subdivision (e) within 60 days of receipt of the report and itemized billing.

(B) The employer prevails.

(b)(1) If the provider contests the amount paid, the provider may request a second review within 90 days of the service of the explanation of review. The request for a second review shall be submitted to the employer on a form prescribed by the administrative director and shall include all of the following:

(A) The date of the explanation of review and the claim number or other unique identifying number provided on the explanation of review.

(B) The party or parties requesting the service.

(C) Any item and amount in dispute.

(D) The additional payment requested and the reason therefor.

(E) Any additional information requested in the original explanation of review and any other information provided in support of the additional payment requested.

(2) If the provider does not request a second review within 90 days, the bill will be deemed satisfied and neither the employer nor the employee shall be liable for any further payment.

(3) Within 14 days of the request for second review, the employer shall respond with a final written determination on each of the items or amounts in dispute, including whether additional payment will be made.

(4) If the provider contests the amount paid, after receipt of the second review, the provider shall request an independent bill review as provided for in Section 4603.6.

(c) If the employer denies all or a portion of the amount billed for any reason other than the amount to be paid pursuant to the fee schedules in effect on the date of service, the provider may object to the denial within 90 days of the service of the explanation of review. If the provider does not object to the denial within 90 days, neither the employer nor the employee shall be liable for the amount that was denied. If the provider objects to the denial within 90 days of the service of the explanation of review, the employer shall file a petition and a declaration of readiness to proceed with the appeals board within 60 days of service of the objection. If the employer prevails before the appeals board, the appeals board shall order the physician to reimburse the employer for the amount of the paid charges found to be unreasonable.

(d) If requested by the employee, or the dependents of a deceased employee, within 20 days from the filing of an order of the appeals board directing payment, and where payment is not made within that period, that portion of the billed sum then unpaid shall be increased by 10 percent, together with interest thereon at the rate of 7 percent per annum retroactive to the date of the filing of the order of the board directing payment.

(e)(1) Using the explanation of review as described in Section 4603.3, the employer shall notify the provider of the services, the employee, or if represented, his or her attorney, if the employer contests the reasonableness or necessity of incurring these expenses, and shall indicate the reasons therefor.

(2) The appeals board shall promulgate all necessary and reasonable rules and regulations to insure compliance with this section, and shall take such further steps as may be necessary to guarantee that the rules and regulations are enforced.

(3) The provisions of Sections 5800 and 5814 shall not apply to this section.

(f) Nothing contained in this section shall be construed to create a rebuttable presumption of entitlement to payment of an expense upon receipt by the employer of the required reports and documents. This section is not applicable unless there has been compliance with Sections 4620 and 4621. **Leg.H.** 1993 ch. 4, effective April 3, 1993, 2012 ch. 363 (SB 863) §53.

2012 Note: For legislative findings, declarations, and applicability of Stats. 2012 ch. 363, see the 2012 Notes following Lab C §62.5.

Ref.: 8 C.C.R. §§9793, 9794, 9795, 10101, 10101.1, 10102, 10111, 10111.1, 10111.2, 10771; Hanna §§ 5.04[2][c], 10.43, 22.09[2], [3], 27.01[8][b][iv], 27.12[3]; Herlick Handbook §§ 4.10[3], 4.18[1], [2], 9.5, 10.02[3], 10.05, 10.08[1], [5], 14.33.

§4625. Prompt payment of all reasonable charges for reports.

(a) Effective for services provided on or after January 1, 2017, all bills for medical-legal evaluation or medical-legal expense shall be submitted to the employer within 12 months of the date of service in the manner prescribed by the administrative director. The administrative director shall adopt rules to define circumstances that constitute good cause for an exception to the 12-month period. Bills for medical-legal charges are barred unless timely submitted.

(b) Notwithstanding subdivision (d) of Section 4628, all charges for medical-legal expenses for which the employer is liable that are not in excess of those set forth in the official medical-legal fee schedule adopted pursuant to Section 5307.6 shall be paid promptly pursuant to Section 4622.

(c) If the employer contests the reasonableness of the charges it has paid, the employer may file a petition with the appeals board to obtain reimbursement of the charges from the physician that are considered to be unreasonable. **Leg.H.** 1993 ch. 4, effective April 3, 1993, 2016 ch. 214 (SB 1175) §3.

Ref.: 8 C.C.R. §§9793, 9794, 9795, 10111, 10111.1, 10111.2, 10771; Herlick Handbook §§ 4.18[1], 10.03[7].

§4626. Billing of diagnostic tests in accordance with official medical fee schedule.

All charges for X-rays, laboratory services, and other diagnostic tests provided in connection with an industrial medical-legal evaluation shall be billed in accordance with the official medical fee schedule adopted by the administrative director pursuant to Section 5307.1 and shall be itemized separately in accordance with rules promulgated by the administrative director.

Ref.: 8 C.C.R. §§9794, 9795; Herlick Handbook § 4.17[1].

§4627. Appeals board and administrative director may promulgate rules and regulations.

The board and the administrative director may promulgate such reasonable rules and regulations as may be necessary to interpret this article and compel compliance with its provisions.

Ref.: Herlick Handbook §§ 14.26, 14.42.

§4628. Responsibilities of physician signing medical-legal report; information required in report; billable amounts; admissibility of report; civil penalty; contempt; declaration by physician; provision of physician's curriculum vitae.

(a) Except as provided in subdivision (c), no person, other than the physician who signs the medical-legal report, except a nurse performing those functions routinely performed by a nurse, such as taking blood pressure, shall examine the injured employee or participate in the nonclerical preparation of the report, including all of the following:

(1) Taking a complete history.

Labor

(2) Reviewing and summarizing prior medical records.

(3) Composing and drafting the conclusions of the report.

(b) The report shall disclose the date when and location where the evaluation was performed; that the physician or physicians signing the report actually performed the evaluation; whether the evaluation performed and the time spent performing the evaluation was in compliance with the guidelines established by the administrative director pursuant to paragraph (5) of subdivision (j) of Section 139.2 or Section 5307.6 and shall disclose the name and qualifications of each person who performed any services in connection with the report, including diagnostic studies, other than its clerical preparation. If the report discloses that the evaluation performed or the time spent performing the evaluation was not in compliance with the guidelines established by the administrative director, the report shall explain, in detail, any variance and the reason or reasons therefor.

(c) If the initial outline of a patient's history or excerpting of prior medical records is not done by the physician, the physician shall review the excerpts and the entire outline and shall make additional inquiries and examinations as are necessary and appropriate to identify and determine the relevant medical issues.

(d) No amount may be charged in excess of the direct charges for the physician's professional services and the reasonable costs of laboratory examinations, diagnostic studies, and other medical tests, and reasonable costs of clerical expense necessary to producing the report. Direct charges for the physician's professional services shall include reasonable overhead expense.

(e) Failure to comply with the requirements of this section shall make the report inadmissible as evidence and shall eliminate any liability for payment of any medical-legal expense incurred in connection with the report.

(f) Knowing failure to comply with the requirements of this section shall subject the physician to a civil penalty of up to one thousand dollars ($1,000) for each violation to be assessed by a workers' compensation judge or the appeals board. All civil penalties collected under this section shall be deposited in the Workers' Compensation Administration Revolving Fund.

(g) A physician who is assessed a civil penalty under this section may be terminated, suspended, or placed on probation as a qualified medical evaluator pursuant to subdivisions (k) and (*l*) of Section 139.2.

(h) Knowing failure to comply with the requirements of this section shall subject the physician to contempt pursuant to the judicial powers vested in the appeals board.

(i) Any person billing for medical-legal evaluations, diagnostic procedures, or diagnostic services performed by persons other than those employed by the reporting physician or physicians, or a medical corporation owned by the reporting physician or physicians shall specify the amount paid or to be paid to those persons for the evaluations, procedures, or services. This subdivision shall not apply to any procedure or service defined or valued pursuant to Section 5307.1.

(j) The report shall contain a declaration by the physician signing the report, under penalty of perjury, stating:

"I declare under penalty of perjury that the information contained in this report and its attachments, if any, is true and correct to the best of my knowledge and belief, except as to information that I have indicated I received from others. As to that information, I declare under penalty of perjury that the information accurately describes the information provided to me and, except as noted herein, that I believe it to be true."

The foregoing declaration shall be dated and signed by the reporting physician and shall indicate the county wherein it was signed.

(k) The physician shall provide a curriculum vitae upon request by a party and include a statement concerning the percent of the physician's total practice time that is annually devoted to medical treatment. **Leg.H.** 1992 ch. 1352, effective September 30, 1992, 1993 ch. 120, effective July 16, 1993, 2002 ch. 6 (AB 749), 2003 ch. 639 (SB 228).

1989 Note: This section is applicable only to injuries occurring on or after January 1, 1990. Stats. 1989 ch. 893 §6.

Ref.: 8 C.C.R. §§43, 49, 49.2, 49.4, 49.6, 49.8, 49.9, 9774, 9793, 9794, 9795, 10606, 10634; Hanna §§ 22.09[5], 26.06[12]; Herlick Handbook §§ 1.02, 4.07[3], 4.08[4], 10.08[4], [5], 14.20, 14.23; Lawyer's Guide to AMA *Guides* and Calif. Workers' Comp. § 3.03.

ARTICLE 3
Disability Payments

§4650. Timing of payments; when employer obligated to reimburse insurer.

(a) If an injury causes temporary disability, the first payment of temporary disability indemnity shall be made not later than 14 days after knowledge of the injury and disability, on which date all indemnity then due shall be paid, unless liability for the injury is earlier denied.

(b)(1) If the injury causes permanent disability, the first payment shall be made within 14 days after the date of last payment of temporary disability indemnity, except as provided in paragraph (2). When the last payment of temporary disability indemnity has been made pursuant to subdivision (c) of Section 4656, and regardless of whether the extent of permanent disability can be determined at that date, the employer nevertheless shall commence the timely payment required by this subdivision and shall continue to make these payments until the employer's reasonable estimate of permanent disability indemnity due has been paid, and if the amount of permanent disability indemnity due has been determined, until that amount has been paid.

(2) Prior to an award of permanent disability indemnity, a permanent disability indemnity payment shall not be required if the employer has offered the employee a position that pays at least 85 percent of the wages and compensation paid to the employee at the time of injury or if the employee is employed in a position that pays at least 100 percent of the wages and compensation paid to the employee at the time of injury, provided that when an award of permanent disability indemnity is made, the amount then due shall be calculated from the last date for which temporary disability indemnity was paid, or the date the employee's disability became permanent and stationary, whichever is earlier.

(c) Payment of temporary or permanent disability indemnity subsequent to the first payment shall be made as due every two weeks on the day designated with the first payment.

(d) If any indemnity payment is not made timely as required by this section, the amount of the late payment shall be increased 10 percent and shall be paid, without application, to the employee, unless the employer continues the employee's wages under a salary continuation plan, as defined in subdivision (g). No increase shall apply to any payment due prior to or within 14 days after the date the claim form was submitted to the employer under Section 5401. No increase shall apply when, within the 14-day period specified under subdivision (a), the employer is unable to determine whether temporary disability indemnity payments are owed and advises the employee, in the manner prescribed in rules and regulations adopted pursuant to Section 138.4, why payments cannot be made within the 14-day period, what additional information is required to make the decision whether temporary disability indemnity payments are owed, and when the employer expects to have the information required to make the decision.

(e) If the employer is insured for its obligation to provide compensation, the employer shall be obligated to reimburse the insurer for the amount of increase in indemnity payments, made pursuant to subdivision (d), if the late payment which gives rise to the increase in indemnity payments, is due less than seven days after the insurer receives the completed claim form from the employer. Except as specified in this subdivision, an employer shall not be obligated to reimburse an insurer nor shall an insurer be permitted to seek reimbursement, directly or indirectly, for the amount of increase in indemnity payments specified in this section.

(f) If an employer is obligated under subdivision (e) to reimburse the insurer for the amount of increase in indemnity payments, the insurer shall notify the employer in writing, within 30 days of the payment, that the employer is obligated to reimburse the insurer and shall bill and collect the amount of the payment no later than at final audit. However, the insurer shall not be obligated to collect, and the employer shall not be obligated to reimburse, amounts paid pursuant to subdivision (d) unless the aggregate total paid in a policy year exceeds one hundred dollars ($100). The employer shall have 60 days, following notice of the obligation to reimburse, to appeal the decision of the insurer to the Department of Insurance. The notice of the obligation to reimburse shall specify that the employer has the right to appeal the decision of the insurer as provided in this subdivision.

(g) For purposes of this section, "salary continuation plan" means a plan that meets both of the following requirements:

(1) The plan is paid for by the employer pursuant to statute, collective bargaining agreement, memorandum of understanding, or established employer policy.

(2) The plan provides the employee on his or her regular payday with salary not less than the employee is entitled to receive pursuant to statute, collective bargaining agreement, memorandum of understanding, or established employer policy and not less than the employee would otherwise receive in indemnity payments. **Leg.H.** Enacted 1937, amended 1947 ch. 1033 §5, 1949 chs. 408 §1, 705 §1, 1959 ch. 1189 §11, 1971 ch. 1750 §4, operative April 1, 1972, 1973 ch. 1021 §1, operative April 1, 1974, 1989 ch. 892 §34, 1990 ch. 1550 (AB 2910) §41, 2004 ch. 34 (SB 899), effective April 19, 2004, 2012 ch. 363 (SB 863) §54.

2012 Note: For legislative findings, declarations, and applicability of Stats. 2012 ch. 363, see the 2012 Notes following Lab C §62.5.

2004 Note: The amendment to §4650 made by this act shall apply prospectively from the date of enactment of this act, regardless of the date of injury, unless otherwise specified, but shall not constitute good cause to reopen or rescind, alter, or amend any existing order, decision, or award of the Workers' Compensation Appeals Board. Stats. 2004 ch. 34 (SB 899) §47.

1989 Note: This section is applicable only to injuries occurring on or after January 1, 1990. Stats. 1989 ch. 893 §6.

Ref.: 8 C.C.R. §§9793, 9810, 9811, 9812, 9813, 9814, 9815, 9880, 10100, 10100.1, 10100.2, 10101, 10101.1, 10102, 10109, 10111, 10111.1, 10111.2, 10462, 10464, 10466; Hanna §§ 2.62[2][f], 2.72[2], 8.08[1], [4], 10.40[3][b], 32.04[1][a]; Herlick Handbook §§ 5.9, 6.02[6], 6.10[1], [2], 6.11[2], 7.15, 9.5, 10.10[1].

§4650.5. Time of first payment; civil service employees; employees of Regents of University of California; Board of Trustees of California State University.

Notwithstanding Section 4650, in the case of state civil service employees, employees of the Regents of the University of California, and employees of the Board of Trustees of the California State University, the disability payment shall be made from the first day the injured employee leaves work as a result of the injury, if the injury is the result of a criminal act of violence against the employee.

Ref.: Hanna § 7.03[2]; Herlick Handbook § 5.9.

§4651. [First of Two; Repealed January 1, 2023] Payment by written instrument; deposits; applicability of state and federal law; employer disability indemnity payment program.

(a)(1) A disability indemnity payment shall not be made by any written instrument unless it is immediately negotiable and payable in cash, on demand, without discount, at some established place of business in the state.

(2) This section does not prohibit an employer from depositing the disability indemnity payment in an account in any bank, savings and loan association, or credit union of the employee's choice in this state, provided the employee has voluntarily authorized the deposit, nor does it prohibit an employer from electronically depositing the disability indemnity payment in an account in any bank, savings and loan association, or credit union, that the employee has previously authorized to receive electronic deposits of payroll, unless the employee has requested, in writing, that disability indemnity benefits not be electronically deposited in the account.

(3)(A) An employer may commence a program under which disability indemnity payments are deposited in a prepaid card account for the employee. The employee shall provide written consent to the employer to use a prepaid card account for the employee's disability payments. The prepaid card account shall meet the applicable requirements of Section 1339.1 of the Unemployment Insurance Code. For purposes of this section, the terms "prepaid card" and "prepaid card account" have the same meanings as defined in Section 1339.1 of the Unemployment Insurance Code. For purposes of this section, a prepaid card shall also meet all of the following requirements:

(i) Allow the employee to withdraw the entire balance on the card in one transaction without incurring fees.

(ii) Allow the employee reasonable access to in-network automatic teller machines (ATMs).

(iii) Allow the employee to make point-of-sale purchases without incurring fees from the financial institution.

(iv) Prohibit a link to any form of credit, including a loan against future payments or a cash advance on future payments.

(B) The fees associated with the use of the prepaid card shall be disclosed to the employee in writing. The only permissible fees associated with the use of a prepaid card are those for a replacement card provided through expedited delivery, out-of-network ATM fees on the third and subsequent withdrawal per deposit, and fees associated with foreign transactions.

(C) If an employee has consented to use the prepaid card payment system under this section, either the employer or the employee may opt to change the method of payment to another method consistent with this section by providing 30 days' written notice to the other party.

(D) On or before December 1, 2022, the Commission on Health and Safety and Workers' Compensation shall issue a report to the Legislature on payments made to prepaid card accounts. Employers shall provide all necessary aggregated data on their prepaid account programs to the commission upon request. The report shall include, but is not limited to, the following:

(i) The number of employees who elected to receive their disability indemnity payments in a prepaid card account.

(ii) The cash value of the disability benefits sent to prepaid card accounts.

(iii) The number of employees who opted to change the method of payment from a prepaid card account to either a written instrument or electronic deposit.

(E) The report issued pursuant to subparagraph (D) shall comply with Section 9795 of the Government Code.

(b) It is not a violation of this section if either of the following delays occurs in connection with a transaction authorized pursuant to this section, and the delay is caused solely by the application of state or federal banking laws or regulations:

(1) A delay in the negotiation of a written instrument, including a delay in the deposit or electronic deposit of a check to a prepaid card account.

(2) A delay in the deposit of a disability indemnity payment to a prepaid card account.

(c) This section shall remain in effect only until January 1, 2023, and as of that date is repealed. **Leg.H.** 2002 ch. 6 (AB 749), 2018 ch. 730 (SB 880) §1.

1989 Note: This section is applicable only to injuries occurring on or after January 1, 1990. Stats. 1989 ch. 893 §6.

Ref.: 8 C.C.R. §§9880, 10111, 10111.1, 10111.2; Hanna § 10.40[3][b]; Herlick Handbook §§ 5.15, 6.10[3], 6.16.

§4651. [Second of Two; Operative January 1, 2023] Disability indemnity payment.

(a) A disability indemnity payment shall not be made by any written instrument unless it is immediately negotiable and payable in cash, on demand, without discount, at some established place of business in the state.

(b) This section does not prohibit an employer from depositing the disability indemnity payment in an account in any bank, savings and loan association, or credit union of the employee's choice in this state, provided the employee has voluntarily authorized the deposit, nor does it prohibit an employer from electronically depositing the disability indemnity payment in an account in any bank, savings and loan association, or credit union that the employee has previously authorized to receive electronic deposits of payroll, unless the employee has requested, in writing, that disability indemnity benefits not be electronically deposited in the account.

(c) It is not a violation of this section if a delay in the negotiation of a written instrument is caused solely by the application of state or federal banking laws or regulations.

(d) This section shall become operative on January 1, 2023. **Leg.H.** 2018 ch. 730 (SB 880) §2.

§4651.1. Petition alleging disability has decreased or terminated.

Where a petition is filed with the appeals board concerning a continuing award of such appeals board, in which it is alleged that the disability has decreased or terminated, there shall be a rebuttable presumption that such temporary disability continues for at least one week following the filing of such petition. In such case, payment for such week shall be made in accordance with the provisions of Sections 4650 and 4651 of this code.

Where the employee has returned to work at or prior to the date of such filing, however, no such presumption shall apply.

Service of a copy of such petition on the employee shall be made as provided by Section 5316 of this code.

Ref.: 8 C.C.R. §§10462, 10464, 10466; Hanna §§ 20.02[2][i], 23.14[2][i], 35.11[1].

§4651.2. Limitations on filing petition alleging disability has decreased or terminated.

No petitions filed under Section 4651.1 shall be granted while the injured worker is pursuing a rehabilitation plan under Section 139.5 of this code.

§4651.3. Denial of petition alleging disability has decreased or terminated; attorney's fees.

Where a petition is filed with the appeals board pursuant to the provisions of Section 4651.1, and is subsequently denied wholly by the appeals board, the board may determine the amount of attorney's fees reasonably incurred by the applicant in resisting the petition and may assess such reasonable attorney's fees as a cost upon the party filing the petition to decrease or terminate the award of the appeals board.

Ref.: Hanna §§ 20.02[2][i], 31.10[1][c].

§4652. Disability suffered after employee leaves work because of injury.

Except as otherwise provided by Section 4650.5, no temporary disability indemnity is recoverable for the disability suffered during the first three days after the employee leaves work as a result of the injury unless temporary disability continues for more than 14 days or the employee is hospitalized as an inpatient for treatment required by the injury, in either of which cases temporary disability indemnity shall be payable from the date of disability. For purposes of calculating the waiting period, the day of the injury shall be included unless the employee was paid full wages for that day.

1989 Note: This section is applicable only to injuries occurring on or after January 1, 1990. Stats. 1989 ch. 893 §6.

Ref.: Herlick Handbook § 5.9.

§4653. Temporary total disability; amount.

If the injury causes temporary total disability, the disability payment is two-thirds of the average weekly earnings during the period of such disability, consideration being given to the ability of the injured employee to compete in an open labor market.

Ref.: 8 C.C.R. §§9811, 10110; Hanna § 7.04[4]; Herlick Handbook §§ 5.10, 6.16.

§4654. Temporary partial disability; amount.

If the injury causes temporary partial disability, the disability payment is two-thirds of the weekly loss in wages during the period of such disability. However, such disability payment shall be reduced by the sum of unemployment compensation benefits and extended duration benefits received by the employee during the period of temporary partial disability.

Ref.: 8 C.C.R. §9811; Herlick Handbook §§ 5.10, 5.12.

§4655. Temporary disability, both total and partial; amount.

If the injury causes temporary disability which is at times total and at times partial, the weekly disability payment during the period of each total or partial disability is in accordance with sections 4653 and 4654 respectively.

Ref.: Herlick Handbook § 5.10.

§4656. Maximum period for temporary disability payments.

(a) Aggregate disability payments for a single injury occurring prior to January 1, 1979, causing temporary disability shall not extend for more than 240 compensable weeks within a period of five years from the date of the injury.

(b) Aggregate disability payments for a single injury occurring on or after January 1, 1979, and prior to April 19, 2004, causing temporary partial disability shall not extend for more than 240 compensable weeks within a period of five years from the date of the injury.

(c)(1) Aggregate disability payments for a single injury occurring on or after April 19, 2004, causing temporary disability shall not extend for more than 104 compensable weeks within a period of two years from the date of commencement of temporary disability payment.

(2) Aggregate disability payments for a single injury occurring on or after January 1, 2008, causing temporary disability shall not extend for more than 104 compensable weeks within a period of five years from the date of injury.

(3) Notwithstanding paragraphs (1) and (2), for an employee who suffers from the following injuries or conditions, aggregate disability payments for a single injury occurring on or after April 19, 2004, causing temporary disability shall not extend for more than 240 compensable weeks within a period of five years from the date of the injury:

(A) Acute and chronic hepatitis B.

(B) Acute and chronic hepatitis C.

(C) Amputations.

(D) Severe burns.

(E) Human immunodeficiency virus (HIV).

(F) High-velocity eye injuries.

(G) Chemical burns to the eyes.

(H) Pulmonary fibrosis.

(I) Chronic lung disease. **Leg.H.** 2004 ch. 34 (SB 899), effective April 19, 2004, 2007 ch. 595 (AB 338) §1.

2004 Note: The amendment to §4656 made by this act shall apply prospectively from the date of enactment of this act, regardless of the date of injury, unless otherwise specified, but shall not constitute good cause to reopen or rescind, alter, or amend any existing order, decision, or award of the Workers' Compensation Appeals Board. Stats. 2004 ch. 34 (SB 899) §47.

Ref.: Hanna §§ 7.02[1], 7.03[5], 7.04[2], 24.03[3][b]; Herlick Handbook §§ 5.10, 6.10[1], 14.9, 16.5.

§4657. Temporary partial disability; lost wages.

In case of temporary partial disability the weekly loss in wages shall consist of the difference between the average weekly earnings of the injured employee and the weekly amount which the injured employee will probably be able to earn during the disability, to be determined in view of the nature and extent of the injury. In computing such probable earnings, due regard shall be given to the ability of the injured employee to compete in an open labor market. If evidence of exact loss of earnings is lacking, such weekly loss in wages may be computed from the proportionate loss of physical ability or earning power caused by the injury.

Ref.: Hanna §§ 7.02[3][c], 7.04[2]; Herlick Handbook §§ 5.10, 5.12, 16.1.

§4658. Permanent disability; computation.

(a) For injuries occurring prior to January 1, 1992, if the injury causes permanent disability, the percentage of disability to total disability shall be determined, and the disability payment computed and allowed, according to paragraph (1). However, in no event shall the disability payment allowed be less than the disability payment computed according to paragraph (2).

(1)

Column 1—Range of percentage of permanent disability incurred:	Column 2—Number of weeks for which two-thirds of average weekly earnings allowed for each 1 percent of permanent disability within percentage range:
Under 10	3

Labor

10–19.75	4
20–29.75	5
30–49.75	6
50–69.75	7
70–99.75	8

The number of weeks for which payments shall be allowed set forth in column 2 above based upon the percentage of permanent disability set forth in column 1 above shall be cumulative, and the number of benefit weeks shall increase with the severity of the disability. The following schedule is illustrative of the computation of the number of benefit weeks:

Column 1—Percentage of permanent disability incurred:	Column 2—Cumulative number of benefit weeks:
5	15.00
10	30.25
15	50.25
20	70.50
25	95.50
30	120.75
35	150.75
40	180.75
45	210.75
50	241.00
55	276.00
60	311.00
65	346.00
70	381.25
75	421.25
80	461.25
85	501.25
90	541.25
95	581.25
100	for life

(2) Two-thirds of the average weekly earnings for four weeks for each 1 percent of disability, where, for the purposes of this subdivision, the average weekly earnings shall be taken at not more than seventy-eight dollars and seventy-five cents ($78.75).

(b) This subdivision shall apply to injuries occurring on or after January 1, 1992. If the injury causes permanent disability, the percentage of disability to total disability shall be determined, and the disability payment computed and allowed, according to paragraph (1). However, in no event shall the disability payment allowed be less than the disability payment computed according to paragraph (2).

(1)

Column 1—Range of percentage of permanent disability incurred:	Column 2—Number of weeks for which two-thirds of average weekly earnings allowed for each 1 percent of permanent disability within percentage range:
Under 10	3
10–19.75	4
20–24.75	5
25–29.75	6
30–49.75	7
50–69.75	8
70–99.75	9

The numbers set forth in column 2 above are based upon the percentage of permanent disability set forth in column 1 above and shall be cumulative, and shall increase with the severity of the disability in the manner illustrated in subdivision (a).

(2) Two-thirds of the average weekly earnings for four weeks for each 1 percent of disability, where, for the purposes of this subdivision, the average weekly earnings shall be taken at not more than seventy-eight dollars and seventy-five cents ($78.75).

(c) This subdivision shall apply to injuries occurring on or after January 1, 2004. If the injury causes permanent disability, the percentage of disability to total disability shall be determined, and the disability payment computed and allowed as follows:

Column 1—Range of percentage of permanent disability incurred:	Column 2—Number of weeks for which two-thirds of average weekly earnings allowed for each 1 percent of permanent disability within percentage range:
Under 10	4
10–19.75	5
20–24.75	5
25–29.75	6
30–49.75	7
50–69.75	8
70–99.75	9

The numbers set forth in column 2 above are based upon the percentage of permanent disability set forth in column 1 above and shall be cumulative, and shall increase with the severity of the disability in the manner illustrated in subdivision (a).

(d)(1) This subdivision shall apply to injuries occurring on or after January 1, 2005, and as additionally provided in paragraph (4). If the injury causes permanent disability, the percentage of disability to total disability shall be determined, and the basic disability payment computed as follows:

Column 1—Range of percentage of permanent disability incurred:	Column 2—Number of weeks for which two-thirds of average weekly earnings allowed for each 1 percent of permanent disability within percentage range:
0.25–9.75	3
10–14.75	4
15–24.75	5
25–29.75	6
30–49.75	7
50–69.75	8
70–99.75	16

The numbers set forth in column 2 above are based upon the percentage of permanent disability set forth in column 1 above and shall be cumulative, and shall increase with the severity of the disability in the manner illustrated in subdivision (a).

(2) If, within 60 days of a disability becoming permanent and stationary, an employer does not offer the injured employee regular work, modified work, or alternative work, in the form and manner prescribed by the administrative director, for a period of at least 12 months, each disability payment remaining to be paid to the injured employee from the date of the end of the 60-day period shall be paid in accordance with paragraph (1) and in-

creased by 15 percent. This paragraph shall not apply to an employer that employs fewer than 50 employees.

(3)(A) If, within 60 days of a disability becoming permanent and stationary, an employer offers the injured employee regular work, modified work, or alternative work, in the form and manner prescribed by the administrative director, for a period of at least 12 months, and regardless of whether the injured employee accepts or rejects the offer, each disability payment remaining to be paid to the injured employee from the date the offer was made shall be paid in accordance with paragraph (1) and decreased by 15 percent.

(B) If the regular work, modified work, or alternative work is terminated by the employer before the end of the period for which disability payments are due the injured employee, the amount of each of the remaining disability payments shall be paid in accordance with paragraph (1) and increased by 15 percent. An employee who voluntarily terminates employment shall not be eligible for payment under this subparagraph. This paragraph shall not apply to an employer that employs fewer than 50 employees.

(4) For compensable claims arising before April 30, 2004, the schedule provided in this subdivision shall not apply to the determination of permanent disabilities when there has been either a comprehensive medical-legal report or a report by a treating physician, indicating the existence of permanent disability, or when the employer is required to provide the notice required by Section 4061 to the injured worker.

(e) This subdivision shall apply to injuries occurring on or after January 1, 2013. If the injury causes permanent disability, the percentage of disability to total disability shall be determined, and the disability payment computed and allowed as follows:

Column 1—Range of percentage of permanent disability incurred:	Column 2—Number of weeks for which two-thirds of average weekly earnings allowed for each 1 percent of permanent disability within percentage range:
0.25–9.75	3
10–14.75	4
15–24.75	5
25–29.75	6
30–49.75	7
50–69.75	8
70–99.75	16

(1) The numbers set forth in column 2 above are based upon the percentage of permanent disability set forth in column 1 above and shall be cumulative, and shall increase with the severity of the disability in the manner illustrated in subdivision (a).

(2) If the permanent disability directly caused by the industrial injury is total, payment shall be made as provided in Section 4659. **Leg.H.** 2002 ch. 6 (AB 749), 2004 ch. 34 (SB 899), effective April 19, 2004, 2012 ch. 363 (SB 863) §55.

2012 Note: For legislative findings, declarations, and applicability of Stats. 2012 ch. 363, see the 2012 Notes following Lab C §62.5.

2004 Note: The amendment to §4658 made by this act shall apply prospectively from the date of enactment of this act, regardless of the date of injury, unless otherwise specified, but shall not constitute good cause to reopen or rescind, alter, or amend any existing order, decision, or award of the Workers' Compensation Appeals Board. Stats. 2004 ch. 34 (SB 899) §47.

Ref.: 8 C.C.R. §§10110, 10133.53; Hanna §§ 8.02[2], 8.08[1], 32.04[3][a]; Herlick Handbook §§ 5.8, 6.01[1], 6.02[6], [7], [9], 6.03[2], 6.11[1], [2], 6.12, 6.15[7].

§4658.1. Meaning of "regular work," "modified work," and "alternative work"; equivalent wages and compensation; location.

As used in this article, the following definitions apply:

(a) "Regular work" means the employee's usual occupation or the position in which the employee was engaged at the time of injury and that offers wages and compensation equivalent to those paid to the employee at the time of injury, and located within a reasonable commuting distance of the employee's residence at the time of injury.

(b) "Modified work" means regular work modified so that the employee has the ability to perform all the functions of the job and that offers wages and compensation that are at least 85 percent of those paid to the employee at the time of injury, and located within a reasonable commuting distance of the employee's residence at the time of injury.

(c) "Alternative work" means work that the employee has the ability to perform, that offers wages and compensation that are at least 85 percent of those paid to the employee at the time of injury, and that is located within reasonable commuting distance of the employee's residence at the time of injury.

(d) For the purpose of determining whether wages and compensation are equivalent to those paid at the time of injury, the wages and compensation for any increase in working hours over the average hours worked at the time of injury shall not be considered.

(e) For the purpose of determining whether wages and compensation are equivalent to those paid at the time of injury, actual wages and compensation shall be determined without regard to the minimums and maximums set forth in Chapter 1 (commencing with Section 4451).

(f) The condition that regular work, modified work, or alternative work be located within a reasonable distance of the employee's residence at the time of injury may be waived by the employee. The condition shall be deemed to be waived if the employee accepts the regular work, modified work, or alternative work and does not object to the location within 20 days of being informed of the right to object. The condition shall be conclusively deemed to be satisfied if the offered work is at the same location and the same shift as the employment at the time of injury. **Leg.H.** 2004 ch. 34 (SB 899), effective April 19, 2004.

2004 Note: The addition of §4658.1 made by this act shall apply prospectively from the date of enactment of this act, regardless of the date of injury, unless otherwise specified, but shall not constitute good cause to reopen or rescind, alter, or amend any existing order, decision, or award of the Workers' Compensation Appeals Board. Stats. 2004 ch. 34 (SB 899) §47.

Ref.: 8 C.C.R. §§10133.50, 10133.53, 10133.60; Hanna § 32.04[3][a]; Herlick Handbook § 6.11[2].

Labor

§4658.5. Supplemental job displacement benefits—Eligibility; voucher; applicability.

(a) This section shall apply to injuries occurring on or after January 1, 2004, and before January 1, 2013.

(b) Except as provided in Section 4658.6, if the injury causes permanent partial disability and the injured employee does not return to work for the employer within 60 days of the termination of temporary disability, the injured employee shall be eligible for a supplemental job displacement benefit in the form of a nontransferable voucher for education-related retraining or skill enhancement, or both, at state-approved or accredited schools, as follows:

(1) Up to four thousand dollars ($4,000) for permanent partial disability awards of less than 15 percent.

(2) Up to six thousand dollars ($6,000) for permanent partial disability awards between 15 and 25 percent.

(3) Up to eight thousand dollars ($8,000) for permanent partial disability awards between 26 and 49 percent.

(4) Up to ten thousand dollars ($10,000) for permanent partial disability awards between 50 and 99 percent.

(c) The voucher may be used for payment of tuition, fees, books, and other expenses required by the school for retraining or skill enhancement. No more than 10 percent of the voucher moneys may be used for vocational or return-to-work counseling. The administrative director shall adopt regulations governing the form of payment, direct reimbursement to the injured employee upon presentation to the employer of appropriate documentation and receipts, and other matters necessary to the proper administration of the supplemental job displacement benefit.

(d) A voucher issued on or after January 1, 2013, shall expire two years after the date the voucher is furnished to the employee or five years after the date of injury, whichever is later. The employee shall not be entitled to payment or reimbursement of any expenses that have not been incurred and submitted with appropriate documentation to the employer prior to the expiration date.

(e) An employer shall not be liable for compensation for injuries incurred by the employee while utilizing the voucher. **Leg.H.** 2003 ch. 635 (AB 227), 2005 ch. 22 (SB 1108) §144, 2008 ch. 179 (SB 1498) §176, 2011 ch. 544 (AB 335) §5, 2012 ch. 363 (SB 863) §56.

2012 Note: For legislative findings, declarations, and applicability of Stats. 2012 ch. 363, see the 2012 Notes following Lab C §62.5.

Ref.: 8 C.C.R. §§9880, 9881, 10118.1, 10133.50, 10133.51, 10133.52, 10133.53, 10133.54, 10133.55, 10133.56, 10133.57, 10133.58, 10133.59, 10133.60; Hanna Ch. 35; Herlick Handbook Ch. 16.

§4658.6. When employer not liable for supplemental job displacement benefit.

The employer shall not be liable for the supplemental job displacement benefit pursuant to Section 4658.5 if the employer meets either of the following conditions:

(a) Within 30 days of the termination of temporary disability indemnity payments, the employer offers, and the employee rejects, or fails to accept, in the form and manner prescribed by the administrative director, modified work, accommodating the employee's work restrictions, lasting at least 12 months.

(b) Within 30 days of the termination of temporary disability indemnity payments, the employer offers, and the employee rejects, or fails to accept, in the form and manner prescribed by the administrative director, alternative work meeting all of the following conditions:

(1) The employee has the ability to perform the essential functions of the job provided.

(2) The job provided is in a regular position lasting at least 12 months.

(3) The job provided offers wages and compensation that are within 15 percent of those paid to the employee at the time of injury.

(4) The job is located within reasonable commuting distance of the employee's residence at the time of injury. **Leg.H.** 2003 ch. 635 (AB 227), 2012 ch. 363 (SB 863) §57.

2012 Note: For legislative findings, declarations, and applicability of Stats. 2012 ch. 363, see the 2012 Notes following Lab C §62.5.

Ref.: 8 C.C.R. §§9880, 9881, 10118.1, 10133.50, 10133.53, 10133.54, 10133.56, 10133.60; Hanna Ch. 35; Herlick Handbook Ch. 16.

§4658.7. Eligibility for supplemental job displacement for injuries occurring on or after January 1, 2013.

(a) This section shall apply to injuries occurring on or after January 1, 2013.

(b) If the injury causes permanent partial disability, the injured employee shall be entitled to a supplemental job displacement benefit as provided in this section unless the employer makes an offer of regular, modified, or alternative work, as defined in Section 4658.1, that meets both of the following criteria:

(1) The offer is made no later than 60 days after receipt by the claims administrator of the first report received from either the primary treating physician, an agreed medical evaluator, or a qualified medical evaluator, in the form created by the administrative director pursuant to subdivision (h), finding that the disability from all conditions for which compensation is claimed has become permanent and stationary and that the injury has caused permanent partial disability.

(A) If the employer or claims administrator has provided the physician with a job description of the employee's regular work, proposed modified work, or proposed alternative work, the physician shall evaluate and describe in the form whether the work capacities and activity restrictions are compatible with the physical requirements set forth in that job description.

(B) The claims administrator shall forward the form to the employer for the purpose of fully informing the employer of work capacities and activity restrictions resulting from the injury that are relevant to potential regular, modified, or alternative work.

(2) The offer is for regular work, modified work, or alternative work lasting at least 12 months.

(c) The supplemental job displacement benefit shall be offered to the employee within 20 days after the expiration of the time for making an offer of regular, modified, or alternative work pursuant to paragraph (1) of subdivision (b).

(d) The supplemental job displacement benefit shall be in the form of a voucher redeemable as provided in this section up to an aggregate of six thousand dollars ($6,000).

(e) The voucher may be applied to any of the following expenses at the choice of the injured employee:

(1) Payment for education-related retraining or skill enhancement, or both, at a California public school or with a .provider that is certified and on the state's Eligible Training Provider List (EPTL), as authorized by the federal Workforce Investment Act (P.L. 105-220), including payment of tuition, fees, books, and other expenses required by the school for retraining or skill enhancement.

(2) Payment for occupational licensing or professional certification fees, related examination fees, and examination preparation course fees.

(3) Payment for the services of licensed placement agencies, vocational or return-to-work counseling, and résumé preparation, all up to a combined limit of 10 percent of the amount of the voucher.

(4) Purchase of tools required by a training or educational program in which the employee is enrolled.

(5) Purchase of computer equipment, up to one thousand dollars ($1,000).

(6) Up to five hundred dollars ($500) as a miscellaneous expense reimbursement or advance, payable upon request and without need for itemized documentation or accounting. The employee shall not be entitled to any other voucher payment for transportation, travel expenses, telephone or Internet access, clothing or uniforms, or incidental expenses.

(f) The voucher shall expire two years after the date the voucher is furnished to the employee, or five years after the date of injury, whichever is later. The employee shall not be entitled to payment or reimbursement of any expenses that have not been incurred and submitted with appropriate documentation to the employer prior to the expiration date.

(g) Settlement or commutation of a claim for the supplemental job displacement benefit shall not be permitted under Chapter 2 (commencing with Section 5000) or Chapter 3 (commencing with Section 5100) of Part 3.

(h) The administrative director shall adopt regulations for the administration of this section, including, but not limited to, both of the following:

(1) The time, manner, and content of notices of rights under this section.

(2) The form of a mandatory attachment to a medical report to be forwarded to the employer pursuant to paragraph (1) of subdivision (b) for the purpose of fully informing the employer of work capacities and of activity restrictions resulting from the injury that are relevant to potential regular work, modified work, or alternative work.

(i) An employer shall not be liable for compensation for injuries incurred by the employee while utilizing the voucher. **Leg.H.** 2012 ch. 363 (SB 863) §58.

2012 Note: For legislative findings, declarations, and applicability of Stats. 2012 ch. 363, see the 2012 Notes following Lab C §62.5.

Ref.: Hanna § 35.01; Herlick Handbook § 16.1.

§4659. Permanent disability; average weekly earnings; life pensions or total permanent disability.

(a) If the permanent disability is at least 70 percent, but less than 100 percent, 1.5 percent of the average weekly earnings for each 1 percent of disability in excess of 60 percent is to be paid during the remainder of life, after payment for the maximum number of weeks specified in Section 4658 has been made. For the purposes of this subdivision only, average weekly earnings shall be taken at not more than one hundred seven dollars and sixty-nine cents ($107.69). For injuries occurring on or after July 1, 1994, average weekly wages shall not be taken at more than one hundred fifty-seven dollars and sixty-nine cents ($157.69). For injuries occurring on or after July 1, 1995, average weekly wages shall not be taken at more than two hundred seven dollars and sixty-nine cents ($207.69). For injuries occurring on or after July 1, 1996, average weekly wages shall not be taken at more than two hundred fifty-seven dollars and sixty-nine cents ($257.69). For injuries occurring on or after January 1, 2006, average weekly wages shall not be taken at more than five hundred fifteen dollars and thirty-eight cents ($515.38).

(b) If the permanent disability is total, the indemnity based upon the average weekly earnings determined under Section 4453 shall be paid during the remainder of life.

(c) For injuries occurring on or after January 1, 2003, an employee who becomes entitled to receive a life pension or total permanent disability indemnity as set forth in subdivisions (a) and (b) shall have that payment increased annually commencing on January 1, 2004, and each January 1 thereafter, by an amount equal to the percentage increase in the "state average weekly wage" as compared to the prior year. For purposes of this subdivision, "state average weekly wage" means the average weekly wage paid by employers to employees covered by unemployment insurance as reported by the United States Department of Labor for California for the 12 months ending March 31 of the calendar year preceding the year in which the injury occurred. **Leg.H.** 1993 ch. 121, effective July 16, 1993, 2002 ch. 6 (AB 749).

1993 Note: Section 4659, as amended by ch. 121, applies only to injuries occurring on or after January 1, 1994. Stats. 1993 ch. 121 §77.

Ref.: 8 C.C.R. §10110; Hanna §§ 8.08[2], 32.04[3][a]; Herlick Handbook §§ 6.02[15], 6.12, 6.15[7].

§4660. Percentage of permanent disability; schedule.

This section shall only apply to injuries occurring before January 1, 2013.

(a) In determining the percentages of permanent disability, account shall be taken of the nature of the physical injury or disfigurement, the occupation of the injured employee, and his or her age at the time of the injury, consideration being given to an employee's diminished future earning capacity.

(b)(1) For purposes of this section, the "nature of the physical injury or disfigurement" shall incorporate the descriptions and measurements of physical impairments and the corresponding percentages of impairments published in the American Medical Association (AMA) Guides to the Evaluation of Permanent Impairment (5th Edition).

(2) For purposes of this section, an employee's diminished future earning capacity shall be a numeric formula based on empirical data and findings that aggregate the average percentage of long-term loss of income resulting from each type of injury for similarly situated employees. The administrative director shall formulate the adjusted rating schedule based on empirical data and findings from the Evaluation of California's Permanent Disability Rating Schedule, Interim Report (December 2003), prepared by the RAND Institute for Civil Justice, and upon data from additional empirical studies.

(c) The administrative director shall amend the schedule for the determination of the percentage of permanent disability in accordance with this section at least once every five years. This schedule shall be available for public inspection and, without formal introduction in evidence, shall be prima facie evidence of the percentage of permanent disability to be attributed to each injury covered by the schedule.

(d) The schedule shall promote consistency, uniformity, and objectivity. The schedule and any amendment thereto or revision thereof shall apply prospectively and shall apply to and govern only those permanent disabilities that result from compensable injuries received or occurring on and after the effective date of the adoption of the schedule, amendment or revision, as the fact may be. For compensable claims arising before January 1, 2005, the schedule as revised pursuant to changes made in legislation enacted during the 2003-04 Regular and Extraordinary Sessions shall apply to the determination of permanent disabilities when there has been either no comprehensive medical-legal report or no report by a treating physician indicating the existence of permanent disability, or when the employer is not required to provide the notice required by Section 4061 to the injured worker.

(e) On or before January 1, 2005, the administrative director shall adopt regulations to implement the changes made to this section by the act that added this subdivision. **Leg.H.** 1993 ch. 121, effective July 16, 1993, 2004 ch. 34 (SB 899), effective April 19, 2004, 2012 ch. 363 (SB 863) §59.

2012 Note: For legislative findings, declarations, and applicability of Stats. 2012 ch. 363, see the 2012 Notes following Lab C §62.5.

2004 Note: The amendment to §4660 made by this act shall apply prospectively from the date of enactment of this act, regardless of the date of injury, unless otherwise specified, but shall not constitute good cause to reopen or rescind, alter, or amend any existing order, decision, or award of the Workers' Compensation Appeals Board. Stats. 2004 ch. 34 (SB 899) §47.

1993 Note: Section 4660, as amended by ch. 121, applies only to injuries occurring on or after January 1, 1994. Stats. 1993 ch. 121 §77.

Ref.: 8 C.C.R. §§9725, 9726, 9727, 9785, 9785.2, 9785.3, 9785.4, 9805, 9805.1, 10110, 10150, 10152, 10156, 10158, 10160, 10163, 10165.5, 10602; Hanna §§ 8.01, 8.02[3], [4][a], 8.06[5][a], 8.08[1], 32.01[3][a][i], 32.02[2][a], [4], 32.04[3][a]; Herlick Handbook §§ 4.01[1], 6.01[1], [3], 6.02[2], [4], 6.03[1], [8], [9], 6.15[3], 14.20, 16.1; Lawyer's Guide to AMA *Guides* and Calif. Workers' Comp. §§ 2.02, 3.02, 3.03, 5.03.

§4660.1. Percentages of permanent disability for injuries occurring on or after January 1, 2013; how determined; adjusted rating schedule; amendments and revisions to schedule.

This section applies to injuries occurring on or after January 1, 2013.

(a) In determining the percentages of permanent partial or permanent total disability, account shall be taken of the nature of the physical injury or disfigurement, the occupation of the injured employee, and the employee's age at the time of injury.

(b) For purposes of this section, the "nature of the physical injury or disfigurement" shall incorporate the descriptions and measurements of physical impairments and the corresponding percentages of impairments published in the American Medical Association (AMA) Guides to the Evaluation of Permanent Impairment (5th Edition) with the employee's whole person impairment, as provided in the Guides, multiplied by an adjustment factor of 1.4.

(c)(1) Except as provided in paragraph (2), the impairment ratings for sleep dysfunction, sexual dysfunction, or psychiatric disorder, or any combination thereof, arising out of a compensable physical injury shall not increase. This section does not limit the ability of an injured employee to obtain treatment for sleep dysfunction, sexual dysfunction, or psychiatric disorder, if any, that are a consequence of an industrial injury.

(2) An increased impairment rating for psychiatric disorder is not subject to paragraph (1) if the compensable psychiatric injury resulted from either of the following:

(A) Being a victim of a violent act or direct exposure to a significant violent act within the meaning of Section 3208.3.

(B) A catastrophic injury, including, but not limited to, loss of a limb, paralysis, severe burn, or severe head injury.

(d) The administrative director may formulate a schedule of age and occupational modifiers and may amend the schedule for the determination of the age and occupational modifiers in accordance with this section. The Schedule for Rating Permanent Disabilities pursuant to the American Medical Association (AMA) Guides to the Evaluation of Permanent Impairment (5th Edition) and the schedule of age and occupational modifiers shall be available for public inspection and, without formal introduction in evidence, shall be prima facie evidence of the percentage of permanent disability to be attributed to each injury covered by the schedule. Until the schedule of age and occupational modifiers is amended, for injuries occurring on or after January 1, 2013, permanent disabilities shall be rated using the age and occupational modifiers in the permanent disability rating schedule adopted as of January 1, 2005.

(e) The schedule of age and occupational modifiers shall promote consistency, uniformity, and objectivity.

(f) The schedule of age and occupational modifiers and any amendment thereto or revision thereof shall apply prospectively and shall apply to and govern only those permanent disabilities that result from compensable injuries received or occurring on and after the effective date of the adoption of the schedule, amendment, or revision, as the case may be.

(g) This section does not preclude a finding of permanent total disability in accordance with Section 4662.

(h) In enacting the act adding this section, it is not the intent of the Legislature to overrule the holding in Milpitas Unified School District v. Workers' Comp. Appeals Bd. (Guzman) (2010) 187 Cal.App.4th 808.

(i) The Commission on Health and Safety and Workers' Compensation shall conduct a study to compare average loss of earnings for employees who sustained work-related injuries with permanent disability ratings under the schedule, and shall report the results of the study to the appropriate policy and fiscal committees of the Legislature no later than January 1, 2016. **Leg.H.** 2012 ch. 363 (SB 863) §60, 2019 ch. 497 (AB 991) §189.

2012 Note: For legislative findings, declarations, and applicability of Stats. 2012 ch. 363, see the 2012 Notes following Lab C §62.5.

Ref.: Hanna §§ 4.02[3][a], 4.69[1], 8.02[4][c][ii], [5], 32.02[2][a]; Herlick Handbook §§ 4.05[7], 6.01[1], [3], 6.02[1]–[5], [9], [13], [14], 6.03[9].

§4661. Compensation for causing both temporary and permanent disability.

Where an injury causes both temporary and permanent disability, the injured employee is entitled to compensation for any permanent disability sustained by him in addition to any payment received by such injured employee for temporary disability.

Every computation made pursuant to this section shall be made only with reference to disability resulting from an original injury sustained after this section as amended during the 1949 Regular Session of the Legislature becomes effective; provided, however, that all rights presently existing under this section shall be continued in force.

Ref.: Hanna §§ 8.01, 21.01[5][b], 32.04[1][a].

§4661.5. Temporary total disability; payment made two years after injury.

Notwithstanding any other provision of this division, when any temporary total disability indemnity payment is made two years or more from the date of injury, the amount of this payment shall be computed in accordance with the temporary disability indemnity average weekly earnings amount specified in Section 4453 in effect on the date each temporary total disability payment is made unless computing the payment on this basis produces a lower payment because of a reduction in the minimum average weekly earnings applicable under Section 4453.

1989 Note: This section is applicable only to injuries occurring on or after January 1, 1990. Stats. 1989 ch. 893 §6.

Ref.: 8 C.C.R. §§9812, 9813, 9815, 10110: Hanna §§ 7.04[1][b], 35.11[2], [3]; Herlick Handbook §§ 5.2, 5.11, 7.15, 10.10[2], 16.1, 16.5.

§4662. Permanent disability; presumption of total disability.

(a) Any of the following permanent disabilities shall be conclusively presumed to be total in character:

(1) Loss of both eyes or the sight thereof.

(2) Loss of both hands or the use thereof.

(3) An injury resulting in a practically total paralysis.

(4) An injury to the brain resulting in permanent mental incapacity.

(b) In all other cases, permanent total disability shall be determined in accordance with the fact. **Leg.H.** 2007 ch. 31 (AB 1640) §2, 2014 ch. 144 (AB 1847) §46.

2007 Note: It is the intent of the Legislature, in enacting this act, not to adversely affect decisional case law that has previously interpreted, or used, the terms "idiot," "imbecility," or "lunatic," or any variation thereof. Stats. 2007 ch. 31 (AB 1640) §5.

Ref.: 8 C.C.R. §§9725, 9726, 9727, 9785, 9785.2, 9785.3, 9785.4, 9805, 9805.1, 10150, 10152, 10156, 10158, 10160, 10161, 10163, 10165.5; Hanna §§ 8.02[2], 8.06[5][d], 8.07[2][a], [c], 32.03[1]; Herlick Handbook §§ 6.02[5], [15], 6.05[1], 6.07[3].

§4663. Apportionment of permanent disability; causation as basis; physician's report; apportionment determination; disclosure by employee.

(a) Apportionment of permanent disability shall be based on causation.

(b) A physician who prepares a report addressing the issue of permanent disability due to a claimed industrial injury shall address in that report the issue of causation of the permanent disability.

(c) In order for a physician's report to be considered complete on the issue of permanent disability, the report must include an apportionment determination. A physician shall make an apportionment determination by finding what approximate percentage of the permanent disability was caused by the direct result of injury arising out of and occurring in the course of employment and what approximate percentage of the permanent disability was caused by other factors both before and subsequent to the industrial injury, including prior industrial injuries. If the physician is unable to include an apportionment determination in his or her report, the physician shall state the specific reasons why the physician could not make a determination of the effect of that prior condition on the permanent disability arising from the injury. The physician shall then consult with other physicians or refer the employee to another physician from whom the employee is authorized to seek treatment or evaluation in accordance with this division in order to make the final determination.

(d) An employee who claims an industrial injury shall, upon request, disclose all previous permanent disabilities or physical impairments.

(e) Subdivisions (a), (b), and (c) do not apply to injuries or illnesses covered under Sections 3212, 3212.1, 3212.2, 3212.3, 3212.4, 3212.5, 3212.6, 3212.7, 3212.8, 3212.85, 3212.9, 3212.10, 3212.11, 3212.12, 3213, and 3213.2. **Leg.H.** 2004 ch. 34 (SB 899) §34, effective April 19, 2004, 2006 ch. 836 (AB 1368) §1, 2016 ch. 86 (SB 1171) §218.

2006 Note: It is the intent of the Legislature that this act be construed as declaratory of existing law. Stats. 2006 ch. 836 (AB 1368) §2.

2004 Note: The addition of §4663 made by this act shall apply prospectively from the date of enactment of this act, regardless of the date of injury, unless otherwise specified, but shall not constitute good cause to reopen or rescind, alter, or amend any existing order, decision, or award of the Workers' Compensation Appeals Board. Stats. 2004 ch. 34 (SB 899) §47.

Ref.: 8 C.C.R. §§9725, 9726, 9727, 9785, 9785.2, 9785.3, 9785.4, 9805, 9805.1, 10150, 10152, 10156, 10158, 10160, 10161, 10163, 10165.5; Hanna §§ 8.01, 8.05[1]–[3], 8.06[1], [3], [4],

[5][a]; Herlick Handbook §§ 6.02[9], [11], [14], [15], 6.03[2], [4], 6.05[1], [2], 6.07[1], 6.08; Lawyer's Guide to AMA *Guides* and Calif. Workers' Comp. §§ 2.06[3], 5.02, 6.01.

§4664. Liability of employer for percentage of permanent disability directly caused by injury; conclusive presumption from prior award of permanent disability; accumulation of permanent disability awards.

(a) The employer shall only be liable for the percentage of permanent disability directly caused by the injury arising out of and occurring in the course of employment.

(b) If the applicant has received a prior award of permanent disability, it shall be conclusively presumed that the prior permanent disability exists at the time of any subsequent industrial injury. This presumption is a presumption affecting the burden of proof.

(c)(1) The accumulation of all permanent disability awards issued with respect to any one region of the body in favor of one individual employee shall not exceed 100 percent over the employee's lifetime unless the employee's injury or illness is conclusively presumed to be total in character pursuant to Section 4662. As used in this section, the regions of the body are the following:

(A) Hearing.

(B) Vision.

(C) Mental and behavioral disorders.

(D) The spine.

(E) The upper extremities, including the shoulders.

(F) The lower extremities, including the hip joints.

(G) The head, face, cardiovascular system, respiratory system, and all other systems or regions of the body not listed in subparagraphs (A) to (F), inclusive.

(2) Nothing in this section shall be construed to permit the permanent disability rating for each individual injury sustained by an employee arising from the same industrial accident, when added together, from exceeding 100 percent. **Leg.H.** 2004 ch. 34 (SB 899), effective April 19, 2004.

2004 Note: The addition of §4664 made by this act shall apply prospectively from the date of enactment of this act, regardless of the date of injury, unless otherwise specified, but shall not constitute good cause to reopen or rescind, alter, or amend any existing order, decision, or award of the Workers' Compensation Appeals Board. Stats. 2004 ch. 34 (SB 899) §47.

Ref.: 8 C.C.R. §§9725, 9726, 9727, 9785, 9785.2, 9785.3, 9785.4, 9805, 9805.1, 10150, 10152, 10156, 10158, 10160, 10161, 10163, 10165.5; Hanna §§ 8.01, 8.05[1]–[3], 8.06[1], [3], [4], [5][a]; Herlick Handbook §§ 6.02[9], [11], [14], [15], 6.03[2], [4], 6.05[1], 6.07[1], [3], 6.08, 6.16; Lawyer's Guide to AMA *Guides* and Calif. Workers' Comp. § 5.02.

ARTICLE 4
Death Benefits

§4700. Death of employee; employer's liability.

The death of an injured employee does not affect the liability of the employer under Articles 2 (commencing with Section 4600) and 3 (commencing with Section 4650). Neither temporary nor permanent disability payments shall be made for any period of time subsequent to the death of the employee. Any accrued and unpaid compensation shall be paid to the dependents, or, if there are no dependents, to the personal representative of the deceased employee or heirs or other persons entitled thereto, without administration.

Ref.: 8 C.C.R. §§9811, 9812, 9813, 9815, 9880; Hanna §§ 9.01[2], 24.03[5], 27.03[2]; Herlick Handbook §§ 6.13[2], 7.1, 7.3, 7.4, 10.09[2], 14.38.

§4701. Fatal injury; burial expenses; death benefits.

If an injury causes death, either with or without disability, the employer shall be liable, in addition to any other benefits provided by this division, for all of the following:

(a) Reasonable expenses of the employee's burial, in accordance with the following:

(1) Up to two thousand dollars ($2,000) for injuries occurring prior to January 1, 1991.

(2) Up to five thousand dollars ($5,000) for injuries occurring on or after January 1, 1991, and prior to January 1, 2013.

(3) Up to ten thousand dollars ($10,000) for injuries occurring on or after January 1, 2013.

(b) A death benefit, to be allowed to the dependents when the employee leaves any person dependent upon him or her for support. **Leg.H.** 1937, 1943 ch. 678 §1. 1949 ch. 321 §1, 1959 ch. 1189 §15, 1968 ch. 4 (First Extra. Sess.) §7, 1978 ch. 487 §1, 1985 ch. 1567 §1, 1988 ch. 584 (SB 1787) §1, 1989 ch. 892 (AB 276) §39, 2012 ch. 363 (SB 863) §61.

2012 Note: For legislative findings, declarations, and applicability of Stats. 2012 ch. 363, see the 2012 Notes following Lab C §62.5.

1989 Note: This section is applicable only to injuries occurring on or after January 1, 1990. Stats. 1989 ch. 893 §6.

Ref.: 8 C.C.R. §§9811, 9812, 9813, 9815, 10101, 10101.1, 10102, 10109, 10110, 10111, 10111.1, 10111.2, 10115; Hanna § 9.01[3][a], [b]; Herlick Handbook §§ 10.01[2], 10.11.

§4702. Death benefits; computation; payable in installments; no deduction for disability indemnity.

(a) Except as otherwise provided in this section and Sections 4553, 4554, 4557, and 4558, and notwithstanding any amount of compensation paid or otherwise owing to the surviving dependent, personal representative, heir, or other person entitled to a deceased employee's accrued and unpaid compensation, the death benefit in cases of total dependency shall be as follows:

(1) In the case of two total dependents and regardless of the number of partial dependents, for injuries occurring before January 1, 1991, ninety-five thousand dollars ($95,000), for injuries occurring on or after January 1, 1991, one hundred fifteen thousand dollars ($115,000), for injuries occurring on or after July 1, 1994, one hundred thirty-five thousand dollars ($135,000), for injuries occurring on or after July 1, 1996, one hundred forty-five thousand dollars ($145,000), and for injuries occurring on or after January 1, 2006, two hundred ninety thousand dollars ($290,000).

(2) In the case of one total dependent and one or more partial dependents, for injuries occurring before January 1, 1991, seventy thousand dollars ($70,000), for injuries

occurring on or after January 1, 1991, ninety-five thousand dollars ($95,000), for injuries occurring on or after July 1, 1994, one hundred fifteen thousand dollars ($115,000), for injuries occurring on or after July 1, 1996, one hundred twenty-five thousand dollars ($125,000), and for injuries occurring on or after January 1, 2006, two hundred fifty thousand dollars ($250,000), plus four times the amount annually devoted to the support of the partial dependents, but not more than the following: for injuries occurring before January 1, 1991, a total of ninety-five thousand dollars ($95,000), for injuries occurring on or after January 1, 1991, one hundred fifteen thousand dollars ($115,000), for injuries occurring on or after July 1, 1994, one hundred twenty-five thousand dollars ($125,000), for injuries occurring on or after July 1, 1996, one hundred forty-five thousand dollars ($145,000), and for injuries occurring on or after January 1, 2006, two hundred ninety thousand dollars ($290,000).

(3) In the case of one total dependent and no partial dependents, for injuries occurring before January 1, 1991, seventy thousand dollars ($70,000), for injuries occurring on or after January 1, 1991, ninety-five thousand dollars ($95,000), for injuries occurring on or after July 1, 1994, one hundred fifteen thousand dollars ($115,000), for injuries occurring on or after July 1, 1996, one hundred twenty-five thousand dollars ($125,000), and for injuries occurring on or after January 1, 2006, two hundred fifty thousand dollars ($250,000).

(4)(A) In the case of no total dependents and one or more partial dependents, for injuries occurring before January 1, 1991, four times the amount annually devoted to the support of the partial dependents, but not more than seventy thousand dollars ($70,000), for injuries occurring on or after January 1, 1991, a total of ninety-five thousand dollars ($95,000), for injuries occurring on or after July 1, 1994, one hundred fifteen thousand dollars ($115,000), and for injuries occurring on or after July 1, 1996, but before January 1, 2006, one hundred twenty-five thousand dollars ($125,000).

(B) In the case of no total dependents and one or more partial dependents, eight times the amount annually devoted to the support of the partial dependents, for injuries occurring on or after January 1, 2006, but not more than two hundred fifty thousand dollars ($250,000).

(5) In the case of three or more total dependents and regardless of the number of partial dependents, one hundred fifty thousand dollars ($150,000), for injuries occurring on or after July 1, 1994, one hundred sixty thousand dollars ($160,000), for injuries occurring on or after July 1, 1996, and three hundred twenty thousand dollars ($320,000), for injuries occurring on or after January 1, 2006.

(6)(A) In the case of a police officer who has no total dependents and no partial dependents, for injuries occurring on or after January 1, 2003, and prior to January 1, 2004, two hundred fifty thousand dollars ($250,000) to the estate of the deceased police officer.

(B) For injuries occurring on or after January 1, 2004, in the case of no total dependents and no partial dependents, two hundred fifty thousand dollars ($250,000) to the estate of the deceased employee.

(b) A death benefit in all cases shall be paid in installments in the same manner and amounts as temporary total disability indemnity would have to be made to the employee, unless the appeals board otherwise orders. However, no payment shall be made at a weekly rate of less than two hundred twenty-four dollars ($224).

(c) Disability indemnity shall not be deducted from the death benefit and shall be paid in addition to the death benefit when the injury resulting in death occurs after September 30, 1949.

(d) All rights under this section existing prior to January 1, 1990, shall be continued in force. **Leg.H.** 1993 ch. 121, effective July 16, 1993, 1994 ch. 1097, 2002 chs. 6 (AB 749), 866 (AB 486), 2004 ch. 92 (AB 1840), 2006 ch. 119 (AB 2292) §2.

2006 Note: It is the intent of the Legislature to clarify existing statutory requirements governing the payment of death benefits to the survivors of deceased employees under the workers' compensation system when the employee suffered a fatal injury. Stats. 2006 ch. 119 (AB 2292) §1.

2004 Note: It is the intent of the Legislature that the amendment to Section 4702 of the Labor Code made by ch. 92 shall have retroactive effect. Stats. 2004 ch. 92 §2.

1993 Note: Section 4702, as amended by ch. 121, applies only to injuries occurring on or after January 1, 1994. Stats. 1993 ch. 121 §77.

1990 Note: The amendments made by this act to subdivision (c) of Section 139.5 of the Labor Code, pertaining to the payment of additional living expenses, and subdivisions (a) and (c) of Section 4702, of the Labor Code, with respect to the crediting of accrued disability indemnity against the amount of the death benefit, and subdivision (a) of Section 4906 of the Labor Code, with respect to legal services, are not intended by the Legislature to make a change in the law as it existed with respect to these provisions prior to January 1, 1990. Stats. 1990 ch. 1550 §67.

1989 Note: This section is applicable only to injuries occurring on or after January 1, 1990. Stats. 1989 ch. 893 §6.

Ref.: 8 C.C.R. §§9812, 9813, 9815, 9880, 10101, 10101.1, 10102, 10109, 10110, 10111, 10111.1, 10111.2, 10115; Hanna §§ 9.02[3], [4][d.2], [5], 9.03[1], [3], 27.03[2]; Herlick Handbook §§ 5.11, 7.5, 7.6, 7.8–7.10, 7.15.

§4703. Dependent's right to death benefits.

Subject to the provisions of section 4704, this section shall determine the right to a death benefit.

If there is any person wholly dependent for support upon a deceased employee, that person shall receive a full death benefit as set forth in Section 4702 for one total dependent, and any additional partial dependents shall receive a death benefit as set forth in subdivision (b) of Section 4702 to a maximum aggregate amount of twenty-five thousand dollars ($25,000).

If there are two or more persons wholly dependent for support upon a deceased employee, those persons shall receive the death benefit set forth in subdivision (a) of Section 4702, and any person partially dependent shall receive no part thereof.

If there is more than one person wholly dependent for support upon a deceased employee, the death benefit shall be divided equally among them.

If there is more than one person partially dependent for support upon a deceased employee, and no person wholly dependent for support, the amount allowed as a death benefit shall be divided among the persons so partially dependent in proportion to the relative extent of their dependency.

Ref.: 8 C.C.R. §§9812, 9813, 9815, 9880, 10101, 10101.1, 10102, 10109, 10110, 10111, 10111.1, 10111.2, 10115; Hanna § 9.03[1], [2]; Herlick Handbook §§ 7.6, 7.9, 7.13.

§4703.5. Payment of death benefits to dependent children.

(a) In the case of one or more totally dependent children, as defined in Section 3501, after payment of the amount specified in Section 4702, and notwithstanding the maximum limitations specified in Sections 4702 and 4703, payment of death benefits shall continue until the youngest child attains 18 years of age, or until the death of a child physically or mentally incapacitated from earning, in the same manner and amount as temporary total disability indemnity would have been paid to the employee, except that no payment shall be made at a weekly rate of less than two hundred twenty-four dollars ($224).

(b)(1) Notwithstanding the age limitation in subdivision (a), the payment of death benefits shall continue until the youngest child attains 19 years of age if the child is still attending high school and is receiving the death benefits as a child of an active member of a sheriff's office, an active member of a police or fire department of a city, county, city and county, district, or other public or municipal corporation or political subdivision, an individual described in Chapter 4.5 (commencing with Section 830) of Title 3 of Part 2 of the Penal Code who is primarily engaged in active law enforcement activities, active firefighting member of the Department of Forestry and Fire Protection, or an active member of any county forestry or firefighting department or unit killed in the performance of duty.

(2) Paragraph (1) shall not apply with respect to a child of a person whose principal duties are clerical or otherwise do not clearly fall within the scope of active law enforcement or active firefighting services, such as stenographers, telephone operators, and other office workers. **Leg.H.** 2002 ch. 6 (AB 749), 2010 ch. 361 (AB 1696) §1, 2013 ch. 786 (AB 607) §2.

1989 Note: This section is applicable only to injuries occurring on or after January 1, 1990. Stats. 1989 ch. 893 §6.

Ref.: 8 C.C.R. §§9812, 9813, 9815, 10101, 10101.1, 10102, 10109, 10110, 10111, 10111.1, 10111.2, 10115; Hanna §§ 9.02[5], 9.03[3]; Herlick Handbook §§ 5.11, 7.6, 7.7, 7.9, 7.15.

§4703.6. Application of death benefit payments to totally dependent minor child of certain local safety members.

The provisions of Section 4703.5 shall also apply to a totally dependent minor child of a local safety member as defined in Article 4 (commencing with Section 20420) of Chapter 4 of Part 3 of Division 5 of Title 2 of the Government Code, or a safety member as defined in Section 31469.3 of the Government Code, other than a member performing duties related to juvenile hall group counseling and group supervision, or a safety member subject to any public retirement system, or a patrol member as defined in Section 20390 of the Government Code, if that member was killed in the line of duty prior to January 1, 1990, and the totally dependent minor child is otherwise entitled to benefits under Section 4703.5. **Leg.H.** 2001 ch. 589, 2002 ch. 296 (AB 2008), effective August 28, 2002.

2002 Note: The provisions of this act shall apply retroactively to January 1, 2002. Stats. 2002 ch. 296 (AB 2008) §2.

Ref.: Hanna § 9.02[5]; Herlick Handbook § 7.6.

§4704. Control assignment of death benefits.

The appeals board may set apart or reassign the death benefit to any one or more of the dependents in accordance with their respective needs and in a just and equitable manner, and may order payment to a dependent subsequent in right, or not otherwise entitled thereto, upon good cause being shown therefor. The death benefit shall be paid to such one or more of the dependents of the deceased or to a trustee appointed by the appeals board for the benefit of the person entitled thereto, as determined by the appeals board.

Ref.: Hanna §§ 3.115[1], 33.02[5][c]; Herlick Handbook §§ 7.9, 7.13.

§4705. Trustee to application of death benefits to beneficiaries.

The person to whom the death benefit is paid for the use of the several beneficiaries shall apply it in compliance with the findings and directions of the appeals board.

§4706. Death of dependent beneficiary.

(a) If a dependent beneficiary of any deceased employee dies and there is no surviving dependent, the payments of the death benefit accrued and payable at the time of the death of the sole remaining dependent shall be paid upon the order of the appeals board to the heirs of the dependent or, if none, to the heirs of the deceased employee, without administration.

(b) In the event there is no surviving dependent and no surviving heir, the appeals board may order the burial expense of the deceased employee, not to exceed the amount specified in Section 4701, paid to the proper person, without administration.

Ref.: 8 C.C.R. §§10111, 10111.1, 10111.2; Hanna § 9.03[5]; Herlick Handbook § 14.38.

§4706.5. Payment of death benefits where no surviving dependent.

(a) Whenever any fatal injury is suffered by an employee under circumstances that would entitle the employee to compensation benefits, but for his or her death, and the employee does not leave surviving any person entitled to a dependency death benefit, the employer shall pay a sum to the Department of Industrial Relations equal to the total dependency death benefit that would be payable to a surviving spouse with no dependent minor children.

(b) When the deceased employee leaves no surviving dependent, personal representative, heir, or other person entitled to the accrued and unpaid compensation referred to in Section 4700, the accrued and unpaid compensation shall be paid by the employer to the Department of Industrial Relations.

(c) The payments to be made to the Department of Industrial Relations, as required by subdivisions (a) and (b), shall be deposited in the General Fund and shall be credited, as a reimbursement, to any appropriation to the Department of Industrial Relations for payment of the additional compensation for subsequent injury provided in

Article 5 (commencing with Section 4751), in the fiscal year in which the Controller's receipt is issued.

(d) The payments to be made to the Department of Industrial Relations, as required by subdivision (a), shall be paid to the department in a lump sum in the manner provided in subdivision (b) of Section 5101.

(e) The Department of Industrial Relations shall keep a record of all payments due the state under this section, and shall take any steps as may be necessary to collect those amounts.

(f) Each employer, or the employer's insurance carrier, shall notify the administrative director, in any form as the administrative director may prescribe, of each employee death, except when the employer has actual knowledge or notice that the deceased employee left a surviving dependent.

(g) When, after a reasonable search, the employer concludes that the deceased employee left no one surviving who is entitled to a dependency death benefit, and concludes that the death was under circumstances that would entitle the employee to compensation benefits, the employer may voluntarily make the payment referred to in subdivision (a). Payments so made shall be construed as payments made pursuant to an appeals board findings and award. Thereafter, if the appeals board finds that the deceased employee did in fact leave a person surviving who is entitled to a dependency death benefit, upon that finding, all payments referred to in subdivision (a) that have been made shall be forthwith returned to the employer, or if insured, to the employer's workers' compensation carrier that indemnified the employer for the loss.

(h) This section does not apply where there is no surviving person entitled to a dependency death benefit or accrued and unpaid compensation if a death benefit is paid to any person under paragraph (6) of subdivision (a) of Section 4702. **Leg.H.** 2004 ch. 34 (SB 899), effective April 19, 2004, 2006 ch. 119 (AB 2292) §3.

2006 Note: It is the intent of the Legislature to clarify existing statutory requirements governing the payment of death benefits to the survivors of deceased employees under the workers' compensation system when the employee suffered a fatal injury. Stats. 2006 ch. 119 (AB 2292) §1.

2004 Note: The amendment to §4706.5 made by this act shall apply prospectively from the date of enactment of this act, regardless of the date of injury, unless otherwise specified, but shall not constitute good cause to reopen or rescind, alter, or amend any existing order, decision, or award of the Workers' Compensation Appeals Board. Stats. 2004 ch. 34 (SB 899) §47.

Ref.: 8 C.C.R. §§10111, 10111.1, 10111.2, 10501; Hanna §§ 9.03[5], 27.03[2], 28.01[1]; Herlick Handbook §§ 7.18, 12.2.

§4707. Limitation on benefits for member of Public Employees' Retirement System.

(a) Except as provided in subdivision (b), no benefits, except reasonable expenses of burial not exceeding one thousand dollars ($1,000), shall be awarded under this division on account of the death of an employee who is an active member of the Public Employees' Retirement System unless it is determined that a special death benefit, as defined in the Public Employees' Retirement Law, or the benefit provided in lieu of the special death benefit in Sections 21547 and 21548 of the Government Code, will not be paid by the Public Employees' Retirement System to the surviving spouse or children under 18 years of age, of the deceased, on account of the death, but if the total death allowance paid to the surviving spouse and children is less than the benefit otherwise payable under this division the surviving spouse and children are entitled, under this division, to the difference.

The amendments to this section during the 1977–78 Regular Session shall be applied retroactively to July 1, 1976.

(b) The limitation prescribed by subdivision (a) shall not apply to local safety members, or patrol members, as defined in Section 20390 of the Government Code, of the Public Employees' Retirement System. This subdivision shall be applied retroactively. **Leg.H.** 1998 ch. 770, 1999 ch. 83, 2001 ch. 589.

Ref.: Hanna §§ 3.115[1], 9.04[1], 33.02[5][c]; Herlick Handbook §§ 3.21, 7.20, 14.17.

§4708. Joinder of Public Employees' Retirement System.

Upon application of any party in interest for a death benefit provided by this division on the death of an employee member of the Public Employees' Retirement System, the latter shall be joined as a defendant, and the appeals board shall determine whether the death resulted from injury or illness arising out of and in the course of his employment, for the purpose of enabling the appeals board to apply the provision of this division and the board of administration to apply the provisions of the Public Employees' Retirement Law.

Ref.: Hanna §§ 9.04[1], 32.02[5][b], [c].

§4709. Scholarships for dependents of specified employees; "dependent."

(a) Notwithstanding any other law, a dependent of a peace officer, as defined in Section 830.1, 830.2, 830.3, 830.31, 830.32, 830.33, 830.34, 830.35, 830.36, 830.37, 830.38, 830.39, 830.4, 830.5, or 830.6 of the Penal Code, or a Sheriff's Special Officer of the County of Orange, who is killed in the performance of duty or who dies or is totally disabled as a result of an accident or an injury caused by external violence or physical force, incurred in the performance of duty, when the death, accident, or injury is compensable under this division or Division 4.5 (commencing with Section 6100) shall be entitled to a scholarship at any qualifying institution described in subdivision (*l*) of Section 69432.7 of the Education Code. The scholarship shall be in an amount equal to the amount provided a student who has been awarded a Cal Grant scholarship as specified in Chapter 1.7 (commencing with Section 69430) of Part 42 of Division 5 of Title 3 of the Education Code.

(b) A dependent of an officer or employee of the Department of Corrections and Rehabilitation or the Department of Corrections and Rehabilitation, Division of Juvenile Justice, described in Section 20403 of the Government Code, who is killed in the performance of duty, or who dies or is totally disabled as a result of an accident or an injury incurred in the performance of duty, when the death, accident, or injury is caused by the direct action of an inmate, and is compensable under this division or Division 4.5 (commencing with Section 6100), shall also be entitled to a scholarship specified in this section.

(c) Notwithstanding any other law, a dependent of a firefighter employed by a county, city, city and county, district, or other political subdivision of the state, who is killed in the performance of duty or who dies or is totally disabled as a result of an accident or injury incurred in the performance of duty, when the death, accident, or injury is compensable under this division or Division 4.5 (commencing with Section 6100), shall also be entitled to a scholarship specified in this section.

(d) Nothing in this section shall be interpreted to allow the admittance of the dependent into a college or university unless the dependent is otherwise qualified to gain admittance to the college or university.

(e) The scholarship provided for by this section shall be paid out of funds annually appropriated in the Budget Act to the Student Aid Commission established by Article 2 (commencing with Section 69510) of Chapter 2 of Part 42 of Division 5 of Title 3 of the Education Code.

(f) The receipt of a scholarship provided for by this section shall not preclude a dependent from receiving a Cal Grant award pursuant to Chapter 1.7 (commencing with Section 69430) of Part 42 of Division 5 of Title 3 of the Education Code, any other grant, or any fee waivers that may be provided by an institution of higher education. The receipt of a Cal Grant award pursuant to Chapter 1.7 (commencing with Section 69430) of Part 42 of Division 5 of Title 3 of the Education Code, any other grant, or any fee waivers that may be provided by an institution of higher education shall not preclude a dependent from receiving a scholarship provided for by this section.

(g) As used in this section, "dependent" means the children (natural or adopted) or spouse, at the time of the death or injury, of the peace officer, law enforcement officer, or firefighter.

(h) Eligibility for a scholarship under this section shall be limited to a person who demonstrates financial need as determined by the Student Aid Commission pursuant to Article 1.5 (commencing with Section 69503) of Chapter 2 of Part 42 of Division 5 of Title 3 of the Education Code. For purposes of determining financial need, the proceeds of death benefits received by the dependent, including, but not limited to, a continuation of income received from the Public Employees' Retirement System, the proceeds from the federal Public Safety Officers' Benefits Act, life insurance policies, proceeds from Sections 4702 and 4703.5, any private scholarship where receipt is predicated upon the recipient being the survivor of a deceased public safety officer, the scholarship awarded pursuant to Section 68120 of the Education Code, and any interest received from these benefits, shall not be considered. **Leg.H.** 1995 ch. 646, 2001 ch. 806, 2011 ch. 349 (SB 940) §12, 2012 ch. 819 (AB 2069) §1, 2013 ch. 76 (AB 383) §143.

Ref.: Hanna §§ 3.115[2], 9.04[2].

ARTICLE 4.5
Public Official Death Benefits

§4720. "Elected public official"; "assassination."

As used in this article:

(a) "Elected public official" means any person other than the President or Vice President of the United States who holds any federal, state, local, or special district elective office as a result of winning election in California to such office or being appointed to fill a vacancy in such office.

(b) "Assassination" means the killing of an elected public official as a direct result of an intentional act perpetrated by an individual or individuals acting to prevent, or retaliate for, the performance of official duties, acting because of the public position held by the official, or acting because of pathological reasons.

Ref.: Hanna §§ 9.04[3], 33.02[5][c]; Herlick Handbook § 7.22.

§4721. Special death benefits upon assassination of elected public official.

The surviving spouse or dependent minor children of an elected public official who is killed by assassination shall be entitled to a special death benefit which shall be in addition to any other benefits provided for by this division or Division 4.5 (commencing with Section 6100).

§4722. Persons entitled to special death benefits.

If the deceased elected public official is survived by a spouse with or without dependent minor children, such special death benefit shall be payable to the surviving spouse. If the deceased elected public official leaves no surviving spouse but one or more dependent minor children, benefits shall be paid to a guardian ad litem and trustee for such child or children appointed by the Workers' Compensation Appeals Board. In the absence of a surviving spouse and dependent minor children, the benefit shall be payable to any legally recognized dependent parent of the deceased elected public official.

§4723. Types of special death benefits; election.

The person or persons to whom the special death benefit is payable pursuant to Section 4722 shall, within one year of the date of death of the elected public official, choose either of the following benefits:

(a) An annual benefit equal to one-half of the average annual salary paid to the elected public official in his or her elected capacity, less credit for any other death benefit provided for under existing law or by public funds, except benefits payable pursuant to this division or Division 4.5 (commencing with Section 6100). Payments shall be paid not less frequently than monthly, and shall be paid from the date of death until the spouse dies or remarries, or until the youngest minor dependent child reaches the age of 18 years, whichever occurs last. If payments are being made to a dependent parent or parents they shall continue during dependency.

(b) A lump-sum benefit of one hundred fifty thousand dollars ($150,000), less any other death benefit provided for under existing law or by public funds, except benefits payable pursuant to this division or Division 4.5 (commencing with Section 6100).

§4724. Filing claim for special death benefits.

The person or persons to whom the special death benefit is payable pursuant to Section 4722 shall file a claim therefor with the Department of General Services, which shall be processed pursuant to the provisions of Chapter 3 (commencing with Section 900) of Part 2 of Division 3.6 of Title 1 of the Government Code. **Leg.H.** 1979 ch. 983 §1, 1981 ch. 714 §318, 2016 ch. 31 (SB 836) §192, effective June 27, 2016.

§4725. State Compensation Insurance Fund as disbursing agent.

The State Compensation Insurance Fund shall be the disbursing agent for payments made pursuant to this article and shall receive a fee for its services to be negotiated by the Department of General Services. Unless otherwise provided herein, payments shall be made in accordance with the provisions of this division. **Leg.H.** 1979 ch. 983 §1, 2016 ch. 31 (SB 836) §193, effective June 27, 2016.

§4726. Joint adoption of rules to carry out article's provisions.

The Department of General Services and the Administrative Director of the Division of Workers' Compensation shall jointly adopt rules and regulations as may be necessary to carry out the provisions of this article. **Leg.H.** 1994 ch. 146, 2016 ch. 31 (SB 836) §194, effective June 27, 2016.

§4727. Assassin's ineligibility for benefits.

Any person who is convicted of any crime in connection with the assassination of an elected public official shall not be eligible for any benefits pursuant to this article.

§4728. Scholarships for dependents of elected public officials intentionally killed in retaliation for or to prevent their performance of official duties.

(a) A dependent of an elected public official, who was intentionally killed while holding office, in retaliation for, or to prevent the performance of, an official duty, shall be entitled to a scholarship at any institution described in subdivision (k) of Section 69535 of the Education Code. The scholarship shall be in an amount equal to the amount provided a student who has been awarded a Cal Grant scholarship as specified in Article 3 (commencing with Section 69530) of Chapter 2 of Part 42 of the Education Code. Eligibility for a scholarship under this section shall be limited to a person who demonstrates financial need as determined by the Student Aid Commission pursuant to Article 1.5 (commencing with Section 69503) of Chapter 2 of Part 42 of the Education Code.

(b) The scholarship provided for by this section shall be paid out of funds annually appropriated in the Budget Act to the Student Aid Commission established by Article 2 (commencing with Section 69510) of Chapter 2 of Part 42 of the Education Code.

(c) The receipt of a scholarship provided for by this section shall not preclude a dependent from receiving a Cal Grant award pursuant to Article 3 (commencing with Section 69530) of Chapter 2 of Part 42 of the Education Code, any other grant, or any fee waivers that may be provided by an institution of higher education. The receipt of a Cal Grant award pursuant to Article 3 (commencing with Section 69530) of Chapter 2 of Part 42 of the Education Code, any other grant, or any fee waivers that may be provided by an institution of higher education shall not preclude a dependent from receiving a scholarship provided for by this section.

(d) This section shall apply to a student receiving a scholarship on the effective date of the section unless that application would result in the student receiving a scholarship on less favorable terms or in a lesser amount, in which case the student shall continue to receive the scholarship on the same terms and conditions in effect prior to the effective date of this section.

(e) As used in this section, "dependent" means the children (natural or adopted) or spouse, at the time of the death or injury, of the elected public official. **Leg.H.** 1995 ch. 646.

Ref.: Hanna § 3.115[2]; Herlick Handbook § 7.22.

ARTICLE 5
Subsequent Injuries Payments

§4751. Compensation for specified additions to permanent partial disabilities.

If an employee who is permanently partially disabled receives a subsequent compensable injury resulting in additional permanent partial disability so that the degree of disability caused by the combination of both disabilities is greater than that which would have resulted from the subsequent injury alone, and the combined effect of the last injury and the previous disability or impairment is a permanent disability equal to 70 percent or more of total, he shall be paid in addition to the compensation due under this code for the permanent partial disability caused by the last injury compensation for the remainder of the combined permanent disability existing after the last injury as provided in this article; provided, that either (a) the previous disability or impairment affected a hand, an arm, a foot, a leg, or an eye, and the permanent disability resulting from the subsequent injury affects the opposite and corresponding member, and such latter permanent disability, when considered alone and without regard to, or adjustment for, the occupation or age of the employee, is equal to 5 percent or more of total, or (b) the permanent disability resulting from the subsequent injury, when considered alone and without regard to or adjustment for the occupation or the age of the employee, is equal to 35 percent or more of total.

Ref.: 8 C.C.R. §§10940, 10942, 15740, 15741; Hanna § 8.09[2]; Herlick Handbook §§ 6.13[1], 14.17.

§4753. Reduction of additional compensation.

Such additional compensation is not in addition to but shall be reduced to the extent of any monetary payments received by the employee, from any source whatsoever, for or on account of such preexisting disability or impairment, except as to payments being made to the employee or to which he is entitled as a pension or other compensation for disability incurred in service in the armed forces of the United States, and except as to payments being made to him or to which he is entitled as assistance under the provisions of Chapter 2 (commencing with Section 11200), Chapter 3 (commencing with Section 12000), Chapter 4 (commencing with Section 12500), Chapter 5 (commencing with Section 13000), or Chapter 6 (commencing with

Labor

Section 13500) of Part 3, or Part 5 (commencing with Section 17000), of Division 9 of the Welfare and Institutions Code, and excluding from such monetary payments received by the employee for or on account of such preexisting disability or impairment a sum equal to all sums reasonably and necessarily expended by the employee for or on account of attorney's fees, costs and expenses incidental to the recovery of such monetary payments.

All cases under this section and under Section 4751 shall be governed by the terms of this section and Section 4751 as in effect on the date of the particular subsequent injury.

Ref.: 8 C.C.R. §§10940, 10942, 15740, 15741.

§4753.5. Legal representation of state.

In any hearing, investigation, or proceeding, the state shall be represented by the Attorney General, or the attorneys of the Department of Industrial Relations, as appointed by the director. Expenses incident to representation, including costs for investigation, medical examinations, other expert reports, fees for witnesses, and other necessary and proper expenses, but excluding the salary of any of the Attorney General's deputies, shall be reimbursed from the Workers' Compensation Administration Revolving Fund. No witness fees or fees for medical services shall exceed those fees prescribed by the appeals board for the same services in those cases where the appeals board, by rule, has prescribed fees. Reimbursement pursuant to this section shall be in addition to, and in augmentation of, any other appropriations made or funds available for the use or support of the legal representation. **Leg.H.** 1994 ch. 146, 2003 ch. 228 (AB 1756), effective August 11, 2003, 2006 ch. 538 (SB 1852) §489.

Ref.: 8 C.C.R. §§10940, 10942; Hanna § 31.20[4][e]; Herlick Handbook § 6.16.

§4754. Special additional compensation; awards, payment; reimbursement.

The appeals board shall fix and award the amounts of special additional compensation to be paid under this article, and shall direct the State Compensation Insurance Fund to pay the additional compensation so awarded. Such additional compensation may be paid only from funds appropriated for such purpose. Out of any such appropriation the fund may reimburse itself for the cost of service rendered in payment of compensation awards pursuant to this article and maintenance of accounts and records pertaining thereto, which cost shall not exceed 5 percent of the amount of award paid.

Ref.: 8 C.C.R. §§15740, 15741; Herlick Handbook § 6.16.

§4754.5. Compromises and release agreements.

Nothing in this article shall impair the right of the Attorney General or the Department of Industrial Relations to release by compromise any claims brought under the provisions of this article. No such compromise and release agreement is valid unless it is approved by the appeals board; however, the provisions of Sections 5000 to 5004, inclusive, of this code, shall not apply to such compromise and release agreements.

Ref.: 8 C.C.R. §§10940, 10942, 15740, 15741; Herlick Handbook § 6.16.

§4755. Cash revolving funds.

(a) The State Compensation Insurance Fund may draw from the State Treasury out of the Subsequent Injuries Benefits Trust Fund for the purposes specified in Section 4751, without at the time presenting vouchers and itemized statements, a sum not to exceed in the aggregate fifty thousand dollars ($50,000), to be used as a cash revolving fund. The revolving fund shall be deposited in any banks and under any conditions as the Department of Finance determines. The Controller shall draw his or her warrants in favor of the State Compensation Insurance Fund for the amounts so withdrawn and the Treasurer shall pay these warrants.

(b) Expenditures made from the revolving fund in payments on claims for any additional compensation and for adjusting services are exempted from the operation of Section 16003 of the Government Code. Reimbursement of the revolving fund for these expenditures shall be made upon presentation to the Controller of an abstract or statement of the expenditures. The abstract or statement shall be in any form as the Controller requires.

(c) The director shall assign claims adjustment services and legal representation services respecting matters concerning subsequent injuries. The director or his or her representative may make these service assignments within the department, or he or she may contract for these services with the State Compensation Insurance Fund, for a fee in addition to that authorized by Section 4754, except insofar as these matters might conflict with the interests of the State Compensation Insurance Fund. The administrative costs associated with these services shall be reimbursed from the Workers' Compensation Administration Revolving Fund, except when a budget impasse requires advances as provided in subdivision (d) of Section 62.5. To the extent permitted by state law, the director may contract for audits or reports of services under this section. **Leg.H.** 2003 ch. 228 (AB 1756), effective August 11, 2003, 2012 ch. 728 (SB 71) §121.

Ref.: 8 C.C.R. §§15740, 15741.

§4756. No prohibition on receipt of compensation solely because of citizenship or immigration status; legislative intent.

(a) The Legislature finds and declares that it is in the best interest of the State of California to provide a person, regardless of his or her citizenship or immigration status, with the benefits provided pursuant to this article, and therefore enacts this section pursuant to Section 1621(d) of Title 8 of the United States Code.

(b) A person shall not be prohibited from receiving compensation paid or payable from the Subsequent Injuries Benefits Trust Fund solely because of his or her citizenship or immigration status.

(c) It is the intent of the Legislature to override Section 15740 of Article 1 of Subchapter 2.1.1 of Chapter 8 of Division 1 of Title 8 of the California Code of Regulations.

(d) The provisions of this section are declaratory of existing law. **Leg.H.** 2015 ch. 290 (SB 623) §2.

Ref.: Hanna § 3.31; Herlick Handbook § 2.3.

ARTICLE 6
Special Payments to Certain Persons

§4800. Paid leave of absence for specified employees of Department of Justice and San Francisco Port Commission.

(a) Whenever any member of the Department of Justice falling within the "state peace officer/firefighter" class is disabled by injury arising out of and in the course of his or her duties, he or she shall become entitled, regardless of his or her period of service with the Department of Justice to leave of absence while so disabled without loss of salary, in lieu of disability payments under this chapter, for a period not exceeding one year. This section applies only to members of the Department of Justice whose principal duties consist of active law enforcement and does not apply to persons employed in the Department of Justice whose principal duties are those of telephone operator, clerk, stenographer, machinist, mechanic, or otherwise clearly not falling within the scope of active law enforcement service, even though this person is subject to occasional call or is occasionally called upon to perform duties within the scope of active law enforcement service.

(b) This section applies to law enforcement officers employed by the Department of Fish and Wildlife who are described in subdivision (e) of Section 830.2 of the Penal Code.

(c) This section applies to harbor police officers employed by the San Francisco Port Commission who are described in Section 20402 of the Government Code.

(d) This section shall does not apply to periods of disability that occur subsequent to termination of employment by resignation, retirement, or dismissal. When this section does not apply, the employee shall be eligible for those benefits that would apply if this section had not been enacted. **Leg.H.** 1994 ch. 762, effective September 23, 1994, 2012 ch. 559 (AB 2402) §28, 2017 ch. 561 (AB 1516) §175.

2017 Note: It appears the Legislature inadvertently added "does" following "shall" in subdivision (d).

Ref.: 8 C.C.R. §9814; Hanna §§ 3.114[2], [3], 33.02[3][a], 34.03[2]; Herlick Handbook §§ 5.17, 14.17, 16.5.

§4800.5. Paid leave of absence for specified employees of Department of the California Highway Patrol—Limitations; appeals board jurisdiction in determining disability; eligibility of other peace officers.

(a) Whenever any sworn member of the Department of the California Highway Patrol is disabled by a single injury, excluding disabilities that are the result of cumulative trauma or cumulative injuries, arising out of and in the course of his or her duties, he or she shall become entitled, regardless of his or her period of service with the patrol, to leave of absence while so disabled without loss of salary, in lieu of disability payments under this chapter, for a period of not exceeding one year. This section shall apply only to members of the Department of the California Highway Patrol whose principal duties consist of active law enforcement and shall not apply to persons employed in the Department of the California Highway Patrol whose principal duties are those of telephone operator, clerk, stenographer, machinist, mechanic, or otherwise clearly not falling within the scope of active law enforcement service, even though this person is subject to occasional call or is occasionally called upon to perform the duties of active law enforcement service.

(b) Benefits payable for eligible sworn members of the Department of the California Highway Patrol whose disability is solely the result of cumulative trauma or injury shall be limited to the actual period of temporary disability or entitlement to maintenance allowance, or for one year, whichever is less.

(c) This section shall not apply to periods of disability that occur subsequent to termination of employment by resignation, retirement, or dismissal. When this section does not apply, the employee shall be eligible for those benefits that would apply had this section not been enacted.

(d) The appeals board may determine, upon request of any party, whether or not the disability referred to in this section arose out of and in the course of duty. In any action in which a dispute exists regarding the nature of the injury or the period of temporary disability or entitlement to maintenance allowance, or both, and upon the request of any party thereto, the appeals board shall determine when the disability commenced and ceased, and the amount of benefits provided by this division to which the employee is entitled during the period of this disability. The appeals board shall have the jurisdiction to award and enforce payment of these benefits, subject to subdivision (a) or (b), pursuant to Part 4 (commencing with Section 5300). A decision issued by the appeals board under this section is final and binding upon the parties subject to the rights of appeal contained in Chapter 7 (commencing with Section 5900) of Part 4.

(e) Except as provided in subdivision (g), this section shall apply for periods of disability commencing on or after January 1, 1995.

(f) This section does not apply to peace officers designated under subdivision (a) of Section 2250.1 of the Vehicle Code.

(g) Peace officers of the California State Police Division who become sworn members of the Department of the California Highway Patrol as a result of the Governor's Reorganization Plan No. 1 of 1995, other than those officers described in subdivision (f), shall be eligible for injury benefits accruing to sworn members of the Department of the California Highway Patrol under this division only for injuries occurring on or after July 12, 1995. **Leg.H.** 1994 ch. 762, effective September 23, 1994, 1995 Gov. Reorg. Plan 1, effective May 12, 1995, ch. 91, 1996 ch. 305.

Ref.: 8 C.C.R. §10405; Hanna § 3.114[2], [3]; Herlick Handbook § 5.17.

§4801. Disability occurring in course of duty.

It shall be the duty of the appeals board to determine in the case of members of the California Highway Patrol, upon request of the Department of the California Highway Patrol or Department of Justice, and, in the case of the harbor policemen, upon the request of the San Francisco Port Commission, whether or not the disability referred to in Section 4800 arose out of and in the course of duty. The appeals board shall, also, in any disputed case, determine when such disability ceases.

Ref.: 8 C.C.R. §10405; Hanna § 21.07[6].

§4802. Medical, surgical, and hospital benefits.

Any such member of the California Highway Patrol or Department of Justice, or any such harbor policeman, so disabled is entitled from the date of injury and regardless of retirement under the Public Employees' Retirement System, to the medical, surgical and hospital benefits prescribed by this division as part of the compensation for persons injured in the course of and arising out of their employment, at the expense of the Department of the California Highway Patrol, the Department of Justice, or the San Francisco Port Commission, as the case may be, and such expense shall be charged upon the fund out of which the compensation of the member is paid.

Ref.: Hanna § 22.01[5].

§4803. Disability continuing beyond one year.

Whenever such disability of such member of the California Highway Patrol, or Department of Justice, or of such harbor policeman, continues for a period beyond one year, such member or harbor policeman shall thereafter be subject, as to disability indemnity, to the provisions of this division other than Section 4800, which refers to temporary disability only, during the remainder of the disability, except that such compensation shall be paid out of funds available for the support of the Department of the California Highway Patrol, the Department of Justice, or the San Francisco Port Commission, as the case may be, and the leave of absence shall continue.

§4804. Prohibition on temporary disability payments concurrent with salary payments.

No disability indemnity shall be paid to said member of the California Highway Patrol or harbor policeman as temporary disability concurrently with wages or salary payments.

§4804.1. Paid leave of absence for specified University of California fire department employees.

Whenever any member of a University of California fire department specified in Section 3212.4 falling within the active "firefighting and prevention service" class is disabled by injury arising out of and in the course of his duties, he shall become entitled, regardless of his period of service with a University of California fire department, to leave of absence while so disabled without loss of salary, in lieu of disability payments under this chapter, for a period of not exceeding one year. This section shall apply only to members of a University of California fire department whose principal duties consists of active firefighting and prevention service and shall not apply to persons employed in a University of California fire department whose principal duties are those of telephone operator, clerk, stenographer, machinist, mechanic, or otherwise clearly not falling within the scope of active firefighting and prevention service, even though such person is subject to occasional call or is occasionally called upon to perform duties within the scope of active firefighting and prevention service.

Ref.: 8 C.C.R. §9814.

§4804.2. University of California firefighter's disability occurring in course of duty; determination.

It shall be the duty of the appeals board to determine in the case of members of a University of California fire department specified in Section 4804.1, upon request of the Regents of the University of California, whether or not the disability referred to in Section 4804.1 arose out of and in the course of duty. The appeals board shall, also in any disputed case, determine when such disability ceases.

Ref.: 8 C.C.R. §10405.

§4804.3. Medical, surgical, and hospital benefits for University of California firefighters.

Any such member of a University of California fire department specified in Section 4804.1, so disabled is entitled from the date of injury and regardless of retirement under the Public Employees' Retirement System, or other retirement system, to the medical, surgical, and hospital benefits prescribed by this division as part of the compensation for persons injured in the course of and arising out of their employment, at the expense of the Regents of the University of California, and such expense shall be charged upon the fund out of which the compensation of the member is paid.

§4804.4. University of California firefighter's disability continuing beyond one year.

Whenever such disability of such member of a University of California fire department, specified in Section 4804.1, continues for a period beyond one year, such member shall thereafter be subject, as to disability indemnity, to the provisions of this division other than Section 4804.1, which refers to temporary disability only, during the remainder of the disability, except that such compensation shall be paid out of funds available for the support of the Regents of the University of California, and the leave of absence shall continue.

§4804.5. Prohibition on temporary disability payments concurrent with salary payments for University of California firefighters.

No disability indemnity shall be paid to said member of a University of California fire department, specified in Section 4804.1, as temporary disability concurrently with wages or salary payments.

§4806. Paid leave of absence for active law enforcement officers of University of California Police Department.

Whenever any member of the University of California Police Department falling within the "law enforcement" class is disabled by injury arising out of and in the course of his duties, he shall become entitled, regardless of his period of service with the police department, to leave of absence while so disabled without loss of salary, in lieu of disability payments under this chapter, for a period of not exceeding one year. This section shall apply only to members of the University of California Police Department whose principal duties consist of active law enforcement, and shall not apply to persons employed in the University of California Police Department whose principal duties are those of telephone operator, clerk, stenographer, machinist, mechanic or otherwise clearly not falling within the scope of active law enforcement service, even though such person is subject to occasional call or is occasionally called upon to perform duties within the scope of active law enforcement service.

This section shall apply only to those members of the University of California Police Department specified in Section 3213.

Ref.: 8 C.C.R. §9814.

§4807. Appeals board to determine relationship of disability to duty.

It shall be the duty of the appeals board to determine, in the case of members of the University of California Police Department, upon the request of the Regents of the University of California, whether or not the disability referred to in Section 4806 arose out of and in the course of duty. The appeals board shall, also in any disputed case, determine when such disability ceases.

Ref.: 8 C.C.R. §10405; Hanna § 3.114[3]; Herlick Handbook § 14.17.

§4808. Medical, surgical, and hospital benefits for University of California police officers.

Any such member of the University of California Police Department so disabled is entitled from the date of injury, and regardless of retirement under either the University of California Retirement System or Public Employees' Retirement System, to the medical, surgical, and hospital benefits prescribed by this division as part of the compensation for persons injured in the course of and arising out of their employment, at the expense of the Regents of the University of California, and such expense shall be charged upon the fund out of which the compensation of the member is paid.

§4809. University of California police officer's disability continuing beyond one year.

Whenever such disability of such member of the University of California Police Department continues for a period beyond one year, such member shall thereafter be subject, as to disability indemnity, to the provisions of this division other than Section 4806, which refers to temporary disability only, during the remainder of the disability, except that such compensation shall be paid out of funds available for the support of the Regents of the University of California and the leave of absence shall continue.

§4810. Prohibition on temporary disability payments concurrent with salary payments for University of California police officers.

No disability indemnity shall be paid to such member of the University of California Police Department as temporary disability concurrently with wages or salary payments.

§4816. California State University Police Department collective bargaining agreement for enhanced industrial disability leave.

Pursuant to a collective bargaining agreement applicable to members of the California State University Police Department, whenever any member of that police department falling within the "law enforcement" class is disabled by injury or illness arising out of and in the course of his or her duties, he or she shall become entitled, regardless of his or her period of service with the police department, to enhanced industrial disability leave equivalent to the injured employee's net take home salary on the date of occurrence of the injury. For the purposes of this section, "net take home salary" means the amount of salary received after federal income tax, state income tax, and the employee's retirement contribution has been deducted from the employee's gross salary, in lieu of disability payments under this chapter, for a period of not exceeding one year. No benefits shall be paid under this section for any psychiatric disability or any physical disability arising from a psychiatric injury.

This section shall apply only to members of the California State University Police Department whose principal duties consist of active law enforcement, and shall not apply to persons employed in the California State University Police Department whose principal duties are those of telephone operator, clerk, stenographer, machinist, mechanic, or otherwise clearly not falling within the scope of active law enforcement service, even though the person is subject to occasional call or is occasionally called upon to perform duties within the scope of active law enforcement service. **Leg.H.** 1994 ch. 50.

Ref.: Herlick Handbook § 8.21.

§4817. Appeals board to determine relationship of disability to duty.

It shall be the duty of the appeals board to determine, in the case of members of the California State University Police Department, upon the request of the Board of Trustees of the California State University, whether or not the disability referred to in Section 4816 arose out of and in the course of duty. The appeals board shall, also in any disputed case, determine when such disability ceases. **Leg.H.** 1994 ch. 50.

§4819. California State University police officer's disability continuing beyond one year.

Whenever the disability of a member of the California State University Police Department continues for a period beyond one year, that member shall thereafter be subject, as to disability indemnity, to the provisions of this division other than Section 4816, which refers to temporary disability only, during the remainder of the disability. **Leg.H.** 1994 ch. 50.

§4820. Prohibition on temporary disability payments concurrent with salary payments for California State University police officers.

No disability indemnity shall be paid to a member of the California State University Police Department as tempo-

Labor

rary disability concurrently with wages or salary payments. **Leg.H.** 1994 ch. 50.

ARTICLE 7
City Police and Firemen, Sheriffs, and Others

§4850. Paid leave of absence for specified public employees.

(a) Whenever any person listed in subdivision (b), who is employed on a regular, full-time basis, and is disabled, whether temporarily or permanently, by injury or illness arising out of and in the course of his or her duties, he or she shall become entitled, regardless of his or her period of service with the city, county, or district, to a leave of absence while so disabled without loss of salary in lieu of temporary disability payments or maintenance allowance payments, if any, that would be payable under this chapter, for the period of the disability, but not exceeding one year, or until that earlier date as he or she is retired on permanent disability pension, and is actually receiving disability pension payments, or advanced disability pension payments pursuant to Section 4850.3.

(b) The persons eligible under subdivision (a) include all of the following:

(1) City police officers.

(2) City, county, or district firefighters.

(3) Sheriffs.

(4) Officers or employees of any sheriff's offices.

(5) Inspectors, investigators, detectives, or personnel with comparable titles in any district attorney's office.

(6) County probation officers, group counselors, or juvenile services officers.

(7) Officers or employees of a probation office.

(8) Peace officers under Section 830.31 of the Penal Code employed on a regular, full-time basis by a county of the first class.

(9) Lifeguards employed year round on a regular, full-time basis by a county of the first class or by the City of San Diego.

(10) Airport law enforcement officers under subdivision (d) of Section 830.33 of the Penal Code.

(11) Harbor or port police officers, wardens, or special officers of a harbor or port district or city or county harbor department under subdivision (a) of Section 830.1 or subdivision (b) of Section 830.33 of the Penal Code.

(12) Police officers of the Los Angeles Unified School District.

(c) This section shall apply only to persons listed in subdivision (b) who meet the requirements of subdivision (a), and shall not include any of the following:

(1) Employees of a police department whose principal duties are those of a telephone operator, clerk, stenographer, machinist, mechanic, or otherwise, and whose functions do not clearly fall within the scope of active law enforcement service.

(2) Employees of a county sheriff's office whose principal duties are those of a telephone operator, clerk, stenographer, machinist, mechanic, or otherwise, and whose functions do not clearly come within the scope of active law enforcement service.

(3) Employees of a county probation office whose principal duties are those of a telephone operator, clerk, stenographer, machinist, mechanic, or otherwise, and whose functions do not clearly come within the scope of active law enforcement service.

(4) Employees of a city fire department, county fire department, or fire district whose principal duties are those of a telephone operator, clerk, stenographer, machinist, mechanic, or otherwise, and whose functions do not clearly fall within the scope of active firefighting and prevention service.

(d) If the employer is insured, the payments that, except for this section, the insurer would be obligated to make as disability indemnity to the injured, the insurer may pay to the insured.

(e) No leave of absence taken pursuant to this section by a peace officer, as defined by Chapter 4.5 (commencing with Section 830) of Title 3 of Part 2 of the Penal Code, or by a city, county, or district firefighter, shall be deemed to constitute family care and medical leave, as defined in Section 12945.2 of the Government Code, or to reduce the time authorized for family care and medical leave by Section 12945.2 of the Government Code.

(f) This section shall not apply to any persons described in paragraph (1) or (2) of subdivision (b) who are employees of the City and County of San Francisco.

(g) Amendments to subdivision (f) made by the act adding this subdivision shall be applied retroactively to January 1, 2010. **Leg.H.** 1995 ch. 474, 1999 chs. 270, 970 §1.5, 2000 chs. 920, 929 §3, 2001 ch. 791, 2009 ch. 389 (AB 1227) §1, 2010 ch. 74 (AB 586) §1, effective July 15, 2010, 2013 ch. 66 (SB 527) §1.

Ref.: 8 C.C.R. §9814; Hanna §§ 3.114, 7.04[9][a], 21.07[6], 21.08[1], 33.02[3]; Herlick Handbook §§ 5.17, 13.4, 14.17, 16.5.

§4850.3. Advanced disability pension payments—Local safety officer.

A city, county, special district, or harbor district that is a member of the Public Employees' Retirement System, is subject to the County Employees Retirement Law of 1937, or is subject to the Los Angeles City Employees' Retirement System, may make advanced disability pension payments to any local safety officer who has qualified for benefits under Section 4850 and is approved for a disability allowance. The payments shall be no less than 50 percent of the estimated highest average annual compensation earnable by the local safety officer during the three consecutive years of employment immediately preceding the effective date of his or her disability retirement, unless the local safety officer chooses an optional settlement in the permanent disability retirement application process which would reduce the pension allowance below 50 percent. In the case where the local safety officer's choice lowers the disability pension allowance below 50 percent of average annual compensation as calculated, the advanced pension payments shall be set at an amount equal to the disability pension allowance. If a local agency has an adopted policy of paying for any accumulated sick leave after the safety officer is eligible for a disability allowance, the advanced disability pension payments under this section may only be made when the local safety officer has exhausted all sick leave payments. Advanced disability pension payments shall not be considered a salary under this or any other provision of law. All advanced disability pension payments made by a local agency with membership in the Public Employees' Retirement System shall be reimbursed by the Public Employees' Retirement System pursuant to Section 21293.1 of the Government Code. **Leg.H.** 1989 ch. 1464, 2000 ch. 920.

Ref.: 8 C.C.R. §9814; Hanna § 3.114[2]; Herlick Handbook § 5.17.

§4850.4. Advanced disability pension payments.

(a) A city, county, special district, or harbor district that is a member of the Public Employees' Retirement System, is subject to the County Employees Retirement Law of 1937, or is subject to the Los Angeles City Employees' Retirement Systems, shall make advanced disability pension payments in accordance with Section 4850.3 unless any of the following is applicable:

(1) After an examination of the employee by a physician, the physician determines that there is no discernable injury to, or illness of, the employee.

(2) The employee was incontrovertibly outside the course of his or her employment duties when the injury occurred.

(3) There is proof of fraud associated with the filing of the employee's claim.

(b) Any employer described in subdivision (a) who is required to make advanced disability pension payments, shall make the payments commencing no later than 30 days from the date of issuance of the last disbursed of the following:

(1) The employee's last regular payment of wages or salary.

(2) The employee's last payment of benefits under Section 4850.

(3) The employee's last payment for sick leave.

(c) The advanced disability payments shall continue until the claimant is approved or disapproved for a disability allowance pursuant to final adjudication as provided by law.

(d) An employer described in subdivision (a) shall be required to make advanced disability pension payments only if the employee does all of the following:

(1) Files an application for disability retirement at least 60 days prior to the payment of benefits pursuant to subdivision (a).

(2) Fully cooperates in providing the employer with medical information and in attending all statutorily required medical examinations and evaluations set by the employer.

(3) Fully cooperates with the evaluation process established by the retirement plan.

(e) The 30-day period for the commencement of payments pursuant to subdivision (b) shall be tolled by whatever period of time is directly related to the employee's failure to comply with the provisions of subdivision (d).

(f) After final adjudication, if an employee's disability application is denied, the local agency and the employee shall arrange for the employee to repay any advanced disability pension payments received by the employee pursuant to this subdivision. The repayment plan shall take into account the employee's ability to repay the advanced disability payments received. Absent an agreement on repayment, the matter shall be submitted for a local agency administrative appeals remedy that includes an independent level of resolution to determine a reasonable repayment plan. If repayment is not made according to the repayment plan, the local agency may take reasonable steps, including litigation, to recover the payments advanced. **Leg.H.** 2002 chs. 189 (AB 1982), 877 (AB 2131).

Ref.: See Govt. Code §21419; 8 C.C.R. §9814; Hanna § 3.114[2]; Herlick Handbook § 5.17.

§4850.5. Benefits for firefighters, sheriff's and probation office employees, and other specified employees of San Luis Obispo County.

Any firefighter employed by the County of San Luis Obispo, and the sheriff or any officer or employee of the sheriff's office of the County of San Luis Obispo, and any county probation officer, group counselor, or juvenile services officer, or any officer or employee of a probation office, employed by the County of San Luis Obispo, shall, upon the adoption of a resolution of the board of supervisors so declaring, be entitled to the benefits of this article, if otherwise entitled to these benefits, even though the employee is not a member of the Public Employees' Retirement System or subject to the County Employees Retirement Law of 1937 (Chapter 3 (commencing with Section 31450) of Part 3 of Division 4 of Title 3 of the Government Code). **Leg.H.** 1999 ch. 970.

Ref.: 8 C.C.R. §9814; Hanna §§ 3.114[1], 33.02[2][a]; Herlick Handbook § 5.17.

§4850.7. Firefighters' entitlement to benefits.

(a) Any firefighter employed by a dependent or independent fire district may be entitled to the benefits of this article, if otherwise entitled to these benefits, even though the employee is not a member of the Public Employees' Retirement System or subject to the County Employees Retirement Law of 1937 (Chapter 3 (commencing with Section 31450) of Part 3 of Division 4 of Title 3 of the Government Code).

(b) The issue of whether the firefighters employed by a fire district are entitled to the benefits of this article is subject to Article 10 (commencing with Section 3500) of Chapter 3 of Division 4 of Title 1 of the Government Code.

(c) If the governing body of the district agrees that the benefits shall apply, it shall adopt a resolution to that effect.

Ref.: 8 C.C.R. §9814.

§4851. Request to make disability determinations.

The governing body of any city, county, or city and county, in addition to anyone else properly entitled, including the Public Employees' Retirement System, may request the appeals board to determine in any case, and the appeals board shall determine, whether or not the disability referred to in Section 4850 arose out of and in the course of duty. The appeals board shall also, in any disputed case, determine when the disability commenced and ceased, and the

Labor

amount of benefits provided by this division to which the employee is entitled during the period of the disability. The appeals board shall have jurisdiction to award and enforce payment of these benefits pursuant to Part 4 (commencing with Section 5300).

Ref.: 8 C.C.R. §10405; Hanna §§ 3.114[3], 33.02[3][b]; Herlick Handbook §§ 13.4, 14.17.

§4852. Article's effect on medical, surgical, and hospital benefits.

The provisions of this article do not diminish or affect the right of any such officer or employee to the medical, surgical, and hospital benefits prescribed by this division.

Ref.: Hanna §§ 3.114[2], 22.01[5].

§4853. Disability continuing beyond one year.

Whenever such disability of any such officer or employee continues for a period beyond one year, such member shall thereafter be subject as to disability indemnity to the provisions of this division other than Section 4850 during the remainder of the period of said disability or until the effective date of his retirement under the Public Employees' Retirement Act, and the leave of absence shall continue.

Ref.: Hanna §§ 3.114[2], 35.19.

§4854. Prohibition on temporary disability payments concurrent with salary payments.

No disability indemnity shall be paid to any such officer or employee concurrently with wages or salary.

§4855. Non-applicability to reserve public safety employees.

This article shall not be applicable to individuals who are appointed as reserve public safety employees and are deemed to be employees of a county, city, town or district for workers' compensation purposes pursuant to Section 3362.

Ref.: Hanna § 33.02[3][a].

§4856. Continued provision of health benefits to surviving spouse and dependents of deceased firefighter or peace officer; limitations.

(a) Whenever any local employee who is a firefighter, or peace officer as described in Chapter 4.5 (commencing with Section 830) of Title 3 of Part 2 of the Penal Code, or a Sheriff's Special Officer of the County of Orange, is killed in the performance of his or her duty or dies as a result of an accident or injury caused by external violence or physical force incurred in the performance of his or her duty, the employer shall continue providing health benefits to the deceased employee's spouse under the same terms and conditions provided prior to the death, or prior to the accident or injury that caused the death, of the employee unless the surviving spouse elects to receive a lump-sum survivors benefit in lieu of monthly benefits. Minor dependents shall continue to receive benefits under the coverage provided the surviving spouse or, if there is no surviving spouse, until the age of 21 years. However, pursuant to Section 22822 of the Government Code, the surviving spouse may not add the new spouse or stepchildren as family members under the continued health benefits coverage of the surviving spouse.

(b) Subdivision (a) also applies to the employer of any local employee who is a firefighter, or peace officer as described in Chapter 4.5 (commencing with Section 830) of Title 3 of Part 2 of the Penal Code, who was killed in the performance of his or her duty or who died as a result of an accident or injury caused by external violence or physical force incurred in the performance of his or her duty prior to September 30, 1996. **Leg.H.** 1996 ch. 1120, effective September 30, 1996, 1997 ch. 193, 2004 ch. 69 (SB 626), effective June 24, 2004, 2012 ch. 819 (AB 2069) §2.

Ref.: Hanna § 3.115[3]; Herlick Handbook § 7.23.

PART 3
Compensation Claims

CHAPTER 1
PAYMENT AND ASSIGNMENT

§4900. Claim for compensation; assignment.

No claim for compensation, except as provided in Section 96, is assignable before payment, but this provision does not affect the survival thereof.

Ref.: 8 C.C.R. §§10110, 10115; Hanna §§ 7.03[3], 27.05, 30.01; Herlick Handbook §§ 10.01[1], 10.02[1].

§4901. Effect of debts on claims.

No claim for compensation nor compensation awarded, adjudged, or paid, is subject to be taken for the debts of the party entitled to such compensation except as hereinafter provided.

Ref.: Hanna §§ 27.05, 30.01; Herlick Handbook § 10.01[1].

§4902. Payment of claim directly to attorney or agent.

No compensation, whether awarded or voluntarily paid, shall be paid to any attorney at law or in fact or other agent, but shall be paid directly to the claimant entitled thereto unless otherwise ordered by the appeals board. No payment made to an attorney at law or in fact or other agent in violation of this section shall be credited to the employer.

Ref.: 8 C.C.R. §§10110, 10115; Hanna § 30.03[1]; Herlick Handbook § 10.01[1].

§4903. Determination of liens against compensation payable.

The appeals board may determine, and allow as liens against any sum to be paid as compensation, any amount determined as hereinafter set forth in subdivisions (a) through (i). If more than one lien is allowed, the appeals board may determine the priorities, if any, between the liens allowed. The liens that may be allowed hereunder are as follows:

(a) A reasonable attorney's fee for legal services pertaining to any claim for compensation either before the appeals board or before any of the appellate courts, and the reasonable disbursements in connection therewith. No fee for legal services shall be awarded to any representative who is not an attorney, except with respect to those claims for compensation for which an application, pursuant to Section 5501, has been filed with the appeals board on or before December 31, 1991, or for which a disclosure form, pursuant to Section 4906, has been sent to the employer, or insurer or third-party administrator, if either is known, on or before December 31, 1991.

(b) The reasonable expense incurred by or on behalf of the injured employee, as provided by Article 2 (commencing with Section 4600), and to the extent the employee is entitled to reimbursement under Section 4621, medical-legal expenses as provided by Article 2.5 (commencing with Section 4620) of Chapter 2 of Part 2, except those disputes subject to independent medical review or independent bill review.

(c) The reasonable value of the living expenses of an injured employee or of his or her dependents, subsequent to the injury.

(d) The reasonable burial expenses of the deceased employee, not to exceed the amount provided for by Section 4701.

(e) The reasonable living expenses of the spouse or minor children of the injured employee, or both, subsequent to the date of the injury, where the employee has deserted or is neglecting his or her family. These expenses shall be allowed in the proportion that the appeals board deems proper, under application of the spouse, guardian of the minor children, or the assignee, pursuant to subdivision (a) of Section 11477 of the Welfare and Institutions Code, of the spouse, a former spouse, or minor children. A collection received as a result of a lien against a workers' compensation award imposed pursuant to this subdivision for payment of child support ordered by a court shall be credited as provided in Section 695.221 of the Code of Civil Procedure.

(f) The amount of unemployment compensation disability benefits that have been paid under or pursuant to the Unemployment Insurance Code in those cases where, pending a determination under this division there was uncertainty whether the benefits were payable under the Unemployment Insurance Code or payable hereunder; provided, however, that any lien under this subdivision shall be allowed and paid as provided in Section 4904.

(g) The amount of unemployment compensation benefits and extended duration benefits paid to the injured employee for the same day or days for which he or she receives, or is entitled to receive, temporary total disability indemnity payments under this division; provided, however, that any lien under this subdivision shall be allowed and paid as provided in Section 4904.

(h) The amount of family temporary disability insurance benefits that have been paid to the injured employee pursuant to the Unemployment Insurance Code for the same day or days for which that employee receives, or is entitled to receive, temporary total disability indemnity payments under this division, provided, however, that any lien under this subdivision shall be allowed and paid as provided in Section 4904.

(i) The amount of indemnification granted by the California Victims of Crime Program pursuant to Article 1 (commencing with Section 13959) of Chapter 5 of Part 4 of Division 3 of Title 2 of the Government Code. **Leg.H.** 1991 chs. 116, 934, 1993 ch. 876, effective October 6, 1993, 1994 ch. 75, effective May 20, 1994, 1996 ch. 1077, 2003 ch. 797 (SB 727), 2012 ch. 363 (SB 863) §62, 2014 ch. 217 (AB 2732) §3.

2012 Note: For legislative findings, declarations, and applicability of Stats. 2012 ch. 363, see the 2012 Notes following Lab C §62.5.

Ref.: 8 C.C.R. §§9812, 9813, 9815, 10770, 10771, 10772, 10774, 10775, 10776, 10778, 10886, 10888; Hanna §§ 30.01–

30.10, 30.24[3], 30.25[3], 30.27; Herlick Handbook §§ 10.01[2], 10.02[2]–[4], 10.03[2], [4], [8], 10.08[1], 10.09[1], [2], [4], 10.10[1], [3], 10.11, 10.12[1], [3], [5], 10.14, 10.15, 11.09[1], [4].

§4903.05. Filing of written lien claim required; form; fee; required documents to accompany lien filing.

(a) Every lien claimant shall file its lien with the appeals board in writing upon a form approved by the appeals board. The lien shall be accompanied by a full statement or itemized voucher supporting the lien and justifying the right to reimbursement and proof of service upon the injured worker or, if deceased, upon the worker's dependents, the employer, the insurer, and the respective attorneys or other agents of record. For liens filed on or after January 1, 2017, the lien shall also be accompanied by an original bill in addition to either the full statement or itemized voucher supporting the lien. Medical records shall be filed only if they are relevant to the issues being raised by the lien.

(b) Any lien claim for expenses under subdivision (b) of Section 4903 or for claims of costs shall be filed with the appeals board electronically using the form approved by the appeals board. The lien shall be accompanied by a proof of service and any other documents that may be required by the appeals board. The service requirements for Section 4603.2 are not modified by this section.

(c)(1) For liens filed on or after January 1, 2017, any lien claim for expenses under subdivision (b) of Section 4903 that is subject to a filing fee under this section shall be accompanied at the time of filing by a declaration stating, under penalty of perjury, that the dispute is not subject to an independent bill review and independent medical review under Sections 4603.6 and 4610.5, respectively, that the lien claimant satisfies one of the following:

(A) Is the employee's treating physician providing care through a medical provider network.

(B) Is the agreed medical evaluator or qualified medical evaluator.

(C) Has provided treatment authorized by the employer or claims administrator under Section 4610.

(D) Has made a diligent search and determined that the employer does not have a medical provider network in place.

(E) Has documentation that medical treatment has been neglected or unreasonably refused to the employee as provided by Section 4600.

(F) Can show that the expense was incurred for an emergency medical condition, as defined by subdivision (b) of Section 1317.1 of the Health and Safety Code.

(G) Is a certified interpreter rendering services during a medical-legal examination, a copy service providing medical-legal services, or has an expense allowed as a lien under rules adopted by the administrative director.

(2) Lien claimants shall have until July 1, 2017, to file a declaration pursuant to paragraph (1) for any lien claim filed before January 1, 2017, for expenses pursuant to subdivision (b) of Section 4903 that is subject to a filing fee under this section.

(3) The failure to file a signed declaration under this subdivision shall result in the dismissal of the lien with prejudice by operation of law. Filing of a false declaration shall be grounds for dismissal with prejudice after notice.

(d) All liens filed on or after January 1, 2013, for expenses under subdivision (b) of Section 4903 or for claims of costs shall be subject to a filing fee as provided by this subdivision.

(1) The lien claimant shall pay a filing fee of one hundred fifty dollars ($150) to the Division of Workers' Compensation prior to filing a lien and shall include proof that the filing fee has been paid. The fee shall be collected through an electronic payment system that accepts major credit cards and any additional forms of electronic payment selected by the administrative director. If the administrative director contracts with a service provider for the processing of electronic payments, any processing fee shall be absorbed by the division and not added to the fee charged to the lien filer.

(2) On or after January 1, 2013, a lien submitted for filing that does not comply with paragraph (1) shall be invalid, even if lodged with the appeals board, and shall not operate to preserve or extend any time limit for filing of the lien.

(3) The claims of two or more providers of goods or services shall not be merged into a single lien.

(4) The filing fee shall be collected by the administrative director. All fees shall be deposited in the Workers' Compensation Administration Revolving Fund and applied for the purposes of that fund.

(5) The administrative director shall adopt reasonable rules and regulations governing the procedure for the collection of the filing fee, including emergency regulations as necessary to implement this section.

(6) Any lien filed for goods or services that are not the proper subject of a lien may be dismissed upon request of a party by verified petition or on the appeals board's own motion. If the lien is dismissed, the lien claimant will not be entitled to reimbursement of the filing fee.

(7) No filing fee shall be required for a lien filed by a health care service plan licensed pursuant to Section 1349 of the Health and Safety Code, a group disability insurer under a policy issued in this state pursuant to the provisions of Section 10270.5 of the Insurance Code, a self-insured employee welfare benefit plan, as defined in Section 10121 of the Insurance Code, that is issued in this state, a Taft-Hartley health and welfare fund, or a publicly funded program providing medical benefits on a nonindustrial basis. **Leg.H.** 2012 ch. 363 (SB 863) §63, 2016 ch. 868 (SB 1160) §8.

2016 Note: For legislative findings and declarations, see the 2016 Note following Lab C §138.4.

2012 Note: For legislative findings, declarations, and applicability of Stats. 2012 ch. 363, see the 2012 Notes following Lab C §62.5.

Ref.: Hanna § 30.20[1]; Herlick Handbook §§ 10.02[1], [4], 10.03[2], [4], [6], 10.08[2], [3].

§4903.06. Fees for claims filed prior to January 1, 2013.

(a) Any lien filed pursuant to subdivision (b) of Section 4903 prior to January 1, 2013, and any cost that was filed as a lien prior to January 1, 2013, shall be subject to a lien activation fee unless the lien claimant provides proof of having paid a filing fee as previously required by former Section 4903.05 as added by Chapter 639 of the Statutes of 2003.

(1) The lien claimant shall pay a lien activation fee of one hundred dollars ($100) to the Division of Workers' Compensation on or before January 1, 2014. The fee shall be collected through an electronic payment system that accepts major credit cards and any additional forms of electronic payment selected by the administrative director. If the administrative director contracts with a service provider for the processing of electronic payments, any processing fee shall be absorbed by the division and not added to the fee charged to the lien filer.

(2) The lien claimant shall include proof of payment of the filing fee or lien activation fee with the declaration of readiness to proceed.

(3) The lien activation fee shall be collected by the administrative director. All fees shall be deposited in the Workers' Compensation Administration Revolving Fund and applied for the purposes of that fund. The administrative director shall adopt reasonable rules and regulations governing the procedure for the collection of the lien activation fee and to implement this section, including emergency regulations, as necessary.

(4) All lien claimants that did not file the declaration of readiness to proceed and that remain a lien claimant of record at the time of a lien conference shall submit proof of payment of the activation fee at the lien conference. If the fee has not been paid or no proof of payment is available, the lien shall be dismissed with prejudice.

(5) Any lien filed pursuant to subdivision (b) of Section 4903 prior to January 1, 2013, and any cost that was filed as a lien prior to January 1, 2013, for which the filing fee or lien activation fee has not been paid by January 1, 2014, is dismissed by operation of law.

(b) This section shall not apply to any lien filed by a health care service plan licensed pursuant to Section 1349 of the Health and Safety Code, a group disability insurer under a policy issued in this state pursuant to the provisions of Section 10270.5 of the Insurance Code, a self-insured employee welfare benefit plan, as defined in Section 10121 of the Insurance Code, that is issued in this state, a Taft-Hartley health and welfare fund, or a publicly funded program providing medical benefits on a nonindustrial basis. **Leg.H.** 2012 ch. 363 (SB 863) §64.

2012 Note: For legislative findings, declarations, and applicability of Stats. 2012 ch. 363, see the 2012 Notes following Lab C §62.5.

Ref.: Hanna § 30.20[1]; Herlick Handbook §§ 10.02[1], 10.03[4], [6], 10.08[2], [3].

§4903.07. Conditions for entitlement to order or award for reimbursement of lien filing or activation fee.

(a) A lien claimant shall be entitled to an order or award for reimbursement from the employer of a lien filing fee or lien activation fee, together with interest at the rate allowed on civil judgments, only if all of the following conditions are satisfied:

(1) Not less than 30 days before filing the lien for which the filing fee was paid or filing the declaration of readiness for which the lien activation fee was paid, the lien claimant has made written demand for settlement of the lien claim for a clearly stated sum which shall be inclusive of all claims of debt, interest, penalty, or other claims potentially recoverable on the lien.

(2) The defendant fails to accept the settlement demand in writing within 20 days of receipt of the demand for settlement, or within any additional time as may be provide by the written demand.

(3) After submission of the lien dispute to the appeals board or an arbitrator, a final award is made in favor of the lien claimant of a specified sum that is equal to or greater than the amount of the settlement demand. The amount of the interest and filing fee or lien activation fee shall not be considered in determining whether the award is equal to or greater than the demand.

(b) This section shall not preclude an order or award of reimbursement of the filing fee or activation fee pursuant to the express terms of an agreed disposition of a lien dispute. **Leg.H.** 2012 ch. 363 (SB 863) §65, 2014 ch. 217 (AB 2732) §4.

2012 Note: For legislative findings, declarations, and applicability of Stats. 2012 ch. 363, see the 2012 Notes following Lab C §62.5.

Ref.: Hanna § 30.20[1]; Herlick Handbook § 10.03[4].

§4903.1. Determination of reimbursement for benefits paid or services provided.

(a) The appeals board or arbitrator, before issuing an award or approval of any compromise of claim, shall determine, on the basis of liens filed with it pursuant to Section 4903.05, whether any benefits have been paid or services provided by a health care provider, a health care service plan, a group disability policy, including a loss-of-income policy or a self-insured employee welfare benefit plan, and its award or approval shall provide for reimbursement for benefits paid or services provided under these plans as follows:

(1) If the appeals board issues an award finding that an injury or illness arises out of and in the course of employment, but denies the applicant reimbursement for self-procured medical costs solely because of lack of notice to the applicant's employer of his or her need for hospital, surgical, or medical care, the appeals board shall nevertheless award a lien against the employee's recovery, to the extent of benefits paid or services provided, for the effects of the industrial injury or illness, by a health care provider, a health care service plan, a group disability policy or a self-insured employee welfare benefit plan, subject to the provisions described in subdivision (b).

(2) If the appeals board issues an award finding that an injury or illness arises out of and in the course of employment, and makes an award for reimbursement for self-procured medical costs, the appeals board shall allow a lien, to the extent of benefits paid or services provided, for the effects of the industrial injury or illness, by a health care provider, a health care service plan, a group disability policy or a self-insured employee welfare benefit plan, subject to the provisions of subdivision (b). For purposes of this paragraph, benefits paid or services provided by a self-insured employee welfare benefit plan shall be determined notwithstanding the official medical fee schedule adopted pursuant to Section 5307.1.

(3)(A) If the appeals board issues an award finding that an injury or illness arises out of and in the course of employment and makes an award for temporary disability indemnity, the appeals board shall allow a lien as living expense under Section 4903, for benefits paid by a group disability policy providing loss-of-time benefits and for loss-of-time benefits paid by a self-insured employee welfare benefit plan. The lien shall be allowed to the extent that benefits have been paid for the same day or days for which temporary disability indemnity is awarded and shall not exceed the award for temporary disability indemnity. A lien shall not be allowed hereunder unless the group disability policy or self-insured employee welfare benefit plan provides for reduction, exclusion, or coordination of loss-of-time benefits on account of workers' compensation benefits.

(B) For purposes of this paragraph, "self-insured employee welfare benefit plan" means any plan, fund, or program that is established or maintained by an employer or by an employee organization, or by both, to the extent that the plan, fund, or program was established or is maintained for the purpose of providing for its participants or their beneficiaries, other than through the purchase of insurance, either of the following:

(i) Medical, surgical, or hospital care or benefits.

(ii) Monetary or other benefits in the event of sickness, accident, disability, death, or unemployment.

(4) If the parties propose that the case be disposed of by way of a compromise and release agreement, in the event the lien claimant, other than a health care provider, does not agree to the amount allocated to it, then the appeals board shall determine the potential recovery and reduce the amount of the lien in the ratio of the applicant's recovery to the potential recovery in full satisfaction of its lien claim.

(b) Notwithstanding subdivision (a), payment or reimbursement shall not be allowed, whether payable by the employer or payable as a lien against the employee's recovery, for any expense incurred as provided by Article 2 (commencing with Section 4600) of Chapter 2 of Part 2, nor shall the employee have any liability for the expense, if at the time the expense was incurred the provider either knew or in the exercise of reasonable diligence should have known that the condition being treated was caused by the employee's present or prior employment, unless at the time the expense was incurred at least one of the following conditions was met:

(1) The expense was incurred for services authorized by the employer.

(2) The expense was incurred for services furnished while the employer failed or refused to furnish treatment as required by subdivision (c) of Section 5402.

(3) The expense was necessarily incurred for an emergency medical condition, as defined by subdivision (b) of Section 1317.1 of the Health and Safety Code.

(c) The changes made to this section by Senate Bill 457 of the 2011–12 Regular Session do not modify in any way the rights or obligations of the following:

(1) Any health care provider to file and prosecute a lien pursuant to subdivision (b) of Section 4903.

(2) A payer to conduct utilization review pursuant to Section 4610.

(3) Any party in complying with the requirements under Section 4903. **Leg.H.** 1975 ch. 1109 §1, 1979 ch. 855 §1, 1990 ch. 1550 (AB 2910) §45, 2011 ch. 564 (SB 457) §1, 2012 chs. 363 (SB 863) §66, 712 (SB 1105) §1.5.

Ref.: 8 C.C.R. §§10609, 10770, 10771, 10886, 10888; Hanna §§ 23.14[2][l], 29.04[3][c], 30.24[2][b], 30.27; Herlick Handbook §§ 10.02[4], 10.08[3], 10.09[2], 10.10[2], 10.12[4], 11.09[3].

§4903.2. Attorney's fee allowed from lien claimant's recovery.

Where a lien claimant is reimbursed pursuant to subdivision (f) or (g) of Section 4903 or Section 4903.1, for benefits paid or services provided, the appeals board may award an attorney's fee out of the lien claimant's recovery if the appeals board determines that all of the following occurred:

(a) The lien claimant received notice of all hearings following the filing of the lien and received notice of intent to award the applicant's attorney a fee.

(b) An attorney or other representative of the lien claimant did not participate in the proceedings before the appeals board with respect to the lien claim.

(c) There were bona fide issues respecting compensability, or respecting allowability of the lien, such that the services of an attorney were reasonably required to effectuate recovery on the claim of lien and were instrumental in effecting the recovery.

(d) The case was not disposed of by compromise and release.

The amount of the attorney's fee out of the lien claimant's recovery shall be based on the extent of applicant's attorney's efforts on behalf of the lien claimant. The ratio of the amount of the attorney's fee awarded against the lien claimant's recovery to that recovery shall not exceed the ratio of the amount of the attorney's fee awarded against the applicant's award to that award.

Ref.: Hanna § 30.27; Herlick Handbook §§ 10.09[2], 10.12[1], 11.09[2].

§4903.3. Compensation provided from fund.

The director, as administrator of the Uninsured Employers Fund, may, in his discretion, provide compensation, including medical treatment, from the Uninsured Employers Fund in cases to which the director is a party before the issuance of any award, if such compensation is not being provided to the applicant.

The appeals board shall determine and allow as a first lien against any sum to be paid as compensation the amount of compensation, including the cost of medical treatment, provided by the director pursuant to this section.

Ref.: Herlick Handbook §§ 1.08, 10.01[2], 10.13.

§4903.4. Disputes over liens for expenses.

(a) If a dispute arises concerning a lien for expenses incurred by or on behalf of the injured employee as provided by Article 2 (commencing with Section 4600) of Chapter 2 of Part 2, the appeals board may resolve the dispute in a separate proceeding, which may include binding arbitration upon agreement of the employer, lien claimant, and the employee, if the employee remains a party to the dispute, according to the rules of practice and procedure.

(b) If the dispute is heard at a separate proceeding it shall be calendared for hearing or hearings as determined by the appeals board based upon the resources available to the appeals board and other considerations as the appeals board deems appropriate and shall not be subject to Section 5501.5. **Leg.H.** 1989 ch. 892 (AB 276) §42, 1990 ch. 1550 (AB 2910) §46, 2012 ch. 363 (SB 863) §67, 2013 ch. 287 (SB 375) §6.

2012 Note: For legislative findings, declarations, and applicability of Stats. 2012 ch. 363, see the 2012 Notes following Lab C §62.5.

1989 Note: This section is applicable only to injuries occurring on or after January 1, 1990. Stats. 1989 ch. 893 §6.

Ref.: 8 C.C.R. §§10773, 10886; Hanna §§ 22.05[5], 30.26; Herlick Handbook §§ 4.18[1], 10.03[7], 10.08[3].

§4903.5. Limitations period for filing lien claim.

(a) A lien claim for expenses as provided in subdivision (b) of Section 4903 shall not be filed after three years from the date the services were provided, nor more than 18 months after the date the services were provided, if the services were provided on or after July 1, 2013.

(b) Notwithstanding subdivision (a), any health care service plan licensed pursuant to Section 1349 of the Health and Safety Code, group disability insurer under a policy issued in this state pursuant to the provisions of Section 10270.5 of the Insurance Code, self-insured employee welfare benefit plan issued in this state as defined in Section 10121 of the Insurance Code, Taft-Hartley health and welfare fund, or publicly funded program providing medical benefits on a nonindustrial basis, may file a lien claim for expenses as provided in subdivision (b) of Section 4903 within 12 months after the entity first knew or in the exercise of reasonable diligence should have known that an industrial injury is being claimed, but in no event later than five years from the date the services were provided to the employee.

(c) The injured worker shall not be liable for any underlying obligation if a lien claim has not been filed and served within the allowable period. Except when the lien claimant is the applicant as provided in Section 5501 or as otherwise permitted by rules of practice and procedure adopted by the appeals board, a lien claimant shall not file a declaration of readiness to proceed in any case until the case-in-chief has been resolved.

(d) This section shall not apply to civil actions brought under the Cartwright Act (Chapter 2 (commencing with Section 16700) of Part 2 of Division 7 of the Business and Professions Code), the Unfair Practices Act (Chapter 4 (commencing with Section 17000) of Part 2 of Division 7 of the Business and Professions Code), or the federal Racketeer Influenced and Corrupt Organization Act (Chapter 96 (commencing with Section 1961) of Title 18 of the United States Code) based on concerted action with other insurers that are not parties to the case in which the lien or claim is filed. **Leg.H.** 2002 ch. 6 (AB 749), 2012 ch. 363 (SB 863) §68.

2012 Note: For legislative findings, declarations, and applicability of Stats. 2012 ch. 363, see the 2012 Notes following Lab C §62.5.

Ref.: Hanna § 30.21[1]; Herlick Handbook §§ 10.02[2], [4], [6], 10.07, 10.08[1].

§4903.6. Lien claim or application for adjudication; requirements for filing; exemptions.

(a) Except as necessary to meet the requirements of Section 4903.5, a lien claim or application for adjudication shall not be filed or served under subdivision (b) of Section 4903 until both of the following have occurred:

(1) Sixty days have elapsed after the date of acceptance or rejection of liability for the claim, or expiration of the time provided for investigation of liability pursuant to subdivision (b) of Section 5402, whichever date is earlier.

(2) Either of the following:

(A) The time provided for payment of medical treatment bills pursuant to Section 4603.2 has expired and, if the employer objected to the amount of the bill, the reasonable fee has been determined pursuant to Section 4603.6, and, if authorization for the medical treatment has been disputed pursuant to Section 4610, the medical necessity of the medical treatment has been determined pursuant to Sections 4610.5 and 4610.6.

(B) The time provided for payment of medical-legal expenses pursuant to Section 4622 has expired and, if the employer objected to the amount of the bill, the reasonable fee has been determined pursuant to Section 4603.6.

(b) All lien claimants under Section 4903 shall notify the employer and the employer's representative, if any, and the employee and the employee's representative, if any, and the appeals board within five working days of obtaining, changing, or discharging representation by an attorney or nonattorney representative. The notice shall set forth the legal name, address, and telephone number of the attorney or nonattorney representative.

(c) A declaration of readiness to proceed shall not be filed for a lien under subdivision (b) of Section 4903 until the underlying case has been resolved or where the applicant chooses not to proceed with the applicant's case.

(d) With the exception of a lien for services provided by a physician as defined in Section 3209.3, a lien claimant shall not be entitled to any medical information, as defined in subdivision (j) of Section 56.05 of the Civil Code, about an injured worker without prior written approval of the appeals board. Any order authorizing disclosure of medical information to a lien claimant other than a physician shall specify the information to be provided to the lien claimant and include a finding that the information is relevant to the proof of the matter for which the information is sought. The appeals board shall adopt reasonable regulations to ensure compliance with this section, and shall take any further steps as may be necessary to enforce the regulations, including, but not limited to, impositions of sanctions pursuant to Section 5813.

(e) The prohibitions of this section do not apply to lien claims, applications for adjudication, or declarations of readiness to proceed filed by or on behalf of the employee, or to the filings by or on behalf of the employer. **Leg.H.** 2006 ch. 69 (AB 1806) §26, effective July 12, 2006, 2012 ch. 363 (SB 863) §69, 2013 ch. 287 (SB 375) §7, 2019 ch. 497 (AB 991) §190.

2012 Note: For legislative findings, declarations, and applicability of Stats. 2012 ch. 363, see the 2012 Notes following Lab C §62.5.

Ref.: Hanna §§ 30.04, 30.05; Herlick Handbook §§ 10.02[1], 10.03[2], 10.08[1], [3].

§4903.8. Person to whom payment of lien to be made; assignment of lien; multiple assignments; conditions under which lien may not be assigned; invalidity of lien.

(a)(1) Any order or award for payment of a lien filed pursuant to subdivision (b) of Section 4903 shall be made for payment only to the person who was entitled to payment for the expenses as provided in subdivision (b) of Section 4903 at the time the expenses were incurred, who is the lien owner, and not to an assignee unless the person has ceased doing business in the capacity held at the time the expenses were incurred and has assigned all right, title, and interest in the remaining accounts receivable to the assignee.

(2) All liens filed pursuant to subdivision (b) of Section 4903 shall be filed in the name of the lien owner only, and no payment shall be made to any lien claimant without evidence that he or she is the owner of that lien.

(3) Paragraph (1) does not apply to an assignment that was completed prior to January 1, 2013, or that was required by a contract that became enforceable and irrevocable prior to January 1, 2013. This paragraph is declarative of existing law.

(4) For liens filed after January 1, 2017, the lien shall not be assigned unless the person has ceased doing business in the capacity held at the time the expenses were incurred and has assigned all right, title, and interest in the remaining accounts receivable to the assignee. The assignment of a lien, in violation of this paragraph is invalid by operation of law.

(b) If there has been an assignment of a lien, either as an assignment of all right, title, and interest in the accounts receivable or as an assignment for collection, a true and correct copy of the assignment shall be filed and served.

(1) If the lien is filed on or after January 1, 2013, and the assignment occurs before the filing of the lien, the copy of the assignment shall be served at the time the lien is filed.

(2) If the lien is filed on or after January 1, 2013, and the assignment occurs after the filing of the lien, the copy of the assignment shall be served within 20 days of the date of the assignment.

(3) If the lien is filed before January 1, 2013, the copy of the assignment shall be served by January 1, 2014, or with the filing of a declaration of readiness or at the time of a lien hearing, whichever is earliest.

(c) If there has been more than one assignment of the same receivable or bill, the appeals board may set the matter for hearing on whether the multiple assignments constitute bad-faith actions or tactics that are frivolous, harassing, or intended to cause unnecessary delay or expense. If so found by the appeals board, appropriate sanctions, including costs and attorney's fees, may be awarded against the assignor, assignee, and their respective attorneys.

(d) At the time of filing of a lien on or after January 1, 2013, or in the case of a lien filed before January 1, 2013, at the earliest of the filing of a declaration of readiness, a lien hearing, or January 1, 2014, supporting documentation shall be filed including one or more declarations under penalty of perjury by a natural person or persons competent to testify to the facts stated, declaring both of the following:

(1) The services or products described in the bill for services or products were actually provided to the injured employee.

(2) The billing statement attached to the lien truly and accurately describes the services or products that were provided to the injured employee.

(e) A lien submitted for filing on or after January 1, 2013, for expenses provided in subdivision (b) of Section 4903, that does not comply with the requirements of this section shall be deemed to be invalid, whether or not accepted for filing by the appeals board, and shall not operate to preserve or extend any time limit for filing of the lien.

(f) This section shall take effect without regulatory action. The appeals board and the administrative director may promulgate regulations and forms for the implementation of this section. **Leg.H.** 2012 ch. 363 (SB 863) §70, 2014 ch. 217 (AB 2732) §5, 2016 ch. 868 (SB 1160) §9.

2016 Notes: The amendment of paragraphs (1) and (2) of subdivision (a) of Section 4903.8 of the Labor Code made by this act does not constitute a change in, but is declaratory of, existing law. Stats. 2016 ch. 868 (SB 1160) §15.

For legislative findings and declarations, see the 2016 Note following Lab C §138.4.

2012 Note: For legislative findings, declarations, and applicability of Stats. 2012 ch. 363, see the 2012 Notes following Lab C §62.5.

Ref.: Hanna § 30.25[1]; Herlick Handbook §§ 10.02[4], 10.03[2], [8].

§4904. Adjustment and disallowance of liens; liens on unemployment compensation benefits.

(a) If notice is given in writing to the insurer, or to the employer if uninsured, setting forth the nature and extent of any claim that is allowable as a lien in favor of the Employment Development Department, the claim is a lien against any amount thereafter payable as temporary or permanent disability compensation, subject to the determination of the amount and approval of the lien by the appeals board. When the Employment Development Department has served an insurer or employer with a lien claim, the insurer or employer shall notify the Employment Development Department, in writing, as soon as possible, but in no event later than 15 working days after commencing disability indemnity payments. When a lien has been served on an insurer or an employer by the Employment Development Department, the insurer or employer shall notify the Employment Development Department, in writing, within 10 working days of filing an application for adjudication, a stipulated award, or a compromise and release with the appeals board.

(b)(1) In determining the amount of lien to be allowed for unemployment compensation disability benefits under subdivision (f) of Section 4903, the appeals board shall allow the lien in the amount of benefits which it finds were paid for the same day or days of disability for which an award of compensation for any permanent disability indemnity resulting solely from the same injury or illness or temporary disability indemnity, or both, is made and for which the employer has not reimbursed the Employment Development Department pursuant to Section 2629.1 of the Unemployment Insurance Code.

(2) In determining the amount of lien to be allowed for unemployment compensation benefits and extended duration benefits under subdivision (g) of Section 4903, the appeals board shall allow the lien in the amount of benefits which it finds were paid for the same day or days for which an award of compensation for temporary total disability is made.

(3) In determining the amount of lien to be allowed for family temporary disability insurance benefits under subdivision (h) of Section 4903, the appeals board shall allow the lien in the amount of benefits that it finds were paid for the same day or days for which an award of compensation for temporary total disability is made and for which the employer has not reimbursed the Employment Development Department pursuant to Section 2629.1 of the Unemployment Insurance Code.

(c) In the case of agreements for the compromise and release of a disputed claim for compensation, the applicant and defendant may propose to the appeals board, as part of the compromise and release agreement, an amount out of the settlement to be paid to any lien claimant claiming under subdivision (f), (g), or (h) of Section 4903. If the lien claimant objects to the amount proposed for payment of its lien under a compromise and release settlement or stipulation, the appeals board shall determine the extent of the lien claimant's entitlement to reimbursement on its lien and make and file findings on all facts involved in the controversy over this issue in accordance with Section 5313. The appeals board may approve a compromise and release agreement or stipulation which proposes the disallowance of a lien, in whole or in part, only where there is proof of service upon the lien claimant by the defendant, not less than 15 days prior to the appeals board action, of all medical and rehabilitation documents and a copy of the proposed compromise and release agreement or stipulation. The determination of the appeals board, subject to petition for reconsideration and to the right of judicial review, as to the amount of lien allowed under subdivision (f), (g), or (h) of Section 4903, whether in connection with an award of compensation or the approval of a compromise and release agreement, shall be binding on the lien claimant, the applicant, and the defendant, insofar as the right to benefits paid under the Unemployment Insurance Code for which the lien was claimed. The appeals board may order the amount of any lien claim, as determined and allowed by it, to be paid directly to the person entitled, either in a lump sum or in installments.

(d) Where unemployment compensation disability benefits, including family temporary disability insurance benefits, have been paid pursuant to the Unemployment Insurance Code while reconsideration of an order, decision, or award is pending, or has been granted, the appeals board shall determine and allow a final amount on the lien as of the date the board is ready to issue its decision denying a petition for reconsideration or affirming, rescinding, altering or amending the original findings, order, decision, or award.

(e) The appeals board shall not be prohibited from approving a compromise and release agreement on all other issues and deferring to subsequent proceedings the determination of a lien claimant's entitlement to reimbursement if the defendant in any of these proceedings agrees to pay the amount subsequently determined to be due under the lien claim.

(f) The amendments made to this section by the act adding this subdivision are declaratory of existing law, and shall not constitute good cause to reopen, rescind, or amend any final order, decision, or award of the appeals board. **Leg.H.** 1993 ch. 748, 2003 ch. 797 (SB 727), 2012 ch. 363 (SB 863) §71.

2012 Note: For legislative findings, declarations, and applicability of Stats. 2012 ch. 363, see the 2012 Notes following Lab C §62.5.

Ref.: 8 C.C.R. §§10772, 10886, 10888; Hanna §§ 30.08, 30.24[1], [3]; Herlick Handbook §§ 10.01[2], 10.02[6], 10.12[1], [5], [6], 10.14, 11.09[4].

§4904.1. Lien does not affect payment of balance of award.

The payment of liens as provided in Section 4904, shall in no way affect the commencement of immediate payments on any balance of the award to the injured claimant where an installment payment for his disability has been determined.

Ref.: 8 C.C.R. §10886; Herlick Handbook § 10.12[5].

§4905. Determination when lien not duly requested.

Except with regard to liens as permitted by subdivision (b) of Section 4903, if it appears in any proceeding pending before the appeals board that a lien should be allowed if it had been duly requested by the party entitled thereto, the appeals board may, without any request for such lien having been made, order the payment of the claim to be made directly to the person entitled, in the same manner and with the same effect as though the lien had been regularly requested, and the award to such person shall constitute a lien against unpaid compensation due at the time of service of the award. **Leg.H.** 1937, 1965 ch. 1513 §105, operative January 15, 1966, 2012 ch. 363 (SB 863) §72.

2012 Note: For legislative findings, declarations, and applicability of Stats. 2012 ch. 363, see the 2012 Notes following Lab C §62.5.

Ref.: 8 C.C.R. §10886; Hanna §§ 20.04[3], 30.23; Herlick Handbook § 10.15; Herlick Handbook § 5.17.

§4906. Reasonableness of charges or claims; attorney fees; disclosures.

(a) A charge, claim, or agreement for the legal services or disbursements mentioned in subdivision (a) of Section 4903, or for the expense mentioned in subdivision (b) of Section 4903, is not enforceable, valid, or binding in excess of a reasonable amount. The appeals board may determine what constitutes a reasonable amount, but payment pursuant to subdivision (a) of Section 4903 or Section 5710 shall not be allowed for any services or expenses incurred prior to the filing of the disclosure form described in subdivision (e) with the appeals board and the sending of that form to the employer, or to the insurer or third-party administrator, if either is known, by the attorney.

Labor

(b) An attorney or agent shall not demand or accept any fee from an employee or dependent of an employee for the purpose of representing the employee or dependent of an employee in any proceeding of the division, appeals board, or any appellate procedure related thereto until the amount of the fee has been approved or set by the appeals board.

(c) Any fee agreement shall be submitted to the appeals board for approval within 10 days after the agreement is made.

(d) In establishing a reasonable attorney's fee, consideration shall be given to the responsibility assumed by the attorney, the care exercised in representing the applicant, the time involved, and the results obtained.

(e) At the initial consultation, an attorney shall furnish the employee a written disclosure form promulgated by the administrative director which shall clearly and prominently describe the procedures available to the injured employee or his or her dependents. The disclosure form shall describe this section, the range of attorney's fees customarily approved by the appeals board, and the attorney's fees provisions of Section 4064 and the extent to which an employee may receive compensation without incurring attorney's fees. The disclosure form shall include the telephone number of the administrative director together with the statement that the employee may receive answers at that number to questions concerning entitlement to compensation or the procedures to follow to receive compensation. A copy of the disclosure form shall be signed by the employee and the attorney and filed with the appeals board and sent to the employer, or insurer or third-party administrator, if either is known, by the attorney within 15 days of the employee's and attorney's execution thereof.

(f) The disclosure form set forth in subdivision (e) shall contain, prominently stated, the following statement: "Any person who makes or causes to be made any knowingly false or fraudulent material statement or representation for the purpose of obtaining or denying workers' compensation benefits or payments is guilty of a felony."

(g)(1) The disclosure form described in subdivision (e) shall also contain a paragraph setting forth the exact location of the district office of the appeals board at which the employee's case will be filed. This paragraph shall also contain, prominently displayed, the following statement:

"The employee has been advised of the district office at which his or her case will be filed and that he or she may be required to attend conferences or hearings at this location at his or her own expense."

(2) The disclosure form may not be signed by the employee until he or she has been advised of the location at which his or her case will be filed, has met with or personally spoken with an attorney licensed by the State Bar of California who is regularly employed by the firm by which the employee will be represented, and has been advised of his or her rights as set forth in subdivision (e) and the provisions of paragraph (1). The name of this individual shall be clearly and legibly set forth on the disclosure form.

(3) The disclosure form shall include the actual date the disclosure form was signed by both the employee and the attorney and shall be signed under penalty of perjury by the attorney representing the employee, or an attorney licensed by the State Bar of California who is regularly employed by his or her firm. A copy of the disclosure form containing all of the required information shall be given to the employee when he or she signs the disclosure form.

(h) In addition to the disclosure form, the employee, the insurer, the employer, and the attorneys for each party shall sign under penalty of perjury and file with the board a statement, with the complete application or answer, and in addition to the disclosure required pursuant to subdivision (g), that they have not violated Section 139.3 and that they have not offered, delivered, received, or accepted any rebate, refund, commission, preference, patronage dividend, discount, or other consideration, whether in the form of money or otherwise, as compensation or inducement for any referred examination or evaluation.

(i) An attorney who subsequently assumes the representation of the employee in the same action or proceeding shall complete a disclosure form that meets all of the requirements of this section and the statement required by subdivision (h). Both the form and the statement shall be signed under penalty of perjury by the attorney or an attorney licensed by the State Bar of California who is regularly employed by his or her firm. Both the disclosure form and the statement shall be filed with the appeals board and sent to the employer, or insurer or third-party administrator, if either is known, by the attorney within 15 days of the employee's and attorney's execution of the form and statement. Payment pursuant to subdivision (a) of Section 4903 or Section 5710 shall not be allowed for any services or expenses incurred prior to the filing of the disclosure form described in subdivision (e) with the appeals board and the sending of that form to the employer, or to the insurer or third-party administrator, if either is known, by the attorney. **Leg.H.** 1991 ch. 934, 1993 ch. 120, effective July 16, 1993, ch. 1241, 2016 ch. 852 (AB 1244) §2.

1990 Note: The amendments made by this act to subdivision (c) of Section 139.5 of the Labor Code, pertaining to the payment of additional living expenses, and subdivisions (a) and (c) of Section 4702, of the Labor Code, with respect to the crediting of accrued disability indemnity against the amount of the death benefit, and subdivision (a) of Section 4906 of the Labor Code, with respect to legal services, are not intended by the Legislature to make a change in the law as it existed with respect to these provisions prior to January 1, 1990. Stats. 1990 ch. 1550 §67.

1989 Note: This section is applicable only to injuries occurring on or after January 1, 1990. Stats. 1989 ch. 893 §6.

Ref.: 8 C.C.R. §§10134, 10135, 10135.1, 10404, 10774, 10775, 10776, 10778, 10886; Hanna §§ 20.02[1][b], 22.06[6][b], 25.01[4], 30.03[2]; Herlick Handbook §§ 9.18, 10.09[1]–[3], 14.11, 14.13, 16.16.

§4907. Removal of privilege to represent party.

(a) The privilege of any person, except attorneys admitted to practice in the Supreme Court of the state, to appear in any proceeding as a representative of any party before the appeals board, or any of its workers' compensation administrative law judges, may, after a hearing, be removed, denied, or suspended by the appeals board for either of the following:

(1) For a violation of this chapter, the Rules of the Workers' Compensation Appeals Board, or the Rules of the Administrative Director.

(2) For other good cause, including, but not limited to, failure to pay final order of sanctions, attorney's fees, or costs issued under Section 5813.

(b) For purposes of this section, nonattorney representatives shall be held to the same professional standards of conduct as attorneys. **Leg.H.** 1937, 1965 ch. 1513 §107, operative January 15, 1966, 2012 ch. 363 (SB 863) §73.

2012 Note: For legislative findings, declarations, and applicability of Stats. 2012 ch. 363, see the 2012 Notes following Lab C §62.5.

Ref.: 8 C.C.R. §§10773, 10779; Hanna §§ 20.01[2], 21.09[5]; Herlick Handbook §§ 10.03[1], 10.09[2].

§4908. Compensation claim's equal preference over other debts.

A claim for compensation for the injury or death of any employee, or any award or judgment entered thereon, has the same preference over the other debts of the employer, or his estate and of the insurer which is given by the law to claims for wages. Such preference is for the entire amount of the compensation to be paid. This section shall not impair the lien of any previous award.

§4909. Effect of employer's payment of benefits before settlement.

Any payment, allowance, or benefit received by the injured employee during the period of his incapacity, or by his dependents in the event of his death, which by the terms of this division was not then due and payable or when there is any dispute or question concerning the right to compensation, shall not, in the absence of any agreement, be an admission of liability for compensation on the part of the employer, but any such payment, allowance, or benefit may be taken into account by the appeals board in fixing the amount of the compensation to be paid. The acceptance of any such payment, allowance, or benefit shall not operate as a waiver of any right or claim which the employee or his dependents has against the employer.

Ref.: Hanna § 7.04[6], [8], [9][b]; Herlick Handbook § 11.01.

§4909.1. State fund may administer benefits.

Authorized representatives of the Department of Corrections, and the Department of the Youth Authority may request the State Compensation Insurance Fund to provide any payment, allowance, or benefit as described in Section 4909. When requested by an authorized representative, the State Compensation Insurance Fund shall administer the benefits in a timely fashion.

CHAPTER 2 COMPROMISE AND RELEASE

§5000. Limitations of this division.

No contract, rule, or regulation shall exempt the employer from liability for the compensation fixed by this division, but nothing in this division shall:

(a) Impair the right of the parties interested to compromise, subject to the provisions herein contained, any liability which is claimed to exist under this division on account of injury or death.

(b) Confer upon the dependents of any injured employee any interest which the employee may not release by compromise or for which he, or his estate is in the event of such compromise by him accountable to dependents.

Ref.: 8 C.C.R. §§10878, 10882; Hanna §§ 29.01[1], 29.04[4]; Herlick Handbook §§ 7.19, 11.01.

§5001. "Compensation"; validity of compromise and release.

Compensation is the measure of the responsibility which the employer has assumed for injuries or deaths which occur to employees in his employment when subject to this division. No release of liability or compromise agreement is valid unless it is approved by the appeals board or referee.

Ref.: 8 C.C.R. §§10608, 10870, 10874, 10878, 10882, 10888, 10890; Hanna §§ 29.01[2], 29.04[1], 29.05[1]; Herlick Handbook §§ 11.01, 11.05, 11.11, 14.5.

§5002. Appeals board's power to enter award once copy of compromise and release filed.

A copy of the release or compromise agreement signed by both parties shall forthwith be filed with the appeals board. Upon filing with and approval by the appeals board, it may, without notice, of its own motion or on the application of either party, enter its award based upon the release or compromise agreement.

Ref.: 8 C.C.R. §§10870, 10874, 10878, 10882, 10888, 10890; Herlick Handbook § 11.05.

§5003. Required information for compromise and release.

Every release or compromise agreement shall be in writing and duly executed, and the signature of the employee or other beneficiary shall be attested by two disinterested witnesses or acknowledged before a notary public. The document shall specify:

(a) The date of the accident.

(b) The average weekly wages of the employee, determined according to Chapter 1 of Part 2 of this division.

(c) The nature of the disability, whether total or partial, permanent or temporary.

(d) The amount paid, or due and unpaid, to the employee up to the date of the release or agreement or death, and the amount of the payment or benefits then or thereafter to be made.

(e) The length of time such payment or benefit is to continue.

(f) In the event a claim of lien under subdivision (f) or (g) of Section 4903 has been filed, the number of days and the amount of temporary disability indemnity which should be allowed to the lien claimant.

Ref.: 8 C.C.R. §§10874, 10878, 10882; Hanna § 29.03[1], [6]; Herlick Handbook §§ 10.03[7], 11.03.

§5004. Additional required information for compromise and release agreements in case of death.

In case of death there shall also be stated in the release or compromise agreement:

(a) The date of death.

(b) The name of the widow.
(c) The names and ages of all children.
(d) The names of all other dependents.
(e) Whether the dependents are total or partial.
(f) The amount paid or to be paid as a death benefit and to whom payment is to be made.

Ref.: 8 C.C.R. §§10874, 10878, 10882; Hanna § 29.03[1]; Herlick Handbook § 11.03.

§5005. Compromises and release agreements; occupational disease or cumulative injury.

In any case involving a claim of occupational disease or cumulative injury, as set forth in Section 5500.5, the employee and any employer, or any insurance carrier for any employer, may enter into a compromise and release agreement settling either all or any part of the employee's claim, including a part of his claim against any employer. Such compromise and release agreement, upon approval by the appeals board or a referee, shall be a total release as to such employer or insurance carrier for the portion or portions of the claim released, but shall not constitute a bar to a recovery from any one or all of the remaining employers or insurance carriers for the periods of exposure not so released.

In any case where a compromise and release agreement of a portion of a claim has been made and approved, the employee may elect to proceed as provided in Section 5500.5 against any one or more of the remaining employers, or against an employer for that portion of his exposure not so released; in any such proceeding after election following compromise and release, that portion of liability attributable to the portion or portions of the exposure so released shall be assessed and deducted from the liability of the remaining defendant or defendants, but any such defendant shall receive no credit for any moneys paid by way of compromise and release in excess of the liability actually assessed against the released employments and the employee shall not receive any further benefits from the released employments for any liability assessed to them above what was paid by way of compromise and release.

In approving a compromise and release agreement under this section, the appeals board or referee shall determine the adequacy of the compromise and release agreement as it shall then reflect the potential liability of the released exposure after apportionment, but need not make a final actual determination of the potential liability of the employer or employers for that portion of the exposure being released.

Ref.: 8 C.C.R. §§10878, 10882; Hanna § 29.06; Herlick Handbook §§ 8.23, 11.10, 14.35.

§5006. Board's findings as having no collateral estoppel effect on subsequent criminal proceedings.

A determination of facts by the appeals board under this chapter has no collateral estoppel effect on a subsequent criminal prosecution and does not preclude litigation of those same facts in the criminal proceeding. **Leg.H.** 1995 ch. 158.

CHAPTER 3
LUMP SUM PAYMENTS

§5100. Lump sum payments; commutation.

At the time of making its award, or at any time thereafter, the appeals board, on its own motion either upon notice, or upon application of either party with due notice to the other, may commute the compensation payable under this division to a lump sum and order it to be paid forthwith or at some future time if any of the following conditions appear:

(a) That such commutation is necessary for the protection of the person entitled thereto, or for the best interest of the applicant. In determining what is in the best interest of the applicant, the appeals board shall consider the general financial condition of the applicant, including but not limited to, the applicant's ability to live without periodic indemnity payments and to discharge debts incurred prior to the date of injury.

(b) That commutation will avoid inequity and will not cause undue expense or hardship to the applicant.

(c) That the employer has sold or otherwise disposed of the greater part of his assets or is about to do so.

(d) That the employer is not a resident of this state.

Ref.: 8 C.C.R. §§10169, 10169.1; Hanna §§ 9.03[4], 27.02[1]–[5][a], 27.10[2][b]; Herlick Handbook §§ 6.13[1], 7.17.

§5100.5. When commutation not possible.

Notwithstanding the provisions of Section 5100, the appeals board shall not commute the compensation payable under this division to a lump sum when such compensation is payable under Section 4751 of the Labor Code.

Ref.: 8 C.C.R. §10169.1; Hanna § 27.02[2]; Herlick Handbook § 6.13[1].

§5100.6. No commutation or settlement of rehabilitation benefits.

Notwithstanding the provisions of Section 5100, the appeals board shall not permit the commutation or settlement of prospective compensation or indemnity payments or other benefits to which the employee is entitled under vocational rehabilitation. **Leg.H.** 1998 ch. 524.

1998 Note: The amendments made by this act do not constitute a change in, but are declaratory of, existing law. Stats. 1998 ch. 524 §3.

Ref.: 8 C.C.R. §§10169.1, 10870; Hanna §§ 29.03[3], 35.03[1], 35.54; Herlick Handbook §§ 16.5, 16.15.

§5101. Determination of lump sum amount.

The amount of the lump sum shall be determined as follows:

(a) If the injury causes temporary disability, the appeals board shall estimate the probable duration thereof and the probable amount of the temporary disability payments therefor, in accordance with Chapter 2 of Part 2 of this division, and shall fix the lump sum at the amount so determined.

(b) If the injury causes permanent disability or death, the appeals board shall fix the total amount of the permanent disability payment or death benefit payable therefor in accordance with Chapter 2 of Part 2 of this division, and shall estimate the present value thereof, assuming interest at the rate of 3 percent per annum and disregarding the probability of the beneficiary's death in all cases except where the percentage of permanent disability is such as to entitle the beneficiary to a life pension, and then taking into consideration the probability of the beneficiary's death only in estimating the present value of such life pension.

Ref.: 8 C.C.R. §§10169, 10169.1; Hanna § 27.02[2], [6]; Herlick Handbook § 6.13[1], [2].

§5102. Method of payment of lump sums.

The appeals board may order the lump sum paid directly to the injured employee or his dependents, or deposited with any savings bank or trust company authorized to transact business in this state, which agrees to accept the same as a deposit bearing interest; or the appeals board may order the lump sum deposited with the State Compensation Insurance Fund. Any lump sum so deposited, together with all interest derived therefrom, shall thereafter be held in trust for the injured employee, or in the event of his death, for his dependents. In the event of the employee's death, his dependents shall have no further recourse against the employer under this chapter.

Ref.: Herlick Handbook § 6.13[1].

§5103. Trustee's payments from deposited lump sum.

Payments from the lump sum so deposited shall be made by the trustee only in the amounts and at the time fixed by order of the appeals board and until the lump sum and interest thereon are exhausted.

Ref.: Herlick Handbook § 6.13[1].

§5104. Preference in trustee appointment.

In the appointment of the trustee, preference may be given to the choice of the injured employee or his dependents.

Ref.: Herlick Handbook § 6.13[1].

§5105. Receipt and certificate for lump sum payment.

Upon the payment of a lump sum, the employer shall present to the appeals board a proper receipt evidencing the same, executed either by the injured employee or his dependents, or by the trustee. The appeals board shall thereupon issue its certificate in proper form evidencing such payment. Such certificate, upon filing with the clerk of the superior court in which any judgment upon an award has been entered, operates as a satisfaction of the award and fully discharges the employer from any further liability on account thereof.

Ref.: 8 C.C.R. §§10820, 10825, 10828.

§5106. Present worth of uninsured employer's future payments.

The appeals board shall, upon the request of the Director of Industrial Relations, where the employer is uninsured and the installments of compensation awarded are to be paid in the future, determine the present worth of the future payments, discounted at the rate of 3 percent per annum, and order the present worth paid into the Uninsured Employers Fund, which fund shall thereafter pay to the beneficiaries of the award the future payments as they become due.

Ref.: Herlick Handbook § 6.13[1].

Labor

PART 3.5
Arbitration

§5270. Representation.

This part shall not apply in cases where an injured employee or dependent is involved unless the employee or dependent is represented by an attorney.

1989 Note: This section is applicable only to injuries occurring on or after January 1, 1990. Stats. 1989 ch. 893 §6.

Ref.: 8 C.C.R. §§10995, 10996, 10997; Hanna § 33.01[6]; Herlick Handbook §§ 1.01[2], 14.4, 14.32, 15.1, 16.1.

§5270.5. List of eligible arbitrators.

(a) The presiding workers' compensation judge at each district office shall prepare a list of all eligible attorneys who apply to be placed on the list of eligible arbitrators. Attorneys are eligible to become arbitrators if they are active members of the California State Bar Association and are one of the following:

(1) A certified specialist in workers' compensation, or eligible to become certified.

(2) A retired workers' compensation judge.

(3) A retired appeals board member.

(4) An attorney who has been certified to serve as a judge pro tempore.

(b) No attorney shall be included in a panel of arbitrators, if he or she has served as a judge in any proceeding involving the same case, or has represented, or whose firm has represented, any party in the same case.

1989 Note: This section is applicable only to injuries occurring on or after January 1, 1990. Stats. 1989 ch. 893 §6.

Ref.: 8 C.C.R. §§10995, 10996, 10997; Herlick Handbook §§ 1.01[2], 14.32.

§5271. Selection of arbitrator.

(a) The parties to a dispute submitted for arbitration may select any eligible attorney from the list prepared by the presiding workers' compensation judge to serve as arbitrator. However, when the disputed issue involves insurance coverage, the parties may select any attorney as arbitrator upon agreement of the parties.

(b) If the parties cannot select an arbitrator by agreement, either party may request the presiding workers' compensation judge to assign a panel of five arbitrators selected at random from the list of eligible attorneys. No more than three arbitrators on a five-member panel may be defense attorneys, no more than three may be applicant's attorneys, and no more than two may be retired workers' compensation judges or appeals board commissioners.

(c) For each party in excess of one party in the capacity of employer and one party in the capacity of injured employee or lien claimant, the presiding judge shall randomly select two additional arbitrators to add to the panel. For each additional party in the capacity of employer, the presiding judge shall assign a retired workers' compensation judge or retired appeals board commissioner and an applicant's attorney. For each additional party in the capacity of injured employee or lien claimant, the presiding judge shall assign a retired workers' compensation judge or retired appeals board commissioner and a defense attorney. For each additional other party, the presiding judge shall assign two arbitrators to the panel, in order of rotation from case to case, as follows: a retired workers' compensation judge or retired appeals board commissioner, an applicant's attorney, a defense attorney.

(d) A party may petition the presiding workers' compensation judge to remove a member from the panel pursuant to Section 170.1 of the Code of Civil Procedure. The presiding workers' compensation judge shall assign another eligible attorney to replace any member removed under this subdivision.

(e) Each party or lien claimant shall strike two members from the panel, and the remaining attorney shall serve as arbitrator.

1989 Note: This section is applicable only to injuries occurring on or after January 1, 1990. Stats. 1989 ch. 893 §6.

Ref.: 8 C.C.R. §§10995, 10996, 10997, 10998; Herlick Handbook § 1.01[2].

§5272. Arbitrators' duties and limits of power.

Arbitrators shall have all of the statutory and regulatory duties and responsibilities of a workers' compensation judge, as set forth in Chapter 1 (commencing with Section 5300) of Part 4, except for the following:

(a) Arbitrators shall have no power to order the injured worker to be examined by a qualified medical evaluator pursuant to Sections 5701 and 5703.5.

(b) Arbitrators shall not have power of contempt.

1989 Note: This section is applicable only to injuries occurring on or after January 1, 1990. Stats. 1989 ch. 893 §6.

Ref.: 8 C.C.R. §§10995, 10996, 10997; Herlick Handbook § 1.01[2].

§5273. Payment of costs of proceedings.

(a) In disputes between an employee and an employer, the employer shall pay all costs related to the arbitration proceeding, including use of facilities, hearing reporter per diems and transcript costs.

(b) In all other disputes, the costs of the arbitration proceedings, including the arbitrator's compensation, shall be paid as follows:

(1) By the parties equally in any dispute between an employer and an insurer, or an employer and a lien claimant.

(2) By the parties equally in proceedings subject to Section 5500.5.

(3) By the dependents in accordance with their proportionate share of death benefits, where there is no dispute as to the injury causing death.

(c) Disputes regarding the costs or fees for arbitration shall be within the exclusive jurisdiction of the appeals board, and shall be determined initially by the presiding judge of the district office.

1989 Note: This section is applicable only to injuries occurring on or after January 1, 1990. Stats. 1989 ch. 893 §6.

Ref.: 8 C.C.R. §§10995, 10996, 10997, 10999; Herlick Handbook § 1.01[2].

§5275. Types of disputes submitted.

(a) Disputes involving the following issues shall be submitted for arbitration:

(1) Insurance coverage.

(2) Right of contribution in accordance with Section 5500.5.

(b) By agreement of the parties, any issue arising under Division 1 (commencing with Section 50) or Division 4 (commencing with Section 3200) may be submitted for arbitration, regardless of the date of injury. **Leg.H.** 1993 ch. 121, effective July 16, 1993, 1994 ch. 470, 2002 ch. 6 (AB 749).

1993 Note: Section 5275, as amended by ch. 121, applies only to injuries occurring on or after January 1, 1994. Stats. 1993 ch. 121 §77.

1989 Note: This section is applicable only to injuries occurring on or after January 1, 1990. Stats. 1989 ch. 893 §6.

Ref.: 8 C.C.R. §§10166, 10866, 10867, 10995, 10996, 10997, 10999; Hanna § 33.01[1][a.1], [6]; Herlick Handbook §§ 1.01[2], 8.23, 10.03[7], 14.32, 15.2, 16.1, 16.8.

§5276. Date, time, and place of proceedings.

(a) Arbitration proceedings may commence at any place and time agreed upon by all parties.

(b) If the parties cannot agree on a time or place to commence arbitration proceedings, the arbitrator shall order the date, time and place for commencement of the proceeding. Unless all parties agree otherwise, arbitration proceedings shall commence not less than 30 days nor more than 60 days from the date an arbitrator is selected.

(c) Ten days before the arbitration, each party shall submit to the arbitrator and serve on the opposing party reports, records and other documentary evidence on which that party intends to rely. If a party intends to rely upon excerpts of records or depositions, only copies of the excerpts shall be submitted to the arbitrator.

1989 Note: This section is applicable only to injuries occurring on or after January 1, 1990. Stats. 1989 ch. 893 §6.

Ref.: 8 C.C.R. §§10995, 10996, 10997; Herlick Handbook § 1.01[2].

§5277. Findings and award.

(a) The arbitrator's findings and award shall be served on all parties within 30 days of submission of the case for decision.

(b) The arbitrator's award shall comply with Section 5313 and shall be filed with the appeals board office pursuant to venue rules published by the appeals board.

(c) The findings of fact, award, order, or decision of the arbitrator shall have the same force and effect as an award, order, or decision of a workers' compensation judge.

(d) Use of an arbitrator for any part of a proceeding or any issue shall not bind the parties to the use of the same arbitrator for any subsequent issues or proceedings.

(e) Unless all parties agree to a longer period of time, the failure of the arbitrator to submit the decision within 30 days shall result in forfeiture of the arbitrator's fee and shall vacate the submission order and all stipulations.

(f) The presiding workers' compensation judge may submit supplemental proceedings to arbitration pursuant to this part. **Leg.H.** 1989 ch. 892 §44, 2006 ch. 538 (SB 1852) §490.

1989 Note: This section is applicable only to injuries occurring on or after January 1, 1990. Stats. 1989 ch. 893 §6.

Ref.: 8 C.C.R. §§10866, 10867, 10995, 10996, 10997; Hanna § 33.01[4]; Herlick Handbook §§ 1.01[2], 14.4, 14.32, 15.1.

§5278. Disclosure of settlement to arbitrator prior to award prohibited.

(a) No disclosure of any offers of settlement made by any party shall be made to the arbitrator prior to the filing of the award.

(b) Article 7 (commencing with Section 11430.10) of Chapter 4.5 of Part 1 of Division 3 of Title 2 of the Government Code applies to a communication to the arbitrator or a potential arbitrator. **Leg.H.** 1995 ch. 938, operative July 1, 1997.

Ref.: Hanna § 33.01[4]; Herlick Handbook §§ 1.01[2], 14.32.

Labor

PART 4
Compensation Proceedings

CHAPTER 1
JURISDICTION

§5300. Proceedings to be handled by appeals board.

All the following proceedings shall be instituted before the appeals board and not elsewhere, except as otherwise provided in Division 4:

(a) For the recovery of compensation, or concerning any right or liability arising out of or incidental thereto.

(b) For the enforcement against the employer or an insurer of any liability for compensation imposed upon the employer by this division in favor of the injured employee, his or her dependents, or any third person.

(c) For the determination of any question as to the distribution of compensation among dependents or other persons.

(d) For the determination of any question as to who are dependents of any deceased employee, or what persons are entitled to any benefit under the compensation provisions of this division.

(e) For obtaining any order which by Division 4 the appeals board is authorized to make.

(f) For the determination of any other matter, jurisdiction over which is vested by Division 4 in the Division of Workers' Compensation, including the administrative director and the appeals board. **Leg.H.** 1994 ch. 146.

Ref.: 8 C.C.R. §§9768.6, 9768.16, 10181, 10364, 10952; Hanna §§ 2.02[3], 11.01[5], 34.01; Herlick Handbook §§ 1.01[2], 3.11, 16.13.

§5301. Appeals board power and jurisdiction.

The appeals board is vested with full power, authority and jurisdiction to try and determine finally all the matters specified in Section 5300 subject only to the review by the courts as specified in this division.

Ref.: 8 C.C.R. §10952; Hanna § 34.01.

§5302. Presumptions regarding all appeals board decisions.

All orders, rules, findings, decisions, and awards of the appeals board shall be prima facie lawful and conclusively presumed to be reasonable and lawful, until and unless they are modified or set aside by the appeals board or upon a review by the courts within the time and in the manner specified in this division.

Ref.: 8 C.C.R. §10950; Hanna § 27.10[2][a].

§5303. Separate cause of action; joined claims.

There is but one cause of action for each injury coming within the provisions of the division. All claims brought for medical expense, disability payments, death benefits, burial expense, liens, or any other matter arising out of such injury may, in the discretion of the appeals board, be joined in the same proceeding at any time; provided, however, that no injury, whether specific or cumulative, shall, for any purpose whatsoever, merge into or form a part of another injury; nor shall any award based on a cumulative injury include disability caused by any specific injury or by any other cumulative injury causing or contributing to the existing disability, need for medical treatment or death.

Ref.: 8 C.C.R. §§10364, 10589, 10590, 10591, 10592; Hanna §§ 7.05[2], 8.02[3], 26.10[2], 31.01; Herlick Handbook § 8.23.

§5304. Appeals board jurisdiction over medical, surgical, and hospital treatment.

The appeals board has jurisdiction over any controversy relating to or arising out of Sections 4600 to 4605 inclusive, unless an express agreement fixing the amounts to be paid for medical, surgical or hospital treatment as such treatment is described in those sections has been made between the persons or institutions rendering such treatment and the employer or insurer.

Ref.: Hanna §§ 5.05[10][d], 30.04; Herlick Handbook §§ 4.18[1], 13.4.

§5305. Jurisdiction of resident's out-of-state injuries.

The Division of Workers' Compensation, including the administrative director, and the appeals board have jurisdiction over all controversies arising out of injuries suffered outside the territorial limits of this state in those cases where the injured employee is a resident of this state at the time of the injury and the contract of hire was made in this state. Any employee described by this section, or his or her dependents, shall be entitled to the compensation or death benefits provided by this division. **Leg.H.** 1994 ch. 146, 2002 ch. 6 (AB 749).

Ref.: Hanna §§ 3.22[2], 21.06, 21.07[5]; Herlick Handbook § 13.2.

§5306. Employee's rights against employer's estate.

The death of an employer subsequent to the sustaining of an injury by an employee shall not impair the right of the employee to proceed before the appeals board against the estate of the employer, and the failure of the employee or his dependents to cause the claim to be presented to the executor or administrator of the estate shall not in any way bar or suspend such right.

§5307. Appeals board powers; procedure for adopting, amending or rescinding regulations.

(a) The appeals board may, by an order signed by four members, do all of the following:

(1) Adopt reasonable and proper rules of practice and procedure.

(2) Regulate and provide the manner in which, and by whom, minors and incompetent persons are to appear and be represented before it.

(3) Regulate and prescribe the kind and character of notices, where not specifically prescribed by this division, and the service thereof.

(4) Regulate and prescribe the nature and extent of the proofs and evidence.

(b) No rule or regulation of the appeals board pursuant to this section shall be adopted, amended, or rescinded without public hearings. Any written request filed with the appeals board seeking a change in its rules or regulations shall be deemed to be denied if not set by the appeals board for public hearing to be held within six months of the date on which the request is received by the appeals board. **Leg.H.** 2002 ch. 6 (AB 749), 2011 ch. 559 (AB 1426) §11, effective October 7, 2011.

Ref.: 8 C.C.R. §§10250, 10301, 10304, 10450, 10602, 10869, 10946; Hanna § 1.11[6][a].

§5307.1. Official medical fee schedule.

(a)(1) The administrative director, after public hearings, shall adopt and revise periodically an official medical fee schedule that shall establish reasonable maximum fees paid for medical services other than physician services, drugs and pharmacy services, health care facility fees, home health care, and all other treatment, care, services, and goods described in Section 4600 and provided pursuant to this section. Except for physician services, all fees shall be in accordance with the fee-related structure and rules of the relevant Medicare and Medi-Cal payment systems, provided that employer liability for medical treatment, including issues of reasonableness, necessity, frequency, and duration, shall be determined in accordance with Section 4600. Commencing January 1, 2004, and continuing until the time the administrative director has adopted an official medical fee schedule in accordance with the fee-related structure and rules of the relevant Medicare payment systems, except for the components listed in subdivision (j), maximum reasonable fees shall be 120 percent of the estimated aggregate fees prescribed in the relevant Medicare payment system for the same class of services before application of the inflation factors provided in subdivision (g), except that for pharmacy services and drugs that are not otherwise covered by a Medicare fee schedule payment for facility services, the maximum reasonable fees shall be 100 percent of fees prescribed in the relevant Medi-Cal payment system. Upon adoption by the administrative director of an official medical fee schedule pursuant to this section, the maximum reasonable fees paid shall not exceed 120 percent of estimated aggregate fees prescribed in the Medicare payment system for the same class of services before application of the inflation factors provided in subdivision (g). Pharmacy services and drugs shall be subject to the requirements of this section, whether furnished through a pharmacy or dispensed directly by the practitioner pursuant to subdivision (b) of Section 4024 of the Business and Professions Code.

(2)(A) The administrative director, after public hearings, shall adopt and review periodically an official medical fee schedule based on the resource-based relative value scale for physician services and nonphysician practitioner services, as defined by the administrative director, provided that all of the following apply:

(i) Employer liability for medical treatment, including issues of reasonableness, necessity, frequency, and duration, shall be determined in accordance with Section 4600.

(ii) The fee schedule is updated annually to reflect changes in procedure codes, relative weights, and the adjustment factor provided in subdivision (g).

(iii) The maximum reasonable fees paid shall not exceed 120 percent of estimated annualized aggregate fees prescribed in the Medicare payment system for physician services as it appeared on July 1, 2012, before application of the adjustment factor provided in subdivision (g). For purposes of calculating maximum reasonable fees, any service provided to injured workers that is not covered under the federal Medicare program shall be included at its rate of payment established by the administrative director pursuant to subdivision (d).

(iv) There shall be a four-year transition between the estimated aggregate maximum allowable amount under the official medical fee schedule for physician services prior to January 1, 2014, and the maximum allowable amount based on the resource-based relative value scale at 120 percent of the Medicare conversion factors as adjusted pursuant to this section.

(B) The official medical fee schedule shall include payment ground rules that differ from Medicare payment ground rules, including, as appropriate, payment of consultation codes and payment evaluation and management services provided during a global period of surgery.

(C) Commencing January 1, 2014, and continuing until the time the administrative director has adopted an official medical fee schedule in accordance with the resource-based relative value scale, the maximum reasonable fees for physician services and nonphysician practitioner services, including, but not limited to, physician assistant, nurse practitioner, and physical therapist services, shall be in accordance with the fee-related structure and rules of the Medicare payment system for physician services and nonphysician practitioner services, except that an average statewide geographic adjustment factor of 1.078 shall apply in lieu of Medicare's locality-specific geographic adjustment factors, and shall incorporate the following conversion factors:

(i) For dates of service in 2014, forty-nine dollars and five thousand three hundred thirteen ten thousandths cents ($49.5313) for surgery, fifty-six dollars and two thousand three hundred twenty-nine ten thousandths cents ($56.2329) for radiology, thirty dollars and six hundred forty-seven ten thousandths cents ($30.0647) for anesthesia, and thirty-seven dollars and one thousand seven hundred twelve ten thousandths cents ($37.1712) for all other before application of the adjustment factor provided in subdivision (g).

(ii) For dates of service in 2015, forty-six dollars and six thousand three hundred fifty-nine ten thousandths cents ($46.6359) for surgery, fifty-one dollars and one thousand thirty-six ten thousandths cents ($51.1036) for radiology, twenty-eight dollars and six thousand sixty-seven ten thousandths cents ($28.6067) for anesthesia, and thirty-eight dollars and three thousand nine hundred fifty-eight ten thousandths cents ($38.3958) for all other before application of the adjustment factor provided in subdivision (g).

(iii) For dates of service in 2016, forty-three dollars and seven thousand four hundred five ten thousandths cents ($43.7405) for surgery, forty-five dollars and nine thousand seven hundred forty-four ten thousandths cents ($45.9744) for radiology, twenty-seven dollars and one thousand four hundred eighty-seven thousandths cents ($27.1487) for anesthesia, and thirty-nine dollars and six thousand two hundred five ten thousandths cents ($39.6205) for all other before application of the adjustment factor provided in subdivision (g).

(iv) For dates of service on or after January 1, 2017, 120 percent of the 2012 Medicare conversion factor as updated pursuant to subdivision (g).

(b) In order to comply with the standards specified in subdivision (f), the administrative director may adopt different conversion factors, diagnostic-related group weights, and other factors affecting payment amounts from those used in the Medicare payment system, provided estimated aggregate fees do not exceed 120 percent of the estimated aggregate fees paid for the same class of services in the relevant Medicare payment system.

(c)(1) Notwithstanding subdivisions (a) and (d), the maximum facility fee for services performed in a hospital outpatient department, shall not exceed 120 percent of the fee paid by Medicare for the same services performed in a hospital outpatient department, and the maximum facility fee for services performed in an ambulatory surgical center shall not exceed 80 percent of the fee paid by Medicare for the same services performed in a hospital outpatient department.

(2) The department shall study the feasibility of establishing a facility fee for services that are performed in an ambulatory surgical center and are not subject to a fee paid by Medicare for services performed in an outpatient department, set at 85 percent of the diagnostic-related group (DRG) fee paid by Medicare for the same services performed in a hospital inpatient department. The department shall report the finding to the Senate Labor Committee and Assembly Insurance Committee no later than July 1, 2013.

(d) If the administrative director determines that a medical treatment, facility use, product, or service is not covered by a Medicare payment system, the administrative director shall establish maximum fees for that item, provided that the maximum fee paid shall not exceed 120 percent of the fees paid by Medicare for services that require comparable resources. If the administrative director determines that a pharmacy service or drug is not covered by a Medi-Cal payment system, the administrative director shall establish maximum fees for that item. However, the maximum fee paid shall not exceed 100 percent of the fees paid by Medi-Cal for pharmacy services or drugs that require comparable resources.

(e)(1) Prior to the adoption by the administrative director of a medical fee schedule pursuant to this section, for any treatment, facility use, product, or service not covered by a Medicare payment system, including acupuncture services, the maximum reasonable fee paid shall not exceed the fee specified in the official medical fee schedule in effect on December 31, 2003, except as otherwise provided in this subdivision.

(2) Any compounded drug product shall be billed by the compounding pharmacy or dispensing physician at the ingredient level, with each ingredient identified using the applicable National Drug Code (NDC) of the ingredient and the corresponding quantity, and in accordance with regulations adopted by the California State Board of Pharmacy. Ingredients with no NDC shall not be separately reimbursable. The ingredient-level reimbursement shall be equal to 100 percent of the reimbursement allowed by the Medi-Cal payment system and payment shall be based on the sum of the allowable fee for each ingredient plus a dispensing fee equal to the dispensing fee allowed by the Medi-Cal payment systems. If the compounded drug product is dispensed by a physician, the maximum reimbursement shall not exceed 300 percent of documented paid costs, but in no case more than twenty dollars ($20) above documented paid costs.

(3) For a dangerous drug dispensed by a physician that is a finished drug product approved by the federal Food and Drug Administration, the maximum reimbursement shall be according to the official medical fee schedule adopted by the administrative director.

(4) For a dangerous device dispensed by a physician, the reimbursement to the physician shall not exceed either of the following:

(A) The amount allowed for the device pursuant to the official medical fee schedule adopted by the administrative director.

(B) One hundred twenty percent of the documented paid cost, but not less than 100 percent of the documented paid cost plus the minimum dispensing fee allowed for dispensing prescription drugs pursuant to the official medical fee schedule adopted by the administrative director, and not more than 100 percent of the documented paid cost plus two hundred fifty dollars ($250).

(5) For any pharmacy goods dispensed by a physician not subject to paragraph (2), (3), or (4), the maximum reimbursement to a physician for pharmacy goods dispensed by the physician shall not exceed any of the following:

(A) The amount allowed for the pharmacy goods pursuant to the official medical fee schedule adopted by the administrative director or pursuant to paragraph (2), as applicable.

(B) One hundred twenty percent of the documented paid cost to the physician.

(C) One hundred percent of the documented paid cost to the physician plus two hundred fifty dollars ($250).

(6) For the purposes of this subdivision, the following definitions apply:

(A) "Administer" or "administered" has the meaning defined by Section 4016 of the Business and Professions Code.

(B) "Compounded drug product" means any drug product subject to Article 4.5 (commencing with Section 1735) of Division 17 of Title 16 of the California Code of Regulations or other regulation adopted by the State Board of Pharmacy to govern the practice of compounding.

(C) "Dispensed" means furnished to or for a patient as contemplated by Section 4024 of the Business and Professions Code and does not include "administered."

(D) "Dangerous drug" and "dangerous device" have the meanings defined by Section 4022 of the Business and Professions Code.

(E) "Documented paid cost" means the unit price paid for the specific product or for each component used in the product as documented by invoices, proof of payment, and inventory records as applicable, or as documented in accordance with regulations that may be adopted by the administrative director, net of rebates, discounts, and any other immediate or anticipated cost adjustments.

(F) "Pharmacy goods" has the same meaning as set forth in Section 139.3.

(7) To the extent that any provision of paragraphs (2) to (6), inclusive, is inconsistent with any provision of the official medical fee schedule adopted by the administrative director on or after January 1, 2012, the provision adopted by the administrative director shall govern.

(8) Notwithstanding paragraph (7), the provisions of this subdivision concerning physician-dispensed pharmacy goods shall not be superseded by any provision of the official medical fee schedule adopted by the administrative director unless the relevant official medical fee schedule provision is expressly applicable to physician-dispensed pharmacy goods.

(f) Within the limits provided by this section, the rates or fees established shall be adequate to ensure a reasonable standard of services and care for injured employees.

(g)(1)(A) Notwithstanding any other law, the official medical fee schedule shall be adjusted to conform to any relevant changes in the Medicare and Medi-Cal payment systems no later than 60 days after the effective date of those changes, subject to the following provisions:

(i) The annual inflation adjustment for facility fees for inpatient hospital services provided by acute care hospitals and for hospital outpatient services shall be determined solely by the estimated increase in the hospital market basket for the 12 months beginning October 1 of the preceding calendar year.

(ii) The annual update in the operating standardized amount and capital standard rate for inpatient hospital services provided by hospitals excluded from the Medicare prospective payment system for acute care hospitals and the conversion factor for hospital outpatient services shall be determined solely by the estimated increase in the hospital market basket for excluded hospitals for the 12 months beginning October 1 of the preceding calendar year.

(iii) The annual adjustment factor for physician services shall be based on the product of one plus the percentage change in the Medicare Economic Index and any relative value scale adjustment factor.

(B) The update factors contained in clauses (i) and (ii) of subparagraph (A) shall be applied beginning with the first update in the Medicare fee schedule payment amounts after December 31, 2003, and the adjustment factor in clause (iii) of subparagraph (A) shall be applied beginning with the first update in the Medicare fee schedule payment amounts after December 31, 2012.

(C) The maximum reasonable fees paid for pharmacy services and drugs shall not include any reductions in the relevant Medi-Cal payment system implemented pursuant to Section 14105.192 of the Welfare and Institutions Code.

(2) The administrative director shall determine the effective date of the changes, and shall issue an order, exempt from Sections 5307.3 and 5307.4 and the rulemaking provisions of the Administrative Procedure Act (Chapter 3.5 (commencing with Section 11340) of Part 1 of Division 3 of Title 2 of the Government Code), informing the public of the changes and their effective date. All orders issued pursuant to this paragraph shall be published on the Internet Web site of the Division of Workers' Compensation.

(3) For the purposes of this subdivision, the following definitions apply:

(A) "Medicare Economic Index" means the input price index used by the federal Centers for Medicare and Medicaid Services to measure changes in the costs of a providing physician and other services paid under the resource-based relative value scale.

(B) "Hospital market basket" means the input price index used by the federal Centers for Medicare and Medicaid Services to measure changes in the costs of providing inpatient hospital services provided by acute care hospitals that are included in the Medicare prospective payment system.

(C) "Hospital market basket for excluded hospitals" means the input price index used by the federal Centers for Medicare and Medicaid Services to measure changes in the costs of providing inpatient services by hospitals that are excluded from the Medicare prospective payment system.

(D) "Relative value scale adjustment factor" means the annual factor applied by the federal Centers for Medicare and Medicaid Services to the Medicare conversion factor to make changes in relative value units for the physician fee schedule budget neutral.

(h) This section does not prohibit an employer or insurer from contracting with a medical provider for reimbursement rates different from those prescribed in the official medical fee schedule.

(i) Except as provided in Section 4626, the official medical fee schedule shall not apply to medical-legal expenses, as that term is defined by Section 4620.

(j) The following Medicare payment system components shall not become part of the official medical fee schedule until January 1, 2005:

(1) Inpatient skilled nursing facility care.

(2) Home health agency services.

(3) Inpatient services furnished by hospitals that are exempt from the prospective payment system for general acute care hospitals.

(4) Outpatient renal dialysis services.

(k) Except as revised by the administrative director, the official medical fee schedule rates for physician services in effect on December 31, 2012, shall remain in effect until January 1, 2014.

(*l*) Notwithstanding subdivision (a), any explicit reductions in the Medi-Cal fee schedule for pharmacy services and drugs to meet the budgetary targets provided in Section 14105.192 of the Welfare and Institutions Code shall not be reflected in the official medical fee schedule.

(m) On or before July 1, 2013, the administrative director shall adopt a regulation specifying an additional reimbursement for MS-DRGs Medicare Severity Diagnostic Related Groups (MS-DRGs) 028, 029, 030, 453, 454, 455, and 456 to ensure that the aggregate reimbursement is sufficient to cover costs, including the implantable medical device, hardware, and instrumentation. This regulation shall be repealed as of January 1, 2014, unless extended by the administrative director. **Leg.H.** 2003 ch. 639 (SB 228) §35, 2006 ch. 538 (SB 1852) §491, 2007 ch. 697 (AB 1269) §1, 2011 ch. 545 (AB 378) §4, 2012 ch. 363 (SB 863) §74.

2012 Note: For legislative findings, declarations, and applicability of Stats. 2012 ch. 363, see the 2012 Notes following Lab C §62.5.

Ref.: 8 C.C.R. §§9768.17, 9789.10, 9789.11, 9789.20, 9789.21, 9789.22, 9789.24, 9789.30, 9789.31, 9789.32, 9789.33, 9789.34, 9789.35, 9789.36, 9789.37, 9789.38, 9789.40, 9789.50, 9789.60, 9789.70, 9789.110, 9789.111, 9790, 9790.1, 9791, 9791.1, 9792, 9792.1, 9792.5, 9900, 10100, 10100.1, 10100.2; Hanna §§ 5.05[6][b], 22.05[2]; Herlick Handbook §§ 4.17[1], 4.18[1], 10.08[3].

§5307.11. Permissible contracts for reimbursement rates outside official fee schedule.

A health care provider or health facility licensed pursuant to Section 1250 of the Health and Safety Code, and a contracting agent, employer, or carrier may contract for reimbursement rates different from those in the fee schedule adopted and revised pursuant to Section 5307.1. When a health care provider or health facility licensed pursuant to Section 1250 of the Health and Safety Code, and a contracting agent, employer, or carrier contract for reimbursement rates different from those in the fee schedule, the medical fee schedule for that health care provider or health facility licensed pursuant to Section 1250 of the Health and Safety Code shall not apply to the contracted reimbursement rates. Except as provided in subdivision (b) of Section 5307.1, the official medical fee schedule shall establish maximum reimbursement rates for all medical services for injuries subject to this division provided by a health care provider or health care facility licensed pursuant to Section 1250 of the Health and Safety Code other than those specified in contracts subject to this section. **Leg.H.** 2001 ch. 252.

Ref.: Hanna §§ 5.05[10][d], 22.05[2]; Herlick Handbook §§ 4.10[3], 4.17[1], 4.18[1].

§5307.12. [Operative July 1, 2021] Written disclosure when contract for reimbursement is more than 20 percent below the official medical fee schedule.

(a) If a health care provider or health facility, licensed pursuant to Section 1250 of the Health and Safety Code, and an entity that provides physician network services, as defined in subdivision (b) of Section 4616.5, or an entity that provides ancillary network services, as defined in subdivision (c) of Section 4616.5, contract for a reimbursement rate that is more than 20 percent below the official medical fee schedule, excluding goods and pharmaceuticals, the entity that provides physician or ancillary network services shall provide the payor with a written disclosure, on a form promulgated by the administrative director, of the reimbursement amount paid to the provider.

(b) Before providing the disclosure required pursuant to subdivision (a), the entity that provides physician or ancillary network services may require the payor to sign a nondisclosure agreement with the entity that provides physician or ancillary network services agreeing to maintain the confidentiality of the disclosed information.

(c) A nondisclosure agreement signed pursuant to subdivision (b) shall not prohibit the division from obtaining the information disclosed pursuant to subdivision (a). This subdivision is declaratory of existing law.

(d) This section does not apply to an entity that provides physician or ancillary network services that discloses, or arranges for the disclosure of, the same pricing and payment information to both the health care provider or health facility and the person or entity paying for the services.

(e) This section shall become operative on July 1, 2021. **Leg.H.** 2019 ch. 647 (SB 537) §9.

Ref.: Herlick Handbook § 4.10[3].

§5307.2. Study of access to medical treatment, quality health care or products, including prescription drugs and pharmacy services, for injured workers; authority of administrative director to adjust medical and facilities' fees.

The administrative director shall contract with an independent consulting firm, to the extent permitted by state law, to perform an annual study of access to medical treatment for injured workers. The study shall analyze whether there is adequate access to quality health care and products, including prescription drugs and pharmacy services, for injured workers and make recommendations to ensure continued access. If the administrative director determines, based on this study, that there is insufficient access to quality health care or products for injured workers, including access to prescription drugs and pharmacy services, the administrative director may make appropriate adjustments to medical, prescription drugs and pharmacy services, and facilities' fees. When there has been a determination that substantial access problems exist, the administrative director may, in accordance with the notification and hearing requirements of Section 5307.1, adopt fees in excess of 120 percent of the applicable Medicare payment system fee, or in excess of 100 percent of the fees prescribed in the relevant Medi-Cal payment system, for the applicable services or products. **Leg.H.** 2003 ch. 639 (SB 228) §37, 2008 ch. 193 (AB 2091) §1.

Ref.: Hanna § 22.05[2]; Herlick Handbook § 4.17[1].

§5307.27. Adoption of medical treatment utilization schedule; evidence-based updates; inclusion of drug formulary.

(a) The administrative director, in consultation with the Commission on Health and Safety and Workers' Compensation, shall adopt, after public hearings, a medical treatment utilization schedule, that shall incorporate the evidence-based, peer-reviewed, nationally recognized standards of care recommended by the commission pursuant to Section 77.5, and that shall address, at a minimum, the frequency, duration, intensity, and appropriateness of all treatment procedures and modalities commonly performed in workers' compensation cases. Evidence-based updates to the utilization schedule shall be made through an order exempt from Sections 5307.3 and 5307.4, and the rulemaking provisions of the Administrative Procedure Act (Chapter 3.5 (commencing with Section 11340) of Part 1 of Division 3 of Title 2 of the Government Code), but the administrative director shall allow at least a 30-day period for public comment and a public hearing. The administrative director shall provide responses to submitted comments prior to the effective date of the updates. All orders issued pursuant to this subdivision shall be published on the Internet Web site of the Division of Workers' Compensation.

(b) On or before July 1, 2017, the medical treatment utilization schedule adopted by the administrative director shall include a drug formulary using evidence-based medicine. Nothing in this section shall prohibit the authorization of medications that are not in the formulary when the variance is demonstrated, consistent with subdivision (a) of Section 4604.5.

(c) The drug formulary shall include a phased implementation for workers injured prior to July 1, 2017, in order to ensure injured workers safely transition to medications pursuant to the formulary.

(d) This section shall apply to all prescribers and dispensers of medications serving injured workers under the workers' compensation system. **Leg.H.** 2003 ch. 639 (SB 228), 2015 ch. 525 (AB 1124) §4, 2016 ch. 868 (SB 1160) §10.

2016 Note: For legislative findings and declarations, see the 2016 Note following Lab C §138.4.

2015 Note: For legislative intent, see the 2015 Note following Lab C §4600.1.

Ref.: 8 C.C.R. §§9767.6, 9768.11, 9768.12; Hanna § 22.05[6][b]; Herlick Handbook §§ 4.01[3], 4.04[4], 4.05[1], [3], 4.09[2], 4.11[4], [8].

§5307.28. Consultation with stakeholders regarding establishment of drug formulary; interim reports.

(a) Prior to the adoption of a drug formulary as required by Section 5307.27, the administrative director shall meet and consult regarding the establishment of a formulary with stakeholders, including, but not limited to, employers, insurers, private sector employee representatives, public sector employee representatives, treating physicians actively practicing medicine, pharmacists, pharmacy benefit managers, attorneys who represent applicants, and injured workers.

(b) Commencing July 1, 2016, and concluding with the implementation of the formulary, the administrative director shall publish at least two interim reports on the Internet Web site of the Division of Workers' Compensation describing the status of the creation of the formulary. **Leg.H.** 2015 ch. 525 (AB 1124) §5.

§5307.29. Quarterly updates to drug formulary; issuance of order for changes; independent pharmacy and therapeutics committee.

(a) The administrative director shall make provision for no less than quarterly updates to the drug formulary to allow for the provision of all appropriate medications, including those new to the market.

(b) Changes made to the list of drugs in the drug formulary described in Section 5307.27 shall be made through an order exempt from Sections 5307.3 and 5307.4, and the rulemaking provisions of the Administrative Procedure Act (Chapter 3.5 (commencing with Section 11340) of Part 1 of Division 3 of Title 2 of the Government Code), informing the public of the changes and their effective date. All orders issued pursuant to this subdivision shall be published on the Internet Web site of the Division of Workers' Compensation.

(c) The administrative director shall establish an independent pharmacy and therapeutics committee to review and consult with the administrative director on available evidence of the relative safety, efficacy, and effectiveness of drugs within a class of drugs in the updating of an evidence-based drug formulary, as required by Section 5307.27.

(1) The committee shall consist of six members and the Executive Medical Director of the Division of Workers' Compensation. The committee shall consist of medical doctors or doctors of osteopathy holding a physician and surgeon license pursuant to Chapter 5 (commencing with Section 2000) of Division 2 of the Business and Professions Code, and pharmacists licensed pursuant to Chapter 9 (commencing with Section 4000) of Division 2 of the Business and Professions Code. A committee member shall have knowledge or expertise in one or more of the following:

(A) Clinically appropriate prescribing of covered drugs.

(B) Clinically appropriate dispensing and monitoring of covered drugs.

(C) Drug use review.

(D) Evidence-based medicine.

(2) Committee members shall not be employed by a pharmaceutical manufacturer, a pharmacy benefits management company, or a company engaged in the development of a pharmaceutical formulary for commercial sale during his or her term, and shall not have been so employed for 12 months prior to his or her appointment.

(3) A committee member shall not have a substantial financial conflict of interest pursuant to standards established by the administrative director. The administrative director may, in his or her sole discretion, disqualify a potential or current member of the committee if the administrative director determines that a substantial conflict of interest exists.

(4) A committee member shall agree to keep all proprietary information confidential to the extent required by existing law. **Leg.H.** 2015 ch. 525 (AB 1124) §6.

§5307.3. Administrative director's powers; changing regulations.

The administrative director may adopt, amend, or repeal any rules and regulations that are reasonably necessary to enforce this division, except where this power is specifically reserved to the appeals board.

No rule or regulation of the administrative director pursuant to this section shall be adopted, amended, or rescinded without public hearings. Any written request filed with the administrative director seeking a change in its rules or regulations shall be deemed to be denied if not set by the administrative director for public hearing to be held within six months of the date on which the request is received by the administrative director. **Leg.H.** 2003 ch. 639 (SB 228), 2011 ch. 559 (AB 1426) §12, effective October 7, 2011.

1989 Note: This section is applicable only to injuries occurring on or after January 1, 1990. Stats. 1989 ch. 893 §6.

Ref.: 8 C.C.R. §§10.5, 9900; Herlick Handbook § 1.01[3][b].

§5307.4. Public hearings.

(a) Public hearings required under Section 5307 and 5307.3 shall be subject to the provisions of this section

Labor

except to the extent that there is involved a matter relating to the management, or to personnel, or to public property, loans, grants, benefits, or to contracts, of the appeals board or the administrative director.

(b) Notice of the rule of regulation proposed to be adopted, amended, or rescinded, shall be given to such business and labor organizations and firms or individuals who have requested notice thereof. The notice shall include all the following:

(1) A statement of the time, place, and nature of the public hearings.

(2) Reference to the legal authority under which the rule is proposed.

(3) Either the terms or substance of the proposed rule, or a description of the subjects and the issues involved.

(c) Except where the proposed rule or regulation has a significant impact on the public, this section shall not apply to interpretive rules, general statements of policy, or rules of agency organization.

(d) After notice required by this section, the appeals board or the administrative director shall give interested persons the opportunity to participate in the rulemaking through submission of written data, views, or arguments, with opportunity for oral presentation. If, after consideration of the relevant matter presented, the appeals board or the administrative director adopts a rule, it or he shall publish a concise, general statement of reasons for the adoption of the rule. The rule and statement of reasons shall be given to the same individuals and organizations who have requested notice of hearings.

(e) The notice required under this section shall be made not less than 30 days prior to the public hearing date.

Ref.: 8 C.C.R. §§10.5, 10300; Hanna §§ 1.11[4], 1.12[6], 23.10[3].

§5307.5. Appeals board or workers' compensation judge's powers.

The appeals board or a workers' compensation judge may:

(a) Appoint a trustee or guardian ad litem to appear for and represent any minor or incompetent upon the terms and conditions which it deems proper. The guardian or trustee shall, if required by the appeals board, give a bond in the form and of the character required by law from a guardian appointed by a superior court and in the amount which the appeals board determines. The bond shall be approved by the appeals board, and the guardian or trustee shall not be discharged from the liability until he or she files an account with the appeals board or with the superior court and the account is approved. The trustee or guardian shall receive the compensation for his or her services fixed and allowed by the appeals board or by the superior court.

(b) Provide for the joinder in the same proceeding of all persons interested therein, whether as employer, insurer, employee, dependent, creditor, or otherwise.

Ref.: 8 C.C.R. §§10360, 10364, 10380, 10402, 10570, 10718; Hanna § 1.11[4]; Herlick Handbook § 14.11.

§5307.6. Director to adopt fee schedule for medical-legal expenses.

(a) The administrative director shall adopt and revise a fee schedule for medical-legal expenses as defined by Section 4620, which shall be prima facie evidence of the reasonableness of fees charged for medical-legal expenses at the same time he or she adopts and revises the medical fee schedule pursuant to Section 5307.1.

The schedule shall consist of a series of procedure codes, relative values, and a conversion factor producing fees which provide remuneration to physicians performing medical-legal evaluations at a level equivalent to that provided to physicians for reasonably comparable work, and which additionally recognizes the relative complexity of various types of evaluations, the amount of time spent by the physician in direct contact with the patient, and the need to prepare a written report.

(b) A provider shall not be paid fees in excess of those set forth in the fee schedule established under this section unless the provider provides an itemization and explanation of the fee that shows that it is both a reasonable fee and that extraordinary circumstances relating to the medical condition being evaluated justify a higher fee; provided, however, that in no event shall a provider charge in excess of his or her usual fee. The employer and employee shall have standing to contest fees in excess of those set forth in the fee schedule.

(c) In the event of a dispute between the provider and the employer, employee, or carrier concerning the fees charged, the provider may be allowed a reasonable fee for testimony if the provider testified pursuant to the employer's or carrier's subpoena and the judge or referee determines that the fee charged was reasonable and justified by extraordinary circumstances.

(d)(1) No provider may request nor accept any compensation, including, but not limited to, any kind of remuneration, discount, rebate, refund, dividend, distribution, subsidy, or other form of direct or indirect payment, whether in money or otherwise, from any source for medical-legal expenses if such compensation is in addition to the fees authorized by this section. In addition to being subject to discipline pursuant to the provisions of subdivision (k) of Section 139.2, any provider violating this subdivision is subject to disciplinary action by the appropriate licensing board.

(2) This subdivision does not apply to medical-legal expenses for which the administrative director has not adopted a fee schedule. **Leg.H.** 1993 ch. 4, effective April 3, 1993, ch. 121, effective July 16, 1993, ch. 1242.

1993 Note: Section 5307.6, as amended by ch. 121, applies only to injuries occurring on or after January 1, 1994. Stats. 1993 ch. 121 §77.

Ref.: 8 C.C.R. §§9793, 9794, 9795; Hanna § 5.04[2][b], [c].

§5307.7. Vocational expert fees.

(a) On or before January 1, 2013, the administrative director shall adopt, after public hearings, a fee schedule that shall establish reasonable fees paid for services provided by vocational experts, including, but not limited to, vocational evaluations and expert testimony determined to be reasonable, actual, and necessary by the appeals board.

(b) A vocational expert shall not be paid, and the appeals board shall not allow, vocational expert fees in excess of those that are reasonable, actual, and necessary, or that are not consistent with the fee schedule adopted by the administrative director. **Leg.H.** 2011 ch. 555 (AB 1168) §1, 2012 ch. 363 (SB 863) §75.

2012 Note: For legislative findings, declarations, and applicability of Stats. 2012 ch. 363, see the 2012 Notes following Lab C §62.5.

Ref.: Hanna § 23.13[2][a]; Herlick Handbook § 4.17[2].

§5307.8. Schedule of fees for services not covered by Medicare or by Section 5307.1.

(a) Notwithstanding Section 5307.1, the administrative director shall adopt, after public hearings, a schedule for payment of home health care services provided in accordance with Section 4600 that are not covered by a Medicare fee schedule and are not otherwise covered by the official medical fee schedule adopted pursuant to Section 5307.1. The schedule shall set forth fees and requirements for service providers, and may be based upon, but is not limited to, being based upon, either of the following:

(1) The maximum service hours and fees as set forth in regulations adopted pursuant to Article 7 (commencing with Section 12300) of Chapter 3 of Part 3 of Division 9 of the Welfare and Institutions Code.

(2) A state or federal home health care services fee schedule other than the schedule described in paragraph (1), including a fee schedule authorized for purposes of the Medi-Cal program or a fee schedule administered by the federal Office of Workers' Compensation Programs.

(b) Fees shall not be provided for any services, including any services provided by a member of the employee's household, to the extent the services had been regularly performed in the same manner and to the same degree prior to the date of injury. If appropriate, attorney's fees for recovery of home health care services fees under this section may be awarded in accordance with Section 4906 and any applicable rules or regulations. **Leg.H.** 2012 ch. 363 (SB 863) §76, 2015 ch. 542 (SB 542) §5.

2012 Note: For legislative findings, declarations, and applicability of Stats. 2012 ch. 363, see the 2012 Notes following Lab C §62.5.

Ref.: Hanna § 5.04[6][b]; Herlick Handbook §§ 4.06[3], 4.17[2].

§5307.9. Schedule of fees for copy and related services.

On or before December 31, 2013, the administrative director, in consultation with the Commission on Health and Safety and Workers' Compensation, shall adopt, after public hearings, a schedule of reasonable maximum fees payable for copy and related services, including, but not limited to, records or documents that have been reproduced or recorded in paper, electronic, film, digital, or other format. The schedule shall specify the services allowed and shall require specificity in billing for these services, and shall not allow for payment for services provided within 30 days of a request by an injured worker or his or her authorized representative to an employer, claims administrator, or workers' compensation insurer for copies of records in the employer's, claims administrator's, or workers' compensation insurer's possession that are relevant to the employee's claim. The schedule shall be applicable regardless of whether payments of copy service costs are claimed under the authority of Section 4600, 4620, or 5811, or any other authority except a contract between the employer and the copy service provider. **Leg.H.** 2012 ch. 363 (SB 863) §77.

2012 Note: For legislative findings, declarations, and applicability of Stats. 2012 ch. 363, see the 2012 Notes following Lab C §62.5.

Ref.: Hanna § 27.01[8][a], [b]; Herlick Handbook §§ 4.17[2], 14.42.

§5308. Appeals board jurisdiction over insurance controversies involving self-employed persons.

The appeals board has jurisdiction to determine controversies arising out of insurance policies issued to self-employing persons, conferring benefits identical with those prescribed by this division.

The appeals board may try and determine matters referred to it by the parties under the provisions of Title 9 (commencing with Section 1280) of Part 3 of the Code of Civil Procedure, with respect to controversies arising out of insurance issued to self-employing persons under the provisions of this division. Such controversies may be submitted to it by the signed agreement of the parties, or by the application of one party and the submission of the other to its jurisdiction, with or without an express request for arbitration.

The State Compensation Insurance Fund, when the consent of the other party is obtained, shall submit to the appeals board all controversies susceptible of being arbitrated under this section.

In acting as arbitrator under this section, the appeals board has all the powers which it may lawfully exercise in compensation cases, and its findings and award upon such arbitration have the same conclusiveness and are subject to the same mode or reopening, review, and enforcement as in compensation cases. No fee or cost shall be charged by the appeals board for arbitrating the issues presented under this section.

Ref.: Hanna § 21.07[2]; Herlick Handbook § 1.01[2].

§5309. Appeals board power over workers' compensation judge.

The appeals board may, in accordance with rules of practice and procedure which it shall adopt and upon the agreement of the parties, on the application of either, or of its own motion, and with or without notice, direct and order a workers' compensation judge:

(a) To try the issues in any proceeding before it, whether of fact or of law, and make and file a finding, order, decision, or award based thereon.

(b) To hold hearings and ascertain facts necessary to enable the appeals board to determine any proceeding or to make any order, decision, or award that the appeals board is authorized to make under Divisions 4 or 5, or necessary for the information of the appeals board.

(c) To issue writs or summons, warrants of attachment, warrants of commitment, and all necessary process in proceedings for direct and hybrid contempt in a like manner and to the same extent as courts of record. For the purposes of this section, "hybrid contempt" means a charge of contempt which arises from events occurring in the immediate presence of the workers' compensation judge for reasons which occur outside the presence of the workers' compensation judge.

Ref.: 8 C.C.R. §§10302, 10346, 10347, 10348, 10349, 10350, 10351, 10352, 10858, 10862; Herlick Handbook §§ 1.01[2], 14.5.

§5310. Workers' compensation administrative law judges appointed by appeals board or administrative director.

The appeals board may appoint one or more workers' compensation administrative law judges in any proceeding, as it may deem necessary or advisable, and may refer, remove to itself, or transfer to a workers' compensation administrative law judge the proceedings on any claim. The administrative director may appoint workers' compensation administrative law judges. Any workers' compensation administrative law judge appointed by the administrative director has the powers, jurisdiction, and authority granted by law, by the order of appointment, and by the rules of the appeals board. **Leg.H.** 2002 ch. 6 (AB 749), 2011 ch. 559 (AB 1426) §13, effective October 7, 2011.

Ref.: 8 C.C.R. §§10302, 10346, 10347, 10348, 10349, 10350, 10351, 10352, 10417, 10420, 10452, 10453, 10454, 10591, 10843, 10850; Herlick Handbook §§ 14.32, 15.3, 15.5.

§5311. Objections to particular workers' compensation judges.

Any party to the proceeding may object to the reference of the proceeding to a particular workers' compensation judge upon any one or more of the grounds specified in Section 641 of the Code of Civil Procedure and the objection shall be heard and disposed of by the appeals board. Affidavits may be read and witnesses examined as to the objections.

Ref.: 8 C.C.R. §§10340, 10347, 10417, 10452, 10453, 10850; Herlick Handbook § 14.19.

§5311.5. Requirement that workers' compensation administrative law judges participate in continuing education.

The administrative director shall require all workers' compensation administrative law judges to participate in continuing education to further their abilities as workers' compensation administrative law judges, including courses in ethics and conflict of interest. The director may coordinate the requirements with those imposed upon attorneys by the State Bar in order that the requirements may be consistent. **Leg.H.** 1993 ch. 483, effective September 27, 1993, 2002 ch. 6 (AB 749), 2011 ch. 559 (AB 1426) §14, effective October 7, 2011.

§5312. Swearing in of workers' compensation judge.

Before entering upon his or her duties, the workers' compensation judge shall be sworn, before an officer authorized to administer oaths, faithfully and fairly to hear and determine the matters and issues referred to him or her, to make just findings and to report according to his or her understanding.

Ref.: 8 C.C.R. §10302.

§5313. Decisions of appeals board or workers' compensation judge.

The appeals board or the workers' compensation judge shall, within 30 days after the case is submitted, make and file findings upon all facts involved in the controversy and an award, order, or decision stating the determination as to the rights of the parties. Together with the findings, decision, order or award there shall be served upon all the parties to the proceedings a summary of the evidence received and relied upon and the reasons or grounds upon which the determination was made.

Ref.: 8 C.C.R. §§9710, 9711, 9712, 9713, 9714, 9714.5, 9715, 10566, 10862; Hanna §§ 22.06[9], 24.11[2], 26.08, 27.01[1][b], 31.14[4]; Herlick Handbook §§ 10.09[2], 14.5, 14.28.

§5315. Time limits for appeals board to act on decision of workers' compensation judge.

Within 60 days after the filing of the findings, decision, order or award, the appeals board may confirm, adopt, modify or set aside the findings, order, decision, or award of a workers' compensation judge and may, with or without further proceedings, and with or without notice, enter its order, findings, decision, or award based upon the record in the case.

Ref.: Herlick Handbook § 15.5.

§5316. Method of service.

Any notice, order, or decision required by this division to be served upon any person either before, during, or after the institution of any proceeding before the appeals board, may be served in the manner provided by Chapter 5, Title 14 of Part 2 of the Code of Civil Procedure, unless otherwise directed by the appeals board. In the latter event the document shall be served in accordance with the order or direction of the appeals board. The appeals board may, in the cases mentioned in the Code of Civil Procedure, order service to be made by publication of notice of time and place of hearing. Where service is ordered to be made by publication the date of the hearing may be fixed at more than 30 days from the date of filing the application.

Ref.: 8 C.C.R. §§10380, 10400, 10417, 10500, 10505, 10506, 10507, 10510, 10514, 10520, 10590, 10591, 10592.

§5317. Service of public official.

Any such notice, order or decision affecting the State or any county, city, school district, or public corporation therein, shall be served upon the person upon whom the service of similar notices, orders, or decisions is authorized by law.

CHAPTER 2 LIMITATIONS OF PROCEEDINGS

§5400. Time limits for notice of injury.

Except as provided by sections 5402 and 5403, no claim to recover compensation under this division shall be maintained unless within thirty days after the occurrence of the injury which is claimed to have caused the disability or death, there is served upon the employer notice in writing, signed by the person injured or someone in his behalf, or in case of the death of the person injured, by a dependent or someone in the dependent's behalf.

Ref.: 8 C.C.R. §9770; Hanna §§ 24.01[1], 24.04[6], 25.03[1]; Herlick Handbook §§ 4.02[1], 8.17, 8.21, 9.4, 14.2.

§5401. Claim form and notice of potential eligibility for benefits; form and content; when and where to file claim form.

(a) Within one working day of receiving notice or knowledge of injury under Section 5400 or 5402, which injury results in lost time beyond the employee's work shift at the time of injury or which results in medical treatment beyond first aid, the employer shall provide, personally or by first-class mail, a claim form and a notice of potential eligibility for benefits under this division to the injured employee, or in the case of death, to his or her dependents. As used in this subdivision, "first aid" means any one-time treatment, and any followup visit for the purpose of observation of minor scratches, cuts, burns, splinters, or other minor industrial injury, which do not ordinarily require medical care. This one-time treatment, and followup visit for the purpose of observation, is considered first aid even though provided by a physician or registered professional personnel. "Minor industrial injury" shall not include serious exposure to a hazardous substance as defined in subdivision (i) of Section 6302. The claim form shall request the injured employee's name and address, social security number, the time and address where the injury occurred, and the nature of and part of the body affected by the injury. Claim forms shall be available at district offices of the Employment Development Department and the division. Claim forms may be made available to the employee from any other source.

(b) Insofar as practicable, the notice of potential eligibility for benefits required by this section and the claim form shall be a single document and shall instruct the injured employee to fully read the notice of potential eligibility. The form and content of the notice and claim form shall be prescribed by the administrative director after consultation with the Commission on Health and Safety and Workers' Compensation. The notice shall be easily understandable and available in both English and Spanish. The content shall include, but not be limited to, the following:

(1) The procedure to be used to commence proceedings for the collection of compensation for the purposes of this chapter.

(2) A description of the different types of workers' compensation benefits.

(3) What happens to the claim form after it is filed.

(4) From whom the employee can obtain medical care for the injury.

(5) The role and function of the primary treating physician.

(6) The rights of an employee to select and change the treating physician pursuant to subdivision (e) of Section 3550 and Section 4600.

(7) How to get medical care while the claim is pending.

(8) The protections against discrimination provided pursuant to Section 132a.

(9) The following written statements:

(A) You have a right to disagree with decisions affecting your claim.

(B) To obtain important information about the workers' compensation claims process and your rights and obligations, go to [applicable Internet Web site(s)], or contact an information and assistance (I&A) officer of the state Division of Workers' Compensation. You can also hear recorded information and a list of local I&A offices by calling [applicable information and assistance telephone number(s)].

(C) You can consult an attorney. Most attorneys offer one free consultation. If you decide to hire an attorney, his or her fee will be taken out of some of your benefits. For names of workers' compensation attorneys, call the State Bar of California at [telephone number of the State Bar of California's legal specialization program, or its equivalent].

(c) The completed claim form shall be filed with the employer by the injured employee, or, in the case of death, by a dependent of the injured employee, or by an agent of the employee or dependent. Except as provided in subdivision (d), a claim form is deemed filed when it is personally delivered to the employer or received by the employer by first-class or certified mail. A dated copy of the completed form shall be provided by the employer to the employer's insurer and to the employee, dependent, or agent who filed the claim form.

(d) The claim form shall be filed with the employer prior to the injured employee's entitlement to late payment supplements under subdivision (d) of Section 4650, or prior to the injured employee's request for a medical evaluation under Section 4060, 4061, or 4062. Filing of the claim form with the employer shall toll, for injuries occurring on or after January 1, 1994, the time limitations set forth in Sections 5405 and 5406 until the claim is denied by the employer or the injury becomes presumptively compensable pursuant to Section 5402. For purposes of this subdivision, a claim form is deemed filed when it is personally delivered to the employer or mailed to the employer by first-class or certified mail. **Leg.H.** 1993 ch. 121, effective July 16, 1993, ch. 1242, 1994 ch. 1118, 2002 ch. 6 (AB 749), 2011 ch. 544 (AB 335) §6.

1993 Note: Section 5401, as amended by ch. 121, applies only to injuries occurring on or after January 1, 1994. Stats. 1993 ch. 121 §77.

1989 Note: This section is applicable only to injuries occurring on or after January 1, 1990. Stats. 1989 ch. 893 §6.

Ref.: 8 C.C.R. §§9767.6, 9770, 10101, 10101.1, 10102, 10103, 10103.1, 10103.2, 10111, 10111.1, 10111.2, 10116, 10116.1, 10117.1, 10118.1, 10119, 10120, 10121, 10430, 10530, 14001, 14005; Hanna §§ 22.05[4], 24.01[1], 25.20[2]; Herlick Handbook §§ 4.04[3], [4], 4.18[1], 6.10[2], 7.3, 8.26, 14.2.

§5401.7. Statement required on claim form; optional statements.

The claim form shall contain, prominently stated, the following statement:

"Any person who makes or causes to be made any knowingly false or fraudulent material statement or material representation for the purpose of obtaining or denying workers' compensation benefits or payments is guilty of a felony."

The statements required to be printed or displayed pursuant to Sections 1871.2 and 1879.2 of the Insurance Code may, but are not required to, appear on the claim form. **Leg.H.** 1991 chs. 116, 934, 1993 ch. 121, effective July 16, 1993, 1997 ch. 346.

1993 Note: Section 5401.7, as amended by ch. 121, applies only to injuries occurring on or after January 1, 1994. Stats. 1993 ch. 121 §77.

Ref.: 8 C.C.R. §§10116, 10117.1, 10118.1, 10120, 10121, 14005, 14006, 14007; Herlick Handbook §§ 9.18, 14.2.

§5402. Employer's knowledge equivalent to notice; employer's notice to employee or employee's dependents.

(a) Knowledge of an injury, obtained from any source, on the part of an employer, his or her managing agent, superintendent, foreman, or other person in authority, or knowledge of the assertion of a claim of injury sufficient to afford opportunity to the employer to make an investigation into the facts, is equivalent to service under Section 5400.

(b) If liability is not rejected within 90 days after the date the claim form is filed under Section 5401, the injury shall be presumed compensable under this division. The presumption of this subdivision is rebuttable only by evidence discovered subsequent to the 90-day period.

(c) Within one working day after an employee files a claim form under Section 5401, the employer shall authorize the provision of all treatment, consistent with Section 5307.27, for the alleged injury and shall continue to provide the treatment until the date that liability for the claim is accepted or rejected. Until the date the claim is accepted or rejected, liability for medical treatment shall be limited to ten thousand dollars ($10,000).

(d) Treatment provided under subdivision (c) shall not give rise to a presumption of liability on the part of the employer. **Leg.H.** 1990 ch. 1550, 2000 ch. 883, 2004 ch. 34 (SB 899), effective April 19, 2004, 2012 ch. 363 (SB 863) §79.

2012 Note: For legislative findings, declarations, and applicability of Stats. 2012 ch. 363, see the 2012 Notes following Lab C §62.5.

2004 Note: The amendment to §5402 made by this act shall apply prospectively from the date of enactment of this act, regardless of the date of injury, unless otherwise specified, but shall not constitute good cause to reopen or rescind, alter, or amend any existing order, decision, or award of the Workers' Compensation Appeals Board. Stats. 2004 ch. 34 (SB 899) §47.

1989 Note: This section is applicable only to injuries occurring on or after January 1, 1990. Stats. 1989 ch. 893 §6.

Ref.: 8 C.C.R. §§9770, 9793, 9812, 9813, 9815, 9884, 10100, 10100.1, 10100.2, 10109, 10111, 10111.1, 10111.2, 10116, 10117.1, 10118.1, 10119, 10120; Hanna §§ 4.02[3][d], 5.05[3][a], 24.01[1], [4], 25.03[2], 25.20[2], [4]; Herlick Handbook §§ 4.02[1], 4.04[4], [5], 6.10[1], 8.26, 10.02[3], 10.08[1], [3], 14.2, 14.3, 14.7, 14.20, 14.34, 14.40.

§5403. Effect of failure to give notice or of defective notice.

The failure to give notice under section 5400, or any defect or inaccuracy in a notice is not a bar to recovery under this division if it is found as a fact in the proceedings for the collection of the claim that the employer was not in fact misled or prejudiced by such failure.

Ref.: Herlick Handbook § 9.4.

§5404. Barring of untimely claims; further claims barred by timely filing.

Unless compensation is paid within the time limited in this chapter for the institution of proceedings for its collection, the right to institute such proceedings is barred. The timely filing of an application with the appeals board by any party in interest for any part of the compensation defined by Section 3207 renders this chapter inoperative as to all further claims by such party against the defendants therein named for compensation arising from that injury, and the right to present such further claims is governed by Sections 5803 to 5805, inclusive.

Ref.: Hanna §§ 24.02[2], 35.50[2]; Herlick Handbook §§ 14.7–14.9.

§5404.5. Dismissal of claims with no activity for 180 days.

(a) Where a claim form has been filed prior to January 1, 1994, and where the claim is denied by the employer, the claim may be dismissed if there has been no activity for the previous 180 days and if the claims adjuster has served notice pursuant to Article 3 (commencing with Section 415.10) of Chapter 4 of Title 5 of the Code of Civil Procedure. The notice shall specify that the claim will be dismissed by operation of law unless an application for adjudication of the claim is filed within 180 days of service of the notice.

(b) Where a claim form has been filed prior to January 1, 1994, and where benefits have been furnished by the employer, the claim may be dismissed if there has been no activity for the previous 180 days and if the claims adjuster has served notice pursuant to Article 3 (commencing with Section 415.10) of Chapter 4 of Title 5 of the Code of Civil Procedure. The notice shall specify that the claim will be dismissed by operation of law unless an application for adjudication of the claim is filed within five years of the date of injury or within one year of the last furnishing of benefits, whichever is later.

(c) The administrative director may adopt rules of practice and procedure consistent with this section.

(d) The provisions of subdivisions (a) and (b) do not limit the jurisdiction of the appeals board.

(e) This section is applicable to injuries occurring before January 1, 1994. **Leg.H.** 1993 ch. 121, effective July 16, 1993, ch. 1242.

Ref.: 8 C.C.R. §§10116, 10120, 10562, 10583; Hanna § 25.20[2]; Herlick Handbook § 14.2.

§5405. Time limits for benefits collection proceedings.

The period within which proceedings may be commenced for the collection of the benefits provided by

Article 2 (commencing with Section 4600) or Article 3 (commencing with Section 4650), or both, of Chapter 2 of Part 2 is one year from any of the following:

(a) The date of injury.

(b) The expiration of any period covered by payment under Article 3 (commencing with Section 4650) of Chapter 2 of Part 2.

(c) The last date on which any benefits provided for in Article 2 (commencing with Section 4600) of Chapter 2 of Part 2 were furnished. **Leg.H.** 2002 ch. 6 (AB 749).

Ref.: 8 C.C.R. §§10102, 10852; Hanna §§ 24.03[1], [3][c], 24.04[2], [3], 31.03[3], 31.05[3]; Herlick Handbook §§ 14.2, 14.7.

§5406. Time limits for commencement of benefits collection proceedings; generally.

(a) Except as provided in Section 5406.5, 5406.6, or 5406.7, the period within which may be commenced proceedings for the collection of the benefits provided by Article 4 (commencing with Section 4700) of Chapter 2 of Part 2 is one year from:

(1) The date of death if death occurs within one year from date of injury.

(2) The date of last furnishing of any benefits under Chapter 2 (commencing with Section 4550) of Part 2, if death occurs more than one year from the date of injury.

(3) The date of death, if death occurs more than one year after the date of injury and compensation benefits have been furnished.

(b) Proceedings shall not be commenced more than one year after the date of death, nor more than 240 weeks from the date of injury. **Leg.H.** 1999 ch. 358, 2014 ch. 15 (AB 1035) §2, 2015 ch. 303 (AB 731) §378.

Ref.: 8 C.C.R. §10852; Hanna §§ 9.01[4], 24.03[5]; Herlick Handbook §§ 7.14, 14.2, 14.7.

§5406.5. Time limits for commencement of benefits collection proceedings; asbestosis.

In the case of the death of an asbestos worker or firefighter from asbestosis, the period within which proceedings may be commenced for the collection of the benefits provided by Article 4 (commencing with Section 4700) of Chapter 2 of Part 2 is one year from the date of death. **Leg.H.** 2003 ch. 831 (AB 149).

Ref.: Hanna § 24.03[5]; Herlick Handbook § 7.4.

§5406.6. Limitations period for claim for workers' compensation benefits for death from HIV-related disease.

(a) In the case of the death of a health care worker, a worker described in Section 3212, or a worker described in Section 830.5 of the Penal Code from an HIV-related disease, the period within which proceedings may be commenced for the collection of benefits provided by Article 4 (commencing with Section 4700) of Chapter 2 of Part 2 is one year from the date of death, providing that one or more of the following events has occurred:

(1) A report of the injury or exposure was made to the employer or to a governmental agency authorized to administer industrial injury claims, within one year of the date of the injury.

(2) The worker has complied with the notice provisions of this chapter and the claim has not been finally determined to be noncompensable.

(3) The employer provided, or was ordered to provide, workers' compensation benefits for the injury prior to the date of death.

(b) For the purposes of this section, "health care worker" means an employee who has direct contact, in the course of his or her employment, with blood or other bodily fluids contaminated with blood, or with other bodily fluids identified by the Division of Occupational Safety and Health as capable of transmitting HIV, who is either (1) any person who is an employee of a provider of health care, as defined in Section 56.05 of the Civil Code, including, but not limited to, a registered nurse, licensed vocational nurse, certified nurse aide, clinical laboratory technologist, dental hygienist, physician, janitor, or housekeeping worker, or (2) an employee who provides direct patient care. **Leg.H.** 1999 ch. 358, 2013 ch. 444 (SB 138) §21.

Ref.: Hanna §§ 9.01[4], 24.03[5].

§5406.7. Limitations period for commencement of proceedings to collect dependency death benefits.

(a) In addition to the timelines established pursuant to Section 5406, proceedings for the collection of the benefits provided by Article 4 (commencing with Section 4700) of Chapter 2 of Part 2 may be commenced after 240 weeks from the date of injury and no later than 420 weeks from the date of injury, but in no event more than one year after the date of death, if all of the following criteria are met:

(1) The proceedings are brought for the collection of benefits by, or on behalf of, a person who was a dependent on the date of death. The extent of dependency shall be determined in accordance with the facts as they existed at the time of death of the employee.

(2) The injury causing death is one of the following:

(A) An injury as defined in Section 3212.1 to a person described in Section 3212.1.

(B) An injury as defined in Section 3212.6 to a person described in Section 3212.6.

(C) An injury as defined in Section 3212.8 to a person described in Section 3212.8.

(3) The date of injury is during the person's active service in applicable capacities described in Section 3212.1, 3212.6, or 3212.8.

(b) This section does not apply to claims for the collection of benefits pursuant to Article 4 (commencing with Section 4700) of Chapter 2 of Part 2 that have already been adjudicated, or otherwise finalized, or for which the commencement period lapsed on or before December 31, 2014.

(c) No dependency death benefit shall be payable pursuant to proceedings commenced more than 240 weeks from the date of injury unless either no proceedings were commenced within 240 weeks from the date of injury, or, if proceedings were commenced within that period, it has been finally determined that no person is entitled to dependency death benefits pursuant to the proceedings that were commenced within that period. **Leg.H.** 2014 ch. 15 (AB 1035) §3, 2018 ch. 734 (SB 1086) §2.

2014 Note: It is the intent of the Legislature that the Administrative Director of the Division of Workers' Compensation collect data pursuant to subdivision (a) of Section 3702.2 of the Labor Code for the purpose of determining whether the extended statute of limitations established by this act provides an adequate timeline for the families of fallen firefighters and peace officers to commence proceedings for the collection of death benefits as provided for in this act, such that the Legislature and the Governor, when considering any extension of the date of repeal of Section 5406.7 of the Labor Code, be informed of the facts surrounding the mortality rate of public safety officers who succumb to these job-related diseases. Stats. 2014 ch. 15 (AB 1035) §1; Stats. 2015 ch. 303 (AB 731) §642.

Ref.: Hanna § 9.01[4]; Herlick Handbook § 7.14.

§5407. Time limits for commencement of compensation collection proceedings in case of misconduct.

The period within which may be commenced proceedings for the collection of compensation on the ground of serious and willful misconduct of the employer, under provision of Section 4553, is as follows:

Twelve months from the date of injury. This period shall not be extended by payment of compensation, agreement therefor, or the filing of application for compensation benefits under other provisions of this division.

Ref.: Herlick Handbook § 14.7.

§5407.5. Time limits for commencement of compensation reduction proceedings in case of employee misconduct.

The period within which may be commenced proceedings for the reduction of compensation on the ground of serious and willful misconduct of the employee, under provisions of Section 4551, is as follows:

Twelve months from the date of injury. However, this limitation shall not apply in any case where the employee has commenced proceedings for the increase of compensation on the ground of serious and willful misconduct of the employer.

Ref.: Herlick Handbook § 14.7.

§5408. Guardian/conservator to exercise minor's or incompetent's rights.

If an injured employee or, in the case of the employee's death, any of the employee's dependents, is under 18 years of age or incompetent at any time when any right or privilege accrues to such employee or dependent under this division, a guardian or conservator of the estate, appointed by the court, or a guardian ad litem or trustee appointed by the appeals board may, on behalf of the employee or dependent, claim and exercise any right or privilege with the same force and effect as if no disability existed.

No limitation of time provided by this division shall run against any person under 18 years of age or any incompetent unless and until a guardian or conservator of the estate or trustee is appointed. The appeals board may determine the fact of the minority or incompetency of any injured employee and may appoint a trustee to receive and disburse compensation payments for the benefit of such minor or incompetent and his family.

Ref.: Hanna §§ 9.01[4], 24.03[5], 24.05[1], 31.03[3], 31.21[1]; Herlick Handbook § 14.7.

§5409. Statute of limitations is affirmative defense.

The running of the period of limitations prescribed by this chapter is an affirmative defense and operates to bar the remedy and not to extinguish the right of the employee. Such defense may be waived. Failure to present such defense prior to the submission of the cause for decision is a sufficient waiver.

Ref.: Herlick Handbook §§ 14.7, 14.9, 14.18.

§5410. Time limits; proceedings for aggravated disabilities.

Nothing in this chapter shall bar the right of any injured worker to institute proceedings for the collection of compensation within five years after the date of the injury upon the ground that the original injury has caused new and further disability. The jurisdiction of the appeals board in these cases shall be a continuing jurisdiction within this period. This section does not extend the limitation provided in Section 5407. **Leg.H.** 2014 ch. 217 (AB 2732) §6.

1989 Note: This section is applicable only to injuries occurring on or after January 1, 1990. Stats. 1989 ch. 893 §6.

Ref.: 8 C.C.R. §10133.60; Hanna §§ 8.07[2][d][ii], 24.03[2], [3][c], 24.04[2][a], 31.05[1]–[5]; Herlick Handbook §§ 14.7–14.9.

§5410.1. Attorney's fee for defendant in action to reduce permanent disability benefits.

Should any party to a proceeding institute proceedings to reduce the amount of permanent disability awarded to an applicant by the appeals board and be unsuccessful in such proceeding, the board may make a finding as to the amount of a reasonable attorney's fee incurred by the applicant in resisting such proceeding to reduce permanent disability benefits previously awarded by the appeals board and assess the same as costs upon the party instituting the proceeding for the reduction of permanent disability benefits.

Ref.: Herlick Handbook § 14.19.

§5411. Date of injury.

The date of injury, except in cases of occupational disease or cumulative injury, is that date during the employment on which occurred the alleged incident or exposure, for the consequences of which compensation is claimed.

Ref.: Herlick Handbook §§ 5.2, 8.17, 14.7.

§5412. Date of injury for occupational diseases or cumulative injuries.

The date of injury in cases of occupational diseases or cumulative injuries is that date upon which the employee first suffered disability therefrom and either knew, or in the exercise of reasonable diligence should have known, that such disability was caused by his present or prior employment.

Ref.: Hanna §§ 24.03[4], [7][a], 31.04[3]; Herlick Handbook §§ 6.10[4], 14.7, 14.35.

§5413. Board's findings as having no collateral estoppel effect on subsequent criminal proceedings.

A determination of facts by the appeals board under this chapter has no collateral estoppel effect on a subsequent criminal prosecution and does not preclude litigation of those same facts in the criminal proceeding. **Leg.H.** 1995 ch. 158.

Ref.: Herlick Handbook § 9.18.

CHAPTER 2.3 WORKERS' COMPENSATION— TRUTH IN ADVERTISING

§5430. Title.

This chapter shall be known and may be cited as the Workers' Compensation Truth in Advertising Act of 1992. **Leg.H.** 1992 ch. 904.

Ref.: 8 C.C.R. §§9820, 9821, 9822, 9823, 9824, 9825, 9826, 9827, 9828, 9829, 9830, 9831, 9832, 9833, 9834, 9835, 9836, 9837; Herlick Handbook § 9.18.

§5431. Purpose.

The purpose of this chapter is to assure truthful and adequate disclosure of all material and relevant information in the advertising which solicits persons to file workers' compensation claims or to engage or consult counsel or a medical care provider or clinic to consider a workers' compensation claim. **Leg.H.** 1992 ch. 904.

Ref.: 8 C.C.R. §§9820, 9821, 9822, 9823, 9824, 9825, 9826, 9827, 9828, 9829, 9830, 9831, 9832, 9833, 9834, 9835, 9836, 9837; Hanna § 20.07.

§5432. Notice requirements.

(a) Any advertisement which solicits persons to file workers' compensation claims or to engage or consult counsel or a medical care provider or clinic to consider a workers' compensation claim in any newspaper, magazine, circular, form letter, or open publication, published, distributed, or circulated in this state, or on any billboard, card, label, transit advertisement or other written advertising medium shall state at the top or bottom on the front side or surface of the document in at least 12-point roman boldface type font, except for any billboard which shall be in type whose letters are 12 inches in height or any transit advertisement which shall be in type whose letters are seven inches in height and for any television announcement which shall be in 12-point roman boldface type font and appear in a dark background and remain on the screen for a minimum of five seconds and for any radio announcement which shall be read at an understandable pace with no loud music or sound effects, or both, to compete for the listener's attention, the following:

NOTICE

Making a false or fraudulent workers' compensation claim is a felony subject to up to 5 years in prison or a fine of up to $50,000 or double the value of the fraud, whichever is greater, or by both imprisonment and fine.

(b) Any television or radio announcement published or disseminated in this state which solicits persons to file workers' compensation claims or to engage or consult counsel to consider a workers' compensation claim under this code shall include the following spoken statement by the announcer of the advertisement:

"Making a false or fraudulent workers' compensation claim is a felony subject to up to 5 years in prison or a fine of up to $50,000 or double the value of the fraud, whichever is greater, or by both imprisonment and fine."

(c) This chapter does not supersede or repeal any regulation which governs advertising under this code and those regulations shall continue to be in force in addition to this chapter.

(d) For purposes of subdivisions (a) and (b), the notice or statement shall be written or spoken in English. In those cases where the preponderance of the listening or reading public receives information other than in the English language, the written notice or spoken statement shall be in those other languages. **Leg.H.** 1992 ch. 904.

Ref.: 8 C.C.R. §§9820, 9821, 9822, 9823, 9824, 9825, 9826, 9827, 9828, 9829, 9830, 9831, 9832, 9833, 9834, 9835, 9836, 9837.

§5433. Disclosure requirements.

(a) Any advertisement or other device designed to produce leads based on a response from a person to file a workers' compensation claim or to engage or consult counsel or a medical care provider or clinic shall disclose that an agent may contact the individual if that is the fact. In addition, an individual who makes contact with a person as a result of acquiring that individual's name from a lead generating device shall disclose that fact in the initial contact with that person.

(b) No person shall solicit persons to file a workers' compensation claim or to engage or consult counsel or a medical care provider or clinic to consider a workers' compensation claim through the use of a true or fictitious name which is deceptive or misleading with regard to the status, character, or proprietary or representative capacity of the entity or person, or to the true purpose of the advertisement.

(c) For purposes of this section, an advertisement includes a solicitation in any newspaper, magazine, circular, form letter, or open publication, published, distributed, or circulated in this state, or on any billboard, card, label, transit advertisement, or other written advertising medium, and includes envelopes, stationery, business cards, or other material designed to encourage the filing of a workers' compensation claim.

(d) Advertisements shall not employ words, initials, letters, symbols, or other devices which are so similar to those used by governmental agencies, a nonprofit or charitable institution, or other entity that they could have the capacity or tendency to mislead the public. Examples of misleading materials include, but are not limited to, those that imply any of the following:

(1) The advertisement is in some way provided by or is endorsed by a governmental agency or charitable institution.

(2) The advertiser is the same as, is connected with, or is endorsed by a governmental agency or charitable institution.

(e) Advertisements may not use the name of a state or political subdivision thereof in an advertising solicitation.

(f) Advertisements may not use any name, service mark, slogan, symbol, or any device in any manner which implies that the advertiser, or any person or entity associated with the advertiser, or that any agency who may call upon the person in response to the advertisement, is connected with a governmental agency.

(g) Advertisements may not imply that the reader, listener, or viewer may lose a right or privilege or benefits under federal, state, or local law if he or she fails to respond to the advertisement. **Leg.H.** 1992 ch. 904, 1998 ch. 485, 1999 ch. 83.

Ref.: 8 C.C.R. §§9820, 9821, 9822, 9823, 9824, 9825, 9826, 9827, 9828, 9829, 9830, 9831, 9832, 9833, 9834, 9835, 9836, 9837; Hanna § 20.07.

§5434. Penalty for violation; "advertiser" defined.

(a) Any advertiser who violates Section 5431 or 5432 is guilty of a misdemeanor.

(b) For the purposes of this chapter, "advertiser" means any person who provides workers' compensation claims services which are described in the written or broadcast advertisements, any person to whom persons solicited by the advertisements are directed to for inquiries or the provision of workers' compensation claims related services, or any person paying for the preparation, broadcast, printing, dissemination, or placement of the advertisements. **Leg.H.** 1992 ch. 904.

Ref.: 8 C.C.R. §§9820, 9821, 9822, 9823, 9824, 9825, 9826, 9827, 9828, 9829, 9830, 9831, 9832, 9833, 9834, 9835, 9836, 9837; Herlick Handbook § 9.18.

CHAPTER 2.5
ADMINISTRATIVE ASSISTANCE

§5450. Assistance from Division of Workers' Compensation.

The Division of Workers' Compensation shall make available to employees, employers and other interested parties information, assistance, and advice to assure the proper and timely furnishing of benefits and to assist in the resolution of disputes on an informal basis. **Leg.H.** 1994 chs. 146, 1097.

Ref.: 8 C.C.R. §§9900, 9922, 9923, 9924, 9925, 9926, 9927, 9928; Herlick Handbook § 1.06.

§5451. Duties of information and assistance officer.

Any party may consult with, or seek the advice of, an information and assistance officer within the Division of Workers' Compensation as designated by the administrative director. If no application is filed, if the employee is not represented, or upon agreement of the parties, the information and assistance officer shall consider the contentions of the parties and may refer the matter to the appropriate bureau or unit within the Division of Workers' Compensation for review and recommendations. The information and assistance officer shall advise the employer and the employee of their rights, benefits, and obligations under this division. Upon making a referral, the information and assistance officer shall arrange for a copy of any pertinent material submitted to be served upon the parties or their representatives, if any. The procedures to be followed by the information and assistance officer shall be governed by the rules and regulations of the administrative director adopted after public hearings. **Leg.H.** 1994 chs. 146, 1097.

Ref.: 8 C.C.R. §§9900, 9922, 9923, 9924, 9925, 9926, 9927, 9928, 9928.1, 10166; Herlick Handbook § 1.06.

§5453. Recommendation of information and assistance officer.

After consideration of the information submitted, including the reports of any bureau or unit within the Division of Workers' Compensation which have been received, the information and assistance officer shall make a recommendation which shall be served on the parties or their representatives, if any. **Leg.H.** 1994 chs. 146, 1097.

Ref.: 8 C.C.R. §§9900, 9922, 9923, 9924, 9925, 9926, 9927, 9928; Herlick Handbook § 1.06.

§5454. Statute of limitations tolled by submission to information and assistance officer.

Submission of any matter to an information and assistance officer of the Division of Workers' Compensation shall toll any applicable statute of limitations for the period that the matter is under consideration by the information and assistance officer, and for 60 days following the issuance of his or her recommendation. **Leg.H.** 1994 chs. 146, 1097.

Ref.: 8 C.C.R. §§9900, 9922, 9923, 9924, 9925, 9926, 9927, 9928; Hanna § 23.03[2][f]; Herlick Handbook § 1.06.

§5455. Application for benefits; admissible evidence.

Nothing in this chapter shall prohibit any party from filing an application for benefits under this division. In any proceeding pursuant to such application, the admissibility of written evidence or reports submitted by any party pursuant to this chapter, or Section 5502, shall be governed by Chapter 5 (commencing with Section 5700).

Ref.: 8 C.C.R. §§9900, 9922, 9923, 9924, 9925, 9926, 9927, 9928; Herlick Handbook § 1.06.

CHAPTER 3
APPLICATIONS AND ANSWERS

§5500. Required pleadings.

No pleadings other than the application and answer shall be required. Both shall be in writing and shall conform to forms prescribed by the appeals board in its rules of practice and procedure, simply but clearly and completely delineating all relevant matters of agreement and all issues of disagreement within the jurisdiction of the appeals board, and providing for the furnishing of any additional information as the appeals board may properly determine necessary to expedite its hearing and determination of the claim.

The amendment of this section made during the 1993 portion of the 1993-94 Regular Session shall apply to all applications filed on or after January 1, 1994.

Notwithstanding Section 5401, except where a claim form has been filed for an injury occurring on or after January 1, 1990, and before January 1, 1994, the filing of an application for adjudication and not the filing of a claim form shall establish the jurisdiction of the appeals board and shall commence proceedings before the appeals board for the collection of benefits. **Leg.H.** 1993 ch. 121, effective July 16, 1993, 1994 ch. 1118.

1993 Note: Section 5500, as amended by ch. 121, applies only to injuries occurring on or after January 1, 1994. Stats. 1993 ch. 121 §77.

1989 Note: This section is applicable only to injuries occurring on or after January 1, 1990. Stats. 1989 ch. 893 §6.

Ref.: 8 C.C.R. §§10353, 10364, 10400, 10401, 10402, 10408, 10480, 10484, 10490, 10878, 10955; Hanna §§ 25.05[1], 25.22[1]; Herlick Handbook §§ 14.2, 14.11.

§5500.3. Uniformity among offices.

(a) The appeals board shall establish uniform district office procedures, uniform forms, and uniform time of court settings for all district offices of the appeals board. No district office of the appeals board or workers' compensation administrative law judge shall require forms or procedures other than as established by the appeals board. A workers' compensation administrative law judge who violates this section may be subject to disciplinary proceedings.

(b) The appeals board shall establish uniform court procedures and uniform forms for all other proceedings of the appeals board. **Leg.H.** 2002 ch. 6 (AB 749), 2011 ch. 559 (AB 1426) §15, effective October 7, 2011.

Ref.: Herlick Handbook § 14.5.

§5500.5. Employers liable for occupational disease or cumulative injury.

(a) Except as otherwise provided in Section 5500.6, liability for occupational disease or cumulative injury claims filed or asserted on or after January 1, 1978, shall be limited to those employers who employed the employee during a period of four years immediately preceding either the date of injury, as determined pursuant to Section 5412, or the last date on which the employee was employed in an occupation exposing him or her to the hazards of the occupational disease or cumulative injury, whichever occurs first. Commencing January 1, 1979, and thereafter on the first day of January for each of the next two years, the liability period for occupational disease or cumulative injury shall be decreased by one year so that liability is limited in the following manner:

For claims filed or asserted on or after:	The period shall be:
January 1, 1979	three years
January 1, 1980	two years
January 1, 1981 and thereafter	one year

In the event that none of the employers during the above referenced periods of occupational disease or cumulative injury are insured for workers' compensation coverage or an approved alternative thereof, liability shall be imposed upon the last year of employment exposing the employee to the hazards of the occupational disease or cumulative injury for which an employer is insured for workers' compensation coverage or an approved alternative thereof.

Any employer held liable for workers' compensation benefits as a result of another employer's failure to secure the payment of compensation as required by this division shall be entitled to reimbursement from the employers who were unlawfully uninsured during the last year of the employee's employment, and shall be subrogated to the rights granted to the employee against the unlawfully uninsured employers under the provisions of Article 1 (commencing with Section 3700) of Chapter 4 of Part 1 of Division 4.

If, based upon all the evidence presented, the appeals board or workers' compensation judge finds the existence of cumulative injury or occupational disease, liability for the cumulative injury or occupational disease shall not be apportioned to prior or subsequent years; however, in determining the liability, evidence of disability due to specific injury, disability due to nonindustrial causes, or disability previously compensated for by way of a findings and award or order approving compromise and release, or a voluntary payment of disability, may be admissible for purposes of apportionment.

(b) Where a claim for compensation benefits is made on account of an occupational disease or cumulative injury which may have arisen out of more than one employment, the application shall state the names and addresses of all employers liable under subdivision (a), the places of employment, and the approximate periods of employment where the employee was exposed to the hazards of the occupational disease or cumulative injury. If the application is not so prepared or omits necessary and proper employers, any interested party, at or prior to the first hearing, may request the appeals board to join as defendant any necessary or proper party. If the request is made prior to the first hearing on the application, the appeals board shall forthwith join the employer as a party defendant and cause a copy of the application together with a notice of the time and place of hearing to be served upon the omitted employer; provided, the notice can be given within the time specified in this division. If the notice cannot be timely given or if the motion for joinder is made at the time of the first hearing, then the appeals board or the workers' compensation judge before whom the hearing is held, if it is found that the omitted employer named is a necessary or proper party, may order a joinder of the party and continue the hearing so that proper notice may be given to the party or parties so joined. Only one continuance shall be allowed for the purpose of joining additional parties. Subsequent to the first hearing the appeals board shall join as a party defendant any additional employer when it appears that the employer is a proper party, but the liability of the employer shall not be determined until supplemental proceedings are instituted.

(c) In any case involving a claim of occupational disease or cumulative injury occurring as a result of more than one employment within the appropriate time period set forth in subdivision (a), the employee making the claim, or his or her dependents, may elect to proceed against any one or more of the employers. Where such an election is made, the employee must successfully prove his or her

Labor

claim against any one of the employers named, and any award which the appeals board shall issue awarding compensation benefits shall be a joint and several award as against any two or more employers who may be held liable for compensation benefits. If, during the pendency of any claim wherein the employee or his or her dependents has made an election to proceed against one or more employers, it should appear that there is another proper party not yet joined, the additional party shall be joined as a defendant by the appeals board on the motion of any party in interest, but the liability of the employer shall not be determined until supplemental proceedings are instituted. Any employer joined as a defendant subsequent to the first hearing or subsequent to the election provided herein shall not be entitled to participate in any of the proceedings prior to the appeal board's final decision, nor to any continuance or further proceedings, but may be permitted to ascertain from the employee or his or her dependents such information as will enable the employer to determine the time, place, and duration of the alleged employment. On supplemental proceedings, however, the right of the employer to full and complete examination or cross-examination shall not be restricted.

(d)(1) In the event a self-insured employer which owns and operates a work location in the State of California, sells or has sold the ownership and operation of the work location pursuant to a sale of a business or all or part of the assets of a business to another self-insured person or entity after January 1, 1974, but before January 1, 1978, and all the requirements of subparagraphs (A) to (D), inclusive, exist, then the liability of the employer-seller and employer-buyer, respectively, for cumulative injuries suffered by employees employed at the work location immediately before the sale shall, until January 1, 1986, be governed by the provisions of this section which were in effect on the date of that sale.

(A) The sale constitutes a material change in ownership of such work location.

(B) The person or entity making the purchase continues the operation of the work location.

(C) The person or entity becomes the employer of substantially all of the employees of the employer-seller.

(D) The agreement of sale makes no special provision for the allocation of liabilities for workers' compensation between the buyer and the seller.

(2) For purposes of this subdivision:

(A) "Work location" shall mean any fixed place of business, office, or plant where employees regularly work in the trade or business of the employer.

(B) A "material change in ownership" shall mean a change in ownership whereby the employer-seller does not retain, directly or indirectly, through one or more corporate entities, associations, trusts, partnerships, joint ventures, or family members, a controlling interest in the work location.

(3) This subdivision shall have no force or effect on or after January 1, 1986, unless otherwise extended by the Legislature prior to that date, and it shall not have any force or effect as respects an employee who, subsequent to the sale described in paragraph (1) and prior to the date of his or her application for compensation benefits has been filed, is transferred to a different work location by the employer-buyer.

(4) If any provision of this subdivision or the application thereof to any person or circumstances is held invalid, that invalidity shall not affect other provisions or applications of this subdivision which can be given effect without the invalid provision or application, and to this end the provisions of this subdivision are severable.

(e) At any time within one year after the appeals board has made an award for compensation benefits in connection with an occupational disease or cumulative injury, any employer held liable under the award may institute proceedings before the appeals board for the purpose of determining an apportionment of liability or right of contribution. The proceeding shall not diminish, restrict, or alter in any way the recovery previously allowed the employee or his or her dependents, but shall be limited to a determination of the respective contribution rights, interest or liabilities of all the employers joined in the proceeding, either initially or supplementally; provided, however, if the appeals board finds on supplemental proceedings for the purpose of determining an apportionment of liability or of a right of contribution that an employer previously held liable in fact has no liability, it may dismiss the employer and amend its original award in such manner as may be required.

(f) In any proceeding before the appeals board for the purpose of determining an apportionment of liability or of a right of contribution where any employee incurred a disability or death resulting from silicosis in underground metal mining operations, the determination of the respective rights and interests of all of the employers joined in the proceedings either initially or supplementally shall be as follows:

(1) All employers whose underground metal mining operations resulted in a silicotic exposure during the period of the employee's employment in those operations shall be jointly and severally liable for the payment of compensation and of medical, surgical, legal and hospital expense which may be awarded to the employee or his or her estate or dependents as the result of disability or death resulting from or aggravated by the exposure.

(2) In making its determination in the supplemental proceeding for the purpose of determining an apportionment of liability or of a right of contribution of percentage liabilities of the various employers engaged in underground metal mining operations the appeals board shall consider as a rebuttable presumption that employment in underground work in any mine for a continuous period of more than three calendar months will result in a silicotic exposure for the employee so employed during the period of employment if the underground metal mine was driven or sunk in rock having a composition which will result in dissemination of silica or silicotic dust particles when drilled, blasted, or transported.

(g) Any employer shall be entitled to rebut the presumption by showing to the satisfaction of the appeals board, or the workers' compensation judge, that the mining methods used by the employer in the employee's place of employment did not result during his or her employment in the creation of silica dust in sufficient amount or concentration to constitute a silicotic hazard. Dust counts, competently made, at intervals and in locations as meet the requirements of the Division of Occupational Safety and Health for safe working conditions may be received as evidence of the amount and concentration of silica dust in the workings where the counts have been made at the time when they were made. The appeals board may from time to time, as its experience may indicate proper, promulgate orders as to the frequency with which dust counts shall be taken in different types of workings in order to justify their acceptance as evidence of the existence or nonexistence of a silicotic hazard in the property where they have been taken.

(h) The amendments to this section adopted at the 1959 Regular Session of the Legislature shall operate retroactively, and shall apply retrospectively to any cases pending before the appeals board or courts. From and after the date this section becomes effective no payment shall be made out of the fund used for payment of the additional compensation provided for in Section 4751, or out of any other state funds, in satisfaction of any liability heretofore incurred or hereafter incurred, except awards which have become final without regard to the continuing jurisdiction of the appeals board on that effective date, and the state and its funds shall be without liability therefor. This subdivision shall not in any way effect a reduction in any benefit conferred or which may be conferred upon any injured employee or his dependents.

(i) The amendments to this section adopted at the 1977 Regular Session of the Legislature shall apply to any claims for benefits under this division which are filed or asserted on or after January 1, 1978, unless otherwise specified in this section.

Ref.: Hanna §§ 8.06[2], 25.05[6], 26.01[2][c], 31.13[2][a]–[d]; Herlick Handbook §§ 6.16, 8.22, 8.23, 8.27, 14.35.

§5500.6. Employers liable for occupational disease or cumulative injury; household employee.

Liability for occupational disease or cumulative injury which results from exposure solely during employment as an employee, as defined in subdivision (d) of Section 3351, shall be limited to those employers in whose employment the employee was exposed to the hazards of the occupational disease or cumulative injury during the last day on which the employee was employed in an occupation exposing the employee to the hazards of the disease or injury. In the event that none of the employers of the last day of hazardous employment is insured for workers' compensation liability, that liability, shall be imposed upon the last employer exposing the employee to the hazards of the occupational disease or cumulative injury who has secured workers' compensation insurance coverage or an approved alternative thereto. If, based upon all the evidence presented, the appeals board or the workers' compensation judge finds the existence of cumulative injury or occupational disease, liability for the cumulative injury or occupational disease shall not be apportioned to prior employers. However, in determining liability, evidence of disability due to specific injury, disability due to non-work-related causes, or disability previously compensated for by way of a findings and award or order approving compromise and release, or a voluntary payment of disability, may be admissible for purposes of apportionment.

§5501. Filing of application; subsequent procedure.

The application may be filed with the appeals board by any party in interest, his attorney, or other representative authorized in writing. A representative who is not an attorney licensed by the State Bar of this state shall notify the appeals board in writing that he or she is not an attorney licensed by the State Bar of this state. Upon the filing of the application, the appeals board shall, where the applicant is represented by an attorney or other representative, serve a conformed copy of the application showing the date of filing and the case number upon applicant's attorney or representative. The applicant's attorney or representative shall, upon receipt of the conformed copy, forthwith serve a copy of the conformed application upon all other parties to the claim. If the applicant is unrepresented, a copy thereof shall forthwith be served upon all adverse parties by the appeals board. **Leg.H.** 1991 ch. 934.

Ref.: Hanna § 23.14[1][b], [2][b]; Herlick Handbook §§ 10.03[2], [7], 10.07, 10.08[3], 10.09[4], 14.11, 14.12.

§5501.5. Where application for adjudication of claim may be filed.

(a) The application for adjudication of claim shall be filed in any of the following locations:

(1) In the county where the injured employee or dependent of a deceased employee resides on the date of filing.

(2) In the county where the injury allegedly occurred, or, in cumulative trauma and industrial disease claims, where the last alleged injurious exposure occurred.

(3) In the county where the employee's attorney maintains his or her principal place of business, if the employee is represented by an attorney.

(b) If the county selected for filing has more than one office of the appeals board, the application shall be filed at any location of the appeals board within that county that meets the criteria specified in subdivision (a). The written consent of the employee, or dependent of a deceased employee, to the selected venue site shall be filed with application.

(c) If the venue site where the application is to be filed is the county where the employee's attorney maintains his or her principal place of business, the attorney for the employee shall indicate that venue site when forwarding the information request form required by Section 5401.5. The employer shall have 30 days from receipt of the information request form to object to the selected venue site. Where there is an employer objection to a venue site under paragraph (3) of subdivision (a), then the application shall be filed pursuant to either paragraph (1) or (2) of subdivision (a).

(d) If there is no appeals board office in the county where venue is permitted under subdivision (a), the application shall be filed at the appeals board office nearest the residence on the date of filing of the injured employee or dependent of a deceased employee, or the nearest place where the injury allegedly occurred, or, in cumulative trauma and industrial disease claims, where the last injurious exposure occurred, or nearest the location where the attorney of the employee maintains his or her principal place of business, unless the employer objects under subdivision (c).

Ref.: 8 C.C.R. §§10408, 10410, 15740; Herlick Handbook §§ 10.02[3], 14.15.

§5501.6. Petition for change of venue.

(a) An applicant or defendant may petition the appeals board for a change of venue and a change of venue shall be granted for good cause. The reasons for the change of venue shall be specifically set forth in the request for change of venue.

(b) If a change of venue is requested for the convenience of witnesses, the names and addresses of these witnesses and the substance of their testimony shall be specifically set forth in the request for change of venue.

Ref.: 8 C.C.R. §§10411, 10412; Hanna § 25.27.

§5502. Time for hearing; priority calendar; mandatory settlement conference.

(a) Except as provided in subdivisions (b) and (d), the hearing shall be held not less than 10 days, and not more than 60 days, after the date a declaration of readiness to proceed, on a form prescribed by the appeals board, is filed. If a claim form has been filed for an injury occurring on or after January 1, 1990, and before January 1, 1994, an application for adjudication shall accompany the declaration of readiness to proceed.

(b) The administrative director shall establish a priority calendar for issues requiring an expedited hearing and decision. A hearing shall be held and a determination as to the rights of the parties shall be made and filed within 30 days after the declaration of readiness to proceed is filed if the issues in dispute are any of the following, provided that if an expedited hearing is requested, no other issue may be heard until the medical provider network dispute is resolved:

(1) The employee's entitlement to medical treatment pursuant to Section 4600, except for treatment issues determined pursuant to Sections 4610 and 4610.5.

(2) Whether the injured employee is required to obtain treatment within a medical provider network.

(3) A medical treatment appointment or medical-legal examination.

(4) The employee's entitlement to, or the amount of, temporary disability indemnity payments.

(5) The employee's entitlement to compensation from one or more responsible employers when two or more employers dispute liability as among themselves.

(6) Any other issues requiring an expedited hearing and determination as prescribed in rules and regulations of the administrative director.

(c) The administrative director shall establish a priority conference calendar for cases in which the employee is represented by an attorney or is or was employed by an illegally uninsured employer and the issues in dispute are employment or injury arising out of employment or in the course of employment. The conference shall be conducted by a workers' compensation administrative law judge within 30 days after the declaration of readiness to proceed. If the dispute cannot be resolved at the conference, a trial shall be set as expeditiously as possible, unless good cause is shown why discovery is not complete, in which case status conferences shall be held at regular intervals. The case shall be set for trial when discovery is complete, or when the workers' compensation administrative law judge determines that the parties have had sufficient time in which to complete reasonable discovery. A determination as to the rights of the parties shall be made and filed within 30 days after the trial.

(d)(1) In all cases, a mandatory settlement conference, except a lien conference or a mandatory settlement lien conference, shall be conducted not less than 10 days, and not more than 30 days, after the filing of a declaration of readiness to proceed. If the dispute is not resolved, the regular hearing, except a lien trial, shall be held within 75 days after the declaration of readiness to proceed is filed.

(2) The settlement conference shall be conducted by a workers' compensation administrative law judge or by a referee who is eligible to be a workers' compensation administrative law judge or eligible to be an arbitrator under Section 5270.5. At the mandatory settlement conference, the referee or workers' compensation administrative law judge shall have the authority to resolve the dispute, including the authority to approve a compromise and release or issue a stipulated finding and award, and if the dispute cannot be resolved, to frame the issues and stipulations for trial. The appeals board shall adopt any regulations needed to implement this subdivision. The presiding workers' compensation administrative law judge shall supervise settlement conference referees in the performance of their judicial functions under this subdivision.

(3) If the claim is not resolved at the mandatory settlement conference, the parties shall file a pretrial conference statement noting the specific issues in dispute, each party's proposed permanent disability rating, and listing the exhibits, and disclosing witnesses. Discovery shall close on the date of the mandatory settlement conference. Evidence not disclosed or obtained thereafter shall not be admissible unless the proponent of the evidence can demonstrate that it was not available or could not have been discovered by the exercise of due diligence prior to the settlement conference.

(e) In cases involving the Director of Industrial Relations in his or her capacity as administrator of the Uninsured Employers Fund, this section shall not apply unless proof of service, as specified in paragraph (1) of subdivision (d) of Section 3716, has been filed with the appeals board and provided to the Director of Industrial Relations, valid jurisdiction has been established over the employer, and the fund has been joined.

(f) Except as provided in subdivision (a), this section shall apply irrespective of the date of injury. **Leg.H.** 1992 ch. 1226, 1993 ch. 121, effective July 16, 1993, 1994 ch. 1118, 2002 chs. 6 (AB 749), 866 (AB 486), 2011 ch. 559 (AB 1426) §16, effective October 7, 2011, 2012 chs. 363 (SB 863) §80, 728 (SB 71) §122 (ch. 363 prevails; ch. 728 not effective), 2013 ch. 76 (AB 383) §144, 2014 chs. 71 (SB 1304) §112, 156 (AB 1746) §1.

2012 Note: For legislative findings, declarations, and applicability of Stats. 2012 ch. 363, see the 2012 Notes following Lab C §62.5.

1993 Note: Section 5502, as amended by ch. 121, applies only to injuries occurring on or after January 1, 1994. Stats. 1993 ch. 121 §77.

1989 Note: This section is applicable only to injuries occurring on or after January 1, 1990. Stats. 1989 ch. 893 §6.

Ref.: 8 C.C.R. §§10136, 10137, 10166, 10353, 10414, 10415, 10417, 10555, 10562, 10563, 10590, 10591, 10601, 10607, 10608; Hanna § 26.04[2]; Herlick Handbook §§ 4.11[4], 10.03[7], 10.04[1], 11.01, 14.8, 14.11, 14.18, 14.20, 14.30, 14.40.

§5502.5. Hearing continuance—Good cause required.

A continuance of any conference or hearing required by Section 5502 shall not be favored, but may be granted by a workers' compensation judge upon any terms as are just upon a showing of good cause. When determining a request for continuance, the workers' compensation judge shall take into consideration the complexity of the issues, the diligence of the parties, and the prejudice incurred on the part of any party by reasons of granting or denying a continuance.

Ref.: 8 C.C.R. §§10353, 10548.

§5503. "Applicant"; "defendant."

The person so applying shall be known as the applicant and the adverse party shall be known as the defendant.

Ref.: 8 C.C.R. §§10360, 10364.

§5504. Service of notice of hearing.

A notice of the time and place of hearing shall be served upon the applicant and all adverse parties and may be served either in the manner of service of a summons in a civil action or in the same manner as any notice that is authorized or required to be served under the provisions of this division.

Ref.: 8 C.C.R. §§10500, 10544.

§5505. Defendant's answer.

If any defendant desires to disclaim any interest in the subject matter of the claim in controversy, or considers that the application is in any respect inaccurate or incomplete, or desires to bring any fact, paper, or document to the attention of the appeals board as a defense to the claim or otherwise, he may, within 10 days after the service of the application upon him, file with or mail to the appeals board his answer in such form as the appeals board may prescribe, setting forth the particulars in which the application is inaccurate or incomplete, and the facts upon which he intends to rely. A copy of the answer shall be forthwith served upon all adverse parties. Evidence upon matters not pleaded by answer shall be allowed only upon the terms and conditions imposed by the appeals board or referee holding the hearing.

Ref.: 8 C.C.R. §§10484, 10544; Herlick Handbook § 14.18.

§5506. Defendant's failure to appear or answer.

If the defendant fails to appear or answer, no default shall be taken against him, but the appeals board shall proceed to the hearing of the matter upon the terms and conditions which it deems proper. A defendant failing to appear or answer, or subsequently contending that no service was made upon him, or claiming to be aggrieved in any other manner by want of notice of the pendency of the proceedings, may apply to the appeals board for relief substantially in accordance with the provisions of Section 473 of the Code of Civil Procedure. The appeals board may afford such relief. No right to relief, including the claim that the findings and award of the appeals board or judgment entered thereon are void upon their face, shall accrue to such defendant in any court unless prior application is made to the appeals board in accordance with this section. In no event shall any petition to any court be allowed except as prescribed in Sections 5950 and 5951.

Ref.: Herlick Handbook § 14.43.

§5507. Dismissal of application without hearing.

If an application shows upon its face that the applicant is not entitled to compensation, the appeals board may, after opportunity to the applicant to be heard orally or to submit his claim or argument in writing dismiss the application without any hearing thereon. Such dismissal may be upon the motion of the appeals board or upon motion of the adverse party. The pendency of such motion or notice of intended dismissal shall not, unless otherwise ordered by the appeals board, delay the hearing on the application upon its merits.

Ref.: 8 C.C.R. §10780; Herlick Handbook § 14.43.

CHAPTER 4 ATTACHMENTS

§5600. Appeals board authority to order writs of attachment.

The appeals board may, upon the filing of an application by or on behalf of an injured employee, the employee's dependents, or any other party in interest, direct the clerk of the superior court of any county to issue writs of attachment authorizing the sheriff to attach the property of the defendant as security for the payment of any compensation which may be awarded in any of the following cases:

(a) In any case mentioned in Section 415.50 of the Code of Civil Procedure.

(b) Where the employer has failed to secure the payment of compensation as required by Article 1 (commencing with Section 3700) of Chapter 4 of Part 1.

The attachment shall be in an amount fixed by the appeals board, not exceeding the greatest probable award against the defendant in the matter. **Leg.H.** 2002 ch. 784 (SB 1316).

§5601. Procedure for attachment proceedings.

The provisions of Title 6.5 (commencing with Section 481.010) of Part 2 of the Code of Civil Procedure, as far as applicable, shall govern the proceedings upon attachment, the appeals board being substituted therein for the proper court.

§5602. Issuance and discharge of attachment.

No writ of attachment shall be issued except upon the order of the appeals board. Such order shall not be made where it appears from the application or affidavit in support thereof that the employer was, at the time of the injury to the employee, insured against liability imposed by this division by any insurer. If, at any time after the levying of an attachment, it appears that such employer was so insured, and the requisites for dismissing the employer from the proceeding and substituting the insurer as defendant under any method prescribed by this division are established, the appeals board shall forthwith discharge the attachment.

§5603. Preference when attachments levied.

In levying attachments preference shall be given to the real property of the employer.

CHAPTER 5 HEARINGS

§5700. Adjournment of hearing; parties permitted at hearing.

The hearing on the application may be adjourned from time to time and from place to place in the discretion of the appeals board or the workers' compensation judge holding the hearing. Any hearing adjourned by the workers' compensation judge shall be continued to be heard by and shall be concluded and the decision made by the workers' compensation judge who previously heard it. Either party may be present at any hearing, in person, by attorney, or by any other agent, and may present testimony pertinent under the pleadings.

Ref.: Herlick Handbook §§ 10.09[4], 14.5.

§5701. Appeals board authority to take testimony or direct examination.

The appeals board may, with or without notice to either party, cause testimony to be taken, or inspection of the premises where the injury occurred to be made, or the timebooks and payroll of the employer to be examined by any member of the board or a workers' compensation judge appointed by the appeals board. The appeals board may also from time to time direct any employee claiming compensation to be examined by a regular physician. The testimony so taken and the results of any inspection or examination shall be reported to the appeals board for its consideration.

Ref.: 8 C.C.R. §§10156, 10166, 10718; Herlick Handbook §§ 4.13, 14.22, 14.40.

§5702. Stipulations.

The parties to a controversy may stipulate the facts relative thereto in writing and file such stipulation with the appeals board. The appeals board may thereupon make its findings and award based upon such stipulation, or may set the matter down for hearing and take further testimony or make the further investigation necessary to enable it to determine the matter in controversy.

Ref.: 8 C.C.R. §§10492, 10496, 10497, 10578, 10878, 10882, 10888, 10890; Hanna §§ 23.11[3], 26.06[2]; Herlick Handbook § 14.44.

§5703. Specified additional evidence allowed.

The appeals board may receive as evidence either at or subsequent to a hearing, and use as proof of any fact in dispute, the following matters, in addition to sworn testimony presented in open hearing:

(a) Reports of attending or examining physicians.

(1) Statements concerning any bill for services are admissible only if made under penalty of perjury that they are true and correct to the best knowledge of the physician.

(2) In addition, reports are admissible under this subdivision only if the physician has further stated in the body of the report that there has not been a violation of Section 139.3 and that the contents of the report are true and correct to the best knowledge of the physician. The statement shall be made under penalty of perjury.

(b) Reports of special investigators appointed by the appeals board or a workers' compensation judge to investigate and report upon any scientific or medical question.

(c) Reports of employers, containing copies of timesheets, book accounts, reports, and other records properly authenticated.

(d) Properly authenticated copies of hospital records of the case of the injured employee.

(e) All publications of the Division of Workers' Compensation.

(f) All official publications of the State of California and United States governments.

(g) Excerpts from expert testimony received by the appeals board upon similar issues of scientific fact in other cases and the prior decisions of the appeals board upon similar issues.

(h) Relevant portions of medical treatment protocols published by medical specialty societies. To be admissible, the party offering such a protocol or portion of a protocol shall concurrently enter into evidence information regarding how the protocol was developed, and to what extent the protocol is evidence-based, peer-reviewed, and nationally recognized. If a party offers into evidence a portion of a treatment protocol, any other party may offer into evidence additional portions of the protocol. The party offering a protocol, or portion thereof, into evidence shall either make a printed copy of the full protocol available for review and copying, or shall provide an Internet address at which the entire protocol may be accessed without charge.

(i) The medical treatment utilization schedule in effect pursuant to Section 5307.27 or the guidelines in effect pursuant to Section 4604.5.

(j) Reports of vocational experts. If vocational expert evidence is otherwise admissible, the evidence shall be produced in the form of written reports. Direct examination of a vocational witness shall not be received at trial except upon a showing of good cause. A continuance may be granted for rebuttal testimony if a report that was not served sufficiently in advance of the close of discovery to permit rebuttal is admitted into evidence.

(1) Statements concerning any bill for services are admissible only if they comply with the requirements applicable to statements concerning bills for services pursuant to subdivision (a).

(2) Reports are admissible under this subdivision only if the vocational expert has further stated in the body of the report that the contents of the report are true and correct to

the best knowledge of the vocational expert. The statement shall be made in compliance with the requirements applicable to medical reports pursuant to subdivision (a). **Leg.H.** 1993 ch. 120, effective July 16, 1993, 1994 ch. 146, 2003 ch. 639 (SB 228), 2004 ch. 34 (SB 899), effective April 19, 2004, 2012 ch. 363 (SB 863) §81.

2012 Note: For legislative findings, declarations, and applicability of Stats. 2012 ch. 363, see the 2012 Notes following Lab C §62.5.

2004 Note: The amendment to §5703 made by this act shall apply prospectively from the date of enactment of this act, regardless of the date of injury, unless otherwise specified, but shall not constitute good cause to reopen or rescind, alter, or amend any existing order, decision, or award of the Workers' Compensation Appeals Board. Stats. 2004 ch. 34 (SB 899) §47.

Ref.: 8 C.C.R. §§10430, 10600, 10601, 10604, 10606, 10608, 10616; Hanna § 26.06[12]; Herlick Handbook §§ 4.13, 4.17[2], 6.02[5], 14.40.

§5703.5. Examination of injured employee by QME.

(a) The appeals board, at any time after an application is filed and prior to the expiration of its jurisdiction may, upon the agreement of a party to pay the cost, direct an unrepresented employee to be examined by a qualified medical evaluator selected by the appeals board, within the scope of the qualified medical evaluator's professional training, upon any clinical question then at issue before the appeals board.

(b) The administrative director or his or her designees, upon the submission of a matter to an information and assistance officer, may, upon the agreement of a party to pay the cost, and with the consent of an unrepresented employee direct the injured employee to be examined by a qualified medical evaluator selected by the medical director, within the scope of the qualified medical evaluator's professional training, upon any clinical question, other than those issues specified in Section 4061, then pertinent to the investigation of the information and assistance officer.

(c) The 1989 and 1990 amendments to this section shall become operative for injuries occurring on and after January 1, 1991.

Ref.: 8 C.C.R. §§10166, 10700, 10718; Hanna §§ 22.07[4], 23.03[2][c]; Herlick Handbook § 14.22.

§5704. Transcripts of testimony.

Transcripts of all testimony taken without notice and copies of all reports and other matters added to the record, otherwise than during the course of an open hearing, shall be served upon the parties to the proceeding, and an opportunity shall be given to produce evidence in explanation or rebuttal thereof before decision is rendered.

Ref.: 8 C.C.R. §10580; Herlick Handbook § 14.40.

§5705. Burden of proof; affirmative defenses.

The burden of proof rests upon the party or lien claimant holding the affirmative of the issue. The following are affirmative defenses, and the burden of proof rests upon the employer to establish them:

(a) That an injured person claiming to be an employee was an independent contractor or otherwise excluded from the protection of this division where there is proof that the injured person was at the time of his or her injury actually performing service for the alleged employer.

(b) Intoxication of an employee causing his or her injury.

(c) Willful misconduct of an employee causing his or her injury.

(d) Aggravation of disability by unreasonable conduct of the employee.

(e) Prejudice to the employer by failure of the employee to give notice, as required by Sections 5400 and 5401. **Leg.H.** 1993 ch. 4, effective April 3, 1993.

Ref.: 8 C.C.R. §10541; Hanna §§ 3.03, 3.05, 3.61, 5.05[9][b], 21.03[4][c]; Herlick Handbook §§ 4.02[3], 10.03[2], 14.6, 14.18.

§5706. Appeals board authority to order autopsy.

Where it is represented to the appeals board, either before or after the filing of an application, that an employee has died as a result of injuries sustained in the course of his employment, the appeals board may require an autopsy. The report of the physician performing the autopsy may be received in evidence in any proceedings theretofore or thereafter brought. If at the time the autopsy is requested, the body of the employee is in the custody of the coroner, the coroner shall, upon the request of the appeals board or of any party interested, afford reasonable opportunity for the attendance of any physicians named by the appeals board at any autopsy ordered by him. If the coroner does not require, or has already performed the autopsy, he shall permit an autopsy or reexamination to be performed by physicians named by the appeals board. No fee shall be charged by the coroner for any service, arrangement, or permission given by him.

Ref.: 8 C.C.R. §10342; Hanna § 22.07[5]; Herlick Handbook §§ 9.15, 14.20, 14.38.

§5707. Appeals board limited authority to order autopsy when body not in coroner's custody.

If the body of a deceased employee is not in the custody of the coroner, the appeals board may authorize the performance of such autopsy and, if necessary, the exhumation of the body therefor. If the dependents, or a majority thereof, of any such deceased employee, having the custody of the body refuse to allow the autopsy, it shall not be performed. In such case, upon the hearing of any application for compensation it is a disputable presumption that the injury or death was not due to causes entitling the claimants to benefits under this division.

Ref.: 8 C.C.R. §10342; Hanna § 31.12[1]; Herlick Handbook §§ 9.15, 14.38.

§5708. Appeals board authority to conduct hearings by own rules.

All hearings and investigations before the appeals board or a workers' compensation judge are governed by this division and by the rules of practice and procedures adopted by the appeals board. In the conduct thereof they shall not be bound by the common law or statutory rules of evidence and procedure, but may make inquiry in the manner, through oral testimony and records, which is best calculated to ascertain the substantial rights of the parties and carry out justly the spirit and provisions of this division. All oral testimony, objections, and rulings shall be taken down in shorthand by a competent phonographic reporter.

Ref.: 8 C.C.R. §§10324, 10490, 10541, 10560, 10562, 10563, 10589, 10591, 10600, 10601, 10602, 10604, 10605, 10606, 10607, 10608, 10609, 10610, 10616, 10618, 10622, 10727, 10740, 10750, 10754, 10762, 10957, 10958; Hanna §§ 23.10[1], 25.41[2], 26.06[4]; Herlick Handbook §§ 6.03[10], 10.06[1], 14.5.

§5709. Informality in proceedings; no effect on validity.

No informality in any proceeding or in the manner of taking testimony shall invalidate any order, decision, award, or rule made and filed as specified in this division. No order, decision, award, or rule shall be invalidated because of the admission into the record, and use as proof of any fact in dispute, of any evidence not admissible under the common law or statutory rules of evidence and procedure.

Ref.: 8 C.C.R. §§10541, 10600, 10601, 10604, 10606, 10608, 10609, 10616, 10618, 10619, 10620, 10622, 10957, 10958; Hanna § 26.06[1]; Herlick Handbook § 6.03[10].

§5710. Deposition of witnesses.

(a) The appeals board, a workers' compensation judge, or any party to the action or proceeding, may, in any investigation or hearing before the appeals board, cause the deposition of witnesses residing within or without the state to be taken in the manner prescribed by law for like depositions in civil actions in the superior courts of this state under Title 4 (commencing with Section 2016.010) of Part 4 of the Code of Civil Procedure. To that end the attendance of witnesses and the production of records may be required. Depositions may be taken outside the state before any officer authorized to administer oaths. The appeals board or a workers' compensation judge in any proceeding before the appeals board may cause evidence to be taken in other jurisdictions before the agency authorized to hear workers' compensation matters in those other jurisdictions.

(b) If the employer or insurance carrier requests a deposition to be taken of an injured employee, or any person claiming benefits as a dependent of an injured employee, the deponent is entitled to receive in addition to all other benefits:

(1) All reasonable expenses of transportation, meals, and lodging incident to the deposition.

(2) Reimbursement for any loss of wages incurred during attendance at the deposition.

(3) One copy of the transcript of the deposition, without cost.

(4) A reasonable allowance for attorney's fees for the deponent, if represented by an attorney licensed by the State Bar of this state. The fee shall be discretionary with, and, if allowed, shall be set by, the appeals board, but shall be paid by the employer or his or her insurer. The administrative director shall, on or before July 1, 2018, determine the range of reasonable fees to be paid.

(5) If interpretation services are required because the injured employee or deponent does not proficiently speak or understand the English language, upon a request from either, the employer shall pay for the services of a language interpreter certified or deemed certified pursuant to Article 8 (commencing with Section 11435.05) of Chapter 4.5 of Part 1 of Division 3 of Title 2 of, or Section 68566 of, the Government Code. The fee to be paid by the employer shall be in accordance with the fee schedule adopted by the administrative director and shall include any other deposition-related events as permitted by the administrative director. **Leg.H.** 1991 ch. 116, 1993 ch. 121, effective July 16, 1993, 1995 ch. 938, operative July 1, 1997, 1998 ch. 931, effective September 28, 1998, 2004 ch. 182 (AB 3081), operative July 1, 2005, 2012 ch. 363 (SB 863) §82, 2016 ch. 868 (SB 1160) §11.

2016 Note: For legislative findings and declarations, see the 2016 Note following Lab C §138.4.

2012 Note: For legislative findings, declarations, and applicability of Stats. 2012 ch. 363, see the 2012 Notes following Lab C §62.5.

1993 Note: Section 5710, as amended by ch. 121, applies only to injuries occurring on or after January 1, 1994. Stats. 1993 ch. 121 §77.

Ref.: 8 C.C.R. §§9795.1, 9795.2, 9795.3, 9795.4, 10536, 10564, 10890; Hanna § 25.41[2]; Herlick Handbook §§ 10.03[1], 10.09[4], [5], 14.20, 14.33, 14.40, 14.43.

CHAPTER 6
FINDINGS AND AWARDS

§5800. Interest on compensation or death benefit payments.

All awards of the appeals board either for the payment of compensation or for the payment of death benefits, shall carry interest at the same rate as judgments in civil actions on all due and unpaid payments from the date of the making and filing of said award. Such interest shall run from the date of making and filing of an award, as to amounts which by the terms of the award are payable forthwith. As to amounts which under the terms of the award subsequently become due in installments or otherwise, such interest shall run from the date when each such amount becomes due and payable.

Ref.: 8 C.C.R. §§10111, 10111.1, 10111.2; Hanna § 27.01[7]; Herlick Handbook §§ 9.12, 14.41.

§5800.5. Clarification of §5313.

The 30-day period specified in Section 5313, shall run from the date of the submission of the application for decision and the provisions requiring the decision within such 30-day period shall be deemed mandatory and not merely directive.

§5801. Appeals board determination of payment matters; attorney's fees.

The appeals board in its award may fix and determine the total amount of compensation to be paid and specify the manner of payment, or may fix and determine the weekly disability payment to be made and order payment thereof during the continuance of disability.

In the event the injured employee or the dependent of a deceased employee prevails in any petition by the employer for a writ of review from an award of the appeals board and the reviewing court finds that there is no reasonable basis for the petition, it shall remand the cause to the appeals board for the purpose of making a supplemental award awarding to the injured employee or his attorney, or the dependent of a deceased employee or his attorney a reasonable attorney's fee for services rendered in connection with the petition for writ of review. Any such fee shall be in addition to the amount of compensation otherwise recoverable and shall be paid as part of the award by the party liable to pay such award.

Ref.: Hanna §§ 20.02[2][l], 34.24; Herlick Handbook §§ 10.08[3], 10.09[2], [5], 10.09, 14.42, 15.6.

§5802. Nominal disability indemnity.

If, in any proceeding under this division, it is proved that an injury has been suffered for which the employer would be liable to pay compensation if disability had resulted therefrom, but it is not proved that any disability has resulted, the appeals board may, instead of dismissing the application, award a nominal disability indemnity, if it appears that disability is likely to result at a future time.

§5803. Appeals board continuing jurisdiction.

The appeals board has continuing jurisdiction over all its orders, decisions, and awards made and entered under the provisions of this division, and the decisions and orders of the rehabilitation unit established under Section 139.5. At any time, upon notice and after an opportunity to be heard is given to the parties in interest, the appeals board may rescind, alter, or amend any order, decision, or award, good cause appearing therefor.

This power includes the right to review, grant or regrant, diminish, increase, or terminate, within the limits prescribed by this division, any compensation awarded, upon the grounds that the disability of the person in whose favor the award was made has either recurred, increased, diminished, or terminated.

Ref.: 8 C.C.R. §§10454, 10455, 10458; Hanna §§ 21.08[1], 26.01[3], 29.05[3], 31.04[2][a]; Herlick Handbook §§ 11.11, 14.7, 14.9.

§5803.5. Grounds for reconsideration of order, decision, or award.

Any conviction pursuant to Section 1871.4 of the Insurance Code that materially affects the basis of any order, decision, or award of the appeals board shall be sufficient grounds for a reconsideration of that order, decision, or award. **Leg.H.** 1991 ch. 116.

Ref.: Hanna § 28.02; Herlick Handbook §§ 9.18, 14.18, 15.4.

§5804. Altering award after five years.

No award of compensation shall be rescinded, altered, or amended after five years from the date of the injury except upon a petition by a party in interest filed within such five years and any counterpetition seeking other relief filed by the adverse party within 30 days of the original petition raising issues in addition to those raised by such original petition. Provided, however, that after an award has been made finding that there was employment and the time to petition for a rehearing or reconsideration or review has expired or such petition if made has been determined, the appeals board upon a petition to reopen shall not have the power to find that there was no employment.

Ref.: 8 C.C.R. §10102; Hanna §§ 24.03[4], 24.13[2], 31.04[1][a], [c], [3]; Herlick Handbook §§ 11.11, 14.34, 15.3, 15.4, 16.14.

§5805. Effect of altered decision.

Any order, decision, or award rescinding, altering or amending a prior order, decision, or award shall have the effect herein provided for original orders, decisions, and awards.

Ref.: Herlick Handbook §§ 14.9, 14.44, 16.14.

§5806. Certified copy of decision; filing.

Any party affected thereby may file a certified copy of the findings and order, decision, or award of the appeals board with the clerk of the superior court of any county. Judgment shall be entered immediately by the clerk in conformity therewith. The words "any party affected thereby" include the Uninsured Employers Fund. In any case in which the findings and order, decision, or award of the appeals board is against an employer that has failed to secure the payment of compensation, the State of California on behalf of the Uninsured Employers Fund shall be entitled to have judgment entered not only against the employer, but also against any person found to be parents or substantial shareholders under Section 3717. **Leg.H.** 1992 ch. 1226.

Ref.: 8 C.C.R. §§10820, 10825, 10828; Hanna § 27.11[2][a].

§5807. Certified copy as judgment roll.

The certified copy of the findings and order, decision, or award of the appeals board and a copy of the judgment constitute the judgment-roll. The pleadings, all orders of the appeals board, its original findings and order, decision, or award, and all other papers and documents filed in the cause shall remain on file in the office of the appeals board.

Ref.: 8 C.C.R. §§10820, 10825, 10828.

§5808. Stay of execution of appeals board decision.

The appeals board or a member thereof may stay the execution of any judgment entered upon an order, decision, or award of the appeals board, upon good cause appearing therefor and may impose the terms and conditions of the stay of execution. A certified copy of such order shall be filed with the clerk entering judgment. Where it is desirable to stay the enforcement of an order, decision, or award and a certified copy thereof and of the findings has not been issued, the appeals board or a member thereof may order the certified copy to be withheld with the same force and under the same conditions as it might issue a stay of execution if the certified copy had been issued and judgment entered thereon.

Ref.: 8 C.C.R. §§10820, 10825, 10828; Hanna §§ 27.10[3][b], 27.11[3][a], [b].

§5809. Satisfaction of judgment in fact.

When a judgment is satisfied in fact, otherwise than upon an execution, the appeals board may, upon motion of either party or of its own motion, order the entry of satisfaction of

Labor

the judgment. The clerk shall enter satisfaction of judgment only upon the filing of a certified copy of such order.

Ref.: 8 C.C.R. §§10820, 10825, 10828; Hanna § 27.11[4][a].

§5810. Court review.

The orders, findings, decisions, or awards of the appeals board made and entered under this division may be reviewed by the courts specified in Sections 5950 and 5956 within the time and in the manner therein specified and not otherwise.

Ref.: Hanna § 34.03[1]; Herlick Handbook § 14.41.

§5811. Limited fees; appeals board allowance of costs; interpreter fees.

(a) No fees shall be charged by the clerk of any court for the performance of any official service required by this division, except for the docketing of awards as judgments and for certified copies of transcripts thereof. In all proceedings under this division before the appeals board, costs as between the parties may be allowed by the appeals board.

(b)(1) It shall be the responsibility of any party producing a witness requiring an interpreter to arrange for the presence of a qualified interpreter.

(2) A qualified interpreter is a language interpreter who is certified, or deemed certified, pursuant to Article 8 (commencing with Section 11435.05) of Chapter 4.5 of Part 1 of Division 3 of Title 2 of, or Section 68566 of, the Government Code. The duty of an interpreter is to accurately and impartially translate oral communications and transliterate written materials, and not to act as an agent or advocate. An interpreter shall not disclose to any person who is not an immediate participant in the communications the content of the conversations or documents that the interpreter has interpreted or transliterated unless the disclosure is compelled by court order. An attempt by any party or attorney to obtain disclosure is a bad faith tactic that is subject to Section 5813.

Interpreter fees that are reasonably, actually, and necessarily incurred shall be paid by the employer under this section, provided they are in accordance with the fee schedule adopted by the administrative director.

A qualified interpreter may render services during the following:

(A) A deposition.

(B) An appeals board hearing.

(C) A medical treatment appointment or medical-legal examination.

(D) During those settings which the administrative director determines are reasonably necessary to ascertain the validity or extent of injury to an employee who does not proficiently speak or understand the English language.

(c) The administrative director shall promulgate regulations establishing criteria to verify the identity and credentials of individuals who provide interpreter services in all necessary settings and proceedings within the workers' compensation system. Those regulations shall be adopted no later than January 1, 2018. **Leg.H.** 1993 ch. 121, effective July 16, 1993, 1995 ch. 938, operative July 1, 1997, 2012 ch. 363 (SB 863) §83, 2016 ch. 868 (SB 1160) §12.

2016 Note: For legislative findings and declarations, see the 2016 Note following Lab C §138.4.

2012 Note: For legislative findings, declarations, and applicability of Stats. 2012 ch. 363, see the 2012 Notes following Lab C §62.5.

1993 Note: Section 5811, as amended by ch. 121, applies only to injuries occurring on or after January 1, 1994. Stats. 1993 ch. 121 §77.

Ref.: 8 C.C.R. §§9795.1, 9795.2, 9795.3, 9795.4, 10322, 10564; Hanna §§ 23.13[3], [4], 27.01[8][a], 34.23; Herlick Handbook §§ 4.06[5], 10.03[4], 10.09[1], 14.33, 14.42.

§5813. Sanctions for bad-faith actions or tactics.

(a) The workers' compensation referee or appeals board may order a party, the party's attorney, or both, to pay any reasonable expenses, including attorney's fees and costs, incurred by another party as a result of bad-faith actions or tactics that are frivolous or solely intended to cause unnecessary delay. In addition, a workers' compensation referee or the appeals board, in its sole discretion, may order additional sanctions not to exceed two thousand five hundred dollars ($2,500) to be transmitted to the General Fund.

(b) The determination of sanctions shall be made after written application by the party seeking sanctions or upon the appeal board's own motion.

(c) This section shall apply to all applications for adjudication that are filed on or after January 1, 1994. **Leg.H.** 1993 ch. 121, effective July 16, 1993, ch. 1242.

Ref.: 8 C.C.R. §§10414, 10416, 10561, 10592; Hanna § 23.15; Herlick Handbook §§ 3.2, 10.02[5], 10.03[2], [6], 10.08[2], [3], 10.09[4], 10.10[1], 14.33[1], 14.42.

§5814. Unreasonable delay or refusal of payment of compensation; increase; self-imposed penalty; conclusive presumption on approval of compromise and release, etc.; actions; applicability.

(a) When payment of compensation has been unreasonably delayed or refused, either prior to or subsequent to the issuance of an award, the amount of the payment unreasonably delayed or refused shall be increased up to 25 percent or up to ten thousand dollars ($10,000), whichever is less. In any proceeding under this section, the appeals board shall use its discretion to accomplish a fair balance and substantial justice between the parties.

(b) If a potential violation of this section is discovered by the employer prior to an employee claiming a penalty under this section, the employer, within 90 days of the date of the discovery, may pay a self-imposed penalty in the amount of 10 percent of the amount of the payment unreasonably delayed or refused, along with the amount of the payment delayed or refused. This self-imposed penalty shall be in lieu of the penalty in subdivision (a).

(c) Upon the approval of a compromise and release, findings and awards, or stipulations and orders by the appeals board, it shall be conclusively presumed that any accrued claims for penalty have been resolved, regardless of whether a petition for penalty has been filed, unless the claim for penalty is expressly excluded by the terms of the order or award. Upon the submission of any issue for determination at a regular trial hearing, it shall be conclusively presumed that any accrued claim for penalty in connection with the benefit at issue has been resolved, regardless of whether a petition for penalty has been filed, unless the issue of penalty is also submitted or is expressly excluded in the statement of issues being submitted.

(d) The payment of any increased award pursuant to subdivision (a) shall be reduced by any amount paid under subdivision (d) of Section 4650 on the same unreasonably delayed or refused benefit payment.

(e) No unreasonable delay in the provision of medical treatment shall be found when the treatment has been authorized by the employer in a timely manner and the only dispute concerns payment of a billing submitted by a physician or medical provider as provided in Section 4603.2.

(f) Nothing in this section shall be construed to create a civil cause of action.

(g) Notwithstanding any other provision of law, no action may be brought to recover penalties that may be awarded under this section more than two years from the date the payment of compensation was due.

(h) This section shall apply to all injuries, without regard to whether the injury occurs before, on, or after the operative date of this section.

(i) This section shall become operative on June 1, 2004. **Leg.H.** 2004 ch. 34 (SB 899) §43, effective April 19, 2004.

2004 Note: The addition of §5814 made by this act shall apply prospectively from the date of enactment of this act, regardless of the date of injury, unless otherwise specified, but shall not constitute good cause to reopen or rescind, alter, or amend any existing order, decision, or award of the Workers' Compensation Appeals Board. Stats. 2004 ch. 34 (SB 899) §47.

Ref.: 8 C.C.R. §§10109, 10111, 10111.1, 10111.2; Hanna §§ 10.40[1], [3]–[6], 27.12[2][a], [c], [d]; Herlick Handbook §§ 4.06[1], 4.16[2], 9.5, 10.01[1], 10.08[3], 10.10[1].

§5814.1. Employer's penalty paid to director.

When the payment of compensation has been unreasonably delayed or refused prior to the issuance of an award, and the director has provided discretionary compensation pursuant to Section 4903.3, the appeals board shall award to the director a penalty to be paid by the employer in the amount of 10 percent of the compensation so provided by the director, such penalty to be in addition to the penalty imposed by Section 5814. The question of delay and the reasonableness of the cause therefor shall be determined by the appeals board in accordance with the facts.

Ref.: Herlick Handbook § 3.19.

§5814.5. Reasonable attorneys' fees awarded when payment of compensation delayed or refused.

When the payment of compensation has been unreasonably delayed or refused subsequent to the issuance of an award by an employer that has secured the payment of compensation pursuant to Section 3700, the appeals board shall, in addition to increasing the order, decision, or award pursuant to Section 5814, award reasonable attorneys' fees incurred in enforcing the payment of compensation awarded. **Leg.H.** 2002 ch. 6 (AB 749).

Ref.: Hanna §§ 10.42, 27.12[5]; Herlick Handbook § 10.09[5].

§5814.6. Administrative penalties for knowing violation of §5814.

(a) Any employer or insurer that knowingly violates Section 5814 with a frequency that indicates a general business practice is liable for administrative penalties of not to exceed four hundred thousand dollars ($400,000). Penalty payments shall be imposed by the administrative director and deposited into the Return-to-Work Fund established pursuant to Section 139.48.

(b) The administrative director may impose a penalty under either this section or subdivision (e) of Section 129.5.

(c) This section shall become operative on June 1, 2004. **Leg.H.** 2004 ch. 34 (SB 899), effective April 19, 2004.

2004 Note: The addition of §5814.6 made by this act shall apply prospectively from the date of enactment of this act, regardless of the date of injury, unless otherwise specified, but shall not constitute good cause to reopen or rescind, alter, or amend any existing order, decision, or award of the Workers' Compensation Appeals Board. Stats. 2004 ch. 34 (SB 899) §47.

Ref.: Hanna §§ 10.40[1], 27.12[2][b]; Herlick Handbook § 9.5.

§5815. Statement of determination of issues raised.

Every order, decision or award, other than an order merely appointing a trustee or guardian, shall contain a determination of all issues presented for determination by the appeals board prior thereto and not theretofore determined. Any issue not so determined will be deemed decided adversely as to the party in whose interest such issue was raised.

§5816. No collateral estoppel effect on subsequent criminal proceedings.

A determination of facts by the appeals board under this chapter has no collateral estoppel effect on a subsequent criminal prosecution and does not preclude litigation of those same facts in the criminal proceeding. **Leg.H.** 1995 ch. 158.

Ref.: Herlick Handbook § 9.18.

CHAPTER 7 RECONSIDERATION AND JUDICIAL REVIEW

ARTICLE 1 Reconsideration

§5900. Reconsideration; petition.

(a) Any person aggrieved directly or indirectly by any final order, decision, or award made and filed by the appeals board or a workers' compensation judge under any provision contained in this division, may petition the appeals board for reconsideration in respect to any matters determined or covered by the final order, decision, or award, and specified in the petition for reconsideration. The petition shall be made only within the time and in the manner specified in this chapter.

(b) At any time within 60 days after the filing of an order, decision, or award made by a workers' compensation judge and the accompanying report, the appeals board may, on its own motion, grant reconsideration.

Ref.: 8 C.C.R. §§10352, 10840, 10842, 10848, 10860, 10864, 10866, 10867; Hanna §§ 28.01[1]–[3], 28.05, 28.20, 34.10; Herlick Handbook §§ 15.1, 15.3, 15.5.

§5901. Accrual of cause of action in court.

No cause of action arising out of any final order, decision or award made and filed by the appeals board or a workers' compensation judge shall accrue in any court to any person until and unless the appeals board on its own motion sets aside the final order, decision, or award and removes the proceeding to itself or if the person files a petition for reconsideration, and the reconsideration is granted or denied. Nothing herein contained shall prevent the enforcement of any final order, decision, or award, in the manner provided in this division.

Ref.: 8 C.C.R. §§10352, 10866, 10867.

§5902. Requirements of petition for reconsideration.

The petition for reconsideration shall set forth specifically and in full detail the grounds upon which the petitioner considers the final order, decision or award made and filed by the appeals board or a workers' compensation judge to be unjust or unlawful, and every issue to be considered by the appeals board. The petition shall be verified upon oath in the manner required for verified pleadings in courts of record and shall contain a general statement of any evidence or other matters upon which the applicant relies in support thereof.

Ref.: 8 C.C.R. §§10352, 10842, 10846, 10850, 10852, 10856, 10866, 10867; Herlick Handbook § 15.4.

§5903. Grounds for reconsideration.

At any time within 20 days after the service of any final order, decision, or award made and filed by the appeals board or a workers' compensation judge granting or denying compensation, or arising out of or incidental thereto, any person aggrieved thereby may petition for reconsideration upon one or more of the following grounds and no other:

(a) That by the order, decision, or award made and filed by the appeals board or a the workers' compensation judge, the appeals board acted without or in excess of its powers.

(b) That the order, decision, or award was procured by fraud.

(c) That the evidence does not justify the findings of fact.

(d) That the petitioner has discovered new evidence material to him or her, which he or she could not, with reasonable diligence, have discovered and produced at the hearing.

(e) That the findings of fact do not support the order, decision, or award.

Nothing contained in this section shall limit the grant of continuing jurisdiction contained in Sections 5803 to 5805, inclusive.

Ref.: 8 C.C.R. §§10352, 10850, 10852, 10856, 10866, 10867; Hanna §§ 28.02, 28.22[1], [2], 28.25; Herlick Handbook §§ 14.34, 15.4.

§5904. Waiver of irregularities.

The petitioner for reconsideration shall be deemed to have finally waived all objections, irregularities, and illegalities concerning the matter upon which the reconsideration is sought other than those set forth in the petition for reconsideration.

Ref.: 8 C.C.R. §§10352, 10866, 10867; Hanna §§ 28.06, 34.20; Herlick Handbook § 15.4.

§5905. Petition for reconsideration; service; answer.

A copy of the petition for reconsideration shall be served forthwith upon all adverse parties by the person petitioning for reconsideration. Any adverse party may file an answer thereto within 10 days thereafter. Such answer shall likewise be verified. The appeals board may require the petition for reconsideration to be served on other persons designated by it.

Ref.: 8 C.C.R. §§10352, 10840, 10866, 10867; Hanna §§ 28.23, 28.24; Herlick Handbook § 15.3.

§5906. Petition for reconsideration; notice of hearings on reconsideration.

Upon the filing of a petition for reconsideration, or having granted reconsideration upon its own motion, the appeals board may, with or without further proceedings and with or without notice affirm, rescind, alter, or amend the order, decision, or award made and filed by the appeals board or the workers' compensation judge on the basis of the evidence previously submitted in the case, or may grant reconsideration and direct the taking of additional evidence. Notice of the time and place of any hearing on reconsideration shall be given to the petitioner and adverse parties and to other persons as the appeals board orders.

Ref.: 8 C.C.R. §§10352, 10859, 10860, 10866, 10867; Herlick Handbook §§ 4.13, 15.3, 15.4.

§5907. Decision without hearing.

If, at the time of granting reconsideration, it appears to the satisfaction of the appeals board that no sufficient reason exists for taking further testimony, the appeals board may affirm, rescind, alter, or amend the order, decision, or award made and filed by the appeals board or the workers' compensation judge and may, without further proceedings, without notice, and without setting a time and place for further hearing, enter its findings, order, decision, or award based upon the record in the case. **Leg.H.** 1937 ch. 90, 1951 ch. 778 §21, 1965 ch. 1513 §177, operative January 15, 1966, 1985 ch. 326 §32, 2006 ch. 538 (SB 1852) §492.

Ref.: 8 C.C.R. §§10352, 10859, 10866, 10867; Hanna §§ 28.33[2], 28.36[2][b].

§5908. Effect of order on reconsideration.

(a) After the taking of additional evidence and a consideration of all of the facts the appeals board may affirm, rescind, alter, or amend the original order, decision, or award. An order, decision, or award made following reconsideration which affirms, rescinds, alters, or amends the original order, decision, or award shall be made by the appeals board but shall not affect any right or the enforcement of any right arising from or by virtue of the original order, decision, or award, unless so ordered by the appeals board.

(b) In any case where the appeals board rescinds or reduces an order, decision, or award on the grounds specified in paragraph (b) of Section 5903, the appeals board shall refer the case to the Bureau of Fraudulent Claims pursuant to Article 4 (commencing with Section 12990) of Chapter 2 of Division 3 of the Insurance Code, if the employer is insured, or to the district attorney of the county in which the fraud occurred if the employer is self-insured.

1989 Note: This section is applicable only to injuries occurring on or after January 1, 1990. Stats. 1989 ch. 893 §6.

Ref.: 8 C.C.R. §§10352, 10866, 10867; Herlick Handbook §§ 9.18, 15.3.

§5908.5. Decision on reconsideration.

Any decision of the appeals board granting or denying a petition for reconsideration or affirming, rescinding, altering, or amending the original findings, order, decision, or award following reconsideration shall be made by the appeals board and not by a workers' compensation judge and shall be in writing, signed by a majority of the appeals board members assigned thereto, and shall state the evidence relied upon and specify in detail the reasons for the decision.

The requirements of this section shall in no way be construed so as to broaden the scope of judicial review as provided for in Article 2 (commencing with Section 5950) of this chapter.

Ref.: 8 C.C.R. §§10352, 10859, 10866, 10867; Hanna §§ 28.36[2][c], 34.17[1]; Herlick Handbook §§ 10.09[2], 15.3.

§5909. Denial of reconsideration.

A petition for reconsideration is deemed to have been denied by the appeals board unless it is acted upon within 60 days from the date of filing. **Leg.H.** 1992 ch. 1226.

Ref.: 8 C.C.R. §§10352, 10866, 10867; Hanna § 28.32; Herlick Handbook § 15.4.

§5910. Filing petition for reconsideration.

The filing of a petition for reconsideration shall suspend for a period of 10 days the order, decision, or award affected, in so far as it applies to the parties to the petition, unless otherwise ordered by the appeals board. The appeals board upon the terms and conditions which it by order directs, may stay, suspend, or postpone the order, decision, or award during the pendency of the reconsideration.

Ref.: 8 C.C.R. §§10352, 10864, 10866, 10867; Hanna § 27.10[2][d].

§5911. Limitations on article.

Nothing contained in this article shall be construed to prevent the appeals board, on petition of an aggrieved party or on its own motion, from granting reconsideration of an original order, decision, or award made and filed by the appeals board within the same time specified for reconsideration of an original order, decision, or award.

Ref.: 8 C.C.R. §§10352, 10864, 10866, 10867; Hanna § 24.12[2]; Herlick Handbook § 15.3.

ARTICLE 2
Judicial Review

§5950. Writ of review; time limit for filing.

Any person affected by an order, decision, or award of the appeals board may, within the time limit specified in this section, apply to the Supreme Court or to the court of appeal for the appellate district in which he resides, for a writ of review, for the purpose of inquiring into and determining the lawfulness of the original order, decision, or award or of the order, decision, or award following reconsideration. The application for writ of review must be made within 45 days after a petition for reconsideration is denied, or, if a petition is granted or reconsideration is had on the appeals board's own motion, within 45 days after the filing of the order, decision, or award following reconsideration.

Ref.: Hanna §§ 28.32, 34.10[3], 34.11[1], 34.12[1]; Herlick Handbook § 15.6.

§5951. Writ of review; based on record of appeals board.

The writ of review shall be made returnable at a time and place then or thereafter specified by court order and shall direct the appeals board to certify its record in the case to the court within the time therein specified. No new or additional evidence shall be introduced in such court, but the cause shall be heard on the record of the appeals board, as certified to by it.

Ref.: Herlick Handbook § 15.6.

§5952. Extent of review.

The review by the court shall not be extended further than to determine, based upon the entire record which shall be certified by the appeals board, whether:

(a) The appeals board acted without or in excess of its powers.

(b) The order, decision, or award was procured by fraud.

(c) The order, decision, or award was unreasonable.

(d) The order, decision, or award was not supported by substantial evidence.

(e) If findings of fact are made, such findings of fact support the order, decision, or award under review.

Nothing in this section shall permit the court to hold a trial de novo, or take evidence, or to exercise its independent judgment on the evidence.

Ref.: Hanna §§ 27.01[1][c], 34.16[1], [2], 34.18[1], [2]; Herlick Handbook § 15.6.

Labor

§5953. Appeals board's findings of fact are final; right to appear at hearing.

The findings and conclusions of the appeals board on questions of fact are conclusive and final and are not subject to review. Such questions of fact shall include ultimate facts and the findings and conclusions of the appeals board. The appeals board and each party to the action or proceeding before the appeals board shall have the right to appear in the review proceeding. Upon the hearing, the court shall enter judgment either affirming or annulling the order, decision, or award, or the court may remand the case for further proceedings before the appeals board.

Ref.: Herlick Handbook § 15.6.

§5954. Code of Civil Procedure governs proceedings; service of pleadings.

The provisions of the Code of Civil Procedure relating to writs of review shall, so far as applicable, apply to proceedings in the courts under the provisions of this article. A copy of every pleading filed pursuant to the terms of this article shall be served on the appeals board and upon every party who entered an appearance in the action before the appeals board and whose interest therein is adverse to the party filing such pleading.

§5955. Exclusive jurisdiction of Supreme Court or appellate courts.

No court of this state, except the Supreme Court and the courts of appeal to the extent herein specified, has jurisdiction to review, reverse, correct, or annul any order, rule, decision, or award of the appeals board, or to suspend or delay the operation or execution thereof, or to restrain, enjoin, or interfere with the appeals board in the performance of its duties but a writ of mandate shall lie from the Supreme Court or a court of appeal in all proper cases.

Ref.: Hanna §§ 34.02, 34.03[2], [3].

§5956. Stay of appeals board decision not automatic.

The filing of a petition for, or the pendency of, a writ of review shall not of itself stay or suspend the operation of any order, rule, decision, or award of the appeals board, but the court before which the petition is filed may stay or suspend, in whole or in part, the operation of the order, decision, or award of the appeals board subject to review, upon the terms and conditions which it by order directs, except as provided in Article 3 of this chapter.

Ref.: 8 C.C.R. §10828.

ARTICLE 3
Undertaking on Stay Order

§6000. Limitations on authority of reviewing court to issue stay order.

The operation of any order, decision, or award of the appeals board under the provisions of this division or any judgment entered thereon, shall not at any time be stayed by the court to which petition is made for a writ of review, unless an undertaking is executed on the part of the petitioner.

Ref.: 8 C.C.R. §§10342, 10344, 10820, 10825, 10828.

§6001. Undertaking.

The undertaking shall provide that:

(a) The petitioner and sureties are bound in double the amount named in such order, decision, or award.

(b) If the order, decision, or award appealed from, or any part thereof, is affirmed, or the proceeding upon review is dismissed, the petitioner will pay the amount directed to be paid by the order, decision, or award or the part of such amount as to which the order, decision, or award is affirmed, and all damages and costs which are awarded against the petitioner.

(c) If the petitioner does not make such payment within 30 days after the filing with the appeals board of the remittitur from the reviewing court, judgment in favor of the adverse party may be entered on motion of the adverse party, and the undertaking shall apply to any judgment entered thereon. Such judgment may be entered in any superior court in which a certified copy of the order, decision, or award is filed, against the sureties for such amount, together with interest that is due thereon, and the damages and costs which are awarded against the petitioner. The provisions of the Code of Civil Procedure, except insofar as they are inconsistent with this division, are applicable to the undertaking.

Ref.: 8 C.C.R. §§10342, 10344, 10820, 10825, 10828.

§6002. Filing of undertaking with appeals board.

The undertaking shall be filed with the appeals board. The certificate of the appeals board or any proper officer thereof, of the filing and approval of such undertaking, is sufficient evidence of the compliance of the petitioner with the provisions of this article.

Ref.: 8 C.C.R. §§10342, 10344, 10346, 10820, 10825, 10828.

DIVISION 4.5 WORKERS' COMPENSATION AND INSURANCE: STATE EMPLOYEES NOT OTHERWISE COVERED

CHAPTER 1 GENERAL PROVISIONS

§6100. Purpose of division.

The purpose of this division is to effect economy, efficiency and continuity in the public service by providing means for increasing the willingness of competent persons to assume the risk of injuries or death in State employment and for restoring experienced employees to productive work at the earliest possible moment following injury in the course of and arising out of State employment, irrespective of fault, in circumstances which make the injury or resulting death non-compensable under the provisions of Division 4 of this code.

§6101. Definitions.

Unless the context otherwise requires, as used in this division:

(a) "State agency" means any agency, department, division, commission, board, bureau, officer, or other authority of the State of California.

(b) "Fund" means State Compensation Insurance Fund.

(c) "Appeals board" means the Workers' Compensation Appeals Board.

CHAPTER 2 DIRECT PAYMENTS

§6110. Voluntary offering of benefits.

Any State agency may, by appropriate action, undertake to provide hospitalization, medical treatment and indemnity, including death benefits, to its employees and to their dependents for injury or death suffered from accident, irrespective of fault, occurring in the course of and arising out of the employment with such State agency, where the injury or death is not compensable under the provisions of Division 4 of this code.

§6111. State Compensation Insurance Fund; master agreement to dispose of claims.

The State Compensation Insurance Fund may enter into a master agreement with the State Department of Finance to render services in accordance with the agreement in the adjustment and disposition of claims against any State agency arising under this chapter.

§6112. Master agreement; uniform rates for state agencies.

The master agreement shall provide for the rendition of services at a uniform rate to all State agencies.

§6113. Authorization for fund to make expenditures.

The fund may make all expenditures, including payments to claimants for medical care or for adjustment or settlement of claims.

§6114. Reimbursement of expenditures by claimant's agency.

The agreement shall provide that the State agency whose officer or employee is a claimant shall reimburse the fund for the expenditures and for the actual cost of services rendered.

§6115. Right of fund to recover from third parties.

The fund may in its own name, or in the name of the State agency for which services are performed, do any and all things necessary to recover on behalf of the State agency any and all amounts which an employer might recover from third persons under Chapter 5 of Part 1 of Division 4 of this code, or which an insurer might recover pursuant to Section 11662 of the Insurance Code, including the rights to commence and prosecute actions or to intervene in other court proceedings, or to compromise claims before or after commencement of suit.

CHAPTER 3 INSURANCE

§6130. Insurance from other insurer.

In lieu of direct payments pursuant to Chapter 2 of this division, any State agency may obtain by insurance from the State Compensation Insurance Fund, if the fund accepts the risk when the application for insurance is made, otherwise from any other insurer, hospitalization, medical treatment, and indemnity, including death benefits, on behalf of its employees and of their dependents for injury or death suffered from accident, irrespective of fault, occurring in the course of and arising out of the employment with such State agency, where the injury or death is not compensable under the provisions of Division 4 of this Code.

§6131. Payment of premium.

The premium for such insurance shall be a proper charge against any moneys appropriated for the support of or expenditure by such State agency. In case such State agency is supported by or authorized to expend moneys appropriated out of more than one fund, it may, with the approval of the Director of Finance, determine the proportion of such premium to be paid out of each such fund.

CHAPTER 4
BENEFITS AND PROCEDURE

§6140. Benefits employees entitled to.

The hospitalization, medical treatment, and indemnity, including death benefits, provided pursuant to this division shall be the same as provided by Division 4 of this code for employees entitled to the benefits of that division.

§6141. Applicable procedure and limitations.

Except as otherwise provided in this chapter, the provisions of Division 4 of this code, relating to benefits, procedure, and limitations, and all other provisions of that division, so far as they are consistent with the intent and purpose of this division, are made a part hereof the same as if set forth herein verbatim.

§6142. Exceptions.

The provisions of Sections 3212, 3212.5, 3361, 4458, 4800 to 4855, inclusive, of this code, as well as of other sections of Division 4 of this code, which are restrictive to particular persons or occupations, are excepted from this division and its operation.

§6143. Powers of appeals board.

The appeals board is vested with all power not inconsistent with Article VI of the Constitution of the State of California to hear and determine any dispute or matter arising out of an obligation under this division to provide directly, or through the medium of insurance, benefits identical with those prescribed by Division 4 of this code, with such limitations as are authorized, in the case of insurance, by Section 11657 of the Insurance Code.

§6144. Trial and determination of controversies.

The appeals board may try and determine controversies under this division referred to it by the parties under the provisions of Part 3, Title 10, of the Code of Civil Procedure, when such controversies are submitted to it by the signed agreement of the parties, or by the application of one party and the submission of the other to its jurisdiction, with or without an express request for arbitration.

§6145. Submission of controversies for arbitration.

The state, acting by or through any state agency or when the consent of the opposing party is obtained, shall submit to the appeals board all controversies under this division susceptible of being arbitrated.

§6146. Powers of appeals board as arbitrator.

In acting as arbitrator, the appeals board has all the powers which it has in compensation cases, and its findings and award upon an arbitration have the same conclusiveness and are subject to the same mode of reopening, review, and enforcement as in compensation cases.

No fee or cost shall be charged by the appeals board for acting as arbitrator.

§6147. Benefits received by state agency.

No state agency, either directly or through its adjusting agency, the State Compensation Insurance Fund, shall pay or provide any benefit authorized by this division unless and until the claimant makes and delivers to such state agency or to the fund an agreement in writing that if he, or his dependents in the event of his death, elects or elect to bring suit against the state with respect to the injury or death, except an action before the appeals board pursuant to the provisions of this division, or an action against the state for damages resulting from the negligence of an employee of another state agency, he or they will allow, and take all proper measures to effect, a credit to the reasonable value of all benefits which he or they have received under the provisions of this division, deductible from any verdict or judgment obtained in such suit, and from the date of commencement of suit will forego further benefits under this division.

§6148. Payment of benefits by insurer.

The insurer, when insurance exists, shall not pay or provide any benefit authorized by this division unless and until the claimant makes and delivers to the insurer an agreement in writing that if he, or his dependents in the event of his death, elects or elect to bring suit against the state or the insurer with respect to the injury or death, except an action before the appeals board pursuant to the provisions of this division, or an action against the state for damages resulting from the negligence of an employee of another state agency, he or they will allow, and take all proper measures to effect, a credit to the reasonable value of all benefits which he or they have received under the provisions of this division, deductible from any verdict or judgment obtained in such suit, and from the date of commencement of suit will forego further benefits under such insurance.

§6149. Negotiation of agreement.

Nothing shall preclude an employee from negotiating the agreement mentioned in Sections 6147 and 6148 prior to the occurrence of injury.

DIVISION 4.7
RETRAINING AND REHABILITATION

§6200. Rehabilitation procedures; purpose of division.

Every public agency, its insurance carrier, and the State Department of Rehabilitation shall jointly formulate procedures for the selection and orderly referral of injured full-time public employees who may be benefited by rehabilitation services and retrained for other positions in public service. The State Department of Rehabilitation shall cooperate in both designing and monitoring results of rehabilitation programs for the disabled employees. The primary purpose of this division is to encourage public agencies to reemploy their injured employees in suitable and gainful employment.

Ref.: Hanna § 35.19.

§6201. Availability of rehabilitation services; notice to employee.

The employer or insurance carrier shall notify the injured employee of the availability of rehabilitation services in those cases where there is continuing disability of 28 days and beyond. Notification shall be made at the time the employee is paid retroactively for first day of disability (in cases of 28 days of continuing disability or hospitalization) which has previously been uncompensated. A copy of said notification shall be forwarded to the State Department of Rehabilitation.

§6202. Initiation of rehabilitation plan.

The initiation of a rehabilitation plan shall be the joint responsibility of the injured employee, and the employer or the insurance carrier.

§6203. Subsistence allowance.

If a rehabilitation plan requires an injured employee to attend an educational or medical facility away from his home, the injured employee shall be paid a reasonable and necessary subsistence allowance in addition to temporary disability indemnity. The subsistence allowance shall be regarded neither as indemnity nor as replacement for lost earnings, but rather as an amount reasonable and necessary to sustain the employee. The determination of need in a particular case shall be established as part of the rehabilitation plan.

§6204. Rehabilitation plan; employee cooperation.

An injured employee agreeing to a rehabilitation plan shall cooperate in carrying it out. On his unreasonable refusal to comply with the provisions of the rehabilitation plan, the injured employee's rights to further subsistence shall be suspended until compliance is obtained, except that the payment of temporary or permanent disability indemnity, which would be payable regardless of the rehabilitation plan, shall not be suspended.

§6205. Rehabilitation plan without state approval.

The injured employee may agree with his employer or insurance carrier upon a rehabilitation plan without submission of such plan for approval to the State Department of Rehabilitation. Provision of service under such plans shall be at no cost to the State General Fund.

§6206. Rehabilitative services; extent.

The injured employee shall receive such medical and vocational rehabilitative services as may be reasonably necessary to restore him to suitable employment.

§6207. Rehabilitative benefits; nature.

The injured employee's rehabilitation benefit is an additional benefit and shall not be converted to or replace any workers' compensation benefit available to him.

§6208. Initiation and acceptance of rehabilitation program.

The initiation and acceptance of a rehabilitation program shall be voluntary and not compulsory upon the employer, the insurance carrier, or the injured employee.

Ref.: Hanna § 35.19.

Labor

DIVISION 5
SAFETY IN EMPLOYMENT

PART 1
Occupational Safety and Health

CHAPTER 1
JURISDICTION AND DUTIES

§6300. Purpose.

The California Occupational Safety and Health Act of 1973 is hereby enacted for the purpose of assuring safe and healthful working conditions for all California working men and women by authorizing the enforcement of effective standards, assisting and encouraging employers to maintain safe and healthful working conditions, and by providing for research, information, education, training, and enforcement in the field of occupational safety and health.

Ref.: Herlick Handbook §§ 2.5, 9.10, 12.11.

§6301. Construction and interpretation.

The definitions set forth in this chapter shall govern the construction and interpretation of this part.

Ref.: Herlick Handbook § 12.11.

§6302. Definitions.

As used in this division:

(a) "Director" means the Director of Industrial Relations.

(b) "Department" means the Department of Industrial Relations.

(c) "Insurer" includes the State Compensation Insurance Fund and any private company, corporation, mutual association, and reciprocal or interinsurance exchange, authorized under the laws of this state to insure employers against liability for compensation under this part and under Division 4 (commencing with Section 3201), and any employer to whom a certificate of consent to self-insure has been issued.

(d) "Division" means the Division of Occupational Safety and Health.

(e) "Standards board" means the Occupational Safety and Health Standards Board, within the department.

(f) "Appeals board" means the Occupational Safety and Health Appeals Board, within the department.

(g) "Aquaculture" means a form of agriculture as defined in Section 17 of the Fish and Game Code.

(h) "Serious injury or illness" means any injury or illness occurring in a place of employment or in connection with any employment that requires inpatient hospitalization, for other than medical observation or diagnostic testing, or in which an employee suffers an amputation, the loss of an eye, or any serious degree of permanent disfigurement, but does not include any injury or illness or death caused by an accident on a public street or highway, unless the accident occurred in a construction zone.

(i) "Serious exposure" means any exposure of an employee to a hazardous substance when the exposure occurs as a result of an incident, accident, emergency, or exposure over time and is in a degree or amount sufficient to create a realistic possibility that death or serious physical harm in the future could result from the actual hazard created by the exposure. **Leg.H.** 1973 ch. 993 §44, effective October 1, 1973, 1979 ch. 72 §25, 1982 ch. 1486 §27, 1983 ch. 131 §29, effective June 27, 1983, 1984 ch. 1317 §1, 2019 ch. 200 (AB 1805) §1.

Ref.: Herlick Handbook § 12.11.

§6303. "Place of employment" and "employment."

(a) "Place of employment" means any place, and the premises appurtenant thereto, where employment is carried on, except a place where the health and safety jurisdiction is vested by law in, and actively exercised by, any state or federal agency other than the division.

(b) "Employment" includes the carrying on of any trade, enterprise, project, industry, business, occupation, or work, including all excavation, demolition, and construction work, or any process or operation in any way related thereto, in which any person is engaged or permitted to work for hire, except household domestic service.

(c) "Employment," for purposes of this division only, also includes volunteer firefighting when covered by Division 4 (commencing with Section 3200) pursuant to Section 3361.

(d) Subdivision (c) shall become operative on January 1, 2004. **Leg.H.** 2001 ch. 807, 2002 ch. 368 (AB 2118), effective September 5, 2002.

Ref.: Herlick Handbook § 12.11.

§6303.5. Unlimited jurisdiction of state where federal law authorizes concurrent jurisdiction.

Nothing in this division shall be construed to limit the jurisdiction of the state over any employment or place of employment by reason of the exercise of occupational safety and health jurisdiction by any federal agency if federal jurisdiction is being exercised under a federal law which expressly authorizes concurrent state jurisdiction over occupational safety or health issues.

§6304. "Employer."

"Employer" shall have the same meaning as in Section 3300.

Ref.: Herlick Handbook §§ 12.7, 12.12.

§6304.1. "Employee."

(a) "Employee" means every person who is required or directed by any employer to engage in any employment or to go to work or be at any time in any place of employment.

(b) "Employee" also includes volunteer firefighters covered by Division 4 (commencing with Section 3200) pursuant to Section 3361.

(c) Subdivision (b) shall become operative on January 1, 2004.

(d) This act does not affect claims that arose pursuant to Division 5 of this code between January 1, 2002, and the effective date of this act. **Leg.H.** 2001 ch. 807, 2002 ch. 368 (AB 2118), effective September 5, 2002.

§6304.2. State prisoners as employees; Department of Corrections as employer.

Notwithstanding Section 6413, and except as provided in Sections 6304.3 and 6304.4, any state prisoner engaged in correctional industry, as defined by the Department of Corrections, shall be deemed to be an "employee," and the Department of Corrections shall be deemed to be an "employer," with regard to such prisoners for the purposes of this part.

§6304.3. Correctional Industry Safety Committee; establishment and duties.

(a) A Correctional Industry Safety Committee shall be established in accordance with Department of Corrections administrative procedures at each facility maintaining a correctional industry, as defined by the Department of Corrections. The Division of Occupational Safety and Health shall promulgate, and the Department of Corrections shall implement, regulations concerning the duties and functions which shall govern the operation of each such committee.

(b) All complaints alleging unsafe or unhealthy working conditions in a correctional industry shall initially be directed to the Correctional Industry Safety Committee of the facility prison. The committee shall attempt to resolve all complaints.

If a complaint is not resolved by the committee within 15 calendar days, the complaint shall be referred by the committee to the division where it shall be reviewed. When the division receives a complaint which, in its determination, constitutes a bona fide allegation of a safety or health violation, the division shall summarily investigate the same as soon as possible, but not later than three working days after receipt of a complaint charging a serious violation, as defined in Section 6309, and not later than 14 calendar days after receipt of a complaint charging a nonserious violation.

(c) Except as provided in subdivision (b) and in Section 6313, the inspection or investigation of a facility maintaining a correctional industry, as defined by the Department of Corrections, shall be discretionary with the division.

(d) Notwithstanding Section 6321, the division may give advance notice of an inspection or investigation and may postpone the same if such action is necessary for the maintenance of security at the facility where the inspection or investigation is to be held, or for insuring the safety and health of the division's representative who will be conducting such inspection or investigation.

§6304.4. When prisoners are not "employees."

A prisoner engaged in correctional industry, as defined by the Department of Corrections, shall not be considered an employee for purposes of the provisions relating to appeal proceedings set forth in Chapter 7 (commencing with Section 6600).

§6304.5. Applicability.

It is the intent of the Legislature that the provisions of this division, and the occupational safety and health standards and orders promulgated under this code, are applicable to proceedings against employers for the exclusive purpose of maintaining and enforcing employee safety.

Neither the issuance of, or failure to issue, a citation by the division shall have any application to, nor be considered in, nor be admissible into, evidence in any personal injury or wrongful death action, except as between an employee and his or her own employer. Sections 452 and 669 of the Evidence Code shall apply to this division and to occupational safety and health standards adopted under this division in the same manner as any other statute, ordinance, or regulation. The testimony of employees of the division shall not be admissible as expert opinion or with respect to the application of occupational safety and health standards. It is the intent of the Legislature that the amendments to this section enacted in the 1999–2000 Regular Session shall not abrogate the holding in *Brock v. State of California* (1978) 8l Cal.App.3d 752. **Leg.H.** 1999 ch. 615.

Ref.: Hanna § 11.22[5]; Herlick Handbook § 12.12.

§6305. Definitions.

(a) "Occupational safety and health standards and orders" means standards and orders adopted by the standards board pursuant to Chapter 6 (commencing with Section 140) of Division 1 and general orders heretofore adopted by the Industrial Safety Board or the Industrial Accident Commission.

(b) "Special order" means any order written by the chief or the chief's authorized representative to correct an unsafe condition, device, or place of employment which poses a threat to the health or safety of an employee and which cannot be made safe under existing standards or orders of the standards board. These orders shall have the same effect as any other standard or order of the standards board, but shall apply only to the employment or place of employment described in the written order of the chief's authorized representative.

§6306. Definitions.

(a) "Safe," "safety," and "health" as applied to an employment or a place of employment mean such freedom from danger to the life, safety, or health of employees as the nature of the employment reasonably permits.

(b) "Safety device" and "safeguard" shall be given a broad interpretation so as to include any practicable method of mitigating or preventing a specific danger, including the danger of exposure to potentially injurious levels of ionizing radiation or potentially injurious quantities of radioactive materials.

Ref.: Herlick Handbook § 12.7.

§6307. Scope of power and jurisdiction.

The division has the power, jurisdiction, and supervision over every employment and place of employment in this state, which is necessary to adequately enforce and administer all laws and lawful standards and orders, or special orders requiring such employment and place of employment to be safe, and requiring the protection of the life, safety, and health of every employee in such employment or place of employment.

Ref.: Herlick Handbook § 1.09.

§6307.1. Role of State Department of Health Services.

The State Department of Health Services shall assist the division in the enforcement of Section 25910 of the Health and Safety Code in the manner prescribed by a written agreement between the State Department of Health Services and the Department of Industrial Relations, pursuant to Section 144.

§6308. Enforcement powers.

The division, in enforcing occupational safety and health standards and orders and special orders may do any of the following:

(a) Declare and prescribe what safety devices, safeguards, or other means or methods of protection are well adapted to render the employees of every employment and place of employment safe as required by law or lawful order.

(b) Enforce Section 25910 of the Health and Safety Code and standards and orders adopted by the standards board pursuant to Chapter 6 (commencing with Section 140) of Division 1 of the Labor Code, for the installation, use, maintenance, and operation of reasonable uniform safety devices, safeguards, and other means or methods of protection, which are necessary to carry out all laws and lawful standards or special orders relative to the protection of the life and safety of employees in employments and places of employment.

(c) Require the performance of any other act which the protection of the life and safety of the employees in employments and places of employment reasonably demands.

An employer may request a hearing on a special order or action ordered pursuant to this section, at which the employer, owner, or any other person may appear. The appeals board shall conduct the hearing at the earliest possible time.

All orders, rules, regulations, findings, and decisions of the division made or entered under this part, except special orders and action orders, may be reviewed by the Supreme Court and the courts of appeal as may be provided by law.

§6308.5. Hearings.

Hearings conducted by the division pursuant to this part shall give any affected employer or other affected person the opportunity to submit facts or arguments, but may be conducted informally, either orally or in writing.

§6309. Investigation procedures.

(a) If the division learns or has reason to believe that an employment or place of employment is not safe or is injurious to the welfare of an employee, it may, on its own motion, or upon complaint, summarily investigate the employment or place of employment, with or without notice or hearings. However, if the division receives a complaint from an employee, an employee's representative, including, but not limited to, an attorney, health or safety professional, union representative, or government agency representative, or an employer of an employee directly involved in an unsafe place of employment, that their employment or place of employment is not safe, it shall, with or without notice or hearing, summarily investigate the complaint as soon as possible, but not later than three working days after receipt of a complaint charging a serious violation, and not later than 14 calendar days after receipt of a complaint charging a nonserious violation. The division shall attempt to determine the period of time in the future that the complainant believes the unsafe condition may continue to exist, and shall allocate inspection resources so as to respond first to those situations in which time is of the essence. For purposes of this section, a complaint is deemed to allege a serious violation if the division determines that the complaint charges that there is a realistic possibility that death or serious physical harm could result from the actual hazard created by a condition that exists, or from one or more practices, means, methods, operations, or processes that have been adopted or are in use in a place of employment. When a complaint charging a serious violation is received from a state or local prosecutor, or a local law enforcement agency, the division shall summarily investigate the employment or place of employment within 24 hours of receipt of the complaint. All other complaints are deemed to allege nonserious violations. The division may enter and serve any necessary order relative thereto. The division is not required to respond to a complaint within this period where, from the facts stated in the complaint, it determines that the complaint is intended to willfully harass an employer or is without any reasonable basis.

(b) The division shall keep complete and accurate records of all complaints, whether verbal or written, and shall inform the complainant, whenever their identity is known, of any action taken by the division in regard to the subject matter of the complaint, and the reasons for the action, within 14 calendar days of taking any action. The records of the division shall include the dates on which any action was taken on the complaint, or the reasons for not taking any action on the complaint. The division shall, pursuant to authorized regulations, conduct an informal review of any refusal by a representative of the division to issue a citation with respect to an alleged violation. The division shall furnish the employee or the representative of employees requesting the review a written statement of the reasons for the division's final disposition of the case.

(c) The name of a person who submits to the division a complaint regarding the unsafe condition of an employment or place of employment shall be kept confidential by the division, unless that person requests otherwise.

(d) The division shall annually compile and release on its internet website data pertaining to complaints received and citations issued.

(e) The requirements of this section do not relieve the division of its requirement to inspect and assure that all places of employment are safe and healthful for employees. The division shall maintain the capability to receive and act upon complaints at all times. However, the division shall prioritize investigations of reports of accidents involving death or serious injury or illness and complaints that allege a serious violation over investigations of complaints that allege a nonserious violation. **Leg.H.** 1999 ch. 615, 2002 ch. 885 (AB 2837), 2003 ch. 884 (AB 1719), 2015 ch. 25 (SB 84) §43, effective June 24, 2015, 2019 ch. 200 (AB 1805) §2.

§6310. Discrimination against employee for filing complaint or otherwise exercising rights; employer prohibited from retaliation.

(a) No person shall discharge or in any manner discriminate against any employee because the employee has done any of the following:

(1) Made any oral or written complaint to the division, other governmental agencies having statutory responsibility for or assisting the division with reference to employee safety or health, [1] **their** employer, or [2] **their** representative.

(2) Instituted or caused to be instituted any proceeding under or relating to [3] **their** rights or has testified or is about to testify in the proceeding or because of the exercise by the employee on behalf of [4] **themselves**, or others of any rights afforded [5] **to them**.

(3) Participated in an occupational health and safety committee established pursuant to Section 6401.7.

(4) Reported a work-related fatality, injury, or illness, requested access to occupational injury or illness reports and records that are made or maintained pursuant to Subchapter 1 (commencing with Section 14000) of Chapter 1 of Division 1 of Title 8 of the California Code of Regulations, or exercised any other rights protected by the federal Occupational Safety and Health Act (29 U.S.C. Sec. 651 et seq.), except in cases where the employee alleges [6] **they have** been retaliated against because [7] **they have** filed or made known [8] **their** intention to file a workers' compensation claim pursuant to Section 132a, which is under the exclusive jurisdiction of the Workers' Compensation Appeals Board.

(b) Any employee who is discharged, threatened with discharge, demoted, suspended, or in any other manner discriminated against in the terms and conditions of employment by [9] **their** employer because the employee has made a bona fide oral or written complaint to the division, other governmental agencies having statutory responsibility for or assisting the division with reference to employee safety or health, [10] **their** employer, or [11] **their** representative, of unsafe working conditions, or work practices, in [12] **their** employment or place of employment, or has participated in an employer-employee occupational health and safety committee, shall be entitled to reinstatement and reimbursement for lost wages and work benefits caused by the acts of the employer. Any employer who willfully refuses to rehire, promote, or otherwise restore an employee or former employee who has been determined to be eligible for rehiring or promotion by a grievance procedure, arbitration, or hearing authorized by law, is guilty of a misdemeanor.

(c) An employer, or a person acting on behalf of the employer, shall not retaliate against an employee because the employee is a family member of a person who has, or is perceived to have, engaged in any acts protected by this section.

(d) For purposes of this section, "employer" or "a person acting on behalf of the employer" includes, but is not limited to, a client employer as defined in paragraph (1) of subdivision (a) of Section 2810.3 and an employer listed in subdivision (b) of Section 6400.

(e) Notwithstanding Section 6303 or other law, as used in this section, "employee" includes a domestic work employee, except for a person who performs household domestic service that is publicly funded, including publicly funded household domestic service provided to a recipient, client, or beneficiary with a share of cost in that service. Leg.H. 2015 ch. 792 (AB 1509) §4, 2017 ch. 28 (SB 96) §29, effective June 27, 2017, 2020 ch. 288 (AB 2658) §1.

§6310. 2020 Deletes. [1] his or her **[2]** his or her **[3]** his or her **[4]** himself, herself **[5]** him or her **[6]** he or she has **[7]** he or she has **[8]** his or her **[9]** his or her **[10]** his or her **[11]** his or her **[12]** his or her

Ref.: 8 C.C.R. §14300.36.

§6311. Employee's refusal to work when health or safety threatened.

No employee shall be laid off or discharged for refusing to perform work in the performance of which this code, including Section 6400, any occupational safety or health standard, or any safety order of the division or standards board will be violated, where the violation would create a real and apparent hazard to the employee or [1] **their** fellow employees. Any employee who is laid off or discharged in violation of this section or is otherwise not paid because [2] **the employee** refused to perform work in the performance of which this code, any occupational safety or health standard, or any safety order of the division or standards board will be violated and where the violation would create a real and apparent hazard to the employee or [3] **their** fellow employees shall have a right of action for wages for the time the employee is without work as a result of the layoff or discharge. **Notwithstanding Section 6303 or other law, as used in this section, "employee" includes a domestic work employee, except for a person who performs household domestic service that is publicly funded, including publicly funded household domestic service provided to a recipient, client, or beneficiary with a share of cost in that service. Leg.H.** 1973 ch. 993 §61, effective October 1, 1973, 1982 ch. 1384 §1, 1985 ch. 1479 §6, 2020 ch. 288 (AB 2658) §2.

§6311. 2020 Deletes. [1] his or her **[2]** he or she **[3]** his or her

Ref.: 8 C.C.R. §14300.36.

§6311.5. Willful and knowing direction of employee to remain in, or enter, an area closed due to public health or safety menace; exemption.

(a)(1) Except as noted in paragraph (2), a person who, after receiving notice to evacuate or leave, willfully and knowingly directs an employee to remain in, or enter, an area closed due to a menace to the public health or safety

Labor

as set forth in Section 409.5 of the Penal Code shall be guilty of a misdemeanor.

(2) This section shall not apply to persons authorized to close an area, or to enter an area that has been closed, pursuant to subdivision (a) or (b) of Section 409.5 of the Penal Code. This exemption includes persons listed in subdivision (d) of Section 409.5 of the Penal Code.

(b) Notwithstanding Section 6303 or other law, as used in this section, the term "employee" includes a person employed for household domestic service, including a person who performs household domestic service that is publicly funded, including publicly funded household domestic service provided to a recipient, client, or other beneficiary with a share of cost in that service. **Leg.H.** 2020 ch. 288 (AB 2658) §3.

§6312. Employee's recourse for violation of §6310 or §6311.

Any employee who believes that he or she has been discharged or otherwise discriminated against by any person in violation of Section 6310 or 6311 may file a complaint with the Labor Commissioner pursuant to Section 98.7.

§6313. Cases for investigation.

(a) The division shall investigate the causes of any employment accident that is fatal to one or more employees or that results in a serious injury or illness, or a serious exposure, unless it determines that an investigation is unnecessary. If the division determines that an investigation of an accident is unnecessary, it shall summarize the facts indicating that the accident need not be investigated and the means by which the facts were determined. The division shall establish guidelines for determining the circumstances under which an investigation of these accidents and exposures is unnecessary.

(b) The division may investigate the causes of any other industrial accident or occupational illness which occurs within the state in any employment or place of employment, or which directly or indirectly arises from or is connected with the maintenance or operation of the employment or place of employment, and shall issue any orders necessary to eliminate the causes and to prevent reoccurrence. The orders may not be admitted as evidence in any action for damages, or any proceeding to recover compensation, based on or arising out of injury or death caused by the accident or illness. **Leg.H.** 2002 ch. 885 (AB 2837).

§6313.5. Transmission of contractor citations to State License Board.

The division, after consultation with the Contractors' State License Board, shall transmit to the Contractors' State License Board copies of any citations or other actions taken by the division against a contractor as defined in the Contractors' State License Law (Chapter 9 (commencing with Section 7000) of Division 3 of the Business and Professions Code). **Leg.H.** 1973 ch. 993 §66, effective October 1, 1973, 2016 ch. 372 (SB 465) §4.

§6314. Access to place of employment for investigative purposes.

(a) To make an investigation or inspection, the chief of the division and all qualified divisional inspectors and investigators authorized by him or her shall, upon presenting appropriate credentials to the employer, have free access to any place of employment to investigate and inspect during regular working hours, and at other reasonable times when necessary for the protection of safety and health, and within reasonable limits and in a reasonable manner. The chief or his or her authorized representative may, during the course of any investigation or inspection, obtain any statistics, information, or any physical materials in the possession of the employer that are directly related to the purpose of the investigation or inspection, conduct any tests necessary to the investigation or inspection, and take photographs. Photographs taken by the division during the course of any investigation or inspection shall be considered to be confidential information pursuant to the provisions of Section 6322, and shall not be deemed to be public records for purposes of the California Public Records Act.

(b) If permission to investigate or inspect the place of employment is refused, or the facts or circumstances reasonably justify the failure to seek permission, the chief or his or her authorized representative may obtain an inspection warrant pursuant to the provisions of Title 13 (commencing with Section 1822.50) of the Code of Civil Procedure. Cause for the issuance of a warrant shall be deemed to exist if there has been an industrial accident, injury, or illness reported, if any complaint that violations of occupational safety and health standards exist at the place of employment has been received by the division, or if the place of employment to be inspected has been chosen on the basis of specific neutral criteria contained in a general administrative plan for the enforcement of this division.

(c) The chief and his or her authorized representatives may issue subpoenas to compel the attendance of witnesses and the production of books, papers, records, and physical materials, administer oaths, examine witnesses under oath, take verification or proof of written materials, and take depositions and affidavits for the purpose of carrying out the duties of the division.

(d) In the course of any investigation or inspection of an employer or place of employment by an authorized representative of the division, a representative of the employer and a representative authorized by his or her employees shall have an opportunity to accompany him or her on the tour of inspection. Any employee or employer, or their authorized representatives, shall have the right to discuss safety and health violations or safety and health problems with the inspector privately during the course of an investigation or inspection. Where there is no authorized employee representative, the chief or his or her authorized representatives shall consult with a reasonable number of employees concerning matters of health and safety of the place of employment.

(e) During any investigation of an industrial accident or occupational illness conducted by the division pursuant to the provisions of Section 6313, the chief or his or her authorized representative may issue an order to preserve physical materials or the accident site as they were at the time the accident or illness occurred if, in the opinion of the division, it is necessary to do so in order to determine the cause or causes of the accident or illness, and the evidence is in potential danger of being removed, altered, or tampered with. Under these circumstances, the division shall issue that order in a manner that will avoid, to the extent possible, any interference with normal business operations.

A conspicuous notice that an order has been issued shall be prepared by the division and shall be posted by the employer in the area or on the article to be preserved. The order shall be limited to the immediate area and the machines, devices, apparatus, or equipment directly associated with the accident or illness.

Any person who knowingly violates an order issued by the division pursuant to this subdivision shall, upon conviction, be punished by a fine of not more than five thousand dollars ($5,000). **Leg.H.** 1993 ch. 998.

§6314.1. High hazardous industries.

(a) The division shall establish a program for targeting employers in high hazardous industries with the highest incidence of preventable occupational injuries and illnesses and workers' compensation losses. The employers shall be identified from any or all of the following data sources: the California Work Injury and Illness program, the Occupational Injuries and Illness Survey, the federal hazardous employers' list, experience modification and other relevant data maintained and furnished by all rating organizations as defined in Section 11750.1 of the Insurance Code, histories of violations of Occupational Safety and Health Act standards, and any other source deemed to be appropriate that identifies injury and illness rates.

(b) The division shall establish procedures for ensuring that the highest hazardous employers in the most hazardous industries are inspected on a priority basis. The division may send a letter to the high hazard employers who are identified pursuant to this section informing them of their status and directing them to submit a plan, including the establishment of joint labor-management health and safety committees, within a time determined by the division for reducing their occupational injury and illness rates. Employers who submit plans that meet the requirements of the division may be placed on a secondary inspection schedule. Employers on that schedule shall be inspected on a random basis as determined by the division. Employers who do not submit plans meeting the requirements of the division within the time specified by the division shall be placed on the primary inspection list. Every employer on the primary inspection list shall be subject to an inspection. The division shall employ sufficient personnel to meet minimum federal targeted inspection standards.

(c) The division shall establish and maintain regional plans for allocating the division's resources for the targeted inspection program in addition to the inspections required or authorized in Section 6309, 6313, and 6320. Each regional plan shall focus on industries selected from the targeted inspection program as well as any other scheduled inspections that the division determines to be appropriate to the region, including the cleanup of hazardous waste sites. All targeted inspections shall be conducted on a priority basis, targeting the worst employers first.

(d) In order to maximize the impact of the regional plans, the division shall coordinate its education, training, and consulting services with the priorities established in the regional plans. **Leg.H.** 1993 ch. 121 §68, effective July 16, 1993.

§6314.5. Scope of inspection.

(a) Every inspection conducted by the division shall include an evaluation of the employer's injury prevention program established pursuant to Section 6401.7. The division shall evaluate injury prevention programs using the criteria for substantial compliance determined by the standards board. The evaluation shall include interviews with a sample of employees and the members of any employer-employee occupational safety and health committee. In any inspection which includes work for which a permit is required pursuant to Section 6500 and for which a permit has been issued pursuant to Section 6502, the evaluation of the employer's injury prevention program shall be limited to the implementation of the plan approved by the division in the issuance of the permit. Before any inspection is concluded, the division shall notify the employer of the services available from the department to assist the employer to establish, maintain, improve, and evaluate the employer's injury prevention program.

(b) Inspections also shall include an evaluation of the following:

(1) The condition or conditions alleged in the complaint if the inspection is conducted pursuant to Section 6309.

(2) The condition or conditions involved in the accident if the inspection is conducted pursuant to Section 6313.

(3) The condition or conditions involving work for which a permit is required pursuant to Section 6500, for which notification of asbestos related work is required pursuant to Section 6501.5, or for which a report of use of a carcinogen is required pursuant to Section 9030.

(4) The condition or conditions related to significant safety or health hazards in the industries identified in the regional plans developed pursuant to Section 6314.1.

(5) The condition or conditions involved in abatement of previous violations, special orders, or action orders if the inspection is conducted pursuant to Section 6320.

(c) The scope of any inspection may be expanded beyond the evaluations specified in subdivisions (a) and (b) whenever, in the opinion of the division, a more complete inspection is warranted.

Ref.: 8 C.C.R. §§15353, 15354.

§6315. Bureau of Investigations.

(a) There is within the division a Bureau of Investigations. The bureau is responsible for directing accident investigations involving violations of standards, orders, special orders, or Section 25910 of the Health and Safety Code, in which there is a serious injury to five or more employees, death, or request for prosecution by a division representative. The bureau shall review inspection reports involving a serious violation where there have been serious injuries to one to four employees or a serious exposure, and may investigate those cases in which the bureau finds criminal violations may have occurred. The bureau is responsible for preparing cases for the purpose of prosecution, including evidence and findings.

(b) The division shall provide the bureau with all of the following:

(1) All initial accident reports.

(2) The division's inspection report for any inspection involving a serious violation where there is a fatality, and the reports necessary for the bureau's review required pursuant to subdivision (a).

(3) Any other documents in the possession of the division requested by the bureau for its review or investigation of any case or which the division determines will be helpful to the bureau in its investigation of the case.

(c) The supervisor of the bureau is the administrative chief of the bureau, and shall be an attorney.

(d) The bureau shall be staffed by as many attorneys and investigators as are necessary to carry out the purposes of this chapter. To the extent possible, the attorneys and investigators shall be experienced in criminal law.

(e) The supervisor of the bureau and bureau representatives designated by the supervisor have a right of access to all places of employment necessary to the investigation, may collect any evidence or samples they deem necessary to an investigation, and have all of the powers enumerated in Section 6314.

(f) The supervisor of the bureau and bureau representatives designated by the supervisor may serve all processes and notices throughout the state.

(g) In any case where the bureau is required to conduct an investigation, and in which there is a serious injury or death, the results of the investigation shall be referred in a timely manner by the bureau to the appropriate prosecuting authority having jurisdiction for appropriate action, unless the bureau determines that there is legally insufficient evidence of a violation of the law. If the bureau determines that there is legally insufficient evidence of a violation of the law, the bureau shall notify the appropriate prosecuting authority, if the prosecuting authority requests notice.

(h) The bureau may communicate with the appropriate prosecuting authority at any time the bureau deems appropriate.

(i) Upon the request of a county district attorney, the department may develop a protocol for the referral of cases that may involve criminal conduct to the appropriate prosecuting authority in lieu of or in cooperation with an investigation by the bureau. The protocol shall provide for the voluntary acceptance of referrals after a review of the case by the prosecuting authority. In cases accepted for investigation by the prosecuting authority, the protocol shall provide for cooperation between the prosecuting authority, the division, and the bureau. Where a referral is declined by the prosecuting authority, the bureau shall comply with subdivisions (a) to (h), inclusive. **Leg.H.** 2002 ch. 885 (AB 2837), 2003 ch. 884 (AB 1719).

§6315.3. Submission of report of bureau activities.

The bureau shall, not later than February 15, annually submit to the division for submission to the director a report on the activities of the bureau, including, but not limited to, the following:

(a) Totals of each type of report provided the bureau under each category in subdivision (b) of Section 6315.

(b) Totals of each type of case reflecting the number of investigations and court cases in progress at the start of the calendar year being reported, investigations completed in the calendar year, cases referred to appropriate prosecuting authorities in the calendar year, and investigations and court cases in progress at the end of the calendar year. The types of cases shall include the following:

(1) Those that the bureau is required to investigate, divided into fatalities, serious injuries to five or more employees, and requests for prosecution from a division representative.

(2) Those that were initiated by the bureau following the review required in subdivision (a) of Section 6315, divided into serious injuries to fewer than five employees and serious exposures.

(c) A summary of the dispositions in the calendar year of cases referred by the bureau to appropriate prosecuting authorities. The summary shall be divided into the types of cases, as described in subdivision (b), and shall show at least the violation, the statute for which the case was referred for prosecution, and the dates of referral to the bureau for investigation, referral from the bureau for prosecution, and the final court action if the case was prosecuted.

(d) A summary of investigations completed in the calendar year that did not result in a referral for prosecution, divided into the types of cases as described in subdivision (b), showing the violation and the reasons for nonreferral.

(e) A summary of the use of the bureau's resources in accomplishing the bureau's mission. **Leg.H.** 1984 ch. 1317 §6, 2006 ch. 538 (SB 1852) §493.

§6315.5. Admissibility as evidence of division's standards, findings, etc.

All occupational safety and health standards and orders, rules, regulations, findings, and decisions of the division made and entered pursuant to this part are admissible as evidence in any prosecution for the violation of any provision of this part, and shall, in every such prosecution, be presumed to be reasonable and lawful and to fix a reasonable and proper standard and requirement of safety unless, prior to the institution of the prosecution for such violation, proceedings for a hearing on a special order are instituted, or a petition is filed under Section 11426 of the Government Code.

§6316. Limitations on powers of other governing bodies.

Except as limited by Chapter 6 (commencing with Section 140) of Division 1, nothing in this part shall deprive the governing body of any county, city, or public corporation, board, or department, of any power or jurisdiction over or relative to any place of employment.

§6317. Steps taken against employers violating regulations.

If, upon inspection or investigation, the division believes that an employer has violated Section 25910 of the Health and Safety Code or any standard, rule, order, or regulation established pursuant to Chapter 6 (commencing with Section 140) of Division 1 of the Labor Code, or any standard, rule, order, or regulation established pursuant to this part, it shall with reasonable promptness issue a citation to the employer. Each citation shall be in writing and shall describe with particularity the nature of the violation, including a reference to the provision of the code, standard, rule, regulation, or order alleged to have been violated. In addition, the citation shall fix a reasonable time for the abatement of the alleged violation. The period specified for abatement shall not commence running until the date the citation or notice is received by certified mail and the certified mail receipt is signed, or if not signed, the date the return is made to the post office. If the division officially and directly delivers the citation or notice to the employer, the period specified for abatement shall commence running on the date of the delivery.

A "notice" in lieu of citation may be issued with respect to violations found in an inspection or investigation which meet either of the following requirements:

(1) The violations do not have a direct relationship upon the health or safety of an employee.

(2) The violations do not have an immediate relationship to the health or safety of an employee, and are of a general or regulatory nature. A notice in lieu of a citation may be issued only if the employer agrees to correct the violations within a reasonable time, as specified by the division, and agrees not to appeal the finding of the division that the violations exist. A notice issued pursuant to this paragraph shall have the same effect as a citation for purposes of establishing repeat violations or a failure to abate. Every notice shall clearly state the abatement period specified by the division, that the notice may not be appealed, and that the notice has the same effect as a citation for purposes of establishing a repeated violation or a failure to abate. The employer shall indicate agreement to the provisions and conditions of the notice by his or her signature on the notice.

A notice shall not be issued in lieu of a citation if the violations are serious, repeated, willful, or arise from a failure to abate.

The director shall prescribe guidelines for the issuance of these notices.

The division may impose a civil penalty against an employer as specified in Chapter 4 (commencing with Section 6423) of this part. A notice in lieu of a citation may not be issued if the number of first instance violations found in the inspection (other than serious, willful, or repeated violations) is 10 or more violations.

A citation or notice shall not be issued by the division more than six months after the occurrence of the violation. For purposes of issuing a citation or notice for a violation of subdivision (b) or (c) of Section 6410, including any implementing related regulations, an "occurrence" continues until it is corrected, or the division discovers the violation, or the duty to comply with the violated requirement ceases to exist. Nothing in this paragraph is intended to alter the meaning of the term "occurrence" for violations of health and safety standards other than the recordkeeping requirements set forth in subdivision (b) or (c) of Section 6410, including any implementing related regulations.

The director shall prescribe procedures for the issuance of a citation or notice.

The division shall prepare and maintain records capable of supplying an inspector with previous citations and notices issued to an employer. **Leg.H.** 1991 ch. 599, effective October 5, 1991, 2018 ch. 538 (AB 2334) §4.

§6317.5. Employer's falsification of materials posted or distributed in workplace—Notice of violation; posting of citation.

(a) If, upon inspection or investigation, the division finds that an employer has falsified any materials posted in the workplace or distributed to employees related to the California Occupational Safety and Health Act, the division shall issue a citation to the employer.

(b) Each citation issued pursuant to this section, or a copy or copies thereof, shall be prominently posted, as prescribed in regulations issued by the director.

(c) Any employer served with a citation pursuant to subdivision (a) may appeal to the appeals board pursuant to the provisions of Chapter 7 (commencing with Section 6600). The appeal shall be subject to the timeframes and procedures set forth in that chapter.

(d) The provisions of this section are in addition to, and not in lieu of, all other criminal penalties and civil remedies that may be applicable to any act leading to issuance of a citation pursuant to this section. **Leg.H.** 1993 ch. 580.

§6317.7. Notice of no violations.

If, upon inspection or investigation, the division finds no violations pursuant to this chapter, the division with reasonable promptness shall issue a written notice to the employer specifying the areas inspected and stating that no violations were found.

The director shall prescribe procedures for the issuance of this notice. **Leg.H.** 1993 ch. 580.

§6318. Posting of citations.

(a) Each citation issued under Section 6317, and each special order or action ordered pursuant to Section 6308, or a copy or copies thereof, shall be prominently posted, as prescribed in regulations issued by the director, at or near each place a violation referred to in the citation or order occurred. All postings shall be maintained for three working days, or until the unsafe condition is abated, whichever is longer. Following each investigation of an industrial accident or occupational illness, if no violations are found, the employer shall post a notice prepared by the division so indicating for three working days.

(b) When the division verifies abatement of a serious violation or an order at the time of inspection or upon reinspection, the employer shall post a notice prepared by the division so indicating for three working days. In all other cases of abatement of serious violations, the employer shall post the signed statement confirming abatement prepared pursuant to Section 6320.

§6319. Procedures for citation or order issuance; appeal; setting of penalties.

(a) If, after an inspection or investigation, the division issues a citation pursuant to Section 6317 or an order pursuant to Section 6308, it shall, within a reasonable time

Labor

after the termination of the inspection or investigation, notify the employer by certified mail of the citation or order, and that the employer has 15 working days from receipt of the notice within which to notify the appeals board that he or she wishes to contest the citation or order for any reason set forth in Section 6600 or 6600.5.

(b) An employer served by certified mail with a notice of civil penalty may appeal to the appeals board within 15 working days from receipt of that notice for any reason set forth in Section 6600. If the citation is issued for a violation involving the condition or operation of any machine, device, apparatus, or equipment, and a person other than the employer is obligated to the employer to repair the machine, device, apparatus, or equipment and to pay any penalties assessed against the employer, the other person may appeal to the appeals board within 15 working days of the receipt of the citation by the employer for any reasons set forth in Section 6600.

(c) The director shall promulgate regulations covering the assessment of civil penalties under this chapter which give due consideration to the appropriateness of the penalty with respect to the following factors:

(1) The size of the business of the employer being charged.

(2) The gravity of the violation.

(3) The good faith of the employer, including timely abatement.

(4) The history of previous violations.

(d) Notwithstanding subdivision (c), if serious injury, illness, exposure, or death is caused by a serious, willful, or repeated violation, or by a failure to correct a serious violation within the time permitted for its correction, the penalty shall not be reduced for a reason other than the size of the business of the employer being charged. Whenever the division issues a citation for a violation covered by this subdivision, it shall notify the employer of its determination that serious injury, illness, exposure or death was caused by the violation and shall, upon request, provide the employer with a copy of the inspection report.

(e) The employer is not liable for a civil penalty under this part for any citation issued by a division representative providing consulting services pursuant to Sections 6354 and 6355.

(f) Whenever a citation of a self-insured employer for a willful or repeat serious violation of the standard adopted pursuant to Section 6401.7 becomes final, the division shall notify the director so that a hearing may be held to determine whether good cause exists to revoke the employer's certificate of consent to self-insure as provided in Section 3702.

(g) Based upon the evidence, the division may propose appropriate modifications concerning the characterization of violations and corresponding modifications to civil penalties as a result thereof. For serious violations, the division shall not grant a proposed modification to civil penalties for abatement or credit for abatement unless the employer has done any of the following:

(1) Abated the violation at the time of the initial inspection.

(2) Abated the violation at the time of a subsequent inspection prior to the issuance of a citation.

(3) Submitted a signed statement under penalty of perjury and supporting evidence, when necessary to prove abatement, in accordance with subdivision (b) of Section 6320. **Leg.H.** 2014 ch. 497 (AB 1634) §1, 2015 ch. 303 (AB 731) §379.

Ref.: 8 C.C.R. §§15210.1, 15353, 15354.

§6319.3. Civil penalty assessed against new employer.

(a) Except as provided in subdivision (b) of this section and subdivision (j) of Section 6401.7, no civil penalty shall be assessed against any new employer in the state for a violation of any standard developed pursuant to subdivision (a) of Section 6401.7 for a period of one year after the date the new employer establishes a business in the state.

(b) Subdivision (a) shall only apply to an employer who has made a good faith effort to comply with any standard developed pursuant to subdivision (a) of Section 6401.7, but shall not apply if the employer is found to have committed a serious, willful, or repeated violation of that standard, or fails to abate the violation and is assessed a penalty pursuant to Section 6430. **Leg.H.** 1993 ch. 928.

§6319.5. Employer's showing of good-faith compliance effort.

Upon a showing by an employer of a good-faith effort to comply with the abatement requirement of a citation, and that abatement has not been completed because of factors beyond his reasonable control, the division, after an opportunity for a hearing, shall issue an order affirming or modifying the abatement requirements in such citation.

§6320. Reinspection.

(a) If, after inspection or investigation, the division issues a special order, order to take special action, or a citation for a serious violation, and if at the time of inspection the order is not complied with or the violation is not abated, the division shall conduct a reinspection in the following cases:

(1) All inspections or investigations involving a serious violation of a standard adopted pursuant to Section 6401.7, a special order or order to take special action, serious violations of those orders, and serious violations characterized as repeat or willful or with abatement periods of less than six days. These reinspections shall be conducted at the end of the period fixed for compliance with the order or abatement of the violation or within 30 days thereafter.

(2) At least 20 percent of the inspections or investigations involving a serious violation not otherwise scheduled for reinspection. These inspections shall be randomly selected and shall be conducted at the end of the period fixed for abatement of the violation or within a reasonable time thereafter.

(b) Whenever a serious violation is not abated at the time of the initial or subsequent inspection, the division shall require the employer to submit a signed statement, with supporting evidence, where necessary to prove abatement, under penalty of perjury, that he or she has complied with the abatement terms within the period fixed for abatement of the violation. The division may grant a modification pursuant to subdivision (g) of Section 6319 only if the employer has abated the violation at the time of the initial or subsequent inspection or the statement, signed under penalty of perjury, and supporting evidence are received within 10 working days after the end of the period fixed for abatement. At no time shall the period for abatement be fixed prior to the issuance of a citation. The submission of a signed abatement statement shall not be considered as evidence of a violation during an appeal. The division shall include on the initial notice of civil penalty a clear warning of reinspection for failure to submit the required statement in the time allotted, and of an additional, potentially substantial monetary penalty for failure to abate the violation. If the division fails to receive evidence of abatement or the statement within 10 working days after the end of the abatement period, the division shall notify the employer that the additional civil penalty for failure to abate, as provided in Section 6430, will be assessed retroactive to the end of the abatement period unless the employer can provide sufficient evidence that the violation was abated prior to that date. The division shall conduct a reinspection of serious violations within 45 days following the end of the abatement period whenever it still has no evidence of abatement. **Leg.H.** 2014 ch. 497 (AB 1634) §2.

§6321. Limitation on advance warning; penalties for violation.

No person or employer shall be given advance warning of an inspection or investigation by any authorized representative of the division unless authorized under provisions of this part.

Only the chief or, in the case of his absence, his authorized representatives shall have the authority to permit advance notice of an inspection or investigation. The director shall, as soon as practicable, set down limitations under which an employer may be granted advance notice by the chief. In no case, except an imminent danger to the health or safety of an employee or employees, is advance notice to be authorized when the investigation or inspection is to be made as a result of an employee complaint.

Any person who gives advance notice of any inspection to be conducted, without authority from the chief or his designees, is guilty of a misdemeanor and shall, upon conviction, be punished by a fine of not more than one thousand dollars ($1,000) or by imprisonment for not more than six months, or by both.

§6322. Confidentiality of information obtained.

All information reported to or otherwise obtained by the chief or his representatives in connection with any inspection or proceeding of the division which contains or which might reveal a trade secret referred to in Section 1905 of Title 18 of the United States Code, or other information that is confidential pursuant to Chapter 3.5 (commencing with Section 6250) of Division 7 of Title 1 of the Government Code, shall be considered confidential, except that such information may be disclosed to other officers or employees of the division concerned with carrying out the purposes of the division or when relevant in any proceeding of the division. The appeals board, standards board, the courts, or the director shall in any such proceeding issue such orders as may be appropriate to protect the confidentiality of trade secrets. Violation of this section is a misdemeanor.

§6323. Injunctions.

If the condition of any employment or place of employment or the operation of any machine, device, apparatus, or equipment constitutes a serious menace to the lives or safety of persons about it, the division may apply to the superior court of the county in which such place of employment, machine, device, apparatus, or equipment is situated, for an injunction restraining the use or operation thereof until such condition is corrected.

§6324. Temporary restraining orders.

The application to the superior court accompanied by affidavit showing that such place of employment, machine, device, apparatus, or equipment is being operated in violation of a safety order or standard, or in violation of Section 25910 of the Health and Safety Code, and that such use or operation constitutes a menace to the life or safety of any person employed thereabout and accompanied by a copy of the order or standard applicable thereto is a sufficient prima facie showing to warrant, in the discretion of the court, the immediate granting of a temporary restraining order. No bond shall be required from the division as a prerequisite to the granting of any restraining order.

§6325. [First of Two; Repealed January 1, 2023] Prohibition of entry into dangerous place or use of dangerous equipment.

(a) When, in the opinion of the division, a place of employment, machine, device, apparatus, or equipment or any part thereof is in a dangerous condition, is not properly guarded or is dangerously placed so as to constitute an imminent hazard to employees, entry therein, or the use thereof, as the case may be, shall be prohibited by the division, and a conspicuous notice to that effect shall be attached thereto. Such prohibition of use shall be limited to the immediate area in which the imminent hazard exists, and the division shall not prohibit any entry in or use of a place of employment, machine, device, apparatus, or equipment, or any part thereof, which is outside such area of imminent hazard. Such notice shall not be removed except by an authorized representative of the division, nor until the place of employment, machine, device, apparatus, or equipment is made safe and the required safeguards or safety appliances or devices are provided. This [1] **subdivision** shall not prevent the entry or use with the division's knowledge and permission for the sole purpose of eliminating the dangerous conditions.

(b) When, in the opinion of the division, a place of employment, operation, or process, or any part thereof, exposes workers to the risk of infection with severe acute respiratory syndrome coronavirus 2 (SARS-CoV-2) so as to constitute an imminent hazard to employees, the performance of such operation or process, or entry into such place of employment, as the case may be, may be prohibited by the division, and a notice thereof shall be provided to the employer and posted in a conspicuous place at the place of employment. Such prohibition of use shall be limited to the immediate area

Labor

in which the imminent hazard exists, and the division shall not prohibit the performance of any operation or process, entry into or use of a place of employment, or any part thereof, which is not exposing employees to, or is outside such area of imminent hazard. In addition, this prohibition shall be issued in a manner so as not to materially interrupt the performance of critical governmental functions essential to ensuring public health and safety functions or the delivery of electrical power or water. This notice shall not be removed except by an authorized representative of the division, nor until the place of employment, operation, or process is made safe and the required safeguards or safety appliances or devices are provided. This subdivision shall not prevent the entry or use with the division's knowledge and permission for the sole purpose of eliminating the dangerous conditions.

(c) This section shall remain in effect only until January 1, 2023, and as of that date is repealed. Leg.H. 1973 ch. 993 §86, effective October 1, 1973; 2020 ch. 84 (AB 685) §2.

§6325. 2020 Deletes. [1] section

§6325. [Second of Two; Operative January 1, 2023] Prohibition of entry into dangerous place or use of dangerous equipment.

(a) When, in the opinion of the division, a place of employment, machine, device, apparatus, or equipment or any part thereof is in a dangerous condition, is not properly guarded or is dangerously placed so as to constitute an imminent hazard to employees, entry therein, or the use thereof, as the case may be, shall be prohibited by the division, and a conspicuous notice to that effect shall be attached thereto. Such prohibition of use shall be limited to the immediate area in which the imminent hazard exists, and the division shall not prohibit any entry in or use of a place of employment, machine, device, apparatus, or equipment, or any part thereof, which is outside such area of imminent hazard. Such notice shall not be removed except by an authorized representative of the division, nor until the place of employment, machine, device, apparatus, or equipment is made safe and the required safeguards or safety appliances or devices are provided. This section shall not prevent the entry or use with the division's knowledge and permission for the sole purpose of eliminating the dangerous conditions.

(b) This section shall become operative on January 1, 2023. **Leg.H.** 2020 ch. 84 (AB 685) §3.

§6325.5. Order prohibiting use of workplace containing friable asbestos.

If the division has reasonable cause to believe that any workplace contains friable asbestos, and if there appears to be inadequate protection for employees at that workplace to the hazards from airborne asbestos fibers, the division may issue an order prohibiting use.

§6326. Penalties for violation of no-entry or no-use orders.

Every person who, after such notice is attached as provided in Section 6325, enters any such place of employment, or uses or operates any such place of employment, machine, device, apparatus, or equipment before it is made safe and the required safeguards or safety appliances or devices are provided, or who defaces, destroys or removes any such notice without the authority of the division, is guilty of a misdemeanor punishable by a fine of up to one thousand dollars ($1,000), or up to one year in the county jail, or both.

§6327. Contesting prohibition of use or entry.

Once an authorized representative of the division has prohibited entry in or use of a place of employment, machine device, apparatus, or equipment, as specified in Section 6325, the employer may contest the order and shall be granted, upon request, a hearing by the division to review the validity of the representative's order. The hearing shall be held within 24 hours following the employer's request.

§6327.5. Employee action if division fails to act.

If the division arbitrarily or capriciously fails to take action to prevent or prohibit any conditions or practices in any employment or place of employment which are such that danger exists which could reasonably be expected to cause death or serious physical harm immediately or before the imminence of such danger can be eliminated through other available means, any employee who may be injured by reason of such failure, or the representatives of such employees, may bring an action against the chief of the division in any appropriate court for a writ of mandate to compel the division to prevent or prohibit the condition. Nothing contained in this section shall be deemed to prevent the bringing of a writ of mandate against any appropriate person or entity as may be provided by law.

§6328. Informational notices.

The division shall prepare a notice containing pertinent information regarding safety rules and regulations. The notice shall contain the address and telephone number of the nearest division office; a clear explanation of an employee's right to report any unsafe working conditions; the right to request a safety inspection by the division for unsafe conditions; the right to refuse to work under conditions which endanger his life or health; the right to receive information under the Hazardous Substances Information and Training Act (Ch. 2.5 (commencing with Section 6360)); posting and notice requirements of employers and the division; and any other information the division deems necessary. It shall be supplied to employers as soon as practical. The division shall promulgate regulations on the content and the required location and number of notices which must be posted by employers. Sufficient posters in both English and Spanish shall be printed to supply employers in this state.

§6329. Payment of money collected from employers.

All money collected for violation of standards, orders, or special orders of, or for fees paid pursuant to this division shall be paid into the state treasury to the credit of the General Fund.

The Department of Industrial Relations shall account to the Department of Finance and the State Controller for all moneys so received and furnish proper vouchers therefor.

§6330. Annual report to Legislature.

The director shall prepare and submit to the Legislature, not later than March 1, an annual report on the division activities. The report shall include, but need not be limited to, the following information for the previous calendar year:

(a) The amount of funds allocated and spent in enforcement, education and research, and administration by the division.

(b) Total inspections made, and citations issued by the division.

(c) The number of civil penalties assessed, total amount of fines collected and the number of appeals heard.

(d) The number of contractors referred to the Contractor's State License Board for hearing, pursuant to Section 7109.5 of the Business and Professions Code, and the total number of these cases resulting in suspension or revocation of a license.

(e) The report from the division prepared by the Bureau of Investigations for submission to the director pursuant to Section 6315.3.

(f) Recommendations for legislation which improves the ability of the division to provide safety in places of employment.

The report shall be made to the Speaker of the Assembly and the Chairman of the Rules Committee of the Senate, for assignment to the appropriate committee or committees for evaluation.

§6331. Testing of self-contained breathing apparatus.

The division shall enter into a contract for the development and execution of tests to define safety standards for the use of positive pressure, closed circuit, breathing apparatus in interior structural fires. The testing shall define numerically what constitutes positive pressure in breathing apparatus. The testing shall also address the issues of the heat of the oxygen coming into the mask, the condensation inside the mask, the possibility of, and effect of, moisture condensation in the lungs of the wearer of the mask, and the risks associated with a dislodgement of the mask in an interior structural fire situation. The development of these tests shall utilize the resources of recognized specialists in fire research to design, conduct, and execute the tests and develop the standards. The standards board shall adopt or revise safety standards based on the results of these tests.

The test parameters, the location where the testing will take place, and the level of expertise required shall be determined by the Cal-OSHA Self Contained Breathing Apparatus Advisory Committee.

§6332. Employers to keep record of violence committed against community health care worker.

(a) For purposes of this section, the following terms have the following meanings:

(1) "Community health care worker" means an individual who provides health care or health care-related services to clients in home settings.

(2) "Employer" means a person or entity that employs a community health care worker. "Employer" does not include an individual who is a recipient of home-based services and who is responsible for hiring his or her own community health care worker.

(3) "Violence" means a physical assault or a threat of a physical assault.

(b) Every employer shall keep a record of any violence committed against a community health care worker and shall file a copy of that record with the department in the form and detail and within the time limits prescribed by the department. **Leg.H.** 2000 ch. 493, 2012 ch. 46 (SB 1038) §107, effective June 27, 2012.

CHAPTER 2
EDUCATION AND RESEARCH
[Selected Provisions]

§6350. Educational and research program.

The division shall maintain an education and research program for the purpose of providing in-service training of division personnel, safety education for employees and employers, research and consulting safety services.

§6351. Preparation and distribution of health and safety information.

The division shall be responsible for preparation and distribution of information concerning occupational safety and health programs, methods, techniques or devices. Such information may include but is not limited to safety publications, films and audiovisual material, speeches and conferences on safety.

§6352. Safety training programs; priority of program development.

The division shall provide safety training programs, upon request, for employees and employers. Priority for the development of safety training programs shall be in those occupations which pose the greatest hazard to the safety and health of employees.

§6353. Continuing research.

The division shall conduct continuing research into methods, means, operations, techniques, processes and practices necessary for improvement of occupational safety and health of employees.

§6354. Consulting services.

The division shall, upon request, provide a full range of occupational safety and health consulting services to any employer or employee group. These consulting services shall include:

(a) A program for identifying categories of occupational safety and health hazards causing the greatest number and most serious preventable injuries and illnesses and workers' compensation losses and the places of employment where they are occurring. The hazards, industries, and places of employment shall be identified from the data system that is used in the targeted inspection program pursuant to Section 6314.1. The division shall develop procedures for offering consultation services to high hazard employers who are identified pursuant to this section. The services may include the development of educational material and procedures for reducing or eliminating safety and health hazards, conducting workplace surveys to identify health and safety problems, and development of plans to improve employer health and safety loss records.

The program shall include a component for reducing the number of work-related, repetitive motion injuries, including, but not limited to, back injuries. The division may formulate recommendations for reducing repetitive motion injuries after conducting a survey of the workplace of the employer who accepts services of the division. The recommendations shall include, wherever appropriate, the application of generally accepted ergonomic and engineering principles to eliminate repetitive motions that are generally expected to result in injuries to workers. The recommendations shall also include, wherever appropriate, training programs to instruct workers in methods for performing job-related movements, such as lifting heavy objects, in a manner that minimizes strain and provides safeguards against injury.

The division shall establish model injury and illness prevention training programs to prevent repetitive motion injuries, including recommendations for the minimum qualifications of instructors. The model programs shall be made available to employers, employer associations, workers' compensation insurers, and employee organizations on request.

(b) A program for providing assistance in the development of injury prevention programs for employees and employers. The highest priority for the division's consulting services shall be given to development of these programs for businesses with fewer than 250 employees in industries identified in the regional plans developed pursuant to subdivision (b) of Section 6314.1.

(c) A program for providing employers or employees with information, advice, and recommendations on maintaining safe employment or place of employment, and on applicable occupational safety and health standards, techniques, devices, methods, practices, or programs. **Leg.H.** 1993 ch. 121, effective July 16, 1993, 1995 ch. 903.

§6354.5. Insurer's provision of occupational safety and health loss control consultation services; standards; insurance loss control services coordinator.

(a) Any insurer desiring to write workers' compensation insurance shall maintain or provide occupational safety and health loss control consultation services. The insurer may employ qualified personnel to provide these services or provide the services through another entity.

(b) The program of an insurer for furnishing loss control consultation services shall be adequate to meet minimum standards prescribed by this section. Required loss control consultation services shall be adequate to identify the hazards exposing the insured to, or causing the insured, significant workers' compensation losses, and to advise the insured of steps needed to mitigate the identified workers' compensation losses or exposures. The program of an insurer for furnishing loss control consultation services shall provide all of the following:

(1) A workplace survey, including discussions with management and, where appropriate, nonmanagement personnel with permission of the employer.

(2) A review of injury records with appropriate personnel.

(3) The development of a plan to improve the employer's health and safety loss control experience, which shall include, where appropriate, modifications to the employer's injury and illness prevention program established pursuant to Section 6401.7. At the time that an insurance policy is issued and annually thereafter, and again when notified by Cal-OSHA that an insured employer has been identified as a targeted employer pursuant to Section 6314.1, the insurer shall provide each insured employer with a written description of the consultation services together with a notice that the services are available at no additional charge to the employer. These notices to the employer shall appear in at least 10-point bold type.

(c) The insurer shall not charge any fee in addition to the insurance premium for safety and health loss control consultation services.

(d) Nothing in this section shall be construed to require insurers to provide loss control services to places of employment that do not pose significant preventable hazards to workers.

(e) The director shall establish an insurance loss control services coordinator position in the Department of Industrial Relations. The coordinator shall provide information to employers about the availability of loss control consultation services and respond to employers' questions and complaints about loss control consultation services provided by their insurer. The coordinator shall notify the insurer of every complaint concerning loss control consultation services. If the employer and the insurer are unable to agree on a mutually satisfactory solution to the complaint, the coordinator shall investigate the complaint. Whenever the coordinator determines that the loss control consultation services provided by the insurer are inadequate or inappropriate, he or she shall recommend to the employer and the insurer the actions required to bring the loss control program into compliance. If the employer and the insurer are unable to agree on a mutually satisfactory solution to the complaint, the coordinator shall forward his or her recommendations to the director. The cost of providing the coordinator services shall be paid out of the Workers' Occupational Safety and Health Education Fund created by subdivision (a) of Section 6354.7. However, no more than 20 percent of that fund may be expended for this purpose each year. **Leg.H.** 1995 ch. 556, 2002 ch. 6 (AB 749).

Ref.: Herlick Handbook § 3.15.

§6354.7. Workers' Occupational Safety and Health Education Fund; development of worker safety and health training and education program.

(a) The Workers' Occupational Safety and Health Education Fund is hereby created as a special account in the State Treasury. Proceeds of the fund may be expended, upon appropriation by the Legislature, by the Commission on Health and Safety and Workers' Compensation for the purpose of establishing and maintaining a worker occupational safety and health training and education program and an insurance loss control services coordinator. The director shall levy and collect fees to fund these purposes from insurers subject to Section 6354.5. However, the fee assessed against any insurer shall not exceed the greater of one hundred dollars ($100) or 0.0286 percent of paid workers' compensation indemnity amounts for claims as reported for the previous calendar year to the designated rating organization for the analysis required under subdivisions (b) and (c) of Section 11759.1 of the Insurance Code. All fees shall be deposited in the fund.

(b) The commission shall establish and maintain a worker safety and health training and education program. The purpose of the worker occupational safety and health training and education program shall be to promote awareness of the need for prevention education programs, to develop and provide injury and illness prevention education programs for employees and their representatives, and to deliver those awareness and training programs through a network of providers throughout the state. The commission may conduct the program directly or by means of contracts or interagency agreements.

(c) The commission shall establish an employer and worker advisory board for the program. The advisory board shall guide the development of curricula, teaching methods, and specific course material about occupational safety and health, and shall assist in providing links to the target audience and broadening the partnerships with worker-based organizations, labor studies programs, and others that are able to reach the target audience.

(d) The program shall include the development and provision of a needed core curriculum addressing competencies for effective participation in workplace injury and illness prevention programs and on joint labor-management health and safety committees. The core curriculum shall include an overview of the requirements related to injury and illness prevention programs and hazard communication.

(e) The program shall include the development and provision of additional training programs for any or all of the following categories:

(1) Industries on the high hazard list.

(2) Hazards that result in significant worker injuries, illnesses, or compensation costs.

(3) Industries or trades in which workers are experiencing numerous or significant injuries or illnesses.

(4) Occupational groups with special needs, such as those who do not speak English as their first language, workers with limited literacy, young workers, and other traditionally underserved industries or groups of workers. Priority shall be given to training workers who are able to train other workers and workers who have significant health and safety responsibilities, such as those workers serving on a health and safety committee or serving as designated safety representatives.

(f) The program shall operate one or more libraries and distribution systems of occupational safety and health training material, which shall include, but not be limited to, all material developed by the program pursuant to this section.

(g) The advisory board shall annually prepare a written report evaluating the use and impact of programs developed.

(h) The payment of administrative costs incurred by the commission in conducting the program shall be made from the Workers' Occupational Safety and Health Education Fund. **Leg.H.** 2002 ch. 866 (AB 486).

Ref.: Hanna § 1.18; Herlick Handbook § 3.15.

§6355. Employer's immunity from prosecution or penalties.

If the employer requests or accepts consulting services offered pursuant to Section 6354, the division in providing such services at the employer's employment or place of employment shall neither institute any prosecution under Section 6423 nor issue any citations for a violation of any standard or order adopted pursuant to Chapter 6 (commencing with Section 140) of Division 1. In any instance in which the division representative providing the consulting service finds that the conditions of employment, place of employment, any work procedure, or the operation of any machine, device, apparatus, or equipment constitutes an imminent hazard or danger, within the meaning of Section 6325, to the lives, safety, or health of employees, entry therein, or the use thereof, as the case may be, shall be prohibited by the division pursuant to Section 6325. The employer shall not, however, be liable to prosecution under Section 6423, nor shall the division issue any citations or assess any civil penalties, except in any case where the employer fails to comply with the division's prohibition of entry or use, or in any case where the provisions of Section 6326 apply. **Leg.H.** 1993 ch. 121, effective July 16, 1993.

§6356. Worker Safety Bilingual Investigative Support, Enforcement, and Training Account.

(a) There is hereby created, in the General Fund, the Worker Safety Bilingual Investigative Support, Enforcement, and Training Account. The moneys in the account may be expended by the department, upon appropriation by the Legislature, for the purposes of this part.

(b) The department may receive and accept a contribution of funds from an individual or private organization, including the proceeds from a judgment in a state or federal court, if the contribution is made to carry out the purposes of this part. The department shall immediately deposit the contribution in the account established by subdivision (a).

(c) The department may not receive or accept a contribution of funds under this section made from the proceeds of a judgment in a criminal action filed pursuant to Section 6423 or 6425 of the Labor Code. **Leg.H.** 2002 ch. 885 (AB 2837).

§6357. Adoption of standards for ergonomics in the workplace.

On or before January 1, 1995, the Occupational Safety and Health Standards Board shall adopt standards for ergonomics in the workplace designed to minimize the instances of injury from repetitive motion. **Leg.H.** 1993 ch. 121, effective July 16, 1993.

CHAPTER 2.5 HAZARDOUS SUBSTANCES INFORMATION AND TRAINING

ARTICLE 3 Hazardous Substances [Selected Provisions]

§6380. List of hazardous substances.

For the purposes of this chapter, the director, pursuant to Section 6382, shall establish a list of hazardous substances and shall make the list available to manufacturers, employers, and the public. Substances on the list shall be designated by their chemical and common name or names. The director shall adopt, amend, and repeal regulations for the establishment of the list of hazardous substances pursuant to the provisions of Chapter 3.5 (commencing with Section 11340) of Part 1 of Division 3 of Title 2 of the Government Code. **Leg.H.** 1980 ch. 874 § 1.

ARTICLE 4 Duties

§6390. Preparation and provision of MSDS.

The manufacturer of any hazardous substance listed pursuant to the provisions of Section 6380 shall prepare and provide its direct purchasers of the hazardous substance with an MSDS containing the information specified in Section 6391 which, to the best of the manufacturer's knowledge, is current, accurate, and complete, based on information then reasonably available to the manufacturer. For purposes of this section, a substance, mixture, or product shall not be considered a hazardous substance if present in a physical state, volume, or concentration for which there is no valid and substantial evidence that any adverse acute or chronic risk to human health may occur from exposure. The manufacturer shall revise an MSDS on a timely basis as appropriate to the importance of any new information which would affect the contents of the existing MSDS, and in any event within one year of such information becoming available to the manufacturer. If the new information indicates significantly increased risks to, or measures necessary to protect, employee health, as compared to those stated on the MSDS previously provided, the manufacturer shall provide such new information to persons who have purchased the product directly from the manufacturer within the last year. **Leg.H.** 1980 ch. 874.

§6390.2. Manufacturers or importers of cosmetics or disinfectants with hazardous substances to post and maintain safety data sheet (SDS) on website accessible to public.

(a) An entity that manufactures or imports a hazardous substance or mixture of substances that constitutes a cosmetic, as defined in Section 109900 of the Health and Safety Code, not excluded by Section 6385, or any substance or mixture of substances that constitutes a disinfectant, as defined in Section 977 of Article 12 of Division 9 of Title 16 of the California Code of Regulations, that is required to develop or obtain an SDS in accordance with this chapter and Section 5194 of Title 8 of the California Code of Regulations, shall post and maintain the SDS in accordance with Section 6390 on the entity's internet website by its brand name or other commonly known name in a manner generally accessible to the public. If a separate SDS based on color or tint exists, the entity shall post and translate each SDS. The entity shall translate the SDS into Spanish, Vietnamese, Chinese, and Korean, and other languages that the director may determine to be common for the beauty care industry. These translations shall also be publicly available on the entity's internet website.

(b) This section shall become operative on July 1, 2020. **Leg.H.** 2019 ch. 305 (AB 647) §1.

§6390.5. Labeling.

The manufacturer, importer, and distributor of any hazardous substance, and the employer, shall label each container of a hazardous substance in a manner consistent with the federal Hazard Communication Standard (29 C.F.R. Sec. 1910.1200) and as set forth in applicable occupational safety and health standards adopted by the standards board. **Leg.H.** 1985 ch. 1000 §4.

§6391. Information manufacturers must provide purchasers.

The information which manufacturers shall provide to their purchasers pursuant to the provisions of Section 6390 shall include the following, if pertinent:

(a) The chemical name, any common names, and the CAS number of the hazardous substance.

(b) The hazards or other risks in the use of the hazardous substance, including all of the following:

(1) The potential for fire, explosion, and reactivity.

(2) The acute and chronic health effects or risks from exposure.

(3) The potential routes of exposure and symptoms of overexposure.

(c) The hazards or other risks of exposure to the combustion products of the hazardous substance.

(d) The proper precautions, handling practices, necessary personal protective equipment, and other safety precautions in the use of or exposure to the hazardous substance, and its combustion products.

(e) The emergency procedures for spills, fire, disposal, and first aid.

(f) A description in lay terms, if not otherwise provided, on either a separate sheet or with the body of the information specified in this section, of the specific potential health risks posed by the hazardous substance and its combustion products intended to alert any person reading the information.

(g) The month and year that the information was compiled and, for an MSDS issued after January 1, 1981, the name and address of the manufacturer responsible for preparing the information. **Leg.H.** 1988 ch. 423 §1.

§6392. Proof of compliance—Federal MSDS.

Provision of a federal Material Safety Data Sheet or equivalent shall constitute prima facie proof of compliance with Section 6390. **Leg.H.** 1980 ch. 874, 1992 ch. 1214.

§6393. Relief of obligation to provide MSDS.

The manufacturer shall be relieved of the obligation to provide a specific purchaser of a hazardous substance with an MSDS pursuant to Section 6390 if the manufacturer has a record of having provided the specific purchaser with the most current version of the MSDS, or if the product is one sold at retail and is incidentally sold to an employer or the employer's employees, in the same form, approximate amount, concentration, and manner as it is sold to consumers, and, to the seller's knowledge, employee exposure to the product is not significantly greater than the consumer exposure occurring during the principal consumer use of the product. Except for products so labeled, this section does not relieve the manufacturer of the requirement to provide direct purchasers with new, revised, or later information or an MSDS pursuant to Section 6390. **Leg.H.** 1991 ch. 274 §3, 1992 ch. 427.

§6394. Transmission of copy of MSDS to department.

The preparer of an MSDS shall provide the department with a copy of the MSDS on each hazardous substance it manufactures. The preparer may transmit the MSDS to the department in either paper or electronic form. In the electronic filing of an MSDS, it is the responsibility of the preparer to protect any trade secret information contained in the MSDS during transmission to the department. Upon receipt by the department of the MSDS, it is the responsibility of the department to protect any trade secret information. **Leg.H.** 1980 ch. 874, 1999 ch. 366.

§6395. MSDS for entire product mixture.

(a) The manufacturer may provide the information required by Section 6390 on an entire product mixture, instead of on each hazardous substance in it, when all of the following conditions exist:

(1) Hazard test information exists on the mixture itself, or adequate information exists to form a valid judgment of the hazardous properties of the mixture itself and the MSDS indicates that the information presented and the conclusions drawn are from some source other than direct test data on the mixture itself, and that an MSDS on each constituent hazardous substance identified on the MSDS is available upon request.

(2) Provision of information on the mixture will be as effective in protecting employee health as information on the ingredients.

(3) The hazardous substances in the mixture are identified on the MSDS unless it is either unfeasible to describe all the ingredients in the mixture or the identity of the ingredients is itself a valid trade secret, in either case the reason why the hazardous substances in the mixture are not identified shall be stated on the MSDS.

(b) A single mixture MSDS may be provided for more than one formulation of a product mixture if the information provided pursuant to Section 6390 does not vary for the formulation. **Leg.H.** 1980 ch. 874.

§6396. Protection from disclosure of trade secrets.

(a) The Director of Industrial Relations shall protect from disclosure any and all trade secrets coming into his or her possession, as defined in subdivision (d) of Section 6254.7 of the Government Code, when requested in writing or by appropriate stamping or marking of documents by the manufacturer or producer of a mixture.

(b) Any information reported to or otherwise obtained by the Director of Industrial Relations, or any of his or her representatives or employees, which is exempt from disclosure under subdivision (a), shall not be disclosed to anyone except an officer or employee of the state or of the United States of America, in connection with the official duties of that officer or employee under any law for the protection of health, or to contractors with the state and their employees if in the opinion of the director the disclosure is necessary and required for the satisfactory performance of a contract for performance of work in connection with this act.

(c) Any officer or employee of the state, or former officer or employee, who by virtue of that employment or official position has obtained possession of or has access to material the disclosure of which is prohibited by this section, and who, knowing that disclosure of the material is prohibited, knowingly and willfully discloses the material in any manner to any person not entitled to receive it, is guilty of a misdemeanor. Any contractor with the state and any employee of that contractor, who has been furnished information as authorized by this section, shall be considered to be an employee of the state for purposes of this section.

(d) Information certified to by appropriate officials of the United States, as necessarily kept secret for national defense purposes, shall be accorded the full protections against disclosure as specified by that official or in accordance with the laws of the United States.

(e)(1) The director, upon his or her own initiative, or upon receipt of a request pursuant to the California Public Records Act, (Chapter 3.5 (commencing with Section 6250) of Division 7 of Title 1 of the Government Code) for the release of data submitted and designated as a trade secret by an employer, manufacturer, or producer of a mixture, shall determine whether any or all of the data so submitted are a properly designated trade secret.

(2) If the director determines that the data is not a trade secret, the director shall notify the employer, manufacturer, or producer of a mixture by certified mail.

(3) The employer, manufacturer, or producer of a mixture shall have 15 days after receipt of notification to provide the director with a complete justification and statement of the grounds on which the trade secret privilege is claimed. This justification and statement shall be submitted by certified mail.

(4) The director shall determine whether the data are protected as a trade secret within 15 days after receipt of the justification and statement, or if no justification and statement is filed, within 30 days of the original notice, and shall notify the employer or manufacturer and any party who has requested the data pursuant to the California Public Records Act of that determination by certified mail. If the director determines that the data are not protected as a trade secret, the final notice shall also specify a date, not sooner than 15 days after the date of mailing of the final notice, when the data shall be available to the public.

(5) Prior to the date specified in the final notice, an employer, manufacturer, or producer of a mixture may institute an action in an appropriate superior court for a declaratory judgment as to whether the data are subjected to protection under subdivision (a).

(f) This section does not authorize a manufacturer to refuse to disclose information required pursuant to this chapter to the director. **Leg.H.** 1983 ch. 142 §112, 1995 ch. 91.

§6397. Provision of MSDS to direct purchaser at time of sale.

(a) Any person other than a manufacturer who sells a mixture or any hazardous substance shall provide its direct purchasers of the mixture or hazardous substance at the time of sale with a copy of the most recent MSDS or equivalent information prepared and supplied to the person pursuant to either Section 6390 or subdivision (b) whenever it is foreseeable that the provisions of this chapter may apply to the purchaser.

(b) Any person who produces a mixture may, for the purposes of this section, prepare and use a mixture MSDS, subject to the provisions of Section 6395.

(c) Any person subject to the provisions of subdivision (a) shall be relieved of the obligation to provide a specific purchaser of a hazardous substance with an MSDS if he or she has a record of having provided the specific purchaser with the most recent version of the MSDS, or if the product is one sold at retail and is incidentally sold to an employer or the employer's employees, in the same form, approximate amount, concentration, and manner as it is sold to consumers, and, to the seller's knowledge, employee exposure to the product is not significantly greater than the consumer exposure occurring during the principal consumer use of the product. **Leg.H.** 1991 ch. 274 §4.

§6398. Employer's duties toward employees.

The Occupational Safety and Health Standards Board shall adopt a standard setting forth an employer's duties toward its employees under this chapter, on or before July 1, 1981, consistent with the following guidelines:

(a) An MSDS shall be available to an employee, collective bargaining representative, or the employee's physician, on a timely and reasonable basis, on substances in the workplace.

(b) Employers shall furnish employees who may be exposed to a hazardous substance with information on the contents of the MSDS for the hazardous substances or equivalent information, either in written form or through training programs, which may be generic to the extent appropriate and related to the job.

(c) Provision shall be made for employees to be informed of their rights under this chapter and under the standard to be adopted. **Leg.H.** 1980 ch. 874.

§6398.5. Availability of printable information on certain cleaning product ingredients and nonfunctional constituents.

An employer that is required to maintain safety data sheets and ensure that those safety data sheets are readily accessible in accordance with this chapter and Section 5194 of Title 8 of the California Code of Regulations shall, in the same manner and to the same persons, make readily available the printable information described in subdivision (c) of Section 108954.5 of the Health and Safety Code for designated products, as defined in subdivision (f) of Section 108952 of the Health and Safety Code, in the workplace. **Leg.H.** 2017 ch. 830 (SB 258) §2.

§6399. Availability of MSDS to employees.

Upon request, the manufacturer of a hazardous substance or the producer of a mixture who has produced a mixture MSDS pursuant to the provisions of subdivision (b) of Section 6397 shall make available to any employer, whose employees may be exposed to its product in the workplace, an MSDS on its product. If the employer does not already have an MSDS and has not already made written inquiry within 12 months as to whether a substance or product is subject to the requirements of this chapter or if the employer has not already made written inquiry within 6 months as to whether any new, revised, or later information has been issued for a hazardous substance, the employer shall do so within seven working days of a request to do so by an employee or employee's collective bargaining representative or physician. The employer may adopt reasonable procedures for acting upon such employee requests to avoid interruption of normal work operations. The manufacturer or the producer of a mixture MSDS pursuant to the provisions of Section 6397 shall answer such inquiries within 15 working days of their receipt, stating that the substance or product is subject to the requirements of this chapter and furnishing the most current MSDS or a statement that the MSDS is under development and the estimated completion date, or stating that it is not subject to the requirements of this chapter, with a brief explanation of why the chapter is not applicable. If an employer has not received a response from a manufacturer within 25 working days of the date the request was made, the employer shall send a copy of the request made of the manufacturer to the director with the notation that no response has been received. **Leg.H.** 1980 ch. 874.

§6399.1. Compliance with Food and Agricultural Code §12981.

Compliance with regulations of the Director of Pesticide Regulation issued pursuant to Section 12981 of the Food and Agricultural Code shall be deemed compliance with the obligations of an employer toward his or her employees under this chapter. **Leg.H.** 1980 ch. 874, 1991 Gov. Reorg. Plan 1, effective July 17, 1991.

§6399.2. Operative date of article.

This article shall become operative 180 days after adoption of the initial list of hazardous substances pursuant to Article 3 (commencing with Section 6380). **Leg.H.** 1980 ch. 874.

1982 Note: Section 339 of Title 8 of the California Code of Regulations, as filed August 25, 1982, contains a hazardous substances list.

CHAPTER 3
RESPONSIBILITIES AND DUTIES OF EMPLOYERS AND EMPLOYEES

§6400. Employer to furnish safe and healthy workplace; employer categories that may be issued citations when employee exposed to hazard on multiemployer worksites.

(a) Every employer shall furnish employment and a place of employment that is safe and healthful for the employees therein.

(b) On multiemployer worksites, both construction and nonconstruction, citations may be issued only to the following categories of employers when the division has evidence that an employee was exposed to a hazard in violation of any requirement enforceable by the division:

(1) The employer whose employees were exposed to the hazard (the exposing employer).

(2) The employer who actually created the hazard (the creating employer).

(3) The employer who was responsible, by contract or through actual practice, for safety and health conditions on the worksite, which is the employer who had the authority for ensuring that the hazardous condition is corrected (the controlling employer).

(4) The employer who had the responsibility for actually correcting the hazard (the correcting employer).

The employers listed in paragraphs (2) to (4), inclusive, of this subdivision may be cited regardless of whether their own employees were exposed to the hazard.

(c) It is the intent of the Legislature, in adding subdivision (b) to this section, to codify existing regulations with respect to the responsibility of employers at multiemployer worksites. Subdivision (b) of this section is declaratory of existing law and shall not be construed or interpreted as creating a new law or as modifying or changing an existing law. **Leg.H.** 1999 ch. 615.

Ref.: Herlick Handbook §§ 9.6, 9.10, 12.7, 12.12.

§6401. Safe and healthy equipment and practices requirement.

Every employer shall furnish and use safety devices and safeguards, and shall adopt and use practices, means, methods, operations, and processes which are reasonably adequate to render such employment and place of employment safe and healthful. Every employer shall do every other thing reasonably necessary to protect the life, safety, and health of employees.

Ref.: Herlick Handbook § 9.10.

§6401.5. Prohibition against salvaging materials during demolition.

No salvage of materials shall be permitted while demolition is in progress on any building, structure, falsework, or scaffold more than three stories high or the equivalent height for which a permit is required under subdivision (c) of Section 6500. For this purpose salvage does not include removal of material from premises solely for the purpose of clearing the area to facilitate the continuation of the demolition.

Ref.: Herlick Handbook § 12.7.

§6401.7. Injury prevention programs.

(a) Every employer shall establish, implement, and maintain an effective injury prevention program. The program shall be written, except as provided in subdivision (e), and shall include, but not be limited to, the following elements:

(1) Identification of the person or persons responsible for implementing the program.

(2) The employer's system for identifying and evaluating workplace hazards, including scheduled periodic inspections to identify unsafe conditions and work practices.

(3) The employer's methods and procedures for correcting unsafe or unhealthy conditions and work practices in a timely manner.

(4) An occupational health and safety training program designed to instruct employees in general safe and healthy work practices and to provide specific instruction with respect to hazards specific to each employee's job assignment.

(5) The employer's system for communicating with employees on occupational health and safety matters, including provisions designed to encourage employees to inform the employer of hazards at the worksite without fear of reprisal.

(6) The employer's system for ensuring that employees comply with safe and healthy work practices, which may include disciplinary action.

(b) The employer shall correct unsafe and unhealthy conditions and work practices in a timely manner based on the severity of the hazard.

(c) The employer shall train all employees when the training program is first established, all new employees, and all employees given a new job assignment, and shall train employees whenever new substances, processes, procedures, or equipment are introduced to the workplace and represent a new hazard, and whenever the employer receives notification of a new or previously unrecognized hazard. An employer in the construction industry who is required to be licensed under Chapter 9 (commencing with Section 7000) of Division 3 of the Business and Professions Code may use employee training provided to the employer's employees under a construction industry occupational safety and health training program approved by the division to comply with the requirements of subdivision (a) relating to employee training, and shall only be required to provide training on hazards specific to an employee's job duties.

(d) The employer shall keep appropriate records of steps taken to implement and maintain the program. An employer in the construction industry who is required to be licensed under Chapter 9 (commencing with Section 7000) of Division 3 of the Business and Professions Code may use records relating to employee training provided to the employer in connection with an occupational safety and health training program approved by the division to comply with this subdivision, and shall only be required to keep

Labor

records of those steps taken to implement and maintain the program with respect to hazards specific to an employee's job duties.

(e)(1) The standards board shall adopt a standard setting forth the employer's duties under this section, on or before January 1, 1991, consistent with the requirements specified in subdivisions (a), (b), (c), and (d). The standards board, in adopting the standard, shall include substantial compliance criteria for use in evaluating an employer's injury prevention program. The board may adopt less stringent criteria for employers with few employees and for employers in industries with insignificant occupational safety or health hazards.

(2) Notwithstanding subdivision (a), for employers with fewer than 20 employees who are in industries that are not on a designated list of high hazard industries and who have a workers' compensation experience modification rate of 1.1 or less, and for any employers with fewer than 20 employees who are in industries that are on a designated list of low hazard industries, the board shall adopt a standard setting forth the employer's duties under this section consistent with the requirements specified in subdivisions (a), (b), and (c), except that the standard shall only require written documentation to the extent of documenting the person or persons responsible for implementing the program pursuant to paragraph (1) of subdivision (a), keeping a record of periodic inspections pursuant to paragraph (2) of subdivision (a), and keeping a record of employee training pursuant to paragraph (4) of subdivision (a). To any extent beyond the specifications of this subdivision, the standard shall not require the employer to keep the records specified in subdivision (d).

(3)(A) The division shall establish a list of high hazard industries using the methods prescribed in Section 6314.1 for identifying and targeting employers in high hazard industries. For purposes of this subdivision, the "designated list of high hazard industries" shall be the list established pursuant to this paragraph.

(B) For the purpose of implementing this subdivision, the Department of Industrial Relations shall periodically review, and as necessary revise, the list.

(4) For the purpose of implementing this subdivision, the Department of Industrial Relations shall also establish a list of low hazard industries, and shall periodically review, and as necessary revise, that list.

(f) The standard adopted pursuant to subdivision (e) shall specifically permit employer and employee occupational safety and health committees to be included in the employer's injury prevention program. The board shall establish criteria for use in evaluating employer and employee occupational safety and health committees. The criteria shall include minimum duties, including the following:

(1) Review of the employer's periodic, scheduled worksite inspections; investigation of causes of incidents resulting in injury, illness, or exposure to hazardous substances; and investigation of any alleged hazardous condition brought to the attention of any committee member. When determined necessary by the committee, the committee may conduct its own inspections and investigations.

(2)(A) Upon request from the division, verification of abatement action taken by the employer as specified in division citations.

(B) If an employer's occupational safety and health committee meets the criteria established by the board, it shall be presumed to be in substantial compliance with paragraph (5) of subdivision (a).

(g) The division shall adopt regulations specifying the procedures for selecting employee representatives for employer-employee occupational health and safety committees when these procedures are not specified in an applicable collective bargaining agreement. No employee or employee organization shall be held liable for any act or omission in connection with a health and safety committee.

(h) The employer's injury prevention program, as required by this section, shall cover all of the employer's employees and all other workers who the employer controls or directs and directly supervises on the job to the extent these workers are exposed to worksite and job assignment specific hazards. Nothing in this subdivision shall affect the obligations of a contractor or other employer that controls or directs and directly supervises its own employees on the job.

(i) When a contractor supplies its employee to a state agency employer on a temporary basis, the state agency employer may assess a fee upon the contractor to reimburse the state agency for the additional costs, if any, of including the contract employee within the state agency's injury prevention program.

(j)(1) The division shall prepare a Model Injury and Illness Prevention Program for Non-High-Hazard Employment, and shall make copies of the model program prepared pursuant to this subdivision available to employers, upon request, for posting in the workplace. An employer who adopts and implements the model program prepared by the division pursuant to this paragraph in good faith shall not be assessed a civil penalty for the first citation for a violation of this section issued after the employer's adoption and implementation of the model program.

(2) For purposes of this subdivision, the division shall establish a list of non-high-hazard industries in California. These industries, identified by their Standard Industrial Classification Codes, as published by the United States Office of Management and Budget in the Manual of Standard Industrial Classification Codes, 1987 Edition, are apparel and accessory stores (Code 56), eating and drinking places (Code 58), miscellaneous retail (Code 59), finance, insurance, and real estate (Codes 60–67), personal services (Code 72), business services (Code 73), motion pictures (Code 78) except motion picture production and allied services (Code 781), legal services (Code 81), educational services (Code 82), social services (Code 83), museums, art galleries, and botanical and zoological gardens (Code 84), membership organizations (Code 86), engineering, accounting, research, management, and related services (Code 87), private households (Code 88), and miscellaneous services (Code 89). To further identify industries that may be included on the list, the division shall also consider data from a rating organization, as defined in Section 11750.1 of the Insurance Code, and all other appropriate information. The list shall be established by June 30, 1994, and shall be reviewed, and as necessary revised, biennially.

(3) The division shall prepare a Model Injury and Illness Prevention Program for Employers in Industries with Intermittent Employment, and shall determine which industries have historically utilized seasonal or intermittent employees. An employer in an industry determined by the division to have historically utilized seasonal or intermittent employees shall be deemed to have complied with the requirements of subdivision (a) with respect to a written injury prevention program if the employer adopts the model program prepared by the division pursuant to this paragraph and complies with any instructions relating thereto.

(k) With respect to any county, city, city and county, or district, or any public or quasi-public corporation or public agency therein, including any public entity, other than a state agency, that is a member of, or created by, a joint powers agreement, subdivision (d) shall not apply.

(*l*) Every workers' compensation insurer shall conduct a review, including a written report as specified below, of the injury and illness prevention program (IIPP) of each of its insureds with an experience modification of 2.0 or greater within six months of the commencement of the initial insurance policy term. The review shall determine whether the insured has implemented all of the required components of the IIPP, and evaluate their effectiveness. The training component of the IIPP shall be evaluated to determine whether training is provided to line employees, supervisors, and upper level management, and effectively imparts the information and skills each of these groups needs to ensure that all of the insured's specific health and safety issues are fully addressed by the insured. The reviewer shall prepare a detailed written report specifying the findings of the review and all recommended changes deemed necessary to make the IIPP effective. The reviewer shall be or work under the direction of a licensed California professional engineer, certified safety professional, or a certified industrial hygienist. **Leg.H.** 1991 ch. 964, 1993 chs. 927, 928, 929 §4, 2003 ch. 639 (SB 228), 2004 ch. 34 (SB 899), effective April 19, 2004, 2012 ch. 46 (SB 1038) §108, effective June 27, 2012.

2004 Note: The amendment to §6401.7 made by this act shall apply prospectively from the date of enactment of this act, regardless of the date of injury, unless otherwise specified, but shall not constitute good cause to reopen or rescind, alter, or amend any existing order, decision, or award of the Workers' Compensation Appeals Board. Stats. 2004 ch. 34 (SB 899) §47.

Ref.: 8 C.C.R. §§15203, 15210.1, 15353, 15354; Herlick Handbook §§ 3.20, 9.10, 12.7.

§6401.8. Adoption of workplace violence prevention plan by certain licensed hospitals; duty of hospital to report violent incidents.

(a) The standards board, no later than July 1, 2016, shall adopt standards developed by the division that require a hospital licensed pursuant to subdivision (a), (b), or (f) of Section 1250 of the Health and Safety Code, except as exempted by subdivision (d), to adopt a workplace violence prevention plan as a part of its injury and illness prevention plan to protect health care workers and other facility personnel from aggressive and violent behavior.

(b) The standards adopted pursuant to subdivision (a) shall include all of the following:

(1) A requirement that the workplace violence prevention plan be in effect at all times in all patient care units, including inpatient and outpatient settings and clinics on the hospital's license.

(2) A definition of workplace violence that includes, but is not limited to, both of the following:

(A) The use of physical force against a hospital employee by a patient or a person accompanying a patient that results in, or has a high likelihood of resulting in, injury, psychological trauma, or stress, regardless of whether the employee sustains an injury.

(B) An incident involving the use of a firearm or other dangerous weapon, regardless of whether the employee sustains an injury.

(3) A requirement that a workplace violence prevention plan include, but not be limited to, all of the following:

(A) Personnel education and training policies that require all health care workers who provide direct care to patients to, at least annually, receive education and training that is designed to provide an opportunity for interactive questions and answers with a person knowledgeable about the workplace violence prevention plan. The education and training shall cover topics that include, but are not limited to, the following topics:

(i) How to recognize potential for violence, and when and how to seek assistance to prevent or respond to violence.

(ii) How to report violent incidents to law enforcement.

(iii) Any resources available to employees for coping with incidents of violence, including, but not limited to, critical incident stress debriefing or employee assistance programs.

(B) A system for responding to, and investigating violent incidents and situations involving violence or the risk of violence.

(C) A system to, at least annually, assess and improve upon factors that may contribute to, or help prevent workplace violence, including, but not limited to, the following factors:

(i) Staffing, including staffing patterns and patient classification systems that contribute to, or are insufficient to address, the risk of violence.

(ii) Sufficiency of security systems, including alarms, emergency response, and security personnel availability.

(iii) Job design, equipment, and facilities.

(iv) Security risks associated with specific units, areas of the facility with uncontrolled access, late-night or early morning shifts, and employee security in areas surrounding the facility such as employee parking areas.

(4) A requirement that all workplace violence prevention plans be developed in conjunction with affected employees, including their recognized collective bargaining agents, if any.

(5) A requirement that all temporary personnel be oriented to the workplace violence prevention plan.

(6) Provisions prohibiting hospitals from disallowing an employee from, or taking punitive or retaliatory action against an employee for, seeking assistance and intervention from local emergency services or law enforcement when a violent incident occurs.

(7) A requirement that hospitals document, and retain for a period of five years, a written record of any violent incident against a hospital employee, regardless of whether the employee sustains an injury, and regardless of whether the report is made by the employee who is the subject of the violent incident or any other employee.

(8) A requirement that a hospital report violent incidents to the division. If the incident results in injury, involves the use of a firearm or other dangerous weapon, or presents an urgent or emergent threat to the welfare, health, or safety of hospital personnel, the hospital shall report the incident to the division within 24 hours. All other incidents of violence shall be reported to the division within 72 hours.

(c) By January 1, 2017, and annually thereafter, the division, in a manner that protects patient and employee confidentiality, shall post a report on its Internet Web site containing information regarding violent incidents at hospitals, that includes, but is not limited to, the total number of reports, and which specific hospitals filed reports, pursuant to paragraph (8) of subdivision (b), the outcome of any related inspection or investigation, the citations levied against a hospital based on a violent incident, and recommendations of the division on the prevention of violent incidents at hospitals.

(d) This section shall not apply to a hospital operated by the State Department of State Hospitals, the State Department of Developmental Services, or the Department of Corrections and Rehabilitation.

(e) This section does not limit the authority of the standards board to adopt standards to protect employees from workplace violence. Nothing in this section shall be interpreted to preclude the standards board from adopting standards that require other employers, including, but not limited to, employers exempted from this section by subdivision (d), to adopt plans to protect employees from workplace violence. Nothing in this section shall be interpreted to preclude the standards board from adopting standards that require an employer subject to this section, or any other employer, to adopt a workplace violence prevention plan that includes elements or requirements additional to, or broader in scope than, those described in this section. **Leg.H.** 2014 ch. 842 (SB 1299) §1.

§6402. Allowing employee to work in unsafe conditions prohibited.

No employer shall require, or permit any employee to go or be in any employment or place of employment which is not safe and healthful.

Ref.: Herlick Handbook § 12.7.

§6403. Requirements of employer.

No employer shall fail or neglect to do any of the following:

(a) To provide and use safety devices and safeguards reasonably adequate to render the employment and place of employment safe.

(b) To adopt and use methods and processes reasonably adequate to render the employment and place of employment safe.

(c) To do every other thing reasonably necessary to protect the life, safety, and health of employees.

Ref.: Herlick Handbook § 12.7.

§6403.1. Health care employer personal protective equipment inventory requirements.

(a) The Legislature hereby finds that having access to a health care employer-level inventory of personal protective equipment in the event of a pandemic or other health emergency is vital to the health and safety of its health care workforce, as well as the general population, who both rely on the state's health care workforce for care and are susceptible to disease transmission should members of the health care workforce needlessly be infected with transmissible disease.

(b) For purposes of this section:

(1) "Department" means the Department of Industrial Relations.

(2)(A) "Health care employer" means a person or organization that employs workers in the public or private sector to provide direct patient care in a general acute care hospital setting as defined in subdivision (a) of Section 1250 of the Health and Safety Code, a health facility as defined in paragraphs (1) and (2) of subdivision (c) of Section 1250 of the Health and Safety Code, a medical practice that is operated or maintained as part of an integrated health system or health facility, or a dialysis clinic licensed in accordance with paragraph (2) of subdivision (b) of Section 1204 of the Health and Safety Code.

(B) "Health care employer" does not include an independent medical practice that is owned and operated, or maintained as a clinic or office, by one or more licensed physicians and used as an office for the practice of their profession, within the scope of their license, regardless of the name used publicly to identify the place or establishment unless the medical practice is operated or maintained exclusively as part of an integrated health system or health facility or is an entity described in subdivision (*l*) of Section 1206 of the Health and Safety Code.

(3) "PPE" and "health care worker" have the same meanings as defined in subdivision (c) of Section 131021 of the Health and Safety Code.

(c) Except as provided in paragraphs (1) and (2) of subdivision (h), a health care employer shall maintain an inventory of unexpired PPE, as specified in this section, for use in the event of a state of emergency declaration by the Governor, or a local emergency for a pandemic or other health emergency. Personal protective equipment in the inventory shall be new and not previously worn or used. A health care employer who violates the requirement to maintain an inventory of unexpired personal protective equipment prescribed by this section shall be assessed a civil penalty of up to twenty-five thousand dollars ($25,000) for each violation, as specified in Section 6428.

(d)(1) Commencing January 1, 2023, or 365 days after regulations are adopted pursuant to subdivision (h), whichever is later, health care employers shall have an inventory at least sufficient for 45 days of surge consumption, as determined by those regulations. The regulations shall not establish policies or standards that are less protective or prescriptive than any federal, state, or local law on PPE standards.

(2) A health care employer shall provide an inventory of its PPE to the Division of Occupational Safety and

Health upon request. An employer who violates this requirement shall be assessed a civil penalty of up to twenty-five thousand dollars ($25,000) for each violation. This subdivision does not apply to a health care employer that provides services in a facility or other setting controlled or owned by another health care employer that is obligated to maintain a PPE inventory and report that inventory pursuant to this subdivision for all its owned or controlled facilities and settings.

(e)(1) If a health care employer provides services in a facility or other setting controlled or owned by another health care employer who is obligated to maintain a PPE inventory, the health care employer who controls or owns the facility or other setting shall be required to maintain the required PPE for the health care employer providing services in that facility or setting.

(2) A health care employer may apply for a waiver of some or all of the PPE inventory requirements of subdivision (d) by writing to the department, which may approve the waiver if the facility has 25 or fewer employees and the employer agrees to close in-person operations during a public health emergency in which increased use of PPE is recommended by the public health officer until sufficient PPE becomes available to return to in-person operations. This provision does not apply to health facilities as described in subdivisions (a), (b), and (c) of Section 1250 of the Health and Safety Code.

(3) If a health care employer's inventory of a type of PPE dips below the mandated level of supplies as a result of the health care employer's distribution of that type of PPE to its health care workers or another health care employer's workers during a state of emergency declared by the Governor or a declared local emergency for a pandemic or other health emergency, the health care employer shall not be subject to the civil penalty established by subdivision (c) for 30 days, provided the health care employer replenishes its inventory to the mandated level within 30 days if the department has determined there is not a supply limitation.

(f) The department may exempt a health care employer from a civil penalty prescribed by subdivision (c) if the department determines that supply chain limitations make meeting the mandated level of supplies infeasible and a health care employer has made a reasonable attempt, in the discretion of the department, to obtain PPE, or if the health care employer makes a showing that meeting the mandated level of supplies is not possible due to issues beyond their control, such as if the equipment was ordered from a manufacturer or distributor but the order was not fulfilled, or if the equipment was damaged or stolen.

(g) Consistent with existing law, a designated health care employer shall supply appropriate PPE to its health care workers, ensure that its health care workers use the PPE supplied to them, and provide appropriate PPE to its health care workers upon their request. This paragraph is declaratory of existing law.

(h) The department, by regulation and in consultation with the State Department of Public Health, shall set forth requirements for determining 45-day surge capacity levels for health care employer inventory as required by paragraph (1) of subdivision (d), including, but not limited to, the types and amount of PPE to be maintained by the health care employer based on the type and size of each health care employer, as well as the composition of health care workers in its workforce. The regulations shall require each health care employer to maintain sufficient PPE for all health care workers. The regulations shall consider the recommendations of the Personal Protective Equipment Advisory Committee established pursuant to Section 6403.2. **Leg.H.** 2020 ch. 301 (SB 275) §2.

§6403.3. Definitions; personal protective equipment stockpile requirements.

(a) For purposes of this section:

(1) "Employer" means a person or organization that employs workers in the public or private sector to provide direct patient care in a general acute care hospital, as defined in subdivision (a) of Section 1250 of the Health and Safety Code.

(2) "Personal protective equipment" means the equipment and devices necessary to comply with Sections 3380 and 5199 of Title 8 of the California Code of Regulations, provided that those requirements are at least as protective as those sections read on May 4, 2020.

(b) An employer shall supply personal protective equipment to employees who provide direct patient care or provide services that directly support patient care in a general acute care hospital. An employer shall ensure that employees use the personal protective equipment supplied to them.

(c)(1) Beginning April 1, 2021, an employer shall maintain a stockpile of the following equipment in the amount equal to three months of normal consumption:

(A) N95 filtering facepiece respirators.

(B) Powered air-purifying respirators with high efficiency particulate air filters.

(C) Elastomeric air-purifying respirators and appropriate particulate filters or cartridges.

(D) Surgical masks.

(E) Isolation gowns.

(F) Eye protection.

(G) Shoe coverings.

(2) Single use equipment in the stockpile shall be unexpired, new, and not previously worn or used. An employer shall provide an inventory of its stockpile and a copy of its written procedures required pursuant to subdivision (f) to the Division of Occupational Safety and Health upon request. An employer who violates the requirement to maintain a supply of equipment prescribed by this subdivision shall be assessed a civil penalty of up to twenty-five thousand dollars ($25,000) for each violation, unless the department determines that the employer could not meet the requirement due to issues beyond their control, such as the employer can demonstrate that equipment needed to meet the requirements of this section has been ordered from their manufacturer or distributor and not fulfilled, or has been damaged or stolen. The exemption from a civil penalty shall apply only to the type of equipment listed in paragraph (1) that is affected by issues beyond the employer's control. An employer shall still maintain the equipment that is not affected by issues beyond the employer's control.

(d) If an employer provides health care services in a facility or other setting controlled by another employer who is obligated to maintain a stockpile pursuant to

Labor

subdivision (c), the employer who controls the facility or other setting shall maintain the required equipment for the employer providing health care services in that facility or setting.

(e) On or before January 15, 2021, an employer licensed under subdivision (a) of Section 1250 of the Health and Safety Code shall be prepared to report to the department, under penalty of perjury, its highest seven-day consecutive daily average consumption of personal protective equipment during the 2019 calendar year, upon request by the department. General acute care hospitals under the jurisdiction of the State Department of State Hospitals are exempt from this requirement. State hospitals shall make their highest seven-day consecutive daily average consumption of personal protective equipment during the 2019 calendar year available upon request to the Division of Occupational Safety and Health.

(f) An employer shall establish and implement effective written procedures for periodically determining the quantity and types of equipment used in its normal consumption.

(g) The division may enforce an alleged violation of this section through the issuance of a citation, pursuant to Section 6317.

(h) Subdivision (b) is declaratory of existing law. **Leg.H.** 2020 ch. 313 (AB 2537) §2.

§6403.5. Adoption of patient protection and health care worker back and musculoskeletal injury prevention plan; safe patient handling policy; training; duties of coordinator of care; disciplinary action.

(a) As part of the injury and illness prevention programs required by Section 3203 of Title 8 of the California Code of Regulations, or any successor law or regulation, employers shall adopt a patient protection and health care worker back and musculoskeletal injury prevention plan. The plan shall include a safe patient handling policy component reflected in professional occupational safety guidelines for the protection of patients and health care workers in health care facilities.

(b) An employer shall maintain a safe patient handling policy at all times for all patient care units, and shall provide trained lift teams or other support staff trained in safe lifting techniques in each general acute care hospital. The employer shall provide training to health care workers that includes, but is not limited to, the following:

(1) The appropriate use of lifting devices and equipment.

(2) The five areas of body exposure: vertical, lateral, bariatric, repositioning, and ambulation.

(3) The use of lifting devices to handle patients safely.

(c) As the coordinator of care, the registered nurse shall be responsible for the observation and direction of patient lifts and mobilization, and shall participate as needed in patient handling in accordance with the nurse's job description and professional judgment.

(d) For purposes of this section, "lift team" means hospital employees specifically trained to handle patient lifts, repositionings, and transfers using patient transfer, repositioning, or lifting devices as appropriate for the specific patient. Lift team members may perform other duties as assigned during their shifts. A general acute care hospital shall not be required by this section to hire new staff to comprise the lift team so long as direct patient care assignments are not compromised.

(e) For purposes of this section, "health care worker" means a lift team member or other staff responsible for assisting in lifting patients who is a hospital employee specifically trained to handle patient lifts, repositioning, and transfers using patient transfer, repositioning, and lifting devices as appropriate for the specific patient.

(f) For the purposes of this section, "safe patient handling policy" means a policy that requires replacement of manual lifting and transferring of patients with powered patient transfer devices, lifting devices, and lift teams, as appropriate for the specific patient and consistent with the employer's safety policies and the professional judgment and clinical assessment of the registered nurse.

(g) A health care worker who refuses to lift, reposition, or transfer a patient due to concerns about patient or worker safety or the lack of trained lift team personnel or equipment shall not, based upon the refusal, be the subject of disciplinary action by the hospital or any of its managers or employees.

(h) This section shall not apply to general acute care hospitals within the Department of Corrections and Rehabilitation or the State Department of Developmental Services. **Leg.H.** 2011 ch. 554 (AB 1136) §3.

2011 Note: This act shall be known and cited as the Hospital Patient and Health Care Worker Injury Protection Act. Stats. 2011 ch. 554 (AB 1136) §1.

§6404. Prohibition against unsafe or unhealthy work sites.

No employer shall occupy or maintain any place of employment that is not safe and healthful.

Ref.: Herlick Handbook § 12.7.

§6404.5. Prohibition against smoking in the workplace.

(a) The Legislature finds and declares that regulation of smoking in the workplace is a matter of statewide interest and concern. It is the intent of the Legislature in enacting this section to prohibit the smoking of tobacco products in all (100 percent of) enclosed places of employment in this state, as covered by this section, thereby eliminating the need of local governments to enact workplace smoking restrictions within their respective jurisdictions. It is further the intent of the Legislature to create a uniform statewide standard to restrict and prohibit the smoking of tobacco products in enclosed places of employment, as specified in this section, in order to reduce employee exposure to environmental tobacco smoke to a level that will prevent anything other than insignificantly harmful effects to exposed employees, and also to eliminate the confusion and hardship that can result from enactment or enforcement of disparate local workplace smoking restrictions. Notwithstanding any other provision of this section, it is the intent of the Legislature that an area not defined as a "place of employment" pursuant to subdivision (e) is subject to local regulation of smoking of tobacco products.

(b) For purposes of this section, an "owner-operated business" shall mean a business having no employees, independent contractors, or volunteers, in which the owner-operator of the business is the only worker. "Enclosed space" includes covered parking lots, lobbies, lounges, waiting areas, elevators, stairwells, and restrooms that are a structural part of the building and not specifically defined in subdivision (e).

(c) An employer or owner-operator of an owner-operated business shall not knowingly or intentionally permit, and a person shall not engage in, the smoking of tobacco products at a place of employment or in an enclosed space.

(d) For purposes of this section, an employer or owner-operator of an owner-operated business who permits any nonemployee access to his or her place of employment or owner-operated business on a regular basis has not acted knowingly or intentionally in violation of this section if he or she has taken the following reasonable steps to prevent smoking by a nonemployee:

(1) Posted clear and prominent signs, as follows:

(A) Where smoking is prohibited throughout the building or structure, a sign stating "No smoking" shall be posted at each entrance to the building or structure.

(B) Where smoking is permitted in designated areas of the building or structure, a sign stating "Smoking is prohibited except in designated areas" shall be posted at each entrance to the building or structure.

(2) Has requested, when appropriate, that a nonemployee who is smoking refrain from smoking in the enclosed workplace or owner-operated business.

For purposes of this subdivision, "reasonable steps" does not include (A) the physical ejection of a nonemployee from the place of employment or owner-operated business or (B) any requirement for making a request to a nonemployee to refrain from smoking, under circumstances involving a risk of physical harm to the employer or any employee or owner-operator.

(e) For purposes of this section, "place of employment" does not include any of the following:

(1) Twenty percent of the guestroom accommodations in a hotel, motel, or similar transient lodging establishment.

(2) Retail or wholesale tobacco shops and private smokers' lounges. For purposes of this paragraph:

(A) "Private smokers' lounge" means any enclosed area in or attached to a retail or wholesale tobacco shop that is dedicated to the use of tobacco products, including, but not limited to, cigars and pipes.

(B) "Retail or wholesale tobacco shop" means any business establishment, the main purpose of which is the sale of tobacco products, including, but not limited to, cigars, pipe tobacco, and smoking accessories.

(3) Cabs of motortrucks, as defined in Section 410 of the Vehicle Code, or truck tractors, as defined in Section 655 of the Vehicle Code, if nonsmoking employees are not present.

(4) Theatrical production sites, if smoking is an integral part of the story in the theatrical production.

(5) Medical research or treatment sites, if smoking is integral to the research and treatment being conducted.

(6) Private residences, except for private residences licensed as family day care homes where smoking is prohibited pursuant to Section 1596.795 of the Health and Safety Code.

(7) Patient smoking areas in long-term health care facilities, as defined in Section 1418 of the Health and Safety Code.

(f) The smoking prohibition set forth in this section constitutes a uniform statewide standard for regulating the smoking of tobacco products in enclosed places of employment and owner-operated businesses and supersedes and renders unnecessary the local enactment or enforcement of local ordinances regulating the smoking of tobacco products in enclosed places of employment and owner-operated businesses. Insofar as the smoking prohibition set forth in this section is applicable to all (100 percent) places of employment and owner-operated businesses within this state and, therefore, provides the maximum degree of coverage, the practical effect of this section is to eliminate the need of local governments to enact enclosed workplace smoking restrictions within their respective jurisdictions.

(g) This section does not prohibit an employer or owner-operator of an owner-operated business from prohibiting smoking of tobacco products in an enclosed place of employment or owner-operated business for any reason.

(h) The enactment of local regulation of smoking of tobacco products in enclosed places of employment or owner-operated businesses by local governments shall be suspended only for as long as, and to the extent that, the (100 percent) smoking prohibition provided for in this section remains in effect. In the event this section is repealed or modified by subsequent legislative or judicial action so that the (100 percent) smoking prohibition is no longer applicable to all enclosed places of employment and owner-operated businesses in California, local governments shall have the full right and authority to enforce previously enacted, and to enact and enforce new, restrictions on the smoking of tobacco products in enclosed places of employment and owner-operated businesses within their jurisdictions, including a complete prohibition of smoking. Notwithstanding any other provision of this section, an area not defined as a "place of employment" or in which smoking is not regulated pursuant to subdivision (e), is subject to local regulation of smoking of tobacco products.

(i) A violation of the prohibition set forth in subdivision (c) is an infraction, punishable by a fine not to exceed one hundred dollars ($100) for a first violation, two hundred dollars ($200) for a second violation within one year, and five hundred dollars ($500) for a third and for each subsequent violation within one year. This subdivision shall be enforced by local law enforcement agencies, including, but not limited to, local health departments, as determined by the local governing body.

(j) Notwithstanding Section 6309, the division is not required to respond to any complaint regarding the smoking of tobacco products in an enclosed space at a place of employment, unless the employer has been found guilty pursuant to subdivision (i) of a third violation of subdivision (c) within the previous year.

(k) If a provision of this section or the application thereof to any person or circumstances is held invalid, that invalidity shall not affect other provisions or applications of the section that can be given effect without the invalid

Labor

provision or application, and to this end the provisions of this section are severable.

(*l*) For purposes of this section, "smoking" has the same meaning as in subdivision (c) of Section 22950.5 of the Business and Professions Code.

(m) For purposes of this section, "tobacco product" means a product or device as defined in subdivision (d) of Section 22950.5 of the Business and Professions Code. **Leg.H.** 1994 ch. 310, 1995 ch. 91, 1996 ch. 989, 1998 ch. 606, 2006 ch. 736 (AB 2067) §2, 2014 ch. 459 (AB 1819) §2, 2015 ch. 303 (AB 731) §380, 2015–2016 2d Ex Sess ch. 4 (ABX2 7) §1, effective June 9, 2016, 2015–2016 2d Ex Sess ch. 7 (SBX2 5) §23.5, effective June 9, 2016.

2016 Note: This act does not affect any laws or regulations regarding medical cannabis. 2015–2016 2d Ex Sess ch. 7 (SBX2 5) §28.

§6405. Prohibition against construction of unhealthy or unsafe work sites.

No employer, owner, or lessee of any real property shall construct or cause to be constructed any place of employment that is not safe and healthful.

§6406. Prohibition against interfering with or neglecting to provide safe or healthful equipment or practices.

No person shall do any of the following:

(a) Remove, displace, damage, destroy or carry off any safety device, safeguard, notice, or warning, furnished for use in any employment or place of employment.

(b) Interfere in any way with the use thereof by any other person.

(c) Interfere with the use of any method or process adopted for the protection of any employee, including himself, in such employment, or place of employment.

(d) Fail or neglect to do every other thing reasonably necessary to protect the life, safety, and health of employees.

Ref.: Herlick Handbook § 9.6.

§6407. Employer's and employee's obligation to comply with regulations.

Every employer and every employee shall comply with occupational safety and health standards, with Section 25910 of the Health and Safety Code, and with all rules, regulations, and orders pursuant to this division which are applicable to his own actions and conduct.

§6408. Obligation to provide specified information to employees.

All employers shall provide information to employees in the following ways, as prescribed by authorized regulations:

(a) Posting of information regarding protections and obligations of employees under occupational safety and health laws.

(b) Posting prominently each citation issued under Section 6317, or a copy or copies thereof, at or near each place a violation referred to in the notice of violation occurred.

(c) The opportunity for employees or their representatives to observe monitoring or measuring of employee exposure to hazards conducted pursuant to standards promulgated under Section 142.3.

(d) Allow access by employees or their representatives to accurate records of employee exposures to potentially toxic materials or harmful physical agents.

(e) Notification of any employee who has been or is being exposed to toxic materials or harmful physical agents in concentrations or at levels exceeding those prescribed by an applicable standard, order, or special order, and informing any employee so exposed of corrective action being taken.

§6409. Requirements of physicians treating injured employees; "occupational illness."

(a) Every physician as defined in Section 3209.3 who attends any injured employee shall file a complete report of that occupational injury or occupational illness in a manner prescribed by the administrative director of the Division of Workers' Compensation. The report shall include a diagnosis, the injured employee's description of how the injury or illness occurred, any treatment rendered at the time of the examination, any work restrictions resulting from the injury or illness, a treatment plan, and other content as prescribed by the administrative director. The form shall be filed electronically with the Division of Workers' Compensation and the employer, or if insured, with the employer's insurer, within five days of the initial examination. If the treatment is for pesticide poisoning or a condition suspected to be pesticide poisoning, the physician shall also, within 24 hours of the initial examination, file a complete report with the local health officer by facsimile transmission or other means. If the treatment is for pesticide poisoning or a condition suspected to be pesticide poisoning, the physician shall not be compensated for the initial diagnosis and treatment unless the report is filed with the Division of Workers' Compensation, the employer, or if insured, with the employer's insurer, and includes or is accompanied by a signed affidavit which certifies that a copy of the report was filed with the local health officer pursuant to this section.

(b) As used in this section, "occupational illness" means any abnormal condition or disorder caused by exposure to environmental factors associated with employment, including acute and chronic illnesses or diseases which may be caused by inhalation, absorption, ingestion, or direct contact. **Leg.H.** 1994 ch. 667, 2012 ch. 46 (SB 1038) §109, effective June 27, 2012, 2016 ch. 868 (SB 1160) §13.

2016 Note: For legislative findings and declarations, see the 2016 Note following Lab C §138.4.

Ref.: 8 C.C.R. §§10101, 10101.1, 10181, 14000, 14001, 14002, 14003; Hanna § 22.08[2]; Herlick Handbook §§ 3.6, 4.08[2], 9.18, 14.2.

§6409.1. Requirements of employers when employee is occupationally injured or ill; subsequent death of employee.

(a) Every employer shall file a complete report of every occupational injury or occupational illness, as defined in subdivision (b) of Section 6409, of each employee which results in lost time beyond the date of the injury or illness, or which requires medical treatment beyond first aid, with the Department of Industrial Relations or, if an insured employer, with the insurer, on a form prescribed for that purpose by the department. A report shall be filed concerning each injury and illness which has, or is alleged to have, arisen out of and in the course of employment, within five days after the employer obtains knowledge of the injury or illness. Each report of occupational injury or occupational illness shall indicate the social security number of the injured employee. In the case of an insured employer, the insurer shall file with the division immediately upon receipt, a copy of the employer's report, which has been received from the insured employer. In the event an employer has filed a report of injury or illness pursuant to this subdivision and the employee subsequently dies as a result of the reported injury or illness, the employer shall file an amended report indicating the death with the department or, if an insured employer, with the insurer, within five days after the employer is notified or learns of the death. A copy of any amended reports received by the insurer shall be filed with the division immediately upon receipt.

(b) In every case involving a serious injury or illness, or death, in addition to the report required by subdivision (a), a report shall be made immediately by the employer to the Division of Occupational Safety and Health by telephone or through a specified online mechanism established by the division for this purpose. Until the division has made such an online mechanism available, the employer shall be permitted to make the report required by this subdivision by telephone or email. An employer who violates this subdivision may be assessed a civil penalty of not less than five thousand dollars ($5,000). Nothing in this subdivision shall be construed to increase the maximum civil penalty, pursuant to Sections 6427 to 6430, inclusive, that may be imposed for a violation of this section. **Leg.H.** 1992 ch. 386, 2002 ch. 885 (AB 2837), 2008 ch. 740 (AB 2181) §1, 2012 ch. 46 (SB 1038) §110, effective June 27, 2012, 2014 ch. 91 (AB 326) §1, 2019 ch. 199 (AB 1804) §1.

2008 Note: The changes to subdivision (a) of Section 6409.1 and Section 6410 of the Labor Code made by Stats. 2008 ch. 740 shall become effective upon the effective date of regulations adopted by the administrative director to implement the changes made to subdivision (a) of Section 6409.1 of the Labor Code by this act, provided that the regulations specify a transition period of no less than 180 days and no more than 545 days in which the employer or insurer may continue to comply with Section 6409.1 as it was last amended by Chapter 885 of the Statutes of 2002. Stats. 2008 ch. 740 §3.

Stats. 2008 ch. 740 § 1 (AB 2181) purported to amend this section contingent on adoption of regulations by the administrative director to implement the changes made to the section provided that the regulations specified a transition period of no less than 180 days and no more than 545 days in which the employer or insurer would continue to comply with the section as it was last amended by Stats. 2002 ch. 885. That contingency apparently did not occur and so the amendment by the 2008 act was not given effect.

Ref.: 8 C.C.R. §§10101, 10101.1, 10181, 14001, 14002, 14004, 14005; Hanna § 25.20[3]; Herlick Handbook §§ 4.04[7], 14.2.

§6409.2. Notification when fire or police are called to serious or fatal accident.

Whenever a state, county, or local fire or police agency is called to an accident involving an employee covered by this part in which a serious injury or illness, or death occurs, the responding agency shall immediately notify the nearest office of the Division of Occupational Safety and Health by telephone. Thereafter, the division shall immediately notify the appropriate prosecuting authority of the accident. **Leg.H.** 2002 ch. 885 (AB 2837).

§6409.3. Pesticide poisoning treatment.

In no case shall the treatment administered for pesticide poisoning or a condition suspected as pesticide poisoning be deemed to be first aid treatment.

Ref.: 8 C.C.R. §14003.

§6409.5. Notification of Division of Occupational Safety and Health and Division of Labor Standards Enforcement regarding garment manufacturing hazards—Investigation by local public fire agency.

(a) Whenever any local public fire agency has knowledge that a place of employment where garment manufacturing operations take place contains fire or safety hazards for which fire and injury prevention measures have not been taken in accordance with local fire and life safety ordinances, the agency may notify the Division of Occupational Safety and Health. This referral shall be made only after the garment manufacturing employer has been given a reasonable amount of time to correct violations.

(b) Whenever the Division of Occupational Safety and Health has knowledge or reasonable suspicion that a place of employment where garment manufacturing operations take place contains fire or safety hazards for which fire and injury prevention measures have not been taken in accordance with local fire and life safety ordinances, the division shall notify the appropriate local public fire agency.

(c) Whenever the Division of Occupational Safety and Health receives a referral by a local public fire agency pursuant to subdivision (a) which informs the division that a place of employment where garment manufacturing operations take place is not safe or is injurious to the welfare of any employee, it shall constitute a complaint for purposes of Section 6309 and shall be investigated.

(d) Whenever a local public fire agency receives a referral by the Division of Occupational Safety and Health pursuant to subdivision (b) which informs the local public fire agency that a place of employment where garment manufacturing operations take place is not safe or is injurious to the welfare of any employee, the local public fire agency may investigate the referral at its discretion.

(e)(1) If the Division of Occupational Safety and Health acquires knowledge that the garment manufacturing employer is not currently registered, it shall notify the Division of Labor Standards Enforcement.

(2) Local public fire agencies may make referrals of individuals not registered as garment manufacturers to the Division of Labor Standards Enforcement.

(3) Whenever the Division of Labor Standards Enforcement is informed by the Division of Occupational Safety

and Health or by a local public fire agency that a garment manufacturing employer is unregistered, the Division of Labor Standards Enforcement shall take measures it deems appropriate to obtain compliance. **Leg.H.** 1991 ch. 7, effective December 13, 1990, operative January 1, 1991.

§6409.6. COVID-19 employer notice requirements.

(a) If an employer or representative of the employer receives a notice of potential exposure to COVID-19, the employer shall take all of the following actions within one business day of the notice of potential exposure:

(1) Provide a written notice to all employees, and the employers of subcontracted employees, who were on the premises at the same worksite as the qualifying individual within the infectious period that they may have been exposed to COVID-19 in a manner the employer normally uses to communicate employment-related information. Written notice may include, but is not limited to, personal service, email, or text message if it can reasonably be anticipated to be received by the employee within one business day of sending and shall be in both English and the language understood by the majority of the employees.

(2) Provide a written notice to the exclusive representative, if any, of employees under paragraph (1).

(3) Provide all employees who may have been exposed and the exclusive representative, if any, with information regarding COVID-19-related benefits to which the employee may be entitled under applicable federal, state, or local laws, including, but not limited to, workers' compensation, and options for exposed employees, including COVID-19-related leave, company sick leave, state-mandated leave, supplemental sick leave, or negotiated leave provisions, as well as antiretaliation and antidiscrimination protections of the employee.

(4) Notify all employees, and the employers of subcontracted employees and the exclusive representative, if any, on the disinfection and safety plan that the employer plans to implement and complete per the guidelines of the federal Centers for Disease Control.

(b) If an employer or representative of the employer is notified of the number of cases that meet the definition of a COVID-19 outbreak, as defined by the State Department of Public Health, within 48 hours, the employer shall notify the local public health agency in the jurisdiction of the worksite of the names, number, occupation, and worksite of employees who meet the definition in subdivision (d) of a qualifying individual. An employer shall also report the business address and NAICS code of the worksite where the qualifying individuals work. An employer that has an outbreak subject to this section shall continue to give notice to the local health department of any subsequent laboratory-confirmed cases of COVID-19 at the worksite.

(c) The notice required pursuant to paragraph (2) of subdivision (a) shall contain the same information as would be required in an incident report in a Cal/OSHA Form 300 injury and illness log unless the information is inapplicable or unknown to the employer. This requirement shall apply regardless of whether the employer is required to maintain a Cal/OSHA Form 300 injury and illness log. Notifications required by this section shall not impact any determination of whether or not the illness is work related.

(d) For purposes of this section, the following definitions apply:

(1) "COVID-19" means severe acute respiratory syndrome coronavirus 2 (SARS-CoV-2).

(2) "Infectious period" means the time a COVID-19-positive individual is infectious, as defined by the State Department of Public Health.

(3) "Notice of potential exposure" means any of the following:

(A) Notification to the employer or representative from a public health official or licensed medical provider that an employee was exposed to a qualifying individual at the worksite.

(B) Notification to the employer or representative from an employee, or their emergency contact, that the employee is a qualifying individual.

(C) Notification through the testing protocol of the employer that the employee is a qualifying individual.

(D) Notification to an employer or representative from a subcontracted employer that a qualifying individual was on the worksite of the employer receiving notification.

(4) "Qualifying individual" means any person who has any of the following:

(A) A laboratory-confirmed case of COVID-19, as defined by the State Department of Public Health.

(B) A positive COVID-19 diagnosis from a licensed health care provider.

(C) A COVID-19-related order to isolate provided by a public health official.

(D) Died due to COVID-19, in the determination of a county public health department or per inclusion in the COVID-19 statistics of a county.

(5) "Worksite" means the building, store, facility, agricultural field, or other location where a worker worked during the infectious period. It does not apply to buildings, floors, or other locations of the employer that a qualified individual did not enter. In a multiworksite environment, the employer need only notify employees who were at the same worksite as the qualified individual.

(e) An employer shall not require employees to disclose medical information unless otherwise required by law.

(f) An employer shall not retaliate against a worker for disclosing a positive COVID-19 test or diagnosis or order to quarantine or isolate. Workers who believe they have been retaliated against in violation of this section may file a complaint with the Division of Labor Standards Enforcement pursuant to Section 98.6. The complaint shall be investigated as provided in Section 98.7.

(g) The State Department of Public Health shall make workplace industry information received from local public health departments pursuant to this section available on its internet website in a manner that allows the public to track the number and frequency of COVID-19 outbreaks and the number of COVID-19 cases and outbreaks by industry reported by any workplace in accordance with subdivision (b). Local public health departments and the division shall provide a link to this page on their internet websites. No personally identifiable employee information shall be made public or posted.

(h) This section shall apply to both private and public employers, except that subdivision (b) shall not apply to a "health facility," as defined in Section 1250 of the Health and Safety Code.

(i) This section shall not apply to employees who, as part of their duties, conduct COVID-19 testing or screening or provide direct patient care or treatment to individuals who are known to have tested positive for COVID-19, are persons under investigation, or are in quarantine or isolation related to COVID-19, unless the qualifying individual is an employee at the same worksite.

(j) No personally identifiable employee information shall be subject to a California Public Records Act request or similar request, posted on a public internet website, or shared with any other state or federal agency.

(k) An employer shall maintain records of the written notifications required in subdivision (a) for a period of at least three years.

(*l*) The division shall enforce paragraphs (1), (2), and (4) of subdivision (a) by the issuance of a citation alleging a violation of these paragraphs and a notice of civil penalty in a manner consistent with Section 6317. Any person who receives a citation and penalty may appeal the citation and penalty to the appeals board in a manner consistent with Section 6319. **Leg.H.** 2020 ch. 84 (AB 685) §4.

§6410. Requirements for reports and records.

(a) The reports required by subdivision (a) of Section 6409 and Section 6413 shall be made in the form and detail and within the time limits prescribed by reasonable rules and regulations adopted by the Department of Industrial Relations in accordance with Chapter 3.5 (commencing with Section 11340) of Part 1 of Division 3 of Title 2 of the Government Code.

(b) Nothing in this chapter requiring recordkeeping and reporting by employers shall relieve the employer of maintaining records and making reports to the assistant secretary, United States Department of Labor, as required under the federal Occupational Safety and Health Act of 1970 (P.L. 91–596). The Division of Occupational Safety and Health shall prescribe and provide the forms necessary for maintenance of the required records, and shall enforce by citation and penalty assessment any violation of the recordkeeping requirements of this chapter.

(c) All state and local government employers shall maintain records and make reports in the same manner and to the same extent as required of other employers by this section. **Leg.H.** 2008 ch. 740 (AB 2181) §2, 2012 ch. 46 (SB 1038) §111, effective June 27, 2012.

2008 Note: The changes to subdivision (a) of Section 6409.1 and Section 6410 of the Labor Code made by Stats. 2008 ch. 740 shall become effective upon the effective date of regulations adopted by the administrative director to implement the changes made to subdivision (a) of Section 6409.1 of the Labor Code by this act, provided that the regulations specify a transition period of no less than 180 days and no more than 545 days in which the employer or insurer may continue to comply with Section 6409.1 as it was last amended by Chapter 885 of the Statutes of 2002. Stats. 2008 ch. 740 §3.

Stats. 2008 ch. 740 § 2 (AB 2181) purported to amend this section contingent on adoption of regulations by the administrative director to implement the changes made to the section provided that the regulations specified a transition period of no less than 180 days and no more than 545 days in which the employer or insurer would continue to comply with the section as it was last amended by Stats. 2002 ch. 885. That contingency apparently did not occur and so the amendment by the 2008 act was not given effect.

Ref.: 8 C.C.R. §§14300, 14300.1, 14300.2, 14300.3, 14300.4, 14300.5, 14300.6, 14300.7, 14300.8, 14300.9, 14300.10, 14300.11, 14300.12, 14300.29, 14300.30, 14300.31, 14300.32, 14300.33, 14300.34, 14300.35, 14300.36, 14300.38, 14300.40, 14300.41, 14300.42, 14300.43, 14300.44, 14300.46, 14300.47, 14300.48; Herlick Handbook §§ 8.28, 9.10.

§6410.1. Legislative intent.

It is the intent of the Legislature that the division maintain strong workplace injury and illness reporting standards. **Leg.H.** 2018 ch. 538 (AB 2334) §5.

§6410.2. Track and implement changes consistent with Occupational Safety and Health Administration's Improve Tracking of Workplace Injuries and Illnesses rule.

(a) The division shall monitor rulemaking and implementation of the United States Department of Labor's Occupational Safety and Health Administration's Improve Tracking of Workplace Injuries and Illnesses rule as published in the federal Register (81 FR 29624) with respect to the electronic submission of workplace injury and illness data.

(b) If the division determines that the Occupational Safety and Health Administration (OSHA) has eliminated or substantially diminished the requirement that employers electronically submit OSHA injury and illness data pursuant to 81 FR 29624, the division shall, within 120 days of the determination, convene an advisory committee to evaluate how to implement the changes necessary to protect the goals of the Improve Tracking of Workplace Injuries and Illnesses rule, as issued May 12, 2016. The committee shall be composed of parties in both management and labor and include parties that are required to keep injury and illness records under Article 2 (commencing with Section 14300) of Subchapter 1 of Chapter 7 of Division 1 of Title 8 of the California Code of Regulations.

(c) This section does not require the disclosure of information prohibited under Section 6412. **Leg.H.** 2018 ch. 538 (AB 2334) §6.

§6410.5. Statement must accompany reports.

The reports required by subdivision (a) of Section 6409, subdivision (a) of Section 6409.1, and Section 6413 shall contain, prominently stated, the statement set forth in Section 5401.7. **Leg.H.** 1991 ch. 116.

Ref.: Herlick Handbook §§ 9.18, 14.2.

§6411. Requirement to fully and accurately complete forms.

Every employer or insurer receiving forms with directions from the Department of Industrial Relations to complete them shall cause them to be properly filled out so as to answer fully and correctly each question propounded therein. In case of inability to answer any questions, a good and sufficient reason shall be given for such failure. **Leg.H.** 1973 ch. 993 §96, effective October 1, 1973, 2012 ch. 46 (SB 1038) §112, effective June 27, 2012.

§6412. Report's confidentiality and admissibility as evidence.

No report of injury or illness required by subdivision (a) of Section 6409.1 shall be open to public inspection or made public, nor shall those reports be admissible as evidence in any adversary proceeding before the Workers' Compensation Appeals Board. However, the reports required of physicians by subdivision (a) of Section 6409 shall be admissible as evidence in the proceeding, except that no physician's report shall be admissible as evidence to bar proceedings for the collection of compensation, and the portion of any physician's report completed by an employee shall not be admissible as evidence in any proceeding before the Workers' Compensation Appeals Board.

Ref.: Herlick Handbook §§ 3.6, 4.04[7], 4.08[2], 14.2.

§6413. Requirements when state prisoner is injured.

(a) The Department of Corrections and Rehabilitation, and every physician or surgeon who attends any injured state prisoner, shall file with the Division of Occupational Safety and Health a complete report, on forms prescribed under Sections 6409 and 6409.1, of every injury to each state prisoner, resulting from any labor performed by the prisoner unless disability resulting from such injury does not last through the day or does not require medical service other than ordinary first aid treatment.

(b) Where the injury results in death a report, in addition to the report required by subdivision (a), shall forthwith be made by the Department of Corrections and Rehabilitation to the Division of Occupational Safety and Health by telephone or telegraph.

(c) Except as provided in Section 6304.2, nothing in this section or in this code shall be deemed to make a prisoner an employee, for any purpose, of the Department of Corrections and Rehabilitation.

(d) Notwithstanding subdivision (a), no physician or surgeon who attends any injured state prisoner outside of a Department of Corrections and Rehabilitation institution shall be required to file the report required by subdivision (a), but the Department of Corrections and Rehabilitation shall file the report. **Leg.H.** 1992 ch. 386, 2012 ch. 46 (SB 1038) §113, effective June 27, 2012.

Ref.: Herlick Handbook § 9.18.

§6413.2. Division's powers regarding Department of Corrections and Rehabilitation.

(a) With regard to any report required by Section 6413, the Division of Occupational Safety and Health may make recommendations to the Department of Corrections and Rehabilitation of ways in which the department might improve the safety of the working conditions and work areas of state prisoners, and other safety matters. The Department of Corrections and Rehabilitation shall not be required to comply with these recommendations.

(b) With regard to any report required by Section 6413, the Division of Occupational Safety and Health may, in any case in which the Department of Corrections and Rehabilitation has not complied with recommendations made by the division pursuant to subdivision (b), or in any other case in which the division deems the safety of any state prisoner shall require it, conduct hearings and, after these hearings, adopt special orders, rules, or regulations or otherwise proceed as authorized in Chapter 1 (commencing with Section 6300) of this part as it deems necessary. The Department of Corrections and Rehabilitation shall comply with any order, rule, or regulation so adopted by the Division of Occupational Safety and Health. **Leg.H.** 1973 ch. 1067 §3, 1980 ch. 676 §237, 2012 ch. 46 (SB 1038) §114, effective June 27, 2012.

§6413.5. Penalties for violation of reporting requirements.

Any employer or physician who fails to comply with any provision of subdivision (a) of Section 6409, or Section 6409.1, 6409.2, 6409.3, or 6410 may be assessed a civil penalty of not less than fifty dollars ($50) nor more than two hundred dollars ($200) by the director or his or her designee if he or she finds a pattern or practice of violations, or a willful violation of any of these provisions. Penalty assessments may be contested in the manner provided in Section 3725. Penalties assessed pursuant to this section shall be deposited in the General Fund.

Ref.: Herlick Handbook §§ 4.08[2], 14.2.

CHAPTER 4
PENALTIES

§6423. Violations as misdemeanors; penalties.

(a) Except where another penalty is specifically provided, every employer and every officer, management official, or supervisor having direction, management, control, or custody of any employment, place of employment, or of any other employee, who does any of the following is guilty of a misdemeanor:

(1) Knowingly or negligently violates any standard, order, or special order, or any provision of this division, or of any part thereof in, or authorized by, this part the violation of which is deemed to be a serious violation pursuant to Section 6432.

(2) Repeatedly violates any standard, order, or special order, or provision of this division, or any part thereof in, or authorized by, this part, which repeated violation creates a real and apparent hazard to employees.

(3) Knowingly fails to report to the division a death, as required by subdivision (b) of Section 6409.1.

(4) Fails or refuses to comply, after notification and expiration of any abatement period, with any such standard, order, special order, or provision of this division, or any part thereof, which failure or refusal creates a real and apparent hazard to employees.

(5) Directly or indirectly, knowingly induces another to commit any of the acts in paragraph (1), (2), (3), or (4) of subdivision (a).

(b) Any violation of paragraph (1) of subdivision (a) is punishable by imprisonment in the county jail for a period not to exceed six months, or by a fine not to exceed five thousand dollars ($5,000), or by both that imprisonment and fine.

(c) Any violation of paragraph (3) of subdivision (a) is punishable by imprisonment in county jail for up to one year, or by a fine not to exceed fifteen thousand dollars ($15,000), or by both that imprisonment and fine. If the violator is a corporation or a limited liability company, the fine prescribed by this subdivision may not exceed one hundred fifty thousand dollars ($150,000).

(d) Any violation of paragraph (2), (4), or (5) of subdivision (a) is punishable by imprisonment in a county jail for a term not exceeding one year, or by a fine not exceeding fifteen thousand dollars ($15,000), or by both that imprisonment and fine. If the defendant is a corporation or a limited liability company, the fine may not exceed one hundred fifty thousand dollars ($150,000).

(e) In determining the amount of fine to impose under this section, the court shall consider all relevant circumstances, including, but not limited to, the nature, circumstance, extent, and gravity of the violation, any prior history of violations by the defendant, the ability of the defendant to pay, and any other matters the court determines the interests of justice require. **Leg.H.** 1999 ch. 615, 2002 ch. 885 (AB 2837).

Ref.: Herlick Handbook § 9.6.

§6425. Penalties for willful violations causing death or serious bodily impairment; violations within 7 years of first conviction.

(a) Any employer and any employee having direction, management, control, or custody of any employment, place of employment, or of any other employee, who willfully violates any occupational safety or health standard, order, or special order, or Section 25910 of the Health and Safety Code, and that violation caused death to any employee, or caused permanent or prolonged impairment of the body of any employee, is guilty of a public offense punishable by imprisonment in a county jail for a term not exceeding one year, or by a fine not exceeding one hundred thousand dollars ($100,000), or by both that imprisonment and fine; or by imprisonment in the state prison for 16 months, or two or three years, or by a fine of not more than two hundred fifty thousand dollars ($250,000), or by both that imprisonment and fine; and in either case, if the defendant is a corporation or a limited liability company, the fine may not exceed one million five hundred thousand dollars ($1,500,000).

(b) If the conviction is for a violation committed within seven years after a conviction under subdivision (b), (c), or (d) of Section 6423 or subdivision (c) of Section 6430, punishment shall be by imprisonment in state prison for a term of 16 months, two, or three years, or by a fine not exceeding two hundred fifty thousand dollars ($250,000), or by both that fine and imprisonment, but if the defendant is a corporation or limited liability company, the fine may not be less than five hundred thousand dollars ($500,000) or more than two million five hundred thousand dollars ($2,500,000).

(c) If the conviction is for a violation committed within seven years after a first conviction of the defendant for any crime involving a violation of subdivision (a), punishment shall be by imprisonment pursuant to subdivision (h) of Section 1170 of the Penal Code for two, three, or four years, or by a fine not exceeding two hundred fifty thousand dollars ($250,000), or by both that fine and imprisonment, but if the defendant is a corporation or a limited liability company, the fine shall not be less than one million dollars ($1,000,000) but may not exceed three million five hundred thousand dollars ($3,500,000).

(d) In determining the amount of fine to be imposed under this section, the court shall consider all relevant circumstances, including, but not limited to, the nature, circumstance, extent, and gravity of the violation, any prior history of violations by the defendant, the ability of the defendant to pay, and any other matters the court determines the interests of justice require.

(e) As used in this section, "willfully" has the same definition as it has in Section 7 of the Penal Code. This subdivision is intended to be a codification of existing law.

(f) This section does not prohibit a prosecution under Section 192 of the Penal Code. **Leg.H.** 1991 ch. 599, effective October 5, 1991, 1999 ch. 615, 2011 ch. 15 (AB 109) §222, effective April 4, 2011, operative October 1, 2011.

2011 Notes: This act is titled and may be cited as the 2011 Realignment Legislation addressing public safety. Stats. 2011 ch. 15 (AB 109) §1.

This act will become operative no earlier than October 1, 2011, and only upon creation of a community corrections grant program to assist in implementing this act and upon an appropriation to fund the grant program. Stats. 2011 ch. 15 (AB 109) §636; Stats. 2011 ch. 39 (AB 117) §68.

The Community Corrections Grant Program referred to in Stats. 2011 ch. 15 §636, as amended by Stats. 2011 ch. 39 §68, was created by Stats. 2011 ch. 40 §3, operative October 1, 2011.

§6426. Penalties for knowingly falsifying reports or records.

Whoever knowingly makes any false statement, representation, or certification in any application, record, report, plan, or other document filed or required to be maintained pursuant to this division shall, upon conviction, be punished by a fine of not more than seventy thousand dollars ($70,000), or by imprisonment for not more than six months, or by both. **Leg.H.** 1991 ch. 599, effective October 5, 1991.

§6427. Civil penalty for non-serious violations.

(a) Any employer who violates any occupational safety or health standard, order, or special order, or Section 25910 of the Health and Safety Code, and the violation is specifically determined not to be of a serious nature, may be assessed a civil penalty of up to twelve thousand four hundred seventy-one dollars ($12,471) for each violation.

(b) Commencing on January 1, 2018, and each January 1 thereafter, the maximum penalty amount specified in this section shall be increased based on the percentage increase in the Consumer Price Index for All Urban Consumers (CPI-U), not seasonally adjusted, for the month of October immediately preceding the date of the adjustment, as compared to the prior year's October CPI-U. Any regulation issued pursuant to this section increasing penalty amounts based on the annual increase in the CPI-U shall be exempt from the rulemaking provisions of the Administrative Procedure Act (Chapter 3.5 (commencing with Section 11340) of Part 1 of Division 3 of Title 2 of the Government Code), except that the regulation shall be filed with the Office of Administrative Law for publication in the Cali-

Labor

fornia Code of Regulations. Any penalty shall be calculated using the penalty amounts in effect during the calendar year in which the citation was issued. **Leg.H.** 1991 ch. 599, effective October 5, 1991, 1993 ch. 928, 2017 ch. 28 (SB 96) §30, effective June 27, 2017.

§6428. Civil penalty for serious violations.

Any employer who violates any occupational safety or health standard, order, or special order, or Section 25910 of the Health and Safety Code, if that violation is a serious violation, shall be assessed a civil penalty of up to twenty-five thousand dollars ($25,000) for each violation. Employers who do not have an operative injury prevention program shall receive no adjustment for good faith of the employer or history of previous violations as provided in paragraphs (3) and (4) of subdivision (c) of Section 6319. **Leg.H.** 1991 ch. 599, effective October 5, 1991, 1999 ch. 615.

§6428.5. Criteria for "operative" injury prevention program.

An employer's injury prevention program shall be deemed to be operative for the purposes of Sections 6427 and 6428 if it meets the criteria for substantial compliance established by the standards board pursuant to Section 6401.7.

§6429. Civil penalties for willful or repetitious violations.

(a)(1) Any employer who willfully or repeatedly violates any occupational safety or health standard, order, or special order, or Section 25910 of the Health and Safety Code, may be assessed a civil penalty of not more than one hundred twenty-four thousand seven hundred nine dollars ($124,709) for each violation, but in no case less than eight thousand nine hundred eight dollars ($8,908) for each willful violation.

(2) Commencing on January 1, 2018, and each January 1 thereafter, the penalty amounts specified in this section shall be increased based on the percentage increase in the Consumer Price Index for All Urban Consumers (CPI-U), not seasonally adjusted, for the month of October immediately preceding the date of the adjustment, as compared to the prior year's October CPI-U. Any regulation issued pursuant to this section increasing penalty amounts based on the annual increase in the CPI-U shall be exempt from the rulemaking provisions of the Administrative Procedure Act (Chapter 3.5 (commencing with Section 11340) of Part 1 of Division 3 of Title 2 of the Government Code), except that the regulation shall be filed with the Office of Administrative Law for publication in the California Code of Regulations. Any penalty shall be calculated using the penalty amounts in effect during the calendar year in which the citation was issued.

(b) Any employer who repeatedly violates any occupational safety or health standard, order, or special order, or Section 25910 of the Health and Safety Code, shall not receive any adjustment of a penalty assessed pursuant to this section on the basis of the regulations promulgated pursuant to subdivision (c) of Section 6319 pertaining to the good faith of the employer or the history of previous violations of the employer.

(c) The division shall preserve and maintain records of its investigations and inspections and citations for a period of not less than seven years. **Leg.H.** 1991 ch. 599, effective October 5, 1991, 1999 ch. 615, 2000 ch. 135, 2017 ch. 28 (SB 96) §31, effective June 27, 2017.

§6430. Civil penalties for failure to correct violations.

(a) Any employer who fails to correct a violation of any occupational safety or health standard, order, or special order, or Section 25910 of the Health and Safety Code, within the period permitted for its correction shall be assessed a civil penalty of not more than fifteen thousand dollars ($15,000) for each day during which the failure or violation continues.

(b) Notwithstanding subdivision (a), for any employer who submits a signed statement affirming compliance with the abatement terms pursuant to Section 6320, and is found upon a reinspection not to have abated the violation, any adjustment to the civil penalty based on abatement shall be rescinded and the additional civil penalty assessed for failure to abate shall not be adjusted for good faith of the employer or history of previous violations as provided in paragraphs (3) and (4) of subdivision (c) of Section 6319.

(c) Notwithstanding subdivision (a), any employer who submits a signed statement affirming compliance with the abatement terms pursuant to subdivision (b) of Section 6320, and is found not to have abated the violation, is guilty of a public offense punishable by imprisonment in a county jail for a term not exceeding one year, or by a fine not exceeding thirty thousand dollars ($30,000), or by both that fine and imprisonment; but if the defendant is a corporation or a limited liability company the fine shall not exceed three hundred thousand dollars ($300,000). In determining the amount of the fine to be imposed under this section, the court shall consider all relevant circumstances, including, but not limited to, the nature, circumstance, extent, and gravity of the violation, any prior history of violations by the defendant, the ability of the defendant to pay, and any other matters the court determines the interests of justice require. Nothing in this section shall be construed to prevent prosecution under any law that may apply. **Leg.H.** 1991 ch. 599, effective October 5, 1991, 1999 ch. 615.

§6431. Civil penalty for violation of posting or recordkeeping requirements.

(a) Any employer who violates any of the posting or recordkeeping requirements as prescribed by regulations adopted pursuant to Sections 6408 and 6410, or who fails to post any notice required by Section 3550, shall be assessed a civil penalty of up to twelve thousand four hundred seventy-one dollars ($12,471) for each violation.

(b) Commencing on January 1, 2018, and each January 1 thereafter, the maximum penalty amount specified in this section shall be increased based on the percentage increase in the Consumer Price Index for All Urban Consumers (CPI-U), not seasonally adjusted, for the month of October immediately preceding the date of the adjustment, as compared to the prior year's October CPI-U. Any regulation issued pursuant to this section increasing maximum penalty amounts based on the annual increase in the CPI-U shall be exempt from the rulemaking provisions of the Administrative Procedure Act (Chapter 3.5 (commencing with Section 11340) of Part 1 of Division 3 of Title 2 of the Government Code), except that the regulation shall be filed with the Office of Administrative Law for publication in the California Code of Regulations. Any penalty shall be calculated using the penalty amounts in effect during the calendar year in which the citation was issued. **Leg.H.** 1991 ch. 599, effective October 5, 1991, 2017 ch. 28 (SB 96) §32, effective June 27, 2017.

Ref.: Herlick Handbook § 14.3.

§6432. [First of Two; Repealed January 1, 2023] Rebuttable presumption of "serious violation"; considerations prior to issuance of violation; "serious physical harm."

(a) There shall be a rebuttable presumption that a "serious violation" exists in a place of employment if the division demonstrates that there is a realistic possibility that death or serious physical harm could result from the actual hazard created by the violation. The demonstration of a violation by the division is not sufficient by itself to establish that the violation is serious. The actual hazard may consist of, among other things:

(1) A serious exposure exceeding an established permissible exposure limit.

(2) The existence in the place of employment of one or more unsafe or unhealthful practices, means, methods, operations, or processes that have been adopted or are in use.

(b)(1) Before issuing a citation alleging that a violation is serious, the division shall make a reasonable attempt to determine and consider, among other things, all of the following:

(A) Training for employees and supervisors relevant to preventing employee exposure to the hazard or to similar hazards.

(B) Procedures for discovering, controlling access to, and correcting the hazard or similar hazards.

(C) Supervision of employees exposed or potentially exposed to the hazard.

(D) Procedures for communicating to employees about the employer's health and safety rules and programs.

(E) Information that the employer wishes to provide, at any time before citations are issued, including, any of the following:

(i) The employer's explanation of the circumstances surrounding the alleged violative events.

(ii) Why the employer believes a serious violation does not exist.

(iii) Why the employer believes its actions related to the alleged violative events were reasonable and responsible so as to rebut, pursuant to subdivision (c), any presumption established pursuant to subdivision (a).

(iv) Any other information that the employer wishes to provide.

(2) The division shall satisfy its requirement to determine and consider the facts specified in paragraph (1) if, not less than 15 days prior to issuing a citation for a serious violation, the division delivers to the employer a standardized form containing the alleged violation descriptions ("AVD") it intends to cite as serious and clearly soliciting the information specified in this subdivision. The director shall prescribe the form for the alleged violation descriptions and solicitation of information. Any forms issued pursuant to this section shall be exempt from the rulemaking provisions of the Administrative Procedure Act (Chapter 3.5 (commencing with Section 11340) of Part 1 of Division 3 of Title 2 of the Government Code).

(c) If the division establishes a presumption pursuant to subdivision (a) that a violation is serious, the employer may rebut the presumption and establish that a violation is not serious by demonstrating that the employer did not know and could not, with the exercise of reasonable diligence, have known of the presence of the violation. The employer may accomplish this by demonstrating both of the following:

(1) The employer took all the steps a reasonable and responsible employer in like circumstances should be expected to take, before the violation occurred, to anticipate and prevent the violation, taking into consideration the severity of the harm that could be expected to occur and the likelihood of that harm occurring in connection with the work activity during which the violation occurred. Factors relevant to this determination include, but are not limited to, those listed in subdivision (b).

(2) The employer took effective action to eliminate employee exposure to the hazard created by the violation as soon as the violation was discovered.

(d) If the employer does not provide information in response to a division inquiry made pursuant to subdivision (b), the employer shall not be barred from presenting that information at the hearing and no negative inference shall be drawn. The employer may offer different information at the hearing than what was provided to the division and may explain any inconsistency, but the trier of fact may draw a negative inference from the prior inconsistent factual information. The trier of fact may also draw a negative inference from factual information offered at the hearing by the division that is inconsistent with factual information provided to the employer pursuant to subdivision (b), or from a failure by the division to provide the form setting forth the descriptions of the alleged violation and soliciting information pursuant to subdivision (b).

(e) "Serious physical harm," as used in this part, means any injury or illness, specific or cumulative, occurring in the place of employment or in connection with any employment, that results in any of the following:

(1) Inpatient hospitalization for purposes other than medical observation.

(2) The loss of any member of the body.

(3) Any serious degree of permanent disfigurement.

(4) Impairment sufficient to cause a part of the body or the function of an organ to become permanently and significantly reduced in efficiency on or off the job, including, but not limited to, depending on the severity, second-degree or worse burns, crushing injuries including internal injuries even though skin surface may be intact, respiratory illnesses, or broken bones.

(f) Serious physical harm may be caused by a single, repetitive practice, means, method, operation, or process.

(g) A division safety engineer or industrial hygienist who can demonstrate, at the time of the hearing, that [1]

their division-mandated training is current shall be deemed competent to offer testimony to establish each element of a serious violation, and may offer evidence on the custom and practice of injury and illness prevention in the workplace that is relevant to the issue of whether the violation is a serious violation.

(h) Paragraph (2) of subdivision (b) and subdivision (d) shall not apply to a citation alleging a serious violation relating to the severe acute respiratory syndrome coronavirus 2 (SARS-CoV-2).

(i) This section shall remain in effect only until January 1, 2023, and as of that date is repealed. Leg.H. 2010 ch. 692 (AB 2774) §2, 2020 ch. 84 (AB 685) §5.

§6432. 2020 Deletes. [1] his or her

§6432. [Second of Two; Operative January 1, 2023] Rebuttable presumption of "serious violation"; considerations prior to issuance of violation; "serious physical harm."

(a) There shall be a rebuttable presumption that a "serious violation" exists in a place of employment if the division demonstrates that there is a realistic possibility that death or serious physical harm could result from the actual hazard created by the violation. The demonstration of a violation by the division is not sufficient by itself to establish that the violation is serious. The actual hazard may consist of, among other things:

(1) A serious exposure exceeding an established permissible exposure limit.

(2) The existence in the place of employment of one or more unsafe or unhealthful practices, means, methods, operations, or processes that have been adopted or are in use.

(b)(1) Before issuing a citation alleging that a violation is serious, the division shall make a reasonable attempt to determine and consider, among other things, all of the following:

(A) Training for employees and supervisors relevant to preventing employee exposure to the hazard or to similar hazards.

(B) Procedures for discovering, controlling access to, and correcting the hazard or similar hazards.

(C) Supervision of employees exposed or potentially exposed to the hazard.

(D) Procedures for communicating to employees about the employer's health and safety rules and programs.

(E) Information that the employer wishes to provide, at any time before citations are issued, including, any of the following:

(i) The employer's explanation of the circumstances surrounding the alleged violative events.

(ii) Why the employer believes a serious violation does not exist.

(iii) Why the employer believes its actions related to the alleged violative events were reasonable and responsible so as to rebut, pursuant to subdivision (c), any presumption established pursuant to subdivision (a).

(iv) Any other information that the employer wishes to provide.

(2) The division shall satisfy its requirement to determine and consider the facts specified in paragraph (1) if, not less than 15 days prior to issuing a citation for a serious violation, the division delivers to the employer a standardized form containing the alleged violation descriptions ("AVD") it intends to cite as serious and clearly soliciting the information specified in this subdivision. The director shall prescribe the form for the alleged violation descriptions and solicitation of information. Any forms issued pursuant to this section shall be exempt from the rulemaking provisions of the Administrative Procedure Act (Chapter 3.5 (commencing with Section 11340) of Part 1 of Division 3 of Title 2 of the Government Code).

(c) If the division establishes a presumption pursuant to subdivision (a) that a violation is serious, the employer may rebut the presumption and establish that a violation is not serious by demonstrating that the employer did not know and could not, with the exercise of reasonable diligence, have known of the presence of the violation. The employer may accomplish this by demonstrating both of the following:

(1) The employer took all the steps a reasonable and responsible employer in like circumstances should be expected to take, before the violation occurred, to anticipate and prevent the violation, taking into consideration the severity of the harm that could be expected to occur and the likelihood of that harm occurring in connection with the work activity during which the violation occurred. Factors relevant to this determination include, but are not limited to, those listed in subdivision (b).

(2) The employer took effective action to eliminate employee exposure to the hazard created by the violation as soon as the violation was discovered.

(d) If the employer does not provide information in response to a division inquiry made pursuant to subdivision (b), the employer shall not be barred from presenting that information at the hearing and no negative inference shall be drawn. The employer may offer different information at the hearing than what was provided to the division and may explain any inconsistency, but the trier of fact may draw a negative inference from the prior inconsistent factual information. The trier of fact may also draw a negative inference from factual information offered at the hearing by the division that is inconsistent with factual information provided to the employer pursuant to subdivision (b), or from a failure by the division to provide the form setting forth the descriptions of the alleged violation and soliciting information pursuant to subdivision (b).

(e) "Serious physical harm," as used in this part, means any injury or illness, specific or cumulative, occurring in the place of employment or in connection with any employment, that results in any of the following:

(1) Inpatient hospitalization for purposes other than medical observation.

(2) The loss of any member of the body.

(3) Any serious degree of permanent disfigurement.

(4) Impairment sufficient to cause a part of the body or the function of an organ to become permanently and significantly reduced in efficiency on or off the job, including, but not limited to, depending on the severity, second-degree or worse burns, crushing injuries including internal injuries even though skin surface may be intact, respiratory illnesses, or broken bones.

(f) Serious physical harm may be caused by a single, repetitive practice, means, method, operation, or process.

(g) A division safety engineer or industrial hygienist who can demonstrate, at the time of the hearing, that their division-mandated training is current shall be deemed competent to offer testimony to establish each element of a serious violation, and may offer evidence on the custom and practice of injury and illness prevention in the workplace that is relevant to the issue of whether the violation is a serious violation.

(h) This section shall become operative on January 1, 2023. **Leg.H.** 2020 ch. 84 (AB 685) §6.

§6433. Civil penalties distinguished.

The civil penalties set forth in Sections 6427 to 6431, inclusive, shall not be considered as other penalties specifically provided within the meaning of Section 6423.

§6434. Civil or administrative penalties assessed against educational entities to be deposited with fund; application for refund upon abatement—Time limit.

(a) Any civil or administrative penalty assessed pursuant to this chapter against a school district, county board of education, county superintendent of schools, charter school, community college district, California State University, University of California, or joint powers agency performing education functions shall be deposited with the Workplace Health and Safety Revolving Fund established pursuant to Section 78.

(b) Any school district, county board of education, county superintendent of schools, charter school, community college district, California State University, University of California, or joint powers agency performing education functions may apply for a refund of their civil penalty, with interest, if all conditions previously cited have been abated, they have abated any other outstanding citation, and if they have not been cited by the division for a serious violation at the same school within two years of the date of the original violation. Funds not applied for within two years and six months of the time of the original violation shall be expended as provided for in Section 78 to assist schools in establishing effective occupational injury and illness prevention programs. **Leg.H.** 1991 ch. 599, effective October 5, 1991, 1999 ch. 615, 2000 ch. 135.

§6434.5. Refund plan for civil and administrative penalties.

(a) Any civil or administrative penalty assessed pursuant to this chapter against a public police or city, county, or special district fire department or the California Department of Forestry and Fire Protection shall be deposited into the Workers' Compensation Administration Revolving Fund established pursuant to Section 62.5.

(b) Any public police or city, county, or special district fire department or the California Department of Forestry and Fire Protection may apply for a refund of any civil or administrative penalty assessed pursuant to this chapter, with interest, if all conditions previously cited have been abated, the department has abated any other outstanding citation, and the department has not been cited by the division for a serious violation within two years of the date of the original violation. Funds received as a result of a penalty, for which a refund is not applied for within two years and six months of the time of the original violation, shall be expended in accordance with Section 78 as follows:

(1) Funds received as a result of a civil or administrative penalty imposed on a city, county, or special district fire department or the California Department of Forestry and Fire Protection shall be allocated to the California Firefighter Joint Apprenticeship Program for the purpose of establishing and maintaining effective occupational injury and illness prevention programs.

(2) Funds received as a result of a civil or administrative penalty imposed on a police department shall be allocated to the Office of Criminal Justice Planning, or any succeeding agency, for the purpose of establishing and maintaining effective occupational injury and illness prevention programs.

(c) This section does not apply to that portion of any civil or administrative penalty that is distributed directly to an aggrieved employee or employees pursuant to the provisions of Section 2699. **Leg.H.** 2005 ch. 141 (AB 186) §1.

§6435. Civil penalty for violation of permit requirements.

(a) Any employer who violates any of the requirements of Chapter 6 (commencing with Section 6500) of this part shall be assessed a civil penalty under the appropriate provisions of Sections 6427 to 6430, inclusive.

(b) This section shall become inoperative on January 1, 1987, and shall remain inoperative until January 1, 1991, at which time it shall become operative, unless a later enacted statute, which becomes effective on or before January 1, 1991, deletes or extends that date.

§6436. Jurisdiction of actions involving asbestos-related complaints.

The criminal complaint regarding a violation of Section 6505.5 may be brought by the Attorney General or by the district attorney or prosecuting attorney of any city, in the superior court of any county in the state with jurisdiction over the contractor or employer, by reason of the contractor's or employer's act or failure to act within that county. Any penalty assessed by the court shall be paid to the office of the prosecutor bringing the complaint, but if the case was referred to the prosecutor by the division, or some other governmental unit, one-half of the civil or criminal penalty assessed shall be paid to that governmental unit. **Leg.H.** 2003 ch. 449 (AB 1712).

CHAPTER 5 TEMPORARY VARIANCES

§6450. Temporary order for variance from health and safety standards.

(a) Any employer may apply to the division for a temporary order granting a variance from an occupational safety or health standard. Such temporary order shall be granted only if the employer files an application which meets the requirements of Section 6451, and establishes that (1) he is unable to comply with a standard by its effective date because of unavailability of professional or technical personnel or of materials and equipment needed to come into compliance with the standard or because necessary construction or alteration of facilities cannot be completed by the effective date, (2) he is taking all available steps to safeguard his employees against the hazards covered by the standard, and (3) he has an effective program for coming into compliance with the standard as quickly as practicable.

(b) Any temporary order issued under this section shall prescribe the practices, means, methods, operations, and processes which the employer must adopt and use while the order is in effect and state in detail his program for coming into compliance with the standard. Such a temporary order may be granted only after notice to employees and an opportunity for a hearing. However, the division may issue one interim order for a temporary variance upon submission of an application showing that the employment or place of employment will be safe for employees pending a hearing on the application for a temporary variance. No temporary order may be in effect for longer than the period needed by the employer to achieve compliance with the standard or one year, whichever is shorter, except that such an order may be renewed not more than twice provided that the requirements of this section are met and an application for renewal is filed prior to the expiration date of the order. No single renewal of an order may remain in effect for longer than 180 days.

§6451. Information needed for temporary variance application.

An application for a temporary order under Section 6450 shall contain all of the following:

(a) A specification of the standard or portion thereof from which the employer seeks a variance.

(b) A representation by the employer, supported by representations from qualified persons having firsthand knowledge of the facts represented, that he is unable to comply with the standard or portion thereof and a detailed statement of the reasons therefor.

(c) A statement of the steps he has taken and will take, with specific dates, to protect employees against the hazard covered by the standard.

(d) A statement of when he expects to be able to comply with the standard and what steps he has taken and what steps he will take, with dates specified, to come into compliance with the standard.

(e) A certification that he has informed his employees of the application by giving a copy thereof to their authorized representative, posting a statement giving a summary of the application and specifying where a copy may be examined at the place or places where notices to employees are normally posted, and by other appropriate means. A description of how employees have been informed shall be contained in the certification. The information to employees shall also inform them of their right to petition the division for a hearing.

§6452. Temporary variance to test new techniques.

The division is authorized to grant a temporary variance from any standard or portion thereof whenever it determines such variance is necessary to permit an employer to participate in an experiment approved by the director designed to demonstrate or validate new and improved techniques to safeguard the health or safety of workers.

§6454. Rules for temporary variances.

The division may, in accordance with Chapter 3.5 (commencing with Section 11340) of Part 1 of Division 3 of Title 2 of the Government Code, make such rules and regulations as are reasonably necessary to carry out the provisions of this chapter and to establish rules and regulations relating to the granting or denial of temporary variances.

§6455. Time limits to appeal temporary variance.

Any employer or other person adversely affected by the granting or denial of a temporary variance may appeal to the standards board within 15 working days from receipt of the notice granting or denying the variance. The 15-day period may be extended by the standards board for good cause.

§6456. Temporary variance decisions binding on parties.

A decision of the standards board on a variance appeal is binding on the director and the division with respect to the parties involved in the particular appeal. The director shall have the right to seek judicial review of a standards board decision irrespective of whether he appeared or participated in the appeal to the standards board.

§6457. Standards board decisions.

The standards board shall conduct hearings and render decisions on appeals of decisions of the division relating to allowance or denial of temporary variances. All board decisions on such variance appeals shall be in writing and shall be final except for any rehearing or judicial review.

CHAPTER 6
PERMIT REQUIREMENTS

§6500. Permit requirement for dangerous employment or place of employment; application to certain construction, demolition, and underground activities and motion picture, television, and theater stages or sets on and after January 1, 2000.

(a) For those employments or places of employment that by their nature involve a substantial risk of injury, the division shall require the issuance of a permit prior to the initiation of any practices, work, method, operation, or process of employment. The permit requirement of this section is limited to employment or places of employment that are any of the following:

(1) Construction of trenches or excavations that are five feet or deeper and into which a person is required to descend.

(2) The construction of any building, structure, falsework, or scaffolding more than three stories high or the equivalent height.

(3) The demolition of any building, structure, falsework, or scaffold more than three stories high or the equivalent height.

(4) The underground use of diesel engines in work in mines and tunnels.

This subdivision does not apply to motion picture, television, or theater stages or sets, including, but not limited to, scenery, props, backdrops, flats, greenbeds, and grids.

(b) On or after January 1, 2000, this subdivision shall apply to motion picture, television, or theater stages or sets, if there has occurred within any one prior calendar year in any combination at separate locations three serious injuries, fatalities, or serious violations related to the construction or demolition of sets more than 36 feet in height for the motion picture, television, and theatrical production industry.

An annual permit shall be required for employers who construct or dismantle motion picture, television, or theater stages or sets that are more than three stories or the equivalent height. A single permit shall be required under this subdivision for each employer, regardless of the number of locations where the stages or sets are located. An employer with a currently valid annual permit issued under this subdivision shall not be required to provide notice to the division prior to commencement of any work activity authorized by the permit. The division may adopt procedures to permit employers to renew by mail the permits issued under this subdivision. For purposes of this subdivision, "motion picture, television, or theater stages or sets" include, but are not limited to, scenery, props, backdrops, flats, greenbeds, and grids. **Leg.H.** 1996 ch. 664, 1997 ch. 17.

§6501. Permit information required of employer.

Any employer subject to Section 6500 shall apply to the division for a permit pursuant to Section 6500. Such application for a permit shall contain such information as the division may deem necessary to evaluate the safety of the proposed employment or place of employment.

An application by an employer shall include a provision that the applicant has knowledge of applicable occupational safety and health standards and will comply with such standards and any other lawful order of the division.

§6501.5. Employer registration of asbestos-related work.

Effective January 1, 1987, any employer or contractor who engages in asbestos-related work, as defined in Section 6501.8, and which involves 100 square feet or more of surface area of asbestos-containing material, shall register with the division.

The division may grant registration based on a determination that the employer has demonstrated evidence that the conditions, practices, means, methods, operations, or processes used, or proposed to be used, will provide a safe and healthful place of employment. This section is not intended to supersede existing laws and regulations under Title 8, California Administrative Code, Section 5208.

An application for registration shall contain such information and attachments, given under penalty of perjury, as the division may deem necessary to evaluate the safety and health of the proposed employment or place of employment. It shall include, but not be limited to, all of the following:

(a) Every employer shall meet each of the following criteria:

(1) If the employer is a contractor, the contractor shall be certified pursuant to Section 7058.5 of the Business and Professions Code.

(2) Provide health insurance coverage to cover the entire cost of medical examinations and monitoring required by the law and be insured for workers' compensation, or provide a five hundred dollar ($500) trust account for each employee engaged in asbestos-related work. The health insurance coverage may be provided through a union, association, or employer.

(3) Train and certify all employees in accordance with all training required by law and Title 8 of the California Administrative Code.

(4) Be proficient and have the necessary equipment to safely do asbestos-related work.

(b) Provide written notice to the division of each separate job or phase of work, where the work process used is different or the work is performed at noncontiguous locations, noting all of the following:

(1) The address of the job.

(2) The exact physical location of the job at that address.

(3) The start and projected completion date.

(4) The name of a certified supervisor with sufficient experience and authority who shall be responsible for the asbestos-related work at that job.

(5) The name of a qualified person, who shall be responsible for scheduling any air sampling, laboratory calibration of air sampling equipment, evaluation of sampling results, and conducting respirator fit testing and evaluating the results of those tests.

(6) The type of work to be performed, the work practices that will be utilized, and the potential for exposure.

Should any change be necessary, the employer or contractor shall so inform the division at or before the time of the change. Any oral notification shall be confirmed in writing.

(c) Post the location where any asbestos-related work occurs so as to be readable at 20 feet stating, "Danger—Asbestos. Cancer and Lung Hazard. Keep Out."

(d) A copy of the registration shall be provided before the start of the job to the prime contractor or other employers on the site and shall be posted on the jobsite beside the Cal-OSHA poster.

(e) The division shall obtain the services of three industrial hygienists and one clerical employee to implement and to enforce the requirements of this section unless the director makes a finding that these services are not necessary or that the services are not obtainable due to a lack of qualified hygienists applying for available positions. Funding may, at the director's discretion, be appropriated from the Asbestos Abatement Fund.

(f) Not later than January 1, 1987, the Division of Occupational Safety and Health shall propose to the Occupational Safety and Health Standards Board for review and adoption a regulation concerning asbestos-related work, as defined in Section 6501.8, which involves 100 square feet or more of surface area of asbestos-containing material. The regulation shall protect most effectively the health and safety of employees and shall include specific requirements for certification of employees, supervisors with sufficient experience and authority to be responsible for asbestos-related work, and a qualified person who shall be responsible for scheduling any air sampling, for arranging for calibration of the air sampling equipment and for analysis of the air samples by a NIOSH approved method, for conducting respirator fit testing, and for evaluating the results of the air sampling.

The Division of Occupational Safety and Health shall also propose a regulation to the Occupational Safety and Health Standards Board for review and adoption specifying sampling methodology for use in taking air samples.

§6501.7. Definition of "asbestos."

"Asbestos" means fibrous forms of various hydrated minerals, including chrysotile (fibrous serpentine), crocidolite (fibrous riebecktite), amosite (fibrous cummingtonite—grunerite), fibrous tremolite, fibrous actinolite, and fibrous anthophyllite.

§6501.8. "Asbestos-related work" and "asbestos containing construction material."

(a) For purposes of this chapter, "asbestos-related work" means any activity which by disturbing asbestos-containing construction materials may release asbestos fibers into the air and which is not related to its manufacture, the mining or excavation of asbestos-bearing ore or materials, or the installation or repair of automotive materials containing asbestos.

(b) For purposes of this chapter, "asbestos containing construction material" means any manufactured construction material that contains more than one-tenth of 1 percent asbestos by weight.

(c) For purposes of this chapter, "asbestos-related work" does not include the installation, repair, maintenance, or nondestructive removal of asbestos cement pipe used outside of buildings, if the installation, repair, maintenance, or nondestructive removal of asbestos cement pipe does not result in asbestos exposures to employees in excess of the action level determined in accordance with Sections 1529 and 5208 of Title 8 of the California Code of Regulations, and if the employees and supervisors involved in the operation have received training through a task-specific training program, approved pursuant to Section 9021.9, with written certification of completion of that training by the training entity responsible for the training. **Leg.H.** 1993 ch. 1075.

§6501.9. Employer or contractor shall determine if asbestos is present.

The owner of a commercial or industrial building or structure, employer, or contractor who engages in, or contracts for, asbestos-related work shall make a good faith effort to determine if asbestos is present before the work is begun. The contractor or employer shall first inquire of the owner if asbestos is present in any building or structure built prior to 1978.

§6502. Division's issuance of permits.

The division may issue a permit based on a determination the employer has demonstrated evidence that the conditions, practices, means, methods, operations or processes used or proposed to be used will provide a safe and healthful place of employment. The division may issue a single permit for two or more projects to be performed by a single employer if similar conditions exist on each project and the chief or his representative is satisfied an adequate safety program has been developed for all the projects. The division may, upon its motion, conduct any investigation or hearing it deems necessary for the purpose of this section, and may require a safety conference prior to the start of actual work.

§6503. Safety conferences.

A safety conference shall include representatives of the owner or contracting agency, the contractor, the employer, employees and employee representatives. The safety conference shall include a discussion of the employer's safety program and such means, methods, devices, processes, practices, conditions or operations as he intends to use in providing safe employment and a safe place of employment.

§6503.5. Safety conference for all asbestos handling jobs.

A safety conference shall be held for all asbestos handling jobs prior to the start of actual work. It shall include representatives of the owner or contracting agency, the contractor, the employer, employees, and employee representatives. It shall include a discussion of the employer's safety program and such means, methods, devices, processes, practices, conditions, or operations as the employer intends to use in providing a safe place of employment.

§6504. Employers to post copies of permits.

Any employer issued a permit pursuant to this chapter shall post a copy or copies of the permit pursuant to subdivision (a) of Section 6408.

§6505. Revocation of permits.

The division may at any time, upon good cause being shown therefor, and after notice and an opportunity to be heard revoke any permit issued pursuant to this chapter.

§6505.5. Penalties for failure to determine if asbestos is present.

(a) The division may, upon good cause shown, and after notice to the employer or contractor by the division and an opportunity to be heard, revoke or suspend any registration issued to the employer or contractor to do asbestos-related work until certain specified written conditions are met.

(b) Any person who owns a commercial or industrial building or structure, any employer who engages in or contracts for asbestos-related work, any contractor, public agency, or any employee acting for any of the foregoing, who, contracts for, or who begins, asbestos-related work in any commercial or industrial building or structure built prior to 1978 without first determining if asbestos-containing material is present, and thereby fails to comply with the applicable laws and regulations, is subject to one of the following penalties:

(1) For a knowing or negligent violation, a fine of not more than five thousand dollars ($5,000) or imprisonment in the county jail for not more than six months, or both the fine and imprisonment.

(2) For a willful violation which results in death, serious injury or illness, or serious exposure, a fine of not more than ten thousand dollars ($10,000) or imprisonment in the county jail for not more than one year, or both the fine and imprisonment. A second or subsequent conviction under this paragraph may be punishable by a fine of not more than twenty thousand dollars ($20,000) or by imprisonment in the county jail for not more than one year, or by both the fine and imprisonment.

(c) It is a defense to an action for violation of this section if the owner, contractor, employer, public agency, or agent thereof, proves, by a preponderance of the evidence, that he or she made a reasonable effort to determine whether asbestos was present. **Leg.H.** 1985 ch. 1587 §14, effective October 2, 1985, 1986 ch. 1451 §13, effective September 30, 1986, 2017 ch. 28 (SB 96) §33, effective June 27, 2017.

§6506. Appeal of permit denial or revocation.

(a) Any employer denied a permit upon application, or whose permit is revoked, may appeal such denial or revocation to the director.

(b) The filing of an appeal to the director from a permit revocation by the division shall not stay the revocation. Upon application by the employer with proper notice to the division, and after an opportunity for the division to respond to the application, the director may issue an order staying the revocation while the appeal is pending.

§6507. Permit and registration fees.

The division shall set fees to be charged for permits and registrations in amounts reasonably necessary to cover the costs involved in administering the permitting and registration programs in this chapter. All permit and registration fees collected under this chapter shall be deposited in the Occupational Safety and Health Fund. **Leg.H.** 1973 ch. 993 §100, effective October 1, 1973, 2016 ch. 31 (SB 836) §195, effective June 27, 2016.

§6508. Entities exempt from permit requirements.

No permit shall be required of the State of California, a city, city and county, county, district, or public utility subject to the jurisdiction of the Public Utilities Commission.

§6508.5. No exemption from registration.

No entity shall be exempt from registration. The State of California, a city, city and county, county, district, or public utility subject to the jurisdiction of the Public Utilities Commission, shall be required to apply for a registration through the designated chief executive officer of that body. No registration fees shall be required of any public agencies.

§6509. Penalty for permit violations.

Any person, or agent or officer thereof, who violates this chapter is guilty of a misdemeanor.

§6509.5. Asbestos consultant may not require contract for corrective work as condition to performing inspection.

(a) If an asbestos consultant has made an inspection for the purpose of determining the presence of asbestos or the need for related remedial action with knowledge that the report has been required by a person as a condition of making a loan of money secured by the property, or is required by a public entity as a condition of issuing a permit concerning the property, the asbestos consultant or any employee, subsidiary, or any company with common ownership, shall not require, as a condition of performing the inspection, that the consultant also perform any corrective work on the property that was recommended in the report.

(b) This section does not prohibit an asbestos consultant that has contracted to perform corrective work after the report of another company has indicated the presence of asbestos or the need for related remedial action from making its own inspection prior to performing that corrective work or from making an inspection to determine whether the corrective measures were successful and, if not, thereafter performing additional corrective work.

(c) A violation of this section is grounds for disciplinary action against any asbestos consultant who engages in that work pursuant to any license from a state agency.

(d) A violation of this section is a misdemeanor punishable by a fine of not less than three thousand dollars ($3,000) and not more than five thousand dollars ($5,000), or by imprisonment in the county jail for not more than one year, or both.

(e) For the purpose of this section:

(1) "Asbestos consultant" means any person who, for compensation, inspects property to identify asbestos containing materials, determining the risks, or the need for related remedial action.

(2) "Asbestos" has the meaning set forth in Section 6501.7.

§6510. Temporary restraining order for permit violation.

(a) If, after inspection or investigation, the division finds that an employer, without a valid permit, is engaging in activity for which a permit is required, it may, through its attorneys, apply to the superior court of the county in which such activity is taking place for an injunction restraining such activity.

(b) The application to the superior court, accompanied by an affidavit showing that the employer, without a valid permit, is engaging in activity for which a permit is required, is a sufficient prima facie showing to warrant, in the discretion of the court, the immediate granting of a temporary restraining order. No bond shall be required of the division as a prerequisite to the granting of any restraining order.

CHAPTER 7
APPEAL PROCEEDINGS

§6600. Time limit for appeal of citation or penalty.

Any employer served with a citation or notice pursuant to Section 6317, or a notice of proposed penalty under this part, or any other person obligated to the employer as specified in subdivision (b) of Section 6319, may appeal to the appeals board within 15 working days from the receipt of such citation or such notice with respect to violations alleged by the division, abatement periods, amount of proposed penalties, and the reasonableness of the changes required by the division to abate the condition.

§6600.5. Time limit for appeal of special order or action order.

Any employer served with a special order or any action order by the division pursuant to Section 6308, or any other person obligated to the employer as specified in subdivision (b) of Section 6319, may appeal to the appeals board within 15 working days from the receipt of the order with respect to the action ordered by the division, abatement periods, the reasonableness of the changes required by the division to abate the condition.

§6601. Failure to act within time limit for appeal of citation or penalty.

If within 15 working days from receipt of the citation or notice of civil penalty issued by the division, the employer fails to notify the appeals board that he intends to contest the citation or notice of proposed penalty, and no notice contesting the abatement period is filed by any employee or representative of the employee within such time, the citation or notice of proposed penalty shall be deemed a final order of the appeals board and not subject to review by any court or agency. The 15-day period may be extended by the appeals board for good cause.

§6601.5. Failure to act within time limit for appeal of special order or action order.

If, within 15 working days from receipt of a special order, or action order by the division, the employer fails to notify the appeals board that he or she intends to contest the order, and no notice contesting the abatement period is filed by any employee or representative of the employee within that time, the order shall be deemed a final order of the appeals board and not subject to review by any court or agency. The 15-day period may be extended by the appeals board for good cause.

§6602. Appeal procedures.

If an employer notifies the appeals board that he or she intends to contest a citation issued under Section 6317, or notice of proposed penalty issued under Section 6319, or order issued under Section 6308, or if, within 15 working days of the issuance of a citation or order any employee or representative of an employee files a notice with the division or appeals board alleging that the period of time fixed in the citation or order for the abatement of the violation is unreasonable, the appeals board shall afford an opportunity for a hearing. The appeals board shall thereafter issue a decision, based on findings of fact, affirming, modifying or vacating the division's citation, order, or proposed penalty, or directing other appropriate relief.

§6603. Appeals board rules of practice and procedure.

(a) The rules of practice and procedure adopted by the appeals board shall be consistent with Article 8 (commencing with Section 11435.05) of Chapter 4.5 of Part 1 of Division 3 of Title 2 of, and Sections 11507, 11507.6, 11507.7, 11513, 11514, 11515, and 11516 of, the Government Code, and shall provide affected employees or representatives of affected employees an opportunity to participate as parties to a hearing under Section 6602.

(b) The superior courts shall have jurisdiction over contempt proceedings, as provided in Article 12 (commencing with Section 11455.10) of Chapter 4.5 of Part 1 of Division 3 of Title 2 of the Government Code. **Leg.H.** 1995 ch. 938, operative July 1, 1997;

§6604. Duties of hearing officer.

The appeals board may, in accordance with rules of practice and procedure which it shall adopt, direct and order a hearing officer:

(a) To try the issues in any proceeding before it, whether of fact or of law, and make and file a finding, order or decision based thereon.

(b) To hold hearings and ascertain facts necessary to enable the appeals board to determine any proceeding or to make any order or decision that the appeals board is authorized to make, or necessary for the information of the appeals board.

§6605. Powers of hearing officer.

The appeals board may appoint one or more hearing officers in any proceeding, as it may deem necessary or advisable, and may defer, remove to itself, or transfer to a hearing officer the proceedings on any appeal. Any hearing officer appointed by the appeals board has the powers, jurisdiction, and authority granted by law, by the order of appointment, and by the rules of the appeals board.

§6606. Objection to hearing officer.

Any party to the proceeding may object to the reference of the proceeding to a particular hearing officer upon any one or more of the grounds specified in Section 641 of the Code of Civil Procedure and such objection shall be heard and disposed of by the appeals board. Affidavits may be read and witnesses examined as to such objections.

§6607. Hearing officer must be sworn.

Before entering upon his duties, the hearing officer shall be sworn, before an officer authorized to administer oaths, faithfully and fairly to hear and determine the matters and issues referred to him, to make just findings and to report according to his understanding. In any proceedings under this chapter, the hearing officer shall have the power to administer oaths and affirmations and to certify official acts.

§6608. Findings; decision.

The appeals board or a hearing officer shall, within 30 days after the case is submitted, make and file findings upon all facts involved in the appeal and file an order or decision. Together with the findings or the decision, there shall be served upon all the parties to the proceedings a summary of the evidence received and relied upon and the reasons or grounds upon which the decision was made.

§6609. Appeals board's action on decision.

Within 30 days after the filing of the findings, decision, or order, the appeals board may confirm, adopt, modify or set aside the findings, order, or decision of a hearing officer and may, with or without further proceedings, and with or without notice, enter its order, findings, or decision based upon the record in the case.

§6610. Service of notice, order, decision.

Any notice, order, or decision required by this part to be served upon any person either before, during, or after the institution of any proceeding before the appeals board, shall be served in the manner provided by Chapter 5 (commencing with Section 1010) of Title 14 of Part 2 of the Code of Civil Procedure, unless otherwise directed by the appeals board. In the latter event the document shall be served in accordance with the order or direction of the appeals board. The appeals board may, in the cases mentioned in the Code of Civil Procedure, order service to be made by publication of notice of time and place of hearing. Where service is ordered to be made by publication the date of the hearing shall be fixed at more than 30 days from the date of filing the application.

§6611. Employer's failure to appear at appeal.

(a) If the employer fails to appear, the appeals board may dismiss the appeal or may take action upon the employer's express admissions or upon other evidence, and affidavits may be used without any notice to the employer. Where the burden of proof is upon the employer to establish the appeals board action sought, the appeals board may act without taking evidence. Nothing in this section shall be construed to deprive the employer of the right to make any showing by way of mitigation.

(b) The appeal may be reinstated by the appeals board upon a showing of good cause by the employer for his failure to appear.

§6612. Informality of proceedings does not affect decision.

No informality in any proceeding or in the manner of taking testimony shall invalidate any order, decision, or finding made and filed as specified in this division. No order, decision, or finding shall be invalidated because of the admission into the record, and use as proof of any fact in dispute of any evidence not admissible under the common law or statutory rules of evidence and procedure.

§6613. Use of depositions on appeal.

The appeals board, a hearing officer, or any party to the action or proceeding, may, in any investigation or hearing before the appeals board, cause the deposition of witnesses residing within or without the state to be taken in the manner prescribed by law for like depositions in civil actions in the superior courts of this state under Title 4 (commencing with Section 2016.010) of Part 4 of the Code of Civil Procedure. To that end the attendance of witnesses and the production of records may be required. Depositions may be taken outside the state before any officer authorized to administer oaths. The appeals board or a hearing officer in any proceeding before the appeals board may cause evidence to be taken in other jurisdictions before the agency authorized to hear similar matters in such other jurisdictions. **Leg.H.** 1998 ch. 931, effective September 28, 1998, 2004 ch. 182 (AB 3081), operative July 1, 2005.

§6614. Time for reconsideration.

(a) At any time within 30 days after the service of any final order or decision made and filed by the appeals board or a hearing officer, any party aggrieved directly or indirectly by any final order or decision, made and filed by the appeals board or a hearing officer under any provision contained in this division, may petition the appeals board for reconsideration in respect to any matters determined or covered by the final order or decision and specified in the petition for reconsideration. Such petition shall be made only within the time and in the manner specified in this chapter.

(b) At any time within 30 days after the filing of an order or decision made by a hearing officer and the accompanying report, the appeals board may, on its own motion, grant reconsideration.

§6615. Accrual of cause of action; role of appeals board.

No cause of action arising out of any final order or decision made and filed by the appeals board or a hearing officer shall accrue in any court to any person until and unless the appeals board on its own motion sets aside such final order or decision and removes such proceeding to itself or such person files a petition for reconsideration, and such reconsideration is granted or denied. Nothing herein contained shall prevent the enforcement of any such final order or decision, in the manner provided in this division.

§6616. Information required in petition for reconsideration.

The petition for reconsideration shall set forth specifically and in full detail the grounds upon which the petitioner considers the final order or decision made and filed by the appeals board or a hearing officer to be unjust or unlawful, and every issue to be considered by the appeals board. The petition shall be verified upon oath in the manner required for verified pleadings in courts of record and shall contain a general statement of any evidence or other matters upon which the applicant relies in support thereof.

§6617. Grounds for reconsideration.

The petition for reconsideration may be based upon one or more of the following grounds and no other:

(a) That by such order or decision made and filed by the appeals board or hearing officer, the appeals board acted without or in excess of its powers.

(b) That the order or decision was procured by fraud.

(c) That the evidence does not justify the findings of fact.

(d) That the petitioner has discovered new evidence material to him, which he could not, with reasonable diligence, have discovered and produced at the hearing.

(e) That the findings of fact do not support the order or decision.

§6618. Waiver of objections not set forth in petition for reconsideration.

The petitioner for reconsideration shall be deemed to have finally waived all objections, irregularities, and illegalities concerning the matter upon which the reconsideration is sought other than those set forth in the petition for reconsideration.

§6619. Service petition for reconsideration; answer.

A copy of the petition for reconsideration shall be served forthwith upon all parties by the person petitioning for reconsideration. Any party may file an answer thereto within 30 days thereafter. Such answer shall likewise be verified. The appeals board may require the petition for reconsideration to be served on other persons designated by it.

§6620. Appeals board's power to reconsider; notice of hearing.

Upon the filing of a petition for reconsideration, or having granted reconsideration upon its own motion, the appeals board may, with or without further proceedings and with or without notice affirm, rescind, alter, or amend the order or decision made and filed by the appeals board or hearing officer on the basis of the evidence previously submitted in the case, or may grant reconsideration and direct the taking of additional evidence. Notice of the time and place of any hearing on reconsideration shall be given to the petitioner and adverse parties and to such other persons as the appeals board orders.

§6621. Decision based on record without further hearing.

If at the time of granting reconsideration, it appears to the satisfaction of the appeals board that no sufficient reason exists for taking further testimony, the appeals board may affirm, rescind, alter or amend the order or decision made and filed by the appeals board or hearing officer and may, without further proceedings, without notice, and without setting a time and place for further hearing, enter its findings, order or decision based upon the record in the case.

§6622. Effect of appeals board's alteration of decision.

After the taking of additional evidence and a consideration of all of the facts the appeals board may affirm, rescind, alter, or amend the original order or decision. An order or decision made following reconsideration which affirms, rescinds, alters, or amends the original order or decision shall be made by the appeals board but shall not affect any right or the enforcement of any right arising from or by virtue of the original order or decision unless so ordered by the appeals board.

§6623. Procedure for decisions.

Any decision of the appeals board granting or denying a petition for reconsideration or affirming, rescinding, altering, or amending the original findings, order, or decision following reconsideration shall be made by the appeals board and not by a hearing officer and shall be in writing, signed by a majority of the appeals board members assigned thereto, and shall state the evidence relied upon and specify in detail the reasons for the decision.

§6624. Denial of reconsideration; presumption.

A petition for reconsideration is deemed to have been denied by the appeals board unless it is acted upon within 45 days from the date of filing. The appeals board may, upon good cause being shown therefor, extend the time within which it may act upon that petition for not exceeding 15 days. **Leg.H.** 1991 ch. 734.

§6625. Filing for reconsideration; effect on original decision.

(a)(1) Except as provided in subdivision (b), the filing of a petition for reconsideration suspends for a period of 10 days the order or decision affected, insofar as it applies to the parties to the petition, unless otherwise ordered by the appeals board.

(2) Except as provided in subdivision (b), the appeals board, upon the terms and conditions which it by order directs, may stay, suspend, or postpone the order or decision during the pendency of the reconsideration.

(b) The filing of a petition for, or the pendency of, reconsideration of a final order or decision involving a citation classified as serious, repeat serious, or willful serious does not stay or suspend the requirement to abate the hazards affirmed by the decision or order unless the employer demonstrates by a preponderance of the evidence that a stay or suspension of abatement will not adversely affect the health and safety of employees. The employer must request a stay or suspension of abatement by filing a written, verified petition with supporting declarations within 10 days after the issuance of the order or decision. **Leg.H.** 2014 ch. 497 (AB 1634) §3, 2015 ch. 303 (AB 731) §381.

§6626. Time for reconsideration of appeals board order.

Nothing contained in this chapter shall be construed to prevent the appeals board, on petition of an aggrieved party or on its own motion, from granting reconsideration of an original order or decision made and filed by the appeals board within the same time specified for reconsideration of an original order or decision.

§6627. Writ of mandate in superior court.

Any person affected by an order or decision of the appeals board may, within the time limit specified in this section, apply to the superior court of the county in which he resides, for a writ of mandate, for the purpose of inquiring into and determining the lawfulness of the original order or decision or of the order or decision following reconsideration. The application for writ of mandate must be made within 30 days after a petition for reconsideration is denied, or, if a petition is granted or reconsideration is had on the appeals board's own motion, within 30 days after the filing of the order or decision following reconsideration.

§6628. Procedure for superior court's consideration.

The writ of mandate shall be made returnable at a time and place then or thereafter specified by court order and shall direct the appeals board to certify its record in the case to the court within the time therein specified. No new or additional evidence shall be introduced in such court, but the cause shall be heard on the record of the appeals board, as certified to by it.

§6629. Scope of superior court review.

The review by the court shall not be extended further than to determine, based upon the entire record which shall be certified by the appeals board, whether:

(a) The appeals board acted without or in excess of its powers.

(b) The order or decision was procured by fraud.

(c) The order or decision was unreasonable.

(d) The order or decision was not supported by substantial evidence.

(e) If findings of fact are made, such findings of fact support the order or decision under review.

Nothing in this section shall permit the court to hold a trial de novo, to take evidence, or to exercise its independent judgment on the evidence.

§6630. Appeals board's factual findings and conclusions as controlling.

The findings and conclusions of the appeals board on questions of fact are conclusive and final and are not subject to review. Such questions of fact shall include ultimate facts and the findings and conclusions of the appeals board. The appeals board and each party to the action or proceeding before the appeals board shall have the right to appear in the mandate proceeding. Upon the hearing, the court shall enter judgment either affirming or annulling the order or decision, or the court may remand the case for further proceedings before the appeals board.

§6631. Procedure for writ of mandate.

The provisions of the Code of Civil Procedure relating to writs of mandate shall, so far as applicable, apply to proceedings in the courts under the provisions of this part. A copy of every pleading filed pursuant to the terms of this part shall be served on the appeals board and upon every party who entered an appearance in the action before the appeals board and whose interest therein is adverse to the party filing such pleading.

§6632. Courts having jurisdiction over appeals board decisions.

No court of this state, except the Supreme Court, the courts of appeal, and the superior court to the extent herein specified, has jurisdiction to review, reverse, correct, or annul any order or rule, or decision of the appeals board, or to suspend or delay the operation or execution thereof, or to restrain, enjoin, or interfere with the appeals board in the performance of its duties.

§6633. Court's power to postpone operation of appeals board decision.

The filing of a petition for, or the pendency of, a writ of mandate shall not of itself stay or suspend the operation of any order, rule or decision of the appeals board, but the court before which the petition is filed may stay or suspend, in whole or in part, the operation of the order or decision of the appeals board subject to review, upon the terms and conditions which it by order directs.

CHAPTER 8
ENFORCEMENT OF CIVIL PENALTIES

§6650. Procedures for unpaid civil penalty.

(a) After the expiration of the period during which a penalty may be appealed, no appeal having been filed, the department may file with the clerk of the superior court in any county a certified copy of the citation and notice of civil penalty, the certification by the department that the penalty remains unpaid, and the division's proof of service on the employer of the items filed with the clerk of the court.

(b) After the exhaustion of the review procedures provided for in Chapter 7 (commencing with Section 6600), an appeal having been filed, the department may file with the clerk of the superior court in any county a certified copy of the citation and notice of civil penalty, a certified copy of the order, findings or decision of the appeals board, the certification of the department that the penalty remains unpaid, and proof of service on the employer at the employer's address as shown on the official address record by the appeals board.

(c) The clerk, immediately upon the filing of a notice of civil penalty by the department pursuant to subdivision (a) or (b), shall enter judgment for the state against the person assessed the civil penalty in the amount of the penalty, plus interest due for each day from the date of issuance of the notice of civil penalty that the penalty remains unpaid.

(d) The department shall serve the notice of entry of judgment provided by Section 664.5 of the Code of Civil Procedure on the employer.

Labor

(e) A judgment entered pursuant to this section shall bear the same rate of interest, have the same effect as other judgments, and be given the same preference allowed by law on other judgments rendered for claims for taxes pursuant to Section 7170 of the Government Code.

(f) No fees shall be charged by the clerk of any court for the performance of any official service required by this chapter. **Leg.H.** 1991 ch. 1210, 2000 ch. 135.

§6651. Deadline to commence action to collect civil penalty.

(a) Notwithstanding Section 340 of the Code of Civil Procedure, an action to collect any civil penalty, fee, or penalty fee under this division shall be commenced within three years from the date the penalty or fee became final.

(b) The amendments made to this section by the act adding this subdivision shall only apply to penalty assessments or fees for which the three-year period prescribed in this section for the commencement of an action to collect a civil penalty or fee has not expired on the effective date of the act adding this subdivision. **Leg.H.** 1991 ch. 1210 §3, 1993 ch. 998.

§6652. Notice to Contractors' State License Board of civil penalty.

The division shall provide the Contractors' State License Board with a certified copy of every notice of civil penalty deemed to be a final order pursuant to Section 6601 or after the exhaustion of all other review procedures pursuant to Chapter 7 (commencing with Section 6600) when both of the following have occurred:

(a) The employer served with the notice of civil penalty is, or is thought to be, a licensee licensed by the Contractors' State License Board.

(b) The employer referred to in subdivision (a) has failed to pay the civil penalty after a period of 60 days following that employer's receipt of the notice of civil penalty.

(c) When the employer has paid the civil penalty referenced in the certified copy of notice of civil penalty that was provided to the Contractors' State License Board, including all interest owed thereon, then the division shall provide to the employer who was the subject of the certified copy of notice a written confirmation or receipt stating that the employer has paid the amount owed that was the subject of the certified notice provided to the board. **Leg.H.** 1991 ch. 1210.

CHAPTER 9 MISCELLANEOUS SAFETY PROVISIONS

§6700. Gas pipelines; conclusive presumptions.

(a) Any employer who causes or allows the use of any flammable or combustible material for the installation acceptance pressure test of any gas houseline or piping shall be conclusively presumed to be maintaining an unsafe place of employment.

(b) Any employer who causes or allows gas pipelines to be tested with gas at pressures in excess of that permitted by applicable sections of the American Society of Mechanical Engineers Code for Pressure Piping shall be conclusively presumed to be maintaining an unsafe place of employment.

§6701. Internal combustion engines used within structures.

It shall be the duty of the standards board to determinc by the maximum allowable standards of emissions of contaminants from portable and from mobile internal combustion engines used inside factories, manufacturing plants, warehouses, buildings and other enclosed structures, which standards are compatible with the safety and health of employees.

§6702. Exhaust purifier devices.

All portable and all mobile internal combustion engines that are used inside factories, manufacturing plants, warehouses, buildings and other enclosed structures shall be equipped with a certified exhaust purifier device after the certification of the device by the State Air Resources Board.

The Division of Occupational Safety and Health shall be responsible for the enforcement of the provisions of this section.

§6703. Exceptions to rules for internal combustion engines used within structures.

Sections 6701 and 6702 shall apply to all portable and all mobile internal combustion engines used inside factories, manufacturing plants, warehouses, buildings and other enclosed structures unless the operation of such an engine used inside a particular factory, plant, warehouse, building or enclosed structure does not result in harmful exposure to concentrations of dangerous gases or fumes in excess of maximum acceptable concentrations as determined by the standards board.

§6704. Boomstops for crawler and wheel cranes.

All crawler and wheel cranes with cable-controlled booms and with rated lifting capacity of more than 10 tons sold or operated in this state shall be equipped with boomstops that meet standards that shall be established therefor by the standards board.

§6705. Restrictions on contracts involving trench excavations.

No contract for public works involving an estimated expenditure in excess of twenty-five thousand dollars ($25,000), for the excavation of any trench or trenches five feet or more in depth, shall be awarded unless it contains a clause requiring submission by the contractor and acceptance by the awarding body or by a registered civil or structural engineer, employed by the awarding body, to whom authority to accept has been delegated, in advance of excavation, of a detailed plan showing the design of shoring, bracing, sloping, or other provisions to be made for worker protection from the hazard of caving ground during the excavation of such trench or trenches. If such plan varies from the shoring system standards, the plan shall be prepared by a registered civil or structural engineer.

Nothing in this section shall be deemed to allow the use of a shoring, sloping, or protective system less effective than that required by the Construction Safety Orders.

Nothing in this section shall be construed to impose tort liability on the awarding body or any of its employees.

The terms "public works" and "awarding body", as used in this section, shall have the same meaning as in Sections 1720 and 1722, respectively, of the Labor Code.

§6705.5. Application of shoring, bracing, and sloping regulations to swimming pool excavations found unsafe.

Regulations of the department requiring the shoring, bracing, or sloping of excavations, or which contain similar requirements for excavations, shall only apply to the excavation of swimming pools where a reasonable examination by a qualified person reveals recognizable conditions which would expose employees to injury from possible moving ground. If these conditions are found to exist with respect to a swimming pool excavation, employees shall not be permitted to enter the excavation until the condition is abated or otherwise no longer exists.

§6706. One permit per project; exceptions.

For the purposes of subdivision (a) of Section 6500, only one permit shall be required for a project involving several trenches or excavations. The provisions of Section 6500 shall not apply to the construction of trenches or excavations for the purpose of performing emergency repair work to underground facilities, or the construction of swimming pools, or the construction of "graves" as defined in Section 7014 of the Health and Safety Code or to the construction or final use of excavations or trenches where the construction or final use does not require a person to descend into the excavations or trenches.

§6707. Bids for local government projects involving trenches or open excavations.

Whenever the state, a county, city and county, or city issues a call for bids for the construction of a pipeline, sewer, sewage disposal system, boring and jacking pits, or similar trenches or open excavations, which are five feet or deeper, such call shall specify that each bid submitted in response thereto shall contain, as a bid item, adequate sheeting, shoring, and bracing, or equipment method, for the protection of life or limb, which shall conform to applicable safety orders. Nothing in this section shall be construed to impose tort liability on the body awarding the contract or any of its employees. This section shall not apply to contracts awarded pursuant to the provisions of Chapter 3 (commencing with Section 14250) of Part 5 of Division 3 of Title 2 of the Government Code.

§6708. Adequate emergency first aid treatment; requirement.

Every contractor on a construction project, including, but not limited to any public works, shall maintain adequate emergency first aid treatment for his employees. As used in this section, "adequate" shall be construed to mean sufficient to comply with the Federal Occupational Safety and Health Act of 1970 (P.L. 91–596).

Ref.: Herlick Handbook § 9.10.

§6709. Valley Fever; awareness training.

(a) The Legislature finds and declares that Valley Fever is caused by a microscopic fungus known as Coccidioides immitis, which lives in the top 2 to 12 inches of soil in many parts of the state. When soil is disturbed by activities such as digging, grading, **or** driving, or is disturbed by environmental conditions such as [1] high winds, fungal spores can become airborne and can potentially be inhaled.

(b) This section applies to a construction employer with employees working at worksites in counties where Valley Fever is highly endemic, including, but not limited to, the Counties of Fresno, Kern, Kings, Madera, Merced, Monterey, San Joaquin, San Luis Obispo, Santa Barbara, Tulare, and Ventura, where work activities disturb the soil, including, but not limited to, digging, grading, or other earth moving operations, or vehicle operation on dirt roads, or high winds. Highly endemic means that the annual incidence rate of Valley Fever is greater than 20 cases per 100,000 persons per year.

(c) An employer subject to this section pursuant to subdivision (b) shall provide effective awareness training on Valley Fever to all employees by May 1, 2020, and annually by that date thereafter, and before an employee begins work that is reasonably anticipated to cause exposure to substantial dust disturbance. Substantial dust disturbance means visible airborne dust for a total duration of one hour or more on any day. The training may be included in the employer's injury and illness prevention program training or as a standalone training program. The training shall include all of the following topics:

(1) What Valley Fever is and how it is contracted.

(2) High risk areas and types of work and environmental conditions during which the risk of contracting Valley Fever is highest.

(3) Personal risk factors that may create a higher risk for some individuals, including pregnancy, diabetes, having a compromised immune system due to causes including, but not limited to, human immunodeficiency virus (HIV) or acquired immunodeficiency syndrome (AIDS), having received an organ transplant, or taking immunosuppressant drugs such as corticosteroids or tumor necrosis factor inhibitors.

(4) Personal and environmental exposure prevention methods that may include, but are not limited to, water-based dust suppression, good hygiene when skin and clothing is soiled by dust, limiting contamination of drinks and food, working upwind from dusty areas when feasible, wet cleaning dusty equipment when feasible, and wearing a respirator when exposure to dust cannot be avoided.

(5) The importance of early detection, diagnosis, and treatment to help prevent the disease from progressing. Early diagnosis and treatment are important because the effectiveness of medication is greatest in early stages of the disease.

(6) Recognizing common signs and symptoms of Valley Fever, which include fatigue, cough, fever, shortness of breath, headache, muscle aches or joint pain, rash on upper

body or legs, and symptoms similar to influenza that linger longer than usual.

(7) The importance of reporting symptoms to the employer and seeking medical attention from a physician and surgeon for appropriate diagnosis and treatment.

(8) Common treatment and prognosis for Valley Fever.

(d) Training materials may include existing material on Valley Fever developed by a federal, state, or local agency, including, but not limited to, the federal Centers for Disease Control and Prevention, the State Department of Public Health, or a local health department.

(e) In the event that a county which has not been previously identified as being highly endemic is determined to be highly endemic per the annual report published by the State Department of Public Health, this section [2] **does** not apply in the initial year of that county's listing in the report. However, this section [3] **applies** to employers in that county in the year subsequent to the department's publication that initially identified the county as being highly endemic.

(f) This section [4] **applies** to an employer whenever employment exists in connection with the construction, alteration, painting, repairing, construction maintenance, renovation, removal, or wrecking of any fixed structure or its parts. **Leg.H.** 2019 ch. 712 (AB 203) §1, 2020 ch. 370 (SB 1371) §225.

§6709. 2020 Deletes. [1] or **[2]** shall **[3]** shall begin to apply **[4]** shall apply

§6710. Explosives.

(a) At every place of employment where explosives are used in the course of employment, there shall be a person licensed pursuant to the provisions of Chapter 3 (commencing with Section 7990) of Part 9 of Division 5, to supervise and visually direct the blasting operation.

(b) For the purposes of this section, "explosives" shall include, but not be limited to, class A and B explosives, blasting caps, detonating cord, and charges or projectiles used in the control of avalanches. For the purposes of this section, "explosives" shall not include small arms ammunition or class C explosives such as explosive powerpacks in the form of explosive cartridges or explosive-charged construction devices, explosive rivets, bolts, and charges for driving pins and studs, and cartridges for explosive-actuated power devices.

This section shall not apply to persons, firms, or corporations licensed pursuant to Part 2 (commencing with Section 12500) of Division 11 of the Health and Safety Code.

§6711. Examination of persons using explosives for snow avalanche blasting.

(a) The division shall develop and administer an oral and written examination for persons using explosives, as defined in Section 6710, while engaged in snow avalanche blasting. Any person engaged in snow avalanche blasting shall pass this examination prior to being licensed by the division.

(b) The division shall select an advisory committee to assist the division in preparing the data and information for the written and oral qualifying examination. The advisory committee shall consist of not less than seven members, nor more than nine members, with at least one representative from explosive manufacturers, snow avalanche blasting consultants, the recreational snow ski industry, a public recreation area, the California Department of Transportation, and the division.

§6712. Occupational safety and health standard for field sanitation.

(a) The standards board shall, no later than December 1, 1991, adopt an occupational safety and health standard for field sanitation. The standard shall comply with all of the following:

(1) The standard shall be at least as effective as the federal field sanitation standard contained in Section 1928.110 of Title 29 of the Code of Federal Regulations.

(2) The standard shall be at least as effective as California field sanitation requirements in effect as of July 1, 1990, pursuant to Article 4 (commencing with Section 113310) of Chapter 11 of Part 6 of Division 104 of the Health and Safety Code, Article 1 (commencing with Section 118375) of Chapter 1 of Part 15 of Division 104 of the Health and Safety Code, and Section 2441 of this code.

(3) The standard shall apply to all agricultural places of employment.

(4) The standard shall require that toilets are serviced and maintained in a clean, sanitary condition and kept in good repair at all times, including written records of that service and maintenance.

(b) Consistent with its mandatory investigation and reinspection duties under Sections 6309, 6313, and 6320, the division shall develop and implement a special emphasis program for enforcement of the standard for at least two years following its adoption. Not later than March 15, 1995, the division shall also develop a written plan to coordinate its enforcement program with other state and local agencies. The division shall be the lead enforcement agency. Other state and local agencies shall cooperate with the division in the development and implementation of the plan. The division shall report to the Legislature, not later than January 1, 1994, on its enforcement program. The plan shall provide for coordination between the division and local officials in counties where the field sanitation facilities required by the standard adopted pursuant to subdivision (a) are registered by the county health officer or other appropriate official of the county where the facilities are located. The division shall establish guidelines to assist counties that choose to register sanitation facilities pursuant to this section, for developing service charges, fees, or assessments to defray the costs of registering the facilities, taking into consideration the differences between small and large employers.

(c)(1) Past violations by a fixed-site or nonfixed-site employer, occurring anywhere in the state within the previous five years, of one or more field sanitation regulations established pursuant to this section, or of Section 1928.110 of Title 29 of the Code of Federal Regulations, shall be considered for purposes of establishing whether a current violation is a repeat violation under Section 6429.

(2) Past violations by a fixed-site or nonfixed-site employer, occurring anywhere in the state within the previous five years, of one or more field sanitation regulations established pursuant to this section, Article 4 (com-

mencing with Section 113310) of Chapter 11 of Part 6 of Division 104 of the Health and Safety Code, Article 1 (commencing with Section 118375) of Part 15 of Division 104 of the Health and Safety Code, or Section 2441 of this code, or of Section 1928.110 of Title 29 of the Code of Federal Regulations, shall constitute evidence of willfulness for purposes of Section 6429.

(d)(1) Notwithstanding Sections 6317 and 6434, any employer who fails to provide the facilities required by the field sanitation standard shall be assessed a civil penalty under the appropriate provisions of Sections 6427 to 6430, inclusive, except that in no case shall the penalty be less than seven hundred fifty dollars ($750) for each violation.

(2) Abatement periods fixed by the division pursuant to Section 6317 for violations shall be limited to one working day. However, the division may, pursuant to Section 6319.5, modify the period in cases where a good faith effort to comply with the abatement requirement is shown. The filing of an appeal with the appeals board pursuant to Sections 6319 and 6600 shall not stay the abatement period.

(3) An employer cited pursuant to paragraph (1) of this subdivision shall be required to annually complete a field sanitation compliance form which shall list the estimated peak number of employees, the toilets, washing, and drinking water facilities to be provided by the employer, any rental and maintenance agreements, and any other information considered relevant by the division for a period of five years following the citation. The employer shall be required to annually submit the completed form, subscribed under penalty of perjury, to the division, or to an agency designated by the division.

(e) The division shall notify the State Department of Health Services and the appropriate local health officers whenever a violation of the standard adopted pursuant to this section may result in the adulteration of food with harmful bacteria or other deleterious substances within the meaning of Article 5 (commencing with Section 110545) of Chapter 5 of Part 5 of Division 104 of the Health and Safety Code.

(f) Pending final adoption and approval of the standard required by subdivision (a), the division may enforce the field sanitation standards prescribed by Section 1928.110 of Title 29 of the Code of Federal Regulations, except subdivision (a) of Section 1928.110, in the same manner as other standards contained in this division. **Leg.H.** 1994 ch. 1203, 1996 ch. 1023, effective September 29, 1996.

§6716. "Lead-related construction work."

For the purposes of this division, "lead-related construction work" means any of the following:

(a) Any construction, alteration, painting, demolition, salvage, renovation, repair, or maintenance of any building or structure, including preparation and cleanup, that, by using or disturbing lead-containing material or soil, may result in significant exposure of employees to lead as determined by the standard adopted pursuant to Section 6717.

(b) The transportation, disposal, storage, or containment of materials containing lead on site or at a location at which construction activities are performed. "Lead-related construction work" does not include any activity related to the manufacture or mining of lead or the installation or repair of automotive materials containing lead. **Leg.H.** 1993 ch. 1122.

§6717. Standard that protects employees engaged in lead-related construction.

(a) On or before February 1, 1994, the division shall propose to the standards board for its review and adoption, a standard that protects the health and safety of employees who engage in lead-related construction work and meets all requirements imposed by the federal Occupational Safety and Health Administration. The standards board shall adopt the standard on or before December 31, 1994. The standard shall at least prescribe protective measures appropriate to the work activity and the lead content of materials to be disturbed by the activity, and shall include requirements and specifications pertaining to the following:

(1) Sampling and analysis of surface coatings and other materials that may contain significant amounts of lead.

(2) Concentrations and amounts of lead in surface coatings and other materials that may constitute a health hazard to employees engaged in lead-related construction work.

(3) Engineering controls, work practices, and personal protective equipment, including respiratory protection, fit-testing requirements, and protective clothing and equipment.

(4) Washing and showering facilities.

(5) Medical surveillance and medical removal protection.

(6) Establishment of regulated areas and appropriate posting and warning requirements.

(7) Recordkeeping.

(8) Training of employees engaged in lead-related construction work and their supervisors, that shall consist of current certification as required by regulations adopted under subdivision (c) of Section 105250 of the Health and Safety Code and include training with respect to at least the following:

(A) Health effects of lead exposure, including symptoms of overexposure.

(B) The construction activities, methods, processes, and materials that can result in lead exposure.

(C) The requirements of the lead standard promulgated pursuant to this section.

(D) Appropriate engineering controls, work practices, and personal protection for lead-related work.

(E) The necessity for fit-testing for respirator use and how fit-testing is conducted. **Leg.H.** 1993 ch. 1122, 1996 ch. 1023, effective September 29, 1996.

1993 Note: Section 6717 has no subsection (b).

§6717.5. Cal/OSHA to submit to Occupational Safety and Health Standards Board rulemaking proposal to revise lead standards for purposes of general industry safety orders and construction safety orders.

The division shall submit to the board a rulemaking proposal to revise the lead standards of the general industry safety orders, found at Section 5198 of Title 8 of the

California Code of Regulations, and the construction safety orders, found at Section 1532.1 of Title 8 of the California Code of Regulations, consistent with scientific research and findings. The board shall vote on the proposed changes on or before September 30, 2020. **Leg.H.** 2019 ch. 24 (SB 83) §34, effective June 27, 2019.

§6718. Restrictions on test procedures for vapor emission from vehicles transporting gasoline.

Notwithstanding any other provision of law, any test procedures adopted by a state agency to determine compliance with vapor emission standards, by vapor recovery systems of cargo tanks on tank vehicles used to transport gasoline, shall not require any person to climb upon the cargo tank during loading operations. **Leg.H.** 1997 ch. 84.

§6719. Concern over repetitive motion injuries.

The Legislature reaffirms its concern over the prevalence of repetitive motion injuries in the workplace and reaffirms the Occupational Safety and Health Standards Board's continuing duty to carry out Section 6357. **Leg.H.** 1999 ch. 615.

§6720. Standard that minimizes heat-related illness and injury among indoor workers.

By January 1, 2019, the division shall propose to the standards board for the board's review and adoption a standard that minimizes heat-related illness and injury among workers working in indoor places of employment. The standard shall be based on environmental temperatures, work activity levels, and other factors. In developing the standard, the division shall take into consideration heat stress and heat strain guidelines in the 2016 Threshold Limit Values and Biological Exposure Indices developed by the American Conference of Governmental Industrial Hygienists. This section does not prohibit the division from proposing, or the standards board from adopting, a standard that limits the application of high heat provisions to certain industry sectors. **Leg.H.** 2016 ch. 839 (SB 1167) §1.

§6721. Maria Isabel Vasquez Jimenez heat illness standard.

The heat illness prevention standards set forth in Section 3395 of Title 8 of the California Code of Regulations shall be known, and may be cited, as the Maria Isabel Vasquez Jimenez heat illness standard. **Leg.H.** 2018 ch. 718 (AB 2751) §4.

§6725. [See Subdivision (e) for Repeal Information] Dissemination of best practices for COVID-19 infection prevention among agricultural employees.

(a) For purposes of this section, the following terms have the following meanings:

(1) The term "agricultural employee" means a person employed in any of the following:

(A) An agricultural occupation, as defined in Wage Order No. 14 of the Industrial Welfare Commission.

(B) An industry preparing agricultural products for the market, on the farm, as defined in Wage Order No. 13 of the Industrial Welfare Commission.

(C) An industry handling products after harvest, as defined in Wage Order No. 8 of the Industrial Welfare Commission.

(2) "Guidance Documents" means the following documents available on the division's internet website:

(A) Cal/OSHA Interim General Guidelines on Protecting Workers from COVID-19.

(B) Cal/OSHA Safety and Health Guidance: COVID-19 Infection Prevention for Agricultural Employers and Employees.

(C) COVID-19 Industry Guidance: Food Packing and Processing, issued by the division, the State Department of Public Health, and the Department of Food and Agriculture.

(D) COVID-19 Industry Guidance: Agriculture and Livestock, issued by the division, the State Department of Public Health, and the Department of Food and Agriculture.

(E) Any other guidance or guidelines made available on the division's internet website pertaining to novel coronavirus (COVID-19) infection prevention for agricultural employees.

(b) Commencing on the effective date of this section, the division shall disseminate, in both English and Spanish, information on best practices for COVID-19 infection prevention, consistent with the Guidance Documents. The information shall be designed to be easily understood by agricultural employees from a variety of ethnic and cultural backgrounds, including by using pictograms. The information shall, where possible, provide contact information for the division that employees can use to report workplace safety complaints. The information shall be made widely and easily accessible, including in both digital and physical formats and via the division's internet website.

(c) The division, working collaboratively with community organizations and organizations representing employees and employers, shall conduct a statewide outreach campaign, targeted at agricultural employees, to assist with the statewide dissemination of the best practices information described in subdivision (b) and to educate employees on any COVID-19-related employment benefits to which they are entitled, including access to paid sick leave and workers' compensation. The campaign shall include, but shall not be limited to, public service announcements on local Spanish radio stations and the distribution of workplace signs. Nothing in this subdivision shall authorize access to the worksite by an individual who is not employed by the division.

(d) The division shall routinely compile and report, via its internet website, information relating to the subject matter, findings, and results of any investigation by the division relating to practices or conditions prescribed in the Guidance Documents or a COVID-19 illness or injury at a workplace of agricultural employees. This information shall include, but shall not be limited to, all of the following:

(1) Across all investigations, statistical information, including, but not limited to, the number of investigations in each county.

(2) For each investigation, summary descriptive information.

(3) For each investigation, a description of the division's response, including, but not limited to, whether the response involved an onsite inspection of the facility, a virtual or remote inspection, a letter to the employer, or any other type of action by the division.

(e) This section shall remain in effect until the state of emergency has been terminated by proclamation of the Governor or by concurrent resolution of the Legislature declaring it at an end, pursuant to Section 8629 of the Government Code, and as of that date is repealed. **Leg.H.** 2020 ch. 212 (AB 2043) §2, effective September 28, 2020.

2020 Note: The California Legislature directs the Division of Occupational Safety and Health, within the Department of Industrial Relations, to enforce Guidance Documents, as defined in Section 6725 of the Labor Code, to the extent any specific Guidance Document applies to any specific workplace and to the extent the division has authority under Title 8 of the California Code of Regulations. Stats. 2020 ch. 212 (AB 2043) §1.

Labor

PART 3
Safety on Buildings

CHAPTER 1
BUILDINGS UNDER CONSTRUCTION OR REPAIR

ARTICLE 1
Floors and Walls

§7100. "Building."

As used in this article, "building" means any multifloor building, other than structural steel framed building, more than two stories high in the course of construction.

§7101. Protective flooring.

Every building shall have the joists, beams, or girders of floors below the floor or level where any work is being done, or about to be done, covered with flooring laid close together, or with other suitable material to protect workers engaged in such building from falling through joists or girders, and from falling substances, whereby life or safety is endangered.

§7102. Protective flooring in concrete buildings.

Every building which is of reinforced concrete construction, with reinforced concrete floors, shall have the floor filled in, either with forms or concrete, on each floor before the commencement of work upon the walls of the second floor above or the commencement of work upon the floor of the next floor above.

§7103. Protective wooden flooring.

Every building having wooden floors other than a steel frame building shall have the underflooring, if double flooring is to be used, laid on each floor within the time prescribed above for reinforced concrete floors. Where single wooden floors are to be used, each floor shall be planked over within the time prescribed above for reinforced concrete floors.

§7104. Supportive intermediate beams.

If a span of a floor on a building exceeds 13 feet, an intermediate beam shall be used to support the temporary flooring, but spans not to exceed 16 feet may be covered by three-inch planks without an intermediate beam. The intermediate beam shall be of a sufficient strength to sustain a live load of 50 pounds per square foot of the area supported.

§7105. Replanking.

If building operations are suspended and the temporary flooring required by this article is removed, the building shall be replanked upon the resumption of work so that every man at work has a covered floor not more than two stories below.

§7106. Building sections as "buildings."

Where a building is being constructed in sections each section constitutes a building for the purpose of this article.

§7107. Planked floors.

Planked floors on buildings shall be tightly laid together of proper thickness, grade and span to carry the working load; such working load to be assumed as at least 25 pounds per square foot.

§7108. Safety belts and nets.

Safety belts and nets shall be required in accordance with Article 24 (commencing with Section 1669) of subchapter 4 of Chapter 4 of Part 1 of Title 8 of the California Administrative Code, Construction Safety Orders of the Division of Occupational Safety and Health.

§7109. Working without required planking or nets.

No person shall proceed with any work assigned to or undertaken by him, or require or permit any other person to proceed with work assigned to or undertaken by either, unless the planking or nets required by this article are in place. Violation of this section is a misdemeanor.

§7110. Enforcement by Division.

The Division of Occupational Safety and Health shall enforce this article.

ARTICLE 2
Scaffolding

§7150. "Scaffolding."

As used in this article, "scaffolding" includes scaffolding and staging.

§7151. Suspended scaffolding.

If the working platform of any scaffolding swung or suspended from an overhead support is more than 10 feet above the ground, floor or area to which an employee on the scaffolding might fall, it shall have a safety rail of wood or other equally rigid material of adequate strength. The rail shall comply with the applicable orders of the Division of Occupational Safety and Health.

Suspended scaffolding shall be fastened so as to prevent the scaffolding from swaying from the building, or structure, or other object being worked on from the scaffolding. All parts of the scaffolding shall be of sufficient strength to support, bear, or withstand with safety any weight of persons, tools, appliances, or materials which might reasonably be placed on it or which are to be supported by it.

§7152. Employers using scaffolding.

In addition to the duties imposed by any law regulating or relating to scaffolding, an employer who uses or permits the use of scaffolding described in Section 7151 in connection with construction, alteration, repairing, painting, cleaning or doing of any work upon any building or structure, shall:

(a) Furnish safety lines to tie all hooks and hangers back on the roof of such building or structure.

(b) Provide safety lines hanging from the roof, securely tied thereto, for all swinging scaffolds which rely upon stirrups of the single point suspension type to support the working platform. One such line shall be provided for each workman with a minimum of one line between each pair of hangers or falls.

The standards board may adopt occupational safety and health standards different from the requirements of this section or grant variances from these requirements if the standards or variances provide equivalent or superior safety for employees.

§7153. Scaffolding platforms or floors.

Platforms or floors of such scaffolding shall be not less than 14 inches in width and shall be free from knots or fractures impairing their strength.

§7154.1. Prohibition of lean-to scaffolds.

The use of lean-to scaffolds, sometimes known as jack scaffolds, as support for scaffolds is hereby prohibited.

§7155. Penalty for scaffolding requirement violations.

Violation of any provision of sections 7151 to 7154 inclusive is a misdemeanor.

§7156. Employer violations and penalty.

Any person employing or directing another to do or perform any labor in the construction, alteration, repairing, painting, or cleaning of any house, building, or structure within this state is guilty of a misdemeanor who does any of the following:

(a) Knowingly or negligently furnishes or erects, or causes to be furnished or erected for the performance of that labor, unsafe or improper scaffolding, slings, hammers, blocks, pulleys, stays, braces, ladders, irons, ropes, or other mechanical contrivances.

(b) Hinders or obstructs any officer or inspector of the Division of Occupational Safety and Health attempting to inspect such equipment under the provisions of this article or any law or safety order of this state.

(c) Destroys or defaces, or removes any notice posted thereon by any division officer or inspector, or permits the use thereof, after the equipment has been declared unsafe by the officer or inspector.

§7157. Division's power regarding safety orders.

The division may make and enforce safety orders in the manner prescribed by law, to supplement and carry into effect the purposes and provisions of this article.

§7158. Enforcement by division.

The division shall enforce the provisions of this article.

ARTICLE 3
Construction Elevators

§7200. "Construction elevator" and "building."

As used in this article:

(a) "Construction elevator" includes any means used to hoist persons or material of any kind on a building under course of construction, when operated by any power other than muscular power.

(b) "Building" includes structures of all kinds during the course of construction, regardless of the purposes for which they are intended and whether such construction be below or above the level of the ground.

§7201. Signals for construction elevators.

Every construction elevator used in buildings shall have a system of signals for the purpose of signaling the person operating or controlling the machinery which operates or controls the construction elevator.

§7202. Employee to give signals.

The person in charge of a building shall appoint one or more persons to give such signals. Such person shall be selected from those most familiar with the work for which the construction elevator is being used. The signaling devices provided shall be protected against unauthorized or accidental operation.

§7203. Board's regulation of signals.

The board shall make, and may from time to time amend, general safety orders in the manner prescribed by law. Such orders shall specify and fix the nature and methods of signals and signaling devices and uniform signals to be used in this State under this article.

§7204. Inspection of construction elevators.

The division shall inspect all construction elevators. If any part of the construction or system of signals used on a construction elevator is defective or endangers the lives of the persons working in the immediate vicinity of the construction elevator, the division shall direct the person in charge thereof to remedy such defect. Such construction elevator shall not be used again until the order of the division is complied with.

§7205. Penalties for violation.

Any person, or the agent or officer thereof, who violates any provision of this article is guilty of a misdemeanor, punishable by a fine of not less than one hundred dollars ($100) and not more than one thousand dollars ($1,000), or imprisonment in the county jail for not less than thirty days and not more than six months, or both.

ARTICLE 4
Structural Steel Framed Buildings

§7250. "Building."

As used in this article "building" means any multifloor structural steel framed building more than two stories high in the course of construction.

§7251. Buildings affected.

As defined above, these provisions shall apply to buildings erected in tiers or stories and shall not apply to steel framed buildings having large open spans or areas such as, mill buildings, gymnasiums, auditoriums, hangars, arenas, or stadiums.

§7252. Decking of derricks or working floors.

The derrick or working floor of every building shall be solidly decked over its entire surface except for access openings.

§7253. Temporary floor and safety belt protection.

There shall be a tight and substantial temporary floor within two floors below and directly under that portion of each tier of beams on which erection, riveting, bolting, welding or painting is being done. For operations of short duration of exposure to falling, safety belts shall be required as set forth in Section 7265.

§7254. Temporary floors.

Temporary floors shall be wood planking of proper thickness, grade and span to carry the working load, but shall not be less than two inches thick, full size undressed.

§7255. Protection against temporary floor displacement.

Provision shall be made to secure temporary flooring against displacement by strong winds or other forces.

§7256. Plank extension.

Planks shall extend a minimum of 12 inches beyond centerline of their supports at each end.

§7257. Covering openings by columns.

Wire mesh or plywood (exterior grade) shall be used to cover openings adjacent to columns where planks do not fit tightly.

§7258. Metal decking instead of wood planking.

Metal decking where used in lieu of wood planking shall be of equivalent strength and shall be laid tightly and secured to prevent movement.

§7259. Replacement of floor planks.

Floor planks that are temporarily removed for any reason whatsoever shall be replaced as soon as work requiring their removal is completed or the open area shall be properly guarded.

§7260. Employee instruction before planking removed.

Prior to removal of temporary floor plank, employees shall be instructed by assigned supervision the steps to be taken to perform the work safely and in proper sequence.

§7261. Removing temporary planking.

When gathering and stacking temporary floor plank on a lower floor, in preparation for transferring such plank for use on an upper working floor, the steel erector's personnel shall remove such plank successively, working toward the last panel of such floor, so that the work is always being done from the planked floor.

§7262. Protection while removing temporary planking.

When gathering and stacking temporary floor planks from the last panel, the steel erector's personnel assigned to such work shall be protected by safety belts with life lines attached to a catenary line or other substantial anchorage.

§7263. Constantly maintaining structural frame's stability.

The sequence of erection, bolting, temporary guying, riveting and welding shall be such as to maintain the stability of the structural frame at all times during construction. This applies to the dead weight of the structure, plus weight and working reactions of all construction equipment placed thereon plus any external forces that may be applied.

§7264. Section as "building."

Where a building is being constructed in sections, each section constitutes a building as defined in Section 7250.

§7265. Safety belts and nets.

Safety belts and nets shall be required in accordance with Article 24 (commencing with Section 1669) of subchapter 4 of Chapter 4 of Part 1 of Title 8 of the California Administrative Code, Construction Safety Orders of the Division of Occupational Safety and Health.

§7266. Penalty for violation.

No person shall proceed with any work assigned to or undertaken by him, or require or permit any other person to proceed with work assigned to or undertaken by either, unless the planking or nets required by this article are in place. Violation of this section is a misdemeanor.

§7267. Enforcement by Division.

The Division of Occupational Safety and Health shall enforce this article.

CHAPTER 2 ELEVATORS, ESCALATORS, PLATFORM AND STAIRWAY CHAIR LIFTS, DUMBWAITERS, MOVING WALKS, AUTOMATED PEOPLE MOVERS, AND OTHER CONVEYANCES

§7300. Standards to promote public safety awareness.

The Legislature finds and declares all of the following:

(a) It is the purpose of this chapter to promote public safety awareness and to assure, to the extent feasible, the safety of the public and of workers with respect to conveyances covered by this chapter.

(b) The use of unsafe or defective conveyances imposes a substantial probability of serious and preventable injury to employees and the public. The prevention of these injuries and protection of employees and the public from unsafe conditions is in the best interest of the people of this state. Therefore, this chapter also establishes minimum standards for persons operating or maintaining conveyances covered by this chapter. These standards include familiarity with the operation and safety functions of the components and equipment, and documented training or experience or both, which shall include, but not be limited to, recognizing the safety hazards and performing the procedures to which they are assigned in conformance with all legal requirements.

(c) This chapter is not intended to prevent the division from implementing regulations, nor to prevent the use of systems, methods, or devices of equivalent or superior quality, strength, fire resistance, code effectiveness, durability, and safety to those required by the law, provided that there is technical documentation to demonstrate that the equivalency of the system, method, or device, is at least as effective as that prescribed in ASME A17.1, ASME A17.3, ASME A18.1, or ASCE 21. **Leg.H.** 2002 ch. 1149 (SB 1886) §3.

§7300.1. Definitions.

As used in this chapter:

(a) "ASCE 21" means the Automated People Mover Standards, as adopted by the American Society of Civil Engineers.

(b) "ASME A17.1" means the Safety Code for Elevators and Escalators, an American National Standard, as adopted by the American Society of Mechanical Engineers.

(c) "ASME A17.3" means the Safety Code for Existing Elevators and Escalators, an American National Standard, as adopted by the American Society of Mechanical Engineers.

(d) "ASME A18.1" means the Safety Standard for Platform Lifts and Stairway Chairlifts, an American National Standard, as adopted by the American Society of Mechanical Engineers.

(e) "Automated people mover" has the same meaning as defined in ASCE 21.

(f) "Board" or "standards board" means the Occupational Safety and Health Standards Board.

(g) "Certified qualified conveyance company" means any person, firm, or corporation that (1) possesses a valid contractor's license if required by Chapter 9 (commencing with Section 7000) of Division 3 of the Business and Professions Code and (2) is certified as a qualified conveyance company by the division in accordance with this chapter.

(h) "Certified competent conveyance mechanic" means any person who has been determined by the division to have the qualifications and ability of a competent journey-level conveyance mechanic and is so certified by the division in accordance with this chapter.

(i) "Conveyance" means any elevator, dumbwaiter, escalator, moving platform lift, stairway chairlift, material lift or dumbwaiter with automatic transfer device, automated people mover, or other equipment subject to this chapter.

(j) "Division" means the Division of Occupational Safety and Health.

(k) "Dormant elevator, dumbwaiter, or escalator" means an installation placed out of service as specified in ASME A17.1 and ASME A18.1.

(*l*) "Elevator" means an installation defined as an "elevator" in ASME A17.1.

(m) "Conveyance inspector" means any conveyance safety inspector of the division or other conveyance inspector determined by the division to be qualified pursuant to this chapter.

(n) "Escalator" means an installation defined as an "escalator" in ASME A17.1.

(o) "Existing installation" means an installation defined as an "installation, existing" in ASME A17.1.

(p) "Full maintenance service contract" means an agreement by a certified competent conveyance company and the person owning or having the custody, management, or control of the operation of the conveyance, if the agreement provides that the certified competent conveyance company is responsible for effecting repairs necessary to the safe operation of the equipment and will provide services as frequently as is necessary, but no less often than monthly.

(q) "Material alteration" means an alteration as defined in ASME A17.1 or A18.1.

(r) "Moving walk" or "moving sidewalk" means an installation defined as a "moving walk" in ASME A17.1.

(s) "Permit" means a document issued by the division that indicates that the conveyance has had the required safety inspection and tests and fees have been paid as set forth in this chapter.

(t) "Temporary permit" means a document issued by the division which permits the use of a noncompliant conveyance by the general public for a limited time while minor repairs are being completed or until permit fees are paid.

(u) "Repair" has the same meaning as defined in ASME A17.1 or A18.1. A "repair" does not require a permit.

(v) "Temporarily dormant elevator, dumbwaiter, or escalator" means a conveyance, the power supply of which has been disconnected by removing fuses and placing a padlock on the mainline disconnect switch in the "off" position. In the case of an elevator or dumbwaiter, the car shall be parked and the hoistway doors shall be in the closed and latched position. A wire seal shall be installed on the mainline disconnect switch by a conveyance inspector of the division. The wire seal and padlock shall not be removed for any purpose without permission from a conveyance inspector of the division. A temporarily dormant elevator, dumbwaiter, or escalator shall not be used again until it has been put in safe running order and is in condition for use. Annual inspections by a conveyance inspector shall continue for the duration of the temporarily dormant status. Temporarily dormant status may be renewed annually, but shall not exceed five years. After each inspection, the conveyance inspector shall file a report with the chief of the division describing the current condition of the conveyance.

(w) The meanings of building transportation terms not otherwise defined in this section shall be as defined in the latest editions of ASME A17.1 and ASME A18.1. **Leg.H.** 2002 ch. 1149 (SB 1886), 2004 ch. 503 (AB 2350).

§7300.2. Equipment covered.

Except as provided in Section 7300.3, this chapter covers the design, erection, construction, installation, material alteration, inspection, testing, maintenance, repair, service, and operation of the following conveyances and their associated parts and hoistways:

(a) Hoisting and lowering mechanisms equipped with a car or platform which move between two or more landings. This equipment includes, but is not limited to, the following:

(1) Elevators.

(2) Platform lifts and stairway chair lifts.

(b) Power-driven stairways and walkways for carrying persons between landings. This equipment includes, but is not limited to, the following:

(1) Escalators.

(2) Moving walks.

(c) Hoisting and lowering mechanisms equipped with a car which serve two or more landings and are restricted to the carrying of material by limited size or limited access to the car. This equipment includes, but is not limited to, the following:

(1) Dumbwaiters.

(2) Material lifts and dumbwaiters with automatic transfer devices.

(d) Automatic guided transit vehicles on guideways with an exclusive right-of-way. This equipment includes, but is not limited to, automated people movers. **Leg.H.** 2002 ch. 1149 (SB 1886).

§7300.3. Equipment not covered.

Equipment not covered by this chapter includes the following:

(a) Material hoists within the scope of standard A10.5 as adopted by the American National Standards Institute.

(b) Mobile scaffolds, towers, and platforms within the scope of standard A92 as adopted by the American National Standards Institute.

(c) Powered platforms and equipment for exterior and interior maintenance within the scope of standard 120.1 as adopted by the American National Standards Institute.

(d) Cranes, derricks, hoists, hooks, jacks, and slings within the scope of standard B30 as adopted by the American Society of Mechanical Engineers.

(e) Industrial trucks within the scope of standard B56 as adopted by the American Society of Mechanical Engineers.

(f) Portable equipment, except for portable escalators that are covered by standard A17.1 as adopted by the American National Standards Institute.

(g) Tiering or piling machines used to move materials to and from storage located and operating entirely within one story.

(h) Equipment for feeding or positioning materials, including that equipment used with machine tools or printing presses.

(i) Skip or furnace hoists.

(j) Wharf ramps.

(k) Railroad car lifts or dumpers.

(*l*) Line jacks, false cars, shafters, moving platforms, and similar equipment used for installing a conveyance by a contractor licensed in this state. **Leg.H.** 2002 ch. 1149 (SB 1886), 2004 ch. 503 (AB 2350).

§7300.4. Work exemptions.

This chapter does not apply to work that is not related to standards for conveyances that are (a) incorporated in codes promulgated by the American National Standards Institute or the American Society of Mechanical Engineers or (b) included in regulations of the division, in effect immediately prior to January 1, 2003, prescribing conveyance safety orders. Work exempted pursuant to this section includes, but is not limited to, routine nonmechanical maintenance, such as cleaning panels and changing light fixtures. **Leg.H.** 2002 ch. 1149 (SB 1886), 2004 ch. 503 (AB 2350).

§7301. Permit required for conveyance operation.

No conveyance shall be operated in this state unless a permit for its operation is issued by or in behalf of the division, and unless the permit remains in effect and is kept posted conspicuously on the conveyance. Operation of a conveyance without a permit or failure to post the permit conspicuously shall constitute cause for the division to prohibit use of the conveyance, unless it can be shown that a request for issuance or renewal of a permit has been made and the request has not been acted upon by the division. **Leg.H.** 1991 ch. 258, 2002 ch. 1149 (SB 1886).

§7301.1. Requirements for permit.

(a) On and after June 30, 2003, no conveyance may be erected, constructed, installed, or materially altered, as defined by regulation of the division, unless a permit has been obtained from the division before the work is commenced. A copy of the permit shall be kept at the construction site at all times while the work is in progress and shall be made available for inspection upon request. This section shall not apply to platform lifts and stairway chairlifts installed in a private residence as provided in paragraph (2) or (3) of subdivision (a) of Section 7317.

(b) Before March 1, 2003, the division shall establish an application procedure and all requirements for a permit under this section, which shall include the following:

(1) At a minimum, the applicant for a permit under this section shall meet all of the following requirements:

(A) The applicant shall hold a current elevator contractor's license issued pursuant to Chapter 9 (commencing with Section 7000) of Division 3 of the Business and Professions Code.

(B) The applicant shall be a certified qualified conveyance company.

(C) The applicant shall submit proof of the following types of insurance coverage, in the form of certified copies of policies or certificates of insurance:

(i) Liability insurance to provide general liability coverage of not less than one million dollars ($1,000,000) for the injury or death of any one person or persons in any one occurrence, with coverage of not less than five hundred thousand dollars ($500,000) for property damage in any one occurrence.

(ii) Workers' compensation insurance coverage.

(D) In the event of any material alteration, nonrenewal, or cancellation of any insurance required by this subparagraph, the applicant or permitholder shall submit written notice thereof to the division within five working days.

(2) At a minimum, each application for a permit under this section shall include all of the following:

(A) Copies of specifications and accurately scaled and fully dimensioned plans showing the location of the installation in relation to the plans and elevation of the building; the location of the machinery room and the equipment to be installed, relocated, or altered; and all structural supporting members thereof, including foundations. The plans and specifications shall identify all materials to be employed and all loads to be supported or conveyed. The plans and specifications shall be sufficiently complete to illustrate all details of construction and design.

(B) The name, residence, and business address of the applicant and each partner, or for a corporation, the principal officers and anyone who is authorized to accept service of process or official notices; the number of years the applicant has engaged in the business of constructing, erecting, installing, or altering conveyances; and the approximate number of persons to be employed on the permitted job.

(C) The permit fee.

(3) The division shall establish, and may from time to time amend, a fee for a permit under this section in an amount sufficient to defray the division's actual costs in administering the permit process, including the costs of investigation, revocation, or other associated costs. Permit fees collected by the division are nonrefundable.

(c)(1) The permit shall expire when the work authorized by that permit is not commenced within six months after the date of issuance, or within a shorter period as the division may specify at the time the permit is issued.

(2) The permit shall expire following commencement of work, if the permitholder suspends or abandons the work for a period of 60 days, or for a shorter period of time as the division may specify at the time the permit is issued.

(3) Upon application and for good cause shown, the division may extend a permit that would otherwise expire under this subdivision.

(d) The division may revoke any permit at any time, upon good cause, and after notice and an opportunity to be heard. **Leg.H.** 2002 ch. 1149 (SB 1886), 2004 ch. 503 (AB 2350).

§7301.5. Adoption of fire and emergency regulations for conveyance operation; emergency certification.

(a) The standards board shall adopt regulations pertaining to conveyances, including, but not limited to, conveyance emergency and signal devices, and the operation of conveyances under fire and other emergency conditions.

(b) Before January 1, 2003, the division shall establish an application procedure and all requirements for certification under this subdivision as an emergency certified competent conveyance mechanic. To ensure the safety of the public when a disaster or other emergency exists within the state and the number of certified competent conveyance mechanics in the state is insufficient to cope with the emergency, any certified qualified conveyance company may, within five business days after commencing work requiring certified competent conveyance mechanics, apply to the division, on behalf of all persons performing the work who are not certified competent conveyance mechanics, for certification as emergency certified competent conveyance mechanics. Any person for whom emergency certification is sought under this subdivision shall be certified by a certified qualified conveyance company to have an acceptable combination of documented experience and education to perform work covered by this chapter without direct and immediate supervision. The certified qualified conveyance company shall furnish proof of competency as the division may require. The division shall issue an emergency certified competent conveyance mechanic certificate upon receipt of acceptable documentation and payment of the required fee. Each certificate issued pursuant to this subdivision shall recite that it is valid for a period of 30 days from the date of issuance and for those particular conveyances and geographical areas as the division may designate, and otherwise shall entitle the person being certified to the rights and privileges of a certified competent conveyance mechanic as set forth in this chapter. The division shall renew an emergency certified competent conveyance mechanic certificate during the existence of the emergency.

(c) Before January 1, 2004, the division shall establish an application procedure and all requirements for certification under this subdivision as a temporary certified competent conveyance mechanic. If there are no certified qualified conveyance mechanics available to perform elevator work, a certified qualified conveyance company may apply to the division for certification of one or more temporary certified competent conveyance mechanics. Any person seeking to work as a temporary certified competent conveyance mechanic shall, before beginning work, be approved by the division as having an acceptable combination of documented experience and education to perform work covered by this chapter without direct and immediate supervision. The certified qualified conveyance company shall furnish proof of competency as the division may require. The division may issue a temporary certified competent conveyance mechanic certificate upon acceptable documentation and payment of the required fee. Each certificate issued pursuant to this subdivision shall recite that it is valid for a period of 30 days from the date of issuance and while the certificate holder is employed by the certified qualified conveyance company that certified the individual as competent. The certificate shall be renewable as long as the shortage of certified competent conveyance mechanics continues. **Leg.H.** 2002 ch. 1149 (SB 1886), 2004 ch. 503 (AB 2350).

§7302. Conveyance operation without permit.

The operation of a conveyance without a permit by any person owning or having the custody, management, or control of the operation of the conveyance, is a misdemeanor, punishable by a fine of not more than one thousand dollars ($1,000), imprisonment in the county jail for not more than 10 days, or by both that fine and imprisonment. Each day of operation for each conveyance without a permit is a separate offense. Any person who has requested the issuance or renewal of a permit if the request has not been acted upon by the division may not be prosecuted for a violation of this section. **Leg.H.** 2002 ch. 1149 (SB 1886) §12.

§7302.1. Conveyance authorization without permit.

(a) Any person who contracts for or authorizes the erection, construction, installation, or material alteration of a conveyance without a permit in violation of Section 7301.1 is guilty of a misdemeanor punishable by a fine of not more than seventy thousand dollars ($70,000), imprisonment in the county jail for not more than one year, or by both that fine and imprisonment.

(b) Any employer or contractor who contracts for or engages in the erection, construction, installation, or material alteration of a conveyance without a permit in violation of Section 7301.1 is guilty of a misdemeanor punishable by a fine of not more than seventy thousand dollars ($70,000), imprisonment in the county jail for not more than one year, or by both that fine and imprisonment. **Leg.H.** 2002 ch. 1149 (SB 1886).

§7302.2. Assessment of penalty.

The division may assess a civil penalty of not more than seventy thousand dollars ($70,000) against any person, and against any employer or contractor, who contracts for or authorizes the erection, construction, installation, or material alteration of a conveyance without a permit issued pursuant to Section 7301.1. **Leg.H.** 2002 ch. 1149 (SB 1886).

§7303. Remedies for dangerous operation without permit.

(a) Whenever any conveyance is operated without a current valid permit issued pursuant to Section 7304, and is in a condition that its use is dangerous to the life or safety of any person, the division or any affected person may apply to the superior court of the county in which the conveyance is located for an injunction restraining the operation of the conveyance until the condition is corrected. Proof by certification of the division that a permit has not been issued, has expired, or has been revoked, together with the affidavit of any safety inspector of the division or other expert that the operation of the conveyance is dangerous to the life or safety of any person, is sufficient ground, in the discretion of the court, for the immediate granting of a temporary restraining order.

(b) No bond shall be required from the division as a prerequisite for the division to seek or obtain any restraining order under subdivision (a).

(c) Any person who intentionally violates any injunction prohibiting the operation of the conveyance issued pursuant to subdivision (a) shall be liable for a civil penalty, to be assessed by the division, not to exceed seven thousand dollars ($7,000) for each violation. Each day of operation for each conveyance is a separate violation. **Leg.H.** 2002 ch. 1149 (SB 1886).

§7304. Conveyance inspection and permit issuance.

(a) Except as provided in subdivision (b), the division shall cause all conveyances to be inspected at least once each year. If a conveyance is found upon inspection to be in a safe condition for operation, a permit for operation for not longer than one year shall be issued by the division.

(b) If a conveyance is subject to a full maintenance service contract, the division may, after investigation and inspection, issue a permit for operation for not longer than two years. **Leg.H.** 2002 ch. 1149 (SB 1886), 2004 ch. 183 (AB 3082).

§7305. Division's power over unsafe conveyances.

If inspection shows that a conveyance is in an unsafe condition, the division may issue a preliminary order requiring repairs or alterations to be made to the conveyance that are necessary to render it safe, and may prohibit its operation or use until the repairs or alterations are made or the unsafe conditions are removed. **Leg.H.** 2002 ch. 1149 (SB 1886).

§7306. Challenging division orders.

Unless the preliminary order is complied with, a hearing before the division shall be allowed, upon request, at which the owner, operator, or other person in charge of the conveyance may appear and show cause why he or she should not comply with the order. **Leg.H.** 2002 ch. 1149 (SB 1886).

§7307. Procedural choices of division; later review.

(a) If it thereafter appears to the division that the conveyance is unsafe and that the requirements contained in the preliminary order should be complied with, or that other things should be done to make the conveyance safe, the division may order or confirm the withholding of the permit and may impose requirements as it deems proper for the repair or alteration of the conveyance or for the correction of the unsafe condition. The order may thereafter be reheard by the division or reviewed by the courts in the manner specified for safety orders by Part 1 (commencing with Section 6300) of this division, and not otherwise.

(b) The operation of a conveyance by any person owning or having the custody, management, or control of the operation thereof, while an order to repair is outstanding pursuant to subdivision (a), is a misdemeanor punishable by a fine of not more than seven thousand dollars ($7,000), by imprisonment in the county jail for not more than 30 days, or by both that fine and imprisonment. Each day of operation for each conveyance without a permit is a separate offense. **Leg.H.** 2002 ch. 1149 (SB 1886).

§7308. Temporary permits.

If the operation of a conveyance during the making of repairs or alterations is not immediately dangerous to the safety of persons, the division may issue a temporary permit for its operation for a period not to exceed 30 days during the making of repairs or alterations. **Leg.H.** 2002 ch. 1149 (SB 1886).

§7309. Inspectors.

The division may cause the inspection herein provided for to be made either by its safety inspectors or by any qualified elevator inspector employed by an insurance company.

§7309.1. Requirements for certification of inspectors.

(a) On and after June 30, 2003, no conveyance subject to this chapter shall be reinspected by any person unless the person is a conveyance inspector employed by the division or certified as qualified by the division.

(b) Before March 1, 2003, the division shall establish an application procedure and all requirements for the certification of conveyance inspectors. Each application for certification shall include information as the division may require and the applicable fee. At a minimum, the applicant shall present proof of certification as a qualified conveyance inspector by the American Society of Mechanical Engineers or proof of education and experience equivalent to what is required to obtain that certification from the American Society of Mechanical Engineers. **Leg.H.** 2002 ch. 1149 (SB 1886), 2004 ch. 503 (AB 2350).

§7310. Division's acceptance of other inspections.

The division may also issue its permit or a permit may be issued on its behalf based upon a certificate of inspection issued by a conveyance inspector of any municipality, upon proof to the satisfaction of the division that the safety requirements of the municipality are equal to the minimum safety requirements for conveyances adopted by the board. **Leg.H.** 1991 ch. 258, 2002 ch. 1149 (SB 1886), 2004 ch. 503 (AB 2350).

§7311. Requirements for inspectors.

All persons inspecting conveyances shall first secure from the division a certificate of competency to make those inspections. The division may determine the competency of any applicant for the certificate, either by examination or by other satisfactory proof of qualifications. The division may rescind at any time, upon good cause being shown therefor, and after hearing, if requested, any certificate of competency issued by it to a conveyance inspector. **Leg.H.** 2002 ch. 1149 (SB 1886), 2004 ch. 503 (AB 2350).

§7311.1. Certified qualified conveyance company—Application and certification.

(a) On and after June 30, 2003, no conveyance subject to this chapter shall be erected, constructed, installed, materially altered, tested, maintained, repaired, or serviced by any person, firm, or corporation unless the person, firm, or corporation is certified by the division as a certified qualified conveyance company. A copy of the certificate shall be kept at the site of the conveyance at all times while any work is in progress, and shall be made available for inspection upon request. However, certification under this section is not required for removing or dismantling conveyances that are destroyed as a result of the complete demolition of a secured building or structure or where the hoistway or wellway is demolished back to the basic support structure and no access is permitted that would endanger the safety of any person. This section does not apply to platform lifts and stairway chairlifts installed in a private residence as provided in paragraph (2) or (3) of subdivision (a) of Section 7317.

(b) Before March 1, 2003, the division shall establish an application procedure and all requirements for certification under this section as a certified qualified conveyance company, consistent with this section. At a minimum, the individual qualifying on behalf of a corporation, the owner on behalf of a sole ownership, or the partners on behalf of a partnership, shall meet either of the following requirements:

(1) Five years' work experience at a journeyperson level in the conveyance industry in construction, installation, alteration, testing, maintenance, and service and repair of conveyances covered by this chapter. This experience shall be verified by current and previously licensed elevator contractors or by current and previously certified qualified conveyance companies.

(2) Satisfactory completion of a written examination administered by the division on the most recent applicable codes and standards.

(c) At a minimum, each application for certification as a certified qualified conveyance company shall include:

(1) The name, residence and business address, and telephone numbers and other means to contact the sole owner or each partner, or for a corporation of the principal officers and the individual qualifying for the corporation; the number of years the applicant business has engaged in the business of constructing, maintaining, and service and repair of conveyances; and other information as the division may require.

(2) The fee required by this chapter.

(d) Before bidding for or engaging in any work covered by this chapter, a certified qualified conveyance company shall submit proof to the division by certified copies of policies or certificates of insurance, of all of the following:

(1) Liability insurance providing general liability coverage of not less than one million dollars ($1,000,000) for injury or death of any one person or persons in any one occurrence, with coverage of not less than five hundred thousand dollars ($500,000) for property damage of any one person or persons in any one occurrence.

(2) Workers' compensation insurance coverage.

(3) In the event of any material alteration or cancellation of any policy specified in paragraph (1) or (2), the certified qualified conveyance company shall provide written notice thereof to the division within five working days.

(e) An elevator company subject to this chapter shall disclose its status as a certified qualified conveyance company prior to bidding on a project or prior to contracting for services. The disclosure shall be in writing and located in a conspicuous place on the bid documents or contract in at least 10-point type. **Leg.H.** 2002 ch. 1149 (SB 1886), 2004 ch. 503 (AB 2350), 2009 ch. 196 (SB 478) §1.

§7311.2. Certified competent conveyance mechanic.

(a) On and after June 30, 2003, except as provided in subdivisions (b) and (c) of Section 7301.5, any person who, without supervision, erects, constructs, installs, alters, tests, maintains, services or repairs, removes, or dismantles any conveyance covered by this chapter, shall be certified as a certified competent conveyance mechanic by the division. This section does not apply to platform lifts and stairway chairlifts installed in a private residence as provided in paragraph (2) or (3) of subdivision (a) of Section 7317.

(b) Before March 1, 2003, the division shall establish an application procedure and all requirements for certification under this section as a certified competent conveyance mechanic, consistent with all of the following:

(1) At a minimum, a certified competent conveyance mechanic applicant shall meet both of the following requirements:

(A) Three years' work experience in the conveyance industry in construction, maintenance, and service and repair of conveyances covered by this chapter. This experience shall be verified by current and previously licensed elevator contractors or by current and previously certified qualified conveyance companies, as required by the division.

(B) One of the following:

(i) Satisfactory completion of a written examination administered by the division on the most recent applicable codes and standards.

(ii) A certificate of completion and successfully passing the mechanic examination of a nationally recognized training program for the conveyance industry, such as the National Elevator Industry Educational Program or its equivalent.

(iii) A certificate of completion of an apprenticeship program for elevator mechanic, having standards substantially equal to those of this chapter, and which program shall be registered with the Bureau of Apprenticeship and Training of the United States Department of Labor or a state apprenticeship council.

(iv) A certificate or license from another state having standards substantially equal to or more comprehensive than those of this chapter.

(v) The applicant applies on or before December 31, 2003, and within the three years immediately prior to January 1, 2003, has documented at least three years of actual work experience in the conveyance industry in construction, maintenance, and service and repair of conveyances covered by this chapter. This experience shall be as a journey-level mechanic working without direct and immediate supervision, and shall be verified by currently and previously licensed conveyance contractors or by current and previously certified qualified conveyance companies, as required by the division.

(2) At a minimum, each application for certification as a certified competent conveyance mechanic shall include the information required by the division and the fee required by this chapter. **Leg.H.** 2002 ch. 1149 (SB 1886), 2004 ch. 503 (AB 2350).

§7311.25. Exception to certified competent conveyance mechanic requirement for certain agricultural production, processing, and handling facilities.

(a) The following meanings apply for purposes of this section:

(1) "Agricultural production, processing, and handling facilities" includes grain elevators, feed mills, flour mills, rice mills, rice dryers, and other similar facilities.

(2) "Applicable Elevator Safety Orders" means the Elevator Safety Orders referenced in Subchapter 6 (commencing with Section 3000) of Chapter 4 of Division 1 of Title 8 of the California Code of Regulations, and any successors to those orders.

(b) Notwithstanding Section 7311.2 or any other provision of this chapter, an owner or operator of agricultural production, processing, and handling facilities may designate a competent person in his or her employ to maintain, repair, service, lubricate, or test manlifts installed and used at the facilities if the manlifts are maintained and inspected in accordance with applicable Elevator Safety Orders. The designated competent person need not be a certified competent conveyance mechanic. **Leg.H.** 2009 ch. 196 (SB 478) §2.

§7311.3. Certificate—2-year term; renewal—Continuing education of certificate holders.

(a) A certificate issued by the division to the certified qualified conveyance inspector, certified qualified conveyance company, or certified competent conveyance mechanic as set forth in Sections 7309.1, 7311.1, and 7311.2, shall have a term of two years. The fee for biennial renewal shall be established by the division in an amount sufficient to defray the division's costs of administering this chapter.

(b) The renewal of all certificates issued under this chapter shall be conditioned upon the submission of a certificate of completion of a course designed to ensure the continuing education of certificate holders on new and existing provisions of the regulations of the board. This continuing education course shall consist of not less than eight hours of instruction that shall be attended and completed within one year immediately preceding any certificate renewal.

(c) The courses shall be taught by instructors through continuing education providers that may include, but not be limited to, division programs, association seminars, and joint labor-management apprenticeship and journeyman upgrade training programs. The division shall approve the continuing education providers and curriculum. All instructors shall be approved by the division and shall be exempt from the requirements of subdivision (b), provided that the applicant is qualified as an instructor at any time during the one-year period immediately preceding the scheduled date for renewal.

(d) A certificate holder who is unable to complete the continuing education course required under this section prior to the expiration of his or her certificate due to a temporary disability may apply for a waiver from the division. Waiver applications shall be submitted to the division on a form provided by the division. Waiver applications shall be signed and accompanied by a declaration signed by a competent physician attesting to the applicant's temporary disability. Upon the termination of the temporary disability, the certificate holder shall submit to the division a declaration from the same physician, if practicable, attesting to the termination of the temporary disability, and a waiver sticker, valid for 90 days, shall be issued to the certificate holder and affixed to his or her certificate.

(e) Continuing education providers approved by the division shall keep uniform records, for a period of 10 years, of attendance of certificate holders, following a format approved by the division. These records shall be available for inspection by the division at its request. Approved continuing education providers shall keep secure all attendance records and certificates of completion. Falsifying or knowingly allowing another to falsify attendance records or certificates of completion of continuing education provided pursuant to this section shall constitute grounds for suspension or revocation of the approval required under this section. **Leg.H.** 2002 ch. 1149 (SB 1886), 2004 ch. 503 (AB 2350).

§7311.4. Certification fees.

(a) The division shall establish fees for initial and renewal applications for certification under this chapter as a certified qualified conveyance inspector, certified qualified conveyance company, or certified competent conveyance mechanic based upon the costs to the division of administering the certification and licensing program in this chapter, including the cost of developing and administering any tests as well as any costs related to continuing education, investigation, revocation, or other associated costs. In fixing the amount of these fees, the division may include direct costs and a reasonable percentage attributable to the indirect costs of the division for administering this chapter.

(b) Fees collected pursuant to this chapter are nonrefundable. **Leg.H.** 2002 ch. 1149 (SB 1886), 2004 ch. 503 (AB 2350), 2016 ch. 31 (SB 836) §196, effective June 27, 2016.

§7311.5. Persons maintaining certain personnel elevators on marine terminal cranes; experiential requirements; proscriptions.

(a) A person, firm, or corporation that maintains and repairs solely special purpose personnel elevators on cranes that utilize a rack and pinion system in marine terminals as part of crane maintenance activities qualifies as a certified qualified conveyance company under Section 7311.1 if the individual qualifying individually or on behalf of the firm or corporation has five years' work experience at a journeyperson level in the crane maintenance industry, including experience in the maintenance and repair of crane elevators. This experience shall be verified by a person, firm, or corporation in the business of maintaining and repairing cranes in marine terminals.

(b) A person qualifies as a certified competent conveyance mechanic under Section 7311.2 if the person has three years' work experience in the crane maintenance industry, including experience in the maintenance and repair of crane elevators, as a journey-level mechanic without direct and immediate supervision. This experience shall be verified by a crane maintenance company approved as a certified qualified conveyance company pursuant to subdivision (a).

(c) The certifications obtained pursuant to this section may only be used for the limited purposes of maintaining and repairing special purpose personnel elevators on cranes that utilize a rack and pinion system in marine terminals.

(d) A person, firm, or corporation that qualifies for certification as a certified qualified conveyance company or certified competent conveyance mechanic is not authorized to perform any of the following procedures:

(1) Any work on a conveyance other than a special purpose personnel elevator on cranes that utilize a rack and pinion system in marine terminals.

(2) Any work related to new elevator installations.

(3) Any modifications or alterations of existing elevator systems.

(4) Testing or replacing of emergency brakes, centrifugal brakes, emergency safety devices, or electrical systems.

(5) Annual certifications of any type of conveyance or elevator.

(e) The certifications authorized by this section require experience but do not require an examination because the general examination given pursuant to this chapter is inapplicable to the work described in this section. The division is not required to set up specialty examinations to certify persons pursuant to this chapter.

(f) For purposes of this section, the following terms shall have the following meanings:

(1) "Special purpose personnel elevators" shall have the same meaning as defined in Section 3085 of Title 8 of the California Code of Regulations.

(2) "Marine terminal" shall have the same meaning as used in Section 3460 of Title 8 of the California Code of Regulations.

(g) Nothing in this section exempts a person, firm, or corporation applying for certification as a certified qualified conveyance company or a certified competent conveyance mechanic under this section from paying the administration fees required under this chapter. **Leg.H.** 2006 ch. 448 (SB 727) §1.

§7312. Revocation of conveyance operation permit.

The division may at any time, upon good cause being shown therefor, and after notice and an opportunity to be heard, revoke any permit to operate a conveyance. **Leg.H.** 2002 ch. 1149 (SB 1886).

§7313. Requirements for inspection reports.

Each conveyance inspector shall, within 21 days after he or she makes an inspection, forward to the division on forms provided by it, a report of the inspection. Failure to comply with this section shall be grounds for the division to cancel his or her certificate. **Leg.H.** 2002 ch. 1149 (SB 1886), 2004 ch. 503 (AB 2350).

§7314. Inspection fees.

(a) The division shall, subject to subdivision (f), fix and collect fees for the inspection of conveyances as it determines to be necessary to cover the costs to the division of administering the inspection and permitting programs in this chapter, including fees for necessary subsequent inspections to determine if applicable safety orders have been complied with and for field consultations. In fixing the amount of these fees, the division may include direct costs and a reasonable percentage attributable to the indirect costs of the division for administering this chapter, including the costs related to regulatory development as required by Section 7323.

(b) Notwithstanding Section 6103 of the Government Code, the division may collect the fees authorized by subdivision (a) from the state or any county, city, district, or other political subdivision.

(c) Whenever a person owning or having the custody, management, or operation of a conveyance fails to pay the fees required under this chapter within 60 days after the date of notification, he or she shall pay, in addition to the fees required under this chapter, a penalty fee equal to 100 percent of the fee. Failure to pay fees within 60 days after the date of notification constitutes cause for the division to prohibit use of the conveyance.

(d)(1) Any fees required pursuant to this section shall, except as otherwise provided in paragraph (2), be set forth in regulations that shall be adopted as emergency regulations. These emergency regulations shall not be subject to the review and approval of the Office of Administrative Law pursuant to the Administrative Procedure Act (Chapter 3.5 (commencing with Section 11340) of Part 1 of Division 3 of Title 2 of the Government Code). These regulations shall become effective immediately upon filing with the Secretary of State.

(2) A suspension or reduction of fees pursuant to subdivision (f) is not required to be set forth in a regulation.

(e) For purposes of this section, the date of the invoice assessing a fee pursuant to this section shall be considered the date of notification.

(f)(1) For the 2015–16 fiscal year, the fees for the annual and biennial inspection of conveyances required by Section 7304 are suspended on a one-time basis.

(2) For the 2016–17 fiscal year, and for every fiscal year thereafter, the Director of Industrial Relations, upon concurrence of the Department of Finance, may suspend or reduce the fees for the annual and biennial inspections of conveyances required by Section 7304 on a one-time basis for that fiscal year in order to reduce the amount of moneys in the Elevator Safety Account. **Leg.H.** 1993 ch. 998, 2002 ch. 1149 (SB 1886), 2007 ch. 179 (SB 86) §30, effective August 24, 2007, 2015 ch. 25 (SB 84) §44, effective June 24, 2015, 2016 ch. 31 (SB 836) §197, effective June 27, 2016.

§7315. Payment of inspection fees; temporary permit issuance; fees—Exceptions.

Fees shall be paid before the issuance of any permit to operate a conveyance, but a temporary permit may be issued pending receipt of fee payment. The division shall not charge an inspection fee if an inspection has been made by an inspector of an insurance company or municipality who holds a certificate as a conveyance inspector and an inspection report is filed with the division within 21 days after inspection is made. The division may charge a fee for processing and issuing the permit to operate. **Leg.H.** 2002 ch. 1149 (SB 1886), 2004 ch. 503 (AB 2350), 2016 ch. 31 (SB 836) §198, effective June 27, 2016.

§7316. Disposition and reporting requirements for inspection fee funds.

All fees collected by the division under this chapter shall be paid into the Elevator Safety Account which is hereby created for the administration of the division's conveyance safety program. The division shall establish criteria upon which fee charges are based and prepare an annual report concerning revenues obtained and expenditures appropriated for the conveyance safety program. The division shall file the report with the Legislative Analyst, the Joint Legislative Audit Committee, and the Department of Finance. **Leg.H.** 2002 ch. 1149 (SB 1886), 2004 ch. 503 (AB 2350).

§7317. Exempted conveyances.

(a) Except as provided in subdivision (b), the following conveyances are exempt from this chapter:

(1) Conveyances under the jurisdiction of the United States government.

(2) Conveyances located in a single-unit private home and not accessible to the public.

(3) Conveyances located in a multiunit residential building serving no more than two dwelling units and not accessible to the public.

(b) Conveyances otherwise exempted pursuant to paragraph (3) of subdivision (a) shall be inspected by the division upon completion of installation prior to being placed in service or after major alterations. The inspection shall be for safety and compliance with orders or regulations applicable to the type of conveyance installed. **Leg.H.** 2002 ch. 1149 (SB 1886).

§7318. Division's authority over safety orders.

Nothing in this chapter limits the authority of the division to prescribe or enforce general or special safety orders. **Leg.H.** 2002 ch. 1149 (SB 1886).

§7319. Seat for elevator operator; penalty for violation.

All elevators used for the carriage of passengers shall be provided with a suitable seat for the operator in charge. Failure to comply with this section is a misdemeanor punishable by a fine not exceeding fifty dollars ($50) for each offense.

§7320. Penalty for failure to display permit.

The division may assess a civil penalty not to exceed one thousand dollars ($1,000) against any person owning or having custody, management, or control of the operation of a conveyance, who operates the conveyance without a permit or who fails to conspicuously post the permit in the conveyance. No penalty shall be assessed against any person who has requested the issuance or renewal of a permit and the request has not been acted upon by the division. **Leg.H.** 2002 ch. 1149 (SB 1886).

§7321. Penalty for operation of unsafe conveyance.

(a) The division may assess a civil penalty not to exceed seventy thousand dollars ($70,000) against any person owning or having custody, management, or control of the operation of a conveyance, who operates or permits the operation of the conveyance in a condition that is dangerous to the life or safety of any person, or who operates or permits the operation of the conveyance in violation of an order prohibiting use issued pursuant to Section 7301, 7305, or 7314.

(b) The division shall issue an order prohibiting use and may assess a civil penalty not to exceed seventy thousand dollars ($70,000) against any person who constructs, installs, or materially alters a conveyance without a permit issued pursuant to Section 7301.1 that is dangerous to the life or safety of any person. **Leg.H.** 2002 ch. 1149 (SB 1886).

§7321.5. Enforcement of penalties; appeals.

The division shall enforce Sections 7320 and 7321 by issuance of a citation and notice of civil penalty in a manner consistent with Sections 6317 and 6319. Any person owning or having custody, management, or control of the operation of a conveyance who receives a citation and notice of civil penalty may appeal to the Occupational Safety and Health Appeals Board in a manner consistent with Section 6319. **Leg.H.** 2002 ch. 1149 (SB 1886).

§7322. Hearing on order prohibiting use of conveyance.

(a) Once an authorized representative of the division has issued an order prohibiting the use of a conveyance as specified in Sections 7301, 7305, 7314, or subdivision (b) of Section 7321, the person owning or having custody, management, or operation of the conveyance may contest the order and shall be granted, upon request, a hearing to review the validity of the order. The hearing shall be held no later than 10 working days following receipt of the request for hearing.

(b) After a notice is attached as provided in Section 7305 or subdivision (b) of Section 7321, every person who enters or uses, or directs or causes another to enter or use, any conveyance before it is made safe, or who defaces, destroys, or removes the notice without the authority of the division, is guilty of a misdemeanor punishable by a fine of not more than seventy thousand dollars ($70,000), by imprisonment in the county jail for not more than one year, or by both that fine and imprisonment.

(c) After a notice is attached for failure to comply with the requirements of Section 7301 or 7314, every person who enters or uses, or directs or causes another to enter or use, any conveyance before it is made safe, or who defaces, destroys, or removes the notice without the authority of the division, is guilty of a misdemeanor punishable by a fine of not more than seven thousand dollars ($7,000), imprisonment in the county jail for not more than six months, or by both that fine and imprisonment. **Leg.H.** 2002 ch. 1149 (SB 1886).

§7323. Regulations for equipment.

The division shall propose to the standards board for review, and the standards board shall adopt, regulations for the equipment covered by this chapter. Not later than December 31, 2003, the division shall propose final rulemaking proposals to the standards board for review and adoption, which shall include provisions at least as effective as ASME A17.1, ASME A17.3, ASME A18.1, and ASCE 21, as in effect prior to September 30, 2002. Not later than nine months after the effective date of any revision or any substantive revision to any addendum to these codes, the division shall propose additional final rulemaking proposals to the standards board for review and adoption at least as effective as those in the revised code or addendum. The standards board shall notice the division's final rulemaking proposals for public hearing within three months of their receipt and shall adopt the proposed regulations promptly and in accordance with subdivision (b) of Section 11346.4 of the Government Code. **Leg.H.** 2002 ch. 1149 (SB 1886).

§7324. Compliance with State Fire Prevention and Building Code.

Individuals, firms, or companies certified as described in this chapter shall ensure that installation, service, and maintenance of conveyances are performed in compliance with the provisions contained in the State Fire Prevention and Building Code and with generally accepted standards referenced in that code. **Leg.H.** 2002 ch. 1149 (SB 1886), 2004 ch. 503 (AB 2350).

§7324.1. Responsibility and liability of persons, firms or corporations.

This chapter shall not be construed to relieve or lessen the responsibility or liability of any person, firm, or corporation owning, operating, controlling, maintaining, erecting, constructing, installing, altering, testing, or repairing any conveyance or other related mechanisms covered by this chapter for damages to any person or property caused by any defect therein. **Leg.H.** 2002 ch. 1149 (SB 1886).

§7324.2. Requirements not retroactive.

The provisions of this chapter added or amended by the act enacting this section shall not be applied retroactively. Equipment subject to this chapter shall be required to comply with the applicable standards in effect on the date of its installation or within the period determined by the board for compliance with ASME A17.3, whichever is more stringent. **Leg.H.** 2002 ch. 1149 (SB 1886).

CHAPTER 3 SAFETY DEVICES UPON BUILDINGS TO SAFEGUARD WINDOW CLEANERS

§7325. "Building."

"Building," as used in this chapter, means any building three stories or more in height, and whether heretofore constructed or hereafter to be constructed, including com-

Labor

mercial buildings of all types, office buildings, apartment houses, hotels and buildings used for manufacturing purposes, but excluding dwelling houses occupied by not more than three families, and excluding all buildings constructed with windows that may be, and are, entirely washed and cleaned from the inside of the building or from a sitting position on the window sill in the manner provided by safety orders issued, or which may be issued from time to time, by the division.

§7326. Window sill or frame fixtures.

There shall be securely attached to the outside window sills or frames of the window of any building, rings, bolts, lugs, fittings, or other devices to which may be fastened safety belts or other devices to be used, or which may hereafter be used by persons engaged in cleaning windows. The division shall, prior to the installation of any such bolts, lugs, rings, fittings, or other devices, approve such bolts, lugs, rings, fittings, or other devices as to their design, durability, and safety. Except as provided in Section 18930 of the Health and Safety Code, the division shall by appropriate rules and orders designate the manner in which said safety devices are to be attached, installed, and used.

§7327. Approval of alternative fixtures.

In lieu of the safety devices enumerated in Section 7326, the division may approve the installation or use of any other devices or means which will effectively safeguard persons engaged in cleaning windows.

§7328. Penalty for employer violation.

Any person employing, directing or permitting another to do or perform any labor upon any windows which have not the safety devices as provided for in Sections 7326 and 7327 shall be guilty of a misdemeanor.

§7329. Obligation to install and maintain safety fixtures; penalty for violation.

Every person owning or entitled to possession, under any lease, sublease, or agreement for a longer period than one year, or under any renewal lease, sublease, or agreement for a period of less than one year, of any building heretofore constructed shall, within six months following the effective date of this chapter, install and provide the safety devices as provided for in this chapter, and thereafter maintain such safety devices in good condition. Any person failing to install or provide and maintain said safety devices as provided for in this chapter shall be guilty of a misdemeanor.

§7330. Penalty for failure to provide safety devices.

Every person who fails to provide the safety devices as set forth in this chapter upon any building hereafter to be constructed, and who thereafter fails to maintain such devices in good condition, shall be guilty of a misdemeanor.

§7331. Division's powers.

The division may make and enforce such safety orders and rules as it considers necessary and proper to carry into effect the purposes and provisions of this chapter.

The division shall give notice to the owner or person entitled to possession of any building that is existing in violation of this chapter or of any rules issued under this chapter. Failure of the person so notified to comply with this chapter and rules issued under it, within 15 days, shall be authority for the division to proceed against such person as authorized in this chapter.

§7332. Enforcement by division.

The division shall enforce the provisions of this chapter.

CHAPTER 4
PASSENGER TRAMWAYS

§7340. "Passenger tramway" and "permit."

As used in this chapter:

(a) "Passenger tramway" includes any method or device used primarily for the purpose of transporting persons by means of cables or ropes suspended between two or more points or structures.

(b) "Permit" means a permit issued by the division to operate a passenger tramway in any place. **Leg.H.** 1965 ch. 1047 §1, 1972 ch. 479 §1, 2016 ch. 31 (SB 836) §200, effective June 27, 2016.

§7341. Permit requirement.

A passenger tramway shall not be operated in any place in this state unless a permit for the operation of the tramway is issued by the division, and unless the permit remains in effect and is kept posted conspicuously in the main operating terminal of the tramway. **Leg.H.** 1965 ch. 1047 §1, 1972 ch. 479 §2, 2016 ch. 31 (SB 836) §201, effective June 27, 2016.

§7342. Violation by operation without permit.

The operation of a passenger tramway by any person owning or having the custody, management, or operation thereof without a permit is a misdemeanor, and each day of operation without a permit is a separate offense. No prosecution shall be maintained where the issuance or renewal of a permit has been requested and remains unacted upon. **Leg.H.** 1965 ch. 1047 §1, 2016 ch. 31 (SB 836) §202, effective June 27, 2016.

§7343. Remedies for dangerous operation.

Whenever a passenger tramway in any place is being operated without the permit herein required, and is in such condition that its use is dangerous to the life or safety of any person, the division, or any person affected thereby, may apply to the superior court of the county in which the passenger tramway is located for an injunction restraining the operation of the passenger tramway until the condition is corrected. Proof by certification of the division that a permit has not been issued, together with the affidavit of any safety engineer of the division that the operation of the passenger tramway is dangerous to the life or safety of any person, is sufficient ground, in the discretion of the court, for the immediate granting of a temporary restraining order. **Leg.H.** 1965 ch. 1047 §1, 1972 ch. 479 §3, 1982 ch. 517 §312, 2016 ch. 31 (SB 836) §203, effective June 27, 2016.

§7344. Inspection and permit issuance.

(a) The division shall cause all passenger tramways to be inspected at least two times each year.

(b) At least one of the inspections required by subdivision (a) shall take place between November 15 of each year and March 15 of the succeeding year.

(c) If a passenger tramway is found upon inspection to be in a safe condition for operation, a permit for operation for not longer than one year shall be issued by the division. **Leg.H.** 1965 ch. 1047 §1, 1972 ch. 478 §1, 2016 ch. 31 (SB 836) §204, effective June 27, 2016.

§7345. Division's powers when tramways are unsafe.

If inspection shows a passenger tramway to be in an unsafe condition, the division may issue a preliminary order requiring repairs or alterations to be made to the passenger tramway that are necessary to render it safe, and may order the operation or use thereof discontinued until the repairs or alterations are made or the unsafe conditions are removed. **Leg.H.** 1965 ch. 1047 §1, 2016 ch. 31 (SB 836) §205, effective June 27, 2016.

§7346. Procedure to challenge division orders.

Unless the preliminary order is complied with, a hearing before the division shall be allowed, upon request, at which the owner, operator, or other person in charge of the passenger tramway may appear and show cause why he should not comply with the order. **Leg.H.** 1965 ch. 1047 §1, 2016 ch. 31 (SB 836) §206, effective June 27, 2016.

§7347. Procedural choices of division; later review.

If it thereafter appears to the division that the passenger tramway is unsafe and that the requirements contained in the preliminary order should be complied with, or that other things should be done to make the passenger tramway safe, the division may order or confirm the withholding of the permit and may make requirements as it determines to be proper for its repair or alteration or for the correction of the unsafe condition. The order may thereafter be reheard by the division or reviewed by the courts only in the manner specified for safety orders by Part 1 (commencing with Section 6300). **Leg.H.** 1965 ch. 1407 §1, 2016 ch. 31 (SB 836) §207, effective June 27, 2016.

§7348. Temporary permits.

If the operation of a passenger tramway during the making of repairs or alterations is not immediately dangerous to the safety of employees or others, the division may issue a temporary permit for the operation of the tramway for a term not to exceed 30 days during the making of repairs or alterations. **Leg.H.** 1965 ch. 1047 §1, 1972 ch. 479 §4, 2016 ch. 31 (SB 836) §208, effective June 27, 2016.

§7349. Inspectors; temporary permits.

The inspection herein provided for shall be made by a division safety engineer or, on ski lifts, by a certified tramway inspector qualified under Section 7354.5 and employed by a licensed insurance company. A temporary permit for operation may be issued by a division engineer or by the qualified insurance inspector, on a form furnished by the division, under conditions of Sections 7348 and 7351.

§7350. Fees.

(a) The division shall fix and collect fees for the inspection of passenger tramways as it deems necessary to cover the costs of the division in administering this chapter. In fixing the amount of these fees, the division may include direct costs and a reasonable percentage attributable to the indirect costs of the division for administering this chapter. The division shall not charge an inspection fee for inspections performed by certified insurance inspectors, but may charge a fee for processing the permit when issued by the division as a result of the inspection. Notwithstanding Section 6103 of the Government Code, the division may collect the fees authorized by this section from the state or any county, city, district, or other political subdivision.

(b) Whenever a person owning or having custody, management, or operation of a passenger tramway fails to pay any fee required under this chapter within 60 days after the date of notification by the division, the division shall assess a penalty fee equal to 100 percent of the initial fee. For purposes of this section, the date of the invoice fixing the fee shall be considered the date of notification. **Leg.H.** 1993 ch. 998, 2007 ch. 179 (SB 86) §31, effective August 24, 2007, 2016 ch. 31 (SB 836) §209, effective June 27, 2016.

§7351. Payment of fees; temporary permit exception.

Fees shall be paid before issuance of a permit to operate a passenger tramway, except that the division, at its own discretion, may issue a temporary operating permit not to exceed 30 days, pending receipt of payment of fees. **Leg.H.** 1965 ch. 1047 §1, 2016 ch. 31 (SB 836) §210, effective June 27, 2016.

§7352. Disposition of fees.

(a) All fees collected by the division under this chapter shall be deposited into the Occupational Safety and Health Fund to support the division's passenger tramway inspection program.

(b) On the effective date of the statute adding this subdivision, any moneys in the Elevator Safety Account that, before that date, were deposited pursuant to this section, subdivision (a) of Section 7904, or subdivision (b) of Section 7929 shall be transferred to the Occupational Safety and Health Fund, together with any assets, liabilities, revenues, expenditures, and encumbrances of that fund that are attributable to the division's passenger tramway inspection program under this chapter, the portable amusement ride inspection program under Part 8 (commencing with Section 7900), and the Permanent Amusement Ride Safety Inspection Program (Part 8.1 (commencing with Section 7920)). **Leg.H.** 2007 ch. 179 (SB 86) §32, effective

August 24, 2007, 2016 ch. 31 (SB 836) §211, effective June 27, 2016.

§7353. Certification of construction and repair plans.

(a) A passenger tramway shall not be constructed or altered until the plans and design information have been properly certified to the division by an engineer qualified under the Professional Engineers Act (Chapter 7 (commencing with Section 6700) of Division 3 of the Business and Professions Code).

(b) Any person who owns, has custody of, manages, or operates a passenger tramway shall notify the division prior to any major repair of the tramway. **Leg.H.** 1965 ch. 1047 §1, 1971 ch. 1033 §1, 2016 ch. 31 (SB 836) §212, effective June 27, 2016.

§7354. Certification.

The division shall not issue an operating permit to operate a passenger tramway until it receives certification in writing by an engineer qualified under the Professional Engineers Act (Chapter 7 (commencing with Section 6700) of Division 3 of the Business and Professions Code) that the erection work on the tramway has been completed in accordance with the design and erection plans for the tramway. **Leg.H.** 1965 ch. 1047 §1, 2016 ch. 31 (SB 836) §213, effective June 27, 2016.

§7354.5. Ski lift inspections.

(a) Notwithstanding any other provision of this chapter, in any case in which an insurer admitted to transact insurance in this state has inspected or caused to be inspected, by a qualified, licensed professional engineer registered in California pursuant to Chapter 7 (commencing with Section 6700) of Division 3 of the Business and Professions Code, any passenger tramway used as a ski lift, the division may, if it finds those inspections were made according to subdivisions (a) and (b) of Section 7344, accept the inspections in lieu of any other inspections for that year, except that the initial inspection of a new ski lift or of a major alteration to an existing ski lift shall be performed by a division safety engineer. A private inspector shall, before commencing his or her duties therein, secure from the division a certificate of competency to make inspections. The division may determine the competency of any applicant for a certificate, either by examination or by other satisfactory proof of qualification.

(b) The division may rescind at any time, upon good cause being shown therefor, and after hearing, if requested, any certificate of competency issued by it to a ski lift inspector. The inspection reports made to the division shall be in a form and content as the division finds necessary for acceptance as a proper inspection made by a private inspector. **Leg.H.** 1974 ch. 61 §1, effective March 12, 1974, 1974 ch. 863 §3, 1975 ch. 678 §54, 2016 ch. 31 (SB 836) §214, effective June 27, 2016.

§7355. Division's authority.

Nothing in the foregoing sections of this chapter shall limit the authority of the division to prescribe or enforce general or special safety orders.

§7356. Report of tramway injury.

The division shall, under the authority of Section 7355, promulgate and cause to be published safety orders directing each owner or operator of a passenger tramway to report to the division each known incident where the maintenance, operation, or use of the tramway results in injury to any person, unless the injury does not require medical service other than ordinary first aid treatment. **Leg.H.** 1972 ch. 477 §1, 2016 ch. 31 (SB 836) §215, effective June 27, 2016.

§7357. Qualification of tramway operators.

The division shall establish standards for the qualification of persons engaged in the operation of passenger tramways, whether as employees or otherwise. The standards shall be consistent with the general objective of this chapter in providing for the safety of members of the public who use passenger tramways and those engaged in their operation. **Leg.H.** 1972 ch. 519 §1, 2016 ch. 31 (SB 836) §216, effective June 27, 2016.

CHAPTER 5 CRANES

ARTICLE 1 Permits for Tower Cranes

§7370. Legislative declaration; priority of tower crane safety inspections.

(a) The Legislature finds and declares that recent statewide spot inspections of cranes have uncovered a pattern of numerous safety violations so serious and pervasive that safety inspections shall be a continuing priority with regard to all tower cranes in the state.

1990 Note: It appears the Legislature inadvertently enacted a subsection (a) designation without enacting subsection (b).

§7371. Definitions.

As used in this chapter, the following definitions shall apply:

(a) "Crane" means a machine for lifting or lowering a load and moving it horizontally, in which the hoisting mechanism is an integral part of the machine. It may be driven manually or by power and may be a fixed or a mobile machine, but does not include stackers, lift trucks, power shovels, backhoes, excavators, concrete pumping equipment, or straddle type mobile boat hoists.

(b) "Straddle type mobile boat hoist" means a straddle type carrier supported by four wheels with pneumatic tires capable of straddling and carrying boats with high masts and superstructure.

(c) "Tower crane" means a crane in which a boom, swinging jib, or other structural member is mounted on a vertical mast or tower.

(d) "Mobile tower crane" means a tower crane which is mounted on a crawler, truck, or similar carrier for travel or transit.

(e) "Crane employer" means an employer who is responsible for the maintenance and operation of a tower crane.

(f) "Certificating agency" shall have the same definition as in Section 4885 of Title 8 of the California Code of Regulations. **Leg.H.** 1992 ch. 254.

§7372. Employment of safety inspectors; establishment of safety inspection program.

(a) The division shall employ safety engineers trained to inspect tower cranes.

(b) The division shall establish a safety inspection program for all tower cranes operated in the state. This safety program shall include:

(1) Safety inspection of tower cranes twice a year.

(2) Increased penalties for the violation of tower crane safety orders and standards.

(3) Permit fees as described in Section 7373.

§7373. Issuance and validity of permits.

(a) A tower crane shall not be operated at any worksite unless an employer obtains a permit from the division. The division shall conduct an investigation for purposes of issuing a permit in an expeditious manner. If the division does not issue a permit within 10 days after being requested to do so by a crane employer, the crane employer may operate the crane without a permit.

(b) The division shall set fees to be charged for these permits in an amount sufficient to cover the costs of administering this article. In fixing the amount of these fees, the division may include direct costs and a reasonable percentage attributable to the indirect costs of the division for administering this article.

(c) The permit for a fixed tower crane shall be valid for the period of time that the tower crane is fixed to the site.

(d) The permit for a mobile tower crane shall be valid for one calendar year. **Leg.H.** 1990 ch. 1033 (AB 3826) §1, 2016 ch. 31 (SB 836) §217, effective June 27, 2016.

§7374. Suspension or revocation of permit.

(a) The division may suspend or revoke the permit of a crane where the employer engages in gross negligence, gross incompetence, or willful or repeated disregard of any occupational safety standard or order involving the crane.

(b) The permit of the crane shall be suspended or revoked for a six-month period for first-time suspensions or revocations, and for a one-year period for each subsequent suspension or revocation. The division shall establish a suspension and revocation hearing procedure and appeal process.

ARTICLE 2
Certification
[Selected Provisions]

§7376. Suspension or revocation of license to certify crane safety.

(a) The division shall suspend or revoke a license to certify for the following reasons:

(1) Gross negligence, gross incompetency, a pattern of incompetence, or fraud in the certification of a crane.

(2) Willful or deliberate disregard of any occupational safety standard while certifying a crane.

(3) Misrepresentation of a material fact in applying for, or obtaining, a license to certify under this chapter.

(4) Upon a showing of good cause.

(b) The period of suspension or revocation shall be for six months for a first suspension or revocation, and one year for each subsequent suspension or revocation. The certificating agency shall obtain a new license from the division following a suspension or revocation. The division shall establish a hearing procedure and an appeal process for license suspensions and revocations.

§7377. Appeal of revocation of license.

Revocation of a license to certify may be appealed to the Director of Industrial Relations.

§7378. Penalties for fraudulent certification.

A licensed certifier who fraudulently certifies that a crane is in compliance with the criteria established by the division under subdivision (a) of Section 7375 is guilty of a misdemeanor punishable by imprisonment in the county jail for a period not to exceed six months, or by a fine not to exceed one thousand dollars ($1,000), or both.

§7379. Penalties for certifying without license.

It shall be a misdemeanor for an individual to engage in the certification of a crane as specified in this chapter if that individual is not licensed pursuant to this chapter. Any violation of this section shall be punishable by imprisonment in the county jail for a period not to exceed six months, or by a fine not to exceed one thousand dollars ($1,000), or both.

§7380. Collection of fees.

(a) The division shall set fees for the examination and licensing of crane certifiers as necessary to cover the costs of administering this article. In fixing the amount of these fees, the division may include direct costs and a reasonable percentage attributable to the indirect costs of the division for administering this article.

(b) All fees collected by the division under this chapter shall be deposited into the Occupational Safety and Health Fund. **Leg.H.** 2016 ch. 31 (SB 836) §219, effective June 27, 2016.

§7381. Penalties for violation of safety standards if serious injury or death results; penalties for serious violations.

(a) Notwithstanding Sections 6319 and 6425, if serious injury or death is caused by any serious or willful repeated violation of a crane standard, order, or special order, or by any failure to correct a serious violation of a crane standard, order, or special order within the time specified for its correction, the employer shall be assessed a civil penalty in an amount equal to double the maximum penalty allowable for each violation contributing to the injury or death.

(b) Notwithstanding any provision of this division, any employer who violates any tower crane standard, order, or special order, if that violation is a serious violation, shall be assessed a civil penalty of not less than one thousand dollars ($1,000) for each serious violation. The penalty shall not be reduced for any of the reasons listed in Section 6319. **Leg.H.** 1990 ch. 1033 (AB 3826) §1, 2017 ch. 28 (SB 96) §34, effective June 27, 2017.

§7382. Presence of safety representative required while installing, dismantling, or "jumping" crane.

No person shall install or dismantle a tower crane, or increase the height of a crane, known in the construction trade as "jumping or climbing a crane," without a safety representative of the crane manufacturer, distributor, or a representative of a licensed crane certifier being present on site for consultation during the procedure. The standards board shall adopt a regulation making failure to provide the designated safety representative a serious violation of a safety order. Local governmental entities may restrict the hours during which these procedures may be performed.

PART 6
Tanks and Boilers

CHAPTER 6
MISMANAGEMENT OF STEAM BOILERS

§7770. Penalty for undue quantity of steam endangering human life.

Every engineer or other person having charge of any steam-boiler, steam-engine, or other apparatus for generating or employing steam, used in any manufactory, railway, or other mechanical works, who wilfully, or from ignorance or from gross neglect, creates, or allows to be created, such an undue quantity of steam as to burst or break the boiler, engine or apparatus, or to cause any other accident whereby human life is endangered, is guilty of a felony.

1945 Note: It appears the Legislature inadvertently substituted "wilfully" for "willfully".

§7771. Imprisonment for causing death.

Every person having charge of any steam boiler, steam engine, or other apparatus for generating or employing steam, used in any manufactory, railroad, vessel, or other mechanical works, who willfully, or from ignorance or neglect, creates, or allows to be created, such an undue quantity of steam as to burst or break the boiler, engine, or apparatus, or to cause any other accident whereby the death of a human being is caused, is punishable by imprisonment pursuant to subdivision (h) of Section 1170 of the Penal Code for two, three, or four years. **Leg.H.** 1945 ch. 1142 §2, 1976 ch. 1139 §95, operative July 1, 1977, 2011 ch. 15 (AB 109) §223, effective April 4, 2011, operative October 1, 2011.

2011 Notes: This act is titled and may be cited as the 2011 Realignment Legislation addressing public safety. Stats. 2011 ch. 15 (AB 109) §1.

This act will become operative no earlier than October 1, 2011, and only upon creation of a community corrections grant program to assist in implementing this act and upon an appropriation to fund the grant program. Stats. 2011 ch. 15 (AB 109) §636; Stats. 2011 ch. 39 (AB 117) §68.

The Community Corrections Grant Program referred to in Stats. 2011 ch. 15 §636, as amended by Stats. 2011 ch. 39 §68, was created by Stats. 2011 ch. 40 §3, operative October 1, 2011.

PART 7
Volatile Flammable Liquids
[Selected Provisions]

§7800. "Volatile flammable liquids."

"Volatile flammable liquids" as used in this part means any petroleum or liquid product of petroleum or natural gas having a flash point below 100 degrees Fahrenheit, and includes any petroleum or liquid product of petroleum or natural gas while at a temperature above its flash point. Flash points shall be as determined by means of the Tag Closed Tester, Designation D56–36 American Society for Testing Materials, or the Pensky-Martens Closed Tester, Designation D93–42 American Society for Testing Materials.

§7803. Means of flame extinguishment.

Every employer who engages in any business requiring any employee to handle or use any volatile flammable liquid or to work in the close proximity of any such liquid in sufficient quantity and under conditions affording opportunity for the person or clothing becoming ignited shall provide adequate means of extinguishment whereby such employee may extinguish flames on his person or clothing.

PART 7.5
Refinery and Chemical Plants

CHAPTER 1
GENERAL

§7850. Title of part.

This part shall be known and cited as the California Refinery and Chemical Plant Worker Safety Act of 1990.

§7851. Legislative declaration.

The Legislature finds and declares that because of the potentially hazardous nature of handling large quantities of chemicals and recent disasters involving chemical handling in other states, a greater state effort is required to assure worker safety. The Legislature also recognizes that a key element for assuring workplace safety is adequate employee training. The potential consequences of explosions, fires, and releases of dangerous chemicals may be catastrophic; thus immediate and comprehensive government action must be taken to ensure that workers in petroleum refineries, chemical plants, and other related facilities are thoroughly trained and that adequate process safety management practices are implemented.

§7852. Legislative intent.

(a) It is the intent of the Legislature, in enacting this part, that the Occupational Safety and Health Standards Board and the Division of Occupational Health and Safety (OSHA) promote worker safety through implementation of training and process safety management practices in petroleum refineries and chemical plants and other facilities deemed appropriate.

(b) To the maximum extent practicable, the board and the division shall minimize duplications with other state statutory programs and business reporting requirements when developing standards pursuant to Chapter 2 (commencing with Section 7855).

(c) It is further the intent of the Legislature, in enacting this part, that in the interest of promoting worker safety, standards be adopted by March 31, 2014. **Leg.H.** 2013 ch. 28 (SB 71) §42, effective June 27, 2013.

§7853. "Process safety management" defined.

For the purposes of this part, "process safety management" means the application of management programs, which are not limited to engineering guidelines, when dealing with the risks associated with handling or working near hazardous chemicals. Process safety management is intended to prevent or minimize the consequences of catastrophic releases of acutely hazardous, flammable, or explosive chemicals.

CHAPTER 2
PROCESS SAFETY MANAGEMENT STANDARDS

§7855. Purpose of chapter.

The purpose of this chapter is to prevent or minimize the consequences of catastrophic releases of toxic, flammable, or explosive chemicals. The establishment of process safety management standards are intended to eliminate, to a substantial degree, the risks to which workers are exposed in petroleum refineries, chemical plants, and other related manufacturing facilities.

§7856. Process safety management standards—Adoption of federal standards; facilities not covered under federal rules.

By March 31, 2014, the board shall adopt process safety management standards for refineries, chemical plants, and other manufacturing facilities, as specified in Codes 28 (Chemical and Allied Products) and 29 (Petroleum Refining and Related Industries) of the Manual of Standard Industrial Classification Codes, published by the United States Office of Management and Budget, 1987 Edition, that handle regulated substances as defined in subdivision (j) of Section 25532 of the Health and Safety Code and pose a significant likelihood of accident risk, as determined by the board. Alternately, upon making a finding that there is a significant likelihood of risk to employees at a facility not included in Codes 28 and 29 resulting from the presence of acutely hazardous materials or explosives as identified in Part 172 (commencing with Section 172.1) of Title 49 of the Code of Federal Regulations, the board may require that these facilities be subject to the jurisdiction of the standards provided for in this section. When adopting these standards, the board shall give priority to facilities and areas of facilities where the potential is greatest for preventing severe or catastrophic accidents because of the size or nature of the process or business. The standards adopted pursuant to this section shall require that injury prevention programs of employers subject to this part and implemented pursuant to Section 6401.7 include the requirements of this part. **Leg.H.** 2013 ch. 28 (SB 71) §43, effective June 27, 2013, 2018 ch. 59 (SB 1502) §4.

§7857. Standards to include prescribed items.

The process safety management standards shall include provisions dealing with the items prescribed by Sections 7858 to 7868, inclusive, of this chapter.

§7858. Written safety information; employee participation; content and availability.

The employer shall develop and maintain a compilation of written safety information to enable the employer and the employees operating the process to identify and understand the hazards posed by processes involving acutely hazardous and flammable material. The employer shall provide for employee participation in this process. This safety information shall be communicated to employees involved in the processes, and shall include information pertaining to hazards of acutely hazardous and flammable materials used in the process, information pertaining to the technology of the process, and information pertaining to the equipment in the process. A copy of this information and communication shall be accessible to all workers who perform any duties in or near the process area.

§7859. Hazard analysis; availability of risk management prevention program information.

The employer shall perform a hazard analysis for identifying, evaluating, and controlling hazards involved in the process. The employer shall provide for the participation of knowledgeable operating employees in these analyses. The final report containing the results of the hazardous analysis for each process shall be available, in the respective work area, for review by any person working in that area. Upon request of any worker or any labor union representative of any worker in the area, the employer shall provide or make available a copy of any risk management prevention program prepared for that facility pursuant to Article 2 (commencing with Section 25531) of Chapter 6.95 of Division 20 of the Health and Safety Code. The board, when adopting a standard or standards pertaining to this section, may authorize employers to submit risk management prevention programs prepared pursuant to Article 2 (commencing with Section 25531) of Chapter 6.95 of Division 20 of the Health and Safety Code to satisfy related requirements in whole or in part.

§7860. Written operating procedures; availability; review.

(a) The employer shall develop and implement written operating procedures that provide clear instructions for safely conducting activities involved in each process consistent with the process safety information.

(b) A copy of the operating procedures shall be readily accessible to employees or to any other person who works in or near the process area.

(c) The operating procedures shall be reviewed as often as necessary to assure that they reflect current operating practice, including changes that result from changes in process chemicals, technology, and equipment, and changes to facilities.

§7861. Safety and health hazard training; refresher courses; employer duty to train; training certification and testing.

(a) Each employee whose primary duties include the operating or maintenance of a process, and each employee prior to assuming operations and maintenance duties in a newly assigned process, shall be trained in an overview of the process and in the operating procedures as specified in Section 7860. The training shall include emphasis on the specific safety and health hazards, procedures, and safe practices applicable to the employee's job tasks.

(b) Refresher and supplemental training shall be provided to each operating or maintenance employee, or both, and other worker necessary to ensure safe operation of the facility and on a recurring regular schedule as determined adequate by the board.

(c) The employer shall ensure that each worker necessary to ensure safe operation of the facility has received and successfully completed training as specified by this section. The employer, after the initial or refresher training shall prepare a certification record which contains the identity of the employee, the date of training, and the signature of the person conducting the training. Testing procedures shall be established by each employer to ensure competency in job skill levels and safe and healthy work practices.

§7862. Contractor's employees working near potential hazard.

(a) The employer shall inform contractors performing work on, or near, a process of the known potential fire, explosion, or toxic release hazards related to the contractor's work and the process, and require that contractors have trained their employees to a level adequate to safely perform their job. The employer shall also inform contractors of any applicable safety rules of the facility, and assure that the contractors have so informed their employees.

(b) The employer shall explain to contractors the applicable provisions of the emergency action plan required by Section 7868.

(c) Contractors shall assure that their employees have received training to safely perform their jobs and that these employees will adhere to all applicable work practices and safety rules of the facility.

§7863. Prestartup safety review for new and modified facilities.

The employer shall perform a prestartup safety review for new facilities and for modified facilities for which the modification necessitates a change in the process safety information. These reviews shall include knowledgeable operating employees.

§7864. Inspection and testing procedures.

The employer shall establish and implement written procedures and inspection and testing programs to maintain the ongoing integrity of process equipment. These programs shall include a process for allowing employees to identify and report potentially faulty or unsafe equipment, and to record their observations and suggestions in writing. The employer shall respond regarding the disposition of the employee's concerns contained in the reports in a timely manner.

§7865. Permits for "hot work."

The employer shall develop and implement a written procedure governing the issuance of "hot work" permits. "Hot work" includes electric or gas welding, cutting, brazing, or similar flame- or spark-producing operations.

§7866. Procedure for managing changes.

The employer shall establish and implement written procedures to manage changes, except for replacements in kind, to process chemicals, technology, and equipment, and to make changes to facilities.

§7867. Procedure for investigating incidents and potential incidents.

The employer shall establish a written procedure for investigating every incident which results in, or, as determined by board criteria, could reasonably have resulted in, a major accident in the workplace. The procedure shall, at a minimum, require that a written report be prepared and be provided to all employees whose work assignments are within the facility where the incident occurred at the time the incident occurred and shall also include establishing a method for dealing with findings and recommendations.

§7868. Emergency action plan.

The employer shall establish and implement an emergency action plan. The employer may use the business plan for emergency response submitted pursuant to subdivision (a) of Section 25503.5 and subdivision (b) of Section 25505 of the Health and Safety Code if it meets the standards adopted by the board.

§7870. Collection of fees.

Notwithstanding the availability of federal funds to carry out the purposes of this part, the division shall annually fix and collect reasonable fees for consultation, inspection, adoption of standards, and other duties conducted pursuant to this part. The fees shall be adopted by March 31, 2014. All revenue collected from these fees shall be deposited into the Occupational Safety and Health Fund. The fees shall be sufficient to support, at a minimum, the annual cost of 15 positions. The expenditure of these funds shall be subject to appropriation by the Legislature in the annual Budget Act or other measure. **Leg.H.** 2013 ch. 28 (SB 71) §44, effective June 27, 2013.

§7872. Petroleum refinery turnaround—Definition; when required; review of records.

(a) As used in this section and in Section 7873, "turnaround" means a planned, periodic shutdown, total or partial, of a refinery process unit or plant to perform maintenance, overhaul, and repair operations and to inspect, test, and replace process materials and equipment. "Turnaround" does not include unplanned shutdowns that occur due to emergencies or other unexpected maintenance matters in a process unit or plant. "Turnaround" also does not include routine maintenance, where routine maintenance consists of regular, periodic maintenance on one or more pieces of equipment at a refinery process unit or plant that may require shutdown of such equipment.

(b) Every September 15, every petroleum refinery employer shall submit to the division a full schedule of planned turnarounds for all affected units for the following calendar year.

(c) At the request of the division, at least 60 days prior to the shutdown of a process unit or plant as part of a planned turnaround, a petroleum refinery employer shall provide access onsite and allow the division to review the following documentation for the process unit or plant scheduled to be shut down for that turnaround:

(1) All corrosion reports and risk-based inspection reports generated since the last turnaround.

(2) Process hazard analyses generated since the last turnaround.

(3) Boiler permit schedules.

(4) All management of change records related to repairs, design modifications, and process changes implemented since the last turnaround or scheduled to be completed in the planned turnaround referenced in this subdivision and identified in subdivision (b).

(5) Work orders scheduled to be completed in the planned turnaround referenced in this subdivision and identified in subdivision (b).

(6) All temporary repairs made since the last turnaround, including, but not limited to, clamps and encapsulations. As used in this section, "temporary repairs" means repairs made to piping systems in order to restore sufficient integrity to continue safe operation until permanent repairs can be scheduled.

(7) Notification and description of all repairs, design modifications, or process changes described in a corrosion report, risk-based inspection report, process hazard analysis, boiler permit schedule, management of change record, work order, or other document listed in paragraphs (1) to (6), inclusive, that the petroleum refinery employer has deferred to a subsequent operational period or turnaround.

(d) The division may request additional information as necessary to perform its responsibilities in this part pursuant to Section 6314.

(e) At the request of the division, at least 30 days before the shutdown of a process unit or plant as part of a planned turnaround, a petroleum refinery employer shall provide access onsite and allow the division to review any changes to the information or documents reviewed by the division pursuant to subdivision (c) and relevant supporting documents.

(f) At the division's request, a petroleum refinery employer shall provide the division with physical copies, or, at the division's discretion, electronic copies if available, of the documentation reviewed by the division pursuant to subdivisions (c), (d), and (e).

(g) By agreement with a petroleum refinery employer, the division may modify the reporting period as to any individual item of information.

(h) This section is not intended to limit or increase the division's authority in Part 1 (commencing with Section 6300) to prohibit use of a place of employment, machine, device, apparatus, or equipment or any part thereof that constitutes an imminent hazard to employees.

(i) The Legislature finds and declares that the purpose of this section is to improve the ability of the state to conduct inspections of petroleum refining operations. **Leg.H.** 2014 ch. 519 (SB 1300) §1.

§7873. When petroleum refinery turnaround information is trade secret; protected information; conditions for release of information to public; court orders; notification.

(a) As used in this section, "trade secret" means a trade secret as defined in subdivision (d) of Section 6254.7 of the Government Code or Section 1061 of the Evidence Code, and shall include the schedule submitted to the division pursuant to subdivision (b) of Section 7872 of this code, and the scheduling, duration, layout, configuration, and type of work to be performed during a turnaround. Upon completion of a turnaround, the scheduling and duration of that turnaround shall no longer be considered a trade secret. The wages, hours, benefits, job classifications, and training standards for employees performing work for petroleum refinery employers is not a trade secret.

(b)(1) If a petroleum refinery employer believes that information submitted to the division pursuant to Section 7872 may involve the release of a trade secret, the petroleum refinery employer shall nevertheless provide this information to the division. The petroleum refinery em-

Labor

ployer may, at the time of submission, identify all or a portion of the information submitted to the division as trade secret and, to the extent feasible, segregate records designated as trade secret from the other records.

(2) Subject to subdivisions (c), (d), and (g), the division shall not release to the public any information designated as a trade secret by the petroleum refinery employer pursuant to paragraph (1).

(c)(1) Upon the receipt of a request for the release of information to the public that includes information that the petroleum refinery employer has notified the division is a trade secret pursuant to paragraph (1) of subdivision (b), the division shall notify the petroleum refinery employer in writing of the request by certified mail, return receipt requested.

(2) The division shall release the requested information to the public, unless both of the following occur:

(A) Within 30 days of receipt of the notice of the request for information, the petroleum refinery employer files an action in an appropriate court for a declaratory judgment that the information is subject to protection as a trade secret, as defined in subdivision (a), and promptly notifies the division of that action.

(B) Within 120 days of receipt of the notice of the request for information, the petroleum refinery employer obtains an order prohibiting disclosure of the information to the public and promptly notifies the division of that action.

(3) This subdivision shall not be construed to allow a petroleum refinery employer to refuse to disclose the information required pursuant to this section to the division.

(d) Except as provided in subdivision (c), any information that has been designated as a trade secret by a petroleum refinery employer shall not be released to any member of the public, except that such information may be disclosed to other officers or employees of the division when relevant in any proceeding of the division.

(e)(1) The petroleum refinery employer filing an action pursuant to paragraph (2) of subdivision (c) shall provide notice of the action to the person requesting the release of the information at the same time that the defendant in the action is served.

(2) A person who has requested the release of information that includes information that the petroleum refinery employer has notified the division is a trade secret pursuant to paragraph (1) of subdivision (b) may intervene in an action by the petroleum refinery employer filed pursuant to paragraph (2) of subdivision (c). The court shall permit that person to intervene.

(f) The public agency shall not bear the court costs for any party named in litigation filed pursuant to this section.

(g) This section shall not be construed to prohibit the exchange of trade secrets between local, state, or federal public agencies or state officials when those trade secrets are relevant and reasonably necessary to the exercise of their authority.

(h) If the person requesting the release of information identified by a petroleum refinery employer as a trade secret files an action against the division to order disclosure of that information, the division shall promptly notify the petroleum refinery employer in writing of the action by certified mail, return receipt requested. The petroleum refinery employer may intervene in an action filed by the person requesting the release of trade secrets identified by the petroleum refinery employer. The court shall permit the petroleum refinery employer to intervene.

(i) An officer or employee of the division who, by virtue of that employment or official position, has possession of, or has access to, trade secret information, and who, knowing that disclosure of the information to the general public is prohibited by this section, knowingly and willfully discloses the information in any manner to a person he or she knows is not entitled to receive it, is guilty of a misdemeanor. A contractor with the division and an employee of the contractor, who has been furnished information as authorized by this section, shall be considered an employee of the division for purposes of this section. **Leg.H.** 2014 ch. 519 (SB 1300) §2, 2015 chs. 303 (AB 731) §382, 314 (SB 421) §1.

PART 9
Tunnel and Mine Safety

CHAPTER 1
TUNNELS AND MINES

§7950. Citation of part.

This part shall be known and may be cited as "The Tom Carrell Memorial Tunnel and Mine Safety Act of 1972."

§7951. Definitions.

As used in this part:

(a) Tunnel shall include excavation, construction, alteration, repairing, renovating, or demolishing of any tunnel except tunnel work covered under the compressed air safety orders adopted by the Occupational Safety and Health Standards Board and manhole construction.

(b) "Tunnel" means an underground passageway, excavated by men and equipment working below the earth's surface, that provides a subterranean route along which men, equipment, or substances can move.

(c) "Mine" means any excavation or opening above or below ground used for removal of ore, minerals, gravel, sand, rock, or other materials intended for manufacturing or sale. It shall include quarries and open pit operations, other than a gravel pit or other pit where material is removed by a contractor or other person for his own use and not for sale to others. The term "mine" shall not include a mine that is operated exclusively by persons having a proprietary interest in such mine or by persons who are paid only a share of the profits from the mine, nor shall it include during any calendar year, any mine that produced less than five thousand dollars ($5,000) in ore, minerals, sand, rock, or other material during the preceding calendar year.

(d) "Access shaft" means a vertical shaft used as a regular means of worker access to underground mines and tunnels under construction, renovation, or demolition.

(e) "Lower explosive limit" means the lowest concentration at which a gas or vapor can be ignited or will explode.

(f) "Face" means the head of the tunnel where soil is being removed, or that area in a mine where digging is underway.

(g) "Muck" means excavated dirt, rock, or other material.

(h) "Permissible equipment" means equipment tested and approved by the U.S. Bureau of Mines or acceptable to other authorities recognized by the division, and acceptable by the division, which is safe for use in gassy or extrahazardous tunnels or underground mines.

(i) "Division" means the Division of Occupational Safety and Health.

(j) "Board" means the Occupational Safety and Health Standards Board.

(k) "Underground mine" means a mine that consists of a subterranean excavation.

§7952. Safety engineers unit.

There shall be within the division a separate unit of safety engineers trained to inspect all tunnel construction and mine operations.

§7953. Inspection of mines and tunnels.

Sufficient manpower shall be maintained to provide for four annual inspections of underground mines, one inspection of surface mines or quarries annually, and six inspections of tunnels under construction annually.

§7954. Availability of additional personnel, facilities, and services.

To assist the unit of safety engineers in determining the safety of tunnel construction and mine operation, the division shall make available at least one industrial hygiene engineer and one chemist. A laboratory for analysis of dust, gas, vapors, soil, or other materials shall be available to members of this unit. Contracts to provide for geological and other services may be signed by the division whenever it is necessary to assure safety for employees engaged in mining or tunnel work.

§7955. Notification before operation or construction; prejob safety conferences; classification of tunnels and underground mines; reclassification.

The division and the owner of a mine, if he is not the operator of the mine, shall be notified before any initial mining operation or construction may be started at any mines or tunnels. A prejob safety conference shall be held with an authorized representative of the division for all underground operations. Representatives of the tunnel or mine owner, the employer, and employees shall be included in the prejob safety conference.

The division shall classify all tunnels or underground mines operating on the effective date of this section, or which commence operation thereafter, as one of the classifications set forth in subdivisions (a) to (d), inclusive. Such classification shall be made prior to the request for bids on all public works projects, whenever possible. This shall not, however, prevent the division from reclassifying such mines or tunnels when conditions warrant it.

(a) Nongassy, which classification shall be applied to tunnels or underground mines where there is little likelihood of encountering gas during the construction of the tunnel or operation of an underground mine. Such tunnels shall be constructed or underground mines operated under regulations, rules, and orders developed by the division and board and approved by the board. This subdivision shall not prohibit the division chief or his representatives from establishing any special orders that they feel are necessary for safety.

(b) Potentially gassy, which classification shall be applied to tunnels or underground mines where there exists a possibility gas will be encountered.

Labor

(c) Gassy, which classification shall be applied to tunnels or underground mines where it is likely gas will be encountered. Special safety measures, including those set forth in Sections 7965 to 7976, inclusive, those established by the division and board and adopted by the board, or special orders written by the chief or his representatives shall be observed in construction of gassy tunnels in addition to regular rules, orders, special orders, or regulations.

(d) Extrahazardous, which classification may, when the division finds that there is a serious danger to the safety of the employees, be applied to tunnels or underground mines where gas or vapors have caused an explosion or fire, where the likelihood of encountering petroleum vapors exists, or where tests show, with normal ventilation, a concentration of hydrocarbon petroleum vapors in excess of 20 percent of the lower explosive limit within three inches of the roof, face, floor, or walls of any open workings. Construction in extrahazardous tunnels or operation in extrahazardous underground mines shall conform to safety measures set forth in Sections 7977 to 7985, inclusive, any rules, regulations, orders, or special orders of the division, or any special rules, orders, or regulations adopted by the board.

The division shall not be required to reclassify any tunnel or underground mine that is shut down seasonally, when such tunnel or underground mine is put back into operation in not less than six months after date of the shutdown.

§7956. Posting of classification and special regulations.

All personnel, including both employees working above ground and those in the tunnel or underground mine, shall be informed of the classification designated by the division for that job. A notice of the classification and any special orders, rules, or regulations to be used in construction, remodeling, demolition, or operation of the tunnel or underground mine shall be prominently posted at the site.

§7957. Emergency rescue plans.

An emergency rescue plan shall be developed by the employer for every tunnel or underground mine. Such plan, including a current map of the tunnel or underground mine, shall be provided to local fire and rescue units, to the division, and to every employee at the place of employment.

§7958. Trained rescue crews.

A trained rescue crew of at least five men shall be provided at underground mines with more than 25 men or tunnels with 10 or more men underground at any one time. Smaller mines shall have one man for each 10 men underground who receives annual training in the use of breathing apparatus. Two trained crews shall be provided at mines with more than 50 men underground and at tunnels with more than 25 men underground.

§7959. Rescue crews: equipment familiarity, regular practices, placement.

Rescue crews shall be familiar with all emergency equipment necessary to effect a rescue or search for missing employees in case of an accident or explosion. Such rescue crews shall hold practices with equipment and using emergency rescue plan procedures at least once monthly during construction or operation of the tunnel or underground mines. At least one rescue crew shall be maintained above ground at all times and within 30 minutes travel of the tunnel or underground mine site classified as gassy or extrahazardous.

§7960. Tests in potentially gassy tunnels and mines.

In any tunnel or underground mine classified as potentially gassy, tests for gas or vapors shall be made prior to start of work at each shift. If any concentration of gas at or above 10 percent of the lower explosive limit is recorded, the division shall be notified immediately.

§7961. Investigation of specified gas readings.

The division shall investigate immediately any notification of a gas reading 10 percent of the lower explosive limit or higher by an employer in a tunnel or underground mine classified as potentially gassy. If the inspection determines the likelihood of encountering more gas or vapor, the division may halt operations until the tunnel or mine can be reclassified.

§7962. Safety representatives.

A safety representative qualified to recognize hazardous conditions and certified by the division shall be designated by the employer in any tunnel or underground mine. He shall have the authority to correct unsafe conditions and unsafe practices, and shall be responsible for directing the required safety programs.

§7963. Communication systems.

All underground mines and tunnels with more than five men underground at one time shall have telephone or other communication systems to the surface in operation at any time there are persons underground. Such systems shall be installed in such a manner that destruction or removal of one phone or communication device does not make other phones or communication devices inoperative.

§7964. Fireproof access shafts.

Whenever an access shaft is used as the normal means of entrance or exit to an underground mine or tunnel, it shall be constructed of fireproof material or fireproofed by chemical or other means.

§7964.5. Division's authority.

Nothing contained in this part shall restrict the division in contracting with the Secretary of the Interior for an approved state plan for mines under P.L. 89–577 (30 U.S.C. 721 et seq.).

CHAPTER 2 GASSY AND EXTRAHAZARDOUS TUNNELS

§7965. Operational procedures for gassy tunnels and mines.

Any tunnel or underground mine classified by the division as gassy shall operate under special procedures adopted by the board, as well as rules, regulations, special orders, or general orders for nongassy underground mines and tunnels.

§7966. Gas tests and probe holes.

In any tunnel classified as gassy by the division, there shall be tests for gas or vapors taken prior to each shift and at least hourly during actual operation. If a mechanical excavator is used, gas tests shall be made prior to removal of muck or material and before any cutting or drilling in tunnels or underground mines where explosives are used. A log shall be maintained for inspection by the division showing results of each test. Whenever a tunnel excavation or underground mine operation approaches a geologic formation in which there is a likelihood of encountering gas or water, a probe hole at least 20 feet ahead of the tunnel face or area where material is being mined shall be maintained.

§7967. Division notification of specified gas levels.

Whenever gas levels in excess of 10 percent of the lower explosive limit are encountered initially in a tunnel or underground mine classified as gassy, the division shall be notified immediately by telephone or telegraph. The chief of the division or his authorized representative may waive subsequent notification for gas readings less than 20 percent of the lower explosive limits upon a finding that adequate ventilation and other safety measures are provided to assure employee safety.

§7968. Shutdown orders for gas or vapor testing.

In any gassy tunnel or underground mine, the division may order work halted until adequate testing can be completed to determine the level of hazard from gases or vapors. A notice of such shutdown shall be filed by the division inspector with his superiors as soon as practicable. Any overruling of such order must be made by the chief or his designated representative and must be in writing. An onsite inspection must be made by the person overruling an inspector's order prior to resumption of work.

§7969. Review of electric plans for gassy tunnels and mines.

In any gassy tunnel or underground mine the division shall review plans for electrical lighting and power for equipment. When it is necessary for safety, the inspector may require changes in the amount and type of lighting, and may require permissive-type wiring, switches, tools, and equipment.

§7970. Smoking and ignition sources prohibited in gassy mines; employer's responsibility.

In any tunnel or underground mine classified gassy, smoking shall be prohibited and the employer shall be responsible for collecting all personal sources of ignition such as lighters and matches from employees entering the tunnel.

§7971. Procedures when gas or vapor ignites.

Whenever there is any ignition of gas or vapor in a tunnel or underground mine, all work shall cease, employees shall be removed, and reentry except for rescue purposes shall be prohibited until the division has conducted an inspection and authorized reentry for maintenance or production in writing.

§7972. Removal of workers at specified gas levels.

If the level of gas in any tunnel or underground mine reaches 20 percent of its lower explosive limit at any time all men shall be removed, the division notified immediately by telephone or telegram, and no one shall reenter the tunnel or underground mine until approval is given by the division.

§7973. Employee notification and posting of special orders following inspection.

In any tunnel or underground mine classified as gassy, all employees shall be informed of any special orders made by the division following an inspection. Such notice shall be given before entering the tunnel or underground mine. A copy of any orders subsequently written by the division shall be posted and all employees shall be notified at a safety meeting called by the safety representative before they are permitted to start work.

§7974. Ventilation in gassy tunnels.

In any tunnel classified as gassy by the division, ventilation shall include continuous exhausting of fumes and air, unless an alternative ventilation plan which is as effective or better is approved by the division. Fans for this purpose shall be located at the surface, and shall be reversible from a single switch at the portal or shaft. These requirements shall not preclude the use of auxiliary fans to supply more air or greater exhaust to a tunnel or underground mine.

§7975. "Kill" buttons for electrical equipment; procedures.

A "kill" button capable of cutting off all electrical equipment shall be maintained in any gassy tunnel or underground mine. The safety representative or his designated representative shall cut off power at any time gas or vapor levels reach 20 percent of the lower explosive limit or more. Before work is restarted every employee underground shall be informed of the level of gas or vapor recorded, and a permanent record shall be called to the surface and retained in a special log.

§7976. Fire extinguishers in gassy tunnels and mines.

In any tunnel or underground mine classified as gassy, the division shall determine the number of fire extinguishers necessary and their locations.

§7977. Extrahazardous tunnels and mines.

Any tunnel or underground mine classified as extrahazardous by the division shall comply with the provisions for gassy tunnels in this chapter, as well as regulations, rules, special orders, and general orders of the division or board.

§7978. Smoking or open flame in extrahazardous tunnel or mine; welding or cutting.

In any extrahazardous tunnel or underground mine smoking by employees or open flame shall be prohibited. Welding or cutting with arc or flame underground in other than fresh air shall be done under the direct supervision of qualified persons who shall test for gas and vapors before welding or cutting starts and continuously during such an operation. No cutting or welding shall be permitted in atmospheres where any concentration of gas or vapor reaches 20 percent of the lower explosive limit or more while a probe hole is being drilled or when the tunnel face or material from a mine is being excavated.

§7979. Air composition of extrahazardous tunnels and mines.

In tunnels or underground mines classified extrahazardous, sufficient air shall be supplied to maintain an atmosphere of all of the following conditions:

(a) Not less than 19 percent oxygen.

(b) Not more than 0.5 percent carbon dioxide.

(c) Not more than 5 parts per million nitrogen dioxide.

(d) No petroleum vapors or toxic gases in concentrations exceeding the threshold limit values established annually by the American Conference of Governmental Industrial Hygienists.

§7980. Equipment in extrahazardous tunnels and mines.

All electrical equipment and machines, including diesel engines, used in tunnels or underground mines classified extrahazardous shall be permissible equipment. The division may, however, permit the use of nonpermissive equipment in a tunnel or underground mine in areas where it finds there is no longer danger from gas or other hazards.

§7981. Escape chambers and routes; rescue equipment.

An escape chamber or alternate escape route shall be maintained within 5,000 feet of the tunnel face or areas being used to excavate material in an underground mine classified as gassy or extrahazardous. Workers shall be provided with emergency rescue equipment and trained in its use.

§7982. Employer's obligation to record air flow and air samples.

Records of air flow and air sample tests to assure compliance with required standards shall be maintained by the employer at the site of any tunnel or underground mine classified extrahazardous. Such records shall be made available to any division representative upon request.

§7983. Main fan lines.

The main fan line used for ventilation in any tunnel or underground mine classified extrahazardous shall contain a cutoff switch capable of halting all machinery underground automatically should the fan fail or its performance fall below minimum power needed to maintain a safe atmosphere.

§7984. Testing for gases or vapors using mechanical excavation.

In any tunnel or underground mine classified extrahazardous a device or devices which automatically and continuously test the atmosphere for gases or vapors shall be maintained. Such device or devices shall be placed as near the face or area of operation as practical, but never more than 50 feet from such point. The division shall determine if additional monitors are necessary and where they should be located. This requirement shall apply only to tunnels or underground mines where excavation of material is by mechanical means.

§7985. Testing device requirements; permissible levels.

All such testing device or devices shall be U.S. Bureau of Mines approved or acceptable to other authorities recognized by the division and shall automatically sound an alarm and activate flashing red signals visible to employees underground whenever the concentration of gases or vapors reaches or exceeds permissible levels. Permissible levels may be established lower than the limits set in division rules, regulations, or general orders whenever a division inspector considers such action necessary to make the operation safe for employees.

CHAPTER 3
LICENSING AND PENALTIES
[Selected Provisions]

§7990. Limitation on explosive use.

In any tunnel or mine under jurisdiction of the division, the use of explosives shall be limited to persons licensed by the division.

§7991. License to use explosives.

(a) To obtain a license under Section 7990, and to renew that license, a person shall pass an oral and written examination given by the division. The division shall offer the examination in Spanish, or any other language, when requested by the applicant. The division shall administer an examination orally when requested by an applicant who cannot write. Licenses shall be renewable every five years.

(b) The division shall set a nonrefundable fee for processing applications for licenses required by Section 7990 and a fee for administering examinations under this section. In fixing the amount of these fees, the division may include direct costs and a reasonable percentage attributable to the indirect costs of the division for administering this chapter. Those fees shall be deposited into the Occupational Safety and Health Fund. **Leg.H.** 1972 ch. 1430 §1, 1974 ch. 1284 §31, 2016 ch. 31 (SB 836) §226, effective June 27, 2016.

§7996. Acceptable safety equipment.

All safety equipment required to provide safe employment in tunnels or underground mines shall be U.S. Bureau of Mines approved, or acceptable to other authorities recognized by the division, and acceptable by the division.

§7997. General orders; review; update; suggested changes.

The board shall review and update general orders for tunnels and mines at least every two years. Representatives of the unit inspecting tunnels and mines shall be consulted during each review and shall be permitted to submit suggested changes to the general orders at any time.

UNEMPLOYMENT INSURANCE CODE
[Selected Provisions]

SYNOPSIS

DIVISION 1
UNEMPLOYMENT AND DISABILITY COMPENSATION

PART 1
Unemployment Compensation

CHAPTER 1
GENERAL PROVISIONS

ARTICLE 2
General Definitions
[Selected Provisions]

§128. "Benefits."
§140.5. "Unemployment compensation disability benefits."
§144. Contributions to Disability Fund.

CHAPTER 4
CONTRIBUTIONS AND REPORTS

ARTICLE 3
Contribution Rates
[Selected Provisions]

§984. Worker's contribution percentage.

CHAPTER 5
UNEMPLOYMENT COMPENSATION BENEFITS

ARTICLE 1
Eligibility and Disqualifications
[Selected Provisions]

§1255.5. Ineligibility when interim cash payments made.

ARTICLE 4
Overpayments
[Selected Provisions]

§1375.3. Liability for overpayment of benefits.

PART 2
Disability Compensation

CHAPTER 2
DISABILITY BENEFITS

ARTICLE 1
Eligibility
[Selected Provisions]

§2626. "Disability" or "disabled."
§2629. Eligibility while receiving specified "other benefits."
§2629.1. Determination of entitlement to workers' compensation benefits; notice; assessment of employer for liability; penalty.

ARTICLE 5
Overpayments
[Selected Provisions]

§2741. Satisfaction by payment of lien claim.

ARTICLE 7
Rights of Industrially Disabled Persons

§2775. Industrially disabled persons; rights.
§2776. "Industrially disabled person"; "industrial disability."
§2777. Determining quarters of base period.
§2778. Actions before disability; effect.

CHAPTER 2.4
NONINDUSTRIAL DISABILITY INSURANCE FOR STATE EMPLOYEES

§2781. State employees; eligibility for benefits.
§2782. Limitations on this chapter.
§2783. Payment; publishing information; records.

CHAPTER 6
VOLUNTARY PLANS

§3251. Voluntary plans.
§3252. Worker contributions.
§3253. Simultaneous voluntary plan and Disability Fund benefits.
§3254. Requirements for voluntary plan approval.
§3254.1. Approval of single voluntary plan for small-business-third-party administrator clients and employees; adoption of application forms and procedures.
§3254.5. Acquisition by other employing unit; effect.
§3255. Voluntary plans; several employers.
§3256. Deductions under §3255.
§3257. Establishment and coverage of voluntary plans.
§3258. Employer's surety required.
§3259. Substituted liability of insurer.
§3260. Deductions from employee wages.
§3260.5. Remittance of excess wage deductions to Disability Fund; assessments for noncompliance; increase in amount deducted.
§3261. Employee contributions treated as voluntary plan trust fund.
§3262. Termination of voluntary plan by director; remittance of moneys for deposit into Disability Fund; assessments for noncompliance; appeal.

§3263. Cessation of coverage; availability of benefits from Fund.
§3264. Appeal procedure when benefits under approved plan are denied.
§3265. Director's intercession on failure to pay.
§3266. Determination of credits and refunds.
§3267. Availability of information.
§3268. Director's obligation to furnish information.
§3269. Director's obligation to determine administrative costs.
§3270. Operative date for selection of risks.
§3271. Amendment of voluntary plans.
§3272. Applicability of specified article.

CHAPTER 7
PAID FAMILY LEAVE

§3300. Legislative findings and declarations.
§3301. Family temporary disability insurance program.
§3302. Definitions.
§3302.1. "Covered active duty" and "disability benefit period."
§3302.2. Qualifying exigency related to the covered active duty or call to covered active duty of the individual's spouse, domestic partner, child, or parent in the Armed Forces of the United States.
§3303. Individual eligibility.
§3303.1. Ineligibility under certain circumstances; taking of FMLA and CFRA leave concurrently; use of vacation leave.
§3304. Receiving benefits under this division.
§3305. Penalty for false certification of medical condition.
§3306. Director may request additional evidence; care recipient to submit to examinations to determine care provider's participation.
§3307. Information in support of request for leave because of qualifying exigency.
§3308. Application for family temporary disability insurance benefits; mandatory languages [Operative January 1, 2025].

SELECTED PROVISIONS Of The UNEMPLOYMENT INSURANCE CODE

DIVISION 1 UNEMPLOYMENT AND DISABILITY COMPENSATION

PART 1 Unemployment Compensation

CHAPTER 1 GENERAL PROVISIONS

ARTICLE 2 General Definitions [Selected Provisions]

§128. "Benefits."

"Benefits" means the money payments payable to an individual, pursuant to this division, with respect to his unemployment and includes unemployment compensation benefits, federal-state extended benefits, or extended duration benefits, or disability benefits, or all of them.

§140.5. "Unemployment compensation disability benefits."

"Unemployment compensation disability benefits" or "disability benefits" refers to money payments payable under Part 2 (commencing with Section 2601) to either of the following:

(a) An eligible unemployed individual with respect to his or her wage losses due to unemployment as a result of illness or other disability, resulting in that individual being unavailable or unable to work.

(b) An eligible individual with respect to his or her wage losses who is unable to work due to caring for a seriously ill or injured family member or bonding with a minor child within one year of the birth or placement of the child in connection with foster care or adoption. **Leg.H.** 2003 ch. 797 (SB 727).

2003 Note: This act shall become operative on January 1, 2004, except that benefits shall be payable for family temporary disability insurance claims commencing on or after July 1, 2004. Stats. 2003 ch. 797 (SB 727) §28.

§144. Contributions to Disability Fund.

"Worker contributions," "contributions by workers," "employee contributions," or "contributions by employees" mean contributions to the Disability Fund.

CHAPTER 4 CONTRIBUTIONS AND REPORTS

ARTICLE 3 Contribution Rates [Selected Provisions]

§984. Worker's contribution percentage.

(a)(1) Each worker shall pay worker contributions at the rate determined by the director pursuant to this section with respect to wages, as defined by Sections 926, 927, and 985. On or before October 31 of each calendar year, the director shall prepare a statement, which shall be a public record, declaring the rate of worker contributions for the calendar year and shall notify promptly all employers of employees covered for disability insurance of the rate.

(2)(A) Except as provided in paragraph (3), the rate of worker contributions for calendar year 1987 and for each subsequent calendar year shall be 1.30 times the amount disbursed from the Disability Fund during the 12-month period ending September 30 and immediately preceding the calendar year for which the rate is to be effective, less the amount in the Disability Fund on that September 30, with the resulting figure divided by total wages paid pursuant to Sections 926, 927, and 985 during the same 12-month period, and then rounded to the nearest one-tenth of 1 percent.

(B) The director shall increase the rate of worker contributions by .08 percent for the 2004 and 2005 calendar

Unemployment Ins.

years to cover the initial cost of family temporary disability insurance benefits provided in Chapter 7 (commencing with Section 3300) of Part 2.

(3) The rate of worker contributions shall not exceed 1.5 percent or be less than 0.1 percent. The rate of worker contributions shall not decrease from the rate in the previous year by more than two-tenths of 1 percent.

(b) Worker contributions required under Sections 708 and 708.5 shall be at a rate determined by the director to reimburse the Disability Fund for unemployment compensation disability benefits paid and estimated to be paid to all employers and self-employed individuals covered by those sections. On or before November 30th of each calendar year, the director shall prepare a statement, which shall be a public record, declaring the rate of contributions for the succeeding calendar year for all employers and self-employed individuals covered under Sections 708 and 708.5 and shall notify promptly the employers and self-employed individuals of the rate. The rate shall be determined by dividing the estimated benefits and administrative costs paid in the prior year by the product of the annual remuneration deemed to have been received under Sections 708 and 708.5 and the estimated number of persons who were covered at any time in the prior year. The resulting rate shall be rounded to the next higher one-hundredth percentage point. The rate may also be reduced or increased by a factor estimated to maintain as nearly as practicable a cumulative zero balance in the funds contributed pursuant to Sections 708 and 708.5. Estimates made pursuant to this subdivision may be made on the basis of statistical sampling, or another method determined by the director.

(c) The director's action in determining a rate under this section shall not constitute an authorized regulation.

(d)(1) Notwithstanding subdivision (a), and except as provided in paragraph (2), the director may, at the director's discretion, increase or decrease, by not to exceed 0.1 percent, the rate of worker contributions determined pursuant to subdivision (a), up to a maximum worker contribution rate of 1.5 percent, if the director determines the adjustment is necessary to reimburse the Disability Fund for disability benefits paid or estimated to be paid to individuals covered by this section or to prevent the accumulation of funds in excess of those needed to maintain an adequate fund balance.

(2) Notwithstanding paragraph (1), for the 2004, 2005, and 2006 calendar years, the director may not decrease the rate of worker contributions, regardless of whether the director determines that a decrease is necessary to prevent the accumulation of funds in excess of those needed to maintain the adequacy of the Disability Fund during program implementation.

(e) The amendment to this section by the act adding this subdivision shall become operative on July 1, 2019. **Leg.H.** 1991 ch. 793 §1, 1993 chs. 747, 748, 2002 ch. 901 (SB 1661), operative January 1, 2004, 2003 ch. 797 (SB 727), 2019 ch. 24 (SB 83) §35, effective June 27, 2019, operative July 1, 2019.

2003 Note: This act shall become operative on January 1, 2004, except that benefits shall be payable for family temporary disability insurance claims commencing on or after July 1, 2004. Stats. 2003 ch. 797 (SB 727) §28.

2002 Note: This act shall become operative on January 1, 2004, except that benefits shall be payable for periods of family temporary disability leave commencing on or after July 1, 2004. Stats. 2002 ch. 901 §7.

CHAPTER 5 UNEMPLOYMENT COMPENSATION BENEFITS

ARTICLE 1 Eligibility and Disqualifications [Selected Provisions]

§1255.5. Ineligibility when interim cash payments made.

(a) An individual is not eligible for unemployment compensation benefits or extended duration benefits for the same day or days of unemployment for which he is allowed by the Workmen's Compensation Appeals Board, or for which he receives, benefits in the form of cash payments for temporary total disability indemnity, under a workmen's compensation law, or employer's liability law of this state, or of any other state, or of the federal government, except that if such cash payments are less than the amount he would otherwise receive as unemployment compensation benefits or extended duration benefits under this division, he shall be entitled to receive for such day or days, if otherwise eligible, unemployment compensation benefits or extended duration benefits reduced by the amount of such cash payments.

(b) Notwithstanding any other provision of this division, an individual who is ineligible to receive unemployment compensation benefits or extended duration benefits under subdivision (a) of this section for one or more days of a week of unemployment and who is eligible to receive unemployment compensation benefits or extended duration benefits for the other days of that week is, with respect to that week, entitled to an amount of unemployment compensation benefits or extended duration benefits computed by reducing his weekly benefit amount by the amount of temporary total disability indemnity received for that week.

(c) The amount determined under subdivision (a) or (b), if not a multiple of one dollar ($1), shall be computed to the next higher multiple of one dollar ($1).

ARTICLE 4 Overpayments [Selected Provisions]

§1375.3. Liability for overpayment of benefits.

No determination of overpayment shall be based upon the disallowance by the Workmen's Compensation Appeals Board of a claim of lien filed under subdivision (g) of Section 4903 of the Labor Code, or the allowance of such lien for less than the amount claimed as a lien, or upon the approval by the said appeals board of a compromise and release agreement providing for the allowance of such lien in an amount less than the amount claimed as a lien.

PART 2
Disability Compensation

CHAPTER 2
DISABILITY BENEFITS

ARTICLE 1
Eligibility
[Selected Provisions]

§2626. "Disability" or "disabled."

(a) An individual shall be deemed disabled on any day in which, because of his or her physical or mental condition, he or she is unable to perform his or her regular or customary work.

(b) For purposes of this section, "disability" or "disabled" includes:

(1) Illness or injury, whether physical or mental, including any illness or injury resulting from pregnancy, childbirth, or related medical condition.

(2) Inability to work because of a written order from a state or local health officer to an individual infected with, or suspected of being infected with, a communicable disease.

(3) Acute alcoholism being medically treated or, to the extent specified in Section 2626.1, resident status in an alcoholic recovery home.

(4) Acute drug-induced illness being medically treated or, to the extent specified in Section 2626.2, resident status in a drug-free residential facility. **Leg.H.** 1993 ch. 748, 2010 ch. 392 (AB 2538) §5.

§2629. Eligibility while receiving specified "other benefits."

(a) Except as provided in this section, an individual is not eligible for disability benefits under this part for any day of unemployment and disability for which he or she has received, or is entitled to receive, "other benefits" in the form of cash payments.

(b) "Other benefits," as used in this section and Section 2629.1, means any of the following:

(1) Temporary disability indemnity under a workers' compensation law of this state or of any other state or of the federal government.

(2) Temporary disability benefits under any employer's liability law of this state or of any other state or of the federal government.

(3) Permanent disability benefits for the same injury or illness under the workers' compensation law of this state, any other state, or the federal government.

(c) If these "other benefits" are less than the amount an individual would otherwise receive as disability benefits under this part, he or she shall be entitled to receive, for that day, if otherwise eligible, disability benefits under this part reduced by the amount of these "other benefits."

(d) An individual shall be entitled to receive, for any day, if otherwise eligible, disability benefits under this part reduced by the amount of the permanent disability indemnity if the permanent disability indemnity is less than the amount an individual would otherwise receive as disability benefits under this part. **Leg.H.** 1953, 1957 ch. 1977 §6 p. 3526, 1972 ch. 833 §11, 1973 ch. 86 §2, effective June 12, 1973, 1980 ch. 1040 §2, 1989 ch. 1280 §3, 1990 ch. 1550 §64 (AB 2910), 1993 ch. 748 §8 (SB 4), 2010 ch. 392 (AB 2538) §6.

§2629.1. Determination of entitlement to workers' compensation benefits; notice; assessment of employer for liability; penalty.

(a) Nothing in Section 2629 shall be construed to authorize the delay of payment of unemployment compensation disability benefits except where the claimant is currently in receipt of other benefits or where the department has received notice that the claimant's employer or insurer has agreed to commence the payment of other benefits.

(b) Notwithstanding Section 2701.5, payments shall commence within 14 days after notice to the employer or insurer under this section unless the employer or insurer has either paid or has agreed to commence the payment of other benefits.

(c) Upon the filing of a claim for unemployment compensation disability benefits, the department shall make an initial determination as to the claimant's entitlement to other benefits for purposes of Section 2629.

(1) The department shall notify the claimant and the claimant's employer if it determines that the claimant is entitled to other benefits.

(2) The notice to the claimant shall inform the claimant that disability benefits will be paid pending receipt of other benefits if the employer fails to agree to pay these other benefits within 14 days of notification of industrial injury and shall advise the claimant of the provisions of Section 2629.

(3) The department shall also include with the claimant's notice a pamphlet to be provided by the Department of Industrial Relations which meets the criteria specified in subdivision (b) of Section 139.6 of the Labor Code.

(4) The notice to the employer shall constitute a claim for compensation and knowledge of an injury for purposes of Section 5402 of the Labor Code, and shall inform the employer of its potential liability for interest and penalties under this section.

(d) If the employer or the insurance carrier disputes liability for the payment of other benefits, or the extent thereof, the department's right to reimbursement shall be subject to the jurisdiction of the Workers' Compensation Appeals Board in accordance with Part 4 (commencing with Section 5300) of Division 4 of the Labor Code.

(e) An employer or insurance carrier who subsequently assumes liability or is determined to be liable for reimbursement to the department for unemployment compensation disability benefits which the department has paid in lieu of other benefits shall be assessed for this liability by the department. In addition, the employer shall pay the department interest on the disability benefits at the annual rate provided in Section 19521 of the Revenue and Taxation Code. The employer shall also pay a penalty of 10 percent of the amount reimbursed to the department if the Workers' Compensation Appeals Board finds that the failure of the employer to pay other benefits upon notice by the department under this section was unreasonable and a penalty has not been awarded for the delay under Section 5814 of the Labor Code. All funds received by the department pursuant to this section shall be deposited in the Disability Fund.

(f) The employer shall reimburse the department in accordance with subdivision (e) within 60 days of either voluntarily accepting liability for other benefits or after a final award, order, or decision of the Workers' Compensation Appeals Board. **Leg.H.** 1989 ch. 1280 §5, 1993 ch. 877 §95 (SB 673), effective October 6, 1993, operative January 1, 1994.

ARTICLE 5
Overpayments
[Selected Provisions]

§2741. Satisfaction by payment of lien claim.

Any claim of lien filed with the Workers' Compensation Appeals Board under the provisions of Section 4903 of the Labor Code shall be fully discharged and satisfied by payment of the amount of such lien allowed by the said appeals board under the provisions of Section 4904 of said code or the amount specified in any compromise and release agreement filed and approved by the said appeals board pursuant to Sections 5000 through 5004 of said code.

ARTICLE 7
Rights of Industrially Disabled Persons

§2775. Industrially disabled persons; rights.

Notwithstanding any inconsistent provisions of this part, the benefit rights of industrially disabled persons shall be determined in accordance with the provisions of this article for the period and with respect to the matters specified in this article. Except as otherwise provided in this article, all of the provisions of this part shall continue to be applicable in connection with such benefits.

§2776. "Industrially disabled person"; "industrial disability."

As used in this article:

(a) "Industrially disabled person" means an individual who has received or is entitled to receive benefits under Division 4 (commencing with Section 3201) of the Labor Code, and who is unable to perform his regular or customary work for 60 consecutive days or more, but not to exceed two calendar years from the date of commencement of his industrial disability.

(b) "Industrial disability" means a disability compensable under Division 4 (commencing with Section 3201) of the Labor Code.

§2777. Determining quarters of base period.

Except as provided in subdivision (b) of Section 2611, in determining the benefit rights of any industrially disabled person the disability base period shall exclude those quarters during which such person was industrially disabled for 60 days or more. For all quarters so excluded there shall be substituted an equal number of quarters immediately preceding the commencement of his or her industrial disability. In the event the base period so determined includes wages in calendar quarters for which the records have been destroyed under proper approval, a claimant may establish the amount of wages by affidavit in accordance with authorized regulations. The quarter of commencement of an industrial disability shall be counted as a completed quarter if the director finds that the inclusion thereof would be more equitable to the industrially disabled person.

§2778. Actions before disability; effect.

No disqualification shall be applied to any industrially disabled person after the termination of his industrial disability, by reason of any act or course of action on his part prior to the date on which his industrial disability commenced.

CHAPTER 2.4
NONINDUSTRIAL DISABILITY INSURANCE FOR STATE EMPLOYEES

§2781. State employees; eligibility for benefits.

Except as provided in this chapter and Chapter 2.5 (commencing with Section 19878) of Part 2.6 of Division 5 of Title 2 of the Government Code, a state employee shall be eligible for nonindustrial disability benefits on the same terms and conditions as are specified by this part. Except as inconsistent with the provisions of this chapter and Chapter 2.6 (commencing with Section 19878) of Part 2.6 of Division 5 of Title 2 of the Government Code, the provisions of this division and authorized regulations shall apply to any matter arising pursuant to this chapter. **Leg.H.** 1976 ch. 341 §14, effective July 7, 1976, operative July 1, 1976, 2005 ch. 152 (AB 1577) §26.

§2782. Limitations on this chapter.

(a) The provisions of Chapter 4 (commencing with Section 2901), Chapter 5 (commencing with Section 3001), and Chapter 6 (commencing with Section 3251) of Part 2 do not apply to this chapter.

(b) The provisions of Article 2 (commencing with Section 2652), Article 6 (commencing with Section 2765) and Article 7 (commencing with Section 2775) of Chapter 2 of Part 2 do not apply to this chapter.

(c) Sections 2609, 2610, 2611, 2625, 2712, and 2712.5 do not apply to this chapter.

§2783. Payment; publishing information; records.

(a) Nonindustrial disability benefits are payable by the Controller upon authorization by the Employment Development Department to individuals who are eligible to receive such benefit payments under this chapter.

(b) In lieu of the contributions required of employees, the State of California shall pay into the Disability Fund in the State Treasury at the times and in the manner provided in subdivision (c), an amount equal to the additional cost to the Disability Fund for added administrative work arising out of nonindustrial disability insurance for state employees.

(c) In making the payments prescribed by subdivision (b), there shall be paid or credited to the Disability Fund, either in advance or by way of reimbursement, as may be determined by the director, such sums as he estimates the Disability Fund will be entitled to receive from the State of California under this section for each fiscal year, reduced or increased by any sum by which he finds that his estimates for any prior fiscal year were greater or less than the amounts which should have been paid to the fund. Such estimates may be made upon the basis of statistical sampling, or other method as may be determined by the director.

Upon making such determination, the director shall certify to the Controller the amount determined with respect to the State of California. The Controller shall pay to the Disability Fund the contributions due from the State of California.

(d) The director may require from each state agency such employment, wage, financial, statistical, or other information and reports, properly verified, as may be deemed necessary by the director to carry out his duties under this chapter, which shall be filed with the director at the time and in the manner prescribed by him.

(e) The director may tabulate and publish information obtained pursuant to this chapter in statistical form and may divulge the name of the employing unit.

(f) Each state agency shall keep such work records as may be prescribed by the director for the proper administration of this chapter.

CHAPTER 6 VOLUNTARY PLANS

§3251. Voluntary plans.

An employer, a majority of the employees employed in this state of an employer, or both, may apply to the Director of Employment Development for approval of a voluntary plan for the payment of disability benefits to the employees so electing. The benefits payable as indemnification for loss of wages under any voluntary plan shall be separately stated and designated in the plan "unemployment compensation disability benefits" separate and distinct from other benefits, if any.

§3252. Worker contributions.

(a) Except as provided by subdivision (b) of this section, neither an employee nor his or her employer shall be liable for the worker contributions required under this division with respect to wages paid by the employer while the employee is covered by an approved voluntary plan.

(b) Each voluntary plan shall pay to the department for the Disability Fund 14 percent of the product obtained by multiplying the rate of worker contributions, as determined in Section 984, by the amount of the taxable wages paid to employees covered by the voluntary plan for disability benefit coverage for each calendar year. Such payments shall not constitute a part of the voluntary plan premium for purposes of any tax under any provision of law. Payments under this section shall be deposited in the Disability Fund.

(c) The payments made under subdivision (b) of this section in excess of the credit to the unemployed disabled account made pursuant to Section 3012 shall reimburse the Disability Fund for the amounts paid for administrative costs arising out of voluntary plans as determined pursuant to Section 3269, and the aggregate amount paid as refunds and credits made to employees applicable to voluntary plans pursuant to Section 1176 as determined pursuant to Section 3266.

(d) Each voluntary plan shall file with the director within the time required for payments under subdivision (e) of this section, a return containing the employer's business name, address, and account number, and such other information as the director shall prescribe. The director shall prescribe the form for the return.

(e) Payments required under this section are due and payable on the first day of the calendar month following the close of each calendar quarter and shall become delinquent if not paid on or before the last day of such month.

(f) The provisions of Article 8 (commencing with Section 1126) of Chapter 4 of Part 1 of this division with respect to the assessment of contributions and the provisions of Chapter 7 (commencing with Section 1701) of Part 1 of this division with respect to the collection of contributions shall apply to payments required by this section.

(g) Whenever the director believes that a change in the percentage rate of payment specified in subdivision (b) may be necessary, he or she shall inform the Governor and the Legislature thereof and make recommendations accordingly.

§3253. Simultaneous voluntary plan and Disability Fund benefits.

Except as provided in this part, an employee covered by an approved voluntary plan at the commencement of a disability benefit period shall not be entitled to benefits from the Disability Fund. Benefits payable to that employee shall be the liability of the approved voluntary plan under which the employee was covered at the commencement of the disability benefit period, regardless of any subsequent disabling condition which may occur during that disability benefit period. The Director of Employment Development shall prescribe authorized regulations to allow benefits to individuals simultaneously covered by one or more approved voluntary plans and the Disability Fund. **Leg.H.** 2003 ch. 797 (SB 727).

2003 Note: This act shall become operative on January 1, 2004, except that benefits shall be payable for family temporary disability insurance claims commencing on or after July 1, 2004. Stats. 2003 ch. 797 (SB 727) §28.

§3254. Requirements for voluntary plan approval.

The Director of Employment Development shall approve any voluntary plan, except one filed pursuant to Section 3255, as to which he or she finds that there is at least one employee in employment and all of the following exist:

(a) The rights afforded to the covered employees are greater than those provided for in Chapter 2 (commencing with Section 2625), including those provided for in Chapter 7 (commencing with Section 3300).

(b) The plan has been made available to all of the employees of the employer employed in this state or to all employees at any one distinct, separate establishment maintained by the employer in this state. "Employees" as used in this subdivision includes those individuals in partial or other forms of short-time employment and employees not in employment as the Director of Employment Development shall prescribe by authorized regulations.

(c) A majority of the employees of the employer employed in this state or a majority of the employees employed at any one distinct, separate establishment maintained by the employer in this state have consented to the plan.

(d) If the plan provides for insurance the form of the insurance policies to be issued have been approved by the Insurance Commissioner and are to be issued by an admitted disability insurer.

(e) The employer has consented to the plan and has agreed to make the payroll deductions required, if any, and transmit the proceeds to the plan insurer, if any.

(f) The plan provides for the inclusion of future employees.

(g) The plan will be in effect for a period of not less than one year and, thereafter, continuously unless the Director of Employment Development finds that the employer or a majority of its employees employed in this state covered by the plan have given notice of withdrawal from the plan. The notice shall be filed in writing with the Director of Employment Development and shall be effective only on the anniversary of the effective date of the plan next following the filing of the notice, but in any event not less than 30 days from the time of the filing of the notice; except that the plan may be withdrawn on the operative date of any law increasing the benefit amounts provided by Sections 2653 and 2655 or the operative date of any change in the rate of worker contributions as determined by Section 984, if notice of the withdrawal from the plan is transmitted to the Director of Employment Development not less than 30 days prior to the operative date of that law or change. If the plan is not withdrawn on the 30 days' notice because of the enactment of a law increasing benefits or because of a change in the rate of worker contributions as determined by Section 984, the plan shall be amended to conform to that increase or change on the operative date of the increase or change.

(h) The amount of deductions from the wages of an employee in effect for any plan shall not be increased on other than an anniversary of the effective date of the plan except to the extent that any increase in the deductions from the wages of an employee allowed by Section 3260 permits that amount to exceed the amount of deductions in effect.

(i) The approval of the plan or plans will not result in a substantial selection of risks adverse to the Disability Fund. **Leg.H.** 2002 chs. 52 (SB 467), 901 (SB 1661), operative January 1, 2004, 2003 ch. 797 (SB 727).

2003 Note: This act shall become operative on January 1, 2004, except that benefits shall be payable for family temporary disability insurance claims commencing on or after July 1, 2004. Stats. 2003 ch. 797 (SB 727) §28.

2002 Note: This act shall become operative on January 1, 2004, except that benefits shall be payable for periods of family temporary disability leave commencing on or after July 1, 2004. Stats. 2002 ch. 901 §7.

§3254.1. Approval of single voluntary plan for small-business-third-party administrator clients and employees; adoption of application forms and procedures.

(a) For the purposes of this section, "small-business-third-party administrator" (hereafter SBTPA), means an applicant that the director finds meets all of the following criteria at the time of application:

(1) The SBTPA administers voluntary disability plans on behalf of its clients pursuant to a written agreement in a form and manner approved by the director.

(2) The SBTPA has at least 1,000 California domiciled clients, 80 percent of whom have fewer than 20 employees.

(3) The SBTPA processes payroll for its California domiciled clients.

(4) The SBTPA offers workers' compensation insurance to its California domiciled clients through an affiliated California domiciled insurance company.

(b) Except as modified by this section, "voluntary plan" shall be defined as, and shall be subject to the same provisions as, a "voluntary plan," as set forth in this chapter.

(c) The director may approve a single voluntary plan for all of an SBTPA's clients and their employees where all of the following criteria are met:

(1) The plan is administered by the SBTPA.

(2) The plan establishes a master trust account that is administered by the SBTPA, and requires the SBTPA to maintain a separate accounting ledger for each individual employer that is a client of the SBTPA to reflect each client's specific plan contributions. The master trust account shall be held in a federally insured bank.

(3) If the plan does not provide for the assumption by an admitted disability insurer of the liability of the employer to pay the benefits afforded by the plan, the director shall not approve it unless the SBTPA meets the financial security requirements of Section 3258 on behalf of the SBTPA clients and their employees.

(4)(A) The single voluntary plan will be in effect for a period of not less than one year and, thereafter, continuously, unless the Director of Employment Development finds that the SBTPA has given notice of withdrawal of the plan. The notice filed by the SBTPA shall be filed in writing with the Director of Employment Development and shall be effective on the anniversary of the effective date of the plan next following the filing of the notice, but in any event shall not be less than 30 days from the time of the filing of the notice; except that the plan may be withdrawn on the operative date of any law increasing the benefit amounts provided by Sections 2653 and 2655 or the operative date of any change in the rate of worker contributions as determined by Section 984, if notice of the withdrawal from the plan is transmitted to the Director of Employment

Development not less than 30 days prior to the operative date of that law or change. If the plan is not withdrawn on the 30 days' notice because of the enactment of a law increasing benefits or because of a change in the rate of worker contributions as determined by Section 984, the plan shall be amended to conform to that increase or change on the operative date of the increase or change.

(B) Any individual employer who is a client of the SBTPA, or a majority of that client's employees employed in this state covered by the plan, may also terminate their participation in the plan by giving written notice of withdrawal from the plan to the SBTPA and to the Director of Employment Development not less than 30 days prior to the date of withdrawal.

(C) The Director of Employment Development may terminate the participation of an individual employer client of the SBTPA from the plan for cause, and the employer's voluntary plan assets shall be recovered from the SBTPA and not from the employer as referenced in Section 3262.

(5) The rights afforded to the covered employees are greater than those provided for in Chapter 2 (commencing with Section 2625), including those provided for in Chapter 7 (commencing with Section 3300).

(6) The plan has been made available to all of the employees of the employer employed in this state or to all employees at any one distinct, separate establishment maintained by the employer in this state. "Employees" as used in this paragraph includes those individuals in partial or other forms of short-time employment and employees not in employment as the director shall prescribe by authorized regulations.

(7) A majority of the employees of the client employed in this state or a majority of the employees employed at any one distinct, separate establishment maintained by the client in this state have consented to the plan.

(8) If the plan provides for insurance, the form of the insurance policies to be issued has been approved by the Insurance Commissioner and is to be issued by an admitted disability insurer.

(9) The client has consented to the plan and has authorized the SBTPA to make the payroll deductions required, if any, and deposit the proceeds into the master account administered by the SBTPA as referenced in paragraph (2).

(10) The plan provides for the inclusion of future employees.

(11) The amount of deductions from the wages of an employee of any client in effect for the plan shall not be increased on other than an anniversary of the effective date of the plan except to the extent that any increase in the deductions from the wages of an employee allowed by Section 3260 permits that amount to exceed the amount of deductions in effect.

(12) The approval of the plan or plans will not result in a substantial selection of risks adverse to the Disability Fund.

(d) The department may adopt application forms and procedures as deemed necessary to ensure compliance with this section.

(e) It is the intent of the Legislature in enacting paragraph (3) of subdivision (c) that, in the event of the insolvency of an employer-client of the SBTPA, or of the SBTPA, the disability claims against the subaccount of any employer-client arising prior to the date of the insolvency shall be satisfied by first accessing the security of the SBTPA, as described in paragraph (3) of subdivision (c), rather than satisfying the claims from the Disability Fund. **Leg.H.** 2010 ch. 399 (AB 2778) §2, 2014 ch. 150 (AB 2733) §1, effective July 18, 2014.

§3254.5. Acquisition by other employing unit; effect.

A voluntary plan in force and effect at the time a successor employing unit acquires the organization, trade, or business, or substantially all the assets thereof, or a distinct and severable portion of the organization, trade, or business, and continues its operation without substantial reduction of personnel resulting from the acquisition, shall not withdraw without specific request for withdrawal thereof. The successor employing unit and the insurer shall be deemed to have consented to the provisions of the plan unless written request for withdrawal, effective as of the date of acquisition, is transmitted to the Director of Employment Development, by the employer or the insurer, within 30 days after the acquisition date, or within 30 days after notification from the Director of Employment Development that the plan is to continue, whichever is later. Unless the plan is withdrawn as of the date of acquisition by the successor employer or the insurer, a written request for withdrawal shall be effective only on the anniversary of the effective date of the plan next occurring on or after the date of acquisition, except that the plan may be withdrawn on the operative date of any law increasing the benefit amounts provided by Sections 2653 and 2655 or the operative date of any change in the rate of worker contributions as determined by Section 984, if notice of the withdrawal of the plan is transmitted to the Director of Employment Development not less than 30 days prior to the operative date of law or change. If the plan is not withdrawn on 30 days' notice because of the enactment of a law increasing benefits or because of a change in the rate of worker contributions as determined by Section 984, the plan shall be amended to conform to the increase or change on the operative date of the increase or change. Promptly, upon notice of change in ownership, any insurer of a plan shall prepare and issue policy forms and amendments as required, unless the plan is withdrawn. Nothing contained in this section shall prevent future withdrawal of any plans on an anniversary of the effective date of the plan upon 30 days' notice, except that the plan may be withdrawn on the operative date of any law increasing the benefit amounts provided by Sections 2653 and 2655 or the operative date of any change in the rate of worker contributions as determined by Section 984, if notice of the withdrawal of the plan is transmitted to the Director of Employment Development not less than 30 days prior to the operative date of the law or change. If the plan is not withdrawn on 30 days' notice because of the enactment of a law increasing benefits or because of a change in the rate of worker contributions as determined by Section 984, the plan shall be amended to conform to the increase or change on the operative date of the increase or change. **Leg.H.** 1957 ch. 2107 §9, operative January 1, 1958, 1961 ch. 1905 §2, operative January 1, 1962, 1963 ch. 1864 §1.5, 1973 ch. 1212 §275, operative July 1, 1974, 1977 ch. 1143 §12,

1980 ch. 1308 §5, 2005 ch. 152 (AB 1577) §27, 2006 ch. 538 (SB 1852) §647.

§3255. Voluntary plans; several employers.

When workers are engaged in an employment that normally involves working for several employers in the same industry interchangeably, and several employers or some of them cooperate to establish a plan for the payment of wages at a central place or places, and have appointed an agent under Section 1096, that agent, or a majority of workers regularly paid through a central place or places, or both, may apply to the Director of Employment Development for approval of a voluntary plan for the payment of disability benefits applicable to all employees whose wages are paid at one or more central place or places. The Director of Employment Development shall approve any voluntary plan under this section as to which he or she finds that all of the following exist:

(a) The rights afforded to the covered employees are greater than those provided for in Chapter 2 (commencing with Section 2625) of this part, and are separately stated and designated "unemployment compensation disability benefits" separate and distinct from other benefits, if any.

(b) The plan applies to all employees whose wages are paid at a central place or places with respect to all employment for which wages are paid at central place or places.

(c) Seventy-five percent of the workers regularly paid at the central place or places have consented to the plan prior to the filing of the initial application for approval.

(d) If the plan provides for insurance the form of the insurance policies to be issued have been approved by the Insurance Commissioner and are to be issued by an admitted disability insurer.

(e) All employers paying wages through the central place or places have agreed to participate in the plan and the agent appointed under Section 1096 has agreed to make the payroll deductions required, if any, and transmit the proceeds to the plan insurer, if any.

(f) The plan provides for the inclusion of all future employees paid at the central place or places.

(g) The plan is to be in effect for a period of not less than one year and, thereafter, continuously unless the Director of Employment Development finds that the agent or a majority of the employees regularly paid at the central place or places has given written notice of withdrawal from the plan. The notice shall be filed in writing with the Director of Employment Development at least 30 days before it is to become effective and, upon the filing, will be effective only as to wages paid after the beginning of the calendar quarter next occurring on or after the anniversary of the effective date of the plan; except that the plan may be withdrawn on the operative date of any law increasing the benefit amounts provided by Sections 2653 and 2655 or the operative date of any change in the rate of worker contributions as determined by Section 984, if notice of the withdrawal from the plan is transmitted to the Director of Employment Development not less than 30 days prior to the operative date of that law or change. If the plan is not withdrawn on 30 days' notice because of the enactment of a law increasing benefits or because of a change in the rate of worker contributions as determined by Section 984, the plan shall be amended to conform to that increase or change on the operative date of the increase or change.

(h) The amount of deductions from the wages of an employee in effect for any plan shall not be increased on other than an anniversary of the effective date of the plan except to the extent that any increase in the deductions from the wages of an employee allowed by Section 3260 permits that amount to exceed the amount of deductions in effect.

(i) The approval of the plan or plans will not result in a substantial selection of risks adverse to the Disability Fund. **Leg.H.** 2002 ch. 52 (SB 467).

§3256. Deductions under §3255.

During the effective period of a plan approved under Section 3255 the employer, or his agent appointed under Section 1096, may make the pay roll deductions provided for by the plan, with respect to all employment covered by the plan.

§3257. Establishment and coverage of voluntary plans.

Whenever eighty-five percent (85%) of the employees to whom a plan is available have consented to the plan, the employer, or seventy-five percent (75%) of the employees who have consented to the plan, or both, may elect to make the plan applicable to all employees to whom it is available, except those who reject the plan. In such case, there shall be filed with the Director of Employment Development a notice stating that the requisite percentage of employees has consented to the plan and fixing the date upon which the plan will become applicable to all employees to whom it is available. At least 10 days before the date fixed in the notice, a notice shall be posted and circulated in a manner reasonably calculated to bring it to the attention of all employees to whom the plan is available but who have not consented thereto. The notice to such employees shall set forth the date the plan is to become applicable and the manner in which an employee may reject it.

From the time fixed in the notice filed with the Director of Employment Development all employees to whom the plan is available shall be deemed to have elected to be covered by the plan, except those who advise the employer in writing of their rejection within the time fixed.

Every person employed after the date the plan becomes applicable and to whom the plan is available, shall be deemed to have elected to be covered by the plan from the time of employment unless he rejects the plan prior to or at the time of employment. Each employee at the time of employment shall be given a written notice specifying his right to consent to or to reject such plan and a written statement setting forth the essential features of the plan.

Any employee covered by a plan may withdraw from the plan as of the beginning of any calendar quarter upon giving reasonable notice in writing directed to the employer.

The form of the statement and the forms of the notices required under this Section shall be approved by the Director of Employment Development.

§3258. Employer's surety required.

If a voluntary plan does not provide for the assumption by an admitted disability insurer of the liability of the employer to pay the benefits afforded by the plan, the director shall not approve it unless the employer files with the director the bond of an admitted surety insurer conditioned on the payment by the employer of its obligations under the plan, deposits with the director securities approved by the director to secure the payment of the obligations, or deposits with the director an irrevocable letter of credit. The penal sum of the bond or the amount of the deposit of securities or letter of credit shall be determined by the director and shall be not less than the product obtained by multiplying the rate of worker contributions in the ensuing year, as determined in Section 984, by 0.5 of the estimated taxable wages prescribed by Section 985 to be paid to the employees for the ensuing year. Upon approval, the bond, money, or securities shall upon the director's written order be deposited with the Treasurer for the purpose specified in this section. The Treasurer shall give a receipt for the deposits and the state shall be responsible for the custody and safe return of any securities so deposited. **Leg.H.** 1994 ch. 960, operative May 31, 1995.

§3259. Substituted liability of insurer.

Whenever an approved voluntary plan is insured by an admitted disability insurer, the insurer shall be substituted for the employer with respect to any assessments under this part which relate to the portion of the voluntary plan insured by such insurer.

§3260. Deductions from employee wages.

An employer may, but need not, assume all or part of the cost of the plan, and may deduct from the wages of an employee covered by the plan, for the purpose of providing the disability benefits specified in this part, an amount not in excess of that which would be required by Sections 984 and 985 if the employee were not covered by the plan. **Leg.H.** 2002 ch. 52 (SB 467).

§3260.5. Remittance of excess wage deductions to Disability Fund; assessments for noncompliance; increase in amount deducted.

(a) All deductions from the wages of an employee remaining in the possession of the employer upon its voluntary withdrawal of the plan as a result of plan contributions being in excess of plan costs, that are not disposed of in conformity with authorized regulations of the Director of Employment Development, shall be remitted to the department and deposited in the Disability Fund. If an employer fails to remit any deductions to the Disability Fund, the Director of Employment Development shall assess the amount thereof against the employer.

(b) The provisions of Article 8 (commencing with Section 1126) of Chapter 4 of Part 1, with respect to the assessment of contributions, and the provisions of Chapter 7 (commencing with Section 1701) of Part 1, with respect to the collection of contributions, shall apply to assessments provided by this section, except that interest may not accrue until 30 days after issuance of the notice of assessment.

(c) With respect to individuals covered by a voluntary plan on January 1 of any calendar year for which the limitation on wages under Section 985 is increased or the tax rate under Section 984 is increased, the amount of the deduction on or after that date may be increased to apply to not more than the maximum limitation on taxable wages or to not more than the maximum tax rate, as applicable, without any further consent of the individual or approval of the Director of Employment Development, but only if such increase in the amount of the deductions is made effective as of January 1 of the affected calendar year. **Leg.H.** 2002 ch. 52 (SB 467).

§3261. Employee contributions treated as voluntary plan trust fund.

All employee contributions and income arising therefrom received or retained by an employer under an approved voluntary plan are trust funds that are not considered to be part of an employer's assets. An employer shall either maintain a separate, specifically identifiable account for voluntary plan trust funds in a financial institution, or an employer may transmit voluntary plan trust funds, including any earned interest or income, directly to the admitted disability insurer. If an employer, with prior approval from the Director of Employment Development, invests voluntary plan trust funds in securities purchased through a commercial bank under Article 4 of Chapter 10 of Division 1 of the Financial Code, the securities account shall be separately identifiable from any other securities accounts maintained by the employer. In the event of commingling of voluntary plan trust funds, or the bankruptcy or insolvency of the employer, or the appointment of a receiver for the business of the employer, those voluntary plan trust funds are entitled to the same preference as are the claims of the state under Sections 1701 and 1702. **Leg.H.** 2002 ch. 52 (SB 467).

§3262. Termination of voluntary plan by director; remittance of moneys for deposit into Disability Fund; assessments for noncompliance; appeal.

(a) The Director of Employment Development may terminate any voluntary plan if the director finds that there is danger that the benefits accrued or to accrue will not be paid, that the security for the payment is insufficient, or for other good cause shown. The Director of Employment Development shall give notice of his or her intention to terminate a plan to the employer, employee group, and insurer. The notice shall state the effective date and the reason for the withdrawal. The Director of Employment Development may change or stay the effective date of the termination.

(b) Notwithstanding Section 3260.5, on the effective date of the termination of a plan by the Director of Employment Development, all moneys in the plan, including moneys paid by the employer, moneys paid by the employee, moneys owed to the voluntary plan by the employer but not yet paid to the plan, and any interest accrued on all these moneys, shall be remitted to the department and deposited into the Disability Fund.

(c) If an employer fails to remit all moneys owed to the Disability Fund after termination of the plan, the Director of Employment Development shall make an assessment against the employer equal to the amount of the moneys owed. The Director of Employment Development shall also make an assessment against the employer for all benefits paid from the Disability Fund after the termination of the plan, less any moneys received from the employer after the termination of the plan.

(d) The provisions of Article 8 (commencing with Section 1126) of Chapter 4 of Part 1, with respect to the assessment of moneys, and the provisions of Chapter 7 (commencing with Section 1701) of Part 1, with respect to the collection of moneys owed, shall apply to assessments authorized under this section, except that interest may not accrue until 30 days after issuance of the notice of assessment.

(e) The employer, employee group or insurer may, within 10 days from mailing or personal service of the notice, appeal to the Appeals Board. The 10-day period may be extended for good cause. The Appeals Board may prescribe by regulation the time, manner, method and procedure through which it may determine appeals under this section.

(f) The payment of benefits from the Disability Fund and the transfer of moneys in the voluntary plan may not be delayed during an employer's appeal of the termination of a voluntary plan. **Leg.H.** 2002 ch. 52 (SB 467).

§3263. Cessation of coverage; availability of benefits from Fund.

(a) An employee is no longer covered by an approved voluntary plan if a disability arose after the employment relationship with the voluntary plan employer ends, or if the Director of Employment Development terminates a voluntary plan in accordance with Section 3262.

(b) An employee who has ceased to be covered by an approved voluntary plan shall, if otherwise eligible, thereupon immediately become entitled to benefits from the Disability Fund to the same extent as though there had been no exemption from contributions as provided in this chapter. **Leg.H.** 2002 ch. 52 (SB 467).

§3264. Appeal procedure when benefits under approved plan are denied.

If any employer or insurer wholly or partially denies liability upon the claim of an employee for disability benefits under an approved plan, the employee may appeal the denial in the manner provided by law and authorized regulations for an appeal on a claim for benefits payable out of the Disability Fund. All decisions of the Appeals Board denying benefits under this section shall be subject to review by the courts of this State by the exclusive remedy of filing a petition for writ of mandate. No such petition may be filed, however, until the employee exhausts the administrative remedies provided for in this division, nor may any other action be commenced by an employee upon a denial of his claim by his employer or insurer, as the case may be, other than that prescribed herein.

§3265. Director's intercession on failure to pay.

(a) If, on appeal, it is decided that an employee is entitled to receive disability benefits under an approved voluntary plan and the employer or insurer fails to pay the same within 15 days after notice of a decision by an administrative law judge or the appeals board, the director shall pay such benefits and shall assess the amount thereof against the employer or the insurer, and the provisions of Article 8 (commencing with Section 1126) of Chapter 4 of Part 1 of this division with respect to the assessment of contributions and the provisions of Chapter 7 (commencing with Section 1701) of Part 1 of this division with respect to the collection of contributions shall apply to the recovery of such benefit payments. Amounts so collected shall be deposited in the Disability Fund.

(b) If an approved voluntary plan is not terminated because of the enactment of any law increasing the benefit amounts provided by Sections 2653 and 2655, and the employer or insurer fails to pay such increase under the plan, the director shall pay such benefits to an employee, if otherwise eligible, and shall assess the amount thereof against the employer or the insurer and the provisions of Article 8 (commencing with Section 1126) of Chapter 4 of Part 1 of this division with respect to the assessment of contributions and the provisions of Chapter 7 (commencing with Section 1701) of Part 1 of this division with respect to the collection of contributions shall apply to the recovery of such benefit payments. Amounts so collected shall be deposited in the Disability Fund.

§3266. Determination of credits and refunds.

The director shall in accordance with his or her authorized regulations determine the portion of the aggregate amount of refunds and credits to employees made under Section 1176 during any calendar year which is applicable to voluntary plans for which deductions were made under Section 3260, such determination to be based upon the relation during the preceding calendar year of the amount of wages subject to contributions to the Disability Fund to the amount of wages exempt from contributions to the Disability Fund under Section 3252.

§3267. Availability of information.

Employers whose employees are participating in an approved voluntary plan and any insurer of an approved plan shall furnish such reports and information and make available to the department such records as the director may by authorized regulations require for the proper administration of this part.

§3268. Director's obligation to furnish information.

The Director of Employment Development shall, in accordance with his authorized regulations, promptly furnish to employers, employees, or insurers, such information as may be required for the proper administration of an approved voluntary plan.

§3269. Director's obligation to determine administrative costs.

The director shall in accordance with his or her authorized regulations, determine each fiscal year the total amount expended for added administrative work arising out of voluntary plans.

§3270. Operative date for selection of risks.

The provisions of subdivision (i) of Section 3254 and subdivision (i) of Section 3255, dealing with substantial selection of risks adverse to the Disability Fund, shall be operative as of January 1, 1962.

§3271. Amendment of voluntary plans.

(a) The director shall approve any amendment to a voluntary plan adjusting the provisions thereof as to periods after the effective date of the amendment as to which he or she finds that the plan, as amended, will conform to the standards set forth in Section 3254, and that any of the following exist:

(1) A majority of the employees covered by the plan have consented in writing to the amendment.

(2) All of the employees covered by the plan who are adversely affected by the amendment have consented in writing to the amendment.

(3) The insurer of such plan, if any, has certified to the director that notice of the amendment either separately or as a part of a new certificate or statement of coverage, has, at least 10 days prior to the effective date of the proposed amendment, been delivered to the employer for distribution to his or her employees within 10 days thereafter and has further certified that such notice specifically included notification to the employees covered by the plan of their right to withdraw from the plan.

(b) Nothing contained in this section is intended to deny or limit the right of the director to make regulations supplementary thereto, nor on the general subject of requirements for amendments of voluntary plans.

§3272. Applicability of specified article.

The provisions of Article 9 (commencing with Section 1176) of Chapter 4 of Part 1 of this division shall apply to amounts collected under Sections 3252, 3260, and 3265, to amounts remitted to the Disability Fund under Section 3260, and to amounts paid to an employee by an employer or insurer after a final decision on appeal under Section 3264 to an administrative judge or the appeals board that the employee is entitled to disability benefits.

CHAPTER 7
PAID FAMILY LEAVE

§3300. Legislative findings and declarations.

The Legislature finds and declares all of the following:

(a) It is in the public benefit to provide family temporary disability insurance benefits to workers to care for their family members. The need for family temporary disability insurance benefits has intensified as the participation of both parents in the workforce has increased, and the number of single parents in the workforce has grown. The need for partial wage replacement for workers taking family care leave will be exacerbated as the population of those needing care, both children and parents of workers, increases in relation to the number of working age adults.

(b) Family Temporary Disability Insurance shall be known as Paid Family Leave.

(c) Developing systems that help families adapt to the competing interests of work and home not only benefits workers, but also benefits employers by increasing worker productivity and reducing employee turnover.

(d) The federal Family and Medical Leave Act (FMLA) and California's Family Rights Act (CFRA) entitle eligible employees working for covered employers to take unpaid, job-protected leave for up to 12 workweeks in a 12-month period. Under the FMLA and the CFRA, unpaid leave may be taken for the birth, adoption, or foster placement of a new child; to care for a seriously ill child, parent, or spouse; or for the employee's own serious health condition.

(e) State disability insurance benefits currently provide wage replacement for workers who need time off due to their own nonwork-related injuries, illnesses, or conditions, including pregnancy, that prevent them from working, but do not cover leave to care for a sick or injured child, spouse, parent, grandparent, grandchild, sibling, or domestic partner, or leave to bond with a new child.

(f) The majority of workers in this state are unable to take family care leave because they are unable to afford leave without pay. When workers do not receive some form of wage replacement during family care leave, families suffer from the worker's loss of income, increasing the demand on the state unemployment insurance system and dependence on the state's welfare system.

(g) It is the intent of the Legislature to create a family temporary disability insurance program to help reconcile the demands of work and family. The family temporary disability insurance program shall be a component of the state's unemployment compensation disability insurance program, shall be funded through employee contributions, and shall be administered in accordance with the policies of the state disability insurance program created pursuant to this part. Initial and ongoing administrative costs associated with the family temporary disability insurance program shall be payable from the Disability Fund. **Leg.H.** 2002 ch. 901 (SB 1661), operative January 1, 2004, 2003 ch. 797 (SB 727), 2013 ch. 350 (SB 770) §3.

2003 Note: This act shall become operative on January 1, 2004, except that benefits shall be payable for family temporary disability insurance claims commencing on or after July 1, 2004. Stats. 2003 ch. 797 (SB 727) §28.

2002 Note: This act shall become operative on January 1, 2004, except that benefits shall be payable for periods of family temporary disability leave commencing on or after July 1, 2004. Stats. 2002 ch. 901 §7.

§3301. Family temporary disability insurance program.

(a)(1) The purpose of this chapter is to establish, within the state disability insurance program, a family temporary disability insurance program. Family temporary disability insurance shall provide up to eight weeks of wage replacement benefits to workers who take time off work to care for a seriously ill child, spouse, parent, grandparent, grandchild, sibling, or domestic partner, to bond with a minor child within one year of the birth or placement of the child in connection with foster care or adoption, or to participate in a qualifying exigency related to the covered active duty or call to covered active duty of the individual's spouse, domestic partner, child, or parent in the Armed Forces of the United States.

(2) Nothing in this chapter shall be construed to abridge the rights and responsibilities conveyed under the CFRA or pregnancy disability leave.

(b) An individual's "weekly benefit amount" shall be the amount provided in Section 2655. An individual is eligible to receive family temporary disability insurance benefits equal to one-seventh of the individual's weekly benefit amount for each full day during which the individual is unable to work due to caring for a seriously ill or injured family member, bonding with a minor child within one year of the birth or placement of the child in connection with foster care or adoption, or participating in a qualifying exigency related to the covered active duty or call to covered active duty of the individual's spouse, domestic partner, child, or parent in the Armed Forces of the United States.

(c) The maximum amount payable to an individual during any disability benefit period for family temporary disability insurance shall be eight times the individual's "weekly benefit amount," but in no case shall the total amount of benefits payable be more than the total wages paid to the individual during the individual's disability base period. If the benefit is not a multiple of one dollar ($1), it shall be computed to the next higher multiple of one dollar ($1).

(d) No more than eight weeks of family temporary disability insurance benefits shall be paid within any 12-month period.

(e) An individual shall file a claim for family temporary disability insurance benefits not later than the 41st consecutive day following the first compensable day with respect to which the claim is made for benefits, which time shall be extended by the department upon a showing of good cause. If a first claim is not complete, the claim form shall be returned to the claimant for completion and it shall be completed and returned not later than the 10th consecutive day after the date it was mailed by the department to the claimant, except that such time shall be extended by the department upon a showing of good cause.

(f) This section shall become operative on January 1, 2021. **Leg.H.** 2018 ch. 849 (SB 1123) §2, 2019 ch. 24 (SB 83) §40, effective June 27, 2019.

2019 Note: With regard to Sections 38, 39, and 40 of ch. 24, the Legislature finds and declares all of the following:

(a) The expansion of the Family Temporary Disability Insurance program, also known as the Paid Family Leave program, has the goal of ensuring that newborns and newly adopted babies can be cared for by a parent or close family member for the first six months of their lives.

(b) Public health shows that providing up to six months of paid parental leave leads to positive health and educational outcomes for children. We now know, for example, that a baby's interactions with parents in the very first months of the infant's life is critical to help the baby's brain develop. In fact, during the first 1,000 days of a child's life, over 700 neural connections are formed every second, but these connections are dependent on the baby interacting with loving parents, close family members and caretakers. Bonding with a newly adopted baby has also demonstrated lasting long-term mental health benefits.

(c) Economic research demonstrates that paid parental leave provides greater economic security for parents by increasing labor force attachment overall, and reducing the economic strain on finding and affording infant childcare. In California, infant childcare averages over $16,400 per infant per year for care at a childcare center or over $10,600 per infant per year for a family-based childcare provider.

(d) Allowing parents to stay at home by providing paid family leave achieves the dual goal of allowing parents to help their children with essential early brain development and improve their family economic security.

(e) Take up rates for the Paid Family Leave program vary by income. Special attention must be paid to allow low wage workers opportunities to access the benefits they finance, including the amount of their wages replaced and the job protection they have to return to their employment.

(f) The Paid Family Leave program is an integral program that already supports California's workers, their families, and early childhood development. The program currently provides parents with up to six weeks of paid leave to bond with a new minor child. Collectively, these paid leave benefits provide families with approximately three months of paid leave when used consecutively. The expansion of the program would double this availability to a total of six months so that infant children can stay with their parent or a close family member for the first six months of the child's life.

(g) A birth mother may take an additional six weeks of leave to recover from childbirth under California's Disability Insurance program, further extending bonding time with her newborn baby.

(h) This legislation represents an initial step forward by increasing paid family leave for parents to bond with their new child from six weeks to eight weeks, thereby providing families up to one additional month to care for and bond with their newborn or newly adopted child.

(i) By November 2019, the Office of the Governor, through consultation with a task force, will develop a proposal to increase paid family leave duration to a full six months by 2021–22, for parents to care for and bond with their newborn or newly adopted child. This proposal must assess and address job protections for employees, wage replacement rates up to 90 percent for low wage workers and provide a plan to implement and fund expanded paid family leave benefits, as well as other findings and recommendations of interest. The Office of the Governor will present task force findings and observations to the Legislature by November 2019.

(j) It is the intent of the Legislature that the task force consult with representatives from employer groups, labor, early education representatives, other employment experts, and the Legislature when developing the proposal.

(k) It is the intent of the Legislature that the task force review and build upon prior reports and research, including those produced by the Legislative Analyst's Office, the Employment Development Department, and the Legislature. Stats. 2019 ch. 24 (SB 83) §43.

Former Sections: Former Unemp Ins C §3301 was added by 2013 ch. 350 (SB 770) §5 and repealed operative July 1, 2020, by its own provisions. 2019 ch. 24 (SB 83) §38.

Former Unemp Ins C §3301 was added by 2019 ch. 24 (SB 83) §39, operative July 1, 2020, and repealed operative January 1, 2021, by its own provisions. 2019 ch. 24 (SB 83) §39.

§3302. Definitions.

On and after July 1, 2014, for purposes of this part:

(a) "Care recipient" means the family member who is receiving care for a serious health condition or the new child with whom the care provider is bonding. **For the purposes of a qualifying exigency as set forth in Section 3302.2, "care recipient" also includes the military member, or child or parent of the military member, who is receiving assistance, or the employee who is participating in a qualifying exigency.**

(b) "Care provider" means the family member who is providing the required care for a serious health condition [1]; the family member who is bonding with the new child; **or the employee who is participating in a qualifying exigency as provided in Section 3302.2**.

(c) "Child" means a biological, adopted, or foster son or daughter, a stepson or stepdaughter, a legal ward, a son or daughter of a domestic partner, or the person to whom the employee stands in loco parentis.

(d) "Domestic partner" has the same meaning as defined in Section 297 of the Family Code.

(e) "Family care leave" means any of the following:

(1) Leave to bond with a minor child within the first year of the child's birth or placement in connection with foster care or adoption.

(2) Leave to care for a child, parent, grandparent, grandchild, sibling, spouse, or domestic partner who has a serious health condition.

(3) Leave to participate in a qualifying exigency as provided in Section 3302.2.

(f) "Family member" means child, parent, grandparent, grandchild, sibling, spouse, or domestic partner as defined in this section.

(g) "Grandchild" means a child of the employee's child.

(h) "Grandparent" means a parent of the employee's parent.

(i) **"Military member" means a child, spouse, domestic partner, or parent of the employee, where the military member is on covered active duty or call to active duty in the Armed Forces of the United States as defined in subdivision (a) of Section 3302.1**

(j) "Parent" means a biological, foster, or adoptive parent, a parent-in-law, a stepparent, a legal guardian, or other person who stood in loco parentis to the employee when the employee was a child.

[2] **(k)** "Parent-in-law" means the parent of a spouse or a domestic partner.

[3] **(*l*)** "Serious health condition" means an illness, injury, impairment, or physical or mental condition that involves inpatient care in a hospital, hospice, or residential health care facility, or continuing treatment or continuing supervision by a health care provider, as defined in Section 12945.2 of the Government Code.

[4] **(m)** "Sibling" means a person related to another person by blood, adoption, or affinity through a common legal or biological parent.

[5] **(n)** "Spouse" means a partner to a lawful marriage.

[6] **(o)** "Valid claim" means any claim for family temporary disability insurance benefits made in accordance with the provisions of this code, and any rules and regulations adopted thereunder, if the individual claiming benefits is unemployed and has been paid the necessary wages in employment for employers to qualify for benefits under Section 2652 and is caring for a seriously ill family member, or bonding with a minor child during the first year after the birth or placement of the child in connection with foster care or adoption.

[7] **(p)** "Twelve-month period," with respect to any individual, means the 365 consecutive days that begin with the first day the individual first establishes a valid claim for family temporary disability benefits. **Leg.H.** 2013 ch. 350 (SB 770) §7, 2020 ch. 348 (AB 2399) §1.

§3302. 2020 Deletes. [1] or **[2]** (j) **[3]** (k) **[4]** (*l*) **[5]** (m) **[6]** (n) **[7]** (o)

§3302.1. "Covered active duty" and "disability benefit period."

(a) For purposes of this chapter:

(1) "Covered active duty" means, with respect to a member of the regular Armed Forces of the United States, duty during the deployment of the member with the regular armed forces to a foreign country and, with respect to a member of the reserve components of the Armed Forces of the United States, duty during the deployment of the member of those reserve components to a foreign country under a federal call or order to active duty.

(2) "Disability benefit period" with respect to any individual, means the period of unemployment beginning with the first day an individual establishes a valid claim for family temporary disability insurance benefits to care for a seriously ill family member, to bond with a minor child during the first year after the birth or placement of the child in connection with foster care or adoption, or to participate in a qualifying exigency related to the covered active duty or call to covered active duty of the individual's spouse, domestic partner, child, or parent in the Armed Forces of the United States.

(A) Periods of family care leave for the same care recipient within a 12-month period shall be considered one disability benefit period.

(B) Periods of disability for pregnancy, as defined in Section 2608, and periods of family care leave for bonding associated with the birth of that child shall be considered one disability benefit period.

(b) This section shall become operative on January 1, 2021. **Leg.H.** 2018 ch. 849 (SB 1123) §4, 2019 ch. 497 (AB 991) §270.

Former Sections: Former Unemp Ins C §3302.1 was added in 2003 and repealed operative January 1, 2021, by its own provisions. 2019 ch. 497 (AB 991) §269.

§3302.2. Qualifying exigency related to the covered active duty or call to covered active duty of the individual's spouse, domestic partner, child, or parent in the Armed Forces of the United States.

For purposes of this chapter, a "qualifying exigency related to the covered active duty or call to covered active duty of the individual's spouse, domestic partner, child, or parent in the Armed Forces of the United States" means any of the following:

(a) Activities undertaken within seven calendar days from the date that a spouse, domestic partner, child, or parent has been notified of an impending call or order to covered active duty in the Armed Forces of the United States to address any issue that arises from the call or order.

(b) Attendance in either or both of the following:

(1) An official ceremony, program, or event sponsored by the military that is related to the covered active duty or call to covered active duty of the spouse, domestic partner, child, or parent.

(2) A family support or assistance program and informational briefing sponsored or promoted by the military, military service organizations, or the American Red Cross that is related to the covered active duty or call to covered active duty of the spouse, domestic partner, child, or parent.

(c) Any of the following activities related to the biological, adopted, or foster child, stepchild, legal ward, or child for whom the spouse, domestic partner, child, or parent in the Armed Forces of the United States stands in loco parentis, who is either not more than 18 years of age or, if equal to or more than 18 years of age, is incapable of self-care because of a disability at the time that the paid leave is to commence:

(1) Arranging for alternative childcare for the child when the covered active duty or call to covered active duty of the spouse, domestic partner, child, or parent in the Armed Forces of the United States necessitates a change in the existing childcare arrangement.

(2) Providing childcare for the child on an urgent, immediate need basis when the need to provide this care arises from the covered active duty or call to covered active duty of the spouse, domestic partner, child, or parent in the Armed Forces of the United States.

(3) Enrolling or transferring the child to a new school or day care facility when enrollment or transfer is necessitated by the covered active duty or call to covered active duty of the spouse, domestic partner, child, or parent in the Armed Forces of the United States.

(4) Attending meetings with staff at the child's school or day care facility, including, but not limited to, meetings with school officials regarding disciplinary measures, parent-teacher conferences, or meetings with school counselors, when these meetings are necessary due to circumstances arising from the covered active duty or call to covered active duty of the spouse, domestic partner, child, or parent in the Armed Forces of the United States.

(d) To make financial and legal arrangements for either or both of the following purposes:

(1) Making or updating financial or legal arrangements to address the absence of the spouse, domestic partner, child, or parent in the Armed Forces of the United States while on covered active duty or call to covered active duty, including, but not limited to, preparing and executing financial and healthcare powers of attorney, transferring bank account signature authority, enrolling in the Defense Enrollment Eligibility Reporting System (DEERS), obtaining military identification cards, or preparing or updating a will or living trust.

(2) Acting as the representative of the spouse, domestic partner, child, or parent in the Armed Forces of the United States before a federal, state, or local agency for purposes of obtaining, arranging, or appealing military service benefits while the spouse, domestic partner, child, or parent in the Armed Forces of the United States is on covered active duty or call to covered active duty, and for a period of ninety days following the termination of the covered active duty.

(e) Attending counseling provided by someone other than a health care provider, for oneself, for the spouse, domestic partner, child, or parent in the Armed Forces of the United States, or for the biological, adopted, or foster child, a stepchild, or a legal ward of the spouse, domestic partner, child, or parent in the Armed Forces of the United States, or a child for whom this person stands in loco parentis, who is either not more than 18 years of age, or equal to or more than 18 years of age and incapable of self-care because of a disability at the time that paid family leave is to commence, provided that the need for counseling arises from the covered active duty or call to covered active duty of the spouse, domestic partner, child, or parent in the Armed Forces of the United States.

(f) Accompanying a spouse, domestic partner, child, or parent in the Armed Forces of the United States while that individual is on short-term, temporary, rest and recuperation leave during the period of deployment in a foreign country, provided that any leave taken for this purpose is for not more than 15 calendar days beginning on the date of commencement for the rest and recuperation leave.

(g) Attending arrival ceremonies, reintegration briefings and events, and any other official ceremony or program sponsored by the military for a period of 90 days following the termination of the covered active duty of the spouse, domestic partner, child, or parent in the Armed Forces of the United States.

(h) Addressing issues that arise from the death of the spouse, domestic partner, child, or parent in the Armed Forces of the United States while on covered active duty status, including meeting and recovering the body of the spouse, domestic partner, child, or parent in the Armed Forces of the United States, making funeral arrangements, and attending funeral services.

(i)(1) Any of the following activities related to the parent of the spouse, domestic partner, child, or parent in the Armed Forces of the United States while the parent of the spouse, domestic partner, child, or parent in the armed forces during covered active duty is incapable of self-care by requiring active assistance or supervision over daily self-care in three or more of the activities of daily living or instrument activities of daily living:

(A) Arranging for alternative care for the parent of the spouse, domestic partner, child, or parent in the Armed Forces of the United States when the covered active duty or call to covered active duty of the spouse, domestic partner, child, or parent in the Armed Forces of the United States necessitates a change in the existing care arrangement for the parent.

(B) Providing care for the parent who is incapable of self-care on an urgent, immediate need basis when the need to provide this care arises from the covered active duty or call to covered active duty of the spouse, domestic partner, child, or parent in the Armed Forces of the United States.

(C) Admitting or transferring the parent to a care facility when admission or transfer is necessitated by the covered active duty or call to covered active duty of the spouse, domestic partner, child, or parent in the Armed Forces of the United States.

(D) Attending meetings with staff at the parent's care facility, including, but not limited to, meetings with hospice or social service providers of the parent of the spouse, domestic partner, child, or parent in the Armed Forces of the United States when these meetings are necessary due to circumstances arising from the covered active duty or call to covered active duty of the spouse, domestic partner, child, or parent in the Armed Forces of the United States.

(2) For purposes of this subdivision, "activities of daily living" include adaptive activities, such as caring appropriately for one's grooming and hygiene, bathing, dressing, and eating. Instrumental activities of daily living include, but are not limited to, cooking, cleaning, shopping, taking public transportation, paying bills, maintaining a residence, using telephones and directories, and using a post office.

(j) Any other activities to address other events that arise out of the covered active duty or call to covered active duty of the spouse, domestic partner, child, or parent in the Armed Forces of the United States, provided that the employer and employee agree that this leave shall qualify as an exigency, and agree to both the timing and duration of this leave.

(k) This section shall become operative on January 1, 2021. **Leg.H.** 2018 ch. 849 (SB 1123) §5.

§3303. Individual eligibility.

(a) On and after July 1, 2014, only if the director makes both of the findings described in subdivision (b), an individual shall be deemed eligible for family temporary disability insurance benefits equal to one-seventh of his or her weekly benefit amount on any day in which he or she is unable to perform his or her regular or customary work because of any of the following:

(1) The individual is bonding with a minor child during the first year after the birth or placement of the child in connection with foster care or adoption.

(2) The individual is caring for a seriously ill child, parent, grandparent, grandchild, sibling, spouse, or domestic partner.

(3) The individual is participating in a qualifying exigency related to the covered active duty or call to covered active duty of the individual's spouse, domestic partner, child, or parent in the Armed Forces of the United States.

(b) An individual shall be deemed eligible for family temporary disability insurance benefits described in subdivision (a) only if the directors finds both of the following:

(1) The individual has made a claim for temporary disability benefits as required by authorized regulations.

(2) The individual has filed a certificate, as required by Sections 2708 and 2709, or for purposes of participating in a qualifying exigency related to the covered active duty or call to covered active duty of the individual's spouse, domestic partner, child, or parent in the Armed Forces of the United States, has provided the information requested pursuant to Section 3307.

(c) This section shall become operative on January 1, 2021. **Leg.H.** 2018 ch. 849 (SB 1123) §7.

Former Sections: Former Unemp Ins C §3303 was added by 2016 ch. 5 (AB 908) §4 and repealed operative January 1, 2021, by its own provisions. 2018 ch. 849 (SB 1123) §6.

§3303.1. Ineligibility under certain circumstances; taking of FMLA and CFRA leave concurrently; use of vacation leave.

(a) An individual is not eligible for family temporary disability insurance benefits with respect to any day that any of the following apply:

(1) The individual has received, or is entitled to receive, unemployment compensation benefits under Part 1 (commencing with Section 100) or under an unemployment compensation act of any other state or of the federal government.

(2) The individual has received, or is entitled to receive, "other benefits" in the form of cash benefits as defined in Section 2629.

(3) The individual has received, or is entitled to receive, state disability insurance benefits under Part 2 (commencing with Section 2601) or under a disability insurance act of any other state.

(4) Another family member, as defined in Section 3302, is ready, willing, and able and available for the same period of time in a day that the individual is providing the required care or participating in a qualifying exigency related to the covered active duty or call to covered active duty of the individual's spouse, domestic partner, child, or parent in the Armed Forces of the United States.

(b) An individual who is entitled to leave under the FMLA and the CFRA shall take Family Temporary Disability Insurance (FTDI) leave concurrent with leave taken under the FMLA and the CFRA.

(c) As a condition of an employee's initial receipt of family temporary disability insurance benefits during any 12-month period in which an employee is eligible for these benefits, an employer may require an employee to take up to two weeks of earned but unused vacation leave prior to the employee's initial receipt of these benefits. This subdivision may not be construed in a manner that relieves an employer of any duty of collective bargaining the employer may have with respect to the subject matter of this subdivision.

(d) This section shall become operative on January 1, 2021. **Leg.H.** 2018 ch. 849 (SB 1123) §9.

Former Sections: Former Unemp Ins C §3303.1 was added by 2003 ch. 797 (SB 727) and repealed operative January 1, 2021, by its own provisions. 2018 ch. 849 (SB 1123) §8.

§3304. Receiving benefits under this division.

Eligible workers shall receive benefits in accordance with provisions established under this division. **Leg.H.** 2002 ch. 901 (SB 1661), operative January 1, 2004.

2002 Note: This act shall become operative on January 1, 2004, except that benefits shall be payable for periods of family temporary disability leave commencing on or after July 1, 2004. Stats. 2002 ch. 901 §7.

§3305. Penalty for false certification of medical condition.

If the director finds that any individual falsely certifies the medical condition of any person in order to obtain family temporary disability insurance benefits, with the intent to defraud, whether for the maker or for any other person, the director shall assess a penalty against the individual in the amount of 25 percent of the benefits paid as a result of the false certification. The provisions of Article 8 (commencing with Section 1126) of Chapter 4 of Part 1, with respect to assessments, the provisions of Article 9 (commencing with Section 1176) of Chapter 4 of Part 1, with respect to refunds, and the provisions of Chapter 7 (commencing with Section 1701) of Part 1, with respect to collections, shall apply to the assessments provided by this section. Penalties collected under this section shall be deposited in the contingent fund. **Leg.H.** 2002 ch. 901 (SB 1661), operative January 1, 2004, 2003 ch. 797 (SB 727), 2004 ch. 183 (AB 3082).

2003 Note: This act shall become operative on January 1, 2004, except that benefits shall be payable for family temporary disability insurance claims commencing on or after July 1, 2004. Stats. 2003 ch. 797 (SB 727) §28.

2002 Note: This act shall become operative on January 1, 2004, except that benefits shall be payable for periods of family temporary disability leave commencing on or after July 1, 2004. Stats. 2002 ch. 901 §7.

§3306. Director may request additional evidence; care recipient to submit to examinations to determine care provider's participation.

(a) The director may request additional medical evidence to supplement the first or any continued claim if the additional evidence can be procured without additional cost to the care recipient. The director may require that the additional evidence include any or all of the following information:

(1) Identification of diagnoses.

(2) Identification of symptoms.

(3) A statement setting forth the facts of the care recipient's serious health condition that warrants the participation of the employee. The statement shall be completed by any of the following people:

(A) The physician or practitioner treating the care recipient.

(B) The registrar, authorized medical officer, or other duly authorized official of the hospital or health facility treating the care recipient.

(C) An examining physician or other representative of the department.

(b) Except as provided in Section 2709, the director may require the care recipient to submit to reasonable examinations for the purpose of determining all of the following:

(1) Whether a serious health condition exists.

(2) Whether a care provider's participation is warranted.

(3) The period of time that the care provider's participation is warranted. **Leg.H.** 2003 ch. 797 (SB 727).

2003 Note: This act shall become operative on January 1, 2004, except that benefits shall be payable for family temporary disability insurance claims commencing on or after July 1, 2004. Stats. 2003 ch. 797 (SB 727) §28.

§3307. Information in support of request for leave because of qualifying exigency.

(a) When an employee requests for the first time leave because of a qualifying exigency arising out of the covered active duty or call to covered active duty or notification of an impending call or order to covered active duty of the employee's spouse, domestic partner, child, or parent in the Armed Forces of the United States, the department may require the employee to provide a copy of the covered active duty orders or other documentation issued by the military that indicates that the employee's spouse, domestic partner, child, or parent is in the Armed Forces of the United States, is on covered active duty or call to covered active duty status, and the dates of the covered active duty service. This information need only be provided to the department. A copy of new active duty orders or other documentation issued by the military may be required by the department if the need for leave because of a qualifying exigency arises out of a different covered active duty or call to covered active duty or notification of an impending call or order to covered active duty of the same or a different **eligible** family member.

(b) The department may require that a request for paid family leave for any qualifying exigency specified in Section 3302.2 be supported by sufficient information from the employee that sets forth the following:

(1) A statement or description, signed by the employee, of appropriate facts regarding the qualifying exigency for which paid family leave is requested. The facts shall be sufficient to support the need for leave and may include information on the type of qualifying exigency for which leave is requested and any available written documentation that supports the request for leave. For example, this information may include a copy of a meeting announcement for informational briefings sponsored by the military, a document confirming an appointment with a counselor or school official, or a copy of a bill for services for the handling of legal or financial affairs.

(2) The approximate date of the commencement or pending commencement of the qualifying exigency.

(3) If an employee requests leave because of a qualifying exigency for a single, continuous period of time, the beginning and end dates for that leave.

(4) If an employee requests leave because of a qualifying exigency on an intermittent basis, an estimate of the frequency and duration of the qualifying exigency.

(5) If the qualifying exigency involves meeting with a third party, appropriate contact information for the individual or entity with whom the employee is meeting, including, but not limited to, the name, title, organization, address, telephone number, fax number, and email address, if available, and a brief description of the purpose of the meeting.

(6) If the qualifying exigency involves rest and recuperation leave, a copy of the rest and recuperation orders for the employee's spouse, domestic partner, child, or parent in the Armed Forces of the United States, or other documentation issued by the military that indicates that this person has been granted rest and recuperation leave, and the dates of that rest and recuperation leave.

(c) If an employee submits complete and sufficient information to support [1] **the employee's** request for leave because of a qualifying exigency, the department may not request additional information from the employee. However, if the qualifying exigency involves meeting with a third party, the department may contact the individual or entity with whom the employee is meeting for purposes of verifying a meeting or appointment schedule and the nature of the meeting between the employee and the specified individual or entity. The employee's permission is not required in order to verify meetings or appointments with third parties, but no additional information may be requested by the department. The department also may contact an appropriate unit of the Department of Defense to request verification that an individual is on covered active duty or call to covered active duty or has been notified of an impending call or order to covered active duty. No additional information may be requested, and the employee's permission is not required.

(d) This section shall become operative on January 1, 2021. **Leg.H.** 2018 ch. 849 (SB 1123) §10, 2020 ch. 348 (AB 2399) §2.

§3307. 2020 Deletes. [1] his or her

§3308. [Operative January 1, 2025] Application for family temporary disability insurance benefits; mandatory languages.

(a) In addition to English, the department shall distribute the application for family temporary disability insurance benefits in all non-English languages spoken by a substantial number of non-English-speaking applicants. As used in this section, "substantial number of non-English-speaking applicants" has the same meaning as "substantial number of non-English-speaking people" is defined in Section 7296.2 of the Government Code.

(b) This section shall become operative on January 1, 2025. **Leg.H.** 2019 ch. 386 (AB 406) §1.

MISCELLANEOUS PROVISIONS

SYNOPSIS

CALIFORNIA CONSTITUTION

ARTICLE XIV
LABOR RELATIONS
[Selected Provisions]

§1. Minimum wages; general welfare of employees.
§4. Workers' compensation system.
§5. Convicts' labor; state benefit.

BUSINESS AND PROFESSIONS CODE

DIVISION 3
PROFESSIONS AND VOCATIONS GENERALLY

CHAPTER 2.7
ADVERTISING FOR WORKERS' COMPENSATION LEGAL SERVICES

§5499.30. Name of attorney required in advertisement for workers' compensation legal services.

CHAPTER 9
CONTRACTORS

ARTICLE 7
Disciplinary Proceedings
[Selected Provisions]

§7110. Grounds for disciplinary action.

ARTICLE 7.5
Workers' Compensation Insurance Reports

§7125. Certificate of Workers' Compensation Insurance or Certification of Self-Insurance required for licensure; exceptions; report to registrar.
§7125.1. License reinstatement retroactive to effective date of certificate if submitted within 90 days; exception.
§7125.2. Failure to obtain or maintain insurance—Automatic license suspension; registrar notice and citation; reinstatement.
§7125.3. Periods of licensure.
§7125.4. Causes for disciplinary action.
§7125.5. Renewal of license; exemption for workers' compensation insurance; recertification; retroactive renewal.
§7126. Misdemeanor violations.
§7127. Stop order prohibiting use of employee labor for failure to secure workers' compensation insurance coverage—Failure to comply; protest; hearing; findings.

CHAPTER 10.5
APP-BASED DRIVERS AND SERVICES

ARTICLE 1
Title, Findings and Declarations, and Statement of Purpose

§7448. Title.
§7449. Findings and declarations.
§7450. Statement of purpose.

ARTICLE 2
App-Based Driver Independence

§7451. Protecting independence.
§7452. Contract and termination provisions.
§7452.5. Independence unaffected.

ARTICLE 3
Compensation

§7453. Earnings guarantee.

ARTICLE 4
Benefits

§7454. Healthcare subsidy.
§7455. Loss and liability protection.

ARTICLE 5
Antidiscrimination and Public Safety

§7456. Antidiscrimination.
§7457. Sexual harassment prevention.
§7458. Criminal background checks.
§7459. Safety training.
§7460. Zero tolerance policies.
§7460.5. Law enforcement information requests.
§7461. App-based driver rest.
§7462. Impersonating an app-based driver.

ARTICLE 6
Definitions

§7463. Definitions.

ARTICLE 7
Uniform Work Standards

§7464. State preemption.

ARTICLE 8
Income Reporting

§7464.5. Information return requirements.

ARTICLE 9
Amendment

§7465. Amendment to chapter.

ARTICLE 10
Regulations

§7466. Emergency regulations.

ARTICLE 11
Severability

§7467. Severability.

CHAPTER 14
STRUCTURAL PEST CONTROL OPERATORS

ARTICLE 7
Disciplinary Proceedings
[Selected Provisions]

§8636. Grounds for disciplinary action.

DIVISION 7
GENERAL BUSINESS REGULATIONS

PART 1
Licensing for Revenue and Regulation

CHAPTER 6
NOTICE TO LICENSEES

§16545. Business license application form.

CIVIL CODE

DIVISION 1
PERSONS

PART 2.6
Confidentiality of Medical Information

CHAPTER 1
DEFINITIONS
[Selected Provisions]

§56.05. Definitions.

CHAPTER 2
DISCLOSURE OF MEDICAL INFORMATION BY PROVIDERS

§56.10. When medical information may be disclosed.
§56.1007. Disclosure to family member, partner, or friend; disclosure for notification purposes; disaster relief efforts.
§56.101. Preservation of confidentiality of medical information.
§56.102. Pharmaceutical company cannot require patient to sign form permitting disclosure of medical information as condition of receiving pharmaceuticals; exceptions.
§56.103. Disclosure of minor's medical information for purpose of coordinating health care services and medical treatment.
§56.104. Release of information on psychotherapy.
§56.105. Authorization to disclose medical information in connection with settlement or compromise of medical malpractice case.
§56.106. Disclosure or release of information on minor removed from physical custody of parent or guardian; restrictions; applicability.
§56.107. Requirements for maintaining confidentiality of medical information.
§56.11. Requirements for authorizing release of medical information.
§56.12. Furnishing copy of authorization to patient.
§56.13. Confidentiality of released medical information.
§56.14. Provider non-liability for unauthorized use of medical information.
§56.15. Cancellation or modification of authorization.
§56.16. Disclosure of nonmedical information permitted.

CHAPTER 2.5
DISCLOSURE OF GENETIC TEST RESULTS BY A HEALTH CARE SERVICE PLAN

§56.17. Insurers prohibited from offering or providing different terms, conditions, or benefits based on genetic characteristics; penalties; disclosure of test results for genetic characteristic—Civil and criminal liability.

CHAPTER 3
USE AND DISCLOSURE OF MEDICAL INFORMATION BY EMPLOYERS
[Selected Provisions]

§56.20. Employer's duty to ensure confidentiality of medical information; employee's right to refuse release of such information.
§56.21. Requirements for authorized release of medical information.

CHAPTER 6
RELATIONSHIP TO EXISTING LAW
[Selected Provisions]

§56.30. Disclosure of medical information not subject to limitations of Part 2.6.
§56.31. Disclosure of human immunodeficiency virus.

DIVISION 3
OBLIGATIONS

PART 3
Obligations Imposed by Law
[Selected Provisions]

§1708.8. Physical and constructive invasion of privacy—Obtaining visual image, sound recording, or other physical impression; liability for damages; civil fines.

DIVISION 4
GENERAL PROVISIONS

PART 1
Relief

TITLE 2
COMPENSATORY RELIEF

CHAPTER 2
MEASURE OF DAMAGES

ARTICLE 2
Damages for Wrongs
[Selected Provisions]

§3333.1. Introduction of evidence of amount payable as benefit in action for personal injury—Health care provider defined—Professional negligence defined.

CODE OF CIVIL PROCEDURE

PART 2
OF CIVIL ACTIONS

TITLE 9
Enforcement of Judgments

DIVISION 2
ENFORCEMENT OF MONEY JUDGMENTS

CHAPTER 2
LIENS

ARTICLE 2
Judgment Lien on Real Property
[Selected Provisions]

§697.330. Creation and duration of judgment lien based on workers' compensation award.

CHAPTER 4
EXEMPTIONS

ARTICLE 3
Exempt Property
[Selected Provisions]

§704.160. Workers' compensation claim, award, or payment—Application to support judgment.

TITLE 14
Miscellaneous Provisions

CHAPTER 5
NOTICES, AND FILING AND SERVICE OF PAPERS
[Selected Provisions]

§1013. Service by mail, Express Mail, overnight delivery, or facsimile transmission—Method of service.

PART 4
Miscellaneous Provisions

TITLE 4
CIVIL DISCOVERY ACT

CHAPTER 1
GENERAL PROVISIONS

§2016.010. Short title.
§2016.020. Definitions.
§2016.030. Modification by written stipulation.
§2016.040. What meet and confer declaration in support of motion to show.
§2016.050. Applicability of Sections 1011 and 1013.
§2016.060. Specified date falling on Saturday, Sunday or holiday; extension of time limit.
§2016.070. Applicability of title to enforcement of money judgment.
§2016.080. Informal discovery conference [Repealed January 1, 2023].
§2016.090. Applicability to civil action; initial disclosure.

CHAPTER 2
SCOPE OF DISCOVERY
[Selected Provisions]

ARTICLE 1
General Provisions

§2017.010. What matters may be subject to discovery.
§2017.020. When court may limit scope of discovery; motion for protective order; monetary sanction.

ARTICLE 2
Scope of Discovery in Specific Contexts

§2017.210. Information concerning insurance.
§2017.220. Discovery regarding plaintiff's sexual conduct in certain actions; showing of good cause; monetary sanction.

CHAPTER 4
ATTORNEY WORK PRODUCT

§2018.010. Meaning of "client" for purposes of chapter.
§2018.020. Policy of state.
§2018.030. Certain writings not discoverable; when other work product may be subject to discovery.
§2018.040. Restatement of existing law.
§2018.050. Work product enabling commission of crime not protected in official investigations.
§2018.060. Right to request in camera hearing.
§2018.070. Discovery for purposes of State Bar disciplinary proceedings; protective order; client approval.
§2018.080. No privilege when work product relevant to issue of breach of attorney-client relationship.

CHAPTER 5
METHODS AND SEQUENCE OF DISCOVERY

ARTICLE 1
General Provisions

§2019.010. Methods of discovery.
§2019.020. Sequence and timing of discovery.
§2019.030. When frequency or extent of discovery may be restricted; motion for protective order; monetary sanction.
§2019.040. Electronically stored information.

ARTICLE 2
Methods and Sequence of Discovery in Specific Contexts

§2019.210. Misappropriation of trade secret.

CHAPTER 6
NONPARTY DISCOVERY

ARTICLE 1
General Provisions

§2020.010. Methods for discovery within state from nonparty.
§2020.020. What deposition subpoena may command.
§2020.030. Provisions applicable to deposition subpoena.

ARTICLE 2
Procedures Applicable to All Types of Deposition Subpoenas

§2020.210. Issuance of deposition subpoena by clerk of court or attorney of record.

§2020.220. Service of deposition subpoena.
§2020.230. Witness fee and mileage.
§2020.240. Punishment for disobeying deposition subpoena; contempt; forfeiture and damages.

ARTICLE 3
Subpoena Commanding Only Attendance and Testimony of the Deponent

§2020.310. Rules applicable to deposition subpoena commanding only attendance and testimony.

ARTICLE 4
Subpoena Commanding Only Production of Business Records for Copying

§2020.410. What deposition subpoena commanding only production of business records to contain; description of records; records pertaining to consumer.
§2020.420. Deposition officer.
§2020.430. Delivery to deposition officer; copy of records and affidavit; duties of custodian; date for delivery; applicability of specified provisions.
§2020.440. Deposition officer to provide copies to specified parties.

ARTICLE 5
Subpoena Commanding Both Production of Business Records and Attendance and Testimony of the Deponent

§2020.510. Requirements for deposition subpoena that commands attendance, testimony and production of business records, etc.; records pertaining to consumer or employee.

CHAPTER 7
SANCTIONS

§2023.010. Misuses of discovery process.
§2023.020. Monetary sanction for failure to confer.
§2023.030. Sanctions which may be imposed for misuse of discovery process.
§2023.040. Request for sanction and notice of motion; what to be included therein.
§2023.050. Sanctions.

CHAPTER 9
ORAL DEPOSITION INSIDE CALIFORNIA
[Selected Provisions]

ARTICLE 2
Deposition Notice

§2025.210. Time for service of notice.
§2025.220. Contents of deposition notice.
§2025.230. Contents of deposition notice if deponent not a natural person.
§2025.240. Notice to parties to the action; duties of subpoenaing party if deponent to produce personal records of consumer or employment records.
§2025.250. Place of taking deposition.
§2025.260. Motion for deposition at more distant place; monetary sanction.
§2025.270. Date of oral deposition; motion to shorten or extend time or for stay.
§2025.280. Effect of service of deposition notice; when deposition subpoena is required; access to password protected or otherwise inaccessible information.
§2025.290. Appropriate time limit for depositions; additional time; exclusion; construction.
§2025.295. Deposition examination; time limitation of testimony when deponent suffers from mesothelioma or silicosis.

ARTICLE 3
Conduct of Deposition

§2025.310. Taking of deposition by telephone or other remote electronic means; procedures.
§2025.320. Supervision of deposition by deposition officer; qualifications and requirements; objections; penalty for violations.
§2025.330. Deponents to be under oath; taking of testimony and objections stenographically; recording of testimony; examination and cross-examination; written questions.
§2025.340. Procedure for audio or video recording of deposition; notice and objections.

ARTICLE 4
Objections, Sanctions, Protective Orders, Motions to Compel, and Suspension of Depositions

§2025.410. Service of written objection; time for serving; motion for stay; monetary sanction; exception.
§2025.420. Motion for protective order; what order may include; discovery of electronically stored information; denial of protective order; monetary sanction.
§2025.430. Imposition of monetary sanction for failure of party giving notice of deposition to attend or proceed; exception.
§2025.440. Imposition of monetary sanction where deponent does not appear due to failure to be served deposition subpoena; sanction where deponent who has been served fails to appear or refuses to be sworn in.
§2025.450. Failure to comply with deposition notice; motion for order compelling compliance; requirements; discovery of electronically stored information; monetary and other sanctions.
§2025.460. Privileged and protected information; waiver absent objection; objection to errors and irregularities; certain matters not waived by failure to object.
§2025.470. Suspension of taking of testimony; stipulation; motion for protective order.
§2025.480. Motion for order compelling answer or production; time for motion; notice; discovery of electronically stored information; certified copy of relevant parts of transcript; monetary and other sanctions.

ARTICLE 5
Transcript or Recording

§2025.510. Transcription of testimony; costs; who may obtain copies and when; retention of stenographic notes; access to recorded testimony; stenographic testimony as official record.
§2025.520. Written notice when original transcript becomes available for reading, correcting and signing; exception; time period for deponent to change answers and approve or refuse to approve transcript; motion to suppress transcript; monetary sanction.

§2025.530. Written notice when audio or video recording becomes available for review; exception; time period for deponent to change answers; identification of deposition as deponent's own or failure to do so; motion to suppress deposition; monetary sanction.
§2025.540. Certification by deposition officer; use of rough draft transcript not permitted.
§2025.550. Transmittal of transcript to attorney; time period for retention.
§2025.560. Retention of audio or video recording of deposition testimony by operator; access of parties to hearing or viewing or copy of recording; cost; timeframe for retention.
§2025.570. Furnishing of copies of transcript or recording by deposition officer; charge; notice to parties of right to seek protective order; applicability of section.

ARTICLE 6
Post-Deposition Procedures

§2025.610. Subsequent depositions; when permitted.
§2025.620. Use of deposition as evidence; requirements.

CHAPTER 10
ORAL DEPOSITION OUTSIDE CALIFORNIA
[Selected Provisions]

§2026.010. Taking of oral deposition in another state or in a territory or insular possession; procedures and process; issuance of commission.
§2027.010. Taking of oral deposition in foreign nation; procedures and process; issuance of commission.

CHAPTER 14
INSPECTION, COPYING, TESTING, SAMPLING, AND PRODUCTION OF DOCUMENTS, ELECTRONICALLY STORED INFORMATION, TANGIBLE THINGS, LAND, AND OTHER PROPERTY
[Selected Provisions]

ARTICLE 1
Inspection Demand

§2031.010. Right to discovery by inspecting, copying, testing, or sampling documents, tangible things, land or other property, and electronically stored information.
§2031.020. Demand for inspection, copying, testing, or sampling by defendant authorized at any time; when plaintiff may make demand for inspection, copying, testing, or sampling.
§2031.030. Format and requirements for demands for inspection, copying, testing, or sampling.
§2031.040. Service of demand for inspection, copying, testing, or sampling.
§2031.050. When supplemental demand may be propounded.
§2031.060. Motion for protective order; what protective order may provide; denial of protective order; monetary sanction.

ARTICLE 2
Response to Inspection Demand

§2031.210. Nature and format of response to demand for inspection, copying, testing, or sampling.
§2031.220. Statement regarding compliance in whole or in part.
§2031.230. Representation of inability to comply.
§2031.240. Statements regarding demand that is objectionable in whole or in part.
§2031.250. Signing of response to demand.
§2031.260. Time for service of response; unlawful detainer action.
§2031.270. Extension of date for inspection or time for service of response; written confirmation of agreement.
§2031.280. Production of documents—Form; date specified; production of electronically stored information; translation; expense.
§2031.285. Production of electronically stored information—Claim of privilege or of protection as attorney work product; notification to receiving party; receiving party's responsibilities; preclusion from using or disclosing specified information; resolution.
§2031.290. Retention of demand for inspection, copying, testing, or sampling, proof of service, and response by demanding party.
§2031.300. Effect of failure to serve timely response to demand for inspection, copying, testing, or sampling; motion for order; monetary and other sanctions.
§2031.310. Motion for order compelling further response; grounds; notice; waiver; monetary and other sanctions.
§2031.320. Motion for order compelling compliance on failure to permit inspection, copying, testing, or sampling in accordance with response; monetary and other sanctions.

CHAPTER 18
SIMULTANEOUS EXCHANGE OF EXPERT WITNESS INFORMATION

ARTICLE 3
Deposition of Expert Witness
[Selected Provisions]

§2034.430. Payment of certain experts' reasonable and customary hourly or daily fees for time spent at deposition; tardy counsel; workers' compensation cases.

EDUCATION CODE

TITLE 1
GENERAL EDUCATION CODE PROVISIONS

DIVISION 1
General Education Code Provisions

PART 2
COUNTY EDUCATIONAL AGENCIES

CHAPTER 2
COUNTY SUPERINTENDENT OF SCHOOLS

ARTICLE 2
Duties, Responsibilities, and General Powers
[Selected Provisions]

§1252. Workers' compensation insurance for schools.

ARTICLE 3
Staff
[Selected Provisions]

§1297. Extent of coverage; payment of costs.

PART 13
STATE TEACHERS' RETIREMENT SYSTEM

CHAPTER 30
SUBROGATION

§24500. Board's right of subrogation.
§24501. Board may contract with SCIF or AG to act as agent.
§24502. Actions board may take to enforce subrogation right.
§24503. Board may compromise claims.
§24504. Application of recovery.
§24505. Three-year limitation period.

PART 19
MISCELLANEOUS

CHAPTER 3
MISCELLANEOUS

ARTICLE 6
District Liability on Loaned Equipment

§32350. Liability for loaned equipment or services; "public entity."

TITLE 2
ELEMENTARY AND SECONDARY EDUCATION

DIVISION 3
Local Administration

PART 25
EMPLOYEES

CHAPTER 1
EMPLOYEES

ARTICLE 1
General Provisions
[Selected Provisions]

§44017. Possible payment to surviving spouse.

ARTICLE 2
Rights and Duties
[Selected Provisions]

§44043. Restrictions on salary and paid leave when temporary disability benefits received.

CHAPTER 4
EMPLOYMENT—CERTIFICATED EMPLOYEE

ARTICLE 3
Resignations, Dismissals, and Leaves of Absence
[Selected Provisions]

§44977. Salaries for those on extended leave and substitutes.
§44977.5. Salary deductions during absence from duties on account of parental leave for employee requiring certification.
§44983. Salary deductions for those on extended leave.
§44984. Rules for industrial accident or illness leave.

CHAPTER 5
CLASSIFIED EMPLOYEES

ARTICLE 4
Resignation and Leaves of Absence
[Selected Provisions]

§45192. Rules for industrial accident or illness leave of classified service employees.

TITLE 3
POSTSECONDARY EDUCATION

DIVISION 8
California State University

PART 55
CALIFORNIA STATE UNIVERSITY

CHAPTER 5
PERSONNEL

ARTICLE 1.1
Industrial Disability Leave

§89529. Application of article.
§89529.01. Resolution of conflicts with memorandum of understanding.
§89529.02. Definitions.
§89529.03. Industrial disability leave: entitlement; amount; frequency; deductions.
§89529.04. Continuation of other employee benefits.
§89529.05. Coordination of industrial disability leave and temporary disability indemnity.
§89529.06. Inapplicability of article.
§89529.07. Continuation of disability after expiration of industrial disability leave.
§89529.08. Commencement of industrial disability leave.
§89529.09. Contingencies that must be satisfied to receive payments.
§89529.10. Rules and regulations.
§89529.11. Effective date.

EVIDENCE CODE

DIVISION 2
WORDS AND PHRASES DEFINED
[Selected Provisions]

§110. Burden of producing evidence defined.
§115. Burden of proof defined.
§140. Evidence defined.
§240. Unavailable as a witness defined.
§250. Writing defined.

DIVISION 4
JUDICIAL NOTICE
[Selected Provisions]

§450. General provision.
§451. Mandatory judicial notice.
§452. Permissive judicial notice.

DIVISION 6
WITNESSES

CHAPTER 5
METHOD AND SCOPE OF EXAMINATION

ARTICLE 2
Examination of Witnesses
[Selected Provisions]

§776. Adverse witnesses.
§777. Exclusion of witnesses from courtroom.

DIVISION 8
PRIVILEGES

CHAPTER 1
DEFINITIONS

§900. Applicability.
§901. Proceeding defined.
§902. Civil proceeding defined.
§903. Criminal proceeding defined.
§905. Presiding officer defined.

CHAPTER 2
APPLICABILITY OF DIVISION

§910. Applicability of division.

CHAPTER 3
GENERAL PROVISIONS RELATING TO PRIVILEGES

§911. General provision.
§912. Waiver by disclosure—Joint holders of privilege.
§913. Comment on exercise of privilege prohibited—No presumption or inference.
§914. Determination of claim of privilege—Contempt for failure to disclose information.
§915. Disclosure of information to determine claim—Official information—Identity of informer—Trade secrets.
§916. Exclusion of information where holder of privilege not a party.
§917. Presumption of confidential nature of communication; electronic communication retains privileged character.
§918. Error in disallowing claim.
§919. Inadmissibility of privileged information erroneously disclosed.
§920. Construction against repeal by implication.

CHAPTER 4
PARTICULAR PRIVILEGES

ARTICLE 3
Lawyer-Client Privilege
[Selected Provisions]

§953. "Holder of privilege" defined.

ARTICLE 3.5
Lawyer Referral Service-Client Privilege

§965. Definitions.
§966. Privilege of confidential communication between client and lawyer referral service; who may claim privilege.
§967. When lawyer referral service must claim privilege.
§968. Disclosure necessary when services sought to enable crime or fraud, or to prevent criminal act likely to result in death or bodily harm.

ARTICLE 4
Privilege Not to Testify Against Spouse
[Selected Provisions]

§971. Spouse of party called as witness by adverse party.
§972. Exceptions to privilege.
§973. Waiver—Proceeding brought or defended for benefit of spouse.

ARTICLE 5
Privilege for Confidential Marital Communications
[Selected Provisions]

§980. General provision.

ARTICLE 6
Physician-Patient Privilege
[Selected Provisions]

§996. Condition of patient in issue.

ARTICLE 7
Psychotherapist-Patient Privilege
[Selected Provisions]

§1010. "Psychotherapist" defined.
§1010.5. Application of privilege to educational psychologist.
§1011. "Patient" defined.
§1012. "Confidential communication between patient and psychotherapist" defined.
§1013. "Holder of privilege" defined.
§1014. Who may claim privilege.
§1015. When psychotherapist must claim privilege.
§1016. Condition of patient in issue.

ARTICLE 9
Official Information and Identity of Informer
[Selected Provisions]

§1043. Investigation of citizens' complaints—Discovery or disclosure of peace or custodial officer personnel records.

DIVISION 10
HEARSAY EVIDENCE

CHAPTER 2
EXCEPTIONS TO THE HEARSAY RULE

ARTICLE 7
Business Records

§1270. "Business" defined.
§1271. Record as evidence.
§1272. Absence of record as evidence.

DIVISION 11
WRITINGS

CHAPTER 2
SECONDARY EVIDENCE OF WRITINGS

ARTICLE 3
Photographic Copies and Printed Representations of Writings

§1550. Business records [First of Two; Operative Until Amendment by Stats. 2002 Ch. 124 Becomes Operative].
§1550. Business records [Second of Two; See Note for Operative Information].
§1550.1. Admissibility of reproductions of files, records, writings, photographs, fingerprints or other instruments.
§1551. Lost or destroyed writings.
§1552. Printed representations of computer information.
§1553. Printed representation of images stored on video or digital medium.

ARTICLE 4
Production of Business Records

§1560. Copies—Transmittal.
§1561. Affidavit accompanying record.
§1562. Admissibility of copies and affidavits.
§1563. Witness fees.
§1564. Personal attendance of custodian or witness.
§1565. Custodian as witness of party serving first subpoena.
§1566. Applicable proceedings.
§1567. Admissibility of certain income and benefit information provided by employer in proceeding to modify or terminate order for child, family, or spousal support.

GOVERNMENT CODE

GENERAL PROVISIONS
[Selected Provisions]

§24. "Workmen's compensation" changed to "workers' compensation."

TITLE 1
GENERAL

DIVISION 7
Miscellaneous

CHAPTER 5
JOINT EXERCISE OF POWERS

ARTICLE 1
Joint Powers Agreements
[Selected Provisions]

§6516. Public agencies' joint powers agreement for insurance and risk pooling; reserve fund.

TITLE 2
GOVERNMENT OF THE STATE OF CALIFORNIA

DIVISION 1
General

CHAPTER 7
CALIFORNIA EMERGENCY SERVICES ACT

ARTICLE 3.5
Oil Spills
[Selected Provisions]

§8574.3. Volunteers of state agencies; entitlement to benefits.

ARTICLE 5
Office of Emergency Services
[Selected Provisions]

§8585.5. Office of Emergency Services; classes of disaster workers; procedures for payment of benefits.

ARTICLE 9.8
Disaster Preparedness
[Selected Provisions]

§8609. Volunteer workers.

ARTICLE 10
Local Disaster Councils
[Selected Provisions]

§8610. Authority to create local disaster councils.
§8612. Certification of accredited disaster councils.

ARTICLE 17
Privileges and Immunities
[Selected Provisions]

§8656. Public employees; privileges applying in territory apply outside territory.
§8657. Liability for damages suffered by volunteer engaged in emergency preparedness training or relief activity; responsibilities and immunities of California Earthquake Prediction Evaluation Council.
§8659. Limitations on liability of specified healing arts practitioners who render services during emergency.
§8660. Limitations on liability; other state rendering aid in emergency.

DIVISION 3
Executive Department

PART 1
STATE DEPARTMENTS AND AGENCIES

CHAPTER 4.5
ADMINISTRATIVE ADJUDICATION: GENERAL PROVISIONS

ARTICLE 8
Language Assistance
[Selected Provisions]

§11435.30. State Personnel Board list of certified

administrative hearing interpreters; other classes of interpreters deemed certified.

§11435.35. State Personnel Board list of certified medical examination interpreters; other classes of interpreters deemed certified.

PART 2.8
DEPARTMENT OF FAIR EMPLOYMENT AND HOUSING

CHAPTER 4
DEFINITIONS
[Selected Provisions]

§12925. Definitions.
§12926. Definitions regarding unlawful practices.
§12926.05. Right of employee of nonprofit sheltered workshop, day program, or rehabilitation facility to bring action for harassment or discrimination; affirmative defense.
§12926.1. Physical and mental disabilities.
§12926.2. Definitions.

CHAPTER 6
DISCRIMINATION PROHIBITED

ARTICLE 1
Unlawful Practices, Generally
[Selected Provisions]

§12940. Unlawful employment practices.

DIVISION 5
Personnel

PART 2.6
PERSONNEL ADMINISTRATION

CHAPTER 2
ADMINISTRATION OF SALARIES

ARTICLE 1
Claims for Reimbursement
[Selected Provisions]

§19820. Adoption of general rules and regulations by the director.

PART 3
PUBLIC EMPLOYEES' RETIREMENT SYSTEM

CHAPTER 1
GENERAL PROVISIONS AND DEFINITIONS

ARTICLE 2
Definitions
[Selected Provisions]

§20046. "Industrial"; death or disability of members.

CHAPTER 2
ADMINISTRATION OF SYSTEM

ARTICLE 2
Powers and Duties of the Board
[Selected Provisions]

§20130. Representation of retirement system before Appeals Board; determination of disability.

ARTICLE 8
Subrogation

§20250. Right of subrogation—Limitation.
§20251. "State fund."
§20252. Amounts recoverable from third person.
§20253. Contracts with state fund or Attorney General for third-party recovery.
§20254. Application of amounts recovered by subrogation.
§20255. Statute of limitations.

CHAPTER 12
RETIREMENT FROM EMPLOYMENT

ARTICLE 6
Disability Retirement
[Selected Provisions]

§21150. Retirement of incapacitated member.
§21151. Members subject to mandatory retirement for incapacity resulting from industrial disability.
§21153. Required application by employer.
§21154. Application for retirement for disability.
§21155. Medical examination; reimbursement for expenses.
§21156. When board to retire member for disability; retirement for service in lieu of retirement for disability; competent medical evidence; appeal.
§21157. Time limit for contracting agency to make determination as to local safety member.
§21158. Time allowed for determination relating to state peace officer/firefighter, state patrol member, or state safety member.
§21163. Retirement of member granted or entitled to sick leave or entitled to compensating time off for overtime.
§21164. Disability retirement of local safety member.
§21166. Determination of industrial disability; limitation on Appeals Board jurisdiction.
§21167. Petition for rehearing; grounds.
§21168. Petition for rehearing denied or granted; application for writ of review.
§21169. Evidence on writ of review; Appeals Board record.
§21170. Scope of review.
§21171. Appeals Board continuing jurisdiction.
§21173. Delegation of authority.
§21174. Subsequent determination that disability is industrial.
§21175. Refusal to submit to medical examination.

ARTICLE 7
Reinstatement from Retirement

§21190. Reinstatement and employment of retiree.
§21191. Reinstatement of person retired for disability.
§21192. Disability retirement recipient under minimum age for voluntary retirement; medical examination; application for reinstatement.
§21193. Cancellation of allowance and reinstatement to position, on determination that recipient not incapacitated.
§21194. Reinstatement from partial retirement.
§21195. Reinstatement requirements.
§21196. Reinstatement procedure.
§21197. Reinstatement procedure for person retired for disability.

§21198. Reinstatement after involuntary termination of employment.
§21199. Reinstatement if person will be appointed to position by Governor.
§21200. Cancellation of retirement allowance; crediting account; future rate of contribution and allowance.
§21201. Cancellation of allowance for person reinstated from disability retirement.
§21202. Reinstatement of unlawfully employed retiree.
§21203. Reinstatement of employee with special qualifications.

CHAPTER 13
RETIREMENT BENEFITS

ARTICLE 1
General Provisions
[Selected Provisions]

§21257. No modification due to workers' compensation benefits received.

ARTICLE 5
Disability Retirement Benefits
[Selected Provisions]

§21413. Local safety member retired for industrial disability.
§21416. Disability allowance for state safety member; retroactive payments.
§21419. Deduction of advanced disability payments from retroactive disability allowance.
§21430. Increased industrial disability allowance of local members based on percentage disability determined by Workers' Compensation Appeals Board subject to employer election.

CHAPTER 14
DEATH BENEFITS

ARTICLE 2
Preretirement Death Benefits
[Selected Provisions]

§21537. Special death benefit; industrial death; determination by Appeals Board; limitations on jurisdiction; applicability.
§21537.5. Special death benefit for state miscellaneous member in State Bargaining Unit 12 [See Subdivision (c) for Operative Information].
§21538. Special death benefit for appointed state member.
§21540. Special death benefit for appointed state member—Death resulting from conduct of correctional institution inmate.
§21540.5. Special death benefit for state, school, or local miscellaneous member or local or state safety member; conditions; jurisdiction and determination of Workers' Compensation Appeals Board; inapplicability of section.
§21541. Special death benefit.
§21541.5. Benefits terminated upon adoption.
§21542. Special death benefit—Accrual; election to receive death benefit in lieu of special death benefit.
§21543. Special death benefit payment—Conditions for lump sum payment; accumulated additional contributions.
§21544. Special death benefit—Determination of death as industrial in nature.
§21546. Death of qualified member while in state service and before retirement; beneficiaries; monthly allowance; application.
§21547. Monthly allowance in lieu of basic death benefit for members in state bargaining units subject to memoranda of understanding.
§21547.5. Adjustment of monthly allowance that began prior to specified date.
§21547.7. Monthly allowance in lieu of basic death benefit.
§21548. Allowance to surviving spouse of member eligible pursuant to specified provision; application.
§21551. Surviving spouse benefits.
§21552. Effect of remarriage by surviving spouse of firefighter or peace officer.
§21553. Restoration of allowance to remarried surviving spouse of firefighter or peace officer.

TITLE 3
GOVERNMENT OF COUNTIES

DIVISION 2
Officers

PART 2
BOARD OF SUPERVISORS

CHAPTER 3
FINANCIAL POWERS
[Selected Provisions]

§25263. County workers' compensation reserve account.

DIVISION 4
Employees

PART 1
GENERAL
[Selected Provisions]

§31000.8. Self-insured county; definitions.

PART 3
RETIREMENT SYSTEMS

CHAPTER 3
COUNTY EMPLOYEES RETIREMENT LAW OF 1937

ARTICLE 3
Retirement Board
[Selected Provisions]

§31520.4. Benefits for retirement board member injured or killed.

ARTICLE 14
Subrogation
[Selected Provisions]

§31820. Recovery of value of benefits from third party.

CHAPTER 5
COUNTY FIRE SERVICE RETIREMENT LAW

ARTICLE 5
Contributions
[Selected Provisions]

§32338. Contributions by member absent from employment due to incapacity.

TITLE 5
LOCAL AGENCIES

DIVISION 1
Cities and Counties

PART 1
POWERS AND DUTIES COMMON TO CITIES AND COUNTIES

CHAPTER 4
POLICE OFFICERS' PENSION FUND AND FIREMEN'S PENSION FUND

ARTICLE 5
Extraterritorial Activities of County and City Peace Officers
[Selected Provisions]

§50920. "Peace officer."
§50921. Peace officer performing duty, not under direction of employer.

ARTICLE 6
Extraterritorial Activities of Firemen
[Selected Provisions]

§50926. Public firefighter performing duty, not under direction of employer.

DIVISION 2
Cities, Counties, and Other Agencies

PART 1
POWERS AND DUTIES COMMON TO CITIES, COUNTIES, AND OTHER AGENCIES

CHAPTER 1
GENERAL

ARTICLE 2
Emergency Powers
[Selected Provisions]

§53023. Privileges and immunities of local agent apply extraterritorially.

CHAPTER 6
REVENUE BOND LAW OF 1941

ARTICLE 5
Additional Powers to Secure Bonds
[Selected Provisions]

§54462. Provision for amount and kind of insurance.

TITLE 8
THE ORGANIZATION AND GOVERNMENT OF COURTS

CHAPTER 2
THE JUDICIAL COUNCIL

ARTICLE 4
Court Interpreter Services
[Selected Provisions]

§68562. Certification of court interpreters—Procedures, standards, and guidelines.

HARBORS AND NAVIGATION CODE

DIVISION 8
HARBOR AND PORT DISTRICTS

PART 4
PORT DISTRICTS

CHAPTER 2
BOARD OF PORT COMMISSIONERS

ARTICLE 2
Jurisdiction and Powers of the Board
[Selected Provisions]

§6276. Stevedore employee workers' compensation benefits.

PART 6
RIVER PORT DISTRICTS

CHAPTER 2
PORT COMMISSION

ARTICLE 2
Jurisdiction and Powers of the Board
[Selected Provisions]

§6869. Federal benefits in lieu of state benefits.

HEALTH AND SAFETY CODE

DIVISION 13
HOUSING

PART 1.5
Regulation of Buildings Used for Human Habitation

CHAPTER 2
RULES AND REGULATIONS
[Selected Provisions]

§17922.5. Building permits from state or local agencies.

MILITARY AND VETERANS CODE

DIVISION 2
THE MILITARY FORCES OF THE STATE

PART 1
The State Militia

CHAPTER 5
COMPENSATION, ALLOWANCE, AND INSURANCE

ARTICLE 3
Casualty Insurance

§340. Members of National Guard, organized or unorganized militia injured in line of duty.
§340.1. Disability for those wounded in service of state.
§340.2. Disability for those transferred under mutual aid or interagency agreements.
§341. Member of militia; determination of average yearly earnings; "injury suffered in line of duty."
§342. Jurisdiction of Appeals Board.

ARTICLE 4
State Militia Disability Equality Act

§345. Citation of article.
§346. Disability benefits.

PART 2
California Cadet Corps and Voluntary Organizations

CHAPTER 1
CALIFORNIA CADET CORPS
[Selected Provisions]

§520. Right to compensation; determination of average yearly earnings.

CHAPTER 3
STATE MILITARY RESERVE ACT
[Selected Provisions]

§562. Members of State Guard; right to compensation; determination of average yearly earnings; "injury suffered in line of duty."

PENAL CODE

PART 1
Of Crimes and Punishments

TITLE 10
OF CRIMES AGAINST THE PUBLIC HEALTH AND SAFETY
[Selected Provisions]

§385. "High voltage"; "overhead conductor"; penalty for activity within specified distance of high voltage overhead conductor and for failure to post warning sign; exceptions.

TITLE 13
OF CRIMES AGAINST PROPERTY

CHAPTER 10
CRIMES AGAINST INSURED PROPERTY AND INSURERS
[Selected Provisions]

§549. Solicitation or referral for purposes of insurance fraud.
§550. Making false or fraudulent claims—Punishment.

PART 2
Of Criminal Procedure

TITLE 3
ADDITIONAL PROVISIONS REGARDING CRIMINAL PROCEDURE

CHAPTER 2
TIME OF COMMENCING CRIMINAL ACTIONS
[Selected Provisions]

§803. Limitation not tolled or extended—Does not commence until discovery of offense.

TITLE 12
OF SPECIAL PROCEEDINGS OF A CRIMINAL NATURE

CHAPTER 3
OF SEARCH WARRANTS
[Selected Provisions]

§1524. Grounds for issuance.

PART 3
Of Imprisonment and the Death Penalty

TITLE 4
COUNTY JAILS, FARMS AND CAMPS

CHAPTER 1
COUNTY JAILS
[Selected Provisions]

§4017. Prisoner labor for firefighting; benefits for injuries; "labor on the public works."
§4017.5. Work required of persons imprisoned for contempt.

CHAPTER 2
COUNTY INDUSTRIAL FARMS AND ROAD CAMPS

ARTICLE 1
County Industrial Farms
[Selected Provisions]

§4125.1. Credit for fire suppression work.

TITLE 7
ADMINISTRATION OF THE STATE CORRECTIONAL SYSTEM

CHAPTER 2
THE SECRETARY OF THE DEPARTMENT OF CORRECTIONS AND REHABILITATION
[Selected Provisions]

§5069. Rehabilitation for injured inmates; notice to inmate.

VEHICLE CODE

DIVISION 13
TOWING AND LOADING EQUIPMENT

CHAPTER 5
TRANSPORTING OTHER LOADS

ARTICLE 2
Vehicles Transporting Workmen
[Selected Provisions]

§31402. Operation of farm labor vehicle after notice that vehicle is in unsafe condition.

§31403. Transportation of passengers in unsafe farm labor vehicles.

WELFARE AND INSTITUTIONS CODE

DIVISION 2
CHILDREN

PART 1
Delinquents and Wards of the Juvenile Court

CHAPTER 2
JUVENILE COURT LAW

ARTICLE 1
General Provisions
[Selected Provisions]

§219. Ward of juvenile court engaged in rehabilitative work; right to benefits.

ARTICLE 24
Wards and Dependent Children—Juvenile Homes, Ranches and Camps
[Selected Provisions]

§883. Wards of juvenile homes, ranches, or camps; right to benefits.

DIVISION 9
PUBLIC SOCIAL SERVICES

PART 3
Aid and Medical Assistance

CHAPTER 3
STATE SUPPLEMENTARY PROGRAM FOR AGED, BLIND AND DISABLED

ARTICLE 7
In-Home Supportive Services
[Selected Provisions]

§12302.2. Performance of statutory compensation and benefit obligations when direct payment made to provider or recipient; payment of administrative costs.

§12302.21. Workers' compensation coverage for employees of nonprofit and proprietary agencies who contract with counties to provide in-home supportive services.

§12302.5. Establishment of agents for employers in order to comply with federal and state laws.

CHAPTER 7
BASIC HEALTH CARE

ARTICLE 1
General Provisions
[Selected Provisions]

§14011. Verification of income required to obtain benefits.

ARTICLE 3
Administration
[Selected Provisions]

§14101.7. Reimbursement from Appeals Board.

DIVISION 10
STATE DEPARTMENT OF REHABILITATION

PART 1
General Provisions

CHAPTER 1
POWERS AND DUTIES
[Selected Provisions]

§19005.5. Federal targeted jobs tax credit eligibility.

SELECTED PROVISIONS Of The CALIFORNIA CONSTITUTION

ARTICLE XIV LABOR RELATIONS [Selected Provisions]

§1. Minimum wages; general welfare of employees.

The Legislature may provide for minimum wages and for the general welfare of employees and for those purposes may confer on a commission legislative, executive, and judicial powers. **Leg.H.** Adopted June 8, 1976.

§4. Workers' compensation system.

The Legislature is hereby expressly vested with plenary power, unlimited by any provision of this Constitution, to create, and enforce a complete system of workers' compensation, by appropriate legislation, and in that behalf to create and enforce a liability on the part of any or all persons to compensate any or all of their workers for injury or disability, and their dependents for death incurred or sustained by the said workers in the course of their employment, irrespective of the fault of any party. A complete system of workers' compensation includes adequate provisions for the comfort, health and safety and general welfare of any and all workers and those dependent upon them for support to the extent of relieving from the consequences of any injury or death incurred or sustained by workers in the course of their employment, irrespective of the fault of any party; also full provision for securing safety in places of employment; full provision for such medical, surgical hospital and other remedial treatment as is requisite to cure and relieve from the effects of such injury; full provision for adequate insurance coverage against liability to pay or furnish compensation; full provision for regulating such insurance coverage in all its aspects, including the establishment and management of a State compensation insurance fund; full provision for otherwise securing the payment of compensation; and full provision for vesting power, authority and jurisdiction in an administrative body with all the requisite governmental functions to determine any dispute or matter arising under such legislation, to the end that the administration of such legislation shall accomplish substantial justice in all cases expeditiously, inexpensively, and without incumbrance of any character; all of which matters are expressly declared to be the social public policy of this State, binding upon all departments of the State government.

The Legislature is vested with plenary powers, to provide for the settlement of any disputes arising under such legislation by arbitration, or by an industrial accident commission, by the courts, or by either, any, or all of these agencies, either separately or in combination, and may fix and control the method and manner of trial of any such dispute, the rules of evidence and the manner of review of decisions rendered by the tribunal or tribunals designated by it; provided, that all decisions of any such tribunal shall be subject to review by the appellate court of this State. The Legislature may combine in one statute all the provisions for a complete system of workers' compensation, as herein defined.

The Legislature shall have power to provide for the payment of an award to the state in the case of the death, arising out of and in the course of the employment, of an employee without dependents, and such awards may be used for the payment of extra compensation for subsequent injuries beyond the liability of a single employer for awards to employees of the employer.

Nothing contained herein shall be taken or construed to impair or render ineffectual in any measure the creation and existence of the industrial accident commission of this State or the State compensation insurance fund, the creation and existence of which, with all the functions vested in them, are hereby ratified and confirmed. **Leg.H.** Adopted June 8, 1976.

Ref.: 8 C.C.R. §§10109, 10548, 10560, 10562, 10727; Herlick Handbook § 1.01[1].

§5. Convicts' labor; state benefit.

(a) The Director of Corrections or any county Sheriff or other local government official charged with jail operations, may enter into contracts with public entities, nonprofit or for profit organizations, entities, or businesses for the purpose of conducting programs which use inmate labor. Such programs shall be operated and implemented pursuant to statutes enacted by or in accordance with the provisions of the Prison Inmate Labor Initiative of 1990, and by rules and regulations prescribed by the Director of Corrections and, for county jail programs, by local ordinances.

(b) No contract shall be executed with an employer that will initiate employment by inmates in the same job classification as non-inmate employees of the same employer who are on strike, as defined in Section 1132.6 of the Labor Code, as it reads on January 1, 1990, or who are subject to lockout, as defined in Section 1132.8 of the Labor Code, as it reads on January 1, 1990. Total daily hours worked by inmates employed in the same job classification as non-inmate employees of the same employer who are on strike, as defined in Section 1132.6 of the Labor Code, as it reads on January 1, 1990, or who are subject to lockout, as defined in Section 1132.8 of the Labor Code, as it reads on January 1, 1990, shall not exceed, for the duration of the strike, the average daily hours worked for the preceding six months, or if the program has been in operation for less than six months, the average for the period of operation.

(c) Nothing in this section shall be interpreted as creating a right of inmates to work. **Leg.H.** Former section repealed operative November 7, 1990; new section adopted operative November 7, 1990.

SELECTED PROVISIONS Of The BUSINESS AND PROFESSIONS CODE

DIVISION 3 PROFESSIONS AND VOCATIONS GENERALLY

CHAPTER 2.7 ADVERTISING FOR WORKERS' COMPENSATION LEGAL SERVICES

§5499.30. Name of attorney required in advertisement for workers' compensation legal services.

(a) Any individual, firm, corporation, partnership, organization, or association which prints, displays, publishes, distributes, or broadcasts or causes or permits to be advertised, printed, displayed, published, distributed, or broadcast any advertising which purports to provide legal services for obtaining workers' compensation benefits shall include the name of at least one attorney associated with the individual, firm, corporation, partnership, organization, or association in all such advertising.

(b) As used in this section, the term "legal services" includes any service which refers potential clients to any attorney.

(c) A violation of this section is a misdemeanor, punishable by imprisonment in the county jail for not more than one year, or by a fine not exceeding ten thousand dollars ($10,000), or both. **Leg.H.** 1993 ch. 120, effective July 16, 1993.

CHAPTER 9 CONTRACTORS

ARTICLE 7 Disciplinary Proceedings [Selected Provisions]

§7110. Grounds for disciplinary action.

Willful or deliberate disregard and violation of the building laws of the state, or of any political subdivision thereof, or of Section 8550 or 8556 of this code, or of Sections 1689.5 to 1689.15, inclusive, of the Civil Code, or of the safety laws or labor laws or compensation insurance laws or Unemployment Insurance Code of the state, or of the Subletting and Subcontracting Fair Practices Act (Chapter 4 (commencing with Section 4100) of Part 1 of Division 2 of the Public Contract Code), or violation by any licensee of any provision of the Health and Safety Code or Water Code, relating to the digging, boring, or drilling of water wells, or Article 2 (commencing with Section 4216) of Chapter 3.1 of Division 5 of Title 1 of the Government Code, constitutes a cause for disciplinary action. **Leg.H.** 1994 ch. 362, 2002 ch. 1013 (SB 2026), 2010 ch. 415 (SB 1491) §22.

ARTICLE 7.5 Workers' Compensation Insurance Reports

§7125. Certificate of Workers' Compensation Insurance or Certification of Self-Insurance required for licensure; exceptions; report to registrar.

(a) Except as provided in subdivision (b), the board shall require as a condition precedent to the issuance, reinstatement, reactivation, renewal, or continued maintenance of a license, that the applicant or licensee have on file at all times a current and valid Certificate of Workers' Compensation Insurance or Certification of Self-Insurance in the applicant's or licensee's business name. A Certificate of Workers' Compensation Insurance shall be issued and filed, electronically or otherwise, by an insurer duly licensed to write workers' compensation insurance in this state. A Certification of Self-Insurance shall be issued and filed by the Director of Industrial Relations. If reciprocity conditions exist, as provided in Section 3600.5 of the Labor Code, the registrar shall require the information deemed necessary to ensure compliance with this section.

(b) This section does not apply to an applicant or licensee who meets both of the following conditions:

(1) Has no employees provided that he or she files a statement with the board on a form prescribed by the registrar prior to the issuance, reinstatement, reactivation, or continued maintenance of a license, certifying that he or she does not employ any person in any manner so as to become subject to the workers' compensation laws of

Misc. Provisions

California or is not otherwise required to provide for workers' compensation insurance coverage under California law.

(2) Does not hold a C-39 license, as defined in Section 832.39 of Title 16 of the California Code of Regulations.

(c) No Certificate of Workers' Compensation Insurance, Certification of Self-Insurance, or exemption certificate is required of a holder of a license that has been inactivated on the official records of the board during the period the license is inactive.

(d)(1) The insurer, including the State Compensation Insurance Fund, shall report to the registrar the following information for any policy required under this section: name, license number, policy number, dates that coverage is scheduled to commence and lapse, and cancellation date if applicable.

(2) A workers' compensation insurer shall also report to the registrar a licensee whose workers' compensation insurance policy is canceled by the insurer if all of the following conditions are met:

(A) The insurer has completed a premium audit or investigation.

(B) A material misrepresentation has been made by the insured that results in financial harm to the insurer.

(C) No reimbursement has been paid by the insured to the insurer.

(3) Willful or deliberate disregard and violation of workers' compensation insurance laws constitutes a cause for disciplinary action by the registrar against the licensee.

(e)(1) For any license that, on January 1, 2013, is active and includes a C-39 classification in addition to any other classification, the registrar shall, in lieu of the automatic license suspension otherwise required under this article, remove the C-39 classification from the license unless a valid Certificate of Workers' Compensation Insurance or Certification of Self-Insurance is received by the registrar.

(2) For any licensee whose license, after January 1, 2013, is active and has had the C-39 classification removed as provided in paragraph (1), and who is found by the registrar to have employees and to lack a valid Certificate of Workers' Compensation Insurance or Certification of Self-Insurance, that license shall be automatically suspended as required under this article.

(f) The information reported pursuant to paragraph (2) of subdivision (d) shall be confidential, and shall be exempt from disclosure under the California Public Records Act (Chapter 3.5 (commencing with Section 6250) of Division 7 of Title 1 of the Government Code). **Leg.H.** 1991 ch. 1160, 1995 ch. 467, 1996 ch. 331, 2002 ch. 311 (AB 264), 2006 ch. 38 (AB 881) §1, 2010 ch. 423 (AB 2305) §1, 2011 ch. 686 (AB 878) §1, 2012 ch. 389 (AB 2219) §1.

2011 Note: The Legislature finds and declares that Sections 1 and 2 of this act, which amend Section 7125 of the Business and Professions Code, impose a limitation on the public's right of access to the meetings of public bodies or the writings of public officials and agencies within the meaning of Section 3 of Article I of the California Constitution. Pursuant to that constitutional provision, the Legislature makes the following findings to demonstrate the interest protected by this limitation and the need for protecting that interest:

In order to allow the Contractors' State License Board to fully implement the Contractors' State License Law, it is imperative to protect the interests of those persons submitting information to the board to ensure that any personal or sensitive business information that this act requires those persons to submit is protected as confidential information. Stats. 2011 ch. 686 (AB 878) §3.

Ref.: Hanna § 3.134; Herlick Handbook § 3.23.

§7125.1. License reinstatement retroactive to effective date of certificate if submitted within 90 days; exception.

(a) The registrar shall accept a certificate required by Section 7125 as of the effective date shown on the certificate, if the certificate is received by the registrar within 90 days after that date, and shall reinstate the license to which the certificate pertains, if otherwise eligible, retroactive to the effective date of the certificate.

(b) Notwithstanding subdivision (a), the registrar shall accept the certificate as of the effective date shown on the certificate, even if the certificate is not received by the registrar within 90 days after that date, upon a showing by the licensee, on a form acceptable to the registrar, that the failure to have a certificate on file was due to circumstances beyond the control of the licensee. The registrar shall reinstate the license to which the certificate pertains, if otherwise eligible, retroactive to the effective date of the certificate. **Leg.H.** 1995 ch. 467 §18.

§7125.2. Failure to obtain or maintain insurance—Automatic license suspension; registrar notice and citation; reinstatement.

The failure of a licensee to obtain or maintain workers' compensation insurance coverage, if required under this chapter, shall result in the automatic suspension of the license by operation of law in accordance with the provisions of this section, but this suspension shall not affect, alter, or limit the status of the licensee as an employer for purposes of Section 3716 of the Labor Code.

(a) The license suspension imposed by this section is effective upon the earlier of either of the following:

(1) On the date that the relevant workers' compensation insurance coverage lapses.

(2) On the date that workers' compensation coverage is required to be obtained.

(b) A licensee who is subject to suspension under paragraph (1) of subdivision (a) shall be provided a notice by the registrar that includes all of the following:

(1) The reason for the license suspension and the effective date.

(2) A statement informing the licensee that a pending suspension will be posted to the license record for not more than 45 days prior to the posting of any license suspension periods required under this article.

(3) The procedures required to reinstate the license.

(c) Reinstatement may be made at any time following the suspension by showing proof of compliance as specified in Sections 7125 and 7125.1.

(d) In addition, with respect to an unlicensed individual acting in the capacity of a contractor who is not otherwise exempted from the provisions of this chapter, a citation may be issued by the registrar under Section 7028.7 for failure to comply with this article and to maintain workers' compensation insurance. An opportunity for a hearing as specified in Section 7028.10 will be granted if requested within 15 working days after service of the citation. **Leg.H.** 1995 ch. 467 §20, 2002 ch. 311 (AB 264).

§7125.3. Periods of licensure.

A contractor shall be considered duly licensed during all periods in which the registrar is required to accept the certificate prescribed by Section 7125, provided the licensee has otherwise complied with the provisions of this chapter. **Leg.H.** 2002 ch. 311 (AB 264).

§7125.4. Causes for disciplinary action.

(a) The filing of the exemption certificate prescribed by this article that is false, or the employment of a person subject to coverage under the workers' compensation laws after the filing of an exemption certificate without first filing a Certificate of Workers' Compensation Insurance or Certification of Self-Insurance in accordance with the provisions of this article, or the employment of a person subject to coverage under the workers' compensation laws without maintaining coverage for that person, constitutes cause for disciplinary action.

(b) Any qualifier for a license who, under Section 7068.1, is responsible for assuring that a licensee complies with the provisions of this chapter is also guilty of a misdemeanor for committing or failing to prevent the commission of any of the acts that are cause for disciplinary action under this section. **Leg.H.** 2002 ch. 311 (AB 264), 2005 ch. 205 (SB 488) §2, 2015 ch. 389 (SB 560) §3.

§7125.5. Renewal of license; exemption for workers' compensation insurance; recertification; retroactive renewal.

(a) At the time of renewal, all active licensees with an exemption for workers' compensation insurance on file with the board, submitted pursuant to subdivision (b) of Section 7125, shall either recertify the licensee's exemption by completing a recertification statement on the license renewal form, as provided by the board, or shall provide a current and valid Certificate of Workers' Compensation Insurance or Certificate of Self-Insurance, whichever is applicable.

(b) The license shall not be renewed unless a licensee with an exemption for workers' compensation insurance on file with the board recertifies the exemption status or provides a current and valid Certificate of Workers' Compensation Insurance or Certificate of Self-Insurance in conjunction with the license renewal.

(c) If the documentation required by subdivision (a) is not provided with the license renewal but is received within 30 days after notification by the board of the renewal rejection, the registrar shall grant a retroactive renewal pursuant to Section 7141.5 back to the date of the postmark of the otherwise acceptable renewal. A renewal that is still incomplete for any reason after 30 days after notification of rejection shall not be eligible for retroactive renewal under this subdivision. **Leg.H.** 2011 ch. 546 (AB 397) §1.

Ref.: Hanna § 3.134.

§7126. Misdemeanor violations.

(a) Any licensee or agent or officer thereof, who violates, or omits to comply with, any of the provisions of this article is guilty of a misdemeanor.

(b) Any person not licensed in accordance with this chapter who is acting as a contractor and who violates, or omits to comply with, Section 3700 of the Labor Code is guilty of a misdemeanor.

(c) Prosecution of any offense under this section shall be commenced within two years after commission of the offense as provided in Section 802 of the Penal Code. **Leg.H.** 1943 ch. 132 §1, 2018 ch. 323 (AB 2705) §1.

§7127. Stop order prohibiting use of employee labor for failure to secure workers' compensation insurance coverage—Failure to comply; protest; hearing; findings.

(a)(1) If an employer subject to licensure under this chapter has failed to secure the payment of compensation as required by Section 3700 of the Labor Code, and whether that employer is or is not licensed under this chapter, the registrar may, in addition to any other administrative remedy, issue and serve on that employer a stop order prohibiting the use of employee labor. The stop order shall become effective immediately upon service. An employee affected by the work stoppage shall be paid by the employer for his or her time lost, not exceeding 10 days, pending compliance by the employer.

(2) Failure of any employer, officer, or any person having direction, management, or control of any place of employment or of employees to observe a stop order issued and served upon him or her pursuant to this section is a misdemeanor punishable by imprisonment in the county jail not exceeding 60 days or by a fine not exceeding ten thousand dollars ($10,000), or both.

(b) An employer who is subject to this section may protest the stop order by making and filing with the registrar a written request for a hearing within 20 days after service of the stop order. The hearing shall be held within five days from the date of filing the request. The registrar shall notify the employer of the time and place of the hearing by mail. At the conclusion of the hearing, the stop order shall be immediately affirmed or dismissed, and within 24 hours thereafter the registrar shall issue and serve on all parties to the hearing by registered or certified mail a written notice of findings and findings. A writ of mandate may be taken from the findings to the appropriate superior court. Such writ must be taken within 45 days after the mailing of the notice of findings and findings. **Leg.H.** 2010 ch. 643 (SB 1254) §1.

Ref.: Herlick Handbook § 7.6.

CHAPTER 10.5 APP-BASED DRIVERS AND SERVICES

ARTICLE 1 Title, Findings and Declarations, and Statement of Purpose

§7448. Title.

This chapter shall be known, and may be cited, as the Protect App-Based Drivers and Services Act. **Leg.H.** Adopted by voters, Prop. 22 §1, effective November 3, 2020.

§7449. Findings and declarations.

The people of the State of California find and declare as follows:

(a) Hundreds of thousands of Californians are choosing to work as independent contractors in the modern economy using app-based rideshare and delivery platforms to transport passengers and deliver food, groceries, and other goods as a means of earning income while maintaining the flexibility to decide when, where, and how they work.

(b) These app-based rideshare and delivery drivers include parents who want to work flexible schedules while children are in school; students who want to earn money in between classes; retirees who rideshare or deliver a few hours a week to supplement fixed incomes and for social interaction; military spouses and partners who frequently relocate; and families struggling with California's high cost of living that need to earn extra income.

(c) Millions of California consumers and businesses, and our state's economy as a whole, also benefit from the services of people who work as independent contractors using app-based rideshare and delivery platforms. App-based rideshare and delivery drivers are providing convenient and affordable transportation for the public, reducing impaired and drunk driving, improving mobility for seniors and individuals with disabilities, providing new transportation options for families who cannot afford a vehicle, and providing new affordable and convenient delivery options for grocery stores, restaurants, retailers, and other local businesses and their patrons.

(d) However, recent legislation has threatened to take away the flexible work opportunities of hundreds of thousands of Californians, potentially forcing them into set shifts and mandatory hours, taking away their ability to make their own decisions about the jobs they take and the hours they work.

(e) Protecting the ability of Californians to work as independent contractors throughout the state using app-based rideshare and delivery platforms is necessary so people can continue to choose which jobs they take, to work as often or as little as they like, and to work with multiple platforms or companies, all the while preserving access to app-based rideshare and delivery services that are beneficial to consumers, small businesses, and the California economy.

(f) App-based rideshare and delivery drivers deserve economic security. This chapter is necessary to protect their freedom to work independently, while also providing these workers new benefits and protections not available under current law. These benefits and protections include a healthcare subsidy consistent with the average contributions required under the Affordable Care Act (ACA); a new minimum earnings guarantee tied to 120 percent of minimum wage with no maximum; compensation for vehicle expenses; occupational accident insurance to cover on-the-job injuries; and protection against discrimination and sexual harassment.

(g) California law and rideshare and delivery network companies should protect the safety of both drivers and consumers without affecting the right of app-based rideshare and delivery drivers to work as independent contractors. Such protections should, at a minimum, include criminal background checks of drivers; zero tolerance policies for drug- and alcohol-related offenses; and driver safety training. **Leg.H.** Adopted by voters, Prop. 22 §1, effective November 3, 2020.

§7450. Statement of purpose.

The purposes of this chapter are as follows:

(a) To protect the basic legal right of Californians to choose to work as independent contractors with rideshare and delivery network companies throughout the state.

(b) To protect the individual right of every app-based rideshare and delivery driver to have the flexibility to set their own hours for when, where, and how they work.

(c) To require rideshare and delivery network companies to offer new protections and benefits for app-based rideshare and delivery drivers, including minimum compensation levels, insurance to cover on-the-job injuries, automobile accident insurance, health care subsidies for qualifying drivers, protection against harassment and discrimination, and mandatory contractual rights and appeal processes.

(d) To improve public safety by requiring criminal background checks, driver safety training, and other safety provisions to help ensure app-based rideshare and delivery drivers do not pose a threat to customers or the public. **Leg.H.** Adopted by voters, Prop. 22 §1, effective November 3, 2020.

ARTICLE 2
App-Based Driver Independence

§7451. Protecting independence.

Notwithstanding any other provision of law, including, but not limited to, the Labor Code, the Unemployment Insurance Code, and any orders, regulations, or opinions of the Department of Industrial Relations or any board, division, or commission within the Department of Industrial Relations, an app-based driver is an independent contractor and not an employee or agent with respect to the app-based driver's relationship with a network company if the following conditions are met:

(a) The network company does not unilaterally prescribe specific dates, times of day, or a minimum number of hours during which the app-based driver must be logged into the network company's online-enabled application or platform.

(b) The network company does not require the app-based driver to accept any specific rideshare service or delivery service request as a condition of maintaining access to the network company's online-enabled application or platform.

(c) The network company does not restrict the app-based driver from performing rideshare services or delivery services through other network companies except during engaged time.

(d) The network company does not restrict the app-based driver from working in any other lawful occupation or business. **Leg.H.** Adopted by voters, Prop. 22 §1, effective November 3, 2020.

§7452. Contract and termination provisions.

(a) A network company and an app-based driver shall enter into a written agreement prior to the driver receiving access to the network company's online-enabled application or platform.

(b) A network company shall not terminate a contract with an app-based driver unless based upon a ground specified in the contract.

(c) Network companies shall provide an appeals process for app-based drivers whose contracts are terminated by the network company. **Leg.H.** Adopted by voters, Prop. 22 §1, effective November 3, 2020.

§7452.5. Independence unaffected.

Nothing in Article 3 (commencing with Section 7453) to Article 11 (commencing with Section 7467), inclusive, of this chapter shall be interpreted to in any way alter the relationship between a network company and an app-based driver for whom the conditions set forth in Section 7451 are satisfied. **Leg.H.** Adopted by voters, Prop. 22 §1, effective November 3, 2020.

ARTICLE 3
Compensation

§7453. Earnings guarantee.

(a) A network company shall ensure that for each earnings period, an app-based driver is compensated at not less than the net earnings floor as set forth in this section. The net earnings floor establishes a guaranteed minimum level of compensation for app-based drivers that cannot be reduced. In no way does the net earnings floor prohibit app-based drivers from earning a higher level of compensation.

(b) For each earnings period, a network company shall compare an app-based driver's net earnings against the net earnings floor for that app-based driver during the earnings period. In the event that the app-based driver's net earnings in the earnings period are less than the net earnings floor for that earnings period, the network company shall include an additional sum accounting for the difference in the app-based driver's earnings no later than during the next earnings period.

(c) No network company or agent shall take, receive, or retain any gratuity or a part thereof that is paid, given to, or left for an app-based driver by a customer or deduct any amount from the earnings due to an app-based driver for a ride or delivery on account of a gratuity paid in connection with the ride or delivery. A network company that permits customers to pay gratuities by credit card shall pay the app-based driver the full amount of the gratuity that the customer indicated on the credit card receipt, without any deductions for any credit card payment processing fees or costs that may be charged to the network company by the credit card company.

(d) For purposes of this chapter, the following definitions apply:

(1) "Applicable minimum wage" means the state mandated minimum wage for all industries or, if a passenger or item is picked up within the boundaries of a local government that has a higher minimum wage that is generally applicable to all industries, the local minimum wage of that local government. The applicable minimum wage shall be determined at the location where a passenger or item is picked up and shall apply for all engaged time spent completing that rideshare request or delivery request.

(2) "Earnings period" means a pay period, set by the network company, not to exceed 14 consecutive calendar days.

(3) "Net earnings" means all earnings received by an app-based driver in an earnings period, provided that the amount conforms to both of the following standards:

(A) The amount does not include gratuities, tolls, cleaning fees, airport fees, or other customer pass-throughs.

(B) The amount may include incentives or other bonuses.

(4) "Net earnings floor" means, for any earnings period, a total amount that is comprised of:

(A) For all engaged time, the sum of 120 percent of the applicable minimum wage for that engaged time.

(B)(i) The per-mile compensation for vehicle expenses set forth in this subparagraph multiplied by the total number of engaged miles.

(ii) After the effective date of this chapter and for the 2021 calendar year, the per-mile compensation for vehicle expenses shall be thirty cents ($0.30) per engaged mile. For calendar years after 2021, the amount per engaged mile shall be adjusted pursuant to clause (iii).

(iii) For calendar years following 2021, the per-mile compensation for vehicle expenses described in clause (ii) shall be adjusted annually to reflect any increase in inflation as measured by the Consumer Price Index for All Urban Consumers (CPI-U) published by the United States Bureau of Labor Statistics. The Treasurer's Office shall calculate and publish the adjustments required by this subparagraph.

(e) Nothing in this section shall be interpreted to require a network company to provide a particular amount of compensation to an app-based driver for any given rideshare or delivery request, as long as the app-based driver's net earnings for each earnings period equals or exceeds that app-based driver's net earnings floor for that earnings period as set forth in subdivision (b). For clarity, the net earnings floor in this section may be calculated on an average basis over the course of each earnings period. **Leg.H.** Adopted by voters, Prop. 22 §1, effective November 3, 2020.

ARTICLE 4
Benefits

§7454. Healthcare subsidy.

(a) Consistent with the average contributions required under the Affordable Care Act (ACA), a network company shall provide a quarterly health care subsidy to qualifying app-based drivers as set forth in this section. An app-based driver that averages the following amounts of engaged time per week on a network company's platform during a calendar quarter shall receive the following subsidies from that network company:

(1) For an average of 25 hours or more per week of engaged time in the calendar quarter, a payment greater

than or equal to 100 percent of the average ACA contribution for the applicable average monthly Covered California premium for each month in the quarter.

(2) For an average of at least 15 but less than 25 hours per week of engaged time in the calendar quarter, a payment greater than or equal to 50 percent of the average ACA contribution for the applicable average monthly Covered California premium for each month in the quarter.

(b) At the end of each earnings period, a network company shall provide to each app-based driver the following information:

(1) The number of hours of engaged time the app-based driver accrued on the network company's online-enabled application or platform during that earnings period.

(2) The number of hours of engaged time the app-based driver has accrued on the network company's online-enabled application or platform during the current calendar quarter up to that point.

(c) Covered California may adopt or amend regulations as it deems appropriate to permit app-based drivers receiving subsidies pursuant to this section to enroll in health plans through Covered California.

(d)(1) As a condition of providing the health care subsidy set forth in subdivision (a), a network company may require an app-based driver to submit proof of current enrollment in a qualifying health plan. Proof of current enrollment may include, but is not limited to, health insurance membership or identification cards, evidence of coverage and disclosure forms from the health plan, or claim forms and other documents necessary to submit claims.

(2) An app-based driver shall have not less than 15 calendar days from the end of the calendar quarter to provide proof of enrollment as set forth in paragraph (1).

(3) A network company shall provide a health care subsidy due for a calendar quarter under subdivision (a) within 15 days of the end of the calendar quarter or within 15 days of the app-based driver's submission of proof of enrollment as set forth in paragraph (1), whichever is later.

(e) For purposes of this section, a calendar quarter refers to the following four periods of time:

(1) January 1 through March 31.

(2) April 1 through June 30.

(3) July 1 through September 30.

(4) October 1 through December 31.

(f) Nothing in this section shall be interpreted to prevent an app-based driver from receiving a health care subsidy from more than one network company for the same calendar quarter.

(g) On or before December 31, 2020, and on or before each September 1 thereafter, Covered California shall publish the average statewide monthly premium for an individual for the following calendar year for a Covered California bronze health insurance plan.

(h) This section shall become inoperative in the event the United States or the State of California implements a universal health care system or substantially similar system that expands coverage to the recipients of subsidies under this section. **Leg.H.** Adopted by voters, Prop. 22 §1, effective November 3, 2020.

§7455. Loss and liability protection.

No network company shall operate in California for more than 90 days unless the network company carries, provides, or otherwise makes available the following insurance coverage:

(a) For the benefit of app-based drivers, occupational accident insurance to cover medical expenses and lost income resulting from injuries suffered while the app-based driver is online with a network company's online-enabled application or platform. Policies shall at a minimum provide the following:

(1) Coverage for medical expenses incurred, up to at least one million dollars ($1,000,000).

(2)(A) Disability payments equal to 66 percent of the app-based driver's average weekly earnings from all network companies as of the date of injury, with minimum and maximum weekly payment rates to be determined in accordance with subdivision (a) of Section 4453 of the Labor Code for up to the first 104 weeks following the injury.

(B) "Average weekly earnings" means the app-based driver's total earnings from all network companies during the 28 days prior to the covered accident divided by four.

(b) For the benefit of spouses, children, or other dependents of app-based drivers, accidental death insurance for injuries suffered by an app-based driver while the app-based driver is online with the network company's online-enabled application or platform that result in death. For purposes of this subdivision, burial expenses and death benefits shall be determined in accordance with Section 4701 and Section 4702 of the Labor Code.

(c) For the purposes of this section, "online" means the time when an app-based driver is utilizing a network company's online-enabled application or platform and can receive requests for rideshare services or delivery services from the network company, or during engaged time.

(d) Occupational accident insurance or accidental death insurance under subdivisions (a) and (b) shall not be required to cover an accident that occurs while online but outside of engaged time where the injured app-based driver is in engaged time on one or more other network company platforms or where the app-based driver is engaged in personal activities. If an accident is covered by occupational accident insurance or accidental death insurance maintained by more than one network company, the insurer of the network company against whom a claim is filed is entitled to contribution for the pro-rata share of coverage attributable to one or more other network companies up to the coverages and limits in subdivisions (a) and (b).

(e) Any benefits provided to an app-based driver under subdivision (a) or (b) of this section shall be considered amounts payable under a worker's compensation law or disability benefit for the purpose of determining amounts payable under any insurance provided under Article 2 (commencing with Section 11580) of Chapter 1 of Part 3 of Division 2 of the Insurance Code.

(f)(1) For the benefit of the public, a DNC as defined in Section 7463 shall maintain automobile liability insurance of at least one million dollars ($1,000,000) per occurrence to compensate third parties for injuries or losses proximately caused by the operation of an automobile by an app-based driver during engaged time in instances where the automobile is not otherwise covered by a policy that complies with subdivision (b) of Section 11580.1 of the Insurance Code.

(2) For the benefit of the public, a TNC as defined in Section 7463 shall maintain liability insurance policies as required by Article 7 (commencing with Section 5430) of Chapter 8 of Division 2 of the Public Utilities Code.

(3) For the benefit of the public, a TCP as defined in Section 7463 shall maintain liability insurance policies as required by Article 4 (commencing with Section 5391) of Chapter 8 of Division 2 of the Public Utilities Code. **Leg.H.** Adopted by voters, Prop. 22 §1, effective November 3, 2020.

ARTICLE 5
Antidiscrimination and Public Safety

§7456. Antidiscrimination.

(a) It is an unlawful practice, unless based upon a bona fide occupational qualification or public or app-based driver safety need, for a network company to refuse to contract with, terminate the contract of, or deactivate from the network company's online-enabled application or platform, any app-based driver or prospective app-based driver based upon race, color, ancestry, national origin, religion, creed, age, physical or mental disability, sex, gender, sexual orientation, gender identity or expression, medical condition, genetic information, marital status, or military or veteran status.

(b) Claims brought pursuant to this section shall be brought solely under the procedures established by the Unruh Civil Rights Act (Section 51 of the Civil Code) and will be governed by its requirements and remedies. **Leg.H.** Adopted by voters, Prop. 22 §1, effective November 3, 2020.

§7457. Sexual harassment prevention.

(a) A network company shall develop a sexual harassment policy intended to protect app-based drivers and members of the public using rideshare services or delivery services. The policy shall be available on the network company's internet website. The policy shall, at a minimum, do all of the following:

(1) Identify behaviors that may constitute sexual harassment, including the following: unwanted sexual advances; leering, gestures, or displaying sexually suggestive objects, pictures, cartoons, or posters; derogatory comments, epithets, slurs, or jokes; graphic comments, sexually degrading words, or suggestive or obscene messages or invitations; and physical touching or assault, as well as impeding or blocking movements.

(2) Indicate that the network company, and in many instances the law, prohibits app-based drivers and customers utilizing rideshare services or delivery services from committing prohibited harassment.

(3) Establish a process for app-based drivers, customers, and rideshare passengers to submit complaints that ensures confidentiality to the extent possible; an impartial and timely investigation; and remedial actions and resolutions based on the information collected during the investigation process.

(4) Provide an opportunity for app-based drivers and customers utilizing rideshare services or delivery services to submit complaints electronically so complaints can be resolved quickly.

(5) Indicate that when the network company receives allegations of misconduct, it will conduct a fair, timely, and thorough investigation to reach reasonable conclusions based on the information collected.

(6) Make clear that neither app-based drivers nor customers utilizing rideshare services or delivery services shall be retaliated against as a result of making a good faith complaint or participating in an investigation against another app-based driver, customer, or rideshare passenger.

(b) Prior to providing rideshare services or delivery services through a network company's online-enabled application or platform, an app-based driver shall do both of the following:

(1) Review the network company's sexual harassment policy.

(2) Confirm to the network company, for which electronic confirmation shall suffice, that the app-based driver has reviewed the network company's sexual harassment policy.

(c) Claims brought pursuant to this section shall be brought solely under the procedures established by the Unruh Civil Rights Act (Section 51 of the Civil Code) and will be governed by its requirements and remedies. **Leg.H.** Adopted by voters, Prop. 22 §1, effective November 3, 2020.

§7458. Criminal background checks.

(a) A network company shall conduct, or have a third party conduct, an initial local and national criminal background check for each app-based driver who uses the network company's online-enabled application or platform to provide rideshare services or delivery services. The background check shall be consistent with the standards contained in subdivision (a) of Section 5445.2 of the Public Utilities Code. Notwithstanding any other provision of law to the contrary, after an app-based driver's consent is obtained by a network company for an initial background check, no additional consent shall be required for the continual monitoring of that app-based driver's criminal history if the network company elects to undertake such continual monitoring.

(b) A network company shall complete the initial criminal background check as required by subdivision (a) prior to permitting an app-based driver to utilize the network company's online-enabled application or platform. The network company shall provide physical or electronic copies or summaries of the initial criminal background check to the app-based driver.

(c) An app-based driver shall not be permitted to utilize a network company's online-enabled application or platform if one of the following applies:

(1) The driver has ever been convicted of any crime listed in subparagraph (B) of paragraph (2) of subdivision (a) of Section 5445.2 of the Public Utilities Code, any serious felony as defined by subdivision (c) of Section 1192.7 of the Penal Code, or any hate crime as defined by Section 422.55 of the Penal Code.

(2) The driver has been convicted within the last seven

years of any crime listed in paragraph (3) of subdivision (a) of Section 5445.2 of the Public Utilities Code.

(d)(1) The ability of an app-based driver to utilize a network company's online-enabled application or platform may be suspended if the network company learns the driver has been arrested for any crime listed in either of the following:

(A) Subparagraph (B) of paragraph (2), or paragraph (3), of subdivision (a) of Section 5445.2 of the Public Utilities Code.

(B) Subdivision (c) of this section.

(2) The suspension described in paragraph (1) may be lifted upon the disposition of an arrest for any crime listed in subparagraph (B) of paragraph (2), or paragraph (3), of subdivision (a) of Section 5445.2 of the Public Utilities Code that does not result in a conviction. Such disposition includes a finding of factual innocence from any relevant charge, an acquittal at trial, an affidavit indicating the prosecuting attorney with jurisdiction over the alleged offense has declined to file a criminal complaint, or an affidavit indicating all relevant time periods described in Chapter 2 (commencing with Section 799) of Title 3 of Part 2 of the Penal Code have expired.

(e) Nothing in this section shall be interpreted to prevent a network company from imposing additional standards relating to criminal history.

(f) Notwithstanding Section 1786.12 of the Civil Code, an investigative consumer reporting agency may furnish an investigative consumer report to a network company about a person seeking to become an app-based driver, regardless of whether the app-based driver is to be an employee or an independent contractor of the network company. **Leg.H.** Adopted by voters, Prop. 22 §1, effective November 3, 2020.

§7459. Safety training.

(a) A network company shall require an app-based driver to complete the training described in this section prior to allowing the app-based driver to utilize the network company's online-enabled application or platform.

(b) A network company shall provide each app-based driver safety training. The safety training required by this section shall include the following subjects:

(1) Collision avoidance and defensive driving techniques.

(2) Identification of collision-causing elements such as excessive speed, DUI, and distracted driving.

(3) Recognition and reporting of sexual assault and misconduct.

(4) For app-based drivers delivering prepared food or groceries, food safety information relevant to the delivery of food, including temperature control.

(c) The training may, at the discretion of the network company, be provided via online, video, or in-person training.

(d) Notwithstanding subdivision (a), any app-based driver that has entered into a contract with a network company prior to January 1, 2021, to provide rideshare services or delivery services shall have until July 1, 2021, to complete the safety training required by this section, and may continue to provide rideshare services or delivery services through the network company's online-enabled application or platform until that date. On and after July 1, 2021, app-based drivers described in this subdivision must complete the training required by this section in order to continue providing rideshare services and delivery services.

(e) Any safety product, feature, process, policy, standard, or other effort undertaken by a network company, or the provision of equipment by a network company, to further public safety is not an indicia of an employment or agency relationship with an app-based driver. **Leg.H.** Adopted by voters, Prop. 22 §1, effective November 3, 2020.

§7460. Zero tolerance policies.

(a) A network company shall institute a "zero tolerance policy" that mandates prompt suspension of an app-based driver's access to the network company's online-enabled application or platform in any instance in which the network company receives a report through its online-enabled application or platform, or by any other company-approved method, from any person who reasonably suspects the app-based driver is under the influence of drugs or alcohol while providing rideshare services or delivery services.

(b) Upon receiving a report described in subdivision (a), a network company shall promptly suspend the app-based driver from the company's online-enabled application or platform for further investigation.

(c) A network company may suspend access to the network company's online-enabled application or platform for any app-based driver or customer found to be reporting an alleged violation of a zero tolerance policy as described in subdivision (a) where that driver or customer knows the report to be unfounded or based the report on an intent to inappropriately deny a driver access to the online-enabled application or platform. **Leg.H.** Adopted by voters, Prop. 22 §1, effective November 3, 2020.

§7460.5. Law enforcement information requests.

A network company shall make continuously and exclusively available to law enforcement a mechanism to submit requests for information to aid in investigations related to emergency situations, exigent circumstances, and critical incidents. **Leg.H.** Adopted by voters, Prop. 22 §1, effective November 3, 2020.

§7461. App-based driver rest.

An app-based driver shall not be logged in and driving on a network company's online-enabled application or platform for more than a cumulative total of 12 hours in any 24-hour period, unless that driver has already logged off for an uninterrupted period of 6 hours. If an app-based driver has been logged on and driving for more than a cumulative total of 12 hours in any 24-hour period, without logging off for an uninterrupted period of 6 hours, the driver shall be prohibited from logging back into the network company's online-enabled application or platform for an uninterrupted period of at least 6 hours. **Leg.H.** Adopted by voters, Prop. 22 §1, effective November 3, 2020.

§7462. Impersonating an app-based driver.

(a) Any person who fraudulently impersonates an app-based driver while providing or attempting to provide rideshare or delivery services shall be guilty of a misdemeanor, and is punishable by imprisonment in a county jail for up to six months, or a fine of up to ten thousand dollars ($10,000), or both. Nothing in this subdivision precludes prosecution under any other law.

(b) In addition to any other penalty provided by law, any person who fraudulently impersonates an app-based driver while providing or attempting to provide rideshare services or delivery services in the commission or attempted commission of an offense described in Section 207, 209, 220, 261, 264.1, 286, 287, 288, or 289 of the Penal Code shall be sentenced to an additional term of five years.

(c) In addition to any other penalty provided by law, any person who fraudulently impersonates an app-based driver while providing or attempting to provide rideshare services or delivery services in the commission of a felony or attempted felony and in so doing personally inflicts great bodily injury to another person other than an accomplice shall be sentenced to an additional term of five years.

(d) In addition to any other penalty provided by law, any person who fraudulently impersonates an app-based driver while providing or attempting to provide rideshare services or delivery services in the commission of a felony or attempted felony and in so doing causes the death of another person other than an accomplice shall be sentenced to an additional term of 10 years. **Leg.H.** Adopted by voters, Prop. 22 §1, effective November 3, 2020.

ARTICLE 6
Definitions

§7463. Definitions.

For purposes of this chapter, the following definitions shall apply:

(a) "App-based driver" means an individual who is a DNC courier, TNC driver, or TCP driver or permit holder; and for whom the conditions set forth in subdivisions (a) to (d), inclusive, of Section 7451 are satisfied.

(b) "Average ACA contribution" means 82 percent of the dollar amount of the average monthly Covered California premium.

(c) "Average monthly Covered California premium" equals the dollar amount published pursuant to subdivision (g) of Section 7454.

(d) "Covered California" means the California Health Benefit Exchange, codified in Title 22 (commencing with Section 100500) of the Government Code.

(e) "Customer" means one or more natural persons or business entities.

(f) "Delivery network company" (DNC) means a business entity that maintains an online-enabled application or platform used to facilitate delivery services within the State of California on an on-demand basis, and maintains a record of the amount of engaged time and engaged miles accumulated by DNC couriers. Deliveries are facilitated on an on-demand basis if DNC couriers are provided with the option to accept or decline each delivery request and the DNC does not require the DNC courier to accept any specific delivery request as a condition of maintaining access to the DNC's online-enabled application or platform.

(g) "Delivery network company courier" (DNC courier) means an individual who provides delivery services through a DNC's online-enabled application or platform.

(h) "Delivery services" means the fulfillment of delivery requests, meaning the pickup from any location of any item or items and the delivery of the items using a passenger vehicle, bicycle, scooter, walking, public transportation, or other similar means of transportation, to a location selected by the customer located within 50 miles of the pickup location. A delivery request may include more than one, but not more than 12, distinct orders placed by different customers. Delivery services may include the selection, collection, or purchase of items by a DNC courier provided that those tasks are done in connection with a delivery that the DNC courier has agreed to deliver. Delivery services do not include deliveries that are subject to Section 26090, as that section read on October 29, 2019.

(i) "Engaged miles" means all miles driven during engaged time in a passenger vehicle that is not owned, leased, or rented by the network company.

(j)(1) "Engaged time" means, subject to the conditions set forth in paragraph (2), the period of time, as recorded in a network company's online-enabled application or platform, from when an app-based driver accepts a rideshare request or delivery request to when the app-based driver completes that rideshare request or delivery request.

(2)(A) Engaged time shall not include the following:

(i) Any time spent performing a rideshare service or delivery service after the request has been cancelled by the customer.

(ii) Any time spent on a rideshare service or delivery service where the app-based driver abandons performance of the service prior to completion.

(B) Network companies may also exclude time if doing so is reasonably necessary to remedy or prevent fraudulent use of the network company's online-enabled application or platform.

(k) "Local government" means a city, county, city and county, charter city, or charter county.

(*l*) "Network company" means a business entity that is a DNC or a TNC.

(m) "Passenger vehicle" means a passenger vehicle as defined in Section 465 of the Vehicle Code.

(n) "Qualifying health plan" means a health insurance plan in which the app-based driver is the subscriber, that is not sponsored by an employer, and that is not a Medicare or Medicaid plan.

(o) "Rideshare service" means the transportation of one or more persons.

(p) "Transportation network company" (TNC) has the same meaning as the definition contained in subdivision (c) of Section 5431 of the Public Utilities Code.

(q) "Transportation network company driver" (TNC driver) has the same meaning as the definition of driver contained in subdivision (a) of Section 5431 of the Public Utilities Code.

(r) "Charter-party carrier of passengers" (TCP) shall have the same meaning as the definition contained in

Section 5360 of the Public Utilities Code, provided the driver is providing rideshare services using a passenger vehicle through a network company's online-enabled application or platform. **Leg.H.** Adopted by voters, Prop. 22 §1, effective November 3, 2020.

ARTICLE 7
Uniform Work Standards

§7464. State preemption.

(a) The performance of a single rideshare service or delivery service frequently requires an app-based driver to travel across the jurisdictional boundaries of multiple local governments. California has over 500 cities and counties, which can lead to overlapping, inconsistent, and contradictory local regulations for cross-jurisdictional services.

(b) In light of the cross-jurisdictional nature of the rideshare services and delivery services, and in addition to the other requirements and standards established by this chapter, the state hereby occupies the field in the following areas:

(1) App-based driver compensation and gratuity, except as provided in Section 7453.

(2) App-based driver scheduling, leave, health care subsidies, and any other work-related stipends, subsidies, or benefits.

(3) App-based driver licensing and insurance requirements.

(4) App-based driver rights with respect to a network company's termination of an app-based driver's contract.

(c) Notwithstanding subdivision (b), nothing in this section shall limit a local government's ability to adopt local ordinances necessary to punish the commission of misdemeanor and felony crimes or to enforce local ordinances and regulations enacted prior to October 29, 2019. **Leg.H.** Adopted by voters, Prop. 22 §1, effective November 3, 2020.

ARTICLE 8
Income Reporting

§7464.5. Information return requirements.

(a) A network company that is acting as a third-party settlement organization shall prepare an information return for each participating payee who is an app-based driver with a California address that has a gross amount of reportable payment transactions equal to or greater than six hundred dollars ($600) during a calendar year, irrespective of the number of transactions between the third-party settlement organization and the payee. A third-party settlement organization must report these amounts to the Franchise Tax Board and furnish a copy to the payee, even if it does not have a federal reporting obligation. The information return shall identify the following:

(1) The name, address, and tax identification number of the participating payee.

(2) The gross amount of the reportable payment transactions with respect to the participating payee.

(b) Within 30 days following the date such an information return would be due to the Internal Revenue Service, a network company shall file a copy of any information return required by subdivision (a) with the Franchise Tax Board and shall provide a copy to the participating payee.

(c) A network company may fulfill this requirement by submitting a copy of Internal Revenue Service Form 1099-K or by submitting a form provided by the Franchise Tax Board that includes the same information as that on Cal-1099-K.

(d) For purposes of this section:

(1) "Participating payee" has the same meaning as provided in Section 6050W(d)(1)(A)(ii) of Title 26 of the United States Code.

(2) "Reportable payment transaction" has the same meaning as provided in Section 6050W(c)(1) of Title 26 of the United States Code.

(3) "Third-party settlement organization" has the same meaning as provided in Section 6050W(b)(3) of Title 26 of the United States Code.

(e) This section shall not apply in instances where the gross amount of reportable payment transactions for a participating payee in a calendar year is less than six hundred dollars ($600) or where the participating payee is not an app-based driver.

(f) This section shall apply to reportable payment transactions occurring on or after January 1, 2021. **Leg.H.** Adopted by voters, Prop. 22 §1, effective November 3, 2020.

ARTICLE 9
Amendment

§7465. Amendment to chapter.

(a) After the effective date of this chapter, the Legislature may amend this chapter by a statute passed in each house of the Legislature by rollcall vote entered into the journal, seven-eighths of the membership concurring, provided that the statute is consistent with, and furthers the purpose of, this chapter. No bill seeking to amend this chapter after the effective date of this chapter may be passed or ultimately become a statute unless the bill has been printed and distributed to members, and published on the internet, in its final form, for at least 12 business days prior to its passage in either house of the Legislature.

(b) No statute enacted after October 29, 2019, but prior to the effective date of this chapter, that would constitute an amendment of this chapter, shall be operative after the effective date of this chapter unless the statute was passed in accordance with the requirements of subdivision (a).

(c)(1) The purposes of this chapter are described in Article 1 (commencing with Section 7448).

(2) Any statute that amends Section 7451 does not further the purposes of this chapter.

(3) Any statute that prohibits app-based drivers from performing a particular rideshare service or delivery service while allowing other individuals or entities to perform the same rideshare service or delivery service, or otherwise imposes unequal regulatory burdens upon app-based drivers based on their classification status, constitutes an amendment of this chapter and must be enacted in compliance with the procedures governing amendments consistent

with the purposes of this chapter as set forth in subdivisions (a) and (b).

(4) Any statute that authorizes any entity or organization to represent the interests of app-based drivers in connection with drivers' contractual relationships with network companies, or drivers' compensation, benefits, or working conditions, constitutes an amendment of this chapter and must be enacted in compliance with the procedures governing amendments consistent with the purposes of this chapter as set forth in subdivisions (a) and (b).

(d) Any statute that imposes additional misdemeanor or felony penalties in order to provide greater protection against criminal activity for app-based drivers and individuals using rideshare services or delivery services may be enacted by the Legislature by rollcall vote entered into the journal, a majority of the membership of each house concurring, without complying with subdivisions (a) and (b). **Leg.H.** Adopted by voters, Prop. 22 §1, effective November 3, 2020.

ARTICLE 10
Regulations

§7466. Emergency regulations.

(a) Emergency regulations may be adopted by Covered California in order to implement and administer subdivisions (c) and (g) of Section 7454.

(b) Any emergency regulation adopted pursuant to this section shall be adopted in accordance with Chapter 3.5 (commencing with Section 11340) of Part 1 of Division 3 of Title 2 of the Government Code, and, for purposes of that chapter, including Section 11349.6 of the Government Code, the adoption of the regulation is an emergency and shall be considered by the Office of Administrative Law as necessary for the immediate preservation of the public peace, health and safety, and general welfare. Notwithstanding any other provision of law, the emergency regulations adopted by Covered California may remain in effect for two years from the date of adoption. **Leg.H.** Adopted by voters, Prop. 22 §1, effective November 3, 2020.

ARTICLE 11
Severability

§7467. Severability.

(a) Subject to subdivision (b), the provisions of this chapter are severable. If any portion, section, subdivision, paragraph, clause, sentence, phrase, word, or application of this chapter is for any reason held to be invalid by a decision of any court of competent jurisdiction, that decision shall not affect the validity of the remaining portions of this chapter. The people of the State of California hereby declare that they would have adopted this chapter and each and every portion, section, subdivision, paragraph, clause, sentence, phrase, word, and application not declared invalid or unconstitutional without regard to whether any other portion of this chapter or application thereof would be subsequently declared invalid.

(b) Notwithstanding subdivision (a), if any portion, section, subdivision, paragraph, clause, sentence, phrase, word, or application of Section 7451 of Article 2 (commencing with Section 7451), as added by the voters, is for any reason held to be invalid by a decision of any court of competent jurisdiction, that decision shall apply to the entirety of the remaining provisions of this chapter, and no provision of this chapter shall be deemed valid or given force of law. **Leg.H.** Adopted by voters, Prop. 22 §1, effective November 3, 2020.

CHAPTER 14
STRUCTURAL PEST CONTROL OPERATORS

ARTICLE 7
Disciplinary Proceedings
[Selected Provisions]

§8636. Grounds for disciplinary action.

Disregard and violation of the buildings laws of the state, or of any of its political subdivisions, or of the safety laws, labor laws, health laws, or compensation insurance laws of the state relating to the practice of structural pest control is a ground for disciplinary action.

DIVISION 7
GENERAL BUSINESS REGULATIONS

PART 1
Licensing for Revenue and Regulation

CHAPTER 6
NOTICE TO LICENSEES

§16545. Business license application form.

Every state agency which licenses any kind of business transacted or carried on within their respective jurisdictions shall require applications filed to designate the name of the applicant's workers' compensation insurance carrier, if any. This section does not apply to licensing under the Outdoor Advertising Act. The license application form shall contain a statement substantially as follows: "I am aware of the provisions of Section 3700 of the Labor Code which requires every employer to be insured against liability for workers' compensation."

SELECTED PROVISIONS Of The CIVIL CODE

DIVISION 1 PERSONS

PART 2.6 Confidentiality of Medical Information

CHAPTER 1 DEFINITIONS [Selected Provisions]

§56.05. Definitions.

For purposes of this part:

(a) "Authorization" means permission granted in accordance with Section 56.11 or 56.21 for the disclosure of medical information.

(b) "Authorized recipient" means any person who is authorized to receive medical information pursuant to Section 56.10 or 56.20.

(c) "Confidential communications request" means a request by a subscriber or enrollee that health care service plan communications containing medical information be communicated to him or her at a specific mail or email address or specific telephone number, as designated by the subscriber or enrollee.

(d) "Contractor" means any person or entity that is a medical group, independent practice association, pharmaceutical benefits manager, or a medical service organization and is not a health care service plan or provider of health care. "Contractor" does not include insurance institutions as defined in subdivision (k) of Section 791.02 of the Insurance Code or pharmaceutical benefits managers licensed pursuant to the Knox-Keene Health Care Service Plan Act of 1975 (Chapter 2.2 (commencing with Section 1340) of Division 2 of the Health and Safety Code).

(e) "Endanger" means that the subscriber or enrollee fears that disclosure of his or her medical information could subject the subscriber or enrollee to harassment or abuse.

(f) "Enrollee" has the same meaning as that term is defined in Section 1345 of the Health and Safety Code.

(g) "Health care service plan" means any entity regulated pursuant to the Knox-Keene Health Care Service Plan Act of 1975 (Chapter 2.2 (commencing with Section 1340) of Division 2 of the Health and Safety Code).

(h) "Licensed health care professional" means any person licensed or certified pursuant to Division 2 (commencing with Section 500) of the Business and Professions Code, the Osteopathic Initiative Act or the Chiropractic Initiative Act, or Division 2.5 (commencing with Section 1797) of the Health and Safety Code.

(i) "Marketing" means to make a communication about a product or service that encourages recipients of the communication to purchase or use the product or service. "Marketing" does not include any of the following:

(1) Communications made orally or in writing for which the communicator does not receive direct or indirect remuneration, including, but not limited to, gifts, fees, payments, subsidies, or other economic benefits, from a third party for making the communication.

(2) Communications made to current enrollees solely for the purpose of describing a provider's participation in an existing health care provider network or health plan network of a Knox-Keene licensed health plan to which the enrollees already subscribe; communications made to current enrollees solely for the purpose of describing if, and the extent to which, a product or service, or payment for a product or service, is provided by a provider, contractor, or plan or included in a plan of benefits of a Knox-Keene licensed health plan to which the enrollees already subscribe; or communications made to plan enrollees describing the availability of more cost-effective pharmaceuticals.

(3) Communications that are tailored to the circumstances of a particular individual to educate or advise the individual about treatment options, and otherwise maintain the individual's adherence to a prescribed course of medical treatment, as provided in Section 1399.901 of the Health and Safety Code, for a chronic and seriously debilitating or life-threatening condition as defined in subdivisions (d) and (e) of Section 1367.21 of the Health and Safety Code, if the health care provider, contractor, or health plan receives direct or indirect remuneration, including, but not limited to, gifts, fees, payments, subsidies, or other economic benefits, from a third party for making the communication, if all of the following apply:

Misc. Provisions

(A) The individual receiving the communication is notified in the communication in typeface no smaller than 14-point type of the fact that the provider, contractor, or health plan has been remunerated and the source of the remuneration.

(B) The individual is provided the opportunity to opt out of receiving future remunerated communications.

(C) The communication contains instructions in typeface no smaller than 14-point type describing how the individual can opt out of receiving further communications by calling a toll-free number of the health care provider, contractor, or health plan making the remunerated communications. No further communication may be made to an individual who has opted out after 30 calendar days from the date the individual makes the opt out request.

(j) "Medical information" means any individually identifiable information, in electronic or physical form, in possession of or derived from a provider of health care, health care service plan, pharmaceutical company, or contractor regarding a patient's medical history, mental or physical condition, or treatment. "Individually identifiable" means that the medical information includes or contains any element of personal identifying information sufficient to allow identification of the individual, such as the patient's name, address, electronic mail address, telephone number, or social security number, or other information that, alone or in combination with other publicly available information, reveals the individual's identity.

(k) "Patient" means any natural person, whether or not still living, who received health care services from a provider of health care and to whom medical information pertains.

(*l*) "Pharmaceutical company" means any company or business, or an agent or representative thereof, that manufactures, sells, or distributes pharmaceuticals, medications, or prescription drugs. "Pharmaceutical company" does not include a pharmaceutical benefits manager, as included in subdivision (c), or a provider of health care.

(m) "Provider of health care" means any person licensed or certified pursuant to Division 2 (commencing with Section 500) of the Business and Professions Code; any person licensed pursuant to the Osteopathic Initiative Act or the Chiropractic Initiative Act; any person certified pursuant to Division 2.5 (commencing with Section 1797) of the Health and Safety Code; any clinic, health dispensary, or health facility licensed pursuant to Division 2 (commencing with Section 1200) of the Health and Safety Code. "Provider of health care" does not include insurance institutions as defined in subdivision (k) of Section 791.02 of the Insurance Code.

(n) "Sensitive services" means all health care services described in Sections 6924, 6925, 6926, 6927, 6928, and 6929 of the Family Code, and Sections 121020 and 124260 of the Health and Safety Code, obtained by a patient at or above the minimum age specified for consenting to the service specified in the section.

(o) "Subscriber" has the same meaning as that term is defined in Section 1345 of the Health and Safety Code. **Leg.H.** 1981 ch. 782, 1984 ch. 1391, 1999 ch. 526, 2000 ch. 1067, 2002 ch. 853 (AB 2191), 2003 ch. 562 (AB 715), 2013 ch. 444 (SB 138) §2.

Ref.: Hanna § 22.02[6].

CHAPTER 2
DISCLOSURE OF MEDICAL INFORMATION BY PROVIDERS

§56.10. When medical information may be disclosed.

(a) A provider of health care, health care service plan, or contractor shall not disclose medical information regarding a patient of the provider of health care or an enrollee or subscriber of a health care service plan without first obtaining an authorization, except as provided in subdivision (b) or (c).

(b) A provider of health care, a health care service plan, or a contractor shall disclose medical information if the disclosure is compelled by any of the following:

(1) By a court pursuant to an order of that court.

(2) By a board, commission, or administrative agency for purposes of adjudication pursuant to its lawful authority.

(3) By a party to a proceeding before a court or administrative agency pursuant to a subpoena, subpoena duces tecum, notice to appear served pursuant to Section 1987 of the Code of Civil Procedure, or any provision authorizing discovery in a proceeding before a court or administrative agency.

(4) By a board, commission, or administrative agency pursuant to an investigative subpoena issued under Article 2 (commencing with Section 11180) of Chapter 2 of Part 1 of Division 3 of Title 2 of the Government Code.

(5) By an arbitrator or arbitration panel, when arbitration is lawfully requested by either party, pursuant to a subpoena duces tecum issued under Section 1282.6 of the Code of Civil Procedure, or another provision authorizing discovery in a proceeding before an arbitrator or arbitration panel.

(6) By a search warrant lawfully issued to a governmental law enforcement agency.

(7) By the patient or the patient's representative pursuant to Chapter 1 (commencing with Section 123100) of Part 1 of Division 106 of the Health and Safety Code.

(8) By a medical examiner, forensic pathologist, or coroner, when requested in the course of an investigation by a medical examiner, forensic pathologist, or coroner's office for the purpose of identifying the decedent or locating next of kin, or when investigating deaths that may involve public health concerns, organ or tissue donation, child abuse, elder abuse, suicides, poisonings, accidents, sudden infant deaths, suspicious deaths, unknown deaths, or criminal deaths, or upon notification of, or investigation of, imminent deaths that may involve organ or tissue donation pursuant to Section 7151.15 of the Health and Safety Code, or when otherwise authorized by the decedent's representative. Medical information requested by a medical examiner, forensic pathologist, or coroner under this paragraph shall be limited to information regarding the patient who is the decedent and who is the subject of the investigation or who is the prospective donor and shall be disclosed to a medical examiner, forensic pathologist, or coroner without delay upon request. A medical examiner, forensic pathologist, or coroner shall not disclose the information contained in the medical record obtained

pursuant to this paragraph to a third party without a court order or authorization pursuant to paragraph (4) of subdivision (c) of Section 56.11.

(9) When otherwise specifically required by law.

(c) A provider of health care or a health care service plan may disclose medical information as follows:

(1) The information may be disclosed to providers of health care, health care service plans, contractors, or other health care professionals or facilities for purposes of diagnosis or treatment of the patient. This includes, in an emergency situation, the communication of patient information by radio transmission or other means between emergency medical personnel at the scene of an emergency, or in an emergency medical transport vehicle, and emergency medical personnel at a health facility licensed pursuant to Chapter 2 (commencing with Section 1250) of Division 2 of the Health and Safety Code.

(2) The information may be disclosed to an insurer, employer, health care service plan, hospital service plan, employee benefit plan, governmental authority, contractor, or other person or entity responsible for paying for health care services rendered to the patient, to the extent necessary to allow responsibility for payment to be determined and payment to be made. If (A) the patient is, by reason of a comatose or other disabling medical condition, unable to consent to the disclosure of medical information and (B) no other arrangements have been made to pay for the health care services being rendered to the patient, the information may be disclosed to a governmental authority to the extent necessary to determine the patient's eligibility for, and to obtain, payment under a governmental program for health care services provided to the patient. The information may also be disclosed to another provider of health care or health care service plan as necessary to assist the other provider or health care service plan in obtaining payment for health care services rendered by that provider of health care or health care service plan to the patient.

(3) The information may be disclosed to a person or entity that provides billing, claims management, medical data processing, or other administrative services for providers of health care or health care service plans or for any of the persons or entities specified in paragraph (2). However, information so disclosed shall not be further disclosed by the recipient in a way that would violate this part.

(4) The information may be disclosed to organized committees and agents of professional societies or of medical staffs of licensed hospitals, licensed health care service plans, professional standards review organizations, independent medical review organizations and their selected reviewers, utilization and quality control peer review organizations as established by Congress in Public Law 97-248 in 1982, contractors, or persons or organizations insuring, responsible for, or defending professional liability that a provider may incur, if the committees, agents, health care service plans, organizations, reviewers, contractors, or persons are engaged in reviewing the competence or qualifications of health care professionals or in reviewing health care services with respect to medical necessity, level of care, quality of care, or justification of charges.

(5) The information in the possession of a provider of health care or a health care service plan may be reviewed by a private or public body responsible for licensing or accrediting the provider of health care or a health care service plan. However, no patient-identifying medical information may be removed from the premises except as expressly permitted or required elsewhere by law, nor shall that information be further disclosed by the recipient in a way that would violate this part.

(6) The information may be disclosed to a medical examiner, forensic pathologist, or county coroner in the course of an investigation by a medical examiner, forensic pathologist, or coroner's office when requested for all purposes not included in paragraph (8) of subdivision (b). A medical examiner, forensic pathologist, or coroner shall not disclose the information contained in the medical record obtained pursuant to this paragraph to a third party without a court order or authorization pursuant to paragraph (4) of subdivision (c) of Section 56.11.

(7) The information may be disclosed to public agencies, clinical investigators, including investigators conducting epidemiologic studies, health care research organizations, and accredited public or private nonprofit educational or health care institutions for bona fide research purposes. However, no information so disclosed shall be further disclosed by the recipient in a way that would disclose the identity of a patient or violate this part.

(8) A provider of health care or health care service plan that has created medical information as a result of employment-related health care services to an employee conducted at the specific prior written request and expense of the employer may disclose to the employee's employer that part of the information that:

(A) Is relevant in a lawsuit, arbitration, grievance, or other claim or challenge to which the employer and the employee are parties and in which the patient has placed in issue his or her medical history, mental or physical condition, or treatment, provided that information may only be used or disclosed in connection with that proceeding.

(B) Describes functional limitations of the patient that may entitle the patient to leave from work for medical reasons or limit the patient's fitness to perform his or her present employment, provided that no statement of medical cause is included in the information disclosed.

(9) Unless the provider of health care or a health care service plan is notified in writing of an agreement by the sponsor, insurer, or administrator to the contrary, the information may be disclosed to a sponsor, insurer, or administrator of a group or individual insured or uninsured plan or policy that the patient seeks coverage by or benefits from, if the information was created by the provider of health care or health care service plan as the result of services conducted at the specific prior written request and expense of the sponsor, insurer, or administrator for the purpose of evaluating the application for coverage or benefits.

(10) The information may be disclosed to a health care service plan by providers of health care that contract with the health care service plan and may be transferred among providers of health care that contract with the health care service plan, for the purpose of administering the health care service plan. Medical information shall not otherwise be disclosed by a health care service plan except in accordance with this part.

(11) This part does not prevent the disclosure by a provider of health care or a health care service plan to an insurance institution, agent, or support organization, subject to Article 6.6 (commencing with Section 791) of Chapter 1 of Part 2 of Division 1 of the Insurance Code, of medical information if the insurance institution, agent, or support organization has complied with all of the requirements for obtaining the information pursuant to Article 6.6 (commencing with Section 791) of Chapter 1 of Part 2 of Division 1 of the Insurance Code.

(12) The information relevant to the patient's condition, care, and treatment provided may be disclosed to a probate court investigator in the course of an investigation required or authorized in a conservatorship proceeding under the Guardianship-Conservatorship Law as defined in Section 1400 of the Probate Code, or to a probate court investigator, probation officer, or domestic relations investigator engaged in determining the need for an initial guardianship or continuation of an existing guardianship.

(13) The information may be disclosed to an organ procurement organization or a tissue bank processing the tissue of a decedent for transplantation into the body of another person, but only with respect to the donating decedent, for the purpose of aiding the transplant. For the purpose of this paragraph, "tissue bank" and "tissue" have the same meanings as defined in Section 1635 of the Health and Safety Code.

(14) The information may be disclosed when the disclosure is otherwise specifically authorized by law, including, but not limited to, the voluntary reporting, either directly or indirectly, to the federal Food and Drug Administration of adverse events related to drug products or medical device problems, or to disclosures made pursuant to subdivisions (b) and (c) of Section 11167 of the Penal Code by a person making a report pursuant to Sections 11165.9 and 11166 of the Penal Code, provided that those disclosures concern a report made by that person.

(15) Basic information, including the patient's name, city of residence, age, sex, and general condition, may be disclosed to a state-recognized or federally recognized disaster relief organization for the purpose of responding to disaster welfare inquiries.

(16) The information may be disclosed to a third party for purposes of encoding, encrypting, or otherwise anonymizing data. However, no information so disclosed shall be further disclosed by the recipient in a way that would violate this part, including the unauthorized manipulation of coded or encrypted medical information that reveals individually identifiable medical information.

(17) For purposes of disease management programs and services as defined in Section 1399.901 of the Health and Safety Code, information may be disclosed as follows: (A) to an entity contracting with a health care service plan or the health care service plan's contractors to monitor or administer care of enrollees for a covered benefit, if the disease management services and care are authorized by a treating physician, or (B) to a disease management organization, as defined in Section 1399.900 of the Health and Safety Code, that complies fully with the physician authorization requirements of Section 1399.902 of the Health and Safety Code, if the health care service plan or its contractor provides or has provided a description of the disease management services to a treating physician or to the health care service plan's or contractor's network of physicians. This paragraph does not require physician authorization for the care or treatment of the adherents of a well-recognized church or religious denomination who depend solely upon prayer or spiritual means for healing in the practice of the religion of that church or denomination.

(18) The information may be disclosed, as permitted by state and federal law or regulation, to a local health department for the purpose of preventing or controlling disease, injury, or disability, including, but not limited to, the reporting of disease, injury, vital events, including, but not limited to, birth or death, and the conduct of public health surveillance, public health investigations, and public health interventions, as authorized or required by state or federal law or regulation.

(19) The information may be disclosed, consistent with applicable law and standards of ethical conduct, by a psychotherapist, as defined in Section 1010 of the Evidence Code, if the psychotherapist, in good faith, believes the disclosure is necessary to prevent or lessen a serious and imminent threat to the health or safety of a reasonably foreseeable victim or victims, and the disclosure is made to a person or persons reasonably able to prevent or lessen the threat, including the target of the threat.

(20) The information may be disclosed as described in Section 56.103.

(21)(A) The information may be disclosed to an employee welfare benefit plan, as defined under Section 3(1) of the Employee Retirement Income Security Act of 1974 (29 U.S.C. Sec. 1002(1)), which is formed under Section 302(c)(5) of the Taft-Hartley Act (29 U.S.C. Sec. 186(c)(5)), to the extent that the employee welfare benefit plan provides medical care, and may also be disclosed to an entity contracting with the employee welfare benefit plan for billing, claims management, medical data processing, or other administrative services related to the provision of medical care to persons enrolled in the employee welfare benefit plan for health care coverage, if all of the following conditions are met:

(i) The disclosure is for the purpose of determining eligibility, coordinating benefits, or allowing the employee welfare benefit plan or the contracting entity to advocate on the behalf of a patient or enrollee with a provider, a health care service plan, or a state or federal regulatory agency.

(ii) The request for the information is accompanied by a written authorization for the release of the information submitted in a manner consistent with subdivision (a) and Section 56.11.

(iii) The disclosure is authorized by and made in a manner consistent with the Health Insurance Portability and Accountability Act of 1996 (Public Law 104-191).

(iv) Any information disclosed is not further used or disclosed by the recipient in any way that would directly or indirectly violate this part or the restrictions imposed by Part 164 of Title 45 of the Code of Federal Regulations, including the manipulation of the information in any way that might reveal individually identifiable medical information.

(B) For purposes of this paragraph, Section 1374.8 of the Health and Safety Code shall not apply.

(22) Information may be disclosed pursuant to subdivision (a) of Section 15633.5 of the Welfare and Institu-

tions Code by a person required to make a report pursuant to Section 15630 of the Welfare and Institutions Code, provided that the disclosure under subdivision (a) of Section 15633.5 concerns a report made by that person. Covered entities, as they are defined in Section 160.103 of Title 45 of the Code of Federal Regulations, shall comply with the requirements of the Health Insurance Portability and Accountability Act (HIPAA) privacy rule pursuant to subsection (c) of Section 164.512 of Title 45 of the Code of Federal Regulations if the disclosure is not for the purpose of public health surveillance, investigation, intervention, or reporting an injury or death.

(d) Except to the extent expressly authorized by a patient, enrollee, or subscriber, or as provided by subdivisions (b) and (c), a provider of health care, health care service plan, contractor, or corporation and its subsidiaries and affiliates shall not intentionally share, sell, use for marketing, or otherwise use medical information for a purpose not necessary to provide health care services to the patient.

(e) Except to the extent expressly authorized by a patient or enrollee or subscriber or as provided by subdivisions (b) and (c), a contractor or corporation and its subsidiaries and affiliates shall not further disclose medical information regarding a patient of the provider of health care or an enrollee or subscriber of a health care service plan or insurer or self-insured employer received under this section to a person or entity that is not engaged in providing direct health care services to the patient or his or her provider of health care or health care service plan or insurer or self-insured employer.

(f) For purposes of this section, a reference to a "medical examiner, forensic pathologist, or coroner" means a coroner or deputy coroner as described in subdivision (c) of Section 830.35 of the Penal Code, or a licensed physician who currently performs official autopsies on behalf of a county coroner's office or a medical examiner's office, whether as a government employee or under contract to that office. **Leg.H.** 2000 ch. 1068 §1.16, 2002 ch. 123 (AB 1958), 2003 ch. 562 (AB 715), 2006 ch. 874 (SB 1430) §2, 2007 chs. 506 (AB 1178) §1, 552 (AB 1687) §2, 553 (AB 1727) §1.9, 2008 ch. 179 (SB 1498) §27, 2009 ch. 493 (AB 952) §1, 2010 ch. 540 (AB 2028) §1, 2013 ch. 341 (AB 1297) §1, 2016 ch. 690 (AB 2119) §1.

2016 Note: The Legislature finds and declares that this act imposes a limitation on the public's right of access to the meetings of public bodies or the writings of public officials and agencies within the meaning of Section 3 of Article I of the California Constitution. Pursuant to that constitutional provision, the Legislature makes the following findings to demonstrate the interest protected by this limitation and the need for protecting that interest:

The privacy rights of the decedent would be impaired if the records released to a medical examiner, forensic pathologist, or coroner regarding the decedent were released to the public. Stats. 2016 ch. 690 (AB 2119) §4.

2006 Note: This act shall be known, and may be cited as the Local Pandemic and Emergency Health Preparedness Act of 2006. Stats. 2006 ch. 874 (SB 1430) §1.

Ref.: Hanna § 22.02[5].

§56.1007. Disclosure to family member, partner, or friend; disclosure for notification purposes; disaster relief efforts.

(a) A provider of health care, health care service plan, or contractor may, in accordance with subdivision (c) or (d), disclose to a family member, other relative, domestic partner, or a close personal friend of the patient, or any other person identified by the patient, the medical information directly relevant to that person's involvement with the patient's care or payment related to the patient's health care.

(b) A provider of health care, health care service plan, or contractor may use or disclose medical information to notify, or assist in the notification of, including identifying or locating, a family member, a personal representative of the patient, a domestic partner, or another person responsible for the care of the patient of the patient's location, general condition, or death. Any use or disclosure of medical information for those notification purposes shall be in accordance with the provisions of subdivision (c), (d), or (e), as applicable.

(c)(1) Except as provided in paragraph (2), if the patient is present for, or otherwise available prior to, a use or disclosure permitted by subdivision (a) or (b) and has the capacity to make health care decisions, the provider of health care, health care service plan, or contractor may use or disclose the medical information if it does any of the following:

(A) Obtains the patient's agreement.

(B) Provides the patient with the opportunity to object to the disclosure, and the patient does not express an objection.

(C) Reasonably infers from the circumstances, based on the exercise of professional judgment, that the patient does not object to the disclosure.

(2) A provider of health care who is a psychotherapist, as defined in Section 1010 of the Evidence Code, may use or disclose medical information pursuant to this subdivision only if the psychotherapist complies with subparagraph (A) or (B) of paragraph (1).

(d) If the patient is not present, or the opportunity to agree or object to the use or disclosure cannot practicably be provided because of the patient's incapacity or an emergency circumstance, the provider of health care, health care service plan, or contractor may, in the exercise of professional judgment, determine whether the disclosure is in the best interests of the patient and, if so, disclose only the medical information that is directly relevant to the person's involvement with the patient's health care. A provider of health care, health care service plan, or contractor may use professional judgment and its experience with common practice to make reasonable inferences of the patient's best interest in allowing a person to act on behalf of the patient to pick up filled prescriptions, medical supplies, X-rays, or other similar forms of medical information.

(e) A provider of health care, health care service plan, or contractor may use or disclose medical information to a public or private entity authorized by law or by its charter to assist in disaster relief efforts, for the purpose of coordinating with those entities the uses or disclosures permitted by subdivision (b). The requirements in subdivisions (c) and (d) apply to those uses and disclosures to the extent that the provider of health care, health care service plan, or contractor, in the exercise of professional judgment, determines that the requirements do not interfere with the ability to respond to the emergency circumstances.

(f) Nothing in this section shall be construed to interfere with or limit the access authority of Protection and Advocacy, Inc., the Office of Patients' Rights, or any county patients' rights advocates to access medical information pursuant to any state or federal law. **Leg.H.** 2006 ch. 833 (AB 3013) §1.

§56.101. Preservation of confidentiality of medical information.

(a) Every provider of health care, health care service plan, pharmaceutical company, or contractor who creates, maintains, preserves, stores, abandons, destroys, or disposes of medical information shall do so in a manner that preserves the confidentiality of the information contained therein. Any provider of health care, health care service plan, pharmaceutical company, or contractor who negligently creates, maintains, preserves, stores, abandons, destroys, or disposes of medical information shall be subject to the remedies and penalties provided under subdivisions (b) and (c) of Section 56.36.

(b)(1) An electronic health record system or electronic medical record system shall do the following:

(A) Protect and preserve the integrity of electronic medical information.

(B) Automatically record and preserve any change or deletion of any electronically stored medical information. The record of any change or deletion shall include the identity of the person who accessed and changed the medical information, the date and time the medical information was accessed, and the change that was made to the medical information.

(2) A patient's right to access or receive a copy of his or her electronic medical records upon request shall be consistent with applicable state and federal laws governing patient access to, and the use and disclosures of, medical information.

(c) This section shall apply to an "electronic medical record" or "electronic health record" that meets the definition of "electronic health record," as that term is defined in Section 17921(5) of Title 42 of the United States Code. **Leg.H.** 1999 ch. 526, 2000 ch. 1067, 2002 ch. 853 (AB 2191), 2011 ch. 714 (SB 850) §1.

§56.102. Pharmaceutical company cannot require patient to sign form permitting disclosure of medical information as condition of receiving pharmaceuticals; exceptions.

(a) A pharmaceutical company may not require a patient, as a condition of receiving pharmaceuticals, medications, or prescription drugs, to sign an authorization, release, consent, or waiver that would permit the disclosure of medical information that otherwise may not be disclosed under Section 56.10 or any other provision of law, unless the disclosure is for one of the following purposes:

(1) Enrollment of the patient in a patient assistance program or prescription drug discount program.

(2) Enrollment of the patient in a clinical research project.

(3) Prioritization of distribution to the patient of a prescription medicine in limited supply in the United States.

(4) Response to an inquiry from the patient communicated in writing, by telephone, or by electronic mail.

(b) Except as provided in subdivision (a) or Section 56.10, a pharmaceutical company may not disclose medical information provided to it without first obtaining a valid authorization from the patient. **Leg.H.** 2002 ch. 853 (AB 2191).

§56.103. Disclosure of minor's medical information for purpose of coordinating health care services and medical treatment.

(a) A provider of health care may disclose medical information to a county social worker, a probation officer, a foster care public health nurse acting pursuant to Section 16501.3 of the Welfare and Institutions Code, or any other person who is legally authorized to have custody or care of a minor for the purpose of coordinating health care services and medical treatment provided to the minor, including, but not limited to, the sharing of information related to screenings, assessments, and laboratory tests necessary to monitor the administration of psychotropic medications.

(b) For purposes of this section, health care services and medical treatment includes one or more providers of health care providing, coordinating, or managing health care and related services, including, but not limited to, a provider of health care coordinating health care with a third party, consultation between providers of health care and medical treatment relating to a minor, or a provider of health care referring a minor for health care services to another provider of health care.

(c) For purposes of this section, a county social worker, a probation officer, foster care public health nurse, or any other person who is legally authorized to have custody or care of a minor shall be considered a third party who may receive any of the following:

(1) Medical information described in Sections 56.05 and 56.10.

(2) Protected health information described in Section 160.103 of Title 45 of the Code of Federal Regulations.

(d) Medical information disclosed to a county social worker, probation officer, foster care public health nurse, or any other person who is legally authorized to have custody or care of a minor shall not be further disclosed by the recipient unless the disclosure is for the purpose of coordinating health care services and medical treatment of the minor and the disclosure is authorized by law. Medical information disclosed pursuant to this section may not be admitted into evidence in any criminal or delinquency proceeding against the minor. Nothing in this subdivision shall prohibit identical evidence from being admissible in a criminal proceeding if that evidence is derived solely from lawful means other than this section and is permitted by law.

(e)(1) Notwithstanding Section 56.104, if a provider of health care determines that the disclosure of medical information concerning the diagnosis and treatment of a mental health condition of a minor is reasonably necessary for the purpose of assisting in coordinating the treatment and care of the minor, that information may be disclosed to a county social worker, probation officer, foster care public health nurse, or any other person who is legally authorized to have custody or care of the minor. The information shall not be further disclosed by the recipient unless the disclosure is for the purpose of coordinating mental health services and treatment of the minor and the disclosure is authorized by law.

(2) As used in this subdivision, "medical information" does not include psychotherapy notes as defined in Section 164.501 of Title 45 of the Code of Federal Regulations.

(f) The disclosure of information pursuant to this section is not intended to limit the disclosure of information when that disclosure is otherwise required by law.

(g) For purposes of this section, "minor" means a minor taken into temporary custody or as to whom a petition has been filed with the court, or who has been adjudged to be a dependent child or ward of the juvenile court pursuant to Section 300 or 601 of the Welfare and Institutions Code.

(h)(1) Except as described in paragraph (1) of subdivision (e), nothing in this section shall be construed to limit or otherwise affect existing privacy protections provided for in state or federal law.

(2) Nothing in this section shall be construed to expand the authority of a social worker, probation officer, foster care public health nurse, or custodial caregiver beyond the authority provided under existing law to a parent or a patient representative regarding access to medical information. **Leg.H.** 2007 ch. 552 (AB 1687) §3, 2008 chs. 699 (SB 1241) §1, 700 (AB 2352) §1, 2015 ch. 535 (SB 319) §1.

§56.104. Release of information on psychotherapy.

(a) Notwithstanding subdivision (c) of Section 56.10, except as provided in subdivision (e), no provider of health care, health care service plan, or contractor may release medical information to persons or entities who have requested that information and who are authorized by law to receive that information pursuant to subdivision (c) of Section 56.10, if the requested information specifically relates to the patient's participation in outpatient treatment with a psychotherapist, unless the person or entity requesting that information submits to the patient pursuant to subdivision (b) and to the provider of health care, health care service plan, or contractor a written request, signed by the person requesting the information or an authorized agent of the entity requesting the information, that includes all of the following:

(1) The specific information relating to a patient's participation in outpatient treatment with a psychotherapist being requested and its specific intended use or uses.

(2) The length of time during which the information will be kept before being destroyed or disposed of. A person or entity may extend that timeframe, provided that the person or entity notifies the provider, plan, or contractor of the extension. Any notification of an extension shall include the specific reason for the extension, the intended use or uses of the information during the extended time, and the expected date of the destruction of the information.

(3) A statement that the information will not be used for any purpose other than its intended use.

(4) A statement that the person or entity requesting the information will destroy the information and all copies in the person's or entity's possession or control, will cause it to be destroyed, or will return the information and all copies of it before or immediately after the length of time specified in paragraph (2) has expired.

(b) The person or entity requesting the information shall submit a copy of the written request required by this section to the patient within 30 days of receipt of the information requested, unless the patient has signed a written waiver in the form of a letter signed and submitted by the patient to the provider of health care or health care service plan waiving notification.

(c) For purposes of this section, "psychotherapist" means a person who is both a "psychotherapist" as defined in Section 1010 of the Evidence Code and a "provider of health care" as defined in Section 56.05.

(d) This section does not apply to the disclosure or use of medical information by a law enforcement agency or a regulatory agency when required for an investigation of unlawful activity or for licensing, certification, or regulatory purposes, unless the disclosure is otherwise prohibited by law.

(e) This section shall not apply to any of the following:

(1) Information authorized to be disclosed pursuant to paragraph (1) of subdivision (c) of Section 56.10.

(2) Information requested from a psychotherapist by law enforcement or by the target of the threat subsequent to a disclosure by that psychotherapist authorized by paragraph (19) of subdivision (c) of Section 56.10, in which the additional information is clearly necessary to prevent the serious and imminent threat disclosed under that paragraph.

(3) Information disclosed by a psychotherapist pursuant to paragraphs (14) and (22) of subdivision (c) of Section 56.10 and requested by an agency investigating the abuse reported pursuant to those paragraphs.

(f) Nothing in this section shall be construed to grant any additional authority to a provider of health care, health care service plan, or contractor to disclose information to a person or entity without the patient's consent. **Leg.H.** 1999 ch. 527, 2004 ch. 463 (SB 598), 2009 ch. 464 (AB 681) §1, 2010 ch. 540 (AB 2028) §2, 2013 ch. 444 (SB 138) §3.

§56.105. Authorization to disclose medical information in connection with settlement or compromise of medical malpractice case.

Whenever, prior to the service of a complaint upon a defendant in any action arising out of the professional negligence of a person holding a valid physician's and surgeon's certificate issued pursuant to Chapter 5 (commencing with Section 2000) of Division 2 of the Business and Professions Code, a person holding a valid license as a marriage and family therapist issued pursuant to Chapter 13 (commencing with Section 4980) of Division 2 of the Business and Professions Code, a person holding a valid license as a clinical social worker issued pursuant to Chapter 14 (commencing with Section 4991) of Division 2 of the Business and Professions Code, or a person holding a valid license as a professional clinical counselor issued pursuant to Chapter 16 (commencing with Section 4999.10) of Division 2 of the Business and Professions Code, a demand for settlement or offer to compromise is made on a patient's behalf, the demand or offer shall be accompanied by an authorization to disclose medical information to persons or organizations insuring, responsible for, or defending professional liability that the certificate holder may incur. The authorization shall be in accordance with Section 56.11 and shall authorize disclosure of that information that is necessary to investigate issues of liability and extent of potential damages in evaluating the merits of the demand for settlement or offer to compromise.

Notice of any request for medical information made pursuant to an authorization as provided by this section shall be given to the patient or the patient's legal representative. The notice shall describe the inclusive subject matter and dates of the materials requested and shall also authorize the patient or the patient's legal representative to receive, upon request, copies of the information at his or her expense.

Nothing in this section shall be construed to waive or limit any applicable privileges set forth in the Evidence Code except for the disclosure of medical information subject to the patient's authorization. Nothing in this section shall be construed as authorizing a representative of any person from whom settlement has been demanded to communicate in violation of the physician-patient privilege with a treating physician, or to communicate in violation of the psychotherapist-patient privilege with a treating licensed marriage and family therapist, licensed clinical social worker, or licensed professional clinical counselor, except for the medical information request.

The requirements of this section are independent of the requirements of Section 364 of the Code of Civil Procedure. **Leg.H.** 1985 ch. 484, 1991 ch. 591, 2013 ch. 58 (SB 282) §1, 2018 ch. 389 (AB 2296) §8.

§56.106. Disclosure or release of information on minor removed from physical custody of parent or guardian; restrictions; applicability.

(a) Notwithstanding Section 3025 of the Family Code, paragraph (2) of subdivision (c) of Section 56.11, or any other provision of law, a psychotherapist who knows that a minor has been removed from the custody of his or her parent or guardian pursuant to Article 6 (commencing with Section 300) to Article 10 (commencing with Section 360), inclusive, of Chapter 2 of Part 1 of Division 2 of the Welfare and Institutions Code shall not release the mental health records of the minor patient and shall not disclose mental health information about that minor patient based upon an authorization to release those records signed by the minor's parent or guardian. This restriction shall not apply if the juvenile court has issued an order authorizing the parent or guardian to sign an authorization for the release of the mental health records or the information about the minor patient after finding that such an order would not be detrimental to the minor patient.

(b) For purposes of this section, the following definitions apply:

(1) "Mental health records" means mental health records as defined by subdivision (b) of Section 123105 of the Health and Safety Code.

(2) "Psychotherapist" means a provider of health care as defined in Section 1010 of the Evidence Code.

(c) When the juvenile court has issued an order authorizing the parent or guardian to sign an authorization for the release of the mental health records or information about that minor patient under the circumstances described in subdivision (a), the parent or guardian seeking the release of the minor's records or information about the minor shall present a copy of the court order to the psychotherapist before any records or information may be released pursuant to the signed authorization.

(d) Nothing in this section shall be construed to prevent or limit a psychotherapist's authority under subdivision (a) of Section 123115 of the Health and Safety Code to deny a parent's or guardian's written request to inspect or obtain copies of the minor patient's mental health records, notwithstanding the fact that the juvenile court has issued an order authorizing the parent or guardian to sign an authorization for the release of the mental health records or information about that minor patient. Liability for a psychotherapist's decision not to release the mental health records of the minor patient or not to disclose information about the minor patient pursuant to the authority of subdivision (a) of Section 123115 of the Health and Safety Code shall be governed by that section.

(e) Nothing in this section shall be construed to impose upon a psychotherapist a duty to inquire or investigate whether a child has been removed from the physical custody of his or her parent or guardian pursuant to Article 6 (commencing with Section 300) to Article 10 (commencing with Section 360), inclusive, of Chapter 2 of Part 1 of Division 2 of the Welfare and Institutions Code when a parent or guardian presents the minor's psychotherapist with an authorization to release information or the mental health records regarding the minor patient. **Leg.H.** 2012 ch. 657 (SB 1407) §1.

§56.107. Requirements for maintaining confidentiality of medical information.

(a) Notwithstanding any other law, and to the extent permitted by federal law, a health care service plan shall take the following steps to protect the confidentiality of a subscriber's or enrollee's medical information on and after January 1, 2015:

(1) A health care service plan shall permit subscribers and enrollees to request, and shall accommodate requests for, communication in the form and format requested by the individual, if it is readily producible in the requested form and format, or at alternative locations, if the subscriber or enrollee clearly states either that the communication discloses medical information or provider name and address relating to receipt of sensitive services or that disclosure of all or part of the medical information or provider name and address could endanger the subscriber or enrollee.

(2) A health care service plan may require the subscriber or enrollee to make a request for a confidential communication described in paragraph (1), in writing or by electronic transmission.

(3) A health care service plan may require that a confidential communications request contain a statement that the request pertains to either medical information

related to the receipt of sensitive services or that disclosure of all or part of the medical information could endanger the subscriber or enrollee. The health care service plan shall not require an explanation as to the basis for a subscriber's or enrollee's statement that disclosure could endanger the subscriber or enrollee.

(4) The confidential communication request shall be valid until the subscriber or enrollee submits a revocation of the request or a new confidential communication request is submitted.

(5) For the purposes of this section, a confidential communications request shall be implemented by the health care service plan within seven calendar days of receipt of an electronic transmission or telephonic request or within 14 calendar days of receipt by first-class mail. The health care service plan shall acknowledge receipt of the confidential communications request and advise the subscriber or enrollee of the status of implementation of the request if a subscriber or enrollee contacts the health care service plan.

(b) Notwithstanding subdivision (a), the provider of health care may make arrangements with the subscriber or enrollee for the payment of benefit cost sharing and communicate that arrangement with the health care service plan.

(c) A health care service plan shall not condition enrollment or coverage on the waiver of rights provided in this section. **Leg.H.** 2013 ch. 444 (SB 138) §4.

§56.11. Requirements for authorizing release of medical information.

Any person or entity that wishes to obtain medical information pursuant to subdivision (a) of Section 56.10, other than a person or entity authorized to receive medical information pursuant to subdivision (b) or (c) of Section 56.10, except as provided in paragraph (21) of subdivision (c) of Section 56.10, shall obtain a valid authorization for the release of this information.

An authorization for the release of medical information by a provider of health care, health care service plan, pharmaceutical company, or contractor shall be valid if it:

(a) Is handwritten by the person who signs it or is in a typeface no smaller than 14-point type.

(b) Is clearly separate from any other language present on the same page and is executed by a signature which serves no other purpose than to execute the authorization.

(c) Is signed and dated by one of the following:

(1) The patient. A patient who is a minor may only sign an authorization for the release of medical information obtained by a provider of health care, health care service plan, pharmaceutical company, or contractor in the course of furnishing services to which the minor could lawfully have consented under Part 1 (commencing with Section 25) or Part 2.7 (commencing with Section 60).

(2) The legal representative of the patient, if the patient is a minor or an incompetent. However, authorization may not be given under this subdivision for the disclosure of medical information obtained by the provider of health care, health care service plan, pharmaceutical company, or contractor in the course of furnishing services to which a minor patient could lawfully have consented under Part 1 (commencing with Section 25) or Part 2.7 (commencing with Section 60).

(3) The spouse of the patient or the person financially responsible for the patient, where the medical information is being sought for the sole purpose of processing an application for health insurance or for enrollment in a nonprofit hospital plan, a health care service plan, or an employee benefit plan, and where the patient is to be an enrolled spouse or dependent under the policy or plan.

(4) The beneficiary or personal representative of a deceased patient.

(d) States the specific uses and limitations on the types of medical information to be disclosed.

(e) States the name or functions of the provider of health care, health care service plan, pharmaceutical company, or contractor that may disclose the medical information.

(f) States the name or functions of the persons or entities authorized to receive the medical information.

(g) States the specific uses and limitations on the use of the medical information by the persons or entities authorized to receive the medical information.

(h) States a specific date after which the provider of health care, health care service plan, pharmaceutical company, or contractor is no longer authorized to disclose the medical information.

(i) Advises the person signing the authorization of the right to receive a copy of the authorization. **Leg.H.** 1981 ch. 782, 1999 ch. 526, 2000 ch. 1066, 2002 ch. 853 (AB 2191), 2003 ch. 562 (AB 715), 2009 ch. 493 (AB 952) §2.

§56.12. Furnishing copy of authorization to patient.

Upon demand by the patient or the person who signed an authorization, a provider of health care, health care service plan, pharmaceutical company, or contractor possessing the authorization shall furnish a true copy thereof. **Leg.H.** 1981 ch. 782, 1999 ch. 526, 2002 ch. 853 (AB 2191).

§56.13. Confidentiality of released medical information.

A recipient of medical information pursuant to an authorization as provided by this chapter or pursuant to the provisions of subdivision (c) of Section 56.10 may not further disclose that medical information except in accordance with a new authorization that meets the requirements of Section 56.11, or as specifically required or permitted by other provisions of this chapter or by law. **Leg.H.** 1981 ch. 782.

§56.14. Provider non-liability for unauthorized use of medical information.

A provider of health care, health care service plan, or contractor that discloses medical information pursuant to the authorizations required by this chapter shall communicate to the person or entity to which it discloses the medical information any limitations in the authorization regarding the use of the medical information. No provider of health care, health care service plan, or contractor that has attempted in good faith to comply with this provision shall be liable for any unauthorized use of the medical information by the person or entity to which the provider, plan, or contractor disclosed the medical information. **Leg.H.** 1981 ch. 782, 1999 ch. 526.

§56.15. Cancellation or modification of authorization.

Nothing in this part shall be construed to prevent a person who could sign the authorization pursuant to subdivision (c) of Section 56.11 from cancelling or modifying an authorization. However, the cancellation or modification shall be effective only after the provider of health care actually receives written notice of the cancellation or modification. **Leg.H.** 1981 ch. 782.

§56.16. Disclosure of nonmedical information permitted.

For disclosures not addressed by Section 56.1007, unless there is a specific written request by the patient to the contrary, nothing in this part shall be construed to prevent a general acute care hospital, as defined in subdivision (a) of Section 1250 of the Health and Safety Code, upon an inquiry concerning a specific patient, from releasing at its discretion any of the following information: the patient's name, address, age, and sex; a general description of the reason for treatment (whether an injury, a burn, poisoning, or some unrelated condition); the general nature of the injury, burn, poisoning, or other condition; the general condition of the patient; and any information that is not medical information as defined in Section 56.05. **Leg.H.** 1981 ch. 782, 2006 ch. 833 (AB 3013) §2, 2013 chs. 76 (AB 383) §10, 444 (SB 138) §5.

Ref.: Hanna § 22.02[5].

CHAPTER 2.5
DISCLOSURE OF GENETIC TEST RESULTS BY A HEALTH CARE SERVICE PLAN

§56.17. Insurers prohibited from offering or providing different terms, conditions, or benefits based on genetic characteristics; penalties; disclosure of test results for genetic characteristic—Civil and criminal liability.

(a) This section shall apply to the disclosure of genetic test results contained in an applicant's or enrollee's medical records by a health care service plan.

(b) Any person who negligently discloses results of a test for a genetic characteristic to any third party in a manner that identifies or provides identifying characteristics of the person to whom the test results apply, except pursuant to a written authorization as described in subdivision (g), shall be assessed a civil penalty in an amount not to exceed one thousand dollars ($1,000) plus court costs, as determined by the court, which penalty and costs shall be paid to the subject of the test.

(c) Any person who willfully discloses the results of a test for a genetic characteristic to any third party in a manner that identifies or provides identifying characteristics of the person to whom the test results apply, except pursuant to a written authorization as described in subdivision (g), shall be assessed a civil penalty in an amount not less than one thousand dollars ($1,000) and no more than five thousand dollars ($5,000) plus court costs, as determined by the court, which penalty and costs shall be paid to the subject of the test.

(d) Any person who willfully or negligently discloses the results of a test for a genetic characteristic to a third party in a manner that identifies or provides identifying characteristics of the person to whom the test results apply, except pursuant to a written authorization as described in subdivision (g), that results in economic, bodily, or emotional harm to the subject of the test, is guilty of a misdemeanor punishable by a fine not to exceed ten thousand dollars ($10,000).

(e) In addition to the penalties listed in subdivisions (b) and (c), any person who commits any act described in subdivision (b) or (c) shall be liable to the subject for all actual damages, including damages for economic, bodily, or emotional harm which is proximately caused by the act.

(f) Each disclosure made in violation of this section is a separate and actionable offense.

(g) The applicant's "written authorization," as used in this section, shall satisfy the following requirements:

(1) Is written in plain language and is in a typeface no smaller than 14-point type.

(2) Is dated and signed by the individual or a person authorized to act on behalf of the individual.

(3) Specifies the types of persons authorized to disclose information about the individual.

(4) Specifies the nature of the information authorized to be disclosed.

(5) States the name or functions of the persons or entities authorized to receive the information.

(6) Specifies the purposes for which the information is collected.

(7) Specifies the length of time the authorization shall remain valid.

(8) Advises the person signing the authorization of the right to receive a copy of the authorization. Written authorization is required for each separate disclosure of the test results.

(h) This section shall not apply to disclosures required by the Department of Health Services necessary to monitor compliance with Chapter 1 (commencing with Section 124975) of Part 5 of Division 106 of the Health and Safety Code, nor to disclosures required by the Department of Managed Care necessary to administer and enforce compliance with Section 1374.7 of the Health and Safety Code.

(i) For purposes of this section, "genetic characteristic" has the same meaning as that set forth in subdivision (d) of Section 1374.7 of the Health and Safety Code. **Leg.H.** 1995 ch. 695, 1996 ch. 1023, effective September 29, 1996, ch. 532, operative January 1, 1997 (ch. 532 prevails), 1999 chs. 311, 525, operative July 1, 2000, 2000 chs. 857, 941, 2003 ch. 562 (AB 715).

CHAPTER 3
USE AND DISCLOSURE OF MEDICAL INFORMATION BY EMPLOYERS
[Selected Provisions]

§56.20. Employer's duty to ensure confidentiality of medical information; employee's right to refuse release of such information.

(a) Each employer who receives medical information shall establish appropriate procedures to ensure the confidentiality and protection from unauthorized use and disclosure of that information. These procedures may include, but are not limited to instruction regarding confidentiality of employees and agents handling files containing medical information, and security systems restricting access to files containing medical information.

(b) No employee shall be discriminated against in terms or conditions of employment due to that employee's refusal to sign an authorization under this part. However, nothing in this section shall prohibit an employer from taking such action as is necessary in the absence of medical information due to an employee's refusal to sign an authorization under this part.

(c) No employer shall use, disclose, or knowingly permit its employees or agents to use or disclose medical information which the employer possesses pertaining to its employees without the patient having first signed an authorization under Section 56.11 or Section 56.21 permitting such use or disclosure, except as follows:

(1) The information may be disclosed if the disclosure is compelled by judicial or administrative process or by any other specific provision of law.

(2) That part of the information which is relevant in a lawsuit, arbitration, grievance, or other claim or challenge to which the employer and employee are parties and in which the patient has placed in issue his or her medical history, mental or physical condition, or treatment may be used or disclosed in connection with that proceeding.

(3) The information may be used only for the purpose of administering and maintaining employee benefit plans, including health care plans and plans providing short-term and long-term disability income, workers' compensation and for determining eligibility for paid and unpaid leave from work for medical reasons.

(4) The information may be disclosed to a provider of health care or other health care professional or facility to aid the diagnosis or treatment of the patient, where the patient or other person specified in subdivision (c) of Section 56.21 is unable to authorize the disclosure.

(d) If an employer agrees in writing with one or more of its employees or maintains a written policy which provides that particular types of medical information shall not be used or disclosed by the employer in particular ways, the employer shall obtain an authorization for such uses or disclosures even if an authorization would not otherwise be required by subdivision (c). **Leg.H.** 1981 ch. 782.

§56.21. Requirements for authorized release of medical information.

An authorization for an employer to disclose medical information shall be valid if it complies with all of the following:

(a) Is handwritten by the person who signs it or is in a typeface no smaller than 14-point type.

(b) Is clearly separate from any other language present on the same page and is executed by a signature that serves no purpose other than to execute the authorization.

(c) Is signed and dated by one of the following:

(1) The patient, except that a patient who is a minor may only sign an authorization for the disclosure of medical information obtained by a provider of health care in the course of furnishing services to which the minor could lawfully have consented under Part 1 (commencing with Section 25) or Part 2.7 (commencing with Section 60) of Division 1.

(2) The legal representative of the patient, if the patient is a minor or incompetent. However, authorization may not be given under this subdivision for the disclosure of medical information that pertains to a competent minor and that was created by a provider of health care in the course of furnishing services to which a minor patient could lawfully have consented under Part 1 (commencing with Section 25) or Part 2.7 (commencing with Section 60) of Division 1.

(3) The beneficiary or personal representative of a deceased patient.

(d) States the limitations, if any, on the types of medical information to be disclosed.

(e) States the name or functions of the employer or person authorized to disclose the medical information.

(f) States the names or functions of the persons or entities authorized to receive the medical information.

(g) States the limitations, if any, on the use of the medical information by the persons or entities authorized to receive the medical information.

(h) States a specific date after which the employer is no longer authorized to disclose the medical information.

(i) Advises the person who signed the authorization of the right to receive a copy of the authorization. **Leg.H.** 1981 ch. 782, 2003 ch. 562 (AB 715), 2006 ch. 538 (SB 1852) §39.

CHAPTER 6
RELATIONSHIP TO EXISTING LAW
[Selected Provisions]

§56.30. Disclosure of medical information not subject to limitations of Part 2.6.

The disclosure and use of the following medical information shall not be subject to the limitations of this part:

(a) (Mental health and developmental disabilities) Information and records obtained in the course of providing services under Division 4 (commencing with Section 4000), Division 4.1 (commencing with Section 4400), Division 4.5 (commencing with Section 4500), Division 5 (commencing with Section 5000), Division 6 (commencing with Section 6000), or Division 7 (commencing with Section 7100) of the Welfare and Institutions Code.

(b) (Public social services) Information and records that are subject to Sections 10850, 14124.1, and 14124.2 of the Welfare and Institutions Code.

(c) (State health services, communicable diseases, developmental disabilities) Information and records maintained pursuant to former Chapter 2 (commencing with Section 200) of Part 1 of Division 1 of the Health and Safety Code and pursuant to the Communicable Disease Prevention and Control Act (subdivision (a) of Section 27 of the Health and Safety Code).

(d) (Licensing and statistics) Information and records maintained pursuant to Division 2 (commencing with Section 1200) and Part 1 (commencing with Section 102100) of Division 102 of the Health and Safety Code;

pursuant to Chapter 3 (commencing with Section 1200) of Division 2 of the Business and Professions Code; and pursuant to Section 8608, 8817, or 8909 of the Family Code.

(e) (Medical survey, workers' safety) Information and records acquired and maintained or disclosed pursuant to Sections 1380 and 1382 of the Health and Safety Code and pursuant to Division 5 (commencing with Section 6300) of the Labor Code.

(f) (Industrial accidents) Information and records acquired, maintained, or disclosed pursuant to Division 1 (commencing with Section 50), Division 4 (commencing with Section 3200), Division 4.5 (commencing with Section 6100), and Division 4.7 (commencing with Section 6200) of the Labor Code.

(g) (Law enforcement) Information and records maintained by a health facility which are sought by a law enforcement agency under Chapter 3.5 (commencing with Section 1543) of Title 12 of Part 2 of the Penal Code.

(h) (Investigations of employment accident or illness) Information and records sought as part of an investigation of an on-the-job accident or illness pursuant to Division 5 (commencing with Section 6300) of the Labor Code or pursuant to Section 105200 of the Health and Safety Code.

(i) (Alcohol or drug abuse) Information and records subject to the federal alcohol and drug abuse regulations (Part 2 (commencing with Section 2.1) of Subchapter A of Chapter 1 of Title 42 of the Code of Federal Regulations) or to Section 11845.5 of the Health and Safety Code dealing with alcohol and drug abuse.

(j) (Patient discharge data) Nothing in this part shall be construed to limit, expand, or otherwise affect the authority of the California Health Facilities Commission to collect patient discharge information from health facilities.

(k) Medical information and records disclosed to, and their use by, the Insurance Commissioner, the Director of the Department of Managed Health Care, the Division of Industrial Accidents, the Workers' Compensation Appeals Board, the Department of Insurance, or the Department of Managed Health Care.

(*l*) Medical information and records related to services provided on and after January 1, 2006, disclosed to, and their use by, the Managed Risk Medical Insurance Board to the same extent that those records are required to be provided to the board related to services provided on and after July 1, 2009, to comply with Section 403 of the federal Children's Health Insurance Program Reauthorization Act of 2009 (Public Law 111-3), applying subdivision (c) of Section 1932 of the federal Social Security Act. **Leg.H.** 1981 ch. 782, 1990 ch. 1363, operative July 1, 1991, 1992 ch. 163, operative January 1, 1994, 1993 ch. 1004, 1996 ch. 1023, effective September 29, 1996, 1999 ch. 526, 2000 ch. 1067, 2010 ch. 717 (SB 853) §1, effective October 19, 2010, 2014 ch. 71 (SB 1304) §14.

§56.31. Disclosure of human immunodeficiency virus.

Notwithstanding any other provision of law, nothing in subdivision (f) of Section 56.30 shall permit the disclosure or use of medical information regarding whether a patient is infected with or exposed to the human immunodeficiency virus without the prior authorization from the patient unless the patient is an injured worker claiming to be infected with or exposed to the human immunodeficiency virus through an exposure incident arising out of and in the course of employment. **Leg.H.** 1999 ch. 766.

1999 Note: The addition of Section 56.31 to the Civil Code by Chapter 766 is not intended either to abrogate the holdings in *Allison v. Workers' Comp. Appeals Bd.* (1999) 72 Cal.App.4th 654, or to prohibit a redaction decision by a workers' compensation judge from being appealed to the Workers' Compensation Appeals Board. Stats. 1999 ch. 766 §3.

DIVISION 3
OBLIGATIONS

PART 3
Obligations Imposed by Law
[Selected Provisions]

§1708.8. Physical and constructive invasion of privacy—Obtaining visual image, sound recording, or other physical impression; liability for damages; civil fines.

(a) A person is liable for physical invasion of privacy when the person knowingly enters onto the land or into the airspace above the land of another person without permission or otherwise commits a trespass in order to capture any type of visual image, sound recording, or other physical impression of the plaintiff engaging in a private, personal, or familial activity and the invasion occurs in a manner that is offensive to a reasonable person.

(b) A person is liable for constructive invasion of privacy when the person attempts to capture, in a manner that is offensive to a reasonable person, any type of visual image, sound recording, or other physical impression of the plaintiff engaging in a private, personal, or familial activity, through the use of any device, regardless of whether there is a physical trespass, if this image, sound recording, or other physical impression could not have been achieved without a trespass unless the device was used.

(c) An assault or false imprisonment committed with the intent to capture any type of visual image, sound recording, or other physical impression of the plaintiff is subject to subdivisions (d), (e), and (h).

(d) A person who commits any act described in subdivision (a), (b), or (c) is liable for up to three times the amount of any general and special damages that are proximately caused by the violation of this section. This person may also be liable for punitive damages, subject to proof according to Section 3294. If the plaintiff proves that the invasion of privacy was committed for a commercial purpose, the person shall also be subject to disgorgement to the plaintiff of any proceeds or other consideration obtained as a result of the violation of this section. A person who comes within the description of this subdivision is also subject to a civil fine of not less than five thousand dollars ($5,000) and not more than fifty thousand dollars ($50,000).

(e) A person who directs, solicits, actually induces, or actually causes another person, regardless of whether there is an employer-employee relationship, to violate any provision of subdivision (a), (b), or (c) is liable for any general, special, and consequential damages resulting from each said violation. In addition, the person that directs, solicits, actually induces, or actually causes another person, regardless of whether there is an employer-employee relationship, to violate this section shall be liable for punitive damages to the extent that an employer would be subject to punitive damages pursuant to subdivision (b) of Section 3294. A person who comes within the description of this subdivision is also subject to a civil fine of not less than five thousand dollars ($5,000) and not more than fifty thousand dollars ($50,000).

(f)(1) The transmission, publication, broadcast, sale, offer for sale, or other use of any visual image, sound recording, or other physical impression that was taken or captured in violation of subdivision (a), (b), or (c) shall not constitute a violation of this section unless the person, in the first transaction following the taking or capture of the visual image, sound recording, or other physical impression, publicly transmitted, published, broadcast, sold, or offered for sale the visual image, sound recording, or other physical impression with actual knowledge that it was taken or captured in violation of subdivision (a), (b), or (c), and provided compensation, consideration, or remuneration, monetary or otherwise, for the rights to the unlawfully obtained visual image, sound recording, or other physical impression.

(2) For the purposes of paragraph (1), "actual knowledge" means actual awareness, understanding, and recognition, obtained prior to the time at which the person purchased or acquired the visual image, sound recording, or other physical impression, that the visual image, sound recording, or other physical impression was taken or captured in violation of subdivision (a), (b), or (c). The plaintiff shall establish actual knowledge by clear and convincing evidence.

(3) Any person that publicly transmits, publishes, broadcasts, sells, or offers for sale, in any form, medium, format, or work, a visual image, sound recording, or other physical impression that was previously publicly transmitted, published, broadcast, sold, or offered for sale by another person, is exempt from liability under this section.

(4) If a person's first public transmission, publication, broadcast, or sale or offer for sale of a visual image, sound recording, or other physical impression that was taken or captured in violation of subdivision (a), (b), or (c) does not constitute a violation of this section, that person's subsequent public transmission, publication, broadcast, sale, or offer for sale, in any form, medium, format, or work, of the visual image, sound recording, or other physical impression, does not constitute a violation of this section.

(5) This section applies only to a visual image, sound recording, or other physical impression that is captured or taken in California in violation of subdivision (a), (b), or (c) after January 1, 2010, and shall not apply to any visual image, sound recording, or other physical impression taken or captured outside of California.

(6) Nothing in this subdivision shall be construed to impair or limit a special motion to strike pursuant to Section 425.16, 425.17, or 425.18 of the Code of Civil Procedure.

(7) This section shall not be construed to limit all other rights or remedies of the plaintiff in law or equity, including, but not limited to, the publication of private facts.

(g) This section shall not be construed to impair or limit any otherwise lawful activities of law enforcement personnel or employees of governmental agencies or other entities, either public or private who, in the course and scope of their employment, and supported by an articulable suspicion, attempt to capture any type of visual image, sound recording, or other physical impression of a person during an investigation, surveillance, or monitoring of any conduct to obtain evidence of suspected illegal activity or other misconduct, the suspected violation of any administrative rule or regulation, a suspected fraudulent conduct, or any activity involving a violation of law or business practices or conduct of public officials adversely affecting the public welfare, health, or safety.

(h) In any action pursuant to this section, the court may grant equitable relief, including, but not limited to, an injunction and restraining order against further violations of subdivision (a), (b), or (c).

(i) The rights and remedies provided in this section are cumulative and in addition to any other rights and remedies provided by law.

(j) It is not a defense to a violation of this section that no image, recording, or physical impression was captured or sold.

(k) For the purposes of this section, "for a commercial purpose" means any act done with the expectation of a sale, financial gain, or other consideration. A visual image, sound recording, or other physical impression shall not be found to have been, or intended to have been, captured for a commercial purpose unless it is intended to be, or was in fact, sold, published, or transmitted.

(*l*)(1) For the purposes of this section, "private, personal, and familial activity" includes, but is not limited to:

(A) Intimate details of the plaintiff's personal life under circumstances in which the plaintiff has a reasonable expectation of privacy.

(B) Interaction with the plaintiff's family or significant others under circumstances in which the plaintiff has a reasonable expectation of privacy.

(C) If and only after the person has been convicted of violating Section 626.8 of the Penal Code, any activity that occurs when minors are present at any location set forth in subdivision (a) of Section 626.8 of the Penal Code.

(D) Any activity that occurs on a residential property under circumstances in which the plaintiff has a reasonable expectation of privacy.

(E) Other aspects of the plaintiff's private affairs or concerns under circumstances in which the plaintiff has a reasonable expectation of privacy.

(2) "Private, personal, and familial activity" does not include illegal or otherwise criminal activity as delineated in subdivision (g). However, "private, personal, and familial activity" shall include the activities of victims of crime in circumstances under which subdivision (a), (b), or (c) would apply.

(m)(1) A proceeding to recover the civil fines specified in subdivision (d) or (e) may be brought in any court of competent jurisdiction by a county counsel or city attorney.

(2) Fines collected pursuant to this subdivision shall be allocated, as follows:

(A) One-half shall be allocated to the prosecuting agency.

(B) One-half shall be deposited in the Arts and Entertainment Fund, which is hereby created in the State Treasury.

(3) Funds in the Arts and Entertainment Fund created pursuant to paragraph (2) may be expended by the California Arts Council, upon appropriation by the Legislature, to issue grants pursuant to the Dixon-Zenovich-Maddy California Arts Act of 1975 (Chapter 9 (commencing with Section 8750) of Division 1 of Title 2 of the Government Code).

(4) The rights and remedies provided in this subdivision are cumulative and in addition to any other rights and remedies provided by law.

(n) The provisions of this section are severable. If any provision of this section or its application is held invalid, that invalidity shall not affect other provisions or applications that can be given effect without the invalid provision or application. **Leg.H.** 1998 ch. 1000, 2005 ch. 424 (AB 381) §1, 2009 ch. 449 (AB 524) §2, 2010 ch. 685 (AB 2479) §1, 2014 chs. 852 (AB 1256) §1, 858 (AB 2306) §1.5, 2015 ch. 521 (AB 856) §1.

DIVISION 4
GENERAL PROVISIONS

PART 1
Relief

TITLE 2
COMPENSATORY RELIEF

CHAPTER 2
MEASURE OF DAMAGES

ARTICLE 2
Damages for Wrongs
[Selected Provisions]

§3333.1. Introduction of evidence of amount payable as benefit in action for personal injury—Health care provider defined—Professional negligence defined.

(a) In the event the defendant so elects, in an action for personal injury against a health care provider based upon professional negligence, he may introduce evidence of any amount payable as a benefit to the plaintiff as a result of the personal injury pursuant to the United States Social Security Act, any state or federal income disability or worker's compensation act, any health, sickness or income-disability insurance, accident insurance that provides health benefits or income-disability coverage, and any contract or agreement of any group, organization, partnership, or corporation to provide, pay for, or reimburse the cost of medical, hospital, dental, or other health care services. Where the defendant elects to introduce such evidence, the plaintiff may introduce evidence of any amount which the plaintiff has paid or contributed to secure his right to any insurance benefits concerning which the defendant has introduced evidence.

(b) No source of collateral benefits introduced pursuant to subdivision (a) shall recover any amount against the plaintiff nor shall it be subrogated to the rights of the plaintiff against a defendant.

(c) For the purposes of this section:

(1) "Health care provider" means any person licensed or certified pursuant to Division 2 (commencing with Section 500) of the Business and Professions Code, or licensed pursuant to the Osteopathic Initiative Act, or the Chiropractic Initiative Act, or licensed pursuant to Chapter 2.5 (commencing with Section 1440) of Division 2 of the Health and Safety Code; and any clinic, health dispensary, or health facility, licensed pursuant to Division 2 (commencing with Section 1200) of the Health and Safety Code. "Health care provider" includes the legal representatives of a health care provider;

(2) "Professional negligence" means a negligent act or omission to act by a health care provider in the rendering of professional services, which act or omission is the proximate cause of a personal injury or wrongful death, provided that such services are within the scope of services for which the provider is licensed and which are not within any restriction imposed by the licensing agency or licensed hospital.

SELECTED PROVISIONS Of The CODE OF CIVIL PROCEDURE

PART 2
OF CIVIL ACTIONS

TITLE 9
Enforcement of Judgments

DIVISION 2
ENFORCEMENT OF MONEY JUDGMENTS

CHAPTER 2
LIENS

ARTICLE 2
Judgment Lien on Real Property
[Selected Provisions]

§697.330. Creation and duration of judgment lien based on workers' compensation award.

(a) In the case of a money judgment entered on an order, decision, or award made under Division 4 (commencing with Section 3200) of the Labor Code (workers' compensation):

(1) If the judgment is for a lump sum, a judgment lien on real property is created by recording an abstract of the judgment as provided in Section 697.310 and, except as otherwise provided in Division 4 (commencing with Section 3200) of the Labor Code, the judgment lien is governed by the provisions applicable to a judgment lien created under Section 697.310.

(2) If the judgment is for the payment of money in installments, a judgment lien on real property is created by recording a certified copy of the judgment as provided in Section 697.320 and, except as otherwise provided in Division 4 (commencing with Section 3200) of the Labor Code, the lien is governed by the provisions applicable to a judgment lien created under Section 697.320.

(b) Nothing in this section limits or affects any provision of Division 4 (commencing with Section 3200) of the Labor Code.

CHAPTER 4
EXEMPTIONS

ARTICLE 3
Exempt Property
[Selected Provisions]

§704.160. Workers' compensation claim, award, or payment—Application to support judgment.

(a) Except as provided by Chapter 1 (commencing with Section 4900) of Part 3 of Division 4 of the Labor Code, before payment, a claim for workers' compensation or workers' compensation awarded or adjudged is exempt without making a claim. Except as specified in subdivision (b), after payment, the award is exempt.

(b) Notwithstanding any other provision of law, during the payment of workers' compensation temporary disability benefits described in subdivision (a) to a support judgment debtor, the support judgment creditor may, through the appropriate local child support agency, seek to apply the workers' compensation temporary disability benefit payment to satisfy the support judgment as provided by Section 17404 of the Family Code.

(c) Notwithstanding any other provision of law, during the payment of workers' compensation temporary disability benefits described in subdivision (a) to a support judgment debtor under a support judgment, including a judgment for reimbursement of public assistance, the judgment creditor may, directly or through the appropriate local child support agency, seek to apply the temporary disability benefit payments to satisfy the support judgment by an earnings assignment order for support, as defined in Section 5208 of the Family Code, or any other applicable enforcement procedure. The amount to be withheld pursuant to the earnings assignment order for support or other enforcement procedure shall be 25 percent of the amount of each periodic payment or any lower amount specified in writing by the judgment creditor or court order, rounded down to the nearest dollar. Otherwise, the amount to be withheld shall be the amount the court determines under subdivision (c) of Section 703.070. The paying entity may deduct from each payment made pursuant to an order assigning earnings under this subdivision an amount reflecting the actual cost of administration of this assignment, up to two dollars ($2) for each payment.

(d) Unless the provision or context otherwise requires, the following definitions govern the construction of this section.

(1) "Judgment debtor" or "support judgment debtor" means a person who is owing a duty of support.

(2) "Judgment creditor" or "support judgment creditor" means the person to whom support has been ordered to be paid.

(3) "Support" refers to an obligation owing on behalf of a child, spouse, or family; or an amount owing pursuant to Section 17402 of the Family Code. It also includes past due support or arrearage when it exists. **Leg.H.** 1982 ch. 1364, operative July 1, 1983, 1992 ch. 848, effective September 22, 1992, 1993 ch. 219, 2000 ch. 808, effective September 28, 2000.

TITLE 14
Miscellaneous Provisions

CHAPTER 5
NOTICES, AND FILING AND SERVICE OF PAPERS
[Selected Provisions]

§1013. Service by mail, Express Mail, overnight delivery, or facsimile transmission—Method of service.

(a) In case of service by mail, the notice or other paper shall be deposited in a post office, mailbox, subpost office, substation, or mail chute, or other like facility regularly maintained by the United States Postal Service, in a sealed envelope, with postage paid, addressed to the person on whom it is to be served, at the office address as last given by that person on any document filed in the cause and served on the party making service by mail; otherwise at that party's place of residence. Service is complete at the time of the deposit, but any period of notice and any right or duty to do any act or make any response within any period or on a date certain after service of the document, which time period or date is prescribed by statute or rule of court, shall be extended five calendar days, upon service by mail, if the place of address and the place of mailing is within the State of California, 10 calendar days if either the place of mailing or the place of address is outside the State of California but within the United States, and 20 calendar days if either the place of mailing or the place of address is outside the United States, but the extension shall not apply to extend the time for filing notice of intention to move for new trial, notice of intention to move to vacate judgment pursuant to Section 663a, or notice of appeal. This extension applies in the absence of a specific exception provided for by this section or other statute or rule of court.

(b) The copy of the notice or other paper served by mail pursuant to this chapter shall bear a notation of the date and place of mailing or be accompanied by an unsigned copy of the affidavit or certificate of mailing.

(c) In case of service by Express Mail, the notice or other paper must be deposited in a post office, mailbox, subpost office, substation, or mail chute, or other like facility regularly maintained by the United States Postal Service for receipt of Express Mail, in a sealed envelope, with Express Mail postage paid, addressed to the person on whom it is to be served, at the office address as last given by that person on any document filed in the cause and served on the party making service by Express Mail; otherwise at that party's place of residence. In case of service by another method of delivery providing for overnight delivery, the notice or other paper must be deposited in a box or other facility regularly maintained by the express service carrier, or delivered to an authorized courier or driver authorized by the express service carrier to receive documents, in an envelope or package designated by the express service carrier with delivery fees paid or provided for, addressed to the person on whom it is to be served, at the office address as last given by that person on any document filed in the cause and served on the party making service; otherwise at that party's place of residence. Service is complete at the time of the deposit, but any period of notice and any right or duty to do any act or make any response within any period or on a date certain after service of the document served by Express Mail or other method of delivery providing for overnight delivery shall be extended by two court days. The extension shall not apply to extend the time for filing notice of intention to move for new trial, notice of intention to move to vacate judgment pursuant to Section 663a, or notice of appeal. This extension applies in the absence of a specific exception provided for by this section or other statute or rule of court.

(d) The copy of the notice or other paper served by Express Mail or another means of delivery providing for overnight delivery pursuant to this chapter shall bear a notation of the date and place of deposit or be accompanied by an unsigned copy of the affidavit or certificate of deposit.

(e) Service by facsimile transmission shall be permitted only where the parties agree and a written confirmation of that agreement is made. The Judicial Council may adopt rules implementing the service of documents by facsimile transmission and may provide a form for the confirmation of the agreement required by this subdivision. In case of service by facsimile transmission, the notice or other paper must be transmitted to a facsimile machine maintained by the person on whom it is served at the facsimile machine telephone number as last given by that person on any document which he or she has filed in the cause and served on the party making the service. Service is complete at the time of transmission, but any period of notice and any right or duty to do any act or make any response within any period or on a date certain after service of the document, which time period or date is prescribed by statute or rule of court, shall be extended, after service by facsimile transmission, by two court days, but the extension shall not apply to extend the time for filing notice of intention to move for new trial, notice of intention to move to vacate judgment pursuant to Section 663a, or notice of appeal. This extension applies in the absence of a specific exception provided for by this section or other statute or rule of court.

(f) The copy of the notice or other paper served by facsimile transmission pursuant to this chapter shall bear a notation of the date and place of transmission and the facsimile telephone number to which transmitted, or to be accompanied by an unsigned copy of the affidavit or certificate of transmission which shall contain the facsimile telephone number to which the notice or other paper was transmitted.

(g) Electronic service shall be permitted pursuant to Section 1010.6 and the rules on electronic service in the California Rules of Court.

(h) Subdivisions (b), (d), and (f) are directory. **Leg.H.** 1872, 1874 p. 343, 1907 p. 602, 1929 p. 845, 1931 ch. 739, 1949 ch. 456, 1967 ch. 169, 1968 ch. 166, 1974 ch. 281,

282 §2, 1980 ch. 196, 1992 ch. 339, 1995 ch. 576, 2001 ch. 812, 2010 ch. 156 (SB 1274) §2.

PART 4
Miscellaneous Provisions

TITLE 4
CIVIL DISCOVERY ACT

CHAPTER 1
GENERAL PROVISIONS

§2016.010. Short title.

This title may be cited as the "Civil Discovery Act." **Leg.H.** 2004 ch. 182 (AB 3081), operative July 1, 2005.

Ref.: Herlick Handbook § 14.20.

§2016.020. Definitions.

As used in this title:

(a) "Action" includes a civil action and a special proceeding of a civil nature.

(b) "Court" means the trial court in which the action is pending, unless otherwise specified.

(c) "Document" and "writing" mean a writing, as defined in Section 250 of the Evidence Code.

(d) "Electronic" means relating to technology having electrical, digital, magnetic, wireless, optical, electromagnetic, or similar capabilities.

(e) "Electronically stored information" means information that is stored in an electronic medium. **Leg.H.** 2004 ch. 182 (AB 3081), operative July 1, 2005, 2009 ch. 5 (AB 5) §3, effective June 29, 2009.

2009 Note: This act shall be known as the Electronic Discovery Act. Stats. 2009 ch. 5 (AB 5) §1.

Ref.: Hanna § 25.45; Herlick Handbook §§ 14.20, 14.20A.

§2016.030. Modification by written stipulation.

Unless the court orders otherwise, the parties may by written stipulation modify the procedures provided by this title for any method of discovery permitted under Section 2019.010. **Leg.H.** 2004 ch. 182 (AB 3081), operative July 1, 2005.

Ref.: Herlick Handbook § 14.20.

§2016.040. What meet and confer declaration in support of motion to show.

A meet and confer declaration in support of a motion shall state facts showing a reasonable and good faith attempt at an informal resolution of each issue presented by the motion. **Leg.H.** 2004 ch. 182 (AB 3081), operative July 1, 2005.

Ref.: Herlick Handbook § 14.20.

§2016.050. Applicability of Sections 1011 and 1013.

Sections 1011 and 1013 apply to any method of discovery or service of a motion provided for in this title. **Leg.H.** 2004 ch. 182 (AB 3081), operative July 1, 2005, 2017 ch. 64 (SB 543) §2.

Ref.: Herlick Handbook § 14.20.

§2016.060. Specified date falling on Saturday, Sunday or holiday; extension of time limit.

When the last day to perform or complete any act provided for in this title falls on a Saturday, Sunday, or holiday as specified in Section 10, the time limit is extended until the next court day closer to the trial date. **Leg.H.** 2004 ch. 182 (AB 3081) §23.5, operative July 1, 2005.

Ref.: Herlick Handbook § 14.20.

§2016.070. Applicability of title to enforcement of money judgment.

This title applies to discovery in aid of enforcement of a money judgment only to the extent provided in Article 1 (commencing with Section 708.010) of Chapter 6 of Title 9 of Part 2. **Leg.H.** 2004 ch. 182 (AB 3081), operative July 1, 2005.

Ref.: Herlick Handbook § 14.20.

§2016.080. [Repealed January 1, 2023] Informal discovery conference.

(a) If an informal resolution is not reached by the parties, as described in Section 2016.040, the court may conduct an informal discovery conference upon request by a party or on the court's own motion for the purpose of discussing discovery matters in dispute between the parties.

(b) If a party requests an informal discovery conference, the party shall file a declaration described in Section 2016.040 with the court. Any party may file a response to a declaration filed pursuant to this subdivision. If a court is in session and does not grant, deny, or schedule the party's request within 10 calendar days after the initial request, the request shall be deemed denied.

(c)(1) If a court grants or orders an informal discovery conference, the court may schedule and hold the conference no later than 30 calendar days after the court granted the request or issued its order, and before the discovery cutoff date.

(2) If an informal discovery conference is granted or ordered, the court may toll the deadline for filing a discovery motion or make any other appropriate discovery order.

(d) If an informal discovery conference is not held within 30 calendar days from the date the court granted the request, the request for an informal discovery conference shall be deemed denied, and any tolling period previously ordered by the court shall continue to apply to that action.

(e) The outcome of an informal discovery conference does not bar a party from filing a discovery motion or prejudice the disposition of a discovery motion.

(f) This section does not prevent the parties from stipulating to the timing of discovery proceedings as described in Section 2024.060.

(g) This section shall remain in effect only until January 1, 2023, and as of that date is repealed, unless a later enacted statute that is enacted before January 1, 2023, deletes or extends that date. **Leg.H.** 2017 ch. 189 (AB 383) §1, 2018 ch. 92 (SB 1289) §44.

§2016.090. Applicability to civil action; initial disclosure.

(a) The following shall apply only to a civil action upon an order of the court following stipulation by all parties to the action:

(1) Within 45 days of the order of the court, a party shall, without awaiting a discovery request, provide to the other parties an initial disclosure that includes all of the following information:

(A) The names, addresses, telephone numbers, and email addresses of all persons likely to have discoverable information, along with the subjects of that information, that the disclosing party may use to support its claims or defenses, unless the use would be solely for impeachment.

(B) A copy, or a description by category and location, of all documents, electronically stored information, and tangible things that the disclosing party has in its possession, custody, or control and may use to support its claims or defenses, unless the use would be solely for impeachment.

(C) Any agreement under which an insurance company may be liable to satisfy, in whole or in part, a judgment entered in the action or to indemnify or reimburse for payments made to satisfy the judgment.

(D) Any agreement under which a person, as defined in Section 175 of the Evidence Code, may be liable to satisfy, in whole or in part, a judgment entered in the action or to indemnify or reimburse for payments made to satisfy the judgment. Only those provisions of an agreement that are material to the terms of the insurance, indemnification, or reimbursement are required to be included in the initial disclosure. Material provisions include, but are not limited to, the identities of parties to the agreement and the nature and limits of the coverage.

(2) A party shall make its initial disclosures based on the information then reasonably available to it. A party is not excused from making its initial disclosures because it has not fully investigated the case, because it challenges the sufficiency of another party's disclosures, or because another party has not made its disclosures.

(3) A party that has made its initial disclosures, as described in paragraph (1), or that has responded to another party's discovery request, shall supplement or correct a disclosure or response in the following situations:

(A) In a timely manner if the party learns that in some material respect the disclosure or response is incomplete or incorrect and the additional or corrective information has not otherwise been made known to the other parties during the disclosure or discovery process.

(B) As ordered by the court.

(4) A party's obligations under this section may be enforced by a court on its own motion or the motion of a party to compel disclosure.

(5) A party's disclosures under this section shall be verified under penalty of perjury as being true and correct to the best of the party's knowledge.

(b) Notwithstanding subdivision (a), this section does not apply to the following actions:

(1) An unlawful detainer action, as defined in Section 1161.

(2) An action in the small claims division of a court, as defined in Section 116.210. **Leg.H.** 2019 ch. 836 (SB 17) §1.

CHAPTER 2
SCOPE OF DISCOVERY
[Selected Provisions]

ARTICLE 1
General Provisions

§2017.010. What matters may be subject to discovery.

Unless otherwise limited by order of the court in accordance with this title, any party may obtain discovery regarding any matter, not privileged, that is relevant to the subject matter involved in the pending action or to the determination of any motion made in that action, if the matter either is itself admissible in evidence or appears reasonably calculated to lead to the discovery of admissible evidence. Discovery may relate to the claim or defense of the party seeking discovery or of any other party to the action. Discovery may be obtained of the identity and location of persons having knowledge of any discoverable matter, as well as of the existence, description, nature, custody, condition, and location of any document, electronically stored information, tangible thing, or land or other property. **Leg.H.** 2004 ch. 182 (AB 3081), operative July 1, 2005, 2012 ch. 72 (SB 1574) §8.

§2017.020. When court may limit scope of discovery; motion for protective order; monetary sanction.

(a) The court shall limit the scope of discovery if it determines that the burden, expense, or intrusiveness of that discovery clearly outweighs the likelihood that the information sought will lead to the discovery of admissible evidence. The court may make this determination pursuant to a motion for protective order by a party or other affected person. This motion shall be accompanied by a meet and confer declaration under Section 2016.040.

(b) The court shall impose a monetary sanction under Chapter 7 (commencing with Section 2023.010) against any party, person, or attorney who unsuccessfully makes or opposes a motion for a protective order, unless it finds that the one subject to the sanction acted with substantial justification or that other circumstances make the imposition of the sanction unjust.

(c)(1) Notwithstanding subdivision (b), or any other section of this title, absent exceptional circumstances, the court shall not impose sanctions on a party or any attorney of a party for failure to provide electronically stored information that has been lost, damaged, altered, or overwritten as the result of the routine, good faith operation of an electronic information system.

(2) This subdivision shall not be construed to alter any obligation to preserve discoverable information. **Leg.H.** 2004 ch. 182 (AB 3081), operative July 1, 2005, 2012 ch. 72 (SB 1574) §9.

ARTICLE 2
Scope of Discovery in Specific Contexts

§2017.210. Information concerning insurance.

A party may obtain discovery of the existence and contents of any agreement under which any insurance carrier may be liable to satisfy in whole or in part a judgment that may be entered in the action or to indemnify or reimburse for payments made to satisfy the judgment. This discovery may include the identity of the carrier and the nature and limits of the coverage. A party may also obtain discovery as to whether that insurance carrier is disputing the agreement's coverage of the claim involved in the action, but not as to the nature and substance of that dispute. Information concerning the insurance agreement is not by reason of disclosure admissible in evidence at trial. **Leg.H.** 2004 ch. 182 (AB 3081), operative July 1, 2005.

§2017.220. Discovery regarding plaintiff's sexual conduct in certain actions; showing of good cause; monetary sanction.

(a) In any civil action alleging conduct that constitutes sexual harassment, sexual assault, or sexual battery, any party seeking discovery concerning the plaintiff's sexual conduct with individuals other than the alleged perpetrator shall establish specific facts showing that there is good cause for that discovery, and that the matter sought to be discovered is relevant to the subject matter of the action and reasonably calculated to lead to the discovery of admissible evidence. This showing shall be made by a noticed motion, accompanied by a meet and confer declaration under Section 2016.040, and shall not be made or considered by the court at an ex parte hearing.

(b) The court shall impose a monetary sanction under Chapter 7 (commencing with Section 2023.010) against any party, person, or attorney who unsuccessfully makes or opposes a motion for discovery under subdivision (a), unless it finds that the one subject to the sanction acted with substantial justification or that other circumstances make the imposition of the sanction unjust. **Leg.H.** 2004 ch. 182 (AB 3081), operative July 1, 2005.

CHAPTER 4
ATTORNEY WORK PRODUCT

§2018.010. Meaning of "client" for purposes of chapter.

For purposes of this chapter, "client" means a "client" as defined in Section 951 of the Evidence Code. **Leg.H.** 2004 ch. 182 (AB 3081), operative July 1, 2005.

§2018.020. Policy of state.

It is the policy of the state to do both of the following:

(a) Preserve the rights of attorneys to prepare cases for trial with that degree of privacy necessary to encourage them to prepare their cases thoroughly and to investigate not only the favorable but the unfavorable aspects of those cases.

(b) Prevent attorneys from taking undue advantage of their adversary's industry and efforts. **Leg.H.** 2004 ch. 182 (AB 3081), operative July 1, 2005.

§2018.030. Certain writings not discoverable; when other work product may be subject to discovery.

(a) A writing that reflects an attorney's impressions, conclusions, opinions, or legal research or theories is not discoverable under any circumstances.

(b) The work product of an attorney, other than a writing described in subdivision (a), is not discoverable unless the court determines that denial of discovery will unfairly prejudice the party seeking discovery in preparing that party's claim or defense or will result in an injustice. **Leg.H.** 2004 ch. 182 (AB 3081), operative July 1, 2005.

§2018.040. Restatement of existing law.

This chapter is intended to be a restatement of existing law relating to protection of work product. It is not intended to expand or reduce the extent to which work product is discoverable under existing law in any action. **Leg.H.** 2004 ch. 182 (AB 3081), operative July 1, 2005.

§2018.050. Work product enabling commission of crime not protected in official investigations.

Notwithstanding Section 2018.040, when a lawyer is suspected of knowingly participating in a crime or fraud, there is no protection of work product under this chapter in any official investigation by a law enforcement agency or proceeding or action brought by a public prosecutor in the name of the people of the State of California if the services of the lawyer were sought or obtained to enable or aid anyone to commit or plan to commit a crime or fraud. **Leg.H.** 2004 ch. 182 (AB 3081), operative July 1, 2005.

§2018.060. Right to request in camera hearing.

Nothing in this chapter is intended to limit an attorney's ability to request an in camera hearing as provided for in People v. Superior Court (Laff) (2001) 25 Cal.4th 703. **Leg.H.** 2004 ch. 182 (AB 3081), operative July 1, 2005.

§2018.070. Discovery for purposes of State Bar disciplinary proceedings; protective order; client approval.

(a) The State Bar may discover the work product of an attorney against whom disciplinary charges are pending when it is relevant to issues of breach of duty by the lawyer and requisite client approval has been granted.

(b) Where requested and for good cause, discovery under this section shall be subject to a protective order to ensure the confidentiality of the work product except for its use by the State Bar in disciplinary investigations and its consideration under seal in State Bar Court proceedings.

(c) For purposes of this chapter, whenever a client has initiated a complaint against an attorney, the requisite client approval shall be deemed to have been granted. **Leg.H.** 2004 ch. 182 (AB 3081), operative July 1, 2005.

§2018.080. No privilege when work product relevant to issue of breach of attorney-client relationship.

In an action between an attorney and a client or a former client of the attorney, no work product privilege under this chapter exists if the work product is relevant to an issue of breach by the attorney of a duty to the client arising out of the attorney-client relationship. **Leg.H.** 2004 ch. 182 (AB 3081), operative July 1, 2005.

CHAPTER 5
METHODS AND SEQUENCE OF DISCOVERY

ARTICLE 1
General Provisions

§2019.010. Methods of discovery.

Any party may obtain discovery by one or more of the following methods:

(a) Oral and written depositions.

(b) Interrogatories to a party.

(c) Inspections of documents, things, and places.

(d) Physical and mental examinations.

(e) Requests for admissions.

(f) Simultaneous exchanges of expert trial witness information. **Leg.H.** 2004 ch. 182 (AB 3081), operative July 1, 2005.

§2019.020. Sequence and timing of discovery.

(a) Except as otherwise provided by a rule of the Judicial Council, a local court rule, or a local uniform written policy, the methods of discovery may be used in any sequence, and the fact that a party is conducting discovery, whether by deposition or another method, shall not operate to delay the discovery of any other party.

(b) Notwithstanding subdivision (a), on motion and for good cause shown, the court may establish the sequence and timing of discovery for the convenience of parties and witnesses and in the interests of justice. **Leg.H.** 2004 ch. 182 (AB 3081), operative July 1, 2005.

§2019.030. When frequency or extent of discovery may be restricted; motion for protective order; monetary sanction.

(a) The court shall restrict the frequency or extent of use of a discovery method provided in Section 2019.010 if it determines either of the following:

(1) The discovery sought is unreasonably cumulative or duplicative, or is obtainable from some other source that is more convenient, less burdensome, or less expensive.

(2) The selected method of discovery is unduly burdensome or expensive, taking into account the needs of the case, the amount in controversy, and the importance of the issues at stake in the litigation.

(b) The court may make these determinations pursuant to a motion for a protective order by a party or other affected person. This motion shall be accompanied by a meet and confer declaration under Section 2016.040.

(c) The court shall impose a monetary sanction under Chapter 7 (commencing with Section 2023.010) against any party, person, or attorney who unsuccessfully makes or opposes a motion for a protective order, unless it finds that the one subject to the sanction acted with substantial justification or that other circumstances make the imposition of the sanction unjust. **Leg.H.** 2004 ch. 182 (AB 3081), operative July 1, 2005.

§2019.040. Electronically stored information.

(a) When any method of discovery permits the production, inspection, copying, testing, or sampling of documents or tangible things, that method shall also permit the production, inspection, copying, testing, or sampling of electronically stored information.

(b) All procedures available under this title to compel, prevent, or limit the production, inspection, copying, testing, or sampling of documents or tangible things shall be available to compel, prevent, or limit the production, inspection, copying, testing, or sampling of electronically stored information. **Leg.H.** 2012 ch. 72 (SB 1574) §14.

ARTICLE 2
Methods and Sequence of Discovery in Specific Contexts

§2019.210. Misappropriation of trade secret.

In any action alleging the misappropriation of a trade secret under the Uniform Trade Secrets Act (Title 5 (commencing with Section 3426) of Part 1 of Division 4 of the Civil Code), before commencing discovery relating to the trade secret, the party alleging the misappropriation shall identify the trade secret with reasonable particularity subject to any orders that may be appropriate under Section 3426.5 of the Civil Code. **Leg.H.** 2004 ch. 182 (AB 3081), operative July 1, 2005.

CHAPTER 6
NONPARTY DISCOVERY

ARTICLE 1
General Provisions

§2020.010. Methods for discovery within state from nonparty.

(a) Any of the following methods may be used to obtain discovery within the state from a person who is not a party to the action in which the discovery is sought:

(1) An oral deposition under Chapter 9 (commencing with Section 2025.010).

(2) A written deposition under Chapter 11 (commencing with Section 2028.010).

(3) A deposition for production of business records and things under Article 4 (commencing with Section 2020.410) or Article 5 (commencing with Section 2020.510).

(b) Except as provided in subdivision (a) of Section 2025.280, the process by which a nonparty is required to provide discovery is a deposition subpoena. **Leg.H.** 2004 ch. 182 (AB 3081), operative July 1, 2005.

§2020.020. What deposition subpoena may command.

(a) Only the attendance and the testimony of the deponent, under Article 3 (commencing with Section 2020.310).

(b) Only the production of business records for copying, under Article 4 (commencing with Section 2020.410).

(c) The attendance and the testimony of the deponent, as well as the production of business records, other documents, electronically stored information, and tangible things, under Article 5 (commencing with Section 2020.510). **Leg.H.** 2004 ch. 182 (AB 3081), operative July 1, 2005, 2012 ch. 72 (SB 1574) §15.

§2020.030. Provisions applicable to deposition subpoena.

Except as modified in this chapter, the provisions of Chapter 2 (commencing with Section 1985) of Title 3 of Part 4 of this code, and of Article 4 (commencing with Section 1560) of Chapter 2 of Division 11 of the Evidence Code, apply to a deposition subpoena. **Leg.H.** 2004 ch. 182 (AB 3081), operative July 1, 2005.

ARTICLE 2
Procedures Applicable to All Types of Deposition Subpoenas

§2020.210. Issuance of deposition subpoena by clerk of court or attorney of record.

(a) The clerk of the court in which the action is pending shall issue a deposition subpoena signed and sealed, but otherwise in blank, to a party requesting it, who shall fill it in before service.

(b) Instead of a court-issued deposition subpoena, an attorney of record for any party may sign and issue a deposition subpoena. A deposition subpoena issued under this subdivision need not be sealed. A copy may be served on the nonparty, and the attorney may retain the original. **Leg.H.** 2004 ch. 182 (AB 3081), operative July 1, 2005.

§2020.220. Service of deposition subpoena.

(a) Subject to subdivision (c) of Section 2020.410, service of a deposition subpoena shall be effected a sufficient time in advance of the deposition to provide the deponent a reasonable opportunity to locate and produce any designated business records, documents, electronically stored information, and tangible things, as described in Article 4 (commencing with Section 2020.410), and, where personal attendance is commanded, a reasonable time to travel to the place of deposition.

(b) Any person may serve the subpoena by personal delivery of a copy of it as follows:

(1) If the deponent is a natural person, to that person.

(2) If the deponent is an organization, to any officer, director, custodian of records, or to any agent or employee authorized by the organization to accept service of a subpoena.

(c) Personal service of any deposition subpoena is effective to require all of the following of any deponent who is a resident of California at the time of service:

(1) Personal attendance and testimony, if the subpoena so specifies.

(2) Any specified production, inspection, testing, and sampling.

(3) The deponent's attendance at a court session to consider any issue arising out of the deponent's refusal to be sworn, or to answer any question, or to produce specified items, or to permit inspection or photocopying, if the subpoena so specifies, or specified testing and sampling of the items produced.

(d) Unless the subpoenaing party and the subpoenaed person otherwise agree or the court otherwise orders, the following shall apply:

(1) If a subpoena requiring production of electronically stored information does not specify a form or forms for producing a type of electronically stored information, the person subpoenaed shall produce the information in the form or forms in which it is ordinarily maintained or in a form that is reasonably usable.

(2) A subpoenaed person need not produce the same electronically stored information in more than one form.

(e) The subpoenaed person opposing the production, inspection, copying, testing, or sampling of electronically stored information on the basis that the information is from a source that is not reasonably accessible because of undue burden or expense shall bear the burden of demonstrating that the information is from a source that is not reasonably accessible because of undue burden or expense.

(f) If the person from whom discovery of electronically stored information is subpoenaed establishes that the information is from a source that is not reasonably accessible because of undue burden or expense, the court may nonetheless order discovery if the subpoenaing party shows good cause, subject to any limitations imposed under subdivision (i).

(g) If the court finds good cause for the production of electronically stored information from a source that is not reasonably accessible, the court may set conditions for the discovery of the electronically stored information, including allocation of the expense of discovery.

(h) If necessary, the subpoenaed person, at the reasonable expense of the subpoenaing party, shall, through detection devices, translate any data compilations included in the subpoena into a reasonably usable form.

(i) The court shall limit the frequency or extent of discovery of electronically stored information, even from a source that is reasonably accessible, if the court determines that any of the following conditions exists:

(1) It is possible to obtain the information from some other source that is more convenient, less burdensome, or less expensive.

(2) The discovery sought is unreasonably cumulative or duplicative.

(3) The party seeking discovery has had ample opportunity by discovery in the action to obtain the information sought.

(4) The likely burden or expense of the proposed discovery outweighs the likely benefit, taking into account the amount in controversy, the resources of the parties, the

importance of the issues in the litigation, and the importance of the requested discovery in resolving the issues.

(j) If a subpoenaed person notifies the subpoenaing party that electronically stored information produced pursuant to a subpoena is subject to a claim of privilege or of protection as attorney work product, as described in Section 2031.285, the provisions of Section 2031.285 shall apply.

(k) A party serving a subpoena requiring the production of electronically stored information shall take reasonable steps to avoid imposing undue burden or expense on a person subject to the subpoena.

(*l*) An order of the court requiring compliance with a subpoena issued under this section shall protect a person who is neither a party nor a party's officer from undue burden or expense resulting from compliance.

(m)(1) Absent exceptional circumstances, the court shall not impose sanctions on a subpoenaed person or any attorney of a subpoenaed person for failure to provide electronically stored information that has been lost, damaged, altered, or overwritten as the result of the routine, good faith operation of an electronic information system.

(2) The subdivision shall not be construed to alter any obligation to preserve discoverable information. **Leg.H.** 2004 ch. 182 (AB 3081), operative July 1, 2005, 2012 ch. 72 (SB 1574) §16.

§2020.230. Witness fee and mileage.

(a) If a deposition subpoena requires the personal attendance of the deponent, under Article 3 (commencing with Section 2020.310) or Article 5 (commencing with Section 2020.510), the party noticing the deposition shall pay to the deponent in cash or by check the same witness fee and mileage required by Chapter 1 (commencing with Section 68070) of Title 8 of the Government Code for attendance and testimony before the court in which the action is pending. This payment, whether or not demanded by the deponent, shall be made, at the option of the party noticing the deposition, either at the time of service of the deposition subpoena, or at the time the deponent attends for the taking of testimony.

(b) Service of a deposition subpoena that does not require the personal attendance of a custodian of records or other qualified person, under Article 4 (commencing with Section 2020.410), shall be accompanied, whether or not demanded by the deponent, by a payment in cash or by check of the witness fee required by paragraph (6) of subdivision (b) of Section 1563 of the Evidence Code. **Leg.H.** 2004 ch. 182 (AB 3081), operative July 1, 2005.

§2020.240. Punishment for disobeying deposition subpoena; contempt; forfeiture and damages.

A deponent who disobeys a deposition subpoena in any manner described in subdivision (c) of Section 2020.220 may be punished for contempt under Chapter 7 (commencing with Section 2023.010) without the necessity of a prior order of court directing compliance by the witness. The deponent is also subject to the forfeiture and the payment of damages set forth in Section 1992. **Leg.H.** 2004 ch. 182 (AB 3081), operative July 1, 2005.

ARTICLE 3
Subpoena Commanding Only Attendance and Testimony of the Deponent

§2020.310. Rules applicable to deposition subpoena commanding only attendance and testimony.

The following rules apply to a deposition subpoena that commands only the attendance and the testimony of the deponent:

(a) The subpoena shall specify the time when and the place where the deponent is commanded to attend the deposition.

(b) The subpoena shall set forth a summary of all of the following:

(1) The nature of a deposition.

(2) The rights and duties of the deponent.

(3) The penalties for disobedience of a deposition subpoena, as described in Section 2020.240.

(c) If the deposition will be recorded using audio or video technology by, or at the direction of, the noticing party under Section 2025.340, the subpoena shall state that it will be recorded in that manner.

(d) If the deposition testimony will be conducted using instant visual display, the subpoena shall state that it will be conducted in that manner.

(e) If the deponent is an organization, the subpoena shall describe with reasonable particularity the matters on which examination is requested. The subpoena shall also advise the organization of its duty to make the designation of employees or agents who will attend the deposition, as described in Section 2025.230. **Leg.H.** 2004 ch. 182 (AB 3081), operative July 1, 2005.

ARTICLE 4
Subpoena Commanding Only Production of Business Records for Copying

§2020.410. What deposition subpoena commanding only production of business records to contain; description of records; records pertaining to consumer.

(a) A deposition subpoena that commands only the production of business records for copying shall designate the business records to be produced either by specifically describing each individual item or by reasonably particularizing each category of item, and shall specify the form in which any electronically stored information is to be produced, if a particular form is desired.

(b) Notwithstanding subdivision (a), specific information identifiable only to the deponent's records system, like a policy number or the date when a consumer interacted with the witness, is not required.

(c) A deposition subpoena that commands only the production of business records for copying need not be accompanied by an affidavit or declaration showing good cause for the production of the business records designated in it. It shall be directed to the custodian of those records or another person qualified to certify the records. It shall command compliance in accordance with Section 2020.430

on a date that is no earlier than 20 days after the issuance, or 15 days after the service, of the deposition subpoena, whichever date is later.

(d) If, under Section 1985.3 or 1985.6, the one to whom the deposition subpoena is directed is a witness, and the business records described in the deposition subpoena are personal records pertaining to a consumer, the service of the deposition subpoena shall be accompanied either by a copy of the proof of service of the notice to the consumer described in subdivision (e) of Section 1985.3, or subdivision (b) of Section 1985.6, as applicable, or by the consumer's written authorization to release personal records described in paragraph (2) of subdivision (c) of Section 1985.3, or paragraph (2) of subdivision (c) of Section 1985.6, as applicable. **Leg.H.** 2004 ch. 182 (AB 3081), operative July 1, 2005, 2012 ch. 72 (SB 1574) §17.

§2020.420. Deposition officer.

The officer for a deposition seeking discovery only of business records for copying under this article shall be a professional photocopier registered under Chapter 20 (commencing with Section 22450) of Division 8 of the Business and Professions Code, or a person exempted from the registration requirements of that chapter under Section 22451 of the Business and Professions Code. This deposition officer shall not be financially interested in the action, or a relative or employee of any attorney of the parties. Any objection to the qualifications of the deposition officer is waived unless made before the date of production or as soon thereafter as the ground for that objection becomes known or could be discovered by reasonable diligence. **Leg.H.** 2004 ch. 182 (AB 3081), operative July 1, 2005.

§2020.430. Delivery to deposition officer; copy of records and affidavit; duties of custodian; date for delivery; applicability of specified provisions.

(a) Except as provided in subdivision (e), if a deposition subpoena commands only the production of business records for copying, the custodian of the records or other qualified person shall, in person, by messenger, or by mail, deliver both of the following only to the deposition officer specified in the subpoena:

(1) A true, legible, and durable copy of the records.

(2) An affidavit in compliance with Section 1561 of the Evidence Code.

(b) If the delivery required by subdivision (a) is made to the office of the deposition officer, the records shall be enclosed, sealed, and directed as described in subdivision (c) of Section 1560 of the Evidence Code.

(c) If the delivery required by subdivision (a) is made at the office of the business whose records are the subject of the deposition subpoena, the custodian of those records or other qualified person shall do one of the following:

(1) Permit the deposition officer specified in the deposition subpoena to make a copy of the originals of the designated business records during normal business hours, as defined in subdivision (e) of Section 1560 of the Evidence Code.

(2) Deliver to the deposition officer a true, legible, and durable copy of the records on receipt of payment in cash or by check, by or on behalf of the party serving the deposition subpoena, of the reasonable costs of preparing that copy, together with an itemized statement of the cost of preparation, as determined under subdivision (b) of Section 1563 of the Evidence Code. This copy need not be delivered in a sealed envelope.

(d) Unless the parties, and if the records are those of a consumer as defined in Section 1985.3 or 1985.6, the consumer, stipulate to an earlier date, the custodian of the records shall not deliver to the deposition officer the records that are the subject of the deposition subpoena prior to the date and time specified in the deposition subpoena. The following legend shall appear in boldface type on the deposition subpoena immediately following the date and time specified for production: "Do not release the requested records to the deposition officer prior to the date and time stated above."

(e) This section does not apply if the subpoena directs the deponent to make the records available for inspection or copying by the subpoenaing party's attorney or a representative of that attorney at the witness' business address under subdivision (e) of Section 1560 of the Evidence Code.

(f) The provisions of Section 1562 of the Evidence Code concerning the admissibility of the affidavit of the custodian or other qualified person apply to a deposition subpoena served under this article. **Leg.H.** 2004 ch. 182 (AB 3081), operative July 1, 2005.

§2020.440. Deposition officer to provide copies to specified parties.

Promptly on or after the deposition date and after the receipt or the making of a copy of business records under this article, the deposition officer shall provide that copy to the party at whose instance the deposition subpoena was served, and a copy of those records to any other party to the action who then or subsequently, within a period of six months following the settlement of the case, notifies the deposition officer that the party desires to purchase a copy of those records. **Leg.H.** 2004 ch. 182 (AB 3081), operative July 1, 2005.

ARTICLE 5
Subpoena Commanding Both Production of Business Records and Attendance and Testimony of the Deponent

§2020.510. Requirements for deposition subpoena that commands attendance, testimony and production of business records, etc.; records pertaining to consumer or employee.

(a) A deposition subpoena that commands the attendance and the testimony of the deponent, as well as the production of business records, documents, electronically stored information, and tangible things, shall:

(1) Comply with the requirements of Section 2020.310.

(2) Designate the business records, documents, electronically stored information, and tangible things to be produced either by specifically describing each individual item or by reasonably particularizing each category of item.

(3) Specify any testing or sampling that is being sought.

(4) Specify the form in which any electronically stored information is to be produced, if a particular form is desired.

(b) A deposition subpoena under subdivision (a) need not be accompanied by an affidavit or declaration showing good cause for the production of the documents and things designated.

(c) If, as described in Section 1985.3, the person to whom the deposition subpoena is directed is a witness, and the business records described in the deposition subpoena are personal records pertaining to a consumer, the service of the deposition subpoena shall be accompanied either by a copy of the proof of service of the notice to the consumer described in subdivision (e) of Section 1985.3, or by the consumer's written authorization to release personal records described in paragraph (2) of subdivision (c) of Section 1985.3.

(d) If, as described in Section 1985.6, the person to whom the deposition subpoena is directed is a witness and the business records described in the deposition subpoena are employment records pertaining to an employee, the service of the deposition subpoena shall be accompanied either by a copy of the proof of service of the notice to the employee described in subdivision (e) of Section 1985.6, or by the employee's written authorization to release personal records described in paragraph (2) of subdivision (c) of Section 1985.6. **Leg.H.** 2004 ch. 182 (AB 3081), operative July 1, 2005, 2007 ch. 113 (AB 1126) §4, 2012 ch. 72 (SB 1574) §18.

CHAPTER 7 SANCTIONS

§2023.010. Misuses of discovery process.

Misuses of the discovery process include, but are not limited to, the following:

(a) Persisting, over objection and without substantial justification, in an attempt to obtain information or materials that are outside the scope of permissible discovery.

(b) Using a discovery method in a manner that does not comply with its specified procedures.

(c) Employing a discovery method in a manner or to an extent that causes unwarranted annoyance, embarrassment, or oppression, or undue burden and expense.

(d) Failing to respond or to submit to an authorized method of discovery.

(e) Making, without substantial justification, an unmeritorious objection to discovery.

(f) Making an evasive response to discovery.

(g) Disobeying a court order to provide discovery.

(h) Making or opposing, unsuccessfully and without substantial justification, a motion to compel or to limit discovery.

(i) Failing to confer in person, by telephone, or by letter with an opposing party or attorney in a reasonable and good faith attempt to resolve informally any dispute concerning discovery, if the section governing a particular discovery motion requires the filing of a declaration stating facts showing that an attempt at informal resolution has been made. **Leg.H.** 2004 ch. 182 (AB 3081), operative July 1, 2005.

§2023.020. Monetary sanction for failure to confer.

Notwithstanding the outcome of the particular discovery motion, the court shall impose a monetary sanction ordering that any party or attorney who fails to confer as required pay the reasonable expenses, including attorney's fees, incurred by anyone as a result of that conduct. **Leg.H.** 2004 ch. 182 (AB 3081), operative July 1, 2005.

§2023.030. Sanctions which may be imposed for misuse of discovery process.

To the extent authorized by the chapter governing any particular discovery method or any other provision of this title, the court, after notice to any affected party, person, or attorney, and after opportunity for hearing, may impose the following sanctions against anyone engaging in conduct that is a misuse of the discovery process:

(a) The court may impose a monetary sanction ordering that one engaging in the misuse of the discovery process, or any attorney advising that conduct, or both pay the reasonable expenses, including attorney's fees, incurred by anyone as a result of that conduct. The court may also impose this sanction on one unsuccessfully asserting that another has engaged in the misuse of the discovery process, or on any attorney who advised that assertion, or on both. If a monetary sanction is authorized by any provision of this title, the court shall impose that sanction unless it finds that the one subject to the sanction acted with substantial justification or that other circumstances make the imposition of the sanction unjust.

(b) The court may impose an issue sanction ordering that designated facts shall be taken as established in the action in accordance with the claim of the party adversely affected by the misuse of the discovery process. The court may also impose an issue sanction by an order prohibiting any party engaging in the misuse of the discovery process from supporting or opposing designated claims or defenses.

(c) The court may impose an evidence sanction by an order prohibiting any party engaging in the misuse of the discovery process from introducing designated matters in evidence.

(d) The court may impose a terminating sanction by one of the following orders:

(1) An order striking out the pleadings or parts of the pleadings of any party engaging in the misuse of the discovery process.

(2) An order staying further proceedings by that party until an order for discovery is obeyed.

(3) An order dismissing the action, or any part of the action, of that party.

(4) An order rendering a judgment by default against that party.

(e) The court may impose a contempt sanction by an order treating the misuse of the discovery process as a contempt of court.

(f)(1) Notwithstanding subdivision (a), or any other section of this title, absent exceptional circumstances, the court shall not impose sanctions on a party or any attorney of a party for failure to provide electronically stored information that has been lost, damaged, altered, or overwritten as the result of the routine, good faith operation of an electronic information system.

(2) This subdivision shall not be construed to alter any obligation to preserve discoverable information. **Leg.H.** 2004 ch. 182 (AB 3081), operative July 1, 2005, 2012 ch. 72 (SB 1574) §19.

§2023.040. Request for sanction and notice of motion; what to be included therein.

A request for a sanction shall, in the notice of motion, identify every person, party, and attorney against whom the sanction is sought, and specify the type of sanction sought. The notice of motion shall be supported by a memorandum of points and authorities, and accompanied by a declaration setting forth facts supporting the amount of any monetary sanction sought. **Leg.H.** 2004 ch. 182 (AB 3081), operative July 1, 2005.

§2023.050. Sanctions.

(a) Notwithstanding any other law, and in addition to any other sanctions imposed pursuant to this chapter, a court shall impose a two hundred and fifty dollar ($250) sanction, payable to the requesting party, upon a party, person, or attorney if, upon reviewing a request for a sanction made pursuant to Section 2023.040, the court finds any of the following:

(1) The party, person, or attorney did not respond in good faith to a request for the production of documents made pursuant to Section 2020.010, 2020.410, 2020.510, or 2025.210, or to an inspection demand made pursuant to Section 2031.010.

(2) The party, person, or attorney produced requested documents within seven days before the court was scheduled to hear a motion to compel production of the records pursuant to Section 2025.450, 2025.480, or 2031.320 that is filed by the requesting party as a result of the other party, person, or attorney's failure to respond in good faith.

(3) The party, person, or attorney failed to confer in person, by telephone, letter, or other means of communication in writing, as defined in Section 250 of the Evidence Code, with the party or attorney requesting the documents in a reasonable and good faith attempt to resolve informally any dispute concerning the request.

(b) Notwithstanding paragraph (3) of subdivision (o) of Section 6068 of the Business and Professions Code, the court may, in its discretion, require an attorney who is sanctioned pursuant to subdivision (a) to report the sanction, in writing, to the State Bar within 30 days of the imposition of the sanction.

(c) The court may excuse the imposition of the sanction required by subdivision (a) if the court makes written findings that the one subject to the sanction acted with substantial justification or that other circumstances make the imposition of the sanction unjust.

(d) Sanctions pursuant to this section shall be imposed only after notice to the party, person, or attorney against whom the sanction is proposed to be imposed and opportunity for that party, person, or attorney to be heard.

(e) For purposes of this section, there is a rebuttable presumption that a natural person acted in good faith if that person was not represented by an attorney in the action at the time the conduct that is sanctionable under subdivision (a) occurred. This presumption may only be overcome by clear and convincing evidence. **Leg.H.** 2019 ch. 836 (SB 17) §2.

CHAPTER 9
ORAL DEPOSITION INSIDE CALIFORNIA
[Selected Provisions]

ARTICLE 2
Deposition Notice

§2025.210. Time for service of notice.

Subject to Sections 2025.270 and 2025.610, an oral deposition may be taken as follows:

(a) The defendant may serve a deposition notice without leave of court at any time after that defendant has been served or has appeared in the action, whichever occurs first.

(b) The plaintiff may serve a deposition notice without leave of court on any date that is 20 days after the service of the summons on, or appearance by, any defendant. On motion with or without notice, the court, for good cause shown, may grant to a plaintiff leave to serve a deposition notice on an earlier date. **Leg.H.** 2004 ch. 182 (AB 3081) §23, operative July 1, 2005.

§2025.220. Contents of deposition notice.

(a) A party desiring to take the oral deposition of any person shall give notice in writing. The deposition notice shall state all of the following, in at least 12-point type:

(1) The address where the deposition will be taken.

(2) The date of the deposition, selected under Section 2025.270, and the time it will commence.

(3) The name of each deponent, and the address and telephone number, if known, of any deponent who is not a party to the action. If the name of the deponent is not known, the deposition notice shall set forth instead a general description sufficient to identify the person or particular class to which the person belongs.

(4) The specification with reasonable particularity of any materials or category of materials, including any electronically stored information, to be produced by the deponent.

(5) Any intention by the party noticing the deposition to record the testimony by audio or video technology, in addition to recording the testimony by the stenographic method as required by Section 2025.330 and any intention to record the testimony by stenographic method through the instant visual display of the testimony. If the deposition will be conducted using instant visual display, a copy of the deposition notice shall also be given to the deposition officer. Any offer to provide the instant visual display of the testimony or to provide rough draft transcripts to any party which is accepted prior to, or offered at, the deposition shall also be made by the deposition officer at the deposition to all parties in attendance. Any party or attorney requesting the provision of the instant visual display of the testimony, or rough draft transcripts, shall pay the reasonable cost of those services, which may be no greater than the costs charged to any other party or attorney.

(6) Any intention to reserve the right to use at trial a video recording of the deposition testimony of a treating or consulting physician or of an expert witness under subdi-

vision (d) of Section 2025.620. In this event, the operator of the video camera shall be a person who is authorized to administer an oath, and shall not be financially interested in the action or be a relative or employee of any attorney of any of the parties.

(7) The form in which any electronically stored information is to be produced, if a particular form is desired.

(8)(A) A statement disclosing the existence of a contract, if any is known to the noticing party, between the noticing party or a third party who is financing all or part of the action and either of the following for any service beyond the noticed deposition:

(i) The deposition officer.

(ii) The entity providing the services of the deposition officer.

(B) A statement disclosing that the party noticing the deposition, or a third party financing all or part of the action, directed his or her attorney to use a particular officer or entity to provide services for the deposition, if applicable.

(b) Notwithstanding subdivision (a), where under Article 4 (commencing with Section 2020.410) only the production by a nonparty of business records for copying is desired, a copy of the deposition subpoena shall serve as the notice of deposition. **Leg.H.** 2004 ch. 182 (AB 3081) §23, operative July 1, 2005, 2012 ch. 72 (SB 1574) §20, 2015 ch. 346 (AB 1197) §2, 2018 ch. 268 (AB 3019) §1.

§2025.230. Contents of deposition notice if deponent not a natural person.

If the deponent named is not a natural person, the deposition notice shall describe with reasonable particularity the matters on which examination is requested. In that event, the deponent shall designate and produce at the deposition those of its officers, directors, managing agents, employees, or agents who are most qualified to testify on its behalf as to those matters to the extent of any information known or reasonably available to the deponent. **Leg.H.** 2004 ch. 182 (AB 3081) §23, operative July 1, 2005.

§2025.240. Notice to parties to the action; duties of subpoenaing party if deponent to produce personal records of consumer or employment records.

(a) The party who prepares a notice of deposition shall give the notice to every other party who has appeared in the action. The deposition notice, or the accompanying proof of service, shall list all the parties or attorneys for parties on whom it is served.

(b) If, as defined in subdivision (a) of Section 1985.3 or subdivision (a) of Section 1985.6, the party giving notice of the deposition is a subpoenaing party, and the deponent is a witness commanded by a deposition subpoena to produce personal records of a consumer or employment records of an employee, the subpoenaing party shall serve on that consumer or employee all of the following:

(1) A notice of the deposition.

(2) The notice of privacy rights specified in subdivision (e) of Section 1985.3 or in subdivision (e) of Section 1985.6.

(3) A copy of the deposition subpoena.

(c) If the attendance of the deponent is to be compelled by service of a deposition subpoena under Chapter 6 (commencing with Section 2020.010), an identical copy of that subpoena shall be served with the deposition notice. **Leg.H.** 2004 ch. 182 (AB 3081) §23, operative July 1, 2005, 2007 ch. 113 (AB 1126) §5.

§2025.250. Place of taking deposition.

(a) Unless the court orders otherwise under Section 2025.260, the deposition of a natural person, whether or not a party to the action, shall be taken at a place that is, at the option of the party giving notice of the deposition, either within 75 miles of the deponent's residence, or within the county where the action is pending and within 150 miles of the deponent's residence.

(b) The deposition of an organization that is a party to the action shall be taken at a place that is, at the option of the party giving notice of the deposition, either within 75 miles of the organization's principal executive or business office in California, or within the county where the action is pending and within 150 miles of that office.

(c) Unless the organization consents to a more distant place, the deposition of any other organization shall be taken within 75 miles of the organization's principal executive or business office in California.

(d) If an organization has not designated a principal executive or business office in California, the deposition shall be taken at a place that is, at the option of the party giving notice of the deposition, either within the county where the action is pending, or within 75 miles of any executive or business office in California of the organization. **Leg.H.** 2004 ch. 182 (AB 3081) §23, operative July 1, 2005, 2005 ch. 294 (AB 333) §7.

§2025.260. Motion for deposition at more distant place; monetary sanction.

(a) A party desiring to take the deposition of a natural person who is a party to the action or an officer, director, managing agent, or employee of a party may make a motion for an order that the deponent attend for deposition at a place that is more distant than that permitted under Section 2025.250. This motion shall be accompanied by a meet and confer declaration under Section 2016.040.

(b) In exercising its discretion to grant or deny this motion, the court shall take into consideration any factor tending to show whether the interests of justice will be served by requiring the deponent's attendance at that more distant place, including, but not limited to, the following:

(1) Whether the moving party selected the forum.

(2) Whether the deponent will be present to testify at the trial of the action.

(3) The convenience of the deponent.

(4) The feasibility of conducting the deposition by written questions under Chapter 11 (commencing with Section 2028.010), or of using a discovery method other than a deposition.

(5) The number of depositions sought to be taken at a place more distant than that permitted under Section 2025.250.

(6) The expense to the parties of requiring the deposition to be taken within the distance permitted under Section 2025.250.

source that is not reasonably accessible because of undue burden or expense and that the deponent will not search the source in the absence of an agreement with the deposing party or court order, the deponent shall identify in its objection the types or categories of sources of electronically stored information that it asserts are not reasonably accessible. By objecting and identifying information of a type or category of source or sources that are not reasonably accessible, the deponent preserves any objections it may have relating to that electronically stored information.

(e) If a deponent fails to answer any question or to produce any document, electronically stored information, or tangible thing under the deponent's control that is specified in the deposition notice or a deposition subpoena, the party seeking that answer or production may adjourn the deposition or complete the examination on other matters without waiving the right at a later time to move for an order compelling that answer or production under Section 2025.480.

(f) Notwithstanding subdivision (a), if a deponent notifies the party that took a deposition that electronically stored information produced pursuant to the deposition notice or subpoena is subject to a claim of privilege or of protection as attorney work product, as described in Section 2031.285, the provisions of Section 2031.285 shall apply. **Leg.H.** 2004 ch. 182 (AB 3081) §23, operative July 1, 2005, 2012 ch. 72 (SB 1574) §25.

§2025.470. Suspension of taking of testimony; stipulation; motion for protective order.

The deposition officer may not suspend the taking of testimony without the stipulation of all parties present unless any party attending the deposition, including the deponent, demands that the deposition officer suspend taking the testimony to enable that party or deponent to move for a protective order under Section 2025.420 on the ground that the examination is being conducted in bad faith or in a manner that unreasonably annoys, embarrasses, or oppresses that deponent or party. **Leg.H.** 2004 ch. 182 (AB 3081) §23, operative July 1, 2005.

§2025.480. Motion for order compelling answer or production; time for motion; notice; discovery of electronically stored information; certified copy of relevant parts of transcript; monetary and other sanctions.

(a) If a deponent fails to answer any question or to produce any document, electronically stored information, or tangible thing under the deponent's control that is specified in the deposition notice or a deposition subpoena, the party seeking discovery may move the court for an order compelling that answer or production.

(b) This motion shall be made no later than 60 days after the completion of the record of the deposition, and shall be accompanied by a meet and confer declaration under Section 2016.040.

(c) Notice of this motion shall be given to all parties and to the deponent either orally at the examination, or by subsequent service in writing. If the notice of the motion is given orally, the deposition officer shall direct the deponent to attend a session of the court at the time specified in the notice.

(d) In a motion under subdivision (a) relating to the production of electronically stored information, the deponent objecting to or opposing the production, inspection, copying, testing, or sampling of electronically stored information on the basis that the information is from a source that is not reasonably accessible because of the undue burden or expense shall bear the burden of demonstrating that the information is from a source that is not reasonably accessible because of undue burden or expense.

(e) If the deponent from whom discovery of electronically stored information is sought establishes that the information is from a source that is not reasonably accessible because of the undue burden or expense, the court may nonetheless order discovery if the deposing party shows good cause, subject to any limitations imposed under subdivision (g).

(f) If the court finds good cause for the production of electronically stored information from a source that is not reasonably accessible, the court may set conditions for the discovery of the electronically stored information, including allocation of the expense of discovery.

(g) The court shall limit the frequency or extent of discovery of electronically stored information, even from a source that is reasonably accessible, if the court determines that any of the following conditions exists:

(1) It is possible to obtain the information from some other source that is more convenient, less burdensome, or less expensive.

(2) The discovery sought is unreasonably cumulative or duplicative.

(3) The party seeking discovery has had ample opportunity by discovery in the action to obtain the information sought.

(4) The likely burden or expense of the proposed discovery outweighs the likely benefit, taking into account the amount in controversy, the resources of the parties, the importance of the issues in the litigation, and the importance of the requested discovery in resolving the issues.

(h) Not less than five days prior to the hearing on this motion, the moving party shall lodge with the court a certified copy of any parts of the stenographic transcript of the deposition that are relevant to the motion. If a deposition is recorded by audio or video technology, the moving party is required to lodge a certified copy of a transcript of any parts of the deposition that are relevant to the motion.

(i) If the court determines that the answer or production sought is subject to discovery, it shall order that the answer be given or the production be made on the resumption of the deposition.

(j) The court shall impose a monetary sanction under Chapter 7 (commencing with Section 2023.010) against any party, person, or attorney who unsuccessfully makes or opposes a motion to compel an answer or production, unless it finds that the one subject to the sanction acted with substantial justification or that other circumstances make the imposition of the sanction unjust.

(k) If a deponent fails to obey an order entered under this section, the failure may be considered a contempt of court. In addition, if the disobedient deponent is a party to the action or an officer, director, managing agent, or employee of a party, the court may make those orders that are just against the disobedient party, or against the party with whom the disobedient deponent is affiliated, including the imposition of an issue sanction, an evidence sanction, or a terminating sanction under Chapter 7 (commencing with Section 2023.010). In lieu of or in addition to this sanction, the court may impose a monetary sanction under Chapter 7 (commencing with Section 2023.010) against that party deponent or against any party with whom the deponent is affiliated.

(*l*)(1) Notwithstanding subdivisions (j) and (k), absent exceptional circumstances, the court shall not impose sanctions on a deponent or any attorney of a deponent for failure to provide electronically stored information that has been lost, damaged, altered, or overwritten as the result of the routine, good faith operation of an electronic information system.

(2) This subdivision shall not be construed to alter any obligation to preserve discoverable information. **Leg.H.** 2004 ch. 182 (AB 3081) §23, operative July 1, 2005, 2005 chs. 22 (SB 1108) §21, 294 (AB 333) §21, 2012 ch. 72 (SB 1574) §26.

ARTICLE 5
Transcript or Recording

§2025.510. Transcription of testimony; costs; who may obtain copies and when; retention of stenographic notes; access to recorded testimony; stenographic testimony as official record.

(a) Unless the parties agree otherwise, the testimony at a deposition recorded by stenographic means shall be transcribed.

(b) The party noticing the deposition shall bear the cost of the transcription, unless the court, on motion and for good cause shown, orders that the cost be borne or shared by another party.

(c) Notwithstanding subdivision (b) of Section 2025.320, any other party or the deponent, at the expense of that party or deponent, may obtain a copy of the transcript.

(d) If the deposition officer receives a request from a party for an original or a copy of the deposition transcript, or any portion thereof, and the full or partial transcript will be available to that party prior to the time the original or copy would be available to any other party, the deposition officer shall immediately notify all other parties attending the deposition of the request, and shall, upon request by any party other than the party making the original request, make that copy of the full or partial deposition transcript available to all parties at the same time.

(e) Stenographic notes of depositions shall be retained by the reporter for a period of not less than eight years from the date of the deposition, where no transcript is produced, and not less than one year from the date on which the transcript is produced. The notes may be either on paper or electronic media, as long as it allows for satisfactory production of a transcript at any time during the periods specified.

(f) At the request of any other party to the action, including a party who did not attend the taking of the deposition testimony, any party who records or causes the recording of that testimony by means of audio or video technology shall promptly do both of the following:

(1) Permit that other party to hear the audio recording or to view the video recording.

(2) Furnish a copy of the audio or video recording to that other party on receipt of payment of the reasonable cost of making that copy of the recording.

(g) If the testimony at the deposition is recorded both stenographically and by audio or video technology, the stenographic transcript shall be the official record of that testimony for the purpose of the trial and any subsequent hearing or appeal.

(h)(1) The requesting attorney or party appearing in propria persona shall timely pay the deposition officer or the entity providing the services of the deposition officer for the transcription or copy of the transcription described in subdivision (b) or (c), and any other deposition product or service that is requested either orally or in writing.

(2) This subdivision shall apply unless responsibility for the payment is otherwise provided by law or unless the deposition officer or entity is notified in writing at the time the services or products are requested that the party or another identified person will be responsible for payment.

(3) This subdivision does not prohibit or supersede an agreement between an attorney and a party allocating responsibility for the payment of deposition costs to the party.

(4) Nothing in the case of Serrano v. Stefan Merli Plastering Co., Inc. (2008) 162 Cal.App.4th 1014 shall be construed to alter the standards by which a court acquires personal jurisdiction over a nonparty to an action.

(5) The requesting attorney or party appearing in propria persona, upon the written request of a deposition officer who has obtained a final judgment for payment of services provided pursuant to this subdivision, shall provide to the deposition officer an address that can be used to effectuate service for the purpose of Section 708.110 in the manner specified in Section 415.10.

(i) For purposes of this section, "deposition product or service" means any product or service provided in connection with a deposition that qualifies as shorthand reporting, as described in Section 8017 of the Business and Professions Code, and any product or service derived from that shorthand reporting. **Leg.H.** 2004 ch. 182 (AB 3081) §23, operative July 1, 2005, 2007 ch. 115 (AB 1211) §1, 2012 ch. 125 (AB 2372) §1, 2014 ch. 913 (AB 2747) §12.

§2025.520. Written notice when original transcript becomes available for reading, correcting and signing; exception; time period for deponent to change answers and approve or refuse to approve transcript; motion to suppress transcript; monetary sanction.

(a) If the deposition testimony is stenographically recorded, the deposition officer shall send written notice to the deponent and to all parties attending the deposition when the original transcript of the testimony for each session of the deposition is available for reading, correcting, and signing, unless the deponent and the attending parties agree on the record that the reading, correcting, and signing of the transcript of the testimony will be waived or that the reading, correcting, and signing of a transcript of the testimony will take place after the entire deposition has been concluded or at some other specific time.

(b) For 30 days following each notice under subdivision (a), unless the attending parties and the deponent agree on the record or otherwise in writing to a longer or shorter time period, the deponent may change the form or the substance of the answer to a question, and may either approve the transcript of the deposition by signing it, or refuse to approve the transcript by not signing it.

(c) Alternatively, within this same period, the deponent may change the form or the substance of the answer to any question and may approve or refuse to approve the transcript by means of a letter to the deposition officer signed by the deponent which is mailed by certified or registered mail with return receipt requested. A copy of that letter shall be sent by first-class mail to all parties attending the deposition.

(d) For good cause shown, the court may shorten the 30-day period for making changes, approving, or refusing to approve the transcript.

(e) The deposition officer shall indicate on the original of the transcript, if the deponent has not already done so at the office of the deposition officer, any action taken by the deponent and indicate on the original of the transcript, the deponent's approval of, or failure or refusal to approve, the transcript. The deposition officer shall also notify in writing the parties attending the deposition of any changes which the deponent timely made in person.

(f) If the deponent fails or refuses to approve the transcript within the allotted period, the deposition shall be given the same effect as though it had been approved, subject to any changes timely made by the deponent.

(g) Notwithstanding subdivision (f), on a seasonable motion to suppress the deposition, accompanied by a meet and confer declaration under Section 2016.040, the court may determine that the reasons given for the failure or refusal to approve the transcript require rejection of the deposition in whole or in part.

(h) The court shall impose a monetary sanction under Chapter 7 (commencing with Section 2023.010) against any party, person, or attorney who unsuccessfully makes or opposes a motion to suppress a deposition under this section, unless the court finds that the one subject to the sanction acted with substantial justification or that other circumstances make the imposition of the sanction unjust. **Leg.H.** 2004 ch. 182 (AB 3081) §23, operative July 1, 2005.

§2025.530. Written notice when audio or video recording becomes available for review; exception; time period for deponent to change answers; identification of deposition as deponent's own or failure to do so; motion to suppress deposition; monetary sanction.

(a) If there is no stenographic transcription of the deposition, the deposition officer shall send written notice to the deponent and to all parties attending the deposition that the audio or video recording made by, or at the direction of, any party, is available for review, unless the deponent and all these parties agree on the record to waive the hearing or viewing of the audio or video recording of the testimony.

(b) For 30 days following a notice under subdivision (a), the deponent, either in person or by signed letter to the deposition officer, may change the substance of the answer to any question.

(c) The deposition officer shall set forth in a writing to accompany the recording any changes made by the deponent, as well as either the deponent's signature identifying the deposition as the deponent's own, or a statement of the deponent's failure to supply the signature, or to contact the officer within the period prescribed by subdivision (b).

(d) When a deponent fails to contact the officer within the period prescribed by subdivision (b), or expressly refuses by a signature to identify the deposition as the deponent's own, the deposition shall be given the same effect as though signed.

(e) Notwithstanding subdivision (d), on a reasonable motion to suppress the deposition, accompanied by a meet and confer declaration under Section 2016.040, the court may determine that the reasons given for the refusal to sign require rejection of the deposition in whole or in part.

(f) The court shall impose a monetary sanction under Chapter 7 (commencing with Section 2023.010) against any party, person, or attorney who unsuccessfully makes or opposes a motion to suppress a deposition under this section, unless it finds that the one subject to the sanction acted with substantial justification or that other circumstances make the imposition of the sanction unjust. **Leg.H.** 2004 ch. 182 (AB 3081) §23, operative July 1, 2005.

§2025.540. Certification by deposition officer; use of rough draft transcript not permitted.

(a) The deposition officer shall certify on the transcript of the deposition, or in a writing accompanying an audio or video record of deposition testimony, as described in Section 2025.530, that the deponent was duly sworn and that the transcript or recording is a true record of the testimony given.

(b) When prepared as a rough draft transcript, the transcript of the deposition may not be certified and may not be used, cited, or transcribed as the certified transcript of the deposition proceedings. The rough draft transcript may not be cited or used in any way or at any time to rebut or contradict the certified transcript of deposition proceedings as provided by the deposition officer. **Leg.H.** 2004 ch. 182 (AB 3081) §23, operative July 1, 2005.

§2025.550. Transmittal of transcript to attorney; time period for retention.

(a) The certified transcript of a deposition shall not be filed with the court. Instead, the deposition officer shall securely seal that transcript in an envelope or package endorsed with the title of the action and marked: "Deposition of (here insert name of deponent)," and shall promptly transmit it to the attorney for the party who noticed the deposition. This attorney shall store it under conditions that will protect it against loss, destruction, or tampering.

(b) The attorney to whom the transcript of a deposition is transmitted shall retain custody of it until six months after final disposition of the action. At that time, the transcript may be destroyed, unless the court, on motion of any party and for good cause shown, orders that the transcript be preserved for a longer period. **Leg.H.** 2004 ch. 182 (AB 3081) §23, operative July 1, 2005.

§2025.560. Retention of audio or video recording of deposition testimony by operator; access of parties to hearing or viewing or copy of recording; cost; timeframe for retention.

(a) An audio or video recording of deposition testimony made by, or at the direction of, any party, including a certified recording made by an operator qualified under subdivisions (b) to (f), inclusive, of Section 2025.340, shall not be filed with the court. Instead, the operator shall retain custody of that recording and shall store it under conditions that will protect it against loss, destruction, or tampering, and preserve as far as practicable the quality of the recording and the integrity of the testimony and images it contains.

(b) At the request of any party to the action, including a party who did not attend the taking of the deposition testimony, or at the request of the deponent, that operator shall promptly do both of the following:

(1) Permit the one making the request to hear or to view the recording on receipt of payment of a reasonable charge for providing the facilities for hearing or viewing the recording.

(2) Furnish a copy of the audio or video recording to the one making the request on receipt of payment of the reasonable cost of making that copy of the recording.

(c) The attorney or operator who has custody of an audio or video recording of deposition testimony made by, or at the direction of, any party, shall retain custody of it until six months after final disposition of the action. At that time, the audio or video recording may be destroyed or erased, unless the court, on motion of any party and for good cause shown, orders that the recording be preserved for a longer period. **Leg.H.** 2004 ch. 182 (AB 3081) §23, operative July 1, 2005, 2009 ch. 88 (AB 176) §18.

§2025.570. Furnishing of copies of transcript or recording by deposition officer; charge; notice to parties of right to seek protective order; applicability of section.

(a) Notwithstanding subdivision (b) of Section 2025.320, unless the court issues an order to the contrary, a copy of the transcript of the deposition testimony made by, or at the direction of, any party, or an audio or video recording of the deposition testimony, if still in the possession of the deposition officer, shall be made available by the deposition officer to any person requesting a copy, on payment of a reasonable charge set by the deposition officer.

(b) If a copy is requested from the deposition officer, the deposition officer shall mail a notice to all parties attending the deposition and to the deponent at the deponent's last known address advising them of all of the following:

(1) The copy is being sought.

(2) The name of the person requesting the copy.

(3) The right to seek a protective order under Section 2025.420.

(c) If a protective order is not served on the deposition officer within 30 days of the mailing of the notice, the deposition officer shall make the copy available to the person requesting the copy.

(d) This section shall apply only to recorded testimony taken at depositions occurring on or after January 1, 1998. **Leg.H.** 2004 ch. 182 (AB 3081) §23, operative July 1, 2005.

ARTICLE 6
Post-Deposition Procedures

§2025.610. Subsequent depositions; when permitted.

(a) Once any party has taken the deposition of any natural person, including that of a party to the action, neither the party who gave, nor any other party who has been served with a deposition notice pursuant to Section 2025.240 may take a subsequent deposition of that deponent.

(b) Notwithstanding subdivision (a), for good cause shown, the court may grant leave to take a subsequent deposition, and the parties, with the consent of any deponent who is not a party, may stipulate that a subsequent deposition be taken.

(c) This section does not preclude taking one subsequent deposition of a natural person who has previously been examined under either or both of the following circumstances:

(1) The person was examined as a result of that person's designation to testify on behalf of an organization under Section 2025.230.

(2) The person was examined pursuant to a court order under Section 485.230, for the limited purpose of discovering pursuant to Section 485.230 the identity, location, and value of property in which the deponent has an interest.

(d) This section does not authorize the taking of more than one subsequent deposition for the limited purpose of Section 485.230. **Leg.H.** 2004 ch. 182 (AB 3081) §23, operative July 1, 2005.

§2025.620. Use of deposition as evidence; requirements.

At the trial or any other hearing in the action, any part or all of a deposition may be used against any party who was present or represented at the taking of the deposition, or who had due notice of the deposition and did not serve a valid objection under Section 2025.410, so far as admissible under the rules of evidence applied as though the deponent were then present and testifying as a witness, in accordance with the following provisions:

(a) Any party may use a deposition for the purpose of contradicting or impeaching the testimony of the deponent as a witness, or for any other purpose permitted by the Evidence Code.

(b) An adverse party may use for any purpose, a deposition of a party to the action, or of anyone who at the time of taking the deposition was an officer, director, managing agent, employee, agent, or designee under Section 2025.230 of a party. It is not ground for objection to the use of a deposition of a party under this subdivision by an adverse party that the deponent is available to testify, has testified, or will testify at the trial or other hearing.

(c) Any party may use for any purpose the deposition of any person or organization, including that of any party to the action, if the court finds any of the following:

(1) The deponent resides more than 150 miles from the place of the trial or other hearing.

(2) The deponent, without the procurement or wrongdoing of the proponent of the deposition for the purpose of preventing testimony in open court, is any of the following:

(A) Exempted or precluded on the ground of privilege from testifying concerning the matter to which the deponent's testimony is relevant.

(B) Disqualified from testifying.

(C) Dead or unable to attend or testify because of existing physical or mental illness or infirmity.

(D) Absent from the trial or other hearing and the court is unable to compel the deponent's attendance by its process.

(E) Absent from the trial or other hearing and the proponent of the deposition has exercised reasonable diligence but has been unable to procure the deponent's attendance by the court's process.

(3) Exceptional circumstances exist that make it desirable to allow the use of any deposition in the interests of justice and with due regard to the importance of presenting the testimony of witnesses orally in open court.

(d) Any party may use a video recording of the deposition testimony of a treating or consulting physician or of any expert witness even though the deponent is available to testify if the deposition notice under Section 2025.220 reserved the right to use the deposition at trial, and if that party has complied with subdivision (m) of Section 2025.340.

(e) Subject to the requirements of this chapter, a party may offer in evidence all or any part of a deposition, and if the party introduces only part of the deposition, any other party may introduce any other parts that are relevant to the parts introduced.

(f) Substitution of parties does not affect the right to use depositions previously taken.

(g) When an action has been brought in any court of the United States or of any state, and another action involving the same subject matter is subsequently brought between the same parties or their representatives or successors in interest, all depositions lawfully taken and duly filed in the initial action may be used in the subsequent action as if originally taken in that subsequent action. A deposition previously taken may also be used as permitted by the Evidence Code. **Leg.H.** 2004 ch. 182 (AB 3081) §23, operative July 1, 2005.

CHAPTER 10
ORAL DEPOSITION OUTSIDE CALIFORNIA
[Selected Provisions]

§2026.010. Taking of oral deposition in another state or in a territory or insular possession; procedures and process; issuance of commission.

(a) Any party may obtain discovery by taking an oral deposition, as described in Section 2025.010, in another state of the United States, or in a territory or an insular possession subject to its jurisdiction. Except as modified in this section, the procedures for taking oral depositions in California set forth in Chapter 9 (commencing with Section 2025.010) apply to an oral deposition taken in another state of the United States, or in a territory or an insular possession subject to its jurisdiction.

(b) If a deponent is a party to the action or an officer, director, managing agent, or employee of a party, the service of the deposition notice is effective to compel that deponent to attend and to testify, as well as to produce any document, electronically stored information, or tangible thing for inspection, copying, testing, or sampling. The deposition notice shall specify a place in the state, territory, or insular possession of the United States that is within 75 miles of the residence or a business office of a deponent.

(c) If the deponent is not a party to the action or an officer, director, managing agent, or employee of a party, a party serving a deposition notice under this section shall use any process and procedures required and available under the laws of the state, territory, or insular possession where the deposition is to be taken to compel the deponent to attend and to testify, as well as to produce any document, electronically stored information, or tangible thing for inspection, copying, testing, sampling, and any related activity.

(d) A deposition taken under this section shall be conducted in either of the following ways:

(1) Under the supervision of a person who is authorized to administer oaths by the laws of the United States or those of the place where the examination is to be held, and who is not otherwise disqualified under Section 2025.320 and subdivisions (b) to (f), inclusive, of Section 2025.340.

(2) Before a person appointed by the court.

(e) An appointment under subdivision (d) is effective to authorize that person to administer oaths and to take testimony.

(f) On request, the clerk of the court shall issue a commission authorizing the deposition in another state or place. The commission shall request that process issue in the place where the examination is to be held, requiring attendance and enforcing the obligations of the deponents to produce documents and electronically stored information and answer questions. The commission shall be issued by the clerk to any party in any action pending in its venue without a noticed motion or court order. The commission may contain terms that are required by the foreign jurisdiction to initiate the process. If a court order is required by the foreign jurisdiction, an order for a commission may be obtained by ex parte application. **Leg.H.** 2004 ch. 182 (AB 3081) §23, operative July 1, 2005, 2012 ch. 72 (SB 1574) §27.

§2027.010. Taking of oral deposition in foreign nation; procedures and process; issuance of commission.

(a) Any party may obtain discovery by taking an oral deposition, as described in Section 2025.010, in a foreign nation. Except as modified in this section, the procedures for taking oral depositions in California set forth in Chapter 9 (commencing with Section 2025.010) apply to an oral deposition taken in a foreign nation.

(b) If a deponent is a party to the action or an officer, director, managing agent, or employee of a party, the service of the deposition notice is effective to compel the deponent to attend and to testify, as well as to produce any document, electronically stored information, or tangible thing for inspection, copying, testing, or sampling.

(c) If a deponent is not a party to the action or an officer, director, managing agent or employee of a party, a party serving a deposition notice under this section shall use any process and procedures required and available under the laws of the foreign nation where the deposition is to be taken to compel the deponent to attend and to testify, as well as to produce any document, electronically stored information, or tangible thing for inspection, copying, testing, sampling, and any related activity.

(d) A deposition taken under this section shall be conducted under the supervision of any of the following:

(1) A person who is authorized to administer oaths or their equivalent by the laws of the United States or of the foreign nation, and who is not otherwise disqualified under Section 2025.320 and subdivisions (b) to (f), inclusive, of Section 2025.340.

(2) A person or officer appointed by commission or under letters rogatory.

(3) Any person agreed to by all the parties.

(e) On motion of the party seeking to take an oral deposition in a foreign nation, the court in which the action is pending shall issue a commission, letters rogatory, or a letter of request, if it determines that one is necessary or convenient. The commission, letters rogatory, or letter of request may include any terms and directions that are just and appropriate. The deposition officer may be designated by name or by descriptive title in the deposition notice and in the commission. Letters rogatory or a letter of request may be addressed: "To the Appropriate Judicial Authority in [name of foreign nation]." **Leg.H.** 2004 ch. 182 (AB 3081) §23, operative July 1, 2005, 2012 ch. 72 (SB 1574) §28.

CHAPTER 14 INSPECTION, COPYING, TESTING, SAMPLING, AND PRODUCTION OF DOCUMENTS, ELECTRONICALLY STORED INFORMATION, TANGIBLE THINGS, LAND, AND OTHER PROPERTY [Selected Provisions]

ARTICLE 1 Inspection Demand

§2031.010. Right to discovery by inspecting, copying, testing, or sampling documents, tangible things, land or other property, and electronically stored information.

(a) Any party may obtain discovery within the scope delimited by Chapter 2 (commencing with Section 2017.010), and subject to the restrictions set forth in Chapter 5 (commencing with Section 2019.010), by inspecting, copying, testing, or sampling documents, tangible things, land or other property, and electronically stored information in the possession, custody, or control of any other party to the action.

(b) A party may demand that any other party produce and permit the party making the demand, or someone acting on the demanding party's behalf, to inspect and to copy a document that is in the possession, custody, or control of the party on whom the demand is made.

(c) A party may demand that any other party produce and permit the party making the demand, or someone acting on the demanding party's behalf, to inspect and to photograph, test, or sample any tangible things that are in the possession, custody, or control of the party on whom the demand is made.

(d) A party may demand that any other party allow the party making the demand, or someone acting on the demanding party's behalf, to enter on any land or other property that is in the possession, custody, or control of the party on whom the demand is made, and to inspect and to measure, survey, photograph, test, or sample the land or other property, or any designated object or operation on it.

(e) A party may demand that any other party produce and permit the party making the demand, or someone acting on the demanding party's behalf, to inspect, copy, test, or sample electronically stored information in the possession, custody, or control of the party on whom demand is made. **Leg.H.** 2004 ch. 182 (AB 3081), operative July 1, 2005, 2009 ch. 5 (AB 5) §4, effective June 29, 2009, 2016 ch. 86 (SB 1171) §42.

2009 Note: This act shall be known as the Electronic Discovery Act. Stats. 2009 ch. 5 (AB 5) §1.

Ref.: Hanna § 25.45; Herlick Handbook §§ 14.20, 14.20A.

§2031.020. Demand for inspection, copying, testing, or sampling by defendant authorized at any time; when plaintiff may make demand for inspection, copying, testing, or sampling.

(a) A defendant may make a demand for inspection, copying, testing, or sampling without leave of court at any time.

(b) A plaintiff may make a demand for inspection, copying, testing, or sampling without leave of court at any time that is 10 days after the service of the summons on, or appearance by, the party to whom the demand is directed, whichever occurs first.

(c) Notwithstanding subdivision (b), in an unlawful detainer action or other proceeding under Chapter 4 (commencing with Section 1159) of Title 3 of Part 3, a plaintiff may make a demand for inspection, copying, testing, or sampling without leave of court at any time that is five days after service of the summons on, or appearance by, the party to whom the demand is directed, whichever occurs first.

(d) Notwithstanding subdivisions (b) and (c), on motion with or without notice, the court, for good cause shown, may grant leave to a plaintiff to make a demand for inspection, copying, testing, or sampling at an earlier time. **Leg.H.** 2004 ch. 182 (AB 3081), operative July 1, 2005, 2007 ch. 113 (AB 1126) §9, 2009 ch. 5 (AB 5) §5, effective June 29, 2009.

2009 Note: This act shall be known as the Electronic Discovery Act. Stats. 2009 ch. 5 (AB 5) §1.

Ref.: Hanna § 25.45; Herlick Handbook §§ 14.20, 14.20A.

§2031.030. Format and requirements for demands for inspection, copying, testing, or sampling.

(a)(1) A party demanding inspection, copying, testing, or sampling shall number each set of demands consecutively.

(2) A party demanding inspection, copying, testing, or sampling of electronically stored information may specify the form or forms in which each type of electronically stored information is to be produced.

(b) In the first paragraph immediately below the title of the case, there shall appear the identity of the demanding party, the set number, and the identity of the responding party.

(c) Each demand in a set shall be separately set forth, identified by number or letter, and shall do all of the following:

(1) Designate the documents, tangible things, land or other property, or electronically stored information to be inspected, copied, tested, or sampled either by specifically describing each individual item or by reasonably particularizing each category of item.

(2) Specify a reasonable time for the inspection, copying, testing, or sampling that is at least 30 days after service of the demand, unless the court for good cause shown has granted leave to specify an earlier date. In an unlawful detainer action or other proceeding under Chapter 4 (commencing with Section 1159) of Title 3 of Part 3, the demand shall specify a reasonable time for the inspection, copying, testing, or sampling that is at least five days after service of the demand, unless the court, for good cause shown, has granted leave to specify an earlier date.

(3) Specify a reasonable place for making the inspection, copying, testing, or sampling, and performing any related activity.

(4) Specify any inspection, copying, testing, sampling, or related activity that is being demanded, as well as the manner in which that activity will be performed, and whether that activity will permanently alter or destroy the item involved. **Leg.H.** 2004 ch. 182 (AB 3081), operative July 1, 2005, 2007 ch. 113 (AB 1126) §10, 2009 ch. 5 (AB 5) §6, effective June 29, 2009.

2009 Note: This act shall be known as the Electronic Discovery Act. Stats. 2009 ch. 5 (AB 5) §1.

Ref.: Hanna § 25.45; Herlick Handbook §§ 14.20, 14.20A.

§2031.040. Service of demand for inspection, copying, testing, or sampling.

The party making a demand for inspection, copying, testing, or sampling shall serve a copy of the demand on the party to whom it is directed and on all other parties who have appeared in the action. **Leg.H.** 2004 ch. 182 (AB 3081), operative July 1, 2005, 2009 ch. 5 (AB 5) §7, effective June 29, 2009.

2009 Note: This act shall be known as the Electronic Discovery Act. Stats. 2009 ch. 5 (AB 5) §1.

Ref.: Hanna § 25.45; Herlick Handbook §§ 14.20, 14.20A.

§2031.050. When supplemental demand may be propounded.

(a) In addition to the demands for inspection, copying, testing, or sampling permitted by this chapter, a party may propound a supplemental demand to inspect, copy, test, or sample any later acquired or discovered documents, tangible things, land or other property, or electronically stored information in the possession, custody, or control of the party on whom the demand is made.

(b) A party may propound a supplemental demand for inspection, copying, testing, or sampling twice before the initial setting of a trial date, and, subject to the time limits on discovery proceedings and motions provided in Chapter 8 (commencing with Section 2024.010), once after the initial setting of a trial date.

(c) Notwithstanding subdivisions (a) and (b), on motion, for good cause shown, the court may grant leave to a party to propound an additional number of supplemental demands for inspection, copying, testing, or sampling. **Leg.H.** 2004 ch. 182 (AB 3081), operative July 1, 2005, 2009 ch. 5 (AB 5) §8, effective June 29, 2009.

2009 Note: This act shall be known as the Electronic Discovery Act. Stats. 2009 ch. 5 (AB 5) §1.

Ref.: Hanna § 25.45; Herlick Handbook §§ 14.20, 14.20A.

§2031.060. Motion for protective order; what protective order may provide; denial of protective order; monetary sanction.

(a) When an inspection, copying, testing, or sampling of documents, tangible things, places, or electronically stored information has been demanded, the party to whom the demand has been directed, and any other party or affected person, may promptly move for a protective order. This motion shall be accompanied by a meet and confer declaration under Section 2016.040.

(b) The court, for good cause shown, may make any order that justice requires to protect any party or other person from unwarranted annoyance, embarrassment, or oppression, or undue burden and expense. This protective order may include, but is not limited to, one or more of the following directions:

(1) That all or some of the items or categories of items in the demand need not be produced or made available at all.

(2) That the time specified in Section 2030.260 to respond to the set of demands, or to a particular item or category in the set, be extended.

(3) That the place of production be other than that specified in the demand.

(4) That the inspection, copying, testing, or sampling be made only on specified terms and conditions.

(5) That a trade secret or other confidential research, development, or commercial information not be disclosed, or be disclosed only to specified persons or only in a specified way.

(6) That the items produced be sealed and thereafter opened only on order of the court.

(c) The party or affected person who seeks a protective order regarding the production, inspection, copying, testing, or sampling of electronically stored information on the basis that the information is from a source that is not reasonably accessible because of undue burden or expense shall bear the burden of demonstrating that the information is from a source that is not reasonably accessible because of undue burden or expense.

(d) If the party or affected person from whom discovery of electronically stored information is sought establishes that the information is from a source that is not reasonably accessible because of undue burden or expense, the court may nonetheless order discovery if the demanding party shows good cause, subject to any limitations imposed under subdivision (f).

(e) If the court finds good cause for the production of electronically stored information from a source that is not reasonably accessible, the court may set conditions for the discovery of the electronically stored information, including allocation of the expense of discovery.

(f) The court shall limit the frequency or extent of discovery of electronically stored information, even from a source that is reasonably accessible, if the court determines that any of the following conditions exist:

(1) It is possible to obtain the information from some other source that is more convenient, less burdensome, or less expensive.

(2) The discovery sought is unreasonably cumulative or duplicative.

(3) The party seeking discovery has had ample opportunity by discovery in the action to obtain the information sought.

(4) The likely burden or expense of the proposed discovery outweighs the likely benefit, taking into account the amount in controversy, the resources of the parties, the importance of the issues in the litigation, and the importance of the requested discovery in resolving the issues.

(g) If the motion for a protective order is denied in whole or in part, the court may order that the party to whom the demand was directed provide or permit the discovery against which protection was sought on terms and conditions that are just.

(h) Except as provided in subdivision (i), the court shall impose a monetary sanction under Chapter 7 (commencing with Section 2023.010) against any party, person, or attorney who unsuccessfully makes or opposes a motion for a protective order, unless it finds that the one subject to the sanction acted with substantial justification or that other circumstances make the imposition of the sanction unjust.

(i)(1) Notwithstanding subdivision (h), absent exceptional circumstances, the court shall not impose sanctions on a party or any attorney of a party for failure to provide electronically stored information that has been lost, damaged, altered, or overwritten as the result of the routine, good faith operation of an electronic information system.

(2) This subdivision shall not be construed to alter any obligation to preserve discoverable information. **Leg.H.** 2004 ch. 182 (AB 3081), operative July 1, 2005, 2009 ch. 5 (AB 5) §9, effective June 29, 2009.

2009 Note: This act shall be known as the Electronic Discovery Act. Stats. 2009 ch. 5 (AB 5) §1.

Ref.: Hanna § 25.45; Herlick Handbook §§ 14.20, 14.20A.

ARTICLE 2
Response to Inspection Demand

§2031.210. Nature and format of response to demand for inspection, copying, testing, or sampling.

(a) The party to whom a demand for inspection, copying, testing, or sampling has been directed shall respond separately to each item or category of item by any of the following:

(1) A statement that the party will comply with the particular demand for inspection, copying, testing, or sampling by the date set for the inspection, copying, testing, or sampling pursuant to paragraph (2) of subdivision (c) of Section 2031.030 and any related activities.

(2) A representation that the party lacks the ability to comply with the demand for inspection, copying, testing, or sampling of a particular item or category of item.

(3) An objection to the particular demand for inspection, copying, testing, or sampling.

(b) In the first paragraph of the response immediately below the title of the case, there shall appear the identity of the responding party, the set number, and the identity of the demanding party.

(c) Each statement of compliance, each representation, and each objection in the response shall bear the same number and be in the same sequence as the corresponding item or category in the demand, but the text of that item or category need not be repeated.

(d) If a party objects to the discovery of electronically stored information on the grounds that it is from a source that is not reasonably accessible because of undue burden or expense and that the responding party will not search the source in the absence of an agreement with the demanding party or court order, the responding party shall identify in its response the types or categories of sources of electronically stored information that it asserts are not reasonably accessible. By objecting and identifying information of a type or category of source or sources that are not reasonably accessible, the responding party preserves any objections it may have relating to that electronically stored information. **Leg.H.** 2004 ch. 182 (AB 3081), operative July 1, 2005, 2007 ch. 738 (AB 1248) §7, 2009 ch. 5 (AB 5) §10, effective June 29, 2009.

2009 Note: This act shall be known as the Electronic Discovery Act. Stats. 2009 ch. 5 (AB 5) §1.

Ref.: Hanna § 25.45; Herlick Handbook §§ 14.20, 14.20A.

§2031.220. Statement regarding compliance in whole or in part.

A statement that the party to whom a demand for inspection, copying, testing, or sampling has been directed will comply with the particular demand shall state that the production, inspection, copying, testing, or sampling, and related activity demanded, will be allowed either in whole or in part, and that all documents or things in the demanded category that are in the possession, custody, or control of that party and to which no objection is being made will be included in the production. **Leg.H.** 2004 ch. 182 (AB 3081), operative July 1, 2005, 2009 ch. 5 (AB 5) §11, effective June 29, 2009.

2009 Note: This act shall be known as the Electronic Discovery Act. Stats. 2009 ch. 5 (AB 5) §1.

Ref.: Hanna § 25.45; Herlick Handbook §§ 14.20, 14.20A.

§2031.230. Representation of inability to comply.

A representation of inability to comply with the particular demand for inspection, copying, testing, or sampling shall affirm that a diligent search and a reasonable inquiry has been made in an effort to comply with that demand. This statement shall also specify whether the inability to comply is because the particular item or category has never existed, has been destroyed, has been lost, misplaced, or stolen, or has never been, or is no longer, in the possession, custody, or control of the responding party. The statement shall set forth the name and address of any natural person or organization known or believed by that party to have possession, custody, or control of that item or category of item. **Leg.H.** 2004 ch. 182 (AB 3081), operative July 1, 2005, 2009 ch. 5 (AB 5) §12, effective June 29, 2009.

2009 Note: This act shall be known as the Electronic Discovery Act. Stats. 2009 ch. 5 (AB 5) §1.

Ref.: Hanna § 25.45; Herlick Handbook §§ 14.20, 14.20A.

§2031.240. Statements regarding demand that is objectionable in whole or in part.

(a) If only part of an item or category of item in a demand for inspection, copying, testing, or sampling is objectionable, the response shall contain a statement of compliance, or a representation of inability to comply with respect to the remainder of that item or category.

(b) If the responding party objects to the demand for inspection, copying, testing, or sampling of an item or category of item, the response shall do both of the following:

(1) Identify with particularity any document, tangible thing, land, or electronically stored information falling within any category of item in the demand to which an objection is being made.

(2) Set forth clearly the extent of, and the specific ground for, the objection. If an objection is based on a claim of privilege, the particular privilege invoked shall be stated. If an objection is based on a claim that the information sought is protected work product under Chapter 4 (commencing with Section 2018.010), that claim shall be expressly asserted.

(c)(1) If an objection is based on a claim of privilege or a claim that the information sought is protected work product, the response shall provide sufficient factual information for other parties to evaluate the merits of that claim, including, if necessary, a privilege log.

(2) It is the intent of the Legislature to codify the concept of a privilege log as that term is used in California case law. Nothing in this subdivision shall be construed to constitute a substantive change in case law. **Leg.H.** 2004 ch. 182 (AB 3081), operative July 1, 2005, 2009 ch. 5 (AB 5) §13, effective June 29, 2009, 2012 ch. 232 (AB 1354) §1.

2009 Note: This act shall be known as the Electronic Discovery Act. Stats. 2009 ch. 5 (AB 5) §1.

Ref.: Hanna § 25.45; Herlick Handbook §§ 14.20, 14.20A.

§2031.250. Signing of response to demand.

(a) The party to whom the demand for inspection, copying, testing, or sampling is directed shall sign the response under oath unless the response contains only objections.

(b) If that party is a public or private corporation or a partnership or association or governmental agency, one of its officers or agents shall sign the response under oath on behalf of that party. If the officer or agent signing the response on behalf of that party is an attorney acting in that capacity for a party, that party waives any lawyer-client privilege and any protection for work product under Chapter 4 (commencing with Section 2018.010) during any subsequent discovery from that attorney concerning the identity of the sources of the information contained in the response.

(c) The attorney for the responding party shall sign any responses that contain an objection. **Leg.H.** 2004 ch. 182 (AB 3081), operative July 1, 2005, 2009 ch. 5 (AB 5) §14, effective June 29, 2009.

2009 Note: This act shall be known as the Electronic Discovery Act. Stats. 2009 ch. 5 (AB 5) §1.

Ref.: Hanna § 25.45; Herlick Handbook §§ 14.20, 14.20A.

§2031.260. Time for service of response; unlawful detainer action.

(a) Within 30 days after service of a demand for inspection, copying, testing, or sampling, the party to whom the demand is directed shall serve the original of the response to it on the party making the demand, and a copy of the response on all other parties who have appeared in the action, unless on motion of the party making the demand, the court has shortened the time for response, or unless on motion of the party to whom the demand has been directed, the court has extended the time for response.

(b) Notwithstanding subdivision (a), in an unlawful detainer action or other proceeding under Chapter 4 (commencing with Section 1159) of Title 3 of Part 3, the party to whom a demand for inspection, copying, testing, or sampling is directed shall have at least five days from the date of service of the demand to respond, unless on motion of the party making the demand, the court has shortened the time for the response, or unless on motion of the party to whom the demand has been directed, the court has extended the time for response. **Leg.H.** 2004 ch. 182 (AB 3081), operative July 1, 2005, 2007 ch. 113 (AB 1126) §11, 2009 ch. 5 (AB 5) §15, effective June 29, 2009.

2009 Note: This act shall be known as the Electronic Discovery Act. Stats. 2009 ch. 5 (AB 5) §1.

Ref.: Hanna § 25.45; Herlick Handbook §§ 14.20, 14.20A.

§2031.270. Extension of date for inspection or time for service of response; written confirmation of agreement.

(a) The party demanding inspection, copying, testing, or sampling and the responding party may agree to extend the date for the inspection, copying, testing, or sampling or the time for service of a response to a set of demands, or to particular items or categories of items in a set, to a date or dates beyond those provided in Sections 2031.030, 2031.210, 2031.260, and 2031.280.

(b) This agreement may be informal, but it shall be confirmed in a writing that specifies the extended date for inspection, copying, testing, or sampling, or for the service of a response.

(c) Unless this agreement expressly states otherwise, it is effective to preserve to the responding party the right to respond to any item or category of item in the demand to which the agreement applies in any manner specified in Sections 2031.210, 2031.220, 2031.230, 2031.240, and 2031.280. **Leg.H.** 2004 ch. 182 (AB 3081), operative July 1, 2005, 2007 ch. 738 (AB 1248) §8, 2009 ch. 5 (AB 5) §16, effective June 29, 2009.

2009 Note: This act shall be known as the Electronic Discovery Act. Stats. 2009 ch. 5 (AB 5) §1.

Ref.: Hanna § 25.45; Herlick Handbook §§ 14.20, 14.20A.

§2031.280. Production of documents or category of documents—Identification; date specified; form; production of electronically stored information; translation; expense.

(a) Any documents or category of documents produced in response to a demand for inspection, copying, testing, or sampling shall be identified with the specific request number to which the documents respond.

(b) The documents shall be produced on the date specified in the demand pursuant to paragraph (2) of subdivision (c) of Section 2031.030, unless an objection has been made to that date. If the date for inspection has been extended pursuant to Section 2031.270, the documents shall be produced on the date agreed to pursuant to that section.

(c) If a party responding to a demand for production of electronically stored information objects to a specified form for producing the information, or if no form is specified in the demand, the responding party shall state in its response the form in which it intends to produce each type of information.

(d) Unless the parties otherwise agree or the court otherwise orders, the following shall apply:

(1) If a demand for production does not specify a form or forms for producing a type of electronically stored information, the responding party shall produce the information in the form or forms in which it is ordinarily maintained or in a form that is reasonably usable.

(2) A party need not produce the same electronically stored information in more than one form.

(e) If necessary, the responding party at the reasonable expense of the demanding party shall, through detection devices, translate any data compilations included in the demand into reasonably usable form. **Leg.H.** 2004 ch. 182 (AB 3081), operative July 1, 2005, 2007 ch. 738 (AB 1248) §9, 2009 ch. 5 (AB 5) §17, effective June 29, 2009, 2019 ch. 208 (SB 370) §1.

2009 Note: This act shall be known as the Electronic Discovery Act. Stats. 2009 ch. 5 (AB 5) §1.

Ref.: Hanna § 25.45; Herlick Handbook §§ 14.20, 14.20A.

§2031.285. Production of electronically stored information—Claim of privilege or of protection as attorney work product; notification to receiving party; receiving party's responsibilities; preclusion from using or disclosing specified information; resolution.

(a) If electronically stored information produced in discovery is subject to a claim of privilege or of protection as attorney work product, the party making the claim may notify any party that received the information of the claim and the basis for the claim.

(b) After being notified of a claim of privilege or of protection under subdivision (a), a party that received the information shall immediately sequester the information and either return the specified information and any copies that may exist or present the information to the court conditionally under seal for a determination of the claim.

(c)(1) Prior to the resolution of the motion brought under subdivision (d), a party shall be precluded from using or disclosing the specified information until the claim of privilege is resolved.

(2) A party who received and disclosed the information before being notified of a claim of privilege or of protection under subdivision (a) shall, after that notification, immediately take reasonable steps to retrieve the information.

(d)(1) If the receiving party contests the legitimacy of a claim of privilege or protection, he or she may seek a determination of the claim from the court by making a motion within 30 days of receiving the claim and presenting the information to the court conditionally under seal.

(2) Until the legitimacy of the claim of privilege or protection is resolved, the receiving party shall preserve the information and keep it confidential and shall be precluded from using the information in any manner. **Leg.H.** 2009 ch. 5 (AB 5) §18, effective June 29, 2009.

2009 Note: This act shall be known as the Electronic Discovery Act. Stats. 2009 ch. 5 (AB 5) §1.

Ref.: Hanna § 25.45; Herlick Handbook §§ 14.20, 14.20A.

§2031.290. Retention of demand for inspection, copying, testing, or sampling, proof of service, and response by demanding party.

(a) The demand for inspection, copying, testing, or sampling, and the response to it, shall not be filed with the court.

(b) The party demanding an inspection, copying, testing, or sampling shall retain both the original of the demand, with the original proof of service affixed to it, and the original of the sworn response until six months after final disposition of the action. At that time, both originals may be destroyed, unless the court, on motion of any party and for good cause shown, orders that the originals be preserved for a longer period. **Leg.H.** 2004 ch. 182 (AB 3081), operative July 1, 2005, 2009 ch. 5 (AB 5) §19, effective June 29, 2009.

2009 Note: This act shall be known as the Electronic Discovery Act. Stats. 2009 ch. 5 (AB 5) §1.

Ref.: Hanna § 25.45; Herlick Handbook §§ 14.20, 14.20A.

§2031.300. Effect of failure to serve timely response to demand for inspection, copying, testing, or sampling; motion for order; monetary and other sanctions.

If a party to whom a demand for inspection, copying, testing, or sampling is directed fails to serve a timely response to it, the following rules shall apply:

(a) The party to whom the demand for inspection, copying, testing, or sampling is directed waives any objection to the demand, including one based on privilege or on the protection for work product under Chapter 4 (commencing with Section 2018.010). The court, on motion, may relieve that party from this waiver on its determination that both of the following conditions are satisfied:

(1) The party has subsequently served a response that is in substantial compliance with Sections 2031.210, 2031.220, 2031.230, 2031.240, and 2031.280.

(2) The party's failure to serve a timely response was the result of mistake, inadvertence, or excusable neglect.

(b) The party making the demand may move for an order compelling response to the demand.

(c) Except as provided in subdivision (d), the court shall impose a monetary sanction under Chapter 7 (commencing with Section 2023.010) against any party, person, or attorney who unsuccessfully makes or opposes a motion to compel a response to a demand for inspection, copying, testing, or sampling, unless it finds that the one subject to the sanction acted with substantial justification or that other circumstances make the imposition of the sanction unjust. If a party then fails to obey the order compelling a response, the court may make those orders that are just, including the imposition of an issue sanction, an evidence sanction, or a terminating sanction under Chapter 7 (commencing with Section 2023.010). In lieu of or in addition to this sanction, the court may impose a monetary sanction under Chapter 7 (commencing with Section 2023.010).

(d)(1) Notwithstanding subdivision (c), absent exceptional circumstances, the court shall not impose sanctions on a party or any attorney of a party for failure to provide electronically stored information that has been lost, damaged, altered, or overwritten as a result of the routine, good faith operation of an electronic information system.

(2) This subdivision shall not be construed to alter any obligation to preserve discoverable information. **Leg.H.** 2004 ch. 182 (AB 3081), operative July 1, 2005, 2005 ch. 22 (SB 1108) §23, 2009 ch. 5 (AB 5) §20, effective June 29, 2009.

2009 Note: This act shall be known as the Electronic Discovery Act. Stats. 2009 ch. 5 (AB 5) §1.

Ref.: Hanna § 25.45; Herlick Handbook §§ 14.20, 14.20A.

§2031.310. Motion for order compelling further response; grounds; notice; waiver; monetary and other sanctions.

(a) On receipt of a response to a demand for inspection, copying, testing, or sampling, the demanding party may move for an order compelling further response to the demand if the demanding party deems that any of the following apply:

(1) A statement of compliance with the demand is incomplete.

(2) A representation of inability to comply is inadequate, incomplete, or evasive.

(3) An objection in the response is without merit or too general.

(b) A motion under subdivision (a) shall comply with each of the following:

(1) The motion shall set forth specific facts showing good cause justifying the discovery sought by the demand.

(2) The motion shall be accompanied by a meet and confer declaration under Section 2016.040.

(3) In lieu of a separate statement required under the California Rules of Court, the court may allow the moving party to submit a concise outline of the discovery request and each response in dispute.

(c) Unless notice of this motion is given within 45 days of the service of the verified response, or any supplemental verified response, or on or before any specific later date to which the demanding party and the responding party have agreed in writing, the demanding party waives any right to compel a further response to the demand.

(d) In a motion under subdivision (a) relating to the production of electronically stored information, the party or affected person objecting to or opposing the production, inspection, copying, testing, or sampling of electronically stored information on the basis that the information is from a source that is not reasonably accessible because of the undue burden or expense shall bear the burden of demonstrating that the information is from a source that is not reasonably accessible because of undue burden or expense.

(e) If the party or affected person from whom discovery of electronically stored information is sought establishes that the information is from a source that is not reasonably accessible because of the undue burden or expense, the court may nonetheless order discovery if the demanding party shows good cause, subject to any limitations imposed under subdivision (g).

(f) If the court finds good cause for the production of electronically stored information from a source that is not reasonably accessible, the court may set conditions for the discovery of the electronically stored information, including allocation of the expense of discovery.

(g) The court shall limit the frequency or extent of discovery of electronically stored information, even from a source that is reasonably accessible, if the court determines that any of the following conditions exists:

(1) It is possible to obtain the information from some other source that is more convenient, less burdensome, or less expensive.

(2) The discovery sought is unreasonably cumulative or duplicative.

(3) The party seeking discovery has had ample opportunity by discovery in the action to obtain the information sought.

(4) The likely burden or expense of the proposed discovery outweighs the likely benefit, taking into account the amount in controversy, the resources of the parties, the importance of the issues in the litigation, and the importance of the requested discovery in resolving the issues.

(h) Except as provided in subdivision (j), the court shall impose a monetary sanction under Chapter 7 (commencing with Section 2023.010) against any party, person, or attorney who unsuccessfully makes or opposes a motion to compel further response to a demand, unless it finds that the one subject to the sanction acted with substantial justification or that other circumstances make the imposition of the sanction unjust.

(i) Except as provided in subdivision (j), if a party fails to obey an order compelling further response, the court may make those orders that are just, including the imposition of an issue sanction, an evidence sanction, or a terminating sanction under Chapter 7 (commencing with Section 2023.010). In lieu of, or in addition to, that sanction, the court may impose a monetary sanction under Chapter 7 (commencing with Section 2023.010).

(j)(1) Notwithstanding subdivisions (h) and (i), absent exceptional circumstances, the court shall not impose sanctions on a party or any attorney of a party for failure to provide electronically stored information that has been lost, damaged, altered, or overwritten as the result of the routine, good faith operation of an electronic information system.

(2) This subdivision shall not be construed to alter any obligation to preserve discoverable information. **Leg.H.** 2004 ch. 182 (AB 3081), operative July 1, 2005, 2009 ch. 5 (AB 5) §21, effective June 29, 2009, 2013 ch. 18 (AB 1183) §2, 2018 ch. 317 (AB 2230) §4, operative January 1, 2020.

§2031.320. Motion for order compelling compliance on failure to permit inspection, copying, testing, or sampling in accordance with response; monetary and other sanctions.

(a) If a party filing a response to a demand for inspection, copying, testing, or sampling under Sections 2031.210, 2031.220, 2031.230, 2031.240, and 2031.280 thereafter fails to permit the inspection, copying, testing, or sampling in accordance with that party's statement of compliance, the demanding party may move for an order compelling compliance.

(b) Except as provided in subdivision (d), the court shall impose a monetary sanction under Chapter 7 (commencing with Section 2023.010) against any party, person, or attorney who unsuccessfully makes or opposes a motion to compel compliance with a demand, unless it finds that the one subject to the sanction acted with substantial justification or that other circumstances make the imposition of the sanction unjust.

(c) Except as provided in subdivision (d), if a party then fails to obey an order compelling inspection, copying, testing, or sampling, the court may make those orders that are just, including the imposition of an issue sanction, an evidence sanction, or a terminating sanction under Chapter 7 (commencing with Section 2023.010). In lieu of or in addition to that sanction, the court may impose a monetary sanction under Chapter 7 (commencing with Section 2023.010).

(d)(1) Notwithstanding subdivisions (b) and (c), absent exceptional circumstances, the court shall not impose sanctions on a party or any attorney of a party for failure to provide electronically stored information that has been lost, damaged, altered, or overwritten as the result of the routine, good faith operation of an electronic information system.

(2) This subdivision shall not be construed to alter any obligation to preserve discoverable information. **Leg.H.** 2004 ch. 182 (AB 3081), operative July 1, 2005, 2009 ch. 5 (AB 5) §22, effective June 29, 2009.

2009 Note: This act shall be known as the Electronic Discovery Act. Stats. 2009 ch. 5 (AB 5) §1.

Ref.: Hanna § 25.45; Herlick Handbook §§ 14.20, 14.20A.

CHAPTER 18
SIMULTANEOUS EXCHANGE OF EXPERT WITNESS INFORMATION

ARTICLE 3
Deposition of Expert Witness
[Selected Provisions]

§2034.430. Payment of certain experts' reasonable and customary hourly or daily fees for time spent at deposition; tardy counsel; workers' compensation cases.

(a) Except as provided in subdivision (f), this section applies to an expert witness, other than a party or an employee of a party, who is any of the following:

(1) An expert described in subdivision (b) of Section 2034.210.

(2) A treating physician and surgeon or other treating health care practitioner who is to be asked during the deposition to express opinion testimony, including opinion or factual testimony regarding the past or present diagnosis or prognosis made by the practitioner or the reasons for a particular treatment decision made by the practitioner, but not including testimony requiring only the reading of words and symbols contained in the relevant medical record or, if those words and symbols are not legible to the deponent, the approximation by the deponent of what those words or symbols are.

(3) An architect, professional engineer, or licensed land surveyor who was involved with the original project design or survey for which that person is asked to express an opinion within the person's expertise and relevant to the action or proceeding.

(b) A party desiring to depose an expert witness described in subdivision (a) shall pay the expert's reasonable and customary hourly or daily fee for any time spent at the deposition from the time noticed in the deposition subpoena, or from the time of the arrival of the expert witness should that time be later than the time noticed in the deposition subpoena, until the time the expert witness is dismissed from the deposition, regardless of whether the expert is actually deposed by any party attending the deposition.

(c) If any counsel representing the expert or a nonnoticing party is late to the deposition, the expert's reasonable and customary hourly or daily fee for the time period determined from the time noticed in the deposition subpoena until the counsel's late arrival, shall be paid by that tardy counsel.

(d) Notwithstanding subdivision (c), the hourly or daily fee charged to the tardy counsel shall not exceed the fee charged to the party who retained the expert, except where the expert donated services to a charitable or other nonprofit organization.

(e) A daily fee shall only be charged for a full day of attendance at a deposition or where the expert was required by the deposing party to be available for a full day and the expert necessarily had to forgo all business that the expert would otherwise have conducted that day but for the request that the expert be available all day for the scheduled deposition.

(f) In a worker's compensation case arising under Division 4 (commencing with Section 3201) or Division 4.5 (commencing with Section 6100) of the Labor Code, a party desiring to depose any expert on another party's expert witness list shall pay the fee under this section. **Leg.H.** 2004 ch. 182 (AB 3081), operative July 1, 2005, 2008 ch. 303 (AB 2619) §2.

SELECTED PROVISIONS Of The EDUCATION CODE

TITLE 1 GENERAL EDUCATION CODE PROVISIONS

DIVISION 1 General Education Code Provisions

PART 2 COUNTY EDUCATIONAL AGENCIES

CHAPTER 2 COUNTY SUPERINTENDENT OF SCHOOLS

ARTICLE 2 Duties, Responsibilities, and General Powers [Selected Provisions]

§1252. Workers' compensation insurance for schools.

The county superintendent of schools of any county may, with the approval of the State Compensation Insurance Fund, insure the liability for compensation of any school districts and community college districts in the territory under his or her jurisdiction, the governing boards of which consent thereto, with the State Compensation Insurance Fund under one policy or contract of insurance and pay the premium for the insurance from the county school service fund. Immediately following the payment of the final premium the county superintendent of schools shall transfer from the funds of each insured district to the county school service fund an amount which bears the same ratio to the premium as the payroll of each district bears to the total payroll of all the insured districts.

Any dividends earned on the premiums paid under this section shall be credited to the individual districts in proportion to the amount of the premium charged to each district.

The expenses of the county superintendent of schools incurred under this section shall be charged to and paid from the county school service fund, which fund shall be reimbursed for those expenses from the general funds of the school districts and community college districts on whose behalf the expenditures are incurred.

ARTICLE 3 Staff [Selected Provisions]

§1297. Extent of coverage; payment of costs.

For the purpose of insurance under the workers' compensation laws of this state, any person employed by a county superintendent of schools to supervise instruction or to give instruction in the school districts or community college districts located in the territory under the jurisdiction of the county superintendent of schools shall be deemed an employee of the county. The cost of insuring any person employed to supervise instruction shall be paid by the county superintendent of schools from the county school service fund. The cost of insuring any person employed by the county superintendent of schools to give instruction shall be paid by the county superintendent of schools from the county school service fund.

PART 13 STATE TEACHERS' RETIREMENT SYSTEM

CHAPTER 30 SUBROGATION

§24500. Board's right of subrogation.

If a disability retirement allowance, disability allowance, family allowance, or survivor benefit allowance is payable under this part due to the injury to or death of a member and the injury or death is the proximate consequence of the act of a third person or entity, other than the member's employer, the board may recover from that person or entity on behalf of the plan, an amount equal to the actuarial equivalent of benefits the system paid and became obligated to pay under the plan because of the injury to or death of the member less any amounts the system may be

Misc. Provisions

obligated to pay under the plan without regard to the actions of the third party. In determining the amount the system may be obligated to pay without regard to the actions of the third party, the system shall base the actuarial equivalent only on creditable compensation and service credit earned by the member prior to the date the disability retirement allowance, disability allowance, family allowance, or survivor benefit allowance becomes payable. This chapter shall be deemed to create a right of subrogation only to amounts the system paid and became obligated to pay as disability retirement allowances, disability allowances, family allowances, or survivor benefit allowances. **Leg.H.** 1993 ch. 893, 1996 ch. 634, 2017 ch. 298 (AB 1325) §13.

§24501. Board may contract with SCIF or AG to act as agent.

The board may act on its own or contract with the State Compensation Insurance Fund or Attorney General for recovery on behalf of the plan of any amounts recoverable from third persons under this chapter, Chapter 5 (commencing with Section 3850) of Part 1 of Division 4 of the Labor Code, Section 11662 of the Insurance Code, or otherwise. **Leg.H.** 1993 ch. 893, 1996 ch. 634.

§24502. Actions board may take to enforce subrogation right.

In the exercise of its rights under this part, the board or the agent under contract may commence or prosecute actions, file liens, intervene in court proceedings, join parties to the action and consolidate actions all in the same manner and to the same extent provided in Chapter 5 (commencing with Section 3850) of Part 1 of Division 4 of the Labor Code except that recovery shall not be made from benefits payable under this part because of the injury or death. **Leg.H.** 1993 ch. 893.

§24503. Board may compromise claims.

The board may compromise claims before or after commencement of suit or entry of judgment for an amount as may be approved by a person duly authorized by the board for that purpose. **Leg.H.** 1993 ch. 893, 2017 ch. 298 (AB 1325) §14.

§24504. Application of recovery.

Any amount recovered by way of subrogation by the board on behalf of the member, shall be applied first to the amount which the plan paid or is obligated to pay including court costs, attorney fees, and expenses. **Leg.H.** 1993 ch. 893, 1996 ch. 634.

§24505. Three-year limitation period.

Actions brought by the board or its agent under contract pursuant to this chapter shall be commenced within three years after the liability of the system to pay benefits under the plan is fixed. Liability of the plan is fixed at the time the board approves the payment of benefits under this plan. **Leg.H.** 1993 ch. 893, 1996 ch. 634, 1998 ch. 965.

PART 19
MISCELLANEOUS

CHAPTER 3
MISCELLANEOUS

ARTICLE 6
District Liability on Loaned Equipment

§32350. Liability for loaned equipment or services; "public entity."

Any person, corporation, firm, or public entity, or employee thereof, who gratuitously loans equipment of any description or the services of an employee to a school district or community college district shall not be liable, and the school district or community college district shall be liable, for damages because of personal injuries to, or the death of any person or damage to property resulting from the operation of such equipment or an act or omission of such employee occurring while such equipment or employee is under the supervision and control of the district.

This section does not apply to any person, corporation, firm, or public entity who gratuitously loans mechanically defective equipment of any description or who gratuitously loans the services of an employee who is not fully qualified to perform such service, and such defect or lack of qualification is the cause of any damage or injury.

An employee whose services are loaned to a school district or community college district pursuant to this section remains an employee of his employer for all purposes, including the application of the provisions of the Labor Code relating to workers' compensation.

For the purposes of this section, "public entity" includes the state, the Regents of the University of California, a county, city, city and county, district, public authority, public agency, or any other political subdivision or public corporation in this state.

TITLE 2
ELEMENTARY AND SECONDARY EDUCATION

DIVISION 3
LOCAL ADMINISTRATION

PART 25
EMPLOYEES

CHAPTER 1
EMPLOYEES

ARTICLE 1
General Provisions
[Selected Provisions]

§44017. Possible payment to surviving spouse.

Notwithstanding any provision of law to the contrary, a school district may, from funds under its jurisdiction, pay the surviving spouse of any employee who is murdered while in the course of his employment the amount that the deceased would have received if he had lived to complete the time remaining in his contract with the district.

This section shall be applicable to the surviving spouse of any such employee who was murdered during or after the 1973–74 school year.

ARTICLE 2
Rights and Duties
[Selected Provisions]

§44043. Restrictions on salary and paid leave when temporary disability benefits received.

Any school employee of a school district who is absent because of injury or illness which arose out of and in the course of the person's employment, and for which the person is receiving temporary disability benefits under the workers' compensation laws of this state, shall not be entitled to receive wages or salary from the district which, when added to the temporary disability benefits, will exceed a full day's wages or salary.

During such periods of temporary disability so long as the employee has available for the employee's use sick leave, vacation, compensating time off or other paid leave of absence, the district shall require that temporary disability checks be endorsed payable to the district. The district shall then cause the employee to receive the person's normal wage or salary less appropriate deductions including but not limited to employee retirement contributions.

When sick leave, vacation, compensating time off or other available paid leave is used in conjunction with temporary disability benefits derived from workers' compensation, as provided in this section, it shall be reduced only in that amount necessary to provide a full day's wage or salary when added to the temporary disability benefits.

CHAPTER 4
EMPLOYMENT—CERTIFICATED EMPLOYEE

ARTICLE 3
Resignations, Dismissals, and Leaves of Absence
[Selected Provisions]

§44977. Salaries for those on extended leave and substitutes.

(a) During each school year, when a person employed in a position requiring certification qualifications has exhausted all available sick leave, including all accumulated sick leave, and continues to be absent from his or her duties on account of illness or accident for an additional period of five school months, whether or not the absence arises out of or in the course of the employment of the employee, the amount deducted from the salary due him or her for any of the additional five months in which the absence occurs shall not exceed the sum that is actually paid a substitute employee employed to fill his or her position during his or her absence or, if no substitute employee was employed, the amount that would have been paid to the substitute had he or she been employed. The school district shall make every reasonable effort to secure the services of a substitute employee.

(b) For purposes of subdivision (a):

(1) The sick leave, including accumulated sick leave, and the five-month period shall run consecutively.

(2) An employee shall not be provided more than one five-month period per illness or accident. However, if a school year terminates before the five-month period is exhausted, the employee may take the balance of the five-month period in a subsequent school year.

(c) The governing board of every school district shall adopt a salary schedule for substitute employees. The salary schedule shall indicate a salary for a substitute for all categories or classes of certificated employees of the district.

(d) Excepting in a district the governing board of which has adopted a salary schedule for substitute employees of the district, the amount paid the substitute employee during any month shall be less than the salary due the employee absent from his or her duties.

(e) When a person employed in a position requiring certification qualifications is absent from his or her duties on account of illness for a period of more than five school months, or when a person is absent from his or her duties for a cause other than illness, the amount deducted from the salary due him or her for the month in which the absence occurs shall be determined according to the rules and regulations established by the governing board of the

Misc. Provisions

district. The rules and regulations shall not conflict with rules and regulations of the State Board of Education.

(f) Nothing in this section shall be construed so as to deprive any district, city, or city and county of the right to make any reasonable rule for the regulation of accident or sick leave or cumulative accident or sick leave without loss of salary for persons acquiring certification qualifications.

(g) This section shall be applicable whether or not the absence from duty is by reason of a leave of absence granted by the governing board of the employing district. **Leg.H.** 1998 ch. 30.

§44977.5. Salary deductions during absence from duties on account of parental leave for employee requiring certification.

(a)(1) Notwithstanding any other law, during each school year, a person employed in a position requiring certification qualifications may use his or her sick leave for purposes of parental leave for a period of up to 12 workweeks.

(2) In school districts that use the differential pay system described in Section 44977, when a person employed in a position requiring certification qualifications has exhausted all available sick leave, including all accumulated sick leave, and continues to be absent from his or her duties on account of parental leave pursuant to Section 12945.2 of the Government Code, the amount deducted from the salary due him or her for any of the remaining portion of the 12-workweek period in which the absence occurs shall not exceed the sum that is actually paid a substitute employee employed to fill his or her position during his or her absence or, if no substitute employee was employed, the amount that would have been paid to a substitute had he or she been employed. The school district shall make every reasonable effort to secure the services of a substitute employee.

(3) In school districts that use the differential pay system described in Section 44983, when a person employed in a position requiring certification qualifications has exhausted all available sick leave, including all accumulated sick leave, and continues to be absent from his or her duties on account of parental leave pursuant to Section 12945.2 of the Government Code, the person shall be compensated at no less than 50 percent of his or her regular salary for the remaining portion of the 12-workweek period of parental leave.

(4) Regardless of the type of differential pay system used by the school district pursuant to paragraphs (2) and (3), the compensation a person employed in a position requiring certification qualifications shall receive shall be no less than 50 percent of his or her regular salary for the remaining portion of the 12-workweek period of parental leave.

(b) For purposes of subdivision (a), all of the following apply:

(1) The 12-workweek period shall be reduced by any period of sick leave, including accumulated sick leave, taken during a period of parental leave.

(2) A person employed in a position requiring certification qualifications shall not be provided more than one 12-week period for parental leave during any 12-month period.

(3) Parental leave taken pursuant to this section shall run concurrently with parental leave taken pursuant to Section 12945.2 of the Government Code. The aggregate amount of parental leave taken pursuant to this section and Section 12945.2 of the Government Code shall not exceed 12 workweeks in a 12-month period.

(c) This section shall be applicable whether or not the absence from duty is by reason of a leave of absence granted by the governing board of the employing school district.

(d) Notwithstanding subdivision (a) of Section 12945.2 of the Government Code, a person employed in a position requiring certification qualifications is not required to have 1,250 hours of service with the employer during the previous 12-month period in order to take parental leave pursuant to this section.

(e) Nothing in this section shall be construed to diminish the obligation of a public school employer to comply with any collective bargaining agreement entered into by a public school employer and an exclusive bargaining representative pursuant to Chapter 10.7 (commencing with Section 3540) of Division 4 of Title 1 of the Government Code that provides greater parental leave rights to employees than the rights established under this section.

(f) For purposes of this section, "parental leave" means leave for reason of the birth of a child of the employee, or the placement of a child with an employee in connection with the adoption or foster care of the child by the employee. **Leg.H.** 2015 ch. 400 (AB 375) §1, 2016 chs. 86 (SB 1171) §61, 883 (AB 2393) §1, 2018 ch. 994 (AB 2012) §1.

§44983. Salary deductions for those on extended leave.

Section 44977 shall not apply to any school district which adopts and maintains in effect a rule which provides that when a person employed in a position requiring certification qualifications is absent from his duties on account of illness or accident for a period of five school months or less whether or not the absence arises out of or in the course of the employment of the employee, he shall receive 50 percent or more of his regular salary during the period of such absence and nothing in Section 44977 shall be construed as preventing the governing board of any district from adopting any such rule.

Notwithstanding the foregoing, when a person employed in a position requiring certification qualifications is absent from his duties on account of illness for a period of more than five school months, or when a person is absent from his duties for a cause other than illness, the amount deducted from the salary due him for the month in which the absence occurs shall be determined according to the rules and regulations established by the governing board of the district. Such rules and regulations shall not conflict with rules and regulations of the State Board of Education.

Nothing in this section shall be construed so as to deprive any district, city, or city and county of the right to make any reasonable rule for the regulation of accident or sick leave or cumulative accident or sick leave without loss of salary for persons requiring certification qualifications.

This section shall be applicable whether or not the absence from duty is by reason of a leave of absence granted by the governing board of the employing district.

§44984. Rules for industrial accident or illness leave.

(a) The governing board of a school district shall provide by rules and regulations for industrial accident and illness leaves of absence for all certificated employees. The governing board of a school district that is created or whose boundaries or status is changed by an action to organize or reorganize school districts completed after the effective date of this section shall provide by rules and regulations for these leaves of absence on or before the date on which the organization or reorganization of the school district becomes effective for all purposes.

(b) The rules or regulations shall include the following provisions:

(1) Allowable leave shall be for not less than 60 days during which the schools of the school district are required to be in session or when the employee would otherwise have been performing work for the school district in any one fiscal year for the same accident.

(2) Allowable leave shall not be accumulated from year to year.

(3) Industrial accident or illness leave shall commence on the first day of absence.

(4)(A) If a certificated employee is absent from his or her duties on account of an industrial accident or illness, he or she shall be paid the portion of the salary due him or her for any month in which the absence occurs as, when added to his or her temporary disability indemnity under Division 4 or Division 4.5 of the Labor Code, will result in a payment to him or her of not more than his or her full salary.

(B) The phrase "full salary" as used in this subdivision shall be computed so that it shall not be less than the employee's "average weekly earnings" as that phrase is used in Section 4453 of the Labor Code. For purposes of this section, however, the maximum and minimum average weekly earnings set forth in Section 4453 of the Labor Code shall otherwise not be deemed applicable.

(5) Industrial accident or illness leave shall be reduced by one day for each day of authorized absence regardless of a temporary disability indemnity award.

(6) When an industrial accident or illness leave overlaps into the next fiscal year, the employee shall be entitled to only the amount of unused leave due him or her for the same illness or injury.

(c) Upon termination of the industrial accident or illness leave, the employee shall be entitled to the benefits provided in Sections 44977, 44978, and 44983, and for purposes of each of these sections, the employee's absence shall be deemed to have commenced on the date of termination of the industrial accident or illness leave, provided that if the employee continues to receive temporary disability indemnity, the employee may elect to take as much of his or her accumulated sick leave as, when added to his or her temporary disability indemnity, will result in a payment to him or her of not more than his or her full salary.

(d) The governing board of a school district may, by rule or regulation, provide for an additional leave of absence for industrial accident or illness as it deems appropriate.

(e) During a paid leave of absence, the employee may endorse to the school district the temporary disability indemnity checks received on account of the employee's industrial accident or illness. The school district, in turn, shall issue the employee appropriate salary warrants for payment of the employee's salary and shall deduct normal retirement, other authorized contributions, and the temporary disability indemnity, if any, actually paid to and retained by the employee for periods covered by the salary warrants.

(f) In the absence of rules and regulations adopted by the governing board of a school district pursuant to this section, an employee shall be entitled to industrial accident or illness leave as provided in this section but without limitation as to the number of days of that leave. **Leg.H.** 2015 ch. 58 (AB 915) §1, 2016 ch. 86 (SB 1171) §62.

CHAPTER 5
CLASSIFIED EMPLOYEES

ARTICLE 4
Resignation and Leaves of Absence
[Selected Provisions]

§45192. Rules for industrial accident or illness leave of classified service employees.

(a) The governing board of a school district shall provide by rules and regulations for industrial accident or illness leaves of absence for employees who are a part of the classified service. The governing board of a school district that is created or whose boundaries or status is changed by an action to organize or reorganize school districts completed after the effective date of this section shall provide by rules and regulations for these leaves of absence on or before the date on which the organization or reorganization of the school district becomes effective for all purposes.

(b) The rules and regulations shall include the following provisions:

(1) Allowable leave shall not be for less than 60 working days in any one fiscal year for the same accident.

(2) Allowable leave shall not be accumulative from year to year.

(3) Industrial accident or illness leave will commence on the first day of absence.

(4) Payment for wages lost on any day shall not, when added to an award granted the employee under the workers' compensation laws of this state, exceed the normal wage for the day.

(5) Industrial accident leave will be reduced by one day for each day of authorized absence regardless of a compensation award made under workers' compensation.

(6) When an industrial accident or illness occurs at a time when the full 60 days will overlap into the next fiscal year, the employee shall be entitled to only that amount remaining at the end of the fiscal year in which the injury or illness occurred, for the same illness or injury.

(c) The industrial accident or illness leave of absence is to be used in lieu of entitlement acquired under Section 45191. When entitlement to industrial accident or illness leave has been exhausted, entitlement or other sick leave will then be used, but if an employee is receiving workers' compensation, the employee shall be entitled to use only so much of his or her accumulated or available sick leave, accumulated compensating time, vacation, or other available leave as, when added to the workers' compensation award, will provide for a full day's wage or salary.

(d) The governing board of a school district may, by rule or regulation, provide for as much additional leave of absence, paid or unpaid, as it deems appropriate and during this leave the employee may return to his or her position without suffering any loss of status or benefits. The employee shall be notified, in writing, that available paid leave has been exhausted, and shall be offered an opportunity to request additional leave.

(e) A period of leave of absence, paid or unpaid, shall not be considered to be a break in service of the employee.

(f) During a paid leave of absence, whether industrial accident leave as provided in this section, sick leave, vacation, compensated time off, or other available leave provided by law or the action of the governing board of a school district, the employee shall endorse to the school district wage loss benefit checks received under the workers' compensation laws of this state. The school district, in turn, shall issue the employee appropriate warrants for payment of wages or salary and shall deduct normal retirement and other authorized contributions. Reduction of entitlement to leave shall be made only in accordance with this section.

(g) When all available leaves of absence, paid or unpaid, have been exhausted and if the employee is not medically able to assume the duties of his or her position, the employee shall, if not placed in another position, be placed on a reemployment list for a period of 39 months. When available, during the 39-month period, the employee shall be employed in a vacant position in the class of the employee's previous assignment over all other available candidates except for a reemployment list established because of lack of work or lack of funds, in which case the employee shall be listed in accordance with appropriate seniority regulations.

(h) The governing board of a school district may require that an employee serve or have served continuously a specified period of time with the school district before the benefits provided by this section are made available to the employee but this period shall not exceed three years and all service of the employee before the effective date of this section shall be credited in determining compliance with the requirement.

(i) In the absence of rules and regulations adopted by the governing board of a school district, pursuant to this section, an employee shall be entitled to industrial and accident or illness leave as provided in this section but without limitation as to the number of days of this leave and without any requirement of a specified period of service.

(j) An employee who has been placed on a reemployment list, as provided in this section, who has been medically released for return to duty and who fails to accept an appropriate assignment shall be dismissed.

(k) This section applies to school districts that have adopted the merit system in the same manner and effect as if it were a part of Article 6 (commencing with Section 45240). **Leg.H.** 2015 ch. 58 (AB 915) §2, 2016 ch. 86 (SB 1171) §63.

TITLE 3
POSTSECONDARY EDUCATION

DIVISION 8
California State University

PART 55
CALIFORNIA STATE UNIVERSITY

CHAPTER 5
PERSONNEL

ARTICLE 1.1
Industrial Disability Leave

§89529. Application of article.

(a) This article applies to employees of the trustees who are members of the Public Employees' Retirement System or the State Teachers' Retirement System in compensated employment on and after July 1, 1974.

(b) This article also applies to a participant in the optional retirement program pursuant to Chapter 5.5 (commencing with Section 89600), provided that he or she would otherwise be eligible to participate in the Public Employees' Retirement System except for the election to participate in the optional retirement program.

(c) This article does not apply to employees of the trustees who are included in the provisions of Article 6 (commencing with Section 4800) of Chapter 2 of Part 2 of Division 4 of the Labor Code. **Leg.H.** 1996 ch. 385.

§89529.01. Resolution of conflicts with memorandum of understanding.

If the provisions of this article are in conflict with the provisions of a memorandum of understanding reached pursuant to Chapter 12 (commencing with Section 3560) of Division 4 of Title 1 of the Government Code, the memorandum of understanding shall be controlling without further legislative action, except that if the provisions of a memorandum of understanding require the expenditure of funds, the provisions shall not become effective unless approved by the Legislature in the annual Budget Act.

§89529.02. Definitions.

As used in this article:

(a) "Industrial disability leave" means temporary disability as defined in Division 4 (commencing with Section 3200) and 4.5 (commencing with Section 6100) of the Labor Code and includes any period in which the disability is permanent and stationary and the disabled employee is undergoing vocational rehabilitation.

(b) "Full pay" means the gross base pay earnable by the employee and subject to retirement contribution if he or she had not vacated his or her position.

§89529.03. Industrial disability leave: entitlement; amount; frequency; deductions.

If an employee is temporarily disabled by illness or injury arising out of and in the course of state employment, he or she shall become entitled, regardless of his or her period of service, to receive industrial disability leave and payments, in lieu of workers' compensation temporary disability payments and payment under Section 89527, for a period not exceeding 52 weeks within two years from the first day of disability. The payments shall be in the amount of the employee's full pay less withholding based on his or her exemptions in effect on the date of his or her disability for federal income taxes, state income taxes, and social security taxes not to exceed 22 working days of disability subject to Section 89529.08. Thereafter, the payment shall be two-thirds of full pay. Payments shall be additionally adjusted to offset disability benefits, excluding those disability benefits payable from the State Teachers' Retirement System, the employee may receive from other employer-subsidized programs, except that no adjustment will be made for benefits to which the employee's family is entitled up to a maximum of three-quarters of full pay. Contributions to the Public Employees' Retirement System or the State Teachers' Retirement System shall be deducted in the amount based on full pay. Discretionary deductions of the employee including those for coverage under a state health benefits plan in which the employee is enrolled shall continue to be deducted unless canceled by the employee. State employer contributions to the Public Employees' Retirement System and state employer normal retirement contributions to the State Teachers' Retirement System shall be made on the basis of full pay and state contributions pursuant to Sections 22871 and 22885 of the Government Code because of the employee's enrollment in a health benefits plan shall continue. **Leg.H.** 2004 ch. 69 (SB 626), effective June 24, 2004.

§89529.04. Continuation of other employee benefits.

An employee who is receiving industrial disability leave benefits shall continue to receive all employee benefits which he or she would have received had he or she not incurred disability.

§89529.05. Coordination of industrial disability leave and temporary disability indemnity.

The disabled employee shall not receive temporary disability indemnity or sick leave or annual leave with pay for any period for which he or she receives industrial disability leave; however, he or she may elect to waive the provisions of this article and to receive disability indemnity pursuant to Divisions 4 (commencing with Section 3200) and 4.5 (commencing with Section 6100) of the Labor

Code and to receive payments under Section 89527 in lieu of the benefits provided in this article. If the amount of the employee's benefits payable under this article is less than the amount he or she would receive under Divisions 4 (commencing with Section 3200) and 4.5 (commencing with Section 6100) of the Labor Code, the employee shall be deemed to have rejected the benefits of this article and shall be paid benefits pursuant to Divisions 4 (commencing with Section 3200) and 4.5 (commencing with Section 6100) of the Labor Code.

§89529.06. Inapplicability of article.

Division 4.7 (commencing with Section 6200) of the Labor Code shall not apply to employees to which this article applies.

§89529.07. Continuation of disability after expiration of industrial disability leave.

If an employee continues to be temporarily disabled after termination of benefits under this article, he or she shall be entitled to the benefits provided by Division 4 (commencing with Section 3200) and 4.5 (commencing with Section 6100) of the Labor Code and to payments under Section 89527.

§89529.08. Commencement of industrial disability leave.

(a) If an illness or injury causes temporary disability, the employee shall be placed on industrial disability leave on the fourth calendar day after the injured employee leaves work as the result of the illness or injury, except that in case the injury causes disability of more than 14 days or necessitates hospitalization, the employee shall be placed on industrial disability leave from the first day he or she leaves work or is hospitalized as a result of the injury.

(b) Notwithstanding subdivision (a), the disability payment shall be made from the first day the injured employee leaves work as a result of the injury, if the injury is the result of a criminal act of violence against the employee.

§89529.09. Contingencies that must be satisfied to receive payments.

Payments shall be contingent on the complete medical certification of the illness or injury including diagnosis and any prognosis of recovery. Further, payments shall be contingent on the employee's agreement to cooperate and participate in a reasonable and appropriate vocational rehabilitation plan when furnished by the state subject to appropriate medical approval as determined by the trustees.

§89529.10. Rules and regulations.

The trustees or its designee shall adopt any rules and regulations necessary for the administration of this article for its employees.

§89529.11. Effective date.

(a) This article shall be effective upon the adoption of applicable rules and regulations, but not later than January 1, 1975.

(b) The reenactment of this article at the 1987–88 Regular Session of the Legislature does not constitute a change in, but is declaratory of, the existing law.

SELECTED PROVISIONS Of The EVIDENCE CODE

DIVISION 2
WORDS AND PHRASES DEFINED
[Selected Provisions]

§110. Burden of producing evidence defined.

"Burden of producing evidence" means the obligation of a party to introduce evidence sufficient to avoid a ruling against him on the issue. **Leg.H.** 1965 ch. 299, operative January 1, 1967.

§115. Burden of proof defined.

"Burden of proof" means the obligation of a party to establish by evidence a requisite degree of belief concerning a fact in the mind of the trier of fact or the court. The burden of proof may require a party to raise a reasonable doubt concerning the existence or nonexistence of a fact or that he establish the existence or nonexistence of a fact by a preponderance of the evidence, by clear and convincing proof, or by proof beyond a reasonable doubt.

Except as otherwise provided by law, the burden of proof requires proof by a preponderance of the evidence. **Leg.H.** 1965 ch. 299, operative January 1, 1967.

Ref.: Hanna § 26.06[6].

§140. Evidence defined.

"Evidence" means testimony, writings, material objects, or other things presented to the senses that are offered to prove the existence or nonexistence of a fact. **Leg.H.** 1965 ch. 299, operative January 1, 1967.

§240. Unavailable as a witness defined.

(a) Except as otherwise provided in subdivision (b), "unavailable as a witness" means that the declarant is any of the following:

(1) Exempted or precluded on the ground of privilege from testifying concerning the matter to which his or her statement is relevant.

(2) Disqualified from testifying to the matter.

(3) Dead or unable to attend or to testify at the hearing because of then-existing physical or mental illness or infirmity.

(4) Absent from the hearing and the court is unable to compel his or her attendance by its process.

(5) Absent from the hearing and the proponent of his or her statement has exercised reasonable diligence but has been unable to procure his or her attendance by the court's process.

(6) Persistent in refusing to testify concerning the subject matter of the declarant's statement despite having been found in contempt for refusal to testify.

(b) A declarant is not unavailable as a witness if the exemption, preclusion, disqualification, death, inability, or absence of the declarant was brought about by the procurement or wrongdoing of the proponent of his or her statement for the purpose of preventing the declarant from attending or testifying.

(c) Expert testimony that establishes that physical or mental trauma resulting from an alleged crime has caused harm to a witness of sufficient severity that the witness is physically unable to testify or is unable to testify without suffering substantial trauma may constitute a sufficient showing of unavailability pursuant to paragraph (3) of subdivision (a). As used in this section, the term "expert" means a physician and surgeon, including a psychiatrist, or any person described by subdivision (b), (c), or (e) of Section 1010.

The introduction of evidence to establish the unavailability of a witness under this subdivision shall not be deemed procurement of unavailability, in absence of proof to the contrary. **Leg.H.** 1965 ch. 299, operative January 1, 1967, 1984 ch. 401, 1988 ch. 485, 2010 ch. 537 (AB 1723) §1.

§250. Writing defined.

"Writing" means handwriting, typewriting, printing, photostating, photographing, photocopying, transmitting by electronic mail or facsimile, and every other means of recording upon any tangible thing, any form of communication or representation, including letters, words, pictures, sounds, or symbols, or combinations thereof, and any record thereby created, regardless of the manner in which the record has been stored. **Leg.H.** 1965 ch. 299, operative January 1, 1967, 2002 ch. 945 (AB 1962).

DIVISION 4
JUDICIAL NOTICE
[Selected Provisions]

§450. General provision.

Judicial notice may not be taken of any matter unless authorized or required by law. **Leg.H.** 1965 ch. 299, operative January 1, 1967.

Ref.: Hanna § 26.06[8].

§451. Mandatory judicial notice.

Judicial notice shall be taken of the following:

(a) The decisional, constitutional, and public statutory law of this state and of the United States and the provisions of any charter described in Section 3, 4, or 5 of Article XI of the California Constitution.

(b) Any matter made a subject of judicial notice by Section 11343.6, 11344.6, or 18576 of the Government Code or by Section 1507 of Title 44 of the United States Code.

(c) Rules of professional conduct for members of the bar adopted pursuant to Section 6076 of the Business and Professions Code and rules of practice and procedure for the courts of this state adopted by the Judicial Council.

(d) Rules of pleading, practice, and procedure prescribed by the United States Supreme Court, such as the Rules of the United States Supreme Court, the Federal Rules of Civil Procedure, the Federal Rules of Criminal Procedure, the Admiralty Rules, the Rules of the Court of Claims, the Rules of the Customs Court, and the General Orders and Forms in Bankruptcy.

(e) The true signification of all English words and phrases and of all legal expressions.

(f) Facts and propositions of generalized knowledge that are so universally known that they cannot reasonably be the subject of dispute. **Leg.H.** 1965 ch. 299, operative January 1, 1967, 1971 ch. 438, 1972 ch. 764, 1982 ch. 454, 1985 ch. 106, 1986 ch. 248.

Ref.: Hanna § 26.06[8].

§452. Permissive judicial notice.

Judicial notice may be taken of the following matters to the extent that they are not embraced within Section 451:

(a) The decisional, constitutional, and statutory law of any state of the United States and the resolutions and private acts of the Congress of the United States and of the Legislature of this state.

(b) Regulations and legislative enactments issued by or under the authority of the United States or any public entity in the United States.

(c) Official acts of the legislative, executive, and judicial departments of the United States and of any state of the United States.

(d) Records of (1) any court of this state or (2) any court of record of the United States or of any state of the United States.

(e) Rules of court of (1) any court of this state or (2) any court of record of the United States or of any state of the United States.

(f) The law of an organization of nations and of foreign nations and public entities in foreign nations.

(g) Facts and propositions that are of such common knowledge within the territorial jurisdiction of the court that they cannot reasonably be the subject of dispute.

(h) Facts and propositions that are not reasonably subject to dispute and are capable of immediate and accurate determination by resort to sources of reasonably indisputable accuracy. **Leg.H.** 1965 ch. 299, operative January 1, 1967.

Ref.: Hanna § 26.06[8].

DIVISION 6 WITNESSES

CHAPTER 5 METHOD AND SCOPE OF EXAMINATION

ARTICLE 2 Examination of Witnesses [Selected Provisions]

§776. Adverse witnesses.

(a) A party to the record of any civil action, or a person identified with such a party, may be called and examined as if under cross-examination by any adverse party at any time during the presentation of evidence by the party calling the witness.

(b) A witness examined by a party under this section may be cross-examined by all other parties to the action in such order as the court directs; but, subject to subdivision (e), the witness may be examined only as if under redirect examination by:

(1) In the case of a witness who is a party, his own counsel and counsel for a party who is not adverse to the witness.

(2) In the case of a witness who is not a party, counsel for the party with whom the witness is identified and counsel for a party who is not adverse to the party with whom the witness is identified.

(c) For the purpose of this section, parties represented by the same counsel are deemed to be a single party.

(d) For the purpose of this section, a person is identified with a party if he is:

(1) A person for whose immediate benefit the action is prosecuted or defended by the party.

(2) A director, officer, superintendent, member, agent, employee, or managing agent of the party or of a person specified in paragraph (1), or any public employee of a public entity when such public entity is the party.

(3) A person who was in any of the relationships specified in paragraph (2) at the time of the act or omission giving rise to the cause of action.

(4) A person who was in any of the relationships specified in paragraph (2) at the time he obtained knowledge of the matter concerning which he is sought to be examined under this section.

(e) Paragraph (2) of subdivision (b) does not require counsel for the party with whom the witness is identified and counsel for a party who is not adverse to the party with whom the witness is identified to examine the witness as if under redirect examination if the party who called the witness for examination under this section:

(1) Is also a person identified with the same party with whom the witness is identified.

(2) Is the personal representative, heir, successor, or assignee of a person identified with the same party with whom the witness is identified.

§777. Exclusion of witnesses from courtroom.

(a) Subject to subdivisions (b) and (c), the court may exclude from the courtroom any witness not at the time under examination so that such witness cannot hear the testimony of other witnesses.

(b) A party to the action cannot be excluded under this section.

(c) If a person other than a natural person is a party to the action, an officer or employee designated by its attorney is entitled to be present.

DIVISION 8
PRIVILEGES

CHAPTER 1
DEFINITIONS

§900. Applicability.

Unless the provision or context otherwise requires, the definitions in this chapter govern the construction of this division. They do not govern the construction of any other division. **Leg.H.** 1965 ch. 299, operative January 1, 1967.

Ref.: Herlick Handbook § 14.40.

§901. Proceeding defined.

"Proceeding" means any action, hearing, investigation, inquest, or inquiry (whether conducted by a court, administrative agency, hearing officer, arbitrator, legislative body, or any other person authorized by law) in which, pursuant to law, testimony can be compelled to be given. **Leg.H.** 1965 ch. 299, operative January 1, 1967.

Ref.: Herlick Handbook § 14.40.

§902. Civil proceeding defined.

"Civil proceeding" means any proceeding except a criminal proceeding. **Leg.H.** 1965 ch. 299, operative January 1, 1967.

Ref.: Herlick Handbook § 14.40.

§903. Criminal proceeding defined.

"Criminal proceeding" means:

(a) A criminal action; and

(b) A proceeding pursuant to Article 3 (commencing with Section 3060) of Chapter 7 of Division 4 of Title 1 of the Government Code to determine whether a public officer should be removed from office for willful or corrupt misconduct in office. **Leg.H.** 1965 ch. 299, operative January 1, 1967.

Ref.: Herlick Handbook § 14.40.

§905. Presiding officer defined.

"Presiding officer" means the person authorized to rule on a claim of privilege in the proceeding in which the claim is made. **Leg.H.** 1965 ch. 299, operative January 1, 1967.

Ref.: Herlick Handbook § 14.40.

CHAPTER 2
APPLICABILITY OF DIVISION

§910. Applicability of division.

Except as otherwise provided by statute, the provisions of this division apply in all proceedings. The provisions of any statute making rules of evidence inapplicable in particular proceedings, or limiting the applicability of rules of evidence in particular proceedings, do not make this division inapplicable to such proceedings. **Leg.H.** 1965 ch. 299, operative January 1, 1967.

Ref.: Herlick Handbook § 14.40.

CHAPTER 3
GENERAL PROVISIONS RELATING TO PRIVILEGES

§911. General provision.

Except as otherwise provided by statute:

(a) No person has a privilege to refuse to be a witness.

(b) No person has a privilege to refuse to disclose any matter or to refuse to produce any writing, object, or other thing.

(c) No person has a privilege that another shall not be a witness or shall not disclose any matter or shall not produce any writing, object, or other thing. **Leg.H.** 1965 ch. 299, operative January 1, 1967.

Ref.: Herlick Handbook § 14.40.

§912. Waiver by disclosure—Joint holders of privilege.

(a) Except as otherwise provided in this section, the right of any person to claim a privilege provided by Section 954 (lawyer-client privilege), 966 (lawyer referral service-client privilege), 980 (privilege for confidential marital communications), 994 (physician-patient privilege), 1014 (psychotherapist-patient privilege), 1033 (privilege of penitent), 1034 (privilege of clergy member), 1035.8 (sexual assault counselor-victim privilege), 1037.5 (domestic violence counselor-victim privilege), or 1038 (human trafficking caseworker-victim privilege) is waived with respect to a communication protected by the privilege if any holder of the privilege, without coercion, has disclosed a significant part of the communication or has consented to disclosure made by anyone. Consent to disclosure is manifested by any statement or other conduct of the holder of the privilege indicating consent to the disclosure, including failure to claim the privilege in any proceeding in which the holder has legal standing and the opportunity to claim the privilege.

(b) Where two or more persons are joint holders of a privilege provided by Section 954 (lawyer-client privilege), 966 (lawyer referral service-client privilege), 994 (physician-patient privilege), 1014 (psychotherapist-patient privilege), 1035.8 (sexual assault counselor-victim privilege), 1037.5 (domestic violence counselor-victim privilege), or 1038 (human trafficking caseworker-victim privilege), a waiver of the right of a particular joint holder of the privilege to claim the privilege does not affect the right of another joint holder to claim the privilege. In the case of the privilege provided by Section 980 (privilege for confidential marital communications), a waiver of the right of one spouse to claim the privilege does not affect the right of the other spouse to claim the privilege.

(c) A disclosure that is itself privileged is not a waiver of any privilege.

(d) A disclosure in confidence of a communication that is protected by a privilege provided by Section 954 (lawyer-client privilege), 966 (lawyer referral service-client privilege), 994 (physician-patient privilege), 1014 (psychotherapist-patient privilege), 1035.8 (sexual assault counselor-victim privilege), 1037.5 (domestic violence counselor-victim privilege), or 1038 (human trafficking caseworker-victim privilege), when disclosure is reasonably necessary for the accomplishment of the purpose for which the lawyer, lawyer referral service, physician, psychotherapist, sexual assault counselor, domestic violence counselor, or human trafficking caseworker was consulted, is not a waiver of the privilege. **Leg.H.** 1965 ch. 299, operative January 1, 1967, 1980 ch. 917, 2002 ch. 72 (SB 2061), 2004 ch. 405 (SB 1796), 2013 ch. 123 (AB 267) §1, 2014 ch. 913 (AB 2747) §13.

Ref.: Herlick Handbook § 14.40.

§913. Comment on exercise of privilege prohibited—No presumption or inference.

(a) If in the instant proceeding or on a prior occasion a privilege is or was exercised not to testify with respect to any matter, or to refuse to disclose or to prevent another from disclosing any matter, neither the presiding officer nor counsel may comment thereon, no presumption shall arise because of the exercise of the privilege, and the trier of fact may not draw any inference therefrom as to the credibility of the witness or as to any matter at issue in the proceeding.

(b) The court, at the request of a party who may be adversely affected because an unfavorable inference may be drawn by the jury because a privilege has been exercised, shall instruct the jury that no presumption arises because of the exercise of the privilege and that the jury may not draw any inference therefrom as to the credibility of the witness or as to any matter at issue in the proceeding. **Leg.H.** 1965 ch. 299, operative January 1, 1967.

Ref.: Herlick Handbook § 14.40.

§914. Determination of claim of privilege—Contempt for failure to disclose information.

(a) The presiding officer shall determine a claim of privilege in any proceeding in the same manner as a court determines such a claim under Article 2 (commencing with Section 400) of Chapter 4 of Division 3.

(b) No person may be held in contempt for failure to disclose information claimed to be privileged unless he has failed to comply with an order of a court that he disclose such information. This subdivision does not apply to any governmental agency that has constitutional contempt power, nor does it apply to hearings and investigations of the Industrial Accident Commission, nor does it impliedly repeal Chapter 4 (commencing with Section 9400) of Part 1 of Division 2 of Title 2 of the Government Code. If no other statutory procedure is applicable, the procedure prescribed by Section 1991 of the Code of Civil Procedure shall be followed in seeking an order of a court that the person disclose the information claimed to be privileged. **Leg.H.** 1965 ch. 299, operative January 1, 1967.

Ref.: Herlick Handbook § 14.40.

§915. Disclosure of information to determine claim—Official information—Identity of informer—Trade secrets.

(a) Subject to subdivision (b), the presiding officer may not require disclosure of information claimed to be privileged under this division or attorney work product under subdivision (a) of Section 2018.030 of the Code of Civil Procedure in order to rule on the claim of privilege; provided, however, that in any hearing conducted pursuant to subdivision (c) of Section 1524 of the Penal Code in which a claim of privilege is made and the court determines that there is no other feasible means to rule on the validity of the claim other than to require disclosure, the court shall proceed in accordance with subdivision (b).

(b) When a court is ruling on a claim of privilege under Article 9 (commencing with Section 1040) of Chapter 4 (official information and identity of informer) or under Section 1060 (trade secret) or under subdivision (b) of Section 2018.030 of the Code of Civil Procedure (attorney work product) and is unable to do so without requiring disclosure of the information claimed to be privileged, the court may require the person from whom disclosure is sought or the person authorized to claim the privilege, or both, to disclose the information in chambers out of the presence and hearing of all persons except the person authorized to claim the privilege and any other persons as the person authorized to claim the privilege is willing to have present. If the judge determines that the information is privileged, neither the judge nor any other person may ever disclose, without the consent of a person authorized to permit disclosure, what was disclosed in the course of the proceedings in chambers. **Leg.H.** 1965 ch. 299, operative January 1, 1967, 1979 ch. 1034, 2001 ch. 812, 2004 ch. 182 (AB 3081), operative July 1, 2005.

Ref.: Herlick Handbook § 14.40.

§916. Exclusion of information where holder of privilege not a party.

(a) The presiding officer, on his own motion or on the motion of any party, shall exclude information that is subject to a claim of privilege under this division if:

(1) The person from whom the information is sought is not a person authorized to claim the privilege; and

(2) There is no party to the proceeding who is a person authorized to claim the privilege.

(b) The presiding officer may not exclude information under this section if:

(1) He is otherwise instructed by a person authorized to permit disclosure; or

(2) The proponent of the evidence establishes that there is no person authorized to claim the privilege in existence. **Leg.H.** 1965 ch. 299, operative January 1, 1967.

Ref.: Herlick Handbook § 14.40.

§917. Presumption of confidential nature of communication; electronic communication retains privileged character.

(a) If a privilege is claimed on the ground that the matter sought to be disclosed is a communication made in confidence in the course of the lawyer-client, lawyer referral service-client, physician-patient, psychotherapist-patient, clergy-penitent, marital or domestic partnership, sexual assault counselor-victim, domestic violence counselor-victim, or human trafficking caseworker-victim relationship, the communication is presumed to have been made in confidence and the opponent of the claim of privilege has the burden of proof to establish that the communication was not confidential.

(b) A communication between persons in a relationship listed in subdivision (a) does not lose its privileged character for the sole reason that it is communicated by electronic means or because persons involved in the delivery, facilitation, or storage of electronic communication may have access to the content of the communication.

(c) For purposes of this section, "electronic" has the same meaning provided in Section 1633.2 of the Civil Code. **Leg.H.** 1965 ch. 299, operative January 1, 1967, 2002 ch. 72 (SB 2061), 2003 ch. 468 (SB 851), 2004 ch. 183 (AB 3082), 2006 ch. 689 (SB 1743) §2, 2014 ch. 913 (AB 2747) §14, 2016 ch. 50 (SB 1005) §33.

2016 Note: It is the intent of the Legislature that the changes made by this act have only technical and nonsubstantive effect. Hence, no change made by this act shall create any new right, duty, or other obligation that did not exist immediately preceding the effective date of this act, or result in the limitation or termination of any right, duty, or other obligation that existed immediately preceding the effective date of this act. Stats. 2016 ch. 50 (SB 1005) §125.

Ref.: Herlick Handbook § 14.40.

§918. Error in disallowing claim.

A party may predicate error on a ruling disallowing a claim of privilege only if he is the holder of the privilege, except that a party may predicate error on a ruling disallowing a claim of privilege by his spouse under Section 970 or 971. **Leg.H.** 1965 ch. 299, operative January 1, 1967.

Ref.: Herlick Handbook § 14.40.

§919. Inadmissibility of privileged information erroneously disclosed.

(a) Evidence of a statement or other disclosure of privileged information is inadmissible against a holder of the privilege if:

(1) A person authorized to claim the privilege claimed it but nevertheless disclosure erroneously was required to be made; or

(2) The presiding officer did not exclude the privileged information as required by Section 916.

(b) If a person authorized to claim the privilege claimed it, whether in the same or a prior proceeding, but nevertheless disclosure erroneously was required by the presiding officer to be made, neither the failure to refuse to disclose nor the failure to seek review of the order of the presiding officer requiring disclosure indicates consent to the disclosure or constitutes a waiver and, under these circumstances, the disclosure is one made under coercion. **Leg.H.** 1965 ch. 299, operative January 1, 1967, 1974 ch. 227.

Ref.: Herlick Handbook § 14.40.

§920. Construction against repeal by implication.

Nothing in this division shall be construed to repeal by implication any other statute relating to privileges. **Leg.H.** 1965 ch. 299, operative January 1, 1967.

Ref.: Herlick Handbook § 14.40.

CHAPTER 4
PARTICULAR PRIVILEGES

ARTICLE 3
Lawyer-Client Privilege
[Selected Provisions]

§953. "Holder of privilege" defined.

As used in this article, "holder of the privilege" means:

(a) The client, if the client has no guardian or conservator.

(b)(1) A guardian or conservator of the client, if the client has a guardian or conservator, except as provided in paragraph (2).

(2) If the guardian or conservator has an actual or apparent conflict of interest with the client, then the guardian or conservator does not hold the privilege.

(c) The personal representative of the client if the client is dead, including a personal representative appointed pursuant to Section 12252 of the Probate Code.

(d) A successor, assign, trustee in dissolution, or any similar representative of a firm, association, organization, partnership, business trust, corporation, or public entity that is no longer in existence. **Leg.H.** 1965 ch. 299, operative January 1,1967, 2009 ch. 8 (AB 1163) §1, 2018 ch. 475 (AB 1290) §1.

ARTICLE 3.5
Lawyer Referral Service-Client Privilege

§965. Definitions.

For purposes of this article, the following terms have the following meanings:

(a) "Client" means a person who, directly or through an authorized representative, consults a lawyer referral service for the purpose of retaining, or securing legal services or advice from, a lawyer in his or her professional capacity, and includes an incompetent who consults the lawyer referral service himself or herself or whose guardian or conservator consults the lawyer referral service on his or her behalf.

(b) "Confidential communication between client and lawyer referral service" means information transmitted between a client and a lawyer referral service in the course of that relationship and in confidence by a means that, so far as the client is aware, does not disclose the information to third persons other than those who are present to further the interests of the client in the consultation or those to whom disclosure is reasonably necessary for the transmission of the information or the accomplishment of the purpose for which the lawyer referral service is consulted.

(c) "Holder of the privilege" means any of the following:

(1) The client, if the client has no guardian or conservator.

(2) A guardian or conservator of the client, if the client has a guardian or conservator.

(3) The personal representative of the client if the client is dead, including a personal representative appointed pursuant to Section 12252 of the Probate Code.

(4) A successor, assign, trustee in dissolution, or any similar representative of a firm, association, organization, partnership, business trust, corporation, or public entity that is no longer in existence.

(d) "Lawyer referral service" means a lawyer referral service certified under, and operating in compliance with, Section 6155 of the Business and Professions Code or an enterprise reasonably believed by the client to be a lawyer referral service certified under, and operating in compliance with, Section 6155 of the Business and Professions Code. **Leg.H.** 2013 ch. 123 (AB 267) §2.

§966. Privilege of confidential communication between client and lawyer referral service; who may claim privilege.

(a) Subject to Section 912 and except as otherwise provided in this article, the client, whether or not a party, has a privilege to refuse to disclose, and to prevent another from disclosing, a confidential communication between client and lawyer referral service if the privilege is claimed by any of the following:

(1) The holder of the privilege.

(2) A person who is authorized to claim the privilege by the holder of the privilege.

(3) The lawyer referral service or a staff person thereof, but the lawyer referral service or a staff person thereof may not claim the privilege if there is no holder of the privilege in existence or if the lawyer referral service or a staff person thereof is otherwise instructed by a person authorized to permit disclosure.

(b) The relationship of lawyer referral service and client shall exist between a lawyer referral service, as defined in Section 965, and the persons to whom it renders services, as well as between such persons and anyone employed by the lawyer referral service to render services to such persons. The word "persons" as used in this subdivision includes partnerships, corporations, limited liability companies, associations, and other groups and entities. **Leg.H.** 2013 ch. 123 (AB 267) §2.

§967. When lawyer referral service must claim privilege.

A lawyer referral service that has received or made a communication subject to the privilege under this article shall claim the privilege if the communication is sought to be disclosed and the client has not consented to the disclosure. **Leg.H.** 2013 ch. 123 (AB 267) §2.

§968. Disclosure necessary when services sought to enable crime or fraud, or to prevent criminal act likely to result in death or bodily harm.

There is no privilege under this article if either of the following applies:

(a) The services of the lawyer referral service were sought or obtained to enable or aid anyone to commit or plan to commit a crime or a fraud.

(b) A staff person of the lawyer referral service who receives a confidential communication in processing a request for legal assistance reasonably believes that disclosure of the confidential communication is necessary to prevent a criminal act that the staff person of the lawyer referral service reasonably believes is likely to result in the death of, or substantial bodily harm to, an individual. **Leg.H.** 2013 ch. 123 (AB 267) §2.

ARTICLE 4
Privilege Not to Testify Against Spouse
[Selected Provisions]

§971. Spouse of party called as witness by adverse party.

Except as otherwise provided by statute, a married person whose spouse is a party to a proceeding has a privilege not to be called as a witness by an adverse party to that proceeding without the prior express consent of the spouse having the privilege under this section unless the party calling the spouse does so in good faith without knowledge of the marital relationship. **Leg.H.** 1965 ch. 299, operative January 1, 1967.

Ref.: Herlick Handbook § 14.40.

§972. Exceptions to privilege.

A married person does not have a privilege under this article in:

(a) A proceeding brought by or on behalf of one spouse against the other spouse.

(b) A proceeding to commit or otherwise place his or her spouse or his or her spouse's property, or both, under the control of another because of the spouse's alleged mental or physical condition.

(c) A proceeding brought by or on behalf of a spouse to establish his or her competence.

(d) A proceeding under the Juvenile Court Law, Chapter 2 (commencing with Section 200) of Part 1 of Division 2 of the Welfare and Institutions Code.

(e) A criminal proceeding in which one spouse is charged with:

(1) A crime against the person or property of the other spouse or of a child, parent, relative, or cohabitant of either, whether committed before or during marriage.

(2) A crime against the person or property of a third person committed in the course of committing a crime against the person or property of the other spouse, whether committed before or during marriage.

(3) Bigamy.

(4) A crime defined by Section 270 or 270a of the Penal Code.

(f) A proceeding resulting from a criminal act which occurred prior to legal marriage of the spouses to each other regarding knowledge acquired prior to that marriage if prior to the legal marriage the witness spouse was aware that his or her spouse had been arrested for or had been formally charged with the crime or crimes about which the spouse is called to testify.

(g) A proceeding brought against the spouse by a former spouse so long as the property and debts of the marriage have not been adjudicated, or in order to establish, modify, or enforce a child, family or spousal support obligation arising from the marriage to the former spouse; in a proceeding brought against a spouse by the other parent in order to establish, modify, or enforce a child support obligation for a child of a nonmarital relationship of the spouse; or in a proceeding brought against a spouse by the guardian of a child of that spouse in order to establish, modify, or enforce a child support obligation of the spouse. The married person does not have a privilege under this subdivision to refuse to provide information relating to the issues of income, expenses, assets, debts, and employment of either spouse, but may assert the privilege as otherwise provided in this article if other information is requested by the former spouse, guardian, or other parent of the child.

Any person demanding the otherwise privileged information made available by this subdivision, who also has an obligation to support the child for whom an order to establish, modify, or enforce child support is sought, waives his or her marital privilege to the same extent as the spouse as provided in this subdivision. **Leg.H.** 1965 ch. 299, 1975 ch. 71, 1982 ch. 256, 1983 ch. 244, 1986 ch. 769, 1989 ch. 1359.

Ref.: Herlick Handbook § 14.40.

§973. Waiver—Proceeding brought or defended for benefit of spouse.

(a) Unless erroneously compelled to do so, a married person who testifies in a proceeding to which his spouse is a party, or who testifies against his spouse in any proceeding, does not have a privilege under this article in the proceeding in which such testimony is given.

(b) There is no privilege under this article in a civil proceeding brought or defended by a married person for the immediate benefit of his spouse or of himself and his spouse. **Leg.H.** 1965 ch. 299, operative January 1, 1967.

Ref.: Herlick Handbook § 14.40.

ARTICLE 5
Privilege for Confidential Marital Communications
[Selected Provisions]

§980. General provision.

Subject to Section 912 and except as otherwise provided in this article, a spouse (or his or her guardian or conservator when he or she has a guardian or conservator), whether or not a party, has a privilege during the marital or domestic partnership relationship and afterwards to refuse to disclose, and to prevent another from disclosing, a communication if he or she claims the privilege and the communication was made in confidence between him or her and the other spouse while they were spouses. **Leg.H.** 1965 ch. 299, operative January 1, 1967, 2016 chs. 50 (SB

1005) §34, 86 (SB 1171) §125 (ch. 50 prevails; ch. 86 not effective).

2016 Note: For legislative intent, see the 2016 Note following Ev C §917.

Ref.: Herlick Handbook § 14.40.

ARTICLE 6 Physician-Patient Privilege [Selected Provisions]

§996. Condition of patient in issue.

There is no privilege under this article as to a communication relevant to an issue concerning the condition of the patient if such issue has been tendered by:

(a) The patient;

(b) Any party claiming through or under the patient;

(c) Any party claiming as a beneficiary of the patient through a contract to which the patient is or was a party; or

(d) The plaintiff in an action brought under Section 376 or 377 of the Code of Civil Procedure for damages for the injury or death of the patient.

ARTICLE 7 Psychotherapist-Patient Privilege [Selected Provisions]

§1010. "Psychotherapist" defined.

As used in this article, "psychotherapist" means a person who is, or is reasonably believed by the patient to be:

(a) A person authorized to practice medicine in any state or nation who devotes, or is reasonably believed by the patient to devote, a substantial portion of his or her time to the practice of psychiatry.

(b) A person licensed as a psychologist under Chapter 6.6 (commencing with Section 2900) of Division 2 of the Business and Professions Code.

(c) A person licensed as a clinical social worker under Chapter 14 (commencing with Section 4991) of Division 2 of the Business and Professions Code, when he or she is engaged in applied psychotherapy of a nonmedical nature.

(d) A person who is serving as a school psychologist and holds a credential authorizing that service issued by the state.

(e) A person licensed as a marriage and family therapist under Chapter 13 (commencing with Section 4980) of Division 2 of the Business and Professions Code.

(f) A person registered as a psychological assistant who is under the supervision of a licensed psychologist or board certified psychiatrist as required by Section 2913 of the Business and Professions Code, or a person registered as an associate marriage and family therapist who is under the supervision of a licensed marriage and family therapist, a licensed clinical social worker, a licensed professional clinical counselor, a licensed psychologist, or a licensed physician and surgeon certified in psychiatry, as specified in Section 4980.44 of the Business and Professions Code.

(g) A person registered as an associate clinical social worker who is under supervision as specified in Section 4996.23 of the Business and Professions Code.

(h) A person registered with the Board of Psychology as a registered psychologist who is under the supervision of a licensed psychologist or board certified psychiatrist.

(i) A psychological intern as defined in Section 2911 of the Business and Professions Code who is under the supervision of a licensed psychologist or board certified psychiatrist.

(j) A trainee, as defined in subdivision (c) of Section 4980.03 of the Business and Professions Code, who is fulfilling his or her supervised practicum required by subparagraph (B) of paragraph (1) of subdivision (d) of Section 4980.36 of, or subdivision (c) of Section 4980.37 of, the Business and Professions Code and is supervised by a licensed psychologist, a board certified psychiatrist, a licensed clinical social worker, a licensed marriage and family therapist, or a licensed professional clinical counselor.

(k) A person licensed as a registered nurse pursuant to Chapter 6 (commencing with Section 2700) of Division 2 of the Business and Professions Code, who possesses a master's degree in psychiatric-mental health nursing and is listed as a psychiatric-mental health nurse by the Board of Registered Nursing.

(*l*) An advanced practice registered nurse who is certified as a clinical nurse specialist pursuant to Article 9 (commencing with Section 2838) of Chapter 6 of Division 2 of the Business and Professions Code and who participates in expert clinical practice in the specialty of psychiatric-mental health nursing.

(m) A person rendering mental health treatment or counseling services as authorized pursuant to Section 6924 of the Family Code.

(n) A person licensed as a professional clinical counselor under Chapter 16 (commencing with Section 4999.10) of Division 2 of the Business and Professions Code.

(o) A person registered as an associate professional clinical counselor who is under the supervision of a licensed professional clinical counselor, a licensed marriage and family therapist, a licensed clinical social worker, a licensed psychologist, or a licensed physician and surgeon certified in psychiatry, as specified in Sections 4999.42 to 4999.48, inclusive, of the Business and Professions Code.

(p) A clinical counselor trainee, as defined in subdivision (g) of Section 4999.12 of the Business and Professions Code, who is fulfilling his or her supervised practicum required by paragraph (3) of subdivision (c) of Section 4999.32 of, or paragraph (3) of subdivision (c) of Section 4999.33 of, the Business and Professions Code, and is supervised by a licensed psychologist, a board-certified psychiatrist, a licensed clinical social worker, a licensed marriage and family therapist, or a licensed professional clinical counselor. **Leg.H.** 1965 ch. 299, operative January 1, 1967, 1967 ch. 1677, 1970 chs. 1396, 1397 §1.5, 1972 ch. 888, 1974 ch. 546, 1983 ch. 928, 1987 ch. 724, 1988 ch. 488, 1989 ch. 1104, 1990 ch. 662, 1992 ch. 308, 1994 ch. 1270, 2001 chs. 142, 420, effective October 2, 2001, §1, operative until January 1, 2002, §1.5, operative January 1,

2002, 2009 ch. 26 (SB 33) §21, 2011 ch. 381 (SB 146) §21, 2015 ch. 529 (AB 1374) §4, 2016 ch. 86 (SB 1171) §126, 2017 ch. 573 (SB 800) §75, 2018 ch. 389 (AB 2296) §10.

§1010.5. Application of privilege to educational psychologist.

A communication between a patient and an educational psychologist, licensed under [1] **Chapter 13.5** (commencing with Section [2] **4989.10**) of Division 2 of the Business and Professions Code, shall be privileged to the same extent, and subject to the same limitations, as a communication between a patient and a psychotherapist described in subdivisions (c), (d), and (e) of Section 1010. **Leg.H.** 1985 ch. 545, 2020 ch. 370 (SB 1371) §113.

§1010.5. 2020 Deletes. [1] Article 5 **[2]** 4986) of Chapter 13

Ref.: Herlick Handbook § 14.40.

§1011. "Patient" defined.

As used in this article, "patient" means a person who consults a psychotherapist or submits to an examination by a psychotherapist for the purpose of securing a diagnosis or preventive, palliative, or curative treatment of his mental or emotional condition or who submits to an examination of his mental or emotional condition for the purpose of scientific research on mental or emotional problems. **Leg.H.** 1965 ch. 299, operative January 1, 1967.

Ref.: Herlick Handbook § 14.40.

§1012. "Confidential communication between patient and psychotherapist" defined.

As used in this article, "confidential communication between patient and psychotherapist" means information, including information obtained by an examination of the patient, transmitted between a patient and his psychotherapist in the course of that relationship and in confidence by a means which, so far as the patient is aware, discloses the information to no third persons other than those who are present to further the interest of the patient in the consultation, or those to whom disclosure is reasonably necessary for the transmission of the information or the accomplishment of the purpose for which the psychotherapist is consulted, and includes a diagnosis made and the advice given by the psychotherapist in the course of that relationship. **Leg.H.** 1965 ch. 299, operative January 1, 1967, 1967 ch. 650, 1970 chs. 1396, 1397.

Ref.: Herlick Handbook § 14.40.

§1013. "Holder of privilege" defined.

As used in this article, "holder of the privilege" means:

(a) The patient when he has no guardian or conservator.

(b) A guardian or conservator of the patient when the patient has a guardian or conservator.

(c) The personal representative of the patient if the patient is dead. **Leg.H.** 1965 ch. 299, operative January 1, 1967.

Ref.: Herlick Handbook § 14.40.

§1014. Who may claim privilege.

Subject to Section 912 and except as otherwise provided in this article, the patient, whether or not a party, has a privilege to refuse to disclose, and to prevent another from disclosing, a confidential communication between patient and psychotherapist if the privilege is claimed by:

(a) The holder of the privilege.

(b) A person who is authorized to claim the privilege by the holder of the privilege.

(c) The person who was the psychotherapist at the time of the confidential communication, but the person may not claim the privilege if there is no holder of the privilege in existence or if he or she is otherwise instructed by a person authorized to permit disclosure.

The relationship of a psychotherapist and patient shall exist between a psychological corporation as defined in Article 9 (commencing with Section 2995) of Chapter 6.6 of Division 2 of the Business and Professions Code, a marriage and family therapist corporation as defined in Article 6 (commencing with Section 4987.5) of Chapter 13 of Division 2 of the Business and Professions Code, a licensed clinical social workers corporation as defined in Article 5 (commencing with Section 4998) of Chapter 14 of Division 2 of the Business and Professions Code, or a professional clinical counselor corporation as defined in Article 7 (commencing with Section 4999.123) of Chapter 16 of Division 2 of the Business and Professions Code, and the patient to whom it renders professional services, as well as between those patients and psychotherapists employed by those corporations to render services to those patients. The word "persons" as used in this subdivision includes partnerships, corporations, limited liability companies, associations, and other groups and entities. **Leg.H.** 1965 ch. 299, operative January 1, 1967, 1969 ch. 1436, 1972 ch. 1286, 1989 ch. 1104, 1990 ch. 605, 1994 ch. 1010, 2002 ch. 1013 (SB 2026), 2011 ch. 381 (SB 146) §22.

Ref.: Herlick Handbook § 14.40.

§1015. When psychotherapist must claim privilege.

The psychotherapist who received or made a communication subject to the privilege under this article shall claim the privilege whenever he is present when the communication is sought to be disclosed and is authorized to claim the privilege under subdivision (c) of Section 1014. **Leg.H.** 1965 ch. 299, operative January 1, 1967.

Ref.: Herlick Handbook § 14.40.

§1016. Condition of patient in issue.

There is no privilege under this article as to a communication relevant to an issue concerning the mental or emotional condition of the patient if such issue has been tendered by:

(a) The patient;

(b) Any party claiming through or under the patient;

(c) Any party claiming as a beneficiary of the patient through a contract to which the patient is or was a party; or

(d) The plaintiff in an action brought under Section 376 or 377 of the Code of Civil Procedure for damages for the injury or death of the patient. **Leg.H.** 1965 ch. 299, operative January 1, 1967.

Ref.: Herlick Handbook § 14.40.

ARTICLE 9
Official Information and Identity of Informer [Selected Provisions]

§1043. Investigation of citizens' complaints—Discovery or disclosure of peace or custodial officer personnel records.

(a) In any case in which discovery or disclosure is sought of peace or custodial officer personnel records or records maintained pursuant to Section 832.5 of the Penal Code or information from those records, the party seeking the discovery or disclosure shall file a written motion with the appropriate court or administrative body upon written notice to the governmental agency that has custody and control of the records, as follows:

(1) In a civil action, the written notice shall be given at the times prescribed by subdivision (b) of Section 1005 of the Code of Civil Procedure.

(2) In a criminal action, the written notice shall be served and filed at least 10 court days before the hearing. All papers opposing a motion so noticed shall be filed with the court at least five court days, and all reply papers at least two court days, before the hearing. Proof of service of the notice shall be filed no later than five court days before the hearing.

(b) The motion shall include all of the following:

(1) Identification of the proceeding in which discovery or disclosure is sought, the party seeking discovery or disclosure, the peace or custodial officer whose records are sought, the governmental agency that has custody and control of the records, and the time and place at which the motion for discovery or disclosure shall be heard.

(2) A description of the type of records or information sought.

(3) Affidavits showing good cause for the discovery or disclosure sought, setting forth the materiality thereof to the subject matter involved in the pending litigation and stating upon reasonable belief that the governmental agency identified has the records or information from the records.

(c) Upon receipt of a notice served pursuant to subdivision (a), the governmental agency shall immediately notify the individual whose records are sought.

(d) No hearing upon a motion for discovery or disclosure shall be held without full compliance with the notice provisions of this section except upon a showing by the moving party of good cause for noncompliance, or upon a waiver of the hearing by the governmental agency identified as having the records. **Leg.H.** 1978 ch. 630, 1989 ch. 693, 2002 ch. 391 (AB 2040), 2019 ch. 585 (AB 1600) §2.

Ref.: Herlick Handbook § 14.40.

DIVISION 10
HEARSAY EVIDENCE

CHAPTER 2
EXCEPTIONS TO THE HEARSAY RULE

ARTICLE 7
Business Records

§1270. "Business" defined.

As used in this article, "a business" includes every kind of business, governmental activity, profession, occupation, calling, or operation of institutions, whether carried on for profit or not. **Leg.H.** 1965 ch. 299, operative January 1, 1967.

§1271. Record as evidence.

Evidence of a writing made as a record of an act, condition, or event is not made inadmissible by the hearsay rule when offered to prove the act, condition, or event if:

(a) The writing was made in the regular course of a business;

(b) The writing was made at or near the time of the act, condition, or event;

(c) The custodian or other qualified witness testifies to its identity and the mode of its preparation; and

(d) The sources of information and method and time of preparation were such as to indicate its trustworthiness. **Leg.H.** 1965 ch. 299, operative January 1, 1967.

§1272. Absence of record as evidence.

Evidence of the absence from the records of a business of a record of an asserted act, condition, or event is not made inadmissible by the hearsay rule when offered to prove the nonoccurrence of the act or event, or the nonexistence of the condition, if:

(a) It was the regular course of that business to make records of all such acts, conditions, or events at or near the time of the act, condition, or event and to preserve them; and

(b) The sources of information and method and time of preparation of the records of that business were such that the absence of a record of an act, condition, or event is a trustworthy indication that the act or event did not occur or the condition did not exist. **Leg.H.** 1965 ch. 299, operative January 1, 1967.

DIVISION 11
WRITINGS

CHAPTER 2
SECONDARY EVIDENCE OF WRITINGS

ARTICLE 3
Photographic Copies and Printed Representations of Writings

§1550. [First of Two; Operative Until Amendment by Stats. 2002 Ch. 124 Becomes Operative] Business records.

A nonerasable optical image reproduction provided that additions, deletions, or changes to the original document are not permitted by the technology, a photostatic, microfilm, microcard, miniature photographic, or other photographic copy or reproduction, or an enlargement thereof, of a writing is as admissible as the writing itself if the copy or reproduction was made and preserved as a part of the records of a business (as defined by Section 1270) in the regular course of that business. The introduction of the copy, reproduction, or enlargement does not preclude admission of the original writing if it is still in existence. A court may require the introduction of a hard copy printout of the document. **Leg.H.** 1965 ch. 299, operative January 1, 1967, 1992 ch. 876.

§1550. [Second of Two; See Note for Operative Information] Business records.

(a) If made and preserved as a part of the records of a business, as defined in Section 1270, in the regular course of that business, the following types of evidence of a writing are as admissible as the writing itself:

(1) A nonerasable optical image reproduction or any other reproduction of a public record by a trusted system, as defined in Section 12168.7 of the Government Code, if additions, deletions, or changes to the original document are not permitted by the technology.

(2) A photostatic copy or reproduction.

(3) A microfilm, microcard, or miniature photographic copy, reprint, or enlargement.

(4) Any other photographic copy or reproduction, or an enlargement thereof.

(b) The introduction of evidence of a writing pursuant to subdivision (a) does not preclude admission of the original writing if it is still in existence. A court may require the introduction of a hard copy printout of the document. **Leg.H.** 1965 ch. 299, operative January 1, 1967, 1992 ch. 876, 2002 ch. 124 (AB 2033).

2002 Note: This act shall become operative on the date the Secretary of State adopts uniform standards for storing and recording permanent and nonpermanent documents in electronic media, as required by Section 12168.7 of the Government Code. Stats. 2002 ch. 124 (AB 2033) §2.

§1550.1. Admissibility of reproductions of files, records, writings, photographs, fingerprints or other instruments.

Reproductions of files, records, writings, photographs, fingerprints or other instruments in the official custody of a criminal justice agency that were microphotographed or otherwise reproduced in a manner that conforms with the provisions of Section 11106.1, 11106.2, or 11106.3 of the Penal Code shall be admissible to the same extent and under the same circumstances as the original file, record, writing or other instrument would be admissible. **Leg.H.** 2004 ch. 65 (AB 883).

2004 Note: The addition of §1550.1 is declarative of existing law. Stats. 2004 ch. 65 (AB 883) §3.

§1551. Lost or destroyed writings.

A print, whether enlarged or not, from a photographic film (including a photographic plate, microphotographic film, photostatic negative, or similar reproduction) of an original writing destroyed or lost after such film was taken is as admissible as the original writing itself if, at the time of the taking of such film, the person under whose direction and control it was taken attached thereto, or to the sealed container in which it was placed and has been kept, or incorporated in the film, a certification complying with the provisions of Section 1531 and stating the date on which, and the fact that, it was so taken under his direction and control.

§1552. Printed representations of computer information.

(a) A printed representation of computer information or a computer program is presumed to be an accurate representation of the computer information or computer program that it purports to represent. This presumption is a presumption affecting the burden of producing evidence. If a party to an action introduces evidence that a printed representation of computer information or computer program is inaccurate or unreliable, the party introducing the printed representation into evidence has the burden of proving, by a preponderance of evidence, that the printed representation is an accurate representation of the existence and content of the computer information or computer program that it purports to represent.

(b) Subdivision (a) applies to the printed representation of computer-generated information stored by an automated traffic enforcement system.

(c) Subdivision (a) shall not apply to computer-generated official records certified in accordance with Section 452.5 or 1530. **Leg.H.** 1998 ch. 100, 2012 ch. 735 (SB 1303) §1.

1998 Note: Stats. 1998 ch. 100 applies in an action or proceeding commenced before, on, or after January 1, 1999. Stats. 1998 ch. 100 §9(b).

§1553. Printed representation of images stored on video or digital medium.

(a) A printed representation of images stored on a video or digital medium is presumed to be an accurate representation of the images it purports to represent. This presumption is a presumption affecting the burden of producing evidence. If a party to an action introduces evidence that a printed representation of images stored on a video or digital medium is inaccurate or unreliable, the party introducing the printed representation into evidence has the burden of proving, by a preponderance of evidence, that the printed representation is an accurate representation of the existence and content of the images that it purports to represent.

(b) Subdivision (a) applies to the printed representation of video or photographic images stored by an automated traffic enforcement system. **Leg.H.** 1998 ch. 100, 2012 ch. 735 (SB 1303) §2.

1998 Note: Stats. 1998 ch. 100 applies in an action or proceeding commenced before, on, or after January 1, 1999. Stats. 1998 ch. 100 §9(b).

ARTICLE 4
Production of Business Records

§1560. Copies—Transmittal.

(a) As used in this article:

(1) "Business" includes every kind of business described in Section 1270.

(2) "Record" includes every kind of record maintained by a business.

(b) Except as provided in Section 1564, when a subpoena duces tecum is served upon the custodian of records or other qualified witness of a business in an action in which the business is neither a party nor the place where any cause of action is alleged to have arisen, and the subpoena requires the production of all or any part of the records of the business, it is sufficient compliance therewith if the custodian or other qualified witness delivers by mail or otherwise a true, legible, and durable copy of all of the records described in the subpoena to the clerk of the court or to another person described in subdivision (d) of Section 2026.010 of the Code of Civil Procedure, together with the affidavit described in Section 1561, within one of the following time periods:

(1) In any criminal action, five days after the receipt of the subpoena.

(2) In any civil action, within 15 days after the receipt of the subpoena.

(3) Within the time agreed upon by the party who served the subpoena and the custodian or other qualified witness.

(c) The copy of the records shall be separately enclosed in an inner envelope or wrapper, sealed, with the title and number of the action, name of witness, and date of subpoena clearly inscribed thereon; the sealed envelope or wrapper shall then be enclosed in an outer envelope or wrapper, sealed, and directed as follows:

(1) If the subpoena directs attendance in court, to the clerk of the court.

(2) If the subpoena directs attendance at a deposition, to the officer before whom the deposition is to be taken, at the place designated in the subpoena for the taking of the deposition or at the officer's place of business.

(3) In other cases, to the officer, body, or tribunal conducting the hearing, at a like address.

(d) Unless the parties to the proceeding otherwise agree, or unless the sealed envelope or wrapper is returned to a witness who is to appear personally, the copy of the records shall remain sealed and shall be opened only at the time of trial, deposition, or other hearing, upon the direction of the judge, officer, body, or tribunal conducting the proceeding, in the presence of all parties who have appeared in person or by counsel at the trial, deposition, or hearing. Records that are original documents and that are not introduced in evidence or required as part of the record shall be returned to the person or entity from whom received. Records that are copies may be destroyed.

(e) As an alternative to the procedures described in subdivisions (b), (c), and (d), the subpoenaing party in a civil action may direct the witness to make the records available for inspection or copying by the party's attorney, the attorney's representative, or deposition officer as described in Section 2020.420 of the Code of Civil Procedure, at the witness' business address under reasonable conditions during normal business hours. Normal business hours, as used in this subdivision, means those hours that the business of the witness is normally open for business to the public. When provided with at least five business days' advance notice by the party's attorney, attorney's representative, or deposition officer, the witness shall designate a time period of not less than six continuous hours on a date certain for copying of records subject to the subpoena by the party's attorney, attorney's representative, or deposition officer. It shall be the responsibility of the attorney's representative to deliver any copy of the records as directed in the subpoena. Disobedience to the deposition subpoena issued pursuant to this subdivision is punishable as provided in Section 2020.240 of the Code of Civil Procedure.

(f) If a search warrant for business records is served upon the custodian of records or other qualified witness of a business in compliance with Section 1524 of the Penal Code regarding a criminal investigation in which the business is neither a party nor the place where any crime is alleged to have occurred, and the search warrant provides that the warrant will be deemed executed if the business causes the delivery of records described in the warrant to the law enforcement agency ordered to execute the warrant, it is sufficient compliance therewith if the custodian or other qualified witness delivers by mail or otherwise a true, legible, and durable copy of all of the records described in the search warrant to the law enforcement agency ordered to execute the search warrant, together with the affidavit described in Section 1561, within five days after the receipt of the search warrant or within such other time as is set forth in the warrant. This subdivision does not abridge or limit the scope of search warrant procedures set forth in Chapter 3 (commencing with Section 1523) of Title 12 of Part 2 of the Penal Code or invalidate otherwise duly executed search warrants. **Leg.H.** 1965 ch. 299, operative January 1, 1967, 1969 ch. 199, 1982 ch. 452, 1984 ch. 481, 1986 ch. 603, 1991 ch. 1090, 1997 ch. 442, 1999 ch. 444, 2000 ch. 287, 2004 chs. 162 (AB 1249), 182 (AB 3081), operative July 1, 2005 (ch. 162 prevails; ch. 182 not effective), 2005 ch. 294 (AB 333) §18, 2006 ch. 538 (SB 1852) §155, 2016 ch. 85 (SB 1087) §1.

§1561. Affidavit accompanying record.

(a) The records shall be accompanied by the affidavit of the custodian or other qualified witness, stating in substance each of the following:

(1) The affiant is the duly authorized custodian of the records or other qualified witness and has authority to certify the records.

(2) The copy is a true copy of all the records described in the subpoena duces tecum or search warrant, or pursuant to subdivision (e) of Section 1560, the records were delivered to the attorney, the attorney's representative, or deposition officer for copying at the custodian's or witness' place of business, as the case may be.

(3) The records were prepared by the personnel of the business in the ordinary course of business at or near the time of the act, condition, or event.

(4) The identity of the records.

(5) A description of the mode of preparation of the records.

(b) If the business has none of the records described, or only part thereof, the custodian or other qualified witness shall so state in the affidavit, and deliver the affidavit and those records that are available in one of the manners provided in Section 1560.

(c) If the records described in the subpoena were delivered to the attorney or his or her representative or deposition officer for copying at the custodian's or witness' place of business, in addition to the affidavit required by subdivision (a), the records shall be accompanied by an affidavit by the attorney or his or her representative or deposition officer stating that the copy is a true copy of all the records delivered to the attorney or his or her representative or deposition officer for copying. **Leg.H.** 1965 ch. 299, operative January 1, 1967, 1969 ch. 199, 1986 ch. 603, 1987 ch. 19, effective May 12, 1987, 1996 ch. 146, 1999 ch. 444, 2016 ch. 85 (SB 1087) §2.

§1562. Admissibility of copies and affidavits.

If the original records would be admissible in evidence if the custodian or other qualified witness had been present and testified to the matters stated in the affidavit, and if the requirements of Section 1271 have been met, the copy of the records is admissible in evidence. The affidavit is admissible as evidence of the matters stated therein pursuant to Section 1561 and the matters so stated are presumed true. When more than one person has knowledge of the facts, more than one affidavit may be made. The presumption established by this section is a presumption affecting the burden of producing evidence. **Leg.H.** 1965 ch. 299, operative January 1, 1967, 1989 ch. 1416, 1996 ch. 146.

§1563. Witness fees.

(a) This article does not require tender or payment of more than one witness fee and one mileage fee or other charge, to a witness or witness' business, unless there is an agreement to the contrary between the witness and the requesting party.

(b) All reasonable costs incurred in a civil proceeding by a witness who is not a party with respect to the production of all or any part of business records requested pursuant to a subpoena duces tecum shall be charged against the party serving the subpoena duces tecum.

(1) "Reasonable costs," as used in this section, includes, but is not limited to, the following specific costs: ten cents ($0.10) per page for standard reproduction of documents of a size 8½ by 14 inches or less; twenty cents ($0.20) per page for copying of documents from microfilm; actual costs for the reproduction of oversize documents or the reproduction of documents requiring special processing which are made in response to a subpoena; reasonable clerical costs incurred in locating and making the records available to be billed at the maximum rate of twenty-four dollars ($24) per hour per person, computed on the basis of six dollars ($6) per quarter hour or fraction thereof; actual postage charges; and the actual cost, if any, charged to the witness by a third person for the retrieval and return of records held offsite by that third person.

(2) The requesting party, or the requesting party's deposition officer, shall not be required to pay the reasonable costs or any estimate thereof before the records are available for delivery pursuant to the subpoena, but the witness may demand payment of costs pursuant to this section simultaneous with actual delivery of the subpoenaed records, and until payment is made, the witness is under no obligation to deliver the records.

(3) The witness shall submit an itemized statement for the costs to the requesting party, or the requesting party's deposition officer, setting forth the reproduction and clerical costs incurred by the witness. If the costs exceed those authorized in paragraph (1), or if the witness refuses to produce an itemized statement of costs as required by paragraph (3), upon demand by the requesting party, or the requesting party's deposition officer, the witness shall furnish a statement setting forth the actions taken by the witness in justification of the costs.

(4) The requesting party may petition the court in which the action is pending to recover from the witness all or a part of the costs paid to the witness, or to reduce all or a part of the costs charged by the witness, pursuant to this subdivision, on the grounds that those costs were excessive. Upon the filing of the petition the court shall issue an order to show cause and from the time the order is served on the witness the court has jurisdiction over the witness. The court may hear testimony on the order to show cause and if it finds that the costs demanded and collected, or charged but not collected, exceed the amount authorized by this subdivision, it shall order the witness to remit to the requesting party, or reduce its charge to the requesting party by an amount equal to, the amount of the excess. If the court finds the costs were excessive and charged in bad faith by the witness, the court shall order the witness to remit the full amount of the costs demanded and collected, or excuse the requesting party from any payment of costs charged but not collected, and the court shall also order the witness to pay the requesting party the amount of the reasonable expenses incurred in obtaining the order, including attorney's fees. If the court finds the costs were not

excessive, the court shall order the requesting party to pay the witness the amount of the reasonable expenses incurred in defending the petition, including attorney's fees.

(5) If a subpoena is served to compel the production of business records and is subsequently withdrawn, or is quashed, modified, or limited on a motion made other than by the witness, the witness shall be entitled to reimbursement pursuant to paragraph (1) for all reasonable costs incurred in compliance with the subpoena to the time that the requesting party has notified the witness that the subpoena has been withdrawn or quashed, modified, or limited. If the subpoena is withdrawn or quashed, if those costs are not paid within 30 days after demand therefor, the witness may file a motion in the court in which the action is pending for an order requiring payment, and the court shall award the payment of expenses and attorney's fees in the manner set forth in paragraph (4).

(6) If records requested pursuant to a subpoena duces tecum are delivered to the attorney, the attorney's representative, or the deposition officer for inspection or photocopying at the witness' place of business, the only fee for complying with the subpoena shall not exceed fifteen dollars ($15), plus the actual cost, if any, charged to the witness by a third person for retrieval and return of records held offsite by that third person. If the records are retrieved from microfilm, the reasonable costs, as defined in paragraph (1), applies.

(c) If the personal attendance of the custodian of a record or other qualified witness is required pursuant to Section 1564, in a civil proceeding, he or she shall be entitled to the same witness fees and mileage permitted in a case where the subpoena requires the witness to attend and testify before a court in which the action or proceeding is pending and to any additional costs incurred as provided by subdivision (b). **Leg.H.** 1965 ch. 299, operative January 1, 1967, 1972 ch. 396, 1981 ch. 1014, 1982 ch. 452, 1986 ch. 603, 1987 ch. 19, effective May 12, 1987, 1997 ch. 442, 1999 ch. 444, 2016 ch. 85 (SB 1087) §3.

§1564. Personal attendance of custodian or witness.

The personal attendance of the custodian or other qualified witness and the production of the original records is not required unless, at the discretion of the requesting party, the subpoena duces tecum contains a clause which reads:

"The personal attendance of the custodian or other qualified witness and the production of the original records are required by this subpoena. The procedure authorized pursuant to subdivision (b) of Section 1560, and Sections 1561 and 1562, of the Evidence Code will not be deemed sufficient compliance with this subpoena."

§1565. Custodian as witness of party serving first subpoena.

If more than one subpoena duces tecum is served upon the custodian of records or other qualified witness and the personal attendance of the custodian or other qualified witness is required pursuant to Section 1564, the witness shall be deemed to be the witness of the party serving the first such subpoena duces tecum.

§1566. Applicable proceedings.

This article applies in any proceeding in which testimony can be compelled.

§1567. Admissibility of certain income and benefit information provided by employer in proceeding to modify or terminate order for child, family, or spousal support.

A completed form described in Section 3664 of the Family Code for income and benefit information provided by the employer may be admissible in a proceeding for modification or termination of an order for child, family, or spousal support if both of the following requirements are met:

(a) The completed form complies with Sections 1561 and 1562.

(b) A copy of the completed form and notice was served on the employee named therein pursuant to Section 3664 of the Family Code. **Leg.H.** 1995 ch. 506.

SELECTED PROVISIONS Of The GOVERNMENT CODE

GENERAL PROVISIONS [Selected Provisions]

§24. "Workmen's compensation" changed to "workers' compensation."

The Legislature hereby declares its intent that the term "workmen's compensation" shall hereafter also be known as "workers' compensation." In furtherance of this policy it is the desire of the Legislature that references to the term "workmen's compensation" in this code be changed to "workers' compensation" when such code sections are being amended for any purpose. This act is declaratory and not amendatory of existing law.

Misc. Provisions

TITLE 1
GENERAL

DIVISION 7
Miscellaneous

CHAPTER 5
JOINT EXERCISE OF POWERS

ARTICLE 1
Joint Powers Agreements
[Selected Provisions]

§6516. Public agencies' joint powers agreement for insurance and risk pooling; reserve fund.

Public agencies conducting agricultural, livestock, industrial, cultural, or other types of fairs or exhibitions may enter into a joint powers agreement to form an insurance pooling arrangement for the payment of workers' compensation, unemployment compensation, tort liability, public liability, or other losses incurred by those agencies. An insurance and risk pooling arrangement formed in accordance with a joint powers agreement pursuant to this section is not subject to Section 11007.7 of the Government Code. The Department of Food and Agriculture may enter into such a joint powers agreement for the California Exposition and State Fair, district agricultural associations, or citrus fruit fairs, and the department shall have authority to contract with the California Exposition and State Fair, district agricultural associations, or citrus fruit fairs with respect to such a joint powers agreement entered into on behalf of the California Exposition and State Fair, district agricultural association, or citrus fruit fair. Any county contracting with a nonprofit corporation to conduct a fair pursuant to Sections 25905 and 25906 of the Government Code may enter into such a joint powers agreement for a fair conducted by the nonprofit corporation, and shall have authority to contract with a nonprofit corporation with respect to such a joint powers agreement entered into on behalf of the fair of the nonprofit corporation.

Any county contracting with a nonprofit corporation to conduct a fair shall assume all workers' compensation and liability obligations accrued prior to the dissolution or nonrenewal of the nonprofit corporation's contract with the county.

Any public entity entering into a joint powers agreement under this section shall establish or maintain a reserve fund to be used to pay losses incurred under the agreement. The reserve fund shall contain sufficient moneys to maintain the fund on an actuarially sound basis. **Leg.H.** 1996 ch. 373.

TITLE 2
GOVERNMENT OF THE STATE OF CALIFORNIA

DIVISION 1
General

CHAPTER 7
CALIFORNIA EMERGENCY SERVICES ACT

ARTICLE 3.5
Oil Spills
[Selected Provisions]

§8574.3. Volunteers of state agencies; entitlement to benefits.

State agencies granted authority to implement a plan adopted under this article may use volunteer workers. The volunteers shall be deemed employees of the state for the purpose of workers' compensation under Article 2 (commencing with Section 3350) of Chapter 2 of Part 1 of Division 4 of the Labor Code. Any payments for workers' compensation under this section shall be made from the account specified in Section 8574.4.

ARTICLE 5
Office of Emergency Services
[Selected Provisions]

§8585.5. Office of Emergency Services; classes of disaster workers; procedures for payment of benefits.

The office shall establish by rule and regulation various classes of disaster service workers and the scope of the duties of each class. The office shall also adopt rules and regulations prescribing the manner in which disaster service workers of each class are to be registered. All of the rules and regulations shall be designed to facilitate the payment of workers' compensation. **Leg.H.** 1970 ch. 1454 §2, 1981 ch. 714 §171, 2006 ch. 502 (AB 1889) §4 (amended & renumbered from §8580), 2010 ch. 618 (AB 2791) §31, 2013 ch. 352 (AB 1317) §123, effective September 26, 2013, operative July 1, 2013.

ARTICLE 9.8
Disaster Preparedness
[Selected Provisions]

§8609. Volunteer workers.

State agencies granted authority by the Governor, the Business Continuity Task Force, the Emergency Preparedness Task Force, or the Executive Committee established by Executive Order D-3-99 to implement any type of disaster, contingency, or business continuity plan may use volunteer workers. The volunteers shall be deemed disaster service workers for the purpose of workers' compensation under Chapter 3 (commencing with Section 3600) of Part 1 of Division 4 of the Labor Code. **Leg.H.** 1999 ch. 784, effective October 10, 1999.

ARTICLE 10
Local Disaster Councils
[Selected Provisions]

§8610. Authority to create local disaster councils.

(a) Counties, cities and counties, and cities may create disaster councils by ordinance. A disaster council shall develop plans for meeting any condition constituting a local emergency or state of emergency, including, but not limited to, earthquakes, natural or manmade disasters specific to that jurisdiction, or state of war emergency; those plans shall provide for the effective mobilization of all of the resources within the political subdivision, both public and private. The disaster council shall supply a copy of any plans developed pursuant to this section to the Office of Emergency Services. The governing body of a county, city and county, or city may, in the ordinance or by resolution adopted pursuant to the ordinance, provide for the organization, powers and duties, divisions, services, and staff of the emergency organization. The governing body of a county, city and county, or city may, by ordinance or resolution, authorize public officers, employees, and registered volunteers to command the aid of citizens when necessary in the execution of their duties during a state of war emergency, a state of emergency, or a local emergency.

(b) Counties, cities and counties, and cities may enact ordinances and resolutions and either establish rules and regulations or authorize disaster councils to recommend to the director of the local emergency organization rules and regulations for dealing with local emergencies that can be adequately dealt with locally; and further may act to carry out mutual aid on a voluntary basis and, to this end, may enter into agreements.

(c)(1) The Office of Emergency Services shall annually review, at a minimum, 10 emergency plans submitted to the office.

(2) The Office of Emergency Services shall determine if a plan reviewed pursuant to this subdivision substantially conforms to or exceeds the recommendations described in the Federal Emergency Management Agency's Comprehensive Preparedness Guide 101, or other successor emergency operations planning guidance.

(3) The Office of Emergency Services shall prioritize, in complying with paragraph (1), a plan submitted from a county determined to be at high risk of wildfire disaster. **Leg.H.** 2007 ch. 130 (AB 299) §110, 2010 ch. 618 (AB 2791) §71, see this section as modified in

Misc. Provisions

Governor's Reorganization Plan No. 2 §137 of 2012, 2013 ch. 352 (AB 1317) §170, effective September 26, 2013, operative July 1, 2013, 2020 ch. 254 (AB 2386) §1.

2013 Note: Stats. 2013 ch. 352 (AB 1317) enacted the statutory changes necessary to reflect the changes made by the Governor's Reorganization Plan No. 2 of 2012.

2012 Note: 2012 Governor's Reorganization Plan No. 2 was submitted to the Legislature on May 3, 2012, and became effective July 3, 2012, pursuant to Gov C §12080.5, and substantively operative July 1, 2013.

§8612. Certification of accredited disaster councils.

Any disaster council that both agrees to follow the rules and regulations established by the Office of Emergency Services pursuant to Section 8585.5 and substantially complies with those rules and regulations shall be certified by the office. Upon that certification, and not before, the disaster council becomes an accredited disaster council. **Leg.H.** 1970 ch. 1454 §2, 2006 ch. 502 (AB 1889) §7, 2010 ch. 618 (AB 2791) §73, see this section as modified in Governor's Reorganization Plan No. 2 §139 of 2012, 2013 ch. 352 (AB 1317) §173, effective September 26, 2013, operative July 1, 2013.

2013 Note: Stats. 2013 ch. 352 (AB 1317) enacted the statutory changes necessary to reflect the changes made by the Governor's Reorganization Plan No. 2 of 2012.

2012 Note: 2012 Governor's Reorganization Plan No. 2 was submitted to the Legislature on May 3, 2012, and became effective July 3, 2012, pursuant to Gov C §12080.5, and substantively operative July 1, 2013.

ARTICLE 17
Privileges and Immunities
[Selected Provisions]

§8656. Public employees; privileges applying in territory apply outside territory.

All of the privileges and immunities from liability; exemptions from laws, ordinances, and rules; all pension, relief, disability, workers' compensation, and other benefits which apply to the activity of officers, agents, or employees of any political subdivision when performing their respective functions within the territorial limits of their respective political subdivisions, shall apply to them to the same degree and extent while engaged in the performance of any of their functions and duties extraterritorially under this chapter.

§8657. Liability for damages suffered by volunteer engaged in emergency preparedness training or relief activity; responsibilities and immunities of California Earthquake Prediction Evaluation Council.

(a) Volunteers duly enrolled or registered with the Office of Emergency Services or any disaster council of any political subdivision, or unregistered persons duly impressed into service during a state of war emergency, a state of emergency, or a local emergency, in carrying out, complying with, or attempting to comply with, any order or regulation issued or promulgated pursuant to the provisions of this chapter or any local ordinance, or performing any of their authorized functions or duties or training for the performance of their authorized functions or duties, shall have the same degree of responsibility for their actions and enjoy the same immunities as officers and employees of the state and its political subdivisions performing similar work for their respective entities.

(b) No political subdivision or other public agency under any circumstances, nor the officers, employees, agents, or duly enrolled or registered volunteers thereof, or unregistered persons duly impressed into service during a state of war emergency, a state of emergency, or a local emergency, acting within the scope of their official duties under this chapter or any local ordinance shall be liable for personal injury or property damage sustained by any duly enrolled or registered volunteer engaged in or training for emergency preparedness or relief activity, or by any unregistered person duly impressed into service during a state of war emergency, a state of emergency, or a local emergency and engaged in such service. The foregoing shall not affect the right of any such person to receive benefits or compensation which may be specifically provided by the provisions of any federal or state statute nor shall it affect the right of any person to recover under the terms of any policy of insurance.

(c) The California Earthquake Prediction Evaluation Council, an advisory committee established pursuant to Section 8590 of this chapter, may advise the Governor of the existence of an earthquake or volcanic prediction having scientific validity. In its review, hearings, deliberations, or other validation procedures, members of the council, jointly and severally, shall have the same degree of responsibility for their actions and enjoy the same immunities as officers and employees of the state and its political subdivisions engaged in similar work in their respective entities. Any person making a presentation to the council as part of the council's validation process, including presentation of a prediction for validation, shall be deemed a member of the council until the council has found the prediction to have or not have scientific validity. **Leg.H.** 2010 ch. 618 (AB 2791) §78, see this section as modified in Governor's Reorganization Plan No. 2 §144 of 2012, 2013 ch. 352 (AB 1317) §179, effective September 26, 2013, operative July 1, 2013.

2013 Note: Stats. 2013 ch. 352 (AB 1317) enacted the statutory changes necessary to reflect the changes made by the Governor's Reorganization Plan No. 2 of 2012.

2012 Note: 2012 Governor's Reorganization Plan No. 2 was submitted to the Legislature on May 3, 2012, and became effective July 3, 2012, pursuant to Gov C §12080.5, and substantively operative July 1, 2013.

§8659. Limitations on liability of specified healing arts practitioners who render services during emergency.

(a) Any physician or surgeon (whether licensed in this state or any other state), hospital, pharmacist, respiratory care practitioner, nurse, or dentist who renders services during any state of war emergency, a state of emergency, or a local emergency at the express or implied request of any responsible state or local official or agency shall have no liability for any injury sustained by any person by reason of those services, regardless of how or under what circumstances or by what cause those injuries are sustained; provided, however, that the immunity herein granted shall not apply in the event of a willful act or omission.

(b) Any veterinarian or registered veterinary technician who renders services during any state of war emergency, a state of emergency, or a local emergency at the express or implied request of any responsible state or local official or agency shall have no liability for any injury sustained by any animal by reason of those services, regardless of how or under what circumstances or by what cause those injuries are sustained; provided, however, that the immunity herein granted shall not apply in the event of a willful act or omission. **Leg.H.** 2009 ch. 308 (SB 819) §91, 2010 ch. 538 (AB 1980) §21.

§8660. Limitations on liability; other state rendering aid in emergency.

No other state or its officers or employees rendering aid in this state pursuant to any interstate arrangement, agreement, or compact shall be liable on account of any act or omission in good faith on the part of such state or its officers or employees while so engaged, or on account of the maintenance or use of any equipment or supplies in connection with an emergency.

DIVISION 3
Executive Department

PART 1
STATE DEPARTMENTS AND AGENCIES

CHAPTER 4.5
ADMINISTRATIVE ADJUDICATION: GENERAL PROVISIONS

ARTICLE 8
Language Assistance [Selected Provisions]

§11435.30. State Personnel Board list of certified administrative hearing interpreters; other classes of interpreters deemed certified.

(a) The State Personnel Board shall establish, maintain, administer, and publish annually an updated list of certified administrative hearing interpreters it has determined meet the minimum standards in interpreting skills and linguistic abilities in languages designated pursuant to Section 11435.40. Any interpreter so listed may be examined by each employing agency to determine the interpreter's knowledge of the employing agency's technical program terminology and procedures.

(b) Court interpreters certified pursuant to Section 68562, and interpreters listed on the State Personnel Board's recommended lists of court and administrative hearing interpreters prior to July 1, 1993, shall be deemed certified for purposes of this section.

(c)(1) In addition to the certification procedure provided pursuant to subdivision (a), the Administrative Director of the Division of Workers' Compensation may establish, maintain, administer, and publish annually an updated list of certified administrative hearing interpreters who, based on testing by an independent organization designated by the administrative director, have been determined to meet the minimum standards in interpreting skills and linguistic abilities in languages designated pursuant to Section 11435.40, for purposes of administrative hearings conducted pursuant to proceedings of the Workers' Compensation Appeals Board. The independent testing organization shall have no financial interest in the training of interpreters or in the employment of interpreters for administrative hearings.

(2)(A) A fee, as determined by the administrative director, shall be collected from each interpreter seeking certification. The fee shall not exceed the reasonable regulatory costs of administering the testing and certification program and of publishing the list of certified administrative hearing interpreters on the Division of Workers' Compensation' Internet Web site.

(B) The Legislature finds and declares that the services described in this section are of such a special and unique nature that they may be contracted out pursuant to paragraph (3) of subdivision (b) of Section 19130. The Legislature further finds and declares that the services described in this section are a new state function pursuant to paragraph (2) of subdivision (b) of Section 19130. **Leg.H.** 1995 ch. 938, operative July 1, 1997, 2012 ch. 363 (SB 863) §2.

2012 Notes: The Legislature finds and declares all of the following:

(a) That Section 4 of Article XIV of the California Constitution authorizes the creation of a workers' compensation system that includes adequate provision for the comfort, health and safety, and general welfare of workers and their dependents to relieve them of the consequences of any work-related injury or death, irrespective of the fault of any party and requires the administration of the workers' compensation system to accomplish substantial justice in all cases expeditiously, inexpensively, and without encumbrance of any character, all of which matters are expressly declared to be the social public policy of this state.

(b) That the current system of determining permanent disability has become excessively litigious, time consuming, procedurally burdensome and unpredictable, and that the provisions of this act will produce the necessary uniformity, consistency, and objectivity of outcomes, in accordance with the constitutional mandate to accomplish substantial justice in all cases expeditiously, inexpensively, and without encumbrance of any character, and that in enacting subdivision (c) of Section 4660.1 of the Labor Code, the Legislature intends to eliminate questionable claims of disability when alleged to be caused by a disabling physical injury arising out of and in the course of employment while guaranteeing medical treatment as required by Division 4 (commencing with Section 3200) of the Labor Code.

(c) That in enacting this act, it is not the intent of the Legislature to overrule the holding in Milpitas Unified School District v. Workers Comp. Appeals Bd. (Guzman) (2010) 187 Cal.App.4th 808.

(d) That the current system of resolving disputes over the medical necessity of requested treatment is costly, time consuming, and does not uniformly result in the provision of treatment that adheres to the highest standards of evidence-based medicine, adversely affecting the health and safety of workers injured in the course of employment.

(e) That having medical professionals ultimately determine the necessity of requested treatment furthers the social policy of this state in reference to using evidence-based medicine to provide injured workers with the highest quality of medical care and that the provision of the act establishing independent medical review are necessary to implement that policy.

(f) That the performance of independent medical review is a service of such a special and unique nature that it must be contracted pursuant to paragraph (3) of subdivision (b) of Section 19130 of the Government Code, and that independent medical review is a new state function pursuant to paragraph (2) of subdivision (b) of Section 19130 of the Government Code that will be more expeditious, more economical, and more scientifically sound than the existing function of medical necessity determinations performed by qualified medical evaluators appointed pursuant to Section 139.2 of the Labor Code. The existing process of appointing qualified medical evaluators to examine patients and resolve treatment disputes is costly and time-consuming, and it prolongs disputes and causes delays in medical treatment for injured workers. Additionally, the process of selection of qualified medical evaluators can bias the outcomes. Timely and medically sound determinations of disputes over appropriate medical treatment require the independent and unbiased medical expertise of specialists that are not available through the civil service system.

(g) That the establishment of independent medical review and provision for limited appeal of decisions resulting from independent medical review are a necessary exercise of the Legislature's plenary power to provide for the settlement of any disputes arising under the workers' compensation laws of this state and to control the manner of review of such decisions.

(h) That the performance of independent bill review is a service of such a special and unique nature that it must be contracted pursuant to paragraph (3) of subdivision (b) of Section 19130 of the Government Code, and that independent bill review is a new state function pursuant to paragraph (2) of subdivision (b) of Section 19130 of the Government Code. Existing law provides no method of medical billing dispute resolution short of litigation. Existing law does not provide for medical billing and payment experts to resolve billing disputes, and billing issues are frequently submitted to workers' compensation judges without the benefit of independent and unbiased findings on these issues. Medical billing and payment systems are a field of technical and specialized expertise, requiring services that are not available through the civil service system. The need for independent and unbiased findings and determinations requires that this new function be contracted pursuant to subdivision (b) of Section 19130 of the Government Code. Stats. 2012 ch. 363 (SB 863) §1.

This act shall apply to all pending matters, regardless of date of injury, unless otherwise specified in this act, but shall not be a basis to rescind, alter, amend, or reopen any final award of workers' compensation benefits. Stats. 2012 ch. 363 (SB 863) §84.

It appears the Legislature inadvertently substituted "Compensation' Internet" for "Compensation's Internet" in the second sentence of subdivision (c)(2)(A).

§11435.35. State Personnel Board list of certified medical examination interpreters; other classes of interpreters deemed certified.

(a) The State Personnel Board shall establish, maintain, administer, and publish annually, an updated list of certified medical examination interpreters it has determined meet the minimum standards in interpreting skills and linguistic abilities in languages designated pursuant to Section 11435.40.

(b) Court interpreters certified pursuant to Section 68562 and administrative hearing interpreters certified pursuant to Section 11435.30 shall be deemed certified for purposes of this section.

(c)(1) In addition to the certification procedure provided pursuant to subdivision (a), the Administrative Director of the Division of Workers' Compensation may establish, maintain, administer, and publish annually an updated list of certified medical examination interpreters who, based on testing by an independent organization designated by the administrative director, have been determined to meet the minimum standards in interpreting skills and linguistic abilities in languages designated pursuant to Section 11435.40, for purposes of medical examinations conducted pursuant to proceedings of the Workers' Compensation Appeals Board, and medical examinations conducted pursuant to Division 4 (commencing with Section 3200) of the Labor Code. The independent testing organization shall have no financial interest in the training of interpreters or in the employment of interpreters for medical examinations.

(2)(A) A fee, as determined by the administrative director, shall be collected from each interpreter seeking certification. The fee shall not exceed the reasonable regulatory costs of administering the testing and certification program and of publishing the list of certified medical examination interpreters on the Division of Workers' Compensation's Internet Web site.

(B) The Legislature finds and declares that the services described in this section are of such a special and unique nature that they may be contracted out pursuant to paragraph (3) of subdivision (b) of Section 19130. The Legislature further finds and declares that the services described in this section are a new state function pursuant to paragraph (2) of subdivision (b) of Section 19130. **Leg.H.** 1995 ch. 938, operative July 1, 1997, 2012 ch. 363 (SB 863) §3, 2013 ch. 287 (SB 375) §1.

2012 Note: For legislative findings, declarations, and applicablity of Stats. 2012 ch. 363 (SB 863), see 2012 Notes following Gov C §11435.30.

PART 2.8 DEPARTMENT OF FAIR EMPLOYMENT AND HOUSING

CHAPTER 4 DEFINITIONS [Selected Provisions]

§12925. Definitions.

As used in this part, unless a different meaning clearly appears from the context:

(a) "Council" means the Fair Employment and Housing Council and "council member" means a member of the council.

(b) "Department" means the Department of Fair Employment and Housing.

(c) "Director" means the Director of Fair Employment and Housing.

(d) "Person" includes one or more individuals, partnerships, associations, corporations, limited liability companies, legal representatives, trustees, trustees in bankruptcy, and receivers or other fiduciaries. **Leg.H.** 1980 ch. 992 §4, 1994 ch. 1010 (SB 2053) §142, 2012 ch. 46 (SB 1038) §34, effective June 27, 2012, operative January 1, 2013.

§12926. Definitions regarding unlawful practices.

As used in this part in connection with unlawful practices, unless a different meaning clearly appears from the context:

(a) "Affirmative relief" or "prospective relief" includes the authority to order reinstatement of an employee, awards of backpay, reimbursement of out-of-pocket expenses, hiring, transfers, reassignments, grants of tenure, promotions, cease and desist orders, posting of notices, training of personnel, testing, expunging of records, reporting of records, and any other similar relief that is intended to correct unlawful practices under this part.

(b) "Age" refers to the chronological age of any individual who has reached a 40th birthday.

(c) Except as provided by Section 12926.05, "employee" does not include any individual employed by that person's parent, spouse, or child or any individual employed under a special license in a nonprofit sheltered workshop or rehabilitation facility.

(d) "Employer" includes any person regularly employing five or more persons, or any person acting as an agent of an employer, directly or indirectly, the state or any political or civil subdivision of the state, and cities, except as follows:

"Employer" does not include a religious association or corporation not organized for private profit.

(e) "Employment agency" includes any person undertaking for compensation to procure employees or opportunities to work.

(f) "Essential functions" means the fundamental job duties of the employment position the individual with a disability holds or desires. "Essential functions" does not include the marginal functions of the position.

(1) A job function may be considered essential for any of several reasons, including, but not limited to, any one or more of the following:

(A) The function may be essential because the reason the position exists is to perform that function.

(B) The function may be essential because of the limited number of employees available among whom the performance of that job function can be distributed.

(C) The function may be highly specialized, so that the incumbent in the position is hired based on expertise or the ability to perform a particular function.

(2) Evidence of whether a particular function is essential includes, but is not limited to, the following:

(A) The employer's judgment as to which functions are essential.

(B) Written job descriptions prepared before advertising or interviewing applicants for the job.

(C) The amount of time spent on the job performing the function.

(D) The consequences of not requiring the incumbent to perform the function.

(E) The terms of a collective bargaining agreement.

(F) The work experiences of past incumbents in the job.

(G) The current work experience of incumbents in similar jobs.

(g)(1) "Genetic information" means, with respect to any individual, information about any of the following:

(A) The individual's genetic tests.

(B) The genetic tests of family members of the individual.

(C) The manifestation of a disease or disorder in family members of the individual.

(2) "Genetic information" includes any request for, or receipt of, genetic services, or participation in clinical research that includes genetic services, by an individual or any family member of the individual.

(3) "Genetic information" does not include information about the sex or age of any individual.

(h) "Labor organization" includes any organization that exists and is constituted for the purpose, in whole or in part, of collective bargaining or of dealing with employers concerning grievances, terms or conditions of employment, or of other mutual aid or protection.

(i) "Medical condition" means either of the following:

(1) Any health impairment related to or associated with a diagnosis of cancer or a record or history of cancer.

(2) Genetic characteristics. For purposes of this section, "genetic characteristics" means either of the following:

(A) Any scientifically or medically identifiable gene or chromosome, or combination or alteration thereof, that is known to be a cause of a disease or disorder in a person or that person's offspring, or that is determined to be associated with a statistically increased risk of development of a disease or disorder, and that is presently not associated with any symptoms of any disease or disorder.

(B) Inherited characteristics that may derive from the individual or family member, that are known to be a cause of a disease or disorder in a person or that person's offspring, or that are determined to be associated with a statistically increased risk of development of a disease or disorder, and that are presently not associated with any symptoms of any disease or disorder.

(j) "Mental disability" includes, but is not limited to, all of the following:

(1) Having any mental or psychological disorder or condition, such as intellectual disability, organic brain syndrome, emotional or mental illness, or specific learning disabilities, that limits a major life activity. For purposes of this section:

(A) "Limits" shall be determined without regard to mitigating measures, such as medications, assistive devices, or reasonable accommodations, unless the mitigating measure itself limits a major life activity.

(B) A mental or psychological disorder or condition limits a major life activity if it makes the achievement of the major life activity difficult.

(C) "Major life activities" shall be broadly construed and shall include physical, mental, and social activities and working.

(2) Any other mental or psychological disorder or condition not described in paragraph (1) that requires special education or related services.

(3) Having a record or history of a mental or psychological disorder or condition described in paragraph (1) or (2), which is known to the employer or other entity covered by this part.

(4) Being regarded or treated by the employer or other entity covered by this part as having, or having had, any mental condition that makes achievement of a major life activity difficult.

(5) Being regarded or treated by the employer or other entity covered by this part as having, or having had, a mental or psychological disorder or condition that has no present disabling effect, but that may become a mental disability as described in paragraph (1) or (2).

"Mental disability" does not include sexual behavior disorders, compulsive gambling, kleptomania, pyromania, or psychoactive substance use disorders resulting from the current unlawful use of controlled substances or other drugs.

(k) "[1] **Veteran or military** status" means a member or veteran of the United States Armed Forces, United States

Armed Forces Reserve, the United States National Guard, and the California National Guard.

(*l*) "On the bases enumerated in this part" means or refers to discrimination on the basis of one or more of the following: race, religious creed, color, national origin, ancestry, physical disability, mental disability, medical condition, genetic information, marital status, sex, age, sexual orientation, or [2] **veteran or military** status.

(m) "Physical disability" includes, but is not limited to, all of the following:

(1) Having any physiological disease, disorder, condition, cosmetic disfigurement, or anatomical loss that does both of the following:

(A) Affects one or more of the following body systems: neurological, immunological, musculoskeletal, special sense organs, respiratory, including speech organs, cardiovascular, reproductive, digestive, genitourinary, hemic and lymphatic, skin, and endocrine.

(B) Limits a major life activity. For purposes of this section:

(i) "Limits" shall be determined without regard to mitigating measures such as medications, assistive devices, prosthetics, or reasonable accommodations, unless the mitigating measure itself limits a major life activity.

(ii) A physiological disease, disorder, condition, cosmetic disfigurement, or anatomical loss limits a major life activity if it makes the achievement of the major life activity difficult.

(iii) "Major life activities" shall be broadly construed and includes physical, mental, and social activities and working.

(2) Any other health impairment not described in paragraph (1) that requires special education or related services.

(3) Having a record or history of a disease, disorder, condition, cosmetic disfigurement, anatomical loss, or health impairment described in paragraph (1) or (2), which is known to the employer or other entity covered by this part.

(4) Being regarded or treated by the employer or other entity covered by this part as having, or having had, any physical condition that makes achievement of a major life activity difficult.

(5) Being regarded or treated by the employer or other entity covered by this part as having, or having had, a disease, disorder, condition, cosmetic disfigurement, anatomical loss, or health impairment that has no present disabling effect but may become a physical disability as described in paragraph (1) or (2).

(6) "Physical disability" does not include sexual behavior disorders, compulsive gambling, kleptomania, pyromania, or psychoactive substance use disorders resulting from the current unlawful use of controlled substances or other drugs.

(n) Notwithstanding subdivisions (j) and (m), if the definition of "disability" used in the federal Americans with Disabilities Act of 1990 (Public Law 101-336) would result in broader protection of the civil rights of individuals with a mental disability or physical disability, as defined in subdivision (j) or (m), or would include any medical condition not included within those definitions, then that broader protection or coverage shall be deemed incorporated by reference into, and shall prevail over conflicting provisions of, the definitions in subdivisions (j) and (m).

(o) "Race, religious creed, color, national origin, ancestry, physical disability, mental disability, medical condition, genetic information, marital status, sex, age, sexual orientation, or [3] **veteran or military** status" includes a perception that the person has any of those characteristics or that the person is associated with a person who has, or is perceived to have, any of those characteristics.

(p) "Reasonable accommodation" may include either of the following:

(1) Making existing facilities used by employees readily accessible to, and usable by, individuals with disabilities.

(2) Job restructuring, part-time or modified work schedules, reassignment to a vacant position, acquisition or modification of equipment or devices, adjustment or modifications of examinations, training materials or policies, the provision of qualified readers or interpreters, and other similar accommodations for individuals with disabilities.

(q) "Religious creed," "religion," "religious observance," "religious belief," and "creed" include all aspects of religious belief, observance, and practice, including religious dress and grooming practices. "Religious dress practice" shall be construed broadly to include the wearing or carrying of religious clothing, head or face coverings, jewelry, artifacts, and any other item that is part of an individual observing a religious creed. "Religious grooming practice" shall be construed broadly to include all forms of head, facial, and body hair that are part of an individual observing a religious creed.

(r)(1) "Sex" includes, but is not limited to, the following:

(A) Pregnancy or medical conditions related to pregnancy.

(B) Childbirth or medical conditions related to childbirth.

(C) Breastfeeding or medical conditions related to breastfeeding.

(2) "Sex" also includes, but is not limited to, a person's gender. "Gender" means sex, and includes a person's gender identity and gender expression. "Gender expression" means a person's gender-related appearance and behavior whether or not stereotypically associated with the person's assigned sex at birth.

(s) "Sexual orientation" means heterosexuality, homosexuality, and bisexuality.

(t) "Supervisor" means any individual having the authority, in the interest of the employer, to hire, transfer, suspend, lay off, recall, promote, discharge, assign, reward, or discipline other employees, or the responsibility to direct them, or to adjust their grievances, or effectively to recommend that action, if, in connection with the foregoing, the exercise of that authority is not of a merely routine or clerical nature, but requires the use of independent judgment.

(u) "Undue hardship" means an action requiring significant difficulty or expense, when considered in light of the following factors:

(1) The nature and cost of the accommodation needed.

(2) The overall financial resources of the facilities involved in the provision of the reasonable accommoda-

tions, the number of persons employed at the facility, and the effect on expenses and resources or the impact otherwise of these accommodations upon the operation of the facility.

(3) The overall financial resources of the covered entity, the overall size of the business of a covered entity with respect to the number of employees, and the number, type, and location of its facilities.

(4) The type of operations, including the composition, structure, and functions of the workforce of the entity.

(5) The geographic separateness or administrative or fiscal relationship of the facility or facilities.

(v) "National origin" discrimination includes, but is not limited to, discrimination on the basis of possessing a driver's license granted under Section 12801.9 of the Vehicle Code.

(w) "Race" is inclusive of traits historically associated with race, including, but not limited to, hair texture and protective hairstyles.

(x) "Protective hairstyles" includes, but is not limited to, such hairstyles as braids, locks, and twists. **Leg.H.** 1980 ch. 992 §4, 1985 ch. 1151 §1, 1990 ch. 15 (SB 1027) §1, 1992 ch. 911 (AB 311) §3, ch. 912 (AB 1286) §3, ch. 913 (AB 1077) §21.3, 1993 ch. 1214 (AB 551) §5, 1998 ch. 99 (SB 654) §1, 1999 ch. 311 (SB 1185) §2, ch. 591 (AB 1670) §5.1, ch. 592 (AB 1001) §3.7, 2000 ch. 1049 (AB 2222) §5, 2003 ch. 164 (AB 196), 2004 ch. 700 (SB 1234), 2011 chs. 261 (SB 559) §9, 719 (AB 887) §14.5, 2012 chs. 287 (AB 1964) §1, 448 (AB 2370) §16, 457 (SB 1381) §16, 701 (AB 2386) §1.5, 2013 chs. 76 (AB 383) §86, 691 (AB 556) §3, 2014 ch. 452 (AB 1660) §1, 2016 ch. 683 (AB 488) §1, 2017 ch. 799 (AB 1556) §3, 2019 ch. 58 (SB 188) §3, 2020 chs. 36 (AB 3364) §32, 370 (SB 1371) §139 (ch. 36 prevails; ch. 370 not effective).

§12926. 2020 Deletes. [1] Military and veteran **[2]** military and veteran **[3]** military and veteran

2012 Note: The amendment of Section 12926 of the Government Code made by this act does not constitute a change in, but is declaratory of, existing law. Stats. 2012 ch. 701 (AB 2386) §2.

Ref.: Hanna § 10.60[4]; Herlick Handbook § 10.70[2], [3][a][i], [b].

§12926.05. Right of employee of nonprofit sheltered workshop, day program, or rehabilitation facility to bring action for harassment or discrimination; affirmative defense.

(a) An individual employed under a special license pursuant to Section 1191 or 1191.5 of the Labor Code in a nonprofit sheltered workshop, day program, or rehabilitation facility may bring an action under this part for any form of harassment or discrimination prohibited by this part.

(b) If an individual specified in subdivision (a) brings an action against an employer for any form of harassment or discrimination prohibited by this part, the employer has an affirmative defense to the action by proving, by a preponderance of evidence, both of the following:

(1) The challenged activity was permitted by statute or regulation.

(2) The challenged activity was necessary to serve employees with disabilities under a special license pursuant to Section 1191 or 1191.5 of the Labor Code.

(c) Nothing in this part relating to discrimination on account of disability shall subject an employer to legal liability for obtaining a license pursuant to Section 1191.5 of the Labor Code or paying an individual with a physical or mental disability less than minimum wage pursuant to either Section 1191 or Section 1191.5 of the Labor Code.

(d) The Legislature finds and declares that the definition of employee in subdivision (c) of Section 12926 was not intended to permit the harassment of, or discrimination against, an individual employed under a special license pursuant to Section 1191 or 1191.5 of the Labor Code in a nonprofit sheltered workshop, day program, or rehabilitation facility. **Leg.H.** 2016 ch. 683 (AB 488) §2.

§12926.1. Physical and mental disabilities.

The Legislature finds and declares as follows:

(a) The law of this state in the area of disabilities provides protections independent from those in the federal Americans with Disabilities Act of 1990 (P.L. 101-336). Although the federal act provides a floor of protection, this state's law has always, even prior to passage of the federal act, afforded additional protections.

(b) The law of this state contains broad definitions of physical disability, mental disability, and medical condition. It is the intent of the Legislature that the definitions of physical disability and mental disability be construed so that applicants and employees are protected from discrimination due to an actual or perceived physical or mental impairment that is disabling, potentially disabling, or perceived as disabling or potentially disabling.

(c) Physical and mental disabilities include, but are not limited to, chronic or episodic conditions such as HIV/AIDS, hepatitis, epilepsy, seizure disorder, diabetes, clinical depression, bipolar disorder, multiple sclerosis, and heart disease. In addition, the Legislature has determined that the definitions of "physical disability" and "mental disability" under the law of this state require a "limitation" upon a major life activity, but do not require, as does the federal Americans with Disabilities Act of 1990, a "substantial limitation." This distinction is intended to result in broader coverage under the law of this state than under that federal act. Under the law of this state, whether a condition limits a major life activity shall be determined without respect to any mitigating measures, unless the mitigating measure itself limits a major life activity, regardless of federal law under the Americans with Disabilities Act of 1990. Further, under the law of this state, "working" is a major life activity, regardless of whether the actual or perceived working limitation implicates a particular employment or a class or broad range of employments.

(d) Notwithstanding any interpretation of law in Cassista v. Community Foods (1993) 5 Cal.4th 1050, the Legislature intends (1) for state law to be independent of the federal Americans with Disabilities Act of 1990, (2) to require a "limitation" rather than a "substantial limitation" of a major life activity, and (3) by enacting paragraph (4) of subdivision (j) and paragraph (4) of subdivision (*l*) of Section 12926, to provide protection when an individual is erroneously or mistakenly believed to have any physical or mental condition that limits a major life activity.

(e) The Legislature affirms the importance of the interactive process between the applicant or employee and the employer in determining a reasonable accommodation, as this requirement has been articulated by the Equal Employment Opportunity Commission in its interpretive guidance of the federal Americans with Disabilities Act of 1990. **Leg.H.** 2000 ch. 1049 (AB 2222) §6, 2011 ch. 261 (SB 559) §10.

§12926.2. Definitions.

As used in this part in connection with unlawful practices, unless a different meaning clearly appears from the context:

(a) "Religious corporation" means any corporation formed under, or otherwise subject to, Part 4 (commencing with Section 9110) or Part 6 (commencing with Section 10000) of Division 2 of Title 1 of the Corporations Code, and also includes a corporation that is formed primarily or exclusively for religious purposes under the laws of any other state to administer the affairs of an organized religious group and that is not organized for private profit.

(b) "Religious duties" means duties of employment connected with carrying on the religious activities of a religious corporation or association.

(c) Notwithstanding subdivision (d) of Section 12926 and except as otherwise provided in subdivision (d) of this section, "employer" includes a religious corporation or association with respect to persons employed by the religious association or corporation to perform duties, other than religious duties, at a health care facility operated by the religious association or corporation for the provision of health care that is not restricted to adherents of the religion that established the association or corporation.

(d) "Employer" does not include a religious corporation with respect to either the employment, including promotion, of an individual of a particular religion, or the application of the employer's religious doctrines, tenets, or teachings, in any work connected with the provision of health care.

(e) Notwithstanding subdivision (d) of Section 12926, "employer" does not include a nonprofit public benefit corporation incorporated to provide health care on behalf of a religious organization under Part 2 (commencing with Section 5110) of Division 2 of Title 1 of the Corporations Code, with respect to employment, including promotion, of an individual of a particular religion in an executive or pastoral-care position connected with the provision of health care.

(f)(1) Notwithstanding any other provision of law, a nonprofit public benefit corporation formed by, or affiliated with, a particular religion and that operates an educational institution as its sole or primary activity, may restrict employment, including promotion, in any or all employment categories to individuals of a particular religion.

(2) Notwithstanding paragraph (1) or any other provision of law, employers that are nonprofit public benefit corporations specified in paragraph (1) shall be subject to the provisions of this part in all other respects, including, but not limited to, the prohibitions against discrimination made unlawful employment practices by this part. **Leg.H.** 1999 ch. 913 (AB 1541) §2, 2001 ch. 910 (SB 504) §1.

CHAPTER 6
DISCRIMINATION PROHIBITED

ARTICLE 1
Unlawful Practices, Generally
[Selected Provisions]

§12940. Unlawful employment practices.

It is an unlawful employment practice, unless based upon a bona fide occupational qualification, or, except where based upon applicable security regulations established by the United States or the State of California:

(a) For an employer, because of the race, religious creed, color, national origin, ancestry, physical disability, mental disability, medical condition, genetic information, marital status, sex, gender, gender identity, gender expression, age, sexual orientation, or [1] **veteran or military** status of any person, to refuse to hire or employ the person or to refuse to select the person for a training program leading to employment, or to bar or to discharge the person from employment or from a training program leading to employment, or to discriminate against the person in compensation or in terms, conditions, or privileges of employment.

(1) This part does not prohibit an employer from refusing to hire or discharging an employee with a physical or mental disability, or subject an employer to any legal liability resulting from the refusal to employ or the discharge of an employee with a physical or mental disability, if the employee, because of a physical or mental disability, is unable to perform the employee's essential duties even with reasonable accommodations, or cannot perform those duties in a manner that would not endanger the employee's health or safety or the health or safety of others even with reasonable accommodations.

(2) This part does not prohibit an employer from refusing to hire or discharging an employee who, because of the employee's medical condition, is unable to perform the employee's essential duties even with reasonable accommodations, or cannot perform those duties in a manner that would not endanger the employee's health or safety or the health or safety of others even with reasonable accommodations. Nothing in this part shall subject an employer to any legal liability resulting from the refusal to employ or the discharge of an employee who, because of the employee's medical condition, is unable to perform the employee's essential duties, or cannot perform those duties in a manner that would not endanger the employee's health or safety or the health or safety of others even with reasonable accommodations.

(3) Nothing in this part relating to discrimination on account of marital status shall do either of the following:

(A) Affect the right of an employer to reasonably regulate, for reasons of supervision, safety, security, or morale, the working of spouses in the same department, division, or facility, consistent with the rules and regulations adopted by the commission.

(B) Prohibit bona fide health plans from providing additional or greater benefits to employees with dependents than to those employees without or with fewer dependents.

(4) Nothing in this part relating to discrimination on account of sex shall affect the right of an employer to use veteran status as a factor in employee selection or to give special consideration to Vietnam-era veterans.

(5)(A) This part does not prohibit an employer from refusing to employ an individual because of the individual's age if the law compels or provides for that refusal. Promotions within the existing staff, hiring or promotion on the basis of experience and training, rehiring on the basis of seniority and prior service with the employer, or hiring under an established recruiting program from high schools, colleges, universities, or trade schools do not, in and of themselves, constitute unlawful employment practices.

(B) The provisions of this part relating to discrimination on the basis of age do not prohibit an employer from providing health benefits or health care reimbursement plans to retired persons that are altered, reduced, or eliminated when the person becomes eligible for Medicare health benefits. This subparagraph applies to all retiree health benefit plans and contractual provisions or practices concerning retiree health benefits and health care reimbursement plans in effect on or after January 1, 2011.

(b) For a labor organization, because of the race, religious creed, color, national origin, ancestry, physical disability, mental disability, medical condition, genetic information, marital status, sex, gender, gender identity, gender expression, age, sexual orientation, or [2] **veteran or military** status of any person, to exclude, expel, or restrict from its membership the person, or to provide only second-class or segregated membership or to discriminate against any person because of the race, religious creed, color, national origin, ancestry, physical disability, mental disability, medical condition, genetic information, marital status, sex, gender, gender identity, gender expression, age, sexual orientation, or [3] **veteran or military** status of the person in the election of officers of the labor organization or in the selection of the labor organization's staff or to discriminate in any way against any of its members or against any employer or against any person employed by an employer.

(c) For any person to discriminate against any person in the selection, termination, training, or other terms or treatment of that person in any apprenticeship training program, any other training program leading to employment, an unpaid internship, or another limited duration program to provide unpaid work experience for that person because of the race, religious creed, color, national origin, ancestry, physical disability, mental disability, medical condition, genetic information, marital status, sex, gender, gender identity, gender expression, age, sexual orientation, or [4] **veteran or military** status of the person discriminated against.

(d) For any employer or employment agency to print or circulate or cause to be printed or circulated any publication, or to make any nonjob-related inquiry of an employee or applicant, either verbal or through use of an application form, that expresses, directly or indirectly, any limitation, specification, or discrimination as to race, religious creed, color, national origin, ancestry, physical disability, mental disability, medical condition, genetic information, marital status, sex, gender, gender identity, gender expression, age, sexual orientation, or [5] **veteran or military** status, or any intent to make any such limitation, specification, or discrimination. This part does not prohibit an employer or employment agency from inquiring into the age of an applicant, or from specifying age limitations, if the law compels or provides for that action.

(e)(1) Except as provided in paragraph (2) or (3), for any employer or employment agency to require any medical or psychological examination of an applicant, to make any medical or psychological inquiry of an applicant, to make any inquiry whether an applicant has a mental disability or physical disability or medical condition, or to make any inquiry regarding the nature or severity of a physical disability, mental disability, or medical condition.

(2) Notwithstanding paragraph (1), an employer or employment agency may inquire into the ability of an applicant to perform job-related functions and may respond to an applicant's request for reasonable accommodation.

(3) Notwithstanding paragraph (1), an employer or employment agency may require a medical or psychological examination or make a medical or psychological inquiry of a job applicant after an employment offer has been made but prior to the commencement of employment duties, provided that the examination or inquiry is job related and consistent with business necessity and that all entering employees in the same job classification are subject to the same examination or inquiry.

(f)(1) Except as provided in paragraph (2), for any employer or employment agency to require any medical or psychological examination of an employee, to make any medical or psychological inquiry of an employee, to make any inquiry whether an employee has a mental disability, physical disability, or medical condition, or to make any inquiry regarding the nature or severity of a physical disability, mental disability, or medical condition.

(2) Notwithstanding paragraph (1), an employer or employment agency may require any examinations or inquiries that it can show to be job related and consistent with business necessity. An employer or employment agency may conduct voluntary medical examinations, including voluntary medical histories, which are part of an employee health program available to employees at that worksite.

(g) For any employer, labor organization, or employment agency to harass, discharge, expel, or otherwise discriminate against any person because the person has made a report pursuant to Section 11161.8 of the Penal Code that prohibits retaliation against hospital employees who report suspected patient abuse by health facilities or community care facilities.

(h) For any employer, labor organization, employment agency, or person to discharge, expel, or otherwise discriminate against any person because the person has opposed any practices forbidden under this part or because the person has filed a complaint, testified, or assisted in any proceeding under this part.

(i) For any person to aid, abet, incite, compel, or coerce the doing of any of the acts forbidden under this part, or to attempt to do so.

(j)(1) For an employer, labor organization, employment agency, apprenticeship training program or any training program leading to employment, or any other person, because of race, religious creed, color, national origin, ancestry, physical disability, mental disability, medical condition, genetic information, marital status, sex, gender, gender identity, gender expression, age, sexual orientation, or [6] **veteran or military** status, to harass an employee, an applicant, an unpaid intern or volunteer, or a person providing services pursuant to a contract. Harassment of an employee, an applicant, an unpaid intern or volunteer, or a person providing services pursuant to a contract by an employee, other than an agent or supervisor, shall be unlawful if the entity, or its agents or supervisors, knows or should have known of this conduct and fails to take immediate and appropriate corrective action. An employer may also be responsible for the acts of nonemployees, with respect to harassment of employees, applicants, unpaid interns or volunteers, or persons providing services pursuant to a contract in the workplace, if the employer, or its agents or supervisors, knows or should have known of the conduct and fails to take immediate and appropriate corrective action. In reviewing cases involving the acts of nonemployees, the extent of the employer's control and any other legal responsibility that the employer may have with respect to the conduct of those nonemployees shall be considered. An entity shall take all reasonable steps to prevent harassment from occurring. Loss of tangible job benefits shall not be necessary in order to establish harassment.

(2) The provisions of this subdivision are declaratory of existing law, except for the new duties imposed on employers with regard to harassment.

(3) An employee of an entity subject to this subdivision is personally liable for any harassment prohibited by this section that is perpetrated by the employee, regardless of whether the employer or covered entity knows or should have known of the conduct and fails to take immediate and appropriate corrective action.

(4)(A) For purposes of this subdivision only, "employer" means any person regularly employing one or more persons or regularly receiving the services of one or more persons providing services pursuant to a contract, or any person acting as an agent of an employer, directly or indirectly, the state, or any political or civil subdivision of the state, and cities. The definition of "employer" in subdivision (d) of Section 12926 applies to all provisions of this section other than this subdivision.

(B) Notwithstanding subparagraph (A), for purposes of this subdivision, "employer" does not include a religious association or corporation not organized for private profit, except as provided in Section 12926.2.

(C) For purposes of this subdivision, "harassment" because of sex includes sexual harassment, gender harassment, and harassment based on pregnancy, childbirth, or related medical conditions. Sexually harassing conduct need not be motivated by sexual desire.

(5) For purposes of this subdivision, "a person providing services pursuant to a contract" means a person who meets all of the following criteria:

(A) The person has the right to control the performance of the contract for services and discretion as to the manner of performance.

(B) The person is customarily engaged in an independently established business.

(C) The person has control over the time and place the work is performed, supplies the tools and instruments used in the work, and performs work that requires a particular skill not ordinarily used in the course of the employer's work.

(k) For an employer, labor organization, employment agency, apprenticeship training program, or any training program leading to employment, to fail to take all reasonable steps necessary to prevent discrimination and harassment from occurring.

(*l*)(1) For an employer or other entity covered by this part to refuse to hire or employ a person or to refuse to select a person for a training program leading to employment or to bar or to discharge a person from employment or from a training program leading to employment, or to discriminate against a person in compensation or in terms, conditions, or privileges of employment because of a conflict between the person's religious belief or observance and any employment requirement, unless the employer or other entity covered by this part demonstrates that it has explored any available reasonable alternative means of accommodating the religious belief or observance, including the possibilities of excusing the person from those duties that conflict with the person's religious belief or observance or permitting those duties to be performed at another time or by another person, but is unable to reasonably accommodate the religious belief or observance without undue hardship, as defined in subdivision (u) of Section 12926, on the conduct of the business of the employer or other entity covered by this part. Religious belief or observance, as used in this section, includes, but is not limited to, observance of a Sabbath or other religious holy day or days, reasonable time necessary for travel prior and subsequent to a religious observance, and religious dress practice and religious grooming practice as described in subdivision (q) of Section 12926. This subdivision shall also apply to an apprenticeship training program, an unpaid internship, and any other program to provide unpaid experience for a person in the workplace or industry.

(2) An accommodation of an individual's religious dress practice or religious grooming practice is not reasonable if the accommodation requires segregation of the individual from other employees or the public.

(3) An accommodation is not required under this subdivision if it would result in a violation of this part or any other law prohibiting discrimination or protecting civil rights, including subdivision (b) of Section 51 of the Civil Code and Section 11135 of this code.

(4) For an employer or other entity covered by this part to, in addition to the employee protections provided pursuant to subdivision (h), retaliate or otherwise discriminate against a person for requesting accommodation under this subdivision, regardless of whether the request was granted.

(m)(1) For an employer or other entity covered by this part to fail to make reasonable accommodation for the known physical or mental disability of an applicant or employee. Nothing in this subdivision or in paragraph (1) or (2) of subdivision (a) shall be construed to require an accommodation that is demonstrated by the employer or other covered entity to produce undue hardship, as defined in subdivision (u) of Section 12926, to its operation.

(2) For an employer or other entity covered by this part to, in addition to the employee protections provided pur-

suant to subdivision (h), retaliate or otherwise discriminate against a person for requesting accommodation under this subdivision, regardless of whether the request was granted.

(n) For an employer or other entity covered by this part to fail to engage in a timely, good faith, interactive process with the employee or applicant to determine effective reasonable accommodations, if any, in response to a request for reasonable accommodation by an employee or applicant with a known physical or mental disability or known medical condition.

(o) For an employer or other entity covered by this part, to subject, directly or indirectly, any employee, applicant, or other person to a test for the presence of a genetic characteristic.

(p) Nothing in this section shall be interpreted as preventing the ability of employers to identify members of the military or veterans for purposes of awarding a veteran's preference as permitted by law. **Leg.H.** 1980 ch. 992 §4, 1981 ch. 11 §1, ch. 270 §1, 1982 ch. 1184 §1, ch. 1193 §2, 1984 ch. 1754 §2, 1985 ch. 1151 §2, 1987 ch. 605 §1, 1989 ch. 1309 §3, 1992 ch. 912 (AB 1286) §5, ch. 913 (AB 1077) §23.1, 1993 ch. 711 (AB 675) §2, 1998 ch. 485 (AB 2803) §85, 1999 chs. 591 (AB 1670) §8, 592 (AB 1001) §7.5, 2000 chs. 1047 (AB 1856) §1, 1049 (AB 2222) §7.5, 2001 ch. 909 (AB 1475) §1, 2002 chs. 525 (AB 1599), 664 (AB 3034) (ch. 525 prevails; ch. 664 not effective), 2003 ch. 671 (AB 76), 2010 ch. 130 (AB 1814) §1, 2011 chs. 261 (SB 559) §14, 719 (AB 887) §18.5, 2012 ch. 287 (AB 1964) §2, 2013 chs. 88 (SB 292) §1, 691 (AB 556) §4.5, 2014 ch. 302 (AB 1443) §1, 2015 ch. 122 (AB 987) §2, 2017 ch. 799 (AB 1556) §6, 2018 ch. 955 (SB 1300) §2, 2020 ch. 36 (AB 3364) §33.

§12940. 2020 Deletes. **[1]** military and veteran **[2]** military and veteran **[3]** military and veteran **[4]** military and veteran **[5]** military and veteran **[6]** military and veteran

2003 Note: It is the intent of the Legislature in enacting this act to construe and clarify the meaning and effect of existing law and to reject the interpretation given to the law in *Salazar v. Diversified Paratransit, Inc.* (2002) 103 Cal.App.4th 131. Stats. 2003 ch. 671 (AB 76) §2.

2002 Note: It is the intent of the Legislature in enacting this act to construe and clarify the meaning and effect of existing law and to reject the interpretation given to the law in *Esberg v. Union Oil Company of California*, 87 Cal.App.4th 378 (2001). Stats. 2002 ch. 525 (AB 1599) §4.

Ref.: Hanna §§ 10.60[4], 11.05[4], 21.03[2][d], 21.07[7]; Herlick Handbook §§ 3.15, 9.12, 10.70[2], [3][a][i], [b], 12.11, 12.13.

DIVISION 5
Personnel

PART 2.6
PERSONNEL ADMINISTRATION

CHAPTER 2
Administration of Salaries

ARTICLE 1
Claims for Reimbursement
[Selected Provisions]

§19820. Adoption of general rules and regulations by the director.

The director shall adopt general rules and regulations doing all of the following:

(a) Limiting the amount, time, and place of expenses and allowances to be paid to officers, employees, experts, and agents of the state while traveling on official state business. The rules and regulations shall provide for reasonable reimbursement to an officer, employee, expert, or agent of the state for expenses incurred by him or her to repair a privately owned vehicle which was damaged through no fault of the officer, employee, expert, or agent, if the damage occurred while the vehicle was used on official state business with the permission or authorization of an employing agency.

As used in this subdivision, "officers and employees of the state" means all officers and employees of the state other than elected state officers, officers and employees of the state provided for in Article VI of the California Constitution, and officers and employees of the California State University. "Officers and employees of the state" is not limited by subdivision (d) of Section 19815.

(b) Governing such matters as are specifically committed to the jurisdiction of the department.

(c) Governing the computation of pay in the case of any employee on a monthly basis salary who is entitled to less than a full month's pay.

If this section is in conflict with a memorandum of understanding reached pursuant to Section 3517.5, the memorandum of understanding shall be controlling without further legislative action, except that if any conflicting provision of a memorandum of understanding requires the expenditure of funds, that provision shall not become effective unless approved by the Legislature in the annual Budget Act. **Leg.H.** 1981 ch. 230 §55, 1982 ch. 1095 §14, 1987 ch. 351 §1.

PART 3
PUBLIC EMPLOYEES' RETIREMENT SYSTEM

CHAPTER 1
GENERAL PROVISIONS AND DEFINITIONS

ARTICLE 2
Definitions
[Selected Provisions]

§20046. "Industrial"; death or disability of members.

"Industrial," in reference to the death or disability of any member of this system who is in a membership category under which special benefits are provided by this part because the death or disability is industrial, means disability or death as a result of injury or disease arising out of and in the course of his or her employment as such a member. **Leg.H.** 1995 ch. 379 §2 (former §20038).

CHAPTER 2
ADMINISTRATION OF SYSTEM

ARTICLE 2
Powers and Duties of the Board
[Selected Provisions]

§20130. Representation of retirement system before Appeals Board; determination of disability.

The board may enter into an agreement with the State Compensation Insurance Fund under which the latter shall represent this system, as its agent, or the Attorney General under which the latter shall represent this system, in proceedings instituted or to be instituted before the Workers' Compensation Appeals Board as may be referred to it by the board to determine whether the death or disability of a member is industrial. The agreed cost of this service and the expenses incidental thereto shall be paid from the retirement fund, except that there shall be no charge to this system by the Attorney General in cases involving members of this system who are employees of the General Fund state agencies. **Leg.H.** 1995 ch. 379 §2 (former §20126).

ARTICLE 8
Subrogation

§20250. Right of subrogation—Limitation.

The provisions of this article shall be deemed to create a right of subrogation only to amounts paid as disability retirement allowances and special death benefits. **Leg.H.** 1995 ch. 379 §2 (former §21456).

§20251. "State fund."

As used in this article, "state fund" means the State Compensation Insurance Fund. **Leg.H.** 1995 ch. 379 §2 (former §21450).

§20252. Amounts recoverable from third person.

If benefits are payable under this part because of an injury to or the death of a member and the injury or death is the proximate consequence of the act of a person other than his or her employer (the state or the employing contracting agency), the board may on behalf of this system recover from that person an amount that is the lesser of the following:

(1) An amount that is equal to one-half of the actuarial equivalent of the benefits for which this system is liable because of such injury or death.

(2) An amount that is equal to one-half of the remaining balance of the amount recovered after allowance of that amount that the employer or its insurance carrier have paid or become obligated to pay. **Leg.H.** 1995 ch. 379 §2 (former §21451).

§20253. Contracts with state fund or Attorney General for third-party recovery.

The board may contract with the state fund or the Attorney General for the recovery on behalf of this system of any amounts that the board might recover from third persons under this article or Chapter 5 (commencing with Section 3850) of Part 1 of Division 4 of the Labor Code, or that an insurer might recover under Section 11662 of the Insurance Code, or otherwise.

Under the contract, the state fund, in its own name or in the name of the board, or the Attorney General for the board, may, to recover the amounts regardless of whether the injury or death is industrial, commence and prosecute actions, file liens, or intervene in court proceedings all in the same manner and to the same extent, provided in Chapter 5 (commencing with Section 3850) of Part 1 of Division 4 of the Labor Code, for the state fund or employer, except that the recovery shall not be made from benefits payable under this part because of the injury or death. The state fund or the Attorney General, as the case may be, may compromise claims before or after commencement of suit or entry of judgment for the amount as may be approved by a person duly authorized by the board for that purpose. The agreed cost of the service and the expense incidental thereto is a proper charge against the retirement fund. **Leg.H.** 1995 ch. 379 §2 (former §21452).

§20254. Application of amounts recovered by subrogation.

Any amount recovered by way of subrogation by the employer, workers' compensation insurer or this system shall be applied first to the amounts that the employer or its insurer has paid or become obligated to pay. The balance of the amount recovered as specified in Section 20252 shall be paid to, or retained by, this system. **Leg.H.** 1995 ch. 379 §2 (former §21454).

§20255. Statute of limitations.

Actions brought by the board under this article shall be commenced within three years after the liability of this system to pay benefits is fixed. Liability of this system is fixed at the time the board approves the payment of benefits under this part. **Leg.H.** 1995 ch. 379 §2 (former §21455).

CHAPTER 12
RETIREMENT FROM EMPLOYMENT

ARTICLE 6
Disability Retirement
[Selected Provisions]

§21150. Retirement of incapacitated member.

(a) A member incapacitated for the performance of duty shall be retired for disability pursuant to this chapter if he or she is credited with five years of state service, regardless of age, unless the person has elected to become subject to Section 21076, 21076.5, or 21077.

(b) A member subject to Section 21076, 21076.5, or 21077 who becomes incapacitated for the performance of duty shall be retired for disability pursuant to this chapter if he or she is credited with 10 years of state service, regardless of age, except that a member may retire for disability if he or she had five years of state service prior to January 1, 1985.

(c) For purposes of this section, "state service" includes service to the state for which the member, pursuant to Section 20281.5, did not receive credit. **Leg.H.** 1995 ch. 379 (SB 541) §2, 2006 ch. 118 (AB 2244) §9, 2007 ch. 130 (AB 299) §124, 2013 ch. 526 (SB 220) §23.

§21151. Members subject to mandatory retirement for incapacity resulting from industrial disability.

(a) Any patrol, state safety, state industrial, state peace officer/firefighter, or local safety member incapacitated for the performance of duty as the result of an industrial disability shall be retired for disability, pursuant to this chapter, regardless of age or amount of service.

(b) This section also applies to local miscellaneous members if the contracting agency employing those members elects to be subject to this section by amendment to its contract.

(c) This section also applies to all of the following:

(1) State miscellaneous members employed by the Department of Justice who perform the duties now performed in positions with the class title of Criminalist (Class Code 8466), or Senior Criminalist (Class Code 8478), or

Criminalist Supervisor (Class Code 8477), or Criminalist Manager (Class Code 8467), Latent Print Analyst I (Class Code 8460), Latent Print Analyst II (Class Code 8472), or Latent Print Supervisor (Class Code 8473).

(2) State miscellaneous members employed by the Department of the California Highway Patrol who perform the duties now performed in positions with the class title of Communications Operator I, California Highway Patrol (Class Code 1663), Communications Operator II, California Highway Patrol (Class Code 1664), Communications Supervisor I, California Highway Patrol (Class Code 1662), or Communications Supervisor II, California Highway Patrol (Class Code 1665).

(3) State miscellaneous members whose disability resulted under the conditions specified in Sections 20046.5 and 20047.

(4) State miscellaneous members in State Bargaining Unit 12 employed by the Department of Transportation, if a memorandum of understanding has been agreed to by the state employer and the recognized employee organization making this paragraph applicable to those members.

(d) This section does not apply to local safety members described in Section 20423.6, unless this section has been made applicable to local miscellaneous members pursuant to subdivision (b).

(e) This section does not apply to state safety members described in Section 20401.5. **Leg.H.** 1995 ch. 379 (SB 541) §2, 1996 chs. 906 (SB 1859) §137, 907 (SB 2039) §7, 1997 ch. 951 (AB 1595) §5, 2002 chs. 1152 (AB 2023), 1153 (SB 1984) §1.5, 2005 ch. 328 (AB 1166) §7.

Ref.: Hanna §§ 3.116[1], 33.02[4][a].

§21153. Required application by employer.

Notwithstanding any other provision of law, an employer may not separate because of disability a member otherwise eligible to retire for disability but shall apply for disability retirement of any member believed to be disabled, unless the member waives the right to retire for disability and elects to withdraw contributions or to permit contributions to remain in the fund with rights to service retirement as provided in Section 20731. **Leg.H.** 1995 ch. 379 (SB 541) §2.

§21154. Application for retirement for disability.

The application shall be made only (a) while the member is in state service, or (b) while the member for whom contributions will be made under Section 20997, is absent on military service, or (c) within four months after the discontinuance of the state service of the member, or while on an approved leave of absence, or (d) while the member is physically or mentally incapacitated to perform duties from the date of discontinuance of state service to the time of application or motion. On receipt of an application for disability retirement of a member, other than a local safety member with the exception of a school safety member, the board shall, or of its own motion it may, order a medical examination of a member who is otherwise eligible to retire for disability to determine whether the member is incapacitated for the performance of duty. On receipt of the application with respect to a local safety member other than a school safety member, the board shall request the governing body of the contracting agency employing the member to make the determination. **Leg.H.** 1995 ch. 379 §2 (former §21024).

§21155. Medical examination; reimbursement for expenses.

If the board requests a person to submit to a medical examination, he or she shall be entitled to reimbursement for expenses of transportation, and meals and lodging incident to the examination if he or she is required to travel more than 50 miles one way. Standard per diem rates in effect for state employees as authorized by current law shall be used for the reimbursement; provided, that higher costs of lodging may be paid if supported by receipt and determined necessary by the board. "Expenses of transportation" with respect to the use of private transportation includes mileage fees from the person's home to the place of examination and back to a maximum of 300 miles round trip or within the state at the appropriate current rate per mile authorized to state employees for use of private vehicles in accordance with current law plus bridge tolls. The per diem and mileage may be paid to the person by this system at the time he or she is given notification of the time and place of examination. **Leg.H.** 1995 ch. 379 §2 (former §21024.1), 1996 chs. 320, 907.

§21156. When board to retire member for disability; retirement for service in lieu of retirement for disability; competent medical evidence; appeal.

(a)(1) If the medical examination and other available information show to the satisfaction of the board, or in case of a local safety member, other than a school safety member, the governing body of the contracting agency employing the member, that the member in the state service is incapacitated physically or mentally for the performance of his or her duties and is eligible to retire for disability, the board shall immediately retire him or her for disability, unless the member is qualified to be retired for service and applies therefor prior to the effective date of his or her retirement for disability or within 30 days after the member is notified of his or her eligibility for retirement on account of disability, in which event the board shall retire the member for service.

(2) In determining whether a member is eligible to retire for disability, the board or governing body of the contracting agency shall make a determination on the basis of competent medical opinion and shall not use disability retirement as a substitute for the disciplinary process.

(b)(1) The governing body of a contracting agency upon receipt of the request of the board pursuant to Section 21154 shall certify to the board its determination under this section that the member is or is not incapacitated.

(2) The local safety member may appeal the determination of the governing body. Appeal hearings shall be conducted by an administrative law judge of the Office of Administrative Hearings pursuant to Chapter 5 (commencing with Section 11500) of Part 1 of Division 3 of this title. **Leg.H.** 1995 ch. 379 (SB 541), 2006 ch. 118 (AB 2244) §10, 2008 ch. 370 (AB 2023) §3.

Ref.: Hanna § 3.114[2].

§21157. Time limit for contracting agency to make determination as to local safety member.

The governing body of a contracting agency shall make its determination within six months of the date of the receipt by the contracting agency of the request by the board pursuant to Section 21154 for a determination with respect to a local safety member.

A local safety member may waive the requirements of this section. **Leg.H.** 1995 ch. 379 (SB 541) §2.

§21158. Time allowed for determination relating to state peace officer/firefighter, state patrol member, or state safety member.

Upon the receipt by the board of an application for disability retirement with respect to a state peace officer/firefighter member, state patrol member, or a state safety member, the board shall inform both the employer and the member of all information required for the board to make its determination. The board shall make its determination within three months of the receipt by the board of all information required to make a determination for disability retirement on an application submitted by a state peace officer/firefighter member, state patrol member, or a state safety member for disability retirement pursuant to this article. **Leg.H.** 1995 ch. 379 (SB 541) §2.

§21163. Retirement of member granted or entitled to sick leave or entitled to compensating time off for overtime.

Notwithstanding any other provision of this article, the retirement of a member who has been granted or is entitled to sick leave or who is entitled to compensating time off for overtime, shall not become effective until the expiration of the sick leave with compensation and the expiration of the compensating time off with compensation, unless the member applies for or consents to his or her retirement as of an earlier date, or unless, with respect to sick leave, the provisions of a local ordinance or resolution or the rules or regulations of the employer provide to the contrary. This section shall also be applicable to a state member who participates in the annual leave program and who has been granted annual leave for the reasons applicable to sick leave. **Leg.H.** 1995 ch. 379 (SB 541) §2.

§21164. Disability retirement of local safety member.

Notwithstanding any other provision of this article, the retirement for disability of a local safety member, other than a school safety member, shall not be effective without the member's consent earlier than the date upon which leave of absence without loss of salary under Section 4850 of the Labor Code because of the disability terminates, or the earlier date during the leave as of which the disability is permanent and stationary as found by the Workers' Compensation Appeals Board. **Leg.H.** 1995 ch. 379 §2 (former §21025.4).

§21166. Determination of industrial disability; limitation on Appeals Board jurisdiction.

If a member is entitled to a different disability retirement allowance according to whether the disability is industrial or nonindustrial and the member claims that the disability as found by the board, or in the case of a local safety member by the governing body of his or her employer, is industrial and the claim is disputed by the board, or in case of a local safety member by the governing body, the Workers' Compensation Appeals Board, using the same procedure as in workers' compensation hearings, shall determine whether the disability is industrial.

The jurisdiction of the Workers' Compensation Appeals Board shall be limited solely to the issue of industrial causation, and this section shall not be construed to authorize the Workers' Compensation Appeals Board to award costs against this system pursuant to Section 4600, 5811, or any other provision of the Labor Code. **Leg.H.** 1995 ch. 379 §2 (former §21026).

§21167. Petition for rehearing; grounds.

At any time within 20 days after the service of any findings of fact by the Workers' Compensation Appeals Board under this part, any party aggrieved thereby, or the board, may petition for a rehearing upon one or more of the following grounds, and no other:

(a) That the Workers' Compensation Appeals Board acted without or in excess of its powers.

(b) That the findings of fact were procured by fraud.

(c) That the evidence does not justify the findings of fact.

(d) That the petitioner has discovered new evidence material to him or her, that he or she could not, with reasonable diligence, have discovered and produced at the hearing. **Leg.H.** 1995 ch. 379 §2 (former §21026.1).

§21168. Petition for rehearing denied or granted; application for writ of review.

Within 30 days after the petition for rehearing is denied, or, if the petition is granted, within 30 days after the rendition of amended findings of fact on rehearing, any person affected thereby, including this system, may apply to the Supreme Court or to the court of appeal of the appellate district in which he or she resides, for a writ of review, for the purpose of inquiring into and determining the lawfulness of the findings of the Workers' Compensation Appeals Board. **Leg.H.** 1995 ch. 379 §2 (former §21026.2).

§21169. Evidence on writ of review; Appeals Board record.

The writ of review shall be made returnable not later than 30 days after the date of issuance thereof, and shall direct the Workers' Compensation Appeals Board to certify its record in the case to the court. On the return day the cause shall be heard in the court unless continued for good cause. No new or additional evidence shall be introduced in the court, but the cause shall be heard on the record of the appeals board, as certified to by it. **Leg.H.** 1995 ch. 379 §2 (former §21026.3).

§21170. Scope of review.

The review by the court shall not be extended further than to determine whether the Workers' Compensation Appeals Board acted without or in excess of its powers, or unreasonably, or whether its act was procured by fraud. **Leg.H.** 1995 ch. 379 §2 (former §21026.4).

§21171. Appeals Board continuing jurisdiction.

The Workers' Compensation Appeals Board shall have continuing jurisdiction over its determinations made under Section 21166 and may at any time within five years of the date of injury, upon notice and after an opportunity to be heard is given to the parties in interest, rescind, alter, or amend the determination, good cause appearing therefor. **Leg.H.** 1995 ch. 379 §2 (former §21026.5).

§21173. Delegation of authority.

The governing body of a contracting agency may delegate any authority or duty conferred or imposed under this article to a subordinate officer subject to conditions it may impose. **Leg.H.** 1995 ch. 379 (SB 541) §2.

§21174. Subsequent determination that disability is industrial.

If it is not claimed that the disability is industrial or if the claim is made and the member so requests, the board shall proceed with retirement and with the payment of the benefits as are payable when disability is not industrial. If the Workers' Compensation Appeals Board subsequently determines that disability is industrial, an amount equal to the benefits paid shall be deducted from the benefits payable under this system because of the determination. No additional benefits shall be payable, however, because disability is determined to be industrial unless the application for that determination is filed with the Workers' Compensation Appeals Board or in the office of this system in Sacramento, for transmission to the Workers' Compensation Appeals Board within two years after the effective date of the member's retirement. **Leg.H.** 1995 ch. 379 §2 (former §21027).

§21175. Refusal to submit to medical examination.

If any recipient of a disability retirement allowance under the minimum age for voluntary retirement for service applicable to members of his or her class refuses to submit to medical examination the pension portions of his or her allowance may be discontinued until his or her withdrawal of the refusal. If the refusal continues for one year his or her disability retirement allowance may be canceled. **Leg.H.** 1995 ch. 379 (SB 541) §2.

ARTICLE 7
Reinstatement from Retirement

§21190. Reinstatement and employment of retiree.

A person who has been retired under this system for service may be reinstated from retirement by the board as provided in this article, and thereafter may be employed by the state or by a contracting agency in accordance with the laws governing that service, in the same manner as a person who has not been so retired. **Leg.H.** 1995 ch. 379 (SB 541) §2.

§21191. Reinstatement of person retired for disability.

Subject to Sections 21197 and 21201, notwithstanding any other provision of law to the contrary, a person who has been retired under this system for industrial disability shall be reinstated from retirement pursuant to this article, upon his or her application to the board, if, upon reinstatement, he or she will be employed by the state or any contracting agency as a state or local miscellaneous member. **Leg.H.** 1995 ch. 379 (SB 541) §2.

§21192. Disability retirement recipient under minimum age for voluntary retirement; medical examination; application for reinstatement.

The board, or in case of a local safety member, other than a school safety member, the governing body of the employer from whose employment the person was retired, may require any recipient of a disability retirement allowance under the minimum age for voluntary retirement for service applicable to members of his or her class to undergo medical examination, and upon his or her application for reinstatement, shall cause a medical examination to be made of the recipient who is at least six months less than the age of compulsory retirement for service applicable to members of the class or category in which it is proposed to employ him or her. The board, or in case of a local safety member, other than a school safety member, the governing body of the employer from whose employment the person was retired, shall also cause the examination to be made upon application for reinstatement to the position held at retirement or any position in the same class, of a person who was incapacitated for performance of duty in the position at the time of a prior reinstatement to another position. The examination shall be made by a physician or surgeon, appointed by the board or the governing body of the employer, at the place of residence of the recipient or other place mutually agreed upon. Upon the basis of the examination, the board or the governing body shall determine whether he or she is still incapacitated, physically or mentally, for duty in the state agency, the university, or contracting agency, where he or she was employed and in the position held by him or her when retired for disability, or in a position in the same classification, and for the duties of the position with regard to which he or she has applied for reinstatement from retirement. **Leg.H.** 1995 ch. 379 (SB 541) §2.

§21193. Cancellation of allowance and reinstatement to position, on determination that recipient not incapacitated.

If the determination pursuant to Section 21192 is that the recipient is not so incapacitated for duty in the position held when retired for disability or in a position in the same classification or in the position with regard to which he or she has applied for reinstatement and his or her employer offers to reinstate that employee, his or her disability retirement allowance shall be canceled immediately, and he or she shall become a member of this system.

If the recipient was an employee of the state or of the university and is so determined to be not incapacitated for duty in the position held when retired for disability or in a position in the same class, he or she shall be reinstated, at

Misc. Provisions

his or her option, to that position. However, in that case, acceptance of any other position shall immediately terminate any right to reinstatement. A recipient who is found to continue to be incapacitated for duty in his or her former position and class, but not incapacitated for duty in another position for which he or she has applied for reinstatement and who accepts employment in the other position, shall upon subsequent discontinuance of incapacity for service in his or her former position or a position in the same class, as determined by the board under Section 21192, be reinstated at his or her option to that position.

If the recipient was an employee of a contracting agency other than a local safety member, with the exception of a school safety member, the board shall notify it that his or her disability has terminated and that he or she is eligible for reinstatement to duty. The fact that he or she was retired for disability does not prejudice any right to reinstatement to duty which he or she may claim. **Leg.H.** 1995 ch. 379 (SB 541) §2.

Ref.: Hanna § 3.116[3].

§21194. Reinstatement from partial retirement.

A person who has been partially retired under this system pursuant to Article 1.7 (commencing with Section 19996.30) of Chapter 7 of Part 2.6 or pursuant to Sections 21110 through 21115 may be reinstated from partial retirement by the board as provided in this article, and thereafter may continue to be employed on a full-time basis by the state, in the same manner as a person who has not been so retired. **Leg.H.** 1995 ch. 379 (SB 541) §2.

§21195. Reinstatement requirements.

(a) Notwithstanding any other section in Article 6 (commencing with Section 21150) or in this article, the Department of Human Resources may reinstate a person who has retired for industrial disability pursuant to Section 21410, within 12 months after the effective date of retirement, if it has identified an available position with duties that the employee is able to perform. Upon reinstatement, the person shall become entitled to benefits under the partial disability retirement program pursuant to Section 21160.

(b) This section shall not apply to any job-related or job-incurred illness or injury that occurs on or after January 1, 2000. **Leg.H.** 1995 ch. 379 (SB 541) §2, 2000 ch. 402 (AB 649) §18, effective September 11, 2000, see this section as modified in Governor's Reorganization Plan No. 1 §147 of 2011, 2012 ch. 665 (SB 1308) §130.

2012 Note: Stats. 2012 ch. 665 (SB 1308) enacts the statutory changes necessary to reflect the changes made by the Governor's Reorganization Plan No. 1 of 2011.

2011 Note: 2011 Governor's Reorganization Plan No. 1 was submitted to the Legislature on June 9, 2011, and became effective September 9, 2011, pursuant to Gov C §12080.5, and substantively operative July 1, 2012.

§21196. Reinstatement procedure.

The board may reinstate a person from retirement upon (a) his or her application to the board for reinstatement and (b) the determination of the board that his or her age at the date of application for reinstatement is at least six months less than the age of compulsory retirement for service applicable to members of the class or category in which it is proposed to employ him or her. The provisions of clause (b) of this section shall apply only to patrol, state peace officer/firefighters, and safety members. The effective date of reinstatement for purposes of this article shall be the first day of compensated employment following approval of reinstatement. **Leg.H.** 1995 chs. 379 (SB 541), 850 (SB 860), 1996 ch. 906 (SB 1859) §135 (former §21101).

§21197. Reinstatement procedure for person retired for disability.

The board may reinstate a person from industrial disability retirement to a miscellaneous member position upon all of the following:

(a) His or her application to the board for reinstatement.

(b) The determination of the board, based upon medical examination, that he or she is not incapacitated for the duties to be assigned to him or her.

(c) The determination of the board that the employer from whose employment the person was retired for industrial disability has been furnished a notice of intent to reinstate that person, that contains information that he or she may be entitled to resume an industrial disability retirement allowance using the salaries earnable under the miscellaneous member position upon termination of the miscellaneous member employment. **Leg.H.** 1995 ch. 379 (SB 541) §2.

§21198. Reinstatement after involuntary termination of employment.

A person who has been retired under this system for service following an involuntary termination of his or her employment, and who is subsequently reinstated to that employment pursuant to an administrative or judicial proceeding, shall be reinstated from retirement. The requirements of Section 21196 shall not apply to that reinstatement. Reinstatement shall be effective as of the date from which salary is awarded in the administrative or judicial proceedings, and his or her rights and obligations shall be as specified in this article. However, amounts paid to the person during retirement for any period after the date from which salary is awarded, shall be repaid by him or her to this system, and contributions shall be made for any period for which salary is awarded in the administrative or judicial proceedings in the amount that he or she would have contributed had his or her employment not been terminated, and he or she shall receive credit as state service for the period for which salary is awarded. **Leg.H.** 1995 ch. 379 (SB 541) §2, 1996 ch. 906 (SB 1859) §142.

§21199. Reinstatement if person will be appointed to position by Governor.

A person who has been retired under this system for service may be reinstated from retirement pursuant to this article, without regard to the requirements of Section 21196, upon his or her application to the board, if, upon reinstatement, he or she will be appointed by the Governor to any state office or employment. **Leg.H.** 1995 ch. 379 (SB 541) §2.

§21200. Cancellation of retirement allowance; crediting account; future rate of contribution and allowance.

When any person is reinstated from retirement under this article, his or her retirement allowance shall be canceled immediately, and he or she shall become a member of this system as of the date of reinstatement. His or her individual account shall be credited with an amount that is the actuarial equivalent of his or her annuity at the date of reinstatement, not to exceed the amount of his or her accumulated contributions as it was at the date of retirement. His or her future rate of contributions and his or her retirement allowance upon subsequent retirement shall be determined in accordance with Chapter 8 (commencing with Section 20670) and Chapter 13 (commencing with Section 21250), respectively.

The actuarial equivalent under this section shall be adjusted by the board every 10 years, or more frequently, to agree with the interest rate and mortality tables in effect at the commencement of each such 10-year or succeeding interval. **Leg.H.** 1995 ch. 379 (SB 541) §2, 1996 ch. 906 (SB 1859) §143.

§21201. Cancellation of allowance for person reinstated from disability retirement.

When any person is reinstated from industrial disability retirement under Sections 21191 and 21197, his or her retirement allowance shall be canceled immediately, and he or she shall become a member of this system as of the date of reinstatement. His or her individual account shall be credited with an amount that is the actuarial equivalent of his or her annuity at the date of reinstatement, not to exceed the amount of his or her accumulated contributions as it was at the date of retirement. Upon subsequent retirement, the board shall resume the payment of his or her previous industrial disability retirement allowance using the highest compensation earnable during any period of membership, notwithstanding Section 20036, to recalculate the industrial disability retirement allowance. The member shall receive, in addition to the disability retirement allowance from the employment in which he or she was granted the industrial disability retirement, an annuity purchased with his or her accumulated normal contributions made in respect to other employment covered by this system. If the member is qualified for service retirement, he or she shall receive his or her service retirement allowance, in lieu of the industrial retirement allowance, if the service retirement allowance is greater. **Leg.H.** 1995 ch. 379 (SB 541) §2, 1999 ch. 785 (AB 813) §7.

§21202. Reinstatement of unlawfully employed retiree.

A person employed in violation of Section 21220 shall be reinstated to membership in the category in which, and on the date on which, the unlawful employment occurred. **Leg.H.** 1995 ch. 379 (SB 541) §2.

§21203. Reinstatement of employee with special qualifications.

A person who has been retired under this system for service may be reinstated from retirement pursuant to this article, without regard to the requirements of Section 21196, upon his or her application to the board if both of the following conditions occur:

(a) Upon reinstatement, he or she will be appointed by a state board or commission to the position to which the board or commission is entitled to appoint an employee exempt from civil service under the provisions of Article VII of the California Constitution.

(b) In the judgment of the board or commission he or she has special knowledge, experience and qualifications respecting the activities of the board or commission. **Leg.H.** 1995 ch. 379 (SB 541) §2.

CHAPTER 13
RETIREMENT BENEFITS

ARTICLE 1
General Provisions
[Selected Provisions]

§21257. No modification due to workers' compensation benefits received.

The benefits payable after August 4, 1943 under this system shall not be modified on account of any amounts paid to a retired member or beneficiary under Division 4 (commencing with Section 3200) of the Labor Code. **Leg.H.** 1995 ch. 379 §2 (former §21202).

ARTICLE 5
Disability Retirement Benefits
[Selected Provisions]

§21413. Local safety member retired for industrial disability.

Upon retirement of a local safety member for industrial disability he or she shall receive a disability retirement allowance of 50 percent of his or her final compensation plus an annuity purchased with his or her accumulated additional contributions, if any, or, if qualified for service retirement, he or she shall receive his or her service retirement allowance if the allowance, after deducting the annuity, is greater. **Leg.H.** 1995 ch. 379 (SB 541) §2.

§21416. Disability allowance for state safety member; retroactive payments.

Notwithstanding any provision of this part, a state safety member employed by the Department of Corrections or the Department of the Youth Authority with 25 years or more of service credit as such, shall, upon retirement on or after January 1, 1982, for industrial disability, receive the disability allowance provided for in Section 21411 or a disability allowance equal to 1/50th of final compensation multiplied by the number of years of state safety member service in the Department of Corrections or the Department of the Youth Authority with which the member is credited at retirement.

This section shall not become operative for any eligible member, until it is first agreed to in a memorandum of understanding reached between the state and the exclusive representatives of the employees in State Bargaining Unit No. 6 pursuant to Chapter 10.3 (commencing with Section

3512) of Division 4 of Title 1, and approved by the Legislature pursuant to law.

Payment of benefits pursuant to this section for any eligible member shall be retroactive to the effective date of the retirement of the member. **Leg.H.** 1995 ch. 379 §2 (former §21292.51).

§21419. Deduction of advanced disability payments from retroactive disability allowance.

This system shall deduct the amount of advanced disability pension payments made to a local safety member pursuant to Section 4850.3 or 4850.4 of the Labor Code from the member's retroactive disability allowance, and reimburse the local agency that has made the advanced disability pension payments. If the retroactive disability allowance is not sufficient to reimburse the total advanced disability pension payments, an amount no greater than 10 percent of the member's monthly disability allowance shall be deducted and reimbursed to the local agency until the total advanced disability pension payments have been repaid. The local safety member and this system may agree to any other arrangement or schedule for the member to repay the advanced disability pension payments. **Leg.H.** 1995 ch. 379 (SB 541), 2002 ch. 877 (AB 2131).

Ref.: See Labor Code § 4850.4; Hanna § 3.114[2].

§21430. Increased industrial disability allowance of local members based on percentage disability determined by Workers' Compensation Appeals Board subject to employer election.

Upon retirement of a local safety member for industrial disability, the member shall receive in lieu of the allowance otherwise provided by this article a disability retirement allowance in the amount of the percentage of final compensation equal to the percentage of permanent disability determined by the Workers' Compensation Appeals Board for the purposes of permanent disability payments pursuant to Article 3 (commencing with Section 4650) of Chapter 2 of Part 2 of the Labor Code with respect solely to the injury resulting in the disability retirement and giving effect to Section 4750 of the Labor Code, but not less than 50 percent nor in excess of 90 percent of the member's final compensation.

This section shall not apply to any contracting agency nor to the employees of any contracting agency unless and until the agency elects to be subject to the provisions of this section by amendment to its contract made in the manner prescribed for approval of contracts, or in the case of contracts made after June 14, 1975, by express provision in such contract making the contracting agency subject to the provisions of this section.

This section shall only apply to members who retire for disability on and after the date the agency elects to be subject to this section. **Leg.H.** 1995 ch. 379 (SB 541) §2.

Ref.: Hanna § 33.02[4][a].

CHAPTER 14
DEATH BENEFITS

ARTICLE 2
Preretirement Death Benefits
[Selected Provisions]

§21537. Special death benefit; industrial death; determination by Appeals Board; limitations on jurisdiction; applicability.

(a) The special death benefit is payable if the deceased was a patrol, state peace officer/firefighter, state safety, state industrial, or local safety member, if his or her death was industrial and if there is a survivor who qualifies under subdivision (b) of Section 21541. The Workers' Compensation Appeals Board, using the same procedures as in workers' compensation hearings, shall in disputed cases determine whether the death of a member was industrial.

(b) The jurisdiction of the Workers' Compensation Appeals Board shall be limited solely to the issue of industrial causation, and this section shall not be construed to authorize the Workers' Compensation Appeals Board to award costs against this system pursuant to Section 4600, 5811, or any other provision of the Labor Code.

(c) This section does not apply to state safety members described in Section 20401.5 or local safety members described in Section 20423.6.

(d)(1) For purposes of this section, the special death benefit is payable as of the effective date of the industrial disability retirement of the member if the death of the member occurred from a single event injury arising out of and in the course of his or her official duties which, based on competent medical opinion, rendered the member into a persistent vegetative state devoid of cognitive function at the time of injury until the time of death.

(2) This subdivision applies only to a member who retired and then died on or after July 3, 2006. **Leg.H.** 1995 ch. 379 §2 (former §21363), 2002 ch. 1152 (AB 2023), 2008 ch. 74 (AB 2156) §1.

§21537.5. [See Subdivision (c) for Operative Information] Special death benefit for state miscellaneous member in State Bargaining Unit 12.

(a) The special death benefit is payable if the deceased was a state miscellaneous member in State Bargaining Unit 12 employed by the Department of Transportation, if his or her death occurred as a direct result of injury arising out of and in the course of his or her official duties with the department working on the California highway system performing highway maintenance, and if there is a survivor who qualifies under subdivision (b) of Section 21541. The Workers' Compensation Appeals Board, using the same procedures as in workers' compensation hearings, shall in disputed cases determine whether the death of the member occurred as a result of that injury.

(b) The jurisdiction of the Workers' Compensation Appeals Board shall be limited solely to the issue of industrial causation, and this section may not be construed to authorize the Workers' Compensation Appeals Board to award costs against this system pursuant to Section 4600, 5811, or any other provision of the Labor Code.

(c) This section shall not become operative unless and until a memorandum of understanding has been agreed to by the state employer and the recognized employee organization making this section applicable to those members described in subdivision (a). **Leg.H.** 2002 ch. 1153 (SB 1984), 2006 ch. 210 (SB 357) §6, effective September 6, 2006.

§21538. Special death benefit for appointed state member.

The special death benefit is also payable if the deceased was a state member appointed by the Governor, the Director of Corrections, or the Board of Prison Terms, if his or her death occurred as a result of injury or disease arising out of and in the course of his or her official duties within a state prison or facility of the Department of Corrections, and if there is a survivor who qualifies under subdivision (b) of Section 21541. The Workers' Compensation Appeals Board, using the same procedure as in workers' compensation hearings, shall in disputed cases determine whether the death of the member occurred as a result of the injury or disease.

The jurisdiction of the Workers' Compensation Appeals Board shall be limited solely to the issue of industrial causation, and this section shall not be construed to authorize the Workers' Compensation Appeals Board to award costs against this system pursuant to Section 4600 or 5811 or any other provision of the Labor Code. **Leg.H.** 1995 ch. 379 §2 (former §21363.3).

§21540. Special death benefit for appointed state member—Death resulting from conduct of correctional institution inmate.

The special death benefit is also payable if the deceased was the Secretary of the Youth and Adult Corrections Agency, or was a state member appointed by the Secretary of the Youth and Adult Corrections Agency, the Department of the Youth Authority, the Superintendent of the California Institution for Women, or the Women's Board of Terms and Paroles, the Board of Corrections, or was a member of the Board of Corrections or the Department of the Youth Authority not already classified as a prison member, provided that his or her death occurred as a result of misconduct of an inmate of a state prison, correctional school, or facility of the Department of Corrections or the Department of the Youth Authority, or a parolee therefrom.

The special death benefit provided by this section is not payable unless the death of the member arose out of and was in the course of his or her official duties and unless there is a survivor who qualifies under subdivision (b) of Section 21541. The Workers' Compensation Appeals Board, using the same procedure as in workers' compensation hearings, shall, in disputed cases, determine whether the member's death arose out of and in the course of his or her official duties.

A natural parent of surviving children eligible to receive an allowance payable under this section shall not be required to become the guardian of surviving unmarried children under 18 years of age in order to be paid the benefits prescribed for those children.

The jurisdiction of the Workers' Compensation Appeals Board shall be limited solely to the issue of industrial causation, and this section shall not be construed to authorize the Workers' Compensation Appeals Board to award costs against this system pursuant to Section 4600 or 5811 or any other provision of the Labor Code. **Leg.H.** 1995 ch. 379 §2 (former §21363.6).

§21540.5. Special death benefit for state, school, or local miscellaneous member or local or state safety member; conditions; jurisdiction and determination of Workers' Compensation Appeals Board; inapplicability of section.

(a) The special death benefit is also payable if the deceased was a state, school, or local miscellaneous member, a local safety member described in Section 20423.6, or a state safety member described in Section 20401.5, if the death of the member was a direct consequence of a violent act perpetrated on his or her person that arose out of and was in the course of his or her official duties and there is a survivor who qualifies under paragraph (2) of subdivision (a) of Section 21541. The Workers' Compensation Appeals Board, using the same procedure as in workers' compensation hearings, shall, in disputed cases determine whether the member's death was a direct consequence of a violent act perpetrated on his or her person that arose out of and in the course of his or her official duties.

(b) A natural parent of surviving children eligible to receive an allowance payable under this section is not required to become the guardian of surviving unmarried children under 18 years of age in order to be paid the benefits prescribed for those children.

(c) The jurisdiction of the Workers' Compensation Appeals Board shall be limited solely to the issue of industrial causation, and this section may not be construed to authorize the Workers' Compensation Appeals Board to award costs against this system pursuant to Section 4600 or 5811 or any other provision of the Labor Code.

(d) This section does not apply to a contracting agency nor its employees unless and until the agency elects to be subject to it by amendment to its contract made in the manner prescribed for approval of contracts, or in the case of a new contract, by express provision of the contract. **Leg.H.** 1995 ch. 379 §2 (former §21363.7), 1997 ch. 386, 2002 ch. 1152 (AB 2023), 2005 ch. 328 (AB 1166) §16.

1997 Note: The amendments to Section 21540.5 of the Government Code during the 1997–98 Regular Session shall not be construed to affect the liability of the Public Employees' Retirement System for any acts respecting state or local miscellaneous members that occurred prior to July 1, 1993, nor any acts respecting school members that occurred prior to January 1, 1998. Stats. 1997 ch. 386 §5.

§21541. Special death benefit.

(a) The special death benefit consists of the following:

(1) An amount equal to and derived from the same source as the basic death benefit exclusive of the contributions from which the annuity provided under paragraph (4) is paid.

(2) An amount sufficient, when added to the amount provided under paragraph (1), to provide, when applied according to tables adopted by the board, a monthly death allowance equal to one-half of his or her final compensation in the membership category applicable to him or her at the time of the injury, or the onset of the disease, causing death, as adjusted pursuant to subdivision (b), which amount shall be payable to the surviving spouse to whom he or she was married either continuously for at least one year prior to death, or prior to sustaining the injury or disease resulting in death, as long as the surviving spouse lives; or, if there is no surviving spouse or if the spouse dies before all children of the deceased member attain the age of 22 years, to his or her children under the age of 22 years collectively until every child shall have died, married, or attained the age of 22 years. However, no child shall receive any part of the allowance after marrying or attaining the age of 22 years. The increases described in this section shall only apply to spouses of deceased members who would have been less than 50 years of age, if still living on January 1, 2001.

(3) During the lifetime of the surviving spouse, an additional percentage of the death benefit allowed by this section, exclusive of the annuity under paragraph (4), shall be paid to the spouse of a member who is killed in the performance of his or her duty or who dies as a result of an accident or an injury caused by external violence or physical force, incurred in the performance of his or her duty, for each of his or her children during the lifetime of the child, or until the child marries or reaches the age of 22 years, as follows: for one child, 25 percent; for two children, 40 percent; and for three or more children, 50 percent.

(4) An annuity that is the actuarial equivalent, assuming monthly payments for life to the surviving spouse, of the deceased's accumulated additional contributions at the date of his or her death, plus his or her accumulated contributions at that date based on compensation earned in any membership category other than the category applicable to him or her at the time of the injury or the onset of the disease causing death.

(b) For purposes of this section only, the deceased member's final compensation shall be deemed to increase, and the death benefit under paragraph (2) of subdivision (a) shall be increased correspondingly, at any time and to the extent the compensation is increased for then-active members employed in the job classification and membership category that was applicable to the deceased member at the time of the injury, or the onset of the disease, causing death. The deceased member's final compensation shall be deemed to be subject to further increases hereunder only until the earlier of (1) the death of the surviving spouse or (2) the date that the deceased member would have attained the age of 50 years.

(c) Monthly allowances shall be adjusted annually for time commencing on the first day of September and effective with the monthly allowance regularly payable on the first day of the October beginning with October 1, 2001. The employer of the deceased member shall be responsible for reporting and certifying top range salary rates by the first day of July, beginning with July 1, 2001.

(d) If the surviving spouse does not have custody of the member's children, the additional amount payable pursuant to this section shall be payable to the person having custody of the children for each child during the lifetime of the child, or until the child marries or reaches the age of 22 years.

(e) The computation for time prior to entering the membership category applicable to the deceased at the time of the injury, or the onset of the disease, causing death shall be based on the compensation earnable by him or her in the position first held by him or her in that category.

(f) For purposes of this section:

(1) "Child" means a natural or adopted child of the deceased member, or a stepchild living or domiciled with the deceased member at the time of his or her death.

(2) "Spouse" means a wife or husband.

(g) This section shall apply to all contracting agencies and to the employees of all contracting agencies.

(h) For purposes of Section 21313, the base allowance shall be the allowance as increased under this section. The base year for annual adjustments of allowances increased by this section shall be the calendar year preceding the year of the adjustment.

(i) The amount of the death benefit payable pursuant to this section on and after January 1, 2001, with respect to any member who died prior to that date, shall be recalculated on and after that date pursuant to subdivision (b). **Leg.H.** 1945 ch. 123 §1, as Gov C §21364, 1949 ch. 298 §41, 1953 ch. 1186 §30, effective October 1, 1953, 1955 ch. 1766 §1, 1961 ch. 2197 §1, 1965 ch. 977 §5, operative October 1, 1965, ch. 1772 §1, ch. 1773 §1, operative October 1, 1965, 1967 ch. 1699 §2, 1974 ch. 92 §1, 1976 ch. 1436 §16, 1980 ch. 1102 §22, 1981 ch. 609 §27, ch. 963 §7, 1982 ch. 432 §10, 1995 chs. 379 (SB 541) §1, 850 (SB 860) §11, 1996 ch. 906 (SB 1859) §166 (amended & renumbered from §21364), 1999 ch. 800 (AB 232) §1.6, 2000 ch. 1031 (AB 2621) §1, 2003 ch. 840 (AB 933).

2003 Note: This act shall apply retroactively to the survivors of a deceased person who dies or is killed in the line of duty on or after January 1, 2001. Stats. 2003 ch. 840 (AB 933) §4.

Ref.: Hanna §§ 3.115[1], 9.04[1].

§21541.5. Benefits terminated upon adoption.

Any child whose benefits under Section 21541 were terminated upon his or her adoption, pursuant to that section as it read prior to January 1, 2001, shall have those benefits restored as follows:

(a) The child shall receive a lump-sum payment in the amount that would have paid, if he or she had not been adopted, from the date of adoption to the earlier of (1) the date his or her eligibility for benefits under Section 21541 would have otherwise terminated had he or she not been adopted or (2) January 1, 2001.

(b) If on January 1, 2001, the child is eligible for benefits under Section 21541, he or she shall receive benefits from and after that date pursuant to Section 21541. **Leg.H.** 2000 ch. 1031 (AB 2621) §2.

§21542. Special death benefit—Accrual; election to receive death benefit in lieu of special death benefit.

The special death benefit shall begin to accrue on the day next following the date of the member's death, and shall be paid in monthly installments to the surviving spouse and children as prescribed in Section 21541. The surviving spouse or the guardian of the minor child or children entitled to the special death benefit may elect, before the first payment, to receive the basic death benefit in lieu of the special death benefit. The election precludes a claim to benefits under Section 4707 of the Labor Code as the special death benefit is deemed payable by this system and is irrevocable. **Leg.H.** 1995 ch. 379 §2.

§21543. Special death benefit payment—Conditions for lump sum payment; accumulated additional contributions.

If payment of the special death benefit is stopped because of death of the surviving spouse or death, marriage, or attainment of the age of 22 years by a child before the sum of the monthly payment made, exclusive of the annuity derived from the accumulated additional contribution of the deceased, equals the basic death benefit, a lump sum equal to the difference shall be paid to the surviving children of the deceased member, share and share alike, or if there are no children, to the estate of the person last entitled to the allowance. In that event, the accumulated additional contributions of the deceased, as they were at his or her death, less the annuity paid as derived from those contributions, and plus interest credited to the accumulated additional contributions, shall be paid in the manner provided in this article for the payments of amounts due in the absence of a designated beneficiary. **Leg.H.** 1995 ch. 379 (SB 541) §2, 2004 ch. 231 (SB 1603).

§21544. Special death benefit—Determination of death as industrial in nature.

Upon notice of a death as a result of which the special death benefit may be payable, and when there is a survivor who would qualify under subdivision (b) of Section 21541, the board, or in disputed cases, the Workers' Compensation Appeals Board, shall determine whether the death was industrial, and pending final determination of the issue, the board shall temporarily pay special death benefits. The temporary payments shall be deducted from any other death benefits otherwise payable if the death is determined not to be industrial. **Leg.H.** 1995 ch. 379 §2 (former §21367).

§21546. Death of qualified member while in state service and before retirement; beneficiaries; monthly allowance; application.

(a) Upon the death of a member who has attained the minimum age for voluntary service retirement applicable to the member in his or her last employment preceding death, and who is eligible to retire and in circumstances in which the basic death benefit is payable other than solely that of membership in a county retirement system, or a retirement system maintained by the university, a monthly allowance shall be payable as follows:

(1) To the member's surviving spouse as long as the spouse lives.

(2) To the children under the age of 18 years collectively if there is no surviving spouse or if the surviving spouse dies before all children of the deceased member attain the age of 18 years, until every child dies or attains the age of 18 years. No child shall receive any allowance after marrying or attaining the age of 18 years.

(b) The monthly allowance under this section shall be equal to one-half of, and derived from the same source as, the unmodified retirement allowance the member would have been entitled to receive if he or she had retired for service on the date of death. If, however, the member made a specific beneficiary designation under Section 21490, the monthly allowance shall be equal to one-half of that portion of the member's unmodified retirement allowance that would have been derived from the nonmember spouse's community property interest in the member's contributions and service credit.

(c) If a member does not have a surviving spouse nor any children under the age of 18 years at the time of death, no allowance shall be payable under this section.

(d) No allowance shall be payable under this section if a special death benefit is payable.

(e)(1) The allowance provided by this section shall be paid in lieu of the basic death benefit but a surviving spouse qualifying for the allowance may elect, before the first payment on account of it, to receive the basic death benefit in lieu of the allowance.

(2) The allowance provided by this section shall be paid in lieu of the basic death benefit but the guardian of the minor child or children qualifying for the allowance may elect, before the first payment on account of it, to receive the basic death benefit in lieu of the allowance. If an election of the basic death benefit is made, the basic death benefit shall be paid to all the member's surviving children, regardless of age or marital status, in equal shares.

(f) If the total of the payments made pursuant to this section are less than the basic death benefit that was otherwise payable on account of the member's death, the amount of the basic death benefit less any payments made pursuant to this section shall be paid in a lump sum to the surviving children of the member, share and share alike, or if there are no children, to the estate of the person last entitled to the allowance.

(g) The board shall compute the amount by which benefits paid pursuant to this section exceed the benefits that would otherwise be payable and shall charge any excess against the contributions of the state so that there shall be no increase in contributions of members by reason of benefits paid pursuant to this section.

(h) As used in this section, "a surviving spouse" means a spouse who was either married to the member for at least one year prior to the member's death, or was married to the member prior to the occurrence of the injury or the onset of the illness that resulted in death, and "child" includes a posthumously born child of the member.

(i) On and after April 1, 1972, this section shall apply to all contracting agencies and to the employees of those agencies with respect to deaths occurring after April 1, 1972, whether or not the agencies have previously elected to be subject to this section. **Leg.H.** 1995 ch. 379 (SB 541) §2, 1999 ch. 800 (AB 232) §2, 2000 ch. 1002 (SB 1998) §8.

§21547. Monthly allowance in lieu of basic death benefit for members in state bargaining units subject to memoranda of understanding.

(a) Notwithstanding any other provision of this article requiring attainment of the minimum age for voluntary service retirement to the member in his or her last employment preceding death, upon the death of a state member on or after January 1, 1993, who is credited with 20 years or more of state service, the surviving spouse, or eligible children if there is no surviving spouse, may receive a monthly allowance in lieu of the basic death benefit. The board shall notify the eligible survivor, as defined in Section 21546, of this alternate death benefit. The board shall calculate the monthly allowance that shall be payable as follows:

(1) To the member's surviving spouse, an amount equal to the amount the member would have received if the member had retired for service at minimum retirement age on the date of death and had elected the optional settlement in Section 21456 and Section 21459.

(2) If the member made a specific beneficiary designation under Section 21490, the monthly allowance shall be based only on that portion of the amount the member would have received described in paragraph (1) that would have been derived from the nonmember spouse's community property interest in the member's contributions and service credit.

(3) If there is no surviving spouse or the spouse dies before all of the children of the deceased member attain the age of 18 years, to the surviving children, under the age of 18 years, collectively, an amount equal to one-half of, and derived from the same source as, the unmodified allowance the member would have received if he or she had retired for service at minimum retirement age on the date of death. No child shall receive any allowance after marrying or attaining the age of 18 years. As used in this paragraph, "surviving children" includes a posthumously born child or children of the member.

(b) This section shall only apply to members employed in state bargaining units for which a memorandum of understanding has been agreed to by the state employer and the recognized employee organization to become subject to this section, members who are excluded from the definition of state employees in subdivision (c) of Section 3513, and members employed by the executive branch of government who are not members of the civil service.

(c) For purposes of this section, "state service" means service rendered as a state employee, as defined in Section 19815. This section shall not apply to any contracting agency nor to the employees of any contracting agency.

(d) For purposes of this section, "state service" includes service to the state for which the member, pursuant to Section 20281.5, did not receive credit. **Leg.H.** 1995 ch. 379 (SB 541) §2, 1999 ch. 457 (SB 401) §14, effective September 21, 1999, 2000 ch. 1002 (SB 1998) §9, 2004 ch. 214 (SB 1105), effective August 11, 2004, 2016 ch. 199 (AB 2404) §28.

Ref.: Herlick Handbook § 7.20.

§21547.5. Adjustment of monthly allowance that began prior to specified date.

For any survivor receiving a monthly allowance pursuant to Section 21547 prior to January 1, 2000, that allowance shall be adjusted as of January 1, 2000, to equal the amount that the survivor would have been entitled to receive if the member's death had occurred on or after January 1, 2000. The adjusted allowance shall be payable only on and after January 1, 2000. **Leg.H.** 1999 ch. 457 (SB 401) §15, effective September 21, 1999.

§21547.7. Monthly allowance in lieu of basic death benefit.

(a) Notwithstanding any other provision of this article requiring attainment of the minimum age for voluntary service retirement applicable to him or her in his or her last employment preceding death, upon the death of a local firefighter member while in the employ of an agency subject to this section on or after January 1, 2001, who is credited with 20 years or more of state service, the surviving spouse, or eligible children, if there is no eligible spouse, may receive a monthly allowance in lieu of the basic death benefit. The board shall notify the eligible survivor, as defined in Section 21546, of this alternate death benefit. The board shall calculate the monthly allowance that shall be payable as follows:

(1) To the member's surviving spouse, an amount equal to the amount the member would have received if he or she had retired for service at the minimum retirement age on the date of death and had elected the optional settlement in Section 21456 and Section 21459. The retirement allowance shall be calculated using all service earned by the member in this system.

(2) If the member made a specific beneficiary designation under Section 21490, the monthly allowance shall be based only on that portion of the amount the member would have received described in paragraph (1) that would have been derived from the nonmember spouse's community property interest in the member's contributions and service credit.

(3) If there is no surviving spouse or the spouse dies before all of the children of the deceased member attain the age of 18 years, to the surviving children, under the age of 18 years, collectively, an amount equal to one-half of, and derived from the same source as, the unmodified allowance the member would have received if he or she had retired for service at the minimum retirement age on the date of death. No child shall receive any allowance after marrying or attaining the age of 18 years. As used in this paragraph, "surviving children" includes a posthumously born child or children of the member. The retirement allowance shall be calculated using all service earned by the member in this system.

(4) The cost of the allowance paid pursuant to this subdivision shall be paid from the assets of the employer at the member's date of death. All member contributions made by the member to this system shall be transferred to the plan assets of the employer liable for the funding of this benefit.

(b)(1) Upon the death of a local firefighter member while in the employ of an agency subject to this section on or after January 1, 2001, who is credited with 20 years or more of state service and who has attained the minimum age for voluntary service retirement applicable to him or her in his or her last employment preceding death, the surviving spouse may elect to receive a monthly allowance that is equal to the amount that member would have received if the member had been retired from service on the date of death and had elected the optional settlement in Section 21456 and Section 21459 in lieu of the basic death benefit. The retirement allowance shall be calculated using all service earned by the member in this system.

(2) If the member made a specific beneficiary designation under Section 21490, the monthly allowance shall be based only on that portion of the amount the member would have received described in paragraph (1) that would have been derived from the nonmember spouse's community property interest in the member's contributions and service credit.

(3) If there is no surviving spouse or the spouse dies before all of the children of the deceased member attain the age of 18 years, the allowance shall continue to the surviving children, under the age of 18 years, collectively, in an amount equal to one-half of, and derived from the same source as, the unmodified allowance the member would have received if he or she had been retired from service on the date of death. No child shall receive any allowance after marrying or attaining the age of 18 years. As used in this paragraph, "surviving children" includes a posthumously born child or children of the member. The retirement allowance will be calculated using all service earned by the member in this system.

(4) The cost of the increase in service allowance paid pursuant to this subdivision shall be paid from the assets of the employer at the member's date of death.

(c) This section shall not apply to any contracting agency, nor to the employees of any contracting agency, unless and until the agency elects to be subject to this section by amendment to its contract made in the manner prescribed for approval of contracts, except that an election among the employees is not required. **Leg.H.** 2000 ch. 855 (SB 1695) §1, 2001 chs. 159 (SB 662) §114, 793 (AB 1683) §31, 2016 ch. 199 (AB 2404) §29.

§21548. Allowance to surviving spouse of member eligible pursuant to specified provision; application.

(a) The surviving spouse of a member who has attained the minimum age for voluntary service retirement applicable to the member in his or her last employment preceding death, and who is eligible to receive an allowance pursuant to Section 21546, shall instead receive an allowance that is equal to the amount that the member would have received if the member had been retired from service on the date of death and had elected the optional settlement in Section 21456 and Section 21459.

(b) The surviving spouse of a member who has attained the minimum age for voluntary service retirement applicable to the member in his or her last employment preceding death, and who is eligible to receive a special death benefit in lieu of an allowance under Section 21546, may elect to instead receive an allowance that is equal to the amount that the member would have received if the member had been retired from service on the date of death and had elected the optional settlement in Section 21456 and Section 21459.

(c) If the member made a specific beneficiary designation under Section 21490, the allowance under this section shall be based only on that portion of the amount the member would have received described in subdivision (a) or (b) that would have been derived from the nonmember spouse's community property interest in the member's contributions and service credit.

(d) The allowance provided by this section shall be payable as long as the surviving spouse lives. Upon the death of the surviving spouse, the benefit shall be continued to minor children, as defined in Section 6500 of the Family Code, or a lump sum shall be paid as provided under circumstances specified in Section 21546 or in Sections 21541 and 21543, as the case may be.

(e) The allowance provided by this section shall be paid in lieu of the basic death benefit, but the surviving spouse qualifying for the allowance may elect before the first payment on account of it to receive the basic death benefit in lieu of the allowance.

(f) This section shall apply with respect to state members whose death occurs on and after July 1, 1976.

(g) All references in this code to Section 21546 shall be deemed to include this section in the alternative.

(h) This section shall not apply to any contracting agency nor to the employees of any contracting agency unless and until the agency elects to be subject to this section by amendment to its contract made in the manner prescribed for approval of contracts, except that an election among the employees is not required, or, in the case of contracts made after January 1, 1985, by express provision in the contract making the contracting agency subject to this section. **Leg.H.** 1995 ch. 379 (SB 541) §2, 1999 ch. 800 (AB 232) §3, 2000 ch. 1002 (SB 1998) §10, 2016 ch. 199 (AB 2404) §30.

Ref.: Herlick Handbook § 7.20.

§21551. Surviving spouse benefits.

Notwithstanding any other provision of this part, the benefits payable to a surviving spouse pursuant to Sections 21541, 21546, 21547, 21548, and Article 3 (commencing with Section 21570), do not cease upon remarriage if the remarriage occurs on or after September 19, 1989, for surviving spouses of deceased state members, January 1, 1991, for surviving spouses of deceased school members, upon the date a contracting agency elected to be subject to this section for deceased local members, or January 1, 2000, for spouses of deceased local members if the contracting agency has not elected to be subject to this section. Any surviving spouse who elected the reduction specified in Section 21500 as it read prior to January 1, 2000, shall be restored to the lifetime allowance to which he or she was originally entitled effective September 19, 1989, for state members, January 1, 1991, for school members, upon the date a contracting agency elected to be subject to this section, or January 1, 2000, if the contracting agency has not elected to be subject to this section.

Pursuant to Section 22822, the surviving spouse who remarries may not enroll his or her new spouse or stepchildren as family members under the continued health benefits coverage of the surviving spouse.

(c) Any surviving spouse whose allowance has been discontinued as a result of remarriage prior to the effective date of this section shall have that allowance restored and resumed on January 1, 2000, or the first of the month, following receipt by the board of a written application from the spouse for resumption of the allowance, whichever is later. The amount of the benefits due shall be calculated as though the allowance had never been reduced or discontinued because of remarriage, and is not payable for the period between the date of discontinuance because of remarriage and January 1, 2000. The board has no duty to identify, locate, or notify a spouse who previously had his or her allowance discontinued because of remarriage. **Leg.H.** 1989 ch. 497 §4, effective September 19, 1989, as Gov C §21373, 1990 ch. 862 §2, 1995 chs. 379 (SB 541) §1, 850 (SB 860) §12, 1996 chs. 906 (SB 1859) §168, 1120 (AB 3478) §1, effective September 30, 1996 (amended & renumbered from §21373), 1999 ch. 800 (AB 232) §5, 2004 ch. 69 (SB 626), effective June 24, 2004.

§21552. Effect of remarriage by surviving spouse of firefighter or peace officer.

Notwithstanding any other provision of this part, on and after the effective date of this section, the remarriage of any surviving spouse of any deceased local safety member who was a firefighter, or peace officer as described in Chapter 4.5 (commencing with Section 830) of Title 3 of Part 2 of the Penal Code, who died in the line of duty, shall not result in the reduction or cessation of any monthly allowance the spouse was receiving pursuant to Section 21541 and Article 3 (commencing with Section 21570). **Leg.H.** 1996 ch. 1120 (AB 3478) §2, effective September 30, 1996.

§21553. Restoration of allowance to remarried surviving spouse of firefighter or peace officer.

(a) The monthly allowance pursuant to Section 21541 and Article 3 (commencing with Section 21570), paid to the surviving spouse of any deceased local safety member who was a firefighter, or peace officer as described in Chapter 4.5 (commencing with Section 830) of Title 3 of Part 2 of the Penal Code, who died in the line of duty, shall be restored if that allowance has been reduced or discontinued upon the spouse's remarriage. The allowance shall be resumed on the effective date of this section, or the first of the month, following receipt by the board of a written application from the spouse for resumption of the allowance, whichever is later.

(b) The amount of the benefits due shall be calculated as though the allowance had never been reduced or discontinued because of remarriage, and shall not be payable for the period between the date of reduction or discontinuance and the effective date of resumption.

(c) The board has no duty to identify, locate, or notify a spouse who previously had his or her allowance reduced or discontinued because of remarriage.

(d) Any surviving spouse shall be entitled to restoration of terminated or diminished benefits upon application to the system if he or she previously qualified for special death benefits because his or her spouse died in the line of duty. **Leg.H.** 1996 ch. 1120 (AB 3478) §3, effective September 30, 1996.

TITLE 3
GOVERNMENT OF COUNTIES

DIVISION 2
Officers

PART 2
BOARD OF SUPERVISORS

CHAPTER 3
FINANCIAL POWERS
[Selected Provisions]

§25263. County workers' compensation reserve account.

Notwithstanding any other law to the contrary, the board of supervisors of a county may, by resolution, establish and maintain a reserve account to insure against its liability or the liability of its employees for injuries, for liability under the workers' compensation laws, for casualty losses incurred by the county, and for providing health and welfare benefits for its employees. In such event, a county may elect to be wholly or partially self-insured, and if such reserves are established, the board of supervisors shall prescribe procedures whereby the reserves may be used to pay for settlement of claims; payment of property losses; payment of attorney and investigator fees; and payment of insurance and broker fees if the county elects to be partially insured. If such reserves are established, appropriations shall be made to such reserves, and payments may be made from such reserves for the above purposes without specific appropriation. All interest earned by the reserve shall be credited to the reserve.

The board of supervisors may authorize any district for which the board is the governing body to establish and maintain the reserves authorized by this section.

Misc. Provisions

DIVISION 4
Employees

PART 1
GENERAL
[Selected Provisions]

§31000.8. Self-insured county; definitions.

Notwithstanding any other law to the contrary, the board of supervisors of a county which is wholly or partially self-insured under the workers' compensation laws, which is wholly or partially self-insured against public liability, or which is wholly or partially self-insured for employee health and welfare benefits, may contract with a qualified firm for the purpose of having such firm render investigative, administrative, and claims adjustment services relating to workers' compensation and public liability and employee health and welfare benefit claims against the county. The contract may provide that the contracting firm may reject, settle, compromise and approve workers' compensation, and public liability and employee health and welfare benefit claims against the county, its officers or employees, within such limits and for such amounts as the board of supervisors may specify, and may provide that the contracting firm may execute and issue checks in payment of such claims, which checks shall be payable only from a trust fund which may be established by the board of supervisors. Funds in the trust fund established by the board pursuant to the provisions of this section shall not exceed a sum sufficient to provide for the settlement of claims for a 30–day period as determined by the board of supervisors or the sum of twenty thousand dollars ($20,000), whichever is larger, at any one time. The rejection or settlement and approval of a claim by the contracting firm in accordance with the terms of the contract shall have the same effect as would the rejection or settlement and approval of such a claim by the board of supervisors and the county auditor. The contract may also provide that the contracting firm may employ legal counsel, subject to such terms and limitations as the board may prescribe, to advise such contracting firm concerning the legality and advisability of rejecting, settling, compromising and paying claims referred to said contracting firm by the county for investigation and adjustment, or to represent the county in litigation concerning such claims. The compensation and expenses of such attorney for services rendered to the county shall be county charges.

The contract provided for in this section may contain such other terms and conditions as the board of supervisors may consider necessary or desirable to effectuate the county's self-insured programs.

In lieu of, or in addition to, contracting for the services described in this section, the board of supervisors may authorize a county employee to perform any or all of the services and functions which the board may contract for under the provisions of this section.

As used in this section:

(a) "Firm" includes a person, corporation, or other legal entity.

(b) "Board of supervisors" includes governing boards of districts and other public agencies for which the board of supervisors acts as the governing board.

(c) "County" includes such districts and other public agencies for which the board of supervisors acts as the governing board.

PART 3
RETIREMENT SYSTEMS

CHAPTER 3
COUNTY EMPLOYEES RETIREMENT LAW OF 1937

ARTICLE 3
Retirement Board
[Selected Provisions]

§31520.4. Benefits for retirement board member injured or killed.

In any county with a board of retirement composed of nine members pursuant to Section 31520.1, if the second, third, seventh, or alternate seventh member of the board is injured or killed while performing his or her duties as a member of the board, that member shall be deemed to have been acting in the course and scope of his or her duties as an employee of the county or district employing the member, for the limited purpose of determining eligibility for workers' compensation benefits or disability or death benefits from the retirement system.

This section shall not be operative in any county until the board of supervisors, by resolution adopted by a majority vote, makes this section operative in that county. **Leg.H.** 1989 ch. 91 §1, 2011 ch. 124 (SB 203) §4.

ARTICLE 14
Subrogation
[Selected Provisions]

§31820. Recovery of value of benefits from third party.

If benefits are payable under this chapter because of any injury to, or the death of, a member of the retirement association, and such injury or death is the proximate consequence of the act of any person other than his employer, the board on behalf of the retirement association may recover from such person an amount which is the lesser of the following:

(1) An amount which is equal to one-half of the actuarial equivalent of the benefits for which the association is liable because of such injury or death; or

(2) An amount which is equal to one-half of the remaining balance of the amount recovered after allowance of that amount which the employer or its insurance carrier have paid or become obligated to pay. The right shall be

determined under the subrogation provisions of any workmen's compensation law.

CHAPTER 5
COUNTY FIRE SERVICE RETIREMENT LAW

ARTICLE 5
Contributions
[Selected Provisions]

§32338. Contributions by member absent from employment due to incapacity.

If any member is compelled to be absent from his employment because temporarily incapacitated for the performance of duty as the result of injury or disease occurring in and arising out of his employment, because of which he becomes entitled to workmen's compensation, within 90 days after his return to active employment, or within 90 days after the effective date of this section, whichever first occurs, or within such further time as may be granted by the board, he may pay into the fund an amount equal to that which would have been deducted had he remained in active employment. Upon the making of such payment, such time, whether before or after the effective date of this section, shall be considered as time served as a county forester, firewarden, or fireman.

Misc. Provisions

TITLE 5
LOCAL AGENCIES

DIVISION 1
Cities and Counties

PART 1
POWERS AND DUTIES COMMON TO CITIES AND COUNTIES

CHAPTER 4
POLICE OFFICERS' PENSION FUND AND FIREMEN'S PENSION FUND

ARTICLE 5
Extraterritorial Activities of County and City Peace Officers
[Selected Provisions]

§50920. "Peace officer."

As used in this article, the term "peace officer" means a sheriff, undersheriff, deputy sheriff, marshal, or deputy marshal of a county or city and county, or a marshal or police officer of a city or town, employed and compensated as such, whether the members are volunteer, partly paid, or fully paid, except those whose principal duties are clerical, such as stenographers, telephone operators, and other workers not engaged in law enforcement operations, or the protection or preservation of life or property, and not under suspension or otherwise lacking in good standing. **Leg.H.** 1998 ch. 931, effective September 28, 1998, 2002 ch. 784 (SB 1316).

1989 Note: This section is applicable only to injuries occurring on or after January 1, 1990. Stats. 1989 ch. 893 §6.

§50921. Peace officer performing duty, not under direction of employer.

Whenever any peace officer of a city, county, or city and county of this state is injured, dies or is disabled from performing his or her duties as a peace officer by reason of engaging in the apprehension or attempted apprehension of law violators or suspected law violators or protection or preservation of life or property, or the preservation of the peace anywhere in this state, including the local jurisdiction in which he or she is employed, but is not at the time acting under the immediate direction of his or her employer, he, she, or his or her dependents, as the case may be, shall be accorded by his or her employer all of the same benefits including the benefits of the Workers' Compensation Law, which he, she, or they would have received had that peace officer been acting under the immediate direction of his or her employer. Any injury, disability or death incurred under the circumstances described in this section shall be deemed to have arisen out of and been sustained in the course of employment for purposes of workers' compensation and all other benefits.

ARTICLE 6
Extraterritorial Activities of Firemen
[Selected Provisions]

§50926. Public firefighter performing duty, not under direction of employer.

Whenever any fireman of a city, county, city and county, district, or other public or municipal corporation or political subdivision is injured, dies or is disabled from performing his duties as a fireman by reason of his proceeding to or engaging in a fire suppression or rescue operation, or the protection or preservation of life or property, anywhere in this state, including the local jurisdiction in which he is employed, but is not at the time acting under the immediate direction of his employer, he or his dependents, as the case may be, shall be accorded by his employer all of the same benefits of the Workers' Compensation Law, which he or they would have received had that fireman been acting under the immediate direction of his employer. Any injury, disability or death incurred under the circumstances described in this section shall be deemed to have arisen out of and been sustained in the course of employment for purposes of workers' compensation and all other benefits.

DIVISION 2
Cities, Counties, and Other Agencies

PART 1
POWERS AND DUTIES COMMON TO CITIES, COUNTIES, AND OTHER AGENCIES

CHAPTER 1
GENERAL

ARTICLE 2
Emergency Powers
[Selected Provisions]

§53023. Privileges and immunities of local agent apply extraterritorially.

Notwithstanding any other provisions of law or any local ordinance all the privileges and immunities from liability, exemptions from laws and rules, all pension, relief, disability, workmen's compensation, and other benefits, which apply to officers, agents, or employees of the local agency when performing functions within the local agency's limits apply to them to the same extent while performing functions extraterritorially pursuant to this article.

CHAPTER 6
REVENUE BOND LAW OF 1941

ARTICLE 5
Additional Powers to Secure Bonds
[Selected Provisions]

§54462. Provision for amount and kind of insurance.

The legislative body may provide for the amount and kind of insurance on the enterprise including insurance against:

(a) Accident to or destruction of any enterprise from any or all risks.

(b) Loss of revenues from an enterprise.

(c) Public liability or property damage and workmen's compensation.

Misc. Provisions

TITLE 8
THE ORGANIZATION AND GOVERNMENT OF COURTS

CHAPTER 2
THE JUDICIAL COUNCIL

ARTICLE 4
Court Interpreter Services
[Selected Provisions]

§68562. Certification of court interpreters—Procedures, standards, and guidelines.

(a) The Judicial Council shall designate the languages for which certification programs shall be established under subdivision (b). The language designations shall be based on (1) the courts' needs as determined by the language and interpreter use and need studies under Section 68563, (2) the language needs of non-English-speaking persons in the courts, and (3) other information the Judicial Council deems relevant.

(b) By July 1, 1996, the Judicial Council shall approve one or more entities to certify Spanish language interpreters and interpreters for as many other languages designated under subdivision (a) as practicable by that date. The Judicial Council may give provisional approval to an entity to examine interpreters and establish a list of recommended court interpreters pending final approval of one or more certification entities. Certification entities may include educational institutions, testing organizations, joint powers agencies, or public agencies.

The Judicial Council shall adopt and publish guidelines, standards, and procedures to determine which certification entities will be approved to test and certify interpreters.

(c) The Judicial Council shall develop and implement procedures to administer the list of recommended court interpreters previously established by the State Personnel Board and the list established by an entity provisionally approved under subdivision (b).

The Judicial Council shall develop procedures and standards for certifying without reexamination interpreters on the list of recommended court interpreters (1) previously established by the State Personnel Board, or (2) established by an entity provisionally approved under subdivision (b). Certification of these interpreters shall be based on criteria determined by the Judicial Council, such as recent interpreting experience, performance in court or at administrative hearings, training, and continuing education.

(d) The Judicial Council shall adopt standards and requirements for interpreter proficiency, continuing education, certification renewal, and discipline. The Judicial Council shall adopt standards of professional conduct for court interpreters.

(e) The Judicial Council shall adopt programs for interpreter recruiting, training, and continuing education and evaluation to ensure that an adequate number of interpreters is available and that they interpret competently.

(f) The Judicial Council shall establish guidelines for fees or shall set and charge fees for applications to take the court interpreter examinations, for renewal of certifications, for certification of interpreters on the list of recommended court interpreters, for maintaining interpreters on the recommended list until January 1, 1996, and for other functions and services provided under this article. All fees and other revenues received by the Judicial Council under this article shall be transferred promptly to the Controller, and shall be placed in the Court Interpreters' Fund, which is hereby created, the moneys in which shall be available to carry out the purposes of this article upon appropriation by the Legislature.

(g) Each superior court may adopt local rules to impose additional requirements, standards, examinations, and programs as necessary for equity or to recognize local conditions. **Leg.H.** 1992 ch. 770, 1995 ch. 143, effective July 18, 1995, 2002 ch. 784 (SB 1316).

Ref.: 8 C.C.R. §9795.4.

SELECTED PROVISIONS Of The HARBORS AND NAVIGATION CODE

DIVISION 8 HARBOR AND PORT DISTRICTS

PART 4 PORT DISTRICTS

CHAPTER 2 BOARD OF PORT COMMISSIONERS

ARTICLE 2 Jurisdiction and Powers of the Board [Selected Provisions]

§6276. Stevedore employee workers' compensation benefits.

(a) In lieu of the benefits afforded pursuant to Division 4 (commencing with Section 3200) and Division 4.7 (commencing with Section 6200) of the Labor Code, the district may agree to provide workers' compensation benefits to its stevedore employees in amounts, and under such conditions, as would be payable to stevedore employees of private employers pursuant to the Longshoremen's and Harbor Workers' Compensation Act (33 U.S.C. 901, et seq.).

(b) Such an agreement shall be binding upon the parties only if it is in writing and signed by the employee and by a representative of the district. It shall acknowledge, in writing, that the benefits agreed upon are authorized by this section and are expressly in lieu of any benefits available under Division 4 (commencing with Section 3200) and Division 4.7 (commencing with Section 6200) of the Labor Code.

(c) All claims for benefits against the district which are authorized by this section shall be determined pursuant to law and the rules and regulations of the Workers' Compensation Appeals Board. To the fullest extent possible, the Workers' Compensation Appeals Board shall attempt to apply the Longshoremen's and Harbor Workers' Compensation Act to employees covered by this section in the same manner as applicable to private employees.

(d) Notwithstanding the provisions of Sections 11779 and 11870 of the Insurance Code or any other provision of law, the State Compensation Insurance Fund or any private insurer may provide insurance coverage for the benefits authorized by this section.

Misc. Provisions

PART 6
RIVER PORT DISTRICTS

CHAPTER 2
PORT COMMISSION

ARTICLE 2
Jurisdiction and Powers of the Board
[Selected Provisions]

§6869. Federal benefits in lieu of state benefits.

(a) In lieu of the benefits afforded pursuant to Division 4 (commencing with Section 3200) and Division 4.7 (commencing with Section 6200) of the Labor Code, the district may agree to provide workers' compensation benefits to its stevedore employees in amounts, and under such conditions, as would be payable to stevedore employees of private employers pursuant to the Longshoremen's and Harbor Workers' Compensation Act (33 U.S.C. 901, et seq.).

(b) Such an agreement shall be binding upon the parties only if it is in writing and signed by the employee and by a representative of the district. It shall acknowledge, in writing, that the benefits agreed upon are authorized by this section and are expressly in lieu of any benefits available under Division 4 (commencing with Section 3200) and Division 4.7 (commencing with Section 6200) of the Labor Code.

(c) All claims for benefits against the district which are authorized by this section shall be determined pursuant to law and the rules and regulations of the Workers' Compensation Appeals Board. To the fullest extent possible, the Workers' Compensation Appeals Board shall attempt to apply the Longshoremen's and Harbor Workers' Compensation Act to employees covered by this section in the same manner as applicable to private employees.

(d) Notwithstanding the provisions of Section 11779 of the Insurance Code or any other provision of law, the State Compensation Insurance Fund may provide insurance coverage for the benefits authorized by this section.

SELECTED PROVISIONS
Of The
HEALTH AND SAFETY CODE

DIVISION 13
HOUSING

PART 1.5
Regulation of Buildings Used for Human Habitation

CHAPTER 2
RULES AND REGULATIONS
[Selected Provisions]

§17922.5. Building permits from state or local agencies.

Any state or local agency which issues building permits shall require, as a condition of issuing any building permit where the working conditions of the construction would require an employer to obtain a permit from the Division of Occupational Safety and Health pursuant to Chapter 6 (commencing with Section 6500) of Part 1 of Division 5 of the Labor Code, that proof be submitted showing that the employer has received such a permit from the Division of Occupational Safety and Health.

An employer may apply for a building permit prior to receiving the permit from the Division of Occupational Safety and Health.

SELECTED PROVISIONS
Of The
MILITARY AND VETERANS CODE

DIVISION 2
THE MILITARY FORCES OF THE STATE

PART 1
The State Militia

CHAPTER 5
COMPENSATION, ALLOWANCE, AND INSURANCE

ARTICLE 3
Casualty Insurance

§340. Members of National Guard, organized or unorganized militia injured in line of duty.

(a) Subject to Section 340.1, whenever any officer, warrant officer, or enlisted member of the California National Guard, the organized militia, or the unorganized militia, when called into the active service of the state, pursuant to Section 142, 143, or 146, is wounded, injured, disabled, or killed in the active service of the state in the line of duty, the member or the member's dependents shall receive compensation under Division 4 (commencing with Section 3201) of the Labor Code. For these purposes, the member is deemed to be an employee of the state. The compensation shall be based on the member's average income from all sources during the year immediately preceding the date of wounding, injury, death, or the commencement of disability and shall not exceed the maximum prescribed in Division 4 (commencing with Section 3200) of the Labor Code.

(b) For the purposes of this article, any officer, warrant officer, or enlisted member performing military duty of any nature pursuant to Title 32 or Title 10 of the United States Code shall not be entitled to benefits described in subdivision (a) or in Section 340.1.

(c) Notwithstanding subdivision (a), any officer, warrant officer, or enlisted member on full-time active duty with the Office of the Adjutant General who suffers disability or death in the line of duty from either injury or disease is entitled to receive, from the state, benefits or compensation for that disability or death comparable to that provided to members of the United States armed forces on active duty. **Leg.H.** 1993 ch. 287, 2006 ch. 538 (SB 1852) §496.

§340.1. Disability for those wounded in service of state.

(a) Any officer, warrant officer, or enlisted member of the California National Guard, the organized militia, or the unorganized militia, when called into the active service of the state, pursuant to Sections 142, 143, or 146, except an officer, warrant officer, or enlisted member on full-time duty with the Office of the Adjutant General, who is wounded, injured, or disabled in the active service of the state in the line of duty shall be retained on active duty and shall receive regular military pay and allowances for not to exceed 52 weeks from the date of wounding, injury, or disability, regardless of the date of expiration of the period of state active duty, unless any of the following occurs:

(1) The member becomes entitled to disability compensation through any private or other public employer.

(2) The member is able to return to his or her regular civilian employment, as determined by proper authority.

(3) The member requests an earlier release from active duty.

(b) A member who has received benefits under subdivision (a) and who is unable to return to his or her regular civilian employment following 52 weeks after the date of wounding, injury, or disability is entitled to compensation under Division 4 (commencing with Section 3201) of the Labor Code, pursuant to Section 340. **Leg.H.** 1993 ch. 287.

§340.2. Disability for those transferred under mutual aid or interagency agreements.

Any officer, warrant officer, or enlisted member of the California National Guard, the organized militia, or the unorganized militia, when called into the active service of the state, pursuant to Sections 142, 143, or 146, who, while in that active service, is transferred by the California National Guard or other military authority to any other state or local agency for purposes of fulfilling active

Misc. Provisions

service requirements pursuant to either a mutual aid agreement or an interagency agreement and is wounded, injured, or disabled in the line of duty, is entitled to the benefits provided under Section 340.1. **Leg.H.** 1993 ch. 287.

§341. Member of militia; determination of average yearly earnings; "injury suffered in line of duty."

In the determination of the benefits to be awarded any member of the militia or his dependents under the provisions of Section 340, it shall be conclusively presumed that the average yearly earning of such injured or deceased member is not less than two thousand five hundred dollars ($2,500). Any injury, death, or disability shall be deemed to have been suffered in line of duty unless the same resulted from misconduct or disobedience of lawful orders by the injured or deceased member.

§342. Jurisdiction of Appeals Board.

The appeals board is empowered to hear and determine all issues concerning any obligation of the State of California to provide to any officer, warrant officer, or enlisted person on active duty with the Office of the Adjutant General any rights or benefits provided in Section 3, Public Law 108, Chapter 225, 81st Congress, First Session, and any and all issues arising under or in connection with that law. In doing so, the appeals board shall follow the same procedures in all respects as are provided in Division 4 (commencing with Section 3200) of the Labor Code for the determination of workers' compensation claims. The orders, decisions, and awards of the appeals board issued in exercising this jurisdiction are subject to review and rehearing in the manner provided in Sections 5900 to 5956, inclusive, of the Labor Code. **Leg.H.** 1994 ch. 114, 2018 ch. 118 (SB 1501) §29.

Note: Section 3 of this law (63 Stats. 201, approved June 20, 1949) reads as follows:

All officers, warrant officers, and enlisted men of the National Guard of the United States, both ground and air, the federal recognized National Guard of the several States, Territories, and the District of Columbia—

(1) if engaged for periods in excess of thirty days in any type of training or active duty under sections 5, 81, 92, 94, 97 or 99 of the National Defense Act, as amended, suffer disability or death in line of duty from disease while so engaged; or

(2) if engaged for any period of time in any type of training or inactive duty under such sections of the National Defense Act as amended, suffer disability or death in line of duty from injury while so employed.

shall be in all respects entitled to receive the same pensions, compensation, death gratuity, retirement pay, hospital benefits, and pay and allowances as are now or may hereafter be provided by law or regulation for officers and enlisted men of corresponding grades and length of service of the Regular Army.

ARTICLE 4
State Militia Disability Equality Act

§345. Citation of article.

This article shall be known and may be cited as the State Militia Disability Equality Act. **Leg.H.** 2005 ch. 319 (AB 980) §2.

2005 Note: It is the intent of the Legislature to ensure that all California National Guard reservists and military personnel, when called into federal active status, receive the same military combat disability compensation that is provided to regular active military service personnel that are injured in combat. Stats. 2005 ch. 319 (AB 980) §1.

§346. Disability benefits.

(a) When any officer, warrant officer, or enlisted member of the California National Guard or the organized militia who is not in active service in this state is wounded, injured, or disabled in the line of duty when performing military duty of any nature under Title 10 or Title 32 of the United States Code, the Military Department shall determine both of the following amounts:

(1) The amount of disability benefits to which a member of the United States Armed Forces of the same or equivalent rank would be entitled from the federal government as a result of a comparable wound, injury, or disability.

(2) The amount of disability benefits to which the officer, warrant officer, or enlisted member is entitled from the federal government as a result of the wound, injury, or disability.

(b) If the Military Department determines that the amount described in paragraph (1) of subdivision (a) is greater than the amount described in paragraph (2) of subdivision (a), that department shall, upon an appropriation of funds to the department by the Legislature for this purpose, provide to the officer, warrant officer, or enlisted member an amount equal to the difference between those two amounts. **Leg.H.** 2005 ch. 319 (AB 980) §2.

2005 Note: It is the intent of the Legislature to ensure that all California National Guard reservists and military personnel, when called into federal active status, receive the same military combat disability compensation that is provided to regular active military service personnel that are injured in combat. Stats. 2005 ch. 319 (AB 980) §1.

PART 2
California Cadet Corps and Voluntary Organizations

CHAPTER 1
CALIFORNIA CADET CORPS
[Selected Provisions]

§520. Right to compensation; determination of average yearly earnings.

Any executive officer, assistant executive officer, regional advisor, or officer, warrant officer, or noncommissioned officer appointed or detailed pursuant to Sections 502, 502.1, 512, 513, 515, or 516.1, who is wounded, injured, disabled, or killed in the performance of ordered duty shall be entitled to receive compensation from the state in accordance with the provisions of Division 4 (commencing with Section 3200) of the Labor Code. In all such cases, these individuals shall be deemed to be employees of the state. The compensation for any such individual shall be ascertained, determined, and fixed upon the basis of his or her average income from all sources during the year immediately preceding the date of such injury or death, or the commencement of such disability, but such compensation shall in no case exceed the maximum prescribed in Division 4 (commencing with Section 3200) of the Labor Code.

In determining the benefits awarded to an individual under the provisions of this section, it shall be conclusively presumed that the average yearly earning of such injured or deceased individual is not less than ten thousand dollars ($10,000). Any injury, death, or disability shall be deemed to have been suffered in line of duty unless the injury, death, or disability resulted from misconduct or disobedience of lawful orders by the injured or deceased individual. **Leg.H.** 1957 ch. 1890 §4, 2011 ch. 630 (SB 537) §29.

CHAPTER 3
STATE MILITARY RESERVE ACT
[Selected Provisions]

§562. Members of State Guard; right to compensation; determination of average yearly earnings; "injury suffered in line of duty."

In all cases in which any officer, warrant officer or enlisted person of the [1] **State Guard**, when organized or authorized as a cadre or otherwise, when in the performance of ordered duty, or when ordered into the active service of the state, is wounded, injured, disabled, or killed in active service, or in the performance of ordered duty and in line of duty, the officer or warrant officer or enlisted person or the dependents of that officer or warrant officer or enlisted person shall be entitled to receive compensation from the state in accordance with the provisions of Division 4 (commencing with Section 3201) of the Labor Code. In all such cases, an officer, warrant officer, enlisted person shall be held and deemed to be an employee of the state. The compensation to be awarded to any such officer, warrant officer, enlisted person shall be ascertained, determined, and fixed upon the basis of [2] **the person's** average income from all sources during the year immediately preceding the date of the injury or death or the commencement of the disability, but the compensation shall in no case exceed the maximum prescribed in Division 4 (commencing with Section 3201) of the Labor Code.

In the determination of the benefits to be awarded any member of the [3] **State Guard or the member's** dependents under the provisions of this section it shall be conclusively presumed that the average yearly earning of the injured or deceased member is not less than two thousand five hundred dollars ($2,500). Any injury, death, or disability shall be deemed to have been suffered in line of duty unless the same resulted from misconduct or disobedience of lawful orders by the injured or deceased member. **Leg.H.** 1949 ch. 678 §1, 3d Ex Sess 1950 ch. 27 §10, effective October 13, 1950, 1951 ch. 394 §6, effective May 10, 1951, 1st Ex Sess 1952 ch. 22 §3, effective April 19, 1952, 1953 ch 493 §2, 1955 ch. 706 §3, effective May 25, 1955, 1963 ch. 94 §14, 1982 ch. 454 §144, 2018 ch. 118 (SB 1501) §45, 2020 ch. 97 (AB 2193) §33.

§562. 2020 Deletes. [1] State Military Reserve **[2]** his or her **[3]** State Military Reserve or his or her

SELECTED PROVISIONS Of The PENAL CODE

PART 1 Of Crimes and Punishments

TITLE 10 OF CRIMES AGAINST THE PUBLIC HEALTH AND SAFETY [Selected Provisions]

§385. "High voltage"; "overhead conductor"; penalty for activity within specified distance of high voltage overhead conductor and for failure to post warning sign; exceptions.

(a) The term "high voltage" as used in this section means, a voltage in excess of 750 volts, measured between conductors or measured between the conductor and the ground.

The term "overhead conductor" as used in this section means any electrical conductor (either bare or insulated) installed above the ground except such conductors as are enclosed in iron pipe or other metal covering of equal strength.

(b) Any person who either personally or through an employee or agent, or as an employee or agent of another operates, places, erects or moves any tools, machinery, equipment, material, building or structure within six feet of a high voltage overhead conductor is guilty of a misdemeanor.

(c) It shall be a misdemeanor to own, operate or to employ any person to operate, any crane, derrick, power shovel, drilling rig, hay loader, hay stacker, piledriver, or similar apparatus, any part of which is capable of vertical, lateral, or swinging motion, unless there is posted and maintained in plain view of the operator thereof, a durable warning sign legible at 12 feet, reading: "Unlawful to operate this equipment within six feet of high voltage lines."

Each day's failure to post or maintain such sign shall constitute a separate violation.

(d) The provisions of this section shall not apply to (1) the construction, reconstruction, operation or maintenance of any high voltage overhead conductor, or its supporting structures or appurtenances by persons authorized by the owner, or (2) the operation of standard rail equipment which is normally used in the transportation of freight or passengers, or the operation of relief trains or other emergency railroad equipment by persons authorized by the owner, or (3) any construction, reconstruction, operation or maintenance of any overhead structures covered by the rules for overhead line construction prescribed by the Public Utilities Commission of the State of California.

Misc. Provisions

TITLE 13
OF CRIMES AGAINST PROPERTY

CHAPTER 10
CRIMES AGAINST INSURED PROPERTY AND INSURERS
[Selected Provisions]

§549. Solicitation or referral for purposes of insurance fraud.

Any firm, corporation, partnership, or association, or any person acting in his or her individual capacity, or in his or her capacity as a public or private employee, who solicits, accepts, or refers any business to or from any individual or entity with the knowledge that, or with reckless disregard for whether, the individual or entity for or from whom the solicitation or referral is made, or the individual or entity who is solicited or referred, intends to violate Section 550 of this code or Section 1871.4 of the Insurance Code is guilty of a crime, punishable upon a first conviction by imprisonment in the county jail for not more than one year or by imprisonment pursuant to subdivision (h) of Section 1170 for 16 months, two years, or three years, or by a fine not exceeding fifty thousand dollars ($50,000) or double the amount of the fraud, whichever is greater, or by both that imprisonment and fine. A second or subsequent conviction is punishable by imprisonment pursuant to subdivision (h) of Section 1170 or by that imprisonment and a fine of fifty thousand dollars ($50,000). Restitution shall be ordered, including restitution for any medical evaluation or treatment services obtained or provided. The court shall determine the amount of restitution and the person or persons to whom the restitution shall be paid. **Leg.H.** 1991 chs. 116, 934, 1992 ch. 1352, effective September 30, 1992, 1993 ch. 589, 1994 chs. 841, 1031, 2000 ch. 843, 2003–04 ch. 2 (Fourth Extra. Sess.) (SB 2 (Fourth Extra. Sess.)), effective March 6, 2005, 2011 ch. 15 (AB 109) §391, effective April 4, 2011, operative October 1, 2011.

2011 Notes: This act is titled and may be cited as the 2011 Realignment Legislation addressing public safety. Stats. 2011 ch. 15 (AB 109) §1.

This act will become operative no earlier than October 1, 2011, and only upon creation of a community corrections grant program to assist in implementing this act and upon an appropriation to fund the grant program. Stats. 2011 ch. 15 (AB 109) §636; Stats. 2011 ch. 39 (AB 117) §68.

The Community Corrections Grant Program referred to in Stats. 2011 ch. 15 §636, as amended by Stats. 2011 ch. 39 §68, was created by Stats. 2011 ch. 40 §3, operative October 1, 2011.

§550. Making false or fraudulent claims—Punishment.

(a) It is unlawful to do any of the following, or to aid, abet, solicit, or conspire with any person to do any of the following:

(1) Knowingly present or cause to be presented any false or fraudulent claim for the payment of a loss or injury, including payment of a loss or injury under a contract of insurance.

(2) Knowingly present multiple claims for the same loss or injury, including presentation of multiple claims to more than one insurer, with an intent to defraud.

(3) Knowingly cause or participate in a vehicular collision, or any other vehicular accident, for the purpose of presenting any false or fraudulent claim.

(4) Knowingly present a false or fraudulent claim for the payments of a loss for theft, destruction, damage, or conversion of a motor vehicle, a motor vehicle part, or contents of a motor vehicle.

(5) Knowingly prepare, make, or subscribe any writing, with the intent to present or use it, or to allow it to be presented, in support of any false or fraudulent claim.

(6) Knowingly make or cause to be made any false or fraudulent claim for payment of a health care benefit.

(7) Knowingly submit a claim for a health care benefit that was not used by, or on behalf of, the claimant.

(8) Knowingly present multiple claims for payment of the same health care benefit with an intent to defraud.

(9) Knowingly present for payment any undercharges for health care benefits on behalf of a specific claimant unless any known overcharges for health care benefits for that claimant are presented for reconciliation at that same time.

(10) For purposes of paragraphs (6) to (9), inclusive, a claim or a claim for payment of a health care benefit also means a claim or claim for payment submitted by or on the behalf of a provider of any workers' compensation health benefits under the Labor Code.

(b) It is unlawful to do, or to knowingly assist or conspire with any person to do, any of the following:

(1) Present or cause to be presented any written or oral statement as part of, or in support of or opposition to, a claim for payment or other benefit pursuant to an insurance policy, knowing that the statement contains any false or misleading information concerning any material fact.

(2) Prepare or make any written or oral statement that is intended to be presented to any insurer or any insurance claimant in connection with, or in support of or opposition to, any claim or payment or other benefit pursuant to an insurance policy, knowing that the statement contains any false or misleading information concerning any material fact.

(3) Conceal, or knowingly fail to disclose the occurrence of, an event that affects any person's initial or continued right or entitlement to any insurance benefit or payment, or the amount of any benefit or payment to which the person is entitled.

(4) Prepare or make any written or oral statement, intended to be presented to any insurer or producer for the purpose of obtaining a motor vehicle insurance policy, that the person to be the insured resides or is domiciled in this state when, in fact, that person resides or is domiciled in a state other than this state.

(c)(1) Every person who violates paragraph (1), (2), (3), (4), or (5) of subdivision (a) is guilty of a felony punishable by imprisonment pursuant to subdivision (h) of Section 1170 for two, three, or five years, and by a fine not exceeding fifty thousand dollars ($50,000), or double the amount of the fraud, whichever is greater.

(2) Every person who violates paragraph (6), (7), (8), or (9) of subdivision (a) is guilty of a public offense.

(A) When the claim or amount at issue exceeds nine hundred fifty dollars ($950), the offense is punishable by imprisonment pursuant to subdivision (h) of Section 1170 for two, three, or five years, or by a fine not exceeding fifty thousand dollars ($50,000) or double the amount of the fraud, whichever is greater, or by both that imprisonment and fine, or by imprisonment in a county jail not to exceed one year, by a fine of not more than ten thousand dollars ($10,000), or by both that imprisonment and fine.

(B) When the claim or amount at issue is nine hundred fifty dollars ($950) or less, the offense is punishable by imprisonment in a county jail not to exceed six months, or by a fine of not more than one thousand dollars ($1,000), or by both that imprisonment and fine, unless the aggregate amount of the claims or amount at issue exceeds nine hundred fifty dollars ($950) in any 12-consecutive-month period, in which case the claims or amounts may be charged as in subparagraph (A).

(3) Every person who violates paragraph (1), (2), (3), or (4) of subdivision (b) shall be punished by imprisonment pursuant to subdivision (h) of Section 1170 for two, three, or five years, or by a fine not exceeding fifty thousand dollars ($50,000) or double the amount of the fraud, whichever is greater, or by both that imprisonment and fine, or by imprisonment in a county jail not to exceed one year, or by a fine of not more than ten thousand dollars ($10,000), or by both that imprisonment and fine.

(4) Restitution shall be ordered for a person convicted of violating this section, including restitution for any medical evaluation or treatment services obtained or provided. The court shall determine the amount of restitution and the person or persons to whom the restitution shall be paid.

(d) Notwithstanding any other provision of law, probation shall not be granted to, nor shall the execution or imposition of a sentence be suspended for, any adult person convicted of felony violations of this section who previously has been convicted of felony violations of this section or Section 548, or of Section 1871.4 of the Insurance Code, or former Section 556 of the Insurance Code, or former Section 1871.1 of the Insurance Code as an adult under charges separately brought and tried two or more times. The existence of any fact that would make a person ineligible for probation under this subdivision shall be alleged in the information or indictment, and either admitted by the defendant in an open court, or found to be true by the jury trying the issue of guilt or by the court where guilt is established by plea of guilty or nolo contendere or by trial by the court sitting without a jury.

Except when the existence of the fact was not admitted or found to be true or the court finds that a prior felony conviction was invalid, the court shall not strike or dismiss any prior felony convictions alleged in the information or indictment.

This subdivision does not prohibit the adjournment of criminal proceedings pursuant to Division 3 (commencing with Section 3000) or Division 6 (commencing with Section 6000) of the Welfare and Institutions Code.

(e) Except as otherwise provided in subdivision (f), any person who violates subdivision (a) or (b) and who has a prior felony conviction of an offense set forth in either subdivision (a) or (b), in Section 548, in Section 1871.4 of the Insurance Code, in former Section 556 of the Insurance Code, or in former Section 1871.1 of the Insurance Code shall receive a two-year enhancement for each prior felony conviction in addition to the sentence provided in subdivision (c). The existence of any fact that would subject a person to a penalty enhancement shall be alleged in the information or indictment and either admitted by the defendant in open court, or found to be true by the jury trying the issue of guilt or by the court where guilt is established by plea of guilty or nolo contendere or by trial by the court sitting without a jury. Any person who violates this section shall be subject to appropriate orders of restitution pursuant to Section 13967 of the Government Code.

(f) Any person who violates paragraph (3) of subdivision (a) and who has two prior felony convictions for a violation of paragraph (3) of subdivision (a) shall receive a five-year enhancement in addition to the sentence provided in subdivision (c). The existence of any fact that would subject a person to a penalty enhancement shall be alleged in the information or indictment and either admitted by the defendant in open court, or found to be true by the jury trying the issue of guilt or by the court where guilt is established by plea of guilty or nolo contendere or by trial by the court sitting without a jury.

(g) Except as otherwise provided in Section 12022.7, any person who violates paragraph (3) of subdivision (a) shall receive a two-year enhancement for each person other than an accomplice who suffers serious bodily injury resulting from the vehicular collision or accident in a violation of paragraph (3) of subdivision (a).

(h) This section shall not be construed to preclude the applicability of any other provision of criminal law or equitable remedy that applies or may apply to any act committed or alleged to have been committed by a person.

(i) Any fine imposed pursuant to this section shall be doubled if the offense was committed in connection with any claim pursuant to any automobile insurance policy in an auto insurance fraud crisis area designated by the Insurance Commissioner pursuant to Article 4.6 (commencing with Section 1874.90) of Chapter 12 of Part 2 of Division 1 of the Insurance Code. **Leg.H.** 1992 ch. 675, 1993 ch. 120, effective July 16, 1993, ch. 605, 1994 chs. 841, 1008 §3.1, 1995 ch. 573 §2, effective October 4, 1995, ch. 574 §4, 1998 ch. 189, 1999 ch. 83, 2000 ch. 867, 2003–04 ch. 2 (Fourth Extra. Sess.) (SB 2 (Fourth Extra. Sess.)), effective March 6, 2005, 2009–10 ch. 28 (Third Extra. Sess.) (SB 18 (Third Extra. Sess.)) §29, effective January 25, 2010, 2011 ch. 15 (AB 109) §392, effective April 4, 2011, operative October 1, 2011.

2011 Notes: This act is titled and may be cited as the 2011 Realignment Legislation addressing public safety. Stats. 2011 ch. 15 (AB 109) §1.

This act will become operative no earlier than October 1, 2011, and only upon creation of a community corrections grant program to assist in implementing this act and upon an appropriation to fund the grant program. Stats. 2011 ch. 15 (AB 109) §636; Stats. 2011 ch. 39 (AB 117) §68.

The Community Corrections Grant Program referred to in Stats. 2011 ch. 15 §636, as amended by Stats. 2011 ch. 39 §68, was created by Stats. 2011 ch. 40 §3, operative October 1, 2011.

Ref.: Hanna § 2.03[2].

PART 2
Of Criminal Procedure

TITLE 3
ADDITIONAL PROVISIONS REGARDING CRIMINAL PROCEDURE

CHAPTER 2
TIME OF COMMENCING CRIMINAL ACTIONS
[Selected Provisions]

§803. Limitation not tolled or extended—Does not commence until discovery of offense.

(a) Except as provided in this section, a limitation of time prescribed in this chapter is not tolled or extended for any reason.

(b) [1] **The** time during which prosecution of the same person for the same conduct is pending in a court of this state is **not** a part of a limitation of time prescribed in this chapter.

(c) A limitation of time prescribed in this chapter does not commence to run until the discovery of an offense described in this subdivision. This subdivision applies to an offense punishable by imprisonment in the state prison or imprisonment pursuant to subdivision (h) of Section 1170, a material element of which is fraud or breach of a fiduciary obligation, the commission of the crimes of theft or embezzlement upon an elder or dependent adult, or the basis of which is misconduct in office by a public officer, employee, or appointee, including, but not limited to, the following offenses:

(1) Grand theft of any type, forgery, falsification of public records, or acceptance of, or asking, receiving, or agreeing to receive, a bribe, by a public official or a public employee, including, but not limited to, a violation of Section 68, 86, or 93.

(2) A violation of Section 72, 118, 118a, 132, 134, or 186.10.

(3) A violation of Section 25540, of any type, or Section 25541 of the Corporations Code.

(4) A violation of Section 1090 or 27443 of the Government Code.

(5) Felony welfare fraud or Medi-Cal fraud in violation of Section 11483 or 14107 of the Welfare and Institutions Code.

(6) Felony insurance fraud in violation of Section 548 or 550 of this code or former Section 1871.1, or Section 1871.4, of the Insurance Code.

(7) A violation of Section 580, 581, 582, 583, or 584 of the Business and Professions Code.

(8) A violation of Section 22430 of the Business and Professions Code.

(9) A violation of Section 103800 of the Health and Safety Code.

(10) A violation of Section 529a.

(11) A violation of subdivision (d) or (e) of Section 368.

(d) If the defendant is out of the state when or after the offense is committed, the prosecution may be commenced as provided in Section 804 within the limitations of time prescribed by this chapter, and no time up to a maximum of three years during which the defendant is not within the state shall be a part of those limitations.

(e) A limitation of time prescribed in this chapter does not commence to run until the offense has been discovered, or could have reasonably been discovered, with regard to offenses under Division 7 (commencing with Section 13000) of the Water Code, under Chapter 6.5 (commencing with Section 25100) of, Chapter 6.7 (commencing with Section 25280) of, or Chapter 6.8 (commencing with Section 25300) of, Division 20 of, or Part 4 (commencing with Section 41500) of Division 26 of, the Health and Safety Code, or under Section 386, or offenses under Chapter 5 (commencing with Section 2000) of Division 2 of, Chapter 9 (commencing with Section 4000) of Division 2 of, Section 6126 of, Chapter 10 (commencing with Section 7301) of Division 3 of, or Chapter 19.5 (commencing with Section 22440) of Division 8 of, the Business and Professions Code.

(f)(1) Notwithstanding any other limitation of time described in this chapter, if subdivision (b) of Section 799 does not apply, a criminal complaint may be filed within one year of the date of a report to a California law enforcement agency by a person of any age alleging that [2] **the person**, while under 18 years of age, was the victim of a crime described in Section 261, 286, 287, 288, 288.5, or 289, former Section 288a, or Section 289.5, as enacted by Chapter 293 of the Statutes of 1991 relating to penetration by an unknown object.

(2) This subdivision applies only if all of the following occur:

(A) The limitation period specified in Section 800, 801, or 801.1, whichever is later, has expired.

(B) The crime involved substantial sexual conduct, as described in subdivision (b) of Section 1203.066, excluding masturbation that is not mutual.

(C) There is independent evidence that corroborates the victim's allegation. If the victim was 21 years of age or older at the time of the report, the independent evidence shall clearly and convincingly corroborate the victim's allegation.

(3) [3] Evidence may **not** be used to corroborate the victim's allegation **if** that [4] **evidence** would **otherwise** be inadmissible during trial. Independent evidence [5] **excludes** the opinions of mental health professionals.

(4)(A) In a criminal investigation involving any of the crimes listed in paragraph (1) committed against a child, when the applicable limitations period has not expired, that period shall be tolled from the time a party initiates litigation challenging a grand jury subpoena until the end of the litigation, including any associated writ or appellate proceeding, or until the final disclosure of evidence to the investigating or prosecuting agency, if that disclosure is ordered pursuant to the subpoena after the litigation.

(B) [6] This subdivision [7] **does not affect** the definition or applicability of any evidentiary privilege.

(C) This subdivision shall not apply if a court finds that the grand jury subpoena was issued or caused to be issued in bad faith.

(g)(1) Notwithstanding any other limitation of time described in this chapter, a criminal complaint may be filed within one year of the date on which the identity of the suspect is conclusively established by DNA testing, if both of the following conditions are met:

(A) The crime is one that is described in subdivision (c) of Section 290.

(B) The offense was committed [8] **before** January 1, 2001, and biological evidence collected in connection with the offense is analyzed for DNA type no later than January 1, 2004, or the offense was committed on or after January 1, 2001, and biological evidence collected in connection with the offense is analyzed for DNA type no later than two years from the date of the offense.

(2) For purposes of this section, "DNA" means deoxyribonucleic acid.

(h) For any crime, the proof of which depends substantially upon evidence that was seized under a warrant, but which is unavailable to the prosecuting authority under the procedures described in People v. Superior Court (Laff) (2001) 25 Cal.4th 703, People v. Superior Court (Bauman & Rose) (1995) 37 Cal.App.4th 1757, or subdivision (c) of Section 1524, relating to claims of evidentiary privilege or attorney work product, the limitation of time prescribed in this chapter shall be tolled from the time of the seizure until final disclosure of the evidence to the prosecuting authority. [9] This section **does not** otherwise [10] **affect** the definition or applicability of any evidentiary privilege or attorney work product.

(i) Notwithstanding any other limitation of time described in this chapter, a criminal complaint may be filed within one year of the date on which a hidden recording is discovered related to a violation of paragraph (2) or (3) of subdivision (j) of Section 647.

(j) Notwithstanding any other limitation of time described in this chapter, if a person flees the scene of an accident that caused death or permanent, serious injury, as defined in subdivision (d) of Section 20001 of the Vehicle Code, a criminal complaint brought pursuant to paragraph (2) of subdivision (b) of Section 20001 of the Vehicle Code may be filed within the applicable time period described in Section 801 or 802 or one year after the person is initially identified by law enforcement as a suspect in the commission of the offense, whichever is later, but in no case later than six years after the commission of the offense.

(k) Notwithstanding any other limitation of time described in this chapter, if a person flees the scene of an accident, a criminal complaint brought pursuant to paragraph (1) or (2) of subdivision (c) of Section 192 may be filed within the applicable time period described in Section 801 or 802, or one year after the person is initially identified by law enforcement as a suspect in the commission of that offense, whichever is later, but in no case later than six years after the commission of the offense.

(*l*) A limitation of time prescribed in this chapter does not commence to run until the discovery of an offense involving the offering or giving of a bribe to a public official or public employee, including, but not limited to, a violation of Section 67, 67.5, 85, 92, or 165, or Section 35230 or 72530 of the Education Code.

(m) Notwithstanding any other limitation of time prescribed in this chapter, if a person actively conceals or attempts to conceal an accidental death in violation of Section 152, a criminal complaint may be filed within one year after the person is initially identified by law enforcement as a suspect in the commission of that offense, provided, however, that in any case a complaint may not be filed more than four years after the commission of the offense.

(n)(1) Notwithstanding any other limitation of time described in this chapter, a criminal complaint brought pursuant to a violation of Section 367g may be filed within one year of the discovery of the offense or within one year after the offense could have reasonably been discovered.

(2) This subdivision applies to crimes that were committed on or after January 1, 2021, and to crimes for which the statute of limitations that was in effect before January 1, 2021, has not run as of January 1, 2021. Leg.H. 2005 chs. 2 (SB 16) §3, effective February 28, 2005, 479 (SB 111) §3, 2007 ch. 579 (SB 172) §41, effective October 13, 2007, 2011 ch. 15 (AB 109) §447, effective April 4, 2011, operative October 1, 2011, ch. 211 (AB 708) §1.5, 2013 ch. 765 (AB 184) §1, 2014 ch. 191 (SB 950) §1, 2015 ch. 338 (AB 835) §1, 2016 ch. 777 (SB 813) §3, 2017 ch. 74 (SB 610) §2, 2018 ch. 423 (SB 1494) §79, 2020 ch. 244 (AB 2014) §1.

§803. 2020 Deletes. [1] No **[2]** he or she **[3]** No **[4]** otherwise **[5]** does not include **[6]** Nothing in **[7]** affects **[8]** prior to **[9]** Nothing in **[10]** affects

2017 Note: This act shall be known and may be cited as Erica's Law. Stats. 2017 ch. 74 (SB 610) §1.

2011 Notes: This act is titled and may be cited as the 2011 Realignment Legislation addressing public safety. Stats. 2011 ch. 15 (AB 109) §1.

This act will become operative no earlier than October 1, 2011, and only upon creation of a community corrections grant program to assist in implementing this act and upon an appropriation to fund the grant program. Stats. 2011 ch. 15 (AB 109) §636; Stats. 2011 ch. 39 (AB 117) §68.

The Community Corrections Grant Program referred to in Stats. 2011 ch. 15 §636, as amended by Stats. 2011 ch. 39 §68, was created by Stats. 2011 ch. 40 §3, operative October 1, 2011.

2005 Note: This act shall be known, and may be cited, as the Child Sexual Abuse Prevention Act. Stats. 2005 ch. 479 (SB 111) §1.

TITLE 12
OF SPECIAL PROCEEDINGS OF A CRIMINAL NATURE

CHAPTER 3
OF SEARCH WARRANTS
[Selected Provisions]

§1524. Grounds for issuance.

(a) A search warrant may be issued upon any of the following grounds:

(1) When the property was stolen or embezzled.

(2) When the property or things were used as the means of committing a felony.

(3) When the property or things are in the possession of any person with the intent to use them as a means of committing a public offense, or in the possession of another to whom that person may have delivered them for the purpose of concealing them or preventing them from being discovered.

(4) When the property or things to be seized consist of an item or constitute evidence that tends to show a felony has been committed, or tends to show that a particular person has committed a felony.

(5) When the property or things to be seized consist of evidence that tends to show that sexual exploitation of a child, in violation of Section 311.3, or possession of matter depicting sexual conduct of a person under 18 years of age, in violation of Section 311.11, has occurred or is occurring.

(6) When there is a warrant to arrest a person.

(7) When a provider of electronic communication service or remote computing service has records or evidence, as specified in Section 1524.3, showing that property was stolen or embezzled constituting a misdemeanor, or that property or things are in the possession of any person with the intent to use them as a means of committing a misdemeanor public offense, or in the possession of another to whom that person may have delivered them for the purpose of concealing them or preventing their discovery.

(8) When the property or things to be seized include an item or evidence that tends to show a violation of Section 3700.5 of the Labor Code, or tends to show that a particular person has violated Section 3700.5 of the Labor Code.

(9) When the property or things to be seized include a firearm or other deadly weapon at the scene of, or at the premises occupied or under the control of the person arrested in connection with, a domestic violence incident involving a threat to human life or a physical assault as provided in Section 18250. This section does not affect warrantless seizures otherwise authorized by Section 18250.

(10) When the property or things to be seized include a firearm or other deadly weapon that is owned by, or in the possession of, or in the custody or control of, a person described in subdivision (a) of Section 8102 of the Welfare and Institutions Code.

(11) When the property or things to be seized include a firearm that is owned by, or in the possession of, or in the custody or control of, a person who is subject to the prohibitions regarding firearms pursuant to Section 6389 of the Family Code, if a prohibited firearm is possessed, owned, in the custody of, or controlled by a person against whom a protective order has been issued pursuant to Section 6218 of the Family Code, the person has been lawfully served with that order, and the person has failed to relinquish the firearm as required by law.

(12) When the information to be received from the use of a tracking device constitutes evidence that tends to show that either a felony, a misdemeanor violation of the Fish and Game Code, or a misdemeanor violation of the Public Resources Code has been committed or is being committed, tends to show that a particular person has committed a felony, a misdemeanor violation of the Fish and Game Code, or a misdemeanor violation of the Public Resources Code, or is committing a felony, a misdemeanor violation of the Fish and Game Code, or a misdemeanor violation of the Public Resources Code, or will assist in locating an individual who has committed or is committing a felony, a misdemeanor violation of the Fish and Game Code, or a misdemeanor violation of the Public Resources Code. A tracking device search warrant issued pursuant to this paragraph shall be executed in a manner meeting the requirements specified in subdivision (b) of Section 1534.

(13) When a sample of the blood of a person constitutes evidence that tends to show a violation of Section 23140, 23152, or 23153 of the Vehicle Code and the person from whom the sample is being sought has refused an officer's request to submit to, or has failed to complete, a blood test as required by Section 23612 of the Vehicle Code, and the sample will be drawn from the person in a reasonable, medically approved manner. This paragraph is not intended to abrogate a court's mandate to determine the propriety of the issuance of a search warrant on a case-by-case basis.

(14) Beginning January 1, 2016, the property or things to be seized are firearms or ammunition or both that are owned by, in the possession of, or in the custody or control of a person who is the subject of a gun violence restraining order that has been issued pursuant to Division 3.2 (commencing with Section 18100) of Title 2 of Part 6, if a prohibited firearm or ammunition or both is possessed, owned, in the custody of, or controlled by a person against whom a gun violence restraining order has been issued, the person has been lawfully served with that order, and the person has failed to relinquish the firearm as required by law.

(15) Beginning January 1, 2018, the property or things to be seized include a firearm that is owned by, or in the possession of, or in the custody or control of, a person who is subject to the prohibitions regarding firearms pursuant to Section 29800 or 29805, and the court has made a finding pursuant to subdivision (c) of Section 29810 that the person has failed to relinquish the firearm as required by law.

(16) When the property or things to be seized are controlled substances or a device, contrivance, instrument, or paraphernalia used for unlawfully using or administering a controlled substance pursuant to the authority described in Section 11472 of the Health and Safety Code.

(17)(A) When all of the following apply:

(i) A sample of the blood of a person constitutes evidence that tends to show a violation of subdivision (b), (c), (d), (e), or (f) of Section 655 of the Harbors and Navigation Code.

(ii) The person from whom the sample is being sought has refused an officer's request to submit to, or has failed to complete, a blood test as required by Section 655.1 of the Harbors and Navigation Code.

(iii) The sample will be drawn from the person in a reasonable, medically approved manner.

(B) This paragraph is not intended to abrogate a court's mandate to determine the propriety of the issuance of a search warrant on a case-by-case basis.

(18) When the property or things to be seized consists of evidence that tends to show that a violation of paragraph (1), (2), or (3) of subdivision (j) of Section 647 has occurred or is occurring.

(19)(A) When the property or things to be seized are data, from a recording device installed by the manufacturer of a motor vehicle, that constitutes evidence that tends to show the commission of a felony or misdemeanor offense involving a motor vehicle, resulting in death or serious bodily injury to any person. The data accessed by a warrant pursuant to this paragraph shall not exceed the scope of the data that is directly related to the offense for which the warrant is issued.

(B) For the purposes of this paragraph, "recording device" has the same meaning as defined in subdivision (b) of Section 9951 of the Vehicle Code. The scope of the data accessible by a warrant issued pursuant to this paragraph shall be limited to the information described in subdivision (b) of Section 9951 of the Vehicle Code.

(C) For the purposes of this paragraph, "serious bodily injury" has the same meaning as defined in paragraph (4) of subdivision (f) of Section 243 of the Penal Code.

(20) When the property or things to be seized consists of evidence that tends to show that a violation of Section 647.9 has occurred or is occurring. Evidence to be seized pursuant to this paragraph shall be limited to evidence of a violation of Section 647.9 and shall not include evidence of a violation of a departmental rule or guideline that is not a public offense under California law.

(b) The property, things, person, or persons described in subdivision (a) may be taken on the warrant from any place, or from any person in whose possession the property or things may be.

(c) Notwithstanding subdivision (a) or (b), a search warrant shall not be issued for any documentary evidence in the possession or under the control of any person who is a lawyer as defined in Section 950 of the Evidence Code, a physician as defined in Section 990 of the Evidence Code, a psychotherapist as defined in Section 1010 of the Evidence Code, or a member of the clergy as defined in Section 1030 of the Evidence Code, and who is not reasonably suspected of engaging or having engaged in criminal activity related to the documentary evidence for which a warrant is requested unless the following procedure has been complied with:

(1) At the time of the issuance of the warrant, the court shall appoint a special master in accordance with subdivision (d) to accompany the person who will serve the warrant. Upon service of the warrant, the special master shall inform the party served of the specific items being sought and that the party shall have the opportunity to provide the items requested. If the party, in the judgment of the special master, fails to provide the items requested, the special master shall conduct a search for the items in the areas indicated in the search warrant.

(2)(A) If the party who has been served states that an item or items should not be disclosed, they shall be sealed by the special master and taken to court for a hearing.

(B) At the hearing, the party searched shall be entitled to raise any issues that may be raised pursuant to Section 1538.5 as well as a claim that the item or items are privileged, as provided by law. The hearing shall be held in the superior court. The court shall provide sufficient time for the parties to obtain counsel and make motions or present evidence. The hearing shall be held within three days of the service of the warrant unless the court makes a finding that the expedited hearing is impracticable. In that case, the matter shall be heard at the earliest possible time.

(C) If an item or items are taken to court for a hearing, any limitations of time prescribed in Chapter 2 (commencing with Section 799) of Title 3 of Part 2 shall be tolled from the time of the seizure until the final conclusion of the hearing, including any associated writ or appellate proceedings.

(3) The warrant shall, whenever practicable, be served during normal business hours. In addition, the warrant shall be served upon a party who appears to have possession or control of the items sought. If, after reasonable efforts, the party serving the warrant is unable to locate the person, the special master shall seal and return to the court, for determination by the court, any item that appears to be privileged as provided by law.

(d)(1) As used in this section, a "special master" is an attorney who is a member in good standing of the California State Bar and who has been selected from a list of qualified attorneys that is maintained by the State Bar particularly for the purposes of conducting the searches described in this section. These attorneys shall serve without compensation. A special master shall be considered a public employee, and the governmental entity that caused the search warrant to be issued shall be considered the employer of the special master and the applicable public entity, for purposes of Division 3.6 (commencing with Section 810) of Title 1 of the Government Code, relating to claims and actions against public entities and public employees. In selecting the special master, the court shall make every reasonable effort to ensure that the person selected has no relationship with any of the parties involved in the pending matter. Information obtained by the special master shall be confidential and may not be divulged except in direct response to inquiry by the court.

(2) In any case in which the magistrate determines that, after reasonable efforts have been made to obtain a special master, a special master is not available and would not be available within a reasonable period of time, the magistrate may direct the party seeking the order to conduct the search in the manner described in this section in lieu of the special master.

(e) Any search conducted pursuant to this section by a special master may be conducted in a manner that permits the party serving the warrant or that party's designee to accompany the special master as the special master conducts the search. However, that party or that party's designee may not participate in the search nor shall they examine any of the items being searched by the special master except upon agreement of the party upon whom the warrant has been served.

(f) As used in this section, "documentary evidence" includes, but is not limited to, writings, documents, blueprints, drawings, photographs, computer printouts, microfilms, X-rays, files, diagrams, ledgers, books, tapes, audio and video recordings, films, and papers of any type or description.

(g) No warrant shall issue for any item or items described in Section 1070 of the Evidence Code.

(h) Notwithstanding any other law, no claim of attorney work product as described in Chapter 4 (commencing with Section 2018.010) of Title 4 of Part 4 of the Code of Civil Procedure shall be sustained where there is probable cause to believe that the lawyer is engaging or has engaged in criminal activity related to the documentary evidence for which a warrant is requested unless it is established at the hearing with respect to the documentary evidence seized under the warrant that the services of the lawyer were not sought or obtained to enable or aid anyone to commit or plan to commit a crime or a fraud.

(i) Nothing in this section is intended to limit an attorney's ability to request an in-camera hearing pursuant to the holding of the Supreme Court of California in People v. Superior Court (Laff) (2001) 25 Cal.4th 703.

(j) In addition to any other circumstance permitting a magistrate to issue a warrant for a person or property in another county, when the property or things to be seized consist of any item or constitute evidence that tends to show a violation of Section 530.5, the magistrate may issue a warrant to search a person or property located in another county if the person whose identifying information was taken or used resides in the same county as the issuing court.

(k) This section shall not be construed to create a cause of action against any foreign or California corporation, its officers, employees, agents, or other specified persons for providing location information. **Leg.H.** 1872, 1899 p. 87, 1957 ch. 1884, 1978 ch. 1054, 1979 ch. 1034, 1980 ch. 441, 1982 ch. 438, 1996 chs. 1078, 1079 §11, 2002 chs. 864 (SB 1980), 1059 (AB 2055), effective September 29, 2002, §3 operative until January 1, 2003, §3.2, operative January 1, 2003, 2003 ch. 137 (AB 1773), 2004 ch. 182 (AB 3081), operative July 1, 2005, 2003–04 ch. 2 (SB 2 Fourth Extra. Sess.), effective March 6, 2005, 2005 chs. 279 (SB 1107) §12, 294 (AB 333) §24, 2006 ch. 538 (SB 1852) §507, 2009 chs. 450 (AB 532) §1, 473 (AB 789) §1.5, 2010 ch. 178 (SB 1115) §79, operative January 1, 2012, 2012 ch. 818 (AB 2055) §1, 2013 ch. 317 (SB 717) §1, effective September 20, 2013, 2014 ch. 872 (AB 1014) §1, 2015 chs. 118 (AB 539) §1, 124 (AB 1104) §1.5, amended by electorate (Prop. 63 §10.1) at the November 8, 2016, General Election, effective November 9, 2016, 2017 ch. 342 (AB 539) §1, 2019 ch. 196 (AB 1638) §1, 2020 ch. 219 (AB 2655) §2.

2009 Note: It is not the intent of the Legislature in enacting this act to authorize the seizure of any firearms not owned by, or in the possession of, or under the custody or control of, any person not subject to the provisions of Section 6389 of the Family Code. Stats. 2009 ch. 473 (AB 789) §2.

PART 3
Of Imprisonment and the Death Penalty

TITLE 4
COUNTY JAILS, FARMS AND CAMPS

CHAPTER 1
COUNTY JAILS
[Selected Provisions]

§4017. Prisoner labor for firefighting; benefits for injuries; "labor on the public works."

All persons confined in the county jail, industrial farm, road camp, or city jail under a final judgment of imprisonment rendered in a criminal action or proceeding and all persons confined in the county jail, industrial farm, road camp, or city jail as a condition of probation after suspension of imposition of a sentence or suspension of execution of sentence may be required by an order of the board of supervisors or city council to perform labor on the public works or ways in the county or city, respectively, and to engage in the prevention and suppression of forest, brush and grass fires upon lands within the county or city, respectively, or upon lands in adjacent counties where the suppression of fires would afford fire protection to lands within the county.

Whenever any such person so in custody shall suffer injuries or death while working in the prevention or suppression of forest, brush or grass fires he shall be considered to be an employee of the county or city, respectively, for the purposes of compensation under the provisions of the Labor Code regarding workers' compensation and such work shall be performed under the direct supervision of a local, state or federal employee whose duties include fire prevention and suppression work. A regularly employed member of an organized fire department shall not be required to directly supervise more than 20 such persons so in custody.

As used in this section, "labor on the public works" includes clerical and menial labor in the county jail, industrial farm, camps maintained for the labor of such persons upon the ways in the county, or city jail.

§4017.5. Work required of persons imprisoned for contempt.

In any case in which a person is confined to a city or county jail for a definite period of time for contempt pursuant to an action or proceeding other than a criminal action or proceeding, all of the provisions of law authorizing, requiring, or otherwise relating to, the performance of labor or work by persons sentenced to such facilities for like periods of time under a judgment of imprisonment, or a fine and imprisonment until the fine is paid or as a condition of probation after suspension of imposition of a sentence or suspension of execution of sentence, in a criminal action or proceeding, shall apply.

Nothing in this section shall be construed to authorize the confinement of any prisoner contrary to the provisions of Section 4001.

CHAPTER 2
COUNTY INDUSTRIAL FARMS AND ROAD CAMPS

ARTICLE 1
County Industrial Farms
[Selected Provisions]

§4125.1. Credit for fire suppression work.

The board of supervisors may contract with the United States or the State of California, or any department or agency thereof, for the performance of work and labor by any person in custody on any county industrial farm or industrial road camp or confined in the county jail or branch thereof under a final judgment of imprisonment rendered in a criminal action or proceeding or as a condition of probation in the suppression of fires within and upon the national forests, state parks, or other lands of the United States or the State of California, or within and upon such other lands, of whatever ownership, contiguous to, or adjacent to said state or federal lands, the suppression of fires upon which other lands affords fire protection to said state or federal lands. Such payments as may be so contracted for and to be paid by the United States or by the State of California for the work and labor so performed by any person so in custody may, by order of the board of supervisors, be credited in full or in part, and upon such terms and conditions as the board shall determine, to any such person so in custody and performing such work and labor, and all in addition to those credits hereinbefore provided in Section 4125 of this code.

Whenever any such person so in custody shall perform the services herein specified he shall be subject to workmen's compensation benefits to the same extent as a county employee, and the board of supervisors shall provide and cover any such person so in custody, while performing such services, with accident, death and compensation insurance as is otherwise regularly provided for employees of the county.

The term "suppression of fires" as herein used shall include the construction of fire-breaks and other works of improvement for the prevention and suppression of fire whether or not constructed in the actual course of suppression of existing fires.

TITLE 7
ADMINISTRATION OF THE STATE CORRECTIONAL SYSTEM

CHAPTER 2
THE SECRETARY OF THE DEPARTMENT OF CORRECTIONS AND REHABILITATION
[Selected Provisions]

§5069. Rehabilitation for injured inmates; notice to inmate.

(a) The administrative director of the Division of Industrial Accidents shall formulate procedures for the selection and orderly referral of injured inmates of state penal or correctional institutions who may be benefited by rehabilitation services and retrained for other positions upon release from incarceration. The State Department of Rehabilitation shall cooperate in both designing and monitoring results of rehabilitation programs for the disabled inmates. The primary purpose of this section is to rehabilitate injured inmates in order that they might engage in suitable and gainful employment upon their release.

(b) The director shall notify the injured inmate of the availability of rehabilitation services in those cases where there is continuing disability of 28 days and beyond. A copy of such notification shall be forwarded to the State Department of Rehabilitation.

(c) The initiation of a rehabilitation plan shall be the responsibility of the director.

(d) Upon establishment of a rehabilitation plan, the injured inmate shall cooperate in carrying it out.

(e) The injured inmate shall receive such medical and vocational rehabilitative services as may be reasonably necessary to restore him to suitable employment.

(f) The injured inmates rehabilitation benefit is an additional benefit and shall not be converted to or replace any workers' compensation benefit available to him.

TITLE V

(d) Upon establishment of a rehabilitation plan, the inmate is the chief component in carrying it out.

CHAPTER 3

SELECTED PROVISIONS Of The VEHICLE CODE

DIVISION 13 TOWING AND LOADING EQUIPMENT

CHAPTER 5 TRANSPORTING OTHER LOADS

ARTICLE 2 Vehicles Transporting Workmen [Selected Provisions]

§31402. Operation of farm labor vehicle after notice that vehicle is in unsafe condition.

(a) No person may operate any farm labor vehicle except as may be necessary to return the unladen vehicle or combination of vehicles to the residence or place of business of the owner or driver, or to a garage, after notice by the department to the owner that the vehicle is in an unsafe condition or is not equipped as required by this code, or any regulations adopted thereunder, until the vehicle and its equipment have been made to conform with the requirements of this code, or any regulations adopted thereunder, and approved by the department.

(b)(1) A person who operates a farm labor vehicle in violation of this section while the vehicle is in a condition that presents an immediate safety hazard is guilty of a misdemeanor punishable by a fine of not less than one thousand dollars ($1,000) and not more than five thousand dollars ($5,000), or both that fine and a sentence of confinement for not more than six months in the county jail. No part of any fine imposed under this subdivision may be suspended.

(2) As used in this subdivision, an "immediate safety hazard" is any equipment violation described in subdivision (a) of Section 31401 or Section 31405, including any violation of a regulation adopted pursuant to that provision or those provisions.

(c) Any member of the Department of the California Highway Patrol may impound a farm labor vehicle operated in violation of this section pursuant to Section 34506.4. A farm labor vehicle shall not be impounded unless a member of that department determines that a person has failed to comply with subdivision (a) or a person fails to comply with a lawful out-of-service order, as described in subdivision (b) of Section 2800. **Leg.H.** 1974 ch. 1447, effective September 26, 1974, 1980 ch. 676, 2000 ch. 873.

§31403. Transportation of passengers in unsafe farm labor vehicles.

A farm labor vehicle known to an owner, farm labor contractor, or driver, to be unsafe, or not equipped as required by this code, or any regulations adopted thereunder, shall not be used for transporting any passengers until it is examined and repaired or equipped as required by this code, or any regulations adopted thereunder, and certified by a competent mechanic to be safe and lawfully equipped.

SELECTED PROVISIONS Of The WELFARE AND INSTITUTIONS CODE

DIVISION 2 CHILDREN

PART 1 Delinquents and Wards of the Juvenile Court

CHAPTER 2 JUVENILE COURT LAW

ARTICLE 1 General Provisions [Selected Provisions]

§219. Ward of juvenile court engaged in rehabilitative work; right to benefits.

The board of supervisors of a county may provide a ward of the juvenile court engaged in rehabilitative work without pay, under an assignment by order of the juvenile court to a work project in a county department, with workers' compensation benefits for injuries sustained while performing such rehabilitative work, in accordance with Section 3364.55 of the Labor Code.

ARTICLE 24 Wards and Dependent Children—Juvenile Homes, Ranches and Camps [Selected Provisions]

§883. Wards of juvenile homes, ranches, or camps; right to benefits.

The wards committed to ranches, camps, or forestry camps may be required to labor on the buildings and grounds thereof, on the making of forest roads for fire prevention or firefighting, on forestation or reforestation of public lands, or on the making of firetrails or firebreaks, or to perform any other work or engage in any studies or activities on or off of the grounds of those ranches, camps, or forestry camps prescribed by the probation department, subject to such approval as the county board of supervisors by ordinance requires.

Wards may not be required to labor in fire suppression when under the age of 16 years.

Wards between the ages of 16 years and 18 years may be required to labor in fire suppression if all of the following conditions are met:

(a) The parent or guardian of the ward has given permission for that labor by the ward.

(b) The ward has completed 80 hours of training in forest firefighting and fire safety, including, but not limited to, the handling of equipment and chemicals, survival techniques, and first aid.

Whenever any ward committed to a camp is engaged in fire prevention work or the suppression of existing fires, he or she shall be subject to worker's compensation benefits to the same extent as a county employee, and the board of supervisors shall provide and cover any ward committed to a camp while performing that service, with accident, death and compensation insurance as is otherwise regularly provided for employees of the county. **Leg.H.** 1998 ch. 694.

DIVISION 9
PUBLIC SOCIAL SERVICES

PART 3
Aid and Medical Assistance

CHAPTER 3
STATE SUPPLEMENTARY PROGRAM FOR AGED, BLIND AND DISABLED

ARTICLE 7
In-Home Supportive Services
[Selected Provisions]

§12302.2. Performance of statutory compensation and benefit obligations when direct payment made to provider or recipient; payment of administrative costs.

(a)(1) If the state or a county makes or provides for direct payment to a provider chosen by a recipient or to the recipient for the purchase of in-home supportive services, the department shall perform or ensure the performance of all rights, duties, and obligations of the recipient relating to those services as required for purposes of unemployment compensation, unemployment compensation disability benefits, workers' compensation, retirement savings accounts, including payroll deduction IRA arrangements offered pursuant to the CalSavers Retirement Savings Program (Title 21 (commencing with Section 100000) of the Government Code), federal and state income tax, and federal old-age, survivors, and disability insurance benefits. Those rights, duties, and obligations include, but are not limited to, registration and obtaining employer account numbers, providing information, notices, and reports, making applications and returns, and withholding in trust from the payments made to or on behalf of a recipient amounts to be withheld from the wages of the provider by the recipient as an employer, including the sales tax extended to support services by Article 4 (commencing with Section 6150) of Chapter 2 of Part 1 of Division 2 of the Revenue and Taxation Code, and transmitting those amounts along with amounts required for all contributions, premiums, and taxes payable by the recipient as the employer to the appropriate person or state or federal agency. The department may ensure the performance of any or all of these rights, duties, and obligations by contract with any person, or any public or private agency.

(2) Contributions, premiums, and taxes shall be paid or transmitted on the recipient's behalf as the employer for any period commencing on or after January 1, 1978, except that contributions, premiums, and taxes for federal and state income taxes and federal old-age, survivors, and disability insurance contributions shall be paid or transmitted pursuant to this section commencing with the first full month that begins 90 days after the effective date of this section.

(3) Contributions, premiums, and taxes paid or transmitted on the recipient's behalf for unemployment compensation, workers' compensation, and the employer's share of federal old-age, survivors, and disability insurance benefits shall be payable in addition to the maximum monthly amount established pursuant to Section 12303.5 or subdivision (a) of Section 12304 or other amount payable to or on behalf of a recipient. Contributions, premiums, or taxes resulting from liability incurred by the recipient as employer for unemployment compensation, workers' compensation, and federal old-age, survivors, and disability insurance benefits with respect to any period commencing on or after January 1, 1978, and ending on or before the effective date of this section shall also be payable in addition to the maximum monthly amount established pursuant to Section 12303.5 or subdivision (a) of Section 12304 or other amount payable to or on behalf of the recipient. Nothing in this section shall be construed to permit any interference with the recipient's right to select the provider of services or to authorize a charge for administrative costs against any amount payable to or on behalf of a recipient.

(b) If the state makes or provides for direct payment to a provider chosen by a recipient, the Controller shall make any deductions from the wages of in-home supportive services personnel that are authorized by Sections 1152 and 1153 of the Government Code, as limited by Section 3515.6 of the Government Code, and for the sales tax extended to support services by Article 4 (commencing with Section 6150) of Chapter 2 of Part 1 of Division 2 of the Revenue and Taxation Code.

(c) Funding for the costs of administering this section and for contributions, premiums, and taxes paid or transmitted on the recipient's behalf as an employer pursuant to this section shall qualify, where possible, for the maximum federal reimbursement. To the extent that federal funds are inadequate, notwithstanding Section 12306, the state shall provide funding for the purposes of this section. **Leg.H.** 1978 ch. 463, effective July 18, 1978, 2002 ch. 1135 (AB 2235), 2010 ch. 725 (AB 1612) §22, effective October 19, 2010, 2016 ch. 804 (SB 1234) §20, 2018 ch. 37 (AB 1817) §62, effective June 27, 2018.

2010 Note: Sections 7, 8, 22, and 26 of this act shall not be interpreted to alter the employer and employee relationship between any provider of in-home supportive services and any governmental agency, except in regard to the collection and disbursement of funds required by this act. Stats. 2010 ch. 725 (AB 1612) §32.

§12302.21. Workers' compensation coverage for employees of nonprofit and proprietary agencies who contract with counties to provide in-home supportive services.

(a) For purposes of providing cost-efficient workers' compensation coverage for in-home supportive services providers under this article, the department shall assume responsibility for providing workers' compensation coverage for employees of nonprofit agencies and proprietary agencies who provide in-home supportive services pursuant to contracts with counties. The workers' compensation coverage provided for these employees shall be provided on the same terms as provided to providers under Section 12302.2 and 12302.5.

(b) A county that has existing contracts with nonprofit agencies or proprietary agencies whose employees will be provided workers' compensation coverage by the department pursuant to subdivision (a), shall reduce the contract hourly rate by fifty cents ($0.50) per hour, effective on the date that the department implements this section. **Leg.H.** 2003 ch. 209 (AB 632), effective August 11, 2003, 2012 ch. 439 (AB 1471) §33, effective September 22, 2012.

2017 Note: This version became inoperative on September 22, 2012, upon operation of the amendment by Stats. 2012 ch. 439, and resumed operation on June 27, 2017, when Stats. 2017 ch. 25 §17, repealed that amended version.

Ref.: Hanna § 3.36[3].

§12302.5. Establishment of agents for employers in order to comply with federal and state laws.

(a) Counties may establish entities or agents to act on behalf of the employers for those recipients who are designated as the employer of the in-home supportive services worker and who elect not to, or who are unable to, ensure compliance with all applicable federal, state, and county wage, hour, and workplace laws.

(b) Any entity or agent established pursuant to this section shall not restrict or interfere with the right of a recipient to select, replace, and terminate the employment of his or her own provider of in-home supportive services and to set his or her own service schedule. **Leg.H.** 1994 ch. 1006 (SB 1484).

CHAPTER 7
BASIC HEALTH CARE

ARTICLE 1
General Provisions
[Selected Provisions]

§14011. Verification of income required to obtain benefits.

(a) Each applicant who is not a recipient of aid under the provisions of Chapter 2 (commencing with Section 11200) or Chapter 3 (commencing with Section 12000) shall be required to file an affirmation setting forth such facts about his annual income and other resources and qualifications for eligibility as may be required by the department. Such statements shall be on forms prescribed by the department.

(b) To the extent permitted by federal law, eligibility for medical assistance for such applicants shall not be granted until the applicant or designated representative provides independent documentation verifying statements of gross income by type and source; income amounts withheld for taxes, health care benefits available through employment, retirement, military service, work related injuries or settlements from prior injuries, employee retirement contributions, and other employee benefit contributions, deductible expenses for maintenance or improvement of income-producing property and status and value of property owned, other than property exempt under Section 14006. The director may prescribe those items of exempt property which the director deems should be verified as to status and value in order to reasonably assure a correct designation of those items as exempt.

(c) The verification requirements of subdivision (b) apply to income, income deductions and property both of applicants for medical assistance (other than applicants for public assistance) and to persons whose income, income deductions, expenses or property holdings must be considered in determining the applicant's eligibility and share of cost.

(d) A determination of eligibility and share of cost may be extended beyond otherwise prescribed time frames if, in the county department's judgment, and subject to standards of the director, the applicant or designated representative has good cause for failure to provide the required verification and continues to make a good faith effort to provide such verification.

(e) To the extent permitted by federal law, in addition to the other verification requirements of this section, a county department may require verification of any other applicant statements, or conduct a full and complete investigation of the statements, whenever a verification or investigation is warranted in the judgment of the county department.

(f) If documentation is unavailable, as defined in regulations promulgated by the department, the applicant's signed statement as to the value or amount shall be deemed to constitute verification.

ARTICLE 3
Administration
[Selected Provisions]

§14101.7. Reimbursement from Appeals Board.

The Workers' Compensation Appeals Board and the department shall exchange information and cooperate to assure that health services provided by Medi-Cal which are reimbursable by Workers' Compensation are identified, and that Workers' Compensation reimburses the department for those services.

DIVISION 10
STATE DEPARTMENT OF REHABILITATION

PART 1
General Provisions

CHAPTER 1
POWERS AND DUTIES
[Selected Provisions]

§19005.5. Federal targeted jobs tax credit eligibility.

(a) The Department of Rehabilitation shall establish a program authorizing rehabilitation professionals serving industrially injured workers under the provisions of Labor Code Section 139.5 to refer clients to the Department of Rehabilitation for federal targeted jobs tax credit eligibility determination. The Department shall set forth the specific requirements, procedures, and eligibility criteria. The Department shall not be required to certify, for purposes of the federal targeted jobs tax credit, industrially injured workers who do not meet the eligibility requirements set forth in the federal Rehabilitation Act.

(b) The Department shall be authorized to collect a fee from the insurer or self-insured employer in the amount necessary to determine eligibility and to certify the industrially injured worker for this program.

CALIFORNIA CODE OF REGULATIONS

SYNOPSIS

TITLE 2
ADMINISTRATION

DIVISION 1
Administrative Personnel

CHAPTER 3
DEPARTMENT OF PERSONNEL ADMINISTRATION

SUBCHAPTER 1
GENERAL CIVIL SERVICE RULES

ARTICLE 2
Traveling Expenses

§599.631. Transportation by Privately Owned Automobile—Excluded Employees.

TITLE 8
INDUSTRIAL RELATIONS

DIVISION 1
Department of Industrial Relations

CHAPTER 1
DIVISION OF WORKERS' COMPENSATION—QUALIFIED MEDICAL EVALUATOR REGULATIONS

ARTICLE 1
General

§1. Definitions.

ARTICLE 2
QME Eligibility

§10. Appointment of QMEs.
§10.2. The QME Fee Assessment Notice Form.
§11. Eligibility Requirements for Initial Appointment as a QME.
§11.5. Disability Evaluation Report Writing Course.
§12. Recognition of Specialty Boards.
§13. Physician's Specialty.
§14. Doctors of Chiropractic: Certification in Workers' Compensation Evaluation.
§15. Appointment of Retired or Teaching Physicians.
§16. Determination of Fees for QME Eligibility.
§17. Fee Schedule for QME.
§18. QME Fee Due Dates.
§19. Certificate of QME Status.

ARTICLE 2.5
Time Periods for Processing Applications for QME Status

§20. Time Periods.

ARTICLE 2.6
QME Office Locations

§26. QME Office Locations and Changes of Office Locations.

ARTICLE 3
Assignment of Qualified Medical Evaluators, Evaluation Procedure

§29. Specified Financial Interests That May Affect Assignment to QME Panels.
§30. QME Panel Requests.
§30.5. Specialist Designation.
§31. QME Panel Selection.
§31.1. QME Panel Selection Disputes in Represented Cases.
§31.3. Scheduling Appointment with Panel QME.
§31.5. QME Replacement Requests.
§31.7. Obtaining Additional QME Panel in a Different Specialty.
§32. Acupuncture Referrals.
§32.6. Additional QME Evaluations Ordered by the Appeals Board.
§33. Unavailability of QME.
§34. Appointment Notification and Cancellation.
§35. Exchange of Information and Ex Parte Communications.
§35.5. Compliance by AMEs and QMEs with Administrative Director Evaluation and Reporting Guidelines.
§36. Service of Comprehensive Medical–Legal Evaluation Reports by Medical Evaluators Including Reports Under Labor Code Section 4061.
§36.5. Service of Comprehensive Medical/Legal Report in Claims of Injury to the Psyche.
§36.7. QME Electronic Service Emergency Regulation in Response to COVID-19.
§37. Request for Factual Correction of a Comprehensive Medical-Legal Report from a Panel QME.
§38. Medical Evaluation Time Frames; Extensions for QMEs and AMEs.
§39. Destruction of Records by the Medical Director.
§39.5. Retention of Records by QMEs.

ARTICLE 4
Evaluation Procedures

§40. Disclosure Requirements: Injured Workers.
§41. Ethical Requirements.
§41.5. Conflicts of Interest by Medical Evaluators.
§41.6. Procedures After Notice of Conflict of Interest

and Waivers of Conflicts of Interest of an Evaluator.
§41.7. Gifts to Medical Evaluators.
§43. Method of Evaluation of Psychiatric Disability.
§44. Method of Evaluation of Pulmonary Disability.
§45. Method of Evaluation of Cardiac Disability.
§46. Method of Evaluation of Neuromusculoskeletal Disability.
§46.1. Guidelines for the Evaluation of Foot and Ankle Disability.
§46.2. QME Emergency Regulation in Response to COVID-19.
§47. Method of Evaluation of Immunologic Disability.

ARTICLE 4.5
Minimum Time Guidelines

§49. Definitions.
§49.2. Neuromusculoskeletal Evaluation.
§49.4. Cardiovascular Evaluation.
§49.6. Pulmonary Evaluation.
§49.8. Psychiatric Evaluation.
§49.9. Other Evaluation.

ARTICLE 5
QME Reappointment

§50. Reappointment: Requirements and Application Form.
§51. Reappointment: Failure to Comply with Time Frames.
§52. Reappointment: Unavailability Notification.
§54. Reappointment: Evaluations Rejected by Appeals Board.
§55. Reappointment: Continuing Education Programs.
§56. Reappointment: Failure to Comply with WCAB Order or Ruling.
§57. Reappointment: Professional Standard—Violation of Business and Professions Code Section 730.

ARTICLE 6
QME Discipline

§60. Discipline.
§61. Hearing Procedure.
§62. Probation.
§63. Denial of Appointment or Reappointment.
§65. Sanction Guidelines for Qualified Medical Evaluators.

ARTICLE 10
QME Application Forms

§100. The Application for Appointment as Qualified Medical Evaluator Form.
§102. The Application for QME Competency Examination Form.
§103. The QME Fee Assessment Form.
§104. The Reappointment Application as Qualified Medical Evaluator Form.

ARTICLE 10.5
QME Process Forms

§105. The Request for Qualified Medical Evaluator Panel — Unrepresented Form.
§106. The Request for Qualified Medical Evaluator Panel — Represented Form — for Injuries Occurring Prior to January 1, 2005.
§107. The Qualified Medical Evaluator Panel Selection Form.
§108. The Qualified Medical Evaluator Panel Selection Instruction Form.
§109. The Qualified Medical Evaluator Notice of Unavailability Form.
§110. The Appointment Notification Form.
§111. The Qualified Medical Evaluator's Findings Summary Form.
§112. The QME/AME Time Frame Extension Request Form.
§113. Notice of Denial of Request for Time Extension Form.
§116. Notice of Late QME/AME Report — No Extension Requested Form.
§117. Qualified Medical Evaluator Course Evaluation Form.
§118. Application for Accreditation or Re–Accreditation As Education Provider.
§119. Faculty Disclosure of Commercial Interest.
§120. Voluntary Directive for Alternate Service of Medical–Legal Evaluation Report on Disputed Injury to Psyche.
§121. Declaration Regarding Protection of Mental Health Record.
§122. AME or QME Declaration of Service of Medical–Legal Report.
§123. QME/AME Conflict of Interest Disclosure and Objection or Waiver by Represented–Parties Form.
§124. Specified Financial Interest Attachment to QME Forms 100, 103 or 104 ("SFI Form 124").

ARTICLE 15
Fraudulent or Misleading Advertising

§150. Definitions.
§151. Filing of Documents.
§152. Statement of Intent.
§153. False or Misleading Advertising Copy Prohibited.
§154. Permissible Advertising Content.
§155. Filing of Complaints.
§156. Requests to Review Advertising Copy.
§157. Determinations.
§158. Penalties.
§159. Severability.

CHAPTER 4.5
DIVISION OF WORKERS' COMPENSATION

SUBCHAPTER 1
ADMINISTRATIVE DIRECTOR—ADMINISTRATIVE RULES

ARTICLE 1.1
Workers' Compensation Information System

§9700. Authority.
§9701. Definitions.
§9702. Electronic Data Reporting.
§9703. Access to Individually Identifiable Information.
§9704. WCIS Advisory Committee.

ARTICLE 1.3
Public Disability Accommodations

§9708.1. Definitions.
§9708.2. Disability Accommodations Request Process.
§9708.3. Confidentiality.
§9708.4. Disability Accommodation Requests in Division of Workers' Compensation Hearings.
§9708.5. Decision-Making Process.
§9708.6. Appeal Procedure.

ARTICLE 1.5
Receipt of Salary by Workers' Compensation Administrative Law Judge

§9710. Authority.
§9711. Operative Date.
§9712. Definitions.
§9713. Receipt of Salary.
§9714. Procedures for Compliance With Labor Code Section 123.5(a).
§9714.5. Affidavit.
§9715. Procedures for Submitting a Cause for Decision.

ARTICLE 1.6
Ethical Standards of Workers' Compensation Administrative Law Judges; Enforcement of Standards

§9720.1. Authority.
§9720.2. Definitions.
§9721.1. Code of Judicial Ethics.
§9721.2. Gifts, Honoraria and Travel.
§9721.11. Requirement for Disclosure.
§9721.12. Disqualification.
§9721.13. What Are Not Grounds for Disqualification.
§9721.14. Manner of Disclosure.
§9721.21. Restriction on Investments.
§9721.31 Financial Interests in Educational Programs.
§9721.32. Duty to Report Ethics Violations.
§9721.33. Previously Earned Compensation.
§9722. The Workers' Compensation Ethics Advisory Committee.
§9722.1. Commencing an Investigation.
§9722.2. Investigation and Action by the Administrative Director or Court Administrator.
§9723. Miscellaneous Provisions.

ARTICLE 2
Disabilities, Description of

§9725. Method of Measurement.
§9726. Method of Measurement (Psychiatric).
§9727. Subjective Disability.

ARTICLE 3.5
Medical Provider Network

§9767.1. Medical Provider Networks—Definitions.
§9767.2. Review of Medical Provider Network Application or Plan for Reapproval.
§9767.3. Requirements for a Medical Provider Network Plan.
§9767.4. Cover Page for Medical Provider Network Application or Plan for Reapproval.
§9767.5. Access Standards.
§9767.5.1. Physician Acknowledgments.
§9767.6. Treatment and Change of Physicians Within MPN.
§9767.7. Second and Third Opinions.
§9767.8. Modification of Medical Provider Network Plan.
§9767.9. Transfer of Ongoing Care into the MPN.
§9767.10. Continuity of Care Policy.
§9767.11. Economic Profiling Policy.
§9767.12. Employee Notification.
§9767.13. Denial of Approval of Application or Reapproval; Re-Evaluation.
§9767.14. Probation, Suspension or Revocation of Medical Provider Network Plan; Hearing.
§9767.15. Compliance with Current MPN Regulations; Reapproval.
§9767.16. Medical Provider Network Complaints.
§9767.16.5. DWC Medical Provider Network Complaint Form 9767.16.5.
§9767.17. Petition for Suspension or Revocation of a Medical Provider Network.
§9767.17.5. DWC Petition for Suspension or Revocation of a Medical Provider Network Form 9767.17.5 [new].
§9767.18. Random Reviews.
§9767.19. Administrative Penalty Schedule; Hearing, Mitigation and Appeal.

ARTICLE 3.6
Independent Medical Review

§9768.1. Definitions.
§9768.2. Conflicts of Interest.
§9768.3. Qualifications of Independent Medical Reviewers.
§9768.4. IMR Contract Application Procedures.
§9768.5. Physician Contract Application Form.
§9768.6. Administrative Director's Action on Contract Application Submitted by Physician.
§9768.7. IMR Request to Be Placed on Voluntary Inactive Status.
§9768.8. Removal of Physicians from Independent Medical Reviewer List.
§9768.9. Procedure for Requesting an Independent Medical Review.
§9768.10. Independent Medical Review Application (Form).
§9768.11. In-Person Examination or Record Review IMR Procedure.
§9768.12. Contents of Independent Medical Review Reports.
§9768.13. Destruction of Records by the Administrative Director.
§9768.14. Retention of Records by Independent Medical Reviewer.
§9768.15. Charges for Independent Medical Reviewers.
§9768.16. Adoption of Decision.
§9768.17. Treatment Outside the Medical Provider Network.

ARTICLE 4
Certification Standards for Health Care Organizations

§9770. Definitions.
§9771. Applications for Certification.
§9771.1. Updating Applications.
§9771.2. Information to Be Furnished as it Becomes Available.
§9771.6. Application of Regulations Concerning Workers' Compensation Health Care Provider Organizations.
§9771.60. Further Definitions.
§9771.61. Prohibition of Bonuses or Gratuities in Solicitations.
§9771.62. Application for Authorization as a Workers'

Compensation Health Care Provider Organization.
§9771.63. Individual Information Sheet (WCHCPO 2).
§9771.64. Organization Assurances Prior to Solicitation.
§9771.65. Filing of Advertising and Disclosure Forms.
§9771.66. Deceptive Advertising.
§9771.67. Disclosure Form.
§9771.68. Deceptive Workers' Compensation Health Care Provider Organization Names.
§9771.69. Workers' Compensation Health Care Contracts.
§9771.70. Contracts with Providers.
§9771.71. Disclosure of Conflicts of Interest.
§9771.72. Contracts with Solicitor Firms.
§9771.73. Fiscal Soundness, Insurance, and Other Arrangements.
§9771.74. Fidelity Bond.
§9771.75. Reimbursements on a Fee-for-Services Basis: Determination of Status of Claims.
§9771.76. Medical Survey Procedure.
§9771.77. Medical Survey: Report of Correction of Deficiencies.
§9771.78. Removal of Books and Records from State.
§9771.79. Examination Procedure.
§9771.80. Additional or Nonroutine Examinations and Surveys.
§9771.81. Financial Statements.
§9771.82. Books and Records.
§9771.83. Retention of Books and Records.
§9772. General Standards.
§9773. Treatment Standards.
§9773.1. Referrals to Chiropractors.
§9774. Quality of Care.
§9775. Grievance and Dispute Resolution Procedure.
§9776. Workplace Safety and Health.
§9776.1. Return to Work Coordination.
§9777. Patient Assistance and Notification.
§9778. Evaluation.
§9779. Certification.
§9779.1. On-Site Surveys.
§9779.2. Suspension; Revocation; Hearing.
§9779.3. Obligations of Employer Covered by a Contract with a Health Care Organization.
§9779.4. DWC Form 1194.
§9779.45. Minimum Periods of Enrollment.
§9779.5. Reimbursement of Costs to the Administrative Director; Obligation to Pay Share of Administrative Expense.
§9779.8. Copies of Documents.

ARTICLE 5
Predesignation of Personal Physician; Request for Change of Physician; Reporting Duties of the Primary Treating Physician; Petition for Change of Primary Treating Physician

§9780. Definitions.
§9780.1. Employee's Predesignation of Personal Physician.
§9781. Employee's Request for Change of Physician.
§9782. Notice to Employee of Right to Choose Physician.
§9783. DWC Form 9783 Predesignation of Personal Physician.
§9783.1. DWC Form 9783.1 Notice of Personal Chiropractor or Personal Acupuncturist.
§9785. Reporting Duties of the Primary Treating Physician.
§9785.2. Form PR-2 "Primary Treating Physician's Progress Report."
§9785.2.1. Form PR-2 "Primary Treating Physician Progress Report" — Services On or After October 1, 2015.
§9785.3. Form PR-3 "Primary Treating Physician's Permanent and Stationary Report."
§9785.3.1. Form PR-3 "Primary Treating Physician's Permanent and Stationary Report" — Services On or After October 1, 2015.
§9785.4. Form PR-4 "Primary Treating Physician's Permanent and Stationary Report."
§9785.4.1. Form PR-4 "Primary Treating Physician's Permanent and Stationary Report" — Services On or After October 1, 2015.
§9785.5. Request for Authorization Form, DWC Form RFA.
§9786. Petition for Change of Primary Treating Physician.
§9786.1. Petition for Change of Primary Treating Physician; Response to Petition for Change of Primary Treating Physician (DWC Form 280 (Parts A and B)).
§9787. Appeal from Administrative Director's Order Granting or Denying Petition for Change of Primary Treating Physician.

ARTICLE 5.1
Provider Suspension Procedure

§9788.1. Notice of Provider Suspension.
§9788.2. Provider Request for Hearing.
§9788.3. Suspension Hearing.
§9788.4. Suspension Notification.
§9788.5. Amendment of the Order of Suspension or Determination and Order re: Suspension.
§9788.6. Service and Computation of Time.

ARTICLE 5.3
Official Medical Fee Schedule

§9789.10. Physician Services Rendered on or After July 1, 2004, but Before January 1, 2014 — Definitions.
§9789.11. Physician Services Rendered on or After July 1, 2004, but Before January 1, 2014.
§9789.12.1. Physician Fee Schedule: Official Medical Fee Schedule for Physician and Non–Physician Practitioner Services — For Services Rendered On or After January 1, 2014.
§9789.12.2. Calculation of the Maximum Reasonable Fee — Services Other than Anesthesia.
§9789.12.3. Status Codes C, I, N and R.
§9789.12.4. "By Report" — Reimbursement for Unlisted Procedures/Procedures Lacking RBRVUs.
§9789.12.5. Conversion Factors.
§9789.12.6. Geographic Health Professional Shortage Area Bonus Payment: Primary Care; Mental Health.
§9789.12.7. CMS' National Physician Fee Schedule Relative Value File / Relative Value Units (RVUs).
§9789.12.8. Status Codes.
§9789.12.9. Professional Component (PC)/Technical Component (TC) Indicator.
§9789.12.10. Coding; Current Procedural Terminology©, Fourth Edition.
§9789.12.11. Evaluation and Management: Coding — New Patient; Documentation.
§9789.12.12. Consultation Services Coding — Use of Visit Codes.
§9789.12.13. Correct Coding Initiative.
§9789.12.14. California Specific Codes.
§9789.12.15. California Specific Modifier.

§9789.13.1. Supplies.
§9789.13.2. Physician–Administered Drugs, Biologicals, Vaccines, Blood Products.
§9789.13.3. Physician–Dispensed Drugs.
§9789.14. Reimbursement for Reports, Duplicate Reports, Chart Notes.
§9789.15.1. Non–Physician Practitioner (NPP) — Payment Methodology.
§9789.15.2. Non–Physician Practitioner (NPP) — "Incident To" Services.
§9789.15.3. Qualified Non–Physician Anesthetist Services.
§9789.15.4. Physical Medicine/Chiropractic/Acupuncture Multiple Procedure Payment Reduction; Pre–Authorization for Specified Procedure/ Modality Services.
§9789.15.5. Ophthalmology Multiple Procedure Reduction.
§9789.15.6. Diagnostic Cardiovascular Procedures — Multiple Procedure Reduction.
§9789.16.1. Surgery — Global Fee.
§9789.16.2. Surgery — Billing Requirements for Global Surgeries.
§9789.16.3. Surgery — Global Fee — Miscellaneous Rules.
§9789.16.4. Surgery — Global Fee; Exception: Circumstances Allowing E&M Code During the Global Period; Primary Treating Physician's Progress Report (PR-2).
§9789.16.5. Surgery — Multiple Surgeries and Endoscopies.
§9789.16.6. Surgery — Bilateral Surgeries.
§9789.16.7. Surgery — Co–Surgeons and Team Surgeons.
§9789.16.8. Surgery — Assistants–at–Surgery.
§9789.17.1. Radiology Diagnostic Imaging Multiple Procedures.
§9789.17.2. Radiology Consultations.
§9789.17.3. Additional Payment Reductions for Certain Diagnostic Imaging Services.
§9789.18.1. Payment for Anesthesia Services — General Payment Rule.
§9789.18.2. Anesthesia — Personally Performed Rate.
§9789.18.3. Anesthesia — Medically Directed Rate.
§9789.18.4. Anesthesia — Definition of Concurrent Medically Directed Anesthesia Procedures.
§9789.18.5. Anesthesia — Medically Supervised Rate.
§9789.18.6. Anesthesia — Multiple Anesthesia Procedures.
§9789.18.7. Anesthesia — Medical and Surgical Services Furnished in Addition to Anesthesia Procedure.
§9789.18.8. Anesthesia — Time and Calculation of Anesthesia Time Units.
§9789.18.9. Anesthesia — Base Unit Reduction for Concurrent Medically Directed Procedures.
§9789.18.10. Anesthesia — Monitored Anesthesia Care.
§9789.18.11. Anesthesia Claims Modifiers.
§9789.18.12. Anesthesia and Medical/Surgical Service Provided by the Same Physician.
§9789.19. Update Table.
§9789.19.1. Table A.
§9789.20. General Information for Inpatient Hospital Fee Schedule — Discharge on or After July 1, 2004.
§9789.21. Definitions for Inpatient Hospital Fee Schedule.
§9789.22. Payment of Inpatient Hospital Services.
§9789.23. Hospital Cost to Charge Ratios, Hospital Specific Outliers, and Hospital Composite Factors.
§9789.24. Diagnostic Related Groups, Relative Weights, Geometric Mean Length of Stay.
§9789.25. Federal Regulations, Federal Register Notices, and Payment Impact File by Date of Discharge.
§9789.30. Hospital Outpatient Departments and Ambulatory Surgical Centers — Definitions.
§9789.31. Hospital Outpatient Departments and Ambulatory Surgical Centers — Adoption of Standards.
§9789.32. Outpatient Hospital Departments and Ambulatory Surgical Centers Fee Schedule — Applicability.
§9789.33. Hospital Outpatient Departments and Ambulatory Surgical Centers Fee Schedule — Determination of Maximum Reasonable Fee.
§9789.34. Table A.
§9789.35. Table B.
§9789.36. Update of Rules to Reflect Changes in the Medicare Payment System.
§9789.37. DWC Form 15 Election for High Cost Outlier.
§9789.38. Appendix X.
§9789.39. Update Table by Date of Service.
§9789.40. Pharmacy.
§9789.50. Pathology and Laboratory.
§9789.60. Durable Medical Equipment, Prosthetics, Orthotics, Supplies.
§9789.70. Ambulance Services.
§9789.110. Update of Rules to Reflect Changes in the Medicare Payment System.
§9789.111. Effective Date of Fee Schedule Provisions.

ARTICLE 5.5
Application of the Official Medical Fee Schedule (Treatment)

§9790. Authority.
§9790.1. Definitions.
§9791. Services Covered.
§9791.1. Medical Fee Schedule.
§9792. Determination of the Fee.
§9792.1. Payment of Inpatient Services of Health Facilities.
§9792.5. Payment for Medical Treatment.

ARTICLE 5.5.0
Rules for Medical Treatment Billing and Payment on or After October 15, 2011

§9792.5.0. Definitions.
§9792.5.1. Medical Billing and Payment Guide; Electronic Medical Billing and Payment Companion Guide; Various Implementation Guides.
§9792.5.2. Standardized Medical Treatment Billing Forms/Formats, Billing Rules, Requirements for Completing and Submitting Form CMS 1500, Form CMS 1450 (or UB-04), American Dental Association Form, Version 2006, NCPDP Workers' Compensation / Property & Casualty Universal Claim Form, Payment Requirements.
§9792.5.3. Medical Treatment Bill Payment Rules.
§9792.5.4. Second Review and Independent Bill Review — Definitions.
§9792.5.5. Second Review of Medical Treatment Bill or Medical–Legal Bill.
§9792.5.6. Provider's Request for Second Bill Review — Form.
§9792.5.7. Requesting Independent Bill Review.

§9792.5.8. Request for Independent Bill Review Form.
§9792.5.9. Initial Review and Assignment of Request for Independent Bill Review to IBRO.
§9792.5.10. Independent Bill Review — Document Filing.
§9792.5.11. Withdrawal of Independent Bill Review.
§9792.5.12. Independent Bill Review — Consolidation or Separation of Requests.
§9792.5.13. Independent Bill Review — Review.
§9792.5.14. Independent Bill Review — Determination.
§9792.5.15. Independent Bill Review — Implementation of Determination and Appeal.

ARTICLE 5.5.1
Utilization Review Standards

§9792.6. Utilization Review Standards—Definitions — For Utilization Review Decisions Issued Prior to July 1, 2013 for Injuries Occurring Prior to January 1, 2013.
§9792.6.1. Utilization Review Standards—Definitions — On or After January 1, 2013.
§9792.7. Utilization Review Standards—Applicability.
§9792.8. Utilization Review Standards—Medically-Based Criteria.
§9792.9. Utilization Review Standards—Timeframe, Procedures and Notice Content — For Injuries Occurring Prior to January 1, 2013, Where the Request for Authorization is Received Prior to July 1, 2013.
§9792.9.1. Utilization Review Standards—Timeframe, Procedures and Notice — On or After January 1, 2013.
§9792.10. Utilization Review Standards—Dispute Resolution — For Utilization Review Decisions Communicated Prior to July 1, 2013 for Injuries Occurring Prior to January 1, 2013.
§9792.10.1. Utilization Review Standards—Dispute Resolution — On or After January 1, 2013.
§9792.10.2. Application for Independent Medical Review, DWC Form IMR.
§9792.10.3. Independent Medical Review — Initial Review of Application.
§9792.10.4. Independent Medical Review — Assignment and Notification.
§9792.10.5. Independent Medical Review — Medical Records.
§9792.10.6. Independent Medical Review — Standards and Timeframes.
§9792.10.7. Independent Medical Review — Implementation of Determination and Appeal.
§9792.10.8. Independent Medical Review — Payment for Review.
§9792.10.9. Independent Medical Review — Publishing of Determinations.
§9792.11. Investigation Procedures: Labor Code §4610 Utilization Review Violations.
§9792.12. Administrative Penalty Schedule for Utilization Review and Independent Medical Review Violations.
§9792.13. Assessment of Administrative Penalties — Penalty Adjustment Factors.
§9792.14. Liability for Penalty Assessments.
§9792.15. Administrative Penalties Pursuant to Labor Code §§4610, 4610.5, and 4610.6 — Order to Show Cause, Notice of Hearing, Determination and Order, and Review Procedure.

ARTICLE 5.5.2
Medical Treatment Utilization Schedule

§9792.20. Medical Treatment Utilization Schedule—Definitions.
§9792.21. Medical Treatment Utilization Schedule.
§9792.21.1. Medical Evidence Search Sequence.
§9792.22. General Approaches.
§9792.23. Clinical Topics.
§9792.23.1. Cervical and Thoracic Spine Disorders Guideline.
§9792.23.2. Shoulder Disorders Guideline.
§9792.23.3. Elbow Disorders Guideline.
§9792.23.4. Hand, Wrist, and Forearm Disorders Guideline.
§9792.23.5. Low Back Disorders Guideline.
§9792.23.6. Knee Disorders Guideline.
§9792.23.7. Ankle and Foot Disorders Guideline.
§9792.23.8. Workplace Mental Health Guideline.
§9792.23.9. Eye Disorders Guideline.
§9792.23.10. Hip and Groin Disorders Guideline.
§9792.23.11. Occupational/Work-Related Asthma Guideline.
§9792.23.12. Occupational Interstitial Lung Disease Guideline.
§9792.24. Special Topics.
§9792.24.1. Acupuncture Medical Treatment Guidelines.
§9792.24.2. Chronic Pain Guidelines.
§9792.24.3. Postoperative Rehabilitation Guidelines.
§9792.24.4. Opioids Guidelines.
§9792.24.5. Traumatic Brain Injury Guideline.
§9792.25. Quality and Strength of Evidence — Definitions.
§9792.25.1. MTUS Methodology for Evaluating Medical Evidence.
§9792.26. Medical Evidence Evaluation Advisory Committee.
§9792.27.1. Medical Treatment Utilization Schedule (MTUS) Drug Formulary — Definitions.
§9792.27.2. MTUS Drug Formulary; MTUS Drug List; Scope of Coverage; Effective Date.
§9792.27.3. MTUS Drug Formulary Transition.
§9792.27.4. MTUS Drug Formulary — Pharmacy Networks; Pharmacy Benefit Manager Contracts.
§9792.27.5. MTUS Drug Formulary — Off-Label Use.
§9792.27.6. MTUS Drug Formulary — Access to Drugs Not Listed as an Exempt Drug on the MTUS Drug List.
§9792.27.7. MTUS Drug Formulary — Brand Name Drugs; Generic Drugs.
§9792.27.8. Physician-Dispensed Drugs.
§9792.27.9. Compounded Drugs.
§9792.27.10. MTUS Drug List; Exempt Drugs, Non-Exempt Drugs, Unlisted Drugs, Prospective Review.
§9792.27.11. Waiver of Prospective Review.
§9792.27.12. MTUS Drug List — Special Fill.
§9792.27.13. MTUS Drug List — Perioperative Fill.
§9792.27.14. Treatment Provided Under Applicable Health and Safety Regulations.
§9792.27.15. MTUS Drug List.
§9792.27.16. National Drug Codes, Unique Pharmaceutical Identifier — MTUS Drug List.
§9792.27.17. Formulary — Dispute Resolution.
§9792.27.18. Pharmacy and Therapeutics Committee — Composition; Application for Appointment; Term of Service.
§9792.27.19. Pharmacy and Therapeutics Committee — Application for Appointment to Committee Form.

§9792.27.20. Pharmacy and Therapeutics Committee — Conflict of Interest.
§9792.27.21. Pharmacy and Therapeutics Committee — Conflict of Interest Disclosure Form.
§9792.27.22. Pharmacy and Therapeutics Committee — Meetings.
§9792.27.23. MTUS Drug List Updates.

ARTICLE 5.6

Medical-Legal Expenses and Comprehensive Medical-Legal Evaluations

§9793. Definitions.
§9794. Reimbursement of Medical-Legal Expenses.
§9795. Reasonable Level of Fees for Medical-Legal Expenses, Follow-up, Supplemental and Comprehensive Medical-Legal Evaluations and Medical-Legal Testimony.

ARTICLE 5.7

Fees for Interpreter Services

§9795.1. Definitions.
§9795.1.5. Interpreters for Hearings, Depositions or Arbitrations.
§9795.1.6. Interpreters for Medical Treatment Appointments or Medical Legal Exams.
§9795.2. Notice of Right to Interpreter.
§9795.3. Fees for Interpreter Services.
§9795.4. Time for Payment; Effective Date.
§9795.5. Interpreter Directories.

ARTICLE 6

Consulting Physician, Certification of

§9796. Certification of Consulting Physician. How Initiated.
§9799. Criterion for Certifying Competence.
§9802. Notification by Administrative Director.

ARTICLE 7

Schedule for Rating Permanent Disabilities

§9805. Schedule for Rating Permanent Disabilities, Adoption, Amendment.
§9805.1. Data Collection, Evaluation, and Revision of Schedule.

ARTICLE 8

Benefit Notices; Claims Administrator's Duties and Responsibilities; Claim Form and Notice of Potential Eligibility for Benefits; Regulatory Authority of the Administrative Director

§9810. General Provisions.
§9811. Definitions.
§9812. Benefit Payment and Notice.
§9813.1. Notice of Offer of Modified or Alternative Work. For Injuries Between January 1, 2004 and December 31, 2012, Inclusive.
§9813.2. Return to Work Notices. For Injuries Occurring on or After January 1, 2005.
§9814. Salary Continuation.
§9815. Corrected Notice.

ARTICLE 8.1

Workers' Compensation Advertising by Non-Attorneys and Non-Physicians; Prohibition of False or Misleading Advertising

§9820. Definitions.
§9821. Coverage and Exclusions.
§9822. Severability.
§9823. General Workers' Compensation Advertising Rules.
§9824. Identification as Representative.
§9825. Representative's WCAB Qualification.
§9826. Advertisement by Unlicensed Attorney.
§9827. Advertisement by Unlicensed Medical Provider.
§9828. Use of Terms "Medical", "Legal", or Comparable Terms.
§9829. Information Required from Referral Panelists.
§9830. Information Supplied to Referral Panelists.
§9831. Registration Statement.
§9832. Maintenance of and Access to Records.
§9833. Right to Conduct Investigation.
§9834. Order to Produce Documents or Provide Information.
§9835. Compliance Orders.
§9836. Other Remedies; Cumulative Remedies.
§9837. Hearing.

ARTICLE 8.5

Employee Information

§9880. Written Notice to New Employees.
§9881. Posting of Notice to Employees.
§9881.1. Notice to Employees Poster.
§9883. Publication of Information, Approval, Spanish Translation.
§9884. Exceptions.

ARTICLE 10

Employee Death, Notice of

§9900. Employer.
§9905. Notice.
§9910. DIA Form 510: Notice of Employee Death.
§9914. Reproduction of Form 510, Notice of Employee Death.
§9918. Service on Administrative Director.

ARTICLE 10.5

Operation of the Information and Assistance Program of the Division of Workers' Compensation

§9921. Operative Date.
§9922. Purpose.
§9923. Designation.
§9924. Scope of Duties.
§9925. Use of Other Division Facilities.
§9926. Referrals to a Qualified Medical Evaluator.
§9927. Jurisdiction.
§9928. Procedures for Mediation and Recommendations.
§9928.1. Procedures for Asbestos Workers.
§9929. Costs.

ARTICLE 12

Document Copy and Electronic Transaction Fees

§9980. Definitions.
§9981. Bills for Copy Services.
§9982. Allowable Services.
§9983. Fees for Copy and Related Services.
§9990. Division Fees for Transcripts; Copies of Documents; Certifications; Case File Inspection; Electronic Transactions.
§9991. Payment of Fees in Advance to the Division.

SUBCHAPTER 1.5
INJURIES ON OR AFTER JANUARY 1, 1990

ARTICLE 1
Audit, General Definitions

§10100. Definitions—Prior to January 1, 1994.
§10100.1. Definitions—On or After January 1, 1994.
§10100.2. Definitions.

ARTICLE 2
Claims Administration and Recordkeeping

§10101. Claim File—Contents.
§10101.1. Claim File—Contents.
§10102. Retention of Claim Files.
§10103. Claim Log—Contents and Maintenance.
§10103.1. Claim Log—Contents and Maintenance.
§10103.2. Claim Log—Contents and Maintenance.
§10104. Annual Report of Inventory.

ARTICLE 3
Auditing

§10105. Auditing, Discretion of the Administrative Director.
§10106. Random and Non-Random Audit Subject Selection; Complaint/Information Investigation.
§10106.1. Routine and Targeted Audit Subject Selection; Complaint Tracking; Appeal of Targeted Audit Selection.
§10106.5. Civil Penalty Investigation.
§10107. Notice of Audit; Claim File Selection; Production of Claim Files; Auditing Procedure.
§10107.1. Notice of Audit; Claim File Selection; Production of Claim Files; Auditing Procedure.
§10108. Audit Violations—General Rules.
§10109. Duty to Conduct Investigation; Duty of Good Faith.

ARTICLE 4
Notices of Compensation Due

§10110. Notice of Intention to Issue a Notice of Compensation Due; Notice of Compensation Due; Review by Workers' Compensation Appeals Board.

ARTICLE 5
Administrative Penalties

§10111. Schedule of Administrative Penalties for Injuries on or After January 1, 1990, but Before January 1, 1994.
§10111.1. Schedule of Administrative Penalties for Injuries On or After January 1, 1994.
§10111.2. Full Compliance Audit Penalty Schedules; Target Audit Penalty Schedule.
§10112. Liability for Penalty Assessments.

ARTICLE 5.5
Administrative Penalties Pursuant to Labor Code Section 5814.6

§10112.1. Definitions.
§10112.2. Schedule of Administrative Penalties Pursuant to Labor Code §5814.6.
§10112.3. Notice of Administrative Penalty Assessment, Appeal Hearing Procedures and Review.

ARTICLE 6
Civil Penalty
[First Enacted Version]

§10113. Order to Show Cause Re: Assessment of Civil Penalty and Notice of Hearing.
§10113.1. Answer to Order to Show Cause.
§10113.2. Amended Complaint or Supplemental Order to Show Cause Before Submission of Case.
§10113.3. Administrative Director's Designation of Hearing Officer.
§10113.4. Written Statement and Supporting Evidence.
§10113.5. Prehearing Conference; Subject Matter; Prehearing Order.
§10113.6. Subpoenas.
§10114. Hearing.
§10114.1. Evidence; Examination of Witnesses.
§10114.2. Affidavits.
§10114.3. Oaths.
§10114.4. Determination.

ARTICLE 7
Appeals

§10115. Appeal of Notice of Compensation Due.
§10115.1. Appeal of Notice of Penalty Assessment—Filing and Contents.
§10115.2. Appeal of Notice of Penalty Assessment; Conference Process and Delegation of Authority; Notice of Findings, Service.

ARTICLE 6
Retraining and Return to Work—Definitions and General Provisions
[Second Enacted Version]

§10116. Applicability of Article.
§10116.1. Filing and Reporting Requirements.
§10116.2. Electronic Filing Exemption.
§10116.3. Incomplete Filings.
§10116.5. Technical Problems and Unavailability of EAMS.
§10116.6. Retraining and Return to Work File Retention.
§10116.7. Misfiled or Misdirected Documents.
§10116.8. Jurisdiction Where the Issue of Injury Has Not Been Resolved.
§10116.9. Definitions for Articles 6.5 and 7.5.

ARTICLE 6.5
Return to Work

§10117. Offer of Work; Adjustment of Permanent Disability Payments.
§10118. Form [DWC AD 10118 "Notice of Offer of Work for Injuries Occurring Between 1/1/05—12/31/12, Inclusive."].

ARTICLE 7.5
Supplemental Job Displacement Benefit

§10133.31. Supplemental Job Displacement Nontransferable Voucher for Injuries Occurring on or After January 1, 2013.
§10133.32. Form [DWC-AD 10133.32 "Supplemental Job Displacement Nontransferable Voucher For Injuries Occurring on or After 1/1/13."]
§10133.33. Form [DWC-AD 10133.33 "Description of Employee's Job Duties Form."]
§10133.34. Offer of Work for Injuries Occurring on or After January 1, 2013.
§10133.35. Form [DWC-AD 10133.35 "Notice of Offer

of Regular, Modified, or Alternative Work For Injuries Occurring on or After 1/1/13."]
§10133.36. Form [DWC-AD 10133.36 "Physician's Return-to-Work & Voucher Report."]
§10133.53. Form [DWC-AD 10133.53 "Notice of Offer of Modified or Alternative Work for Injuries Occurring Between 1/1/04 — 12/31/12, Inclusive."]
§10133.54. Dispute Resolution.
§10133.55. Form [DWC-AD 10133.55 "Request for Dispute Resolution Before the Administrative Director."]
§10133.56. Requirement to Issue Supplemental Job Displacement Nontransferable Training Voucher.
§10133.57. Form [DWC-AD 10133.57 "Supplemental Job Displacement Nontransferable Training Voucher Form for Injuries Occurring Between 1/1/04 — 12/31/12, Inclusive."]
§10133.58. State Approved or Accredited Schools.
§10133.59. The Administrative Director's List of Vocational Return to Work Counselors.
§10133.60. Termination of Claims Administrator's Liability for the Supplemental Job Displacement Benefit.

ARTICLE 8
Attorney Fee Disclosure Statement

§10134. Attorney Fee Disclosure Statement Form.
§10135. Required Use of Form.
§10135.1. Service of Form.

ARTICLE 9
Claim Form: Availability, Filing, Acknowledgement of Receipt, Dismissal

§10136. General: Definitions.
§10137. General: Employer Obligation.
§10138. Claim Form and Notice of Potential Eligibility for Benefits.
§10139. Workers' Compensation Claim Form (DWC 1) and Notice of Potential Eligibility.
§10140. Employer's Responsibility to Process Claim Form, Claims Administrator's Duty to Provide Claim Form.
§10141. Dismissal of Inactive Claim by Operation of Law After Notice.
§10142. Date of Denial for Purposes of End of Tolling of Limitations Period.

SUBCHAPTER 1.6
PERMANENT DISABILITY RATING DETERMINATION

§10150. Disability Evaluation Unit.
§10150.1. Signature Disputes and the Signatures of Consultants.
§10150.2. Technical Unavailability of EAMS.
§10150.3. Disability Evaluation Unit File Retention.
§10150.4. Misfiled or Misdirected Documents.
§10151. Filing Requirements.
§10151.1. Electronic Filing Exemption.
§10152. Disability, When Considered Permanent.
§10156. Formal Rating Determinations.
§10158. Formal Rating Determinations As Evidence.
§10159. Time Period for Issuing a Summary Rating Determination Pursuant to Labor Code §4061(e).
§10160. Summary Rating Determinations, Comprehensive Medical Evaluation of Unrepresented Employee.
§10160.1. Summary Rating Determinations, Report of Primary Treating Physician for Unrepresented Employee.
§10160.5. Summary Rating Determinations, Represented Employees.
§10161. Forms.
§10161.1. Reproduction of Forms.
§10162. Summary Rating Determinations, Apportionment.
§10163. Apportionment Referral.
§10164. Summary Rating Determinations, Reconsideration if Employee is Unrepresented.
§10165. Service of Summary Rating Determination and Notice of Options Following Permanent Disability Rating.
§10165.5. Notice of Options Following Disability Rating (DEU Form 110).
§10166. Consultative Ratings Determinations.
§10166.1. Form (Request for Consultative Rating).
§10167. Informal Ratings.
§10169. Commutation Tables and Instructions.
§10169.1. Commutation of Life Pension and Permanent Disability Benefits.

SUBCHAPTER 1.8
COLLECTIVE BARGAINING AGREEMENTS UNDER LABOR CODE SECTIONS 3201.5 AND 3201.7

§10200. Definitions
§10201. Procedure for Determining Eligibility Under Labor Code Section 3201.5.
§10202. Procedure for Recognizing Labor-Management Agreements Under Labor Code Section 3201.7.
§10202.1. Petition for Permission to Negotiate a Section 3201.7 Labor-Management Agreement (DWC Form RGS-1).
§10203. Reporting Data.
§10203.1. Aggregate Employer Annual Report (DWC Form GV-1).
§10203.2. Individual Employer Annual Report (DWC Form GV-2).
§10204. Annual Reports.

SUBCHAPTER 1.8.5
ELECTRONIC ADJUDICATION MANAGEMENT SYSTEM RULES

ARTICLE 1
Definitions and General Provisions

§10205. Definitions.
§10205.1. District Office Records Not Subject to Subpoena.
§10205.2. Compromise and Release Forms and Stipulations with Request for Award Forms.

ARTICLE 1.2
Electronic Filing

§10205.3. Case Names and Case Index.
§10205.4. Adjudication Files.
§10205.5. Official Participant Record and Duty to Furnish Correct Address.
§10205.6. Designated Preferred Method of Service.

§10205.7. Failure to Comply with the Electronic Adjudication Management System Rules.
§10205.8. Corrective Measures for Misfiled or Misdirected Documents into the Case Management System.
§10205.9. Extended System Unavailability.

ARTICLE 1.3
Filing of Documents by Parties or Lien Claimants

§10205.10. Manner of Filing Documents.
§10205.11. Electronic Filing Exemption.
§10205.12. Form and Size Requirements for Filed Documents.
§10205.13. Document Cover Sheet Form.
§10205.14. Document Separator Sheet Form.

ARTICLE 2
Electronic Filing System Rules

§10206. Electronic Document Filing; Electronic Adjudication Management System (EAMS) Reference Guide and Instructional Manual for E-Form Filers; Incorporation.
§10206.1. Electronic Document Filing; Electronic Adjudication Management System Business Rules for JET Filers; Incorporation.
§10206.2. Electronic Filing Exemption

ARTICLE 3
Manner of Filing of Electronic Documents

§10206.3. Time of Filing of Documents.
§10206.4. Uniform Assigned Names.
§10206.5. Form and Size Requirements for Electronic Filed Documents.

ARTICLE 4
DWC E-Forms, DWC Unstructured Forms, and DWC JET Forms

§10206.14. DWC E-Forms and DWC Unstructured Forms.
§10206.15. DWC JET Forms.

ARTICLE 5
The Form of Minutes of Hearing and Electronically Filed Decisions, Findings, Awards, and Orders

§10206.20. Minutes of Hearing Form.

ARTICLE 6
Initial Lien Filing and Lien Activation Fees

§10207. Initial Lien Filing Fees.
§10208. Lien Activation Fees.
§10208.1. Lien Fee Refunds.

ARTICLE 7
Declarations of Readiness to Proceed, Expedited Hearing and Pre-Trial Conference Statement Forms

§10208.2. Declaration of Readiness to Proceed Form.
§10208.3. Expedited Hearing Form.
§10208.4. Pre-Trial Conference Statement Form.

ARTICLE 8
Access to Records and Retention of Records

§10208.5. Access to and Viewing Adjudication Files.
§10208.6. Prohibitions on Document Inspection.
§10208.7. Retention, Return and Destruction of Records and Exhibits.

ARTICLE 9
Review of Administrative Orders Issued by the Administrative Director

§10208.8. Petition Appealing Order Granting or Denying Petition for Order Requiring Employee to Select Employer-Designated Physician.
§10208.9. Petition Appealing Notice of Compensation Due.
§10208.10. Petition Appealing Order of the Rehabilitation Unit.
§10208.11. Petition Appealing Determination Regarding Supplemental Job Displacement Benefits.

ARTICLE 10
Arbitration Submittal Form

§10208.12. Arbitration Submittal Form.

SUBCHAPTER 2
WORKERS' COMPENSATION APPEALS BOARD—RULES AND PRACTICE PROCEDURE

ARTICLE 1
General

§10300. Construction of Rules.
§10302. Rulemaking Notices.
§10305. Definitions.

ARTICLE 2
Powers, Duties and Responsibilities

§10320. Appeals Board Decisions and Orders.
§10325. En Banc and Significant Panel Decisions.
§10330. Authority of Workers' Compensation Judges.
§10338. Authority of Commissioners of the Appeals Board.
§10344. Authority of Commissioners, Deputy Commissioners and Presiding Workers' Compensation Judges.
§10346. Authority of Presiding Workers' Compensation Judge to Assign or Transfer Cases.
§10355. Appointment and Authority of Pro Tempore Workers' Compensation Judges.
§10360. Testimony of Judicial or Quasi-Judicial Officers.
§10370. Extensions Of Time During Public Emergencies.

ARTICLE 3
Parties, Joinder and Consolidation

§10380. Necessary Parties.
§10382. Joinder of Parties.
§10390. Proper Identification of Parties.
§10396. Consolidation of Cases.
§10398. Assignment of Consolidated Cases.

ARTICLE 4
Conduct of Parties, Attorneys and Non-Attorney Representatives

§10400. Attorney Representatives.
§10401. Non-Attorney Representatives.
§10402. Substitution or Dismissal of Attorneys and Non-Attorney Representatives.
§10403. Complaints Regarding Violations of Labor Code Section 4907.
§10404. Suspension and Removal of a Non-Attorney Representative's Privilege to Appear Before

the Workers' Compensation Appeals Board Under Labor Code Section 4907.
§10410. Ex Parte Communications.
§10421. Sanctions.
§10430. Vexatious Litigants.
§10440. Contempt.
§10445. Disbarred and Suspended Attorneys.

ARTICLE 5
Applications and Answers

§10450. Invoking the Jurisdiction of the Workers' Compensation Appeals Board.
§10455. Applications.
§10460. Request for Findings of Fact.
§10462. Subsequent Injuries Benefits Trust Fund Application.
§10465. Answers.
§10470. Labor Code Section 4906(h) Statement.

ARTICLE 6
Venue

§10480. Venue.
§10482. Venue When Applicant is Employee of Division of Workers' Compensation.
§10488. Objection to Venue Based on an Attorney's Principal Place of Business.
§10490. Petition for Change of Venue for Good Cause.

ARTICLE 7
Petitions, Pleadings and Forms

§10500. Form Pleadings.
§10510. Petitions and Answers to Petitions.
§10515. Demurrer, Judgment on the Pleadings and Summary Judgment Not Permitted.
§10517. When Pleadings Deemed Amended.
§10520. Special Requirements for Pleadings Filed or Served by Representatives.
§10525. Petition for Increased or Decreased Compensation — Serious and Willful Misconduct.
§10528. Petition for Increased Compensation — Discrimination Under Labor Code Section 132a.
§10530. Emergency Petition for Stay.
§10534. Petition to Reopen.
§10536. Petition for New and Further Disability.
§10540. Petition to Terminate Liability for Continuing Temporary Disability.
§10545. Petition for Costs.
§10547. Petition for Labor Code Section 5710 Attorney's Fees.
§10550. Petition to Dismiss Inactive Cases.
§10555. Petition for Credit.

ARTICLE 8
Petitions Related to Administrative Orders

§10560. Petitions Related to Orders Issued by the Division of Workers' Compensation Administrative Director or the Director of Industrial Relations.
§10565. Petition Appealing Denial of Return-to-Work Supplement.
§10567. Petition Appealing Independent Bill Review Determination.
§10570. Petition to Enforce an Administrative Director Determination.
§10575. Petition Appealing Independent Medical Review Determination.
§10580. Petition Appealing Medical Provider Network Determination of the Administrative Director.
§10590. Petition Appealing Audit Penalty Assessment — Labor Code Section 129.5(g).

ARTICLE 9
Filing and Service of Documents

§10600. Time for Actions.
§10605. Time Within Which to Act When a Document is Served by Mail, Fax or E-Mail.
§10610. Filing and Service of Documents.
§10615. Filing of Documents.
§10617. Restrictions on the Rejection for Filing of Documents Subject to a Statute of Limitations or a Jurisdictional Time Limitation.
§10620. Filing Proposed Exhibits.
§10625. Service.
§10628. Service by the Workers' Compensation Appeals Board.
§10629. Designated Service.
§10632. Service on the Division of Workers' Compensation and the Director of Industrial Relations.
§10635. Duty to Serve Documents.
§10637. Service of Medical Reports, Medical-Legal Reports, and other Medical Information on a Non-Physician Lien Claimant.

ARTICLE 10
Subpoenas

§10640. Subpoenas.
§10642. Notice to Appear or Produce.
§10644. Subpoenas of Electronic Records.
§10647. Witness Fees and Subpoenas.
§10650. Subpoena for Medical Witness.
§10655. Subpoenas for Medical Information by Non-Physician Lien Claimants.
§10660. X-Rays.

ARTICLE 11
Evidence

§10670. Documentary Evidence.
§10672. Evidence Taken Without Notice.
§10675. Formal Permanent Disability Rating Determinations.
§10677. Oversized Exhibits, Diagnostic Imaging, Physical Exhibits and Exhibits on Media.
§10680. Reproductions of Documents.
§10682. Physicians' Reports as Evidence.
§10683. Specific Finding of Fact — Labor Code Section 139.2(d)(2).
§10685. Vocational Experts' Reports as Evidence.

ARTICLE 12
Settlements

§10700. Approval of Settlements.
§10702. Service of Settlements on Lien Claimants.
§10705. Procedures — Labor Code Section 3761.

ARTICLE 13
Hearings

§10742. Declaration of Readiness to Proceed.
§10744. Objection to Declaration of Readiness to Proceed.
§10745. Setting the Case.

§10748. Continuances.
§10750. Notice of Hearing.
§10751. Appearances by Non-Attorney Representatives Not Identified on Notice of Representation.
§10752. Appearances Required.
§10755. Failure to Appear at Mandatory Settlement Conference in Case in Chief.
§10756. Failure to Appear at Trial in Case in Chief.
§10757. Appearances in Settled Cases.
§10758. Status Conferences.
§10759. Mandatory Settlement Conferences.
§10761. Submission at Conference.
§10782. Expedited Hearings.
§10785. Priority Conferences.
§10786. Determination of Medical-Legal Expense Dispute.
§10787. Trials.
§10788. Petition for Automatic Reassignment of Trial or Expedited Hearing to Another Workers' Compensation Judge.
§10789. Walk-Through Documents.
§10790. Interpreters.

ARTICLE 14
Record of Proceedings

§10800. Transcripts.
§10803. Record of Proceedings Maintained in Adjudication File.
§10807. Inspection of Workers' Compensation Appeals Board Records.
§10811. Destruction of Records.
§10813. Sealed Documents.
§10818. Recording of Proceedings.
§10820. When Certified Copies Will Issue.
§10825. Withholding Certified Copies.

ARTICLE 15
Findings, Awards and Orders

§10832. Notices of Intention and Orders after Notices of Intention.
§10833. Minute Orders.
§10835. Effect of Stipulations.
§10840. Approval of Attorney's Fee by Workers' Compensation Appeals Board Required.
§10842. Request for Increase of Attorney's Fee
§10844. Reasonable Attorney's Fee.
§10850. Order Dismissing Application.

ARTICLE 16
Liens

§10862. Filing and Service of Lien Claims and Supporting Documents.
§10863. Verification of Compliance with Labor Code Section 4903.6 on Filing of Lien Claim or Application by Lien Claimant.
§10868. Notices of Representation for Lien Claimants.
§10872. Notification of Resolution or Withdrawal of Lien Claims.
§10873. Lien Claimant Declarations of Readiness to Proceed.
§10874. Verification to Filing of Declaration of Readiness to Proceed by or on Behalf of Lien Claimant.
§10875. Lien Conferences.
§10876. Fees Required at Lien Conference.
§10878. Submission at Lien Conferences.
§10880. Lien Trials.
§10888. Dismissal of Lien Claims.
§10899. Unemployment Compensation Disability Liens.

ARTICLE 17
Arbitration

§10900. Mandatory Arbitration.
§10905. Voluntary Arbitration.
§10910. Selection of Arbitrator.
§10912. Disqualification of Arbitrator.
§10914. Record of Arbitration Proceeding.
§10920. Arbitrator Fee and Cost Disputes.

ARTICLE 18
Reconsideration, Removal and Disqualification

§10940. Filing and Service of Petitions for Reconsideration, Removal, Disqualification and Answers.
§10945. Required Content of Petitions for Reconsideration, Removal, Disqualification and Answers.
§10955. Petitions for Removal and Answers.
§10960. Petition for Disqualification of Workers' Compensation Judge.
§10961. Actions by Workers' Compensation Judge After Petition for Reconsideration is Filed.
§10962. Report of Workers' Compensation Judge.
§10964. Supplemental Petitions.
§10966. Correction of Errors.
§10972. Skeletal Petitions.
§10974. Allegations of Newly Discovered Evidence and Fraud.
§10984. Hearing After Reconsideration Granted.
§10986. Authority of Workers' Compensation Judge After Decision After Reconsideration.
§10990. Reconsideration of Arbitration Decisions Made Pursuant to Labor Code Sections 3201.5 and 3201.7.
§10995. Reconsideration of Arbitrator's Decisions or Awards Made Pursuant to the Mandatory or Voluntary Arbitration Provisions of Labor Code Sections 5270 through 5275.

CHAPTER 7
DEPARTMENT OF INDUSTRIAL RELATIONS

SUBCHAPTER 1
OCCUPATIONAL INJURY OR ILLNESS REPORTS AND RECORDS

ARTICLE 1
Reporting of Occupational Injury or Illness

§14000. Definitions.
§14001. Employer.
§14002. Insurer.
§14003. Physician.
§14004. Employer's Report of Occupational Injury or Illness, Form 5020, Rev. 7.
§14005. Reproduction of the Employer's Report.
§14006. Form 5021, Rev. 4, Doctor's First Report of Occupational Injury or Illness.
§14006.1. DIR Form 5021 (Rev. 5) 2015, Doctor's First Report of Occupational Injury or Illness.
§14007. Reproduction of the Doctor's Report.

ARTICLE 2
Employer Records of Occupational Injury or Illness

§14300. Purpose.

§14300.1. Partial Exemption for Employers with 10 or Fewer Employees.
§14300.2. Partial Exemption for Establishments in Certain Industries.
§14300.3. Keeping Records for More than One Agency.
§14300.4. Recording Criteria.
§14300.5. Determination of Work-Relatedness.
§14300.6. Determination of New Cases.
§14300.7. General Recording Criteria.
§14300.8. Recording Criteria for Needlestick and Sharps Injuries.
§14300.9. Recording Criteria for Cases Involving Medical Removal Under Cal/OSHA Standards.
§14300.10. Recording Criteria for Cases Involving Occupational Hearing Loss.
§14300.11. Recording Criteria for Work-Related Tuberculosis Cases.
§14300.12. Recording Criteria for Cases Involving Work-Related Musculoskeletal Disorders.
§14300.29. Forms.
§14300.30. Multiple Establishments.
§14300.31. Covered Employees.
§14300.32. Annual Summary.
§14300.33. Retention and Updating.
§14300.34. Change in Establishment Ownership.
§14300.35. Employee Involvement.
§14300.36. Prohibition Against Discrimination.
§14300.38. Variances from the Recordkeeping Rule.
§14300.40. Providing Records to Government Representatives.
§14300.41. Electronic Submission of Injury and Illness Records to OSHA.
§14300.42. Requests from the Bureau of Labor Statistics for Data.
§14300.43. Annual Summary and Posting of the 2001 Data.
§14300.44. Retention and Updating of Old Forms.
§14300.46. Definitions.
§14300.47. Recordkeeping Requirements for Employers Covered by the Federal Mine Safety and Health Act.
§14300.48. Effective Date.

SUBCHAPTER 2
REPORTS OF INJURY TO BE FILED BY THE CALIFORNIA DEPARTMENT OF CORRECTIONS

ARTICLE 1
Prison Labor

§14900. Prison Labor.

ARTICLE 2
Reports to Be Filed by Department of Corrections

§14901. Department of Corrections' Report of Injury (Form 5030).
§14902. Agreement Between Parties.
§14903. Color of Form 5030.
§14904. Time of Filing.
§14910. Physician or Surgeon (Report Form 5031).
§14911. Agreement Between Parties.
§14912. Color of Form 5031.
§14913. Time of Filing Form 5031.
§14920. Effective Date.

CHAPTER 8
OFFICE OF THE DIRECTOR

SUBCHAPTER 2
ADMINISTRATION OF SELF-INSURANCE PLANS

ARTICLE 1
Definitions

§15201. Definitions.
§15202. Advisory Committee.

ARTICLE 2
Certificate of Consent to Self-Insure

§15203. Applications and Required Forms.
§15203.1. Agreement of Assumption and Guarantee of Subsidiary's or Affiliate's Liabilities.
§15203.2. Continuing Financial Capacity for Individual Private Self-Insurers.
§15203.3. Resolution To Authorize Self-Insurance for an Individual Private Employer.
§15203.4. Resolution to Self Insure for Public Entities.
§15203.5. Agreement and Undertaking for Security Deposit.
§15203.6. Delayed Start-up of a Self-Insurance Program.
§15203.7. Documentation of Consent to Self-Insure and Notice to Employees of Self-Insured Status.
§15203.8. Change in Status.
§15203.9. Validity of Certificate of Consent to Self Insure.
§15203.10. Reinstatement of a Certificate of Consent to Self-Insure.
§15203.11. Continuing Financial Capacity for Public Self-Insurers.
§15204. Application Filing Fee.
§15205. Interim Certificates.

ARTICLE 3
Security Deposit Requirements

§15209. Actuarial Studies and Summaries.
§15210. Security Deposit.
§15210.1. Adjustments in the Amount of Security Deposit.
§15210.2. Deposit Adjustment Upon Revocation of Certificate to Self-Insure.
§15210.3. Insurance Coverage.
§15211. Allocation of the Security Deposit for Private Individual Self-Insurers.
§15211.1. Appeals to Increase in Security Deposit Due to Impaired Financial Condition of Self-Insurer.
§15211.2. Guaranty of Workers' Compensation Liabilities.
§15211.3. Agreement and Undertaking For Security Deposit.
§15212. Surety Bonds.
§15213. Approved Securities.
§15214. Cash in Trust.
§15215. Letters of Credit.
§15216. Administration of Defaulted Self-Insurer's Claims.

ARTICLE 3.1
Alternative Composite Deposits

§15220. Participation in Alternative Composite Deposits.
§15220.1. Financial Information.
§15220.2. Listing of Security Deposit Amount Required.
§15220.3. Alternative Composite Deposits.
§15220.4. Deposit Assessments by the Security Fund for Participants of the Alternative Composite Deposit.
§15220.5. Deposit Assessments; Failure to Pay; Assessment Liability.
§15220.6. New Self Insurers Fair Share Contribution Surcharge Fee.
§15220.7. Appeals of Deposit Assessments and Appeals of Deposit Assessment Penalties.
§15220.8. Requirements for Use and Investment of Cash Generated from Deposit Assessments.

ARTICLE 4
Assessments

§15230. Private Sector License Fee Assessment.
§15231. Public Sector License Fee.
§15232. User Funding Assessment.
§15233. Fraud Investigation and Prosecution Assessment.
§15234. Cal/OSHA Targeted Inspection and Consultation Assessment.

ARTICLE 5
Self-Insurer's Annual Report

§15251. Self-Insurer's Annual Report.

ARTICLE 6
Estimating Work Injury Claims and Medical Reports

§15300. Estimating and Reporting Work Injury Claims.
§15301. Revision of Estimates.
§15302. Medical Reports.
§15303. Medical, Surgical, Hospital Contract.

ARTICLE 7
Injury and Illness Prevention Program

§15353. Injury and Illness Prevention Program.
§15354. Willful or Repeat Violation of Injury Prevention Program by a Self Insurer.

ARTICLE 8
Transfer of Liabilities

§15360. Transfer of Claim Liabilities.

ARTICLE 9
Recordkeeping and Audits

§15400. Claim File.
§15400.1. Claim Log.
§15400.2. Maintenance of Records.
§15402. Notice of Change of Administrator and Location of Records.
§15402.1. Self Insurer's Interim Report.
§15402.2. Report of Transfer of Records.
§15402.3. Notice of Change of Membership in a Joint Powers Authority or in a Private Group Self Insurer.
§15402.4. Transfer of Claim Files and Computerized Claim File Data Information.
§15403. Audits.
§15403.1. Notice of Special Audit.
§15404. Expense of Out-of-State Audit.
§15404.1. Expense of Revoked Certificate Audit.
§15404.2. Expense of Special Audit.
§15405. Confidentiality.

ARTICLE 10
Revocation of a Certificate to Self-Insure or Certificate to Administer and Continuing Jurisdiction

§15420. Compliance with Statutes and Regulatory Requirements.
§15422. Voluntary Revocation.
§15423. Revocation.
§15424. Revoked Certificate Report.
§15425. Revoked Certificate Audit.
§15426. Release of Security Deposit.
§15427. Continuing Jurisdiction.
§15428. Administration of Claims After Revocation.

ARTICLE 11
Hearing and Appeal Procedures

§15430. Hearing.
§15430.1. Definitions.
§15431. Delegation of Authority.
§15431.1. Appeals and/or Requests for Hearings.
§15431.2. Complaints.
§15432. Hearings; Special Requirements: Failure to Appear.
§15433. Hearing Officer: Appointment and Delegation of Authority.
§15434. Hearing Procedures.
§15435. Decision.
§15436. Reconsideration.
§15437. Appellate Review.
§15438. Severability.

ARTICLE 12
Claims Administration

§15450. Certificate to Administer.
§15450.1. Third Party Claims Administration for New Private Self Insurers.
§15452. Administrator Competence.
§15454. Certificate to Administer: Fees.
§15458. Claims Administration and Recordkeeping.
§15459. Notification of Willful Failure to Pay Benefits.
§15463. Revocation of Certificate.

ARTICLE 13
Group Self-Insurance

§15470. General.
§15471. Initial Feasibility Study.
§15472. Minimum Financial Requirements for a Group Self-Insurer.
§15473. Homogeneity of Group Members.
§15474. Reporting Periods.
§15475. Board of Trustees.
§15475.1. Separation Among Service Providers.
§15475.2. Restriction on Use of Funds.
§15475.3. Investment of Funds.
§15476. Advanced Contribution Discounts.
§15477. Surplus or Insufficient Funding.
§15478. Excess Insurance.
§15479. Indemnity Agreement and Power of Attorney.
§15480. Termination of Membership in a Group Self-Insurer.
§15481. Actuarial Studies and Summaries.
§15482. Private Group Application.
§15482.1. Private Group Member Application.

§15482.2. Interim Certificates to Group Members.
§15483. Agreement of Assumption and Guarantee of Group Member's Liabilities.
§15484. Continuing Financial Capacity of Group Self-Insurers.
§15485. Resolution to Authorize Self Insurance for a Group Self Insurer or Group Member.
§15486. Agreement and Undertaking for Director to Utilize Security Deposit to Pay Benefits Due.
§15486.1. Group Self-Insurer Injury and Illness Prevention Program.
§15487. Delayed Start-Up of a Group Self-Insurer or Group Member Participation in Group Self-Insurance.
§15488. Initial Issuance of the Certificate of Consent to Self Insure and Notice to Employees of Self Insured Status.
§15489. Reporting Group Charter Amendments.
§15489.1. Change in Status.
§15490. Validity of Certificate to Group Self Insurer or Group Member.
§15490.1. Reinstatement of a Certificate or Affiliate Certificate of Consent to Self Insure.
§15491. Group Self-Insurer and Group Member Application Filing Fees.
§15496. Group Self-Insurer's Security Deposit.
§15497. Adjustments in the Amount of a Group Self-Insurer's Security Deposit.
§15497.1. Security Deposit Adjustment upon Revocation of Group Self Insurer or Group Member Certificates.
§15498. Insurance Coverage.
§15499. Allocation of the Security Deposit for a Group Self Insurer.
§15499.5. Appeals of Increases in Security Deposits Based on Impaired Group Self Insurer Financial Condition.

SUBCHAPTER 2.05 ENFORCEMENT OF WORKERS' COMPENSATION COVERAGE, PENALTY ASSESSMENT ORDERS, STOP ORDERS AND POSTING AND NOTICE REQUIREMENTS

ARTICLE 1 Delegation of Enforcement Authority

§15550. Delegation of Enforcement Authority.

ARTICLE 2 Definitions

§15551. Direction to File Verified Statement.
§15552. Director.
§15553. Division.
§15554. Findings.
§15555. Issue.
§15556. Notice of Findings on Penalty Assessment Order or Stop Order.
§15557. Penalty Assessment Order.
§15558. Special Judgment.
§15559. Stop Order.
§15560. Uninsured Employer.
§15561. Verified Statement.
§15562. Verified Petition.

ARTICLE 3 Investigation of Employer's Workers' Compensation Status

§15563. Access to Places of Labor.
§15564. Inquiry Into Workers' Compensation Status.
§15565. Posting Notice of Workers' Compensation Carrier.

ARTICLE 4 Penalties

§15566. Assessment of Penalty.
§15567. Penalty Assessment Orders.
§15568. Types of Penalty Assessment Orders.
§15569. Maximum Penalties.
§15570. Number of Employees.

ARTICLE 5 Stop Order

§15571. When Issued.
§15571.5. When Effective.
§15572. Failure to Observe Stop Order Constitutes Misdemeanor.
§15573. Injunctive Relief.

ARTICLE 6 Contents of Orders, of Direction to File Verified Statement and of Verified Statement

§15574. Stop Order.
§15575. Penalty Assessment Orders.
§15576. Direction to File Verified Statement.
§15577. Verified Statement.

ARTICLE 7 Service of Stop Order and Penalty Assessment Order

§15578. Service.

ARTICLE 8 Review of Proceedings and Withdrawal Proceedings

§15579. Review of Proceedings to Correct Designation of Legal Entity or Clerical Error.
§15580. Withdrawal of Orders.

ARTICLE 9 Appeal Procedures

§15581. Stop Order.
§15582. Penalty Assessment Orders.
§15583. Grounds of Objection.
§15584. Matters Not Grounds for Objection.

ARTICLE 10 Hearing

§15585. Proceedings Under Oath.
§15586. Proceedings Shall Be Recorded.
§15587. Conduct of Hearing.
§15588. Right to Subpoenas and Subpoenas Duces Tecum.
§15589. Custody of Papers Filed With the Division.
§15590. Decision of the Division.

ARTICLE 11 Writ of Review

§15591. Employer's Right to Writ of Review.

ARTICLE 12 Special Judgment Procedure as to Penalty Assessment Orders

§15592. Procedures After Hearing or in the Absence of a Hearing.

§15593. Procedures Subsequent to Entry of Judgment.

ARTICLE 14
Penalty Liens

§15594. Recording of Penalty Lien.
§15595. Cancellation of Penalty Lien.

ARTICLE 15
Notice of Right to Benefits

§15596. Notice of Employee's Right to Workers' Compensation Benefits.

SUBCHAPTER 2.06 WORKERS' COMPENSATION—ADMINISTRATION REVOLVING FUND ASSESSMENT, UNINSURED EMPLOYERS BENEFITS TRUST FUND ASSESSMENT, SUBSEQUENT INJURIES BENEFITS TRUST FUND ASSESSMENTS, LABOR ENFORCEMENT AND COMPLIANCE FUND ASSESSMENT, OCCUPATIONAL SAFETY AND HEALTH FUND ASSESSMENT, AND FRAUD SURCHARGE

ARTICLE 1
Definitions

§15600. Definitions.

ARTICLE 2
Determination of Assessments and/or Surcharge

§15601. Determination of Revolving Fund, Subsequent Injuries Fund, Labor Enforcement and Compliance Fund, Occupational Safety and Health Fund, and Uninsured Employers Fund Total Assessment.
§15601.5. Ascertainment of State Fraud Investigation and Prosecution Surcharge.
§15601.7. Determination of Self Insured Employers Subject to the Targeted Inspection Assessment.
§15601.8. Determination of Insured Employers' Payroll and Premium Data.
§15602. Allocation of Revolving Fund Assessment, Subsequent Injuries Fund Assessment, Labor Enforcement and Compliance Fund Assessment, Occupational Safety and Health Fund Assessment, Uninsured Employers Fund Assessment, and/or Fraud Surcharge Among Insured and Self–Insured Employers.
§15603. Determination of Insured and Self–Insured Employer Revolving Fund Assessment, Subsequent Injuries Fund Assessment, Labor Enforcement and Compliance Fund Assessment, Occupational Safety and Health Fund Assessment, Uninsured Employers Fund Assessment, and Fraud Surcharge Factors.
§15604. Surplus in Funding.

ARTICLE 3
Collection of Assessments and/or Surcharges

§15605. Collection of the Revolving Fund Assessment, Subsequent Injuries Fund Assessment, Labor Enforcement and Compliance Fund Assessment, Occupational Safety and Health Fund Assessment, Uninsured Employers Fund Assessment, and Fraud Surcharge from Self–Insured Employers.
§15606. Collection of Advances Against Insured Employers.
§15607. Collection of Revolving Fund Assessment, Subsequent Injuries Fund Assessment, Labor Enforcement and Compliance Fund Assessment, Occupational Safety and Health Fund Assessment, Uninsured Employers Fund Assessment, and Fraud Surcharge from Insured Employers.
§15608. Assessment and/or Surcharge Collection in Excess of Insured Employer Assessment Advance.
§15609. Credit for Undercollection.
§15611. Collection of Interim Assessments.

SUBCHAPTER 2.1 ILLEGALLY UNINSURED EMPLOYERS. DETERMINATIONS BY THE DIRECTOR: PRIMA FACIE ILLEGALLY UNINSURED, CORPORATE PARENT AND SUBSTANTIAL SHAREHOLDER; NOTICE; HEARINGS; APPEALS

ARTICLE 1
General

§15710. Definitions.
§15711. Delegation of Authority.

ARTICLE 2
Determinations by Director

§15720. Determinations.
§15721. Negative Inferences.
§15722. Reconsideration of Section 3715(c) Determinations; Finality.
§15723. Reconsideration of Section 3720.1(a) Determinations; Finality.

ARTICLE 3
Hearings Under Code Section 3720.1

§15730. Administrative Hearing.
§15731. Delegation of Authority.
§15732. Conduct of Hearing.

SUBCHAPTER 2.1.1 UNINSURED EMPLOYERS FUND AND SUBSEQUENT INJURIES FUND BENEFITS TO ALIENS

ARTICLE 1
Limitations on Benefits

§15740. Limitations on Uninsured Employers Fund and Subsequent Injuries Fund Benefits for Aliens.
§15741. Statement of Citizenship, Alienage, and Immigration Status for State Public Benefits, Form UEF-1.

SUBCHAPTER 7 RETURN-TO-WORK SUPPLEMENT

ARTICLE 1

§17300. General, Scope and Application of Article.
§17301. Definitions.

§17302. Eligibility.
§17303. Notice.
§17304. Deadline for Application.
§17305. Method of Application.
§17306. Application Contents.
§17307. Processing of Applications and Decision on Applications.
§17308. Supplement Payment.
§17309. Appeal to the WCAB.
§17310. False Claims.

TITLE 10
INVESTMENTS

CHAPTER 5
INSURANCE COMMISSIONER

SUBCHAPTER 3
INSURERS

ARTICLE 20
Standards Applicable to Workers' Compensation Claims Adjusters and Medical Billing Entities and Certification of Those Standards by Insurers

§2592. Authority and Purpose.
§2592.01. Definitions.
§2592.02. Training Required for Claims Adjusters and Medical-Only Claims Adjusters.
§2592.03. Curriculum.
§2592.04. Training Required for Medical Bill Reviewers.
§2592.05. Designation
§2592.06. Maintenance of Records.
§2592.07. Certification and Submission of Documents.
§2592.08. Insurer Annual Certification Form—Claims Adjusters and Medical-Only Claims Adjusters.
§2592.09. Insurer Annual Certification Form—Medical Bill Reviewers.
§2592.10. Designation—Claims Adjuster and Medical-Only Claims Adjuster.
§2592.11. Designation—Medical Bill Reviewer.
§2592.12. Designation—Experienced Claims Adjuster and Medical-Only Claims Adjuster.
§2592.13. Designation—Experienced Medical Bill Reviewer.
§2592.14. Post-Designation Training Form.

ARTICLE 21
Workers' Compensation Rating Organization Internet Web Sites

§2593. Authority and Purpose.
§2593.1. Definitions.
§2593.2. Employer Query Identifying Information.
§2593.3. Web Site Access Restrictions.
§2593.4. Disclaimers.
§2593.5. Updating Coverage Information.
§2593.6. Disputes.
§2593.7. Statistics To Be Maintained by the Rating Organization.

TITLE 16
PROFESSIONAL AND VOCATIONAL REGULATIONS

DIVISION 4
State Board of Chiropractic Examiners

ARTICLE 2
Practice of Chiropractic

§310. Change of Name.
§310.1. Replacement License.
§310.2. Use of Title by Unlicensed Persons.
§311. Advertisements.
§311.1. Chiropractic Specialties.
§312. Illegal Practice.
§312.1. Ownership of a Chiropractic Practice.
§312.2. Ownership of Practice upon the Death or Incapacity of a Licensee.
§313. Inducing Student to Practice Chiropractic.
§314. Law Violators.
§315. Mental Illness.
§316. Responsibility for Conduct on Premises.
§317. Unprofessional Conduct.
§317.1. Chiropractic Referral Services.
§317.5. Investigation and Enforcement Costs; Payment by Licentiate.
§318. Chiropractic Patient Records/Accountable Billings.
§318.1. Standard of Care Regarding Manipulation Under Anesthesia (MUA).
§319. Free or Discount Services.
§319.1. Informed Consent.

SELECTED PROVISIONS Of The CALIFORNIA CODE OF REGULATIONS

TITLE 2
ADMINISTRATION

DIVISION 1
Administrative Personnel

CHAPTER 3
DEPARTMENT OF PERSONNEL ADMINISTRATION

SUBCHAPTER 1
GENERAL CIVIL SERVICE RULES

ARTICLE 2
Traveling Expenses

§599.631. Transportation by Privately Owned Automobile—Excluded Employees.

(a) Where the employee is authorized to use a privately owned automobile on official state business the reimbursement rate shall be 34 cents per mile. Claims for reimbursement for private vehicle expenses must include the vehicle license number and the name of each state officer, employee or board, commission or authority member transported on the trip. No reimbursement of transportation expense shall be allowed any passenger in any vehicle operated by another state officer, employee or member.

(1) Expenses arising from travel between home and headquarters or garage shall not be allowed, except as provided in section 599.626(d)(2) or 599.626.1(c) of these regulations, regardless of the employee's normal mode of transportation.

(2) When a trip is commenced or terminated at a claimant's home on a regularly scheduled work day, the distance traveled shall be computed from either his/her residence or headquarters, whichever shall result in the lesser distance except as provided in section 599.626.1(c) of these regulations.

(3) However, if the employee commences or terminates travel on a regularly scheduled day off, mileage may be computed from his/her residence.

(b) Where the employee's use of a privately owned automobile is authorized for travel to or from a common carrier terminal, and the automobile is not parked at the terminal during the period of travel, the employee may claim double the number of miles between the terminal and the employee's headquarters or residence, whichever is less, at a rate as defined in section 599.631(a) of these regulations, while the employee occupies the automobile for the distance between the terminal and his/her residence or headquarters. If the employee commences or terminates travel one hour before or after his/her regularly scheduled work day, or on a regularly scheduled day off, mileage may be computed from his/her residence.

(c) All ferry, bridge, or toll road charges will be allowed with any required receipts.

(d) All necessary parking charges while on state business will be allowed, with any required receipts, for:

(1) Day parking on trips away from the headquarters office and excluded employee's primary residence.

(2) Overnight public parking on trips away from the headquarters and excluded employee's primary residence, except that parking shall not be claimed if expense-free overnight parking is available.

(3) Day parking adjacent to either a headquarters office, a temporary job site or training site, but only if the excluded employee had other reimbursable private or state automobile expenses for the same day. An employee may not prorate weekly or monthly parking fees.

(e) Gasoline, maintenance and automobile repair expenses will not be allowed.

(f) The mileage reimbursement rates include the cost of maintaining liability insurance at the minimum amount prescribed by a law and collision insurance sufficient to cover the reasonable value of the automobile, less a deductible. When a privately owned automobile operated by a state officer, agent or excluded employee is damaged by collision or is otherwise accidentally damaged, reimbursement for repair or the deductible to a maximum of $500 will be allowed if:

(1) the damage occurred while the automobile was used on official state business by permission or authorization of the employing agency; and

(2) the automobile was damaged through no fault of the state officer, agent or excluded employee; and

(3) the amount claimed is an actual loss to the state officer, agent or excluded employee, and is not recoverable directly from or through the insurance coverage of any party involved in the accident; and

(4) the loss claimed does not result from a decision of a state officer, agent or excluded employee not to maintain collision coverage; and

(5) the claim is processed in accordance with the procedures prescribed by the Department.

(g) Specialized Vehicles. An employee with a physical disability who must operate a motor vehicle on official state business and who can operate only specially equipped or modified vehicles may claim a rate of 34 cents per mile without certification and up to 37 cents per mile with certification. Where travel is authorized to and from a common carrier terminal, as specified in section 599.631(b) of these regulations the employee may compute the mileage as defined in section 599.631(b) of these regulations. Supervisors approving these claims must determine the employee's need for the use of such vehicles.

Note: Authority cited: Sections 3539.5, 18502, 19815.4(d) and 19820, Government Code. Reference: Section 11030, Government Code.

History: 1. Amendment of subsections (a)-(c) and (h) filed by the Department of Personnel Administration with the Secretary of State on 8-20-84; effective upon filing. Submitted to OAL for printing only pursuant to Government Code section 11343.8 (Register 85, No. 18).

2. Amendment filed by the Department of Personnel Administration with the Secretary of State on 7-8-87; operative 7-8-87. Submitted to OAL for printing only pursuant to Government Code section 11343.8 (Register 87, No. 32).

3. Amendment filed by the Department of Personnel Administration with the Secretary of State on 6-27-88 pursuant to Government Code section 3539.5. Submitted to OAL for printing only pursuant to Government Code section 11343.8 (Register 88, No. 31).

4. Amendment filed by the Department of Personnel Administration with the Secretary of State on 6-30-89; operative 6-30-89. Submitted to OAL for printing only pursuant to Government Code section 11343.8 (Register 89, No. 33).

5. Amendment filed 12-31-91 with Secretary of State by Department of Personnel Administration; operative 12-31-91. Submitted to OAL for printing only pursuant to Government Code section 3539.5 (Register 92, No. 12).

6. Amendment of section heading and section filed 12-27-95; operative 1-1-96. Submitted to OAL for printing only pursuant to Government Code section 3539.5 (Register 95, No. 52).

7. Amendment of subsection (a)(1) filed 1-10-96; operative 1-10-96. Submitted to OAL for printing only pursuant to Government Code section 3539.5 (Register 96, No. 38).

8. Editorial correction of subsection (g) (Register 96, No. 38).

9. Amendment of subsection (a) filed 7-1-97; operative 7-1-97 pursuant to Government Code section 11343.4(d). Submitted to OAL for printing only pursuant to Government Code section 3539.5 (Register 97, No. 27).

10. Amendment of subsections (a), (a)(2) and (g) filed 10-28-99; operative 11-2-99. Submitted to OAL for printing only (Register 99, No. 51). At the request of DPA pursuant to Government Code section 3539.5, OAL is directing the printing of this regulation in the CCR. Title 1, CCR, section 6(b)(2)(F)1 defines "print only" regulations as "regulations *adopted pursuant to the requirements of the APA*, but which are expressly exempted by statute from OAL review …" (Emphasis added.) In complying with DPA's request, OAL makes no determination concerning whether or not DPA has met the statutory requirements for adoption of regulations set forth in Government Code sections 11346-11347.3, including but not limited to public notice and comment. See 1998 OAL Determination No. 40 (Department of Personnel Administration, 96-008, December 9, 1998), California Regulatory Notice Register 99, No. 3-Z, January 15, 1999, p. 139, at p. 145; typewritten version, p. 18.

11. Amendment of subsections (a) and (g) filed 10-1-2001; operative 10-1-2001. Submitted to OAL for printing only pursuant to Government Code section 3539.5 (Register 2001, No. 46).

12. Change without regulatory effect amending section and Note filed 10-13-2014 pursuant to section 100, title 1, California Code of Regulations (Register 2014, No. 42).

Ref.: Hanna §§ 5.04[1], 22.07[2][a].

TITLE 8
INDUSTRIAL RELATIONS

DIVISION 1
Department of Industrial Relations

CHAPTER 1
DIVISION OF WORKERS' COMPENSATION—QUALIFIED MEDICAL EVALUATOR REGULATIONS

ARTICLE 1
General

§1. Definitions.

As used in the regulations in Chapter 1:

(a) "Accreditation" means the conferring of recognized status as a provider of physician education by the Administrative Director.

(b) "Administrative Director" means the administrative director of the Division of Workers' Compensation of the State of California Department of Industrial Relations, and includes his or her designee.

(c) "Agreed Panel QME" means the Qualified Medical Evaluator described in Labor Code section 4062.2(c), that the claims administrator, or if none the employer, and a represented employee agree upon and select from a QME panel list issued by the Medical Director without using the striking process. An Agreed Panel QME shall be entitled to be paid at the same rate as an Agreed Medical Evaluator under section 9795 of Title 8 of the California Code of Regulations for medical/legal evaluation procedures and medical testimony.

(d) "AMA Guides" means American Medical Association, Guides to the Evaluation of Permanent Impairment [Fifth Edition].

(e) "AME" means Agreed Medical Evaluator, a physician selected by agreement between the claims administrator, or if none the employer, and a represented employee to resolve disputed medical issues referred by the parties in a workers' compensation proceeding.

(f) "Appeals Board" means the Workers' Compensation Appeals Board within the State of California Department of Industrial Relations.

(g) "Audit" means a formal evaluation of a continuing education program, disability evaluation report writing course, or an accredited education provider which is conducted at the request of the Medical Director.

(h) "Comprehensive Medical-Legal Evaluation" means a medical evaluation performed pursuant to Labor Code Sections 4060, 4061, 4062, 4062.1, 4062.2 or 4067 and meeting the requirements of section 9793(c) of Title 8 of the California Code of Regulations.

(i) "Claims Administrator" means the person or entity responsible for the payment of compensation for any of the following: a self-administered insurer providing security for the payment of compensation required by Divisions 4 and 4.5 of the Labor Code, a self-administered self-insured employer, a group self-insurer, an insured employer, the director of the Department of Industrial Relations as administrator for the Uninsured Employers Benefits Trust Fund (UEBTF) and for the Subsequent Injuries Benefit Trust Fund (SIBTF), a third-party claims administrator for a self-insured employer, insurer, legally uninsured employer, group self-insurer, or joint powers authority, and the California Insurance Guarantee Association (CIGA). The UEBTF shall only be subject to these regulations after proper service has been made on the uninsured employer and the Appeals Board has obtained jurisdiction over the UEBTF by joinder as a party.

(j) "Continuing Education Program" means a systematic learning experience (such as a course, seminar, or audiovisual or computer learning program) which serves to develop, maintain, or increase the knowledge, skills and professional performance of physicians who serve as Qualified Medical Evaluators in the California workers' compensation system.

(k) "Course" means the 12 hours of instruction in disability evaluation report writing which is required of a Qualified Medical Evaluator prior to appointment. A course must be approved by the Administrative Director.

(*l*) "Credit Hour" means a sixty minute hour. A credit hour may include time for questions and answers related to the presentation.

(m) "Direct medical treatment" means that special phase of the physician-patient relationship during which the physician: (1) attempts to clinically diagnose and to alter or modify the expression of a non-industrial illness, injury or pathological condition; or (2) attempts to cure or relieve the effects of an industrial injury.

(n) "Distance Learning" means an education program in which the instructor and student are in different locations, as in programs based on audio or video tapes, computer programs, or printed educational material.

(o) "DEU" is the Disability Evaluation Unit under the Administrative Director responsible for issuing summary disability ratings.

(p) "Education Provider" means the individual or organization which has been accredited by the Administrative Director to offer physician education programs. There are two categories of providers: (1) the Administrative Director; and (2) individuals, partnerships, or corporations, hospitals, clinics or other patient care facilities, educational institutions, medical or health-related organizations whose membership includes physicians as defined in Labor Code section 3209.3, organizations of non-medical participants in the California workers' compensation system, and governmental agencies. In the case of a national organization seeking accreditation, the California Chapter or organization affiliated with the national organization shall be accredited by the Administrative Director in lieu of the national organization.

(q) "Employer" means any employer within the meaning of Labor Code section 3300, including but not limited to, any of the following: (1) an uninsured employer and the Uninsured Employers Benefits Trust Fund (UEBTF) pursuant to Labor Code Section 3716, (2) an insured employer, (3) a self-insured employer and (4) a lawfully uninsured employer. The UEBTF shall only be subject to these regulations after proper service has been made on the uninsured employer and the Appeals Board has obtained jurisdiction over the UEBTF by joinder as a party.

(r) "Evaluator" means any of the following: "Qualified Medical Evaluator", "Agreed Medical Evaluator", "Agreed Panel QME" or "Panel QME", as appropriate in a specific case.

(s) "Follow-up comprehensive medical-legal evaluation" means a medical evaluation performed pursuant to Labor Code sections 4060, 4061, 4062, 4062.1, 4062.2 or 4067 and meeting the requirements of Section 9793(f) of Title 8 of the California Code of Regulations.

(t) "Future medical care" means medical treatment as defined in Labor Code section 4600 that is reasonably required to cure or relieve an injured worker of the effects of the industrial injury after an injured worker has reached maximum medical improvement or permanent and stationary status including a description of the type of the medical treatment that might be necessary in the future.

(u) "Medical Treatment Utilization Schedule" or "MTUS" means the treatment utilization scheduled adopted by the Administrative Director of the Division of Workers' Compensation as required by Labor Code section 5307.27 and sections 9792.20 *et seq* of Title 8 of the California Code of Regulations.

(v) "Medical Director" means the Medical Director appointed by the Administrative Director pursuant to Labor Code section 122 and includes any Associate Medical Directors when acting as his or her designee.

(w) "Mental health record" means a medical treatment or evaluation record created or reviewed by a licensed physician as defined in Labor Code section 3209.3 in the course of treating or evaluating a mental disorder.

(x) "Panel QME" means the physician, from a QME panel list provided by the Medical Director, who is selected under Labor Code section 4062.1(c) when the injured worker is not represented by an attorney, and when the injured worker is represented by an attorney, the physician whose name remains after completion of the striking process or who is otherwise selected as provided in Labor Code section 4062.2(c) when the parties are unable to agree on an Agreed Panel QME.

(y) "Physician's office" means a bona fide office facility which is identified by a street address and any other more specific designation such as a suite or room number and which contains the usual and customary equipment for the evaluation and treatment appropriate to the physician's medical specialty or practice.

(z) "Qualified Medical Evaluator (QME)" means a physician licensed by the appropriate licensing body for the state of California and appointed by the Administrative Director pursuant to Labor Code section 139.2, provided, however, that acupuncturist QMEs shall not perform comprehensive medical-legal evaluations to determine disability.

(aa) "QME competency examination" means an examination administered by the Administrative Director for the purpose of demonstrating competence in evaluating medical-legal issues in the workers' compensation system. This examination shall be given at least as often as twice annually.

(bb) "QME competency examination for acupuncturists" means an examination administered by the Administrative Director for the purpose of demonstrating competence in evaluating medical-legal issues in the workers' compensation system which are not pertinent to the determination of disability, but should be understood by acupuncturist QMEs. This examination shall be given at least as often as twice annually.

(cc) "Request for factual correction" means a request by an unrepresented injured worker or a claims administrator, or their representative, to a panel QME to change an incorrect statement or assertion of fact contained in a comprehensive medical-legal evaluation to a statement or assertion of fact that is capable of verification from written records submitted to a panel QME pursuant to section 35 of title 8 of the California Code of Regulations.

(dd) "Significant Financial Interest or Affiliation Held by Faculty", as used in sections 11.5, 14, 55, 118 and 119 pertaining to faculty of approved disability report writing or continuing education courses under these regulations, means grant or research support; status as a consultant, member of a speakers' bureau, or major stock shareholder; or other financial or material interest for the program faculty member or his or her family.

(ee) "Specified Financial Interests" means having a shared financial interest that must be reported or disclosed pursuant to sections 11, 17, 29, 50 or on the "SFI Form 124" attached to QME Form 100, 103 or 104 as required by these regulations.

(ff) "Supplemental medical-legal evaluation" means a medical evaluation performed pursuant to Labor Code sections 4060, 4061, 4062, 4062.1, 4062.2 or 4067 and meeting the requirements of section 9793(*l*) of Title 8 of the California Code of Regulations.

(gg) "Treating physician" means a physician who has provided direct medical treatment to an employee which is reasonably required to cure or relieve the effects of an industrial injury pursuant to section 4600 of the Labor Code.

(hh) "Unrepresented employee" means an employee not represented by an attorney.

Note: Authority cited: Sections 53, 133, 139.2, 4060, 4061, 4062, 4062.1, 4062.2 and 5307.3, Labor Code. Reference: Sections 139.2, 139.3, 139.31, 139.4, 139.43, 3716, 4060, 4061, 4061.5, 4062, 4062.1, 4062.2, 4062.3, 4062.5, 4067, 4600, 4604.5 and 4660-4664, Labor Code.

History: 1. Repealer and new section filed 8-1-94; operative 8-31-94 (Register 94, No. 31). For prior history, see Register 93, No. 38.

2. Change without regulatory effect amending subsections (c), (g), (h), (k) and (p) filed 9-19-94 pursuant to section 100, title 1, California Code of Regulations (Register 94, No. 38).

3. Amendment of subsections (d) and (f), repealer and new subsection (m), amendment of subsections (n) and (o), new subsections (p) and (q) and subsection relettering, and amendment of newly designated subsection (r) filed 8-23-96; operative 9-22-96 (Register 96, No. 34).

4. New subsection (s) and subsection relettering filed 6-3-97; operative 7-3-97 (Register 97, No. 23).

5. Amendment of subsections (f) and (r) filed 4-14-2000; operative 5-14-2000 (Register 2000, No. 15).

6. New subsections (a) and (e), repealer of former subsection (f), new subsections (h), (j), (k), (m), (r) and (x) and subsection relettering filed 10-16-2000 as an emergency; operative 1-1-2001 (Register 2000, No. 42). A Certificate of Compliance must be transmitted to OAL by 5-1-2001 or emergency language will be repealed by operation of law on the following day.

7. New subsections (a) and (e), repealer of former subsection (f), new subsections (h), (j), (k), (r) and (x) and subsection relettering refiled 5-2-2001 as an emergency; operative 5-2-2001 (Register 2001, No. 18). A Certificate of Compliance must be transmitted to OAL by 8-30-2001 or emergency language will be repealed by operation of law on the following day.

8. Certificate of Compliance as to 5-2-2001 order, including further amendment of section, transmitted to OAL 7-12-2001 and filed 8-23-2001 (Register 2001, No. 34).

9. Amendment of chapter heading, section and Note filed 1-13-2009; operative 2-17-2009 (Register 2009, No. 3).

10. Repealer of subsection (b), new subsections (t) and (cc) and subsection relettering filed 12-31-2012 as an emergency; operative 1-1-2013 pursuant to Government Code section 11346.1(d) (Register 2013, No. 1). A Certificate of Compliance must be transmitted to OAL by 7-1-2013 or emergency language will be repealed by operation of law on the following day.

11. Repealer of subsection (b), new subsections (t) and (cc) and subsection relettering refiled 7-1-2013 as an emergency; operative 7-1-2013 (Register 2013, No. 27). A Certificate of Compliance must be transmitted to OAL by 9-30-2013 or emergency language will be repealed by operation of law on the following day.

12. Certificate of Compliance as to 7-1-2013 order, including amendment of subsections (t) and (cc), transmitted to OAL 8-2-2013 and filed 9-16-2013; amendments operative 9-16-2013 pursuant to Government Code section 11343.4(b)(3) (Register 2013, No. 38).

Ref.: Hanna §§ 1.12[2A][b]–[h], 22.11[1]–[16]; Herlick Handbook §§ 1.02, 14.22.

ARTICLE 2
QME Eligibility

§10. Appointment of QMEs.

(a) Applications for appointment as a QME shall be submitted on the form in section 100 (QME Form 100). The completed application form, and any supporting documentation as required by the application, shall be filed at the Administrative Director's office listed on the form in section 100. Upon his or her approval of each application form and supporting documentation, the Administrative Director shall certify, as eligible to sit for the QME competency examination, those applicants who meet all of the statutory and regulatory eligibility requirements. Any application for appointment may be rejected if it is incomplete, contains false information or does not contain the required supporting documentation listed in section 11.

(b) The Administrative Director may deny appointment or reappointment to any physician who has performed a QME evaluation or examination without valid QME certification at the time of examining the injured worker or the time of signing the initial or follow-up evaluation report. An applicant serving a period of probation imposed by the applicant's professional licensing board or agency may be allowed to take the QME examination while on probationary license status. Applications for appointment or reappointment from physicians who are on probationary license status with a California licensing board or agency while the QME application is pending shall be reviewed by the Medical Director on a case-by-case basis consistent with the provisions of Labor Code section 139.2(m).

(c) No physician who has been convicted of a felony or misdemeanor related to his or her practice shall be appointed or reappointed as a QME. An applicant who has been convicted of any other type of felony or misdemeanor may be denied appointment or reappointment.

(d) Any physician who, while under investigation or after the service of a statement of issues or accusation for alleged violations of these regulations or the Labor Code, withdraws his or her application for appointment or reappointment, resigns or fails to seek reappointment as a QME, shall be subject to having the disciplinary process reactivated whenever an application for appointment or re-appointment is subsequently filed. In the event any of the alleged violations are found to have occurred, the physician's application for appointment or reappointment may be denied by the Administrative Director.

NOTE: Form is available at no charge by downloading from the web at www.dir.ca.gov/dwc/forms.html or by requesting at 1-800-794-6900.

Note: Authority cited: Sections 133, 139.2 and 5307.3, Labor Code; and Section 730, Business and Professions Code. Reference: Sections 139.2, 4060, 4061, 4062, 4062.1 and 4062.2, Labor Code; and Section 730, Business and Professions Code.

History: 1. Relocation of article 2 heading and new section filed 8-1-94; operative 8-31-94 (Register 94, No. 31).

2. Amendment of section filed 8-23-96; operative 9-22-96 (Register 96, No. 34).

3. Amendment filed 4-14-2000; operative 5-14-2000 (Register 2000, No. 15).

4. Amendment of section and Note filed 1-13-2009; operative 2-17-2009 (Register 2009, No. 3).

Ref.: Hanna §§ 1.12[2A][b]–[h], 22.11[1]–[16]; Herlick Handbook §§ 1.02, 14.22.

§10.1. The Application for Appointment as Qualified Medical Evaluator Form. [Repealed]

Note: Authority cited: Sections 133, 139 and 139.2, Labor Code. Reference: Sections 139.2, 4060, 4061 and 4062, Labor Code.

History: 1. New section filed 8-1-94; operative 8-31-94 (Register 94, No. 31).

2. Change without regulatory effect updating QME Application Form filed 6-27-95 pursuant to section 100, title 1, California Code of Regulations (Register 95, No. 26).

3. Change without regulatory effect amending specialty codes filed 10-11-95 pursuant to section 100, title 1, California Code of Regulations (Register 95, No. 41).

4. Change without regulatory effect amending QME Application form and adding MAP specialty code filed 12-27-95 pursuant to section 100, title 1, California Code of Regulations (Register 95, No. 52).

5. Change without regulatory effect amending MD/DO specialty codes filed 6-19-97 pursuant to section 100, title 1, California Code of Regulations (Register 97, No. 25).

6. Change without regulatory effect amending MD/DO specialty codes and updating form revision date filed 4-15-98 pursuant to section 100, title 1, California Code of Regulations (Register 98, No. 16).

7. Change without regulatory effect amending QME appointment application form filed 8-19-98 pursuant to section 100, title 1, California Code of Regulations (Register 98, No. 34).

8. Change without regulatory effect amending MD/DO specialty codes and updating form revision date filed 7-12-99 pursuant to section 100, title 1, California Code of Regulations (Register 99, No. 29).

9. Repealer filed 4-14-2000; operative 5-14-2000 (Register 2000, No. 15).

§10.1A. Reappointment Application as Qualified Medical Evaluator Form. [Repealed]

History: 1. Change without regulatory effect adding new section filed 6-20-96 pursuant to section 100, title 1, California Code of Regulations (Register 96, No. 25).

2. Change without regulatory effect repealing section and adding new section filed 4-16-98 pursuant to section 100, title 1, California Code of Regulations (Register 98, No. 16).

3. Change without regulatory effect amending block 2, item 3 and verification statement in block 5 filed 8-12-98 pursuant to section 100, title 1, California Code of Regulations (Register 98, No. 33).

4. Change without regulatory effect amending block 5 filed 10-30-98 pursuant to section 100, title 1, California Code of Regulations (Register 98, No. 44).

5. Repealer filed 4-14-2000; operative 5-14-2000 (Register 2000, No. 15).

§10.2. The QME Fee Assessment Notice Form.

[Form Not Reproduced]

Editor's Note: To acquire a copy of IMC Form 5 (Rev. 4/99), please contact the local I&A office. *See* Reference Directory, p. xi, for phone numbers.

Note: Authority cited: Sections 133, 139 and 139.2, Labor Code. Reference: Sections 139.2, 4060, 4061 and 4062, Labor Code.

History: 1. New section filed 8-1-94; operative 8-31-94 (Register 94, No. 31).

2. Repealer and new section filed 6-7-99 as an emergency; operative 6-7-99 (Register 99, No. 24). A Certificate of Compliance must be transmitted to OAL by 10-5-99 or emergency language will be repealed by operation of law on the following day.

3. Repealed by operation of Government Code section 11346.1(g) (Register 2000, No. 3).

4. New section filed 1-19-2000; operative 1-19-2000 pursuant to Government Code section 11343.4(d) (Register 2000, No. 3).

§10.5. Limitations on Certification as Qualified Medical Evaluators. [Repealed]

Note: Authority cited: Sections 139 and 139.2. Reference: 8 U.S.C. Sections 1621, 1641 and 1642; Sections 139.2, 5307.3 and 5307.4, Labor Code; and Section 11507 et seq., Government Code.

History: 1. New section filed 11-5-98; operative 12-5-98 (Register 98, No. 45).

2. Change without regulatory effect repealing and adding new Form 10.5, Rev. 5/99 (incorporated by reference) filed 7-12-99 pursuant to section 100, title 1, California Code of Regulations (Register 99, No. 29).

3. Amendment of subsections (e)(1), (e)(3) and (i) and repealer of subsections (i)(1)-(6) filed 4-14-2000; operative 5-14-2000 (Register 2000, No. 15).

4. Repealer filed 1-13-2009; operative 2-17-2009 (Register 2009, No. 3).

§11. Eligibility Requirements for Initial Appointment as a QME.

The Administrative Director shall appoint as QMEs all applicants who meet the requirements set forth in Labor Code Section 139.2(b) and all applicants:

(a) Shall submit the required supporting documentation:

(1) Copy of current license to practice in California;

(2) For Medical Doctors, or Doctors of Osteopathy:

(A) A copy of the applicant's certificate of completion of postgraduate specialty training at an institution recognized by the Accreditation Council for Graduate Medical Education or the osteopathic equivalent as defined pursuant to Section 12, or;

(B) A copy of the applicant's Board certification by a specialty board recognized by the Administrative Director or as defined pursuant to Section 12, or;

(C) A declaration under penalty of perjury accompanied by supporting documentation that the physician has qualifications that the Administrative Director and the Medical Board of California or the Osteopathic Medical Board of California both deem to be equivalent to board certification in a specialty.

(3) If a psychologist, (i) a copy of a doctoral degree in psychology or a doctoral degree deemed equivalent for licensure by the Board of Psychology pursuant to Section 2914 of the Business and Professions Code, and has not had less than five years postdoctoral experience in the treatment of emotional and mental disorders or (ii) served as an AME on eight or more occasions prior to January 1, 1990 and has not less than five years postdoctoral experience in the diagnosis and treatment of emotional and mental disorders.

(4) For Doctors of Chiropractic, the physician shall provide a copy of a current or otherwise valid certificate in California Workers Compensation Evaluation by either a California professional chiropractic association or an accredited California college recognized by the Administrative Director (i.e. Workers' Compensation Evaluation Certificate with a minimum 44 hours completed).

(5) Or, for other physicians, a copy of the physician's professional diploma.

(b)(1) Shall, prior to appointment as a QME, complete a course of at least twelve (12) hours in disability evaluation report writing pursuant to section 11.5 of this Article. Doctors of Chiropractic who submit documentation showing compliance with section 11(a)(4)(1) are exempt from this requirement; and

(2) Shall accurately and fully report on the SFI Form 124 attached to the application (QME Form 100) to the best of the applicant's knowledge the information required by section 29 of Title 8 of the California Code of Regulations, regarding applicant's specified financial interests.

(c) Shall provide supplemental information and/or documentation to the Administrative Director after an application, QME Form 100 (see, 8 Cal. Code Regs. §100), is submitted if requested to verify an applicant's eligibility for appointment.

(d) Shall agree that during a QME evaluation exam he or she will not treat or offer or solicit to provide medical treatment for that injury for which he or she has done a QME evaluation for an injured worker unless a medical emergency arises as defined under subdivision (a) or (b) of section 1317.1 of the Health and Safety Code. A QME may also provide treatment if requested by the employee pursuant to section 4600 of the Labor Code, but he or she shall not offer or solicit to provide it. A QME who solicits an injured worker to receive direct medical treatment or to become the primary treating physician of that employee shall be subject to disciplinary action pursuant to section 60.

(e) Shall declare under penalty of perjury on the QME application that he or she:

(1) Has an unrestricted California license and is not currently on probation from the state licensing board, or, if the applicant has a California restricted license or is currently on probation, state all the restrictions on the license and all terms of probation; and

(2) Devotes at least one-third of his or her total practice time to providing direct medical treatment during each year of the applicant's term of appointment. This requirement shall not apply if the applicant qualifies for appointment because the applicant served as an AME on 8 or more occasions in the year prior to application and in each year of the applicant's term; or if the applicant meets the requirements of section 15; and

(3) Has not performed a QME evaluation without QME certification;

(4) Has accurately and fully reported on QME Form 124 to the best of the applicant's knowledge the specified financial interest information required by section 29 of Title 8 of the California Code of Regulations.

(f) Shall pass the QME Competency Examination, or if an acupuncturist, shall pass the QME Competency Examination for acupuncturists.

(1) In order to take this examination, a physician who is not currently appointed as a QME and not exempt pursuant to Labor Code section 139(b)(1), shall be considered to have applied to take the QME competency examination upon submitting the properly-completed Application for Appointment Form in Section 100 (see, 8 Cal. Code Regs. section 100), and the Registration Form for the QME Competency Examination in section 102 (see, 8 Cal. Code Regs. §102) and the appropriate fee as specified in section 11(f)(2).

(2) The fee for applying to take or retake the QME competency examination is $ 125.00 and may be waived by the Administrative Director at his or her discretion for first time applicants.

(3) The Administrative Director shall give appropriate public notice of the date, time and location of the examination no fewer than sixty (60) calendar days before a competency examination is to be given.

(4) An applicant must submit the properly completed forms as required in section 11(f)(1) to the Administrative Director at least thirty (30) calendar days prior to the date of the next scheduled competency examination unless the Administrative Director finds good cause to grant an extension to the physician(s).

(5) The Administrative Director shall inform the applicant in writing whether he or she shall be allowed to take the examination within fifteen (15) calendar days from the date the Administrative Director receives the properly-completed forms and appropriate fee.

(6) The Administrative Director shall inform the applicant in writing whether or not he or she passed the examination within sixty (60) calendar days from the date the applicant takes the competency examination.

(7) An applicant who passes the QME competency examination shall file the QME Fee Assessment Form in Section 103 (see, 8 Cal. Code Regs. section 103) including the appropriate fee within thirty (30) days of the date of the notice. The physician shall not be appointed to the official QME list until the appropriate fee is paid and has completed a disability evaluation report writing course pursuant to section 11.5. Appointments shall be for two-year terms beginning with the date of appointment by the Administrative Director.

(8) Any applicant, who upon good cause shown by the test administrator, is suspected of cheating may be disqualified from the examination and, upon a finding that the applicant did cheat in that exam, the applicant will be denied further admittance to any QME examination for a period of at least five years thereafter. Any applicant who fails to follow test instructions and/or proctor instructions either before or during or at the conclusion of an examination shall be disqualified from the examination procedure and the applicant's exam shall be nullified.

(9) If an applicant fails the competency examination or fails to appear for a noticed QME examination for which the applicant has submitted a QME Exam Registration Form 102 (see, 8 Cal. Code Regs. § 102), the applicant may apply to take any subsequent examinations, upon submission of a new test application form and a fee of $125. An applicant who fails the exam three times shall show proof of having completed six (6) hours continuing education from a course approved by the Administrative Director prior to taking the examination again.

(10) Any applicant who receives a failing grade on a competency exam may appeal the failing grade to the Administrative Director. Appeals shall be considered on a case by case basis. Appeals will be accepted immediately after a candidate has completed the examination and until ten (10) days after the date of the examination results letter. The appeal shall state specific facts as to why the failing grade should be overturned. Pursuant to Section 6254(g) of the Government Code, the Administrative Director will

consider appeals of test questions and will base his or her decision solely on the written appeal including any supporting documentation submitted by the physician. Appeals will only be accepted for the current examination period. Grounds for appeal are:

(A) Significant procedural error in the examination process;

(B) Unfair Discrimination;

(C) Bias or fraud.

(g) Each applicant shall pay the annual fee required by section 17 of this Article prior to appointment.

NOTE: Forms referred to above are available at no charge by downloading from the web at www.dir.ca.gov/dwc/forms.html or by requesting at 1-800-794-6900.

Note: Authority cited: Sections 133, 139.2, 4060, 4062 and 5307.3, Labor Code. Reference: Section 139.2, Labor Code; and Section 6254, Government Code.

History: 1. New section filed 8-1-94; operative 8-31-94 (Register 94, No. 31).

2. New subsections (a)-(c) and subsection relettering, amendment of newly designated subsections (d)-(f)(6), new subsections (f)(7) and (f)(8) and subsection renumbering, amendment of newly designated subsections (f)(9) and (f)(10), and new subsection (g) filed 8-23-96; operative 9-22-96 (Register 96, No. 34).

3. Change without regulatory effect amending section (f)(5) filed 6-20-97 pursuant to section 100, title 1, California Code of Regulations (Register 97, No. 25).

4. Amendment filed 4-14-2000; operative 5-14-2000 (Register 2000, No. 15).

5. Amendment of section heading and section filed 8-23-2001; operative 8-23-2001 pursuant to Government Code section 11343.4 (Register 2001, No. 34).

6. Amendment of section and Note filed 1-13-2009; operative 2-17-2009 (Register 2009, No. 3).

7. Amendment of subsection (a)(4) and Note filed 12-31-2012 as an emergency; operative 1-1-2013 pursuant to Government Code section 11346.1(d) (Register 2013, No. 1). A Certificate of Compliance must be transmitted to OAL by 7-1-2013 or emergency language will be repealed by operation of law on the following day.

8. Amendment of subsection (a)(4) and Note refiled 7-1-2013 as an emergency; operative 7-1-2013 (Register 2013, No. 27). A Certificate of Compliance must be transmitted to OAL by 9-30-2013 or emergency language will be repealed by operation of law on the following day.

9. Certificate of Compliance as to 7-1-2013 order transmitted to OAL 8-2-2013 and filed 9-16-2013 (Register 2013, No. 38).

Ref.: Hanna §§ 1.12[2A][b]–[h], 22.11[1]–[16]; Herlick Handbook §§ 1.02, 14.22.

§11.1. Application for QME Competency Examination Form. [Repealed]

Note: Authority cited: Section 139.2, Labor Code. Reference: Section 139.2, Labor Code.

History: 1. New section filed 8-1-94; operative 8-31-94 (Register 94, No. 31).

2. Change without regulatory effect amending form filed 3-11-96 pursuant to section 100, title 1, California Code of Regulations (Register 96, No. 11).

3. Change without regulatory effect amending form filed 7-23-96 pursuant to section 100, title 1, California Code of Regulations (Register 96, No. 30).

4. Amendment of form filed 3-15-99; operative 4-14-99 (Register 99, No. 12).

5. Repealer filed 4-14-2000; operative 5-14-2000 (Register 2000, No. 15).

§11.5. Disability Evaluation Report Writing Course.

Prior to appointment as a QME, a physician shall complete a course of at least twelve hours of instruction in disability evaluation report writing. The course curriculum shall be specified by the Administrative Director. Only report writing courses which are offered by education providers as defined in subdivision 1(p) of Title 8 of the California Code of Regulations shall qualify to satisfy this requirement.

(a) An education provider applicant shall submit:

(1) a completed QME Form 118 (Application for Accreditation) (see, 8 Cal. Code Regs. §118) which contains:

(A) the applicant's name; address; director of education with contact information; type of organization; length of time in business; nature of business; and past experience providing continuing education courses (including a list of other accrediting agencies that have approved such courses);

(B) a description of the proposed education program or course which includes the title; type (continuing education program or disability evaluation report writing course); location(s); date(s); length of training in clock hours; educational objectives; a complete description of the program or course content; faculty; and the names of other accrediting agencies that have approved the program.

(2) A curriculum vitae for each proposed instructor. A proposed instructor shall have education and/or training and recent work experience relevant to the subject of his/her presentation.

(3) The application for accreditation as an education provider, along with all required supporting documents, shall be submitted to the Administrative Director, at least 60 calendar days before any public advertisement of the applicant's course.

(b) The Administrative Director shall accredit an applicant that: meets the definition of an education provider; submits a completed, signed and dated application which demonstrates past experience in providing continuing education programs; and proposes a program which meets the requirements of section 55(c) or a course which meets the requirements of section 11.5(a) and (i). The applicant must demonstrate that adequate time is allocated to the curriculum set forth in section 11.5(i) for the course to be approved by the Administrative Director. Proposed content for continuing education program credit must relate directly to disability evaluation or California workers' compensation-related medical dispute evaluation. No credit shall be recognized by the Administrative Director for material primarily discussing the business aspects of workers' compensation medical practice, including but not limited to billing, coding and marketing.

(c) The Administrative Director shall notify the applicant within 20 calendar days after receipt of the application containing all the information listed in section 11.5(a) whether that education provider has been accredited for a two year period and the proposed course has been approved. Incomplete applications will be returned to the applicant.

(d) Each education provider that has been accredited by the Administrative Director will be given a number which must be displayed on course promotional material.

(e) On or before the date the course is first presented, the education provider shall submit the program syllabus (all program handouts) to the Administrative Director.

(f) An approved course may be offered for two (2) years. An accredited education provider shall notify the Administrative Director in writing of any change to the faculty in an approved course. The provider shall send the Administrative Director the program outline, promotional material and faculty for each offering of the program at least 45 days prior to the date of the presentation of the program. The Administrative Director may require submission of the program syllabi. The Administrative Director may require changes in the program based on its review of the program outline, program syllabi, promotional material or faculty if the Administrative Director finds that any aspect of the program is not in compliance with these regulations.

(g) To apply for re-accreditation, the education provider applicant must submit a completed QME Form 118 (Application for Accreditation) (see, 8 Cal. Code Regs. §118), using the application process in 11.5(a). The applicant may complete section 2 of the form using a new program or course or one which was given by the applicant during the recent accreditation period. The Administrative Director shall give the provider 90 days' notice of the need to seek re-accreditation.

(h) Promotional materials for a course must state the education provider's educational objectives; the professional qualifications of course faculty (at the least, all relevant professional degrees); the content of course activities; and the intended audience.

(i) The minimum of 12 hours of instruction in disability evaluation report writing shall include:

(1) The Qualified Medical Evaluator's Role in the Disability Evaluation Process (minimum recommended 1 hour)

How disability evaluation reports are used

The reasons why reports must be clear, complete and timely

The QME's role as an expert witness

Impact of the QME's report on the injured worker

QME ethics and the Confidentiality of Medical Information Act

(2) Elements of the Medical-Legal Report (minimum recommended 1 hour)

The Labor Code and regulatory requirements for medical-legal reports

(3) The Language of Reports (minimum recommended 4 hours)

Evaluation of disability in California (impairment and disability)

The occupational history

The physician examination and the role of testing

The Medical Treatment Utilization Schedule (MTUS) adopted by the Administrative Director pursuant to Labor Code section 5307.27, found in section 9792.20 *et seq* of Title 8 of the California Code of Regulations

Providing opinions that resolve disputed medical treatment issues consistent with the evaluation criteria specified in section 35.5 (d) of Title 8 of the California Code of Regulations

Packard Thurber's Evaluation of Industrial Disability, section 43 through 47 and section 9725 through 9727 of Title 8 of the California Code of Regulations (for cases with dates of injury not subject to the AMA guide-based impairment rating system, described below)

Factors of disability, including subjective and objective factors, loss of pre-injury capacity and work restrictions, for cases involving dates of injury not subject to the AMA guide-based impairment rating system

Activities of Daily Living, for cases subject to the AMA Guides

Work restrictions

Work Capabilities

American Medical Association, Guides to the Evaluation of Permanent Impairment, [Fifth Edition] (AMA Guides) and its use in determining permanent disability in accordance with the Schedule for Rating Permanent Disabilities [effective January 1, 2005] (for all claims with dates of injury on or after January 1, 2005, and for those compensable claims arising before January 1, 2005, in which either there is no comprehensive medical-legal report or no report by a treating physician indicating the existence of permanent disability, or when the employer is not required to provide the notice to the injured worker required by Labor Code section 4061)

Causation

Determination of permanent and stationary status

Apportionment including the requirements of Labor Code sections 4660, 4663 and 4664 added by SB 899 (Stats. 2004, ch. 34)

Future medical care

Review of records

Providing sufficient support for conclusions

(4) The Administrative Director's Disability Evaluation Protocols (minimum recommended 1 hour)

An overview of the Neuromusculoskeletal, Pulmonary, Cardiac, Immunologic, or Psychiatric protocols, and an in-depth discussion of measurement of impairment, calculations and rationale for rating under the AMA Guides, as relevant.

(5) The Third Party Perspective (minimum recommended 1 hour)

The report from the perspective of those who read it: Judge(s), attorney(ies), insurer(s), rater(s), employer(s), qualified rehabilitation representative(s).

(6) Anatomy of a Good Report (small group or other interactive sessions — minimum recommended 3 hours)

Discussion of examples of good reports and identification of weaknesses in reports

Opportunities for the practitioner to critique and/or correct reports.

If feasible, physician should have the opportunity to write a sample report.

Review of results of Administrative Director's annual report review and identification of common problems with reports.

(7) Mechanics of Report Writing (minimum recommended 1 hour)

The QME Process

Face to face time

Timelines for submission of report

Completion of required forms

Service of reports

Final questions and answers

(8) Submission and Critique of Written Medical/legal Report. As a condition of completion of the course taken to satisfy the requirements of this section, each physician enrollee shall draft at least one practice written medical/legal report, based on a sample case library of materials, which written report shall be critiqued with notations by the course education provider.

(j) All audio or video tapes, computer programs and printed educational material used in the course must be submitted to the Administrative Director on or before the date the course is first given. Up to the full twelve hours of instruction may be completed by distance learning whenever the Administrative Director has approved the submitted course prior to the first day the course is given. All distance learning materials shall bear a date of release and shall be updated yearly. The education provider shall notify the Administrative Director in writing of the revision.

(k) No one shall recruit members or promote commercial products or services in the instruction room immediately before, during, or immediately after the presentation of a course. Education providers or vendors may display/sell educational materials related to workers' compensation or applications for membership in an area adjoining a course. A course provider or faculty member shall disclose on QME Form 119 (Faculty Disclosure of Commercial Interest) (see, 8 Cal. Code Regs. §119) any significant financial interest held by faculty in or affiliation with any commercial product or service which is discussed in a course and that interest or affiliation must be disclosed to all attendees. An education provider shall file every Form 119 in its possession with the Administrator Director.

(*l*) The provider shall maintain attendance records for each disability evaluation report writing course for a period of no less than three years after the course is given. A physician attending the course must be identified by signature. The provider must submit a copy of the signature list to the Administrative Director within 60 days of completion of the course.

(m) The provider is required to give the QME Evaluation Form 117 (Qualified Medical Evaluator Continuing Education Response Form) (see, 8 Cal. Code Regs. §117) to course attendees and request they submit the form to the Administrative Director. This information shall not be used in lieu of a certification of completion given by the provider, as specified pursuant to section (n). Destruction by a provider or its employee of a QME's Evaluation Form or failure by such provider or its employee to distribute Form 117 as part of its course shall constitute grounds for revocation of a provider's accredited status. The Administrative Director shall tabulate the responses and return a summary to the provider within 90 days of completion of the course.

(n) The provider shall issue a certificate of completion to the physician that states the name of the provider, the provider's number, the date(s) and location and title of the course. To be eligible for appointment as a QME, a physician must complete no less than 12 hours of the curriculum specified in Section 11.5(i) and must submit a copy of that certificate to the Administrative Director.

(o) Joint sponsorship of courses (as between an accredited and an unaccredited provider) must be approved by the Administrative Director prior to presentation of the course.

(p) The Administrative Director may audit a provider's course(s) at the request of the medical director to determine if the provider meets the criteria for accreditation. The Administrative Director may audit courses given by providers randomly, when a complaint is received, or on the basis of responses on QME Form 117 (Qualified Medical Evaluator Continuing Education Response Form) (see, 8 Cal. Code Regs. §117). An auditor shall not receive QME credit for auditing a course. The Administrative Director shall make written results of the audit available to the provider no more than 30 days after the audit is completed.

(q) Accredited providers that cease to offer disability evaluation report writing courses shall notify the Administrative Director in writing no later than 60 days prior to the discontinuing an approved course.

(r) The Administrative Director may withdraw accreditation of a provider or deny such a provider's application for accreditation on the following grounds (in addition to failure to meet the relevant requirements of subsections 11.5(a):

(1) Conviction of a felony or any offense substantially related to the activities of the provider.

(2) Any material misrepresentation of fact made by the provider.

(3) Failure to comply with Administrative Director regulations.

(4) False or misleading advertising.

(5) Failure to comply with Administrative Director's recommendations following an audit.

(6) Failure to distribute QME Form 117 (Qualified Medical Evaluator Continuing Education Response Form) (see, 8 Cal. Code Regs. §117) cards to course attendees.

NOTE: Forms referred to above are available at no charge by downloading from the web at www.dir.ca.gov/dwc/forms.html or by requesting at 1-800-794-6900.

Note: Authority cited: Sections 133, 139.2, 4060, 4061, 4062, 4062.1, 4062.2 and 5307.3, Labor Code. Reference: Sections 139.2, 4060, 4061, 4061.5, 4062, 4062.1, 4062.2, 4062.3 and 4067, Labor Code.

History: 1. New section filed 10-16-2000 as an emergency; operative 1-1-2001 (Register 2000, No. 42). A Certificate of Compliance must be transmitted to OAL by 5-1-2001 or emergency language will be repealed by operation of law on the following day.

2. New section refiled 5-2-2001 as an emergency; operative 5-2-2001 (Register 2001, No. 18). A Certificate of Compliance must be transmitted to OAL by 8-30-2001 or emergency language will be repealed by operation of law on the following day.

3. Certificate of Compliance as to 5-2-2001 order, including further amendment of section, transmitted to OAL 7-12-2001 and filed 8-23-2001 (Register 2001, No. 34).

4. Amendment of section and Note filed 1-13-2009; operative 2-17-2009 (Register 2009, No. 3).

5. Amendment of subsection (i)(3) filed 12-31-2012 as an emergency; operative 1-1-2013 pursuant to Government Code section 11346.1(d) (Register 2013, No. 1). A Certificate of Compliance must be transmitted to OAL by 7-1-2013 or emergency language will be repealed by operation of law on the following day.

6. Amendment of subsection (i)(3) refiled 7-1-2013 as an emergency; operative 7-1-2013 (Register 2013, No. 27). A Certificate of Compliance must be transmitted to OAL by 9-30-2013 or emergency language will be repealed by operation of law on the following day.

7. Certificate of Compliance as to 7-1-2013 order, including amendment of first paragraph, transmitted to OAL 8-2-2013 and filed 9-16-2013; amendment operative 9-16-2013 pursuant to Government Code section 11343.4(b)(3) (Register 2013, No. 38).

Ref.: Hanna §§ 1.12[2A][b]–[h], 22.11[1]–[16]; Herlick Handbook § 14.22.

§12. Recognition of Specialty Boards.

The Administrative Director shall recognize only those specialty boards recognized by the respective California licensing boards for physicians as defined in Labor Code section 3209.3.

Note: Authority cited: Sections 133, 139.2, 139.4, 139.43, 139.45 and 5307.3, Labor Code. Reference: Sections 139.2(b)(3)(A) and 3209.3, Labor Code; Section 651(i), Business and Professions Code.

History: 1. New section filed 8-1-94; operative 8-31-94 (Register 94, No. 31).

2. Amendment of section filed 8-23-96; operative 9-22-96 (Register 96, No. 34).

3. Amendment of section and Note filed 1-13-2009; operative 2-17-2009 (Register 2009, No. 3).

Ref.: Hanna §§ 1.12[2A][b]–[h], 22.11[1]–[16]; Herlick Handbook § 14.22.

§13. Physician's Specialty.

(a) A physician's specialty(ies) is one for which the physician is board certified or, one for which a medical doctor or doctor of osteopathy has completed a postgraduate specialty training as defined in Section 11(a)(2)(A) or held an appointment as a QME in that specialty on June 30, 2000, pursuant to Labor Code Section 139.2. To be listed as a QME in a particular specialty, the physician's licensing board must recognize the designated specialty board and the applicant for QME status must have provided to the Administrative Director documentation from the relevant board of certification or qualification.

(b) All requests by a physician to add or remove a medical specialty shall be in writing. A physician seeking to add or change specialties shall include the documentation specified in subdivision (a) that establishes the physician is board certified in the specialty or the subspecialty recognized by the Administrative Director that the physician wishes to add. The failure to provide proof of board certification shall be grounds to deny the request.

Note: Authority cited: Sections 133, 139.2, 139.4, 139.43, 139.45 and 5307.3, Labor Code. Reference: Section 139.2(b)(3)(A), Labor Code; and Section 651(i), Business and Professions Code.

History: 1. New section filed 8-1-94; operative 8-31-94 (Register 94, No. 31).

2. Amendment of section filed 8-23-96; operative 9-22-96 (Register 96, No. 34).

3. Amendment filed 4-14-2000; operative 5-14-2000 (Register 2000, No. 15).

4. Amendment filed 8-23-2001; operative 8-23-2001 pursuant to Government Code section 11343.4 (Register 2001, No. 34).

5. Amendment of section and Note filed 1-13-2009; operative 2-17-2009 (Register 2009, No. 3).

6. New subsection (a) designator and subsection (b) filed 9-16-2013; operative 9-16-2013 pursuant to Government Code section 11343.4(b)(3) (Register 2013, No. 38).

Ref.: Hanna §§ 1.12[2A][b]–[h], 22.11[1]–[16]; Herlick Handbook § 14.22.

§13.5. Chiropractic Certification in Workers' Compensation Evaluation. [Renumbered]

Note: Authority cited: Sections 139, 139.2 and 139.3, Labor Code. Reference: Sections 139.2, 4060, 4061 and 4062, Labor Code.

History: 1. New section filed 8-1-94; operative 8-31-94 (Register 94, No. 31).

2. Change without regulatory effect amending subsection (a) filed 12-2-96 pursuant to section 100, title 1, California Code of Regulations (Register 96, No. 49).

3. Amendment filed 3-15-99; operative 4-14-99 (Register 99, No. 12).

4. Renumbering of former section 13.5 to section 14 filed 4-14-2000, operative 5-14-2000 (Register 2000, No. 15).

§13.7. Appointment of Retired or Teaching Physicians. [Renumbered]

Note: Authority cited: Sections 139 and 139.2, Labor Code. Reference: Sections 139.2, 4060, 4061 and 4062, Labor Code.

History: 1. New section filed 8-1-94; operative 8-31-94 (Register 94, No. 31).

2. Amendment of opening paragraph and subsections (c)(2) and (c)(3) and new subsection (e) filed 8-23-96; operative 9-22-96 (Register 96, No. 34).

3. Renumbering of former section 13.7 to section 15 filed 4-14-2000; operative 5-14-2000 (Register 2000, No. 15).

§14. Doctors of Chiropractic: Certification in Workers' Compensation Evaluation.

(a) All doctors of chiropractic shall be certified in workers' compensation evaluation by either a California professional chiropractic association, or an accredited California college recognized by the Administrative Director. The certification program shall include instruction in disability evaluation report writing that meets the standards set forth in section 11.5.

(b) California professional chiropractic associations or accredited California colleges applying to be recognized by the Administrative Director for the purpose of providing these required courses to chiropractors in California workers' compensation evaluation, shall meet the following criteria:

(1) The provider's courses shall be administered and taught by a California professional chiropractic association or a California chiropractic college accredited by the

Council on Chiropractic Education. Instructors shall be licensed or certified in their profession or if a member of a non-regulated profession have at least two years experience in their area of instruction regarding workers' compensation issues.

(2) The provider's method of instruction and testing shall include all of the following:

(A) Lecture, didactic sessions and group discussion including an initial 8 hours of overview of the workers' compensation system and 36 additional hours in medical-legal issues for total minimum class time of 44 hours. Up to 4 hours of the instruction covering the regulations affecting QMEs and/or writing ratable reports may be satisfied by distance learning. The initial 8 hours of overview are transferable to any other approved program provider for credit;

(B) Passing a written test at the completion of the program to determine proficiency and application of course material;

(C) Writing a narrative conclusion to medical-legal issues in response to facts presented or a narrative report, in appropriate format, which would meet the standards of a ratable report;

(3) The initial 8 hours of the course material shall cover the following information:

(A) Overview of California Labor Code, DWC (Division of Workers' Compensation of the California Department of Industrial Relations) and the regulations of the Division of Workers' Compensation and of the Workers' Compensation Appeals Board governing QMEs, medical-legal reports and evaluations;

(B) Obligations of the treating and evaluating physicians;

(C) Review of appropriate workers' compensation terminology;

(4) The remaining 36 hours shall include but not be limited to the following:

(A) History and examination procedure requirements, including all relevant treatment, treatment utilization and evaluation guidelines and regulations adopted by the Administrative Director;

(B) The subjects outlined in subdivision 11.5(i) not already addressed in the first 8 hours, including, but not limited to, proper use of the AMA Guides, and the medical treatment utilization schedule (MTUS) adopted pursuant to Labor Code section 5307.27;

(C) Apportionment, including the changes in Labor Code sections 4660, 4663 and 4664 by SB 899 (Stats. 2004, ch. 34);

(D) Future medical care.

(5) The provider's course material and tests shall be submitted to the Administrative Director for annual review and the Administrative Director shall monitor a provider's course as necessary to determine if the provider meets the criteria for recognition.

(6) The provider's course advertising shall clearly state whether or not the course is recognized to satisfy the requirement for chiropractic California workers' compensation evaluation by the Administrative Director.

(c) Course Material shall also cover at a minimum, the material within the text of the "Physicians Guide to Medical Practice in the California Workers' Compensation System (Current Edition)."

(d) No one shall recruit members or promote commercial products or services in the instruction room immediately before, during, or immediately after the presentation of a course. Education providers or vendors may display/sell educational materials related to workers' compensation or applications for membership in an area adjoining a course. A course provider or faculty member shall disclose on QME Form 119 (Faculty Disclosure of Commercial Interest) (see, 8 Cal. Code Regs. §119) any significant financial interest held by faculty in or affiliation with any commercial product or service which is discussed in a course and that interest or affiliation must be disclosed to all attendees. An education provider shall file every Form 119 in its possession with the Administrator Director.

NOTE: The "Physicians' Guide" does not appear as a part of this regulation. Copies are available through the Medical Director Division of Workers' Compensation, Attention: Medical Unit, P. O. Box 71010, Oakland, CA 94612.

Note: Authority cited: Sections 122, 133, 139.2, 139.3 and 5307.3, Labor Code. Reference: Sections 139.2, 4060, 4061, 4062, 4062.1, 4062.2, 4062.3 and 4067, Labor Code.

History: 1. New section filed 4-9-93 as an emergency; operative 4-9-93 (Register 93, No. 15). A Certificate of Compliance must be transmitted to OAL 8-9-93 or emergency language will be repealed by operation of law on the following day.

2. Editorial correction amending subsections (a)(1) and (b) and Note (Register 93, No. 17).

3. New section refiled 9-16-93 with amendment of subsections (a)(1)-(b) as an emergency; operative 9-16-93 (Register 93, No. 38). A Certificate of Compliance must be transmitted to OAL by 1-14-94 or emergency language will be repealed by operation of law on the following day.

4. Certificate of Compliance as to 9-16-93 order including amendment of subsections (b) and (c) transmitted to OAL 10-28-93 and filed 12-14-93 (Register 93, No. 51).

5. Relocation of article 2 filed 8-1-94; operative 8-31-94 (Register 94, No. 31).

6. Amendment of subsections (a)(1) and (a)(2), repealer of subsections (b)-(b)(2) and subsection relettering, and amendment of newly designated subsections (b) and (c) filed 8-23-96; operative 9-22-96 (Register 96, No. 34).

7. Amendment filed 6-7-99 as an emergency; operative 6-7-99 (Register 99, No. 24). A Certificate of Compliance must be transmitted to OAL by 10-5-99 or emergency language will be repealed by operation of law on the following day.

8. Reinstatement of section as it existed prior to 6-7-99 emergency amendment by operation of Government Code section 11346.1(f) (Register 2000, No. 3).

9. Amendment filed 1-19-2000; operative 1-19-2000 pursuant to Government Code section 11343.4(d) (Register 2000, No. 3).

10. Renumbering of former section 14 to section 16 filed 4-14-2000 pursuant to section 100, title 1, California Code of Regulations (Register 2000, No. 15).

11. Renumbering and amendment of former section 13.5 to section 14 filed 4-14-2000; operative 5-14-2000 (Register 2000, No. 15).

12. Amendment of subsections (a), (b), (b)(4) and (b)(6) and redesignation and amendment of former subsection (b)(7) as new subsection (c) filed 8-23-2001; operative 8-23-2001 pursuant to Government Code section 11343.4 (Register 2001, No. 34).

13. Amendment of section and Note filed 1-13-2009; operative 2-17-2009 (Register 2009, No. 3).

14. Amendment of subsection (b)(4)(B), repealer of subsection (b)(4)(D), subsection relettering and amendment of newly designated subsection (b)(4)(D) filed 12-31-2012 as an emergency; operative 1-1-2013 pursuant to Government Code section 11346.1(d) (Register 2013, No. 1). A Certificate of Compliance must be transmitted to OAL by 7-1-2013 or emergency language will be repealed by operation of law on the following day.

15. Amendment of subsection (b)(4)(B), repealer of subsection (b)(4)(D), subsection relettering and amendment of newly designated subsection (b)(4)(D) refiled 7-1-2013 as an emergency; operative 7-1-2013 (Register 2013, No. 27). A Certificate of Compliance must be transmitted to OAL by 9-30-2013 or emergency language will be repealed by operation of law on the following day.

16. Certificate of Compliance as to 7-1-2013 order transmitted to OAL 8-2-2013 and filed 9-16-2013 (Register 2013, No. 38).

Ref.: Hanna §§ 1.12[2A][b]–[h], 22.11[1]–[16]; Herlick Handbook § 14.22.

§15. Appointment of Retired or Teaching Physicians.

In order to be considered for appointment as a QME pursuant to Labor Code Section 139.2(c), a physician shall pass the QME competency examination and submit written documentation to the Administrative Director that he or she meets either (a), (b) or (c) of this section.

The physician shall:

(a) Be a current salaried faculty member at an accredited university or college, have a current license to practice as a physician and be engaged in teaching, lecturing, published writing or medical research at that university or college in the area of his or her specialty for not less than one-third of his or her professional time. The physician's practice in the three consecutive years immediately preceding the time of application shall not have been devoted solely to the forensic evaluation of disability.

(b) Be retired from full-time practice; retain a current license to practice in California as a physician with his or her licensing board; and

(1) Have a minimum of 25 years' experience in his or her practice as a physician; and

(2) Have had a minimum of 10 years' experience in workers' compensation medical issues; and

(3) Be practicing currently fewer than 10 hours per week on direct medical treatment as a physician; and

(4) Not have engaged in a practice devoted solely to the forensic evaluation of disability during the three consecutive years immediately preceding the time of application.

(c) Be retired from active practice due to a documented medical or physical disability as defined pursuant to Government Code section 12926 and currently practice in his or her specialty fewer than 10 hours per week. The physician shall have 10 years experience in workers' compensation medical issues as a physician. The physician's practice in the three consecutive years immediately preceding the time of application shall not have been devoted solely to the forensic evaluation of disability.

(d) A physician appointed under section 11 of Title 8 of the California Code of Regulations or this section shall, notify the Administrative Director of changes in his or her status and shall complete the requirements for continuing education pursuant to section 55 of Title 8 of the California Code of Regulations prior to reappointment.

Note: Authority cited: Sections 133, 139.2 and 5307.3, Labor Code. Reference: Section 139.2, Labor Code.

History: 1. New section filed 4-9-93 as an emergency; operative 4-9-93 (Register 93, No. 15). A Certificate of Compliance must be transmitted to OAL 8-9-93 or emergency language will be repealed by operation of law on the following day.

2. Editorial correction amending subsection (b) and Note (Register 93, No. 17).

3. New section refiled 9-16-93 with amendment of subsections (a)(1)-(b) as an emergency; operative 9-16-93 (Register 93, No. 38). A Certificate of Compliance must be transmitted to OAL by 1-14-94 or emergency language will be repealed by operation of law on the following day.

4. Certificate of Compliance as to 9-16-93 order including amendment of subsection (b) transmitted to OAL 10-28-93 and filed 12-14-93 (Register 93, No. 51).

5. Amendment filed 6-7-99 as an emergency; operative 6-7-99 (Register 99, No. 24). A Certificate of Compliance must be transmitted to OAL by 10-5-99 or emergency language will be repealed by operation of law on the following day.

6. Reinstatement of section as it existed prior to 6-7-99 emergency amendment by operation of Government Code section 11346.1(f) (Register 2000, No. 3).

7. Amendment filed 1-19-2000; operative 1-19-2000 pursuant to Government Code section 11343.4(d) (Register 2000, No. 3).

8. Renumbering of former section 15 to section 17 filed 4-14-2000 pursuant to section 100, title 1, California Code of Regulations (Register 2000, No. 15).

9. Renumbering and amendment former section 13.7 to section 15 filed 4-14-2000; operative 5-14-2000 (Register 2000, No. 15).

10. Amendment of section and Note filed 1-13-2009; operative 2-17-2009 (Register 2009, No. 3).

Ref.: Hanna §§ 1.12[2A][b]–[h], 22.11[1]–[16]; Herlick Handbook §§ 1.02, 14.22.

§16. Determination of Fees for QME Eligibility.

(a) For purposes of establishing the annual fee for any qualified medical evaluator pursuant to Article 2, physicians (as defined under Section 3209.3 of the Labor Code) shall be classified into one of three categories:

(1) QMEs who meet all applicable requirements under Article 2 and 5 and who have conducted 0-10 comprehensive medical-legal evaluations in the twelve months prior to the assessment of the fee. Comprehensive medical-legal evaluations are evaluations as defined under Section (1)(i) of this Chapter performed by a physician.

(2) QMEs who meet all applicable requirements under Article 2 and 5 and who have conducted 11-24 comprehensive medical-legal evaluations in the twelve months prior to assessment of the fee. Comprehensive medical-legal evaluations are evaluations as defined under Section (1)(i) of this Chapter performed by a physician.

(3) QMEs who meet all applicable requirements under Article 2 and 5 and who have conducted 25 or more comprehensive medical-legal evaluations in the twelve months prior to assessment of the fee. Comprehensive medical-legal evaluations are evaluations as defined under Section (1)(i) of this Chapter performed by a physician.

(b) The evaluations shall be conducted in compliance with all applicable statutes and regulations.

(c) Verification of the number of examinations shall be made by the Administrative Director using The Qualified or Agreed Medical Evaluator Findings Summary Form in section 111 (See, 8 Cal. Code Regs. § 111), as well as any other relevant records or sources of information. Misrepresentation of the number of evaluations performed for purposes of establishing a physician's QME fee shall constitute grounds for disciplinary proceedings under section 60 of this chapter.

NOTE: Form referred to above is available at no charge by downloading from the web at www.dir.ca.gov/dwc/forms.html or by requesting at 1-800-794-6900.

Note: Authority cited: Sections 133, 139.2 and 5307.3, Labor Code. Reference: Section 139.2, Labor Code.

History: 1. New section filed 4-9-93 as an emergency; operative 4-9-93 (Register 93, No. 15). A Certificate of Compliance must be transmitted to OAL 8-9-93 or emergency language will be repealed by operation of law on the following day.

2. Editorial correction amending Note (Register 93, No. 17).

3. New section refiled 9-16-93 with amendment of subsection (a) as an emergency; operative 9-16-93 (Register 93, No. 38). A Certificate of Compliance must be transmitted to OAL by 1-14-94 or emergency language will be repealed by operation of law on the following day.

4. Certificate of Compliance as to 9-16-93 order including amendments transmitted to OAL 10-28-93 and filed 12-14-93 (Register 93, No. 51).

5. Amendment of section filed 8-23-96; operative 9-22-96 (Register 96, No. 34).

6. Amendment filed 6-7-99 as an emergency; operative 6-7-99 (Register 99, No. 24). A Certificate of Compliance must be transmitted to OAL by 10-5-99 or emergency language will be repealed by operation of law on the following day.

7. Reinstatement of section as it existed prior to 6-7-99 emergency amendment by operation of Government Code section 11346.1(f) (Register 2000, No. 3).

8. Amendment filed 1-19-2000; operative 1-19-2000 pursuant to Government Code section 11343.4(d) (Register 2000, No. 3).

9. Renumbering of former section 16 to section 18 and renumbering of former section 14 to number 16 filed 4-14-2000 pursuant to section 100, title 1, California Code of Regulations (Register 2000, No. 15).

10. Amendment of subsection (c) and Note filed 1-13-2009; operative 2-17-2009 (Register 2009, No. 3).

Ref.: Hanna §§ 1.12[2A][b]–[h], 22.11[1]–[16]; Herlick Handbook §§ 1.02, 14.22.

§17. Fee Schedule for QME.

(a) All physicians seeking QME status shall be required to pay to the Workers' Compensation Administration Revolving Fund, the following fee:

(1) QMEs performing 0–10 comprehensive medical-legal evaluations, $110 during each of the years or any part of a year the physician retains his or her eligibility on the approved QME list.

(2) QMEs performing 11–24 comprehensive medical-legal evaluations, $125 during each of the years or any part of a year the physician retains his or her eligibility on the approved QME list.

(3) QMEs performing 25 or more comprehensive medical-legal evaluations, $250 during each of the years or any part of a year the physician retains his or her eligibility on the approved QME list.

(b) The Administrative Director may waive or return the statutory fee in the amount of $110 for the completion of a survey of QMEs to validate the QME competency examination. The term "completion of the survey" means the return of the survey to the testing agency designated by the Administrative Director on or before the date for the return of the survey.

(c) At the time of paying the appropriate QME annual fee, each QME shall also complete and forward to the Medical Director with the annual fee a completed QME SFI Form 124, providing updated information about the QME's specified financial interests as defined in section 29 of Title 8 of the California Code of Regulations.

Note: Authority cited: Section 133, 139.2 and 5307.3, Labor Code. Reference: Section139.2, Labor Code.

History: 1. New section filed 4-9-93 as an emergency; operative 4-9-93 (Register 93, No. 15). A Certificate of Compliance must be transmitted to OAL 8-9-93 or emergency language will be repealed by operation of law on the following day.

2. Editorial correction amending Note (Register 93, No. 17).

3. New section refiled 9-16-93 with amendments as an emergency; operative 9-16-93 (Register 93, No. 38). A Certificate of Compliance must be transmitted to OAL by 1-14-94 or emergency language will be repealed by operation of law on the following day.

4. Certificate of Compliance as to 9-16-93 order including amendments transmitted to OAL 10-28-93 and filed 12-14-93 (Register 93, No. 51).

5. Renumbering former section 17 to new section 19 filed 4-14-2000; operative 5-14-2000 (Register 2000, No. 15).

6. Renumbering of former section 15 to section 17 filed 4-14-2000 pursuant to section 100, title 1, California Code of Regulations (Register 2000, No. 15).

7. New subsection (c) and amendment of Note filed 2-14-2002 as an emergency; operative 2-14-2002 (Register 2002, No. 7). A Certificate of Compliance must be transmitted to OAL by 6-14-2002 or emergency language will be repealed by operation of law on the following day.

8. Amendment of section and Note filed 1-13-2009; operative 2-17-2009 (Register 2009, No. 3).

9. Amendment of subsection (b) filed 12-31-2012 as an emergency; operative 1-1-2013 pursuant to Government Code section 11346.1(d) (Register 2013, No. 1). A Certificate of Compliance must be transmitted to OAL by 7-1-2013 or emergency language will be repealed by operation of law on the following day.

10. Amendment of subsection (b) refiled 7-1-2013 as an emergency; operative 7-1-2013 (Register 2013, No. 27). A Certificate of Compliance must be transmitted to OAL by 9-30-2013 or emergency language will be repealed by operation of law on the following day.

11. Certificate of Compliance as to 7-1-2013 order, including repealer of subsection (b) and subsection relettering, transmitted to OAL 8-2-2013 and filed 9-16-2013; amendment operative 9-16-2013 pursuant to Government Code section 11343.4(b)(3) (Register 2013, No. 38).

Ref.: Hanna §§ 1.12[2A][b]–[h], 22.11[1]–[16]; Herlick Handbook § 14.22.

§18. QME Fee Due Dates.

(a) All physicians, regardless of the number of comprehensive medical-legal evaluations performed under section 17 of Title 8 of the California Code of Regulations shall pay the required QME fees at yearly intervals within 30 days of receipt of notice from the Administrative Director that the QME fee for the next 12 months is due and payable. No physician who has passed the competency examination shall be placed on the active QME roster until the appropriate fee under section 17 has been paid.

(b) Any QME who fails to pay the required statutory fee within 30 days of receipt of a final notice that the fee is due shall be notified that he or she shall be terminated from the official QME roster of physicians within 30 days and shall not perform any panel QME or represented QME comprehensive medical-legal evaluation until the fee is paid.

(c) If the QME fee is not paid within two years from the due date in the final fee notice from the Administrative Director to the QME or QME applicant that the fee is due, then the physician shall resubmit a new application pursuant to Sections 10 and 11 of Title 8 of the California Code of Regulations, pass the QME competency examination and pay the appropriate fee prior to regaining or obtaining QME active status.

Note: Authority cited: Sections 133, 139.2 and 5307.3, Labor Code. Reference: Section 139.2, Labor Code.

History: 1. New section filed 4-9-93 as an emergency; operative 4-9-93 (Register 93, No. 15). A Certificate of Compliance must be transmitted to OAL 8-9-93 or emergency language will be repealed by operation of law on the following day.

2. Editorial correction amending subsections (b) and (b)(1) and Note (Register 93, No. 17).

3. New section refiled 9-16-93 with amendment of section heading and text as an emergency; operative 9-16-93 (Register 93, No. 38). A Certificate of Compliance must be transmitted to OAL by 1-14-94 or emergency language will be repealed by operation of law on the following day.

4. Certificate of Compliance as to 9-16-93 order including amendments transmitted to OAL 10-28-93 and filed 12-14-93 (Register 93, No. 51).

5. Repealer filed 8-23-96; operative 9-22-96 (Register 96, No. 34).

6. Renumbering of former section 16 to section 18 filed 4-14-2000 pursuant to section 100, title 1, California Code of Regulations (Register 2000, No. 15).

7. Amendment of section and Note filed 1-13-2009; operative 2-17-2009 (Register 2009, No. 3).

Ref.: Hanna §§ 1.12[2A][b]–[h], 22.11[1]–[16]; Herlick Handbook § 14.22.

§19. Certificate of QME Status.

(a) Upon receipt of the QME fees and review by the Administrative Director to ensure current compliance with section 139.2 of Labor Code and any other applicable regulations promulgated by the Administrative Director concerning QME eligibility, the Administrative Director shall within 45 days send to the physician a Qualified Medical Evaluator certificate. The QME certificate shall be displayed in a conspicuous manner at the QME's office location at all times during the period the QME is appointed by the Administrative Director to conduct evaluations.

(b) It shall be unlawful for any physician who has been terminated or suspended from the QME list or who has failed to pay the required QME fee pursuant to sections 17 and 18 of Title 8 of the California Code of Regulations to display a Qualified Medical Evaluator certificate.

Note: Authority cited: Sections 133, 139.2 and 5307.3, Labor Code. Reference: Section 139.2, Labor Code.

History: 1. Renumbering and amendment of former section 17 to new section 19 filed 4-14-2000; operative 5-14-2000 (Register 2000, No. 15).

2. Amendment of section and Note filed 1-13-2009; operative 2-17-2009 (Register 2009, No. 3).

Ref.: Hanna §§ 1.12[2A][b]–[h], 22.11[1]–[16]; Herlick Handbook §§ 1.02, 14.22.

ARTICLE 2.5
Time Periods for Processing Applications for QME Status

§20. Time Periods.

(a) Within 45 days of receipt of an application for QME status, the Administrative Director shall either inform the applicant, in writing, that the application is complete and accepted for filing, or that the application is deficient and what specific information is required.

(b) Within 45 days of receipt of a completed application, the Administrative Director shall inform the applicant, in writing, of its decision to allow or not to allow the applicant to proceed to take the required QME competency examination as per Section 11(f) of Title 8 of the California Code of Regulations.

(c) Within 45 days of receipt of a completed application, the Administrative Director must inform the applicant, in writing, of its decision to grant or deny the application.

Note: Authority cited: Sections 133, 139.2 and 5307.3, Labor Code. Reference: Sections 4060, 4061, 4062, 4062.1, 4062.2 and 4067, Labor Code.

History: 1. New article 2.5 and section filed 8-1-94; operative 8-31-94 (Register 94, No. 31).

2. Amendment of section and Note filed 1-13-2009; operative 2-17-2009 (Register 2009, No. 3).

Ref.: Hanna §§ 1.12[2A][b]–[h], 22.11[1]–[16]; Herlick Handbook § 14.22.

ARTICLE 2.6
QME Office Locations

§26. QME Office Locations and Changes of Office Locations.

(a) Subject to the restriction in Labor Code section 139.2(h)(3)(B) of 10 offices for conducting comprehensive medical-legal evaluations, QMEs who perform comprehensive medical-legal evaluations at more than one physician's office location shall be required to pay an additional $ 100 annually per additional office location. Each physician's office listed with the Medical Director must be located within California, be identified by a street address and any other more specific location such as a suite or room number, and must contain the usual and customary equipment for the type of evaluation appropriate to the QME's medical specialty or scope of practice. Nothing in this section shall prevent a QME from adding additional offices up to the maximum set forth in Labor Code section 139.2 (h)(3) (B).

(b) An office location shall be maintained by a QME at least 180 days from the date the Medical Unit lists the office as available to perform comprehensive medical-legal evaluations, except upon a showing of good cause to the Medical Director. For purposes of this section the term "good cause" includes, but is not limited to:

(1) natural disasters or other community catastrophes that interrupt the operation of the evaluator's business;

(2) the expiration of a written lease agreement of not less than 12 months duration for an office location defined in subdivision (a);

(3) the sale of real property by the QME of an office location defined in subdivision (a) where the QME vacates the property.

(c) All changes of office location or requests to change office locations, except in the case of natural disaster or community catastrophes, shall be communicated to the Medical Unit at least 30 days in advance.

Note: Authority cited: Sections 133, 139.2 and 5307.3, Labor Code. Reference: Section 139.2, Labor Code.

History: 1. New article 2.6 (section 26) and section filed 9-16-2013; operative 9-16-2013 pursuant to Government Code section 11343.4(b)(3) (Register 2013, No. 38).

Ref.: Hanna § 1.12[2A]; Herlick Handbook §§ 1.02, 14.22.

ARTICLE 3
Assignment of Qualified Medical Evaluators, Evaluation Procedure

§29. Specified Financial Interests That May Affect Assignment to QME Panels.

(a) Every physician seeking appointment or reappointment as a Qualified Medical Evaluator shall disclose specified financial interests, as defined in section 1(dd) and 29(b) of Title 8 of the California Code of Regulations.

(b) "Specified Financial Interests" means being a general partner or limited partner in, or having an interest of five (5) percent or more in, or receiving or being legally entitled to receive a share of five (5) percent or more of the profits from, any medical practice, group practice, medical group, professional corporation, limited liability corporation, clinic or other entity that provides treatment or medical evaluation, goods or services for use in the California workers' compensation system.

(c) "SFI Form 124", as used in sections 1 though 159 of Title 8 of the California Code of Regulations, means the QME SFI Form 124 that is completed and filed as an attachment to QME Form 100, 103 or 104 by the physician or QME with the Medical Director of the Division of Workers' Compensation.

(d) Specified financial interests shall be disclosed on QME SFI Form 124, respectively, when applying for appointment on QME Form 100, at the time of paying the annual fee on QME Form 103 or when applying for reappointment on QME Form 104.

(e) The completed QME SFI Form 124 shall be filed along with the QME Form 100, 103 or 104, respectively, when the form is filed with the Medical Director of the Division of Workers' Compensation.

(f) Failure of a Qualified Medical Evaluator to complete and file a QME SFI Form 124 with the Medical Director when required by this section shall be grounds for disciplinary action pursuant to section 60 of Title 8 of the California Code of Regulations.

(g) The Administrative Director shall use the information provided by physicians pursuant to this section to avoid assigning QMEs who share specified financial interests to the same QME panel. If two or more QMEs assigned to a panel share specified financial interests as defined in this section, any party may request a replacement QME. If three QMEs share specified financial interests as defined in this section, two of the QMEs shall be replaced. If two QMEs share specified financial interests as defined in this section, one of the QMEs shall be replaced. The QMEs that must be replaced shall be randomly selected by the Medical Director.

NOTE: Forms referred to above are available at no charge by downloading from the web at www.dir.ca.gov/dwc/forms.html or by requesting at 1-800-794-6900.

Note: Authority cited: Sections 133, 139.2 and 5307.3, Labor Code. Reference: Sections 139.2, 4060, 4061, 4062, 4062.1, 4062.2 and 4067, Labor Code.

History: 1. New section filed 1-13-2009; operative 2-17-2009 (Register 2009, No. 3).

Ref.: Hanna §§ 1.12[2A][b]–[h], 22.11[1]–[16]; Herlick Handbook §§ 1.02, 14.22.

§30. QME Panel Requests.

(a) Unrepresented cases. Whenever an employee is not represented by an attorney and either the employee or the claims administrator requests a QME panel pursuant to Labor Code section 4062.1, the request shall be submitted on the Request for Qualified Medical Evaluator Panel Form (Unrepresented Employee), QME Form 105, in section 105.

(1) For disputes covered by Labor Code section 4060, the requesting party shall attach the claims administrator's notice that the claim was denied or a copy of the claims administrator's request for an examination to determine compensability to the QME Form 105;

(2) For disputes covered by Labor Code section 4061 or 4062, if the requesting party is the claims administrator, the claims administrator shall attach a written objection indicating the identity of the primary treating physician, the date of the primary treating physician's report that is the subject of the objection and a description of the medical determination that requires a comprehensive medical-legal report to resolve to the QME Form 105.

(3) The claims administrator (or if none the employer) shall provide QME Form 105 to the unrepresented employee pursuant to Labor Code sections 4060, 4061, and 4062, by means of personal delivery or by first class or certified mailing.

(4) If the form is incomplete, so that a QME panel selection cannot be made, the request form shall be returned to the requesting party with an explanation of why the QME panel selection could not be made. The Medical Director may delay issuing a QME panel until the Medical Director receives additional information, requested from a party or both parties, needed to resolve the panel request.

(b) Represented cases. Effective October 1, 2015, requests for an initial QME panel in a represented case, for all cases with a date of injury on or after January 1, 2005, shall be submitted electronically utilizing the Division of Workers' Compensation internet site at www.dwc.ca.gov. The Medical Unit will not accept or process panel requests on the QME Form 106 postmarked after September 3, 2015, except as to those cases with dates of injury prior to January 1, 2005 where represented parties agree to obtain a panel of Qualified Medical Evaluators pursuant to the process in Labor Code section 4062.2.

(1) The party requesting a QME panel online shall:

(A) Identify the following elements in the appropriate sections:

1. Panel Request Information Section

i. Date of Injury

ii. Claim Number

iii. Requesting Party

iv. Reason QME Panel is being Requested

v. Dispute type

vi. Name of primary treating physician

vii. Date of report being objected to

viii. Date of objection communication

ix. Specialty of treating physician

x. QME Specialty Requested

xi. Opposing Party's QME Specialty Preferred (if known)

2. Employee Information Section

i. Employee First Name

ii. Employee Middle Name

iii. Employee Last Name

iv. Mailing Address

v. City

vi. Zip Code

vii. State

3. Applicant's Attorney Information Section

i. First Name

ii. Last Name

iii. Address

iv. City

v. State Zip

vi. Phone Number

vii. Electronic Adjudication Management System (EAMS) Uniform Assigned Names (UAN)

viii. Firm Name

4. Employee and Claims Administrator Information Section

i. Employer Name

ii. Claims Administrator First Name

iii. Claims Administrator Last Name

iv. Claims Administrator Company Name

v. Address

vi. City

vii. State

viii. Zip

ix. Phone Number

x. Electronic Adjudication Management System (EAMS) Uniform Assigned Names (UAN)

5. Defense Attorney Information Section

i. First name

ii. Last name

iii. Defense Attorney Firm Name

iv. Address/P.O. Box

v. City

vi. State Zip

vii. Phone Number

viii. EAMS UAN Number

(B) Scan and upload the following supporting documentation when prompted:

1. a written request for an examination to determine compensability for disputes covered by Labor Code section 4060; or

2. a written objection indicating the identity of the primary treating physician, the date of the primary treating physician's report that is the subject of the objection and a description of the medical determination that requires a comprehensive medical - legal report to resolve, for disputes covered by Labor Code sections 4061 and 4062;

(C) Print and serve a paper copy of the online request, the panel list, and a copy of any supporting documentation that was submitted online, upon the opposing party with a proof of service, within 1 (one) working day after generating the QME panel list. Within 10 (ten) days of service of the panel, each party may strike one name from the panel.

(2) Requests may be made twenty-four hours a day, seven days a week. For determining the timeliness of requests under Labor Code section 4062.2, requests made on Saturday, Sunday or a holiday will be deemed to have been made at 8:00 a.m. on the next business day. Requests made Monday through Friday after 5:00 p.m. and before 12:00 a.m. will be deemed to have been made at 8:00 a.m. on the next business day, and requests made between 12:00 a.m. and 8:00 a.m. will be deemed to have been made at 8:00 a.m. on the same business day.

(3) Upon submission of the request online, the QME panel selection will be generated automatically. After issuance of a panel, any subsequent request on the same claim, whether made on the same day or not, is a duplicate request. In the event of technical difficulties, such that a panel QME selection cannot be generated on-line, the requesting party may contact the Medical Unit and shall reference the error code or message.

(c) If after the issuance of a panel it appears to the satisfaction of the Medical Director that the panel was issued by mistake, misrepresentation of fact contained in the forms or document filed in support of the request, or the parties have agreed to resolve their dispute using an AME or by other agreement, the issued panel may be revoked. Notice of the revocation shall be sent to parties listed on the panel request.

(d)(1) After a claim form has been filed, the claims administrator, or if none the employer, may request a panel of Qualified Medical Evaluators only as provided in Labor Code section 4060, to determine whether to accept or reject a claim within the ninety (90) day period for rejecting liability in Labor Code section 5402(b), and only after providing evidence of compliance with Labor Code Section 4062.1 or 4062.2.

(2) Once the claims administrator, or if none, the employer, has accepted as compensable injury to any body part in the claim, a request for a panel QME may only be filed based on a dispute arising under Labor Code section 4061 or 4062.

(e) If the request is submitted by or on behalf of an employee who does not reside within the state of California, the geographic area of the QME panel selection within the state shall be determined by agreement between the claims administrator, or if none the employer, and the employee. If no agreement can be reached, the geographic area of the QME panel selection shall be determined for an unrepresented employee by the employee's former residence within the state or, if the employee never resided in the state, by the geographic location of the employer's place of business where the employee was employed, and for a represented employee by the office of the employee's attorney.

(f) To compile a panel list of three (3) independent QMEs randomly selected from the specialty designated by the party holding the legal right to request a QME panel, the Medical Director shall exclude from the panel, to the extent feasible, any QME who is listed by another QME as a business partner or as having a shared specified financial interest, as those terms are defined in sections 1 and 29 of Title 8 of the California Code of Regulations.

(g) The time periods specified in Labor Code sections 4062.1(c) and 4062.2(c), respectively, for selecting an evaluator from a QME panel and for scheduling an appointment, shall be tolled whenever the Medical Director asks a party for additional information needed to resolve the panel request. These time periods shall remain tolled until the date the Medical Director issues either a new QME panel or a decision on the panel request.

NOTE: Forms referred to above are available at no charge by downloading from the web at www.dir.ca.gov/dwc/forms.html or by requesting at 1-800-794-6900.

Note: Authority cited: Sections 133, 139.2, 4061, 4062 and 5307.3, Labor Code. Reference: Sections 139.2, 4060, 4061, 4062, 4062.1, 4062.2, 4062.3, 4064 and 4067, Labor Code.

History: 1. New article 3 and section filed 8-1-94; operative 8-31-94 (Register 94, No. 31).

2. Amendment of subsection (b) and new subsections (d)-(e) filed 8-23-96; operative 9-22-96 (Register 96, No. 34).

3. Amendment of subsections (a), (c) and (d)(1) filed 4-14-2000; operative 5-14-2000 (Register 2000, No. 15).

4. Amendment of section and Note filed 1-13-2009; operative 2-17-2009 (Register 2009, No. 3).

5. Amendment of subsection (b)(1), repealer of subsection (b)(2), subsection renumbering, amendment of newly designated subsection (b)(4) and repealer of subsections (d)(3)-(4) filed 12-31-2012 as an emergency; operative 1-1-2013 pursuant to Government Code section 11346.1(d) (Register 2013, No. 1). A Certificate of Compliance must be transmitted to OAL by 7-1-2013 or emergency language will be repealed by operation of law on the following day.

6. Amendment of subsection (b)(1), repealer of subsection (b)(2), subsection renumbering, amendment of newly designated subsection (b)(4) and repealer of subsections (d)(3)-(4) refiled 7-1-2013 as an emergency; operative 7-1-2013 (Register 2013, No. 27). A Certificate of Compliance must be transmitted to OAL by 9-30-2013 or emergency language will be repealed by operation of law on the following day.

7. Certificate of Compliance as to 7-1-2013 order, including further amendment of section, transmitted to OAL 8-2-2013 and filed 9-16-2013; amendments operative 9-16-2013 pursuant to Government Code section 11343.4(b)(3) (Register 2013, No. 38).

8. Amendment of section and Note filed 8-12-2015; operative 9-1-2015 pursuant to Government Code section 11343.4(b)(3) (Register 2015, No. 33).

Ref.: See Labor Code §4060; Hanna §§ 1.12[2A][b]–[h], 22.11[1]–[16]; Herlick Handbook § 14.22.

§30.1. The Request for Qualified Medical Evaluator Form. [Repealed]

Note: Authority cited: Sections 133, 139 and 139.2, Labor Code. Reference: Sections 139.2, 4060, 4061 and 4062, Labor Code.

History: 1. New section filed 8-1-94; operative 8-31-94 (Register 94, No. 31).

2. Change without regulatory effect amending specialty codes filed 6-27-95 pursuant to section 100, title 1, California Code of Regulations (Register 95, No. 26).

3. Editorial correction adding History 3 and including previously filed amendments (Register 95, No. 41).

4. Change without regulatory effect amending specialty code MPT, repealing specialty codes DDS and DMD and adding specialty code DEN filed 10-11-95 pursuant to section 100, title 1, California Code of Regulations (Register 95, No. 41).

5. Change without regulatory effect adding MAP specialty code filed 12-27-95 pursuant to section 100, title 1, California Code of Regulations (Register 95, No. 52).

6. Change without regulatory effect amending form filed 6-20-96 pursuant to section 100, title 1, California Code of Regulations (Register 96, No. 25).

7. Change without regulatory effect amending form filed 2-25-97 pursuant to section 100, title 1, California Code of Regulations (Register 97, No. 9).

8. Change without regulatory effect amending MD/DO specialty codes filed 6-19-97 pursuant to section 100, title 1, California Code of Regulations (Register 97, No. 25).

9. Change without regulatory effect amending MD/DO specialty codes and updating form revision date filed 4-15-98 pursuant to section 100, title 1, California Code of Regulations (Register 98, No. 16).

10. Change without regulatory effect amending MD/DO specialty codes and updating form revision date filed 7-12-99 pursuant to section 100, title 1, California Code of Regulations (Register 99, No. 29).

11. Repealer filed 4-14-2000; operative 5-14-2000 (Register 2000, No. 15).

§30.2. The Request for Qualified Medical Evaluator Instruction Form. [Repealed]

Note: Authority cited: Sections 4061 and 4062, Labor Code. Reference: Sections 4061 and 4062, Labor Code.

History: 1. New section filed 8-1-94; operative 8-31-94 (Register 94, No. 31).

2. Change without regulatory effect amending third paragraph filed 2-25-97 pursuant to section 100, title 1, California Code of Regulations (Register 97, No. 9).

3. Repealer filed 4-14-2000; operative 5-14-2000 (Register 2000, No. 15).

4. Editorial correction reinstating inadvertently deleted section (Register 2013, No. 44).

§30.5. Specialist Designation.

The Medical Director shall utilize in the QME panel selection process the type of specialist(s) indicated by the requestor online or on the Request for Qualified Medical Evaluator Form 105 or 106 of Title 8 of the California

Code of Regulations, unless otherwise provided in these regulations.

Note: Authority cited: Sections 133, 139.2, 4061, 4062 and 5307.3, Labor Code. Reference: Sections 139.2, 4060, 4061, 4062, 4062.1, 4062.2, 4064 and 4067, Labor Code.

History: 1. Renumbering and amendment of former section 32 to new section 30.5 filed 4-14-2000; operative 5-14-2000 (Register 2000, No. 15).

2. Amendment of section and Note filed 1-13-2009; operative 2-17-2009 (Register 2009, No. 3).

3. Editorial correction reinstating inadvertently deleted section (Register 2013, No. 44).

4. Amendment of section and Note filed 8-12-2015; operative 9-1-2015 pursuant to Government Code section 11343.4(b)(3) (Register 2015, No. 33).

Ref.: Hanna §§ 1.12[2A][b]–[h], 22.11[1]–[16]; Herlick Handbook § 14.22.

§31. QME Panel Selection.

(a) The panels shall be selected randomly from the appropriate specialty identified by the party who holds the legal right to designate the specialty, with consideration given to the proximity of the QME's medical office to the employee's residence.

(b) The Medical Director shall exclude from the panel selection process any QME who has informed the Medical Director that he or she is unavailable pursuant to section 33 of Title 8 of the California Code of Regulations.

(c) Any physician who has served as a primary treating physician or secondary physician and who has provided treatment to the employee in accordance with section 9785 of Title 8 of the California Code of Regulations for the disputed injury shall not perform a QME evaluation on that employee. Whenever that physician's name appears on a QME panel, he or she shall disqualify him or herself if contacted by a party to perform the evaluation. Either party may request a replacement QME for this reason pursuant to section 31.5 of Title 8 of the California Code of Regulations.

(d) To issue a panel in a selected specialty there shall be at least five active QMEs in the specialty at the time the panel selection is requested. In the event less than five QMEs are active in a requested specialty, the Medical Director shall contact the party who holds the legal right to designate the specialty for an alternate specialty selection.

Note: Authority cited: Sections 133, 139.2, 4061, 4062 and 5307.3, Labor Code. Reference: Sections 139.2, 4060, 4061, 4062, 4062.1, 4062.2, 4064 and 4067, Labor Code.

History: 1. New section filed 8-1-94; operative 8-31-94 (Register 94, No. 31).

2. Repealer of subsection (d) and subsection relettering, and amendment of newly designated subsection (d) filed 8-23-96; operative 9-22-96 (Register 96, No. 34).

3. Amendment of subsections (b) and (d) filed 4-14-2000; operative 5-14-2000 (Register 2000, No. 15).

4. Amendment of section and Note filed 1-13-2009; operative 2-17-2009 (Register 2009, No. 3).

5. Editorial correction reinstating inadvertently deleted section (Register 2013, No. 44).

Ref.: Hanna §§ 1.12[2A][b]–[h], 22.11[1]–[16]; Herlick Handbook § 14.22.

§31.1. QME Panel Selection Disputes in Represented Cases.

(a) Disputes regarding the validity of panel requests shall be resolved by a Workers' Compensation Administrative Law Judge.

(b) Disputes regarding the appropriateness of the specialty designated shall be resolved pursuant to section 31.5(a)(10) of Title 8 of the California Code of Regulations. Either party may appeal the Medical Director's decision as to the appropriateness of the specialty to a Workers' Compensation Administrative Law Judge.

(c) In the event the Medical Director is unable to issue a QME panel in a represented case within thirty (30) calendar days of receiving the request, either party may seek an order from a Workers' Compensation Administrative Law Judge that a QME panel be issued. Any such order shall specify the specialty of the QME panel or the party to be designated to select the specialty.

Note: Authority cited: Sections 133, 139.2 and 5307.3, Labor Code. Reference: Sections 4060, 4061, 4062, 4062.2, 4064 and 4067, Labor Code.

History: 1. New section filed 1-13-2009; operative 2-17-2009 (Register 2009, No. 3). For prior history, see Register 2000, No. 15.

2. Editorial correction reinstating inadvertently deleted section (Register 2013, No. 44).

3. Amendment filed 8-12-2015; operative 9-1-2015 pursuant to Government Code section 11343.4(b)(3) (Register 2015, No. 33).

Ref.: Hanna §§ 1.12[2A][b]–[h], 22.11[1]–[16], Herlick Handbook § 14.22.

§31.2. QME Office Locations. [Repealed]

Note: Authority cited: Sections 133, 139.2 and 5307.3, Labor Code. Reference: Sections 139.2, 4060, 4061, 4062, 4062.1, 4062.2, 4062.5 and 4067, Labor Code.

History: 1. New section filed 12-31-2012 as an emergency; operative 1-1-2013 pursuant to Government Code section 11346.1(d) (Register 2013, No. 1). A Certificate of Compliance must be transmitted to OAL by 7-1-2013 or emergency language will be repealed by operation of law on the following day. For prior history, see Register 2000, No. 15.

2. New section refiled 7-1-2013 as an emergency; operative 7-1-2013 (Register 2013, No. 27). A Certificate of Compliance must be transmitted to OAL by 9-30-2013 or emergency language will be repealed by operation of law on the following day.

3. Certificate of Compliance as to 7-1-2013 order, including repealer of section, transmitted to OAL 8-2-2013 and filed 9-16-2013; repealer operative 9-16-2013 pursuant to Government Code section 11343.4(b)(3) (Register 2013, No. 38).

§31.3. Scheduling Appointment with Panel QME.

(a) When the employee is not represented by an attorney, the unrepresented employee shall, within ten (10) days of having been furnished with the form, select a QME from the panel list, contact the QME to schedule an appointment and inform the claims administrator of the QME selection and the appointment.

(b) Neither the employer, nor the claims administrator nor any other representative of the employer shall discuss the selection of the QME with an unrepresented worker who has the legal right to select the QME.

(c) If, within ten (10) days of the issuance of a QME panel, the unrepresented employee fails to select a QME from the QME panel or fails to schedule an appointment with the selected QME, the claims administrator may schedule an appointment with a panel QME only as provided in Labor Code section 4062.1(c), and shall notify the employee of the appointment as provided in that section.

(d) Whenever the employee is represented by an attorney and the parties have completed the striking processes described in Labor Code section 4062.2(c), the represented employee shall schedule the appointment with the physician selected from the QME panel. If the represented employee fails to do so within ten (10) business days of the date a QME is selected from the panel, the claims administrator or administrator's attorney may arrange the appointment and notify the employee and employee's attorney.

(e) If a party with the legal right to schedule an appointment with a QME is unable to obtain an appointment with a selected QME within sixty (60) days of the date of the appointment request, that party may waive the right to a replacement in order to accept an appointment no more than ninety (90) days after the date of the party's initial appointment request. When the selected QME is unable to schedule the evaluation within ninety (90) days of the date of that party's initial appointment request, either party may report the unavailability of the QME and the Medical Director shall issue a replacement pursuant to section 31.5 of Title 8 of the California Code of Regulations upon request, unless both parties agree in writing to waive the ninety (90) day time limit for scheduling the initial evaluation.

Note: Authority cited: Sections 133, 139.2 and 5307.3, Labor Code. Reference: Sections 4060, 4061, 4062, 4062.1, 4062.2, 4064 and 4067, Labor Code.

History: 1. New section filed 1-13-2009; operative 2-17-2009 (Register 2009, No. 3).

2. Amendment of subsection (d) and new subsection (e) filed 9-16-2013; operative 9-16-2013 pursuant to Government Code section 11343.4(b)(3) (Register 2013, No. 38).

Ref.: Hanna §§ 1.12[2A][b]–[h], 22.11[1]–[16]; Herlick Handbook § 14.22.

§31.5. QME Replacement Requests.

(a) A replacement QME to a panel, or at the discretion of the Medical Director a replacement of an entire panel of QMEs, shall be selected at random by the Medical Director and provided upon request whenever any of the following occurs:

(1) A QME on the panel issued does not practice in the specialty requested by the party holding the legal right to request the panel.

(2) A QME on the panel issued cannot schedule an examination for the employee within sixty (60) days of the initial request for an appointment, or if the 60 day scheduling limit has been waived pursuant to section 31.3(e) of Title 8 of the California Code of Regulations, the QME cannot schedule the examination within ninety (90) days of the date of the initial request for an appointment.

(3) The injured worker has changed his or her residence address since the QME panel was issued and prior to date of the initial evaluation of the injured worker.

(4) A physician on the QME panel is a member of the same group practice as defined by Labor Code section 139.3 as another QME on the panel.

(5) The QME is unavailable pursuant to section 33 (Unavailability of the QME).

(6) The evaluator who previously reported in the case is no longer available.

(7) A QME named on the panel is currently, or has been, the employee's primary treating physician or secondary physician as described in section 9785 of Title 8 of the California Code of Regulations for the injury currently in dispute.

(8) The claims administrator, or if none the employer, and the employee agree in writing, for the employee's convenience only, that a new panel may be issued in the geographic area of the employee's work place and a copy of the employee's agreement is submitted with the panel replacement request.

(9) The Medical Director, upon written request, finds good cause that a replacement QME or a replacement panel is appropriate for reasons related to the medical nature of the injury. For purposes of this subsection, "good cause" is defined as a documented medical or psychological impairment.

(10) The Medical Director, upon written request, filed with a copy of the Doctor's First Report of Occupational Injury or Illness (Form DLSR 5021 [see 8 Cal. Code Regs. §§14006 and 14007]) and the most recent DWC Form PR-2 ("Primary Treating Physician's Progress Report" [See 8 Cal. Code Regs. §9785.2]) or narrative report filed in lieu of the PR-2, determines after a review of all appropriate records that the specialty chosen by the party holding the legal right to designate a specialty is medically or otherwise inappropriate for the disputed medical issue(s). The Medical Director may request either party to provide additional information or records necessary for the determination.

(11) The evaluator has violated section 34 (Appointment Notification and Cancellation) of Title 8 of the California Code of Regulations, except that the evaluator will not be replaced for this reason whenever the request for a replacement by a party is made more than fifteen (15) calendar days from either the date the party became aware of the violation of section 34 of Title 8 of the California Code of Regulations or the date the report was served by the evaluator, whichever is earlier.

(12) The evaluator failed to meet the deadlines specified in Labor Code section 4062.5 and section 38 (Medical Evaluation Time Frames) of Title 8 of the California Code of Regulations and the party requesting the replacement objected to the report on the grounds of lateness prior to the date the evaluator served the report. A party requesting a replacement on this ground shall attach to the request for a replacement a copy of the party's objection to the untimely report.

(13) The QME has a disqualifying conflict of interest as defined in section 41.5 of Title 8 of the California Code of Regulations.

(14) The Administrative Director has issued an order pursuant to section 10164(c) of Title 8 of the California Code of Regulations (order for additional QME evaluation).

(15) The selected medical evaluator, who otherwise appears to be qualified and competent to address all disputed medical issues refuses to provide, when requested by a party or by the Medical Director, either: A) a complete medical evaluation as provided in Labor Code sections 4062.3(i) and 4062.3(k), or B) a written statement that explains why the evaluator believes he or she is not medically qualified or medically competent to address one or more issues in dispute in the case.

(16) The QME panel list was issued more than twenty four (24) months prior to the date the request for a replacement is received by the Medical Unit, and none of the QMEs on the panel list have examined the injured worker.

(b) Whenever the Medical Director determines that a request made pursuant to subdivision 31.5(a) for a QME replacement or QME panel replacement is valid, the time limit for an unrepresented employee to select a QME and schedule an appointment under section Labor Code section 4062.1(c) and the time limit for a represented employee to strike a QME name from the QME panel under Labor Code section 4062.2(c), shall be tolled until the date the replacement QME name or QME panel is issued.

(c) In the event the parties in a represented case have struck two QME names from a panel and subsequently a valid ground under subdivision 31.5 arises to replace the remaining QME, none of the QMEs whose names appeared on the earlier QME panel shall be included in the replacement QME panel.

(d) Form 31.5 shall be used to request a replacement QME.

[QME Form 31.5 (10/2013) Not Reproduced]

NOTE: Forms referred to above are available at no charge by downloading from the web at http://www.dir.ca.gov/dwc/forms.html or by requesting at 1-800-794-6900.

Note: Authority cited: Sections 133, 139.2, 4061, 4062, 4062.3, 4062.5, 5307.3 and 5703.5, Labor Code. Reference: Sections 139.2, 4060, 4061, 4062, 4062.1, 4062.2, 4062.3, 4064 and 4067, Labor Code.

History: 1. New section filed 8-23-96; operative 9-22-96 (Register 96, No. 34).

2. Amendment of subsections (b), (b)(1) and (b)(3) and new subsections (b)(4)-(5) filed 4-14-2000; operative 5-14-2000 (Register 2000, No. 15).

3. Amendment of section and Note filed 1-13-2009; operative 2-17-2009 (Register 2009, No. 3).

4. New subsection (d), including new Form 31.5, filed 9-16-2013; operative 9-16-2013 pursuant to Government Code section 11343.4(b)(3) (Register 2013, No. 38).

5. Amendment filed 4-6-2020; operative 4-6-2020 pursuant to Government Code section 11343.4(b). Submitted to OAL for filing and printing only pursuant to Labor Code section 142.3(a)(3) (Register 2020, No. 15).

Ref.: Hanna §§ 1.12[2A][b]–[h], 22.11[1]–[16]; Herlick Handbook § 14.22.

§31.7. Obtaining Additional QME Panel in a Different Specialty.

(a) Once an Agreed Medical Evaluator, an Agreed Panel QME, or a panel Qualified Medical Evaluator has issued a comprehensive medical-legal report in a case and a new medical dispute arises, the parties, to the extent possible, shall obtain a follow-up evaluation or a supplemental evaluation from the same evaluator.

(b) Upon a showing of good cause that a panel of QME physicians in a different specialty is needed to assist the parties reach an expeditious and just resolution of disputed medical issues in the case, the Medical Director shall issue an additional panel of QME physicians selected at random in the specialty requested. For the purpose of this section, good cause means:

(1) A written agreement by the parties in a represented case that there is a need for an additional comprehensive medical-legal report by an evaluator in a different specialty and the specialty that the parties have agreed upon for the additional evaluation; or

(2) Where an acupuncturist has referred the parties to the Medical Unit to receive an additional panel because disability is in dispute in the matter; or

(3) An order by a Workers' Compensation Administrative Law Judge for a panel of QME physicians that also either designates a party to select the specialty or states the specialty to be selected and the residential or employment-based zip code from which to randomly select evaluators; or

(4) In an unrepresented case, that the parties have conferred with an Information and Assistance Officer, have explained the need for an additional QME evaluator in another specialty to address disputed issues and, as noted by the Information and Assistance Officer on the panel request form, the parties have reached agreement in the presence of and with the assistance of the Officer on the specialty requested for the additional QME panel. The parties may confer with the Information and Assistance Officer in person or by conference call.

(c) Form 31.7 shall be used to request an additional QME panel in a different specialty.

[QME Form 31.7 (New 9/2013) Not Reproduced]

NOTE: Forms referred to above are available at no charge by downloading from the web at www.dir.ca.gov/dwc/forms.html or by requesting at 1-800-794-6900.

Note: Authority cited: Sections 133, 139.2, 4061, 4062, 4062.3, 4062.5, 5307.3 and 5703.5, Labor Code. Reference: Sections 139.2, 4061, 4062, 4062.1, 4062.2, 4062.3, 4064 and 4067, Labor Code.

History: 1. New section filed 1-13-2009; operative 2-17-2009 (Register 2009, No. 3).

2. Amendment of subsections (b)(1) and (b)(3) filed 12-31-2012 as an emergency; operative 1-1-2013 pursuant to Government Code section 11346.1(d) (Register 2013, No. 1). A Certificate of Compliance must be transmitted to OAL by 7-1-2013 or emergency language will be repealed by operation of law on the following day.

3. Amendment of subsections (b)(1) and (b)(3) refiled 7-1-2013 as an emergency; operative 7-1-2013 (Register 2013, No. 27). A Certificate of Compliance must be transmitted to OAL by 9-30-2013 or emergency language will be repealed by operation of law on the following day.

4. Certificate of Compliance as to 7-1-2013 order, including amendment of subsections (a) and (b)(1)-(2) and new subsection (c) and Form 31.7, transmitted to OAL 8-2-2013 and filed

9-16-2013; amendments operative 9-16-2013 pursuant to Government Code section 11343.4(b)(3) (Register 2013, No. 38).

Ref.: Hanna §§ 1.12[2A][b]–[h], 22.11[1]–[16]; Herlick Handbook § 14.22.

§32. Acupuncture Referrals.

(a) In any case where an acupuncturist has been selected by the injured worker from a three-member panel and an issue of disability is in dispute, the acupuncturist shall notify the parties to the examination that another specialty is required to determine disability and refer the parties to the Medical Unit to request an additional panel pursuant to section 31.7(b) (2). The acupuncturist shall evaluate all other issues as required for a complete evaluation.

(b) Except as provided in subdivision 32(a) above, no QME may obtain a consultation for the purpose of obtaining an opinion regarding permanent disability and apportionment consistent with the requirements of Labor Code sections 4660 through 4664 and the AMA Guides.

NOTE: Form referred to above is available at no charge by downloading from the web at www.dir.ca.gov/dwc/forms.html or by requesting at 1-800-794-6900.

Note: Authority cited: Sections 133, 139.2, 4061, 4062, 4064, 5307.3 and 5703.5, Labor Code. Reference: Sections 3209.3, 4061, 4062, 4062.1, 4062.2, 4064, 4067 and 5703.5, Labor Code.

History: 1. New section filed 8-1-94; operative 8-31-94 (Register 94, No. 31).

2. Renumbering of former section 32 to new section 30.5 and renumbering and amendment of former section 32.5 to section 32 filed 4-14-2000; operative 5-14-2000 (Register 2000, No. 15).

3. Amendment of section and Note filed 1-13-2009; operative 2-17-2009 (Register 2009, No. 3).

4. Amendment of section heading and section filed 9-16-2013; operative 9-16-2013 pursuant to Government Code section 11343.4(b)(3) (Register 2013, No. 38).

Ref.: Hanna §§ 1.12[2A][b]–[h], 22.11[1]–[16]; Herlick Handbook § 14.22.

§32.5. Rebuttal QME Examinations. [Repealed]

Note: Authority cited: Sections 139.2, 4061, 4062 and 4064, Labor Code. Reference: Sections 4061 and 4062, Labor Code.

History: 1. New section filed 8-23-96; operative 9-22-96 (Register 96, No. 34).

2. Renumbering of former section 32.5 to section 32 and renumbering and amendment of former section 32.7 to section 32.5 filed 4-14-2000; operative 5-14-2000 (Register 2000, No. 15).

3. Repealer filed 1-13-2009; operative 2-17-2009 (Register 2009, No. 3).

§32.6. Additional QME Evaluations Ordered by the Appeals Board.

The Medical Director shall issue a panel of Qualified Medical Evaluators upon receipt of an order of a Workers' Compensation Administrative Law Judge or the Appeals Board, that includes a finding that an additional evaluation is reasonable and necessary to resolve disputed issues under Labor Code sections 4060, 4061 or 4062. The order shall specify the residential or employment-based zip code from which to randomly select evaluators, specify the specialty for the QME panel or designate the party who shall select the specialty of the QME panel, and specify who shall select a new specialty in the event there are too few QMEs in the specialty initially selected to issue a panel in accordance with section 31(d) of Title 8 of the California Code of Regulations.

Note: Authority cited: Sections 133, 139.2, 4061, 4062, 4064, 5307.3, 5703 and 5703.5, Labor Code. Reference: Sections 139.2, 4060, 4061, 4062, 4062.1, 4062.2 and 4064, Labor Code.

History: 1. New section filed 1-13-2009; operative 2-17-2009 (Register 2009, No. 3).

Ref.: Hanna §§ 1.12[2A][b]–[h], 22.11[1]–[16]; Herlick Handbook § 14.22.

§32.7. Rebuttal QME Examinations. [Renumbered]

Note: Authority cited: Sections 139.2, 4061 and 4062, Labor Code. Reference: Sections 4061 and 4064, Labor Code.

History: 1. New section filed 8-23-96; operative 9-22-96 (Register 96, No. 34).

2. Renumbering of former section 32.7 to section 32.5 filed 4-14-2000; operative 5-14-2000 (Register 2000, No. 15).

§33. Unavailability of QME.

(a) A QME who will be unavailable to schedule or perform comprehensive medical evaluations as an Agreed Panel QME or as a Panel QME for a period of 14 days, or up to a maximum of 90 days during a calendar year, for any reason shall notify the Medical Director by submitting the form in Section 109 (Notice of Qualified Medical Evaluator Unavailability) (see, 8 Cal. Code Regs. §109) at least 30 days before the period of unavailability is to begin. The Medical Director may, in his or her discretion, grant unavailable status within the 30-day notice period for good cause, including but not limited to medical or family emergency.

(b) At the time of requesting unavailable status, the QME shall provide the Medical Director with a list of any and all comprehensive medical/legal evaluation examinations already scheduled during the time requested for unavailable status. The QME shall indicate whether each such examination is being rescheduled or the QME plans to complete the exam and report while in unavailable status.

(c) A QME who is unavailable as provided in subdivision (a) shall not perform any new evaluation examinations as a QME until the physician returns to active QME status. Such a QME may complete medical-legal examinations and reports already scheduled and reported to the Medical Director, as well as reports for evaluation examinations performed prior to becoming unavailable under subdivision (a). Such a QME also may complete supplemental reports.

(d) It shall not be an acceptable reason for unavailability that a QME does not intend to perform comprehensive medical-legal evaluations for unrepresented workers. A QME who has filed notifications for unavailability totaling more than ninety (90) days during the QME calendar year without good cause may be denied reappointment subject to section 52 of Title 8 of the California Code of Regulations. Good cause includes, but is not limited to, sabbaticals, or death or serious illness of an immediate family member.

(e) If a QME fails to notify the Medical Director, by submitting the form in section 109 (Notice of Qualified Medical Evaluator Unavailability) (see, 8 Cal. Code Regs. §109), of his or her unavailability at a medical office at least thirty (30) days prior to the period the evaluator becomes unavailable, the Medical Director may designate the QME to be unavailable at that location for thirty (30) days from the date the Medical Director learns of the unavailability.

(f) Whenever the Medical Director is notified by a party seeking an appointment with a Qualified Medical Evaluator, or otherwise becomes aware, that the QME is not available and not responding to calls or mail at a location listed for the QME, a certified letter will be sent to the QME by the Medical Director regarding his/her unavailability. If the Medical Director does not receive a response within fifteen (15) days of the date the certified letter is mailed, then the QME will be made unavailable at that location. The time a QME is placed on unavailable status pursuant to this subdivision shall count toward the ninety (90) day limit in subdivision 33(a) of Title 8 of the California Code of Regulations.

NOTE: Form referred to above is available at no charge by downloading from the web at www.dir.ca.gov/dwc/forms.html or by requesting at 1-800-794-6900.

Note: Authority cited: Sections 133, 139.2 and 5307.3, Labor Code. Reference: Sections 139.2, 4060, 4061, 4062, 4062.1, 4062.2, 4062.5 and 4067, Labor Code.

History: 1. New section filed 8-1-94; operative 8-31-94 (Register 94, No. 31).

2. Amendment filed 4-14-2000; operative 5-14-2000 (Register 2000, No. 15).

3. Amendment of section and Note filed 1-13-2009; operative 2-17-2009 (Register 2009, No. 3).

4. New subsection (h) filed 12-31-2012 as an emergency; operative 1-1-2013 pursuant to Government Code section 11346.1(d) (Register 2013, No. 1). A Certificate of Compliance must be transmitted to OAL by 7-1-2013 or emergency language will be repealed by operation of law on the following day.

5. New subsection (h) refiled 7-1-2013 as an emergency; operative 7-1-2013 (Register 2013, No. 27). A Certificate of Compliance must be transmitted to OAL by 9-30-2013 or emergency language will be repealed by operation of law on the following day.

6. Certificate of Compliance as to 7-1-2013 order, including amendment of subsections (a) and (d), repealer of subsections (e) and (h) and subsection relettering, transmitted to OAL 8-2-2013 and filed 9-16-2013; amendments operative 9-16-2013 pursuant to Government Code section 11343.4(b)(3) (Register 2013, No. 38).

Ref.: Hanna §§ 1.12[2A][b]–[h], 22.11[1]–[16]; Herlick Handbook §§ 1.02, 14.22.

§33.1. The Notice of QME Unavailability Form. [Repealed]

Note: Authority cited: Sections 139 and 139.2, Labor Code. Reference: Sections 139.2, 4061 and 4062, Labor Code.

History: 1. New section filed 8-1-94; operative 8-31-94 (Register 94, No. 31).

2. Amendment of section heading, repealer and new section filed 8-23-96; operative 9-22-96 (Register 96, No. 34).

3. Repealer filed 4-14-2000; operative 5-14-2000 (Register 2000, No. 15).

§34. Appointment Notification and Cancellation.

(a) Whenever an appointment for a comprehensive medical evaluation is made with a QME, the QME shall complete an appointment notification form by submitting the form in Section 110 (QME Appointment Notification Form)(See, 8 Cal. Code Regs. §110). The completed form shall be postmarked or sent by facsimile to the employee and the claims administrator, or if none the employer, within 5 business days of the date the appointment was made. In a represented case, a copy of the completed form shall also be sent to the attorney who represents each party, if known. Failure to comply with this requirement shall constitute grounds for denial of reappointment under section 51 of Title 8 of the California Code of Regulations.

(b) The QME shall schedule an appointment for the first comprehensive medical-legal examination which shall be conducted only at the medical office listed on the panel selection form. Any subsequent evaluation appointments may be performed at another medical office of the selected QME if it is listed with the Medical Director and is within a reasonable geographic distance from the injured worker's residence.

(c) The QME shall include within the notification whether a Certified Interpreter, as defined by Labor Code Section 5811 and subject to the provisions of section 9795.3 of Title 8 of the California Code of Regulations, is required and specify the language. The interpreter shall be arranged by the party who is to pay the cost as provided for in Section 5811 of the Labor Code.

(d) An evaluator, whether an AME, Agreed Panel QME or QME, shall not cancel a scheduled appointment less than six (6) business days prior to the appointment date, except for good cause. Whenever an evaluator cancels a scheduled appointment, the evaluator shall advise the parties in writing of the reason for the cancellation. The Appeals Board shall retain jurisdiction to resolve disputes among the parties regarding whether an appointment cancellation pursuant to this subdivision was for good cause. The Administrative Director shall retain jurisdiction to take appropriate disciplinary action against any Agreed Panel QME or QME for violations of this section.

(e) An Agreed Panel QME or a QME who cancels a scheduled appointment shall reschedule the appointment to a date within thirty (30) calendar days of the date of cancellation. The re-scheduled appointment date may not be more than sixty (60) calendar days from the date of the initial request for an appointment, unless the parties agree in writing to accept the date beyond the sixty (60) day limit.

(f) An Agreed Medical Evaluator who cancels a scheduled appointment shall reschedule the appointment within sixty (60) calendar days of the date of the cancellation, unless the parties agree in writing to accept an appointment date no more than thirty (30) calendar days beyond the sixty (60) day limit.

(g) Failure to receive relevant medical records, as provided in section 35 of Title 8 of the California Code of Regulations and section 4062.3 of the Labor Code, prior to a scheduled appointment shall not constitute good cause under this section for the evaluator to cancel the appointment, unless the evaluator is a psychiatrist or psychologist performing an evaluation regarding a disputed injury to the psyche who states in the evaluation report that receipt of relevant medical records prior to the evaluation was necessary to conduct a full and fair evaluation.

(h) An appointment scheduled with an evaluator, whether an AME, Agreed Panel QME or QME shall not be cancelled or rescheduled by a party or the party's attorney less than six (6) business days before the appointment date, except for good cause. Whenever the claims administrator, or if none the employer, or the injured worker, or either party's attorney, cancels an appointment scheduled by an evaluator, the cancellation shall be made in writing, state the reason for the cancellation and be served on the opposing party. Oral cancellations shall be followed with a written confirming letter that is faxed or mailed by first class U.S. mail within twenty four hours of the verbal cancellation and that complies with this section. An injured worker shall not be liable for any missed appointment fee whenever an appointment is cancelled for good cause. The Appeals Board shall retain jurisdiction to resolve disputes regarding whether an appointment cancellation by a party pursuant to this subdivision was for good cause.

(i) The date of cancellation shall be determined from the date of postmark, if mailed, or from the facsimile receipt date as shown on the recipient's fax copy.

NOTE: Form referred to above is available at no charge by downloading from the web at www.dir.ca.gov/dwc/forms.html or by requesting at 1-800-794-6900.

Note: Authority cited: Sections , 133, 139.2 and 5307.3, Labor Code. Reference: Sections 4060, 4061, 4062, 4062.1, 4062.2 and 4067, Labor Code.

History: 1. New section filed 8-1-94; operative 8-31-94 (Register 94, No. 31).

2. Amendment of subsections (a) and (c) filed 4-14-2000; operative 5-14-2000 (Register 2000, No. 15).

3. Amendment of section heading, section and Note filed 1-13-2009; operative 2-17-2009 (Register 2009, No. 3).

4. Amendment of subsection (b) filed 9-16-2013; operative 9-16-2013 pursuant to Government Code section 11343.4(b)(3) (Register 2013, No. 38).

Ref.: Hanna §§ 1.12[2A][b]–[h], 22.11[1]–[16]; Herlick Handbook §§ 1.02, 14.22.

§34.1. The Appointment Notification Form. [Repealed]

Note: Authority cited: Sections 139 and 139.2, Labor Code. Reference: Sections 139.2, 4061 and 4062, Labor Code.

History: 1. New section filed 8-1-94; operative 8-31-94 (Register 94, No. 31).

2. Repealer filed 4-14-2000; operative 5-14-2000 (Register 2000, No. 15).

§35. Exchange of Information and Ex Parte Communications.

(a) The claims administrator, or if none the employer, shall provide, and the injured worker may provide, the following information to the evaluator, whether an AME, Agreed panel QME or QME:

(1) All records prepared or maintained by the employee's treating physician or physicians;

(2) Other medical records, including any previous treatment records or information, which are relevant to determination of the medical issue(s) in dispute;

(3) A letter outlining the medical determination of the primary treating physician or the compensability issue(s) that the evaluator is requested to address in the evaluation, which shall be served on the opposing party no less than 20 days in advance of the evaluation;

(4) Where the evaluation is for injuries that occurred before January 1, 2013, concerning a dispute over a utilization review decision if the decision is communicated to the requesting physician on or before June 30, 2013, whenever the treating physician's recommended medical treatment is disputed, a copy of the treating physician's report recommending the medical treatment with all supporting documents, a copy of claims administrator's, or if none the employer's, decision to approve, delay, deny or modify the disputed treatment with the documents supporting the decision, and all other relevant communications about the disputed treatment exchanged during the utilization review process required by Labor Code section 4610;

(5) Non-medical records, including films and videotapes, which are relevant to determination of medical issue(s) in dispute, after compliance with subdivision 35(c) of Title 8 of the California Code of Regulations.

(b)(1) Except as expressly provided in Labor Code section 4062.3(f) concerning communications with an agreed medical evaluator, all communications by the parties with the evaluator shall be in writing and sent simultaneously to the opposing party when sent to the medical evaluator, except as otherwise provided in subdivisions (c), (k) and (*l*) of this section. Labor Code section 4062.3(f) allows oral or written communications with an AME physician or the physician's staff relative to nonsubstantive matters such as the scheduling of appointments, missed appointments, the furnishing of records and reports, and the availability of the report, unless the appeals board has made a specific finding of an impermissible ex parte communication.

(2) Represented parties who have selected an Agreed Medical Evaluator or an Agreed Panel QME shall, as part of their agreement, agree on what information is to be provided to the AME or the Agreed Panel QME, respectively.

(c) At least twenty (20) days before the information is to be provided to the evaluator, the party providing such medical and non-medical reports and information shall serve it on the opposing party. Mental health records that are subject to the protections of Health and Safety Code section 123115(b) shall not be served directly on the injured employee, but may be provided to a designated health care provider as provided in section 123115(b)(2), and the injured employee shall be notified in writing of this option for each such record to be provided to the evaluator. In both unrepresented and represented cases the claims administrator shall attach a log to the front of the records and information being sent to the opposing party that identifies each record or other information to be sent to the evaluator and lists each item in the order it is attached to or appears on the log. In a represented case, the injured worker's attorney shall do the same for any records or other information to be sent to the evaluator directly from the attorney's office, if any. The claims administrator, or if none the employer, shall include a cover letter or other document when providing such information to the employee which shall clearly and conspicuously include the following language: "Please look carefully at the enclosed information. It may be used by the doctor who is evaluating your medical condition as it relates to your workers' compensation claim. If you do not want the doctor to see this information, you must let me know within 10 days."

(d) If the opposing party objects within 10 days to any non-medical records or information proposed to be sent to an evaluator, those records and that information shall not be provided to the evaluator unless so ordered by a Workers' Compensation Administrative Law Judge.

(e) In no event shall any party forward to the evaluator: (1) any medical/legal report which has been rejected by a party as untimely pursuant to Labor Code section 4062.5; (2) any evaluation or consulting report written by any physician other than a treating physician, the primary treating physician or secondary physician, or an evaluator through the medical-legal process in Labor Code sections 4060 through 4062, that addresses permanent impairment, permanent disability or apportionment under California workers' compensation laws, unless that physician's report has first been ruled admissible by a Workers' Compensation Administrative Law Judge; or (3) any medical report or record or other information or thing which has been stricken, or found inadequate or inadmissible by a Workers' Compensation Administrative Law Judge, or which otherwise has been deemed inadmissible to the evaluator as a matter of law.

(f) Either party may use discovery to establish the accuracy or authenticity of non-medical records or information prior to the evaluation.

(g) Copies of all records being sent to the evaluator shall be sent to all parties except as otherwise provided in section (d) and (e). Failure to do so shall constitute ex parte communication within the meaning of subdivision (k) below by the party transmitting the information to the evaluator.

(h) In the event that the unrepresented employee schedules an appointment within 20 days of receipt of the panel, the employer or if none, the claims administrator shall not be required to comply with the 20 day time frame for sending medical information in subsection (c) provided, however, that the unrepresented employee is served all non-medical information in subdivision (c) 20 days prior to the information being served on the QME so the employee has an opportunity to object to any non-medical information.

(i) In the event that a party fails to provide to the evaluator any relevant medical record which the evaluator deems necessary to perform a comprehensive medical-legal evaluation, the evaluator may contact the treating physician or other health care provider, to obtain such record(s). If the party fails to provide relevant medical records within 10 days after the date of the evaluation, and the evaluator is unable to obtain the records, the evaluator shall complete and serve the report to comply with the statutory time frames under section 38 of Title 8 of the California Code of Regulations. The evaluator shall note in the report that the records were not received within the required time period. Upon request by a party, or the Appeals Board, the evaluator shall complete a supplemental evaluation when the relevant medical records are received. For a supplemental report the evaluator need not conduct an additional physical examination of the employee if the evaluator believes a review of the additional records is sufficient.

(j) The evaluator and the employee's treating physician(s) may consult as necessary to produce a complete and accurate report. The evaluator shall note within the report new or additional information received from the treating physician.

(k) The Appeals Board shall retain jurisdiction in all cases to determine disputes arising from objections and whether ex parte contact in violation of Labor Code section 4062.3 or this section of Title 8 of the California Code of Regulations has occurred. If any party communicates with an evaluator in violation of Labor Code section 4062.3, the Medical Director shall provide the aggrieved party with a new panel in which to select a new QME or the aggrieved party may elect to proceed with the original evaluator. Oral or written communications by the employee, or if the employee is deceased by the employee's dependent, made in the course of the examination or made at the request of the evaluator in connection with the examination shall not provide grounds for a new evaluator unless the Appeals Board has made a specific finding of an impermissible ex parte communication.

(*l*) In claims involving a date of injury prior to 1/1/2005 where the injured worker is represented by an attorney and the parties have decided to each select a separate Qualified Medical Evaluator, the provisions of this section shall not apply to the communications between a party and the QME selected by that party.

Note: Authority cited: Sections 133, 139.2 and 5307.3, Labor Code. Reference: Sections 139.2, 4060, 4061, 4062, 4062.1, 4062.2, 4062.3, 4064 and 4067, Labor Code.

History: 1. New section filed 8-1-94; operative 8-31-94 (Register 94, No. 31).

2. New subsection (c) and subsection relettering, amendment of newly designated subsections (d) and (e) and new subsection (f) filed 8-23-96; operative 9-22-96 (Register 96, No. 34).

3. New subsection (b)(3) and amendment of subsection (e) filed 4-14-2000; operative 5-14-2000 (Register 2000, No. 15).

4. Amendment of section heading, section and Note filed 1-13-2009; operative 2-17-2009 (Register 2009, No. 3).

5. Amendment of subsections (a)(4) and (b)(1) filed 12-31-2012 as an emergency; operative 1-1-2013 pursuant to Government Code section 11346.1(d) (Register 2013, No. 1). A Certificate of Compliance must be transmitted to OAL by 7-1-2013 or emergency language will be repealed by operation of law on the following day.

6. Amendment of subsections (a)(4) and (b)(1) refiled 7-1-2013 as an emergency; operative 7-1-2013 (Register 2013, No. 27). A Certificate of Compliance must be transmitted to OAL by 9-30-2013 or emergency language will be repealed by operation of law on the following day.

7. Certificate of Compliance as to 7-1-2013 order, including amendment of subsections (a)(3)-(4), transmitted to OAL 8-2-2013 and filed 9-16-2013; amendments operative 9-16-2013 pursuant to Government Code section 11343.4(b)(3) (Register 2013, No. 38).

Ref.: Hanna §§ 1.12[2A][b]–[h], 22.11[1]–[16]; Herlick Handbook §§ 4.14[3], 6.04[1], 14.22.

§35.5. Compliance by AMEs and QMEs with Administrative Director Evaluation and Reporting Guidelines.

(a) Each evaluation examination and report completed pursuant to Labor Code sections 4060, 4061, 4062, 4062.1, 4062.2, 4064, 4067 or 5703.5 shall be performed in compliance with all appropriate evaluation procedures pursuant to this Chapter.

(b) Each reporting evaluator shall state in the body of the comprehensive medical-legal report the date the examination was completed and the street address at which the examination was performed. If the evaluator signs the report on any date other than the date the examination was completed, the evaluator shall enter the date the report is signed next to or near the signature on the report.

(c)(1) The evaluator shall address all contested medical issues arising from all injuries reported on one or more claim forms prior to the date of the employee's appointment with the medical evaluator that are issues within the evaluator's scope of practice and areas of clinical competence. The reporting evaluator shall attempt to address each question raised by each party in the issue cover letter sent to the evaluator as provided in subdivision 35(a)(3).

(2) If the evaluator declares the injured worker permanent and stationary for the body part evaluated and the evaluator finds injury has caused permanent partial disability, the evaluator shall complete the Physician's Report of Permanent and Stationary Status and Work Capacity (DWC-AD Form 10133.36) and serve it on the claims administrator together with the medical report.

(d) At the evaluator's earliest opportunity and no later than the date the report is served, the evaluator shall advise the parties in writing of any disputed medical issues outside of the evaluator's scope of practice and area of clinical competency in order that the parties may initiate the process for obtaining an additional evaluation pursuant to section 4062.1 or 4062.2 of the Labor Code and these regulations in another specialty. In the case of an Agreed Panel QME or a panel QME, the evaluator shall send a copy of the written notification provided to the parties to the Medical Director at the same time. However, only a party's request for an additional panel, with the evaluator's written notice under this section attached, or an order by a Workers' Compensation Administrative Law Judge, will be acted upon by the Medical Director to issue a new QME panel in another specialty in the claim.

(e) In the event a new injury or illness is claimed involving the same type of body part or body system and the parties are the same, or in the event either party objects to any new medical issue within the evaluator's scope of practice and clinical competence, the parties shall utilize to the extent possible the same evaluator who reported previously.

(f) Unless the Appeals Board or a Workers' Compensation Administrative Law Judge orders otherwise or the parties agree otherwise, whenever a party is legally entitled to depose the evaluator, the evaluator shall make himself or herself available for deposition within at least one hundred twenty (120) days of the notice of deposition and, upon the request of the unrepresented injured worker and whenever consistent with Labor Code section 5710, the deposition shall be held at the location at which the evaluation examination was performed, or at a facility or office chosen by the deposing party that is not more than 20 miles from the location of the evaluation examination.

(g)(1) Where the evaluation is performed for injuries that occurred before January 1, 2013, concerning a dispute over a utilization review decision if the decision is communicated to the requesting physician on or before June 30, 2013, whenever an Agreed Medical Evaluator or Qualified Medical Evaluator provides an opinion in a comprehensive medical/legal report on a disputed medical treatment issue, the evaluator's opinion shall be consistent with and apply the standards of evidence-based medicine set out in Division 1, Chapter 4.5, Subchapter 1, sections 9792.20 *et seq* of Title 8 of the California Code of Regulations (Medical Treatment Utilization Schedule). In the event the disputed medical treatment, condition or injury is not addressed by the Medical Treatment Utilization Schedule, the evaluator's medical opinion shall be consistent with and refer to other evidence-based medical treatment guidelines, peer reviewed studies and articles, if any, and otherwise shall explain the medical basis for the evaluator's reasoning and conclusions.

(2) For any evaluation performed on or after July 1, 2013, and regardless of the date of injury, an Agreed Medical Evaluator or Qualified Medical Evaluator shall not provide an opinion on any disputed medical treatment issue, but shall provide an opinion about whether the injured worker will need future medical care to cure or relieve the effects of an industrial injury.

Note: Authority cited: Sections 133, 139.2, 4062.3 and 5307.3, Labor Code. Reference: Sections 139.2, 4060, 4061, 4062, 4062.1, 4062.2, 4064, 4067, 4604.5, 4610.5, 4628, 5703.5, 5307.27 and 5710, Labor Code.

History: 1. New section filed 4-14-2000; operative 5-14-2000 (Register 2000, No. 15).

2. Amendment of section heading and section and new Note filed 1-13-2009; operative 2-17-2009 (Register 2009, No. 3).

3. Redesignation of former subsection (c) as subsection (c)(1), new subsection (c)(2), redesignation and amendment of former subsection (g) as new subsection (g)(1), new subsection (g)(2) and amendment of Note filed 12-31-2012 as an emergency; operative 1-1-2013 pursuant to Government Code section 11346.1(d) (Register 2013, No. 1). A Certificate of Compliance must be transmitted to OAL by 7-1-2013 or emergency language will be repealed by operation of law on the following day.

4. Redesignation of former subsection (c) as subsection (c)(1), new subsection (c)(2), redesignation and amendment of former subsection (g) as new subsection (g)(1), new subsection (g)(2) and amendment of Note refiled 7-1-2013 as an emergency; operative 7-1-2013 (Register 2013, No. 27). A Certificate of Compliance must be transmitted to OAL by 9-30-2013 or emergency language will be repealed by operation of law on the following day.

5. Certificate of Compliance as to 7-1-2013 order, including amendment of subsections (c)(2) and (g)(1)-(2), transmitted to OAL 8-2-2013 and filed 9-16-2013; amendments operative 9-16-2013 pursuant to Government Code section 11343.4(b)(3) (Register 2013, No. 38).

Ref.: Hanna §§ 1.12[2A][b]–[h], 22.11[1]–[16]; Herlick Handbook §§ 1.02, 4.14[3], 14.22.

§36. Service of Comprehensive Medical–Legal Evaluation Reports by Medical Evaluators Including Reports Under Labor Code Section 4061.

(a)(1) Whenever an injured worker is represented by an attorney, the evaluator shall serve each comprehensive medical-legal evaluation report, follow-up comprehensive medical-legal evaluation report and supplemental evaluation report on the injured worker, his or her attorney and on the claims administrator, or if none the employer, by completing QME Form 122 (AME or QME Declaration of Service of Medical-Legal Report Form)(See, 8 Cal. Code Regs. §122) and attaching QME Form 122 to the report, unless section 36.5 of Title 8 of the California Code of Regulations applies.

(2) If applicable in a claim involving disputed injury to the psyche, the evaluator shall comply with the requirements of section 36.5 of Title 8 of the California Code of Regulations (Service of Comprehensive Medical-Legal Report in Claims of Injury to the Psyche)(See, 8 Cal. Code Regs. §§36.5, 120 and 121).

(b)(1) Whenever an injured worker is not represented by an attorney, the Qualified Medical Evaluator shall serve each comprehensive medical-legal evaluation report, follow-up evaluation report or supplemental report that addresses only disputed issues outside of the scope of Labor Code section 4061, by completing the questions and declaration of service on the QME Form 111 (QME Findings Summary Form) (See, 8 Cal. Code Regs. §111), and by serving the report with the QME Form 111 attached, on the injured worker and the claims administrator, or if none on the employer, unless section 36.5 of Title 8 of the California Code of Regulations applies.

(2) If applicable in a claim involving disputed injury to the psyche, the evaluator shall comply with the requirements of section 36.5 of Title 8 of the California Code of Regulations (Service of Comprehensive Medical-Legal Report in Claims of Injury to the Psyche)(See, 8 Cal. Code Regs. §§36.5, 120 and 121.)

(c)(1) Whenever the evaluator is serving a medical-legal evaluation report that addresses or describes findings and conclusions pertaining to permanent impairment, permanent disability or apportionment of an unrepresented injured worker, the evaluator shall serve the following documents:

A. the evaluation report with a separator sheet, DWC-CA Form 10232.2 (see, 8 Cal. Code Regs. §10205.14), as required by Title 8, California Code of Regulations section 10160(d)(4);

B. the completed QME Form 111 (QME Findings Summary Form) (See, 8 Cal. Code Regs. §111) with a separator sheet, DWC-CA Form 10232.2 (see, 8 Cal. Code Regs. §10205.14), as required by Title 8, California Code of Regulations section 10160(d)(4);

C. the DWC-AD Form 100 (DEU) (Employee's Disability Questionnaire)(See, 8 Cal. Code Regs. §§10160 and 10161) with a separator sheet, DWC-CA Form 10232.2 (see, 8 Cal. Code Regs. §10205.14), as required by Title 8, California Code of Regulations section 10160(d)(4);

D. the DWC-AD Form 101 (DEU) (Request for Summary Rating Determination of Qualified Medical Evaluator's Report)(See, 8 Cal. Code Regs. §§10160 and 10161), with a separator sheet, DWC-CA Form 10232.2 (see, 8 Cal. Code Regs. § 10205.14), as required by Title 8, California Code of Regulations section 10160(d)(4); and

E. A document cover sheet, DWC-CA Form 10232.1 (see, 8 Cal. Code Regs. §10205.13).

The documents listed above shall be simultaneously served on the local DEU office, at the same time as serving the report on the claims administrator, or if none the employer, and on the unrepresented employee within the time frames specified in section 38 of Title 8 of the California Code of Regulations, unless section 36.5 of Title 8 of the California Code of Regulations applies.

(2) If applicable, in cases involving disputed injury to the psyche, the evaluator shall follow the procedures described in section 36.5 of Title 8 of the California Code of Regulations (Service of Comprehensive Medical-Legal Report in Claims of Injury to the Psyche)(See, 8 Cal. Code Regs.§§36.5, 120 and 121).

(d) If an evaluation report is completed for an unrepresented employee, in which the QME determines that the employee's condition has not become permanent and stationary as of the date of the evaluation, the parties shall request any further evaluation from the same QME if the QME is currently an active QME and available at the time of the request for the additional evaluation. If the QME is unavailable, a new panel may be issued to resolve any disputed issue(s). If the evaluator is no longer a QME, he/she may issue a supplemental report as long as a face-to-face evaluation (as defined in section 49(b) of Title 8 of the California Code of Regulations) with the injured worker is not required. In no event shall a physician who is not a QME or no longer a QME perform a follow up evaluation on an unrepresented injured worker.

(e) Except as provided in Section 37 concerning a request for factual correction, after a Qualified Medical Evaluator has served a comprehensive medical-legal report that finds and describes permanent impairment, permanent disability or apportionment in the case of an unrepresented injured worker, the QME shall not issue any supplemental report on any of those issues in response to a party's request until after the Disability Evaluation Unit has issued an initial summary rating report, or unless the evaluator is otherwise directed to issue a supplemental report by the Disability Evaluation Unit, by the Administrative Director or by a Workers' Compensation Administrative Law Judge. A party wishing to request a supplemental report pursuant to subdivision 10160(f) of Title 8 of the California Code of Regulations, based on the party's objection to or need for clarification of the evaluator's discussion of permanent impairment, permanent disability or apportionment, may do so only by sending the detailed request, within the time limits of subdivision 10160(f), directly to the DEU office where the report was served by the evaluator and not to the evaluator until after the initial summary rating has been issued.

NOTE: Forms referred to above are available at no charge by downloading from the web at www.dir.ca.gov/dwc/forms.html or by requesting at 1-800-794-6900.

Note: Authority cited: Sections 133, 139.2 and 5307.3, Labor Code. Reference: Sections 4060, 4061, 4062, 4062.1, 4062.2, 4064, 4067, 4600 and 4660-4664, Labor Code.

History: 1. New section filed 8-1-94; operative 8-31-94 (Register 94, No. 31).

2. Amendment of section heading, section and Note filed 4-14-2000; operative 5-14-2000 (Register 2000, No. 15).

3. Amendment of section heading, section and Note filed 1-13-2009; operative 2-17-2009 (Register 2009, No. 3).

4. Amendment of subsection (e) filed 12-31-2012 as an emergency; operative 1-1-2013 pursuant to Government Code section 11346.1(d) (Register 2013, No. 1). A Certificate of Compliance must be transmitted to OAL by 7-1-2013 or emergency language will be repealed by operation of law on the following day.

5. Amendment of subsection (e) refiled 7-1-2013 as an emergency; operative 7-1-2013 (Register 2013, No. 27). A Certificate of Compliance must be transmitted to OAL by 9-30-2013 or emergency language will be repealed by operation of law on the following day.

6. Certificate of Compliance as to 7-1-2013 order, including amendment of section, transmitted to OAL 8-2-2013 and filed 9-16-2013; amendments operative 9-16-2013 pursuant to Government Code section 11343.4(b)(3) (Register 2013, No. 38).

Ref.: Hanna §§ 1.12[2A][b]–[h], 22.11[1]–[16]; Herlick Handbook § 14.22.

§36.1. The Qualified or Agreed Medical Evaluator's Findings Summary Form. [Repealed]

Note: Authority cited: Sections 139, 139.2, 4061 and 4062, Labor Code. Reference: Sections 139.2, 4061 and 4062, Labor Code.

History: 1. New section filed 8-1-94; operative 8-31-94 (Register 94, No. 31).

2. Change without regulatory effect amending section filed 11-9-94 pursuant to section 100, title 1, California Code of Regulations (Register 94, No. 45).

3. Amendment of section filed 8-23-96; operative 9-22-96 (Register 96, No. 34).

4. Repealer filed 4-14-2000; operative 5-14-2000 (Register 2000, No. 15).

§36.5. Service of Comprehensive Medical/Legal Report in Claims of Injury to the Psyche.

(a) For any evaluation involving a claimed or disputed injury to the psyche, the injured worker shall be advised by the evaluator that the employee's copy of the comprehensive medical-legal report, and any follow up or supplemental reports, from the evaluation may be served either directly on the injured worker or instead on a physician designated in writing by the injured worker prior to leaving the evaluator's office, for the purpose of reviewing and discussing the evaluation report with the injured worker. The evaluator shall explain that the designated physician may be but need not be the injured worker's primary treating physician in the workers' compensation claim and that the employer will be responsible for payment for one office visit with the designated physician for this purpose.

(b) Whenever injury to the psyche is claimed and in the course of the evaluation, the evaluator makes a determination pursuant to Health and Safety Code section 123115(b) that there is a substantial risk of significant adverse or detrimental medical consequences to the injured worker from seeing or receiving a copy of part or all of evaluation report which is a mental health record, the evaluator shall do all of the following:

(1) Complete QME Form 121 (Declaration Regarding Protection of Mental Health Record);

(2) Advise the injured worker that the determination under Health and Safety Code 123115(b) has been made regarding the evaluation report as a mental health record and that the evaluator only may serve the injured worker's copy of the evaluation report on a person who is a licensed physician, as defined in Labor Code section 3209.3, whose name the injured worker may designate in writing prior to leaving the evaluator's office, or on the employee's attorney, if any;

(3) Permit inspection and copying of the mental health record(s) subject to the Health and Safety Code section 123115(b) determination, only by a licensed physician as defined in Labor Code section 3209.3 or another health care provider as defined in Health and Safety Code section 123105(a);

(4) Complete the QME Form 121 and enter the name and address of the physician designated in writing by the injured worker on this form;

(5) Attach a completed copy of QME Form 121 (Declaration Regarding Protection of Mental Health Record) to the copy of the evaluation report in the injured worker's medical or medical-legal file;

(6) Serve the completed comprehensive medical-legal evaluation report, follow-up medical-legal report or supplemental medical-legal report(s) subject to the provisions of this section, with the completed QME Form 121 (Declaration Regarding Protection of Mental Health Record) attached, on the licensed physician designated by the injured worker on QME Form 121, and on the claims administrator, and on each party's attorney, if any, as provided in section 36, and within the time periods in section 38, of Title 8 of the California Code of Regulations. In the event the injured worker designates a physician on QME Form 121 other than the current primary treating physician in his or her workers' compensation claim, the evaluator shall also serve a copy of the report with the QME Form 121 attached on the primary treating physician;

(7) Whenever the report addresses any permanent impairment, permanent disability or apportionment and the injured worker is not represented by an attorney, a copy of the report with the completed QME Form 121 attached shall also be served on the appropriate office of the Disability Evaluation Unit, along with the QME Form 111 (QME's Findings Summary Form), and DWC-AD form 100 (DEU) (Employee's Disability Questionnaire) (See, 8 Cal. Code Regs. §§ 10160 and 10161) and DWC-AD form 101 (DEU) (Request for Summary Rating Determination of Qualified Medical Evaluator's Report) (See, 8 Cal. Code Regs. §§10160 and 10161), with the document cover sheet, DWC-CA form 10232.1 (see, 8 Cal. Code Regs. § 10232.1), and separator sheet, DWC-CA form 10232.2 (see, 8 Cal. Code Regs. § 10232.2), as required by Title 8, California Code of Regulations section 10160(d)(4);

(8) Whenever the report addresses permanent impairment, permanent disability or apportionment and the injured worker is represented by an attorney, a copy of the report with the completed QME Form 121 attached shall be served with QME Form 122 (AME or QME Declaration of

Service of Medical-Legal Report) on the physician designated by the injured worker, the injured worker's attorney and on the claims administrator's attorney, or if none on the claims administrator.

(c) "Mental health record" for the purposes of this subdivision means a medical treatment or evaluation record created by or received and reviewed by a licensed physician, as defined in Labor Code section 3209.3, in the course of treating or evaluating the injured worker in a workers' compensation claim, and includes for the purposes of this subdivision but is not limited to, treatment records and comprehensive medical-legal reports.

(d) Upon serving the employee's copy of the medical-legal report in compliance with subdivisions 36.5(b)(6), 36.5(b)(7) or 36.5(b)(8) of Title 8 of the California Code of Regulations on the physician designated by the employee on the QME Form 121 (Declaration Regarding Protection of Mental Health Record), the evaluator's obligation to serve the report on the injured worker under Labor Code sections 139.2(j)(1) and 4061(c), and section 36 of Title 8 of the California Code of Regulation, shall be deemed satisfied.

(e) Mental health records subject to a determination under Health and Safety Code section 123115(b) and this subdivision shall be kept confidential by the claims administrator and all parties' attorneys in the case unless ordered otherwise by a Workers' Compensation Administrative Law Judge. Whenever such a mental health record is filed by a party at the Workers' Compensation Appeals Board, the party filing such a record shall request and obtain a protective order from a Workers' Compensation Administrative Law Judge that shall specify in what manner the mental health record may be inspected, copied and entered into evidence.

(f) Whenever the injured worker advises the evaluator that he or she prefers to have the evaluation report served on a designated physician as provided in subdivision 36.5(b) above, and the evaluator does not make a determination pursuant to Health and Safety Code section 123115(b), the evaluator shall provide QME Form 120 (Voluntary Directive for Alternate Service of Medical-Legal Report) (See, 8 Cal. Code Regs. § 120) to the injured worker and shall request the injured worker to complete the form before leaving the evaluator's office.

(g) Upon receipt by the evaluator of a QME Form 120 completed by the injured worker, the evaluator shall attach the original executed QME Form 120 to the original medical-legal report for service on the claims administrator, or if none on the employer. The evaluator shall serve the evaluation report with QME Form 120 attached by completing the questions and the declaration of proof of service on QME Form 111 (Qualified Medical Evaluator's Findings Summary Form) (See, 8 Cal. Code Regs. § 111). In the case of an unrepresented injured worker, the evaluator shall serve the report with the required forms as provided in subdivision 36.5(b)(7) of Title 8 of the California Code of Regulations. In the case of a represented injured worker, the evaluator shall serve the report with QME Form 120 attached, by completing the declaration of service on QME Form 122 (AME or QME Declaration of Service of Medical-Legal Report) (See, 8 Cal. Code § 122) and serving it with the report.

(h) Whenever an evaluation report is being served on a designated physician with QME Form 120 (Voluntary Directive for Alternate Service of Medical-Legal Report) (See, 8 Cal. Code Regs. § 120), the evaluator shall serve two copies of the medical-legal report with the QME Form 120 attached on the physician designated on the form by the injured worker, at the same time as serving the copies of the medical-legal report on the claims administrator, or if none on the employer, and on the injured worker's attorney if any. Service of a medical-legal report by an evaluator in compliance with this subdivision shall satisfy the evaluator's obligation to serve a copy of the report on the employee under Labor Code sections 139.2(j)(1) and 4061(c,) and section 36 of Title 8 of the California Code of Regulations.

(i) The physician designated by the injured worker in writing and listed on QME Form 120 or QME Form 121 shall not be limited to the primary treating physician in the disputed workers' compensation claim. As an additional medical treatment expense incurred in the claim within the meaning of section 4600 of the Labor Code, the claims administrator, or if none the employer, shall reimburse the physician designated by the injured worker and listed on either the QME Form 121 (Declaration Regarding Protection of Mental Health Record) or the QME Form 120 (Voluntary Directive for Alternate Service of Medical-Legal Evaluation Report on Disputed Injury to the Psyche), for one office visit, when used, for the purpose of reviewing and discussing the evaluator's report with injured worker, at the applicable rate under section 9789.11 (Physician Services Rendered on or After July 1, 2004) of Title 8 of the California Code of Regulations for an office visit and may include, as appropriate, record review, any necessary face-to-face time during the visit in excess of that specified in the applicable CPT office visit code, and charges, for time required to prepare a treatment report pertaining to the office visit, if necessary.

(j) Whenever the comprehensive medical-legal report is served by the evaluator on a physician pursuant to subdivision 36.5(f) with the QME Form 120 (Voluntary Directive for Alternate Service of Medical-Legal Report on Disputed Injury to the Psyche) attached, one of the two copies of the medical-legal report served on the designated physician shall be provided to the injured worker by the designated physician during the office visit.

(k) In the event the injured worker refuses or fails to designate a physician in writing to be listed on either QME Form 120 or QME Form 121, the evaluator shall serve the report as appropriate under section 36 or section 36.5, and within the time periods under section 38, of Title 8 of the California Code of Regulations, except that the injured worker's copy of the report which is subject to a finding under Health and Safety Code § 123115(b) shall then be served only on the injured worker's attorney, if represented, or if not represented on the injured worker's primary treating physician.

NOTE: Forms referred to above are available at no charge by downloading from the web at www.dir.ca.gov/dwc/forms.html or by requesting at 1-800-794-6900.

Note: Authority cited: Sections 133, 139.2 and 5307.3, Labor Code. Reference: Sections 56-56.37, Civil Code; Sections 4060, 4061, 4062, 4062.1, 4062.2, 4064, 4067, 4600 and 4660-4664, Labor Code; Section 123115(b), Health and Safety Code.

History: 1. New section filed 1-13-2009; operative 2-17-2009 (Register 2009, No. 3).

Ref.: Hanna §§ 1.12[2A][b]–[h], 22.11[1]–[16]; Herlick Handbook § 14.22.

§36.7. QME Electronic Service Emergency Regulation in Response to COVID-19.

(a) During the period that this emergency regulation is in effect, a QME, AME, or other medical-legal report and required documents may be served electronically as follows:

(1) For purposes of this section:

(A) "Electronic service" means service of the medical-legal report and all documents required by section 36, on a party or other person, by either electronic transmission or electronic notification. Electronic service may be performed directly by the physician or by an agent of the physician, or through an electronic service provider.

(B) "Electronic transmission" means the transmission of a document by electronic means to the electronic service address at or through which a party or other person has authorized electronic service.

(C) "Electronic notification" means the notification of the party or other person that a document is served by sending an electronic message to the electronic address at or through which the party or other person has authorized electronic service, specifying the exact name of the document served, and providing a hyperlink at which the served document may be viewed and downloaded.

(2) Electronic service shall be permitted only where the parties agree and a written confirmation of that agreement is made. At the time of giving consent to electronic service, a party or entity shall provide the party's electronic address for the purpose of receiving electronic service.

(3) Electronic service shall not be permitted on any unrepresented party or unrepresented injured worker.

(4) For purposes of electronic service, the medical-legal report or other papers must be transmitted to an electronic address maintained by the person or entity on whom it is served, using the most recent electronic address provided to the physician by the party who consented to accept service electronically.

(5) Service is complete at the time of transmission. Any period of notice and any right or duty to act or make any response within any period or on a date certain after service of the document, shall be extended by two business days.

(b) For purposes of service of a medical-legal report in claims of injury to the psyche, all of the terms of section 36.5 shall apply to electronic service, except the service requirements in section 36.5(b)(6) may be accomplished by electronic service pursuant to the terms of this regulation.

(c) For purposes of service of all medical-legal reports, all of the terms of section 36 shall apply to electronic service, except that the manner of service of the report may be accomplished by electronic transmission, where appropriate, pursuant to the terms of this regulation.

(d) For purposes of electronic service of all medical-legal reports, the mandatory form 122 (AME or QME Declaration of Service of Medical-Legal Report, see 8 Cal. Code Regs. § 122) may be replaced by an Affidavit of Proof of Electronic Service. The Affidavit of Proof of Electronic Service shall set forth the exact title of the document served in the action, showing (A) the name and residence or business address of the person making the service, (B) that he or she is a resident of, or employed in, the county where the electronic service occurs, (C) that he or she is over the age of 18 years, (D) that he or she is readily familiar with the business' practice for serving electronically, and (E) that the document would be electronically served that same day in the ordinary course of business following ordinary business practices. The Affidavit of Proof of Electronic Service shall be signed under penalty of perjury under the laws of the State of California. The Affidavit of Proof of Electronic Service shall also include all of the following:

(1) The electronic service address and the residence or business address of the person making the electronic service.

(2) The date of electronic service.

(3) The name and electronic service address of the person or entity served.

(4) A statement that the document was served electronically.

(e) For purposes of electronic service, the physician shall maintain an original copy of all documents electronically served, pursuant to the terms of section 39.5 of title 8, California Code of Regulations. The documents maintained by the physician pursuant to this section shall contain an original signature.

Note: Authority cited: Sections 133, 139.2, 4627 and 5307.3, Labor Code.

History: 1. New section filed 5-14-2020 as an emergency; operative 5-14-2020 (Register 2020, No. 20). A Certificate of Compliance must be transmitted to OAL by 11-10-2020 or emergency language will be repealed by operation of law on the following day.

2. Emergency filed 5-14-2020 extended 60 days (Executive Order N-40-20) (Register 2020, No. 20). A Certificate of Compliance must be transmitted to OAL by 1-11-2021 or emergency language will be repealed by operation of law on the following day.

3. Emergency filed 5-14-2020 extended an additional 60 days pursuant to Executive Order N-66-20 (Register 2020, No. 40). A Certificate of Compliance must be transmitted to OAL by 3-12-2021 or emergency language will be repealed by operation of law on the following day.

§37. Request for Factual Correction of a Comprehensive Medical–Legal Report from a Panel QME.

(a) An unrepresented employee or the claims administrator may request the factual correction of a comprehensive medical-legal report within 30 days of the receipt of a comprehensive medical-legal report from a panel Qualified Medical Evaluator that is required to be filed with the DEU pursuant to Labor Code section 4061(e).

(b) A request for factual correction using the form in subdivision (f) shall be served on the panel Qualified Medical Evaluator who examined the injured worker, the party who did not file the request, and the Disability Evaluation Unit office where the comprehensive medical-legal report was served. If the claims administrator serves the request for factual correction on the Qualified Medical Evaluator, the injured worker shall have five (5) days after the service of the request for factual correction to respond to the corrections mentioned in the request. The injured workers' response shall be served on the panel Qualified Medical Evaluator and the claims administrator.

(c) If the request for factual correction is filed by the injured worker, the panel Qualified Medical Evaluator shall have ten (10) days after service of the request to review the corrections requested in the form and determine if factual corrections are necessary to ensure the factual accuracy of the comprehensive medical-legal report. If the request for factual correction is filed by the claims administrator or by both parties, the time to review the request for correction shall be extended to fifteen (15) days after the service of the request for correction.

(d) At the end of the period for the panel QME to review the request for factual correction in subdivision (c), the panel QME shall file a supplemental report with the DEU office where the original comprehensive medical-legal report was filed indicating whether the factual correction of the comprehensive medical-legal report is necessary to ensure the factual accuracy of the report and, where factual corrections are necessary, if the factual corrections change the opinions of the panel QME stated in the report.

(e) In no event shall a party file any documents with the panel QME other than the form indicating the facts that should be corrected; nor shall the panel QME review any documents not previously filed with the panel QME pursuant to Section 35 of these rules.

(f) Request for Factual Correction of an Unrepresented Panel QME report form. [Form 37]

[QME Form 37 (Rev. 9/2013) Not Reproduced]

NOTE: Form is available at no charge by downloading from the web at www.dir.ca.gov/dwc/forms.html or by requesting at 1-800-794-6900.

Note: Authority cited: Sections 133 and 4061, Labor Code. Reference: Section 4061, Labor Code.

History: 1. New section and new QME Form 37 filed 12-31-2012 as an emergency; operative 1-1-2013 pursuant to Government Code section 11346.1(d) (Register 2013, No. 1). A Certificate of Compliance must be transmitted to OAL by 7-1-2013 or emergency language will be repealed by operation of law on the following day. For prior history, see Register 2009, No. 3.

2. New section and new QME Form 37 refiled 7-1-2013 as an emergency; operative 7-1-2013 (Register 2013, No. 27). A Certificate of Compliance must be transmitted to OAL by 9-30-2013 or emergency language will be repealed by operation of law on the following day.

3. Certificate of Compliance as to 7-1-2013 order, including amendment of subsections (a), (b) and (f), transmitted to OAL 8-2-2013 and filed 9-16-2013; amendments operative 9-16-2013 pursuant to Government Code section 11343.4(b)(3) (Register 2013, No. 38).

Ref.: Hanna § 22.11; Herlick Handbook §§ 6.04[5], 14.22.

§38. Medical Evaluation Time Frames; Extensions for QMEs and AMEs.

(a) The time frame for an initial or a follow-up comprehensive medical-legal evaluation report to be prepared and submitted shall not exceed thirty (30) days after the QME, Agreed Panel QME or AME has seen the employee or otherwise commenced the comprehensive medical-legal evaluation procedure.

(b) If an evaluator fails to prepare and serve the initial or follow-up comprehensive medical-legal evaluation report within thirty (30) days and the evaluator has failed to obtain approval from the Medical Director for an extension of time pursuant to this section, the employee or the employer may request a QME replacement pursuant to section 31.5 of Title 8 of the California Code of Regulations. Neither the employee nor the employer shall have any liability for payment for the medical evaluation which was not completed within the timeframes required under this section unless the employee and the employer each waive the right to a new evaluation and elect to accept the original evaluation, in writing or by signing and returning to the Medical Director either QME Form 113 (Notice of Denial of Request For Time Extension) or QME Form 116 (Notice of Late QME/AME Report - No Extension Requested) (See, 8 Cal. Code Regs. §§113 and 116).

(c) All requests by an evaluator for extensions of time shall be made on form 112 (QME/AME Time Frame Extension Request) (See, 8 Cal. Code Regs. §112). If the evaluation will not be completed on the original due date, the evaluator may request an extension from the Medical Director, not to exceed an additional 30 days. An extension of the time for completing the report shall be approved, as follows:

(1) When the evaluator has not received test results or the report of a consulting physician, necessary to address all disputed medical issues in time to meet the initial 30 day deadline, an extension of up to thirty (30) days shall be granted;

(2) When the evaluator has good cause, as defined in Labor Code section 139.2(j)(1)(B), an extension of fifteen (15) days shall be granted.

(d) Not later than 5 days before the initial 30-day period to complete and serve the report expires, the evaluator shall notify the Medical Director, the employee and the claims administrator, or if none, the employer, of the request for an extension by use of QME Form 112 (QME/AME Time Extension Request) (See, 8 Cal. Code Regs. §112).

(e) The Medical Director shall notify the requesting evaluator and the parties of the decision on the extension request by completion of the box at the bottom of QME Form 112 (QME/AME Time Frame Extension Request)(See, 8 Cal. Code Regs. §112). In the event that a request for an extension of time is denied, the Medical Director shall also send the parties QME Form 113 (Notice of Denial of Request for Time Extension)(See, 8 Cal. Code Regs. §113) to be used by each party to state whether the party wishes to request a new evaluator or to accept the late report of the original evaluator.

(f) Whenever the Medical Director becomes aware that the report of a Qualified Medical Evaluator or an Agreed Medical Evaluator has not been completed within the required time under section 38 and no extension of time was requested by the evaluator, the Medical Director shall send the parties a Notice of Late QME/AME Report - No Extension Requested (QME Form 116) (Sec, 8 Cal. Code Regs. §116). Each party shall complete the form and return it to the Medical Director in order to indicate whether or not the party wishes to accept the late report.

(g) Good cause, as defined in Labor Code section 139.2(j)(1)(B) and section 38(b)(2) of Title 8 of the California Code of Regulations, means:

(1) medical emergencies of the evaluator or the evaluator's family;

(2) death in the evaluator's family;

(3) natural disasters or other community catastrophes that interrupt the operation of the evaluator's office operations;

(h) Extensions shall not be granted because relevant medical information/records (including Disability Evaluation Form 101 (Request for Summary Determination of Qualified Medical Evaluator's Report) (See, 8 Cal. Code Regs. §10161)) have not been received. The evaluator shall complete the report based on the information available and state that the opinions and/or conclusions may or may not change after review of the relevant medical information/records.

(i) Except as provided in Section 37 with respect to a request for factual correction, the time frame for supplemental reports shall be no more than sixty (60) days from the date of a written or electronically transmitted request to the physician by a party. The request for a supplemental report, except for requests for factual correction, shall be accompanied by any new medical records that were unavailable to the evaluator at the time of the original evaluation and which were properly served on the opposing party as required by Labor Code section 4062.3. An extension of the sixty (60) day time frame for completing the supplemental report, of no more than thirty (30) days, may be agreed to by the parties without the need to request an extension from the Medical Director.

(j) Evaluators requesting time extensions will be monitored and advised by the Medical Director when such a request appears unreasonable or excessive. Failure to comply with this section may constitute grounds for denial of the QME's request for reappointment pursuant to section 51 of Title 8 of the California Code of Regulations.

NOTE: Forms referred to above are available at no charge by downloading from the web at www.dir.ca.gov/dwc/forms.html or by requesting at 1-800-794-6900.

Note: Authority cited: Sections 133, 139.2(j)(1), 4061, 4062 and 5307.3, Labor Code. Reference: Sections 139.2, 4061, 4062, 4062.1, 4062.2, 4062.5, 4064 and 4067, Labor Code.

History: 1. New section filed 8-1-94; operative 8-31-94 (Register 94, No. 31).

2. Amendment of subsections (a) and (b), new subsections (c)-(c)(3) and subsection relettering, and amendment of newly designated subsection (d) filed 8-23-96; operative 9-22-96 (Register 96, No. 34).

3. Amendment filed 4-14-2000; operative 5-14-2000 (Register 2000, No. 15).

4. Amendment of section and Note filed 1-13-2009; operative 2-17-2009 (Register 2009, No. 3).

5. Amendment of subsection (h) filed 12-31-2012 as an emergency; operative 1-1-2013 pursuant to Government Code section 11346.1(d) (Register 2013, No. 1). A Certificate of Compliance must be transmitted to OAL by 7-1-2013 or emergency language will be repealed by operation of law on the following day.

6. Amendment of subsection (h) refiled 7-1-2013 as an emergency; operative 7-1-2013 (Register 2013, No. 27). A Certificate of Compliance must be transmitted to OAL by 9-30-2013 or emergency language will be repealed by operation of law on the following day.

7. Certificate of Compliance as to 7-1-2013 order, including redesignation of portion of subsection (a) as subsection (b) and subsection relettering, transmitted to OAL 8-2-2013 and filed 9-16-2013; amendments operative 9-16-2013 pursuant to Government Code section 11343.4(b)(3) (Register 2013, No. 38).

Ref.: Hanna §§ 1.12[2A][b]–[h], 22.11[1]–[16]; Herlick Handbook §§ 1.02, 14.22.

§38.1. The QME and AME Time Frame Extension Request Form. [Repealed]

Note: Authority cited: Sections 139 and 139.2, Labor Code. Reference: Sections 139.2, 4060, 4061, 4062 and 4062.5, Labor Code.

History: 1. New section filed 8-1-94; operative 8-31-94 (Register 94, No. 31).

2. Change without regulatory effect amending form filed 4-2-96 pursuant to section 100, title 1, California Code of Regulations (Register 96, No. 14).

3. Repealer filed 4-14-2000; operative 5-14-2000 (Register 2000, No. 15).

§38.2. "The Time Extension Approval" Form. [Repealed]

Note: Authority cited: Sections 139 and 139.2, Labor Code. Reference: Sections 139.2, 4060, 4061, 4062 and 4062.5, Labor Code.

History: 1. New section filed 8-1-94; operative 8-31-94 (Register 94, No. 31).

2. Change without regulatory effect amending section filed 3-28-96 pursuant to section 100, title 1, California Code of Regulations (Register 96, No. 13).

3. Repealer filed 4-14-2000; operative 5-14-2000 (Register 2000, No. 15).

§38.3. The "Denial of Time Extension" Form. [Repealed]

Note: Authority cited: Sections 139 and 139.2, Labor Code. Reference: Sections 139.2, 4060, 4061, 4062 and 4062.5, Labor Code.

History: 1. New section filed 8-1-94; operative 8-31-94 (Register 94, No. 31).

2. Amendment of section heading and repealer and new section filed 8-23-96; operative 9-22-96 (Register 96, No. 34).

3. Repealer filed 4-14-2000; operative 5-14-2000 (Register 2000, No. 15).

§38.4. The "Notice of Late QME Report" Form. [Repealed]

Note: Authority cited: Sections 139 and 139.2, Labor Code. Reference: Sections 139.2, 4060, 4061, 4062 and 4062.5, Labor Code.

History: 1. New section filed 8-1-94; operative 8-31-94 (Register 94, No. 31).

2. Repealer filed 4-14-2000; operative 5-14-2000 (Register 2000, No. 15).

§39. Destruction of Records by the Medical Director.

The Medical Director may destroy any forms filed pursuant to these regulations five years after the date of receipt, provided that the completed "Application for Appointment as Qualified Medical Evaluator" form shall be preserved for each QME during the period(s) of his or her appointment as a QME. The "Request for Qualified Medical Evaluator" forms may be destroyed by the Medical Director two years after the date of receipt.

Note: Authority cited: Sections 133, 139.2 and 5307.3, Labor Code. Reference: Sections 139.2, 4060, 4061 and 4062, Labor Code; and Section 14755, Government Code.

History: 1. New section filed 8-1-94; operative 8-31-94 (Register 94, No. 31).

2. Amendment of section heading, section and Note filed 1-13-2009; operative 2-17-2009 (Register 2009, No. 3).

Ref.: Hanna §§ 1.12[2A][b]–[h], 22.11[1]–[16]; Herlick Handbook § 14.22.

§39.5. Retention of Records by QMEs.

(a) All QMEs shall retain a copy of all comprehensive medical-legal reports completed by the QME for a period of five years from the date of each evaluation report. A QME may satisfy this requirement by retaining only an electronic copy of the report, as long as the electronic copy retained is a true and correct copy of the original, showing the QME signature, that was served on the parties. Upon written request, a QME is required to return original radiological films, imaging studies and original medical records to the person who supplied the original records to the QME or to the injured worker.

(b) An evaluator shall submit all comprehensive medical/legal reports performed as a QME under this article to the Medical Director upon request for a review by the Medical Director. Failure to submit evaluations upon request by the Medical Director may constitute grounds for disciplinary action pursuant to Section 60.

Note: Authority cited: Sections 133, 139.2(j)(1) and 5307.3, Labor Code. Reference: Sections 139.2, 4060, 4061, 4062, 4062.1, 4062.2, 4064 and 4062.5, Labor Code; and Section 14755, Government Code.

History: 1. New section filed 8-23-96; operative 9-22-96 (Register 96, No. 34).

2. Amendment filed 4-14-2000; operative 5-14-2000 (Register 2000, No. 15).

3. Amendment of section heading, section and Note filed 1-13-2009; operative 2-17-2009 (Register 2009, No. 3).

Ref.: Hanna §§ 1.12[2A][b]–[h], 22.11[1]–[16]; Herlick Handbook § 14.22.

ARTICLE 4
Evaluation Procedures

§40. Disclosure Requirements: Injured Workers.

(a) An evaluator selected from a QME panel shall advise an injured worker prior to or at the time of the actual evaluation of the following:

(1) That he or she is entitled to ask the evaluator and the evaluator shall promptly answer questions about any matter concerning the evaluation process in which the QME and the injured worker are involved;

(2) That subject to section 41(g), the injured worker may discontinue the evaluation based on good cause. Good cause includes: (A) discriminatory conduct by the evaluator towards the worker based on race, sex, national origin, religion, or sexual preference, (B) abusive, hostile or rude behavior including behavior that clearly demonstrates a bias against injured workers, and (C) instances where the evaluator requests the worker to submit to an unnecessary exam or procedure.

(b) When required as a condition of probation by the Administrative Director or his/her licensing authority, the QME shall disclose his/her probationary status. The QME shall be entitled to explain any circumstances surrounding the probation. If at that time, the injured worker declines to proceed with the evaluation, such termination shall be considered by the Administrative Director to have occurred for good cause.

(c) If the injured worker declines to ask any questions relating to the evaluation procedure as set forth in section 40(a), and does not otherwise object on the grounds of good cause to the exam proceedings under section 41(a) during the exam itself, the injured worker shall have no right to object to the QME comprehensive medical-legal evaluation based on a violation of this section.

Note: Authority cited: Sections 133, 139.2 and 5307.3, Labor Code. Reference: Sections 139.2, 4060, 4061, 4062, 4062.1, 4062.2 and 4067, Labor Code.

History: 1. New article 4 heading and section filed 4-11-95; operative 5-11-95 (Register 95, No. 15).

2. Amendment of article 4 heading filed 4-14-2000; operative 5-14-2000 (Register 2000, No. 15).

3. Amendment of section heading, section and Note filed 1-13-2009; operative 2-17-2009 (Register 2009, No. 3).

Ref.: Hanna §§ 1.12[2A][b]–[h], 22.11[1]–[16]; Herlick Handbook § 14.22.

§41. Ethical Requirements.

(a) All QMEs, regardless of whether the injured worker is represented by an attorney, shall:

(1) Maintain a clean, professional physician's office (as defined in section 1(y) at all times which shall contain functioning medical instruments and equipment appropriate to conducting the evaluation within the physician's scope of practice and a functioning business office phone with the phone number listed with the Medical Director for that location which a party may use to schedule an examination or to handle other matters related to a comprehensive medical/legal evaluation.

(2) Schedule all appointments for comprehensive medical-legal evaluations without regard to whether a worker is unrepresented or represented by an attorney. A QME shall not refuse to schedule an appointment with an injured worker solely because the worker is not represented by an attorney or because a promise to reimburse or reimbursement is not made prior to the evaluation.

(3) Not request the employee to submit to an unnecessary exam or procedure.

(4) Refrain from treating or soliciting to provide medical treatment, medical supplies or medical devices to the injured worker.

(5) Communicate with the injured worker in a respectful, courteous and professional manner.

(6) Refrain from violating section 41.5 of Title 8 of the California Code of Regulations.

(7) Refrain from unilaterally rescheduling a panel QME examination more than two times in the same case.

(8) Refrain from cancelling a QME examination less than six (6) business days from the date the exam is scheduled without good cause and without providing a new examination date within thirty (30) calendar days of the date of cancellation.

(b) Evaluators selected from a QME panel provided by the Administrative Director shall not engage in ex parte communication in violation of Labor Code section 4062.3.

(c) All QMEs, regardless of whether the injured worker is represented by an attorney, shall with respect to his or her comprehensive medical-legal evaluation:

(1) Refuse any compensation from any source contingent upon writing an opinion that in any way could be construed as unfavorable to a party to the case.

(2) Review all available relevant medical and non-medical records and/or facts necessary for an accurate and objective assessment of the contested medical issues in an injured worker's case before generating a written report. The report must list and summarize all medical and non-medical records reviewed as part of the evaluation.

(3) Render expert opinions or conclusions without regard to an injured worker's race, sex, national origin, religion or sexual preference.

(4) Render expert opinions or conclusions only on issues which the evaluator has adequate qualifications, education, and training. All conclusions shall be based on the facts and on the evaluator's training and specialty-based knowledge and shall be without bias either for or against the injured worker or the claims administrator, or if none the employer.

(5) Present a report that addresses all relevant and contested medical issues as presented on one or more claim forms, is ratable by the DEU, if applicable, and complies with all relevant guidelines of the Administrative Director.

(6) Date the report on the date it is completed and ready for signature and service on the parties. No report shall be dated on the date of the evaluation examination unless the full written text of the report is completed and ready for signature and service on that same date.

(7) Write all portions of the report that contain discussion of medical issues, medical research used as the basis for medical determinations, and medical conclusions made by the evaluator. In the event more than one evaluator signs a single report, each signing physician shall clearly state those parts of the employee evaluation examination performed and the portions of the report discussion and conclusion drafted by the signing evaluator. Where a consultation report is obtained by an evaluator from a physician in a different specialty, the consultation report shall be incorporated by reference into the final report and appended to the referring QME's report.

(8) Serve the report as provided in these regulations at the same time on the employee and the claims administrator, or if none the employer, and on each of their attorneys, respectively.

(d) All aspects of all physical and/or psychological comprehensive medical-legal evaluations, including history taking, shall be directly related to contested medical issues as presented by any party or addressed in the reports of treating physician(s). No evaluator shall engage in any physical contact with the injured worker which is unnecessary to complete the examination.

(e) No physician certified by the Administrative Director as a QME, or his or her agent, shall contact an evaluator for the purpose of influencing that evaluator's opinions or conclusions in any comprehensive medical-legal evaluation or report.

(f) No evaluator shall schedule appointments to the extent that any injured worker will be required to wait for more than one hour at the evaluator's office prior to being seen for the previously agreed upon appointment time for an evaluation. An injured worker who is not seen by the evaluator within one hour may terminate the exam and request a replacement evaluator from the Administrative Director. No party shall be liable for the terminated exam. The evaluator may explain any reasons for the delay to the injured worker and, provided both parties agree, the evaluation may proceed or be rescheduled for a later date. If the evaluation is rescheduled, the evaluator shall provide notice of the new date of the evaluation to the parties within 5 business days after rescheduling the appointment.

(g) If the injured worker terminates the examination process based on an alleged violation of section 35(k), 40, 41(a) or 41.5 of Title 8 of the California Code of Regulations, and the Appeals Board later determines that good cause did not exist for the termination, the cost of the evaluation shall be deducted from the injured worker's award. A violation of section 40 or of any part of section 41(a) or 41.5 by the evaluator shall constitute good cause for purposes of an Appeals Board determination. No party shall be liable for any cost for medical reports or medical services delivered as a result of an exam terminated for good cause.

(h) Nothing in this section shall require an evaluator to undertake or continue a comprehensive medical-legal evaluation where the injured worker or his/her representative uses abusive language towards the evaluator or evaluator's staff or deliberately attempts to disrupt the operation of the evaluator's office in any way. The evaluator shall state under penalty of perjury, the facts supporting the termination of the evaluation process. Upon request, the Medical Director shall investigate the facts and make a final determination of the issue(s).

(i) Nothing in this section shall require an evaluator selected from a panel to undertake or continue a comprehensive medical-legal evaluation where the injured worker is intoxicated or under the influence of any medication which impairs the injured worker's ability to participate in the evaluation process. The evaluator shall state under penalty of perjury, the facts supporting the termination of the evaluation process. Upon request, the Medical Director shall investigate the facts and make a final determination of the issue(s).

Note: Authority cited: Sections 133, 139.2, 5307.3 and 5307.6, Labor Code. Reference: Sections 139.2, 4060, 4061, 4062, 4062.1, 4062.2, 4062.3, 4062.5, 4067 and 4628, Labor Code.

History: 1. New section filed 4-11-95; operative 5-11-95 (Register 95, No. 15).

2. New subsection (b), subsection relettering, and amendment of redesignated subsection (b)(1) filed 7-18-95 as an emergency; operative 7-18-95 (Register 95, No. 29). A Certificate of Compliance must be transmitted to OAL by 11-15-95 or emergency language will be repealed by operation of law on the following day.

3. Certificate of Compliance as to 7-18-95 order including amendment of subsection (b), deletion of subsection (b)(1) designator, and amendment of Note transmitted to OAL 11-14-95 and filed 12-21-95 (Register 95, No. 51).

4. Amendment filed 4-14-2000; operative 5-14-2000 (Register 2000, No. 15).

5. Amendment of section and Note filed 1-13-2009; operative 2-17-2009 (Register 2009, No. 3).

Ref.: Hanna §§ 1.12[2A][b]–[h], 22.11[1]–[16]; Herlick Handbook §§ 4.08[4], 6.04[1], 14.22.

§41.5. Conflicts of Interest by Medical Evaluators.

(a) An evaluator shall not request or accept any compensation or other thing of value from any source that does or could create a conflict with his or her duties as an evaluator under the Labor Code or the regulations of the Administrative Director (Title 8 of the California Code of Regulations, Chapters 1 through 1.8, section 1 et seq) or of the Workers' Compensation Appeals Board (Title 8 of the California Code of Regulations, Chapters 1.9, sections 10600 through 10727).

(b) A conflict with the duties of an evaluator as used in Labor Code section 139.2(o) means having a disqualifying conflict of interest with one or more of the persons or entities described in subdivision (c) and failing to disclose the fact of the conflict.

(c) The persons or entities with whom a disqualifying conflict of interest can exist are:

(1) The injured worker, or his or her attorney;

(2) The employer, or the employer's attorney;

(3) The claims adjuster or insurer or third party administrator, or their attorney, respectively;

(4) Any primary treating physician or secondary physician for the employee, if the treatment provided by that physician is disputed in the case;

(5) The utilization review physician reviewer or expert reviewer, or utilization review organization, only if the opinion of that reviewer or that utilization review organization is disputed in the case;

(6) The surgical center in which the injured worker had, or is proposed to be used to have, surgery, only if the need for surgery is disputed in the case.

(7) Other purveyor of medical goods or medical services, only if the medical necessity for using such goods or services is in dispute in the case.

(d) "Disqualifying Conflict of Interest" means the evaluator has any of the following relationships or interests with a person or entity listed in subdivision 41.5(c):

(1) A familial relationship of parent, child, grandparent, grandchild, sibling, uncle, aunt, nephew, niece, spouse, financee or cohabitant;

(2) A significant disqualifying financial interest, as defined below, including:

(A) Employment or a promise of employment;

(B) An interest of five (5) % or more in the fair market value of any form of business entity involved in workers' compensation matters, or of private real property or personal property, or in a leasehold interest;

(C) Five (5) % or more of the evaluator's income is received from direct referrals by or from one or more contracts with a person or entity listed in subdivision 41.5(c), except that contracts for participation in a Medical Provider Network as defined under Labor Code section 4616 et seq shall be excluded;

(D) A financial interest as defined in Labor Code section 139.3 that would preclude referral by the evaluator to such a person or entity;

(E) A financial interest as defined under the Physician Ownership and Referral Act of 1993 (PORA) set out in Business and Professions Code sections 650.01 and 650.02 that would preclude referral by the evaluator to such a person or entity.

(3) A professional affiliation which means the evaluator performs services in the same medical group or other business entity comprised of medical evaluators who specialize in workers' compensation medical-legal evaluations;

(4) Any other relationship or interest not addressed by subdivisions (d)(1) through (d)(3) which would cause a person aware of the facts to reasonably entertain a doubt that the evaluator would be able to act with integrity and impartiality.

(e) An Agreed Medical Evaluator or a Qualified Medical Evaluator may disqualify himself or herself on the basis of a conflict of interest pursuant to this section whenever the evaluator has a relationship with a person or entity in a specific case, including doctor-patient, familial, financial or professional, that causes the evaluator to decide it would be unethical to perform a comprehensive medical-legal evaluation examination or to write a report in the case.

(f) An Agreed Medical Evaluator or Qualified Medical Evaluator who knows, or should know, that he or she has a disqualifying conflict of interest with any person or entity listed in subdivision 41.5(c), that also is involved in the specific workers' compensation claim identified to the evaluator, shall send written notification to the injured worker and the claims administrator, or if none the employer, or their respective attorneys if any, within five (5) business days of the evaluator becoming aware of the conflict. The written notice shall include, at a minimum: 1) disclosure that a disqualifying conflict of interest exists; 2) the person or entity with whom the conflict arises; and 3) the category of conflict, such as familial, significant financial, or other type of ethical conflict. Whenever the evaluator declines to perform an evaluation due to disqualifying himself or herself pursuant to subdivision 41.5(e), the parties shall be entitled to a replacement QME or, in represented cases a replacement panel pursuant to section 31.5 of Title 8 of the California Code of Regulations. Whenever the evaluator notifies the parties of a conflict without stating that he or she declines to perform the evaluation, the parties shall follow the procedures set out in section 41.6 of Title 8 of the California Code of Regulations. In any case in which the injured worker is not represented by an attorney, the evaluator shall fax a copy of the notice of conflict to the Medical Unit of the Division of

Workers' Compensation at the same time it is sent to the parties.

(g) Any injured worker or claims administrator or if none the employer, including his or her attorney respectively, who knows of, or becomes aware of, a potential disqualifying conflict of interest, as defined under this section, with a specific evaluator selected to perform a comprehensive medical/legal examination and report or a follow up examination and report, shall notify the selected evaluator in writing at the earliest opportunity and no later than within five (5) business days of becoming aware of the potential conflict, to enable the evaluator to determine whether the disqualifying conflict exists. The notice shall include the person with whom the alleged conflict exists and the nature of the conflict. A copy of this notice shall be served on the opposing party at the same time as it is sent to the evaluator. The evaluator shall review the information provided and advise the parties in writing within five (5) business days of receipt of the notice whether the evaluator has a conflict of interest as specified in this section.

Note: Authority cited: Sections 133, 139.2(o) and 5307.3, Labor Code. Reference: Sections 139.2 and 139.3, Labor Code; and Sections 650.01 and 650.02, Business and Professions Code.

History: 1. New section filed 1-13-2009; operative 2-17-2009 (Register 2009, No. 3).

Ref.: Hanna §§ 1.12[2A][b]–[h], 22.11[1]–[16]; Herlick Handbook § 14.22.

§41.6. Procedures After Notice of Conflict of Interest and Waivers of Conflicts of Interest of an Evaluator.

(a) Whenever an Agreed or Qualified Medical Evaluator notifies the parties that a disqualifying conflict of interest exists, and even if it arises after the evaluator has performed an initial or follow up comprehensive medical-legal evaluation, the parties shall use the following procedures.

(b) An evaluator shall proceed with any scheduled evaluation involving a physical examination or supplemental report in the case, unless either the evaluator declines to proceed due to disqualifying himself or herself pursuant to section 41.5(e) of Title 8 of the California Code of Regulations or unless, pursuant to this section, the injured worker or the claims administrator is entitled to a replacement QME.

(c) Within five (5) business days of receipt of the evaluator's notice of conflict:

(1) If the injured worker is not represented by an attorney, the parties shall obtain a new evaluator by following the procedure provided under section 31.5 of Title 8 of the California Code of Regulations and a replacement QME, or when necessary replacement QME panel, shall be issued.

(2) If the injured worker is represented by an attorney, each party shall notify the evaluator and the opposing party in writing of the party's decision either to waive the conflict or to object to the evaluator on the basis of the evaluator's conflict. Whenever either party objects to the evaluator due to a conflict, the parties shall obtain a new evaluator by following the procedures provided in Labor Code section 4062.2 and section 31.5 of Title 8 of the California Code of Regulations.

(3) In the event the parties in a represented case wish to waive a conflict of interest, any such waiver shall be valid only if the general nature of the conflict of interest is disclosed in writing and on the same document, or duplicate copies of the same document, each party has signed a statement indicating that the signing party understands that the evaluator has a conflict of interest, the party understands the nature of the conflict, and the party wishes to waive the opportunity to obtain another evaluator. The signature of an attorney shall have the same effect as the signature of the party represented by the attorney, if a copy of the document signed by the attorney is served on the represented party by the attorney or by any other party or attorney. It shall be the duty of the attorney to serve a copy of the signed document on the party-client.

(d) Any dispute over whether a conflict of interest of an evaluator may affect the integrity and impartiality of the evaluator with respect to an evaluation report or supplemental report, and any dispute over waiver of an evaluator's conflict under this section, shall be determined by a Workers' Compensation Administrative Law Judge.

Note: Authority cited: Sections 133, 139.2(o) and 5307.3, Labor Code. Reference: Sections 139.2, 4060, 4061, 4062, 4062.1, 4062.2, 4064 and 4067, Labor Code.

History: 1. New section filed 1-13-2009; operative 2-17-2009 (Register 2009, No. 3).

Ref.: Hanna §§ 1.12[2A][b]–[h], 22.11[1]–[16]; Herlick Handbook § 14.22.

§41.7. Gifts to Medical Evaluators.

(a) No physician reporting as an Agreed Medical Evaluator or a Qualified Medical Evaluator shall accept gifts that have a total fair market value in the aggregate of three hundred sixty dollars ($ 360) or more, from any single source that handles California workers' compensation matters, in the course of any consecutive twelve months. The sources include, but are not limited to, one or more attorneys, physicians, employers, claims administrators, medical or health care or insurance or utilization review business entities. This prohibition shall not include reasonable and appropriate income earned from a Medical Provider Network as defined in Labor Code sections 4616 et seq, from a Health Care Organization as defined in Labor Code sections 4600.3 et seq, from a Preferred Provider Organization or managed care organization as defined in Health and Safety Code sections 1340 et seq for services performed as a treating physician nor for reasonable and appropriate income paid for services performed as reviewing physician or medical director pursuant to Labor Code section 4610, or for services performed as an Agreed Medical Evaluator or Qualified Medical Evaluator.

(b) For the purposes of this section, "Gift" means any payment to the extent that consideration of equal or greater value is not received. It includes any rebate or discount in the price of anything of value, unless the rebate or discount is also made in the regular course of business to members of the public, and any loan, forgiveness or other thing of value having a fair market value in excess of $ 360 in the aggregate.

(c) Any person who claims that a payment, rebate, discount, loan, forgiveness, or other thing of value is not a gift by reason of receipt of consideration has the burden of proving that the consideration received is of equal or greater value.

(d) A Qualified Medical Evaluator who violates any portion of this section shall be subject to disciplinary action pursuant to section 60 et seq of these regulations.

Note: Authority cited: Sections 133, 139.2(o) and 5307.3, Labor Code. Reference: Sections 139.2 and 139.3, Labor Code.

History: 1. New section filed 1-13-2009; operative 2-17-2009 (Register 2009, No. 3).

Ref.: Hanna §§ 1.12[2A][b]–[h], 22.11[1]–[16]; Herlick Handbook § 14.22.

§42. Disciplinary Proceedings. [Repealed]

Note: Authority cited: Sections 139.2 and 5307.3, Labor Code; Section 11370 et seq., Government Code; and Section 11500 et seq., Government Code. Reference: Sections 139, 139.2, 4060, 4061 and 4062, Labor Code.

History: 1. New section filed 4-11-95; operative 5-11-95 (Register 95, No. 15).

2. Repealer filed 4-14-2000; operative 5-14-2000 (Register 2000, No. 15).

§43. Method of Evaluation of Psychiatric Disability.

(a) For all claims arising before January 1, 2005, not subject to section 43(b), the method of measuring the psychiatric elements of a disability shall be as set forth below in the "Psychiatric Protocols" as adopted by the Industrial Medical Council on July 16, 1992, and amended on March 18 and October 25, 1993. The full text of this document is available at no charge on the web at www.dir.ca.gov/IMC/guidelines.html or by calling the Medical Unit at 1-800-794-6900.

(b) For all claims having dates of injury on or after January 1, 2005, and for those compensable claims arising before January 1, 2005, where there has been either no comprehensive medical-legal report or no report by a treating physician indicating the existence of permanent disability, or when the claims administrator, or if none the employer, is not required to provide the notice required by section 4061 to the injured worker, the method of evaluating the psychiatric elements of impairment shall include describing the employee's symptoms, social, occupational and, if relevant, school functioning, and describing the rationale for the evaluator's assignment to a level of impairment as published in the Permanent Disability Rating Schedule adopted by the Administrative Director on or after January 2005 pursuant to section 9805 of Title 8 of the California Code of Regulations.

[Psychiatric Protocols Not Reproduced]

Note: Authority cited: Sections 133, 139.2(j)(4) and 5307.3, Labor Code. Reference: Sections 139.2(j)(4), 4060, 4061, 4062, 4062.1, 4062.2, 4067, 4628 and 4660, Labor Code, and Section 9805 of Title 8 of the California Code of Regulations.

History: 1. New section filed 12-7-93; operative 1-6-94 (Register 93, No. 50).

2. Change without regulatory effect amending section filed 3-15-94 pursuant to title 1, section 100, California Code of Regulations (Register 94, No. 11).

3. Change without regulatory effect amending section filed 9-7-95 pursuant to section 100, title 1, California Code of Regulations (Register 95, No. 36).

4. Change without regulatory effect amending section filed 7-12-2001 pursuant to section 100, title 1, California Code of Regulations (Register 2001, No. 28). Pursuant to this filing, material adopted pursuant to the Administrative Procedure Act that had previously been incorporated by reference in the California Code of Regulations was instead printed in full in the California Code of Regulations.

5. Amendment of section heading, section and Note filed 1-13-2009; operative 2-17-2009 (Register 2009, No. 3).

Ref.: Hanna §§ 1.12[2A][b]–[h], 22.11[1]–[16]; Herlick Handbook § 14.22, 14.23.

§44. Method of Evaluation of Pulmonary Disability.

(a) For all claims arising before January 1, 2005, not subject to section 44(b), the method of measuring the pulmonary elements of disability shall be as set forth below in the "Guidelines for Evaluation of Pulmonary Disability" as adopted by the Industrial Medical Council on December 4, 1997. The full text of this document is available at no charge on the web at www.dir.ca.gov/IMC/guidelines.html or by calling the Medical Unit at 1-800-794-6900.

(b) For all claims having dates of injury on or after January 1, 2005, and for those compensable claims arising before January 1, 2005, where there has been either no comprehensive medical-legal report or no report by a treating physician indicating the existence of permanent disability, or when the claims administrator, or if none the employer, is not required to provide the notice required by section 4061 to the injured worker, the method of measuring the pulmonary elements of impairment shall be as described in the American Medical Association, Guides to the Evaluation of Permanent Impairment [Fifth Edition] (AMA Guides). Permanent disability shall be described by applying the provisions of the Permanent Disability Rating Schedule adopted by the Administrative Director pursuant to section 9805 of Title 8 of the California Code of Regulations.

[Guidelines for Evaluation of Pulmonary Disability Not Reproduced]

Note: Authority cited: Sections 133, 139.2(j)(2) and 5307.3, Labor Code. Reference: Sections 139.2(j)(2), 4060, 4061, 4062, 4062.1, 4062.2, 4067, 4628 and 4660, Labor Code.

History: 1. New section filed 5-23-94; operative 6-22-94 (Register 94, No. 21).

2. Amendment of section and Note filed 6-19-98; operative 7-19-98 (Register 98, No. 25).

3. Change without regulatory effect amending section filed 7-12-2001 pursuant to section 100, title 1, California Code of Regulations (Register 2001, No. 28). Pursuant to this filing, material adopted pursuant to the Administrative Procedure Act that had previously been incorporated by reference in the California Code of Regulations was instead printed in full in the California Code of Regulations.

4. Amendment of section and Note filed 1-13-2009; operative 2-17-2009 (Register 2009, No. 3).

Ref.: Hanna §§ 1.12[2A][b]–[h], 22.11[1]–[16]; Herlick Handbook § 14.22, 14.23.

§45. Method of Evaluation of Cardiac Disability.

(a) For all claims arising before January 1, 2005, not subject to section 45(b), the method of measuring the cardiac elements of disability shall be set forth below in the "Guidelines for Evaluation of Cardiac Disability" as adopted by the Industrial Medical Council on December 4, 1997 and updated on July 19, 1998. The full text of this document is available at no charge on the web at www.dir.ca.gov/IMC/guidelines.html or by calling the Medical Unit at 1-800-794-6900.

(b) For all claims having dates of injury on or after January 1, 2005, and for those compensable claims arising before January 1, 2005, where there has been either no comprehensive medical-legal report or no report by a treating physician indicating the existence of permanent disability, or when the claims administrator, or if none the employer, is not required to provide the notice required by section 4061 to the injured worker, the method of measuring the cardiac elements of impairment shall be as described in the American Medical Association, Guides to the Evaluation of Permanent Impairment [Fifth Edition] (AMA Guides). Permanent disability shall be described by applying the provisions of the Permanent Disability Rating Schedule adopted by the Administrative Director pursuant to section 9805 of Title 8 of the California Code of Regulations.

[Guidelines for Evaluation of Cardiac Disability Not Reproduced]

Note: Authority cited: Sections 133, 139.2(j)(2) and 5307.3, Labor Code. Reference: Sections 139.2(j)(2), 4060, 4061, 4062, 4062.1, 4062.2, 4067, 4628 and 4660, Labor Code.

History: 1. New section filed 5-23-94; operative 6-22-94 (Register 94, No. 21).

2. Amendment of section and Note filed 6-19-98; operative 7-19-98 (Register 98, No. 25).

3. Change without regulatory effect amending section filed 7-12-2001 pursuant to section 100, title 1, California Code of Regulations (Register 2001, No. 28). Pursuant to this filing, material adopted pursuant to the Administrative Procedure Act that had previously been incorporated by reference in the California Code of Regulations was instead printed in full in the California Code of Regulations.

4. Amendment of section and Note filed 1-13-2009; operative 2-17-2009 (Register 2009, No. 3).

Ref.: Hanna §§ 1.12[2A][b]–[h], 22.11[1]–[16]; Herlick Handbook § 14.22, 14.23.

§46. Method of Evaluation of Neuromusculoskeletal Disability.

(a) For all claims arising before January 1, 2005, not subject to section 46(b), the method of measuring the neuromusculoskeletal elements of disability shall be as set forth below in the "Guidelines for Evaluation of Neuromusculoskeletal Disability" as adopted by the Industrial Medical Council on October 20, 1994. The full text of this document is available on the web at no charge at www.dir.ca.gov/IMC/guidelines.html or by calling the Medical Unit at 1-800-794-6900.

(b) For all claims having dates of injury on or after January 1, 2005, and for those compensable claims arising before January 1, 2005, where there has been either no comprehensive medical-legal report or no report by a treating physician indicating the existence of permanent disability, or when the claims administrator, or if none the employer, is not required to provide the notice required by section 4061 to the injured worker, the method of measuring the neuromusculoskeletal elements of impairment shall be as described in the American Medical Association, Guides to the Evaluation of Permanent Impairment [Fifth Edition] (AMA Guides). Permanent disability shall be described by applying the provisions of the Permanent Disability Rating Schedule adopted by the Administrative Director pursuant to section 9805 of Title 8 of the California Code of Regulations.

[Guidelines for Evaluation of Neuromusculoskeletal Disability Not Reproduced]

Note: Authority cited: Sections 133, 139.2(j)(2) and 5307.3, Labor Code. Reference: Sections 139.2, 4060, 4061, 4062, 4062.1, 4062.2, 4067, 4628 and 4660, Labor Code.

History: 1. New section filed 4-18-96; operative 4-18-96 pursuant to Government Code section 11343.4(d) (Register 96, No. 16).

2. Change without regulatory effect amending "Guidelines for Evaluation of Neuromusculoskeletal Disability, 2nd Ed." (incorporated by reference) filed 6-6-96 pursuant to section 100, title 1, California Code of Regulations (Register 96, No. 23).

3. Change without regulatory effect amending Note filed 8-1-96 pursuant to section 100, title 1, California Code of Regulations (Register 96, No. 31).

4. Amendment of section and Note filed 4-14-2000; operative 5-14-2000 (Register 2000, No. 15).

5. Change without regulatory effect amending section filed 7-12-2001 pursuant to section 100, title 1, California Code of Regulations (Register 2001, No. 28). Pursuant to this filing, material adopted pursuant to the Administrative Procedure Act that had previously been incorporated by reference in the California Code of Regulations was instead printed in full in the California Code of Regulations.

6. Amendment of section and Note filed 1-13-2009; operative 2-17-2009 (Register 2009, No. 3).

Ref.: Hanna §§ 1.12[2A][b]–[h], 22.11[1]–[16]; Herlick Handbook § 14.22, 14.23.

§46.1. Guidelines for the Evaluation of Foot and Ankle Disability.

(a) For all claims before January 1, 2005, not subject to section 46.1(b), the method of measuring the elements of foot and ankle shall be set forth below in the "Guidelines for Evaluation of Foot and Ankle Disability" as adopted by the Industrial Medical Council on October 28, 2000. The full text of this document is available on the web at no charge at www.dir.ca.gov/IMC/guidelines.html or by calling the Medical Unit at 1-800-794-6900.

(b) For all claims having dates of injury on or after January 1, 2005, and for those compensable claims arising before January 1, 2005, where there has been either no comprehensive medical-legal report or no report by a treating physician indicating the existence of permanent disability, or when the claims administrator, or if none the employer, is not required to provide the notice required by section 4061 to the injured worker, the method of measuring the elements of foot and ankle impairment shall be described in the American Medical Association, Guides to the Evaluation of Permanent Impairment [Fifth Edition] (AMA Guides). Permanent disability shall be described by applying the provisions of the Permanent Disability Rating Schedule adopted by the Administrative Director pursuant to section 9805 of Title 8 of the California Code of Regulations.

Note: Authority cited: Sections 139, 139.2, 4060, 4061 and 4062, Labor Code. Reference: Sections 139, 139.2, 4060, 4061, 4061.5 and 4062, Labor Code.

History: 1. New section and appendices A-C filed 1-8-2003; operative 2-7-2003 (Register 2003, No. 2).

2. Repealer of section and Appendices A-C and new section filed 1-13-2009; operative 2-17-2009 (Register 2009, No. 3).

Ref.: Hanna §§ 1.12[2A][b]–[h], 22.11[1]–[16]; Herlick Handbook § 14.22.

§46.2. QME Emergency Regulation in Response to COVID-19.

(a) During the period that this emergency regulation is in effect a QME, AME, or other medical-legal evaluation may be performed as follows:

(1) A QME or AME may reschedule in-person medical-legal appointments currently calendared. When a currently calendared in-person medical-legal appointment is rescheduled, the physician shall reschedule the evaluation to take place within 90 days after the date that both the statewide stay-at-home order limiting travel outside one's home, and any similar local order in the jurisdiction where the injured worker resides or the visit will occur, if applicable, are lifted; or

(2) A QME or AME may provide a record review and injured worker electronic interview summary report. The physician may interview the injured worker either by telephone or by any form of video conferencing. Once the statewide stay-at-home order, and any similar local order in the jurisdiction where the visit will occur, are lifted, the QME may then schedule a face-to-face evaluation taking all necessary precautions.

(A) The QME or AME shall schedule the electronic interview appointment by sending notice of the appointment with the information necessary for the injured worker to make the telephone call or initiate the videoconferencing for the appointment. The notice shall contain all the information ordinarily provided by the form 110 (QME: Appointment Notification Form See 8 Cal. Code Regs. §110) in addition to the information to complete the telephone or videoconference connection. The notice of electronic interview shall be transmitted in the manner required by 8 CCR section 34(a). Upon service of the notice of electronic interview, the parties to the action shall provide the QME or AME with the records for review at least 10 days prior to the scheduled appointment and in accordance with the provisions of Labor Code section 4062.3.

(3) A QME or AME may complete a medical-legal evaluation through telehealth when a physical examination is not necessary and all of the following conditions are met:

(A) The injured worker is not required to travel outside of their immediate household to accomplish the telehealth evaluation; and

(B) There is a medical issue in dispute which involves whether or not the injury is AOE/COE (Arising Out of Employment / Course of Employment), or the physician is asked to address the termination of an injured worker's indemnity benefit payments or address a dispute regarding work restrictions; and

(C) There is agreement in writing to the telehealth evaluation by the injured worker, the carrier or employer, and the QME. Agreement to the telehealth evaluation cannot be unreasonably denied. If a party to the action believes that agreement to the telehealth evaluation has been unreasonably denied under this section, they may file an objection with the Workers' Compensation Appeals Board, along with a Declaration of Readiness to Proceed to set the matter for a hearing;

(D) The telehealth visit under the circumstances is consistent with appropriate and ethical medical practice, as determined by the QME; and

(E) The QME attests in writing that the evaluation does not require a physical exam.

(4) For purposes of evaluations pursuant to subdivision (3) of this emergency regulation, telehealth means remote visits via video-conferencing, video-calling, or similar such technology that allows each party to see the other via a video connection.

(b) During the time this regulation is in effect, section 31.3 (e) of title 8 of the California Code of Regulations, is suspended and the following is effective:

(1) If a party with the legal right to schedule an appointment with a QME is unable to obtain an appointment with a selected QME within 90 days of the date of the appointment request, that party may waive the right to a replacement QME in order to accept an appointment that is no more than 120 days after the date of the party's initial appointment request. When the selected QME is unable to schedule the evaluation within 120 days of the date of that party's initial appointment request, either party may report the unavailability of the QME and the Medical Director shall issue a replacement pursuant to section 31.5 of title 8 of the California Code of Regulations upon request, unless both parties agree in writing to waive the 120-day time limit for scheduling the initial evaluation.

(c) During the time this regulation is in effect, all of the time periods enumerated in section 38 of title 8 of the California Code of Regulations are extended by a period of 15 days.

(d) During the time this regulation is in effect, section 34(b) of title 8 of the California Code of Regulations is suspended and the following is effective:

The QME shall schedule an appointment for the first comprehensive medical-legal evaluation which shall be conducted at a medical office listed on the panel selection form or any office listed with the Medical Director provided there is agreement by the parties. Any subsequent evaluation appointments may be performed at another medical office of the selected QME if it is listed with the Medical Director and is within a reasonable geographic distance from the injured worker's residence.

(e) Upon the lifting or termination of Governor Gavin Newsom's Executive Order N-33-20, and when there is no longer any stay-at-home order in the jurisdiction where the injured workers resides or evaluation will occur, QME evaluations may take place under the provisions of the non-emergency QME regulations (title 8 Cal. Code of Regs. Articles 3, 4 and 4.5) or via the emergency regulations while they are in effect.

(f) Nothing in this emergency regulation is intended to encourage or to authorize any individual, group, or business to violate any provision of Governor Gavin Newsom's Executive Order N-33-20 and related stay-at-home and social distancing protocols, or any similar such orders applicable in local jurisdictions.

Note: Authority cited: Sections 133, 139.2, 4627, 5307.3, 5307.6, 4061 and 4062, Labor Code.

History: 1. New section filed 5-14-2020 as an emergency; operative 5-14-2020 (Register 2020, No. 20). A Certificate of Compliance must be transmitted to OAL by 11-10-2020 or emergency language will be repealed by operation of law on the following day.

2. Emergency filed 5-14-2020 extended 60 days (Executive Order N-40-20) (Register 2020, No. 20). A Certificate of Compliance must be transmitted to OAL by 1-11-2021 or emergency language will be repealed by operation of law on the following day.

3. Emergency filed 5-14-2020 extended an additional 60 days pursuant to Executive Order N-66-20 (Register 2020, No. 40). A Certificate of Compliance must be transmitted to OAL by 3-12-2021 or emergency language will be repealed by operation of law on the following day.

§47. Method of Evaluation of Immunologic Disability.

(a) For all claims before January 1, 2005, not subject to section 47(b), the method of measuring the immunologic elements of disability shall be set forth below in the "Guidelines for Immunologic Testing" as adopted by the Industrial Medical Council on March 17, 1994. The full text of this document id available on the web at no charge at www.dir.ca.gov/IMC/guidelines.html or by calling the Medical Unit at 1-800-794-6900.

(b) For all claims having dates of injury on or after January 1, 2005, and for those compensable claims arising before January 1, 2005, where there has been either no comprehensive medical-legal report or no report by a treating physician indicating the existence of permanent disability, or when the employer is not required to provide the notice required by section 4061 to the injured worker, the method of measuring the immunological elements of impairment shall be described in the American Medical Association, Guides to the Evaluation of Permanent Impairment [Fifth Edition] (AMA Guides). Permanent disability shall be described by applying the provisions of the Permanent Disability Rating Schedule adopted by the Administrative Director pursuant to section 9805 of Title 8 of the California Code of Regulations.

[Guidelines for Immunologic Testing Not Reproduced]

Note: Authority cited: Section 139.2(j)(2), Labor Code. Reference: Sections 139.2(j)(2), 4060, 4061 and 4062, Labor Code.

History: 1. New section filed 5-23-94; operative 6-22-94 (Register 94, No. 21).

2. Amendment of Note filed 4-14-2000; operative 5-14-2000 (Register 2000, No. 15).

3. Change without regulatory effect amending section filed 7-12-2001 pursuant to section 100, title 1, California Code of Regulations (Register 2001, No. 28). Pursuant to this filing, material adopted pursuant to the Administrative Procedure Act that had previously been incorporated by reference in the California Code of Regulations was instead printed in full in the California Code of Regulations.

4. Amendment filed 1-13-2009; operative 2-17-2009 (Register 2009, No. 3).

Ref.: Hanna §§ 1.12[2A][b]–[h], 22.11[1]–[16]; Herlick Handbook § 14.22, 14.23.

§48. QME Ethical Guidelines. [Repealed]

Note: Authority cited: Sections 139.2(j)(2) and (3) and 5307.3, Labor Code. Reference: Sections 139.2(j)(2) and (3), 4060, 4061 and 4062, Labor Code.

History: 1. New section filed 5-23-94; operative 6-22-94 (Register 94, No. 21).

2. Repealer filed 4-11-95; operative 5-11-95 (Register 95, No. 15).

ARTICLE 4.5
Minimum Time Guidelines

§49. Definitions.

The following definitions apply to this Article:

(a) Cardiovascular evaluation. "Cardiovascular evaluation" means the determination of disability due to pathological changes of the heart and/or the central circulatory system.

(b) Face to Face time. "Face to face time" means only that time the evaluator is present with an injured worker. This includes the time in which the evaluator performs such tasks as taking a history, performing a physical examination or discussing the worker's medical condition with the worker. Face to face time excludes time spent on research, records review and report writing. Any time spent by the injured worker with clinical or clerical staff who perform diagnostic or laboratory tests (including blood tests or x-rays) or time spent by the injured worker in a waiting room or other area outside the evaluation room is not included in face to face time.

(c) Medical evaluation. "Medical evaluation" means a comprehensive medical-legal evaluation as defined under section 9793 of Article 5.6, Subchapter 1, Chapter 4.5 of Title 8 of the California Code of Regulations.

(d) Neuromusculoskeletal evaluation. "Neuromusculoskeletal evaluation" means the determination of disability due to injury to the central nervous systems, the spine and extremities, and the various muscle groups of the body.

(e) Psychiatric evaluation. "Psychiatric evaluation" means the determination of disability due to psychopathology, by either a psychiatrist or psychologist following the Method of Measurement of Psychiatric Disability set out in section 43 of Title 8 of the California Code of Regulations.

(f) Pulmonary evaluation. "Pulmonary evaluation" means the determination of disability due to pathological changes of the lungs and/or other components of the respiratory system.

(g) QME. "QME" means Qualified Medical Evaluator appointed by the Administrative Director pursuant to Labor Code section 139.2.

(h) Uncomplicated evaluation. "Uncomplicated evaluation" means a face to face evaluation in which all of the following are recorded in the medical report: Minimal or no review of records, minimal or no diagnostic studies or laboratory testing, minimal or no research, and minimal or no medical history taking.

Note: Authority cited: Sections 133, 139.2 and 5307.3, Labor Code. Reference: Sections 139.2, 4060, 4061, 4062, 4062.1, 4062.2, 4067, 4628 and 4660, Labor Code.

History: 1. Change without regulatory effect relocating article 4.5 heading and renumbering former section 149 to new section 49 filed 8-31-94 pursuant to section 100, title 1, California Code of Regulations (Register 94, No. 35).

2. Change without regulatory effect amending article heading filed 9-28-94 pursuant to section 100, title 1, California Code of Regulations (Register 94, No. 39).

3. Amendment of subsection (b) filed 4-14-2000; operative 5-14-2000 (Register 2000, No. 15).

4. Amendment of section and Note filed 1-13-2009; operative 2-17-2009 (Register 2009, No. 3).

Ref.: Hanna §§ 1.12[2A][b]–[h], 22.11[1]–[16]; Herlick Handbook § 14.22.

§49.2. Neuromusculoskeletal Evaluation.

A medical evaluation concerning a claim for neuromusculoskeletal injury (whether specific or cumulative in nature) shall not be completed by a QME in fewer than 20 minutes of face to face time. Twenty minutes is the minimum allowable face to face time for an uncomplicated evaluation. The evaluator shall state in the evaluation report the amount of face to face time actually spent with the injured worker and explain in detail any variance below the minimum amount of face to face time stated in this regulation.

Note: Authority cited: Sections 133, 139.2(j) and 5307.3, Labor Code. Reference: Sections 139.2, 4060, 4061, 4062, 4062.1, 4062.2, 4067, 4628 and 4660, Labor Code.

History: 1. Change without regulatory effect renumbering former section 149.2 to new section 49.2 filed 8-31-94 pursuant to section 100, title 1, California Code of Regulations (Register 94, No. 35).

2. Amendment of section and Note filed 1-13-2009; operative 2-17-2009 (Register 2009, No. 3).

Ref.: Hanna §§ 1.12[2A][b]–[h], 22.11[1]–[16]; Herlick Handbook § 14.22.

§49.4. Cardiovascular Evaluation.

A medical evaluation concerning a claim for cardiovascular injury (whether specific or cumulative in nature) shall not be completed by a QME in fewer than 30 minutes of face to face time. Thirty minutes is the minimum allowable face to face time for an uncomplicated evaluation. The evaluator shall state in the evaluation report the amount of face to face time actually spent with the injured worker and explain in detail any variance below the minimum amount of face to face time stated in this regulation.

Note: Authority cited: Sections 133, 139.2(j) and 5307.3, Labor Code, Reference: Sections 139.2, 4060, 4061, 4062, 4062.1, 4062.2, 4067, 4628 and 4660, Labor Code.

History: 1. Change without regulatory effect renumbering former section 149.4 to new section 49.4 filed 8-31-94 pursuant to section 100, title 1, California Code of Regulations (Register 94, No. 35).

2. Amendment of section and Note filed 1-13-2009; operative 2-17-2009 (Register 2009, No. 3).

Ref.: Hanna §§ 1.12[2A][b]–[h], 22.11[1]–[16]; Herlick Handbook § 14.22.

§49.6. Pulmonary Evaluation.

A medical evaluation concerning a claim for pulmonary injury (whether specific or cumulative in nature) shall not be completed by a QME in fewer than 30 minutes of face to face time. Thirty minutes is the minimum allowable face to face time for an uncomplicated evaluation. The evaluator shall state in the evaluation report the amount of face to face time actually spent with the injured worker and explain in detail any variance below the minimum amount of face to face time stated in this regulation.

Note: Authority cited: Sections 133, 139.2(j) and 5307.3, Labor Code. Reference: Sections 139.2, 4060, 4061, 4062, 4062.1, 4062.2, 4067, 4628 and 4660, Labor Code.

History: 1. Change without regulatory effect renumbering former section 149.6 to new section 49.6 filed 8-31-94 pursuant to section 100, title 1, California Code of Regulations (Register 94, No. 35).

2. Amendment of section and Note filed 1-13-2009; operative 2-17-2009 (Register 2009, No. 3).

Ref.: Hanna §§ 1.12[2A][b]–[h], 22.11[1]–[16]; Herlick Handbook § 14.22.

§49.8. Psychiatric Evaluation.

A medical evaluation concerning a claim for psychiatric injury (whether specific or cumulative in nature) shall not be completed by a QME in less than one hour of face to face time. One hour is considered the minimum allowable face to face time for an uncomplicated evaluation. The evaluator shall state in the evaluation report the amount of face to face time actually spent with the injured worker and explain in detail any variance below the minimum amount of face to face time stated in this regulation.

Note: Authority cited: Sections 133, 139.2(j) and 5307.3, Labor Code. Reference: Sections 139, 139.2, 4060, 4061, 4062, 4062.1, 4062.2, 4067, 4628 and 4660, Labor Code.

History: 1. Change without regulatory effect renumbering former section 149.8 to new section 49.8 filed 8-31-94 pursuant to section 100, title 1, California Code of Regulations (Register 94, No. 35).

2. Amendment of section and Note filed 1-13-2009; operative 2-17-2009 (Register 2009, No. 3).

Ref.: Hanna §§ 1.12[2A][b]–[h], 22.11[1]–[16]; Herlick Handbook § 14.22.

§49.9. Other Evaluation.

A medical evaluation concerning a claim for any injury (whether specific or cumulative in nature) not specifically included in this article shall not be completed by a QME in fewer than 30 minutes of face to face time. Thirty minutes is the minimum allowable face to face time for an uncomplicated evaluation. The evaluator shall state in the evaluation report the amount of face to face time actually spent with the injured worker and explain in detail any variance below the minimum amount of face to face time stated in this regulation.

Note: Authority cited: Sections 133, 139.2(j) and 5307.3, Labor Code. Reference: Sections 139.2, 4060, 4061, 4062, 4062.1, 4062.2, 4067, 4628 and 4660, Labor Code.

History: 1. Change without regulatory effect renumbering former section 149.9 to new section 49.9 filed 8-31-94 pursuant to section 100, title 1, California Code of Regulations (Register 94, No. 35).

2. Amendment of section and Note filed 1-13-2009; operative 2-17-2009 (Register 2009, No. 3).

Ref.: Hanna §§ 1.12[2A][b]–[h], 22.11[1]–[16]; Herlick Handbook § 14.22.

ARTICLE 5
QME Reappointment

§50. Reappointment: Requirements and Application Form.

(a) In addition to the eligibility requirements set forth in section 11, a physician may seek reappointment on the basis that he or she was an active QME on June 30, 2000. For all physicians, applications for reappointment shall include a Reappointment Application Form in section 104, and the appropriate fee under section 17. The reappointment application and the appropriate fee shall be filed at the Administrative Director's headquarters office listed on the reappointment form.

(b) Any Reappointment Application Form may be rejected if it is incomplete or does not contain the required supporting documentation listed in section 11 and on the Reappointment Application Form. As part of the approval of the Reappointment Application Form, the Administrative Director shall verify that the QME has complied with all requirements under this Article.

(c) When a QME applies for reappointment, he or she shall submit a statement signed under penalty of perjury:

(1) attesting that he or she has completed the applicable QME continuing education requirement; and

(2) listing the dates, locations, and titles of the continuing education programs and the names of the providers of those programs which he or she has taken to meet the requirement of Labor Code section 139.2(d)(3), as well as the number of hours of attendance at each program. The Administrative Director may randomly audit QMEs for documentation of program attendance, which supports compliance with this requirement; and

(3) attesting that the physician has accurately reported on the QME SFI Form 124 to the best of the QME's knowledge the information required by section 29 regarding the QME's specified financial interests; and

(4) attesting that the physician's license to practice as a physician, as defined under Labor Code section 3209.3, is neither restricted nor encumbered by suspension or probation, nor has the physician been convicted of a misdemeanor or felony related to the physician's practice or a crime of moral turpitude, and that the physician will notify the Administrative Director if the physician's license to practice is subsequently suspended or placed on probation or if the physician is convicted of a misdemeanor or felony related to the physician's practice or of a crime of moral turpitude; and

(5) attesting that the physician shall abide by all regulations of the Administrative Director and shall refrain from making referrals in violation of those regulations; and

(6) attesting that the physician has not performed a QME evaluation during a time when the physician was not appointed as a QME.

Note: Authority cited: Sections 133, 139.2 and 5307.3, Labor Code. Reference: Sections 139.2, Labor Code.

History: 1. New article 5 and repealer and new section filed 8-1-94; operative 8-31-94 (Register 94, No. 31). For prior history, see Register 91, No. 26.

2. Change without regulatory effect amending first paragraph and subsection (i) filed 4-19-95 pursuant to section 100, title 1, California Code of Regulations (Register 95, No. 16).

3. Amendment of article 5 heading and renumbering of former section 50 to new section 53 and new section filed 8-23-96; operative 9-22-96 (Register 96, No. 34).

4. Amendment filed 4-14-2000; operative 5-14-2000 (Register 2000, No. 15).

5. Amendment of section heading and section and new Note filed 9-6-2001; operative 10-6-2001 (Register 2001, No. 36).

6. Amendment of section and Note filed 1-13-2009; operative 2-17-2009 (Register 2009, No. 3).

Ref.: Hanna §§ 1.12[2A][b]–[h], 22.11[1]–[16]; Herlick Handbook §§ 1.02, 14.22.

§50.1. Reappointment: Failure to Comply with Time Frames. [Renumbered]

Note: Authority cited: Section 139.2, Labor Code. Reference: Section 139.2(d)(1), Labor Code.

History: 1. New section filed 8-1-94; operative 8-31-94 (Register 94, No. 31).

2. Change without regulatory effect amending section filed 12-2-96 pursuant to section 100, title 1, California Code of Regulations (Register 96, No. 49).

3. Renumbering of former section 50.1 to section 51 filed 4-14-2000; operative 5-14-2000 (Register 2000, No. 15).

§50.2. Reappointment: Unavailability Notification. [Renumbered]

Note: Authority cited: Section 139.2, Labor Code. Reference: Sections 139.2(d) and 139.2(j)(6), Labor Code.

History: 1. New section filed 8-1-94; operative 8-31-94 (Register 94, No. 31).

2. Change without regulatory effect amending section filed 12-2-96 pursuant to section 100, title 1, California Code of Regulations (Register 96, No. 49).

3. Renumbering of former section 50.2 to section 52 filed 4-14-2000; operative 5-14-2000 (Register 2000, No. 15).

§50.3. Reappointment: Evaluations Rejected by Appeals Board. [Renumbered]

Note: Authority cited: Section 139.2, Labor Code. Reference: Sections 139.2(d) and 139.2(j)(6), Labor Code.

History: 1. New section filed 8-1-94; operative 8-31-94 (Register 94, No. 31).

2. Renumbering of former section 50.3 to new section 52 filed 8-23-96; operative 9-22-96 (Register 96, No. 34).

§51. Reappointment: Failure to Comply with Time Frames.

All QMEs shall comply with the time frames in sections 34 and 38 as a condition for reappointment. The Administrative Director may deny reappointment to any QME who has failed to comply with the evaluation time frames in sections 34 and 38 on at least three occasions during the calendar year.

Note: Authority cited: Sections 133, 139.2 and 5307.3, Labor Code. Reference: Section 139.2(d)(1), Labor Code.

History: 1. Repealer and new section filed 8-1-94; operative 8-31-94 (Register 94, No. 31). For prior history, see Register 91, No. 26.

2. Renumbering of former section 51 to new section 60 and new section filed 8-23-96; operative 9-22-96 (Register 96, No. 34).

3. Renumbering of former section 51 to section 53 and renumbering of former section 50.1 to section 51 filed 4-14-2000; operative 5-14-2000 (Register 2000, No. 15).

4. Amendment of section and Note filed 1-13-2009; operative 2-17-2009 (Register 2009, No. 3).

Ref.: Hanna §§ 1.12[2A][b]–[h], 22.11[1]–[16]; Herlick Handbook §§ 1.02, 14.22.

§52. Reappointment: Unavailability Notification.

All QMEs shall comply with the unavailability notification requirements in section 33 as a condition for reappointment. The Administrative Director may deny reappointment of any QME who has filed notification for unavailability under section 33 for more than 90 calendar days during the calendar year, or who has on any single occasion refused without good cause to perform a medical-legal evaluation.

Note: Authority cited: Sections 133, 139.2 and 5307.3, Labor Code. Reference: Sections 139.2(d) and 139.2(j)(6), Labor Code.

History: 1. Repealer and new section filed 8-1-94; operative 8-31-94 (Register 94, No. 31). For prior history, see Register 91, No. 26.

2. Renumbering of former section 52 to new section 61, renumbering of former section 50.3 to new section 52 and amendment of section filed 8-23-96; operative 9-22-96 (Register 96, No. 34).

3. Renumbering of former section 52 to section 54 and renumbering of former section 50.2 to section 52 filed 4-14-2000; operative 5-14-2000 (Register 2000, No. 15).

4. Amendment of section and Note filed 1-13-2009; operative 2-17-2009 (Register 2009, No. 3).

Ref.: Hanna §§ 1.12[2A][b]–[h], 22.11[1]–[16]; Herlick Handbook §§ 1.02, 14.22.

§53. Reappointment: Failure of Board Certification Examination. [Repealed]

History: 1. Repealer and new section filed 8-1-94; operative 8-31-94 (Register 94, No. 31). For prior history, see Register 91, No. 26.

2. Renumbering of former section 53 to new section 62, renumbering of former section 50 to new section 53 and amendment of section filed 8-23-96; operative 9-22-96 (Register 96, No. 34).

3. Amendment filed 3-15-99; operative 4-14-99 (Register 99, No. 12).

4. Renumbering of former section 53 to section 55 and renumbering of former section 51 to section 53 filed 4-14-2000; operative 5-14-2000 (Register 2000, No. 15).

5. Repealer filed 1-13-2009; operative 2-17-2009 (Register 2009, No. 3).

§53.1. QME Continuing Education Response Form. [Repealed]

Note: Authority cited: Section 139.2, Labor Code. Reference: Section 139.2, Labor Code.

History: 1. New section filed 3-15-99; operative 4-14-99 (Register 99, No. 12).

2. Repealer filed 4-14-2000; operative 5-14-2000 (Register 2000, No. 15).

§54. Reappointment: Evaluations Rejected by Appeals Board.

The Administrative Director may deny reappointment to any QME who has had more than five evaluations rejected by a Workers' Compensation Judge or the Appeals Board originally submitted at a contested hearing. The rejection shall be based on the failure of the QME's evaluation to prove or disprove a contested issue or failure to comply with guidelines promulgated by the Administrative Director pursuant to Labor Code section 139.2(j)(2), (3), (4) or (5). A specific finding must become final and the time for appeal must have expired before any rejected evaluation shall be counted as one of the five rejections.

Note: Authority cited: Sections 133, 139.2 and 5307.3, Labor Code. Reference: Sections 139.2(d) and 139.2(j)(6), Labor Code.

History: 1. New section filed 5-9-91; operative 5-9-91 (Register 91, No. 26). New section is exempt from review by OAL pursuant to Government Code section 11351(a).

2. Repealer filed 8-1-94; operative 8-31-94 (Register 94, No. 31).

3. Renumbering of former section 52 to section 54 filed 4-14-2000; operative 5-14-2000 (Register 2000, No. 15).

4. Amendment of section and Note filed 1-13-2009; operative 2-17-2009 (Register 2009, No. 3).

Ref.: Hanna §§ 1.12[2A][b]–[h], 22.11[1]–[16]; Herlick Handbook §§ 1.02, 14.22.

§55. Reappointment: Continuing Education Programs.

A QME shall complete within the previous 24 months of his or her term of appointment 12 hours of continuing education in disability evaluation or workers' compensation related medical dispute evaluation given by a provider accredited by the Administrative Director.

(a) There are two types of continuing education programs:

(1) On-site programs, in which the instructor and QME are in the same location; and

(2) Distance learning programs.

(A) Providers of distance learning programs shall give either a pre- or post-course self-examination based on the program material. The provider shall grade the QME's test. Credit for the course can be given only for a passing rate of no lower than 70 percent correct responses. The Administrative Director may audit physicians' examinations and scores.

(B) Credit for distance learning courses shall be granted for the actual time spent viewing, listening to or participating in the program and for the reasonable and necessary time to take the examinations for up to six hours per program. Credit for the same distance learning program may be taken only once.

(C) All distance learning materials shall bear a date of release and shall be updated every three years. The provider shall notify the Administrative Director in writing of the revision.

(b) In addition to granting credit for attending a course or program which it gives, the Administrative Director may grant credit for:

(1) Participating in a panel on the development or review of the QME competency examination. A physician may receive one hour credit for each hour of participation on a panel. The QME shall obtain documentation of participation from the test administrator for submission to the Administrative Director.

(2) Instructing in a program given for QME credit by a provider accredited by the Administrative Director. The instructor may receive two hours of credit for each hour of instruction in an accredited provider's program or one hour of credit for each hour of participation on a panel. Credit for the same presentation may be taken only once during each calendar year. The QME shall submit documentation of participation from the program provider to the Administrative Director.

(3) Attending a program which is accepted by the QME's licensing board for renewal of his or her professional license, provided the subject matter is directly related to California impairment evaluation or workers' compensation medical dispute evaluation.

To request credit for this type of course, the QME must submit:

(A) proof of attendance;

(B) written material which describes the program content and program faculty; and

(C) documentation that the program is for continuing education credit by the physician's licensing board.

(4) Passing the QME competency examination. A QME may be granted six hours of continuing education credit for passing this examination for the purpose of receiving an initial appointment as a QME.

(c) To apply to the Administrative Director for accreditation, a provider shall submit to the Administrative Director, at least 60 calendar days before any public advertisement of the applicant's program or course is made:

(1) a completed form 118, in section 118 of these regulations.

(2) A curriculum vitae for each proposed instructor or author (for paper-based programs). A proposed instructor or author shall have education and/or training and recent work experience relevant to the subject of his/her presentation.

(3) The proposed promotional material for the program.

(4) An outline of course content, or actual course content, consistent with the topics in section 11.5(c) of Title 8 of the California Code of Regulations.

(d) The Administrative Director shall accredit an applicant who meets the definition of an education provider in Section 1(q); submits a completed, signed and dated application which demonstrates past experience in providing continuing education programs; and proposes a program which meets the requirements of section 55(c) or a course which meets the requirements of section 11.5(a) and (i). Proposed content for continuing education program credit must relate directly to disability evaluation or California workers' compensation-related medical dispute evaluation. No credit shall be recognized by the Administrative Director for material solely discussing the business aspects of workers' compensation medical practice such as billing, coding and marketing.

(e) The Administrative Director shall notify the applicant within 30 calendar days after receipt of the application containing all the information listed in section 55(c) whether that provider has been accredited for a two year period. Incomplete applications will be returned to the applicant.

(f) A provider that has been accredited by the Administrative Director will be given a number which must be displayed on any public advertisements of QME continuing education programs for that provider with the statement "Accredited by the Administrative Director of the California Division of Workers' Compensation for Qualified Medical Evaluator continuing education. Physicians may report up to _____ hours of credit for QME reappointment."

(g) On or before the date the program is first presented or distributed, the provider shall submit the program syllabus (all program handouts) to the Administrative Director. Each distance learning program shall also submit one copy of the examinations and one copy of the audio/video tapes, computer program or each issue of the journal or newsletter for which credit is to be granted.

(h) A provider may offer different QME continuing education programs during the two-year accreditation period provided the subject matter is in disability evaluation or workers' compensation related medical dispute resolution. The provider shall send the Administrative Director the program outlined and faculty for each new program at least forty-five (45) days prior to the date of presentation of the new program. The Administrative Director may require submission of program syllabi. The Administrative Director may require changes in the program based on its review of the program outline, program syllabi, promotional material or faculty if the Administrative Director finds that any aspect of the program is not in compliance with these regulations.

(i) Promotional materials for a program must state the educational objectives; the professional qualifications of program faculty (at least all relevant professional degrees); the content of program activities; the maximum number of credit hours to be granted; and the intended audience.

(j) Joint sponsorship of education programs (as between an accredited and an unaccredited provider) must be approved by the Administrative Director prior to presentation of the program.

(k) Accredited providers that cease to offer education programs shall notify the Administrative Director in writing.

(*l*) Instructors shall not recruit members or promote commercial products or services immediately before, during or after a course. Providers or vendors may display/sell educational related to workers' compensation or applications for membership in an area adjoining a course. A course provider or faculty member shall disclose on QME Form 119 (Faculty Disclosure of Commercial Interest), located in section 119 of Title 8 of the California Code of Regulations, any significant financial interest in or affiliation with any commercial product or service held by faculty and discussed in a course and that interest or affiliation must be disclosed to all attendees. A provider shall file every Form 119 in its possession or in its control with the Administrative Director.

(m) The provider shall issue a certificate of completion to each QME who successfully completes a continuing education program. The certificate must list the provider; provider number; date(s); location and title of the continuing education program; and the number of hours in attendance for which credit is to be granted. Credit shall be granted only for the actual time of attendance at or participation in a program. Each accredited provider may in its sole discretion limit the amount of credit hours that a course will be granted to less than the amount of time actually spent in attendance in the course.

(n) To apply for re-accreditation, a provider must submit a completed QME Form 118 (Application for Accreditation or Re-Accreditation as Education Provider) (See, 8 Cal. Code Regs. § 118). The provider may complete section 2 of the form using a new program or course or one which was given by the provider during the recent accreditation period. The Administrative Director shall give the provider ninety (90) days' notice of the need to seek re-accreditation.

(o) The provider shall maintain attendance records for each continuing education program for a period of no less than three (3) years after the program is given. A physician attending the program must be identified by signature. The provider must submit a copy of the signature list to the Administrative Director within sixty (60) days of completion of the program.

(p) The provider is required to give the QME's Evaluation Form 117 (Qualified Medical Evaluator Continuing Education Response Form) (See, 8 Cal. Code Regs. § 117) to program attendees and request they submit the form to the Administrative Director. This information shall not be used in lieu of a certification of completion given by the provider, as specified pursuant to section (m). Destruction by a provider or its employee of a QME's Evaluation Form or failure by such provider or its employee to distribute Form 117 as part of its program shall constitute grounds for revocation of a provider's accredited status. The Administrative Director shall tabulate the responses and return a summary to the provider within ninety (90) days of completion of the program.

(q) The Administrative Director may audit a provider's program(s) at the request of the medical director to determine if the provider meets the criteria for accreditation. The Administrative Director may audit programs randomly, when a complaint is received, or on the basis of responses on QME Form 117 (Qualified Medical Evaluator Continuing Education Response Form) (See, 8 Cal. Code Regs. § 117). An auditor shall not receive QME credit for an audited program. The Administrative Director shall make written results of the audit available to the provider no more than thirty (30) days after the audit is completed.

(r) The Administrative Director may withdraw accreditation of a provider or deny such a provider's application for accreditation on the following grounds (in addition to failure to meet the relevant requirements of subdivision 11.5(a) or 55(c) of Title 8 of the California Code of Regulations):

(1) Conviction of a felony or any offense substantially related to the activities of the provider.

(2) Any material misrepresentation of fact made by the provider.

(3) Failure to comply with Administrative Director regulations.

(4) False or misleading advertising.

(5) Failure to comply with Administrative Director recommendations following an audit.

(6) Failure to distribute QME Form 117 (Qualified Medical Evaluator Continuing Education Response Form) (See, 8 Cal. Code Regs. § 117) cards to program attendees.

NOTE: Forms referred to above are available at no charge by downloading from the web at www.dir.ca.gov/dwc/forms.html or by requesting at 1-800-794-6900.

Note: Authority cited: Sections 133, 139.2 and 5307.3, Labor Code. Reference: Sections 139.2, 4060, 4061, 4062, 4062.1, 4062.2, 4062.3, 4067 and 4628, Labor Code.

History: 1. New section filed 5-9-91; operative 5-9-91 (Register 91, No. 26). New section is exempt from review by OAL pursuant to Government Code section 11351(a).

2. Repealer filed 8-1-94; operative 8-31-94 (Register 94, No. 31).

3. Renumbering of former section 53 to section 55 filed 4-14-2000; operative 5-14-2000 (Register 2000, No. 15).

4. Amendment of section heading and section filed 9-6-2001; operative 10-6-2001 (Register 2001, No. 36).

5. Amendment of section and Note filed 1-13-2009; operative 2-17-2009 (Register 2009, No. 3).

Ref.: Hanna §§ 1.12[2A][b]–[h], 22.11[1]–[16]; Herlick Handbook §§ 1.02, 14.22.

§56. Reappointment: Failure to Comply with WCAB Order or Ruling.

The Administrative Director may deny reappointment to any QME who has been found in violation of any order or ruling by a Workers' Compensation Judge or the Appeals Board.

Note: Authority cited: Sections 133, 139.2 and 5307.3, Labor Code. Reference: Sections 139.2(d) and 139.2(j)(6), Labor Code.

History: 1. New section filed 4-14-2000; operative 5-14-2000 (Register 2000, No. 15). For prior history see Register 94, No. 31.

2. Amendment of section and Note filed 1-13-2009; operative 2-17-2009 (Register 2009, No. 3).

Ref.: Hanna §§ 1.12[2A][b]–[h], 22.11[1]–[16]; Herlick Handbook §§ 1.02, 14.22.

§57. Reappointment: Professional Standard—Violation of Business and Professions Code Section 730.

The Administrative Director may deny appointment or reappointment to any physician who has performed a QME evaluation or examination without valid QME certification at the time of examining the injured worker or the time of signing the initial or follow-up evaluation report.

Note: Authority cited: Sections 133, 139.2 and 5307.3, Labor Code; and Section 730, Business and Professions Code. Reference: Sections 139.2(d) and 139.2(j)(6), Labor Code; and Section 730, Business and Professions Code.

History: 1. New section filed 4-14-2000; operative 5-14-2000 (Register 2000, No. 15).

2. Amendment of section and Note filed 1-13-2009; operative 2-17-2009 (Register 2009, No. 3).

Ref.: Hanna §§ 1.12[2A][b]–[h], 22.11[1]–[16]; Herlick Handbook §§ 1.02, 14.22.

ARTICLE 6
QME Discipline

§60. Discipline.

(a) The Administrative Director may, in his or her discretion, suspend or terminate any physician from the QME list without hearing:

(1) whose license has been revoked;

(2) whose license has been suspended or terminated by the relevant licensing board so as to preclude practice;

(3) who has been convicted of a misdemeanor or felony related to the conduct of his or her practice or who has been suspended or placed on probation by his or her licensing board;

(4) based on a stipulation or a decision by the physician's licensing board that the physician has been placed on probation;

(5) who has failed to pay timely the appropriate fee as required under section 17 of Title 8 of the California Code of Regulations.

(b) The Administrative Director may, based on a complaint by the Medical Director, and following a hearing pursuant to section 61 of Title 8 of the California Code of Regulations, suspend, terminate or place on probation a QME found in violation of a statutory or administrative duty as described in the Administrative Director Sanction Guidelines for QMEs under section 65 of Title 8 of the California Code of Regulations. Such violations include, but are not limited to:

(1) one violation of Labor Code section 139.3 or 4628;

(2) failure to follow the medical procedures established by the Administrative Director pursuant to Labor Code section 139.2(j)(1)(2)(3)(4)(5) or (6);

(3) failure to comply with the requirements of Labor Code section 139.2(b) or (c) and/or section 10, 10.5, 11 or 12 of Title 8 of the California Code of Regulations;

(4) failure to comply with the unavailability notification requirements pursuant to section 33 of Title 8 of the California Code of Regulations.

(5) failure to comply with the disclosure, ethical or conflict of interest requirements pursuant to sections 40, 41 or 41.5, respectively, of Title 8 of the California Code of Regulations;

(6) failure to complete accurate and complete reports pursuant to Labor Code section 139.2(i) or to comply with section 39.5 of Title 8 of the California Code of Regulations.

(7) one finding by the Appeals Board of ex parte contact by the QME prohibited by Labor Code section 4062.3.

(8) one finding by the Administrative Director that the QME solicited an injured worker to take over that worker's treatment for his or her workers compensation claim.

(9) failure to disclose a disqualifying conflict of interest as required by section 41.5 of Title 8 of the California Code of Regulations;

(10) failure to disclose a significant financial interest, as defined in sections 1(cc) and 29 of Title 8 of the California Code of Regulations.

(c) The Medical Director may file a complaint with the Administrative Director against a QME on any of the grounds listed in subsection (b) based on a complaint from a member of the public and/or the Medical Director's own initiative. The Medical Director may assign legal counsel and investigators to conduct all matters related to this Article.

(d) The powers and discretion of the Administrative Director are hereby delegated to the Medical Director of the Division, or his or her designee Associate Medical Director, with respect to:

(1) Conducting investigations and assigning investigators;

(2) Issuing subpoenas for testimony and/or production of documents;

(3) Propounding interrogatories;

(4) Receiving and filing requests for hearing and notices of defense;

(5) Setting and calendaring cases for hearing;

(6) Issuing notices of hearing;

(7) Assigning counsel; and

(8) Performing all other functions related to QME discipline under this Article, except for issuing statements of issues, issuing accusations and issuing disciplinary orders after hearing.

(e) A report prepared by a QME which has not been completed and served on one or more parties prior to the date of the final decision taken by the licensing board or the date of the conviction, whichever is earlier, shall be inadmissible before the Appeals Board and no party shall have liability for payment for the report.

Note: Authority cited: Sections 11180-11191, Government Code; Sections 111, 133, 139.2 and 5307.3, Labor Code. Reference: Sections 139.2 and 4062.3, Labor Code.

History: 1. New article 6 (sections 60-62), renumbering of former section 51 to new section 60, repealer and new subsection (a), amendment of subsection (b), new subsection (b)(6) and subsection renumbering, and new subsections (b)(8) and (d) filed 8-23-96; operative 9-22-96 (Register 96, No. 34).

2. Amendment filed 4-14-2000; operative 5-14-2000 (Register 2000, No. 15).

3. Amendment of section and Note filed 1-13-2009; operative 2-17-2009 (Register 2009, No. 3).

Ref.: Hanna §§ 1.12[2A][b]–[h], 22.11[1]–[16]; Herlick Handbook §§ 1.02, 6.04[1], 14.22.

§61. Hearing Procedure.

(a) Where the Medical Director determines that there is prima facie evidence of any violation of section 60 of

Title 8 of the California Code of Regulations, he or she shall make and submit a prima facie case of the violation to the Administrative Director.

(b) If the Administrative Director sustains the Medical Director's prima facie case, the QME shall be notified in writing of the determination and shall also be notified of his or her right to a hearing in accordance with Chapter 4 (commencing with Section 11370) and Chapter 5 (commencing with section 11500) and Part 1 of Division 3 of the Government Code.

(1) The Administrative Director may, notwithstanding Government Code section 11502, assign the hearing to a hearing officer designated by the Medical Director who shall act as an Administrative Law Judge for the purposes of Government Code sections 11370 et seq. and 11500 et seq., or may delegate in whole or in part to an Administrative Law Judge the authority to conduct the hearing and decide the case. In the event of a hearing, the hearing officer or Administrative Law Judge shall fix the time and place of the hearing and notify interested parties in writing no fewer than 10 days in advance of the hearing and in accordance with Code of Civil Procedure sections 1013(a) and 2015.5 specifying the time and place of the hearing.

(2) If an Administrative Law Judge conducts a hearing, the Administrative Law Judge selected to preside over the hearing shall hear the case alone, and exercise all powers related to the conduct of the hearing.

(3) At the conclusion of the hearing, the Administrative Law Judge or hearing officer shall file a written statement of findings and proposed decision with the Administrative Director. The decision made pursuant to this action shall include specific findings in accordance with section 60(b) of Title 8 of the California Code of Regulations, and under section 65 of Title 8 of the California Code of Regulations shall recommend, but defer to the Administrative Director the final decision with respect to sanctions.

(4) The Administrative Director's decision on which sanction(s) to impose on a QME, pursuant to Labor Code section 139.2(k) or any other statute giving the Administrative Director disciplinary authority, shall be in accordance with the Sanction Guidelines for Qualified Medical Evaluators under section 65 of Title 8 of the California Code of Regulations.

(5) In accordance with Government Code section 11517(c), if the proposed decision is not adopted by the Administrative Director, the Administrative Director shall determine whether or not to decide the case, based on the record and transcript, and/or whether or not to take additional evidence or to refer the case back to the Administrative Law Judge to take additional evidence on any issue or issues requested by the Administrative Director.

(6) Within thirty (30) days of the date the written decision is served upon the QME, the QME may file a petition for reconsideration with the Administrative Director. The petition shall be governed by Government Code section 11521 and shall set forth any legal or factual basis as to why the decision should not be confirmed.

(c) Judicial Review of the Administrative Director's decision may be had by the filing of a petition for writ of mandate pursuant to Government Code Section 11523 no later than thirty (30) days after the last day on which the Administrative Director can order reconsideration in accordance with (b)(6) of this section.

Note: Authority cited: Sections 133, 139.2, 5307.3 and 5307.4, Labor Code; and Sections 11370 *et seq.* and 11500 *et seq.*, Government Code. Reference: Section 139.2, Labor Code; and Sections 11502 *et seq.*, Government Code.

History: 1. Renumbering of former section 52 to new section 61, and amendment of subsections (c) and (d) filed 8-23-96; operative 9-22-96 (Register 96, No. 34).

2. Repealer and new section and amendment of Note filed 4-14-2000; operative 5-14-2000 (Register 2000, No. 15).

3. Amendment of section and Note filed 1-13-2009; operative 2-17-2009 (Register 2009, No. 3).

Ref.: Hanna §§ 1.12[2A][b]–[h], 22.11[1]–[16]; Herlick Handbook §§ 1.02, 14.22.

§62. Probation.

(a) A physician on probationary status from his or her licensing authority may be placed on probationary status by the Administrative Director in its discretion in accordance with Sanction Guidelines for Qualified Medical Evaluators under section 65 of Title 8 of the California Code of Regulations.

(b) A QME on probationary status may be required to report periodically to the Medical Director to ensure compliance with any conditions of probation that have been imposed by the Administrative Director. These conditions may include the completion of specific courses and training.

(c) A QME shall be deemed to have passed probation and be eligible for reappointment if he or she has complied with the conditions imposed by the Administrative Director during the probation period, and meets the requirements for reappointment in accordance with Article 5.

(d) A QME shall be deemed to have failed probation if upon completion of the probation period it is determined that he or she has not complied with the conditions imposed by the Administrative Director during the probation period, and/or has failed to meet the requirements for reappointment in accordance with Article 5.

(e) The Administrative Director shall terminate probation, which shall be equivalent to a failure to pass probation, before completion of the probation period if during the probation period it is determined that a QME has not complied with the conditions of probation.

Note: Authority cited: Sections 133, 139.2 and 5307.3, Labor Code. Reference: Sections 139.2, 4060, 4061, 4062, 4062.1, 4062.2, 4067 and 4628, Labor Code.

History: 1. Renumbering of former section 53 to new section 62, new subsection (a) and subsection relettering, and amendment of subsections (c) and (d) filed 8-23-96; operative 9-22-96 (Register 96, No. 34).

2. Amendment of subsections (a), (c) and (d) filed 4-14-2000; operative 5-14-2000 (Register 2000, No. 15).

3. Amendment of section and Note filed 1-13-2009; operative 2-17-2009 (Register 2009, No. 3).

Ref.: Hanna §§ 1.12[2A][b]–[h], 22.11[1]–[16]; Herlick Handbook §§ 1.02, 14.22.

§63. Denial of Appointment or Reappointment.

(a) Whenever the Administrative Director determines that an application for appointment or reappointment as a Qualified Medical Evaluator will be denied, the Administrative Director shall:

(1) Notify the applicant in writing of the decision to deny the application and the reasons for the denial; and

(2) Provide notice that if the applicant submits a specific, written response to the notice of denial within thirty (30) days, the Administrative Director will review the decision to deny the application, and within sixty (60) days of receipt of the response notify the applicant of the Administrative Director's final decision.

(b) If the applicant fails to submit a specific, written response to the notice of denial within thirty (30) days, the decision to deny shall become final without any further notice.

(c) If the applicant submits a specific, written response, and the Administrative Director's final decision is that the application should be denied, notice of the final decision shall be provided to the applicant by means of a statement of issues and notice of right to hearing under Chapter 5 (commencing with section 11500) of Title 2 of the Government Code.

(d) All notices and response under this section shall be made by certified mail.

Note: Authority cited: Sections 133, 139.2(f) and 5307.3, Labor Code; Section 11500 *et seq.*, Government Code. Reference: Section 139.2, Labor Code.

History: 1. New section filed 1-13-2009; operative 2-17-2009 (Register 2009, No. 3).

Ref.: Hanna §§ 1.12[2A][b]–[h], 22.11[1]–[16]; Herlick Handbook §§ 1.02, 14.22.

§65. Sanction Guidelines for Qualified Medical Evaluators.

The guidelines for determining appropriate sanctions for physicians licensed as Qualified Medical Evaluators shall be set forth in the Sanction Guidelines for Qualified Medical Evaluators as adopted by the Industrial Medical Council on October 21, 1999, and re-adopted and enforced by the Administrative Director.

[Sanction Guidelines for Qualified Medical Evaluators Not Reproduced]

Note: Authority cited: Sections 133, 139.2 and 5307.3, Labor Code. Reference: Section 139.2, Labor Code.

History: 1. New section filed 4-14-2000; operative 5-14-2000 (Register 2000, No. 15).

2. Change without regulatory effect amending section filed 10-29-2001 pursuant to section 100, title 1, California Code of Regulations (Register 2001, No. 44). Pursuant to this filing, material adopted pursuant to the Administrative Procedure Act that had previously been incorporated by reference in the California Code of Regulations was instead printed in full in the California Code of Regulations.

3. Amendment of section heading, section and Note filed 1-13-2009; operative 2-17-2009 (Register 2009, No. 3).

Ref.: Hanna §§ 1.12[2A][b]–[h], 22.11[1]–[16]; Herlick Handbook §§ 1.02, 14.22.

ARTICLE 7
Practice Parameters for the Treatment of Common Industrial Injuries [Repealed]

§70. Treatment Guideline for Low Back Problems. [Repealed]

Note: Authority cited: Section 139(e)(8), Labor Code. Reference: Section 139(e)(8) Labor Code.

History: 1. Editorial correction changing placement of article 7 heading (Register 97, No. 23).

2. New section filed 6-3-97; operative 7-3-97 (Register 97, No. 23).

3. Amendment filed 4-14-2000; operative 5-14-2000 (Register 2000, No. 15).

4. Change without regulatory effect amending section filed 7-12-2001 pursuant to section 100, title 1, California Code of Regulations (Register 2001, No. 28). Pursuant to this filing, material adopted pursuant to the Administrative Procedure Act that had previously been incorporated by reference in the California Code of Regulations was instead printed in full in the California Code of Regulations.

5. Repealer of article 7 (sections 70-77) and section filed 1-13-2009; operative 2-17-2009 (Register 2009, No. 3).

§71. Treatment Guideline for Industrial Neck Injuries. [Repealed]

Note: Authority cited: Section 139(e)(8), Labor Code. Reference: Section 139(e)(8), Labor Code.

History: 1. New section filed 7-18-97; operative 8-17-97 (Register 97, No. 29).

2. Amendment filed 4-14-2000; operative 5-14-2000 (Register 2000, No. 15).

3. Change without regulatory effect amending section filed 7-12-2001 pursuant to section 100, title 1, California Code of Regulations (Register 2001, No. 28). Pursuant to this filing, material adopted pursuant to the Administrative Procedure Act that had previously been incorporated by reference in the California Code of Regulations was instead printed in full in the California Code of Regulations.

4. Repealer filed 1-13-2009; operative 2-17-2009 (Register 2009, No. 3).

§72. Treatment Guideline for Occupational Asthma. [Repealed]

Note: Authority cited: Section 139(e)(8), Labor Code. Reference: Section 139(e)(8), Labor Code.

History: 1. New section filed 9-18-95; operative 10-18-95 (Register 95, No. 38).

2. Change without regulatory effect amending section heading and section filed 9-25-95 pursuant to section 100, title 1, California Code of Regulations (Register 95, No. 39).

3. Amendment filed 4-14-2000; operative 5-14-2000 (Register 2000, No. 15).

4. Change without regulatory effect amending section filed 7-12-2001 pursuant to section 100, title 1, California Code of Regulations (Register 2001, No. 28). Pursuant to this filing, material adopted pursuant to the Administrative Procedure Act that had previously been incorporated by reference in the California Code of Regulations was instead printed in full in the California Code of Regulations.

5. Repealer filed 1-13-2009; operative 2-17-2009 (Register 2009, No. 3).

§73. Treatment Guideline for Contact Dermatitis. [Repealed]

Note: Authority cited: Section 139(e)(8), Labor Code. Reference: Section 139(e)(8), Labor Code.

History: 1. New section filed 9-18-95; operative 10-18-95 (Register 95, No. 38).

2. Change without regulatory effect amending section heading and section filed 9-25-95 pursuant to section 100, title 1, California Code of Regulations (Register 95, No. 39).

3. Amendment filed 4-14-2000; operative 5-14-2000 (Register 2000, No. 15).

4. Change without regulatory effect amending section filed 7-12-2001 pursuant to section 100, title 1, California Code of Regulations (Register 2001, No. 28). Pursuant to this filing, material adopted pursuant to the Administrative Procedure Act that had previously been incorporated by reference in the California Code of Regulations was instead printed in full in the California Code of Regulations.

5. Repealer filed 1-13-2009; operative 2-17-2009 (Register 2009, No. 3).

§74. Treatment Guideline for Post–Traumatic Stress Disorder. [Repealed]

Note: Authority cited: Section 139(e)(8), Labor Code. Reference: Section 139 and 139.2, Labor Code.

History: 1. New section filed 1-24-97; operative 2-23-97 (Register 97, No. 4).

2. Change without regulatory effect amending section filed 7-12-2001 pursuant to section 100, title 1, California Code of Regulations (Register 2001, No. 28). Pursuant to this filing, material adopted pursuant to the Administrative Procedure Act that had previously been incorporated by reference in the California Code of Regulations was instead printed in full in the California Code of Regulations.

3. Repealer filed 1-13-2009; operative 2-17-2009 (Register 2009, No. 3).

§75. Treatment Guidelines for Shoulder Problems. [Repealed]

Note: Authority cited: Section 139(e)(8), Labor Code. Reference: Section 139(e)(8), Labor Code.

History: 1. New section filed 7-16-97; operative 8-15-97 (Register 97, No. 29).

2. Amendment filed 4-14-2000; operative 5-14-2000 (Register 2000, No. 15).

3. Change without regulatory effect amending section filed 7-12-2001 pursuant to section 100, title 1, California Code of Regulations (Register 2001, No. 28). Pursuant to this filing, material adopted pursuant to the Administrative Procedure Act that had previously been incorporated by reference in the California Code of Regulations was instead printed in full in the California Code of Regulations.

4. Repealer filed 1-13-2009; operative 2-17-2009 (Register 2009, No. 3).

§76. Treatment Guideline for Knee Problems. [Repealed]

Note: Authority cited: Section 139(e)(8), Labor Code. Reference: Section 139(e)(8), Labor Code.

History: 1. New article 7 (section 76) and section filed 5-13-97; operative 6-12-97 (Register 97, No. 20).

2. Amendment filed 4-14-2000; operative 5-14-2000 (Register 2000, No. 15).

3. Change without regulatory effect amending section filed 7-12-2001 pursuant to section 100, title 1, California Code of Regulations (Register 2001, No. 28). Pursuant to this filing, material adopted pursuant to the Administrative Procedure Act that had previously been incorporated by reference in the California Code of Regulations was instead printed in full in the California Code of Regulations.

4. Repealer filed 1-13-2009; operative 2-17-2009 (Register 2009, No. 3).

§76.5. Treatment Guideline for Elbow Problems. [Repealed]

Note: Authority cited: Section 139(e)(8), Labor Code. Reference: Section 139(e)(8), Labor Code.

History: 1. New section filed 7-17-97; operative 8-16-97 (Register 97, No. 29).

2. Amendment filed 4-14-2000; operative 5-14-2000 (Register 2000, No. 15).

3. Change without regulatory effect amending section filed 7-12-2001 pursuant to section 100, title 1, California Code of Regulations (Register 2001, No. 28). Pursuant to this filing, material adopted pursuant to the Administrative Procedure Act that had previously been incorporated by reference in the California Code of Regulations was instead printed in full in the California Code of Regulations.

4. Repealer filed 1-13-2009; operative 2-17-2009 (Register 2009, No. 3).

§77. Treatment Guideline for Problems of the Hand and Wrist. [Repealed]

Note: Authority cited: Section 139(e)(8), Labor Code. Reference: Section 139(e)(8), Labor Code.

History: 1. New section filed 7-18-97; operative 8-17-97 (Register 97, No. 29).

2. Change without regulatory effect amending section filed 7-12-2001 pursuant to section 100, title 1, California Code of Regulations (Register 2001, No. 28). Pursuant to this filing, material adopted pursuant to the Administrative Procedure Act that had previously been incorporated by reference in the California Code of Regulations was instead printed in full in the California Code of Regulations.

3. Repealer filed 1-13-2009; operative 2-17-2009 (Register 2009, No. 3).

ARTICLE 10
QME Application Forms

§100. The Application for Appointment as Qualified Medical Evaluator Form.

[QME Form 100 (Rev. 9/1/2015) Not Reproduced]

NOTE: Form is available at no charge by downloading from the web at www.dir.ca.gov/dwc/forms.html or by requesting at 1-800-794-6900.

Note: Authority cited: Sections 53, 133, 139.2 and 5307.3, Labor Code. Reference: Sections 139.2, 4060, 4061, 4062, 4062.1

and 4062.2, Labor Code; Sections 1798 *et seq.*, Civil Code; and Sections 6250 *et seq.*, Government Code.

History: 1. Renumbering of former article 10 to new article 15, new article 10 (sections 100-104) and new section filed 4-14-2000; operative 5-14-2000 (Register 2000, No. 15). For prior history see Register 94, No. 31.

2. Amendment filed 8-23-2001; operative 8-23-2001 pursuant to Government Code section 11343.4 (Register 2001, No. 34).

3. Change without regulatory effect amending section filed 5-2-2002 pursuant to section 100, title 1, California Code of Regulations (Register 2002, No. 18).

4. Change without regulatory effect amending section filed 1-27-2006 pursuant to section 100, title 1, California Code of Regulations (Register 2006, No. 4).

5. Repealer and new section and new Note filed 1-13-2009; operative 2-17-2009 (Register 2009, No. 3).

6. Repealer and new QME Form 100 filed 12-31-2012 as an emergency; operative 1-1-2013 pursuant to Government Code section 11346.1(d) (Register 2013, No. 1). A Certificate of Compliance must be transmitted to OAL by 7-1-2013 or emergency language will be repealed by operation of law on the following day.

7. Repealer and new QME Form 100 refiled 7-1-2013 as an emergency; operative 7-1-2013 (Register 2013, No. 27). A Certificate of Compliance must be transmitted to OAL by 9-30-2013 or emergency language will be repealed by operation of law on the following day.

8. Certificate of Compliance as to 7-1-2013 order transmitted to OAL 8-2-2013 and filed 9-16-2013 (Register 2013, No. 38).

9. Amendment filed 8-12-2015; operative 9-1-2015 pursuant to Government Code section 11343.4(b)(3) (Register 2015, No. 33).

Ref.: Hanna §§ 1.12[2A][b]–[h], 22.11[1]–[16]; Herlick Handbook §§ 1.02, 14.22.

§101. The Alien Application Form. [Repealed]

History: 1. New section filed 4-14-2000; operative 5-14-2000 (Register 2000, No. 15). For prior history see Register 94, No. 31.

2. Repealer filed 1-13-2009; operative 2-17-2009 (Register 2009, No. 3).

§102. The Application for QME Competency Examination Form.

[QME Form 102 (Rev. 2/2009) Not Reproduced]

NOTE: Form is available at no charge by downloading from the web at www.dir.ca.gov/dwc/forms.html or by requesting at 1-800-794-6900.

Note: Authority cited: Sections 53, 133, 139.2 and 5307.3, Labor Code. Reference: Section 139.2, Labor Code.

History: 1. New section filed 4-14-2000; operative 5-14-2000 (Register 2000, No. 15). For prior history see Register 94, No. 31.

2. Change without regulatory effect amending section filed 1-27-2006 pursuant to section 100, title 1, California Code of Regulations (Register 2006, No. 4).

3. Repealer and new section and new Note filed 1-13-2009; operative 2-17-2009 (Register 2009, No. 3).

Ref.: Hanna §§ 1.12[2A][b]–[h], 22.11[1]–[16]; Herlick Handbook §§ 1.02, 14.22.

§103. The QME Fee Assessment Form.

[QME Form 103 (Rev. 2/2009) Not Reproduced]

NOTE: Form is available at no charge by downloading from the web at www.dir.ca.gov/dwc/forms.html or by requesting at 1-800-794-6900.

Note: Authority cited: Sections 53, 133, 139.2 and 5307.3, Labor Code. Reference: Section 139.2, Labor Code.

History: 1. New section filed 4-14-2000; operative 5-14-2000 (Register 2000, No. 15). For prior history see Register 94, No. 31.

2. Change without regulatory effect amending section filed 6-27-2000 pursuant to section 100, title 1, California Code of Regulations (Register 2000, No. 26).

3. Repealer and new section and new Note filed 1-13-2009; operative 2-17-2009 (Register 2009, No. 3).

Ref.: Hanna §§ 1.12[2A][b]–[h], 22.11[1]–[16]; Herlick Handbook §§ 1.02, 14.22.

§104. The Reappointment Application as Qualified Medical Evaluator Form.

[QME Form 104 (Rev. 9/1/2015) Not Reproduced]

NOTE: Form is available at no charge by downloading from the web at www.dir.ca.gov/dwc/forms.html or by requesting at 1-800-794-6900.

Note: Authority cited: Sections 53, 133, 139.2 and 5307.3, Labor Code. Reference: Sections 139.2, 4060, 4061, 4061.5, 4062, 4062.1 and 4062.2, Labor Code; Sections 1798 et seq., Civil Code; and Sections 6250 et seq., Government Code.

History: 1. New section filed 4-14-2000; operative 5-14-2000 (Register 2000, No. 15). For prior history see Register 94, No. 31.

2. Amendment filed 9-6-2001; operative 10-6-2001 (Register 2001, No. 36).

3. Repealer and new section and new Note filed 1-13-2009; operative 2-17-2009 (Register 2009, No. 3).

4. Repealer and new Form 104 filed 9-16-2013; operative 9-16-2013 pursuant to Government Code section 11343.4(b)(3) (Register 2013, No. 38).

5. Amendment filed 8-12-2015; operative 9-1-2015 pursuant to Government Code section 11343.4(b)(3) (Register 2015, No. 33).

Ref.: Hanna §§ 1.12[2A][b]–[h], 22.11[1]–[16]; Herlick Handbook §§ 1.02, 14.22.

ARTICLE 10.5
QME Process Forms

§105. The Request for Qualified Medical Evaluator Panel — Unrepresented Form.

[QME Form 105 (Rev. 9/1/2015) Not Reproduced]

NOTE: Forms are available at no charge by downloading from the web at http://www.dir.ca.gov/dwc/forms.html or by requesting at 1-800-794-6900.

Note: Authority cited: Sections 53, 133, 139.2 and 5307.3, Labor Code. Reference: Sections 139.2, 4060, 4061, 4061.5, 4062, 4062.1, 4062.2, 4064 and 4067, Labor Code.

History: 1. New article 10.5 (sections 105-117) and new section filed 4-14-2000; operative 5-14-2000 (Register 2000, No. 15). For prior history see Register 94, No. 31.

2. Amendment of section heading, repealer and new section and new Note filed 1-13-2009; operative 2-17-2009 (Register 2009, No. 3).

3. Amendment of section heading, new QME Form 105a and amendment of informational note filed 12-31-2012 as an emergency; operative 1-1-2013 pursuant to Government Code section 11346.1(d) (Register 2013, No. 1). A Certificate of Compliance must be transmitted to OAL by 7-1-2013 or emergency language will be repealed by operation of law on the following day.

4. Amendment of section heading, new QME Form 105a and amendment of informational note refiled 7-1-2013 as an emergency; operative 7-1-2013 (Register 2013, No. 27). A Certificate of Compliance must be transmitted to OAL by 9-30-2013 or emergency language will be repealed by operation of law on the following day.

5. Certificate of Compliance as to 7-1-2013 order, including amendment of section heading and repealer and new Form 105, transmitted to OAL 8-2-2013 and filed 9-16-2013; amendments operative 9-16-2013 pursuant to Government Code section 11343.4(b)(3) (Register 2013, No. 38).

6. Change without regulatory effect amending form and explanatory Note filed 11-6-2013 pursuant to section 100, title 1, California Code of Regulations (Register 2013, No. 45).

7. Amendment filed 8-12-2015; operative 9-1-2015 pursuant to Government Code section 11343.4(b)(3) (Register 2015, No. 33).

Ref.: Hanna §§ 1.12[2A][b]–[h], 22.11[1]–[16]; Herlick Handbook § 14.22.

§106. The Request for Qualified Medical Evaluator Panel — Represented Form — for Injuries Occurring Prior to January 1, 2005.

[QME Form 106 (Rev. 9/1/2015) Not Reproduced]

NOTE: Form is available at no charge by downloading from the web at www.dir.ca.gov/dwc/forms.html or by requesting at 1-800-794-6900.

Note: Authority cited: Sections 53, 133, 139.2 and 5307.3, Labor Code. Reference: Sections 139.2, 4060, 4061, 4062, 4062.1, 4062.2, 4064 and 4067, Labor Code.

History: 1. New section filed 4-14-2000; operative 5-14-2000 (Register 2000, No. 15). For prior history see Register 94, No. 31.

2. Change without regulatory effect amending section filed 5-2-2002 pursuant to section 100, title 1, California Code of Regulations (Register 2002, No. 18).

3. Amendment of section heading, repealer and new section and new Note filed 1-13-2009; operative 2-17-2009 (Register 2009, No. 3).

4. Amendment of section heading, new QME Form 106a and amendment of informational note filed 12-31-2012 as an emergency; operative 1-1-2013 pursuant to Government Code section 11346.1(d) (Register 2013, No. 1). A Certificate of Compliance must be transmitted to OAL by 7-1-2013 or emergency language will be repealed by operation of law on the following day.

5. Amendment of section heading, new QME Form 106a and amendment of informational note refiled 7-1-2013 as an emergency; operative 7-1-2013 (Register 2013, No. 27). A Certificate of Compliance must be transmitted to OAL by 9-30-2013 or emergency language will be repealed by operation of law on the following day.

6. Certificate of Compliance as to 7-1-2013 order, including amendment of section heading and repealer and new Form 106, transmitted to OAL 8-2-2013 and filed 9-16-2013; amendments operative 9-16-2013 pursuant to Government Code section 11343.4(b)(3) (Register 2013, No. 38).

7. Amendment of section heading and section filed 8-12-2015; operative 9-1-2015 pursuant to Government Code section 11343.4(b)(3) (Register 2015, No. 33).

Ref.: Hanna §§ 1.12[2A][b]–[h], 22.11[1]–[16]; Herlick Handbook § 14.22.

§107. The Qualified Medical Evaluator Panel Selection Form.

[QME Form 107 (Rev. 2/2009) Not Reproduced]

NOTE: Form is available at no charge by downloading from the web at www.dir.ca.gov/dwc/forms.html or by requesting at 1-800-794-6900.

Note: Authority cited: Sections 53, 133, 139.2 and 5307.3, Labor Code. Reference: Sections 139.2, 4060, 4061, 4062, 4062.1, 4062.2, 4064 and 4067, Labor Code.

History: 1. New section filed 4-14-2000; operative 5-14-2000 (Register 2000, No. 15). For prior history see Register 94, No. 31.

2. Repealer and new section and new Note filed 1-13-2009; operative 2-17-2009 (Register 2009, No. 3).

Ref.: Hanna §§ 1.12[2A][b]–[h], 22.11[1]–[16]; Herlick Handbook § 14.22.

§108. The Qualified Medical Evaluator Panel Selection Instruction Form.

[QME Form 108 (Rev. 2/2009) Not Reproduced]

NOTE: Form is available at no charge by downloading from the web at www.dir.ca.gov/dwc/forms.html or by requesting at 1-800-794-6900.

Note: Authority cited: Sections 53, 133, 139.2 and 5307.3, Labor Code. Reference: Sections 139.2, 4060, 4061, 4062, 4062.1, 4062.2, 4064 and 4067, Labor Code.

History: 1. New section filed 4-14-2000; operative 5-14-2000 (Register 2000, No. 15). For prior history see Register 94, No. 31.

2. Amendment of section heading, repealer and new section and new Note filed 1-13-2009; operative 2-17-2009 (Register 2009, No. 3).

Ref.: Hanna §§ 1.12[2A][b]–[h], 22.11[1]–[16]; Herlick Handbook § 14.22.

§109. The Qualified Medical Evaluator Notice of Unavailability Form.

[QME Form 109 (Rev. 9/1/2015) Not Reproduced]

NOTE: Form is available at no charge by downloading from the web at www.dir.ca.gov/dwc/forms.html or by requesting at 1-800-794-6900.

Note: Authority cited: Sections 53, 133, 139.2 and 5307.3, Labor Code. Reference: Sections 139.2, 4060, 4061, 4062, 4062.1, 4062.2, 4064 and 4067, Labor Code.

History: 1. New section filed 4-14-2000; operative 5-14-2000 (Register 2000, No. 15). For prior history see Register 94, No. 31.

2. Amendment of section heading, repealer and new section and new Note filed 1-13-2009; operative 2-17-2009 (Register 2009, No. 3).

3. Repealer and new Form 109 filed 9-16-2013; operative 9-16-2013 pursuant to Government Code section 11343.4(b)(3) (Register 2013, No. 38).

4. Amendment filed 8-12-2015; operative 9-1-2015 pursuant to Government Code section 11343.4(b)(3) (Register 2015, No. 33).

Ref.: Hanna §§ 1.12[2A][b]–[h], 22.11[1]–[16]; Herlick Handbook § 14.22.

§110. The Appointment Notification Form.

[QME Form 110 (New 10/2013) Not Reproduced]

NOTE: Form is available at no charge by downloading from the web at www.dir.ca.gov/dwc/forms.html or by requesting at 1-800-794-6900.

Note: Authority cited: Sections 53, 133, 139.2 and 5307.3, Labor Code. Reference: Sections 139.2, 4060, 4061, 4062, 4062.1, 4062.2, 4064 and 4067, Labor Code.

History: 1. New section filed 4-14-2000; operative 5-14-2000 (Register 2000, No. 15). For prior history see Register 94, No. 31.

2. Repealer and new section and new Note filed 1-13-2009; operative 2-17-2009 (Register 2009, No. 3).

3. Repealer and new Form 110 filed 9-16-2013; operative 9-16-2013 pursuant to Government Code section 11343.4(b)(3) (Register 2013, No. 38).

Ref.: Hanna §§ 1.12[2A][b]–[h], 22.11[1]–[16]; Herlick Handbook § 14.22.

§111. The Qualified Medical Evaluator's Findings Summary Form.

[QME Form 111 (Rev. 2/2009) Not Reproduced]

NOTE: Form is available at no charge by downloading from the web at www.dir.ca.gov/dwc/forms.html or by requesting at 1-800-794-6900.

Note: Authority cited: Sections 53, 133, 139.2 and 5307.3, Labor Code. Reference: Sections 139.2, 4060, 4061, 4062, 4062.1, 4062.2, 4064, 4067 and 4660-4664, Labor Code.

History: 1. New section filed 4-14-2000; operative 5-14-2000 (Register 2000, No. 15).

2. Amendment of section heading, repealer and new section and new Note filed 1-13-2009; operative 2-17-2009 (Register 2009, No. 3).

Ref.: Hanna §§ 1.12[2A][b]–[h], 22.11[1]–[16]; Herlick Handbook § 14.22.

§112. The QME/AME Time Frame Extension Request Form.

[QME Form 112 (New 10/2013) Not Reproduced]

NOTE: Form is available at no charge by downloading from the web at www.dir.ca.gov/dwc/forms.html or by requesting at 1-800-794-6900.

Note: Authority cited: Sections 53, 133, 139.2 and 5307.3, Labor Code. Reference: Sections 139.2, 4060, 4061, 4062, 4062.1, 4062.2, 4064 and 4067, Labor Code.

History: 1. New section filed 4-14-2000; operative 5-14-2000 (Register 2000, No. 15).

2. Amendment of section heading, repealer and new section and new Note filed 1-13-2009; operative 2-17-2009 (Register 2009, No. 3).

3. Repealer and new Form 112 filed 9-16-2013; operative 9-16-2013 pursuant to Government Code section 11343.4(b)(3) (Register 2013, No. 38).

Ref.: Hanna §§ 1.12[2A][b]–[h], 22.11[1]–[16]; Herlick Handbook § 14.22.

§113. Notice of Denial of Request for Time Extension Form.

[QME Form 113 (Rev. 2/2009) Not Reproduced]

NOTE: Form is available at no charge by downloading from the web at www.dir.ca.gov/dwc/forms.html or by requesting at 1-800-794-6900.

Note: Authority cited: Sections 53, 133, 139.2 and 5307.3, Labor Code. Reference: Sections 139.2, 4060, 4061, 4062, 4062.1, 4062.2, 4064 and 4067, Labor Code.

History: 1. New section filed 4-14-2000; operative 5-14-2000 (Register 2000, No. 15).

2. Amendment of section heading, repealer and new section and new Note filed 1-13-2009; operative 2-17-2009 (Register 2009, No. 3).

Ref.: Hanna §§ 1.12[2A][b]–[h], 22.11[1]–[16]; Herlick Handbook § 14.22.

§114. The Denial of Time Extension Form. [Repealed]

Note: Authority cited: Sections 139 and 139.2, Labor Code. Reference: Sections 139.2, 4060, 4061, 4062 and 4062.5, Labor Code.

History: 1. New section filed 4-14-2000; operative 5-14-2000 (Register 2000, No. 15).

2. Repealer filed 1-13-2009; operative 2-17-2009 (Register 2009, No. 3).

§115. The Notice of Late Qualified Medical Evaluator Report Form. [Repealed]

Note: Authority cited: Sections 139 and 139.2, Labor Code. Reference: Sections 139.2, 4060, 4061, 4062 and 4062.5, Labor Code.

History: 1. New section filed 4-14-2000; operative 5-14-2000 (Register 2000, No. 15).

2. Repealer filed 1-13-2009; operative 2-17-2009 (Register 2009, No. 3).

§116. Notice of Late QME/AME Report — No Extension Requested Form.

[QME Form 116 (Rev. 2/2009) Not Reproduced]

NOTE: Form is available at no charge by downloading from the web at www.dir.ca.gov/dwc/forms.html or by requesting at 1-800-794-6900.

Note: Authority cited: Sections 53, 133, 139.2 and 5307.3, Labor Code. Reference: Sections 139.2, 4060, 4061, 4062, 4062.1, 4062.2, 4064 and 4067, Labor Code.

History: 1. New section filed 4-14-2000; operative 5-14-2000 (Register 2000, No. 15).

2. Amendment of section heading, repealer and new section and new Note filed 1-13-2009; operative 2-17-2009 (Register 2009, No. 3).

Ref.: Hanna §§ 1.12[2A][b]–[h], 22.11[1]–[16]; Herlick Handbook § 14.22.

§117. Qualified Medical Evaluator Course Evaluation Form.

[QME Form 117 (New 10/2013) Not Reproduced]

NOTE: Form is available at no charge by downloading from the web at www.dir.ca.gov/dwc/forms.html or by requesting at 1-800-794-6900.

Note: Authority cited: Sections 53, 133, 139.2 and 5307.3, Labor Code. Reference: Sections 139.2, 4060, 4061, 4062, 4062.1, 4062.2, 4064 and 4067, Labor Code.

History: 1. New section filed 4-14-2000; operative 5-14-2000 (Register 2000, No. 15).

2. Change without regulatory effect amending section filed 5-2-2002 pursuant to section 100, title 1, California Code of Regulations (Register 2002, No. 18).

3. Amendment of section heading, repealer and new section and new Note filed 1-13-2009; operative 2-17-2009 (Register 2009, No. 3).

4. Repealer and new Form 117 filed 9-16-2013; operative 9-16-2013 pursuant to Government Code section 11343.4(b)(3) (Register 2013, No. 38).

Ref.: Hanna §§ 1.12[2A][b]–[h], 22.11[1]–[16]; Herlick Handbook § 14.22.

§118. Application for Accreditation or Re–Accreditation As Education Provider.

[QME Form 118 (Rev. 2/2009) Not Reproduced]

NOTE: Form is available at no charge by downloading from the web at www.dir.ca.gov/dwc/forms.html or by requesting at 1-800-794-6900.

Note: Authority cited: Sections 53, 133, 139.2 and 5307.3, Labor Code. Reference: Sections 139.2, 4060, 4061, 4062, 4062.1, 4062.2, 4064 and 4067, Labor Code.

History: 1. New section filed 10-16-2000 as an emergency; operative 1-1-2001 (Register 2000, No. 42). A Certificate of Compliance must be transmitted to OAL by 5-1-2001 or emergency language will be repealed by operation of law on the following day.

2. New section refiled 5-2-2001 as an emergency; operative 5-2-2001 (Register 2001, No. 18). A Certificate of Compliance must be transmitted to OAL by 8-30-2001 or emergency language will be repealed by operation of law on the following day.

3. Certificate of Compliance as to 5-2-2001 order, including further amendment of section, transmitted to OAL 7-12-2001 and filed 8-23-2001 (Register 2001, No. 34).

4. Repealer and new section and new Note filed 1-13-2009; operative 2-17-2009 (Register 2009, No. 3).

Ref.: Hanna §§ 1.12[2A][b]–[h], 22.11[1]–[16]; Herlick Handbook § 14.22.

§119. Faculty Disclosure of Commercial Interest.

[QME Form 119 (Rev. 2/2009) Not Reproduced]

NOTE: Form is available at no charge by downloading from the web at www.dir.ca.gov/dwc/forms.html or by requesting at 1-800-794-6900.

Note: Authority cited: Sections 53, 133, 139.2 and 5307.3, Labor Code. Reference: Sections 139.2, 4060, 4061, 4062, 4062.1, 4062.2, 4064 and 4067, Labor Code.

History: 1. New section filed 10-16-2000 as an emergency; operative 1-1-2001 (Register 2000, No. 42). A Certificate of Compliance must be transmitted to OAL by 5-1-2001 or emergency language will be repealed by operation of law on the following day.

2. New section refiled 5-2-2001 as an emergency; operative 5-2-2001 (Register 2001, No. 18). A Certificate of Compliance must be transmitted to OAL by 8-30-2001 or emergency language will be repealed by operation of law on the following day.

3. Certificate of Compliance as to 5-2-2001 order, including further amendment of section, transmitted to OAL 7-12-2001 and filed 8-23-2001 (Register 2001, No. 34).

4. Repealer and new section and new Note filed 1-13-2009; operative 2-17-2009 (Register 2009, No. 3).

Ref.: Hanna §§ 1.12[2A][b]–[h], 22.11[1]–[16]; Herlick Handbook § 14.22.

§120. Voluntary Directive for Alternate Service of Medical–Legal Evaluation Report on Disputed Injury to Psyche.

[QME Form 120 (Rev. 2/2009) Not Reproduced]

NOTE: Form is available at no charge by downloading from the web at www.dir.ca.gov/dwc/forms.html or by requesting at 1-800-794-6900.

Note: Authority cited: Sections 53, 133, 139.2 and 5307.3, Labor Code. Reference: Sections 139.2, 4060, 4061, 4062, 4062.1, 4062.2, 4064 and 4067, Labor Code.

History: 1. New section filed 1-13-2009; operative 2-17-2009 (Register 2009, No. 3).

Ref.: Hanna §§ 1.12[2A][b]–[h], 22.11[1]–[16]; Herlick Handbook § 14.22.

§121. Declaration Regarding Protection of Mental Health Record.

[QME Form 121 (Rev. 2/2009) Not Reproduced]

NOTE: Form is available at no charge by downloading from the web at www.dir.ca.gov/dwc/forms.html or by requesting at 1-800-794-6900.

Note: Authority cited: Sections 53, 133, 139.2 and 5307.3, Labor Code. Reference: Sections 139.2, 4060, 4061, 4062, 4062.1, 4062.2, 4064 and 4067, Labor Code.

History: 1. New section filed 1-13-2009; operative 2-17-2009 (Register 2009, No. 3).

Ref.: Hanna §§ 1.12[2A][b]–[h], 22.11[1]–[16]; Herlick Handbook § 14.22.

§122. AME or QME Declaration of Service of Medical–Legal Report.

[QME Form 122 (Rev. 2/2009) Not Reproduced]

NOTE: Form is available at no charge by downloading from the web at www.dir.ca.gov/dwc/forms.html or by requesting at 1-800-794-6900.

Note: Authority cited: Sections 53, 133, 139.2 and 5307.3, Labor Code. Reference: Sections 139.2, 4060, 4061, 4062, 4062.1, 4062.2, 4064 and 4067, Labor Code.

History: 1. New section filed 1-13-2009; operative 2-17-2009 (Register 2009, No. 3).

Ref.: Hanna §§ 1.12[2A][b]–[h], 22.11[1]–[16]; Herlick Handbook § 14.22.

§123. QME/AME Conflict of Interest Disclosure and Objection or Waiver by Represented–Parties Form.

[QME Form 123 (Rev. 2/2009) Not Reproduced]

NOTE: Form is available at no charge by downloading from the web at www.dir.ca.gov/dwc/forms.html or by requesting at 1-800-794-6900.

Note: Authority cited: Sections 53, 133, 139.2 and 5307.3, Labor Code. Reference: Sections 139.2, 4060, 4061, 4062, 4062.1, 4062.2, 4064 and 4067, Labor Code.

History: 1. New section filed 1-13-2009; operative 2-17-2009 (Register 2009, No. 3).

Ref.: Hanna §§ 1.12[2A][b]–[h], 22.11[1]–[16]; Herlick Handbook § 14.22.

§124. Specified Financial Interest Attachment to QME Forms 100, 103 or 104 ("SFI Form 124").

Any physician who files a QME Form 100 (Application for Appointment), 103 (QME Fee Assessment Form) or 104 (Reappointment Application) with the Administrative Director also shall complete the QME SFI Form 124, in order to disclose specified financial interests that may affect the fairness of QME panels, and append it to the form 100, 103 or 104 being submitted when the form is filed.

[QME SFI Form 124 (Rev. 2/2009) Not Reproduced]

NOTE: Form is available at no charge by downloading from the web at www.dir.ca.gov/dwc/forms.html or by requesting at 1-800-794-6900.

Note: Authority cited: Sections 53, 133, 139.2 and 5307.3, Labor Code. Reference: Section 139.2, Labor Code.

History: 1. New section filed 1-13-2009; operative 2-17-2009 (Register 2009, No. 3).

Ref.: Hanna §§ 1.12[2A][b]–[h], 22.11[1]–[16]; Herlick Handbook § 14.22.

§125. [Reserved]

§149. Definitions. [Renumbered]

Note: Authority cited: Section 139, Labor Code. Reference: Sections 139, 139.2 and 4628, Labor Code.

History: 1. New article 4.5 and section filed 7-8-94; operative 8-8-94 (Register 94, No. 27).

2. Change without regulatory effect relocating article 4.5 heading and renumbering former section 149 to new section 49 filed 8-31-94 pursuant to section 100, title 1, California Code of Regulations (Register 94, No. 35).

§149.2. Neuromusculoskeletal Evaluation. [Renumbered]

Note: Authority cited: Sections 139 and 139.2(j), Labor Code. Reference: Sections 139, 139.2 and 4628, Labor Code.

History: 1. New section filed 7-8-94; operative 8-8-94 (Register 94, No. 27).

2. Change without regulatory effect renumbering former section 149.2 to new section 49.2 filed 8-31-94 pursuant to section 100, title 1, California Code of Regulations (Register 94, No. 35).

§149.4. Cardiovascular Evaluation. [Renumbered]

Note: Authority cited: Sections 139 and 139.2(j), Labor Code. Reference: Sections 139, 139.2 and 4628, Labor Code.

History: 1. New section filed 7-8-94; operative 8-8-94 (Register 94, No. 27).

2. Change without regulatory effect renumbering former section 149.4 to new section 49.4 filed 8-31-94 pursuant to section 100, title 1, California Code of Regulations (Register 94, No. 35).

§149.6. Pulmonary Evaluation. [Renumbered]

Note: Authority cited: Sections 139 and 139.2(j), Labor Code. Reference: Sections 139, 139.2 and 4628, Labor Code.

History: 1. New section filed 7-8-94; operative 8-8-94 (Register 94, No. 27).

2. Change without regulatory effect renumbering former section 149.6 to new section 49.6 filed 8-31-94 pursuant to section 100, title 1, California Code of Regulations (Register 94, No. 35).

§149.8. Psychiatric Evaluation. [Renumbered]

Note: Authority cited: Sections 139 and 139.2(j), Labor Code. Reference: Sections 139, 139.2 and 4628, Labor Code.

History: 1. New section filed 7-8-94; operative 8-8-94 (Register 94, No. 27).

2. Change without regulatory effect renumbering former section 149.8 to new section 49.8 filed 8-31-94 pursuant to section 100, title 1, California Code of Regulations (Register 94, No. 35).

§149.9. Other Evaluation. [Renumbered]

Note: Authority cited: Sections 139 and 139.2(j), Labor Code. Reference: Sections 139, 139.2 and 4628, Labor Code.

History: 1. New section filed 7-8-94; operative 8-8-94 (Register 94, No. 27).

2. Change without regulatory effect renumbering former section 149.9 to new section 49.9 filed 8-31-94 pursuant to section 100, title 1, California Code of Regulations (Register 94, No. 35).

ARTICLE 15
Fraudulent or Misleading Advertising

§150. Definitions.

As used in this Article:

(a) Administrative Director — means the Administrative Director of the Division of Workers' Compensation of the State of California, Department of Industrial Relations, and includes his or her designee.

(b) Advertising copy — includes any "public communication" as defined in Business and Professions Code Section 651, or any other communication of any message in any form or medium regarding the availability for professional employment of any physician, which is made by or on behalf of any physician to the general public or any substantial portion thereof.

Advertising concerning medical services regarding industrial injuries or illnesses which benefits any physician, and which is placed by any medical clinic, medical service organization or other non-physician third party shall be deemed advertising copy subject to these regulations.

(c) Medical Board — means the Medical Board of California as established in Business and Professions Code Section 2001.

(d) Medical Director — means the physician appointed pursuant to Labor Code Section 122 or such person as he or she may designate.

(e) Physician — has the meaning defined in Labor Code Section 3209.3.

(f) QME — means a Qualified Medical Evaluator as defined in Labor Code Section 139.2. **Note:** Authority cited: Sections 133, 139.4, 139.45 and 5307.3, Labor Code. Reference: Sections 139.2, 139.4 and 139.45, Labor Code.

History: 1. New article 10 and section filed 3-31-93; operative 4-30-93 (Register 93, No. 14).

2. Renumbering of article 10 to article 15 filed 4-14-2000; operative 5-14-2000 (Register 2000, No. 15).

3. New subsection (a), repealer of subsection (b), subsection relettering and amendment of Note filed 1-13-2009; operative 2-17-2009 (Register 2009, No. 3).

Ref.: Hanna §§ 1.12[2A][b]–[h], 22.11[1]–[16]; Herlick Handbook § 14.22.

§151. Filing of Documents.

Any document filed under these regulations shall be deemed filed on the date when it is received by the Administrative Director.

Note: Authority cited: Sections 133, 139.4, 139.45 and 5307.3, Labor Code. Reference: Sections 133, 139.4 and 139.45, Labor Code.

History: 1. New section filed 3-31-93; operative 4-30-93 (Register 93, No. 14).

2. Amendment of section and Note filed 1-13-2009; operative 2-17-2009 (Register 2009, No. 3).

Ref.: Hanna §§ 1.12[2A][b]–[h], 22.11[1]–[16]; Herlick Handbook § 14.22.

§152. Statement of Intent.

Nothing in these regulations is intended to alter the interpretation or application of Business and Professions Code section 651. These regulations are promulgated under the authority of Labor Code sections 139.4 and 139.45 and are intended to reflect the Administrative Director's understanding of the Legislature's intent that the Administrative Director apply a higher and independent standard, pursuant to those Sections, to physician advertising which relates to industrial injuries or illnesses.

Note: Authority cited: Sections 133, 139.4, 139.45 and 5307.3, Labor Code. Reference: Sections 28, 139.4 and 139.45, Labor Code.

History: 1. New section filed 3-31-93; operative 4-30-93 (Register 93, No. 14).

2. Amendment of section and Note filed 1-13-2009; operative 2-17-2009 (Register 2009, No. 3).

Ref.: Hanna §§ 1.12[2A][b]–[h], 22.11[1]–[16]; Herlick Handbook § 14.22.

§153. False or Misleading Advertising Copy Prohibited.

No physician subject to these regulations, or any person acting on his or her behalf or for his or her benefit, shall use, cause to be used, or allow to be used:

(a) Any advertising copy which, through endorsements, testimonials or other representations, makes or implies any guarantee, warranty, or prediction that is intended, or is likely, to create a false or unjustified expectation of favorable results concerning the outcome of the employment of the physician.

(b) Any advertising copy which by use of a firm name, trade name, fictitious business name, or other professional designation states or implies a relationship between any physician in private practice and any governmental agency or entity, with the exception that, as provided in section 154 below, a physician currently or previously certified by the Administrative Director as a Qualified Medical Evaluator may state this fact in advertising copy, a curriculum vitae or in descriptive text, only for the period of time that is true and correct.

(c) Any advertising copy which states or implies that a medical-legal report written by any physician, or group or association of physicians enjoys any special degree of credibility by any workers' compensation judge or judges.

(d) Any advertising copy which advises or recommends the securing of any medical-legal examination, or which suggests that a tactical advantage may be secured by obtaining any medical-legal evaluation.

(e) Any advertising copy which contains the phrase "Qualified Medical Evaluator" or the designation "QME" unless such phrase is used to identify individual physicians who are currently certified as QMEs by the Administrative Director in accordance with Labor Code section 139.2.

(f) Any advertising copy which contains a firm name, trade name, or fictitious business name which contains the phrases "Qualified Medical Evaluator," "Qualified Medical Examiner", "Agreed Medical Evaluator", "Agreed Medical Examiner", "Independent Medical Examiner", "Independent Medical Evaluator" or the designations "QME", "AME" or "IME."

(g) Any advertising copy which states or implies that any physician has an ongoing appointment, title or professional status as an "Agreed Medical Examiner," "Agreed Medical Evaluator", "Independent Medical Examiner," "AME," or "IME."

(h) Any advertising copy which states or implies that the physician is currently an "Agreed Medical Examiner" or "Independent Medical Examiner" in the California Workers' Compensation system.

Note: Authority cited: Sections 133, 139.4, 139.45 and 5307.3, Labor Code. Reference: Sections 28, 139.2, 139.4 and 139.45, Labor Code.

History: 1. New section filed 3-31-93; operative 4-30-93 (Register 93, No. 14).

2. Amendment of subsections (b), (e) and (f), new subsection (h) and amendment of Note filed 1-13-2009; operative 2-17-2009 (Register 2009, No. 3).

Ref.: Hanna §§ 1.12[2A][b]–[h], 22.11[1]–[16]; Herlick Handbook § 14.22.

§154. Permissible Advertising Content.

(a) A physician subject to these regulations, or any person acting on his or her behalf, may use, disseminate, or cause to be disseminated to the public, or any portion of the public, advertising copy which relates to any industrial injury or illness which accurately states:

(1) The name of each physician affiliated with or participating in the physician's practice.

(2) The address, telephone number and business hours of the office or offices.

(3) The areas of practice each physician engages in.

(4) An individual physician's appointment as a QME. A physician who is not currently certified by the Administrative Director as a Qualified Medical Evaluator may, in a curriculum vitae or descriptive text, state any periods in the past during which the physician was certified as a Qualified Medical Evaluator.

(5) A statement that the physician is Board Certified or limits his or her practice to specific fields as authorized by Business and Professions Code Section 651. Any statement of Board Certification shall include the name of the certifying board.

(6) Any languages spoken fluently by the physician or his or her staff.

(7) A description of any diagnostic or therapeutic facilities available.

(8) The availability of surgery or hospitalization on a lien basis.

(9) The usual time frame for scheduling appointments or producing medical reports.

(10) That all billings are made in compliance with the Official Medical Fee Schedule promulgated by the Administrative Director.

(11) Biographic information concerning the physician's educational background, internships and residencies, hospital affiliations, professional affiliations and professional publications.

(b) Any physician who wishes to use, disseminate, or cause to be disseminated to the public, or any portion of the public, any advertising copy which relates to any industrial injury or illness which contains any material not specified in subsection (a) above, shall apply in writing to the Administrative Director for approval before using such material. The Administrative Director shall approve all requests which do not contain material which is false or likely to mislead the public with respect to workers' compensation. No advertising copy submitted to the Council pursuant to this subsection shall be used until the Administrative Director has given his/her written approval.

Note: Authority cited: Sections 133, 139.4, 139.45 and 5307.3, Labor Code. Reference: Sections 139.2, 139.4 and 139.45, Labor Code.

History: 1. New section filed 3-31-93; operative 4-30-93 (Register 93, No. 14).

2. Amendment of subsections (a)(4), (a)(10) and (b) and amendment of Note filed 1-13-2009; operative 2-17-2009 (Register 2009, No. 3).

Ref.: Hanna §§ 1.12[2A][b]–[h], 22.11[1]–[16]; Herlick Handbook § 14.22.

§155. Filing of Complaints.

(a) Any person may file a complaint with the Medical Director, alleging that any physician is using advertising copy which violates the provisions of Business and Professions Code Section 651, or the provisions of these regulations.

(b) Complaints filed with the Medical Director shall be in writing and contain the following:

(1) The full name and address of the party filing the complaint.

(2) The full name and address of the physician against whom the complaint is made, or if the complainant is unable to identify the physician using the advertising, as much information as the complainant can provide to assist the Administrative Director in identifying the physician who used the advertisement.

(3) A copy, if available to the complaining party, of the advertising copy against which the complaint is made, or a description of the medium in which the advertising copy appeared. Such description should contain sufficient details regarding the manner and form in which the advertising copy was published to allow a copy of the advertising copy to be obtained by the Administrative Director.

(4) A detailed statement of the grounds on which the advertising copy is alleged to violate Business and Professions Code Section 651 or these regulations.

(5) All complaints filed under this section shall be filed with the Medical Director, at Division of Workers' Compensation, P.O. Box 71010, Attention: Medical Unit, Oakland, CA 94612.

(6) Nothing in these regulations shall prevent the Administrative Director or Medical Director from acting independently, and without receipt of a complaint, to initiate an investigation and issue a complaint on the Administrative Director's own motion whenever the Administrative Director or Medical Director has reason to believe that there has been a violation of Business and Professions Code section 651 or these regulations.

Note: Authority cited: Sections 133, 139.4, 139.45 and 5307.3, Labor Code. Reference: Sections 139.4 and 139.45, Labor Code.

History: 1. New section filed 3-31-93; operative 4-30-93 (Register 93, No. 14).

2. Amendment of subsections (b)(2)-(3) and (b)(5)-(6) and amendment of Note filed 1-13-2009; operative 2-17-2009 (Register 2009, No. 3).

Ref.: Hanna §§ 1.12[2A][b]–[h], 22.11[1]–[16]; Herlick Handbook § 14.22.

§156. Requests to Review Advertising Copy.

(a) Upon receipt of a complaint under Section 155 of these regulations, the Administrative Director shall serve a written notice of complaint on the physician against whom the complaint was filed. Such notice shall direct the physician to file a copy of his or her advertising with the Medical Director within 15 working days of the date on which the notice was served.

(b) The Medical Director may take such steps as he or she deems necessary to determine whether the complaint has merit.

(1) The Medical Director shall respond to the complaint within fifteen (15) working days of the Administrative Director's receipt of the physician's response and notify the complainant that the Administrative Director:

(A) will investigate the complaint; or

(B) will require additional time to ascertain whether the complaint has merit; or

(C) will refer a copy of the complaint to another agency which also has jurisdiction over the subject matter of the complaint; or

(D) will take no further action on the complaint because the Administrative Director lacks jurisdiction over the person or conduct complained of; or

(E) will take no further action on the complaint because the allegations of the complaint do not warrant further action by the Administrative Director for the reasons stated in the response.

(c) At the time of filing the advertising copy with the Medical Director, the physician shall also file an answer to the complaint, briefly setting forth the grounds on which the physician believes the copy to be in compliance with Business and Professions Code Section 651, and the provisions of these regulations. Nothing contained in the answer shall preclude the right of the physician to present further or different grounds of defense before the Administrative Director or appropriate licensing board. Upon reviewing the physician's answer, the Medical Director may dismiss or informally resolve the complaint where he or she deems such action appropriate.

(d) The Administrative Director may, without receipt of a complaint, request a physician to provide a copy of any advertising used by that physician for review. Such a request shall be made in writing, and shall be personally served on the physician.

(e) If a physician who has been appointed as a QME fails to deliver a copy of the advertising used to the Administrative Director within fifteen (15) working days of receipt of the notice, the Administrative Director may infer from the failure to comply that the advertising material used by the QME is in violation of Business and Professions Code Section 651, or these regulations. The maximum penalty that the Administrative Director may impose for a finding of violation based solely on the negative inference created by this provision shall be suspension of the physician's appointment as a Qualified Medical Evaluator for a period of six months followed by a period of probation not to exceed one year.

(f) If a non-QME physician fails to deliver a copy of the advertising used to the Administrative Director within fifteen (15) working days of receipt of the request, the Administrative Director shall refer the matter to that physician's licensing board for such proceedings as that board may deem proper.

Note: Authority cited: Sections 133, 139.4, 139.45 and 5307.3, Labor Code. Reference: Sections 139.4 and 139.45, Labor Code.

History: 1. New section filed 3-31-93; operative 4-30-93 (Register 93, No. 14).

2. Amendment of section heading, section and Note filed 1-13-2009; operative 2-17-2009 (Register 2009, No. 3).

Ref.: Hanna §§ 1.12[2A][b]–[h], 22.11[1]–[16]; Herlick Handbook § 14.22.

§157. Determinations.

(a) If, after reviewing the physician's advertising copy and the physician's answer to the complaint, the Medical Director determines that the advertising copy violates Business and Professions Code section 651, or these regulations and that the physician is currently a Qualified Medical Evaluator, the disciplinary and hearing procedures set forth in sections 60 through 65 of Title 8 of the California Code of Regulations shall apply. The Medical Director shall forward a copy of any final decision of such violations to the physician's licensing board for such proceedings as that board may deem proper.

(b) If the Medical Director determines that the physician subject to the investigation currently is not a QME, the Medical Director shall forward a copy of the preliminary determination, the complaint, and all supporting documentation to the appropriate physician's licensing board for such proceedings as that board may deem proper.

Note: Authority cited: Sections 133, 139.4, 139.45 and 5307.3, Labor Code. Reference: Sections 139.4 and 139.45, Labor Code.

History: 1. New section filed 3-31-93; operative 4-30-93 (Register 93, No. 14).

2. Amendment of subsections (a) and (b), repealer of subsections (c)-(d)(6) and amendment of Note filed 1-13-2009; operative 2-17-2009 (Register 2009, No. 3).

Ref.: Hanna §§ 1.12[2A][b]–[h], 22.11[1]–[16]; Herlick Handbook § 14.22.

§158. Penalties.

(a) A QME who is found to have violated any provision of Business and Professions Code section 651, or these regulations may have his or her QME status terminated, suspended, or placed on probation by the Administrative Director. Any probation imposed may have such conditions as the Administrative Director deems reasonable, including, but not limited to the publication of corrective advertising and the submission of future advertising copy for the Administrative Director's approval before its use.

(b) The Administrative Director shall consider the following factors in determining the appropriate penalty for a violation of Business and Professions Code section 651, or these regulations:

1. the seriousness or materiality of the misrepresentation,

2. whether the physician cooperated with the investigation,

3. whether the violation was a single event, or appeared to be part of a pattern sufficient to demonstrate a business practice,

4. whether the violator has a record of prior discipline by the Administrative Director, Medical Board, or other appropriate licensing board or authority,

5. whether the violator has a record of contempt reprimands or adjudications issued by the Workers' Compensation Appeals Board.

Note: Authority cited: Sections 133, 139.4, 139.45 and 5307.3, Labor Code. Reference: Sections 139.4 and 139.45, Labor Code.

History: 1. New section filed 3-31-93; operative 4-30-93 (Register 93, No. 14).

2. Amendment of subsections (a), (b) and (b)4. and amendment of Note filed 1-13-2009; operative 2-17-2009 (Register 2009, No. 3).

Ref.: Hanna §§ 1.12[2A][b]–[h], 22.11[1]–[16]; Herlick Handbook § 14.22.

§159. Severability.

If any portion of this chapter or the application of any part thereof to any person, individual, party, entity, or circumstance is held invalid, the remainder of the chapter and its application to any other person, individual, party, entity, or circumstance, shall not be affected thereby.

Note: Authority cited: Sections 133, 139.4, 139.45 and 5307.3, Labor Code. Reference: Sections 139.4 and 139.45, Labor Code.

History: 1. New section filed 3-31-93; operative 4-30-93 (Register 93, No. 14).

2. Amendment of Note filed 1-13-2009; operative 2-17-2009 (Register 2009, No. 3).

Ref.: Hanna §§ 1.12[2A][b]–[h], 22.11[1]–[16]; Herlick Handbook § 14.22.

CHAPTER 4.5 DIVISION OF WORKERS' COMPENSATION

SUBCHAPTER 1 ADMINISTRATIVE DIRECTOR— ADMINISTRATIVE RULES

ARTICLE 1 Payment and Conduct of Workers' Compensation Judges [Repealed]

Note: Authority cited: Sections 123, 123.5, 123.6 and 133, Labor Code. Reference: Chapters 402 and 414, Statutes of 1980.

History: 1. New Article 1 (Sections 9700-9703) filed 1-16-81; effective thirtieth day thereafter (Register 81, No. 3).

2. Repealer of Article 1 (Sections 9700-9703) filed 8-29-84; effective thirtieth day thereafter (Register 84, No. 35).

ARTICLE 1.1 Workers' Compensation Information System

§9700. Authority.

This article is adopted to implement the Workers' Compensation Information System mandated by Sections 138.6 and 138.7 of the Labor Code.

Note: Authority cited: Sections 133, 138.6 and 138.7, Labor Code. Reference: Sections 138.6 and 138.7, Labor Code.

History: 1. New article 1.1 (sections 9700-9704) and section filed 10-6-99; operative 11-5-99 (Register 99, No. 41).

Ref.: Herlick Handbook § 1.01[3][b].

§9701. Definitions.

The following definitions apply in this article:

(a) Bona Fide Statistical Research. The analysis of existing workers' compensation data for the purpose of developing or contributing to basic knowledge regarding the California workers' compensation system.

(b) California EDI Implementation Guide for First and Subsequent Reports of Injury. Contains California specific reporting requirements and information excerpted from the IAIABC EDI Implementation Guide for First, Subsequent, Acknowledgment Detail, Header & Trailer Records, Release 1, issued February 15, 2002, by the International Association of Industrial Accident Boards and Commissions. The California EDI Implementation Guide for First and Subsequent Reports of Injury is posted on the Division's Web site at http://www.dir.ca.gov/dwc/WCIS.htm, and is available from the Division of Workers' Compensation upon request.

(1) For reporting prior to November 15, 2011, use the California EDI Implementation Guide for First and Subsequent Reports of Injury, Version 2.1, dated February 2006, which is incorporated by reference.

(2) For reporting on or after November 15, 2011, but before the date of the California EDI Implementation Guide for First and Subsequent Reports of Injury, Version 3.1, dated March 27, 2018, use the California EDI Implementation Guide for First and Subsequent Reports of Injury, Version 3.0, dated November 15, 2011, which is incorporated by reference.

(3) For reporting on or after March 27, 2018, use the California EDI Implementation Guide for First and Subsequent Reports of Injury, Version 3.1, dated March 27, 2018, which is incorporated by reference.

(c) California EDI Implementation Guide for Medical Bill Payment Records. Contains the California-specific protocols and excerpts from the IAIABC EDI Implementation Guide for Medical Bill Payment Records, explains the technical design and functionality of the WCIS system, testing options for the trading partners, instructions regarding the medical billing data elements, and reporting standards and requirements. The California EDI Implementation Guide for Medical Bill Payment Records is posted on the Division's Web site at http://www.dir.ca.gov/dwc/WCIS.htm, and is available from the Division of Workers' Compensation upon request.

(1) For reporting prior to April 6, 2016, use the California EDI Implementation Guide for Medical Bill Payment Records, Version 1.1, dated November 15, 2011, which is incorporated by reference.

(2) For reporting prior to September 27, 2017, use the California EDI Implementation Guide for Medical Bill Payment Records, Version 2.0, dated April 6, 2016, which is incorporated by reference. For reporting on or after September 27, 2017, use the California EDI Implementation Guide for Medical Bill Payment Records, Version 2.0, dated September 27, 2017, which is incorporated by reference. This Guide adopts ASC (Accredited Standards Committee) X12 Implementation Acknowledgement for Health Care insurance (999) dated February 2011.

(d) California Jurisdiction Code. A California-specific code that identifies a medical procedure, service, or product that is not identified by a current HCPCS code. California

Jurisdiction Codes are either set forth and/or incorporated by reference in California Code of Regulations, title 8, section 9795, regarding reasonable fees for medical-legal expenses, section 9789.11, regarding fees for physician services rendered on or after July 1, 2004, and before January 1, 2014, sections 9789.12.1–9789.19, regarding fees for physician services rendered on or after January 1, 2014, or in California EDI Implementation Guide for Medical Bill Payment, Release 1.1.

(e) Claim. An injury as defined in Division 4 of the Labor Code, occurring on or after March 1, 2000, that has resulted in the receipt of one or more of the following by a claims administrator:

(1) Employer's Report of Occupational Injury or Illness, as required by California Code of Regulations, title 8, sections 14004-14005.

(2) Doctor's First Report of Occupational Injury or Illness, as required by California Code of Regulations, title 8, sections 14006-14007.

(3) Application for Adjudication filed with the Workers' Compensation Appeals Board under Labor Code section 5500 and California Code of Regulations, title 8, section 10408.

(4) Any information indicating that the injury requires medical treatment by a physician as defined in Labor Code section 3209.3.

(f) Claims Administrator. A self-administered insurer providing security for the payment of compensation required by Divisions 4 and 4.5 of the Labor Code, a self-administered self-insured employer, California Insurance Guarantee Association (CIGA), or a third-party claims administrator for a self-insured employer, insurer, legally uninsured employer, or joint powers authority.

(g) Claims Administrator's Agents. Any entity contracted by the claims administrator to assist in adjusting the claim(s) including third party administrators, bill reviewers, utilization review vendors, and electronic data interchange vendors.

(h) Closed Claim. A claim in which future payment of indemnity benefits and/or provision of medical benefits cannot be reasonably expected to be due.

(i) Data Elements. Information identified by data number (DN) and defined in the dictionary of the IAIABC EDI Implementation Guide, Release 1. Data elements set forth in California Code of Regulations, title 8, section 9702 must be transmitted on all claims, where applicable, as indicated in section 9702. The data elements set forth in the IAIABC EDI Implementation Guide, Release 1 that are not enumerated in section 9702 are optional and may, but need not be, submitted on any or all claims.

(j) Electronic Data Interchange. ("EDI"). A computer to computer exchange of data or information in a standardized format acceptable to the Administrative Director.

(k) Health Care Organization ("HCO"). Any entity certified as a health care organization by the Administrative Director pursuant to Labor Code sections 4600.5 and 4600.6.

(*l*) HCPCS. Acronym for the Healthcare Common Procedure Coding System.

(m) IAIABC EDI Implementation Guide, Release 1. EDI Implementation Guide for First, Subsequent, Acknowledgment Detail, Header & Trailer Records, Release 1, issued February 15, 2002, by the International Association of Industrial Accident Boards and Commissions. The IAIABC EDI Implementation Guide, Release 1, can be obtained from the IAIABC at either the IAIABC website at http://www.iaiabc.org, or the IAIABC office located at 7780 Elmwood Avenue, Suite 207, Middleton, Wisconsin 53562; Telephone: (608) 663-6355.

(n) IAIABC Workers' Compensation Medical Bill Data Reporting Implementation Guide, Release 2.0, by the International Association of Industrial Accident Boards and Commissions. The IAIABC Workers' Compensation Medical Bill Data Reporting Implementation Guide, Release 2.0, February 1, 2015 Publication can be obtained from the IAIABC at either the IAIABC website at http://www.iaiabc.org, or the IAIABC office located at 7780 Elmwood Avenue, Suite 207, Middleton, Wisconsin 53562; Telephone: (608) 663-6355.

(1) For reporting prior to the designated effective date (see subdivision (c)(1)), use the IAIABC EDI Implementation Guide for Medical Bill Payment Records, Release 1.1, July 1, 2009, which is incorporated by reference.

(2) For reporting on or after the designated effective date (see subdivision (c)(2)), use the IAIABC Workers' Compensation Medical Bill Data Reporting Implementation Guide, Release 2.0, February 1, 2015 Publication, which is incorporated by reference.

(o) Indemnity Benefits. Payments conferred, including those made by settlement, for any of the following: temporary disability indemnity, permanent disability indemnity, death benefits, vocational rehabilitation maintenance allowance, and employer-paid salary in lieu of compensation.

(p) Individually Identifiable Information. Any data concerning an injury or claim that is linked to a uniquely identifiable employee, employer, claims administrator, or any other person or entity.

(q) International Association of Industrial Accident Boards and Commissions ("IAIABC"). A professional association of workers' compensation specialists, located at 7780 Elmwood Avenue, Suite 207, Middleton, Wisconsin 53562, which is, in addition to other activities, engaged in the production and publication of EDI standards for filing workers' compensation information. Note: IAIABC asserts ownership of such EDI standards which are published in various ways and include Implementation Guides with instructions on their use, technical and business specifications and coding information to permit the transfer of data between regulatory bodies and regulated entities in a uniform and consistent manner.

(r) WCIS. The Workers' Compensation Information System established pursuant to sections 138.6 and 138.7 of the Labor Code.

Note: Authority cited: Sections 133, 138.6 and 138.7, Labor Code. Reference: Sections 138.6 and 138.7, Labor Code.

History: 1. New section filed 10-6-99; operative 11-5-99 (Register 99, No. 41).

2. Amendment filed 3-22-2006; operative 4-21-2006 (Register 2006, No. 12).

3. Amendment filed 11-15-2010; operative 11-15-2011 (Register 2010, No. 47).

4. Repealer of subsection (c)(1), subsection renumbering, amendment of newly designated subsection (c)(1), new subsection (c)(2),

amendment of subsections (d) and (n), repealer and new subsection (n)(1) and amendment of subsection (n)(2) filed 4-6-2015; operative 4-6-2016 (Register 2015, No. 15).

5. Amendment of subsection (b)(2), new subsection (b)(3) and amendment of subsections (c)(2), (m), (n), (n)(2) and (q) filed 3-27-2017; operative 9-27-2017 (Register 2017, No. 13).

Ref.: Herlick Handbook § 1.01[3][b].

§9702. Electronic Data Reporting.

(a) Each claims administrator shall transmit data elements, by electronic data interchange in the manner set forth in the California EDI Implementation Guide for First and Subsequent Reports of Injury and the California EDI Implementation Guide for Medical Bill Payment Records, to the WCIS by the dates specified in this section. Each claims administrator shall, at a minimum, provide complete, valid, accurate data for the data elements set forth in this section. The data elements required in subdivisions (b), (c), (d) and (e) are taken from California EDI Implementation Guide for First and Subsequent Reports of Injury and the California EDI Implementation Guide for Medical Bill Payment Records. Claims administrators shall only transmit the data elements that are set forth in the California EDI Implementation Guide for First and Subsequent Reports of Injury and the California EDI Implementation Guide for Medical Bill Payment Records. Each transmission of data elements shall include appropriate header and trailer records as set forth in the California EDI Implementation Guide for First and Subsequent Reports of Injury and the California EDI Implementation Guide for Medical Bill Payment Records.

(b) Each claims administrator shall submit to the WCIS on each claim, within ten (10) business days of knowledge of the claim, each of the following data elements known to the claims administrator:

Data Element Name	*DN*
ACCIDENT DESCRIPTION/CAUSE	38
CAUSE OF INJURY CODE	37
CLAIM ADMINISTRATOR ADDRESS LINE 1	10
CLAIM ADMINISTRATOR ADDRESS LINE 2	11
CLAIM ADMINISTRATOR CITY	12
CLAIM ADMINISTRATOR CLAIM NUMBER	15
CLAIM ADMINISTRATOR FEIN	8
CLAIM ADMINISTRATOR NAME	9
CLAIM ADMINISTRATOR POSTAL CODE	14
CLAIM ADMINISTRATOR STATE	13
CLASS CODE(3)	59
DATE DISABILITY BEGAN	56
DATE LAST DAY WORKED	65
DATE OF HIRE(1)	61
DATE OF INJURY	31
DATE OF RETURN TO WORK	68
DATE REPORTED TO CLAIM ADMINISTRATOR	41
DATE REPORTED TO EMPLOYER	40
EMPLOYEE ADDRESS LINE 1(1)	46
EMPLOYEE ADDRESS LINE 2(1)	47
EMPLOYEE CITY(1)	48
EMPLOYEE DATE OF BIRTH	52
EMPLOYEE DATE OF DEATH	57
EMPLOYEE FIRST NAME	44
EMPLOYEE LAST NAME	43
EMPLOYEE MIDDLE INITIAL(1)	45
EMPLOYEE PHONE(1)	51
EMPLOYEE POSTAL CODE(1)	50
EMPLOYEE STATE(1)	49
EMPLOYER ADDRESS LINE 1	19
EMPLOYER ADDRESS LINE 2	20
EMPLOYER CITY	21
EMPLOYER FEIN	16
EMPLOYER NAME	18
EMPLOYER POSTAL CODE	23
EMPLOYER STATE	22
EMPLOYMENT STATUS CODE(1)	58
GENDER CODE	53
INDUSTRY CODE	25
INITIAL TREATMENT CODE	39
INSURED REPORT NUMBER	26
INSURER FEIN	6
INSURER NAME	7
JURISDICTION	4
MAINTENANCE TYPE CODE	2
MAINTENANCE TYPE CODE DATE	3
MARITAL STATUS CODE(2)	54
NATURE OF INJURY CODE	35
NUMBER OF DEPENDENTS(2)	55
OCCUPATION DESCRIPTION	60
PART OF BODY INJURED CODE	36
POLICY EFFECTIVE DATE	29
POLICY EXPIRATION DATE	30
POLICY NUMBER	28
POSTAL CODE OF INJURY SITE	33
SALARY CONTINUED INDICATOR	67
SELF INSURED INDICATOR	24
SOCIAL SECURITY NUMBER(4)	42
TIME OF INJURY	32
WAGE(1)	62
WAGE PERIOD(1)	63

(1) Required only when provided to the claims administrator.

(2) Death Cases Only.

(3) Required for insured claims only; optional for self-insured claims.

(4) If the Social Security Number (DN 42) is not known, use a string of eight zeros followed by a six.

Data elements omitted under this subsection because they were not known by the claims administrator shall be submitted within sixty (60) days from the date of the first report under this subsection.

(c) Each transmission of data elements listed under subdivisions (b), (d), (e), (f), or (g) of this section shall also include the following elements for data linkage:

Data Element Name	*DN*
AGENCY/JURISDICTION CLAIM NUMBER(2) (3)	5
CLAIM ADMINISTRATOR CLAIM NUMBER(4)	15
CLAIM ADMINISTRATOR FEIN(8)	8
DATE OF INJURY(5)	31
EMPLOYEE DATE OF BIRTH(6)	52
EMPLOYEE FIRST NAME(7)	44
EMPLOYEE FEIN(7)	16
INSURER FEIN(4)	6
JURISDICTION(1)	4

Data Element Name	DN
MAINTENANCE TYPE CODE[1]	2
MAINTENANCE TYPE CODE DATE[1]	3
TIME OF INJURY[9]	32
TRANSACTION SET ID[1]	1

[1] Jurisdiction (DN 4), Maintenance Type Code (DN 2), Maintenance Type Code Date (DN 3), and Transaction Set ID (DN 1) are required for transmissions under subdivisions (b), (d), (f), and (g).

[2] The Agency/Jurisdiction Claim Number (DN 5) will be provided by WCIS upon acceptance of the first report under subdivision (b).

[3] The Agency/Jurisdiction Claim Number (DN 5) is required on all transmissions under subdivision (b), except for original, denied and acquired reports. The Agency/Jurisdiction Claim Number (DN 5) is required on all transmissions under subdivisions (d), (e), (f) and (g).

[4] The Insurer FEIN (DN 6) and Claim Administrator Claim Number (DN 15) are required on all transmissions under subdivisions (b), (d), (e), (f) and (g).

[5] The Date of Injury (DN 31) is required on all transmissions under subdivisions (b), (d) and (g), except acquired and cancel first report transmissions under subdivision (b).

[6] The Employee Date of Birth (DN 52) is required on all first report transmissions under subdivision (b), except cancel first report transmissions under subdivision (b).

[7] The Employer FEIN (DN 16) and Employee First Name (DN 44) are required on all first report transmissions under subdivision (b) except for transmissions to cancel a first report.

[8] The Claims Administrator FEIN (DN 8) is required on all transmissions under subdivisions (b), (d), (e), (f) and (g).

[9] The Time of Injury (DN 32) is required on all non-cumulative trauma first report transmissions except acquired transmissions and denied, changed and corrected transmissions for claims that have been previously submitted as acquired under subdivision (b) with a Date of Injury (DN 31) on or after the implementation date of the California EDI Implementation Guide for First and Subsequent Reports of Injury, Version 3.1.

(d) Each claims administrator shall submit to the WCIS within fifteen (15) business days the following data elements, whenever indemnity benefits of a particular type and amount are started, changed, suspended, restarted, stopped, delayed, or denied, or when a claim is closed, or when the claims administrator is notified of a change in employee representation. Submissions under this subsection are required only for claims with a date of injury on or after July 1, 2000, and shall not include data on routine payments made during the course of an uninterrupted period of indemnity benefits.

Data Element Name	DN
BENEFIT ADJUSTMENT CODE	92
BENEFIT ADJUSTMENT START DATE	94
BENEFIT ADJUSTMENT WEEKLY AMOUNT	93
CLAIM ADMINISTRATOR POSTAL CODE	14
CLAIM STATUS	73
CLAIM TYPE	74
DATE DISABILITY BEGAN	56
DATE OF MAXIMUM MEDICAL IMPROVEMENT	70
DATE OF REPRESENTATION	76
DATE OF RETURN/RELEASE TO WORK	72
EMPLOYEE DATE OF DEATH	57
INSURED REPORT NUMBER	26
LATE REASON CODE	77
NUMBER OF BENEFIT ADJUSTMENTS	80
NUMBER OF DEATH DEPENDENT/ PAYEE RELATIONSHIPS	82
NUMBER OF DEPENDENTS	55
NUMBER OF PAID TO DATE/ REDUCED EARNINGS/ RECOVERIES	81
NUMBER OF PAYMENTS/ ADJUSTMENTS	79
NUMBER OF PERMANENT IMPAIRMENTS	78
PAID TO DATE/REDUCED EARNINGS/ RECOVERIES AMOUNT	96
PAID TO DATE/REDUCED EARNINGS/ RECOVERIES CODE	95
PAYMENT/ADJUSTMENT CODE	85
PAYMENT/ADJUSTMENT DAYS PAID	91
PAYMENT/ADJUSTMENT END DATE	89
PAYMENT/ADJUSTMENT PAID TO DATE	86
PAYMENT/ADJUSTMENT START DATE	88
PAYMENT/ADJUSTMENT WEEKLY AMOUNT	87
PAYMENT/ADJUSTMENT WEEKS PAID	90
PERMANENT IMPAIRMENT BODY PART CODE[1] [2]	83
PERMANENT IMPAIRMENT PERCENTAGE[2]	84
RETURN TO WORK QUALIFIER	71
SALARY CONTINUED INDICATOR	67
WAGE	62
WAGE PERIOD	63

[1] May use Code 90 (Multiple Body Parts) to reflect combined rating for any/all impairments.

[2] Use actual permanent disability rating at the time of initial payment of permanent disability benefits. For compromise and release cases and stipulated settlements, use permanent disability estimate as reported to the appropriate rating organization established under Insurance Code § 11750, et seq.

(e) Claims administrators handling one hundred and fifty (150) or more total claims per year shall submit to the WCIS on each claim the following data elements for all medical services for which the claims administrator has received a billing or other report of provided medical services. The California EDI Implementation Guide for Medical Bill Payment Records sets forth the specific California reporting requirements.

Data Element Name	DN
ACKNOWLEDGMENT TRANSACTION SET ID	0110
ADA PROCEDURE BILLED CODE	0719
ADA PROCEDURE PAID CODE	0722
ADMISSION DATE	0513
ADMISSION HOUR	0622
ADMISSION TYPE CODE	0577
ADMITTING DIAGNOSIS CODE	0535
APPLICATION ACKNOWLEDGMENT	

Data Element Name	DN
CODE	0111
BILL ADJUSTMENT AMOUNT	0545
BILL ADJUSTMENT GROUP CODE	0543
BILL ADJUSTMENT REASON CODE	0544
BILL ADJUSTMENT UNITS	0546
BILL FREQUENCY TYPE CODE	0505
BILL SUBMISSION REASON CODE	0508
BILLED DRG CODE	0548
BILLING FORMAT CODE	0503
BILLING PROVIDER CITY	0540
BILLING PROVIDER COUNTRY CODE	0569
BILLING PROVIDER FEIN	0629
BILLING PROVIDER FIRST NAME	0529
BILLING PROVIDER LAST/GROUP NAME	0528
BILLING PROVIDER NATIONAL PROVIDER ID	0634
BILLING PROVIDER POSTAL CODE	0542
BILLING PROVIDER PRIMARY ADDRESS	0538
BILLING PROVIDER PRIMARY SPECIALTY CODE	0537
BILLING PROVIDER SECONDARY ADDRESS	0539
BILLING PROVIDER STATE CODE	0541
BILLING PROVIDER STATE LICENSE NUMBER	0630
BILLING PROVIDER UNIQUE BILL IDENTIFICATION NUMBER	0523
BILLING TYPE CODE	0502
CLAIM ADMINISTRATOR CLAIM NUMBER	0015
CLAIM ADMINISTRATOR FEIN	0187
CLAIM ADMINISTRATOR MAILING POSTAL CODE	0014
CLAIM ADMINISTRATOR NAME	0188
COMPOUND DRUG INDICATOR	0762
CONDITION CODE	0556
CONTRACT LINE TYPE CODE	0741
CONTRACT TYPE CODE	0515
DATE INSURER PAID BILL	0512
DATE INSURER RECEIVED BILL	0511
DATE OF BILL	0510
DATE OF INJURY	0031
DATE PROCESSED	0108
DATE TRANSMISSION SENT	0100
DAYS/UNITS BILLED	0554
DAYS/UNITS CODE	0553
DAY(S)/UNIT(S) PAID	0580
DIAGNOSIS CODE	0522
DIAGNOSIS POINTER	0557
DISCHARGE DATE	0514
DISCHARGE HOUR	0623
DISPENSE AS WRITTEN CODE	0562
DRUG NAME	0563
DRUGS/SUPPLIES BILLED AMOUNT	0572
DRUGS/SUPPLIES DISPENSING FEE	0579
DRUGS/SUPPLIES NUMBER OF DAYS	0571
DRUGS/SUPPLIES QUANTITY DISPENSED	0570
ELEMENT ERROR NUMBER	0116
ELEMENT NUMBER	0115
EMPLOYEE FIRST NAME	0044
EMPLOYEE LAST NAME	0043
EMPLOYEE MAILING CITY	0048
EMPLOYEE MAILING POSTAL CODE	0050
EMPLOYEE MIDDLE NAME/INITIAL	0045
EMPLOYEE SOCIAL SECURITY NUMBER	0042
EMPLOYER FEIN	0016
EMPLOYER NAME	0018
FACILITY CITY	0686
FACILITY CODE	0504
FACILITY COUNTRY CODE	0689
FACILITY NAME	0678
FACILITY NATIONAL PROVIDER ID	0682
FACILITY POSTAL CODE	0688
FACILITY PRIMARY ADDRESS	0684
FACILITY SECONDARY ADDRESS	0685
FACILITY STATE CODE	0687
FACILITY STATE LICENSE NUMBER	0680
HCPCS LINE PROCEDURE BILLED CODE	0714
HCPCS LINE PROCEDURE PAID CODE	0726
HCPCS MODIFIER BILLED CODE	0717
HCPCS MODIFIER PAID CODE	0727
HIPPS RATE CODE	0625
INSURER FEIN	0006
INSURER NAME	0007
INSURER POSTAL CODE	0616
JURISDICTION CLAIM NUMBER	0005
JURISDICTION MODIFIER BILLED CODE	0718
JURISDICTION MODIFIER PAID CODE	0730
JURISDICTION PROCEDURE BILLED CODE	0715
JURISDICTION PROCEDURE PAID CODE	0729
JURISDICTION TRACKING NUMBER	0743
LINE ITEM PRIOR ACTUAL AMOUNT PAID	0761
LINE NUMBER	0547
LUMP SUM PAYMENT SETTLEMENT CODE	0293
MANAGED CARE ORGANIZATION FEIN	0704
MANAGED CARE ORGANIZATION IDENTIFICATION NUMBER	0208
MANAGED CARE ORGANIZATION NAME	0209
NDC BILLED CODE	0721
NDC PAID CODE	0728
ORIGINATOR TRANSACTION IDENTIFICATION BATCH CONTROL NUMBER	0532
ORIGINAL TRANSMISSION DATE	0102
ORIGINAL TRANSMISSION TIME	0103
OTHER PROCEDURE CODE	0736
OUTPATIENT REASON FOR VISIT CODE	0520
PAID DRG CODE	0549
PLACE OF SERVICE BILL CODE	0555
PLACE OF SERVICE LINE CODE	0600
PRESCRIPTION DATE(S) RANGE	0527
PRESCRIPTION LINE DATE	0604
PRESCRIPTION LINE NUMBER	0561
PRESENT ON ADMISSION INDICATOR	0533
PRINCIPAL DIAGNOSIS CODE	0521
PRINCIPAL PROCEDURE CODE	0525
PRINCIPLE PROCEDURE DATE	0550
PRIOR ACTUAL AMOUNT PAID	0760
PROCEDURE DATE	0524
PROCEDURE DESCRIPTION	0551
PROVIDER AGREEMENT CODE	0507

Data Element Name	*DN*
PROVIDER AGREEMENT LINE CODE	0742
RECEIVER ID	0099
REFERRING PROVIDER FIRST NAME	0691
REFERRING PROVIDER LAST/GROUP NAME	0690
REFERRING PROVIDER NATIONAL PROVIDER ID	0699
RENDERING BILL PROVIDER FIRST NAME	0639
RENDERING BILL PROVIDER LAST/ GROUP NAME	0638
RENDERING BILL PROVIDER NATIONAL PROVIDER ID	0647
RENDERING BILL PROVIDER PRIMARY SPECIALTY CODE	0651
RENDERING BILL PROVIDER STATE LICENSE NUMBER	0643
RENDERING LINE PROVIDER NATIONAL PROVIDER ID	0592
RENDERING LINE PROVIDER FIRST NAME	0587
RENDERING LINE PROVIDER LAST/ GROUP NAME	0589
RENDERING LINE PROVIDER PRIMARY SPECIALTY CODE	0595
RENDERING LINE PROVIDER STATE LICENSE NUMBER	0599
REPORTING PERIOD	0615
REVENUE BILLED CODE	0559
REVENUE PAID CODE	0576
SENDER ID	0098
SERVICE ADJUSTMENT AMOUNT	0733
SERVICE ADJUSTMENT GROUP CODE	0731
SERVICE ADJUSTMENT REASON CODE	0732
SERVICE ADJUSTMENT UNITS	0734
SERVICE BILL DATE(S) RANGE	0509
SERVICE LINE DATE(S) RANGE	0605
SUPERVISING PROVIDER FIRST NAME	0659
SUPERVISING PROVIDER LAST/ GROUP NAME	0658
SUPERVISING PROVIDER NATIONAL PROVIDER ID	0667
SUPERVISING PROVIDER PRIMARY SPECIALTY CODE	0671
TEST/PRODUCTION INDICATOR	0104
TIME PROCESSED	0109
TIME TRANSMISSION SENT	0101
TOTAL AMOUNT PAID PER BILL	0516
TOTAL AMOUNT PAID PER LINE	0574
TOTAL CHARGE PER BILL	0501
TOTAL CHARGE PER LINE	0552
TRANSACTION TRACKING NUMBER	0266
UNIQUE BILL ID NUMBER	0500

(1) Each claims administrator shall submit all medical bills data including interpreter bills within ninety (90) calendar days of the medical bill payment or the date of the final determination that payment for billed medical services will be denied.

(2) Each claims administrator shall submit all medical lien lump sum payments or settlements following the filing of a lien claim for the payment of such medical services pursuant to Labor Code sections 4903 and 4903.1 within ninety (90) calendar days of the medical lien lump sum payment or settlement.

(3) Data transmission shall follow the requirements set forth in IAIABC Workers' Compensation Medical Bill Data Reporting Implementation Guide, Release 2.0, February 1, 2015 Publication. California Specific requirements are included in the California EDI Implementation Guide for Medical Bill payment Records Version 2.0, dated the designated effective date (see Section 9701(c)(2)).

(f)(1) Notwithstanding the requirement in Subsection (b) to submit data elements omitted from the first report within 60 days from the date of transmission of the first report, when a claims administrator becomes aware of an error, the claims administrator shall transmit the corrected data to WCIS within 60 calendar days from the date of transmission of the error acknowledgment.

(2) Notwithstanding the requirement in Subsection (b) to submit data elements omitted from the first report within 60 days from the date of transmission of the first report, when a claims administrator becomes aware of a need to update data elements previously transmitted, or learns of information that was previously omitted, the claims administrator shall transmit the updated or omitted data to WCIS no later than the next submission of data for the affected claim.

(g) No later than January 31 of every year, claims administrators shall report for each claim the total paid in any payment category in the previous calendar year by submitting the following data elements:

Data Element Name	*DN*
PAID TO DATE/REDUCED EARNINGS/ RECOVERIES AMOUNT	96
PAID TO DATE/REDUCED EARNINGS/ RECOVERIES CODE	95
PAYMENT/ADJUSTMENT CODE	85
PAYMENT/ADJUSTMENT END DATE	89
PAYMENT/ADJUSTMENT DAYS PAID	91
PAYMENT/ADJUSTMENT PAID TO DATE	86
PAYMENT/ADJUSTMENT START DATE	88
PAYMENT/ADJUSTMENT WEEKLY AMOUNT	87
PAYMENT/ADJUSTMENT WEEKS PAID	90

(h) Final reports (MTC = FN) are required only for claims where indemnity benefits are paid or claims where no benefits are paid. For medical-only claims or claims with only non-indemnity benefit payments, the final report may be reported under this section or on the annual report (MTC = AN) with Claim Status (DN0073) = "closed."

(i)(1) A claims administrator's obligation to submit copies of benefit notices to the Administrative Director pursuant to Labor Code section 138.4 is satisfied upon written determination by the Administrative Director that the claims administrator has demonstrated the capability to submit complete, valid, and accurate data as required under subdivision (d) and continued compliance with that subsection.

(2) Reserved.

(3) On and after September 22, 2006, a claims administrator's obligation to submit an Annual Report of Inventory pursuant to California Code of Regulations, title 8, section 10104 is satisfied upon determination by the

Administrative Director that the claims administrator has demonstrated the capability to submit complete, valid, and accurate data as required under subdivisions (b), (d), (e), and (g), and continued compliance with those subsections.

(j) The data submitted pursuant to this section shall not have any application to, nor be considered in, nor be admissible into, evidence in any personal injury or wrongful death action, except as between an employee and the employee's employer. Nothing in this subdivision shall be construed to expand access to information held in the WCIS beyond that authorized in California Code of Regulations, title 8, section 9703 and Labor Code section 138.7.

(k) Each claims administrator required to submit data under this section shall submit to the Administrative Director an EDI Trading Partner Profile at least thirty days prior to its first transmission of EDI data. Each claims administrator shall advise the Administrative Director of any subsequent changes and/or corrections made to the information provided in the EDI Trading Partner Profile by filing a corrected copy of the EDI Trading Partner Profile with the Administrative Director.

(*l*)(1) The Administrative Director may grant a claims administrator either a partial or total variance in reporting all or part of the data elements required under this section upon a documented showing that compliance with the reporting deadlines would cause undue hardship to the claims administrator.

(2) "Undue hardship" shall be determined based upon a review of the documentation submitted by the claims administrator. The documentation shall include:

(A) A statement explaining why the claims administrator is unable to transmit required data elements to the WCIS.

(B) The claims administrator's estimated expenses necessary to meet the reporting requirements of this section.

(C) The reporting cost per claim if transmitted directly by the claims administrator and the total cost per claim if reported by a vendor.

(D) Submission of a plan documenting the means by which the claims administrator will ensure full compliance with the data reporting within six months from the date of the request.

(3) Any variance granted by the Administrative Director under this subdivision shall be set forth in writing and shall be for a period of six (6) months.

(4) The variance period for reporting data elements under this subdivision may be extended for additional six (6) month period if the claims administrator resubmits a written request for an extension of the variance.

(5) Upon expiration of the variance period, a claims administrator granted a variance shall submit to the WCIS all data elements that were required to be submitted under this section during the variance period except for data elements that were not known to the claims administrator, the claims administrator's agents, or not captured on the claims administrator's electronic data systems. The data shall be submitted in an electronic format acceptable to the Division.

Note: Authority cited: Sections 133, 138.4, 138.6 and 138.7, Labor Code. Reference: Sections 138.4, 138.6 and 138.7, Labor Code.

History: 1. New section filed 10-6-99; operative 11-5-99 (Register 99, No. 41).

2. Amendment filed 3-22-2006; operative 4-21-2006 (Register 2006, No. 12).

3. Amendment filed 11-15-2010; operative 11-15-2011 (Register 2010, No. 47).

4. Repealer of subsections (a)(1)-(3), amendment of subsection (e) and new subsections (e)(1)-(3) and (*l*)(1)-(5) filed 4-6-2015; operative 4-6-2016 (Register 2015, No. 15).

5. Amendment of subsections (b)–(e) and (e)(3), redesignation and amendment of subsection (f) as new subsection (f)(1), new subsection (f)(2) and amendment of subsections (g)–(h) filed 3-27-2017; operative 9-27-2017 (Register 2017, No. 13).

Ref.: Herlick Handbook § 1.01[3][b].

§9703. Access to Individually Identifiable Information.

(a) No person shall have access to individually identifiable data held in the WCIS except as provided in this section and subdivision (c) of section 138.7 of the Labor Code.

(b) The Division of Workers' Compensation may obtain and use individually identifiable information for the following purposes:

(1) To create and maintain the WCIS, including the selection of claims to survey in order to obtain information not available from the data elements provided by claims administrators.

(2) To help select claims administrators for audits under section 129 of the Labor Code.

(3) To report the promptness with which claims administrators make payments.

(4) To electronically import names, addresses, and other information into Division of Workers' Compensation case files which would otherwise have to be key entered by agency staff.

(5) To conduct research related to the workers' compensation system for the purpose of carrying out the duties of the Division of Workers' Compensation or the Administrative Director.

(c) The following agencies may obtain individually identifiable information from the WCIS, in the manner set forth in a memorandum of understanding between the Administrative Director and the agency, for the purposes specified:

(1) The Division of Occupational Safety and Health may use individually identifiable information to help select employers for health and safety consultations and inspections.

(2) The Division of Labor Statistics and Research may use individually identifiable information to carry out its research and reporting responsibilities under Labor Code sections 150 and 156.

(3) The Department of Health Services may use individually identifiable information to carry out its occupational health and occupational disease prevention responsibilities under section 105175 of the Health and Safety Code.

(d) Upon written request to the Administrative Director, researchers employed by or under contract to the Commission on Health and Safety and Workers' Compensation (CHSWC) may obtain individually identifiable information from the WCIS, in the manner set forth in a memorandum of understanding between the Administrative Director, the commission, and the person or entity conducting research, for the purpose of bona fide statistical research.

(1) Any request from the CHSWC for individually identifiable information under this subdivision shall include the identity of the person or entity conducting the research, the purpose of the research, the research protocol, the need for individually identifiable WCIS data, and an anticipated completion date for the research.

(2) Researchers under contract to the CHSWC seeking individually identifiable WCIS data under this subdivision shall also submit to the Administrative Director written approval of the research protocol by an Institutional Review Board in the same manner as required under subdivision (e). If the researcher under contract to the CHSWC is the University of California or a non profit educational institution, the researcher shall comply with the provisions of Civil Code section 1789.24 subdivision (t).

(3) Individually identifiable information obtained under this subdivision shall not be disclosed to the members of the CHSWC.

(4) No individually identifiable information obtained by researchers under this subdivision may be disclosed to any other person or entity, public or private, for a use other than that research project for which the information was obtained.

(5) Researchers obtaining individually identifiable information under this subdivision shall notify the Administrative Director when the research has been completed. Except as required by researchers subject to subdivision (f), within 30 days thereafter, the CHSWC shall present evidence to the Administrative Director that the data collected has been modified in a manner so that the subjects cannot be identified, directly or through identifiers linked to the subjects.

(e) Individually identifiable information may be provided to other persons or public or private entities for the purpose of bona fide statistical research which does not divulge individually identifiable information concerning any employee, employer, claims administrator, or any other person or entity. Any request for individually identifiable information for this purpose shall include the identity of the requester, the purpose of the research, the methods of research, and the need for individually identifiable WCIS data. The requester shall also submit written approval of the research protocol by an Institutional Review Board, under Title 45, Code of Federal Regulations, Part 46, Subpart A. "Approval" means a determination by the Institutional Review Board that the research protocol was reviewed and provides sufficient safeguards to ensure the confidentiality of individually identifiable information. Any agreement to permit use of the data shall be in writing between the requester and the Administrative Director. Note: The Division shall make available upon request a list of Institutional Review Boards known to the Division that have the authority to grant the required approval and that expressed willingness to review research proposals under this section.

(f) The University of California or any non profit educational institution conducting scientific research must comply with the provisions of Civil Code section 1798.24 subdivision (t).

(g) Each agreement or memorandum of understanding entered concerning the use of individually identifiable information by any agency, entity, or person shall specify the methods to be used to protect the information from unlawful disclosure, and shall include a warning to the receiving party that it is unlawful for any person who has received individually identifiable information from the Division of Workers' Compensation under this section to provide the information to any person who is not entitled to it under this section and Labor Code § 138.7.

(h) Nothing in this section shall be construed to exempt from disclosure any public record contained in an individual's file once an Application for Adjudication has been filed with the Workers' Compensation Appeals Board. This includes any data from an individual's file that are converted to or stored in an electronic format for the purpose of case processing and tracking.

(i) Nothing in this section shall be construed to exempt from disclosure WCIS data in a format that does not contain individually identifiable information.

Note: Authority cited: Sections 127, 133, 138.4, 138.6 and 138.7, Labor Code. Reference: Sections 129, 138.4, 138.6 and 138.7, Labor Code; and Section 1798.24, Civil Code.

History: 1. New section filed 10-6-99; operative 11-5-99 (Register 99, No. 41).

2. Amendment filed 3-22-2006, operative 4-21-2006 (Register 2006, No. 12).

Ref.: Herlick Handbook § 1.01[3][b].

§9704. WCIS Advisory Committee.

(a) The Administrative Director shall maintain a Workers' Compensation Information System Advisory Committee, which shall include, but not be limited to, representatives of claims administrators (including self-insured employers, insurers, and third party administrators), insured employers, organized labor, attorneys, physicians as defined in Labor Code § 3209.3, vocational rehabilitation counselors, academic researchers, the Department of Insurance statistical agent, and appropriate legislative committees and state agencies with jurisdiction over workers' compensation, occupational health, and related areas, including the Commission on Health and Safety and Workers' Compensation and the Employment Development Department.

(b) The advisory committee shall meet at least annually on the call of the Administrative Director, and may provide advice on all aspects of WCIS. The Administrative Director, or his or her designee, shall present to the advisory committee any plan to collect survey data, including any expanded collection of the data elements specified in subdivision (d) of section 9702.

Note: Authority cited: Sections 133 and 138.6, Labor Code. Reference: Sections 138.6 and 138.7, Labor Code.

History: 1. New section filed 10-6-99; operative 11-5-99 (Register 99, No. 41).

Ref.: Herlick Handbook § 1.01[3][b].

ARTICLE 1.3
Public Disability Accommodations

§9708.1. Definitions.

(a) Auxiliary aids: services or devices that enable persons with impaired sensory, manual, or speaking skills to have an equal opportunity to participate in, and enjoy the benefits of, programs or activities.

(b) Braille: written text for use by the blind.

(c) Computer-Aided Realtime Translation (CART): a form of captioning in which spoken words are translated onto a computer screen as the words are spoken.

(d) Disability: any mental or physical disability or medical condition as defined in California Government Code section 12926 *et seq.*, California Civil Code section 51 *et seq.*, the Americans with Disabilities Act of 1990 (42 U.S.C. § 12101 *et seq.*), or other applicable state and federal law.

(e) Disability Accommodation: actions that result in services, programs or activities being readily accessible to and useable by an individual with a disability. Reasonable disability accommodations that may be provided include physical equipment such as wheelchair ramps or other accommodations for physical access and the use of auxiliary aids and services, such as, but not limited to, assistive listening devices, texts in Braille or large print, audio recordings, or Computer Aided Realtime Translation (CART) reporters. Reasonable disability accommodations may also include reasonable modification of policies and procedures.

(f) Disability Accommodation Request: a written or oral request for an accommodation that is needed for a disability.

(g) Disability Coordinator: An individual who handles disability accommodation issues for the public on behalf of the Division of Workers' Compensation.

(h) Division of Workers' Compensation ("Division"): The Division of the Department of Industrial Relations overseeing the state's workers' compensation system. The Division includes its headquarters, administrative offices, the district offices servicing workers' compensation cases and includes other offices and locations used by the Division when conducting business, including but not limited to, the holding of public hearings.

(i) Individual with a Disability: an individual seeking to access or participate in the Division's services, programs or activities who has a physical or mental impairment that limits one or more major life activities, or has a record of such impairment, or is regarded as having such an impairment, as covered by California Government Code section 12926 *et seq.*, California Civil Code section 51 *et seq.*, the Americans with Disabilities Act of 1990 (42 U.S.C. § 12101 *et seq.*), or other applicable state and federal law.

(j) Requestor: a member of the public, a representative, relative or friend of a member of the public, or any other participant who requests disability accommodation on behalf of himself, herself, or another individual with a disability to use or participate in a program, activity or service of the Division.

(k) Statewide Disability Coordinator: The individual who handles disability accommodation issues for the public statewide on behalf of the Division of Workers' Compensation.

Note: Authority: Sections 111(a), 133, 138.2 and 5307.3, Labor Code; and Section 11138 Government Code. Reference: Sections 51, 54, 54.1 and 54.8, Civil Code; Sections 11135 and 11351(c), Government Code; and 42 USC Sections 12102, 12111, 12112, 12113, 12131 and 12132.

History: 1. New article 1.3 (sections 9708.1–9708.6) and section filed 1-19-2012; operative 2-18-2012 (Register 2012, No. 3).

Ref.: Herlick Handbook § 1.01[3][a], [b].

§9708.2. Disability Accommodations Request Process.

(a) The Division will provide reasonable accommodations to individuals with disabilities to promote equal access to and equal participation in the Division's programs, activities and services.

(b) A request for a disability accommodation to participate in the Division's programs, activities, or services may be made in writing on an optional disability accommodation request form, or orally to a Disability Coordinator. If the request concerns activities, programs or services provided at a Division district office, then the request should be directed to the Disability Coordinator located in each district office. If the request concerns other Division activities, programs or services, then the request should be directed to the Division's Statewide Disability Coordinator.

(c) Written notice of how to request a disability accommodation shall be posted and made available to the public.

(d) Disability accommodation requests shall include a statement regarding the limitation or impairment necessitating the accommodation; what accommodation is requested; how the requested accommodation would mitigate the impact of the disability or impairment in accessing the program; and the location, date and time the accommodation is needed.

(e) Disability accommodation requests shall not address substantive issues involved in a legal proceeding.

(f) Additional information, including medical documentation, may be requested by the Division as support for the accommodation request.

(g) In general, requests should be made with as much notice as possible. If the request is made less than five days before the date it is needed, the Division will provide a reasonable accommodation by that date unless it is unreasonable to do so.

(h) Upon submitting a request, the requestor must enter an interactive process to assist in determining what, if any, reasonable accommodation may be provided. The interactive process includes providing additional information and timely correspondence with the Division as needed to address the accommodation request.

Note: Authority: Sections 111(a), 133 and 5307.3, Labor Code; and Section 11138, Government Code. Reference: Section 11138, Government Code; Sections 51, 54, 54.1, 54.8, 4450, 4451 and 4452, Civil Code; Sections 11135 and 11351(c), Government Code; and 42 USC Sections 12101, 12102, 12111, 12112, 12113, 12131, 12132 and 12133.

History: 1. New section filed 1-19-2012; operative 2-18-2012 (Register 2012, No. 3).

Ref.: Herlick Handbook § 1.01[3][a], [b].

§9708.3. Confidentiality.

Information concerning a disability accommodation request will be kept confidential to the extent possible, unless confidentiality is waived by the individual with a disability or disclosure is required by law. Confidential information may be disclosed to other Division staff involved in the accommodation process to the extent necessary.

Note: Authority: Sections 111(a), 133 and 5307.3, Labor Code; and Section 11138, Government Code. Reference: Section 123.6(a), Labor Code; Sections 51, 54 and 54.1, Civil Code; Sections 11135 and 11351(c), Government Code; and 42 USC Sections 12101, 12112 and 12132.

History: 1. New section filed 1-19-2012; operative 2-18-2012 (Register 2012, No. 3).

Ref.: Herlick Handbook § 1.01[3][a], [b].

§9708.4. Disability Accommodation Requests in Division of Workers' Compensation Hearings.

(a) Disability accommodations requests are considered to be non-substantive requests that are separate from the merits of a legal case.

(b) Disability accommodation requests should be raised with and handled by a Disability Coordinator. If an immediate need for a disability accommodation arises during the course of a hearing and is more expeditiously handled by the hearing officer or the workers' compensation administrative law judge, the request for an accommodation may be made directly to the hearing officer or the workers' compensation administrative law judge.

(c) Disability accommodation requests are permitted communications. Only impermissible *ex parte* communications shall be disclosed to the other parties.

Note: Authority: Sections 111(a), 133 and 5307.3, Labor Code; and Section 11138, Government Code. Reference: Section 123.6(a), Labor Code; Sections 51, 54 and 54.1, Civil Code; Sections 11135 and 11351(c), Government Code; and 42 USC Sections 12101 and 12132.

History: 1. New section filed 1-19-2012; operative 2-18-2012 (Register 2012, No. 3).

Ref.: Herlick Handbook § 1.01[3][a], [b].

§9708.5. Decision-Making Process.

(a) Each disability accommodation request shall be considered on a case-by-case basis.

(b) In determining whether to grant a request for disability accommodation and what disability accommodation may be provided, the Division shall consider, California Civil Code section 51 *et seq.*, the provisions of the Americans with Disabilities Act of 1990, and other applicable state and federal laws.

(c) For each disability accommodation request, the Division shall, either:

(1) Issue a decision to provide the requested disability accommodation in whole or in part, or to provide a reasonable alternative accommodation; or

(2) Issue a decision denying the request for a disability accommodation.

(d) The Division will make a decision on an accommodation request before the date the requested accommodation is needed.

(e) If the Division is informed that the provided accommodation is not effective, the Division will seek to provide an effective alternative reasonable accommodation.

(f) Unless otherwise specified, the disability accommodation is provided only for the specific appearance or proceeding for which the accommodation was requested.

(g) A request for a disability accommodation may be denied if it is determined that:

(1) The individual who would receive the disability accommodation is not legally entitled to a disability accommodation; or

(2) The requestor has failed to satisfy the requirements for requesting a disability accommodation, including failing to engage in a good faith interactive process; or

(3) The requested disability accommodation would create an undue financial and administrative burden; or

(4) The requested disability accommodation would fundamentally alter the nature of the service, program, or activity provided by the Division; or

(5) The requested disability accommodation is unreasonable, including requesting an accommodation that is not within the Division's jurisdiction to grant under the law.

(h) The decision to deny a disability accommodation shall be issued by the Administrative Director or the designee of the Administrative Director.

(i) A denial of a disability accommodation shall be in writing and shall set forth the reasons for denial and sent to the requestor. A Disability Coordinator may also verbally inform the requestor of the denial.

(j) If the Division denies a requested disability accommodation, the Division shall seek to provide a reasonable alternative disability accommodation, unless a reasonable accommodation is not available or any provision under subdivision (g) of this section is met.

Note: Authority: Sections 111(a), 133 and 5307.3, Labor Code; and Section 11138, Government Code. Reference: Sections 51, 54 and 54.1, Civil Code; Sections 11135 and 11351(c), Government Code; and 42 USC Sections 12101, 12102, 12111, 12113, 12131, 12132 and 12133.

History: 1. New section filed 1-19-2012; operative 2-18-2012 (Register 2012, No. 3).

Ref.: Herlick Handbook § 1.01[3][a], [b].

§9708.6. Appeal Procedure.

(a) A requestor may seek review of an accommodation decision within 15 calendar days of the date the accommodation decision is received.

(b) A requestor seeking review of an accommodation decision shall submit a request to the Division's Statewide Disability Coordinator setting forth the disability accommodation requested, the accommodation decision to be reviewed, and the reasons for review, with any relevant documentation provided.

(c) The Division's Administrative Director or a designee shall issue a decision within 30 calendar days from the date the request for review is received.

(d) If circumstances require a more expedited review, a request to expedite the review process shall be submitted to the Division's Statewide Disability Coordinator along with the appeal requirements under section (b) within five calendar days of the date the accommodation decision was received and before any pending proceeding is scheduled for which the accommodation is requested. The request shall include a detailed explanation of the justification for an expedited review, the time frame requested, and the reasons for the appeal, with any relevant documentation provided. The Division will address the appeal and issue a decision no later than 15 calendar days from the date the requested for expedited review was received.

Note: Authority: Sections 111(a), 133 and 5307.3, Labor Code; and Section 11138, Government Code. Reference: Sections 51, 54 and 54.1, Civil Code; Sections 11135 and 11351(c), Government Code; and 42 USC Sections 12101, 12132 and 12133.

History: 1. New section filed 1-19-2012; operative 2-18-2012 (Register 2012, No. 3).

Ref.: Herlick Handbook § 1.01[3][a], [b].

ARTICLE 1.5
Receipt of Salary by Workers' Compensation Administrative Law Judge

§9710. Authority.

The rules and regulations contained in Article 1.5 are adopted pursuant to the authority contained in Sections 123, 123.5(a) and 133 of the California Labor Code.

Note: Authority cited: Sections 123, 123.5(a) and 133, Labor Code. Reference: Sections 123.5(a) and 5313, Labor Code.

History: 1. New Article 1.5 (Sections 9710-9715) filed 1-16-81; effective thirtieth day thereafter (Register 81, No. 3).

2. Amendment of article heading, section and Note filed 1-12-99; operative 2-11-99 (Register 99, No. 3).

Ref.: Herlick Handbook § 1.01[3][b].

§9711. Operative Date.

The provisions of this Article shall first apply to cases submitted after January 1, 1981, and the affidavit shall first be required for the April 1981 pay period. For the purposes of this Article, all cases submitted prior to January 1, 1981 shall be deemed to have been submitted on January 2, 1981.

Note: Authority cited: Sections 123, 123.5(a) and 133, Labor Code. Reference: Sections 123.5(a) and 5313, Labor Code.

History: 1. New Note filed 1-12-99; operative 2-11-99 (Register 99, No. 3).

Ref.: Herlick Handbook § 1.01[3][b].

§9712. Definitions.

For the purposes of this Article and Section 123.5(a) of the Labor Code, the following definitions shall apply:

(a) "Salary" shall include ordinary pay, but shall not include sick leave pay, industrial disability leave or non-industrial disability insurance substantiated by a physician's report.

(b) "Cause" shall mean a cause of action arising out of the substantive rights, liabilities and duties provided for in Sections 132(a) and 139.5, and in Divisions 4 and 4.5 of the Labor Code which is pending before a Workers' Compensation Administrative Law Judge for decision. "Cause" shall not include Compromise and Release agreements, Stipulations with Request for Award, or petitions and motions which have been filed ex parte and are not part of a submission ordered by a Workers' Compensation Administrative Law Judge.

(c) "Pending and Undetermined" means that the Workers' Compensation Administrative Law Judge's decision has not been filed in the record.

(d) "Submitted" means the closing of the record for the receipt of further evidence or argument.

Note: Authority cited: Sections 123, 123.5(a) and 133, Labor Code. Reference: Sections 123.5(a) and 5313, Labor Code.

History: 1. Amendment of section and new Note filed 1-12-99; operative 2-11-99 (Register 99, No. 3).

Ref.: Herlick Handbook § 1.01[3][b].

§9713. Receipt of Salary.

Note: *See Executive Order N-63-20 (2019 CA EO 63-20), issued in response to the COVID-19 pandemic, which extends certain deadlines related to the filing of Workers' Compensation decisions.*

A Workers' Compensation Administrative Law Judge may not receive his or her salary while any cause before the Workers' Compensation Administrative Law Judge remains pending and undetermined for ninety (90) days after it has been submitted for decision.

Note: Authority cited: Sections 123, 123.5(a) and 133, Labor Code. Reference: Sections 123.5(a) and 5313, Labor Code.

History: 1. Amendment of section and new Note filed 1-12-99; operative 2-11-99 (Register 99, No. 3).

2. Governor Newsom issued Executive Order N-63-20 (2019 CA EO 63-20), dated May 7, 2020, which extended certain deadlines related to the filing of Workers' Compensation decisions, due to the COVID-19 pandemic.

Ref.: Herlick Handbook § 1.01[3][b].

§9714. Procedures for Compliance With Labor Code Section 123.5(a).

Note: *See Executive Order N-63-20 (2019 CA EO 63-20), issued in response to the COVID-19 pandemic, which extends certain deadlines related to the filing of Workers' Compensation decisions.*

(a) In order to receive his or her salary for each pay period, at some time before 5:00 p.m. on the last working day of each State payroll period, the Workers' Compensation Administrative Law Judge shall submit to the Division of Workers' Compensation an affidavit based upon information and belief in the form prescribed by Section 9714.5, and executed under penalty of perjury, declaring that no cause submitted before him or her remains pending and undetermined for a period of ninety (90) days or more.

(b) When a Workers' Compensation Administrative Law Judge who receives salary by automatic direct deposit does not timely submit the affidavit required by subsection (a), he or she shall, before 5:00 p.m. on the next working day following the direct deposit of salary into his or her account, deliver to the Presiding Workers' Compensation Administrative Law Judge of the district office to which the judge is assigned a money order or cashier's check for the amount of salary automatically deposited.

Note: Authority cited: Section 133, Labor Code. Reference: Sections 123.5(a) and 5313, Labor Code.

History: 1. Amendment of section heading and section and new Note filed 1-12-99; operative 2-11-99 (Register 99, No. 3).

2. Amendment of subsection (a) and Note filed 5-23-2001; operative 6-22-2001 (Register 2001, No. 21).

3. Governor Newsom issued Executive Order N-63-20 (2019 CA EO 63-20), dated May 7, 2020, which extended certain deadlines related to the filing of Workers' Compensation decisions, due to the COVID-19 pandemic.

Ref.: Herlick Handbook § 1.01[3][b].

§9714.5. Affidavit.

Note: *See Executive Order N-63-20 (2019 CA EO 63-20), issued in response to the COVID-19 pandemic, which extends certain deadlines related to the filing of Workers' Compensation decisions.*

Department of Industrial Relations
Division of Workers' Compensation
Workers' Compensation Appeals Board

AFFIDAVIT
(Labor Code Section 123.5(a))

I, __________, (Name) Workers' Compensation Administrative Law Judge in the __________ (City) office of the Division of Workers' Compensation/Workers' Compensation Appeals Board, Department of Industrial Relations, State of California, declare that I have made a reasonable and diligent inquiry concerning those matters submitted to me, and based on information and belief, state that no cause remains pending and undetermined that has been submitted to me for the period of ninety (90) days prior to the first day of __________, 20____. (Date) (Year)

Executed on __________ (Date) at __________ (City), California. I declare under penalty of perjury that the foregoing is true and correct.

____
(Signature)
Workers' Compensation Administrative Law Judge

Note: Authority cited: Section 133, Labor Code. Reference: Sections 123.5(a) and 5313, Labor Code.

History: 1. Amendment filed 1-12-99; operative 2-11-99 (Register 99, No. 3).

2. Amendment of section and new Note filed 5-23-2001; operative 6-22-2001 (Register 2001, No. 21).

3. Governor Newsom issued Executive Order N-63-20 (2019 CA EO 63-20), dated May 7, 2020, which extended certain deadlines related to the filing of Workers' Compensation decisions, due to the COVID-19 pandemic.

Ref.: Herlick Handbook § 1.01[3][b].

§9715. Procedures for Submitting a Cause for Decision.

Minutes of Hearing must be prepared at the conclusion of each hearing and filed in the record. Workers' Compensation Administrative Law Judges are to follow the provisions of Rules of Practice and Procedure Section 10566. Each set of minutes must include a disposition which includes the time and action, if any, required for submissions.

Thereafter, any change in or modification of the disposition must be served on all parties forthwith, together with the statement of the reasons for the change of disposition.

A hearing has not been concluded if the disposition includes an order taking off calendar or an order of continuance for further hearing with or without notice. Continuances and further hearings are governed by Rules of Practice and Procedure Sections 10548 and 10560.

Note: Authority cited: Sections 123, 123.5(a) and 133, Labor Code. Reference: Sections 123.5(a) and 5313, Labor Code.

History: 1. Amendment of first paragraph and new Note filed 1-12-99; operative 2-11-99 (Register 99, No. 3).

Ref.: Herlick Handbook § 1.01[3][b].

ARTICLE 1.6
Ethical Standards of Workers' Compensation Administrative Law Judges; Enforcement of Standards

§9720.1. Authority.

The rules and regulations contained in Article 1.6 are adopted pursuant to the authority contained in Sections 123.6, 133, and 5307.3 of the Labor Code. This article is designed to enforce the highest ethical standards among workers' compensation administrative law judges and to provide all parties with an independent, impartial investigation into allegations of ethics violations by workers' compensation administrative law judges.

Note: Authority cited: Sections 123.6, 133 and 5307.3, Labor Code. Reference: Sections 111 and 123.6, Labor Code.

History: 1. New article 1.6 and section filed 11-30-95; operative 12-1-95. Submitted to OAL for printing only pursuant to Government Code section 11351 (Register 95, No. 48).

2. Amendment of article heading and section filed 8-25-2008; operative 9-24-2008 (Register 2008, No. 35).

Ref.: Herlick Handbook § 1.01[3][b].

§9720.2. Definitions.

For purposes of this Article and Section 123.6 of the Labor Code, the following definitions shall apply:

(a) "Code of Judicial Ethics" shall mean the Code of Judicial Ethics adopted by the Supreme Court pursuant to subdivision (m) of Section 18 of Article VI of the California Constitution and any subsequent revision thereof.

(b) "Committee" shall mean the Workers' Compensation Ethics Advisory Committee specified in Section 9722 of these regulations.

(c) "Complaint" shall mean a statement alleging facts that, if true, might constitute an ethics violation.

(d) "Ethics violation" shall mean any conduct of a workers' compensation administrative law judge that is contrary to the Code of Judicial Ethics or to the other rules of conduct that apply to workers' compensation administrative law judges.

(e) "Financial interest" shall mean a legal or equitable interest of either more than one per cent (1%) or a fair market value in excess of two thousand dollars ($2,000). Ownership in a mutual fund or other common investment fund that holds securities is not a "financial interest" in those securities unless the judge participates in the management of the fund.

(f) "Gift" means any payment or furnishing of value to the extent that consideration of equal or greater value is not given and includes a rebate or discount in the price of anything of value unless the rebate or discount is made in the regular course of business to members of the public without regard to official status. Any person who claims that a payment is not a gift by reason of the giving of consideration has the burden of proving that the consideration received is of equal or greater value. The term "gift" does not include:

(1) Informational material such as books, reports, pamphlets, calendars, periodicals, cassettes and discs, or free or reduced-price admission, tuition, or registration, for informational conferences or seminars. No payment for travel or reimbursement for any expenses shall be deemed "informational material."

(2) Gifts which are not used and which, within 30 days after receipt, are returned to the donor or delivered to a charitable organization without being claimed as a charitable contribution for tax purposes.

(3) Gifts from a judge's spouse, fiancée, child, parent, grandparent, grandchild, brother, sister, parent-in-law, brother-in-law, sister-in-law, nephew, niece, aunt, uncle, or first cousin or the spouse of any such person; provided that a gift from any such person shall be considered a gift if the donor is acting as an agent or intermediary for any person not covered by this paragraph.

(4) Campaign contributions required to be reported under Chapter 4 (commencing with Section 84100) of Title 9 of the Government Code.

(5) Gifts of comestible items of nominal value that are not directed to a particular judge, such as holiday baskets of candy or fruit delivered to a District office of the Division, and placed in public areas for consumption by members of the public.

(6) Any devise, inheritance, or other transfer to the judge occurring as a result of death or distribution from an irrevocable trust.

(7) Personalized plaques and trophies with an individual value of less than the amount specified from time to time in Government Code § 82028 (which at the time of this amendment is two hundred fifty dollars ($ 250).

(8) Admission to events and refreshments and similar non-cash nominal benefits provided to a judge during the entire event at which the judge gives a speech, participates in a panel or seminar, or provides a similar service, and payments, advances, or reimbursements for actual transportation and any reasonably necessary lodging and subsistence provided directly in connection with the speech, panel, seminar, or service, provided that the lodging and subsistence expenses are limited to the day immediately preceding, the day of, and the day immediately following the speech, panel participation or seminar, and the travel is within the United States.

(9) Complimentary admission to events and refreshments and similar non-cash nominal benefits, at legal educational events at which the judge is not a speaker or participant in a panel, if:

A. the educational event is open to the public who wish to purchase admission;

B. continuing legal education credits are available for attorneys who attend; and

C. the free admission is offered to all workers' compensation administrative law judges;

"Complimentary admission to events" does not include admission to non-educational functions, such as golf tournaments, excursions, picnics, and dances. "Refreshments" does not include meals other than meals served contemporaneously with an educational presentation, and is limited to those refreshments offered to all who pay admission to the event.

(g) "Honorarium" shall mean any payment made in consideration for any speech given, article published, or attendance at any public or private conference, convention, meeting, social event, meal, or like gathering.

(1) "Honorarium" does not include earned income for personal services which are customarily provided in connection with the practice of a bona fide business, trade, or profession, such as teaching or writing for a publisher.

(2) For purposes of this article, "teaching" includes presentations to impart educational information to students in bona fide educational institutions, to associations or groups of judges, and to presentations of the State Bar of California or a section of the State Bar of California. An individual is presumed to be engaged in the bona fide profession of teaching in any of the following circumstances:

(A) The individual receives payment for teaching students at a bona fide educational institution.

(B) The individual receives payment for teaching students enrolled in an examination preparation program, such as a bar examination review course.

(C) The individual receives payment for teaching or making a presentation or participating in a panel presentation at an educational program offered by an association or group of judges, or at an educational program of the State Bar of California or of a section of the State Bar of California.

(h) "Judge" shall mean a worker's compensation administrative law judge and presiding workers' compensation administrative law judge employed by the Administrative Director and supervised by the Court Administrator pursuant to Section 123.5 of the Labor Code. The term shall also include Vocational Rehabilitation Consultants, Regional Managers (Associate Chief Judges) the Chief Judge, the Court Administrator, the Administrative Director, pro tem administrative law judges, and the Administrative Director's designees, but only while they are exercising judicial or quasi-judicial powers. The term does not include Information and Assistance Officers, Workers' Compensation Compliance Officers (Auditors), nor Disability Evaluation Specialists.

(i) "Previously earned compensation" shall mean legal fees and other compensation to which a workers' compensation administrative law judge may be entitled arising out of the practice of law, engaged in before the judge was appointed to be a judge. Previously earned compensation includes compensation to which the judge was contingently entitled as of the time of appointment, but which became fixed in amount after appointment.

(j) "Spouse" shall include "domestic partner".

(k) "Third degree of relationship" shall mean the following persons: great-grandparent, grandparent, parent, uncle, aunt, brother, sister, child, grandchild, great-grandchild, nephew, and niece.

Note: Authority cited: Sections 123.6, 133 and 5307.3, Labor Code. Reference: Sections 111 and 123.6, Labor Code.

History: 1. New section filed 11-30-95; operative 12-1-95. Submitted to OAL for printing only pursuant to Government Code section 11351 (Register 95, No. 48).

2. Amendment filed 8-25-2008; operative 9-24-2008 (Register 2008, No. 35).

Ref.: Herlick Handbook § 1.01[3][b].

§9721.1. Code of Judicial Ethics.

Every workers' compensation administrative law judge shall abide by the Code of Judicial Ethics.

Note: Authority cited: Sections 123.6, 133 and 5307.3, Labor Code. Reference: Sections 111 and 123.6, Labor Code.

History: 1. New section filed 11-30-95; operative 12-1-95. Submitted to OAL for printing only pursuant to Government Code section 11351 (Register 95, No. 48).

2. Amendment of section heading and section filed 8-25-2008; operative 9-24-2008 (Register 2008, No. 35).

Ref.: Herlick Handbook § 1.01[3][b].

§9721.2. Gifts, Honoraria and Travel.

(a) No workers' compensation administrative law judge shall accept any gift or favor, the acceptance of which is prohibited by the Code of Judicial Ethics, or the transmission of which is prohibited by the Rules of Professional Conduct of the State Bar of California.

(b) No workers' compensation administrative law judge shall accept gifts from any single source in any calendar year with a total value of more than the greater of three hundred ninety dollars ($390) and the amount specified for that year in regulations of the Fair Political Practices Commission interpreting Government Code § 89503 (currently Title 2, Regulation § 18940.2). This section shall not be construed to authorize the receipt of gifts that would otherwise be prohibited by the Code of Judicial Ethics, Government Code section 19990, the Political Reform Act of 1974 and any amendment thereto, the Rules of Professional Conduct of the State Bar of California, or any other provision of law.

(c) The limitation of subdivision (b) shall not apply to or limit the following:

(1) Payments, advances, or reimbursements for travel and related lodging and subsistence described in subdivision (d).

(2) Wedding gifts and gifts exchanged between individuals on birthdays, holidays and other similar occasions, provided that the gifts exchanged are not substantially disproportionate in value.

(3) A gift from any person whose pre-existing relationship with a judge would disqualify the judge under the Code of Judicial Ethics from hearing a case involving that person.

(d) Payments, advances, or reimbursements, for travel, including actual transportation and related lodging and subsistence which is reasonably related to a judicial or governmental purpose, or to an issue of state, national, or international public policy, are excluded from the limits prescribed by subdivision (b) if any of the following apply:

(1) The travel is provided by a government, a governmental agency or authority, a foreign government, a bona fide public or private educational institution, as defined in Section 203 of the Revenue and Taxation Code, a nonprofit organization which is exempt from taxation under Section 501(c)(3) of the Internal Revenue Code, or by a person domiciled outside the United States who substantially satisfies the requirements for tax exempt status under Section 501(c)(3) of the Internal Revenue Code.

(2) The travel is provided by the California State Bar or a section of the California State Bar, a state bar association, or professional association of judges in connection with testimony before a governmental body or attendance at any professional function hosted by the bar, bar association or professional association of judges, and the lodging and subsistence expenses are limited to the day immediately preceding, the day of, and the day immediately following the professional function.

(e) Payments, advances, and reimbursements for travel not described in either subdivision (c) of this Section or subdivision (f)(8) of Section 9720.2 are subject to the limit in subdivision (b).

(f) No workers' compensation administrative law judge shall accept any honorarium unless allowed in writing by the Court Administrator, if either:

(1) the cost of the honorarium is significantly paid for by attorneys who practice before the Workers' Compensation Appeals Board; or

(2) the judge would be required to report the receipt of income or gifts from the source of payment for the honorarium on the judge's statement of economic interests

(g) This section does not apply to any honorarium that is not used and within 30 days after receipt, is either returned to the donor or delivered to the Controller for deposit in the General Fund without being claimed as a deduction from income for tax purposes.

(h) The Court Administrator shall enforce the prohibitions of this section.

(i) Judges may not accept honoraria or travel allowed by the Court Administrator, and not otherwise prohibited by this section in connection with any public or private conference, convention, meeting, social event, or like gathering, the cost of which is significantly paid for by attorneys who practice before the board, unless the Court Administrator, or his or her designee, has provided prior approval in writing to the workers' compensation administrative law judge allowing him or her to accept the payments. This section shall not be construed to authorize the acceptance of an honorarium, as defined by Government Code section 89501, the acceptance of which is prohibited by Government Code section 89502.

(j) Honoraria to give a speech, participate in a panel or seminar, or provide a similar service, are allowed within the meaning of Labor Code section 123.6 where the event is sponsored by one of the following:

A professional association of judges, the State Bar of California, a section of the State Bar of California, a government, a governmental agency or authority, a foreign government, a state, national or local bar association not comprised primarily of either defense or applicant workers' compensation attorneys, a foreign bar association, an international service organization, a bona fide public or private educational institution as defined in Section 203 of the Revenue and Taxation Code, a nonprofit organization which is exempt from taxation under Section 501(c)(3) of the Internal Revenue Code, or by a person domiciled outside the United States who substantially satisfies the requirements for tax exempt status under Section 501(c)(3) of the Internal Revenue Code.

(k) Upon request to the Court Administrator by a judge, the Court Administrator may approve honoraria and travel reimbursement to give a speech, participate in a panel or seminar, or provide a similar service, where the event is sponsored by a person or entity not listed in subdivision (j) of this section.

(*l*) Payment, provision, or reimbursement for travel in connection with a judge's speech, participation in a panel or seminar, or provision of a similar service, if the event is sponsored by a professional association of judges, the State Bar of California, or a section of the State Bar of California, a government, a governmental agency or authority, a foreign government, a foreign bar association, a bona fide public or private educational institution as defined in Section 203 of the Revenue and Taxation Code, a nonprofit organization which is exempt from taxation under Section 501(c)(3) of the Internal Revenue Code, or by a person domiciled outside the United States who substantially satisfies the requirements for tax exempt status under Section 501(c)(3) of the Internal Revenue Code, is allowed within the meaning of Labor Code section 123.6 for actual transportation and any reasonably necessary lodging and subsistence provided directly in connection with the speech, panel, seminar, or service, provided that the lodging and subsistence expenses are limited to the day immediately preceding, the day of, and the day immediately following the speech, panel participation or seminar, and the travel is within the United States.

(m) Payment, provision, or reimbursement for a judge's travel, including actual transportation and related lodging and subsistence, that is reasonably related to a legislative or governmental purpose, or to an issue of state, national, or international public policy, that is provided by a government, a governmental agency or authority, a foreign government, a bona fide public or private educational institution as defined in Section 203 of the Revenue and Taxation Code, a nonprofit organization which is exempt from taxation under Section 501(c)(3) of the Internal Revenue Code, or by a person domiciled outside the United States who substantially satisfies the requirements for tax exempt status under Section 501(c)(3) of the Internal Revenue Code, is allowed within the meaning of Labor Code section 123.6, and may also be accepted when prior approval of the Court Administrator is not required.

(n) Upon approval by the Court Administrator, payment, provision, or reimbursement for a judge's travel in connection with a speech, participation in a panel or seminar, or provision of a similar service, if the event is sponsored by, or if the payment or reimbursement is to be made by, an association or group of attorneys who practice before the appeals board, will be allowed for the following:

Refreshments and similar non-cash nominal benefits provided to a judge during the entire event at which the judge gives a speech, participates in a panel or seminar, or provides a similar service, actual transportation and any reasonably necessary lodging and subsistence provided directly in connection with the speech, panel, seminar, or service. Reasonably necessary subsistence is limited to meals and beverages served contemporaneously with a breakfast, dinner, or luncheon speech, panel participation or seminar, and to meals consumed while traveling to or from the activity, limited to the days of necessary travel.

(o) When prior approval of the Court Administrator is not required, payment or reimbursement for travel in connection with a speech, participation in a panel or seminar, or provision of a similar service, if the event is sponsored by a professional association of judges, the State Bar of California, or a section of the State Bar of California, a government, a governmental agency or authority, a foreign government, a foreign bar association, an international service organization, a bona fide public or private educational institution as defined in Section 203 of the Revenue and Taxation Code, a nonprofit organization which is exempt from taxation under Section 501(c)(3) of the Internal Revenue Code, or by a person domiciled outside the United States who substantially satisfies the requirements for tax exempt status under Section 501(c)(3) of the Internal Revenue Code, may be accepted for actual transportation and any reasonably necessary lodging and subsistence provided directly in connection with the speech, panel, seminar, or service, provided that the lodging and subsistence expenses are limited to the day immediately preceding, the day of, and the day immediately following the speech, panel participation or seminar, and the travel is within the United States.

Note: Authority cited: Sections 123.6, 133 and 5307.3, Labor Code. Reference: Sections 111 and 123.6, Labor Code.

History: 1. New section filed 11-30-95; operative 12-1-95. Submitted to OAL for printing only pursuant to Government Code section 11351 (Register 95, No. 48).

2. Amendment filed 8-25-2008; operative 9-24-2008 (Register 2008, No. 35).

Ref.: Hanna § 1.11[3][a]; Herlick Handbook § 1.01[3][b].

§9721.11. Requirement for Disclosure.

A judge shall disclose to all parties or attorneys in a case, at the time the judge first becomes aware of the existence of the facts, any and all of the following:

(a) That the judge served as a lawyer for a party at any time within the three years before being assigned to the case. "Serving as a lawyer" includes having interviewed a prospective client and learned confidential information, although the judge did not become a lawyer for the prospective client. A judge shall use the resources reasonably available to the judge to ascertain the identity of the judge's former clients.

(b) That the judge provided legal advice on the specific issue presently at bar to a party involved in the instant action or proceeding.

(c) That within the past two years, a party, officer, director, or trustee of a party was a client of the judge or of a lawyer with whom the judge was associated in private practice, as an employee or on a contract basis.

(d) That a lawyer, associate of the lawyer in private practice, or spouse of a lawyer in the proceeding is a spouse, former spouse, child, sibling, or parent of the judge or of the judge's spouse.

(e) That the judge has, as a lawyer or public official, participated in the drafting of enacted laws or actively participated in the effort to pass or defeat laws, the meaning, effect, or application of which is in issue in the proceeding. "Actively participated" means the judge has engaged in lobbying, or made other substantial efforts to change law. Mere membership in an organization which advocates or has advocated change in law does not constitute active participation.

(f) Any information that the workers' compensation administrative law judge believes would be relevant to the issue of disqualification, such that a person aware of the facts might reasonably entertain a doubt as to the workers' compensation administrative law judge's ability to be impartial.

(g) Any situation known to the judge, disclosure of which is required by the Code of Judicial Ethics.

(h) That the judge has a disputed workers' compensation claim against a party.

Note: Authority cited: Sections 123.6, 133 and 5307.3, Labor Code. Reference: Sections 111 and 123.6, Labor Code.

History: 1. New section filed 8-25-2008; operative 9-24-2008 (Register 2008, No. 35).

Ref.: Herlick Handbook § 1.01[3][b].

§9721.12. Disqualification.

(a) A judge is disqualified in a workers' compensation case if any of the following is true:

(1) The judge has personal knowledge of disputed evidentiary facts.

(2) The judge served as lawyer for a party in the past two years.

(3) The judge has actual bias in favor of or against any party and the judge has substantial doubt as to his or her capacity to be impartial.

(4) Because of physical impairment, the judge is unable to perceive evidence or properly conduct proceedings.

(5) Within the past two years, the judge served as a lawyer for an officer, director, trustee of a party.

(6) Within the past two years, the judge was associated in private practice, as an employee or on a contract basis, with a lawyer in the proceedings.

(7) The judge, the judge's spouse, or minor child of the judge, personally or as a fiduciary, has a financial interest in the subject matter in a proceeding or in a party to the proceeding, or has a relationship of director, advisor, or active participant to a party to the proceeding.

(8) The judge, the judge's spouse, a relative of either within the third degree of relationship, or spouse of such relative, is likely to be a material witness.

(9) A party to the action before the judge, or the party's spouse, is related within the third degree of relationship to either the judge or to the judge's spouse.

(10) The judge believes that recusal would further the interests of justice or believes there is a substantial doubt as to his or her capacity to be impartial.

(11) The judge has actual bias against or in favor of an attorney for a party and the judge has a substantial doubt as to his or her capacity to be impartial. A judge is not disqualified as to other members or associates in a law firm, or as to the law firm itself, solely because of actual bias against or in favor of individual attorneys in or associated with the firm. Actual bias in favor of or against an attorney does not in itself create the appearance of bias as to a law firm of which the attorney is a member or associate. A doubt of a person aware of the facts that a judge could be impartial towards a law firm or other members or associates of a law firm, based only on knowledge of a judge's bias in favor of or against an individual attorney or attorneys, is not a doubt which is reasonably entertained. If the workers' compensation appeals board, on a petition for disqualification alleging bias against or in favor of an attorney, determines that a judge is disqualified because of the appearance of bias or because a person aware of the facts might reasonably entertain a doubt that the judge could be impartial, it shall not be presumed, as to a law firm of which the attorney is a member or associate, or as to other members or associates of the law firm:

A. that there is the appearance of bias; or

B. that a person aware of the facts might reasonably entertain a doubt that the judge could be impartial.

(b) The parties may waive the disqualification of a judge after written disclosure of the facts constituting a ground of disqualification. A judge who believes he or she is disqualified shall recuse or shall state in writing the basis of disqualification. All waivers shall be in writing and shall be made part of the file, or shall be made on the record. The judge may ask the parties and their attorneys whether they wish to waive the disqualification. The judge may not request the parties or attorneys to waive the disqualification The parties and any attorney for the employee shall execute any waiver. An attorney for a party other than the employee may execute the waiver on behalf of the attorney's clients. Such a waiver shall state that the attorney has advised the client of the disqualification information, and that the client has agreed to waive the disqualification.

(c) Disqualification for the following circumstances cannot be waived:

(1) The judge, the judge's spouse, a relative of either within the third degree of relationship, or spouse of such relative, is likely to be a material witness

(2) The judge served as a lawyer in the case.

Note: Authority cited: Sections 123.6, 133 and 5307.3, Labor Code. Reference: Sections 111 and 123.6, Labor Code.

History: 1. New section filed 8-25-2008; operative 9-24-2008 (Register 2008, No. 35).

Ref.: Herlick Handbook § 1.01[3][b].

§9721.13. What Are Not Grounds for Disqualification.

The following factors do not in themselves disqualify a judge:

(a) That the judge is or is not a member of a racial, ethnic, religious, gender, or sexual orientation classification, and the proceedings involve the rights of a person of the same classification.

(b) That the judge has, in any capacity, expressed a view on a legal or factual issue presented in the proceeding, except if the judge has formed or expressed an unqualified opinion or belief as to the merits of the particular action before the judge.

(c) That the judge has a policy of insurance with an insurance company that is a party or is a carrier of a party in the proceeding, unless the judge also has a pending claim or dispute with the insurance company.

(d) That the judge has a currently disputed or recently finalized workers' compensation claim against a party.

Note: Authority cited: Sections 123.6, 133 and 5307.3, Labor Code. Reference: Sections 111 and 123.6, Labor Code.

History: 1. New section filed 8-25-2008; operative 9-24-2008 (Register 2008, No. 35).

Ref.: Herlick Handbook § 1.01[3][b].

§9721.14. Manner of Disclosure.

(a) Facts or circumstances which are required to be disclosed pursuant to §9721.11 or §9721.12, except for those which must be disclosed pursuant to subdivision (a) of §9721.11, shall be disclosed on the record.

(b) Facts or circumstances which are required to be disclosed pursuant to subdivision (a) of §9721.11 may be disclosed by the judge by providing a list of former clients. The posting in the courtroom of a list of the judge's former clients will satisfy this requirement as to former clients who were not employee workers' compensation claimants. A judge shall not post a list of former clients who were employee workers' compensation claimants, but shall make a list available to the parties in a case, and shall disclose the availability of the list.

Note: Authority cited: Sections 123.6, 133 and 5307.3, Labor Code. Reference: Sections 111 and 123.6, Labor Code.

History: 1. New section filed 8-25-2008; operative 9-24-2008 (Register 2008, No. 35).

Ref.: Herlick Handbook § 1.01[3][b].

§9721.21. Restriction on Investments.

(a) A workers' compensation administrative law judge may not have an ownership interest in, either in his individual capacity or as a fiduciary, and may not purchase an interest in, an insurance carrier which either writes policies of workers' compensation insurance to employers in the state of California or is authorized to write policies of workers' compensation insurance to employers in the state of California.

(b) A workers' compensation administrative law judge who, as of the date this regulation becomes effective, has an interest in an insurance company described in subdivision (a), shall dispose of the interest or terminate the fiduciary relationship within one year of the date this regulation becomes effective.

(c) A workers' compensation administrative law judge who acquires an interest in an insurance company described in subdivision (a) through gift, inheritance or devise, or by becoming a fiduciary for a person, estate, or trust which has an interest in such an insurance company, shall dispose of the acquired interest or terminate the fiduciary relationship within one year.

(d) Upon application by a workers' compensation administrative law judge who acquired an interest in an insurance company described in subdivision (a) through gift, inheritance or devise, or by becoming a fiduciary for a person, estate, or trust which has an interest in such an insurance company, and upon the showing of hardship to the judge or to the person, trust, or estate for whom the judge is serving as fiduciary, the Administrative Director may grant an extension of time to dispose of the acquired interest or to terminate the fiduciary relationship or may grant an exemption if the value of the interest is de minimus.

(e) The obligation of a workers' compensation administrative law judge under the California Code of Judicial Ethics to "manage personal investments and financial activities so as to minimize the necessity for disqualification" includes the obligation not to acquire or hold investments in self-insured employers who are reasonably likely to be defendant employers in cases at the district office where the judge is usually employed.

(f) An ownership interest in a corporation which owns, wholly or in part, an insurance carrier which either writes policies of workers' compensation insurance to employers in the state of California or is authorized to write policies of workers' compensation insurance to employers in the state of California, is not an ownership interest in that insurance carrier. This subdivision shall not affect a judge's disqualification or obligation to disclose.

Note: Authority cited: Sections 123.6, 133 and 5307.3, Labor Code. Reference: Sections 111 and 123.6, Labor Code.

History: 1. New section filed 8-25-2008; operative 9-24-2008 (Register 2008, No. 35).

Ref.: Herlick Handbook § 1.01[3][b].

§9721.31. Financial Interests in Educational Programs.

(a) A workers' compensation administrative law judge may not have an ownership interest in, nor may the workers' compensation administrative law judge receive a percentage of revenue or any other contingent economic interest relating to, educational programs servicing the workers' compensation community.

(b) As used in this section, "percentage of revenues or any other contingent financial interest" does not include:

(1) Usual and customary royalties or residuals paid by commercial publishers in the normal course of business, provided that the publisher does not appear before the workers' compensation administrative law judge in question.

(2) Usual and customary royalties or residuals earned by a workers' compensation administrative law judge who self-publishes or owns the company that publishes his or her work, provided that the book is not available for purchase or delivery at any office of the Division of Workers' Compensation and is not sold or distributed by any Division of Workers' Compensation employee on behalf of the workers' administrative law judge. Any workers' compensation administrative law judge who self-publishes or owns the company that publishes his or her work has the responsibility to submit to the Court Administrator, or his or her designee, for approval a proposed plan that complies with this subdivision. If there is no Court Administrator, then the workers' compensation administrative law judge shall submit the proposed plan to the Administrative Director.

Note: Authority cited: Sections 123.6, 133 and 5307.3, Labor Code. Reference: Sections 111 and 123.6, Labor Code.

History: 1. New section filed 11-30-95; operative 12-1-95. Submitted to OAL for printing only pursuant to Government Code section 11351 (Register 95, No. 48).

2. Amendment filed 8-25-2008; operative 9-24-2008 (Register 2008, No. 35).

Ref.: Hanna § 1.11[3][a]; Herlick Handbook § 1.01[3][b].

§9721.32. Duty to Report Ethics Violations.

When circumstances warrant, a workers' compensation administrative law judge shall take or initiate appropriate corrective action, which may include reporting to the appropriate authority, in respect to a workers' compensation administrative law judge, lawyer, party, or other person who engages in unprofessional, fraudulent or other improper conduct of which the workers' compensation administrative law judge becomes aware through personal knowledge or based upon information the judge reasonably believes to be competent and reliable.

Note: Authority cited: Sections 123.6, 133 and 5307.3, Labor Code. Reference: Sections 111 and 123.6, Labor Code.

History: 1. New section filed 11-30-95; operative 12-1-95. Submitted to OAL for printing only pursuant to Government Code section 11351 (Register 95, No. 48).

2. Amendment of section heading and section filed 8-25-2008; operative 9-24-2008 (Register 2008, No. 35).

Ref.: Hanna § 1.11[3][a]; Herlick Handbook § 1.01[3][b].

§9721.33. Previously Earned Compensation.

A Workers' Compensation Administrative Law Judge may receive previously earned compensation.

Note: Authority cited: Sections 123.6, 133 and 5307.3, Labor Code. Reference: Sections 111 and 123.6, Labor Code.

History: 1. New section filed 8-25-2008; operative 9-24-2008 (Register 2008, No. 35).

Ref.: Herlick Handbook § 1.01[3][b].

§9722. The Workers' Compensation Ethics Advisory Committee.

(a) There shall be a Workers' Compensation Ethics Advisory Committee consisting of nine members appointed by the Administrative Director or by his/her designee:

(1) a member of the public representing organized labor,

(2) a member of the public representing insurers,

(3) a member of the public representing self-insured employers,

(4) an attorney who formerly practiced before the Workers' Compensation Appeals Board and who usually represented insurers or employers,

(5) an attorney who formerly practiced before the Workers' Compensation Appeals Board and who usually represented applicants,

(6) a presiding workers' compensation administrative law judge,

(7) a workers' compensation administrative law judge or retired workers' compensation administrative law judge,

(8) and (9) two members of the public outside the workers' compensation community.

Members shall serve for a term of four years. However, to create staggered terms, the first term of members in odd-numbered categories above shall be two years. The Administrative Director shall designate a chairperson.

(b) The Committee shall meet as necessary to carry out its responsibilities under this article. State employees shall meet on state time and at state expense.

(c) The Committee may do the following:

(1) Receive complaints made against workers' compensation administrative law judges,

(2) Forward those complaints to the Administrative Director or Court Administrator with a recommendation to investigate or not to investigate,

(3) Monitor the outcome of complaints, and

(4) Make reports and recommendations to the Administrative Director, the Court Administrator, the legislature and the public concerning the integrity of the workers' compensation adjudicatory process. The Committee shall make a public report on or before April 15 or each year, summarizing the activities of the Committee in the previous calendar year. The report shall not contain personally identifiable information concerning complainants or workers' compensation administrative law judges, unless the information is already public.

(d) The Administrative Director shall make staff available to the Committee to assist it in carrying out its functions.

(e) The Committee may receive information that is not available to the public. The Committee shall hold such information strictly confidential from public disclosure. However, this rule of confidentiality shall not prevent the Administrative Director or Court Administrator from disclosing information to the workers' compensation administrative law judge, if the workers' compensation administrative law judge is otherwise entitled to the information.

Note: Authority cited: Sections 123.6, 133 and 5307.3, Labor Code. Reference: Sections 111 and 123.6, Labor Code.

History: 1. New section filed 11-30-95; operative 12-1-95. Submitted to OAL for printing only pursuant to Government Code section 11351 (Register 95, No. 48).

2. Amendment filed 8-25-2008; operative 9-24-2008 (Register 2008, No. 35).

Ref.: Hanna § 1.11[3][a]; Herlick Handbook § 1.01[3][b].

§9722.1. Commencing an Investigation.

(a) Any person may file a complaint concerning an ethics violation by a workers' compensation administrative law judge with the Committee. The Committee or the Administrative Director may require complaints to be filed in a particular form. Nothing in these regulations prohibits any person from complaining directly to a presiding workers' compensation administrative law judge, the Chief Judge, the Court Administrator or to the Administrative Director. The presiding workers' compensation administrative law judge, the Chief Judge, and Court Administrator or the Administrative Director may, but is not required to, refer such complaints to the Committee.

(b) The Committee shall review the complaint. The Committee may make inquiries to obtain information needed to clarify the complaint and/or to obtain additional information necessary to determine if the complaint might have merit.

(c) If the Committee determines that the complaint does not allege facts that might constitute an ethics violation, or if the complaint is merely conjectural or conclusory, specious, obviously unfounded, or stale, or alleges only legal error by the workers' compensation administrative law judge, the Committee shall forward the complaint to the Administrative Director or Court Administrator with a recommendation not to proceed with the complaint.

(d) If the Committee determines that the complaint might have merit, the Committee shall refer the complaint to the Administrative Director or Court Administrator. Complaints against the Administrative Director or Court Administrator shall be referred to the Director of Industrial Relations.

(e) Except as otherwise provided in subdivision (c) of section 9722.2, reports and recommendations of the Committee regarding individual complaints shall remain confidential.

Note: Authority cited: Sections 123.6, 133 and 5307.3, Labor Code. Reference: Sections 111 and 123.6, Labor Code.

History: 1. New section filed 11-30-95; operative 12-1-95. Submitted to OAL for printing only pursuant to Government Code section 11351 (Register 95, No. 48).

2. Amendment filed 8-25-2008; operative 9-24-2008 (Register 2008, No. 35).

Ref.: Hanna § 1.11[3][a]; Herlick Handbook § 1.01[3][b].

§9722.2. Investigation and Action by the Administrative Director or Court Administrator.

(a) Upon receiving a complaint from the Committee, the Administrative Director or Court Administrator shall investigate whether a workers' compensation administrative law judge has committed an ethics violation.

(b) If the Administrative Director or Court Administrator determines after investigation that misconduct has occurred, he or she shall take appropriate disciplinary or other action against the workers' compensation administrative law judge. The Administrative Director's or Court Administrator's action shall be in the form required by Government Code section 19574 or section 19590(b), or other applicable laws governing the ethics violation.

(c) The Administrative Director or Court Administrator shall provide the Committee with a copy of his or her decision and shall inform the complaining party whether an ethical violation occurred, and whether corrective action was taken.

Note: Authority cited: Sections 123.6, 133 and 5307.3, Labor Code. Reference: Sections 111 and 123.6, Labor Code.

History: 1. New section filed 11-30-95; operative 12-1-95. Submitted to OAL for printing only pursuant to Government Code section 11351 (Register 95, No. 48).

2. Amendment of section heading and section filed 8-25-2008; operative 9-24-2008 (Register 2008, No. 35).

Ref.: Hanna § 1.11[3][a]; Herlick Handbook § 1.01[3][b].

§9723. Miscellaneous Provisions.

(a) This article does not replace or diminish the procedural rights of a workers' compensation administrative law judge under the State Civil Service Act. Documentation of unfounded or unsubstantiated complaints shall not be retained in the employee's personnel file.

(b) This article does not replace or diminish the authority of the Administrative Director or Court Administrator to investigate allegations of ethics violations, to impose appropriate discipline, or to take any other action authorized by law.

(c) Nothing in this article shall affect the rights and obligations of the Administrative Director or Court Administrator and workers' compensation administrative law judges concerning the probationary period under Government Code sections 19170 through 19180.

(d) Pursuant to Government Code section 19574.5, the Administrative Director or Court Administrator may place a workers' compensation administrative law judge on leave of absence pending investigation of the accusations listed in that section.

(e) A workers' compensation administrative law judge or other interested person may request the Administrative Director or Court Administrator to issue an advisory opinion on the application of the Code or other rules to a particular situation. The Administrative Director or Court Administrator may, in his or her sole discretion, issue an advisory opinion. The Administrative Director or Court Administrator may issue an advisory opinion on his or her own initiative.

Note: Authority cited: Sections 123.6, 133 and 5307.3, Labor Code. Reference: Sections 111 and 123.6, Labor Code.

History: 1. New section filed 11-30-95; operative 12-1-95. Submitted to OAL for printing only pursuant to Government Code section 11351 (Register 95, No. 48).

2. Amendment filed 8-25-2008; operative 9-24-2008 (Register 2008, No. 35).

Ref.: Herlick Handbook § 1.01[3][b].

ARTICLE 2
Disabilities, Description of

§9725. Method of Measurement.

The method of measuring physical elements of a disability should follow the Report of the Joint Committee of the California Medical Association and Industrial Accident Commission, as contained in "*Evaluation of Industrial Disability*" edited by Packard Thurber, Second Edition, Oxford University Press, New York, 1960. This section shall not apply to any permanent disability evaluations performed pursuant to the permanent disability rating schedule adopted on or after January 1, 2005.

Note: Authority cited: Sections 133 and 5307.3, Labor Code. Reference: Sections 4660, 4662, 4663 and 4664, Labor Code.

History: 1. New Subchapter (§§9725, 9727, 9732, 9735, 9738, 9739, 9742-9744, 9750, 9753, 9756-9760, 9770, 9773, 9775, 9778, 9784, 9787, 9790, 9796, 9799, 9802 and 9805) filed 4-18-66; effective thirtieth day thereafter (Register 65, No. 10).

2. Amendment of section and Note filed 12-31-2004 as an emergency; operative 1-1-2005 (Register 2004, No. 53). A Certificate of Compliance must be transmitted to OAL by 5-2-2005 or emergency language will be repealed by operation of law on the following day.

3. Certificate of Compliance as to 12-31-2004 order transmitted to OAL 4-29-2005 and filed 6-10-2005 (Register 2005, No. 23).

Editor's Note: *"Evaluation of Industrial Disability"* is available in major law libraries in California.

Ref.: Hanna §§ 22.08[5][b], 32.02[2][b]; Herlick Handbook §§ 1.01[3][b], 14.23.

§9726. Method of Measurement (Psychiatric).

The method of measuring the psychiatric elements of a disability shall follow the Report of the Subcommittee on Permanent Psychiatric Disability to the Medical Advisory Committee of the California Division of Industrial Accidents, entitled "The Evaluation of Permanent Psychiatric Disability," (hereinafter referred to as the "Psychiatric Protocols") as adopted, forwarded for adoption on July 10, 1987, and subsequent amendments and/or revisions thereto adopted after a public hearing. This section shall not apply to any permanent disability evaluations performed pursuant to the permanent disability rating schedule adopted on or after January 1, 2005.

Note: The Report (which contains these Protocols) of the Subcommittee on Permanent Psychiatric Disability, as adopted, does not appear as a printed part of the Administrative Director's Regulations (8 California Code of Regulations, Section 9726); copies will be available through the Medical Director of the Division of Industrial Accidents.

Note: Authority cited: Sections 133 and 5307.3, Labor Code. Reference: Sections 4660, 4662, 4663 and 4664, Labor Code.

History: 1. New section filed 8-24-87; operative 8-24-87 (Register 87, No. 36). This regulation was filed pursuant to Government Code Section 11351 and thus this filing is exempted from compliance with Article 5 (commencing with Section 11346), (except subdivision (e) of Section 11346.4), Article 6 (commencing with Section 11349), and Article 7 (commencing with Section 11350) of Chapter 3.5 of the Government Code. The provisions of Government Code Section 11343.6 are not applicable to this filing.

2. Amendment filed 6-30-88; operative 7-1-88 (Register 88, No. 28). The amendment was filed pursuant to Government Code Section 11351.

3. Amendment of section and Note filed 12-31-2004 as an emergency; operative 1-1-2005 (Register 2004, No. 53). A Certificate of Compliance must be transmitted to OAL by 5-2-2005 or emergency language will be repealed by operation of law on the following day.

4. Certificate of Compliance as to 12-31-2004 order transmitted to OAL 4-29-2005 and filed 6-10-2005 (Register 2005, No. 23).

Ref.: Hanna §§ 4.69[3][a], [c], 8.02[4][c][i], 22.08[5][c], 32.02[5][b][i], [ii]; Herlick Handbook §§ 1.01[3][b], 14.23; Lawyer's Guide to AMA *Guides* and Calif. Workers' Comp. §§ 2.06, 13.14.

§9727. Subjective Disability.

Subjective Disability should be identified by:

1. A description of the activity which produces the disability.

2. The duration of the disability.

3. The activities which are precluded and those which can be performed with the disability.

4. The means necessary for relief. The terms shown below are presumed to mean the following:

1. A *severe* pain would preclude the activity precipitating the pain.

2. A *moderate* pain could be tolerated, but would cause marked handicap in the performance of the activity precipitating the pain.

3. A *slight* pain could be tolerated, but would cause some handicap in the performance of the activity precipitating the pain.

4. A *minimal* (mild) pain would constitute an annoyance, but causing no handicap in the performance of the particular activity, would be considered as nonratable permanent disability.

This section shall not apply to any permanent disability evaluations performed pursuant to the permanent disability rating schedule adopted on or after January 1, 2005.

Note: Authority cited: Sections 133 and 5307.3, Labor Code. Reference: Sections 4660, 4662, 4663 and 4664, Labor Code.

History: 1. New last paragraph and new Note filed 12-31-2004 as an emergency; operative 1-1-2005 (Register 2004, No. 53). A Certificate of Compliance must be transmitted to OAL by 5-2-2005 or emergency language will be repealed by operation of law on the following day.

2. Certificate of Compliance as to 12-31-2004 order transmitted to OAL 4-29-2005 and filed 6-10-2005 (Register 2005, No. 23).

Ref.: Hanna §§ 8.02[4][b], 22.08[5][b], 32.02[2][c][i], [ii]; Herlick Handbook §§ 1.01[3][b], 6.15[2], [5].

ARTICLE 3
Permanent Disability Ratings and Evaluations [Repealed]

History: 1. Repealer of article 3 (sections 9732-9766, nonconsecutive) and section filed 12-27-96; operative 12-27-96. Submitted to OAL for printing only pursuant to Government Code section 11351 (Register 96, No. 52).

ARTICLE 3.5
Medical Provider Network

§9767.1. Medical Provider Networks—Definitions.

(a) As used in this article:

(1) "Ancillary services" means any provision of medical services or goods as allowed in Labor Code section 4600 by a non-physician, including, but not limited to, interpreter services, physical therapy and pharmaceutical services.

(2) "Covered employee" means an employee or former employee whose employer has ongoing workers' compensation obligations and whose employer or employer's insurer is using a Medical Provider Network for the provision of medical treatment to injured employees unless:

(A) the injured employee has properly designated a personal physician pursuant to Labor Code section 4600(d) by notice to the employer prior to the date of injury, or;

(B) the injured employee's employment with the employer is covered by an agreement providing medical treatment for the injured employee and the agreement is validly established under Labor Code section 3201.5, 3201.7 or 3201.81.

(3) "Division" means the Division of Workers' Compensation.

(4) "Economic profiling" means any evaluation of a particular physician, provider, medical group, or individual practice association based in whole or in part on the economic costs or utilization of services associated with medical care provided or authorized by the physician, provider, medical group, or individual practice association.

(5) "Emergency health care services" means health care services for a medical condition manifesting itself by acute symptoms of sufficient severity such that the absence of immediate medical attention could reasonably be expected to place the patient's health in serious jeopardy.

(6) "Employer" means a self-insured employer, the Self-Insurer's Security Fund, a group of self-insured employers pursuant to Labor Code section 3700(b) and as defined by Title 8, California Code of Regulations, section 15201(s), a joint powers authority, or the state.

(7) "Entity that provides physician network services" means a legal entity employing or contracting with physicians and other medical providers or contracting with physician networks, and may include but is not limited to third party administrators and managed care entities, to deliver medical treatment to injured workers on behalf of one or more insurers, self-insured employers, the Uninsured Employers Benefits Trust Fund, the California Insurance Guaranty Association, or the Self-Insurers Security Fund, and that meets the requirements of this article, Labor Code 4616 et seq., and corresponding regulations.

(8) "Geocoding" means the mapping of addresses within specific geographic location(s) or coordinate space.

(9) "Group Disability Insurance Policy" means an entity designated pursuant to Labor Code section 4616.7(c).

(10) "Health Care Organization" means an entity designated pursuant to Labor Code section 4616.7(a).

(11) "Health Care Service Plan" means an entity designated pursuant to Labor Code section 4616.7(b).

(12) "Health care shortage" means a situation in a geographical area in which the number of physicians in a particular specialty who are available and willing to treat injured workers under the California workers' compensation system is insufficient to meet the Medical Provider Network access standards set forth in 9767.5(a) through (c) to ensure medical treatment is available and accessible at reasonable times. A lack of physicians participating in an MPN does not constitute a health care shortage where a sufficient number of physicians in that specialty are available within the access standards and willing to treat injured workers under the California workers' compensation system.

(13) "Insurer" means an insurer admitted to transact workers' compensation insurance in the state of California, California Insurance Guarantee Association, or the State Compensation Insurance Fund.

(14) "Medical Provider Network" ("MPN") means any entity or group of providers approved as a Medical Provider Network by the Administrative Director pursuant to Labor Code sections 4616 to 4616.7 and this article.

(15) "Medical Provider Network Identification Number" means the unique number assigned by DWC to a Medical Provider Network upon approval or within ninety (90) days of the effective date of these regulations and used to identify each approved Medical Provider Network.

(16) "Medical Provider Network Medical Access Assistant" means an individual in the United States provided by the Medical Provider Network to help injured workers with finding available Medical Provider Network physicians of the injured workers' choice and with scheduling provider appointments.

(17) "Medical Provider Network Geographic Service Area" means the geographic area within California in which medical services will be provided by the Medical Provider Network.

(18) "Medical Provider Network Plan" means an employer's, insurer's, or entity that provides physician network services' detailed description for a Medical Provider Network contained in a complete application submitted according to the the requirements of this article to the Administrative Director by an MPN Applicant.

(19) "MPN Applicant" means an insurer or employer or an entity that provides physician network services as defined in this section who is legally responsible for the Medical Provider Network.

(20) "MPN Contact" means an individual(s) designated by the MPN Applicant in the employee notification who is responsible for responding to complaints, for answering employees' questions about the Medical Provider Network and for assisting the employee in arranging for an MPN independent medical review pursuant to Labor Code section 4616.4.

(21) "Occupational Medicine" means the diagnosis or treatment of any injury or disease arising out of and in the course of employment.

(22) "Primary treating physician" means a primary treating physician within the medical provider network and as defined by section 9785(a)(1).

(23) "Probation" means a Medical Provider Network's approval is conditioned on the completion of specified actions within a stated time frame as required by the Administrative Director for the Medical Provider Network to comply with the requirements of this article and Labor Code sections 4616 et seq.

(24) "Provider" means a physician as described in Labor Code section 3209.3 or other practitioner as described in Labor Code section 3209.5.

(25) "Regional area listing" means either:

(A) a listing of all MPN providers within a 15-mile radius of an employee's worksite or residence; or

(B) a listing of all MPN providers in the county where the employee resides or works if

1. the employer or insurer cannot produce a provider listing based on a mile radius

2. or by choice of the employer or insurer, or upon request of the employee.

(C) If the listing described in either (A) or (B) does not provide a minimum of three physicians of each specialty, then the listing shall be expanded by adjacent counties or by 5-mile increments until the minimum number of physicians per specialty are met.

(26) "Residence" means the covered employee's primary residence.

(27) "Revocation" means the permanent termination of a Medical Provider Network's approval.

(28) "Second Opinion" means an opinion rendered by a medical provider network physician after an in person examination to address an employee's dispute over either the diagnosis or the treatment prescribed by the treating physician, pursuant to Labor Code section 4616.3.

(29) "Suspension" means the temporary discontinuance of MPN coverage for new claims within a specified period as required by the Administrative Director.

(30) "Taft-Hartley health and welfare fund" means an entity designated pursuant to Labor Code section 4616.7(d).

(31) "Termination" means the permanent discontinued use of an implemented MPN that ceases to do business.

(32) "Third Opinion" means an opinion rendered by a medical provider network physician after an in person examination to address an employee's dispute over either the diagnosis or the treatment prescribed by either the treating physician or physician rendering the second opinion, pursuant to Labor Code section 4616.3.

(33) "Treating physician" means any physician within the MPN applicant's medical provider network other than the primary treating physician who examines or provides treatment to the employee, but is not primarily responsible for continuing management of the care of the employee.

(34) "Withdrawal" means the permanent discontinuance of an approved MPN that was never implemented.

(35) "Workplace" means the geographic location where the covered employee is regularly employed.

Note: Authority cited: Sections 133 and 4616(h), Labor Code. Reference: Sections 1063.1, 3208, 3209.3, 3209.5, 3700, 3702, 3743, 4616, 4616.1, 4616.3, 4616.5 and 4616.7, Labor Code; and *California Insurance Guarantee Association v. Division of Workers' Compensation* (April 26, 2005) WCAB No. Misc. #249.

History: 1. New article 3.5 (sections 9767.1–9767.14) and section filed 11-1-2004 as an emergency; operative 11-1-2004 (Register 2004, No. 45). A Certificate of Compliance must be transmitted to OAL by 3-1-2005 or emergency language will be repealed by operation of law on the following day.

2. New article 3.5 (sections 9767.1–9767.14) and section refiled 2-28-2005 as an emergency; operative 3-1-2005 (Register 2005, No. 9). A Certificate of Compliance must be transmitted to OAL by 6-29-2005 or emergency language will be repealed by operation of law on the following day.

3. New article 3.5 (sections 9767.1–9767.14) and section refiled 6-20-2005 as an emergency; operative 6-29-2005 (Register 2005, No. 25). A Certificate of Compliance must be transmitted to OAL by 10-27-2005 or emergency language will be repealed by operation of law on the following day.

4. Certificate of Compliance as to 6-20-2005 order, including amendment of section and Note, transmitted to OAL 7-29-2005 and filed 9-9-2005 (Register 2005, No. 36).

5. New subsections (a)(2) and (a)(25), subsection renumbering and amendment of newly designated subsection (a)(14) filed 12-11-2007; operative 4-9-2008 (Register 2007, No. 50).

6. Amendment of section and Note filed 8-27-2014; operative 8-27-2014 pursuant to Government Code section 11343.4(b)(3) (Register 2014, No. 35).

Ref.: Hanna §§ 5.03[1], 5.05[13]; Herlick Handbook §§ 1.01[3][b], 4.11[5].

§9767.2. Review of Medical Provider Network Application or Plan for Reapproval.

Note: *See Executive Order N-63-20 (2019 CA EO 63-20), issued in response to the COVID-19 pandemic, which extends certain deadlines for action on Medical Provider Network applications or requests for modifications or reapprovals.*

(a) Within 60 days of the Administrative Director's receipt of a complete new application, the Administrative Director shall approve for a four-year period or disapprove a new application based on the requirements of Labor Code section 4616 et seq. and this article. An application shall be considered complete if it includes correct information responsive to each applicable subdivision of section 9767.3. Pursuant to Labor Code section 4616(b), if the Administrative Director has not acted on a new application plan within 60 days of submittal of a complete plan, it shall be deemed approved on the 61st day for a period of four years.

(b) Within 180 days of the Administrative Director's receipt of a complete plan for reapproval, the Administrative Director shall approve for a four-year period or disapprove the complete plan for reapproval based on the requirement of Labor Code section 4616 et seq. and this article. A plan for reapproval shall be considered complete if it includes correct information responsive to each applicable subdivision of section 9767.3. If the Administrative Director has not acted within 180 days of receipt of a complete plan for reapproval, it shall be deemed approved on the 181st day for a period of four years.

(c) The Administrative Director shall provide notification(s) to the MPN applicant: (1) setting forth the date the MPN application or reapproval plan was received by the Division; (2) informing the MPN applicant if the MPN application or reapproval plan is not complete and the item(s) necessary to complete the application or reapproval plan; and (3) if the Administrative Director is aware that the MPN applicant is not eligible to have an MPN.

(d) No additional materials shall be submitted by the MPN applicant or considered by the Administrative Director until the MPN applicant receives the notification described in (c).

(e) The Administrative Director's decision to approve or disapprove an application shall be limited to his/her review of the information provided in the application or reapproval plan.

(f) Upon approval of a new Medical Provider Network Plan, the MPN shall be assigned a unique MPN Identification number. This unique MPN Identification number shall be used in all correspondence with DWC regarding the MPN, including but not limited to future filings and complaints, and shall be included in the complete employee notification, transfer of care notice, continuity of care notice, MPN IMR notice and end of MPN coverage notice.

(g) An MPN applicant may choose to withdraw an approved MPN that has never been implemented by sending a letter signed by the MPN's authorized individual to the Administrative Director with the name and approval number of the MPN to be withdrawn, and a statement verifying that the MPN has never been used and that the MPN applicant will not use the MPN in the future.

Note: Authority cited: Sections 133 and 4616(h), Labor Code. Reference: Section 4616, Labor Code.

History: 1. New section filed 11-1-2004 as an emergency; operative 11-1-2004 (Register 2004, No. 45). A Certificate of Compliance must be transmitted to OAL by 3-1-2005 or emergency language will be repealed by operation of law on the following day.

2. New section refiled 2-28-2005 as an emergency; operative 3-1-2005 (Register 2005, No. 9). A Certificate of Compliance must be transmitted to OAL by 6-29-2005 or emergency language will be repealed by operation of law on the following day.

3. New section refiled 6-20-2005 as an emergency; operative 6-29-2005 (Register 2005, No. 25). A Certificate of Compliance must be transmitted to OAL by 10-27-2005 or emergency language will be repealed by operation of law on the following day.

4. Certificate of Compliance as to 6-20-2005 order, including new subsection (c) and subsection relettering, transmitted to OAL 7-29-2005 and filed 9-9-2005 (Register 2005, No. 36).

5. Amendment of section heading, section and Note filed 8-27-2014; operative 8-27-2014 pursuant to Government Code section 11343.4(b)(3) (Register 2014, No. 35).

6. Governor Newsom issued Executive Order N-63-20 (2019 CA EO 63-20), dated May 7, 2020, which extended certain deadlines for action on Medical Provider Network applications or requests for modifications or reapprovals, due to the COVID-19 pandemic.

Ref.: Hanna §§ 5.03[1], 5.05[13][a]; Herlick Handbook §§ 1.01[3][b], 4.11[2].

§9767.3. Requirements for a Medical Provider Network Plan.

(a) As long as the application for a medical provider network plan meets the requirements of Labor Code section 4616 et seq. and this article, nothing in this section precludes an employer or insurer or entity that provides physician network services from submitting for approval one or more medical provider network applications.

(b) Nothing in this section precludes an MPN applicant from agreeing to submit for approval a medical provider network plan which meets the specific needs of an insured employer considering the experience of the insured employer, the common injuries experienced by the insured employer, the type of occupation and industry in which the insured employer is engaged and the geographic area where the employees are employed.

(c) All MPN applicants shall complete the section 9767.4 Cover Page for Medical Provider Network Application or Plan for Reapproval with an original signature, and an MPN Plan meeting the requirements of this section or the optional MPN Plan Application form. Two copies of the completed, signed Cover Page for Medical Provider Network Application or Plan for Reapproval and the complete MPN Plan shall be submitted to the DWC in compact discs or flash drives in word-searchable PDF format. The hard copy of the completed, signed original Cover Page for Medical Provider Network Application or Plan for Reapproval and the complete MPN Plan shall be maintained by the MPN applicant and made available for review by the Administrative Director upon request. Electronic signatures in compliance with California Government Code section 16.5 are accepted.

(1) An MPN applicant shall submit the MPN provider information and ancillary service provider information required in section 9767.3(d)(8)(G) and (I) in a compact disc(s) or, a flash drive(s). The information shall be submitted as a Microsoft Excel spread sheet unless an alternative format is approved by the Administrative Director. If the MPN applicant is using a valid and currently certified Health Care Organization, then this information must be noted on the application's Cover Page for Medical Provider Network or Plan for Reapproval and only a listing of any additional ancillary service providers is required to be submitted pursuant to the requirements in subsection (3) of this subdivision.

(2) The network provider information shall be submitted in a compact disc(s), or a flash drive(s), and the provider file shall have only the following eight columns. These columns shall be in the following order: (1) physician name (2) specialty (3) physical address (4) city (5) state (6) zip code (7) any MPN medical group affiliations and (8) an assigned provider code for each physician listed. If a physician falls under more than one provider code, the physician shall be listed separately for each applicable provider code. The following are the provider codes to be used: primary treating physician (PTP), orthopedic medicine (ORTHO), chiropractic medicine (DC), occupational medicine (OCCM), acupuncture medicine (LAC), psychology (PSYCH), pain specialty medicine (PM), psychiatry (PSY), neurosurgery (NSG), family medicine (GP), neurology (NEURO), internal medicine (IM), physical medicine and rehabilitation (PMR), or podiatry (DPM). If the specialty does not fall under any one of the previously listed categories, then the specialty shall be clearly identified in the specialty column and the code used shall be (MISC). By submission of its provider listing, the applicant is affirming that all of the physicians listed have been informed that the Medical Treatment Utilization Schedule ("MTUS") is presumptively correct on the issue of the extent and scope of medical treatment and diagnostic services and have a valid and current license number to practice in the State of California.

(3) If an MPN chooses to provide ancillary services, the ancillary service provider file shall have only the following six columns. The columns shall be in the following order: (1) the name of each ancillary service provider (2) specialty or type of service (3) physical address (4) city (5) state (6) zip code of each ancillary service provider. If the ancillary service or ancillary service provider is mobile, list the covered service area within California. By submission of an ancillary provider listing, the applicant is affirming that the providers listed can provide the requested medical services or goods and have a current valid license number or certification to practice, if they are required to have a license or certification by the State of California. If interpreter services are included as an MPN ancillary service, the interpreters listed must be certified pursuant to section 9795.1.6(a)(2)(A) and (B).

(4) An MPN determines which locations are approved for physicians to provide treatment under the MPN. Approved locations are listed in an MPN's provider listing; however, an MPN has the discretion to approve treatment at non-listed locations.

(5) An MPN applicant shall have the exclusive right to determine the members of its network.

(d) A Medical Provider Network application shall include all of the following information:

(1) Type of Eligible MPN applicant. Provide a description of the entity's qualifications to be an eligible MPN Applicant. Attach proof of MPN eligibility. If a self-insured employer or joint powers authority, attach a copy of the current valid certificate of self-insurance. For an insurer, attach a current valid certificate of authority. For an entity providing physician network services, attach documentation of current legal status including, but not limited to, legal licenses or certificates and affirm that the entity employs or contracts with physicians and other medical providers or contracts with physician networks.

(2) Name of MPN applicant.

(3) MPN applicant's Taxpayer Identification Number.

(4) Name of Medical Provider Network.

(5) MPN Liaison to DWC: Provide the name, title, address, e-mail address, and telephone number of the person designated as the liaison for the Division, who is responsible for receiving compliance and informational communications from the Division and for disseminating the same within the MPN.

(6) The application must be verified by an officer or employee of the MPN applicant with the authority to act on behalf of the MPN applicant with respect to the MPN. The verification by the authorized individual shall state: "I, the undersigned officer or employee of the MPN applicant, have read and signed this application and know the contents thereof, and verify that, to the best of my knowledge and belief, the information included in this application is true and correct."

(7) Nothing in this section precludes a network, entity, administrator, or other third-party, upon agreement with a MPN applicant, from preparing a MPN application on behalf of an eligible MPN applicant.

(8) Description of Medical Provider Network Plan:

(A) Affirm that the MPN network is adequate to handle the expected number of claims covered under the MPN and explain how this was determined;

(B) Describe the MPN geographic service area or areas within the State of California to be served;

(C) State the toll-free number, email address, fax number and days and times of availability to reach the MPN's medical access assistants.

(D) State the MPN website address;

(E) State the web address or URL to the roster of all treating physicians in the MPN. Affirm that secondary treating physicians who are counted when determining access standards but can only be seen with an approved referral are clearly designated "by referral only".

(F) Affirm that each MPN physician or medical group in the network has agreed to treat workers under the MPN and that the written acknowledgments are in accordance with the requirements under "Physician Acknowledgments" section 9767.5.1, and are available for review by the Administrative Director upon request;

(G) Provide a listing of the name, specialty, and location of each physician as described in Labor Code Section 3209.3, who will be providing occupational medicine services under the plan. Only individual physicians in the MPN shall be listed, but MPN medical group affiliation(s) may be included with each individual physician listed. By submission of the application, the MPN applicant is confirming that a contractual agreement exists with the physicians, providers or medical group practice in the MPN to provide treatment for injured workers in the workers' compensation system and that the contractual agreement is in compliance with Labor Code section 4609, if applicable.

(H) Provide an electronic copy in Microsoft Excel format of the geocoding results of the MPN provider directory to show estimated compliance with the access standards set forth in section 9767.5. The access standards set forth in section 9767.5 are determined by the injured employee's residence or workplace address and not the center of a zip code. The geocoding results will be used by DWC in reviewing MPN plans to give an approximation of MPN compliance with the access standards set forth in section 9767.5. The geocoding results shall include the following separate files summarizing data reasonably available at the time of compilation: 1) a complete list of all zip codes within the MPN geographic service area; 2) a narrative or graphic report that establishes where there are at least three available primary treating physicians within the fifteen-mile access standard from the center of each zip code within the MPN geographic service area; 3) a narrative or graphic report that establishes where there is a hospital or an emergency health care service provider within the fifteen-mile access standard from the center of each zip code within the MPN geographic service area; 4) a narrative or graphic report that establishes where there are at least three available physicians in each of the specialties commonly required to treat injured workers covered by the MPN within the thirty-mile access standard from the center of each zip code within the MPN geographic service area; 5) a list of all zip codes where access standards are not met in the geographic service area or areas to be served by the MPN for primary treating physicians, for acute care hospitals or emergency facilities, and for each specialty listed to treat common injuries experienced by injured workers covered by the MPN, and a narrative report explaining if medical treatment will be provided according to an approved alternative access standard or according to a written policy permitting out of MPN treatment in those areas; and 6) each physician listed in the MPN provider directory listing shall be assigned at least one provider code as set forth in subdivision (c)(2) of this section to be used in the geocoding reports.

(I) If an MPN chooses to include ancillary services in its network, a listing of the name, specialty or type of service and location of each ancillary service, other than a physician covered under subdivision (d)(8)(G) of this section, who will be providing services or goods within the medical provider network. By submission of the application, the MPN applicant is confirming that a contractual agreement exists with the ancillary service providers to provide services to be used under the MPN and that the ancillary services will be available at reasonable times and within a reasonable geographic area to covered employees;

(J) Describe how the MPN provides ancillary services to its covered employees. Set forth which ancillary services, if any, will be within the MPN. For ancillary services not able to be provided within the MPN pursuant to section 9767.5(d), affirm that referrals will be made to services outside the MPN;

(K) Describe how the MPN complies with the second and third opinion process set forth in section 9767.7;

(L) Describe how the MPN complies with the access standards set forth in section 9767.5 for all covered employees;

(M) Describe the employee notification process, and attach an English and Spanish copy of the required employee notification material and information to be given to covered employees described in section 9767.12(a).

(N) Attach a copy of the written continuity of care policy as described in Labor Code section 4616.2;

(O) Attach a copy of the written transfer of care policy that complies with section 9767.9;

(P) Attach any policy or procedure that is used by the MPN applicant or an entity contracted with the MPN or MPN applicant to conduct "economic profiling of MPN providers" pursuant to Labor Code section 4616.1 and affirm that a copy of the policy or procedure has been provided to the MPN providers or attach a statement that the MPN applicant does not conduct economic profiling of MPN providers;

(Q) Provide an affirmation that the physician compensation is not structured in order to achieve the goal of reducing, delaying, or denying medical treatment or restricting access to medical treatment; and

(R) Describe how the MPN applicant will ensure that no person other than a licensed physician who is competent to evaluate the specific clinical issues involved in the medical treatment services, when these services are within the scope of the physician's practice, will modify, delay, or deny requests for authorization of medical treatment.

(S) Describe the MPN's procedures, criteria and how data is used to continuously review quality of care and performance of medical personnel, utilization of services and facilities, and costs.

(T) Affirm that as of January 1, 2013, every contracting agent that sells, leases, assigns, transfers, or conveys its medical provider networks and their contracted reimbursement rates to an insurer, employer, or entity that provides physician network services, or to another contracting agent shall, upon entering or renewing a provider contract, disclose to the provider whether the medical provider network may be sold, leased, transferred, or conveyed to other insurers, employers, entities providing physician network services, or another contracting agent, and specify whether those insurers, employers, entities providing physician network services, or contracting agents include workers' compensation insurers.

(e) If the entity is a Health Care Service Plan, Group Disability Insurance Policy, or Taft-Hartley Health and Welfare Fund, in addition to the requirements set forth in subdivision (d) of this section, a Medical Provider Network application shall include the following information:

(1) The application shall set forth that the entity has a reasonable number of providers with competency in occupational medicine.

(A) The MPN applicant may show that a physician has competency by confirming that the physician either is Board Certified or was residency trained in that specialty.

(B) If (A) is not applicable, describe any other relevant procedure or process that assures that providers of medical treatment are competent to provide treatment for occupational injuries and illnesses.

(f) If the MPN applicant is providing for ancillary services within the MPN that are in addition to the services provided by the Health Care Organization, Health Care Service Plan, Group Disability Insurance Policy, or Taft-Hartley Health and Welfare Fund, it shall set forth the ancillary services in the application.

(g) If a Health Care Organization, Health Care Service Plan, Group Disability Insurance Policy, or Taft-Hartley Health and Welfare Fund has been approved as a MPN, and the entity does not maintain its certification or licensure or regulated status, then the entity must file a new Medical Provider Network Application pursuant to section 9767.3(d).

(h) If a Health Care Organization, Health Care Service Plan, Group Disability Insurance Policy, or Taft-Hartley Health and Welfare Fund has been modified from its certification or licensure or regulated status, the application shall comply with subdivision (d) of this section.

Note: Authority cited: Sections 133 and 4616(h), Labor Code. Reference: Sections 3209.3, 4609, 4616, 4616.1, 4616.2, 4616.3, 4616.5 and 4616.7, Labor Code; and Section 16.5, Government Code.

History: 1. New section filed 11-1-2004 as an emergency; operative 11-1-2004 (Register 2004, No. 45). A Certificate of Compliance must be transmitted to OAL by 3-1-2005 or emergency language will be repealed by operation of law on the following day.

2. New section refiled 2-28-2005 as an emergency; operative 3-1-2005 (Register 2005, No. 9). A Certificate of Compliance must be transmitted to OAL by 6-29-2005 or emergency language will be repealed by operation of law on the following day.

3. New section refiled 6-20-2005 as an emergency; operative 6-29-2005 (Register 2005, No. 25). A Certificate of Compliance must be transmitted to OAL by 10-27-2005 or emergency language will be repealed by operation of law on the following day.

4. Certificate of Compliance as to 6-20-2005 order, including amendment of section and Note, transmitted to OAL 7-29-2005 and filed 9-9-2005 (Register 2005, No. 36).

5. Amendment of subsections (c)(1)-(3), (d)(6)-(7), (d)(8)(C)-(D), (d)(8)(I), (d)(8)(L), (e)(6)-(7), (e)(11), (e)(14), (f) and (i) filed 8-9-2010; operative 10-8-2010 (Register 2010, No. 33).

6. Change without regulatory effect amending subsections (c)(1), (d)(8)(I) and (e)(11) filed 9-23-2010 pursuant to section 100, title 1, California Code of Regulations (Register 2010, No. 39).

7. Amendment of section heading, section and Note filed 8-27-2014; operative 8-27-2014 pursuant to Government Code section 11343.4(b)(3) (Register 2014, No. 35).

Ref.: Hanna §§ 5.03[1], 5.05[13][a]; Herlick Handbook §§ 1.01[3][b], 4.11[2].

§9767.4. Cover Page for Medical Provider Network Application or Plan for Reapproval.

[DWC Form 9767.4 (Rev. 08/2014) Not Reproduced]

NOTE: Form is available at no charge by downloading from the web at www.dir.ca.gov/dwc/forms.html or by requesting at 1-800-794-6900.

Note: Authority cited: Sections 133 and 4616(h), Labor Code. Reference: Sections 3700, 3743, 4616, 4616.5 and 4616.7, Labor Code.

History: 1. New section filed 11-1-2004 as an emergency; operative 11-1-2004 (Register 2004, No. 45). A Certificate of Compliance must be transmitted to OAL by 3-1-2005 or emergency language will be repealed by operation of law on the following day.

2. New section refiled 2-28-2005 as an emergency; operative 3-1-2005 (Register 2005, No. 9). A Certificate of Compliance must be transmitted to OAL by 6-29-2005 or emergency language will be repealed by operation of law on the following day.

3. New section refiled 6-20-2005 as an emergency; operative 6-29-2005 (Register 2005, No. 25). A Certificate of Compliance must be transmitted to OAL by 10-27-2005 or emergency language will be repealed by operation of law on the following day.

4. Certificate of Compliance as to 6-20-2005 order, including amendment of section and Note, transmitted to OAL 7-29-2005 and filed 9-9-2005 (Register 2005, No. 36).

5. Change without regulatory effect amending section filed 5-23-2007 pursuant to section 100, title 1, California Code of Regulations (Register 2007, No. 21).

6. Amendment of section heading and section (DWC Mandatory Form Section 9767.4) and amendment of Note filed 8-27-2014; operative 8-27-2014 pursuant to Government Code section 11343.4(b)(3) (Register 2014, No. 35).

Ref.: Hanna §§ 5.03[1], 5.05[13][a]; Herlick Handbook § 1.01[3][b].

§9767.5. Access Standards.

(a) A MPN must have at least three available physicians of each specialty to treat common injuries experienced by injured employees based on the type of occupation or industry in which the employee is engaged and within the access standards set forth in (1) and (2).

(1) An MPN must have at least three available primary treating physicians and a hospital for emergency health care services, or if separate from such hospital, a provider of all emergency health care services, within 30 minutes or 15 miles of each covered employee's residence or workplace.

(2) An MPN must have providers of occupational health services and specialists who can treat common injuries experienced by the covered injured employees within 60 minutes or 30 miles of a covered employee's residence or workplace.

(b) If an MPN applicant believes that, given the facts and circumstances with regard to a portion of its service area, specifically areas in which there is a health care shortage, including non-rural areas and rural areas in which health facilities are located at least 30 miles apart, the accessibility standards set forth in subdivisions (a)(1) and/or (a)(2) cannot be met, the MPN applicant may propose alternative standards of accessibility for that portion of its service area. The MPN applicant shall do so by including the proposed alternative standards in writing in its plan application or in a notice of MPN plan modification and shall be reviewed and approved by the Administrative Director before the alternative standard can be used. The applicant shall explain how the proposed alternative standard was determined to be necessary for the specialty(ies) in which there is a health care shortage, including a description of the geographic area(s) affected for each specialty at issue, how the applicant determined a physician shortage exists in each area and specialty how the alternative access distance was determined and why it is necessary. The alternative standards shall provide that all services shall be available and accessible at reasonable times to all covered employees.

(c) If a covered employee is not able to obtain from an MPN physician reasonable and necessary medical treatment within the applicable access standards in subdivisions (a) or (b) and the required time frames in subdivisions (f) and (g), then the MPN shall have a written policy permitting the covered employee to obtain necessary treatment for that injury from an appropriate specialist outside the MPN within a reasonable geographic area. When the MPN is able to provide the necessary treatment through an MPN physician, a covered employee treating outside the MPN may be required to treat with an MPN physician when a transfer is appropriate.

(d) If an MPN provides ancillary services and those services or goods are not available within a reasonable time or a reasonable geographic area to a covered employee, then the employee may obtain necessary ancillary services outside of the MPN within a reasonable geographic area.

(e)(1) The MPN applicant shall have a written policy for arranging or approving non-emergency medical care for: (A) a covered employee authorized by the employer to temporarily work or travel for work outside the MPN geographic service area when the need for medical care arises; (B) a former employee whose employer has ongoing workers' compensation obligations and who permanently resides outside the MPN geographic service area; and (C) an injured employee who decides to temporarily reside outside the MPN geographic service area during recovery.

(2) The written policy shall provide the employees described in subdivision (e)(1) above with a list of at least three physicians outside the MPN geographic service area who either have been referred by the employee's primary treating physician within the MPN or have been selected by the MPN applicant. In addition to physicians within the MPN, the employee may change physicians among the referred physicians and may obtain a second and third opinion from the referred physicians.

(3) The referred physicians shall be located within the access standards described in (a) of this section.

(4) Nothing in this section precludes a covered employee outside the MPN geographic service area from choosing his or her own provider for non-emergency medical care.

(f) For non-emergency services, the MPN applicant shall ensure that an appointment for the first treatment visit under the MPN is available within 3 business days of a covered employee's notice to an MPN medical access assistant that treatment is needed.

(g) For non-emergency specialist services to treat common injuries experienced by the covered employees based on the type of occupation or industry in which the employee is engaged, the MPN applicant shall ensure that an initial appointment with a specialist in an appropriate referred specialty is available within 20 business days of a covered employee's reasonable requests for an appointment through an MPN medical access assistant. If an MPN medical access assistant is unable to schedule a timely medical appointment with an appropriate specialist within ten business days of an employee's request, the employer shall permit the employee to obtain necessary treatment with an appropriate specialist outside of the MPN.

(h) MPN medical access assistants shall be located in the United States and shall be available, at a minimum, from Monday through Saturday from 7 am to 8 pm, Pacific Time, to provide employee assistance with access to medical care under the MPN. The employee assistance shall be available in English and Spanish. The assistance shall include but not be limited to contacting provider offices during regular business hours and scheduling medical appointments for covered employees.

(1) There shall be at least one MPN medical access assistant available to respond at all required times, with the ability for callers to leave a voice message. There shall be enough medical access assistants to respond to calls, faxes or messages by the next day, excluding Sundays and holidays.

(2) MPN medical access assistants have different duties than claims adjusters. MPN medical access assistants

work in coordination with the MPN Contact and the claims adjuster(s) to ensure timely and appropriate medical treatment is provided to the injured worker. Although their duties are different, if the same person performs both, the MPN medical access assistant's contacts must be separately and accurately logged.

(i) If the primary treating physician refers the covered employee to a type of specialist not included in the MPN, the covered employee may select a specialist from outside the MPN.

(j) The MPN applicant shall have a written policy to allow an injured employee to receive emergency health care services from a medical service or hospital provider who is not a member of the MPN.

Note: Authority cited: Sections 133 and 4616(h), Labor Code. Reference: Sections 4616 and 4616.3, Labor Code.

History: 1. New section filed 11-1-2004 as an emergency; operative 11-1-2004 (Register 2004, No. 45). A Certificate of Compliance must be transmitted to OAL by 3-1-2005 or emergency language will be repealed by operation of law on the following day.

2. New section refiled 2-28-2005 as an emergency; operative 3-1-2005 (Register 2005, No. 9). A Certificate of Compliance must be transmitted to OAL by 6-29-2005 or emergency language will be repealed by operation of law on the following day.

3. New section refiled 6-20-2005 as an emergency; operative 6-29-2005 (Register 2005, No. 25). A Certificate of Compliance must be transmitted to OAL by 10-27-2005 or emergency language will be repealed by operation of law on the following day.

4. Certificate of Compliance as to 6-20-2005 order, including amendment of section, transmitted to OAL 7-29-2005 and filed 9-9-2005 (Register 2005, No. 36).

5. Amendment of section and Note filed 8-27-2014; operative 8-27-2014 pursuant to Government Code section 11343.4(b)(3) (Register 2014, No. 35).

Ref.: Hanna §§ 5.03[1], 5.05[13][a]; Herlick Handbook §§ 1.01[3][b], 4.11[4].

§ 9767.5.1. Physician Acknowledgments.

(a) An MPN applicant shall obtain from each physician participating in the MPN a written acknowledgement in which the physician affirmatively elects to be a member of the MPN as provided in this section. This section does not apply to a physician who is a shareholder, partner, or employee of a medical group that elects to participate in the MPN, however this section applies to the medical group that elects to participate in the MPN.

(b) The following persons may execute the acknowledgment:

(1) If the acknowledgment is for one or more physicians, it shall be executed by:

(A) The physician(s); or

(B) An employee of the physician or an employee of the physician's office; or

(C) If authorized by the physician(s), an agent or representative of a medical group.

(2) If a medical group elects to participate in an MPN, an authorized officer or agent of the medical group shall execute the acknowledgment. Unless the acknowledgment is for all physicians who are shareholders, partners, or employees of a medical group, or all physicians in a distinct department or unit of the medical group, the acknowledgement shall include or refer to a list of the participating physicians, and the officer or agent shall update the list within 90 days of any additions to or removals from the list.

(c) A written acknowledgment may be in any of the following forms:

(1) A tangible document bearing an original signature, or a facsimile or electronic image of the original document and signature.

(2) An electronically signed document in compliance with Government Code section 16.5 or Civil Code sections 1633.1 et seq. whichever is applicable.

(3) An electronic acknowledgment using generally accepted means of authentication to confirm the identity of the person making the acknowledgment.

(d) The acknowledgement shall identify the MPN in which the physician or group participates. Multiple MPNs may be identified in a single acknowledgment or separate acknowledgments or in any combination. Any form that presents more than one MPN for the physician's acknowledgment shall enable the physician either to opt in or to opt out of each MPN. The MPN or MPNs may be identified by reference to a website listing where a person described in subdivision (b) is enabled to observe which MPN or MPNs are selected for the physician or group. If permitted by the written acknowledgment, the website listing may be amended without further action by the physician or the group, provided that the website enables the physician or the group to de-select any MPN. If the physician or group is removed from an MPN by anyone other than a person described in subdivision (b), the MPN applicant shall give the physician or group notice of that fact in writing or electronically.

(e) The acknowledgment shall be obtained at the time of the following occurrences:

(1) If, on or after August 27, 2014, the physician or medical group enters into a new contract or renews a contract to participate in the MPN, then the acknowledgment shall be obtained at the time of entering into or renewing the contract.

(2) If, on or after August 27, 2014, the physician joins a medical group that already has a contract to participate in an MPN or MPNs, the acknowledgment shall be obtained at the time of the physician's joining the medical group.

(3) If, on or after January 1, 2014 but before August 27, 2014, the physician or medical group enters into a new contract or renews a contract to participate in the MPN, then the acknowledgment shall be obtained no later than January 1, 2015.

(4) If, on or after January 1, 2014 but before August 27, 2014, the physician joins a medical group that already has a contract to participate in an MPN or MPNs, the acknowledgment shall be obtained no later than January 1, 2015.

(5) If a contract entered prior to August 27, 2014 is continuous or automatically renews without a new execution by or on behalf of the physician, then the acknowledgment shall be obtained no later than January 1, 2016, unless the MPN applicant can satisfy either (A) or (B) below:

(A) The contract identifies the MPN in which the physician or group is participating.

(B) A website address is openly published where a person described in subdivision (b) is enabled to observe which MPN or MPNs have been selected for the physician or group and to de-select any MPN. The means to authenticate a person to access the website and to de-select any MPN shall be made available upon reasonable proof of the requesting person's identity as one of the persons authorized in subdivision (b).

(f) The MPN applicant shall retain a copy of the executed acknowledgment so long as it remains in force and for three years thereafter.

(g) The MPN applicant is responsible for obtaining physician acknowledgments and must ensure that all physician acknowledgments are up to date, meet regulatory requirements, and are readily available for review upon request by the Administrative Director.

Note: Authority cited: Sections 133 and 4616, Labor Code. Reference: Section 4616(a), Labor Code; Section 16.5, Government Code; and Sections 1633.1 et seq., Civil Code.

History: 1. New section filed 8-27-2014; operative 8-27-2014 pursuant to Government Code section 11343.4(b)(3) (Register 2014, No. 35).

Ref.: Hanna § 5.03[1].

§9767.6. Treatment and Change of Physicians Within MPN.

(a) When the injured covered employee notifies the employer or insured employer of the injury or files a claim for workers' compensation with the employer or insured employer, the employer or insurer or entity that provides physician network services shall arrange an initial medical evaluation with a MPN physician in compliance with the access standards set forth in section 9767.5.

(b) Within one working day after an employee files a claim form under Labor Code section 5401, the employer or insurer shall provide for all treatment, consistent with guidelines adopted by the Administrative Director pursuant to Labor Code section 5307.27 and as set forth in title 8, California Code of Regulations, section 9792.20 et seq.

(c) The employer or insurer shall provide for the treatment with MPN providers for the alleged injury and shall continue to provide the treatment until the date that liability for the claim is rejected. Until the date the claim is rejected, liability for the claim shall be limited to ten thousand dollars ($10,000).

(d) The insurer or employer shall notify the employee of his or her right to be treated by a physician of his or her choice within the MPN after the first visit with the MPN physician and the method by which the list of participating providers may be accessed by the employee.

(e) At any point in time after the initial medical evaluation with an MPN physician, the covered employee may select a physician of his or her choice from within the MPN. Selection by the covered employee of a treating physician and any subsequent physicians shall be based on the physician's specialty or recognized expertise in treating the particular injury or condition in question. If a chiropractor is selected as a treating physician, the chiropractor may act as a treating physician only until the 24-visit cap is met unless otherwise authorized by the employer or insurer, after which the covered employee must select another treating physician in the MPN who is not a chiropractor, and if the employee fails to do so, then the insurer or employer may assign another treating physician who is not a chiropractor.

(f) A Petition for Change of Treating Physician, as set forth at section 9786, cannot be utilized to seek a change of physician for a covered employee who is treating with a physician within the MPN.

Note: Authority cited: Sections 133 and 4616(h), Labor Code. Reference: Sections 4604.5, 4616, 4616.3, 5307.27 and 5401, Labor Code.

History: 1. New section filed 11-1-2004 as an emergency; operative 11-1-2004 (Register 2004, No. 45). A Certificate of Compliance must be transmitted to OAL by 3-1-2005 or emergency language will be repealed by operation of law on the following day.

2. New section refiled 2-28-2005 as an emergency; operative 3-1-2005 (Register 2005, No. 9). A Certificate of Compliance must be transmitted to OAL by 6-29-2005 or emergency language will be repealed by operation of law on the following day.

3. New section refiled 6-20-2005 as an emergency; operative 6-29-2005 (Register 2005, No. 25). A Certificate of Compliance must be transmitted to OAL by 10-27-2005 or emergency language will be repealed by operation of law on the following day.

4. Certificate of Compliance as to 6-20-2005 order, including amendment of section, transmitted to OAL 7-29-2005 and filed 9-9-2005 (Register 2005, No. 36).

5. Amendment of subsections (b) and (f) filed 8-9-2010; operative 10-8-2010 (Register 2010, No. 33).

6. Amendment of subsections (a) and (e) and amendment of Note filed 8-27-2014; operative 8-27-2014 pursuant to Government Code section 11343.4(b)(3) (Register 2014, No. 35).

Ref.: Hanna §§ 5.03[1], 5.05[13][d]; Herlick Handbook §§ 1.01[3][b], 4.04[3], 4.11[7], [8].

§9767.7. Second and Third Opinions.

(a) If the covered employee disputes either the diagnosis or the treatment prescribed by the primary treating physician or the treating physician, the employee may obtain a second and third opinion from physicians within the MPN. During this process, the employee is required to continue his or her treatment with the treating physician or a physician of his or her choice within the MPN.

(b) If the covered employee disputes either the diagnosis or the treatment prescribed by primary treating physician or the treating physician, it is the employee's responsibility to: (1) inform the person designated by the employer or insurer that he or she disputes the treating physician's opinion and requests a second opinion (the employee may notify the person designated by the employer or insurer either in writing or orally); (2) select a physician or specialist from a list of available MPN providers; (3) make an appointment with the second opinion physician within 60 days; and (4) inform the person designated by the employer or insurer of the appointment date. It is the employer's or insurer's responsibility to (1) provide at least a regional area listing of MPN providers and/or specialists to the employee for his/her selection based on the specialty or recognized expertise in treating the particular injury or condition in question and inform the employee of his or her right to request a copy of the medical records that will be sent to the second opinion physician; (2) contact the treating physician, provide a copy of the medical records or send the necessary medical records to the second opinion physician prior to the appointment date, and provide a copy of the records to the covered employee upon request; and (3) notify the second opinion physician in writing that he or she has been selected to provide a second opinion and the nature of the dispute with a copy to the employee. If the appointment is not made within 60 days of receipt of the list of the available MPN providers, then the employee shall be deemed to have waived the second opinion process with regard to this disputed diagnosis or treatment of this treating physician.

(c) If, after reviewing the covered employee's medical records, the second opinion physician determines that the employee's injury is outside the scope of his or her practice, the physician shall notify the person designated by the employer or insurer and employee so the employer or insurer can provide a new list of MPN providers and/or specialists to the employee for his/her selection based on the specialty or recognized expertise in treating the particular injury or condition in question.

(d) If the covered employee disagrees with either the diagnosis or treatment prescribed by the second opinion physician, the injured employee may seek the opinion of a third physician within the MPN. It is the employee's responsibility to: (1) inform the person designated by the employer or insurer that he or she disputes the treating physician's opinion and requests a third opinion (the employee may notify the person designated by the employer or insurer either in writing or orally); (2) select a physician or specialist from a list of available MPN providers; and (3) make an appointment with the third opinion physician within 60 days; and (4) inform the person designated by the employer or insurer of the appointment date. It is the employer's or insurer's responsibility to (1) provide at least a regional area listing of MPN providers and/or specialists to the employee for his/her selection based on the specialty or recognized expertise in treating the particular injury or condition in question and inform the employee of his or her right to request a copy of the medical records that will be sent to the third opinion physician; and (2) contact the treating physician, provide a copy of the medical records or send the necessary medical records to the third opinion physician prior to the appointment date, and provide a copy of the records to the covered employee upon request; and (3) notify the third opinion physician in writing that he or she has been selected to provide a third opinion and the nature of the dispute with a copy to the employee. If the appointment is not made within 60 days of receipt of the list of the available MPN providers, then the employee shall be deemed to have waived the third opinion process with regard to this disputed diagnosis or treatment of this treating physician.

(e) If, after reviewing the covered employee's medical records, the third opinion physician determines that the employee's injury is outside the scope of his or her practice, the physician shall notify the person designated by the employer or insurer and employee so the MPN can provide a new list of MPN providers and/or specialists to the employee for his/her selection based on the specialty or recognized expertise in treating the particular injury or condition in question.

(f) The second and third opinion physicians shall each render his or her opinion of the disputed diagnosis or treatment in writing and offer alternative diagnosis or treatment recommendations, if applicable. Any recommended treatment shall be in accordance with Labor Code section 4616(e). The second and third opinion physicians may order diagnostic testing if medically necessary. A copy of the written report shall be served on the employee, the person designated by the employer or insurer, and the treating physician within 20 days of the date of the appointment or receipt of the results of the diagnostic tests, whichever is later.

(g) The employer or insurer shall permit the employee to obtain the recommended treatment within the MPN or if the MPN does not contain a physician who can provide the recommended treatment, the employee may choose a physician outside the MPN within a reasonable geographic area. The covered employee may obtain the recommended treatment by changing physicians to the second opinion physician, third opinion physician, or other MPN physician.

(h) If the injured covered employee disagrees with the diagnosis or treatment of the third opinion physician, the injured employee may file with the Administrative Director a request for an MPN Independent Medical Review, pursuant to Labor Code sections 4616.3, 4616.4 and title 8, California Code of Regulations sections 9768.1 et seq.

Note: Authority cited: Sections 133 and 4616(h), Labor Code. Reference: Sections 4616(a) and 4616.3, Labor Code.

History: 1. New section filed 11-1-2004 as an emergency; operative 11-1-2004 (Register 2004, No. 45). A Certificate of Compliance must be transmitted to OAL by 3-1-2005 or emergency language will be repealed by operation of law on the following day.

2. New section refiled 2-28-2005 as an emergency; operative 3-1-2005 (Register 2005, No. 9). A Certificate of Compliance must be transmitted to OAL by 6-29-2005 or emergency language will be repealed by operation of law on the following day.

3. New section refiled 6-20-2005 as an emergency; operative 6-29-2005 (Register 2005, No. 25). A Certificate of Compliance must be transmitted to OAL by 10-27-2005 or emergency language will be repealed by operation of law on the following day.

4. Certificate of Compliance as to 6-20-2005 order, including amendment of section, transmitted to OAL 7-29-2005 and filed 9-9-2005 (Register 2005, No. 36).

5. Amendment of subsections (b), (d) and (g)-(h) and amendment of Note filed 8-27-2014; operative 8-27-2014 pursuant to Government Code section 11343.4(b)(3) (Register 2014, No. 35).

Ref.: Hanna §§ 5.03[1], 5.05[13][d], [e]; Herlick Handbook §§ 1.01[3][b], 4.11[7], [8].

§9767.8. Modification of Medical Provider Network Plan.

Note: *See Executive Order N-63-20 (2019 CA EO 63-20), issued in response to the COVID-19 pandemic, which extends certain deadlines for action on Medical Provider Network applications or requests for modifications or reapprovals.*

(a) The MPN applicant shall serve the Administrative Director with two copies of the completed, signed Notice of MPN Plan Modification and any necessary documentation in compact discs or flash drives in word-searchable PDF format. The hard copy of the original signed Notice of Medical Provider Network Plan Modification form and any necessary documentation shall be maintained by the MPN applicant and made available for review by the Administrative Director upon request. Electronic signatures in compliance with California Government Code section 16.5 are accepted. The MPN applicant shall serve these documents with the Administrative Director within the stated time frames or if no time frame is stated, then before any of the following changes occur:

(1) Change in the name of the MPN or the name of the MPN applicant. Filing required within (15) fifteen business days of the change. Provide written documentation reflecting date of change.

(2) Change in the eligibility status of the MPN applicant. Filing required within fifteen (15) business days of written knowledge of a change in eligibility. Provide written documentation reflecting date of change.

(3) Change of MPN Liaison or Authorized Individual: Filing required within fifteen (15) business days of change. Provide written documentation reflecting date of change.

(4) Change in MPN geographic service area within the State of California.

(5) A material change in the continuity of care policy.

(6) A material change in the transfer of care policy.

(7) Change in policy or procedure that is used by the MPN or an entity contracted with the MPN or MPN applicant to conduct "economic profiling of MPN providers" pursuant to Labor Code section 4616.1.

(8) Change in how the MPN complies with the access standards.

(9) A material change in any of the employee notification materials, including a change in MPN contact, a change in the Medical Access Assistants contact information, or a change in provider listing access or MPN website information, required by section 9767.12.

(10) Change in use of one of the following deemed entities: Health Care Organization (HCO), Health Care Service Plan, Group Disability Insurer, or Taft-Hartley Health and Welfare Trust Fund.

(11) Revision of any plan section(s) required by section 9767.3(d) due to a change of any MPN administrator(s) listed in the MPN Plan.

(12) Replacement of entire MPN plan application.

(13) Updating to the current regulations pursuant to section 9767.15.

(b) Failure to file a material modification within the requisite time frame may result in administrative actions pursuant to sections 9767.14 and/or 9767.19.

(c) The modification must be verified by an officer or employee of the MPN with the authority to act on behalf of the MPN applicant with respect to the MPN. The verification by the authorized individual shall state: "I, the undersigned officer or employee of the MPN applicant, have read and signed this notice and know the contents thereof, and verify that, to the best of my knowledge and belief, the information included in this modification is true and correct."

(d) Within 60 days of the Administrative Director's receipt of a Notice of MPN Plan Modification, the Administrative Director shall approve or disapprove the plan modification based on information provided in the Notice of MPN Plan Modification. The Administrative Director shall approve or disapprove a plan modification based on the requirements of Labor Code section 4616 et seq. and this article. If the Administrative Director has not acted on a plan within 60 days of submittal of a Notice of MPN Plan Modification, it shall be deemed approved. Except for subdivisions (a)(2), (a)(3) and (b) of this section, modifications shall not be made until the Administrative Director has approved the plan or until 60 days have passed, whichever occurs first. If the Administrative Director disapproves of the MPN plan modification, he or she shall serve the MPN applicant with a Notice of Disapproval within 60 days of the submittal of a Notice of MPN Plan Modification.

(e) A MPN applicant denied approval of a MPN plan modification may either:

(1) Submit a new request addressing the deficiencies; or

(2) Request a re-evaluation by the Administrative Director.

(f) Any MPN applicant may request a re-evaluation of the denial by submitting with the Division, within 20 days of the issuance of the Notice of Disapproval, a written request for a re-evaluation with a detailed statement explaining the basis upon which a re-evaluation is requested. The request for re-evaluation shall be accompanied by supportive documentary material relevant to the specific allegations raised and shall be verified under penalty of perjury. The MPN application and modification at issue shall not be refiled; they shall be made part of the administrative record by incorporation by reference.

(g) The Administrative Director shall, within 45 days of the receipt of the request for a re-evaluation, either:

(1) Issue a Decision and Order affirming or modifying the Notice of Disapproval based on a failure to meet the procedural requirements of this section or based on a failure to meet the requirements of Labor Code section 4616 et seq. and this article; or

(2) Issue a Decision and Order rescinding the Notice of Disapproval and issue an approval of the modification.

(h) The Administrative Director may extend the time specified in subdivision (g) within which to act upon the request for a re-evaluation for a period of 30 days and may order a party to submit additional documents or information.

(i) An MPN applicant may appeal the Administrative Director's decision and order regarding the MPN by filing, within twenty (20) days of the issuance of the decision and order, a "Petition Appealing Administrative Director's Medical Provider Network Determination" with the Workers' Compensation Appeals Board pursuant to WCAB Rule 10959. A copy of the petition shall be concurrently served on the Administrative Director.

(j) The MPN applicant shall use the following Notice of MPN Plan Modification form:

[DWC Mandatory Form — Section 9767.8 — 5/14) Not Reproduced]

NOTE: Form is available at no charge by downloading from the web at www.dir.ca.gov/dwc/forms.html or by requesting at 1-800-794-6900.

Note: Authority cited: Sections 133, 4616(h) and 5300(f), Labor Code. Reference: Sections 3700, 3743, 4616, 4616.2 and 4616.5, Labor Code.

History: 1. New section filed 11-1-2004 as an emergency; operative 11-1-2004 (Register 2004, No. 45). A Certificate of Compliance must be transmitted to OAL by 3-1-2005 or emergency language will be repealed by operation of law on the following day.

2. New section refiled 2-28-2005 as an emergency; operative 3-1-2005 (Register 2005, No. 9). A Certificate of Compliance must be transmitted to OAL by 6-29-2005 or emergency language will be repealed by operation of law on the following day.

3. New section refiled 6-20-2005 as an emergency; operative 6-29-2005 (Register 2005, No. 25). A Certificate of Compliance must be transmitted to OAL by 10-27-2005 or emergency language will be repealed by operation of law on the following day.

4. Certificate of Compliance as to 6-20-2005 order, including amendment of section and Note, transmitted to OAL 7-29-2005 and filed 9-9-2005 (Register 2005, No. 36).

5. Change without regulatory effect amending form filed 5-23-2007 pursuant to section 100, title 1, California Code of Regulations (Register 2007, No. 21).

6. Amendment of subsections (a)(5)-(6) and (a)(9), new subsections (a)(10)-(13) and amendment of subsections (b)-(d), (g)(2) and (j) filed 8-9-2010; operative 10-8-2010 (Register 2010, No. 33).

7. Amendment of section, including amendment of DWC Mandatory Form Section 9767.8, and amendment of Note filed 8-27-2014; operative 8-27-2014 pursuant to Government Code section 11343.4(b)(3) (Register 2014, No. 35).

8. Governor Newsom issued Executive Order N-63-20 (2019 CA EO 63-20), dated May 7, 2020, which extended certain deadlines for action on Medical Provider Network applications or requests for modifications or reapprovals, due to the COVID-19 pandemic.

Ref.: Hanna § 5.03[1]; Herlick Handbook § 1.01[3][b].

§9767.9. Transfer of Ongoing Care into the MPN.

(a) If the injured covered employee's injury or illness does not meet the conditions set forth in (e)(1) through (e)(4), the injured covered employee may be transferred into the MPN for medical treatment, unless otherwise authorized by the employer or insurer.

(b) Until the injured covered employee is transferred into the MPN, the employee's physician may make referrals to providers within or outside the MPN.

(c) Nothing in this section shall preclude an insurer or employer from agreeing to provide medical care with providers outside of the MPN.

(d) If an injured covered employee is being treated for an occupational injury or illness by a physician or provider prior to coverage of a medical provider network, and the injured covered employee's physician or provider becomes a provider within the MPN that applies to the injured covered employee, then the employer, insurer, or entity that provides physician network services shall inform the injured covered employee and his or her physician or provider if his/her treatment is being provided by his/her physician or provider under the provisions of the MPN.

(e) The employer or insurer shall authorize the completion of treatment for injured covered employees who are being treated outside of the MPN for an occupational injury or illness that occurred prior to the coverage of the MPN and whose treating physician is not a provider within the MPN, including injured covered employees who predesignated a physician and do not fall within the Labor Code section 4600(d), for the following conditions:

(1) An acute condition. For purposes of this subdivision, an acute condition is a medical condition that involves a sudden onset of symptoms due to an illness, injury, or other medical problem that requires prompt medical attention and that has a duration of less than 90 days. Completion of treatment shall be provided for the duration of the acute condition.

(2) A serious chronic condition. For purposes of this subdivision, a serious chronic condition is a medical condition due to a disease, illness, catastrophic injury, or other medical problem or medical disorder that is serious in nature and that persists without full cure or worsens over 90 days and requires ongoing treatment to maintain remission or prevent deterioration. Completion of treatment shall be authorized for a period of time necessary, up to one year: (A) to complete a course of treatment approved by the employer or insurer; and (B) to arrange for transfer to another provider within the MPN, as determined by the insurer, employer, or entity that provides physician network services. The one year period for completion of treatment starts from the date of the injured covered employee's receipt of the notification, as required by subdivision (f), of the determination that the employee has a serious chronic condition.

(3) A terminal illness. For purposes of this subdivision, a terminal illness is an incurable or irreversible condition that has a high probability of causing death within one year or less. Completion of treatment shall be provided for the duration of a terminal illness.

(4) Performance of a surgery or other procedure that is authorized by the insurer or employer as part of a documented course of treatment and has been recommended and documented by the provider to occur within 180 days from the MPN coverage effective date.

(f) If the employer or insurer decides to transfer the covered employee's medical care to the medical provider network, the employer, insurer, or entity that provides physician network services shall notify the covered employee of the determination regarding the completion of treatment and the decision to transfer medical care into the medical provider network. The notification shall be sent to the covered employee's address and a copy of the letter shall be sent to the covered employee's primary treating physician. The notification shall be written in English and Spanish and use layperson's terms to the maximum extent possible.

(g) If the injured covered employee disputes the medical determination under this section, the injured covered employee shall request a report from the covered employee's primary treating physician that addresses whether the covered employee falls within any of the conditions set forth in subdivisions (e)(1-4). The treating physician shall provide the report to the covered employee within twenty calendar days of the request. If the treating physician fails to issue the report, then the determination made by the employer or insurer referred to in (f) shall apply.

(h) If the employer or insurer or injured covered employee objects to the medical determination by the treating physician, the dispute regarding the medical determination made by the treating physician concerning the transfer of care shall be resolved pursuant to Labor Code section 4062.

(i) If the treating physician agrees with the employer's or insurer's determination that the injured covered employee's medical condition does not meet the conditions set forth in subdivisions (e)(1) through (e)(4), the transfer of care shall go forward during the dispute resolution process.

(j) If the treating physician does not agree with the employer's or insurer's determination that the injured covered employee's medical condition does not meet the conditions set forth in subdivisions (e)(1) through (e)(4), the transfer of care shall not go forward until the dispute is resolved.

Note: Authority cited: Sections 133, 4616(h) and 4062, Labor Code. Reference: Sections 4616 and 4616.2, Labor Code.

History: 1. New section filed 11-1-2004 as an emergency; operative 11-1-2004 (Register 2004, No. 45). A Certificate of Compliance must be transmitted to OAL by 3-1-2005 or emergency language will be repealed by operation of law on the following day.

2. New section refiled 2-28-2005 as an emergency; operative 3-1-2005 (Register 2005, No. 9). A Certificate of Compliance must be transmitted to OAL by 6-29-2005 or emergency language will be repealed by operation of law on the following day.

3. New section refiled 6-20-2005 as an emergency; operative 6-29-2005 (Register 2005, No. 25). A Certificate of Compliance must be transmitted to OAL by 10-27-2005 or emergency language will be repealed by operation of law on the following day.

4. Certificate of Compliance as to 6-20-2005 order, including amendment of section, transmitted to OAL 7-29-2005 and filed 9-9-2005 (Register 2005, No. 36).

5. Amendment of subsections (a) (d), (e)(2) and (f) and amendment of Note filed 8-27-2014; operative 8-27-2014 pursuant to Government Code section 11343.4(b)(3) (Register 2014, No. 35).

Ref.: Hanna §§ 5.03[1], 5.05[13][c]; Herlick Handbook §§ 1.01[3][b], 4.11[6].

§9767.10. Continuity of Care Policy.

(a) At the request of a covered employee, an insurer, employer, or an entity that provides physician network services that offers a medical provider network shall complete the treatment by a terminated provider as set forth in Labor Code sections 4616.2(d) and (e).

(b) An "acute condition," as referred to in Labor Code section 4616.2(d)(3)(A), shall have a duration of less than ninety days.

(c) "An extended period of time," as referred to in Labor Code section 4616.2(d)(3)(B) with regard to a serious and chronic condition, means a duration of at least ninety days.

(d) The MPN applicant's continuity of care policy shall include a dispute resolution procedure that contains the following requirements:

(1) Following the employer's or insurer's determination of the injured covered employee's medical condition, the employer, insurer, or an entity that provides physician network services shall notify the covered employee of the determination regarding the completion of treatment and whether or not the employee will be required to select a new provider from within the MPN. The notification shall be sent to the covered employee's address and a copy of the letter shall be sent to the covered employee's primary treating physician. The notification shall be written in English and Spanish and use layperson's terms to the maximum extent possible.

(2) If the terminated provider agrees to continue treating the injured covered employee in accordance with Labor Code section 4616.2 and if the injured covered employee disputes the medical determination, the injured covered employee shall request a report from the covered employee's primary treating physician that addresses whether the covered employee falls within any of the conditions set forth in Labor Code section 4616.2(d)(3); an acute condition; a serious chronic condition; a terminal illness; or a performance of a surgery or other procedure that is authorized by the insurer or employer as part of a documented course of treatment and has been recommended and documented by the provider to occur within 180 days of the contract's termination date. The treating physician shall provide the report to the covered employee within twenty calendar days of the request. If the treating physician fails to issue the report, then the determination made by the employer or insurer referred to in (d)(1) shall apply.

(3) If the employer or insurer or injured covered employee objects to the medical determination by the treating physician, the dispute regarding the medical determination made by the treating physician concerning the continuity of care shall be resolved pursuant to Labor Code section 4062.

(4) If the treating physician agrees with the employer's or insurer's determination that the injured covered employee's medical condition does not meet the conditions set forth in Labor Code section 4616.2(d)(3), the employee shall choose a new provider from within the MPN during the dispute resolution process.

(5) If the treating physician does not agree with the employer's or insurer's determination that the injured covered employee's medical condition does not meet the conditions set forth in Labor Code section 4616.2(d)(3), the injured covered employee shall continue to treat with the terminated provider until the dispute is resolved.

Note: Authority cited: Sections 133 and 4616(h), Labor Code. Reference: Section 4616.2, Labor Code.

History: 1. New section filed 11-1-2004 as an emergency; operative 11-1-2004 (Register 2004, No. 45). A Certificate of Compliance must be transmitted to OAL by 3-1-2005 or emergency language will be repealed by operation of law on the following day.

2. New section refiled 2-28-2005 as an emergency; operative 3-1-2005 (Register 2005, No. 9). A Certificate of Compliance must be transmitted to OAL by 6-29-2005 or emergency language will be repealed by operation of law on the following day.

3. New section refiled 6-20-2005 as an emergency; operative 6-29-2005 (Register 2005, No. 25). A Certificate of Compliance must be transmitted to OAL by 10-27-2005 or emergency language will be repealed by operation of law on the following day.

4. Certificate of Compliance as to 6-20-2005 order, including amendment of section, transmitted to OAL 7-29-2005 and filed 9-9-2005 (Register 2005, No. 36).

5. Amendment of subsections (a) and (d)(1) and amendment of Note filed 8-27-2014; operative 8-27-2014 pursuant to Government Code section 11343.4(b)(3) (Register 2014, No. 35).

Ref.: Hanna §§ 5.03[1], 5.05[13][c]; Herlick Handbook §§ 1.01[3][b], 4.11[6].

§9767.11. Economic Profiling Policy.

(a) An MPN applicant's filing of its economic profiling policies and procedures shall include:

(1) An overall description of the profiling methodology, data used to create the profile and risk adjustment;

(2) A description of how economic profiling is used in utilization review;

(3) A description of how economic profiling is used in peer review; and

(4) A description of any incentives and penalties used in the program and in provider retention and termination decisions.

Note: Authority cited: Sections 133 and 4616(h), Labor Code. Reference: Section 4616.1, Labor Code.

History: 1. New section filed 11-1-2004 as an emergency; operative 11-1-2004 (Register 2004, No. 45). A Certificate of Compliance must be transmitted to OAL by 3-1-2005 or emergency language will be repealed by operation of law on the following day.

2. New section refiled 2-28-2005 as an emergency; operative 3-1-2005 (Register 2005, No. 9). A Certificate of Compliance must be transmitted to OAL by 6-29-2005 or emergency language will be repealed by operation of law on the following day.

3. New section refiled 6-20-2005 as an emergency; operative 6-29-2005 (Register 2005, No. 25). A Certificate of Compliance must be transmitted to OAL by 10-27-2005 or emergency language will be repealed by operation of law on the following day.

4. Certificate of Compliance as to 6-20-2005 order transmitted to OAL 7-29-2005 and filed 9-9-2005 (Register 2005, No. 36).

5. Amendment of subsection (a) and Note filed 8-27-2014; operative 8-27-2014 pursuant to Government Code section 11343.4(b)(3) (Register 2014, No. 35).

Ref.: Hanna §§ 5.03[1], 5.05[13][b]; Herlick Handbook §§ 1.01[3][b], 4.11[5].

§9767.12. Employee Notification.

(a) When an injury is reported or an employer has knowledge of an injury that is subject to an MPN or when an employee with an existing injury is required to transfer treatment to an MPN, a complete written MPN employee notification with the information specified in paragraph (2) of this subdivision, shall be provided to the covered employee by the employer or the insurer for the employer. This MPN notification shall be provided to employees in English and also in Spanish if the employee primarily speaks Spanish.

(1) A complete MPN notification with the information specified in paragraph (2) of this subdivision may be sent electronically in lieu of by mail, if the covered employee has regular electronic access to email at work to receive this notice at the time of injury or when the employee is being transferred into the MPN. If the employee cannot receive this notice electronically at work, then the employer shall ensure this information is provided to the employee in writing at the time of injury or when the employee is being transferred into the MPN.

(2) The complete written MPN employee notification shall include the following information:

(A) The unique MPN Identification number. How to contact the person designated by MPN applicant to be the MPN Contact for covered employees to answer questions about the use of MPNs and to address MPN complaints. The employer or insurer shall provide a toll-free telephone number with access to the MPN Contact if the MPN geographic service area includes more than one area code. A toll-free number must also be listed for MPN Medical Access Assistants, with a description of the access assistance they provide, including finding available MPN physicians of the injured workers' choice and scheduling and confirming physician appointments, and the times they are available to assist workers with obtaining access to medical treatment under the MPN;

(B) A description of MPN services as well as the MPN's web address for more information about the MPN and the web address that includes a roster of all treating physicians in the MPN;

(C) How to review, receive or access the MPN provider directory. An employer, insurer, or entity that provides physician network services shall ensure covered employees have access to, at minimum, a regional area listing of MPN providers in addition to maintaining and making available its complete provider directory listing in writing and/or on the MPN's website. The MPN's website address shall be clearly listed. If an employee requests an electronic provider directory listing, it shall be provided electronically on a CD, flash drive, via email or on a website. The URL address for the provider directory shall be listed with any additional information needed to access the directory online including any necessary instructions and passcodes. MPN applicants are responsible for updating an MPN's provider listings, at minimum, on a quarterly basis with the date of the last update provided on the listing given to the employee. Each provider directory listing shall include a phone number and an email address for reporting of provider listing inaccuracies. If a listed provider becomes deceased or is no longer treating workers' compensation patients at the listed address, the provider shall be taken off the provider directory within 45 days of notice to the MPN through the contact method stated on the provider directory listing to report inaccuracies.

(D) How to access initial care and subsequent medical care and how to contact the medical access assistants if an employee needs help in finding a physician or scheduling an appointment;

(E) The mileage, time requirements and alternative access standards required under section 9767.5;

(F) How to access treatment if (A) the employee is authorized by the employer to temporarily work or travel for work outside the MPN's geographic service area; (B) a former employee whose employer has ongoing workers' compensation obligations permanently resides outside the MPN geographic service area; and (C) an injured employee decides to temporarily reside outside the MPN geographic service area during recovery;

(G) How to choose a physician within the MPN;

(H) What to do if a covered employee has trouble getting an appointment with a provider within the MPN and how to use the medical access assistants for help;

(I) How to change a physician within the MPN;

(J) How to obtain a referral to a specialist within the MPN or outside the MPN, if needed;

(K) How to use the second and third opinion process;

(L) How to request and receive an MPN independent medical review;

(M) A description of the standards for the transfer of care policy and a notification that a copy of the policy in English or in Spanish if the employee speaks Spanish shall be provided to an employee upon request; and

(N) A description of the standards for the continuity of care policy and a notification that a copy of the policy in English or in Spanish if the employee speaks Spanish shall be provided to an employee upon request.

(b) When MPN coverage will end, the employer or the insurer for the employer shall ensure each injured covered employee who is treating under its MPN is given written notice of the date the employee will no longer be able to use its MPN. The notice required by this section shall be provided in English and also in Spanish if the employee speaks Spanish.

(1) The employer or the insurer for the employer shall ensure that every affected injured covered employee using its MPN is provided the following information prior to the date its MPN coverage ends:

(A) The effective date the employee can no longer use the MPN. The unique MPN Identification number shall be stated in the notice.

(B) Whether the MPN will still be used for injuries arising before the date MPN coverage ends.

(C) The address(es), telephone number(s), and email address(es) of the MPN Contact and MPN Medical Access Assistants who can address MPN questions, and an MPN website.

(D) For periods when an employee is not covered by a MPN, an employee may choose a physician 30 days after the date the employee notified the employer of his or her injury.

(2) The following language may be provided in writing to injured covered employees to give the required notice of the end of coverage under an MPN: "The <Insert MPN Name> Medical Provider Network (MPN), under the unique MPN Identification number <Insert MPN Identification number> will no longer be used for injuries arising after <Insert Date MPN Coverage Ends>. You will/will not <Select Whichever is Appropriate> continue to use this MPN to obtain care for work injuries occurring before this date. For new injuries that occur when you are not covered by a MPN, you have the right to choose your physician 30 days after you notify your employer of your injury. For more information contact <Insert MPN Contact and Medical Access Assistants toll free number(s), MPN Address(es), MPN Email Address(es), and MPN Website."

(3) This required notice may be provided by mail or included on or with an employee's paystub, paycheck or sent electronically in lieu of mail, if the employee has regular electronic access to email at work to receive this notice prior to the end of MPN coverage. If the employee cannot receive this notice electronically at work within the required time frame, then the employer shall ensure this information is provided to the employee in writing prior to the end of MPN coverage.

(4) Any pending MPN Independent Medical Review will end with the employee's coverage under the MPN.

(c) At the time of the selection of the physician for a third opinion, the covered employee shall be notified about the MPN Independent Medical Review process, as set forth in section 9768.9(a).

Note: Authority cited: Sections 133 and 4616, Labor Code. Reference: Sections 4616, 4616.2 and 4616.3, Labor Code.

History: 1. New section filed 11-1-2004 as an emergency; operative 11-1-2004 (Register 2004, No. 45). A Certificate of Compliance must be transmitted to OAL by 3-1-2005 or emergency language will be repealed by operation of law on the following day.

2. New section refiled 2-28-2005 as an emergency; operative 3-1-2005 (Register 2005, No. 9). A Certificate of Compliance must be transmitted to OAL by 6-29-2005 or emergency language will be repealed by operation of law on the following day.

3. New section refiled 6-20-2005 as an emergency; operative 6-29-2005 (Register 2005, No. 25). A Certificate of Compliance must be transmitted to OAL by 10-27-2005 or emergency language will be repealed by operation of law on the following day.

4. Certificate of Compliance as to 6-20-2005 order, including amendment of section, transmitted to OAL 7-29-2005 and filed 9-9-2005 (Register 2005, No. 36).

5. Amendment filed 8-9-2010; operative 10-8-2010 (Register 2010, No. 33).

6. Amendment filed 8-27-2014; operative 8-27-2014 pursuant to Government Code section 11343.4(b)(3) (Register 2014, No. 35).

Ref.: Hanna §§ 5.03[1], 5.05[13][c]; Herlick Handbook §§ 1.01[3][b], 4.11[3], [7].

§9767.13. Denial of Approval of Application or Reapproval; Re-Evaluation.

(a) The Administrative Director shall deny approval or reapproval of a plan if the MPN applicant does not satisfy the requirements of this article and Labor Code section 4616 et seq. and shall state the reasons for disapproval in writing in a Notice of Disapproval, and shall transmit the Notice to the MPN applicant by U.S. Mail.

(b) An MPN applicant denied approval may either:

(1) Submit a corrected application or plan for reapproval addressing the deficiencies; or

(2) Request a re-evaluation by the Administrative Director.

(c) Any MPN applicant may request a re-evaluation by submitting with the Division, within 20 days of the issuance of the Notice of Disapproval, a written request for re-evaluation with a detailed statement explaining the basis upon which a re-evaluation is requested. The request for a re-evaluation shall be accompanied by supportive documentary material relevant to the specific allegations raised and shall be verified under penalty of perjury. The MPN application at issue shall not be re-filed; it shall be made part of the administrative record by incorporation by reference.

(d) The Administrative Director shall, within 45 days of the receipt of the request for a re-evaluation, either:

(1) Issue a Decision and Order affirming or modifying the Notice of Disapproval based on a failure to meet the procedural requirements of this section or based on a failure to meet the requirements of Labor Code section 4616 et seq. and this article; or

(2) Issue a Decision and Order recinding the Notice of Disapproval and issue an approval of the MPN.

(e) The Administrative Director may extend the time specified in subdivision (d) within which to act upon the request for a re-evaluation for a period of 30 days and may order a party to submit additional documents or information.

(f) An MPN applicant may appeal the Administrative Director's decision and order regarding the MPN by filing, within twenty (20) days of the issuance of the decision and order, a "Petition Appealing Administrative Director's Medical Provider Network Determination" with the Workers' Compensation Appeals Board pursuant to WCAB Rule 10959. A copy of the petition shall be concurrently served on the Administrative Director.

Note: Authority cited: Sections 133, 4616(h) and 5300(f), Labor Code. Reference: Section 4616, Labor Code.

History: 1. New section filed 11-1-2004 as an emergency; operative 11-1-2004 (Register 2004, No. 45). A Certificate of Compliance must be transmitted to OAL by 3-1-2005 or emergency language will be repealed by operation of law on the following day.

2. New section refiled 2-28-2005 as an emergency; operative 3-1-2005 (Register 2005, No. 9). A Certificate of Compliance must be transmitted to OAL by 6-29-2005 or emergency language will be repealed by operation of law on the following day.

3. New section refiled 6-20-2005 as an emergency; operative 6-29-2005 (Register 2005, No. 25). A Certificate of Compliance must be transmitted to OAL by 10-27-2005 or emergency language will be repealed by operation of law on the following day.

4. Certificate of Compliance as to 6-20-2005 order, including amendment of section heading, section and Note, transmitted to OAL 7-29-2005 and filed 9-9-2005 (Register 2005, No. 36).

5. Amendment of section heading, section and Note filed 8-27-2014; operative 8-27-2014 pursuant to Government Code section 11343.4(b)(3) (Register 2014, No. 35).

Ref.: Hanna §§ 5.03[1], 5.05[13][a]; Herlick Handbook § 1.01[3][b].

§9767.14. Probation, Suspension or Revocation of Medical Provider Network Plan; Hearing.

(a) The Administrative Director may place on probation, suspend or revoke a Medical Provider Network if:

(1) Service under the MPN is not being provided according to the terms of the approved MPN plan.

(2) The MPN fails to meet the requirements of Labor Code section 4616 et seq. and this article.

(3) The MPN fails to meet the requirements for reapproval under Labor Code section 4616 et seq. or this article.

(4) False or misleading information is knowingly or repeatedly submitted by the MPN or a participating provider or the MPN knowingly or repeatedly fails to report information required by this article.

(5) The MPN knowingly continues to use the services of a provider or medical reviewer whose license, registration, or certification has been suspended or revoked or who is otherwise ineligible to provide treatment to an injured worker under California law.

(6) The MPN applicant no longer meets the eligibility requirements to have an MPN, including but not limited to the following situations: the MPN applicant is no longer recognized as a self-insured entity with the Office of Self-Insurance Plans for any period of time during which the MPN applicant has an MPN or if the MPN applicant is no longer properly licensed to provide workers' compensation insurance by the Department of Insurance for any period of time during which the MPN applicant has an MPN or is no longer an entity that provides physician network services.

(A) Once an MPN applicant is no longer eligible to have an MPN, by operation of law, the MPN is automatically suspended and MPN coverage will not be deemed valid for new claims during the period of suspension, pending revocation by the Administrative Director. During the effective dates of suspension, any injured worker with a new claim shall be informed of the employee's right to be treated by a physician of his or her own choice or at a facility of his or her own choice within a reasonable geographic area 30 days after reporting the injury, pursuant to Labor Code section 4600(c). After a suspension has ended, any transfer of the employee's care back into the MPN shall be subject to the MPN transfer of care requirements.

(7) The MPN fails to respond to at least two or more repeated requests or inquiries by the Administrative Director to comply with the requirements of this article or Labor Code sections 4616 et seq.

(b) If one of the circumstances in subdivision (a) exists, the Administrative Director shall notify the MPN applicant in writing of the specific violations alleged. The Administrative Director shall allow the MPN applicant an opportunity to correct the violation or to respond within ten days with a plan of action to correct the violation in a timely manner. If the Administrative Director determines that the violations have not been cured in a timely manner, he or she shall issue a Notice of Action to the MPN applicant that specifies the time period in which probation, the suspension or revocation will take effect and shall transmit the Notice of Action to the MPN applicant by U.S. Mail.

(c) An MPN applicant may request a re-evaluation of the probation, suspension or revocation by submitting to the Administrative Director, within 20 days of the issuance of the Notice of Action, a written notice of the request for a re-evaluation with a detailed statement explaining the basis upon which a re-evaluation is requested. The request for a re-evaluation shall be accompanied by supportive documentary material relevant to the specific allegations raised and shall be verified under penalty of perjury. The MPN application at issue shall not be re-filed; it shall be made part of the administrative record and incorporated by reference.

(d) The Administrative Director shall, within 45 days of the receipt of the request for a re-evaluation, either:

(1) Issue a Decision and Order affirming or modifying the Notice of Action based on a failure to meet the procedural requirements of this section or based on a failure to meet the requirements of Labor Code section 4616 et seq. and this article;

(2) Issue a Decision and Order rescinding the Notice of Action;

(e) The Administrative Director may extend the time specified in subdivision (d) within which to act upon the request for a re-evaluation for a period of 30 days and may order a party to submit additional documents or information.

(f) An MPN applicant may appeal the Administrative Director's decision and order regarding the MPN by filing, within twenty (20) days of the issuance of the decision and order, a "Petition Appealing Administrative Director's Medical Provider Network Determination" with the Workers' Compensation Appeals Board pursuant to WCAB Rule 10959. A copy of the petition shall be concurrently served on the Administrative Director.

Note: Authority cited: Sections 133, 4616(h) and 5300(f), Labor Code. Reference: Section 4616, Labor Code.

History: 1. New section filed 11-1-2004 as an emergency; operative 11-1-2004 (Register 2004, No. 45). A Certificate of Compliance must be transmitted to OAL by 3-1-2005 or emergency language will be repealed by operation of law on the following day.

2. New section refiled 2-28-2005 as an emergency; operative 3-1-2005 (Register 2005, No. 9). A Certificate of Compliance must be transmitted to OAL by 6-29-2005 or emergency language will be repealed by operation of law on the following day.

3. New section refiled 6-20-2005 as an emergency; operative 6-29-2005 (Register 2005, No. 25). A Certificate of Compliance must be transmitted to OAL by 10-27-2005 or emergency language will be repealed by operation of law on the following day.

4. Certificate of Compliance as to 6-20-2005 order, including amendment of section, transmitted to OAL 7-29-2005 and filed 9-9-2005 (Register 2005, No. 36).

5. Amendment of section heading, section and Note filed 8-27-2014; operative 8-27-2014 pursuant to Government Code section 11343.4(b)(3) (Register 2014, No. 35).

Ref.: Hanna § 5.03[1]; Herlick Handbook § 1.01[3][b].

§9767.15. Compliance with Current MPN Regulations; Reapproval.

(a) MPNs approved prior to January 1, 2014 that are not in compliance with the current MPN regulations must file a modification and update to comply with the current regulations no later than January 1, 2018. If the MPN is required to apply for reapproval before January 1, 2018 based on the four-year approval period, then the MPN shall update to the current regulations with its reapproval filing, whichever is sooner.

(b) The MPN applicant shall file a new complete application for reapproval no later than six months prior to the expiration of the MPN's four-year date of approval.

(1) For MPNs approved prior to January 1, 2014, the four-year date of approval begins from the most recent approved filing prior to January 1, 2014.

(2) For MPNs approved after January 1, 2014, the first four-year date of approval begins from the date the original application is approved.

(3) After an MPN has been reapproved, the expiration of reapproval will be four years from the date of the last complete plan reapproval.

(4) Each application for reapproval shall meet all requirements for a new MPN original application.

(5) Each filing for reapproval shall meet the requirements for geocoding as follows: Provide an electronic copy in Microsoft Excel format of the geocoding results of the MPN provider directory to show estimated compliance with the access standards set forth in section 9767.5. The access standards set forth in section 9767.5 are determined by the injured employee's residence or workplace address and not the center of a zip code. The geocoding results will be used by DWC in reviewing MPN plans to give an approximation of MPN compliance with the access standards set forth in section 9767.5. The geocoding results shall include the following separate files summarizing data reasonably available at the time of compilation: 1) a complete list of all zip codes within the MPN geographic service area; 2) a narrative or graphic report that establishes where there are at least three available primary treating physicians within the fifteen-mile access standard from the center of each zip code within the MPN geographic service area; 3) a narrative or graphic report that establishes where there is a hospital or an emergency health care service provider within the fifteen-mile access standard from the center of each zip code within the MPN geographic service area; 4) a narrative or graphic report that establishes-where there are at least three available physicians in each of the specialties commonly required to treat injured workers covered by the MPN within the thirty-mile access standard from the center of each zip code within the MPN geographic service area; 5) a list of all zip codes where access standards are not met in the geographic service area or areas to be served by the MPN for primary treating physicians, for acute care hospitals or emergency facilities, and for each specialty listed to treat common injuries experienced by injured workers covered by the MPN, and a narrative report explaining if medical treatment will be provided according to an approved alternative access standard or according to a written policy permitting out of MPN treatment in those areas; and 6) each physician listed in the MPN provider directory shall be assigned at least one provider code as set forth in section 9767.3(c)(2) of this section to be used in the geocoding reports.

(6) The time frames for the review process for a plan for reapproval are as stated in section 9767.2(b).

(7) If the filing for reapproval is not filed within the requisite six months prior to the expiration of approval, then the MPN may be subject to penalties or other administrative actions. If an application for reapproval is filed less than 60 days prior to the approval expiration date, then the MPN may be subject to penalties and MPN approval will be suspended after the date of expiration if the review is not completed prior to the expiration of the MPN plan's approval.

Note: Authority cited: Sections 133, 4616(h) and 5300(f), Labor Code. Reference: Sections 4609, 4616, 4616.2 and 4616.3, Labor Code.

History: 1. New section filed 9-9-2005; operative 9-9-2005 (Register 2005, No. 36).

2. Amendment of section heading, section and Note filed 8-27-2014; operative 8-27-2014 pursuant to Government Code section 11343.4(b)(3) (Register 2014, No. 35).

Ref.: Hanna § 5.03[1]; Herlick Handbook § 1.01[3][b].

§9767.16. Medical Provider Network Complaints.

(a) Any person contending a Medical Provider Network is in violation of the requirements of this article or Labor Code sections 4616 through 4616.7 shall submit a written complaint directly with the MPN Contact.

(1) The written complaint shall provide an explanation to the MPN with sufficient detail of the MPN's alleged violation under this article or any of Labor Code sections

4616 through 4616.7. The written complaint shall include, but not be limited to, the following information:

(A) Citation of the specific statutory or regulatory provision(s) violated;

(B) When the alleged violation occurred;

(C) If the alleged violation is still occurring;

(D) What attempts the complainant has made with the MPN to address the violation;

(E) What, if any, impact there has been on an injured worker; and

(F) What remedy is sought for the alleged violation.

(2) The MPN applicant shall have thirty (30) calendar days from the date the complaint was received to respond in writing to the complainant.

(A) For purposes of this section, the complaint shall be deemed to have been received by the MPN Contact by e-mail on the e-mail receipt confirmation date or on the delivery status notification date indicating successful delivery of an e-mail to the MPN Contact, whichever is earliest.

(B) Where the complaint is made by facsimile, the complaint shall be deemed to have been received by the MPN Contact on the date the receiving facsimile electronically date stamps the transmission was successfully sent. If there is no electronically stamped date recorded, then the date the request was transmitted.

(C) Where the complaint is made by mail, and a proof of service by mail exists, the request shall be deemed to have been received by the MPN Contact five (5) days after the deposit in the mail at a facility regularly maintained by the United States Postal Service. Where the complaint is delivered via certified mail, return receipt mail, the request shall be deemed to have been received by the MPN Contact on the receipt date entered on the return receipt. In the absence of a proof of service by mail or a dated return receipt, the complaint shall be deemed to have been received by the MPN Contact on the date stamped as received on the document.

(3) Within (30) calendar days from the date the complaint was received, the MPN applicant shall respond to the complainant by:

(A) Taking reasonable actions to remedy the violation in a timely manner and stating any additional actions it will be taking if more than thirty (30) calendar days are needed to address the violation, or

(B) Verifying in writing to the complainant that the MPN is disputing the complaint and denying there is a violation.

(b) If the MPN applicant has not remedied the violation or has not taken reasonable action to remedy the violation within thirty (30) calendar days from the date the complaint was received or the MPN has confirmed in writing it is disputing the complaint and denying there is a violation, the complainant may file a written complaint with the Division of Workers' Compensation against the MPN. If the complainant can show imminent and serious threat to the health of an injured worker, including but not limited to potential loss of life, limb or other major bodily function, he or she may file a written complaint with the Division of Workers' Compensation against the MPN concurrently with the written complaint under subdivision (a) submitted on the MPN.

(1) The written complaint filed with the DWC must be made on the DWC Medical Provider Network Complaint Form, as contained in title 8, California Code of Regulations, section 9767.16.5. The complainant shall provide written details of the MPN's violation along with documentary evidence that the MPN has been notified according to subdivision (a) of this section. A copy of the DWC Medical Provider Network Complaint Form 9767.16.5 shall be served on the MPN Contact.

(2) The Administrative Director shall have the discretion to limit investigations to complaints which provide credible evidence that a violation exists.

(A) The Administrative Director may make reasonable requests for information or documentary evidence from the MPN applicant or the complainant in order to conduct an investigation to determine the validity of the allegations. The MPN applicant or the complainant shall have thirty (30) calendar days from receipt of the Administrative Director's request, as determined by the parameters set forth in (a)(2)(A) through (C) of this section, to provide DWC with the requested information or documentary evidence.

(3) If the investigation confirms a violation or if other violations are found as a result of the investigation, the Administrative Director shall notify the MPN's authorized individual and MPN Contact in writing of the specific violation(s) found and shall follow the procedures set forth in §9767.14 and/or §9767.19, if the MPN fails to remedy the violation as required.

Note: Authority cited: Sections 133 and 4616, Labor Code. Reference: Sections 4616(b)(4) and 4616(b)(5), Labor Code.

History: 1. New section filed 12-11-2007; operative 4-9-2008 (Register 2007, No. 50).

2. Amendment of section heading, section and Note filed 8-9-2010; operative 10-8-2010 (Register 2010, No. 33).

3. Repealer and new section heading and section and amendment of Note filed 8-27-2014; operative 8-27-2014 pursuant to Government Code section 11343.4(b)(3) (Register 2014, No. 35).

Ref.: Hanna §§ 5.03[1], 5.05[13][f]; Herlick Handbook §§ 1.01[3][b], 4.11[9].

§9767.16.5. DWC Medical Provider Network Complaint Form 9767.16.5.

[DWC Form 9767.16.5 (New 8/2014) Not Reproduced]

NOTE: Form is available at no charge by downloading from the web at www.dir.ca.gov/dwc/forms.html or by requesting at 1-800-794-6900.

Note: Authority cited: Sections 133 and 4616, Labor Code. Reference: Sections 4616(b) and 4616, Labor Code.

History: 1. New section filed 8-27-2014; operative 8-27-2014 pursuant to Government Code section 11343.4(b)(3) (Register 2014, No. 35).

§ 9767.17. Petition for Suspension or Revocation of a Medical Provider Network.

(a) The DWC Petition for Suspension or Revocation of a Medical Provider Network Form 9767.17.5, as contained in title 8, California Code of Regulations, section 9767.17.5, may be filed with the Division of Workers' Compensation by any person who can show:

(1) The employer, insurer or entity that provides physician network services failed to maintain its qualifying status to have an MPN, or

(2) That an MPN has systematically failed to meet access standards under 9767.5, at minimum, on more than one occasion in at least two specific access locations within the MPN geographic service area. Additionally, the MPN failed to ensure in each instance that a worker received necessary medical treatment within the MPN or failed to authorize treatment outside of the MPN within the required time frames and access standards.

(b) The failure of an MPN to accept or retain a particular provider in its network shall not be grounds to file a DWC Petition for Suspension or Revocation of a Medical Provider Network.

(c) The petitioner shall complete the DWC Petition for Suspension or Revocation of a Medical Provider Network Form 9767.17.5, include all supporting documentation and file the petition verified under penalty of perjury and with proof of service, directly with the Administrative Director. The petitioner shall concurrently serve a copy of the completed DWC Petition for Suspension or Revocation of a Medical Provider Network Form 9767.17.5 along with a copy of all supporting documentation on the MPN's authorized individual. The petition shall include details that show an MPN no longer meets the eligibility requirements to have a Medical Provider Network and/or an MPN systemically fails to meet the access standards. A petition for suspension or revocation of an MPN shall include but not be limited to the following:

(1) Documentation showing all attempts made to contact the MPN to address the violations that form the basis for the petition.

(2) Results of any and all attempts by petitioner to determine if the MPN has met the access standards on more than one occasion for the specific locations within the geographic service area or areas described in its plan.

(3) What, if any, impact the violation has had on injured workers.

(d) The MPN applicant has thirty (30) calendar days to respond to the petition after the date of service of the petition. The verified response shall include but not be limited to addressing the alleged violations and providing any supporting documentation to establish that no violation has occurred or that all specified violations have been remedied in a timely manner. Any response shall be served concurrently on the Administrative Director and on the petitioner.

(e) Within thirty (30) calendar days of the last day for the MPN applicant to file a response to the DWC Petition for Suspension or Revocation of a Medical Provider Network, the Administrative Director or his/her designee may make reasonable requests for information or additional evidence from the MPN or the petitioner.

(1) The MPN applicant or petitioner shall have thirty (30) calendar days from receipt of the Administrative Director's request, as determined by the parameters set forth in 9767.16(a)(2)(A) through (C), to provide DWC with the requested information or documentary evidence.

(f) Within sixty (60) calendar days of receipt of all the requested information or additional evidence, the Administrative Director shall issue an administrative Decision and Order either granting or denying the petition and setting forth the reasons for the Decision.

(g) Once the Administrative Director issues a Decision and Order, the procedures set forth in section 9767.14 and/or section 9767.19 may apply.

Note: Authority cited: Sections 133 and 4616, Labor Code. Reference: Section 4616(b)(5), Labor Code.

History: 1. New section filed 8-27-2014; operative 8-27-2014 pursuant to Government Code section 11343.4(b)(3) (Register 2014, No. 35).

Ref.: Hanna § 5.03[7].

§ 9767.17.5. DWC Petition for Suspension or Revocation of a Medical Provider Network Form 9767.17.5 [new].

[DWC Form 9767.17.5 (Part A) (New 8/2014) Not Reproduced]

[DWC Form 9767.17.5 (Part B) (New 8/2014) Not Reproduced]

NOTE: Form is available at no charge by downloading from the web at www.dir.ca.gov/dwc/forms.html or by requesting at 1-800-794-6900.

Note: Authority cited: Sections 133 and 4616, Labor Code. Reference: Section 4616(b)(5), Labor Code.

History: 1. New section filed 8-27-2014; operative 8-27-2014 pursuant to Government Code section 11343.4(b)(3) (Register 2014, No. 35).

Ref.: Hanna § 5.03[7].

§ 9767.18. Random Reviews.

(a) The Administrative Director may conduct random reviews of any approved Medical Provider Network to determine if the requirements of this article and Labor Code sections 4616 through 4616.7 are being satisfied.

(1) An MPN will not be randomly reviewed more than once in a two-year period. However, an MPN may be subject to investigation for good cause.

(2) To initiate a random review, the Division of Workers' Compensation shall:

(A) Issue a "Notice of Random Review" to a Medical Provider Network's authorized individual specifying the parameters of the review, including the time frame and scope of the review.

(B) Make reasonable requests in writing for information or documentary evidence from the MPN in order to conduct the review. MPN applicants shall be prepared to respond to reasonable requests for information or documentary evidence by the DWC including, but not limited to, the following items:

(i) Documentary proof the MPN applicant meets the eligibility requirements to have an MPN, that the MPN name or MPN applicant name is legally correct and consistent with the approved MPN plan, or that the MPN status is still valid and approved.

(ii) A complete copy of the MPN's most recent approved plan submission (new MPN application, reapproval plan or modification) including a copy of the most recent employee notification and MPN notices given to covered employees, and a listing of all plan filings to date after the effective date of this section.

(iii) A copy of the most recent network provider listing, the URL address of the MPN's network provider listing, documentary evidence of quarterly updates to the provider listing for the past year and documentary evidence of timely corrections to the provider listing for inaccuracies reported to the MPN within a reasonable time period.

(iv) A copy of any MPN complaints or petitions for suspension or revocation received by the MPN and the MPN's responses. In addition, documentation of any administrative actions taken by the Administrative Director against the MPN within a reasonable time period may be requested.

(v) A copy of the telephone call logs tracking the calls and the contents of the calls made to and by the MPN medical access assistants and the MPN Contact within a reasonable time period.

(vi) Copies of the written MPN physician acknowledgments.

(3) The MPN applicant shall have thirty (30) calendar days from receipt of the Administrative Director's request, as determined by the parameters set forth in 9767.16(a)(2)(A) through (C), to provide DWC with the requested information and or documentary evidence.

(4) If the review reveals that the MPN has violated or is in violation of a provision of this article or of Labor Code sections 4616 through 4616.7, the Administrative Director shall notify the MPN applicant in writing of the specific violation(s) found and may follow the procedures set forth in section 9767.14 and/or section 9767.19.

Note: Authority cited: Sections 122 and 4616(h), Labor Code. Reference: Sections 4616(b)(4) and 4616(b)(5), Labor Code.

History: 1. New section filed 8-27-2014; operative 8-27-2014 pursuant to Government Code section 11343.4(b)(3) (Register 2014, No. 35).

Ref.: Hanna § 5.03[6].

§ 9767.19. Administrative Penalty Schedule; Hearing, Mitigation and Appeal.

(a) A penalty may be assessed against an MPN applicant for each failure of an MPN to comply with the Medical Provider Network requirements in Labor Code sections 4616 through 4616.7 and Title 8, California Code of Regulations, sections 9767.1 et seq. For MPN applicants who have multiple MPNs and for multiple MPNs using the same network, if a specific violation affects more than one MPN, multiple penalties will not be assessed against the MPN applicant(s) provided that the violation is remedied for all affected MPNs within a reasonable time period, as determined by the Administrative Director based on the nature and extent of the violation. Penalties may be assessed against an MPN applicant for the following violations:

(1) MPN filing requirements with DWC:

(A) Failure to file a Notice of MPN Plan Modification within fifteen (15) business days of a change in the name of the MPN or the MPN applicant, $500 initially and for each seven calendar days thereafter if the failure continues, up to $5,000.

(B) Failure to file a Notice of MPN Plan Modification within fifteen (15) business days of a change in the MPN applicant's eligibility status, $2,500.

(C) Failure to file a Notice of MPN Plan Modification within fifteen (15) business days of a change in DWC liaison or authorized individual, $500 initially and for each seven calendar days thereafter if the failure continues, up to $5,000.

(D) Failure to file a Notice of MPN Plan Modification for a material change in any of the employee notification materials, including but not limited to a change in MPN contact or MPN medical access assistant information or a change in provider listing access or website information required by section 9767.12, $2,500.

(E) Failure to file a Notice of MPN Plan Modification for all other material changes that require the filing of a Modification of MPN plan as set forth in section 9767.8, $1,000.

(F) Failure to file a complete plan for MPN reapproval within the time frames set forth in section 9767.15, $2,500.

(G) Failure to include geocoding of its current provider listing with the MPN reapproval application, $500 for each 30 days or part thereof that the failure continues after the date of submission of the reapproval plan.

(2) Network access requirements:

(A) Failure to perform the required quarterly provider listing updates pursuant to section 9767.12(a)(2)(C), for each inaccurate entry, $250 up to a total of $10,000 per quarter.

(B) Failure to update reported inaccuracies in the network provider online listing within forty-five (45) days of notice to the MPN through the contact method stated on the provider listings, $250 for each occurrence up to a total of $10,000, per quarter.

(C) Failure of an MPN medical access assistant to respond to calls by the next day, excluding Sunday and holidays, $250 for each occurrence and $50 for each additional day a response is not provided, up to a total of $1,000 per occurrence.

(D) Failure of an MPN Applicant to permit an injured covered employee to obtain necessary non-emergency services for an initial MPN treatment from an out-of-network physician when the Medical Access Assistant fails to schedule an appointment within 3 business days of receipt of request from the injured covered employee, $500 for each occurrence.

(E) Failure of an MPN Applicant to permit an injured covered employee to obtain necessary medical treatment from an appropriate out-of-network specialists requested by the primary treating physician when, within 10 business days of receipt of request from the injured covered employee, the MPN Medical Access Assistant has failed to schedule or offer an appointment with an appropriate specialist to occur within 20 days of the receipt of the request, $500 for each occurrence.

(F) Failure to meet the physician acknowledgment requirements pursuant to section 9767.5.1; $250 per non-compliant acknowledgment.

(3) MPN cooperation with DWC's requests for information or documentary evidence:

(A) Failure to respond to a request for information or documentary evidence pursuant to an MPN complaint, petition for suspension or revocation of an MPN, random review or investigation, within thirty (30) calendar days of DWC's request, $2,500.

(b) Penalties may be assessed against the employer or insurer responsible for these notices violations:

(1) Failure to provide the complete MPN employee notification pursuant to section 9767.12 to an injured covered employee, $500 per occurrence up to $10,000.

(2) Failure to provide the entire or correct complete MPN employee notification notice required under section 9767.12 to an injured covered employee, $250 per occurrence up to $10,000.

(3) Failure to provide an injured covered employee who is still treating under an MPN written notice of the date the employee will no longer be able to use the MPN, $1,000 per occurrence.

(4) Failure to provide the MPN Independent Medical Review notice, $250 per occurrence.

(5) Failure to provide the Transfer of Care notice to an injured covered employee, $250 per occurrence up to $10,000.

(6) Failure to provide the Continuity of Care notice to an injured covered employee, $250 per occurrence up to $10,000.

(c) If a violation of any of the requirements of this article and or Labor Code section 4616 through 4616.7 is found, the Administrative Director shall notify the MPN applicant in writing of the specific violation. The Administrative Director shall allow the MPN applicant an opportunity to correct the violation or to respond within ten days with a plan of action to correct the violation in a timely manner. If the Administrative Director determines that the violation has not been cured in a timely manner, he or she shall issue a Notice of Action to the MPN applicant that specifies the time period in which the administrative penalty will take effect and shall transmit the Notice of Action to the MPN applicant by U.S. Mail.

(d) Penalty amounts may be mitigated upon written request to the Administrative Director by the MPN applicant within twenty-one days of the date of the Notice of Action. Mitigation will be determined based on the MPN's documented attempts to address the violation(s) of Labor Code sections 4616.1 through 4616.7 or of this article resulting in the penalties at issue, the responsiveness and good faith of the MPN in taking actions to prevent the violations from reoccurring, whether it is the first violation of its type, the frequency of violations found, the history of violations by the MPN, the medical harm or consequences of the violation(s) on an injured worker(s), and any extraordinary circumstances that may be relevant to mitigation of the penalties, when strict application of this mitigation provision would be clearly inequitable.

(e) An MPN applicant may request a re-evaluation of the administrative penalty, by submitting to the Administrative Director, within 20 days of the issuance of the Notice of Action, a written notice of the request for a re-evaluation with a detailed statement explaining the basis upon which a re-evaluation is requested. The request for a re-evaluation shall be accompanied by supportive documentary material relevant to the specific allegations raised and shall be verified under penalty of perjury.

(f) The Administrative Director shall, within 45 days of the receipt of the request for a reevaluation, either:

(1) Issue a Decision and Order affirming the Notice of Action based on a failure to meet the procedural requirements of this section or based on a failure to meet the requirements of Labor Code section 4616 through 4616.7 and this article;

(2) Issue a Decision and Order rescinding the Notice of Action;

(g) The Administrative Director may extend the time specified in subdivision (f) within which to act upon the request for a re-evaluation for a period of 30 days and may order a party to submit additional documents or information.

(h) An MPN applicant may appeal the Administrative Director's decision and order regarding the MPN by filing, within twenty (20) days of the issuance of the decision and order, a "Petition Appealing Administrative Director's Medical Provider Network Determination" with the Workers' Compensation Appeals Board pursuant to WCAB Rule 10959. A copy of the petition shall be concurrently served on the Administrative Director.

Note: Authority cited: Sections 133 and 4616, Labor Code. Reference: Sections 4616(b)(4) and 4616(b)(5), Labor Code.

History: 1. New section filed 8-27-2014; operative 8-27-2014 pursuant to Government Code section 11343.4(b)(3) (Register 2014, No. 35).

Ref.: Hanna § 5.03[6].

ARTICLE 3.6
Independent Medical Review

§9768.1. Definitions.

(a) As used in this article, the following definitions apply:

(1) "American College of Occupational and Environmental Medicine's Occupational Medicine Practice Guidelines" ("ACOEM") means the American College of Occupational and Environmental Medicine's Occupational Medicine Practice Guidelines, 2nd Edition (2004), published by OEM Press. The Administrative Director incorporates ACOEM by reference. A copy may be obtained from OEM Press, 8 West Street, Beverly Farms, Massachusetts 01915 (www.oempress.com).

(2) "Appropriate specialty" means a medical specialty in an area or areas appropriate to the condition or treatment under review.

(3) "Independent Medical Reviewer" ("IMR") means the physician who is randomly selected pursuant to subdivision (b) of Labor Code section 4616.4.

(4) "In-person examination" means an examination of an injured employee by a physician which involves more than a review of records, and may include a physical examination, discussing the employee's medical condition with the employee, taking a history and performing an examination.

(5) "Material familial affiliation" means a relationship in which one of the persons or entities listed in section 9768.2 is the parent, child, grandparent, grandchild, sibling, uncle, aunt, nephew, niece, spouse, or cohabitant of the Independent Medical Reviewer.

(6) "Material financial affiliation" means a financial interest (owns a legal or equitable interest of more than 1% interest in the party, or a fair market value in excess of $2000, or relationship of director, advisor, or active participant) in any person or entity listed in section 9768.2. It also means any gift or income of more than $300 in the preceding year except for income for services as a second opinion physician, third opinion physician, treating physician, Agreed Medical Evaluator, Qualified Medical Evaluator, or Independent Medical Reviewer.

(7) "Material professional affiliation" means any relationship in which the Independent Medical Reviewer shares office space with, or works in the same office of, any person or entity listed in section 9768.2.

(8) "Medical emergency" means a medical condition manifesting itself by acute symptoms of sufficient severity such that the absence of immediate medical attention could reasonably be expected to place the patient's health in serious jeopardy.

(9) "Medical Provider Network Contact" ("MPN Contact") means the individual(s) designated by the MPN Applicant in the employee notification who is responsible for answering employees' questions about the Medical Provider Network and is responsible for assisting the employee in arranging for an Independent Medical Review.

(10) "Panel" means the contracted providers in a specific specialty.

(11) "Relevant medical records" means all information that was considered in relation to the disputed treatment or diagnostic service, including: (A) a copy of all correspondence from, and received by, any treating physician who provided a treatment or diagnostic service to the injured employee in connection with the injury; (B) a complete and legible copy of all medical records and other information used by the physicians in making a decision regarding the disputed treatment or diagnostic service; (C) the treating physician's report with the disputed treatment or diagnosis; and (D) the second and third opinion physicians' reports.

(12) "Residence" means the covered employee's primary residence.

Note: Authority cited: Sections 133 and 4616, Labor Code. Reference: Section 4616.4, Labor Code.

History: 1. New article 3.6 (sections 9768.1-9768.17) and section filed 12-31-2004 as an emergency; operative 1-1-2005 (Register 2004, No. 53). A Certificate of Compliance must be transmitted to OAL by 5-2-2005 or emergency language will be repealed by operation of law on the following day.

2. Certificate of Compliance as to 12-31-2004 order, including amendment of section, transmitted to OAL 4-29-2005 and filed 6-10-2005 (Register 2005, No. 23).

Ref.: Hanna § 5.05[13][e]; Herlick Handbook §§ 1.01[3][b], 4.11[7], [8].

§9768.2. Conflicts of Interest.

(a) The IMR shall not have any material, professional, familial, or financial affiliation with any of the following:

(1) The injured employee's employer or employer's workers' compensation insurer;

(2) Any officer, director, management employee, or attorney of the injured employee's medical provider network, employer or employer's workers' compensation insurer;

(3) Any treating health care provider proposing the service or treatment;

(4) The institution at which the service or treatment would be provided, if known;

(5) The development or manufacture of the principal drug, device, procedure, or other therapy proposed for the injured employee whose treatment is under review; or

(6) The injured employee, the injured employee's immediate family, or the injured employee's attorney.

(b) The IMR shall not have a contractual agreement to provide physician services for the injured employee's MPN if the IMR is within a 35 mile radius of the treating physician.

(c) The IMR shall not have previously treated or examined the injured employee.

Note: Authority cited: Sections 133 and 4616, Labor Code. Reference: Section 4616.4, Labor Code.

History: 1. New section filed 12-31-2004 as an emergency; operative 1-1-2005 (Register 2004, No. 53). A Certificate of Compliance must be transmitted to OAL by 5-2-2005 or emergency language will be repealed by operation of law on the following day.

2. Certificate of Compliance as to 12-31-2004 order transmitted to OAL 4-29-2005 and filed 6-10-2005 (Register 2005, No. 23).

Ref.: Hanna § 5.05[13][e]; Herlick Handbook §§ 1.01[3][b], 4.11[8].

§9768.3. Qualifications of Independent Medical Reviewers.

(a) To qualify to be on the Administrative Director's list of Independent Medical Reviewers, a physician shall file a Physician Contract Application pursuant to section 9768.5 that demonstrates to the satisfaction of the Administrative Director that the physician:

(1) Is board certified. For physicians, the Administrative Director shall recognize only specialty boards recognized by the appropriate California licensing board.

(2) Has an unrestricted license as a physician in California under the appropriate licensing Board;

(3) Is not currently under accusation by any governmental licensing agency for a quality of care violation, fraud related to medical practice, or felony conviction or conviction of a crime related to the conduct of his or her practice of medicine;

(4) Has not been terminated or had discipline imposed by the Industrial Medical Council or Administrative Director in relation to the physician's role as a Qualified Medical Evaluator; is not currently under accusation by the Industrial Medical Council or Administrative Director; has not been denied renewal of Qualified Medical Evaluator status, except for non-completion of continuing education or for non-payment of fees; has neither resigned nor failed to renew Qualified Medical Evaluator status while under accusation or probation by the Industrial Medical Council or Administrative Director or after notification that reappointment as a Qualified Medical Evaluator may or would be denied for reasons other than non-completion of continuing education or non-payment of fees; and has not filed any applications or forms with the Industrial Medical Council or Administrative Director which contained any untrue material statements;

(5) Has not been convicted of a felony crime or a crime related to the conduct of his or her practice of medicine; and

(6) Has no history of disciplinary action or sanction, including but not limited to, loss of staff privileges or participation restrictions taken or pending by any hospital, government or regulatory body.

Note: Authority cited: Sections 133 and 4616, Labor Code. Reference: Section 4616.4, Labor Code.

History: 1. New section filed 12-31-2004 as an emergency; operative 1-1-2005 (Register 2004, No. 53). A Certificate of Compliance must be transmitted to OAL by 5-2-2005 or emergency language will be repealed by operation of law on the following day.

2. Certificate of Compliance as to 12-31-2004 order, including amendment of subsections (a) and (a)(3), transmitted to OAL 4-29-2005 and filed 6-10-2005 (Register 2005, No. 23).

Ref.: Hanna § 5.05[13][e]; Herlick Handbook §§ 1.01[3][b], 4.11[8].

§9768.4. IMR Contract Application Procedures.

(a) A physician seeking to serve as an Independent Medical Reviewer shall:

(1) Apply to the Administrative Director on the Physician Contract Application set forth in section 9768.5.

(2) Furnish a certified copy of his or her board certification, a copy of his or her current license to practice medicine, and submit other documentation of his or her qualifications as the Administrative Director may require.

(3) Designate specialties based on each of his or her board certifications.

(4) Designate the address(es) of the physician's office with necessary medical equipment where in-person examinations will be held.

(5) Agree to see any injured worker assigned to him or her within 30 days unless there is a conflict of interest as defined in section 9768.2.

(6) During the application process and after being notified by the Administrative Director that the contract application has been accepted, the physician shall keep the Administrative Director informed of any change of address, telephone, email address or fax number, and of any disciplinary action taken by a licensing board.

(b) The contract application, completed by the physician, and any supporting documentation included with the contract application, shall be filed at the Administrative Director's office listed on the form. The contract application submitted by the physician may be rejected if it is incomplete, contains false information or does not contain the required supporting documentation listed in this section.

(c) The Administrative Director shall maintain a list of physicians who have applied, and whom the Administrative Director has contracted with to conduct Independent Medical Reviews under Labor Code section 4616.4.

(d) The IMR contract term is two years. A physician may apply to serve for subsequent two year terms by following the procedure set forth in subdivision (a).

Note: Authority cited: Sections 133 and 4616, Labor Code. Reference: Section 4616.4, Labor Code.

History: 1. New section filed 12-31-2004 as an emergency; operative 1-1-2005 (Register 2004, No. 53). A Certificate of Compliance must be transmitted to OAL by 5-2-2005 or emergency language will be repealed by operation of law on the following day.

2. Certificate of Compliance as to 12-31-2004 order, including amendment of subsections (a) and (c), transmitted to OAL 4-29-2005 and filed 6-10-2005 (Register 2005, No. 23).

Ref.: Hanna § 5.05[13][e]; Herlick Handbook §§ 1.01[3][b], 4.11[8].

§9768.5. Physician Contract Application Form.

[DWC Form 9768.5 (Rev. May 2007) Not Reproduced]

NOTE: Form is available at no charge by downloading from the web at www.dir.ca.gov/dwc/forms.html or by requesting at 1-800-794-6900.

Note: Authority cited: Sections 133 and 4616, Labor Code. Reference: Section 4616.4, Labor Code.

History: 1. New section filed 12-31-2004 as an emergency; operative 1-1-2005 (Register 2004, No. 53). A Certificate of Compliance must be transmitted to OAL by 5-2-2005 or emergency language will be repealed by operation of law on the following day.

2. Certificate of Compliance as to 12-31-2004 order, including amendment of section, transmitted to OAL 4-29-2005 and filed 6-10-2005 (Register 2005, No. 23).

3. Change without regulatory effect amending form filed 10-18-2006 pursuant to section 100, title 1, California Code of Regulations (Register 2006, No. 42).

4. Change without regulatory effect amending form filed 5-21-2007 pursuant to section 100, title 1, California Code of Regulations (Register 2007, No. 21).

Ref.: Hanna § 5.05[13][e]; Herlick Handbook §§ 1.01[3][b], 4.11[8].

§9768.6. Administrative Director's Action on Contract Application Submitted by Physician.

(a) After reviewing a completed contract application submitted by a physician, if the Administrative Director finds that the physician meets the qualifications, he/she shall accept the contract application made by the physician to be an Independent Medical Reviewer by executing the IMR contract, notify the physician by mail, and add the physician's name to the list of Independent Medical Reviewers. The contract term shall be for a two-year term beginning with the date of acceptance by the Administrative Director.

(b) If the Administrative Director determines that a physician does not meet the qualifications, he/she shall notify the physician by mail that the physician's contract application is not accepted and the reason for the rejection.

(c) A physician whose contract application has not been accepted may reapply.

(d) If the Administrative Director denies a physician's contract application following at least two subsequent submissions, the physician may seek further review of the Administrative Director's decision by filing an appeal with the Workers' Compensation Appeals Board, and serving a copy on the Administrative Director, within twenty days after receipt of the denial.

Note: Authority cited: Sections 133 and 4616, Labor Code. Reference: Sections 4616.4 and 5300(f), Labor Code.

History: 1. New section filed 12-31-2004 as an emergency; operative 1-1-2005 (Register 2004, No. 53). A Certificate of Compliance must be transmitted to OAL by 5-2-2005 or emergency language will be repealed by operation of law on the following day.

2. Certificate of Compliance as to 12-31-2004 order, including amendment of subsection (a), transmitted to OAL 4-29-2005 and filed 6-10-2005 (Register 2005, No. 23).

Ref.: Hanna § 5.05[13][e]; Herlick Handbook §§ 1.01[3][b], 4.11[8].

§9768.7. IMR Request to Be Placed on Voluntary Inactive Status.

A physician may request to be placed on the inactive list during the IMR contract term. The physician shall submit the request to the Administrative Director and specify the time period that he or she is requesting to be on voluntary inactive status. The two-year contract term is not extended due to a physician's request to be placed on voluntary inactive status.

Note: Authority cited: Sections 133 and 4616, Labor Code. Reference: Section 4616.4, Labor Code.

History: 1. New section filed 12-31-2004 as an emergency; operative 1-1-2005 (Register 2004, No. 53). A Certificate of Compliance must be transmitted to OAL by 5-2-2005 or emergency language will be repealed by operation of law on the following day.

2. Certificate of Compliance as to 12-31-2004 order transmitted to OAL 4-29-2005 and filed 6-10-2005 (Register 2005, No. 23).

Ref.: Herlick Handbook § 1.01[3][b].

§9768.8. Removal of Physicians from Independent Medical Reviewer List.

(a) The Administrative Director may cancel the IMR contract and remove a physician from the Independent Medical Reviewer list if the Administrative Director determines based upon the Administrative Director's monitoring of reports:

(1) That the physician, having been notified by the Administrative Director of the physician's selection to render an Independent Medical Review, has not issued the Independent Medical Review report in a case within the time limits prescribed in these regulations on more than one occasion; or

(2) That the physician has not met the reporting requirements on more than one occasion; or

(3) That the physician has at any time failed to disclose to the Administrative Director that the physician had a conflict of interest pursuant to section 9768.2; or

(4) That the physician has failed to schedule appointments within the time frame required by these regulations on more than one occasion; or

(5) That the physician has failed to maintain the confidentiality of medical records and the review materials consistent with the applicable state and federal law.

(b) The Administrative Director shall cancel the IMR contract and remove a physician from the Independent Medical Reviewer list if the Administrative Director determines:

(1) That the physician no longer meets the qualifications to be on the list; or

(2) That the physician's contract application to be on the list contained material statements which were not true.

(c) The Administrative Director shall place a physician on an inactive list for up to the end of the two year contract term whenever the Administrative Director determines that the appropriate licensing Board from whom the physician is licensed has filed an accusation for a quality of care violation, fraud related to medical practice, or conviction of a felony crime or a crime related to the conduct of his or her practice of medicine against the physician or taken other action restricting the physician's medical license. If the accusation or action is later withdrawn, dismissed or determined to be without merit during the two year contract term, the physician shall advise the Administrative Director who will then remove the physician's name from the inactive list. If the accusation or action is withdrawn, dismissed or determined to be without merit after the expiration of the two year contract term, the physician may reapply to serve as an Independent Medical Reviewer pursuant to section 9768.4.

(d) Upon removal of a physician from the Independent Medical Reviewer list or placement on the inactive list, the Administrative Director shall advise the physician by mail of the removal or placement on the inactive list, the Administrative Director's reasons for such action, and the right to request a hearing on the removal from the IMR list or placement on the inactive list.

(e) A physician who has been mailed a notice of removal from the list or placement on the inactive list, may, within 30 calendar days of the mailing of the notice, request a hearing by filing a written request for hearing with the Administrative Director. If a written request for hearing is not received by the Administrative Director within 30 calendar days of the mailing of the notice, the physician shall be deemed to have waived any appeal or request for hearing.

(f) Upon receipt of a written request for hearing, the Administrative Director shall prepare an accusation and serve the applicant physician with the accusation, as provided in Government Code section 11503.

(g) Hearings shall be held by the Administrative Director or his or her designee under the procedures of Chapter 5 of Part 1 of Division 3 of Title 2 of the Government Code (commencing with section 11500) and the regulations of the Office of Administrative Hearings (Title 1, California Code of Regulations, section 1000 et seq.).

(h) Failure to timely file a notice of defense or failure to appear at a noticed hearing or conference shall constitute a waiver of a right to a hearing.

(i) A physician who has been removed from the list may petition for reinstatement after one year has elapsed since the effective date of the Administrative Director's decision on the physician's removal. The provisions of Government Code section 11522 shall apply to such petition.

Note: Authority cited: Sections 133 and 4616, Labor Code; and Section 11400.20, Government Code. Reference: Section 4616.4, Labor Code; and Sections 11415.10, 11503 and 11522, Government Code.

History: 1. New section filed 12-31-2004 as an emergency; operative 1-1-2005 (Register 2004, No. 53). A Certificate of Compliance must be transmitted to OAL by 5-2-2005 or emergency language will be repealed by operation of law on the following day.

2. Certificate of Compliance as to 12-31-2004 order, including amendment of section, transmitted to OAL 4-29-2005 and filed 6-10-2005 (Register 2005, No. 23).

Ref.: Hanna § 5.05[13][e]; Herlick Handbook §§ 1.01[3][b], 4.11[8].

§9768.9. Procedure for Requesting an Independent Medical Review.

(a) If a covered employee disputes the diagnostic service, diagnosis, or medical treatment prescribed by the second opinion physician, the injured employee may seek the opinion of a third physician in the MPN. The covered employee and the employer or insurer shall comply with the requirements of section 9767.7(d). Additionally, at the time of the selection of the physician for a third opinion, the MPN Contact shall notify the covered employee about the Independent Medical Review process and provide the covered employee with an "Independent Medical Review Application" form set forth in section 9768.10. The MPN Contact shall fill out the "MPN Contact Section" of the form and list the specialty of the treating physician and an alternative specialty, if any, that is different from the specialty of the treating physician.

(b) If a covered employee disputes either the diagnostic service, diagnosis or medical treatment prescribed by the third opinion physician, the covered employee may request an Independent Medical Review by filing the completed Independent Medical Review Application form with the Administrative Director. The covered employee shall complete the "employee section" of the form, indicate on the form whether he or she requests an in-person examination or record review, and may list an alternative specialty, if any, that is different from the specialty of the treating physician.

(c) The Administrative Director shall select an IMR with an appropriate specialty within ten business days of receiving the Independent Medical Review Application form. The Administrative Director's selection of the IMR shall be based on the specialty of the treating physician, the alternative specialties listed by the covered employee and the MPN Contact, and the information submitted with the Independent Medical Review Application.

(d) If the covered employee requests an in-person examination, the Administrative Director shall randomly select a physician from the panel of available Independent Medical Reviewers, with an appropriate specialty, who has an office located within thirty miles of the employee's residence address, to be the Independent Medical Reviewer. If there is only one physician with an appropriate specialty within thirty miles of the employee's residence address, that physician shall be selected to be the Independent Medical Reviewer. If there are no physicians with an appropriate specialty who have offices located within thirty miles of the employee's residence address, the Administrative Director shall search in increasing five mile increments, until one physician is located. If there are no available physicians with this appropriate specialty, the Administrative Director may choose another specialty based on the information submitted.

(e) If the covered employee requests a record review, then the Administrative Director shall randomly select a physician with an appropriate specialty from the panel of available Independent Medical Reviewers to be the IMR. If there are no physicians with an appropriate specialty, the Administrative Director may choose another specialty based on the information submitted.

(f) The Administrative Director shall send written notification of the name and contact information of the IMR to the covered employee, the employee's attorney, if any, the MPN Contact and the IMR. The Administrative Director shall send a copy of the completed Independent Medical Review Application to the IMR.

(g) The covered employee, MPN Contact, or the selected IMR can object within 10 calendar days of receipt of the name of the IMR to the selection if there is a conflict of interest as defined by section 9768.2. If the IMR determines that he or she does not practice the appropriate specialty, the IMR shall withdraw within 10 calendar days of receipt of the notification of selection. If this conflict is verified or the IMR withdraws, the Administrative Director shall select another IMR from the same specialty. If there are no available physicians with the same specialty, the Administrative Director may select an IMR with another specialty based on the information submitted and in accordance with the procedure set forth in subdivision (d) for an in-person examination and subdivision (e) for a record review.

(h) If the covered employee requests an in-person exam, within 60 calendar days of receiving the name of the IMR, the covered employee shall contact the IMR to arrange an appointment. If the covered employee fails to contact the IMR for an appointment within 60 calendar days of receiving the name of the IMR, then the employee shall be deemed to have waived the IMR process with regard to this disputed diagnosis or treatment of this treating physician. The IMR shall schedule an appointment with the covered employee within 30 calendar days of the request for an appointment, unless all parties agree to a later date. The IMR shall notify the MPN Contact of the appointment date.

(i) The covered employee shall provide written notice to the Administrative Director and the MPN Contact if the covered employee decides to withdraw the request for an Independent Medical Reviewer.

(j) During this process, the employee shall remain within the MPN for treatment pursuant to section 9767.6.

Note: Authority cited: Sections 133 and 4616, Labor Code. Reference: Sections 4616.3 and 4616.4, Labor Code.

History: 1. New section filed 12-31-2004 as an emergency; operative 1-1-2005 (Register 2004, No. 53). A Certificate of Compliance must be transmitted to OAL by 5-2-2005 or emergency language will be repealed by operation of law on the following day.

2. Certificate of Compliance as to 12-31-2004 order, including amendment of section, transmitted to OAL 4-29-2005 and filed 6-10-2005 (Register 2005, No. 23).

Ref.: Hanna § 5.05[13][e]; Herlick Handbook §§ 1.01[3][b], 4.11[7], [8].

§9768.10. Independent Medical Review Application (Form).

[DWC Form 9768.10 (Rev. May 2007) Not Reproduced]

NOTE: Form is available at no charge by downloading from the web at www.dir.ca.gov/dwc/forms.html or by requesting at 1-800-794-6900.

Note: Authority cited: Sections 133 and 4616, Labor Code. Reference: Sections 4616.3 and 4616.4, Labor Code.

History: 1. New section filed 12-31-2004 as an emergency; operative 1-1-2005 (Register 2004, No. 53). A Certificate of Compliance must be transmitted to OAL by 5-2-2005 or emergency language will be repealed by operation of law on the following day.

2. Certificate of Compliance as to 12-31-2004 order, including amendment of section heading and section, transmitted to OAL 4-29-2005 and filed 6-10-2005 (Register 2005, No. 23).

3. Change without regulatory effect amending form filed 10-18-2006 pursuant to section 100, title 1, California Code of Regulations (Register 2006, No. 42).

4. Change without regulatory effect amending section filed 5-23-2007 pursuant to section 100, title 1, California Code of Regulations (Register 2007, No. 21).

Ref.: Hanna § 5.05[13][e]; Herlick Handbook §§ 1.01[3][b], 4.11[7], [8].

§9768.11. In-Person Examination or Record Review IMR Procedure.

(a) The MPN Contact shall send all relevant medical records to the IMR. The MPN Contact shall also send a copy of the documents to the covered employee. The employee may furnish any relevant medical records or additional materials to the Independent Medical Reviewer, with a copy to the MPN Contact. If an in-person examination is requested and if a special form of transportation is required because of the employee's medical condition, it is the obligation of the MPN Contact to arrange for it. The MPN Contact shall furnish transportation and arrange for an interpreter, if necessary, in advance of the in-person examination. All reasonable expenses of transportation shall be incurred by the insurer or employer pursuant to Labor Code section 4600. Except for the in-person examination itself, the Independent Medical Reviewer shall have no ex parte contact with any party. Except for matters dealing with scheduling appointments, scheduling medical tests and obtaining medical records, all communications between the Independent Medical Reviewer and any party shall be in writing, with copies served on all parties.

(b) If the IMR requires further tests, the IMR shall notify the MPN Contact within one working day of the appointment. All tests shall be consistent with the medical treatment utilization schedule adopted pursuant to Labor Code section 5307.27 or, prior to the adoption of this schedule, the ACOEM guidelines, and for all injuries not covered by the medical treatment utilization schedule or the ACOEM guidelines, in accordance with other evidence based medical treatment guidelines generally recognized by the national medical community and that are scientifically based.

(c) The IMR may order any diagnostic tests necessary to make his or her determination regarding medical treatment or diagnostic services for the injury or illness but shall not request the employee to submit to an unnecessary exam or procedure. If a test duplicates a test already given, the IMR shall provide justification for the duplicative test in his or her report.

(d) If the employee fails to attend an examination with the IMR and fails to reschedule the appointment within five business days of the missed appointment, the IMR shall perform a review of the record and make a determination based on those records.

(e) The IMR shall serve the report on the Administrative Director, the MPN Contact, the employee and the employee's attorney, if any, within 20 days after the in-person examination or completion of the record review.

(f) If the disputed health care service has not been provided and the IMR certifies in writing that an imminent and serious threat to the health of the injured employee exists, including, but not limited to, the potential loss of life, limb, or bodily function, or the immediate and serious deterioration of the injured employee, the report shall be expedited and rendered within three business days of the in-person examination by the IMR.

(g) Subject to approval by the Administrative Director, reviews not covered under subdivision (f) may be extended for up to three business days in extraordinary circumstances or for good cause.

(h) Extensions for good cause shall be granted for:

(1) Medical emergencies of the IMR or the IMR's family;

(2) Death in the IMR's family; or

(3) Natural disasters or other community catastrophes that interrupt the operation of the IMR's office operations.

(i) Utilizing the medical treatment utilization schedule established pursuant to Labor Code section 5307.27 or, prior to the adoption of this schedule, the ACOEM guidelines, and taking into account any reports and information provided, the IMR shall determine whether the disputed health care service is consistent with the recommended standards. For injuries not covered by the medical treatment utilization schedule or by the ACOEM guidelines, the treatment rendered shall be in accordance with other evidence-based medical treatment guidelines which are generally recognized by the national medical community and scientifically based.

(j) The IMR shall not treat or offer to provide medical treatment for that injury or illness for which he or she has done an Independent Medical Review evaluation for the employee unless a medical emergency arises during the in-person examination.

(k) Neither the employee nor the employer nor the insurer shall have any liability for payment for the Independent Medical Review which was not completed within the required timeframes unless the employee and the employer each waive the right to a new Independent Medical Review and elect to accept the original evaluation.

Note: Authority cited: Sections 133 and 4616, Labor Code. Reference: Sections 4616.4 and 5307.27, Labor Code.

History: 1. New section filed 12-31-2004 as an emergency; operative 1-1-2005 (Register 2004, No. 53). A Certificate of Compliance must be transmitted to OAL by 5-2-2005 or emergency language will be repealed by operation of law on the following day.

2. Certificate of Compliance as to 12-31-2004 order, including amendment of subsections (a), (e), (j) and (k), transmitted to OAL 4-29-2005 and filed 6-10-2005 (Register 2005, No. 23).

Ref.: Hanna § 5.05[13][e]; Herlick Handbook §§ 1.01[3][b], 4.11[8].

§9768.12. Contents of Independent Medical Review Reports.

(a) Reports of Independent Medical Reviewers shall include:

(1) The date of the in-person examination or record review;

(2) The patient's complaint(s);

(3) A listing of all information received from the parties reviewed in preparation of the report or relied upon for the formulation of the physician's opinion;

(4) The patient's medical history relevant to the diagnostic services, diagnosis or medical treatment;

(5) Findings on record review or in-person examination;

(6) The IMR's diagnosis;

(7) The physician's opinion whether or not the proposed treatment or diagnostic services are appropriate and indicated. If the proposed treatment or diagnostic services are not appropriate or indicated, any alternative diagnosis or treatment recommendation consistent with the medical treatment utilization schedule shall be included;

(8) An analysis and determination whether the disputed health care service is consistent with the medical treatment utilization schedule established pursuant to Labor Code section 5307.27 or, prior to the adoption of this schedule, the ACOEM guidelines. For injuries not covered by the medical treatment utilization schedule or by the ACOEM guidelines, an analysis and determination whether the treatment rendered is in accordance with other evidence-based medical treatment guidelines which are generally recognized by the national medical community and scientifically based; and

(9) The signature of the physician.

(b) The report shall be in writing and use layperson's terms to the maximum extent possible.

(c) An Independent Medical Reviewer shall serve with each report the following executed declaration made under penalty of perjury:

"I declare under penalty of perjury that this report is true and correct to the best of my knowledge and that I have not violated Labor Code section 139.3.

______________ ______________"

Date Signature

Note: Authority cited: Sections 133 and 4616, Labor Code. Reference: Sections 139.3, 4616.4 and 5307.27, Labor Code.

History: 1. New section filed 12-31-2004 as an emergency; operative 1-1-2005 (Register 2004, No. 53). A Certificate of Compliance must be transmitted to OAL by 5-2-2005 or emergency language will be repealed by operation of law on the following day.

2. Certificate of Compliance as to 12-31-2004 order, including amendment of subsections (a) and (c), transmitted to OAL 4-29-2005 and filed 6-10-2005 (Register 2005, No. 23).

Ref.: Hanna § 5.05[13][e]; Herlick Handbook §§ 1.01[3][b], 4.11[8].

§9768.13. Destruction of Records by the Administrative Director.

The Administrative Director may destroy any forms or documents submitted to the Administrative Director as part of the IMR process two years after the date of receipt.

Note: Authority cited: Sections 133 and 4616, Labor Code. Reference: Section 4616.4, Labor Code.

History: 1. New section filed 12-31-2004 as an emergency; operative 1-1-2005 (Register 2004, No. 53). A Certificate of Compliance must be transmitted to OAL by 5-2-2005 or emergency language will be repealed by operation of law on the following day.

2. Certificate of Compliance as to 12-31-2004 order transmitted to OAL 4-29-2005 and filed 6-10-2005 (Register 2005, No. 23).

Ref.: Herlick Handbook § 1.01[3][b].

§9768.14. Retention of Records by Independent Medical Reviewer.

Each Independent Medical Reviewer shall retain all comprehensive medical reports completed by the Independent Medical Reviewer for a period of five years from the date of the IMR report.

Note: Authority cited: Sections 133 and 4616, Labor Code. Reference: Section 4616.4, Labor Code.

History: 1. New section filed 12-31-2004 as an emergency; operative 1-1-2005 (Register 2004, No. 53). A Certificate of Compliance must be transmitted to OAL by 5-2-2005 or emergency language will be repealed by operation of law on the following day.

2. Certificate of Compliance as to 12-31-2004 order, including amendment of section, transmitted to OAL 4-29-2005 and filed 6-10-2005 (Register 2005, No. 23).

Ref.: Herlick Handbook § 1.01[3][b].

§9768.15. Charges for Independent Medical Reviewers.

(a) Payment for the services of the Independent Medical Reviewers shall be made by the employer or insurer.

(b) The fee shall be based on the Official Medical Fee Schedule using confirmatory consultation codes (99271 through 99275 for in-person examinations or 99271 through 99273 for evaluations not requiring an in-person examination), 99080 for reports, and 99358 for record reviews, and any other appropriate codes or modifiers.

(c) An IMR shall not accept any additional compensation from any source for his or her services as an IMR except for services provided to treat a medical emergency that arose during an in-person examination pursuant to section 9768.11(j).

Note: Authority cited: Sections 133 and 4616, Labor Code. Reference: Section 4616.4, Labor Code.

History: 1. New section filed 12-31-2004 as an emergency; operative 1-1-2005 (Register 2004, No. 53). A Certificate of Compliance must be transmitted to OAL by 5-2-2005 or emergency language will be repealed by operation of law on the following day.

2. Certificate of Compliance as to 12-31-2004 order, including amendment of subsections (a) and (b), transmitted to OAL 4-29-2005 and filed 6-10-2005 (Register 2005, No. 23).

Ref.: Hanna § 5.05[13][e]; Herlick Handbook §§ 1.01[3][b], 4.11[8].

§9768.16. Adoption of Decision.

(a) The Administrative Director shall immediately adopt the determination of the Independent Medical Reviewer and issue a written decision within 5 business days of receipt of the report.

(b) The parties may appeal the Administrative Director's written decision by filing a petition with the Workers' Compensation Appeals Board and serving a copy on the Administrative Director, within twenty days after receipt of the decision.

Note: Authority cited: Sections 133 and 4616, Labor Code. Reference: Sections 4616.4 and 5300(f), Labor Code.

History: 1. New section filed 12-31-2004 as an emergency; operative 1-1-2005 (Register 2004, No. 53). A Certificate of Compliance must be transmitted to OAL by 5-2-2005 or emergency language will be repealed by operation of law on the following day.

2. Certificate of Compliance as to 12-31-2004 order, including amendment of subsection (a), transmitted to OAL 4-29-2005 and filed 6-10-2005 (Register 2005, No. 23).

Ref.: Hanna § 5.05[13][e]; Herlick Handbook §§ 1.01[3][b], 4.11[8].

§9768.17. Treatment Outside the Medical Provider Network.

(a) If the IMR agrees with the diagnosis, diagnostic service or medical treatment prescribed by the treating physician, the covered employee shall continue to receive medical treatment from physicians within the MPN.

(b) If the IMR does not agree with the disputed diagnosis, diagnostic service or medical treatment prescribed by the treating physician, the covered employee shall seek medical treatment with a physician of his or her choice either within or outside the MPN. If the employee chooses to receive medical treatment with a physician outside the MPN, the treatment is limited to the treatment recommended by the IMR or the diagnostic service recommended by the IMR.

(c) The medical treatment shall be consistent with the medical treatment utilization schedule established pursuant to Labor Code section 5307.27 or, prior to the adoption of this schedule, the ACOEM guidelines. For injuries not covered by the medical treatment utilization schedule or by the ACOEM guidelines, the treatment rendered shall be in accordance with other evidence-based medical treatment guidelines which are generally recognized by the national medical community and scientifically based.

(d) The employer or insurer shall be liable for the cost of any approved medical treatment in accordance with Labor Code section 5307.1 or 5307.11.

Note: Authority cited: Sections 133 and 4616, Labor Code. Reference: Sections 4616.4, 5307.1, 5307.11 and 5307.27, Labor Code.

History: 1. New section filed 12-31-2004 as an emergency; operative 1-1-2005 (Register 2004, No. 53). A Certificate of Compliance must be transmitted to OAL by 5-2-2005 or emergency language will be repealed by operation of law on the following day.

2. Certificate of Compliance as to 12-31-2004 order, including amendment of Note, transmitted to OAL 4-29-2005 and filed 6-10-2005 (Register 2005, No. 23).

Ref.: Hanna § 5.05[13][e]; Herlick Handbook §§ 1.01[3][b], 4.11[8].

ARTICLE 4
Certification Standards for Health Care Organizations

§9770. Definitions.

(a) "Administrative Director" means the administrative director of the Division of Workers' Compensation.

(b) "Claims Administrator" means a self-administered insurer providing security for the payment of compensation required by Divisions 4 and 4.5 of the Labor Code, a self-administered self-insured employer, or a third-party claims administrator for a self-insured employer, insurer, legally uninsured employer, or joint powers authority.

(c) "Division" means the Division of Workers' Compensation.

(d) "Employer" means an employer as defined in Section 3300 of the Labor Code.

(e) "HCO Enrollee" means a person who is eligible to receive services from an HCO.

(f) "Health care organization" ("HCO") means any entity certified as a health care organization by the administrative director pursuant to Section 4600.5 of the Labor Code and this article.

(g) "Material": A factor is "material" with respect to a matter if it is one to which a reasonable person would attach importance in determining the action to be taken upon the matter.

(h) "Participating provider" means a provider who is employed by or under contract with an HCO for purposes of providing occupational medical or health services or services required by this article.

(i) "Patient" means an HCO enrollee who is currently obtaining treatment or services for a work-related injury or illness.

(j) "Primary treating physician" means the treating physician primarily responsible for managing the care of the injured worker in accordance with Section 9785.5.

(k) "Professionally recognized standards of care" means health care practice encompassing the learning, skill and clinical judgment ordinarily possessed and and used by a provider of good standing in similar circumstances.

(*l*) "Provider" means any professional person, organization, health facility, or other person or institution licensed by the state to deliver or furnish health care services.

(m) "Revocation" means the termination of a health care organization's certification to provide services pursuant to Section 4600.5 of the Labor Code and this article.

(n) "Standard Industrial Classification code" means the 4 digit number which identifies the primary type of economic activity which the employer is engaged in that corresponds to the numeric classifications and descriptions listed in The Standard Industrial Classification Manual 1987, Office of Management and Budget, Washington DC: Superintendent of Documents, US Government Printing Office, 1989, and updated successor revised manuals.

(o) "Suspension" means the health care organization's authority to enter into new, renewed, or amended contracts with claims administrators has been suspended by the administrative director for a specific period of time.

(p) "Utilization review" or "Utilization Management" is the system used to manage, assess, improve, or review patient care and decision-making through case by case assessments of the medical reasonableness or medical necessity of the frequency, duration, level and appropriateness of medical care and services, based upon professionally recognized standards of care. Utilization review may include, but is not limited to, prospective, concurrent, and retrospective review of a request for authorization of medical treatment.

Note: Authority cited: Sections 133, 4600.5, 4603.5 and 5307.3, Labor Code. Reference: Sections 3300, 4061.5, 4600.5, 5400, 5401 and 5402, Labor Code.

History: 1. New article 4 and section filed 12-31-93; operative 1-1-94. Submitted to OAL for printing only pursuant to Government Code section 11351 (Register 93, No. 53). For prior history, see Register 84, No. 35.

2. New subsection (h) and subsection relettering filed 2-14-96; operative 2-14-96. Submitted to OAL for printing only pursuant to Government Code section 11351 (Register 96, No. 7).

3. Repealer of subsection (g) and subsection relettering filed 9-21-2015; operative 10-1-2015 pursuant to Government Code section 11343.4(b)(3) (Register 2015, No. 39).

Ref.: Herlick Handbook §§ 1.01[3][b], 4.08[2], [3], 4.12.

§9771. Applications for Certification.

(a) Any of the following entities may apply for certification as a health care organization:

(1) A disability insurer licensed by the Department of Insurance to transact health insurance or disability income insurance pursuant to Part 2 of Division 2 of the Insurance Code.

(2) Any workers compensation health care provider organization.

(b) An applicant must meet all of the requirements set forth in this article in order to be certified as a health care organization by the administrative director. Applicants must initially submit to the administrative director, as part of the application, a plan which will provide a clear and concise description of how occupational medical and health care services are to be provided and how each of the requirements in this article are met, and, where specified, in the manner required under each section. HCOs must include all documentation necessary to demonstrate that they meet the requirements for certification.

(c) Health care service plans must provide written certification that at the time of application the applicant is not in violation of any provision of law or rules or orders of the Director of the Department of Managed Health Care, and that there are no outstanding orders, undertakings, or deficiency letters which involve the applicant. Disability insurers must provide written certification that at the time of application they are in good standing with the Department of Insurance. The requirement of this subdivision may be satisfied by verified statement under penalty of perjury by the president or managing officer of an applicant that the applicant meets the requirements of this subdivision, subject to verification by the administrative director.

(d) An applicant who is in compliance with requirements for certification by the Department of Insurance may submit copies of any relevant exhibits, sections or other documents submitted as part of the primary certification application to meet any of the requirements of this article, provided that the applicant (1) verifies that the Department of Insurance has fully reviewed and approved the submitted information, (2) provides a concise narrative identifying any manner in which HCO services will be provided differently from those provided under the primary certification, and (3) provides a concise description for each requirement of this article, specifying how occupational medical and health care services or other services specifically and exclusively required by this article will be met.

(e) Applications must be in writing in the form and manner prescribed by the administrative director, and must be submitted on or after January 1, 1994. The original plus one copy of the application shall be submitted together with a fee as specified in subdivision (c). Each application shall provide, in addition to the plan specified in subdivision (b), the following information:

(1) The names of all directors and officers of the health care organization;

(2) The title and name of the person designated to be the day-to-day administrator of the health care organization.

(3) The title and name of the person designated to be the administrator of the financial affairs of the health care organization.

(4) The name, medical specialty, if any, board certification, if any, and any unrestricted licenses (including states where licensed), of the medical director.

(5) The name, address, and telephone number of a person designated to serve as a liaison for the Division, who is responsible for receiving compliance and informational communications from the Division and for disseminating the same within the HCO organization.

(6) A sample of each type of contract with participating providers, claims administrators, and insurers, and any entities specifically providing services required by this article; and a list of contractors for each type of contract. Copies of contracts shall be made available to the administrative director upon request. The Division will maintain as confidential information pertaining to provider rates and other financial information in accordance with Government Code Section 6254(d)(1).

(7) An organizational chart demonstrating the structural relationships between the medical director, fiscal or financial administrator, and executive officers and administrators.

(8) The identity of any worker's compensation insurer that controls or is controlled by the applicant, as defined by Section 1215 of the Insurance Code.

(f) Each application for certification must be accompanied by a non refundable fee of $2,500.

(g) In lieu of an application for certification, an entity licensed as a full service health care service plan under Section 1353 of the Health and Safety Code (a Knox-Keene Health Care Service Plan Act) and deemed to be an HCO pursuant to Labor Code Section 4600.5(c) shall submit to the administrative director:

(1) a concise description of how the health plan will satisfy the requirements of Labor Code Section

4600.5(c)(1–5) and Sections 9772 through 9778, inclusive, of these regulations. At the time the materials required by this subsection are submitted to the administrative director for review, the health plan shall pay a nonrefundable documentation processing and review fee of $1,000; and,

(2) written certification that the health plan is not in violation of any provisions of law or rules or orders of the Director of the Department of Managed Health Care, and that there are no outstanding orders, undertakings, or deficiency letters which involve the health plan. The requirements of this subdivision may be satisfied by verified statement under penalty of perjury by the president or managing officer of the health plan that the plan meets the requirements of this subdivision, subject to verification by the administrative director.

Note: Authority cited: Sections 133, 4600.5, 4600.7, 4603.5 and 5307.3, Labor Code. Reference: Sections 4600 and 4600.5, Labor Code.

History: 1. New section filed 12-31-93; operative 1-1-94. Submitted to OAL for printing only pursuant to Government Code section 11351 (Register 93, No. 53).

2. Amendment of subsection (d), new subsection (e)(8) and amendment of subsection (f) filed 2-14-96; operative 2-14-96. Submitted to OAL for printing only pursuant to Government Code section 11351 (Register 96, No. 7).

3. Repealer of subsection (a)(1), subsection renumbering, amendment of newly designated subsection (a)(2) and subsections (c), (d) and (f), new subsections (g)-(g)(2) and amendment of Note filed 1-9-2003; operative 1-9-2003 pursuant to Government Code section 11343.4 (Register 2003, No. 2).

4. Amendment of subsections (f) and (g)(1) filed 11-4-2009; operative 1-1-2010 (Register 2009, No. 45).

Ref.: Hanna § 22.01[6]; Herlick Handbook §§ 1.01[3][b], 4.12.

§9771.1. Updating Applications.

(a) Every application submitted under Section 9771(e) shall be kept current to reflect accurately the actual operation of the HCO. An applicant or a certified HCO shall file an amendment to its application to show any change in any information contained in the application. Amendments include changes, deletions, additions and variations to the original application and its exhibits, including sample contracts. Amendments shall be filed as set forth in this section. However, the administrative director may approve an alternative form of submitting an amendment if it substantially accomplishes the purposes of this section.

(b) An original and one copy of an amendment shall be submitted to the administrative director as follows:

(1) Submit an Execution Page of the application, indicating it is an "Amendment to Pending Application" or "Amendment to Application of a Certified Organization";

(2) Furnish only those pages of the application and/or those exhibits which are changed by the amendment.

(3) If a page of the application is amended, complete all items on that page and "redline" or otherwise clearly designated the changed item. At the lower left-hand corner of each page, type "Rev. [date]", giving the effective date of the amendment.

(4) If an exhibit is being amended:

(A) Furnish the complete exhibit as amended, bearing the same number as the original exhibit, with the changed portions of the exhibit "redlined" or otherwise clearly designated, or

(B) Furnish the pages of the exhibit which are amended, each page to be marked with the exhibit number and the page number of the exhibit, and with the changed portions "redlined" or otherwise clearly designated. At the lower left-hand corner of each page, type "Rev. [date]", giving the effective date of the amendment. If this method of amendment is employed, the applicant shall refile the entire exhibit as amended whenever more than 10 percent if its pages have been amended.

(2) In the event that it is impossible to submit a proposed material change in the application 30 days before the change is implemented, the applicant shall submit the change as soon as the applicant becomes aware that a change is required. If, in the opinion of the administrative director, the change or proposed changed raises a question as to the ability of a certified HCO to meet the requirements of this article, the administrative director may, within 30 days of receiving notice of the change inform the HCO of the question. When the administrative director informs the HCO that a question exists, the HCO may not implement the proposed change, or shall cease implementing the change. The HCO may submit whatever materials it deems appropriate to justify the amendment and may meet with the administrative director or staff to discuss the question. Within 30 days after informing the HCO of the question, the administrative director shall inform the HCO whether the amendment is approved or disapproved.

(d) Amendments making non-material changes shall be filed quarterly on dates specified by the administrative director. However, a list of providers need be amended only when 10 percent or more of the names contained in the list for a service area have been changed or when the sole or principal provider for a particular health care service in a service area is added or deleted. When amended, the complete list (or the list for the service area) shall be furnished following the instructions for the particular item, with each added "redlined" or otherwise clearly designated and the names of persons deleted from the list shown at the end under the heading "deletions."

(e) Review of amendments submitted under section 9771.1, except quarterly updates under section 9771.1(e)(2), will be charged based on the actual cost for performing the review. The amount shall include the actual salaries or compensation paid to the persons reviewing amendment; the expenses incurred in the course thereof, and overhead costs in connection therewith as fixed by the Administrative Director. Overhead costs shall be based on the total expenditure for operating expenses and equipment, except travel, of the managed care unit of the Division of Workers' Compensation for the previous fiscal year. The invoice will be sent upon the completion of the review and shall be paid within 30 calendar days.

Note: Authority: Sections 133, 4600.5, 4600.7, 5307.3, Labor Code. Reference: Sections 4600.3, 4600.5, Labor Code.

History: 1. New section filed 2-14-96; operative 2-14-96. Submitted to OAL for printing only pursuant to Government Code section 11351 (Register 96, No. 7).

1996 Note: It appears that the subsection preceding subsection (d) should be designated as subsection (c).

Ref.: Herlick Handbook §§ 1.01[3][b], 4.12.

§9771.2. Information to Be Furnished as it Becomes Available.

(a) If an HCO, or any person listed in section 9771(e)(8), is named as a defendant in a lawsuit that is materially related to the provision of medical treatment under Labor Code section 4600, the HCO shall inform the administrative director within 5 days of the day it becomes aware the suit is filed and shall provide a copy of the complaint.

(b)(1) If a certified HCO is a health care services plan and if the Director of the Department of Managed Health Care begins proceedings against the plan under Articles 7 or 8 of the Knox-Keene Health Care Service Plan Act of 1975, the certified HCO shall inform the administrative director within 5 days of the day it becomes aware of the proceedings. The requirements of this subdivision shall also apply to an HMO deemed an HCO pursuant to Labor Code Section 4600.5(c) while the administrative director is reviewing the documentation required by Section 9771 subdivisions (g)(1) and (2) prior to issuing the HMO its certification.

(2) If an applicant or a certified HCO is a disability insurer and if the Commissioner of Insurance begins proceedings against the insurer under Insurance Code section 704 or an examination under section 730, the applicant or certified HCO shall inform the administrative director within 5 days of the day it becomes aware of the proceedings or examination.

(c) A change in the information required by Section 9771(e)(1), (2), (3), (4), (5), and (8) shall be submitted within 5 days of the change.

(d) If an applicant or an affiliate of an applicant enters a contract whereby the applicant is to be purchased by or otherwise come under the control of another entity, the applicant shall notify the administrative director within 5 days of entry into the contract.

Note: Authority: Sections 133, 4600.5, 5307.3, Labor Code. Reference: Sections 4600.3, 4600.5, Labor Code.

History: 1. New section filed 2-14-96; operative 2-14-96. Submitted to OAL for printing only pursuant to Government Code section 11351 (Register 96, No. 7).

2. Amendment of subsection (b)(2) and repealer of subsection (b)(3) filed 1-9-2003; operative 1-9-2003 pursuant to Government Code section 11343.4 (Register 2003, No. 2).

Ref.: Herlick Handbook §§ 1.01[3][b], 4.12.

§9771.6. Application of Regulations Concerning Workers' Compensation Health Care Provider Organizations.

Sections 9771.6 through 9771.83 apply only to workers' compensation health care organizations as defined by Section 9771.60(m).

Note: Authority cited: Stats. 1997, Ch. 346, Section 5. Reference: Sections 4600.3, 4500.5 and 4600.6, Labor Code.

History: 1. New section filed 4-15-98; operative 4-15-98. Submitted to OAL for printing only pursuant to Stats. 1997, Ch. 346, Section 5 (Register 98, No. 16).

Ref.: See Labor Code §4600.5; Herlick Handbook §§ 1.01[3][b], 4.12.

§9771.60. Further Definitions.

The following definitions apply to the interpretation of these rules and the Act:

(a) "Act" means Sections 4600.3, 4600.5 and 4600.6 of the Code.

(b) "Advertisement" includes the disclosure form required pursuant to Section 4600.6(e) of the Code.

(c)(1) An "affiliate" of a person is a person controlled by, under common control with, or controlling such person.

(2) A person's relationship with another person is that of an "affiliated person" if such person is, as to such other person, a director, trustee or a member of its executive committee or other governing board or committee, or that of an officer or general partner, or holds any other position involving responsibility and authority similar to that of a principal officer or general partner; or who is the holder of 5 percent or more of its outstanding equity securities; or who has any such relationship with an affiliate of such person. An affiliate is also an affiliated person.

(d) The term "control" (including the terms "controlling," "controlled by" and "under common control with") means the possession, direct or indirect, of the power to direct or cause the direction of the management and policies of a person, whether through the ownership of voting shares, debt, by contract, or otherwise.

(e) The term "certified" or "audited," when used in regard to financial statements, means examined and reported upon with an opinion expressed by an independent public or certified public accountant.

(f) "Code" means the California Labor Code.

(g) "Administrative Director" means the Administrative Director of the Division of Workers' Compensation.

(h) "Facility" means (1) any premises owned, leased, used or operated directly or indirectly by or for the benefit of an organization or any affiliate thereof, and (2) any premises maintained by a provider to provide services on behalf of an organization.

(i) "Material": A factor is "material" with respect to a matter if it is one to which a reasonable person would attach importance in determining the action to be taken upon the matter.

(j) "Principal creditor" means (1) a person who has loaned funds to another for the operation of such other person's business, and (2) a person who has, directly or indirectly, 20 percent or more of the outstanding debts of a person.

(k) "Principal officer" means a president, vice-president, secretary, treasurer or chairman of the board of a corporation, a sole proprietor, the managing general partner of a partnership, or a person having similar responsibilities or functions.

(*l*) The term "generally accepted accounting principles," when used in regard to financial statements, assets, liabilities and other accounting items, means generally accepted accounting principles as used by business enterprises organized for profit. Accordingly, Financial Accounting Standards Board statements, Accounting Principles Board opinions, accounting research bulletins and other authoritative pronouncements of the accounting profession should be applied in determining generally accepted accounting principles unless such statements, opinions, bulletins and pronouncements are inapplicable. Section 510.05

of the AICPA Professional Standards, in and of itself, shall not be sufficient reason for determining inapplicability of statements, opinions, bulletins and pronouncements.

(m) "Workers' compensation health care provider organization" or "organization" means an entity authorized by the Administrative Director to be a health care organization pursuant to Section 4600.5(e) and 4600.6, or an entity applying for such authorization.

Note: Authority cited: Stats. 1997, Ch. 346, Section 5. Reference: Sections 4600.3, 4500.5 and 4600.6, Labor Code.

History: 1. New section filed 4-15-98; operative 4-15-98. Submitted to OAL for printing only pursuant to Stats. 1997, Ch. 346, Section 5 (Register 98, No. 16).

Ref.: See Labor Code §4600.5; Herlick Handbook §§ 1.01[3][b], 4.12.

§9771.61. Prohibition of Bonuses or Gratuities in Solicitations.

No person subject to the provisions of the Act shall offer or otherwise distribute any bonus or gratuity to a potential self-insured employer, group of self-insured employers, or insurer of an employer for the purpose of inducing enrollment or to an existing self-insured employer, group of self-insured employers, or insurer of an employer for the purpose of inducing the continuation of enrollment.

Note: Authority cited: Stats. 1997, Ch. 346, Section 5. Reference: Sections 4600.3, 4500.5 and 4600.6, Labor Code.

History: 1. New section filed 4-15-98; operative 4-15-98. Submitted to OAL for printing only pursuant to Stats. 1997, Ch. 346, Section 5 (Register 98, No. 16).

Ref.: See Labor Code §4600.5; Herlick Handbook §§ 1.01[3][b], 4.12.

§9771.62. Application for Authorization as a Workers' Compensation Health Care Provider Organization.

(a) An application for authorization as a workers' compensation health care provider organization shall be filed in the form specified in subsection (c) and contain the information specified in this section.

(b) Applications will be processed in the order in which they are filed; provided however, that applications under Section 4600.5(f)(2) shall have priority.

(c) Application Form (WHWCPO-1).

DIVISION OF WORKERS' COMPENSATION SUPPLEMENTARY APPLICATION UNDER LABOR CODE SECTION 4600.6.

Date of Application:

WORKERS' COMPENSATION HEALTH CARE PROVIDER ORGANIZATION AUTHORIZATION APPLICATION LABOR CODE SECTION 4600.6 (EXECUTION PAGE)

Identification of Organization.

Name of Applicant.

a. Legal name: ______________________

b. Please list all fictitious names you intend to use

A. Type of Filing: Indicate the type of filing by checking and completing the appropriate items:

1. ( ) Original application for organization authorization.

2. ( ) Amendment #__ to a pending application dated ________ for organization authorization. (Complete Item A-5 below.)

3. ( ) Notice of a proposed material modification (Complete Item A-5 below.)

4. ( ) Amendment filed by an organization because of a change in the information contained in the original application. (Complete Item A-5 below.)

5. Item numbers being amended

Exhibit numbers being amended

B. Other Agencies.

1. If applicant has made or intends to make any filing relating to its plan of operation to any other state or federal agency, check here ______, and attach Exhibit B-1 identifying each such agency, and the nature, purpose and (projected) date of each such filing.

Additional Exhibits: An original application for organization authorization must include the completed form specified in this subsection and the exhibits required.

C. Summary of Information in Application.

1. Summary Description of Organization and Operation. Provide as Exhibit C-1 a summary description of the organization and operation of applicant's business as a workers' compensation health care provider organization, covering the highlights and essential features of the information provided in response to the other portions of this application which is essential or desirable to an effective overview of the applicant's workers' compensation health care business, including a summary of the applicant's experience in the provision of workers' compensation health care.

2. Summary Description of Start-up. Provide as Exhibit C-2 a concise description of applicant's start-up program and its assumptions, including such program's operating, capitalization and financial assumptions. Indicate applicant's projected date for the beginning of operations, and discuss the factors which require such date.

D. Organization and Affiliated Persons.

1. Type of Organization.

a. Corporation. If applicant is a corporation, attach as Exhibits D-1-a-I, D-1-a-ii, D-1-a-iii and D-1-a-iv respectively, the Articles of Incorporation, Bylaws, the Corporation Information Form (Form WCHCPO 1-A) and any other organizational documents or agreements relating to the internal affairs of the applicant.

b. Partnership. If applicant is a partnership, attach as Exhibits D-1-b-I, D-1-b-ii and D-1-b-iii respectively, the Partnership Agreement, the Partnership Information Form (Form WCHCPO 1-B) and any other organizational documents or agreements relating to the internal affairs of the applicant.

c. Sole Proprietor. If applicant is a sole proprietorship, attach as Exhibit D-1-c the Sole Proprietorship Information Form. (Form WCHCPO 1-C)

d. Other Organization. If applicant is any other type of organization, attach as Exhibit D-1-d Articles of Association, trust agreement, or any other applicable documents, and any other organizational documents or agreements relating to the conduct of the internal affairs of the applicant, and attach as Exhibit D-1-d-ii the Information Form for other than Corporations, Partnerships, and Sole Proprietorships. (Form WCHCPO 1-D)

e. Individual Information Sheet. Attach as Exhibit D-1-e, an Individual Information Sheet (Form WCHCPO 2) for each natural person named in any exhibit in Item D-1.

2. Contracts with Affiliated Persons, Principal Creditors and Providers of Administrative Services.

a. Persons to Be Identified. Attach as Exhibit D-2-a, a list identifying each individual or entity who is a party to a contract with applicant, if such contract is one for the provision of administrative services to the applicant or any such party is an Affiliated Person or Principal Creditor (Rule 9771.60(c) and (j)) of the applicant. As to each such person, show the following information in columnar form:

(i) The names in alphabetical order.

(ii) The exhibit and page number of the contract (including loans and other obligations).

(iii) The type of contract or loan.

(iv) Each relationship which such individual or entity bears to the applicant (officer, director, partner, trustee, member, Principal Creditor, employee, administrative services provider, health care services provider, or shareholder).

3. Other Controlling Persons. Does any individual or entity not named as a contracting party in Item D-2 or any exhibit thereto have any power, directly or indirectly, to manage, influence, or administer the operation, or to control the operations or decisions, of applicant?

If the appropriate response to this item is "yes," attach as Exhibit D-3 a statement identifying each such person or entity and explaining fully such person's power or control, and summarizing every contract or other arrangement or understanding (if any) with each such person. (Each such contract should be submitted pursuant to Subsection D-2.)

4. Criminal, Civil and Administrative Proceedings. Within the preceding 10 years, has the applicant, its management company, or any Affiliate of the applicant (Rule 9771.60(c)), or any controlling person, officer, director or other person occupying a principal management or supervisory position in such organization, management company or Affiliate, or any person intended to hold such a relationship or position, been convicted of or pleaded nolo contendere to a crime, or been held to have committed any act involving dishonesty, fraud or deceit in a judicial or administrative proceeding to which such person was a party?

If "yes," attach a separate exhibit as to each such person designated Exhibit D-4, identifying such person and fully explaining the crime or act committed. Also, attach a copy of the exhibit to any Individual Information Sheet required by Item D-1-e for such individual.

5. Employment of Barred Persons. Has the organization engaged or does the organization intend to engage, as an officer, director, employee, associate, or provider, any person named in (i) any order of the Commissioner pursuant to Section 1386(c) or Section 1388(d) of the Knox-Keene Health Care Service Plan Act of 1975, (ii) any similar order of the Insurance Commissioner under the Insurance Code barring or otherwise prohibiting such person from being employed or otherwise engaged as an officer, director, employee, associate or provider of any entity subject to the jurisdiction of the Insurance Commissioner, or (iii) any administrative orders issued by a professional licensing board or by the Department of Industrial Relations? If the appropriate response to this item is "yes," attach as Exhibit D-5 a statement identifying each such person and explaining fully the scope of, and the circumstances giving rise to, such order.

E. Contracts with Providers.

1. Compliance with Requirements. Attach as Exhibit E a statement in tabular form for each provider contract, and for each standard form contract and its variations, if any, specifying the provisions of such contract which comply with the following provisions of the Act and rules:

Section 4600.6(g)
4600.6(I)(8)
4600.6(n)
Rules 9771.69
9771.70
9772 through 9778

2. The provisions describing the mechanism by which payments are to be rendered to the provider clearly identified by the name of the provider.

F. Workers' Compensation Health Care Contracts.

Compliance with Requirements. Attach as Exhibit F a schedule in tabular form for each workers' compensation health care contract and each standard form workers' compensation contract, identifying the particular provision of such contract which complies with the sections listed below, covering also any variations made in standard form contracts. As to any provision which varies from the applicable provision of the Act or rules, identify such provision in Exhibit F.

Section 4600.5(e)(7)(B)
4600.6(e)
Rules 9771.67
9771.69
9772 – 9778

G. Advertising.

Attach as Exhibit G a copy of any advertising which is subject to Section 4600.6 of the Code and which applicant proposes to use. With respect to each proposed advertisement indicate the contract(s) by name and by exhibit number(s) to which such advertisement relates and identify the employer segment to which the advertisement is directed.

H. Marketing of Workers' Compensation Health Care Contracts.

Attach as Exhibit H a statement describing the methods by which applicant proposes to market workers' compensation health care contracts, including the use of employees, or contracting solicitors or solicitor firms, their method or form of compensation, and the methods by which applicant will obtain compliance with Rules 9771.64, 9771.65, and 9771.83.

I. Supervision of Marketing.

Attach as Exhibit I a statement setting forth applicant's internal arrangements to supervise the marketing of its workers' compensation health care contracts, including the name and title of each person who has primary management responsibility for the employment and qualification of solicitors, advertising, contracts with solicitors and solicitor firms and for monitoring and supervising compliance with contractual and regulatory provisions.

J. Solicitation Contracts.

1. Attach as Exhibit J-1 a list of all persons (other than any employee of the organization whose only compensation is by salary) soliciting or agreeing to solicit the sale of workers' compensation health care contracts on behalf of the applicant. For each such person, identify by exhibit number that person's contract furnished pursuant to Item K-2 and, if such contract does not show the rate of compensation to be paid, specify the person's rate of compensation.

2. Attach as Exhibit J-2, a copy of each contract or proposed contract between applicant and the persons named in Exhibit J-1 for soliciting the sale of or selling workers' compensation health care contracts on behalf of applicant. If a standard form contract is used, furnish a specimen of the form, identify the provision and terms of the form which may be varied and include a copy of each variation.

K. Workers' Compensation Health Care Contract Enrollment Projections.

NOTE: All projections are to cover the period commencing from the applicant's commencement of operations as an authorized and certified workers' compensation health care provider organization for two years.

1. Projections. Attach as Exhibit K-1 projections of applicant's enrollments under workers' compensation health care provider contracts with self-insured employers, groups of self-insured employers, or insurers of employers (individually, "Employer"; collectively, "Employers") for the periods specified in the above note. Exhibit K-1 is to contain the following information with respect to each anticipated workers' compensation health care contract:

a. The name of the Employer.

b. The number of potential employees eligible to receive workers' compensation health care from the organization who are employed by the Employer.

c. The locations within and around applicant's service area in which the potential employees live and work.

d. The estimated date (or period after authorization by the Administrative Director and certification by the Workers' Compensation Division of the Department of Industrial Relations) for entry into the workers' compensation health care contract.

e. Identification of the workers' compensation health care contract anticipated with the Employer, by reference to Exhibit F. If more than one type of workers' compensation health care contract is expected with an Employer, each contract must be covered separately.

f. The projected number of employees on a monthly basis for the initial period specified in the Note, above, and quarterly for the following year.

2. Substantiation of Projections. Attach as Exhibit K-2 for each workers' compensation health care contract specified in Exhibit K-1 a description of the facts and assumptions used in connection with the information specified in that exhibit and include documentation of the source and validity of such facts and assumptions.

3. Letters of Interest. Attach as Exhibit K-3 letters of interest or intent from each Employer listed in Exhibit K-1, on the letterhead of the Employer and signed by its representative.

L. (Reserved for future use.)

M. Current Viability.

1. Financial Statements.

a. Attach as Exhibit M-1-a the most recent audited financial statements of applicant, accompanied by a report, certificate, or opinion of an independent certified public accountant, together with all footnotes to such financial statements.

b. If the financial statements attached as Exhibit M-1-a are for a period ended more than 60 days before the date of filing of this application, also attach as Exhibit M-1-b financial statements prepared as of date no later than 60 days prior to the filing of this application consisting of at least a balance sheet, a statement of income and expenses, and any accompanying footnotes; these more recent financial statements need not be audited, so long as they are prepared in accordance with generally accepted accounting principles.

2. Provision for Extraordinary Losses. The following requirements require an initial applicant to submit legible copies of the actual policies of insurance (including any riders or endorsements) or specimen copies of the policies of insurance which show all of the terms and conditions of coverage, or with respect to those items expressly allowing for self-insurance, allow applicant to provide evidence of self-insurance at least as adequate as insurance coverage.

a. Attach as Exhibit M-2-a evidence of adequate insurance coverage or self- insurance to respond to claims for damages arising out of furnishing workers' compensation health care (malpractice insurance).

b. Attach as Exhibit M-2-b evidence of adequate insurance coverage or self-insurance (e.g., appropriate reserve set aside to fund likely liabilities associated with uninsured costs) to respond to claims for tort claims, other than with respect to claims for damages arising out of furnishing health care services.

c. Attach as Exhibit M-2-c evidence of adequate insurance coverage or self-insurance to protect applicant against losses of facilities upon which it has the risk of loss due to fire or other causes. Identify facilities covered by individual policies and indicate the basis upon which applicant believes that the insurance thereon is adequate.

d. Attach as Exhibit M-2-d, evidence of fidelity bond coverage for at least the amounts specified in Rule 9771.74, in the form of a primary commercial blanket bond or a blanket position bond written by an insurer licensed by the California Insurance Commissioner, providing 30 days' notice to the Administrative Director prior to cancellation, and covering each officer, director, trustee, partner and employee of the organization, whether or not compensated.

e. Attach as Exhibit M-2-e evidence of adequate workers' compensation insurance coverage against claims which may arise against applicant.

N. Fiscal Arrangements.

1. Maintenance of Financial Viability. Attach as Exhibit N-1 a statement describing applicant's arrangements to comply with Section 4600.6(m) of the Code and Rule 9771/73.

2. Provider Claims. Attach as Exhibit N-2 a statement describing applicant's system for processing claims from providers for payment, including the rules defining applicant's obligation to reimburse, the standards and proce-

dures for applicant's claims processing system (including receipt, identification, handling, screening, and payment of claims), the timetable for processing claims, and procedures for monitoring the claims processing system.

3. Other Business. If the applicant is or will engage in any business other than as a workers' compensation health care provider organization, attach as Exhibit N-3 a statement describing such other business, its relationship to applicant's business as an organization, and the anticipated financial risks and liabilities of such other business. If the financial statements and projections in Exhibits M-1-a, do not include such other business, explain.

(d) Information Forms Required by Item D-1:

(1) Corporation Information Form (WCHCPO 1-A).

STATE OF CALIFORNIA
DIVISION OF WORKERS' COMPENSATION

D-1-a-iii CORPORATION
INFORMATION FORM

To be used in response to Item D-1-a of Form WCHCPO 1.

1. Name of Applicant (as in Item 1-a) ______

2. State of Incorporation. ______

3. Date of Incorporation. ______

4. Is applicant a nonprofit corporation?
( ) Yes ( ) No

5. Is applicant exempted from taxation as a nonprofit corporation? ( ) Yes ( ) No

6. Names of principal officers, directors and shareholders: List (a) each person who is a director or principal officer or who performs similar functions or duties and (b) each person who holds of record or beneficially 5 percent or more of the voting securities of applicant or 5 percent or more of applicant's equity securities. If this is an amended exhibit, place an asterisk (*) before the names for whom a change in title, status or stock ownership is being reported and a double asterisk (**) before the names of persons which are added to those furnished in the most recent previous filing.

Full Name Last First Middle	Relationship Beginning Date Mo. Year	Class of Equity Title or Security Status	Percent of Class

7. If this is an amended exhibit, list below the names reported in the most recent filing of this exhibit which are deleted by this amendment:

______

______

(2) Partnership Information Form (WCHCPO 1-B)

STATE OF CALIFORNIA
DIVISION OF WORKERS' COMPENSATION

EXHIBIT D-1-ii PARTNERSHIP
INFORMATION FORM.

To be used in response to Item D-1-b of Form WCHCPO 1.

1. Name of Applicant (as in Item 1-a). ______

2. State of organization. ______

3. Date of organization. ______

4. Names of Partners and Principal Management: List all general, limited and special partners and all persons who perform principal management functions. If this is an amended exhibit, place an asterisk (*) before the names of persons for whom a change in title, status or partnership interest is being reported and place a double asterisk (**) before the names of persons which are added to those furnished in the most recent previous filing.

Full Name Last First Middle	Beginning Date Mo. Year	Type of Partner	Capital Contribution (percentage)	Title or Duties

5. If this is an amended exhibit, list below the names reported in the most recent filing of this exhibit which are deleted by this amendment:

______

______

(3) Sole Proprietor Information Form (WCHCPO 1-C).

STATE OF CALIFORNIA
DIVISION OF WORKERS' COMPENSATION

EXHIBIT D-1-c SOLE PROPRIETORSHIP
INFORMATION FORM

To be used in response to Item D-1-c of Form WCHCPO 1

1. Name of Applicant (as in Item 1-a). ______

2. Residence Address. ______

3. Names of persons performing principal management functions: List each person who occupies a principal management position or who performs principal management functions for the applicant. If this is an amended exhibit, place an asterisk (*) before the names of persons for whom a change in title or duties is being reported and place a double asterisk (**) before the names of persons which are being added to those furnished in the most recent previous filing of this exhibit.

Full Name Last First Middle	Beginning Date Mo. Year	Title and Duties

4. If this is an amended exhibit, list below the names reported in the most recent filing of this exhibit which are deleted by this amendment:

______

______

(4) Information Form for Miscellaneous Types of Entities (WCHCPO 1-D).

STATE OF CALIFORNIA
DIVISION OF WORKERS' COMPENSATION

EXHIBIT D-1-d INFORMATION FORM FOR
MISCELLANEOUS TYPES OF ENTITIES.

To be used in response to Item D-1-d of Form WCHCPO 1.

1. Name of Applicant (as in Item 1-a) ______________________________

2. State of Organization ______________________
3. Date of Organization ______________________
4. Form of Organization (describe briefly)

5. Names of Principal Officers and Beneficial Owners: List below the names of (a) each person who is a principal officer or trustee of the applicant or who performs principal management functions, and (b) each person who owns of record or beneficially over 5 percent of any class of equity security of the applicant. If this is an amended exhibit, place an asterisk (*) before the name of each person for whom a change in title, status or interest is reported, and a double asterisk (**) before the name of persons which are added to those reported in the most recent previous filing.

Full Name Last First	Beginning Date Mo. Year	Class of Equity Security	Percent of Class	Title and Duties

6. If this is an amended exhibit, list below the names reported in the most recent filing of this exhibit which are deleted by this amendment:

____

____

Note: Authority cited: Stats. 1997, Ch. 346, Section 5. Reference: Sections 4600.3, 4500.5 and 4600.6, Labor Code.

History: 1. New section filed 4-15-98; operative 4-15-98. Submitted to OAL for printing only pursuant to Stats. 1997, Ch. 346, Section 5 (Register 98, No. 16).

Ref.: See Labor Code §4600.5; Herlick Handbook §§ 1.01[3][b], 4.12.

§9771.63. Individual Information Sheet (WCHCPO 2).

An individual information sheet required pursuant to these rules shall be in the following form:

CONFIDENTIAL
DIVISION OF WORKERS' COMPENSATION
State of California
INDIVIDUAL INFORMATION SHEET
under Labor Code Section 4600.6

1. Name of Applicant: __________ File No. __________

2. Exact full name of person completing this statement:

____
First Middle Last

3. Have you ever had a certificate, license, permit registration or exemption issued pursuant to the Business and Professions Code, Health and Safety Code, Insurance Code, or Labor Code denied, revoked or suspended or been otherwise subject to disciplinary action, while you were in the employ of the applicant, or while you had a contract with the applicant as a provider or otherwise? [ ] Yes [ ] No

If "yes" state the date of the action and the administrative body taking such action.

____

____

4. Have you ever been convicted or pled nolo contendere to a misdemeanor involving moral turpitude or any felony, other than traffic violations? [ ] Yes [ ] No

If the answer is "yes" give details:

____

____

5. Have you ever changed your name or ever been known by any name other than that herein listed? (Including a married person's prior surname, if any.) [ ] Yes [ ] No

If so, explain. Change in name through marriage or court order should also be listed. EXACT DATE OF EACH NAME CHANGE MUST BE LISTED.

____

____

6. Have you ever engaged in business under a fictitious firm name either as an individual or in the partnership or corporate form?
[ ] Yes [ ] No

If the answer is "yes" set forth particulars:

____

____

____

VERIFICATION

I, the undersigned, state that I am the person named in the foregoing Individual Information Sheet, that I have read and signed said Individual Information Sheet and know the contents thereof, including all exhibits attached thereto; and that the statements made therein, including any exhibits attached thereto, are true and correct.

I certify (or declare) under penalty of perjury under the laws of the State of California that I have read this Individual Information Sheet and the exhibits thereto and know the contents thereto, and that the statements therein are true and correct.

Executed at __________ (Place) on __________ (Date)

____
(Signature of Declarant)

NOTE: If this form is signed outside California complete the verification before a notary public in the space provided below.

State of ______________________________
County of ______________________________
Dated, ______________________________
at ______________________________

____
(Signature of Affiant)

Subscribed and sworn to before me,

____
Notary Public in and for said
County and State

Note: Authority cited: Stats. 1997, Ch. 346, Section 5. Reference: Sections 4600.3, 4500.5 and 4600.6, Labor Code.

History: 1. New section filed 4-15-98; operative 4-15-98. Submitted to OAL for printing only pursuant to Stats. 1997, Ch. 346, Section 5 (Register 98, No. 16).

Ref.: See Labor Code §4600.5; Herlick Handbook §§ 1.01[3][b], 4.12.

§9771.64. Organization Assurances Prior to Solicitation.

Prior to allowing any person to engage in acts of solicitation on its behalf, each organization shall reasonably assure itself that such person has sufficient knowledge of its organization, procedures, workers' compensation health care contracts, and the provisions of the Act and these rules to do so lawfully.

Note: Authority cited: Stats. 1997, Ch. 346, Section 5. Reference: Sections 4600.3, 4500.5 and 4600.6, Labor Code.

History: 1. New section filed 4-15-98; operative 4-15-98. Submitted to OAL for printing only pursuant to Stats. 1997, Ch. 346, Section 5 (Register 98, No. 16).

Ref.: See Labor Code §4600.5; Herlick Handbook §§ 1.01[3][b], 4.12.

§9771.65. Filing of Advertising and Disclosure Forms.

(a) Two copies of a proposed advertisement shall be filed. To minimize the expense of changes in advertising copy, it may be submitted in draft form for preliminary review subject to the later filing of a proof or final copy, and the later filing of a proof or final copy may be waived when the draft copy is presented in a manner reasonably representing the final appearance of the advertisement. The text of audio or audio/visual advertising should indicate any directions for presentation, including voice qualities and the juxtaposition of the visual materials with the text.

(b) The Administrative Director will not issue letters of nondisapproval of advertising. If the person submitting the advertisement requests an order shortening the 30-day waiting period under Section 4600.6(d) of the Code, such order will be issued when an appropriate showing of the need therefor is made.

Note: Authority cited: Stats. 1997, Ch. 346, Section 5. Reference: Sections 4600.3, 4500.5 and 4600.6, Labor Code.

History: 1. New section filed 4-15-98; operative 4-15-98. Submitted to OAL for printing only pursuant to Stats. 1997, Ch. 346, Section 5 (Register 98, No. 16).

Ref.: See Labor Code §4600.5; Herlick Handbook §§ 1.01[3][b], 4.12.

§9771.66. Deceptive Advertising.

Without limitation upon the meaning of Section 4600.6 of the Code, an advertisement or other consumer information is untrue, misleading or deceptive if:

(a) It represents that payment is provided in full for the charge for workers' compensation health care other than in accordance with what is required under the Labor Code.

(b) It represents that payment is provided for the customary charges for workers' compensation health care other than in accordance with what is required under the Labor Code.

(c) It represents that the organization, firm or solicitor or any provider or other person associated therewith is licensed or regulated by the Department of Managed Health Care or Administrative Director or other governmental agency, unless such statement is required by law or regulation or unless such statement is accompanied by a satisfactory statement which counters any inference that such licensing or regulation is an assurance of financial soundness or the quality or extent of workers' compensation health care.

Note: Authority cited: Stats. 1997, Ch. 346, Section 5. Reference: Sections 4600.3, 4500.5 and 4600.6, Labor Code.

History: 1. New section filed 4-15-98; operative 4-15-98. Submitted to OAL for printing only pursuant to Stats. 1997, Ch. 346, Section 5 (Register 98, No. 16).

2. Amendment of subsection (c) filed 1-9-2003; operative 1-9-2003 pursuant to Government Code section 11343.4 (Register 2003, No. 2).

Ref.: See Labor Code §4600.5; Herlick Handbook §§ 1.01[3][b], 4.12.

§9771.67. Disclosure Form.

(a) The disclosure form required under subdivision (a) of Section 4600.6(e) of the Code and made available to employers and employees shall conform to the requirements established by the Administrative Director of the Division of Workers' Compensation of the Department of Industrial Relations (Cal. Code Regs., Tit. 8, Sec. 9770 et seq.).

Note: Authority cited: Stats. 1997, Ch. 346, Section 5. Reference: Sections 4600.3, 4500.5 and 4600.6, Labor Code.

History: 1. New section filed 4-15-98; operative 4-15-98. Submitted to OAL for printing only pursuant to Stats. 1997, Ch. 346, Section 5 (Register 98, No. 16).

Ref.: See Labor Code §4600.5; Herlick Handbook §§ 1.01[3][b], 4.12.

§9771.68. Deceptive Workers' Compensation Health Care Provider Organization Names.

(a) A change of organization name is a "material modification".

(b) An organization name will be considered deceptive if it suggests the quality of care furnished by the organization or if it suggests that the cost of workers' compensation health care provided to employees is lower than the cost of similar health care purchased elsewhere, and in any such case the express or implied representation contained in the organization name is demonstrably untrue or is not supported by substantial evidence at all times while such name is used by the organization. Nothing in this subsection limits or restricts the Administrative Director from a determination that an organization or solicitor firm name is deceptive for reasons other than those stated herein.

Note: Authority cited: Stats. 1997, Ch. 346, Section 5. Reference: Sections 4600.3, 4500.5 and 4600.6, Labor Code.

History: 1. New section filed 4-15-98; operative 4-15-98. Submitted to OAL for printing only pursuant to Stats. 1997, Ch. 346, Section 5 (Register 98, No. 16).

Ref.: See Labor Code §4600.5; Herlick Handbook §§ 1.01[3][b], 4.12.

§9771.69. Workers' Compensation Health Care Contracts.

(a) All workers' compensation health care contracts and endorsements and amendments shall be printed legibly and shall include at least the following:

(1) The information required to be included on disclosure forms by Section 4600.6(e) of the Code and the information required to be included on disclosure forms by Rule 9771.67.

(2) Definitions of all terms contained in the contract which:

(A) Are defined by the Act, relevant Labor Code provisions, and the Regulations of the Administrative Director.

(B) Require definition in order to be understood by a reasonable person not possessing special knowledge of law, medicine, or organizations;

(C) Specifically describes the eligibility of employees.

(3) Appropriate captions, in boldface type, regarding the provision of workers' compensation health care, consistent with the requirements of the certification standards for health care organizations promulgated by the Administrative Director of the Division of Workers' Compensation of the Department of Industrial Relations (Cal. Code Regs., Tit. 8, Sec. 9770, et seq.).

(A) A benefit afforded by the contract shall not be subject to any limitation, exclusion, exception, reduction, deductible, or copayment, if any, which renders the benefit illusory.

(4) Provisions relating to cancellation under appropriate caption, in boldface type, which provisions shall include a statement of the time when a notice of cancellation becomes effective.

(5) A provision requiring the organization to provide written notice within a reasonable time to the other party of any termination or breach of contract by, or inability to perform of, any contracting provider if the other party may be materially and adversely affected thereby.

(6) A provision requiring a self-insured employer, group of self-insured employers, or insurer of an employer to mail promptly to each employee a legible, true copy of any notice of cancellation of the organization contract which may be received from the organization and to provide promptly to the organization proof of such mailing and the date thereof.

(7) A provision that (i) the organization is subject to the requirements of the Labor Code, the Regulations of the Administrative Director, and (ii) any provision required to be in the contract by the above shall bind the organization whether or not provided in the contract.

(b) For the purposes of this section:

(1) "Other party" means (A) in the case of a group of self-insured employers, the group representative designated in the contract, and (B) in the case of a self-insured employer or issuer of an employer, the self-insured employer or insurer of an employer and the insured employer.

(2) Any express or implied requirement of notice to the other party, in the context of a contract with a group of self-insured employers, requires notice to the group representative designated in the contract and, with respect to material matters, to the employers and employees under the contract. An organization may fulfill any obligation imposed by this section to notify employers and employees under such contract if the organization provider notice to the group representative designated in the contract, and the contract requires the group representative to disseminate such notice to employers and employees by the next regular communication to the group, but in no event later than 30 days after the receipt thereof.

Note: Authority cited: Stats. 1997, Ch. 346, Section 5. Reference: Sections 4600.3, 4500.5 and 4600.6, Labor Code.

History: 1. New section filed 4-15-98; operative 4-15-98. Submitted to OAL for printing only pursuant to Stats. 1997, Ch. 346, Section 5 (Register 98, No. 16).

Ref.: See Labor Code §4600.5; Herlick Handbook §§ 1.01[3][b], 4.12.

§9771.70. Contracts with Providers.

Written contracts must be executed between the organization and each provider of workers' compensation health care which regularly furnishes health care under the organization. All contracts with providers shall be subject to the following requirements:

(a) A written contract shall be prepared or arranged in a manner which permits confidential treatment by the Administrative Director of payment rendered or to be rendered to the provider without concealment or misunderstanding of other terms and provisions of the contract.

(b) The contract shall require that the provider submit claims for workers' compensation health care services to the organization within a reasonable period of time following the delivery of health care services to an employee.

Contracts which contain the following language shall be deemed to meet the timing requirements of this subsection (b), and there shall be no other agreements or other language in the contract which negates or diminishes the effect of the following language:

"[Name of Provider] shall submit claims for the cost of workers' compensation health care services to [Organization] according to the compensation provisions of [Section and paragraph] of this agreement, within 60 days after [Name of Provider] has rendered the workers' compensation health care services to the employee. However, failure to submit claims within 60 days does not alter the obligation of the organization to pay claims of contracting providers for which the organization has received payment."

(c) The contract shall provide that the organization shall forward claims from providers to the self-insured employer, group of self-insured employers or insurers of employers within 30 days after receipt of the claim from the provider, and that the organization shall pay the provider's claim no later than 30 days after receiving payment from the self-insured employer, group of self-insured employers or insurer of employers.

(d) The contract shall require that the provider maintain such records and provide such information to the organization or to the Administrative Director as may be necessary for compliance by the organization with the provisions of the Code and the rules thereunder, that such records will be retained by the provider for at least five years, and that such obligation is not terminated upon a termination of the agreement, whether by rescission or otherwise. (See Rule 9771.83) Contracts which contain the following language shall be deemed to meet the requirements of this subsection (d), and there shall be no other agreements or other language in the contract which negates or diminishes the effect of the following language:

"[Name of Provider] shall maintain all books, records of account, medical records, reports and papers as may be necessary for compliance by the organization with the provisions of Labor Code Section 4600.6 and the rules thereunder. All such books, records and reports shall be available to the organization or to the Administrative Director, as necessary or required, under the Act and Rules.

All such books, records, reports and papers must be maintained for at least five years after the initial date of delivery of health care services under this Agreement. The obligation of [Name of Provider] to maintain books, records, reports and papers and to make them available shall not terminate upon the termination of [this Agreement]."

(e) The contract shall require that the organization shall have access at reasonable times upon demand to the books, records and papers of the provider relating to the workers' compensation health care provided to employees, to the cost thereof, to payments received by the provider from the organization, self-insured employer, group of self-insured employers, an insurer of an employer, employee, or from others on the behalf of the foregoing.

Contracts which contain the following language shall be deemed to meet the requirements of this subsection (e), and there shall be no other agreements or other language in the contract which negates or diminishes the effect of the following language:

"The [Organization] shall have access during regular business hours to all administrative, financial and medical books, records reports and papers relating to the delivery of workers' compensation health care to employees, and to the cost of such delivery, payments received by [the Provider] from [the Organization] and/or any self-insured employer, group of self-insured employers, or insurer of an employer, an employee, or others."

(f) The contract shall prohibit surcharges or other payments in violation of the Labor Code for workers' compensation health care services and shall provide that whenever the organization receives notice of any such surcharge it shall take appropriate action.

(g) The contract shall disclose whether there are any other agreements between the organization and the provider, and shall incorporate by reference all such other agreements. Contracts which contain the following language shall be deemed to meet the requirements of this subsection (g):

"This [Agreement], including all addenda, supersedes any and all other agreements between [the Organization] and [the Provider] which are not attached hereto and incorporated herein and which are related to the delivery of, or to the compensation for, workers' compensation health care services. No future statements or promises relating to the delivery of workers' compensation health care services shall be valid or binding unless written and incorporated herein as addenda, subject to the approval of the Administrative Director".

(h) The contract shall contain provisions complying with Section 4600.6(n) of the Code and shall comply with the provisions of subsection (a)(7) of Rule 9771.69.

(i) The contract shall require that the provider cooperate with the organization's quality assurance and utilization review system established pursuant to Section 4600.6(k) of the Code, and cooperate with the Administrative Director in accordance with the provisions of Section 4600.6(o) of the Code and Sections 9771.76 and 9771.77 of the Rules.

Note: Authority cited: Stats. 1997, Ch. 346, Section 5. Reference: Sections 4600.3, 4500.5 and 4600.6, Labor Code.

History: 1. New section filed 4-15-98; operative 4-15-98. Submitted to OAL for printing only pursuant to Stats. 1997, Ch. 346, Section 5 (Register 98, No. 16).

Ref.: See Labor Code §4600.5; Herlick Handbook §§ 1.01[3][b], 4.12.

§9771.71. Disclosure of Conflicts of Interest.

(a) An organization shall not enter into any transaction with a person currently named in Item D of its application under Rule 9771.62 unless, prior thereto, each of the following conditions is met:

(1) The material facts concerning the transaction and the person's interest therein are disclosed to the governing body of the organization.

(2) The transaction is approved by a disinterested majority of the governing body.

(3) Such facts and such approval are made a part of the minutes of such governing body or, if no minutes are required of such governing body, otherwise retained as a record of the organization.

(b) An organization shall promptly give written notice to the Administrative Director if a transaction with a person currently named in Item D of its application under Rule 9771.62 is entered into otherwise than in conformity with the terms of this section.

(c) For the purposes of this section, "governing body" means the board of directors, all general partners, the sole proprietor, the board of trustees, and any other persons occupying a similar position or performing similar functions.

Note: Authority cited: Stats. 1997, Ch. 346, Section 5. Reference: Sections 4600.3, 4500.5 and 4600.6, Labor Code.

History: 1. New section filed 4-15-98; operative 4-15-98. Submitted to OAL for printing only pursuant to Stats. 1997, Ch. 346, Section 5 (Register 98, No. 16).

Ref.: See Labor Code §4600.5; Herlick Handbook §§ 1.01[3][b], 4.12.

§9771.72. Contracts with Solicitor Firms.

An organization shall not permit a solicitor firm to solicit self-insured employers, groups of self-insured employers, or insurers of an employer on its behalf except pursuant to a written contract which meets all of the following minimum requirements:

(a) The solicitor firm shall comply, and shall cause its principal persons and employees to comply, with all applicable provisions of the Act and the rules thereunder.

(b) The solicitor firm shall promptly notify the organization of the institution of any disciplinary proceedings against it or against any of its principal persons or employees relating to any license issued to any such person by the California Insurance Commissioner.

Note: Authority cited: Stats. 1997, Ch. 346, Section 5. Reference: Sections 4600.3, 4500.5 and 4600.6, Labor Code.

History: 1. New section filed 4-15-98; operative 4-15-98. Submitted to OAL for printing only pursuant to Stats. 1997, Ch. 346, Section 5 (Register 98, No. 16).

Ref.: See Labor Code §4600.5; Herlick Handbook §§ 1.01[3][b], 4.12.

§9771.73. Fiscal Soundness, Insurance, and Other Arrangements.

(a) An organization shall demonstrate fiscal soundness as follows:

Demonstrate an approach to the risk of insolvency which allows for the continuation of health care services for the duration of the contract period, the continuation of health care services to employees who are under treatment or confined on the date of insolvency in an in-patient facility until their discharge, and payments to unaffiliated providers for health care services rendered.

(b) In passing upon an organization's showing pursuant to this section, the Administrative Director will consider all relevant factors, including but not limited to:

(1) The method of compensating providers and the terms of provider contracts, especially as to the obligations of providers to employees in the event of the organization's insolvency.

(2) The methods by which the organization controls and monitors the utilization of health care services.

Note: Authority cited: Stats. 1997, Ch. 346, Section 5. Reference: Sections 4600.3, 4500.5 and 4600.6, Labor Code.

History: 1. New section filed 4-15-98; operative 4-15-98. Submitted to OAL for printing only pursuant to Stats. 1997, Ch. 346, Section 5 (Register 98, No. 16).

Ref.: See Labor Code §4600.5; Herlick Handbook §§ 1.01[3][b], 4.12.

§9771.74. Fidelity Bond.

(a) Each organization shall at all times maintain a fidelity bond covering each officer, director, trustee, partner and employee of the organization, whether or not they are compensated. The fidelity bond may be either a primary commercial blanket bond or a blanket position bond written by an insurer licensed by the California Insurance Commissioner, and it shall provide for 30 days' notice to the Administrative Director prior to cancellation. The fidelity bond shall provide at least the minimum coverage for the organization determined by the following schedule:

Annual Gross Income	*Minimum Coverage*
Up to $ 100,000	$ 10,000
100,000 to 300,000	20,000
300,000 to 500,000	30,000
500,000 to 750,000	50,000
750,000 to 1,000,000	75,000
1,000,000 to 2,000,000	100,000
2,000,000 to 4,000,000	200,000
4,000,000 to 6,000,000	400,000
6,000,000 to 10,000,000	600,000
10,000,000 to 20,000,000	1,000,000
20,000,000 and over	2,000,000

(b) The fidelity bond required pursuant to subsection (a) may contain a provision for a deductible amount from any loss which, except for such deductible provision, would be recoverable from the insurer. A deductible provision shall not be in excess of 10 percent of the required minimum bond coverage, but in no event shall the deductible amount be in excess of $100,000.

Note: Authority cited: Stats. 1997, Ch. 346, Section 5. Reference: Sections 4600.3, 4500.5 and 4600.6, Labor Code.

History: 1. New section filed 4-15-98; operative 4-15-98. Submitted to OAL for printing only pursuant to Stats. 1997, Ch. 346, Section 5 (Register 98, No. 16).

Ref.: See Labor Code §4600.5; Herlick Handbook §§ 1.01[3][b], 4.12.

§9771.75. Reimbursements on a Fee-for-Services Basis: Determination of Status of Claims.

Every organization shall institute procedures whereby all claim forms received by the organization from providers of workers' compensation health care for reimbursement on a fee-for-service basis are maintained and accounted for in a manner which permits the determination of the date of receipt of any claim, the status of any claim, the dollar amount of unpaid claims at any time, and rapid retrieval of any claim. Although any categories for status-determination held unobjectionable by the Administrative Director may be used, for the purposes of this section, the following status-determination categories, as a group, shall be presumptively reasonable:

(1) to be processed,

(2) processed, waiting for payment,

(3) pending, waiting for approval for payment or denial,

(4) pending, waiting for additional information,

(5) denied,

(6) paid, and, if appropriate,

(7) other.

These procedures shall involve the use of either a claims log, claims numbering system, electronic data processing records, and/or any other method held unobjectionable by the Administrative Director.

Note: Authority cited: Stats. 1997, Ch. 346, Section 5. Reference: Sections 4600.3, 4500.5 and 4600.6, Labor Code.

History: 1. New section filed 4-15-98; operative 4-15-98. Submitted to OAL for printing only pursuant to Stats. 1997, Ch. 346, Section 5 (Register 98, No. 16).

Ref.: See Labor Code §4600.5; Herlick Handbook §§ 1.01[3][b], 4.12.

§9771.76. Medical Survey Procedure.

(a) Unless the Administrative Director in his discretion determines that advance notice will render the survey less useful, an organization will be notified approximately four weeks in advance of the date for commencement of an onsite medical survey. The Administrative Director may, without prior notice, conduct inspections of organization facilities or other elements of a medical survey, either in conjunction with the medical survey or as part of an unannounced inspection program.

(b) The onsite medical survey of an organization shall include, but not be limited to, the following procedures to the extent considered necessary based upon prior experience with the organization and in accordance with the procedures and standards developed by the Administrative Director.

(1) Review of the procedures for obtaining workers' compensation health care including, but not limited to, the scope of health care.

(A) The availability and adequacy of facilities for telephone communication with health personnel, emergency health care facilities, out-of-the-area coverage, referral procedures, and medical encounters.

(B) The means of advising employees of the procedures to obtain health care, including the hours of operation, location and nature of facilities, types of health care, telephone and other arrangements for appointment setting.

(C) The availability of qualified personnel at each facility referred to in Section 4600.6(j) of the Code to receive and handle inquiries concerning health care and grievances.

(2) Review of the design and implementation of procedures for reviewing and regulating utilization of health care and facilities.

(3) Review of the design and implementation of procedures to review and control costs.

(4) Review of the design, implementation and effectiveness of the internal quality of care review systems, including review of medical records and medical records systems. A review of medical records and medical records systems may include, but is not limited to, determining whether:

(A) The entries establish the diagnosis stated, including an appropriate history and physical findings;

(B) The therapies noted reflect an awareness of current therapies;

(C) The important diagnoses are summarized or highlighted; (Important are those conditions that have a bearing on future clinical management.)

(D) Drug allergies and idiosyncratic medical problems are conspicuously noted;

(E) Pathology, laboratory and other reports are recorded;

(F) The health professional responsible for each entry is identifiable;

(G) Any necessary consultation and progress notes are evidenced as indicated;

(H) The maintenance of an appropriate system for coordination and availability of the medical records of the employee, including out-patient, in-patient and referral services and significant telephone consultations.

(5) Review of the overall performance of the organization in providing workers' compensation health care, by consideration of the following:

(A) The numbers and qualifications of health professional and other personnel;

(B) The provision of, incentives for, and participation in, continuing education for health personnel and the provision for access to current medical literature;

(C) The adequacy of all physical facilities, including lighting, cleanliness, maintenance, equipment, furnishings, and convenience to employees, organization personnel and visitors;

(D) The practice of health professionals and allied personnel in a functionally integrated manner, including the extent of shared responsibility for patient care and coordinated use of equipment, medical records and other facilities and services;

(E) The appropriate functioning of health professionals and other health personnel, including specialists, consultants and referrals;

(F) Nursing practices, including reasonable supervision;

(G) Written nondiscriminatory personnel practices which attract and retain qualified health professionals and other personnel;

(H) The adequacy and utilization of pathology and other laboratory facilities, including the quality, efficiency and appropriateness of laboratory procedures and records and quality control procedures;

(I) X-ray and radiological services, including staffing, utilization, equipment, and the promptness of interpretation of X-ray films by a qualified provider;

(J) The handling and adequacy of medical record systems, including filing procedures, provisions for maintenance of confidentiality, the efficiency of procedures for retrieval and transmittal, and the utilization of sampling techniques for medical records audits and quality of care review;

(K) The adequacy, including convenience and readiness of availability to employees, of all provided health care;

(L) How the organization is organized and its mechanisms for furnishing workers' compensation health care, including the supervision of health professionals and other personnel;

(M) The extent to which individual medical decisions by qualified medical personnel are unduly constrained by fiscal or administrative personnel, policies or considerations;

(N) The adequacy of staffing, including medical specialties.

(6) Review of the overall performance of the organization in meeting the health needs of employees.

(A) Accessibility of facilities and workers' compensation health care, based upon location of facilities, hours of operation, waiting periods for health care and appointments, the availability of parking and transportation;

(B) Continuity of health care, including the ability of employees to select a primary treating physician, staffing in medical specialties or arrangements therefor; the referral system (including instructions, monitoring and follow-up); the maintenance and ready availability of medical records; and the availability of health care education to employees;

(C) The grievance procedure required by Section 4600.6(j) of the Code, including the availability to employees of grievance procedure information, the time required for and the adequacy of the response to grievances and the utilization of grievance information by the organization's management.

(7) In considering the above and in pursuit of the survey objectives, the survey team may perform any or all of the following procedures:

(A) Private interviews and group conferences with employees, physicians and other health care professionals and providers, and members of its administrative staff including, but not limited to, persons in principal management positions.

(B) Examination of any records, books, reports and papers of the organization and of any management company, provider or subcontractor providing workers' compensation health care or other services to the organization including, but not limited to, the minutes of medical staff meetings, peer review, and quality of care review records, duty rosters of medical personnel, surgical logs, appointment records, the written procedures for the internal operation of the organization, and contracts and correspondence with employees and with providers of workers' compensation health care and of other services to the organization, and such additional documentation the Administrative Director may specifically direct the surveyors to examine.

(C) Physical examination of facilities, including equipment.

(D) Investigation of grievances or complaints from employees, or from the general public.

Note: Authority cited: Stats. 1997, Ch. 346, Section 5. Reference: Sections 4600.3, 4500.5 and 4600.6, Labor Code.

History: 1. New section filed 4-15-98; operative 4-15-98. Submitted to OAL for printing only pursuant to Stats. 1997, Ch. 346, Section 5 (Register 98, No. 16).

Ref.: See Labor Code §4600.5; Herlick Handbook §§ 1.01[3][b], 4.12.

§9771.77. Medical Survey: Report of Correction of Deficiencies.

Prior to or immediately upon the expiration of the 30-day period following notice to an organization of a deficiency as provided in subdivision (8) of Section 4600.6(o) of the Code, the organization shall file a written statement with the Administrative Director identifying the deficiency and describing the action taken to correct the deficiency and the results of such action. The report shall be signed by a principal officer of the organization.

Where such deficiencies reasonably may be adjudged to require long-term corrective action or to be of a nature which reasonably may be expected to require a period longer than 30 days to remedy, evidence that the organization has initiated remedial action and is on the way to achieving acceptable levels of compliance may be submitted for review by the Administrative Director.

Note: Authority cited: Stats. 1997, Ch. 346, Section 5. Reference: Sections 4600.3, 4500.5 and 4600.6, Labor Code.

History: 1. New section filed 4-15-98; operative 4-15-98. Submitted to OAL for printing only pursuant to Stats. 1997, Ch. 346, Section 5 (Register 98, No. 16).

Ref.: See Labor Code §4600.5; Herlick Handbook §§ 1.01[3][b], 4.12.

§9771.78. Removal of Books and Records from State.

The books and records of an organization, management company, solicitor firm, and any provider or subcontractor providing workers' compensation health care or other services to an organization, management company, or solicitor firm shall not be removed from this state without the prior written consent of the Administrative Director.

Note: Authority cited: Stats. 1997, Ch. 346, Section 5. Reference: Sections 4600.3, 4500.5 and 4600.6, Labor Code.

History: 1. New section filed 4-15-98; operative 4-15-98. Submitted to OAL for printing only pursuant to Stats. 1997, Ch. 346, Section 5 (Register 98, No. 16).

Ref.: See Labor Code §4600.5; Herlick Handbook §§ 1.01[3][b], 4.12.

§9771.79. Examination Procedure.

Regular and additional or nonroutine examinations conducted by the Administrative Director pursuant to Section 4600.6(q) of the Code will ordinarily be commenced on an unannounced basis. To the extent feasible, deficiencies noted will be called to the attention of the responsible officers of the company under examination during the course of the examination, and in that event the company should take the corrective action indicated. When deemed appropriate, the company will be advised by letter of the deficiencies noted upon the examination. If the deficiency letter requires a report from the organization, such report must be furnished within 15 days or such additional time as may be allowed.

Note: Authority cited: Stats. 1997, Ch. 346, Section 5. Reference: Sections 4600.3, 4500.5 and 4600.6, Labor Code.

History: 1. New section filed 4-15-98; operative 4-15-98. Submitted to OAL for printing only pursuant to Stats. 1997, Ch. 346, Section 5 (Register 98, No. 16).

Ref.: See Labor Code §4600.5; Herlick Handbook §§ 1.01[3][b], 4.12.

§9771.80. Additional or Nonroutine Examinations and Surveys.

(a) An examination or survey is additional or nonroutine for good cause for the purposes of Section 4600.6(q) of the Code when the reason for such examination or survey is any of the following:

(1) The organization's noncompliance with written instructions from the Administrative Director;

(2) The organization has violated, or the Administrative Director has reason to believe that the organization has violated, any of the provisions of Sections 4600.3, 4600.5, or 4600.6 of the Code or regulations referring to those sections.

(3) The organization has committed, or the Administrative Director has reason to believe that the organization has committed, any of the acts or omissions enumerated in Section 4600.5(k) of the Code.

(4) The Administrative Director deems such additional or nonroutine examination or survey necessary to verify representations made to the Administrative Director by an organization in response to a deficiency letter.

(b) Each situation giving rise to an additional or nonroutine examination or survey shall be evaluated on a case-by-case basis as to the seriousness of the violation, or lack of timely or adequate response by the organization to the Administrative Director's request to correct the violation. The organization shall be notified in writing of the provisions of the Act or regulations which have been, or may have been, violated and which therefore caused such additional or nonroutine examination or survey to be performed. The expense of such examinations and surveys shall be charged to the organization being examined or surveyed in accordance with Section 4600.6(q) of the Code.

Note: Authority cited: Stats. 1997, Ch. 346, Section 5. Reference: Sections 4600.3, 4500.5 and 4600.6, Labor Code.

History: 1. New section filed 4-15-98; operative 4-15-98. Submitted to OAL for printing only pursuant to Stats. 1997, Ch. 346, Section 5 (Register 98, No. 16).

Ref.: See Labor Code §4600.5; Herlick Handbook §§ 1.01[3][b], 4.12.

§9771.81. Financial Statements.

(a) Whenever pursuant to these rules or pursuant to an order or request of the Administrative Director under the Code a financial statement or other report is required to be audited or be accompanied by the opinion of a certified public accountant, such accountant shall be independent of the licensee, determined in accordance with Section 602.02 of Financial Reporting Release No. 1 issued by the Securities and Exchange Commission (Securities Act Release 6395, April 15, 1982).

(b) The financial statements shall be audited by an independent accountant in accordance with Rule 9771.60(e).

(c) Except as provided in subsection (d), financial statements of an organization required pursuant to these rules must be on a combining basis with an affiliate, if the organization or such affiliate is substantially dependent upon the other for the provision of workers' compensation health care, management or other services. An affiliate will normally be required to be combined, regardless of its form of organization, if the following conditions exist:

(1) The affiliate controls, is controlled by, or is under common control with, the organization, either directly or indirectly (see subsections (c) and (d) of Rule 9771.60), and

(2) The organization or the affiliate is substantially dependent, either directly or indirectly, upon the other for services or revenue.

(d) Upon written request of an organization, the Administrative Director may waive the requirement that an affiliate be combined in financial statements required pursuant to these rules. Normally, a waiver will be granted only when

(1) the affiliate is not directly engaged in the delivery of workers' compensation health care or

(2) the affiliate is operating under an authority granted by a governmental agency pursuant to which the affiliate is required to submit periodic financial reports in a form prescribed by such governmental agency that cannot practicably be reformatted into the form prescribed by these rules (such as an insurance company).

(e) When combined financial statements are required by this section, the independent accountant's report or opinion must cover all the entities included in the combined financial statements. If the accountant's report or opinion makes reference to the fact that a part of the examination was performed by another auditor, the organization shall also file the individual financial statements and report or opinion issued by the other auditor.

(f) Organizations which have subsidiaries that are required to be consolidated under generally accepted accounting principles must present either

(1) consolidating financial statements, or

(2) consolidating schedules for the balance sheet and statement of operations, which in either case must show the organization separate from the other entities included in the consolidated balances.

(g) This section shall not apply to an organization which is a public entity or political subdivision.

(h) All filings of financial statements required pursuant to these rules must include an original and one copy.

Note: Authority cited: Stats. 1997, Ch. 346, Section 5. Reference: Sections 4600.3, 4500.5 and 4600.6, Labor Code.

History: 1. New section filed 4-15-98; operative 4-15-98. Submitted to OAL for printing only pursuant to Stats. 1997, Ch. 346, Section 5 (Register 98, No. 16).

Ref.: See Labor Code §4600.5; Herlick Handbook §§ 1.01[3][b], 4.12.

§9771.82. Books and Records.

(a) Each organization, solicitor firm, and solicitor shall keep and maintain their books of account and other records on a current basis.

(b) Each organization shall make or cause to be made and retain books and records which accurately reflect:

(1) The names and last known addresses of all employees eligible to receive workers' compensation health care, and all contracting self-insured employers, groups of self-insured employers and insurers of employers.

(2) All contracts required to be submitted to the Administrative Director and all other contracts entered into by the organization.

(3) All requests made to the organization for payment of moneys for workers' compensation health care, the date of such requests, and the dispositions thereof.

(4) A current list of the names and addresses of all individuals employed by the organization as solicitors.

(5) A current list of the names and addresses of all solicitor firms with which the organization contracts.

(6) A current list of the names and addresses of all of the organization's officers, directors, principal shareholders, general managers, and other principals.

(7) The amount of any commissions paid to persons who obtain self-insured employers, groups of self-insured employers, and insurers of employers for workers' compensation health care provider organizations, and the manner in which said commissions are determined.

(c) Each solicitor firm shall make and retain books and records which include a current list of the names and addresses of its partners, if any, and all of its employees who make act as solicitors.

Note: Authority cited: Stats. 1997, Ch. 346, Section 5. Reference: Sections 4600.3, 4500.5 and 4600.6, Labor Code.

History: 1. New section filed 4-15-98; operative 4-15-98. Submitted to OAL for printing only pursuant to Stats. 1997, Ch. 346, Section 5 (Register 98, No. 16).

Ref.: See Labor Code §4600.5; Herlick Handbook §§ 1.01[3][b], 4.12.

§9771.83. Retention of Books and Records.

Every organization and solicitor firm shall preserve for a period of not less than five years, the last two years of which shall be in an easily accessible place at the offices of the organization or solicitor firm, the books of account and other records required under the provisions, and for the purposes, of the Act. After such books and records have been preserved for two years, they may be warehoused or stored, or microfilmed, subject to their availability to the Administrative Director within not more than 5 days after request therefore.

Note: Authority cited: Stats. 1997, Ch. 346, Section 5. Reference: Sections 4600.3, 4500.5 and 4600.6, Labor Code.

History: 1. New section filed 4-15-98; operative 4-15-98. Submitted to OAL for printing only pursuant to Stats. 1997, Ch. 346, Section 5 (Register 98, No. 16).

Ref.: See Labor Code §4600.5; Herlick Handbook §§ 1.01[3][b], 4.12.

§9772. General Standards.

(a) HCOs must demonstrate that they meet the following requirements:

(1) All facilities located in this state including, but not limited to, clinics, hospitals, laboratories, and skilled nursing facilities to be utilized by the HCO for the delivery of occupational medical and health care services or other services specifically required by this article shall be licensed by the State Department of Health Services, if such licensure is required by law, and shall meet any other relevant certification requirements. Facilities not located in this state shall conform to all licensing and other requirements of the jurisdiction in which they are located.

(2) All personnel employed by or under contract to the HCO shall be licensed or certified by their respective board or agency, where such licensure or certification is required by law.

(3) All equipment required to be licensed or registered by law shall be so licensed or registered and the operating personnel for such equipment shall be licensed or certified as required by law.

(4) The HCO shall provide continuity of care and timely referral of patients to other providers in a manner consistent with professionally recognized standards of care.

(5) All services shall be available and accessible at reasonable times to all HCO enrollees.

(6) The HCO may employ and utilize allied health personnel for the furnishing of occupational health services to the extent permitted by law and provided such use is consistent with professionally recognized standards of care; however, any course of treatment beyond first aid, as defined in subdivision (c) of Section 14311, shall provide for at least one face to face visit with a primary treating physician.

(7) The HCO shall have the organizational, financial, and administrative capacity to provide services to employers, claims administrators, and HCO enrollees. The HCO shall be able to demonstrate to the Division that medical decisions are rendered by qualified providers unhindered by fiscal and administrative management, and that such decisions adhere to professionally recognized standards of care.

Any applicant that is owned in whole or in part or controlled by a workers' compensation insurer or self-insured employer shall, in addition to the requirements set forth above, further demonstrate that the organization's claims function shall have no influence or control over medical decision-making. The applicant shall further demonstrate that the clear authority of its Medical Director over all medical decisions is reflected both in its organizational chart and any internal procedure manual or other internal description of HCO operations.

(8) All contracts with claims administrators, employers, providers and other persons or entities furnishing services specifically required by this article shall be consistent with the requirements of this article and Division 4 of the Labor Code.

Note: Authority cited: Sections 133, 4600.5, 4603.5 and 5307.3, Labor Code. Reference: Section 4600.5, Labor Code.

History: 1. New section filed 12-31-93; operative 1-1-94. Submitted to OAL for printing only pursuant to Government Code section 11351 (Register 93, No. 53).

2. Amendment of subsection (b)(7) filed 1-9-2003; operative 1-9-2003 pursuant to Government Code section 11343.4 (Register 2003, No. 2).

Ref.: Hanna § 22.01[6]; Herlick Handbook §§ 1.01[3][b], 4.12.

§9773. Treatment Standards.

(a) HCOs shall provide all HCO enrollees with access to all medical, surgical, chiropractic, and hospital treatment which is reasonably required to cure or relieve the effects of an injury in accordance with Section 4600 of the Labor Code. This treatment must be provided without payment of any co-payment, deductible, or premium share by an HCO enrollee. HCOs must provide a description of the method for providing treatment required under the code, including a list of its physical facilities. The description must include the occupational health care delivery capabilities of the HCO, including the number of primary treating physicians and specialists, the number and types of licensed or state-certified health care support staff, the number of hospital beds, and the arrangements and the methods by which occupational health care services will be provided, which shall include the following:

(1) Provider services, including consultation and referral. HCOs must identify the total number of full time equivalent physicians and providers of each different specialty type available to provide treatment for work injuries or illnesses on a regular basis.

(2) Inpatient hospital services, which shall include acute hospital services, general nursing care, use of operating room and related facilities, intensive care unit and services, diagnostic laboratory and x-ray services, special duty nursing as medically necessary, physical therapy, respiratory therapy, administration of blood and blood products, and other diagnostic, therapeutic and rehabilitative services as medically reasonable or medically necessary, and coordinated discharge planning including planning of such continuing care as may be necessary, both medically and as a means of preventing possible rehospitalization.

(3) Ambulatory care services, (including outpatient hospital services) which shall include diagnostic and treatment services, physical therapy, speech therapy, occupational therapy services as appropriate, and those hospital services which can reasonably be provided on an ambulatory basis.

(4) Emergency services, including ambulance services and out-of-area coverage for emergency care.

(5) Diagnostic laboratory services, diagnostic and therapeutic radiological services, and other diagnostic services.

(6) Home health service, which shall include, where medically appropriate, health services provided at the home of an HCO enrollee as provided or prescribed by a physician or osteopath licensed to practice in California. Such home health services shall be provided in the home, including nursing care, performed by a registered nurse, public health nurse, licensed vocational nurse or licensed home health aide.

(b) HCOs shall provide a description of the times, places and manner of providing services under the HCO, including a description of the geographical service area. The geographical service area shall be designated by a list of the postal zip codes in the service area, and a map indicating the type and number of facilities within the service area. The following requirements must be met unless the HCO shows that a lack of a type of provider exists in an area and that the minimum number is not available:

(1) At least one full-time equivalent primary treating physician shall be available within the geographical proximity specified in paragraph (2) for every 1,200 expected injuries or illnesses. The HCO shall provide information on expected case-load and the methodology, data and assumptions used in the calculations.

(2) HCO enrollees must have a residence or workplace within 30 minutes or 15 miles of (i) a primary treating physician or (ii) a contracting or HCO-operating hospital, or if separate from such hospital, a contracting or HCO-operated provider of all emergency health care services. Enrollees must have a residence or workplace within 60 minutes or 30 miles of all other occupational health services listed in subdivision (a).

(3) The HCO must provide a description of how access to any of the basic health services listed in subdivision (a) will be provided to HCO enrollees who reside outside the HCO's geographical service area such that the requirements of this subdivision are met.

(4) Initial treatment for non-emergency services must be made available by an HCO within 24 hours of the HCO's receipt of a request for treatment.

(5) The HCO must describe how treatment is initiated and how an HCO enrollee is assigned a primary treating physician.

(6) Enrollees shall be entitled to at least one change of physician for an injury. The HCO shall provide the employee, within five days of a request by an HCO enrollee, with a choice of any other available participating provider in the appropriate specialty.

(7) HCO enrollees shall be provided with a second opinion, upon request, from a participating provider.

(8) The HCO must describe how it will make available interpreter's services, as required, for the treatment or evaluation of patients.

(9) The HCO must describe how the HCO will treat an injury or illness pending a claims administrator's decision concerning liability for treatment.

(10) HCOs must maintain and make available or insure that their contracted medical providers maintain and make available medical records to treating or evaluating physicians in a timely manner.

(c) The HCO shall describe its process for coordinating all aspects of medical treatment, including the coordination and monitoring of referrals to consultants, therapeutic or diagnostic facilities, reporting of treatment, being responsive to the HCO patient's request for change of physician or physician referrals as may be required by this article, and for ensuring timeliness of referrals and timely response to the primary treating physician.

(d) The HCO must include at least one full-time equivalent board-certified occupational medicine employed or contracting physician to provide expertise on workplace health and safety issues and prevention and treatment of occupational injuries and illnesses. The HCO shall describe its ongoing educational program to ensure that all primary treating physicians receive education, training or experience in occupational medicine and workers compensation, including but not limited to, the following:

(1) The regulatory requirements for primary treating physicians in workers' compensation;

(2) Familiarity with workplace hazards, causes of workplace injury, work restrictions, and vocational rehabilitation;

(3) The requirements of medical-legal reports in workers compensation.

Note: Authority cited: Sections 133, 4600.5, 4603.5 and 5307.3, Labor Code. Reference: Sections 3209.3, 4600 and 4600.5, Labor Code.

History: 1. New section filed 12-31-93; operative 1-1-94. Submitted to OAL for printing only pursuant to Government Code section 11351 (Register 93, No. 53).

Ref.: Herlick Handbook §§ 1.01[3][b], 4.12.

§9773.1. Referrals to Chiropractors.

HCOs shall maintain guidelines for chiropractor care in accordance with paragraph (2) of subdivision (1) of Section 4600.5 of the Labor Code. The HCO must include a description of the HCO's guidelines and utilization review process for chiropractic care, including the HCO's definition of "neuromusculoskeletal condition", and the procedure whereby enrollees may be referred to chiropractors in accordance with the HCO's guidelines.

Note: Authority cited: Sections 133, 4600.5, 4603.5 and 5307.3, Labor Code. Reference: Section 3209.3, 4600 and 4600.5, Labor Code.

History: 1. New section filed 12-31-93; operative 1-1-94. Submitted to OAL for printing only pursuant to Government Code section 11351 (Register 93, No. 53).

Ref.: Herlick Handbook §§ 1.01[3][b], 4.12.

§9774. Quality of Care.

(a) An HCO must include a written program designed to ensure a level of care for occupational injuries and illnesses which meets professionally recognized standards of care. The program must be designed and directed by providers to document that the quality of care provided is reviewed, that problems are identified, that effective action is taken to improve care where deficiencies are identified, that follow-up measures are planned where indicated, and that all of the requirements of this division are met. The plans must describe the goals and objectives of the program and organizational arrangements, including staffing, the methodology for on-going monitoring and evaluation of health services, the scope of the program, and required levels of activity. Quality of care problems must be identified and corrected. The program must demonstrate that the HCO's utilization review activities are designed to improve the quality of care provided.

The HCO shall describe and implement a program, including the following:

(1) A description of the process whereby the medical reasonableness or medical necessity of requests for authorization are reviewed and decisions on such requests are made by the HCO. The description shall include the specific criteria utilized in the review and throughout the decision-making process, including treatment protocols or standards in any software, database, or other resource used in the process. Treatment protocols must be consistent with any guidelines adopted pursuant to paragraph (8) of subdivision (e) of Section 139 of the Labor Code.

(2) A description of the qualifications of the personnel involved in reviewing and making decisions concerning requests for authorization, including the professional qualifications of the personnel, and the manner in which such personnel are involved in the review process. Medical decisions must be rendered by physicians with licenses unrestricted by their licensing board.

(3) A description of manual and automated data storage and retrieval systems for medical and utilization review; and the types of data analyses, reports, and manner in which results are communicated to providers.

(b) The HCO's quality assurance committee shall meet on at least a quarterly basis or more frequently if problems have been identified, to oversee its quality assurance program responsibilities. Reports to the HCO's governing body shall be sufficiently detailed to include findings and actions taken as a result of the quality assurance program and to identify those internal or contracting provider components which the quality assurance program had identified as presenting significant or chronic quality of care issues.

(c) The HCO is responsible for establishing a quality assurance program to monitor and evaluate the care provided by each contracting provider group or facility. Medical groups or other provider entities may have active quality assurance programs which the HCO may use. However, the HCO must retain responsibility for reviewing the overall quality of care delivered to HCO enrollees. To the extent that the HCO's quality assurance responsibilities are delegated within the HCO or to a contracting provider or facility, the HCO shall provide evidence of an oversight mechanism for ensuring that delegated quality assurance functions are adequately performed.

(d) Physicians must be an integral part of the quality assurance program. Design and implementation of the quality assurance program shall be supervised by designated physicians. Physician participation in quality assurance activity must be adequate to monitor the full scope of clinical services rendered, resolve problems and ensure that corrective action is taken when indicated. Specialist providers must also be involved in peer review of like specialties.

(e) The HCO may delegate inpatient quality assurance functions to hospitals, however in such case a HCO must fully describe and monitor that hospital's quality assurance program.

(f) The HCO must insure that all comprehensive medical-legal reports are prepared in an objective, fair, and unbiased manner, and that such reports are prepared in accordance with Section 4628 of the Labor Code, any applicable procedures promulgated under Section 139.2 of the Labor Code, and the requirements of Section 10606. The HCO or physician shall retain, for no less than three years, copies of all comprehensive medical evaluation reports which are prepared by any of its physicians to determine an employee's eligibility for compensation. These reports shall be made available to the administrative director upon request. The administrative director may review such reports as he or she deems necessary to insure compliance with this subdivision, and the results of this review may be used to deny recertification if it is determined that a significant number of an HCO's reports show bias or are legally inadequate.

(g) The HCO must describe how it will assess its activities as required by Sections 9776 and 9776.1 and the HCO's system for assuring data quality.

Note: Authority cited: Sections 133, 4600.5, 4603.5 and 5307.3, Labor Code. Reference: Sections 4600, 4600.5 and 4628, Labor Code.

History: 1. New section filed 12-31-93; operative 1-1-94. Submitted to OAL for printing only pursuant to Government Code section 11351 (Register 93, No. 53).

Ref.: Herlick Handbook §§ 1.01[3][b], 4.12.

§9775. Grievance and Dispute Resolution Procedure.

(a) HCOs must maintain a grievance procedure under which HCO enrollees or participating providers may submit grievances to the HCO. Each HCO must include a system for resolving disputes which shall include HCO enrollee disputes with a provider and a provider's dispute with the HCO. The HCO must provide that either an HCO enrollee or a provider shall be able to initiate a grievance. Each HCO must provide reasonable procedures which insure adequate consideration of enrollee and provider grievances or disputes and which provide prompt rectification when appropriate.

(b) Compliant forms and a copy of the grievance procedure shall be readily available through each provider facility and through the claims administrator, and shall be furnished promptly upon receipt of a verbal or written request.

(c) If a grievance or dispute concerns the medical reasonableness or medical necessity of treatment recommended by a provider, the HCO must provide for an expedited procedure for review of the grievance or dispute by physicians or qualified professional providers not previously involved in the grievance or dispute and who possess the specialty which is appropriate to the medical nature of the disputed treatment. Under no circumstance may the appeal decision be made by a registered nurse. The HCO must issue a written decision as to the grievance or dispute within 30 days unless the HCO enrollee's medical condition requires a more expedited decision.

(d) Each HCO shall inform providers and HCO enrollees, or their representatives, that they may file a written complaint to the administrative director

(e) The HCO shall annually provide to the administrative director a summary of written grievances received concerning the provision of occupational health services, including the number of total grievances received and processed. Records of all written grievances concerning the provision of occupational health services, including the name of the grievant, the nature of the complaint or grievance, and the manner in which the grievance was resolved or referred for further action, shall be kept by the HCO for a period of not less than 3 years and shall be made available by the HCO to the administrative director as he or she deems necessary.

Note: Authority cited: Sections 133, 4600.5, 4603.5 and 5307.3, Labor Code. Reference: Sections 4600 and 4600.5, Labor Code.

History: 1. New section filed 12-31-93; operative 1-1-94. Submitted to OAL for printing only pursuant to Government Code section 11351 (Register 93, No. 53).

Ref.: Herlick Handbook §§ 1.01[3][b], 4.12.

§9776. Workplace Safety and Health.

(a) The HCO must maintain the capability to work cooperatively and in conjunction with claims administrators, employers, and employees to promote workplace health and safety and to detect workplace exposures and hazards, including:

(1) education of employees and employers on health and medical aspects of workplace health and safety issues;

(2) consultation on employee medical screening for early detection of occupational disease, and assessment of workplace risk factors.

(b) An HCO shall include in contracts with claims administrators a provision which enables the HCO to obtain upon request information to allow appropriate provider decision-making regarding diagnoses, patient medical restrictions, early disease detection, or return-to-work, which may include:

(1) the employer's written Injury and Illness Prevention Plan, including the name and title of individual responsible for implementing the plan.

(2) information concerning exposure levels for specified materials, and information, including Material Safety Data Sheets, concerning health, safety, and ergonomic risk factors in the workplace.

(3) the name and title of the individual responsible for loss control services for each employer.

(c) The HCO shall have in place a program for prompt reporting, to the employer or insurer loss control program and to the employer's designee responsible for the Injury and Illness Prevention Plan, of the following occupational injuries and illnesses: occupational asthma; cumulative trauma disorders of the upper extremities; lead poisoning; amputations (excluding amputations of the distal phalanges); noise-induced hearing loss; pesticide illness; electrocutions; asphyxiation; and burns and falls from heights requiring hospitalization.

(d) The HCO shall annually report to the insurer loss control program or to the employer's designee responsible for the Injury and Illness Prevention Plan as designated in the contract between the HCO and the claims administrator, aggregate data on injuries and illnesses.

History: 1. New section filed 12-31-93; operative 1-1-94. Submitted to OAL for printing only pursuant to Government Code section 11351 (Register 93, No. 53).

Ref.: Herlick Handbook § 4.12.

§9776.1. Return to Work Coordination.

An HCO shall maintain a return to work program in conjunction with the employer and claims administrator to facilitate and coordinate returning injured workers to the workplace, to assess the feasibility and availability of modified work or modified duty, and to minimize risk of employee exposure after return to work to risk factors which may aggravate or cause recurrence of injury. The duties of the HCO shall be specified in the contract between the HCO and the claims administrator.

History: 1. New section filed 12-31-93; operative 1-1-94. Submitted to OAL for printing only pursuant to Government Code section 11351 (Register 93, No. 53).

Ref.: Herlick Handbook §§ 1.01[3][b], 4.12.

§9777. Patient Assistance and Notification.

(a) The HCO shall inform HCO enrollees upon enrollment in the plan and annually thereafter of the details of their coverage, and their rights and options under the HCO including: (1) how HCO enrollees are informed of the procedure for processing and resolving grievances, including the location(s) and telephone number where grievances may be submitted; and (2) how HCO enrollees are informed of their right to file a complaint with the administrative director in accordance with subdivision (d) of Section 9775.

(b) The HCO shall provide patient education specifically designed for injured workers with work-related injuries or illnesses.

(c) HCO enrollees must be able to receive information on a 24-hour basis regarding the availability of necessary medical services available within the HCO. The information may be provided through recorded telephone message after normal working hours. It must include information on how the enrollee can obtain emergency services or other urgently needed care and how the employee can access an evaluation within 24 hours of the injury as required under paragraph 4 of subdivision (b) of section 9773.

(d) Informational materials must be in a form understandable to all enrollees and available in Spanish. HCOs must provide in their application a description of how the information specified in subdivisions (a) through (c) will be provided to HCO enrollees. A copy of the informational material provided to HCO enrollees, including the text of phone messages, shall be made available to the administrative director upon request.

(e) The HCO shall provide for periodic evaluation of the HCO by enrollees. The HCO must provide a survey to HCO enrollees and patients, which shall be in the form and manner prescribed by the administrative director. The HCO must describe its method for incorporating the results of the survey in its quality assurance program. The completed forms and any data extracted from such forms shall be made available to the administrative director upon request.

Note: Authority cited: Sections 133, 4600.5, 4603.5 and 5307.3, Labor Code. Reference: Sections 4600 and 4600.5, Labor Code.

History: 1. New section filed 12-31-93; operative 1-1-94. Submitted to OAL for printing only pursuant to Government Code section 11351 (Register 93, No. 53).

Ref.: Herlick Handbook §§ 1.01[3][b], 4.12.

§9778. Evaluation.

(a) The HCO must include a timely and accurate method to report to the administrative director the following information, in a standardized format to be prescribed by the administrative director:

(1) Aggregated information on the number of HCO enrollees and their age, sex, geographical distribution, occupation, and SIC, by federal employer identification number.

(2) Information required to be provided pursuant to this section shall be made available by the HCO to the administrative director, in a form and manner to be prescribed by the administrative director, annually, on March 1.

(b) Information regarding medical and health care service cost and utilization, rates of return to work, and average time in medical treatment shall be submitted by the claims administrator in the format specified in Article 1.1 (commencing with section 9700).

Note: Authority cited: Sections 133, 4600.5, 4603.5 and 5307.3, Labor Code. Reference: Sections 4600 and 4600.5, Labor Code.

History: 1. New section filed 12-31-93; operative 1-1-94. Submitted to OAL for printing only pursuant to Government Code section 11351 (Register 93, No. 53).

2. New subsections (c)-(c)(2) filed 10-7-99; operative 3-1-2000 (Register 99, No. 41).

3. Amendment filed 11-4-2009; operative 1-1-2010 (Register 2009, No. 45).

Ref.: Herlick Handbook §§ 1.01[3][b], 4.12.

§9779. Certification.

(a) Once an applicant has completed an application and submitted a fee in accordance with Section 9771 and has demonstrated to the administrative director that its organization has met all of the criteria for certification, the administrative director will certify the organization as an HCO for a period of three years, unless earlier revoked or suspended.

(b) Once the Administrative Director has determined that an entity licensed as a full service health care service plan under Section 1353 of the Health and Safety Code (a Knox-Keene Health Care Service Plan Act) and deemed to be an HCO pursuant to Labor Code Section 4600.5(c) has complied with the requirements of Section 9771 subsections (g)(1) and (2) the administrative director shall certify the organization as an HCO, pursuant to Section 4600.5(c), for a period of three years unless earlier revoked or suspended.

(c) A certification shall state that a particular entity is certified as a health care organization to provide health care to injured employees for injuries and diseases and other services in accordance with the terms of the entity's application. The certification shall also state: (1) the geographic service area in which the health care organization is permitted to provide health care, (2) the maximum number of enrollees, (3) the name or names under which the health care organization is permitted to provide health care, (4) the date of expiration of the certification, and (5) any other conditions or limitations.

(d) The HCO will be recertified at the expiration of each subsequent three year period, provided it continues to meet the requirements of this article and timely pays a recertification fee of $1,000.

Note: Authority cited: Sections 133, 4600.5, 4600.7, 4603.5 and 5307.3, Labor Code. Reference: Sections 4600, 4600.5 and 4600.7, Labor Code.

History: 1. New section filed 12-31-93; operative 1-1-94. Submitted to OAL for printing only pursuant to Government Code section 11351 (Register 93, No. 53).

2. Amendment of subsection (a), repealer and new subsection (b), amendment of subsection (c), repealer and new subsection (d), repealer of subsection (e), and amendment of Note filed 2-14-96; operative 2-14-96. Submitted to OAL for printing only pursuant to Government Code section 11351 (Register 96, No. 7).

3. New subsection (b), repealer of subsection (d) and subsection relettering filed 1-9-2003; operative 1-9-2003 pursuant to Government Code section 11343.4 (Register 2003, No. 2).

4. Amendment of subsection (d) filed 11-4-2009; operative 1-1-2010 (Register 2009, No. 45).

Ref.: Herlick Handbook §§ 1.01[3][b], 4.12.

§9779.1. On-Site Surveys.

(a) The HCO must ensure that it will be available for and cooperate with on-site surveys as the administrative director deems necessary to insure compliance with this article, including during the initial certification process. The administrative director will coordinate on-site surveys with the Department of Managed Health Care to the extent feasible.

(b) The administrative director will notify the HCO of deficiencies found by the survey team. The administrative director will provide the HCO a reasonable time to correct the deficiencies. Failure on the part of the HCO to timely correct noted deficiencies may result in suspension or revocation of an HCO's certification in accordance with Section 9779.2.

(c) Reports of all surveys shall be open to public inspection, except that no survey shall be made public unless the HCO has had an opportunity to review the survey and file a statement in response within 30 days, to be attached to the report. Deficiencies shall not be made public if they are corrected within 30 days of the date that the HCO was notified.

(d) Non-routine audits will be charged based on the actual cost for performing the audit. The amount shall include the actual salaries or compensation paid to the persons making the audit, the expenses incurred in the course thereof, and overhead costs in connection therewith as fixed by the Administrative Director. Overhead costs shall be based on the total expenditure for operating expenses and equipment, except travel, of the managed care unit of the Division of Workers' Compensation for the previous fiscal year. The invoice will be sent upon the completion of the audit and shall be paid within 30 calendar days.

Note: Authority cited: Sections 133, 4600.5, 4600.7, 4603.5 and 5307.3, Labor Code. Reference: Sections 4600, 4600.5 and 4600.7, Labor Code.

History: 1. New section filed 12-31-93; operative 1-1-94. Submitted to OAL for printing only pursuant to Government Code section 11351 (Register 93, No. 53).

2. Editorial correction of section heading (Register 96, No. 7).

3. New subsection (d) and amendment of Note filed 2-14-96; operative 2-14-96. Submitted to OAL for printing only pursuant to Government Code section 11351 (Register 96, No. 7).

4. Amendment of subsection (a) filed 1-9-2003; operative 1-9-2003 pursuant to Government Code section 11343.4 (Register 2003, No. 2).

Ref.: Herlick Handbook §§ 1.01[3][b], 4.12.

§9779.2. Suspension; Revocation; Hearing.

(a) Complaints pertaining to an HCO's violations of this article may be directed in writing to the administrative director. Upon receipt of a complaint, or in the course of monitoring the HCO's operations, the administrative director may investigate an alleged violation. The investigation may include, but not be limited to, a request for and review of pertinent HCO records, interviewing medical and administrative personnel, or an on-site medical survey. If the investigation reveals reasonable cause to belive that the HCO has violated a requirement of this article, the administrative director may initiate proceedings to suspend or revoke an HCO's certification.

(b) Certification of an HCO may be suspended or revoked if:

(1) Service under the HCO is not being provided according to the terms of the certified HCO.

(2) The HCO fails to meet the requirements of this article, the Labor Code, or other applicable law.

(3) False or misleading information is knowingly or repeatedly submitted by the HCO or a participating provider or the HCO knowingly or repeatedly fails to report information required by this article.

(4) The HCO knowingly continues to use the services of a provider or medical reviewer whose license, registration, or certification has been suspended or revoked or who is otherwise ineligible to provide treatment to an inured worker under California law.

(c) In the event an HCO or organization is formally notified of the administrative director's intention to revoke or suspend the HCO's certification, or to refuse certification or recertification as an HCO, the HCO or organization shall be entitled to a hearing before the administrative director or an administrative law judge which shall be shall be held in accordance with the Administrative Procedure Act (Chapter 5 (commencing with Section 11500), of Part 1 of Division 3 of Title 2 of the Government Code), and the administrative director shall have all of the powers granted under that act.

Note: Authority cited: Sections 133, 4600.5, 4603.5 and 5307.3, Labor Code. Reference: Sections 4600 and 4600.5, Labor Code.

History: 1. New section filed 12-31-93; operative 1-1-94. Submitted to OAL for printing only pursuant to Government Code section 11351 (Register 93, No. 53).

Ref.: Herlick Handbook §§ 1.01[3][b], 4.12.

§9779.3. Obligations of Employer Covered by a Contract with a Health Care Organization.

(a) When an insurer or employers, a group of self-insured employers, or self-insured employers have contracted with a health care organization certified pursuant to Section 4600.5 of the Labor Code the employer shall provide information to all employees who are eligible to be enrolled in the health care organization as follows:

(1) a new employee shall be provided with the choice of enrolling in an HCO or designating the employee's own personal physician or personal chiropractor no later than 30 days following the employee's date of hire.

(2) a current employee shall be provided with the choice of enrolling in an HCO or designating the employee's own personal physician or personal chiropractor no later than 30 days before the initial enrollment period ends;

(3) an employer must provide information concerning the HCO it is offering to its employees no later than 30 days prior to the final date for enrollment. Information shall be provided in written form, in no less than twelve (12) point typeface, and in a language understandable to employees. The information provided must include, at a minimum, the following:

(i) the name of the HCO offered;

(ii) the corporate or business name of all entities which own or control the HCO offered; and indication of relationship, if any, of the HCO to workers' compensation carrier or self-insured employer;

(iii) the services offered by the HCO;

(iv) a complete listing of all primary treating physicians, specialist physicians, and clinics participating in the HCO who would be reasonably accessible to the employee for the provision of occupational health services. Primary treating physicians who are not accepting new patients must be clearly identified;

(v) If the HCO is also the provider of group health coverage for non-occupational health services, the HCO policy regarding enrollees' ability to use their personal physician (for non-occupational health services) for treatment of work injuries.

(vi) any provider risk-sharing arrangements related to utilization of services.

(4) Within fifteen days following enrollment, the HCO must provide to each enrollee complete information regarding HCO services and processes, including but not limited to:

(i) the services offered, including interpreters services, how such services are obtained, hours of services;

(ii) the definition of emergency care, how to obtain out-of-service treatment, how to obtain after-hours services;

(iii) case management and medical management processes, selection of the primary treating physician, and method for obtaining second opinions, change of physician, or referrals to chiropractors, physical therapists, or specialists;

(iv) the grievance and dispute resolution procedures;

(v) additional services offered, including return to work, health and safety, patient assistance, and patient education.

(b) Employees shall designate their enrollment option on form DWC 1194. This form must be maintained in the employee's personnel file for a minimum of three (3) years, and be made available to the employee or employee's representative on request.

Employees who designate on form DWC 1194 that they do not wish to enroll in an HCO and wish to pre-designate their own personal physician or personal chiropractor or personal acupuncturist shall pre-designate that personal physician or personal chiropractor or personal acupuncturist on the form 1194. At least once each year the employer shall provide the employee with a notice informing the employee of his or her right to continue as an enrollee of the HCO, change to another HCO if another HCO is offered by the employer, or designate the employee's own personal physician, personal chiropractor or personal acupuncturist instead of the HCO. If another HCO is offered by the employer and the employee chooses to change to another HCO, or if the employee chooses to designate a personal physician, personal chiropractor or personal acupuncturist, the employee shall designate such choice on a form DWC 1194, which shall be provided by the employer.

Note: Authority cited: Sections 133, 4600.3, 4600.5, 4603.5 and 5307.3, Labor Code. Reference: Sections 4600, 4600.3 and 4600.5, Labor Code.

History: 1. New section filed 3-27-95; operative 3-27-95. Submitted to OAL for printing only pursuant to Government Code section 11351 (Register 95, No. 13).

2. Amendment filed 5-17-99; operative 5-17-99 pursuant to Government Code section 11343.4(d) (Register 99, No. 21).

3. Amendment of section heading and section filed 1-9-2003; operative 1-9-2003 pursuant to Government Code section 11343.4 (Register 2003, No. 2).

Ref.: Hanna § 22.01[6]; Herlick Handbook §§ 1.01[3][b], 4.12.

§9779.4. DWC Form 1194.

CHOOSING MEDICAL CARE FOR WORK-RELATED INJURIES and ILLNESSES

California law requires your employer to provide and pay for medical treatment if you are injured at work. Your employer has chosen to provide this medical care by using a health plan called a Workers' Compensation Health Care Organization, or HCO. This form gives you information about the HCO program, and describes your rights in choosing medical care for work-related injuries and illnesses.

What is an HCO?

A Workers' Compensation Health Care Organization is an organization which has been certified by the State of California Division of Workers' Compensation to provide health care to injured workers. HCOs must meet the quality and service standards set by the Division of Workers' Compensation. They must have health care providers who understand the workers' compensation system and occupational health care. The HCO must be able to work with employers and workers to improve worksite health and safety. If you choose an HCO, the HCO will coordinate all aspects of the care for your work injury, including working with your employer to help you get back to work in a job that will not make the injury worse. The HCO must provide information on the services they provide to injured workers and must answer your questions and complaints. By choosing an HCO, you may help your employer save money. There is no cost to you in choosing an HCO.

Choosing an HCO

Your employer has offered you enrollment in an HCO. If your employer's workers' compensation insurance company owns or controls this HCO, your employer must tell you this during the enrollment process. Your employer must give you information about the HCO before you make a choice.

If you choose to enroll in the HCO, you must use the HCO for any medical treatment you need as a result of a work injury for at least 90 days after the injury. If you choose an HCO and your employer pays for at least one-half of your health insurance (for non-work injuries), then you must use the HCO for at least 180 days after a work injury. In some HCOs, your own personal physician, personal chiropractor or personal acupuncturist for your regular health care is available to treat you for work injuries/illnesses.

Choosing Your Own Doctor—Not in an HCO

If you do not want to be treated by the HCO after a work injury, you can "designate" your own personal physician, personal chiropractor or personal acupuncturist who has treated you before and who has your medical records. If you choose your own personal physician, personal chiropractor or personal acupuncturist, you may go to him or her any time for treatment of a work injury.

DWC Form 1194: front (rev. 1/03)

MAKING YOUR CHOICE
For Workers' Compensation Health Care

Use this form to choose how you want to get medical care if you have a work-related injury or illness. You may choose the Workers' Compensation Health Care Organization offered by your employer, or you may designate your own personal physician, personal chiropractor or personal acupuncturist. If you choose to designate your own personal physician, personal chiropractor or personal acupuncturist, you should do so in the space provided below. If you do not make one of these choices, your employer will enroll you in the HCO in order for you to receive treatment for a work injury or illness.

If you have questions about HCOs or medical treatment after a work injury, you may call an Information and Assistance officer. Find the telephone number in the phone book listed under State of California, Department of Industrial Relations, Division of Workers Compensation. If you have concerns, complaints or questions regarding a specific HCO or the enrollment process you can call 1-800-277-1767.

THIS IS AN IMPORTANT LEGAL DOCUMENT THAT AFFECTS YOUR RIGHTS IF YOU HAVE A WORK INJURY.

☐ I want to enroll in an HCO for my medical care for any work-related injury or illness. I have received information about the Health Care Organization offered by my employer and want to enroll in that HCO.

☐ I do not want to enroll in an HCO. I want my personal physician, personal chiropractor or personal acupuncturist to treat me for any work-related injury or illness. My personal physician, personal chiropractor or personal acupuncturist is:

____

(Write in the name, and address and telephone number of your personal physician, personal chiropractor or personal acupuncturist.)

☐ I do not want to enroll in an HCO or designate a personal physician, personal chiropractor or personal acupuncturist to treat me for any work-related injury or illness. I understand that my employer will enroll me in the HCO for treatment of any work-related injury or illness.

____________________ ____________________

(Print) Name of Employee Signature

____

Date Signed DWC Form 1194: back (rev. 1/03)

Note: Authority cited: Sections 133, 4600.5, 4603.5 and 5307.3, Labor Code. Reference: Sections 4600 and 4600.5, Labor Code.

History: 1. New section filed 3-27-95; operative 3-27-95. Submitted to OAL for printing only pursuant to Government Code section 11351 (Register 95, No. 13).

2. Amendment filed 1-9-2003; operative 1-9-2003 pursuant to Government Code section 11343.4 (Register 2003, No. 2).

Ref.: Hanna § 22.01[6]; Herlick Handbook §§ 1.01[3][b], 4.12.

§9779.45. Minimum Periods of Enrollment.

Pursuant to Labor Code Section 4600.3:

(a) An employee whose employer does not offer non-occupational health coverage under a plan established pursuant to collective bargaining, and does not offer to pay more than one-half the cost of non-occupational health coverage for that employee under another plan, may be treated for occupational injuries and illnesses by a physician of the employee's choosing after 90 days from the date the injury was reported.

(b) An employee whose employer offers non-occupational health coverage under a plan established pursuant to collective bargaining, or offers to pay more than one-half the cost of non-occupational health coverage for that employee under another plan, may be treated for occupational injuries and illnesses by a physician of the employee's choosing after 180 days from the date the injury was reported or upon the date of contract renewal or open enrollment of the health care organization, whichever occurs first, but in no case until 90 days from the date the injury was reported.

Note: Authority cited: Sections 133, 4600.3, 4600.5, 4603.5 and 5307.3, Labor Code. Reference: Sections 4600, 4600.3 and 4600.5, Labor Code.

History: 1. New section filed 5-17-99; operative 5-17-99 pursuant to Government Code section 11343.4(d) (Register 99, No. 21).

2. Repealer of subsection (c) filed 1-9-2003; operative 1-9-2003 pursuant to Government Code section 11343.4 (Register 2003, No. 2).

Ref.: Herlick Handbook §§ 1.01[3][b], 4.12.

§9779.5. Reimbursement of Costs to the Administrative Director; Obligation to Pay Share of Administrative Expense.

(a) Each organization certified under this article shall pay to the administrative director an amount as estimated by the administrative director for the ensuing fiscal year, as a reimbursement of a share of all costs and expenses, including routine on-site surveys, data collection and dissemination and overhead, reasonably incurred in the administration of this article and not otherwise recovered by the administrative director under this article or from the Worker's Compensation Managed Care Fund. The amount shall be assessed annually on or before April 15 and may be paid to the Workers' Compensation Managed Care Fund in two equal installments. The first installment shall be paid on or before July 1 of each year and the second installment shall be paid on or before December 15 of each year.

(1) Annual Assessment: The assessment shall be calculated on the basis of the number of enrollees in each individual HCO. Based on the number of enrollees enrolled in the HCO on December 31 of the prior calendar year, the annual assessment shall be $250.00 for 0 to 1000 enrollees, $350 for 1001 to 5000 enrollees, and $500 for 5001 or more enrollees.

(b) Non-routine audits conducted in response to complaints will be charged based on the actual cost for performing the audit. The invoice will be sent within sixty days of the completion of the audit and shall be paid within 30 calendar days after the billing date.

(c) In no case shall the reimbursement, payment, or other fee authorized by this section exceed the cost, including overhead, reasonably incurred in the administration of this article.

Note: Authority cited: Sections 133, 4600.5, 4600.7, 4603.5 and 5307.3, Labor Code. Reference: Sections 4600 and 4600.5, Labor Code.

History: 1. New section filed 2-14-96; operative 2-14-96. Submitted to OAL for printing only pursuant to Government Code section 11351 (Register 96, No. 7).

2. Amendment of subsection (a)(1) and repealer and new subsection (a)(2) filed 5-17-99; operative 5-17-99 pursuant to Government Code section 11343.4(d) (Register 99, No. 21).

3. Amendment of subsection (a)(1) and repealer of subsection (a)(2) filed 11-4-2009; operative 1-1-2010 (Register 2009, No. 45).

Ref.: Herlick Handbook §§ 1.01[3][b], 4.12.

§9779.8. Copies of Documents.

Fees for copies of documents will be charged as set forth in Section 9990. Any request for copies of documents must include payment of fees by check or money order made payable to the Workers' Compensation Managed Care Fund.

Note: Authority: Sections 133, 4600.5, 4600.7, 4603.5, 5307.3, Labor Code. Reference: Sections 4600, 4600.5, Labor Code.

History: 1. New section filed 2-14-96; operative 2-14-96. Submitted to OAL for printing only pursuant to Government Code section 11351 (Register 96, No. 7).

Ref.: Herlick Handbook §§ 1.01[3][b], 4.12.

§9779.9. Late Payment. [Repealed]

Note: Authority: Sections 133, 4600.5, 4600.7, 4603.5, 5307.3, Labor Code. Reference: Sections 4600, 4600.5, Labor Code.

History: 1. New section filed 2-14-96; operative 2-14-96. Submitted to OAL for printing only pursuant to Government Code section 11351 (Register 96, No. 7).

2. Repealer filed 11-4-2009; operative 1-1-2010 (Register 2009, No. 45).

Ref.: Herlick Handbook §§ 1.01[3][b], 4.12.

ARTICLE 5
Predesignation of Personal Physician; Request for Change of Physician; Reporting Duties of the Primary Treating Physician; Petition for Change of Primary Treating Physician

§9780. Definitions.

As used in this Article:

(a) "Claims Administrator" means a self-administered insurer providing security for the payment of compensation required by Divisions 4 and 4.5 of the Labor Code, a self-administered self-insured employer, a self-administered joint powers authority, a self-administered legally uninsured, or a third-party claims administrator for a self-insured employer, insurer, legally uninsured employer, or joint powers authority.

(b) "Emergency health care services" means health care services for a medical condition manifesting itself by acute symptoms of sufficient severity such that the absence of immediate medical attention could reasonably be expected to place the patient's health in serious jeopardy.

(c) "Facility" means a hospital, clinic or other institution capable of providing the medical, surgical, chiropractic or hospital treatment which is reasonably required to cure or relieve the employee from the effects of the injury.

(d) "First aid" is any one-time treatment, and a follow-up visit for the purpose of observation of minor scratches, cuts, burns, splinters, etc., which do not ordinarily require medical care. Such one-time treatment, and follow-up visit for the purpose of observation, is considered first aid, even though provided by a physician or registered professional personnel.

(e) "Personal Physician" means (1) the employee's regular physician and surgeon, licensed pursuant to Chapter 5 (commencing with section 2000) of Division 2 of the Business and Professions Code, (2) who has been the employee's primary care physician, and has previously directed the medical treatment of the employee, and (3) who retains the employee's medical records, including the employee's medical history. "Personal physician" includes a medical group, if the medical group is a single corporation or partnership composed of licensed doctors of medicine or osteopathy, which operates an integrated multispecialty medical group providing comprehensive medical services predominantly for nonoccupational illnesses and injuries.

(f) "Primary Care Physician" means a physician who has the responsibility for providing initial and primary care to patients, for maintaining the continuity of patient care, and for initiating referral for specialist care. A primary care physician shall be either a physician who has limited his or her practice of medicine to general practice or who is a board-certified or board-eligible internist, pediatrician, obstetrician-gynecologist, or family practitioner.

(g) "Reasonable geographic area" within the context of Labor Code section 4600 shall be determined by giving consideration to:

(1) The employee's place of residence, place of employment and place where the injury occurred; and

(2) The availability of physicians in the fields of practice, and facilities offering treatment reasonably required to cure or relieve the employee from the effects of the injury;

(3) The employee's medical history;

(4) The employee's primary language.

Note: Authority cited: Sections 59, 133 and 4603.5, Labor Code. Reference: Section 4600, Labor Code.

History: 1. Repealer of Article 5 (Sections 9783-9785, 9787 and 9788) and new Article 5 (Sections 9780-9787) filed 1-28-76 as an emergency; effective upon filing (Register 76, No. 5). For prior history, see Register 70, No. 49, and Register 72, No. 51.

2. Certificate of Compliance filed 1-29-76 (Register 76, No. 5).

3. New subsections (f)-(i) filed 11-7-78; effective thirtieth day thereafter (Register 78, No. 45).

4. Repealer and new article 5 heading and amendment of section and Note filed 3-14-2006; operative 3-14-2006 pursuant to Government Code section 11343.4 (Register 2006, No. 11).

5. Editorial correction of subsection (f) (Register 2007, No. 7).

6. Change without regulatory effect amending subsection (f) filed 2-21-2007 pursuant to section 100, title 1, California Code of Regulations (Register 2007, No. 8).

7. Repealer of subsection (e) and subsection relettering filed 2-12-2014; operative 7-1-2014 pursuant to Government Code section 11343.4 (Register 2014, No. 7).

Ref.: Hanna §§ 5.02[1], [4], 5.05[6][a], 22.01[4], 22.02[1], [2], 22.03[2]; Herlick Handbook §§ 1.01[3][b], 4.04[1].

§9780.1. Employee's Predesignation of Personal Physician.

(a) An employee may be treated for an industrial injury in accordance with section 4600 of the Labor Code by a personal physician that the employee predesignates prior to the industrial injury if the following three conditions are met:

(1) Notice of the predesignation of a personal physician is in writing, and is provided to the employer prior to the industrial injury for which treatment by the personal physician is sought. The notice shall include the personal physician's name and business address, and the name of the plan, policy, or fund providing the employee with health care coverage for nonoccupational injuries or illnesses as required by subdivision (a)(2) of this section. The employee may use the optional predesignation form (DWC Form 9783) in section 9783 for this purpose.

(2) The employee has health care coverage for nonoccupational injuries or illnesses on the date of injury in a plan, policy, or fund as described in subdivisions (b), (c), and (d) of Labor Code section 4616.7.

(3) The employee's personal physician agrees to be predesignated prior to the injury. The personal physician may sign the optional predesignation form (DWC Form 9783) in section 9783 as documentation of such agreement. The physician may authorize a designated employee of the physician to sign the optional predesignation form on his or her behalf. If the personal physician or the designated employee of the physician does not sign a predesignation form, there must be other documentation that the physician agrees to be predesignated prior to the injury in order to satisfy this requirement.

(b) If an employee has predesignated a personal physician prior to the effective date of these regulations, such predesignation shall be considered valid if the conditions in subdivision (a) have been met.

(c) Where an employer or an employer's insurer has a Medical Provider Network pursuant to section 4616 of the Labor Code, an employee's predesignation which has been made in accordance with this section shall be valid and the employee shall not be subject to the Medical Provider Network.

(d) Where an employee has made a valid predesignation pursuant to this section, and where the employer or employer's insurer has a Medical Provider Network, any referral to another physician for other treatment need not be within the Medical Provider Network.

(e) Unless the employee agrees, neither the employer nor the claims administrator shall contact the predesignated personal physician to confirm predesignation status or contact the personal physician regarding the employee's medical information or medical history prior to the personal physician's commencement of treatment for an industrial injury.

(f) Where the employer has been notified of an employee's predesignation of a personal physician in accordance with this section and where the employer becomes liable for an employee's medical treatment, the claims administrator shall:

(1) authorize the predesignated physician to provide all medical treatment reasonably required to cure or relieve the injured employee from the effects of his or her injury;

(2) furnish the name and address of the person to whom billing for treatment should be sent;

(3) where there has been treatment of an injury prior to commencement of treatment by the predesignated physician, arrange for the delivery to the predesignated physician of all medical information relating to the claim, all X-rays, the results of all laboratory studies done in relation to the injured employee's treatment; and

(4) provide the physician with (1) the fax number, if available, to be used to request authorization of treatment plans; (2) the complete requirements of section 9785; and (3) the forms set forth in sections 9785.2, 9785.4, and 9785.5. In lieu of providing the materials required in (2) and (3) immediately above, the claims administrator may refer the physician to the Division of Workers' Compensation's website where the applicable information and forms can be found at http://www.dir.ca.gov/DWC/dwc_home_page.htm.

(g) Notwithstanding subdivision (f), the employer shall provide first aid and appropriate emergency health care services reasonably required by the nature of the injury or illness. Thereafter, if further medical treatment is reasonably required to cure or relieve the injured employee from the effects of his or her injury, the claims administrator shall authorize treatment with the employee's predesignated personal physician in accordance with subdivision (f).

(h) If documentation of a physician's agreement to be predesignated has not been provided to the employer as of the time of injury, treatment shall be provided in accordance with Labor Code section 4600, or Labor Code section 4616, if the employer or insurer has established or contracted for a Medical Provider Network, as though no predesignation had occurred. Upon provision of the documented agreement that was made prior to injury that meets the conditions of Labor Code section 4600(d), the employer or claims administrator shall authorize treatment with the employee's predesignated physician as set forth in subdivision (f).

Note: Authority cited: Sections 59, 133 and 4603.5, Labor Code. Reference: Sections 3551, 4600 and 4616, Labor Code.

History: 1. New section filed 11-7-78; effective thirtieth day thereafter (Register 78, No. 45).

2. Amendment of section heading, repealer and new section and amendment of Note filed 3-14-2006; operative 3-14-2006 pursuant to Government Code section 11343.4 (Register 2006, No. 11).

3. Amendment of subsection (a)(1), repealer and new subsection (a)(2), repealer of subsection (e), subsection relettering and amendment of newly designated subsections (f)(4)-(h) filed 2-12-2014; operative 7-1-2014 pursuant to Government Code section 11343.4 (Register 2014, No. 7).

Ref.: Hanna § 5.05[1]; Herlick Handbook §§ 1.01[3][b], 4.04[1].

§9780.2. Employer's Duty to Provide First Aid and Emergency Treatment. [Repealed]

Note: Authority cited: Sections 124, 127, 133, 138.2, 138.3, 138.4, 139, 139.5, 139.6, 4600, 4601, 4602, 4603, 4603.2, 4603.5, 5307.3, 5450, 5451, 5452, 5453, 5454, and 5455, Labor Code. Reference: Chapters 442, 709, and 1172, Statutes of 1977; Chapter 1017, Statutes of 1976.

History: 1. New section filed 11-7-78; effective thirtieth day thereafter (Register 78, No. 45).

2. Repealer filed 3-14-2006; operative 3-14-2006 pursuant to Government Code section 11343.4 (Register 2006, No. 11).

§9781. Employee's Request for Change of Physician.

(a) This section shall not apply to self-insured and insured employers who offer a Medical Provider Network pursuant to section 4616 of the Labor Code.

(b) Pursuant to section 4601 of the Labor Code, and notwithstanding the 30 day time period specified in subdivision (c), the employee may request a one time change of physician at any time.

(1) An employee's request for change of physician pursuant to this subdivision need not be in writing. The claims administrator shall respond to the employee in the manner best calculated to inform the employee, and in no event later than 5 working days from receipt of said request, the claims administrator shall provide the employee an alternative physician, or if the employee so requests, a chiropractor or acupuncturist.

(2) Notwithstanding subdivision (a) of section 9780.1, if an employee requesting a change of physician pursuant to this subdivision has notified his or her employer in writing prior to the date of injury that he or she has either a personal chiropractor or a personal acupuncturist, and where the employee so requests, the alternative physician tendered by the claims administrator to the employee shall be the employee's personal chiropractor or personal acupuncturist as defined in subdivisions (b) and (c), respectively, of Labor Code section 4601. The notification to the employer must include the name and business address of the chiropractor or acupuncturist. The employer shall notify its employees of the requirements of this subdivision and provide its employees with an optional form for notification of a personal chiropractor or acupuncturist, in accordance with section 9880. DWC Form 9783.1 in section 9783.1 may be used for this purpose.

(3) Except where the employee is permitted to select a personal chiropractor or acupuncturist as defined in subdivisions (b) and (c), respectively, of Labor Code section 4601, the claims administrator shall advise the employee of the name and address of the alternative physician, or chiropractor or acupuncturist if requested, the date and time of an initial scheduled appointment, and any other pertinent information.

(c) Pursuant to section 4600, after 30 days from the date the injury is reported, the employee shall have the right to be treated by a physician or at a facility of his or her own choice within a reasonable geographic area.

(1) The employee shall notify the claims administrator of the name and address of the physician or facility selected pursuant to this subdivision. However, this notice requirement will be deemed to be satisfied if the selected physician or facility gives notice to the claims administrator of the commencement of treatment or if the claims administrator receives this information promptly from any source.

(2) If so requested by the selected physician or facility, the employee shall sign a release permitting the selected physician or facility to report to the claims administrator as required by section 9785.

(d) When the claims administrator is notified of the name and address of an employee-selected physician or facility pursuant to subdivision (c), or of a personal chiropractor or acupuncturist pursuant to paragraph (2) of subdivision (b), the claims administrator shall:

(1) authorize such physician or facility or personal chiropractor or acupuncturist to provide all medical treatment reasonably required pursuant to section 4600 of the Labor Code;

(2) furnish the name and address of the person to whom billing for treatment should be sent;

(3) arrange for the delivery to the selected physician or facility of all medical information relating to the claim, all X-rays and the results of all laboratory studies done in relation to the injured employee's treatment; and

(4) provide the physician or facility with (1) the fax number, if available, to be used to request authorization of treatment plans; (2) the complete requirements of section 9785; and (3) the forms set forth in sections 9785.2 and 9785.4. In lieu of providing the materials required in (2) and (3) immediately above, the claims administrator may refer the physician or facility to the Division of Workers' Compensation's website where the applicable information and forms can be found at http://www.dir.ca.gov/DWC/dwc_home_page.htm.

Note: Authority cited: Sections 133 and 4603.5, Labor Code. Reference: Sections 3551, 4600 and 4601, Labor Code.

History: 1. Repealer and new section filed 11-9-77; effective thirtieth day thereafter (Register 77, No. 46).

2. Repealer and new section and amendment of Note filed 3-14-2006; operative 3-14-2006 pursuant to Government Code section 11343.4 (Register 2006, No. 11).

Ref.: Hanna §§ 5.05[7][a], 22.03[1]; Herlick Handbook § 1.01[3][b].

§9782. Notice to Employee of Right to Choose Physician.

(a) Except for an employer who has established a Medical Provider Network, or an employer whose insurer has established a Medical Provider Network, every employer shall advise its employees in writing of an employee's right (1) to request a change of treating physician if the original treating physician is selected initially by the employer pursuant to Labor Code section 4601, and (2) to be treated by a physician of his or her own choice 30 days after reporting an injury pursuant to subdivision (c) of Labor Code 4600.

(b) Every employer shall advise its employees in writing of an employee's right to predesignate a personal physician pursuant to subdivision (d) of Labor Code section 4600, and section 9780.1.

(c) The notices required by this section shall be provided in accordance with section 9880 and posted in accordance with section 9881.

Note: Authority cited: Sections 133 and 4603.5, Labor Code. Reference: Sections 3550, 3551, 4600, 4601 and 4616, Labor Code.

History: 1. Repealer and new section filed 11-9-77; effective thirtieth day thereafter (Register 77, No. 46).

2. Repealer and new section filed 11-7-78; effective thirtieth day thereafter (Register 78, No. 45).

3. Amendment of section and Note filed 3-14-2006; operative 3-14-2006 pursuant to Government Code section 11343.4 (Register 2006, No. 11).

Ref.: Hanna § 5.05[2]; Herlick Handbook § 1.01[3][b].

§9783. DWC Form 9783 Predesignation of Personal Physician.

[DWC Form 9783 (Rev. 7/2014) Not Reproduced]

NOTE: Form is available at no charge by downloading from the web at www.dir.ca.gov/dwc/forms.html or by requesting at 1-800-794-6900.

Note: Authority cited: Sections 133, 4603.5 and 5307.3, Labor Code. Reference: Section 4600, Labor Code.

History: 1. Amendment filed 11-11-78; effective thirtieth day thereafter (Register 78, No. 45).

2. Repealer and new section heading, section and Note filed 3-14-2006; operative 3-14-2006 pursuant to Government Code section 11343.4 (Register 2006, No. 11).

3. Change without regulatory effect amending section filed 2-21-2007 pursuant to section 100, title 1, California Code of Regulations (Register 2007, No. 8).

4. Amendment filed 2-12-2014; operative 7-1-2014 pursuant to Government Code section 11343.4 (Register 2014, No. 7).

Ref.: Hanna §§ 5.05[6][b], 22.02[2], 25.10[4]; Herlick Handbook § 1.01[3][b].

§9783.1. DWC Form 9783.1 Notice of Personal Chiropractor or Personal Acupuncturist.

[DWC Form 9783.1 (Rev. 7/2014) Not Reproduced]

NOTE: Form is available at no charge by downloading from the web at www.dir.ca.gov/dwc/forms.html or by requesting at 1-800-794-6900.

Note: Authority cited: Sections 133, 4603.5 and 5307.3, Labor Code. Reference: Sections 4600 and 4601, Labor Code.

History: 1. New section filed 3-14-2006; operative 3-14-2006 pursuant to Government Code section 11343.4 (Register 2006, No. 11).

2. Amendment filed 2-12-2014; operative 7-1-2014 pursuant to Government Code section 11343.4 (Register 2014, No. 7).

Ref.: Herlick Handbook § 1.01[3][b].

§9784. Duties of the Employer. [Repealed]

Note: Authority cited: Sections 124, 127, 133, 138.2, 138.3, 138.4, 139, 139.5, 139.6, 4600, 4601, 4602, 4603, 4603.2, 4603.5, 5307.3, 5450, 5451, 5452, 5453, 5454, and 5455, Labor Code.

Reference: Chapters 442, 709, and 1172, Statutes of 1977; Chapter 1017, Statutes of 1976.

History: 1. Repealer and new section filed 11-9-77; effective thirtieth day thereafter (Register 77, No. 46).

2. Amendment filed 11-11-78; effective thirtieth day thereafter (Register 78, No. 45).

3. Repealer filed 3-14-2006; operative 3-14-2006 pursuant to Government Code section 11343.4 (Register 2006, No. 11).

§9785. Reporting Duties of the Primary Treating Physician.

(a) For the purposes of this section, the following definitions apply:

(1) The "primary treating physician" is the physician who is primarily responsible for managing the care of an employee, and who has examined the employee at least once for the purpose of rendering or prescribing treatment and has monitored the effect of the treatment thereafter. The primary treating physician is the physician selected by the employer, the employee pursuant to Article 2 (commencing with section 4600) of Chapter 2 of Part 2 of Division 4 of the Labor Code, or under the contract or procedures applicable to a Health Care Organization certified under section 4600.5 of the Labor Code, or in accordance with the physician selection procedures contained in the medical provider network pursuant to Labor Code section 4616. For injuries on or after January 1, 2004, a chiropractor shall not be a primary treating physician after the employee has received 24 chiropractic visits, unless the employer has authorized additional visits in writing. This prohibition shall not apply to the provision of postsurgical physical medicine prescribed by the employee's surgeon, or physician designated by the surgeon pursuant to the postsurgical component of the medical treatment utilization schedule adopted by the Administrative Director pursuant to Labor Code section 5307.27. For purposes of this subdivision, the term "chiropractic visit" means any chiropractic office visit, regardless of whether the services performed involve chiropractic manipulation or are limited to evaluation and management.

(2) A "secondary physician" is any physician other than the primary treating physician who examines or provides treatment to the employee, but is not primarily responsible for continuing management of the care of the employee. For injuries on or after January 1, 2004, a chiropractor shall not be a secondary treating physician after the employee has received 24 chiropractic visits, unless the employer has authorized, in writing, additional visits. This prohibition shall not apply to the provision of postsurgical physical medicine prescribed by the employee's surgeon, or physician designated by the surgeon pursuant to the postsurgical component of the medical treatment utilization schedule adopted by the Administrative Director pursuant to Labor Code section 5307.27. For purposes of this subdivision, the term "chiropractic visit" means any chiropractic office visit, regardless of whether the services performed involve chiropractic manipulation or are limited to evaluation and management.

(3) "Claims administrator" is a self-administered insurer providing security for the payment of compensation required by Divisions 4 and 4.5 of the Labor Code, a self-administered self-insured employer, or a third-party administrator for a self-insured employer, insurer, legally uninsured employer, or joint powers authority.

(4) "Medical determination" means, for the purpose of this section, a decision made by the primary treating physician regarding any and all medical issues necessary to determine the employee's eligibility for compensation. Such issues include but are not limited to the scope and extent of an employee's continuing medical treatment, the decision whether to release the employee from care, the point in time at which the employee has reached permanent and stationary status, and the necessity for future medical treatment.

(5) "Released from care" means a determination by the primary treating physician that the employee's condition has reached a permanent and stationary status with no need for continuing or future medical treatment.

(6) "Continuing medical treatment" is occurring or presently planned treatment that is reasonably required to cure or relieve the employee from the effects of the injury.

(7) "Future medical treatment" is treatment which is anticipated at some time in the future and is reasonably required to cure or relieve the employee from the effects of the injury.

(8) "Permanent and stationary status" is the point when the employee has reached maximal medical improvement, meaning his or her condition is well stabilized, and unlikely to change substantially in the next year with or without medical treatment.

(b)(1) An employee shall have no more than one primary treating physician at a time.

(2) An employee may designate a new primary treating physician of his or her choice pursuant to Labor Code §§ 4600 or 4600.3 provided the primary treating physician has determined that there is a need for:

(A) continuing medical treatment; or

(B) future medical treatment. The employee may designate a new primary treating physician to render future medical treatment either prior to or at the time such treatment becomes necessary.

(3) If the employee disputes a medical determination made by the primary treating physician, including a determination that the employee should be released from care, the dispute shall be resolved under the applicable procedures set forth at Labor Code sections 4060, 4061 4062, 4600.5, 4616.3, or 4616.4. If the employee objects to a decision made pursuant to Labor Code section 4610 to modify, delay, or deny a treatment recommendation, the dispute shall be resolved by independent medical review pursuant to Labor Code section 4610.5, if applicable, or otherwise pursuant to Labor Code section 4062.

(4) If the claims administrator disputes a medical determination made by the primary treating physician, the dispute shall be resolved under the applicable procedures set forth at Labor Code sections 4060, 4061, 4062, and 4610.

(c) The primary treating physician, or a physician designated by the primary treating physician, shall make reports to the claims administrator as required in this section. A primary treating physician has fulfilled his or her reporting duties under this section by sending one copy of a required report to the claims administrator. A claims administrator may designate any person or entity to be the recipient of its copy of the required report.

(d) The primary treating physician shall render opinions on all medical issues necessary to determine the employee's eligibility for compensation in the manner prescribed in subdivisions (e), (f) and (g) of this section. The primary treating physician may transmit reports to the claims administrator by mail or FAX or by any other means satisfactory to the claims administrator, including electronic transmission.

(e)(1) Within 5 working days following initial examination, a primary treating physician shall submit a written report to the claims administrator on the form entitled "Doctor's First Report of Occupational Injury or Illness," Form 5021. Emergency and urgent care physicians shall also submit a Form 5021 to the claims administrator following the initial visit to the treatment facility. On line 24 of the Doctor's First Report, or on the reverse side of the form, the physician shall (A) list methods, frequency, and duration of planned treatment(s), (B) specify planned consultations or referrals, surgery or hospitalization and (C) specify the type, frequency and duration of planned physical medicine services (e.g., physical therapy, manipulation, acupuncture). For dates of service prior to October 1, 2015, use Form 5021 (Rev. 4 1992). For dates of service on or after October 1, 2015, use Form 5021 (Rev. 5 2015). Although ICD-10 coding is required on or after October 1, 2015, for a twelve-month period ending October 1, 2016, no medical treatment or medical-legal bill shall be denied based solely on an error in the level of specificity of the ICD-10 diagnosis code(s) used. Providers may use either version of the form until December 31, 2015. As of January 1, 2016, providers must use the 2015 version of the form.

(2) Each new primary treating physician shall submit a Form 5021 following the initial examination in accordance with subdivision (e)(1).

(3) Secondary physicians, physical therapists, and other health care providers to whom the employee is referred shall report to the primary treating physician in the manner required by the primary treating physician.

(4) The primary treating physician shall be responsible for obtaining all of the reports of secondary physicians and shall, unless good cause is shown, within 20 days of receipt of each report incorporate, or comment upon, the findings and opinions of the other physicians in the primary treating physician's report and submit all of the reports to the claims administrator.

(f) A primary treating physician shall, unless good cause is shown, within 20 days report to the claims administrator when any one or more of the following occurs:

(1) The employee's condition undergoes a previously unexpected significant change;

(2) There is any significant change in the treatment plan reported, including, but not limited to, (A) an extension of duration or frequency of treatment, (B) a new need for hospitalization or surgery, (C) a new need for referral to or consultation by another physician, (D) a change in methods of treatment or in required physical medicine services, or (E) a need for rental or purchase of durable medical equipment or orthotic devices;

(3) The employee's condition permits return to modified or regular work;

(4) The employee's condition requires him or her to leave work, or requires changes in work restrictions or modifications;

(5) The employee is released from care;

(6) The primary treating physician concludes that the employee's permanent disability precludes, or is likely to preclude, the employee from engaging in the employee's usual occupation or the occupation in which the employee was engaged at the time of the injury;

(7) The claims administrator reasonably requests appropriate additional information that is necessary to administer the claim. "Necessary" information is that which directly affects the provision of compensation benefits as defined in Labor Code Section 3207.

(8) When continuing medical treatment is provided, a progress report shall be made no later than forty-five days from the last report of any type under this section even if no event described in paragraphs (1) to (7) has occurred. If an examination has occurred, the report shall be signed and transmitted within 20 days of the examination.

Except for a response to a request for information made pursuant to subdivision (f)(7), reports required under this subdivision shall be submitted on the "Primary Treating Physician's Progress Report" form (Form PR-2) contained in Section 9785.2, or in the form of a narrative report. If a narrative report is used, it must be entitled "Primary Treating Physician's Progress Report" in bold-faced type, must indicate clearly the reason the report is being submitted, and must contain the same information using the same subject headings in the same order as Form PR-2. A response to a request for information made pursuant to subdivision (f)(7) may be made in letter format. A narrative report and a letter format response to a request for information must contain the same declaration under penalty of perjury that is set forth in the Form PR-2: "I declare under penalty of perjury that this report is true and correct to the best of my knowledge and that I have not violated Labor Code § 139.3."

For dates of service prior to October 1, 2015, use Form PR-2 (Rev. 06-05). For dates of service on or after October 1, 2015, use Form PR-2 (Rev. 2015). Although ICD-10 coding is required on or after October 1, 2015, for a twelve-month period ending October 1, 2016, no medical treatment or medical-legal bill shall be denied based solely on an error in the level of specificity of the ICD-10 diagnosis code(s) used. Providers may use either version of the form until December 31, 2015. As of January 1, 2016, providers must use the 2015 version of the form.

By mutual agreement between the physician and the claims administrator, the physician may make reports in any manner and form.

(g) As applicable in section 9792.9.1, a written request for authorization of medical treatment for a specific course of proposed medical treatment, or a written confirmation of an oral request for a specific course of proposed medical treatment, must be set forth on the "Request for Authorization," DWC Form RFA, contained in section 9785.5. A written confirmation of an oral request shall be clearly marked at the top that it is written confirmation of an oral request. The DWC Form RFA must include as an attachment documentation substantiating the need for the requested treatment.

(h) When the primary treating physician determines that the employee's condition is permanent and stationary, the physician shall, unless good cause is shown, report within 20 days from the date of examination any findings concerning the existence and extent of permanent impairment and limitations and any need for continuing and/or future medical care resulting from the injury. The information may be submitted on the "Primary Treating Physician's Permanent and Stationary Report" form (DWC Form PR-3 or DWC Form PR-4) contained in section 9785.3 or section 9785.4, or in such other manner which provides all the information required by Title 8, California Code of Regulations, section 10606. For permanent disability evaluation performed pursuant to the permanent disability evaluation schedule adopted on or after January 1, 2005, the primary treating physician's reports concerning the existence and extent of permanent impairment shall describe the impairment in accordance with the AMA Guides to the Evaluation on Permanent Impairment, 5th Edition (DWC Form PR-4). Qualified Medical Evaluators and Agreed Medical Evaluators may not use DWC Form PR-3 or DWC Form PR-4 to report medical-legal evaluations.

For dates of service prior to October 1, 2015, use Form PR-3 (Rev. 06-05) or PR-4 (Rev. 06-05), as applicable. For dates of service on or after October 1, 2015, use Form PR-3 (Rev. 2015) or PR-4 (Rev. 2015), as applicable. Although ICD-10 coding is required on or after October 1, 2015, for a twelve-month period ending October 1, 2016, no medical treatment or medical-legal bill shall be denied based solely on an error in the level of specificity of the ICD-10 diagnosis code(s) used. Providers may use either version of the form until December 31, 2015. As of January 1, 2016, providers must use the 2015 version of the form.

(i) The primary treating physician, upon finding that the employee is permanent and stationary as to all conditions and that the injury has resulted in permanent partial disability, shall complete the "Physician's Return-to-Work & Voucher Report" (DWC-AD 10133.36) and attach the form to the report required under subdivision (h).

(j) Any controversies concerning this section shall be resolved pursuant to Labor Code Section 4603 or 4604, whichever is appropriate.

(k) Claims administrators shall reimburse primary treating physicians for their reports submitted pursuant to this section as required by the Official Medical Fee Schedule.

Note: Authority cited: Sections 133, 4603.5 and 5307.3, Labor Code. Reference: Sections 4061, 4061.5, 4062, 4600, 4600.3, 4603.2, 4604.5, 4610.5, 4658.7, 4660, 4662, 4663 and 4664, Labor Code.

History: 1. Amendment filed 11-9-77; effective thirtieth day thereafter (Register 77, No. 46).

2. Amendment of subsection (b) filed 11-11-78; effective thirtieth day thereafter (Register 78, No. 45).

3. Amendment of subsections (c) and (d) and new subsection (e) filed 7-11-89; operative 10-1-89 (Register 89, No. 28).

4. Amendment of section and Note filed 8-31-93; operative 8-31-93. Submitted to OAL for printing only pursuant to Government Code section 11351 (Register 93, No. 36).

5. New subsection (e) and subsection relettering filed 3-27-95; operative 3-27-95. Submitted to OAL for printing only pursuant to Government Code section 11351 (Register 95, No. 13).

6. Repealer and new section filed 11-9-98; operative 1-1-99 (Register 98, No. 46).

7. Amendment of subsections (e)(1), (f)(8) and (g) filed 12-22-2000; operative 1-1-2001 pursuant to Government Code section 11343.4(d) (Register 2000, No. 51).

8. Amendment of section and Note filed 5-20-2003; operative 6-19-2003 (Register 2003, No. 21).

9. Amendment of subsections (a)(1), (a)(8), (b)(3)-(4) and (g) and amendment of Note filed 12-31-2004 as an emergency; operative 1-1-2005 (Register 2004, No. 53). A Certificate of Compliance must be transmitted to OAL by 5-2-2005 or emergency language will be repealed by operation of law on the following day.

10. Certificate of Compliance as to 12-31-2004 order, including further amendment of subsections (a)(1) and (g), transmitted to OAL 4-29-2005 and filed 6-10-2005 (Register 2005, No. 23).

11. Amendment of subsections (b)(3) and (f)(6), new subsections (g) and (i), subsection relettering and amendment of Note filed 12-31-2012 as an emergency; operative 1-1-2013 pursuant to Government Code section 11346.1(d) (Register 2013, No. 1). A Certificate of Compliance must be transmitted to OAL by 7-1-2013 or emergency language will be repealed by operation of law on the following day.

12. Amendment of subsections (b)(3) and (f)(6), new subsections (g) and (i), subsection relettering and amendment of Note refiled 7-1-2013 as an emergency; operative 7-1-2013 (Register 2013, No. 27). A Certificate of Compliance must be transmitted to OAL by 9-30-2013 or emergency language will be repealed by operation of law on the following day.

13. Amendment of subsections (b)(3) and (f)(6), new subsections (g) and (i), subsection relettering and amendment of Note refiled 9-30-2013 as an emergency; operative 10-1-2013 (Register 2013, No. 40). A Certificate of Compliance must be transmitted to OAL by 12-30-2013 or emergency language will be repealed by operation of law on the following day.

14. Certificate of Compliance as to 9-30-2013 order, including amendment of subsections (b)(3)-(4) and (g), transmitted to OAL 12-30-2013 and filed 2-12-2014; amendments effective 2-12-2014 pursuant to Government Code section 11343.4(b)(3) (Register 2014, No. 7).

15. Amendment of subsections (a)(1)-(2) filed 2-12-2014; operative 7-1-2014 pursuant to Government Code section 11343.4 (Register 2014, No. 7).

16. Amendment of subsections (e)(1)-(2), (f)(8) and (h) filed 9-21-2015; operative 10-1-2015 pursuant to Government Code section 11343.4(b)(3) (Register 2015, No. 39).

Ref.: Hanna §§ 5.05[6][b], [7][b], 22.02[4], [5], 22.03[2], 22.08[3][b], 22.10; Herlick Handbook §§ 1.01[3][b], 4.08[1], [2], [3], [4], 6.04[5], 10.08[3]; Lawyer's Guide to AMA *Guides* and Calif. Workers' Comp. § 3.03.

§9785.2. Form PR-2 "Primary Treating Physician's Progress Report."

[DWC Form PR-2 (Rev. 06/2005) Not Reproduced]

NOTE: Form is available at no charge by downloading from the web at www.dir.ca.gov/dwc/forms.html or by requesting at 1-800-794-6900.

Note: Authority cited: Sections 133, 4603.5 and 5307.3, Labor Code. Reference: Sections 4061.5, 4600, 4603.2, 4610, 4636, 4660, 4662, 4663 and 4664, Labor Code.

History: 1. New section filed 11-9-98; operative 1-1-99 (Register 98, No. 46).

2. Repealer and new form filed 12-22-2000; operative 1-1-2001 pursuant to Government Code section 11343.4(d) (Register 2000, No. 51).

3. Amendment of form filed 5-20-2003; operative 6-19-2003 (Register 2003, No. 21).

4. Amendment of section and Note filed 12-31-2004 as an emergency; operative 1-1-2005 (Register 2004, No. 53). A Certificate of Compliance must be transmitted to OAL by 5-2-2005 or emergency language will be repealed by operation of law on the following day.

5. Certificate of Compliance as to 12-31-2004 order, including further amendment of section, transmitted to OAL 4-29-2005 and filed 6-10-2005 (Register 2005, No. 23).

Ref.: Hanna §§ 5.05[6][b], 22.02[5]; Herlick Handbook § 1.01[3][b].

§9785.2.1. Form PR-2 "Primary Treating Physician Progress Report" — Services On or After October 1, 2015.

[DWC Form PR-2 (Rev. 10/2015) Not Reproduced]

NOTE: Form is available at no charge by downloading from the web at www.dir.ca.gov/dwc/forms.html or by requesting at 1-800-794-6900.

Note: Authority cited: Sections 133, 4603.5 and 5307.3, Labor Code. Reference: Sections 4061.5, 4600, 4603.2, 4610, 4636, 4660, 4662, 4663 and 4664, Labor Code.

History: 1. New section filed 9-21-2015; operative 10-1-2015 pursuant to Government Code section 11343.4(b)(3) (Register 2015, No. 39).

Ref.: Herlick Handbook § 4.08[2], [3].

§9785.3. Form PR-3 "Primary Treating Physician's Permanent and Stationary Report."

[DWC Form PR-3 (Rev. 06/2005) Not Reproduced]

NOTE: Form is available at no charge by downloading from the web at www.dir.ca.gov/dwc/forms.html or by requesting at 1-800-794-6900.

Note: Authority cited: Sections 133, 4603.5 and 5307.3, Labor Code. Reference: Sections 4061.5, 4600, 4603.2, 4636, 4660, 4662, 4663 and 4664, Labor Code.

History: 1. New section filed 11-9-98; operative 1-1-99 (Register 98, No. 46).

2. Change without regulatory effect amending DWC Form PR-3, page 3, last sentence in the "Precipitating activity" narrative under the "Subjective Findings" section filed 12-30-98 pursuant to section 100, title 1, California Code of Regulations (Register 99, No. 1).

3. Repealer and new form filed 12-22-2000; operative 1-1-2001 pursuant to Government Code section 11343.4(d) (Register 2000, No. 51).

4. Amendment of form filed 5-20-2003; operative 6-19-2003 (Register 2003, No. 21).

5. Amendment of section and Note filed 12-31-2004 as an emergency; operative 1-1-2005 (Register 2004, No. 53). A Certificate of Compliance must be transmitted to OAL by 5-2-2005 or emergency language will be repealed by operation of law on the following day.

6. Certificate of Compliance as to 12-31-2004 order, including further amendment of section, transmitted to OAL 4-29-2005 and filed 6-10-2005 (Register 2005, No. 23).

Ref.: Hanna §§ 5.05[6][b], 22.02[5]; Herlick Handbook § 1.01[3][b].

§9785.3.1. Form PR-3 "Primary Treating Physician's Permanent and Stationary Report" — Services On or After October 1, 2015

[DWC Form PR-3 (Rev. 10/2015) Not Reproduced]

NOTE: Form is available at no charge by downloading from the web at www.dir.ca.gov/dwc/forms.html or by requesting at 1-800-794-6900.

Note: Authority cited: Sections 133, 4603.5 and 5307.3, Labor Code. Reference: Sections 4061.5, 4600, 4603.2, 4636, 4660, 4662, 4663 and 4664, Labor Code.

History: 1. New section filed 9-21-2015; operative 10-1-2015 pursuant to Government Code section 11343.4(b)(3) (Register 2015, No. 39).

Ref.: Herlick Handbook § 4.08[2], [3].

§9785.4. Form PR-4 "Primary Treating Physician's Permanent and Stationary Report."

[DWC Form PR-4 (Rev. 06/2005) Not Reproduced]

NOTE: Form is available at no charge by downloading from the web at www.dir.ca.gov/dwc/forms.html or by requesting at 1-800-794-6900.

Note: Authority cited: Sections 133 and 5307.3, Labor Code. Reference: Sections 4061.5, 4600, 4603.2, 4636, 4604.5, 4660, 4662, 4663 and 4664, Labor Code.

History: 1. New section filed 12-31-2004 as an emergency; operative 1-1-2005 (Register 2004, No. 53). A Certificate of Compliance must be transmitted to OAL by 5-2-2005 or emergency language will be repealed by operation of law on the following day.

2. Certificate of Compliance as to 12-31-2004 order, including amendment of section, transmitted to OAL 4-29-2005 and filed 6-10-2005 (Register 2005, No. 23).

3. Amendment of Note filed 9-21-2015; operative 10-1-2015 pursuant to Government Code section 11343.4(b)(3) (Register 2015, No. 39).

Ref.: Hanna § 22.02[5]; Herlick Handbook § 1.01[3][b], 4.08[2], [3].

§ 9785.4.1. Form PR-4 "Primary Treating Physician's Permanent and Stationary Report" — Services On or After October 1, 2015.

[DWC Form PR-4 (Rev. 02/2016) Not Reproduced]

NOTE: Form is available at no charge by downloading from the web at www.dir.ca.gov/dwc/forms.html or by requesting at 1-800-794-6900.

Note: Authority cited: Sections 133 and 5307.3, Labor Code. Reference: Sections 4061.5, 4600, 4603.2, 4604.5, 4636, 4660, 4662, 4663 and 4664, Labor Code.

History: 1. New section filed 9-21-2015; operative 10-1-2015 pursuant to Government Code section 11343.4(b)(3) (Register 2015, No. 39).

2. Change without regulatory effect updating form filed 3-4-2016 pursuant to section 100, title 1, California Code of Regulations (Register 2016, No. 10).

§9785.5. Request for Authorization Form, DWC Form RFA.

[DWC Form RFA (New 2/2014) Not Reproduced]

NOTE: Form is available at no charge by downloading from the web at www.dir.ca.gov/dwc/forms.html or by requesting at 1-800-794-6900.

Note: Authority cited: Sections 133, 4603.5 and 5307.3, Labor Code. Reference: Sections 4061, 4061.5, 4062, 4600, 4604.5, 4610, 4610.5 and 4610.6, Labor Code.

History: 1. New section filed 12-31-2012 as an emergency; operative 1-1-2013 pursuant to Government Code section 11346.1(d) (Register 2013, No. 1). A Certificate of Compliance must be transmitted to OAL by 7-1-2013 or emergency language will be repealed by operation of law on the following day. For prior history, see Register 98, No. 46.

2. New section refiled 7-1-2013 as an emergency; operative 7-1-2013 (Register 2013, No. 27). A Certificate of Compliance must be transmitted to OAL by 9-30-2013 or emergency language will be repealed by operation of law on the following day.

3. New section refiled 9-30-2013 as an emergency; operative 10-1-2013 (Register 2013, No. 40). A Certificate of Compliance must be transmitted to OAL by 12-30-2013 or emergency language will be repealed by operation of law on the following day.

4. Certificate of Compliance as to 9-30-2013 order, including repealer and new section, transmitted to OAL 12-30-2013 and filed 2-12-2014; new section effective 2-12-2014 pursuant to Government Code section 11343.4(b)(3) (Register 2014, No. 7).

Ref.: Herlick Handbook §§ 1.01[3][b], 4.08[5].

§9786. Petition for Change of Primary Treating Physician.

(a) A claims administrator desiring a change of primary treating physician pursuant to Labor Code Section 4603 shall file with the Administrative Director a petition, verified under penalty of perjury, on the "Petition for Change of Primary Treating Physician" form (DWC-Form 280 (Part A)) contained in Section 9786.1.

The petition shall be accompanied by supportive documentary evidence relevant to the specific allegations raised. A proof of service by mail declaration shall be attached to the petition indicating that (1) the completed petition (Part A), (2) the supportive documentary evidence and (3) a blank copy of the "Response to Petition for Change of Primary Treating Physician", (DWC-Form 280 (Part B)), were served on the employee or, the employee's attorney, and the employee's current primary treating physician.

(b) Good cause to grant the petition shall be clearly shown by verified statement of facts, and, where appropriate, supportive documentary evidence. Good cause includes, but is not limited to any of the following:

(1) The primary treating physician has failed to comply with Section 9785, subdivisions (e), (f)(1-7), or (g) by not timely submitting a required report or submitting a report which is inadequate due to material omissions or deficiencies;

(2) The primary treating physician has failed to comply with subdivision (f)(8) of Section 9785 by failing to submit timely or complete progress reports on two or more occasions within the 12-month period immediately preceding the filing of the petition;

(3) A clear showing that the current treatment is not consistent with the treatment plan submitted pursuant to Section 9785, subdivisions (e) or (f);

(4) A clear showing that the primary treating physician or facility is not within a reasonable geographic area as determined by Section 9780(e).

(5) A clear showing that the primary treating physician has a possible conflict of interest, including but not limited to a familial, financial or employment relationship with the employee, which has a significant potential for interfering with the physician's ability to engage in objective and impartial medical decision making.

(c)(1) Where good cause is based on inadequate reporting under subdivisions (b)(1) or (b)(2), the petition must show, by documentation and verified statement, that the claims administrator notified the primary treating physician or facility in writing of the complete requirements of Section 9785 prior to the physician's failure to properly report.

(2) Good cause shall not include a showing that current treatment is inappropriate or that there is no present need for medical treatment to cure or relieve from the effects of the injury or illness. The claims administrator's contention that current treatment is inappropriate, or that the employee is no longer in need of medical treatment to cure or relieve from the effects of the injury or illness should be directed to the Workers' Compensation Appeals Board, not the Administrative Director, in support of a Petition for Change of Primary Treating Physician.

(3) Where an allegation of good cause is based upon failure to timely issue the "Doctor's First Report of Occupational Injury or Illness," Form DLSR 5021, within 5 working days of the initial examination pursuant to Section 9785(e)(1) or (e)(2), the petition setting forth such allegation shall be filed within 90 days of the initial examination.

(4) The failure to verify a letter response to a request for information made pursuant to Section 9785(f)(7), failure to verify a narrative report submitted pursuant to Section 9785(f)(8), or failure of the narrative report to conform to the format requirements of Section 9785(f)(8) shall not constitute good cause to grant the petition unless the claims administrator submits documentation showing that the physician was notified of the deficiency in the verification or reporting format and allowed a reasonable time to correct the deficiency.

(d) The employee, his or her attorney, and/or the primary treating physician may file with the Administrative Director a response to said petition, provided the response is verified under penalty of perjury and is filed and served on the claims administrator and all other parties no later than 20 days after service of the petition. The response may be accompanied by supportive documentary evidence relevant to the specific allegations raised in the petition. The response may be filed using the "Response to Petition for

Change of Primary Treating Physician" form (DWC-Form 280 (Part B)) contained in Section 9786.1. Where the petition was served by mail, the time for filing a response shall be extended pursuant to the provisions of Code of Civil Procedure Section 1013. Unless good cause is shown, no other document will be considered by the Administrative Director except for the petition, the response, and supportive documentary evidence.

(e) The Administrative Director shall, within 45 days of the receipt of the petition, either:

(1) Dismiss the petition, without prejudice, for failure to meet the procedural requirements of this Section;

(2) Deny the petition pursuant to a finding that there is no good cause to require the employee to select a primary treating physician from the panel of physicians provided in the petition;

(3) Grant the petition and issue an order requiring the employee to select a physician from the panel of physicians provided in the petition, pursuant to a finding that good cause exists therefor;

(4) Refer the matter to the Workers' Compensation Appeals Board for hearing and determination by a Workers' Compensation Administrative Law Judge of such factual determinations as may be requested by the Administrative Director; or

(5) Issue a Notice of Intention to Grant the petition and an order requiring the submission of additional documents or information.

(f) The claims administrator's liability to pay for medical treatment by the primary treating physician shall continue until an order of the Administrative Director issues granting the petition.

(g) The Administrative Director may extend the time specified in Subsection (e) within which to act upon the claims administrator's petition for a period of 30 days and may order a party to submit additional documents or information.

Note: Authority cited: Sections 133, 139.5, 4603, 4603.2, 4603.5 and 5307.3, Labor Code. Reference: Sections 4600, 4603 and 4603.2, Labor Code.

History: 1. Repealer and new section filed 11-9-77; effective thirtieth day thereafter (Register 77, No. 46).

2. Amendment of subsections (a), (c), (d)(4), (e), and (f) filed 11-11-78; effective thirtieth day thereafter (Register 78, No. 45).

3. Amendment of subsection (a) filed 8-9-84; effective thirtieth day thereafter (Register 84, No. 35).

4. Change without regulatory effect of subsection (c) filed 7-11-86; effective upon filing (Register 86, No. 28).

5. Amendment of section and Note filed 8-31-93; operative 8-31-93. Submitted to OAL for printing only pursuant to Government Code section 11351 (Register 93, No. 36).

6. Amendment of subsections (b)(5), (d), and (g) filed 3-27-95; operative 3-27-95. Submitted to OAL for printing only pursuant to Government Code section 11351 (Register 95, No. 13).

7. Editorial correction of subsection (h) (Register 95, No. 29).

8. Editorial correction of inadvertently omitted subsection (d)(2) (Register 96, No. 52).

9. Amendment of subsection (f) and repealer and new subsection (g) filed 12-27-96; operative 12-27-96. Submitted to OAL for printing only pursuant to Government Code section 11351 (Register 96, No. 52).

10. Amendment of section heading and section filed 12-22-2000; operative 1-1-2001 pursuant to Government Code section 11343.4(d) (Register 2000, No. 51).

11. Amendment filed 5-20-2003; operative 6-19-2003 (Register 2003, No. 21).

Ref.: Hanna §§ 5.05[6][b], [7][b], 22.03[2]; Herlick Handbook §§ 1.01[3][b], 4.11[7].

§9786.1. Petition for Change of Primary Treating Physician; Response to Petition for Change of Primary Treating Physician (DWC Form 280 (Parts A and B)).

[DWC Form 280 (Part A) (New 1/2001) Not Reproduced]

[DWC Form 280 (Part B) (New 1/2001) Not Reproduced]

NOTE: Form is available at no charge by downloading from the web at www.dir.ca.gov/dwc/forms.html or by requesting at 1-800-794-6900.

Note: Authority cited: Sections 133, 139.5, 4603, 4603.2, 4603.5, and 5307.3, Labor Code. Reference: Sections 4600, 4603 and 4603.2, Labor Code.

History: 1. New section (DWC form 280) filed 12-22-2000; operative 1-1-2001 pursuant to Government Code section 11343.4(d) (Register 2000, No. 51).

Ref.: Herlick Handbook § 1.01[3][b].

§9787. Appeal from Administrative Director's Order Granting or Denying Petition for Change of Primary Treating Physician.

Any order denying or granting the claims administrator's petition whether issued with or without hearing, shall be final and binding upon the parties unless within 20 days from service thereof the aggrieved party petitions the Workers' Compensation Appeals Board for relief in the manner prescribed by Section 10950 of the Board's Rules of Practice and Procedure.

Note: Authority cited: Sections 133, 139.5, 4603.2, 4603.5 and 5307.3, Labor Code. Reference: Sections 4600, 4603 and 4603.2, Labor Code.

History: 1. Repealer and new section filed 11-9-77; effective thirtieth day thereafter (Register 77, No. 46).

2. Amendment of section heading and section filed 12-22-2000; operative 1-1-2001 pursuant to Government Code section 11343.4(d) (Register 2000, No. 51).

3. Amendment of section and new Note filed 5-20-2003; operative 6-19-2003 (Register 2003, No. 21).

Ref.: Hanna § 22.03[2]; Herlick Handbook §§ 1.01[3][b], 15.2.

ARTICLE 5.1
Provider Suspension Procedure

§9788.1. Notice of Provider Suspension.

(a) The Administrative Director shall issue a notice of suspension to a physician, practitioner, or provider who has met one of the criteria set forth under Labor Code section 139.21(a)(1).

(b) The term "suspension from participation" means the physician, practitioner, or provider is prohibited from providing any goods or services related to an occupational injury or illness that is either for pay or required by Labor Code sections 4060, 4061, 4062, 4062.1, 4062.2, 4600, 4600.3, 4610, 4610.5, 4610.6, 4616, and 4620. The term "suspension from participation" also precludes a physician's continued certification as a qualified medical evaluator pursuant to Labor Code section 139.2.

(c) The physician, practitioner, or provider is prohibited from seeking payment or reimbursement, either directly or indirectly, for any goods or services related to an occupational injury or illness that is provided on or after the date of their suspension.

(d) The notice required under subdivision (a) shall be in writing and shall include all of the following:

(1) Notice that the physician, practitioner, or provider is subject to suspension from participating in the workers' compensation system;

(2) The basis for the suspension under Labor Code section 139.21(a)(1);

(3) A statement that the suspension is effective 30 days from the date the notice is mailed, unless the physician, practitioner, or provider requests a hearing and, in that hearing, provides proof that Labor Code section 139.21(a)(1) is not applicable;

(4) A statement that the physician, practitioner, or provider may request a hearing within 10 days from the date the notice is served, which will stay the suspension pending the outcome of the hearing, and that the failure to request a hearing will result in suspension pursuant to section 9788.2(b); and

(5) A description of the method for requesting the hearing, including instructions on how the request should be filed and served.

(e) The notice shall be served by registered or certified mail.

Note: Authority: Sections 133 and 139.21, Labor Code. Reference: Section 139.21, Labor Code.

History: 1. Amendment of article heading, new article 5.1 (sections 9788.1-9788.4) and new section filed 1-6-2017 as an emergency; operative 1-6-2017 (Register 2017, No. 1). A Certificate of Compliance must be transmitted to OAL by 7-5-2017 or emergency language will be repealed by operation of law on the following day. For prior history of article 5.1 (sections 9788.01-9788.91), see Register 2014, No. 16.

2. Amendment of article heading, new article 5.1 (sections 9788.1-9788.4) and new section refiled 6-29-2017 as an emergency; operative 7-6-2017 pursuant to Government Code section 11346.1(d) (Register 2017, No. 26). A Certificate of Compliance must be transmitted to OAL by 10-4-2017 or emergency language will be repealed by operation of law on the following day.

3. Amendment of article heading, new article 5.1 (sections 9788.1-9788.4) and new section refiled 9-28-2017 as an emergency; operative 10-5-2017 pursuant to Government Code section 11346.1(d) (Register 2017, No. 39). A Certificate of Compliance must be transmitted to OAL by 1-3-2018 or emergency language will be repealed by operation of law on the following day.

4. Certificate of Compliance as to 9-28-2017 order, including amendment of subsections (d)(4) and (e), transmitted to OAL 12-29-2017 and filed 2-7-2018; amendments operative 2-7-2018 pursuant to Government Code section 11343.4(b)(3) (Register 2018, No. 6).

Ref.: Hanna § 30.22[1].

§9788.2. Provider Request for Hearing.

(a) Within 10 days after the date the notice of suspension is served, the physician, practitioner, or provider may request a hearing as the respondent with the Administrative Director, in which the respondent may contest the allegation that Labor Code section 139.21(a)(1) is applicable and the basis for suspension. The respondent must set forth the legal and factual reason for the request for hearing.

(b) Failure to timely file a request for hearing shall constitute a waiver of the physician's, practitioner's, or provider's right to an evidentiary hearing. If a request for hearing is not timely filed, the Order of Suspension shall become effective 30 days after the date that the notice of suspension was mailed. The Administrative Director shall serve an Order of Suspension on the physician, practitioner, or provider after 30 days from the date the notice of suspension is mailed. The Order of Suspension shall provide the written notification required by section 9788.4. The Order of Suspension shall be served upon the physician, practitioner, or provider by registered or certified mail. All appeals from the Order of Suspension issued pursuant to this subdivision shall be made to the Superior Court of California by writ as provided in the Code of Civil Procedure.

(c) The request for hearing shall be in writing and signed by the respondent, or the respondent's legal representative on behalf of the respondent, and shall state the respondent's mailing address.

(d) The respondent must file the original and one copy of the request for hearing on the Administrative Director and serve one copy on the Department of Industrial Relations Anti-fraud Unit at the address stated in the notice of suspension. The original and all copies of any filings required by this section shall have a proof of service attached.

Note: Authority: Sections 133 and 139.21, Labor Code. Reference: Section 139.21, Labor Code.

History: 1. New section filed 1-6-2017 as an emergency; operative 1-6-2017 (Register 2017, No. 1). A Certificate of Compliance must be transmitted to OAL by 7-5-2017 or emergency language will be repealed by operation of law on the following day. For prior history, see Register 2014, No. 16.

2. New section refiled 6-29-2017 as an emergency; operative 7-6-2017 pursuant to Government Code section 11346.1(d) (Register 2017, No. 26). A Certificate of Compliance must be transmitted to OAL by 10-4-2017 or emergency language will be repealed by operation of law on the following day.

3. New section refiled 9-28-2017 as an emergency; operative 10-5-2017 pursuant to Government Code section 11346.1(d) (Register 2017, No. 39). A Certificate of Compliance must be transmitted to OAL by 1-3-2018 or emergency language will be repealed by operation of law on the following day.

4. Certificate of Compliance as to 9-28-2017 order, including amendment of subsections (a), (b) and (d), transmitted to OAL 12-29-2017 and filed 2-7-2018; amendments operative 2-7-2018 pursuant to Government Code section 11343.4(b)(3) (Register 2018, No. 6).

Ref.: Hanna § 30.22[1].

§9788.3. Suspension Hearing.

(a) Upon receipt by the Administrative Director of the respondent's timely request for hearing, the Administrative Director shall issue a notice of hearing setting forth the date, time, and place of a hearing to determine whether the respondent shall be suspended from participating in the workers' compensation system. The date of the hearing shall be no later than 30 days after the receipt of the request for hearing, which shall be stated on the notice of hearing. The notice shall be served on the respondent by registered or certified mail.

(b) The Administrative Director shall designate a hearing officer to preside over the hearing, which need not be conducted according to the technical rules relating to evidence and witnesses. Any relevant evidence shall be admitted if it is the sort of evidence on which reasonable persons are accustomed to rely in the conduct of serious affairs, regardless of the existence of any common law or statutory rule which might make the admission of the evidence improper over objection in civil actions. Oral testimony shall be taken only on oath or affirmation.

(c) The designated hearing officer shall issue a written recommended Determination and Order re: Suspension, including a statement of the basis for the Determination, within ten (10) days of the date the case was submitted for decision, which shall be served on the Administrative Director. The time requirement of this subdivision is directory and not jurisdictional.

(d) The Administrative Director shall have ten (10) days from the date of receipt to adopt or modify the recommended Determination and Order re: Suspension issued by the designated hearing officer. In the event the recommended Determination and Order of the designated hearing officer is modified, the Administrative Director shall include a statement of the basis for the Determination and Order re: Suspension signed and served by the Administrative Director, or his or her designee. If the Administrative Director does not act within ten (10) days from the date of receipt of the recommended Determination and Order re: Suspension, then the recommended Determination and Order re: Suspension of the hearing officer shall become the Determination and Order re: Suspension on the eleventh (11th) day.

(e) The Determination and Order re: Suspension shall be served on the respondent by registered or certified mail by the Administrative Director, and shall become final on the day it is mailed.

(f) All appeals from the Determination and Order re: Suspension shall be made to the Superior Court of California by writ as provided in the Code of Civil Procedure.

Note: Authority: Sections 133 and 139.21, Labor Code. Reference: Section 139.21, Labor Code.

History: 1. New section filed 1-6-2017 as an emergency; operative 1-6-2017 (Register 2017, No. 1). A Certificate of Compliance must be transmitted to OAL by 7-5-2017 or emergency language will be repealed by operation of law on the following day. For prior history, see Register 2014, No. 16.

2. New section refiled 6-29-2017 as an emergency; operative 7-6-2017 pursuant to Government Code section 11346.1(d) (Register 2017, No. 26). A Certificate of Compliance must be transmitted to OAL by 10-4-2017 or emergency language will be repealed by operation of law on the following day.

3. New section refiled 9-28-2017 as an emergency; operative 10-5-2017 pursuant to Government Code section 11346.1(d) (Register 2017, No. 39). A Certificate of Compliance must be transmitted to OAL by 1-3-2018 or emergency language will be repealed by operation of law on the following day.

4. Certificate of Compliance as to 9-28-2017 order, including amendment of subsection (d), transmitted to OAL 12-29-2017 and filed 2-7-2018; amendments operative 2-7-2018 pursuant to Government Code section 11343.4(b)(3) (Register 2018, No. 6).

Ref.: Hanna § 30.22[1].

§9788.4. Suspension Notification.

(a) Following the date that the Determination and Order re: Suspension is final, the Administrative Director shall provide written notification of the physician's, practitioner's, or provider's suspension from participating in the workers' compensation system to:

(1) The Chief Judge of the Division of Workers' Compensation. Upon notification, the Chief Judge shall provide written notification of the suspension to the district offices of the Division of Workers' Compensation and all Administrative Law Judges employed by the Division.

(2) The special lien proceeding attorney designated under Labor Code section 139.21(f), if one is appointed.

(3) The physician's, practitioner's, or provider's state licensing, certifying, or registering authority.

(b) Following the date that the Determination and Order re: Suspension is final, the Administrative Director shall further:

(1) Update the Division's qualified medical evaluator and medical provider network databases, as appropriate, to indicate the physician's, practitioner's, or provider's suspension; and

(2) Post notification of the physician, practitioner, or provider's suspension on the Division's website.

Note: Authority: Sections 133 and 139.21, Labor Code. Reference: Section 139.21, Labor Code.

History: 1. New section filed 1-6-2017 as an emergency; operative 1-6-2017 (Register 2017, No. 1). A Certificate of Compliance must be transmitted to OAL by 7-5-2017 or emergency language will be repealed by operation of law on the following day. For prior history, see Register 2014, No. 16.

2. New section refiled 6-29-2017 as an emergency; operative 7-6-2017 pursuant to Government Code section 11346.1(d) (Register 2017, No. 26). A Certificate of Compliance must be transmitted to OAL by 10-4-2017 or emergency language will be repealed by operation of law on the following day.

3. New section refiled 9-28-2017 as an emergency; operative 10-5-2017 pursuant to Government Code section 11346.1(d) (Register 2017, No. 39). A Certificate of Compliance must be transmitted to OAL by 1-3-2018 or emergency language will be repealed by operation of law on the following day.

4. Certificate of Compliance as to 9-28-2017 order transmitted to OAL 12-29-2017 and filed 2-7-2018 (Register 2018, No. 6).

Ref.: Hanna § 30.22[1].

§9788.5. Amendment of the Order of Suspension or Determination and Order re: Suspension.

If the Administrative Director becomes aware that a suspended physician, practitioner, or provider would be subject to suspension under Labor Code section 139.21(a)(1) for a criminal conviction or other statutory basis that did not serve as the basis for the suspension in the original Order of Suspension or Determination and Order re: Suspension, the Administrative Director may issue an amended Order of Suspension or amended Determination and Order re: Suspension following written notice to the physician, practitioner, or provider pursuant to section 9788.1 and an opportunity for hearing pursuant to sections 9788.2 and 9788.3.

Note: Authority cited: Sections 133 and 139.21, Labor Code. Reference: Section 139.21, Labor Code.

History: 1. New section filed 2-7-2018; operative 2-7-2018 pursuant to Government Code section 11343.4(b)(3) (Register 2018, No. 6).

Ref.: Hanna § 30.22[1].

§9788.6. Service and Computation of Time.

(a) In the case of service by mail, the notice or other paper shall be complete at the time of mailing.

(b) All documents shall be considered "filed" when the original is actually received by the Division of Workers' Compensation or the hearing officer designated to hear the case, where appropriate.

(c) A five day extension of time shall apply to any filing made in response to documents served by mail if the place of address is within the State of California, ten days if the place of address is outside the State of California but within the United States, and twenty days if the place of address is outside the United States.

Note: Authority cited: Sections 133 and 139.21, Labor Code. Reference: Section 139.21, Labor Code; and Section 1013, Code of Civil Procedure.

History: 1. New section filed 2-7-2018; operative 2-7-2018 pursuant to Government Code section 11343.4(b)(3) (Register 2018, No. 6).

Ref.: Hanna § 30.22[1].

ARTICLE 5.3
Official Medical Fee Schedule

Physician Services Rendered on or after July 1, 2004.

Inpatient Hospital Services for Services Rendered for an Admission with Date of Discharge on or after July 1, 2004.

Outpatient Services Rendered on or after July 1, 2004.

Pharmacy Services Rendered after January 1, 2004

Pathology and Laboratory Services Rendered after January 1, 2004

Durable Medical Equipment, Prosthetics, Orthotics, Supplies Services after January 1, 2004

Ambulance Services Rendered after January 1, 2004

§9789.10. Physician Services Rendered on or After July 1, 2004, but Before January 1, 2014 — Definitions.

(a) "Basic value" means the unit value for an anesthesia procedure that is set forth in the Official Medical Fee Schedule 2003.

(b) "CMS" means the Centers for Medicare & Medicaid Services of the United States Department of Health and Human Services.

(c) "Conversion factor" or "CF" means the factor set forth below for the applicable OMFS section:

Evaluation and Management	$8.50
Medicine	$6.15
Surgery	$153.00
Radiology	$12.50
Pathology	$1.50
Anesthesia	$34.50

(d) "CPT®" means the procedure codes set forth in the American Medical Association's *Physicians' Current Procedural Terminology (CPT) 1997*, copyright 1996, American Medical Association, or the *Physicians' Current Procedural Terminology (CPT) 1994*, copyright 1993, American Medical Association.

(e) "Medicare rate" means the physician fee schedule rate derived from the Resource Based Relative Value Scale and related data, adopted for the Calendar Year 2004, published in the Federal Register on January 7, 2004, Volume 69, No. 4, pages 1117 through 1242 (CMS-1372-IFC), as amended by CMS Manual System, Pub. 100-04 Medicare Claims Processing, Transmittal 105 (February 20, 2004). The Medicare rate for each procedure is derived by the Administrative Director utilizing the non-facility rate (or facility rate if no non-facility rate exists), and a weighted average geographic adjustment factor of 1.063.

(f) "Modifying units" means the anesthesia modifiers and qualifying circumstances as set forth in the Official Medical Fee Schedule 2003.

(g) "Official Medical Fee Schedule" or "OMFS" means Article 5.3 of Subchapter 1 of Chapter 4.5 of Title 8, California Code of Regulations (Sections 9789.10 – 9789.111), adopted pursuant to Section 5307.1 of the Labor Code for all medical services, goods, and treatment provided pursuant to Labor Code Section 4600.

(h) "Official Medical Fee Schedule 2003" or "OMFS 2003" means the Official Medical Fee Schedule incorporated into Section 9791.1 in effect on December 31, 2003, which consists of the OMFS book revised April 1, 1999 and as amended for dates of service on or after July 12, 2002.

(i) "Percentage reduction calculation" means the factor set forth in Table A for each procedure code which will result in a reduction of the OMFS 2003 rate by 5%, or a lesser percent so that the reduction results in a rate that is no lower than the Medicare rate.

(j) "Physician service" means professional medical service that can be provided by a physician, as defined in Section 3209.3 of the Labor Code, and is subject to reimbursement under the Official Medical Fee Schedule. For purposes of the OMFS, "physician service" includes service rendered by a physician or by a non-physician who is acting under the supervision, instruction, referral or prescription of a physician, including but not limited to a physician assistant, nurse practitioner, clinical nurse specialist, and physical therapist.

(k) "RVU" means the relative value unit for a particular procedure that is set forth in the Official Medical Fee Schedule 2003.

(*l*) "Time value" means the unit of time indicating the duration of an anesthesia procedure that is set forth in the Official Medical Fee Schedule 2003.

Note: Authority cited: Sections 133, 4603.5, 5307.1 and 5307.3, Labor Code. Reference: Sections 4600, 4603.2 and 5307.1, Labor Code.

History: 1. New article 5.3 (sections 9789.10-9789.110) and section filed 1-2-2004 as an emergency; operative 1-2-2004 (Register 2004, No. 2). A Certificate of Compliance must be transmitted to OAL by 5-3-2004 or emergency language will be repealed by operation of law on the following day.

2. Certificate of Compliance as to 1-2-2004 order, including amendment of article heading, new introductory paragraph and amendment of subsections (d), (e) and (g), transmitted to OAL 4-30-2004 and filed 6-15-2004 (Register 2004, No. 25).

3. Amendment of section heading filed 2-4-2015; operative 3-5-2015. Submitted to OAL for printing only pursuant to Government Code section 11340.9 (Register 2015, No. 6).

Ref.: Hanna § 22.05[2]; Herlick Handbook §§ 1.01[3][b], 4.17[1].

§9789.11. Physician Services Rendered on or After July 1, 2004, but Before January 1, 2014.

(a) Except as specified below, or otherwise provided in this Article, the ground rule materials set forth in each individual section of the OMFS 2003 are applicable to physician services rendered on or after July 1, 2004, but before January 1, 2014.

(1) The OMFS 2003's "General Information and Instructions" section is not applicable. The "General Information and Instructions, Effective for Dates of Service on or after July 1, 2004," are incorporated by reference and will be made available on the Division of Workers' Compensation Internet site http://www.dir.ca.gov/DWC/OMFS9904.htm or upon request to the Administrative Director at:

DIVISION OF WORKERS' COMPENSATION
(ATTENTION: OMFS – PHYSICIAN SERVICES)
P.O. BOX 420603
SAN FRANCISCO, CA 94142

(b) Except as specified in this section, or otherwise provided in this Article, for physician services rendered on or after July 1, 2004, but before January 1, 2014, the maximum allowable reimbursement amount set forth in the OMFS 2003 for each procedure code is reduced by five (5) percent, except that those procedures that are reimbursed under OMFS 2003 at a rate between 100% and 105% of the Medicare rate will be reduced between zero and 5% so that the OMFS reimbursement will not fall below the Medicare rate. The reduction rate for each procedure is set forth as the adjustment factor in Table A. Reimbursement for procedures that are reimbursed under OMFS 2003 at a rate below the Medicare rate will not be reduced.

(c)(1) Table A, "OMFS Physician Services Fees for Services Rendered on or after July 1, 2004," which sets forth each individual procedure code with its corresponding relative value, conversion factor, percentage reduction calculation (between 0 and 5.0%), and maximum reimbursable fee, is incorporated by reference.

(2) Table A, "OMFS Physician Services Fees for Services Rendered on or after January 14, 2005," which sets forth each individual procedure code with its corresponding relative value, conversion factor, percentage reduction calculation (between 0 and 5.0%), and maximum reimbursable fee, is incorporated by reference.

(3) Table A, "OMFS Physician Services Fees for Services Rendered on or after May 14, 2005," which sets forth each individual procedure code with its corresponding relative value, conversion factor, percentage reduction calculation (between 0 and 5.0%), and maximum reimbursable fee, is incorporated by reference.

(4) Table A and its addenda may be obtained from the Division of Workers' Compensation Internet site http://www.dir.ca.gov/DWC/OMFS9904.htm or upon request to the Administrative Director at:

DIVISION OF WORKERS' COMPENSATION
(ATTENTION: OMFS – PHYSICIAN SERVICES)
P.O. BOX 420603
SAN FRANCISCO, CA 94142

(d)(1) Except as specified in this section, or otherwise provided in this Article, except for anesthesia services, to determine the maximum allowable reimbursement for a physician service rendered on or after July 1, 2004, but before January 1, 2014, the following formula is utilized: RVU x conversion factor × percentage reduction calculation = maximum reasonable fee before application of ground rules. Applicable ground rules set forth in the OMFS 2003 and the "General Information and Instructions, Effective for Dates of Service on or after July 1, 2004," are then applied to calculate the maximum reasonable fee.

(2) Except as specified in this section, or otherwise provided in this Article, to determine the maximum allowable reimbursement for anesthesia services (CPT Codes 00100 through 01999) rendered after January 1, 2004, but before January 1, 2014, the following formula is utilized: (basic value + modifying units (if any) + time value) × (conversion factor x .95) = maximum reasonable fee.

(e) Except as specified in this section, or otherwise provided in this Article, the following procedures in the Pathology and Laboratory section (both professional and technical component), rendered after January 1, 2004, but before January 1, 2014, will be reimbursed under this section: CPT Codes 80500, 80502; 85060 through 85102; 86077 through 86079; 87164; and 88000 through 88399. All other pathology and laboratory services will be reimbursed pursuant to Section 9789.50, including but not limited to: CPT Codes 80002 through 80440; 81000 through 85048; 85130 through 86063; 86140 through 87163; 87166 through 87999; and 89050 through 89399.

(f) Except as specified in this section, or otherwise provided in this Article, for physician services rendered on or after February 15, 2007, but before January 1, 2014, the maximum allowable reimbursement amounts for procedure codes 99201 through 99205 and 99211 through 99215 are set forth in the February, 2007 Addendum to Table A, "OMFS Physician Services Fees for Services Rendered on or after February 15, 2007." The February, 2007 Addendum to Table A, "OMFS Physician Services Fees for Services Rendered on or after February 15, 2007", which sets forth individual procedure codes with the corresponding maximum reimbursable fees, is incorporated by reference.

Note: Authority cited: Sections 133, 4603.5, 5307.1 and 5307.3, Labor Code. Reference: Sections 4600, 4603.2 and 5307.1, Labor Code.

History: 1. New section filed 1-2-2004 as an emergency; operative 1-2-2004 (Register 2004, No. 2). A Certificate of

Compliance must be transmitted to OAL by 5-3-2004 or emergency language will be repealed by operation of law on the following day.

2. Certificate of Compliance as to 1-2-2004 order, including amendment of section heading and section, transmitted to OAL 4-30-2004 and filed 6-15-2004 (Register 2004, No. 25).

3. Amendment of subsection (a)(1), redesignation and amendment of former subsection (c) as new subsections (c)(1) and (c)(3), new subsection (c)(2) and adoption of new revision of Table A (incorporated by reference) filed 12-15-2004 as an emergency; operative 1-14-2005 (Register 2004, No. 51). A Certificate of Compliance must be transmitted to OAL by 5-16-2005 or emergency language will be repealed by operation of law on the following day.

4. Readoption of 12-15-2004 order, with additional amendments, filed 5-12-2005 as an emergency; operative 5-14-2005 (Register 2005, No. 19). A Certificate of Compliance must be transmitted to OAL by 9-12-2005 or emergency language will be repealed by operation of law on the following day.

5. Certificate of Compliance as to 5-12-2005 order transmitted to OAL 8-22-2005 and filed 9-29-2005 (Register 2005, No. 39).

6. Amendment of subsection (c)(4) and new subsection (f) submitted to the Office of Administrative Law for printing only as exempt from the Administrative Procedure Act and review by the Office of Administrative Law pursuant to section 11340.9(g) of the Government Code (Register 2007, No. 7).

7. Editorial correction of History 6 (Register 2013, No. 39).

8. Amendment of section heading and section filed 2-4-2015; operative 3-5-2015. Submitted to OAL for printing only pursuant to Government Code section 11340.9 (Register 2015, No. 6).

Ref.: Hanna § 22.05[2]; Herlick Handbook §§ 1.01[3][b], 4.17[1].

§9789.12.1. Physician Fee Schedule: Official Medical Fee Schedule for Physician and Non–Physician Practitioner Services — For Services Rendered On or After January 1, 2014.

(a) Maximum reasonable fees for physician and non-physician practitioner medical treatment provided pursuant to Labor Code section 4600, which is rendered on or after January 1, 2014, shall be no more than the amount determined by the Official Medical Fee Schedule for Physician and Non-Physician Practitioners, consisting of the regulations set forth in Sections 9789.12.1 through 9789.19.1 ("Physician Fee Schedule.") Maximum fees for services rendered prior to January 1, 2014 shall be determined in accordance with the fee schedule in effect at the time the service was rendered. The Physician Fee Schedule shall not govern fees for services covered by a contract setting such fees as permitted by Labor Code section 5307.11.

(b) Maximum fees for services of a physician or non-physician practitioner are governed by the Physician Fee Schedule, regardless of specialty, for services performed within his or her scope of practice or license as defined by California law, except:

(1) Evaluation and management codes are to be used only by physicians (as defined by Labor Code §3209.3), as well as physician assistants and nurse practitioners who are acting within the scope of their practice and are under the direction of a supervising physician.

(2) Osteopathic Manipulation Codes (98925–98929) are to be used only by licensed Doctors of Osteopathy and Medical Doctors.

(c) Physicians and non-physician practitioners shall utilize other applicable parts of the OMFS to determine maximum fees for services or goods not covered by the Physician Fee Schedule, such as pharmaceuticals (section 9789.40), pathology and clinical laboratory (section 9789.50) and durable medical equipment, prosthetics, orthotics, supplies (section 9789.60), except: 1) where such services or goods are bundled into the Physician Fee Schedule payment, and/or 2) as otherwise specified in the Physician Fee Schedule.

Note: Authority: Sections 133, 4603.5, 5307.1 and 5307.3, Labor Code. Reference: Sections 4600, 5307.1 and 5307.11, Labor Code.

History: 1. New section filed 9-24-2013; operative 1-1-2014. Submitted to OAL for filing and printing only pursuant to Government Code section 11340.9(g) (Register 2013, No. 39).

2. Amendment of subsection (a) filed 11-6-2018; operative 1-1-2019. Submitted to OAL for filing and printing only pursuant to Government Code section 11340.9(g) (Register 2018, No. 45).

Ref.: Herlick Handbook § 1.01[3][b].

§9789.12.2. Calculation of the Maximum Reasonable Fee—Services Other than Anesthesia.

Except for fees determined pursuant to §9789.18.1 et seq., (Anesthesia), the base maximum reasonable fee for physician and non-physician professional medical practitioner services shall be the non-facility or facility fee calculated as follows:

(a) Non-facility site of service fee calculation:

For dates of service on or after January 1, 2014, but before January 1, 2019:

[(Work RVU * Statewide Work GAF) + (Non-Facility PE RVU * Statewide PE GAF) + (MP RVU * Statewide MP GAF)] * Conversion Factor (CF) = Base Maximum Fee

Key: RVU = Relative Value Unit
GAF = Average Statewide Geographic Adjustment Factor
Work = Physician Work
PE = Practice Expense
MP = Malpractice Expense

For dates of service on or after January 1, 2019:

[(Work RVU * Work GPCI) + (Non-Facility PE RVU * PE GPCI) + (MP RVU * MP GPCI)] * Conversion Factor (CF) = Base Maximum Fee

Key: RVU = Relative Value Unit
GPCI = Geographic Practice Cost Index (by locality corresponding to the county where service was provided)
Work = Physician Work
PE = Practice Expense
MP = Malpractice Expense

The base maximum fee for the procedure code is the maximum reasonable fee, except as otherwise provided by applicable provisions of this fee schedule, including but not limited to the application of ground rules and modifiers that affect reimbursement.

(b) Facility site of service fee calculation:

For dates of service on or after January 1, 2014, but before January 1, 2019:
[(Work RVU * Statewide Work GAF) + (Facility PE RVU * Statewide PE GAF) + (MP RVU * Statewide MP GAF)] * Conversion Factor = Base Maximum Fee

Key: RVU = Relative Value Unit
GAF = Average Statewide Geographic Adjustment Factor
Work = Physician Work
PE = Practice Expense
MP = Malpractice Expense

For dates of service on or after January 1, 2019:
[(Work RVU * Work GPCI) + (Facility PE RVU * PE GPCI) + (MP RVU * MP GPCI)] * Conversion Factor (CF) = Base Maximum Fee

Key: RVU = Relative Value Unit
GPCI = Geographic Practice Cost Index (by locality corresponding to the county where service was provided)
Work = Physician Work
PE = Practice Expense
MP = Malpractice Expense

The base maximum fee for the procedure code is the maximum reasonable fee, except as otherwise provided by applicable provisions of this fee schedule, including but not limited to the application of ground rules and modifiers that affect reimbursement.

(c) "Facility RVUs" shall be used where the place of service is listed as facility ("F") in subdivision (d). "Non-Facility Total RVUs" shall be used where the place of service is listed as nonfacility ("NF") in subdivision (d).

(d)(1) The place of service code (POS) is used to identify where the procedure is furnished. All services shall be assigned the POS code for the setting in which the patient received the face-to-face service. In cases where the face-to-face requirement is obviated such as those when a physician/practitioner provides the PC/interpretation of a diagnostic test, from a distant site, the POS code assigned by the physician/practitioner shall be the setting in which the patient received the Technical Component (TC) of the service.

(2) This face-to-face rule does not apply where the patient is receiving care as a registered inpatient or an outpatient of a hospital. The correct POS code assignment will be for the setting in which the patient is receiving inpatient care or outpatient care from a hospital, including the inpatient hospital (POS code 21) or the outpatient hospital (POS 19 or POS 22).

POS Code and Name Description	*Payment Rate Facility = F Nonfacility = NF*
01 Pharmacy A facility or location where drugs and other medically related items and services are sold, dispensed, or otherwise provided directly to patients.	NF
02 Telehealth The location where health services and health related services are provided or received, through a telecommunication system. (Effective for services on or after March 1, 2017)	F
03 School A facility whose primary purpose is education.	NF
04 Homeless Shelter A facility or location whose primary purpose is to provide temporary housing to homeless individuals (e.g., emergency shelters, individual or family shelters).	NF
09 Prison/Correctional Facility A prison, jail, reformatory, work farm, detention center, or any other similar facility maintained by either Federal, State or local authorities for the purpose of confinement or rehabilitation of adult or juvenile criminal offenders.	NF
11 Office Location, other than a hospital, skilled nursing facility (SNF), military treatment facility, community health center, State or local public health clinic, or intermediate care facility (ICF), where the health professional routinely provides health examinations, diagnosis, and treatment of illness or injury on an ambulatory basis.	NF
12 Home or Private Residence of Patient Location, other than a hospital or other facility, where the patient receives care in a private residence.	NF
13 Assisted Living Facility Congregate residential facility with self-contained living units providing assessment of each resident's needs and on-site support 24 hours a day, 7 days a week, with the capacity to deliver or arrange for services including some health care and other services.	NF
14 Group Home A residence, with shared living areas, where clients receive supervision and other services such as social and/or behavioral services, custodial service, and minimal services (e.g., medication administration).	NF
15 Mobile Unit A facility/unit that moves from place-to-place equipped to provide preventive, screening, diagnostic, and/or treatment services.	NF

POS Code and Name Description	*Payment Rate Facility = F Nonfacility = NF*
16 Temporary Lodging A short-term accommodation such as a hotel, camp ground, hostel, cruise ship or resort where the patient receives care, and which is not identified by any other POS code.	NF
17 Walk-in Retail Health Clinic A walk-in health clinic, other than an office, urgent care facility, pharmacy or independent clinic and not described by any other Place of Service code, that is located within a retail operation and provides, on an ambulatory basis, preventive and primary care services.	NF
18 Place of Employment/ Worksite A location, not described by any other POS code, owned or operated by a public or private entity where the patient is employed, and where a health professional provides on-going or episodic occupational medical, therapeutic or rehabilitative services to the individual.	NF
19 Off Campus— Outpatient Hospital A portion of an off-campus hospital provider based department which provides diagnostic, therapeutic (both surgical and nonsurgical), and rehabilitation services to sick or injured persons who do not require hospitalization or institutionalization. (Effective for Services on or after January 1, 2016)	F
20 Urgent Care Facility Location, distinct from a hospital emergency room, an office, or a clinic, whose purpose is to diagnose and treat illness or injury for unscheduled, ambulatory patients seeking immediate medical attention.	NF
21 Inpatient Hospital A facility, other than psychiatric, which primarily provides diagnostic, therapeutic (both surgical and nonsurgical), and rehabilitation services by, or under, the supervision of physicians to patients admitted for a variety of medical conditions.	F
22 Outpatient Hospital A portion of a hospital which provides diagnostic, therapeutic (both surgical and nonsurgical), and rehabilitation services to sick or injured persons who do not require hospitalization or institutionalization. (Effective for Services prior to January 1, 2016)	F
22 On Campus— Outpatient Hospital A portion of a hospital's main campus which provides diagnostic, therapeutic (both surgical and nonsurgical), and rehabilitation services to sick or injured persons who do not require hospitalization or institutionalization. (Effective for Services on or after January 1, 2016)	F
23 Emergency Room— Hospital A portion of a hospital where emergency diagnosis and treatment of illness or injury is provided.	F
24 Ambulatory Surgical Center A freestanding facility, other than a physician's office, where surgical and diagnostic services are provided on an ambulatory basis.	F
31 Skilled Nursing Facility A facility which primarily provides inpatient skilled nursing care and related services to patients who require medical, nursing, or rehabilitative services but does not provide the level of care or treatment available in a hospital.	F
32 Nursing Facility A facility which primarily provides to residents skilled nursing care and related services for the rehabilitation of injured, disabled, or sick persons, or, on a regular basis, health-related care services above the level of custodial care to other than mentally retarded individuals.	NF
33 Custodial Care Facility A facility which provides room, board and other personal assistance services, generally on a longterm basis, and which does not include a medical component.	NF
34 Hospice — for inpatient care A facility, other than a patient's home, in which palliative and supportive care for terminally ill patients and their families are provided.	F
41 Ambulance—Land A land vehicle specifically designed, equipped and staffed for lifesaving and transporting the sick or injured.	F
42 Ambulance—Air or Water An air or water vehicle specifically designed, equipped and staffed for lifesaving and transporting the sick or injured.	F

POS Code and Name Description	Payment Rate Facility = F Nonfacility = NF
49 Independent Clinic A location, not part of a hospital and not described by any other Place of Service code, that is organized and operated to provide preventive, diagnostic, therapeutic, rehabilitative, or palliative services to outpatients only.	NF
51 Inpatient Psychiatric Facility A facility that provides inpatient psychiatric services for the diagnosis and treatment of mental illness on a 24-hour basis, by or under the supervision of a physician.	F
52 Psychiatric Facility—Partial Hospitalization A facility for the diagnosis and treatment of mental illness that provides a planned therapeutic program for patients who do not require full time hospitalization, but who need broader programs than are possible from outpatient visits to a hospital-based or hospital-affiliated facility.	F
53 Community Mental Health Center A facility that provides the following services: outpatient services, including specialized outpatient services for children, the elderly, individuals who are chronically ill, and residents of the CMHC's mental health services area who have been discharged from inpatient treatment at a mental health facility; 24 hour a day emergency care services; day treatment, other partial hospitalization services, or psychosocial rehabilitation services; screening for patients being considered for admission to State mental health facilities to determine the appropriateness of such admission; and consultation and education services.	F
54 Intermediate Care Facility/Mentally Retarded A facility which primarily provides health-related care and services above the level of custodial care to mentally retarded individuals but does not provide the level of care or treatment available in a hospital or skilled nursing facility (SNF).	NF
55 Residential Substance Abuse Treatment Facility A facility which provides treatment for substance (alcohol and drug) abuse to live-in residents who do not require acute medical care. Services include individual and group therapy and counseling, family counseling, laboratory tests, drugs and supplies, psychological testing, and room and board.	NF
56 Psychiatric Residential Treatment Center A facility or distinct part of a facility for psychiatric care which provides a total 24-hour therapeutically planned and professionally staffed group living and learning environment.	F
57 Non-residential Substance Abuse Treatment Facility A location which provides treatment for substance (alcohol and drug) abuse on an ambulatory basis. Services include individual and group therapy and counseling, family counseling, laboratory tests, drugs and supplies, and psychological testing.	NF
60 Mass Immunization Center A location where providers administer pneumococcal pneumonia and influenza virus vaccinations and submit these services as electronic media claims, paper claims, or using the roster billing method. This generally takes place in a mass immunization setting, such as, a public health center, pharmacy, or mall but may include a physician office setting.	NF
61 Comprehensive Inpatient Rehabilitation Facility A facility that provides comprehensive rehabilitation services under the supervision of a physician to inpatients with physical disabilities. Services include physical therapy, occupational therapy, speech pathology, social or psychological services, and orthotics and prosthetics services.	F
62 Comprehensive Outpatient Rehabilitation Facility	NF

POS Code and Name Description	*Payment Rate Facility = F Nonfacility = NF*
A facility that provides comprehensive rehabilitation services under the supervision of a physician to outpatients with physical disabilities. Services include physical therapy, occupational therapy, and speech pathology services.	
65 End-Stage Renal Disease Treatment Facility	NF
A facility other than a hospital, which provides dialysis treatment, maintenance, and/or training to patients or caregivers on an ambulatory or home-care basis.	
71 State or Local Public Health Clinic	NF
A facility maintained by either State or local health departments that provides ambulatory primary medical care under the general direction of a physician.	
72 Rural Health Clinic	NF
A certified facility which is located in a rural medically underserved area that provides ambulatory primary medical care under the general direction of a physician.	
81 Independent Laboratory	NF
A laboratory certified to perform diagnostic and/or clinical tests independent of an institution or a physician's office.	
99 Other Place of Service	NF
Other place of service not identified above.	

(e)(1) For dates of service on or after January 1, 2014, but before January 1, 2019, see section 9789.19, by date of service, for the average statewide GAFs.

(2) For dates of service on or after January 1, 2019, see section 9789.19, by date of service, for reference to the Geographic Practice Code Index (GPCI) values by payment locality.

(A) Determination of Payment Locality: The payment locality is based upon the county in which the service was provided, determined by the ZIP code of the location where the service is actually performed and not necessarily the physical locality of the provider's office, except as otherwise specified in subdivisions (e)(2)(B) and (e)(2)(C).

(i) For purposes of determining the appropriate payment locality, the name and address, including the ZIP code, for each service code must be included on the bill, in accordance with the medical treatment billing regulations at 9792.5.0 et seq.

(ii) See section 9789.19, by date of service, for reference to: counties included in locality file; the zip code to payment locality file; and the zip codes requiring +4 extension file. For zip codes that span more than one county, the 9-digit zip code is required to map to the payment locality.

(B) Determination of Payment Locality for Radiology Services, Pathology Services, and Other Diagnostic Procedures:

(i) Global Service Code — If the global diagnostic code (no modifier TC and no modifier -26) is billed, the provider must report the name and address, including the ZIP code, of where the test was furnished on the bill for the global diagnostic service code. For example, when the global diagnostic service code is billed for chest x-ray as described by CPT code 71045 (no modifier TC and no modifier -26), the locality is determined by the ZIP code applicable to the testing facility.

In order to bill for a global diagnostic service code, the same physician or supplier entity must furnish both the TC and the PC of the diagnostic service and the TC and PC must be furnished within the same payment locality.

(ii) Separate Billing of Professional Interpretation:

If the physician or supplier entity does not furnish both the TC and PC of the diagnostic service, or if the physician or supplier entity furnishes both the TC and PC but the professional interpretation was furnished in a different payment locality from where the TC was furnished, the professional interpretation of a diagnostic test must be separately billed with modifier -26 by the interpreting physician. The interpreting physician must report the name and address, including ZIP code, of the location where professional interpretation was furnished on the bill. If the professional interpretation was furnished at an unusual and infrequent location, for example, a hotel, the locality of the professional interpretation is determined based on where the interpreting physician most commonly practices.

(C) Global Surgical Package — Determination of Payment Locality When Services are Provided in Different Payment Localities:

If portions of the global period are provided in different payment localities, the physician must report the name and address, including ZIP code, of the location where the service was rendered. The procedure code for the surgery is billed with modifier -54; and the postoperative care is billed with the procedure code for the surgery with modifier -55. For example, if the surgery is performed in one GPCI locality and the postoperative care is provided in another GPCI locality, the surgery is billed with modifier "-54" and the payment locality would be where the surgery was performed. The postoperative care is billed with modifier "-55" and the payment locality would be where the postoperative care was performed. This is true whether the services were performed by the same physician/group or different physicians/groups. See sections 9789.16.2, et seq. for additional billing requirements for global surgeries.

(f) The maximum fee for physician and non-physician practitioner services shall be the lesser of the actual charge or the calculated rate established by this fee schedule.

Note: Authority: Sections 133, 4603.5, 5307.1 and 5307.3, Labor Code. Reference: Sections 4600, 5307.1 and 5307.11, Labor Code.

History: 1. New section filed 9-24-2013; operative 1-1-2014. Submitted to OAL as a file and print only pursuant to Government Code section 11340.9(g) (Register 2013, No. 39).

2. Amendment of subsection (b) filed 12-26-2013; operative 1-1-2014. Submitted to OAL as a file and print only pursuant to Government Code section 11340.9(g) (Register 2013, No. 52).

3. Amendment of subsection (d)(2) filed 3-23-2016; operative 1-1-2016 pursuant to Labor Code section 5307.1(g)(2). Submitted to OAL for filing and printing only pursuant to Labor Code section 5307.1(g)(2) (Register 2016, No. 13).

4. Editorial correction of subsection (d)(2) (Register 2017, No. 5).

5. Editorial correction of subsection (d)(2) (Register 2017, No. 14).

6. Editorial correction of subsection (d)(2) (Register 2017, No. 19).

7. Amendment of subsection (d)(2) filed 7-18-2017; operative 3-1-2017. Submitted to OAL as a file and print only pursuant to Labor Code section 5307.1(g)(2) (Register 2017, No. 29).

8. Amendment of subsections (a)-(b), redesignation and amendment of former subsection (e) as new subsection (e)(1) and new subsections (e)(2)-(e)(2)(C) filed 11-6-2018; operative 1-1-2019. Submitted to OAL for filing and printing only pursuant to Government Code section 11340.9(g) (Register 2018, No. 45).

Ref.: Herlick Handbook § 1.01[3][b].

§9789.12.3. Status Codes C, I, N and R.

(a) Except as otherwise provided in this fee schedule, for physician and nonphysician practitioner services billed using Current Procedural Terminology (CPT) codes, the RVUs listed in the Centers for Medicare and Medicaid Services (CMS') National Physician Fee Schedule Relative Value File will be utilized regardless of status code.

(b) When procedures with status indicator codes C, N, or R, do not have RVUs assigned under the CMS' National Physician Fee Schedule Relative Value File, these services shall be reimbursed By Report.

(c)(1) CPT codes with status indicator code I, where Medicare uses another CPT code for reporting and payment for these services shall be reimbursed according to the other CPT code used by Medicare.

(2) Healthcare Common Procedure Coding System (HCPCS) "J" procedures with status indicator I shall be reimbursed according to section 9789.13.2.

(3) CPT codes with status indicator code I, where Medicare uses HCPCS "J" code for reporting and payment for these services, shall be reimbursed according to section 9789.13.2.

(4) Maximum reasonable fee for procedures with status indicator code I, that do not meet the criteria of subdivisions (c)(1), (c)(2), or (c)(3) shall be determined as follows:

(A) use the RVUs listed in the CMS' National Physician Fee Schedule Relative Value File;

(B) If (c)(4)(A) is not applicable, use the applicable fee schedule contained in sections 9789.30–9789.70;

(C) If (c)(4)(A) or (B) are not applicable, payable By Report.

Note: Authority: Sections 133, 4603.5, 5307.1 and 5307.3, Labor Code. Reference: Sections 4600, 5307.1 and 5307.11, Labor Code.

History: 1. New section filed 9-24-2013; operative 1-1-2014. Submitted to OAL as a file and print only pursuant to Government Code section 11340.9(g) (Register 2013, No. 39).

2. Amendment filed 12-26-2013; operative 1-1-2014. Submitted to OAL as a file and print only pursuant to Government Code section 11340.9(g) (Register 2013, No. 52).

Ref.: Herlick Handbook § 1.01[3][b].

§9789.12.4. "By Report" — Reimbursement for Unlisted Procedures/Procedures Lacking RBRVUs.

(a) An unlisted procedure shall be billed using the appropriate unlisted procedure code from the CPT. The procedure shall be billed by report (report not separately reimbursable), justifying that the service was reasonable and necessary to cure or relieve from the effects of the industrial injury or illness. Pertinent information should include an adequate definition or description of the nature, extent, and need for the procedure, and the time, effort and equipment necessary to provide the service.

(b)(1) In accordance with section 9789.12.3, when procedures with status indicator codes C, N, or R, do not have RVUs assigned under the CMS' National Physician Fee Schedule Relative Value File, these services shall be billed by report, justifying that the service was reasonable and necessary to cure or relieve from the effects of the industrial injury or illness. Pertinent information should include an adequate definition or description of the nature, extent, and need for the procedure, and the time, effort and equipment necessary to provide the service.

(2) CPT codes that: 1) appear in the CMS' National Physician Fee Schedule Relative Value File, and 2) do not have an RVU assigned for the service, and 3) that are payable under a fee schedule contained in section 9789.30 – 9789.70, are not payable under the physician fee schedule on a "By Report" basis.

(c) In determining the value of a By Report procedure, consideration may be given to the value assigned to a comparable procedure or analogous code. The comparable procedure or analogous code should reflect similar amount of resources, such as practice expense, time, complexity, expertise, etc. as required for the procedure performed.

Note: Authority: Sections 133, 4603.5, 5307.1 and 5307.3, Labor Code. Reference: Sections 4600, 5307.1 and 5307.11, Labor Code.

History: 1. New section filed 9-24-2013; operative 1-1-2014. Submitted to OAL as a file and print only pursuant to Government Code section 11340.9(g) (Register 2013, No. 39).

2. Amendment of subsection (b)(1) filed 12-26-2013; operative 1-1-2014. Submitted to OAL as a file and print only pursuant to Government Code section 11340.9(g) (Register 2013, No. 52).

Ref.: Herlick Handbook § 1.01[3][b].

§9789.12.5. Conversion Factors.

(a) The conversion factors to be used for determining maximum reasonable fees are set forth in section 9789.19, by date of service.

(b)(1) Commencing January 1, 2014, there shall be a four-year transition between:

"OMFS Budget Neutral CF": the estimated aggregate maximum allowable amount under the official medical fee schedule for physician services prior to January 1, 2014, and

"120% RBRVS 2012 CF": the maximum allowable amount based on the resource-based relative value scale at 120 percent of the Medicare conversion factor in effect in July 2012.

(2) During the transition, the conversion factors before adjustment shall be as follows:

Type of Service	*OMFS Budget–Neutral CF*	*120% 2012 Medicare*	*2014 (75 Percent OMFS/25 Percent 120 % Medicare)*	*2015 (50 Percent OMFS/50 Percent 120 % Medicare)*	*2016 (25 Percent OMFS/75 Percent 120 % Medicare)*	*2017 (120% Medicare)*
Anesthesia	34.5903	25.6896	32.3651	30.1400	27.9148	25.6896
Surgery	55.6849	40.8451	51.9750	48.2650	44.5551	40.8451
Radiology	52.9434	40.8451	49.9188	46.8943	43.8697	40.8451
All other services	34.4566	40.8451	36.0537	37.6509	39.2480	40.8451

(3) The conversion factors specified in subdivision (b)(2) shall be adjusted by the cumulative changes in MEI and the Relative Value Scale Adjustment Factor, if any, between 2012 and each transition year. See section 9789.19 for annual and cumulative MEI, and Relative Value Scale Adjustment Factor, by date of service.

(4)(A) During years 2014 through 2016:

(1) The anesthesia conversion factor shall be applied to CPT codes in the Anesthesia section of the CPT;

(2) The surgery conversion factor shall be applied to CPT codes in the Surgery section of the CPT;

(3) The radiology conversion factor shall be applied to CPT codes in the Radiology section of the CPT;

(4) The "other services" conversion factor shall be applied to CPT codes in the Evaluation and Management, Medicine, and Pathology and Laboratory sections of the CPT, to the extent the services are payable under this fee schedule.

(B) In 2017, and thereafter, there will be two conversion factors: Anesthesia and Other Services.

(c) For calendar year 2018, and annually thereafter, the Anesthesia conversion factor and the Other Services conversion factor in effect in the prior calendar year shall be updated by the Medicare Economic Index inflation rate and by the Relative Value Scale Adjustment Factor, if any.

Note: Authority: Sections 133, 4603.5, 5307.1 and 5307.3, Labor Code. Reference: Sections 4600, 5307.1 and 5307.11, Labor Code.

History: 1. New section filed 9-24-2013; operative 1-1-2014. Submitted to OAL as a file and print only pursuant to Government Code section 11340.9(g) (Register 2013, No. 39).

2. Editorial correction of subsection (b)(2) (Register 2015, No. 12).

Ref.: Herlick Handbook § 1.01[3][b].

§9789.12.6. Geographic Health Professional Shortage Area Bonus Payment: Primary Care; Mental Health.

(a) Physicians who provide professional services in a Geographic Health Professional Shortage Area (HPSA) are eligible for a 10-percent bonus payment. Eligibility for receiving the 10 percent bonus payment is based on whether the specific location at which the service is furnished is within an area that is designated as a Geographic HPSA by the Health Resources and Services Administration (HRSA), within the United States Department of Health & Human Services.

Physicians, including psychiatrists, furnishing services in a primary medical care Geographic HPSA are eligible to receive bonus payments. In addition, psychiatrists furnishing services in mental health Geographic HPSAs are eligible to receive bonus payments.

It is not enough for the physician merely to have his/her office or primary service location in a Geographic HPSA, nor must the injured worker reside in a Geographic HPSA. Eligibility for the bonus is determined by where the service is actually provided (place of service). For example, a physician providing a service in his/her office, the patient's home, or in a hospital qualifies for the incentive payment as long as the specific location of the service is within an area designated as a Geographic HPSA. On the other hand, a physician may have an office in a Geographic HPSA but go outside the office (and the designated Geographic HPSA area) to provide the service. In this case, the physician would not be eligible for the incentive payment.

(b) Only services provided in areas that are designated as of December 31 of the prior year are eligible for the Geographic HPSA bonus payment. Physicians providing services in areas that were designated as of December 31 of the prior year but not on the automated file shall use the AQ modifier. Only services provided in areas that were designated as of December 31 of the prior year but not on the automated file may use the modifier. Services provided in areas that are designated during the year will not be eligible for the Geographic HPSA bonus payment until the following year, provided they are still designated on December 31. Services provided in areas that are de-designated during the year will continue to be eligible for the Geographic HPSA bonus through the end of the calendar year.

(c) The claims administrator shall automatically pay bonuses for services rendered in ZIP Code areas that fully fall within a designated primary care or mental health full county Geographic HPSA; are considered to fully fall in the county based on a determination of dominance made by the United States Postal Service (USPS); or are fully within a partial county Geographic HPSA area.

(d) Should a ZIP Code fall within both a primary care and mental health Geographic HPSA, only one bonus will be paid on the service. Bonuses for mental health Geographic HPSAs will only be paid when performed by the provider specialty of 26 — psychiatry.

(e) For services rendered in ZIP Code areas that do not fall within a designated full county Geographic HPSA; are not considered to fall within the county based on a determination of dominance made by the USPS; or are partially within a partial county Geographic HPSA, physicians must submit an AQ modifier to receive payment.

To determine whether a modifier is needed, physicians must review the information provided on the CMS web site or the HRSA web site for Geographic HPSA designations to determine if the location where they render services is within a Geographic HPSA bonus area. Physicians may also base the determinations on letters of designations received from HRSA. They must be prepared to provide these letters as documentation upon the request of the claims administrator.

For services rendered in ZIP Code areas that cannot automatically receive the bonus, it will be necessary to know the census tract of the area to determine if a bonus should be paid and a modifier submitted. Census tract data can be retrieved by visiting the U.S. Census Bureau Web site at http://www.census.gov/ or the Federal Financial Institutions Examination Council (FFIEC) Web site at http://www.ffiec.gov/geocode/. Instructions on how to use these Web sites can be found on the CMS Web site at http://www.cms.gov/Medicare/Medicare-Fee-for-Service-Payment/HPSAPSAPhysicianBonuses/index.html?redirect=/hpsapsaphysicianbonuses/.

(f) The claims administrator shall pay the 10% bonus together with the payment for the service performed in the Geographic HPSA designated area. The Geographic HPSA bonus pertains only to physician's professional services. Should a service be billed that has both a professional and technical component, only the professional component will receive the bonus payment.

(g) See section 9789.19, by date of service, for:

(1) The links for the Primary Care HPSA zip code file and the Mental Health HPSA zip code file listing zip codes that will automatically receive the Geographic HPSA bonus;

(2) The HRSA web link to determine if a particular address is in a Primary Care Geographic HPSA and/or a Mental Health Geographic HPSA;

(3) The HRSA web link to find Primary Care Geographic HPSA and Mental Health Geographic HPSA by State & County.

Note: Authority: Sections 133, 4603.5, 5307.1 and 5307.3, Labor Code. Reference: Sections 4600, 5307.1 and 5307.11, Labor Code.

History: 1. New section filed 9-24-2013; operative 1-1-2014. Submitted to OAL as a file and print only pursuant to Government Code section 11340.9(g) (Register 2013, No. 39).

2. Amendment of subsection (e) filed 3-23-2016; operative 1-1-2016 pursuant to Labor Code section 5307.1(g)(2). Submitted to OAL for filing and printing only pursuant to Labor Code section 5307.1(g)(2) (Register 2016, No. 13).

3. Amendment of section heading and section filed 11-6-2018; operative 1-1-2019. Submitted to OAL for filing and printing only pursuant to Government Code section 11340.9(g) (Register 2018, No. 45).

Ref.: Herlick Handbook § 1.01[3][b].

§9789.12.7. CMS' National Physician Fee Schedule Relative Value File / Relative Value Units (RVUs).

The National Physician Fee Schedule Relative Value File which is published on the CMS website shall be utilized to determine the maximum reasonable fees. See section 9789.19 for Relative Value File by date of service.

Note: Authority: Sections 133, 4603.5, 5307.1 and 5307.3, Labor Code. Reference: Sections 4600, 5307.1 and 5307.11, Labor Code.

History: 1. New section filed 9-24-2013; operative 1-1-2014. Submitted to OAL as a file and print only pursuant to Government Code section 11340.9(g) (Register 2013, No. 39).

Ref.: Herlick Handbook § 1.01[3][b].

§9789.12.8. Status Codes.

The Medicare Status Codes have been adapted for workers' compensation and have the following meanings:

A = Active Code. These codes are paid separately under the physician fee schedule. There will be RVUs for codes with this status.

B = Bundled Code. Payment for covered services are always bundled into payment for other services not specified. If RVUs are shown, they are not used for payment. If these services are covered, payment for them is subsumed by the payment for the services to which they are incident. (An example is a telephone call from a hospital nurse regarding care of a patient).

C = If payable, these codes will be paid using the RVUs listed in the Centers for Medicare and Medicaid Services (CMS') National Physician Fee Schedule Relative Value File, or if no RVUs are assigned, then by "By Report," generally following review of documentation such as an operative report.

E = If payable:
(a) HCPCS codes beginning with "J" or "P", maximum fee is determined according section 9789.13.2.
(b) Other codes are paid under the applicable fee schedule contained in Section 9789.30-9789.70, or if none of those schedules is applicable the code is payable "By Report."

I = Except as otherwise provided, not valid code for workers' compensation physician billing. See section 9789.12.3.

J = Anesthesia Services. The intent of this value is to facilitate the identification of anesthesia services. There are no RVUs and no payment amounts for these codes in the National Physician Fee Schedule Relative Value File. Instead, the Anesthesia Base Units file is to be used to determine the base units for these codes.

M = Measurement codes. Used for reporting purposes only.

N = If payable, these CPT codes are paid using the listed RVUs; but if no RVUs are listed, then By Report. See section 9789.12.3.

P = Bundled/Excluded Codes. There are no RVUs and no payment amounts for these services. No separate payment should be made for them under the fee schedule.
—If the item or service is covered as incident to a physician service and is provided on the same day as a physician service, payment for it is bundled into the payment for the physician service to which it is incident. (An example is an elastic bandage furnished by a physician incident to physician service.)
—If the item or service is covered as other than incident to a physician service, it is excluded from the fee schedule (i.e., colostomy supplies) and should be paid under the other portions of the fee schedule.

Q = Therapy functional information code (used for required Medicare reporting purposes only; not used for workers' compensation).

R = If payable, these codes will be paid pursuant to section 9789.12.3.

T = Injections. There are RVUS and payment amounts for these services, but they are only paid if there are no other services payable under the physician fee schedule billed on the same date by the same provider. If any other services payable under the physician fee schedule are billed on the same date by the same provider, these services are bundled into the physician services for which payment is made.

X = No RVUS or payment amounts are shown for these codes. If payable, these codes are paid under the applicable fee schedule contained in Sections 9789.30 – 9789.70, or if none of those schedules is applicable the code is payable "By Report."
(Examples of services payable under another fee schedule are ambulance services and clinical diagnostic laboratory services.)

Note: Authority: Sections 133, 4603.5, 5307.1 and 5307.3, Labor Code. Reference: Sections 4600, 5307.1 and 5307.11, Labor Code.

History: 1. New section filed 9-24-2013; operative 1-1-2014. Submitted to OAL as a file and print only pursuant to Government Code section 11340.9(g) (Register 2013, No. 39).

2. Amendment of table — items C and N filed 12-26-2013; operative 1-1-2014. Submitted to OAL as a file and print only pursuant to Government Code section 11340.9(g) (Register 2013, No. 52).

3. Amendment of table adding new item Q filed 3-23-2016; operative 1-1-2016 pursuant to Labor Code section 5307.1(g)(2). Submitted to OAL for filing and printing only pursuant to Labor Code section 5307.1(g)(2) (Register 2016, No. 13).

4. Amendment filed 11-6-2018; operative 1-1-2019. Submitted to OAL for filing and printing only pursuant to Government Code section 11340.9(g) (Register 2018, No. 45).

Ref.: Herlick Handbook § 1.01[3][b].

§9789.12.9. Professional Component (PC)/ Technical Component (TC) Indicator.

The Medicare PC/TC Indicators have been adapted for workers' compensation and have the following meanings:

0 = Physician Service Codes—Identifies codes that describe physician services. Examples include visits, consultations, and surgical procedures. The concept of PC/TC does not apply since physician services cannot be split into professional and technical components. Modifiers 26 and TC cannot be used with these codes. The RVUS include values for physician work, practice expense and malpractice expense. There are some codes with no work RVUs.

1 = Diagnostic Tests for Radiology Services—Identifies codes that describe diagnostic tests. Examples are pulmonary function tests or therapeutic radiology procedures, e.g., radiation therapy. These codes have both a professional and technical component. Modifiers 26 and TC can be used with these codes. The total RVUs for codes reported with a 26 modifier include values for physician work, practice expense, and malpractice expense. The total RVUs for codes reported with a TC modifier include values for practice expense and malpractice expense only. The total RVUs for codes reported without a modifier include values for physician work, practice expense, and malpractice expense.

2 = Professional Component Only Codes—This indicator identifies stand-alone codes that describe the physician work portion of selected diagnostic tests for which there is an associated code that describes the technical component of the diagnostic test only and another associated code that describes the global test. An example of a professional component only code is CPT code 93010—Electrocardiogram; Interpretation and Report. Modifiers 26 and TC cannot be used with these codes. The total RVUs for professional component only codes include values for physician work, practice expense, and malpractice expense.

3 = Technical Component Only Codes—This indicator identifies stand-alone codes that describe the technical component (i.e., staff and equipment costs) of selected diagnostic tests for which there is an associated code that describes the professional component of the diagnostic test only. An example of a technical component only code is CPT code 93005-Electrocardiogram; Tracing Only, without interpretation and report. It also identifies codes that are covered only as diagnostic tests and therefore do not have a related professional code. Modifiers 26 and TC cannot be used with these codes. The total RVUs for technical component only codes include values for practice expense and malpractice expense only.

4 = Global Test Only Codes—This indicator identifies stand-alone codes that describe selected diagnostic tests for which there are associated codes that describe (a) the professional component of the test only, and (b) the technical component of the test only. Modifiers 26 and TC cannot be used with these codes. The total RVUs for global procedure only codes include values for physician work, practice expense, and malpractice expense. The total RVUs for global procedure only codes equals the sum of the total RVUs for the professional and technical components only codes combined.

5 = Incident To Codes—This indicator identifies codes that describe services covered incident to a physician's service when they are provided by auxiliary personnel employed by the physician and working under his or her direct personal supervision. These services are not payable when they are provided to hospital inpatients or patients in a hospital outpatient department. Modifiers 26 and TC cannot be used with these codes.

6 = Laboratory Physician Interpretation Codes—This indicator identifies clinical laboratory codes for which separate payment for interpretations by laboratory physicians may be made. Actual performance of the tests is paid for under the lab fee schedule. Modifier TC cannot be used with these codes. The total RVUs for laboratory physician interpretation codes include values for physician work, practice expense, and malpractice expense.

7 = Physical therapy service, for which payment may not be made--Payment may not be made if the service is provided to either a patient in a hospital outpatient department or to an inpatient of the hospital by an independently practicing physical or occupational therapist.

8 = Physician interpretation codes—This indicator identifies the professional component of clinical laboratory codes for which separate payment may be made only if the physician interprets an abnormal smear for hospital inpatient. This applies to CPT codes 88141 and 85060. No TC billing is recognized because payment for the underlying clinical laboratory test is made to the hospital, generally through the Hospital Fee Schedule payment rate.

No payment is recognized for CPT codes 88141 and 85060 furnished to hospital outpatients or non-hospital patients. The physician interpretation is paid through the clinical laboratory fee schedule payment for the clinical laboratory test.

9 = Not Applicable—Concept of a professional/technical component does not apply.

Note: Authority: Sections 133, 4603.5, 5307.1 and 5307.3, Labor Code. Reference: Sections 4600, 5307.1 and 5307.11, Labor Code.

History: 1. New section filed 9-24-2013; operative 1-1-2014. Submitted to OAL as a file and print only pursuant to Government Code section 11340.9(g) (Register 2013, No. 39).

Ref.: Herlick Handbook § 1.01[3][b].

§9789.12.10. Coding; Current Procedural Terminology©, Fourth Edition.

(a) The coding, modifiers, guidelines, appendices and all other provisions of *Current Procedural Terminology©*, Fourth Edition ("*CPT*"), published by the American Medical Association are applicable to the bills submitted for physician and non-physician practitioner services, except: (1) any provision in the Physician Fee Schedule that conflicts with a provision in *CPT* will take precedence over the *CPT*, and (2) as otherwise specified in regulation. See section 9789.19 for the version of the CPT by date of service.

(b) Copies of *Current Procedural Terminology©*, Fourth Edition may be purchased from the American Medical Association:

Order Department
American Medical Association
P.O. Box 930876
Atlanta, GA 31193-0876

Or over the internet at:

www.amapress.com or https://commerce.ama-assn.org/store/

Or through the American Medical Association's toll free order line: (800) 621-8335.

(c) See section 9789.19 for CPT codes that shall not be used for reporting of or payment for physician services, by date of service.

(d) For coding requirements for physician-administered drugs, biologicals, blood products, and vaccines, see section 9789.13.2.

(e) For HCPCS codes to bill splint and cast materials, see section 9789.19, by date of service.

Note: Authority: Sections 133, 4603.5, 5307.1 and 5307.3, Labor Code. Reference: Sections 4600, 5307.1 and 5307.11, Labor Code.

History: 1. New section filed 9-24-2013; operative 1-1-2014. Submitted to OAL as a file and print only pursuant to Government Code section 11340.9(g) (Register 2013, No. 39).

Ref.: Herlick Handbook § 1.01[3][b].

§9789.12.11. Evaluation and Management: Coding — New Patient; Documentation.

(a) For purposes of workers' compensation billing, the following definitions of "new patient" and "established patient" will be used instead of the CPT definitions:

(1) A "new patient" is one who is new to the physician or medical group or an established patient with a new industrial injury or illness. Only one new patient visit is reimbursable to a single physician or medical group per specialty for evaluation of the same patient relating to the same incident, injury or illness.

(2) An "established patient" is a patient who has been seen previously for the same industrial injury or illness by the physician or medical group.

(b) To properly document and determine the appropriate level of evaluation and management service, physicians and qualified non-physician practitioners must use either one of the following guidelines but not a combination of the two guidelines for a patient encounter. If the physician's or qualified non-physician practitioner's documentation for a medically necessary service conforms to either one of the guidelines, the maximum reasonable fee shall be according to the documented level of service:

(1) The "1995 Documentation Guidelines for Evaluation & Management Services," or

(2) The "1997 Documentation Guidelines for Evaluation and Management Services."

Both guidelines are incorporated by reference and are available on Medicare's website, or will be made available upon request to the Administrative Director.

The 1995 version is available at https://www.cms.gov/Outreach-and-Education/Medicare-Learning-Network-MLN/MLNEdWebGuide/Downloads/95Docguidelines.pdf

The 1997 version is available at https://www.cms.gov/Outreach-and-Education/Medicare-Learning-Network-MLN/MLNEdWebGuide/Downloads/97Docguidelines.pdf.

Note: Authority: Sections 133, 4603.5, 5307.1 and 5307.3, Labor Code. Reference: Sections 4600, 5307.1 and 5307.11, Labor Code.

History: 1. New section filed 9-24-2013; operative 1-1-2014. Submitted to OAL as a file and print only pursuant to Government Code section 11340.9(g) (Register 2013, No. 39).

Ref.: Herlick Handbook § 1.01[3][b].

§9789.12.12. Consultation Services Coding — Use of Visit Codes.

(a) Maximum fees for physicians and qualified non-physician practitioners performing consultation services shall be determined utilizing the appropriate RVU for a patient evaluation and management visit and the RVU(s) for prolonged service codes if warranted under CPT guidelines. Physicians and qualified non-physician practitioners shall code consultation visits as patient evaluation and management visits utilizing the CPT Evaluation and Management codes that represent where the visit occurs and that identify the complexity of the visit performed. CPT consultation codes shall not be utilized.

(1) In the inpatient hospital setting and the nursing facility setting consulting physicians (and qualified non-physician practitioners where permitted) who perform an initial evaluation may bill the initial hospital care codes (99221–99223) or nursing facility care codes (99304–99306).

Follow-up consultation visits in the inpatient hospital setting shall be billed as subsequent hospital care visits (99231–99233) and subsequent nursing facility care visits (99307–99310.)

(2) In the office or other outpatient setting where a consultation / evaluation is performed, physicians and qualified non-physician practitioners shall use the CPT visit codes (99201–99215) depending on the complexity of the visit and whether the patient is a new or established patient to that physician, as defined in section 9789.12.11.

(b) Consultation reports are bundled into the underlying evaluation and management visit code or hospital care code, and are not separately payable, except as specified in subdivision (c).

(c) The following consultation reports are separately reimbursable:

(1) Consultation reports requested by the Workers' Compensation Appeals Board or the Administrative Director. Use WC007, modifier -32.

(2) Consultation reports requested by the Qualified Medical Evaluator ("QME") or Agreed Medical Evaluator ("AME") in the context of a medical-legal evaluation. Use WC007, modifier -30.

Note: Authority: Sections 133, 4603.5, 5307.1 and 5307.3, Labor Code. Reference: Sections 4600, 5307.1 and 5307.11, Labor Code.

History: 1. New section filed 9-24-2013; operative 1-1-2014. Submitted to OAL as a file and print only pursuant to Government Code section 11340.9(g) (Register 2013, No. 39).

2. Amendment of subsection (b) filed 11-6-2018; operative 1-1-2019. Submitted to OAL for filing and printing only pursuant to Government Code section 11340.9(g) (Register 2018, No. 45).

Ref.: Herlick Handbook § 1.01[3][b].

§9789.12.13. Correct Coding Initiative.

(a) The National Correct Coding Initiative Edits ("NCCI") adopted by the CMS shall apply to payments for medical services under the Physician Fee Schedule. Except where payment ground rules differ from the Medicare ground rules, claims administrators shall apply the NCCI physician coding edits (Practitioner PTP Edits and Medically Unlikely Edits, excluding codes with an MUE value of zero) to bills to determine appropriate payment. Claims Administrators shall utilize the National Correct Coding Initiative Coding Policy Manual for Medicare Services. If a billing is reduced or denied reimbursement because of application of the NCCI, the claims administrator must notify the physician or qualified non-physician practitioner of the basis for the denial, including the fact that the determination was made in accordance with the NCCI.

(b) The National Correct Coding Initiative Coding Policy Manual may be obtained from the CMS website: http://www.cms.hhs.gov/NationalCorrectCodInitEd/. See section 9789.19 for the adopted version of the NCCI Coding Policy Manual, by date of service.

(c) Medically Unlikely Edits are published by CMS on its website at: http://www.cms.gov/Medicare/Coding/NationalCorrectCodInitEd/MUE.html in the document "Practitioner Services MUE Table." See section 9789.19 for the adopted version of the Practitioner Services MUE Table, by date of service. For services on or after July 1, 2018, see section 9789.19 for the excerpt of the adopted Practitioner Services MUE Table (which excludes codes with zero value), by date of service.

(d) Physician NCCI Edits are published by CMS on its website at: http://www.cms.gov/Medicare/Coding/NationalCorrectCodInitEd/NCCI-Coding-Edits. html in the documents "Practitioner PTP Edits." See section 9789.19 for the adopted version of the Practitioner PTP Edits, by date of service.

Note: Authority: Sections 133, 4603.5, 5307.1 and 5307.3, Labor Code. Reference: Sections 4600, 5307.1 and 5307.11, Labor Code.

History: 1. New section filed 9-24-2013; operative 1-1-2014. Submitted to OAL as a file and print only pursuant to Government Code section 11340.9(g) (Register 2013, No. 39).

2. Amendment of subsection (b) filed 3-23-2016; operative 1-1-2016 pursuant to Labor Code section 5307.1(g)(2). Submitted to OAL for filing and printing only pursuant to Labor Code section 5307.1(g)(2) (Register 2016, No. 13).

3. Amendment filed 11-6-2018; operative 1-1-2019. Submitted to OAL for filing and printing only pursuant to Government Code section 11340.9(g) (Register 2018, No. 45).

Ref.: Herlick Handbook § 1.01[3][b].

§9789.12.14. California Specific Codes.

Physicians and non-physician practitioners shall use the "California Specific Codes" listed below. Maximum reasonable fees for services performed by physicians and non-physician practitioners within their scope of practice shall be no more than the fee listed in section 9789.19, by date of service. The fees shall be updated annually in accordance with the Medicare Economic Index.

CA Code	*Procedure*
WC001	Doctor's First Report of Occupational Illness or Injury (Form 5021) (Section 9789.14(a)(1))
WC002	Treating Physician's Progress Report (PR-2 or narrative equivalent in accordance with §9785) (Section 9789.14(b)(1))
WC003	Primary Treating Physician's Permanent and Stationary Report (Form PR-3) (Section 9789.14(b)(2))
WC004	Primary Treating Physician's Permanent and Stationary Report (Form PR-4) (Section 9789.14(b)(3))
WC005	Psychiatric Report requested by the WCAB or the Administrative Director, other than medical-legal report. Use modifier -32 (Section 9789.14(b)(4))

WC006	[Reserved]
WC007	Consultation Reports Requested by the Workers' Compensation Appeals Board or the Administrative Director (Use modifier -32) Consultation Reports requested by the QME or AME in the context of a medical-legal evaluation (Section 9789.14(b)(5)). (Use modifier -30)
WC008	Chart Notes (Section 9789.14(c))
WC009	Duplicate Reports (Section 9789.14(d))
WC010	Duplication of X-Ray
WC011	Duplication of Scan
WC012	Missed Appointments. This code is designated for communication only. It does not imply that compensation is owed.

Note: Authority: Sections 133, 4603.5, 5307.1 and 5307.3, Labor Code. Reference: Sections 4600, 5307.1 and 5307.11, Labor Code.

History: 1. New section filed 9-24-2013; operative 1-1-2014. Submitted to OAL as a file and print only pursuant to Government Code section 11340.9(g) (Register 2013, No. 39).

Ref.: Herlick Handbook § 1.01[3][b].

§9789.12.15. California Specific Modifier.

The following modifier is to be appended to the applicable CPT Code or California Specific code in addition to any applicable CPT modifier.

-30 Consultation Service During Medical-Legal Evaluation: Services or procedures performed by a consultant at the request of a QME or AME in the context of a medical-legal evaluation where those services are paid under the Physician Fee Schedule.

Note: Authority: Sections 133, 4603.5, 5307.1 and 5307.3, Labor Code. Reference: Sections 4600, 5307.1 and 5307.11, Labor Code.

History: 1. New section filed 9-24-2013; operative 1-1-2014. Submitted to OAL as a file and print only pursuant to Government Code section 11340.9(g) (Register 2013, No. 39).

Ref.: Herlick Handbook § 1.01[3][b].

§9789.13.1. Supplies.

(a) Separate payment for routinely bundled supplies is not allowed.

(b) See section 9789.13.2 regarding payment for physician-administered drugs/biological/vaccines/blood products.

(c) Splints and casting supplies are payable separately in addition to payment for the procedure for applying the splint or cast, performed in a physician's office. See section 9789.19 for the splint and cast HCPCS codes and maximum payment amounts, by date of service. For services on or after April 1, 2014, maximum fees for splints and casting supplies are determined by the Durable Medical Equipment, Prosthetics, Orthotics, Supplies fee schedule.

Note: Authority: Sections 133, 4603.5, 5307.1 and 5307.3, Labor Code. Reference: Sections 4600, 5307.1 and 5307.11, Labor Code.

History: 1. New section filed 9-24-2013; operative 1-1-2014. Submitted to OAL as a file and print only pursuant to Government Code section 11340.9(g) (Register 2013, No. 39).

2. Amendment of subsection (c) filed 3-23-2016; operative 1-1-2016 pursuant to Labor Code section 5307.1(g)(2). Submitted to OAL for filing and printing only pursuant to Labor Code section 5307.1(g)(2) (Register 2016, No. 13).

Ref.: Herlick Handbook § 1.01[3][b].

§9789.13.2. Physician–Administered Drugs, Biologicals, Vaccines, Blood Products.

(a) Physician-administered drugs, biologicals, vaccines, or blood products are separately payable.

(1) Vaccines shall be reported using the NDC and CPT-codes for the vaccine. Other physician-administered drugs, biological and blood products shall be reported using the NDC and J-codes assigned to the product.

(2) The maximum reimbursement shall be determined using the "Basic Rate" for the HCPCS code contained on the Medi-Cal Rates file for the date of service. The Medi-Cal fee schedule reimburses drug products, vaccines and immunizations at the Medicare rate of reimbursement when established and published by the Centers for Medicare & Medicaid Services (CMS) or the Medi-Cal pharmacy rate of reimbursement when the Medicare rate is not available. The Medicare rate is currently defined as average sales price (ASP) plus 6 percent. The pharmacy rate is currently defined as the lower of (1) the average wholesale price (AWP) minus 17 percent; (2) the federal upper limit (FUL); or (3) the maximum allowable ingredient cost (MAIC).

(3) The "Basic Rate" price listed on the Medi-Cal rates page of the Medi-Cal website for each physician-administered drug includes an injection administration fee of $4.46. This injection administration fee should be subtracted from the published rate because payment for the injection administration fee will be determined under the RBRVS. See section 9789.19 for a link to the Department of Health Care Services' Medi-Cal rates file.

(4) For a physician-administered drug, biological, vaccine or blood product not contained in the Medi-Cal Rates file referenced in subdivision (a)(2), the maximum reimbursement is the amount prescribed in the Medi-Cal Pharmacy Fee Schedule as adopted by the Division of Workers' Compensation in section 9789.40 and posted on the Division website as the Pharmaceutical Fee Schedule. See section 9789.19 for a link to the Division of Workers' Compensation Pharmaceutical Fee Schedule.

(b) The physician fee schedule shall be used to determine the maximum reimbursement for the drug administration fee.

(1) Injection services (codes 96365 through 96379) are not paid for separately, if the physician is paid for any other physician fee schedule service furnished at the same time. Pay separately for those injection services only if no other physician fee schedule service is being paid.

(2) Pay separately for cancer chemotherapy injections (CPT codes 96401–96549) in addition to the visit furnished on the same day.

(c) Physician-administered radiopharmaceuticals. When furnished to patients in settings in which a technical component is payable, separate payments may be made for low osmolar contrast material used during intrathecal radiologic procedures (HCPCS Q-codes Q9965–9967), pharmacologic stressing agents used in connection with nuclear medicine and cardiovascular stress testing procedures HCPCS A-codes A4641, A4642, A9500–A9507, A9600), radionuclide used in connection nuclear medicine procedures furnished to beneficiaries in settings in which TCs are payable.

Low-osmolar contrast media is reported using HCPCS Q-codes.

(d) All claims for a physician-administered drug, biological, vaccine, or blood product must include the specific name of the drug and dosage.

(e) "Administer" means the direct application of a drug or device to the body of a patient by injection, inhalation, ingestion, or other means.

Note: Authority: Sections 133, 4603.5, 5307.1 and 5307.3, Labor Code. Reference: Sections 4600, 5307.1 and 5307.11, Labor Code.

History: 1. New section filed 9-24-2013; operative 1-1-2014. Submitted to OAL as a file and print only pursuant to Government Code section 11340.9(g) (Register 2013, No. 39).

2. Amendment of subsection (b) filed 11-6-2018; operative 1-1-2019. Submitted to OAL for filing and printing only pursuant to Government Code section 11340.9(g) (Register 2018, No. 45).

Ref.: Herlick Handbook § 1.01[3][b].

§9789.13.3. Physician–Dispensed Drugs.

The maximum reimbursement for physician-dispensed drugs is determined pursuant to the Pharmaceutical Fee Schedule set forth in section 9789.40 and pursuant to the provisions of Labor Code section 5307.1.

Note: Authority: Sections 133, 4603.5, 5307.1 and 5307.3, Labor Code. Reference: Sections 4600, 5307.1 and 5307.11, Labor Code.

History: 1. New section filed 9-24-2013; operative 1-1-2014. Submitted to OAL as a file and print only pursuant to Government Code section 11340.9(g) (Register 2013, No. 39).

Ref.: Herlick Handbook § 1.01[3][b].

§9789.14. Reimbursement for Reports, Duplicate Reports, Chart Notes.

This section governs reimbursement of all reports other than those which are payable under the medical-legal fee schedule, found at section 9793 et seq.

(a) Treatment Reports Not Separately Reimbursable.

The following treatment reports are not separately reimbursable as the appropriate fee is included within the underlying Evaluation and Management service, Physical Therapy Evaluation service or Occupational Therapy Evaluation service for an office visit:

(1) Doctor's First Report of Occupational Illness or Injury (Form 5021) issued in accordance with section 9785(e). Use Code WC001;

(2) Consultation Reports, except as specified in subdivision (b)(5).

(3) Report by a secondary physician to the primary treating physician.

(4) Physician's Return-to-Work & Voucher Report (DWC-AD 10133.36) issued in accordance with section 9785 subdivision (i) (reimbursement is bundled into payment for PR-3 or PR-4).

(b) Treatment Reports That Are Separately Reimbursable.

The following treatment reports are separately reimbursable.

(1) Primary Treating Physician's Progress Report (Form PR-2), issued in accordance with section 9785(f), using DWC form PR-2, its narrative equivalent, or letter format where allowed by section 9785. Use Code WC002.

(2) Primary Treating Physician's Permanent and Stationary Report (Form PR-3) issued in accordance with section 9785(h). Use Code WC003.

(3) Primary Treating Physician's Permanent and Stationary Report (Form PR-4) issued in accordance with section 9785(h). Use Code WC004.

(4) Psychiatric Report Requested by the WCAB or the Administrative Director, other than a medical-legal report. Use Code WC005, modifier -32.

(5) Consultation Reports that are separately reimbursable. The following reports are separately reimbursable.

(A) Consultation reports requested by the Workers' Compensation Appeals Board or the Administrative Director. Use WC007, modifier -32.

(B) Consultation reports requested by the Qualified Medical Evaluator ("QME") or Agreed Medical Evaluator ("AME") in the context of a medical-legal evaluation. Use WC007, modifier -30.

(c) Chart Notes. Requests for chart notes shall be in writing and shall be separately reimbursable. Chart note requests shall be made only by the claims administrator. Use Code WC008 to bill for requested chart notes "By Report".

(d) Duplicate Reports. A primary treating physician has fulfilled his or her reporting duties by sending one copy of a required report to the claims administrator or to a person designated by the claims administrator to be the recipient of the required report. Requests for duplicate reports related to billings shall be made only by the claims administrator and shall be in writing. Duplicate reports are separately reimbursable. Use Code WC009 to bill for duplicate reports "By Report".

Note: Authority: Sections 133, 4603.5, 5307.1 and 5307.3, Labor Code. Reference: Sections 4600, 5307.1 and 5307.11, Labor Code.

History: 1. New section filed 9-24-2013; operative 1-1-2014. Submitted to OAL as a file and print only pursuant to Government Code section 11340.9(g) (Register 2013, No. 39).

Ref.: Herlick Handbook § 1.01[3][b].

§9789.15.1. Non-Physician Practitioner (NPP) — Payment Methodology.

(a) For purposes of this section, NPP services means services provided by physician assistants, nurse practitioners, clinical nurse specialists, and clinical social workers.

(b) Except for clinical social workers, maximum fees for NPP services shall be 85 percent of what a physician is paid under the Official Medical Fee Schedule — Physician Fee Schedule. Maximum fees for clinical social workers shall be 75 percent of what a physician is paid under the Official Medical Fee Schedule-Physician Fee Schedule.

Maximum fees for NPP assistant-at-surgery services are set according to Section 9789.15.1(c). Maximum fees for services provided by NPPs employed by the physician that are incident to the physician service shall be at 100 percent of the physician fee schedule amount as though the physician personally performed the services.

(c) When a NPP actively assists a physician in performing a surgical procedure and furnishes more than just ancillary services, the NPP's services are eligible for payment as assistant-at-surgery services. Maximum fees for covered NPP assistant-at-surgery services shall be 85 percent of what a physician is paid under the Official Medical Fee Schedule — Physician Fee Schedule. Since physicians are paid at 16 percent of the surgical payment amount for assistant-at-surgery services, the actual payment amount that NPPs receive for assistant-at-surgery services is 13.6 percent of the amount paid to physicians. The AS modifier must be reported when billing NPP assistant-at-surgery services.

Note: Authority: Sections 133, 4603.5, 5307.1 and 5307.3, Labor Code. Reference: Sections 4600, 5307.1 and 5307.11, Labor Code.

History: 1. New section filed 9-24-2013; operative 1-1-2014. Submitted to OAL as a file and print only pursuant to Government Code section 11340.9(g) (Register 2013, No. 39).

Ref.: Herlick Handbook § 1.01[3][b].

§9789.15.2. Non–Physician Practitioner (NPP) — "Incident To" Services.

(a) Non-institutional Setting.

For purposes of this section a non-institutional setting means all settings other than a hospital or skilled nursing facility.

(1) Services that are furnished incident to a physician's are commonly included in the physician's bills, and for which no separate payment is made. Diagnostic tests and pneumococcal, influenza, and hepatitis B vaccines need not also meet the incident to requirement in this section.

(2) NPPs may provide services without direct physician supervision and bill directly for these services. When their services are provided under direct physician supervision, their services may be covered as incident to services, in which case the incident to requirements would apply.

(3) To be covered incident to the services of a physician, services must be:

(A) An integral, although incidental, part of the physician's professional service;

(B) Commonly rendered without charge or included in the physician's bill;

(C) Of a type that are commonly furnished in physician's offices or clinics;

(D) Furnished by the physician or by auxiliary personnel under the physician's direct supervision.

(b) Institutional Setting.

Hospital services incident to physician's services rendered to outpatients and partial hospitalization services incident to such services are subject to the incident to requirements. Payment for these services is made to a hospital.

(c) Incident To Physician's Professional Services

Incident to a physician's professional services means that the services are furnished as an integral, although incidental, part of the physician's personal professional services in the course of diagnosis or treatment of an injury or illness. See section 9789.19 for "incident to" codes by date of service.

(1) Services Commonly Furnished in Physicians' Offices.

Services commonly furnished in physicians' offices are covered under the incident to provision. Charges for such services must be included in the physicians' bills. Where services are of a type not considered medically appropriate to provide in the office setting, they would not be covered under the incident to provision.

(2) Direct Personal Supervision.

(A) Services incident to the professional services of a physician in private practice is limited to situations in which there is direct physician supervision of auxiliary/NPP personnel. The incident to services must represent an expense incurred by the physician or legal entity billing for the services.

(B) Where a physician supervises auxiliary/NPP personnel to assist him/her in rendering services to patients and includes the charges for their services in his/her own bills, the services of such personnel are considered incident to the physician's service if there is a physician's service rendered to which the services of such personnel are an incidental part and there is direct supervision by the physician.

(C) To be considered incident to, each occasion of service by auxiliary/NPP personnel needs also to always be the occasion of the actual rendition of a personal professional service by the physician. Such a service could be considered to be incident to when furnished during a course of treatment where the physician performs an initial service and subsequent services of a frequency which reflect his/her active participation in and management of the course of treatment. However, the direct supervision requirement must still be met with respect to every nonphysician service.

(D) Direct supervision in the office setting does not mean that the physician must be present in the same room with his or her aide. However, the physician must be present in the office suite and immediately available to provide assistance and direction throughout the time the aide is performing services.

(E) If auxiliary/NPP personnel perform services outside the office setting, e.g., in a patient's home or in an institution (other than hospital or skilled nursing facility (SNF)), their services are covered incident to a physician's service only if there is direct supervision by the physician. For example, if a nurse accompanied the physician on house calls and administered an injection, the nurse's services are covered. If the same nurse made the calls alone and administered the injection, the services are not covered (even when billed by the physician) since the physician is not providing direct supervision.

(F) The availability of the physician by telephone and the presence of the physician somewhere in the institution does not constitute direct supervision for services provided by auxiliary/NPP personnel in an institution (e.g., nursing, or convalescent home).

(G) There is no payment for services of physician-employed auxiliary/NPP personnel as services incident to physician service.

(H) A NPP who performs a specific medical procedure without physician supervision may receive separate payment for the service as a NPP's service.

(d) Incident to physician's services in clinic.

Services incident to a physician's service in a physician directed clinic or group association are generally the same as those described in this subsection.

A physician directed clinic is one where:

(1) A physician (or a number of physicians) is present to perform medical (rather than administrative) services at all times the clinic is open;

(2) Each patient is under the care of a clinic physician; and

(3) The non-physician services are under medical supervision.

(4) In highly organized clinics, particularly those that are departmentalized, direct physician supervision may be the responsibility of several physicians as opposed to an individual attending physician. In this situation, medical management of all services provided in the clinic is assured. The physician ordering a particular service need not be the physician who is supervising the service.

(5) When the auxiliary/NPP personnel perform services outside the clinic premises, the services are covered only if performed under the direct supervision of a clinic physician. If the clinic refers a patient for auxiliary/NPP services performed by personnel who are not supervised by clinic physicians, such services are not incident to a physician's service.

Note: Authority: Sections 133, 4603.5, 5307.1 and 5307.3, Labor Code. Reference: Sections 4600, 5307.1 and 5307.11, Labor Code.

History: 1. New section filed 9-24-2013; operative 1-1-2014. Submitted to OAL as a file and print only pursuant to Government Code section 11340.9(g) (Register 2013, No. 39).

Ref.: Herlick Handbook § 1.01[3][b].

§9789.15.3. Qualified Non–Physician Anesthetist Services.

(a) This subsection applies to certified registered nurse anesthetists (CRNAs) and certified anesthesiologist assistants (AAs). The term "qualified non-physician anesthetist" refers to both CRNAs and AAs.

(b) The maximum fee for anesthesia services furnished by qualified non-physician anesthetists is the fee determined by this section and section 9789.18.1.

(c) Anesthesia time means the time during which a qualified non-physician anesthetist is present with the patient. It starts when the qualified non-physician anesthetist begins to prepare the patient for anesthesia services in the operating room or an equivalent area and ends when the qualified non-physician anesthetist is no longer furnishing anesthesia services to the patient, that is, when the patient may be placed safely under postoperative care. Anesthesia time is a continuous time period from the start of anesthesia to the end of an anesthesia service. In counting anesthesia time, the qualified non-physician anesthetist can add blocks of time around an interruption in anesthesia time as long as the qualified non-physician anesthetist is furnishing continuous anesthesia care within the time periods around the interruption.

(d) The following modifiers are used when billing for anesthesia services:

(1) QX — Qualified non-physician anesthetist with medical direction by a physician.

(2) QZ — CRNA without medical direction by a physician.

(3) QS — Monitored anesthesiology care services (can be billed by a qualified non-physician anesthetist or a physician).

(4) QY — Medical direction of one qualified non-physician anesthetist by an anesthesiologist.

(e) Where a single anesthesia procedure involves both a physician medical direction service and the service of the medically directed qualified non-physician anesthetist, the payment amount for the service of each is 50 percent of the allowance otherwise recognized had the service been furnished by the anesthesiologist alone. The modifier to be used for current procedure identification is QX.

Where the qualified non-physician anesthetist and the anesthesiologist are involved in a single anesthesia case, and the physician is performing medical direction, the service is billed in accordance with the following procedures:

(1) For the single medically directed service, the physician will use the modifier "QY" (Medical Direction Of One Qualified Non-physician Anesthetist By An Anesthesiologist).

(2) For the anesthesia service furnished by the medically directed qualified non-physician anesthetist, the qualified non-physician anesthetist will use the current modifier "QX."

(3) In unusual circumstances when it is medically necessary for both the qualified non-physician anesthetist and the anesthesiologist to be completely and fully involved during a procedure, full payment for the services of each provider is allowed. The physician would report using the "AA" modifier and the qualified non-physician anesthetist would use "QZ," or the modifier for a nonmedically directed case.

Documentation must be submitted by each physician and qualified non-physician practitioner to support payment of the full fee.

(f) Payment can be made to a teaching CRNA who supervises a single case involving a student nurse anesthetist where the CRNA is continuously present. The CRNA reports the service using the usual "QZ" modifier. This modifier designates that the teaching CRNA is not medically directed by an anesthesiologist. No payment shall be made for the service provided by a student nurse anesthetist.

(g) The teaching CRNA, not under the medical direction of a physician, can be paid for his/her involvement in each of two concurrent cases with student nurse anesthetists. Payment is allowed at the regular fee schedule rate if the teaching CRNA is involved with two concurrent student nurse anesthetist cases. The CRNA reports the anesthesia service using the "QZ" modifier.

To bill the anesthesia base units, the CRNA must be present with the student nurse anesthetist during the pre and post anesthesia care for each of the two cases.

To bill anesthesia time for each case, the teaching CRNA must continue to devote his/her time to the two concurrent cases and not be involved in other activities. The teaching CRNA can decide how to allocate his or her time to optimize patient care in the two cases based on the complexity of the anesthesia case, the experience and skills of the student nurse anesthetist, the patient's health status and other factors.

The teaching CRNA must document his/her involvement in the cases with the student nurse anesthetists.

Note: Authority: Sections 133, 4603.5, 5307.1 and 5307.3, Labor Code. Reference: Sections 4600, 5307.1 and 5307.11, Labor Code.

History: 1. New section filed 9-24-2013; operative 1-1-2014. Submitted to OAL as a file and print only pursuant to Government Code section 11340.9(g) (Register 2013, No. 39).

Ref.: Herlick Handbook § 1.01[3][b].

§9789.15.4. Physical Medicine/Chiropractic/ Acupuncture Multiple Procedure Payment Reduction; Pre-Authorization for Specified Procedure/Modality Services.

(a)(1) The Medicare Multiple Procedure Payment Reduction ("MPPR") for "Always Therapy" Codes shall be applied when more than one of the following codes is billed on the same day: codes on the Medicare "Always Therapy" list, acupuncture codes, chiropractic manipulation codes.

(2) Many therapy services are time-based codes, i.e., multiple units may be billed for a single procedure. The MPPR applies to the Practice Expense ("PE") payment when more than one unit or procedure is provided to the same patient on the same day, i.e., the MPPR applies to multiple units as well as multiple procedures. Full payment is made for the unit or procedure with the highest PE payment. Full payment is made for the work and malpractice components and 50 percent payment is made for the PE for subsequent units and procedures, furnished to the same patient on the same day.

(3) For therapy services furnished by a group practice or "incident to" a physician's service, the MPPR applies to all services furnished to a patient on the same day, regardless of whether the services are provided in one therapy discipline or multiple disciplines, for example, physical therapy, occupational therapy, or speech-language pathology.

(4) The MPPR applies to acupuncture codes and chiropractic manipulation codes and to the procedures listed in the "Separately Payable Always Therapy Services Subject to the Multiple Procedure Payment Reduction (MPPR)" file of the Medicare Physician Fee Schedule Final Rule. The listed procedures will also have a Multiple Procedure value of "5" on the National Physician Fee Schedule Relative Value File.

(5) See section 9789.19 for the location of the list of codes on the Medicare "Always Therapy" code list, by date of service.

(b) In addition to the MPPR, the following caps are presumed reasonable limitations on reimbursement for services provided at one visit unless pre-authorization and a pre-negotiated fee arrangement has been obtained. The pre-authorization must be provided by an authorized agent of the claims administrator to the physician or qualified non-physician practitioner. The fee agreement and pre-authorization must be memorialized in writing prior to performing the medical services.

(1) When billing for treatment consisting of physical medicine modalities only: no more than two codes on the same visit;

(2) When billing for physical medicine modality, procedure, or acupuncture codes, no more than 60 minutes on the same visit;

(3) Where modalities and procedures are billed: no more than 4 codes total on the same visit.

For the purpose of this subdivision "modality" means a service that is listed in the CPT Medicine section, Physical Medicine and Rehabilitation under the sub-heading of "Modalities". For the purpose of this subdivision "procedure" means a service that is listed in the CPT Medicine section, Physical Medicine and Rehabilitation under the sub-headings "Therapeutic Procedures," "Other Procedures," and under the headings "Acupuncture" and "Chiropractic Manipulative Treatment."

Note: Authority: Sections 133, 4603.5, 5307.1 and 5307.3, Labor Code. Reference: Sections 4600, 5307.1 and 5307.11, Labor Code.

History: 1. New section filed 9-24-2013; operative 1-1-2014. Submitted to OAL as a file and print only pursuant to Government Code section 11340.9(g) (Register 2013, No. 39).

2. Amendment of subsection (a)(4) filed 3-23-2016; operative 1-1-2016 pursuant to Labor Code section 5307.1(g)(2). Submitted to OAL for filing and printing only pursuant to Labor Code section 5307.1(g)(2) (Register 2016, No. 13).

Ref.: Herlick Handbook § 1.01[3][b].

§9789.15.5. Ophthalmology Multiple Procedure Reduction.

(a) The Multiple Procedure Payment Reduction (MPPR) on ophthalmology procedures applies when multiple services are furnished to the same patient on the same day. The MPPRs apply to Technical Component (TC)-only services, and to the TC of global services. Full payment is made for the TC service with the highest payment. Payment is made at 80 percent for subsequent TC services furnished by the same physician (or by multiple physicians in the same group practice, i.e., same Group National Provider Identifier (NPI)) to the same patient on the same day. The MPPR does not apply to professional component (PC) services. See section 9789.19 for the location of the list of codes subject to the MPPR on ophthalmology procedures, by date of service.

(b) For services subject to both the multiple procedure payment reduction and the OPPS cap on imaging, the MPPR shall be applied first, then the reduced amount will be compared with the OPPS cap, and the lower amount shall be used.

Note: Authority: Sections 133, 4603.5, 5307.1 and 5307.3, Labor Code. Reference: Sections 4600, 5307.1 and 5307.11, Labor Code.

History: 1. New section filed 9-24-2013; operative 1-1-2014. Submitted to OAL as a file and print only pursuant to Government Code section 11340.9(g) (Register 2013, No. 39).

Ref.: Herlick Handbook § 1.01[3][b].

§9789.15.6. Diagnostic Cardiovascular Procedures — Multiple Procedure Reduction.

(a) The Multiple Procedure Payment Reduction (MPPR) on diagnostic cardiovascular procedures applies when multiple services are furnished to the same patient on the same day. The MPPR applies to Technical Component (TC)-only services, and to the TC of global services. Full payment is made for the TC service with the highest payment. Payment is made at 75 percent for subsequent TC services furnished by the same physician (or by multiple physicians in the same group practice, i.e., same Group National Provider Identifier (NPI)) to the same patient on the same day. The MPPR does not apply to professional component (PC) services. See section 9789.19 for the location of the list of codes subject to the MPPR on diagnostic cardiovascular procedures, by date of service.

(b) For services subject to both the multiple procedure payment reduction and the OPPS cap on imaging, the MPPR shall be applied first, then the reduced amount will be compared with the OPPS cap, and the lower amount shall be used.

Note: Authority: Sections 133, 4603.5, 5307.1 and 5307.3, Labor Code. Reference: Sections 4600, 5307.1 and 5307.11, Labor Code.

History: 1. New section filed 9-24-2013; operative 1-1-2014. Submitted to OAL as a file and print only pursuant to Government Code section 11340.9(g) (Register 2013, No. 39).

Ref.: Herlick Handbook § 1.01[3][b].

§9789.16.1. Surgery — Global Fee.

(a) Global Surgical Package.

A global surgical package refers to a payment policy of bundling payment for the various services associated with a surgical procedure into a single payment covering the operation and these other services.

(1) Definition of a Global Surgical Package. The National Physician Fee Schedule Relative Value File, Global Days column (labeled "Glob Days"), provides the postoperative periods that apply to each surgical procedure. The payment rules for surgical procedures apply to codes with entries of 000, 010, 090. For workers' compensation, the global period will not apply to codes with "YYY".

(A) Codes with "000" in the Global Days column are minor procedures or endoscopies with related preoperative and postoperative relative values on the day of the procedure only included in the fee schedule payment amount; evaluation and management services on the day of the procedure are generally not payable.

(B) Codes with "010" in the Global Days column are minor procedures or endoscopies with preoperative relative values on the day of the procedure and postoperative relative values during a 10 day postoperative period included in the fee schedule amount; evaluation and management services on the day of the procedure and during the 10-day postoperative period generally not payable.

(C) Codes with "090" in the Global Days column are major surgeries with a 1-day preoperative period and 90-day postoperative period included in the fee schedule amount.

(D) Codes with "ZZZ" are surgical codes related to another service and are always included in the global period of the other service. They are add-on codes that are always billed with another service. There is no postoperative work included in the fee schedule payment for the "ZZZ" codes. Payment is made for both the primary and the add-on codes, and the global period assigned is applied to the primary code.

(2) Components of a Global Surgical Package. A global surgical package is applied to all procedures with the appropriate entry in the Global Days column of the National Physician Fee Schedule Relative Value File. The services included in the global surgical package may be furnished in any setting, e.g., in hospitals, ASCs, physicians' offices. Visits to a patient in an intensive care or critical care unit are also included if made by the surgeon. However, critical care services (99291 and 99292) are payable separately in some situations.

The global fee includes payment for the following services related to the surgery when furnished by the physician who performs the surgery:

(A) Preoperative Visits — Preoperative visits after the decision is made to operate beginning with the day before the day of surgery for major procedures and the day of surgery for minor procedures;

(B) Intra-operative Services — Intra-operative services that are normally a usual and necessary part of a surgical procedure;

(C) Complications Following Surgery — All additional medical or surgical services required of the surgeon during the postoperative period of the surgery because of complications which do not require additional trips to the operating room (OR). For the purposes of this section, an operating room is defined as a place of service specifically equipped and staffed for the sole purpose of performing procedures. The term includes a cardiac catheterization suite, a laser suite, and an endoscopy suite. It does not include a patient's room, a minor treatment room, a recovery room, or an intensive care unit (unless the patient's condition was so critical there would be insufficient time for transportation to an OR);

(D) Postoperative Visits — Follow-up visits during the postoperative period of the surgery that are related to recovery from the surgery;

(E) Postsurgical Pain Management — By the surgeon;

(F) Supplies — Except for those identified as exclusions; and

(G) Miscellaneous Services — Items such as dressing changes; local incisional care; removal of operative pack; removal of cutaneous sutures and staples, lines, wires, tubes, drains, casts, and splints; insertion, irrigation and removal of urinary catheters, routine peripheral intravenous lines, nasogastric and rectal tubes; and changes and removal of tracheostomy tubes.

(3) Services Not Included in the Global Surgical Package. The services listed below may be paid for separately:

(A) The initial evaluation of the problem by the surgeon to determine the need for a major surgical procedure. (The initial evaluation is always included in the allowance for a minor surgical procedure and is not separately payable);

(B) Services of other physicians except where the surgeon and the other physician(s) agree on the transfer of care; this agreement may be in the form of a letter or an annotation in the discharge summary, hospital record, or ASC record;

(C) Visits unrelated to the diagnosis for which the surgical procedure is performed, unless the visits occur due to complications of the surgery;

(D) Treatment for the underlying condition or an added course of treatment which is not part of normal recovery from surgery;

(E) Diagnostic tests and procedures, including diagnostic radiological procedures;

(F) Clearly distinct surgical procedures during the postoperative period which are not re-operations or treatment for complications. (A new postoperative period begins with the subsequent procedure.) This includes procedures done in two or more parts for which the decision to stage the procedure is made prospectively or at the time of the first procedure. Examples of this are procedures to diagnose and treat epilepsy (codes 61533, 61534–61536, 61539, 61541, and 61543) which may be performed in succession within 90 days of each other;

(G) Treatment for postoperative complications which requires a return trip to the operating room (OR);

(H) If a less extensive procedure fails, and a more extensive procedure is required, the second procedure is payable separately;

(I) Splints and casting supplies are payable separately;

(J) Immunosuppressive therapy for organ transplants; and

(K) Critical care services (codes 99291 and 99292) unrelated to the surgery where a seriously injured or burned patient is critically ill and requires constant attendance of the physician.

(L) Services that fall within section 9789.16.4 (Primary Treating Physician's Progress Reports, and specified Evaluation and Management visits.)

(4) Minor Surgeries and Endoscopies. Visits by the same physician on the same day as a minor surgery or endoscopy are included in the payment for the procedure, unless a significant, separately identifiable service is also performed. A postoperative period of 10 days applies to some minor surgeries. The postoperative period for these procedures is indicated in the Global Days column of the National Physician Fee Schedule Relative Value File. If the Global Days column entry is "010", no separate payment is allowed for postoperative visits or services within 10 days of the surgery that are related to recovery from the procedure. If a diagnostic biopsy with a 10-day global period precedes a major surgery on the same day or in the 10-day period, the major surgery is payable separately. Services by other physicians are not included in the global fee for a minor procedure except as otherwise excluded. If the Global Days column entry is "000", postoperative visits beyond the day of the procedure are not included in the payment amount for the surgery. Separate payment is made in this instance.

(5) Physicians Furnishing Less Than the Full Global Package. There are occasions when more than one physician provides services included in the global surgical package. It may be the case that the physician who performs the surgical procedure does not furnish the follow-up care. Payment for the postoperative, postdischarge care is split between two or more physicians where the physicians agree on the transfer of care. When more than one physician furnishes services that are included in the global surgical package, the sum of the amount approved for all physicians may not exceed what would have been paid if a single physician provides all services, except where permitted. When either modifier "-54" or "-55" is used, a percentage of the fee schedule is applied as appropriate. The percentages for pre-, intra-, and postoperative care of the total RVUs for major surgical procedures and for minor surgeries with a postoperative period of 10 days may be found in the columns Preoperative Percentage ("Pre Op"), Intraoperative Percentage ("Intra Op"), and Postoperative Percentage ("Post Op"), respectively, of the National Physician Fee Schedule Relative Value File. The intra-operative percentage includes postoperative hospital visits. Split global care does apply to procedures with "000" in the Global Days column of the National Physician Fee Schedule Relative Value File.

(6) Determining the Duration of a Global Period. To determine the global period for major surgeries, count 1 day immediately before the day of surgery, the day of surgery, and the 90 days immediately following the day of surgery. To determine the global period for minor procedures, count the day of surgery and the appropriate number of days (either 0 or 10 days) immediately following the date of surgery.

Note: Authority: Sections 133, 4603.5, 5307.1 and 5307.3, Labor Code. Reference: Sections 4600, 5307.1 and 5307.11, Labor Code.

History: 1. New section filed 9-24-2013; operative 1-1-2014. Submitted to OAL as a file and print only pursuant to Government Code section 11340.9(g) (Register 2013, No. 39).

2. Amendment of subsection (a)(1) filed 3-23-2016; operative 1-1-2016 pursuant to Labor Code section 5307.1(g)(2). Submitted to OAL for filing and printing only pursuant to Labor Code section 5307.1(g)(2) (Register 2016, No. 13).

3. Amendment of subsections (a)(1)(C) and (a)(5) filed 11-6-2018; operative 1-1-2019. Submitted to OAL for filing and printing only pursuant to Government Code section 11340.9(g) (Register 2018, No. 45).

Ref.: Herlick Handbook § 1.01[3][b].

§9789.16.2. Surgery — Billing Requirements for Global Surgeries.

To ensure the proper identification of services that are, or are not, included in the global package, the following procedures apply.

(a) Procedure Codes and Modifiers

Use of the modifiers in this section apply to both major procedures with a 90-day postoperative period and minor procedures with a 10-day postoperative period (and/or a zero day postoperative period in the case of modifiers "-22" and "-25").

(1) Physicians Who Furnish the Entire Global Surgical Package.

Physicians who perform the surgery and furnish all of the usual pre-and postoperative work bill for the global package by entering the appropriate CPT code for the surgical procedure only. Billing is not allowed for visits or other services that are included in the global package.

(2) Physicians in Group Practice.

When different physicians in a group practice participate in the care of the patient, the group bills for the entire global package if the physicians reassign benefits to the group. The physician who performs the surgery is shown as the performing (rendering) physician.

(3) Physicians Who Furnish Part of a Global Surgical Package

Where physicians agree on the transfer of care during the global period, the following modifiers are used:

- "-54" for surgical care only; or
- "-55" for postoperative management only.

Both the bill for the surgical care only and the bill for the postoperative care only, will contain the same date of service and the same surgical procedure code, with the services distinguished by the use of the appropriate modifier.

Physicians need not specify on the claim that care has been transferred. However, the date on which care was relinquished or assumed, as applicable, must be shown on the claim. This should be indicated in the remarks field/free text segment on the claim form/format. Both the surgeon and the physician providing the postoperative care must keep a copy of the written transfer agreement in the beneficiary's medical record.

Where a transfer of postoperative care occurs, the receiving physician cannot bill for any part of the global services until he/she has provided at least one service. Once the physician has seen the patient, that physician may bill for the period beginning with the date on which he/she assumes care of the patient.

EXCEPTIONS:

- Where a transfer of care does not occur, occasional post-discharge services of a physician other than the surgeon are reported by the appropriate evaluation and management code. No modifiers are necessary on the claim.
- If the transfer of care occurs immediately after surgery, the physician other than the surgeon who provides the in-hospital postoperative care bills using subsequent hospital care codes for the inpatient hospital care and the surgical code with the "-55" modifier for the post-discharge care. The surgeon bills the surgery code with the "-54" modifier.
- Physicians who provide follow-up services for minor procedures performed in emergency departments bill the appropriate level of office visit code. The physician who performs the emergency room service bills for the surgical procedure without a modifier.
- If the services of a physician other than the surgeon are required during a postoperative period for an underlying condition or medical complication, the other physician reports the appropriate evaluation and management code. No modifiers are necessary on the claim. An example is a cardiologist who manages underlying cardiovascular conditions of a patient.

(4) Evaluation and Management Service Resulting in the Initial Decision to Perform Surgery.

Evaluation and management services on the day before major surgery or on the day of major surgery that result in the initial decision to perform the surgery are not included in the global surgery payment for the major surgery and, therefore, may be paid separately.

In addition to the CPT evaluation and management code, modifier "-57" (decision for surgery) is used to identify a visit which results in the initial decision to perform surgery.

If evaluation and management services occur on the day of surgery, use modifier "-57," not "-25." The "-57" modifier is not used with minor surgeries because the global period for minor surgeries does not include the day prior to the surgery. Moreover, where the decision to perform the minor procedure is typically done immediately before the service, it is considered a routine preoperative service and a visit is not separately payable in addition to the procedure.

(5) Return Trips to the Operating Room During the Postoperative Period for Treatment of Complications.

When treatment for complications requires a return trip to the operating room, physicians must bill the CPT code that describes the procedure(s) performed during the return trip. If no such code exists, use the unlisted procedure code in the correct series, e.g., 47999 or 64999. The procedure code for the original surgery is not used except when the identical procedure is repeated. In addition to the CPT code, use CPT modifier "-78" for return trips (return to the operating room for a related procedure during a postoperative period).

The physician may also need to indicate that another procedure was performed during the postoperative period of the initial procedure. When this subsequent procedure is related to the first procedure, and requires the use of the operating room, report this circumstance by adding the modifier "78" to the related procedure.

(6) Staged or Related Procedures. Use modifier "-58" for staged or related surgical procedures done during the postoperative period of the first procedure. This modifier is not used to report the treatment of a problem that requires a return to the operating room.

Modifier "-58" is added to the staged procedure when the performance of a procedure or service during the postoperative period was:

(A) Planned prospectively or at the time of the original procedure;

(B) More extensive than the original procedure; or

(C) For therapy following a diagnostic surgical procedure.

A new postoperative period begins when the next procedure in the series is billed.

(7) Unrelated Procedures or Visits During the Postoperative Period.

CPT modifiers "-79" and "-24" are used for visits and other procedures which are furnished during the postoperative period of a surgical procedure, but which are not included in the payment for the surgical procedure.

(A) Modifier "-79" reports an unrelated procedure by the same physician during a postoperative period. A new postoperative period begins with the unrelated procedure.

(B) Modifier "-24" reports an unrelated evaluation and management service by same physician during a postoperative period. Services submitted with the "-24" modifier must be sufficiently documented to establish that the visit was unrelated to the surgery. A diagnosis code that clearly indicates that the reason for the encounter was unrelated to the surgery is acceptable documentation. A physician who is responsible for postoperative care using modifier "-55" should also use modifier "-24" to report any unrelated visits.

(8) Significant Evaluation and Management on the Day of a Procedure. Modifier "-25" is used for evaluation and management services on the day of a procedure for which separate payment may be made. It is used to report a significant, separately identifiable evaluation and management service by the same physician on the day of a procedure. The physician may need to indicate that on the day a procedure or service that is identified with a CPT code was performed, the patient's condition required a significant, separately identifiable evaluation and management service above and beyond the usual preoperative and postoperative care associated with the procedure or service that was performed. This circumstance may be reported by adding the modifier "-25" to the appropriate level of evaluation and management service.

(9) Critical Care. Critical care services provided during a global surgical period for a seriously injured or burned patient are not considered related to a surgical procedure and may be paid separately under the following circumstances. Preoperative and postoperative critical care may be paid in addition to a global fee if:

(A) The patient is critically ill and requires the constant attendance of the physician; and

(B) The critical care is above and beyond, and, in most instances, unrelated to the specific anatomic injury or general surgical procedure performed. Such patients are potentially unstable or have conditions that could pose a significant threat to life or risk of prolonged impairment.

In order for these services to be paid, two reporting requirements must be met:

- Codes 99291/99292 and modifier "-25" (for preoperative care) or "-24" (for postoperative care) must be used; and
- Documentation that the critical care was unrelated to the specific anatomic injury or general surgical procedure performed must be submitted. A diagnosis which clearly indicates that the critical care was unrelated to the surgery, is acceptable documentation.

(10) Unusual Circumstances. Surgeries for which services performed are significantly greater than usually required may be billed with the "-22" modifier added to the CPT code for the procedure. Surgeries for which services performed are significantly less than usually required may be billed with the "-52" modifier. The biller must provide:

- A concise statement about how the service differs from the usual; and
- An operative report with the claim.

Modifier "-22" should only be reported with procedure codes that have a global period of 0, 10, or 90 days. There is no such restriction on the use of modifier "-52."

(b) Date(s) of Service

Physicians, who bill for the entire global surgical package or for only a portion of the care, must enter the date on which the surgical procedure was performed in the "From/To" date of service field. This will enable the claims administrator to relate all appropriate billings to the correct surgery. Physicians who share postoperative management with another physician must submit additional information showing when they assumed and relinquished responsibility for the postoperative care. If the physician who performed the surgery relinquishes care at the time of discharge, he or she need only show the date of surgery when billing with modifier "-54."

However, if the surgeon also cares for the patient for some period following discharge, the surgeon must show the date of surgery and the date on which postoperative care was relinquished to another physician. The physician providing the remaining postoperative care must show the date care was assumed. This information should be shown in Item 19 on the paper Form CMS-1500, or as specified in the ANSI ASC X12N 005010X222A1 Health Care Claim Payment/Advice (837) for electronic claims.

Note: Authority: Sections 133, 4603.5, 5307.1 and 5307.3, Labor Code. Reference: Sections 4600, 5307.1 and 5307.11, Labor Code.

History: 1. New section filed 9-24-2013; operative 1-1-2014. Submitted to OAL as a file and print only pursuant to Government Code section 11340.9(g) (Register 2013, No. 39).

2. Amendment of subsections (a)(7)(B) and (a)(9)(B) filed 3-23-2016; operative 1-1-2016 pursuant to Labor Code section 5307.1(g)(2). Submitted to OAL for filing and printing only pursuant to Labor Code section 5307.1(g)(2) (Register 2016, No. 13).

Ref.: Herlick Handbook § 1.01[3][b].

§9789.16.3. Surgery — Global Fee — Miscellaneous Rules.

(a) Relationship to Correct Coding Initiative (CCI)

The CCI edits allow the claims administrator to detect instances of fragmented billing for certain intra-operative services and other services furnished on the same day as the surgery that are considered to be components of the surgical procedure and, therefore, included in the global surgical fee. When both correct coding and global surgery edits apply to the same claim, the claims administrator shall first apply the correct coding edits, then, apply the global surgery edits to the correctly coded services.

(b) Claims From Physicians Who Furnish Less Than the Global Package (Split Global Care)

(1) For surgeries that are billed with either modifier "-54" or "-55," the claims administrator shall pay the applicable percentage of the fee schedule payment. Columns labeled "Pre Op", "Intra Op" and "Post Op" of the National Physician Fee Schedule Relative Value File, list the percentages for pre-, intra-, and postoperative care of the total RVUs for major surgical procedures and for minor surgeries with a postoperative period of 10 days. The intra-operative percentage includes postoperative hospital visits.

(2) Where more than one physician bills for the postoperative care, the claims administrator will apportion the postoperative percentage according to the number of days each physician was responsible for the patient's care by dividing the postoperative allowed amount by the number of post-op days and that amount is multiplied by the number of days each physician saw the patient.

EXAMPLE

Dr. Jones bills for procedure "42145-54" performed on March 1 and states that he cared for the patient through April 29. Dr. Smith bills for procedure "42145-55" and states that she assumed care of the patient on April 30. The percentage of the total fee amount for the postoperative care for this procedure is determined to be 17 percent and the length of the global period is 90 days. Since Dr. Jones provided postoperative care for the first 60 days, he will receive 66 2/3 percent of the total fee of 17 percent since 60/90 = .6666. Dr. Smith's 30 days of service entitle her to 30/90 or .3333 of the fee.

6666 × .17 = .11333 or 11.3%; and

3338 × .17 = .057 or 5.7%.

Thus, Dr. Jones will be paid at a rate of 11.3 percent (66.7 percent of 17 percent). Dr. Smith will be paid at a rate of 5.7 percent (33.3 percent of 17 percent).

(3) Procedures with a "000" entry in "Glob Days" column have an entry of "0.0000" in the Pre Op, Intra Op and Post Op columns. Split global care does not apply to these procedures.

(c) Payment for Return Trips to the Operating Room for Treatment of Complications

When a CPT code billed with modifier "-78" describes the services involving a return trip to the operating room to deal with complications, the claims administrator shall pay the value of the intra-operative services of the code that describes the treatment of the complications. Refer to the Intra Op column of the National Physician Fee Schedule Relative Value File to determine the percentage of the global package for the intra-operative services. The fee schedule amount is multiplied by this percentage and rounded to the nearest cent.

When a procedure with a "000" global period is billed with a modifier "-78," representing a return trip to the operating room to deal with complications, the claims administrator shall pay the full value for the procedure, since these codes have no pre-, post-, or intra-operative values.

When an unlisted procedure is billed because no code exists to describe the treatment for complications, the claims administrator shall base payment on a maximum of 50 percent of the value of the intra-operative services originally performed. If multiple surgeries were originally performed, the claims administrator shall base payment on no more than 50 percent of the value of the intra-operative services of the surgery for which the complications occurred. The claims administrator shall multiply the fee schedule amount for the original surgery by the intra-operative percentage for the procedure, and then multiply that figure by 50 percent to obtain the maximum payment amount. [.50 X (fee schedule amount × intra-operative percentage)]. Round to the nearest cent.

If additional procedures are performed during the same operative session as the original surgery to treat complications which occurred during the original surgery, the claims administrator shall pay the additional procedures as multiple surgeries. Only surgeries that require a return to the operating room are paid under the complications rules.

If the patient is returned to the operating room after the initial operative session, but on the same day as the original surgery for one or more additional procedures as a result of complications from the original surgery, the complications rules apply to each procedure required to treat the complications from the original surgery. The multiple surgery rules would not also apply.

If the patient is returned to the operating room during the postoperative period of the original surgery, not on the same day of the original surgery, for multiple procedures that are required as a result of complications from the original surgery, the complications rules would apply. The multiple surgery rules would also not apply.

If the patient is returned to the operating room during the postoperative period of the original surgery, not on the same day of the original surgery, for bilateral procedures that are required as a result of complications from the original surgery, the complication rules would apply. The bilateral rules would not apply.

Note: Authority: Sections 133, 4603.5, 5307.1 and 5307.3, Labor Code. Reference: Sections 4600, 5307.1 and 5307.11, Labor Code.

History: 1. New section filed 9-24-2013; operative 1-1-2014. Submitted to OAL as a file and print only pursuant to Government Code section 11340.9(g) (Register 2013, No. 39).

Ref.: Herlick Handbook § 1.01[3][b].

§9789.16.4. Surgery — Global Fee; Exception: Circumstances Allowing E&M Code During the Global Period; Primary Treating Physician's Progress Report (PR-2).

(a) Notwithstanding sections 9789.16.2 - 9789.16.3, where a surgical code is subject to a global period, the provider may separately bill an E&M service during the global period in the following circumstance.

The provider may bill one or more evaluation and management codes for medically necessary services that exceed the number of visits that are listed for the global surgical code in the Medicare Physician Fee Schedule's "Physician Time File". See section 9789.19 for the Physician Time File, by date of service.

Calculation shall be made as follows: For the surgical procedure subject to the global days, add the number of visits for all E&M services shown on that row in the Physician Time File. Round up if the total number of visits includes a half visit. If the physician provides E&M services in excess of the total number of E&M visits shown for the surgical code, medically necessary E&M services in excess of that number may be separately billed.

(b) The Primary Treating Physician's Progress reports (PR-2 or the equivalent allowed by section 9785) are separately reimbursable even if the change in the patient's condition or treatment warranting a progress report occurs during the surgical global follow-up period.

Note: Authority: Sections 133, 4603.5, 5307.1 and 5307.3, Labor Code. Reference: Sections 4600, 5307.1 and 5307.11, Labor Code.

History: 1. New section filed 9-24-2013; operative 1-1-2014. Submitted to OAL as a file and print only pursuant to Government Code section 11340.9(g) (Register 2013, No. 39).

Ref.: Herlick Handbook § 1.01[3][b].

§9789.16.5. Surgery — Multiple Surgeries and Endoscopies.

(a) General

Multiple surgeries are separate procedures performed by a single physician or physicians in the same group practice on the same patient at the same operative session or on the same day for which separate payment may be allowed. Co-surgeons, surgical teams, or assistants-at-surgery may participate in performing multiple surgeries on the same patient on the same day.

Multiple surgeries are distinguished from procedures that are components of or incidental to a primary procedure. These intra-operative services, incidental surgeries, or components of more major surgeries are not separately billable.

(b) Billing Instructions

The following procedures apply when billing for multiple surgeries by the same physician on the same day.

- Report the more major surgical procedure without the multiple procedures modifier "-51."

- Report additional surgical procedures performed by the surgeon on the same day with modifier "-51."

There may be instances in which two or more physicians each perform distinctly different, unrelated surgeries on the same patient on the same day (e.g., in some multiple trauma cases). When this occurs, the payment adjustment rules for multiple surgeries may not be appropriate. In such cases, the physician does not use modifier "-51" unless one of the surgeons individually performs multiple surgeries.

(c) Determining Maximum Payment for Multiple Surgeries

The Multiple Procedure ("Mult Proc") column of the National Physician Fee Schedule Relative Value File contains a "2" to indicate procedures that are subject to the surgery multiple procedure payment reduction.

If a procedure is performed on the same day as another procedure, base the payment on the lower of (a) the actual charge, or (b) the fee schedule amount for the procedure reduced by the applicable percentage.

Rank the procedures subject to the multiple surgery rule (indicator "2") in descending order by fee schedule amount and apply the appropriate reduction to this code:

(A) 100 percent of the fee schedule amount for the highest valued procedure; and

(B) 50 percent of the fee schedule amount for the second through the fifth highest valued procedures; or

(C) if more than five procedures with indicator "2" are billed, pay for the first five according to (A) and (B) above and pay "by report" for the sixth and subsequent procedures. Payment determined on a "by report" basis should never be lower than 50 percent of the full payment amount. Pay by the unit for services that are already reduced (e.g. 17003).

In cases of multiple interventional radiological procedures, both the radiology code and the primary surgical code are paid at 100 percent of the fee schedule amount. The subsequent surgical procedures are paid at the standard multiple surgical percentages (50 percent, 50 percent, 50 percent and 50 percent).

(d) Determining Maximum Payment for Endoscopies

Endoscopy

The Multiple Procedure ("Mult Proc") column of the National Physician Fee Schedule Relative Value File contains a "3" to indicate procedures that are subject to special rules for multiple endoscopic procedures. For each endoscopic procedure with an indicator of "3", the Endoscopic Base Code ("Endo Base") column indicates the related base endoscopy code. Those codes that share a base code are in the same "family" and are "related."

Two codes billed: Endoscopic procedure and related base endoscopic procedure billed

If an endoscopic procedure is reported with only its base procedure, the base procedure is not separately payable. Payment for the base procedure is included in the payment for the other endoscopy.

Multiple Related Endoscopic procedures billed

If Multiple Procedure column contains an indicator of "3," and multiple endoscopies are billed, pay the full value of the highest valued endoscopy, plus the difference between the next highest and the base endoscopy. Access the Endo Base column to determine the base endoscopy.

EXAMPLE [dollar amounts are for illustration only]

In the course of performing a fiber optic colonoscopy (CPT code 45378), a physician performs a biopsy on a lesion (code 45380) and removes a polyp (code 45385) from a different part of the colon. The physician bills for codes 45380 and 45385. The value of codes 45380 and 45385 have the value of the diagnostic colonoscopy (45378) built in. Rather than paying 100 percent for the highest valued procedure (45385) and 50 percent for the next (45380), pay the full value of the higher valued endoscopy (45385), plus the difference between the next highest endoscopy (45380) and the base endoscopy (45378).

Assume the following fee schedule amounts for these codes:

45378 — $255.40
45380 — $285.98
45385 — $374.56

Pay the full value of 45385 ($374.56), plus the difference between 45380 and 45378 ($30.58), for a total of $405.14.

Multiple Related and Unrelated Endoscopies or Other Surgical Procedures Billed

Apply the following rules where endoscopies are performed on the same day as unrelated endoscopies or other surgical procedures:

- Two unrelated endoscopies (e.g., 46606 and 43217): Apply the usual multiple surgery rules;

- Two sets of unrelated endoscopies (e.g., 43202 and 43217; 46606 and 46608): Apply the special endoscopy rules to each series and then apply the multiple surgery rules. Consider the total payment for each set of endoscopies as one service;

- Two related endoscopies and a third, unrelated procedure: Apply the special endoscopic rules to the related endoscopies, and, then apply the multiple surgery rules. Consider the total payment for the related endoscopies as one service and the unrelated endoscopy as another service.

(e) Multiple Procedures of Equal Value

If two or more multiple surgeries are of equal value, rank them in descending dollar order billed and base payment on the percentages listed above (i.e., 100 percent for the first billed procedure, 50 percent for the second, etc.)

(f) Multiple Procedures Including Bilateral Surgeries

If any of the multiple surgeries are bilateral surgeries, consider the bilateral procedure at 150 percent as one payment amount, rank this with the remaining procedures, and apply the appropriate multiple surgery reductions.

(g) Multiple Surgical Procedures and Multiple Interventional Radiological Procedures

In cases of multiple interventional radiological procedures, both the radiology code and the primary surgical code are paid at 100 percent of the fee schedule amount. The subsequent surgical procedures are paid at the standard multiple surgical percentages (50 percent, 50 percent, 50 percent and 50 percent.)

(h) Ranking of Same Day Multiple Surgeries When One Surgery Has a "-22" Modifier and Additional Payment is Allowed

If the patient returns to the operating room after the initial operative session on the same day as a result of complications from the original surgery, the complications rules apply to each procedure required to treat the complications from the original surgery. The multiple surgery rules would not apply.

However, if the patient is returned to the operating room during the postoperative period of the original surgery, not on the same day of the original surgery, for multiple procedures that are required as a result of complications from the original surgery, the complications rules would apply. The multiple surgery rules would also not apply.

Multiple surgeries are defined as separate procedures performed by a single physician or physicians in the same group practice on the same patient at the same operative session or on the same day for which separate payment may be allowed. Co-surgeons, surgical teams, or assistants-at-surgery may participate in performing multiple surgeries on the same patient on the same day.

Multiple surgeries are distinguished from procedures that are components of or incidental to a primary procedure. These intra-operative services, incidental surgeries, or components of more major surgeries are not separately billable.

Note: Authority: Sections 133, 4603.5, 5307.1 and 5307.3, Labor Code. Reference: Sections 4600, 5307.1 and 5307.11, Labor Code.

History: 1. New section filed 9-24-2013; operative 1-1-2014. Submitted to OAL as a file and print only pursuant to Government Code section 11340.9(g) (Register 2013, No. 39).

Ref.: Herlick Handbook § 1.01[3][b].

§9789.16.6. Surgery — Bilateral Surgeries.

(a) Bilateral surgeries are procedures performed on both sides of the body during the same operative session or on the same day.

The terminology for some procedure codes includes the terms "bilateral" (e.g., code 27395; Lengthening of the hamstring tendon; multiple, bilateral) or "unilateral or bilateral" (e.g., code 52290; cystourethroscopy; with ureteral meatotomy, unilateral or bilateral). The payment adjustment rules for bilateral surgeries do not apply to procedures identified by CPT as "bilateral" or "unilateral or bilateral" since the fee schedule reflects any additional work required for bilateral surgeries. The Bilateral Surgery ("Bilat Surg") column of the National Physician Fee Schedule Relative Value File indicates whether the bilateral payment adjustment rules apply to a surgical procedure.

(b) Billing Instructions for Bilateral Surgeries

(1) If a procedure is not identified by its terminology as a bilateral procedure (or unilateral or bilateral), report the procedure with modifier "-50." (NOTE: This differs from the CPT coding guidelines which indicate that bilateral procedures should be billed as two line items.)

If a procedure is identified by the terminology as bilateral (or unilateral or bilateral), as in codes 27395 and 52290, do not report the procedure with modifier "-50".

(A) If the Bilateral Surgery column of the National Physician Fee Schedule Relative Value File contains an indicator of "0," "2," or "3," the payment adjustment rules for bilateral surgeries do not apply. Payment is determined by the lower of the billed amount or 100 percent of the fee schedule amount unless other payment adjustment rules apply.

Note: Some codes which have a bilateral indicator of "0" in the Bilateral Surgery column may be performed more than once on a given day. These are services that would never be considered bilateral and thus should not be billed with modifier "-50." Where such a code is billed on multiple line items or with more than 1 in the units field and the claims administrator has determined that the code may be reported more than once, bypass the "0" bilateral indicator and refer to the multiple surgery field for pricing.

(B) If Bilateral Surgery column of the National Physician Fee Schedule Relative Value File contains an indicator of "1," the standard payment adjustment for bilateral procedures apply. Payment is determined by the lower of the billed amount or 150 percent of the fee schedule amount. (Multiply the payment amount for the surgery by 150 percent.)

(c) The global surgery rules are applicable to bilateral procedures.

Note: Authority: Sections 133, 4603.5, 5307.1 and 5307.3, Labor Code. Reference: Sections 4600, 5307.1 and 5307.11, Labor Code.

History: 1. New section filed 9-24-2013; operative 1-1-2014. Submitted to OAL as a file and print only pursuant to Government Code section 11340.9(g) (Register 2013, No. 39).

Ref.: Herlick Handbook § 1.01[3][b].

§9789.16.7. Surgery — Co-Surgeons and Team Surgeons.

(a) General

Under some circumstances, the individual skills of two or more surgeons are required to perform surgery on the same patient during the same operative session. This may be required because of the complex nature of the procedure(s) and/or the patient's condition. In these cases, the additional physicians are not acting as assistants-at-surgery.

(b) Billing Instructions/Determination of Maximum Payment

The following billing procedures apply when billing for a surgical procedure or procedures that required the use of two surgeons or a team of surgeons:

(1) If two surgeons (each in a different specialty) are required to perform a specific procedure, each surgeon bills for the procedure with a modifier "-62." Co-surgery also refers to surgical procedures involving two surgeons performing the parts of the procedure simultaneously, i.e., heart transplant or bilateral knee replacements. Documentation of the medical necessity for two surgeons is required for certain services identified in the Co-Surgeons ("Co Surg") column of the National Physician Fee Schedule Relative Value File. If the surgery is billed with a "-62"

modifier and the Co-Surgeons column contains an indicator of "1," any documentation submitted with the claim should be reviewed to identify support for the need for co-surgeons. If the documentation supports the need for co-surgeons, base payment for each physician on the lower of the billed amount or 62.5 percent of the fee schedule amount. If the surgery is billed with a "-62" modifier and the Co-Surgeons column contains an indicator of "2," payment rules for two surgeons apply. The claims administrator shall base payment for each physician on the lower of the billed amount or 62.5 percent of the fee schedule amount. If the surgery is billed with a "-62" modifier and the Co-Surgeons column contains an indicator of "0," payment for co-surgeons is not allowed.

(2) If a team of surgeons (more than 2 surgeons of different specialties) is required to perform a specific procedure, each surgeon bills for the procedure with a modifier "-66." The Team Surgery ("Team Surg") column of the National Physician Fee Schedule Relative Value File identifies certain services submitted with a "-66" modifier which must be sufficiently documented to establish that a team was medically necessary.

If the surgery is billed with a "-66" modifier and the Team Surgery column contains an indicator of "1," the claim should be reviewed to identify support for the need for a team of surgeons. If the claims administrator determines that team surgeons were medically necessary, each physician is paid on a "by report" basis.

If the surgery is billed with a "-66" modifier and the Team Surgery column contains an indicator of "2," the claims administrator shall pay "by report".

All claims for team surgeons must contain sufficient information to allow pricing "by report."

(3) If surgeons of different specialties are each performing a different procedure (with specific CPT codes), neither co-surgery nor multiple surgery rules apply (even if the procedures are performed through the same incision). If one of the surgeons performs multiple procedures, the multiple procedure rules apply to that surgeon's services.

(4) For co-surgeons (modifier 62), the fee schedule amount applicable to the payment for each co-surgeon is 62.5 percent of the global surgery fee schedule amount. Team surgery (modifier 66) is paid for on a "By Report" basis.

Note: A fee may have been established for some surgical procedures that are billed with the "-66" modifier. In these cases, all physicians on the team must agree on the percentage of the payment amount each is to receive. If the claims administrator receives a bill with a "-66" modifier after the claims administrator has paid one surgeon the full payment amount (on a bill without the modifier), deny the subsequent claim.

(5) Apply the rules relating to global surgical packages to each of the physicians participating in a co-or team surgery.

Note: Authority: Sections 133, 4603.5, 5307.1 and 5307.3, Labor Code. Reference: Sections 4600, 5307.1 and 5307.11, Labor Code.

History: 1. New section filed 9-24-2013; operative 1-1-2014. Submitted to OAL as a file and print only pursuant to Government Code section 11340.9(g) (Register 2013, No. 39).

2. Amendment of subsection (b)(1) filed 11-6-2018; operative 1-1-2019. Submitted to OAL for filing and printing only pursuant to Government Code section 11340.9(g) (Register 2018, No. 45).

Ref.: Herlick Handbook § 1.01[3][b].

§9789.16.8. Surgery — Assistants–at–Surgery.

For assistant-at-surgery services performed by physicians, the fee schedule amount equals 16 percent of the amount otherwise applicable for the surgical payment.

Procedures billed with the assistant-at-surgery physician modifiers -80, -81, -82, or the AS modifier for physician assistants, nurse practitioners and clinical nurse specialists, are subject to the assistant-at-surgery policy.

If the Assistant at Surgery ("Asst Surg") column of the National Physician Fee Schedule Relative Value File contains an indicator of "0" the physician or non-physician practitioner must submit documentation to establish medical necessity for use of an assistant at surgery. If the Assistant at Surgery column contains an indicator of "1", assistant-at-surgery is not payable. If the Assistant at Surgery column contains indicator "2", the assistant at surgery may be paid.

Payment is not generally allowed for an assistant surgeon when payment for either two surgeons (modifier "-62") or team surgeons (modifier "-66") is appropriate.

Note: Authority: Sections 133, 4603.5, 5307.1 and 5307.3, Labor Code. Reference: Sections 4600, 5307.1 and 5307.11, Labor Code.

History: 1. New section filed 9-24-2013; operative 1-1-2014. Submitted to OAL as a file and print only pursuant to Government Code section 11340.9(g) (Register 2013, No. 39).

Ref.: Herlick Handbook § 1.01[3][b].

§9789.17.1. Radiology Diagnostic Imaging Multiple Procedures.

(a) Specified diagnostic imaging procedures are designated in the "Diagnostic Imaging Service Subject to the Multiple Procedure Payment Reduction (MPPR)" file of the CMS Physician Fee Schedule final rule, and in the CMS National Physician Fee Schedule Relative Value excel file, to indicate that the Multiple Procedure Payment Reduction (MPPR) shall be applied to the professional component (PC) and technical component (TC) of the procedure, when multiple services are furnished to the same patient, in the same session, on the same day, by one or more physicians in the same group practice. The MPPR shall apply to both PC-only services, TC-only services, and to the PC and TC of global services. If the procedure is reported in the same session, on the same day, and furnished to the same patient, by one or more physicians in the same group practice (same Group National Provider Identifier (NPI)), the maximum reimbursement shall be determined as follows:

(1) Full payment is made for each PC and TC with the highest payment under the physician fee schedule.

(2)(A) For services rendered prior to March 1, 2017 payment is made at 75 percent for subsequent PC services furnished to the same patient, in the same session, on the same day, by one or more physicians in the same group practice (NPI).

(B) For services rendered on or after March 1, 2017, payment is made at 95 percent for subsequent PC services furnished to the same patient, in the same session, on the same day, by one or more physicians in the same group practice (NPI).

(3) Payment is made at 50 percent for subsequent TC services furnished to the same patient, in the same session, on the same day, by one or more physicians in the same group practice (NPI).

(4) The individual PC and TC services with the highest payments under the physician fee schedule of globally billed services must be determined in order to calculate the MPPR.

(b) See section 9789.19 for the diagnostic imaging procedures subject to the radiology diagnostic imaging multiple procedures discount, description of the diagnostic imaging family indicators, and diagnostic imaging family indicators for procedure, by date of service.

Note: Authority: Sections 133, 4603.5, 5307.1 and 5307.3, Labor Code. Reference: Sections 4600, 5307.1 and 5307.11, Labor Code

History: 1. New section filed 9-24-2013; operative 1-1-2014. Submitted to OAL as a file and print only pursuant to Government Code section 11340.9(g) (Register 2013, No. 39).

2. Amendment of subsection (a) filed 3-23-2016; operative 1-1-2016 pursuant to Labor Code section 5307.1(g)(2). Submitted to OAL for filing and printing only pursuant to Labor Code section 5307.1(g)(2) (Register 2016, No. 13).

3. Redesignation and amendment of subsection (a)(2) as new subsection (a)(2)(A) and new subsection (a)(2)(B) filed 7-18-2017; operative 3-1-2017. Submitted to OAL as a file and print only pursuant to Labor Code section 5307.1(g)(2) (Register 2017, No. 29).

Ref.: Herlick Handbook § 1.01[3][b].

§9789.17.2. Radiology Consultations.

(a)(1) Only one interpretation of an x ray procedure shall be reimbursed. This interpretation of an x-ray procedure must directly contribute to the diagnosis and treatment of the patient. The physician must prepare a signed written report of his or her interpretation of the results of the x-ray. The professional component of the x-ray procedure shall be paid using modifier -26. A professional component billing based on a review of the findings of these x-ray procedures, without a complete written report similar to that which would be prepared by a specialist in the field, does not meet the conditions for separate payment of the service.

(2) Reimbursement for a second interpretation shall only be allowed under unusual circumstances (for which documentation is provided), such as a questionable finding for which the physician performing the initial interpretation believes another physician's expertise is needed or a changed diagnosis resulting from a second interpretation of the results of the procedure. This second interpretation shall be identified through the use of modifier "-77".

(b) Do not use CPT 76140 (consultation on X-ray examination made elsewhere, written report).

Note: Authority: Sections 133, 4603.5, 5307.1 and 5307.3, Labor Code. Reference: Sections 4600, 5307.1 and 5307.11, Labor Code.

History: 1. New section filed 9-24-2013; operative 1-1-2014. Submitted to OAL as a file and print only pursuant to Government Code section 11340.9(g) (Register 2013, No. 39).

Ref.: Herlick Handbook § 1.01[3][b].

§9789.17.3. Additional Payment Reductions for Certain Diagnostic Imaging Services.

(a) For services rendered on or after March 1, 2017, payment of X-ray imaging services that are taken using film is made at:

(1) 80 percent of a technical component-only service;

(2) 80 percent of the technical component of a global service.

Services for X-rays using film must be identified through the use of modifier "FX." For services subject to both the multiple procedure payment reduction (MPPR) set forth in section 9789.17.1, and the "FX" modifier reduction on imaging, the "FX" modifier reduction should be applied before the MPPR for radiology diagnostic imaging procedures.

(b) For services rendered on or after January 1, 2018, payment for imaging services that are X-rays taken using computed radiography is made at:

(1) 93 percent of a technical component-only service;

(2) 93 percent of the technical component of a global service.

Imaging services that are X-rays taken using computed radiography must be identified through the use of the modifier "FY." For services subject to both the multiple procedure payment reduction (MPPR) set forth in section 9789.17.1, and the "FY" modifier reduction on imaging, the "FY" modifier reduction should be applied before the MPPR for radiology diagnostic imaging procedures. Computed radiography technology is defined for purposes of this subdivision as cassette-based imaging which utilizes an imaging plate to create the image involved.

Note: Authority: Sections 133, 4603.5, 5307.1 and 5307.3, Labor Code. Reference: Sections 4600, 5307.1 and 5307.11, Labor Code.

History: 1. New section filed 7-18-2017; operative 3-1-2017. Submitted to OAL as a file and print only pursuant to Labor Code section 5307.1(g)(2) (Register 2017, No. 29).

2. Designation of first paragraph as subsection (a) and new subsection (b) filed 12-28-2017; operative 1-1-2018. Submitted to OAL for filing and printing only pursuant to Labor Code section 5307-1(g)(2) (Register 2017, No. 52).

§9789.18.1. Payment for Anesthesia Services — General Payment Rule.

(a) For dates of service on or after January 1, 2014, but before January 1, 2019:

The fee schedule amount for physician anesthesia services is, with the exceptions noted, based on allowable base and time units multiplied by an anesthesia conversion factor and statewide anesthesia GAF.

The maximum reasonable fee for physician and non-physician practitioner anesthesia services shall be calculated as follows:

[Base Unit + Time Unit] * CF * Statewide Anesthesia GAF = Base Maximum Fee

The base maximum fee for the procedure code is the maximum reasonable fee, except as otherwise provided by applicable provisions of this fee schedule, including but not limited to the application of ground rules and modifiers that affect reimbursement.

(1) Base Unit: The base unit for each anesthesia procedure is listed in a file entitled "Anesthesia Base Units by CPT Code," which is adopted and incorporated by reference. See Section 9789.19 for reference to the "Anesthesia Base Units by CPT Code" file, by date of service.

(2) Time Units: The way in which time units are to be calculated is set forth in Section 9789.18.8.

(3) Anesthesia Conversion Factor and Statewide Anesthesia GAF: See Section 9789.19 for the anesthesia conversion factor and statewide anesthesia GAF, by date of service.

(b) For dates of service on or after January 1, 2019:

The fee schedule amount for physician anesthesia services is, with the exceptions noted, based on allowable base and time units multiplied by an anesthesia conversion factor adjusted by the anesthesia shares and Geographic Practice Cost Index (GPCIs) specific to a locality where the service was provided.

The maximum reasonable fee for physician and nonphysician practitioner anesthesia services shall be calculated as follows:

[Base Unit + Time Unit] * Adjusted CF by locality = Base Maximum Fee

The base maximum fee for the procedure code is the maximum reasonable fee, except as otherwise provided by applicable provisions of this fee schedule, including but not limited to the application of ground rules and modifiers that affect reimbursement.

(1) Base Unit: The base unit for each anesthesia procedure is listed in a file entitled "Anesthesia Base Units by CPT Code", which is adopted and incorporated by reference. See Section 9789.19 for reference to the "Anesthesia Base Units by CPT Code" file, by date of service.

(2) Time Units: The way in which time units are to be calculated is set forth in Section 9789.18.8.

(3) Adjusted Anesthesia Conversion Factor is set forth in 9789.19.1, Table A applicable to the date of service.

The adjusted conversion factor for the locality corresponding to the county where the service is provided, is determined as follows:

[(Work GPCI by locality * Anesthesia Work Share) + (Practice Expense GPCI by locality * Anesthesia Practice Expense Share) + (Malpractice GPCI by locality * Anesthesia Malpractice Share)] * Anesthesia Conversion Factor].

The appropriate payment locality will be determined according to subdivision (e)(2) of section 9789.12.2.

Note: Authority: Sections 133, 4603.5, 5307.1 and 5307.3, Labor Code. Reference: Sections 4600, 5307.1 and 5307.11, Labor Code.

History: 1. New section filed 9-24-2013; operative 1-1-2014. Submitted to OAL as a file and print only pursuant to Government Code section 11340.9(g) (Register 2013, No. 39).

2. Amendment filed 11-6-2018; operative 1-1-2019. Submitted to OAL for filing and printing only pursuant to Government Code section 11340.9(g) (Register 2018, No. 45).

Ref.: Herlick Handbook § 1.01[3][b].

§9789.18.2. Anesthesia — Personally Performed Rate.

The anesthesia fee calculation will recognize the base unit for the anesthesia code and time units as calculated in accordance with section 9789.18.8 in any of the following circumstances:

(a) The physician personally performed the entire anesthesia service alone;

(b) The physician is involved with one anesthesia case with a resident and the physician is a teaching physician. A teaching physician is a physician (other than another resident) who involves residents in the care of his or her patients. The teaching physician must document in the medical records that he/she was present during all critical (or key) portions of the procedure. The teaching physician's physical presence during only the preoperative or postoperative visits with the patient is not sufficient;

(c) The physician is involved in the training of physician residents in a single anesthesia case, two concurrent anesthesia cases involving residents or a single anesthesia case involving a resident that is concurrent to another case paid under the medical direction rules. The teaching anesthesiologist, or different anesthesiologists in the same anesthesia group, must be present during all critical or key portions of the anesthesia service or procedure involved. The teaching anesthesiologist (or another anesthesiologist with whom the teaching physician has entered into an arrangement) must be immediately available to furnish anesthesia services during the entire procedure. The documentation in the patient's medical records must indicate the teaching physician's presence during all critical or key portions of the anesthesia procedure and the immediate availability of another teaching anesthesiologist as necessary;

(d) The physician is continuously involved in a single case involving a student nurse anesthetist;

(e) The physician is continuously involved in one anesthesia case involving a CRNA (or AA). If the physician is involved with a single case with a CRNA (or AA) the physician service and the CRNA (or AA) service may be paid in accordance with the medical direction payment policy; or

(f) The physician and the CRNA (or AA) are involved in one anesthesia case and the services of each are found to be medically necessary. Documentation must be submitted by both the CRNA and the physician to support payment of the full fee for each of the two providers. The physician reports the "AA" modifier and the CRNA reports the "QZ" modifier for a nonmedically directed case.

Note: Authority: Sections 133, 4603.5, 5307.1 and 5307.3, Labor Code. Reference: Sections 4600, 5307.1 and 5307.11, Labor Code.

History: 1. New section filed 9-24-2013; operative 1-1-2014. Submitted to OAL as a file and print only pursuant to Government Code section 11340.9(g) (Register 2013, No. 39).

2. Amendment of first paragraph filed 11-6-2018; operative 1-1-2019. Submitted to OAL for filing and printing only pursuant to Government Code section 11340.9(g) (Register 2018, No. 45).

Ref.: Herlick Handbook § 1.01[3][b].

§9789.18.3. Anesthesia — Medically Directed Rate.

(a) Payment for the physician's medical direction service is determined on the basis of 50 percent of the allowance for the service performed by the physician alone. Medical direction occurs if the physician medically directs qualified individuals (all of whom could be CRNAs, AAs, interns, residents, or combinations of these individuals) in two, three, or four concurrent cases and the physician performs all the following activities:

(1) Performs a pre-anesthetic examination and evaluation;

(2) Prescribes the anesthesia plan;

(3) Personally participates in the most demanding procedures in the anesthesia plan, including, if applicable, induction and emergence;

(4) Ensures that any procedures in the anesthesia plan that he or she does not perform are performed by a qualified anesthetist;

(5) Monitors the course of anesthesia administration at frequent intervals;

(6) Remains physically present and available for immediate diagnosis and treatment of emergencies; and

(7) Provides indicated-post-anesthesia care.

(b) The physician must participate only in the most demanding procedures of the anesthesia plan, including, if applicable, induction and emergence. The physician must document in the medical record that he or she performed the pre-anesthetic examination and evaluation. Physicians must also document that they provided indicated post-anesthesia care, were present during some portion of the anesthesia monitoring, and were present during the most demanding procedures, including induction and emergence, where indicated.

(c) The physician can medically direct two, three, or four concurrent procedures involving qualified individuals, all of whom could be CRNAs, AAs, interns, residents or combinations of these individuals. The medical direction rules apply to cases involving student nurse anesthetists if the physician directs two concurrent cases, each of which involves a student nurse anesthetist, or the physician directs one case involving a student nurse anesthetist and another involving a CRNA, AA, intern or resident.

(d) The medical direction rules do not apply to a single resident case that is concurrent to another anesthesia case paid under the medical direction rules or to two concurrent anesthesia cases involving residents.

(e) If anesthesiologists are in a group practice, one physician member may provide the pre-anesthesia examination and evaluation while another fulfills the other criteria. Similarly, one physician member of the group may provide post-anesthesia care while another member of the group furnishes the other component parts of the anesthesia service. However, the medical record must indicate that the services were furnished by physicians and identify the physicians who furnished them.

(f) A physician who is concurrently directing the administration of anesthesia to not more than four surgical patients cannot ordinarily be involved in furnishing additional services to other patients. However, addressing an emergency of short duration in the immediate area, administering an epidural or caudal anesthetic to ease labor pain, or periodic, rather than continuous, monitoring of an obstetrical patient does not substantially diminish the scope of control exercised by the physician in directing the administration of anesthesia to surgical patients. It does not constitute a separate service for the purpose of determining whether the medical direction criteria are met. Further, while directing concurrent anesthesia procedures, a physician may receive patients entering the operating suite for the next surgery, check or discharge patients in the recovery room, or handle scheduling matters without affecting fee schedule payment. However, if the physician leaves the immediate area of the operating suite for other than short durations or devotes extensive time to an emergency case or is otherwise not available to respond to the immediate needs of the surgical patients, the physician's services to the surgical patients are supervisory in nature. See section 9789.18.4 for a definition of concurrent anesthesia procedures.

Note: Authority: Sections 133, 4603.5, 5307.1 and 5307.3, Labor Code. Reference: Sections 4600, 5307.1 and 5307.11, Labor Code.

History: 1. New section filed 9-24-2013; operative 1-1-2014. Submitted to OAL as a file and print only pursuant to Government Code section 11340.9(g) (Register 2013, No. 39).

2. Amendment of subsections (a) and (a)(3) filed 11-6-2018; operative 1-1-2019. Submitted to OAL for filing and printing only pursuant to Government Code section 11340.9(g) (Register 2018, No. 45).

Ref.: Herlick Handbook § 1.01[3][b].

§9789.18.4. Anesthesia — Definition of Concurrent Medically Directed Anesthesia Procedures.

Concurrency is defined with regard to the maximum number of procedures that the physician is medically directing within the context of a single procedure and whether these other procedures overlap each other.

Note: Authority: Sections 133, 4603.5, 5307.1 and 5307.3, Labor Code. Reference: Sections 4600, 5307.1 and 5307.11, Labor Code.

History: 1. New section filed 9-24-2013; operative 1-1-2014. Submitted to OAL as a file and print only pursuant to Government Code section 11340.9(g) (Register 2013, No. 39).

Ref.: Herlick Handbook § 1.01[3][b].

§9789.18.5. Anesthesia — Medically Supervised Rate.

Only three base units per procedure is allowed when the anesthesiologist is involved in furnishing more than four procedures concurrently or is performing other services while directing the concurrent procedures. An additional time unit may be recognized if the physician can document he or she was present at induction.

Note: Authority: Sections 133, 4603.5, 5307.1 and 5307.3, Labor Code. Reference: Sections 4600, 5307.1 and 5307.11, Labor Code.

History: 1. New section filed 9-24-2013; operative 1-1-2014. Submitted to OAL as a file and print only pursuant to Government Code section 11340.9(g) (Register 2013, No. 39).

Ref.: Herlick Handbook § 1.01[3][b].

§9789.18.6. Anesthesia — Multiple Anesthesia Procedures.

(a) Physicians and non-physician practitioners shall bill for the anesthesia services associated with multiple bilateral surgeries by reporting the anesthesia procedure with the highest base unit value with the multiple procedure modifier "-51." The total time for all procedures shall be reported in the line item with the highest base unit value.

(b) If the same anesthesia CPT code applies to two or more of the surgical procedures, billers enter the anesthesia code with the "-51" modifier and the number of surgeries to which the modified CPT code applies.

(c) Payment can be made under the fee schedule for anesthesia services associated with multiple surgical procedures or multiple bilateral procedures. The maximum fee is determined based on the base unit of the anesthesia procedure with the highest base unit value and time units based on the actual anesthesia time of the multiple procedures.

Note: Authority: Sections 133, 4603.5, 5307.1 and 5307.3, Labor Code. Reference: Sections 4600, 5307.1 and 5307.11, Labor Code.

History: 1. New section filed 9-24-2013; operative 1-1-2014. Submitted to OAL as a file and print only pursuant to Government Code section 11340.9(g) (Register 2013, No. 39).

Ref.: Herlick Handbook § 1.01[3][b].

§9789.18.7. Anesthesia — Medical and Surgical Services Furnished in Addition to Anesthesia Procedure.

Payment may be made under the fee schedule for specific medical and surgical services furnished by the anesthesiologist as long as these services are reasonable and medically necessary and provided that other rebundling and ground rule provisions do not preclude separate payment. These services may be furnished in conjunction with the anesthesia procedure to the patient or may be furnished as single services, e.g., during the day of or the day before the anesthesia service. These services include the insertion of a Swan Ganz catheter, the insertion of central venous pressure lines, emergency intubation, and critical care visits.

Note: Authority: Sections 133, 4603.5, 5307.1 and 5307.3, Labor Code. Reference: Sections 4600, 5307.1 and 5307.11, Labor Code.

History: 1. New section filed 9-24-2013; operative 1-1-2014. Submitted to OAL as a file and print only pursuant to Government Code section 11340.9(g) (Register 2013, No. 39).

Ref.: Herlick Handbook § 1.01[3][b].

§9789.18.8. Anesthesia — Time and Calculation of Anesthesia Time Units.

(a) Anesthesia time is defined as the period during which an anesthesia practitioner is present with the patient. It starts when the anesthesia practitioner begins to prepare the patient for anesthesia services in the operating room or an equivalent area and ends when the anesthesia practitioner is no longer furnishing anesthesia services to the patient, that is, when the patient may be placed safely under postoperative care. Anesthesia time is a continuous time period from the start of anesthesia to the end of an anesthesia service. In counting anesthesia time, the anesthesia practitioner can add blocks of time around an interruption in anesthesia time as long as the anesthesia practitioner is furnishing continuous anesthesia care within the time periods around the interruption.

(b) Time units are computed by dividing the actual reported anesthesia time by 15 minutes. Round the time unit to one decimal place.

(c) Time units are not allowed for CPT code 01996.

For purposes of this section, "anesthesia practitioner" means a physician who performs the anesthesia service alone, a CRNA who is not medically directed, or a CRNA or AA, who is medically directed. The physician who medically directs the CRNA or AA would ordinarily report the same time as the CRNA or AA reports for the CRNA service.

Note: Authority: Sections 133, 4603.5, 5307.1 and 5307.3, Labor Code. Reference: Sections 4600, 5307.1 and 5307.11, Labor Code.

History: 1. New section filed 9-24-2013; operative 1-1-2014. Submitted to OAL as a file and print only pursuant to Government Code section 11340.9(g) (Register 2013, No. 39).

Ref.: Herlick Handbook § 1.01[3][b].

§9789.18.9. Anesthesia — Base Unit Reduction for Concurrent Medically Directed Procedures.

If the physician medically directs concurrent medically directed procedures, reduce the number of base units for each concurrent procedure as follows.

(a) For two concurrent procedures, the base unit on each procedure is reduced 10 percent.

(b) For three concurrent procedures, the base unit on each procedure is reduced 25 percent.

(c) For four concurrent procedures, the base on each concurrent procedure is reduced 40 percent.

(d) If the physician medically directs concurrent procedures and any of the concurrent procedures are cataract or iridectomy anesthesia, reduce the base units for each cataract or iridectomy procedure by 10 percent.

Note: Authority: Sections 133, 4603.5, 5307.1 and 5307.3, Labor Code. Reference: Sections 4600, 5307.1 and 5307.11, Labor Code.

History: 1. New section filed 9-24-2013; operative 1-1-2014. Submitted to OAL as a file and print only pursuant to Government Code section 11340.9(g) (Register 2013, No. 39).

Ref.: Herlick Handbook § 1.01[3][b].

§9789.18.10. Anesthesia — Monitored Anesthesia Care.

The physician or non-physician practitioner shall be reimbursed for reasonable and medically necessary monitored anesthesia care services on the same basis as other anesthesia services. Anesthesiologists use modifier QS to report monitored anesthesia care cases. Monitored anesthesia care involves the intra-operative monitoring by a physician or qualified individual under the medical direction of a physician or of the patient's vital physiological signs in anticipation of the need for administration of general anesthesia or of the development of adverse physiological patient reaction to the surgical procedure. It also includes the performance of a pre-anesthetic examination and evaluation, prescription of the anesthesia care required, administration of any necessary oral or parenteral medications (e.g., atropine, demerol, valium) and provision of indicated postoperative anesthesia care. Payment is made under the fee schedule using the payment rules in section 9789.18.2 if the physician personally performs the monitored anesthesia care case or under the rules in section 9789.18.3 if the physician medically directs four or fewer concurrent cases and monitored anesthesia care represents one or more of these concurrent cases.

Note: Authority: Sections 133, 4603.5, 5307.1 and 5307.3, Labor Code. Reference: Sections 4600, 5307.1 and 5307.11, Labor Code.

History: 1. New section filed 9-24-2013; operative 1-1-2014. Submitted to OAL as a file and print only pursuant to Government Code section 11340.9(g) (Register 2013, No. 39).

Ref.: Herlick Handbook § 1.01[3][b].

§9789.18.11. Anesthesia Claims Modifiers.

Physicians shall report the appropriate anesthesia modifier to denote whether the service was personally performed, medically directed, or medically supervised in addition to any applicable CPT modifier.

Specific anesthesia modifiers include:

AA — Anesthesia Services performed personally by the anesthesiologist;

AD — Medical Supervision by a physician; more than 4 concurrent anesthesia procedures;

G8 — Monitored anesthesia care (MAC) for deep complex complicated, or markedly invasive surgical procedures;

G9 — Monitored anesthesia care for patient who has a history of severe cardio-pulmonary condition;

QK — Medical direction of two, three or four concurrent anesthesia procedures involving qualified individuals;

QS — Monitored anesthesia care service — The QS modifier is for informational purposes. Providers must report actual anesthesia time and payment modifier on the claim;

QX — CRNA service; with medical direction by a physician;

QY — Medical direction of one qualified non-physician anesthetist by an anesthesiologist;

QZ — CRNA service: without medical direction by a physician; and

GC — these services have been performed by a resident under the direction of a teaching physician. The GC modifier is reported by the teaching physician to indicate he/she rendered the service in compliance with the teaching physician requirements in section 9789.18.2. One of the payment modifiers must be used in conjunction with the GC modifier.

Note: Authority: Sections 133, 4603.5, 5307.1 and 5307.3, Labor Code. Reference: Sections 4600, 5307.1 and 5307.11, Labor Code.

History: 1. New section filed 9-24-2013; operative 1-1-2014. Submitted to OAL as a file and print only pursuant to Government Code section 11340.9(g) (Register 2013, No. 39).

2. Amendment filed 11-6-2018; operative 1-1-2019. Submitted to OAL for filing and printing only pursuant to Government Code section 11340.9(g) (Register 2018, No. 45).

Ref.: Herlick Handbook § 1.01[3][b].

§9789.18.12. Anesthesia and Medical/Surgical Service Provided by the Same Physician.

(a) For services rendered before March 1, 2017, conscious sedation codes 99143 to 99145 may be billed as long as the procedure it is billed with is not listed in Appendix G of CPT (Summary of Codes that Include Moderate Conscious Sedation.)

(b) For services rendered before March 1, 2017, when a second physician other than the health care professional performing the diagnostic or therapeutic services provides moderate sedation in the facility setting for the procedures listed in Appendix G, the second physician may bill 99148 to 99150. When these services are performed by the second physician in the nonfacility setting, CPT codes 99148 to 99150 are not to be reported.

(c) If the anesthesiologist or CRNA provides anesthesia for diagnostic or therapeutic nerve blocks or injections and a different provider performs the block or injection, then the anesthesiologist or CRNA may report the anesthesia service using CPT code 01991. The service must meet the criteria for monitored anesthesia care. If the anesthesiologist or CRNA provides both the anesthesia service and the block or injection, then the anesthesiologist or CRNA may report the anesthesia service using the conscious sedation code and the injection or block. However, the anesthesia service must meet the requirements for conscious sedation and if a lower level complexity anesthesia service is provided, then the conscious sedation code shall not be reported.

(d) If the physician performing the medical or surgical procedure also provides a level of anesthesia lower in intensity than moderate or conscious sedation, such as a local or topical anesthesia, then the conscious sedation code shall not be reported and no payment shall be allowed. There is no CPT code for the performance of local anesthesia as payment for this service is considered to be bundled into the payment for the underlying medical or surgical service.

Note: Authority: Sections 133, 4603.5, 5307.1 and 5307.3, Labor Code. Reference: Sections 4600, 5307.1 and 5307.11, Labor Code.

History: 1. New section filed 9-24-2013; operative 1-1-2014. Submitted to OAL as a file and print only pursuant to Government Code section 11340.9(g) (Register 2013, No. 39).

2. Amendment of subsections (a) and (b) filed 7-18-2017; operative 3-1-2017. Submitted to OAL as a file and print only pursuant to Labor Code section 5307.1(g)(2) (Register 2017, No. 29).

Ref.: Herlick Handbook § 1.01[3][b].

§9789.19. Update Table.

(a) Services Rendered On or After 1/1/2014. Documents listed in the following table are incorporated by reference and will be made available upon request to the Administrative Director.

Document	*Services Rendered On or After 1/1/2014*
Adjustment Factors (These factors have been incorporated into the conversion factors listed below)	For all services other than anesthesia: 2014 Total RVS adjustment factor: 1.0477 2014 RVU budget neutrality factor: 1.00046 2014 RVU rescaling adjustment factor: 1.04718 2014 Annual increase in the MEI: 1.008 2014 Cumulative adjustment factor: 1.0638

Document	*Services Rendered On or After 1/1/2014*
	For anesthesia services: 2014 Total RVS adjustment factor: 1.0291 2014 RVU budget neutrality factor: 1.00046 2014 RVU rescaling adjustment factor: 1.04718 2014 anesthesia practice expense adjustment factor: 0.9823 2014 Annual increase in the MEI: 1.008 2014 Cumulative adjustment factor: 1.0449
Anesthesia Base Units by CPT Code	2014anesBASEfin
California-Specific Codes	WC001 — Not reimbursable WC002 — $11.91 WC003 — $38.68 for first page $23.80 each additional page. Maximum of six pages absent mutual agreement ($157.68) WC004 — $38.68 for first page $23.80 each additional page. Maximum of seven pages absent mutual agreement ($181.48) WC005 — $38.68 for first page, $23.80 each additional page. Maximum of six pages absent mutual agreement ($157.68) WC007 — $38.68 for first page $23.80 each additional page. Maximum of six pages absent mutual agreement ($157.68) WC008 — $10.26 for up to the first 15 pages. $0.25 for each additional page after the first 15 pages. WC009 — $10.26 for up to the first 15 pages. $0.25 for each additional page after the first 15 pages. WC010 — $5.13 per x-ray WC011 — $10.26 per scan WC012 — No Fee Prescribed/Non Reimbursable absent agreement
CCI Edits: Medically Unlikely Edits	For services rendered on or after 1/1/2014, use: "Practitioner Services MUE Table — Updated 10/1/2013." For services rendered on or after 1/23/2014, use: "Practitioner Services MUE Table — Updated 1/1/2014." For services rendered on or after 4/1/2014, use: "Practitioner Services MUE Table — Updated 4/1/2014." For services rendered on or after 7/1/2014, use: "Practitioner Services MUE Table — Updated 7/1/2014." For services rendered on or after 10/1/2014, use: "Practitioner Services MUE Table – Updated 10/1/2014." Copies of the MUE Tables are posted on the DWC website: http://www.dir.ca.gov/dwc/OMFS9904.htm CMS posts only the most recent version of the Practitioner Services MUE Table on the web at: http://www.cms.gov/Medicare/Coding/NationalCorrectCodInitEd/MUE.html .
CCI Edits: National Correct Coding Initiative Policy Manual for Medicare Services	NCCI Policy Manual for Medicare Services — Effective January 1, 2014 [ZIP, 749KB] Copy of the 1/1/2014 Manual is posted on the DWC website: http://www.dir.ca.gov/dwc/OMFS9904.htm
CCI Edits: Physician CCI Edits	For services rendered on or after January 1, 2014: Physician CCI Edits v19.3 (819,852 records). The last row contains edit column 1 = 39599 and column 2 = 49570 Physician CCI Edits v19.3 (710,236 records). The first row contains edit column 1 = 40490 and column 2 = C8950 For services rendered on or after April 15, 2014:

Document	*Services Rendered On or After 1/1/2014*
	Physician CCI Edits v20.1 effective April 1, 2014 (851,137 records). The last row contains edit column 1 = 39599 and column 2 = 49570 Physician CCI Edits v20.1 effective April 1, 2014 (744,393 records). The first row contains edit column 1 = 40490 and column 2 = C8950 For services rendered on or after July 1, 2014: Physician CCI Edits v20.2 effective July 1, 2014 (863,712 records). The last row contains edit column 1 = 39599 and column 2 = 49570 Physician CCI Edits v20.2 effective July 1, 2014 (752,547 records). The first row contains edit column 1 = 40490 and column 2 = C8950 For services rendered on or after October 1, 2014: Physician CCI Edits v20.3 effective October 1, 2014 (864,930 records). The last row contains edit column 1 = 39599 and column 2 = 49570 Physician CCI Edits v20.3 effective October 1, 2014 (756,576 records). The first row contains edit column 1 = 40490 and column 2 = C8950
CMS' Medicare National Physician Fee Schedule Relative Value File [Zip]	For services rendered on or after January 1, 2014: RVU14A [Zip] • RVUPUF14 (Excluding Attachment A) • PPRRVU14_V1219 • OPPSCAP_V1219 Excluding: 14LOCCO ANES 2014_V0103 CY 2014 GPCI _12172013 For services rendered on or after April 15, 2014: RVU14B [Zip] • RVUPUF14 (Excluding Attachment A) • PPRRVU14_V0324 • OPPSCAP_V0324 Excluding: 14LOCCO ANES_2014_V0103 CY 2014 GPCI_12172013 For services rendered on or after July 1, 2014: RVU14C [Zip 3MB] • RVUPUF14 (Excluding Attachment A) • PPRRVU14_V0515 • OPPSCAP_V0515 Excluding: 14LOCCO ANES 2014_V0103 CY 2014 GPCI_12172013 For services rendered on or after October 1, 2014: RVU14D [Zip 3MB] • RVUPUF14 (Excluding Attachment A) • PPRRVU14_V0815_v4 • OPPSCAP_V0815 Excluding: 14LOCCO ANES 2014_V0103 CY 2014 GPCI_12172013
CMS Pub 100-04 Medicare Claims Processing: Casting and Splint Supplies	For services rendered on or after 1/1/2014, use: Transmittal 2837 (Change Request 8523) For services rendered on or after 4/1/2014, use: the OMFS Durable Medical Equipment, Prosthetics, Orthotics, Supplies (DMEPOS) Fee Schedule applicable to the date of service

Document	*Services Rendered On or After 1/1/2014*
Conversion Factors adjusted for MEI and Relative Value Scale adjustment factor, if any	Anesthesia Conversion Factor: $33.8190 Surgery Conversion Factor: $55.2913 Radiology Conversion Factor: $53.1039 Other Services Conversion Factor: $38.3542
Current Procedural Terminology (CPT®)	CPT 2014 https://commerce.ama-assn.org/store/
Current Procedural Terminology CPT codes that shall not be used	Do not use CPT codes: 27215 (Use G0412 and Surgery CF) 27216 (Use G0413 and Surgery CF) 27217 (Use G0414 and Surgery CF) 27218 (Use G0415 and Surgery CF) 76140 (see §9789.17.2) 80100 through 80104 (see clinical lab fee schedule, § 9789.50) 90889 (See §9789.14. Use code WC005 code) 97014 (Use G0283 and Other Services CF) 99075 (see Medical-Legal fee schedule, §9795) 99080 (see §9789.14) 99241 through 99245 (see §9789.12.12) 99251 through 99255 (see §9789.12.12) 99455 and 99456.
Diagnostic Cardiovascular Procedure CPT codes subject to the MPPR	For services rendered on or after January 1, 2014: RVU14A, PPRRVU14_V1219, Number "6" in Column labeled "Mult Proc" (Modifier 51) also Addendum I, Diagnostic Cardiovascular Services Subject to The Multiple Procedure Payment Reduction (MPPR) CY 2014 CMS 1600 FC: http://www.cms.gov/Medicare/Medicare-Fee-for-Service-Payment/ PhysicianFeeSched/PFS-Federal-Regulation- Notices-Items/CMS-1600-FC.html?DLPage=1&DLSort=3&DLSortDir=descending For services rendered on or after April 15, 2014: RVU14B, PPRRVU14_V0324, Number "6" in Column labeled "Mult Proc" (Modifier 51) also Addendum I, Diagnostic Cardiovascular Services Subject to The Multiple Procedure Payment Reduction (MPPR) CY 2014 CMS 1600 FC For services rendered on or after July 1, 2014: RVU14C, PPRRVU14_V0515, Number "6" in Column labeled "Mult Proc" (Modifier 51) also Addendum I, Diagnostic Cardiovascular Services Subject to The Multiple Procedure Payment Reduction (MPPR) CY 2014 CMS 1600 FC For services rendered on or after October 1, 2014: RVU14D, PPRRVU14_V0815_v4, Number "6" in Column labeled "Mult Proc" (Modifier 51) also Addendum I, Diagnostic Cardiovascular Services Subject to The Multiple Procedure Payment Reduction (MPPR) CY 2014 CMS 1600 FC
Diagnostic Imaging Family Indicator Description	For services rendered on or after January 1, 2014: National Physician Fee Schedule Relative Value File Calendar Year 2014 http://www.cms.gov/Medicare/Medicare-Fee-for- Service-Payment/PhysicianFeeSched/PFS-Relative- Value-Files-Items/RVU14A.html?DLPage=1&DLSort=0&DLSortDir=descending RVUPUF14 (PDF document) For services rendered on or after April 15, 2014: RVU14B, PPRRVU14_V0324, RVUPUF14 (PDF document) For services rendered on or after July 1, 2014: RVU14C, PPRRVU14_V0515, RVUPUF14 (PDF document) For services rendered on or after October 1, 2014: RVU14D, PPRRVU14_V0815_v4, RVUPUF14 (PDF document)
Diagnostic Imaging Family Indicator for Procedure	For services rendered on or after January 1, 2014: RVU14A, PPRRVU14_V1219, column AB, labeled, "Diagnostic Imaging Family Indicator". Also Addendum F, Diagnostic Imaging Service Subject to the Multiple Procedure Payment Reduction (MPPR) CY2014 CMS 1600 FC

Document	*Services Rendered On or After 1/1/2014*
	For services rendered on or after April 15, 2014: RVU14B, PPRRVU14_V0324, column AB, labeled, "Diagnostic Imaging Family Indicator". Also Addendum F, Diagnostic Imaging Service Subject to the Multiple Procedure Payment Reduction (MPPR) CY2014 CMS 1600 FC
	For services rendered on or after July 1, 2014: RVU14C, PPRRVU14_V0515, column AB, labeled, "Diagnostic Imaging Family Indicator". Also Addendum F, Diagnostic Imaging Service Subject to the Multiple Procedure Payment Reduction (MPPR) CY2014 CMS 1600 FC
	For services rendered on or after October 1, 2014: RVU14D, PPRRVU14_V0815_v4, column AB, labeled, "Diagnostic Imaging Family Indicator". Also Addendum F, Diagnostic Imaging Service Subject to the Multiple Procedure Payment Reduction (MPPR) CY2014 CMS 1600 FC
DWC Pharmaceutical Fee Schedule	http://www.dir.ca.gov/dwc/OMFS9904.htm#8
Geographic Health Professional	2014 Primary Care HPSA [ZIP, 97KB]
Shortage Area zip code data files	2014 Mental Health HPSA [ZIP, 222KB]
Health Resources and Services Administration: Geographic HPSA shortage area query	
(By State & County)	http://hpsafind.hrsa.gov/
(By Address)	http://datawarehouse.hrsa.gov/geoHPSAAdvisor/GeographicHPSAAdvisor.aspx
Incident To Codes	For services rendered on or after January 1, 2014: RVU14A, PPRRVU14_V1219, with PC/TC indicator number "5"
	For services rendered on or after April 15, 2014: RVU14B, PPRRVU14_V0324, with PC/TC indicator number "5"
	For services rendered on or after July 1, 2014: RVU14C, PPRRVU14_V0515, with PC/TC indicator number "5"
	For services rendered on or after October 1, 2014: RVU14D, PPRRVU14_V0815_v4, with PC/TC indicator number "5"
Medi-Cal Rates — DHCS	For services rendered on or after 1/1/2014, use: Medi-Cal Rates file — Updated 12/15/2013
	For services rendered on or after 1/23/2014, use: Medi-Cal Rates file — Updated 1/15/2014
	For services rendered on or after 2/15/2014, use: Medi-Cal Rates file — Updated 2/15/2014
	For services rendered on or after 3/15/2014, use: Medi-Cal Rates file — Updated 3/15/2014
	For services rendered on or after 6/15/2014, use: Medi-Cal Rates file — Updated 6/15/2014
	For services rendered on or after 7/15/2014, use: Medi-Cal Rates file — Updated 7/15/2014
	For services rendered on or after 8/15/2014, use: Medi-Cal Rates file — Updated 8/15/2014
	For services rendered on or after 9/15/2014, use: Medi-Cal Rates file — Updated 9/15/2014
	For services rendered on or after 10/15/2014, use: Medi-Cal Rates file — Updated 10/15/2014

Document	*Services Rendered On or After 1/1/2014*
	For services rendered on or after 11/15/2014, use: Medi-Cal Rates file — Updated 11/15/2014 For services rendered on or after 12/15/2014, use: Medi-Cal Rates file — Updated 12/15/2014 For services rendered on or after 1/15/2015, use: Medi-Cal Rates file — Updated 1/15/2015 For services rendered on or after 2/15/2015, use: Medi-Cal Rates file — Updated 2/15/2015 Copies of the Medi-Cal Rates files (without CPT descriptors) are posted on the DWC website: http://www.dir.ca.gov/dwc/OMFS9904.htm
Ophthalmology Procedure CPT codes subject to the MPPR	For services rendered on or after January 1, 2014: RVU14A, PPRRVU14_V1219, Number "7" in Column labeled "Multiple Procedure" (Modifier 51). Also Addendum J, Diagnostic Ophthalmology Services Subject to the Multiple Procedure Payment Reduction (MPPR) CY 2014 CMS 1600 FC For services rendered on or after April 15, 2014: RVU14B, PPRRVU14_V0324, Number "7" in Column labeled "Multiple Procedure" (Modifier 51). Also Addendum J, Diagnostic Ophthalmology Services Subject to the Multiple Procedure Payment Reduction (MPPR) CY 2014 CMS 1600 FC For services rendered on or after July 1, 2014: RVU14C, PPRRVU14_V0515, Number "7" in Column labeled "Multiple Procedure" (Modifier 51). Also Addendum J, Diagnostic Ophthalmology Services Subject to the Multiple Procedure Payment Reduction (MPPR) CY 2014 CMS 1600 FC For services rendered on or after October 1, 2014: RVU14D, PPRRVU14_V0815_v4, Number "7" in Column labeled "Multiple Procedure" (Modifier 51). Also Addendum J, Diagnostic Ophthalmology Services Subject to the Multiple Procedure Payment Reduction (MPPR) CY 2014 CMS 1600 FC
Physical Therapy Multiple Procedure Payment Reduction: "Always Therapy" Codes; and Acupuncture and Chiropractic Codes	For services rendered on or after January 1, 2014: RVU14A, PPRRVU14_V1219, Number "5" in Column labeled "Mult Proc". Also Addendum H, Separately Payable Always Therapy Services Subject to the Multiple Procedure Payment Reduction (MPPR) CY 2014 CMS 1600 FC In addition, CPT codes: 97810, 97811, 97813, 97814, 98940, 98941, 98942, 98943 For services rendered on or after April 15, 2014: RVU14B, PPRRVU14_V0324, Number "5" in Column labeled "Mult Proc". Also Addendum H, Separately Payable Always Therapy Services Subject to the Multiple Procedure Payment Reduction (MPPR) CY 2014 CMS 1600 FC In addition, CPT codes: 97810, 97811, 97813, 97814, 98940, 98941, 98942, 98943 For services rendered on or after July 1, 2014: RVU14C, PPRRVU14_V0515, Number "5" in Column labeled "Mult Proc". Also Addendum H, Separately Payable Always Therapy Services Subject to the Multiple Procedure Payment Reduction (MPPR) CY 2014 CMS 1600 FC In addition, CPT codes: 97810, 97811, 97813, 97814, 98940, 98941, 98942, 98943 For services rendered on or after October 1, 2014: RVU14D, PPRRVU14_V0815_v4, Number "5" in Column labeled "Mult Proc". Also Addendum H, Separately Payable Always Therapy Services Subject to the Multiple Procedure Payment Reduction (MPPR) CY 2014 CMS 1600 FC In addition, CPT codes: 97810, 97811, 97813, 97814, 98940, 98941, 98942, 98943
Physician Time	CY 2014 PFS Physician Time [ZIP, 504KB]

Document	*Services Rendered On or After 1/1/2014*
Radiology Diagnostic Imaging Multiple Procedures	For services rendered on or after January 1, 2014: RVU14A, PPRRVU14_V1219, number "4" in column S, labeled, "Mult Proc". For services rendered on or after April 15, 2014: RVU14B, PPRRVU14_V0324, number "4" in column S, labeled, "Mult Proc" For services rendered on or after July 1, 2014: RVU14C, PPRRVU14_V0515, number "4" in column S, labeled, "Mult Proc" For services rendered on or after October 1, 2014: RVU14D, PPRRVU14_V0815_v4, number "4" in column S, labeled, "Mult Proc"
Statewide GAFs (Other than anesthesia)	Average Statewide Work GAF: 1.040 Average Statewide Practice Expense GAF: 1.1606 Average Statewide Malpractice Expense GAF: 0.6636
Statewide GAF (Anesthesia)	Average Statewide Anesthesia GAF: 1.0313
The 1995 Documentation Guidelines for Evaluation & Management Services	https://www.cms.gov/Outreach-and-Education/Medicare-Learning-Network-MLN/MLNEdWebGuide/Downloads/95Docguidelines.pdf
The 1997 Documentation Guidelines for Evaluation and Management Services	https://www.cms.gov/Outreach-and-Education/Medicare-Learning-Network-MLN/MLNEdWebGuide/Downloads/97Docguidelines.pdf.

(b) Services Rendered On or After 3/1/2015. Documents listed in the following table are incorporated by reference and will be made available upon request to the Administrative Director.

Document/Data	*Services Rendered On or After March 1, 2015 & Mid-year Updates*
Adjustment Factors (These factors have been incorporated into the conversion factors listed below)	For all services other than anesthesia: 2015 Cumulative Relative Value Scale adjustment factor: 1.0703 [2015 annual adjustment factor x 2014 cumulative adjustment factor = 2015 cumulative adjustment factor (1.006 x 1.0638 = 1.0703)] 2015 RVS adjustment factor†: 0.9981 2015 Annual increase in the MEI: 1.008 2015 Annual adjustment factor: 1.006 (0.9981 x 1.008) For anesthesia services: 2015 Anesthesia cumulative adjustment factor: 1.0461 [2015 anesthesia annual adjustment factor x 2014 anesthesia cumulative adjustment factor = 2015 cumulative adjustment factor (1.001 x 1.0449 = 1.0461)] 2015 Total RVS adjustment factor†: 0.9932 2015 RVU budget neutrality factor: 0.9981 2015 Anesthesia practice expense adjustment factor: 0.99506 2015 Annual increase in the MEI: 1.008 2015 Anesthesia annual adjustment factor: 1.001 [BN RVU x Anesthesia PE Adjustment x MEI = (0.9981 x 0.99506 x 1.008) = 1.001] †RVS adjustment factor for 2015 is 1) the RVU budget neutrality adjustment factor for "all services other than anesthesia"; and 2) the product of RVU budget neutrality adjustment factor and the anesthesia practice expense adjustment factor for anesthesia services.
Anesthesia Base Units by CPT Code	2014anesBASEfin
California-Specific Codes	WC001 — Not reimbursable WC002 — $ 12.01 WC003 — $38.99 for first page $23.99 each additional page. Maximum of six pages absent mutual agreement ($158.94) WC004 — $38.99 for first page

Document/Data	*Services Rendered On or After March 1, 2015 & Mid-year Updates*
	$23.99 each additional page. Maximum of seven pages absent mutual agreement ($182.93) WC005 — $38.99 for first page, $23.99 each additional page. Maximum of six pages absent mutual agreement ($158.94) WC007 — $38.99 for first page $23.99 each additional page. Maximum of six pages absent mutual agreement ($158.94) WC008 — $10.34 for up to the first 15 pages. $0.25 for each additional page after the first 15 pages. WC009 — $10.34 for up to the first 15 pages. $0.25 for each additional page after the first 15 pages. WC010 — $5.17 per x-ray WC011 — $10.34 per scan WC012 — No Fee Prescribed / Non Reimbursable absent agreement
CCI Edits: Medically Unlikely Edits	For services rendered on or after March 1, 2015, use: "Practitioner Services MUE Table — Effective 1/1/2015." For services rendered on or after April 1, 2015, use: "Practitioner Services MUE Table — Effective 4/1/2015." For services rendered on or after July 1, 2015, use: "Practitioner Services MUE Table — Effective 7/1/2015." For services rendered on or after October 1, 2015, use: "Practitioner Services MUE Table — Effective 10/1/2015." Copies of the MUE Tables are posted on the DWC website: http://www.dir.ca.gov/dwc/OMFS9904.htm CMS posts only the most recent version of the Practitioner Services MUE Table on the web at: http://www.cms.gov/Medicare/Coding/NationalCorrectCodInitEd/MUE.html .
CCI Edits: National Correct Coding Initiative Policy Manual for Medicare Services	For services rendered on or after March 1, 2015: "NCCI Policy Manual for Medicare Services — Effective January 1, 2015 [ZIP, 1MB]" Copy of the 2015 Manual is posted on the DWC website: http://www.dir.ca.gov/dwc/OMFS9904.htm#7
CCI Edits: Physician CCI Edits (Practitioner PTP Edits)	For services rendered on or after March 1, 2015: Physician CCI Edits v21.0 effective January 1, 2015 (898,800 records). The last row contains edit column 1 = 39599 and column 2 = 49570 Physician CCI Edits v21.0 effective January 1, 2015 (787,357 records). The first row contains edit column 1 = 40490 and column 2 = C8950 For services rendered on or after April 1, 2015: Practitioner PTP Edits v21.1 effective April 1, 2015 (899,747 records). The last row contains edits column 1 = 39599 and column 2 = 49570 Practitioner PTP Edits v21.1 effective April 1, 2015 (787,520 records). The first row contains edits column 1 = 40490 and column 2 = C8950 For services rendered on or after July 1, 2015: Practitioner PTP Edits v21.2 effective July 1, 2015 (872,404 records). The last row contains edits column 1 = 39599 and column 2 = 49570 Practitioner PTP Edits v21.2 effective July 1, 2015 (821,537 records). The first row contains edits column 1 = 40490 and column 2 = 00170 For services rendered on or after October 1, 2015: Practitioner PTP Edits v21.3 effective October 1, 2015 (880,855 records). The last row contains edits column 1 = 39599 and column 2 = 49570 Practitioner PTP Edits v21.3 effective October 1, 2015 (832,093 records). The first row contains edits column 1 = 40490 and column 2 = 00170

Document/Data	*Services Rendered On or After March 1, 2015 & Mid-year Updates*
	Access the Physician CCI Edits on the CMS website: http://www.cms.gov/Medicare/Coding/NationalCorrectCodInitEd/NCCI-Coding-Edits.html Note: the Physician CCI Edits excel file maintained by CMS contains effective date and deletion date (if any) for each column 1/column 2 pair. Therefore, the most recent file is the only file posted on the CMS website, and covers all time periods.
CMS' Medicare National Physician Fee Schedule Relative Value File [Zip]	For services rendered on or after March 1, 2015: RVU15A (Updated 01/08/15) [ZIP, 2MB] • RVUPUF15 (Excluding Attachment A) • PPRRVU15_V1223c • OPPSCAP_V1223 Excluding: 15LOCCO ANES 2015_V122314 CY2015_GPCIs For services rendered on or after May 1, 2015: RVU15B [ZIP, 3MB] • RVUPUF15 (Excluding Attachment A) • PPRRVU15_V0213_Current • OPPSCAP_V0217 Excluding: 15LOCCO Anes_2015_122314 Anes_Conv_122314_fmt CY2015_GPCIs For services rendered on or after July 1, 2015: RVU15C [ZIP, 5MB] (Except the 0.5% update is not adopted) • RVUPUF15 (Excluding Attachment A) • PPRRVU15_UP05_V0622 • OPPSCAP_UP05_V0619 Excluding: 15LOCCO Anes_2015_122314 ANES_2015_UP05_V0701 CY2015_GPCIs PPRRVU15_UP0.V0515 OPPSCAP_UP0_V0515 For services rendered on or after October 1, 2015: RVU15D [ZIP, 5MB] (Except the 0.5% update is not adopted) • RVUPUF15 (Excluding Attachment A) • PPRRVU15_OCT05_V1001 • OPPSCAP_UP05_V0815 Excluding: 15LOCCO Anes_2015_122314 ANES_2015_UP05_V0701 CY2015_GPCIs OPPSCAP_UP0_V0815 PPRRVU15_OCT_V1001
Conversion Factors adjusted for MEI and Relative Value Scale adjustment factor	Anesthesia Conversion Factor: $31.5290 Surgery Conversion Factor: $51.6570 Radiology Conversion Factor: $50.1900 Other Services Conversion Factor: $40.2970
Current Procedural Terminology (CPT®)	CPT 2015 https://commerce.ama-assn.org/store/
Current Procedural Terminology CPT codes that shall not be used	Do not use CPT codes: 27215 (Use G0412 and Surgery CF) 27216 (Use G0413 and Surgery CF) 27217 (Use G0414 and Surgery CF) 27218 (Use G0415 and Surgery CF)

Document/Data	*Services Rendered On or After March 1, 2015 & Mid-year Updates*
	76140 (see §9789.17.2) 90889 (See §9789.14. Use code WC005 code) 97014 (Use G0283 and Other Services CF) 99075 (see Medical-Legal fee schedule, §9795) 99080 (see §9789.14) 99241 through 99245 (see §9789.12.12) 99251 through 99255 (see §9789.12.12) 99455 and 99456.
Diagnostic Cardiovascular Procedure CPT codes subject to the MPPR	For services rendered on or after March 1, 2015: RVU15A, PPRRVU15_V1223c, Number "6" in Column labeled "Mult Proc" (Modifier 51), also listed in CY 2015 PFS Final Rule Multiple Procedure Payment Reduction Files [Zip, 44KB], in the document CY_2015_PFS_1612-F_ Diagnostic Cardiovascular Services Subject To the Multiple Procedure Payment Reduction (MPPR) For services rendered on or after May 1, 2015: RVU15B, PPRRVU15_V0213_Current, Number "6" in Column labeled "Mult Proc" (Modifier 51), also listed in CY 2015 PFS Final Rule Multiple Procedure Payment Reduction Files [Zip, 44KB], in the document CY_2015_PFS_1612-F_ Diagnostic Cardiovascular Services Subject To the Multiple Procedure Payment Reduction (MPPR) For services rendered on or after July 1, 2015: RVU15C, PPRRVU15_UP05_V0622, Number "6" in Column labeled "Mult Proc" (Modifier 51), also listed in CY 2015 PFS Final Rule Multiple Procedure Payment Reduction Files [Zip, 44KB], in the document CY_2015_PFS_1612-F_ Diagnostic Cardiovascular Services Subject To the Multiple Procedure Payment Reduction (MPPR) For services rendered on or after October 1, 2015: RVU15D, PPRRVU15_OCT05_V1001, Number "6" in Column labeled "Mult Proc" (Modifier 51), also listed in CY 2015 PFS Final Rule Multiple Procedure Payment Reduction Files [Zip, 44KB], in the document CY_2015_PFS_1612-F_ Diagnostic Cardiovascular Services Subject To the Multiple Procedure Payment Reduction (MPPR)
Diagnostic Imaging Family Indicator Description	For services rendered on or after March 1, 2015: Diagnostic Imaging Family Indicator: 88 = Subject to the reduction 99 = Concept does not apply RVU15A, RVUPUF15 (PDF document) For services rendered on or after May 1, 2015: Diagnostic Imaging Family Indicator: 88 = Subject to the reduction 99 = Concept does not apply RVU15B, RVUPUF15 (PDF document) For services rendered on or after July 1, 2015: Diagnostic Imaging Family Indicator: 88 = Subject to the reduction 99 = Concept does not apply RVU15C, RVUPUF15 (PDF document) For services rendered on or after October 1, 2015: Diagnostic Imaging Family Indicator: 88 = Subject to the reduction 99 = Concept does not apply RVU15D, RVUPUF15 (PDF document)
Diagnostic Imaging Family Procedures Subject to the MPPR	For services rendered on or after March 1, 2015: RVU15A, PPRRVU15_V1223c, number "88" in column AB, labeled, "Diagnostic Imaging Family Indicator", also listed in CY 2015 PFS Final Rule Multiple Procedure Payment Reduction File [Zip, 44KB], in the document CY_2015_PFS_1612-F_Diagnostic Imaging Services Subject To the Multiple Procedure Payment Reduction (MPPR)

Document/Data	*Services Rendered On or After March 1, 2015 & Mid-year Updates*
	For services rendered on or after May 1, 2015: RVU15B, PPRRVU15_V0213_Current, number "88" in column AB, labeled, "Diagnostic Imaging Family Indicator", also listed in CY 2015 PFS Final Rule Multiple Procedure Payment Reduction File [Zip, 44KB], in the document CY_2015_PFS_1612-F_Diagnostic Imaging Services Subject To the Multiple Procedure Payment Reduction (MPPR) For services rendered on or after July 1, 2015: RVU15C, PPRRVU15_UP05_V0622, number "88" in column AB, labeled, "Diagnostic Imaging Family Indicator", also listed in CY 2015 PFS Final Rule Multiple Procedure Payment Reduction File [Zip, 44KB], in the document CY_2015_PFS_1612-F_Diagnostic Imaging Services Subject To the Multiple Procedure Payment Reduction (MPPR) For services rendered on or after October 1, 2015: RVU15D, PPRRVU15_OCT05_V1001, number "88" in column AB, labeled, "Diagnostic Imaging Family Indicator", also listed in CY 2015 PFS Final Rule Multiple Procedure Payment Reduction File [Zip, 44KB], in the document CY_2015_PFS_1612-F_Diagnostic Imaging Services Subject To the Multiple Procedure Payment Reduction (MPPR)
Diagnostic Imaging Multiple Procedures Subject to the MPPR	For services rendered on or after March 1, 2015: RVU15A, PPRRVU15_V1223c, number "4" in column S, labeled, "Mult Proc", also listed in CY 2015 PFS Final Rule Multiple Procedure Payment Reduction File [Zip, 44KB], in the document CY_2015_PFS_1612-F_Diagnostic Imaging Services Subject To the Multiple Procedure Payment Reduction (MPPR) For services rendered on or after May 1, 2015: RVU15B, PPRRVU15_V0213_Current, number "4" in column S, labeled, "Mult Proc", also listed in CY 2015 PFS Final Rule Multiple Procedure Payment Reduction File [Zip, 44KB], in the document CY_2015_PFS_1612-F_Diagnostic Imaging Services Subject To the Multiple Procedure Payment Reduction (MPPR) For services rendered on or after July 1, 2015: RVU15C, PPRRVU15_UP05_V0622, number "4" in column S, labeled, "Mult Proc", also listed in CY 2015 PFS Final Rule Multiple Procedure Payment Reduction File [Zip, 44KB], in the document CY_2015_PFS_1612-F_Diagnostic Imaging Services Subject To the Multiple Procedure Payment Reduction (MPPR) For services rendered on or after October 1, 2015: RVU15D, PPRRVU15_OCT05_V1001, number "4" in column S, labeled, "Mult Proc", also listed in CY 2015 PFS Final Rule Multiple Procedure Payment Reduction File [Zip, 44KB], in the document CY_2015_PFS_1612-F_Diagnostic Imaging Services Subject To the Multiple Procedure Payment Reduction (MPPR)
DWC Pharmaceutical Fee Schedule	http://www.dir.ca.gov/dwc/OMFS9904.htm#8
Geographic Health Professional Shortage Area zip code data files	2015 Primary Care HPSA [ZIP, 88KB] 2015 Mental Health HPSA [ZIP, 185KB]
Health Resources and Services Administration: Geographic HPSA shortage area query	
(By State & County)	http://hpsafind.hrsa.gov/
(By Address)	http://datawarehouse.hrsa.gov/geoHPSAAdvisor/GeographicHPSAAdvisor.aspx
Incident To Codes	For services rendered on or after March 1, 2015: RVU15A, PPRRVU15_V1223c, with PC/TC indicator number "5" For services rendered on or after May 1, 2015: RVU15B, PPRRVU15_V0213_Current, with PC/TC indicator number "5" For services rendered on or after July 1, 2015:

Document/Data	*Services Rendered On or After March 1, 2015 & Mid-year Updates*
	RVU15C, PPRRVU15_UP05_V0622, with PC/TC indicator number "5" For services rendered on or after October 1, 2015: RVU15D, PPRRVU15_OCT05_V1001, with PC/TC indicator number "5"
Medi-Cal Rates - DHCS	Pursuant to section 9789.13.2, the Medi-Cal Rates file's "Basic Rate" is used in calculating maximum fee for physician-administered drugs, biologicals, vaccines or blood products, by date of service. For services rendered on or after March 1, 2015, use: Medi-Cal Rates file — Updated 2/15/2015 For services rendered on or after March 15, 2015, use: Medi-Cal Rates file — Updated 3/15/2015 For services rendered on or after April 15, 2015, use: Medi-Cal Rates file — Updated 4/15/2015 For services rendered on or after May 15, 2015, use: Medi-Cal Rates file — Updated 5/15/2015 For services rendered on or after June 15, 2015, use: Medi-Cal Rates file — Updated 6/15/2015 For services rendered on or after July 15, 2015, use: Medi-Cal Rates file — Updated 7/15/2015 For services rendered on or after August 15, 2015, use: Medi-Cal Rates file — Updated 8/15/2015 For services rendered on or after September 15, 2015, use: Medi-Cal Rates file — Updated 9/15/2015 For services rendered on or after October 15, 2015, use: Medi-Cal Rates file — Updated 10/15/2015 For services rendered on or after November 15, 2015, use: Medi-Cal Rates file — Updated 11/15/2015 For services rendered on or after December 15, 2015, use: Medi-Cal Rates file — Updated 12/15/2015 Copies of the Medi-Cal Rates files (without CPT descriptors) are posted on the DWC website: http://www.dir.ca.gov/dwc/OMFS9904.htm
Ophthalmology Procedure CPT codes subject to the MPPR	For services rendered on or after March 1, 2015: RVU15A, PPRRVU15_V1223c, Number "7" in Column labeled "Mult Proc" (Modifier 51). Also listed in CY 2015 PFS Final Rule Multiple Procedure Payment Reduction File [Zip, 44KB], in the document CY_2015_PFS_1612-F Diagnostic Ophthalmology Services Subject to the Multiple Procedure Payment Reduction (MPPR) For services rendered on or after May 1, 2015: RVU15B, PPRRVU15_V0213_Current, Number "7" in Column labeled "Mult Proc" (Modifier 51). Also listed in CY 2015 PFS Final Rule Multiple Procedure Payment Reduction File [Zip, 44KB], in the document CY_2015_PFS_1612-F Diagnostic Ophthalmology Services Subject to the Multiple Procedure Payment Reduction (MPPR) For services rendered on or after July 1, 2015: RVU15C, PPRRVU15_UP05_V0622, Number "7" in Column labeled "Mult Proc" (Modifier 51). Also listed in CY 2015 PFS Final Rule Multiple Procedure Payment Reduction File [Zip, 44KB], in the document CY_2015_PFS_1612-F Diagnostic Ophthalmology Services Subject to the Multiple Procedure Payment Reduction (MPPR) For services rendered on or after October 1, 2015:

Document/Data	*Services Rendered On or After March 1, 2015 & Mid-year Updates*
	RVU15D, PPRRVU15_OCT05_V1001, Number "7" in Column labeled "Mult Proc" (Modifier 51). Also listed in CY 2015 PFS Final Rule Multiple Procedure Payment Reduction File [Zip, 44KB], in the document CY_2015_PFS_1612-F Diagnostic Ophthalmology Services Subject to the Multiple Procedure Payment Reduction (MPPR)
Physical Therapy Multiple Procedure Payment Reduction: "Always Therapy" Codes; and Acupuncture and Chiropractic Codes	For services rendered on or after March 1, 2015: RVU15A, PPRRVU15_V1223c, Number "5" in Column labeled "Mult Proc". Also listed in the CY 2015 PFS Final Rule Multiple Procedure Payment Reduction File [Zip, 44KB] in the document CY_2015_PFS_1612-F Separately Payable Always Therapy Services Subject to the Multiple Procedure Payment Reduction (MPPR) In addition, CPT codes: 97810, 97811, 97813, 97814, 98940, 98941, 98942, 98943 For services rendered on or after May 1, 2015: RVU15B, PPRRVU15_V0213_Current, Number "5" in Column labeled "Mult Proc". Also listed in the CY 2015 PFS Final Rule Multiple Procedure Payment Reduction File [Zip, 44KB] in the document CY_2015_PFS_1612-F Separately Payable Always Therapy Services Subject to the Multiple Procedure Payment Reduction (MPPR) In addition, CPT codes: 97810, 97811, 97813, 97814, 98940, 98941, 98942, 98943 For services rendered on or after July 1, 2015: RVU15C, PPRRVU15_UP05_V0622, Number "5" in Column labeled "Mult Proc". Also listed in the CY 2015 PFS Final Rule Multiple Procedure Payment Reduction File [Zip, 44KB] in the document CY_2015_PFS_1612-F Separately Payable Always Therapy Services Subject to the Multiple Procedure Payment Reduction (MPPR) In addition, CPT codes: 97810, 97811, 97813, 97814, 98940, 98941, 98942, 98943 For services rendered on or after October 1, 2015: RVU15D, PPRRVU15_OCT05_V1001, Number "5" in Column labeled "Mult Proc". Also listed in the CY 2015 PFS Final Rule Multiple Procedure Payment Reduction File [Zip, 44KB] in the document CY_2015_PFS_1612-F Separately Payable Always Therapy Services Subject to the Multiple Procedure Payment Reduction (MPPR) In addition, CPT codes: 97810, 97811, 97813, 97814, 98940, 98941, 98942, 98943
Physician Time	CY 2015 PFS Final Rule Physician Time Updated 01/20/15 [ZIP 478KB]
Statewide GAFs (Other than anesthesia)	Average Statewide Work GAF: 1.0420 Average Statewide Practice Expense GAF: 1.1621 Average Statewide Malpractice Expense GAF: 0.7388
Statewide GAF (Anesthesia)	Average Statewide Anesthesia GAF: 1.0391
Splints and Casting Supplies	For services rendered on or after March 1, 2015, use: The OMFS Durable Medical Equipment, Prosthetics, Orthotics, Supplies (DMEPOS) Fee Schedule applicable to the date of service.
The 1995 Documentation Guidelines for Evaluation & Management Services	https://www.cms.gov/Outreach-and-Education/ Medicare-Learning-Network-MLN/MLNEdWebGuide/Downloads/95Docguidelines.pdf
The 1997 Documentation Guidelines for Evaluation and Management Services	https://www.cms.gov/Outreach-and-Education/ Medicare-Learning-Network-MLN/MLNEdWebGuide/Downloads/97Docguidelines.pdf.

(c) Services Rendered On or After 1/1/2016. Documents listed in the following table are incorporated by reference and will be made available upon request to the Administrative Director.

Document/Data	*Services Rendered On or After January 1, 2016 & Mid-year Updates*
Adjustment Factors (These factors have been incorporated into the	For services rendered on or after January 1, 2016: For all services other than anesthesia:

Document/Data	*Services Rendered On or After January 1, 2016 & Mid-year Updates*
conversion factors listed below)	2016 Cumulative adjustment factor: 1.0818 2016 RVU budget neutrality adjustment factor: 0.9998 2016 Annual increase in the MEI: 1.011 2015 Cumulative "other than anesthesia" adjustment 1.0703 For anesthesia services: 2016 Cumulative anesthesia adjustment factor: 1.0527 2016 RVU budget neutrality adjustment factor: 0.9998 2016 Anesthesia Practice Expense and Malpractice adjustment factor: 0.99555 2016 Annual increase in the MEI: 1.011 2015 Cumulative anesthesia adjustment: 1.0461 For services rendered on or after April 1, 2016: For all services other than anesthesia: 2016 Cumulative adjustment factor: 1.0812 2016 RVU budget neutrality adjustment factor: 0.99924 2016 Annual increase in the MEI: 1.011 2015 Cumulative "other than anesthesia" adjustment 1.0703 For anesthesia services: 2016 Cumulative anesthesia adjustment factor: 1.0317 2016 RVU budget neutrality adjustment factor: 0.99924 2016 Anesthesia Practice Expense and Malpractice adjustment factor: 0.97628 2016 Annual increase in the MEI: 1.011 2015 Cumulative anesthesia adjustment: 1.0461
Anesthesia Base Units by CPT Code	2014anesBASEfin
California-Specific Codes	WC001 — Not reimbursable WC002 — $ 12.14 WC003 — $39.42 for first page $24.25 each additional page. Maximum of six pages absent mutual agreement ($160.69) WC004 — $39.42 for first page $24.25 each additional page. Maximum of seven pages absent mutual agreement ($184.94) WC005 — $39.42 for first page, $24.25 each additional page. Maximum of six pages absent mutual agreement ($160.69) WC007 — $39.42 for first page $24.25 each additional page. Maximum of six pages absent mutual agreement ($160.69) WC008 — $10.45 for up to the first 15 pages. $0.25 for each additional page after the first 15 pages. WC009 — $10.45 for up to the first 15 pages. $0.25 for each additional page after the first 15 pages. WC010 — $5.23 per x-ray WC011 — $10.45 per scan WC012 — No Fee Prescribed / Non Reimbursable absent agreement
CCI Edits: Medically Unlikely Edits	For services rendered on or after January 1, 2016, use: "Practitioner Services MUE Table — Effective 1/1/2016." For services rendered on or after April 1, 2016, use: "Practitioner Services MUE Table — Effective 4/1/2016." For services rendered on or after July 1, 2016, use: "Practitioner Services MUE Table — Effective 7/1/2016." For services rendered on or after October 1, 2016, use: "Practitioner Services MUE Table — Effective 10/1/2016." Copies of the MUE Tables are posted on the DWC website: http://www.dir.ca.gov/dwc/OMFS9904.htm

Document/Data	*Services Rendered On or After January 1, 2016 & Mid-year Updates*
	CMS posts only the most recent version of the Practitioner Services MUE Table on the web at: http://www.cms.gov/Medicare/Coding/NationalCorrectCodInitEd/MUE.html
CCI Edits: National Correct Coding Initiative Policy Manual for Medicare Services	For services rendered on or after January 1, 2016: "NCCI Policy Manual for Medicare Services — Effective January 1, 2016 [ZIP, 761MB]" Copy of the 2016 Manual is posted on the DWC website: http://www.dir.ca.gov/dwc/OMFS9904.htm#7
CCI Edits: Physician CCI Edits (Practitioner PTP Edits)	For services rendered on or after January 1, 2016: Practitioner PTP Edits v22.0 effective January 1, 2016 (903,287 records). The last row contains edits column 1 = 39599 and column 2 = 49570 Practitioner PTP Edits v22.0 effective January 1, 2016 (866,823 records). The first row contains edits column 1 = 40490 and column 2 = 00170 For services rendered on or after April 1, 2016: Practitioner PTP Edits v22.1 effective April 1, 2016 (914,985 records). The last row contains edits column 1 = 39599 and column 2 = 49570 Practitioner PTP Edits v22.1 effective April 1, 2016 (877,109 records). The first row contains edits column 1 = 40490 and column 2 = 00170 For services rendered on or after July 1, 2016: Practitioner PTP Edits v22.2 effective July 1, 2016 (915,436 records). The last row contains edits column 1 = 39599 and column 2 = 49570 Practitioner PTP Edits v22.2 effective July 1, 2016 (877,847 records). The first row contains edits column 1 = 40490 and column 2 = 00170 For services rendered on or after October 1, 2016: Practitioner PTP Edits v22.3 effective October 1, 2016 (668,511 records) 0001M/36591 - 29999/G0354 Practitioner PTP Edits v22.3 effective October 1, 2016 (498,018 records) 30000/0213T - 49999/49570 Practitioner PTP Edits v22.3 effective October 1, 2016 (489,682 records) 50010/0213T - 79999/90784 Practitioner PTP Edits v22.3 effective October 1, 2016 (179,162 records) 80003/80002 - R0075/R0070 Access the Physician CCI Edits on the CMS website: http://www.cms.gov/Medicare/Coding/NationalCorrectCodInitEd/NCCI-Coding-Edits.html Note: the Physician CCI Edits excel file maintained by CMS contains effective date and deletion date (if any) for each column 1/column 2 pair. Therefore, the most recent file is the only file posted on the CMS website, and covers all time periods.
CMS' Medicare National Physician Fee Schedule Relative Value File [Zip]	For services rendered on or after January 1, 2016: RVU16A (Released January 2016) [ZIP, 3MB] • RVUPUF16 (Excluding Attachment A) • PPRRVU16_V0122 • OPPSCAP_V0105 • Excluding: 16LOCCO ANES_V0105 CY2016_GPCIs For services rendered on or after April 1, 2016:

Document/Data	*Services Rendered On or After January 1, 2016 & Mid-year Updates*
	RVU16B (April 2016 release) [ZIP, 3MB] • RVUPUF16 (Excluding Attachment A) • PPRRVU16_April_V0202 • OPPSCAP_V0215 Excluding: 16LOCCO ANES_V0105 CY2016_GPCIs For services rendered on or after July 1, 2016: RVU16C (July 2016 release) [ZIP, 3MB] • RVUPUF16 (Excluding Attachment A) • PPRRVU16_V0517 • OPPSCAP_V0515 Excluding: 16LOCCO ANES_V0105 CY2016_GPCIs For services rendered on or after October 1, 2016: RVU16D [ZIP, 3MB] • RVUPUF16 (Excluding Attachment A) • PPRRVU16_V0804 • OPPSCAP_V0815 Excluding: 16LOCCO ANES_V0105 CY2016_GPCIs
Conversion Factors adjusted for MEI and Relative Value Scale adjustment factor	For services rendered on or after January 1, 2016: Anesthesia Conversion Factor: $29.3852 Surgery Conversion Factor: $48.2013 Radiology Conversion Factor: $47.4598 Other Services Conversion Factor: $42.4599 For services rendered on or after April 1, 2016: Anesthesia Conversion Factor: $28.8003 Surgery Conversion Factor: $48.1743 Radiology Conversion Factor: $47.4332 Other Services Conversion Factor: $42.4361
Current Procedural Terminology (CPT®)	CPT 2016 https://commerce.ama-assn.org/store/
Current Procedural Terminology CPT codes that shall not be used	Do not use CPT codes: 27215 (Use G0412 and Surgery CF) 27216 (Use G0413 and Surgery CF) 27217 (Use G0414 and Surgery CF) 27218 (Use G0415 and Surgery CF) 76140 (see §9789.17.2) 90889 (See §9789.14. Use codeWC005 code) 97014 (Use G0283 and Other Services CF) 99075 (see Medical-Legal fee schedule, §9795) 99080 (see §9789.14) 99241 through 99245 (see §9789.12.12) 99251 through 99255 (see §9789.12.12) 99455 and 99456
Diagnostic Cardiovascular Procedure CPT codes subject to the MPPR	For services rendered on or after January 1, 2016: RVU16A, PPRRVU16_V0122, Number "6" in column S, labeled "Mult Proc" (Modifier 51), also listed in CY 2016 PFS Final Rule Multiple Procedure Payment Reduction Files [Zip, 39KB], in the document CMS-1631-FC_Diagnostic Cardiovascular Services Subject to MPPR For services rendered on or after April 1, 2016:

Document/Data	*Services Rendered On or After January 1, 2016 & Mid-year Updates*
	RVU16B, PPRRVU16_April_V0202, Number "6" in column S, labeled "Mult Proc" (Modifier 51), also listed in CY 2016 PFS Final Rule Multiple Procedure Payment Reduction Files [Zip, 39KB], in the document CMS-1631-FC_Diagnostic Cardiovascular Services Subject to MPPR For services rendered on or after July 1, 2016: RVU16C, PPRRVU16_V0517, Number "6" in column S, labeled "Mult Proc" (Modifier 51), also listed in CY 2016 PFS Final Rule Multiple Procedure Payment Reduction Files [Zip, 39KB], in the document CMS-1631-FC_Diagnostic Cardiovascular Services Subject to MPPR For services rendered on or after October 1, 2016: RVU16D, PPRRVU16_V0804, Number "6" in column S, labeled "Mult Proc" (Modifier 51), also listed in CY 2016 PFS Final Rule Multiple Procedure Payment Reduction Files [Zip, 39KB], in the document CMS-1631-FC_Diagnostic Cardiovascular Services Subject to MPPR
Diagnostic Imaging Family Indicator Description	For services rendered on or after January 1, 2016: Diagnostic Imaging Family Indicator: 88 = Subject to the reduction 99 = Concept does not apply RVU16A, RVUPUF16 (PDF document) For services rendered on or after April 1, 2016: Diagnostic Imaging Family Indicator: 88 = Subject to the reduction 99 = Concept does not apply RVU16B, RVUPUF16 (PDF document) For services rendered on or after July 1, 2016: Diagnostic Imaging Family Indicator: 88 = Subject to the reduction 99 = Concept does not apply RVU16C, RVUPUF16 (PDF document) For services rendered on or after October 1, 2016: Diagnostic Imaging Family Indicator: 88 = Subject to the reduction 99 = Concept does not apply RVU16D, RVUPUF16 (PDF document)
Diagnostic Imaging Family Procedures Subject to the MPPR	For services rendered on or after January 1, 2016: RVU16A, PPRRVU16_V0122, number "88" in column AB, labeled, "Diagnostic Imaging Family Indicator", also listed in CY 2016 PFS Final Rule Multiple Procedure Payment Reduction File [Zip, 39KB], in the document CMS-1631-FC_Diagnostic Imaging Services Subject to MPPR For services rendered on or after April 1, 2016: RVU16B, PPRRVU16l_V0202, number "88" in column AB, lableled, "Diagnostic Imaging Family Indicator", also listed in CY 2016 PFS Final Rule Multiple Procedure Payment Reduction File [ZIP, 39 KB], in the document CMS-1631-FC_Diagnostic Imaging Services Subject to MPPR For services rendered on or after July 1, 2016: RVU16C, PPRRVU16_V0517, number "88" in column AB, lableled, "Diagnostic Imaging Family Indicator", also listed in CY 2016 PFS Final Rule Multiple Procedure Payment Reduction File [ZIP, 39 KB], in the document CMS-1631-FC_Diagnostic Imaging Services Subject to MPPR For services rendered on or after October 1, 2016: RVU16D, PPRRVU16_V0804, number "88" in column AB, lableled, "Diagnostic Imaging Family Indicator", also listed in CY 2016 PFS Final Rule Multiple Procedure Payment Reduction File [ZIP, 39 KB], in the document CMS-1631-FC_Diagnostic Imaging Services Subject to MPPR
Diagnostic Imaging Multiple	For services rendered on or after January 1, 2016:

Document/Data	*Services Rendered On or After January 1, 2016 & Mid-year Updates*
Procedures Subject to the MPPR	RVU16A, PPRRVU16_V0122, number "4" in column S, labeled, "Mult Proc", also listed in CY 2016 PFS Final Rule Multiple Procedure Payment Reduction File [Zip, 39KB], in the document CMS-1631-FC_Diagnostic Imaging Services Subject to MPPR For services rendered on or after April 1, 2016: RVU16B, PPRRVU16_April_V0202, number "4" in column S, labled, "Mult Proc", also listed in CY 2016 PFS Final Rule Multiple Procedure Payment Reduction File [Zip, 39KB], in the document CMS-1631-FC_Diagnostic Imaging Services Subject to MPPR For services rendered on or after July 1, 2016: RVU16C, PPRRVU16_V0517, number "4" in column S, labled, "Mult Proc", also listed in CY 2016 PFS Final Rule Multiple Procedure Payment Reduction File [Zip, 39KB], in the document CMS-1631-FC_Diagnostic Imaging Services Subject to MPPR For services rendered on or after October 1, 2016: RVU16D, PPRRVU16_V0804, number "4" in column S, labled, "Mult Proc", also listed in CY 2016 PFS Final Rule Multiple Procedure Payment Reduction File [Zip, 39KB], in the document CMS-1631-FC_Diagnostic Imaging Services Subject to MPPR
DWC Pharmaceutical Fee Schedule	http://www.dir.ca.gov/dwc/OMFS9904.htm#8
Geographic Health Professional Shortage Area zip code data files	2016 Primary Care HPSA [ZIP, 99KB] 2016 Mental Health HPSA [ZIP, 239KB] Access the files on the CMS website: https://www.cms.gov/Medicare/Medicare-Fee-for- Service-Payment/ HPSAPSAPhysicianBonuses/index.html?redirect=/hpsapsaphysicianbonuses/
Health Resources and Services Administration: Geographic HPSA shortage area query	
(By State & County)	http://hpsafind.hrsa.gov/
(By Address)	http://datawarehouse.hrsa.gov/geoHPSAAdvisor/GeographicHPSAAdvisor.aspx
Incident To Codes	For services rendered on or after January 1, 2016: RVU16A, PPRRVU16_V0122, number "5" in column N, labeled, "PCTC IND", (PC/TC Indicator) For services rendered on or after April 1, 2016: RVU16B, PPRRVU16_April_V0202, number "5" in column N, labeled, "PCTC IND", (PC/TC Indicator) For services rendered on or after July 1, 2016: RVU16C, PPRRVU16_V0517, number "5" in column N, labeled, "PCTC IND", (PC/TC Indicator) For services rendered on or after October 1, 2016: RVU16D, PPRRVU16_V0804, number "5" in column N, labeled, "PCTC IND", (PC/TC Indicator)
Medi-Cal Rates - DHCS	Pursuant to section 9789.13.2, the Medi-Cal Rates file's "Basic Rate" is used in calculating maximum fee for physician-administered drugs, biologicals, vaccines or blood products, by date of service. For services rendered on or after January 1, 2016, use: Medi-Cal Rates file — Updated 12/15/2015 For services rendered on or after January 15, 2016, use: Medi-Cal Rates file — Updated 1/15/2016 For services rendered on or after February 15, 2016, use: Medi-Cal Rates file — Updated 2/15/2016

Document/Data	*Services Rendered On or After January 1, 2016 & Mid-year Updates*
	For services rendered on or after March 15, 2016, use: Medi-Cal Rates file — Updated 3/15/2016 For services rendered on or after April 15, 2016, use: Medi-Cal Rates file — Updated 4/15/2016 For services rendered on or after May 15, 2016, use: Medi-Cal Rates file — Updated 5/15/2016 For services rendered on or after June 15, 2016, use: Medi-Cal Rates file — Updated 6/15/2016 For services rendered on or after July 15, 2016, use: Medi-Cal Rates file — Updated 7/15/2016 For services rendered on or after August 15, 2016, use: Medi-Cal Rates file — Updated 8/15/2016 For services rendered on or after September 15, 2016, use: Medi-Cal Rates file — Updated 9/15/2016 For services rendered on or after October 15, 2016, use: Medi-Cal Rates file — Updated 10/15/2016 For services rendered on or after November 15, 2016, use: Medi-Cal Rates file — Updated 11/15/2016 For services rendered on or after December 15, 2016, use: Medi-Cal Rates file — Updated 12/15/2016 For services rendered on or after January 15, 2017, use: Medi-Cal Rates file — Updated 1/15/2017 For services rendered on or after February 15, 2017, use: Medi-Cal Rates file — Updated 2/15/2017 Copies of the Medi-Cal Rates files (without CPT descriptors) are posted on the DWC website: http://www.dir.ca.gov/dwc/OMFS9904.htm
Ophthalmology Procedure CPT codes subject to the MPPR	For services rendered on or after January 1, 2016: RVU16A, PPRRVU16_V0122, Number "7" in column S, labeled "Mult Proc" (Modifier 51). Also MPPR listed in CY 2016 PFS Final Rule Multiple Procedure Payment Reduction File [Zip, 39KB], in the CMS-1631-FC_Diagnostic Ophthalmology Services Subject to MPPR For services rendered on or after April 1, 2016: RVU16B, PPRRVU16_April_V0202, Number "7" in column S, labeled "Mult Proc" (Modifier 51). Also listed in CY 2016 PFS Final Rule Multiple Procedure Payment Reduction File [Zip, 39KB], in the CMS-1631-FC_Diagnostic Ophthalmology Services Subject to MPPR For services rendered on or after July 1, 2016: RVU16C, PPRRVU16_V0517, Number "7" in column S, labeled "Mult Proc" (Modifier 51). Also listed in CY 2016 PFS Final Rule Multiple Procedure Payment Reduction File [Zip, 39KB], in the CMS-1631-FC_Diagnostic Ophthalmology Services Subject to MPPR For services rendered on or after October 1, 2016: RVU16D, PPRRVU16_V0804, Number "7" in column S, labeled "Mult Proc" (Modifier 51). Also listed in CY 2016 PFS Final Rule Multiple Procedure Payment Reduction File [Zip, 39KB], in the CMS-1631-FC_Diagnostic Ophthalmology Services Subject to MPPR
Physical Therapy Multiple Procedure Payment Reduction: "Always Therapy" Codes; and Acupuncture and Chiropractic Codes	For services rendered on or after January 1, 2016: RVU16A, PPRRVU16_V0122, Number "5" in column S, labeled "Mult Proc". Also listed in the CY 2016 PFS Final Rule Multiple Procedure Payment Reduction File [Zip, 39KB] in the document CMS-1631-FC_Separately Payable Therapy Services Subject to MPPR

Document/Data	*Services Rendered On or After January 1, 2016 & Mid-year Updates*
	In addition, CPT codes: 97810, 97811, 97813, 97814, 98940, 98941, 98942, 98943
	For services rendered on or after April 1, 2016: RVU16B, PPRRVU16_April_V0202, Number "5" in column S, labeled "Mult Proc". Also listed in the CY 2016 PFS Final Rule Multiple Procedure Payment Reduction File [Zip, 39KB] in the document CMS-1631-FC_Separately Payable Therapy Services Subject to MPPR
	In addition, CPT codes: 97810, 97811, 97813, 97814, 98940, 98941, 98942, 98943
	For services rendered on or after July 1, 2016: RVU16C, PPRRVU16_V0517, Number "5" in column S, labeled "Mult Proc". Also listed in the CY 2016 PFS Final Rule Multiple Procedure Payment Reduction File [Zip, 39KB] in the document CMS-1631-FC_Separately Payable Therapy Services Subject to MPPR
	In addition, CPT codes: 97810, 97811, 97813, 97814, 98940, 98941, 98942, 98943
	For services rendered on or after October 1, 2016: RVU16D, PPRRVU16_V0804, Number "5" in column S, labeled "Mult Proc". Also listed in the CY 2016 PFS Final Rule Multiple Procedure Payment Reduction File [Zip, 39KB] in the document CMS-1631-FC_Separately Payable Therapy Services Subject to MPPR
	In addition, CPT codes: 97810, 97811, 97813, 97814, 98940, 98941, 98942, 98943
Physician Time	CY 2016 PFS Final Rule Work Time [ZIP 220KB]
Statewide GAFs (Other than anesthesia)	Average Statewide Work GAF: 1.0420 Average Statewide Practice Expense GAF: 1.1621 Average Statewide Malpractice Expense GAF: 0.7388
Statewide GAF (Anesthesia)	Average Statewide Anesthesia GAF: 1.0487
Splints and Casting Supplies	For services rendered on or after January 1, 2016, use: The OMFS Durable Medical Equipment, Prosthetics, Orthotics, Supplies (DMEPOS) Fee Schedule applicable to the date of service.
The 1995 Documentation Guidelines for Evaluation & Management Services	https://www.cms.gov/Outreach-and-Education/Medicare-Learning-Network-MLN/MLNEdWebGuide/Downloads/95Docguidelines.pdf
The 1997 Documentation Guidelines for Evaluation and Management Services	https://www.cms.gov/Outreach-and-Education/Medicare-Learning-Network-MLN/MLNEdWebGuide/Downloads/97Docguidelines.pdf

(d) Services Rendered On or After 3/1/2017. Documents listed in the following table are incorporated by reference and will be made available upon request to the Administrative Director.

Document/Data	*Services Rendered On or After March 1, 2017 & Mid-year Updates*
Adjustment Factors (These factors have been incorporated into the conversion factors listed below)	For services rendered on or after March 1, 2017: For all services other than anesthesia: 2017 Cumulative adjustment factor: 1.0933 2017 RVU budget neutrality adjustment factor: 0.99987 2017 Imaging MPPR adjustment factor: 0.9993 2017 Annual increase in the MEI: 1.012 2016 Cumulative "other than anesthesia" adjustment: 1.0812 For anesthesia services: 2017 Cumulative anesthesia adjustment factor: 1.0433 2017 RVU budget neutrality adjustment factor: 0.99987 2017 Imaging MPPR adjustment factor: 0.9993 2017 Annual increase in the MEI: 1.012 2016 Cumulative anesthesia adjustment: 1.0317

Document/Data	*Services Rendered On or After March 1, 2017 & Mid-year Updates*
Anesthesia Base Units by CPT Code	2014anesBASEfin
California-Specific Codes	WC001 — Not reimbursable WC002 — $12.29 WC003 — $39.89 for first page $24.54 each additional page. Maximum of six pages absent mutual agreement ($162.59) WC004 — $39.89 for first page $24.54 each additional page. Maximum of seven pages absent mutual agreement ($187.13) WC005 — $39.89 for first page, $24.54 each additional page. Maximum of six pages absent mutual agreement ($162.59) WC007 — $39.89 for first page $24.54 each additional page. Maximum of six pages absent mutual agreement ($162.59) WC008 — $10.58 for up to the first 15 pages. $0.25 for each additional page after the first 15 pages. WC009 — $10.58 for up to the first 15 pages. $0.25 for each additional page after the first 15 pages. WC010 — $5.29 per x-ray WC011 — $10.58 per scan WC012 — No Fee Prescribed /Non Reimbursable absent agreement
CCI Edits: Medically Unlikely Edits	For services rendered on or after March 1, 2017, use: "Practitioner Services MUE Table — Effective 1/1/2017." Copies of the MUE Tables are posted on the DWC website: http://www.dir.ca.gov/dwc/OMFS9904.htm For services rendered on or after April 1, 2017, use: "Practitioner Services MUE Table — Effective 4/1/2017." Copies of the MUE Tables are posted on the DWC website: http://www.dir.ca.gov/dwc/OMFS9904.htm For services rendered on or after July 1, 2017, use: "Practitioner Services MUE Table — Effective 7/1/2017." Copies of the MUE Tables are posted on the DWC website: http://www.dir.ca.gov/dwc/OMFS9904.htm For services rendered on or after October 1, 2017, use: "Practitioner Services MUE Table — Effective 10/1/2017." Copies of the MUE Tables are posted on the DWC website: http://www.dir.ca.gov/dwc/OMFS9904.htm CMS posts only the most recent version of the Practitioner Services MUE Table on the web at: http://www.cms.gov/Medicare/Coding/NationalCorrectCodInitEd/MUE.html
CCI Edits: National Correct Coding Initiative Policy Manual for Medicare Services	For services rendered on or after March 1, 2017: "NCCI Policy Manual for Medicare Services — Effective January 1, 2017 [ZIP, 770KB]" Copy of the 2017 Manual is posted on the DWC website: http://www.dir.ca.gov/dwc/OMFS9904.htm#7
CCI Edits: Physician CCI Edits (Practitioner PTP Edits)	For services rendered on or after March 1, 2017: Practitioner PTP Edits v23.0 effective January 1, 2017 (422,052 records) 0001M/36591 - 24940/G0471 Practitioner PTP Edits v23.0 effective January 1, 2017 (574,135 records) 25000/01810 - 39599/49570 Practitioner PTP Edits v23.0 effective January 1, 2017 (436,857 records) 40490/00170 - 59897/G0347 Practitioner PTP Edits v23.0 effective January 1, 2017 (501,820 records) 60000/0213T - R0075/R0070 For services rendered on or after April 1, 2017: Practitioner PTP Edits v23.1 effective April 1, 2017 (474,500 records) 0001M/36591 - 25931/G0471

Document/Data	*Services Rendered On or After March 1, 2017 & Mid-year Updates*
	Practitioner PTP Edits v23.1 effective April 1, 2017 (502,046 records) 26010/01810 - 36909/J2001 Practitioner PTP Edits v23.1 effective April 1, 2017 (495,097 records) 37140/0213T - 60650/G0471 Practitioner PTP Edits v23.1 effective April 1, 2017 (501,223 records) 61000/0213T - R0075/R0070 For services rendered on or after July 1, 2017: Practitioner PTP Edits v23.2 effective July 1, 2017 (476,159 records) 0001M/36591 - 25931/G0471 [ZIP, 13MB] Practitioner PTP Edits v23.2 effective July 1, 2017 (502,166 records) 26010/01810 - 36909/J2001 [ZIP, 13MB] Practitioner PTP Edits v23.2 effective July 1, 2017 (495,291 records) 37140/0213T - 60650/G0471 [ZIP, 13MB] Practitioner PTP Edits v23.2 effective July 1, 2017 (503,693 records) 61000/0213T - R0075/R0070 [ZIP, 13MB] For services rendered on or after October 1, 2017: Practitioner PTP Edits v23.3 effective October 1, 2017 (476,064 records) 0001M/36591 - 25931/G0471 Practitioner PTP Edits v23.3 effective October 1, 2017 (502,759 records) 26010/01810 - 36909/J2001 Practitioner PTP Edits v23.3 effective October 1, 2017 (495,446 records) 37140/0213T - 60650/G0471 Practitioner PTP Edits v23.3 effective October 1, 2017 (504,589 records) 61000/0213T - R0075/R0070 Access the Physician CCI Edits on the CMS website: http://www.cms.gov/Medicare/Coding/ NationalCorrectCodInitEd/NCCI-Coding-Edits.html Note: the Physician CCI Edits excel file maintained by CMS contains effective date and deletion date (if any) for each column 1/column 2 pair. Therefore, the most recent file is the only file posted on the CMS website, and covers all time periods.
CMS' Medicare National Physician Fee Schedule Relative Value File [Zip]	For services rendered on or after March 1, 2017: RVU17A (January 2017 release) [ZIP, 3MB] • RVU17A (Excluding Attachment A) • PPRRVU17_V1219 • OPPSCAP_V1219 Excluding: 17LOCCO ANES_V0101 CY2017_GPCIs For services rendered on or after April 1, 2017: RVU17B [ZIP, 3MB] • RVU17B (Excluding Attachment A) • PPRRVU17_V0209 • OPPSCAP_V0215 Excluding: 17LOCCO ANES_V0101 CY2017_GPCIs For services rendered on or after July 1, 2017: RVU17C [ZIP, 3MB] • RVU17C (Excluding Attachment A) • PPRRVU17_JULY_V0503 • OPPSCAP_V0515 Excluding: 17LOCCO ANES_V0101 CY2017_GPCIs For services rendered on or after October 1, 2017: RVU17D [ZIP, 3MB] • RVUPUF17 (Excluding Attachment A)

Document/Data	*Services Rendered On or After March 1, 2017 & Mid-year Updates*
	• PPRRVU17_OCT • OPPSCAP_OCT Excluding: 17LOCCO ANES_OCT CY2017_GPCIs
Conversion Factors adjusted for MEI and Relative Value Scale adjustment factor	For services rendered on or after March 1, 2017: Anesthesia Conversion Factor: $26.8011 Other Services Conversion Factor: $ 44.6572
Current Procedural Terminology (CPT®)	CPT 2017 https://commerce.ama-assn.org/store/
Current Procedural Terminology CPT codes that shall not be used	Do not use CPT codes: 27215 (Use G0412) 27216 (Use G0413) 27217 (Use G0414) 27218 (Use G0415) 76140 (see §9789.17.2) 90889 (See §9789.14. Use code WC005) 97014 (Use G0283) 99075 (see Medical-Legal fee schedule, §9795) 99080 (see §9789.14) 99241 through 99245 (see §9789.12.12) 99251 through 99255 (see §9789.12.12) 99455 and 99456
Diagnostic Cardiovascular Procedure CPT codes subject to the MPPR	For services rendered on or after March 1, 2017: RVU17A, PPRRVU17_V1219, Number "6" in column S, labeled "Mult Proc" (Modifier 51), also listed in CY 2017 PFS Final Rule Multiple Procedure Payment Reduction File [Zip, 42KB], in the document CMS-1654-F_Diagnostic Cardiovascular Services Subject to MPPR For services rendered on or after April 1, 2017: RVU17B, PPRRVU17_V0209, Number "6" in column S, labeled "Mult Proc" (Modifier 51), also listed in CY 2017 PFS Final Rule Multiple Procedure Payment Reduction File [Zip, 42KB], in the document CMS-1654-F_Diagnostic Cardiovascular Services Subject to MPPR For services rendered on or after July 1, 2017: RVU17C, PPRRVU17_JULY_V0503, Number "6" in column S, labeled "Mult Proc" (Modifier 51), also listed in CY 2017 PFS Final Rule Multiple Procedure Payment Reduction File [Zip, 42KB], in the document CMS-1654-F_Diagnostic Cardiovascular Services Subject to MPPR For services rendered on or after October 1, 2017: RVU17D, PPRRVU17_OCT, Number "6" in column S, labeled "Mult Proc" (Modifier 51), also listed in CY 2017 PFS Final Rule Multiple Procedure Payment Reduction File [Zip, 42KB], in the document CMS-1654-F_Diagnostic Cardiovascular Services Subject to MPPR
Diagnostic Imaging Family Indicator Description	For services rendered on or after March 1, 2017: Diagnostic Imaging Family Indicator: 88 = Subject to the reduction 99 = Concept does not apply RVU17A, RVU17A (PDF document) For services rendered on or after April 1, 2017: Diagnostic Imaging Family Indicator: 88 = Subject to the reduction 99 = Concept does not apply RVU17B, RVU17B (PDF document) For services rendered on or after July 1, 2017: Diagnostic Imaging Family Indicator: 88 = Subject to the reduction 99 = Concept does not apply

Document/Data	*Services Rendered On or After March 1, 2017 & Mid-year Updates*
	RVU17C, RVU17C (PDF document) For services rendered on or after October 1, 2017: Diagnostic Imaging Family Indicator: 88 = Subject to the reduction 99 = Concept does not apply RVU17D, RVUPUF17 (PDF document)
Diagnostic Imaging Family Procedures Subject to the MPPR	For services rendered on or after March 1, 2017: RVU17A, PPRRVU17_V1219, number "88" in column AB, labeled, "Diagnostic Imaging Family Indicator", also listed in CY 2017 PFS Final Rule Multiple Procedure Payment Reduction File [Zip, 42KB], in the document CMS-1654-F _Diagnostic Imaging Services Subject to MPPR For services rendered on or after April 1, 2017: RVU17B, PPRRVU17_V0209, number "88" in column AB, labeled, "Diagnostic Imaging Family Indicator", also listed in CY 2017 PFS Final Rule Multiple Procedure Payment Reduction File [Zip, 42KB], in the document CMS-1654-F _Diagnostic Imaging Services Subject to MPPR For services rendered on or after July 1, 2017: RVU17C, PPRRVU17_JULY_V0503, number "88" in column AB, labeled, "Diagnostic Imaging Family Indicator", also listed in CY 2017 PFS Final Rule Multiple Procedure Payment Reduction File [Zip, 42KB], in the document CMS-1654-F _Diagnostic Imaging Services Subject to MPPR For services rendered on or after October 1, 2017: RVU17D, PPRRVU17_OCT, number "88" in column AB, labeled, "Diagnostic Imaging Family Indicator," also listed in CY 2017 PFS Final Rule Multiple Procedure Payment Reduction File [Zip, 42KB], in the document CMS-1654-F _Diagnostic Imaging Services Subject to MPPR
Diagnostic Imaging Multiple Procedures Subject to the MPPR	For services rendered on or after March 1, 2017: RVU17A, PPRRVU17_V1219, number "4" in column S, labeled, "Mult Proc", also listed in CY 2017 PFS Final Rule Multiple Procedure Payment Reduction File [Zip, 42KB], in the document CMS-1654-F_Diagnostic Imaging Services Subject to MPPR For services rendered on or after April 1, 2017: RVU17B, PPRRVU17_V0209, number "4" in column S, labeled, "Mult Proc", also listed in CY 2017 PFS Final Rule Multiple Procedure Payment Reduction File [Zip, 42KB], in the document CMS-1654-F_Diagnostic Imaging Services Subject to MPPR For services rendered on or after July 1, 2017: RVU17C, PPRRVU17_JULY_V0503, number "4" in column S, labeled, "Mult Proc", also listed in CY 2017 PFS Final Rule Multiple Procedure Payment Reduction File [Zip, 42KB], in the document CMS-1654-F_Diagnostic Imaging Services Subject to MPPR For services rendered on or after October 1, 2017: RVU17D, PPRRVU17_OCT, number "4" in column S, labeled, "Mult Proc," also listed in CY 2017 PFS Final Rule Multiple Procedure Payment Reduction File [Zip, 42KB], in the document CMS-1654-F_Diagnostic Imaging Services Subject to MPPR
DWC Pharmaceutical Fee Schedule	http://www.dir.ca.gov/dwc/OMFS9904.htm#8
Geographic Health Professional Shortage Area zip code data files	2017 Primary Care HPSA [ZIP, 99KB] 2017 Mental Health HPSA [ZIP, 237KB] Access the files on the CMS website: https://www.cms.gov/Medicare/Medicare-Fee-for- Service-Payment/HPSAPSAPhysicianBonuses/index.html?redirect=/hpsapsaphysicianbonuses/
Health Resources and Services Administration: Geographic HPSA shortage area query (By State & County)	http://hpsafind.hrsa.gov/

Document/Data	*Services Rendered On or After March 1, 2017 & Mid-year Updates*
(By Address)	http://datawarehouse.hrsa.gov/geoHPSAAdvisor/GeographicHPSAAdvisor.aspx
Incident To Codes	For services rendered on or after March 1, 2017: RVU17A, PPRRVU17_V1219, number "5" in column N, labeled, "PCTC IND", (PC/TC Indicator) For services rendered on or after April 1, 2017: RVU17B, PPRRVU17_V0209, number "5" in column N, labeled, "PCTC IND", (PC/TC Indicator) For services rendered on or after July 1, 2017: RVU17C, PPRRVU17_JULY_V0503, number "5" in column N, labeled, "PCTC IND", (PC/TC Indicator) For services rendered on or after October 1, 2017: RVU17D, PPRRVU17_OCT, number "5" in column N, labeled, "PCTC IND," (PC/TC Indicator)
Medi-Cal Rates - DHCS	Pursuant to section 9789.13.2, the Medi-Cal Rates file's "Basic Rate" is used in calculating maximum fee for physician-administered drugs, biologicals, vaccines or blood products, by date of service. For services rendered on or after March 1, 2017 use: Medi-Cal Rates file — Updated 2/15/2017 For services rendered on or after March 15, 2017, use: Medi-Cal Rates file — Updated 3/15/2017 For services rendered on or after April 15, 2017, use: Medi-Cal Rates file — Updated 4/15/2017 For services rendered on or after May 15, 2017, use. Medi-Cal Rates file — Updated 5/15/2017 For services rendered on or after June 15, 2017, use: Medi-Cal Rates file — Updated 6/15/2017 For services rendered on or after July 15, 2017, use: Medi-Cal Rates file — Updated 7/15/2017 For services rendered on or after August 15, 2017, use: Medi-Cal Rates file — Updated 8/15/2017 For services rendered on or after September 15, 2017, use: Medi-Cal Rates file — Updated 9/15/2017 For services rendered on or after October 15, 2017, use: Medi-Cal Rates file — Updated 10/15/2017 For services rendered on or after November 15, 2017, use: Medi-Cal Rates file — Updated 11/15/2017 For services rendered on or after December 15, 2017, use: Medi-Cal Rates file — Updated 12/15/2017 Copies of the Medi-Cal Rates files (without CPT descriptors) are posted on the DWC website: http://www.dir.ca.gov/dwc/OMFS9904.htm
Ophthalmology Procedure CPT codes subject to the MPPR	For services rendered on or after March 1, 2017: RVU17A, PPRRVU17_V1219, Number "7" in column S, labeled "Mult Proc" (Modifier 51). Also listed in CY 2017 PFS Final Rule Multiple Procedure Payment Reduction File [Zip, 42KB], in the CMS-1654-F_Diagnostic Ophthalmology Services Subject to MPPR For services rendered on or after April 1, 2017:

Document/Data	Services Rendered On or After March 1, 2017 & Mid-year Updates
	RVU17B, PPRRVU17_V0209, Number "7" in column S, labeled "Mult Proc" (Modifier 51). Also listed in CY 2017 PFS Final Rule Multiple Procedure Payment Reduction File [Zip, 42KB], in the CMS-1654-F_Diagnostic Ophthalmology Services Subject to MPPR For services rendered on or after July 1, 2017: RVU17C, PPRRVU17_JULY_V0503, Number "7" in column S, labeled "Mult Proc" (Modifier 51). Also listed in CY 2017 PFS Final Rule Multiple Procedure Payment Reduction File [Zip, 42KB], in the CMS-1654-F_Diagnostic Ophthalmology Services Subject to MPPR For services rendered on or after October 1, 2017: RVU17D, PPRRVU17_OCT, Number "7" in column S, labeled "Mult Proc" (Modifier 51). Also listed in CY 2017 PFS Final Rule Multiple Procedure Payment Reduction File [Zip, 42KB], in the CMS-1654-F_Diagnostic Ophthalmology Services Subject to MPPR
Physical Therapy Multiple Procedure Payment Reduction: "Always Therapy" Codes; and Acupuncture and Chiropractic Codes	For services rendered on or after March 1, 2017: RVU17A, PPRRVU17_V1219, Number "5" in column S, labeled "Mult Proc". Also listed in the CY 2017 PFS Final Rule Multiple Procedure Payment Reduction File [Zip, 42KB] in the document Therapy" Codes; and CMS-1654-F_Separately Payable Therapy Services Subject to MPPR In addition, CPT codes: 97810, 97811, 97813, 97814, 98940, 98941, 98942, 98943 For services rendered on or after April 1, 2017: RVU17B, PPRRVU17_V0209, Number "5" in column S, labeled "Mult Proc". Also listed in the CY 2017 PFS Final Rule Multiple Procedure Payment Reduction File [Zip, 42KB] in the document CMS-1654-F_Separately Payable Therapy Services Subject to MPPR In addition, CPT codes: 97810, 97811, 97813, 97814, 98940, 98941, 98942, 98943 For services rendered on or after July 1, 2017: RVU17C, PPRRVU17_JULY_V0503, Number "5" in column S, labeled "Mult Proc". Also listed in the CY 2017 PFS Final Rule Multiple Procedure Payment Reduction File [Zip, 42KB] in the document CMS-1654-F_Separately Payable Therapy Services Subject to MPPR In addition, CPT codes: 97810, 97811, 97813, 97814, 98940, 98941, 98942, 98943 For services rendered on or after October 1, 2017: RVU17D, PPRRVU17_OCT, Number "5" in column S, labeled "Mult Proc." Also listed in the CY 2017 PFS Final Rule Multiple Procedure Payment Reduction File [Zip, 42KB] in the document CMS-1654-F_Separately Payable Therapy Services Subject to MPPR In addition, CPT codes: 97810, 97811, 97813, 97814, 98940, 98941, 98942, 98943
Physician Time	CY 2017 PFS Final Rule Physician Time [ZIP, 628KB]
Statewide GAFs (Other than anesthesia)	Average Statewide Work GAF: 1.0417 Average Statewide Practice Expense GAF: 1.1632 Average Statewide Malpractice Expense GAF: 0.6632
Statewide GAF (Anesthesia)	Average Statewide Anesthesia GAF: 1.0374
Splints and Casting Supplies	For services rendered on or after March 1, 2017, use: The OMFS Durable Medical Equipment, Prosthetics, Orthotics, Supplies (DMEPOS) Fee Schedule applicable to the date of service.
The 1995 Documentation Guidelines for Evaluation & Management Services	https://www.cms.gov/Outreach-and-Education/Medicare-Learning-Network-MLN/MLNEdWebGuide/Downloads/95Docguidelines.pdf
The 1997 Documentation Guidelines for Evaluation	https://www.cms.gov/Outreach-and-Education/Medicare-Learning-Network-MLN/MLNEdWebGuide/

Document/Data	*Services Rendered On or After March 1, 2017 & Mid-year Updates*
and Management Services	Downloads/97Docguidelines.pdf

(e) Services Rendered On or After 1/1/2018. Documents listed in the following table are incorporated by reference and will be made available upon request to the Administrative Director.

Document/Data	*Services Rendered On or After January 1, 2018 & Mid-year Updates*
Adjustment Factors (These factors have been incorporated into the conversion factors listed below)	For services rendered on or after January 1, 2018: For all services other than anesthesia: 2018 Cumulative adjustment factor: 1.1075 2018 RVU budget neutrality adjustment factor: 0.9990 2018 Annual increase in the MEI: 1.014 2017 Cumulative "other than anesthesia" adjustment: 1.0933 For anesthesia services: 2018 Cumulative anesthesia adjustment factor: 1.0604 2018 RVU budget neutrality adjustment factor: 0.9990 2018 Annual increase in the MEI: 1.014 2018 Anesthesia practice expense and malpractice adjustment factor: 1.0034 2017 Cumulative anesthesia adjustment: 1.0433
Anesthesia Base Units by CPT Code	cms1676f_cy_2018_anesthesia_base_units.xlsx
California-Specific Codes	WC001 — Not reimbursable WC002 — $12.46 WC003 — $40.45 for first page $24.88 each additional page. Maximum of six pages absent mutual agreement ($164.85) WC004 — $40.45 for first page $24.88 each additional page. Maximum of seven pages absent mutual agreement ($189.73) WC005 — $40.45 for first page, $24.88 each additional page. Maximum of six pages absent mutual agreement ($164.85) WC007 — $40.45 for first page $24.88 each additional page. Maximum of six pages absent mutual agreement ($164.85) WC008 — $10.73 for up to the first 15 pages. $0.25 for each additional page after the first 15 pages. WC009 — $10.73 for up to the first 15 pages. $0.25 for each additional page after the first 15 pages. WC010 — $5.36 per x-ray WC011 — $10.73 per scan WC012 — No Fee Prescribed/Non Reimbursable absent agreement
CCI Edits: Medically Unlikely Edits	For services rendered on or after January 1, 2018, use: "Practitioner Services MUE Table - Effective 1/1/18." Copy of the MUE Table is posted on the DWC website: http://www.dir.ca.gov/dwc/OMFS9904.htm For services rendered on or after April 1, 2018, use: "Practitioner Services MUE Table - Effective 4/1/18" Copy of the MUE Table is posted on the DWC website: http://www.dir.ca.gov/dwc/OMFS9904.htm For services rendered on or after July 1, 2018, use: "Practitioner Services MUE Table - Effective 07-01-2018 [ZIP, 346KB]," excluding all codes listed with Practitioner Services MUE Value of "0" (zero). Excerpts of the MUE Table is posted on the DWC website: http://www.dir.ca.gov/dwc/OMFS9904.htm For services rendered on or after October 1, 2018, use: "Practitioner Services MUE Table - Effective 10-01-2018 [ZIP, 348KB]," excluding all codes listed with Practitioner Services MUE Value of "0" (zero).

Document/Data	*Services Rendered On or After January 1, 2018 & Mid-year Updates*
	Excerpts of the MUE Table is posted on the DWC website: http://www.dir.ca.gov/dwc/OMFS9904.htm
CCI Edits: National Correct Coding Initiative Policy Manual for Medicare Services	For services rendered on or after January 1, 2018: "NCCI Policy Manual for Medicare Services Effective January 1, 2018 [ZIP, 851KB]" Copy of the 2018 Manual is posted on the DWC website: http://www.dir.ca.gov/dwc/OMFS9904.htm#7
CCI Edits: Practitioner Procedure to Procedure (PTP) Edits	For services rendered on or after January 1, 2018: Practitioner PTP Edits v24.0 effective January 1, 2018 (511,599 records) 0001M/36591 - 25931/G0471 Practitioner PTP Edits v24.0 effective January 1, 2018 (507,927 records) 26010/01810 - 36909/J2001 Practitioner PTP Edits v24.0 effective January 1, 2018 (474,903 records) 37140/0213T - 60650/G0471 Practitioner PTP Edits v24.0 effective January 1, 2018 (514,837 records) 61000/0213T - R0075/R0070 For services rendered on or after April 1, 2018: Practitioner PTP Edits v24.1 effective April 1, 2018 (537,183 records) 0001M/36591 - 25931/G0471 Practitioner PTP Edits v24.1 effective April 1, 2018 (482,358 records) 26010/01810 - 36909/J2001 Practitioner PTP Edits v24.1 effective April 1, 2018 (523,111 records) 37140/0213T - 60650/G0471 Practitioner PTP Edits v24.1 effective April 1, 2018 (466,820 records) 61000/0213T - R0075/R0070 For services rendered on or after July 1, 2018: Practitioner PTP Edits v24.2 effective July 1, 2018 (539,120 records) 0001M/36591 - 26992/G0471 Practitioner PTP Edits v24.2 effective July 1, 2018 (482,378 records) 27000/01995 - 37790/G0471 Practitioner PTP Edits v24.2 effective July 1, 2018 (523,129 records) 38100/0213T - 61888/G0471 Practitioner PTP Edits v24.2 effective July 1, 2018 (467,725 records) 62000/0213T - R0075/R0070 For services rendered on or after October 1, 2018: Practitioner PTP Edits v24.3 effective October 1, 2018 (539,717 records) 0001M/36591 - 26992/G0471 Practitioner PTP Edits v24.3 effective October 1, 2018 (482,493 records) 27000/01995 - 37790/G0471 Practitioner PTP Edits v24.3 effective October 1, 2018 (523,504 records) 38100/0213T - 61888/G0471 Practitioner PTP Edits v24.3 effective October 1, 2018 (467,777 records) 62000/0213T - R0075/R0070 Access the Practitioner PTP Edits on the CMS website: http://www.cms.gov/Medicare/Coding/ NationalCorrectCodInitEd/NCCI-Coding-Edits.html

Document/Data	*Services Rendered On or After January 1, 2018 & Mid-year Updates*
	Note: the Practitioner PTP Edits excel file maintained by CMS contains effective date and deletion date (if any) for each column 1/column 2 pair. Therefore, the most recent file is the only file posted on the CMS website, and covers all time periods.
CMS' Medicare National Physician Fee Schedule Relative Value File [Zip]	For services rendered on or after January 1, 2018: RVU18A (Updated 12/20/2017) [ZIP, 3MB] • RVU18A (Excluding Attachment A) • PPRRVU18_JAN • OPPSCAP_JAN Excluding: 18LOCCO ANES2018 GPCI2018 For services rendered on or after April 1, 2018: RVU18B [ZIP, 3MB] • RVU18B (Excluding Attachment A) • PRRVU18_APR • OPPSCAP_APR Excluding: 18LOCCO ANES2018 GPCI2018 For services rendered on or after July 1, 2018: RVU18C1 [ZIP, 3MB] • RVU18C (Excluding Attachment A) • PPRRVU18_JUL • OPPSCAP_JUL Excluding: 18LOCCO ANES2018 GPCI2018 For services rendered on or after October 1, 2018: RVU18D [ZIP, 3MB] • RVU18D (Excluding Attachment A) • PPRRVU18_OCT • OPPSCAP_OCT Excluding: 18LOCCO ANES2018 GPCI2018
Conversion Factors adjusted for MEI and Relative Value Scale adjustment factor	For services rendered on or after January 1, 2018: Anesthesia Conversion Factor: \$27.2415 Other Services Conversion Factor: \$45.2371
Current Procedural Terminology (CPT®)	CPT 2018 https://commerce.ama-assn.org/store/
Current Procedural Terminology CPT codes that shall not be used	Do not use CPT codes: 27215 (Use G0412) 27216 (Use G0413) 27217 (Use G0414) 27218 (Use G0415) 76140 (see §9789.17.2) 90889 (See §9789.14. Use codeWC005 code) 97014 (Use G0283) 97127 (Use G0515) 99075 (see Medical-Legal fee schedule, §9795) 99080 (see §9789.14) 99241 through 99245 (see §9789.12.12) 99251 through 99255 (see §9789.12.12) 99455 and 99456
Diagnostic Cardiovascular	For services rendered on or after January 1, 2018:

Document/Data	*Services Rendered On or After January 1, 2018 & Mid-year Updates*
Procedure CPT codes subject to the MPPR	RVU18A, PPRRVU18_JAN, number "6" in column S, labeled "Mult Proc" (Modifier 51), also listed in CY 2018 PFS Final Rule Multiple Procedure Payment Reduction Files [ZIP, 42KB], in the document CMS-1676-F_Diagnostic Cardiovascular Services Subject to MPPR For services rendered on or after April 1, 2018: RVU18B, PPRRVU18_APR, number "6" in column S, labeled "Mult Proc" (Modifier 51), also listed in CY 2018 PFS Final Rule Multiple Procedure Payment Reduction Files [ZIP, 42KB], in the document CMS-1676-F_Diagnostic Cardiovascular Services Subject to MPPR For services rendered on or after July 1, 2018: RVU18C1, PPRRVU18_JUL, number "6" in column S, labeled "Mult Proc" (Modifier 51), also listed in CY 2018 PFS Final Rule Multiple Procedure Payment Reduction Files [ZIP, 42KB], in the document CMS-1676-F_Diagnostic Cardiovascular Services Subject to MPPR For services rendered on or after October 1, 2018: RVU18D, PPRRVU18_OCT, number "6" in column S, labeled "Mult Proc" (Modifier 51), also listed in CY 2018 PFS Final Rule Multiple Procedure Payment Reduction Files [ZIP, 42KB], in the document CMS-1676-F_Diagnostic Cardiovascular Services Subject to MPPR
Diagnostic Imaging Family Indicator Description	For services rendered on or after January 1, 2018: Diagnostic Imaging Family Indicator: 88 = Subject to the reduction 99 = Concept does not apply RVU18A, RVU18A (PDF document) For services rendered on or after April 1, 2018: Diagnostic Imaging Family Indicator: 88 = Subject to the reduction 99 = Concept does not apply RVU18B, RVU18B (PDF document) For services rendered on or after July 1, 2018: Diagnostic Imaging Family Indicator: 88 = Subject to the reduction 99 = Concept does not apply RVU18C1, RVU18C (PDF document) For services rendered on or after October 1, 2018: Diagnostic Imaging Family Indicator: 88 = Subject to the reduction 99 = Concept does not apply RVU18D, RVU18D (PDF document)
Diagnostic Imaging Family Procedures Subject to the MPPR	For services rendered on or after January 1, 2018: RVU18A, PPRRVU18_JAN, number "88" in column AB, labeled, "Diagnostic Imaging Family Indicator," also listed in CY 2018 PFS Final Rule Multiple Procedure Payment Reduction Files [ZIP, 42KB], in the document CMS-1676-F_Diagnostic Imaging Services Subject to MPPR For services rendered on or after April 1, 2018: RVU18B, PPRRVU18_APR, number "88" in column AB, labeled, "Diagnostic Imaging Family Indicator," also listed in CY 2018 PFS Final Rule Multiple Procedure Payment Reduction Files [ZIP, 42KB], in the document CMS-1676-F_Diagnostic Imaging Services Subject to MPPR For services rendered on or after July 1, 2018: RVU18C1, PPRRVU18_JUL, number "88" in column AB, labeled, "Diagnostic Imaging Family Indicator," also listed in CY 2018 PFS Final Rule Multiple Procedure Payment Reduction Files [ZIP, 42KB], in the document CMS-1676-F_Diagnostic Imaging Services Subject to MPPR For services rendered on or after October 1, 2018:

Document/Data	*Services Rendered On or After January 1, 2018 & Mid-year Updates*
	RVU18D, PPRRVU18_OCT, number "88" in column AB, labeled, "Diagnostic Imaging Family Indicator," also listed in CY 2018 PFS Final Rule Multiple Procedure Payment Reduction Files [ZIP, 42KB], in the document CMS-1676-F_Diagnostic Imaging Services Subject to MPPR
Diagnostic Imaging Multiple Procedures Subject to the MPPR	For services rendered on or after January 1, 2018: RVU18A, PPRRVU18_JAN, number "4" in column S, labeled, "Mult Proc," also listed in CY 2018 PFS Final Rule Multiple Procedure Payment Reduction Files [ZIP, 42KB], in the document CMS-1676-F_Diagnostic Imaging Services Subject to MPPR For services rendered on or after April 1, 2018: RVU18B, PPRRVU18_APR, number "4" in column S, labeled, "Mult Proc," also listed in CY 2018 PFS Final Rule Multiple Procedure Payment Reduction Files [ZIP, 42KB], in the document CMS-1676-F_Diagnostic Imaging Services Subject to MPPR For services rendered on or after July 1, 2018: RVU18C1, PPRRVU18_JUL, number "4" in column S, labeled, "Mult Proc," also listed in CY 2018 PFS Final Rule Multiple Procedure Payment Reduction Files [ZIP, 42KB], in the document CMS-1676-F_Diagnostic Imaging Services Subject to MPPR For services rendered on or after October 1, 2018: RVU18D, PPRRVU18_OCT, number "4" in column S, labeled, "Mult Proc," also listed in CY 2018 PFS Final Rule Multiple Procedure Payment Reduction Files [ZIP, 42KB], in the document CMS-1676-F_Diagnostic Imaging Services Subject to MPPR
DWC Pharmaceutical Fee Schedule	http://www.dir.ca.gov/dwc/OMFS9904.htm#8
Geographic Health Professional Shortage Area zip code data files	2018 Primary Care HPSA [ZIP, 98KB] 2018 Mental Health HPSA [ZIP, 218KB] Access the files on the CMS website: https://www.cms.gov/Medicare/Med icare-Fee-for-Service-Payment/ HPSAPSAPhysicianBonuses/index.html?redirect=/ hpsapsaphysicianbonuses/
Health Resources and Services Administration: Geographic HPSA shortage area query	
(By State & County)	http://hpsafind.hrsa.gov/
(By Address)	http: //datawarehouse.hrsa.gov/geoHPSAAdvisor/GeographicHPSAAdvisor.aspx
Incident To Codes	For services rendered on or after January 1, 2018: RVU18A, PPRRVU18_JAN, number "5" in column N, labeled, "PCTC IND," (PC/TC Indicator) For services rendered on or after April 1, 2018: RVU18B, PPRRVU18_APR, number "5" in column N, labeled, "PCTC IND," (PC/TC Indicator) For services rendered on or after July 1, 2018: RVU18C1, PPRRVU18_JUL, number "5" in column N, labeled, "PCTC IND," (PC/TC Indicator) For services rendered on or after October 1, 2018: RVU18D, PPRRVU18_OCT, number "5" in column N, labeled, "PCTC IND," (PC/TC Indicator)
Medi-Cal Rates — DHCS	Pursuant to section 9789.13.2, the Medi-Cal Rates file's "Basic Rate" is used in calculating maximum fee for physician-administered drugs, biologicals, vaccines or blood products, by date of service. For services rendered on or after January 1, 2018, use: Medi-Cal Rates file — Updated 12/15/2017 For services rendered on or after January 15, 2018, use:

Document/Data	*Services Rendered On or After January 1, 2018 & Mid-year Updates*
	Medi-Cal Rates file — Updated 1/15/2018 For services rendered on or after February 15, 2018, use: Medi-Cal Rates file — Updated 2/15/2018 For services rendered on or after March 15, 2018, use: Medi-Cal Rates file — Updated 3/15/2018 For services rendered on or after April 15, 2018, use: Medi-Cal Rates file — Updated 4/15/2018 For services rendered on or after May 15, 2018, use: Medi-Cal Rates file — Updated 5/15/2018 For services rendered on or after June 15, 2018, use: Medi-Cal Rates file — Updated 6/15/2018 For services rendered on or after July 15, 2018, use: Medi-Cal Rates file — Updated 7/15/2018 For services rendered on or after August 15, 2018, use: Medi-Cal Rates file — Updated 8/15/2018 For services rendered on or after September 15, 2018, use: Medi-Cal Rates file — Updated 9/15/2018 For services rendered on or after October 15, 2018, use: Medi-Cal Rates file — Updated 10/15/2018 For services rendered on or after November 15, 2018, use: Medi-Cal Rates file — Updated 11/15/2018 For services rendered on or after December 15, 2018, use: Medi-Cal Rates file — Updated 12/15/2018 Copies of the Medi-Cal Rates files (without CPT descriptors) are posted on the DWC website: http://www.dir.ca.gov/dwc/OMFS9904.htm
Ophthalmology Procedure CPT codes subject to the MPPR	For services rendered on or after January 1, 2018: RVU18A, PPRRVU18_JAN, number "7" in column S, labeled "Mult Proc" (Modifier 51). Also listed in CY 2018 PFS Final Rule Multiple Procedure Payment Reduction Files [ZIP, 42KB], in the document CMS-1676-F_Diagnostic Ophthalmology Services Subject to MPPR For services rendered on or after April 1, 2018: RVU18B, PPRRVU18_APR, number "7" in column S, labeled "Mult Proc" (Modifier 51). Also listed in CY 2018 PFS Final Rule Multiple Procedure Payment Reduction Files [ZIP, 42KB], in the document CMS-1676-F_Diagnostic Ophthalmology Services Subject to MPPR For services rendered on or after July 1, 2018: RVU18C1, PPRRVU18_JUL, number "7" in column S, labeled "Mult Proc" (Modifier 51). Also listed in CY 2018 PFS Final Rule Multiple Procedure Payment Reduction Files [ZIP, 42KB], in the document CMS-1676-F_Diagnostic Ophthalmology Services Subject to MPPR For services rendered on or after October 1, 2018: RVU18D, PPRRVU18_OCT, number "7" in column S, labeled "Mult Proc" (Modifier 51). Also listed in CY 2018 PFS Final Rule Multiple Procedure Payment Reduction Files [ZIP, 42KB], in the document CMS-1676-F_Diagnostic Ophthalmology Services Subject to MPPR
Physical Therapy Multiple Procedure Payment Reduction: "Always Therapy" Codes; and Acupuncture and Chiropractic Codes	For services rendered on or after January 1, 2018: RVU18A, PPRRVU18_JAN, number "5" in column S, labeled "Mult Proc." Also listed in CY 2018 PFS Final Rule Multiple Procedure Payment Reduction Files [ZIP, 42KB], in the document CMS-1676-F_Separately Payable Therapy Services Subject to MPPR

Document/Data	*Services Rendered On or After January 1, 2018 & Mid-year Updates*
	In addition, CPT codes: 97810, 97811, 97813, 97814, 98940, 98941, 98942, 98943
	For services rendered on or after April 1, 2018: RVU18B, PPRRVU18_APR, number "5" in column S, labeled "Mult Proc." Also listed in CY 2018 PFS Final Rule Multiple Procedure Payment Reduction Files [ZIP, 42KB], in the document CMS-1676-F_Separately Payable Therapy Services Subject to MPPR
	In addition, CPT codes: 97810, 97811, 97813, 97814, 98940, 98941, 98942, 98943
	For services rendered on or after July 1, 2018: RVU18C1, PPRRVU18_JUL, number "5" in column S, labeled "Mult Proc." Also listed in CY 2018 PFS Final Rule Multiple Procedure Payment Reduction Files [ZIP, 42KB], in the document CMS-1676-F_Separately Payable Therapy Services Subject to MPPR
	In addition, CPT codes: 97810, 97811, 97813, 97814, 98940, 98941, 98942, 98943
	For services rendered on or after October 1, 2018: RVU18D, PPRRVU18_OCT, number "5" in column S, labeled "Mult Proc." Also listed in CY 2018 PFS Final Rule Multiple Procedure Payment Reduction Files [ZIP, 42KB], in the document CMS-1676-F_Separately Payable Therapy Services Subject to MPPR
	In addition, CPT codes: 97810, 97811, 97813, 97814, 98940, 98941, 98942, 98943
Physician Time	CY 2018 PFS Final Rule Physician Time [ZIP, 591KB]
Statewide GAFs (Other than anesthesia)	Average Statewide Work GAF: 1.041 Average Statewide Practice Expense GAF: 1.166 Average Statewide Malpractice Expense GAF: 0.605
Statewide GAF (Anesthesia)	Average Statewide Anesthesia GAF: 1.034
Splints and Casting Supplies	For services rendered on or after January 1, 2018, use: The OMFS Durable Medical Equipment, Prosthetics, Orthotics, Supplies (DMEPOS) Fee Schedule applicable to the date of service.
The 1995 Documentation Guidelines for Evaluation & Management Services	https://www.cms.gov/Outreach-and-Education/Medicare-Learning-Network-MLN/MLNEdWebGuide/Downloads/95Docguidelines.pdf
The 1997 Documentation Guidelines for Evaluation & Management Services	https://www.cms.gov/Outreach-and-Education/Medicare-Learning-Network-MLN/MLNEdWebGuide/Downloads/97Docguidelines.pdf

(f) Services Rendered On or After January 1, 2019. Documents listed in the following table are incorporated by reference and will be made available upon request to the Administrative Director.

Document/Data	*Services Rendered On or After January 1, 2019 & Mid-year Updates*
Adjustment Factors (These factors have been incorporated into the conversion factors listed below)	For all services other than anesthesia: 2019 Cumulative adjustment factor: 1.1226 2019 RVU budget neutrality adjustment factor: 0.9986 2019 Annual increase in the MEI: 1.015 2018 Cumulative "other than anesthesia" adjustment: 1.1075 For anesthesia services: 2019 Cumulative anesthesia adjustment factor: 1.0777 2019 RVU budget neutrality adjustment factor: 0.9986 2019 Annual increase in the MEI: 1.015 2019 Anesthesia practice expense and malpractice adjustment factor: 1.0027 2018 Cumulative anesthesia adjustment: 1.0604
Anesthesia Base Units by	cms1676f_cy_2018_anesthesia_base_units.xlsx

Document/Data	*Services Rendered On or After January 1, 2019 & Mid-year Updates*
CPT Code	
California-Specific Codes	WC001 — Not reimbursable WC002 — $12.65 WC003 — $41.06 for first page $25.25 each additional page. Maximum of six pages absent mutual agreement ($167.31) WC004 — $41.06 for first page $25.25 each additional page. Maximum of seven pages absent mutual agreement ($192.56) WC005 — $41.06 for first page, $25.25 each additional page. Maximum of six pages absent mutual agreement ($167.31) WC007 — $41.06 for first page $25.25 each additional page. Maximum of six pages absent mutual agreement ($167.31) WC008 — $10.89 for up to the first 15 pages. $0.25 for each additional page after the first 15 pages. WC009 — $10.89 for up to the first 15 pages. $0.25 for each additional page after the first 15 pages. WC010 — $5.44 per x-ray WC011 — $10.89 per scan WC012 — No Fee Prescribed/Non Reimbursable absent agreement
CCI Edits: Medically Unlikely Edits	For services rendered on or after January 1, 2019, use: "Practitioner Services MUE Table — Effective 01/01/2019 [ZIP, 350KB]," excluding all codes listed with Practitioner Services MUE Value of "0" (zero). Excerpts of the MUE Tables are posted on the DWC website: http://www.dir.ca.gov/dwc/OMFS9904.htm
CCI Edits: National Correct Coding Initiative Policy Manual for Medicare Services	"NCCI Policy Manual for Medicare Services — Effective January 1, 2019 [ZIP, 1MB]" Copy of the 2019 Manual is posted on the DWC website: http://www.dir.ca.gov/dwc/OMFS9904.htm#7
CCI Edits: Practitioner Procedure to Procedure (PTP) Edits	For services rendered on or after January 1, 2019: Practitioner PTP Edits v25.0 effective January 1, 2019 (556,965 records) 0001M/36591 — 26992/G0471 Practitioner PTP Edits v25.0 effective January 1, 2019 (489,643 records) 27000/01995 — 37790/G0471 Practitioner PTP Edits v25.0 effective January 1, 2019 (529,244 records) 38100/0213T — 61888/G0471 Practitioner PTP Edits v25.0 effective January 1, 2019 (483,364 records) 62000/0213T — R0075/R0070 Access the Practitioner PTP Edits on the CMS website: http://www.cms.gov/Medicare/Coding/NationalCorrectCodInitEd/NCCI-Coding-Edits.html Note: the Practitioner PTP Edits excel file maintained by CMS contains effective date and deletion date (if any) for each column 1/column 2 pair. Therefore, the most recent file is the only file posted on the CMS website, and covers all time periods.
CMS' Medicare National Physician Fee Schedule Relative Value File [Zip]	For services rendered on or after January 1, 2019: RVU19A [ZIP, 3MB] • RVU19A-508 (Excluding Attachment A) • PPRRVU19_Jan • OPPSCAP_Jan • 19LOCCO • GPCI2019 Excluding: ANES2019

Document/Data	*Services Rendered On or After January 1, 2019 & Mid-year Updates*
	Access the Relative Value File on the CMS website: https://www.cms.gov/Medicare/Medicare-Fee-for-Service-Payment/PhysicianFeeSched/PFS-Relative-Value-Files.html
Conversion Factors adjusted for MEI and Relative Value Scale adjustment factor	Anesthesia Conversion Factor: $27.6859 Other Services Conversion Factor: $45.8513
Current Procedural Terminology (CPT®)	CPT 2019 https://commerce.ama-assn.org/store/
Current Procedural Terminology CPT codes that shall not be used	Do not use CPT codes: 27215 (Use G0412) 27216 (Use G0413) 27217 (Use G0414) 27218 (Use G0415) 76140 (see §9789.17.2) 90889 (See §9789.14. Use codeWC005 code) 97014 (Use G0283) 97127 (Use G0515) 99075 (see Medical-Legal fee schedule, §9795) 99080 (see §9789.14) 99241 through 99245 (see §9789.12.12) 99251 through 99255 (see §9789.12.12) 99455 and 99456
Diagnostic Cardiovascular Procedure CPT codes subject to the MPPR	For services rendered on or after January 1, 2019: RVU19A, PPRRVU19_Jan, number "6" in column S, labeled "Mult Proc" (Modifier 51), also listed in CY 2019 PFS Final Rule Multiple Procedure Payment Reduction Files [ZIP, 61KB], in the document CMS-1693-F_Diagnostic Cardiovascular Services Subject to MPPR
Diagnostic Imaging Family Indicator Description	For services rendered on or after January 1, 2019: Diagnostic Imaging Family Indicator. 88 = Subject to the reduction 99 = Concept does not apply RVU19A, RVU19A-508 (PDF document)
Diagnostic Imaging Family Procedures Subject to the MPPR	For services rendered on or after January 1, 2019: RVU19A, PPRRVU19_Jan, number "88" in column AB, labeled, "Diagnostic Imaging Family Indicator," also listed in CY 2019 PFS Final Rule Multiple Procedure Payment Reduction Files [ZIP, 61KB], in the document CMS-1693-F_Diagnostic Imaging Services Subject to MPPR
Diagnostic Imaging Multiple Procedures Subject to the MPPR	For services rendered on or after January 1, 2019: RVU19A, PPRRVU19_Jan, number "4" in column S, labeled "Mult Proc," also listed in CY 2019 PFS Final Rule Multiple Procedure Payment Reduction Files [ZIP, 61KB], in the document CMS-1693-F_Diagnostic Imaging Services Subject to MPPR
DWC Pharmaceutical Fee Schedule	http://www.dir.ca.gov/dwc/OMFS9904.htm#8
Geographic Practice Cost Index (GPCI) by locality (Other than anesthesia services)	For services rendered on or after January 1, 2019: RVU19A • GPCI2019 Addendum E — Column B ("Locality Number"), column C ("Locality Name"), column D ("2019 PW GPCI"), column E ("PE GPCI"), and column F ("MP GPCI") for the State of California ("CA") • 19LOCCO — Column B ("Locality Number"), column C ("State"), column D ("Fee Schedule Area"), and column E ("Counties") for the State of California ("CA") Access the Relative Value File on the CMS website: https://www.cms.gov/Medicare/Medicare-Fee-for-Service-Payment/PhysicianFeeSched/PFS-Relative-Value-Files.html Also, see Zip Code mapping files listed below.
Geographic Practice Cost Index (GPCIs) by locality and anesthesia shares (Anesthesia)	For services rendered on or after January 1, 2019: 2019 Anesthesia Conversion Factors [ZIP, 18KB] (These factors have been incorporated into the conversion factors listed on section 9789.19.1, Table A)

Document/Data	*Services Rendered On or After January 1, 2019 & Mid-year Updates*
	• Locality-Adjusted Anesthesia Conversion Factors as a result of the CY 2019 Final Rule, excluding column G labeled, "National Anes CF of 22.2730" • Anesthesia Shares RVU19A (County to locality index) • 19LOCCO — Column B ("Locality Number"), column C ("State"), column D ("Fee Schedule Area"), and column E ("Counties") for the State of California ("CA") Access the Anesthesia Conversion Factors File on the CMS website: https://www.cms.gov/Center/Provider-Type/Anesthesiologists-Center.html Access the Relative Value File on the CMS website: https://www.cms.gov/Medicare/Medicare-Fee-for-Service-Payment/PhysicianFeeSched/PFS-Relative-Value-Files.html Also, see Zip Code mapping files listed below.
Geographic Practice Cost Index (GPCI) locality mapping	For services rendered on or after January 1, 2019: Zip Code to Carrier Locality File — Revised 11/14/2018 [ZIP, 4MB], Column A ("STATE"), column B ("ZIP CODE"), and column D ("LOCALITY") for the State of California ("CA")
Zip Code files mapping zip codes to GPCI locality (for "other than anesthesia services" and anesthesia services)	Zip Codes requiring + 4 extension — Revised 11/14/2018 [ZIP, 1KB], for the State of California ("CA") The Zip Code files can be accessed on the CMS website: https://www.cms.gov/Medicare/Medicare-Fee-for-Service-Payment/FeeScheduleGenInfo/index.html
Geographic Health Professional Shortage Area zip code data files	2019 Primary Care HPSA [ZIP, 100KB] 2019 Mental Health HPSA [ZIP, 218KB] Access the files on the CMS website: https://www.cms.gov/Medicare/Medicare-Fee-for-Service-Payment/HPSAPSAPhysicianBonuses/index.html?redirect=/hpsapsaphysicianbonuses/
Health Resources and Services Administration: Geographic HPSA shortage area query	
(By State & County)	http://hpsafind.hrsa.gov/
(By Address)	http://datawarehouse.hrsa.gov/geoHPSAAdvisor/GeographicHPSAAdvisor.aspx
Incident To Codes	For services rendered on or after January 1, 2019: RVU19A, PPRRVU19_Jan, number "5" in column N, labeled, "PCTC IND," (PC/TC Indicator)
Medi-Cal Rates — DHCS	Pursuant to section 9789.13.2, the Medi-Cal Rates file's "Basic Rate" is used in calculating maximum fee for physician-administered drugs, biologicals, vaccines or blood products, by date of service. For services rendered on or after January 1, 2019, use: Medi-Cal Rates file — Updated 12/15/2018 Copies of the Medi-Cal Rates files (without CPT descriptors) are posted on the DWC website: http://www.dir.ca.gov/dwc/OMFS9904.htm
Ophthalmology Procedure CPT codes subject to the MPPR	For services rendered on or after January 1, 2019: RVU19A, PPRRVU19_Jan, number "7" in column S, labeled "Mult Proc" (Modifier 51). Also listed in CY 2019 PFS Final Rule Multiple Procedure Payment Reduction Files [ZIP, 61KB], in the document CMS-1693-F_Diagnostic Ophthalmology Services Subject to MPPR
Physical Therapy Multiple Procedure Payment Reduction: "Always Therapy" Codes; and Acupuncture	For services rendered on or after January 1, 2019: RVU19A, PPRRVU19_Jan, number "5" in column S, labeled "Mult Proc." Also listed in CY 2019

Document/Data	*Services Rendered On or After January 1, 2019 & Mid-year Updates*
and Chiropractic Codes	PFS Final Rule Multiple Procedure Payment Reduction Files [ZIP, 61KB], in the document CMS-1693-F_Separately Payable Therapy Services Subject to MPPR In addition, CPT codes: 97810, 97811, 97813, 97814, 98940, 98941, 98942, 98943
Physician Time	CY 2019 PFS Final Rule Physician Time [ZIP, 244KB]
Splints and Casting Supplies	The OMFS Durable Medical Equipment, Prosthetics, Orthotics, Supplies (DMEPOS) Fee Schedule applicable to the date of service.
The 1995 Documentation Guidelines for Evaluation & Management Services	https://www.cms.gov/Outreach-and-Education/Medicare-Learning-Network-MLN/MLNEdWebGuide/Downloads/95Docguidelines.pdf
The 1997 Documentation Guidelines for Evaluation & Management Services	https://www.cms.gov/Outreach-and-Education/Medicare-Learning-Network-MLN/MLNEdWebGuide/Downloads/97Docguidelines.pdf

Note: Authority: Sections 133, 4603.5, 5307.1 and 5307.3, Labor Code. Reference: Sections 4600, 5307.1 and 5307.11, Labor Code.

History: 1. New section filed 9-24-2013; operative 1-1-2014. Submitted to OAL as a file and print only pursuant to Government Code section 11340.9(g) (Register 2013, No. 39).

2. Amendment of table filed 12-26-2013; operative 1-1-2014. Submitted to OAL as a file and print only pursuant to Government Code section 11340.9(g) (Register 2013, No. 52).

3. Editorial correction of Table (Register 2015, No. 16).

4. Amendment of subsection (a) and new subsections (b) and (c) filed 3-23-2016; operative 1-1-2016 pursuant to Labor Code section 5307.1(g)(2). Submitted to OAL for filing and printing only pursuant to Labor Code section 5307.1(g)(2) (Register 2016, No. 13).

5. Editorial correction (Register 2017, No. 5).

6. Amendment of subsection (c) and new subsection (d) filed 7-18-2017; operative 3-1-2017. Submitted to OAL as a file and print only pursuant to Labor Code section 5307.1(g)(2) (Register 2017, No. 29).

7. Editorial correction of subsection (c) table headings (Register 2017, No. 30).

8. Amendment of subsection (d) and new subsection (e) filed 12-28-2017; operative 1-1-2018. Submitted to OAL for filing and printing only pursuant to Labor Code section 5307-1(g)(2) (Register 2017, No. 52).

9. Amendment filed 11-6-2018; operative 1-1-2019. Submitted to OAL for filing and printing only pursuant to Government Code section 11340.9(g) (Register 2018, No. 45).

10. Editorial correction of subsection (e) (Register 2018, No. 52).

11. Amendment of subsections (e) and (f) filed 12-26-2018; operative 1-1-2019. Submitted to OAL for filing and printing only pursuant to Labor Code section 5307.1(g)(2) (Register 2018, No. 52).

12. Editorial correction of subsection (f) (Register 2019, No. 22).

Ref.: Herlick Handbook § 1.01[3][b].

§9789.19.1. Table A.

For anesthesia services rendered on or after January 1, 2019, Table A contains the anesthesia conversion factor adjusted by Medicare locality GPCIs and anesthesia shares, which are incorporated by reference, by date of service. Table A will be updated by Administrative Director Order and will be made available at http://www.dir.ca.gov/dwc/OMFS9904.htm, or upon request to the Administrative Director at:

DIVISION OF WORKERS' COMPENSATION (ATTENTION: OMFS)
P.O. BOX 420603
SAN FRANCISCO, CA 94142

Note: Authority cited: Sections 133, 4603.5, 5307.1 and 5307.3, Labor Code. Reference: Sections 4600, 5307.1 and 5307.11, Labor Code.

History: 1. New section filed 11-6-2018; operative 1-1-2019. Submitted to OAL for filing and printing only pursuant to Government Code section 11340.9(g) (Register 2018, No. 45).

§9789.20. General Information for Inpatient Hospital Fee Schedule — Discharge on or After July 1, 2004.

(a) This Inpatient Hospital Fee Schedule section of the Official Medical Fee Schedule covers charges made by a hospital for inpatient services provided by the hospital.

(b) Charges by a hospital for the professional component of medical services for physician services rendered on or after January 1, 2014, shall be paid according to Sections 9789.12.1 through 9789.19. Services rendered on or after July 1, 2004 but before January 1, 2014 shall be paid according to Sections 9789.10 through 9789.11. Services rendered after January 1, 2004 but before July 1, 2004 are governed by the "emergency" regulations that were effective on January 2, 2004. Services rendered on or before January 1, 2004 will be paid according to Section 9790, et seq.

(c) Sections 9789.20 through 9789.25 shall apply to all bills for inpatient services with a date of discharge on or after July 1, 2004. Services for discharges after January 1, 2004, but before July 1, 2004 are governed by the "emergency" regulations that were effective on January 2, 2004. Bills for services with date of admission on or before December 31, 2003 will be reimbursed in accordance with Section 9792.1.

(d) The Inpatient Hospital Fee schedule shall be adjusted to conform to any relevant changes in the Medicare payment schedule, including mid-year changes no later than 60 days after the effective date of those changes. Updates shall be posted on the Division of Workers' Compensation webpage at http://www.dir.ca.gov/DWC/

dwc_home_page.htm. The annual updates to the Inpatient Hospital Fee schedule shall be effective every year on December 1.

(e) Any document incorporated by reference in Sections 9789.20 through 9789.25 is available from the Division of Workers' Compensation Internet site (http://www.dir.ca.gov/DWC/dwc_home_page.htm) or upon request to the Administrative Director at:

DIVISION OF WORKERS' COMPENSATION
(ATTENTION: OMFS)
P.O. BOX 420603
SAN FRANCISCO, CA 94142

Note: Authority cited: Sections 133, 4603.5, 5307.1 and 5307.3, Labor Code. Reference: Sections 4600, 4603.2, 5307.1, and 5318, Labor Code.

History: 1. New section filed 1-2-2004 as an emergency; operative 1-2-2004 (Register 2004, No. 2). A Certificate of Compliance must be transmitted to OAL by 5-3-2004 or emergency language will be repealed by operation of law on the following day.

2. Certificate of Compliance as to 1-2-2004 order, including amendment of section heading and subsections (c) and (d), transmitted to OAL 4-30-2004 and filed 6-15-2004 (Register 2004, No. 25).

3. Amendment of subsections (c), (d) and (e) filed 12-27-2012; operative 1-1-2013 as a file and print only pursuant to Government Code section 11340.9(g) (Register 2012, No. 52).

4. Amendment of subsection (b) filed 2-4-2015; operative 3-5-2015. Submitted to OAL for printing only pursuant to Government Code section 11340.9 (Register 2015, No. 6).

Ref.: Hanna § 22.05[2]; Herlick Handbook §§ 1.01[3][b], 4.17[1].

§9789.21. Definitions for Inpatient Hospital Fee Schedule.

(a) "Average length of stay" means the geometric mean length of stay for a diagnosis-related group assigned by CMS.

(b) "Capital outlier factor" means for discharges occurring after January 1, 2004 and before January 1, 2008, the fixed loss cost outlier threshold × capital wage index × large urban add-on × (capital cost-to-charge ratio/total cost-to-charge ratio).

For discharges on or after January 1, 2008, "Capital outlier factor" means fixed loss cost outlier threshold × capital wage index × (capital cost-to-charge ratio/total cost-to-charge ratio) as modified by Title 42, Code of Federal Regulations, Section 412.316(b), as it is in effect on November 11, 2003, amended October 1, 2004, amended October 1, 2006, and amended as of October 1, 2007, which document is hereby incorporated by reference and will be made available upon request to the Administrative Director.

(1) The capital wage index, also referred to as the capital geographic factor (GAF), is specified in the Federal Register notices announcing revisions in the Medicare payment rates. See Section 9789.25(b) for the Federal Register reference that contains the capital wage index value for a given discharge.

(2) For discharges occurring before January 1, 2008, the "large urban add-on" is an additional 3% of what would otherwise be payable to the hospital, and the large urban add-on is eliminated for discharges occurring on or after January 1, 2008, pursuant to Title 42, Code of Federal Regulations, Section 412.316(b). See Section 9789.25(a) for the Federal Regulation reference to the large urban add-on.

(3) "Fixed loss cost outlier threshold" means the Medicare fixed loss cost outlier threshold for inpatient admissions. The threshold is specified in the Federal Register notices announcing revisions in the Medicare payment rates. See Section 9789.25(b) for the Federal Register reference that defines the fixed loss cost outlier threshold by date of discharge.

(c) "CMS" means the Centers for Medicare & Medicaid Services of the United States Department of Health and Human Services.

(d) For discharges before January 1, 2014, "Complex spinal surgery" is defined by the DRG to which a patient is assigned and is used to determine whether any additional payment is allowed for spinal devices used during the spinal surgery. See Section 9789.25(b) for the DRGs that define complex spinal surgery by date of discharge.

(e) "Composite factor" means the standard OMFS rate calculated by the administrative director for a hospital by adding the hospital-adjusted rates for prospective operating costs and for prospective capital costs. It excludes the DRG weight and any applicable payments for outlier cases, spinal devices used in complex spinal surgery, and new technology.

(1) The hospital-adjusted rate for prospective capital costs is determined by the following formula:

(A) For discharges after January 1, 2004 and before January 1, 2008, the hospital-adjusted rate for prospective capital costs is determined by the following formula: Capital standard federal payment rate × capital geographic adjustment factor × large urban add-on × [1 + capital disproportionate share adjustment factor + capital indirect medical education adjustment factor]

For discharges after January 1, 2008, the hospital-adjusted rate for prospective capital costs is determined by the following formula as modified by Title 42, Code of Federal Regulations, Section 412.316(b), as it is in effect on November 11, 2003, amended October 1, 2004, amended October 1, 2006, and amended as of October 1, 2007, which document is hereby incorporated by reference and will be made available upon request to the Administrative Director: Capital standard federal payment rate × capital geographic adjustment factor × [1 + capital disproportionate share adjustment factor + capital indirect medical education adjustment factor].

(B) The "capital market basket" means the Medicare capital input price index (CIPI). To determine the capital standard federal payment rate, the capital market basket is applied to the preceding capital standard federal payment rate. The capital market basket is specified in the Federal Register notices announcing revisions in the Medicare payment rates. See Section 9789.25(b) for the percentage change in the capital market basket that was applied to the preceding capital standard federal payment rate to establish the applicable capital payment rate for a discharge date.

(C) The "capital standard federal payment rate" is $ 414.18 for discharges occurring on or after January 1, 2004 and before November 29, 2004. For each update in the composite factor, the capital standard federal payment rate for the preceding period is adjusted by the rate of change in the capital market basket. See Section 9789.25(b) for the capital standard federal payment rate for discharges occurring on or after November 29, 2004 by date of discharge.

(D) The "capital geographic adjustment factor" is the post-reclassification geographic adjustment factor that is published in the Payment Impact File for each Medicare payment update. See Section 9789.25(c) for the variable name on the Payment Impact File by date of discharge.

(E) For discharges occurring before January 1, 2008, the "large urban add-on" is an additional 3% of what would otherwise be payable to the hospital, and the large urban add-on is eliminated for discharges occurring on or after January 1, 2008.

(F) The "capital disproportionate share adjustment factor" is published in the Payment Impact File for each Medicare payment update. See Section 9789.25(c) for the variable name on the Payment Impact File by date of discharge.

(G) The "capital indirect medical education adjustment factor" (capital IME adjustment) is published in Payment Impact File for each Medicare payment update. See Section 9789.25(c) for the variable name on the Payment Impact File by date of discharge.

(2) The hospital-adjusted rate for prospective operating costs is determined by the following formula:

(A) [(Labor-related national standardized amount × operating wage index) + nonlabor-related national standardized amount] × [1 + operating disproportionate share adjustment factor + operating indirect medical education adjustment]

For discharges on or after November 29, 2004, the hospital-adjusted rate for prospective operating costs is determined by the following formula as modified by Section 403 of Public Law 108–173 amended Sections 1886(d)(3)(E) of the Social Security Act, and as stated in Title 42, Code of Regulations, Section 412.64(h)(3), which document is hereby incorporated by reference and will be made available upon request to the Administrative Director and in conformance with California Labor Code Section 5307.1(g)(1)(A)(i). See Section 9789.25(a) for the Federal Regulation reference for the effective date, revisions, and amendments by date of discharge:

1. The wage-adjusted standard rate is determined as follows:

If operating wage index >1.0, wage-adjusted rate = labor-related national standard operating rate × (labor-related share × operating wage index + nonlabor-related share).

If operating wage index <=1.0, wage-adjusted rate= labor-related national standard operating rate × (.62 × operating wage index + .38).

2. The wage-adjusted operating rate is further adjusted for any additional payments for teaching and serving a disproportionate share of low-income patients.

OMFS Adjusted operating rate = wage-adjusted standard rate × (1 + operating disproportionate share adjustment factor + operating indirect medical education adjustment).

(B) The "labor-related national standardized amount" is $3,136.39 for discharges occurring on or after January 1, 2004 and before November 29, 2004. For each update in the composite factor, the labor-related national standardized amount for the preceding period is adjusted by the rate of change in the operating market basket. See Section 9789.25(b) for the national standard operating rate for discharges occurring on or after November 29, 2004 by date of discharge.

(C) The "operating wage index" is published in the Payment Impact File for each Medicare payment update. See Section 9789.25(c) for the variable name on the Payment Impact File by date of discharge.

(D) The "nonlabor-related national standardized amount" is $1,274.85, as published by CMS in the Federal Register of October 6, 2003 (correcting the publication of August 1, 2003), at Vol. 68, page 57735, Table 1A, which document is hereby incorporated by reference and will be made available upon request to the Administrative Director and as modified by Medicare Prescription Drug, Improvement, and Modernization Act of 2003, Public Law 108–173, §401, which document is hereby incorporated by reference and will be made available upon request to the Administrative Director.

For discharges on or after November 29, 2004, the nonlabor-related portion is that portion of operating costs attributable to nonlabor costs, and is determined by the following formula as modified by Section 403 of Public Law 108–173 amended sections 1886(d)(3)(E) of the Social Security Act, and as stated in Title 42, Code of Regulations, Section 412.64(h), which documents are hereby incorporated by reference and will be made available upon request to the Administrative Director. See Section 9789.25(a) for the Federal Regulation reference for the effective date, revisions, and amendments by date of discharge:

100% – labor-related portion (%).

(E) The "operating disproportionate share adjustment factor" is published in the Payment Impact File for each Medicare payment update, and as modified by Medicare Prescription Drug, Improvement, and Modernization Act of 2003, Public Law 108–173, §402, which document is hereby incorporated by reference and will be made available upon request to the Administrative Director. See Section 9789.25(c) for the variable name on the Payment Impact File by date of discharge.

For discharges on or after March 5, 2015, the OMFS "operating disproportionate share (DSH) adjustment factor" is determined by the following formula:

OMFS operating DSH adjustment factor equals the sum of a) the Medicare DSH operating adjustment and b) 3 * the Medicare DSH operating adjustment * the Uncompensated Care adjustment).

The Medicare DSH operating adjustment is published in the Payment Impact File for each Medicare payment update, as amended by section 3133 of the Affordable Care Act, and set forth by new section 1886(r) of the Social Security Act, and as implemented in Title 42, Code of Regulations, Section 412.106, which documents are incorporated by reference and will be made available upon request to the Administrative Director. See Section 9789.25(a) for the Federal Regulation reference for the effective date, revisions, and amendments by date of discharge. See Section 9789.25(c) for the variable name on the Payment Impact File by date of discharge.

The Uncompensated Care adjustment factor reflects the change in percentage of uninsured individuals and additional Medicare adjustments, as defined in Section 1886(r) of the Social Security Act, as implemented in Title 42, Code of Regulations, Section 412.106, and as published by CMS in the Federal Register, which documents are incorporated by reference and will be made available upon request to the Administrative Director. See Section 9789.25(a) for the Federal Regulation reference for the effective date, revisions, and amendments by date of discharge. See Section 9789.25(b) for the Uncompensated Care adjustment factor for discharges occurring on or after March 5, 2015, by date of discharge.

(F) The "operating indirect medical education adjustment" is published in the Payment Impact File for each Medicare payment update, and as modified by Medicare Prescription Drug, Improvement, and Modernization Act of 2003, Public Law 108–173, §502, which document is hereby incorporated by reference and will be made available upon request to the Administrative Director. See Section 9789.25(c) for the variable name on the Payment Impact File by date of discharge.

(G) For sole community hospitals, the operating component of the composite rate shall be the higher of the prospective operating costs determined using the formula in Section 9789.21(e)(2) or the hospital-specific rate published in the Payment Impact File for each Medicare payment update. See Section 9789.25(c) for the variable name on the Payment Impact File by date of discharge.

(3) A table of composite factors for each hospital in California is contained in Section 9789.23. The sole community hospital composite factors that incorporate the operating component specified in Section 9789.21(e)(2)(G) are listed in italics in the column headed "Composite" set forth in Section 9789.23.

(f) "Costs" means the total billed charges for an admission, excluding non-medical charges such as television and telephone charges, charges for Durable Medical Equipment for in home use, charges for implantable medical devices, hardware, and/or instrumentation reimbursed under subdivision (g) of Section 9789.22, multiplied by the hospital's total cost-to-charge ratio plus the hospital's documented paid spinal device costs, plus an additional 10% of the hospital's documented paid cost, net of discounts and rebates, not to exceed a maximum of $250.00, plus any sales tax and/or shipping and handling charges actually paid.

(g) "Cost-to-charge ratio" means the sum of the hospital specific operating cost-to-charge ratio and the hospital specific capital cost-to-charge ratio. The operating cost-to-charge ratio and capital cost-to-charge ratio for each hospital are published in the Payment Impact File for each Medicare payment update. See Section 9789.25(c) for the variable names on the Payment Impact File by date of discharge.

(h) "Cost outlier case" means a hospitalization for which the hospital's costs, as defined in subdivision (f) above, exceeds the cost outlier threshold.

(i) "Cost outlier threshold" means the sum of the Inpatient Hospital Fee Schedule payment amount, the payment for new medical services and technologies reimbursed under Section 9789.22(h), the hospital specific outlier factor, and any additional allowance for spinal devices under section 9789.22(g)(2).

(j) "Diagnosis Related Group (DRG)" means the inpatient classification scheme used by CMS for hospital inpatient reimbursement. The DRG system classifies patients based on principal diagnosis, surgical procedure, age, presence of comorbidities and complications and other pertinent data.

(k) "DRG weight" means the weighting factor for a diagnosis-related group assigned by CMS for the purpose of determining payment under Medicare. Section 9789.24 lists the DRG weights and geometric mean lengths of stay as assigned by CMS.

(*l*) "FY" means the CMS fiscal year October 1 through September 30.

(m) "Hospital" means any facility as defined in Section 1250 of the Health and Safety Code.

(n) "Inpatient" means a person who has been admitted to a hospital for the purpose of receiving inpatient services. A person is considered an inpatient when he or she is formally admitted as an inpatient with the expectation that he or she will remain at least overnight and occupy a bed, even if it later develops that such person can be discharged or is transferred to another facility and does not actually remain overnight.

(o) Unless otherwise provided by applicable provisions of this fee schedule, "Inpatient Hospital Fee Schedule maximum payment amount" is that amount determined by multiplying the DRG weight × hospital composite factor × 1.20 and by making any adjustments required in Section 9789.22.

(p) "Labor-related portion" is that portion of operating costs attributable to labor costs, as specified in the Federal Register notices announcing revisions in the Medicare payment rates. See Section 9789.25(b) for the Federal Register reference that defines the labor-related portion by date of discharge.

(q) As stated in Title 42, Code of Federal Regulations, Section 412.316(b), for discharges before January 1, 2008, "Large urban add-on" means an additional 3% of what would otherwise be payable to the hospital located in large urban areas. The "large urban add-on" adjustment was eliminated for discharges on or after January 1, 2008. See Section 9789.25(a) for the Code of Federal Regulations reference for effective date, revisions, and amendments by date of discharge. The "large urban add-on" is indicated in the annual Payment Impact File for each Medicare payment update. See Section 9789.25(c) for the variable name on the Payment Impact File by date of discharge.

(r) "Medical services" means those goods and services provided pursuant to Article 2 (commencing with Section 4600) of Chapter 2 of Part 2 of Division 4 of the Labor Code.

(s) "Operating outlier factor" means ((fixed loss cost outlier threshold × ((labor-related portion × operating wage index) + nonlabor-related portion)) × (operating cost-to-charge ratio/ total cost-to-charge ratio)).

(1) The wage index, also referred to as operating wage index published in the Payment Impact File for each Medicare payment update, is specified as the wage index in the Federal Register notices announcing revisions in the Medicare payment rates. See Section 9789.25(c) for the variable name on the Payment Impact File by date of discharge and see Section 9789.25(b) for the Federal

Register reference that defines the wage index by date of discharge.

(2) The nonlabor-related portion is that portion of operating costs attributable to nonlabor costs as defined in the Federal Register of October 6, 2003 (correcting the publication of August 1, 2003), at Vol. 68, page 57735, Table 1A, which document is hereby incorporated by reference and will be made available upon request to the Administrative Director.

For discharges on or after November 29, 2004, the nonlabor-related portion is determined by the following formula as modified by Section 403 of Public Law 108–173 amended Sections 1886(d)(3)(E) of the Social Security Act, and as stated in Title 42, Code of Regulations, Section 412.64(h), which document is hereby incorporated by reference and will be made available upon request to the Administrative Director. See Section 9789.25(a) for the Federal Regulation reference for the effective date, revisions, and amendments by date of discharge:

100% – labor-related portion (%).

(t) "Outlier factor" means the sum of the capital outlier factor and the operating outlier factor. A table of hospital specific outlier factors for each hospital in California is contained in Section 9789.23.

(u) "Payment Impact File" means the Prospective Payment System Payment Impact File published by CMS, for each Medicare update. See Section 9789.25(c) for references to the Payment Impact File by date of discharge.

(v) "Spinal device" means a medical device that is an instrument, apparatus, implement, machine, contrivance, implant, in vitro reagent, or other similar related article, including a component part, or accessory which is: (1) recognized in the official National Formulary, or the United States Pharmacopoeia, or any supplement to them; (2) intended for use in the cure, mitigation, treatment, or prevention of disease; or (3) intended to affect the structure or any function of the body, and which does not achieve any of its primary intended purposes through chemical action within or on the body and which is not dependent upon being metabolized for the achievement of any of its primary intended purposes.

(w) "Professional Component" means the charges associated with a professional service provided to a patient by a hospital based physician. This component is billed separately from the inpatient charges.

Note: Authority cited: Sections 133, 4603.5, 5307.1 and 5307.3, Labor Code. Reference: Sections 4600, 4603.2, 5307.1 and 5318, Labor Code.

History: 1. New section filed 1-2-2004 as an emergency; operative 1-2-2004 (Register 2004, No. 2). A Certificate of Compliance must be transmitted to OAL by 5-3-2004 or emergency language will be repealed by operation of law on the following day.

2. Certificate of Compliance as to 1-2-2004 order, including amendment of section, transmitted to OAL 4-30-2004 and filed 6-15-2004 (Register 2004, No. 25).

3. Amendment filed 12-27-2012; operative 1-1-2013 as a file and print only pursuant to Government Code section 11340.9(g) (Register 2012, No. 52).

4. Amendment of subsections (b), (e)(1)(A), (e)(2)(E) and (f), new subsection (v) and subsection relettering filed 2-4-2015; operative 3-5-2015. Submitted to OAL for printing only pursuant to Government Code section 11340.9 (Register 2015, No. 6).

5. Amendment of subsection (e)(2)(B) filed 3-14-2016; operative 3-1-2016 pursuant to Labor Code section 5307.1(g)(2). Submitted to OAL for filing and printing only pursuant to Labor Code section 5307.1(g)(2) (Register 2016, No. 12).

6. Editorial correction of subsections (e)(2)(A)1. and (o) (Register 2018, No. 15).

Ref.: Hanna § 22.05[2]; Herlick Handbook §§ 1.01[3][b], 4.17[1].

§9789.22. Payment of Inpatient Hospital Services.

(a) Unless otherwise provided by applicable provisions of this fee schedule, the maximum payment for inpatient medical services shall be determined by multiplying 1.20 by the product of the hospital's composite factor and the applicable DRG weight and by making any adjustments required by this fee schedule. The fee determined under this subdivision shall be a global fee, constituting the maximum reimbursement to a hospital for inpatient medical services not exempted under this section. However, preadmission services rendered by a hospital more than 24 hours before admission are separately reimbursable.

(b) The maximum payment for inpatient medical services includes reimbursement for all of the inpatient operating costs specified in Title 42, Code of Federal Regulations, Section 412.2(c), which is incorporated by reference and will be made available upon request to the Administrative Director, and the inpatient capital-related costs specified in Title 42, Code of Federal Regulations, Section 412.2(d), which is incorporated by reference and will be made available upon request to the Administrative Director. See Section 9789.25(a) for the Code of Federal Regulations reference for the effective date, revisions, and amendments by date of discharge.

(c) The maximum payment shall include the cost items specified in Title 42, Code of Federal Regulations, Section 412.2(e)(1), (2), (3), and (5), which in incorporated by reference and will be made available upon request to the Administrative Director. The maximum allowable fees for cost item set forth at 42 C.F.R. Section 412.2(e)(4), "the acquisition costs of hearts, kidneys, livers, lungs, pancreas, and intestines (or multivisceral organ) incurred by approved transplantation centers," shall be based on the documented paid cost of procuring the organ or tissue. See Section 9789.25(a) for the Code of Federal Regulations reference for the effective date, revisions, and amendments by date of discharge.

(d) The maximum payment shall cover all items and services provided to hospital inpatients other than professional services provided by physicians and other practitioners that are payable under the Official Medical Fee Schedule — physicians fee schedule section in effect at the time the service was rendered (see Section 9789.111(a)). Except for services paid under the physicians fee schedule, all billing for payments shall originate from hospitals and payment may be made only to hospitals for the covered items and services, including any spinal device separately payable under Sections 9789.22(g).

(e) Hospitals billing for fees under this section shall be submitted in accordance with the e-billing regulations beginning with Section 9792.5.0 or the standardized paper billing regulations beginning with Section 9792.5.2.

(f)(1) Cost Outlier cases.

(A) Unless otherwise provided, except for inpatient services provided by a hospital transferring an inpatient to another hospital or post-acute care provider in accordance with section 9789.22(j), inpatient services for cost outlier cases, shall be reimbursed as follows:

Step 1: Determine the Inpatient Hospital Fee Schedule maximum payment amount (DRG weight × 1.2 × hospital specific composite factor).

Step 2: Determine costs according to section 9789.21(f).

Step 3: Determine outlier threshold. Outlier threshold = (Inpatient Hospital Fee Schedule payment amount + hospital specific outlier factor + any new technology pass-through payment determined under Section 9789.22(h) + any additional allowance for spinal devices under Section 9789.22(g)(2)).

(B) Inpatient services provided by a hospital transferring an inpatient to another hospital subject to section 9789.22(j)(1) for cost outlier cases, shall be reimbursed as follows:

Step 1: Determine the Inpatient Hospital Fee Schedule maximum payment amount according to section 9789.22(j)(1).

Step 2: Determine costs according to section 9789.21(f).

Step 3: Determine outlier threshold. Outlier threshold = ((Inpatient Hospital Fee Schedule payment amount + hospital specific outlier factor) geometric length of stay for the DRG × (the actual length of stay for the case + one day)) + any new technology pass-through payment + any additional allowance for spinal devices under Section 9789.22(g)(2). The outlier threshold determined under this subdivision shall not exceed the amount determined under subdivision (A) of this section.

Inpatient services provided by the receiving hospital (final discharging hospital) subject to section 9789.22(j)(1) for cost outlier cases shall be reimbursed according to subdivision (A) of this section.

(C) Inpatient services provided by a hospital transferring an inpatient to a post-acute care provider subject to section 9789.22(j)(2)(A) for cost outlier cases, shall be reimbursed according to subdivision (B).

(D) Inpatient service discharges assigned to a special pay DRG provided by a hospital transferring an inpatient to a post-acute care provider subject to section 9789.22(j)(2)(B) for cost outlier cases, shall be reimbursed as follows:

Step 1: Determine the Inpatient Hospital Fee Schedule maximum payment amount according to section 9789.22(j)(2)(B).

Step 2: Determine costs according to section 9789.21(f).

Step 3: Determine outlier threshold. Outlier threshold = (Inpatient Hospital Fee Schedule payment amount + hospital specific outlier factor) × 0.5 + ((Inpatient Hospital Fee Schedule payment amount + hospital specific outlier factor) × 0.5 the geometric mean length of stay × the actual length of stay plus one day) + any new technology pass-through payment determined under Section 9789.22(h) + any additional allowance for spinal devices under Section 9789.22(g)(2). The outlier threshold determined under this subdivision shall not exceed the amount determined under subdivision (A) of this section.

(2) If costs exceed the outlier threshold, the case is a cost outlier case. The additional allowance for the outlier case equals 0.8 × (costs − cost outlier threshold).

(3) For discharges before January 1, 2013, for purposes of determining whether a case qualifies as a cost outlier case under this subdivision, charges for implantable spinal device and/or instrumentation reimbursed under subsection (g)(1) is excluded from the calculation of costs. If an admission for a complex spinal surgery DRG qualifies as a cost outlier case, any implantable spinal device and/or instrumentation shall be separately reimbursed under subsection (g)(1).

(g) Additional allowance for spinal devices used in complex spinal surgery:

(1) For discharges occurring before January 1, 2013, costs for spinal devices used during complex spinal surgery DRGs shall be separately reimbursed at the hospital's documented paid cost, plus an additional 10% of the hospital's documented paid cost, net of discounts and rebates, not to exceed a maximum of $250.00, plus any sales tax and/or shipping and handling charges actually paid.

(2) For discharges occurring on or after January 1, 2013 but before January 1, 2014, an additional allowance of $9,140 shall be made for spinal devices used during complex spinal surgery MS-DRGs 453, 454, and 455; an additional allowance of $3,170 shall be made for spinal devices used during complex spinal surgery MS-DRG 456; and an additional allowance of $670 shall be made for spinal devices used during complex spinal surgery MS-DRGs 028, 029, and 030.

(3) For discharges occurring on or after January 1, 2014, complex spinal surgery DRGs shall not receive any additional or separate reimbursement for spinal devices, unless the Administrative Director extends section 9789.22(g)(2) to discharges occurring on or after January 1, 2014, in accordance with Labor Code Section 5307.1(m) through a later enacted regulation.

(h) "New technology pass-through": Additional payments will be allowed for new medical services and technologies as provided by CMS and set forth in Title 42, Code of Federal Regulations Section 412.87 and Section 412.88 which document is hereby incorporated by reference and will be made available upon request to the Administrative Director. See Section 9789.25(a) for the Code of Federal Regulations reference for the effective date, revisions, and amendments by date of discharge.

(i) Sole Community Hospitals: If a hospital meets the criteria for sole community hospitals, under Title 42, Code of Federal Regulations §412.92(a), and has been classified by CMS as a sole community hospital, its payment rates are determined under Title 42, Code of Federal Regulations §412.92(d), which document is hereby incorporated by reference and will be made available upon request to the Administrative Director. See Section 9789.25(a) for the Code of Federal Regulations reference for the effective date, revisions, and amendments by date of discharge.

(j) Transfers

(1) Inpatient services provided by a hospital transferring an inpatient to another hospital are exempt from the maximum reimbursement formula set forth in Section 9789.22(a). Maximum reimbursement for inpatient medical services of a hospital transferring an inpatient to another hospital shall be a per diem rate for each day of the patient's stay in that hospital, not to exceed the amount that

would have been paid under Section 9789.22(a). However, the first day of the stay in the transferring hospital shall be reimbursed at twice the per diem amount and the hospital shall receive the additional allowances under Sections 9789.22(g) and (h) when applicable. The per diem rate is determined by dividing the maximum reimbursement as determined under Section 9789.22(a) by the average length of stay (as defined in Section 9789.21(a)) for that specific DRG. However, if an admission to a hospital transferring a patient is exempt from the maximum reimbursement formula set forth in Section 9789.22(a) because it satisfies one or more of the requirements of Section 9789.22(k), this subdivision shall not apply. Inpatient services provided by the hospital receiving the patient shall be reimbursed under the provisions of Section 9789.22(a).

(2) Post-acute care transfers exempt from the maximum reimbursement set forth in Section 9789.22(a).

(A) When an acute care patient is discharged to a post-acute care provider which is a rehabilitation hospital or distinct part rehabilitation unit of an acute care hospital or a long-term hospital, and the patient's discharge is assigned to one of the qualifying DRGs as specified in the Federal Register, payment to the transferring hospital shall be made as set forth in Section 9789.22(j)(1). See Section 9789.25(b) for the Federal Register reference that contains the qualifying DRGs for a given discharge.

(B) When an acute care patient is discharged to a post-acute care provider and the patient's discharge is assigned to one of the qualifying special pay DRGs as specified in the Federal Register, the payment to the transferring hospital is 50% of the amount paid under Section 9789.22(a), plus 50% of the per diem, set forth in Section 9789.22(j)(1) for each day, up to the full DRG amount. See Section 9789.25(b) for the Federal Register reference that contains the qualifying DRGs for a given discharge.

(k) The following are exempt from the maximum reimbursement formula set forth in Section 9789.22(a) and are paid on a reasonable cost basis.

(1) Critical access hospitals;

(2) Children's hospitals that are engaged in furnishing services to inpatients who are predominantly individuals under the age of 18;

(3) Cancer hospitals as defined by Title 42, Code of Federal Regulations, Section 412.23(f) which document is hereby incorporated by reference and will be made available upon request to the Administrative Director. See Section 9789.25(a) for the Code of Federal Regulations reference for the effective date, revisions, and amendments by date of discharge;

(4) Veterans Administration hospitals;

(5) Long term care hospitals as defined by Title 42, Code of Federal Regulations, Section 412.23(e) which document is hereby incorporated by reference and will be made available upon request to the Administrative Director. See Section 9789.25(a) for the Code of Federal Regulations reference for the effective date, revisions, and amendments by date of discharge;

(6) Rehabilitation hospital or distinct part rehabilitation units of an acute care hospital or a psychiatric hospital or distinct part psychiatric unit of an acute care hospital;

(7) The cost of durable medical equipment provided for use at home is exempt from this Inpatient Hospital Fee Schedule. The cost of durable medical equipment shall be paid pursuant to Section 9789.60; and

(8) Out of state hospitals.

(*l*) For discharges occurring before January 1, 2013, a hospital that is not listed on the Medicare Cost Report should notify the Administrative Director and provide in writing the following information: OSHPD Licensure number, Medicare provider number, physical location, number of beds, and, if applicable, avearage [average] FTE residents in approved training programs. If a hospital has been in operation for more than one year, information should also be provided on the precentage [percentage] of inpatient days attributable to Medicaid patients.

For discharges occurring on or after January 1, 2013, a hospital that is not listed in Section 9789.23, may notify the Administrative Director and provide in writing the following Medicare information: Medicare provider number, physical location, county code, hospital specific operating and capital CCRs, and DSH and/or IME adjustments, if applicable.

(m) Any hospital that believes its composite factor or hospital specific outlier factor was erroneously determined because of an error in tabulating data may request the Administrative Director for a re-determination of its composite factor or hospital specific outlier factor. Such requests shall be in writing, shall state the alleged error, and shall be supported by written documentation. Within 30 days after receiving a complete written request, the Administrative Director shall make a redetermination of the composite factor or hospital specific outlier factor or reaffirm the published factor.

Note: Authority cited: Sections 133, 4603.5, 5307.1, 5307.3 and 5318, Labor Code. Reference: Sections 4600, 4603.2, 5307.1 and 5318, Labor Code.

History: 1. New section filed 1-2-2004 as an emergency; operative 1-2-2004 (Register 2004, No. 2). A Certificate of Compliance must be transmitted to OAL by 5-3-2004 or emergency language will be repealed by operation of law on the following day.

2. Certificate of Compliance as to 1-2-2004 order, including amendment of section, transmitted to OAL 4-30-2004 and filed 6-15-2004 (Register 2004, No. 25).

3. Amendment filed 12-27-2012; operative 1-1-2013 as a file and print only pursuant to Government Code section 11340.9(g) (Register 2012, No. 52).

4. Amendment of subsection (d), redesignation and amendment of portion of subsection (f)(1) as new subsection (f)(1)(A), new subsection (f)(1)(B), amendment of subsection (f)(3), repealer of subsection (g)(4) and amendment of subsection (j)(1) filed 2-4-2015; operative 3-5-2015. Submitted to OAL for printing only pursuant to Government Code section 11340.9 (Register 2015, No. 6).

5. Editorial correction of subsection (f)(1)(D) (Register 2018, No. 15).

Ref.: Hanna § 22.05[2]; Herlick Handbook §§ 1.01[3][b], 4.17[1].

§9789.23. Hospital Cost to Charge Ratios, Hospital Specific Outliers, and Hospital Composite Factors.

For discharges on or after January 1, 2004, hospital cost to charge ratios, hospital specific outliers, and hospital composite factors by date of discharge, are incorporated by reference, and are available at http://www.dir.ca.gov/dwc/OMFS9904.htm#4, or upon request to the Administrative Director at:

DIVISION OF WORKERS' COMPENSATION
(ATTENTION: OMFS)
P.O. BOX 420603
SAN FRANCISCO, CA 94142

Full Payment Impact File (impfile04zip) at http://www.cms.gov/providers/hipps/ippsputs.asp (Section 9789.23 reflects the modifications of the Medicare Prescription Drug, Improvement, and Modernization Act of 2003, Public Law 108-173, sections 402, 402 and 502, section 3133 of the Affordable Care Act, and section 1886(r) of the Social Security Act, which documents are hereby incorporated by reference and will be made available upon request to the Administrative Director.)

Record Layout at https://www.cms.gov/Medicare/Medicare-Fee-for-Service-Payment/AcuteInpatientPPS/index.html?redirect=/AcuteInpatientPPS/.

Composite Rate (in italics) reflects Sole Community Hospital adjustment. See Section 9789.25(a) for the Code of Federal Regulations reference for the effective date, revisions, and amendments by date of discharge, and see Section 9789.25(c) for references to the Payment Impact File by date of discharge.

Note: Authority cited: Sections 133, 4603.5, 5307.1, 5307.3 and 5318, Labor Code. Reference: Sections 4600, 4603.2, 5307.1 and 5318, Labor Code.

History: 1. New section filed 1-2-2004 as an emergency; operative 1-2-2004 (Register 2004, No. 2). A Certificate of Compliance must be transmitted to OAL by 5-3-2004 or emergency language will be repealed by operation of law on the following day.

2. Certificate of Compliance as to 1-2-2004 order, including amendment of section heading and repealer and new section, transmitted to OAL 4-30-2004 and filed 6-15-2004 (Register 2004, No. 25).

3. Amendment filed 3-13-2013; operative 3-15-2013. Submitted to OAL for filing and printing only pursuant to Labor Code section 5307.1(g)(2) (Register 2013, No. 11).

4. Amendment filed 2-4-2015; operative 3-5-2015. Submitted to OAL for printing only pursuant to Government Code section 11340.9 (Register 2015, No. 6).

2004 Note: It appears section 402 is cited twice in reference to Public Law 108-173 being incorporated into the revision of this section.

Ref.: Hanna § 22.05[2]; Herlick Handbook §§ 1.01[3][b], 4.17[1].

§9789.24. Diagnostic Related Groups, Relative Weights, Geometric Mean Length of Stay.

For discharges on or after January 1, 2004, diagnostic related groups, relative weights, and geometric mean length of stay by date of discharge, are incorporated by reference, and are available at http://www.dir.ca.gov/dwc/OMFS9904.htm#4, or upon request to the Administrative Director at:

DIVISION OF WORKERS' COMPENSATION
(ATTENTION: OMFS)
P.O. BOX 420603
SAN FRANCISCO, CA 94142

History: 1. New section filed 1-2-2004 as an emergency; operative 1-2-2004 (Register 2004, No. 2). A Certificate of Compliance must be transmitted to OAL by 5-3-2004 or emergency language will be repealed by operation of law on the following day.

2. Certificate of Compliance as to 1-2-2004 order transmitted to OAL 4-30-2004 and filed 6-15-2004 (Register 2004, No. 25).

3. Repealer and new section filed 3-13-2013; operative 3-15-2013. Submitted to OAL for filing and printing only pursuant to Labor Code section 5307.1(g)(2) (Register 2013, No. 11).

Ref.: Hanna § 22.05[2]; Herlick Handbook §§ 1.01[3][b], 4.17[1].

§9789.25. Federal Regulations, Federal Register Notices, and Payment Impact File by Date of Discharge.

(a) Federal Regulations by Date of Discharge

(1) The Federal Regulations can be accessed at: http://www.cms.gov/AcuteInpatientPPS/ and the referenced sections are incorporated by reference and will be made available upon request to the Administrative Director.

	Discharges Occurring On or After 1/1/2004	*Discharges Occurring On or After 11/29/2004*	*Discharges Occurring On or After 12/1/2005*	*Discharges Occurring On or After 12/1/2006*
Title 42, Code of Federal Regulations, §412.2	Effective October 1, 2003			
Title 42, Code of Federal Regulations, §412.23(e)	Effective date October 1, 2002 and revised as of October 1, 2003			
Title 42, Code of Federal Regulations, §412.23(f)	Effective October 1, 2002 and revised as of October 1, 2003			
Title 42, Code of Federal Regulations, Section 412.64	Effective October 1, 2004			
Title 42, Code of Federal Regulations, Section 412.87	Effective September 7, 2001 and revised as of October 1, 2003	Amended; effective October 1, 2004		

Title 42, Code of Federal Regulations, Section 412.88	Effective September 7, 2001 and amended August 1, 2002 and August 1, 2003 and revised as of October 1, 2003	Amended; effective October 1, 2004		
Title 42, Code of Federal Regulations, §412.92(a)	Effective October 1, 2002 and revised as of October 1, 2003		Amended; effective October 1, 2005	
Title 42, Code of Federal Regulations, §412.92(d)	Effective October 1, 2002 and revised as of October 1, 2003		Amended; effective October 1, 2005	
Title 42, Code of Federal Regulations, Section 412.316(b)	Effective November 11, 2003, large urban add-on is an additional 3%	Amended; effective October 1, 2004, large urban add-on is an additional 3%	Amended; effective October 1, 2004, large urban add-on is an additional 3%	Amended; effective October 1, 2006, large urban add-on is an additional 3%
	Discharges Occurring On or After 1/1/2008	*Discharges Occurring On or After 12/1/2008*	*Discharges Occurring On or After 12/1/2009*	*Discharges Occurring On or After 3/01/2011*
Title 42, Code of Federal Regulations, §412.2				Amended; effective October 1, 2010
Title 42, Code of Federal Regulations, §412.23(e)			Amended; effective October 1, 2009	Amended; effective October 1, 2010
Title 42, Code of Federal Regulations, §412.23(f)				
Title 42, Code of Federal Regulations, Section 412.64				
Title 42, Code of Federal Regulations, Section 412.87		Amended; effective October 1, 2008	Amended; effective October 1, 2009	
Title 42, Code of Federal Regulations, Section 412.88	Amended; effective October 1, 2007			
Title 42, Code of Federal Regulations, Section 412.92(a)				
Title 42, Code of Federal Regulations, Section 412.92(d)		Amended; effective October 1, 2008		
Title 42, Code of Federal Regulations, Section 412.316(b)	Amended; effective October 1, 2007, large urban add-on is eliminated			
	Discharges Occurring On or After 12/01/2011	*Discharges Occurring On or After 03/15/2013*	*Discharges Occurring On or After 03/05/2015*	*Discharges Occurring On or After 03/05/2015 (These 2015 factors are updated by AD Order dated 02/05/2015, and supersedes 2014 factors adopted under the OMFS rulemaking filed with the Secretary of State on 02/04/2015)*
Title 42, Code of Federal Regulations, §412.2				Amended; effective October 1, 2010
Title 42, Code of Federal Regulations, §412.23(e)	Amended; effective October 1, 2011			Amended; effective October 1, 2014
Title 42, Code of Federal Regulations, §412.23(f)				Effective October 1, 2002 and revised as of October 1, 2003
Title 42, Code of Federal Regulations, §412.64	Amended; effective October 1, 2011	Amended	Amended	Amended; effective October 1, 2014
Title 42, Code of Federal Regulations, Section 412.87				Amended; effective October 1, 2009
Title 42, Code of Federal Regulations, Section 412.88				Amended; effective October 1, 2007

Title 42, Code of Federal Regulations, Section 412.92(a)				Amended; effective October 1, 2005
Title 42, Code of Federal Regulations, Section 412.92(d)				Amended; effective October 1, 2008
Title 42, Code of Federal Regulations, Section 412.106			Amended; effective October 1, 2013	Amended; effective October 1, 2014
Title 42, Code of Federal Regulations, Section 412.316(b)				Amended; effective October 1, 2007

	Discharges Occurring On or After 3/01/2016	*Discharges Occurring On or After 01/01/2017*	*Discharges Occurring On or After 12/01/2017*	*Discharges Occurring On or After 12/01/2018*
Title 42, Code of Federal Regulations, §412.2	Amended; effective October 1, 2010	Amended; effective October 1, 2010	Amended; effective October 1, 2010	Amended; effective October 1, 2010
Title 42, Code of Federal Regulations, §412.23(e)	Amended; effective October 1, 2015	Amended; effective October 1, 2015	Amended; effective October 1, 2017	Amended; effective October 1, 2018
Title 42, Code of Federal Regulations, §412.23(f)	Effective October 1, 2002 and revised as of October 1, 2003	Effective October 1, 2002 and revised as of October 1, 2003	Effective October 1, 2002 and revised as of October 1, 2003	Effective October 1, 2002 and revised as of October 1, 2003
Title 42, Code of Federal Regulations, §412.64	Amended; effective October 1, 2015	Amended; effective October 1, 2016	Amended; effective October 1, 2017	Amended; effective October 1, 2018
Title 42, Code of Federal Regulations, Section 412.87	Amended; effective October 1, 2009	Amended; effective October 1, 2009	Amended; effective October 1, 2017	Amended; effective October 1, 2017
Title 42, Code of Federal Regulations, Section 412.88	Amended; effective October 1, 2007	Amended; effective October 1, 2007	Amended; effective October 1, 2007	Amended; effective October 1, 2007
Title 42, Code of Federal Regulations, Section 412.92(a)	Amended; effective October 1, 2005	Amended; effective October 1, 2005	Amended; effective October 1, 2005	Amended; effective October 1, 2018
Title 42, Code of Federal Regulations, Section 412.92(d)	Amended; effective October 1, 2008	Amended; effective October 1, 2008	Amended; effective October 1, 2008	Amended; effective October 1, 2018
Title 42, Code of Federal Regulations, Section 412.106	Amended; effective October 1, 2015	Amended; effective October 1, 2016	Amended; effective October 1, 2017	Amended; effective October 1, 2018
Title 42, Code of Federal Regulations, Section 412.316(b)	Amended; effective October 1, 2007	Amended; effective October 1, 2007	Amended; effective October 1, 2007	Amended; effective October 1, 2007

	Discharges Occurring On or After 11/01/2019
Title 42, Code of Federal Regulations, § 412.2	Amended; effective October 1, 2010
Title 42, Code of Federal Regulations, § 412.23(e)	Amended; effective October 1, 2015
Title 42, Code of Federal Regulations, § 412.23(f)	Effective October 1, 2002 and revised as of October 1, 2003
Title 42, Code of Federal Regulations, Section 412.64	Amended effective Octobter 1, 2019
Title 42, Code of Federal Regulations, § 412.87	Amended effiective October 1, 2019
Title 42, Code of Federal Regulations, Section 412.88	Amended effective October 1, 2019
Title 42, Code of Federal Reguiations, Section 412.92(a)	Amended effective October 1, 2005

Title 42, Code of Federal Regulations, Section 412.92(d)	Amended effective October 1, 2008
Title 42, Code of Federal Regulations, Section 412.106	Amended effective October 1, 2019
Title 42, Code of Federal Regulations, Section 412.316(b)	Amended effective October 1, 2007

(b) Federal Register Notices by Date of Discharge

(1) The Federal Register Notices can be accessed at: http://www.cms.gov/AcuteInpatientPPS/ and the referenced sections are incorporated by reference and will be made available upon request to the Administrative Director.

	Discharges Occurring On or After 1/1/2004	*Discharges Occurring On or After 11/29/2004*	*Discharges Occurring On or After 7/1/2005*	*Discharges Occurring On or After 12/1/2005*
Applicable FR Notices	(A) August 1, 2003 (CMS-1470-F; 68 FR 45346) final rule (B) October 6, 2003 (CMS-1470-CN; 68 FR 57732) correction notice	(A) August 11, 2004 (CMS-1428-F; 69 FR 48916) final rule (B) October 7, 2004 (CMS-1428-CN2; 69 FR 60242) correction notice (C) 69 FR 78526 (CMS-1428-F2) correction notice	(A) August 11, 2004 (CMS-1428-F; 69 FR 48916) final rule (B) October 7, 2004 (CMS-1428-CN2; 69 FR 60242) correction notice (C) 69 FR 78526 (CMS-1428-F2) correction notice	(A) August 12, 2005 (CMS-1500-F; 70 FR 47278) final rule (B) September 30, 2005 70 FR 57161 (CMS-1500-CN) correction notice
Capital wage index	Tables 4A–4C beginning on (A) page 57736	Tables $4A_1$–$4C_2$ beginning on (C) page 78619		Tables 4A–4C beginning on (A) page 47580 as corrected by Tables 4A–4C beginning on (B) page 57163
Capital market basket	Not applicable	0.7% ((A) page 49285)		0.8% ((A) page 47500)
Capital standard federal payment rate	$414.18 ((B) page 57735, Table 1D)	$416.73 ($413.83 × 1.007)		$420.06 ($416.73 × 1.008)
Complex Spinal Surgery DRGs	496, 497, 498, 519, 520, 531, 532			496, 497, 498, 519, 520, 531, 532, 546 (page 47308 of (A))
Fixed Loss Outlier Threshold	$31,000 ((A) page 45477)	$25,800 ((A) page 49278)		$23,600 ((A) page 47494)
National Standard Operating Rate	$3,136.39 ((B) page 57735, Table 1A)	$4,569.83 ($4,423.84 × 1.033)		$4,738.91 ($4,569.83 × 1.037)
Operating Wage Index	Tables 4A–4C beginning on (A) page 57736; PIF: Operating Wage Index location (WIGRN)	Tables $4A_1$–$4C_2$ beginning on (C) page 78619; PIF: Final Wage Index location (WIGRN)		Tables 4A–4C beginning on (A) page 47580 as corrected by Tables 4A–4C beginning on (B) page 57163; PIF: Post Reclass Wage Index location
Labor-Related Portion	Table 1A beginning on B page 57735	For wage indexes greater than 1.0, the labor-related portion is 71.066% of the standard operating rate. For wage indexes less than or equal to 1.0, the labor-related portion is 62%. (A) page 49070		For wage indexes greater than 1.0, the labor-related portion is 69.731% of the standard operating rate. For wage indexes less than or equal to 1.0, the labor-related portion is 62%. (A) page 47393
Post-acute care transfer to a rehabilitation hospital or unit or long-term hospital qualifying DRGs	DRGs 12, 14, 24, 25, 89, 90, 113, 121, 122, 130, 131, 236, 239, 243, 263, 264, 277, 278, 296, 297, 320, 321, 429, 462, 483, or 468 (A) beginning at page 45413		DRGs 12, 14, 24, 25, 88, 89, 90, 113, 121, 122, 127, 130, 131, 236, 239, 277, 278, 294, 296, 297, 320, 321, 395, 429, 468, 541 or 542 (B) beginning at page 60246	DRGs designated with a "yes" in "FY06 Final Rule Post-acute Care DRG" column in Table 5 (A) beginning at page 47617 and (B) beginning at page 57163
Post-acute care transfer qualifying DRGs	DRGs 209, 210 or 211 (A) beginning at page 45413			DRGs 7, 8, 210, 211, 233, 234, 471, 497, 498, 544, 545, 549, or 550 (A) beginning at page 47617 and (B) beginning at page 57163

	Discharges Occurring On or After 12/1/2006	*Discharges Occurring On or After 3/1/2007*	*Discharges Occurring On or After 1/1/2008*	*Discharges Occurring On or After 12/1/2008*
Applicable FR Notices	(A) August 18, 2006 (CMS-1488-F; 71 FR 47870) (B) October 11, 2006 (CMS-1488-N; 71 FR 59886) additional notice	(A) August 18, 2006 (CMS-1488-F; 71 FR 47870) (B) October 11, 2006 (CMS-1488-N; 71 FR 59886) additional notice (C) January 5, 2007 (CMS-1488-CN2; 72 fr 569) correction notice	(A) August 22, 2007 (CMS-1533-FC; 72 FR 47130) final rule (B) October 10, 2007 72 FR 57634 (CMS-1533-CN2) correction notice	(A) August 19, 2008 (CMS-1390-F; 73 FR 48434) final rule (B) October 3, 2008 73 FR 57888 (CMS-1390-N) correction notice
Capital wage index	Tables 4A-1–4C-1 (for discharges before 4/1/2007) and Tables 4A-2–4C-2 (for discharges occurring on or after 4/1/2007) beginning on (B) page 59975		Tables 4A–4C beginning on (B) page 57698	Tables 4A–4C beginning on (B) page 57956
Capital market basket	1.10% ((A) page 48163)		1.3% ((A) page 47426)	1.4% ((A) page 48776)
Capital standard federal payment rate	$424.68 ($420.06 × 1.0110)		$430.20 ($424.68 × 1.013)	$436.22 ($430.20 × 1.014)
Complex Spinal Surgery DRGs			028, 029, 030, 453, 454, 455, 456, 457, 458, 459, 460, 471, 472, 473	
Fixed Loss Outlier Threshold	$24,485 ((A) page 59890)		$22,185 ((A) Page 66887)	$20,045 ((A) page 57891)
National Standard Operating Rate	$4,900.03 ($4,738.91 × 1.034)		$5,061.73 ($4,900.03 × 1.033)	$5,243.95 ($5,061.73 × 1.036)
Operating Wage Index	Tables 4A-1–4C-1 (for discharges before 4/1/2007) and Tables 4A-2–4C-2 (for discharges occurring on or after 4/1/2007) beginning on (B) page 59975; PIF: Post Reclass Wage Index_a (for first half FY 2007) and Post Reclass Wage Index_b (for second half FY 2007)		Tables 4A–4C beginning on (B) page 57698; PIF: Post Reclass Wage Index location	Tables 4A–4C beginning on (B) page 57956; PIF: Post Reclass Wage Index location
Labor-Related Portion	For wage indexes greater than 1.0, the labor-related portion is 69.731% of the standard operating rate. For wage indexes less than or equal to 1.0, the labor-related portion is 62%. (A) page 48029		For wage indexes greater than 1.0, the labor-related portion is 69.731% of the standard operating rate. For wage indexes less than or equal to 1.0, the labor-related portion is 62%. (A) page 47344	For wage indexes greater than 1.0, the labor-related portion is 69.731% of the standard operating rate. For wage indexes less than or equal to 1.0, the labor-related portion is 62%. (A) page 48592
Post-acute care transfer to a rehabilitation hospital or unit or long-term hospital qualifying DRGs	DRGs designated with a "yes" in the "FY 07 Final Rule Post-acute Care DRG" column in Table 5 (B) beginning at page 60013	DRGs designated with a "yes" in the "FY 07 Final Rule Post-acute Care DRG" column in Table 5 (B) beginning at page 60013 and (C) beginning at page 573	Medicare Severity DRGs designated with a "yes" in the "FY08 Final Rule Post-Acute DRG" column in Table 5 (A) beginning at page 47539 and (B) at page 57727	Medicare Severity DRGs designated with a "yes" in the "FY09 Final Rule Post-Acute DRG" column in Table 5 (A) beginning at page 48899
Post-acute care transfer qualifying DRGs	DRGs 7, 8, 210, 211, 233, 234, 471, 497, 498, 545, 549, or 550 (B) beginning at page 60013	DRGs 7, 8, 210, 211, 233, 234, 471, 497, 498, 544, 545, 549, or 550 (B) beginning at page 60013 and (C) beginning at page 573	Medicare-Severity DRGs designated with a "yes" in the "FY08 Final Rule Special Pay DRG" column in Table 5 (A) beginning at page 47539 and (B) at page 57727	Medicare-Severity DRGs designated with a "yes" in the "FY09 Final Rule Special Pay DRG" column in Table 5 (A) beginning at page 48899

	Discharges Occurring On or After 12/1/2009	*Discharges Occurring On or After 3/01/2011*	*Discharges Occurring On or After 12/01/2011*	*Discharges Occurring On or After 1/1/2013 but Before 1/1/2014*
Applicable FR Notices	(A) August 27, 2009 (CMS-1406-F; FR 43754) final rule (B) October 7, 2009 (CMS-1406-CN; 74 FR 51496) correction notice	(A) August 16, 2010 (CMS-1498-F; FR 50042) final Rule (B) October 1, 2011 (CMS-1498-F; 75 FR 60640) correction	(A) August 18, 2011 (CMS-1518-F; FR 51476) final Rule (B) September 26, 2011 (CMS-1518-CN3; 76 FR 59263) correction	

Capital wage index	Tables 4A–4C beginning on page (A) 44085 as corrected by Tables 4A–4C beginning on (B) page 51505 for certain areas	Tables 4A–C Beginning on page (A) 50511	Tables 4A–C at https://www.cms.gov/AcuteInpatientPPS/01_overview.asp	
Capital market basket	1.2% ((B) page 51498)	1.2%, (A) page 50442	1.5%, (A) page 51806	
Capital standard federal payment rate	$441.46 ($436.22 × 1.012)	$446.75 ($441.46 × 1.012	$453.46 (446.75 × 1.015)	
Complex Spinal Surgery DRGs				028, 029, 030, 453, 454, 455, 456
Fixed Loss Outlier Threshold	$23,140 ((A) page 44011)	$23,075, (A) page 50441	$22,385, (A) page 51795	
National Standard Operating Rate	$5,354.08 ($5,243.95 × 1.021)	$5,493.28 ($5,354.08 × 1.026)	$5,658.08 ($5,493.28 × 1.03)	
Operating Wage Index	Tables 4A–4C beginning on page (A) 44085 as corrected by Tables 4A–4C beginning on (B) page 51505 for certain areas; PIF: Post Reclass Wage Index location	Tables 4A–C Beginning on page (A) 50511; PIF: FY 2011 Wage Index Location	Tables 4A–C at https://www.cms.gov/AcuteInpatientPPS/01_overview.asp; PIF: FY 2012 Wage Index Location	
Labor-Related Portion	For wage indexes greater than 1.0, the labor-related portion is 68.802% of the standard operating rate. For wage indexes less than or equal to 1.0, the labor-related portion is 62%. (A) page 43856	For wage indexes greater than 1.0, the labor-related portion is 68.8% of the standard operating rate. For wage indexes less than or equal to 1.0, the labor-related portion is 62% (A) page 50422	For wage indexes greater than 1.0, the labor-related portion is 68.8% of the standard operating rate. For wage indexes less than or equal to 1.0, the labor-related portion is 62% (A) page 51786	
Post-acute care transfer to a rehabilitation hospital or unit or long-term hospital qualifying DRGs	Medicare-Severity DRGs designated with a "yes" in the "FY 2010 Final Rule Post-Acute DRG" column in Table 5 (A) beginning at page 44126	Medicare-Severity DRGs designated with a "yes" in the "FY 2011 Final Rule Post-Acute DRG" Column in Table 5 (A) beginning at page 50547	Medicare-Severity DRGs designated with a "yes" in the "FY 2012 Final Rule Post-Acute DRG" Column in Table 5 https://www.cms.gov/AcuteInpatientPPS/	
Post-acute care transfer qualifying DRGs	Medicare-Severity DRGs designated with a "yes" in the "FY2010 Final Rule Special Pay DRG" column in Table 5 (A) beginning at page 44126	Medicare-Severity DRGs designated with a "yes" in the "FY 2011 Final Rule Special Pay DRG" column in Table 5 (A) Beginning at page 50547	Medicare-Severity DRGs designated with a "yes" in the "FY 2012 Final Rule Special Pay DRG" column in Table 5 https://www.cms.gov/AcuteInpatientPPS/	
	Discharges Occurring On or After 3/15/2013	*Discharges Occurring On or After 03/05/2015*	*Discharges Occurring On or After 03/05/2015 (These 2015 factors are updated by AD Order dated 02/05/2015, and supersedes 2014 factors adopted under the OMFS rulemaking filed with the Secretary of State on 02/04/2015)*	*Discharges Occurring On or After 03/01/2016*
Applicable FR Notices	(A) August 31, 2012 (CMS-1588-F; 77 FR 53258) final rule (B) October 3, 2012 (CMS-1588-CN2; 77 FR 60315; correction notice) (C) October 29, 2012 (CMS-1588-CN3; 77 FR 65495; correction notice)	(A) August 19, 2013 (CMS-1599-F; 78 FR 50496) Final Rule (B) October 3, 2013 (CMS-1599-CN2; 78 FR 61197; corrections) (C) October 3, 2013 (CMS-1599-IFC; 78 FR 61191; interim final rule) (D) January 2, 2014 (CMS-1599-CN3; 79 FR 61; corrections)	(A) August 22, 2014 (CMS-1607-F; 79 FR 49854) Final Rule (B) October 3, 2014 (CMS-1607-CN; 79 FR 59675; Corrections)	(A) August 17, 2015 (CMS-1632-F and IFC; 80 FR 49326; Final Rule) (B) October 5, 2015 (CMS-1632-CN; 80 FR 60055; Correction)

		(E) January 10, 2014 (CMS-1599-CN4; 79 FR 1741; corrections) (F) March 18, 2014 (CMS-1599-IFC2; 79 FR 15022; Interim final rule)		
Capital wage index	Tables 4A–C at https://www.cms.gov/AcuteInpatientPPS/01_overview.asp	Tables 4A–4C-CN2 at https://www.cms.gov/AcuteInpatientPPS/01_overview.asp	Tables 4A-1 Through 4C-2CN at https://www.cms.gov/Medicare/Medicare-Fee-for-Service-Payment/AcuteInpatientPPS/index.html	Table 3 at https://www.cms.gov/Medicare/Medicare-Fee-for-Service-Payment/AcuteInpatientPPS/index.html Note: Table 3 contains information by CBSA and information from the following tables that have been provided in previous fiscal years: Tables 3A, 3B, 4A, 4B, 4C, 4D, and 4F.
Capital market basket	1.2% (A) page 53703	1.2% (A) page 50507	1.5% (A) page 50390	1.3% (A) page 49795
Capital standard federal payment rate	$458.90 ($453.46 × 1.012)	$464.41 ($458.90 × 1.012)	$471.37 ($464.41 × 1.015)	$477.50 ($471.37 x 1.013)
Complex Spinal Surgery DRGs			N/A	N/A
Fixed Loss Outlier Threshold	$21,821 ((A) page 53696)	$21,748 ((A) page 50983)	$24,626 (B) page 59680	$22,539 (B) page 60058
National Standard Operating Rate	$5,805.19 ($5,658.08 × 1.026)	$5,950.32 ($5,805.19 × 1.025)	$6,122.88 ($5,950.32 × 1.029)	$6,269.83 ($6,122.88 × 1.024)
Operating Wage Index	Tables 4A–C at https://www.cms.gov/AcuteInpatientPPS/01_overview.asp; PIF: FY 2013 Wage Index Location	Tables 4A–C at https://www.cms.gov/AcuteInpatientPPS/01_overview.asp; PIF: FY 2014 Wage Index Location	Tables 4A-1 Through 4C-2CN at https://www.cms.gov/Medicare/Medicare-Fee-for-Service-Payment/AcuteInpatientPPS/index.html	Table 3 at https://www.cms.gov/Medicare/Medicare-Fee-for-Service-Payment/AcuteInpatientPPS/index.html Note: Table 3 contains information by CBSA and information from the following tables that have been provided in previous fiscal years: Tables 3A, 3B, 4A, 4B, 4C, 4D, and 4F.
Labor-Related Portion	For wage indexes greater than 1.0, the labor-related portion is 68.8% of the standard operating rate. For wage indexes less than or equal to 1.0, the labor-related portion is 62% (A) page 53685	For wage indexes greater than 1.0, the labor-related portion is 69.6% of the standard operating rate. For wage indexes less than or equal to 1.0, the labor-related portion is 62% (A) page 50972	For wage indexes greater than 1.0, the labor-related portion is 69.6% of the standard operating rate. For wage indexes less than or equal to 1.0, the labor-related portion is 62% (A) page 49991	For wage indexes greater than 1.0, the labor-related portion is 69.6% of the standard operating rate. For wage indexes less than or equal to 1.0, the labor-related portion is 62% (A) page 49505
Post-acute care transfer to a rehabilitation hospital or unit or long-term hospital qualifying DRGs	Medicare-Severity DRGs designated with a "yes" in the "FY 2013 Final Rule Post-Acute DRG" Column in Table 5 https://www.cms.gov/AcuteInpatientPPS/	Medicare-Severity DRGs designated with a "yes" in the "FY 2014 FR Post-Acute DRG" Column in Table 5 https://www.cms.gov/AcuteInpatientPPS/	Medicare-Severity DRGs designated with a "yes" in the "FINAL Post-Acute DRG" Column in Table 5 https://www.cms.gov/Medicare/Medicare-Fee-for-Service-Payment/AcuteInpatientPPS/index.html?redirect=/AcuteInpatientPPS/01_overview.asp	Medicare-Severity DRGs designated with a "yes" in the "FY 2016 Final Post-Acute DRG" Column in Table 5 https://www.cms.gov/Medicare/Medicare-Fee-for-Service-Payment/AcuteInpatientPPS/index.html?redirect=/AcuteInpatientPPS/01_overview.asp

Post-acute care transfer qualifying DRGs	Medicare-Severity DRGs designated with a "yes" in the "FY 2013 Final Rule Special Pay DRG" column in Table 5 https://www.cms.gov/AcuteInpatientPPS/	Medicare-Severity DRGs designated with a "yes" in the "FY 2014 FR Special Pay DRG" column in Table 5 https://www.cms.gov/AcuteInpatientPPS/	Medicare-Severity DRGs designated with a "yes" in the "FY 2015 NPRM Special Pay DRG" column in Table 5 https://www.cms.gov/Medicare/Medicare-Fee-for-Service-Payment/AcuteInpatientPPS/index.html?redirect=/AcuteInpatientPPS/01_overview.asp	Medicare-Severity DRGs designated with a "yes" in the "FY 2016 Final Special Pay DRG" column in Table 5 https://www.cms.gov/Medicare/Medicare-Fee-for-Service-Payment/AcuteInpatientPPS/index.html?redirect=/AcuteInpatientPPS/01_overview.asp
Uncompensated Care Adjustment		0.943 (A) page 50634	0.7619 (A) page 50014	0.6369 (A) page 49522

	Discharges Occurring on or After 01/01/2017	*Discharges Occurring on or After 12/01/2017*	*Discharges Occurring on or After 12/01/2018*	*Discharges Occurring on or After 11/01/2019*
Applicable FR Notices	(A) August 22, 2016 (CMS-1655-F; 81 FR 56762) final rule (B) October 5, 2016 (CMS-1655-F; 81 FR 68947; final rule; correction)	(A) August 14, 2017 (CMS-1677-F; 82 FR 37990 (B) October 4, 2017 (CMS-1677-CN; 82 FR 46138; Final rule; correction)	(A) August 17, 2018 (CMS-1694-F; 83 FR 41144) (B) October 3, 2018 (CMS-1694-CN2; 83 FR 49836; Correction)	(A) August 16, 2019 (CMS-1716-F; 84 FR 42044 (B) October 8, 2019 (CMS-1716-CN2; 84 FR 53603; correction)
Capital wage index	Table 3 at https://www.cms.gov/Medicare/Medicare-Fee-for-Service-Payment/AcuteInpatientPPS/index.html	Table 3 at https://www.cms.gov/Medicare/Medicare-Fee-for-Service-Payment/AcuteInpatientPPS/index.html	Table 3 at https://www.cms.gov/Medicare/Medicare-Fee-for-Service-Payment/AcuteInpatientPPS/index.html	Table 3 (CN), at https://www.cms.gov/Medicare/Medicare-Fee-for-Service-Payment/AcuteInpatientPPS/index.html
Capital market basket	1.2% (A) page 57295	1.3% (A) page 38174	1.4% (A) page 41730	1.5% (A) page 42640
Capital standard federal payment rate	$483.23 ($477.50 × 1.012)	$489.51 ($483.23 × 1.013)	$496.36 ($489.51 × 1.014)	$503.81 ($496.36 × 1.015)
Complex Spinal Surgery DRGs	N/A	N/A	N/A	N/A
Fixed Loss Outlier Threshold	$23,573 ((B) page 68952)	$26,537 ((B) page 46143)	$25,743 ((B) page 49844)	$26.552 ((B) page 53609)
National Standard Operating Rate	$6,439.11 ($6,269.83 × 1.027)	$6,612.97 ($6,439.11 × 1.027)	$6,804.75 ($6,612.97 × 1.029)	$7,008.89 ($6,804.75 × 1.030)
Operating Wage Index	Table 3 at https://www.cms.gov/Medicare/Medicare-Fee-for-Service-Payment/AcuteInpatientPPS/index.html	Table 3 at https://www.cms.gov/Medicare/Medicare-Fee-for-Service-Payment/AcuteInpatientPPS/index.html	Table 3 at https://www.cms.gov/Medicare/Medicare-Fee-for-Service-Payment/AcuteInpatientPPS/index.html	Table 3 (CN) at https://www.cms.gov/Medicare/Medicare-Fee-for-Service-Payment/AcuteInpatientPPS/index.html
Labor-Related Portion	For wage indexes greater than 1.0, the labor-related portion is 69.6% of the standard operating rate. For wage indexes less than or equal to 1.0, the labor-related portion is 62% (A) page 57276	For wage indexes greater than 1.0, the labor-related portion is 68.3% of the standard operating rate. For wage indexes less than or equal to 1.0, the labor-related portion is 62% (A) page 38157	For wage indexes greater than 1.0, the labor-related portion is 68.3% of the standard operating rate. For wage indexes less than or equal to 1.0, the labor-related portion is 62% (A) page 41713	For wage indexes greater than 1.0, the labor-related portion is 68.3% of the standard operating rate. For wage indexes less than or equal to 1.0, the labor-related portion is 62% (A) page 42325
Post-acute care transfer to a rehabilitation hospital or unit or long-term hospital qualifying DRGs	Medicare-Severity DRGs designated with a "yes" in the "FY 2017 FINAL Post-Acute DRG" Column in Table 5 https://www.cms.gov/Medicare/Medicare-Fee-for-Service-Payment/AcuteInpatientPPS/index.html?redirect=/AcuteInpatientPPS/01_overview.asp	Medicare-Severity DRGs designated with a "yes" in the "FY 2018 Final Post-Acute DRG" Column in Table 5 https://www.cms.gov/Medicare/Medicare-Fee-for-Service-Payment/AcuteInpatientPPS/index.html?redirect=/AcuteInpatientPPS/01_overview.asp	Medicare-Severity DRGs designated with a "yes" in the "FY 2019 FINAL Post-Acute DRG" Column in Table 5 https://www.cms.gov/Medicare/Medicare-Fee-for-Service-Payment/AcuteInpatientPPS/index.html	Medicare-Severity DRGs designated with a "yes" in the "FY 2020 FINAL Post-Acute DRG" Column in Table 5, (Final Rule and Correction Notice) https://www.cms.gov/Medicare/Medicare-Fee-for-Service-Payment/AcuteInpatientPPS/index.html

Post-acute care transfer qualifying DRGs	Medicare-Severity DRGs designated with a "yes" in the "FY 2017 FINAL Special Pay DRG" column in Table 5 https://www.cms.gov/Medicare/Medicare-Fee-for-Service-Payment/AcuteInpatientPPS/index.html?redirect=/AcuteInpatientPPS/01_overview.asp	Medicare-Severity DRGs designated with a "yes" in the "FY 2018 Final Special Pay DRG" column in Table 5 https://www.cms.gov/Medicare/Medicare-Fee-for-Service-Payment/AcuteInpatientPPS/index.html?redirect=/AcuteInpatientPPS/01_overview.asp	Medicare-Severity DRGs designated with a "yes" in the "FY 2019 FINAL Special Pay DRG" column in Table 5 https://www.cms.gov/Medicare/Medicare-Fee-for-Service-Payment/AcuteInpatientPPS/index.html	Medicare-Severity DRGs designated with a "yes" in the "FY 2020 FINAL Special Pay DRG" column in Table 5, (Final Rule and Correction Notice) https://www.cms.gov/Medicare/Medicare-Fee-for-Service-Payment/AcuteInpatientPPS/index.html
Uncompensated Care Adjustment	0.5536 (A) page 56950	0.5801 (A) page 38200	0.6751 (A) page 41409	0.6714 (A) page 42358

(c) Payment Impact File by Date of Discharge

(1) The Payment Impact File can be accessed at: http://www.cms.gov/AcuteInpatientPPS/ and the referenced sections are incorporated by reference and will be made available upon request to the Administrative Director.

	Discharges Occurring On or After 1/1/2004	*Discharges Occurring On or After 11/29/2004*	*Discharges Occurring On or After 12/1/2005*	*Discharges Occurring On or After 12/1/2006*
Applicable Payment Impact File (PIF)	FY2004 Final Rule Impact File	FY2005 Final Rule Impact File	FY2006 Final Rule Impact File	FY2007 Final Rule Impact File
Capital geographic adjustment factor	PIF: Capital Wage Index	PIF: POST RECLASS GAF	PIF: WICGRN	PIF: Post Reclass GAF_a (for first half FY 2007) and Post Reclass GAF_b (for capital second half FY 2007)
Large Urban Add-on	PIF: Post-Reclassification Urban/Rural location	PIF: Standardized payment location	PIF: URSPA	PIF: URSPA
Capital Disproportionate Share Adjustment Factor	PIF: Capital Disproportionate Share Adjustment location (DSHCPG)	PIF: Capital Disproportionate Share (DSH) Adjustment location (CAPITAL DSH ADJ.)	PIF: Capital Disproportionate Share (DSH) Adjustment location (DSHCPG)	PIF: Capital Disproportionate Share (DSH) Adjustment location (DSHCPG)
Capital Indirect Medical Education Adjustment Factor	PIF: Capital IME Adjustment location (TCHCP)	PIF: IME adjustment factor for capital PPS location (IME ADJUSTMENT-CAPITAL)	PIF: IME adjustment factor for capital PPS location (TCHCP)	PIF: IME adjustment factor for capital PPS location (TCHCP)
Operating Wage Index	Tables 4A–4C beginning on (A) page 57736; PIF: Operating Wage Index location (WIGRN)	Tables $4A_1$–$4C_2$ beginning on (C) page 78619; PIF: Final Wage Index location (WIGRN)	Tables 4A–4C beginning on (A) page 47580 as corrected by Tables 4A–4C beginning on (B) page 57163; PIF: Post Reclass Wage Index location	Tables 4A-1–4C-1 (for discharges before 4/1/2007) and Tables 4A-2–4C-2 (for discharges occurring on or after 4/1/2007) beginning on (B) page 59975; PIF: Post Reclass Wage Index_a (for first half FY 2007) and Post Reclass Wage Index_b (for second half FY 2007)
Operating Disproportionate Share Adjustment Factor	PIF: Operating DSH Adjustment Factor location (DSHOPG)	PIF: Operating Disproportionate Share (DSH) Adjustment Factor location (OPERATING DSH ADJ.)	PIF: Operating Disproportionate Share (DSH) Adjustment Factor location (DSHOPG)	PIF: Operating Disproportionate Share (DSH) Adjustment Factor location (DSHOPG)
Operating Indirect Medical Education Adjustment	PIF: Operating IME Adjustment location (TCHOP)	PIF: IME Adjustment Factor for Operating PPS location (IME ADJUSTMENT OPERATING)	PIF: IME Adjustment Factor for Operating PPS location (TCHOP)	PIF: IME Adjustment Factor for Operating PPS location (TCHOP)
Sole Community Hospital — Hospital Specific Rate	PIF: Hospital — Specific Rate location (HSPPUB)	PIF: Sole Community Hospital Cost/Case 1982/1987 and Sole Community Hospital Cost/Case 1996 locations	PIF: 82/87 Hospital Specific Rate Updated to FY 2006 (OLDHSPPS) and 1996 Hospital Specific Rate Updated to FY 2006 (HSP96) locations	PIF: 82/87/96 Hospital Specific Rate Updated to FY 2007 for SCH Providers location (HSP Rate)

Cost-to-Charge Ratio	PIF: Operating Cost-to-Charge Ratio location (OPCCR) and Capital Cost-to-Charge location (CPCCR)	PIF: Operating Cost-to-Charge Ratio location (OPCCR) and Capital Cost-to-Charge location (CPCCR)	PIF: Operating Cost-to-Charge Ratio location (OPCCR) and Capital Cost-to-Charge location (CPCCR)	PIF: Operating Cost-to-Charge Ratio location (OPCCR) and Capital Cost-to-Charge location (CPCCR)
	Discharges Occurring On or After 1/1/2008	*Discharges Occurring On or After 12/1/2008*	*Discharges Occurring On or After 12/1/2009*	*Discharges Occurring On or After 3/01/2011*
Applicable Payment Impact File (PIF)	FY2008 Final Rule	FY2009 Final Rule	FY2010 Correction Notice	FY 2011 Final Rule
Capital Geographic Adjustment Factor	Post Reclass GAF	Post Reclass GAF	Post Reclass GAF	FY 2011 GAF
Capital Disproportionate Share Adjustment Factor	PIF: Capital Disproportionate Share (DSH) Adjustment location (DSHCPG)	PIF: Capital Disproportionate Share (DSH) Adjustment location (DSHCPG)	PIF: Capital Disproportionate Share (DSH) Adjustment location (DSHCPG)	PIF: Capital Disproportionate Share (DSH) adjustment location (DSHCPG)
Capital Indirect Medical Education Adjustment Factor	PIF: IME adjustment factor for capital PPS location (TCHCP)	PIF: IME adjustment factor for capital PPS location (TCHCP)	PIF: IME adjustment factor for capital PPS location (TCHCP)	PIF: IME adjustment factor for capital PPS location (TCHCP)
Operating Wage Index	Tables 4A–4C beginning on (B) page 57698; PIF: Post Reclass Wage Index location	Tables 4A–4C beginning on (B) page 57956; PIF: Post Reclass Wage Index location	Tables 4A–4C beginning on page (A) 44085 as corrected by Tables 4A–4C beginning on (B) page 51505 for certain areas; PIF: Post Reclass Wage Index location	Tables 4A–C Beginning on page (A) 50511; PIF: FY 2011 Wage Index Location
Operating Disproportionate Share Adjustment Factor	PIF: Operating Disproportionate Share (DSH) Adjustment Factor location (DSHOPG)	PIF: Operating Disproportionate Share (DSH) Adjustment Factor location (DSHOPG)	PIF: Operating Disproportionate Share (DSH) Adjustment Factor location (DSHOPG)	PIF: Operating Disproportionate Share (DSH) Adjustment Factor location (DSHOPG)
Operating Indirect Medical Education Adjustment	PIF: IME Adjustment Factor for Operating PPS location (TCHOP)	PIF: IME Adjustment Factor for Operating PPS location (TCHOP)	PIF: IME Adjustment Factor for Operating PPS location (TCHOP)	PIF: IME Adjustment Factor for Operating PPS location (TCHOP)
Sole Community Hospital — Hospital Specific Rate	PIF: 82/87/96 Hospital Specific Rate Updated to FY 2008 for SCH Providers location (HSP Rate)	PIF: 82/87/96 Hospital Specific Payment (HSP) Rate Updated to FY 2009 for SCH Providers location (HSP Rate)	PIF: 82/87/96/06 Hospital Specific Payment (HSP) Rate Updated to FY 2010 for SCH Providers location (FY10 HSP Rate)	PIF: 82/87/96/06 Hospital Specific Payment (HSP) Rate Updated to FY2011 for SCH Providers location (FY11 HSP Rate)
Cost-to-Charge Ratio	PIF: Operating Cost-to-Charge Ratio location (OPCCR) and Capital Cost-to-Charge location (CPCCR)	PIF: Operating Cost-to-Charge Ratio location (Operating CCR) and Capital Cost-to-Charge location (Capital CCR)	PIF: Operating Cost-to-Charge Ratio location (Operating CCR) and Capital Cost-to-Charge location (Capital CCR)	PIF: Operating Cost-to-Charge Ratio location (Operating CCR) and Capital Cost-to-Charge location (Capital CCR)
	Discharges Occurring On or After 12/01/2011	*Discharges Occurring On or After 03/15/2013*	*Discharges Occurring On or After 03/05/2015*	*Discharges Occurring On or After 03/05/2015 (These 2015 factors are updated by AD Order dated 02/05/2015, and supersedes 2014 factors adopted under the OMFS rulemaking filed with the Secretary of State on 02/04/2015)*
Applicable Payment Impact File (PIF)	FY 2012 Final Rule-IPPS Impact File	FY 13 FR Impact File — updated October 2012	FY 2014 Impact file — updated January 2014 to reflect changes from the September 2013 correction notice and interim final rule with comment	FY 15 Impact File (August 22, 2014 Final Rule and October 3, 2014 Correction Notice)
Capital Geographic Adjustment Factor	FY 2012 GAF	FY 2013 GAF	FY 2014 GAF—Updated September 2013	FY 2015 GAF—Updated October 2014
Capital Disproportionate Share Adjustment Factor	PIF: Capital Disproportionate Share (DSH) adjustment location (DSHCPG)	PIF: Capital Disproportionate Share (DSH) adjustment location (DSHCPG)	PIF: Capital Disproportionate Share (DSH) adjustment location (DSHCPG)	PIF: Capital Disproportionate Share (DSH) adjustment location (DSHCPG)

Capital Indirect Medical Education Adjustment Factor	PIF: IME adjustment factor for capital PPS location (TCHCP)	PIF: IME adjustment factor for capital PPS location (TCHCP)	PIF: IME adjustment factor for capital PPS location (TCHCP)	PIF: IME adjustment factor for capital PPS location (TCHCP)
Operating Wage Index	Tables 4A–C at https://www.cms.gov/AcuteInpatientPPS/01_overview.asp; PIF: FY 2012 Wage Index location	Tables 4A–C at https://www.cms.gov/AcuteInpatientPPS/01_overview.asp; PIF: FY 2013 Wage Index location	Tables 4A–C–CN2 at https://www.cms.gov/AcuteInpatientPPS/01_overview.asp; PIF: FY 2014 Wage Index location	Tables 4A-1 Through 4C-2CN at https://www.cms.gov/Medicare/Medicare-Fee-for-Service-Payment/AcuteInpatientPPS/index.html
Operating Disproportionate Share Adjustment Factor	PIF: Operating Disproportionate Share (DSH) Adjustment Factor location (DSHOPG)	PIF: Operating Disproportionate Share (DSH) Adjustment Factor location (DSHOPG)	PIF: Operating Disproportionate Share Hospital (DSH) Adjustment Factor location (DSHOPG)	PIF: Operating Disproportionate Share Hospital (DSH) Adjustment. Reflects a 75% reduction to the DSH adjustment required under Section 3133 of the Affordable Care Act. Factor location (DSHOPG)
Operating Indirect Medical Education Adjustment	PIF: IME Adjustment Factor for Operating PPS location (TCHOP)	PIF: IME Adjustment Factor for Operating PPS location (TCHOP)	PIF: IME Adjustment Factor for Operating PPS location (TCHOP)	PIF: IME Adjustment Factor for Operating PPS location (TCHOP)
Sole Community Hospital — Hospital Specific Rate	PIF: 82/87/96/06 Hospital Specific Payment (HSP) Rate Updated to FY2012 for SCH Providers location (FY12 HSP Rate)	PIF: 82/87/96/06 Hospital Specific Payment (HSP) Rate Updated to FY2013 for SCH Providers location (FY13 HSP Rate)	PIF: 82/87/96/06 Hospital Specific Payment (HSP) Rate Updated to FY2014 for SCH and MDH Providers with the -0.2% adjustment for presumptive inpatient hospital status policy. Location (FY14 HSP Rate)	PIF: 82/87/96/06 Hospital Specific Payment (HSP) Rate Updated to FY2015 for SCH and MDH Providers. Location (FY14 HSP Rate)
Cost-to-Charge Ratio	PIF: Operating Cost-to-Charge Ratio location (Operating CCR) and Capital Cost-to-Charge location (Capital CCR)	PIF: Operating Cost-to-Charge Ratio location (Operating CCR) and Capital Cost-to-Charge location (Capital CCR)	PIF: Operating Cost-to-Charge Ratio location (Operating CCR) and Capital Cost-to-Charge location (Capital CCR)	PIF: Operating Cost-to-Charge Ratio location (Operating CCR) and Capital Cost-to-Charge location (Capital CCR)
	Discharges Occurring On or After 03/01/2016	*Discharges Occurring On or After 01/01/2017*	*Discharges Occurring On or After 12/01/2017*	*Discharges Occurring On or After 12/01/2018*
Applicable Payment Impact File (PIF)	FY 16 Impact File (August 17, 2015 Final Rule and October 5, 2015 Correction Notice)	FY 17 Impact File (August 22, 2016 Final Rule and October 5, 2016 Correction Notice)	FY 18 Impact File (August 14, 2017 Final Rule and October 4, 2017 Correction Notice)	FY 19 Impact File (August 17, 2018 Final Rule and October 3, 2018 Correction Notice)
Capital Geographic Adjustment Factor	FY 2016 GAF — Updated October 2015	FY 2017 GAF — Updated October 2016	FY 2018 GAF — Updated October 2017	FY 2019 GAF — Updated October 2018
Capital Disproportionate Share Adjustment Factor	PIF: Capital Disproportionate Share (DSH) adjustment location (DSHCPG)	PIF: Capital Disproportionate Share (DSH) adjustment location (DSHCPG)	PIF: FY 2018 Capital Disproportionate Share (DSH) adjustment location (DSHCPG)	PIF: FY 2019 Capital Disproportionate Share Share (DSH) adjustment (DSHCPP)
Capital Indirect Medical Education Adjustment Factor	PIF: IME adjustment factor for capital PPS location (TCHCP)	PIF: IME adjustment factor for capital PPS location (TCHCP)	PIF: IME adjustment factor for capital PPS location (TCHCP)	PIF: IME adjustment factor for capital PPS location (TCHCP)
Operating Wage Index	Table 3 at https://www.csm.gov/Medicare/Medicare-Fee-for-Service-Payment/AcuteInpatientPPS/index.html Note: Table 3 contains information by CBSA and information from the following tables that have been provided in previous fiscal years: Tables 3A, 3B, 4A, 4B, 4C, 4D, and 4F.	Table 3 at https://www.cms.gov/Medicare/Medicare-Fee-for-Service-Payment/AcuteInpatientPPS/index.html	Table 3 at https://www.cms.gov/Medicare/Medicare-Fee-for-Service-Payment/AcuteInpatientPPS/index.html	Table 3 at https://www.cms.gov/Medicare/Medicare-Fee-for-Service-Payment/AcuteInpatientPPS/index.html

Operating Disproportionate Share Adjustment Factor	PIF: Operating Disproportionate Share Hospital (DSH) Adjustment. Reflects a 75% reduction to the DSH adjustment required under section 3133 of the Affordable Care Act. Factor location (DSHOPG)	PIF: Operating Disproportionate Share Hospital (DSH) Adjustment. Reflects a 75% reduction to the DSH adjustment required under Section 3133 of the Affordable Care Act. Factor location (DSHOPG)	PIF: Estimated FY 2018 Operating Disproportionate Share Hospital (DSH) adjustment. Reflects a 75% reduction to the DSH adjustment required under Section 3333 of the Affordable Care Act (DSHOPP)	PIF: Estimated FY 2019 Operating Disproportionate Share Hospital (DSH) adjustment. Reflects a 75% reduction to the DSH adjustment required under Section 3333 of the Affordable Care Act (DSHOPP)
Operating Indirect Medical Education Adjustment	PIF: IME Adjustment Factor for Operating PPS location (TCHOP)	PIF: IME Adjustment Factor for Operating PPS location (TCHOP)	PIF: IME Adjustment Factor for Operating IPPS location (TCHOP)	PIF: IME Adjustment Factor for Operating IPPS location (TCHOP)
Sole Community Hospital — Hospital Specific Rate	PIF: Hospital Specific Payment (HSP) Rate updated to FY 2016 for SCH and MDH providers. HSP Rate is based on the March 2015 update of the Provider Specific File (PSF). Location (HSP Rate)	PIF: Hospital Specific Payment (HSP) Rate updated to FY 2017 for SCH and MDH providers. HSP Rate is based on the March 2016 update of the Provider Specific File (PSF). Location (HSP Rate)	PIF: Hospital Specific Payment (HSP) Rate updated to FY 2018 for SCH providers. HSP Rate is based on the March 2017 update of the Provider Specific File (PSF). Location (HSP Rate)	PIF: Hospital Specific Payment (HSP) Rate updated to FY 2019 for SCH providers. HSP Rate is based on the March 2018 update of the Provider Specific File (PSF). Location (HSP Rate)
Cost-to-Charge Ratio	PIF: Operating Cost-to-Charge Ratio location (Operating CCR) and Capital Cost-to-Charge location (Capital CCR)	PIF: Operating Cost-to-Charge Ratio location (Operating CCR) and Capital Cost-to-Charge location (Captial CCR)	PIF: Operating Cost-to-Charge Ratio location (Operating CCR) and Capital Cost-to-Charge location (Capital CCR)	PIF: Operating Cost-to-Charge Ratio location (Operating CCR) and Capital Cost-to-Charge location (Capital CCR)

	Discharges Occurring On or After 11/01/2019
Applicable Payment Impact File (PIF)	FY 20 Impact File (Final Rule and Correction Notice)
Capital Geographic Adjustment Factor	FY 2020 GAF — Updated October 2019
Capital Disproportionate Share Adjustment Factor	PIF: Capital Disproportionate Share (DSH) adjustment location (DSHCPP)
Capital Indirect Medical Education Adjustment Factor	PIF: IME adjustment factor for capital PPS location (TCHCP)
Operating Wage Index	Table 3 (CN) at https://www.csm.gov/Medicare/Medicare-Fee-for-Service-Payment/AcuteInpatientPPS/index.html
Operating Disproportionate Share Adjustment Factor	PIF: Estimated FY 2020 Operating Disproportionate Share Hospital (DSH) adjustment. Reflects a 75% reduction to the DSH adjustment required under Section 3333 of the Affordable Care Act (DSHOPP)
Operating Indirect Medical Education Adjustment	PIF: IME Adjustment Factor for Operating IPPS location (TCHOP)
Sole Community Hospital — Hospital Specific Rate	PIF: Hospital Specific Payment (HSP) Rate updated to FY 2020 for SCH providers. HSP Rate is based on the March 2019 update of the Provider Specific File (PSF). Location (HSP Rate)

Cost-to-Charge Ratio	PIF: Operating Cost-to-Charge Ratio location (Operating CCR) and Capital Cost-to-Charge location (Capital CCR)

Note: Authority cited: Sections 133, 4603.5, 5307.1, 5307.3 and 5318, Labor Code. Reference: Sections 4600, 4603.2, 5307.1 and 5318, Labor Code.

History: 1. New section filed 12-27-2012; operative 1-1-2013 as a file and print only pursuant to Government Code section 11340.9(g) (Register 2012, No. 52).

2. Amendment filed 3-13-2013; operative 3-15-2013. Submitted to OAL for filing and printing only pursuant to Labor Code section 5307.1(g)(2) (Register 2013, No. 11).

3. Amendment filed 2-4-2015; operative 3-5-2015. Submitted to OAL for printing only pursuant to Government Code section 11340.9 (Register 2015, No. 6).

4. Amendment filed 2-25-2015; operative 3-5-2015 pursuant to Labor Code section 5307.1(g)(2). Submitted to OAL for printing only pursuant to Labor Code section 5307.1(g)(2) (Register 2015, No. 9).

5. Amendment filed 3-14-2016; operative 3-1-2016 pursuant to Labor Code section 5307.1(g)(2). Submitted to OAL for filing and printing only pursuant to Labor Code section 5307.1(g)(2) (Register 2016, No. 12).

6. Editorial correction of subsection (b) (Register 2016, No. 49).

7. Amendment of subsections (a)(1), (b)(1) and (c)(1) filed 1-19-2017; operative 1-1-2017 pursuant to Labor Code section 5307.1(g)(2). Submitted to OAL for printing only pursuant to Labor Code section 5307.1(g)(2) (Register 2017, No. 3).

8. Amendment filed 11-28-2017; operative 12-1-2017 pursuant to Labor Code section 5307.1(g)(2). Submitted to OAL for filing and printing only pursuant to Labor Code section 5307.1(g)(2) (Register 2017, No. 48).

9. Editorial correction of formatting (Register 2018, No. 15).

10. Nonsubstantive action without change filed 4-27-2018 pursuant to section 100, title 1, California Code of Regulations to correct errors in 11-28-2017 filing (Register 2018, No. 17).

11. Editorial correction of subsections (b)(1) and (c)(1) (Register 2018, No. 48).

12. Amendment filed 11-26-2018; operative 12-1-2018 pursuant to Labor Code section 5307.1(g)(2). Submitted to OAL for filing and printing only pursuant to Labor Code section 5307.1(g)(2) (Register 2018, No. 48).

13. Amendment filed 10-16-2019; operative 11-1-2019 pursuant to Labor Code section 5307.1(g)(2). Submitted to OAL for filing and printing only pursuant to Labor Code section 5307.1(g)(2) (Register 2019, No. 42).

14. Amendment of subsections (b)(1) and (c)(1) filed 12-12-2019; operative 11-1-2019 pursuant to Labor Code section 5307.1(g)(2). Submitted to OAL for filing and printing only pursuant to Labor Code section 5307.1(g)(2) (Register 2019, No. 50).

Ref.: Herlick Handbook §§ 1.01[3][b], 4.17[1].

§9789.30. Hospital Outpatient Departments and Ambulatory Surgical Centers — Definitions.

(a) "Adjusted Conversion Factor" is determined as follows: unadjusted conversion factor × (1-labor-related share + (labor-related share × wage index)). For each update, the unadjusted conversion factor for the preceding period is adjusted by the rate of change in the market basket inflation factor. The market basket inflation factor and labor-related share are specified in the Federal Register notices announcing revisions in the Medicare payment rates. See Section 9789.39(b) for the unadjusted conversion factor, market basket inflation factor, and labor-related share by date of service.

For services rendered on or after February 15, 2006, in accordance with Section 411 of Pub. L. 108–173 and the final rule published in the Federal Register of November 10, 2005 (CMS-1501-FC, 70 FR 68516) at page 68556, the "Adjusted Conversion Factor" for a rural Sole Community Hospital (SCH) includes an adjustment factor of 1.071, which document is incorporated by reference and will be made available upon request to the Administrative Director.

(b) "Ambulatory Payment Classifications (APC)" means the Centers for Medicare & Medicaid Services' (CMS) list of ambulatory payment classifications of hospital outpatient services.

(c) "Ambulatory Surgical Center (ASC)" means any surgical clinic as defined in the California Health and Safety Code Section 1204, subdivision (b)(1), any ambulatory surgical center that is certified to participate in the Medicare program under Title XVIII (42 U.S.C. SEC. 1395 et seq.) of the federal Social Security Act, or any surgical clinic accredited by an accrediting agency as approved by the Licensing Division of the Medical Board of California pursuant to Health and Safety Code Sections 1248.15 and 1248.4 to use anesthesia, except local anesthesia or peripheral nerve blocks, or both, in compliance with the community standard of practice, in doses that, when administered have the probability of placing a patient at risk for loss of the patient's life-preserving protective reflexes.

(d) "Ambulatory Surgical Center Payment System" means Medicare's payment system for specific ambulatory surgical center covered surgical procedures published in the Hospital Outpatient Prospective Payment and Ambulatory Surgical Center Payment Systems final rule for the relevant payment year.

(e) "Annual Utilization Report of Specialty Clinics" means the Annual Utilization Report of Clinics that is filed by February 15 of each year with the Office of Statewide Health Planning and Development by the ASCs as required by Section 127285 and Section 1216 of the Health and Safety Code.

(f) "APC Payment Rate" means CMS' hospital outpatient prospective payment system rate. The APC payment rate is specified in the Federal Register notices announcing revisions in the Medicare payment rates. See Section 9789.39(b) for the Federal Register reference to the APC payment rate by date of service.

(g) "APC Relative Weight" means CMS' APC relative weight as set forth in CMS' hospital outpatient prospective payment system. The APC relative weight is specified in the Federal Register notices announcing revisions in the Medicare payment rates. See Section 9789.39(b) for the Federal Register reference to the APC relative weight by date of service.

(h) "CMS" means the Centers for Medicare & Medicaid Services of the United States Department of Health and Human Services.

(i) "Cost to Charge Ratio for ASC" means the ratio of the facility's total operating costs to total gross charges during the preceding calendar year.

(j) "Cost to Charge Ratio for Hospital Outpatient Department" means the hospital cost-to-charge used by the Medicare fiscal intermediary to determine high cost outlier payments.

(k) "Facility Only Services" means services, defined by Medicare, that rarely or are never performed in the non-facility setting, and are not: 1. emergency room visits; 2. Surgical procedures; or 3. An integral part of the emergency room visit or surgical procedure, in accordance with section 9789.32. See section 9789.39(b) for the CMS Physician Fee Schedule Relative Value File which contains the description of the Facility Only Services by date of service.

(*l*) "HCPCS" means CMS' Healthcare Common Procedure Coding System, which describes products, supplies, procedures and health professional services and includes, the American Medical Associations (AMA's) Physician "Current Procedural Terminology", Fourth Edition (CPT-4) codes, alphanumeric codes, and related modifiers.

(m) "HCPCS Level I Codes" are the AMA's CPT-4 codes and modifiers for professional services and procedures.

(n) "HCPCS Level II Codes" are national alphanumeric codes and modifiers maintained by CMS for health care products and supplies, as well as some codes for professional services not included in the AMA's CPT-4.

(o) "Health facility" means any facility as defined in Section 1250 of the Health and Safety Code.

(p) "Hospital Outpatient Department" means any hospital outpatient department of a health facility as defined in the California Health and Safety Code Section 1250 and any hospital outpatient department that is certified to participate in the Medicare program under Title XVIII (42 U.S.C. SEC. 1395 et seq.) of the federal Social Security Act.

(q) "Hospital Outpatient Department Services" means services furnished by any health facility as defined in the California Health and Safety Code Section 1250 and any hospital that is certified to participate in the Medicare program under Title XVIII (42 U.S.C. SEC. 1395 et seq.) of the federal Social Security Act to a patient who has not been admitted as an inpatient but who is registered as an outpatient in the records of the hospital.

(r) "Hospital Outpatient Prospective Payment System (HOPPS)" means Medicare's payment system for outpatient services at hospitals. These outpatient services are classified according to a list of ambulatory payment classifications (APCs).

(s) "Labor-related Share" means the portion of the payment rate that is attributable to labor and labor-related cost determined by CMS, pursuant to Section 1833(t)(2)(D) of the Social Security Act and as specified in the Federal Register notices announcing revisions in the Medicare payment rates. See Section 9789.39(b) for the Federal Register reference that references the labor-related share by date of service.

(t) "Market Basket Inflation Factor" means the market basket percentage change determined by CMS as set forth in the Federal Register notices announcing revisions in the Medicare payment rates. See Section 9789.39(b) for the Federal Register reference to the market basket inflation factor by date of service.

(u) "Other Services" means Hospital Outpatient Department Services rendered on or after September 1, 2014, but before December 15, 2016, to hospital outpatients and payable under the CMS hospital outpatient prospective payment system that are not: 1. Surgical procedures; 2. Emergency room visits; 3. Facility Only Services; or 4. An integral part of the surgical procedure, emergency room visit or Facility Only Service.

For services rendered on or after December 15, 2016, "Other Services" means Hospital Outpatient Department Services rendered to hospital outpatients and payable under the CMS hospital outpatient prospective payment system that are not: 1. Surgical procedures; 2. Emergency room visits; or 3. An integral part of the surgical procedure or emergency room visit.

(v) "Outlier Threshold" means the Medicare outlier threshold used in determining high cost outlier payments.

(w) "Price adjustment" means any and all price reductions, offsets, discounts, rebates, adjustments, and or refunds which accrue to or are factored into the final net cost to the hospital outpatient department or ambulatory surgical center.

(x) "OMFS RBRVS" means the Official Medical Fee Schedule for physician and non-physician practitioner services in accordance with sections 9789.12 through 9789.19.

(y) "Total Gross Charges" means the facility's total usual and customary charges to patients and third-party payers before reductions for contractual allowances, bad debts, courtesy allowances and charity care.

(z) "Total Operating Costs" means the direct cost incurred in providing care to patients. Included in operating cost are: salaries and wages, rent or mortgage, employee benefits, supplies, equipment purchase and maintenance, professional fees, advertising, overhead, etc. It does not include start up costs.

(aa) "Wage Index" means CMS' wage index for urban, rural and hospitals that are reclassified as described in CMS' Hospital Outpatient Prospective Payment System (HOPPS) and wage index values as specified in the Hospital Inpatient Prospective Payment Systems set forth in the Federal Register notices announcing revisions in the Medicare payment rates. See Section 9789.39(b) for the Federal Register reference that contains description of the wage index and wage index values by date of service.

(ab) For services payable under Sections 9789.30 through 9789.39, "Workers' Compensation Multiplier" means the multiplier to the Medicare rate adopted by the AD in accordance with Labor Code Section 5307.1, or the multiplier that includes an extra percentage reimbursement for high cost outlier cases, by date of service.

Date of Service	Hospital Outpatient Department Services that are: Surgical Procedures; Emergency Room visits; or services that are an integral part of the surgical procedure or emergency room visit Multipliers (A) Medicare multiplier; (B) multiplier that includes an extra percentage reimbursement for high cost outlier cases	Ambulatory Surgical Centers Surgical Procedures Multipliers (A) Medicare multiplier; (B) multiplier that includes an extra percentage reimbursement for high cost outlier cases	Hospital Outpatient Department Services (as defined in Section 9789.30(q)) that are Facility Only Services (as defined in Section 9789.30(k)) Multiplier (B) multiplier that includes an extra percentage reimbursement for high cost outlier cases	Hospital Outpatient Department Services (as defined in Section 9789.30(q)) that are Other Services (as defined in Section 9789.30(u)) Multiplier (B) multiplier that includes an extra percentage reimbursement for high cost outlier cases
Before January 1, 2013	(A) 120%; (B) 122%	(A) 120%; (B) 122%	Not applicable. Payable under Sections 9789.10 and 9789.11	Not applicable. Payable under Sections 9789.10 and 9789.11
On or after January 1, 2013, but before September 1, 2014	(A) 120%; (B) 122%	(A) 80%; (B) 82%	Not applicable. Payable under Sections 9789.10 and 9789.11	Not applicable. Payable under Sections 9789.10 and 9789.11
On or after September 1, 2014, but before December 15, 2016	(B) 121.2%	(B) 80.81%	(B) 101.01%	Not applicable. Payable under Section 9789.32(c)
On or after December 15, 2016	(B) 117.8%	(B) 80.81%	Not applicable. These services are payable as "Other Services".	(B) 101.01%

Note: Authority cited: Sections 133, 4603.5, 5307.1 and 5307.3, Labor Code. Reference: Sections 4600, 4603.2 and 5307.1, Labor Code.

History: 1. New section filed 1-2-2004 as an emergency; operative 1-2-2004 (Register 2004, No. 2). A Certificate of Compliance must be transmitted to OAL by 5-3-2004 or emergency language will be repealed by operation of law on the following day.

2. Certificate of Compliance as to 1-2-2004 order, including amendment of subsections (d)-(f), transmitted to OAL 4-30-2004 and filed 6-15-2004 (Register 2004, No. 25).

3. Amendment filed 12-27-2012; operative 1-1-2013 as a file and print only pursuant to Government Code section 11340.9(g) (Register 2012, No. 52).

4. New subsections (j), (s) and (w), subsection relettering, amendment of newly designated subsections (u) and (aa) and repealer of last paragraph filed 6-3-2014; operative 9-1-2014 as a file and print only pursuant to Government Code section 11340.9(g) (Register 2014, No. 23).

5. Editorial correction removing extraneous text from subsection (m) (Register 2016, No. 51).

6. New subsections (d) and (r), repealer of subsection (u), subsection relettering and amendment of newly designated subsections (u) and (ab) filed 12-15-2016; operative 12-15-2016 as a file and print only pursuant to Government Code section 11340.9(g) (Register 2016, No. 51).

Ref.: Hanna § 22.05[2]; Herlick Handbook §§ 1.01[3][b], 4.17[1].

§9789.31. Hospital Outpatient Departments and Ambulatory Surgical Centers — Adoption of Standards.

(a) The Administrative Director incorporates by reference, the Centers for Medicare and Medicaid Services' (CMS) Hospital Outpatient Prospective Payment System (HOPPS) certain addenda published in the Federal Register notices announcing revisions in the Medicare payment rates. See Section 9789.39(b) for the adopted payment system addenda by date of service.

(b) For services rendered on or after July 15, 2005, the Administrative Director incorporates by reference, the Centers for Medicare and Medicaid Services' (CMS) Hospital Inpatient Prospective Payment Systems (IPPS) certain tables published in the Federal Register notices announcing revisions in the Medicare payment rates. See Section 9789.39(b) for the adopted payment system tables by date of service.

(c) For services rendered on or after July 15, 2005, the Administrative Director incorporates by reference, the Hospital Inpatient Prospective Payment Systems (IPPS) "Payment Impact File" published by the federal Centers for Medicare & Medicaid Services (CMS) in effect as of the date the Administrative Director Order becomes effective, which document is found at http://www.cms.hhs.gov/AcuteInpatientPPS/.

(d) For services rendered on or after September 1, 2014, but before December 15, 2016, the Administrative Director incorporates by reference, the Medicare Physician Fee Schedule "Relative Value File" published by the federal Centers for Medicare & Medicaid Services (CMS), which document is found at http://www.cms.gov/ Medicare/Medicare-Fee-for-Service-Payment/PhysicianFeeSched/index.html?redirect=/PhysicianFeeSched/. See Section 9789.39(b) for the adopted Relative Value File by date of service.

(e) For services rendered on or after December 15, 2016, the Administrative Director incorporates by reference the Centers for Medicare and Medicaid Services' (CMS) Ambulatory Surgical Centers Payment System particular columns of certain addenda published in the Federal Register notices announcing revisions in the Medicare payment rates. See Section 9789.39(b) for the adopted payment system addenda by date of service.

(f) The Administrative Director incorporates by reference certain sections of the Centers for Medicare and Medicaid Services' (CMS) Claims Processing Manual, Chapter 4. See Section 9789.39(b) for the adopted sections of Chapter 4, by date of service.

(g) The Administrative Director incorporates by reference certain sections of the Centers for Medicare and Medicaid Services' Integrated Outpatient Code Editor (I/OCE) CMS Specifications. See Section 9789.39(b) for the adopted sections of I/OCE CMS Specifications, by date of service.

(h) The Administrative Director incorporates by reference the American Medical Associations' "Current Procedural Terminology," 4th Edition, annual revision in effect as of the date the Administrative Director Order becomes effective. Copies of the Current Procedural Terminology may be purchased from the American Medical Association:

ORDER DEPARTMENT
AMERICAN MEDICAL ASSOCIATION
P.O. BOX 930876
ATLANTA, GA 31193-0876

Or over the internet at:

WWW.AMAPRESS.COM

Or through the American Medical Association's toll free order line:

(800) 621-8335.

(i) The Administrative Director incorporates by reference CMS' Alphanumeric "Healthcare Common Procedure Coding System (HCPCS)" annual revision in effect as of the date the Administrative Director Order becomes effective. Copies of the Healthcare Common Procedure Coding System (HCPCS) may be purchased from the American Medical Association:

ORDER DEPARTMENT
AMERICAN MEDICAL ASSOCIATION
P.O. BOX 930876
ATLANTA, GA 31193-0876

Or over the internet at:

WWW.AMAPRESS.COM

Or through the American Medical Association's toll free order line:

(800) 621-8335.

Note: Authority cited: Sections 133, 4603.5, 5307.1 and 5307.3, Labor Code. Reference: Sections 4600, 4603.2 and 5307.1, Labor Code.

History: 1. New section filed 1-2-2004 as an emergency; operative 1-2-2004 (Register 2004, No. 2). A Certificate of Compliance must be transmitted to OAL by 5-3-2004 or emergency language will be repealed by operation of law on the following day.

2. Certificate of Compliance as to 1-2-2004 order, including amendment of subsection (a), transmitted to OAL 4-30-2004 and filed 6-15-2004 (Register 2004, No. 25).

3. Amendment filed 12-27-2012; operative 1-1-2013 as a file and print only pursuant to Government Code section 11340.9(g) (Register 2012, No. 52).

4. Amendment of subsections (c)-(e) filed 3-29-2013; operative 4-1-2013 pursuant to Labor Code section 5307.1(g)(2). Submitted to OAL for filing and printing only pursuant to Labor Code section 5307.1(g)(2) (Register 2013, No. 13).

5. New subsection (d) and subsection relettering filed 6-3-2014; operative 9-1-2014 as a file and print only pursuant to Government Code section 11340.9(g) (Register 2014, No. 23).

6. Amendment of subsection (d), new subsection (e) and subsection relettering filed 12-15-2016; operative 12-15-2016 as a file and print only pursuant to Government Code section 11340.9(g) (Register 2016, No. 51).

7. New subsections (f) and (g) and subsection relettering filed 5-8-2018; operative 3-15-2018 pursuant to Labor Code section 5307.1(g)(2). Submitted to OAL for filing and printing only pursuant to Labor Code section 5307.1(g)(2) (Register 2018, No. 19).

Ref.: Hanna § 22.05[2]; Herlick Handbook §§ 1.01[3][b], 4.17[1].

§9789.32. Outpatient Hospital Departments and Ambulatory Surgical Centers Fee Schedule — Applicability.

(a) Sections 9789.30 through 9789.39 shall be applicable to the maximum allowable fees for emergency room visits and surgical procedures provided on an outpatient basis rendered on or after July 1, 2004, but before September 1, 2014. Sections 9789.30 through 9789.39 shall be applicable to the maximum allowable fees for emergency room visits, surgical procedures, and Facility Only Services provided on an outpatient basis rendered on or after September 1, 2014, but before December 15, 2016. Sections 9789.30 through 9789.39 shall be applicable to the maximum allowable fees for services provided on an outpatient basis and payable under the Medicare (CMS) HOPPS rendered on or after December 15, 2016. For purposes of this section, emergency room visits and surgical procedures shall be defined by HCPCS codes set forth in section 9789.39(b) by date of service. A supply, drug, device, blood product and biological is considered an integral part of an emergency room visit, or surgical procedure, or, if applicable, Facility Only Service, or if applicable and only if rendered on or after December 15, 2016, Other Service if:

(1)

Date of Service	Supply, Drug, Device, Blood Product, or Biological
For services rendered before March 1, 2008	The item has a status code N and is packaged into the APC payment for the emergency room visit or surgical procedure (in which case no additional fee is allowable).

For services rendered on or after March 1, 2008 but before March 1, 2009	The item has a status code N or Q and is packaged into the APC payment for the emergency room visit or surgical procedure (in which case no additional fee is allowable).
For services rendered on or after March 1, 2009 but before September 1, 2014	The item has a status code N, Q1, Q2, or Q3 and is packaged into the APC payment for the emergency room visit or surgical procedure (in which case no additional fee is allowable).
For services rendered on or after September 1, 2014 but before December 15, 2016	The item has a status code N, Q1, Q2, or Q3 and is packaged into the APC payment for the emergency room visit, surgical procedure, or Facility Only Service (in which case no additional fee is allowable).
For services rendered on or after December 15, 2016	The item has a status code N, Q1, Q2, or Q3 and is packaged into the APC payment for the emergency room visit, surgical procedure, or Other Service (in which case no additional fee is allowable).

(2)

Date of Service	**Supply, Drug, Device, Blood Product, or Biological**
For services rendered before March 1, 2009	The item is furnished in conjunction with an emergency room visit or surgical procedure and has been assigned Status Code G, H or K.
For services rendered on or after March 1, 2009 but before September 1, 2014	The item is furnished in conjunction with an emergency room visit or surgical procedure and has been assigned status code G, H, K, R, or U.
For services rendered on or after September 1, 2014 but before December 15, 2016	The item is furnished in conjunction with an emergency room visit, surgical procedure, or Facility Only Service, and has been assigned status code G, H, K, R, or U.
For services rendered on or after December 15, 2016	The item is furnished in conjunction with an emergency room visit, surgical procedure, or Other Service and has been assigned status code G, H, K, R, or U.

(b) Sections 9789.30 through 9789.39 apply to any hospital outpatient department as defined in Section 9789.30(p) and any ASC as defined in Section 9789.30(c).

(c) This subsection (c) is inapplicable for dates of services on or after December 15, 2016. Depending on date of service, the maximum allowable fees for services, drugs and supplies furnished by hospitals that do not meet the requirements in (a) for a facility fee payment and are not bundled in the APC payment rate for services in (a) will be determined as follows:

(1)(A) For services rendered before September 1, 2014, the maximum allowable hospital outpatient facility fees for professional medical services which are performed by physicians and other licensed health care providers to hospital outpatients shall be paid according to Section 9789.10 and Section 9789.11.

(B) For Other Services rendered on or after September 1, 2014, but before December 15, 2016, to hospital outpatients, the maximum allowable hospital outpatient facility fees shall be paid according to the OMFS RBRVS.

(i) If the Other Service has a Professional Component/Technical Component under the OMFS RBRVS, the hospital outpatient facility fee shall be the Technical Component amount determined according to the OMFS RBRVS.

(ii) For Other Services, which do not meet the requirement in (i), the hospital outpatient facility fee shall be determined based solely on the non-facility practice expense relative value units applicable under the OMFS RBRVS.

The base facility fee is calculated as follows: Non-Facility Site of Service Practice Expense (PE) Relative Value Unit (RVU) * Statewide Geographic Adjustment Factor (GAF) for PE * RBRVS Conversion Factor (CF) = Base facility fee.

(d) Hospital Outpatient Departments and ASCs should utilize other applicable parts of the OMFS to determine maximum allowable fees for services or goods not covered by the Hospital Outpatient Departments and Ambulatory Surgical Centers fee schedule (Sections 9789.30 through 9789.39).

(1) The fees for any physician and non-physician practitioner professional services shall be determined in accordance with the OMFS RBRVS.

(2) The maximum allowable fees for organ acquisition costs and corneal tissue acquisition costs shall be based on the documented paid cost of procuring the organ or tissue.

(3) The maximum allowable fee for drugs not otherwise covered by a Medicare fee schedule payment for facility services shall be determined pursuant to Labor Code Section 5307.1, or, where applicable, Section 9789.40.

(4) The maximum allowable fee for clinical diagnostic tests shall be determined according to Section 9789.50.

(5) The maximum allowable fee for durable medical equipment, prosthetics and orthotics shall be determined according to Section 9789.60.

(6) The maximum allowable fee for ambulance service shall be determined according to Section 9789.70.

(e) For services rendered before September 1, 2014, only hospitals may charge or collect a facility fee for emergency room visits. Only hospital outpatient departments and ambulatory surgical centers as defined in Section 9789.30(p) and Section 9789.30(c) may charge or collect a facility fee for surgical services provided on an outpatient basis.

For services rendered on or after September 1, 2014, but before December 15, 2016, only hospitals may charge or collect a facility fee for emergency room visits, Facility Only Services, and Other Services. Only hospital outpatient departments and ambulatory surgical centers as defined in Section 9789.30(p) and Section 9789.30(c) may charge or collect a facility fee for surgical services provided on an outpatient basis. Facility fees are not payable to an ambulatory surgical center for any services that are not an integral part of a surgical service.

For services rendered on or after December 15, 2016, only hospitals as defined in Section 9789.30(p) may charge or collect a facility fee for Hospital Outpatient Department Services rendered to a hospital outpatient and payable under the Medicare (CMS) HOPPS. Ambulatory surgical centers as defined in Section 9789.30(c) may charge or collect a facility fee for only surgical services or services that are an integral part of the surgical service provided on an outpatient basis and payable under the Medicare (CMS) HOPPS. Facility fees are not payable to an ambulatory surgical center for any services that are not an integral part of a surgical service. Only ambulatory surgical centers may charge or collect a facility fee for its services.

(f) Hospital outpatient departments and ambulatory surgical centers shall not be reimbursed for procedures on the inpatient only list, referenced in Section 9789.31(a), Addendum E, except that pre-authorized services rendered are payable at the pre-negotiated fee arrangement. The pre-authorization must be provided by an authorized agent of the claims administrator to the provider. The fee agreement and pre-authorization must be memorialized in writing prior to performing the medical services.

(g) Critical access hospitals and hospitals that are excluded from acute PPS are exempt from this fee schedule.

(h) Out of state hospital outpatient departments and ambulatory surgical centers are exempt from this fee schedule.

(i) Hospital outpatient departments and ambulatory surgical centers billing for facility fees and other services under this Section shall be submitted in accordance with the e-billing regulations beginning with Section 9792.5.0 or the standardized paper billing regulations beginning with Section 9792.5.2.

Note: Authority cited: Sections 133, 4603.5, 5307.1 and 5307.3, Labor Code. Reference: Sections 4600, 4603.2 and 5307.1, Labor Code.

History: 1. New section filed 1-2-2004 as an emergency; operative 1-2-2004 (Register 2004, No. 2). A Certificate of Compliance must be transmitted to OAL by 5-3-2004 or emergency language will be repealed by operation of law on the following day.

2. Certificate of Compliance as to 1-2-2004 order, including amendment of section, transmitted to OAL 4-30-2004 and filed 6-15-2004 (Register 2004, No. 25).

3. Amendment of subsections (a), (b), (c)(3), (e) and (h) filed 12-27-2012; operative 1-1-2013 as a file and print only pursuant to Government Code section 11340.9(g) (Register 2012, No. 52).

4. Amendment filed 6-3-2014; operative 9-1-2014 as a file and print only pursuant to Government Code section 11340.9(g) (Register 2014, No. 23).

5. Amendment of subsection (c)(1)(B)(ii) filed 9-23-2014; operative 9-1-2014 as a file and print only pursuant to Government Code section 11340.9(g) (Register 2014, No. 39).

6. Amendment of section heading and section filed 12-15-2016; operative 12-15-2016 as a file and print only pursuant to Government Code section 11340.9(g) (Register 2016, No. 51).

7. Amendment of subsection (a)(1) filed 5-8-2018; operative 3-15-2018 pursuant to Labor Code section 5307.1(g)(2). Submitted to OAL for filing and printing only pursuant to Labor Code section 5307.1(g)(2) (Register 2018, No. 19).

Ref.: Hanna § 22.05[2]; Herlick Handbook §§ 1.01[3][b], 4.17[1].

§9789.33. Hospital Outpatient Departments and Ambulatory Surgical Centers Fee Schedule — Determination of Maximum Reasonable Fee.

(a) In accordance with section 9789.32, the maximum allowable payment for hospital outpatient department or ambulatory surgical center facility fees for services provided on an outpatient basis and payable under the Medicare (CMS) HOPPS, shall be determined based on the following. In accordance with Section 9789.30(ab), an extra percentage reimbursement shall be used in lieu of an additional payment for high cost outlier cases.

Standard payment.

Date of Service	Status Code Indicators	Hospital Outpatient Department Services that are: Surgical procedures; Emergency Room Visits; or services that are an integral part of the surgical procedure or emergency room visit	Ambulatory Surgical Centers surgical procedures	Hospital Outpatient Department Services (as defined in Section 9789.30(q)) that are Facility Only Services (as defined in Section 9789.30(k))	Hospital Outpatient Department Services (as defined in Section 9789.30(q)) that are Other Services (as defined in Section 9789.30(u))

For services rendered before March 1, 2008	"S", "T", "X", or "V"	APC relative weight × adjusted conversion factor × 1.22 workers' compensation multiplier, pursuant to Section 9789.30(ab). See Section 9789.39(b) for the APC relative weight by date of service.	APC relative weight × adjusted conversion factor × 1.22 workers' compensation multiplier, pursuant to Section 9789.30(ab). See Section 9789.39(b) for the APC relative weight by date of service.	Not applicable. Payable under Sections 9789.10 and 9789.11.	Not applicable. Payable under Sections 9789.10 and 9789.11.
For services rendered on or after March 1, 2008 but before March 1, 2009	"S", "T", "X", or "V", or "Q". Status code indicator "Q" must qualify for separate payment.	APC relative weight × adjusted conversion factor × 1.22 workers' compensation multiplier, pursuant to Section 9789.30(ab). See Section 9789.39(b) for the APC relative weight by date of service.	APC relative weight × adjusted conversion factor × 1.22 workers' compensation multiplier, pursuant to Section 9789.30(ab). See Section 9789.39(b) for the APC relative weight by date of service.	Not applicable. Payable under Sections 9789.10 and 9789.11.	Not applicable. Payable under Sections 9789.10 and 9789.11.
For services rendered on or after March 1, 2009 but before January 1, 2013	"S", "T", "X", or "V", "Q1", "Q2", or "Q3". Status code indicators "Q1", "Q2", and "Q3" must qualify for separate payment.	APC relative weight × adjusted conversion factor × 1.22 workers' compensation multiplier, pursuant to Section 9789.30(ab). See Section 9789.39(b) for the APC relative weight by date of service.	APC relative weight × adjusted conversion factor × 1.22 workers' compensation multiplier, pursuant to Section 9789.30(ab). See Section 9789.39(b) for the APC relative weight by date of service.	Not applicable. Payable under Sections 9789.10 and 9789.11.	Not applicable. Payable under Sections 9789.10 and 9789.11.
For services rendered on or after January 1, 2013 but before September 1, 2014	"S", "T", "X", or "V", "Q1", "Q2", or "Q3". Status code indicators "Q1", "Q2", and "Q3" must qualify for separate payment.	APC relative weight × adjusted conversion factor × 1.22 workers' compensation multiplier, pursuant to Section 9789.30(ab). See Section 9789.39(b) for the APC relative weight by date of service.	APC relative weight × adjusted conversion factor × 0.82 workers' compensation multiplier, pursuant to Section 9789.30(ab). See Section 9789.39(b) for the APC relative weight by date of service.	Not applicable. Payable under Sections 9789.10 and 9789.11.	Not applicable. Payable under Sections 9789.10 and 9789.11
For services rendered on or after September 1, 2014 but before December 15, 2016	"S", "T", "X", or "V", "Q1", "Q2", or "Q3". Status code indicators "Q1", "Q2", and "Q3" must qualify for separate payment.	APC relative weight × adjusted conversion factor × 1.212 workers' compensation multiplier, pursuant to Section 9789.30(ab). See Section 9789.39(b) for the APC relative weight by date of service.	APC relative weight × adjusted conversion factor × 0.8081 workers' compensation multiplier, pursuant to Section 9789.30(ab). See Section 9789.39(b) for the APC relative weight by date of service.	APC relative weight × adjusted conversion factor × 1.0101 workers' compensation multiplier, pursuant to Section 9789.30(ab). See Section 9789.39(b) for the APC relative weight by date of service	Payable under Section 9789.32(c)
For services rendered on or after December 15, 2016	"S," "T," "V," "Q1," "Q2," "Q3," "J1," or "J2." Status code indicators must qualify for separate payment.	APC relative weight × adjusted conversion factor × 1.178 workers' compensation multiplier, pursuant to Section 9789.30(ab). See Section 9789.39(b) for the APC relative weight by date of service.	APC relative weight × adjusted conversion factor × 0.8081 workers' compensation multiplier, pursuant to Section 9789.30(ab). See Section 9789.39(b) for the APC relative weight by date of service.	Not applicable. These services are payable as "Other Services".	APC relative weight × adjusted conversion factor × 1.0101 workers' compensation multiplier, pursuant to Section 9789.30(ab). See Section 9789.39(b) for the APC relative weight by date of service.

Table A in Section 9789.34 contains an "adjusted conversion factor" which incorporates the standard conversion factor, wage index and inflation factor. The maximum payment rate for ASCs and non-listed hospitals can be determined according to Table A and subdivision (a).

For services rendered before February 15, 2006, Table B

in Section 9789.35 contains an "adjusted conversion factor" which incorporates the standard conversion factor, wage index and inflation factor.

For services rendered on or after February 15, 2006, table B in Section 9789.35 contains an "adjusted conversion factor" which incorporates the standard conversion factor, wage index, rural SCH adjustment factor, and inflation factor, as described in CMS' 2006 Hospital Outpatient Prospective Payment System final rule of November 10, 2005, published in the Federal Register (CMS-1501-FC, 70 FR 68516), at page 68556.

The maximum payment rate for the listed hospital outpatient departments can be determined according to Table B and subdivision (a).

(1) Procedure codes for drugs and biologicals with status code indicator "G":

APC payment rate × workers' compensation multiplier pursuant to Section 9789.30(ab), by date of service.

(2) Procedure codes for devices with status code indicator "H":

Documented paid cost, plus an additional 10% of the hospital outpatient department's or ASC's documented paid cost, net of immediate and anticipated price adjustments based upon the hospital outpatient department's or ASC's prior calendar year's usage for comparable devices, not to exceed a maximum of $ 250.00, plus any sales tax and/or shipping and handling charges actually paid.

(3) Procedure codes for drugs and biologicals with status code indicator "K," unless rendered on or after December 15, 2016, and packaged into a procedure with a status code indicator "J1" or "J2," in which case no additional fee is allowable:

APC payment rate × workers' compensation multiplier pursuant to Section 9789.30(ab), by date of service.

(4) For services rendered on or after March 1, 2009: Procedure codes for blood and blood products with status code indicator "R," unless rendered on or after December 15, 2016, and packaged into a procedure with a status code indicator "J1" or "J2," in which case no additional fee is allowable:

APC relative weight × adjusted conversion factor × workers' compensation multiplier pursuant to Section 9789.30(ab), by date of service. See section 9789.39(b) for APC relative weight by date of service.

(5) For services rendered on or after March 1, 2009: Procedure codes for brachytherapy services with status code indicator "U":

Documented paid cost, plus an additional 10% of the hospital outpatient department's or ASC's documented paid cost, net of immediate and anticipated price adjustments based upon the hospital outpatient department's or ASC's prior calendar year's usage for comparable devices, not to exceed a maximum of $ 250.00, plus any sales tax and/or shipping and handling charges actually paid.

For services rendered on or after April 15, 2010: Procedure codes for brachytherapy services with status code indicator "U":

APC relative weight × adjusted conversion factor × workers' compensation multiplier pursuant to Section 9789.30(ab), by date of service. See section 9789.39(b) for APC relative weight by date of service.

(b) *This section (b) is inapplicable for dates of service on or after September 1, 2014.* Alternative payment methodology. In lieu of the maximum allowable fees set forth under (a), the maximum allowable fees for a facility meeting the requirements in subdivisions (c)(1) through (c)(5) will be determined as follows:

(1) Standard payment:

(A) For services rendered before March 1, 2008, CTP codes 99281-99285 and CPT codes 10021-69990 with status code indicators "S", "T", "X" or "V":

For services rendered on or after March 1, 2008, use: CPT codes 99281-99285 and CPT codes 10021-69990 with status code indicators "S", "T", "X", "V", or "Q". Status code indicator "Q" must qualify for separate payment.

For services rendered on or after March 1, 2009, use: CPT codes 99281-99285 and CPT codes 10021-69990 with status code indicators "S","T", "X", "V","Q1", "Q2", or "Q3". Status code indicators "Q1", "Q2", and "Q3" must qualify for separate payment.

For services rendered before January 1, 2013: APC relative weight × adjusted conversion factor × 1.20 workers' compensation multiplier, pursuant to Section 9789.30(ab). See Section 9789.39(b) for the APC relative weight by date of service.

For services rendered on or after January 1, 2013 and before September 1, 2014: APC relative weight × adjusted conversion factor × 1.20 workers' compensation multiplier for hospital outpatient departments and 0.80 workers' compensation multiplier for ambulatory surgical centers, pursuant to Section 9789.30(ab).

For services rendered on or after February 15, 2006 and before September 1, 2014, by rural SCH hospitals, use: APC relative weight × adjusted conversion factor × 1.071 × 1.20 workers' compensation multiplier, pursuant to Section 9789.30(ab). See Section 9789.39(b) for the APC relative weight by date of service.

(B) Procedure codes for drugs and biologicals with status code indicator "G":

For services rendered before January 1, 2013: APC payment rate × 1.20 workers' compensation multiplier pursuant to Section 9789.30(ab).

For services rendered on or after January 1, 2013 and before September 1, 2014: APC payment rate × 1.20 workers' compensation multiplier for hospital outpatient departments and 0.80 workers' compensation multiplier for ambulatory surgical centers, pursuant to Section 9789.30(ab).

(C) Procedure codes for devices with status code indicator "H" for services rendered before September 1, 2014:

Documented paid cost, plus an additional 10% of the hospital outpatient department's or ASC's documented paid cost, net of immediate and anticipated price adjustments based upon the hospital outpatient department's or ASC's prior calendar year's usage for comparable devices, not to exceed a maximum of $ 250.00, plus any sales tax and/or shipping and handling charges actually paid.

(D) Procedure codes for drugs and biologicals with status code indicator "K"

For services rendered before January 1, 2013: APC payment rate × 1.20 workers' compensation multiplier pursuant to Section 9789.30(ab).

For services rendered on or after January 1, 2013 and before September 1, 2014: APC payment rate × 1.20 workers' compensation multiplier for hospital outpatient departments and 0.80 workers' compensation multiplier for ambulatory surgical centers, pursuant to Section 9789.30(ab).

(E) For services rendered on or after March 1, 2009: Procedure codes for blood and blood products with status code indicator "R":

For services rendered before January 1, 2013: APC relative weight × adjusted conversion factor × 1.20 workers' compensation multiplier pursuant to Section 9789.30(ab). See section 9789.39(b) for APC relative weight by date of service.

For services rendered on or after January 1, 2013 and before September 1, 2014: APC relative weight × adjusted conversion factor × 1.20 workers' compensation multiplier for hospital outpatient departments and 0.80 workers' compensation multiplier for ambulatory surgical centers, pursuant to Section 9789.30(ab). See section 9789.39(b) for APC relative weight by date of service.

(F) For services rendered on or after March 1, 2009: Procedure codes for brachytherapy services with status code indicator "U":

Documented paid cost, plus an additional 10% of the hospital outpatient department's or ASC's documented paid cost, net of immediate and anticipated price adjustments based upon the hospital outpatient department's or ASC's prior calendar year's usage for comparable devices, not to exceed a maximum of $ 250.00, plus any sales tax and/or shipping and handling charges actually paid.

For services rendered on or after April 15, 2010 and before January 1, 2013: Procedure codes for brachytherapy services with status code indicator "U":

APC relative weight × adjusted conversion factor × 1.20 workers' compensation multiplier pursuant to Section 9789.30(ab). See section 9789.39(b) for APC relative weight by date of service.

For services rendered on or after January 1, 2013 and before September 1, 2014: APC relative weight × adjusted conversion factor × 1.20 workers' compensation multiplier for hospital outpatient departments and 0.80 workers' compensation multiplier for ambulatory surgical centers, pursuant to Section 9789.30(ab). See section 9789.39(b) for APC relative weight by date of service.

(2) Additional payment for high cost outlier case:

[(Facility charges × cost-to-charge ratio) − (standard payment × 2.6)] × .50

For services rendered on or after July 15, 2005, if (Facility charges × cost-to-charge ratio) > (standard payment + outlier threshold), additional payment = [(Facility charges × cost-to-charge ratio) − (standard payment × 1.75)] × .50

For services rendered on or after July 15, 2005, the outlier threshold is specified in the Federal Register notices announcing revisions in the Medicare payment rates. See Section 9789.39(b) for the Federal Register reference that defines the outlier threshold by date of service.

(3) For services rendered before March 1, 2009: In determining the additional payment, the facility's charges and payment for devices with status code indicator "H" shall be excluded from the computation.

For services rendered on or after March 1, 2009: In determining the additional payment, the facility's charges and payment for devices with status code indicator "H" and for brachytherapy services with status code indicator "U" shall be excluded from the computation.

For services rendered on or after April 15, 2010 and before September 1, 2014: In determining the additional payment, the facility's charges and payment for devices with status code indicator "H" shall be excluded from the computation.

(c) *This section (c) is inapplicable for dates of service on or after September 1, 2014.* The following requirements shall be met for election of the alternative payment methodology:

(1) A facility seeking to be paid for high cost outlier cases under subdivision 9789.33(b) must file a written election using DWC Form 15 "Election for High Cost Outlier," contained in Section 9789.37 with the Division of Workers' Compensation, Medical Unit (Attention: OMFS-Outpatient). P.O. Box 71010, Oakland, CA 94612. The form must be post-marked by March 1 of each year and shall be effective for one year commencing with services furnished on or after April 1 of the year in which the election is made.

(2) The maximum allowable fees applicable to a facility that does not file a timely election satisfying the requirements set forth in this subdivision and Section 9789.37 shall be determined under subdivision (a).

(3) The maximum allowable fees applicable to a hospital that does not participate under the Medicare program shall be determined under subdivision (a).

(4) The cost-to-charge ratio applicable to a hospital participating in the Medicare program shall be the hospital's cost-to-charge ratio used by the Medicare fiscal intermediary to determine high cost outlier payments under 42 C.F.R. § 419.43(d), which is incorporated by reference, as contained in Section 9789.38 Appendix X. The cost-to-charge ratio being used by the intermediary for services furnished on February 15 of the year the election is filed shall be included on the hospital's election form.

(5) The cost-to-charge ratio applicable to an ambulatory surgery center shall be the ratio of the facility's total operating costs to total gross charges during the preceding calendar year. Total Operating Costs are the direct costs incurred in providing care to patients. Included in operating cost are: salaries and wages, rent or mortgage, employee benefits, supplies, equipment purchase and maintenance, professional fees, advertising, overhead, etc. It does not include start up costs. Total gross charges are defined as the facility's total usual and customary charges to all patients and third-party party payers before reductions for contractual allowances, bad debts, courtesy allowances and charity care. The facility's election form, as contained in Section 9789.37 shall include a completed Annual Utilization Report of Specialty Clinics filed with Office of Statewide Health Planning and Development (OSHPD) for the preceding calendar year, which is incorporated by reference. The facility's election form shall further include the facility's total operating costs during the preceding calendar year, the facility's total gross charges during the preceding calendar year, and a certification under penalty of perjury signed by the Chief Executive Officer and a Certified Public Accountant, as to the accuracy of the information.

Upon request from the Administrative Director, an independent audit may be conducted at the expense of the ASC. (Note: While ASCs may not typically file Annual Utilization Report of Specialty Clinics with OSHPD, any ASC applying for the alternative payment methodology must file the equivalent, subject to the Division of Workers' Compensation's audit.) A copy of the Annual Utilization Report of Specialty Clinics may be obtained at OSHPD's website at http://www.oshpd.ca.gov/HID/HID/clinic/util/index.htm#Forms or upon request to the Division of Workers' Compensation, Medical Unit (Attention: OMFS-Outpatient), P.O. Box 71010, Oakland, CA 94612.

(6) Before April 1 of each year the AD shall post a list of those facilities that have elected to be paid under this paragraph and the facility-specific cost-to-charge ratio that shall be used to determine additional fees allowable for high cost outlier cases. The list shall be posted on the Division of Workers' Compensation website: http://www.dir.ca.gov/dwc/dwc_home_page.htm or is available upon request to the Division of Workers' Compensation, Medical Unit (Attention: OMFS-Outpatient), P.O. Box 71010, Oakland, CA 94612.

(d) *This section (d) is inapplicable for dates of service on or after September 1, 2014.* Any ambulatory surgical center that believes its cost-to-charge ratio in connection with its election to participate in the alternative payment methodology for high cost outlier cases under Section 9789.33(b) was erroneously determined because of error in tabulating data may request the Administrative Director for a re-determination of its cost-to-charge ratio. Such requests shall be in writing, shall state the alleged error, and shall be supported by written documentation. Within 30 days after receiving a complete written request, the Administrative Director shall make a redetermination of the cost-to-charge ratio or reaffirm the published cost-to-charge ratio.

(e) The OPPS rules in 42 C.F.R § 419.44 regarding reimbursement for multiple procedures are incorporated by reference as contained in Section 9789.38 Appendix X.

(f) The OPPS rules in 42 C.F.R. §§ 419.62, 419.64, and 419.66 regarding transitional pass-through payments for innovative medical devices, drugs and biologicals shall be incorporated by reference, as contained in Section 9789.38 Appendix X, except that payment for these items shall be in accordance with subdivisions (a) or (b) as applicable.

(g) The payment determined under subdivisions (a) and (b) include reimbursement for all of the included cost items specified in 42 CFR §419.2(b)(1)-(12), which is incorporated by reference, as contained in Section 9789.38 Appendix X.

(h) The maximum allowable fee shall be determined without regard to the cost items specified in 42 C.F.R. § 419.2(c)(1), (2), (3), (4), and (6), as contained in Section 9789.38 Appendix X. Cost item set forth at 42 C.F.R. § 419.2(c)(5), as contained in Section 9789.38 Appendix X, is payable pursuant to Section 9789.32(c)(1). Cost items set forth at 42 C.F.R. § 419.2(c)(7) and (8), as contained in Section 9789.38 Appendix X, are payable pursuant to Section 9789.32(c)(2).

(i) The maximum allowable fees shall be determined without regard to the provisions in 42 C.F.R. § 419.70.

Note: Authority cited: Sections 133, 4603.5, 5307.1 and 5307.3, Labor Code. Reference: Sections 4600, 4603.2 and 5307.1, Labor Code.

History: 1. New section filed 1-2-2004 as an emergency; operative 1-2-2004 (Register 2004, No. 2). A Certificate of Compliance must be transmitted to OAL by 5-3-2004 or emergency language will be repealed by operation of law on the following day.

2. Certificate of Compliance as to 1-2-2004 order, including amendment of section, transmitted to OAL 4-30-2004 and filed 6-15-2004 (Register 2004, No. 25).

3. Change without regulatory effect amending subsections (c)(1), (c)(5) and (c)(6) filed 10-18-2006 pursuant to section 100, title 1, California Code of Regulations (Register 2006, No. 42).

4. Amendment filed 12-27-2012; operative 1-1-2013 as a file and print only pursuant to Government Code section 11340.9(g) (Register 2012, No. 52).

5. Amendment filed 6-3-2014; operative 9-1-2014 as a file and print only pursuant to Government Code section 11340.9(g) (Register 2014, No. 23).

6. Amendment of section heading and section filed 12-15-2016; operative 12-15-2016 as a file and print only pursuant to Government Code section 11340.9(g) (Register 2016, No. 51).

Ref.: Hanna § 22.05[2]; Herlick Handbook §§ 1.01[3][b], 4.17[1].

§9789.34. Table A.

For services rendered on or after January 1, 2004, the "adjusted conversion factor" and wage index values are incorporated by reference, for services rendered by hospital outpatient departments not listed in Section 9789.35 (Table B) and services rendered by ambulatory surgical centers on or after the date the Administrative Director Order becomes effective, and are available at http://www.dir.ca.gov/dwc/OMFS9904.htm, or upon request to the Administrative Director at:

DIVISION OF WORKERS' COMPENSATION
(ATTENTION: OMFS)
P.O. BOX 420603
SAN FRANCISCO, CA 94142

Note: Authority cited: Sections 133, 4603.5, 5307.1 and 5307.3, Labor Code. Reference: Sections 4600, 4603.2 and 5307.1, Labor Code.

History: 1. New section filed 1-2-2004 as an emergency; operative 1-2-2004 (Register 2004, No. 2). A Certificate of Compliance must be transmitted to OAL by 5-3-2004 or emergency language will be repealed by operation of law on the following day.

2. Certificate of Compliance as to 1-2-2004 order, including amendment of section, transmitted to OAL 4-30-2004 and filed 6-15-2004 (Register 2004, No. 25).

3. Repealer and new section filed 3-29-2013; operative 4-1-2013 pursuant to Labor Code section 5307.1(g)(2). Submitted to OAL for filing and printing only pursuant to Labor Code section 5307.1(g)(2) (Register 2013, No. 13).

Ref.: Hanna § 22.05[2]; Herlick Handbook §§ 1.01[3][b], 4.17[1].

§9789.35. Table B.

For services rendered on or after January 1, 2004, the "adjusted conversion factor" and hospital-specific wage index values for listed hospital outpatient departments, are incorporated by reference, for services rendered on or after the date the Administrative Director Order becomes effective, and are available at http://www.dir.ca.gov/dwc/OMFS9904.htm, or upon request to the Administrative Director at:

DIVISION OF WORKERS' COMPENSATION
(ATTENTION: OMFS)
P.O. BOX 420603
SAN FRANCISCO, CA 94142

Note: Authority cited: Sections 133, 4603.5, 5307.1 and 5307.3, Labor Code. Reference: Sections 4600, 4603.2 and 5307.1, Labor Code.

History: 1. New section filed 1-2-2004 as an emergency; operative 1-2-2004 (Register 2004, No. 2). A Certificate of Compliance must be transmitted to OAL by 5-3-2004 or emergency language will be repealed by operation of law on the following day.

2. Certificate of Compliance as to 1-2-2004 order, including amendment, transmitted to OAL 4-30-2004 and filed 6-15-2004 (Register 2004, No. 25).

3. Repealer and new section filed 3-29-2013; operative 4-1-2013 pursuant to Labor Code section 5307.1(g)(2). Submitted to OAL for filing and printing only pursuant to Labor Code section 5307.1(g)(2) (Register 2013, No. 13).

Ref.: Hanna § 22.05[2]; Herlick Handbook §§ 1.01[3][b], 4.17[1].

§9789.36. Update of Rules to Reflect Changes in the Medicare Payment System.

Sections 9789.30 through 9789.39 shall be adjusted to conform to any relevant changes in the Medicare payment schedule, including mid-year changes, no later than 60 days after the effective date of those changes. Updates shall be posted on the Division of Workers' Compensation webpage at http://www.dir.ca.gov/dwc/dwc_home_page.htm. The annual updates to the Hospital Outpatient Departments and Ambulatory Surgical Centers Fee Schedule shall be effective every year on March 1.

Note: Authority cited: Sections 133, 4603.5, 5307.1 and 5307.3, Labor Code. Reference: Sections 4600, 4603.2 and 5307.1, Labor Code.

History: 1. New section filed 1-2-2004 as an emergency; operative 1-2-2004 (Register 2004, No. 2). A Certificate of Compliance must be transmitted to OAL by 5-3-2004 or emergency language will be repealed by operation of law on the following day.

2. Certificate of Compliance as to 1-2-2004 order, including amendment of section, transmitted to OAL 4-30-2004 and filed 6-15-2004 (Register 2004, No. 25).

3. Amendment filed 12-27-2012; operative 1-1-2013 as a file and print only pursuant to Government Code section 11340.9(g) (Register 2012, No. 52).

Ref.: Hanna § 22.05[2]; Herlick Handbook §§ 1.01[3][b], 4.17[1].

§9789.37. DWC Form 15 Election for High Cost Outlier.

State of California
Department of Industrial Relations
DIVISION OF WORKERS' COMPENSATION

ELECTION FOR HIGH COST OUTLIER

Labor Code § 5307.1; Title 8, California Code of Regulations § 9789.37
This Section 9789.37 in inapplicable for dates of service on or after September 1, 2014.
For the 12 month period commencing on April 1, 20____

This Election is filed with the Administrative Director pursuant to Labor Code Section 5307.1, and Title 8, California Code of Regulations Section 9789.33. A provider who elects to participate in the alternative payment methodology for high cost outlier cases under Section 9789.33, subdivision (b) in lieu of the maximum allowable fees set forth under Section 9789.33 subdivision (a), shall file this form by March 1 of each year providing the requested information to the Administrative Director. The maximum allowable fees applicable to a facility that does not file a timely election satisfying the requirements set forth in Section 9789.33, subdivision (b), shall be determined under subdivision (a).

1. PROVIDER'S NAME: ____________________
2. OSHPD FACILITY NUMBER: ____________________
3. MEDICARE PROVIDER NUMBER: ____________________
4. CONTACT PERSON AND PHONE NUMBER: ____________________

Hospital Outpatient Department Cost-to-Charge Ratio

Pursuant to Section 9789.33(c)(4), the cost-to-charge ratio applicable to a hospital outpatient department participating in the Medicare program shall be the hospital's cost-to-charge ratio used by the Medicare fiscal intermediary to determine high cost outlier payments under 42 CFR 419.43(d). List below the cost-to-charge ratio being used by the intermediary for services furnished on February 15 of the year this election is filed:

5. Cost-to-charge ratio ____________________

____________________ Signature and Title ____________________ Date

Ambulatory Surgical Center (ASC) Cost-to-Charge Ratio

Pursuant to Section 9789.33(c)(5), the cost-to-charge ratio applicable to an ambulatory surgery center shall be the ratio of the facility's total operating costs to total gross charges during the preceding calendar year. Total gross charges is defined as the facility's total usual and customary charges to patients and third-party payers before reductions for contractual allowances, bad debts, courtesy allowances and charity care.

6. Provide:
   (a) The facility's total operating costs during the preceding calendar year ____________________
   (b) The facility's total gross charges during the preceding calendar year ____________________
   (c) Provide county where facility is located ____________________

7. Attach completed Annual Utilization Report of Specialty Clinics (OSHPD) which is incorporated by reference, and may be obtained at OSHPD's website at http://www.oshpd.ca.gov/HID/HID/clinic/util/index.htm#Forms or is available upon request to the Administrative Director at: Division of Workers' Compensation (Attention: OMFS-Outpatient), P.O. Box 71010, Oakland, CA 94612.

Upon request from the Administrative Director, an independent audit may be conducted at the expense of the ASC.

8. We, the undersigned, declare under penalty of perjury under the laws of the State of California that the foregoing, and attachment(s), are true and correct.

____________________ Signature, Chief Executive Officer ____________________ Date

____________________ Signature, Certified Public Accountant ____________________ Date

DWC Form 15 (rev. 09/01/2014)

Note: Authority cited: Sections 133, 4603.5, 5307.1 and 5307.3, Labor Code. Reference: Sections 4600, 4603.2 and 5307.1, Labor Code.

History: 1. New section filed 1-2-2004 as an emergency; operative 1-2-2004 (Register 2004, No. 2). A Certificate of Compliance must be transmitted to OAL by 5-3-2004 or emergency language will be repealed by operation of law on the following day.

2. Certificate of Compliance as to 1-2-2004 order transmitted to OAL 4-30-2004 and filed 6-15-2004 (Register 2004, No. 25).

3. Amendment filed 12-27-2012; operative 1-1-2013 as a file and print only pursuant to Government Code section 11340.9(g) (Register 2012, No. 52).

4. Amendment filed 6-3-2014; operative 9-1-2014 as a file and print only pursuant to Government Code section 11340.9(g) (Register 2014, No. 23).

Ref.: Hanna § 22.05[2]; Herlick Handbook §§ 1.01[3][b], 4.17[1].

§9789.38. Appendix X.

The federal regulations as incorporated by reference and/or referred to in Sections 9789.30 through 9789.37 are set forth below in numerical order. See Section 9789.39(a), for the Code of Federal Regulations reference for effective date, revisions, and amendments by date of service.

42 C.F.R. § 419.2

Basis of payment.

(a) Unit of payment. Under the hospital outpatient prospective payment system, predetermined amounts are paid for designated services furnished to Medicare beneficiaries. These services are identified by codes established under the Centers for Medicare & Medicaid Services Common Procedure Coding System (HCPCS). The prospective payment rate for each service or procedure for which payment is allowed under the hospital outpatient prospective payment system is determined according to the methodology described in subpart C of this part. The manner in which the Medicare payment amount and the beneficiary copayment amount for each service or procedure are determined is described in subpart D of this part.

(b) Determination of hospital outpatient prospective payment rates: Included costs. The prospective payment system establishes a national payment rate, standardized for geographic wage differences, that includes operating and capital-related costs that are directly related and integral to performing a procedure or furnishing a service on an outpatient basis. In general, these costs include, but are not limited to

(1) Use of an operating suite, procedure room, or treatment room;

(2) Use of recovery room;

(3) Use of an observation bed;

(4) Anesthesia, certain drugs, biologicals, and other pharmaceuticals; medical and surgical supplies and equipment; surgical dressings; and devices used for external reduction of fractures and dislocations;

(5) Supplies and equipment for administering and monitoring anesthesia or sedation;

(6) Intraocular lenses (IOLs);

(7) Incidental services such a venipuncture;

(8) Capital-related costs;

(9) Implantable items used in connection with diagnostic x-ray tests, diagnostic laboratory tests, and other diagnostic tests;

(10) Durable medical equipment that is implantable;

(11) Implantable prosthetic devices (other than dental) which replace all or part of an internal body organ (including colostomy bags and supplies directly related to colostomy care), including replacement of these devices; and;

(12) Costs incurred to procure donor tissue other than corneal tissue.

(c) Determination of hospital outpatient prospective payment rates: Excluded costs. The following costs are excluded from the hospital outpatient prospective payment system.

(1) The costs of direct graduate medical education activities as described in §413.86 of this chapter.

(2) The costs of nursing and allied health programs as described in §413.86 of this chapter.

(3) The costs associated with interns and residents not in approved teaching programs as described in §415.202 of this chapter.

(4) The costs of teaching physicians attributable to Part B services for hospitals that elect cost-based reimbursement for teaching physicians under §415.160.

(5) The reasonable costs of anesthesia services furnished to hospital outpatients by qualified nonphysician anesthetists (certified registered nurse anesthetists and anesthesiologists' assistants) employed by the hospital or obtained under arrangements, for hospitals that meet the requirements under §412.113(c) of this chapter.

(6) Bad debts for uncollectible deductibles and coinsurances as described in §413.80(b) of this chapter.

(7) Organ acquisition costs paid under Part B.

(8) Corneal tissue acquisition costs.

42 C.F.R. § 419.32

Calculation of prospective payment rates for hospital outpatient services.

(a) Conversion factor for 1999. CMS calculates a conversion factor in such a manner that payment for hospital outpatient services furnished in 1999 would have equaled the base expenditure target calculated in § 419.30, taking into account APC group weights and estimated service frequencies and reduced by the amounts that would be payable in 1999 as outlier payments under § 419.43(d) and transitional pass-through payments under § 419.43(e).

(b) Conversion factor for calendar year 2000 and subsequent years.

(1) Subject to paragraph (b)(2) of this section, the conversion factor for a calendar year is equal to the conversion factor calculated for the previous year adjusted as follows:

(i) For calendar year 2000, by the hospital inpatient market basket percentage increase applicable under section 1886(b)(3)(B)(iii) of the Act reduced by one percentage point.

(ii) For calendar year 2001 —

(A) For services furnished on or after January 1, 2001 and before April 1, 2001, by the hospital inpatient market basket percentage increase applicable under section 1886(b)(3)(B)(iii) of the Act reduced by one percentage point; and

(B) For services furnished on or after April 1, 2001 and before January 1, 2002, by the hospital inpatient market basket percentage increase applicable under section 1886(b)(3)(B)(iii) of the Act, and increased by a transitional percentage allowance equal to 0.32 percent.

(iii) For the portion of calendar year 2002 that is affected by these rules, by the hospital inpatient market basket percentage increase applicable under section 1886(b)(3)(B)(iii) of the Act reduced by one percentage point, without taking into account the transitional percentage allowance referenced in § 419.32(b)(ii)(B).

(iv) For calendar year 2003 and subsequent years, by the hospital inpatient market basket percentage increase applicable under section 1886(b)(3)(B)(iii) of the Act.

(2) Beginning in calendar year 2000, CMS may substitute for the hospital inpatient market basket percentage in paragraph (b) of this section a market basket percentage increase that is determined and applied to hospital outpatient services in the same manner that the hospital inpatient market basket percentage increase is determined and applied to inpatient hospital services.

(c) Payment rates. The payment rate for services and procedures for which payment is made under the hospital outpatient prospective payment system is the product of the conversion factor calculated under paragraph (a) or paragraph (b) of this section and the relative weight determined under § 419.31(b).

(d) Budget neutrality.

(1) CMS adjusts the conversion factor as needed to ensure that updates and adjustments under § 419.50(a) are budget neutral.

(2) In determining adjustments for 2004 and 2005, CMS will not take into account any additional expenditures per section 1833(t)(14) of the Act that would not have been made but for enactment of section 621 of the Medicare Prescription Drug, Improvement, and Mordernization [Modernization] Act of 2003.

42 C.F.R. § 419.43

Adjustments to national program payment and beneficiary copayment amounts.

(a) General rule. CMS determines national prospective payment rates for hospital outpatient department services and determines a wage adjustment factor to adjust the portion of the APC payment and national beneficiary copayment amount attributable to labor-related costs for relative differences in labor and labor-related costs across geographic regions in a budget neutral manner.

(b) Labor-related portion of payment and copayment rates for hospital outpatient services. CMS determines the portion of hospital outpatient costs attributable to labor and labor-related costs (known as the "labor-related portion" of hospital outpatient costs) in accordance with § 419.31(c)(1).

(c) Wage index factor. CMS uses the hospital inpatient prospective payment system wage index established in accordance with part 412 of this chapter to make the adjustment referred to in paragraph (a) of this section.

(d) Outlier adjustment —

(1) General rule. Subject to paragraph (d)(4) of this section, CMS provides for an additional payment for a hospital outpatient service (or group of services) not excluded under paragraph (f) of this section for which a hospital's charges, adjusted to cost, exceed the following:

(i) A fixed multiple of the sum of —

(A) The applicable Medicare hospital outpatient payment amount determined under § 419.32(c), as adjusted under § 419.43 (other than for adjustments under this paragraph (d) or paragraph (e) of this section); and

(B) Any transitional pass-through payment under paragraph (e) of this section.

(ii) At the option of CMS, a fixed dollar amount.

(2) Amount of adjustment. The amount of the additional payment under paragraph (d)(1) of this section is determined by CMS and approximates the marginal cost of care beyond the applicable cutoff point under paragraph (d)(1) of this section.

(3) Limit on aggregate outlier adjustments — (i) In general. The total of the additional payments made under this paragraph (d) for covered hospital outpatient department services furnished in a year (as estimated by CMS before the beginning of the year) may not exceed the applicable percentage specified in paragraph (d)(3)(ii) of this section of the total program payments (sum of both the Medicare and beneficiary payments to the hospital) estimated to be made under this part for all hospital outpatient services furnished in that year. If this paragraph is first applied to less than a full year, the limit applies only to the portion of the year.

(ii) Applicable percentage. For purposes of paragraph (d)(3)(i) of this section, the term "applicable percentage" means a percentage specified by CMS up to (but not to exceed) —

(A) For a year (or portion of a year) before 2004, 2.5 percent; and

(B) For 2004 and thereafter, 3.0 percent.

(4) Transitional authority. In applying paragraph (d)(1) of this section for hospital outpatient services furnished before January 1, 2002, CMS may —

(i) Apply paragraph (d)(1) of this section to a bill for these services related to an outpatient encounter (rather than for a specific service or group of services) using hospital outpatient payment amounts and transitional pass-through payments covered under the bill; and

(ii) Use an appropriate cost-to-charge ratio for the hospital or CMHC (as determined by CMS), rather than for specific departments within the hospital.

(e) Budget neutrality. CMS establishes payment under paragraph (d) of this section in a budget-neutral manner excluding services and groups specified in paragraph (f) of this section.

(f) Excluded services and groups. Drugs and biologicals that are paid under a separate APC and devices of branchytherapy, consisting of a seed or seeds (including radioactive source) are excluded from qualification for outlier payments.

42 C.F.R. § 419.44

(a) Multiple surgical procedures. When more than one surgical procedure for which payment is made under the hospital outpatient prospective payment system is performed during a single surgical encounter, the Medicare program payment amount and the beneficiary copayment amount are based on —

(1) The full amounts for the procedure with the highest APC payment rate; and

(2) One-half of the full program and the beneficiary payment amounts for all other covered procedures.

(b) Terminated procedures. When a surgical procedure is terminated prior to completion due to extenuating circumstances or circumstances that threaten the well-being of the patient, the Medicare program payment amount and the beneficiary copayment amount are based on —

(1) The full amounts if the procedure is discontinued after the induction of anesthesia or after the procedure is started; or

(2) One-half of the full program and the beneficiary coinsurance amounts if the procedure is discontinued after the patient is prepared for surgery and taken to the room where the procedure is to be performed but before anesthesia is induced.]

42 C.F.R. § 419.62

Transitional pass-through payments: General rules.

(a) General. CMS provides for additional payments under §§ 419.64 and 419.66 for certain innovative medical devices, drugs, and biologicals.

(b) Budget neutrality. CMS establishes the additional payments under §§ 419.64 and 419.66 in a budget neutral manner.

(c) Uniform prospective reduction of pass-through payments. (1) If CMS estimates before the beginning of a calendar year that the total amount of pass-through payments under §§ 419.64 and 419.66 for the year would exceed the applicable percentage (as described in paragraph (c)(2) of this section) of the total amount of Medicare payments under the outpatient prospective payment system. CMS will reduce, pro rata, the amount of each of the additional payments under §§ 419.64 and 419.66 for that year to ensure that the applicable percentage is not exceeded.

(2) The applicable percentages are as follows:

(i) For a year before CY 2004, the applicable percentage is 2.5 percent.

(ii) For 2004 and subsequent years, the applicable percentage is a percentage specified by CMS up to (but not to exceed) 2.0 percent.

(d) CY 2002 incorporated amount. For the portion of CY 2002 affected by these rules, CMS incorporated 75 percent of the estimated pass-through costs (before the incorporation and any pro rata reduction) for devices into the procedure APCs associated with these devices.

42 C.F.R. § 419.64

Transitional pass-through payments: drugs and biologicals.

(a) Eligibility for pass-through payment. CMS makes a transitional pass-through payment for the following drugs and biologicals that are furnished as part of an outpatient hospital service:

(1) Orphan drugs. A drug or biological that is used for a rare disease or condition and has been designated as an orphan drug under section 526 of the Federal Food, Drug and Cosmetic Act if payment for the drug or biological as an outpatient hospital service was being made on August 1, 2000.

(2) Cancer therapy drugs and biologicals. A drug or biological that is used in cancer therapy, including, but not limited to, a chemotherapeutic agent, an antiemetic, a hematopoietic growth factor, a colony stimulating factor, a biological response modifier, and a bisphosphonate if payment for the drug or biological as an outpatient hospital service was being made on August 1, 2000.

(3) Radiopharmaceutical drugs and biological products. A radiopharmaceutical drug or biological product used in diagnostic, monitoring, and therapeutic nuclear medicine services if payment for the drug or biological as an outpatient hospital service was being made on August 1, 2000.

(4) Other drugs and biologicals. A drug or biological that meets the following conditions:

(i) It was first payable as an outpatient hospital service after December 31, 1996.

(ii) CMS has determined the cost of the drug or biological is not insignificant in relation to the amount payable for the applicable APC (as calculated under § 419.32(c)) as defined in paragraph (b) of this section.

(b) Cost. CMS determines the cost of a drug or biological to be not insignificant if it meets the following requirements:

(1) Services furnished before January 1, 2003. The expected reasonable cost of a drug or biological must exceed 10 percent of the applicable APC payment amount for the service related to the drug or biological.

(2) Services furnished after December 31, 2002. CMS considers the average cost of a new drug or biological to be not insignificant if it meets the following conditions:

(i) The estimated average reasonable cost of the drug or biological in the category exceeds 10 percent of the applicable APC payment amount for the service related to the drug or biological.

(ii) The estimated average reasonable cost of the drug or biological exceeds the cost of the drug or biological portion of the APC payment amount for the related service by at least 25 percent.

(iii) The difference between the estimated reasonable cost of the drug or biological and the estimated portion of the APC payment amount for the drug or biological exceeds 10 percent of the APC payment amount for the related service.

(c) Limited period of payment. CMS limits the eligibility for a pass-through payment under this section to a period of at least 2 years, but not more than 3 years, that begins as follows:

(1) For a drug or biological described in paragraphs (a)(1) through (a)(3) of this section — August 1, 2000.

(2) For a drug or biological described in paragraph (a)(4) of this section — the date that CMS makes its first pass-through payment for the drug or biological.

(d) Amount of pass-through payment. (1) Subject to any reduction determined under § 419.62(b), the pass-through payment for a drug or biological as specified in section 1842(o)(1)(A) and (o)(1)(D)(i) of the Act is 95 percent of the average wholesale price of the drug or biological minus the portion of the APC payment CMS determines is associated with the drug or biological.

(2) Subject to any reduction determined under § 419.62(b), the pass-through payment for a drug or biological as specified in section 1842(o)(1)(B) and (o)(1)(E)(i) of the act is 85 percent of the average wholesale price, determined as of April 1, 2003, of the drug or biological minus the portion of the APC payment CMS determines is associated with the drug or biological.

42 C.F.R. § 419.66

Transitional pass-through payments: medical devices.

(a) General rule. CMS makes a pass-through payment for a medical device that meets the requirements in paragraph (b) of this section and that is described by a category of devices established by CMS under the criteria in paragraph (c) of this section.

(b) Eligibility. A medical device must meet the following requirements:

(1) If required by the FDA, the device must have received FDA approval or clearance (except for a device that has received an FDA investigational device exemption (IDE) and has been classified as a Category B device by the FDA in accordance with §§ 405.203 through 405.207 and 405.211 through 405.215 of this chapter) or another appropriate FDA exemption.

(2) The device is determined to be reasonable and necessary for the diagnosis or treatment of an illness or injury or to improve the functioning of a malformed body part (as required by section 1862(a)(1)(A) of the Act).

(3) The device is an integral and subordinate part of the service furnished, is used for one patient only, comes in contact with human tissue, and is surgically implanted or inserted whether or not it remains with the patient when the patient is released from the hospital.

(4) The device is not any of the following:

(i) Equipment, an instrument, apparatus, implement, or item of this type for which depreciation and financing expenses are recovered as depreciable assets as defined in Chapter 1 of the Medicare Provider Reimbursement Manual (CMS Pub. 15-1).

(ii) A material or supply furnished incident to a service (for example, a suture, customized surgical kit, or clip, other than radiological site marker).

(iii) A material that may be used to replace human skin (for example, a biological or synthetic material).

(c) Criteria for establishing device categories. CMS uses the following criteria to establish a category of devices under this section:

(1) CMS determines that a device to be included in the category is not described by any of the existing categories or by any category previously in effect, and was not being paid for as an outpatient service as of December 31, 1996.

(2) CMS determines that a device to be included in the category has demonstrated that it will substantially improve the diagnosis or treatment of an illness or injury or improve the functioning of a malformed body part compared to the benefits of a device or devices in a previously established category or other available treatment.

(3) Except for medical devices identified in paragraph (e) of this section, CMS determines the cost of the device is not insignificant as described in paragraph (d) of this section.

(d) Cost criteria. CMS considers the average cost of a category of devices to be not insignificant if it meets the following conditions:

(1) The estimated average reasonable cost of devices in the category exceeds 25 percent of the applicable APC payment amount for the service related to the category of devices.

(2) The estimated average reasonable cost of the devices in the category exceeds the cost of the device-related portion of the APC payment amount for the related service by at least 25 percent.

(3) The difference between the estimated average reasonable cost of the devices in the category and the portion of the APC payment amount for the device exceeds 10 percent of the APC payment amount for the related service.

(e) Devices exempt from cost criteria. The following medical devices are not subject to the cost requirements described in paragraph (d) of this section, if payment for the device was being made as an outpatient service on August 1, 2000:

(1) A device of brachytherapy.

(2) A device of temperature-monitored cryoablation.

(f) Identifying a category for a device. A device is described by a category, if it meets the following conditions:

(1) Matches the long descriptor of the category code established by CMS.

(2) Conforms to guidance issued by CMS relating to the definition of terms and other information in conjunction with the category descriptors and codes.

(g) Limited period of payment for devices. CMS limits the eligibility for a pass-through payment established under this section to a period of at least 2 years, but not more than 3 years beginning on the date that CMS establishes a category of devices.

(h) Amount of pass-through payment. Subject to any reduction determined under § 419.62(b), the pass-through payment for a device is the hospital's charge for the device, adjusted to the actual cost for the device, minus the amount included in the APC payment amount for the device.

Note: Authority cited: Sections 133, 4603.5, 5307.1 and 5307.3, Labor Code. Reference: Sections 4600, 4603.2 and 5307.1, Labor Code.

History: 1. New section filed 1-2-2004 as an emergency; operative 1-2-2004 (Register 2004, No. 2). A Certificate of Compliance must be transmitted to OAL by 5-3-2004 or emergency language will be repealed by operation of law on the following day.

2. Certificate of Compliance as to 1-2-2004 order, including amendment of section, transmitted to OAL 4-30-2004 and filed 6-15-2004 (Register 2004, No. 25).

3. Amendment of first paragraph filed 12-27-2012; operative 1-1-2013 as a file and print only pursuant to Government Code section 11340.9(g) (Register 2012, No. 52).

Ref.: Hanna § 22.05[2]; Herlick Handbook §§ 1.01[3][b], 4.17[1].

§9789.39. Update Table by Date of Service.

(a) Federal Regulations by Date of Service

The Federal Regulations can be accessed at: http://www.cms.gov/HospitalOutpatientPPS/ and the referenced sections are incorporated by reference and will be made available upon request to the Administrative Director.

	Services Occurring On or After 7/15/2005	*Services Occurring On or After 2/15/2006*	*Services Occurring On or After 3/1/2007*	*Services Occurring On or After 3/1/2008*
Title 42, Code of Federal Regulations, §419.2				
Title 42, Code of Federal Regulations, §419.32				
Title 42, Code of Federal Regulations, §419.43		As amended; effective January 1, 2006	As amended; effective January 1, 2007	As amended; effective January 1, 2008
Title 42, Code of Federal Regulations, §419.44				Amended; effective January 1, 2008

Title 42, Code of Federal Regulations, §419.62				
Title 42, Code of Federal Regulations, §419.64	As amended; effective January 1, 2005			
Title 42, Code of Federal Regulations, §419.66		As amended; effective January 1, 2006		
	Services Occurring On or After 3/1/2009	*Services Occurring On or After 4/15/2010*	*Services Occurring On or After 9/15/2011*	*Services Occurring On or After 3/1/2012*
Title 42, Code of Federal Regulations, §419.2				
Title 42, Code of Federal Regulations, §419.32			As amended; effective January 1, 2011	As amended; effective January 1, 2012
Title 42, Code of Federal Regulations, §419.43	As amended; effective January 1, 2009		As amended; effective January 1, 2011	As amended; effective January 1, 2012
Title 42, Code of Federal Regulations, §419.44				
Title 42, Code of Federal Regulations, §419.62				
Title 42, Code of Federal Regulations, §419.64		As amended; effective January 1, 2010		
Title 42, Code of Federal Regulations, §419.66		As amended; effective January 1, 2010		
	Services Occurring On or After 4/1/2013	*Services Occurring On or After 12/1/2014*	*Services Occurring On or After December 15, 2016*	*Services Occurring On or After June 1, 2017*
Title 42, Code of Federal Regulations, §419.2	As amended; effective January 1, 2013	As amended; effective January 1, 2014	As amended; effective January 1, 2016	As amended; effective January 1, 2016
Title 42, Code of Federal Regulations, §419.32	As amended; effective January 1, 2013	As amended; effective January 1, 2014	As amended; effective January 1, 2016	As amended; effective January 1, 2017
Title 42, Code of Federal Regulations, §419.43			As amended; effective January 1, 2012	As amended; effective January 1, 2017
Title 42, Code of Federal Regulations, §419.44			As amended; effective January 1, 2016	As amended; effective January 1, 2017
Title 42, Code of Federal Regulations, §419.62			Effective January 1, 2004	Effective January 1, 2004
Title 42, Code of Federal Regulations, §419.64			As amended; effective January 1, 2015	As amended; effective January 1, 2015
Title 42, Code of Federal Regulations, §419.66		As amended; effective January 1, 2014	As amended; effective January 1, 2016	As amended; effective January 1, 2017
	Services Occurring On or After March 15, 2018	*Services Occurring On or After February 15, 2019*		
Title 42, Code of Federal Regulations, §419.2	As amended; effective January 1, 2016	As amended; effective January 1, 2016		
Title 42, Code of Federal Regulations, §419.32	As amended; effective January 1, 2018	As amended; effective January 1, 2019		
Title 42, Code of Federal Regulations, §419.43	As amended; effective January 1, 2017	As amended; effective January 1, 2017		
Title 42, Code of Federal Regulations, §419.44	As amended; effective January 1, 2017	As amended; effective January 1, 2017		
Title 42, Code of Federal Regulations, §419.62	Effective January 1, 2004	Effective January 1, 2004		
Title 42, Code of Federal Regulations, §419.64	As amended; effective January 1, 2015	As amended; effective January 1, 2015		

Title 42, Code of Federal Regulations, §419.66	As amended; effective January 1, 2017	As amended; effective January 1, 2017
Title 42, Code of Federal Regulations, §419.71	Effective January 1, 2018	Effective January 1, 2018

(b) Update factors and Federal Register Notices by Date of Service

The Federal Register Notices can be accessed at: http:// www.cms.gov/HospitalOutpatientPPS/ and the referenced sections are incorporated by reference and will be made available upon request to the Administrative Director.

	Services Occurring On or After 1/1/2004	*Services Occurring On or After 7/15/2005*	*Services Occurring On or After 2/15/2006*	*Services Occurring On or After 3/1/2007*
Applicable FR Notices	(A) November 7, 2003 (CMS-1471-FC; 68 FR 63398); (B) December 31, 2003 (CMS-1471-CN; 68 FR 75442); (C) January 6, 2004 (CMS-1371-IFC; 69 FR 820); (D) August 1, 2003 (CMS-1470-F; 68 FR 45346); (E) August 11, 2003 (CMS-1470-F; 68 FR 47637)	(A) November 15, 2004 (CMS-1427-FC; 69 FR 65681); (B) December 30, 2004 (CMS-1427-CN; 69 FR 78315; (C) August 11, 2004 (CMS-1428-F; 69 FR 48916); (D) December 30, 2004 (CMS-1482-F2; 69 FR 78526	(A) November 10, 2005 (CMS-1501-FC; 70 FR 68515); (B) December 23, 2005 (CMS-1501-CN2; 70 FR 76176); (C) August 12, 2005 (CMS-1500-F; 70 FR 47278); (D) September 30, 2005 (CMS-1500-CN; 70 FR 57161)	(A) November 24, 2006 (CMS-1506-FC; 71 FR 67960); (B) August 18, 2006 (CMS-1488-F; 71 FR 47870) (C) October 11, 2006 (CMS-1488-N; 71 FR 59886)
APC Payment Rate	Addendum B (A) beginning on page 63488 conformed to comply with (B) beginning on page 75442 and (C) beginning on page 820	Addendum B (A) beginning on page 65887	Addendum B (A) beginning on page 68752	Addendum B (A) beginning on page 68283
APC Relative Weight	Addendum B (A) beginning on page 63488 conformed to comply with (B) beginning on page 75442 and (C) beginning on page 820	Addendum B (A) beginning on page 65887	Addendum B (A) beginning on page 68752	Addendum B (A) beginning on page 68283
Emergency Department HCPCS Codes	99281-99285	99281-99285	99281-99285	99281-99285
HOPPS Addenda	Addenda A, B, D1, D2, E, H, I, and J (A) beginning at page 63478; as changed by (B) beginning at page 75442; and (C) beginning at page 820	Addenda A, B, D1, D2, and E (A) beginning at page 65864	Addenda A, B, D1, D2, E and L (A) beginning at page 68729; and correction (B) beginning at page 76176	Addenda A, B, D1, D2, E, and L (A) beginning at page 68231
IPPS Tables		Tables $4A_1$, $4A_2$, $4B_1$, $4B_2$, $4C_1$ $4C_2$ and 4J (D) beginning at page 78619	Tables 4A, 4B, 4C, and 4J (D) beginning at page 57163; and Tables 4A, 4B, 4C, and 4J (C) beginning on page 47580	Tables 4A-1, 4A-2, 4B-1, 4B-2, 4C-1, 4C-2, and 4J (C) beginning at page 59975
Labor-related Share	60% ((A) page 63458)	60% ((A) beginning at page 65842)	60% ((A) beginning at page 68551)	60% ((A) beginning at page 68003)
Market Basket Inflation Factor	3.4% (D) page 45346	3.3% (C) page 49274	3.7% (C) page 47492	3.4% (B) page 48146
Outlier Threshold		$1,175 (A) at page 65846	$1,250 (A) at page 68565	$1,825(A) at page 68012
Surgical Procedure HCPCS	10021-69990	10021-69990	10021-69990	10021-69990
Conversion Factor adjusted for inflation factor	$53.924 (2003 unadjusted conversion factor of 52.151 × estimated inflation factor of 1.034)	$55.703 (2004 unadjusted conversion factor of $53.924 × estimated inflation factor of 1.033)	$57.764 (2005 unadjusted conversion factor of $55.703 × estimated inflation factor of 1.037)	$59.728 (2006 unadjusted conversion factor of $57.764 × estimated inflation factor of 1.034)

Wage Index	Addenda H through J (A) beginning at page 63682	Referenced in Addenda H through J (B) beginning at page 78316; wage index values are specified in Tables $4A_1$ through $4C_2$ (D) beginning at page 78619	Referenced in (A) beginning at page 68551; wage index values are specified in Tables 4A through 4C (D) beginning at page 57163; and as specified in Tables 4A through 4C (C) beginning at page 47580	Referenced in (A) beginning at page 68003; wage index values are specified in Tables 4A-1 through 4C-2 (C) beginning at page 59975
	Services Occurring On or After 3/1/2008	*Services Occurring On or After 3/1/2009*	*Services Occurring On or After 4/15/2010*	*Services Occurring On or After 9/15/2011*
Applicable FR Notices	(A) November 27, 2007 (CMS-1392-FC; CMS-1533-F2; 72 FR 66580); (B) August 22, 2007 (CMS-1533-FC; 72 FR 47130); (C) October 10, 2007 (CMS-1533-CN2; 72 FR 57634); (D) November 6, 2007 (CMS-1533-CN3; 72 FR 62585); (E) November 27, 2007 (CMS-1392-FC; CMS-1533-F2; 72 FR 66580); (F) February 22, 2008 (CMS-1392-CN; CMS-1533-CN)	(A) November 18, 2008 (CMS-1404-FC; 73 FR 68502); (B) August 19, 2008 (CMS-1390-F; 73 FR 48434); (C) October 3, 2008 (CMS-1390-CN; 73 FR 57541); (D) October 3, 2008 (CMS-1390-N; 73 FR 57888); (E) December 3, 2008 (CMS-1390-N2; 73 FR 73656); (F) January 26, 2009 (CMS-1404-CN; 74 FR 4343)	(A) November 20, 2009 (CMS-1414-FC; 74 FR 60316); (B) December 31, 2009 (CMS-1414-CN; 74 FR 69502); (C) August 27, 2009 (CMS-1406-F; 74 FR 43754); (D) October 7, 2009 (CMS-1406-CN; 74 FR 51496)	(A) November 24, 2010 (CMS-1504-FC; 75 FR 71800); (B) March 11, 2011 (CMS-1504-CN; 76 FR 13292); (C) August 16, 2010 (CMS-1498-F; 75 FR 50042); (D) October 1, 2010 (CMS-1498-F; 75 FR 60640)
APC Payment Rate	Addendum B (A) beginning on page 66993 conformed to comply with correction published in (F) beginning on page 9863	Addendum B (A) beginning on page 68934 conformed to comply with correction published in (F) beginning on page 4344	Addendum B (A) beginning on page 60752 conformed to comply with correction published in (B) page 69503	Addendum B (A) beginning on page 72331 conformed to comply with correction published in (B) page 13295
APC Relative Weight	Addendum B (A) beginning on page 66993 conformed to comply with correction published in (F) beginning on page 9863	Addendum B (A) beginning on page 68934 conformed to comply with correction published in (F) beginning on page 4344	Addendum B (A) beginning on page 60752 conformed to comply with correction published in (B) page 69503	Addendum B (A) beginning on page 72331 conformed to comply with correction published in (B) page 13295
Emergency Department HCPCS Codes	99281-99285	99281-99285	99281-99285	99281-99285
HOPPS Addenda	Addenda A, B, D1, D2, E, L, and M (A) beginning at page 66934; and corrections to addenda A, B, D2, and M (F) beginning at page 9862	Addenda A, B, D1, D2, E, L, and M (A) beginning at page 68816; and corrections to addenda A and B (F) beginning at page 4343	Addenda A, B, D1, D2, E, L, and M (A) beginning at page 60682; and corrections to addenda B and E (B) beginning at page 69503	Addenda A, B, D1, D2, E, L, and M (A) beginning at page 72268; and corrections to addendum B (B) on page 13295
IPPS Tables	Tables 4A, 4B, and 4C (C) beginning at page 57698 and Table 4J (B) beginning at page 47531 and correction (C) beginning at page 57726	Tables 4A, 4B, 4C, and 4J (C) beginning at page 57956; and Tables 2 and 4J (E) beginning at page 73657	Tables 2, 4A, 4B, 4C, and 4J (C) beginning at page 44032; as changed by correction to Tables 2, 4A, 4B, 4C, and 4J (D) beginning at page 51499	Tables 2, 4A, 4B, 4C, and 4J (C) beginning at page 50451
Labor-related Share	60% ((A) beginning at page 66678)	60% ((A) beginning at page 68585)	60% ((A) beginning at page 60419)	60% ((A) beginning at page 71877)
Market Basket Inflation Factor	3.3% (B) page 47415	3.6% (B) page 48759	2.1% (C) page 44002	2.6% (C) page 50422
Outlier Threshold	$1,575 (A) at page 66686	$1,800 (A) at page 68594	$2,175 (A) at page 60428	$2,025 (A) at page 71889
Surgical Procedure HCPCS	10021-69990	10021-69990	10021-69990	10021-69990

Conversion Factor adjusted for inflation factor	$61.699 (2007 unadjusted conversion factor of $59.728 × estimated inflation factor of 1.033)	$63.920 (2008 unadjusted conversion factor of $61.699 × estimated inflation factor of 1.036)	$65.262 (2009 unadjusted conversion factor of $63.920 × estimated inflation factor of 1.021)	$66.959 (2010 unadjusted conversion factor of $65.262 × estimated inflation factor of 1.026)
Wage Index	Referenced in (A) beginning at page 66678; wage index values are specified in Tables 4A through 4C (C) beginning at page 57698	Referenced in (A) beginning at page 68585; wage index values are specified in Tables 4A through 4C (D) beginning at page 57956	Referenced in (A) beginning at page 60419; wage index values are specified in Tables 4A through 4C (D) beginning at page 51505; and as specified in Tables 4A through 4C (C) beginning at page 44085	Referenced in (A) beginning at page 71877; wage index values are specified in Tables 4A through 4C (C) beginning at page 50511
	Services Occurring On or After 3/1/2012	*Services Occurring On or After 9/1/2012*	*Services Occurring On or After 4/1/2013*	*Services Occurring On or After 9/1/2014*
Applicable FR Notices	(A) November 30, 2011 (CMS-1525-FC; 76 FR 74122); (B) January 4, 2012 (CMS-1525-CN; 77 FR 217); (C) August 18, 2011 (CMS-1518-F; 76 FR 51476); (D) September 26, 2011 (CMS-1518-CN3; 76 FR 59263)	(A) November 30, 2011 (CMS-1525-FC; 76 FR 74122); (B) January 4, 2012 (CMS-1525-CN; 77 FR 217); (C) August 18, 2011 (CMS-1518-F; 76 FR 51476); (D) September 26, 2011 (CMS-1518-CN3; 76 FR 59263); (E) April 24, 2012 (CMS-1525-CN2; 77 FR 24409)	(A) November 15, 2012 (CMS-1589-FC; 77 FR 68210)	
APC Payment Rate	Addendum B (A) conformed to comply with correction published in (B) found on CMS website at: http://www.cms.gov/HospitalOutpatient PPS	Addendum B (A) conformed to comply with corrections published in (B) and (E) found on CMS website at: http://www.cms.gov/HospitalOutpatient PPS	Addendum B (A) found on CMS website at: http://www.cms.gov/HospitalOutpatientPPS	
APC Relative Weight	Addendum B (A) conformed to comply with correction published in (B) found on CMS website at: http://www.cms.gov/HospitalOutpatient PPS	Addendum B (A) conformed to comply with corrections published in (B) and (E) found on CMS website at: http://www.cms.gov/HospitalOutpatient PPS	Addendum B (A) found on CMS website at: http://www.cms.gov/HospitalOutpatientPPS	
Emergency Department HCPCS Codes	99281-99285	99281-99285	99281-99285	99281-99285, 99291, 99292, G0380-G0384, G0390
Facility Only Services				Services with a "NA" in the column labeled "Non-Facility NA Indicator" of the Medicare Physician Fee Schedule Relative Value File for Calendar Year 2014 (RVU14A), located at: http://www.cms.gov/Medicare/Medicare-Fee-for-Service-Payment/PhysicianFeeSched/PFS-Relative-Value-Files.html
HOPPS Addenda	Addenda A, B, D1, D2, E, L, and M (A) and corrections to addenda (B) found on CMS website at: http://www.cms.gov/HospitalOutpatient PPS	Addenda A, B, D1, D2, E, L, and M (A and E) and corrections to addenda (A) and (B) found on CMS website at: http://www.cms.gov/HospitalOutpatient PPS	Addenda A, B, D1, D2, E, L, and M (A) found on CMS website at: http://www.cms.gov/HospitalOutpatientPPS	
IPPS Tables	Tables 2, 4A, 4B, 4C, and 4J (C) and correction (D) found on CMS website at: http://www.cms.hhs.gov/AcuteInpatientPPS/.		Tables 2, 4A, 4B, 4C, and 4J (C) and correction (D) found on CMS website at: http://www.cms.gov/AcuteInpatientPPS/.	
Labor-related Share	60% ((A) beginning at page 74191)		60% (A) beginning at page 68285	

Market Basket Inflation Factor	3.0% (A) page 74189		2.6% (A) page 68215	
Medicare Physician Fee Schedule Relative Value File				Calendar Year 2014 (RVU14A), located at: http://www.cms.gov/ Medicare/Medicare-Fee-for-Service-Payment/ PhysicianFeeSched/ PFS-Relative-Value-Files.html
Outlier Threshold	$2,025 (B) at page 222		$2,025 (A) page 68297	
Surgical Procedure HCPCS	10021-69990	10021-69990	10021-69990	10021-69990, G0413
Conversion Factor adjusted for inflation factor	$68.968 (2011 unadjusted conversion factor of $66.959 × estimated inflation factor of 1.03)		$70.761 (2012 unadjusted conversion factor of $68.968 × estimated inflation factor of 1.026)	
Wage Index	Referenced in (A) beginning at page 74191; wage index values are specified in Tables 4A through 4C (C) found on the CMS web site at: http://www.cms.gov/ AcuteInpatientPPS/		Referenced in (A) beginning at page 68285; wage index values are specified in Tables 4A through 4C found on CMS website at: http:// www.cms.gov/ AcuteInpatientPPS/	
	Services Occurring On or After 12/1/2014	*Services Occurring On or After December 15, 2016 and Mid-year Updates*	*Services Occurring On or After June 1, 2017 and Mid-year Updates*	*Services Occurring On or After March 15, 2018 and Mid-year Updates*
Applicable FR Notices	(A) December 10, 2013 (CMS-1601-FC; 78 FR 74826) (B) August 19, 2013 (CMS-1599-F; 78 FR 50496) (C) October 3, 2013 (CMS-1599-CN2; 78 FR 61197) (D) October 3, 2013 (CMS-1599-IFC; 78 FR 61191) (E) January 2, 2014 (CMS-1599-CN3; 79 FR 61) (F) January 10, 2014 (CMS-1599-CN4; 79 FR 1741) (G) March 14, 2014 (CMS-1599-IFC2; 79 FR 15022) (H) June 17, 2014; (CMS-1599-N; 79 FR 34444)	(A) November 13, 2015 (CMS-1633-FC; 80 FR 70298) (B) August 17, 2015 (CMS-1632-F; 80 FR 49326) (C) October 5, 2015 (CMS 1632-CN; 80 FR 60055)	(A) November 14, 2016 (CMS-1656-FC; 81 FR 79562) (B) January 3, 2017 (CMS-1656-CN; 82 FR 24) (C) August 22, 2016 (CMS-1655-F; 81 FR 56762) (D) October 5, 2016 (CMS-1655-F Correction; 81 FR 68947)	(A) December 14, 2017 (CMS-1678-FC; 82 FR 59216) Republication) (B) December 27, 2017 (CMS-1678-CN; 82 FR 61184) (C) August 14, 2017 (CMS-1677-F; 82 FR 37990; (D) October 4, 2017 (CMS-1677-CN; 82 FR 46138; Final rule; correction)
Ambulatory Surgical Centers Payment System Addenda		For services rendered on or after December 15, 2016, Column A, of Addendum AA, entitled, "HCPCS Code" and Column A, of Addendum EE, entitled, "HCPCS Code" located in "July 2016 ASC Approved HCPCS Code and Payment Rates" found on CMS website at: https:// www.cms.gov/Medicare/ Medicare-Fee-for-Service-Payment/ASCPayment/ index.html	For services occurring on or after June 1, 2017, Column A, of Addendum AA, entitled, "HCPCS Code" and Column A, of Addendum EE entitled, "HCPCS Code" located in "April 2017 ASC Approved HCPCS Code and Payment Rates" (april_2017_asc_ addenda_rev_ 20170329)	For services occurring on or after March 15 2018, Column A, of Addendum AA, entitled, "HCPCS Code" and Column A, of Addendum EE entitled, "HCPCS Code" located in "Correction Notice Addendum AA, BB, DD1, DD2, EE" (CMS-1678-CN-ASC-Addendum-AA-BB-DD1-DD2-EE.zip)

Regulations

			For services occurring on or after July 1 2017, Column A, of Addendum AA, entitled, "HCPCS Code" and Column A, of Addendum EE, entitled, "HCPCS Code" located in "July 2017 ASC Approved HCPCS Code and Payment Rates" (july_2017_asc_addendal)	For services occurring on or after April 1 2018, Column A, of Addendum AA, entitled, "HCPCS Code" and Column A, of Addendum EE, entitled, "HCPCS Code" located in "April 2018 ASC Approved HCPCS Code and Payment Rates—Updated 03/21/2018" (april_2018_asc_addenda_updated_04_01_2018b.xlsx)
			For services occurring on or after October 1 2017, Column A, of Addendum AA, entitled, "HCPCS Code" and Column A, of Addendum EE, entitled, "HCPCS Code" located in "October 2017 ASC Approved HCPCS Code and Payment Rates" (october_2017_asc_addenda)	For services occurring on or after July 1, 2018, Column A, of Addendum AA, entitled, "HCPCS Code" and Column A, of Addendum EE, entitled, "HCPCS Code" located in "July 2018 ASC Approved HCPCS Code and Payment Rates — Updated 06/28/2018" (july_2018_asc_addenda_updated_06_28_2018.xlsx)
			Access the files on CMS website at: https://www.cms.gov/Medicare/Medicare-Fee-for-Service-Payment/ASCPayment/index.html	For services occurring on or after October 1, 2018, Column A, of Addendum AA, entitled, "HCPCS Code" and Column A, of Addendum EE, entitled, "HCPCS Code" located in "October 2018 ASC Approved HCPCS Code and Payment Rates" (oct_2018_asc_addenda_updated_09_19_2018.09212018cb.xlsx)
				Access the files on CMS website at: https://www.cms.gov/Medicare/Medicare-Fee-for-Service-Payment/ ASCPayment/index.html
APC Payment Rate	Addendum B (A) found on CMS website at: http://www.cms.gov/HospitalOutpatient- PPS	For services rendered on or after December 15, 2016, Addendum B, dated July 2016, (A) found on CMS website at: http://www.cms.gov/HospitalOutpatient PPS	For services occurring on or after June 1, 2017, Addendum B, dated April 2017 (— updated: 03/28/2017; april_2017_web_addendum_ b.03.28.17) — found on CMS website at: http://www.cms.gov/HospitalOutpatient PPS	For services occurring on or after March 15, 2018, Addendum B (CMS-1678-CN-2018-OPPS-Addendum-B.zip; 2018 CN Addendum B.11.29.17)
			For services occurring on or after July 1, 2017, Addendum B, dated July 2017 (july_2017_web_addendum_ b.06.13.17)	For services occurring on or after April 1, 2018, Addendum B, dated April 2018 (2018_april_web_addendum_b.03.19.18final.xlsx)
			For services occurring on or after October 1, 2017, Addendum B, dated October 2017 (october_2017_web_addendum_ a.09.14.17)	For services occurring on or after July 1, 2018, Addendum B — Updated 6/27/2018 (july_addendum_b.07.01.18 revised06272018.xlsx)

			— found on CMSwebsite at: http://www.cms.gov/ HospitalOutpatient PPS/	For services occurring on or after October 1, 2018, Addendum B (2018_october_web_ addendum_b.10.01.18 no340brem.xlsx)
				Access the files on the CMS website at: https:// www.cms.gov/Medicare/ Medicare-Fee-for-Service-Payment HospitalOutpatient PPS/index.html?redirect= /HospitalOutpatient PPS/
APC Relative Weight	Addendum B (A) found on CMS website at: http:// www.cms.gov/ HospitalOutpatient- PPS	For services rendered on or after December 15, 2016, Addendum B, dated July 2016, (A) found on CMS website at: http:// www.cms.gov/ HospitalOutpatient PPS	For services occurring on or after June 1, 2017, Addendum B, dated April 2017 (— updated: 03/28/2017; april_2017_ web_addendum_ b.03.28.17)	For services occurring on or after March 15, 2018, Addendum B (CMS-1678-CN-2018- OPPS-Addendum-B.zip; 2018 CN Addendum B.11.29.17)
			For services occurring on or after July 1, 2017, July 2017 (july_2017_ web_addendum_ b.06.13.17)	For services occurring on or after April 1, 2018, Addendum B, dated April 2018 (2018_april_ web_addendum_ b.03.19.18final.xlsx)
			For services occurring on or after October 1, 2017, Addendum B, dated October 2017 (october_2017_ web_addendum_ a.09.14.17)	For services occurring on or after July 1, 2018, Addendum B — Updated 6/27/2018 (july_addendum_ b.07.01.18 revised0627 2018.xlsx)
			— found on CMSwebsite at: http://www.cms.gov/ HospitalOutpatient PPS	For services occurring on or after October 1, 2018, Addendum B (2018_october_web_ addendum_b.10.01.18 no340brem.xlsx)
				Access the files on CMS website at: https:// www.cms.gov/Medicare/ Medicare-Fee-for-Service-Payment/HospitalOutpatient PPS/index.html?redirect= /HospitalOutpatient PPS/
Composite APCs (codes assigned status indicator "Q1," "Q2," "Q3," or "Q4") payment rules				For services occurring on or after March 15, 2018, payment rules are: • Medicare Claims Processing Manual, Chapter 4, sections 10.2.1, 10.2.2, 10.4, and 10.4.1 • CMS 2018 OPPS Addendum D1 • CMS 2018 OPPS Addendum M (corrected 12/4/2017) • Integrated OCE (IOCE) CMS Specifications V19.0 (effective 01/01/2018), sections 10-12, 20
				For services occurring on or after April 1, 2018, payment rules are:

- Medicare Claims Processing Manual, Chapter 4, sections 10.2.1, 10.2.2, 10.4, and 10.4.1
- CMS 2018 OPPS Addendum D1
- CMS 2018 OPPS Addendum M (corrected 12/4/2017)
- IOCE Quarterly Data Files V19.1 [ZIP, 46MB] (IntegOCEspecs V19.1.pdf), sections 6.4.1, 6.4.3, 6.4.5, and 6.5

For services occurring on or after July 1, 2018, payment rules are:

- Medicare Claims Processing Manual, Chapter 4, sections 10.2.1, 10.2.2, 10.4, and 10.4.1
- CMS 2018 OPPS Addendum D1
- CMS 2018 OPPS Addendum M (corrected 12/4/2017)
- Revised IOCE Quarterly Data Files V19.2.R1 [ZIP, 9MB], sections 5.4.1, 5.4.3, 5.4.5, and 5.5

For services occurring on or after October 1, 2018, payment rules are:

- Medicare Claims Processing Manual, Chapter 4, sections 10.2.1, 10.2.2, 10.4, and 10.4.1
- CMS 2018 OPPS Addendum D1
- CMS 2018 OPPS Addendum M (corrected 12/4/2017)
- IOCE Quarterly Data Files V19.3 [ZIP, 55MB], sections 5.4.1, 5.4.3, 5.4.5, and 5.5

A copy of the IOCE is posted on the DWC website: http://www.dir.ca.gov/dwc/OMFS9904htm#6

Access documents on the CMS website at: https://www.cms.gov/Medicare/Medicare-Fee-for-Service-Payment/HospitalOutpatientPPS/index.html?redirect=/HospitalOutpatient PPS/ and https://www.cms.gov/Regulations-and-Guidance/Guidance/Manuals/Internet-Only-Manuals-IOMs-Items/CMS018912.html

Comprehensive APC's (codes assigned status indicator "J1," or "J2") payment rules	For services occurring onor after March 15, 2018, payment rules are:

- Medicare Claims Processing Manual, Chapter 4, sections 10.2.3, 10.4, 290.5.2, and 290.5.3
- CMS 2018 OPPS Addendum D1
- CMS 2018 OPPS Addendum J (Revised 1/25/2018)
- Integrated OCE (IOCE) CMS Specifications V19.0 (effective 01/01/2018), sections 7, 21, and Appendix L

For services occurring on or after April 1, 2018, payment rules are:

- Medicare Claims Processing Manual, Chapter 4, sections 10.2.3, 10.4, 290.5.2, and 290.5.3
- CMS 2018 OPPS Addendum D1
- CMS 2018 OPPS Addendum J (Revised 1/25/2018)
- IOCE Quarterly Data Files V19.1 [ZIP, 46MB] (IntegOCE-specsV19.1.pdf), sections 6.6.1, 6.6.1.1, 6.6.2, 6.6.3, 6.6.4, 6.6.4.1, and 6.6.4.2

For services occurring on or after July 1, 2018, payment rules are:

- Medicare Claims Processing Manual, Chapter 4, sections 10.2.3, 10.4, 290.5.2, and 290.5.3
- CMS 2018 OPPS Addendum D1
- CMS 2018 OPPS Addendum J (Revised 1/25/2018)
- Revised IOCE Quarterly Data Files V19.2.R1 [ZIP, 9MB], sections 5.6.1, 5.6.1.1, 5.6.2, 5.6.3, 5.6.4, 5.6.4.1, and 5.6.4.2

For services occurring on or after October 1, 2018, payment rules are:

- Medicare Claims Processing Manual, Chapter 4, sections 10.2.3, 10.4, 290.5.2, and 290.5.3
- CMS 2018 OPPS Addendum D1
- CMS 2018 OPPS Addendum J (Revised 1/25/2018)
- IOCE Quarterly Data Files V19.3 [ZIP, 55MB], sections 5.6.1, 5.6.1.1, 5.6.2, 5.6.3, 5.6.4, 5.6.4.1, and 5.6.4.2

				A copy of the IOCE is posted on the DWC website: http://www.dir.ca.gov/dwc/OMFS9904.htm#6 Access documents on the CMS website at: https://www.cms.gov/Medicare/Medicare-Fee-for-Service-Payment/HospitalOutpatientPPS/index.html?redirect=/HospitalOutpatientPPS/ and https://www.cms.gov/Regulations-and-Guidance/Guidance/Manuals/Internet-Only-Manuals-IO Ms-Items/CMS018912.html
Emergency Department HCPCS Codes	99281-99285, 99291, 99292, G0380-G0384, G0390	99281-99285, 99291, 99292, G0380-G0384, G0390	99281-99285, 99291, 99292, G0380-G0384, G0390	99281-99285, 99291, 99292, G0380-G0384, G0390
Facility Only Services	Services with a "NA" in the column labeled "Non-Facility NA Indicator" of the Medicare Physician Fee Schedule Relative Value File, by date of service, as adopted and incorporated by reference in the Official Medical Fee Schedule (OMFS) Physician Fee Schedule (Title 8 CCR sections 9789.12.1, et seq.). The (OMFS) Physician Fee Schedule is located at: http://www.dir.ca.gov/dwc/OMFS9904.htm and the Medicare Physician Fee Schedule Relative Value File is located at: http://www.cms.gov/Medicare/Medicare-Fee-for-Service-Payment/PhysicianFeeSched/PFS-Relative-Value-Files.html	Not applicable for services rendered on or after December 15, 2016	Not applicable for services rendered on or after December 15, 2016	Not applicable for services rendered on or after December 15, 2016
Film X-ray services and X-rays taken using computed radiography technology/cassette-based imaging payment reductions				For services occurring on or after March 15, 2018, use modifier "FX" to report X-rays taken using film, which requires a 20 percent payment reduction for such service. Use modifier "FY" to report X-rays taken using computed radiography technology/cassette-based imaging which requires a 7 percent payment reduction for such service. Apply payment rules set forth in: • December 14, 2017 (CMS-1678-FC; 82 FR 59216, Republished, section X.E., pages 59391 through 59393) • Medicare Claims Processing Manual, Chapter 4, section 20.6.14 (effective 01/01/2018) and section 20.6.15 (effective 01/01/2018) • CFR section 419.71

For services occurring on or after April 1, 2018, use modifier "FX" to report X-rays taken using film, which requires a 20 percent payment reduction for such service. Use modifier "FY" to report X-rays taken using computed radiography technology/cassette-based imaging which requires a 7 percent payment reduction for such service. Apply payment rules set forth in:

- December 14, 2017 (CMS-1678-FC; 82 FR 59216, Republished, section X.E., pages 59391 through 59393)
- Medicare Claims Processing Manual, Chapter 4, section 20.6.14 (effective 01/01/2018) and section 20.6.15 (effective 01/01/2018)
- CFR section 419.71
- CMS' April 2018 Update of the Hospital Outpatient Prospective Payment System (OPPS) CR 10515 Revised March 22, 2018, Transmittal R4005CP, section 6

For services occurring on or after July 1, 2018, use modifier "FX" to report X-rays taken using film, which requires a 20 percent payment reduction for such service. Use modifier "FY" to report X-rays taken using computed radiography technology/cassette-based imaging which requires a 7 percent payment reduction for such service. Apply payment rules set forth in:

- December 14, 2017 (CMS-1678-FC; 82 FR 59216, Republished, section X.E., pages 59391 through 59393)
- Medicare Claims Processing Manual, Chapter 4, section 20.6.14 (effective 01/01/2018) and section 20.6.15 (effective 01/01/2018)
- CFR section 419.71
- CMS' April 2018 Update of the Hospital Outpatient Prospective Payment System (OPPS) CR 10515 Revised March 22, 2018, Transmittal R4005CP, section 6

				For services occurring on or after October 1, 2018, use modifier "FX" to report X-rays taken using film, which requires a 20 percent payment reduction for such service. Use modifier "FY" to report X-rays taken using computed radiography technology/cassette-based imaging which requires a 7 percent payment reduction for such service. Apply payment rules set forth in: • December 14, 2017 (CMS-1678-FC; 82 FR 59216, Republished, section X.E., pages 59391 through 59393) • Medicare Claims Processing Manual, Chapter 4, section 20.6.14 (effective 01/01/2018) and section 20.6.15 (effective 01/01/2018) • CFR section 419.71 • CMS' April 2018 Update of the Hospital Outpatient Prospective Payment System (OPPS) CR 10515 Revised March 22, 2018, Transmittal R4005CP, section 6 Access the Medicare Claims Processing Manual on the CMS website at: https://www.cms.gov/Regulations-and-Guidance/Guidance/Manuals/Internet-Only-Manuals-IO Ms-Items/CMS018912.html
HOPPS Addenda	Addenda A, B, D1, D2, E, L, M, and P (A) found on CMS website at: http://www.cms.gov/HospitalOutpatientPPS	Addenda A, B, D1, D2, E, J, L, and M (A) found on CMS website at: http://www.cms.gov/HospitalOutpatientPPS	For services occurring on or after June 1, 2017, addenda: • A (April 2017 (— updated: 3/20/2017; april_2017_web_addendum_a_03202017) • B (April 2017 (— updated: 3/28/2017; april_2017_web_addendum_b.03.28.17) • D1 (2017 Final Addendum D1.10.11.16) • D2 (2017 Final Addendum D2.10.11.16) • E (2017 Final Addendum E.10.20.16) • J (2017 NFRM Addendum J 2016 12.05.16) • L (2017 Final OPPS Addendum L) • M (2017 Final Addendum	For services occurring on or after March 15, 2018 addenda: • A (2018 CN Addendum A.11.29.17) • B (2018 CN Addendum B.11.29.17) • D1 (2018 Final Addendum 2018, NFRM Addendum D1.10.18.17) • D2 (2018 Final Addendum, 2018 NFRM Addendum D2.10.18.17) • E (2018 Final Addendum, 2018 NFRM Addendum E.10.18.17) • J (2018 NFRM Addendum J Revised 01-25-2018) • L (2018 Final Addendum, 2018 NFRM Addendum L_

M.10.20.16)
- P (2017 Final Addendum P)

For services occurring on or after July 1, 2017, addenda:

- A (July 2017; july_2017_ web_addendum_ a.06.13.17)
- B (July 2017; july_2017_ web_addendum_ b.06.13.17)
- D1 (2017 Final Addendum D1.10.11.16)
- D2 (2017 Final Addendum D2.10.11.16)
- E (2017 Final Addendum E.10.20.16)
- J (2017 NFRM Addendum J 2016 12.05.16)
- L (2017 Final OPPS Addendum L)
- M (2017 Final Addendum M.10.20.16)
- P (2017 Final Addendum P)

For services occurring on or after October 1, 2017, addenda:

- A (October 2017; october_2017_ web_addendum_ a.09.14.17)
- B (October 2017; october_2017_ web_addendum_ b.09.14.17)
- D1 (2017 Final Addendum D1.10.11.16)
- D2 (2017 Final Addendum D2.10.11.16)
- E (2017 Final Addendum E.10.20.16)
- J (2017 NFRM Addendum J 2016 12.05.16)
- L (2017 Final OPPS Addendum L)
- M (2017 Final Addendum M.10.20.16)
- P (2017 Final Addendum P)

final)
- M (2018 CN Addendum M.12.04.17)
- P (2018 NFRM CN Addendum P 11 20 17)

For services occurring on or after April 1, 2018 addenda:

- A (April 2018; 2018_april_ web_addendum_ a.03.19.18 final.xlsx)
- B (April 2018; 2018_april_ web_addendum_ b.03.19.18 final.xlsx)
- D1 (2018 Final Addendum 2018, NFRM Addendum D1.10.18.17)
- D2 (2018 Final Addendum, 2018 NFRM Addendum D2.10.18.17)
- E (2018 Final Addendum, 2018 NFRM Addendum E.10.18.17)
- J (2018 NFRM Addendum J Revised 01-25-2018)
- L (2018 Final Addendum, 2018 NFRM Addendum L_ final)
- M (2018 CN Addendum M.12.04.17)
- P (2018 NFRM CN Addendum P 11 20 17)

For services occurring on or after July 1, 2018 addenda:

- A (July 2018 — Updated 6/27/2018; july_ addendum_ a.07.01.18 revised0627 2018.xlsx)
- B (July 2018 — Updated 6/27/2018; july_ addendum_ b.07.01.18 revised0627 2018.xlsx)
- D1 (2018 Final Addendum 2018, NFRM Addendum D1.10.18.17)
- D2 (2018 Final Addendum, 2018 NFRM Addendum D2.10.18.17)
- E (2018 Final Addendum, 2018 NFRM Addendum E.10.18.17)
- J (2018 NFRM

			Access the files on the CMS website at: http://www.cms.gov/ HospitalOutpatient PPS	Addendum J Revised 01-25-2018) • L (2018 Final Addendum, L_final) • M (2018 CN Addendum M.12.04.17) • P (2018 NFRM CN Addendum P 11 20 17) For services occurring on or after October 1, 2018 addenda: • A (October 2018; 2018_october_web_ addendum_ a.10.01.18 no_340brem.xlsx) • B (October 2018; 2018_october_web_ addendum_ b.10.01.18 no340brem.xlsx) • D1 (2018 Final Addendum 2018, NFRM Addendum D1.10.18.17) • D2 (2018 Final Addendum, 2018 NFRM Addendum D2.10.18.17) • E (2018 Final Addendum, 2018 NFRM Addendum E.10.18.17) • J (2018 NFRM Addendum J Revised 01-25-2018) • L (2018 Final Addendum, 2018 NFRM Addendum L_final) • M (2018 CN Addendum M.12.04.17) • P (2018 NFRM CN Addendum P 11 20 17) Access the files on the CMS website at: https:// www.cms.gov/ Medicare/ Medicare-Fee-for-Service-Payment/HospitalOutpatient PPS/index.html
IPPS Tables	Tables 2, 4A, 4B, 4C, and 4J (B) found on CMS website at: http:// www.cms.hhs.gov/ AcuteInpatientPPS/.	Tables 2 and 3 found on CMS website at: http:// www.cms.hhs.gov/ AcuteInpatientPPS/.	Tables 2 and 3 (CMS 1655-F and CN FY 2017 Tables 2 and 3) found on CMS website at: http:// www.cms.hhs.gov/ AcuteInpatientPPS/	Tables 2 and 3 (CMS-1677-F; CMS-1677-CN) found at: https:// www.cms.gov/Medicare/ Medicare-Fee-for-Service-Payment/ AcuteInpatientPPS/ FY2018-IPPS-Final-Rule-Home-Page.html?DLSort= 0&DLEntries= 10&DLPage= 1&DLSortDir= ascending
Labor-related Share	60% ((A) beginning at page 74950)	60% ((A) beginning at page 70359)	60% ((A) beginning at page 79597)	60% ((A) beginning at page 59258)
Market Basket Inflation Factor	2.5% (A) page 74949	2.4% (A) page 70351	2.7% (A) page 79595	2.7% (A) page 59222)

Regulations

Medicare Physician Fee Schedule Relative Value File	Medicare Physician Fee Schedule Relative Value File, by date of service, as adopted and incorporated by reference in the Official Medical Fee Schedule (OMFS) Physician Fee Schedule (Title 8 CCR sections 9789.12.1, et seq.). The (OMFS) Physician Fee Schedule is located at: http://www.dir.ca.gov/dwc/OMFS9904.htm and the Medicare Physician Fee Schedule Relative Value File is located at: http://www.cms.gov/Medicare/Medicare-Fee-for-Service-Payment/PhysicianFeeSched/PFS-Relative-Value-Files.html	Not applicable for services rendered on or after December 15, 2016	Not applicable for services rendered on or after December 15, 2016	Not applicable for services rendered on or after December 15, 2016
Surgical Procedure HCPCS	10021-69990, G0413	HCPCS codes listed in column A of July 2016 CMS' Ambulatory Surgical Center Payment System (ASC) Addendum AA, column A of July 2016 CMS' ASC Addendum EE, and CPT codes 21811-21813, but, excluding HCPCS codes listed on CMS' HOPPS Addendum E as an inpatient only procedure.	For services rendered on or after June 1, 2017, HCPCS codes listed in column A of April 2017 CMS' Ambulatory Surgical Center Payment System (ASC) Addendum AA, column A of April 2017 CMS' ASC Addendum EE, and CPT codes 21811-21813, and 36415, but, excluding HCPCS codes listed on CMS' 2017 HOPPS Addendum E as an inpatient only procedure.	For services rendered on or after March 15, 2018, HCPCS codes listed in column A of January 2018 CMS' Ambulatory Surgical Center Payment System (ASC) corrected Addendum AA, column A of January 2018 CMS' ASC corrected Addendum EE, and CPT codes 21811-21813, and 36415, but, excluding HCPCS codes listed on CMS' 2018 HOPPS Addendum E as an inpatient only procedure.
			ASC Addenda AA and EE may be found in: April 2017 — april_2017_asc_addenda_rev_ 20170329, at: (https://www.cms.gov/Medicare/Medicare- Fee-for-Service-Payment/ASCPayment/11_Addenda_Updates.html)	ASC Addenda AA and EE may be found in: "Correction Notice Addendum AA, BB, DD1, DD2, EE" (CMS-1678-CN-ASC-Addendum- AA-BB-DD1-DD2-EE.zip) at: https://www.cms.gov/Medicare/Medicare-Fee-for-Service-Payment/ASCPayment/11_Addenda_Updates.html
			2017 HOPPS Addendum E (2017 Final Addendum E.10.20.16) is found at: https://www.cms.gov/Medicare/Medicare-Fee-for-Service-Payment/HospitalOutpatient PPS/Hospital-Outpatient-Regulations-and-Notices-Items/ CMS-1656-FC.html?DLPage=1&DLEntries=10 &DLSort=2&DLSortDir= descending	2018 HOPPS Addendum E (2018 NFRM Addendum E.10.18.17) is found at: https://www.cms.gov/Medicare/Medicare-Fee-for-Service-Payment/HospitalOutpatient PPS/Hospital -Outpatient-Regulations- and-Notices-Items/ CMS-1678-FC.html?DLPage=1 &DLEntries=10 &DLSort =2&DLSort Dir= descending

For services rendered on or after July 1, 2017, HCPCS codes listed in column A of July 2017 CMS' Ambulatory Surgical Center Payment System (ASC) Addendum AA, column A of July 2017 CMS' ASC Addendum EE, and CPT codes 21811-21813, and 36415, but, excluding HCPCS codes listed on CMS' 2017 HOPPS Addendum E as an inpatient only procedure.	For services rendered on or after April 1, 2018, HCPCS codes listed in column A, of April 2018 CMS' Ambulatory Surgical Center Payment System (ASC) Addendum AA, Column A, of April 2018 CMS' ASC Addendum EE, and CPT codes 21811-21813, and 36415, but, excluding HCPCS codes listed on CMS' 2018 HOPPS Addendum E as an inpatient only procedure.
ASC Addenda AA and EE may be found in: July 2017 - July_2017_asc_ addenda1: (https://www.cms.gov/Medicare/Medicare-Fee-for-Service-Payment/ASC Payment/11_Addenda_ Updates.html)	
2017 HOPPS Addendum E (2017 Final Addendum E.10.20.16) is found at: https://www.cms.gov/Medicare/Medicare-Fee-for-Service-Payment/Hospital OutpatientPPS/Hospital-Outpatient-Regulations-and-Notices-Items/CMS- 1656-FC.html? DLPage=1&DL Entries=10&DLSort= 2&DLSortDir= descending	ASC Addenda AA and EE may be found in: "April 2018 ASC Approved HCPCS Code and Payment Rates — Updated 03/21/2018" (april_2018_ asc_addenda_updated_ 04_01_2018b.xlsx) at: https://www.cms.gov/Medicare/Medicare- Fee-for-Service-Payment/ ASCPayment/11_Addenda_ Updates.html
For services rendered on or after October 1, 2017, HCPCS codes listed in column A of October 2017 CMS' Ambulatory Surgical Center Payment System (ASC) Adendum AA, column A of October 2017 CMS' ASC Addendum EE, and CPT codes 21811-21813, and 36415, but, excluding HCPCS codes listed on CMS' 2017 HOPPS Addendum E as an inpatient only procedure.	2018 HOPPS Addendum E (2018 NFRM Addendum E.10.18.17) is found at: https://www.cms.gov/Medicare/Medicare- Fee-for-Service- Payment/ HospitalOutpatient PPS/ Hospital- Outpatient-Regulations-and-Notices-Items/ CMS-1678-FC.html?DLPage= 1&DLEntries= 10 &DLSort= 2&DL SortDir= descending
ASC Addenda AA and EE may be found in: October 2017 — october_2017_ asc_ https:// www.cms.gov/Medicare/Medicare- Fee-for-Service-Payment/ ASCPayment/11_Addenda_ Updates.html)	For services rendered on or after July 1, 2018, HCPCS codes listed in column A, of July 2018 CMS' Ambulatory Surgical Center Payment System (ASC) Addendum AA, Column A, of July 2018 CMS' ASC Addendum EE, and CPT codes 21811-21813, and 36415, but, excluding HCPCS codes listed on CMS' 2018 HOPPS Addendum E as an inpatient only procedure.

			2017 HOPPS Addendum E (2017 Final Addendum E.10.20.16) is found at: https://www.cms.gov/Medicare/Medicare-Fee-for-Service-Payment/HospitalOutpatient PPS/Hospital-Outpatient-Regulations-and-Notices-Items/ CMS-1656-FC.html?DLPage=1&DLEntries= 10&DLSort=2&DLSortDir= descending	ASC Addenda AA and EE may be found in: "July 2018 ASC Approved HCPCS Code and Payment Rates — Updated 06/28/2018" (july_2018_asc_addenda_updated_06_28_2018.xlsx) at: https://www.cms.gov/Medicare/Medicare-Fee-for-Service-Payment/ASCPayment/11_Addenda_Updates.html 2018 HOPPS Addendum E (2018 NFRM Addendum E.10.18.17) is found at: https://www.cms.gov/Medicare/Medicare-Fee-for-Service-Payment/HospitalOutpatient PPS/Hospital- Outpatient-Regulations-and- Notices-Items/ CMS-1678-FC.html?DLPage=1&DLEntries=10&DLSort=2&DLSortDir= descending For services rendered on or after October 1, 2018, HCPCS codes listed in column A, of October 2018 CMS' Ambulatory Surgical Center Payment System (ASC) Addendum AA, Column A, of October 2018 CMS' ASC Addendum EE, and CPT codes 21811-21813, and 36415, but, excluding HCPCS codes listed on CMS' 2018 HOPPS Addendum E as an inpatient only procedure. ASC Addenda AA and EE may be found in: "October 2018 ASC Approved HCPCS Code and Payment Rates" (oct_2018_asc_addenda_updated_09_19_2018.0921 2018cb.xlsx) at: https://www.cms.gov/Medicare/Medicare-Fee-for-Service-Payment/ASCPayment/11_Addenda_ Updates.html 2018 HOPPS Addendum E (2018 NFRM Addendum E.10.18.17) is found at: https://www.cms.gov/Medicare/Medicare-Fee-for-Service-Payment/HospitalOutpatient PPS/Hospital- Outpatient-Regulations-and- Notices-Items/ CMS-1678-FC.html?DLPage=1&DLEntries=10&DLSort=2&DLSortDir= descending
Conversion Factor adjusted for inflation factor	\$72.530 (2013 unadjusted conversion factor of \$70.761 × estimated inflation factor of 1.025)	\$76.424 (2015 unadjusted conversion factor of \$74.633 × estimated inflation factor of 1.024)	\$78.488 (2016 unadjusted conversion factor of \$76.424 × estimated inflation factor of 1.027)	\$80.607 (2017 unadjusted conversion factor of \$78.488 × estimated inflation factor of 1.027)

Wage Index	Referenced in (A) beginning at page 74952; wage index values are specified in Tables 4A through 4C (B) found on the CMS website at: http://www.cms.gov/AcuteInpatientPPS/	Referenced in (A) beginning at page 70359; wage index values are specified in Table 2 (B) found on the CMS website at http://www.cms.gov/AcuteInpatientPPS/	Referenced in (A) beginning at page 79597; wage index values are specified in Table 2 (D) found on the CMS website at http://www.cms.gov/AcuteInpatientPPS/	Referenced in (A) beginning at page 59261; wage index values are specified in Table 2 (D) found on the CMS website at https://www.cms.gov/Medicare/Medicare-Fee-for-Service-Payment/AcuteInpatientPPS/FY2018-IPPS- Final-Rule-Home-Page.html?DLSort=0&DLEntries=10&DLPage=1&DLSortDir= ascending
	Services Occurring On or After February 15, 2019 and Mid-year Updates			
Applicable FR Notices	(A) November 21, 2018 (CMS-1695-FC; 83 FR 58818) (B) December 28, 2018 (CMS-1695-CN2; 83 FR 67083) (C) August 17, 2018 (CMS-1694-F; 83 FR 41144) (D) October 3, 2018 (CMS-1694-CN2; 83 FR 49836)			
Ambulatory Surgical Centers Payment System Addenda	For services occurring on or after February 15, 2019, Column A, of Addendum AA, entitled, "HCPCS Code" and Column A, of Addendum EE, entitled, "HCPCS Code" located in "January 2019 ASC Approved HCPCS Code and Payment Rates - Updated 01/29/2019" (jan_2019_asc_addenda_1_28_19.xlsx) For services occurring on or after April 1, 2019, Column A, of Addendum AA, entitled, "HCPCS Code" and Column A, of Addendum EE, entitled, "HCPCS Code" located in "April 2019 ASC Approved HCPCS Code and Payment Rates - Updated 3/28/2019" (Apr_2019_ASC_Addenda_3_27_2019) For services occurring on or after July 1, 2019, Column A, of Addendum AA, entitled, "HCPCS Code" and Column A, of Addendum EE, entitled, "HCPCS Code" located in "July 2019 ASC Approved HCPCS Code and Payment Rates - Updated 06/27/2019" (July_2019_ASC_Addenda.06262019.xlsx)			

	For services occurring on or after October 1, 2019, Column A, of Addendum AA, entitled, "HCPCS Code" and Column A, of Addendum EE, entitled, "HCPCS Code" located in "October 2019 ASC Approved HCPCS Code and Payment Rates CORRECTIONS - Updated 10/15/2019" (October_2019_ASC_Addenda.CORRECTED.10152019.xlsx)
	Note: Access the files on CMS website at: https://www.cms.gov/Medicare/Medicare-Fee-for-Service-Payment/ASCPayment/index.html
APC Payment Rate	For services occurring on or after February 15, 2019, Addendum B, dated January 2019 (january_2019_opps_web_addendum_b.12312018.xlsx)
	For services occurring on or after April 1, 2019, Addendum B, dated April 2019 (2019_April_Web_Addendum_B.03222019.xlsx)
	For services occurring on or after July 1, 2019, Addendum B, dated July 2019 (July_2019_Web_Addendum_B.06212019.xlsx)
	For services occurring on or after October 1, 2019, Addendum B - Correction, dated October 2019 (2019_October_Web_Addendum_B.CORRECTED.09292019.xlsx)
APC Relative Weight	For services occurring on or after February 15, 2019, Addendum B, dated January 2019 (january_2019_opps_web_addendum_ b.1231 2018.xlsx)
	For services occurring on or after April 1, 2019, Addendum B, dated April 2019 (2019_April_Web_Addendum_B.03222019.xlsx)
	For services occurring on or after July 1, 2019, Addendum B, dated July 2019 (July_2019_Web_Addendum_B.06212019.xlsx)
	For services occurring on or after October 1, 2019, Addendum B - Correction, dated October 2019 (2019_October_Web_Addendum_B.CORRECTED.09292019.xlsx)
Composite APCs (codes assigned status indicator "Q1," "Q2," "Q3," or "Q4")	For services occurring on or after February 15, 2019, payment rules are:

Regulations

payment rules	• Medicare Claims Processing Manual, Chapter 4, sections 10.2.1, 10.2.2, 10.4, and 10.4.1 • CMS 2019 OPPS Addendum D1 • CMS 2019 OPPS Addendum M • IOCE Quarterly Data Files V20.0 [ZIP, 52MB], IntegOCEspecsV20.0.pdf, sections 5.4.1, 5.4.3, 5.4.5, and 5.5 For services occurring on or after April 1, 2019, payment rules are: • Medicare Claims Processing Manual, Chapter 4, sections 10.2.1, 10.2.2, 10.4, and 10.4.1 • CMS 2019 OPPS Addendum D1 • CMS 2019 OPPS Addendum M • IOCE Quarterly Data Files V20.1 [ZIP, 50MB], IntegOCEspecsV20.1.pdf, sections 5.4.1, 5.4.3, 5.4.5, and 5.5 For services occurring on or after July 1, 2019, payment rules are: • Medicare Claims Processing Manual, Chapter 4, sections 10.2.1, 10.2.2, 10.4, and 10.4.1 • CMS 2019 OPPS Addendum D1 • CMS 2019 OPPS Addendum M • IOCE Quarterly Data Files V20.2 [ZIP, 50MB], IntegOCEspecsV20.2.pdf, sections 5.4.1, 5.4.3, 5.4.5, and 5.5 For services occurring on or after October 1, 2019, payment rules are: • Medicare Claims Processing Manual, Chapter 4, sections 10.2.1, 10.2.2, 10.4, and 10.4.1 • CMS 2019 OPPS Addendum D1 • CMS 2019 OPPS Addendum M • IOCE Quarterly Data Files V20.3 [ZIP, 50 MB] IntegOCEspecsV20.3.pdf, sections 4.4.1, 4.4.3, 4.4.5, and 4.5 Note: A copy of the IOCE is posted on the DWC website: http://www.dir.ca.gov/dwc/OMFS9904.htm#6

	Access documents on the CMS website at: https://www.cms.gov/Medicare/Medicare-Fee-for-Service-Payment/HospitalOutpatientPPS/index.html?redirect=/HospitalOutpatientPPS/ and https://www.cms.gov/Regulations-and-Guidance/Guidance/Manuals/Internet-Only-Manuals-IOMs-Items/CMS018912.html
Comprehensive APCs (codes assigned status indicator "J1" or "J2") payment rules	For services occurring on or after February 15, 2019, payment rules are: • Medicare Claims Processing Manual, Chapter 4, sections 10.2.3, 10.4, 290.5.2, and 290.5.3 • CMS 2019 OPPS Addendum D1 • CMS 2019 OPPS Addendum J • IOCE Quarterly Data Files V20.0 [ZIP, 52MB], IntegOCEspecsV20.0.pdf, sections 5.6.1, 5.6.1.1, 5.6.2, 5.6.3, 5.6.4, 5.6.4.1, and 5.6.4.2 For services occurring on or after April 1, 2019, payment rules are: • Medicare Claims Processing Manual, Chapter 4, sections 10.2.1, 10.2.2, 10.4, and 10.4.1 • CMS 2019 OPPS Addendum D1 • CMS 2019 OPPS Addendum M • IOCE Quarterly Data Files V20.1 [ZIP, 50MB], IntegOCEspecsV20.1.pdf, sections 5.4.1, 5.4.3, 5.4.5, and 5.5 For services occurring on or after April 1, 2019, payment rules are: • Medicare Claims Processing Manual, Chapter 4, sections 10.2.1, 10.2.2, 10.4, and 10.4.1 • CMS 2019 OPPS Addendum D1 • CMS 2019 OPPS Addendum M • IOCE Quarterly Data Files V20.2 [ZIP, 50MB], IntegOCEspecsV20.2.pdf, sections 5.4.1, 5.4.3, 5.4.5, and 5.5 For services occurring on or after October 1, 2019, payment rules are: • Medicare Claims Processing Manual, Chapter 4, sections 10.2.1, 10.2.2, 10.4, and 10.4.1 • CMS 2019 OPPS Addendum D1 • CMS 2019 OPPS Addendum M

	• IOCE Quarterly Data Files V20.3 [ZIP, 50 MB] IntegOCEspecsV20.3.pdf, sections 4.4.1, 4.4.3, 4.4.5, and 4.5 Note: A copy of the IOCE is posted on the DWC website: http://www.dir.ca.gov/dwc/OMFS9904.htm#6 Access documents on the CMS website at: https://www.cms.gov/Medicare/Medicare-Fee-for-Service-Payment/HospitalOutpatientPPS/index.html And CMS Claims Processing Manual at: https://www.cms.gov/Regulations-and-Guidance/Guidance/Manuals/Internet-Only-Manuals-IOMs-Items/CMS018912.html? DLPage=1&DLEntries= 10&DLSort=0&DLSortDir= ascending
Emergency Department HCPCS Codes	99281-99285, 99291, 99292, G0380-G0384, G0390
Facility Only Services	Not applicable for services rendered on or after December 15, 2016
Film X-ray services and X-rays taken using computed radiography technology/cassette-based imaging payment reductions	Use modifier "FX" to report X-rays taken using film, which requires a 20 percent payment reduction for such service. Use modifier "FY" to report X-rays taken using computed radiography technology/cassette-based imaging which requires a 7 percent payment reduction for such service. Apply payment rules set forth in: • December 14, 2017 (CMS-1678-FC; 82 FR 59216, Republished, section X.E., pages 59391 through 59393) • Medicare Claims Processing Manual, Chapter 4, section 20.6.14 (effective 01/01/2018) and section 20.6.15 (effective 01/01/2018) • CFR section 419.71 • CMS' April 2018 Update of the Hospital Outpatient Prospective Payment System (OPPS) CR 10515 Revised March 22, 2018, Transmittal R4005CP, section 6 Access the Medicare Claims Processing Manual on the CMS website at: https://www.cms.gov/Regulations-and-Guidance/Guidance/Manuals/Internet-Only-Manuals-IOMs-Items/CMS018912.html

HOPPS Addenda

For services occurring on or after February 15, 2019 addenda:

- A (January 2019; january_2019_opps_web_addendum_a.12312018.xlsx)
- B (January 2019; january_2019_opps_web_addendum_b.12312018.xlsx)
- D1 (CY2019 NFRM OPPS Addenda; CY2019 NFRM Addendum D1.11012018.xlsx)
- D2 (CY2019 NFRM OPPS Addenda; CY2019 NFRM Addendum D2.11012018.xlsm)
- E (CY2019 NFRM OPPS Addenda; CY2019 NFRM Addendum E.11012018.xlsx)
- J (CY2019 NFRM OPPS Addenda; CY2019 NFRM Addendum J.11012018.xls)
- L (CY2019 NFRM OPPS Addenda; CY2019 NFRM Addendum L.11012018.xlsx)
- M (CY2019 NFRM OPPS Addenda; CY2019 NFRM Addendum M.11012018.xlsx)
- P (2019 CN2 OPPS Addenda; 2019 CN2 Addendum P.12212018.xlsx)

For services occurring on or after April 1, 2019 addenda:

- A (April 2019; 2019_April_Web_Addendum_A.03222019.xlsx)
- B (April 2019; 2019_April_Web_Addendum_B.03222019.xlsx)
- D1 (CY2019 NFRM OPPS Addenda; CY2019 NFRM Addendum D1.11012018.xlsx)
- D2 (CY2019 NFRM OPPS Addenda; CY2019 NFRM Addendum D2.11012018.xlsm)
- E (CY2019 NFRM OPPS Addenda; CY2019 NFRM Addendum E.11012018.xlsx)
- J (CY2019 NFRM OPPS Addenda; CY2019 NFRM Addendum J.11012018.xls)
- L (CY2019 NFRM OPPS Addenda; CY2019 NFRM Addendum L.11012018.xlsx)
- M (CY2019 NFRM OPPS Addenda; CY2019 NFRM Addendum M.11012018.xlsx)
- P (2019 CN2 OPPS Addenda; 2019 CN2 Addendum P.12212018.xlsx)

For services occurring on or after July 1, 2019 addenda:

- A (July 2019; July_2019_Web_Addendum_A.06212019.xlsx)
- B (July 2019; July_2019_Web_Addendum_B.06212019.xlsx)
- D1 (CY2019 NFRM OPPS Addenda; CY2019 NFRM Addendum D1.11012018.xlsx)

	• D2 (CY2019 NFRM OPPS Addenda; CY2019 NFRM Addendum D2.11012018.xlsm) • E (CY2019 NFRM OPPS Addenda; CY2019 NFRM Addendum E.11012018.xlsx) • J (CY2019 NFRM OPPS Addenda; CY2019 NFRM Addendum J.11012018.xls) • L (CY2019 NFRM OPPS Addenda; CY2019 NFRM Addendum L.11012018.xlsx) • M (CY2019 NFRM OPPS Addenda; CY2019 NFRM Addendum M.11012018.xlsx) • P (2019 CN2 OPPS Addenda; 2019 CN2 Addendum P.12212018.xlsx) For services occurring on or after October 1, 2019 addenda: • A (October 2019; 2019_October_Web_Addendum_A.CORRECTED.09292019.xlsx) • B (October 2019; 2019_October_Web_Addendum_B.CORRECTED.09292019.xlsx) • D1 (CY2019 NFRM OPPS Addenda; CY2019 NFRM Addendum D1.11012018.xlsx) • D2 (CY2019 NFRM OPPS Addenda; CY2019 NFRM Addendum D2.11012018.xlsm) • E (CY2019 NFRM OPPS Addenda; CY2019 NFRM Addendum E.11012018.xlsx) • J (CY2019 NFRM OPPS Addenda; CY2019 NFRM Addendum J.11012018.xls) • L (CY2019 NFRM OPPS Addenda; CY2019 NFRM Addendum L.11012018.xlsx) • M (CY2019 NFRM OPPS Addenda; CY2019 NFRM Addendum M.11012018.xlsx) • P (2019 CN2 OPPS Addenda; 2019 CN2 Addendum P.12212018.xlsx) Note: Access the files on the CMS website at: https://www.cms.gov/Medicare/Medicare-Fee-for-Service-Payment/HospitalOutpatientPPS/index.html
IPPS Tables	FY 2019 Tables 2, 3 and 4 (Wage Index Tables) (Final Rule and Correction Notice) [ZIP, 1MB] found at: https://www.cms.gov/Medicare/Medicare-Fee-for-Service-Payment/AcuteInpatientPPS/FY2019-IPPS-Final-Rule-Home-Page-Items/FY2019-IPPS-Final-Rule-Tables.html?DLPage=1&DLEntries= 10&DLSort=0&DLSortDir= ascending
Labor-related Share	60% (A) beginning at page 58863

Market Basket Inflation Factor	2.9% (A) page 58822
Medicare Physician Fee Schedule Relative Value File	Not applicable for services rendered on or after December 15, 2016
Surgical Procedure HCPCS	For services rendered on or after February 15, 2019, HCPCS codes listed in column A, of CMS' Ambulatory Surgical Center Payment System (ASC) "Jan 2019 ASC AA," Column A, of CMS' ASC "Jan 2019 ASC EE, and CPT codes 21811-21813, 33289, and 36415, but, excluding HCPCS codes listed on CMS' 2019 HOPPS Addendum E as an inpatient only procedure. ASC Addenda AA and EE may be found in: "January 2019 ASC Approved HCPCS Code and Payment Rates - Updated-01/29/2019" (jan_2019_asc_addenda_1_28_19.xlsx) at: https://www.cms.gov/ Medicare/Medicare-Fee-for-Service-Payment/ ASCPayment/ 11_Addenda_Updates.html 2019 HOPPS Addendum E (CY2019 NFRM Addendum E.11012018.xlsx) is found at: https://www.cms.gov/ Medicare/Medicare-Fee-for-Service-Payment/ HospitalOutpatient PPS/ Hospital- Outpatient-Regulations-and- Notices-Items/ CMS-1695-FC.html?DLPage= 1&DLEntries= 10&DLSort= 2&DLSortDir= descending For services rendered on or after April 1, 2019, HCPCS codes listed in column A, of CMS' Ambulatory Surgical Center Payment System (ASC) "Apr 2019 ASC AA," Column A, of CMS' ASC "Apr 2019 ASC EE," and CPT codes 21811-21813, 33289, and 36415, but, excluding HCPCS codes listed on CMS' 2019 HOPPS Addendum E as an inpatient only procedure. ASC Addenda AA and EE may be found in: "April 2019 ASC Approved HCPCS Code and Payment Rates - Updated 3/28/19" (Apr_2019_ASC_Addenda_3_27_2019) at: https://www.cms.gov/ Medicare/Medicare-Fee-for-Service-Payment/ ASCPayment/ 11_Addenda_Updates.html

2019 HOPPS Addendum E (CY2019 NFRM Addendum E.11012018.xlsx) is found at: https://www.cms.gov/Medicare/Medicare-Fee-for-Service-Payment/HospitalOutpatient PPS/Hospital- Outpatient-Regulations-and- Notices-Items/ CMS-1695-FC.html?DLPage=1&DLEntries= 10&DLSort=2&DLSortDir=descending

For services rendered on or after July 1, 2019, HCPCS codes listed in column A, of CMS' Ambulatory Surgical Center Payment System (ASC) "Jul 2019 ASC AA," Column A, of CMS' ASC "Jul 2019 ASC EE," and CPT codes 21811-21813, 33289, and 36415, but, excluding HCPCS codes listed on CMS' 2019 HOPPS Addendum E as an inpatient only procedure.

ASC Addenda AA and EE may be found in: "July 2019 ASC Approved HCPCS Code and Payment Rates - Updated 06/27/2019" (July_2019_ASC_Addenda.06262019.xlsx) at: https://www.cms.gov/Medicare/Medicare-Fee-for-Service-Payment/ASCPayment/11_Addenda_Updates.html

2019 HOPPS Addendum E (CY2019 NFRM Addendum E.11012018.xlsx) is found at: https://www.cms.gov/Medicare/Medicare-Fee-for-Service-Payment/HospitalOutpatient PPS/Hospital- Outpatient-Regulations-and- Notices-Items/ CMS-1695-FC.html?DLPage=1&DLEntries= 10&DLSort=2&DLSortDir=descending

For services rendered on or after October 1, 2019, HCPCS codes listed in column A, of CMS' Ambulatory Surgical Center Payment System (ASC) "Oct 2019 ASC AA," Column A, of CMS' ASC "Oct 2019 ASC EE," and CPT codes 21811-21813, 3289, and 36415, but, excluding HCPCS codes listed on CMS' 2019 HOPPS Addendum E as an inpatient only procedure.

	ASC Addenda AA and EE may be found in: "October 2019 ASC Approved HCPCS Code and Payment Rates CORRECTIONS - Updated 10/15/2019" (October_2019_ASC_Addenda.CORRECTED.10152019.xlsx) at: https://www.cms.gov/Medicare/Medicare-Fee-for-Service-Payment/ASCPayment/index.html 2019 HOPPS Addendum E (CY2019 NFRM Addendum E.11012018.xlsx) is found at: https://www.cms.gov/Medicare/Medicare-Fee-for-Service-Payment/HospitalOutpatient PPS/Hospital- Outpatient-Regulations-and- Notices-Items/ CMS-1695-FC.html?DLPage=1&DLEntries= 10&DLSort=2&DLSortDir=descending
Conversion Factor adjusted for inflation factor	$82.945 (2018 unadjusted conversion factor of $80.607 × estimated inflation factor of 1.029)
Wage Index	Referenced in (A) beginning at page 58876; wage index values are specified in Table 2 (C) and (D) found on the CMS website at https://www.cms.gov/Medicare/Medicare-Fee-for-Service-Payment/AcuteInpatientPPS/FY2019-IPPS-Final-Rule-Home-Page-Items/FY2019-IPPS-Final-Rule-Tables.html?DLPage=1&DLEntries= 10&DLSort=0&DLSortDir= ascending
	Services Occurring On or After March 1, 2020 and Mid-year Updates
Applicable FR Notices	(A) November 12, 2019 (CMS-1717-FC; 84 FR 61142) (B) January 3, 2020 (CMS-1717-CN; 85 FR 224) (C) August 16, 2019 (CMS-1716-F; 84 FR 42044) (D) October 8, 2019 (CMS-1716-CN2; 84 FR 53603)
Ambulatory Surgical Centers Payment System Addenda	For services occurring on or after March 1, 2020, Column A, of Addendum AA, entitled, "HCPCS Code" and Column A, of Addendum EE, entitled, "HCPCS Code" located in "CY 2020 CN ASC Addenda.12122019" (CY 2020 CN ASC Addenda.12122019.xlsx) Note: Access the files on CMS website at: https://www.cms.gov/Medicare/Medicare-Fee-for-Service-Payment/ASCPayment/index.html

APC Payment Rate	For services occurring on or after March 1, 2020, Addendum B, dated December 2019 (2020 CN Addendum B.12202019.xlsx)
APC Relative Weight	For services occurring on or after March 1, 2020, Addendum B, dated December 2019 (2020 CN Addendum B.12202019.xlsx)
Composite APCs (codes assigned status indicator "Q1," "Q2," "Q3," or "Q4") payment rules	For services occurring on or after March 1, 2020, payment rules are: • Medicare Claims Processing Manual, Chapter 4, sections 10.2.1, 10.2.2, 10.4, and 10.4.1 • CMS 2020 OPPS Addendum D1 • CMS 2020 OPPS Addendum M • IOCE Quarterly Data Files V21.0 [ZIP, 1.17MB], IntegOCEspecsV21.0.pdf, sections 5.4.1, 5.4.3, 5.4.5, and 5.5 Note: A copy of the IOCE is posted on the DWC website: http://www.dir.ca.gov/dwc/OMFS9904.htm#6 Access documents on the CMS website at: https://www.cms. gov/Medicare/Medicare-Fee-for-Service-Payment/HospitalOutpatientPPS/index and CMS Claims Processing Manual at: https://www.cms.gov/Regulations-and-Guidance/Guidance/Manuals/Internet-Only-Manuals-IOMs-Items/CMS018912.html
Comprehensive APCs (codes assigned status indicator "J1" or "J2") payment rules	For services occurring on or after March 1, 2020, payment rules are: • Medicare Claims Processing Manual, Chapter 4, sections 10.2.3, 10.4, 290.5.2, and 290.5.3 • CMS 2020 OPPS Addendum D1 • CMS 2020 OPPS Addendum J • IOCE Quarterly Data Files V21.0 [ZIP, 1.17MB], IntegOCEspecsV21.0.pdf, sections 5.6.1, 5.6.1.1, 5.6.2, 5.6.3, 5.6.4, 5.6.4.1, and 5.6.4.2 Note: A copy of the IOCE is posted on the DWC website: http://www.dir.ca.gov/dwc/OMFS9904.htm#6

	Access documents on the CMS website at: https://www.cms.gov/Medicare/Medicare-Fee-for-Service-Payment/HospitalOutpatientPPS/index and CMS Claims Processing Manual at: https://www.cms.gov/Regulations-and-Guidance/Guidance/Manuals/Internet-Only-Manuals-IOMs-Items/CMS018912.html?DLPage=1&DLEntries=10&DLSort=0&DLSortDir=ascending
Emergency Department HCPCS Codes	99281-99285, 99291, 99292, G0380-G0384, G0390
Facility Only Services	Not applicable for services rendered on or after December 15, 2016
Film X-ray services and X-rays taken using computed radiography technology/cassette-based imaging payment reductions	Use modifier "FX" to report X-rays taken using film, which requires a 20 percent payment reduction for such service. Use modifier X-rays taken using computed "FY" to report X-rays taken using computed radiography technology/cassette-based imaging which requires a 7 percent radiography technology/cassette-payment reduction for such service. Apply payment rules set forth in: • December 14, 2017 (CMS-1678-FC; 82 FR 59216, Republished, section X.E., pages 59391 through 59393) • Medicare Claims Processing Manual, Chapter 4, section 20.6.14 (effective 01/01/2018) and section 20.6.15 (effective 01/01/2018) • CFR section 419.71 • CMS' April 2018 Update of the Hospital Outpatient Prospective Payment System (OPPS) CR 10515 Revised March 22, 2018, Transmittal R4005CP, section 6 Access the Medicare Claims Processing Manual on the CMS website at: https://www.cms.gov/Regulations-and-Guidance/Guidance/Manuals/Internet-Only-Manuals-IOMs-Items/CMS018912.html
HOPPS Addenda	For services occurring on or after March 1, 2020 addenda: • A (CY2020 CN Addendum A; CY2020 Addendum A. 12202019.xlsx) • B (CY2020 CN Addendum B; CY2020 Addendum B. 12202019.xlsx)

	• D1 (CY2020 NFRM OPPS Addenda; CY2020 NFRM Addendum D1.11012019.xlsx) • D2 (CY2020 NFRM OPPS Addenda; CY2020 NFRM Addendum D2.11012019.xlsm) • E (CY2020 NFRM OPPS Addenda; CY2020 NFRM Addendum E.11012019.xlsx) • J (CY2020 NFRM OPPS Addenda; CY2020 NFRM Addendum J.11012019.xls) • L (CY2020 NFRM OPPS Addenda; CY2020 NFRM Addendum L.11012019.xlsx) • M (CY2020 NFRM OPPS Addenda; CY2020 NFRM Addendum M.11012019.xlsx) • P (CY2020 CN Addendum P; CY2020 CN Addendum P.12202019.xlsx) Note: Access the files on the CMS website at: https://www.cms.gov/Medicare/Medicare-Fee-for-Service-Payment/HospitalOutpatientPPS/index.html
IPPS Tables	FY 2020 Tables 2, 3 and 4 (Wage Index Tables) (Final Rule and Correction Notice) [ZIP, 1MB] found at: https://www.cms.gov/Medicare/Medicare-Fee-for-Service Payment/AcuteInpatientPPS/FY2020-IPPS-Final-Rule-Home-Page-Items/FY2020-IPPS-Final-Rule-Tables
Labor-related Share	60% (A) beginning at page 61184
Market Basket Inflation Factor	3% (A) page 61145
Medicare Physician Fee Schedule Relative Value File	Not applicable for services rendered on or after December 15, 2016
Surgical Procedure HCPCS	For services rendered on or after March 1, 2020, HCPCS codes listed in column A, of CMS' Ambulatory Surgical Center Payment System (ASC) "Jan 2020 ASC AA," Column A, of CMS' ASC "Jan 2020 ASC EE, and CPT codes 21811-21813, 33289, and 36415, but, excluding HCPCS codes listed on CMS' 2020 HOPPS Addendum E as an inpatient only procedure.

	ASC Addenda AA and EE may be found in: "January 2020 ASC Approved HCPCS Code and Payment Rates - Updated 01/01/2020" (cy2020_january_asc_addenda.01022020.xlsx) at: https://www.cms.gov/Medicare/Medicare-Fee-for-Service-Payment/ASCPayment/11_Addenda_Updates 2020 HOPPS Addendum E (2020 NFRM Addendum E.11012019.xlsx) is found at: https://www.cms.gov/Medicare/Medicare-Fee-for-Service-Payment/HospitalOutpatient PPS/Hospital- Outpatient-Regulations-and- Notices-Items/ CMS-1695-FC.html?DLPage=1&DLEntries= 10&DLSort=2&DLSortDir=descending
Conversion Factor adjusted for inflation factor	$ 85.433 (2019 unadjusted conversion factor of $82.945 x estimated inflation factor of 1.03)
Wage Index	Referenced in (A) beginning at page 61184; wage index values are specified in Table 2 (C) and (D) found on the CMS website at https://www.cms.gov/Medicare/Medicare-Fee-for-Service-Payment/AcuteInpatientPPS/FY2020-IPPS-Final-Rule-Home-Page-Items/FY2020-IPPS-Final-Rule-Tables

Note: Authority cited: Sections 133, 4603.5, 5307.1 and 5307.3, Labor Code. Reference: Sections 4600, 4603.2 and 5307.1, Labor Code.

History: 1. New section filed 12-27-2012; operative 1-1-2013 as a file and print only pursuant to Government Code section 11340.9(g) (Register 2012, No. 52).

2. Amendment filed 3-29-2013; operative 4-1-2013 pursuant to Labor Code section 5307.1(g)(2). Submitted to OAL for filing and printing only pursuant to Labor Code section 5307.1(g)(2) (Register 2013, No. 13).

3. Amendment of section heading and section filed 6-3-2014; operative 9-1-2014 as a file and print only pursuant to Government Code section 11340.9(g) (Register 2014, No. 23).

4. Amendment filed 12-4-2014; operative 12-1-2014 pursuant to Labor Code section 5307.1(g)(2). Submitted to OAL for filing and printing only pursuant to Labor Code section 5307.1(g)(2) (Register 2014, No. 49).

5. Amendment filed 12-15-2016; operative 12-15-2016 as a file and print only pursuant to Government Code section 11340.9(g) (Register 2016, No. 51).

6. Editorial correction of subsection (b) (Register 2017, No. 18).

7. Amendment filed 6-20-2017; operative 6-1-2017 pursuant to Labor Code section 5307.1(g)(2). Submitted to OAL for filing and printing only pursuant to Labor Code section 5307.1(g)(2) (Register 2017, No. 25).

8. Amendment filed 5-8-2018; operative 3-15-2018 pursuant to Labor Code section 5307.1(g)(2). Submitted to OAL for filing and printing only pursuant to Labor Code section 5307.1(g)(2) (Register 2018, No. 19).

9. Editorial correction (Register 2019, No. 5).

10. Amendment filed 2-14-2019; operative 2-15-2019 pursuant to Labor Code section 5307.1(g)(2). Submitted to OAL for filing and printing only pursuant to Labor Code section 5307.1(g)(2) (Register 2019, No. 7).

11. Editorial correction (Register 2019, No. 33).

12. Amendment of subsection (b) filed 3-19-2020; operative 3-1-2020 pursuant to Labor Code section 5307.1(g)(2). Submitted to OAL for filing and printing only pursuant to Labor Code section 5307.1(g)(2) (Register 2020, No. 12).

Ref.: Herlick Handbook §§ 1.01[3][b], 4.17[1].

§9789.40. Pharmacy.

(a) The maximum reasonable fee for pharmaceuticals and pharmacy services rendered after January 1, 2004 is 100% of the reimbursement prescribed in the relevant Medi-Cal payment system, including the Medi-Cal professional fee for dispensing. Medi-Cal rates will be made available on the Division of Workers' Compensation's Internet Website (http://www.dir.ca.gov/DWC/dwc_home_page.htm) or upon request to the Administrative Director at:

DIVISION OF WORKERS' COMPENSATION
(ATTENTION: OMFS – PHARMACY)

P.O. BOX 420603
SAN FRANCISCO, CA 94142.

(b) For a pharmacy service or drug that is not covered by a Medi-Cal payment system, the maximum reasonable fee paid shall not exceed the drug cost portion of the fee determined in accordance with this subdivision, plus $7.25 professional fee for dispensing or $8.00 if the patient is in a skilled nursing facility or in an intermediate care facility. The maximum fee shall include only a single professional dispensing fee for dispensing for each dispensing of a drug.

(1) If the National Drug Code for the drug product as dispensed is not in the Medi-Cal database, and the National Drug Code for the underlying drug product from the original labeler appears in the Medi-Cal database, then the maximum fee shall be the drug cost portion of the reimbursement allowed pursuant to section 14105.45 of the Welfare and Institutions Code using the National Drug Code for the underlying drug product from the original labeler as it appears in the Medi-Cal database, calculated on a per unit basis, plus the professional fee allowed by subdivision (b) of this section.

(2) If the National Drug Code for the drug product as dispensed is not in the Medi-Cal database and the National Drug Code for the underlying drug product from the original labeler is not in the Medi-Cal database, then the maximum fee shall be 83 percent of the average wholesale price of the lowest priced therapeutically equivalent drug, calculated on a per unit basis, plus the professional fee allowed by subdivision (b) of this section.

(c) For purposes of this section:

(1) "therapeutically equivalent drugs" means drugs that have been assigned the same Therapeutic Equivalent Code starting with the letter "A" in the Food and Drug Administration's publication "Approved Drug Products with Therapeutic Equivalence Evaluations" ("Orange Book".) The Orange Book any be accessed through the Food and Drug Administration's website: http://www.fda.gov/cder/orange/default.htm.;

(2) "National Drug Code for the underlying drug product from the original labeler" means the National Drug Code of the drug product actually utilized by the repackager in producing the repackaged product.

(d) The changes made to this Section in February, 2007, shall be applicable to all pharmaceuticals dispensed or provided on or after March 1, 2007.

Note: Authority cited: Sections 133, 4603.5, 5307.1 and 5307.3, Labor Code. Reference: Sections 4600, 4603.2 and 5307.1, Labor Code.

History: 1. New section filed 1-2-2004 as an emergency; operative 1-2-2004 (Register 2004, No. 2). A Certificate of Compliance must be transmitted to OAL by 5-3-2004 or emergency language will be repealed by operation of law on the following day.

2. Certificate of Compliance as to 1-2-2004 order, including redesignation of existing section as subsection (a) and new subsection (b), transmitted to OAL 4-30-2004 and filed 6-15-2004 (Register 2004, No. 25).

3. Amendment of subsections (a) and (b) and new subsections (b)(1)-(d) filed 2-28-2007; operative 2-28-2007. Submitted to OAL for printing purposes only pursuant to Government Code section 11343.8, as exempt from the APA and OAL review pursuant to Government Code section 11340.9(g) (Register 2007, No. 9).

Ref.: Hanna § 22.05[2]; Herlick Handbook §§ 1.01[3][b], 4.17[1].

§9789.50. Pathology and Laboratory.

(a) Effective for services after January 1, 2004, the maximum reasonable fees for pathology and laboratory services shall not exceed one hundred twenty (120) percent of the rate for the same procedure code in the CMS' Clinical Diagnostic Laboratory Fee Schedule, as established by Sections 1833 and 1834 of the Social Security Act (42 U.S.C. §§ 1395*l* and 1395m) and applicable to California. The Clinical Diagnostic Laboratory Fee Schedule, which can be found on the CMS Internet Website (http://www.cms.gov/Medicare/Medicare-Fee-For-Service-Payment/Clinicallabfeesched/index.html) is incorporated by reference and will be made available on the Division of Workers' Compensation's Internet Website (http://www.dir.ca.gov/DWC/dwc_home_page.htm) or upon request to the Administrative Director at:

DIVISION OF WORKERS' COMPENSATION
(ATTENTION: OMFS)
P.O. BOX 420603
SAN FRANCISCO, CA 94142.

(b) The following procedures in the Special Services and Reports section of the OMFS 2003 will not be valid for services rendered after January 1, 2004: CPT Codes 99000, 99001, 99017, 99019, 99020, 99021, 99026, and 99027.

Note: Authority cited: Sections 133, 4603.5, 5307.1 and 5307.3, Labor Code. Reference: Sections 4600, 4603.2 and 5307.1, Labor Code.

History: 1. New section filed 1-2-2004 as an emergency; operative 1-2-2004 (Register 2004, No. 2). A Certificate of Compliance must be transmitted to OAL by 5-3-2004 or emergency language will be repealed by operation of law on the following day.

2. Certificate of Compliance as to 1-2-2004 order, including new subsection (c), transmitted to OAL 4-30-2004 and filed 6-15-2004 (Register 2004, No. 25).

3. Amendment of subsection (a) and repealer of subsection (c) filed 2-4-2015; operative 3-5-2015. Submitted to OAL for printing only pursuant to Government Code section 11340.9 (Register 2015, No. 6).

Ref.: Hanna § 22.05[2]; Herlick Handbook §§ 1.01[3][b], 4.17[1].

§9789.60. Durable Medical Equipment, Prosthetics, Orthotics, Supplies.

(a) For services, equipment, or goods provided after January 1, 2004, the maximum reasonable reimbursement for durable medical equipment, supplies and materials, orthotics, prosthetics, and miscellaneous supplies and services shall not exceed one hundred twenty (120) percent of the rate set forth in the CMS' Durable Medical Equipment, Prosthetics/Orthotics, and Supplies (DMEPOS) Fee Schedule, as established by Section 1834 of the Social Security Act (42 U.S.C. § 1395m) and applicable to California. The DMEPOS Fee Schedule, which can be found on the CMS Internet Website (http://www.cms.gov/Medicare/Medicare-Fee-for-Service-Payment/DMEPOSFeeSched/DMEPOS-Fee-Schedule.html) is incorporated by reference and will be made available on the Division of Workers' Compensation's Internet Website (http://www.dir.ca.gov/ DWC/

dwc_home_page.htm) or upon request to the Administrative Director at:

DIVISION OF WORKERS' COMPENSATION
(ATTENTION: OMFS)
P.O. BOX 420603
SAN FRANCISCO, CA 94142.

(b) The following procedures in the Special Services and Reports section of the OMFS 2003 will not be valid for services rendered after January 1, 2004: CPT Code 99002.

Note: Authority cited: Sections 133, 4603.5, 5307.1 and 5307.3, Labor Code. Reference: Sections 4600, 4603.2 and 5307.1, Labor Code.

History: 1. New section filed 1-2-2004 as an emergency; operative 1-2-2004 (Register 2004, No. 2). A Certificate of Compliance must be transmitted to OAL by 5-3-2004 or emergency language will be repealed by operation of law on the following day.

2. Certificate of Compliance as to 1-2-2004 order, including amendment of subsection (b) and new subsection (c), transmitted to OAL 4-30-2004 and filed 6-15-2004 (Register 2004, No. 25).

3. Amendment of subsection (a) and repealer of subsection (c) filed 2-4-2015; operative 3-5-2015. Submitted to OAL for printing only pursuant to Government Code section 11340.9 (Register 2015, No. 6).

Ref.: Hanna § 22.05[2]; Herlick Handbook §§ 1.01[3][b], 4.17[1].

§9789.70. Ambulance Services.

(a) The maximum reasonable fee for ambulance services rendered after January 1, 2004 shall not exceed 120% of the applicable fee for the Calendar Year 2004 set forth in CMS's Ambulance Fee Schedule, which is established pursuant to Section 1834 of the Social Security Act (42 U.S.C. §1395m) and applicable to California. The Ambulance Fee Schedule, which can be found at the CMS Internet Website http://www.cms.gov/Medicare/Medicare-Fee-for-Service-Payment/AmbulanceFeeSchedule/) is incorporated by reference and will be made available on the Division of Workers' Compensation's Internet Website (http://www.dir.ca.gov/DWC/dwc_home_page.htm) or upon request to the Administrative Director at:

DIVISION OF WORKERS' COMPENSATION
(ATTENTION: OMFS)
P.O. BOX 420603
SAN FRANCISCO, CA 94142.

(b) This section is not applicable to services provided by any air ambulance provider which at the time of service is an "air carrier" as defined in Title 49 U.S.C.A. Section 40102, a part of the Airline Deregulation Act of 1978 as amended.

Note: Authority cited: Sections 133, 4603.5, 5307.1 and 5307.3, Labor Code. Reference: Sections 4600, 4603.2 and 5307.1, Labor Code.

History: 1. New section filed 1-2-2004 as an emergency; operative 1-2-2004 (Register 2004, No. 2). A Certificate of Compliance must be transmitted to OAL by 5-3-2004 or emergency language will be repealed by operation of law on the following day.

2. Certificate of Compliance as to 1-2-2004 order, including designation and amendment of first paragraph as subsection (a) and new subsection (b), transmitted to OAL 4-30-2004 and filed 6-15-2004 (Register 2004, No. 25).

3. New subsection (c) filed 7-13-2010; operative 7-13-2010. Exempt from the Administrative Procedure Act and OAL review and submitted to OAL for printing only pursuant to Government Code section 11340.9(g) (Register 2010, No. 29).

4. Amendment of subsection (a), repealer of subsection (b) and subsection relettering filed 2-4-2015; operative 3-5-2015. Submitted to OAL for printing only pursuant to Government Code section 11340.9 (Register 2015, No. 6).

Ref.: Hanna § 22.05[2]; Herlick Handbook §§ 1.01[3][b], 4.17[1].

§9789.80. Skilled Nursing Facility. [Reserved]

§9789.90. Home Health Care. [Reserved]

§9789.100. Outpatient Renal Dialysis. [Reserved]

§9789.110. Update of Rules to Reflect Changes in the Medicare Payment System.

The OMFS shall be adjusted within 60 days to conform to any relevant changes in the Medicare and Medi-Cal payment systems as required by law. The Administrative Director shall determine the effective date of the change and issue an order informing the public of the change and the effective date. Such order shall be posted on the Division's Internet Website: http://www.dir.ca.gov/DWC/dwc_home_page.htm.

Note: Authority cited: Sections 133, 4603.5, 5307.1 and 5307.3, Labor Code. Reference: Sections 4600, 4603.2 and 5307.1, Labor Code.

History: 1. New section filed 1-2-2004 as an emergency; operative 1-2-2004 (Register 2004, No. 2). A Certificate of Compliance must be transmitted to OAL by 5-3-2004 or emergency language will be repealed by operation of law on the following day.

2. Certificate of Compliance as to 1-2-2004 order, including amendment of section, transmitted to OAL 4-30-2004 and filed 6-15-2004 (Register 2004, No. 25).

Ref.: Hanna § 22.05[2]; Herlick Handbook §§ 1.01[3][b], 4.17[1].

§9789.111. Effective Date of Fee Schedule Provisions.

(a) The Resource Based Relative Value Scale (RBRVS)-based OMFS for Physician Services (Sections 9789.12.1 – 9789.19) are effective for services rendered on or after January 1, 2014. The OMFS regulations for Physician Services (Sections 9789.10–9789.11) are effective for services rendered on or after July 1, 2004, but before January 1, 2014. Services rendered after January 1, 2004, but before July 1, 2004 are governed by the "emergency" regulations that were effective on January 2, 2004. The OMFS for physician services set forth in Article 5.5 (Sections 9790, et seq.), is applicable only for services rendered on or before January 1, 2004, unless otherwise specified in this Subchapter (Subchapter 1. Administrative Director — Administrative Rules).

(b) The OMFS regulations for Inpatient Services (Sections 9789.20–9789.25) are effective for inpatient hospital admissions with dates of discharge on or after July 1, 2004. Services for discharges after January 1, 2004, but before

July 1, 2004 are governed by the "emergency" regulations that were effective on January 2, 2004. The OMFS for inpatient services set forth in Article 5.5 (Sections 9790, et seq.), is applicable only to bills for services with date of admission on or before December 31, 2003, unless otherwise specified in this Subchapter (Subchapter 1. Administrative Director — Administrative Rules).

(c) The OMFS regulations for Outpatient Services (Sections 9789.30–9789.39) are effective for services rendered on or after July 1, 2004. Services rendered after January 1, 2004, but before July 1, 2004 are governed by the "emergency" regulations that were effective on January 2, 2004.

(d) The OMFS regulation for pharmacy (Section 9789.40) is effective for services rendered after January 1, 2004.

(e) The OMFS regulation for Pathology and Laboratory (Section 9789.50) is effective for services rendered after January 1, 2004.

(f) The OMFS regulation for Durable Medical Equipment, Prosthetics, Orthotics, Supplies (Section 9789.60) is effective for services rendered after January 1, 2004.

(g) The OMFS regulation for Ambulance Services (Section 9789.70) is effective for services rendered after January 1, 2004.

Note: Authority cited: Sections 133, 4603.5, 5307.1 and 5307.3, Labor Code. Reference: Sections 4600, 4603.2 and 5307.1, Labor Code.

History: 1. New section filed 6-15-2004; operative 7-1-2004 (Register 2004, No. 25).

2. Amendment of subsections (a)-(c) and (g) filed 2-4-2015; operative 3-5-2015. Submitted to OAL for printing only pursuant to Government Code section 11340.9 (Register 2015, No. 6).

Ref.: Hanna § 22.05[2]; Herlick Handbook §§ 1.01[3][b], 4.17[1].

ARTICLE 5.5
Application of the Official Medical Fee Schedule (Treatment)

§9790. Authority.

The rules and regulations contained in this Article are adopted pursuant to the authority contained in Sections 133, 4603.5, 307.1 and 5307.3 of the California Labor Code. Sections 9790.1 – 9792.1 and Appendices A-C, contained in this Article, are not applicable for physician services rendered and inpatient hospital facility services for discharges after January 1, 2004, unless otherwise specified in this Subchapter 1. Administrative Director — Administrative Rules.

Note: Authority cited: Sections 133, 4603.5, 5307.1 and 5307.3, Labor Code. Reference: Sections 4600, 4603.2 and 5307.1, Labor Code.

History: 1. New article 5.5 (sections 9790-9792) filed 11-9-77; effective thirtieth day thereafter (Register 77, No. 46).

2. Amendment of section and Note filed 10-7-93; operative 1-1-94 (Register 93, No. 41). This filing is exempt from much of the APA (including OAL review) pursuant to Government Code section 11351.

3. Editorial correction (Register 95, No. 15).

4. Amendment filed 2-4-2015; operative 3-5-2015. Submitted to OAL for printing only pursuant to Government Code section 11340.9 (Register 2015, No. 6).

Ref.: Herlick Handbook § 1.01[3][b].

§9790.1. Definitions.

(a) "Capital outlier factor" means (California fixed loss cost outlier threshold × geographic adjustment factor × large urban add-on × (capital cost-to-charge ratio to total cost-to-charge ratio)). The geographic adjustment factor is specified in the *Federal Register* of August 1, 2000 at Vol. 65, page 47126, Table 1a, which document is hereby incorporated by reference and will be made available upon request to the Administrative Director. The "large urban add-on" is indicated by the post-reclassification urban/rural location published in the Payment Impact File at positions 229-235. As stated in Title 42, Code of Federal Regulations, Section 412.316(b), as it is in effect on September 29, 2000, the "large urban add-on" is an additional 3% of what would otherwise be payable to the health facility.

(b) "California fixed loss cost outlier threshold" means the factor calculated by adjusting the Medicare fixed loss cost outlier threshold for California workers' compensation inpatient admissions. The California fixed loss cost outlier threshold is $14,500.

(c) "Composite factor" means the factor calculated by the administrative director for a health facility by adding the prospective operating costs and the prospective capital costs for the health facility, excluding the DRG weight and any applicable outlier payment, as determined by the federal Health Care Financing Administration for the purpose of determining reimbursement under Medicare.

(1) Prospective capital costs are determined by the following formula:

Capital standard federal payment rate × capital wage index × large urban add-on × [1 + capital disproportionate share adjustment factor + capital indirect medical education adjustment factor]

The "capital standard federal payment rate" is $382.03 as published by HCFA in the *Federal Register* of August 1, 2000, at Vol. 65, page 47127, Table 1d, which document is hereby incorporated by reference and will be made available upon request to the Administrative Director.

The "capital wage index" was published in the Payment Impact File at positions 243-252.

The "large urban add-on" is indicated by the post-reclassification urban/rural location published in the Payment Impact File at positions 229-235. As stated in Title 42, Code of Federal Regulations, Section 412.316(b), as it is in effect on September 29, 2000, the "large urban add-on" is an additional 3% of what would otherwise be payable to the health facility.

The "capital disproportionate share adjustment factor" was published in the Payment Impact File at positions 117-126.

The "capital indirect medical education adjustment factor" (capital IME adjustment) was published in Payment Impact File at positions 202-211.

(2) Prospective operating costs are determined by the following formula:

[(Labor-related national standardized amount × operating wage index) + nonlabor-related national standardized amount] × [1 + operating disproportionate share adjustment factor + operating indirect medical education adjustment]

The "labor-related national standardized amount" is $2,864.19 for large urban areas and $2,818.85 for other areas, as published by the federal Health Care Financing Administration [HCFA] in the *Federal Register* of August 1, 2000, at Vol. 65, page 47126, Table 1a, which document is hereby incorporated by reference and will be made available upon request to the Administrative Director. The "labor-related national standardized amount" is $2,894.99 for large urban area sole community hospitals and $2,849.16 for other areas sole community hospitals, as published by the federal Health Care Financing Administration [HCFA] in the *Federal Register* of August 1, 2000, at Vol. 65, page 47127, Table 1e, which document is hereby incorporated by reference and will be made available upon request to the Administrative Director.

The "operating wage index" was published in the Payment Impact File at positions 253-262.

The "nonlabor-related national standardized amount" is $1,164.21 for large urban areas and $1,145.78 for other areas, as published by HCFA in the *Federal Register* of August 1, 2000, at Vol. 65, page 47126, Table 1a, which document is hereby incorporated by reference and will be made available upon request to the Administrative Director. The "nonlabor-related national standardized amount" is $1,176.73 for large urban area sole community hospitals and $1,158.10 for other areas sole community hospitals as published by the federal Health Care Financing Administration [HCFA] in the *Federal Register* of August 1, 2000, at Vol. 65, page 47127, Table 1e, which document is hereby incorporated by reference and will be made available upon request to the administrative director.

The "operating disproportionate share adjustment factor" was published in the Payment Impact File at positions 127-136.

The "operating indirect medical education adjustment" was published in the Payment Impact File at positions 212-221.

(3) A table of composite factors for each health facility in California is contained in Appendix A to Section 9792.1.

(d) "Costs" means the total billed charges for an admission, excluding non-medical charges such as television and telephone charges, multiplied by the hospital's total cost-to-charge ratio. For DRGs 496 through 500, for purposes of determining whether an admission is a cost outlier, "costs" exclude implantable hardware and/or instrumentation reimbursed under subsection (7) of Section 9792.1.

(e) "Cost-to-charge ratio" means the sum of the hospital specific operating cost-to-charge ratio and the hospital specific capital cost-to-charge ratio. The operating cost-to-charge ratio for each hospital was published in the Payment Impact File at positions 161-168. The capital cost-to-charge ratio for each hospital was published in the Payment Impact File at positions 99-106. A table of hospital specific capital cost-to-charge, operating cost-to-charge and total cost-to-charge ratios for each health facility in California is contained in Appendix A to Section 9792.1.

(f) "Cost outlier case" means a hospitalization for which the hospital's costs, as defined in subdivision (d) above, exceed the Inpatient Hospital Fee Schedule payment amount by the hospital's outlier factor. If costs exceed the cost outlier threshold, the case is a cost outlier case.

(g) "Cost outlier threshold" means the sum of the Inpatient Hospital Fee Schedule payment amount plus the hospital specific outlier factor.

(h) "DRG weight" means the weighting factor for a diagnosis-related group assigned by the Health Care Financing Administration for the purpose of determining reimbursement under Medicare. A table is contained in Appendix B to Section 9792.1. Appendix B shows DRG weights as assigned by HCFA and, where applicable, "Revised DRG weights" in italics.

(i)(1) "Revised DRG weight" means the product of the DRG weight multiplied by the ratio set forth in subsection (i)(2) for 48 specified DRGs to reflect the different resource usage between the workers' compensation population and the Medicare population.

(2) The ratios that were applied to the DRG weights are contained in the column identified as "DWC Revised Ratio" in Appendix B of Section 9792.1.

(j) "Health facility" means any facility as defined in Section 1250 of the Health and Safety Code.

(k) "Inpatient" means a person who has been admitted to a health facility for the purpose of receiving inpatient services. A person is considered an inpatient when he or she is formally admitted as an inpatient with the expectation that he or she will remain at least overnight and occupy a bed, even if it later develops that such person can be discharged or is transferred to another facility and does not actually remain overnight.

(*l*) "Inpatient Hospital Fee Schedule payment amount" is that amount determined by multiplying the DRG weight × hospital composite factor × 1.2.

(m) "Labor-related portion" is that portion of operating costs attributable to labor costs, as specified in the *Federal Register* of August 1, 2000 at Vol. 65, page 47126, Table 1a, which document is hereby incorporated by reference and will be made available upon request to the Administrative Director.

(n) "Medical services" means those goods and services provided pursuant to Article 2 (commencing with Section 4600) of Chapter 2 of Part 2 of Division 4 of the Labor Code.

(o) "Average length of stay" means the geometric mean length of stay for a diagnosis-related group assigned by the Health Care Financing Administration.

(p) "Operating outlier factor" means ((California fixed loss cost outlier threshold × ((labor-related portion × MSA wage index) + nonlabor-related portion)) × (operating cost-to-charge ratio to total cost-to-charge ratio)). The MSA wage index is specified at *Federal Register* of August 1, 2000 at Vol. 65, page 47149, Table 4a, which document is hereby incorporated by reference and will be made available upon request to the Administrative Director. The nonlabor-related portion is that portion of operating costs as defined in the *Federal Register* of August 1, 2000 at Vol. 65, page 47126, Table 1a, which document is hereby incorporated by reference and will be made available upon request to the Administrative Director.

(q) "Outlier factor" means the sum of the capital outlier factor and the operating outlier factor. A table of hospital specific outlier factors for each health facility in California is contained in Appendix A to Section 9792.1.

(r) "Payment Impact File" means the FY 2001 Prospective Payment System Payment Impact File (August 2000 Update) (IMPCTF01.EXE) published by the federal Health Care Financing Administration, which document is hereby incorporated by reference. The description of the file is found at http://www.hcfa.gov/stats/impctf01.doc. The file is accessible through http://www.hcfa.gov/stats/pufiles.htm#ppfexmtp. A paper copy of the Payment Impact File, with explanatory material, is available from the Administrative Director upon request. An electronic copy is available from the Administrative Director at http://www.dir.ca.gov.

Note: Authority cited: Sections 133, 4603.5, 5307.1 and 5307.3, Labor Code. Reference: Sections 4600, 4603.2 and 5307.1, Labor Code.

History: 1. New section filed 10-7-93; operative 1-1-94 (Register 93, No. 41). This filing is exempt from much of the APA (including OAL review) pursuant to Government Code section 11351.

2. New subsections (a)-(c)(2), subsection relettering, and new subsection (g) filed 12-31-96; operative 12-31-96 pursuant to Government Code section 11343.4(d). Submitted to OAL for printing only pursuant to Government Code section 11351 (Register 97, No. 1).

3. New subsections (a)(1)-(3), amendment of subsections (b) and (c)(2) and new subsection (h) filed 2-23-99; operative 4-1-99 (Register 99, No. 9).

4. Amendment filed 5-30-2001; operative 6-29-2001. Submitted to OAL for printing only pursuant to Government Code section 11340.9(g) (Register 2001, No. 23).

Ref.: Hanna § 22.05[2]; Herlick Handbook § 1.01[3][b].

§9791. Services Covered.

Except as provided in this article, the Official Medical Fee Schedule applies to all covered medical services provided, referred or prescribed by physicians (as defined in Section 3209.3 of the Labor Code), regardless of the type of facility in which the medical services are performed, including clinic and hospital-based physicians working on a contract basis. The Schedule shall not apply to inpatient medical services provided by employees of a health facility, medical-legal expenses authorized under Section 4621 of the Labor Code, and medical expenses payable pursuant to Section 9795. Nothing contained in this schedule shall preclude any hospital as defined in subdivisions (a), (b), or (f) of Section 1250 of the Health and Safety Code, or any surgical facility which is licensed under subdivision (b) of Section 1204 of the Health and Safety Code, or any ambulatory surgical center that is certified to participate in the Medicare program under Title XVIII (42 U.S.C. Sec. 1395 et seq.) of the federal Social Security Act, or any surgical clinic accredited by the Accreditation Association for Ambulatory Health Care (AAAHC), from charging and collecting a facility fee for the use of the emergency room or operating room of the facility.

Note: Authority cited: Sections 133, 4603.5, 5307.1 and 5307.3, Labor Code. Reference: Sections 4600, 4603.2 and 5307.1, Labor Code.

History: 1. Amendment of section and new Note filed 10-7-93; operative 1-1-94 (Register 93, No. 41). This filing is exempt from much of the APA (including OAL review) pursuant to Government Code section 11351.

2. Amendment filed 10-11-95; operative 10-11-95. Submitted to OAL for printing only pursuant to Government Code section 11351 (Register 95, No. 41).

Ref.: Hanna § 22.05[2]; Herlick Handbook § 1.01[3][b].

§9791.1. Medical Fee Schedule.

The Official Medical Fee Schedule shall include the procedures, procedure numbers, descriptions, instructions, and unit values adopted by the Administrative Director, effective January 1, 1994; as revised for services on or after January 1, 1996; and as thereafter revised and adopted. The Official California Workers' Compensation Medical Fee Schedule (Revised April 1, 1999, and as amended for dates of service on or after 7/12/02) is hereby incorporated by reference. An order form for purchasing a copy of the Schedule can be obtained by contacting the Division of Workers' Compensation at the following address:

DIVISION OF WORKERS' COMPENSATION
(ATTENTION: OMFS ORDER)
P.O. BOX 420603
SAN FRANCISCO, CA 94142

The amendments of the OMFS for dates of service on or after 7/12/02 may be obtained either by purchasing them from the Division or they may be downloaded at no charge from the Division's website at (http://www.dir.ca.gov/workers'_comp.html).

Note: Authority cited: Sections 133, 4603.5, 5307.1 and 5307.3, Labor Code. Reference: Sections 4600, 4603.2 and 5307.1, Labor Code.

History: 1. New section filed 8-14-81; effective thirtieth day thereafter (Register 81, No. 33).

2. Amendment filed 8-29-84; effective thirtieth day thereafter (Register 84, No. 35).

3. Change without regulatory effect filed 7-11-86; effective upon filing (Register 86, No. 28).

4. Amendment filed 5-18-87; operative 5-18-87 (Register 87, No. 21).

5. Amendment of section and Note filed 10-7-93; operative 1-1-94 (Register 93, No. 41). This filing is exempt from much of the APA (including OAL review) pursuant to Government Code section 11351.

6. Amendment filed 10-11-95; operative 10-11-95. Submitted to OAL for printing only pursuant to Government Code section 11351 (Register 95, No. 41).

7. Amendment of section incorporating by reference "The Official California Workers' Compensation Medical Fee Schedule" (revised April 1, 1999) filed 2-19-99; operative 4-1-99 (Register 99, No. 8).

8. Change without regulatory effect amending section filed 6-12-2002 pursuant to section 100, title 1, California Code of Regulations (Register 2002, No. 24).

Ref.: Hanna § 22.05[2]; Herlick Handbook §§ 1.01[3][b], 4.17[1].

§9792. Determination of the Fee.

(a) The fee is determined by the use of the Official Medical Fee Schedule as defined in Section 9791.1 of these rules. For services provided on and after January 1, 1994, the conversion factors to be applied to unit values in the schedule are as follows:

Determination of the Fee

Evaluation and Management
Services Section $7.15
Medicine Section $6.15
Surgery Section $153.00
Radiology Section $12.50
Pathology Section $1.50
Anesthesia Section $34.50

(b) For services in the Evaluation and Management Services Section provided on and after April 1, 1999, the conversion factor to be applied to unit values in the schedule is $8.50.

(c) The conversion factor shall be multiplied by the listed unit value (also known as relative value) of the procedure as set forth in the Official Medical Fee Schedule to establish the reasonable maximum fee. A medical provider or a licensed health care facility may be paid a fee in excess of the reasonable maximum fees if the fee is reasonable, accompanied by itemization, and justified by an explanation of extraordinary circumstances related to the unusual nature of the services rendered; however, in no event shall a physician charge in excess of his or her usual fee.

Note: Authority cited: Sections 133, 4603.5, 5307.1 and 5307.3, Labor Code. Reference: Sections 4600, 4603.2 and 5307.1, Labor Code.

History: 1. Amendment filed 4-11-79; designated effective 7-1-79 (Register 79, No. 15).

2. Amendment filed 8-14-81; effective thirtieth day thereafter (Register 81, No. 33).

3. Amendment filed 11-5-82; designated effective 1-1-83 (Register 82, No. 45).

4. Amendment filed 11-23-83; effective thirtieth day thereafter (Register 83, No. 48).

5. Amendment filed 8-29-84; effective thirtieth day thereafter (Register 84, No. 35).

6. Editorial correction (Register 84, No. 48).

7. Amendment filed 1-10-85; effective upon filing pursuant to Government Code section 11346.2(d) (Register 85, No. 2).

8. Amendment filed 7-1-87; operative 7-1-87 (Register 87, No. 28).

9. Amendment of section and Note filed 10-7-93; operative 1-1-94 (Register 93, No. 41). This filing is exempt from much of the APA (including OAL review) pursuant to Government Code section 11351.

10. New subsection (a) designator, new subsection (b), and amendment of newly designated subsection (c) filed 2-19-99; operative 4-1-99 (Register 99, No. 8).

Ref.: Hanna §§ 5.05[10][d], 22.05[2]; Herlick Handbook §§ 1.01[3][b], 4.17[1].

§9792.1. Payment of Inpatient Services of Health Facilities.

(a) Maximum reimbursement for inpatient medical services shall be determined by multiplying 1.20 by the product of the health facility's composite factor and the applicable DRG weight or revised DRG weight if a revised weight has been adopted by the administrative director. The fee determined under this subdivision shall be a global fee, constituting the maximum reimbursement to a health facility for inpatient medical services not exempted under this section. However, preadmission services rendered by a health facility more than 24 hours before admission are separately reimbursable.

(b) Health facilities billing for fees under this section shall present with their bill the name and address of the facility, the facility's Medicare ID number, and the applicable DRG codes.

(c) The following are exempt from the maximum reimbursement formula set forth in subdivision (a):

(1) Inpatient services for the following diagnoses: Psychiatry (DRGs 424-432), Substance Abuse (DRGs 433-437), Organ Transplants (DRGs 103, 302, 480, 481, 495), Rehabilitation (DRG 462 and inpatient rehabilitation services provided in any rehabilitation center that is authorized by the Department of Health Services in accordance with Title 22, §§70301, 70595 70603 of the California Code of Regulations to provide rehabilitation services), Tracheostomies (DRGs 482, 483), and Burns (DRGs 475 and 504-511).

(2) Inpatient services provided by a Level I or Level II trauma center, as defined in Title 22, California Code of Regulations sections 100260, 100261, to a patient with an immediately life threatening or urgent injury.

(3) Inpatient services provided by a health facility for which there is no composite factor.

(4) Inpatient services provided by a health facility located outside the State of California.

(5) The cost of durable medical equipment provided for use at home.

(6) Inpatient services provided by a health facility transferring an inpatient to another hospital. Maximum reimbursement for inpatient medical services of a health facility transferring an inpatient to another hospital shall be a per diem rate for each day of the patient's stay in that hospital, not to exceed the amount that would have been paid under Title 8, California Code of Regulations §9792.1(a). However, the first day of the stay in the transferring hospital shall be reimbursed at twice the per diem amount. The per diem rate is determined by dividing the maximum reimbursement as determined under Title 8, California Code of Regulations §9792.1(a) by the average length of stay for that specific DRG. However, if an admission to a health facility transferring a patient is exempt from the maximum reimbursement formula set forth in subdivision (a) because it satisfies one or more of the requirements of Title 8, California Code of Regulations §9792.1(c)(1) through (c)(4), subdivision (c)(6) shall not apply. Inpatient services provided by the hospital receiving the patient shall be reimbursed under the provisions of Title 8, California Code of Regulations §9792.1(a).

(7) Implantable hardware and/or instrumentation for DRGs 496 through 500, where the admission occurs on or after April 13, 2001. Implantable hardware and/or instrumentation for DRGs 496 through 500, where the admission occurs on or after April 13, 2001, shall be separately reimbursed at the provider's documented paid cost, plus an additional 10% of the provider's documented paid cost not to exceed a maximum of $250.00, plus any sales tax and/or shipping and handling charges actually paid.

(8) Cost Outlier cases. Inpatient services for cost outlier cases where the admission occurs on or after June 29, 2001, shall be reimbursed as follows:

Step 1: Determine the Inpatient Hospital Fee Schedule payment amount (DRG relative weight × 1.2 × hospital specific composite factor).

Step 2: Determine costs. Costs = (total billed charges × total cost-to-charge ratio).

Step 3: Determine outlier threshold. Outlier threshold = (Inpatient Hospital Fee Schedule payment amount + hospital specific outlier factor).

If costs exceed the outlier threshold, the case is a cost outlier case and the admission is reimbursed at the Inpatient Hospital Fee Schedule payment amount + (0.8 × (costs - cost outlier threshold)).

NOTE: For purposes of determining whether a case qualifies as a cost outlier case under this subsection, implantable hardware and/or instrumentation reimbursed under subsection (8) below is excluded from the calculation of costs. Once an admission for DRGs 496 through 500 qualifies as a cost outlier case, any implantable hardware and/or instrumentation shall be separately reimbursed under subsection (8) below.

(d) Any health care facility that believes its composite factor or hospital specific outlier factor was erroneously determined because of an error in tabulating data may request the Administrative Director for a re-determination of its composite factor or hospital specific outlier factor. Such requests shall be in writing, shall state the alleged error, and shall be supported by written documentation. Within 30 days after receiving a complete written request, the Administrative Director shall make a redetermination of the composite factor or hospital specific outlier factor or reaffirm the published factor.

(e) This section, except as provided in subsections (c)(7) and (c)(8), shall apply to covered inpatient hospital stays for which the day of admittance is on or after April 1, 1999.

(f) Subsections (c)(7) and (c)(8) shall remain in effect only through December 31, 2001, and shall not apply to admissions occurring on or after January 1, 2002.

AN IMPORTANT NOTE CONCERNING SUBSECTIONS (c)(7) AND (c)(8):

Labor Code Section 5318, (as added by Statutes of 2001, chapter 252, effective January 1, 2002,) provides that: "Notwithstanding any other provision of law, the termination date of December 31, 2001, provided in Section 9792.1(f) of Title 8 of the California Code of Regulations shall be extended until the effective date of new regulations adopted by the administrative director, as required by Section 5307.1, providing for the biennial review of the fee schedule for health care facilities." Sections 9792.1(c)(7) and (c)(8) will therefore remain in effect for admissions on or after January 1, 2002, and will not sunset.

Note: Authority cited: Sections 133, 4603.5, 5307.1, 5307.3 and 5318, Labor Code. Reference: Sections 4600, 4603.2, 5307.1 and 5318, Labor Code.

History: 1. New section filed 12-31-96; operative 12-31-96 pursuant to Government Code section 11343.4(d). Submitted to OAL for printing only pursuant to Government Code section 11351 (Register 97, No. 1).

2. Amendment of section and new appendices A-C filed 2-23-99; operative 4-1-99 (Register 99, No. 9).

3. New subsection (c)(8), amendment of subsection (e) and new subsection (f) filed 3-14-2001; operative 4-13-2001. Submitted to OAL for printing only pursuant to Government Code section 11343(a)(1) (Register 2001, No. 22).

4. Amendment of section and repealer and new Appendices A and B filed 5-30-2001; operative 6-29-2001. Submitted to OAL for printing only pursuant to Government Code section 11340.9(g) (Register 2001, No. 23).

5. Change without regulatory effect adding final two paragraphs and amending Note filed 12-31-2001 pursuant to section 100, title 1, California Code of Regulations (Register 2002, No. 1).

Ref.: Hanna § 22.05[2]; Herlick Handbook §§ 1.01[3][b], 4.18[1].

Appendix A. Hospital Composite Factors and Cost to Charge Rations [Appendix Not Reproduced]

Appendix B. DRG Weights and Revised DRG Weights 2001 Rates (California revisions shown in italics incorporate the DWC Revised Ratios) [Appendix Not Reproduced]

Appendix C. Ratios Applied to Revise Certain DRG Weights in California [Appendix Not Reproduced]

Editor's Note: For text of Appendix A, B, and/or C, please see Barclays *Official California Code of Regulations*.

Ref.: Hanna § 22.05[2]; Herlick Handbook § 1.01[3][b].

§9792.5. Payment for Medical Treatment.

This section is applicable to medical treatment rendered before October 15, 2011.

(a) As used in this section:

(1) "Claims Administrator" has the same meaning specified in Section 9785(a)(3).

(2) "Medical treatment" means the treatment to which an employee is entitled under Labor Code Section 4600.

(3) "Physician" has the same meaning specified in Labor Code Section 3209.3.

(4) "Required report" means a report which must be submitted pursuant to Section 9785.

(5) "Treating physician" means the "primary treating physician" as that term is defined by Section 9785(a)(1).

(b) Any properly documented bill for medical treatment within the planned course, scope and duration of treatment reported under Section 9785 which is provided or authorized by the treating physician shall be paid by the claims administrator within forty five working days from receipt of each separate itemized bill and any required reports, or within sixty working days if the employer is a governmental entity, unless the bill is contested, as specified in subdivisions (d), and (e), within thirty working days of receipt of the bill. Any amount not contested within the thirty working days or not paid within the forty five working day period, or within sixty working days if the employer is a governmental entity, shall be increased 15%, and shall carry interest at the same rate as judgments in civil actions retroactive to the date of receipt of the bill.

For purposes of this Section, treatment which is provided or authorized by the treating physician includes but is not limited to treatment provided by a "secondary physician" as that term is defined by Section 9785(a)(2).

(c) A claims administrator who objects to all or any part of a bill for medical treatment shall notify the physician or other authorized provider of the objection within thirty working days after receipt of the bill and any required report and shall pay any uncontested amount within forty five working days, or within sixty working days if the employer is a governmental entity, after receipt of the bill. If a required report is not received with the bill, the periods to object or pay shall commence on the date of receipt of the bill or report, whichever is received later. If the claims administrator receives a bill and believes that it has not received a required report to support the bill, the claims administrator shall so inform the medical provider within thirty working days of receipt of the bill. An objection will be deemed timely if sent by first class mail and postmarked on or before the thirtieth working day after receipt, or if personally delivered or sent by electronic facsimile on or before the thirtieth working day after receipt. Any notice of objection shall include or be accompanied by all of the following:

(1) An explanation of the basis for the objection to each contested procedure and charge. The original procedure codes used by the physician or authorized provider shall not be altered. If the objection is based on appropriate coding of a procedure, the explanation shall include both the code reported by the provider and the code believed reasonable by the claims administrator.

(2) If additional information is necessary as a prerequisite to payment of the contested bill or portions thereof, a clear description of the information required.

(3) The name, address, and telephone number of the person or office to contact for additional information concerning the objection.

(4) A statement that the treating physician or authorized provider may adjudicate the issue of the contested charges before the Workers' Compensation Appeals Board.

(d) An objection to charges from a hospital, outpatient surgery center, or independent diagnostic facility shall be deemed sufficient if the provider is advised, within the thirty working day period specified in subdivision (d), that a request has been made for an audit of the billing, when the results of the audit are expected, and contains the name, address, and telephone number of the person or office to contact for additional information concerning the audit.

(e) The above provisions are altered for services rendered prior to January 1, 2004, as follows:

(1) Claims administrators shall pay any uncontested amount within sixty days after receipt of the bill, and

(2) Any amount not contested within the thirty working days or not paid within the sixty day period shall be increased 10% and shall carry interest at the same rate as judgments in civil actions retroactive to the date of receipt of the bill.

Note: Authority cited: Sections 133, 4603.5 and 5307.3, Labor Code. Reference: Sections 4603.2 and 5307.1, Labor Code.

History: 1. New section filed 4-13-93; operative 4-13-93. Submitted to OAL for printing only pursuant to Government Code section 11351 (Register 93, No. 16).

2. Amendment of subsections (b), (d), (d)(1), (f) and (g) filed 9-25-95; operative 9-25-95. Submitted to OAL for printing only pursuant to Government Code section 11351 (Register 95, No. 39).

3. Change without regulatory effect amending section and Note filed 6-12-2002 pursuant to section 100, title 1, California Code of Regulations (Register 2002, No. 24).

4. New first paragraph, amendment of subsection (b), repealer of subsection (c), subsection relettering, amendment of newly designated subsection (c) and new subsections (e)-(e)(2) filed 4-18-2011; operative 4-18-2011 pursuant to Government Code section 11343.4 (Register 2011, No. 16).

Ref.: Hanna §§ 5.05[6][b], 22.05[1], [3]; Herlick Handbook §§ 1.01[3][b], 4.18[1].

ARTICLE 5.5.0
Rules for Medical Treatment Billing and Payment on or After October 15, 2011

§9792.5.0. Definitions.

As used in this article:

(a) "Assignee" means a person or entity that has purchased the right to payments for medical goods or services from the health care provider or health care facility and is authorized by law to collect payment from the responsible payer.

(b) "Billing Agent" means a person or entity that has contracted with a health care provider or health care facility to process bills for services provided by the health care provider or health care facility.

(c) "Claims Administrator" means a self-administered insurer providing security for the payment of compensation required by Divisions 4 and 4.5 of the Labor Code, a self-administered self-insured employer, or a third-party administrator for a self-insured employer, insurer, legally uninsured employer, or joint powers authority.

(d) "Health Care Facility" means any facility as defined in Section 1250 of the Health and Safety Code, any surgical facility which is licensed under subdivision (b) of Section 1204 of the Health and Safety Code, any outpatient setting as defined in Section 1248 of the Health and Safety Code, any surgical facility accredited by an accrediting agency approved by the Licensing Division of the Medical Board of California pursuant to Health and Safety Code Sections 1248.15 and 1248.4, or any ambulatory surgical center or hospital outpatient department that is certified to participate in the Medicare program under Title XVIII (42 U.S.C. Sec. 1395 et seq.) of the federal Social Security Act.

(e) "Health Care Provider" means a provider of medical treatment, goods and services provided pursuant to Labor Code section 4600, including but not limited to a physician, a non-physician or any other person or entity who furnishes medical treatment, goods or services in the normal course of business.

(f) "Physician" includes physicians and surgeons holding an M.D. or D.O. degree, psychologists, acupuncturists, optometrists, dentists, podiatrists, and chiropractic practitioners licensed by California state law and within the scope of their practice as defined by California state law.

(1) "Psychologist" means a licensed psychologist with a doctoral degree in psychology, or a doctoral degree deemed equivalent for licensure by the Board of Psychology pursuant to Section 2914 of the Business and Professions Code, and who either has at least two years of clinical experience in a recognized health setting or has met the standards of the National Register of the Health Service Providers in Psychology.

(2) "Acupuncturist" means a person who holds an acupuncturist's certificate issued pursuant to Chapter 12 (commencing with Section 4925) of Division 2 of the Business and Professions Code.

Note: Authority cited: Sections 133, 4603.4, 4603.5 and 5307.3, Labor Code. Reference: Sections 3209.3, 4603.2, 4603.4 and 5307.1, Labor Code.

History: 1. New article 5.5.0 (sections 9792.5.0–9792.5.3) and section filed 4-18-2011; operative 4-18-2011 pursuant to Government Code section 11343.4 (Register 2011, No. 16).

Ref.: Herlick Handbook § 1.01[3][b].

§9792.5.1. Medical Billing and Payment Guide; Electronic Medical Billing and Payment Companion Guide; Various Implementation Guides.

(a) The *California Division of Workers' Compensation Medical Billing and Payment Guide*, versions listed below, which set forth billing, payment and coding rules for paper and electronic medical treatment bill submissions, are incorporated by reference. They may be downloaded from the Division of Workers' Compensation through the Department of Industrial Relations' website at www.dir.ca.gov or may be obtained by writing to:

DIVISION OF WORKERS' COMPENSATION MEDICAL UNIT
ATTN: MEDICAL BILLING AND PAYMENT GUIDE
P.O. BOX 71010
OAKLAND, CA 94612

(1) California Division of Workers' Compensation Medical Billing and Payment Guide 2011, for bills submitted on or after October 15, 2011.

(2) California Division of Workers' Compensation Medical Billing and Payment Guide, Version 1.1, for bills submitted on or after January 1, 2013.

(3) California Division of Workers' Compensation Medical Billing and Payment Guide, Version 1.2.1, for bills submitted on or after February 12, 2014.

(4) California Division of Workers' Compensation Medical Billing and Payment Guide, Version 1.2.2, for bills submitted on or after October 1, 2015.

(b) The *California Division of Workers' Compensation Electronic Medical Billing and Payment Companion Guide*, versions listed below, which set forth billing, payment and coding rules and technical information for electronic medical treatment bill submissions, are incorporated by reference. They may be downloaded from the Division of Workers' Compensation website at www.dir.ca.gov or may be obtained by writing to:

DIVISION OF WORKERS' COMPENSATION MEDICAL UNIT
ATTN: MEDICAL BILLING AND PAYMENT COMPANION GUIDE
P.O. BOX 71010
OAKLAND, CA 94612

(1) California Division of Workers' Compensation Electronic Medical Billing and Payment Companion Guide, Version 1.0, dated 2012, for bills submitted on or after October 18, 2012.

(2) California Division of Workers' Compensation Electronic Medical Billing and Payment Companion Guide, Version 1.1, for bills submitted on or after January 1, 2013.

(3) California Division of Workers' Compensation Electronic Medical Billing and Payment Companion Guide, Version 1.2, for bills submitted on or after February 12, 2014.

Note: Authority cited: Sections 133, 4603.4, 4603.5 and 5307.3, Labor Code. Reference: Sections 4600, 4603.2 and 4603.4, Labor Code.

History: 1. New section filed 4-18-2011; operative 4-18-2011 pursuant to Government Code section 11343.4 (Register 2011, No. 16).

2. Amendment of subsections (a), (b) and (h) filed 12-31-2012 as an emergency; operative 1-1-2013 pursuant to Government Code section 11346.1(d) (Register 2013, No. 1). A Certificate of Compliance must be transmitted to OAL by 7-1-2013 or emergency language will be repealed by operation of law on the following day.

3. Amendment of subsections (a), (b) and (h) refiled 7-1-2013 as an emergency; operative 7-1-2013 (Register 2013, No. 27). A Certificate of Compliance must be transmitted to OAL by 9-30-2013 or emergency language will be repealed by operation of law on the following day.

4. Amendment of subsections (a), (b) and (h) refiled 9-30-2013 as an emergency; operative 10-1-2013 (Register 2013, No. 40). A Certificate of Compliance must be transmitted to OAL by 12-30-2013 or emergency language will be repealed by operation of law on the following day.

5. Certificate of Compliance as to 9-30-2013 order, including amendment of section, transmitted to OAL 12-30-2013 and filed 2-12-2014; amendments effective 2-12-2014 pursuant to Government Code section 11343.4(b)(3) (Register 2014, No. 7).

6. Amendment of subsection (a)(3) filed 9-30-2014; operative 9-30-2014 pursuant to Government Code section 11343.4(b)(3) (Register 2014, No. 40).

7. New subsection (a)(4) filed 9-21-2015; operative 10-1-2015 pursuant to Government Code section 11343.4(b)(3) (Register 2015, No. 39).

Ref.: Hanna § 5.02[2][e]; Herlick Handbook §§ 1.01[3][b], 4.08[2], [3], 4.10[3].

§9792.5.2. Standardized Medical Treatment Billing Forms/Formats, Billing Rules, Requirements for Completing and Submitting Form CMS 1500, Form CMS 1450 (or UB-04), American Dental Association Form, Version 2006, NCPDP Workers' Compensation / Property & Casualty Universal Claim Form, Payment Requirements.

(a) On and after October 15, 2011, all paper bills for medical treatment provided by health care providers and health care facilities shall be submitted on billing forms set forth in the *California Division of Workers' Compensation Medical Billing and Payment Guide*.

(b) On and after October 15, 2011, all medical bills shall conform to the provisions of the *California Division of Workers' Compensation Medical Billing and Payment*

Guide which includes coding, billing standards, timeframes and other rules.

(c) On and after October 18, 2012, all bills for medical treatment provided by health care providers and health care facilities may be electronically submitted to the claims administrator for payment. Electronic bills submitted on or after that date shall conform to the applicable provisions of the *California Division of Workers' Compensation Medical Billing and Payment Guide* and the *California Division of Workers' Compensation Electronic Medical Billing and Payment Companion Guide.*

(d) Except as otherwise specifically provided, legally authorized billing agents and assignees shall submit bills in the same manner as the original rendering provider or facility would be required to do had the bills been submitted by the provider or facility directly and shall conform to applicable provisions of the *California Division of Workers' Compensation Medical Billing and Payment Guide* and the *California Division of Workers' Compensation Medical Billing and Payment Companion Guide.*

Note: Authority cited: Sections 133, 4603.4, 4603.5 and 5307.3, Labor Code. Reference: Sections 4600, 4603.2 and 4603.4, Labor Code.

History: 1. New section filed 4-18-2011; operative 4-18-2011 pursuant to Government Code section 11343.4 (Register 2011, No. 16).

Ref.: Hanna § 5.02[2][e]; Herlick Handbook §§ 1.01[3][b], 4.18[1].

§9792.5.3. Medical Treatment Bill Payment Rules.

(a) On and after October 15, 2011, claims administrators shall conform to the payment, communication, penalty, and other provisions contained in the *California Division of Workers' Compensation Medical Billing and Payment Guide,* except that the provisions relating to the payment of electronic medical bills shall become effective on October 18, 2012. This subdivision does not apply to processing or payment of bills submitted before October 15, 2011.

(b) On and after October 18, 2012, claims administrators shall conform to the payment, communication, penalty, and other provisions contained in the *California Division of Workers' Compensation Electronic Medical Billing and Payment Companion Guide.*

Note: Authority cited: Sections 133, 4603.3, 4603.4, 4603.5 and 5307.3, Labor Code. Reference: Sections 4600, 4603.2, 4603.3 and 4603.4, Labor Code.

History: 1. New section filed 4-18-2011; operative 4-18-2011 pursuant to Government Code section 11343.4 (Register 2011, No. 16).

2. Amendment of Note filed 12-31-2012 as an emergency; operative 1-1-2013 pursuant to Government Code section 11346.1(d) (Register 2013, No. 1). A Certificate of Compliance must be transmitted to OAL by 7-1-2013 or emergency language will be repealed by operation of law on the following day.

3. Amendment of Note refiled 7-1-2013 as an emergency; operative 7-1-2013 (Register 2013, No. 27). A Certificate of Compliance must be transmitted to OAL by 9-30-2013 or emergency language will be repealed by operation of law on the following day.

4. Amendment of Note refiled 9-30-2013 as an emergency; operative 10-1-2013 (Register 2013, No. 40). A Certificate of Compliance must be transmitted to OAL by 12-30-2013 or emergency language will be repealed by operation of law on the following day.

5. Certificate of Compliance as to 9-30-2013 order transmitted to OAL 12-30-2013 and filed 2-12-2014 (Register 2014, No. 7).

Ref.: Hanna § 5.02[2][e]; Herlick Handbook §§ 1.01[3][b], 4.10[3], 4.18[1].

§9792.5.4. Second Review and Independent Bill Review — Definitions.

This section is applicable to medical treatment services and goods rendered under Labor Code section 4600, or medical-legal expenses incurred under Labor Code section 4620, on or after January 1, 2013.

(a) "Amount of payment" means the amount of money paid by the claims administrator for either:

(1) Medical treatment services or goods rendered by a provider or goods supplied in accordance with Labor Code section 4600 that were authorized by Labor Code section 4610, and for which there exists an applicable fee schedule adopted by the Administrative Director for those categories of goods and services, including but not limited to those found at sections 9789.10 to 9789.111, or for which a contract for reimbursement rates exists under Labor Code section 5307.11.

(2) Medical-legal expenses, as defined by Labor Code section 4620, where the payment is determined in accordance with sections 9793–9795 and 9795.1–9795.4.

(b) "Billing Code" means those codes adopted by the Administrative Director for use in the Official Medical Fee Schedule, located at sections 9789.10 to 9789.111, or in the Medical-Legal Fee Schedule, located at sections 9795(c) and 9795(d).

(c) "Claims Administrator" means a self-administered insurer providing security for the payment of compensation required by Divisions 4 and 4.5 of the Labor Code, a self-administered self-insured employer, or a third-party administrator for a self-insured employer, insurer, legally uninsured employer, or joint powers authority.

(d) "Contested liability" means the existence of a good-faith issue which, if resolved against the injured worker, would defeat the right to any workers' compensation benefits or the existence of a good-faith issue that would defeat a provider's right to receive compensation for medical treatment services provided in accordance with Labor Code section 4600 or for medical-legal expenses defined in Labor Code section 4620.

(e) "Consolidation" means combining two or more requests for independent bill review together for the purpose of having the payment reductions contested in each request resolved in a single determination.

(f) "Explanation of review" means the document described in Labor Code section 4603.3 provided by a claims administrator to a provider upon the payment, adjustment, or denial of a complete or incomplete itemization of medical services.

(g) "Independent bill review organization" or "IBRO" means the organization or the organizations designated by the Administrative Director pursuant to Labor Code section 139.5 to perform independent bill review under Labor Code section 4603.6.

(h) "Independent bill reviewer" means an individual retained by the IBRO and subject to the provisions of

Labor Code section 139.5 to review a request for independent bill review, with supporting documentation, and issue a determination under the Article.

(i) "Provider" means a provider of medical treatment services or goods, including a health care facility as defined in Section One of the California Division of Workers' Compensation Medical Billing and Payment Guide as incorporated by reference in section 9792.5.1, whose billing processes are governed by Labor Code section 4603.2 or 4603.4, or a provider of medical-legal services whose billing processes are governed by Labor Code sections 4620 and 4622, that has requested a second bill review and, if applicable, independent bill review to resolve a dispute over the amount of payment for services according to either a fee schedule established by the Administrative Director or a contract for reimbursement rates under Labor Code section 5307.11. A provider may utilize the services of a billing agent, a person or entity that has contracted with the provider to process bills under this article for services or goods rendered by the provider, to request a second bill review or independent bill review.

Note: Authority cited: Sections 133, 4603.6, 5307.3 and 5307.6, Labor Code. Reference: Sections 4060, 4061, 4061.5, 4062, 4600, 4603.2, 4603.3. 4603.4, 4603.6, 4620, 4621, 4622, 4625, 4628 and 5307.6, Labor Code.

History: 1. New section filed 12-31-2012 as an emergency; operative 1-1-2013 pursuant to Government Code section 11346.1(d) (Register 2013, No. 1). A Certificate of Compliance must be transmitted to OAL by 7-1-2013 or emergency language will be repealed by operation of law on the following day.

2. New section refiled 7-1-2013 as an emergency; operative 7-1-2013 (Register 2013, No. 27). A Certificate of Compliance must be transmitted to OAL by 9-30-2013 or emergency language will be repealed by operation of law on the following day.

3. New section refiled 9-30-2013 as an emergency; operative 10-1-2013 (Register 2013, No. 40). A Certificate of Compliance must be transmitted to OAL by 12-30-2013 or emergency language will be repealed by operation of law on the following day.

4. Certificate of Compliance as to 9-30-2013 order, including amendment of first paragraph and subsections (a)(1)-(2), (d) and (i), transmitted to OAL 12-30-2013 and filed 2-12-2014; amendments effective 2-12-2014 pursuant to Government Code section 11343.4(b)(3) (Register 2014, No. 7).

Ref.: Hanna § 5.02[2][e]; Herlick Handbook § 1.01[3][b].

§9792.5.5. Second Review of Medical Treatment Bill or Medical–Legal Bill.

(a) If the provider disputes the amount of payment made by the claims administrator on a bill for medical treatment services or goods rendered on or after January 1, 2013, submitted pursuant to Labor Code section 4603.2, or Labor Code section 4603.4, or bill for medical-legal expenses incurred on or after January 1, 2013, submitted pursuant to Labor Code section 4622, the provider may request the claims administrator to conduct a second review of the bill.

(b) The second review must be requested within 90 days of:

(1) The date of service of the explanation of review provided by a claims administrator in conjunction with the payment, adjustment, or denial of the initially submitted bill, if a proof of service accompanies the explanation of review.

(A) The date of receipt of the explanation of review by the provider is deemed the date of service, if a proof of service does not accompany the explanation of review and the claims administrator has documentation of receipt.

(B) If the explanation of review is sent by mail and if in the absence of a proof of service or documentation of receipt, the date of service is deemed to be five (5) calendar days after the date of the United States postmark stamped on the envelope in which the explanation of review was mailed.

(2) The date of service of an order of the Workers' Compensation Appeal Board resolving any threshold issue that would preclude a provider's right to receive compensation for the submitted bill.

(c) The request for second review shall be made as follows:

(1) For a non-electronic medical treatment bill, the second review shall be requested on either:

(A) The initially reviewed bill submitted on a CMS 1500 or UB04, as modified by this subdivision. The second review bill shall be marked using the National Uniform Billing Committee (NUBC) Condition Code Qualifier "BG" followed by NUBC Condition Code "W3" in the field designated for that information to indicate a request for second review, or, for the ADA Dental Claim Form 2006, or ADA Dental Claim Form (2012), the words "Request for Second Review" will be marked in Field 1, or for the NCPDP WC/PC Claim Form, the words "Request for Second Review" may be written on the form.

(B) The Request for Second Bill Review form, DWC Form SBR-1, set forth at section 9792.5.6. The DWC Form SBR-1 shall be the first page of the request for second review submitted by the provider.

(2) For an electronic medical treatment bills for professional, institutional or dental services, the request for second review shall be submitted on the correct electronic standard format, utilizing the National Uniform Billing Committee (NUBC) Condition Code Qualifier "BG" followed by NUBC Condition Code "W3" as specified in the Division of Workers' Compensation Electronic Medical Billing and Payment Companion Guide.

(3) For an electronic pharmacy bill that used either the NCPDP Telecommunications D.0 or the NCPDP Batch Standard Implementation Guide 1.2, the method for identifying a request for second review may be addressed in the trading partner agreement, or the second review may be requested on the DWC Form SBR-1.

(4) For medical-legal bills, the second review shall be requested on the Request for Second Bill Review form, DWC Form SBR-1, set forth at section 9792.5.6.

(d) The request for second review shall include:

(1) The original dates of service and the same itemized services rendered as the original bill. No new dates of service or additional billing codes may be included.

(2) In addition to the bill as modified in this subdivision, the second review request shall include, as applicable, the following:

(A) The date of the explanation of review and the claim number or other unique identifying number provided on the explanation of review.

(B) The item and amount in dispute.

(C) The additional payment requested and the reason therefor.

(D) The additional information provided in response to a request in the first explanation of review or any other additional information provided in support of the additional payment requested.

(e) If the only dispute is the amount of payment and the provider does not request a second review within the timeframes set forth in subdivision (b), the bill shall be deemed satisfied and neither the claims administrator nor the employee shall be liable for any further payment.

(e) If the only dispute is the amount of payment and the provider does not request a second review within the timeframes set forth in subdivision (b), the bill shall be deemed satisfied and neither the claims administrator nor the employee shall be liable for any further payment.

(f) A claims administrator may respond to a request for second bill review that does not comply with the requirements of subdivision (d). Any response to such a request is not subject to the requirements of subdivisions (g) and (h) of this section.

(g) Within 14 days of receipt of a request for second review that complies with the requirements of subdivision (d), the claims administrator shall respond to the provider with a final written determination on each of the items or amounts in dispute by issuing an explanation of review. The determination shall contain all the information that is required to be set forth in an explanation of review under Labor Code section 4603.3, including an explanation of the time limit to raise any further objection regarding the amount paid for services and how to obtain independent bill review under Labor Code section 4603.6. The 14 day time limit for responding to a request for second review may be extended by mutual written agreement between the provider and the claims administrator.

(h) Based on the results of the second review, payment of any balance no longer in dispute, or payment of any additional amount determined to be payable, shall be made within 21 days of receipt of the request for second review. The 21-day time limit for payment may be extended by mutual written agreement between the provider and the claims administrator.

(i) If the provider further contests the amount paid after receipt of the final written determination following a second review, the provider shall request an independent bill review pursuant to this Article.

Note: Authority cited: Sections 133, 4603.6, 5307.3 and 5307.6, Labor Code. Reference: Sections 4060, 4061, 4061.5, 4062, 4600, 4603.2, 4603.3, 4603.4, 4620, 4621, 4622, 4625, 4628 and 5307.6, Labor Code.

History: 1. New section filed 12-31-2012 as an emergency; operative 1-1-2013 pursuant to Government Code section 11346.1(d) (Register 2013, No. 1). A Certificate of Compliance must be transmitted to OAL by 7-1-2013 or emergency language will be repealed by operation of law on the following day.

2. New section refiled 7-1-2013 as an emergency; operative 7-1-2013 (Register 2013, No. 27). A Certificate of Compliance must be transmitted to OAL by 9-30-2013 or emergency language will be repealed by operation of law on the following day.

3. New section refiled 9-30-2013 as an emergency; operative 10-1-2013 (Register 2013, No. 40). A Certificate of Compliance must be transmitted to OAL by 12-30-2013 or emergency language will be repealed by operation of law on the following day.

4. Certificate of Compliance as to 9-30-2013 order, including amendment of section, transmitted to OAL 12-30-2013 and filed 2-12-2014; amendments effective 2-12-2014 pursuant to Government Code section 11343.4(b)(3) (Register 2014, No. 7).

5. Editorial correction of subsections (b)(1)(A)-(B) (Register 2014, No. 9).

Publisher's Note: The regulation appears as amended by Register 2014, No. 7; duplicated subdivision (e).

Ref.: Hanna § 5.02[2][e]; Herlick Handbook §§ 1.01[3][b], 4.10[3].

§9792.5.6. Provider's Request for Second Bill Review — Form.

Provider's Request for Second Bill Review. DWC Form SBR-1.

[DWC Form SBR-1 (New 2/2014) Not Reproduced]

NOTE: Form is available at no charge by downloading from the web at www.dir.ca.gov/dwc/forms.html or by requesting at 1-800-794-6900.

History: 1. New section filed 12-31-2012 as an emergency; operative 1-1-2013 pursuant to Government Code section 11346.1(d) (Register 2013, No. 1). A Certificate of Compliance must be transmitted to OAL by 7-1-2013 or emergency language will be repealed by operation of law on the following day.

2. New section refiled 7-1-2013 as an emergency; operative 7-1-2013 (Register 2013, No. 27). A Certificate of Compliance must be transmitted to OAL by 9-30-2013 or emergency language will be repealed by operation of law on the following day.

3. New section refiled 9-30-2013 as an emergency; operative 10-1-2013 (Register 2013, No. 40). A Certificate of Compliance must be transmitted to OAL by 12-30-2013 or emergency language will be repealed by operation of law on the following day.

4. Certificate of Compliance as to 9-30-2013 order, including repealer and new DWC Form SBR-1, transmitted to OAL 12-30-2013 and filed 2-12-2014; amendments effective 2-12-2014 pursuant to Government Code section 11343.4(b)(3) (Register 2014, No. 7).

Ref.: Hanna § 5.02[2][e]; Herlick Handbook § 1.01[3][b].

§9792.5.7. Requesting Independent Bill Review.

(a) If the provider further contests the amount of payment made by the claims administrator on a bill for medical treatment services or goods rendered on or after January 1, 2013, submitted pursuant to Labor Code sections 4603.2 or 4603.4, or bill for medical-legal expenses incurred on or after January 1, 2013, submitted pursuant to Labor Code section 4622, following the second review conducted under section 9792.5.5, the provider shall request an independent bill review. Unless consolidated under section 9792.5.12, a request for independent bill review shall only resolve:

(1) For a bill for medical treatment services or goods, a dispute over the amount of payment for services or goods billed by a single provider involving one injured employee, one claims administrator, and either one date of service and one billing code or one hospital stay, under the applicable fee schedule adopted by the Administrative Director or, if applicable, under a contract for reimbursement rates under Labor Code section 5307.11 covering one range of effective dates.

(2) For a bill for medical-legal expenses, a dispute over the amount of payment for services billed by a single provider involving one injured employee, one claims administrator, and one comprehensive, follow-up, or supplemental medical legal evaluation report as defined in section 9794.

(b) Unless as permitted by section 9792.5.12, independent bill review shall only be conducted if the only dispute between the provider and the claims administrator is the amount of payment owed to the provider. Any other issue, including issues of contested liability or the applicability of a contract for reimbursement rates under Labor Code section 5307.11 shall be resolved before seeking independent bill review. Issues that are not eligible for independent bill review shall include:

(1) The determination of a reasonable fee for services where that category of services is not covered by a fee schedule adopted by the Administrative Director or a contract for reimbursement rates under Labor Code section 5307.11.

(2) The proper selection of an analogous code or formula based on a fee schedule adopted by the Administrative Director, or, if applicable, a contract for reimbursement rates under Labor Code section 5307.11, unless the fee schedule or contract allows for such analogous coding.

(c) The request for independent bill review must be made within 30 calendar days of:

(1) The date of service of the final written determination issued by the claims administrator under section 9792.5.5(f), if a proof of service accompanies the final written determination.

(2) The date of receipt of the final written determination by the provider, if a proof of service does not accompany the final written determination and the claims administrator has documentation of receipt.

(3) The date that is five (5) calendar days after the date of the United States postmark stamped on the envelope in which the final written determination was mailed if the final written determination is sent by mail and there is no proof of service or documentation of receipt.

(4) The date of resolution in favor of the provider of any issue of contested liability.

(5) The date of service of an order of the Workers' Compensation Appeal Board resolving in favor of the provider any threshold issue that would have precluded a provider's right to receive compensation for medical treatment services or goods provided in accordance with Labor Code section 4600 or for medical-legal expenses defined in Labor Code section 4620.

(d)(1) The request for independent bill review shall be made in one of the following manners:

(A) Completing and electronically submitting the online Request for Independent Bill Review form, which can be accessed on the Internet at the Division of Workers' Compensation's website. The website link for the online form can be found at http://www.dir.ca.gov/dwc/IBR.htm. Electronic payment of the required fee of $335.00 shall be made at the time the request is submitted.

(B) Mailing the Request for Independent Bill Review form, DWC Form IBR-1, set forth in section 9792.5.8, and simultaneously paying the required fee of $335.00 as instructed on the form.

(2) The provider shall include with the request form submitted under this subdivision, either by electronic upload or by mail, a copy of the following documents which shall be indexed and arranged so that each of the following categories of documents can be separately identified:

(A) The original billing itemization;

(B) Any supporting documents that were furnished with the original billing;

(C) If applicable, the relevant contract provisions for reimbursement rates under Labor Code section 5307.11;

(D) The explanation of review that accompanied the claims administrator's response to the original billing;

(E) The provider's request for second review of the claims administrator's original response to the billing;

(F) Any supporting documentation submitted to the claims administrator with that request for second review;

(G) The final written determination of the second review (explanation of review) issued by the claims administrator to the provider.

(e) The provider may request that two or more disputes that would each constitute a separate request for independent bill review be consolidated for a single determination under section 9792.5.12.

(f) The provider shall concurrently serve a copy of the request for independent bill review upon the claims administrator with a copy of the supporting documents submitted under subdivision (d). Any document that was previously provided to the claims administrator or originated from the claims administrator need not be served if a written description of the document and its date is served.

Note: Authority cited: Sections 133, 4603.6, 5307.3 and 5307.6, Labor Code. Reference: Sections 4060, 4061, 4061.5, 4062, 4600, 4603.2, 4603.3. 4603.4, 4603.6, 4620, 4621, 4622, 4625, 4628 and 5307.6, Labor Code.

History: 1. New section filed 12-31-2012 as an emergency; operative 1-1-2013 pursuant to Government Code section 11346.1(d) (Register 2013, No. 1). A Certificate of Compliance must be transmitted to OAL by 7-1-2013 or emergency language will be repealed by operation of law on the following day.

2. New section refiled 7-1-2013 as an emergency; operative 7-1-2013 (Register 2013, No. 27). A Certificate of Compliance must be transmitted to OAL by 9-30-2013 or emergency language will be repealed by operation of law on the following day.

3. New section refiled 9-30-2013 as an emergency; operative 10-1-2013 (Register 2013, No. 40). A Certificate of Compliance must be transmitted to OAL by 12-30-2013 or emergency language will be repealed by operation of law on the following day.

4. Certificate of Compliance as to 9-30-2013 order, including amendment of subsections (a)-(a)(2), (c), (d)(1)(A) and (d)(2), transmitted to OAL 12-30-2013 and filed 2-12-2014; amendments effective 2-12-2014 pursuant to Government Code section 11343.4(b)(3) (Register 2014, No. 7).

Ref.: Hanna § 5.02[2][e]; Herlick Handbook §§ 1.01[3][b], 4.10[3].

§9792.5.8. Request for Independent Bill Review Form.

Request for Independent Bill Review. DWC Form IBR-1.

[DWC Form IBR-1 (New 2/2014) Not Reproduced]

NOTE: Form is available at no charge by downloading from the web at www.dir.ca.gov/dwc/forms.html or by requesting at 1-800-794-6900.

History: 1. New section filed 12-31-2012 as an emergency; operative 1-1-2013 pursuant to Government Code section 11346.1(d) (Register 2013, No. 1). A Certificate of Compliance must be transmitted to OAL by 7-1-2013 or emergency language will be repealed by operation of law on the following day.

2. New section refiled 7-1-2013 as an emergency; operative 7-1-2013 (Register 2013, No. 27). A Certificate of Compliance must be transmitted to OAL by 9-30-2013 or emergency language will be repealed by operation of law on the following day.

3. New section refiled 9-30-2013 as an emergency; operative 10-1-2013 (Register 2013, No. 40). A Certificate of Compliance must be transmitted to OAL by 12-30-2013 or emergency language will be repealed by operation of law on the following day.

4. Certificate of Compliance as to 9-30-2013 order, including repealer and new DWC Form IBR-1, transmitted to OAL 12-30-2013 and filed 2-12-2014; amendments effective 2-12-2014 pursuant to Government Code section 11343.4(b)(3) (Register 2014, No. 7).

Ref.: Hanna § 5.02[2][e]; Herlick Handbook § 1.01[3][b].

§9792.5.9. Initial Review and Assignment of Request for Independent Bill Review to IBRO.

(a) Upon receipt of the Request for Independent Bill Review under section 9792.5.7, the Administrative Director, or his or her designee, shall conduct a preliminary review to determine whether the request is ineligible for review. In making this determination, the Administrative Director shall consider:

(1) The timeliness and completeness of the request;

(2) The date the medical treatment services or goods were rendered or the medical-legal expenses incurred;

(3) Whether the second request for review of the bill under section 9792.5.5 was timely requested by the provider;

(4) Whether the second review of the bill under section 9792.5.5 was timely completed by the claims administrator;

(5) Whether, for a bill for medical treatment services or goods, the medical treatment was authorized by the claims administrator under Labor Code section 4610.

(6) If the required fee for the review was paid pursuant to section 9792.5.7(d)(1)(A) or (B);

(7) Any previous or duplicate requests for independent bill review of the same bill for medical treatment services or bill for medical-legal expenses.

(8) If the dispute between the provider and the claims administrator is ineligible under section 9792.5.7(b) or contains any other issue than the amount of payment of the bill.

(b) If the request appears eligible for review, the Administrative Director, or his or her designee, shall within fifteen (15) days of the determination, notify the provider and the claims administrator by the most efficient means available that request for independent bill review has been submitted and appears eligible for assignment to an IBRO. The notification shall contain:

(1) An independent bill review case or identification number;

(2) The date the Request for Independent Bill Review, DWC Form IBR-1, was received by the Administrative Director

(3) A statement that the claims administrator may dispute both eligibility of the request for independent bill review under subdivision (a) and the provider's reason for requesting independent bill review by submitting a statement with supporting documents, and that the Administrative Director or his or her designee must receive the statement and supporting documents within fifteen (15) calendar days of the date designated on the notification, if the notification was provided by mail, or within twelve (12) calendar days of the date designated on the notification if the notification was provided electronically.

(c) Any document filed with the Administrative Director, or his or her designee, under subdivision (b)(3) must be concurrently served on the provider. Any document that was previously provided to the provider or originated from the provider need not be served if a written description of the document and its date is served.

(d) Upon receipt of the documents requested in subdivision (b)(3), or, if no documents have been received, upon the expiration of fifteen (15) days of the date designated on the notification, if the notification was provided by mail, or within twelve (12) days of the date designated on the notification if the notification was provided electronically, the Administrative Director, or his or her designee, shall conduct a further review in order to make a determination as to whether the request is ineligible for independent bill review under subdivision (a).

(e) If the review conducted under either subdivision (a) or subdivision (d) finds that the request is ineligible for independent bill review, the Administrative Director shall, within fifteen (15) days following receipt of the documents requested in subdivision (b)(3) or, if no documents are received, the expiration of the time period indicated above, issue a written determination informing the provider and claims administrator that the request is not eligible for independent bill review and the reasons therefor.

(1) If a request is deemed ineligible under this section, the provider shall be reimbursed the amount of $270.00.

(2) The provider or the claims administrator may appeal an eligibility determination by the Administrative Director by filing a petition with the Workers' Compensation Appeals Board and serving a copy on all interested parties, including the Administrative Director, within 30 days of receipt of the determination.

(f) If the Administrative Director or his or her designee determines from the review conducted under subdivision (d), that the request is eligible for independent bill review, the Administrative Director shall assign the request to an IBRO for an independent bill review. Upon assignment of the request, the IBRO shall notify the parties in writing that the request has been assigned to that organization for review. The notification shall contain:

(1) The name and address of the IBRO;

(2) An independent bill review case or identification number;

(3) Identification of the claim and disputed amount of payment made by the claims administrator on a bill for medical treatment services submitted pursuant to Labor Code sections 4603.2 or 4603.4, or bill for medical-legal expenses submitted pursuant to Labor Code section 4622,

(g) After the assignment to the IBRO, the request shall immediately be assigned to an independent bill reviewer who does not have any material professional, familial, or financial affiliation with any of the individuals, institutions, facilities, services or products as described in Labor Code section 139.5(c)(2) to review and resolve the dispute.

(h) If in the course of conducting an independent bill review it is determined that the bill reviewer assigned to the dispute has a prohibited interest as described in in Labor Code Section 139.5(c)(2), the IBRO shall reassign the matter to a different independent bill reviewer.

(i) Upon reassignment under subdivision (h), the IBRO shall immediately notify the Administrative Director, the provider, and claims administrator of the reassignment of the dispute to a different independent bill reviewer.

Note: Authority cited: Sections 133, 4603.6, 5307.3 and 5307.6, Labor Code. Reference: Sections 4060, 4061, 4061.5, 4062, 4600, 4603.2, 4603.3. 4603.4, 4603.6, 4620, 4621, 4622, 4625, 4628 and 5307.6, Labor Code.

History: 1. New section filed 12-31-2012 as an emergency; operative 1-1-2013 pursuant to Government Code section 11346.1(d) (Register 2013, No. 1). A Certificate of Compliance must be transmitted to OAL by 7-1-2013 or emergency language will be repealed by operation of law on the following day.

2. New section refiled 7-1-2013 as an emergency; operative 7-1-2013 (Register 2013, No. 27). A Certificate of Compliance must be transmitted to OAL by 9-30-2013 or emergency language will be repealed by operation of law on the following day.

3. New section refiled 9-30-2013 as an emergency; operative 10-1-2013 (Register 2013, No. 40). A Certificate of Compliance must be transmitted to OAL by 12-30-2013 or emergency language will be repealed by operation of law on the following day.

4. Certificate of Compliance as to 9-30-2013 order, including amendment of section, transmitted to OAL 12-30-2013 and filed 2-12-2014; amendments effective 2-12-2014 pursuant to Government Code section 11343.4(b)(3) (Register 2014, No. 7).

Ref.: Hanna § 5.02[2][e]; Herlick Handbook §§ 1.01[3][b], 4.10[3].

§9792.5.10. Independent Bill Review — Document Filing.

(a) The independent bill reviewer assigned the request shall review all information provided by the parties to determine if any additional information is necessary to resolve the dispute. If the independent bill reviewer determines that additional information is necessary, the independent bill reviewer shall contact the claims administrator and the provider in writing to request the information.

(b) If the independent bill reviewer requests information from either the claims administrator or the provider, or both, the party shall file the documents with the independent bill reviewer at the address listed in the correspondence in Section 9792.5.9(f). The requested documents must be received within 35 days of the request, if the request is made by mail, or 32 days of the request, if the request is made electronically. The filing party shall concurrently serve the non-filing party with the documents requested by the independent bill reviewer.

(C) Except for the documents submitted under this section, and those requested under section 9792.5.12, neither the provider nor the claims administrator shall file any additional documents with the independent bill reviewer.

Note: Authority cited: Sections 133, 4603.6, 5307.3 and 5307.6, Labor Code. Reference: Sections 4060, 4061, 4061.5, 4062, 4600, 4603.2, 4603.3. 4603.4, 4603.6, 4620, 4621, 4622, 4625, 4628 and 5307.6, Labor Code.

History: 1. New section filed 12-31-2012 as an emergency; operative 1-1-2013 pursuant to Government Code section 11346.1(d) (Register 2013, No. 1). A Certificate of Compliance must be transmitted to OAL by 7-1-2013 or emergency language will be repealed by operation of law on the following day.

2. New section refiled 7-1-2013 as an emergency; operative 7-1-2013 (Register 2013, No. 27). A Certificate of Compliance must be transmitted to OAL by 9-30-2013 or emergency language will be repealed by operation of law on the following day.

3. New section refiled 9-30-2013 as an emergency; operative 10-1-2013 (Register 2013, No. 40). A Certificate of Compliance must be transmitted to OAL by 12-30-2013 or emergency language will be repealed by operation of law on the following day.

4. Certificate of Compliance as to 9-30-2013 order, including amendment of subsection (b), transmitted to OAL 12-30-2013 and filed 2-12-2014; amendments effective 2-12-2014 pursuant to Government Code section 11343.4(b)(3) (Register 2014, No. 7).

Ref.: Hanna § 5.02[2][e]; Herlick Handbook §§ 1.01[3][b], 4.10[3].

§9792.5.11. Withdrawal of Independent Bill Review.

The provider may, concurrent with written notice to the claims administrator, withdraw a request for independent bill review at any time prior to the issuance of a final determination on the amount of payment owed under section 9792.5.14.

(a) If the request is withdrawn prior to its assignment to an IBRO for an independent bill review under section 9792.5.9(f), the provider shall be reimbursed the amount of $270.00 from the fee provided with the request under section 9792.5.7(d).

(b) If the request is withdrawn subsequent to its assignment to an IBRO for an independent bill review under section 9792.5.9(f), the provider shall not be reimbursed the fee provided with the request under section 9792.5.7(d).

Note: Authority cited: Sections 133, 4603.6, 5307.3 and 5307.6, Labor Code. Reference: Sections 4060, 4061, 4061.5, 4062, 4600, 4603.2, 4603.3. 4603.4, 4603.6, 4620, 4621, 4622, 4625, 4628 and 5307.6, Labor Code.

History: 1. New section filed 12-31-2012 as an emergency; operative 1-1-2013 pursuant to Government Code section 11346.1(d) (Register 2013, No. 1). A Certificate of Compliance must be transmitted to OAL by 7-1-2013 or emergency language will be repealed by operation of law on the following day.

2. New section refiled 7-1-2013 as an emergency; operative 7-1-2013 (Register 2013, No. 27). A Certificate of Compliance must be transmitted to OAL by 9-30-2013 or emergency language will be repealed by operation of law on the following day.

3. New section refiled 9-30-2013 as an emergency; operative 10-1-2013 (Register 2013, No. 40). A Certificate of Compliance must be transmitted to OAL by 12-30-2013 or emergency language will be repealed by operation of law on the following day.

4. Certificate of Compliance as to 9-30-2013 order, including amendment of section, transmitted to OAL 12-30-2013 and filed 2-12-2014; amendments effective 2-12-2014 pursuant to Government Code section 11343.4(b)(3) (Register 2014, No. 7).

Ref.: Hanna § 5.02[2][e]; Herlick Handbook §§ 1.01[3][b], 4.10[3].

§9792.5.12. Independent Bill Review — Consolidation or Separation of Requests.

(a) With a request for independent bill review submitted under section 9792.5.7, a provider may request combining two or more requests, with a maximum of twenty (20), for independent bill review for the purpose of having the payment reductions contested in each request resolved in a single determination issued under section 9792.5.14.

(b) In applying this section, the following definitions shall be used:

(1) "Common issues of law and fact" means the denial or reduction of the amount of payment in each request was made for similar reasons and arose from a similar fact pattern material to the reason for the denial or reduction.

(2) "Delivery of similar or related services" means like or coordinated medical treatment services or goods, or medical-legal services, provided to one or more injured employees.

(c) Two or more requests, with a maximum of twenty (20), for independent bill review by a single provider may be consolidated if the Administrative Director or the IBRO determines that the requests involve common issues of law and fact or the delivery of similar or related services.

(1) Requests for independent bill review by a single provider involving multiple dates of medical treatment or medical-legal services may be consolidated and treated as one single independent bill review request if the requests involve one injured employee, one claims administrator, and one billing code under an applicable fee schedule adopted by the Administrative Director, or, if applicable, under a contract for reimbursement rates under Labor Code section 5307.11, and the total amount in dispute does not exceed $4,000.00.

(2) Requests for independent bill review by a single provider involving multiple billing codes under applicable fee schedules adopted by the Administrative Director or, if applicable, under a contract for reimbursement rates under Labor Code section 5307.11, may be consolidated with no limit on the total dollar amount in dispute and treated as one request if the request involves one injured employee, one claims administrator, and one date of medical treatment service.

(3) After consultation with the Administrative Director, the IBRO may allow the consolidation of requests or independent bill review by a single provider showing a possible pattern and practice of underpayment by a claims administrator for specific billing codes. Requests to be consolidated under the subdivision shall involve multiple injured employees, one claim administrator, one billing code, one or multiple dates of service, and aggregated amounts in dispute up to $4,000.00 or individual amounts in dispute less than $50.00 each.

(d) Upon filing a request for independent bill review under section 9792.5.7, the provider, if requesting the consolidation of separate requests, shall, in addition to providing the filing fee of $335.00, specify all of the requests for independent bill review sought to be consolidated with a description of how the requests involve common issues of law and fact or delivery of similar or related services. Once consolidation has been granted no other disputes shall be added to the consolidated disputes.

(e) The IBRO may disaggregate into separate independent bill review requests a single request that does not meet the standards set forth in subdivision (c) of this section. For any independent bill review request that must be disaggregated, the same fee shall be charged for each additional independent bill review request as charged for one independent bill review request.

(1) If an independent bill review request must be separated, the IBRO shall immediately provide notice in writing to the provider and claims administrator stating the reasons for disaggregation, and shall inform the provider of the additional fee or fees required to perform the independent bill review.

(2) Within ten (10) days following receipt of the notification informing the provider of the separation of requests, the provider shall submit to the IBRO any additional fee or fees necessary to conduct independent bill review. The failure to provide the additional fee or fees shall subject the request to a determination of ineligibility under section 9792.5.9.

(f) Nothing in this section shall extend the time for issuing a determination required by Labor Code section 4603.6 (e).

Note: Authority cited: Sections 133, 4603.6, 5307.3 and 5307.6, Labor Code. Reference: Sections 4060, 4061, 4061.5, 4062, 4600, 4603.2, 4603.3. 4603.4, 4603.6, 4620, 4621, 4622, 4625, 4628 and 5307.6, Labor Code.

History: 1. New section filed 12-31-2012 as an emergency; operative 1-1-2013 pursuant to Government Code section 11346.1(d) (Register 2013, No. 1). A Certificate of Compliance must be transmitted to OAL by 7-1-2013 or emergency language will be repealed by operation of law on the following day.

2. New section refiled 7-1-2013 as an emergency; operative 7-1-2013 (Register 2013, No. 27). A Certificate of Compliance must be transmitted to OAL by 9-30-2013 or emergency language will be repealed by operation of law on the following day.

3. New section refiled 9-30-2013 as an emergency; operative 10-1-2013 (Register 2013, No. 40). A Certificate of Compliance must be transmitted to OAL by 12-30-2013 or emergency language will be repealed by operation of law on the following day.

4. Certificate of Compliance as to 9-30-2013 order, including amendment of subsections (a), (b)(2)-(c)(1) and (c)(3), transmitted to OAL 12-30-2013 and filed 2-12-2014; amendments effective 2-12-2014 pursuant to Government Code section 11343.4(b)(3) (Register 2014, No. 7).

Ref.: Hanna § 5.02[2][e]; Herlick Handbook §§ 1.01[3][b], 4.10[3].

§9792.5.13. Independent Bill Review — Review.

(a) If the request for independent bill review involves the application of the Official Medical Fee Schedule (OMFS) for the payment of medical treatment services or goods as defined in Labor Code section 4600, the independent bill reviewer shall apply the provisions of sections 9789.10 to 9789.111 to determine the additional amounts, if any, that are to be paid to the provider.

(b) If the request for independent bill review involves the application of a contract for reimbursement rates under Labor Code section 5307.11 for the payment of medical treatment services as defined in Labor Code section 4600, the independent bill reviewer shall apply the contract to determine the additional amounts, if any, that are to be paid to the provider.

(c) If the request for independent bill review involves the application of the Medical-Legal Fee Schedule (M/L Fee Schedule) for services defined in Labor Code section 4620, the independent bill reviewer shall apply the provisions of sections 9793–9795 and 9795.1 to 9795.4 to determine the additional amounts, if any, that are to be paid to the provider.

(d) In applying this section, the independent bill reviewer shall apply the provisions of the OMFS, the M/L Fee Schedule, and, if applicable, the contract for reimbursement rates under Labor Code section 5307.11, as if the bill is being reviewed for the first time. The independent bill review shall also apply as necessary all billing, payment, and coding rules adopted under this Article.

Note: Authority cited: Sections 133, 4603.6, 5307.3 and 5307.6, Labor Code. Reference: Sections 4060, 4061, 4061.5, 4062, 4600, 4603.2, 4603.3. 4603.4, 4603.6, 4620, 4621, 4622, 4625, 4628 and 5307.6, Labor Code.

History: 1. New section filed 12-31-2012 as an emergency; operative 1-1-2013 pursuant to Government Code section 11346.1(d) (Register 2013, No. 1). A Certificate of Compliance must be transmitted to OAL by 7-1-2013 or emergency language will be repealed by operation of law on the following day.

2. New section refiled 7-1-2013 as an emergency; operative 7-1-2013 (Register 2013, No. 27). A Certificate of Compliance must be transmitted to OAL by 9-30-2013 or emergency language will be repealed by operation of law on the following day.

3. New section refiled 9-30-2013 as an emergency; operative 10-1-2013 (Register 2013, No. 40). A Certificate of Compliance must be transmitted to OAL by 12-30-2013 or emergency language will be repealed by operation of law on the following day.

4. Certificate of Compliance as to 9-30-2013 order, including amendment of subsection (d), transmitted to OAL 12-30-2013 and filed 2-12-2014; amendments effective 2-12-2014 pursuant to Government Code section 11343.4(b)(3) (Register 2014, No. 7).

Ref.: Hanna § 5.02[2][e]; Herlick Handbook §§ 1.01[3][b], 4.10[3].

§9792.5.14. Independent Bill Review — Determination.

(a) Within sixty (60) days of the assignment of a dispute to an independent bill reviewer under section 9792.5.9(g), the reviewer shall issue a written determination, in plain language, if any additional amount of money is owed the provider under the request for independent bill review. The determination shall state the reasons for the determination and the information received and relied upon by the independent bill reviewer in rendering the determination.

(b) If the independent bill reviewer finds any additional amount of money is owed to the provider, the determination shall also order the claims administrator to reimburse the provider the amount of the filing fee in addition to any additional payments for services found owing.

(c) The independent bill reviewer shall serve the determination on the provider, the claims administrator and the Administrative Director.

(d) The determination issued by the independent bill reviewer shall be deemed to be the determination of the Administrative Director and shall be binding on all parties.

Note: Authority cited: Sections 133, 4603.6, 5307.3 and 5307.6, Labor Code. Reference: Sections 4060, 4061, 4061.5, 4062, 4600, 4603.2, 4603.3. 4603.4, 4603.6, 4620, 4621, 4622, 4625, 4628 and 5307.6, Labor Code.

History: 1. New section filed 12-31-2012 as an emergency; operative 1-1-2013 pursuant to Government Code section 11346.1(d) (Register 2013, No. 1). A Certificate of Compliance must be transmitted to OAL by 7-1-2013 or emergency language will be repealed by operation of law on the following day.

2. New section refiled 7-1-2013 as an emergency; operative 7-1-2013 (Register 2013, No. 27). A Certificate of Compliance must be transmitted to OAL by 9-30-2013 or emergency language will be repealed by operation of law on the following day.

3. New section refiled 9-30-2013 as an emergency; operative 10-1-2013 (Register 2013, No. 40). A Certificate of Compliance must be transmitted to OAL by 12-30-2013 or emergency language will be repealed by operation of law on the following day.

4. Certificate of Compliance as to 9-30-2013 order transmitted to OAL 12-30-2013 and filed 2-12-2014 (Register 2014, No. 7).

Ref.: Hanna § 5.02[2][e]; Herlick Handbook §§ 1.01[3][b], 4.10[3].

§9792.5.15. Independent Bill Review — Implementation of Determination and Appeal.

(a) Upon receiving the determination of the Administrative Director that an additional amount of money is owed to the provider on a bill for medical treatment services submitted pursuant to Labor Code sections 4603.2 or 4603.4, or bill for medical-legal expenses submitted pursuant to Labor Code section 4622, the claims administrator shall, unless appealed under subdivision (b), pay the additional amounts set forth in the determination per the timely payment requirements set forth in Labor Code sections 4603.2 and 4603.4.

(b) Pursuant to Labor Code section 4603.6(f), the provider or the claims administrator may appeal a determination of the Administrative Director under section 9792.5.14 by filing a petition with the Workers' Compensation Appeals Board.

(c) If the final determination of the Administrative Director is reversed by the Workers' Compensation Appeals Board, the dispute shall be remanded to the Administrative Director. The Administrative Director shall:

(1) Submit the dispute to independent bill review by a different IBRO, if available;

(2) If a different IBRO is not available after remand, the Administrative Director shall submit the dispute to the original IBRO for review by a different reviewer in the organization.

Note: Authority cited: Sections 133, 4603.6, 5307.3 and 5307.6, Labor Code. Reference: Sections 4060, 4061, 4061.5, 4062, 4600, 4603.2, 4603.3. 4603.4, 4603.6, 4620, 4621, 4622, 4625, 4628 and 5307.6, Labor Code.

History: 1. New section filed 12-31-2012 as an emergency; operative 1-1-2013 pursuant to Government Code section 11346.1(d) (Register 2013, No. 1). A Certificate of Compliance must be transmitted to OAL by 7-1-2013 or emergency language will be repealed by operation of law on the following day.

2. New section refiled 7-1-2013 as an emergency; operative 7-1-2013 (Register 2013, No. 27). A Certificate of Compliance must be transmitted to OAL by 9-30-2013 or emergency language will be repealed by operation of law on the following day.

3. New section refiled 9-30-2013 as an emergency; operative 10-1-2013 (Register 2013, No. 40). A Certificate of Compliance must be transmitted to OAL by 12-30-2013 or emergency language will be repealed by operation of law on the following day.

4. Certificate of Compliance as to 9-30-2013 order, including amendment of section, transmitted to OAL 12-30-2013 and filed 2-12-2014; amendments effective 2-12-2014 pursuant to Government Code section 11343.4(b)(3) (Register 2014, No. 7).

Ref.: Hanna § 5.02[2][e]; Herlick Handbook §§ 1.01[3][b], 4.10[3].

ARTICLE 5.5.1 Utilization Review Standards

§9792.6. Utilization Review Standards— Definitions — For Utilization Review Decisions Issued Prior to July 1, 2013 for Injuries Occurring Prior to January 1, 2013.

The following definitions apply to any request for authorization of medical treatment, made under Article 5.5.1 of this Subchapter, for an occupational injury or illness occurring prior to January 1, 2013 if the decision on the request is communicated to the requesting physician prior to July 1, 2013.

(a) "ACOEM Practice Guidelines" means the American College of Occupational and Environmental Medicine's Occupational Medicine Practice Guidelines, Second Edition.

(b) "Authorization" means assurance that appropriate reimbursement will be made for an approved specific course of proposed medical treatment to cure or relieve the effects of the industrial injury pursuant to section 4600 of the Labor Code, subject to the provisions of section 5402 of the Labor Code, based on the "Doctor's First Report of Occupational Injury or Illness," Form DLSR 5021, or on the "Primary Treating Physician's Progress Report," DWC Form PR-2, as contained in section 9785.2, or in narrative form containing the same information required in the DWC Form PR-2.

(c) "Claims Administrator" is a self-administered workers' compensation insurer, an insured employer, a self-administered self-insured employer, a self-administered legally uninsured employer, a self-administered joint powers authority, a third-party claims administrator or other entity subject to Labor Code section 4610. The claims administrator may utilize an entity contracted to conduct its utilization review responsibilities.

(d) "Concurrent review" means utilization review conducted during an inpatient stay.

(e) "Course of treatment" means the course of medical treatment set forth in the treatment plan contained on the "Doctor's First Report of Occupational Injury or Illness," Form DLSR 5021, or on the "Primary Treating Physician's Progress Report," DWC Form PR-2, as contained in section 9785.2 or in narrative form containing the same information required in the DWC Form PR-2.

(f) "Dispute liability" means an assertion by the claims administrator that a factual, medical, or legal basis exists that precludes compensability on the part of the claims administrator for an occupational injury, a claimed injury to any part or parts of the body, or a requested medical treatment.

(g) "Emergency health care services" means health care services for a medical condition manifesting itself by acute symptoms of sufficient severity such that the absence of immediate medical attention could reasonably be expected to place the patient's health in serious jeopardy.

(h) "Expedited review" means utilization review conducted when the injured worker's condition is such that the injured worker faces an imminent and serious threat to his or her health, including, but not limited to, the potential loss of life, limb, or other major bodily function, or the normal timeframe for the decision-making process would be detrimental to the injured worker's life or health or could jeopardize the injured worker's permanent ability to regain maximum function.

(i) "Expert reviewer" means a medical doctor, doctor of osteopathy, psychologist, acupuncturist, optometrist, dentist, podiatrist, or chiropractic practitioner licensed by any state or the District of Columbia, competent to evaluate the specific clinical issues involved in the medical treatment services and where these services are within the individual's scope of practice, who has been consulted by the reviewer or the utilization review medical director to provide specialized review of medical information.

(j) "Health care provider" means a provider of medical services, as well as related services or goods, including but not limited to an individual provider or facility, a health care service plan, a health care organization, a member of a preferred provider organization or medical provider network as provided in Labor Code section 4616.

(k) "Immediately" means within 24 hours after learning the circumstances that would require an extension of the timeframe for decisions specified in subdivisions (b)(1), (b)(2) or (c) and (g)(1) of section 9792.9.

(*l*) "Material modification" is when the claims administrator changes utilization review vendor or makes a change to the utilization review standards as specified in section 9792.7.

(m) "Medical Director" is the physician and surgeon licensed by the Medical Board of California or the Osteopathic Board of California who holds an unrestricted license to practice medicine in the State of California. The Medical Director is responsible for all decisions made in the utilization review process.

(n) "Medical services" means those goods and services provided pursuant to Article 2 (commencing with Labor Code section 4600) of Chapter 2 of Part 2 of Division 4 of the Labor Code.

(o) "Medical Treatment Utilization Schedule" means the standards of care adopted by the Administrative Director pursuant to Labor Code section 5307.27 and set forth in Article 5.5.2 of this Subchapter, beginning with section 9792.20.

(p) "Prospective review" means any utilization review conducted, except for utilization review conducted during an inpatient stay, prior to the delivery of the requested medical services.

(q) "Request for authorization" means a written confirmation of an oral request for a specific course of proposed medical treatment pursuant to Labor Code section 4610(h) or a written request for a specific course of proposed medical treatment. An oral request for authorization must be followed by a written confirmation of the request within seventy-two (72) hours. Both the written confirmation of an oral request and the written request must be set forth on the "Doctor's First Report of Occupational Injury or Illness," Form DLSR 5021, section 14006, or on the Primary Treating Physician Progress Report, DWC Form PR-2, as contained in section 9785.2, or in narrative form containing the same information required in the PR-2 form. If a narrative format is used, the document shall be clearly marked at the top that it is a request for authorization.

(r) "Retrospective review" means utilization review conducted after medical services have been provided and for which approval has not already been given.

(s) "Reviewer" means a medical doctor, doctor of osteopathy, psychologist, acupuncturist, optometrist, dentist, podiatrist, or chiropractic practitioner licensed by any state or the District of Columbia, competent to evaluate the specific clinical issues involved in medical treatment services, where these services are within the scope of the reviewer's practice.

(t) "Utilization review plan" means the written plan filed with the Administrative Director pursuant to Labor Code section 4610, setting forth the policies and procedures, and a description of the utilization review process.

(u) "Utilization review process" means utilization management functions that prospectively, retrospectively, or concurrently review and approve, modify, delay, or deny, based in whole or in part on medical necessity to cure or relieve, treatment recommendations by physicians, as defined in Labor Code section 3209.3, prior to, retrospec tively, or concurrent with the provision of medical treatment services pursuant to Labor Code section 4600. Utilization review does not include determinations of the work-relatedness of injury or disease, or bill review for the purpose of determining whether the medical services were accurately billed.

(v) "Written" includes a facsimile as well as communications in paper form.

Note: Authority cited: Sections 133, 4603.5 and 5307.3, Labor Code. Reference: Sections 3209.3, 4062, 4600, 4600.4, 4604.5, 4610 and 4610.5, Labor Code.

History: 1. New section filed 7-20-95; operative 7-20-95. Submitted to OAL for printing only pursuant to Government Code section 11351 (Register 95, No. 29).

2. Amendment of subsections (a)(4), (c)(1), (c)(3)(iii)-(iv) and (c)(4)(i)-(iii) filed 11-9-98; operative 1-1-99 (Register 98, No. 46).

3. New article 5.5.1 (sections 9792.6-9792.11) and repealer and new section filed 12-9-2004 as an emergency; operative 12-13-2004 (Register 2004, No. 50). A Certificate of Compliance must be transmitted to OAL by 4-12-2005 or emergency language will be repealed by operation of law on the following day.

4. New article 5.5.1 (sections 9792.6-9792.11) and repealer and new section refiled 4-6-2005 as an emergency; operative 4-12-2005 (Register 2005, No. 14). A Certificate of Compliance must be transmitted to OAL by 8-10-2005 or emergency language will be repealed by operation of law on the following day.

5. Certificate of Compliance as to 4-6-2005 order, including amendment of section and Note, transmitted to OAL 8-10-2005 and filed 9-22-2005 (Register 2005, No. 38).

6. Amendment of section heading, repealer and new first paragraph and amendment of Note filed 12-31-2012 as an emergency; operative 1-1-2013 pursuant to Government Code section 11346.1(d) (Register 2013, No. 1). A Certificate of Compliance must be transmitted to OAL by 7-1-2013 or emergency language will be repealed by operation of law on the following day.

7. Amendment of section heading, repealer and new first paragraph and amendment of Note refiled 7-1-2013 as an emergency; operative 7-1-2013 (Register 2013, No. 27). A Certificate of Compliance must be transmitted to OAL by 9-30-2013 or emergency language will be repealed by operation of law on the following day.

8. Amendment of section heading, repealer and new first paragraph and amendment of Note refiled 9-30-2013 as an emergency; operative 10-1-2013 (Register 2013, No. 40). A Certificate of Compliance must be transmitted to OAL by 12-30-2013 or emergency language will be repealed by operation of law on the following day.

9. Certificate of Compliance as to 9-30-2013 order, including new subsections (f) and (o), subsection relettering and amendment of Note, transmitted to OAL 12-30-2013 and filed 2-12-2014; amendments effective 2-12-2014 pursuant to Government Code section 11343.4(b)(3) (Register 2014, No. 7).

Ref.: Herlick Handbook §§ 1.01[3][b], 4.08[5], 4.09[1], [2], [6], 4.16[3].

§9792.6.1. Utilization Review Standards—Definitions — On or After January 1, 2013.

The following definitions apply to any request for authorization of medical treatment, made under Article 5.5.1 of this Subchapter, for either: (1) an occupational injury or illness occurring on or after January 1, 2013; or (2) where the decision on the request for authorization of medical treatment is communicated to the requesting physician on or after July 1, 2013, regardless of the date of injury.

(a) "Authorization" means assurance that appropriate reimbursement will be made for an approved specific course of proposed medical treatment to cure or relieve the effects of the industrial injury pursuant to section 4600 of the Labor Code, subject to the provisions of section 5402 of the Labor Code, based on either a completed "Request for Authorization," DWC Form RFA, as contained in California Code of Regulations, title 8, section 9785.5, or a request for authorization of medical treatment accepted as complete by the claims administrator under section 9792.9.1(c)(2), that has been transmitted by the treating physician to the claims administrator. Authorization shall be given pursuant to the timeframe, procedure, and notice requirements of California Code of Regulations, title 8, section 9792.9.1, and may be provided by utilizing the indicated response section of the "Request for Authorization," DWC Form RFA if that form was initially submitted by the treating physician.

(b) "Claims Administrator" is a self-administered workers' compensation insurer of an insured employer, a self-administered self-insured employer, a self-administered legally uninsured employer, a self-administered joint powers authority, a third-party claims administrator or other entity subject to Labor Code section 4610, the California Insurance Guarantee Association, and the director of the Department of Industrial Relations as administrator for the Uninsured Employers Benefits Trust Fund (UEBTF). "Claims Administrator" includes any utilization review organization under contract to provide or conduct the claims administrator's utilization review responsibilities.

(c) "Concurrent review" means utilization review conducted during an inpatient stay.

(d) "Course of treatment" means the course of medical treatment set forth in the treatment plan contained on the "Doctor's First Report of Occupational Injury or Illness," Form DLSR 5021, found at California Code of Regulations, title 8, section 14006, or on the "Primary Treating Physician's Progress Report," DWC Form PR-2, as contained in section 9785.2 or in narrative form containing the same information required in the DWC Form PR-2.

(e) "Delay" means a determination, based on the need for additional evidence as set forth in section 9792.9.1(f), that the timeframe requirements for the utilization review process provided in section 9792.9.1(c) cannot be met.

(f) "Denial" means a decision by a physician reviewer that the requested treatment or service is is not authorized.

(g) "Dispute liability" means an assertion by the claims administrator that a factual, medical, or legal basis exists, other than medical necessity, that precludes compensability on the part of the claims administrator for an occupational injury, a claimed injury to any part or parts of the body, or a requested medical treatment.

(h) "Disputed medical treatment" means medical treatment that has been modified, or denied by a utilization review decision.

(i) "Emergency health care services" means health care services for a medical condition manifesting itself by acute symptoms of sufficient severity such that the absence of immediate medical attention could reasonably be expected to place the patient's health in serious jeopardy.

(j) "Expedited review" means utilization review or independent medical review conducted when the injured worker's condition is such that the injured worker faces an imminent and serious threat to his or her health, including, but not limited to, the potential loss of life, limb, or other major bodily function, or the normal timeframe for the decision-making process would be detrimental to the injured worker's life or health or could jeopardize the injured worker's permanent ability to regain maximum function.

(k) "Expert reviewer" means a medical doctor, doctor of osteopathy, psychologist, acupuncturist, optometrist, dentist, podiatrist, or chiropractic practitioner licensed by any state or the District of Columbia, competent to evaluate the specific clinical issues involved in the medical treatment services and where these services are within the individual's scope of practice, who has been consulted by the reviewer or the utilization review medical director to provide specialized review of medical information.

(*l*) "Health care provider" means a provider of medical services, as well as related services or goods, including but not limited to an individual provider or facility, a health care service plan, a health care organization, a member of a preferred provider organization or medical provider network as provided in Labor Code section 4616.

(m) "Immediately" means within one business day.

(n) "Material modification" is when the claims administrator changes utilization review vendor or makes a change to the utilization review standards as specified in section 9792.7.

(o) "Medical Director" is the physician and surgeon licensed by the Medical Board of California or the Osteopathic Board of California who holds an unrestricted license to practice medicine in the State of California. The Medical Director is responsible for all decisions made in the utilization review process.

(p) "Medical services" means those goods and services provided pursuant to Article 2 (commencing with Labor Code section 4600) of Chapter 2 of Part 2 of Division 4 of the Labor Code.

(q) "Medical Treatment Utilization Schedule" means the standards of care adopted by the Administrative Director pursuant to Labor Code section 5307.27 and set forth in Article 5.5.2 of this Subchapter, beginning with section 9792.20.

(r) "Modification" means a decision by a physician reviewer that part of the requested treatment or service is not medically necessary.

(s) "Prospective review" means any utilization review conducted, except for utilization review conducted during an inpatient stay, prior to the delivery of the requested medical services

(t) "Request for authorization" means a written request for a specific course of proposed medical treatment.

(1) Unless accepted by a claims administrator under section 9792.9.1(c)(2), a request for authorization must be set forth on a "Request for Authorization (DWC Form RFA)," completed by a treating physician, as contained in California Code of Regulations, title 8, section 9785.5. Prior to March 1, 2014, any version of the DWC Form RFA adopted by the Administrative Director under section 9785.5 may be used by the treating physician to request medical treatment.

(2) "Completed," for the purpose of this section and for purposes of investigations and penalties, means that the request for authorization must identify both the employee and the provider, identify with specificity a recommended treatment or treatments, and be accompanied by documentation substantiating the need for the requested treatment.

(3) The request for authorization must be signed by the treating physician and may be mailed, faxed or e-mailed to, if designated, the address, fax number, or e-mail address designated by the claims administrator for this purpose. By agreement of the parties, the treating physician may submit the request for authorization with an electronic signature.

(u) "Retrospective review" means utilization review conducted after medical services have been provided and for which approval has not already been given.

(v) "Reviewer" means a medical doctor, doctor of osteopathy, psychologist, acupuncturist, optometrist, dentist, podiatrist, or chiropractic practitioner licensed by any state or the District of Columbia, competent to evaluate the specific clinical issues involved in medical treatment services, where these services are within the scope of the reviewer's practice.

(w) "Utilization review decision" means a decision pursuant to Labor Code section 4610 to approve, modify, delay, or deny, a treatment recommendation or recommendations by a physician prior to, retrospectively, or concurrent with the provision of medical treatment services pursuant to Labor Code sections 4600 or 5402(c).

(x) "Utilization review plan" means the written plan filed with the Administrative Director pursuant to Labor Code section 4610, setting forth the policies and procedures, and a description of the utilization review process.

(y) "Utilization review process" means utilization management functions that prospectively, retrospectively, or concurrently review and approve, modify, delay, or deny, based in whole or in part on medical necessity to cure or relieve, treatment recommendations by physicians, as defined in Labor Code section 3209.3, prior to, retrospectively, or concurrent with the provision of medical treatment services pursuant to Labor Code section 4600. The utilization review process begins when the completed DWC Form RFA, or a request for authorization accepted as complete under section 9792.9.1(c)(2), is first received by the claims administrator, or in the case of prior authorization, when the treating physician satisfies the conditions described in the utilization review plan for prior authorization.

(z) "Written" includes a communication transmitted by facsimile or in paper form. Electronic mail may be used by agreement of the parties although an employee's health records shall not be transmitted via electronic mail.

Note: Authority cited: Sections 133, 4603.5 and 5307.3, Labor Code. Reference: Sections 3209.3, 4062, 4600, 4600.4, 4604.5, 4610 and 4610.5, Labor Code.

History: 1. New section filed 12-31-2012 as an emergency; operative 1-1-2013 pursuant to Government Code section 11346.1(d) (Register 2013, No. 1). A Certificate of Compliance must be transmitted to OAL by 7-1-2013 or emergency language will be repealed by operation of law on the following day.

2. New section refiled 7-1-2013 as an emergency; operative 7-1-2013 (Register 2013, No. 27). A Certificate of Compliance must be transmitted to OAL by 9-30-2013 or emergency language will be repealed by operation of law on the following day.

3. New section refiled 9-30-2013 as an emergency; operative 10-1-2013 (Register 2013, No. 40). A Certificate of Compliance must be transmitted to OAL by 12-30-2013 or emergency language will be repealed by operation of law on the following day.

4. Certificate of Compliance as to 9-30-2013 order, including amendment of section, transmitted to OAL 12-30-2013 and filed 2-12-2014; amendments effective 2-12-2014 pursuant to Government Code section 11343.4(b)(3) (Register 2014, No. 7).

Ref.: Herlick Handbook §§ 1.01[3][b], 4.08[5], 4.09[1], [2], [4], 4.16[3].

§9792.7. Utilization Review Standards—Applicability.

(a) Effective January 1, 2004, every claims administrator shall establish and maintain a utilization review process for treatment rendered on or after January 1, 2004, regardless of date of injury, in compliance with Labor Code section 4610. Each utilization review process shall be set forth in a utilization review plan which shall contain:

(1) The name, address, phone number, and medical license number of the employed or designated medical director, who holds an unrestricted license to practice medicine in the state of California issued pursuant to section 2050 or section 2450 of the Business and Professions Code.

(2) A description of the process whereby requests for authorization are reviewed, and decisions on such requests are made, and a description of the process for handling expedited reviews.

(3) A description of the specific criteria utilized routinely in the review and throughout the decision-making process, including treatment protocols or standards used in the process. The treatment protocols or standards governing the utilization review process shall be consistent with the Medical Treatment Utilization Schedule adopted by the Administrative Director pursuant to Labor Code section 5307.27.

(4) A description of the qualifications and functions of the personnel involved in decision-making and implementation of the utilization review plan.

(5) A description of the claims administrator's practice, if applicable, of any prior authorization process, including but not limited to, where authorization is provided without the submission of the request for authorization.

(b)(1) The medical director shall ensure that the process by which the claims administrator reviews and approves, modifies, delays, or denies requests by physicians prior to, retrospectively, or concurrent with the provision of medical services, complies with Labor Code section 4610 and these implementing regulations.

(2) A reviewer who is competent to evaluate the specific clinical issues involved in the medical treatment services, and where these services are within the reviewer's scope of practice, may, except as indicated below, delay, modify or deny, requests for authorization of medical treatment for reasons of medical necessity to cure or relieve the effects of the industrial injury.

(3) A non-physician reviewer may be used to initially apply specified criteria to requests for authorization for medical services. A non-physician reviewer may approve requests for authorization of medical services. A non physician reviewer may discuss applicable criteria with the requesting physician, should the treatment for which authorization is sought appear to be inconsistent with the criteria. In such instances, the requesting physician may voluntarily withdraw a portion or all of the treatment in question and submit an amended request for treatment authorization, and the non-physician reviewer may approve the amended request for treatment authorization. Additionally, a non-physician reviewer may reasonably request appropriate additional information that is necessary to render a decision but in no event shall this exceed the time limitations imposed in section 9792.9(c)(1), (c)(2), or (d), or section 9792.9.1(c) and (d). Any time beyond the time specified in these sections is subject to the provisions of section 9792.9(h) or section 9792.9.1(f).

(c) The complete utilization review plan, consisting of the policies and procedures, and a description of the utilization review process, shall be filed by the claims administrator, or by the external utilization review organization contracted by the claims administrator to perform the utilization review, with the Administrative Director. In lieu of filing the utilization review plan, the claims administrator may submit a letter identifying the external utilization review organization which has been contracted to perform the utilization review functions, provided that the utilization review organization has filed a complete utilization review plan with the Administrative Director. A modified utilization review plan shall be filed with the Administrative Director within 30 calendar days after the claims administrator makes a material modification to the plan.

(d) Upon request by the public, the claims administrator shall make available the complete utilization review plan, consisting of the policies and procedures, and a description of the utilization review process.

(1) The claims administrator may make available the complete utilization review plan, consisting of the policies and procedures and a description of the utilization review process, through electronic means. If a member of the public requests a hard copy of the utilization review plan, the claims administrator may charge reasonable copying and postage expenses related to disclosing the complete utilization review plan. Such charge shall not exceed $0.25 per page plus actual postage costs.

Note: Authority cited: Sections 133, 4603.5 and 5307.3, Labor Code. Reference: Sections 4062, 4600, 4600.4, 4604.5 and 4610, Labor Code.

History: 1. New section filed 12-9-2004 as an emergency; operative 12-13-2004 (Register 2004, No. 50). A Certificate of Compliance must be transmitted to OAL by 4-12-2005 or emergency language will be repealed by operation of law on the following day.

2. New section refiled 4-6-2005 as an emergency; operative 4-12-2005 (Register 2005, No. 14). A Certificate of Compliance must be transmitted to OAL by 8-10-2005 or emergency language will be repealed by operation of law on the following day.

3. Certificate of Compliance as to 4-6-2005 order, including amendment of section, transmitted to OAL 8-10-2005 and filed 9-22-2005 (Register 2005, No. 38).

4. Amendment filed 2-12-2014; operative 2-12-2014 pursuant to Government Code section 11343.4(b)(3) (Register 2014, No. 7).

Ref.: Hanna §§ 5.02[2][c], 22.05[6][c]; Herlick Handbook §§ 1.01[3][b], 4.09[1], [2], 4.16[3].

§9792.8. Utilization Review Standards—Medically-Based Criteria.

(a)(1) The criteria shall be consistent with the schedule for medical treatment utilization adopted pursuant to Labor Code section 5307.27. Prior to adoption of the schedule, the criteria or guidelines used in the utilization review process shall be consistent with the American College of Occupational and Environmental Medicine's (ACOEM) Practice Guidelines, Second Edition. The guidelines set forth in the ACOEM Practice Guidelines shall be presumptively correct on the issue of extent and scope of medical treatment until the effective date of the utilization schedule adopted pursuant to Labor Code section 5307.27. The presumption is rebuttable and may be controverted by a preponderance of the scientific medical evidence establishing that a variance from the guidelines is reasonably required to cure or relieve the injured worker from the effects of his or her injury.

(2) For all conditions or injuries not addressed by the ACOEM Practice Guidelines or by the official utilization schedule after adoption pursuant to Labor Code section 5307.27, authorized treatment shall be in accordance with other evidence-based medical treatment guidelines that are generally recognized by the national medical community and are scientifically based. Treatment may not be denied on the sole basis that the treatment is not addressed by the ACOEM Practice Guidelines until adoption of the medical treatment utilization schedule pursuant to Labor Code section 5307.27. After the Administrative Director adopts a medical treatment utilization schedule pursuant to Labor Code section 5307.27, treatment may not be denied on the sole basis that the treatment is not addressed by that schedule.

(3) The relevant portion of the criteria or guidelines used shall be disclosed in written form to the requesting physician, the injured worker, and if the injured worker is represented by counsel, the injured worker's attorney, if used as the basis of a decision to modify, delay, or deny services in a specific case under review. The claims administrator may not charge an injured worker, the injured worker's attorney or the requesting physician for a copy of the relevant portion of the criteria or guidelines used to modify, delay or deny the treatment request.

(4) Nothing in this section precludes authorization of medical treatment not included in the specific criteria under section 9792.8(a)(3).

Note: Authority cited: Sections 133, 4603.5 and 5307.3, Labor Code. Reference: Sections 4062, 4600, 4600.4, 4604.5 and 4610, Labor Code.

History: 1. New section filed 12-9-2004 as an emergency; operative 12-13-2004 (Register 2004, No. 50). A Certificate of Compliance must be transmitted to OAL by 4-12-2005 or emergency language will be repealed by operation of law on the following day.

2. New section refiled 4-6-2005 as an emergency; operative 4-12-2005 (Register 2005, No. 14). A Certificate of Compliance must be transmitted to OAL by 8-10-2005 or emergency language will be repealed by operation of law on the following day.

3. Certificate of Compliance as to 4-6-2005 order, including amendment of section, transmitted to OAL 8-10-2005 and filed 9-22-2005 (Register 2005, No. 38).

Ref.: Hanna § 22.05[6][c]; Herlick Handbook §§ 1.01[3][b], 4.09[1], [2], 4.16[3].

§9792.9. Utilization Review Standards—Timeframe, Procedures and Notice Content — For Injuries Occurring Prior to January 1, 2013, Where the Request for Authorization is Received Prior to July 1, 2013.

This section applies to any request for authorization of medical treatment, submitted under Article 5.5.1 of this Subchapter, for an occupational injury or illness occurring prior to January 1, 2013 where the request for authorization is received prior to July 1, 2013.

(a) The request for authorization for a course of treatment as defined in section 9792.6(e) must be in written form.

(1) For purposes of this section, the written request for authorization shall be deemed to have been received by the claims administrator by facsimile on the date the request was received if the receiving facsimile electronically date stamps the transmission. If there is no electronically stamped date recorded, then the date the request was transmitted. A request for authorization transmitted by facsimile after 5:30 PM Pacific Time shall be deemed to have been received by the claims administrator on the following business day as defined in Labor Code section 4600.4 and in section 9 of the Civil Code. The copy of the request for authorization received by a facsimile transmission shall bear a notation of the date, time and place of transmission and the facsimile telephone number to which the request was transmitted or be accompanied by an unsigned copy of the affidavit or certificate of transmission

which shall contain the facsimile telephone number to which the request was transmitted. The requesting physician must indicate the need for an expedited review upon submission of the request.

(2) Where the request for authorization is made by mail, and a proof of service by mail exists, the request shall be deemed to have been received by the claims administrator five (5) days after the deposit in the mail at a facility regularly maintained by the United States Postal Service. Where the request for authorization is delivered via certified mail, return receipt mail, the request shall be deemed to have been received by the claims administrator on the receipt date entered on the return receipt. In the absence of a proof of service by mail or a dated return receipt, the request shall be deemed to have been received by the claims administrator on the date stamped as received on the document.

(b) Utilization review of a request for authorization of medical treatment may be deferred if the claims administrator disputes liability for either the occupational injury for which the treatment is recommended or the recommended treatment itself on grounds other than medical necessity.

(1) If the claims administrator disputes its liability for the requested medical treatment under this subdivision, it may, no later than five (5) business days from receipt of the request for authorization, issue a written decision deferring utilization review of the requested treatment, unless the requesting physician has been previously notified under this subdivision of a dispute over liability and an explanation for the deferral of utilization review for a specific course of treatment. The written decision must be sent to the requesting physician, the injured worker, and if the injured worker is represented by counsel, the injured worker's attorney. The written decision shall only contain the following information specific to the request:

(A) The date on which the request for authorization was first received.

(B) A description of the specific course of proposed medical treatment for which authorization was requested.

(C) A clear, concise, and appropriate explanation of the reason for the claims administrator's dispute of liability for either the injury, claimed body part or parts, or the recommended treatment.

(D) A plain language statement advising the injured employee that any dispute under this subdivision shall be resolved either by agreement of the parties or through the dispute resolution process of the Workers' Compensation Appeals Board.

(E) The following mandatory language advising the injured employee:

"You have a right to disagree with decisions affecting your claim. If you have questions about the information in this notice, please call me (insert claims adjuster's name in parentheses) at (insert telephone number). However, if you are represented by an attorney, please contact your attorney instead of me.

and

"For information about the workers' compensation claims process and your rights and obligations, go to www.dwc.ca.gov or contact an information and assistance (I&A) officer of the state Division of Workers' Compensation. For recorded information and a list of offices, call toll-free 1-800-736-7401."

(2) If utilization review is deferred pursuant to this subdivision, and it is finally determined that the claims administrator is liable for treatment of the condition for which treatment is recommended, either by decision of the Workers' Compensation Appeals Board or by agreement between the parties, the time for the claims administrator to conduct retrospective utilization review in accordance with this section shall begin on the date the determination of the claims administrator's liability becomes final. The time for the claims administrator to conduct prospective utilization review shall commence from the date of the claims administrator's receipt of a request for authorization after the final determination of liability.

(c) The utilization review process shall meet the following timeframe requirements:

(1) Prospective or concurrent decisions shall be made in a timely fashion that is appropriate for the nature of the injured worker's condition, not to exceed five (5) working days from the date of receipt of the written request for authorization.

(2) If appropriate information which is necessary to render a decision is not provided with the original request for authorization, such information may be requested by a reviewer or non-physician reviewer within five (5) working days from the date of receipt of the written request for authorization to make the proper determination. In no event shall the determination be made more than 14 days from the date of receipt of the original request for authorization by the health care provider.

(A) If the reasonable information requested by the claims administrator is not received within 14 days of the date of the original written request by the requesting physician, a reviewer may deny the request with the stated condition that the request will be reconsidered upon receipt of the information requested.

(3) Decisions to approve a physician's request for authorization prior to, or concurrent with, the provision of medical services to the injured worker shall be communicated to the requesting physician within 24 hours of the decision. Any decision to approve a request shall be communicated to the requesting physician initially by telephone or facsimile. The communication by telephone shall be followed by written notice to the requesting physician within 24 hours of the decision for concurrent review and within two business days for prospective review.

(4) Decisions to modify, delay or deny a physician's request for authorization prior to, or concurrent with the provision of medical services to the injured worker shall be communicated to the requesting physician initially by telephone or facsimile. The communication by telephone shall be followed by written notice to the requesting physician, the injured worker, and if the injured worker is represented by counsel, the injured worker's attorney within 24 hours of the decision for concurrent review and within two business days of the decision for prospective review. In addition, the non-physician provider of goods or services identified in the request for authorization, and for whom contact information has been included, shall be notified in writing of the decision modifying, delaying, or

denying a request for authorization that shall not include the rationale, criteria or guidelines used for the decision.

(5) For purposes of this section "normal business day" means a business day as defined in Labor Code section 4600.4 and Civil Code section 9.

(d) When review is retrospective, decisions shall be communicated to the requesting physician who provided the medical services and to the individual who received the medical services, and his or her attorney/designee, if applicable, within 30 days of receipt of the medical information that is reasonably necessary to make this determination. In addition, the non-physician provider of goods or services identified in the request for authorization, and for whom contact information has been included, shall be notified in writing of the decision modifying, delaying, or denying a request for authorization that shall not include the rationale, criteria or guidelines used for the decision.

(e) Failure to obtain prior authorization for emergency health care services shall not be an acceptable basis for refusal to cover medical services provided to treat and stabilize an injured worker presenting for emergency health care services. Emergency health care services, however, may be subjected to retrospective review. Documentation for emergency health care services shall be made available to the claims administrator upon request.

(f) Prospective or concurrent decisions related to an expedited review shall be made in a timely fashion appropriate to the injured worker's condition, not to exceed 72 hours after the receipt of the written information reasonably necessary to make the determination. The requesting physician must indicate the need for an expedited review upon submission of the request. Decisions related to expedited review refer to the following situations:

(1) When the injured worker's condition is such that the injured worker faces an imminent and serious threat to his or her health, including, but not limited to, the potential loss of life, limb, or other major bodily function, or

(2) The normal timeframe for the decision-making process, as described in subdivision (b), would be detrimental to the injured worker's life or health or could jeopardize the injured worker's permanent ability to regain maximum function.

(g) The review and decision to deny, delay or modify a request for medical treatment must be conducted by a reviewer, who is competent to evaluate the specific clinical issues involved in the medical treatment services, and where these services are within the scope of the individual's practice.

(h)(1) The timeframe for decisions specified in subdivisions (b)(1), (b)(2) or (c) may only be extended by the claims administrator under the following circumstances:

(A) The claims administrator is not in receipt of all of the necessary medical information reasonably requested.

(B) The reviewer has asked that an additional examination or test be performed upon the injured worker that is reasonable and consistent with professionally recognized standards of medical practice.

(C) The claims administrator needs a specialized consultation and review of medical information by an expert reviewer.

(2) If subdivisions (A), (B) or (C) above apply, the claims administrator shall immediately notify the requesting physician, the injured worker, and if the injured worker is represented by counsel, the injured worker's attorney in writing, that the claims administrator cannot make a decision within the required timeframe, and specify the information requested but not received, the additional examinations or tests required, or the specialty of the expert reviewer to be consulted. The claims administrator shall also notify the requesting physician, the injured worker, and if the injured worker is represented by counsel, the injured worker's attorney of the anticipated date on which a decision will be rendered. This notice shall include a statement that if the injured worker believes that a bona fide dispute exists relating to his or her entitlement to medical treatment, the injured worker or the injured worker's attorney may file an Application for Adjudication of Claim, Form WCAB 1, and a Declaration of Readiness to Proceed (expedited trial), DWC-CA form 10252.1. In addition, the non-physician provider of goods or services identified in the request for authorization, and for whom contact information has been included, shall be notified in writing of the decision to extend the timeframe and the anticipated date on which the decision will be rendered in accordance with this subdivision. The written notification shall not include the rationale, criteria or guidelines used for the decision.

(3) Upon receipt of information pursuant to subdivisions (A), (B), or (C) above, and (b)(2)(A), the claims administrator shall make the decision to approve, and the reviewer shall make a decision to modify or deny the request for authorization within five (5) working days of receipt of the information for prospective or concurrent review. The decision shall be communicated pursuant to subdivisions (b)(3) or (b)(4).

(4) Upon receipt of information pursuant to subdivisions (A), (B), or (C) above, the claims administrator shall make the decision to approve, and the reviewer shall make a decision to modify or deny the request for authorization within thirty (30) days of receipt of the information for retrospective review.

(i) Every claims administrator shall maintain telephone access from 9:00 AM to 5:30 PM Pacific Time, on normal business days, for health care providers to request authorization for medical services. Every claims administrator shall have a facsimile number available for physicians to request authorization for medical services. Every claims administrator shall maintain a process to receive communications from health care providers requesting authorization for medical services after business hours. For purposes of this section "normal business day" means a business day as defined in Labor Code section 4600.4 and Civil Code section 9. In addition, for purposes of this section the requirement that the claims administrator maintain a process to receive communications from requesting physicians after business hours shall be satisfied by maintaining a voice mail system or a facsimile number for after business hours requests.

(j) A written decision approving a request for treatment authorization under this section shall specify the specific medical treatment service approved.

(k) A written decision modifying, delaying or denying treatment authorization under this section, when the decision is communicated prior to July 1, 2013, shall be provided to the requesting physician, the injured worker, and if the injured worker is represented by counsel, the injured worker's attorney and shall contain the following information:

(1) The date on which the decision is made.

(2) A description of the specific course of proposed medical treatment for which authorization was requested.

(3) A specific description of the medical treatment service approved, if any.

(4) A clear and concise explanation of the reasons for the claims administrator's decision.

(5) A description of the medical criteria or guidelines used pursuant to section 9792.8, subdivision (a)(3).

(6) The clinical reasons regarding medical necessity.

(7) A clear statement that any dispute shall be resolved in accordance with the provisions of Labor Code section 4062, and that an objection to the utilization review decision must be communicated by the injured worker or the injured worker's attorney on behalf of the injured worker to the claims administrator in writing within 20 days of receipt of the decision. It shall further state that the 20-day time limit may be extended for good cause or by mutual agreement of the parties. The letter shall further state that the injured worker may file an Application for Adjudication of Claim, Form WCAB 1, and a Declaration of Readiness to Proceed (expedited trial), DWC-CA form 10252.1.

(8)(A) Include the following mandatory language:

Either

"If you want further information, you may contact the local state Information and Assistance office by calling [enter district I & A office telephone number closest to the injured worker] or you may receive recorded information by calling 1-800-736-7401.

or

"If you want further information, you may contact the local state Information and Assistance office closest to you. Please see attached listing (attach a listing of I&A offices and telephone numbers) or you may receive recorded information by calling 1-800-736-7401."

and

"You may also consult an attorney of your choice. Should you decide to be represented by an attorney, you may or may not receive a larger award, but, unless you are determined to be ineligible for an award, the attorney's fee will be deducted from any award you might receive for disability benefits. The decision to be represented by an attorney is yours to make, but it is voluntary and may not be necessary for you to receive your benefits."

(B) Instead of the mandatory language stated in subdivision (k)(8)(A), the following language may be used:

"You have a right to disagree with decisions affecting your claim. If you have questions about the information in this notice, please call me (insert claims adjuster's name in parentheses) at (insert telephone number). However, if you are represented by an attorney, please contact your attorney instead of me.

and

"For information about the workers' compensation claims process and your rights and obligations, go to www.dwc.ca.gov or contact an information and assistance (I&A) officer of the state Division of Workers' Compensation. For recorded information and a list of offices, call toll-free 1-800-736-7401."

In addition, the non-physician provider of goods or services identified in the request for authorization, and for whom contact information has been included, shall be notified in writing of the decision modifying, delaying, or denying a request for authorization that shall not include the rationale, criteria or guidelines used for the decision.

(9) Details about the claims administrator's internal utilization review appeals process, if any, and a clear statement that the appeals process is on a voluntary basis, including the following mandatory statement:

"If you disagree with the utilization review decision and wish to dispute it, you must send written notice of your objection to the claims administrator within 20 days of receipt of the utilization review decision in accordance with Labor Code section 4062. You must meet this deadline even if you are participating in the claims administrator's internal utilization review appeals process."

(*l*) A written decision modifying, delaying or denying treatment authorization under this section, sent on or after July 1, 2013, shall be provided to the requesting physician, the injured worker, and if the injured worker is represented by counsel, the injured worker's attorney and shall contain the following information:

(1) The date on which the decision is made.

(2) A description of the specific course of proposed medical treatment for which authorization was requested.

(3) A list of all medical records reviewed.

(4) A specific description of the medical treatment service approved, if any.

(5) A clear, concise, and appropriate explanation of the reasons for the claims administrator's decision, including the clinical reasons regarding medical necessity and a description of the relevant medical criteria or guidelines used to reach the decision pursuant to section 9792.8. If a utilization review decision to modify, deny or delay a medical service is due to incomplete or insufficient information, the decision shall specify the reason for the decision and specify the information that is needed.

(6) The Application for Independent Medical Review, DWC Form IMR, with all fields, except for the signature of the employee, to be completed by the claims administrator. The written decision provided to the injured worker, and if the injured worker is represented by counsel, the injured worker's attorney, shall include an addressed envelope, which may be postage-paid for mailing to the Administrative Director or his or her designee.

(7) A clear statement advising the injured employee that any dispute shall be resolved in accordance with the independent medical review provisions of Labor Code section 4610.5 and 4610.6, and that an objection to the utilization review decision must be communicated by the injured worker, the injured worker's representative, or the injured worker's attorney on behalf of the injured worker on the enclosed Application for Independent Medical

Review, DWC Form IMR, within 30 calendar days of receipt of the decision.

(8) Include the following mandatory language advising the injured employee:

"You have a right to disagree with decisions affecting your claim. If you have questions about the information in this notice, please call me (insert claims adjuster's or appropriate contact's name in parentheses) at (insert telephone number). However, if you are represented by an attorney, please contact your attorney instead of me.

and

"For information about the workers' compensation claims process and your rights and obligations, go to www.dwc.ca.gov or contact an information and assistance (I&A) officer of the state Division of Workers' Compensation. For recorded information and a list of offices, call toll-free 1-800-736-7401."

(9) Details about the claims administrator's internal utilization review appeals process for the requesting physician, if any, and a clear statement that the internal appeals process is a voluntary process that neither triggers nor bars use of the dispute resolution procedures of Labor Code section 4610.5 and 4610.6, but may be pursued on an optional basis.

(m) The written decision modifying, delaying or denying treatment authorization provided to the requesting physician shall also contain the name and specialty of the reviewer or expert reviewer, and the telephone number in the United States of the reviewer or expert reviewer. The written decision shall also disclose the hours of availability of either the review, the expert reviewer or the medical director for the treating physician to discuss the decision which shall be, at a minimum, four (4) hours per week during normal business hours, 9:00 AM to 5:30 PM., Pacific Time or an agreed upon scheduled time to discuss the decision with the requesting physician. In the vent the reviewer is unavailable, the requesting physician may discuss the written decision with another reviewer who is competent to evaluate the specific clinical issues involved in the medical treatment services.

(n) Authorization may not be denied on the basis of lack of information without documentation reflecting an attempt to obtain the necessary information from the physician or from the provider of goods or services identified in the request for authorization either by facsimile or mail.

(o) A utilization review decision to modify, delay, or deny a request for authorization of medical treatment shall remain effective for 12 months from the date of the decision without further action by the claims administrator with regard to any further recommendation by the same physician for the same treatment unless the further recommendation is supported by a documented change in the facts material to the basis of the utilization review decision.

Note: Authority cited: Sections 133, 4603.5 and 5307.3, Labor Code. Reference: Sections 4062, 4600, 4600.4, 4604.5, 4610 and 4610.5, Labor Code.

History: 1. New section filed 12-9-2004 as an emergency; operative 12-13-2004 (Register 2004, No. 50). A Certificate of Compliance must be transmitted to OAL by 4-12-2005 or emergency language will be repealed by operation of law on the following day.

2. New section refiled 4-6-2005 as an emergency; operative 4-12-2005 (Register 2005, No. 14). A Certificate of Compliance must be transmitted to OAL by 8-10-2005 or emergency language will be repealed by operation of law on the following day.

3. Certificate of Compliance as to 4-6-2005 order, including amendment of section, transmitted to OAL 8-10-2005 and filed 9-22-2005 (Register 2005, No. 38).

4. Amendment of section heading, new first paragraph and new subsections (b)-(b)(2), subsection relettering, amendment of newly designated subsections (h)(2), (k) and (k)(7), new subsections (k)(8)(A)-(B) and (*l*)-(*l*)(9), subsection relettering, new subsection (o) and amendment of Note filed 12-31-2012 as an emergency; operative 1-1-2013 pursuant to Government Code section 11346.1(d) (Register 2013, No. 1). A Certificate of Compliance must be transmitted to OAL by 7-1-2013 or emergency language will be repealed by operation of law on the following day.

5. Amendment of section heading, new first paragraph and new subsections (b)-(b)(2), subsection relettering, amendment of newly designated subsections (h)(2), (k) and (k)(7), new subsections (k)(8)(A)-(B) and (*l*)-(*l*)(9), subsection relettering, new subsection (o) and amendment of Note refiled 7-1-2013 as an emergency; operative 7-1-2013 (Register 2013, No. 27). A Certificate of Compliance must be transmitted to OAL by 9-30-2013 or emergency language will be repealed by operation of law on the following day.

6. Amendment of section heading, new first paragraph and new subsections (b)-(b)(2), subsection relettering, amendment of newly designated subsections (h)(2), (k) and (k)(7), new subsections (k)(8)(A)-(B) and (*l*)-(*l*)(9), subsection relettering, new subsection (o) and amendment of Note refiled 9-30-2013 as an emergency; operative 10-1-2013 (Register 2013, No. 40). A Certificate of Compliance must be transmitted to OAL by 12-30-2013 or emergency language will be repealed by operation of law on the following day.

7. Certificate of Compliance as to 9-30-2013 order, including further amendment of section heading, first paragraph and subsections (b)(1), (b)(2), (k) and (*l*)(6), transmitted to OAL 12-30-2013 and filed 2-12-2014; amendments effective 2-12-2014 pursuant to Government Code section 11343.4(b)(3) (Register 2014, No. 7).

Ref.: Hanna §§ 5.02[2][c], 22.05[6][c][iii], [iv]; Herlick Handbook §§ 1.01[3][b], 4.08[5], 4.09[1], [2], [4]–[7], 4.16[3].

§9792.9.1. Utilization Review Standards—Timeframe, Procedures and Notice — On or After January 1, 2013.

This section applies to any request for authorization of medical treatment, submitted under Article 5.5.1 of this Subchapter, for either: (1) an occupational injury or illness occurring on or after January 1, 2013; or (2) where the decision on the request is communicated to the requesting physician on or after July 1, 2013, regardless of the date of injury.

(a) The request for authorization for a course of treatment as defined in section 9792.6.1(d) must be in written form set forth on the "Request for Authorization (DWC Form RFA)," as contained in California Code of Regulations, title 8, section 9785.5.

(1) For purposes of this section, the DWC Form RFA shall be deemed to have been received by the claims administrator or its utilization review organization by facsimile or by electronic mail on the date the form was received if the receiving facsimile or electronic mail address electronically date stamps the transmission when received. If there is no electronically stamped date recorded, then the date the form was transmitted shall be

deemed to be the date the form was received by the claims administrator or the claims administrator's utilization review organization. A DWC Form RFA transmitted by facsimile after 5:30 PM Pacific Time shall be deemed to have been received by the claims administrator on the following business day, except in the case of an expedited or concurrent review. The copy of the DWC Form RFA or the cover sheet accompanying the form transmitted by a facsimile transmission or by electronic mail shall bear a notation of the date, time and place of transmission and the facsimile telephone number or the electronic mail address to which the form was transmitted or the form shall be accompanied by an unsigned copy of the affidavit or certificate of transmission, or by a fax or electronic mail transmission report, which shall display the facsimile telephone number to which the form was transmitted. The requesting physician must indicate if there is the need for an expedited review on the DWC Form RFA.

(2)(A) Where the DWC Form RFA is sent by mail, the form, absent documentation of receipt, shall be deemed to have been received by the claims administrator five (5) business days after the deposit in the mail at a facility regularly maintained by the United States Postal Service.

(B) Where the DWC Form RFA is delivered via certified mail, with return receipt mail, the form, absent documentation of receipt, shall be deemed to have been received by the claims administrator on the receipt date entered on the return receipt.

(C) In the absence of documentation of receipt, evidence of mailing, or a dated return receipt, the DWC Form RFA shall be deemed to have been received by the claims administrator five days after the latest date the sender wrote on the document.

(3) Every claims administrator shall maintain telephone access and have a representative personally available by telephone from 9:00 AM to 5:30 PM Pacific Time, on business days for health care providers to request authorization for medical services. Every claims administrator shall have a facsimile number available for physicians to request authorization for medical services. Every claims administrator shall maintain a process to receive communications from health care providers requesting authorization for medical services after business hours. For purposes of this section the requirement that the claims administrator maintain a process to receive communications from requesting physicians after business hours shall be satisfied by maintaining a voice mail system or a facsimile number or a designated email address for after business hours requests.

(b) Utilization review of a medical treatment request made on the DWC Form RFA may be deferred if the claims administrator disputes liability for either the occupational injury for which the treatment is recommended or the recommended treatment itself on grounds other than medical necessity.

(1) If the claims administrator disputes liability under this subdivision, it may, no later than five (5) business days from receipt of the DWC Form RFA, issue a written decision deferring utilization review of the requested treatment unless the requesting physician has been previously notified under this subdivision of a dispute over liability and an explanation for the deferral of utilization review for a specific course of treatment. The written decision must be sent to the requesting physician, the injured worker, and if the injured worker is represented by counsel, the injured worker's attorney. The written decision shall contain the following information specific to the request:

(A) The date on which the DWC Form RFA was first received.

(B) A description of the specific course of proposed medical treatment for which authorization was requested.

(C) A clear, concise, and appropriate explanation of the reason for the claims administrator's dispute of liability for either the injury, claimed body part or parts, or the recommended treatment.

(D) A plain language statement advising the injured employee that any dispute under this subdivision shall be resolved either by agreement of the parties or through the dispute resolution process of the Workers' Compensation Appeals Board.

(E) The following mandatory language advising the injured employee:

"You have a right to disagree with decisions affecting your claim. If you have questions about the information in this notice, please call me (insert claims adjuster's name in parentheses) at (insert telephone number). However, if you are represented by an attorney, please contact your attorney instead of me.

and

"For information about the workers' compensation claims process and your rights and obligations, go to www.dwc.ca.gov or contact an information and assistance (I&A) officer of the state Division of Workers' Compensation. For recorded information and a list of offices, call toll-free 1-800-736-7401."

(2) If utilization review is deferred pursuant to this subdivision, and it is finally determined that the claims administrator is liable for treatment of the condition for which treatment is recommended, either by decision of the Workers' Compensation Appeals Board or by agreement between the parties, the time for the claims administrator to conduct retrospective utilization review in accordance with this section shall begin on the date the determination of the claims administrator's liability becomes final. The time for the claims administrator to conduct prospective utilization review shall commence from the date of the claims administrator's receipt of a DWC Form RFA after the final determination of liability.

(c) Unless additional information is requested necessitating an extension under subdivision (f), the utilization review process shall meet the following timeframe requirements:

(1) The first day in counting any timeframe requirement is the day after the receipt of the DWC Form RFA, except when the timeline is measured in hours. Whenever the timeframe requirement is stated in hours, the time for compliance is counted in hours from the time of receipt of the DWC Form RFA.

(2)(A) Upon receipt of a request for authorization as described in subdivision (c)(2)(B), or a DWC Form RFA that does not identify the employee or provider, does not identify a recommended treatment, is not accompanied by documentation substantiating the medical necessity for the requested treatment, or is not signed by the requesting physician, a non-physician reviewer as allowed by section

9792.7 or reviewer must either regard the request as a complete DWC Form RFA and comply with the timeframes for decision set forth in this section or return it to the requesting physician marked "not complete," specifying the reasons for the return of the request no later than five (5) business days from receipt. The timeframe for a decision on a returned request for authorization shall begin anew upon receipt of a completed DWC Form RFA.

(B) The claims administrator may accept a request for authorization for medical treatment that does not utilize the DWC Form RFA, provided that: (1) "Request for Authorization" is clearly written at the top of the first page of the document; (2) all requested medical services, goods, or items are listed on the first page; and (3) the request is accompanied by documentation substantiating the medical necessity for the requested treatment.

(3) Prospective or concurrent decisions to approve, modify, delay, or deny a request for authorization shall be made in a timely fashion that is appropriate for the nature of the injured worker's condition, not to exceed five (5) business days from the date of receipt of the completed DWC Form RFA.

(4) Prospective or concurrent decisions to approve, modify, delay, or deny a request for authorization related to an expedited review shall be made in a timely fashion appropriate to the injured worker's condition, not to exceed 72 hours after the receipt of the written information reasonably necessary to make the determination. The requesting physician must certify in writing and document the need for an expedited review upon submission of the request. A request for expedited review that is not reasonably supported by evidence establishing that the injured worker faces an imminent and serious threat to his or her health, or that the timeframe for utilization review under subdivision (c)(3) would be detrimental to the injured worker's condition, shall be reviewed by the claims administrator under the timeframe set forth in subdivision (c)(3).

(5) Retrospective decisions to approve modify, delay, or deny a request for authorization shall be made within 30 days of receipt of the request for authorization and medical information that is reasonably necessary to make a determination.

(d) Decisions to approve a request for authorization.

(1) All decisions to approve a request for authorization shall specify the specific the date the complete request for authorization was received medical treatment service requested, the specific medical treatment service approved, and the date of the decision.

(2) For prospective, concurrent, or expedited review, approvals shall be communicated to the requesting physician within 24 hours of the decision, and shall be communicated to the requesting physician initially by telephone, facsimile, or electronic mail. The communication by telephone shall be followed by written notice to the requesting physician within 24 hours of the decision for concurrent review and within two (2) business days for prospective review.

(3)(A) For retrospective review, a written decision to approve shall be communicated to the requesting physician who provided the medical services and to the individual who received the medical services, and his or her attorney/designee, if applicable.

(B) Payment, or partial payment consistent with the provisions of California Code of Regulations, title 8, section 9792.5, of a medical bill for services requested on the DWC Form RFA, within the 30-day timeframe set forth in subdivision (c)(5), shall be deemed a retrospective approval, even if a portion of the medical bill for the requested services is contested, denied, or considered incomplete. A document indicating that a payment has been made for the requested services, such as an explanation of review, may be provided to the injured employee who received the medical services, and his or her attorney/designee, if applicable, in lieu of a communication expressly acknowledging the retrospective approval.

(e) Decisions to modify, delay, or deny a request for authorization.

(1) The review and decision to deny, delay, or modify a request for medical treatment must be conducted by a reviewer, who is competent to evaluate the specific clinical issues involved in the medical treatment services, and where these services are within the scope of the individual's practice.

(2) Failure to obtain authorization prior to providing emergency health care services shall not be an acceptable basis for refusal to cover medical services provided to treat and stabilize an injured worker presenting for emergency health care services. Emergency health care services may be subjected to retrospective review. Documentation for emergency health care services shall be made available to the claims administrator upon request.

(3) For prospective, concurrent, or expedited review, a decision to modify, delay, or deny shall be communicated to the requesting physician within 24 hours of the decision, and shall be communicated to the requesting physician initially by telephone, facsimile, or electronic mail. The communication by telephone shall be followed by written notice to the requesting physician, the injured worker, and if the injured worker is represented by counsel, the injured worker's attorney within 24 hours of the decision for concurrent review and within two (2) business days for prospective review and for expedited review within 72 hours of receipt of the request.

(4) For retrospective review, a written decision to deny part or all of the requested medical treatment shall be communicated to the requesting physician who provided the medical services and to the individual who received the medical services, and his or her attorney/designee, if applicable, within 30 days of receipt of request for authorization and medical information that is reasonably necessary to make a determination.

(5) The written decision modifying, delaying or denying treatment authorization shall be provided to the requesting physician, the injured worker, the injured worker's representative, and if the injured worker is represented by counsel, the injured worker's attorney. The written decision shall be signed by either the claims administrator or the reviewer, and shall only contain the following information specific to the request:

(A) The date on which the DWC Form RFA was first received.

(B) The date on which the decision is made.

(C) A description of the specific course of proposed medical treatment for which authorization was requested.

(D) A list of all medical records reviewed.

(E) A specific description of the medical treatment service approved, if any.

(F) A clear, concise, and appropriate explanation of the reasons for the reviewing physician's decision, including the clinical reasons regarding medical necessity and a description of the relevant medical criteria or guidelines used to reach the decision pursuant to section 9792.8. If a utilization review decision to modify, deny or delay a medical service is due to incomplete or insufficient information, the decision shall specify the reason for the decision and specify the information that is needed.

(G) The Application for Independent Medical Review, DWC Form IMR. All fields of the form, except for the signature of the employee, must be completed by the claims administrator. The written decision provided to the injured worker, shall include an addressed envelope, which may be postage-paid for mailing to the Administrative Director or his or her designee. Prior to March 1, 2014, any version of the DWC Form IMR adopted by the Administrative Director under section 9792.10.2 may be used by the claims administrator in a written decision modifying, delaying or denying treatment authorization.

(H) A clear statement advising the injured employee that any dispute shall be resolved in accordance with the independent medical review provisions of Labor Code section 4610.5 and 4610.6, and that an objection to the utilization review decision must be communicated by the injured worker, the injured worker's representative, or the injured worker's attorney on behalf of the injured worker on the enclosed Application for Independent Medical Review, DWC Form IMR, within 30 calendar days after service of the decision.

(I) Include the following mandatory language advising the injured employee:

"You have a right to disagree with decisions affecting your claim. If you have questions about the information in this notice, please call me (insert claims adjuster's or appropriate contact's name in parentheses) at (insert telephone number). However, if you are represented by an attorney, please contact your attorney instead of me.

and

"For information about the workers' compensation claims process and your rights and obligations, go to www.dwc.ca.gov or contact an information and assistance (I&A) officer of the state Division of Workers' Compensation. For recorded information and a list of offices, call toll-free 1-800-736-7401."

(J) Details about the claims administrator's internal utilization review appeals process for the requesting physician, if any, and a clear statement that the internal appeals process is voluntary process that neither triggers nor bars use of the dispute resolution procedures of Labor Code section 4610.5 and 4610.6, but may be pursued on an optional basis.

(K) The written decision modifying, delaying or denying treatment authorization provided to the requesting physician shall also contain the name and specialty of the reviewer or expert reviewer, and the telephone number in the United States of the reviewer or expert reviewer. The written decision shall also disclose the hours of availability of either the reviewer, the expert reviewer or the medical director for the treating physician to discuss the decision which shall be, at a minimum, four (4) hours per week during normal business hours, 9:00 AM to 5:30 PM., Pacific Time or an agreed upon scheduled time to discuss the decision with the requesting physician. In the event the reviewer is unavailable, the requesting physician may discuss the written decision with another reviewer who is competent to evaluate the specific clinical issues involved in the medical treatment services.

(6) The following requirements shall be met prior to a concurrent review decision to deny authorization for medical treatment:

(A) Medical care shall not be discontinued until the requesting physician has been notified of the decision and a care plan has been agreed upon by the requesting physician that is appropriate for the medical needs of the employee.

(B) Medical care provided during a concurrent review shall be treatment that is medically necessary to cure or relieve from the effects of the industrial injury.

(f)(1) The timeframe for decisions specified in subdivision (c) may only be extended under one or more of the following circumstances:

(A) The claims administrator or reviewer is not in receipt of all of the information reasonably necessary to make a determination.

(B) The reviewer has asked that an additional examination or test be performed upon the injured worker that is reasonable and consistent with professionally recognized standards of medical practice.

(C) The reviewer needs a specialized consultation and review of medical information by an expert reviewer.

(2)(A) If the circumstance under subdivision (f)(1)(A) applies, a reviewer or non-physician reviewer shall request the information from the treating physician within five (5) business days from the date of receipt of the request for authorization.

(B) If any of the circumstances set forth in subdivisions (f)(1)(B) or (C) are deemed to apply following the receipt of a DWC Form RFA or accepted request for authorization, the reviewer shall within five (5) business days from the date of receipt of the request for authorization notify the requesting physician, the injured worker, and if the injured worker is represented by counsel, the injured worker's attorney in writing, that the reviewer cannot make a decision within the required timeframe, and request, as applicable, the additional examinations or tests required, or the specialty of the expert reviewer to be consulted. The reviewer shall also notify the requesting physician, the injured worker, and if the injured worker is represented by counsel, the injured worker's attorney of the anticipated date on which a decision will be rendered.

(3)(A) If the information reasonably necessary to make a determination under subdivision (f)(1)(A) that is requested by the reviewer or non-physician reviewer is not received within fourteen (14) days from receipt of the completed request for authorization for prospective or concurrent review, or within thirty (30) days of the request for retrospective review, the reviewer shall deny the request with the stated condition that the request will be reconsidered upon receipt of the information.

(B) If the results of the additional examination or test required under subdivision (f)(1)(B), or the specialized consultation under subdivision (f)(1)(C), that is requested by the reviewer under this subdivision is not received within thirty (30) days from the date of the request for authorization, the reviewer shall deny the treating physician's request with the stated condition that the request will be reconsidered upon receipt of the results of the additional examination or test or the specialized consultation.

(4) Upon receipt of the information requested pursuant to subdivisions (f)(1)(A), (B), or (C), the claims administrator or reviewer, for prospective or concurrent review, shall make the decision to approve, modify, or deny the request for authorization within five (5) business days of receipt of the information. The requesting physician shall be notified by telephone, facsimile or electronic mail within 24 hours of making the decision The written decision shall include the date the information was received and the decision shall be communicated in the manner set out in section 9792.9.1(d) or (e), whichever is applicable.

(5) Upon receipt of the information requested pursuant to subdivisions (f)(1)(A), (B), or (C), the claims administrator or reviewer, for prospective or concurrent decisions related to an expedited review, shall make the decision to approve, modify, or deny the request for authorization within 72 hours of receipt of the information. The requesting physician shall be notified by telephone, facsimile or electronic mail within 24 hours of making the decision. The written notice of decision shall include the date the requested information was received and be communicated pursuant to subdivisions (d)(2) or (e)(3), whichever is applicable.

(6) Upon receipt of the information requested pursuant to subdivisions (f)(1)(A), (B), or (C), the claims administrator or reviewer, for retrospective review, shall make the decision to approve, modify, delay, or deny the request for authorization within thirty (30) calendar days of receipt of the information requested. The decision shall include the date it was made and be communicated pursuant to subdivisions (d)(3) or (e)(4), whichever is applicable.

(g) Whenever a reviewer issues a decision to deny a request for authorization based on the lack of medical information necessary to make a determination, the claims administrator's file must document the attempt by the claims administrator or reviewer to obtain the necessary medical information from the physician either by facsimile, mail, or e-mail.

(h) A utilization review decision to modify, delay, or deny a request for authorization of medical treatment shall remain effective for 12 months from the date of the decision without further action by the claims administrator with regard to any further recommendation by the same physician for the same treatment unless the further recommendation is supported by a documented change in the facts material to the basis of the utilization review decision.

Note: Authority: Sections 133, 4603.5 and 5307.3, Labor Code. Reference: Sections 4062, 4600, 4600.4, 4604.5, 4610 and 4610.5, Labor Code.

History: 1. New section filed 12-31-2012 as an emergency; operative 1-1-2013 pursuant to Government Code section 11346.1(d) (Register 2013, No. 1). A Certificate of Compliance must be transmitted to OAL by 7-1-2013 or emergency language will be repealed by operation of law on the following day.

2. New section refiled 7-1-2013 as an emergency; operative 7-1-2013 (Register 2013, No. 27). A Certificate of Compliance must be transmitted to OAL by 9-30-2013 or emergency language will be repealed by operation of law on the following day.

3. New section refiled 9-30-2013 as an emergency; operative 10-1-2013 (Register 2013, No. 40). A Certificate of Compliance must be transmitted to OAL by 12-30-2013 or emergency language will be repealed by operation of law on the following day.

4. Certificate of Compliance as to 9-30-2013 order, including amendment of section, transmitted to OAL 12-30-2013 and filed 2-12-2014; amendments effective 2-12-2014 pursuant to Government Code section 11343.4(b)(3) (Register 2014, No. 7).

Ref.: Hanna § 5.02[2][c], [d], [f]; Herlick Handbook §§ 1.01[3][b], 4.08[5], 4.09[1], [2], [4]–[6], 4.16[3].

§9792.10. Utilization Review Standards—Dispute Resolution — For Utilization Review Decisions Communicated Prior to July 1, 2013 for Injuries Occurring Prior to January 1, 2013.

This section applies to any request for authorization of medical treatment, made under Article 5.5.1 of this Subchapter, for an occupational injury or illness occurring prior to January 1, 2013 if the decision on the request is communicated to the requesting physician prior to July 1, 2013.

(a)(1) If the request for authorization of medical treatment is not approved, or if the request for authorization for medical treatment is approved in part, any dispute shall be resolved in accordance with Labor Code section 4062.

(2) An objection to a decision disapproving in whole or in part a request for authorization of medical treatment, must be communicated to the claims administrator by the injured worker or the injured worker's attorney in writing within 20 days of receipt of the utilization review decision. The 20-day time limit may be extended for good cause or by mutual agreement of the parties.

(3) Nothing in this paragraph precludes the parties from participating in an internal utilization review appeal process on a voluntary basis provided the injured worker and if the injured worker is represented by counsel, the injured worker's attorney have been notified of the 20-day time limit to file an objection to the utilization review decision in accordance with Labor Code section 4062.

(4) Additionally, the injured worker or the injured worker's attorney may file an Application for Adjudication of Claim and request an expedited hearing and decision on his or her entitlement to medical treatment if the request for medical treatment is not authorized within the time limitations set forth in section 9792.9, or when there exists a bona fide dispute as to entitlement to medical treatment.

(b) The following requirements shall be met prior to a concurrent review decision to deny authorization for medical treatment and to resolve disputes:

(1) In the case of concurrent review, medical care shall not be discontinued until the requesting physician has been notified of the decision and a care plan has been agreed upon by the requesting physician that is appropriate for the medical needs of the injured worker. In addition, the non-physician provider of goods or services identified in the request for authorization, and for whom contact information has been included, shall be notified in writing of the decision modifying, delaying, or denying a request for

authorization that shall not include the rationale, criteria or guidelines used for the decision.

(2) Medical care provided during a concurrent review shall be medical treatment that is reasonably required to cure or relieve from the effects of the industrial injury.

Note: Authority cited: Sections 133, 4603.5 and 5307.3, Labor Code. Reference: Sections 4062, 4600, 4600.4, 4604.5, 4610 and 4610.5, Labor Code.

History: 1. New section filed 12-9-2004 as an emergency; operative 12-13-2004 (Register 2004, No. 50). A Certificate of Compliance must be transmitted to OAL by 4-12-2005 or emergency language will be repealed by operation of law on the following day.

2. New section refiled 4-6-2005 as an emergency; operative 4-12-2005 (Register 2005, No. 14). A Certificate of Compliance must be transmitted to OAL by 8-10-2005 or emergency language will be repealed by operation of law on the following day.

3. Certificate of Compliance as to 4-6-2005 order, including amendment of subsection (b)(1), transmitted to OAL 8-10-2005 and filed 9-22-2005 (Register 2005, No. 38).

4. Amendment of section heading, new first paragraph and amendment of subsection (a)(4) and Note filed 12-31-2012 as an emergency; operative 1-1-2013 pursuant to Government Code section 11346.1(d) (Register 2013, No. 1). A Certificate of Compliance must be transmitted to OAL by 7-1-2013 or emergency language will be repealed by operation of law on the following day.

5. Amendment of section heading, new first paragraph and amendment of subsection (a)(4) and Note refiled 7-1-2013 as an emergency; operative 7-1-2013 (Register 2013, No. 27). A Certificate of Compliance must be transmitted to OAL by 9-30-2013 or emergency language will be repealed by operation of law on the following day.

6. Amendment of section heading, new first paragraph and amendment of subsection (a)(4) and Note refiled 9-30-2013 as an emergency; operative 10-1-2013 (Register 2013, No. 40). A Certificate of Compliance must be transmitted to OAL by 12-30-2013 or emergency language will be repealed by operation of law on the following day.

7. Certificate of Compliance as to 9-30-2013 order, including amendment of section heading and subsection (a)(4), transmitted to OAL 12-30-2013 and filed 2-12-2014; amendments effective 2-12-2014 pursuant to Government Code section 11343.4(b)(3) (Register 2014, No. 7).

Ref.: Hanna § 22.05[6][c]; Herlick Handbook §§ 1.01[3][b], 4.08[5], 4.09[1], [7], 4.16[3].

§9792.10.1. Utilization Review Standards—Dispute Resolution — On or After January 1, 2013.

This section applies to any request for authorization of medical treatment, made under Article 5.5.1 of this Subchapter, for either: (1) an occupational injury or illness occurring on or after January 1, 2013; or (2) where the decision on the request is communicated to the requesting physician on or after July 1, 2013, regardless of the date of injury.

(a) If the request for authorization of medical treatment is not approved, or if the request for authorization for medical treatment is approved in part, any dispute shall be resolved in accordance with Labor Code sections 4610.5 and 4610.6. Neither the employee nor the claims administrator shall have any liability for medical treatment furnished without the authorization of the claims administrator if the treatment is delayed, modified, or denied by a utilization review decision unless the utilization review decision is overturned by independent medical review or the Workers' Compensation Appeals Board under this Article.

(b)(1) A request for independent medical review must be filed by an eligible party by mail, facsimile, or electronic transmission with the Administrative Director, or the Administrative Director's designee, within 30 days of service of the written utilization review determination issued by the claims administrator under section 9792.9.1(e)(5). The request must be made on the Application for Independent Medical Review, DWC Form IMR, and submitted with a copy of the written decision delaying, denying, or modifying the request for authorization of medical treatment. At the time of filing, the employee shall concurrently provide a copy of the signed DWC Form IMR, without a copy of the written decision delaying, denying, or modifying the request for authorization of medical treatment, to the claims administrator.

(2) A party eligible to file a request for independent medical review includes:

(A) The employee or, if the employee is represented, the employee's attorney. If the employee's attorney files the DWC Form IMR, the form must be accompanied by a notice of representation or other document or written designation confirming representation.

(i) An unrepresented employee may designate a parent, guardian, conservator, relative, or other designee of the employee as an agent to act on his or her behalf in filing an application for independent medical review under this subdivision. A designation of an agent executed prior to the utilization review decision shall not be valid.

(ii) The physician whose request for authorization of medical treatment was delayed, denied, or modified may join with or otherwise assist the employee in seeking an independent medical review. The physician may submit documents on the employee's behalf pursuant to section 9792.10.5 (b) and may respond to any inquiry by the independent review organization.

(B) A provider of emergency medical treatment when the employee faced an imminent and serious threat to his or her health, including, but not limited to, the potential loss of life, limb, or other major bodily function, may submit an application for independent medical review under this section on its own behalf within 30 days after the service of the utilization review decision that either delays, denies, or modifies the provider's retrospective request for authorization of the emergency medical treatment.

(3) If expedited review is requested for a utilization review decision eligible for independent medical review, the Application for Independent Medical Review, DWC Form IMR, shall include, unless the initial utilization review decision was made on an expedited basis, written certification from the employee's treating physician with documentation confirming that the employee faces an imminent and serious threat to his or her health as described in section 9792.6.1(j).

(c)(1) If at the time of a utilization review decision the claims administrator is also disputing liability for the treatment for any reason besides medical necessity, the time for the employee to submit an application for independent medical review under subdivision (b)(1) is extended to 30 days after service of a notice to the employee showing that the other dispute of liability has been resolved.

(2) If the claims administrator provides the employee with a written utilization review determination modifying, delaying, or denying a treatment request that does not contain the required elements set forth in section 9792.9(*l*) or section 9792.9.1(e) at the time of notification of its utilization review decision, the time limitations for the employee to submit an application for independent medical review under subdivision (b)(1) shall not begin to run until the claims administrator provides the written decision, with all required elements, to the employee.

(d)(1) Nothing in this section precludes the parties from participating in an internal utilization review appeal process on a voluntary basis provided the employee and, if the employee is represented by counsel, the employee's attorney, have been notified of the 30-day time limit to file an objection to the utilization review decision in accordance with Labor Code sections 4610.5 and 4610.6. Any request by the injured worker or treating physician for an internal utilization review appeal process conducted under this subdivision must be submitted to the claims administrator within ten (10) days after the receipt of the utilization review decision.

(2) A request for an internal utilization review appeal must be completed, and a determination issued, by the claims administrator within thirty (30) days after receipt of the request under subdivision (d)(1). An internal utilization review appeal shall be considered complete upon the issuance of a final independent medical review determination under section 9792.10.6(e) that determines the medical necessity of the disputed treatment.

(3) Any determination by the claims administrator following an internal utilization review appeal that results in a modification of the requested medical treatment shall be communicated to the requesting physician and the injured worker, the injured worker's representative, and if the injured worker is represented by counsel, the injured worker's attorney according to the requirements set forth in section 9792.9.1(e). The Application for Independent Medical Review, DWC Form IMR, that accompanies the written decision letter under section 9792.9.1(e)(5)(G) must indicate that the decision is a modification after appeal.

Note: Authority: Sections 133, 4603.5 and 5307.3, Labor Code. Reference: Sections 4062, 4600, 4600.4, 4604.5, 4610 and 4610.5, Labor Code.

History: 1. New section filed 12-31-2012 as an emergency; operative 1-1-2013 pursuant to Government Code section 11346.1(d) (Register 2013, No. 1). A Certificate of Compliance must be transmitted to OAL by 7-1-2013 or emergency language will be repealed by operation of law on the following day.

2. New section refiled 7-1-2013 as an emergency; operative 7-1-2013 (Register 2013, No. 27). A Certificate of Compliance must be transmitted to OAL by 9-30-2013 or emergency language will be repealed by operation of law on the following day.

3. New section refiled 9-30-2013 as an emergency; operative 10-1-2013 (Register 2013, No. 40). A Certificate of Compliance must be transmitted to OAL by 12-30-2013 or emergency language will be repealed by operation of law on the following day.

4. Certificate of Compliance as to 9-30-2013 order, including amendment of section, transmitted to OAL 12-30-2013 and filed 2-12-2014; amendments effective 2-12-2014 pursuant to Government Code section 11343.4(b)(3) (Register 2014, No. 7).

Ref.: Hanna § 5.02[2][d]; Herlick Handbook §§ 1.01[3][b], 4.08[5], 4.09[1], 4.10[1], [2], 4.16[3].

§9792.10.2. Application for Independent Medical Review, DWC Form IMR.

[DWC Form IMR (New 2/2014) Not Reproduced]

NOTE: Form is available at no charge by downloading from the web at www.dir.ca.gov/dwc/forms.html or by requesting at 1-800-794-6900.

Note: Authority: Sections 133, 4603.5, 4610.5 and 5307.3, Labor Code. Reference: Sections 4600, 4610 and 4610.5, Labor Code.

History: 1. New section filed 12-31-2012 as an emergency; operative 1-1-2013 pursuant to Government Code section 11346.1(d) (Register 2013, No. 1). A Certificate of Compliance must be transmitted to OAL by 7-1-2013 or emergency language will be repealed by operation of law on the following day.

2. New section refiled 7-1-2013 as an emergency, including further amendment of form; operative 7-1-2013 (Register 2013, No. 27). A Certificate of Compliance must be transmitted to OAL by 9-30-2013 or emergency language will be repealed by operation of law on the following day.

3. New section refiled 9-30-2013 as an emergency, including further amendment of form; operative 10-1-2013 (Register 2013, No. 40). A Certificate of Compliance must be transmitted to OAL by 12-30-2013 or emergency language will be repealed by operation of law on the following day.

4. Certificate of Compliance as to 9-30-2013 order, including repealer and new section, transmitted to OAL 12-30-2013 and filed 2-12-2014; new section effective 2-12-2014 pursuant to Government Code section 11343.4(b)(3) (Register 2014, No. 7).

Ref.: Herlick Handbook §§ 1.01[3][b], 4.09[1], 4.10[2], 4.16[3].

§9792.10.3. Independent Medical Review — Initial Review of Application.

(a) Following receipt of the Application for Independent Medical Review, DWC Form IMR, pursuant to section 9792.10.1(b), the Administrative Director shall determine whether the disputed medical treatment identified in the application is eligible for independent medical review. In making this determination, the Administrative Director shall consider:

(1) The timeliness and completeness of the Application;

(2) Any previous application or request for independent medical review of the disputed medical treatment;

(3) Any assertion, other than medical necessity, by the claims administrator that a factual, medical, or legal basis exists that precludes liability on the part of the claims administrator for an occupational injury or a claimed injury to any part or parts of the body.

(4) Any assertion, other than medical necessity, by the claims administrator that a factual, medical, or legal basis exists that precludes liability on the part of the claims administrator for a specific course of treatment requested by the treating physician.

(5) The employee's date of injury.

(6) The failure by the requesting physician to respond to a request by the claims administrator under section

9792.9.1(f) for information reasonably necessary to make a utilization review determination, for additional required examinations or tests, or for a specialized consultation.

(b) The Administrative Director may reasonably request additional appropriate information from the parties in order to make a determination that a disputed medical treatment is eligible for independent medical review. The Administrative Director shall advise the claims administrator, the employee, if the employee is represented by counsel, the employee's attorney, and the requesting physician, as appropriate, by the most efficient means available.

(c) The parties shall respond to any reasonable request made pursuant to subdivision (b) within five (5) business days following receipt of the request. Following receipt of all information necessary to make a determination, the Administrative Director shall either immediately inform the parties in writing that a disputed medical treatment is not eligible for independent medical review and the reasons therefor, or assign the request to independent medical review under section 9792.10.4.

(d) If there appears to be any medical necessity issue, the dispute shall be resolved pursuant to an independent medical review, except that, unless the claims administrator agrees that the case is eligible for independent medical review, a request for independent medical review shall be deferred if at the time of a utilization review decision the claims administrator is also disputing liability for the treatment for any reason besides medical necessity.

(e) The parties may appeal an eligibility determination by the Administrative Director that a disputed medical treatment is not eligible for independent medical review by filing a petition with the Workers' Compensation Appeals Board.

(f) The Administrative Director shall retain the right to determine the eligibility of a request for independent medical review under this section until an appeal of the final independent medical review determination issued under section 9792.10.6(e) that determines the medical necessity of the disputed medical treatment has been filed with the Workers' Compensation Appeals Board, or the time in which to file such an appeal has expired.

Note: Authority: Sections 133, 4603.5 and 5307.3, Labor Code. Reference: Sections 4600, 4600.4, 4604.5, 4610 and 4610.5, Labor Code.

History: 1. New section filed 12-31-2012 as an emergency; operative 1-1-2013 pursuant to Government Code section 11346.1(d) (Register 2013, No. 1). A Certificate of Compliance must be transmitted to OAL by 7-1-2013 or emergency language will be repealed by operation of law on the following day.

2. New section refiled 7-1-2013 as an emergency; operative 7-1-2013 (Register 2013, No. 27). A Certificate of Compliance must be transmitted to OAL by 9-30-2013 or emergency language will be repealed by operation of law on the following day.

3. New section refiled 9-30-2013 as an emergency; operative 10-1-2013 (Register 2013, No. 40). A Certificate of Compliance must be transmitted to OAL by 12-30-2013 or emergency language will be repealed by operation of law on the following day.

4. Certificate of Compliance as to 9-30-2013 order, including amendment of section, transmitted to OAL 12-30-2013 and filed 2-12-2014; amendments effective 2-12-2014 pursuant to Government Code section 11343.4(b)(3) (Register 2014, No. 7).

Ref.: Hanna § 5.02[2][d]; Herlick Handbook §§ 1.01[3][b], 4.09[1], 4.10[2], 4.16[3].

§9792.10.4. Independent Medical Review — Assignment and Notification.

(a) The independent review organization delegated the responsibility by the Administrative Director to conduct independent medical review pursuant to Labor Code section 139.5 (IMRO) may consolidate two or more eligible applications for independent medical review by a single employee for resolution in a single determination if the applications involve the same requesting physician and the same date of injury.

(b) Within one business day following receipt of the Administrative Director's finding that the disputed medical treatment is eligible for independent medical review, the independent review organization delegated the responsibility by the Administrative Director to conduct independent medical review pursuant to Labor Code section 139.5 shall notify the employer, employee, if the employee is represented the employee's attorney, and the requesting physician in writing that the dispute has been assigned to that organization for review. The notification shall contain:

(1) The name and address of the independent review organization;

(2) Identification of the disputed medical treatment, including the date of the request for authorization (if available), the name of the requesting physician, and the date of the claims administrator's utilization review decision.

(3) The date the Application for Independent Medical Review, DWC Form IMR, was received by the Independent Review Organization.

(4) A statement whether the independent medical review will be conducted on a regular or expedited basis.

(5) For regular review, a statement that within fifteen (15) calendar days of the date designated on the notification, if the notification was provided by mail, or within twelve (12) calendar days of the date designated on the notification if the notification was provided electronically, the independent review organization must receive the documents indicated in section 9792.10.5. For the notification provided to the claims administrator, the statement shall provide that, pursuant to Labor Code section 4610.5(i), in addition to any other fines, penalties, and other remedies available to the Administrative Director, the failure to comply with section 9792.10.5 could result in the assessment of administrative penalties up to $5,000.00.

(6) For expedited review, a statement that within twenty-four (24) hours following receipt of the notification the independent review organization must receive the documents indicated in section 9792.10.5. For the notification provided to the claims administrator, the statement shall provide that, pursuant to Labor Code section 4610.5(i), in addition to any other fines, penalties, and other remedies available to the Administrative Director, the failure to comply with section 9792.10.5 could result in the assessment of administrative penalties up to $5,000.00.

(c) Review conducted on a regular basis shall be converted into an expedited review if, subsequent to the receipt of the Application for Independent Medical Review, DWC Form IMR, the independent review organization receives from the employee's treating physician written certification with supporting documentation verifying that the employee faces an imminent and serious threat to his or her health as described in section 9792.6.1(j). The independent review organization shall immediately notify the parties by the most efficient means available that the review has been converted from a regular review to an expedited review.

Note: Authority: Sections 133, 4603.5 and 5307.3, Labor Code. Reference: Sections 4062, 4600, 4600.4, 4604.5, 4610 and 4610.5, Labor Code.

History: 1. New section filed 12-31-2012 as an emergency; operative 1-1-2013 pursuant to Government Code section 11346.1(d) (Register 2013, No. 1). A Certificate of Compliance must be transmitted to OAL by 7-1-2013 or emergency language will be repealed by operation of law on the following day.

2. New section refiled 7-1-2013 as an emergency; operative 7-1-2013 (Register 2013, No. 27). A Certificate of Compliance must be transmitted to OAL by 9-30-2013 or emergency language will be repealed by operation of law on the following day.

3. New section refiled 9-30-2013 as an emergency; operative 10-1-2013 (Register 2013, No. 40). A Certificate of Compliance must be transmitted to OAL by 12-30-2013 or emergency language will be repealed by operation of law on the following day.

4. Certificate of Compliance as to 9-30-2013 order, including amendment of section, transmitted to OAL 12-30-2013 and filed 2-12-2014; amendments effective 2-12-2014 pursuant to Government Code section 11343.4(b)(3) (Register 2014, No. 7).

Ref.: Hanna § 5.02[2][d]; Herlick Handbook §§ 1.01[3][b], 4.09[1], 4.10[2], 4.16[3].

§9792.10.5. Independent Medical Review — Medical Records.

(a)(1) Within fifteen (15) days following the mailing of the notification from the independent review organization that the disputed medical treatment has been assigned for independent medical review, or within twelve (12) days if the notification was sent electronically, or for expedited review within twenty-four (24) hours following receipt of the notification, the independent medical review organization shall receive from the claims administrator all of the following documents:

(A) A copy of all reports of the physician relevant to the employee's current medical condition produced within six months prior to the date of the request for authorization, including those that are specifically identified in the request for authorization or in the utilization review determination. If the requesting physician has treated the employee for less than six months prior to the date of the request for authorization, the claims administrator shall provide a copy of all reports relevant to the employee's current medical condition produced within the described six month period by any prior treating physician or referring physician.

(B) A copy of the written Application for Independent Medical Review, DWC Form IMR, that was included with the written determination, issued under section 9792.9.1(e)(5), which notified the employee that the disputed medical treatment was denied, delayed or modified. Neither the written determination nor the application's instructions should be included.

(C) Other than the written determination by the claims administrator issued under section 9792.9.1(e)(5) , a copy of all information, including correspondence, provided to the employee by the claims administrator concerning the utilization review decision regarding the disputed treatment.

(D) A copy of any materials the employee or the employee's provider submitted to the claims administrator in support of the request for the disputed medical treatment.

(E) A copy of any other relevant documents or information used by the claims administrator in determining whether the disputed treatment should have been provided, and any statements by the claims administrator explaining the reasons for the decision to deny, modify, or delay the recommended treatment on the basis of medical necessity.

(F) The claims administrator's response to any additional issues raised in the employee's application for independent medical review.

(2) The claims administrator shall, concurrent with the provision of documents under subdivision (a), forward to the employee or the employee's representative a notification that lists all of the documents submitted to the independent review organization under subdivision (a). The claims administrator shall provide with the notification a copy of all documents that were not previously provided to the employee or the employee's representative excluding mental health records withheld from the employee pursuant to Health and Safety Code section 123115(b).

(3) Any newly developed or discovered relevant medical records in the possession of the claims administrator after the documents identified in subdivision (a) are provided to the independent review organization shall be forwarded immediately to the independent review organization. The claims administrator shall concurrently provide a copy of medical records required by this subdivision to the employee, or the employee's representative, or the employee's treating physician, unless the offer of medical records is declined or otherwise prohibited by law.

(b)(1) Within fifteen (15) days following the mailing of the notification from the independent review organization that the disputed medical treatment has been assigned for independent medical review, or within twelve (12) days if the notification was sent electronically, or for expedited review, within twenty-four (24) hours following receipt of the notification, independent medical review organization shall receive from the employee, if represented the employee's attorney, or any party identified in section 9792.10.1(b)(2), any of the following documents:

(i) The treating physician's recommendation indicating that the disputed medical treatment is medically necessary for the employee's medical condition.

(ii) Medical information or justification that a disputed medical treatment, on an urgent care or emergency basis, was medically necessary for the employee's medical condition.

(iii) Reasonable information supporting the position that the disputed medical treatment is or was medically necessary, including all information provided by the employee's treating physician, or any additional material that the employee believes is relevant.

(2) The employee, if represented the employee's attorney or any party identified in section 9792.10.1(b)(2) shall, concurrent with the provision of documents under subdivision (b), forward the documents provided under subdivision (b) on the claims administrator, except that documents

previously provided to the claims administrator need not be provided again if a list of those documents is served.

(3) Any newly developed or discovered relevant medical records in the possession of the employee, if represented the employee's attorney, or any party identified in section 9792.10.1(b)(2), after the documents identified in subdivision (b) are provided to the independent review organization shall be forwarded immediately to the independent review organization. The employee, if represented the employee's attorney, or any party identified in section 9792.10.1(b)(2), shall concurrently provide a copy of medical records required by this subdivision to the claims administrator, unless the offer of medical records is declined or otherwise prohibited by law.

(c) At any time following the submission of documents under subdivision (a) and (b), the independent review organization may reasonably request appropriate additional documentation or information necessary to make a determination that the disputed medical treatment is medically necessary. Additional documentation or other information requested under this section shall be sent by the party to whom the request was made, with a copy forwarded to all other parties, within five (5) business days after the request is received in routine cases or one (1) calendar day after the request is received in expedited cases.

(d) The confidentiality of medical records shall be maintained pursuant to applicable state and federal laws.

Note: Authority: Sections 133, 4603.5 and 5307.3, Labor Code. Reference: Sections 4062, 4600, 4600.4, 4604.5, 4610 and 4610.5, Labor Code.

History: 1. New section filed 12-31-2012 as an emergency; operative 1-1-2013 pursuant to Government Code section 11346.1(d) (Register 2013, No. 1). A Certificate of Compliance must be transmitted to OAL by 7-1-2013 or emergency language will be repealed by operation of law on the following day.

2. New section refiled 7-1-2013 as an emergency; operative 7-1-2013 (Register 2013, No. 27). A Certificate of Compliance must be transmitted to OAL by 9-30-2013 or emergency language will be repealed by operation of law on the following day.

3. New section refiled 9-30-2013 as an emergency; operative 10-1-2013 (Register 2013, No. 40). A Certificate of Compliance must be transmitted to OAL by 12-30-2013 or emergency language will be repealed by operation of law on the following day.

4. Certificate of Compliance as to 9-30-2013 order, including amendment of section, transmitted to OAL 12-30-2013 and filed 2-12-2014; amendments effective 2-12-2014 pursuant to Government Code section 11343.4(b)(3) (Register 2014, No. 7).

Ref.: Hanna § 5.02[2][d]; Herlick Handbook §§ 1.01[3][b], 4.09[1], 4.10[2], 4.16[3].

§9792.10.6. Independent Medical Review — Standards and Timeframes.

(a) The independent medical review process may be terminated at any time upon notice by the claims administrator to the independent review organization that the disputed medical treatment has been authorized.

(b)(1) Upon assignment of the disputed medical treatment for independent medical review, the independent review organization shall designate a medical reviewer to conduct an examination of the documents submitted pursuant to section 9792.10.5 and issue a determination, using plain language where possible, as to whether the disputed medical treatment is medically necessary. For the purpose of independent medical review, "medically necessary" means medical treatment that is reasonably required to cure or relieve the employee of the effects of their injury and based on the standards set forth in Labor Code section 4610.5(c)(2).

(2) If a claims administrator fails to submit the documentation required under section 9792.10.5(a)(1), a medical reviewer may, issue a determination as to whether the disputed medical treatment is medically necessary based on both a summary of medical records listed in the utilization review determination issued under section 9792.9.1(e)(5), and documents submitted by the employee or requesting physician under section 9792.10.5(b) or (c). No independent medical review determination shall issue based solely on the information provided by a utilization review determination.

(c) The independent review organization, upon written approval by the Administrative Director, may utilize more than one medical reviewer to reach a determination regarding the medical necessity of a disputed medical treatment if it is found that the employee's condition and the disputed medical treatment is sufficiently complex such that a single reviewer could not reasonably address all disputed issues.

(d) The determination issued by the medical reviewer shall state whether the disputed medical treatment is medically necessary. The determination shall include the employee's medical condition, a list of the documents reviewed, a statement of the disputed medical treatment, references to the specific medical and scientific evidence utilized and the clinical reasons regarding medical necessity.

(e) The independent review organization shall provide the Administrative Director, the claims administrator, the employee, if represented the employee's attorney, and the employee's provider with a final determination regarding the medical necessity of the disputed medical treatment. With the final determination, the independent review organization shall provide a description of the qualifications of the medical reviewer or reviewers and the determination issued by the medical reviewer.

(1) If more than one medical reviewer reviewed the case, the independent review organization shall provide each reviewer's determination.

(2) The recommendation of the majority of medical reviewers shall prevail. If the reviewers are evenly split as to whether the disputed medical treatment should be provided, the decision shall be in favor of providing the treatment.

(f) The independent review organization shall keep the names of the reviewer, or reviewers if applicable, confidential in all communications with entities or individuals outside the independent review organization.

(g) Timeframes for final determinations:

(1) For regular review, the independent review organization shall complete its review and make its final determination within thirty (30) days of the receipt of the Application for Independent Medical Review, DWC Form IMR, and the supporting documentation and information provided under section 9792.10.5.

(A) If two (2) or more requests for independent medical review are consolidated under section 9792.10.4(a), the thirty (30) day period for the independent review organization to complete its review and make its final determination shall begin upon receipt of the last filed application for independent medical review that was consolidated for determination and the supporting documentation and information for that application.

(B) If, under section 9792.10.1(d)(3), an internal utilization review appeal modifies a utilization review determination for which an application for independent medical review was previously filed under section 9792.10.1(b), the thirty (30) day period for the independent review organization to complete its review and make its final determination shall begin upon receipt of the application for independent medical review requesting review of the modified treatment, and the supporting documentation and information for that application.

(2) For expedited review where the disputed medical treatment has not been provided, the independent review organization shall complete its review and make its final determination within three (3) days of the receipt of the Application for Independent Medical Review, DWC Form IMR, and the supporting documentation and information provided under section 9792.10.5.

(3) Subject to the approval of the Administrative Director, the deadlines for final determinations from the independent review organization, involving both regular and expedited reviews, may be extended for up to three days in extraordinary circumstances or for good cause.

(h) The final determination issued by the independent review organization shall be deemed to be the determination of the Administrative Director and shall be binding on all parties.

(i) Upon receipt of credible information that the claims administrator has failed to comply with its obligations under the independent medical review requirements set forth in Labor Code sections 4610.5 or in sections 9792.6 through 9792.10.8 of this Article, the Administrative Director shall, concurrent or subsequent to the issuance of the final determination issued by the independent review organization, issue an order to show cause under section 9792.15 for the assessment of administrative penalties against the claims administrator under section 9792.12(c).

Note: Authority: Sections 133, 4603.5, 4610.5 and 5307.3, Labor Code. Reference: Sections 4062, 4600, 4600.4, 4604.5, 4610 and 4610.5, Labor Code.

History: 1. New section filed 12-31-2012 as an emergency; operative 1-1-2013 pursuant to Government Code section 11346.1(d) (Register 2013, No. 1). A Certificate of Compliance must be transmitted to OAL by 7-1-2013 or emergency language will be repealed by operation of law on the following day.

2. New section refiled 7-1-2013 as an emergency; operative 7-1-2013 (Register 2013, No. 27). A Certificate of Compliance must be transmitted to OAL by 9-30-2013 or emergency language will be repealed by operation of law on the following day.

3. New section refiled 9-30-2013 as an emergency; operative 10-1-2013 (Register 2013, No. 40). A Certificate of Compliance must be transmitted to OAL by 12-30-2013 or emergency language will be repealed by operation of law on the following day.

4. Certificate of Compliance as to 9-30-2013 order, including amendment of section and Note, transmitted to OAL 12-30-2013 and filed 2-12-2014; amendments effective 2-12-2014 pursuant to Government Code section 11343.4(b)(3) (Register 2014, No. 7).

Ref.: Hanna § 5.02[2][d]; Herlick Handbook §§ 1.01[3][b], 4.09[1], 4.10[2], 4.16[3].

§9792.10.7. Independent Medical Review — Implementation of Determination and Appeal.

(a) Upon receiving the final determination of the Administrative Director that a disputed medical treatment is medically necessary, the claims administrator shall, unless an appeal is filed under subdivision (c) or liability for the treatment is disputed as described in subdivision (a)(3), promptly implement the determination.

(1) In the case of reimbursement for services already rendered, the claims administrator shall reimburse the provider or employee, whichever applies, within twenty (20) days after receipt of the final determination, subject to resolution of any remaining issue of the amount of payment pursuant to Labor Code sections 4603.2 to 4603.6, inclusive.

(2) In the case of services not yet rendered, the claims administrator shall authorize the services within five (5) working days of receipt of the final determination, or sooner if appropriate for the nature of the employee's medical condition, and shall inform the employee and provider of the authorization.

(3) If, at the time of receiving the final determination, the claims administrator is disputing liability for the medical treatment on grounds other than medical necessity, implementation of the final determination shall be deferred until the liability dispute has been resolved.

(b) Upon receipt of credible information that the claims administrator has failed to implement the final determination as required in subdivision (a), the Administrative Director shall issue an order to show cause under section 9792.15 for the assessment of administrative penalties against the claims administrator under section 9792.12(c).

(c) The parties may appeal a final determination of the Administrative Director by filing a petition with the Workers' Compensation Appeals Board.

(d) If the final determination of the Administrative Director is reversed by the Workers' Compensation Appeals Board, the dispute shall be remanded to the Administrative Director. The Administrative Director shall:

(1) Submit the dispute to independent medical review by a different independent review organization, if available;

(2) If a different independent medical review organization is not available after remand, the Administrative Director shall submit the dispute to the original independent review organization for review by a different reviewer in the organization.

Note: Authority: Sections 133, 4603.5, 4610.6 and 5307.3, Labor Code. Reference: Sections 4062, 4600, 4600.4, 4604.5, 4610 and 4610.5, Labor Code.

History: 1. New section filed 12-31-2012 as an emergency; operative 1-1-2013 pursuant to Government Code section 11346.1(d) (Register 2013, No. 1). A Certificate of Compliance must be transmitted to OAL by 7-1-2013 or emergency language will be repealed by operation of law on the following day.

2. New section refiled 7-1-2013 as an emergency; operative 7-1-2013 (Register 2013, No. 27). A Certificate of Compliance must be transmitted to OAL by 9-30-2013 or emergency language will be repealed by operation of law on the following day.

3. New section refiled 9-30-2013 as an emergency; operative 10-1-2013 (Register 2013, No. 40). A Certificate of Compliance

must be transmitted to OAL by 12-30-2013 or emergency language will be repealed by operation of law on the following day.

4. Certificate of Compliance as to 9-30-2013 order, including amendment of section and Note, transmitted to OAL 12-30-2013 and filed 2-12-2014; amendments effective 2-12-2014 pursuant to Government Code section 11343.4(b)(3) (Register 2014, No. 7).

Ref.: Herlick Handbook §§ 1.01[3][b], 4.09[1], 4.10[2], 4.16[3].

§9792.10.8. Independent Medical Review — Payment for Review.

(a) The costs of independent medical review and the administration of the independent medical review system shall be borne by claims administrators. For each Application for Independent Medical Review, DWC Form IMR, assigned to an independent review organization for an independent medical review of a disputed medical treatment, the fee for the claims administrator shall be:

(1) For calendar year 2013:

(A) For regular review:

(i) $560.00 for each application where a determination is issued under section 9792.10.6(b) by a medical reviewer who: (1) is a physician as defined by Labor Code section 3209.3; and (2) holds an M.D. or D.O. degree. If the review is conducted and a determination, or determinations if applicable, is issued by two medical reviewers as defined in this provision, the cost is $760.00

(ii) $495.00 for each application where a determination is issued under section 9792.10.6(b) by a medical reviewer who: (1) is a physician as defined by Labor Code section 3209.3; and (2) holds a degree other than an M.D. or D.O. degree. If the review is conducted and a determination, or determinations if applicable, is issued by two medical reviewers as defined in this provision, the cost is $655.00

(B) For expedited review:

(i) $685.00 for each application where a determination is issued under section 9792.10.6(b) by a medical reviewer who: (1) is a physician as defined by Labor Code section 3209.3; and (2) holds an M.D. or D.O. degree. If the review is conducted and a determination, or determinations if applicable, is issued by two medical reviewers as defined in this provision, the cost is $850.00.

(ii) $595.00 for each application where a determination is issued under section 9792.10.6(b) by a medical reviewer who: (1) is a physician as defined by Labor Code section 3209.3; and (2) holds a degree other than an M.D. or D.O. degree. If the review is conducted and a determination, or determinations if applicable, is issued by two medical reviewers as defined in this provision, the cost is $760.00.

(C) For withdrawn reviews:

(i) $215.00 for each application where review is terminated by the independent review organization prior to the receipt of the documentation and information provided under section 9792.10.5 by a medical reviewer.

(ii) If the review of an application and documentation and information provided under section 9792.10.5 is terminated by the independent review organization during or subsequent to the review of by a medical reviewer, the cost will be the same as if a determination under section 9792.10.6(b) had been issued by the medical reviewer.

(2) For calendar year 2014:

(A) For regular review:

(i) $550.00 for each application where a determination is issued under section 9792.10.6(b) by a medical reviewer who: (1) is a physician as defined by Labor Code section 3209.3; and (2) holds a M.D. or D.O. degree. If the review is conducted and a determination, or determinations if applicable, is issued by two medical reviewers as defined in this provision, the cost is $740.00.

(ii) $475.00 for each application where a determination is issued under section 9792.10.6(b) by a medical reviewer who: (1) is a physician as defined by Labor Code section 3209.3; and (2) holds a degree other than an M.D. or D.O. degree. If the review is conducted and a determination, or determinations if applicable, is issued by two medical reviewers as defined in this provision, the cost is $635.00.

(B) For expedited review:

(i) $645.00 for each application where a determination is issued under section 9792.10.6(b) by a medical reviewer who: (1) is a physician as defined by Labor Code section 3209.3; and (2) holds a M.D. or D.O. degree. If the review is conducted and a determination, or determinations if applicable, is issued by two medical reviewers as defined in this provision, the cost is $830.00.

(ii) $575.00 for each application where a determination is issued under section 9792.10.6(b) by a medical reviewer who: (1) is a physician as defined by Labor Code section 3209.3; and (2) holds a degree other than an M.D. or D.O. degree. If the review is conducted and a determination, or determinations if applicable, is issued by two medical reviewers as defined in this provision, the cost is $740.00.

(C) For withdrawn reviews:

(i) $215.00 for each application where review is terminated by the independent review organization prior to the receipt of the documentation and information provided under section 9792.10.5 by a medical reviewer.

(ii) If the review of an application and documentation and information provided under section 9792.10.5 is terminated by the independent review organization subsequent to the receipt of the documentation and information provided under section 9792.10.5 by a medical reviewer, the cost will be the same as if a determination under section 9792.10.6(b) had been issued by the medical reviewer.

(b) The independent medical review organization shall bill each claims administrator for payment in arrears for every independent medical review initiated under this Article that was completed or terminated prior to completion. Invoices shall identify each independent medical review, the fees assessed for each review, and the aggregate total fee owed by the claims administrator.

(c) The aggregate total fee owed by the claims administrator for the prior calendar month shall be paid to the independent medical review organization within thirty (30) days of the billing. If the aggregate total fee is not paid within ten (10) days after it becomes due, there shall be added an additional amount equal to 10 percent, plus interest at the legal rate, which shall be paid at the same time but in addition to the total aggregate fee.

(d) The fees paid by claims administrators for independent medical review under this section are non-refundable and not subject to discount or rebate. Any questions or disputes over the aggregate total fee and additional payments owed by the claims administrator under subdivision (c), late payments, and untimely determinations shall be submitted to the Administrative Director for informal resolution. Any request to resolve a dispute must be accompanied by a written statement setting forth the amount in dispute and the nature of the dispute.

Note: Authority: Sections 133, 4603.5, 5307.3 and 4610.6, Labor Code. Reference: Sections 4610, 4610.5 and 4610.6, Labor Code.

History: 1. New section filed 12-31-2012 as an emergency; operative 1-1-2013 pursuant to Government Code section 11346.1(d) (Register 2013, No. 1). A Certificate of Compliance must be transmitted to OAL by 7-1-2013 or emergency language will be repealed by operation of law on the following day.

2. New section refiled 7-1-2013 as an emergency; operative 7-1-2013 (Register 2013, No. 27). A Certificate of Compliance must be transmitted to OAL by 9-30-2013 or emergency language will be repealed by operation of law on the following day.

3. New section refiled 9-30-2013 as an emergency; operative 10-1-2013 (Register 2013, No. 40). A Certificate of Compliance must be transmitted to OAL by 12-30-2013 or emergency language will be repealed by operation of law on the following day.

4. Certificate of Compliance as to 9-30-2013 order transmitted to OAL 12-30-2013 and filed 2-12-2014 (Register 2014, No. 7).

Ref.: Herlick Handbook §§ 1.01[3][b], 4.09[1], 4.10[2], 4.16[3].

§9792.10.9. Independent Medical Review — Publishing of Determinations.

The Administrative Director may publish the results of independent medical review determinations after removing all individually identifiable information as defined in Labor Code section 138.7, including, but not limited to, the employee, all medical providers, the claims administrator, any of the claims administrator's employees or contractors, or any utilization review organization.

Note: Authority: Sections 133, 4603.5, 5307.3 and 4610.6, Labor Code. Reference: Sections 4610, 4610.5 and 4610.6, Labor Code.

History: 1. New section filed 12-31-2012 as an emergency; operative 1-1-2013 pursuant to Government Code section 11346.1(d) (Register 2013, No. 1). A Certificate of Compliance must be transmitted to OAL by 7-1-2013 or emergency language will be repealed by operation of law on the following day.

2. New section refiled 7-1-2013 as an emergency; operative 7-1-2013 (Register 2013, No. 27). A Certificate of Compliance must be transmitted to OAL by 9-30-2013 or emergency language will be repealed by operation of law on the following day.

3. New section refiled 9-30-2013 as an emergency; operative 10-1-2013 (Register 2013, No. 40). A Certificate of Compliance must be transmitted to OAL by 12-30-2013 or emergency language will be repealed by operation of law on the following day.

4. Certificate of Compliance as to 9-30-2013 order transmitted to OAL 12-30-2013 and filed 2-12-2014 (Register 2014, No. 7).

Ref.: Herlick Handbook §§ 1.01[3][b], 4.09[1], 4.10[2], 4.16[3].

§9792.11. Investigation Procedures: Labor Code §4610 Utilization Review Violations.

(a) To carry out the responsibilities mandated by Labor Code Section 4610(i), the Administrative Director, or his or her designee, shall investigate the utilization review process of any employer, insurer or other entity subject to the provisions of section 4610. The investigation shall include, but not be limited to, review of the practices, files, documents and other records, whether electronic or paper, of the claims administrator, and any other person responsible for utilization review processes for an employer. As used in sections 9792.11 through 9792.15, the phrase 'utilization review organization' includes any person or entity with which the employer, or an insurer, or third party administrator, contracts to fulfill part or all of the employer's utilization review responsibilities under Labor Code section 4610 and Title 8 of the California Code of Regulations, sections 9792.6 through 9792.15.

(b) Notwithstanding Labor Code section 129(a) through (d) and section 129.5 subdivisions (a) through (d), the Administrative Director, or his or her designee, may conduct a utilization review investigation pursuant to Labor Code section 4610, which may include, but is not limited to, an audit of files and other records.

(c) The Administrative Director, or his or her designee, may conduct a utilization review investigation at any location where Labor Code Section 4610 utilization review processes occur, as follows:

(1) For utilization review organizations:

(A) A Routine Investigation shall be initiated at each known utilization review organization at least once every five (5) years. The investigation shall include a review of a random sample of requests for authorization, as defined by section 9792.6(q) or section 9792.6.1(t), received by the utilization review organization during the three most recent full calendar months preceding the date of the issuance of the Notice of Utilization Review Investigation. The investigation may also include a review of any credible complaints received by the Administrative Director since the time of the previous investigation. If there has not been a previous investigation, the investigation may include a review of any credible complaints received by the Administrative Director since the effective date of sections 9792.11 through 9792.15.

(B) Target Investigations:

1. A Return Target Investigation of the same investigation subject shall be conducted within 18 months of the date of the previous investigation if the performance rating was less than eighty-five percent.

2. A Special Target Investigation may be conducted at any time based on credible information indicating the possible existence of a violation of Labor Code section 4610 or sections 9792.6 through 9792.12.

3. The Return Target Investigation and the Special Target Investigation may include: (i) a review of the requests for authorization previously investigated which contained violations; (ii) a review of the file or files pertaining to the complaint or possible violation; (iii) a random sample of requests for authorization received by the utilization review organization during the three most recent full calendar months preceding the date of the issuance of the Notice of Utilization Review Investigation; (iv) a sample of a specific type of request for authorization; and (v) any credible complaints received by the Administrative Director since the time of any prior investigation. If there has not been a previous investigation, the investigation may include a review of any credible complaints received by the Administrative Director since the effective date of sections 9792.11 through 9792.15.

(2) For a claims administrator:

(A) A Routine Investigation shall be initiated at each claims adjusting location at least once every five (5) years concurrent with the profile audit review done pursuant to Labor Code sections 129 and 129.5. The investigation shall include a review of a random sample of requests for authorization, as defined by section 9792.6(q) or section 9792.6.1(t), received by the claims administrator during the three most recent full calendar months preceding the date of the issuance of the Notice of Utilization Review Investigation. The investigation may also include a review of any credible complaints received by the Administrative Director since the time of the previous investigation. If there has not been a previous investigation, the investigation may include a review of any credible complaints received by the Administrative Director since the effective date of sections 9792.11 through 9792.15.

(B) Target Investigations:

1. A Return Target Investigation of the same investigation subject shall be conducted within 18 months of the date of any previous investigation if the performance rating was less than eighty-five percent.

2. A Special Target Investigation may be conducted at any time based on credible information indicating the possible existence of a violation of Labor Code section 4610 or sections 9792.6 through 9792.12.

3. The Return Target Investigation and the Special Target Investigation may include: (i) a review of the requests for authorization previously investigated which contained violations; (ii) a review of the file or files pertaining to the complaint or possible violation; (iii) a random sample of requests for authorization received by the claims administrator during the three most recent full calendar months preceding the date of the issuance of the Notice of Utilization Review Investigation; (iv) a sample of a specific type of request for authorization; and (v) any credible complaints received by the Administrative Director since the time of any prior investigation. If there has not been a previous investigation, the investigation may include a review of any credible complaints received by the Administrative Director since the effective date of sections 9792.11 through 9792.15.

(d) The number of requests for authorization randomly selected for investigation shall be determined based on the following table:

Population of requests for authorization received during a three month calendar period	*Sample Size*
5 or less	all
6-10	1 less than total
11-13	2 less than total
14-16	3 less than total
17-18	4 less than total
19-20	5 less than total
21-23	6 less than total
24	17
25-26	18
27-29	19
30-31	20
32-33	21
34-36	22
37-39	23
40-41	24
42-44	25
45-48	26
49-51	27
52-55	28
56-58	29
59-62	30
63-67	31
68-72	32
73-77	33
78-82	34
83-88	35
89-95	36
96-102	37
103-110	38
111-119	39
120-128	40
129-139	41
140-151	42
152-164	43
165-179	44
180-197	45
198-217	46
218-241	47
242-269	48
270-304	49
305-346	50
347-399	51
400-468	52
469-562	53
563-696	54
697-905	55
906-1,272	56
1,273-2,091	57
2,092-5,530	58
5,531 +	59

(e) Complaints concerning utilization review procedures may be submitted with any supporting documentation to the Division of Workers' Compensation using the sample complaint form that is posted on the Division's website at:

http://www.dir.ca.gov/dwc/FORMS/UtilizationReviewcomplaintform.pdf

Complaints should be mailed to DWC Medical Unit-UR, P.O. Box 71010, Oakland, CA 94612, attention UR Complaints or emailed to DWCManagedCare@dir.ca.gov. Complaints received by the Division of Workers' Compensation will be reviewed and investigated, if necessary, to determine if the complaints are credible and indicate the possible existence of a violation of Labor Code section 4610 or sections 9792.6 through 9792.12.

(f) Administrative penalties may be assessed for any failure to comply with Labor Code section 4610, or sections 9792.6 through 9792.12 of Title 8, California Code of Regulations, except that the penalties listed in section 9792.12(a)(6) through (14) and (b) shall only be imposed if the request was subject to the Labor Code section 4610 utilization review process.

(g) In the event an investigation of utilization review processes is done at the claims administrator's adjusting location, concurrent with a profile audit review done pursuant to Labor Code section 129 or 129.5, the administrative penalty amounts for each violation of Labor Code section 4610 or sections 9792.6 through 9792.12 of Title 8, California Code of Regulations, shall be governed by sections 9792.11 through 9792.15. Any such administrative penalty for utilization review process violations shall apply in lieu of the administrative penalty amount allowed under the audit regulations at section 10111.2(b)(8)[vi] of Title 8, California Code of Regulations. In addition, any report of findings from the investigation and any Order to Show Cause re: Assessment of Administrative Penalties prepared by the Administrative Director, or his or her designee, based on violations of Labor Code section 4610 or sections 9792.6 through 9792.12 of Title 8, California Code of Regulations, shall be prepared separately from any audit report or assessment of administrative penalties made pursuant to Labor Code section 129 and 129.5. The Order to Show Cause re: Assessment of Administrative Penalties for violations of sections 9792.6 et seq of Title 8 of the California Code of Regulations shall be governed by sections 9792.11 through 9792.15.

(h) The Administrative Director, or his or her designee, may also utilize the provisions of Government Code sections 11180 through 11191 to determine whether any violations of the requirements in Labor Code section 4610 or sections 9792.6 through 9792.12 of Title 8, California Code of Regulations, have occurred.

(i) Sections 9792.11 through 9792.15 of Title 8 of the California Code of Regulations shall apply to any Labor Code section 4610 utilization review investigation conducted on or after the effective date of sections 9792.11 through 9792.15 and for conduct which occurred on or after the effective date of sections 9792.11 through 9792.15.

(j) Unless the Administrative Director in his or her discretion determines that advance notice will render a Special Target or Return Target Investigation less useful, the claims administrator or utilization review organization shall be notified of its selection for an Investigation. Claims administrators and utilization review organizations shall be sent a Notice of Utilization Review Investigation. The Notice of Utilization Review Investigation shall require the investigation subject to provide the following:

(1) A description of the system used to identify each request for authorization (if applicable). To the extent the system identifies any of the following information in an electronic format, the claims administrator or utilization review organization shall provide in an electronic format a list of each and every request for authorization received at the investigation site during a three month calendar period specified by the Administrative Director, or his or her designee, and the following data elements: i) a unique identifying number for each request for authorization if one has been assigned; ii) the name of the injured worker; iii) the claim number used by the claims adjuster; iv) the initial date of receipt of the request for authorization; v) the type of review (expedited prospective, prospective, expedited concurrent, concurrent, retrospective, appeal); vi) the disposition (approve, deny, delay, modify, withdrawal); and, vii) if applicable, the type of person who withdrew the request (requesting physician, claims adjuster, injured employee or his or her attorney, or other person). In the event the claims administrator or utilization review organization is not able to provide the list in an electronic format, the list shall be provided in such a form that the listed requests for authorization are sorted in the following order: by type of utilization review, type of disposition, and date of receipt of the initial request;

(2) A description of all media used to transmit, share, record or store information received and transmitted in reference to each request, whether printed copy, electronic, fax, diskette, computer drive or other media;

(3) A legend of any and all numbers, letters and other symbols used to identify the disposition (e.g. approve, deny, modify, delay or withdraw), type of review (expedited prospective, prospective, expedited concurrent, concurrent, retrospective, appeal), and other abbreviations used to document individual requests for authorization and a data dictionary for all data elements provided;

(4) A description of the methods by which the medical director for utilization review ensures that the process by which requests for authorization are reviewed and approved, modified, delayed, or denied is in compliance with Labor Code section 4610 and sections 9792.6 through 9792.10.1 and

(5) The following additional information, may be requested by the Administrative Director or his or her designee, as applicable to the type of entity investigated: i) whether utilization review services are provided externally; ii) the name(s) of the utilization review organization(s); iii) the name and address of the employer; and iv) the name and address of the insurer.

(k) The utilization review organization or claims administrator shall provide the requested information listed in subdivision (j) within fourteen (14) calendar days of receipt of the Notice of Utilization Review Investigation. Based on the information provided, the Administrative Director, or his or her designee, shall provide the claims administrator or utilization review organization with a Notice of Investigation Commencement, which shall include a list of randomly selected requests for authorization from a three month calendar period designated by the Administrative Director and complaint files (if applicable) for investigation.

(*l*) For utilization review organizations: Within fourteen (14) calendar days of receipt from the Administrative Director, or his or her designee, of the Notice of Investigation Commencement, the utilization review organization shall deliver to the Administrative Director, or his or her designee, a true and complete copy of all records, whether electronic or paper, for each request for authorization listed. Copies of the records shall be delivered with a statement signed under penalty of perjury by the custodian of records for the location at which the records are held, attesting that all of the records produced are true, correct and complete copies of the originals, in his or her possession. After reviewing the records, the Administrative Director, or his or her designee, shall determine if an onsite investigation is required. If an onsite investigation is required, fourteen (14) calendar days notice shall be provided to the utilization review organization.

(m) For claims administrators: The Notice of Investigation Commencement shall be provided to the claims administrator at least fourteen (14) calendar days prior to the commencement of the onsite investigation. The claims administrator shall produce for the Administrative Director, or his or her designee, on the first day of commencement of the onsite investigation, the true, correct and complete copies, whether electronic or paper, whether located onsite or offsite, of each request for authorization identified by the Administrative Director or his or her designee, together with a statement signed under penalty of perjury by the custodian of records for the location at which the records are held, attesting that all of the records produced are true, correct and complete copies of the originals.

(n) In the event the Administrative Director, or his or her designee, determines additional records or files are needed for review during the course of an onsite investigation, the claims administrator or utilization review organization shall produce the requested records in the manner described by subdivision 9792.11(k), within one (1) working day when the records are located at the site of investigation, and within five (5) working days when the records are located at any other site. Any such request by the Administrative Director or his or her designee also may include records or files pertaining to any complaint alleging violations of Labor Code sections 4610 or sections 9792.6 through 9792.12 of Title 8 of the California Code of Regulations. The Administrative Director or his or her designee may extend the time for production of the requested records for good cause.

(o) If the date or deadline in sections 9792.9(b) and (c), or section 9792.9.1(c), to perform any act related to utilization review practices falls on a weekend or holiday, for the purposes of assessing penalties, the act may be performed on the next normal business day, as defined by Labor Code section 4600.4 and Civil Code section 9. This subdivision shall not apply in cases involving concurrent or expedited review. The timelines in sections 9792.9(b) shall only be extended as provided under section 9792.9(g); the timelines in sections 9792.9.1(c) shall only be extended as provided under section 9792.9.1(f).

(p) If the claims administrator or utilization review organization does not record the date a document is received, it shall be deemed received by using the method set out in section 9792.9(a)(2) or section 9792.9.1(a)(2), except that:

(1) where the request for authorization is made by mail through the U.S. postal service and no proof of service by mail exists, the request shall be deemed to have been received by the claims administrator, or utilization review organization on whichever date is earlier, either the receipt date stamped by the addressee or within five (5) calendar days of the date stated in the request for authorization or where the addressee can show a delay in mailing by the postmark date on the mailing envelope then: (A) within five (5) calendar days of the postmark date, if the place of mailing and place of address are both within California; (B) within ten (10) calendar days if the place of address is within the United States but outside of California; or (C) within twenty (20) calendar days if the place of address is outside of the United States; and

(2) where the request for authorization is made by express mail, overnight mail or courier without any proof of service, the request shall be deemed received by the addressee on the date specified in any written confirmation of delivery.

(q) Upon initiating a Special Target Investigation, the Administrative Director, or his or her designee, shall provide to the claims administrator or the utilization review organization a written description of the factual information or of the complaint containing factual information or a copy of the complaint that triggered the utilization review investigation, unless the Administrative Director or his or her designee determines that providing the information would make the investigation less useful. The claims administrator or utilization review organization shall have ten (10) business days upon receipt of the written description or copy of the complaint to provide a written response to the Administrative Director or his or her designee. After reviewing the written response, the Administrative Director, or his or her designee, shall either close the investigation without the assessment of administrative penalties or conduct further investigation to determine whether a violation exists and whether to impose penalty assessments.

(r) For utilization review organizations: The files and other records, whether electronic or paper, that pertain to the utilization review process shall be retained for at least three (3) years following either: (1) the most recent utilization review decision for each injured employee, or (2) the date on which any appeal from the assessment of penalties for violations of Labor Code section 4610 or sections 9792.6 through 9792.12 is final, whichever date is later. Claims administrators shall retain their claim files as set forth in section 10102 of Title 8 of the California Code of Regulations.

(s) Upon receipt of a notice of Routine or Target Investigation or any other request from the Administrative Director, or his or her designee, to review all files and other records pertaining to the employer's utilization review process, whether electronic or paper, that are created or held outside of California, the claims administrator or utilization review organization shall either deliver all such requested files and other records to an address in California specified by the Administrative Director, or his or her designee, or reimburse the Administrative Director for the actual expenses of each investigator who travels outside of California to the place where the records are held, including the per diem expenses, travel expenses and compensated overtime of the investigators.

(t) A preliminary investigation report will be provided to the claims administrator or utilization review organization. The preliminary investigation report shall consist of the preliminary notice of utilization review penalty assessments, the performance rating, and may include one or more requests for additional documentation or compliance. A conference to discuss the preliminary investigation report shall be scheduled, if necessary, within twenty-one calendar days from the issuance of the preliminary findings. Following the conference, the Administrative Director or his or her designee shall issue an Order to Show Cause Re: Assessment of Administrative Penalty (which shall include the final investigation report), as set forth in section 9792.15.

(u) The claims administrator or utilization review organization may stipulate to the allegations and final report set forth in the Order to Show Cause.

(v) Within forty-five (45) calendar days of the service of the Order to Show Cause Re: Assessment of Administrative Penalties, if no answer has been filed, or within 15 calendar days after any and all appeals have become final, the claims administrator or utilization review organization shall provide the following:

(1) A notice, which shall include a copy of the final investigation report, the measures actually implemented to

abate such conditions, and the website address for the Division where the performance rating and summary of violations is posted. If a hearing was conducted under section 9792.15, the notice shall include the Final Determination in lieu of the final investigation report.

(2) For utilization review organizations: the notice must be served on any employer or third party claims administrator that contracted with the utilization review organization and whose utilization review process was assessed with a penalty pursuant to section 9792.12, and any insurer whose utilization review process was assessed with a penalty pursuant to section 9792.12.

(3) For claims administrators: the notice must be served on any self-insured employer and any insurer whose utilization review process was assessed with a penalty pursuant to section 9792.12.

(4) The notice shall be served by certified mail.

(5) Documentation of compliance with this section shall be served on the Administrative Director within thirty calendar days from the date the notice was served.

Note: Authority cited: Sections 11180-1191, Government Code; and Sections 133, 4610 and 5307.3, Labor Code. Reference: Sections 129, 129.5, 4062, 4600, 4600.4, 4604.5, 4610 and 4614, Labor Code.

History: 1. New section filed 6-7-2007; operative 6-7-2007 pursuant to Government Code section 11343.4 (Register 2007, No. 23). For prior history, see Register 2005, No. 38.

2. Amendment of subsections (c)(1)(A), (c)(2)(A), (j)(4) and (o)-(p) filed 2-12-2014; operative 2-12-2014 pursuant to Government Code section 11343.4(b)(3) (Register 2014, No. 7).

Ref.: Hanna § 22.05[6][c]; Herlick Handbook §§ 1.01[3][b], 4.09[1], 4.16[1], [3].

§9792.12. Administrative Penalty Schedule for Utilization Review and Independent Medical Review Violations.

(a) Mandatory Utilization Review Administrative Penalties. Notwithstanding Labor Code section 129.5(c)(1) through (c)(3), the penalty amount that shall be assessed for each failure to comply with the utilization review process required by Labor Code section 4610, and sections 9792.6 through 9792.12 of Title 8 of the California Code of Regulations, is:

(1) For failure to establish a Labor Code section 4610 utilization review plan: $50,000;

(2) For failure to include all of the requirements of section 9792.7(a) in the utilization review plan: $5,000;

(3) For failure to file the utilization review plan or a letter in lieu of a utilization review plan with the Administrative Director as required by section 9792.7(c): $10,000;

(4) For failure to file a modified utilization review plan with the Administrative Director within 30 calendar days after the claims administrator makes a material modification to the plan as required by section 9792.7(c): $5,000;

(5) For failure to employ or designate a physician as a medical director, as defined in section 9792.6(*l*), of the utilization review process, as required by section 9792.7(b): $50,000;

(6) For issuance of a decision to modify or deny a request for authorization regarding a medical treatment, procedure, service or product where the requested treatment, procedure or service is not within the reviewer's scope of practice (as set forth by the reviewer's licensing board): $25,000;

(7) For failure to comply with the requirement that only a licensed physician may modify, delay, or deny requests for authorization of medical treatment for reasons of medical necessity to cure or relieve, except as provided for in Labor Code section 4604.5(c): $25,000;

(8) For failure of a non-physician reviewer (person other than a reviewer, expert reviewer or medical director as defined in section 9792.6 of Title 8 of the California Code of Regulations), who approves an amended request without documenting the amended request as provided under section 9792.7(b)(3) when a physician has voluntarily withdrawn a request in order to submit an amended request: $1,000;

(9) For failure to communicate the decision in response to a request for an expedited review, as defined in section 9792.6(g), in a timely fashion, as required by section 9792.9 and section 9792.9.1: $15,000;

(10) For failure to approve the request for authorization solely on the basis that the condition for which treatment was requested is not addressed by the medical treatment utilization schedule adopted pursuant to section 5307.27 of the Labor Code: $5,000;

(11) For failure to discuss or document attempts to discuss reasonable options for a care plan with the requesting physician as required by Labor Code section 4610(g)(3)(B), prior to denying authorization of or discontinuing medical care, in the case of concurrent review: $10,000;

(12) For failure to respond to a complete DWC Form RFA or other request for authorization accepted by a claims administrator under section 9792.9.1(c)(2) submitted by the injured employee's requesting treating physician, in the case of a non-expedited concurrent review: $2,000;

(13) For failure to respond to a complete DWC Form RFA or other request for authorization accepted by a claims administrator under section 9792.9.1(c)(2) submitted for authorization by the injured employee's requesting treating physician, in the case of a non-expedited prospective review: $1,000;

(14) For failure to respond to a complete DWC Form RFA or other request for authorization accepted by a claims administrator under section 9792.9.1(c)(2) submitted by the injured employee's requesting treating physician, in the case of a retrospective review: $500;

(15) For failure to disclose or otherwise to make available, if requested, the Utilization Review criteria or guidelines to the public, as required by Labor Code section 4610, subdivision (f)(5) and section 9792.7(d) of Title 8 of the California Code of Regulations: $100.

(16) For failure to timely serve the Administrative Director with documentation of compliance pursuant to section 9792.11(v)(5): $500.

(17) For failure to timely comply with any compliance requirement listed in the Final Report if no timely answer was filed or any compliance requirement listed in the Determination and Order after any and all appeals have become final: $500.

(b) Additional Utilization Review Penalties and Remediation.

(1) After conducting a Routine or Return Target Investigation, the Administrative Director, or his or her designee, shall calculate the investigation subject's performance rating based on its review of the randomly selected requests. The investigation subject's performance rating may also be calculated after conducting a Special Target Investigation. The performance rating will be calculated as follows:

(A) The factor for failure to make and/or provide a timely response to a request for authorization shall be determined by dividing the number of randomly selected requests with violations involving failure to make or provide a timely response to a request for authorization by the total number of randomly selected requests.

(B) The factor for notice(s) with faulty content shall be determined by dividing the number of requests involving notice(s) with faulty content by the total number of randomly selected requests.

(C) The factor for failure to issue notice(s) to all appropriate parties shall be determined by the number of requests involving the failure to issue notice(s) to all appropriate parties by the total number of randomly selected requests.

(D) The investigation subject's investigation performance rating will be determined by adding the factors calculated pursuant to subsections (b)(1)(A) through (b)(1)(C), dividing the total by three, subtracting from one, and multiplying by one-hundred.

(E) If the investigation subject's performance rating meets or exceeds eighty-five percent, the Administrative Director, or his or her designee, shall assess no penalties for the violations listed in this subdivision. If the performance rating is less than eighty-five percent, the violations shall be assessed as set forth below in (b)(2) through (b)(5):

(2) For the types of violations listed below in (b)(4) and (b)(5), each violation shall have a penalty amount, as specified of $100 in (b)(4) or $50 in (b)(5). The penalty amount specified in (b)(4) and (b)(5) shall be waived if the investigation subject's performance rating meets or exceeds eighty-five percent, or if following a Routine Investigation the claims administrator or utilization review organization agrees in writing to:

(A) Deliver to the Administrative Director, or his or her designee, within no more than thirty (30) calendar days from the date of the agreement or the number of days otherwise specified, written evidence, tendered with a declaration made under penalty of perjury, that explains or demonstrates how the violation has been abated in compliance with the applicable statute or regulations and the terms of abatement specified by the Administrative Director; and

(B) Grant the Administrative Director, or his or her designee, entry, upon request and within the time frame specified in the agreement, to the site at which the violation was found for a Return Target Investigation for the purpose of verifying compliance with the abatement measures reported in subdivision 9792.12(b)(1)(A) above and agree to a review of randomly selected requests for authorization; and

(C) Reinstatement of the penalty amount previously waived for each such instance, in the event the violative condition is not abated within the time period specified by the Administrative Director, or his or her designee, or in the event that such abatement measures are not consistent with abatement terms specified by the Administrative Director, or his or her designee.

(3) In the event the Administrative Director, or his or her designee, returns for a Return Target Investigation, after the initial violation has become final, and the subject fails to meet the performance standard of 85%, the amount of penalty shall be calculated as described below and in no event shall the penalty amount be waived:

(A) The penalty amount for each violation shall be multiplied by two for a second investigation, but in no event shall the total penalties for the violations exceed $100,000;

(B) The penalty amount for each violation shall be multiplied by five for a third investigation, but in no event shall the total penalties for the violations exceed $200,000;

(C) The penalty amount for each violation shall be multiplied by ten for a fourth investigation, but in no event shall the total penalties for the violations exceed $400,000.

(4) For each of the violations listed below, the penalty amount shall be $100.00 for each instance found by the Administrative Director, or his or her designee:

(A) For failure to immediately notify all parties in the manner described in section 9792.9(h)(2) and section 9792.9.1(f)(2) of the basis for extending the decision date for a request for medical treatment;

(B) For failure to document efforts to obtain information from the requesting party prior to issuing a denial of a request for authorization on the basis of lack of reasonable and necessary information;

(C) For failure to make a decision to approve or modify or deny the request for authorization, within five (5) working days of receipt of a complete DWC Form RFA or other request for authorization accepted by a claims administrator under section 9792.9.1(c)(2) submitted by the injured employee's requesting treating physician, or receipt of the requested information for prospective or concurrent review, and to communicate the decision as required by section 9792.9(h)(3) and section 9792.9.1(f)(3) and section 9792.9.1(f)(4);

(D) For failure to make and communicate a retrospective decision to approve, modify, or deny the request, within thirty (30) working days of receipt of a complete DWC Form RFA or other request for authorization accepted by a claims administrator under section 9792.9.1(c)(2) submitted by the injured employee's requesting treating physician, or receipt of the requested information, as required by section 9792.9(h)(4) and section 9792.9.1(e)(4), and (f)(6);

(E) Except as provided in subdivision (a), for failure to include in the written decision that modifies, delays or denies authorization, all of the items required by section 9792.9(k) and(*l*), and section 9792.9.1(e);

(F) For failure to disclose or otherwise to make available, if requested, the Utilization Review criteria or guidelines, to the injured employee whose case is under review, as required by Labor Code section 4610(f)(5) and section 9792.8(a)(3) Title 8 of the California Code of Regulations.

(5) For each of the violations listed below, the penalty amount shall be $50.00 for each instance found by the Administrative Director, or his or her designee:

(A) For failure by a non-physician or physician reviewer to timely notify the requesting physician, as required by section 9792.9(c)(2) or section 9792.9.1(f)(2), that additional information is needed in order to make a decision in compliance with the timeframes contained in section 9792.9(c) or section 9792.9.1(c);

(B) For failure to communicate the decision to approve to the requesting physician in the case of prospective or concurrent review, by phone or fax within 24 hours of the decision, as required by Labor Code section 4610(g)(3)(A) and in accordance with section 9792.9(c)(3) or section 9792.9.1(d)(2);

(C) For failure to send a written notice of the decision to modify, delay or deny to the requesting party, and to the injured employee and to his or her attorney if any, within twenty four (24) hours of making the decision for concurrent review, or within two business days for prospective review, as required by Labor Code section 4610(g)(3)(A) and section 9792.9(c)(4) or section 9792.9.1(e)(3);

(D) For failure to send a written notice of the decision in the case of retrospective review as required by section 9792.9(d) or section 9792.9.1(d)(3) and (e)(4) within thirty (30) days of receipt of the medical information that was reasonably necessary to make the determination;

(E) For failure to document that one of the following events occurred prior to the claims administrator providing written notice for delay under Labor Code section 4610(g)(5):

(1) the claims administrator had not received all of the information reasonably necessary and requested;

(2) the employer or claims administrator has requested a consultation by an expert reviewer;

(3) the physician reviewer has requested an additional examination or test be performed;

(F) Reserved.

(G) For failure to explain in writing the reason for delay as required by section 9792.9(h)(2) or section 9792.9.1(f)(2) of Title 8 of the California Code of Regulations when the decision to delay was made under one of the circumstances listed in section 9792.9(h)(1) or section 9792.9.1(f)(1).

(6) After the time to file an answer to the Order to Show Cause Re: Assessment of Administrative Penalties has elapsed and no answer has been filed or after any and all appeals have become final, the Administrative Director, or his or her designee, shall post on the website for the Division of Workers' Compensation the performance rating and summary of violations for each utilization review investigation.

(c) Independent Medical Review Administrative Penalties. Notwithstanding Labor Code section 129.5(c)(1) through (c)(3), the penalty amount that shall be assessed for each failure to comply with the independent medical review process required by Labor Code sections 4610.5 and 4610.6, and sections 9792.6 through 9792.10.8 of this Article is:

(1) For the failure to provide the Application for Independent Medical Review, DWC Form IMR, set forth at section 9792.10.2, with a written decision modifying, delaying, or denying a treatment authorization under sections 9792.9(*l*) or 9792.9.1: $2,000.

(2) For the failure to complete all applicable fields on the Application for Independent Medical Review, DWC Form IMR, set forth at section 9792.10.2, that is provided with a written decision modifying, delaying, or denying a treatment authorization under sections 9792.9(*l*) or 9792.9.1:

(A) $500 for a failure to provide the Employee Name, Address, Phone Number, and Date of Injury;

(B) $500 for a failure to provide the Requesting Physician Name, Address, Specialty, and Phone Number;

(C) $500 for a failure to provide the Claims Administrator Name, Adjustor/Contact Name, Address, and Phone Number;

(D) $500 for a failure to complete any field under the section heading "Disputed Medical Treatment;"

(E) $100 for a failure to provide any field not identified above.

(3) For the failure to include in a written decision modifying, delaying, or denying a treatment authorization under sections 9792.9(*l*) or 9792.9.1 a clear statement that advising the injured employee that any dispute shall be resolved in accordance with the independent medical review provisions of Labor Code section 4610.5 and 4610.6, and that an objection to the utilization review decision must be communicated by the injured worker, the injured worker's representative, or the injured worker's attorney on behalf of the injured worker on the Application for Independent Medical Review, DWC Form IMR, set forth at section 9792.10.2, within 30 days of service of the utilization review decision: $1,000.

(4) For the failure to include in a written decision modifying, delaying, or denying a treatment authorization under sections 9792.9(*l*) or 9792.9.1 a statement detailing the claims administrator's internal utilization review appeals process for the requesting physician, if any, and a statement that the internal appeals process is a voluntary process that neither triggers nor bars use of the dispute resolution procedures of Labor Code section 4610.5 and 4610.6, but may be pursued on an optional basis: $1,000.

(5) For the failure to timely provide information requested by the Administrative Director under section 9792.10.3(b): $500.00 for each day the response is untimely under section 9792.10.3(c), up to a maximum of $5,000.00.

(6) For the failure to timely provide all information required by section 9792.10.5(a) and (c): $500.00 for each day the response is untimely up to a maximum of $5,000.00.

(7) For the failure to authorize services found to be medically necessary by the independent medical review organization in the final determination issued under section 9792.10.6 within either five (5) business days of receipt of the determination, or sooner if appropriate for the employee's medical condition, or five (5) business days from the date the determination is final, if an appeal of the determination has been filed under Labor Code section 4610.6(h): $1,000.00 for each day up to a maximum of $5,000.00.

(8) For the failure to reimburse for services already rendered that has been found to be medically necessary by the independent medical review organization in the final determination issued under section 9792.10.6 within twenty (20) days after receipt of the final determination, or within twenty (20) days from the date the determination is final if an appeal of the determination has been filed under Labor Code section 4610.6(h), subject to resolution of any remaining issue of the amount of payment pursuant to Labor

Code sections 4603.2 to 4603.6, inclusive: $500.00 for each day up to a maximum of $5,000.00

(9) For the failure to timely pay an invoice sent from the designated independent medical review organization under section 9792.10.8(c): $250.

(d) The Administrative Director, or his or her designee, may assess both an administrative penalty under either Labor Code sections 4610.5 and 4610.6, and a civil penalty under Labor Code section 129.5(e), based on the same violation(s).

(e) The penalty amounts specified for violations under this section may, in the discretion of the Administrative Director, be reduced after consideration of the factors set out in section 9792.13 of Title 8 of the California Code of Regulations. Failure to abate a violation found under section 9792.12(b)(4) and (b)(5), in the time period or in a manner consistent with that specified by the Administrative Director, or his or her designee, shall result in the assessment of the full original penalty amount proposed by the Administrative Director for that violation.

Note: Authority cited: Sections 133, 4610, 4610.5, 4610.6 and 5307.3, Labor Code. Reference: Sections 129, 129.5, 4062, 4600, 4600.4, 4604.5, 4610, 4610.5, 4610.6 and 4614, Labor Code.

History: 1. New section filed 6-7-2007; operative 6-7-2007 pursuant to Government Code section 11343.4 (Register 2007, No. 23).

2. Amendment of section heading and subsections (a), (a)(7) and (a)(9), new subsections (a)-(18)-(25), amendment of subsections (b)(4)(A), (b)(4)(C)-(E), (b)(5)(A)-(B) and (b)(5)(D), repealer of subsection (b)(5)(E), subsection relettering, amendment of subsection (b)(5)(G) and amendment of Note filed 12-31-2012 as an emergency; operative 1-1-2013 pursuant to Government Code section 11346.1(d) (Register 2013, No. 1). A Certificate of Compliance must be transmitted to OAL by 7-1-2013 or emergency language will be repealed by operation of law on the following day.

3. Amendment of section heading and subsections (a), (a)(7) and (a)(9), new subsections (a)-(18)-(25), amendment of subsections (b)(4)(A), (b)(4)(C)-(E), (b)(5)(A)-(B) and (b)(5)(D), repealer of subsection (b)(5)(E), subsection relettering, amendment of newly designated subsection (b)(5)(F) and amendment of Note refiled 7-1-2013 as an emergency; operative 7-1-2013 (Register 2013, No. 27). A Certificate of Compliance must be transmitted to OAL by 9-30-2013 or emergency language will be repealed by operation of law on the following day.

4. Amendment of section heading and subsections (a), (a)(7) and (a)(9), new subsections (a)-(18)-(25), amendment of subsections (b)(4)(A), (b)(4)(C)-(E), (b)(5)(A)-(B) and (b)(5)(D), repealer of subsection (b)(5)(E), subsection relettering, amendment of newly designated subsection (b)(5)(F) and amendment of Note refiled 9-30-2013 as an emergency; operative 10-1-2013 (Register 2013, No. 40). A Certificate of Compliance must be transmitted to OAL by 12-30-2013 or emergency language will be repealed by operation of law on the following day.

5. Certificate of Compliance as to 9-30-2013 order, including amendment of section and Note, transmitted to OAL 12-30-2013 and filed 2-12-2014; amendments effective 2-12-2014 pursuant to Government Code section 11343.4(b)(3) (Register 2014, No. 7).

Ref.: Herlick Handbook §§ 1.01[3][b], 4.09[1], 4.16[1], [2].

§9792.13. Assessment of Administrative Penalties — Penalty Adjustment Factors.

(a) In any investigation that the Administrative Director deems appropriate, the Administrative Director, or his or her designee, may mitigate a penalty amount imposed under section 9792.12 after considering each of these factors:

(1) The medical consequences or gravity of the violation(s);

(2) The good faith of the claims administrator or utilization review organization. Mitigation for good faith shall be determined based on documentation of attempts to comply with the Labor Code and regulations and shall result in a reduction of 20% for each applicable penalty;

(3) The history of previous penalties;

(4) The frequency of violations found during the investigation giving rise to a penalty;

(5) Penalties may be mitigated outside the above mitigation guidelines in extraordinary circumstances, when strict application of the mitigation guidelines would be clearly inequitable; and

(6) In the event an objection or appeal is filed pursuant to subsection 9792.15 of these regulations, whether the claims administrator or utilization review organization abated the alleged violation within the time period specified by the Administrative Director or his or her designee.

(b) The Administrative Director, or his or her designee, may assess both an administrative penalty under Labor Code section 4610 and a civil penalty under subdivision (e) of Labor Code section 129.5 based on the same violation(s).

(c) The Administrative Director, or his or her designee, shall not collect payment for an administrative penalty under Labor Code section 4610 from both the utilization review organization and the claims administrator for an assessment based on the same violation(s).

(d) Where an injured worker's or a requesting provider's refusal to cooperate in the utilization review process has prevented the claims administrator or utilization review organization from determining whether there is a legal obligation to perform an act, the Administrative Director, or his or her designee, may forego a penalty assessment for any related act or omission. The claims administrator or utilization review organization shall have the burden of proof in establishing both the refusal to cooperate and that such refusal prevented compliance with the relevant applicable statute or regulation.

Note: Authority cited: Sections 133, 4610 and 5307.3, Labor Code. Reference: Sections 129, 129.5, 4062, 4600, 4600.4, 4604.5, 4610 and 4614, Labor Code.

History: 1. New section filed 6-7-2007; operative 6-7-2007 pursuant to Government Code section 11343.4 (Register 2007, No. 23).

Ref.: Herlick Handbook §§ 1.01[3][b], 4.16[1], [3], [4].

§9792.14. Liability for Penalty Assessments.

(a) If more than one claims administrator or utilization review organization has been responsible for a claim file, utilization review file or other file that is being investigated, penalties may be assessed against each such entity for the violation(s) that occurred during the time each such entity had responsibility for the file or for the utilization review process.

(b) The claims administrator or utilization review organization is liable for all penalty assessments made against it, except that if the subject of the investigation is acting as an agent, the agent and the principal are jointly and severally liable for all penalty assessments resulting from a given investigation. This paragraph does not prohibit an agent and its principal from allocating the administrative penalty liability between them. Liability for civil penalties assessed pursuant to Labor Code section 129.5(e) for violations under Labor Code section 4610 or sections 9792.6 through 9792.10 of Title 8 of the California Code of Regulations shall not be allocated.

(c) Successor liability may be imposed on a claims administrator or utilization review organization that has merged with, consolidated, or otherwise continued the business of a corporation, other business entity or other person that was cited by the Administrative Director for violations of Labor Code section 4610 or sections 9792.6 through 9792.12. The surviving entity or person responsible for administering the utilization review process for an employer, shall assume and be liable for all the liabilities, obligations and penalties of the prior corporation or business entity. Successor liability will be imposed if there has been a substantial continuity of business operations and/or the new business uses the same or substantially the same work force.

Note: Authority cited: Sections 133, 4610 and 5307.3, Labor Code. Reference: Sections 129, 129.5, 4062, 4600, 4600.4, 4604.5, 4610 and 4614, Labor Code.

History: 1. New section filed 6-7-2007; operative 6-7-2007 pursuant to Government Code section 11343.4 (Register 2007, No. 23).

Ref.: Herlick Handbook §§ 1.01[3][b], 4.16[1], [3].

§9792.15. Administrative Penalties Pursuant to Labor Code §§4610, 4610.5, and 4610.6 — Order to Show Cause, Notice of Hearing, Determination and Order, and Review Procedure.

(a) Pursuant to Labor Code sections 4610(i), 4610.5(i), and 4610.6(k), the Administrative Director shall issue an Order to Show Cause Re: Assessment of Administrative Penalty when the Administrative Director, or his or her designee (the investigating unit of the Division of Workers' Compensation), has reason to believe that an employer, insurer or other entity subject to Labor Code sections 4610(i), 4610.5(i), and 4610.6(k), has failed to meet any of the requirements of this section or of any regulation adopted by the Administrative Director pursuant to the authority of sections 4610(i), 4610.5(i), and 4610.6(k),

(b) The order shall be in writing and shall include all of the following:

(1) Notice that an administrative penalty may be assessed;

(2) For administrative penalties assessed under section 4610(i), the final investigation report, which shall consist of the notice of utilization review penalty assessment, the performance rating, and may include one or more requests for documentation or compliance;

(3) For administrative penalties assessed under sections 4610.5(i) and 4610.6(k), the basis for the penalty assessment, including a statement of the alleged violations and the amount of each proposed penalty.

(4) A description of the methods for paying or appealing the penalty assessment.

(c) The order shall be served personally or by registered or certified mail.

(d) Within thirty (30) calendar days after the date of service of the Order to Show Cause Re: Assessment of Administrative Penalties, the claims administrator or utilization review organization may pay the assessed administrative penalties or file an answer as the respondent with the Administrative Director, in which the respondent may:

(1) Admit or deny in whole or in part any of the allegations set forth in the Order to Show Cause;

(2) Contest the amount of any or all proposed administrative penalties;

(3) Contest the existence of any or all of the violations;

(4) Set forth any affirmative and other defenses;

(5) Set forth the legal and factual bases for each defense.

(e) Any allegation and proposed penalty stated in the Order to Show Cause that is not contested shall be paid within thirty (30) calendar days after the date of service of the Order to Show Cause.

(f) Failure to timely file an answer shall constitute a waiver of the respondent's right to an evidentiary hearing. Unless set forth in the answer, all defenses to the Order to Show Cause shall be deemed waived. If the answer is not timely filed, within ten (10) days of the date for filing the answer, the respondent may file a written request for leave to file an answer. The respondent may also file a written request for leave to assert additional defenses, which the Administrative Director may grant upon a showing of good cause.

(g) The answer shall be in writing and signed by, or on behalf of, the claims administrator or utilization review organization and shall state the respondent's mailing address. It need not be verified or follow any particular form.

(1) The respondent must file the original and one copy of the answer on the Administrative Director and concurrently serve one copy of the answer on the investigating unit of the Division of Workers' Compensation (designated by the Administrative Director). The original and all copies of any filings required by this section shall have a proof of service attached.

(h) Within sixty (60) calendar days of the issuance of the Order to Show Cause Re: Assessment of Administrative Penalty, the Administrative Director shall issue the Notice of the date, time and place of a hearing. The date of the hearing shall be at least ninety calendar days from the date of service of the Notice. The Notice shall be served personally or by registered or certified mail. Continuances will not be allowed without a showing of good cause.

(i) At any time before the hearing, the Administrative Director may file or permit the filing of an amended complaint or supplemental Order to Show Cause. All parties shall be notified thereof. If the amended complaint or supplemental Order to Show Cause presents new charges, the Administrative Director shall afford the respondent a reasonable opportunity to prepare its defense, and the respondent shall be entitled to file an amended answer.

(j) At the Administrative Director's discretion, the Administrative Director may proceed with an informal pre-hearing conference with the respondent in an effort to resolve the contested matters. If any or all of the violations or proposed penalties in the Order to Show Cause, the amended Order or the supplemental Order remain contested, those contested matters shall proceed to an evidentiary hearing.

(k) Whenever the Administrative Director's Order to Show Cause has been contested, the Administrative Director may designate a hearing officer to preside over the hearing. The authority of the Administrative Director or the designated hearing officer shall include, but is not limited to: conducting a pre-hearing settlement conference; setting the date for an evidentiary hearing and any continuances; issuing subpoenas for the attendance of any person residing anywhere within the state as a witness or party at any pre-hearing conference and hearing; issuing subpoenas duces tecum for the production of documents and things at the hearing; presiding at the hearings; administering oaths or affirmations and certifying official acts; ruling on objections and motions; issuing pre-hearing orders; and preparing a Recommended Determination and Opinion based on the hearing.

(*l*) The Administrative Director or the designated hearing officer shall set the time and place for any pre-hearing conference on the contested matters in the Order to Show Cause, and shall give sixty (60) calendar days written notice to all parties.

(m) The pre-hearing conference may address one or more of the following matters:

(1) Exploration of settlement possibilities;

(2) Preparation of stipulations;

(3) Clarification of issues;

(4) Rulings on the identity of witnesses and limitation of the number of witnesses;

(5) Objections to proffers of evidence;

(6) Order of presentation of evidence and cross-examination;

(7) Rulings regarding issuance of subpoenas and protective orders;

(8) Schedules for the submission of written briefs and schedules for the commencement and conduct of the hearing;

(9) Any other matters as shall promote the orderly and prompt conduct of the hearing.

(n) The Administrative Director or the designated hearing officer shall issue a pre-hearing order incorporating the matters determined at the pre-hearing conference. The Administrative Director or the designated hearing officer may direct one or more of the parties to prepare the pre-hearing order.

(o) Not less than thirty (30) calendar days prior to the date of the evidentiary hearing, the respondent shall file and serve the original and one copy of a written statement with the Administrative Director or the designated hearing officer specifying the legal and factual bases for its answer and each defense, listing all witnesses the respondent intends to call to testify at the hearing, and appending copies of all documents and other evidence the respondent intends to introduce into evidence at the hearing. A copy of the written statement and its attachments shall also concurrently be served on the investigating unit of the Division of Workers' Compensation. If the written statement and supporting evidence are not timely filed and served, the Administrative Director or the designated hearing officer shall dismiss the answer and issue a written Determination based on the evidence provided by the investigating unit of the Division of Workers' Compensation. Within ten (10) calendar days of the date for filing the written statement and supporting evidence, the respondent may file a written request for leave to file a written statement and supporting evidence. The Administrative Director or the designated hearing officer may grant the request, upon a showing of good cause. If leave is granted, the written statement and supporting evidence must be filed and served no later than ten (10) calendar days prior to the date of the hearing.

(p) Oral testimony shall be taken only on oath or affirmation.

(q)(1) Each party shall have these rights: to call and examine witnesses, to introduce exhibits; to cross-examine opposing witnesses on any matter relevant to the issues even though that matter was not covered in the direct examination; to impeach any witness regardless of which party first called him or her to testify; and to rebut the evidence.

(2) In the absence of a contrary order by the Administrative Director or the designated hearing officer, the investigating unit of the Division of Workers' Compensation shall present evidence first.

(3) The hearing need not be conducted according to the technical rules relating to evidence and witnesses, except as hereinafter provided. Any relevant evidence shall be admitted if it is the sort of evidence on which responsible persons are accustomed to rely in the conduct of serious affairs, regardless of the existence of any common law or statutory rule which might make the admission of the evidence improper over objection in civil actions.

(4) Hearsay evidence may be used for the purpose of supplementing or explaining other evidence but upon timely objection shall not be sufficient in itself to support a finding unless it would be admissible over objection in civil actions. An objection is timely if made before submission of the case to the Administrative Director or to the designated hearing officer.

(r) The written affidavit or declaration of any witness may be offered and shall be received into evidence provided that (i) the witness was listed in the written statement pursuant to section 9792.15(n); (ii) the statement is made by affidavit or by declaration under penalty of perjury; (iii) copies of the statement have been delivered to all opposing parties at least twenty (20) days prior to the hearing; and (iv) no opposing party has, at least ten (10) days before the hearing, delivered to the proponent of the evidence a written demand that the witness be produced in person to testify at the hearing. The Administrative Director or the designated hearing officer shall disregard any portion of the statement received pursuant to this regulation that would be inadmissible if the witness were testifying in person, but the inclusion of inadmissible matter does not render the entire statement inadmissible. Upon timely demand for production of a witness in lieu of admission of an affidavit or declaration, the proponent of that witness shall ensure the witness appears at the scheduled hearing and the proffered declaration or affidavit from that witness shall not be admitted. If the Administrative Director or the designated hearing officer determines that good cause exists that prevents the witness from appearing at the hearing, the declaration may be introduced in evidence, but it shall be given only the same effect as other hearsay evidence.

(s) The Administrative Director or the designated hearing officer shall issue a written Determination and Order Assessing Penalty, if any, including a statement of the basis for the Determination and each penalty assessed, within sixty (60) days of the date the case was submitted for decision, which shall be served on all parties. This requirement is directory and not jurisdictional.

(t) The Administrative Director shall have sixty (60) calendar days to adopt or modify the Determination and Order Assessing Penalty issued by the Administrative Director or the designated hearing officer. In the event the recommended Determination and Order of the designated hearing officer is modified, the Administrative Director shall include a statement of the basis for the Determination and Order Assessing Penalty signed and served by the Administrative Director, or his or her designee. If the Administrative Director does not act within sixty (60) calendar days, then the recommended Determination and Order shall become the Determination and Order on the sixty-first calendar day.

(u) The Determination and Order Assessing Penalty shall be served on all parties personally or by registered or certified mail by the Administrative Director.

(v) The Determination and Order Assessing Penalty, if any, shall become final on the day it is served, unless the aggrieved party files a timely Petition Appealing the Determination of the Administrative Director. All findings and assessments in the Determination and Order Assessing Penalty not contested in the Petition Appealing the Determination of the Administrative Director shall become final as though no petition were filed.

(w) At any time prior to the date the Determination and Order Assessing Penalty becomes final, the Administrative Director or designated hearing officer may correct the Determination and Order Assessing Penalty for clerical, mathematical or procedural error(s).

(x) Penalties assessed in a Determination and Order Assessing Penalty shall be paid within thirty (30) calendar days of the date the Determination and Order became final. A timely filed Petition Appealing the Determination of the Administrative Director shall toll the period for paying the penalty assessed for the item appealed.

(y) All appeals from any part or the entire Determination and Order Assessing Penalty shall be made in the form of a Petition Appealing the Determination of the Administrative Director, in conformance with the requirements of chapter 7, part 4 of Division 4 of the Labor Code. Any such Petition Appealing the Determination of the Administrative Director shall be filed at the Appeals Board in San Francisco (and not with any district office of the Workers' Compensation Appeals Board), in the same manner specified for petitions for reconsideration.

Note: Authority cited: Sections 133, 4610, 4610.5, 4610.6 and 5307.3, Labor Code. Reference: Sections 129, 129.5, 4062, 4600, 4600.4, 4604.5, 4610, 4610.5, 4610.6, 4614 and 5300, Labor Code.

History: 1. New section filed 6-7-2007; operative 6-7-2007 pursuant to Government Code section 11343.4 (Register 2007, No. 23).

2. Amendment of section heading and subsections (a) and (b)(2), new subsections (b)(3)-(4) and amendment of Note filed 2-12-2014; operative 2-12-2014 pursuant to Government Code section 11343.4(b)(3) (Register 2014, No. 7).

Ref.: Herlick Handbook §§ 1.01[3][b], 4.16[1], [3], [4].

ARTICLE 5.5.2
Medical Treatment Utilization Schedule

§9792.20. Medical Treatment Utilization Schedule—Definitions.

As used in this Article:

(a) "ACOEM" means the American College of Occupational and Environmental Medicine's Occupational Medicine Practice Guidelines published by the Reed Group containing evidenced-based medical treatment guidelines for conditions commonly associated with the workplace. ACOEM guidelines may be obtained from the Reed Group (http://go.reedgroup.com/mtus).

(b) "Chronic pain" means pain lasting three or more months from the initial onset of pain.

(c) "Claims administrator" is a self-administered workers' compensation insurer, a self-administered self-insured employer, a self-administered legally uninsured employer, a self-administered joint powers authority, a third-party claims administrator, or the California Insurance Guarantee Association.

(d) "Evidence-Based Medicine (EBM)" means a systematic approach to making clinical decisions which allows the integration of the best available research evidence with clinical expertise and patient values.

(e) "Functional improvement" means either a clinically significant improvement in activities of daily living or a reduction in work restrictions as measured during the history and physical exam, performed and documented as part of the medical evaluation and treatment; and a reduction in the dependency on continued medical treatment.

(f) "Medical treatment" is care which is reasonably required to cure or relieve the employee from the effects of the industrial injury consistent with the requirements of sections 9792.20–9792.26.

(g) "Medical treatment guidelines" means the most current version of written recommendations which are systematically developed by a multidisciplinary process through a comprehensive literature search to assist in decision-making about the appropriate medical treatment for specific clinical circumstances reviewed and updated within the last five years.

(h) "Nationally recognized" means published in a peer-reviewed medical journal; or developed, endorsed and disseminated by a national organization with affiliates based in two or more U.S. states and is the most current version.

(i) "ODG" means the Official Disability Guidelines published by the Work Loss Data Institute containing evidenced-based medical treatment guidelines for conditions commonly associated with the workplace. ODG guidelines may be obtained from the Work Loss Data Institute, 169 Saxony, #101, Encinitas, California 92024 (www.ODG@worklossdata.com).

(j) "Peer reviewed" means that a study's content, methodology and results have been evaluated and approved prior to publication by an editorial board of qualified experts.

(k) "Scientifically based" means based on scientific literature, wherein the body of literature is identified through performance of a literature search, the identified literature is evaluated, and then used as the basis to support a recommendation.

(*l*) "Strength of Evidence" establishes the relative weight that shall be given to scientifically based evidence.

Note: Authority cited: Sections 133, 4603.5, 5307.3 and 5307.27, Labor Code. Reference: Sections 77.5, 4600, 4604.5 and 5307.27, Labor Code.

History: 1. New article 5.5.2 (sections 9792.20-9792.23) and section filed 6-15-2007; operative 6-15-2007 pursuant to Government Code section 11343.4 (Register 2007, No. 24).

2. Amendment of subsection (b), new subsection (c), subsection relettering and amendment of newly designated subsection (g) filed 6-18-2009; operative 7-18-2009 (Register 2009, No. 25).

3. Editorial correction of operative date in History 2 (Register 2009, No. 30).

4. Amendment filed 4-20-2015; operative 4-20-2015 pursuant to Government Code section 11343.4(b)(3) (Register 2015, No. 17).

5. Amendment of subsection (a) filed 1-11-2018; operative 12-1-2017. Submitted to OAL for filing and printing only pursuant to Labor Code section 5307.27(a) (Register 2018, No. 2).

Ref.: Hanna §§ 5.02[1], 22.05[6][a], [b]; Herlick Handbook §§ 1.01[3][b], 4.01[3].

§9792.21. Medical Treatment Utilization Schedule.

(a) The Administrative Director adopts the Medical Treatment Utilization Schedule (MTUS) consisting of section 9792.20 through section 9792.26.

(b) The MTUS is based on the principals of Evidenced-Based Medicine (EBM). EBM is a systematic approach to making clinical decisions which allows the integration of the best available evidence with clinical expertise and patient values. EBM is a method of improving the quality of care by encouraging practices that work and discouraging those that are ineffective or harmful. EBM asserts that intuition, unsystematic clinical experience, and pathophysiologic rationale are insufficient grounds for making clinical decisions. Instead, EBM requires the evaluation of medical evidence by applying an explicit systematic methodology to determine the quality and strength of evidence used to support the recommendations for a medical condition or injury. The best available evidence is then used to guide clinical decision making.

(c) The recommended guidelines set forth in the MTUS are presumptively correct on the issue of extent and scope of medical treatment. The MTUS constitutes the standard for the provision of medical care in accordance with Labor Code section 4600 for all injured workers diagnosed with industrial conditions because it provides a framework for the most effective treatment of work-related illness or injury to achieve functional improvement, return-to-work, and disability prevention. The MTUS shall be the primary source of guidance for treating physicians and physician reviewers for the evaluation and treatment of injured workers.

(d) Treatment shall not be denied on the sole basis that the condition or injury is not addressed by the MTUS. There are two limited situations that may warrant treatment based on recommendations found outside of the MTUS.

(1) First, if a medical condition or injury is not addressed by the MTUS, medical care shall be in accordance with other medical treatment guidelines or peer-reviewed studies found by applying the Medical Evidence Search Sequence set forth in section 9792.21.1.

(2) Second, if the MTUS' presumption of correctness is successfully challenged. The recommended guidelines set forth in the MTUS are presumptively correct on the issue of extent and scope of medical treatment. The presumption is rebuttable and may be controverted by a preponderance of scientific medical evidence establishing that a variance from the schedule is reasonably required to cure or relieve the injured worker from the effects of his or her injury. The presumption created is one affecting the burden of proof. Therefore, the treating physician who seeks treatment outside of the MTUS bears the burden of rebutting the MTUS' presumption of correctness by a preponderance of scientific medical evidence.

Note: Authority cited: Sections 133, 4603.5, 5307.3 and 5307.27, Labor Code. Reference: Sections 77.5, 4600, 4604.5, 4610.5 and 5307.27, Labor Code.

History: 1. New section filed 6-15-2007; operative 6-15-2007 pursuant to Government Code section 11343.4 (Register 2007, No. 24).

2. Amendment of subsection (a), renumbering of former subsection (a)(1) to section 9792.22, subsection (a), renumbering of former subsections (a)(2)-(a)(2)(E) to new section 9792.24.1 and amendment of subsections (b) and (c) filed 6-18-2009; operative 7-18-2009 (Register 2009, No. 25).

3. Editorial correction of operative date in History 2 (Register 2009, No. 30).

4. Amendment of section and Note filed 4-20-2015; operative 4-20-2015 pursuant to Government Code section 11343.4(b)(3) (Register 2015, No. 17).

Ref.: Hanna §§ 5.02[1], 22.05[6][a], [b], [c][i]; Herlick Handbook §§ 1.01[3][b], 4.01[3].

§9792.21.1. Medical Evidence Search Sequence.

(a) Treating physicians and medical reviewers shall conduct the following medical evidence search sequence for the evaluation and treatment of injured workers.

(1) Search the recommended guidelines set forth in the current MTUS to find a recommendation applicable to the injured worker's medical condition or injury.

(2) In the limited situation where a medical condition or injury is not addressed by the MTUS or if the MTUS' presumption of correctness is being challenged, then:

(A) Search the most current version of ACOEM or ODG to find a recommendation applicable to the injured worker's medical condition or injury. Choose the recommendation that is supported with the best available evidence according to the MTUS Methodology for Evaluating Medical Evidence set forth in section 9792.25.1. If no applicable recommendation is found, or if the treating physician or reviewing physician believes there is another recommendation supported by a higher quality and strength of evidence, then

(B) Search the most current version of other evidence-based medical treatment guidelines that are recognized by the national medical community and are scientifically based to find a recommendation applicable to the injured worker's medical condition or injury. Choose the recommendation that is supported with the best available evidence according to the MTUS Methodology for Evaluating Medical Evidence set forth in section 9792.25.1. Medical treatment guidelines can be found in the National Guideline Clearinghouse that is accessible at the following website address: www.guideline.gov/. If no applicable recommendation is found, or if the treating physician or reviewing physician believes there is another recommendation supported by a higher quality and strength of evidence, then

(C) Search for current studies that are scientifically-based, peer-reviewed, and published in journals that are nationally recognized by the medical community to find a recommendation applicable to the injured worker's medical condition or injury. Choose the recommendation that is supported with the best available evidence according to the MTUS Methodology for Evaluating Medical Evidence set forth in section 9792.25.1. A search for peer-reviewed published studies may be conducted by accessing the U.S. National Library of Medicine's database of biomedical citations and abstracts that is searchable at the following website: www.ncbi.nlm.nih.gov/pubmed. Other searchable databases may also be used.

(b) After conducting the medical evidence search in the sequence specified above:

(1) Treating Physicians

(A) If the medical condition or injury is not addressed by the MTUS, then the treating physician may provide in the Request for Authorization (RFA) or in an attachment to the RFA a citation to the guideline or study containing the recommendation he or she believes guides the reasonableness and necessity of the requested treatment that is applicable to the injured worker's medical condition or injury.

1. The citation provided by the treating physician shall be the primary source relied upon which he or she believes contains the recommendation that guides the reasonableness and necessity of the requested treatment that is applicable to the injured worker's medical condition or injury.

2. If the treating physician provides more than one citation, then a narrative shall be included by the treating physician in the RFA or in an attachment to the RFA explaining how each guideline or study cited provides additional information that guides the reasonableness and necessity of the requested treatment that is applicable to the injured worker's medical condition or injury but is not addressed by the primary source cited.

(B) If the medical condition or injury is addressed by the MTUS but the treating physician is attempting to rebut the MTUS' presumption of correctness, then the treating physician shall provide in the RFA or in an attachment to the RFA the following: a clear and concise statement that the MTUS' presumption of correctness is being challenged; a citation to the guideline or study containing the recommendation he or she believes guides the reasonableness and necessity of the requested treatment that is applicable to the injured worker's medical condition or injury; and a copy of the entire study or the relevant sections of the guideline containing the recommendation he or she believes guides the reasonableness and necessity of the requested treatment that is applicable to the injured worker's medical condition or injury.

1. The citation and copy of the study or copy of the relevant sections of the guideline provided by the treating physician shall be the primary source relied upon which he or she believes contains the recommendation that guides the reasonableness and necessity of the requested treatment that is applicable to the injured worker's medical condition or injury.

2. If the treating physician provides more than one citation, then a copy of the additional study(ies) or copy of the additional relevant sections of the guideline(s) along with a narrative shall be included by the treating physician in the RFA or in an attachment to the RFA explaining how each guideline or study cited provides additional information that guides the reasonableness and necessity of the requested treatment that is applicable to the injured worker's medical condition or injury but is not addressed by the primary source cited.

(2) Utilization Review Physicians

(A) If the RFA is being modified, delayed or denied, then the Utilization Review physician shall provide in the Utilization Review decision, in addition to the requirements set forth in section 9792.9.1(e), a citation to the guideline or study containing the recommendation he or she believes guides the reasonableness and necessity of the requested treatment that is applicable to the injured worker's medical condition or injury.

1. The citation provided by the Utilization Review physician shall be the primary source relied upon which he or she believes contains the recommendation that guides the reasonableness and necessity of the requested treatment that is applicable to the injured worker's medical condition or injury.

2. If the Utilization Review physician provides more than one citation, then a narrative shall be included by the reviewing physician in the Utilization Review decision explaining how each guideline or study cited provides additional information that guides the reasonableness and necessity of the requested treatment that is applicable to the injured worker's medical condition or injury but is not addressed by the primary source cited.

(3) Independent Medical Review Physicians

(A) If the Utilization Review Decision delays, denies or modifies an injured worker's request for treatment and review of that decision is requested through Independent Medical Review, then the Independent Medical Review physician shall provide in the Independent Medical Review decision, in addition to the requirements set forth in section 9792.10.6(d), a citation to the guideline or study containing the recommendation that guides the reasonableness and necessity of the requested treatment that is applicable to the injured worker's medical condition or injury.

1. The citation provided by the Independent Medical Review physician shall be the primary source he or she relied upon which contains the recommendation that guides the reasonableness and necessity of the requested treatment that is applicable to the injured worker's medical condition or injury.

2. If the Independent Medical Review physician provides more than one citation, then a narrative shall be included by the reviewing physician in the Independent Medical Review decision explaining how each guideline or study cited provides additional information that guides the

reasonableness and necessity of the requested treatment that is applicable to the injured worker's medical condition or injury but is not addressed by the primary source cited.

(c) If the treating physician and/or the Utilization Review physician and/or the Independent Medical Review physician cited different guidelines or studies containing recommendations that are at variance with one another, the MTUS Methodology for Evaluating Medical Evidence set forth in section 9792.25.1 shall be applied by the reviewing physician to determine which one of the recommendations is supported by the best available evidence.

(d) The format of the citations provided by the treating physician, Utilization Review physician, and Independent Medical physician, shall include the following

(1) When citing the MTUS:

(A) Indicate the MTUS is being cited and the effective year of the guideline;

(B) Title of chapter (e.g., Low Back Complaints); and

(C) Section of chapter (e.g., Surgical Considerations).

(2) When citing other medical treatment guidelines:

(A) Title of organization publishing the guideline (e.g., ACOEM or ODG);

(B) Year of publication;

(C) Title of chapter; and

(D) Section of chapter.

(3) When citing a peer-reviewed study:

(A) First author's last name and first name initial;

(B) Published article title;

(C) Journal title (standard abbreviations may be used);

(D) Volume number;

(E) Year published; and

(F) Page numbers.

(e) Employers and their representatives, at their discretion, may approve medical treatment beyond what is covered in the MTUS or supported by the best available medical evidence in order to account for medical circumstances warranting an exception. The treating physician should provide clear documentation of the clinical rationale focusing on expected objective functional gains afforded by the requested treatment and impact upon prognosis.

Note: Authority cited: Sections 133, 4603.5, 5307.3 and 5307.27, Labor Code. Reference: Sections 77.5, 4600, 4604.5, 4610.5 and 5307.27, Labor Code.

History: 1. New section filed 4-20-2015; operative 4-20-2015 pursuant to Government Code section 11343.4(b)(3) (Register 2015, No. 17).

Ref.: Hanna § 5.02[1]; Herlick Handbook § 4.01[3].

§9792.22. General Approaches.

(a) The Administrative Director adopts and incorporates by reference into the MTUS specific guidelines set forth below from the American College of Occupational and Environmental Medicine's Occupational Medicine Practice Guidelines (ACOEM Practice Guidelines) for the following chapters.

(1) Prevention (ACOEM May 1, 2011).

(2) General Approach to Initial Assessment and Documentation (ACOEM July 25, 2016).

(3) Initial Approaches to Treatment (ACOEM June 30, 2017).

(4) Cornerstones of Disability Prevention and Management (ACOEM May 1, 2011).

Note: Authority cited: Sections 133, 4603.5, 5307.3 and 5307.27, Labor Code. Reference: Sections 77.5, 4600, 4604.5 and 5307.27, Labor Code.

History: 1. New section filed 6-15-2007; operative 6-15-2007 pursuant to Government Code section 11343.4 (Register 2007, No. 24).

2. Amendment of section heading, renumbering of former section 9792.22 to section 9792.25, renumbering and amendment of former section 9792.21, subsection (a)(1) to section 9792.22, subsection (a) and new subsections (a)(1)-(4) filed 6-18-2009; operative 7-18-2009 (Register 2009, No. 25).

3. Editorial correction of operative date in History 2 (Register 2009, No. 30).

4. Amendment of subsections (a) and (a)(3) filed 1-11-2018; operative 12-1-2017. Submitted to OAL for filing and printing only pursuant to Labor Code section 5307.27(a) (Register 2018, No. 2).

5. Amendment of subsections (a)(1)-(2) and (a)(4) filed 10-30-2018; operative 10-31-2018. Submitted to OAL for filing and printing only pursuant to Labor Code section 5307.27(a) (Register 2018, No. 44).

Ref.: Hanna § 22.05[6][a]; Herlick Handbook §§ 1.01[3][b], 4.01[3].

§9792.23. Clinical Topics.

(a) The Administrative Director adopts and incorporates by reference a series of medical treatment guidelines into the MTUS commencing with section 9792.23.1.

(b) For all conditions or injuries not addressed in the MTUS treatment guidelines, the authorized treatment and diagnostic services shall be in accordance with other scientifically and evidence-based medical treatment guidelines that are nationally recognized by the medical community pursuant to section 9792.21(d)(1).

Note: Authority cited: Sections 133, 4603.5, 5307.3 and 5307.27, Labor Code. Reference: Sections 77.5, 4600, 4604.5 and 5307.27, Labor Code.

History: 1. New section filed 6-15-2007; operative 6-15-2007 pursuant to Government Code section 11343.4 (Register 2007, No. 24).

2. Renumbering of former section 9792.23 to section 9792.26 and new section 9792.23 filed 6-18-2009; operative 7-18-2009 (Register 2009, No. 25).

3. Editorial correction of operative date in History 2 (Register 2009, No. 30).

4. Amendment of subsection (b) filed 4-20-2015; operative 4-20-2015 pursuant to Government Code section 11343.4(b)(3) (Register 2015, No. 17).

5. Amendment of subsection (b)(1) filed 7-28-2016; operative 7-28-2016 pursuant to Government Code section 11343.4(b)(3) (Register 2016, No. 31).

6. Amendment filed 1-11-2018; operative 12-1-2017. Submitted to OAL for filing and printing only pursuant to Labor Code section 5307.27(a) (Register 2018, No. 2).

Ref.: Hanna §§ 5.02[1], 22.05[6][a]; Herlick Handbook §§ 1.01[3][b], 4.01[3].

§9792.23.1. Cervical and Thoracic Spine Disorders Guideline.

The Administrative Director adopts and incorporates by reference the Cervical and Thoracic Spine Disorders Guideline (ACOEM October 17, 2018) into the MTUS from the ACOEM Practice Guidelines.

Note: Authority cited: Sections 133, 4603.5, 5307.3 and 5307.27, Labor Code. Reference: Sections 77.5, 4600, 4604.5 and 5307.27, Labor Code.

History: 1. New section filed 6-18-2009; operative 7-18-2009 (Register 2009, No. 25).

2. Editorial correction of operative date in History 1 (Register 2009, No. 30).

3. Amendment of section heading and repealer and new section filed 1-11-2018; operative 12-1-2017. Submitted to OAL for filing and printing only pursuant to Labor Code section 5307.27(a) (Register 2018, No. 2).

4. Amendment filed 4-11-2019; operative 4-18-2019. Submitted to OAL for filing and printing only pursuant to Labor Code section 5307.27(a) (Register 2019, No. 15).

Ref.: Hanna § 22.05[6][a]; Herlick Handbook §§ 1.01[3][b], 4.01[3].

§9792.23.2. Shoulder Disorders Guideline.

The Administrative Director adopts and incorporates by reference the Shoulder Disorders Guideline (ACOEM August 1, 2016) into the MTUS from the ACOEM Practice Guidelines.

Note: Authority cited: Sections 133, 4603.5, 5307.3 and 5307.27, Labor Code. Reference: Sections 77.5, 4600, 4604.5 and 5307.27, Labor Code.

History: 1. New section filed 6-18-2009; operative 7-18-2009 (Register 2009, No. 25).

2. Editorial correction of operative date in History 1 (Register 2009, No. 30).

3. Amendment of section heading and repealer and new section filed 1-11-2018; operative 12-1-2017. Submitted to OAL for filing and printing only pursuant to Labor Code section 5307.27(a) (Register 2018, No. 2).

Ref.: Hanna § 22.05[6][a]; Herlick Handbook §§ 1.01[3][b], 4.01[3].

§9792.23.3. Elbow Disorders Guideline.

The Administrative Director adopts and incorporates by reference the Elbow Disorders Guideline (ACOEM August 23, 2018) into the MTUS from the ACOEM Practice Guidelines.

Note: Authority cited: Sections 133, 4603.5, 5307.3 and 5307.27, Labor Code. Reference: Sections 77.5, 4600, 4604.5 and 5307.27, Labor Code.

History: 1. New section filed 6-18-2009; operative 7-18-2009 (Register 2009, No. 25).

2. Editorial correction of operative date in History 1 (Register 2009, No. 30).

3. Amendment of section heading and repealer and new section filed 1-11-2018; operative 12-1-2017. Submitted to OAL for filing and printing only pursuant to Labor Code section 5307.27(a) (Register 2018, No. 2).

4. Amendment filed 4-11-2019; operative 4-18-2019. Submitted to OAL for filing and printing only pursuant to Labor Code section 5307.27(a) (Register 2019, No. 15).

Ref.: Hanna § 22.05[6][a]; Herlick Handbook §§ 1.01[3][b], 4.01[3].

§9792.23.4. Hand, Wrist, and Forearm Disorders Guideline.

The Administrative Director adopts and incorporates by reference the Hand, Wrist, and Forearm Disorders Guideline (ACOEM January 7, 2019) into the MTUS from the ACOEM Practice Guidelines.

Note: Authority cited: Sections 133, 4603.5, 5307.3 and 5307.27, Labor Code. Reference: Sections 77.5, 4600, 4604.5 and 5307.27, Labor Code.

History: 1. New section filed 6-18-2009; operative 7-18-2009 (Register 2009, No. 25).

2. Editorial correction of operative date in History 1 (Register 2009, No. 30).

3. Amendment of section heading and repealer and new section filed 1-11-2018; operative 12-1-2017. Submitted to OAL for filing and printing only pursuant to Labor Code section 5307.27(a) (Register 2018, No. 2).

4. Amendment filed 4-11-2019; operative 4-18-2019. Submitted to OAL for filing and printing only pursuant to Labor Code section 5307.27(a) (Register 2019, No. 15).

Ref.: Hanna § 22.05[6][a]; Herlick Handbook §§ 1.01[3][b], 4.01[3].

§9792.23.5. Low Back Disorders Guideline.

The Administrative Director adopts and incorporates by reference the Low Back Disorders Guideline (ACOEM March 7, 2019) into the MTUS from the ACOEM Practice Guidelines.

Note: Authority cited: Sections 133, 4603.5, 5307.3 and 5307.27, Labor Code. Reference: Sections 77.5, 4600, 4604.5 and 5307.27, Labor Code.

History: 1. New section filed 6-18-2009; operative 7-18-2009 (Register 2009, No. 25).

2. Editorial correction of operative date in History 1 (Register 2009, No. 30).

3. Amendment of section heading and repealer and new section filed 1-11-2018; operative 12-1-2017. Submitted to OAL for filing and printing only pursuant to Labor Code section 5307.27(a) (Register 2018, No. 2).

4. Amendment filed 8-28-2019; operative 8-11-2019. Submitted to OAL for filing and printing only pursuant to Labor Code section 5302.27(a) (Register 2019, No. 35).

Ref.: Hanna § 22.05[6][a]; Herlick Handbook §§ 1.01[3][b], 4.01[3].

§9792.23.6. Knee Disorders Guideline.

The Administrative Director adopts and incorporates by reference the Knee Disorders Guideline (ACOEM December 3, 2019) into the MTUS from the ACOEM Practice Guidelines.

Note: Authority cited: Sections 133, 4603.5, 5307.3 and 5307.27, Labor Code. Reference: Sections 77.5, 4600, 4604.5 and 5307.27, Labor Code.

History: 1. New section filed 6-18-2009; operative 7-18-2009 (Register 2009, No. 25).

2. Editorial correction of operative date in History 1 (Register 2009, No. 30).

3. Amendment of section heading and repealer and new section filed 1-11-2018; operative 12-1-2017. Submitted to OAL for filing and printing only pursuant to Labor Code section 5307.27(a) (Register 2018, No. 2).

4. Amendment filed 9-10-2020; operative 9-21-2020. Submitted to OAL for filing and printing only pursuant to Labor Code section 5307.27(a) (Register 2020, No. 37).

Ref.: Hanna § 22.05[6][a]; Herlick Handbook §§ 1.01[3][b], 4.01[3].

§9792.23.7. Ankle and Foot Disorders Guideline.

The Administrative Director adopts and incorporates by reference the Ankle and Foot Disorders Guideline (ACOEM July 16, 2018) into the MTUS from the ACOEM Practice Guidelines.

Note: Authority cited: Sections 133, 4603.5, 5307.3 and 5307.27, Labor Code. Reference: Sections 77.5, 4600, 4604.5 and 5307.27, Labor Code.

History: 1. New section filed 6-18-2009; operative 7-18-2009 (Register 2009, No. 25).

2. Editorial correction of operative date in History 1 (Register 2009, No. 30).

3. Amendment of section heading and repealer and new section filed 1-11-2018; operative 12-1-2017. Submitted to OAL for filing and printing only pursuant to Labor Code section 5307.27(a) (Register 2018, No. 2).

4. Amendment filed 4-11-2019; operative 4-18-2019. Submitted to OAL for filing and printing only pursuant to Labor Code section 5307.27(a) (Register 2019, No. 15).

Ref.: Hanna § 22.05[6][a]; Herlick Handbook §§ 1.01[3][b], 4.01[3].

§9792.23.8. Workplace Mental Health Guideline.

(a) The Administrative Director adopts and incorporates by reference the Introduction to the Workplace Mental Health Guideline (ACOEM March 13, 2019) into the MTUS. The Workplace Mental Health Guideline consists of specific modules set forth below from the ACOEM Practice Guidelines addressing the issue of Workplace Mental Health:

(1) Posttraumatic Stress Disorder and Acute Stress Disorder (ACOEM December 18, 2018).

(2) Depressive Disorders (ACOEM Fedruary 13, 2020).

Note: Authority cited: Sections 133, 4603.5, 5307.3 and 5307.27, Labor Code. Reference: Sections 77.5, 4600, 4604.5 and 5307.27, Labor Code.

History: 1. New section filed 6-18-2009; operative 7-18-2009 (Register 2009, No. 25).

2. Editorial correction of operative date in History 1 (Register 2009, No. 30).

3. Repealer and new section filed 1-11-2018; operative 12-1-2017. Submitted to OAL for filing and printing only pursuant to Labor Code section 5307.27(a) (Register 2018, No. 2).

4. Amendment of section heading and section filed 4-11-2019; operative 4-18-2019. Submitted to OAL for filing and printing only pursuant to Labor Code section 5307.27(a) (Register 2019, No. 15).

5. Amendment filed 8-28-2019; operative 8-11-2019. Submitted to OAL for filing and printing only pursuant to Labor Code section 5302.27(a) (Register 2019, No. 35).

6. New subsection (a)(2) filed 9-10-2020; operative 9-21-2020. Submitted to OAL for filing and printing only pursuant to Labor Code section 5307.27(a) (Register 2020, No. 37).

Ref.: Hanna § 22.05[6][a]; Herlick Handbook §§ 1.01[3][b], 4.01[3].

§9792.23.9. Eye Disorders Guideline.

The Administrative Director adopts and incorporates by reference the Eye Disorders Guideline (ACOEM April 1, 2017) into the MTUS from the ACOEM Practice Guidelines.

Note: Authority cited: Sections 133, 4603.5, 5307.3 and 5307.27, Labor Code. Reference: Sections 77.5, 4600, 4604.5 and 5307.27, Labor Code.

History: 1. New section filed 6-18-2009; operative 7-18-2009 (Register 2009, No. 25).

2. Editorial correction of operative date in History 1 (Register 2009, No. 30).

3. Amendment of section heading and repealer and new section filed 1-11-2018; operative 12-1-2017. Submitted to OAL for filing and printing only pursuant to Labor Code section 5307.27(a) (Register 2018, No. 2).

Ref.: Hanna § 22.05[6][a]; Herlick Handbook §§ 1.01[3][b], 4.01[3].

§9792.23.10. Hip and Groin Disorders Guideline.

The Administrative Director adopts and incorporates by reference the Hip and Groin Disorders Guideline (ACOEM April 24, 2019) into the MTUS from the ACOEM Practice Guidelines.

Note: Authority cited: Sections 133, 4603.5, 5307.3 and 5307.27, Labor Code. Reference: Sections 77.5, 4600, 4604.5 and 5307.27, Labor Code.

History: 1. New section filed 1-11-2018; operative 12-1-2017. Submitted to OAL for filing and printing only pursuant to Labor Code section 5307.27(a) (Register 2018, No. 2).

2. Amendment of section heading, section and Note filed 10-21-2019; operative 10-7-2019. Submitted to OAL for printing only pursuant to Labor Code section 5302.27(a) (Register 2019, No. 43).

§9792.23.11. Occupational/Work-Related Asthma Guideline.

The Administrative Director adopts and incorporates by reference the Occupational/Work-Related Asthma Guideline (ACOEM June 5, 2020) into the MTUS from the ACOEM Practice Guidelines.

Note: Authority cited: Sections 133, 4603.5 and 5307.27, Labor Code. Reference: Sections 77.5, 4600, 4604.5 and 5307.27, Labor Code.

History: 1. New section filed 1-11-2018; operative 12-1-2017. Submitted to OAL for filing and printing only pursuant to Labor Code section 5307.27(a) (Register 2018, No. 2).

2. Amendment of section heading and section filed 9-10-2020; operative 9-21-2020. Submitted to OAL for filing and printing only pursuant to Labor Code section 5307.27(a) (Register 2020, No. 37).

§9792.23.12. Occupational Interstitial Lung Disease Guideline.

The Administrative Director adopts and incorporates by reference the Occupational Interstitial Lung Disease Guideline (ACOEM November 8, 2019) into the MTUS from the ACOEM Practice Guidelines.

Note: Authority cited: Sections 133, 4603.5 and 5307.27, Labor Code. Reference: Sections 77.5, 4600, 4604.5 and 5307.27, Labor Code.

History: 1. New section filed 1-11-2018; operative 12-1-2017. Submitted to OAL for filing and printing only pursuant to Labor Code section 5307.27(a) (Register 2018, No. 2).

2. Amendment filed 9-10-2020; operative 9-21-2020. Submitted to OAL for filing and printing only pursuant to Labor Code section 5307.27(a) (Register 2020, No. 37).

§9792.24. Special Topics.

(a) Special topics refer to clinical topic areas where the Administrative Director has determined that the clinical topic sections of the MTUS require further supplementation.

Note: Authority cited: Sections 133, 4603.5, 5307.3 and 5307.27, Labor Code. Reference: Sections 77.5, 4600, 4604.5 and 5307.27, Labor Code.

History: 1. New section filed 6-18-2009; operative 7-18-2009 (Register 2009, No. 25).

2. Editorial correction of operative date in History 1 (Register 2009, No. 30).

Ref.: Hanna § 22.05[6][a]; Herlick Handbook §§ 1.01[3][b], 4.01[3].

§9792.24.1. Acupuncture Medical Treatment Guidelines.

Guidance for acupuncture treatment and evaluation are contained in the applicable Clinical Topics guidelines, and/or Chronic Pain Guideline, and/or Opioid Guideline.

Note: Authority cited: Sections 133, 4603.5, 5307.3 and 5307.27, Labor Code. Reference: Sections 77.5, 4600, 4604.5 and 5307.27, Labor Code.

History: 1. Renumbering and amendment of former section 9792.21, subsections (a)(2)-(a)(2)(E) to new section 9792.24.1 filed 6-18-2009; operative 7-18-2009 (Register 2009, No. 25).

2. Editorial correction of operative date in History 1 (Register 2009, No. 30).

3. Amendment of subsection (d) filed 4-20-2015; operative 4-20-2015 pursuant to Government Code section 11343.4(b)(3) (Register 2015, No. 17).

4. Repealer and new section filed 1-11-2018; operative 12-1-2017. Submitted to OAL for filing and printing only pursuant to Labor Code section 5307.27(a) (Register 2018, No. 2).

Ref.: Hanna §§ 5.02[1], 22.05[6][a]; Herlick Handbook §§ 1.01[3][b], 4.01[3].

§9792.24.2. Chronic Pain Guidelines.

The Administrative Director adopts and incorporates by reference the Chronic Pain Guideline (ACOEM May 15, 2017) into the MTUS from the ACOEM Practice Guidelines for the treatment and evaluation of patients who have chronic pain as defined in section 9792.20. This guideline addresses a general approach to patients with chronic pain and the psychological and behavioral aspects of chronic pain. This guideline also addresses a few specific chronic pain disorders (i.e., complex regional pain syndrome, fibromyalgia, neuropathic pain). Guidance for treatment and evaluation of chronic pain disorders not specifically addressed in this guideline are contained in the Clinical Topics guidelines and/or Opioid Guideline.

Note: Authority cited: Sections 133, 4603.5, 5307.3 and 5307.27, Labor Code. Reference: Sections 77.5, 4600, 4604.5 and 5307.27, Labor Code.

History: 1. New section filed 6-18-2009; operative 7-18-2009 (Register 2009, No. 25).

2. Editorial correction of operative date in History 1 (Register 2009, No. 30).

3. Amendment filed 7-28-2016; operative 7-28-2016 pursuant to Government Code section 11343.4(b)(3) (Register 2016, No. 31).

4. Amendment of section heading and repealer and new section filed 1-11-2018; operative 12-1-2017. Submitted to OAL for filing and printing only pursuant to Labor Code section 5307.27(a) (Register 2018, No. 2).

Ref.: Hanna § 22.05[6][a]; Herlick Handbook §§ 1.01[3][b], 4.01[3].

§9792.24.3. Postoperative Rehabilitation Guidelines.

Guidance for postoperative rehabilitation treatment and evaluation are contained in the Clinical Topics guidelines, and/or Chronic Pain Guideline and/or Opioid Guideline. The post-operative rehabilitation treatment recommendations apply to visits during the post-operative period only and to surgeries as defined in those guidelines. At the conclusion of the post-operative period, treatment reverts back to the applicable 24-visit limitation for chiropractic, occupational therapy, and physical therapy pursuant to Labor Code section 4604.5(c)(1).

Note: Authority cited: Sections 133, 4603.5, 5307.3 and 5307.27, Labor Code. Reference: Sections 77.5, 4600, 4604.5 and 5307.27, Labor Code.

History: 1. New section filed 6-18-2009; operative 7-18-2009 (Register 2009, No. 25).

2. Editorial correction of operative date in History 1 (Register 2009, No. 30).

3. Amendment of subsection (d)(1) filed 4-20-2015; operative 4-20-2015 pursuant to Government Code section 11343.4(b)(3) (Register 2015, No. 17).

4. Amendment of section heading and repealer and new section filed 1-11-2018; operative 12-1-2017. Submitted to OAL for filing and printing only pursuant to Labor Code section 5307.27(a) (Register 2018, No. 2).

Ref.: Hanna §§ 5.02[1], 22.05[6][a]; Herlick Handbook §§ 1.01[3][b], 4.01[3].

§9792.24.4. Opioids Guidelines.

(a) The Administrative Director adopts and incorporates by reference the Opioids Guideline (ACOEM April 20, 2017) into the MTUS from the ACOEM Practice Guidelines.

(b) The Opioids Guideline describes the appropriate use of opioid medications as part of an overall multidisciplinary treatment regimen for acute, sub-acute, post-operative, and chronic non-cancer pain. This guideline applies when the use of opioid medications is being considered as part of the treatment regimen.

Note: Authority cited: Sections 133, 4603.5, 5307.3 and 5307.27, Labor Code. Reference: Sections 77.5, 4600, 4604.5 and 5307.27, Labor Code.

History: 1. New section filed 7-28-2016; operative 7-28-2016 pursuant to Government Code section 11343.4(b)(3) (Register 2016, No. 31).

2. Amendment of section heading, repealer and new subsection (a) and amendment of subsection (b) filed 1-11-2018; operative 12-1-2017. Submitted to OAL for filing and printing only pursuant to Labor Code section 5307.27(a) (Register 2018, No. 2).

Ref.: Hanna § 5.02[1].

§9792.24.5. Traumatic Brain Injury Guideline.

The Administrative Director adopts and incorporates by reference the Traumatic Brain Injury Guideline (ACOEM November 15, 2017) into the MTUS from the ACOEM Practice Guidelines.

Note: Authority cited: Sections 133, 4603.5, 5307.3 and 5307.27, Labor Code. Reference: Sections 77.5, 4600, 4604.5 and 5307.27, Labor Code.

History: 1. New section filed 10-30-2018; operative 10-31-2018. Submitted to OAL for filing and printing only pursuant to Labor Code section 5307.27(a) (Register 2018, No. 44).

§9792.25. Quality and Strength of Evidence — Definitions.

(a) For purposes of sections 9792.25–9792.26, the following definitions shall apply:

(1) "Appraisal of Guidelines for Research & Evaluation II (AGREE II) Instrument" means a tool designed primarily to help guideline developers and users assess the methodological rigor and transparency in which a guideline is developed. The Administrative Director adopts and incorporates by reference the Appraisal of Guidelines for Research & Evaluation II (AGREE II) Instrument, May 2009 into the MTUS from the following website; www.agreetrust.org. A copy of the Appraisal of Guidelines for Research & Evaluation II (AGREE II) Instrument, May 2009 version may be obtained from the Medical Unit, Division of Workers' Compensation, P.O. Box 71010, Oakland, CA 94612-1486, or from the DWC web site at http://www.dwc.ca.gov.

(2) "Bias" means any tendency to influence the results of a trial (or its interpretation) other than the experimental intervention. Biases include but are not limited to vested interests such as financial interests, academic interests, and industry influence; confounding variables, inadequate generation of the randomization sequence, inadequate concealment of allocation, selection, lack of blinding, selective outcome reporting, failure to do intention-to-treat analysis, early stopping, and publication.

(3) "Biologic plausibility" means the likelihood that existing biological, medical, and toxicological knowledge explains observed effect.

(4) "Blinding" means a technique used in research to eliminate bias by hiding the intervention from the patient, clinician, and any others who are interpreting results.

(5) "Case-control study" means a retrospective observational epidemiologic study of persons with the disease (or other outcome variable) of interest and a suitable control (comparison, reference) group of persons without the disease. The relationship of an attribute to the disease is examined by comparing the diseased and non-diseased with regard to how frequently the attribute is present or, if quantitative, the levels of the attribute, in each of the groups.

(6) "Case report" means a detailed report of the symptoms, signs, diagnosis, treatment, and follow-up of an individual patient. Case reports usually describe an unusual or novel occurrence.

(7) "Case-series" means a group or series of case reports involving patients who were given similar treatment. Reports of case series usually contain detailed information about the individual patients. This includes demographic information (for example, age, gender, ethnic origin) and information on diagnosis, treatment, response to treatment, and follow-up after treatment. This may be done prospectively or retrospectively.

(8) "Cohort study" (also known as "follow-up study" or "prospective study") means an epidemiologic study in which two or more groups of people that are free of disease and that differ according to the extent of exposure to a potential cause of the disease are compared with respect to the incidence (occurrence of the disease) in each of the groups. This may include a comparison of treated and non-treated patients. The main feature of cohort study is observation of large numbers of people over a long period of time (commonly years) with comparison of incidence rates in groups that differ in exposure levels.

(9) "Concealment of allocation" means precautions taken to ensure that the groups to which patients or subjects are assigned as part of a study are not revealed prior to definitively allocating them to their respective groups.

(10) "Confounding variable" means extrinsic factor associated with the exposure under study and cause of the outcome.

(11) "Cross-sectional study" means a study that examines the relationship between diseases (or other health-related characteristics) and other variables of interest as they exist in a defined population at one particular time. Note that disease prevalence rather than disease incidence is normally recorded in a cross-sectional study. The temporal sequence of cause and effect cannot necessarily be determined in a cross-sectional study.

(12) "Diagnostic test" means any medical test performed to confirm, or determine the presence of disease in an individual suspected of having the disease, usually following the report of symptoms, or based on the results of other medical tests. Some examples of diagnostic tests include performing a chest x-ray to diagnose pneumonia, and taking skin biopsy to detect cancerous cells.

(13) "Disease incidence" means new cases of disease or condition over a period of time.

(14) "Disease prevalence" means rate of a disease or condition at any particular point in time.

(15) "Expert opinion" means a determination by experts, through a process of evidenced-based thinking, that a given practice should or should not be recommended, and the opinion is published in a peer-reviewed medical journal.

(16) "Inception cohort study" means a group of individuals identified for subsequent study at an early, uniform point in the course of the specified health condition, or before the condition develops.

(17) "Index test" means the diagnostic procedure or test that is being evaluated in a study.

(18) "Intention to treat" means a procedure in the conduct and analysis of randomized controlled trials. All patients allocated to a given arm of the treatment regimen are included in the analysis whether or not they received or

completed the prescribed regimen. Failure to follow this step defeats the main purpose of random allocation and can invalidate the results.

(19) "Low risk of bias" means those trials or studies that contain methodological safeguards to protect against biases related to vested interests such as financial interests, academic interests, industry influence, or other biases related to the generation of the randomization sequence, concealment of allocation, selection, blinding, selective outcome reporting, early stopping, and intention to treat.

(20) "Meta-analysis" means a mathematical process whereby results from two or more studies are combined using a method that provides a weight to each study that reflects the statistical likelihood (variance) that its results are more likely to be closer to the truth.

(21) "Post-marketing surveillance" means a procedure implemented after a drug has been licensed for public use. The procedure is designed to provide information on the actual use of the drug for a given indication and on the occurrence of side effects, adverse reactions, etc. This is a method for identifying adverse drug reactions, especially rare (< 1% incidence) ones.

(22) "Prognosis" means the prospect of survival and recovery from a disease as anticipated from the usual course of that disease or indicated by special features of the case.

(23) "Randomized trial" means a clinical experiment in which subjects in a population are allocated by chance into groups, usually called study and control groups, to receive or not receive an experimental diagnostic, preventive, or therapeutic procedure, maneuver, or intervention. The results are assessed by comparison of rates of disease, death, recovery, or other appropriate outcome in the study and control groups.

(24) "Reference standard" means the gold standard to which an index test is being compared.

(25) "Risk of bias" means a term that refers to the advertent or inadvertent introduction of bias into trials because of methodological insufficiencies to protect against biases related to vested interests such as financial interests, academic interests, industry influence, or other biases related to the generation of the randomization sequence, concealment of allocation, selection, blinding, selective outcome reporting, early stopping, and intention to treat.

(26) "Selective outcome reporting" means the failure to report all of the outcomes that are assessed in a trial, including a post hoc change in the primary outcome.

(27) "Systematic review" means the application of strategies that limit bias in the assembly, critical appraisal, and synthesis of all relevant studies on a specific topic. Systematic reviews focus on peer-reviewed publications about a specific health problem and use rigorous, standardized methods for selecting and assessing articles. A systematic review differs from a meta-analysis in not including a quantitative summary of the results. However, a meta-analysis may be part of a systematic review.

(28) "Treatment benefits" means positive patient-relevant outcome associated with an intervention, quantifiable by epidemiological measures such as absolute risk reduction and number needed to treat.

(29) "Treatment harms" means an adverse patient-relevant outcome associated with an intervention, identifiable by epidemiological measures such as absolute increased risk of occurrence or number needed to harm if possible, but also identifiable by post-marketing surveillance.

Note: Authority cited: Sections 133, 4603.5, 5307.3 and 5307.27, Labor Code. Reference: Sections 77.5, 4600, 4604.5 and 5307.27, Labor Code.

History: 1. Renumbering and amendment of former section 9792.22 to new section 9792.25 filed 6-18-2009; operative 7-18-2009 (Register 2009, No. 25).

2. Editorial correction of operative date in History 1 (Register 2009, No. 30).

3. Amendment of section heading and repealer and new section filed 4-20-2015; operative 4-20-2015 pursuant to Government Code section 11343.4(b)(3) (Register 2015, No. 17).

Ref.: Hanna § 5.02[1].

§9792.25.1. MTUS Methodology for Evaluating Medical Evidence.

(a) When competing recommendations are cited to guide medical care, Utilization Review and Independent Medical Review physicians shall apply the MTUS Methodology for Evaluating Medical Evidence to evaluate the quality and strength of evidence used to support the recommendations that are at variance with one another. The MTUS Methodology for Evaluating Medical Evidence provides a process to evaluate studies, not guidelines. Therefore, the reviewing physician shall evaluate the underlying study or studies used to support a recommendation found in a guideline. Medical care shall be in accordance with the recommendation supported by the best available evidence. The MTUS Methodology for Evaluating Medical Evidence shall be applied as follows:

(1) The reviewing physician shall determine if different guidelines or studies were cited to guide the injured worker's medical care by the treating physician, the Utilization Review physician and/or the Independent Medical Review physician that contain recommendations that are at variance with one another.

(2) If different guidelines or studies were cited to guide the injured worker's medical care containing recommendations that are at variance with one another, the reviewing physician shall evaluate the quality of evidence by determining if the studies used to support the recommendations are applicable to the injured worker and his or her medical condition or injury. Applicability refers to the extent to which the individual patients, subjects, settings, interventions, and outcome measures of studies used to support a recommendation are similar to the worker and his or her medical condition or injury. A recommendation supported by inapplicable studies should not be used as the source to support, deny, delay or modify an RFA. Reviewing physicians shall provide an explanation of their rationale in the Utilization Review or Independent Medical Review decision if they conclude a recommendation is supported by studies inapplicable to the worker and his or her medical condition or injury.

(A) The evaluation of medical evidence can end after this step if a citation to a guideline or a study contains a recommendation supported by inapplicable studies and the other citation contains a recommendation that is supported by studies applicable to the injured worker's medical condition or injury.

(3) If the guidelines or studies cited contain recommendations supported by studies applicable to the worker and his or her medical condition or injury, then the reviewing physician shall continue to evaluate the quality of evidence by determining what factors, if any, bias may have had in the studies used to support the recommendations. Factors to consider include, but are not limited to, vested interests such as financial interests, academic interests, industry influence, and the methodological safeguards to protect against biases related to the generation of the randomization sequence, concealment of allocation, blinding, selective outcome reporting, early stopping, intention to treat, and confounding bias. A recommendation supported by studies determined to be of poor quality due to the presence of bias should not be used as the source to support, deny, delay or modify an RFA. Reviewing physicians shall provide an explanation of their rationale in the Utilization Review or Independent Medical Review decision if they conclude a recommendation is supported by studies determined to be of poor quality due to the presence of bias.

(A) The evaluation of medical evidence can end after this step if a citation to a guideline or a study contains a recommendation supported by studies determined to be of poor quality due to the presence of bias and the other citation contains a recommendation that is supported by studies determined to be of good quality due to the absence of bias.

(4) If the guidelines or studies cited contain recommendations supported by studies applicable to the worker and his or her medical condition or injury and if the recommendations are supported by studies that are determined to be of good quality due to the absence of bias, then the reviewing physician shall determine the strength of evidence used to support the differing recommendations by applying the Hierarchy of Evidence for Different Clinical Questions set forth in 9792.25.1(b). To apply the Hierarchy of Evidence for Different Clinical Questions, the following steps shall be taken:

(A) Determine the design of the study used to support the recommendation. Study designs are categorized as one of the following categories:

1. Systematic Review of:
(aa) Randomized Controlled Trials
(bb) Prospective or Cohort Studies
2. Randomized Controlled Trials
3. Observational studies:
(aa) Prospective study or Cohort Study
(bb) Cross-sectional study
(cc) Case-control study
(dd) Case-series
(ee) Uncontrolled or observational study
(ff) Case report
4. Published expert opinion

(B) Determine which of the four clinical questions in the MTUS Hierarchy of Evidence for Different Clinical Questions as set forth in Section 9792.25.2(b) the study is answering and then apply the corresponding hierarchy(ies) of evidence. The sequence to be followed for each of the four clinical questions is as follows:

1. If the original study answers the question "How useful is Treatment X in treating patients with Disease Y?" then the hierarchy of evidence set forth under Treatment Benefits shall apply.

2. If the original study answers the question "How useful is Test X in diagnosing patients with Disease Y?" then the hierarchy of evidence set forth under Diagnostic Test shall apply.

3. If the original study answers the question "What will happen to a patient with Disease Y if nothing is done?" then the hierarchy of evidence set forth under Prognosis shall apply.

4. If the original study answers the question "What are the harms of intervention (treatment or diagnostic test) X in patients with Disease Y?" then the hierarchy of evidence set forth under Treatment Harms shall apply.

(C) In each Clinical Question category, the levels of evidence are listed from highest to lowest, as defined by the principles of Evidence-Based Medicine. Levels of evidence shall be applied in the order listed. Recommendation for or against medical treatment based on a lower level of evidence shall be permitted only if every higher ranked level of evidence is inapplicable to the employee's medical condition.

1. The level of evidence for each published study (e.g. 1a, 1b, 2, etc.) shall be documented and included with the citation in the Utilization Review or Independent Medical Review decisions.

2. When relying on lower levels of evidence, a written statement shall be provided that states higher levels of evidence are absent.

(b) MTUS Hierarchy of Evidence for Different Clinical Questions shall apply:

MTUS Hierarchy of Evidence for Different Clinical Questions

Evidence Level	**Treatment Benefits** How useful is Treatment X in treating patients with Disease Y?	**Diagnostic Test** How useful is Test X in diagnosing patients with Disease Y?	**Prognosis** What will happen to a patient with Disease Y if nothing is done?	**Treatment Harms** What are the harms of intervention (treatment or diagnostic test) X in patients with Disease Y?

1a	Systematic review of randomized controlled trials with low risk of bias	Systematic review of high-quality prospective studies (homogeneous sample of patients, consecutively enrolled, all undergoing the index test and reference standard) or systematic review of randomized controlled trials with low risk bias	Systematic review of inception cohort studies or of control arms of randomized controlled trials with low risk of bias	Systematic review of randomized controlled trials with low risk of bias
1b	Randomized controlled trials with low risk of bias	High-quality prospective study or cohort study or randomized controlled trials with low risk of bias	Inception cohort study or control arm from one randomized controlled trial with low risk of bias	Randomized controlled trials with low risk of bias
1c	One or more randomized controlled trials with identified risks of bias (or systematic review of such trials)	Biased cross-sectional study	Cohort study or control arm of randomized controlled trials with identified risks of bias	Prospective study
2	Non-randomized cohort studies that include controls	Case-control study enrolling a broad spectrum of patients and controls with conditions that may be confused with the disease being considered	Case-series or case control studies	Randomized controlled trial(s) with identified risk of bias
3	Case-control studies or historically controlled studies	Case-control study using severe cases and healthy controls		Non-randomized controlled cohort/follow-up study (post-marketing surveillance)
4	Uncontrolled studies (case studies or case reports)		Uncontrolled studies (observational studies, case studies, or case reports)	Consistent case reports (for example, individual case safety reports from US Food and Drug Administration, which are available at the following website: www.fda.gov/ForIndustry/DataStandards/IndividualCaseSafetyReports/default.htm
5	Published expert opinion	Published expert opinion	Published expert opinion	Toxicological or mechanistic data that demonstrate or support biologic plausibility

Note: Authority cited: Sections 133, 4603.5, 5307.3 and 5307.27, Labor Code. Reference: Sections 77.5, 4600, 4604.5, 4610.5 and 5307.27, Labor Code.

History: 1. New section filed 4-20-2015; operative 4-20-2015 pursuant to Government Code section 11343.4(b)(3) (Register 2015, No. 17).

Ref.: Hanna § 5.02[1]; Herlick Handbook § 4.01[3].

§9792.26. Medical Evidence Evaluation Advisory Committee.

(a) The Medical Director shall create a Medical Evidence Evaluation Advisory Committee (MEEAC) to provide recommendations to the Medical Director on matters concerning the MTUS. The recommendations are advisory only and shall not constitute scientifically based evidence.

(1) If the Medical Director position becomes vacant, the Administrative Director shall appoint a competent person to temporarily assume the authority and duties of the Medical Director as set forth in this section, until such time that the Medical Director position is filled.

(2) The members of the MEEAC shall be appointed by the Medical Director, or his or her designee, and shall consist of 19 members of the medical community holding the following licenses: Medical Doctor (M.D.) board certified by an American Board of Medical Specialties (ABMS) approved specialty board; Doctor of Osteopathy (D.O.) board certified by an ABMS or American Osteopathic Association (AOA) approved specialty board; M.D. board certified by a Medical Board of California (MBC) approved specialty board; Doctor of Chiropractic (D.C.); Physical Therapy (P.T.); Occupational Therapy (O.T.); Acupuncture (L.Ac.); Psychology (PhD.); Doctor of Podiatric Medicine (DPM); Pharmacologist (PharmD); Nurse Practitioner (NP) or Registered Nurse (RN), and representing the following specialty fields:

(A) One member shall be from the orthopedic field;

(B) One member shall be from the chiropractic field;

(C) One member shall be from the occupational medicine field;

(D) One member shall be from the acupuncture medicine field;

(E) One member shall be from the physical therapy field;

(F) One member shall be from the psychology field;

(G) One member shall be from the pain specialty field;

(H) One member shall be from the occupational therapy field;

(I) One member shall be from the psychiatry field;

(J) One member shall be from the neurosurgery field;

(K) One member shall be from the family physician field;

(L) One member shall be from the neurology field;

(M) One member shall be from the internal medicine field;

(N) One member shall be from the physical medicine and rehabilitation field;

(O) One member shall be from the podiatrist field;

(P) One member shall be from the pharmacology field;

(Q) One member shall be from the nursing field;

(R) Two additional members shall be appointed at the discretion of the Medical Director or his or her designee.

(3) In addition to the nineteen members of MEEAC appointed under subdivision (a)(2) above, the Medical Director, or his or her designee, may appoint an additional three members to MEEAC as subject matter experts for any given topic.

(b) The Medical Director, or his or her designee, shall serve as the chairperson of MEEAC.

(c) Members of MEEAC shall make advisory recommendations to the Medical Director or his or her designee to revise, update or supplement the MTUS.

(d) The advisory MEEAC recommendations shall be supported by the best available medical evidence found in scientifically and evidenced-based medical treatment guidelines or peer-reviewed published studies that are nationally recognized by the medical community.

(e) To assess the quality and methodological rigors used to develop a medical treatment guideline, members of MEEAC shall use a modified version of the Appraisal of Guidelines for Research & Evaluation II (AGREE II) Instrument, May 2009. The AGREE II Instrument, May 2009, consisting of 23 key items organized within six domains followed by two global rating items was found in the following website: www.agreetrust.org. A copy of the AGREE II Instrument, May 2009 version may be obtained from the Medical Unit, Division of Workers' Compensation, P.O. Box 71010, Oakland, CA 94612-1486, or from the DWC web site at http://www.dwc.ca.gov.

(1) Members of MEEAC shall use a modified AGREE II that uses the same six domains and two global rating items as the AGREE II Instrument, May 2009 version but includes two additional domains and additional key items:

(A) Additional domain in the modified AGREE II Instrument — Conflict of Interest

1. Key Item in this domain — All conflicts of interest of each guideline development group member were reported and discussed by the prospective group prior to the onset of his or her work.

2. Key Item in this domain — Each panel member explained how his or her conflict of interest could influence the clinical practice guideline development process or specific recommendation.

3. Key Item in this domain — The chairperson of the guideline development group had no conflicts of interest.

(B) Additional domain in the modified AGREE II Instrument - Currency of Guideline

1. Key Item in this domain — The guideline is being updated in a timely fashion (typically at least every three years and, if the guideline is more than five years old, it should be considered to be out of date).

(f) Recommendations in guidelines that have a low AGREE II overall score may still be considered, provided that the evidence supporting the recommendations is the best available medical evidence.

(g) To determine the best available medical evidence, members of MEEAC shall rank the medical evidence used to support recommendations found in either guidelines or peer-reviewed published studies by applying the MTUS Methodology for Evaluating Medical Evidence set forth in section 9792.25.1 and shall choose the recommendations supported by the best available medical evidence.

(h) The members of MEEAC, except for the three subject matter experts, shall serve a two-year term, but shall remain in that position until a successor is selected. The subject matter experts shall serve as members of the medical evidence evaluation advisory committee until the evaluation of the subject matter guideline is completed. The members of the committee shall meet as necessary, but no less than three (3) times a year.

(i) The Administrative Director, in consultation with the Medical Director, may revise, update, and supplement the MTUS as necessary.

Note: Authority cited: Sections 133, 4603.5, 5307.3 and 5307.27, Labor Code. Reference: Sections 77.5, 4600, 4604.5 and 5307.27, Labor Code.

History: 1. Renumbering and amendment of former section 9792.23 to new section 9792.26 filed 6-18-2009; operative 7-18-2009 (Register 2009, No. 25).

2. Editorial correction of operative date in History 1 (Register 2009, No. 30).

3. Amendment filed 4-20-2015; operative 4-20-2015 pursuant to Government Code section 11343.4(b)(3) (Register 2015, No. 17).

Ref.: Hanna § 22.05[6][a], [b]; Herlick Handbook §§ 1.01[3][b], 4.01[3].

§9792.27.1. Medical Treatment Utilization Schedule (MTUS) Drug Formulary — Definitions.

For purposes of sections 9792.27.1 through 9792.27.23, the following definitions shall apply:

(a) "Administer" means the direct application of a drug or device to the body of the patient by injection, inhalation, ingestion, or other means.

(b) "Authorization through prospective review" means authorization for proposed treatment obtained through the utilization review process set forth in section 9792.6.1 et seq.

(c) "Brand name drug" means a drug that is produced or distributed under an FDA original New Drug Application (NDA) or Biologic License Application (BLA) approved by the FDA. It also includes a drug product marketed by any cross-licensed producers or distributors operating under the same NDA or BLA.

(d) "Combination drug" means a fixed dose combination of two or more active drug ingredients into a single dosage form that is FDA-approved for marketing.

(e) "Compounded drug" means any drug subject to:

(1) Article 4.5 (commencing with section 1735) or article 7 (commencing with section 1751) of division 17 of title 16 of the California Code of Regulations, or

(2) Other regulation adopted by the State Board of Pharmacy to govern the practice of compounding, or

(3) Federal law governing compounding, including title 21, United State Code, sections 353a, 353a-1, 353b.

(f) "Dispense" means: 1) the furnishing of a drug upon a prescription from a physician or other health care provider acting within the scope of his or her practice, or 2) the furnishing of drugs directly to a patient by a physician acting within the scope of his or her practice.

(g) "Executive Medical Director" means the medical director of the Division of Workers' Compensation.

(h) "Exempt drug" means a drug on the MTUS Drug List which is designated as being a drug that does not require authorization through prospective review prior to dispensing the drug, provided that the drug is prescribed in accordance with the MTUS Treatment Guidelines. The Exempt status of a drug is designated in the column with the heading labeled "Exempt / "Exempt / Non-Exempt."

(i) "Expedited review" means the expedited utilization review conducted prior to the delivery of the requested medical services, in accordance with Labor Code section 4610 and title 8, California Code of Regulations section 9792.6.1 et seq.

(j) "FDA" means the United States Food and Drug Administration within the United States Department of Health & Human Services.

(k) "FDA-approved drug" means a prescription or nonprescription drug that has been approved by the FDA under the federal Food, Drug, and Cosmetic Act, title 21, United States Code, section 301 et seq.

(*l*) "Generic drug" means a drug that is produced or distributed under an FDA Abbreviated New Drug Application (ANDA) approved by the FDA. A generic drug may be substituted for a therapeutic equivalent brand name drug pursuant to applicable state and federal laws and regulations.

(m) "MTUS Drug Formulary" means the MTUS Drug List set forth in section 9792.27.15 and the formulary rules set forth in sections 9792.27.1 through 9792.27.23.

(n) "MTUS Drug List" means the drug list and related information in section 9792.27.15, which sets forth the Exempt or Non-Exempt status of drugs listed by active drug ingredient(s).

(o) "Non-Exempt drug" means a drug on the MTUS Drug List which is designated as requiring authorization through prospective review prior to dispensing the drug. The Non-Exempt Drug status of a drug is designated in the column labeled "Exempt / Non-Exempt."

(p) "Nonprescription drug" or "over-the-counter drug" (OTC drug) means a drug which may be sold without a prescription and which is labeled for use by the consumer without the supervision of a health care professional.

(q) "Off-label use" means use of a drug for a condition, or in a dosage or method of administration, not listed in the drug's FDA-approved labeling for approved use.

(r) "OTC Monograph" means a monograph established by the FDA setting forth acceptable ingredients, doses, formulations, and labeling for a class of OTC drugs.

(s) "Perioperative Fill" means the policy set forth in section 9792.27.13 allowing dispensing of identified Non-Exempt drugs without prospective review where the drug is prescribed within the perioperative period and meets specified criteria.

(t) "P&T Committee" means the Pharmacy and Therapeutics Committee established by the Administrative Director pursuant to Labor Code section 5307.29 to review and consult with the administrative director on available evidence of the relative safety, efficacy, and effectiveness of drugs within a class of drugs in the updating of the evidence-based drug formulary.

(u) "Physician": Notwithstanding the definition in Labor Code section 3209.3, for purposes of the MTUS Drug Formulary, "Physician" means a medical doctor, doctor of osteopathy, or other health care provider whose scope of practice includes the prescription of drugs. However, for purposes of membership on the P&T Committee, "physician" means a medical doctor or doctor of osteopathy licensed pursuant to the California Business and Professions Code.

(v) "Prescription drug" means any drug whose labeling states "Caution: Federal law prohibits dispensing without prescription," "Rx only," or words of similar import.

(w) "Prospective review" means the utilization review conducted prior to the delivery of the requested medical services, in accordance with Labor Code section 4610 and title 8, California Code of Regulations section 9792.6.1 et seq.

(x) "Special Fill" means the policy set forth in section 9792.27.12 allowing dispensing of identified Non-Exempt drugs without prospective review where the drug is prescribed or dispensed in accordance with the criteria set forth in subdivision (b) of section 9792.27.12.

(y) A "therapeutic equivalent" is a drug designated by the FDA as equivalent to a Reference Listed Drug if the two drugs are pharmaceutical equivalents (contain the same active ingredient(s), dosage form, route of administration and strength), and are bioequivalent (comparable availability and rate of absorption of the active ingredient(s).) Drugs that the FDA considers to be therapeutically equivalent products are assigned a Therapeutic Equivalence Evaluation Code beginning with the letter "A" in the FDA publication "Orange Book: Approved Products with Therapeutic Equivalence Evaluations" which is available on the FDA website and accessible via a link provided on the department's website.

(z) "Unlisted drug" means a drug that does not appear on the MTUS Drug List and which is one of the following: an FDA-approved or a nonprescription drug that is marketed pursuant to an FDA OTC Monograph. An "unlisted drug" does not include a compounded drug but does include a combination drug.

Note: Authority cited: Sections 133, 4603.5, 5307.3 and 5307.27, Labor Code. Reference: Sections 4600, 4604.5, 5307.27 and 5307.29, Labor Code.

History: 1. New section filed 12-7-2017; operative 1-1-2018 pursuant to Government Code section 11343.4(b)(3) (Register 2017, No. 49).

§9792.27.2. MTUS Drug Formulary; MTUS Drug List; Scope of Coverage; Effective Date.

(a) Drugs prescribed or dispensed to treat a work related injury or illness fall within Labor Code section 4600's definition of "medical treatment" and are subject to the relevant provisions of the MTUS, including the MTUS Treatment Guidelines, provisions relating to the presumption of correctness, and the methods for rebutting the presumption and for substantiating medical necessity where the MTUS Treatment Guidelines do not address the condition or injury.

(b) Except for continuing drug treatment subject to section 9792.27.3, subdivision (b), a drug dispensed on or after January 1, 2018 for outpatient use shall be subject to the MTUS Drug Formulary, regardless of the date of injury.

(1) A drug is for "outpatient use" if it is dispensed to be taken, applied, or self-administered by the patient at home or outside of a clinical setting, including "take home" drugs dispensed at the time of discharge from a facility. "Home" includes an institutional setting in which the injured worker resides, including but not limited to, an assisted living facility.

(2) The MTUS Drug Formulary does not apply to drugs administered to the patient by a physician. However, the physician administered drug treatment is subject to relevant provisions of the MTUS, including the MTUS Treatment Guidelines.

Note: Authority cited: Sections 133, 4603.5, 5307.3 and 5307.27, Labor Code. Reference: Sections 4600, 4604.5 and 5307.27, Labor Code.

History: 1. New section filed 12-7-2017; operative 1-1-2018 pursuant to Government Code section 11343.4(b)(3) (Register 2017, No. 49).

§9792.27.3. MTUS Drug Formulary Transition.

(a) Except as provided in subdivision (b), the MTUS Drug Formulary applies to drugs dispensed on or after January 1, 2018, regardless of the date of injury.

(b)(1) For injuries occurring prior to January 1, 2018, the MTUS Drug Formulary should be phased in to ensure that injured workers who are receiving ongoing drug treatment are not harmed by an abrupt change to the course of treatment. The physician is responsible for requesting a medically appropriate and safe course of treatment for the injured worker in accordance with the MTUS, which may include use of a Non-Exempt drug or unlisted drug, where that is necessary for the injured worker's condition or necessary for safe weaning, tapering, or transition to a different drug.

(2) If the injured worker with a date of injury prior to January 1, 2018 is receiving a course of treatment that includes a Non-Exempt drug, an unlisted drug, or a compounded drug, the physician shall submit a progress report issued pursuant to section 9785 and a Request for Authorization that shall address the injured worker's ongoing drug treatment plan. The report shall either:

(A) Include a treatment plan setting forth a medically appropriate weaning, tapering, or transitioning of the worker to a drug pursuant to the MTUS, or

(B) Provide supporting documentation, as appropriate, to substantiate the medical necessity of, and to obtain authorization for, the Non-Exempt drug, unlisted drug, or compounded drug, pursuant to the MTUS (via guidelines, Medical Evidence Search Sequence, and/or Methodology for Evaluating Medical Evidence.)

(3) The progress report, including the treatment plan and Request for Authorization provided under this subdivision, shall be submitted at the time the next progress report is due under section 9785, subdivision (f)(8), however, if that is not feasible, no later than April 1, 2018.

(4) Previously approved drug treatment shall not be terminated or denied except as may be allowed by the MTUS and in accordance with applicable utilization review and independent medical review regulations.

(5) The claims administrator shall process the progress report, treatment plan and Request for Authorization in accordance with the standard procedures and timeframes set forth in section 9792.6.1 et seq.

Note: Authority cited: Sections 133, 4603.5, 5307.3 and 5307.27, Labor Code. Reference: Sections 4600, 4604.5 and 5307.27, Labor Code.

History: 1. New section filed 12-7-2017; operative 1-1-2018 pursuant to Government Code section 11343.4(b)(3) (Register 2017, No. 49).

§9792.27.4. MTUS Drug Formulary — Pharmacy Networks; Pharmacy Benefit Manager Contracts.

Where an employer or insurer contracts pursuant to Labor Code section 4600.2 with a pharmacy, a pharmacy benefit manager, or pharmacy network for the provision of drugs for the treatment of injured workers, the drugs available to the injured worker must be consistent with the MTUS Treatment Guidelines and MTUS Drug Formulary for the condition or injury being treated, and may not be restricted pursuant to the contract.

Note: Authority cited: Sections 133, 4603.5, 5307.3 and 5307.27, Labor Code. Reference: Sections 4600, 4600.2, 4604.5 and 5307.27, Labor Code.

History: 1. New section filed 12-7-2017; operative 1-1-2018 pursuant to Government Code section 11343.4(b)(3) (Register 2017, No. 49).

§9792.27.5. MTUS Drug Formulary — Off-Label Use.

(a) Off-label use of a drug shall be in accordance with the MTUS Treatment Guidelines and rules and the MTUS Drug Formulary.

(b) Authorization through prospective review is not required to dispense an Exempt drug for an off-label use if the MTUS Treatment Guideline recommends the off-label use of the drug to treat the condition.

(c) Authorization through prospective review is required prior to dispensing the following drugs for an off-label use:

(1) Non-Exempt drug, or

(2) Unlisted drug, or

(3) Exempt drug lacking recommendation in the MTUS Treatment Guideline for the intended off-label use.

(d) When a physician believes it is medically necessary to prescribe a drug for an off-label use not recommended by the MTUS Treatment Guidelines or not addressed by the MTUS Treatment Guidelines, the permissibility of the treatment outside of the guidelines is governed by section 9792.21 subdivision (d) (condition not addressed by MTUS or seeking to rebut the MTUS), section 9792.21.1 (medical evidence search sequence), section 9792.25 (quality and strength of evidence definitions) and section 9792.25.1 (MTUS methodology for Evaluating Medical Evidence).

Note: Authority cited: Sections 133, 4603.5, 5307.3 and 5307.27, Labor Code. Reference: Sections 4600, 4604.5 and 5307.27, Labor Code.

History: 1. New section filed 12-7-2017; operative 1-1-2018 pursuant to Government Code section 11343.4(b)(3) (Register 2017, No. 49).

§9792.27.6. MTUS Drug Formulary — Access to Drugs Not Listed as an Exempt Drug on the MTUS Drug List.

(a) Drug treatment that is in conformity with the MTUS Treatment Guidelines is presumed correct on the issue of extent and scope of medical treatment pursuant to section 9792.21, subdivision (c), and Labor Code section 4604.5. Although the MTUS Drug List identifies Exempt drugs that do not require prospective review when dispensed in accordance with the MTUS Treatment Guidelines, other medically necessary drugs are available to the injured worker when authorized through prospective review.

(b) Any medically necessary FDA-approved drug, or nonprescription drug that is marketed pursuant to an FDA OTC Monograph, may be authorized through prospective review and dispensed to an injured worker if it is shown in accordance with the MTUS regulations that the drug is required to cure or relieve the injured worker from the effects of the injury. Determination of the medical necessity of treatment based on recommendations found outside of the MTUS Treatment Guidelines is governed by section 9792.21 subdivision (d) (condition not addressed by MTUS or seeking to rebut the MTUS), section 9792.21.1 (medical evidence search sequence), section 9792.25 (quality and strength of evidence definitions) and section 9792.25.1 (MTUS methodology for evaluating medical evidence).

Note: Authority cited: Sections 133, 4603.5, 5307.3 and 5307.27, Labor Code. Reference: Sections 4600, 4604.5 and 5307.27, Labor Code.

History: 1. New section filed 12-7-2017; operative 1-1-2018 pursuant to Government Code section 11343.4(b)(3) (Register 2017, No. 49).

§9792.27.7. MTUS Drug Formulary — Brand Name Drugs; Generic Drugs.

If a physician prescribes a brand name drug when a less costly therapeutically equivalent generic drug exists, and writes "Do Not Substitute" or "Dispense as Written" on the prescription in conformity with Business and Professions Code section 4073, the physician must document the medical necessity for prescribing the brand name drug in the patient's medical chart and in the Doctor's First Report of Injury (Form 5021) or Progress Report (PR-2.) The documentation must include the patient-specific factors that support the physician's determination that the brand name drug is medically necessary. The physician must submit a Request for Authorization and obtain authorization through prospective review before the brand name drug is dispensed.

Note: Authority cited: Sections 133, 4603.5, 5307.3 and 5307.27, Labor Code. Reference: Sections 4600, 4604.5 and 5307.27, Labor Code.

History: 1. New section filed 12-7-2017; operative 1-1-2018 pursuant to Government Code section 11343.4(b)(3) (Register 2017, No. 49).

§9792.27.8. Physician-Dispensed Drugs.

(a) Drugs dispensed by a physician must be authorized through prospective review prior to being dispensed, except as provided in subdivision (b), section 9792.27.12 ("Special Fill"), and section 9792.27.13 ("Perioperative Fill").

(b) A physician may dispense up to a seven-day supply of one or more drugs that are designated as "Exempt" in the MTUS Drug List without obtaining authorization through prospective review, if the drug treatment is in accordance with the MTUS Treatment Guidelines and the up-to-seven-day supply is dispensed at the time of an initial visit that occurs within 7 days of the date of injury.

(c) Nothing in this Article shall invalidate a provision in a Medical Provider Network agreement which restricts physician dispensing by medical providers within the network.

(d) Nothing in this Article shall permit physician dispensing where otherwise prohibited by a pharmacy benefit contract pursuant to subdivision (a) of Labor Code section 4600.2.

Note: Authority cited: Sections 133, 4603.5, 5307.3 and 5307.27, Labor Code. Reference: Sections 4600, 4604.5 and 5307.27, Labor Code.

History: 1. New section filed 12-7-2017; operative 1-1-2018 pursuant to Government Code section 11343.4(b)(3) (Register 2017, No. 49).

§9792.27.9. Compounded Drugs.

(a) Compounded drugs must be authorized through prospective review prior to being dispensed. When it is necessary for medical reasons to prescribe or dispense a compounded drug instead of an FDA-approved drug or over-the-counter drug that complies with an OTC Monograph, the physician must document the medical necessity in the patient's medical chart, and in the Doctor's First Report of Injury (Form 5021) or Progress Report (PR-2) and must submit a Request for Authorization. The documentation must include the patient-specific factors that support the physician's determination that a compounded drug is medically necessary.

(b) Nothing in this Article shall invalidate a provision in a Medical Provider Network agreement which restricts physician dispensing of compounded drugs by medical providers within the network.

(c) Nothing in this Article shall permit physician dispensing of compounded drugs where otherwise prohibited by a pharmacy benefit contract pursuant to subdivision (a) of Labor Code section 4600.2.

Note: Authority cited: Sections 133, 4603.5, 5307.3 and 5307.27, Labor Code. Reference: Sections 4600, 4604.5 and 5307.27, Labor Code.

History: 1. New section filed 12-7-2017; operative 1-1-2018 pursuant to Government Code section 11343.4(b)(3) (Register 2017, No. 49).

§9792.27.10. MTUS Drug List; Exempt Drugs, Non-Exempt Drugs, Unlisted Drugs, Prospective Review.

(a) The MTUS Drug List is set forth by active drug ingredient(s).

(b) A drug that is identified as "Exempt" may be dispensed to the injured worker without obtaining authorization through prospective review if the drug treatment is in accordance with the MTUS Treatment Guidelines, except:

(1) Brand name drugs are subject to section 9792.27.7;

(2) Physician-dispensed drugs are subject to section 9792.27.8.

(3) Compounded drugs are subject to section 9792.27.9 even if one or more of the ingredients is listed as "Exempt" on the MTUS Drug List.

(c) For a drug that is identified as "Non-Exempt," authorization through prospective review must be obtained prior to the time the drug is dispensed. Expedited review should be conducted where it is warranted by the injured worker's condition.

(d) For a drug that is identified as eligible for "Special Fill" or "Perioperative Fill", the usual requirement to obtain authorization through prospective review prior to dispensing the drug is altered for the specified circumstances set forth in sections 9792.27.12 and 9792.27.13. If the requirements set forth in section 9792.27.12 or section 9792.27.13 are not met, then the drug is considered "Non-Exempt" and is subject to the provisions set forth under subdivision (c).

(e) For an unlisted drug, authorization through prospective review must be obtained prior to the time the drug is dispensed. A combination drug that is not on the MTUS Drug List is an unlisted drug even if the individual active ingredients are on the MTUS Drug List.

Note: Authority cited: Sections 133, 4603.5, 5307.3 and 5307.27, Labor Code. Reference: Sections 4600, 4604.5 and 5307.27, Labor Code.

History: 1. New section filed 12-7-2017; operative 1-1-2018 pursuant to Government Code section 11343.4(b)(3) (Register 2017, No. 49).

§9792.27.11. Waiver of Prospective Review.

Nothing in the MTUS Drug Formulary shall prohibit waiver of the prospective review requirement for a Non-Exempt or unlisted drug if the drug falls within a utilization review plan's provision of prior authorization without necessity of a request for authorization, where that provision is adopted pursuant to section 9792.7, subdivision (a)(5).

Note: Authority cited: Sections 133, 4603.5, 5307.3 and 5307.27, Labor Code. Reference: Sections 4600, 4604.5 and 5307.27, Labor Code.

History: 1. New section filed 12-7-2017; operative 1-1-2018 pursuant to Government Code section 11343.4(b)(3) (Register 2017, No. 49).

§9792.27.12. MTUS Drug List — Special Fill.

(a) The MTUS Drug List identifies drugs that are subject to the Special Fill policy. Under this policy, a drug that usually requires prospective review because it is "Non-Exempt" will be allowed without prospective review as specified in subdivision (b).

(b) The drug identified as a Special Fill drug may be dispensed to the injured worker without seeking prospective review if all of the following conditions are met:

(1) The drug is prescribed at the single initial treatment visit following a workplace injury, provided that the initial visit is within 7 days of the date of injury; and

(2) The prescription is for a supply of the drug not to exceed the limit set forth in the MTUS Drug List; and

(3) The prescription for the Special Fill-eligible drug is for:

(A) An FDA-approved generic drug or single source brand name drug, or,

(B) A brand name drug where the physician documents and substantiates the medical need for the brand name drug rather than the FDA-approved generic drug, and

(4) The drug is prescribed in accordance with the MTUS Treatment Guidelines.

(c) When calculating the 7-day period in subdivision (b)(1), the day after the date of injury is "day one."

(d) An employer or insurer that has a contract with a pharmacy, pharmacy network, pharmacy benefit manager, or a medical provider network (MPN) that includes a pharmacy or pharmacies within the MPN, may provide for a longer Special Fill period or may cover additional drugs under the Special Fill policy pursuant to a pharmacy benefit contract or MPN contract.

(e) After the Special Fill provision has been in effect for one year, the Administrative Director shall evaluate the impact of the provision on the use of opioids by injured workers. As part of the evaluation process, the Administrative Director shall solicit feedback from the workers' compensation system participants.

Note: Authority cited: Sections 133, 4603.5, 5307.3 and 5307.27, Labor Code. Reference: Sections 4600, 4604.5 and 5307.27, Labor Code.

History: 1. New section filed 12-7-2017; operative 1-1-2018 pursuant to Government Code section 11343.4(b)(3) (Register 2017, No. 49).

§9792.27.13. MTUS Drug List — Perioperative Fill.

(a) The MTUS Drug List identifies drugs that are subject to the Perioperative Fill policy. Under this policy, the Non-Exempt drug identified as a Perioperative Fill drug may be dispensed to the injured worker without seeking prospective review if all of the following conditions are met:

(1) The drug is prescribed during the perioperative period; and

(2) The prescription is for a supply of the drug not to exceed the limit set forth in the MTUS Drug List; and

(3) The prescription for the Perioperative Fill — eligible drug is for:

(A) An FDA-approved generic drug or single source brand name drug, or,

(B) A brand name drug where the physician documents and substantiates the medical need for the brand name drug rather than the FDA-approved generic drug, and

(4) The drug is prescribed in accordance with the MTUS Treatment Guidelines.

(b) For purposes of this section, the perioperative period is defined as the period from 4 days prior to surgery to 4 days after surgery, with the day of surgery as "day zero".

(c) An employer or insurer that has a contract with a pharmacy, pharmacy network, pharmacy benefit manager, or a medical provider network that includes a pharmacy or pharmacies within the MPN, may provide for a longer Perioperative Fill period or may cover additional drugs under the Perioperative Fill policy pursuant to a pharmacy benefit contract or MPN contract.

Note: Authority cited: Sections 133, 4603.5, 5307.3 and 5307.27, Labor Code. Reference: Sections 4600, 4604.5 and 5307.27, Labor Code.

History: 1. New section filed 12-7-2017; operative 1-1-2018 pursuant to Government Code section 11343.4(b)(3) (Register 2017, No. 49).

§9792.27.14. Treatment Provided Under Applicable Health and Safety Regulations.

The MTUS Drug Formulary and associated regulations do not relieve an employer of any responsibilities pursuant to applicable health and safety regulations such as the requirements of the California occupational Bloodborne Pathogens standard at title 8, California Code of Regulations, section 5193, including the responsibility to provide urgent post-exposure prophylaxis as needed to protect the health of the employee.

Note: Authority cited: Sections 133, 4603.5, 5307.3 and 5307.27, Labor Code. Reference: Sections 4600, 4604.5 and 5307.27, Labor Code.

History: 1. New section filed 12-7-2017; operative 1-1-2018 pursuant to Government Code section 11343.4(b)(3) (Register 2017, No. 49).

§9792.27.15. MTUS Drug List.

[MTUS Drug List Not Reproduced]

NOTE: List is available at no charge by downloading from the web at https://www.dir.ca.gov/dwc/MTUS/MTUS-Formulary.html or by requesting at 1-800-794-6900.

Note: Authority cited: Sections 133, 4603.5, 5307.3 and 5307.27, Labor Code. Reference: Sections 4600, 4604.5 and 5307.27, Labor Code.

History: 1. New section filed 12-7-2017; operative 1-1-2018 pursuant to Government Code section 11343.4(b)(3) (Register 2017, No. 49).

§9792.27.16. National Drug Codes, Unique Pharmaceutical Identifier — MTUS Drug List.

(a) The Administrative Director may maintain and post on the DWC website a listing by National Drug Code, RxCUI (clinical drug concept unique identifier maintained by the National Library of Medicine), or other unique pharmaceutical identifier, of drug products that are embodied in the MTUS Drug List. If posted, the listing will be regularly updated to account for revisions to the MTUS Drug List and for changes in drug products that are marketed for outpatient use.

(b) For each active ingredient on the MTUS Drug List, the product listing shall include brand name and therapeutically equivalent generic versions of outpatient prescription drugs and non-prescription drug products. The listing shall include only drug products that can be self-administered by the patient. Injectable drug products must be packaged and identified for patient self-administration.

(c) The listing shall include combination drugs with multiple active ingredients only if the combination of active ingredients is listed on the MTUS Drug List.

(d) The listing may include, but is not limited to, the following data elements:

(1) National Drug Code, RxCUI, or other pharmaceutical identifier;

(2) Drug ingredient(s);

(3) Therapeutic class;

(4) Strength;

(5) Dosage form;

(6) Exempt or Non-Exempt status, as applicable;

(7) Any applicable Special Fill or Perioperative Fill policies.

Note: Authority cited: Sections 133, 4603.5, 5307.3 and 5307.27, Labor Code. Reference: Sections 4600, 4604.5, 5307.27 and 5307.29, Labor Code.

History: 1. New section filed 12-7-2017; operative 1-1-2018 pursuant to Government Code section 11343.4(b)(3) (Register 2017, No. 49).

§9792.27.17. Formulary — Dispute Resolution.

(a) Medical Necessity Disputes.

Disputes over the medical necessity of pharmaceutical treatment covered by the MTUS Drug Formulary are governed by the utilization review and independent medical review provisions of Labor Code sections 4610, 4610.5, and regulations at section 9792.6.1 et seq, and section 9792.10.1 et seq.

(b) Formulary Rule Medical Treatment Disputes Other than Medical Necessity Disputes.

Disputes over failure to follow formulary rules, other than medical necessity disputes covered by subdivision (a), shall be resolved through the procedure for non-IMR/IBR disputes set forth in WCAB rules, title 8, California Code of Regulations, section 10451.2, Determination of Medical Treatment Disputes.

Note: Authority cited: Sections 133, 4603.5, 5307.3, 5307.1 and 5307.27, Labor Code. Reference: Sections 4600, 4604.5, 5307.1, 5307.27 and 5307.29, Labor Code.

History: 1. New section filed 12-7-2017; operative 1-1-2018 pursuant to Government Code section 11343.4(b)(3) (Register 2017, No. 49).

§9792.27.18. Pharmacy and Therapeutics Committee — Composition; Application for Appointment; Term of Service.

(a) The Administrative Director shall create an independent Pharmacy and Therapeutics Committee (P&T Committee) to review and consult with the Administrative Director on available evidence of the relative safety, efficacy, and effectiveness of drugs within a class of drugs, for purposes of updating the MTUS Drug List.

(b) The P&T Committee shall consist of the Executive Medical Director, and six members appointed by the Administrative Director.

(1) The Executive Medical Director, or his or her designee, shall serve as chairperson of the P&T Committee. If the Executive Medical Director position becomes vacant, the Administrative Director shall appoint a competent person to temporarily assume the authority and duties of the Executive Medical Director on the P&T Committee, until such time that the Executive Medical Director position is filled.

(2) The Administrative Director shall appoint 3 pharmacists and 3 physicians (medical doctors or doctors of osteopathy) to serve on the P&T Committee. At least one of the physicians appointed shall be actively engaged in the treatment of injured workers. At least one of the pharmacists appointed shall be an actively practicing pharmacist.

(3) The members of the P&T Committee shall be appointed to serve a two-year term, but shall remain in the position until a successor is appointed. A member may apply to be reappointed when his or her two-year term ends. The Administrative Director may cancel the appointment of a committee member if a substantial conflict of interest arises, or for other reason constituting good cause.

(c) A person interested in serving on the P&T Committee shall submit an application on the form prescribed by the Administrative Director and a completed Conflict of Interest Disclosure Form. The applicant for P&T Committee appointment shall demonstrate that he or she has knowledge or expertise in one or more of the following:

(1) Clinically appropriate prescribing of covered drugs;

(2) Clinically appropriate dispensing and monitoring of covered drugs;

(3) Drug use review;

(4) Evidence-based medicine.

Note: Authority cited: Sections 133, 4603.5, 5307.3 and 5307.27, Labor Code. Reference: Sections 4600, 4604.5, 5307.27 and 5307.29, Labor Code.

History: 1. New section filed 12-7-2017; operative 1-1-2018 pursuant to Government Code section 11343.4(b)(3) (Register 2017, No. 49).

§9792.27.19. Pharmacy and Therapeutics Committee — Application for Appointment to Committee Form.

[DWC MTUS PT-APP (New 11/17) Not Reproduced]

NOTE: Form is available at no charge by downloading from the web at www.dir.ca.gov/dwc/forms.html or by requesting at 1-800-794-6900.

Note: Authority cited: Sections 133, 4603.5, 5307.3 and 5307.27, Labor Code. Reference: Sections 4600, 4604.5, 5307.27 and 5307.29, Labor Code.

History: 1. New section filed 12-7-2017; operative 1-1-2018 pursuant to Government Code section 11343.4(b)(3) (Register 2017, No. 49).

§9792.27.20. Pharmacy and Therapeutics Committee — Conflict of Interest.

(a) The conflict of interest standards are intended to ensure that the members of the P&T Committee are free from financial interests or other relationships that could compromise the objectivity of the members of the committee as they perform their duties to consult with the Administrative Director on formulary updates based upon the principles of evidence-based medicine. Appointed members of the P&T Committee must impartially perform formulary update review activities, and must be free of conflicts of interest.

(b) Persons applying to be appointed to the P&T Committee shall not be employed by a pharmaceutical manufacturer, a pharmacy benefits management company, or a company engaged in the development of a pharmaceutical formulary for commercial sale, and shall not have been so employed for 12 months prior to the appointment. A P&T Committee member who undertakes such employment during the term of appointment shall not be eligible to continue to serve on the committee.

(c) Members of the P&T Committee shall not have a substantial financial conflict of interest in relation to a pharmaceutical entity.

(1) "Pharmaceutical entity" means a pharmaceutical manufacturer, pharmaceutical repackager, pharmaceutical relabeler, compounding pharmacy, pharmacy benefits management company, biotechnology company, or any other business entity that is involved in manufacturing, packaging, selling or distribution of prescription or nonprescription drugs, drug delivery systems, or biological agents.

(2) For purposes of this section, "substantial financial conflict of interest" means that the applicant or committee member, or his or her immediate family member, has a direct or indirect financial interest in a pharmaceutical entity, including:

(A) Receipt of income within the previous 12 months, amounting to a total of $500 or more from the pharmaceutical entity, including but not limited to salary, wages, speaking fees, consultant fees, expert witness fees, honoraria, gifts, loans, and travel payments;

(B) Receipt of grants or research funding from the pharmaceutical entity within the previous 24 months;

(C) Has had ownership interest in the pharmaceutical entity at any time during the previous 12 months, including but not limited to, a sole proprietorship, partnership, limited liability company, or stock ownership in a corporation that is not publicly traded;

(D) Investment interest worth $2,000 or more in a publicly-traded pharmaceutical entity, not including an investment held through a diversified mutual fund;

(3) "Immediate family member" means spouse, domestic partner, child, son-in-law, daughter-in-law, parent, mother-in-law, father-in-law, brother or sister;

(4)(A) "Direct financial interest" means an interest held by the applicant or committee member.

(B) "Indirect financial interest" means an interest held by the applicant or committee member's immediate family member, or held by a business entity or trust in which the applicant or committee member owns directly or indirectly, or beneficially, a 10-percent interest or greater.

(d) The members of the P&T Committee shall submit an updated Conflict of Interest Disclosure Form annually, and more frequently if there have been changes in circumstances relating to employment by, or financial interests in, a pharmaceutical entity.

Note: Authority cited: Sections 133, 4603.5, 5307.3 and 5307.27, Labor Code. Reference: Sections 4600, 4604.5, 5307.27 and 5307.29, Labor Code.

History: 1. New section filed 12-7-2017; operative 1-1-2018 pursuant to Government Code section 11343.4(b)(3) (Register 2017, No. 49).

§9792.27.21. Pharmacy and Therapeutics Committee — Conflict of Interest Disclosure Form.

[DWC MTUS PT-COI (New 11/17) Not Reproduced]

NOTE: Form is available at no charge by downloading from the web at www.dir.ca.gov/dwc/forms.html or by requesting at 1-800-794-6900.

Note: Authority cited: Sections 133, 4603.5, 5307.3 and 5307.27, Labor Code. Reference: Sections 4600, 4604.5, 5307.27 and 5307.29, Labor Code.

History: 1. New section filed 12-7-2017; operative 1-1-2018 pursuant to Government Code section 11343.4(b)(3) (Register 2017, No. 49).

§9792.27.22. Pharmacy and Therapeutics Committee — Meetings.

(a) The P&T Committee shall meet when deemed necessary by the Executive Medical Director, but no less frequently than quarterly.

(b) P&T Committee meetings shall be conducted in accordance with the Bagley-Keene Open Meeting Act, California Government Code sections 11120 through 11132.

(c) Notice of the regularly scheduled meetings shall be given at least ten days in advance of the meeting as follows:

(1) To persons who have requested notice of the meetings;

(2) To persons on the Administrative Director's mailing list; and

(3) By posting notice on the division's website.

(d) The Executive Medical Director shall include a period to receive public comment during the P&T Committee meetings, in a manner consistent with the orderly and efficient conduct of the business of the committee. Members of the public addressing the P&T Committee shall be limited to three minutes per speaker.

(e) The Executive Medical Director shall maintain a written summary of the meetings and the recommendations made to the Administrative Director in a format determined by the Administrative Director. The written summary shall be posted on the Division's website. It shall include a description of any action taken and the vote or abstention of each P&T Committee member present.

Note: Authority cited: Sections 133, 4603.5, 5307.3 and 5307.27, Labor Code. Reference: Sections 11120-11132, Government Code; and Sections 4600, 4604.5, 5307.27 and 5307.29, Labor Code.

History: 1. New section filed 12-7-2017; operative 1-1-2018 pursuant to Government Code section 11343.4(b)(3) (Register 2017, No. 49).

§9792.27.23. MTUS Drug List Updates.

(a) The Administrative Director shall consult with the P&T Committee as needed on updates to the MTUS Drug List, which may be adopted by the Administrative Director on a quarterly or more frequent basis in order to allow provision for all appropriate medications.

(b) The P&T Committee is responsible for reviewing and consulting with the Administrative Director on available evidence of the relative safety, efficacy, and effectiveness of drugs within a class of drugs. In carrying out these duties the P&T Committee may provide consultation on a variety of relevant issues, including but not limited to the following:

(1) Recommendations on prospective review requirements for drugs;

(2) Recommendations on Special Fill and Perioperative Fill designation and policies;

(3) Review of drug treatment changes adopted into the MTUS Treatment Guidelines to identify needed additions or deletions of drugs from the MTUS Drug List;

(4) Recommendations on establishing a therapeutic interchange program in order to promote safe and appropriate cost effective care.

(c) The P&T Committee serves in an advisory role only. P&T Committee recommendations are not binding on the Administrative Director.

(d) Updates to the MTUS Drug List will be adopted by issuance of an Administrative Director's order specifying the changes and the effective date, and shall be posted on the division's website pursuant to Labor Code section 5307.29.

Note: Authority cited: Sections 133, 4603.5, 5307.3 and 5307.27, Labor Code. Reference: Sections 4600, 4604.5, 5307.27 and 5307.29, Labor Code.

History: 1. New section filed 12-7-2017; operative 1-1-2018 pursuant to Government Code section 11343.4(b)(3) (Register 2017, No. 49).

ARTICLE 5.6
Medical-Legal Expenses and Comprehensive Medical-Legal Evaluations

§9793. Definitions.

As used in this article:

(a) "Claim" means a claim for compensation as evidenced by either the filing of a claim form pursuant to Section 5401 of the Labor Code or notice or knowledge of an injury under Section 5400 or 5402 of the Labor Code.

(b) "Contested claim" means any of the following:

(1) Where the claims administrator has rejected liability for a claimed benefit.

(2) Where the claims administrator has failed to accept liability for a claim and the claim has become presumptively compensable under Section 5402 of the Labor Code.

(3) Where the claims administrator has failed to respond to a demand for the payment of compensation after the expiration of any time period fixed by statute for the payment of indemnity benefits, including where the claims administrator has failed to either commence the payment of temporary disability indemnity or issue a notice of delay within 14 days after knowledge of an employee's injury and disability as provided in Section 4650 of the Labor Code.

(4) Where the claims administrator has accepted liability for a claim and a disputed medical fact exists.

(c) "Comprehensive medical-legal evaluation" means an evaluation of an employee which (A) results in the preparation of a narrative medical report prepared and attested to in accordance with Section 4628 of the Labor Code, any applicable procedures promulgated under Section 139.2 of the Labor Code, and the requirements of Section 10606 and (B) is either:

(1) performed by a Qualified Medical Evaluator pursuant to subdivision (h) of Section 139.2 of the Labor Code, or

(2) performed by a Qualified Medical Evaluator, Agreed Medical Evaluator, or the primary treating physician for the purpose of proving or disproving a contested claim, and which meets the requirements of paragraphs (1) through (5), inclusive, of subdivision (h).

(d) "Claims Administrator" means a self-administered insurer providing security for the payment of compensation required by Divisions 4 and 4.5 of the Labor Code, a self-administered self-insured employer, a group self-insurer, or a third-party claims administrator for a self-insured employer, insurer, legally uninsured employer, group self-insurer, or joint powers authority.

(e) "Disputed medical fact" means an issue in dispute, including an objection under Section 4062 of the Labor Code to a medical determination made by a treating physician concerning: (1) the employee's medical condition, (2) the cause of the employee's medical condition, (3) For injuries that occurred before January 1, 2013, concerning a dispute over a utilization review decision if the decision is communicated to the requesting physician on or before June 30, 2013, treatment for the employee's medical condition; (4) the existence, nature, duration or extent of temporary or permanent disability caused by the employee's medical condition; or (5) the employee's medical eligibility for rehabilitation services.

(f) "Explanation of review" means the document described in Labor Code sections 4603.3(a) and 4622 that is provided to a Qualified Medical Evaluator, Agreed Medical Evaluator, or the primary treating physician when the claims administrator has objected to the cost of a medical-legal expense.

(g) "Follow-up medical-legal evaluation" means an evaluation which includes an examination of an employee which (A) results in the preparation of a narrative medical report prepared and attested to in accordance with Section 4628 of the Labor Code, any applicable procedures promulgated under Section 139.2 of the Labor Code, and the requirements of Section 10606, (B) is performed by a qualified medical evaluator, agreed medical evaluator, or primary treating physician within nine months following the evaluator's examination of the employee in a comprehensive medical-legal evaluation and (C) involves an evaluation of the same injury or injuries evaluated in the comprehensive medical-legal evaluation.

(h) "Medical-legal expense" means any costs or expenses incurred by or on behalf of any party or parties, the administrative director, or the appeals board for X-rays, laboratory fees, other diagnostic tests, medical reports, medical records, medical testimony, and as needed, interpreter's fees, for the purpose of proving or disproving a contested claim. The cost of medical evaluations, diagnostic tests, and interpreters is not a medical-legal expense unless it is incidental to the production of a comprehensive medical-legal evaluation report, follow-up medical-legal evaluation report, or a supplemental medical-legal evaluation report and all of the following conditions exist:

(1) The report is prepared by a physician, as defined in Section 3209.3 of the Labor Code.

(2) The report is obtained at the request of a party or parties, the administrative director, or the appeals board for the purpose of proving or disproving a contested claim and addresses the disputed medical fact or facts specified by the party, or parties or other person who requested the comprehensive medical-legal evaluation report. Nothing in this paragraph shall be construed to prohibit a physician from addressing additional related medical issues.

(3) The report is capable of proving or disproving a disputed medical fact essential to the resolution of a contested claim, considering the substance as well as the form of the report, as required by applicable statutes, regulations, and case law.

(4) The medical-legal examination is performed prior to receipt of notice by the physician, the employee, or the employee's attorney, that the disputed medical fact or facts for which the report was requested have been resolved.

(5) In the event the comprehensive medical-legal evaluation is served on the claims administrator after the disputed medical fact or facts for which the report was requested have been resolved, the report is served within the time frame specified in Section 139.2(j)(1) of the Labor Code.

(i) "Medical-legal testimony" means expert testimony provided by a physician at a deposition or workers' compensation appeals board hearing, regarding the medical opinion submitted by the physician.

(j) "Medical research" is the investigation of medical issues. It includes investigating and reading medical and scientific journals and texts. "Medical research" does not include reading or reading about the *Guides for the Evaluation of Permanent Impairment* (any edition), treatment guidelines (including guidelines of the American College of Occupational and Environmental Medicine), the Labor Code, regulations or publications of the Division of Workers' Compensation (including the *Physicians' Guide*), or other legal materials.

(k) "Primary treating physician" is the treating physician primarily responsible for managing the care of the injured worker in accordance with subdivision (a) of Section 9785.

(*l*) "Reports and documents required by the administrative director" means an itemized billing, a copy of the medical-legal evaluation report, and any verification required under Section 9795(c).

(m) "Supplemental medical-legal evaluation" means an evaluation which (A) does not involve an examination of the patient, (B) is based on the physician's review of records, test results or other medically relevant information which was not available to the physician at the time of the initial examination, or a request for factual correction pursuant to Labor Code section 4061(d), (C) results in the preparation of a narrative medical report prepared and attested to in accordance with Section 4628 of the Labor Code, any applicable procedures promulgated under Section 139.2 of the Labor Code, and the requirements of Section 10606 and (D) is performed by a qualified medical evaluator, agreed medical evaluator, or primary treating physician following the evaluator's completion of a comprehensive medical-legal evaluation.

Note: Authority cited: Sections 133, 4622, 4627, 5307.3 and 5307.6, Labor Code. Reference: Sections 4061, 4061.5, 4062, 4610.5, 4620, 4621, 4622, 4625, 4628, 4650, 5307.6 and 5402, Labor Code.

History: 1. New article 5.6 (sections 9793–9795) filed 1-10-85; designated effective 3-1-85 (Register 85, No. 2).

2. Change without regulatory effect filed 7-11-86; effective upon filing (Register 86, No. 28).

3. Repealer and new section filed 8-3-93; operative 8-3-93. Submitted to OAL for printing only pursuant to Government Code section 11351 (Register 93, No. 32).

4. Amendment of article heading, section and Note filed 12-31-93; operative 1-1-94. Submitted to OAL for printing only pursuant to Government Code section 11351 (Register 93, No. 53).

5. Change without regulatory effect amending subsections (f) and (i) filed 6-12-2002 pursuant to section 100, title 1, California Code of Regulations (Register 2002, No. 24).

6. Amendment of subsections (a) and (b)(3), new subsection (i), subsection relettering and amendment of newly designated subsection (j) filed 6-30-2006; operative 7-1-2006. Submitted to OAL for filing with the Secretary of State and printing only pursuant to Government Code section 11340.9(g) (Register 2006, No. 26).

7. Amendment of subsection (e), new subsection (f), subsection relettering, amendment of newly designated subsection (m) and amendment of Note filed 12-31-2012 as an emergency; operative 1-1-2013 pursuant to Government Code section 11346.1(d) (Register 2013, No. 1). A Certificate of Compliance must be transmitted to OAL by 7-1-2013 or emergency language will be repealed by operation of law on the following day.

8. Amendment of subsection (e), new subsection (f), subsection relettering, amendment of newly designated subsection (m) and amendment of Note refiled 7-1-2013 as an emergency; operative 7-1-2013 (Register 2013, No. 27). A Certificate of Compliance must be transmitted to OAL by 9-30-2013 or emergency language will be repealed by operation of law on the following day.

9. Amendment of subsection (e), new subsection (f), subsection relettering, amendment of newly designated subsection (m) and amendment of Note refiled 9-30-2013 as an emergency; operative 10-1-2013 (Register 2013, No. 40). A Certificate of Compliance must be transmitted to OAL by 12-30-2013 or emergency language will be repealed by operation of law on the following day.

10. Certificate of Compliance as to 9-30-2013 order, including amendment of subsections (c)(2) and (e), transmitted to OAL 12-30-2013 and filed 2-12-2014; amendments effective 2-12-2014 pursuant to Government Code section 11343.4(b)(3) (Register 2014, No. 7).

Ref.: Hanna §§ 5.04[2][a], 22.09[1], [3], 23.13[2][b], [3]; Herlick Handbook §§ 1.01[3][b], 1.02, 10.08[5], 14.33[4].

§9794. Reimbursement of Medical-Legal Expenses.

(a) The cost of comprehensive, follow-up and supplemental medical-legal evaluation reports, diagnostic tests, and medical-legal testimony, regardless of whether incurred on behalf of the employee or claims administrator, shall be billed and reimbursed as follows:

(1) X-rays, laboratory services and other diagnostic tests shall be billed and reimbursed in accordance with the official medical fee schedule adopted pursuant to Labor Code Section 5307.1. In no event shall the claims administrator be liable for the cost of any diagnostic test provided in connection with a comprehensive medical-legal evaluation report unless the subjective complaints and physical findings that warrant the necessity for the test are included in the medical-legal evaluation report. Additionally, the claims administrator shall not be liable for the cost of diagnostic tests, absent prior authorization by the claims administrator, if adequate medical information is already in the medical record provided to the physician.

(2) The cost of comprehensive, follow-up and supplemental medical-legal evaluations, and medical-legal testimony shall be billed and reimbursed in accordance with the schedule set forth in Section 9795.

(b) All medical-legal expenses shall be paid within 60 days after receipt by the employer of the reports and documents required by the administrative director unless the claims administrator, within this period, contests its liability for such payment.

(c) A claims administrator who contests all or any part of a bill for medical-legal expense, or who contests a bill on the basis that the expense does not constitute a medical-legal expense, shall pay any uncontested amount and notify the physician or other provider of the objection within sixty days after receipt of the reports and documents required by the administrative director using an explanation of review. Any notice of objection shall include or be accompanied by all of the following:

(1) An explanation of review shall indicate the basis for the objection to each contested procedure and charge. The original procedure codes used by the physician or other provider shall not be altered. If the objection is based on appropriate coding of a procedure, the explanation of review shall include both the code reported by the provider and the code believed reasonable by the claims administrator, and shall include the claim's administrator's rationale as to why its code more accurately reflects the service provided.

(2) If additional information is necessary as a prerequisite to payment of the contested bill or portions thereof, a clear description of the information required.

(3) The name, address, and telephone number of the person or office to contact for additional information concerning the objection.

(4) A statement pursuant to Labor Code section 4622(b)(1) that the physician may seek a second review by the claims administrator of the reduction of billing of the medical-legal expense. The statement shall also state the request for second review by the physician and completion of the second review process of the medical-legal expense under California Code of Regulations, title 8, section 9792.5.5.

(5) A statement that the request for second review by the physician and completion of the second review process of the medical-legal expense by the claims administrator is a prerequisite to seeking independent bill review provided in Labor Code section 4603.6.

(6) A statement that if the provider does not seek a second review and the only issue in dispute is the amount of payment, the bill shall be deemed satisfied and neither the employer nor the employee shall be liable for any additional payment.

(d) If the provider disputes the amount of payment made by the claims administrator on a bill for medical-legal expenses following the receipt of an explanation of review issued under subdivision (c), the provider must request the claims administrator to conduct a second review of the bill. The second bill review request must be made according to the provisions of California Code of Regulations, title 8, section 9792.5.5.

(e) If after completion of the second review process under Labor Code section 4622 (b)(1) the physician still contests the amount paid for the medical-legal expense, the physician shall only contest the amount to be paid by requesting independent bill review as provided in Labor Code section 4603.6.

A form objection which does not identify the specific deficiencies of the report in question shall not satisfy the requirements of this subdivision.

(f) If the claims administrator denies liability for the medical-legal expense in whole or in part, for any reasons other than the amount to be paid pursuant to the fee schedule set forth in section 9795, the denial shall set forth the legal, medical, or factual basis for the decision in the explanation of review which shall also contain the following statements:

(1) The physician may object to the denial of the medical-legal expense issued under this subdivision by notifying the claims administrator in writing of their objection within ninety (90) days of the service of the explanation of review; and

(2) If the physician does not file a written objection with the claims administrator challenging the denial of the medical-legal expense issued under this subdivision, neither the employer nor the employee shall be liable for the amount of the expense that was denied.

(g) If the claims administrator receives a written objection to the denial of the medical-legal expense under subdivision (d) within ninety (90) days of the service of the explanation of review, the claims administrator shall file a petition to review of the denial of medical-legal expense and a declaration of readiness to proceed pursuant to section 10228 et. seq.

(h) All reports and documents required by the administrative director shall be included in or attached to the medical-legal report when it is filed and served on the parties pursuant to Section 10608 or served on the parties pursuant to Section 4061 or 4062 of the Labor Code.

(i) Physicians shall keep and maintain for five years, and shall make available to the administrative director by date of examination upon request, copies of all billings for medical-legal expense.

(j) A physician may not charge, nor be paid, any fees for services in violation of Sections 139.3 and 139.32 of the Labor Code or subdivision (d) of Section 5307.6 of the Labor Code;

(i) Claims administrator shall retain, for five years, the following information for each comprehensive medical evaluation for which the claims administrator is billed:

(1) name and specialty of medical evaluator;

(2) name of the employee evaluated;

(3) date of examination;

(4) the amount billed for the evaluation;

(5) the date of the bill;

(6) the amount paid for the evaluation, including any penalties and interest;

(7) the date payment was made.

This information may be stored in paper or electronic form and shall be made available to the administrative director upon request. This information shall also be made available, upon request, to any party to a case, where the requested information pertains to an evaluation obtained in the case.

Note: Authority cited: Sections 133, 4622, 4627, 5307.3 and 5307.6, Labor Code. Reference: Sections 139.3, 139.32, 4620, 4621, 4622, 4625, 4626, 4628 and 5307.6, Labor Code.

History: 1. Repealer and new section filed 8-3-93; operative 8-3-93. Submitted to OAL for printing only pursuant to Government Code section 11351 (Register 93, No. 32).

2. Amendment of subsections (a)-(c)(1) and (e), and new subsections (f)-(h) filed 12-31-93; operative 1-1-94. Submitted to OAL for printing only pursuant to Government Code section 11351 (Register 93, No. 53).

3. Repealer of subsection (h) filed 2-14-96; operative 2-14-96. Submitted to OAL for printing only pursuant to Government Code section 11351 (Register 96, No. 7).

4. Editorial correction of subsection (a) (Register 2001, No. 22).

5. Amendment of subsections (c) and (c)(1), repealer and new subsection (c)(4), new subsections (c)(5) and (d)-(e), subsection relettering and amendment of Note filed 12-31-2012 as an emergency; operative 1-1-2013 pursuant to Government Code section 11346.1(d) (Register 2013, No. 1). A Certificate of Compliance must be transmitted to OAL by 7-1-2013 or emergency language will be repealed by operation of law on the following day.

6. Amendment of subsections (c) and (c)(1), repealer and new subsection (c)(4), new subsections (c)(5) and (d)-(e), subsection relettering and amendment of Note refiled 7-1-2013 as an emergency; operative 7-1-2013 (Register 2013, No. 27). A Certificate of Compliance must be transmitted to OAL by 9-30-2013 or emergency language will be repealed by operation of law on the following day.

7. Amendment of subsections (c) and (c)(1), repealer and new subsection (c)(4), new subsections (c)(5) and (d)-(e), subsection relettering and amendment of Note refiled 9-30-2013 as an emergency; operative 10-1-2013 (Register 2013, No. 40). A Certificate of Compliance must be transmitted to OAL by 12-30-2013 or emergency language will be repealed by operation of law on the following day.

8. Certificate of Compliance as to 9-30-2013 order, including amendment of section and Note, transmitted to OAL 12-30-2013 and filed 2-12-2014; amendments effective 2-12-2014 pursuant to Government Code section 11343.4(b)(3) (Register 2014, No. 7).

Publisher's Note: The regulation appears as amended by Register 2014, No. 7; relettering of subdivisions except for the last subdivision (i).

Ref.: Hanna §§ 10.50[2][a], 22.09[2]–[4], 27.01[8][b][ii]; Herlick Handbook §§ 1.01[3][b], 4.18[1], [2], 10.05, 10.08[5].

§9795. Reasonable Level of Fees for Medical-Legal Expenses, Follow-up, Supplemental and Comprehensive Medical-Legal Evaluations and Medical-Legal Testimony.

(a) The schedule of fees set forth in this section shall be prima facie evidence of the reasonableness of fees charged for medical-legal evaluation reports, and fees for medical-legal testimony.

Reports by treating or consulting physicians, other than comprehensive, follow-up or supplemental medical-legal evaluations, regardless of whether liability for the injury has been accepted at the time the treatment was provided or the report was prepared, shall be subject to the Official

Medical Fee Schedule adopted pursuant to Labor Code Section 5307.1 rather than to the fee schedule set forth in this section.

(b) The fee for each evaluation is calculated by multiplying the relative value by $12.50, and adding any amount applicable because of the modifiers permitted under subdivision (d). The fee for each medical-legal evaluation procedure includes reimbursement for the history and physical examination, review of records, preparation of a medical-legal report, including typing and transcription services, and overhead expenses. The complexity of the evaluation is the dominant factor determining the appropriate level of service under this section; the times to perform procedures is expected to vary due to clinical circumstances, and is therefore not the controlling factor in determining the appropriate level of service.

(c) Medical-legal evaluation reports and medical-legal testimony shall be reimbursed as follows:

CODE	*B.R.*	*PROCEDURE DESCRIPTION*
ML100		*Missed Appointment for a Comprehensive or Follow-Up Medical-Legal Evaluation.* This code is designed for communication purposes only. It does not imply that compensation is necessarily owed.

CODE	*RV*	*PROCEDURE DESCRIPTION*
ML101	5	*Follow-up Medical-Legal Evaluation.* Limited to a follow-up medical-legal evaluation by a physician which occurs within nine months of the date on which the prior medical-legal evaluation was performed. The physician shall include in his or her report verification, under penalty of perjury, of time spent in each of the following activities: review of records, face-to-face time with the injured worker, and preparation of the report. Time spent shall be tabulated in increments of 15 minutes or portions thereof, rounded to the nearest quarter hour. The physician shall be reimbursed at the rate of RV 5, or his or her usual and customary fee, whichever is less, for each quarter hour.

CODE	*RV*	*PROCEDURE DESCRIPTION*
ML102	50	*Basic Comprehensive Medical-Legal Evaluation.* Includes all comprehensive medical-legal evaluations other than those included under ML 103 or ML 104.

CODE	*RV*	*PROCEDURE DESCRIPTION*
ML103	75	*Complex Comprehensive Medical-Legal Evaluation.* Includes evaluations which require three of the complexity factors set forth below.

In a separate section at the beginning of the report, the physician shall clearly and concisely specify which of the following complexity factors were required for the evaluation, and the circumstances which made these complexity factors applicable to the evaluation. An evaluator who specifies complexity factor (3) must also provide a list of citations to the sources reviewed, and excerpt or include copies of medical evidence relied upon:

(1) Two or more hours of face-to-face time by the physician with the injured worker;

(2) Two or more hours of record review by the physician;

(3) Two or more hours of medical research by the physician;

(4) Four or more hours spent on any combination of two of the complexity factors (1)-(3), which shall count as two complexity factors. Any complexity factor in (1), (2), or (3) used to make this combination shall not also be used as the third required complexity factor;

(5) Six or more hours spent on any combination of three complexity factors (1)-(3), which shall count as three complexity factors;

(6) Addressing the issue of medical causation, upon written request of the party or parties requesting the report;

(7) Addressing the issue of apportionment, when determination of this issue requires the physician to evaluate the claimant's employment by three or more employers, three or more injuries to the same body system or body region as delineated in the Table of Contents of *Guides to the Evaluation of Permanent Impairment* (Fifth Edition), or two or more or more injuries involving two or more body systems or body regions as delineated in that Table of Contents. The Table of Contents of *Guides to the Evaluation of Permanent Impairment* (Fifth Edition), published by the American Medical Association, 2000, is incorporated by reference.

(8) A psychiatric or psychological evaluation which is the primary focus of the medical-legal evaluation.

(9) Where the evaluation is performed for injuries that occurred before January 1, 2013, concerning a dispute over a utilization review decision if the decision is communicated to the requesting physician on or before June 30 2013, addressing the issue of denial or modification of treatment by the claims administrator following utilization review under Labor Code section 4610.

CODE	*RV*	*PROCEDURE DESCRIPTION*
ML104	5	*Comprehensive Medical-legal Evaluation Involving Extraordinary Circumstances.* The physician shall be reimbursed at the rate of RV 5, or his or her usual and customary hourly fee, whichever is less, for each quarter hour or portion thereof, rounded to the nearest quarter hour, spent by the physician for any of the following:

(1) An evaluation which requires four or more of the complexity factors listed under ML 103; In a separate section at the beginning of the report, the physician shall clearly and concisely specify which four or more of the complexity factors were required for the evaluation, and the circumstances which made these complexity factors applicable to the evaluation. An evaluator who specifies complexity factor (3) must also provide a list of citations to the sources reviewed, and excerpt or include copies of medical evidence relied upon.

(2) An evaluation involving prior multiple injuries to the same body part or parts being evaluated, and which requires three or more of the complexity factors listed under ML 103, including three or more hours of record review by the physician;

(3) A comprehensive medical-legal evaluation for which the physician and the parties agree, prior to the evaluation, that the evaluation involves extraordinary circumstances. When billing under this code for extraordinary circumstances, the physician shall include in his or her report (i) a clear, concise explanation of the extraordinary circumstances related to the medical condition being evaluated which justifies the use of this procedure code, and (ii) verification under penalty of perjury of the total time spent by the physician in each of these activities: reviewing the records, face-to-face time with the injured worker, preparing the report and, if applicable, any other activities.

CODE	*RV*	*PROCEDURE DESCRIPTION*
ML105	5	Fees for medical-legal testimony. The physician shall be reimbursed at the rate of RV 5, or his or her usual and customary fee, whichever is less, for each quarter hour or portion thereof, rounded to the nearest quarter hour, spent by the physician. The physician shall be entitled to fees for all itemized reasonable and necessary time spent related to the testimony, including reasonable preparation and travel time. The physician shall be paid a minimum of one hour for a scheduled deposition.

CODE	*RV*	*PROCEDURE DESCRIPTION*
ML106	5	Fees for supplemental medical-legal evaluations. The physician shall be reimbursed at the rate of RV 5, or his or her usual and customary fee, whichever is less, for each quarter hour or portion thereof, rounded to the nearest quarter hour, spent by the physician. Fees will not be allowed under this section for supplemental reports following the physician's review of (A) information which was available in the physician's office for review or was included in the medical record provided to the physician prior to preparing the initial report or (B) the results of laboratory or diagnostic tests which were ordered by the physician as part of the initial evaluation.

(d) The services described by Procedure Codes ML101 through ML106 may be modified under the circumstances described in this subdivision. The modifying circumstances shall be identified by the addition of the appropriate modifier code, which is reported by a two-digit number placed after the usual procedure number separated by a hyphen. The modifiers available are the following:

–92 Performed by a primary treating physician. This modifier is added solely for identification purposes, and does not change the normal value of the service.

–93 Interpreter needed at time of examination, or other circumstances which impair communication between the physician and the injured worker and significantly increase the time needed to conduct the examination. Requires a description of the circumstance and the increased time required for the examination as a result. Where this modifier is applicable, the value for the procedure is modified by multiplying the normal value by 1.1. This modifier shall only be applicable to ML 102 and ML 103.

–94 Evaluation and medical-legal testimony performed by an Agreed Medical Evaluator. Where this modifier is applicable, the value of the procedure is modified by multiplying the normal value by 1.25. If modifier –93 is also applicable for an ML-102 or ML-103, then the value of the procedure is modified by multiplying the normal value by 1.35.

–95 Evaluation performed by a panel selected Qualified Medical Evaluator. This modifier is added solely for identification purposes, and does not change the normal value of any procedure.

(e) Requests for duplicate reports shall be in writing. Duplicate reports shall be separately reimbursable and shall be reimbursed in the same manner as set forth in the Official Medical Fee Schedule adopted pursuant to Labor Code Section 5307.1.

(f) This section shall apply to medical-legal evaluation reports where the examination occurs on or after the effective date of this section. The 2006 amendments to this section shall apply to: (1) medical-legal evaluation reports where the medical examination to which the report refers occurs on or after the effective date of the 2006 amendments; (2) medical-legal testimony provided on or after the effective date of the 2006 amendments; and (3) supplemental medical legal reports that are requested on or after the effective date of the 2006 amendments regardless of the date of the original examination.

Note: Authority cited: Sections 133, 4627, 5307.3 and 5307.6, Labor Code. Reference: Sections 139.2, 4061, 4061.5, 4062, 4610.5, 4620, 4621, 4622, 4625, 4626, 4628, 5307.6 and 5402, Labor Code.

History: 1. Repealer and new section filed 8-3-93; operative 8-3-93. Submitted to OAL for printing only pursuant to Government Code section 11351 (Register 93, No. 32).

2. Change without regulatory effect amending subsection (a) and subsection (c) medical-legal evaluation procedure code ML104 filed 8-27-93 pursuant to section 100, title 1, California Code of Regulations (Register 93, No. 35).

3. Amendment of section heading, section and Note filed 12-31-93; operative 1-1-94. Submitted to OAL for printing only pursuant to Government Code section 11351 (Register 93, No. 53).

4. Amendment filed 2-24-99; operative 4-1-99 (Register 99, No. 9).

5. Change without regulatory effect amending subsections (b) and (d) filed 6-12-2002 pursuant to section 100, title 1, California Code of Regulations (Register 2002, No. 24).

6. Amendment of section and Note filed 6-30-2006; operative 7-1-2006. Submitted to OAL for filing with the Secretary of State

and printing only pursuant to Government Code section 11340.9(g) (Register 2006, No. 26).

7. Amendment of subsection (c) (medical-legal evaluation procedure code ML103) and amendment of Note filed 12-31-2012 as an emergency; operative 1-1-2013 pursuant to Government Code section 11346.1(d) (Register 2013, No. 1). A Certificate of Compliance must be transmitted to OAL by 7-1-2013 or emergency language will be repealed by operation of law on the following day.

8. Amendment of subsection (c) (medical-legal evaluation procedure code ML103) and amendment of Note refiled 7-1-2013 as an emergency; operative 7-1-2013 (Register 2013, No. 27). A Certificate of Compliance must be transmitted to OAL by 9-30-2013 or emergency language will be repealed by operation of law on the following day.

9. Amendment of subsection (c) (medical-legal evaluation procedure code ML103) and amendment of Note refiled 9-30-2013 as an emergency; operative 10-1-2013 (Register 2013, No. 40). A Certificate of Compliance must be transmitted to OAL by 12-30-2013 or emergency language will be repealed by operation of law on the following day.

10. Certificate of Compliance as to 9-30-2013 order, including further amendment of subsection (c) (medical-legal evaluation code ML103), transmitted to OAL 12-30-2013 and filed 2-12-2014; amendments effective 2-12-2014 pursuant to Government Code section 11343.4(b)(3) (Register 2014, No. 7).

Ref.: Hanna §§ 5.04[2][b], 22.09[3], 23.13[2][b], 27.01[8][b][ii], 30.05; Herlick Handbook §§ 1.01[3][b], 10.08[5].

ARTICLE 5.7
Fees for Interpreter Services

§9795.1. Definitions.

As used in this article:

(a) "Claims Administrator" means the person or entity responsible for the payment of compensation for any of the following: a self-administered insurer providing security for the payment of compensation required by Divisions 4 and 4.5 of the Labor Code, a self-administered self-insured employer, the director of the Department of Industrial Relations as administrator for the Uninsured Employers Benefits Trust Fund (UEBTF) or for the Subsequent Injuries Benefits Trust Fund (SIBTF), a third-party claims administrator for a self-insured employer, insurer, legally uninsured employer, joint powers authority, the Self-Insurers' Security Fund, or the California Insurance Guarantee Association (CIGA).

(b) "Full day" means services performed which exceed one-half day, up to 8 hours.

(c) "One-half day" means:

(1) When appearing at any Workers' Compensation Appeals Board hearing or daytime arbitration, all or any part of a morning or afternoon session.

(2) When appearing at a deposition, all or any part of 3.5 hours.

(3) When appearing at an evening arbitration, all or any part of 3 hours.

(d) "Travel time" means the time an interpreter actually travels to and from the place where service is to be rendered and his or her place of business.

(e) "Market rate" means that amount an interpreter has actually been paid for recent interpreter services provided in connection with the preparation and resolution of an employee's claim.

Note: Authority cited: Sections 133, 5307.3, 5710 and 5811, Labor Code. Reference: Sections 4600, 4620, 4621, 5710 and 5811, Labor Code; and Sections 11435.30, 11435.35 and 68562, Government Code.

History: 1. New article 5.7 (sections 9795.1–9795.4) and section filed 1-28-94; operative 1-28-94. Submitted to OAL for printing only pursuant to Government Code section 11351 (Register 94, No. 4).

2. Repealer of subsection (g), subsection relettering, and new Note filed 12-30-96; operative 12-30-96 pursuant to Government Code section 11343.4(d). Submitted to OAL for printing only pursuant to Government Code section 11351 (Register 97, No. 1).

3. Amendment of section and Note filed 12-27-2012 as an emergency; operative 1-1-2013 pursuant to Government Code section 11340.9(d) (Register 2012, No. 52). A Certificate of Compliance must be transmitted to OAL by 7-1-2013 or emergency language will be repealed by operation of law on the following day.

4. Amendment of section and Note refiled 7-1-2013 as an emergency; operative 7-1-2013 (Register 2013, No. 27). A Certificate of Compliance must be transmitted to OAL by 9-30-2013 or emergency language will be repealed by operation of law on the following day.

5. Certificate of Compliance as to 7-1-2013 order, including further amendment of section and Note, transmitted to OAL 7-1-2013 and filed 8-13-2013; amendments operative 8-13-2013 pursuant to Government Code section 11343.4(b)(3) (Register 2013, No. 33).

Ref.: Hanna § 23.13[2]; Herlick Handbook §§ 1.01[3][b], 14.33.

§9795.1.5. Interpreters for Hearings, Depositions or Arbitrations.

(a) To qualify to be paid for interpreter services at a hearing, deposition or arbitration, the interpreter shall be

(1) certified, which means listed on the State Personnel Board webpage at http://jobs.spb.ca.gov/InterpreterListing/ or the California Courts webpage at http://courts.ca.gov/programs-interpreters.htm; or

(2) provisionally certified, which means deemed qualified to perform interpreter services when a certified interpreter cannot be present, either:

(A) by agreement of the parties, or

(B) based on a finding by the workers' compensation administrative law judge conducting a hearing that the interpreter is qualified to interpret at the hearing, or by the arbitrator conducting the arbitration that the interpreter is qualified to interpret at the arbitration. The finding of the judge or arbitrator and the basis for the finding shall be set forth in the record of proceedings.

Note: Authority cited: Sections 133, 5307.3, 5710 and 5811, Labor Code. Reference: Sections 4600, 4620, 4621, 5710 and 5811, Labor Code; and Sections 11435.30, 11435.35, 11435.55, 11513 and 68562, Government Code.

History: 1. New section filed 8-13-2013; operative 8-13-2013 pursuant to Government Code section 11343.4(b)(3) (Register 2013, No. 33).

Ref.: Hanna § 23.13[2]; Herlick Handbook §§ 1.01[3][b], 14.33[2], [5].

§9795.1.6. Interpreters for Medical Treatment Appointments or Medical Legal Exams.

(a) To qualify to be paid for interpreter services at a medical treatment appointment or medical legal exam, the interpreter shall be certified, certified for medical treatment appointments or medical legal exams, or provisionally certified.

(1) Certified means listed on the State Personnel Board webpage at http://jobs.spb.ca.gov/InterpreterListing/ or the California Courts webpage at http://courts.ca.gov/programs-interpreters.htm; or

(2) Certified for medical treatment appointments or medical legal exams, which means either

(A) passing the Certification Commission for Healthcare Interpreters (CCHI) exam evidenced by a CCHI certification/credential indicating that the interpreter passed the exam and specifying the language, if indicated. The certification procedure is set forth on the CCHI webpage at http://www.healthcareinterpretercertification.org/. The CCHI certification/credentials are valid for four years from the date when CCHI granted/issued the credential. Individuals who are granted a CCHI certification or credential must comply with the CCHI requirements to be recertified within this four year period to maintain their certification/credential. Questions about an application may be sent by email to apply@healthcareinterpretercertification.org or to CCHI, 1725 I Street NW, Suite 300, Washington, DC, 20006 (866-969-6656); or

(B) passing the National Board of Certification for Medical Interpreters (National Board) exams evidenced by a National Board credential indicating that the interpreter passed the exams and specifying the language. The certification procedure is set forth on the National Board webpage at http://www.certifiedmedicalinterpreters.org/. The National Board certification is valid for five years from the date when National Board granted/issued the certification. Individuals who are granted a National Board certification must comply with the National Board requirements to be recertified within this five year period to maintain their certification. Questions about an application may be sent by email to info@certifiedmedicalinterpreters.org or to National Board, P.O. Box 300, Stow, MA 01775 (1-765-633-2378); or

(3) Provisionally certified as an interpreter for purposes of medical treatment appointments or medical legal exams (A) if the claims administrator has given prior written consent to the interpreter who provides the services, or (B) the injured worker requires interpreter services in a language other than Spanish, Tagalog, Arabic, Cantonese, Japanese, Korean, Portuguese, and Vietnamese, in which case the physician may use a provisionally certified interpreter if that fact is noted in the record of the medical evaluation.

Note: Authority cited: Sections 133, 5307.3, 5710 and 5811, Labor Code. Reference: Sections 4600, 4620, 4621, 5710 and 5811, Labor Code; and Sections 11435.30, 11435.35, 11435.40, 11435.55, 11513 and 68562, Government Code.

History: 1. New section filed 8-13-2013; operative 8-13-2013 pursuant to Government Code section 11343.4(b)(3) (Register 2013, No. 33).

Ref.: Hanna § 23.13[2]; Herlick Handbook §§ 1.01[3][b], 14.33[3], [5].

§9795.2. Notice of Right to Interpreter.

The notice of hearing, deposition, or other setting shall include a statement explaining the right to have an interpreter present if they do not proficiently speak or understand the English language. Where a party is designated to serve a notice, it shall be the responsibility of that party to include this statement in the notice.

Note: Authority cited: Sections 133, 5307.3, 5710 and 5811, Labor Code. Reference: Sections 4600, 4620, 4621, 5710 and 5811, Labor Code; and Sections 11513 and 68562, Government Code.

History: 1. New section filed 1-28-94; operative 1-28-94. Submitted to OAL for printing only pursuant to Government Code section 11351 (Register 94, No. 4).

2. New Note filed 12-30-96; operative 12-30-96 pursuant to Government Code section 11343.4(d). Submitted to OAL for printing only pursuant to Government Code section 11351 (Register 97, No. 1).

Ref.: Hanna §§ 23.13[3], 23.14[1][c], 26.04[1], 33.01[4], 35.53[3]; Herlick Handbook §§ 1.01[3][b], 14.33.

§9795.3. Fees for Interpreter Services.

(a) Fees for services performed by a certified or provisionally certified interpreter, upon request of an employee who does not proficiently speak or understand the English language, shall be paid by the claims administrator for any of the following events:

(1) An examination by a physician to which an injured employee submits at the requests of the claims administrator, the administrative director, or the appeals board;

(2) A medical treatment appointment;

(3) A comprehensive medical-legal evaluation as defined in subdivision (c) of Section 9793, a follow-up medical-legal evaluation as defined in subdivision (f) of Section 9793, or a supplemental medical-legal evaluation as defined in subdivision (k) of Section 9793; provided, however, that payment for interpreter's fees by the claims administrator shall not be required under this paragraph unless the medical report to which the services apply is compensable in accordance with Article 5.6. Nothing in this paragraph, however, shall be construed to relieve the party who retains an interpreter from liability to pay the interpreter's fees in the event the claims administrator is not liable.

(4) A deposition of an injured employee or any person claiming benefits as a dependent of an injured employee, at the request of the claims administrator, including the following related events:

(i) Preparation of the deponent immediately prior to the deposition,

(ii) Reading of a deposition to a deponent prior to signing, and,

(iii) Reading of prior volumes to a deponent in preparation for continuation of a deposition.

(5) An appeals board hearing, or arbitration.

(6) A conference held by an information and assistance officer pursuant to Chapter 2.5 (commencing with Section 5450) of Part 4 of Division 4 of the Labor Code to assist in resolving a dispute between an injured employee and a claims administrator.

(7) Other similar settings determined by the Workers' Compensation Appeals Board to be reasonable and neces-

sary to determine the validity and extent of injury to an employee.

(b) The following fees for interpreter services provided by a certified or provisionally certified interpreter shall be presumed to be reasonable:

(1) For an appeals board hearing, arbitration, or deposition: interpreter fees shall be billed and paid at the greater of the following (i) at the rate for one-half day or one full day as set forth in the Superior Court fee schedule for interpreters in the county where the service was provided, or (ii) at the market rate. The interpreter shall establish the market rate for the interpreter's services by submitting documentation to the claims administrator, including a list of recent similar services performed and the amounts paid for those services. Services over 8 hours shall be paid at the rate of one-eighth the full day rate for each hour of service over 8 hours.

(2) For all other events listed under subdivision (a), interpreter fees shall be billed and paid at the rate of $11.25 per quarter hour or portion thereof, with a minimum payment of two hours, or the market rate, whichever is greater. The interpreter shall establish the market rate for the interpreter's services by submitting documentation to the claims administrator, including a list of recent similar services performed and the amounts paid for those services.

(3) The fee in paragraph (1) or (2) shall include, when requested and adequately documented by the interpreter, payment for mileage and travel time where reasonable and necessary to provide the service, and where the distance between the interpreter's place of business and the place where the service was rendered is over 25 miles. Travel time is not deemed reasonable and necessary where a qualified interpreter listed in the master listing for the county where the service is to be provided can be present to provide the service without the necessity of excessive travel.

(i) Mileage shall be paid at the minimum rate adopted by the Director of the Department of Personnel Administration pursuant to Section 19820 of the Government Code for non-represented (excluded) employees at Title 2, CCR § 599.631(a).

(ii) Travel time shall be paid at the rate of $5.00 per quarter hour or portion thereof.

(c) Unless notified of a cancellation at least 24 hours prior to the time the service is to be provided, the interpreter shall be paid no less than the minimum fee.

(d) Nothing in this section shall preclude payment to an interpreter or agency for interpreting services based on an agreement made in advance of services between the interpreter or agency and the claims administrator, regardless of whether or not such payment is less than, or exceeds, the fees set forth in this section.

(e) The fees set forth in subdivision (b) shall be presumed reasonable for services provided by provisionally certified interpreters only if efforts to obtain a certified interpreter are documented and submitted to the claims administrator with the bill for services. Efforts to obtain a certified interpreter shall also be disclosed in any document based in whole or in part on information obtained through a provisionally certified interpreter.

(f) It is the responsibility of the party producing a witness requiring an interpreter to arrange for the presence of the interpreter.

Note: Authority cited: Sections 133, 5307.3, 5710 and 5811, Labor Code. Reference: Sections 4600, 4620, 4621, 5710 and 5811, Labor Code; and Sections 11435.30, 11435.35 and 68562, Government Code.

History: 1. New section filed 1-28-94; operative 1-28-94. Submitted to OAL for printing only pursuant to Government Code section 11351 (Register 94, No. 4).

2. Amendment of subsections (b)(1) and (b)(2), repealer of subsection (b)(3), subsection renumbering, amendment of newly designated subsection (b)(4) and subsection (d), and new Note filed 12-30-96; operative 12-30-96 pursuant to Government Code section 11343.4(d). Submitted to OAL for printing only pursuant to Government Code section 11351 (Register 97, No. 1).

3. New subsection (a)(2), subsection renumbering, repealer of former subsection (a)(5), amendment of newly designated subsection (a)(5) and subsection (b)(1) and amendment of Note filed 12-27-2012 as an emergency; operative 1-1-2013 pursuant to Government Code section 11340.9(d) (Register 2012, No. 52). A Certificate of Compliance must be transmitted to OAL by 7-1-2013 or emergency language will be repealed by operation of law on the following day.

4. New subsection (a)(2), repealer of former subsection (a)(5), subsection renumbering, amendment of newly designated subsection (a)(5) and subsection (b)(1) and amendment of Note refiled 7-1-2013 as an emergency; operative 7-1-2013 (Register 2013, No. 27). A Certificate of Compliance must be transmitted to OAL by 9-30-2013 or emergency language will be repealed by operation of law on the following day.

5. Certificate of Compliance as to 7-1-2013 order, including further amendment of section and Note, transmitted to OAL 7-1-2013 and filed 8-13-2013; amendments operative 8-13-2013 pursuant to Government Code section 11343.4(b)(3) (Register 2013, No. 33).

Ref.: Hanna §§ 22.07[2][a], 23.03[2], 23.13[3], 25.41[2], 27.01[8][a]; Herlick Handbook §§ 1.01[3][b], 14.33.

§9795.4. Time for Payment; Effective Date.

(a) All expenses for interpreter services shall be paid within 60 days after receipt by the claims administrator of the bill for services unless the claims administrator, within this period, contests its liability for such payment, or the reasonableness or the necessity of incurring such expenses. A claims administrator who contests all or any part of a bill for interpreter services shall pay the uncontested amount and notify the interpreter of the objection within 60 days after receipt of the bill. Any notice of objection shall include all of the following:

(1) An explanation of the basis of the objection.

(2) If additional information is needed as a prerequisite to payment of a contested bill or portions thereof, a clear description of the information required.

(3) The name, address and telephone number of the person or office to contact for additional information concerning the objection.

(4) A statement that the interpreter may adjudicate the issue of the contested charge before the Workers' Compensation Appeals Board.

(b) Any bill for interpreter's services which constitutes a medical-legal expense as defined in subdivision (g) of Section 9793 and which is neither paid nor contested within the time limits set forth herein shall be subject to the penalties and interest set forth in Section 4622 of the Labor Code.

(c) This article shall be effective for services provided on and after the effective date of this article which pertain to injuries occurring on or after January 1, 1994. Amendments to this article which became effective in 1996 shall apply to interpreting services provided on or after April 1, 1997.

Note: Authority cited: Sections 133, 5307.3, 5710 and 5811, Labor Code. Reference: Sections 4600, 4620, 4621, 5710 and 5811, Labor Code; and Sections 68562 and 11513, Government Code.

History: 1. New section filed 1-28-94; operative 1-28-94. Submitted to OAL for printing only pursuant to Government Code section 11351 (Register 94, No. 4).

2. Amendment of subsection (c) and Note filed 12-30-96; operative 12-30-96 pursuant to Government Code section 11343.4(d). Submitted to OAL for printing only pursuant to Government Code section 11351 (Register 97, No. 1).

Ref.: Hanna §§ 23.03[2][e], 22.13[3], 33.01[5], 33.53[3][b]; Herlick Handbook §§ 1.01[3][b], 10.05, 14.33.

§9795.5. Interpreter Directories.

a. Interpreters certified in accordance with sections 9795.1.5 (a)(1) and 9795.1.6 (a)(1) are listed at the following websites: http://jobs.spb.ca.gov/InterpreterListing/ and http://www.courts.ca.gov /programs-interpreters.htm.

b. Certified interpreters for the purposes of medical treatment appointments and medical legal exams who meet the qualifications of section 9795.1.6(a)(2) are listed in the registry for Certification Commission for Healthcare Interpreters (CCHI) or National Board of Certification for Medical Interpreters (National Board) at the following websites: https://cchi.learningbuilder.com/Account/Login?ReturnUrl =%2f or http://www.certifiedmedicalinterpreters.org/registry.

(c) Proof of certification may be requested by the claims administrator and shall be provided by the certified interpreter for the purposes of medical treatment appointments and medical legal exams if the interpreter is not listed in the CCHI or National Board website directory.

Note: Authority cited: Sections 133, 5307.3, 5710 and 5811, Labor Code. Reference: Sections 4600, 4620, 4621, 5710 and 5811, Labor Code; and Sections 11435.30, 11435.35 and 68562, Government Code.

History: 1. New section filed 8-13-2013; operative 8-13-2013 pursuant to Government Code section 11343.4(b)(3) (Register 2013, No. 33).

Ref.: Hanna § 23.13[2]; Herlick Handbook §§ 1.01[3][b], 14.33[5].

ARTICLE 6
Consulting Physician, Certification of

§9796. Certification of Consulting Physician, How Initiated.

When an injured employee requests an employer to secure certification of a consulting physician under Labor Code Section 4602, the employer shall direct a letter in triplicate to the Division of Industrial Accidents, attention Medical Director, 525 Golden Gate Avenue, Room 201, San Francisco, California 94102, containing the following information:

(a) The name and address of the injured employee;

(b) The name and address of the consulting physician chosen;

(c) The field of practice of the consulting physician.

Note: Authority cited: Sections 124, 127, 133, 138.2, 138.3, 138.4, 139, 139.5, 139.6, 4600, 4601, 4602, 4603, 4603.2, 4603.5, 5307.3, 5450, 5451, 5452, 5453, 5454 and 5455, Labor Code. Reference: Chapters 442, 709 and 1172, Statutes of 1977; and Chapter 1017, Statutes of 1976.

History: 1. Amendment filed 11-7-78; effective thirtieth day thereafter (Register 78, No. 45).

2. Change without regulatory effect filed 7-11-86; effective upon filing (Register 86, No. 28).

Ref.: Hanna §§ 5.05[8], 22.04; Herlick Handbook § 1.01[3][b].

§9799. Criterion for Certifying Competence.

The criterion to be followed by the Administrative Director in certifying the competence of the consulting physician chosen by the injured employee is that the field of practice is related to the injury or the problem for which consultation was requested.

Ref.: Hanna § 22.04; Herlick Handbook § 1.01[3][b].

§9802. Notification by Administrative Director.

The Administration Director will notify the employer and employee as to the competence of a consulting physician within twelve (12) days of the date of the receipt of the request for such certification.

Ref.: Hanna §§ 5.05[8], 22.04; Herlick Handbook § 1.01[3][b].

ARTICLE 7
Schedule for Rating Permanent Disabilities

§9805. Schedule for Rating Permanent Disabilities, Adoption, Amendment.

The method for the determination of percentages of permanent disability is set forth in the Schedule for Rating Permanent Disabilities, which has been adopted by the Administrative Director effective January 1, 2005, and which is hereby incorporated by reference in its entirety as though it were set forth below. The schedule adopts and incorporates the American Medical Association (AMA) *Guides to the Evaluation of Permanent Impairment 5th Edition*. The schedule shall be effective for dates of injury on or after January 1, 2005 and for dates of injury prior to January 1, 2005, in accordance with subdivision (d) of Labor Code section 4660, and it shall be amended at least once every five years.

The schedule may be downloaded from the Division of Workers' Compensation website at http://www.dir.ca.gov/dwc/dwcrep.htm.

Note: Authority cited: Sections 133 and 5307.3, Labor Code. Reference: Sections 4660, 4662, 4663 and 4664, Labor Code.

History: 1. Amendment filed 12-8-69; designated effective 1-1-70 (Register 69, No. 50).

2. Amendment filed 12-14-72; designated effective 1-1-73 (Register 72, No. 51).

3. Editorial correction (Register 81, No. 31).

4. Amendment filed 7-15-83; effective thirtieth day thereafter (Register 83, No. 30).

5. Editorial correction of 7-15-83 order redesignating effective date to 8-1-83 pursuant to Government Code Section 11346.2(d) filed 7-19-83 (Register 83, No. 30).

6. Amendment of section and Note filed 12-31-2004 as an emergency; operative 1-1-2005 (Register 2004, No. 53). A Certificate of Compliance must be transmitted to OAL by 5-2-2005 or emergency language will be repealed by operation of law on the following day.

7. Certificate of Compliance as to 12-31-2004 order, including further amendment of section, transmitted to OAL 4-29-2005 and filed 6-10-2005 (Register 2005, No. 23).

Ref.: Hanna §§ 1.12[6], 8.02[3], [4][a], 32.01[3][a][i], 32.03[1]; Herlick Handbook § 1.01[3][b]; Lawyer's Guide to AMA *Guides* and Calif. Workers' Comp. §§ 2.02, 2.03, 3.02, 3.03, 6.03.

§9805.1. Data Collection, Evaluation, and Revision of Schedule.

The Administrative Director shall: (1) collect for 18 months permanent disability ratings under the 2005 Permanent Disability Rating Schedule (PDRS) effective for injuries occurring on or after 1/1/05 and effective for injuries occurring on or after 4/19/04 and before 1/1/05 where there has been either no comprehensive medical-legal report or no report by a treating physician indicating the existence of permanent disability, or when the employer is not required to provide the notice required by Labor Code Section 4601 to the injured employee; (2) evaluate the data to determine the aggregate effect of the diminished future earning capacity adjustment on the permanent partial disability ratings under the 2005 PDRS; and (3) revise, if necessary, the diminished future earning capacity adjustment to reflect consideration of an employee's diminished future earning capacity for injuries based on the data collected. If the Administrative Director determines that there is not a sufficient amount of data to perform a statistically valid evaluation, the Administrative Director shall continue to collect data until a valid statistical sample is obtained. If there is a statistically valid sample of data that the Administrative Director determines supports a revision to the diminished future earning capacity adjustment, the Administrative Director shall revise the PDRS before the mandatory five year statutory revision contained in Labor Code section 4660(c).

Note: Authority cited: Sections 133 and 5307.3, Labor Code. Reference: Sections 4660, 4662, 4663 and 4664, Labor Code.

History: 1. New section filed 6-10-2005; operative 6-10-2005 (Register 2005, No. 23).

Ref.: Hanna § 8.02[4][a]; Herlick Handbook § 1.01[3][b]; Lawyer's Guide to AMA *Guides* and Calif. Workers' Comp. §§ 2.02, 2.03, 3.02, 3.03, 6.03.

ARTICLE 8
Benefit Notices; Claims Administrator's Duties and Responsibilities; Claim Form and Notice of Potential Eligibility for Benefits; Regulatory Authority of the Administrative Director

§9810. General Provisions.

(a) This Article applies to benefit notices prepared on or after its effective date. Where a claim is subject to an alternative dispute resolution (ADR) program pursuant to section 3201.5 or 3201.7, the contents of any notice required by this Article that would be inconsistent with the provisions of the ADR agreement shall be modified to be consistent with the ADR agreement.

(b) The Administrative Director may issue and revise from time to time a Benefit Notice Instruction Manual as a guide for completing and serving the notices required by this Article.

(c) Benefit notices, excepting those notices whose language or format is set forth in statute or where a specific notice form has been adopted as a regulation, may be produced on the claims administrator's letterhead.

(1) All notices shall identify the claims administrator's name, mailing address, telephone number and website address if available, the employee's name, employer's name, the claim number, the date the notice was sent to the employee, and the date of injury. All notices shall clearly identify the name and telephone number and mailing address of the individual claims examiner responsible for the payment and adjusting of the claim.

(2) Where the claims administrator has a clearly documented reason to believe that disclosure of the claims examiner's name presents or may present a security concern towards the personal safety of the claims examiner, the claims administrator may identify an alternate but specific claims department name and telephone number in lieu of the claims examiner's name and telephone number.

(3) All notices shall include a notation if one or more attachments are being sent with the notice.

(d) All notices shall clearly state that additional information may be obtained from an Information and Assistance officer with the Division of Workers' Compensation, or on the Division's website: www.dwc.ca.gov. Each benefit notice shall refer the employee (by chapter number and internet url) to the appropriate chapter of the publication "Workers' Compensation in California: A Guidebook for Injured Workers" that addresses the benefit(s) to which the notice pertains, and shall advise the employee that a complete copy of the Guidebook may be obtained on the Division of Workers' Compensation's website at http://www.dir.ca.gov/InjuredWorkerGuidebook/InjuredWorkerGuidebook.html or by contacting an information and assistance (I&A) officer of the Division of Workers' Compensation. If the employer offers additional disability benefits in addition to those provided by law under workers' compensation, the claims administrator may incorporate the information within the notices required by these regulations. A single benefit notice may encompass multiple events. Where a notice is being issued but a check for benefits to which the notice refers is being separately mailed to the employee, the notice shall advise the employee that the check is being mailed separately.

(e) Every benefit notice, excepting those mandatory notices that have been set forth in statute or where a specific notice form has been adopted as a regulation, shall include a mandatory statement of employee's (or claimant's) remedies, as follows:

(1) For claims not subject to an alternative dispute resolution (ADR) program under Labor Code sections 3201.5 or 3201.7, the following language shall be used:

"You have a right to disagree with decisions affecting your claim. If you have any questions about the information provided to you in this notice, please call, [*insert either me, the adjuster's name or a specific claims department name and telephone number*]. You also have the right to be represented by an attorney of your choice. However, if you are represented by an attorney, you should call your attorney, not me.

"For information about the workers' compensation claims process and your rights and obligations, go to www.dwc.ca.gov or contact an information and assistance (I&A) officer of the state Division of Workers' Compensation. For recorded information and a list of offices, call (800) 736-7401."

(2) For claims subject to an alternative dispute resolution (ADR) program under Labor Code sections 3201.5 or 3201.7, the language in paragraph (1) shall be used to the extent that it is consistent with the provisions of the ADR agreement, and the following language shall be substituted in its place to the extent appropriate according to the ADR agreement:

"You have a right to disagree with decisions affecting your claim. If you have any questions regarding the information provided to you in this notice, please call, [*insert either me, the adjuster's name or a specific claims department name and telephone number*], or [*insert name, title, and telephone of ombudsperson or mediator*]. However, if you are represented by an attorney, you should call your attorney, not [insert me, or the specific claims department name], the ombudsperson, or mediator.

NOTE: For employees subject to an alternative dispute resolution (ADR) program under Labor Code section 3201.5, the claims administrator may include the following language if appropriate under the provisions of the ADR program:

"In accordance with the [*insert union name*] agreement, active participation by an attorney is not allowed in the Ombudsman and Mediation stages of the ADR workers' compensation process. However, you have the right to consult with an attorney and your right to obtain legal advice is not limited and you may obtain such at your own expense at any time. If the Ombudsman and Mediation stages of dispute resolution are unsuccessful and a written request for Arbitration has been timely filed, attorney participation is allowed.

"For information about the workers' compensation claims process and your rights and obligations, contact an information and assistance (I&A) officer of the state Division of Workers' Compensation. Be sure to inform the I&A officer that your claim is subject to an alternative dispute resolution program. For a list of offices, go to www.dwc.ca.gov or call (800) 736-7401."

(f) Benefit notices, except those notices where language or format is set forth in statute or specific notice forms adopted by regulation, may be produced in any format developed by the claims administrator. Each such benefit notice shall contain all relevant notice elements required by either statute or regulation. The Administrative Director may make sample notices that comply with these requirements available on the DWC website. Benefit notices using the sample notices devised by the Administrative Director and available on the Division's website are presumed to be adequate notice to the employee and, unless modified, shall not be subject to audit penalties.

(g) Every benefit notice shall have a title at the top of the first page that clearly identifies the subject of the notice. The notice shall also contain the following statement ***in bold font*** at the end of the notice: "Keep this notice. It contains important information about your workers' compensation benefits."

(h) The claims administrator shall provide copies to the employee, upon request, of all medical reports, relevant to any benefit notice issued, or which are not required to be provided along with a notice and have not yet been provided to the employee other than psychiatric reports which the physician has recommended not be provided to the employee.

(i) The claims administrator shall send a copy of each benefit notice, and any enclosures not previously served on the attorney, concurrently to the attorney of any represented employee. Where the claims administrator offers the service, and upon the documented written agreement of the attorney, all benefit notices, including attachments, may be sent electronically in lieu of by mail. An attorney may elect to change the method in which he or she receives benefit notices by giving written notice to the claims administrator.

(j) Any deadline for reply which is measured from the date a notice is sent, and all rights protected within the deadline, are extended if the notice is sent by mail or electronically. The deadline is extended as follows: by 5 days if the place of mailing and the place of address are in the same state of the United States; by 10 days if the place of mailing and the place of address are in different states of the United States; by 20 days if the place of mailing is in and the place of address is outside the United States. All notices shall be mailed from the United States.

(k) Copies of all benefit notices sent to employees shall be maintained by the claims administrator in the claims file. In lieu of retaining a copy of any attachments to the notice, the claims administrator may identify the attachments by name and revision date on the notice. These copies may be maintained in paper or electronic form.

(*l*) All benefit notices shall be made available in English and Spanish, as appropriate.

(m) Where the claims administrator offers the service, and upon the documented written agreement of the employee, all benefit notices, including attachments, may be sent electronically to the employee in lieu of by mail. The employee's agreement may be documented by provision of a personal email address on the claim form (DWC Form 1) and checking the box agreeing to receive benefit notices electronically. An employee may elect to change the form in which he or she receives benefit notices by giving written notice to the claims administrator.

(n) When the method of service of the benefit notice is electronic, in lieu of regular mail, service shall be through the use of a secure, encrypted email system. The claims administrator shall maintain a log of service dates, and receipt acknowledgements, for each benefit notice sent electronically on each claims file, and will produce this log upon demand to the employee, the employee's attorney, if represented and the DWC Audit Unit. If the claims administrator receives notice that an electronic benefit notice was not delivered to the email address provided by the employee, or attorney, if represented, they shall then send the benefit notice to the employee and attorney by regular mail within one (1) business day of receipt of the failed electronic delivery notice.

(o) Electronic delivery of benefit notices by a claims administrator does not constitute consent to accept electronic service of any communications sent to the claims administrator.

Note: Authority cited: Sections 59, 124, 133, 138.3, 138.4, 4061(a), 4061(b), 4061(d) and 5307.3, Labor Code. Reference: Sections 1010.6 and 1013, Code of Civil Procedure; and Sections 138.4, 4061 and 4650(a)-(d), Labor Code.

History: 1. Repealer of article 8 (sections 9810–9878, not consecutive) and new article 8 (sections 9810–9817) filed 7-15-83; effective thirtieth day thereafter (Register 83, No. 30). For prior history, see Registers 81, No. 42; 79, No. 30; 78, No. 45; 73, Nos. 51 and 38; 72, No. 51; and 66, No. 20.

2. Editorial correction of 7-15-83 order redesignating effective date to 8-1-83 pursuant to Government Code section 11346.2(d) filed 7-19-83 (Register 83, No. 30).

3. Editorial correction of 7-15-83 order filed 8-11-83 (Register 83, No. 33).

4. Amendment of article heading, section and Note filed 1-7-94; operative 1-7-94. Submitted to OAL for printing only pursuant to Government Code section 11351 (Register 94, No. 1).

5. Repealer of subsection (d) and subsection relettering filed 7-7-2004; operative 8-1-2004 pursuant to Government Code section 11343.4 (Register 2004, No. 28).

6. Repealer and new article heading and amendment of section and Note filed 12-11-2007; operative 4-9-2008 (Register 2007, No. 50).

7. Amendment of section and Note filed 8-24-2015; operative 1-1-2016 (Register 2015, No. 35).

Ref.: Hanna §§ 1.12[6], 7.03[1], 9.06; Herlick Handbook §§ 1.01[3][b], 4.04[3], 9.3, 14.3.

§9811. Definitions.

As used in this Article:

(a) "Claims Administrator" means a self-administered insurer providing security for the payment of compensation required by Divisions 4 and 4.5 of the Labor Code, a self-administered self-insured employer, a self-administered joint powers authority, a self-administered legally uninsured employer, a third-party claims administrator for a self-insured employer, insurer, legally uninsured employer, or joint powers authority, or an administrator for an alternative dispute resolution (ADR) program established under Labor Code section 3201.5 or 3201.7.

(b) "Date of knowledge of injury" means the date the employer had knowledge of a worker's injury or claim of injury.

(c) "Date of knowledge of injury and disability" means the date the employer had knowledge of (1) a worker's injury or claim of injury, and (2) the worker's inability or claimed inability to work because of the injury.

(d) "Dependent" means any person who may be or is claimed to be entitled to workers' compensation benefits as a result of an employee's death (including compensation which was accrued and unpaid to an injured employee before his or her death), and includes the parent or legal guardian of a minor dependent child.

(e) "Duration" means any known period of time for which benefits are to be paid, or, where benefits will continue for an unknown period of time the event that will occur which will determine when benefits will terminate.

(f) "Employee" includes dependent(s) in the event of any injury which results in death.

(g) "Employee's (or claimant's) remedies" means the statement of the employee's rights, as set forth in subdivision (e) of section 9810, of which an employee or claimant shall be informed in benefit notices when specified in these regulations.

(h) "Employer" means any person or entity defined as an employer by Labor Code section 3300.

(i) "Injury" means any injury as defined in Labor Code section 3208 which results in medical treatment beyond first aid, lost time beyond the date of injury, or death.

(j) "Medical issue" means a dispute or question that is subject to Labor Code section 4060, 4061, or 4062, and does not include a medical treatment issue that is subject to Labor Code section 4610, 4610.5, and 4610.6.

(k) "Permanent and stationary status" means the point when the employee has reached maximal medical improvement his or her condition is well stabilized and unlikely to change substantially in the next year with or without medical treatment.

(*l*) "Salary continuation" means payments made to an employee pursuant to a plan that meets the criteria specified in Labor Code section 4650(g).

(m) "Temporary disability payment" includes salary continuation as defined in subdivision (*l*) of this section.

Note: Authority cited: Sections 59, 133, 138.3, 138.4 and 5307.3, Labor Code. Reference: Sections 138.4, 3201.5, 3201.7, 3208, 3300, 3351, 3351.5, 3700, 3753, 4060, 4061, 4062, 4062.2, 4610, 4610.5, 4610.6, 4650(a)-(d), 4653, 4654, 4700, 4701 and 4850, Labor Code; Sections 11651 and 11652, Insurance Code; Section 19871, Government Code; Section 89529.03, Education Code; and Sections 2330 and 2332, Civil Code.

History: 1. Amendment of section and Note filed 1-7-94; operative 1-7-94. Submitted to OAL for printing only pursuant to Government Code section 11351 (Register 94, No. 1).

2. Amendment of section and Note filed 12-11-2007; operative 4-9-2008 (Register 2007, No. 50).

3. Amendment of section and Note filed 8-24-2015; operative 1-1-2016 (Register 2015, No. 35).

Ref.: Hanna §§ 7.03[1], 9.06, 32.07[1], [4], 35.11[3]; Herlick Handbook §§ 1.01[3][b], 9.3, 14.3.

§9812. Benefit Payment and Notice.

(a) Temporary Disability Notices. When an injury causes or is claimed to cause temporary disability:

(1) Notice of First Temporary Disability Indemnity Payment. The first time the claims administrator pays temporary disability indemnity, the claims administrator shall advise the employee of the amount of temporary disability indemnity due, how it was calculated, and the duration and schedule of indemnity payments. The notice shall be sent no later than the 14th day after the employer's date of knowledge of injury and disability.

(2) Notice of Delay in Any Temporary Disability Indemnity Payment. If the employee's entitlement to any period of temporary disability indemnity cannot be determined within 14 days after the date of knowledge of injury

and disability, the claims administrator shall advise the employee within the 14-day period of the delay, the reasons for it, the need, if any, for additional information required to make a determination, and when a determination is likely to be made. If the claims administrator cannot make a determination by the date specified in a notice to the employee, the claims administrator shall send a subsequent delay notice to the employee, not later than the determination date specified in the previous delay notice, notifying the employee of the revised date by which the claims administrator now expects the determination to be made. A subsequent delay notice shall comply with all requirements for the contents of an original delay notice.

(A) Where the delay is related to a medical issue, and the claims administrator is requesting a comprehensive medical evaluation, and the employee is not represented by an attorney, the notice shall advise the employee of one of the following:

1. If the employee has already received a comprehensive medical evaluation, the employee may be asked to return to that physician for a new evaluation.

2. If no comprehensive medical evaluation has taken place, the notice shall advise the employee that if he or she disagrees with the results of the evaluation, the employee must either:

a. contact the claims administrator within the applicable time limit prescribed in Labor Code section 4062(a) to obtain the form prescribed by the DWC Medical Unit to request assignment of a panel of Qualified Medical Evaluators, or

b. within the applicable time limit prescribed in Labor Code section 4062(a), download the form to request assignment of a panel of Qualified Medical Evaluators from the DWC website. (Note: the notice shall provide the employee with the url to enable the employee to download the applicable form.)

However, if the employee has already received a comprehensive medical evaluation, the notice may instead advise the employee to contact the claims administrator to arrange for the employee to return to that same medical evaluator for a new evaluation if possible.

(B) If the employee is represented by an attorney, the notice shall instruct the employee to contact the attorney with any questions.

(3) Notice of Denial of Any Temporary Disability Indemnity Payment. If the claims administrator denies liability for the payment of any period for which an employee claims temporary disability indemnity, the notice shall advise the employee of the denial and the reasons for it. The notice shall be sent within 14 days after the determination to deny was made. If the claims administrator's determination is based on a medical report, a copy of the medical report(s) shall be provided with the notice, except for psychiatric reports that the psychiatrist has recommended not be provided to the employee.

(A) Where the denial is related to a medical issue and the employee is not represented by an attorney, the notice shall advise the employee of one of the following:

1. If the denial is based on a comprehensive medical evaluation, and the employee disputes the results of the evaluation, the employee may file an Application for Adjudication of Claim with the WCAB.

2. If the denial is based on the treating physician's evaluation of the employee's temporary disability status and the claims administrator agrees with those findings, the notice shall advise the employee that if he or she disagrees with the results of the evaluation, the employee must either:

a. contact the claims administrator within the applicable time limit prescribed in Labor Code section 4062(a) to obtain the form prescribed by the DWC Medical Unit to request assignment of a panel of Qualified Medical Evaluators, or

b. within the applicable time limit prescribed in Labor Code section 4062(a), download the form to request assignment of a panel of Qualified Medical Evaluators from the DWC website. (Note: the notice shall provide the employee with the url to enable the employee to download the applicable form.)

However, if the employee has already received a comprehensive medical evaluation, the notice may instead advise the employee to contact the claims administrator to arrange for the employee to return to that same medical evaluator for a new evaluation if possible.

3. If the denial is based on the treating physician's evaluation of the employee's temporary disability status and the claims administrator disagrees with those findings, the notice shall advise the employee that the claims administrator disputes the result of the evaluation. If the claims administrator's determination is based on a medical report, the notice shall be provided within the applicable time limit prescribed in Labor Code section 4062(a), notwithstanding the 14 days required by this subdivision. The notice shall advise the employee that the claims administrator disputes the results of the evaluation, and advise the employee that if he or she disagrees with the results of the evaluation, the employee must either:

a. contact the claims administrator within the applicable time limit prescribed in Labor Code section 4062(a) to obtain the form prescribed by the DWC Medical Unit to request assignment of a panel of Qualified Medical Evaluators, or

b. within the applicable time limit prescribed in Labor Code section 4062(a), download the form to request assignment of a panel of Qualified Medical Evaluators from the DWC website. (Note: the notice shall provide the employee with the url to enable the employee to download the applicable form.)

However, if the employee has already received a comprehensive medical evaluation, the notice may instead advise the employee to contact the claims administrator to arrange for the employee to return to that same medical evaluator for a new evaluation if possible.

(B) If the employee is represented by an attorney, the notice shall instruct the employee to contact the attorney with any questions or need for clarification.

(b) Notice of Resumed Benefit Payments (TD, PD). If the payment of temporary disability indemnity or permanent disability indemnity is resumed after terminating any of these benefits, the claims administrator shall advise the employee of the amount of indemnity due and the duration and schedule of payments. Notice shall be sent within 14 days after the employer's date of knowledge of the entitlement to additional benefits.

(c) Notice of Changed Benefit Rate, Payment Amount or Schedule (TD, PD). When the claims administrator changes the benefit rate, payment amount or benefit payment schedule for temporary disability indemnity or permanent disability indemnity, the claims administrator shall advise the employee, as applicable, of the amount of the new benefit rate and the reason the rate is being changed, or of the new benefit payment schedule. Notice shall be given before or at the same time as the new payment.

(d) Notice that Benefits Are Ending (TD, PD). At the same time as the last payment of temporary disability indemnity or permanent disability indemnity, the claims administrator shall advise the employee of the ending of indemnity payments and the reason, and shall make an accounting of all compensation paid to or on behalf of the employee in the species of benefit to which the notice refers, including the dates and amounts paid and any related penalties. If the decision to end payment of indemnity was made after the last payment, the claims administrator shall send the notice and accounting within 14 days after the last payment. If the claims administrator's determination is based on a medical report, a copy of the medical report(s) shall be provided with the notice, except for psychiatric reports that the psychiatrist has recommended not be provided to the employee.

(1) Where the determination is related to a medical issue and the employee is not represented by an attorney, the notice shall advise the employee of one of the following:

(A) If the termination of benefits is based on a comprehensive medical evaluation, and the employee disputes the results of the evaluation, the employee may file an Application for Adjudication of Claim with the WCAB.

(B) If the termination of benefits is based on the treating physician's evaluation of the employee's temporary or permanent disability status, the notice shall advise the employee that if he or she disagrees with the results of the evaluation, the employee must either:

1. contact the claims administrator within the applicable time limit prescribed in Labor Code section 4062(a) to obtain the form prescribed by the DWC Medical Unit to request assignment of a panel of Qualified Medical Evaluators, or

2. within the applicable time limit prescribed in Labor Code section 4062(a), download the form to request assignment of a panel of Qualified Medical Evaluators from the DWC website. (Note: the notice shall provide the employee with the url to enable the employee to download the applicable form.)

However, if the employee has already received a comprehensive medical evaluation, the notice may instead advise the employee to contact the claims administrator to arrange for the employee to return to that same medical evaluator for a new evaluation if possible. If the claims administrator's determination is based on a medical report, the notice shall be provided within the applicable time limit prescribed in Labor Code section 4062(a), notwithstanding the 14 days required by this subdivision.

(2) If the employee is represented by an attorney, the notice shall instruct the employee to contact the attorney with any questions.

(e) Permanent Disability Notices:

(1) Condition Not Permanent and Stationary, May Cause Permanent Disability — Notice of Monitoring Until P&S Date. If the injury has resulted or may result in permanent disability but the employee's medical condition is not permanent and stationary, the claims administrator shall advise the employee at the same time as the last payment of temporary disability indemnity, that permanent disability indemnity is or may be payable but that the amount cannot be determined because the employee's medical condition has not yet reached a stationary status. The notice shall advise the employee that his or her medical condition will be monitored until it is permanent and stationary, at which time a medical evaluation will be performed to determine the existence and extent of permanent impairment or limitations and the need for future medical care. The notice shall advise the employee of the estimated date when a determination is likely to be made. If the claims administrator cannot make a determination of A) permanent and stationary status, B) the existence and extent of permanent impairment or limitations, and C) the need for future medical care by the date it specified in a monitoring notice to the employee, the claims administrator shall send a subsequent notice to the employee, not later than the determination date specified in the previous notice, notifying the employee of the date by which the claims administrator now expects the determination to be made. The additional notice shall comply with all requirements of the original notice.

(2) Notice That Permanent Disability Exists. At the same time as the last payment of temporary disability or within 14 days after knowledge that the injury has caused permanent disability, whichever is later, the claims administrator shall inform the employee of the claims administrator's estimate of the amount of permanent disability indemnity payable, the basis for the estimate, whether there will be the need for future medical care, and whether an indemnity payment will be deferred pursuant to paragraph (2) of subdivision (b) of Labor Code section 4650. If the claims administrator's determination is based on a medical report, a copy of the medical report(s) shall be provided with the notice, except for psychiatric reports that the psychiatrist has recommended not be provided to the employee.

(A) Where the employee is not represented by an attorney:

1. If the determination is based on a comprehensive medical evaluation, the notice shall advise the employee that if he or she disputes the results of the evaluation, the employee may file an Application for Adjudication of Claim with the WCAB.

2. If the claims administrator's determination is based on an evaluation by a treating physician, the notice shall inform the employee whether or not the claims administrator is requesting a rating from the Disability Evaluation Unit. If the claims administrator is not requesting a rating from the Disability Evaluation Unit, the notice shall advise the employee that he or she may contact an Information and Assistance office to have the treating physician's evaluation reviewed and rated by the Disability Evaluation Unit.

3. If the claims administrator's determination is based on an evaluation by a treating physician, the notice shall advise the employee that if he or she disagrees with the results of the evaluation, the employee must either:

a. contact the claims administrator within the applicable time limit prescribed by Labor Code section 4062(a) to obtain the form prescribed by the DWC Medical Unit to request assignment of a panel of Qualified Medical Evaluators, or

b. within the applicable time limit prescribed in Labor Code section 4062(a), download the form to request assignment of a panel of Qualified Medical Evaluators from the DWC website. (Note: the notice shall provide the employee with the url to enable the employee to download the applicable form.)

However, if the employee has already received a comprehensive medical evaluation, the notice may instead advise the employee to contact the claims administrator to arrange for the employee to return to that same medical evaluator for a new evaluation if possible.

(B) If the employee is represented by an attorney, the notice shall instruct the employee to contact the attorney with any questions.

(3) Notice That No Permanent Disability Exists. In cases where the employee has sustained compensable lost time from work, if the claims administrator alleges that the injury has caused no permanent disability in a case where either the employee has received payment of temporary disability indemnity or the employee claims permanent disability, the claims administrator shall advise the employee that no permanent disability indemnity is payable. This notice shall be sent at the same time as the last payment of temporary disability indemnity or within 14 days after the claims administrator determines that the injury has caused no permanent disability. If the claims administrator's determination is based on a medical report, a copy of the medical report(s) shall be provided with the notice, except for psychiatric reports that the psychiatrist has recommended not be provided to the employee.

(A) Where the employee is not represented by an attorney, the notice shall advise the employee of one of the following:

1. If the determination is based on a comprehensive medical evaluation, the injured employee may file an Application for Adjudication of Claim with the WCAB.

2. If the claims administrator's determination is based on an evaluation by a treating physician, the notice shall inform the employee whether or not the claims administrator is requesting a rating from the Disability Evaluation Unit. If the claims administrator is not requesting a rating from the Disability Evaluation Unit, the notice shall advise the employee that he or she may contact an Information and Assistance office to have the treating physician's evaluation reviewed and rated by the Disability Evaluation Unit. The notice shall also advise the employee that if he or she disagrees with the results of the evaluation, the employee must either:

a. contact the claims administrator within the time limit prescribed by Labor Code section 4062(a) to obtain the form prescribed by the DWC Medical Unit to request assignment of a panel of Qualified Medical Evaluators, or

b. within the applicable time limit prescribed in Labor Code section 4062(a), download the form to request assignment of a panel of Qualified Medical Evaluators from the DWC website. (Note: the notice shall provide the employee with the url to enable the employee to download the applicable form.)

However, if the employee has already received a comprehensive medical evaluation, the notice may instead advise the employee to contact the claims administrator to arrange for the employee to return to that same medical evaluator for a new evaluation if possible.

(B) If the employee is represented by an attorney, the notice shall instruct the employee to contact the attorney with any questions.

(4) Notice of Permanent Disability Indemnity Payment. At the same time as the first payment of permanent disability indemnity, the claims administrator shall advise the employee of the weekly permanent disability indemnity payment, how it was calculated, the duration and schedule of payments, and the claims administrator's reasonable estimate of permanent disability indemnity to be paid.

(f) Notices to Dependents in Death Cases. In a case of fatal injury which is or is claimed to be compensable under the workers' compensation laws of this state, or involving accrued compensation which was not paid to an injured employee before the employee's death, the claims administrator shall advise the dependent(s) of the status of any benefits to which they may be entitled or which they have claimed as a result of the employee's death. The claims administrator shall send each dependent a copy of all notices concerning benefits claimed by, or which may be payable to, that dependent, including notices sent to a different dependent if the benefits paid to the different dependent affect the amount payable to the other claimant. If the claims administrator discovers a new dependent after having sent a notice, the claims administrator shall send copies of each prior notice which concerned benefits to which the newly-discovered dependent might be entitled, to that dependent.

(1) Benefit Payment Schedule. If the claims administrator pays death benefits (including compensation which was accrued and unpaid to an employee before his or her death), the claims administrator shall advise each affected dependent of the amount of the death benefit payable to the dependent, how it was calculated, the duration and schedule of payments and other pertinent information. Notice is required within 14 days after the claims administrator's date of knowledge both of the death and of the identity and address of the dependent.

(2) Notice of Changed Benefit Rate, Amount or Schedule or that Benefits are Ending. If the claims administrator changes the benefit rate, amount or payment schedule, or ends payment, of a death benefit to a dependent, the claims administrator shall advise the affected dependent of the change and the reason for it, or of the new payment schedule. A notice that benefits are ending shall include an accounting of all compensation paid to the claimant. A notice that payment is ending shall be sent at the same time as the last payment unless the decision to end payment was made after that payment; in that case it shall be sent within 14 days after the last payment. Other notices concerning changed payments shall be sent before or with the changed payment, but not later than 14 days after the last payment which was made before the change.

(3) Delay in Determining Benefits. If the claims administrator cannot determine entitlement to some or all death benefits, the claims administrator shall advise each affected dependent of the delay, the reasons for it, the need, if any, for additional information required to make a

determination, and when a determination is likely to be made. Notice is required within 14 days after the claims administrator's date of knowledge of the death, the identity and address of the affected dependent, and the nature of the benefit claimed or which might be due. If the claims administrator cannot make a determination by the date it specified in a notice to the affected dependent(s), the claims administrator shall send a subsequent notice to the affected dependent(s), not later than the determination date specified in the previous notice, notifying the affected dependent(s) of the date by which the claims administrator now expects the determination to be made. The additional delay notices shall include the employee's remedies and shall comply with all requirements for an original delay notice.

(4) Notices Denying Death Benefits. If the claims administrator denies liability for the payment of any or all death benefits, the claims administrator shall advise the affected dependent(s) of the denial and the reasons for it. The notice shall be sent within 14 days after the determination to deny was made.

(g) Notice of Delay in Determining All Liability. If the claims administrator cannot determine whether the employer has any liability for an injury, other than an injury causing death, within 14 days after the date of knowledge of injury, the claims administrator shall advise the employee within the 14-day period of the delay, the reasons for the delay, the need, if any, for additional information required to make a determination, and when a determination is likely to be made. If the claims administrator cannot make a determination by the date it specified in a notice to the employee, or if the reason for the delay has changed, the claims administrator shall send a subsequent notice to the employee, as soon as is reasonably practical, but in any event not later than the determination date specified in the previous notice. The notice shall inform the employee of the date by which the claims administrator now expects the determination to be made, and shall explain the reason for the additional delay. The additional delay notices shall comply with all requirements for an original delay notice.

(1) For injuries on or after January 1, 1990, if the claims administrator sends a notice of a delay in its decision whether to accept or deny liability for the claim, the notice shall include an explanation that the claim is presumed to be compensable if not denied within 90 days from the filing of the claim form, and that this presumption can be rebutted only with evidence discovered after the 90-day period.

(2) For claims reported on or after April 19, 2004, regardless of the date of injury, if the claims administrator sends a notice of delay in its decision whether to accept or deny liability for the claim, the notice shall include an explanation that Labor Code section 5402(c), provides that within one working day after an employee files a claim form, the employer shall authorize the provision of all treatment, consistent with the applicable treatment guidelines, for the alleged injury and shall continue to provide treatment until the date that liability is rejected. The notice shall advise the employee that the employer's liability for medical treatment under this Labor Code section is limited to ten thousand dollars ($10,000).

(3) For employees who are not represented by an attorney, where the delay is related to a medical issue, and the claims administrator is requesting a comprehensive medical evaluation the notice shall be accompanied by the form prescribed by the DWC Medical Unit to request assignment of a panel of Qualified Medical Evaluators. The notice shall contain the following statement (with the phrase "**10 days**" in bold font as shown):

"Enclosed is a form that you must submit to the state Division of Workers' Compensation (DWC) within **10 days** to request a panel of three Qualified Medical Evaluators (QMEs). If you do not submit the form within **10 days**, we will have the right to submit the form. In addition, within **10 days** after the DWC sends you a panel, you must choose a QME from the panel, make an appointment to be examined by the QME, and inform us of your choice and appointment time. If you inform us of your choice but you do not arrange the appointment, we will arrange the appointment. If you do not inform us of your choice, we may choose the QME who will examine you and arrange the appointment."

(4) If the employee is represented by an attorney, the notice shall instruct the employee to contact the attorney with any questions.

(h) Provision of QME Panel Request Form. An unrepresented employee may object to a medical determination made by a treating physician by requesting the form prescribed by the DWC Medical Unit to request assignment of a panel of Qualified Medical Evaluators. If an unrepresented employee requests the form, within ten business days of receipt of the objection, the claims administrator shall acknowledge receipt of the employee's objection and provide the employee with a copy of the form prescribed by the DWC Medical Unit to request assignment of a panel of Qualified Medical Evaluators.

The notice shall contain the following statement (with the phrase "**10 days**" in bold font as shown): "If you wish to obtain a comprehensive medical evaluation, enclosed is a form that you must submit to the state Division of Workers' Compensation (DWC) within **10 days** to request a panel of three Qualified Medical Evaluators (QMEs). If you do not submit the form within **10 days**, we will have the right to submit the form. In addition, within **10 days** after the DWC sends you a panel, you must choose a QME from the panel, make an appointment to be examined by the QME, and inform me of your choice and appointment time. If you inform us of your choice but you do not arrange the appointment, we will arrange the appointment. If you do not inform us of your choice, we may choose the QME who will examine you and arrange the appointment."

(i) Notice Denying Liability for All Compensation Benefits. If the claims administrator denies liability for the payment of all workers' compensation benefits for any claim except a claim for death benefits, including medical-only claims, the claims administrator shall advise the employee of the denial and the reasons for it. The notice shall be sent no later than 14 days after the determination to deny was made. If the claims administrator's determination is based on a medical report, a copy of the medical report(s) shall be provided with the notice, except for psychiatric reports that the psychiatrist has recommended not be provided to the employee.

(1) Where the employee is not represented by an attorney, and the determination is related to a medical issue, the notice shall advise the employee one of the following:

(A) If the determination is based on a comprehensive medical evaluation, and the employee disputes the results of the evaluation, the employee may file an Application for Adjudication of Claim with the WCAB.

(B) If the employee has not previously received a comprehensive medical evaluation for this claim, the notice shall be accompanied by the form prescribed by the DWC Medical Unit to request assignment of a panel of Qualified Medical Evaluators. The notice shall contain the following statement (with the phrase "**10 days**" in bold font as shown): "If you disagree with the decision to deny your claim and wish to obtain a comprehensive medical evaluation, enclosed is a form that you must submit to the state Division of Workers' Compensation (DWC) within **10 days** to request a panel of three Qualified Medical Evaluators (QMEs). If you do not submit the form within **10 days**, we will have the right to submit the form. In addition, within **10 days** after the DWC sends you a panel, you must choose a QME from the panel, make an appointment to be examined by the QME, and inform us of your choice and appointment time. If you inform us of your choice but you do not arrange the appointment, we will arrange the appointment. If you do not inform us of your choice, we may choose the QME who will examine you and arrange the appointment." However, if the employee has already received a comprehensive medical evaluation and he or she disagrees with the decision to deny the claim, the notice may instead advise the employee to contact the claims administrator to arrange for the employee to return to that same medical evaluator for a new evaluation if possible.

(2) If the employee is represented by an attorney, the notice shall instruct the employee to contact the attorney with any questions.

(3) For claims reported on or after April 19, 2004, if an employee has filed a completed claim form with the employer, the claims administrator shall advise the employee to immediately send for consideration of payment, all bills for medical services provided between the date the completed claim form was given to the employer and the date that liability for the claim is rejected, unless he or she has done so already. The claims administrator shall also advise the employee that the maximum payment for medical services that were provided consistent with the applicable treatment guidelines is $10,000.

(4) A copy of the Notice Denying Liability for All Compensation Benefits shall be served on all lien claimants, all claim for costs claimants, and all persons or entities that have been authorized by the claims administrator to furnish benefits, goods or services for which a lien or claim for costs may be filed under Labor Code sections 4903 through 4906, inclusive.

Note: Authority cited: Sections 59, 124, 133, 138.3, 138.4 and 5307.3, Labor Code. Reference: Sections 138.4, 4060, 4061(a), 4061(b), 4061(d), 4061(f), 4061(g), 4062.1, 4062.2, 4650(a)-(d), 4658(d), 4661.5, 4700, 4701, 4702, 4703, 4703.5, 4903-4906 and 5402, Labor Code.

History: 1. Repealer and new section filed 7-11-89; operative 10-1-89 (Register 89 No. 28).

2. Amendment of section and Note filed 1-7-94; operative 1-7-94. Submitted to OAL for printing only pursuant to Government Code section 11351 (Register 94, No. 1).

3. Amendment of section and Note filed 12-11-2007; operative 4-9-2008 (Register 2007, No. 50).

4. Change without regulatory effect amending subsection (g)(2) filed 12-9-2009 pursuant to section 100, title 1, California Code of Regulations (Register 2009, No. 50).

5. Amendment of section and Note filed 8-24-2015; operative 1-1-2016 (Register 2015, No. 35).

Ref.: Hanna §§ 7.03[1], 9.06, 22.06[2][a], 25.20[4], 35.11[3], 35.12; Herlick Handbook §§ 1.01[3][b], 9.3, 14.3, 16.3.

§9813. Vocational Rehabilitation Notices. [Repealed]

Note: Authority cited: Sections 59, 133, 138.3, 138.4, 139.5(a)(2), 4636(d), 4637 and 5307.3, Labor Code. Reference: Sections 138.4, 139.5, 4061(a), (b), (d), 4636, 4637, 4641, 4643, 4644, 4650(a)-(d), 4661.5, 4700, 4701, 4702, 4703, 4703.5, 4903(a) and 5402, Labor Code.

History: 1. Repealer filed 7-11-89; operative 10-1-89 (Register 89, No. 28).

2. New section filed 1-7-94; operative 1-7-94. Submitted to OAL for printing only pursuant to Government Code section 11351 (Register 94, No. 1). For prior history, see Register 89, No. 28.

3. Amendment of subsections (a)(2)-(a)(3)(C), (c)(2), (c)(2)(B)-(E), (d)(2) and (d)(2)(B)-(E) filed 2-21-95; operative 2-21-95. Submitted to OAL for printing only pursuant to Government Code section 11351 (Register 95, No. 8).

4. Amendment of subsections (a), (a)(2)-(3), (a)(3)(C), (c)(4)-(d)(1), (d)(2)(A) and (d)(4) filed 12-11-2007; operative 4-9-2008 (Register 2007, No. 50).

5. Repealer filed 8-24-2015; operative 1-1-2016 (Register 2015, No. 35).

Ref.: Hanna §§ 35.31[1][a], [b], 35.81; Herlick Handbook §§ 1.01[3][b], 9.3, 14.3, 16.3.

§9813.1. Notice of Offer of Modified or Alternative Work. For Injuries Between January 1, 2004 and December 31, 2012, Inclusive.

Notice of Offer of Modified or Alternative Work. Within 30 days of the termination of temporary disability indemnity payments, the employer may offer, in the form and manner prescribed by section 10133.53 of these regulations, modified or alternative work accommodating the employee's work restrictions, lasting at least 12 months.

Note: Authority cited: Sections 59, 133, 138.3, 138.4, 4658.5 and 5307.3, Labor Code. Reference: Sections 124, 4658.1, 4658.5 and 4658.6, Labor Code.

History: 1. New section filed 12-11-2007; operative 4-9-2008 (Register 2007, No. 50).

2. Amendment of section heading and repealer of subsection (a) and subsection (b) designator filed 12-20-2012 as an emergency; operative 1-1-2013 pursuant to Government Code section 11346.1(d) (Register 2012, No. 51). A Certificate of Compliance must be transmitted to OAL by 7-1-2013 or emergency language will be repealed by operation of law on the following day.

3. Amendment of section heading and repealer of subsection (a) and subsection (b) designator refiled 6-26-2013 as an emergency; operative 7-1-2013 pursuant to Government Code section 11346.1(d) (Register 2013, No. 26). A Certificate of Compliance must be transmitted to OAL by 9-30-2013 or emergency language will be repealed by operation of law on the following day.

4. Certificate of Compliance as to 7-1-2013 order, including amendment of section heading, transmitted to OAL 9-27-2013 and filed 11-8-2013; amendments operative 1-1-2014 (Register 2013, No. 45).

Ref.: Hanna §§ 7.02[3][d][vi], 35.01, 35.110[1]; Herlick Handbook § 1.01[3][b].

§9813.2. Return to Work Notices. For Injuries Occurring on or After January 1, 2005.

Notice of Offer of Regular Work, Notice of Offer of Modified or Alternative Work. Within 60 calendar days from the date that the condition of an injured employee with permanent partial disability becomes permanent and stationary:

(a) If an employer does not serve the employee with a notice of offer of regular work, modified work or alternative work as set forth in section 10002, each payment of permanent partial disability remaining to be paid to the employee from the date of the end of the 60 day period shall be paid in accordance with Labor Code section 4658(d)(1) and increased by 15 percent.

(b) If an employer serves the employee with a notice of offer of regular work, modified work or alternative work as set forth in section 10002(b)(3) and (4), each payment of permanent partial disability remaining to be paid from the date the offer was served on the employee shall be paid in accordance with Labor Code section 4658(d)(1) and decreased by 15 percent, regardless of whether the employee accepts or rejects the offer.

(c) The employer shall use Form DWC-AD 10133.53 (Section 10133.53) to offer modified or alternative work, or Form DWC-AD 10003 (Section 10003) to offer regular work. The claims administrator may serve the offer of work on behalf of the employer.

Note: Authority cited: Sections 59, 133, 138.3, 138.4, 4658 and 5307.3, Labor Code. Reference: Sections 124, 4658 and 4658.1, Labor Code.

History: 1. New section filed 12-11-2007; operative 4-9-2008 (Register 2007, No. 50).

Ref.: Hanna §§ 7.02[3][d][vi], 35.110[1]; Herlick Handbook § 1.01[3][b].

§9814. Salary Continuation.

In relation to periods of temporary disability, where an employer provides salary or other payments in lieu of or in excess of temporary disability indemnity, the claims administrator or employer shall comply with the notice requirements of this article which apply to temporary disability. In addition, the claims administrator or employer shall include a full explanation of the salary continuation plan with the initial notice.

Note: Authority cited: Sections 59, 133, 138.4, 4637 and 5307.3, Labor Code. Reference: Sections 4650(a), 4650(c), 4650(d), 4650(g), 4800, 4804.1, 4806, 4850-4850.7, Labor Code; Sections 11651 and 11652, Insurance Code; Section 19871, Government Code; and Section 89529.03, Education Code.

History: 1. Amendment filed 7-11-89; operative 10-1-89 (Register 89, No. 28).

2. Amendment of section and Note filed 1-7-94; operative 1-7-94. Submitted to OAL for printing only pursuant to Government Code section 11351 (Register 94, No. 1).

3. Amendment of Note filed 8-24-2015; operative 1-1-2016 (Register 2015, No. 35).

Ref.: Hanna § 7.03[1]; Herlick Handbook §§ 1.01[3][b], 9.3, 14.3.

§9815. Corrected Notice.

If information in any notice, or the action taken as reflected in the notice, was incorrect or incomplete, the claims administrator shall provide the employee with a corrected notice within 14 days after knowledge of the error or omission. The notice shall be identified as a "Corrected Notice" and explain the nature and reason for the correction. Any additional benefits due as a result of the error or omission shall be paid or provided with the notice, if not previously provided.

Note: Authority cited: Sections 59, 133, 138.4, 4637 and 5307.3, Labor Code. Reference: Sections 138.4, 4061(a), 4061(b), 4061(d), 4637, 4641, 4643, 4644, 4650(a) through (d), 4661.5, 4700, 4701, 4702, 4703, 4703.5, 4903(a) and 5402, Labor Code; Sections 11651 and 11652, Insurance Code; Section 19871, Government Code; and Section 89529.03, Education Code.

History: 1. Amendment of section and Note filed 1-7-94; operative 1-7-94. Submitted to OAL for printing only pursuant to Government Code section 11351 (Register 94, No. 1).

2. Amendment of section and Note filed 8-24-2015; operative 1-1-2016 (Register 2015, No. 35).

Ref.: Hanna §§ 7.03[1], 32.07[4]; Herlick Handbook §§ 1.01[3][b], 9.3, 14.3, 16.3.

§9816. Enforcement of Reporting Requirements. [Repealed]

Note: Authority cited: Sections 138.3 and 138.4, Labor Code. Reference: Sections 138.3, 138.4 and 5453, Labor Code.

History: 1. Repealer filed 1-7-94; operative 1-7-94. Submitted to OAL for printing only pursuant to Government Code section 11351 (Register 94, No. 1).

§9817. Destruction of Records. [Repealed]

Note: Authority cited: Sections 138.3 and 138.4, Labor Code. Reference: Sections 138.4, 4650, 4651, 4700–4703 and 5402, Labor Code.

History: 1. Repealer filed 1-7-94; operative 1-7-94. Submitted to OAL for printing only pursuant to Government Code section 11351 (Register 94, No. 1).

ARTICLE 8.1
Workers' Compensation Advertising By Non-Attorneys and Non-Physicians; Prohibition of False or Misleading Advertising

§9820. Definitions.

As used in this article:

(a) Administrative Director. The Administrative Director of the Division of Workers' Compensation or the Director's duly authorized representative designee, or delegee.

(b) Advertisement. Any form of communication, in writing, photograph or picture, electronic broadcasting or transmission, that solicits any person to:

(1) file a workers' compensation claim, or,

(2) use any workers' compensation services as defined in subsection (k), or,

(3) engage or consult counsel or a medical care provider or clinic to consider a workers' compensation claim.

The form of advertisement may include, but is not limited to, advertising by newspaper, magazine, circular, form letter, publication, billboard, card, label, placard, transit advertisement, business card, envelope, book, list, directory, radio, motion picture, video, television, or electronic mail.

(c) Advertiser. Any person who sends, publishes, broadcasts, transmits or communicates an advertisement as defined in subsection (b); or who causes or pays in whole or in part for the sending, publishing, broadcasting, transmission or communication of such an advertisement either for himself or on behalf of another person. However, advertiser does not include the following persons if the person's principal business is other than providing workers' compensation services:

(1) a publisher, printer, distributor or circulator of a newspaper, magazine, book, or other writing;

(2) an operator of a broadcasting station, movie or video production company;

(3) an operator of premises where advertisements are displayed;

(4) a person while working as an employee of any persons exempted in paragraphs 1 through 3 of this subsection.

(d) Attorney. A person who holds a valid, active license to practice law in California at the time the advertisement governed by these regulations is published.

(e) False or misleading advertisement. An advertisement that:

(1) Is false or misleading pursuant to Labor Code Section 139.43(a) or 139.45(b).

(2) Violates any provision of Labor Code Section 5433.

(3) Offers or implies that the advertiser can or will dissuade, delay or impede a claimant from pursuing a legitimate work injury claim; or can or will provide false or inaccurate evidence or opinion in support of or in opposition to a work injury claim.

(4) Fails to include the notice as specified in Labor Code Section 5432 or Title 8 CCR Section 9823(b).

(5) Fails to comply with any requirement of this article.

(6) Is placed in furtherance of business operations conducted in violation of law, or when the advertiser has not complied with any requirement of this article.

(f) Him, Himself or His. These terms include "her", "herself" or "hers" when the person is female, and "it", "itself" or "its" when referring to an artificial person.

(g) Owner. A person who has a direct or indirect ownership interest in a business which provides workers' compensation services, or a person who has a direct or indirect claim to all or a portion of the income of a business which provides workers' compensation services.

(h) Person. Any natural or artificial person or combination of persons, including without limitation a corporation, partnership, trust, or unincorporated association.

(i) Physician. A person who holds a valid, active license to practice in California at the time the advertisement governed by these regulations is published, as any of the following medical practitioners: a medical or osteopathic physician and surgeon; a psychologist; a chiropractor; a podiatrist; a dentist; or an optometrist.

(j) Referral panelist. A person who will receive or has agreed to receive referrals of clients from a workers' compensation referral service.

(k) Workers' compensation services means services provided by any of the following:

(1) A workers' compensation medical or medical-legal provider, which means any person who provides medical treatment or evaluation of injuries or alleged injuries, including work injuries.

(2) A workers' compensation non-attorney advisor or representative, which means any person who is not an attorney who advises or represents persons in connection with injuries or alleged injuries, including work injuries.

(3) A workers' compensation referral service, which means any person who refers persons to medical or medical-legal providers, non-attorney advisors or representatives, or attorneys who advise or represent persons in connection with injuries or alleged injuries, including work injuries.

(4) A workers' compensation advertiser, which means any person who advertises or solicits for any or all of the preceding three categories of persons.

This definition includes persons who provide services for several types of injuries, as long as work injuries are included.

Note: Authority cited: Sections 59, 133, 139.43(b) and 5307.3, Labor Code. Reference: Sections 7, 139.43(a), (b), (d), 139.45 and 5430-5434, Labor Code.

History: 1. New article 8.1 and section filed 12-31-93; operative 1-1-94. Submitted to OAL for printing only pursuant to Government Code section 11351 (Register 93, No. 53).

2. Amendment of article 8.1 heading filed 8-7-95; operative 8-7-95. Submitted to OAL for printing only pursuant to Government Code section 11351 (Register 95, No. 32).

Ref.: Hanna § 1.23; Herlick Handbook §§ 1.01[3][b], 9.3, 9.18.

§9821. Coverage and Exclusions.

(a) This article does not apply to attorneys, as defined in Section 9820(d), or physicians, as defined in Section 9820(i). Nothing in this article shall be construed to obviate or lessen the obligations of attorneys or physicians under Labor Code Sections 5430 through 5434, or under other provisions of law. A person who was not licensed to practice in California at the time of the act or omission is not considered an attorney or physician under this article, and these regulations apply to such a person.

(b) This article does not apply to government agencies, labor organizations as defined in Labor Code Section 1117, charitable organizations, or non-profit tax-exempt bar associations whose primary business or purpose is other than providing workers' compensation services as defined in Section 9820(k), or to agents or employees of any of these exempt entities while acting for them.

(c) This article does apply to all other advertisers, as defined in Section 9820(c), even though an advertiser who is subject to this article may also be subject to attorney or physician workers' compensation advertising laws because the person advertises with or for an attorney or physician.

(d) The provisions of this article are not exclusive. The Administrative Director may use the remedies in this article and any other remedies provided by law.

(e) Any waiver of this article is void as against public policy.

(f) This article shall not be construed to authorize the unlawful practice of law or medicine by any person.

Note: Authority cited: Sections 59, 133, 139.43(b) and 5307.3, Labor Code. Reference: Sections 7, 139.43(a), (b), (d), 139.45 and 5430-5434, Labor Code.

History: 1. New section filed 12-31-93; operative 1-1-94. Submitted to OAL for printing only pursuant to Government Code section 11351 (Register 93, No. 53).

2. Amendment of subsection (a) filed 8-7-95; operative 8-7-95. Submitted to OAL for printing only pursuant to Government Code section 11351 (Register 95, No. 32).

Ref.: Hanna § 1.23; Herlick Handbook §§ 1.01[3][b], 9.3, 9.18.

§9822. Severability.

If any portion of this article, or the application of any part of it to any person or circumstance, is held to be invalid, the rest of the article and its application to any other person or circumstance remain valid.

Note: Authority cited: Sections 59, 133, 139.43(b) and 5307.3, Labor Code. Reference: Sections 7, 139.43(a), (b), (d), 139.45 and 5430-5434, Labor Code.

History: 1. New section filed 12-31-93; operative 1-1-94. Submitted to OAL for printing only pursuant to Government Code section 11351 (Register 93, No. 53).

Ref.: Herlick Handbook §§ 1.01[3][b], 9.3, 9.18.

§9823. General Workers' Compensation Advertising Rules.

All advertisements shall comply with the following rules:

(a) No advertisement shall be false or misleading.

(b) All advertisements shall include the written or spoken fraud notices, in the manner set forth in Labor Code Section 5432(a), (b).

(c) If an advertisement includes a testimonial, it must not overstate or distort the facts or results of the person's case, and must qualify the testimonial by stating immediately before or after it: (1) that each person's case is different and that the reader's or viewer's results will not necessarily be the same as the example; (2) in the case of a spoken or pictorial testimonial when the speaker is not relating his or her own experience, that the reader, model or performer is an actor and not the actual person involved in the case. The advertisement must give the qualifying information in a similar manner and with similar emphasis as the testimonial.

(d) The advertiser must identify himself either by his true legal name or by a fictitious business name that was duly filed under Division 7, Part 3, Chapter 5 of the Business & Professions Code before using the fictitious name in an advertisement, and which fictitious name filing had not expired at the time of the advertisement. However, no such advertised name shall violate subsection (e). Notwithstanding the general provisions of the fictitious business name law, an advertiser must file its fictitious business statement before using it in an advertisement.

(e) An advertisement for a person who is not a physician (as defined in Section 9820(i)) may not use the terms "medical", "physician", or "doctor"; nor a term describing a specific area of medical practice such as "surgeon", "osteopath", "psychologist", "chiropractor", "podiatrist", "dentist", "optometrist", etc.; nor their linguistic variants; nor any similar designation implying that the person is a physician; in the advertiser's name or to describe the advertiser's services. In addition, an advertisement for a person who is not licensed as a physician in the specific area of medical practice named in the advertisement may not include a term describing a specific area of medical practice. However, an advertisement for a medical referral service may use the terms as provided in Section 9828(a).

(f) An advertisement for a person who is not an attorney (as defined in Section 9820(d)) may not use the terms "legal", "attorney", "law firm", "law office", "law center", "counselor at law", "specialist in workers' compensation law"; nor their linguistic variants; nor any similar designation implying that the person is an attorney; in the advertiser's name nor to describe the advertiser's services. However, an advertisement for a legal referral service may use the terms as provided in Section 9828(b).

Note: Authority cited: Sections 59, 133, 139.43(b) and 5307.3, Labor Code. Reference: Sections 7, 139.43(a), (b), (d), 139.45 and 5430-5434, Labor Code.

History: 1. New section filed 12-31-93; operative 1-1-94. Submitted to OAL for printing only pursuant to Government Code section 11351 (Register 93, No. 53).

Ref.: Hanna § 1.23; Herlick Handbook §§ 1.01[3][b], 9.3, 9.18.

§9824. Identification as Representative.

An advertisement for a workers' compensation non-attorney advisor or representative shall identify the advertiser as a non-attorney as follows: *"The advertiser is a representative* [or *an advisor] who is not an attorney."* This notice shall be advertised in the same manner (size, typeface, display, etc.) required for the notice specified in Section 9823(b).

Note: Authority cited: Sections 59, 133, 139.43(b) and 5307.3, Labor Code. Reference: Sections 7, 139.43(a), (b), (d), 139.45 and 5430-5434, Labor Code.

History: 1. New section filed 12-31-93; operative 1-1-94. Submitted to OAL for printing only pursuant to Government Code section 11351 (Register 93, No. 53).

Ref.: Hanna § 1.23; Herlick Handbook §§ 1.01[3][b], 9.3, 9.18.

§9825. Representative's WCAB Qualification.

No person shall advertise as or on behalf of a non-attorney advisor or representative whose right to practice before the Workers' Compensation Appeals Board is suspended or revoked when the advertisement is published.

Note: Authority cited: Sections 59, 133, 139.43(b) and 5307.3, Labor Code. Reference: Sections 7, 139.43(a), (b), (d), 139.45 and 5430-5434, Labor Code.

History: 1. New section filed 12-31-93; operative 1-1-94. Submitted to OAL for printing only pursuant to Government Code section 11351 (Register 93, No. 53).

Ref.: Herlick Handbook §§ 1.01[3][b], 9.3, 9.18.

§9826. Advertisement by Unlicensed Attorney.

No person shall advertise as or on behalf of a non-attorney advisor or representative whose California license to practice law is suspended or revoked when the advertisement is published, without stating in the advertisement: *"The advertiser is a representative [*or *an advisor] whose* *license to practice law has been suspended [or revoked]."* This notice shall be advertised in the same manner (size, typeface, display, etc.) required for the notice specified in Section 9823(b). This section does not permit advertising by a person whose right to practice before the WCAB, as well as his license to practice law, is suspended or revoked.

Note: Authority cited: Sections 59, 133, 139.43(b) and 5307.3, Labor Code. Reference: Sections 7, 139.43(a), (b), (d), 139.45 and 5430-5434, Labor Code.

History: 1. New section filed 12-31-93; operative 1-1-94. Submitted to OAL for printing only pursuant to Government Code section 11351 (Register 93, No. 53).

Ref.: Hanna § 1.23; Herlick Handbook §§ 1.01[3][b], 9.3, 9.18.

§9827. Advertisement by Unlicensed Medical Provider.

No person shall advertise medical goods or services whose provision requires a license, by or on behalf of a person who does not hold a valid, active license to provide the goods or services when the advertisement is published.

Note: Authority cited: Sections 59, 133, 139.43(b) and 5307.3, Labor Code. Reference: Sections 7, 139.43(a), (b), (d), 139.45 and 5430-5434, Labor Code.

History: 1. New section filed 12-31-93; operative 1-1-94. Submitted to OAL for printing only pursuant to Government Code section 11351 (Register 93, No. 53).

Ref.: Herlick Handbook §§ 1.01[3][b], 9.3, 9.18.

§9828. Use of Terms "Medical", "Legal", or Comparable Terms.

An advertisement for workers' compensation referral services shall not use any of the following terms or their linguistic variants, nor any similar designation, in its name or to describe its services: (1) "medical", "physician", or "doctor"; (2) a term describing a specific area of medical practice such as "surgeon", "osteopath", "psychologist", "chiropractor", "podiatrist", "dentist", "surgeon", "optometrist", or the like; (3) "legal", "attorney", "law firm", "law office", "law center", "counselor at law", "specialist in workers' compensation law", except:

(a) An advertisement for a medical referral service may use the terms "medical referral" or "physician referral" if the service refers persons who respond to the advertisement only to physicians (as defined in Subsection 9820(i)). It may also use the term "medical referral" if it refers for goods or services by medical providers outside the fields of practice listed in subsection 9820(i), only to persons licensed to provide those other goods or services. It may use the term "referral" preceded by the name of a specific type of physician, such as "chiropractic referral", "podiatric referral", etc., if it restricts its referrals to physicians of the type named.

(b) An advertisement for a legal referral service may use the terms "legal referral" or "attorney referral" if the service refers persons who respond to the advertisement only to attorneys (as defined in Subsection 9820(d)).

Note: Authority cited: Sections 59, 133, 139.43(b) and 5307.3, Labor Code. Reference: Sections 7, 139.43(a), (b), (d), 139.45 and 5430-5434, Labor Code.

History: 1. New section filed 12-31-93; operative 1-1-94. Submitted to OAL for printing only pursuant to Government Code section 11351 (Register 93, No. 53).

Ref.: Herlick Handbook §§ 1.01[3][b], 9.3, 9.18.

§9829. Information Required from Referral Panelists.

Each advertiser of workers' compensation referral services shall require each medical, legal or non-attorney advisor or representative who will receive referrals from the referral service to supply the following information in writing, before receiving any referrals:

(a) In the case of all referral panelists, the information required by Section 9831.

(b) In the case of all referral panelists, an agreement that the panelist will inform the referral service in writing of any change in the information supplied, within 10 days of the change.

(c) In the case of an attorney, physician or other medical care referral panelist, the date the panelist was licensed to practice in California (if a license is required for that field of practice); that the license is then active and in good standing; and the panelist's specialty area of practice, if any, including the name of any specialty board or certification and date of that certification which the panelist holds.

(d) In the case of a non-attorney advisor or representative, a statement that the panelist is then entitled to appear before the Workers' Compensation Appeals Board.

Note: Authority cited: Sections 59, 133, 139.43(b) and 5307.3, Labor Code. Reference: Sections 7, 139.43(a), (b), (d), 139.45 and 5430-5434, Labor Code.

History: 1. New section filed 12-31-93; operative 1-1-94. Submitted to OAL for printing only pursuant to Government Code section 11351 (Register 93, No. 53).

Ref.: Herlick Handbook §§ 1.01[3][b], 9.3, 9.18.

§9830. Information Supplied to Referral Panelists.

Each advertiser of workers' compensation referral services shall give each referral panelist a copy of each advertisement it will use to refer clients to the panelist, on or before the date the advertisement is published. The advertiser shall notify the panelist in writing, with the copy of the advertisement, that the panelist may object to the advertiser's using that advertisement to attract or refer clients to the panelist. If a panelist notifies the service that (s)he objects to the advertisement, the service shall not refer any clients who respond to that advertisement to a panelist who objected to it.

The advertiser shall maintain written records of each objection to an advertisement, containing a copy of the advertisement, the identity of the panelist who objected to it, and the date of the objection. During the period any objection is in force to an advertisement then being published, the advertiser shall ask each respondent to identify the advertisement to which the person is responding, and shall not refer the respondent to any panelist who objected to that advertisement.

Note: Authority cited: Sections 59, 133, 139.43(b) and 5307.3, Labor Code. Reference: Sections 7, 139.43(a), (b), (d), 139.45 and 5430-5434, Labor Code.

History: 1. New section filed 12-31-93; operative 1-1-94. Submitted to OAL for printing only pursuant to Government Code section 11351 (Register 93, No. 53).

Ref.: Herlick Handbook §§ 1.01[3][b], 9.3, 9.18.

§9831. Registration Statement.

Every advertiser shall prepare, retain, and make available to the administrative director upon request a written registration statement. The information in the statement shall be verified by a declaration under penalty of perjury signed by the advertiser (if an individual), or by each owner of the advertiser (if a business entity). Whenever a material change occurs in the information in the statement, the advertiser shall within 10 days of the change revise the statement.

The statement shall contain the following information:

(a) The full legal name of the advertiser, and any other name(s) under which the person will advertise or do business.

(b) The advertiser's business form and place of organization; if the advertiser is a corporation, a copy of its articles of incorporation and bylaws and any amendments to them; if the advertiser is a partnership, a copy of the partnership agreement and any amendments to it; if the advertiser is an unincorporated organization a copy of its written organizational documents and any amendments to them; if the advertiser has filed or uses a fictitious business name, a copy of each fictitious business name statement showing the place(s) of filing.

(c) The complete street address or addresses of all locations at which the advertiser does or proposes to do business, and a designation of one such location in California as its principal place of business in the state.

(d) A listing of all telephone numbers to be used by the advertiser and the address where each telephone using each of these telephone numbers is located.

(e) The name of, and the office held by, the advertiser's officers, directors, trustees, general and limited partners, sole proprietor, and owners, as the case may be, and the names of those persons who have management responsibilities in connection with the advertiser's business activities.

(f) For each person whose name is disclosed under subdivision (e): the complete address of his principal residence; his driver's license number and state of issuance; and the number, licensing agency, and status of each professional license (s)he holds.

(g) A statement identifying any person disclosed under subdivision (e) who:

(1) has been convicted of or has pleaded guilty or no contest to a felony or misdemeanor violation of any offense related to workers' compensation, or of fraud, theft, embezzlement, fraudulent conversion, or misappropriation of property; or

(2) is or has been the subject of any civil or administrative action alleging acts in violation of any workers' compensation law, or of fraud, theft, embezzlement, fraudulent conversion, or misappropriation of property, or of the use of unfair, unlawful, or deceptive business practices.

The statement shall identify the person, court or administrative agency in which the case was filed, the case number, title of the case, and the result of the case.

Note: Authority cited: Sections 59, 133, 139.43(b) and 5307.3, Labor Code. Reference: Sections 7, 139.43(a), (b), (d), 139.45 and 5430-5434, Labor Code.

History: 1. New section filed 12-31-93; operative 1-1-94. Submitted to OAL for printing only pursuant to Government Code section 11351 (Register 93, No. 53).

Ref.: Hanna § 1.23; Herlick Handbook §§ 1.01[3][b], 9.3, 9.18.

§9832. Maintenance of and Access to Records.

Every advertiser shall maintain the following records, at its principal place of business in California, of its business of providing workers' compensation services:

(a) Complete financial records using generally accepted accounting principles, as defined by the American Institute of Certified Public Accountants and the Financial Standards Board.

(b) A copy of all of its workers' compensation advertisements (whether in print, video or audio media) published within the preceding two years. The records shall include a copy of the advertisement and the dates and places of each publication, including as applicable the name and city of publication of a periodical, or the station call letters and city location of any radio or television station.

(c) Its registration statement required by Section 9831.

(d) For workers' compensation referral services, a record of all objections to advertisements as required by Section 9830.

(e) For workers' compensation referral services, a single record listing all referral panelists, including each panelist's: (1) name; (2) address(es) at which (s)he will consult with clients; (3) profession, professional license number and state of issuance; (4) if the panelist works for a business, the name of the business and his status with it (owner, employee or independent contractor); (5) date (s)he became a panelist; and (6) the date (s)he ended the status as a panelist if applicable.

The service shall update the record to show any change in a panelist's status within 10 days of knowledge of the change. The record shall continue to list each panelist who ends his status as such, for two years after the person's status as a panelist ended.

(f) The advertiser shall maintain all records required by this section for at least two years after: (1) for advertisements, the date of its last publication; (2) for financial records, the end of the calendar year to which the records refer in whole or in part; (3) for registration statements or statement changes, the end of the calendar year to which the statement or change relates; (4) for objections to advertisements, the later of the date of the objection or the date the advertisement was last published; (5) for the combined listing of referral panelists required by Subsection (e) (in its current updated form), the date the service publishes its last advertisement.

(g) The advertiser shall make all records required by this section available for inspection and copying by any representative of the Department of Industrial Relations, the Department of Justice, or district or city attorney, during the advertiser's normal business hours but at least between 9:00 a.m. and 5:00 p.m. Monday through Friday (excepting holidays). In addition, if necessary in the judgment of the inspector to protect the integrity of an investigation, the advertiser shall allow, and an inspector may conduct or continue inspection and copying during other hours or days.

Note: Authority cited: Sections 59, 133, 139.43(b) and 5307.3, Labor Code. Reference: Sections 7, 139.43(a), (b), (d), 139.45 and 5430-5434, Labor Code; Sections 11180-11191, Government Code.

History: 1. New section filed 12-31-93; operative 1-1-94. Submitted to OAL for printing only pursuant to Government Code section 11351 (Register 93, No. 53).

Ref.: Hanna § 1.23; Herlick Handbook §§ 1.01[3][b], 9.3, 9.18.

§9833. Right to Conduct Investigation.

The Administrative Director may investigate any violation of this article, of the Workers' Compensation Truth in Advertising Act of 1992 (Labor Code §§5430 et seq.), of Section 139.43 of the Labor Code, or of any other provision of law now or hereafter enacted concerning workers' compensation advertising by persons other than attorneys or physicians. For this purpose (s)he may employ all rights and remedies possessed or delegated under Government Code §§11180 et seq.

Note: Authority cited: Sections 59, 133, 139.43(b) and 5307.3, Labor Code. Reference: Sections 7, 139.43(a), (b), (d), 139.45 and 5430-5434, Labor Code; and Sections 11180-11191, Government Code.

History: 1. New section filed 12-31-93; operative 1-1-94. Submitted to OAL for printing only pursuant to Government Code section 11351 (Register 93, No. 53).

Ref.: Herlick Handbook §§ 1.01[3][b], 9.3, 9.18.

§9834. Order to Produce Documents or Provide Information.

The Administrative Director may issue and serve on any advertiser, or the advertiser's employees or agents, an order requiring the advertiser, employee or agent to provide information, copies and access to any information related to workers' compensation advertising subject to regulation under this article. The advertiser, employee or agent shall comply with the order within the time specified in it. The Administrative Director may serve the order by any method reasonably calculated to give notice to the person served.

Note: Authority cited: Sections 59, 133, 139.43(b) and 5307.3, Labor Code. Reference: Sections 7, 133.49(a), (b), (d), 139.45 and 5430-5434, Labor Code; Sections 11180-11191, Government Code.

History: 1. New section filed 12-31-93; operative 1-1-94. Submitted to OAL for printing only pursuant to Government Code section 11351 (Register 93, No. 53).

2. Editorial correction of Note (Register 98, No. 46).

Ref.: Herlick Handbook §§ 1.01[3][b], 9.3, 9.18.

§9835. Compliance Orders.

(a) The Administrative Director may issue and serve on any advertiser, or the advertiser's employees or agents, a compliance order requiring the advertiser, employee or agent to cease and desist from committing any violation, or to comply with any requirement, of this article. The Administrative Director may serve the order by any method reasonably calculated to give notice to the person served.

(b) The Administrative Director's order may include, but is not limited to, the following provisions: (1) an order to stop using an advertisement or to use it only with specified modifications; (2) an order to advertise or otherwise disseminate corrective information, either by the advertiser at its expense, or by the Administrative Director at the advertiser's expense; (3) an order to pay the Administrative Director's investigation and enforcement costs.

(c) The advertiser, employee or agent shall comply with the order within the time specified in it.

Note: Authority cited: Sections 59, 133, 139.43(b) and 5307.3, Labor Code. Reference: Sections 7, 139.43(a), (b), (d), 139.45 and 5430-5434, Labor Code.

History: 1. New section filed 12-31-93; operative 1-1-94. Submitted to OAL for printing only pursuant to Government Code section 11351 (Register 93, No. 53).

Ref.: Herlick Handbook §§ 1.01[3][b], 9.3, 9.18.

§9836. Other Remedies; Cumulative Remedies.

The Administrative Director may institute civil proceedings against any person for violation of this article or of the statutes which may be investigated under this article, or may refer any violation for civil, criminal or professional disciplinary proceedings to the Attorney General, a district or city attorney, or other authorities having jurisdiction of the matter.

The Administrative Director's remedies in this article are cumulative and not exclusive, and the exercise of any or all of them is discretionary.

Note: Authority cited: Sections 59, 133, 139.43(b) and 5307.3, Labor Code. Reference: Sections 7, 139.43(a), (b), (d), 139.45 and 5430-5434, Labor Code.

History: 1. New section filed 12-31-93; operative 1-1-94. Submitted to OAL for printing only pursuant to Government Code section 11351 (Register 93, No. 53).

Ref.: Herlick Handbook §§ 9.3, 9.18.

§9837. Hearing.

(a) Any person aggrieved by an order issued under Sections 9834 or 9835 may request a hearing before the administrative director or an administrative law judge which shall be shall be held in accordance with the Administrative Procedure Act [Chapter 5, (commencing with Section 11500), of Part 1 of Division 3 of Title 2 of the Government Code], and the administrative director shall have all of the powers granted under that act.

Note: Authority cited: Sections 59, 133, 139.43(b) and 5307.3, Labor Code. Reference: Sections 7, 139.43(a), (b), (d), 139.45 and 5430-5434, Labor Code.

History: 1. New section filed 12-31-93; operative 1-1-94. Submitted to OAL for printing only pursuant to Government Code section 11351 (Register 93, No. 53).

Ref.: Herlick Handbook §§ 1.01[3][b], 9.3, 9.18.

ARTICLE 8.5
Employee Information

§9880. Written Notice to New Employees.

(a) Every employer shall provide to every new employee, either at the time of hire or by the end of the first pay period, the Written Notice to New Employees concerning the rights, benefits and obligations under worker's compensation law. The content of the notice must be approved by the Administrative Director.

(b) The notice shall be easily understandable. It shall be available in both English and Spanish where there are Spanish-speaking employees.

(c) The notice provided shall be in writing, in non-technical terms and shall include the following information:

(1) The name of the current compensation insurance carrier of the employer at the time of distribution, or when such is the fact, that the employer is self-insured, and who is responsible for claims adjustment;

(2) How to get emergency medical treatment, if needed;

(3) The kind of events, injuries and illnesses covered by workers' compensation;

(4) The injured employee's right to receive medical care;

(5) How to obtain appropriate medical care for a job injury;

(6) The role and function of the primary treating physician;

(7) The rights of the employee to select and change the treating physician pursuant to the provisions of Labor Code Sections 4600 to 4601, including the right to predesignate a personal physician or medical group;

(8) A form that the employee may use as an optional method for notifying the employer of the name of the employee's "personal physician," as defined by Labor Code Section 4600, or "personal chiropractor," as defined by Labor Code Section 4601;

(9) The rights of the employee to receive temporary disability indemnity, permanent disability indemnity, supplemental job displacement benefits, and death benefits, as appropriate;

(10) To whom the injuries should be reported;

(11) The existence of time limits for the employer to be notified of an occupational injury;

(12) The protections against discrimination provided pursuant to Section 132a;

(13) The location and telephone number of the nearest information and assistance officer, including an explanation of services available; and

(14) A description about Medical Provider Networks ("MPN") which includes that the employer may be using a MPN, what a MPN is, the predesignation exemption from the MPN, when an employee must begin to use a physician from the MPN, and how to request information about using a MPN.

Note: Authority cited: Sections 133, 138.3, 138.4, 3550, 3551, 4603.5 and 5307.3, Labor Code. Reference: Sections 132(a), 139.6, 3550, 3551, 3600, 4600, 4601, 4603, 4650, 4651, 4656, 4658.5, 4658.6, 4700, 4702, 4703, 5400 and 5401, Labor Code.

History: 1. New Article 8.5 (Sections 9880-9882) filed 1-28-76 as an emergency; effective upon filing (Register 76, No. 5).

2. Certificate of Compliance filed 1-29-76 (Register 76, No. 5).

3. Repealer and new section filed 11-9-77; effective thirtieth day thereafter (Register 77, No. 46).

4. Amendment filed 10-16-81; effective thirtieth day thereafter (Register 81, No. 42).

5. Editorial correction restoring Article 8.5 (Sections 9880-9883), which was inadvertently repealed by a 7-15-83 order (Register 83, No. 33).

6. Repealer and new section filed 7-11-89; operative 10-1-89 (Register 89, No. 28).

7. Amendment of section and Note filed 7-7-2004; operative 8-1-2004 pursuant to Government Code section 11343.4 (Register 2004, No. 28).

8. Amendment of subsections (c)(7), (c)(9) and (c)(12)-(13), new subsection (c)(14) and amendment of Note filed 8-9-2010; operative 10-8-2010 (Register 2010, No. 33).

Ref.: Hanna § 22.01[3]; Herlick Handbook §§ 1.01[3][b], 4.04[3], 9.3.

§9881. Posting of Notice to Employees.

(a) Every employer shall post and keep posted in a conspicuous location frequented by employees during the hours of the workday a Notice to Employees.

(b) The Notice to Employees poster shall be easily understandable. It shall be posted in both English and Spanish where there are Spanish-speaking employees.

(c) The Notice to Employees poster shall include the following information:

(1) The name of the current compensation insurance carrier of the employer, or when such is the fact, that the employer is self-insured, and who is responsible for claims adjustment.

(2) How to get emergency medical treatment, if needed.

(3) Emergency telephone number(s), for hospital, ambulance, police and firefighting services.

(4) The kinds of events, injuries and illnesses covered by workers' compensation.

(5) Advice that the employer may not be responsible for compensation because of an injury due to the employee's voluntary participation in any off-duty recreational, social, or athletic activity that is not a part of the employee's work-related duties.

(6) The injured employee's right to receive medical care.

(7) The rights of the employee to select and change the treating physician pursuant to the provisions of Labor Code Section 4600, including the right to predesignate a personal physician or medical group.

(8) The rights of the employee to receive temporary disability indemnity, permanent disability indemnity, supplemental job displacement benefits, and death benefits, as appropriate.

(9) To whom the injuries should be reported.

(10) The existence of time limits for the employer to be notified of an occupational injury.

(11) The protections against discrimination provided pursuant to Labor Code Section 132a.

(12) The location and telephone number of the nearest information and assistance officer.

(13) A description about Medical Provider Networks ("MPN") which includes what a MPN is, the predesignation exemption from the MPN, when an employee must begin to use a physician from the MPN, and how to request information about using a MPN. The MPN Contact telephone number, address and, if available, the MPN website address/URL shall be included. The effective date of MPN coverage for the MPN being used by the employer to cover current injuries shall also be stated if the employer is using an MPN.

(d) The employer may post the Administrative Director's approved Notice to Employee Poster provided in Section 9881.1. If the employer chooses not to use the Notice to Employee Poster provided in Section 9881.1, the employer may use a poster which meets the posting requirements of Labor Code Section 3550, includes the information required by this regulation, and has been approved by the Administrative Director.

Note: Authority cited: Sections 133, 138.3, 139.6, 3550, 4603.5 and 5307.3, Labor Code. Reference: Sections 132(a), 139.6, 3550, 3600, 4600, 4601, 4603, 4616, 4656, 4658.5, 4658.6, 5400 and 5401, Labor Code.

History: 1. Repealer and new section filed 7-11-89; operative 10-1-89 (Register 89, No. 28).

2. Amendment of section heading, section and Note filed 7-7-2004; operative 8-1-2004 pursuant to Government Code section 11343.4 (Register 2004, No. 28).

3. Amendment of subsections (c)(3) and (c)(7)-(8), new subsection (c)(13), redesignation of second subsection (c) as new subsection (d) and amendment of Note filed 8-9-2010; operative 10-8-2010 (Register 2010, No. 33).

Ref.: Hanna §§ 4.25[5], 22.01[3]; Herlick Handbook §§ 1.01[3][b], 8.7, 9.3.

§9881.1. Notice to Employees Poster.

[DWC Form 7 (Rev. 1/1/2016) Not Reproduced]

NOTE: Form is available at no charge by downloading from the web at www.dir.ca.gov/dwc/forms.html or by requesting at 1-800-794-6900.

Note: Authority cited: Sections 133, 138.3, 139.6, 3550, 4603.5 and 5307.3, Labor Code. Reference: Sections 132(a), 139.6, 3550, 4600, 4600.3, 4601, 4603, 4604.5, 4616, 4656, 4658.5, 4658.6, 5400, 5401 and 5402, Labor Code.

History: 1. New section filed 7-7-2004; operative 8-1-2004 pursuant to Government Code section 11343.4 (Register 2004, No. 28).

2. Amendment of section and Note filed 8-9-2010; operative 10-8-2010 (Register 2010, No. 33).

3. Repealer and new section filed 8-24-2015; operative 1-1-2016 (Register 2015, No. 35).

Ref.: Hanna § 22.01[3]; Herlick Handbook § 1.01[3][b].

§9882. Written Notice to Injured Employees; Pamphlet Contents. [Repealed]

Note: Authority cited: Sections 133, 138.3, 138.4, 139.6, and 5402, Labor Code. Reference: Sections 132(a), 139.5, 3600, 4600, 4601, 4650, 4658, 4700, 4701, 4702, 4703, 4401–4411 and 5400–5412, Labor Code.

History: 1. Repealer and new section filed 7-11-89; operative 10-1-89 (Register 89, No. 28).

2. Repealer filed 7-7-2004; operative 8-1-2004 pursuant to Government Code section 11343.4 (Register 2004, No. 28).

§9883. Publication of Information, Approval, Spanish Translation.

(a) Insurers, employers or private enterprises may prepare and publish for their use or sale the Notice to Employees poster and/or the Written Notice to New Employees required by this Article upon prior approval of the form and content by the Administrative Director. The Notice to Employees poster and/or Written Notice to New Employees may include a logotype. The addition only of a logotype to a previously approved Notice to Employees poster or Written Notice to New Employees does not require additional approval.

(1) Any published Written Notice to New Employees shall be available in English and Spanish and shall include the information specified in Section 9880.

(2) Any published Notice to Employees poster shall be available in English and Spanish, where there are Spanish-speaking employees, and shall include the information specified in Section 9881.

(b) All matter published subsequent to the effective date of this regulation shall indicate that the written informational material has been approved by the Administrative Director.

(c) Publications other than those of the Administrative Director or the Workers' Compensation Appeals Board may reflect the employer, private publisher or insurance carrier identifier or logotype.

Note: Authority cited: Sections 133, 139.6, 3550, 3551 and 5307, Labor Code. Reference: Sections 139.6, 3550 and 3551, Labor Code.

History: 1. New section filed 7-27-79; effective thirtieth day thereafter (Register 79, No. 30).

2. Change without regulatory effect of NOTE filed 7-11-86; effective upon filing (Register 86, No. 28).

3. Repealer and new section filed 7-11-89; operative 10-1-89 (Register 89, No. 28).

4. Amendment of section and Note filed 7-7-2004; operative 8-1-2004 pursuant to Government Code section 11343.4 (Register 2004, No. 28).

Ref.: Hanna § 22.01[3]; Herlick Handbook § 1.01[3][b].

§9884. Exceptions.

The requirements of this article shall not apply to injuries where the employee files an application for adjudication of claim with the appeals board.

Note: Authority cited: Sections 138.4, Labor Code. Reference: Section 5402, Labor Code.

History: 1. New section filed 7-11-89; operative 10-1-89 (Register 89, No. 28).

2. Editorial correction to History 1 (Register 96, No. 52).

Ref.: Hanna § 24.01[2]; Herlick Handbook § 1.01[3][b].

ARTICLE 9
Computation of Life Pensions, Tables For [Repealed]

History: 1. Repealer of article 9 (section 9885) and section filed 1-17-2001; operative 1-17-2001 pursuant to Government Code section 11343.4(c) (Register 2001, No. 3).

ARTICLE 10
Employee Death, Notice of

§9900. Employer.

(a) Each employer shall notify the Administrative Director of the death of every employee, regardless of the cause of death, except where the employer has actual knowledge or notice that the deceased employee left a surviving minor child.

(b) Notification shall be made on the Division of Industrial Accidents Form 510, "Notice of Employee Death" (See Section 9910).

(c) The Notice of Employee Death shall be filed within 60 days of the employer's notice or knowledge of the employee death.

(d) The employer may forward the "Notice of Employee Death" to his workmens' compensation insurer for subsequent submission to the Administrative Director.

Note: Authority cited: Sections 133, 138.2, 138.3, 139.5, 139.6, 4603.2, 4603.5, 5307.1, 5307.3 and 5450–5455, Labor Code.

History: 1. Amendment of subsection (a) filed 11-9-77; effective thirtieth day thereafter (Register 77, No. 46) For prior history, see Register 73, No. 28.

Ref.: Hanna §§ 23.14[2][e], 25.20[6]; Herlick Handbook §§ 1.01[3][b], 7.18.

§9905. Notice.

If the Notice required in Section 9900 is incomplete or otherwise deficient, the Administrative Director may require a further explanation or additional information from the employer, or his insurance carrier.

Ref.: Hanna § 25.20[6]; Herlick Handbook § 1.01[3][b].

§9910. DIA Form 510: Notice of Employee Death.

[DIA Form 510 (Rev. 9/1984) Not Reproduced]

NOTE: Form is available at no charge by downloading from the web at www.dir.ca.gov/dwc/forms.html or by requesting at 1-800-794-6900.

History: 1. Amendment filed 7-11-73 as an emergency; effective upon filing. Certificate of Compliance included (Register 73, No. 28).

2. Amendment filed 11-9-77; effective thirtieth day thereafter (Register 77, No. 46).

3. Repealer and new section filed 8-29-84; effective thirtieth day thereafter (Register 84, No. 35).

Ref.: Herlick Handbook § 1.01[3][b].

§9914. Reproduction of Form 510, Notice of Employee Death.

(a) Employers and insurers may reproduce DIA Form 510, in which the heading may be rearranged to permit printing of:

(1) The insurance carrier's or employer's name, address and telephone number.

(2) Instructions for forwarding the form and number of copies required.

(b) The spacing, arrangement, sequence or language shall not otherwise be altered.

History: 1. Amendment filed 7-11-73 as an emergency; effective upon filing. Certificate of Compliance included (Register 73, No. 28).

Ref.: Hanna § 25.20[6]; Herlick Handbook § 1.01[3][b].

§9918. Service on Administrative Director.

The Notice of Employee Death, DIA Form 510, shall be mailed to the Administrative Director, Division of Industrial Accidents, P.O. Box 422400, San Francisco, California 94142.

This P.O. Box is to be used only for the notices required in Section 9900 and not for any other functions of the Administrative Director or Division of Industrial Accidents.

Ref.: Hanna § 25.20[6]; Herlick Handbook § 1.01[3][b].

ARTICLE 10.5
Operation of the Information and Assistance Program of the Division of Workers' Compensation

§9920. Authority. [Repealed]

Note: Authority cited: Sections 127, 133, 138.2, 138.3, 139.5, 139.6, 4603.2, 4603.5, 5307.1, 5307.3, 5451-5454, Labor Code.

History: 1. New Article 10.5 (Sections 9920-9929) filed 11-9-77; effective thirtieth day thereafter (Register 77, No. 46).

2. Repealer filed 10-16-81; effective thirtieth day thereafter (Register 81, No. 42).

3. Amendment of Article 10.5 heading filed 2-16-95; operative 2-16-95. Submitted to OAL for printing only pursuant to Government Code section 11351 (Register 95, No. 7).

§9921. Operative Date.

The provisions of this Article are effective immediately upon adoption.

Ref.: Herlick Handbook § 1.01[3][b].

§9922. Purpose.

This Article is being adopted to implement Section 139.6 and Article 2.5 of Part 4 of Division 4 of the Labor Code by providing that the State, through the Division of Workers' Compensation, establish an affirmative impartial service to employees, employers, claims administrators, labor unions, medical providers, and all others subject to or interested in the workers' compensation laws of the State of California. This service shall be provided so that all such parties are informed of the provisions of the workers' compensation laws, that benefits due are paid promptly, that disputes and misunderstandings are resolved informally insofar as possible, and that premature and unnecessary litigation be minimized.

Note: Authority cited: Sections 133, 139.6, 5307.3 and 5450, Labor Code. Reference: Sections 5450-5455, Labor Code.

History: 1. Amendment filed 2-16-95; operative 2-16-95. Submitted to OAL for printing only pursuant to Government Code section 11351 (Register 95, No. 7).

Ref.: Hanna §§ 1.12[11], [14], 23.03[1]; Herlick Handbook §§ 1.01[3][b], 1.06.

§9923. Designation.

(a) Pursuant to Labor Code Section 139.6, the Administrative Director shall appoint a person or persons thoroughly familiar with the Workers' Compensation Program in California to be responsible for informing the general public, labor unions, employees, employers, claims administrators, medical providers and all other interested parties of the rights, benefits and obligations of the workers' compensation law, including the creation and existence of the Information and Assistance Program.

(b) In each district office of the Division of Workers' Compensation (Workers' Compensation Appeals Board) and at the Division headquarters the Administrative Director shall appoint an Information and Assistance Officer, and such Deputy Information and Assistance Officers as the work of the district office and headquarters may require. The Administrative Director shall provide office facilities and clerical support appropriate to the functions of such Information and Assistance Officer.

Note: Authority cited: Sections 133, 139.6, 5307.3 and 5450, Labor Code. Reference: Sections 5450-5455, Labor Code.

History: 1. Amendment filed 2-16-95; operative 2-16-95. Submitted to OAL for printing only pursuant to Government Code section 11351 (Register 95, No. 7).

Ref.: Hanna §§ 1.12[11], 23.03[1]; Herlick Handbook §§ 1.01[3][b], 1.06.

§9924. Scope of Duties.

Each Information and Assistance Officer shall be responsible for the performance of the following duties:

(a) Provide continuing information concerning the rights, benefits and obligations under the workers' compensation laws of the State of California to employees, employers, medical providers, claims administrators and other interested parties.

(b) Assist in the prompt resolution of misunderstandings, disputes, and controversies arising out of claims for compensation, without formal proceedings, to the end that full and timely compensation benefits are furnished.

(c) Distribute such information pamphlets in English, Spanish and other languages as needed that have been prepared and approved by the Administrative Director to all inquiring employees and to such other parties that may request copies of the same.

(d) Establish and maintain liaison with the persons located in the geographic area served by the district office, with other affected State agencies, with organizations representing employees, employers, claims administrators and the medical community.

(e) Discharge such other duties consistent with the purposes of this Article as from time to time may be delegated by the Administrative Director.

Note: Authority cited: Sections 133, 139.6, 5307.3 and 5451, Labor Code. Reference: Sections 5450-5455, Labor Code.

History: 1. Amendment of subsections (a), (c) and (d) filed 2-16-95; operative 2-16-95. Submitted to OAL for printing only pursuant to Government Code section 11351 (Register 95, No. 7).

Ref.: Hanna §§ 1.12[11], [14], 23.03[1]; Herlick Handbook §§ 1.01[3][b], 1.06.

§9925. Use of Other Division Facilities.

In undertaking his or her duties, the Information and Assistance Officer may use the services of the Industrial Medical Council, the Disability Evaluation Unit, the Rehabilitation Unit, the Audit Unit and any other unit or units of the Division of Workers' Compensation available to aid in the resolution of disputes.

Copies of medical reports, permanent disability rating evaluations, earnings data and other pertinent information obtained by the Information and Assistance Officer shall be furnished to all parties involved in a dispute.

Note: Authority cited: Sections 133, 136.6, 5307.3 and 5451, Labor Code. Reference: Sections 5450-5455, Labor Code.

History: 1. Amendment filed 2-16-95; operative 2-16-95. Submitted to OAL for printing only pursuant to Government Code section 11351 (Register 95, No. 7).

Ref.: Hanna § 23.03[2][c]; Herlick Handbook §§ 1.01[3][b], 1.06.

§9926. Referrals to a Qualified Medical Evaluator.

Upon the submission of a matter to an Information and Assistance Officer, the Officer, with the agreement of a party to pay the cost and with the consent of an unrepresented employee, may request that the Administrative Director direct the injured employee to be examined by a Qualified Medical Evaluator selected by the Medical Director, within the scope of the qualified medical evaluator's professional training, for the purpose of addressing any pertinent clinical question other than those issues specified in Labor Code Section 4061.

Note: Authority cited: Sections 133, 139.6, 5307.3, 5451 and 5703.5(b), Labor Code. Reference: Sections 5450-5455, Labor Code.

History: 1. Amendment of section heading and section filed 2-16-95; operative 2-16-95. Submitted to OAL for printing only pursuant to Government Code section 11351 (Register 95, No. 7).

Ref.: Hanna §§ 1.12[2][a], 22.07[4], 23.03[2][c]; Herlick Handbook §§ 1.01[3][b], 1.06.

§9927. Jurisdiction.

(a) Any party to a claim may consult with an Information and Assistance Officer at any time to seek advice and assistance in the resolution of any misunderstanding, dispute, or controversy. The request for assistance need not be in writing, or be in any particular form, but it shall apprise the Information and Assistance Officer of the nature of the dispute and any other pertinent information to facilitate an appropriate inquiry by the Information and Assistance Officer. The Information and Assistance Officer shall communicate with the parties and provide information and assistance in resolving disputes.

(b) If an Application for Adjudication of Claim has been filed with the Workers' Compensation Appeals Board, any party may consult with an Information and Assistance Officer to seek assistance in resolving controverted issues or misunderstandings at any time prior to the filing of a Declaration of Readiness to Proceed. If the employee is not represented or by consent of the parties, the Information and Assistance Officer may continue to provide assistance after a filing of a Declaration of Readiness to Proceed.

(c) The Information and Assistance Officer shall provide assistance to asbestos workers in obtaining benefits from the Asbestos Workers' Account and/or the responsible employer pursuant to Section 4410 of the Labor Code.

(d) When the injured worker is not represented by an attorney or other representative, and either a Compromise and Release agreement or Stipulations with Request for Award, other than those presented at or subsequent to a regularly scheduled hearing, has been filed with the Workers' Compensation Appeals Board, the information and assistance officer shall: review the documents; contact the parties when indicated; coordinate with other units within the Division of Workers' Compensation; seek to determine that the employee is aware of the significance of the agreement; and make recommendations to the parties and the workers' compensation judge. The Manager of the Information and Assistance Unit shall notify the Presiding Workers' Compensation Judge when this service cannot be provided timely.

Note: Authority cited: Sections 133, 139.6 and 5307.3, Labor Code. Reference: Sections 5450–5455, Labor Code.

History: 1. Amendment filed 10-16-81; effective thirtieth day thereafter (Register 81, No. 42).

2. Amendment filed 7-15-83; effective thirtieth day thereafter (Register 83, No. 30).

3. Editorial correction of 7-15-83 order redesignating effective date to 8-1-83 pursuant to Government Code Section 11346.2(d) filed 7-19-83 (Register 83, No. 30).

4. Repealer of subsection (d), subsection relettering and amendment of newly designated subsection (d) filed 2-16-95; operative 2-16-95. Submitted to OAL for printing only pursuant to Government Code section 11351 (Register 95, No. 7).

Ref.: Hanna §§ 1.12[11], [12][b], [13], 23.03[2][b], [3]; Herlick Handbook §§ 1.01[3][b], 1.06.

§9928. Procedures for Mediation and Recommendations.

(a) The Information and Assistance Officer is not bound by technical or formal rules of procedure but may make inquiries into any matter referred to him or her in a manner best suited to protect the rights of all parties and to achieve substantial justice.

(b) When there is a dispute regarding the provision of workers' compensation benefits, the employee, claims administrator or any party may request the Information and Assistance Officer to mediate the dispute. The Information and Assistance Officer will attempt to resolve the dispute by mediation, which may include a conference. The officer shall make appropriate inquiries to determine the contentions of the parties, identify the matters which may prevent amicable resolution, and afford all parties an opportunity to present their positions.

(c) In the event a dispute is not resolved through mediation, the Information and Assistance Officer shall issue a recommendation as soon as possible.

(d) In order to toll the statutes of limitations pursuant to Section 5454 of the Labor Code, the Information and Assistance Officer must notify in writing all parties to any misunderstanding, dispute or controversy of the fact that said Information and Assistance Officer has taken under consideration the misunderstanding, dispute or controversy submitted to him or her for a recommendation.

(e) Upon issuing a recommendation, the Officer shall advise the parties of his or her recommendation in a written communication which describes in non-technical terms the nature of the differences, the proposed resolution and the rationale used in arriving at that resolution. The communication shall also advise the parties that the tolling of any applicable statute of limitations will cease 60 days after the issuance of the recommendation, and shall further advise the parties of their right to obtain a decision from the appeals board if the recommendation is not accepted by the parties. In the event a party does not accept the recommendation of the Information and Assistance Officer, the party must notify all other parties in writing within 30 days of receipt of the recommendation. Where the Information and Assistance Officer feels that further mediation may resolve the dispute, he or she will notify the parties of the availability of the Information and Assistance Officer to provide such further mediation.

Note: Authority cited: Sections 133, 139.6, 5307.3, 5451 and 5453, Labor Code. Reference: Sections 5450-5455, Labor Code.

History: 1. Amendment of section heading and subsections (b), (c) and (e) filed 2-16-95; operative 2-16-95. Submitted to OAL for printing only pursuant to Government Code section 11351 (Register 95, No. 7).

Ref.: Hanna §§ 1.12[12][a], [c], 23.03[2][d]; Herlick Handbook §§ 1.01[3][b], 1.06.

§9928.1. Procedures for Asbestos Workers.

When consulted by an asbestos worker or his/her representative, the Information and Assistance Officer shall aid the worker in procuring those records, reports and other information which are necessary for the identification of responsible employers and insurance carriers, and in obtaining information required by the Asbestos Workers' Account before payments may be made pursuant to Section 4406.

Note: Authority cited: Sections 5307.3 and 5451, Labor Code. Reference: Sections 139.6, 4410 and 5451, Labor Code.

History: 1. New section filed 10-16-81; effective thirtieth day thereafter (Register 81, No. 42).

Ref.: Hanna §§ 1.12[13], 23.03[3]; Herlick Handbook §§ 1.01[3][b], 1.06.

§9929. Costs.

(a) Except as otherwise provided by this Section or by Section 5452 of the Labor Code, no fees or costs shall be charged to any party for services provided by the Division of Industrial Accidents under this Article.

(b) If the employee is represented, such representative may request that the Information and Assistance Officer refer the matter to a Workers' Compensation Judge for the determination of the value of the services of such representative. The Information and Assistance Officer shall, thereafter, refer such request to the Presiding Judge of the office which has jurisdiction over the claim.

Ref.: Hanna §§ 1.12[11], 20.02[2][d], 23.03[2][e]; Herlick Handbook §§ 1.01[3][b], 1.06.

ARTICLE 12
Document Copy and Electronic Transaction Fees

§9980. Definitions.

As used in this article:

(a) "Authorization" means a release signed and dated by the injured worker, or the injured worker's representative if the injured worker is a minor or an incompetent or is deceased, to obtain records which states the specific uses and limitations on the types of information to be disclosed, the name of the person or entity that may disclose the information, the name of the person or entity authorized to receive the information, a specific date after which the provider is no longer authorized to disclose the information, and advises the person signing the authorization of the right to receive a copy of the authorization.

(b) "Copy and related services" means all services and expenses that are related to the retrieval and copying of documents that are responsive to a duly issued subpoena or authorization to release documents for a workers' compensation claim.

(c) "Claims administrator" means the person or entity responsible for the payment of compensation for any of the following: a self-administered insurer providing security for the payment of compensation required by Divisions 4 and 4.5 of the Labor Code, a self-administered self-insured employer, the administrator of the Uninsured Employers Benefits Trust Fund (UEBTF), the administrator of the Subsequent Injuries Benefits Trust Fund (SIBTF), a third-party claims administrator for a self-insured employer, insurer, legally uninsured employer, joint powers authority, the Self-Insurers' Security Fund, or the California Insurance Guarantee Association (CIGA) .

(d) "Custodian of records" means the person who has physical custody and control of the books, records, documents or physical evidence and maintains them in the ordinary course of business.

(e) "Set of records" means records or documents that have been recorded in paper, electronic, film, digital, or other format from one custodian of records under one subpoena or authorization.

(f) "Professional photocopier" is defined by section 22450 of the Business and Professions Code.

Note: Authority cited: Section 5307.9, Labor Code. Reference: Section 5307.9, Labor Code.

History: 1. Renumbering of former article 11 to article 12 and new section filed 4-30-2015; operative 7-1-2015 (Register 2015, No. 18). For prior history of article 12 (sections 10001-10021), see Register 2008, No. 47.

Ref.: Hanna § 23.13[1]; Herlick Handbook §§ 4.17[2], 14.42.

§9981. Bills for Copy Services.

(a) This article applies to services provided on and after the effective date of this article regardless of date of injury.

(b) Bills for copy services must specify services provided and include the provider tax identification number and professional photocopier registration number, county of registration, date of billing, case information including employee name, claim number, case number (if applicable), source information including type of records, date of service, description of services, and the number of pages produced.

(1) Bills for records may include billing codes. WC 020 is for Flat Fee of $180, WC 021 is for Cancelled Service of $75, WC 022 is for Certificate of No Record of $75, WC 023 is for Per Page Fee of .10 per page, WC 024 is for records from the Employment Development Department (EDD) of $20, WC 025 is for records from the Workers' Compensation Insurance Rating Bureau of $30, WC 026 is for an Additional Electronic Set of $5, WC 027 is for an Additional Electronic Set of $30, WC 028 is for Duplication of X-Ray or scan of $10.26, WC 029 is for CD of X-rays and scans of $3.

(2) Each bill for services must include a statement that there was no violation of Labor Code section 139.32 with respect to the services described.

Note: Authority cited: Section 5307.9, Labor Code. Reference: Section 5307.9, Labor Code, Section 22462, Business and Professions Code.

History: 1. New section filed 4-30-2015; operative 7-1-2015 (Register 2015, No. 18).

Ref.: Hanna § 23.13[1]; Herlick Handbook §§ 4.17[2], 14.42.

§9982. Allowable Services.

(a) This fee schedule covers copy and related services for records relevant to an injured worker's claim, except services under a contract between the employer and the copy service provider.

(b) If the claims administrator fails to serve records in the employer's or insurer's possession requested by an injured worker or his or her representative within the time frames set forth in Labor Code section 5307.9 or fails to serve a copy of any subsequently-received medical report or medical-legal report within the timeframes set forth in section 10608, this fee schedule applies to obtaining those records.

(c) If the claims administrator fails to provide written notice, pursuant to Labor Code section 4055.2, to the injured worker of records which they are seeking by subpoena, this fee schedule applies to obtaining those records.

(d) There will be no payment for copy and related services that are:

(1) Provided within 30 days of a written request by an injured worker or his or her authorized representative to an employer, claims administrator, or workers' compensation insurer for copies of records in the employer's, claims administrator's, or workers' compensation insurer's possession that are relevant to the employee's claim,

(2) Provided by any person or entity which is not a registered professional photocopier.

(e) The claims administrator is not liable for payment of:

(1) Records previously obtained by subpoena or authorization by the same party and served from the same source, unless the subpoena or authorization is accompanied by a declaration from the party requesting the records setting forth good cause to seek duplicate records.

(A) If there is good cause, the claims administrator is liable for payment. Good cause includes new counsel seeking duplicate records for review, and loss or destruction of records due to natural disaster.

(2) Summaries, tabulations, or for indexing of documents.

(3) Subpoenaed records obtainable from the Workers' Compensation Insurance Rating Bureau, and the Employment Development Department that can be obtained without a subpoena at lower cost.

Note: Authority cited: Section 5307.9, Labor Code. Reference: Section 2019.030, Code of Civil Procedure; and Section 5307.9, Labor Code.

History: 1. New section filed 4-30-2015; operative 7-1-2015 (Register 2015, No. 18).

Ref.: Herlick Handbook §§ 4.17[2], 14.42.

§9983. Fees for Copy and Related Services.

The reasonable maximum fees, not including sales tax, payable for copy and related services are as follows:

(a) A $180 flat fee for a set of records, from a single custodian of records, which includes, but is not limited to mileage, postage, pickup and delivery, phone calls, repeat visits to the record source and records locators, page numbering, witness fees for delivery of records, check fees, fees for release of information services, service of the subpoena, shipping and handling, and subpoena preparation.

(b) $75 in the event of cancellation after a subpoena or request for records by authorization has been issued but before records are produced, or for a certificate of no records.

(c) $20 for records obtained from the Employment Development Department.

(d) $30 for records obtained from the Workers' Compensation Insurance Rating Bureau.

(e) Release of information services of witness costs for the retrieval and return of physical records held offsite by a third party are included in the flat fee. Disputes over the production of records may be resolved by filing a petition with the Workers' Compensation Appeals Board or by filing a petition with the superior court pursuant to Labor Code section 132. Release of information services of witness costs for retrieval and return of physical records held offsite by a third party are governed by Evidence Code Section 1563.

(f) In addition to the flat fee, the following separate fees apply:

(1) Ten cents ($.10) per page for copies above 500 pages.

(2) $5.00 for each additional set of records in electronic form ordered within 30 days of the subpoena, or $30 if ordered after 30 days and the copy is retained by the registered photocopier. If the injured worker requests an additional set of records in electronic form ordered within 30 days of the subpoena , the claims administrator is liable for one additional set of records in electronic form for no more than $5.00 for the additional set of records if ordered within 30 days and for no more than $30 if ordered after 30 days and the copy is retained by the registered photocopier. All other additional sets of records are payable by the party ordering the additional set.

(3) X-rays and scans are to be paid at $10.26 per sheet, and $3 per CD of X-rays and scans.

Note: Authority cited: Section 5307.9, Labor Code. Reference: Section 5307.9, Labor Code; and Section 1563, Evidence Code.

History: 1. New section filed 4-30-2015; operative 7-1-2015 (Register 2015, No. 18).

Ref.: Hanna § 23.13[1]; Herlick Handbook §§ 4.17[2], 14.42.

§9990. Division Fees for Transcripts; Copies of Documents; Certifications; Case File Inspection; Electronic Transactions.

The Division will charge and collect fees for copies of records or documents. For the purposes of this section, "records" includes any writing containing information relating to the conduct of the public's business which is prepared, owned, or used by the Division, regardless of the physical form or characteristics. "Writing" means handwriting, typewriting, printing, photostatting, photographing and every other means of recording any form of communication thereof, and all papers, maps, magnetic tapes, photographic films and prints, electronic facsimiles, any form of stored computer data, magnetic cards or disks, drums, and other documents.

Fees will be charged and collected by the Division as follows:

(a) For copies of papers, records or documents, not certified or otherwise authenticated, one dollar ($1.00) for the first copy and twenty cents ($0.20) for each additional copy of the same page, except to the injured worker to whom the fee will be ten cents ($.10) per page.

(1) State sales tax and postage will be added to this fee.

(b) For certification of copies of official records or documents and orders of evidence taken or proceedings had, ten dollars ($10.00) for each certification.

(1) Where the Division is requested to both copy and certify a document, the fee is the sum of the fees prescribed in (a) and (b) above.

(c) For paper transcripts of any proceeding of record, $100 to order transcripts of 33 pages or less, for transcripts over 33 pages,

(1) An additional charge of three dollars ($3.00) for each page over 33, and for each page of additional copies of the transcript, $1.50 per page, both to be paid prior to the release of the transcripts.

(2) Sales tax and postage will be added to this fee.

(3) Transcripts delivered on a medium other than paper shall be compensated at the same rate set for paper transcripts, except an additional fee shall be charged to cover the cost of the medium and any copies thereof.

(d) For inspection of a case file not stored in the place where the inspection is requested, ten dollars ($10.00) plus any postage or other delivery costs, except when requested by an injured employee or his or her attorney or his or her representative of record.

(e) For electronic records maintained by the Division:

(1) Listing of WCAB new case filings is $85.00 per complete download for WCAB new case opening records transmitted to the requester by direct electronic download.

Paper copies of the WCAB new case opening records provided in addition to the electronic data will be subject to a separate charge of $0.10 per page, plus postage.

(2) Electronic response to an electronic inquiry concerning a case's status, a lien's status, or other case specific information available in electronic form, through EDEX (the Division's Electronic Data Exchange program), twenty cents ($0.20) per transaction.

(3) The Division will provide electronic copies of WCAB new case opening records or EDEX access only pursuant to a written agreement with the administrative director.

(4) Copies of existing electronic records, other than those electronic records set forth in subsections (e)(1) or (e)(2), that constitute disclosable public records, will be provided as required by law, for the Division's actual costs of retrieving and transmitting the data, including staff research, downloading redaction and transfer to storage media time, programming and processing time, storage media, postage or shipping costs and sales tax. All staff

research, downloading redaction and transfer, programming and processing time required to create new data sorts of existing electronically maintained records will be charged at the Division's standard rate of $85.00 per hour, billed in fifteen (15) minute increments.

(f) Copies of Division records containing information that is privileged or otherwise non-disclosable will be redacted before release.

Note: Authority cited: Sections 127, 133, 138.7 and 5307.3, Labor Code. Reference: Sections 127 and 138.7, Labor Code.

History: 1. Amendment of subsection (a) filed 11-7-78; effective thirtieth day thereafter (Register 78, No. 45). For former history, see Registers 77, No. 46; 75, No. 32; and 73, No. 51.

2. Amendment filed 8-29-84; effective thirtieth day thereafter (Register 84, No. 35).

3. Amendment of article and section headings and text filed 1-28-94; operative 1-28-94 (Register 94, No. 4). Submitted to OAL for printing only pursuant to Government Code section 11351.

4. Amendment of section and Note filed 8-22-2000; operative 9-21-2000 (Register 2000, No. 34).

5. Amendment of section heading and subsection (c), new subsection (c)(1), subsection renumbering, amendment of subsection (e)(1), repealer of subsections (e)(1)(A)-(B) and amendment of subsection (e)(4) filed 4-30-2015; operative 7-1-2015 (Register 2015, No. 18).

Ref.: Hanna §§ 23.13[1], 34.21[2]; Herlick Handbook §§ 1.01[3][b], 4.17[2], 14.42.

§9991. Payment of Fees in Advance to the Division.

Payment of fees in Section 9990 must accompany the request, either in cash or by check or money order made payable to the Division of Workers' Compensation, except as otherwise provided in the establishment of payment accounts.

Note: Authority cited: Sections 127, 133 and 5307.3, Labor Code. Reference: Section 127, Labor Code.

History: 1. Renumbering of former section 9992 to new section 9991, including amendment of section heading, filed 4-30-2015; operative 7-1-2015 (Register 2015, No. 18).

Ref.: Hanna §§ 1.12[5][b], 23.13[1]; Herlick Handbook § 1.01[3][b].

§9992. Payment of Fees in Advance. [Renumbered]

Note: Authority cited: Sections 127, 133 and 5307.3, Labor Code. Reference: Section 127, Labor Code.

History: 1. Amendment filed 1-28-94; operative 1-28-94 (Register 94, No. 4). Submitted to OAL for printing only pursuant to Government Code section 11351.

2. Renumbering of former section 9992 to section 9991 filed 4-30-2015; operative 7-1-2015 (Register 2015, No. 18).

§9994. Payment for Transcripts. [Repealed]

Note: Authority cited: Sections 127, 133 and 5307.3, Labor Code. Reference: Section 127, Labor Code.

History: 1. Amendment of section heading and text filed 1-28-94; operative 1-28-94 (Register 94, No. 4). Submitted to OAL for printing only pursuant to Government Code section 11351.

2. Repealer filed 4-30-2015; operative 7-1-2015 (Register 2015, No. 18).

ARTICLE 12
Return to Work

§10001. Definitions. [Renumbered]

Note: Authority cited: Sections 133, 139.48 and 5307.3, Labor Code. Reference: Sections 139.48 and 4658.1, Labor Code; *Henry v. WCAB* (1998) 68 Cal.App.4th 981.

History: 1. New section filed 6-30-2006; operative 7-1-2006. Submitted to OAL for filing with the Secretary of State and printing only pursuant to Government Code section 11340.9(g) (Register 2006, No. 38). For prior history, see Register 96, No. 52.

2. Renumbering of former section 10001 to section 10116.9 filed 11-17-2008; operative 11-17-2008 pursuant to Government Code section 11343.4 (Register 2008, No. 47).

§10002. Offer of Work; Adjustment of Permanent Disability Payments. [Renumbered]

Note: Authority cited: Sections 133, 139.48 and 5307.3, Labor Code. Reference: Sections 139.48 and 4658, Labor Code; *Del Taco v. WCAB* (2000) 79 Cal.App.4th 1437; *Anzelde v. WCAB* (1996) 61 Cal. Comp. Cases 1458 (Writ denied); and *Henry v. WCAB* (1998) 68 Cal.App.4th 981.

History: 1. New section filed 6-30-2006; operative 7-1-2006. Submitted to OAL for filing with the Secretary of State and printing only pursuant to Government Code section 11340.9(g) (Register 2006, No. 38). For prior history, see Register 96, No. 52.

2. Renumbering of former section 10002 to section 10117 filed 11-17-2008; operative 11-17-2008 pursuant to Government Code section 11343.4 (Register 2008, No. 47).

§10003. Form [DWC AD 10003 Notice of Offer of Work]. [Renumbered]

Note: Authority cited: Sections 133, 139.48 and 5307.3, Labor Code. Reference: Sections 139.48 and 4658, Labor Code.

History: 1. New section filed 6-30-2006; operative 7-1-2006. Submitted to OAL for filing with the Secretary of State and printing only pursuant to Government Code section 11340.9(g) (Register 2006, No. 38). For prior history, see Register 96, No. 52.

2. Renumbering of former section 10003 to section 10118 filed 11-17-2008; operative 11-17-2008 pursuant to Government Code section 11343.4 (Register 2008, No. 47).

§10004. Return to Work Program. [Renumbered]

Note: Authority cited: Sections 133, 139.48 and 5307.3, Labor Code. Reference: Sections 62.5, 139.48 and 5814.6, Labor Code.

History: 1. New article 12 (sections 10004-10005) and section filed 7-19-2006; operative 8-18-2006 (Register 2006, No. 29). For prior history of article 12 (sections 10001-10021), see Register 88, No. 21; Register 95, No. 7 and Register 96, No. 52.

2. Renumbering of former section 10004 to section 10119 filed 11-17-2008; operative 11-17-2008 pursuant to Government Code section 11343.4 (Register 2008, No. 47).

§10005. Form [DWC AD 10005 Request for Reimbursement of Accommodation Expenses]. [Renumbered]

Note: Authority cited: Sections 133, 139.48 and 5307.3, Labor Code. Reference: Sections 62.5, 139.48 and 5814.6, Labor Code.

History: 1. New section filed 7-19-2006; operative 8-18-2006 (Register 2006, No. 29). For prior history, see Register 96, No. 52.

2. Renumbering of former section 10005 to section 10120 filed 11-17-2008; operative 11-17-2008 pursuant to Government Code section 11343.4 (Register 2008, No. 47).

§10006. Notice to Employee. [Repealed]

Note: Authority cited: Sections 133, 138.4, 139.5 and 5307.3, Labor Code. Reference: Chapter 1435, 1974 Stats.

History: 1. Repealer and new section filed 5-17-88; operative 7-1-88 (Register 88, No. 21). For prior history, see Register 83, No. 30.

2. Repealer of section filed 12-27-96; operative 12-27-96. Submitted to OAL for printing only pursuant to Government Code section 11351 (Register 96, No. 52).

§10007. Reports to Bureau. [Repealed]

Note: Authority cited: Sections 133, 138.4, 139.5 and 5307.3, Labor Code. Reference: Chapter 1435, 1974 Stats.

History: 1. Repealer and new section filed 5-17-88; operative 7-1-88 (Register 88, No. 21). For prior history, see Register 83, No. 30.

2. Repealer of section filed 12-27-96; operative 12-27-96. Submitted to OAL for printing only pursuant to Government Code section 11351 (Register 96, No. 52).

§10007.1. Entitlement Issues. [Repealed]

Note: Authority cited: Section 139.5, Labor Code. Reference: Section 133, Labor Code.

History: 1. New section filed 6-15-81; effective thirtieth day thereafter (Register 81, No. 25).

2. Repealer filed 5-17-88; operative 7-1-88 (Register 88, No. 21).

§10008. Identification of Need for Vocational Rehabilitation Services. [Repealed]

Note: Authority cited: Sections 133, 138.4, 139.5 and 5307.3, Labor Code. Reference: Chapter 1435, 1974 Stats.

History: 1. Repealer and new section filed 5-17-88; operative 7-1-88 (Register 88, No. 21). For prior history, see Register 83, No. 30.

2. Repealer of section filed 12-27-96; operative 12-27-96. Submitted to OAL for printing only pursuant to Government Code section 11351 (Register 96, No. 52).

§10009. Initiation of Vocational Rehabilitation Services. [Repealed]

Note: Authority cited: Sections 133, 138.4, 139.5 and 5307.3, Labor Code. Reference: Chapter 1435, 1974 Stats.

History: 1. Repealer and new section filed 5-17-88; operative 7-1-88 (Register 88, No. 21). For prior history, see Register 79, No. 30.

2. Repealer of section filed 12-27-96; operative 12-27-96. Submitted to OAL for printing only pursuant to Government Code section 11351 (Register 96, No. 52).

§10010. Independent Vocational Evaluators. [Repealed]

Note: Authority cited: Sections 133, 138.4, 139.5 and 5307.3, Labor Code. Reference: Chapter 1435, 1974 Stats.

History: 1. Repealer and new section filed 5-17-88; operative 7-1-88 (Register 88, No. 21). For prior history, see Register 75, No. 1.

2. Repealer of section filed 12-27-96; operative 12-27-96. Submitted to OAL for printing only pursuant to Government Code section 11351 (Register 96, No. 52).

§10011. Vocational Rehabilitation Plans. [Repealed]

Note: Authority cited: Sections 133, 138.4, 139.5 and 5307.3, Labor Code. Reference: Chapter 1435, 1974 Stats.

History: 1. Repealer and new section filed 5-17-88; operative 7-1-88 (Register 88, No. 21). For prior history, see Register 83, No. 30.

2. Repealer of section filed 12-27-96; operative 12-27-96. Submitted to OAL for printing only pursuant to Government Code section 11351 (Register 96, No. 52).

§10012. Plan Approval. [Repealed]

Note: Authority cited: Sections 133, 138.4, 139.5 and 5307.3, Labor Code. Reference: Chapter 1435, 1974 Stats.

History: 1. Repealer and new section filed 5-17-88; operative 7-1-88 (Register 88, No. 21). For prior history, see Register 79, No. 30.

2. Repealer of section filed 12-27-96; operative 12-27-96. Submitted to OAL for printing only pursuant to Government Code section 11351 (Register 96, No. 52).

§10013. Entitlement Issues. [Repealed]

Note: Authority cited: Sections 133, 138.4, 139.5 and 5307.3, Labor Code. Reference: Chapter 1435, 1974 Stats.

History: 1. Repealer and new section filed 5-17-88; operative 7-1-88 (Register 88, No. 21). For prior history, see Register 83, No. 30.

2. Repealer of section filed 12-27-96; operative 12-27-96. Submitted to OAL for printing only pursuant to Government Code section 11351 (Register 96, No. 52).

§10014. Bureau Resolution of Disputes. [Repealed]

Note: Authority cited: Sections 133, 138.4, 139.5 and 5307.3, Labor Code. Reference: Chapter 1435, 1974 Stats.

History: 1. Repealer and new section filed 5-17-88; operative 7-1-88 (Register 88, No. 21). For prior history, see Register 79, No. 30. (c)

2. Repealer of section filed 12-27-96; operative 12-27-96. Submitted to OAL for printing only pursuant to Government Code section 11351 (Register 96, No. 52).

§10015. Interruption of Services. [Repealed]

Note: Authority cited: Sections 133, 138.4, 139.5 and 5307.3, Labor Code. Reference: Chapter 1435, 1974 Stats.

History: 1. Repealer and new section filed 5-17-88; operative 7-1-88 (Register 88, No. 21). For prior history, see Register 83, No. 30.

2. Repealer of section filed 12-27-96; operative 12-27-96. Submitted to OAL for printing only pursuant to Government Code section 11351 (Register 96, No. 52).

§10016. Conclusion of Vocational Rehabilitation Services. [Repealed]

Note: Authority cited: Sections 133, 138.4, 139.5 and 5307.3, Labor Code. Reference: Chapter 1435, 1974 Stats.

History: 1. Repealer and new section filed 5-17-88; operative 7-1-88 (Register 88, No. 21). For prior history, see Register 83, No. 30.

2. Repealer of section filed 12-27-96; operative 12-27-96. Submitted to OAL for printing only pursuant to Government Code section 11351 (Register 96, No. 52).

§10017. Reinstatement of Vocational Rehabilitation Benefits. [Repealed]

Note: Authority cited: Sections 133, 138.4, 139.5 and 5307.3, Labor Code. Reference: Chapter 1435, 1974 Stats.

History: 1. Repealer and new section filed 5-17-88; operative 7-1-88 (Register 88, No. 21). For prior history, see Register 83, No. 30.

2. Repealer of section filed 12-27-96; operative 12-27-96. Submitted to OAL for printing only pursuant to Government Code section 11351 (Register 96, No. 52).

§10018. Vocational Rehabilitation Temporary Disability Indemnity. [Repealed]

Note: Authority cited Sections 133, 138.4, 139.5 and 5307.3, Labor Code. Reference: Chapter 1435, 1974 Stats.

History: 1. New section filed 5-17-88; operative 7-1-88 (Register 88, No. 21).

2. Repealer of section filed 12-27-96; operative 12-27-96. Submitted to OAL for printing only pursuant to Government Code section 11351 (Register 96, No. 52).

§10019. Bureau File Retention. [Renumbered]

Note: Authority cited: Sections 133, 138.4, 139.5 and 5307.3, Labor Code. Reference: Chapter 1435, 1974 Stats.

History: 1. New section filed 5-17-88; operative 7-1-88 (Register 88, No. 21).

2. Renumbering and amendment of former section 10019 to section 10134 filed 2-16-95; operative 2-16-95. Submitted to OAL for printing only pursuant to Government Code §11351 (Register 95, No. 7).

§10020. Enforcement of Notice and Reporting Requirements. [Repealed]

Note: Authority cited: Sections 133, 138.4, 139.5 and 5307.3, Labor Code. Reference: Chapter 1435, 1974 Stats.

History: 1. New section filed 5-17-88; operative 7-1-88 (Register 88, No. 21).

2. Repealer of section filed 12-27-96; operative 12-27-96. Submitted to OAL for printing only pursuant to Government Code section 11351 (Register 96, No. 52).

§10021. Rehabilitation of Industrially Injured Inmates. [Renumbered]

Note: Authority cited: Sections 133, 138.4, 139.5 and 5307.3, Labor Code. Reference: Chapter 1435, 1974 Stats.

History: 1. New section filed 5-17-88; operative 7-1-88 (Register 88, No. 21).

2. Renumbering of former section 10021 to new section 10133.4 filed 12-27-96; operative 12-27-96. Submitted to OAL for printing only pursuant to Government Code section 11351 (Register 96, No. 52).

SUBCHAPTER 1.5
INJURIES ON OR AFTER JANUARY 1, 1990

ARTICLE 1
Audit, General Definitions

§10100. Definitions—Prior to January 1, 1994.

The following definitions apply in Articles 1 through 7 of this Subchapter for injuries occurring on or after January 1, 1990 and before January 1, 1994.

(a) Adjusting Location. The office where claims are administered.

(b) Administrative Director. The Administrative Director of the Division of Workers' Compensation or his/her duly authorized representative.

(c) Audit. Any audit performed by the Audit Unit of the Division of Workers' Compensation pursuant to Labor Code Sections 129 and 129.5.

(d) Claims Administrator. A self-administered insurer providing security for the payment of compensation required by Divisions 4 and 4.5 of the Labor Code, a self-administered self-insured employer, or a third-party claims administrator for a self-insured employer, insurer, legally uninsured employer, or joint powers authority.

(e) Claim File. A record, either in legible paper or electronic form which can be produced into legible paper, containing all of the information specified in Section 10101 and related documents pertaining to a given work-injury claim.

(f) Claim Log. A handwritten or printed ledger maintained by the claims administrator listing each work injury case by the date the injury was reported to the claims administrator and listing the date of injury. The claim log contents are specified in Section 10103.

(g) Compensation. Compensation as defined in Labor Code Section 3207.

(h) Duly Authorized Representative. A designated employee or unit of the Department of Industrial Relations.

(i) DWC. The Division of Workers' Compensation of the Department of Industrial Relations.

(j) Employee. An employee, his or her dependents or his agent.

(k) Indemnity Case. A work-injury claim which has or may result in any of the following benefits:

(1) Temporary Disability

(2) Permanent Disability

(3) Life Pension

(4) Death Benefits

(5) Vocational Rehabilitation

(*l*) Insurer. Any company, group or entity in, or which has been in, the business of transacting workers' compensation insurance for employers subject to the workers' compensation laws of this state. The term insurer includes the State Compensation Insurance Fund.

(m) Investigation. The process of examining and evaluating a claim to determine the nature and extent of all legally required benefits, if any, which are due under the claim. Investigation may include formal or informal methods of gathering information relevant to evaluating the claim such as: obtaining employment records, obtaining earnings records, informal or formal interviews of the employee, employer, or witnesses, deposition of parties or witnesses, obtaining expert opinion where an issue requires an expert opinion for its resolution, such as obtaining a medical-legal evaluation.

(n) Issue Date. The date upon which a notice of penalty assessment or an order of the Administrative Director is served.

(o) Joint Powers Authority. Any county, city, city and county, municipal corporation, public district, public agency, or political subdivision of the state, but not the state itself, including in a pooling arrangement under a joint exercise of powers agreement for the purpose of securing a certificate of consent to self-insure workers' compensation claims under Labor Code Section 3700(c).

(p) Medical-Only Claim. A work-injury case which requires compensation only for medical treatment by a physician.

(q) Medical Fee Schedule. Official schedule promulgated by the Administrative Director pursuant to Labor Code Section 5307.1. Refer to Title 8 of existing CCR Section 9791.1 through Section 9792.

(r) Non-Random. Any method of selecting an audit subject which is specific to that audit subject, based on any or all of the factors provided in Labor Code Section 129(b).

(s) Notice of Compensation Due. The Notice of Assessment issued pursuant to Labor Code Section 129(c).

(t) Open Claim. A work-injury claim in which future payment of compensation may be due or for which reserves for the future payment of compensation are maintained.

(u) Payment Schedule. The two-week cycle of indemnity payments due on the day designated with the first payment as required by Labor Code Section 4650(c) or 4702(b).

(v) Random. Any method of selecting an audit subject which is not based on factors specific to that audit subject, but instead which chooses subjects from a broad cross-section of possible subjects. Random selection methods may stratify by general groups and need not be statistically precise.

(w) Self-insured Employer. An employer that has been issued a certificate of consent to self-insure as provided by Labor Code Section 3700(b) or (c), including a joint powers authority or the State of California as a legally uninsured employer.

(x) Third-Party Administrator. An agent under contract to administer the workers' compensation claims of an insurer, self-insured employer, or joint powers authority.

(y) VRMA. Vocational rehabilitation maintenance allowance.

(z) Work-Injury Claim. A claim for an injury that is reported or reportable to the Division of Labor Statistics and Research pursuant to Sections 6409, 6409.1 and 6413 of the Labor Code.

Note: Authority cited: Sections 59, 133, 129.5, 138.4 and 5307.3, Labor Code. Reference: Sections 7, 124, 129, 129.5, 3700, 3702.1, 4636, 4650(c), 5307.1 and 5402, Labor Code.

History: 1. New section filed 1-18-90; operative 1-18-90 (Register 90, No. 4). New section is exempt from review by OAL pursuant to Government Code Section 11351.

2. Amendment of section heading, text and Note filed 1-28-94; operative 1-28-94. Submitted to OAL for printing only pursuant to Government Code section 11351 (Register 94, No. 4).

Ref.: Hanna § 10.50[2][b]; Herlick Handbook §§ 1.01[3][b], 9.5.

§10100.1. Definitions—On or After January 1, 1994.

The following definitions apply in Articles 1 through 7 of this Subchapter for injuries occurring on or after January 1, 1994.

(a) Adjusting Location. The office where claims are administered.

(b) Administrative Director. The Administrative Director of the Division of Workers' Compensation or the Director's duly authorized representative, designee, or delegee.

(c) Audit. An audit performed under Labor Code Sections 129 and 129.5.

(d) Audit Subject. A single adjusting location of a claims administrator which has been selected for audit. If a claims administrator has more than one adjusting location, other locations may be selected as separate audit subjects. In its discretion, the Audit Unit may combine more than one adjusting location of a claims administrator as a single non-random audit subject.

(e) Audit Unit. The organizational unit within the Division of Workers' Compensation which audits insurers, self-insured employers and third-party administrators pursuant to Labor Code Sections 129 and 129.5.

(f) Claim. A request for compensation for an injury arising out of and in the course of employment, whether disputed or not, or notice or knowledge that such an injury has occurred or is alleged to have occurred.

(g) Claim File. A record in paper or electronic form, or a combination, containing all of the information specified in Section 10101.1 of these Regulations and all documents or entries related to the provision or denial of benefits.

(h) Claim Log. A handwritten or printed ledger maintained by the claims administrator listing each work-injury claim as specified in Section 10103.1 of these Regulations.

(i) Claims Administrator or Administrator. A self-administered workers' compensation insurer, a self-administered self-insured employer, a self-administered legally uninsured employer, a self-administered joint powers authority, or a third-party claims administrator for an insurer, a self-insured employer, a legally-uninsured employer or a joint powers authority.

(j) Closed Claim. A work-injury claim in which future payment of compensation cannot be reasonably expected to be due.

(k) Compensation. Every benefit or payment, including vocational rehabilitation, medical, and medical-legal expenses, conferred by Divisions 1 and 4 of the Labor Code on an injured employee or the employee's dependents.

(*l*) Date of Knowledge of Injury and Disability. The date the employer had knowledge or reasonably can be expected to have had knowledge of (1) a worker's injury or claim for injury, and (2) the worker's inability or claimed inability to work because of the injury.

(m) Denied Claim. A claim for which all liability has been denied at any time, even if the claim was accepted before or after the denial. A claim which otherwise meets this definition is a denied claim even if medical-legal expenses were paid.

(n) Employee. An employee, or in the case of the employee's death, his or her dependent, as each is defined in Division 4 of the Labor Code, or the employee's or dependent's agent.

(o) First Payment of Temporary Disability Indemnity. (1) The first payment of temporary disability indemnity made to an injured worker for a work injury; or (2) the first resumed payment of temporary disability indemnity following any period of one or more days for which no temporary disability indemnity was payable for that work injury; or (3) the first resumed payment of temporary disability indemnity following issuance of a lawful notice that temporary disability benefits were ending.

(p) Indemnity Claim. A work-injury claim which has resulted or may result in entitlement to any of the following benefits: temporary disability indemnity or salary continuation in lieu of temporary disability indemnity, permanent disability indemnity, death benefits, or vocational rehabilitation.

(q) Insurer. Any company, group, or entity in, or which has been in, the business of transacting workers' compensation insurance for employers subject to the workers' compensation laws of this state. The term insurer includes the State Compensation Insurance Fund.

(r) Investigation. The process of examining and evaluating a claim to determine the nature and extent of all legally required benefits, if any, which are due under the claim. Investigation may include formal or informal methods of gathering information relevant to evaluating the claim such as: obtaining employment records; obtaining earnings records; informal or formal interviews of the employee, employer, or witnesses; deposition of parties or witnesses; obtaining expert opinion where an issue requires an expert opinion for its resolution, such as obtaining a medical-legal evaluation.

(s) Joint Powers Authority. Any county, city, city and county, municipal corporation, public district, public agency, or political subdivision of the state, but not the state itself, included in a pooling arrangement under a joint exercise of powers agreement for the purpose of securing a certificate of consent to self-insure workers' compensation claims under Labor Code Section 3700(c).

(t) Medical-Only Claim. A work-injury claim in which no indemnity benefits are payable.

(u) Non-Random. Any method of selecting an audit subject which is specific to that audit subject, based on any or all of the factors provided in Labor Code Section 129(b).

(v) Notice of Compensation Due. The Notice of Assessment issued pursuant to Labor Code Section 129(c).

(w) Open Claim. A work-injury claim in which future payment of compensation may be due or for which reserves for the future payment of compensation are maintained.

(x) Payment Schedule. Either:

(1) The two-week cycle of indemnity payments due on the day designated with the first payment as required by Labor Code Section 4650(c) or 4702(b), including any lawfully changed payment schedule; or

(2) The two-week cycle of payments of vocational rehabilitation maintenance allowance (VRMA) required by Title 8, California Code of Regulations, Division 1, Chapter 4.5, Subchapter 1.5, Article 7, Section 10125.1.

(y) Random. Any method of selecting an audit subject which is not based on factors specific to that audit subject, but instead which chooses subjects from a broad cross-section of possible subjects. Random selection methods may stratify by general groups and need not be statistically precise.

(z) Record of Payment. An accurate written or electronic record of all compensation payments in a claim file, including but not limited to:

(1) The check number, date the check was issued, name of the payee, amount, and for indemnity payments the time period(s) covered by the payment;

(2) All dates for which salary continuation as defined by Labor Code Section 4650(g) was provided instead of direct indemnity payments; the dates for which salary continuation was authorized; and documentation when applicable that sick leave or other leave credits were restored for any periods for which salary continuation was payable;

(3) A copy of each bill received which included a medical progress or work status report; and either a copy of each other bill received or documentation of the contents of that bill showing the date and description of the service provided, provider's name, amount billed, date the claims administrator received the bill, and date and amount paid.

(aa) Self-insured Employer. An employer, either as an individual employer or as a group of employers, that has been issued a certificate of consent to self-insure as provided by Labor Code Section 3700(b) or (c), including a joint powers authority or the State of California as a legally uninsured employer.

(bb) Third-Party Administrator. An agent under contract to administer the workers' compensation claims of an insurer, self-insured employer, or joint powers authority.

(cc) VRMA. Vocational rehabilitation maintenance allowance.

Note: Authority cited: Sections 59, 133, 129.5, 138.4, 5307.3, Labor Code. Reference: Sections 7, 124(a), 129(a), (b), (c), 129.5(a), (b), 3700, 3702.1, 4636, 4650(c), 5307.1, 5402, Labor Code.

History: 1. New section filed 1-28-94; operative 1-28-94. Submitted to OAL for printing only pursuant to Government Code section 11351 (Register 94, No. 4).

2. Amendment of subsection (i) filed 2-14-96; operative 2-14-96. Submitted to OAL for printing only pursuant to Government Code section 11351 (Register 96, No. 7).

3. Editorial correction of subsection (d) (Register 2000, No. 45).

Ref.: Hanna § 10.50[2][a]; Herlick Handbook §§ 1.01[3][b], 9.5.

§10100.2. Definitions.

The following definitions apply in Articles 1 through 7 of this Subchapter for audits conducted on or after January 1, 2003.

(a) Adjusting Location. The office where claims are administered. Separate underwriting companies, self-administered, self-insured employers, and/or third-party administrators operating at one location shall be combined as one audit subject for the purposes of audits conducted pursuant to Labor Code section 129(b) only if claims are administered under the same local management at that location.

For auditing purposes, any separate office or location whose staff includes local management may be considered a single adjusting location.

(b) Additional claim file. A claim selected for audit in addition to the random sample of claims selected. An additional claim file may include a companion claim file, a file selected for audit because it was incorrectly designated on the claim log, or a claim chosen based on criteria relevant to a target audit but for which no specific complaint has been received.

(c) Administrative Director. The Administrative Director of the Division of Workers' Compensation or the Director's duly authorized representative, designee, or delegee.

(d) Audit. An audit performed under Labor Code sections 129 and 129.5.

(e) Audit Subject. A single adjusting location of a claims administrator which has been selected for audit. If a claims administrator has more than one adjusting location, other locations shall be considered as separate audit subjects for the purposes of implementing Labor Code sections 129(a) and 129(b). However, the Audit Unit at its discretion may combine more than one adjusting location of a claims administrator as a single targeted audit subject, or may designate one insurer, insurer group, or self-insured employer at one or more third-party administrator adjusting locations as a single targeted audit subject.

(f) Audit Unit. The organizational unit within the Division of Workers' Compensation which audits and/or investigates insurers, self-insured employers and third-party administrators pursuant to Labor Code sections 129 and 129.5.

(g) Carve-Out Program.

(1) An alternative dispute resolution (ADR) system for employees and employers engaged in construction (or other enumerated activities), established pursuant to Labor Code section 3201.5.

(2) An alternative dispute resolution (ADR) system for any industry (other than construction), established pursuant to Labor Code section 3201.7.

(h) Claim. A request for compensation, or record of an occurrence in which compensation reasonably would be expected to be payable for an injury arising out of and in the course of employment.

(i) Claim File. A record in paper or electronic form, or a combination, containing all of the information specified in California Code of Regulations, title 8, section 10101.1 and all documents or entries related to the provision, delay, or denial of benefits.

(j) Claim Log. A handwritten, printed, or electronically maintained listing maintained by the claims administrator listing each work-injury claim as specified in California Code of Regulations, title 8, section 10103.2.

(k) Claims Administrator or Administrator. A self-administered workers' compensation insurer, a self-administered self-insured employer, a self-administered legally uninsured employer, a self-administered joint powers authority, or a third-party claims administrator for an insurer, a self-insured employer, a legally-uninsured employer or a joint powers authority.

(*l*) Closed Claim. A work-injury claim in which future payment of compensation cannot be reasonably expected to be due.

(m) Companion claim file. A claim file that is related to a claim file selected for random or targeted audit, in that claims were filed by the same injured worker, and the Audit Unit cannot ascertain the extent to which benefits have been paid on the initial claim selected for audit without auditing the related claim file.

(n) Compensation. Every benefit or payment, including vocational rehabilitation, supplemental job displacement benefits, medical treatment, and medical-legal expenses, conferred by Divisions 1 and 4 of the Labor Code on an injured employee or the employee's dependents.

(o) Complaint claim file. A claim file that is selected for audit because the Audit Unit has received information indicating the existence of possible claims handling violations of the kind which, if found, would be subject to the assessment of an administrative penalty, the issuance of a notice of compensation due, or the assessment of a civil penalty.

(p) Date of Knowledge of Injury and Disability. The date the employer had knowledge or reasonably can be expected to have had knowledge, pursuant to Labor Code section 5402, of (1) a worker's injury or claim for injury, and (2) the worker's inability or claimed inability to work because of the injury.

(q) Denied Claim. A claim for which all liability has been denied at any time, even if the claim was accepted before or after the denial. A claim which otherwise meets this definition is a denied claim even if medical treatment is provided and paid pursuant to Labor Code section 5402(c) or medical-legal expenses were paid.

(r) Employee. An employee, or in the case of the employee's death, his or her dependent, as each is defined in Division 4 of the Labor Code, or the employee's or dependent's agent.

(s) First Payment of Permanent Disability Indemnity. (1) The first payment of permanent disability indemnity made to an injured worker for a work injury; or (2) the resumed payment of permanent disability indemnity following any period of one or more days for which no permanent disability indemnity was payable for that work injury; or (3) the resumed payment of permanent disability indemnity following issuance of a lawful notice that permanent disability benefits were ending.

(t) First Payment of Temporary Disability Indemnity. (1) The first payment of temporary disability indemnity made to an injured worker for a work injury; or (2) the resumed payment of temporary disability indemnity following any period of one or more days for which no temporary disability indemnity was payable for that work injury; or (3) the resumed payment of temporary disability indemnity following issuance of a lawful notice that temporary disability benefits were ending.

(u) First Payment of Vocational Rehabilitation Maintenance Allowance. (1) The first payment of Vocational Rehabilitation Maintenance Allowance made to an injured worker for a work injury; or (2) the resumed payment of Vocational Rehabilitation Maintenance Allowance following any period of one or more days for which no Vocational Rehabilitation Maintenance Allowance was payable for that work injury; or (3) the resumed payment of Vocational Rehabilitation Maintenance Allowance following issuance of a lawful notice that Vocational Rehabilitation Maintenance Allowance benefits were ending.

(v) Frequency. The ratio of the number of claim files with one or more of a specific type of violation divided by the number of claim files with exposure for the same specific type of violation selected for audit at the adjusting location.

(w) General Business Practice. For the purposes of Labor Code section 129.5(e), conduct that can be distinguished by a reasonable person from an isolated event. The conduct can include a single practice and/or separate, discrete acts or omissions in the handling of several claims.

(x) Indemnity Claim. A work-injury claim that has resulted in the payment of any of the following benefits: temporary disability indemnity, including temporary partial disability indemity, or salary continuation in lieu of temporary disability indemnity, permanent disability indemnity, death benefits, or vocational rehabilitation maintenance allowance.

(y) Indemnity Payment. Compensation for any of the following benefits: temporary disability indemnity, including temporary partial disability indemnity, or salary continuation in lieu of temporary disability indemnity, permanent disability indemnity, death benefits, or vocational rehabilitation maintenance allowance. An indemnity payment includes any increase made pursuant to Labor Code section 4650(d), and any interest pursuant to Labor Code section 5800.

(z) Insurer. Any company, group, or entity in, or which has been in, the business of transacting workers' compensation insurance for employers subject to the workers' compensation laws of this state. The term insurer includes the State Compensation Insurance Fund.

(aa) Investigation.

(1) As conducted by a claims administrator, an investigation is the process of examining and evaluating a claim to determine the nature and extent of all legally required benefits, if any, which are due under the claim. Investigation may include formal or informal methods of gathering information relevant to evaluating the claim such as: obtaining employment records; obtaining earnings records; informal or formal interviews of the employee, employer, or witnesses; deposition of parties or witnesses; and, obtaining expert opinion where an issue requires an expert opinion for its resolution, such as obtaining a medical-legal evaluation.

(2) As conducted by the Audit Unit, an investigation is the process of reviewing and evaluating, pursuant to California Code of Regulations, title 8, section 10106.5 and/or Government Code sections 11180 through 11191, the extent to which a claims administrator meets its compensation obligations under the California Labor Code or Administrative Director's regulations. An investigation may be conducted concurrently as part of an on-going audit without separate notice issued by the Audit Unit, or may be conducted independently from a specific audit in order to determine if an audit will be conducted, or to determine the nature and extent of business practices for which one or more civil penalties may be assessed pursuant to Labor Code section 129.5(e).

(bb) Joint Powers Authority. Any county, city, city and county, municipal corporation, public district, public agency, or political subdivision of the state, but not the state itself, included in a pooling arrangement under a joint exercise of powers agreement for the purpose of securing a certificate of consent to self-insure workers' compensation claims under Labor Code section 3700(c).

(cc) Knowingly committed. Acting with knowledge of the facts of the conduct subject to an investigation and/or audit under Labor Code sections 129 and 129.5. A corporation has knowledge of facts any employee receives while acting within the scope of his or her authority. A corporation has knowledge of information contained in its records and of the actions of its employees performed in the course of employment. An employer or insurer has knowledge of information contained in the records of its third party administrator and of the actions of the employees of the third party administrator performed in the scope and course of employment.

(dd) Lawful delay. A delay permitted by law or regulation, and for which the claims administrator has given a proper and timely notice of delay when such a notice is required. Any other delay is an unlawful delay.

(ee) Local Management. Claims personnel, regardless of their job titles, who have supervisory authority at an adjusting location over claims administration.

(ff) Medical-Only Claim. A work-injury claim in which no indemnity benefits have been paid or would reasonably be anticipated or expected to be paid.

(gg) Nontransferable Training Voucher. A document provided to an employee that allows the employee to enroll in education-related training or skills enhancement. The document shall include identifying information for the employee and claims administrator, and specific information regarding the value of the voucher pursuant to Labor Code section 4658.5 and California Code of Regulations, title 8, section 10133.50 et seq.

(hh) Notice of Compensation Due. The Notice of Assessment issued pursuant to Labor Code section 129(c).

(ii) Open Claim. A work-injury claim in which future payment of compensation may be due or for which reserves for the future payment of compensation are maintained.

(jj) Payment Schedule. Either:

(1) The two-week cycle of indemnity payments due on the day designated with the first payment as required by Labor Code sections 4650(c) or 4702(b), including any lawfully changed payment schedule; or

(2) The two-week cycle of payments of vocational rehabilitation maintenance allowance (VRMA) required by California Code of Regulations, title 8, section 10125.1.

(kk) Performance Standard. Criteria developed from historical audit findings data and used as a basis for judgment of quality, quantity, level, and grade to measure claim adjusting performance in the handling of the workers' compensation benefit areas set forth in California Code of Regulations, title 8, section 10107.1, subdivision (c)(3)(A). The standard rating factors will be calculated annually and based on all final audit findings as published in the Annual

DWC Audit Reports over the three calendar years before the year preceding the current audit. The Administrative Director shall determine and publish the performance standards for profile audit reviews and full compliance audits for the following calendar year.

(*ll*) Random sample. For the purpose of audit or investigation, a random sample is a selection of claim files selected pursuant to California Code of Regulations, title 8, section 10107.1, subdivisions (c)(1), (d)(1) or (e)(1).

(mm) Record of Payment. An accurate written or electronic record of all compensation payments in a claim file, including but not limited to:

(1) The check number, date the check was issued, name of the payee, amount, and for indemnity payments, including self-imposed increases, penalties, and/or interest, the time period(s) covered by the payment;

(2) All dates for which salary continuation as defined by Labor Code section 4650(g) was provided instead of direct indemnity payments; the dates for which salary continuation was authorized; and documentation when applicable that sick leave or other leave credits were restored for any periods for which salary continuation was payable;

(3) A copy of each bill received which included as part of the bill a medical progress or work status report; and either a copy of each other bill received or documentation of the contents of that bill showing the date and description of the service provided, provider's name, amount billed, date the claims administrator received the bill, the number of the check providing payment for each bill, including the check number, the date of the check, and the amount paid.

(nn) Self-insured Employer. An employer, either as an individual employer or as a group of employers, that has been issued a certificate of consent to self-insure as provided by Labor Code section 3700(b) or (c), including a joint powers authority or the State of California as a legally uninsured employer.

(oo) Supplemental Job Displacement Benefit. An educational retraining or skills enhancement allowance for injured employees, with dates of injury on or after January 1, 2004, whose employers are unable to provide work consistent with the requirements of Labor Code sections 4658.5 and California Code of Regulations, title 8, section 10133.50 et seq.

(pp) Third-Party Administrator. An agent under contract to administer the workers' compensation claims of an insurer, a self-insured employer, a legally uninsured employer. or a self-insured joint powers authority. The term third-party administrator includes the State Compensation Insurance Fund for locations that administer claims for legally uninsured and self-insured employers, and also includes Managing General Agents.

(qq) VRMA. Vocational rehabilitation maintenance allowance.

(rr) Workers' Compensation Information System (WCIS). The workers' compensation information system established pursuant to Labor Code sections 138.6 and 138.7.

Note: Authority cited: Sections 59, 129, 129.5, 133, 138.4 and 5307.3, Labor Code. Reference: Sections 7, 124(a), 129(a), 129(b), 129(c), 129.5(a), 129.5(b), 138.6, 138.7, 139.5, 3700, 3702.1, 4636, 4650(c), 4658.5, 4658.6, 5307.1 and 5402, Labor Code.

History: 1. New section filed 12-30-2002; operative 1-1-2003 pursuant to Government Code section 11343.4 (Register 2003, No. 1).

2. Amendment of section and Note filed 4-20-2009; operative 5-20-2009 (Register 2009, No. 17).

Ref.: Hanna §§ 1.12[8]–[10], 10.50, 10.51; Herlick Handbook §§ 1.01[3][b], 9.19.

ARTICLE 2
Claims Administration and Recordkeeping

§10101. Claim File—Contents.

This section applies to maintenance of claims files for injuries occurring before January 1, 1994.

Every claims administrator shall maintain a claim file of each work-injury claim including claims which were denied. All open claim files shall be kept at the adjusting location for the file. The file shall contain but not be limited to:

(a) An employer date stamped copy of the Employee's Claim for Workers' Compensation Benefits, DWC Form 1, or documentation of reasonable attempts to obtain the form.

(b) Employers Report of Occupational Injury or Illness, DLSR Form 5020, or documentation of reasonable attempts to obtain it.

(c) Every notice or report sent to the Division of Workers' Compensation.

(d) A copy of every Doctor's First Report of Occupational Injury or Illness, DLSR Form 5021, or documentation of reasonable attempts to obtain them.

(e) The original or a copy of every medical report pertaining to the claim, or documentation of reasonable attempts to obtain them.

(f) All orders or awards of the Workers' Compensation Appeals Board pertaining to the claim.

(g) A record of payment of compensation.

(h) A copy of the application(s) for adjudication of claim filed with the Workers' Compensation Appeals Board, if any.

(i) Copies of all notices sent to the employee pursuant to the requirements of the Benefit Notice Program established by Labor Code Section 138.4 and the notices required by Article 2.6 of Chapter 2 of Part 2 of the Labor Code, commencing with Section 4635.

Note: Authority cited: Sections 59, 129.5, 133, 138.4, 4603.5 and 5307.3, Labor Code. Reference: Sections 124, 129, 129.5, 138.3, 138.4, 139.5, 4061, 4453, 4454, 4600, 4603.2, 4621, 4622, 4636, 4637, 4641, 4643, 4644, 4650, 4701 through 4703.5, 5401, 6409 and 6409.1, Labor Code.

History: 1. New section filed 1-18-90; operative 1-18-90 (Register 90, No. 4). New section is exempt from review by OAL pursuant to Government Code Section 11351.

2. Amendment of article heading, section heading, text and Note filed 1-28-94; operative 1-28-94. Submitted to OAL for printing only pursuant to Government Code section 11351 (Register 94, No. 4).

Ref.: Herlick Handbook §§ 1.01[3][b], 9.5.

§10101.1. Claim File—Contents.

This section applies to maintenance of claim files for injuries occurring on or after January 1, 1994.

Every claims administrator shall maintain a claim file of each work-injury claim including claims which were denied. For injuries reported on or after June 19, 2009 each claims administrator shall maintain a claim file for each indemnity and medical-only claim, including denied claims, and shall ensure that each file is complete and current for each claim. Contents of claim files may be in hard copy, in electronic form, or some combination of hard copy and electronic form. Files maintained in hard copy shall be in chronological order with the most recently dated documents on top, or subdivided into sections such as medical reports, benefit notices, correspondence, claim notes, and vocational rehabilitation. Files or portions of files maintained in electronic form shall be easily retrievable. All open claim files shall be maintained at the adjusting location responsible for administering the claim. The file shall contain but not be limited to:

(a) Either (1) a copy of the Employee's Claim for Workers' Compensation Benefits, DWC Form 1, showing the employer's date of knowledge of injury, the date the employer provided the form to the employee and the date the employer received the completed form from the employee; or (2) if the employee did not return the claim form, documentation of the date the employer provided a claim form to the employee. If the administrator cannot obtain the form or determine that the form was provided to the employee by the employer, the file shall contain documentation that the administrator has provided the claim form to the employee as required by Title 8, California Code of Regulations section 10119.

(b) A copy of the Employer's Report of Occupational Injury or Illness, DLSR Form 5020, or documentation of reasonable attempts to obtain it;

(c) A copy of every notice, correspondence either initiated or received by the claims administrator, or report sent to the Division of Workers' Compensation.

(d) A copy of every Doctor's First Report of Occupational Injury or Illness, DLSR Form 5021, or documentation of reasonable attempts to obtain them.

(e) The original or a copy of every medical report pertaining to the claim, or documentation of reasonable attempts to obtain them.

(f) All orders or awards of the Workers' Compensation Appeals Board or the Rehabilitation Unit pertaining to the claim.

(g) A record of payment of compensation.

(h) A copy of the application(s) for adjudication of claim filed with the Workers' Compensation Appeals Board, if any.

(i) Copies of the following notices sent to the employee:

(1) Benefit notices, including vocational rehabilitation notices and supplemental job displacement benefit notices, required by California Code of Regulations, title 8, section 9810, or by California Code of Regulations, title 8, section 10122 through section 10133.60;

(2) Notices and forms related to the Qualified Medical Evaluation or Agreed Medical Evaluator process required by Labor Code sections 4060 et seq.;

(j) Documentation sufficient to determine the injured worker's average weekly earnings in accordance with Labor Code sections 4453 through 4459. Unless the claims administrator accepts liability to pay the maximum temporary disability rate, including any increased maximum due under Labor Code section 4661.5, the information shall include:

(1) Documentation whether the employee received the following earnings, and if so, the amount or fair market value of each: tips, commissions, bonuses, overtime, and the market value of board, lodging, fuel, or other advantages as part of the worker's remuneration, which can be estimated in money, said documentation to include the period of time, not exceeding one year, as may conveniently be taken to determine an average weekly rate of pay;

(2) Documentation of concurrent earnings from employment other than that in which the injury occurred, or that there were no concurrent earnings, or of reasonable attempts to determine this information;

(3) If earnings at the time of injury were irregular, documentation of earnings from all sources of employment for one year prior to the injury, or of reasonable attempts to determine this information.

(4) If the foregoing information results in less than maximum earnings, documentation of the worker's earning capacity, including documentation of any increase in earnings likely to have occurred but for the injury (such as periodic salary increases or increased earnings upon completion of training status), or of reasonable attempts to determine this information.

(k) Notes, correspondence, and documentation, including correspondence to or from any individual or entity, related to the provision, delay, or denial of benefits.

(*l*) Notes, correspondence, and documentation, including correspondence to or from any individual or entity, related to any utilization review process conducted under Labor Code section 4610.

(m) Notes, correspondence, and documentation, including correspondence to or from any individual or entity, related to a return to regular, modified, or alternative work as defined by Labor Code section 4658.1

(n) Notes, correspondence, and documentation, including correspondence to or from any individual or entity, evidencing the legal, factual, or medical basis for nonpayment or delay in payment of compensation benefits or expenses.

(o) Notes, correspondence, and documentation, including correspondence to or from any individual or entity, describing telephone conversations relating to the claim which are of significance to claims handling, including the dates of calls, substance of calls, and identification of parties to the calls.

Note: Authority cited: Sections 59, 129.5, 133, 138.4, 4603.5 and 5307.3, Labor Code. Reference: Sections 124, 129, 129.5, 138.3, 138.4, 139.48, 139.5, 4060, 4061, 4062, 4453, 4454, 4600, 4603.2, 4616, 4621, 4622, 4636, 4637, 4641, 4643, 4644, 4650, 4658.5, 4658.6, 4701-4703.5, 5401, 6409 and 6409.1, Labor Code.

History: 1. New section filed 1-28-94; operative 1-28-94. Submitted to OAL for printing only pursuant to Government Code section 11351 (Register 94, No. 4).

2. Amendment of section and Note filed 4-20-2009; operative 5-20-2009 (Register 2009, No. 17).

Ref.: Hanna §§ 1.12[8]–[10], 10.50, 10.51; Herlick Handbook §§ 1.01[3][b], 9.5, 9.19.

§10102. Retention of Claim Files.

(a) All claim files shall be maintained at least until the latest of the following dates:

(1) five years from the date of injury;

(2) one year from the date compensation was last provided;

(3) all compensation due or which may be due has been paid;

(4) if an audit has been conducted within the time specified in (a)(1), until the findings of an audit of the file have become final.

(b) Open and closed claim files may be maintained in whole or in part in an electronic or other non-paper storage medium.

Note: Authority cited: Sections 59, 129.5(b), 133, 138.4, 4603.5 and 5307.3, Labor Code. Reference: Sections 124(a), 129(a) through (c), 129.5(a), (b), (d), 138.3, 4061, 4453, 4454, 4600, 4603.2(b), 4621, 4622, 4636, 4637, 4641, 4643, 4644, 4650, 4701 through 4703.5, 5401(a), 5401.6, 5405 and 5804, Labor Code.

History: 1. New section filed 1-18-90; operative 1-18-90 (Register 90, No. 4). New section is exempt from review by OAL pursuant to Government Code section 11351.

2. Renumbering of former section 10103 to section 10102, and renumbering and amendment of former section 10102 to section 10103 filed 1-28-94; operative 1-28-94. Submitted to OAL for printing only pursuant to Government Code section 11351 (Register 94, No. 4).

Ref.: Herlick Handbook §§ 1.01[3][b], 9.5.

§10103. Claim Log—Contents and Maintenance.

This section shall govern claim log maintenance prior to January 1, 1994.

(a) Every claims administrator shall produce a claim log of all work-injury claims maintained at each adjusting location, prepared chronologically in alphanumeric or numeric ascending order, or in a combination thereof.

(b) The claim log shall contain at least the following information:

(1) Name of injured.

(2) The claims administrator's claim number.

(3) Date of injury.

(4) An indication as to whether the work-injury claim is an indemnity or medical-only case.

(5) An entry if all liability for a claim has been denied.

(6) For self-insurer, when a Certificate of Consent to Self-Insure has been issued, an entry identifying the corporation employing the injured.

(c) The claim log of a former self-insurer shall be maintained and made available to the audit unit within 5 days of request.

(d) A claims administrator shall provide a copy of a claim log within 14 days of receiving a written request from the Administrative Director.

Note: Authority cited: Sections 59, 129.5, 133 and 5307.3, Labor Code. Reference: Sections 124, 129, 129.5, 138.4, 3702.8 and 5401, Labor Code.

History: 1. New section filed 1-18-90; operative 1-18-90 (Register 90, No. 4). New section is exempt from review by OAL pursuant to Government Code Section 11351.

2. Renumbering of former section 10102 to section 10103, and renumbering and amendment of former section 10103 to section 10102 filed 1-28-94; operative 1-28-94. Submitted to OAL for printing only pursuant to Government Code section 11351 (Register 94, No. 4).

3. Amendment of subsection (b)(6) filed 2-14-96; operative 2-14-96. Submitted to OAL for printing only pursuant to Government Code section 11351 (Register 96, No. 7).

Ref.: Herlick Handbook §§ 1.01[3][b], 9.5.

§10103.1. Claim Log—Contents and Maintenance.

This section shall govern claim log maintenance on or after January 1, 1994.

(a) The claims administrator shall maintain annual claim logs listing all work-injury claims, open and closed. Each year's log shall be maintained for at least five years from the end of the year covered. Separate claim logs shall be maintained for each self-insured employer and each insurer for each adjusting location.

(b) Each entry in the claim log shall contain at least the following information:

(1) Name of injured worker.

(2) Claims administrator's claim number.

(3) Date of injury.

(4) An indication whether the claim is an indemnity or medical-only claim.

(5) An entry if all liability for a claim has been denied at any time. All liability is considered to have been denied even if the administrator accepted liability for medical-legal expense.

(6) If the claim log is for a self-insured employer and a Certificate of Consent to Self-Insure has been issued, the name of the corporation employing the injured worker. If the claim log consists of claims for two or more members of an insurer group, each entry on the log shall identify the insurer.

(c) The entries on a log provided to the Administrative Director shall reflect current information, to show at least any changes in status of a claim which occurred 45 days or more before the claim log was provided. However, once all liability for a claim has been denied the log shall designate the claim as a denial, even if the claim was later accepted.

(d) The claim log of each former self-insured employer and each self-insured employer which changes or terminates the use of a third-party administrator shall be maintained by that self-insured employer as required by subsection (a).

(e) A claims administrator shall provide a copy of a claim log within 14 days of receiving a written request from the Administrative Director.

Note: Authority cited: Sections 59, 129.5, 133 and 5307.3, Labor Code. Reference: Sections 124, 129, 129.5, 138.4, 3702.8 and 5401, Labor Code.

History: 1. New section filed 1-28-94; operative 1-28-94. Submitted to OAL for printing only pursuant to Government Code section 11351 (Register 94, No. 4).

2. Amendment of subsection (b)(6) filed 2-14-96; operative 2-14-96. Submitted to OAL for printing only pursuant to Government Code section 11351 (Register 96, No. 7).

Ref.: Hanna § 10.50[2][a]; Herlick Handbook §§ 1.01[3][b], 9.5.

§10103.2. Claim Log—Contents and Maintenance.

This section shall govern claim log maintenance on or after January 1, 2003.

(a) The claims administrator shall maintain annual claim logs listing all work-injury claims, open and closed. Each year's log shall be maintained for at least five years from the end of the year covered. Separate claim logs shall be maintained for each self-insured employer and each insurer for each adjusting location.

(b) Each entry in the claim log shall contain at least the following information:

(1) Name of injured worker.

(2) Claims administrator's claim number.

(3) Date of injury.

(4) An indication whether the claim is an indemnity or medical-only claim. Indemnity claims shall be differentiated from medical-only claims or any other claim where no indemnity payment(s) has been made. Claims that only require the provision of first aid, as defined by California Code of Regulations, title 8, section 9780(d), should not be included in the claim log.

(5) An entry if all liability for a claim has been denied at any time. All liability is considered to have been denied even if the administrator accepted liability for medical-legal expense.

(6) If the claim log is for a self-insured employer and a Certificate of Consent to Self-Insure has been issued, the name of the corporation employing the injured worker. If the claim log consists of claims for two or more members of an insurer group, the log shall identify the insurer for each claim.

(7) If the claim has been transferred from one adjusting location to another:

(A) The address of the new location shall be identified on the initial adjusting location's log along with the date of transfer.

(B) Claims that are transferred from one adjusting location to another shall be listed on the claim log of the new adjusting location for the year in which the claim was initially reported, not for the year in which the claim was transferred. The claim log shall also indicate the address of the old adjusting location along with the date of transfer.

(c) The entries on a log provided to the Administrative Director shall reflect current information, to show at least any changes in status of a claim which occurred 45 days or more before the claim log was provided. However, once all liability for a claim has been denied the log shall designate the claim as a denial, even if the claim was later accepted.

(d) The claim log of each former self-insured employer and each self-insured employer that changes or terminates the use of a third-party administrator shall be maintained by that self-insured employer as required by subsection (a).

(e) A claims administrator shall provide a copy of a claim log within 14 days of receiving a written request from the Administrative Director.

Note: Authority cited: Sections 59, 129.5, 133 and 5307.3, Labor Code. Reference: Sections 124, 129, 129.5, 138.4, 3702.8 and 5401, Labor Code.

History: 1. New section filed 12-30-2002; operative 1-1-2003 pursuant to Government Code section 11343.4 (Register 2003, No. 1).

2. Amendment of subsections (b)(4) and (b)(7), including redesignation and amendment of portions of subsection (b)(7) as new subsections (b)(7)(A)-(B), filed 4-20-2009; operative 5-20-2009 (Register 2009, No. 17).

Ref.: Hanna §§ 1.12[8]–[10], 10.50, 10.51; Herlick Handbook §§ 1.01[3][b], 9.19.

§10104. Annual Report of Inventory.

(a) Each claims administrator shall maintain, and shall file with the Administrative Director, an Annual Report of Inventory for each of its adjusting locations. The report shall be filed annually by April 1. It shall include the name, address, and telephone number of the adjusting location and the name and title of the person responsible for audit coordination. Claims administrators shall report, as of the preceding January 1, the numbers of indemnity, denied, and medical-only claims reported to each of its adjusting locations during the preceding calendar year for insurers and private self-insured employers, or public self-insured employers. If the administrator adjusts for more than one entity at that location, the report shall give the total numbers of claims at that location and shall also identify the numbers of claims for each self-insured employer or insurer liable for the payment of compensation. Indemnity claims shall be differentiated on the Annual Report of Inventory from medical-only claims or any other claim where no indemnity payment(s) has been made.

(b) If a claims administrator relocates, opens a new adjusting location, closes an adjusting location, changes contact persons, changes the e-mail address, changes from third-party administered to self-administered or from self-administered to third-party administered, or changes from self-insured to insured, the claims administrator shall advise the Administrative Director by mailing written notice to the manager of the Audit Unit within 45 calendar days of the event.

(c) Adjusting locations that have no indemnity, denied, or medical-only claims reported during the preceding calendar year must file with the Administrative Director a statement indicating whether the location is actively adjusting workers' compensation claims. The statement, which shall be filed annually by April 1, shall contain the name, address, and telephone number of the adjusting location and the name and title of the person responsible for audit coordination.

(d)(1) A claims administrator's obligation to submit an Annual Report of Inventory under subdivision (a) of this section is waived upon a determination by the Administrative Director that the claims administrator is in compliance with the electronic data reporting requirements of the Workers' Compensation Information System, as set forth in California Code of Regulations, title 8, section 9702.

(2) Each claims administrator whose obligation to submit an Annual Report of Inventory is satisfied under subdivision (d)(1) of this section shall maintain and file with the Administrative Director an Annual Report of Adjusting Locations. This report shall be filed annually by

April 1 of each calendar year and shall report, as of the preceding December 31, each of the claims administrator's adjusting locations. The report shall include the name, street and mailing address, physical zip code, e-mail address, fax number, and telephone number for each adjusting location and the name, title, e-mail address, fax number and telephone number of the person responsible for audit coordination.

(3) The claims administrator shall notify the Administrative Director, by mailing written notice to the manager of the Audit Unit, of any change in the information provided in the Annual Report of Adjusting Locations. A reportable change shall include the relocation of the claims administrator or the opening or closing of an adjusting location. The notification shall be made within 45 calendar days after the effective date of the change.

(4) The waiver granted to a claims administrator under subdivision (d)(1) of this section shall be rescinded if the total number of claims reported by the claims administrator to the Audit Unit in a claim log submitted pursuant to California Code of Regulations, title 8, section 10107.1(a) is not within one percent of the total number of claims electronically reported by the claims administrator to the Workers' Compensation Information System for the same period of time as covered in the submitted claim log.

Note: Authority cited: Sections 59, 129.5, 133 and 5307.3, Labor Code. Reference: Sections 129, 129.5 and 138.6, Labor Code.

History: 1. Renumbering of former section 10104 to section 10105 and new section filed 1-28-94; operative 1-28-94. Submitted to OAL for printing only pursuant to Government Code section 11351 (Register 94, No. 4).

2. Amendment filed 12-30-2002; operative 1-1-2003 pursuant to Government Code section 11343.4 (Register 2003, No. 1).

3. Amendment filed 10-6-2003; operative 12-1-2003 (Register 2003, No. 41).

4. Amendment of section and Note filed 4-20-2009; operative 5-20-2009 (Register 2009, No. 17).

Ref.: Hanna §§ 1.12[8]–[10], 10.50[2][a], 10.51; Herlick Handbook §§ 1.01[3][b], 9.5, 9.19.

ARTICLE 3
Auditing

§10105. Auditing, Discretion of the Administrative Director.

To carry out the responsibility pursuant to Labor Code sections 129 or 129.5, the Administrative Director or his/her representative shall audit claims administrators' claim files and claim logs at such reasonable times as he/she deems necessary. The Administrative Director or his/her representative may also utilize the provisions of Government Code sections 11180 through 11191.

Note: Authority cited: Sections 59, 129, 129.5, 133 and 5307.3, Labor Code. Reference: Sections 129 and 129.5, Labor Code.

History: 1. New article 3 heading, repealer of former section 10105 and renumbering and amendment of former section 10104 to section 10105 filed 1-28-94; operative 1-28-94. Submitted to OAL for printing only pursuant to Government Code section 11351 (Register 94, No. 4). For prior history, see Register 90, No. 4.

2. Amendment filed 12-30-2002; operative 1-1-2003 pursuant to Government Code section 11343.4 (Register 2003, No. 1).

3. Amendment of section and Note filed 4-20-2009; operative 5-20-2009 (Register 2009, No. 17).

Ref.: Hanna §§ 1.12[8]–[10], 10.50, 10.51; Herlick Handbook §§ 1.01[3][b], 9.5, 9.19.

§10106. Random and Non-Random Audit Subject Selection; Complaint/Information Investigation.

(a) In its discretion, the Audit Unit may treat an affiliated group of insurers at a single adjusting location as individual insurers, or may combine all or any of them as a single insurer audit subject. In its discretion, the Audit Unit may treat parent and subsidiary self-insured employers at a single adjusting location as individual self-insureds, or may combine all or any of them as a single self-insured audit subject.

(b) The final selection of audit subjects shall be within the discretion of the Audit Unit. The Audit Unit may investigate information or complaints instead of, or in addition to, conducting an audit. Investigations and/or audits may be conducted if complaints or information indicate the possible existence of claims handling practices which would be assessed as a civil penalty under Labor Code Section 129.5(d).

(c) The Audit Unit shall select at least half of its audit subjects at random from any available listing of adjusting locations of workers' compensation insurers, self-insured employers, self-insured joint powers authorities, legally uninsured employers, and third-party administrators. If, after the results of an audit become final, none of the criteria qualifying an audit subject for a return non-random audit pursuant to subsection (f) of this section exist, the audit subject shall be removed from the pool of potential random audit subject selection for three years. However, eligibility under this subsection for removal from the pool for random audit subject selection shall not bar the non-random selection of the audit subject pursuant to this section or Labor Code Section 129(b).

(d) In order to establish priorities for audits pursuant to Labor Code §129(b), the Audit Unit shall review and compile complaints and information that indicate a claims administrator is failing to meet its obligations under Divisions 1 or 4 of the Labor Code or regulations of the administrative director.

(1) The information and complaints shall be tracked and compiled into a list of Claims Administrators Identified for Potential Non-Random Investigation as follows:

(i) Complaints or information available to the Audit Unit which indicate possible violations of the kind which, if found on audit, would be subject to the assessment of administrative penalties or issuance of notices of compensation due shall be retained in potential audit subject files by claims adjusting locations. Factual information and complaints shall be weighted on the basis of apparent severity of the alleged violation, using the assessment categories set forth in the subsections (a) through (d) of §10111 and §10111.1 to set a point value.

An alleged violation that would fall within subsection (a) is given one point, an alleged violation that would fall within subsection (b) is given five points, an alleged violation that would fall within subsection (c) is given ten points, and an alleged violation that would fall within subsection (d) is given fifty points. When multiple violations are alleged in one complaint, each potential violation is given the appropriate point(s).

Points assigned for violations which are evidenced by decisions or findings rendered by the WCAB or Rehabilitation Unit shall be multiplied by ten.

(ii) Periodically, the audit unit shall review and analyze the complaint and information data in order to establish a list of Claims Administrators Identified for Potential Non-Random Investigation. The total number of points assigned to a claims administrator at an adjusting location shall be compared to the total number of claims reported at that claims adjusting location as indicated on the Annual Report of Inventory or the Self Insurer's Annual Report. The claims administrators shall be ranked on the list of Claims Administrators Identified for Potential Non-Random Investigation on the basis of the ratio of weighted complaints to case load size at each adjusting location. It is within the discretion of the Audit Unit to determine when new lists shall be established.

(2) The audit unit shall select any number of the highest ranking claims adjusting locations for investigation from the list of Claims Administrators Identified for Potential Non-Random Investigation.

(i) The Audit Unit shall notify the claims administrator that it will conduct an investigation, and shall specify the files it will review by providing the names of the injured workers. The Audit Unit shall give the claims administrator a minimum of three working days notice of the date of commencement of the investigation. Notice may be given by telephone. The claim files shall be made available to the Audit Unit at the time of the commencement of the investigation. The Audit Unit may examine claim files and require a claims administrator to provide documents and information.

(ii) The Audit Unit shall examine the selected files and shall assign points for each violation found in the files in accordance with the point system set forth in subsection (d)(1)(i), except that there shall be no multiplier for violations evidenced by decisions or findings of the WCAB or Rehabilitation Unit. Points shall be assigned for every violation found in the file, both violations that were alleged in the complaints and additional violations found by the audit unit.

(iii) The Audit Unit shall send a notice to the claims administrator which outlines the violations found in the files investigated. The claims administrator may request copies of the complaints relating to the files investigated. The complaints may be kept confidential by the audit unit if confidentiality is requested by the complainant.

(iv) The claims administrator may present documentation and/or argument to the Audit Unit to disprove any or all of the violations found by the audit unit in the investigated files. The documentation and argument must be post-marked or personally delivered to the Audit Unit within fourteen days of receipt of the letter outlining the violations.

(v) The Audit Unit shall consider documents and argument submitted by the claims administrator to disprove the violations found in the investigated files and determine whether there is a basis to alter any of the points previously assigned.

(vi) The adjusting locations shall then be ranked on a list of Claims Administrators Identified for Potential Non-Random Audit on the basis of the ratio of violation points to the number of claims investigated at each adjusting location.

(e) The Audit Unit shall select non-random audit subjects from the list of Claims Administrators Identified for Potential Non-Random Audit, and shall endeavor to give priority in scheduling audits to those administrators that have been assigned the most points. However, the audit unit may also consider the results and recency of prior audits at the adjusting location, the resources of the audit unit, and the need to conduct random audits, in scheduling investigations and audits. The Audit Unit is not required to investigate or audit every claims administrator on the list, nor is it required to investigate or audit in the order in which claims administrators appear on the list.

If the Audit Unit is able to conduct more non-random audits than the number appearing on the list of Claims Administrators Identified for Potential Non-Random Audit, it may select any number of the next highest ranking adjusting locations appearing on the list of Claims Administrators Identified for Potential Non-Random Investigation. The adjusting locations shall then be investigated and ranked according to subsection (d)(2).

(f) Prior audit results shall be used independently as factual information to support selection of a claims administrator for non-random audit.

(1) The Audit Unit shall return for a repeat non-random audit of denied files of the audit subject within one to three years of the results of an audit becoming final if there is more than one unsupported denial and the number of unsupported denials exceeds 5% of the audited denied claims.

(2) The Audit Unit shall return for a repeat non-random audit of indemnity files of the audit subject within one to three years of the results of an audit becoming final if:

(i) The number of randomly selected audited files with violations involving the failure to pay indemnity exceeds 20% of the audited files in which indemnity is accrued and payable and the average amount of unpaid indemnity exceeds $200.00 per file in which indemnity is accrued and payable, or

(ii) The numbers of randomly selected files with violations involving the late first payments of temporary disability indemnity, permanent disability indemnity, vocational rehabilitation maintenance allowance, late subsequent indemnity payments, and late payments of death benefits, as mitigated for frequency under Section 10111.1(e)(3)(i) through (v), exceeds 30% of the audited files in which those indemnity payments have been made, and the number of audited files with violations involving the failure to issue benefit notices, as assessed under Section 10111.1(a)(7)(ii) of these regulations, exceeds 30% of the files in which there is a requirement to issue those notices.

(g) The Audit Unit shall send a claims administrator selected for non-random audit a Notice of Audit in accordance with §10107. The Notice of Audit for a non-random audit may be appealed as follows:

(i) Within 7 days after receiving a Notice of Audit the claims administrator may appeal its selection for audit by filing and serving a request for an appeals conference or a request for a written decision by the Administrative Director without a conference.

(ii) Within 21 days after the request for a written decision or an appeals conference is filed, the appellant shall file with the Administrative Director and serve a written statement setting forth the legal and factual basis of the appeal, and including documentation or other evidence which supports the appellant's position.

(iii) If a request for an appeals conference or a request for a written decision without conference or if the written statement and documentation are not timely filed and served under Subsections (g)(i) and (g)(ii), the claims administrator shall be deemed to have finally waived the issue of the propriety of its selection for audit. The claims administrator will be precluded from raising the issue at any subsequent appeals of Notices of Penalty Assessment or Notices of Compensation Due.

(iv) Service and filing are timely if the documents are placed in the United States mail, first class postage prepaid, or personally delivered between the hours of 8:00 a.m. and 5:00 p.m., within the periods specified in Subsections (g)(i) and (g)(ii). The original and all copies of any filing shall attach proof of service as provided in Section 10514.

(v) The appeal process shall be governed by Section 10115.2.

Note: Authority cited: Sections 59, 129.5, 133 and 5307.3, Labor Code. Reference: Sections 7, 53, 111, 124, 129 and 129.5, Labor Code; and Sections 11180, 11180.5, 11181 and 11182, Government Code.

History: 1. Relocation of article 3 heading to article 5 and repealer and new section filed 1-28-94; operative 1-28-94. Submitted to OAL for printing only pursuant to Government Code section 11351 (Register 94, No. 4). For prior history, see Register 90, No. 4.

2. Amendment of subsection (b), (d)(2), and (e) filed 2-14-96; operative 2-14-96. Submitted to OAL for printing only pursuant to Government Code section 11351 (Register 96, No. 7).

3. Amendment of section and Note filed 10-26-98; operative 11-25-98 (Register 98, No. 44).

Ref.: Herlick Handbook §§ 1.01[3][b], 9.5.

§10106.1. Routine and Targeted Audit Subject Selection; Complaint Tracking; Appeal of Targeted Audit Selection.

For audits conducted on or after January 1, 2003:

(a) The Division of Workers' Compensation shall maintain and update annually a list of known adjusting locations of California workers' compensation claims. The list will be based on information provided to the Division in Annual Reports of Inventory submitted pursuant to California Code of Regulations, title 8, section 10104, data submitted to the Division's Workers' Compensation Information System pursuant to Labor Code section 138.6, and any other sources of information available. The list shall include all known adjusting locations, located in or out of California, of insurers, self-administered self-insured employers, and third-party administrators that administer California workers' compensation claims.

(b) The Audit Unit shall select each adjusting location from the list of adjusting locations for routine profile audit review pursuant to Labor Code section 129(b)(1) at least once every five years. Audit subjects may be selected in any order, and routine audits may be scheduled by the Audit Unit in a manner to best minimize travel expenses and utilize audit personnel efficiently.

(1) For routine audit subject selection pursuant to Labor Code section 129(b)(1), if the adjusting location includes claims of more than one insurance underwriting company, self-insured employer, or third-party administrator at the location and all claims at that location share the same local management, the location will be considered as one audit subject.

(2) Eligibility under this subsection for removal from the pool for routine audit subject selection shall not bar the targeted selection of the audit subject pursuant to subdivisions (c)(2), (c)(3), (c)(4) of this section, Labor Code section 129(b)(3), or for investigation and/or audit pursuant to California Code of Regulations, title 8, section 10106.5.

(c) Pursuant to Labor Code section 129(b), the Audit Unit may conduct a targeted profile audit review or full compliance audit of targeted audit subjects. An audit subject shall be selected for a targeted audit based on the following target audit criteria:

(1) Prior audit results pursuant to Labor Code section 129(b)(2) shall be used independently as factual information to support selection of a claims administrator for a return, targeted audit as follows:

(A) When a final audit report is issued, the report will include a final performance rating. The final performance rating will be calculated in the same manner as the performance audit review performance rating as set forth in California Code of Regulations, title 8, section 10107.1(c)(3), except that the rating shall be determined based on audit findings from all claim files randomly selected pursuant to section 10107(c)(1), (d)(1), and (e)(1), and selected additional claim files.

(B) If the audit subject's performance rating calculated pursuant to section 10107.1(c)(3) or (d)(3) fails to meet or exceed the worst 10% of performance ratings for all audits conducted in the three calendar years before the year preceding the year in which the current audit was commenced, the Audit Unit will return for a targeted audit of the audit subject within two years of the date the audit findings become final.

(C) In the final audit report, the Audit Unit shall notify the audit subject that a return, targeted audit will be conducted based upon its performance rating.

(D) Any appeal of the audit subject's selection for a targeted audit based upon the audit findings must be made in the same manner as an appeal of the Notice of Penalty Assessment as set forth in California Code of Regulations, title 8, section 10115.1, and must be made within seven days of receipt of the audit findings upon which the selection for targeted audit is based.

(2) Audit subjects may be selected for targeted audit based on final decisions or findings of the WCAB issued pursuant to Labor Code section 5814 as follows:

(A) The Division of Workers' Compensation will regularly submit to the Audit Unit copies of WCAB decisions, findings, and/or awards issued pursuant to Labor Code section 5814, and reports of WCAB cases involving section 5814 violations.

(B) The Audit Unit will establish a list of claims administrators identified for potential targeted audit based on the documentation provided pursuant to subdivision (c)(2)(A). For each adjusting location, the total number of decisions, findings, and/or awards issued pursuant to Labor Code section 5814 shall be compared to the total number of claims reported at that claims adjusting location for the last year for that potential audit subject, as indicated on the Annual Report of Inventory or the Self Insurer's Annual Report, or as indicated in the data reported by the claims administrator to the Division of Workers' Compensation as part of the Workers' Compensation Information System pursuant to Labor Code section 138.6. The Audit Unit may obtain data runs or claim logs from the claims administrator to verify the accuracy of the claims reported.

(C) The Audit Unit may select for target audit the highest-ranking subjects, based on the ratios of decisions, findings, and/or awards issued pursuant to Labor Code section 5814 compared to the number of claims reported at the adjusting location, from the list. The Audit Unit may consider the results and recency of prior audits at the adjusting location, the resources of the Audit Unit, and the need to conduct routine audits in scheduling targeted audits. The Audit Unit is not required to audit every claims administrator on the list, nor is it required to audit in the order in which claims administrators appear on the list.

(3) The Audit Unit may also target audit subjects based on credible complaints and/or information received by the Division of Workers' Compensation that indicate possible claims handling violations, except that the Audit Unit will not target audit subjects based only on anonymous complaints unless the complaint(s) is supported by credible documentation. Complaints received by the Division of Workers' Compensation may be kept confidential if confidentiality is requested by the complaining party. In order to establish priorities for audits pursuant to this subsection, the Audit Unit shall review and compile complaints and information that indicate claims administrator adjusting locations are failing to meet their obligations under Divisions 1 or 4 of the Labor Code or regulations of the Administrative Director. The Audit Unit may contact a claims administrator and request information necessary to determine the validity of a complaint. Complaints and information alleging improper claims handling shall be tracked and compiled into a list of claims administrators identified for potential target audits in two manners:

(A) On the basis of overall gravity and frequency of potential violations as measured by assigned points:

1. Complaints or information indicating possible violations of the kind which, if found on audit, would be subject to the assessment of administrative penalties or issuance of notices of compensation due shall be weighted on the basis of apparent severity of the alleged violation. One point shall be assigned for each $100.00 in penalties assessable under the corresponding violations in California Code of Regulations, title 8, sections 10111 through 10111.2 of these regulations.

2. The Audit Unit may select for target audit the highest-ranking subjects, based on points assigned compared to the number of claims reported at the adjusting location. The Audit Unit may consider the results and recency of prior audits at the adjusting location, the resources of the Audit Unit, and the need to conduct routine audits in scheduling targeted audits. The Audit Unit is not required to audit every claims administrator on the list, nor is it required to audit in the order in which claims administrators appear on the list.

(B) On the basis of credible complaints or information indicating claims handling for which a civil penalty may be assessed pursuant to Labor Code section 129.5(e).

The Audit Unit may select for target audit the highest-ranking subjects based on the ratios of complaints or information regarding specific claims practices compared to the number of claims. In considering the potential for specific poor claims practices, the Audit Unit may consider the results and recency of prior audits at the adjusting location, the resources of the Audit Unit, and the need to conduct routine audits in scheduling targeted audits. The Audit Unit is not required to audit every claims administrator on the list, nor is it required to audit in the order in which claims administrators appear on the list.

(4) The Audit Unit may also select targeted audit subjects based on data from the Workers' Compensation Information System which indicates the claims administrator is failing to meet its obligations, including, but not limited to, high percentages of possible violations compared to other claims administrators. Possible violations include high percentages of apparent late first and/or subsequent indemnity payments, either overall or by class of indemnity, and/or high ratios of denied claims to indemnity claims.

(5) The Audit Unit may also target an audit subject for any of the following:

(A) Failure to produce a claim for the Audit Unit within 30 days of receipt of a written request in a profile audit review conducted pursuant to Labor Code section 129(b).

(B) Failure to pay or appeal pursuant to California Code of Regulations, title 8, section 10115.1 any Notice of Compensation Due issued by the Audit Unit.

(C) Failure to comply with the Workers' Compensation Information System (WCIS) requirements and timelines set forth in Labor Code section 138.6 or California Code of Regulations, title 8,, sections 9700 et seq.

(D) The assessment of or a stipulation to a civil penalty pursuant to Labor Code section 129.5(e).

(d) For targeted audits conducted in accordance with the target audit criteria set forth in subdivision (c) of this section:

(1) The Audit Unit shall send the audit subject selected for targeted audit a Notice of Audit in accordance with section 10107.1(a).

(2) For target audits, the Audit Unit may randomly select claims pursuant to section 10107.1 of these regulations and/or target claims on the basis that the Audit Unit has received information alleging the existence of an improper claim handling practice, and for the purpose of determining whether that practice occurred in those files. Companion claim files or additional claim files as defined

by these regulations may be included for audit with the selected files.

(3) For all types of target audits and/or for targeted claims in any audit, the Audit Unit is not required to audit an entire claim file, but may audit only those parts of the claim file that pertain to the complaint or to a specific type of possible violation(s).

(4) The Notice of Audit for a targeted audit selected pursuant to subdivisions (c)(2) through (c)(5) of this section may be appealed as follows:

(A) Within 7 days after receiving a Notice of Audit the claims administrator may appeal its selection for audit by filing with the Administrative Director and serving on the Audit Unit a request for an appeals conference or a request for a written decision without a conference.

(B) Within 21 days after the request for a written decision or an appeals conference is filed, the appellant shall file with the Administrative Director and serve the Audit Unit with a written statement setting forth the legal and factual basis of the appeal, and including documentation or other evidence which supports the appellant's position.

(C) If a request for an appeals conference or a request for a written decision without conference or if the written statement and documentation are not timely filed and served under California Code of Regulations, title 8, section 10115.1(g)(1) and (g)(2), the claims administrator shall be deemed to have waived any issue concerning its selection for audit. The claims administrator will be precluded from raising the issue at any subsequent appeals of Notices of Penalty Assessment or Notices of Compensation Due.

(D) Service and filing are timely if the documents are placed in the United States mail, first class postage prepaid, or personally delivered between the hours of 8:00 a.m. and 5:00 p.m., within the periods specified in section 10115.1(g). The original and all copies of any filing shall attach proof of service as provided in California Code of Regulations, title 8, section 10975.

(E) The appeal process shall be governed by California Code of Regulations, title 8, section 10115.2.

Note: Authority cited: Sections 59, 129, 129.5, 133, 138.6, 138.7 and 5307.3, Labor Code. Reference: Sections 7, 53, 111, 124, 129, 129.5, 138.6 and 138.7, Labor Code; and Sections 11180, 11181 and 11182, Government Code.

History: 1. New section filed 12-30-2002; operative 1-1-2003 pursuant to Government Code section 11343.4 (Register 2003, No. 1).

2. Change without regulatory effect redesignating and amending former subsections (c)(8)(i)-(v) to subsections (c)(8)(A)-(E) filed 5-1-2003 pursuant to section 100, title 1, California Code of Regulations (Register 2003, No. 18).

3. Amendment of section and Note filed 4-20-2009; operative 5-20-2009 (Register 2009, No. 17).

Ref.: Hanna §§ 1.12[8]–[10], 10.50, 10.51; Herlick Handbook §§ 1.01[3][b], 9.19.

§10106.5. Civil Penalty Investigation.

Notwithstanding California Code of Regulations, title 8, sections 10106.1 and 10107.1, if the Audit Unit has information indicating the possible existence of claims handling practices which would be assessable as a civil penalty under Labor Code section 129.5(e), it may conduct an investigation and/or audit pursuant to Labor Code sections 129 and 129.5. The Audit Unit may also utilize the provisions of Government Code sections 11180 through 11191 as the delagee of the Administrative Director's powers as a department head.

The Audit Unit shall report any suspected fraudulent activity uncovered during an audit and/or investigation to the appropriate law enforcement agencies, including but not limited to the Department of Insurance Fraud Bureau and the appropriate District Attorney having jurisdiction over the audit subject.

Note: Authority cited: Sections 129.5, 133 and 5307.3, Labor Code. Reference: Sections 11180 through 11191, Government Code; and Sections 59, 60, 111, 124, 129 and 129.5, Labor Code.

History: 1. New section filed 10-26-98; operative 11-25-98 (Register 98, No. 44).

2. Amendment filed 12-30-2002; operative 1-1-2003 pursuant to Government Code section 11343.4 (Register 2003, No. 1).

3. Amendment of first paragraph filed 4-20-2009; operative 5-20-2009 (Register 2009, No. 17).

Ref.: Hanna §§ 1.12[8]–[10], 10.50, 10.51; Herlick Handbook §§ 1.01[3][b], 9.5, 9.19.

§10107. Notice of Audit; Claim File Selection; Production of Claim Files; Auditing Procedure.

(a) Once a subject has been selected for an audit, the Audit Unit shall serve a Notice of Audit on the claims administrator. The Notice shall inform the administrator of its selection for audit, and shall include a request to provide the Audit Unit with a claim log or logs. The audit subject shall provide two copies of the specified claim log(s) within fourteen days of the date of the receipt of the Notice. The Audit Unit may select any or all claim files for audit.

(b) The Audit Unit shall send the audit subject a Notice of Audit Commencement identifying the files to be audited, except that no notice need be given to audit claim files which are the subject of inquiries or complaints. The audit shall commence no less than fourteen days from the date the Notice was sent, unless the audit subject agrees to earlier commencement.

(c) The Audit Unit shall randomly select separate samples of indemnity, denied, and medical-only files from two years' of the audit subject's claim logs, except that if the earliest of the last two completed years has already been the subject of an audit, claims will be randomly selected from only the last completed year.

(1) The total number of indemnity files randomly selected for audit will be determined based on the following table:

Population	*Sample Size*
8 or less	all
9-15	1 less than total
16-19	2 less than total
20-23	3 less than total
24-27	4 less than total
28-30	5 less than total
31-33	6 less than total
34-36	7 less than total
37-38	8 less than total

Population	*Sample Size*
39-41	9 less than total
42	32
43-44	33
45	34
46-47	35
48-49	36
50-51	37
52-53	38
54-55	39
56-57	40
58-59	41
60-61	42
62-63	43
64-65	44
66-67	45
68-70	46
71-72	47
73-74	48
75-77	49
78-79	50
80-82	51
83-84	52
85-87	53
88-89	54
90-92	55
93-95	56
96-98	57
99-101	58
102-104	59
105-107	60
108-110	61
111-114	62
115-117	63
118-120	64
121-124	65
125-128	66
129-131	67
132-135	68
136-139	69
140-143	70
144-148	71
149-152	72
153-156	73
157-161	74
162-166	75
167-171	76
172-176	77
177-181	78
182-187	79
188-192	80
193-198	81
199-204	82
205-210	83
211-217	84
218-223	85
224-230	86
231-238	87
239-245	88
246-253	89
254-261	90
262-270	91
271-279	92
280-288	93
289-298	94
299-308	95
309-319	96
320-330	97
331-342	98
343-354	99
355-367	100
368-381	101
382-396	102
397-411	103
412-427	104
428-444	105
445-463	106
464-482	107
483-503	108
504-525	109
526-549	110
550-575	111
576-603	112
604-633	113
634-665	114
666-700	115
701-739	116
740-781	117
782-827	118
828-879	119
880-936	120
937-1,000	121
1,001-1,072	122
1,073-1,154	123
1,155-1,248	124
1,249-1,356	125
1,357-1,483	126
1,484-1,633	127
1,634-1,814	128
1,815-2,036	129
2,037-2,315	130
2,316-2,677	131
2,678-3,163	132
3,164-3,852	133
3,853-4,904	134
4,905-6,710	135
6,711-10,530	136
10,531-23,993	137
23,994 +	138

(2) In conducting the audit, the Audit Unit shall calculate the frequency of files with violations as percentages of the files with exposure for violations after the following number of randomly selected indemnity files are audited:

Population	*Sample Size*
5 or less	all
6-10	1 less than total
11-13	2 less than total
14-16	3 less than total
17-18	4 less than total
19-20	5 less than total

Population	*Sample Size*
21-23	6 less than total
24	17
25-26	18
27-29	19
30-31	20
32-33	21
34-36	22
37-39	23
40-41	24
42-44	25
45-48	26
49-51	27
52-55	28
56-58	29
59-62	30
63-67	31
68-72	32
73-77	33
78-82	34
83-88	35
89-95	36
96-102	37
103-110	38
111-119	39
120-128	40
129-139	41
140-151	42
152-164	43
165-179	44
180-197	45
198-217	46
218-241	47
242-269	48
270-304	49
305-346	50
347-399	51
400-468	52
469-562	53
563-696	54
697-905	55
906-1,272	56
1,273-2,091	57
2.092-5,530	58
5,531 +	59

If any of the following criteria are met after auditing the sample size as set forth in this subsection (c)(2), the Audit Unit will proceed to audit the remaining number of randomly selected indemnity files selected for audit pursuant to subsection (c)(1):

(i) The number of randomly selected audited files with violations involving the failure to pay indemnity exceeds 20% of those files in which indemnity is accrued and payable and the average amount of unpaid indemnity exceeds $200.00 per file in which indemnity is accrued and payable;

(ii) The numbers of randomly selected files with violations involving the late first payments of temporary disability indemnity, permanent disability indemnity, vocational rehabilitation maintenance allowance, late subsequent indemnity payments, and late payments of death benefits, as mitigated for frequency under Section 10111.1(e)(3)(i) through (v), exceeds 30% of the files in which those indemnity payments have been made;

(iii) The number of randomly selected audited files with violations involving the failure to issue benefit notices, as assessed under Section 10111.1(a)(7)(ii) of these regulations, exceeds 30% of those files in which there is a requirement to issue those notices.

The determination of whether or not to audit the number of files selected pursuant to subsection (c)(1) of this section shall not be the subject of appeal, and no preliminary report of findings will be issued to the audit subject before the determination is made.

(d) The total numbers of denied files and medical-only files randomly selected for audit will be determined based on the following table:

Population	*Sample Size*
6 or less	all
7-10	1 less than total
11-14	2 less than total
15-17	3 less than total
18	14
19-20	15
21	16
22-23	17
24-25	18
26-27	19
28-29	20
30-31	21
32-33	22
34-36	23
37-38	24
39-41	25
42-43	26
44-46	27
47-49	28
50-52	29
53-55	30
56-59	31
60-63	32
64-67	33
68-71	34
72-75	35
76-80	36
81-85	37
86-90	38
91-96	39
97-102	40
103-109	41
110-116	42
117-124	43
125-132	44
133-141	45
142-151	46
152-163	47
164-175	48
176-189	49
190-205	50
206-222	51
223-242	52
243-265	53

Population	*Sample Size*
266-292	54
293-323	55
324-360	56
361-405	57
406-461	58
462-531	59
532-623	60
624-749	61
750-931	62
932-1,217	63
1,218-1,731	64
1,732-2,934	65
2,935-8,990	66
8,991 +	67

(e) In addition to randomly selected indemnity, denied, and medical-only files, the Audit Unit may also select for audit any or all files for which the Division of Workers' Compensation has received complaints within the past three years.

(f) The audit subject shall pay all expenses of an audit of an adjusting location outside the State of California, including per diem, travel expense, and compensated overtime of audit personnel.

(g) The audit subject shall make each of the claim files selected for audit available at the audit site at the time of audit commencement. If claim files are maintained in an electronic or other non-paper storage medium, the claims administrator shall, upon request, provide to the Audit Unit direct computer access to electronic claim files and/or legible printed paper copies of the claim files, including all records of compensation payments.

(h) The Audit Unit shall have discretion to audit files in addition to those identified with the Notice of Audit Commencement. The audit subject shall make each of the additional files selected for audit available at the audit site within 14 days of receipt of written notice identifying the additional files.

(i) The audit subject shall provide the auditor(s) an adequate, safe, and healthful work space during the audit, which allows the auditors a reasonable degree of privacy. If this work space is not provided, the Audit Unit may require the audit subject to deliver the files to the nearest Audit Unit office for completion of the audit.

(j) The Audit Unit may obtain and retain copies of documentation or information from claim files to support the assessment of penalties.

(k) The audit subject shall have the opportunity to discuss preliminary findings and provide additional information at a post-audit conference.

(*l*) The Audit Unit may at any time request additional information or documentation in order to complete its audit. Such information may include documentation that, as specified by Labor Code Sections 3751(a) and 3752, compensation has not been reduced or affected by any insurance, contribution, or other benefit due to or received by or from the employee. The audit subject shall provide any requested documentation or other information within thirty days from the Audit Unit's request, unless the Audit Unit extends the time for good cause.

(m) The Audit Unit shall issue a report of audit findings which may include, but is not limited to, the following: one or more requests for additional documentation or compliance, Notices of Intention to Issue Notice of Compensation Due, Preliminary Notices of Penalty Assessments, Notices of Compensation Due, or Notices of Penalty Assessments. If any additional requested documentation is not provided within thirty days of receipt of the report, additional audit penalties may be assessed under Section 10111.1(d)(2) of these Regulations.

Note: Authority cited: Sections 59, 129.5, 133 and 5307.3, Labor Code. Reference: Sections 11180, 11180.5, 11181 and 11182, Government Code; and Sections 111, 124, 129, 129.5, 3751 and 3752, Labor Code.

History: 1. Repealer and new section filed 1-28-94; operative 1-28-94. Submitted to OAL for printing only pursuant to Government Code section 11351 (Register 94, No. 4). For prior history, see Register 90, No. 4.

2. New subsections (c)-(e), subsection relettering, amendment of newly designated subsection (g) and amendment of Note filed 10-26-98; operative 11-25-98 (Register 98, No. 44).

Ref.: Hanna § 10.50[2][a]; Herlick Handbook §§ 1.01[3][b], 9.5.

§10107.1. Notice of Audit; Claim File Selection; Production of Claim Files; Auditing Procedure.

For audits conducted on or after January 1, 2003:

(a) Once a subject has been selected for an audit, the Audit Unit shall serve a Notice of Audit on the claims administrator. The Notice of Audit shall inform the claims administrator of its selection for audit, and may include a request to provide the Audit Unit with a claim log or logs. If the Audit Unit has requested claim logs, the audit subject shall provide two copies of each requested claim log within 14 days of the date of the receipt of the Notice of Audit. Only one copy of the requested claim log or logs shall be provided within 14 days of the date of the receipt of the Notice of Audit by the claims administrator if the copy is provided via electronic submission to the Audit Unit mailbox at DWCAuditUnit@dir.ca.gov.

(b) At least 14 days before the audit is scheduled, the Audit Unit shall send the audit subject a Notice of Audit Commencement identifying the claims to be audited. The audit shall commence no less than 14 days from the date the Notice of Audit Commencement was sent, unless the audit subject and Audit Unit agrees to earlier commencement. Claims selected for audit that are administered at the home of a telecommuting adjuster must be presented for audit at a California office location of the administrator, at a California location of the self insured employer, an Audit Unit office, or a Workers' Compensation Appeals Board district office. Other arrangements may be made as agreed between the audit subject and the Audit Unit.

(c) For profile audit reviews conducted pursuant to Labor Code section 129(b)(1), the Audit Unit shall randomly select samples of indemnity claims from the most recent three years of the audit subject's claim logs or from the list of claims for those years as reported to the Division of Workers' Compensation pursuant to Labor Code section 138.6 as part of the Workers' Compensation Information System. Claim samples randomly selected under this subdivision shall not include claims with a single indemnity payment that cannot be classified under the profile audit review performance standards set forth in subdivision (c)(3)(A) through (C)(3)(E). If any of the years have been the subject of a previous audit, claims will be randomly selected from the most recent unaudited year(s).

(1) The initial number of indemnity claims randomly selected for audit will be determined based on the following table:

Population	*Sample Size*
5 or less	all
6-10	1 less than total
11-13	2 less than total
14-16	3 less than total
17-18	4 less than total
19-20	5 less than total
21-23	6 less than total
24	17
25-26	18
27-29	19
30-31	20
32-33	21
34-36	22
37-39	23
40-41	24
42-44	25
45-48	26
49-51	27
52-55	28
56-58	29
59-62	30
63-67	31
68-72	32
73-77	33
78-82	34
83-88	35
89-95	36
96-102	37
103-110	38
111-119	39
120-128	40
129-139	41
140-151	42
152-164	43
165-179	44
180-197	45
198-217	46
218-241	47
242-269	48
270-304	49
305-346	50
347-399	51
400-468	52
469-562	53
563-696	54
697-905	55
906-1,272	56
1,273-2,091	57
2,092-5,530	58
5,531 +	59

(2) In addition to the randomly selected indemnity claims, the Audit Unit may audit any claims for which it has received a complaint or information over the past three years that indicate a failure to pay indemnity, including any companion claim needed to ascertain the extent to which benefits have been provided. Claims with complaints that are randomly selected will be audited as part of the random sample and included in the performance rating.

Complaints not involving a failure to pay indemnity will be provided to the audit subject, if confidentiality has not been requested, for review and corrective action, if warranted. Within 30 days of receipt of the report of audit findings issued pursuant to subdivision (f) of this section, the audit subject shall provide a written response to the Audit Unit, stating its review findings and corrective actions, if any.

(3) After reviewing the claims selected pursuant to subdivision (c)(1), the Audit Unit shall calculate the audit subject's profile audit review performance rating based on its review of the randomly selected claims. The profile audit review performance rating will be calculated as follows:

(A) The factor for the failure to pay accrued and undisputed indemnity shall be determined by:

1. Dividing the number of randomly selected claims with violations involving the failure to pay indemnity [pursuant to California Code of Regulations, title 8, section 10111.2, subdivisions (a)(1), (a)(2), (a)(3), (a)(4), and (a)(10)] by the number of randomly selected claims with accrued and payable indemnity, to produce a frequency rate.

2. Dividing the total amount of unpaid indemnity in randomly selected claims by the number of randomly selected claims with accrued and payable indemnity, to produce an average amount of unpaid indemnity per file with the obligation to pay indemnity.

3. Dividing the average amount of unpaid indemnity per randomly selected audited claim with the obligation to pay indemnity for the audit subject by the average amount of unpaid indemnity per randomly selected audited claim for all audit subjects for the three calendar years before the year preceding the year in which the current audit was commenced, to produce a severity rate.

4. Multiplying the frequency rate by the severity rate by a modifier of 2 to determine the factor for the failure to pay accrued and undisputed indemnity.

(B) The factor for the late first payment of temporary disability indemnity shall be determined by dividing the number of randomly selected claims with violations involving the late first payment of temporary disability indemnity [pursuant to section 10111.2, subdivisions (a)(5), (a)(8), and (a)(10)], or in claims that involve salary continuation, failure to comply with the requirements for first notices advising the injured employee of the provision of salary continuation in lieu of first temporary disability payments [pursuant to section 10111.2, subdivisions (b)(8)(B) and (b)(8)(C)], by the number of randomly selected claims in which temporary disability payments or first notices advising the injured employee of the provision of salary continuation in lieu of first temporary disability notices were required. In any claim that involves the payment of both salary continuation in lieu of first temporary disability payments and temporary disability payments, each benefit type paid will be considered in calculating this factor.

(C) The factor for the late first payment of permanent disability indemnity, vocational rehabilitation maintenance allowance, and death benefits [pursuant to section 10111.2, subdivisions (a)(6), (a)(7), (a)(8), and (a)(10)] shall be determined by dividing the numbers of randomly selected claims with violations involving late first payments of those benefits by the numbers of randomly selected claims with payments for those benefits. In calculation of this factor, claims shall be counted for each type of exposure and late first payment.

(D) The factor for late subsequent indemnity payments [pursuant to section 10111.2, subdivisions (a)(8), (a)(9), and (a)(10)] shall be determined by dividing the number of randomly selected claims with violations involving late indemnity payments subsequent to first payment by the number of randomly selected claims with subsequent indemnity payments.

(E) The factor for failure to comply with requirements for notices advising injured employees of the process for selecting Agreed Medical Examiners and/or Qualified Medical Examiners, and for injured workers with injuries prior to January 1, 2004, failure to comply with the requirements for notices advising injured workers of potential eligibility for vocational rehabilitation, or for injured workers with injuries on or after January 1, 2004, failure to comply with the requirements for notices advising injured workers of the right to the supplemental job displacement benefit, shall be determined by dividing the numbers of randomly selected claims with violations involving the failure to comply with the applicable requirement to issue the notices by the numbers of randomly selected claims with the requirement to issue the notices. In calculation of this factor, claims shall be counted for each type of exposure and violation.

(F) The audit subject's profile audit review performance rating will be determined by adding the factors calculated pursuant to subdivisions (c)(3)(A) through (c)(3)(E).

(4) If the audit subject's profile audit review performance rating meets or exceeds the worst 20% of performance ratings for all final audit reports issued for audits commenced the three calendar years before the year preceding the year in which the current audit was commenced, the Audit Unit will issue Notices of Compensation Due pursuant to California Code of Regulations, title 8, section 10110 but will assess no administrative penalties for violations found in the profile audit review.

(5) If the audit subject's profile audit review performance rating fails to meet or exceed the rating of the worst 20% of performance ratings as calculated based on all final audit findings as published in the Annual DWC Audit Reports over the three calendar years before the year preceding the year in which the current audit was commenced, the Audit Unit will conduct a full compliance audit by randomly selecting and auditing an additional sample of indemnity claims pursuant to subdivision (d). Written notification of the Audit Unit's findings from the profile audit review, the calculation of the profile audit review performance rating, and intent to proceed to a full compliance audit, will be provided to the audit subject in time for the timely filing of an objection. The audit subject may dispute whether or not a full compliance audit is merited under this subdivision at a post-profile audit review conference. Unless the audit subject demonstrates that the factual basis for the Audit Unit's calculation of the profile audit review performance rating is incorrect within two working days of the receipt of the rating or at the post profile audit review conference, the Audit Unit may complete the full compliance audit. The audit subject may appeal the issues pursuant to California Code of Regulations, title 8, section 10115.1 following the issuance of the final audit report. Failure of the audit subject to raise factual issues related to failing to meet or exceed the profile audit review performance standard within two working days of the receipt of the profile audit review performance rating or during the post-profile audit review conference shall constitute a waiver of appeal on those issues.

(d) If the audit subjects fails to meet or exceed the profile audit review performance standard, the Audit Unit shall conduct a full compliance audit by selecting and auditing an additional sample of indemnity claims.

(1) The total number of indemnity claims randomly selected for audit, including the number audited pursuant to subdivision (c)(1), will be determined based on the following table:

Population	*Sample Size*
8 or less	all
9-15	1 less than total
16-19	2 less than total
20-23	3 less than total
24-27	4 less than total
28-30	5 less than total
31-33	6 less than total
34-36	7 less than total
37-38	8 less than total
39-41	9 less than total
42	32
43-44	33
45	34
46-47	35
48-49	36
50-51	37
52-53	38
54-55	39
56-57	40
58-59	41
60-61	42
62-63	43
64-65	44
66-67	45
68-70	46
71-72	47
73-74	48
75-77	49
78-79	50
80-82	51
83-84	52
85-87	53
88-89	54
90-92	55
93-95	56
96-98	57
99-101	58
102-104	59

Population	*Sample Size*
105-107	60
108-110	61
111-114	62
115-117	63
118-120	64
121-124	65
125-128	66
129-131	67
132-135	68
136-139	69
140-143	70
144-148	71
149-152	72
153-156	73
157-161	74
162-166	75
167-171	76
172-176	77
177-181	78
182-187	79
188-192	80
193-198	81
199-204	82
205-210	83
211-217	84
218-223	85
224-230	86
231-238	87
239-245	88
246-253	89
254-261	90
262-270	91
271-279	92
280-288	93
289-298	94
299-308	95
309-319	96
320-330	97
331-342	98
343-354	99
355-367	100
368-381	101
382-396	102
397-411	103
412-427	104
428-444	105
445-463	106
464-482	107
483-503	108
504-525	109
526-549	110
550-575	111
576-603	112
604-633	113
634-665	114
666-700	115
701-739	116
740-781	117
782-827	118
828-879	119
880-936	120
937-1,000	121
1,001-1,072	122
1,073-1,154	123
1,155-1,248	124
1,249-1,356	125
1,357-1,483	126
1,484-1,633	127
1,634-1,814	128
1,815-2,036	129
2,037-2,315	130
2,316-2,677	131
2,678-3,163	132
3,164-3,852	133
3,853-4,904	134
4,905-6,710	135
6,711-10,530	136
10,531-23,993	137
23,994 +	138

(2) In addition to the randomly selected indemnity claims, the Audit Unit may audit any claims for which it has received a complaint or information over the past three years that indicate a failure to pay indemnity or late-paid indemnity, including any companion claim needed to ascertain the extent to which benefits have been provided.

Complaints not involving a failure to pay indemnity or late paid indemnity will be provided to the audit subject, if confidentiality has not been requested, for self-review and corrective action, if warranted. Within 30 days of receipt of the report of audit findings issued pursuant to subdivision (f) of this section, the audit subject shall provide a written response to the Audit Unit stating its review findings and corrective actions, if any.

(3) After reviewing the claims selected pursuant to subdivision (d)(1), the Audit Unit shall calculate the audit subject's full compliance audit performance rating.

(A) The audit subject's full compliance audit performance rating will be calculated pursuant to subdivision (c)(3), except that it shall be based on the review of all claims selected pursuant to subdivision (d)(1).

(B) If the audit subject's full compliance audit performance rating meets or exceeds the worst 10% of performance ratings for all final audit reports issued for audits commenced in the three calendar years before the year preceding the year in which the current audit was commenced, the Audit Unit will issue Notices of Compensation Due pursuant to section 10110 and will assess administrative penalties only for violations involving unpaid and late paid compensation, pursuant to Labor Code section 129.5(c)(2).

(e) If the audit subject's full compliance audit performance rating fails to meet or exceed the rating of the worst 10% of performance ratings for all final audit reports issued for audits commenced in the three calendar years before the year preceding the year in which the current audit was commenced, the Audit Unit will audit all claims selected for audit for all violations, and also randomly select a sample of denied claims. Written notification of the Audit Unit's findings from the full compliance audit, the calculation of the full compliance audit performance rating, and intent to audit a sample of denied claims and assess penalties pursuant to Labor Code section 129.5(c)(3), will be provided to the audit subject in time for the timely filing of an objection. The audit subject may dispute whether or not it met or exceeded the full compliance audit performance standard at a meet and confer audit review conference. Unless the audit subject demonstrates that the factual basis for the Audit Unit's calculation of the full compliance audit performance rating is incorrect within two working days of the receipt of the rating or at the meet and confer audit review conference, the Audit Unit may complete the full compliance audit. The audit subject may appeal pursuant to section 10115.1 following the issuance of the final audit report. Failure of the audit subject to raise factual issues related to failing to meet or exceed the full compliance audit performance standard within two working days of the receipt of the full compliance audit performance rating or during the meet and confer audit review conference shall constitute a waiver of appeal on those issues.

(1) The number of denied claims randomly selected for audit will be based on the following table:

Population	*Sample Size*
6 or less	all
7-10	1 less than total
11-14	2 less than total
15-17	3 less than total
18	14
19-20	15
21	16
22-23	17
24-25	18
26-27	19
28-29	20
30-31	21
32-33	22
34-36	23
37-38	24
39-41	25
42-43	26
44-46	27
47-49	28
50-52	29
53-55	30
56-59	31
60-63	32
64-67	33
68-71	34
72-75	35
76-80	36
81-85	37
86-90	38
91-96	39
97-102	40
103-109	41
110-116	42
117-124	43
125-132	44
133-141	45
142-151	46
152-163	47
164-175	48
176-189	49
190-205	50
206-222	51
223-242	52
243-265	53
266-292	54
293-323	55
324-360	56
361-405	57
406-461	58
462-531	59
532-623	60
624-749	61
750-931	62
932-1,217	63
1,218-1,731	64
1,732-2,934	65
2,935-8,990	66
8,991 +	67

(2) In addition to the random samples of indemnity and denied claims, the Audit Unit may select for audit all claims for which the Division received complaints or information over the past three years that indicate the possible existence of any claims handling violations, including any companion claim(s) needed to ascertain the extent to which benefits have been provided.

(f) Following the conclusion of the audit, the Audit Unit shall issue a report of audit findings which may include, but is not limited to, the following: one or more requests for additional documentation or compliance, Notices of Intention to Issue Notice of Compensation Due, Preliminary Notices of Penalty Assessments, Notices of Compensation Due, or Notices of Penalty Assessments. If any additional requested documentation is not provided within thirty days of receipt of the report, additional audit penalties may be assessed under California Code of Regulations, title 8, section 10111.2(b)(23) of these Regulations.

(g) The audit subject shall pay all expenses of an audit of an adjusting location outside the State of California, including per diem, travel expense, and compensated overtime of audit personnel.

(h) The audit subject shall make each of the claim files selected for audit available at the audit site at the time of audit commencement. Claims will include but not be limited to the required contents of California Code of Regulations, title 8, section 10101.1. If claim files are maintained in an electronic or other non-paper storage medium, the claims administrator shall, upon request, provide to the Audit Unit, at the Audit Unit's discretion, direct computer access to electronic claim files and/or legible printed paper copies of the claim files, including all records of compensation payments. If a randomly selected indemnity, medical-only, or denied claim has been incorrectly classified as to type by the audit subject, the Audit Unit may randomly select an additional correctly designated claim file for audit, and may also assess penalties as appropriate in the misdesignated claim initially selected. If the audit subject fails to produce a claim selected for audit, the Audit Unit may assess a penalty for failure to produce the claim pursuant to section 10111.2(b)(3) and may also select for audit another claim of the same type to complete the random sample. If, after the issuance of the Notice of Audit Commencement that notified the audit subject that the claim was selected for audit, the audit subject has transferred a claim to a different adjusting location of the company being audited, the audit subject shall nonetheless produce the claim for audit within five working days of request, unless additional time is agreed upon by both the Audit Unit and the audit subject.

(i) The Audit Unit shall have discretion to audit claims in addition to those identified with the Notice of Audit Commencement. The audit subject shall make each of the additional claims selected for audit available at the audit site as follows:

(1) Open claims and closed claims stored on site within one working day of request;

(2) Closed claims stored off site within five working days of request, unless additional time is agreed upon by both the Audit Unit and the audit subject.

(j) The audit subject shall provide the auditor(s) an adequate, safe, and healthful workspace during the audit, which allows the auditors a reasonable degree of privacy. If the Audit Unit determines that this workspace is not provided, the Audit Unit may require the audit subject to deliver the files to another California office location of the audit subject, an Audit Unit office, or a Workers' Compensation Appeals Board district office, for completion of the audit. Other arrangements may be made as agreed between the audit subject and the Audit Unit.

(k) The Audit Unit may obtain and retain copies of documentation or information from claim files to support the assessment of penalties.

(*l*) The audit subject shall have the opportunity to discuss preliminary findings and provide additional information at a post-audit conference.

(m) The Audit Unit may at any time request additional information or documentation related to the claims being audited in order to complete its audit. Such information may include documentation demonstrating that, as specified by Labor Code sections 3751 and 3752, compensation has not been reduced or affected by any insurance, contribution, or other benefit due to or received by or from the employee. The audit subject shall provide any requested documentation or other information within ten working days from the Audit Unit's request, unless the Audit Unit extends the time for good cause.

Note: Authority cited: Sections 59, 129, 129.5, 133 and 5307.3, Labor Code. Reference: Sections 11180, 11180.5, 11181 and 11182, Government Code; and Sections 111, 124, 129, 129.5, 139.5, 3751, 3752, 4658.5 and 4658.6, Labor Code.

History: 1. New section filed 12-30-2002; operative 1-1-2003 pursuant to Government Code section 11343.4 (Register 2003, No. 1).

2. Change without regulatory effect amending subsections (c)(3)(A)(i-a) and (c)(3)(A)(i-c) filed 5-1-2003 pursuant to section 100, title 1, California Code of Regulations (Register 2003, No. 18).

3. Amendment of subsection (c)(3)(A)v. filed 10-6-2003; operative 12-1-2003 (Register 2003, No. 41).

4. Amendment of section and Note filed 4-20-2009; operative 5-20-2009 (Register 2009, No. 17).

Ref.: Hanna §§ 1.12[8]–[10], 10.50, 10.51; Herlick Handbook §§ 1.01[3][b], 9.5, 9.19.

§10108. Audit Violations—General Rules.

The following general rules apply to audits and audit processes under Labor Code sections 129 and 129.5:

(a) If the date or deadline (including any applicable extension) to perform any act falls on a weekend or holiday, the act may be performed on the last business day before or the first business day after the weekend or holiday. A payment date which is changed under this provision shall not change the normal dates for later payments in an existing two-week payment schedule.

(b) For the purpose of imposing audit penalties, if the claims administrator does not record the date it received a document, it shall be deemed received five days after the latest date the sender wrote on the document.

(c) Audit penalties will be based on each claim's status when the claim is audited.

(1) If, at the time of the audit, the claims administrator has failed to perform a required act, but remedies the failure prior to the receipt of the Notice of Audit Commencement, when the claims administrator was notified that the claim was selected for audit, the claims administrator will be accountable for the violation. The penalty for an unlawful delay of more than 30 days in performing an act is the same as the penalty for not performing the act unless these regulations specifically provide otherwise. However the penalty will be mitigated for good faith because the act, though late, was eventually performed.

(2) If the claims administrator remedies a failure to perform a required act only after receipt of the Notice of Audit Commencement, the claims administrator will nonetheless be accountable for the violation as a failure to act and audit findings related to the violation will be based on the failure to perform the act. In cases where there is an unlawful delay of more than 30 days in performing an act and the act was performed only after the audit subject was notified that the claim was selected for audit, penalties will be assessed as though there was a failure to perform the act rather than late performance of the act. There will be no mitigation for good faith if the act was performed after notification to the audit subject that the claim was selected for audit.

(d) Penalties will not be assessed during the period a claims administrator is actively investigating its liability for provision of benefits or payment of compensation, provided that a Notice of Delay has been timely and properly issued in accordance with California Code of Regulations, title 8, sections 9812 or 9813. However, penalties shall still be issued for violations during the period of delay for: the failure to timely pay or object to medical bills for treatment authorized under Labor Code section 5402(c); the failure to timely pay or object to medical treatment bills in accordance with Labor Code section 4603.2, or the failure to timely pay or object to medical legal expenses in accordance with Labor Code section 4620, et seq.

(e) Penalties will not be assessed for an act or omission where an injured worker's unreasonable refusal to cooperate in the investigation has prevented the claims administrator from determining its legal obligation to perform the act.

(f) Where a penalty is provided for failure to pay mileage fees related to medical treatment or evaluation, a penalty will be imposed if payment is not made at a rate that is at least the minimum rate adopted by the Director of the Department of Personnel Administration pursuant to Section 19820 of the Government Code for non-represented (excluded) employees at California Code of Regulations, title 2, section 599.631(a).

(g) Failure, delay, or refusal to pay compensation benefits or expenses shall be subject to the applicable penalties under California Code of Regulations, title 8, sections 10111, 10111.1, or 10111.2 unless the legal, factual, or medical basis for the failure, refusal, or delay is documented in the claim file.

(h) The Audit Unit will not assess penalties for violations of failure to make payment of indemnity due if the total indemnity is less than twenty-five dollars ($25.00) aggregate per claim. Although penalties may not be assessed, the audit subject shall pay all indemnity owed.

(i) Nothing in these regulations will bar the assessment of a civil penalty under Labor Code section 129.5(e), whether or not the audit subject meets or exceeds performance rating standards calculated pursuant to California Code of Regulations, title 8, section 10107.1(c)(3) or (d)(3).

(j) Claims that are randomly selected for audit pursuant to California Code of Regulations, title 8, sections 10107.1(c)(1) and (d)(1) will be considered as randomly selected claims for purposes of determining whether or not an audit subject meets or exceeds performance standards pursuant to sections 10107.1(c)(3) or (d)(3), whether or not complaints or information indicating claims handling violations in those claims have been received by the Audit Unit. If the Audit Unit cannot ascertain the extent to which benefits have been paid on a claim randomly selected for audit without auditing a companion or master claim to that claim, the Audit Unit may add the companion or master claim to the random sample. The companion or master claims will be considered as randomly selected claims for purposes of determining whether or not the audit subject meets or exceeds performance standards pursuant to sections 10107.1(c)(3) and/or (d)(3).

(k) Notwithstanding section 10111.2(a) and (b), penalties may be assessed for failure to timely submit an accurate Annual Report of Inventory regardless of whether or not an audit has been conducted, or, if an audit was conducted, whether or not the audit subject's performance rating in the key performance areas calculated pursuant to section 10107(c) warrants the audit of a full sample of indemnity claims pursuant to section 10107(c)(4), or a return, targeted audit based on performance in those areas pursuant to California Code of Regulations, title 8, section 10106(c)(2).

(*l*) Notwithstanding penalty amounts established pursuant to section 10111.2, penalties for late performance of an act may not exceed penalty amounts for the failure to perform an act.

(m) If more than one claims administrator has adjusted a claim file that is being audited or investigated, penalties will be assessed against the audit subject only for violations that occurred subsequent to the date the audit subject began adjusting the claim file, except that the audit subject will be assessed penalties for the failure to pay compensation due if the claim was open when transferred to the audit subject or re-opened subsequent to its transfer and the compensation remained unpaid. The audit subject is required to correct any failures to issue notices which are still pertinent, to recalculate and correct any improperly calculated payments due to the worker, and to pay any interest and increase due for late paid medical payments.

(n) Successor liability may be imposed on a claims administrator or insurer that has merged with, consolidated, or otherwise continued the business of a corporation or other business entity that is a responsible party and failed to meet its obligations under Divisions 1 and 4 of the Labor Code or regulations of the administrative director. The surviving claims administrator shall assume and be liable for all the liabilities, obligations and penalties of the prior corporation or business entity. Successor liability will be imposed if there has been a substantial continuity of business operations; and/or the new business uses the same or substantially the same work force. In such circumstances, due consideration of the appropriateness of penalties with respect to the history of previous violations pursuant to Labor Code section 129.5(b)(3) will encompass findings related to the last audit of the predecessor claims administrator applied in conjunction with audit results of the successor claims administrator pursuant to California Code of Regulations, title 8, section 10111.2(c)(4).

Note: Authority cited: Sections 59, 129.5, 133, 138.3, 138.4, 138.6 and 5307.3, Labor Code. Reference: Sections 124, 129, 129.5, 138.6, 4600, 4603.2, 4621 and 5402, Labor Code; and Sections 7, 9, 10 and 11, Civil Code.

History: 1. Renumbering of former section 10108 to section 10111 and new section filed 1-28-94; operative 1-28-94. Submitted to OAL for printing only pursuant to Government Code section 11351 (Register 94, No. 4).

2. Amendment of subsection (e) filed 2-14-96; operative 2-14-96. Submitted to OAL for printing only pursuant to Government Code section 11351 (Register 96, No. 7).

3. Amendment of subsection (c) filed 10-26-98; operative 11-25-98 (Register 98, No. 44).

4. Amendment of subsections (c) and (f) and new subsections (h)-(n) filed 12-30-2002; operative 1-1-2003 pursuant to Government Code section 11343.4 (Register 2003, No. 1).

5. Amendment of section and Note filed 4-20-2009; operative 5-20-2009 (Register 2009, No. 17).

Ref.: Hanna §§ 1.12[8]–[10], 10.50, 10.51; Herlick Handbook §§ 1.01[3][b], 9.5, 9.19.

§10109. Duty to Conduct Investigation; Duty of Good Faith.

(a) To comply with the time requirements of the Labor Code and the Administrative Director's regulations, a claims administrator must conduct a reasonable and timely investigation upon receiving notice or knowledge of an injury or claim for a workers' compensation benefit.

(b) A reasonable investigation must attempt to obtain the information needed to determine and timely provide each benefit, if any, which may be due the employee.

(1) The administrator may not restrict its investigation to preparing objections or defenses to a claim, but must fully and fairly gather the pertinent information, whether that information requires or excuses benefit payment. The investigation must supply the information needed to provide timely benefits and to document for audit the administrator's basis for its claims decisions. The claimant's

burden of proof before the Appeal Board does not excuse the administrator's duty to investigate the claim.

(2) The claims administrator may not restrict its investigation to the specific benefit claimed if the nature of the claim suggests that other benefits might also be due.

(c) The duty to investigate requires further investigation if the claims administrator receives later information, not covered in an earlier investigation, which might affect benefits due.

(d) The claims administrator must document in its claim file the investigatory acts undertaken and the information obtained as a result of the investigation. This documentation shall be retained in the claim file and available for audit review.

(e) Insurers, self-insured employers and third-party administrators shall deal fairly and in good faith with all claimants, including lien claimants.

Note: Authority cited: Sections 59, 129.5, 133, 5307.3, Labor Code. Reference: Article 14, Section 4, California Constitution; Sections 124, 129, 133, 4061, 4550, 4600, 4636 through 4638, 4650, 4701 through 4703.5, 5402 and 5814, Labor Code; *Ramirez v. WCAB*, 10 Cal.App.3d 227, 88 CR 865, 35 CCC 383 (1970); and Section 790.03(h)(3), (5), (13), Insurance Code.

History: 1. Relocation of article 4 heading to article 6, renumbering of former section 10109 to section 10113 and new section filed 1-28-94; operative 1-28-94. Submitted to OAL for printing only pursuant to Government Code section 11351 (Register 94, No. 4).

2. Amendment of subsection (d) filed 4-20-2009; operative 5-20-2009 (Register 2009, No. 17).

Ref.: Hanna §§ 1.12[8]–[10], 10.50[2][a], 10.51; Herlick Handbook §§ 1.01[3][b], 9.5, 9.19.

ARTICLE 4
Notices of Compensation Due

§10110. Notice of Intention to Issue a Notice of Compensation Due; Notice of Compensation Due; Review by Workers' Compensation Appeals Board.

(a) If as the result of an audit, the Administrative Director determines that compensation is due and unpaid to an employee, (s)he shall serve on the audit subject, personally or by first class mail, a Notice of Intention to Issue a Notice of Compensation Due specifying the amount, reason and period for which compensation is due. If liability for compensation is clear but the amount cannot be determined from information in the claim file, the Administrative Director may direct the claims administrator to gather the necessary additional information.

(b) The audit subject may file an Objection to the Notice of Intention within 14 days of receipt. The Objection shall state in detail the reasons the compensation found due is disputed and may include supporting documentation and legal argument.

(c) The Administrative Director will review any Objection, and may set the matter for an administrative meeting, which may be included as part of a post audit conference. The administrative meeting or the post audit conference may be set on the Administrative Director's own initiative or at the request of the audit subject. After review, the Administrative Director shall either dismiss the Notice of Intention to Issue a Notice of Compensation Due or issue a Notice of Compensation Due.

(d) If no timely Objection is submitted, the Administration Director may issue a Notice of Compensation Due. A Notice of Compensation Due which was issued without a timely Objection shall be final without right of further review unless the Workers' Compensation Appeals Board agrees to hear an appeal after a late Objection.

(e) A Notice of Compensation Due shall specify the amount, reason and period for which compensation is due and shall order payment of the compensation to the employee or dependent. The Notice of Compensation Due shall be served on the insurer, self-insured employer or third-party administrator personally or by certified or registered mail, and a copy shall be sent by first class mail to the affected employee or dependent. The compensation due must be paid within 15 days of receipt of the Notice of Compensation Due unless appealed to the Workers Compensation Appeals Board in accordance with Section 10115 of these Rules and the applicable rules of the Workers' Compensation Appeals Board.

Note: Authority cited: Sections 59, 129.5, 133, 4603.5 and 5307.3, Labor Code. Reference: Sections 129, 139.5, 3207, 4453, 4550, 4600, 4621, 4636 through 4638, 4639, 4653, 4658, 4659, 4660, 4661.5, 4701-4703.5, 4900 and 4902, Labor Code; and Section 10952, Title 8, California Code of Regulations.

History: 1. New article 4 heading, renumbering of former section 10110 to section 10114 and new section filed 1-28-94; operative 1-28-94. Submitted to OAL for printing only pursuant to Government Code section 11351 (Register 94, No. 4).

Ref.: Hanna §§ 1.12[9][a], [b], 10.50[2][a]; Herlick Handbook §§ 1.01[3][b], 9.5.

ARTICLE 5
Administrative Penalties

§10111. Schedule of Administrative Penalties for Injuries on or After January 1, 1990, but Before January 1, 1994.

The administrative penalties set forth in subsections (a) through (d) of this section will be imposed for injuries occurring on or after January 1, 1990, but before January 1, 1994, subject to any applicable mitigation or exacerbation under subsection (e) of this section.

(a) A penalty of up to $100 for each violation shall be assessed when there is:

(1) Failure to make full payment of 10% self-imposed increase when temporary disability indemnity or permanent disability indemnity is overdue. The penalty for this violation is:

If the self-imposed increase was not paid or was only partially paid, the audit penalty is based on the amount of the underlying indemnity and is as follows:

$25 if the late-paid indemnity totals not more than 3 days;

$50 if the late-paid indemnity totals more than 3 but not more than 7 days;

$75 if the late-paid indemnity totals more than 7 but not more than 14 days;

$100 if the late paid indemnity totals more than 14 days.

(2) Failure to provide first permanent disability payment when due and/or within 14 days after temporary disability payments are terminated. The penalty for this violation is:

$25 if the first payment was made 1 to 2 days late;

$50 if the first payment was made 3 to 7 days late;

$75 if the first payment was made 8 to 14 days late;

$100 if the first payment was made more than 14 days late.

(3) Failure to respond to a written request for medical treatment of injured worker within 20 days of the date of request. The penalty for this violation is:

$25 for a response made from 1 to 7 days late;

$50 for a response made from 8 to 15 days late;

$75 for a response made from 16 to 34 days late;

$100 for failure to respond for more than 35 days.

(4) Failure to provide, upon request, any transportation costs when due to injured worker for medical care. The penalty for this violation is:

$25 for $10 or less in expense;

$50 for more than $10, to $20, in expense;

$75 for more than $20, to $40, in expense;

$100 for more than $40 in expense.

(5) Failure to document average weekly earnings if temporary disability indemnity is being paid at less than the maximum rate. The penalty for this violation is $100.

(6) Failure to make the first payment of temporary disability indemnity not later than 14 days after the date of the employer's knowledge of injury and disability pursuant to Labor Code Section 4650(a). The penalty for this violation is:

$25 if the first payment was made 1 to 2 days late;

$50 if the first payment was made 3 to 7 days late;

$75 if the first payment was made 8 to 14 days late, and/or if all indemnity then due was not paid but was paid with a subsequent payment;

$100 if the first payment was made more than 14 days late, and/or if all indemnity then due was not paid with the first payment and remains unpaid at the time of audit.

(7) Failure to follow the Rules and Regulations established by the Administrative Director for the purpose of carrying out the workers' compensation provisions in Labor Code Section 3200 through Section 6002. The penalty for this violation is:

[i] For each failure to include in a claim file a copy of the Employee's Claim for Worker's Compensation Benefits, DWC Form 1, showing the date the form was provided to and received from the employee, or documentation of the date the claim form was provided to the employee if the employee did not return the form, the penalty is:

$100 if there were any late indemnity payments, or if notice of acceptance of the claim was not issued within 90 days after the employer's date of knowledge of injury and disability, or if the claim was denied.

[ii] For each failure to issue a notice of benefits as required by Title 8, California Code of Regulations, Division 1, Chapter 4.5, Subchapter 1, Article 8, beginning with Section 9810, or by Title 8, California Code of Regulations, Division 1, Chapter 4.5, Subchapter 1.5, Article 7, beginning with Section 10122, unless penalties apply and are assessed under Section 10111(b)(2) of these regulations, the penalty is $100.

[iii] For each notice of benefits which was not issued timely as provided in Title 8, California Code of Regulations, Division 1, Chapter 4.5, Subchapter 1, Article 8, beginning with Section 9810, or as provided in Title 8, California Code of Regulations, Division 1, Chapter 4.5, Subchapter 1.5, Article 7, beginning with Section 10122, the penalty is:

$25 for each notice of first, resumed, changed or final payment of temporary disability indemnity, wage continuation, death benefits, permanent disability indemnity, or VRMA which was issued from 1 to 7 days late;

$50 for each notice of first, resumed, changed or final payment of temporary disability indemnity, wage continuation, death benefits, permanent disability indemnity, or VRMA which was issued more than 7 days late, and for each delay in decision notice or denial notice which was issued from 1 to 7 days late;

$75 for each delay in decision notice or denial notice which was issued more than 7 days late.

[iv] For each Notice of Benefits required by Title 8, California Code of Regulations, Division 1, Chapter 4.5, Subchapter 1, Article 8, beginning with Section 9810, or by Title 8, California Code of Regulations, Division 1, Chapter 4.5, Subchapter 1.5, Article 7, beginning with Section 10122, which was materially inaccurate or incomplete, except an inaccurate or incomplete denial notice, the penalty is $25. For a materially inaccurate or incomplete denial notice the penalty is $100.

[v] For each failure to include in a claim file, or document attempts to obtain, any of the required contents specified in Section 10101, the penalty is $100.

[vi] For each failure to comply with any regulation of the Administrative Director, not otherwise assessed in these Regulations, the penalty is $100.

(8) Failure to pay or object to all documented Medical-Legal expenses within 60 days of receipt of billing and any required reports as provided for in Labor Code 4622. The penalty for this violation is:

$50 for each bill which was paid more than 60 days from receipt with interest and a 10% increase;

$75 for each bill which was paid more than 60 days from receipt where either interest or a 10% increase was not included;

$100 for each bill which was paid more than 60 days from receipt where neither interest nor a 10% increase was paid;

$100 for each bill which was not paid where no timely objection was sent.

(9) Failure to pay or object to expenses for medical treatment within 60 days of receipt of the bill and any required reports. The penalty for this violation is:

$25 for each bill of $100 or less, excluding interest and penalty;

$50 for each bill of more than $100, but no more than $200, excluding interest and penalty;

$75 for each bill of more than $200, but no more than $300, excluding interest and penalty;

$100 for each bill of more than $300, excluding interest and penalty.

(10) Failure to pay within ten days any indemnity due, which is not specified in subsections (a)(1) through (a)(9). The penalty for this violation is:

$25 for late payment of 3 days of indemnity or less;

$50 for late payment of more than 3 but no more than 7 days of indemnity;

$75 for late payment of more than 7 days of indemnity, or failure to pay 3 days of indemnity or less;

$100 for failure to pay more than 3 days of indemnity.

(b) A penalty of up to $500 for each violation shall be assessed when there is:

(1) Failure to maintain and provide a written claim log as defined in Section 10100(g) to the audit unit commencing July 1, 1990, and thereafter. The claim log shall contain all claims received, whether liability has been accepted, and distinguish between Indemnity and Medical-only claims. The penalty for this violation is:

$25 for each failure to list on a claim log one or more of the following: employee's name; claim number; date of injury;

$25 for each misdesignation of an indemnity file as a medical-only file on the claim log;

$100 for each failure to identify subsidiary self-insured employers on the log;

$100 for each failure to identify the underwriting insurance company of an insurance group;

$100 for each failure to designate a denied claim on the log;

$100 for each claim not listed on the log;

$250 for each failure to provide the claim log to the Audit Unit within 14 days of receipt of a written request if the claim log was provided more than 14 but no more than 30 days from receipt of the request;

$500 for each failure for more than 30 days from receipt of a written request, to provide the claim log to the Audit Unit.

(2) Failure to comply with Labor Code Sections 4636, 4637 and 4644. The penalty for this violation is:

[i] The penalty for each failure to assign a qualified rehabilitation representative immediately after 90 days of aggregate temporary disability indemnity is $100 if the assignment was made or the employee returned to his or her usual and customary occupation more than 10 but not more than 20 days after 90 days of aggregate total disability, and an additional $100 for each additional delay of not more than 10 days, to a maximum penalty of $500.

[ii] The penalty for each failure to issue notice of medical eligibility for vocational rehabilitation services (if not previously issued) within 10 days after knowledge of a physician's opinion that the employee is medically eligible, or for failure to issue notice within 10 days after 366 days of aggregate total temporary disability, is $100 if the notice was issued not more than 10 days late, and an additional $100 for each additional delay of not more than 10 days, to a maximum penalty of $500.

[iii] The penalty for each failure to notify an injured employee of the reasons he or she is not entitled to any, or to any further, vocational rehabilitation services, and the procedure for contesting the determination of non-eligibility, is $100 if notification was issued more than 10 but not more than 20 days after the determination, and an additional $100 for each additional delay of not more than 10 days, to a maximum penalty of $500.

(c) A penalty of up to $1,000 for each violation shall be assessed when there is:

(1) Failure to pay or appeal penalties provided for in the Notice of Compensation Due within 15 days of the date of receipt of the Notice. The penalty for this violation is:

$250 for each assessment paid more than 15 but not more than 30 days after receipt;

$500 for each assessment paid more than 30 but not more than 45 days after receipt;

$1,000 for each assessment not paid within 45 days after receipt.

(2) Failure to comply with or appeal any final order of the Workers' Compensation Appeals Board within 30 days of service. The penalty for this violation is:

$250 for full compliance in more than 30 but not more than 45 days from the date of service, or for any late payment or failure to pay interest due;

$500 for full compliance (other than a late interest payment) in more than 45 but not more than 60 days from the date of service;

$750 for full compliance (other than a late interest payment) in more than 60 but not more than 75 days from the date of service;

$1,000 if there was not full compliance (other than failure to pay interest) within 75 days of the date of service.

(d) A penalty of up to $5,000 for each violation shall be assessed when there is:

(1) Failure to produce, on a second request, a legible paper copy of a claim files within 5 days of written notice by the Administrative Director or his representatives. The penalty for this violation is:

$100 if the file was produced not more than 3 days late;

$250 if the file was produced more than 3 but not more than 14 days late;

$500 if the file was produced more than 14 but not more than 29 days late;

$1,000 if the file was produced more than 29 but not more than 40 days late;

$2500 if the file was produced more than 40 days late but not more than 90 days late.

$5000 if the was produced more than 90 days late or was not produced.

(2) Denial of liability for a claim without supporting documentation.

The total penalty shall be determined by applying the penalty assessment amount listed in [i] for gravity, subtracting the amount listed in [ii] for good faith if applicable, and increasing or decreasing the penalty as applicable for history and frequency as set forth in [iii] and [iv]:

[i] For a claim involving potential for medical treatment only the penalty is $3,500;

For a claim involving potential for medical treatment and either temporary or permanent disability the penalty is $4,000;

For a claim involving potential for medical treatment and both temporary and permanent disability the penalty is $4,500;

For a claim involving potential for medical treatment, temporary disability, permanent disability and vocational rehabilitation the penalty is $5,000;

For a claim involving potential for death benefits the penalty is $5,000.

[ii] The penalty will be reduced by $1,000 for good faith if there was a reasonable attempt to investigate the claim.

[iii] Reduction or increase of the penalty for history shall be based on the following:

An audit subject having no prior Audit Unit history will receive a $500 reduction;

An audit subject having a prior Audit Unit history of no more than one audited unsupported denial will receive a $500 reduction;

An audit subject having a prior Audit Unit history of more than one audited unsupported denial but no more than 5% of audited denials as unsupported will receive no reduction or increase for history;

An audit subject having a prior Audit Unit history of more than one audited unsupported denial and more than 5% of audited denials as unsupported will receive a $500 increase.

[iv] Reduction or increase of the penalty for frequency shall be based on the following:

An audit subject having no more than one audited unsupported denial will receive a $500 reduction;

An audit subject having more than one audited unsupported denial but no more than 5% of audited denials which are unsupported will receive no reduction or increase for frequency;

An audit subject having more than one audited unsupported denial and more than 5% of audited denials which are unsupported will receive an increase of $500.

[v] The total amount assessed for a denial shall be reduced by 50% if the claim was accepted after the denial without evidence that the acceptance was the result of litigation or of the claim's selection for audit.

(3) Except as provided in subsection (d)(1) of this section, failure to comply with or appeal any lawful written request or order of the Administrative Director regarding a claim filed within 30 days. The penalty for this violation is:

$500 if there was compliance in more than 30 but not more than 40 days from receipt or order;

$1,000 if there was compliance in more than 40 but not more than 60 days from receipt of the request or order;

$2,500 if there was compliance in more than 60 but not more than 90 days of receipt fo the request or order;

$5,000 for failure to comply within 90 days of receipt of the request or order.

(4) Failure by a claims administrator to provide a claim form within 24 hours upon request of an injured worker or his/her agent. The penalty for this violation is:

$500 if the claim form was provided in more than 1 but not more than 5 working days from receipt of the request, if benefits were being provided to the employee at the time of the request;

$1,000 if the claim form was not provided within 5 working days of receipt of the request, if benefits were being provided to the employee at the time of the request;

$3,000 if the claim form was provided in more than 1 but not more than 5 working days from receipt of the request, if benefits were not being provided to the employee at the time of the request;

$5,000 if the claim form was not provided within 5 working days of receipt of the request, if benefits were not being provided to the employee at the time of the request.

(e) The penalties otherwise applicable under subsections (a) through (d) of this section shall be modified, if warranted, for good faith, history, and frequency in the same manner as penalties are modified for acts or omissions occurring on or after January 1, 1994 by Section 10111.1(e) of this Article.

Note: Authority cited: Sections 59, 129.5, 133, 138.3, 138.4, 139.5, 4603.5, 4627 and 5307.3, Labor Code. Reference: Sections 124, 129, 129.5, 4061, 4453, 4454, 4550, 4600, 4603.2, 4621, 4622, 4625, 4636 through 4638, 4639, 4641, 4642, 4650, 4651, 4701 through 4703.5, 4706, 4706.5, 5401, 5401.6, 5402, 5800 and 5814, Labor Code; and Section 2629.1(e), (f), Unemployment Insurance Code.

History: 1. New section filed 1-18-90; operative 1-18-90 (Register 90, No. 4). New section is exempt from review by OAL pursuant to Government Code Section 11351.

2. Relocation and amendment of article heading, renumbering of former section 10111 to section 10114 subsections (g)-(h) and renumbering and amendment of former section 10108 to section 10111 filed 1-28-94; operative 1-28-94. Submitted to OAL for printing only pursuant to Government Code section 11351 (Register 94, No. 4).

3. Editorial correction by official state publisher of subsection (a)(2) (Register 95, No. 32).

4. Amendment of subsections (a), (a)(6), (a)(7)[ii], (a)(7)[iv] and (b)(1) filed 2-14-96; operative 2-14-96. Submitted to OAL for printing only pursuant to Government Code section 11351 (Register 96, No. 7).

5. Amendment of subsection (b)(1) filed 7-30-96; operative 7-30-96 pursuant to Government Code section 11343.4(d) (Register 96, No. 31).

Ref.: Hanna § 10.50[2][b]; Herlick Handbook §§ 1.01[3][b], 9.5.

§10111.1. Schedule of Administrative Penalties for Injuries On or After January 1, 1994.

The administrative penalties set forth in subdivisions (a) through (d) of this section will be imposed for injuries occurring on or after January 1, 1994, subject to any applicable mitigation or exacerbation under subdivision (e) of this section. Penalties will not be assessed for violations occurring during the period January 1, 1994 through March 31, 1994 for acts or omissions for which there previously existed no audit penalties.

(a) The following Group A violations carry penalties of up to $100:

(1) The penalty for each failure to pay the 10% self-imposed increase with a late indemnity payment in accordance with Labor Code section 4650(d) is:

$25 if the self-imposed increase was paid after the late indemnity payment;

If the self-imposed increase was not paid or was only partially paid, the audit penalty is based on the amount of the underlying indemnity and is as follows:

$25 if the late-paid indemnity totals not more than 3 days;

$50 if the late-paid indemnity totals more than 3 but not more than 7 days;

$75 if the late-paid indemnity totals more than 7 but not more than 14 days;

$100 if the late paid indemnity totals more than 14 days.

(2) The penalty for each failure to make the first payment of permanent disability indemnity within 14 days after the last payment of temporary disability indemnity, or within 14 days of knowledge of the existence of permanent disability when there is no temporary disability, is:

$25 if the first payment was made 1 to 2 days late;

$50 if the first payment was made 3 to 7 days late;

$75 if the first payment was made 8 to 14 days late;

$100 if the first payment was made more than 14 days late;

(3) The penalty for each failure to object or pay to the injured worker, within 60 days of receiving a request, reimbursement for the reasonable expense incurred for self-procured medical treatment in accordance with Labor Code section 4600, is:

$25 for $100 or less in expense;

$50 for more than $100, to $200, in expense;

$75 for more than $200, to $400, in expense;

$100 for more than $400 in expense.

(4) The penalty for each failure to pay mileage fees and bridge tolls when notifying the employee of a medical evaluation scheduled by the claims administrator, in accordance with Labor Code sections 4600 through 4621; or to pay mileage fees and bridge tolls within 14 days of receiving notice of a medical evaluation scheduled by the administrative director or the appeals board; or to object or pay the injured worker for any other transportation, temporary disability, meal or lodging expense incurred to obtain medical treatment or evaluation, within 60 days of receiving a request, is:

$25 for $10 or less in expense;

$50 for more than $10, to $50, in expense;

$75 for more than $50, to $100, in expense;

$100 for more than $100 in expense.

(5) The penalty for each failure to document a factual basis for paying less than the maximum indemnity rate is $100.

(6) The penalty for each failure to make temporary disability, permanent disability, death benefits or VRMA payments according to the payment schedule defined by California Code of Regulations, title 8, section 10100.1(x) of these regulations is:

$25 for each payment made 1 to 2 days late;

$50 for each payment made 3 to 7 days late;

$75 for each payment made 8 to 14 days late;

$100 for each payment made more than 14 days late.

(7) The penalty for each failure to comply with any regulation of the Administrative Director specified in this subdivision is:

[i] For each failure to include in a claim file a copy of the Employee's Claim for Worker's Compensation Benefits, DWC Form 1, showing the date the form was provided to and received from the employee, or documentation of the date the claim form was provided to the employee if the employee did not return the form, the penalty is:

$100 if there was any late indemnity payments, or if notice of acceptance of the claim was not issued within 90 days after the employer's date of knowledge of injury and disability, or if the claim was denied.

[ii] For each failure to issue a notice of benefits as required by California Code of Regulations, title 8, beginning with section 9810, or by California Code of Regulations, title 8, beginning with section 10122, unless penalties apply and are assessed under section 10111.1 subdivisions (b)(2), (b)(3), (b)(4), (b)(5), (b)(6), (b)(7) or (b)(8), the penalty is $100.

[iii] For each Notice of Benefits which was not issued timely as provided in California Code of Regulations, title 8, beginning with section 9810, or as provided in California Code of Regulations, title 8, beginning with section 10122, unless penalties apply and are assessed under section 10111.1 subdivisions (b)(2), (b)(3), (b)(4), (b)(5), (b)(6), (b)(7) or (b)(8), the penalty is:

$25 for each notice of first, resumed, changed or final payment of temporary disability indemnity, wage continuation, death benefits, permanent disability indemnity, or VRMA which was issued from 1 to 7 days late;

$50 for each notice of first, resumed, changed or final payment of temporary disability indemnity, wage continuation, death benefits, permanent disability indemnity, or VRMA which was issued more than 7 days late, and for each delay in decision notice which was issued from 1 to 7 days late;

$75 for each delay in decision notice which was issued more than 7 days late.

[iv] For each notice of benefits required by California Code of Regulations, title 8, beginning with section 9810, (except a materially misleading denial notice assessed under section 10111.1(b)(9)), or by California Code of Regulations, title 8, beginning with section 10122, which is materially inaccurate or incomplete, the penalty is $25.

[v] For each failure to include in a claim file, or document attempts to obtain, any of the required contents specified in section 10101.1 subdivisions (b), (c), (d), (e), (f), (g), (h), (i), (j), the penalty is $100.

[vi] For each failure to comply with any regulation of the Administrative Director, not otherwise assessed in this subchapter, the penalty is $100.

(8) The penalty for each failure to pay or object to a billing for a medical-legal expense, in the manner required by section 9794, within 60 days of receiving the bill and all reports and documents required by the Administrative Director incident to the services, is:

$25 for each bill which was paid more than 60 days from receipt with interest and a 10% increase;

$50 for each bill which was paid more than 60 days from receipt where either interest or a 10% increase was not included;

$75 for each bill which was paid more than 60 days from receipt where neither interest nor a 10% increase was paid.

$100 for each bill which was not paid at the time the audit subject was notified the claim was selected for audit where no timely objection was sent.

(9) The penalty for each failure to pay or object to, in the manner required by Labor Code section 4603.2, a bill for medical treatment provided or authorized by the treating physician, is as follows when the bill remains unpaid at

the time the audit subject is notified that the claim was selected for audit. For the purpose of this penalty the treating physician will be presumed chosen by the employee unless the claims administrator demonstrates otherwise:

$25 for each bill of $100 or less, excluding interest and penalty;

$50 for each bill of more than $100, but no more than $200 excluding interest and penalty;

$75 for each bill of more than $200, but no more than $300, excluding interest and penalty;

$100 for each bill of more than $300, excluding interest and penalty.

(10) The penalty for each failure to pay or object to, in the manner required by Labor Code section 4603.2, a bill for medical treatment provided or authorized by the treating physician, is as follows when the bill was paid before the audit subject was notified that the claim was selected for audit:

$25 for each bill which included an increase and interest with the late payment of any uncontested amount of the bill, in accordance with Labor Code Section 4603.2;

$50 for each bill which included either the increase or interest with the late payment of any uncontested amount of the bill, in accordance with Labor Code Section 4603.2;

$75 for any bill which included neither the increase nor interest with the late payment of any uncontested amount of the bill, in accordance with Labor Code Section 4603.2.

(11) The penalty for each failure to pay or object to a vocational rehabilitation bill within 60 days of receipt, as required by California Code of Regulations, title 8, sections 10132 and 10132.1, is:

$25 for each bill of $100 or less;

$50 for each bill of more than $100, but no more than $200;

$75 for each bill of more than $200, but no more than $300;

$100 for each bill of more than $300.

(12) The penalty for each failure to make a required first payment of temporary disability indemnity within 14 days after the employer's date of knowledge of injury and disability is:

$25 if the first payment was made 1 to 7 days late;

$50 if the first payment was made 8 to 14 days late;

$75 if the first payment was made 15 to 21 days late;

$100 if the first payment was made more than 21 days late.

(13) The penalty for each underpayment of an indemnity payment (including death benefits and VRMA), when the balance of the indemnity was paid late, is:

$25 for late payment of the equivalent of 3 days of indemnity or less;

$50 for late payment of the equivalent of more than 3 but no more than 7 days of indemnity;

$75 for late payment of the equivalent of more than 7 but no more than 14 days of indemnity;

$100 for the late payment of the equivalent of more than 14 days of indemnity.

(14) The penalty for each failure to make a first payment of VRMA or death benefit when due is:

$25 if the first payment was made 1 to 7 days late;

$50 if the first payment was made 8 to 14 days late;

$75 if the first payment was made 15 to 21 days late;

$100 if the first payment was made more than 21 days late.

(b) The following Group B violations carry penalties of up to $500:

(1) The penalty for each failure to maintain or provide to the Audit Unit a claim log which complies with these Regulations is:

$25 for each failure to list on a claim log one or more of the following: employee's name; claim number; date of injury;

$25 for each misdesignation of an indemnity file as a medical-only file on the claim log;

$100 for each failure to identify self-insured employers on the log as required by California Code of Regulations, title 8, section 10103.1(b)(6);

$100 for each failure to identify the underwriting insurance company of an insurance group;

$100 for each failure to designate a denied claim on the log;

$100 for each claim not listed on the log;

$250 for each failure to provide the claim log to the Audit Unit within 14 days of receipt of a written request if the claim log was provided more than 14 but no more than 30 days from receipt of the request;

$500 for each failure for more than 30 days from receipt of a written request, to provide the claim log to the Audit Unit.

(2) The penalty for each failure to provide information regarding the Americans with Disabilities Act, the Fair Employment and Housing Act, and workers' compensation vocational rehabilitation as required by Labor Code section 4636(a) immediately after 90 days of aggregate temporary disability indemnity is $100 if the information was provided or the employee returned to his or her usual and customary occupation more than 10 but not more than 20 days after 90 days of aggregate total disability, and an additional $100 for each additional delay of not more than 10 days, to a maximum penalty of $400 if the notice was issued more than 30 days late, and $500 if the notice was overdue more than 40 days and was not issued at the time the audit subject was notified that the claim was selected for audit.

(3) The penalty for each failure to issue notice of medical eligibility for vocational rehabilitation services (if not previously issued) within 10 days after knowledge of a physician's opinion that the employee is medically eligible, or for failure to issue notice within 10 days after 366 days of aggregate total temporary disability, is $100 if the notice was issued not more than 10 days late, and an additional $100 for each additional delay of not more than 10 days, to a maximum penalty of $400 if the notice was issued more than 30 days late, and $500 if the notice was overdue more than 40 days and was not issued at the time the audit subject was notified that the claim was selected for audit. Where the injured worker is represented by an attorney and documentation in the claim file indicates that the injured worker's attorney has received a copy of the physician's report indicating the employee is medically eligible for vocational rehabilitation, and if the knowledge is of a physician's opinion other than the injured worker's treating

physician, a physician selected from a panel provided by the DWC Medical Unit, or an agreed medical examiner, the penalty shall be assessed at 20% of the amount otherwise assessed under this subdivision and shall not exceed $100.

(4) The penalty for each failure to provide the employee with a copy of the treating physician's final report together with notice of the procedure to contest the treating physician's determination, in accordance with Labor Code section 4636(d), immediately upon receipt of that report, is $100 for compliance more than 10 but not more than 20 days after receipt of the treating physician's final report, and an additional $100 for each additional delay of not more than 10 days, to a maximum penalty of $400 if the notice was issued more than 30 days late, and $500 if the notice was overdue more than 40 days and was not issued at the time the audit subject was notified that the claim was selected for audit.

(5) The penalty for each failure to notify an injured employee of the reasons he or she is not entitled to any, or to any further, vocational rehabilitation services, and the procedure for contesting the determination of non-eligibility, as required by California Code of Regulations, title 8, sections 9813(a)(3) and 10131, is $100 if notification was issued more than 10 but not more than 20 days after the determination, and an additional $100 for each additional delay of not more than 10 days, to a maximum penalty of $400 if the notice was issued more than 30 days late, and $500 if the notice was overdue more than 40 days and was not issued at the time the audit subject was notified that the claim was selected for audit.

(6) The penalty for each failure to notify an injured employee that his or her injury may have caused permanent disability and the procedures for evaluating the permanent disability, or of the employer's position that the injury has caused no permanent disability and the employee's remedies, in the manner provided by California Code of Regulations, title 8, beginning with section 9810; is $100 if the notice was issued up to 10 days late, and an additional $100 for each additional delay of not more than 10 days, to a maximum penalty of $400 if the notice was issued more than 30 days late, and $500 if the notice was overdue more than 40 days and was not issued at the time the audit subject was notified that the claim was selected for audit.

(7) The penalty for each failure to notify a claimant of the denial of all death benefits claimed by that person (except a denial limited to all or any of: burial expense, benefits which were due to the injured worker before his or her death, or medical-legal expense), in the manner provided by California Code of Regulations, title 8, beginning with section 9810, is $100 if the notice was issued up to 10 days late, and an additional $100 for each additional delay of not more than 10 days, to a maximum penalty of $400 if the notice was issued more than 30 days late, and $500 if the notice was overdue more than 40 days and was not issued at the time the audit subject was notified that the claim was selected for audit.

(8) The penalty for each failure to send a notice denying liability for all workers' compensation benefits, in accordance with California Code of Regulations, title 8, beginning with section 9810, is $100 if the notice was issued up to 10 days late, and an additional $100 for each additional delay of not more than 10 days, to a maximum penalty of $400 if the notice was issued more than 30 days late, and $500 if the notice was overdue more than 40 days and was not issued at the time the audit subject was notified that the claim was selected for audit.

(9) The penalty for each notice denying liability for all workers' compensation benefits, which was materially misleading, is $500. The penalty for each materially incomplete denial notice is $100.

(10) The penalty for each failure to pay any uncontested penalty assessment in a Notice of Penalty Assessments within 15 days of receipt of the Notice of Penalty Assessments is:

$100 for each assessment paid more than 15 but not more than 30 days after receipt;

$300 for each assessment paid more than 30 but not more than 45 days after receipt;

$500 for each assessment not paid within 45 days after receipt.

(11) The penalty for each failure to comply with California Code of Regulations, title 8, section 10104 is:

$100 for each period of 1 to 14 days' delay in filing the Annual Report of Inventory, to a maximum penalty of $500 for each Annual Report of Inventory;

$500 for each Annual Report of Inventory that overstates or understates the number of claims by 10% or more.

(c) The following Group C violations carry penalties of up to $1,000:

(1) The penalty for each failure to pay compensation as ordered in a Notice of Compensation Due within 15 days of receipt, if no timely Request for Review of Notice of Compensation Due was filed, is:

$250 if the compensation was paid more than 15 but not more than 30 days from receipt of notice;

$500 if the compensation was paid more than 30 but not more than 45 days from receipt of notice;

$1,000 for failure to pay the compensation within 45 days of receipt of notice.

(2) The penalty for each termination, interruption or deferral of vocational rehabilitation services other than as provided by Labor Code sections 4637(b), 4644(b) is $1,000.

(3) The penalty for each failure to pay or denial of rehabilitation maintenance allowance, temporary disability indemnity, or salary continuation in lieu of temporary disability indemnity, without a factual, medical or legal basis for the failure or denial, is:

$100 for the equivalent of 3 days or less of unpaid indemnity;

$200 for the equivalent of more than 3 but not more than 7 days of unpaid indemnity;

$300 for the equivalent of more than 7 but not more than 14 days of unpaid indemnity;

$500 for the equivalent of more than 14 but not more than 21 days of unpaid indemnity;

$750 for the equivalent of more than 21 but not more than 28 days of unpaid indemnity;

$1,000 for the equivalent of more than 28 days of unpaid indemnity.

(4) The penalty for each failure to pay permanent disability indemnity based on a reasonable estimate of permanent disability, or denial of permanent disability indemnity, without a factual, medical or legal basis, is:

$200 for up to 6 weeks of unpaid indemnity;

$400 for more than 6 but not more than 15 weeks of unpaid indemnity;

$750 for more than 15 but not more than 30 weeks of unpaid indemnity;

$1,000 for more than 30 weeks of unpaid indemnity.

(5) The penalty for each failure to pay or denial of death benefits to any claimant without a factual, medical or legal basis for the failure or denial, is:

$100 for the equivalent of 3 days or less of unpaid indemnity under Labor Code section 4701(b), or for up to $300 of unpaid burial expenses;

$200 for the equivalent of more than 3 but not more than 7 days of unpaid indemnity under Labor Code section 4701(b), or for more than $300, up to $600, of unpaid burial expenses;

$300 for the equivalent of more than 7 but not more than 14 days of unpaid indemnity under Labor Code section 4701(b), or for more than $600, up to $900, of unpaid burial expenses;

$500 for the equivalent of more than 14 but not more than 21 days of unpaid indemnity under Labor Code section 4701(b), or for more than $900, up to $1,500, of unpaid burial expenses;

$750 for the equivalent of more than 21 but not more than 28 days of unpaid indemnity under Labor Code section 4701(b), or for more than $1,500, up to $2,250, of unpaid burial expenses;

$1,000 for the equivalent of more than 28 days of unpaid indemnity under Labor Code section 4701(b), or for more than $2,250 of unpaid burial expenses.

The penalty for each failure to pay or denial of payment to any claimant of compensation which was accrued and unpaid to the injured worker at the time of the worker's death is the same penalty which would apply for failure to pay or denial of payment of that compensation to the injured worker.

The penalty under this subdivision does not supersede the penalty under subdivision 10111.1(d)(1).

(6) The penalty for each failure to investigate a claim as provided by California Code of Regulations, title 8, section 10109 of these regulations is:

$250 if the failure to investigate involved a claim for medical treatment only, with no reasonable expectation of liability for indemnity payments;

$500 if the failure to investigate involved a claim or reasonable expectation of liability for temporary or permanent disability indemnity or vocational rehabilitation benefits;

$1,000 if the failure to investigate involved a claim or reasonable expectation of liability for death benefits, or a combination of two or more of the following classes of benefits temporary or permanent disability indemnity or vocational rehabilitation.

This penalty does not supersede a penalty for denial of claim without an investigation and documentation supporting a factual, medical, or legal basis for denial as set forth in section 10111.1(d)(1).

(d) The following Group D violations carry penalties of up to $5,000:

(1) The penalty for each denial of all liability for a claim without documentation supporting a factual, medical, or legal basis for the denial is specified in this subdivision. In order to avoid a penalty, the denial must state a legal, factual or medical basis recognized by applicable law and documented by information in the claim file. An employee's purported waiver of benefits in a compensable case is not a ground to deny liability.

The gravity portion of the penalty is based on the class or classes of benefits potentially payable if benefits were provided. The total penalty shall be determined by the applying the penalty assessment amount listed in [i] for gravity, subtracting the amount listed in [ii] for good faith if applicable, and increasing or decreasing the penalty as applicable for history and frequency as set forth in [iii] and [iv]:

[i] For a claim involving potential for medical treatment only the penalty is $3,500;

For a claim involving potential for medical treatment and either temporary or permanent disability the penalty is $4,000;

For a claim involving potential for medical treatment and both temporary and permanent disability the penalty is $4,500;

For a claim involving potential for medical treatment, temporary disability, permanent disability and vocational rehabilitation the penalty is $5,000;

For a claim involving potential for death benefits the penalty is $5,000.

[ii] The penalty will be reduced by $1,000 for good faith if there was a reasonable attempt to investigate the claim.

[iii] Reduction or increase of the penalty for history shall be based on the following:

An audit subject having no prior Audit Unit history will receive a $500 reduction;

An audit subject having a prior Audit Unit history of no more than one audited unsupported denial will receive a $500 reduction;

An audit subject having a prior Audit Unit history of more than one audited unsupported denial but no more than 5% of audited denials as unsupported will receive no reduction or increase for history;

An audit subject having a prior Audit Unit history of more than one audited unsupported denial and more than 5% of audited denials as unsupported will receive a $500 increase.

[iv] Reduction of the penalty for frequency shall be based on the following:

An audit subject having no more than one audited unsupported denial will receive a $500 reduction;

An audit subject having more than one audited unsupported denial but no more than 5% of audited denials which are unsupported will receive no reduction or increase for frequency;

An audit subject having more than one audited denial and more than 5% of audited denials which are unsupported will receive an increase of $500.

[v] The total amount assessed for a denial shall be reduced by 50% if the claim was accepted after the denial without evidence that the acceptance was the result of litigation or of the claim's selection for audit.

(2) The penalty for each failure to comply with, show good cause for non-compliance with, or contest, within 30 days of receipt, any written request or order of the Administrative Director or Audit Unit which is not specified in subdivisions (b)(1), (c)(1), or (d)(5) of this section is:

$500 if there was compliance in more than 30 but not more than 40 days from receipt of the request or order;

$1,000 if there was compliance in more than 40 but not more than 60 days from receipt of the request or order;

$2,500 if there was compliance in more than 60 but not more than 90 days of receipt of the request or order;

$5,000 for failure to comply within 90 days of receipt of the request or order.

(3) The penalty for each failure by a claims administrator to provide a claim form within one working day of receipt of a request from an injured worker or the worker's agent is:

$500 if the claim form was provided in more than 1 but not more than 5 working days from receipt of the request, if benefits were being provided to the employee at the time of the request;

$1,000 if the claim form was not provided within 5 working days of receipt of the request, if benefits were being provided to the employee at the time of the request;

$3,000 if the claim form was provided in more than 1 but not more than 5 working days from receipt of the request, if benefits were not being provided to the employee at the time of the request;

$5,000 if the claim form was not provided within 5 working days of receipt of the request, if benefits were not being provided to the employee at the time of the request.

(4) The penalty for each failure to comply in full with any final award or order of the Workers' Compensation Appeals Board or the Rehabilitation Unit within 20 days of service, allowing an additional five days for service by mail, is:

For any failure to pay all amounts payable as awarded or ordered, including interest, when partial nonpayment is due to a miscalculation or oversight and all other amounts have been paid, the penalty amount shall be determined based on the equivalent amount of unpaid indemnity as assessed under subdivision (c)(3) of this section.

For late payment of an award or order, the penalty is:

$500 for compliance in more than 20 but not more than 35 days from the date of service;

$1,000 for compliance (other than a late interest payment) in more than 35 but not more than 60 days from the date of service;

$2,500 for compliance (other than a late interest payment) in more than 60 but not more than 90 days from the date of service;

$5,000 if there was not compliance (other than failure to pay interest) within 90 days of the date of service.

Penalties will be assessed separately for both late payment and the failure to pay a portion of an award or order.

(5) The penalty for each failure to produce a legible paper copy of a claim file as required by California Code of Regulations, title 8, section 10107 or at the time specified by the Administrative Director is:

$100 if the file was produced not more than 3 days late;

$250 if the file was produced more than 3 but not more than 14 days late;

$500 if the file was produced more than 14 but not more than 29 days late;

$1,000 if the file was produced more than 29 days late but not more than 40 days late;

$2,500 if the file was produced more than 40 days late but not more than 90 days late;

$5000 if the was produced more than 90 days late or was not produced.

(6) The penalty for providing a backdated or otherwise altered or fraudulent document to the Audit Unit, or intentionally withholding a document from the Audit Unit, which would have the effect of avoiding liability for the payment of compensation or an audit penalty is:

$5,000 for each backdated, altered, or withheld document. The amount of the penalty is not subject to reduction based on frequency, history, or good faith as set forth in subdivision (e) of this section.

The claims administrator shall not be subjected to penalty under this subdivision if it demonstrates by clear and convincing evidence that the backdating, alteration, or withholding of the document was due solely to unintentional clerical error.

(e) The penalties otherwise applicable under subdivisions (a) through (d) of this section shall be modified by any applicable provision of this subdivision (e). However, the method of modifying penalties for unsupported denials is set forth in section 10111(d)(2) and section 10111.1(d)(1) and is not governed by this subdivision (e).

(1) Modification for the gravity of each violation is included within the penalty assessment amounts listed in subdivisions (a) through (d);

(2) Modification for the good faith of the audit subject shall be determined based on documentation of attempts to comply with requirements of the Labor Code and the Administrative Director's regulations, and may result in a reduction of 20% for each applicable violation.

(3) Modification for frequency shall be considered for each type of violation. Frequency shall be determined by comparing the number of audited files which were randomly selected pursuant to section 10107(c) and (d) of these regulations in which there is an assessment for a specific type of violation to the total number of those randomly selected audited files in which the possibility of that type of violation exists. The frequency of violations in the complaint files selected for audit pursuant to section 10107(e) shall not be used to determine penalty amounts for these categories, except the mitigation or exacerbation of penalty amounts based on frequency of violations in the randomly selected files shall be applied to the audited complaint files.

[i] If there are assessments for late first payments of temporary disability indemnity in 10% or less of the audited files in which payments of temporary disability indemnity are made, the penalty amounts of these assessments will be reduced by 20%. If there are assessments for late first payments of temporary disability indemnity in more than 30% of the audited files in which payments of temporary disability indemnity are made, the penalty amounts of these assessments will be increased by 20%,

[ii] If there are assessments for late first payments of permanent disability indemnity in 10% or less of the audited files in which payments of permanent disability indemnity are made, the penalty amounts of these assessments will be reduced by 20%. If there are assessments for late first payments of permanent disability indemnity in more than 30% of the audited files in which payments of permanent disability indemnity are made, the penalty amounts of these assessments will be increased by 20%.

[iii] If there are assessments for late first payments of vocational rehabilitation maintenance allowance in 10% or less of the audited files in which payments of maintenance allowance in 10% or less of the audited files in which payments of maintenance allowance are made, the penalty amounts of these assessments will be reduced by 20%. If there are assessments for late first payments of vocational rehabilitation maintenance allowance in more than 30% of the audited files in which payments of maintenance allowance are made, the penalty amounts of these assessments will be increased by 20%.

[iv] If there are assessments involving late subsequent payments, including any payment in which all indemnity then due is not paid with that payment but is paid with a subsequent payment as assessed under subdivision (a)(13) of this section, of temporary disability indemnity, permanent disability indemnity, or vocational rehabilitation maintenance allowance in 10% or less of the audited files in which these subsequent payments were made, the penalty amounts of these assessments will be reduced by 20%. If the number of audited files with assessments for late subsequent payments of temporary disability indemnity, permanent disability indemnity, or vocational rehabilitation maintenance allowance exceeds 30% of the total number of audited files with subsequent payments of these benefits, the penalty amounts of these assessments will be increased by 20%.

[v] If there are assessments involving late payments of death benefits in 10% or less of the audited files in which these payments were made, the penalty amounts of these assessments will be reduced by 20%. If the number of audited files with assessments for late payments of death benefits exceeds 30% of the total number of audited files with payments of death benefits, the penalty amounts of these assessments will be increased by 20%.

[vi] If there are assessments involving failure to issue benefit notices (other than notices specifically mentioned elsewhere in this subdivision (3)) in 10% or less of the audited files in which these benefit notices are required, no penalties will be assessed for those violations. If the number of audited files with assessments for failure to issue these notices exceeds 10%, but does not exceed 20%, the penalty amounts of these assessments will be reduced by 20%. If the number of audited files with assessments for failure to issue these notices exceeds 30% of the total number of audited files in which these notices are required, the penalty amounts of these assessments will be increased by 20%.

[vii] If there are assessments involving late provision of benefit notices (other than notices specifically mentioned elsewhere in this subdivision (3)) in 10% or less of the audited files in which these benefit notices are required, no penalties will be assessed for those violations. If the number of audited files with assessments for late issuance of these notices exceeds 10%, but does not exceed 20%, the penalty amounts of these assessments will be reduced by 20%. If the number of audited files with assessments for late issuance of these notices exceeds 30% of the total number of audited files in which these notices were required and issued, the penalty amounts of these assessments will be increased by 20%.

[viii] If there are assessments involving the failure to pay or object to medical expenses within 60 days of receipt of the billing in 10% or less of the audited files with a requirement to pay or object to medical bills within 60 days of receipt of billing, the penalty amounts of these assessments will be reduced by 20%. if the number of audited files with assessments for failure to pay or object to medical expenses within 60 days of receipt of the billing exceeds 30% of the total number of audited files in which there was a requirement to pay or object to medical bills within 60 days of receipt of billing, the penalty amounts of these assessments will be increased by 20%.

[ix] If there are assessments involving the failure to pay or object to medical-legal expenses within 60 days of receipt of the billing in 10% or less of the audited files containing medical-legal expenses, the penalty amounts of these assessments will be reduced by 20%. If the number of audited files with assessments for failure to pay or object to medical-legal expenses within 60 days of receipt of the billing exceeds 30% of the total number of audited files in which there was a requirement to pay or object to medical-legal expenses within 60 days of receipt of billing, the penalty amounts of these assessments will be increased by 20%.

[x] If there are assessments involving the failure to pay or object to vocational rehabilitation expenses within 60 days of receipt of the billing in 10% or less of the audited files containing vocational rehabilitation expenses, the penalty amounts of these assessments will be reduced by 20%. If the number of audited files with assessments for failure to pay or object to vocational rehabilitation expenses within 60 days of receipt of the billing exceeds 30% of the total number of audited files in which there was a requirement to pay or object to vocational rehabilitation expenses within 60 days of receipt of billing, the penalty amounts of these assessments will be increased by 20%.

[xi] For injuries before January 1, 1994, if there are assessments involving the failure to assign a qualified rehabilitation representative within 10 days after 90 days of aggregate total disability in 10% or less of the audited files with 90 or more days of aggregate total disability, the penalty amounts of these assessments will be reduced by 20%. If the number of audited files with assessments involving the failure to assign a qualified rehabilitation representative within 10 days after 90 days of aggregate total disability exceeds 30% of the total number of audited files in which there was a requirement to assign a qualified rehabilitation representative within 10 days after 90 days of aggregate total disability, the penalty amounts of these assessments will be increased by 20%.

[xii] For injuries on or after January 1, 1994, if there are assessments involving the failure to provide information to the employee required by Labor Code section 4636(a) within 10 days after 90 days of aggregate total disability in 10% or less of the audited files with 90 or more days of aggregate total disability, the penalty amounts of

these assessments will be reduced by 20%. If the number of audited files with assessments involving the failure to provide the information specified in section 4636(a) within 10 days after 90 days of aggregate total disability exceeds 30% of the total number of audited files in which there was a requirement to provide the information specified in section 4636(a) within 10 days after 90 days of aggregate total disability, the penalty amounts of these assessments will be increased by 20%.

[xiii] If there are assessments involving the failure to notify an employee in a timely manner of potential eligibility for vocational rehabilitation in 10% or less of the audited files in which these notices are required, the penalty amounts of these assessments will be reduced by 20%. If the number of audited files with assessments involving the failure to notify an employee in a timely manner of potential eligibility for vocational rehabilitation exceeds 30% of the total number of audited files in which these notices are required, the penalty amounts of these assessments will be increased by 20%.

[xiv] If there are assessments involving the failure to notify an employee in a timely manner of non-eligibility for vocational rehabilitation in 10% or less of the audited files in which these notices are required, the penalty amounts of these assessments will be reduced 20%. If the number of audited files with assessments involving the failure to notify an employee in a timely manner of non-eligibility for vocational rehabilitation exceeds 30% of the total number of audited files in which these notices are required, the penalty amounts of these assessments will be increased by 20%.

[xv] If there are assessments involving the failure to notify an employee in a timely manner of the procedure for evaluating the employee's permanent disability, as required by California Code of Regulations, title 8, section 9812(f)(2), (f)(4), (g)(2), and (g)(3), in 10% or less of the audited files in which these notices are required, the penalty amounts of these assessments will be reduced by 20%. If the number of audited files with assessments for failure to issue these notices exceeds 30% of the total number of audited files in which these notices are required, the penalty amounts of these assessments will be increased by 20%.

[xvi] If there are assessments involving the failure to notify an employee or claimant in a timely manner of the denial of all liability for a claim, or of all liability for death benefits, in 10% or less of the audited files in which these notices are required, the penalty amounts of these assessments will be reduced by 20%. If the number of audited files with assessments for failure to issue these notices exceeds 30% of the total number of audited files in which these notices are required, the penalty amounts of these assessments will be increased by 20%.

[xvii] If there is an assessment for the failure to timely respond to a request to provide or authorize medical treatment in no more than one audited file, the penalty amount of that assessment will be reduced by 20%. If the number of audited files with assessments for the failure to timely respond to a request to provide or authorize medical treatment, the penalty amounts for these assessments will be increased by 20%.

[xviii] If there are assessments involving the failure to pay temporary disability indemnity, permanent disability indemnity, death benefits, vocational rehabilitation maintenance allowance, self-imposed increase for late indemnity payment, interest, or penalty in 5% or less of the audited files in which any of these forms of compensation are accrued and payable, the penalty amounts of these assessments will be reduced by 20%. If the number of audited files with assessments for the failure to pay any of these forms of compensation is more than 20% of the audited files in which any of these forms of compensation is accrued and payable, the penalty amounts of these assessments will be increased by 20%.

[xix] If there are assessments for failure to include items or properly designate entries on a claim log, and if no more than ten, or no more than 1%, of the entries on the log are affected, whichever is smaller, the penalty amounts of these assessments will be reduced by 20%. If more than fifty, or more than 5% of the entries on the log are affected, whichever is smaller, the penalty amounts of these assessments will be increased by 20%.

[xx] If there are other violations assessed which are not specified in [i] through [xix] above in 5% or less of the audited files, the penalty amounts of these assessments will be reduced by 20%. If the number of audited files with assessments exceeds 20% of the audited files, the penalty amounts of these assessments will be increased by 20%.

(4) Modification of the history of previous violations, if any, shall be based on prior audits of the audit subject at the current adjusting location. However, no modification for history shall apply if a valid comparison cannot be made between the current and prior audit(s). The penalty shall be modified for history as follows:

[i] There will be a reduction of 20% of any penalty for which there was no increase in the penalty amount based on frequency as described in subdivisions (e)(3)[i] through (3)[xx] above in the previous audit, and for which there was a reduction in the penalty amount based on frequency in the present audit at the audited adjusting location.

[ii] There will be an increase of 20% of any penalty for which there was an increase in the penalty amount based on frequency as described in subdivisions (3)[i] through (3)[xx] above in the previous audit, and for which there was no decrease in the penalty amount based on frequency of violations in the present audit at the audited adjusting location, provided that any increased penalty is limited to the maximum provided by statute and regulation for the violation.

(5) No administrative penalties shall be assessed if the only violations found in an audit are violations which do not involve the denial of a claim without supporting documentation, or failure to pay or late payment of compensation, and the violations are found in 20% or less of the indemnity files audited.

(6) Penalties may be mitigated outside the above mitigation guidelines in extraordinary circumstances, when strict application of the mitigation guidelines would be clearly inequitable.

Note: Authority cited: Sections 59, 129.5, 133, 138.3, 138.4, 139.5, 4603.5, 4627 and 5307.3, Labor Code. Reference: Sections 124, 129, 129.5, 4061, 4453, 4454, 4550, 4600, 4603.2, 4621, 4622, 4625, 4636 through 4638, 4639, 4641, 4642, 4650, 4651, 4701 through 4703.5, 4706, 4706.5, 5401, 5401.6, 5402, 5800 and 5814, Labor Code; and Section 2629.1(e), (f), Unemployment Insurance Code.

History: 1. New section filed 1-28-94; operative 1-28-94. Submitted to OAL for printing only pursuant to Government Code section 11351 (Register 94, No. 4).

2. Editorial correction inserting omitted text in subsection (e)(3)[xviii] (Register 95, No. 32).

3. Amendment of subsections (a)(7)[ii]-(a)(7)[iv], (b)(1), (b)(9), (d)(1) and (e)(3)[xv] filed 2-14-96; operative 2-14-96. Submitted to OAL for printing only pursuant to Government Code section 11351 (Register 96, No. 7).

4. Amendment filed 10-26-98; operative 11-25-98 (Register 98, No. 44).

5. Amendment filed 4-20-2009; operative 5-20-2009 (Register 2009, No. 17).

Ref.: Hanna §§ 1.12[8]–[10], 10.50[2][a], [c], 10.51; Herlick Handbook §§ 1.01[3][b], 9.19.

§10111.2. Full Compliance Audit Penalty Schedules; Target Audit Penalty Schedule.

(a) For full compliance audits conducted on or after January 1, 2003, administrative penalties will be assessed pursuant to subdivision (a) for audit subjects that fail to meet or exceed the profile audit review performance standards calculated pursuant to California Code of Regulations, title 8, section 10107.1(c)(3) but meet or exceed the full compliance audit performance standards calculated pursuant to section 10107.1(d)(3). However, for violations in claims with dates of injury from January 1, 1990 through December 31, 1993, penalty amounts may not exceed the amounts that would be assessed pursuant to California Code of Regulations, title 8, section 10111, and for violations in claims with dates of injury from January 1, 1994 through December 31, 2002, penalty amounts may not exceed the amounts that would be assessed pursuant to Section 10111.1:

(1) The penalty for each failure to pay the 10% self-imposed increase due because of a late indemnity payment is:

If the self-imposed increase was not paid or was only partially paid, the audit penalty is based on the amount of the underlying indemnity and is as follows:

$50 if the late-paid indemnity totals not more than 3 days;

$100 if the late-paid indemnity totals more than 3 but not more than 7 days;

$150 if the late-paid indemnity totals more than 7 but not more than 14 days;

$200 if the late paid indemnity totals more than 14 but not more than 21 days;

$300 if the late paid indemnity totals more than 21 but not more than 28 days;

$500 if the late paid indemnity totals more than 28 days.

(2) The penalty for each failure to pay or denial of rehabilitation maintenance allowance, temporary disability indemnity, or salary continuation in lieu of temporary disability indemnity, without a factual, medical or legal basis for the failure or denial, is:

$200 for the equivalent of 3 days or less of unpaid indemnity;

$400 for the equivalent of more than 3 but not more than 7 days of unpaid indemnity;

$600 for the equivalent of more than 7 but not more than 14 days of unpaid indemnity;

$1,000 for the equivalent of more than 14 but not more than 21 days of unpaid indemnity;

$1,500 for the equivalent of more than 21 but not more than 28 days of unpaid indemnity;

$2,000 for the equivalent of more than 28 but not more than 35 days of unpaid indemnity;

$3,000 for the equivalent of more than 35 but not more than 42 days of unpaid indemnity;

$5,000 for the equivalent of more than 42 days of unpaid indemnity.

(3) The penalty for each failure to pay permanent disability indemnity based on a reasonable estimate of permanent disability, or denial of permanent disability indemnity, without a factual, medical or legal basis, is:

$400 for up to 6 weeks of unpaid indemnity;

$800 for more than 6 but not more than 15 weeks of unpaid indemnity;

$1,500 for more than 15 but not more than 30 weeks of unpaid indemnity;

$2,000 for more than 30 but not more than 50 weeks of unpaid indemnity;

$3,000 for more than 50 but not more than 95 weeks of unpaid indemnity;

$5,000 for more than 95 weeks of unpaid indemnity.

(4) The penalty for each failure to pay death benefits pursuant to Labor Code section 4701 to any claimant without a factual, medical or legal basis for the failure, is:

$200 for the equivalent of 3 days or less of unpaid indemnity or for no more than $300 of unpaid burial expenses;

$400 for the equivalent of more than 3 but not more than 7 days of unpaid indemnity or for more than $300, but not more than $600, of unpaid burial expenses;

$600 for the equivalent of more than 7 but not more than 14 days of unpaid indemnity or for more than $600, but no more than $900, of unpaid burial expenses;

$1,000 for the equivalent of more than 14 but not more than 21 days of unpaid indemnity or for more than $900, but no more than $1,500, of unpaid burial expenses;

$1,500 for the equivalent of more than 21 but not more than 28 days of unpaid indemnity or for more than $1,500, but no more than $2,000, of unpaid burial expenses;

$3,000 for the equivalent of more than 28 but not more than 42 days of unpaid indemnity or for more than $2,250 of unpaid burial expenses;

$5,000 for the equivalent of more than 42 days of unpaid indemnity.

The penalty for each failure to pay to any claimant compensation which was accrued and unpaid to the injured worker at the time of the worker's death is the same penalty which would apply for failure to pay that compensation to the injured worker.

(5) The penalty for each late first payment of temporary disability indemnity is:

$100 if the first payment was made 1 to 3 days late

$200 if the first payment was made 4 to 7 days late

$250 if the first payment was made 8 to 14 days late;

$300 if the first payment was made 15 to 21 days late;

$400 if the first payment was made 22 to 30 days late.

Penalty amounts for payments made over 30 days late are assessed pursuant to California Code of Regulations, title 8, section 10108(c) and subdivision (a)(2) of this section.

(6) The penalty for each late first payment of permanent disability is:

$100 if the first payment was made 1 to 3 days late;

$200 if the first payment was made 4 to 7 days late

$250 if the first payment was made 8 to 14 days late;

$300 if the first payment was made 15 to 21 days late;

$400 if the first payment was made 22 to 30 days late.

Penalty amounts for payments made over 30 days late are assessed pursuant to section 10108(c) and subdivision (a)(3) of this section.

For purposes of this subdivision, the first payment of permanent disability indemnity shall be considered late if not made within 14 days after the last payment of temporary disability indemnity, or within 14 days of knowledge of the existence of permanent disability, whichever last occurs.

(7) The penalty for each late first payment of VRMA or death benefit is:

$100 if the first payment was made 1 to 3 days late;

$200 if the first payment was made 4 to 7 days late

$250 if the first payment was made 8 to 14 days late;

$300 if the first payment was made 15 to 21 days late;

$400 if the first payment was made 22 to 30 days late.

Penalty amounts for payments made over 30 days late are assessed pursuant to section 10108(c) and subdivision (a)(2) of this section.

(8) The penalty for each underpayment of temporary disability, permanent disability, death benefits, or VRMA, when the balance of the indemnity was paid late, or late paid self-imposed increases, not paid together with the late indemnity payment is:

$100 for late payment of the equivalent of 3 days of indemnity or less, except it is $25 for late paid self-imposed increases;

$200 for late payment of the equivalent of more than 3 but no more than 7 days of indemnity, except it is $50 for late paid self-imposed increases;

$250 for late payment of the equivalent of more than 7 but no more than 14 days of indemnity, except it is $75 for late paid self-imposed increases;

$300 for late payment of the equivalent of more than 14 but no more than 21 days of indemnity, except it is $100 for late paid self-imposed increases;

$400 for the late payment of the equivalent of more than 21 days of indemnity, except it is $125 for late paid self-imposed increases.

Penalty amounts for underpayments made more than 30 days late are governed by section 10108(c).

(9) The penalty for each failure to make temporary disability, permanent disability, death benefits or VRMA payments according to the payment schedule defined by section 10100.2(jj) is:

$100 for each payment made 1 to 3 days late

$200 for each payment made 4 to 7 days late

$250 for each payment made 8 to 14 days late;

$300 for each payment made 15 to 21 days late;

$400 for each payment made 22 to 30 days late.

Penalty amounts for payments made more than 30 days late are governed by section 10108(c).

(10) Penalty amounts assessed pursuant to subdivisions (a)(1) through (a)(9) will be increased by 100%, but will not exceed $5000 except as provided by Labor Code section 129.5(c)(3), if the failure to pay or late payment was in violation of an award or order of the Workers' Compensation Appeals Board, the Rehabilitation Unit, or the Administrative Director. When the award or order is not specific to, but only stated as a lump sum, of any benefit pursuant to subdivisions (a)(1) through (a)(9) above, the increased penalty amount of 100% as specified above shall be determined based on the equivalent amount of unpaid indemnity as assessed under subdivision (a)(2), (a)(3), or (a)(4) of this section. Increased penalties under this subdivision will be separately assessed for late compliance and/or the failure to pay any portion of an award or order.

(11) Notwithstanding Labor Code section 129.5(c)(1) and whether or not the audit subject has met or exceeded performance standards calculated pursuant to California Code of Regulations, title 8, section 10107.1(c)(3), penalties will be assessed for failure to pay, or late or partial payment of, a Notice of Compensation Due issued as a result of an audit conducted pursuant to Labor Code section 129(b). Penalties will be assessed as follows:

A penalty in the same amount as the total of the penalties applicable under subdivisions (a)(1) through (a)(4) and (a)(10) will be assessed for any compensation paid more than 15 but not more than 30 days after receipt of the Notice of Compensation Due;

A penalty in the amount of 200% of the total of the penalties applicable under subdivisions (a)(1) through (a)(4) and (a)(10) will be assessed for any compensation paid more than 30 but not more than 60 days late;

A penalty in the amount of 300% of the total of the penalties applicable under subdivisions (a)(1) through (a)(4) and (a)(10) will be assessed for any compensation not paid within 60 days.

(12) Notwithstanding Labor Code section 129.5(c)(2) and whether or not the audit subject has met or exceeded performance standards calculated pursuant to section 10107.1(d)(3), additional penalties will be assessed for late payment or failure of the audit subject to pay any administrative penalties assessed pursuant to this section that are not timely appealed pursuant to California Code of Regulations, title 8, section 10115.1. Penalties will be assessed as follows:

An additional penalty of 50% of the amount of each late paid penalty will be assessed for each penalty paid more than 30 but not more than 60 days from receipt of the Notice of Penalty Assessments;

An additional penalty of 100% of the amount of each applicable penalty will be assessed for each penalty not paid within 60 days of receipt of the Notice of Penalty Assessments.

(b) For full compliance audits conducted on or after January 1, 2003, administrative penalties will be assessed pursuant to subdivision (a) and this subdivision (b) for audit subjects that fail to meet or exceed the full compliance audit performance standards calculated pursuant to section 10107.1(d)(3). However, for violations in claims with dates of injury from January 1, 1990 through December 31, 1993, penalty amounts may not exceed the amounts that would be assessed pursuant to section 10111, and for violations in claims with dates of injury from January 1, 1994 through December 31, 2002, penalty amounts may not exceed the amounts that would be assessed pursuant to section 10111.1:

(1) The penalty for each failure to investigate a claim as provided by California Code of Regulations, title 8, section 10109 is:

$500 if the failure to investigate involved a claim for medical treatment only, with no reasonable expectation of liability for indemnity payments, or if the failure to investigate involved the need for medical treatment or testing, but did not involve uncompensated lost time or permanent disability;

$1,000 if the failure to investigate involved a claim or reasonable expectation of liability for only one of the following classes of benefits: temporary disability; permanent disability indemnity; or, vocational rehabilitation;

$2,500 if the failure to investigate involved a claim or reasonable expectation of liability for any combination two of the following classes of benefits: temporary disability; permanent disability indemnity; or, vocational rehabilitation;

$5,000 if the failure to investigate involved a claim or reasonable expectation of liability for death benefits, or for all of the following classes of benefits: temporary disability; permanent disability indemnity; and, vocational rehabilitation.

(2) The penalty for each denial of all liability for a claim without documentation supporting a factual, medical, or legal basis for the denial is specified in this subdivision.

In order to avoid a penalty, the denial must state a legal, factual or medical basis recognized by applicable law and documented by information in the claim file. An employee's waiver of benefits in an otherwise clearly compensable case is not a ground to deny liability.

The penalty is $2,500 for a claim involving the potential for medical treatment only, with no potential for liability for indemnity payments;

The penalty is $4,000 for a claim involving the potential liability for medical treatment and for only one of the following classes of benefits: temporary disability; permanent disability indemnity; or, vocational rehabilitation;

The penalty is $4,500 for a claim involving the potential liability for medical treatment and for any combination of two of the following classes of benefits: temporary disability; permanent disability indemnity; or, vocational rehabilitation;

The penalty is $5,000 for a claim involving the potential liability for death benefits, or for all of the following classes of benefits: medical treatment, temporary disability; permanent disability indemnity; and, vocational rehabilitation.

The penalty will be reduced by 20% for good faith if there was a reasonable attempt to investigate the claim.

The total amount assessed for a denial shall be reduced by 50% if the claim was accepted after the denial without evidence that the acceptance was the result of litigation or of the claim's selection for audit.

(3) The penalty for each failure to produce a legible paper copy of a claim file as required by California Code of Regulations, title 8, section 10107.1(h) or at the time specified by the Administrative Director is:

$100 if the file was produced not more than 2 days late;

$250 if the file was produced more than 2 but not more than 4 days late;

$500 if the file was produced more than 4 but not more than 7 days late;

$1,000 if the file was produced more than 7 days late but not more than 15 days late;

$2,500 if the file was produced more than 15 days late but not more than 30 days late;

$5000 if the was produced more than 30 days late or was not produced.

(4) The penalty for providing a backdated or otherwise altered or fraudulent document to the Audit Unit, or intentionally withholding a document from the Audit Unit, which would have the effect of avoiding liability for the payment of compensation or an audit penalty is: $5,000 for each backdated, altered, or withheld document.

(5) The penalty for each failure to object to or pay reimbursement to an injured worker for the reasonable expense incurred for self-procured medical treatment, in accordance with the timeframes set forth for the payment of a medical bill in Labor Code section 4603.2(b)(1), is:

$100 for $100 or less in expense;

$200 for more than $100, to $500, in expense;

$300 for more than $500, to $1,000, in expense;

$500 for more than $1,000 in expense.

(6) The penalty for each failure to pay reasonable expenses of transportation, meals, and lodging incident to reporting to an examination, together with one day of temporary disability indemnity for each day of wages lost when submitting to the examination, when notifying the employee of a medical evaluation scheduled by the claims administrator in accordance with Labor Code sections 4600 through 4621; or to pay these expenses within 14 days of receiving notice of a medical evaluation scheduled by the Administrative Director or the appeals board; or to object or pay the injured worker for any reasonable transportation expenses incurred to obtain medical treatment or evaluation, within 60 days of receiving a request, is:

$100 for more than $10, to $100, in expense;

$200 for more than $100, to $300, in expense;

$300 for more than $300, to $500, in expense.

$500 for more than $500 in expense.

(7) The penalty for each failure to document a factual basis for paying less than the maximum indemnity rate is:

$50 if the total indemnity, paid and unpaid, totals not more than 3 days;

$100 if the total indemnity totals more than 3 but not more than 7 days;

$150 if the total indemnity totals more than 7 but not more than 14 days;

$200 if the total indemnity totals more than 14 but not more than 21 days;

$300 if the total indemnity totals more than 21 but not more than 28 days;

$500 if the total indemnity totals more than 28 days.

(8) The penalty for each failure to comply with any regulation of the Administrative Director specified in this subdivision is:

[A] For each failure to include in a claim file a copy of the Employee's Claim for Worker's Compensation Benefits, DWC Form 1, showing the date the form was provided to and received from the employee, or documentation of the date the claim form was provided to the employee if the employee did not return the form, the penalty is:

$100 if there was any late indemnity payments, or if notice of acceptance of the claim was not issued within 90 days after the employer's date of knowledge of injury and disability, or if the claim was denied.

[B] For each failure to issue a notice of benefits as required by California Code of Regulations, title 8, section 9810, or by California Code of Regulations, title 8, beginning with section 10122, unless penalties are assessed pursuant to subdivisions (b)(14) through (b)(20), the penalty is $100.

[C] For each Notice of Benefits that was not issued timely as provided in California Code of Regulations, title 8, beginning with section 9810, or as provided in California Code of Regulations, title 8, beginning with section 10122, unless penalties are assessed pursuant to subdivisions (b)(14) through (b)(20), the penalty is:

$25 for each notice of first, resumed, changed or final payment of temporary disability indemnity, wage continuation, death benefits, permanent disability indemnity, or VRMA that was issued from 1 to 7 days late;

$50 for each notice of first, resumed, changed or final payment of temporary disability indemnity, wage continuation, death benefits, permanent disability indemnity, or VRMA that was issued more than 7 days late, and for each delay in decision notice which was issued from 1 to 7 days late;

$75 for each delay in decision notice that was issued more than 7 days late.

[D] For each notice of benefits required by California Code of Regulations, title 8, beginning with section 9810, [except a materially misleading or materially incomplete denial notice assessed under subdivision (b)(21)] or by California Code of Regulations, title 8, beginning with section 10117, or by California Code of Regulations, title 8, beginning with section 10122, or by California Code of Regulations, title 8, beginning with section 10133.50, [unless penalties are assessed pursuant to subdivision (b)(27)] that is materially inaccurate or incomplete, the penalty is $25.

[E] For each failure to include in a claim file, or document attempts to obtain, any of the required contents specified in section 10101.1(b), (c), (d), (e), (f), (g), (h), (i), (j) of these Regulations, the penalty is $100.

[F] For each failure to comply with any regulation of the Administrative Director, not otherwise assessed in this Subchapter, the penalty is $100.

(9) The penalty for each failure to pay or object to a billing for a medical-legal expense in the manner required by Labor Code section 4622, is:

$100 for each bill that was paid late with interest and increase;

$200 for each bill that was paid late where either interest or increase was not included;

$300 for each bill that was paid late where neither interest nor increase was paid.

$500 for each bill that was not paid at the time the audit subject was notified the claim was selected for audit where no timely objection was sent.

(10) The penalty for each failure to pay or object, in the manner required by law or regulation, to a bill for medical treatment provided or authorized by the treating physician, including medical treatment provided pursuant to Labor Code section 5402(c), is as follows when the bill remains unpaid at the time the audit subject is notified that the claim was selected for audit:

$100 for each bill of $100 or less, excluding interest and penalty;

$200 for each bill of more than $100, but no more than $500 excluding interest and penalty;

$300 for each bill of more than $500, but no more than $1,000, excluding interest and penalty;

$500 for each bill of more than $1,000, excluding interest and penalty.

Any penalty assessed under this subdivision shall be doubled if the medical treatment provided by the physician was authorized by a reviewer, as defined by California Code of Regulations, title 8, section 9792.6(q), through a utilization review process established pursuant to Labor Code section 4610 and California Code of Regulations, title 8, section 9792.7.

(11) The penalty for each failure to pay or object, in the manner required by law or regulation, to a bill for medical treatment provided or authorized by the treating physician, including medical treatment provided pursuant to Labor Code section 5402(c), is as follows when the bill was paid before the audit subject was notified that the claim was selected for audit:

$100 for each bill that included an increase and interest with the late payment of any uncontested amount of the bill, in accordance with Labor Code section 4603.2;

$200 for each bill that included either an increase or interest with the late payment of any uncontested amount of the bill, in accordance with Labor Code section 4603.2;

$300 for each bill that included neither an increase nor interest with the late payment of any uncontested amount of the bill, in accordance with Labor Code section 4603.2.

Any penalty assessed under this subdivision will be no greater than the penalty that would have issued under subdivision (b)(10) of this section had the bill been unpaid at the time the audit subject was notified that the claim was selected for audit.

(12) The penalty for each failure to pay or object to a vocational rehabilitation bill within 60 days of receipt, as required by California Code of Regulations, title 8, sections 10132 and 10132.1, is:

$25 for each bill of $100 or less;

$50 for each bill of more than $100, but no more than $200;

$75 for each bill of more than $200, but no more than $300;

$100 for each bill of more than $300.

(13) The penalty for each failure to maintain or provide to the Audit Unit a claim log that complies with these Regulations is:

$25 for each failure to list on a claim log one or more of the following: employee's name; claim number; date of injury;

$50 for each misdesignation of an indemnity claim as a medical-only claim on the claim log;

$50 for each failure to distinguish on the claim log an indemnity claim that has no payment of indemnity from one that has indemnity payment(s).

$100 for each failure to identify self-insured employers on the log as required by section 10103.1(b)(6) of these Regulations;

$100 for each failure to identify the underwriting insurance company of an insurance group;

$100 for each failure to designate a denied claim on the log;

$100 for each claim not listed on the log;

$250 for each failure to provide the claim log to the Audit Unit within 14 days of receipt of a written request if the claim log was provided more than 14 but no more than 30 days from receipt of the request;

$500 for each failure for more than 30 days from receipt of a written request, to provide the claim log to the Audit Unit.

(14) The penalty for each failure to provide information regarding the Americans with Disabilities Act, the Fair Employment and Housing Act, and workers' compensation vocational rehabilitation as required by Labor Code section 4636(a) immediately after 90 days of aggregate temporary disability indemnity is $100 if the information was provided or the employee returned to his or her usual and customary occupation more than 10 but not more than 20 days after 90 days of aggregate total disability, and an additional $100 for each additional delay of not more than 10 days, to a maximum penalty of $400 if the notice was issued more than 30 days late, and $500 if the notice was overdue more than 40 days and was not issued at the time the audit subject was notified that the claim was selected for audit.

(15) The penalty for each failure to issue notice of medical eligibility for vocational rehabilitation services (if not previously issued) within 10 days after knowledge of a physician's opinion that the employee is medically eligible, or for failure to issue notice within 10 days after 366 days of aggregate total temporary disability, is $100 if the notice was issued not more than 10 days late, and an additional $100 for each additional delay of not more than 10 days, to a maximum penalty of $400 if the notice was issued more than 30 days late, and $500 if the notice was overdue more than 40 days and was not issued at the time the audit subject was notified that the claim was selected for audit. Where the injured worker is represented by an attorney and documentation in the claim file indicates that the injured worker's attorney has received a copy of the physician's report indicating the employee is medically eligible for vocational rehabilitation, and if the knowledge is of a physician's opinion other than the injured worker's treating physician, a physician selected from a panel provided by the DWC Medical Unit, or an agreed medical examiner, the penalty shall be assessed at 20% of the amount otherwise assessed under this subdivision and shall not exceed $100.

(16) The penalty for each failure to provide the employee with a copy of the treating physician's final report together with notice of the procedure to contest the treating physician's determination, in accordance with Labor Code section 4636(d), immediately upon receipt of that report, is $100 for compliance more than 10 but not more than 20 days after receipt of the treating physician's final report, and an additional $100 for each additional delay of not more than 10 days, to a maximum penalty of $400 if the notice was issued more than 30 days late, and $500 if the notice was overdue more than 40 days and was not issued at the time the audit subject was notified that the claim was selected for audit. However, if a separate penalty is assessed under subdivision (b)(17) for the violation, no penalty will be assessed under this subdivision. If the injured worker was notified of the procedure to contest the treating physician's determination, but no copy of the treating physician's final report was provided with the notice, the maximum penalty shall be $100 under this subdivision.

(17) The penalty for each failure to notify an injured employee of the reasons he or she is not entitled to any, or to any further, vocational rehabilitation services, and the procedure for contesting the determination of non-eligibility, as required by California Code of Regulations, title 8, sections 9813(a)(3) and 10131, is $100 if notification was issued more than 10 but not more than 20 days after the determination, and an additional $100 for each additional delay of not more than 10 days, to a maximum penalty of $400 if the notice was issued more than 30 days late, and $500 if the notice was overdue more than 40 days and was not issued at the time the audit subject was notified that the claim was selected for audit.

(18) The penalty for each failure to notify an injured employee that his or her injury may have caused permanent disability and the procedures for evaluating the permanent disability, or of the employer's position that the injury has caused no permanent disability and the employee's remedies, in the manner provided by California Code of Regulations, title 8, beginning with section 9810; is $100 if the notice was issued up to 10 days late, and an additional $100 for each additional delay of not more than 10 days, to a maximum penalty of $400 if the notice was issued more than 30 days late, and $500 if the notice was overdue more than 40 days and was not issued at the time the audit subject was notified that the claim was selected for audit.

(19) The penalty for each failure to notify a claimant of the denial of all death benefits claimed by that person (except a denial limited to all or any of: burial expense, benefits which were due to the injured worker before his or her death, or medical-legal expense), in the manner provided by California Code of Regulations, title 8, beginning with section 9810, is $100 if the notice was issued up to 10 days late, and an additional $100 for each additional delay of not more than 10 days, to a maximum penalty of $400 if the notice was issued more than 30 days late, and $500 if the notice was overdue more than 40 days and was not issued at the time the audit subject was notified that the claim was selected for audit.

(20) The penalty for each failure to send a notice denying liability for all workers' compensation benefits, in accordance with California Code of Regulations, title 8, beginning with section 9810, is $100 if the notice was issued up to 10 days late, and an additional $100 for each additional delay of not more than 10 days, to a maximum

penalty of $400 if the notice was issued more than 30 days late, and $500 if the notice was overdue more than 40 days and was not issued at the time the audit subject was notified that the claim was selected for audit.

(21) The penalty for each notice denying liability for all workers' compensation benefits, which was materially misleading, is $500.

The penalty for each materially incomplete denial notice is $100.

(22) The penalty for each termination, interruption or deferral of vocational rehabilitation services other than as provided by Labor Code sections 4637(b) and 4644(b) is $1,000.

(23) The penalty for each failure to comply with, show good cause for non-compliance with, or contest, within 30 days of receipt, any written request or order of the Administrative Director or Audit Unit which is not specified in subdivisions (a)(10), (a)(12), (b)(3), (b)(13), or (b)(24) of this section is:

$500 if there was compliance in more than 30 but not more than 40 days from receipt of the request or order;

$1,000 if there was compliance in more than 40 but not more than 60 days from receipt of the request or order;

$2,500 if there was compliance in more than 60 but not more than 90 days of receipt of the request or order;

$5,000 for failure to comply within 90 days of receipt of the request or order.

(24) The penalty for each failure to fully and/or timely comply with any final award or order of the Workers' Compensation Appeals Board, or the Rehabilitation Unit, or the Administrative Director which is not assessed pursuant to subdivision (a)(10), is:

$100 for each late payment of interest required pursuant to Labor Code section 5800.

$250 for each failure to pay interest required pursuant to Labor Code section 5800.

$500 for compliance (other than a late interest payment) in more than 20 but not more than 35 days from the date of service

$1,000 for compliance (other than a late interest payment) in more than 35 but not more than 60 days from the date of service;

$2,500 for compliance (other than a late interest payment) in more than 60 but not more than 90 days from the date of service;

$5,000 if there was not compliance (other than failure to pay interest) within 90 days of the date of service.

Penalties will be assessed separately for both late compliance and the failure to pay a portion of an award or order. Compliance with an award or order must be within 20 days of service of the award or order, unless the award or order expressly allows additional time, plus an additional five days for service by mail. If additional time for payment is allowed in the award or order, the penalties set forth under this subdivision will be assessed based on the date the payment is ordered due instead of the date of service.

(25) The penalty for each failure by a claims administrator to provide a claim form within one working day of receipt of a request from an injured worker or the worker's agent is:

$100 in addition to those shown below, if the claim form provided to the injured worker is not the current form required by existing regulation;

$500 if the claim form was provided in more than 1 but not more than 5 working days from receipt of the request, if benefits were being provided to the employee at the time of the request;

$1,000 if the claim form was not provided within 5 working days of receipt of the request, if benefits were being provided to the employee at the time of the request;

$3,000 if the claim form was provided in more than 1 but not more than 5 working days from receipt of the request, if benefits were not being provided to the employee at the time of the request;

$5,000 if the claim form was not provided within 5 working days of receipt of the request, if benefits were not being provided to the employee at the time of the request.

(26) The penalty for each failure to comply with California Code of Regulations, title 8, section 10104 is:

$100 if the Annual Report of Inventory or Annual Report of Adjusting Locations was filed not more than 10 days late, and an additional $100 for each additional delay of not more than 10 days, to a maximum penalty of $500 if the Annual Report of Inventory or Annual Report of Adjusting Locations was filed more than 40 days late, and $1,000 if the Annual Report of Inventory or Annual Report of Adjusting Locations was overdue more than 40 days and was not filed at the time the audit subject was notified that the claim was selected for audit.

$500 for each Annual Report of Inventory that overstates or understates the number of claims by 10% or more.

(27) The penalty for each failure to comply with the supplemental job displacement benefit notice requirements of California Code of Regulations, title 8, section 10133.51 is:

(A) $100 for each materially incomplete or inaccurate notice relating to the supplemental job disability benefit;

(B) $100 for each failure to send the notice of supplemental job displacement benefits by certified mail.

(C) For each failure to issue the notice of supplemental job displacement benefits (if not previously issued) within 10 days of the last payment of temporary disability is:

$100 for each failure to issue the notice of supplemental job displacement benefits within 10 days of the last payment of temporary disability if the notice was issued not more than 10 days late.

$200 for each failure to issue the notice of supplemental job displacement benefits if the notice was issued more than ten but not more than 20 days late;

$300 for each failure to issue the notice of supplemental job displacement benefits if the notice was issued more than 20 but no more than 30 days late;

$400 for each failure to issue the notice of supplemental job displacement benefits if the notice was issued more than 30 but no more than 40 days late;

$500 for each failure to issue the notice of supplemental job displacement if the notice was issued more than 40 days late or was not issued;

(28) For each failure to issue the voucher for education-related retraining/skill enhancement in compliance with California Code of Regulations, title 8, section 10133.56(c),

unless the employer meets the conditions set forth in Labor Code section 4658.6, is:

$100 for each failure to issue the voucher, in the manner required by law and regulations, not more than 10 days late;

$200 for each failure to issue the voucher, in the manner required by law and regulations, more than ten but not more than 20 days late;

$300 for each failure to issue the voucher, in the manner required by law and regulations, more than 20 but not more than 30 days late;

$400 for each failure to issue the voucher, in the manner required by the law and regulations, more than 30 but not more than 40 days late;

$500 for each failure to issue the voucher, in the manner required by the law and regulations, more than 40 but not more than 50 days late;

$1000 for each failure to issue the voucher, in the manner required by the law and regulations, within 51 days.

(29) For failure to pay any properly documented supplemental job displacement benefit voucher billing within the time frames required by California Code of Regulations, title 8, section 10133.56(h) is:

$100 for each bill of $1000 or less;

$200 for each bill of more than $1000, but no more than $2000;

$300 for each bill of more than $2000, but no more than $3000;

$500 for each bill of more than $3000, but no more than $5000;

$1000 for each bill of more than $5000.

(30) For claims reported on or after April 19, 2004, regardless of the date of injury, the penalty for each failure to authorize medical treatment for which the employer is responsible under Labor Code section 5402(c) is $2,500.

(c) Mitigation of penalty amounts pursuant to Labor Code section 129.5(b)(1) through (b)(7) will be applied as follows:

(1) Mitigation for gravity of the violation is included within the penalty amounts set forth in subdivisions (a) and (b).

(2) Mitigation for good faith of the insurer, self-insured employer, or third-party administrator will be determined based on documentation of attempts to comply with requirements of the Labor Code and the Administrative Director's regulations, and will result in a reduction of 20% for each applicable violation. Penalties may be mitigated for good faith in an amount greater than 20% in extraordinary circumstances, when strict application of this mitigation guideline would be clearly inequitable.

(3) Mitigation for frequency is considered as included within the numbers of penalties and their amounts established by this section and in conjunction with the frequency of violations that determines whether or not the audit subject meets or exceeds the profile audit review performance standards and/or full compliance audit performance standards pursuant to sections 10107.1(c)(3) and (d)(3).

(4) Mitigation for history shall be determined as follows:

(A) For audits that meet or exceed the full compliance audit performance standard, penalty amounts will be reduced by 20%, after modification for good faith, if any, in instances in which the audit subject met or exceeded the profile audit review performance standards in the audit preceding the current audit. No reduction shall apply if the preceding audit occurred before January 1, 2003.

(B) For audits that fail to meet or exceed the full compliance audit performance standards, mitigation for history shall be determined pursuant to Labor Code section 129.5(e).

(5) Mitigation based on whether or not the audit subject has met or exceeded the profile audit review performance standard is determined pursuant to Labor Code section 129.5(c)(1) and (c)(2).

(6) Mitigation based on whether or not the audit subject has met or exceeded the full compliance audit performance standard is determined pursuant to Labor Code section 129.5(c)(3).

(7) Consideration of penalty amounts based on the size of the audit subject location pursuant to Labor Code section 129.5(c)(3) shall be based on the number of indemnity claims reported at the audit subject's location for the most recent complete calendar year. For an audit subject location that is handling only run-off claims, the penalty amount shall be based on the number of open run-off claims and claims that were closed at the audit subject location in the most recent complete calendar year. For audit subjects that fail to meet or exceed the full compliance audit performance standards calculated pursuant to section 10107.1(d)(3), after penalty amounts are calculated pursuant to subdivisions (a)(1) through (c)(6) of this section, penalty amounts will be modified based on the size of the adjusting location as follows:

Number of indemnity claims reported at the audit subject location in most recent complete calendar year:	*Multiply the penalty amount calculated pursuant to subdivisions (a)(1) through (c)(6) of this section by the following factor:*
Less than 65:	1.0
65-99	1.2
100-249	1.4
250-499	1.6
500-749	1.8
750-999	2.0
1,000-1,499	2.4
1,500-1,999	2.8
2,000-3,499	3.6
3,500 or more	7.2

(8) The Audit Unit may assess penalties pursuant to subdivisions (a), (b), and (c) in target audits in which the claims were audited to evaluate specific practices but in which full compliance audit samples of claims were not randomly selected pursuant to Section 10107.1(c) through (e).

Note: Authority cited: Sections 59, 129, 129.5, 133, 138.3, 138.4, 138.6, 138.7, 139.5, 4603.5, 4610, 4627, 4658.5, 4658.6 and 5307.3, Labor Code. Reference: Sections 124, 129, 129.5, 138.6, 138.7, 4061, 4453, 4454, 4550, 4600, 4603.2, 4610, 4621, 4622, 4625, 4636-4638, 4639, 4641, 4642, 4650, 4658.5, 4658.6, 4701-4703.5, 4706, 4706.5, 4951, 5401, 5401.6, 5402, 5800 and 5814, Labor Code; and Section 2629.1(e) and (f), Unemployment Insurance Code.

History: 1. New section filed 12-30-2002; operative 1-1-2003 pursuant to Government Code section 11343.4 (Register 2003, No. 1).

2. Change without regulatory effect amending subsection (b)(8)[iv] filed 5-1-2003 pursuant to section 100, title 1, California Code of Regulations (Register 2003, No. 18).

3. Amendment of subsections (a)(1) and (a)(8), new subsection (a)(9), subsection renumbering, amendment of newly designated subsections (a)(10)-(11) and subsection (b)(23), new subsection (b)(24) and subsection renumbering filed 10-6-2003; operative 12-1-2003 (Register 2003, No. 41).

4. Amendment of section and Note filed 4-20-2009; operative 5-20-2009 (Register 2009, No. 17).

5. Change without regulatory effect amending subsection (a)(9) filed 12-9-2009 pursuant to section 100, title 1, California Code of Regulations (Register 2009, No. 50).

Ref.: Hanna §§ 1.12[8]–[10], 10.50[2][b], 10.51; Herlick Handbook §§ 1.01[3][b], 9.19.

§10112. Liability for Penalty Assessments.

The audit subject is liable for all penalty assessments, except that if the audit subject is acting as a third-party administrator, the client of that third-party administrator which secures the payment of compensation is jointly and severally liable with the administrator for all penalty assessments except civil penalties imposed under Labor Code section 129.5(e). Without affecting DWC's rights, a third-party administrator and its client may agree how to allocate the audit penalty expense between them.

Note: Authority cited: Sections 59, 129.5, 133. 5307.3, Labor Code. Reference: Section 129, 129.5, 3200-6002, Labor Code.

History: 1. Renumbering of former section 10112 to section 10115 and new section filed 1-28-94; operative 1-28-94. Submitted to OAL for printing only pursuant to Government Code section 11351 (Register 94, No. 4).

2. Amendment filed 4-20-2009; operative 5-20-2009 (Register 2009, No. 17).

Ref.: See Labor Code §4651; Hanna §§ 1.12[8]–[10], 10.50[1], 10.51; Herlick Handbook §§ 1.01[3][b], 9.5, 9.19, 15.2.

ARTICLE 5.5
Administrative Penalties Pursuant to Labor Code Section 5814.6

§10112.1. Definitions.

As used in this article:

(a) "Adjusting location" means the office where claims are administered. Separate underwriting companies, employers that are both self-administered and self-insured, and/or third-party administrators operating at one location shall be combined as one adjusting location only if claims are administered under the same management at that location. Where claims are administered from an office that includes a satellite office at another location, claims administered at the satellite office(s) will be considered as part of the single adjusting location for investigation and auditing purposes under this article when it is demonstrated that the claims are under the same immediate management.

(b) "Administrative Director" means the Administrative Director of the Division of Workers Compensation, including his or her designee.

(c) "Claim" means a request for compensation, or record of an occurrence in which compensation reasonably would be expected to be payable for an injury arising out of and in the course of employment.

(d) "Claim file" means a record in paper or electronic form, or any combination, containing all of the information specified in section 10101.1 of Title 8 of the California Code of Regulations and all documents or entries related to the provision, payment, delay, or denial of benefits or compensation under Divisions 1, 4 or 4.5 of the Labor Code.

(e) "Claims administrator" means a self-administered workers' compensation insurer; a self-administered self-insured employer; a self-administered legally uninsured employer; a self-administered joint powers authority; or a third-party claims administrator for an insurer, a self-insured employer, a legally uninsured employer or a joint powers authority.

(f) "Compensation" means every benefit or payment, including vocational rehabilitation, supplemental job displacement benefits, medical treatment, medical and medical-legal expenses, conferred by Divisions 1 and 4 of the Labor Code on an injured employee or the employee's dependents.

(g) "Compensation order" means any award, order or decision issued by the Workers' Compensation Appeals Board or the Division of Workers' Compensation vocational rehabilitation unit by which a party is entitled to payment of compensation.

(h) "Concurrent medical treatment authorization" means authorization requested or provided during an inpatient stay.

(i) "Determination and Order" means Determination and Order in re Labor Code § 5814.6 Administrative Penalties.

(j) "Employee" means every person in the service of another, as defined under Article 2 of Chapter 2 of Part 1 of Division 4 of the Labor Code (Sections 3350 et seq.), or in the case of the employee's death, his or her dependent, as each is defined in Division 4 of the Labor Code, or the employee's or dependent's agent or attorney.

(k) "Employer" shall have the same meaning as the word 'employer' as defined in Division 4 of the Labor Code (sections 3300 et seq.).

(*l*) "General business practice" means a pattern of violations of Labor Code section 5814 at a single adjusting location that can be distinguished by a reasonable person from an isolated event. The pattern of violations must occur in the handling of more than one claim. The pattern of violations may consist of one type of act or omission, or separate, discrete acts or omissions in the handling of more than one claim. However, where a claim file with a violation of Labor Code section 5814 has been adjusted at multiple adjusting locations, that claim file may be considered when determining the general business practice of any of the adjusting locations where the conduct that caused the violation occurred even if the file has been transferred to a different adjusting location.

(m) "Indemnity" means payments made directly to an eligible person as a result of a work injury and as required under Division 4 of the Labor Code, including but not limited to temporary disability indemnity, salary continuation in lieu of temporary disability indemnity, permanent disability indemnity, vocational rehabilitation temporary disability indemnity, vocational rehabilitation maintenance allowance, life pension and death benefits.

(n) "Insurer" means any company, group, or entity in, or which has been in, the business of transacting workers' compensation insurance for one or more employers subject to the workers' compensation laws of this state. The term insurer includes the State Compensation Insurance Fund.

(o) "Investigation" means the process used by the Administrative Director, or his or her designee, pursuant to Section 10112.2 and/or Government Code sections 11180 through 11191, to determine whether a violation of Labor Code section 5814.6 has occurred, including but not limited to reviewing, evaluating, copying and preserving electronic and paper records, files, accounts and other things, and interviewing potential witnesses.

(p) "Joint powers authority" means any county, city, city and county, municipal corporation, public district, public agency, or political subdivision of the state, but not the state itself, included in a pooling arrangement under a joint exercise of powers agreement for the purpose of securing a certificate of consent to self-insure workers' compensation claims under Labor Code Section 3700(c).

(q) "Knowingly" means acting with knowledge of the facts of the conduct at issue. For the purposes of this article, a corporation has knowledge of the facts an employee receives while acting within the scope of his or her authority. A corporation has knowledge of information contained in its records and of the actions of its employees performed in the scope and course of employment. An employer or insurer has knowledge of information contained in the records of its third-party administrator and of the actions of the employees of the third-party administrator performed in the scope and course of employment.

(r) "Notice of Assessment" means Notice of Labor Code § 5814.6 Administrative Penalty Assessment.

(s) "Penalty award" means a final order or final award by the Workers' Compensation Appeals Board to pay penalties due to a violation of section 5814 of the Labor Code.

(t) "Petition Appealing Determination and Order" means Petition Appealing Determination and Order of the Administrative Director in re Labor Code § 5814.6 Administrative Penalties.

(u) "Proof of service" means an affidavit or declaration made under penalty of perjury and filed with one or more documents required to be filed, setting out a description of the document(s) being served, the names and addresses of all persons served, whether service was made personally or by mail, the date of service, and the place of service or the address to which mailing was made.

(v) "Prospective medical treatment authorization" means authorization requested or provided prior to the delivery of the medical services.

(w) "Recommended Determination and Order" means Recommended Determination and Order in re Labor Code § 5814.6 Administrative Penalties.

(x) "Retrospective medical treatment authorization" means authorization requested or provided after medical services have been provided and for which services approval has not already been given.

(y) "Salary continuation" means payment made to an injured employee as provided under Division 4 of the Labor Code.

(z) "Serve" means to file or deliver a document or to cause it to be delivered to the Administrative Director or his or her designee, or to such other person as is required under this article.

(aa) "Stipulated Order" means a Notice of Assessment that was timely paid.

(bb) "Supplemental job displacement benefits" means benefits as described under Labor Code section 4658.5 and sections 10133.50–10133.59 of Title 8 of the California Code of Regulations.

(cc) "Third-party administrator" means an agent under contract to administer the workers' compensation claims of an insurer, a self-insured employer, a legally uninsured employer, a self-insured joint powers authority or on behalf of the California Insurance Guarantee Association. The term third-party administrator includes the State Compensation Insurance Fund for locations that administer claims for legally uninsured and self-insured employers, and also includes managing general agents.

(dd) "Utilization review files" means those files, documents or records, whether paper or electronic, containing information that documents an employer or insurer utilization review process required under Division 4 of the Labor Code.

(ee) "Workers' Compensation Appeals Board" means the Appeals Board, commissioners, deputy commissioners, presiding workers' compensation judges and workers' compensation administrative law judges.

Note: Authority cited: Sections 133, 5307.3 and 5814.6, Labor Code. Reference: Sections 129.5, 139.48, 5814 and 5814.6, Labor Code.

History: 1. Change without regulatory effect renumbering former subchapter 1.8, article 1 (sections 10225–10225.2) to subchapter 1.5, article 5.5 (sections 10112.1–10112.3) and renumbering former section 10225 to section 10112.1 filed 4-7-2008 pursuant to section 100, title 1, California Code of Regulations (Register 2008, No. 15).

Ref.: Herlick Handbook § 1.01[3][b].

§10112.2. Schedule of Administrative Penalties Pursuant to Labor Code §5814.6.

(a) Administrative penalties shall only be imposed under this section based on violations of Labor Code section 5814, after more than one penalty award has been issued by the Workers' Compensation Appeals Board on or after June 1, 2004 based on conduct occurring on or after April 19, 2004 for unreasonable delay or refusal to pay compensation within a five year time period. The five year period of time shall begin on the date of issuance of any penalty award not previously subject to an administrative penalty assessment pursuant to Labor Code section 5814.6.

(b) The Division of Workers' Compensation shall at least monthly submit copies of WCAB decisions, findings, and/or awards issued pursuant to Labor Code section 5814 to the Audit Unit.

(c) The Audit Unit shall obtain monthly Labor Code section 5814 activity reports and shall determine if the decisions, findings, and/or awards are final. If more than one final penalty award has been issued on or after June 1,

2004 against a claims administrator at a single adjusting location, the Audit Unit may proceed with an investigation.

(d) To determine whether a violation described in Labor Code section 5814.6 has occurred, and notwithstanding Labor Code section 129(a) through (d) and section 129.5 subdivisions (a) through (c) and sections 10106, 10106.1, 10107 and 10107.1 of Title 8 of the California Code of Regulations, the Administrative Director, or his or her designee, may conduct an investigation, which may include but is not limited to an audit of claims and/or utilization review files. The investigation may be independent of, or may be conducted concurrently with, an audit conducted pursuant to Labor Code section 129 and 129.5.

(e) The Administrative Director, or his or her designee, may also utilize the provisions of Government Code sections 11180 through 11191 to carry out the responsibilities mandated by Labor Code section 5814.6.

(f) The Administrative Director may issue a Notice of Assessment under this article in conjunction with an order to show cause pursuant to section 10113 of Title 8 of the California Code of Regulations, charging both an administrative penalty under this section and a civil penalty under subdivision (e) of Labor Code section 129.5 in the same pleading, however only one penalty may be imposed by the Administrative Director following the hearing on such charges.

(g) Pursuant to Labor Code section 5814.6, the Administrative Director, or his or her designee, shall issue a Notice of Assessment for administrative penalties against an employer and/or insurer as follows:

(1) $100,000 for when the Administrative Director, or his or her designee, has evidence to support a finding that an employer or insurer knowingly violated Labor Code section 5814 with a frequency that indicates a general business practice, and additionally for each applicable penalty award, the following;

(2) $30,000 for each penalty award by the Workers' Compensation Appeals Board for a violation of Labor Code section 5814 for an unreasonable delay or refusal to comply with an existing compensation order;

(3) For each penalty award by the Workers' Compensation Appeals Board for a violation of Labor Code section 5814 for an unreasonable delay or refusal to make a payment of temporary disability benefits or salary continuation payments in lieu of temporary disability; vocational rehabilitation maintenance allowance, life pension, or death benefits:

(A) $5,000 for 14 days or less of indemnity benefits;

(B) $10,000 for 15 days through 42 days of indemnity benefits;

(C) $15,000 for more than 42 days of indemnity benefits.

(4) For each penalty award by the Workers' Compensation Appeals Board for a violation of Labor Code section 5814 for an unreasonable delay or refusal to provide authorization for medical treatment:

(A) $1,000 for retrospective medical treatment authorization;

(B) $5,000 for prospective or concurrent medical treatment authorization;

(C) $15,000 for prospective or concurrent medical treatment authorization when the employee's condition is such that the employee faces an imminent and serious threat to his or her health.

(5) For each penalty award by the Workers' Compensation Appeals Board for a violation of Labor Code section 5814 for an unreasonable delay or refusal to reimburse an employee for self-procured medical treatment costs:

(A) $1,000 for medical treatment costs of $100 or less, excluding interest and penalty;

(B) $2,000 for medical treatment costs of more than $100 to $300, excluding interest and penalty;

(C) $3,000 for medical treatment costs of more than $300 to $500, excluding interest and penalty;

(D) $5,000 for medical treatment costs of more than $500, excluding interest and penalty.

(6) $2,500 for each penalty award by the Workers' Compensation Appeals Board for a violation of Labor Code section 5814 for an unreasonable delay or refusal to provide the the supplemental job displacement benefit, as required by section 10133.51(b) and section 10133.56(c), respectively, of Title 8 of the California Code of Regulations.

(7) $2,500 for each penalty award by the Workers' Compensation Appeals Board for a violation of Labor Code section 5814 for an unreasonable delay or refusal to make payment to an injured worker as reimbursement for payment for services provided for a supplemental job displacement benefit voucher, or where the unreasonable delay or refusal to pay the training provider causes an interruption in the employee's retraining.

(8) For each penalty award by the Workers' Compensation Appeals Board for a violation of Labor Code section 5814 for an unreasonable delay or refusal to make a payment of permanent disability indemnity benefits:

(A) $1,000 for 15 weeks or less of indemnity benefits;

(B) $5,000 for more than 15 but not more than 50 weeks of indemnity benefits;

(C) $7,500 for more than 50 but not more than 95 weeks of indemnity benefits;

(D) $15,000 for more than 95 weeks of indemnity benefits.

(9) $2,500 for any other penalty award by the Workers' Compensation Appeals Board pursuant to Labor Code section 5814 not otherwise specified in this section.

(h) In cases that the Administrative Director deems appropriate, the Administrative Director, or his or her designee, may mitigate a penalty imposed under this section after considering each of these factors:

(1) The consequences and gravity of the violation(s).

(2) The good faith of the claims administrator.

(3) The history of previous penalty awards under Labor Code section 5814.

(4) The number and type of the violations.

(5) The time period in which the violations occurred.

(6) The size of the claims adjusting location.

(i) Each administrative penalty assessed under this section shall be doubled upon a second Order (which may be a Stipulated Order or a final Determination and Order) by the Administrative Director under Labor Code § 5814.6 against the same employer or insurer within a five (5) year period. Each administrative penalty under this section shall be tripled upon a third Order (which may be a Stipulated

Order or a final Determination and Order) by the Administrative Director under Labor Code § 5814.6 against the same employer or insurer within the same five (5) year period.

(j) In no event shall the administrative penalties assessed against a single employer or insurer in a single Stipulated Order or final Determination and Order after doubling or tripling exceed $400,000.

Note: Authority cited: Sections 133, 5307.3 and 5814.6, Labor Code. Reference: Sections 129.5, 139.48, 5814 and 5814.6, Labor Code; and Sections 11180–11191, Government Code.

History: 1. Change without regulatory effect renumbering former section 10225.1 to section 10112.2 filed 4-7-2008 pursuant to section 100, title 1, California Code of Regulations (Register 2008, No. 15).

Ref.: Herlick Handbook § 1.01[3][b].

§10112.3. Notice of Administrative Penalty Assessment, Appeal Hearing Procedures and Review.

(a) Pursuant to Labor Code section 5814.6, the Administrative Director shall issue a Notice of Assessment when the Administrative Director, or his or her designee (the investigating unit of the Division of Workers Compensation), has evidence to support a finding that an employer or insurer has knowingly violated section 5814 with a frequency that indicates a general business practice.

(b) Successor liability may be imposed on a corporation or other business entity that has merged with, consoli dated with, or otherwise continued the business of an employer or insurer that is subject to penalties under Labor Code section 5814.6. The surviving entity shall assume and be liable for all the liabilities, obligations and penalties of the prior employer or insurer. Successor liability will be imposed if there has been a substantial continuity of business operations and/or the new business uses the same or substantially the same work force.

(c) The Notice of Assessment shall be in writing and shall contain all of the following:

(1) The basis for the penalty assessment, including a statement of the alleged violations and the amount of each proposed penalty;

(2) A description of the methods for paying or appealing the penalty assessment.

(d) The Notice of Assessment shall be served personally or by registered or certified mail.

(e) Within thirty (30) calendar days after the date of service of the Notice of Assessment, the employer or insurer may pay the penalties as assessed or file an appeal with the Administrative Director.

(f) If the employer or insurer pays the penalties within thirty (30) calendar days, the Notice of Assessment shall be deemed a Stipulated Order.

(g) If the employer or insurer files an appeal of the Notice of Assessment with the Administrative Director, the appeal shall:

(1) Admit or deny, in whole or in part any of the allegations set forth in the Notice;

(2) Appeal the existence of any or all of the alleged violations;

(3) Appeal the amount of any or all the penalties assessed;

(4) Set forth any affirmative and other defenses;

(5) Set forth the legal and factual bases for each defense and each ground for appeal. Any item listed in the Notice of Assessment but not appealed shall be paid within thirty (30) calendar days after the date of service of the Notice of Assessment.

(h) Failure to timely file an appeal shall constitute a waiver of the appellant's right to an evidentiary hearing. Unless set forth in the appeal, all defenses to the Notice of Assessment shall be deemed waived. The appellant may also file a written request for leave to assert additional defenses which the Administrative Director may grant upon a showing of good cause.

(i) The appeal shall be in writing signed by, or on behalf of, the employer or insurer, and shall state the appellant's mailing address. The appeal shall be verified, under penalty of perjury, by the employer or insurer. If the appellant is a corporation, the verification may be signed by an officer of the corporation. In the event the appellant is not the employer, the employer's address shall be provided and the employer shall be included on the proof of service.

(1) The appellant shall file the original and one copy of the appeal on the Administrative Director and concurrently serve one copy of the appeal on the investigating unit of the Division of Workers Compensation designated by the Administrative Director. The original and all copies of any filings required by this section shall have a proof of service attached.

(j) At any time before the hearing, the Administrative Director may file or permit the filing of an amended Notice of Assessment. All parties shall be notified thereof. If the amended Notice of Assessment presents new allegations or new penalties, the Administrative Director shall afford the Appellant a reasonable opportunity to prepare its defense, and the Appellant shall be entitled to file an amended appeal.

(k) At the Administrative Director's discretion, the Administrative Director may proceed with an informal pre-hearing conference with the appellant in an effort to resolve the contested matters. If any or all of the proposed penalties in Notice of Assessment or the amended Notice of Assessment remain contested, those contested matters shall proceed to an evidentiary hearing.

(*l*) Whenever the Administrative Director's Notice of Assessment has been contested, the Administrative Director may designate a hearing officer to preside over the hearing. The authority of the Administrative Director or any designated hearing officer includes, but is not limited to: conducting a prehearing settlement conference; setting the date for an evidentiary hearing and any continuances; issuing subpoenas for the attendance of any person residing anywhere within the state as a witness or party at any pre-hearing conference and hearing; issuing subpoenas duces tecum for the production of documents and things at the hearing; presiding at hearings; administering oaths or affirmations and certifying official acts; ruling on objections and motions; issuing prehearing orders; and preparing a Recommended Determination and Order based on the hearing.

(m) The Administrative Director, or the designated hearing officer, shall set the time and place for any prehearing conference on the contested matters in a Notice of Hearing and shall give sixty (60) calendar days written notice to all parties.

(n) The prehearing conference may address one or more of the following matters:

(1) Exploration of settlement possibilities.

(2) Preparation of stipulations.

(3) Clarification of issues.

(4) Rulings on identity and limitation of the number of witnesses.

(5) Objections to proffers of evidence.

(6) Order of presentation of evidence and cross-examination.

(7) Rulings regarding issuance of subpoenas and protective orders.

(8) Schedules for the submission of written briefs and schedules for the commencement and conduct of the hearing.

(9) Any other matters as shall promote the orderly and prompt conduct of the hearing.

(o) The Administrative Director, or the designated hearing officer, shall issue a prehearing conference order incorporating the matters determined at the prehearing conference. The Administrative Director, or the designated hearing officer, may direct one or more of the parties to prepare the prehearing conference order.

(p) Not less than 30 calendar days prior to the date of the pre-hearing conference, or if no pre-hearing conference is set, not less than 30 calendar days prior to the date of the evidentiary hearing, the Appellant shall file and serve the original and one copy of a written statement with the Administrative Director, or the designated hearing officer, specifying the legal and factual bases for its appeal and each defense, listing all witnesses the Appellant intends to call to testify at the hearing, and appending copies of all documents and other evidence the Appellant intends to introduce into evidence at the hearing. A copy of the written statement and its attachments shall also concurrently be served on the investigating unit of the Division of Workers' Compensation. If the Appellant's written statement and supporting evidence are not timely filed and served, the Administrative Director, or the designated hearing officer, shall dismiss the appeal and the violations and penalties as stated in the Notice of Assessment shall be final, due and payable. Within ten (10) calendar days of the date for filing the written statement and supporting evidence, the Appellant may file a written request for leave to file a written statement and supporting evidence. The Administrative Director, or the designated hearing officer, may grant the request, upon a showing of good cause. If leave is granted, the written statement and supporting evidence must be filed and served no later than ten (10) calendar days prior to the date of the hearing.

(q) Oral testimony shall be taken only on oath or affirmation.

(r)(1) Each party shall have these rights: to call and examine witnesses, to introduce exhibits; to cross-examine opposing witnesses on any matter relevant to the issues even though that matter was not covered in the direct examination; to impeach any witness regardless of which party first called him or her to testify; and to rebut the evidence.

(2) In the absence of a contrary order by the Administrative Director, or the designated hearing officer, the investigating unit of the Division of Worker's Compensation shall present evidence first.

(3) The hearing need not be conducted according to the technical rules relating to evidence and witnesses, except as hereinafter provided. Any relevant evidence shall be admitted if it is the sort of evidence on which responsible persons are accustomed to rely in the conduct of serious affairs, regardless of the existence of any common law or statutory rule which might make improper the admission of the evidence over objection in civil actions.

(4) Hearsay evidence may be used for the purpose of supplementing or explaining other evidence but over timely objection shall not be sufficient in itself to support a finding unless it would be admissible over objection in civil actions. An objection is timely if made before submission of the case to the Administrative Director, or to the designated hearing officer.

(s) The written affidavit or declaration of any witness may be offered and shall be received into evidence provided that (i) the witness was listed in the written statement pursuant to section 10112.3(p), (ii) the statement is made by affidavit or by declaration under penalty of perjury, (iii) copies of the statement have been delivered to all opposing parties at least 20 calendar days prior to the hearing, and (iv) no opposing party has, at least 10 calendar days before the hearing, delivered to the proponent of the evidence a written demand that the witness be produced in person to testify at the hearing. The Administrative Director, or the designated hearing officer, shall disregard any portion of the statement received pursuant to this regulation that would be inadmissible if the witness were testifying in person, but the inclusion of inadmissible matter does not render the entire statement inadmissible. Upon timely demand for production of a witness in lieu of admission of an affidavit or declaration, the proponent of that witness shall ensure the witness appears at the scheduled hearing and the proffered declaration or affidavit from that witness shall not be admitted. If the Administrative Director, or the designated hearing officer, determines that good cause exists that prevents the witness from appearing at the hearing, the declaration may be introduced in evidence, but it shall be given only the same effect as other hearsay evidence.

(t) The Administrative Director, or the designated hearing officer, shall issue a written Recommended Determination and Order, granting or denying the appeal, in whole or part, and affirming or amending the penalty assessment(s). The Recommended Determination and Order shall include a statement of the basis for the decision and each penalty assessed. It shall be served on all parties within sixty (60) calendar days of the date the case was submitted for determination. This requirement is directory and not jurisdictional.

(u) The Administrative Director shall have up to sixty (60) calendar days to adopt or modify the Recommended Determination and Order issued by the Administrative Director or the designated hearing officer. In the event the Recommended Determination and Order is modified, the Administrative Director shall include a statement of the basis for the Determination and Order. If the Administrative Director does not act within sixty (60) calendar days, then the Recommended Determination and Order shall become the Determination and Order on the sixty-first calendar day.

(v) The Determination and Order shall be served on all parties personally or by registered or certified mail by the Administrative Director.

(w) The Determination and Order, if any, shall become final on the date it was served, unless the aggrieved party files a timely Petition Appealing Determination and Order within twenty (20) days. A timely filed Petition Appealing the Determination and Order tolls the period for paying any disputed penalty. All findings and assessments in the Determination and Order that are not contested in the Petition Appealing Determination and Order shall become final as though no such petition was filed.

(x) At any time prior to the date the Determination and Order becomes final, the Administrative Director may correct the Determination and Order for clerical, mathematical or procedural error.

(y) Penalties assessed in a Determination and Order shall be paid within thirty (30) calendar days of the date the Determination and Order has been served, if no Petition Appealing Determination and Order has been filed. The penalties shall be deposited into the Return-to-Work-Fund.

(z) All appeals from any part or the entire Determination and Order shall be made in the form of a Petition Appealing the Determination and Order, in conformance with the requirements of chapter 7, part 4 of Division 4 of the Labor Code. Any such Petition Appealing the Determination and Order shall be filed at the Workers' Compensation Appeals Board in San Francisco (and not with any district office of the Workers' Compensation Appeals Board), in the same manner specified for petitions for reconsideration.

Note: Authority cited: Sections 133, 5307.3 and 5814.6, Labor Code. Reference: Sections 129.5, 139.48, 5300, 5814, 5814.6 and 5900 et seq., Labor Code.

History: 1. Change without regulatory effect renumbering former section 10225.2 to section 10112.3, including amendment of subsection (s), filed 4-7-2008 pursuant to section 100, title 1, California Code of Regulations (Register 2008, No. 15).

Ref.: Herlick Handbook § 1.01[3][b].

ARTICLE 6
Civil Penalty
[First Enacted Version]

Another Article 6, Retraining and Return to Work—Definitions and General Provisions, precedes Section 10116.

§10113. Order to Show Cause Re: Assessment of Civil Penalty and Notice of Hearing.

(a) If an audit subject fails to meet the full compliance audit performance standards in two consecutive full compliance audits, the Audit Unit shall refer the audit subject to the Administrative Director for the possible assessment of a civil penalty pursuant to Labor Code Section 129.5(e). Nothing in these regulations shall prohibit the Audit Unit from referring any audit subject to the Administrative Director for the possible assessment of a civil penalty under Labor Code Section 129.5(e) for any other reason. If the Administrative Director has reason to believe that an employer, insurer, or third-party administrator has knowingly committed or performed any of the practices set forth in Labor Code Section 129.5(e), (s)he shall issue an Order to Show Cause Re: Assessment of Civil Penalty and Notice of Hearing.

(b) The order shall be in writing and shall contain all of the following:

(1) Notice that a civil penalty not to exceed $100,000 per audit subject named in the order may be assessed;

(2) The basis for the assessment, including a statement of the alleged violations;

(3) Notice of the date, time and place of hearing. Continuances will not be allowed without a showing of good cause.

(c) The order shall be served personally or by registered or certified mail.

Note: Authority cited: Sections 59, 129, 129.5, 133 and 5307.3, Labor Code. Reference: Sections 7, 124, 129 and 129.5, Labor Code.

History: 1. New section filed 1-18-90; operative 1-18-90 (Register 90, No. 4). New section is exempt from review by OAL pursuant to Government Code Section 11351.

2. Relocation and amendment of article heading, renumbering of former section 10113 to section 10115.1 and renumbering and amendment of former section 10109 to section 10113 filed 1-28-94; operative 1-28-94. Submitted to OAL for printing only pursuant to Government Code section 11351 (Register 94, No. 4).

3. Amendment of subsections (a), (b)(2) and Note filed 10-26-98; operative 11-25-98 (Register 98, No. 44).

4. Amendment of section and Note filed 12-30-2002; operative 1-1-2003 pursuant to Government Code section 11343.4 (Register 2003, No. 1).

Ref.: Hanna §§ 1.12[2], [7], 10.51[2][a], [b]; Herlick Handbook §§ 1.01[3][b], 9.5, 15.2.

§10113.1. Answer to Order to Show Cause.

(a) Within 30 days after service of the Order to Show Cause Re Assessment of Civil Penalties the claims administrator may file with the Administrative Director an Answer to the Order to Show Cause in which the claims administrator may:

(1) Admit or deny in whole or in part any of the allegations of set forth in the Order to Show Cause;

(2) Set forth any affirmative defenses.

(b) Failure to timely file an Answer shall constitute a waiver of the claims administrator's right to a hearing. Unless set forth in the Answer, all defenses to the Order to Show cause shall be deemed waived. If the Answer is not timely filed, the claims administrator may file a written request for leave to file an Answer. The claims administrator may also file a written request for leave to assert additional defenses. The Administrative Director may grant relief upon a showing of good cause.

(c) The Answer shall be in writing signed by or on behalf of the claims administrator and shall state the claims administrator's mailing address. It need not be verified or follow any particular form.

(d) The claims administrator must file the original and one copy of the Answer on the Administrative Director and concurrently serve one copy of the Answer on the Audit Unit. The original and all copies of any filings shall have a proof of service.

Note: Authority cited: Sections 59, 129, 129.5, 133 and 5307.3, Labor Code Reference: Sections 129 and 129.5, Labor Code.

History: 1. New section filed 12-30-2002; operative 1-1-2003 pursuant to Government Code section 11343.4 (Register 2003, No. 1).

Ref.: Hanna § 10.51[2][a.1]; Herlick Handbook § 1.01[3][b].

§10113.2. Amended Complaint or Supplemental Order to Show Cause Before Submission of Case.

At any time before the hearing, the Administrative Director may file or permit the filing of an amended complaint or supplemental Order to Show Cause. All parties shall be notified thereof. If the amended or supplemental Order to Show Cause presents new charges, the Administrative Director shall afford the claims administrator a reasonable opportunity to prepare its defense thereto, and it shall be entitled to file an amended Answer.

Note: Authority cited: Sections 59, 129, 129.5, 133 and 5307.3, Labor Code. Reference: Sections 129 and 129.5, Labor Code.

History: 1. New section filed 12-30-2002; operative 1-1-2003 pursuant to Government Code section 11343.4 (Register 2003, No. 1).

Ref.: Hanna § 10.51[2][a.2]; Herlick Handbook §§ 1.01[3][b], 9.5.

§10113.3. Administrative Director's Designation of Hearing Officer.

The Administrative Director may delegate authority to a Workers' Compensation Administrative Law Judge to act as the Hearing Officer. The delegation may include the following authority: to conduct a prehearing conference; to conduct the civil penalty hearing; to issue subpoenas for the attendance of witnesses at the conference; to issue subpoena duces tecum for the production of documents; and to prepare a Recommended Determination.

Note: Authority cited: Sections 59, 129, 129.5, 133 and 5307.3, Labor Code. Reference: Sections 129 and 129.5, Labor Code.

History: 1. New section filed 12-30-2002; operative 1-1-2003 pursuant to Government Code section 11343.4 (Register 2003, No. 1).

Ref.: Hanna § 10.51[2][a.3]; Herlick Handbook § 1.01[3][b].

§10113.4. Written Statement and Supporting Evidence.

(a) Not less than 30 calendar days prior to the date of hearing, the claims administrator shall file and serve a written statement with the Administrative Director specifying its legal and factual bases for its Answer. The written statement shall also include copies of all documents and all other evidence the claims administrator intends on introducing into evidence at the hearing. If the written statement and supporting evidence are not timely filed and served, the Administrative Director shall dismiss the Answer and issue a written Determination. If the written statement and supporting evidence are not timely filed and served, the claims administrator may file a written request for leave to file a written statement and supporting evidence. The written request for leave must be filed and served no later than the date of the hearing. The Administrative Director may grant the request for leave to file the written statement and supporting evidence and continue the hearing, upon a showing of good cause.

(b) The claims administrator must file the original and one copy of the written statement and all supporting evidence on the Administrative Director and concurrently serve one copy of the written statement and all supporting evidence on the Audit Unit. The original and all copies of any filings shall have a proof of service.

Note: Authority cited: Sections 59, 129, 129.5, 133 and 5307.3, Labor Code. Reference: Sections 129 and 129.5, Labor Code.

History: 1. New section filed 12-30-2002; operative 1-1-2003 pursuant to Government Code section 11343.4 (Register 2003, No. 1).

2. Amendment of subsection (a) filed 4-20-2009; operative 5-20-2009 (Register 2009, No. 17).

Ref.: Hanna §§ 1.12[8]–[10], 10.50, 10.51[2][b]; Herlick Handbook §§ 1.01[3][b], 9.19.

§10113.5. Prehearing Conference; Subject Matter; Prehearing Order.

(a) The Administrative Director or designee shall set the time and place for the prehearing conference, and shall give reasonable written notice to all parties.

(b) The prehearing conference may deal with one or more of the following matters:

(1) Exploration of settlement possibilities.

(2) Preparation of stipulations.

(3) Clarification of issues.

(4) Rulings on identity and limitation of the number of witnesses.

(5) Objections to proffers of evidence.

(6) Order of presentation of evidence and cross-examination.

(7) Rulings regarding issuance of subpoenas and protective orders.

(8) Exchange of witness lists and of exhibits or documents to be offered in evidence at the hearing.

(9) Schedules for the submission of written briefs and schedules for the commencement and conduct of the hearing.

(10) Any other matters as shall promote the orderly and prompt conduct of the hearing.

(c) The Administrative Director or designee shall issue a prehearing order incorporating the matters determined at the prehearing conference. The Administrative Director or designee may direct one or more of the parties to prepare a prehearing order.

Note: Authority cited: Sections 59, 129, 129.5, 133 and 5307.3, Labor Code. Reference: Sections 129 and 129.5, Labor Code.

History: 1. New section filed 12-30-2002; operative 1-1-2003 pursuant to Government Code section 11343.4 (Register 2003, No. 1).

2. New subsection (b)(8) and subsection renumbering filed 4-20-2009; operative 5-20-2009 (Register 2009, No. 17).

Ref.: Hanna §§ 1.12[8]–[10], 10.50, 10.51[2][a.5]; Herlick Handbook §§ 1.01[3][b], 9.19.

§10113.6. Subpoenas.

The Administrative Director or designee may issue subpoenas for the attendance of persons and the production of documents or other things, to compel the attendance of persons residing anywhere within the State.

Note: Authority cited: Sections 59, 129, 129.5, 133 and 5307.3, Labor Code. Reference: Sections 129 and 129.5, Labor Code.

History: 1. New section filed 12-30-2002; operative 1-1-2003 pursuant to Government Code section 11343.4 (Register 2003, No. 1).

Ref.: Hanna § 10.51[2][a.3]; Herlick Handbook § 1.01[3][b].

§10114. Hearing.

(a) The hearing shall be held at the place, time and date noticed, unless a continuance has been granted for good cause.

(b) A record of the hearing shall be made.

(c) Any claims administrator that fails to meet the full compliance audit performance standards in two consecutive full compliance audits shall be rebuttably presumed to have engaged in a general business practice of discharging and administering its compensation obligations in a manner causing injury to those dealing with it. With regard to any other bases for the assessment of a civil penalty, the Audit Unit will have the burden to prove a *prima facie* case that a violation of 129.5(e) occurred. The claims administrator may cross-examine the witnesses. The claims administrator may then present any testimony to rebut the Audit Unit's testimony, and the Audit Unit may cross-examine. The Designated Hearing Officer may choose to ask questions for clarification of the record.

Note: Authority cited: Sections 59, 129.5, 133 and 5307.3, Labor Code. Reference: Sections 7, 124 and 129.5, Labor Code.

History: 1. New section filed 1-18-90; operative 1-18-90 (Register 90, No. 4). New section is exempt from review by OAL pursuant to Government Code Section 11351.

2. Renumbering of former section 10114 to section 10115.2 and renumbering and amendment of former sections 10110 and 10111 to section 10114 filed 1-28-94; operative 1-28-94. Submitted to OAL for printing only pursuant to Government Code section 11351 (Register 94, No. 4).

3. Amendment of section heading, repealer of subsections (a), (b), (d), (e), (g) and (h), subsection relettering and new subsection (c) filed 12-30-2002; operative 1-1-2003 pursuant to Government Code section 11343.4 (Register 2003, No. 1).

Ref.: Hanna § 10.51[2][b], [c]; Herlick Handbook §§ 1.01[3][b], 9.5, 15.2.

§10114.1. Evidence; Examination of Witnesses.

(a) Oral evidence shall be taken only on oath or affirmation.

(b) Each party shall have these rights: to call and examine witnesses, to introduce exhibits; to cross-examine opposing witnesses on any matter relevant to the issues even though that matter was not covered in the direct examination; to impeach any witness regardless of which party first called him or her to testify; and to rebut the evidence.

(c) In the absence of a contrary order by the Hearing Officer, the Audit Unit shall present its evidence first.

(d) The hearing need not be conducted according to technical rules relating to evidence and witnesses, except as hereinafter provided. Any relevant evidence shall be admitted if it is the sort of evidence on which responsible persons are accustomed to rely in the conduct of serious affairs, regardless of the existence of any common law or statutory rule which might make improper the admission of the evidence over objection in civil actions.

(e) Hearsay evidence may be used for the purpose of supplementing or explaining other evidence but over timely objection shall not be sufficient in itself to support a finding unless it would be admissible over objection in civil actions. An objection is timely if made before submission of the case or on reconsideration.

(f) The rules of privilege shall be effective to the extent that they are otherwise required by statute to be recognized at the hearing.

Note: Authority cited: Sections 59, 129, 129.5, 133 and 5307.3, Labor Code. Reference: Sections 7, 124 and 129.5, Labor Code.

History: 1. New section filed 12-30-2002; operative 1-1-2003 pursuant to Government Code section 11343.4 (Register 2003, No. 1).

Ref.: Hanna § 10.51[2][b]; Herlick Handbook § 1.01[3][b].

§10114.2. Affidavits.

The written affidavit or declaration of any witness may be offered and shall be received into evidence provided that (i) the witness was named in a witness list exchanged either through agreement of the parties or pursuant to an order issued under section 10113.5(c), (ii) the statement is made by affidavit or by declaration under penalty of perjury, (iii) copies of the statement have been delivered to all opposing parties at least 20 days prior to the hearing, and (iv) no opposing party has, at least 10 days before the hearing, delivered to the proponent of the evidence a written demand that the witness be produced in person to testify at the hearing. The Hearing Officer shall disregard any portion of the statement received pursuant to this regulation that would be inadmissible if the witness were testifying in person, but the inclusion of inadmissible matter does not render the entire statement inadmissible.

Note: Authority cited: Sections 59, 129, 129.5, 133 and 5307.3, Labor Code. Reference: Sections 7, 124 and 129.5, Labor Code.

History: 1. New section filed 12-30-2002; operative 1-1-2003 pursuant to Government Code section 11343.4 (Register 2003, No. 1).

2. Amendment filed 4-20-2009; operative 5-20-2009 (Register 2009, No. 17).

Ref.: Hanna §§ 1.12[8]–[10], 10.50, 10.51[2][b]; Herlick Handbook §§ 1.01[3][b], 9.19.

§10114.3. Oaths.

In any proceedings under this chapter the Administrative Director or his designated hearing officer, has power to administer oaths and affirmations and to certify to official acts.

Note: Authority cited: Sections 59, 129, 129.5, 133 and 5307.3, Labor Code. Reference: Sections 7, 124 and 129.5, Labor Code.

History: 1. New section filed 12-30-2002; operative 1-1-2003 pursuant to Government Code section 11343.4 (Register 2003, No. 1).

Ref.: Hanna § 10.51[2][b]; Herlick Handbook § 1.01[3][b].

§10114.4. Determination.

(a) The Administrative Director shall issue a written Determination, including a statement of the basis for the

Determination, within 60 days of the date the case was submitted for decision. This requirement is directory and not jurisdictional.

(b) The Determination shall be served on the audit subject personally or by registered or certified mail. If the Determination assesses a civil penalty, the Determination shall become final 7 days after the audit subject receives it, and the audit subject shall pay the amount assessed within 30 days after receiving the Determination, but the 30-day period shall be tolled if the audit subject files a timely appeal pursuant to Section 10953.

Note: Authority cited: Sections 59, 129, 129.5, 133 and 5307.3, Labor Code. Reference: Sections 7, 124 and 129.5, Labor Code.

History: 1. New section filed 12-30-2002; operative 1-1-2003 pursuant to Government Code section 11343.4 (Register 2003, No. 1).

Ref.: Hanna § 10.51[2][c]; Herlick Handbook § 1.01[3][b].

ARTICLE 7
Appeals

§10115. Appeal of Notice of Compensation Due.

An audit subject which has filed a timely Objection under California Code of Regulations, title 8, section 10110 may seek further review of a Notice of Compensation Due by filing an appeal with the Workers Compensation Appeals Board pursuant to California Code of Regulations, title 8, section 10952, and serving copies of the appeal on the injured worker, any other person to whom the payment is due as specified in the Notice of Compensation Due, and the Administrative Director, within 15 days of receiving the Notice.

Note: Authority cited: Sections 59, 129.5, 133, 4603.5, 5300 and 5307.3, Labor Code. Reference: Sections 129, 129.5, 3207, 4550, 4600, 4621, 4636–4638, 4639, 4701–4703.5, 4900 and 4902, Labor Code; and California Code of Regulations, title 8, section 10952.

History: 1. Relocation and amendment of article heading, renumbering of former section 10115 to 10115.2 subsections (i)-(*l*) and new section filed 1-28-94; operative 1-28-94. Submitted to OAL for printing only pursuant to Government Code section 11351 (Register 94, No. 4). For prior history, see Register 90, No. 4.

2. Amendment of section and Note filed 4-20-2009; operative 5-20-2009 (Register 2009, No. 17).

Ref.: Hanna §§ 1.12[8]–[10], 10.50, 10.51; Herlick Handbook §§ 1.01[3][b], 9.5, 9.19.

§10115.1. Appeal of Notice of Penalty Assessment—Filing and Contents.

(a) Within 7 days after receiving a Notice of Penalty Assessment issued under Labor Code section 129.5(a) and (c), the claims administrator may appeal all or a portion of the penalty assessments in the Notice by filing with the Administrative Director and serving the Audit Unit with a request for an appeals conference or a request for a written decision without a conference.

(b) If a request for a written decision or request for appeals conference is not timely filed and served, the Notice of Penalty Assessment will become final 7 days after the claims administrator received it, and must be paid in accordance with Labor Code §129.5(d) within 15 days of receipt.

(c) The request shall be in writing in a form specified by the Administrative Director and shall include at least the following information:

(1) The name and address of the person filing the request;

(2) A copy of the Notice of Penalty Assessment which is disputed.

(d) Within 21 days after the request for a written decision or appeals conference is filed, the appellant shall file with the Administrative Director and serve the Audit Unit with a written statement listing the assessments appealed, specifying the legal or factual basis of the appeal, and including documentation or other evidence, if any, which supports the appellant's position. If the written statement and supporting documentation are not timely filed and served, the the Administrative Director shall dismiss the request for written decision or appeals conference. The Notice of Penalty Assessment becomes final on the date of the Administrative Director's notice of dismissal. Penalties shall be paid within 15 days of receipt of the notice of dismissal.

(e) The appellant is deemed to have finally waived any legal or factual basis for appeal which is not stated in a timely filed appeal or timely filed supporting statement. However, the appellant may move the Administrative Director, upon a written showing of good cause filed and served not later than thirty days after its written statement was timely filed, for leave to amend its appeal or statement to add a legal or factual basis for appeal not previously stated. The motion shall attach a copy of the proposed amendment. The motion may include a request to file additional supporting documentation, which shall also be attached. If leave to amend is granted, the proposed amendment shall be deemed filed on the date the Administrative Director's order is served.

(f) Documentation which the appellant did not file with its appeal or supporting statement (including an amended appeal and statement allowed under subdivision (e)) will not be admitted into evidence in support of the appeal without a showing of good cause. Good cause requires the appellant to show that the additional documentation was not reasonably available to accompany its appeal statement, and also requires that the appellant serve a copy of the proposed additional documentation on the Audit Unit before the hearing, as soon as the document becomes available.

(g) The appellant shall mail or deliver an original and one copy of its request under subdivision (a) and its statement, documentation and any motion under subdivisions (d) or (e) to the office of the Administrative Director at the address shown in the report of audit findings. Requests, statements, documentation and motions are timely if they were:

(1) Placed in the United States mail in a fully prepaid, sealed envelope postmarked within the times specified in subdivisions (a), (d) and (e); or,

(2) Delivered to the office of the Administrative Director between the hours of 8:00 a.m. and 5:00 p.m. within the periods specified in subdivisions (a), (d) and (e).

If a date to submit a request under subdivision (a) or to submit a filing under subdivisions (d) or (e) falls on a weekend or holiday, that date is extended to the next business day.

(h) The appellant shall serve two copies of any request, statement, document or motion filed with the Administrative Director concurrently on the Audit Unit, by the same means of delivery as the original which was filed with the Administrative Director. The original and all copies of any filing shall attach proof of service, which may be made as provided in California Code of Regulations, title 8, section 10975.

(i) If a request for a written decision or an appeals conference, or a written statement in support of the appeal, contests only a portion of a Notice of Penalty Assessment, the portions of which are not appealed (or not included in the supporting statement(s)) shall become final on the same date an entire Notice of Penalty Assessment would become final if not timely appealed or supported, and appellant shall pay the uncontested assessments by the date payment would be due under subdivision (b) if an entire Notice of Penalty Assessment were involved.

Note: Authority cited: Sections 59, 129.5, 133 and 5307.3, Labor Code. Reference: Sections 129 and 129.5, Labor Code.

History: 1. Renumbering and amendment of former section 10113 to section 10115.1 filed 1-28-94; operative 1-28-94. Submitted to OAL for printing only pursuant to Government Code section 11351 (Register 94, No. 4).

2. Amendment of subsection (i) filed 2-14-96; operative 2-14-96. Submitted to OAL for printing only pursuant to Government Code section 11351 (Register 96, No. 7).

3. Amendment of subsections (a) and (d) filed 12-30-2002; operative 1-1-2003 pursuant to Government Code section 11343.4 (Register 2003, No. 1).

4. Amendment filed 4-20-2009; operative 5-20-2009 (Register 2009, No. 17).

Ref.: Hanna §§ 1.12[8]–[10], 10.50[3][a], [b][i]–[iii], 10.51; Herlick Handbook §§ 1.01[3][b], 9.5, 9.19.

§10115.2. Appeal of Notice of Penalty Assessment; Conference Process and Delegation of Authority; Notice of Findings, Service.

(a) The Administrative Director may appoint a designee to conduct the appeal conference.

(b) The conference shall be held at the place, time, and date scheduled unless, upon a showing of good cause, a continuance has been granted. Notice of the conference date will be provided to the parties no late than thirty days before the conference.

(c) The appeals conference is an informal hearing in which the parties are given an opportunity to explain their positions and to present evidence in support of their positions. The conference need not be conducted in accordance with the formal rules of evidence, and legal representation is not required.

(d) The conference will be tape recorded, unless a party chooses to have it recorded by a court reporter. Should a party choose to use a court reporter, the party shall: (1) notify the Administrative Director and the opposing party no later than five days before the conference that a court reporter will be provided; and (2) make the arrangements for the reporter and pay the costs of the reporter and transcription, including the cost of a copy of the transcript for the Administrative Director.

(e) Either party may present live testimony or documentary evidence at the conference. The Administrative Director may issue subpoenas for the attendance of witnesses at the conference, or subpoenas duces tecum for the production of documents, if requested by a party in writing within a reasonable time before the conference. Any person who is subpoenaed to appear may, instead of appearing at the time specified in the subpoena, agree with the party at whose request the subpoena was issued to appear at another time or upon agreed notice. Any failure to appear according to that agreement may be treated in all respects as a failure to appear in response to the original subpoena. The facts establishing or disproving the agreement and failure to appear may be proved by an affidavit of any person having personal knowledge of the facts.

(f) All testimony shall be made on oath or affirmation administered by the Administrative Director or designee.

(g) The Administrative Director or the Director's designee shall preside over the conference and shall have authority to admit any relevant testimony or documentary evidence into the record, and to decide any issues which arise during the conference including objections to evidence, privileges, claims and defenses.

(h) If the appellant fails to appear at the conference, the Administrative Director shall dismiss the request for conference and issue an order affirming the notice of penalty assessment.

(i) Within 15 days of the date the appeal is submitted for decision, the Administrative Director shall issue a Notice of Findings. When a written decision without a conference was requested, the date of submission is the date the Administrative Director receives the Audit Unit's written response to the appeal unless that date is extended by the Administrative Director for good cause. The time limits for action by the Administrative Director are directory and not jurisdictional.

(j) The Notice of Findings shall be served on the appellant by registered or certified mail, and is final for purposes of judicial review upon receipt.

(k) The appellant must pay any amount found due by the Administrative Director within 30 days after receiving the Notice of Findings, but the 30-day period shall be tolled if the appellant files a timely petition for writ of mandate, as to any assessment included for review in the petition proceeding, until that proceeding has become final.

(*l*) The appellant may file a petition for a writ of mandate from the Administrative Director's Notice of Findings in accordance with Labor Code section 129.5(f). The deadline for filing the petition for writ is 30 days after receipt of the Notice of Findings.

Note: Authority cited: Sections 59, 129.5, 133 and 5307.3, Labor Code. Reference: Sections 7, 129 and 129.5, Labor Code.

History: 1. Renumbering and amendment of former sections 10114 and 10115 to section 10115.2 filed 1-28-94; operative 1-28-94. Submitted to OAL for printing only pursuant to Government Code section 11351 (Register 94, No. 4).

2. Amendment of subsections (d), (g) and (*l*) filed 4-20-2009; operative 5-20-2009 (Register 2009, No. 17).

Ref.: Hanna §§ 1.12[8]–[10], 10.50[3][b][iv], [v], 10.51; Herlick Handbook §§ 1.01[3][b], 9.5, 9.19.

§10115.3. Appeal of Civil Penalty. [Repealed]

Note: Authority cited: Sections 59, 129.5, 133 and 5307.3, Labor Code. Reference: Sections 7, 124 and 129.5, Labor Code.

History: 1. Renumbering and amendment of former section 10112 to section 10115.3 filed 1-28-94; operative 1-28-94. Submitted to OAL for printing only pursuant to Government Code section 11351 (Register 94, No. 4).

2. Repealer filed 12-30-2002; operative 1-1-2003 pursuant to Government Code section 11343.4 (Register 2003, No. 1).

ARTICLE 6
Retraining and Return to Work—Definitions and General Provisions [Second Enacted Version]

Another Article 6, Civil Penalty, precedes Section 10113.

§10116. Applicability of Article.

The provisions of this article are applicable to Articles 6.5, 7, and 7.5 of these regulations, except for the definitions in section 10116.9. The definitions in section 10116.9 only apply to the provisions of Articles 6.5 and 7.5.

Note: Authority cited: Sections 111, 133, 5307.3 and 5307.4, Labor Code. Reference: Sections 139.5, 4658, 4658.1, 4658.5 and 4658.6, Labor Code.

History: 1. New article 6 (sections 10116-10116.9) and section filed 11-17-2008; operative 11-17-2008 pursuant to Government Code section 11343.4 (Register 2008, No. 47). For prior history of article 6, see Register 2008, No. 15, renumbering article 6, sections 10116-10121 to article 9, sections 10136-10142.

Ref.: Hanna §§ 7.02[3][d], 35.05[4][b]; Herlick Handbook §§ 1.01[3][b], 5.20, 16.23.

§10116.1. Filing and Reporting Requirements.

(a) "Electronic Adjudication Management System" or "EAMS" means the computer case management system used by the Division of Workers' Compensation to electronically store and maintain the Division of Workers' Compensation or appeals board's case files and to perform other case management functions.

(b) All forms, documents or correspondence submitted to the Retraining and Return to Work Unit shall be signed by the filing party and stored in the EAMS:

(1) Except for documents or forms which open a Retraining and Return to Work Unit file, all documents and forms shall contain a case number assigned by the Division of Workers' Compensation.

(2) Case opening documents shall be assigned a case number by the Division of Workers' Compensation after filing where no case number has been previously assigned for the date of injury alleged by the injured worker. The case number shall be preceded by the prefix "VOC" for cases governed by Article 7 of these rules and "RSU" for cases governed by Article 6.5 and 7.5 of these rules. If a case number has been previously assigned by the Division of Workers' Compensation, the prefix "VOC" or "RSU" shall precede the assigned case number on a form or document filed with the Retraining and Return to Work Unit. Documents or forms filed in existing cases without a case number will be returned to the sender with instructions for proper filing.

(3) All documents presented for filing shall conform to the requirements of sections 10217, 10228 and 10232 of title 8 of the California Code of Regulations.

(4) The Division of Workers' Compensation shall scan all documents and forms filed into the EAMS case file and then the paper document or form will be destroyed not less than 30 business days after filing. A properly filed form or document shall be deemed a legal filing for all purposes.

(5) The service of all documents and forms shall conform to the methods of service described in section of 10218 of title 8 of the California Code of Regulation.

(c) All required notices, any documents or forms shall be sent to the employee and his or her attorney, if any, on a timely basis by the claims administrator in the form and manner prescribed in section 10218 of title 8 of the California Code of Regulation. Failure to provide notices timely shall subject the insurer, third party administrator or self-insured employer to administrative or civil penalties. The notices are timely when sent according to the requirements of sections 9813, 9813.1 and 9813.2 of title 8 of the California Code of Regulation.

Note: Authority cited: Sections 133, 139.48, 139.5, 4658, 4658.5 and 5307.3, Labor Code. Reference: Section 139.5, Labor Code; *Godinez v. Buffets, Inc.* (2004, Significant Panel Decision) 69 Cal. Comp. Cases 1311; and *Vulean Materials Co. v. WCAB* (2006, Writ Denied) 71 Cal. Comp. Cases 1346.

History: 1. New section filed 11-17-2008; operative 11-17-2008 pursuant to Government Code section 11343.4 (Register 2008, No. 47).

Ref.: Hanna §§ 7.02[3][d], 35.05[4][b]; Herlick Handbook §§ 1.01[3][b], 5.20, 16.23.

§10116.2. Electronic Filing Exemption.

If a document is filed with EAMS as part of the electronic filing trial, that document does not need to be filed in compliance with sections 10228 and 10232 of title 8 of the California Code of Regulation.

Note: Authority cited: Sections 111, 133, 5307.3 and 5307.4, Labor Code. Reference: Sections 124 and 126, Labor Code.

History: 1. New section filed 11-17-2008; operative 11-17-2008 pursuant to Government Code section 11343.4 (Register 2008, No. 47).

Ref.: Hanna §§ 7.02[3][d], 35.05[4][b]; Herlick Handbook §§ 1.01[3][b], 5.20, 16.23.

§10116.3. Incomplete Filings.

(a) A form filed without the attachments or enclosures required by these rules is deemed incomplete and shall not be deemed filed for any purpose. All incomplete requests will be date stamped by the Division of Workers' Compensation.

(b) The Retraining and Return to Work Unit shall notify the filer and the other parties when a form or document is deemed not filed.

(c) Forms including filing instructions and venue lists shall be provided upon request by the Retraining and Return to Work Unit. Requests shall be submitted to:

Retraining and Return to Work Unit Headquarters
P.O. Box 420603
San Francisco, CA 94142

Or may be found at http://www.dir.ca.gov/dwc/forms.html

Note: Authority cited: Sections 133, 139.48, 139.5, 4658, 4658.5 and 5307.3, Labor Code. Reference: Section 139.5, Labor Code; *Godinez v. Buffets, Inc.* (2004, Significant Panel Decision) 69 Cal. Comp. Cases 1311; and *Vulean Materials Co. v. WCAB* (2006, Writ Denied) 71 Cal. Comp. Cases 1346.

History: 1. New section filed 11-17-2008; operative 11-17-2008 pursuant to Government Code section 11343.4 (Register 2008, No. 47).

Ref.: Hanna §§ 7.02[3][d], 35.05[4][b]; Herlick Handbook §§ 1.01[3][b], 5.20, 16.23.

§10116.4. Reproduction of Forms, Notices. [Repealed]

Note: Authority cited: Sections 133, 139.5 and 5307.3, Labor Code. Reference: Section 139.5, Labor Code; *Godinez v. Buffets, Inc.* (2004, Significant Panel Decision) 69 Cal. Comp. Cases 1311; and *Vulean Materials Co. v. WCAB* (2006, Writ Denied) 71 Cal. Comp. Cases 1346.

History: 1. Renumbering of former section 10123.1 to new section 10116.4, including amendment of section and new Note, filed 11-17-2008; operative 11-17-2008 pursuant to Government Code section 11343.4 (Register 2008, No. 47).

2. Change without regulatory effect repealing section filed 2-25-2009 pursuant to section 100, title 1, California Code of Regulations (Register 2009, No. 9).

§10116.5. Technical Problems and Unavailability of EAMS.

Technical problems with filing documents shall be governed by sections 10223 and 10225 of title 8 of the California Code of Regulation.

Note: Authority cited: Sections 133, 139.48, 139.5, 4658, 4658.5 and 5307.3, Labor Code. Reference: Section 139.5, Labor Code; *Godinez v. Buffets, Inc.* (2004, Significant Panel Decision) 69 Cal. Comp. Cases 1311; and *Vulean Materials Co. v. WCAB* (2006, Writ Denied) 71 Cal. Comp. Cases 1346.

History: 1. New section filed 11-17-2008; operative 11-17-2008 pursuant to Government Code section 11343.4 (Register 2008, No. 47).

Ref.: Hanna §§ 7.02[3][d], 35.05[4][b]; Herlick Handbook §§ 1.01[3][b], 5.20, 16.23.

§10116.6. Retraining and Return to Work File Retention.

(a) Following a period of fifty (50) years after the filing of a document used to open a case or file, the Division of Workers' Compensation may destroy the electronic and/or paper file in each case maintained by the Retraining and Return to Work Unit.

(b) The Division of Workers' Compensation, at any time, may convert a paper file to an electronic file. The Division of Workers' Compensation shall inform the parties when a paper file is converted. If a paper case file has been converted to electronic form, the paper case file may be destroyed no less than 30 business days after the parties have been informed of the conversion.

Note: Authority cited: Sections 133, 138.4, 139.5 and 5307.3, Labor Code. Reference: Section 139.5, Labor Code.

History: 1. New section filed 11-17-2008; operative 11-17-2008 pursuant to Government Code section 11343.4 (Register 2008, No. 47).

Ref.: Hanna §§ 7.02[3][d], 35.05[4][b]; Herlick Handbook §§ 1.01[3][b], 5.20, 16.23.

§10116.7. Misfiled or Misdirected Documents.

(a) A request to move, substitute, or correct a document shall be made in conformity with section 10223 of title 8 of the California Code of Regulation, except that a request to substitute shall be made in lieu of a petition to substitute as allowed under section 10223(b). The authority to approve moving a document from one file to another file shall reside with the Manager of the Retraining and Return to Work Unit or his or her designee.

(b) If a document is not filed in compliance with sections 10217, 10228 and 10232 of title 8 of the California Code of Regulations and these regulations, the administrative director may in his or her discretion take the actions set forth in section 10222 of title 8 of the California Code of Regulations.

Note: Authority cited: Sections 133, 138.4, 139.5 and 5307.3, Labor Code. Reference: Section 139.5, Labor Code.

History: 1. New section filed 11-17-2008; operative 11-17-2008 pursuant to Government Code section 11343.4 (Register 2008, No. 47).

Ref.: Hanna §§ 7.02[3][d], 35.05[4][b]; Herlick Handbook §§ 1.01[3][b], 5.20, 16.23.

§10116.8. Jurisdiction Where the Issue of Injury Has Not Been Resolved.

(a) No forms, notices or reports shall be filed with the Retraining and Return to Work Unit until the claims administrator has accepted liability for the injury or there has been a finding of compensable injury by the appeals board.

(b) Any requests for provision of retraining or return to work services and for intervention/dispute resolution require confirmation on the appropriate form by the employee or his/her representative that liability for the injury has been accepted.

(c) Forms sent to the Retraining and Return to Work Unit when a good faith issue of injury exists or where there has been no confirmation of acceptance of liability for the injury shall be returned to the sender.

Note: Authority cited: Sections 133, 139.48, 139.5, 4658, 4658.5 and 5307.3, Labor Code. Reference: Section 139.5, Labor Code; *Godinez v. Buffets, Inc.* (2004, Significant Panel Decision) 69 Cal. Comp. Cases 1311; and *Vulcan Materials Co. v. WCAB* (2006, Writ Denied) 71 Cal. Comp. Cases 1346.

History: 1. New section filed 11-17-2008; operative 11-17-2008 pursuant to Government Code section 11343.4 (Register 2008, No. 47).

Ref.: Hanna §§ 7.02[3][d], 35.05[4][b]; Herlick Handbook §§ 1.01[3][b], 5.20, 16.23.

§10116.9. Definitions for Articles 6.5 and 7.5.

The following definitions apply to the provisions of Articles 6.5 and 7.5 governing injuries occurring on or after January 1, 2004:

(a) "Alternative work" means work (1) offered either by the employer who employed the injured worker at the time of injury, or by another employer where the previous employment was seasonal work, (2) that the employee has the ability to perform, (3) that offers wages and compensation that are at least 85 percent of those paid to the employee at the time of injury, and (4) that is located within a reasonable commuting distance of the employee's residence at the time of injury.

(b) "Approved training facility" means a training or skills enhancement facility or institution that meets the requirements of section 10133.58.

(c) "Claims administrator" means a self-administered insurer providing security for the payment of compensation required by Divisions 4 and 4.5 of the Labor Code, a self-administered self-insured employer, a self-administered joint powers authority, a self-administered legally uninsured, or a third-party claims administrator for a self-insured employer, insurer, legally uninsured employer, or joint powers authority.

(d) "Employer" means the person or entity that employed the injured employee at the time of injury.

(e) "Essential functions" means job duties considered crucial to the employment position held or desired by the employee. Functions may be considered essential because the position exists to perform the function, the function requires specialized expertise, serious results may occur if the function is not performed, other employees are not available to perform the function or the function occurs at peak periods and the employer cannot reorganize the work flow.

(f) "Furnished" means five days after the date of deposit in the United States mail or the date of personal service.

(g) "Insurer" has the same meaning as in Labor Code section 3211.

(h) "Modified work" means regular work modified so that the employee has the ability to perform all the functions of the job and that offers wages and compensation that are at least 85 percent of those paid to the employee at the time of injury, and located within a reasonable commuting distance of the employee's residence at the time of injury.

(i) "Nontransferable voucher" means a document provided to an employee that allows the employee to enroll in education-related training or skills enhancement. The document shall include identifying information for the employee and claims administrator.

(j) "Notice" means a required letter or form generated by the claims administrator and directed to the injured employee.

(k) "Offer of modified or alternative work" means an offer to the injured employee of medically appropriate employment with the date-of-injury employer through the use of Form DWC-AD 10133.53, Notice of Offer of Modified or Alternative Work for Injuries Occurring Between 1/1/04 — 12/31/12, Inclusive, or Form 10133.35 Notice of Offer of Regular, Modified, or Alternative Work for Injuries Occurring on or after 1/1/13.

(*l*) "Parties" means the employee, the claims administrator and their designated representatives, if any.

(m) "Permanent and stationary" means the point in time when the employee has reached maximal medical improvement, meaning his or her condition is well stabilized, and unlikely to change substantially in the next year with or without medical treatment, based on (1) an opinion from a treating physician, AME, or QME; (2) a judicial finding by a Workers' Compensation Administrative Law Judge, the Workers' Compensation Appeals Board, or a court; or (3) a stipulation that is approved by a Workers' Compensation Administrative Law Judge or the Workers' Compensation Appeals Board.

(n) "Permanent partial disability award" means a final award of permanent partial disability determined by a workers' compensation administrative law judge or the appeals board.

(o) "Receipt" means the date of actual receipt by electronic delivery, personal service, or five days after the date of deposit in the United States mail.

(p) "Regular work" means the employee's usual occupation or the position in which the employee was engaged at the time of injury and that offers wages and compensation equivalent to those paid to the employee at the time of injury, and located within a reasonable commuting distance of the employee's residence at the time of injury.

(q) "Seasonal work" means employment as a daily hire, a project hire, or an annual season hire.

(r) "Supplemental job displacement benefit" means an educational retraining or skills enhancement allowance for injured employees whose employers are unable to provide work consistent with the requirements of Labor Code sections 4658.5, 4658.6 and 4658.7.

(s) "Vocational & return to work counselor (VRTWC)" means a person or entity capable of assisting a person with a disability with development of a return to work strategy and whose regular duties involve the evaluation, counseling and placement of disabled persons. A VRTWC must have at least an undergraduate degree in any field and three or more years full time experience in conducting vocational evaluations, counseling and placement of disabled adults.

(t) "Work restrictions" means permanent medical limitations on employment activity established by the treating physician, qualified medical examiner or agreed medical examiner.

Note: Authority cited: Sections 133, 4658.5, 4658.7 and 5307.3, Labor Code. Reference: Sections 124, 4658.1, 4658.5, 4658.6 and 4658.7, Labor Code; and *Henry v. WCAB* (1998) 68 Cal.App.4th 981.

History: 1. Renumbering of former section 10001 to new section 10116.9, including amendment of section heading, section and Note, filed 11-17-2008; operative 11-17-2008 pursuant to Government Code section 11343.4 (Register 2008, No. 47).

2. Amendment of section heading and first paragraph, new subsections (f) and (o), subsection relettering, amendment of newly designated subsections (i), (k) and (r) and amendment of Note filed 12-20-2012 as an emergency; operative 1-1-2013 pursuant to Government Code section 11346.1(d) (Register 2012, No. 51). A Certificate of Compliance must be transmitted to OAL by 7-1-2013 or emergency language will be repealed by operation of law on the following day.

3. Amendment of section heading and first paragraph, new subsections (f) and (o), subsection relettering, amendment of newly designated subsections (i)-(j) and (r) and amendment of Note refiled 6-26-2013 as an emergency; operative 7-1-2013 pursuant to Government Code section 11346.1(d) (Register 2013, No. 26). A Certificate of Compliance must be transmitted to OAL by 9-30-2013 or emergency language will be repealed by operation of law on the following day.

4. Certificate of Compliance as to 7-1-2013 order, including amendment of subsection (k), transmitted to OAL 9-27-2013 and filed 11-8-2013; amendments operative 1-1-2014 (Register 2013, No. 45).

Ref.: Hanna §§ 7.02[3][d][i]–[iv], 35.05[4][b]; Herlick Handbook §§ 1.01[3][b], 5.20, 16.23.

ARTICLE 6.5
Return to Work

§10117. Offer of Work; Adjustment of Permanent Disability Payments.

(a) This section shall apply to all injuries occurring between January 1, 2005 and December 31, 2012, inclusive and to the following employers:

(1) Insured employers who employed 50 or more employees at the time of the most recent policy inception or renewal date for the insurance policy that was in effect at the time of the employee's injury;

(2) Self-insured employers who employed 50 or more employees at the time of the most recent filing by the employer of the Self-Insurer's Annual Report that was in effect at the time of the employee's injury; and

(3) Legally uninsured employers who employed 50 or more employees at the time of injury.

(b) Within 60 calendar days from the date that the condition of an injured employee with permanent partial disability becomes permanent and stationary:

(1) If an employer does not serve the employee with a notice of offer of regular work, modified work or alternative work for a period of at least 12 months, each payment of permanent partial disability remaining to be paid to the employee from the date of the end of the 60 day period shall be paid in accordance with Labor Code section 4658(d)(1) and increased by 15 percent.

(2) If an employer serves the employee with a notice of offer of regular work, modified work or alternative work for a period of at least 12 months, and in accordance with the requirements set forth in paragraphs (3) and (4), each payment of permanent partial disability remaining to be paid from the date the offer was served on the employee shall be paid in accordance with Labor Code section 4658(d)(1) and decreased by 15 percent, regardless of whether the employee accepts or rejects the offer.

(3) The employer shall use form DWC-AD 10133.53 (Section 10133.53) to offer modified or alternative work, or form DWC-AD 10118 (Section 10118) to offer regular work. The claims administrator may serve the offer of work on behalf of the employer.

(4) The regular, alternative, or modified work that is offered by the employer pursuant to paragraph (2) shall be located within a reasonable commuting distance of the employee's residence at the time of the injury, unless the employee waives this condition. This condition shall be deemed to be waived if the employee accepts the regular, modified, or alternative work, and does not object to the location within 20 calendar days of being informed of the right to object. The condition shall be conclusively deemed to be satisfied if the offered work is at the same location and the same shift as the employment at the time of injury.

(c) If the claims administrator relies upon a permanent and stationary date contained in a medical report prepared by the employee's treating physician, QME, or AME, but there is subsequently a dispute as to an employee's permanent and stationary status, and there has been a notice of offer of work served on the employee in accordance with subdivision (b), the claims administrator may withhold 15% from each payment of permanent partial disability remaining to be paid from the date the notice of offer was served on the employee until there has been a final judicial determination of the date that the employee is permanent and stationary pursuant to Labor Code section 4062.

(1) Where there is a final judicial determination that the employee is permanent and stationary on a date later than the date relied on by the employer in making its offer of work, the employee shall be reimbursed any amount withheld up to the date a new notice of offer of work is served on the employee pursuant to subdivision (b).

(2) Where there is a final judicial determination that the employee is not permanent and stationary, the employee shall be reimbursed any amount withheld up to the date of the determination.

(3) The claims administrator is not required to reimburse permanent partial disability benefit payments that have been withheld pursuant to this subdivision during any period for which the employee is entitled to temporary disability benefit payments.

(d) If the employee's regular work, modified work, or alternative work that has been offered by the employer pursuant to paragraph (1) of subdivision (b) and has been accepted by the employee, is terminated prior to the end of the period for which permanent partial disability benefits are due, the amount of each remaining permanent partial disability payment from the date of the termination shall be paid in accordance with Labor Code section 4658(d)(1), as though no decrease in payments had been imposed, and increased by 15 percent. An employee who voluntarily terminates his or her regular work, modified work, or alternative work shall not be eligible for the 15 percent increase in permanent partial disability payments pursuant to this subdivision.

(e) Nothing in this section shall prevent the parties from settling or agreeing to commute the permanent disability benefits to which an employee may be entitled. However, if the permanent disability benefits are commuted by a workers' compensation administrative law judge or the appeals board pursuant to Labor Code section 5100, the commuted sum shall account for any adjustment that would have been required by this section if payment had been made pursuant to Labor Code section 4658.

(f) If the employer offers regular, modified, or alternative seasonal work to the employee, the offer shall meet the following requirements:

(1) the employee was hired for seasonal work prior to injury;

(2) the offer of regular, modified or alternative seasonal work is of reasonably similar hours and working conditions to the employee's previous employment, and the one year requirement may be satisfied by cumulative periods of seasonal work;

(3) the work must commence within 12 months of the date of the offer; and

(4) The offer meets the conditions set forth in this section.

Note: Authority cited: Sections 133 and 5307.3, Labor Code. Reference: Section 4658, Labor Code; *Del Taco v. WCAB* (2000) 79 Cal.App.4th 1437; *Anzelde v. WCAB* (1996) 61 Cal. Comp.

Cases 1458 (writ denied); and *Henry v. WCAB* (1998) 68 Cal.App.4th 981.

History: 1. New article 6.5 (sections 10117-10120) and renumbering of former section 10002 to new section 10117, including amendment of section, filed 11-17-2008; operative 11-17-2008 pursuant to Government Code section 11343.4 (Register 2008, No. 47).

2. Amendment of subsection (a) and amendment of Note filed 12-20-2012 as an emergency; operative 1-1-2013 pursuant to Government Code section 11346.1(d) (Register 2012, No. 51). A Certificate of Compliance must be transmitted to OAL by 7-1-2013 or emergency language will be repealed by operation of law on the following day.

3. Amendment of subsection (a) and amendment of Note refiled 6-26-2013 as an emergency; operative 7-1-2013 pursuant to Government Code section 11346.1(d) (Register 2013, No. 26). A Certificate of Compliance must be transmitted to OAL by 9-30-2013 or emergency language will be repealed by operation of law on the following day.

4. Certificate of Compliance as to 7-1-2013 order, including amendment of subsection (a), repealer of subsection (f) and subsection relettering, transmitted to OAL 9-27-2013 and filed 11-8-2013; amendments operative 1-1-2014 (Register 2013, No. 45).

Ref.: Hanna §§ 7.02[3][d][i]–[iv], 35.05[4][b]; Herlick Handbook §§ 1.01[3][b], 5.20, 16.23.

§10118. Form [DWC AD 10118 "Notice of Offer of Work for Injuries Occurring Between 1/1/05—12/31/12, Inclusive."].

[DWC-AD Form 10118 (Rev. 1/1/14) Not Reproduced]

NOTE: Form is available at no charge by downloading from the web at www.dir.ca.gov/dwc/forms.html or by requesting at 1-800-794-6900.

Note: Authority cited: Sections 133 and 5307.3, Labor Code. Reference: Section 4658, Labor Code.

History: 1. Renumbering of former section 10003 to new section 10118, including amendment of section heading and repealer and new form, filed 11-17-2008; operative 11-17-2008 pursuant to Government Code section 11343.4 (Register 2008, No. 47).

2. Amendment of section heading, form and Note filed 12-20-2012 as an emergency; operative 1-1-2013 pursuant to Government Code section 11346.1(d) (Register 2012, No. 51). A Certificate of Compliance must be transmitted to OAL by 7-1-2013 or emergency language will be repealed by operation of law on the following day.

3. Amendment of section heading, form and Note refiled 6-26-2013 as an emergency; operative 7-1-2013 pursuant to Government Code section 11346.1(d) (Register 2013, No. 26). A Certificate of Compliance must be transmitted to OAL by 9-30-2013 or emergency language will be repealed by operation of law on the following day.

4. Certificate of Compliance as to 7-1-2013 order, including amendment of section heading and form, transmitted to OAL 9-27-2013 and filed 11-8-2013; amendments operative 1-1-2014 (Register 2013, No. 45).

Ref.: Hanna §§ 7.02[3][d][i]–[iv], 35.05[4][b]; Herlick Handbook §§ 1.01[3][b], 5.20, 16.23.

§10119. Return to Work Program. [Repealed]

Note: Authority cited: Sections 133, 139.48 and 5307.3, Labor Code. Reference: Sections 62.5, 139.48 and 5814.6, Labor Code.

History: 1. Renumbering of former section 10004 to new section 10119, including amendment of section, filed 11-17-2008; operative 11-17-2008 pursuant to Government Code section 11343.4 (Register 2008, No. 47).

2. Change without regulatory effect repealing section filed 6-27-2011 pursuant to section 100, title 1, California Code of Regulations (Register 2011, No. 26).

§10120. Form [DWC AD 10120 Request for Reimbursement of Accommodation Expenses]. [Repealed]

Note: Authority cited: Sections 133, 139.48 and 5307.3, Labor Code. Reference: Sections 62.5, 139.48 and 5814.6, Labor Code.

History: 1. Renumbering of former section 10005 to new section 10120, including amendment of section heading and repealer and new form, filed 11-17-2008; operative 11-17-2008 pursuant to Government Code section 11343.4 (Register 2008, No. 47).

2. Change without regulatory effect repealing section filed 6-27-2011 pursuant to section 100, title 1, California Code of Regulations (Register 2011, No. 26).

§10121. Date of Denial for Purposes of End of Tolling of Limitations Period. [Renumbered]

Note: Authority cited: Sections 133 and 5307.3, Labor Code. Reference: Section 5401, Labor Code.

History: 1. New section filed 12-31-93; operative 1-1-94. Submitted to OAL for printing only pursuant to Government Code section 11351 (Register 93, No. 53).

2. Change without regulatory effect renumbering former section 10121 to section 10142 filed 4-7-2008 pursuant to section 100, title 1, California Code of Regulations (Register 2008, No. 15).

ARTICLE 7
Vocational Rehabilitation [Repealed]

History: 1. Change without regulatory effect repealing article 7 (sections 10122-10133.22) filed 2-25-2009 pursuant to section 100, title 1, California Code of Regulations (Register 2009, No. 9).

ARTICLE 7.5
Supplemental Job Displacement Benefit

§10133.31. Supplemental Job Displacement Nontransferable Voucher for Injuries Occurring on or After January 1, 2013.

(a) This section shall apply to all injuries occurring on or after January 1, 2013.

(b) If the injury causes partial permanent disability, the employee shall be entitled to a Supplemental Job Displacement Benefit unless the employer makes an offer of regular, modified, or alternative work pursuant to section 10133.34 no later than 60 days after receipt by the claims administrator of the Physician's Return to Work & Voucher Report (Form DWC-AD 10133.36) that indicates the work capacities and activity restrictions that are relevant to regular work, modified work, or alternative work.

(1) Upon receipt of the Physician's Return-to-Work & Voucher Report (Form DWC-AD 10133.36), the claims administrator shall forward the form to the employer.

(2) If the claims administrator provides the physician with a job description of the employee's regular work, proposed modified work, or proposed alternative work, the physician shall complete the bottom portion of the Physician's Return-to-Work & Voucher Report (Form DWC-AD10133.36.)

(c) An employee who has lost no time from work or has returned to the same job for the same employer, is deemed to have been offered and accepted regular work in accordance with the criteria set forth in Labor Code section 4658.7(b).

(d) If no offer for regular, modified, or alternative work is made, pursuant to subdivision (b), the claims administrator shall furnish a "Supplemental Job Displacement Nontransferable Voucher For Injuries Occurring on or After 1/1/13" (Form DWC-AD 10133.32) within 20 calendar days from expiration of time for making an offer of regular, modified, or alternative work pursuant to paragraph (1) of subdivision (b).

(e) The voucher shall be redeemable up to an aggregate of six thousand dollars ($6,000)

(f) The voucher may be applied to any of the following expenses at the choice of the injured worker:

(1) Payment for education-related training or skill enhancement, or both, at a California public school or with a provider that is certified on the state's Eligible Training Provider List at http://etpl.edd.ca.gov, including payment of tuition, fees, books, and other expenses required by the school for retraining and skill enhancement.

(2) Payment for occupational licensing or professional certification fees, related examination fees, and examination preparation course fees.

(3) Payment for services of licensed placement agencies, vocational or return-to-work counseling, and resume preparation, all up to a combined limit of six hundred dollars ($600).

(4) Purchase of tools required by a training or educational program in which the employee is enrolled.

(5) Purchase of computer equipment including, but not limited to monitors, software, networking devices, input devices (such as keyboard and mouse), peripherals (such as printers), and tablet computers of up to one thousand dollars ($1,000) payable upon submission of a Request for Purchase of Computer Equipment (page 4 of the DWC-AD Form 10133.32) and submitted with appropriate documentation of either a written invoice payable to a computer retailer or itemized receipts showing the purchase(s) of computer equipment. At the time the voucher is provided, the claims administrator or employer may give the employee the option to obtain computer equipment directly from the employer. The employee shall not be entitled to reimbursement for purchase of games or any entertainment media.

(6) Up to five hundred dollars ($500) as a miscellaneous expense reimbursement or advance, payable upon submission of a Request for Miscellaneous Expenses (page 3 of the DWC-AD Form 10133.32) and without need for itemized documentation or accounting. The claims examiner may provide an email address on Form [DWC-AD 10133.32 "Supplemental Job Displacement Nontransferable Voucher for Injuries Occurring on or After 1/1/13]; if an email address is provided, the employee can submit the request via email or regular mail. The employee shall not be entitled to any other voucher payment for transportation, travel expenses, telephone or internet access, clothing or uniforms or incidental expenses.

(g) The voucher will expire two years after the date it is furnished to the employee, or five years after the date of injury, whichever is later. The employee may not receive payment or reimbursement of any expenses that have not been incurred and submitted with appropriate documentation to the claims administrator prior to the expiration date.

(h) Settlement or commutation of a claim for the supplemental job displacement voucher is not permitted.

(i) An employer shall not be liable for compensation for injuries incurred by the employee while utilizing the voucher.

(j) The claims administrator shall issue the voucher payments to the employee or direct payments to the VRTWC, training providers, and/or computer retailer within 45 calendar days from receipt of the completed voucher, receipts, and documentation. If computer equipment will be provided directly to the employee, the employer must provide the computer equipment along with documentation of the cost of the computer equipment to the employee within 45 days of receipt of the Request for Purchase of Computer Equipment.

Note: Authority cited: Sections 133, 4658.1, 4658.7 and 5307.3, Labor Code. Reference: Sections 4658.6 and 4658.7, Labor Code.

History: 1. New section filed 12-20-2012 as an emergency; operative 1-1-2013 pursuant to Government Code section 11346.1(d) (Register 2012, No. 51). A Certificate of Compliance must be transmitted to OAL by 7-1-2013 or emergency language will be repealed by operation of law on the following day.

2. New section refiled 6-26-2013 as an emergency; operative 7-1-2013 pursuant to Government Code section 11346.1(d) (Register 2013, No. 26). A Certificate of Compliance must be transmitted to OAL by 9-30-2013 or emergency language will be repealed by operation of law on the following day.

3. Certificate of Compliance as to 7-1-2013 order, including amendment of section heading and subsection (b), repealer of subsections (b)(1) and (b)(2), redesignation of former subsections (b)(1)(A)-(B) as new subsections (b)(1)-(2), new subsection (c), subsection relettering and amendment of newly designated subsections (f)(5)-(6), (g) and (j), transmitted to OAL 9-27-2013 and filed 11-8-2013; amendments operative 1-1-2014 (Register 2013, No. 45).

4. Editorial correction of subsection (f)(5) (Register 2013, No. 47).

Ref.: Hanna §§ 35.03, 35.06; Herlick Handbook §§ 1.01[3][b], 11.01.

§10133.32. Form [DWC-AD 10133.32 "Supplemental Job Displacement Nontransferable Voucher For Injuries Occurring on or After 1/1/13."]

This form may be produced without a logo and may be produced on the claim's administrator's letterhead.

[DWC-AD Form 10133.32 (Rev. 10/1/15) Not Reproduced]

NOTE: Form is available at no charge by downloading from the web at www.dir.ca.gov/dwc/forms.html or by requesting at 1-800-794-6900.

Note: Authority cited: Sections 133, 4658.1, 4658.7 and 5307.3, Labor Code. Reference: Sections 4658.6 and 4658.7, Labor Code.

History: 1. New section filed 12-20-2012 as an emergency; operative 1-1-2013 pursuant to Government Code section 11346.1(d) (Register 2012, No. 51). A Certificate of Compliance must be transmitted to OAL by 7-1-2013 or emergency language will be repealed by operation of law on the following day.

2. New section refiled 6-26-2013 as an emergency; operative 7-1-2013 pursuant to Government Code section 11346.1(d) (Register 2013, No. 26). A Certificate of Compliance must be transmitted to OAL by 9-30-2013 or emergency language will be repealed by operation of law on the following day.

3. Certificate of Compliance as to 7-1-2013 order, including amendment of form, transmitted to OAL 9-27-2013 and filed 11-8-2013; amendments operative 1-1-2014 (Register 2013, No. 45).

4. Change without regulatory effect amending section filed 2-5-2014 pursuant to section 100, title 1, California Code of Regulations (Register 2014, No. 6).

5. Change without regulatory effect repealing and adopting new section filed 11-23-2015 pursuant to section 100, title 1, California Code of Regulations (Register 2015, No. 48).

Ref.: Hanna § 35.06; Herlick Handbook § 1.01[3][b].

§10133.33. Form [DWC-AD 10133.33 "Description of Employee's Job Duties Form."]

Prior to any medical evaluation declaring the employee permanent and stationary, the physician may be sent Form [DWC-AD 10133.33, "Description of Employee's Job Duties."]

This form may be produced without a logo and may be produced on the claim's administrator's letterhead.

[DWC-AD Form 10133.33 (New 1/1/14) Not Reproduced]

NOTE: Form is available at no charge by downloading from the web at www.dir.ca.gov/dwc/forms.html or by requesting at 1-800-794-6900.

Note: Authority cited: Sections 133 and 4658.7, Labor Code. Reference: Sections 4658.6 and 4658.7, Labor Code.

History: 1. New section filed 12-20-2012 as an emergency; operative 1-1-2013 pursuant to Government Code section 11346.1(d) (Register 2012, No. 51). A Certificate of Compliance must be transmitted to OAL by 7-1-2013 or emergency language will be repealed by operation of law on the following day.

2. New section refiled 6-26-2013 as an emergency; operative 7-1-2013 pursuant to Government Code section 11346.1(d) (Register 2013, No. 26). A Certificate of Compliance must be transmitted to OAL by 9-30-2013 or emergency language will be repealed by operation of law on the following day.

3. Certificate of Compliance as to 7-1-2013 order, including amendment of form, transmitted to OAL 9-27-2013 and filed 11-8-2013; amendments operative 1-1-2014 (Register 2013, No. 45).

4. Change without regulatory effect amending section filed 2-5-2014 pursuant to section 100, title 1, California Code of Regulations (Register 2014, No. 6).

Ref.: Herlick Handbook § 1.01[3][b].

§10133.34. Offer of Work for Injuries Occurring on or After January 1, 2013.

(a) This section shall apply to all injuries occurring on or after January 1, 2013.

(b) The injured employee shall be entitled to a supplemental job displacement benefit unless the employer makes an offer of regular, modified, or alternative work on Form [DWC-AD10133.35 "Notice of Offer of Regular, Modified, or Alternative Work For injuries occurring on or after 1/1/13" within 60 days after receipt of Form [DWC-AD 10133.36 "Physician's Return-to-Work & Voucher Report."] that indicates the work capacities and activity restrictions that are relevant to regular work, modified work, or alternative work.

(1) The claims administrator may serve the offer of work on behalf of the employer.

(2) The regular, alternative, or modified work that is offered by the employer pursuant to paragraph (1) shall be located within a reasonable commuting distance of the employee's residence at the time of the injury, unless the employee waives this condition. This condition shall be deemed to be waived if the employee accepts the regular, modified, or alternative work, and does not object to the location within 20 calendar days of being informed of the right to object. The condition shall be conclusively deemed to be satisfied if the offered work is at the same location and the same shift as the employment at the time of injury.

(3) The offer of regular, modified, or alternative work must be for work lasting at least 12 months.

(4) If the employer offers regular, modified, or alternative seasonal work to the employee, the offer shall meet the following requirements:

(A) the employee was hired for seasonal work prior to injury;

(B) the offer of regular, modified or alternative seasonal work is of reasonably similar hours and working conditions to the employee's previous employment, and the one year requirement may be satisfied by cumulative periods of seasonal work;

(C) the work must commence within 12 months of the date of the offer; and

(D) The offer meets the conditions set forth in this section.

Note: Authority cited: Sections 133, 4658.7 and 5307.3, Labor Code. Reference: Sections 4658 and 4658.7, Labor Code.

History: 1. New section filed 12-20-2012 as an emergency; operative 1-1-2013 pursuant to Government Code section 11346.1(d) (Register 2012, No. 51). A Certificate of Compliance must be transmitted to OAL by 7-1-2013 or emergency language will be repealed by operation of law on the following day.

2. New section refiled 6-26-2013 as an emergency; operative 7-1-2013 pursuant to Government Code section 11346.1(d) (Register 2013, No. 26). A Certificate of Compliance must be transmitted to OAL by 9-30-2013 or emergency language will be repealed by operation of law on the following day.

3. Certificate of Compliance as to 7-1-2013 order, including amendment of subsection (b), repealer of subsection (b)(4) and

subsection renumbering, transmitted to OAL 9-27-2013 and filed 11-8-2013; amendments operative 1-1-2014 (Register 2013, No. 45).

Ref.: Herlick Handbook § 1.01[3][b].

§10133.35. Form [DWC-AD 10133.35 "Notice of Offer of Regular, Modified, or Alternative Work For Injuries Occurring on or After 1/1/13."]

This form may be produced without a logo and may be produced on the claim's administrator's letterhead.

[DWC-AD Form 10133.35 (New 1/1/14) Not Reproduced]

NOTE: Form is available at no charge by downloading from the web at www.dir.ca.gov/dwc/forms.html or by requesting at 1-800-794-6900.

Note: Authority cited: Sections 133, 4658.7 and 5307.3, Labor Code. Reference: Sections 4658 and 4658.7, Labor Code.

History: 1. New section filed 12-20-2012 as an emergency; operative 1-1-2013 pursuant to Government Code section 11346.1(d) (Register 2012, No. 51). A Certificate of Compliance must be transmitted to OAL by 7-1-2013 or emergency language will be repealed by operation of law on the following day.

2. New section refiled 6-26-2013 as an emergency; operative 7-1-2013 pursuant to Government Code section 11346.1(d) (Register 2013, No. 26). A Certificate of Compliance must be transmitted to OAL by 9-30-2013 or emergency language will be repealed by operation of law on the following day.

3. Certificate of Compliance as to 7-1-2013 order, including amendment of form, transmitted to OAL 9-27-2013 and filed 11-8-2013; amendments operative 1-1-2014 (Register 2013, No. 45).

4. Change without regulatory effect amending section filed 2-5-2014 pursuant to section 100, title 1, California Code of Regulations (Register 2014, No. 6).

Ref.: Herlick Handbook § 1.01[3][b].

§10133.36. Form [DWC-AD 10133.36 "Physician's Return-to-Work & Voucher Report."]

This form may be produced without a logo and may be produced on the claim's administrator's letterhead.

[DWC-AD Form 10133.36 (New 1/1/14) Not Reproduced]

NOTE: Form is available at no charge by downloading from the web at www.dir.ca.gov/dwc/forms.html or by requesting at 1-800-794-6900.

Note: Authority cited: Sections 133, 4658.7 and 5307.3, Labor Code. Reference: Sections 4658 and 4658.7, Labor Code.

History: 1. New section filed 12-20-2012 as an emergency; operative 1-1-2013 pursuant to Government Code section 11346.1(d) (Register 2012, No. 51). A Certificate of Compliance must be transmitted to OAL by 7-1-2013 or emergency language will be repealed by operation of law on the following day.

2. New section refiled 6-26-2013 as an emergency; operative 7-1-2013 pursuant to Government Code section 11346.1(d) (Register 2013, No. 26). A Certificate of Compliance must be transmitted to OAL by 9-30-2013 or emergency language will be repealed by operation of law on the following day.

3. Certificate of Compliance as to 7-1-2013 order, including amendment of form, transmitted to OAL 9-27-2013 and filed 11-8-2013; amendments operative 1-1-2014 (Register 2013, No. 45).

4. Change without regulatory effect amending section filed 2-5-2014 pursuant to section 100, title 1, California Code of Regulations (Register 2014, No. 6).

Ref.: Hanna § 35.06; Herlick Handbook § 1.01[3][b].

§10133.50. Definitions. [Repealed]

Note: Authority cited: Sections 133, 4658.5 and 5307.3, Labor Code. Reference: Sections 124, 4658.1, 4658.5 and 4658.6, Labor Code.

History: 1. New article 7.5 (sections 10133.50-10133.60) and section filed 6-6-2005; operative 8-1-2005 (Register 2005, No. 23).

2. Repealer filed 11-17-2008; operative 11-17-2008 pursuant to Government Code section 11343.4 (Register 2008, No. 47).

§10133.51. Notice of Potential Right to Supplemental Job Displacement Benefit. [Repealed]

Note: Authority cited: Sections 133, 4658.5 and 5307.3, Labor Code. Reference: Section 4658.5, Labor Code.

History: 1. New section filed 6-6-2005; operative 8-1-2005 (Register 2005, No. 23).

2. Repealer filed 12-20-2012 as an emergency; operative 1-1-2013 pursuant to Government Code section 11346.1(d) (Register 2012, No. 51). A Certificate of Compliance must be transmitted to OAL by 7-1-2013 or emergency language will be repealed by operation of law on the following day.

3. Repealer refiled 6-26-2013 as an emergency; operative 7-1-2013 pursuant to Government Code section 11346.1(d) (Register 2013, No. 26). A Certificate of Compliance must be transmitted to OAL by 9-30-2013 or emergency language will be repealed by operation of law on the following day.

4. Certificate of Compliance as to 7-1-2013 order transmitted to OAL 9-27-2013 and filed 11-8-2013 (Register 2013, No. 45).

§10133.52. "Notice of Potential Right to Supplemental Job Displacement Benefit Form." [Repealed]

Note: Authority cited: Sections 133, 4658.5 and 5307.3, Labor Code. Reference: Section 4658.5, Labor Code.

History: 1. New section filed 6-6-2005; operative 8-1-2005 (Register 2005, No. 23).

2. Repealer filed 12-20-2012 as an emergency; operative 1-1-2013 pursuant to Government Code section 11346.1(d) (Register 2012, No. 51). A Certificate of Compliance must be transmitted to OAL by 7-1-2013 or emergency language will be repealed by operation of law on the following day.

3. Repealer refiled 6-26-2013 as an emergency; operative 7-1-2013 pursuant to Government Code section 11346.1(d) (Register 2013, No. 26). A Certificate of Compliance must be transmitted to OAL by 9-30-2013 or emergency language will be repealed by operation of law on the following day.

4. Certificate of Compliance as to 7-1-2013 order transmitted to OAL 9-27-2013 and filed 11-8-2013 (Register 2013, No. 45).

§10133.53. Form [DWC-AD 10133.53 "Notice of Offer of Modified or Alternative Work for Injuries Occurring Between 1/1/04 — 12/31/12, Inclusive."]

[DWC-AD Form 10133.53 (Rev. 1/1/14) Not Reproduced]

NOTE: Form is available at no charge by downloading from the web at www.dir.ca.gov/dwc/forms.html or by requesting at 1-800-794-6900.

Note: Authority cited: Sections 133, 4658 and 5307.3, Labor Code. Reference: Sections 4658, 4658.1, 4658.5 and 4658.6, Labor Code.

History: 1. New section filed 6-6-2005; operative 8-1-2005 (Register 2005, No. 23).

2. Amendment filed 7-19-2006; operative 8-18-2006 (Register 2006, No. 29). For prior history, see Register 96, No. 52.

3. Repealer and new form filed 11-17-2008; operative 11-17-2008 pursuant to Government Code section 11343.4 (Register 2008, No. 47).

4. Amendment of section heading and form filed 12-20-2012 as an emergency; operative 1-1-2013 pursuant to Government Code section 11346.1(d) (Register 2012, No. 51). A Certificate of Compliance must be transmitted to OAL by 7-1-2013 or emergency language will be repealed by operation of law on the following day.

5. Amendment of section heading and form refiled 6-26-2013 as an emergency; operative 7-1-2013 pursuant to Government Code section 11346.1(d) (Register 2013, No. 26). A Certificate of Compliance must be transmitted to OAL by 9-30-2013 or emergency language will be repealed by operation of law on the following day.

6. Certificate of Compliance as to 7-1-2013 order, including amendment of section heading and form, transmitted to OAL 9-27-2013 and filed 11-8-2013; amendments operative 1-1-2014 (Register 2013, No. 45).

Ref.: Hanna §§ 7.02[3][d], 35.05[4][b], 35.110[1]; Herlick Handbook §§ 1.01[3][b], 5.20, 16.22, 16.23.

§10133.54. Dispute Resolution.

(a) This section and section 10133.55 shall only apply to injuries occurring on or after January 1, 2004.

(b) When there is a dispute regarding the Supplemental Job Displacement Benefit, the employee, or claims administrator may request the administrative director to resolve the dispute.

(c) The party requesting the administrative director to resolve the dispute shall:

(1) Complete Form DWC-AD 10133.55 "Request for Dispute Resolution before the Administrative Director;"

(2) Clearly state the issue(s) and identify supporting information for each issue and position;

(3) Attach all pertinent documents;

(4) Submit a copy of the request and all attached documents to the administrative director and serve a copy of the request and all attached documents on all parties; and

(5) Attach a signed and dated proof of service to the Form DWC-AD 10133.55 "Request for Dispute Resolution before the Administrative Director."

(d) The opposing party shall have twenty (20) calendar days from the date of the proof of service of the Request to submit the original response and all attached documents to the administrative director and serve a copy of the response and all attached documents on all parties.

(e) The administrative director or his or her designee may request additional information from the parties.

(f) The administrative director or his or her designee shall issue a written determination and order based solely on the request, response, and any attached documents within thirty (30) calendar days of the date the opposing party's response and supporting information is due. If the administrative director or his or her designee requests additional information, the written determination shall be issued within thirty (30) calendar days from the receipt of the additional information. In the event no decision is issued within sixty (60) calendar days of the date the opposing party's response is due or within sixty (60) calendar days of the administrative director's receipt of the requested additional information, whichever is later, the request shall be deemed to be denied.

(g) Either party may appeal the determination and order of the administrative director by filing a written petition together with a declaration of readiness to proceed pursuant to section 10250 within twenty calendar days of the issuance of the decision or within twenty days after a request is deemed denied pursuant to subdivision (f). The petition shall set forth the specific factual and/or legal reason(s) for the appeal as set forth in section 10294.5 of title 8 of the California Code of Regulations.

Note: Authority cited: Sections 133, 4658.5 and 5307.3, Labor Code. Reference: Sections 4658.5 and 4658.6, Labor Code.

History: 1. New section filed 6-6-2005; operative 8-1-2005 (Register 2005, No. 23).

2. Amendment filed 11-17-2008; operative 11-17-2008 pursuant to Government Code section 11343.4 (Register 2008, No. 47).

Ref.: Hanna §§ 7.02[3][d], 35.05[4][b], 35.110[2]; Herlick Handbook §§ 1.01[3][b], 5.20, 16.22, 16.23.

§10133.55. Form [DWC-AD 10133.55 "Request for Dispute Resolution Before the Administrative Director."]

[DWC-AD Form 10133.55 (Rev. 1/1/14) Not Reproduced]

NOTE: Form is available at no charge by downloading from the web at www.dir.ca.gov/dwc/forms.html or by requesting at 1-800-794-6900.

Note: Authority cited: Sections 133, 4658.5 and 5307.3, Labor Code. Reference: Section 4658.5, Labor Code.

History: 1. New section filed 6-6-2005; operative 8-1-2005 (Register 2005, No. 23).

2. Amendment filed 7-19-2006; operative 8-18-2006 (Register 2006, No. 29). For prior history, see Register 96, No. 52.

3. Repealer and new form filed 11-17-2008; operative 11-17-2008 pursuant to Government Code section 11343.4 (Register 2008, No. 47).

4. Amendment of section heading and form filed 12-20-2012 as an emergency; operative 1-1-2013 pursuant to Government Code section 11346.1(d) (Register 2012, No. 51). A Certificate of Compliance must be transmitted to OAL by 7-1-2013 or emergency language will be repealed by operation of law on the following day.

5. Amendment of section heading and form refiled 6-26-2013 as an emergency; operative 7-1-2013 pursuant to Government Code section 11346.1(d) (Register 2013, No. 26). A Certificate of Compliance must be transmitted to OAL by 9-30-2013 or emergency language will be repealed by operation of law on the following day.

6. Certificate of Compliance as to 7-1-2013 order, including amendment of form, transmitted to OAL 9-27-2013 and filed 11-8-2013; amendments operative 1-1-2014 (Register 2013, No. 45).

Ref.: Hanna §§ 7.02[3][d], 35.05[4][b]; Herlick Handbook §§ 1.01[3][b], 5.20, 16.22, 16.23.

§10133.56. Requirement to Issue Supplemental Job Displacement Nontransferable Training Voucher.

(a) This section and section 10133.57 shall only apply to injuries occurring between January 1, 2004 and December 31, 2012, inclusive.

(b) The employee shall be eligible for the Supplemental Job Displacement Benefit when:

(1) the injury causes permanent partial disability; and

(2) within 30 days of the termination of temporary disability indemnity payments, the claims administrator does not offer modified or alternative work in accordance with Labor Code section 4658.6; and

(3) either the injured employee does not return to work for the employer within 60 days of the termination of temporary disability benefits; or

(4) in the case of a seasonal employee, where the employee is unable to return to work within 60 days of the termination of temporary disability benefits because the work season has ended, the injured employee does not return to work on the next available work date of the next work season.

(c) When the requirements under subdivision (b) have been met, the claims administrator shall provide a nontransferable voucher for education-related retraining or skill enhancement or both to the employee within 25 calendar days from the issuance of the permanent partial disability award by the workers' compensation administrative law judge or the appeals board.

(d) The voucher shall be issued to the employee allowing direct reimbursement to the employee upon the employee's presentation to the claims administrator of documentation and receipts or as a direct payment to the provider of the education related training or skill enhancement and/or to the VRTWC.

(e) The voucher must indicate the appropriate level of money available to the employee in compliance with Labor Code section 4658.5.

(f) The mandatory voucher form is set forth in Section 10133.57.

(g) The voucher shall certify that the school is approved pursuant to section 10133.58.

(h) The claims administrator shall issue the reimbursement payments to the employee or direct payments to the VRTWC and the training providers within 45 calendar days from receipt of the completed voucher, receipts and documentation.

Note: Authority cited: Sections 133, 4658.5, 4658.6 and 5307.3, Labor Code. Reference: Sections 4658.5 and 4658.6, Labor Code.

History: 1. New section filed 6-6-2005; operative 8-1-2005 (Register 2005, No. 23).

2. Amendment of subsections (c) and (g) filed 11-17-2008; operative 11-17-2008 pursuant to Government Code section 11343.4 (Register 2008, No. 47).

3. Amendment of subsections (a) and (g) filed 11-8-2013; operative 1-1-2014 (Register 2013, No. 45).

Ref.: Hanna §§ 7.02[3][d], 35.05[4][b], 35.110[3]; Herlick Handbook §§ 1.01[3][b], 5.20, 16.22, 16.23.

§10133.57. Form [DWC-AD 10133.57 "Supplemental Job Displacement Nontransferable Training Voucher Form for Injuries Occurring Between 1/1/04 — 12/31/12, Inclusive."]

[DWC-AD Form 10133.57 (Rev. 1/1/14) Not Reproduced]

NOTE: Form is available at no charge by downloading from the web at www.dir.ca.gov/dwc/forms.html or by requesting at 1-800-794-6900.

Note: Authority cited: Sections 133, 4658.5 and 5307.3, Labor Code. Reference: Section 4658.5, Labor Code.

History: 1. New section filed 6-6-2005; operative 8-1-2005 (Register 2005, No. 23).

2. Repealer and new form filed 11-17-2008; operative 11-17-2008 pursuant to Government Code section 11343.4 (Register 2008, No. 47).

3. Amendment of section heading and form filed 12-20-2012 as an emergency; operative 1-1-2013 pursuant to Government Code section 11346.1(d) (Register 2012, No. 51). A Certificate of Compliance must be transmitted to OAL by 7-1-2013 or emergency language will be repealed by operation of law on the following day.

4. Amendment of section heading and form refiled 6-26-2013 as an emergency; operative 7-1-2013 (Register 2013, No. 26). A Certificate of Compliance must be transmitted to OAL by 9-30-2013 or emergency language will be repealed by operation of law on the following day.

5. Certificate of Compliance as to 7-1-2013 order, including amendment of section heading and form, transmitted to OAL 9-27-2013 and filed 11-8-2013; amendments operative 1-1-2014 (Register 2013, No. 45).

Ref.: Hanna §§ 7.02[3][d], 35.05[4][b], 35.110[3]; Herlick Handbook §§ 1.01[3][b], 5.20, 16.22, 16.23.

§10133.58. State Approved or Accredited Schools.

(a) This section shall apply to all injuries occurring on or after January 1, 2004.

(b) For injuries between January 1, 2004 and December 31, 2012, inclusive, private providers of education-related retraining or skill enhancement selected to provide training as part of a supplemental job displacement benefit shall be:

(1) approved by the Bureau for Private Postsecondary and Education (www.bppe.ca.gov), or a California state agency that has an agreement with the Bureau for the regulation and oversight of non-degree-granting private postsecondary institutions; or

(2) accredited by one of the Regional Associations of Schools and Colleges authorized by the United States Department of Education; or

(3) by a California State agency that has an agreement with the United States Department of Education or Regional Associations of School and Colleges for the regulation and oversight of non-degree granting private post secondary providers; or

(4) certified by the Federal Aviation Administration.

(c) For injuries on or after January 1, 2013, private providers of education-related retraining or skill enhancement selected to provide training as part of a supplement job displacement benefit shall be certified and on the state's Eligible Training Provider List at http://etpl.edd.ca.gov/wiaetplind.htm.

Note: Authority cited: Sections 133, 4658.5 and 5307.3, Labor Code. Reference: Sections 4658.5 and 4658.7, Labor Code.

History: 1. New section filed 6-6-2005; operative 8-1-2005 (Register 2005, No. 23).

2. Amendment filed 11-17-2008; operative 11-17-2008 pursuant to Government Code section 11343.4 (Register 2008, No. 47).

3. Amendment of section and Note filed 12-20-2012 as an emergency; operative 1-1-2013 pursuant to Government Code section 11346.1(d) (Register 2012, No. 51). A Certificate of Compliance must be transmitted to OAL by 7-1-2013 or emergency language will be repealed by operation of law on the following day.

4. Amendment of section and Note refiled 6-26-2013 as an emergency; operative 7-1-2013 pursuant to Government Code section 11346.1(d) (Register 2013, No. 26). A Certificate of Compliance must be transmitted to OAL by 9-30-2013 or emergency language will be repealed by operation of law on the following day.

5. Certificate of Compliance as to 7-1-2013 order, including amendment of subsection (b), transmitted to OAL 9-27-2013 and filed 11-8-2013; amendments operative 1-1-2014 (Register 2013, No. 45).

Ref.: Hanna §§ 7.02[3][d], 35.03, 35.05[4][b], 35.110[4]; Herlick Handbook §§ 1.01[3][b], 5.20, 16.22, 16.23.

§10133.59. The Administrative Director's List of Vocational Return to Work Counselors.

(a) This section shall only apply to injuries occurring on or after January 1, 2004.

(b) The Administrative Director shall maintain a list of Vocational & Return to Work Counselors (VRTWC) who perform the work of assisting injured employees. A VRTWC who meets the qualifications specified in Section 10133.50(a)(15) must apply to the Administrative Director to be included on the list throughout the year. The list shall be reviewed and revised on a yearly basis, and shall be made available on the website www.dir.ca.gov or upon request.

(c) The injured employee may select a Vocational & Return to Work Counselor whenever the assistance of a Vocational & Return to Work Counselor is needed to facilitate an employee's vocational training or return to work in connection with the Supplemental Job Displacement Benefit set forth in this Article.

(d) The injured employee shall be responsible for providing the VRTWC with any necessary medical reports. However, a claims administrator shall provide a VRTWC with any medical reports, including permanent and stationary medical reports, upon an employee's written request and a signed release waiver.

(e) The VRTWC shall communicate with the injured employee regarding the evaluation.

Note: Authority cited: Sections 133, 4658.5 and 5307.3, Labor Code. Reference: Section 4658.5, Labor Code.

History: 1. New section filed 6-6-2005; operative 8-1-2005 (Register 2005, No. 23).

Ref.: Hanna § 35.110[5]; Herlick Handbook § 1.01[3][b].

§10133.60. Termination of Claims Administrator's Liability for the Supplemental Job Displacement Benefit.

(a) For injuries occurring on or after January 1, 2004, the claims administrator's liability to provide a supplemental job displacement voucher shall end if either (a)(1), (a)(2), or (a)(3) occur:

(1) the employer offers regular, modified or alternative work to the employee, meeting the requirements as set forth in section 10133.34.

(A) If the employer offers regular, modified, or alternative work to the employee for 12 months of seasonal work, the offer shall meet the following requirements:

1. the employee was hired on a seasonal basis prior to injury; and

2. the offer of regular, modified or alternative work is on a similar seasonal basis to the employee's previous employment;

(2) the maximum funds of the voucher have been exhausted. Vouchers issued on or after January 1, 2013, shall expire two years after the date the voucher is furnished to the employee or five years after the date of injury, whichever is later.

(3) Settlement or commutation of a claim for the supplemental job displacement voucher has been approved for dates of injury prior to January 1, 2013.

Note: Authority cited: Sections 133, 4658.7 and 5307.3, Labor Code. Reference: Sections 4658.1, 4658.5, 4658.6, 4658.7 and 5410, Labor Code; and *Henry v. WCAB* (1998) 68 Cal.App.4th 981.

History: 1. New section filed 6-6-2005; operative 8-1-2005 (Register 2005, No. 23).

2. Amendment of section and Note filed 12-20-2012 as an emergency; operative 1-1-2013 pursuant to Government Code section 11346.1(d) (Register 2012, No. 51). A Certificate of Compliance must be transmitted to OAL by 7-1-2013 or emergency language will be repealed by operation of law on the following day.

3. Amendment of section and Note refiled 6-26-2013 as an emergency; operative 7-1-2013 pursuant to Government Code section 11346.1(d) (Register 2013, No. 26). A Certificate of Compliance must be transmitted to OAL by 9-30-2013 or emergency language will be repealed by operation of law on the following day.

4. Certificate of Compliance as to 7-1-2013 order, including amendment of subsections (a)(1) and (a)(3), transmitted to OAL 9-27-2013 and filed 11-8-2013; amendments operative 1-1-2014 (Register 2013, No. 45).

Ref.: Hanna §§ 35.03, 35.110[6]; Herlick Handbook § 1.01[3][b].

ARTICLE 8
Attorney Fee Disclosure Statement

§10134. Attorney Fee Disclosure Statement Form.

[DWC Form 3 (Rev. 1/17) Not Reproduced]

NOTE: Form is available at no charge by downloading from the web at www.dir.ca.gov/dwc/forms.html or by requesting at 1-800-794-6900.

Note: Authority cited: Sections 133 and 5307.3, Labor Code. Reference: Section 4906, Labor Code.

History: 1. New section filed 1-18-90; operative 1-18-90 (Register 90, No. 4). New section is exempt from review by OAL pursuant to Government Code Section 11351.

2. Repealer and new section filed 4-13-93; operative 4-13-93. Submitted to OAL for printing only pursuant to Government Code section 11351 (Register 93, No. 16).

3. Change without regulatory effect amending section and Note filed 2-2-2017 pursuant to section 100, title 1, California Code of Regulations (Register 2017, No. 5).

Ref.: Hanna § 25.01[4]; Herlick Handbook §§ 1.01[3][b], 10.09[1], 16.16.

§10135. Required Use of Form.

Every attorney or his/her agent who consults with an injured worker or dependent is required to furnish the attorney fee disclosure statement form set forth in Section 10134 of this Article to the injured worker or dependent at the initial consultation.

Note: Authority cited: Sections 133 and 5307.3, Labor Code. Reference: Section 4906(e), Labor Code.

History: 1. New section filed 1-18-90; operative 1-18-90 (Register 90, No. 4). New section is exempt from review by OAL pursuant to Government Code Section 11351.

2. Amendment filed 4-13-93; operative 4-13-93. Submitted to OAL for printing only pursuant to Government Code section 11351 (Register 93, No. 16).

Ref.: Hanna §§ 20.01[4], 25.01[4]; Herlick Handbook §§ 1.01[3][b], 10.09[1].

§10135.1. Service of Form.

Within 15 days of the employee's and attorney's execution of the disclosure form, a copy of the disclosure form shall be mailed to the employer or, if known, to the employer's insurer or third-party administrator.

Note: Authority cited: Sections 133 and 5307.3, Labor Code. Reference: Section 4906(e), Labor Code.

History: 1. New section filed 4-13-93; operative 4-13-93. Submitted to OAL for printing only pursuant to Government Code section 11351 (Register 93, No. 16).

Ref.: Hanna §§ 20.01[4], 25.01[4]; Herlick Handbook §§ 1.01[3][b], 10.09[1].

ARTICLE 9
Claim Form: Availability, Filing, Acknowledgement of Receipt, Dismissal

§10136. General: Definitions.

As used in this Article, the following definitions apply:

(a) Claims Administrator. A self-administered workers' compensation insurer, a self-administered self-insured employer, a self-administered joint powers authority, or a third-party claims administrator for an insurer, a self-insured employer, a legally-uninsured employer or a joint powers authority; or an attorney or agent of any of those entities.

(b) Claim Form. The official Division of Workers' Compensation DWC Form 1 Employee's Claim for Workers' Compensation Benefits, as set forth in Section 10139 of this Article.

(c) Employee. An employee, a person claiming to be an employee, his or her dependents, or agent.

Note: Authority cited: Sections 133 and 5307.3, Labor Code. Reference: Sections 5401, 5401.7, 5402 and 5404.5, Labor Code.

History: 1. New section filed 1-18-90; operative 1-18-90 (Register 90, No. 4). New section is exempt from review by OAL pursuant to Government Code Section 11351.

2. Amendment of subsections (b), (b)(3), (b)(4) and (c), repealer of subsections (b)(5), (d), (e) and (f), and new subsection (d) filed 4-13-93; operative 4-13-93. Submitted to OAL for printing only pursuant to Government Code section 11351 (Register 93, No. 16)

3. Change without regulatory effect repealing article 9 heading, renumbering former article 6 to new article 9, renumbering former section 10136 to section 10252 and renumbering former section 10116 to section 10136, including amendment of subsection (b), filed 4-7-2008 pursuant to section 100, title 1, California Code of Regulations (Register 2008, No. 15).

Ref.: Herlick Handbook § 1.01[3][b].

§10137. General: Employer Obligation.

Nothing in this article shall abrogate the duty of an employer to provide timely compensation to an injured worker, even if the employee has not completed and filed the form required by Labor Code Section 5401 and this article.

Note: Authority cited: Sections 133 and 5307.3, Labor Code. Reference: Sections 5401 and 3200–6208, Labor Code.

History: 1. New section filed 1-18-90; operative 1-18-90 (Register 90, No. 4). New section is exempt from review by OAL pursuant to Government Code Section 11351.

2. Repealer and new section filed 4-13-93; operative 4-13-93. Submitted to OAL for printing only pursuant to Government Code section 11351 (Register 93, No. 16)

3. Change without regulatory effect renumbering former section 10137 to section 10252.1 and renumbering former section 10116.1 to section 10137 filed 4-7-2008 pursuant to section 100, title 1, California Code of Regulations (Register 2008, No. 15).

Ref.: Herlick Handbook § 1.01[3][b].

§10138. Claim Form and Notice of Potential Eligibility for Benefits.

The employee's form for filing a workers' compensation claim (DWC 1) and the Notice of Potential Eligibility for Benefits is a mandatory form set forth in Section 10139 of this Article. The employer portion of the form may also include other information pertinent to the claim, including a logo or other employer-identifying information, but such information shall in no way impose additional duties or prohibitions on the employee or delay the processing of the claim. The claim form consists of an original and three (3) copies.

Note: Authority cited: Sections 133 and 5307.3, Labor Code. Reference: Sections 5401, 5401.7 and 5402, Labor Code.

History: 1. Change without regulatory effect renumbering former section 10117.1 to section 10138, including amendment of section, filed 4-7-2008 pursuant to section 100, title 1, California Code of Regulations (Register 2008, No. 15).

Ref.: Herlick Handbook § 1.01[3][b].

§10139. Workers' Compensation Claim Form (DWC 1) and Notice of Potential Eligibility.

[DWC Form 1 (Rev. 1/1/2016) Not Reproduced]

NOTE: Form is available at no charge by downloading from the web at www.dir.ca.gov/dwc/forms.html or by requesting at 1-800-794-6900.

Note: Authority cited: Sections 133, 5307.3 and 5401, Labor Code. Reference: Sections 132(a), 139.48, 139.6, 4600, 4600.3, 4601, 4604.5, 4616, 4650, 4656, 4658.5, 4658.6, 4700, 4701, 4702, 4703, 5400, 5401, 5401.7 and 5402, Labor Code.

History: 1. Change without regulatory effect renumbering former section 10118.1 to section 10139 filed 4-7-2008 pursuant to section 100, title 1, California Code of Regulations (Register 2008, No. 15).

2. Amendment of section and Note filed 8-9-2010; operative 10-8-2010 (Register 2010, No. 33).

3. Repealer and new section filed 8-24-2015; operative 1-1-2016 (Register 2015, No. 35).

Ref.: Herlick Handbook § 1.01[3][b].

§10140. Employer's Responsibility to Process Claim Form, Claims Administrator's Duty to Provide Claim Form.

(a) Within one working day of receipt of a claim form, the employer shall date the claim form and provide a dated copy of the form to the employee and the employer's claims administrator.

(b) If the claims administrator obtains knowledge that the employer has not provided a claim form, it shall provide one to the employee within three working days of its knowledge that the form was not provided.

(c) If the claims administrator cannot determine if the employer has provided a claim form to the employee, the claims administrator shall provide one to the employee within 30 days of the administrator's date of knowledge of the claim.

Note: Authority cited: Sections 133 and 5307.3, Labor Code. Reference: Sections 5401 and 5402, Labor Code.

History: 1. Change without regulatory effect renumbering former section 10119 to section 10140 filed 4-7-2008 pursuant to section 100, title 1, California Code of Regulations (Register 2008, No. 15).

Ref.: Herlick Handbook § 1.01[3][b].

§10141. Dismissal of Inactive Claim by Operation of Law After Notice.

(a) Where a claim form has been filed for an injury that occurred prior to January 1, 1994, the claim has been denied, and there has been no activity for 180 days, the claims administrator may issue a notice of dismissal of the claim as follows:

(1) The notice shall include the following:

NOTICE REGARDING WORKERS' COMPENSATION CLAIM

You applied for workers' compensation benefits. A copy of your claim form is attached. We have not heard from you since we sent you a letter denying your claim on __________ [Date]. Your case has been inactive for at least 180 days. If you are still claiming benefits, you must file an Application for Adjudication of Claim with the Workers' Compensation Appeal Board within 180 days of the date this notice is served on you. The date of service is listed at the bottom of this form. IF YOU DO NOT FILE THE APPLICATION BY THE DEADLINE, THE CLAIM WILL AUTOMATICALLY BE DISMISSED "BY OPERATION OF LAW". This means you will not be able to claim benefits for the injury or illness listed on the claim form unless you file the Application for Adjudication of Claim by the deadline. Please call me at __________ [phone number] if you want more information or help figuring out the deadline for filing an Application.

You can get the Application form, help figuring out the deadline for filing an Application, and information about your claim by calling the State of California Division of Workers' Compensation Information and Assistance Office. [Enter telephone number of district Information and Assistance Office closest to injured workers' residence.] You may hear recorded information by calling 1-800-736-7401. You may also consult an attorney.

[Claims Administrator Representative]

Date Notice Is Served:__________

(2) The blank(s) in the prescribed notice language shall be completed by the claims administrator to specify the information described in brackets. The date of service of the Notice shall be inserted on the Notice by the claims administrator or process server to accurately reflect the date service is effected in accordance with the Code of Civil Procedure as specified in subsection (d).

(b) Where a claim form has been filed for an injury that occurred prior to January 1, 1994, benefits have been furnished, and there has been no activity for 180 days, the claims administrator may issue a notice of dismissal of the claim as follows:

(1) The notice shall include the following:

NOTICE REGARDING WORKERS' COMPENSATION CLAIM

You applied for workers' compensation benefits. A copy of your claim form is attached. Your case has been inactive for at least 180 days.

Your right to workers' compensation benefits will end on __________ [Insert date – either five years from the date of injury or one year from the last furnishing of benefits, whichever is later], unless you file an Application for Adjudication of Claim by that date. That date is __________ [insert either "five years from the date of your injury", or "one year from the date of the last benefit provided to you."]

IF YOU DO NOT FILE THE APPLICATION BY THE DEADLINE, THE CLAIM WILL AUTOMATICALLY BE DISMISSED "BY OPERATION OF LAW". This means you will not be able to claim further benefits for the injury or illness listed on the claim form unless you file the Application for Adjudication of Claim by the deadline. Please call me at ____________ [phone number] if you want more information.

You can get the application form and information about your claim by calling the State of California Division of Workers' Compensation Information and Assistance Office at ________ [Enter telephone number of district Information and Assistance Office closest to injured worker's residence.] You may hear recorded information by calling 1-800-736-7401. You may also consult an attorney.

____

[Claims Administrator Representative]

(2) The date of last furnishing of benefits shall be the latter of: the latest date of receipt by the employee of medical or rehabilitation services, or the latest date that payment of any compensation benefit was mailed or personally delivered to the employee or any service provider.

(3) The blanks in the prescribed notice language shall be completed by the claims administrator to specify the information described in brackets.

(c) The Notice under (a)(2) and (b)(2) shall further contain the date(s) of injury, name of the employee, the name of the employer, identification of the claims administrator, including address and telephone number, and claim number, if any. A copy of the claim form(s) shall be attached to the notice prior to service.

(d) The claims administrator shall serve notice on the employee in the manner prescribed for a summons in a civil action in accordance with Article 3 (commencing with Section 415.10) of Chapter 4 of Title 5 of the Code of Civil Procedure.

If the employee is represented by an attorney, the claims administrator shall in addition serve a copy of the notice on the attorney by personal delivery or first class mail. Where no Application for Adjudication of Claim has been filed, but the Workers' Compensation Appeals Board has assigned a case number to the matter because of a pre-Application filing, the claims administrator shall also serve a copy of the notice on the appeals board. Proof of service shall be made in accordance with Title 8, CCR section 10975.

(e) The occurrence of any of the following during the 180 days prior to service of the notice is evidence that the claim is not inactive and there can be no dismissal under (a)(1) or (a)(2): the employee has made demand for payment or provision of benefits (whether indemnity, medical, or other), the claims administrator has knowledge that there are benefits due and unpaid, there has been treatment rendered for the industrial injury, there has been a medical-legal evaluation of the employee, there has been a deposition in regard to the claim, the claims administrator has other knowledge that the employee is actively pursuing his or her claim.

Note: Authority cited: Sections 133, 5307.3 and 5404.5, Labor Code. Reference: Sections 5401, 5402 and 5404.5, Labor Code.

History: 1. Change without regulatory effect renumbering former section 10120 to section 10141 filed 4-7-2008 pursuant to section 100, title 1, California Code of Regulations (Register 2008, No. 15).

Ref.: Herlick Handbook § 1.01[3][b].

§10142. Date of Denial for Purposes of End of Tolling of Limitations Period.

For purposes of Labor Code Section 5401(c), the date "the claim is denied" for determining when the claim form ceases to toll the specified limitations periods is:

(a) the date the written denial notice is personally served, or

(b) five days after the written denial notice is placed in the mail if the address is within the State of California, ten days if the address is outside the State of California, but within the United States and twenty days if the address is outside of the United States.

The written denial notice must be issued in accordance with the notice regulations in Title 8, CCR, Subchapter 1, Article 8, Sections 9810 et seq. in order to cease the claim form's tolling of the limitations periods.

Note: Authority cited: Sections 133 and 5307.3, Labor Code. Reference: Section 5401, Labor Code.

History: 1. Change without regulatory effect renumbering former section 10121 to section 10142 filed 4-7-2008 pursuant to section 100, title 1, California Code of Regulations (Register 2008, No. 15).

Ref.: Herlick Handbook § 1.01[3][b].

SUBCHAPTER 1.6 PERMANENT DISABILITY RATING DETERMINATION

§10150. Disability Evaluation Unit.

The Disability Evaluation Unit, under the direction and authority of the administrative director, will issue permanent disability ratings as required under this subchapter utilizing the Schedule for Rating Permanent Disabilities adopted by the administrative director. The Disability Evaluation Unit will prepare the following kinds of rating determinations:

(a) Formal rating determinations

(b) Summary rating determinations

(c) Consultative rating determinations

(d) Informal rating determinations.

Note: Authority cited: Sections 133 and 5307.3, Labor Code. Reference: Sections 124, 4061, 4660, 4662, 4663 and 4664, Labor Code.

History: 1. New section filed 4-25-91; operative 4-25-91 (Register 91, No. 26). New section is exempt from review by OAL pursuant to Government Code section 11351.

2. Amendment of subchapter 1.6 heading filed 12-27-96; operative 12-27-96. Submitted to OAL for printing only pursuant to Government Code section 11351 (Register 96, No. 52).

3. Amendment of section heading, section and Note filed 12-31-2004 as an emergency; operative 1-1-2005 (Register 2004, No. 53). A Certificate of Compliance must be transmitted to OAL by 5-2-2005 or emergency language will be repealed by operation of law on the following day.

4. Certificate of Compliance as to 12-31-2004 order transmitted to OAL 4-29-2005 and filed 6-10-2005 (Register 2005, No. 23).

5. Amendment of first paragraph filed 11-17-2008; operative 11-17-2008 pursuant to Government Code section 11343.4 (Register 2008, No. 47).

Ref.: Hanna §§ 1.12[15], 32.01[3][d], [4], 32.05[1]–[6][b]; Herlick Handbook §§ 1.01[3][b], 6.04[2], 14.4, 14.22; Lawyer's Guide to AMA *Guides* and Calif. Workers' Comp. §§ 2.02, 2.06[4].

§10150.1. Signature Disputes and the Signatures of Consultants.

(a) Anyone who disputes the authenticity of any signature must file with the Manager of the Disability Evaluation Unit an objection to the pleading or other document within ten (10) days of the filing of that document. The objection shall contain a complete explanation of the basis for the objection.

(b) The filing of a document, signed with a "/s/ name" or an electronic image of the signature filed with the login and password of the Division of Workers' Compensation consultant assigned to the case shall constitute an original signature for all purposes.

Note: Authority cited: Sections 133 and 5307.3, Labor Code. Reference: Sections 124, 4061, 4062, 4062.1, 4062.2, 4062.5, 4064, 4067, 4660, 4662, 4663 and 4664, Labor Code.

History: 1. New section filed 11-17-2008; operative 11-17-2008 pursuant to Government Code section 11343.4 (Register 2008, No. 47).

Ref.: Hanna §§ 32.01[3][d], [4], 32.05[1]–[6][b]; Herlick Handbook §§ 1.01[3][b], 6.04[2], 14.4, 14.22.

§10150.2. Technical Unavailability of EAMS.

Technical problems with filing documents shall be governed by section 10225 of title 8 of the California Code of Regulation.

Note: Authority cited: Sections 133 and 5307.3, Labor Code. Reference: Sections 5502 and 5700, Labor Code.

History: 1. New section filed 11-17-2008; operative 11-17-2008 pursuant to Government Code section 11343.4 (Register 2008, No. 47).

Ref.: Hanna §§ 32.01[3][d], [4], 32.05[1]–[6][b]; Herlick Handbook §§ 1.01[3][b], 14.4, 14.22.

§10150.3. Disability Evaluation Unit File Retention.

(a) Following a period of fifty (50) years after the filing of a document used to open a case or file, the Division of Workers' Compensation may destroy the electronic and/or paper file in each case maintained by the Disability Evaluation Unit.

(b) The Division of Workers' Compensation, at any time, may convert a paper file to an electronic file. The Division of Workers' Compensation shall inform the parties when a paper file is converted. If a paper case file has been converted to electronic form, the paper case file may be destroyed no less than 30 business days after the parties have been informed of the conversion.

Note: Authority cited: Sections 133 and 5307.3, Labor Code. Reference: Sections 124, 4061, 4062, 4062.1, 4062.2, 4062.5, 4064, 4067, 4660, 4662, 4663 and 4664, Labor Code.

History: 1. New section filed 11-17-2008; operative 11-17-2008 pursuant to Government Code section 11343.4 (Register 2008, No. 47).

Ref.: Hanna §§ 32.01[3][d], [4], 32.05[1]–[6][b]; Herlick Handbook §§ 1.01[3][b], 14.4, 14.22.

§10150.4. Misfiled or Misdirected Documents.

(a) A request to move or substitute a corrected document shall be made in conformity with section 10223 of title 8 of the California Code of Regulation, except that a written request to substitute with the proposed document for substitution appended shall be made in lieu of a petition to substitute as allowed under section 10223(b). The authority to approve moving a document from one file to another file shall reside with the Manager of the Disability Evaluation Unit or his or her designee.

(b) If a document is not filed in compliance with sections 10217, 10228 and 10232 of title 8 of the California Code of Regulations and these regulations, the administrative director may in his or her discretion take the actions set forth in section 10222 of title 8 of the California Code of Regulations.

Note: Authority cited: Sections 133 and 5307.3, Labor Code. Reference: Sections 124, 4061, 4062, 4062.1, 4062.2, 4062.5, 4064, 4067, 4660, 4662, 4663 and 4664, Labor Code.

History: 1. New section filed 11-17-2008; operative 11-17-2008 pursuant to Government Code section 11343.4 (Register 2008, No. 47).

Ref.: Hanna §§ 32.01[3][d], [4], 32.05[1]–[6][b]; Herlick Handbook §§ 1.01[3][b], 14.4, 14.22.

§10151. Filing Requirements.

(a) "Electronic Adjudication Management System" or "EAMS" means the computer case management system used by the Division of Workers' Compensation to electronically store and maintain the Division of Workers' Compensation or the appeals board's case files and to perform other case management functions.

(b) All forms or correspondence submitted to the Disability Evaluation Unit shall be stored in the EAMS:

(1) Except for documents or forms which open a Disability Evaluation Unit file, all documents and forms shall contain a case number assigned by the Division of Workers' Compensation. The case number shall be preceded by the prefix "DEU". Case opening document shall be assigned a case number by the Division of Workers' Compensation after filing. Documents or forms filed without a case number will be returned to the sender with instructions for proper filing.

(2) All documents presented for filing shall conform to the requirements of sections 10217, 10228 and 10232 of title 8 of the California Code of Regulations.

(3) All filed paper documents and forms shall be scanned into the EAMS and then will be destroyed. A properly filed paper document or form shall be deemed a legal filing for all purposes.

(4) The service of all documents and forms shall conform to the receiving party's designated preferred method of service described in section of 10218 of title 8 of the California Code of Regulation.

Note: Authority cited: Sections 133, 4061, 4660, 5307.3 and 5307.4, Labor Code. Reference: Sections 124 and 4061, Labor Code.

History: 1. New section filed 11-17-2008; operative 11-17-2008 pursuant to Government Code section 11343.4 (Register 2008, No. 47). For prior history, see Register 2005, No. 23.

Ref.: Hanna §§ 32.01[3][d], [4], 32.05[1]–[6][b]; Herlick Handbook §§ 1.01[3][b], 14.4, 14.22.

§10151.1. Electronic Filing Exemption.

If a document is filed with EAMS as part of the electronic filing trial, that document does not need to be filed in compliance with sections 10228 and 10232 of title 8 of the California Code of Regulation.

Note: Authority cited: Sections 111, 133, 5307.3 and 5307.4, Labor Code. Reference: Sections 124 and 4061, Labor Code.

History: 1. New section filed 11-17-2008; operative 11-17-2008 pursuant to Government Code section 11343.4 (Register 2008, No. 47).

Ref.: Hanna §§ 32.01[3][d], [4], 32.05[1]–[6][b]; Herlick Handbook §§ 1.01[3][b], 6.04[2], 14.4, 14.22.

§10152. Disability, When Considered Permanent.

A disability is considered permanent when the employee has reached maximal medical improvement, meaning his or her condition is well stabilized, and unlikely to change substantially in the next year with or without medical treatment.

Note: Authority cited: Sections 133 and 5307.3, Labor Code. Reference: Sections 124, 4061, 4062, 4062.01, 4062.1, 4660, 4662, 4663 and 4664, Labor Code.

History: 1. New section filed 4-25-91; operative 4-25-91 (Register 91, No. 26). New section is exempt from review by OAL pursuant to Government Code section 11351.

2. Amendment of section and Note filed 12-31-2004 as an emergency; operative 1-1-2005 (Register 2004, No. 53). A Certificate of Compliance must be transmitted to OAL by 5-2-2005 or emergency language will be repealed by operation of law on the following day.

3. Certificate of Compliance as to 12-31-2004 order transmitted to OAL 4-29-2005 and filed 6-10-2005 (Register 2005, No. 23).

Ref.: Hanna §§ 8.01, 8.03, 32.02[1]; Herlick Handbook §§ 1.01[3][b], 6.01[2], 14.4; Lawyer's Guide to AMA *Guides* and Calif. Workers' Comp. § 3.03.

§10154. Permanent Disability Rating Determinations, Kinds. [Repealed]

Note: Authority cited: Sections 133, 5307.3 and 5307.4, Labor Code. Reference: Sections 124. 4061, 5452, 5701 and 5703.5, Labor Code.

History: 1. New section filed 4-25-91; operative 4-25-91 (Register 91, No. 26). New section is exempt from review by OAL pursuant to Government Code section 11351.

2. New subsection (d) filed 12-27-96; operative 12-27-96. Submitted to OAL for printing only pursuant to Government Code section 11351 (Register 96, No. 52).

3. Repealer filed 12-31-2004 as an emergency; operative 1-1-2005 (Register 2004, No. 53). A Certificate of Compliance must be transmitted to OAL by 5-2-2005 or emergency language will be repealed by operation of law on the following day.

4. Certificate of Compliance as to 12-31-2004 order transmitted to OAL 4-29-2005 and filed 6-10-2005 (Register 2005, No. 23).

§10156. Formal Rating Determinations.

A formal rating determination will be prepared by the Disability Evaluation Unit when requested by the Appeals Board or a Workers' Compensation Judge on a form specified for that purpose by the Administrative Director. The form will provide for a description of the disability to be rated, the occupation of the injured employee, the employee's age at the time of injury, the date of injury, the formula used, and a notice of submission in accordance with Appeals Board Rules of Practice and Procedure.

Note: Authority cited: Sections 133 and 5307.3, Labor Code. Reference: Sections 124, 4061, 4660, 4662, 4663, 4664 and 5701, Labor Code.

History: 1. New section filed 4-25-91; operative 4-25-91 (Register 91, No. 26). New section is exempt from review by OAL pursuant to Government Code section 11351.

2. Amendment of section and Note filed 12-31-2004 as an emergency; operative 1-1-2005 (Register 2004, No. 53). A Certificate of Compliance must be transmitted to OAL by 5-2-2005 or emergency language will be repealed by operation of law on the following day.

3. Certificate of Compliance as to 12-31-2004 order transmitted to OAL 4-29-2005 and filed 6-10-2005 (Register 2005, No. 23).

Ref.: Hanna § 32.05[6][a]; Herlick Handbook §§ 1.01[3][b], 6.04[3], 14.4; Lawyer's Guide to AMA *Guides* and Calif. Workers' Comp. §§ 2.02, 2.06[4].

§10158. Formal Rating Determinations As Evidence.

Formal rating determinations prepared by disability evaluators shall be deemed to constitute evidence only as to the relation between the disability or impairment standard(s) described and the percentage of permanent disability.

Note: Authority cited: Sections 133 and 5307.3, Labor Code. Reference: Sections 124, 4061, 4660, 4662, 4663 and 4664, Labor Code.

History: 1. New section filed 4-25-91; operative 4-25-91 (Register 91, No. 26). New section is exempt from review by OAL pursuant to Government Code section 11351.

2. Amendment of section and Note filed 12-31-2004 as an emergency; operative 1-1-2005 (Register 2004, No. 53). A Certificate of Compliance must be transmitted to OAL by 5-2-2005 or emergency language will be repealed by operation of law on the following day.

3. Certificate of Compliance as to 12-31-2004 order transmitted to OAL 4-29-2005 and filed 6-10-2005 (Register 2005, No. 23).

Ref.: Hanna § 32.05[2]; Herlick Handbook §§ 1.01[3][b], 6.04[3], 14.4; Lawyer's Guide to AMA *Guides* and Calif. Workers' Comp. §§ 2.02, 2.06[4].

§10159. Time Period for Issuing a Summary Rating Determination Pursuant to Labor Code §4061(e).

Following the receipt of a comprehensive medical-legal evaluation from a Qualified Medical Evaluator that is eligible for rating under section 10160, the Disability Evaluation Unit shall issue a summary rating determination pursuant to Labor Code section 4061(e) within 20 days of either the date the time has passed for the filing of a request for factual correction under Labor Code section 4061(d)(1), or the date of receipt of a supplemental report submitted to the Disability Evaluation Unit in response to a request for factual correction under section 37 of title 8 of the California Code of Regulations, whichever is later.

Note: Authority cited: Sections 111, 133, 5307.3 and 5307.4, Labor Code. Reference: Sections 124 and 4061, Labor Code.

History: 1. New section filed 12-31-2012 as an emergency; operative 1-1-2013 pursuant to Government Code section 11346.1(d) (Register 2013, No. 1). A Certificate of Compliance must be transmitted to OAL by 7-1-2013 or emergency language will be repealed by operation of law on the following day.

2. New section refiled 7-1-2013 as an emergency; operative 7-1-2013 (Register 2013, No. 27). A Certificate of Compliance must be transmitted to OAL by 9-30-2013 or emergency language will be repealed by operation of law on the following day.

3. Certificate of Compliance as to 7-1-2013 order, including repealer of subsection (a) designator, transmitted to OAL 8-2-2013 and filed 9-16-2013; amendments operative 9-16-2013 pursuant to Government Code section 11343.4(b)(3) (Register 2013, No. 38).

Ref.: Herlick Handbook §§ 1.01[3][b], 6.04[5].

§10160. Summary Rating Determinations, Comprehensive Medical Evaluation of Unrepresented Employee.

(a) The Disability Evaluation Unit will prepare a summary rating determination upon receipt of a properly prepared request. A properly prepared request shall consist of:

(1) A completed Request for Summary Rating Determination, DWC AD Form 101 (DEU);

(2) A completed Employee's Disability Questionnaire, DWC AD Form 100 (DEU);

(3) A comprehensive medical evaluation of an unrepresented employee from a Qualified Medical Evaluator.

(b) The insurance carrier or self-insured employer shall provide the employee with an Employee's Disability Questionnaire prior to the appointment scheduled with the Qualified Medical Evaluator. The employee will be instructed in the form and manner prescribed by the administrative director to complete the questionnaire and provide it to the Qualified Evaluator at the time of the examination.

(c) The insurance carrier, self-insured employer or injured worker shall complete a Request for Summary Rating Determination of Qualified Medical Evaluator's Report, a copy of which shall be served on the opposing party. The requesting party shall send the request, including proof of service of the request on the opposing party, to the Qualified Medical Evaluator together with all medical reports and medical records relating to the case prior to the scheduled examination with the Qualified Medical Evaluator. The request shall include the appropriate address of the Disability Evaluation Unit. A listing of all of the offices of the Disability Evaluation Unit, with each office's area of jurisdiction, will be provided, upon request, by any office of the Disability Evaluation Unit or any Information and Assistance Office.

(d) When a summary rating determination has been requested, the Qualified Medical Evaluator shall submit all of the following documents to the Disability Evaluation Unit at the location indicated on the DWC AD Form 101 (DEU) and shall concurrently serve copies on the employee and claims administrator:

(1) Request for Summary Rating Determination of Qualified Medical Evaluator's Report as a cover sheet to the evaluation report;

(2) Employee's Disability Questionnaire;

(3) Comprehensive medical evaluation by the Qualified Medical Evaluator, including the Qualified Medical Evaluator's Findings Summary Form (QME Form 111).

(4) A document cover sheet and separator sheet pursuant to section 10205.14 of title 8 of the California Code of Regulation, which shall only be served on the Disability Evaluation Unit.

(e) No request for a summary rating determination shall be considered to be received until the Employee's Disability Questionnaire, the Request for Summary Rating Determination of Qualified Medical Evaluator's Report, and the comprehensive medical evaluation have been received by the office of the Disability Evaluation Unit having jurisdiction over the employee's area of residence. In the event an employee does not have a completed Employee's Disability Questionnaire at the time of his or her appointment with a Qualified Medical Evaluator, the medical evaluator shall provide this form to the employee for completion prior to the evaluation. Any requests received on or after April 1, 1994 without all the required documents will be returned to the sender.

(f) Except when a request for factual correction is filed in compliance with section 37 of title 8 of the California Code of Regulations, any request for the rating of a supplemental comprehensive medical evaluation report shall be made no later than twenty days from the receipt of the report and shall be accompanied by a copy of the correspondence to the evaluator soliciting the supplemental evaluation, together with proof of service of the correspondence on the opposing party.

(g) If a Qualified Medical Evaluator files a correction to the comprehensive medical evaluation previously filed pursuant to section 37(d) of title 8 of the California Code of Regulations, the Disability Evaluation Unit shall consider in its summary rating the corrections indicated by the Qualified Medical Evaluator in the supplemental report.

Note: Authority cited: Sections 133 and 5307.3, Labor Code. Reference: Sections 124, 4061, 4062, 4062.1, 4062.2, 4062.5, 4064, 4067, 4660, 4662, 4663 and 4664, Labor Code.

History: 1. New section filed 4-25-91; operative 4-25-91 (Register 91, No. 26). New section is exempt from review by OAL pursuant to Government Code section 11351.

2. Amendment of section filed 1-28-94; operative 1-28-94. Submitted to OAL for printing only pursuant to Government Code section 11351 (Register 94, No. 4).

3. Amendment of section heading and text filed 2-21-95; operative 2-21-95. Submitted to OAL for printing only pursuant to Government Code section 11351 (Register 95, No. 8).

4. Amendment of subsections (c)-(d) and (f) and amendment of Note filed 12-31-2004 as an emergency; operative 1-1-2005 (Register 2004, No. 53). A Certificate of Compliance must be transmitted to OAL by 5-2-2005 or emergency language will be repealed by operation of law on the following day.

5. Certificate of Compliance as to 12-31-2004 order, including amendment of subsections (a)(2), (b), (d) and (e), transmitted to OAL 4-29-2005 and filed 6-10-2005 (Register 2005, No. 23).

6. Amendment filed 11-17-2008; operative 11-17-2008 pursuant to Government Code section 11343.4 (Register 2008, No. 47).

7. Amendment of subsection (f) and new subsection (g) filed 12-31-2012 as an emergency; operative 1-1-2013 pursuant to Government Code section 11346.1(d) (Register 2013, No. 1). A Certificate of Compliance must be transmitted to OAL by 7-1-2013 or emergency language will be repealed by operation of law on the following day.

8. Amendment of subsection (f) and new subsection (g) refiled 7-1-2013 as an emergency; operative 7-1-2013 (Register 2013, No. 27). A Certificate of Compliance must be transmitted to OAL by 9-30-2013 or emergency language will be repealed by operation of law on the following day.

9. Certificate of Compliance as to 7-1-2013 order, including amendment of subsection (d)(4) and Note, transmitted to OAL 8-2-2013 and filed 9-16-2013; amendments operative 9-16-2013 pursuant to Government Code section 11343.4(b)(3) (Register 2013, No. 38).

Ref.: Hanna §§ 22.06[1][b], 32.01[3][d], [4], 32.05[1]–[6][b]; Herlick Handbook §§ 1.01[3][b], 6.04[5], 14.4, 14.22.

§10160.1. Summary Rating Determinations, Report of Primary Treating Physician for Unrepresented Employee.

(a) For injuries on or after January 1, 1994, the insurance carrier, self-insured employer or the employee may request a summary rating of the primary treating physician's report prepared in accordance with Section 9785.

(b) The request may be made by completing a Request for Summary Rating Determination of Primary Treating Physician's Report (DWC AD Form 102 (DEU)) and filing the request with the Disability Evaluation Unit together with a copy of the primary treating physician's report, if the report has not already been filed in EAMS.

(c) A filed copy of the request form and a copy of the primary treating physician's report shall be served immediately after filing on the non-requesting party, with a proof of service on the non-requesting party.

Note: Authority cited: Sections 133, 5307.3 and 5307.4, Labor Code. Reference: Sections 124, 4061, 4061.5, 4062, 4062.1, 4062.2, 4062.5, 4064 and 4067, Labor Code.

History: 1. New section filed 2-21-95; operative 2-21-95. Submitted to OAL for printing only pursuant to Government Code section 11351 (Register 95, No. 8).

2. Amendment filed 11-17-2008; operative 11-17-2008 pursuant to Government Code section 11343.4 (Register 2008, No. 47).

Ref.: Hanna §§ 32.01[3][d], [4], 32.05[1]–[6][b]; Herlick Handbook §§ 1.01[3][b], 6.04[5], 14.4, 14.22.

§10160.5. Summary Rating Determinations, Represented Employees.

(a) For injuries on or after January 1, 1991 and before January 1, 1994, the Disability Evaluation Unit will prepare a summary rating determination in cases where the injured worker is represented only if requested by a party. A summary rating determination will be prepared only upon receipt of a properly prepared request. A properly prepared request shall consist of:

(1) A completed Request for Summary Rating Determination DWC AD Form 101 (DEU);

(2) An evaluation by a Qualified Medical Evaluator or Agreed Medical Evaluator.

(b) The requesting party shall complete a Request for Summary Rating Determination of Qualified Medical Evaluator's Report and submit it together with all medical reports and medical records concerning the case to the medical evaluator. The medical evaluator shall send the completed medical evaluation report together with the Request for Summary Rating Determination to the office of the Disability Evaluation Unit designated by the administrative director and specific on the Request for Summary Rating Determination of Qualified Medical Evaluator's Report and shall simultaneously serve the party or parties requesting the evaluation.

(c) Notwithstanding the provisions of subdivision (b), a party may request a summary rating determination following receipt of a medical report prepared by a Qualified Medical Evaluator or Agreed Medical Evaluator on a represented case. The party shall file the Request for Summary Rating Determination of Qualified Medical Evaluator's Report and the medical report with the DEU office designated by the administrative director and shall immediately serve a filed copy of the Summary Rating Determination on the other party.

(d) If a case is settled prior to receipt of a summary rating which has been requested, the requesting party shall notify the DEU office of the settlement.

Note: Authority cited: Sections 133, 5307.3 and 5307.4, Labor Code. Reference: Sections 124, 4061, 4062, 4062.1, 4062.2, 4062.5, 4064 and 4067, Labor Code.

History: 1. New section filed 4-25-91; operative 4-25-91 (Register 91, No. 26). New section is exempt from review by OAL pursuant to Government Code section 11351.

2. Amendment of section filed 1-28-94; operative 1-28-94. Submitted to OAL for printing only pursuant to Government Code section 11351 (Register 94, No. 4).

3. Amendment of section heading and subsections (a)-(c), repealer of subsection (d), subsection relettering, and amendment of redesignated subsection (d) filed 2-21-95; operative 2-21-95. Submitted to OAL for printing only pursuant to Government Code section 11351 (Register 95, No. 8).

4. Amendment filed 11-17-2008; operative 11-17-2008 pursuant to Government Code section 11343.4 (Register 2008, No. 47).

Ref.: Hanna §§ 32.01[3][d], [4], 32.05[1]–[6][b]; Herlick Handbook §§ 1.01[3][b], 14.4, 14.22.

§10161. Forms.

(a) Employee's Disability Questionnaire (DWC AD Form 100 (DEU)).

(b) Request for Summary Determination of Qualified Medical Evaluator's Report (DWC AD Form 101 (DEU)).

(c) Request for Summary Determination of Primary Treating Physician's Report (DWC AD Form 102 (DEU)).

[DWC-AD Form 100 (Rev. 11/2008) Not Reproduced]

[DWC-AD Form 101 (Rev. 11/2008) Not Reproduced]

[DWC-AD Form 102 (Rev. 11/2008) Not Reproduced]

NOTE: Forms referred to above are available at no charge by downloading from the web at www.dir.ca.gov/dwc/forms.html or by requesting at 1-800-794-6900.

Note: Authority cited: Sections 133 and 5307.3, Labor Code. Reference: Sections 124, 4061, 4062, 4062.01, 4062.1, 4062.2, 4062.5, 4064, 4067, 4660, 4662, 4663 and 4664, Labor Code.

History: 1. New section filed 4-25-91; operative 4-25-91 (Register 91, No. 26). New section is exempt from review by OAL pursuant to Government Code section 11351.

2. Repealer and new DEU Form 100 filed 1-28-94; operative 1-28-94. Submitted to OAL for printing only pursuant to Government Code section 11351 (Register 94, No. 4).

3. Editorial correction restoring inadvertently omitted subsection (b) (Register 95, No. 8).

4. Amendment of subsections (a), (b) and forms 100 and 101; and new subsection (c) and form 102 filed 2-21-95; operative 2-21-95. Submitted to OAL for printing only pursuant to Government Code section 11351 (Register 95, No. 8).

5. Certificate of Compliance as to 12-31-2004 order, including further amendment of section and forms and amendment of Note, transmitted to OAL 4-29-2005 and filed 6-10-2005 (Register 2005, No. 23).

6. Amendment of section, including repealer and new DEU Form 100, DEU Form 101 and DEU Form 102, filed 11-17-2008; operative 11-17-2008 pursuant to Government Code section 11343.4 (Register 2008, No. 47).

Ref.: Hanna §§ 32.01[3][d], [4], 32.05[1]–[6][b]; Herlick Handbook §§ 1.01[3][b], 14.4, 14.22.

§10161.1. Reproduction of Forms.

The Request for Summary Rating Determination of Qualified Medical Evaluator's Report, the Employee's Disability Questionnaire, and the Request for Summary Rating Determination of the Primary Treating Physician's Report may be reproduced by automated office equipment or other means as long as the printed content and layout of the form are identical to the specified form.

Note: Authority cited: Sections 133 and 5307.3, Labor Code. Reference: Sections 124, 4061, 4062, 4062.01, 4062.1, 4062.2, 4062.5, 4064, 4067, 4660, 4662, 4663 and 4664, Labor Code.

History: 1. New section filed 2-21-95; operative 2-21-95. Submitted to OAL for printing only pursuant to Government Code section 11351 (Register 95, No. 8).

2. Amendment of section number filed 8-8-95; operative 8-8-95. Submitted to OAL for printing only pursuant to Government Code section 11351 (Register 95, No. 32).

3. Amendment of section and new Note filed 11-17-2008; operative 11-17-2008 pursuant to Government Code section 11343.4 (Register 2008, No. 47).

Ref.: Hanna §§ F11.01[2], F11.02[2], F11.03[2], 32.01[3][d], [4], 32.05[1]–[6][b]; Herlick Handbook §§ 1.01[3][b], 14.4, 14.22.

§10162. Summary Rating Determinations, Apportionment.

(a) In cases where the injured worker is not represented and a Qualified Medical Evaluator's formal medical evaluation indicates apportionment of the permanent disability, a summary rating determination will not be made until a workers' compensation administrative law judge has reviewed the medical evaluation to determine if the apportionment is inconsistent with the law. The determination of the workers' compensation administrative law judge will not be admissible in any judicial proceeding.

(b) Upon receipt of a formal medical evaluation which apportions the disability, the Disability Evaluation Unit will transmit the medical evaluation to the presiding workers' compensation administrative law judge of the office of the appeals board designated by the Disability Evaluation Unit, with a request to review the apportionment to determine whether it is inconsistent with the law. The workers' compensation administrative law judge shall make the determination and respond to the Disability Evaluation Unit within 45 days.

(c) If the workers' compensation administrative law judge refers the medical report back to the Qualified Medical Evaluator for correction or clarification, the Qualified Medical Evaluator shall provide a response to the workers' compensation administrative law judge within 30 days of the referral. If no response is received, the workers' compensation administrative law judge shall make a determination whether the apportionment is inconsistent with the law, and a summary rating determination will be made.

(d) In cases where the injured worker is represented and an Agreed Medical Evaluator or Qualified Medical Evaluator apportions the permanent disability, the Disability Evaluation Unit will issue a summary rating determination "Before Apportionment."

Note: Authority cited: Sections 133, 5307.3 and 5307.4, Labor Code. Reference: Sections 124 and 4061, Labor Code.

History: 1. New section filed 4-25-91; operative 4-25-91 (Register 91, No. 26). New section is exempt from review by OAL pursuant to Government Code section 11351.

2. Amendment filed 11-17-2008; operative 11-17-2008 pursuant to Government Code section 11343.4 (Register 2008, No. 47).

Ref.: Hanna §§ 32.01[3][d], [4], 32.05[1]–[6][b]; Herlick Handbook §§ 1.01[3][b], 6.04[5], 14.4, 14.22.

§10163. Apportionment Referral.

[DEU Form 105 (Rev. 6/2005) Not Reproduced]

NOTE: Form is available at no charge by downloading from the web at www.dir.ca.gov/dwc/forms.html or by requesting at 1-800-794-6900.

Note: Authority cited: Sections 133 and 5307.3, Labor Code. Reference: Sections 124, 4061, 4062, 4062.01, 4062.1, 4062.2, 4062.5, 4064, 4067, 4660, 4662, 4663 and 4664, Labor Code.

History: 1. New section filed 4-25-91; operative 4-25-91 (Register 91, No. 26). New section is exempt from review by OAL pursuant to Government Code section 11351.

2. Amendment of section and Note filed 12-31-2004 as an emergency; operative 1-1-2005 (Register 2004, No. 53). A Certificate of Compliance must be transmitted to OAL by 5-2-2005 or emergency language will be repealed by operation of law on the following day.

3. Certificate of Compliance as to 12-31-2004 order, including further amendment of Note, transmitted to OAL 4-29-2005 and filed 6-10-2005 (Register 2005, No. 23).

Ref.: Hanna § F11.06[2]; Herlick Handbook §§ 1.01[3][b], 14.4.

§10164. Summary Rating Determinations, Reconsideration if Employee is Unrepresented.

(a) Requests for reconsideration of the summary rating determination shall be filed with the administrative director in writing within 30 days of receipt of the summary rating determination. The request shall clearly specify the reasons the summary rating determination should be reconsidered and shall include a proof of service on the other party and any other information necessary to support the request. Reconsideration of a summary rating may be granted by the administrative director for one or more of the following reasons:

(1) the summary rating was incorrectly calculated;

(2) the comprehensive medical evaluation failed to address one or more issues;

(3) the comprehensive medical evaluation failed to completely address one or more issues;

(4) the comprehensive medical evaluation was not prepared in accordance with required procedures, including the procedures of the administrative director promulgated under paragraph (2) or (3) of subdivision (j) of Section 139.2.

Requests for reconsideration which are not based on one of the above reasons will be denied.

(b) The administrative director shall not accept or consider, as a basis for a request for reconsideration, a supplemental or follow-up evaluation which was requested by a party after a summary rating determination has already been issued to the parties.

(c) If the administrative director determines that an additional evaluation from another Qualified Medical Evaluator is necessary, the matter shall be referred to the Medical Director of the Medical Unit for the provision of another Qualified Medical Evaluator.

Note: Authority cited: Sections 133, 5307.3 and 5307.4, Labor Code. Reference: Sections 124 and 4061, Labor Code.

History: 1. New section filed 4-25-91; operative 4-25-91 (Register 91, No. 26). New section is exempt from review by OAL pursuant to Government Code section 11351.

2. Amendment of section filed 1-28-94; operative 1-28-94. Submitted to OAL for printing only pursuant to Government Code section 11351 (Register 94, No. 4).

3. Amendment of section heading, repealer of subsection (a), subsection relettering, amendment of redesignated subsection (a), new subsections (a)(1)-(4) and (b) and amendment of subsection (c) filed 2-21-95; operative 2-21-95. Submitted to OAL for printing only pursuant to Government Code section 11351 (Register 95, No. 8).

4. Amendment filed 11-17-2008; operative 11-17-2008 pursuant to Government Code section 11343.4 (Register 2008, No. 47).

Ref.: Hanna §§ 32.01[3][d], [4], 32.05[1]–[6][b]; Herlick Handbook §§ 1.01[3][b], 6.04[5], 14.4, 14.22.

§10165. Service of Summary Rating Determination and Notice of Options Following Permanent Disability Rating.

Within the time specified in Labor Code section 4061(e), the Disability Evaluation Unit shall serve the permanent disability rating determination and the Notice of Options Following Permanent Disability Rating on the employee and employer by the method of service described in section of 10218 of title 8 of the California Code of Regulation.

Note: Authority cited: Sections 133, 5307.3 and 5307.4, Labor Code. Reference: Sections 124 and 4061, Labor Code.

History: 1. New section filed 4-25-91; operative 4-25-91 (Register 91, No. 26). New section is exempt from review by OAL pursuant to Government Code section 11351.

2. Amendment filed 11-17-2008; operative 11-17-2008 pursuant to Government Code section 11343.4 (Register 2008, No. 47).

Ref.: Hanna §§ 32.01[3][d], [4], 32.05[1]–[6][b]; Herlick Handbook §§ 1.01[3][b], 6.04[5], 14.4, 14.22.

§10165.5. Notice of Options Following Disability Rating (DEU Form 110).

[DEU Form 110 (Rev. 6/2005) Not Reproduced]

NOTE: Form is available at no charge by downloading from the web at www.dir.ca.gov/dwc/forms.html or by requesting at 1-800-794-6900.

Note: Authority cited: Sections 133 and 5307.3, Labor Code. Reference: Sections 124, 4061, 4062, 4062.01, 4062.1, 4062.2, 4062.5, 4064, 4067, 4660, 4662, 4663 and 4664, Labor Code.

History: 1. New section filed 4-25-91; operative 4-25-91 (Register 91, No. 26). New section is exempt from review by OAL pursuant to Government Code section 11351.

2. Amendment of section filed 1-28-94; operative 1-28-94. Submitted to OAL for printing only pursuant to Government Code section 11351 (Register 94, No. 4).

3. Amendment of section and Note filed 12-31-2004 as an emergency; operative 1-1-2005 (Register 2004, No. 53). A Certificate of Compliance must be transmitted to OAL by 5-2-2005 or emergency language will be repealed by operation of law on the following day.

4. Certificate of Compliance as to 12-31-2004 order, including further amendment of section and Note, transmitted to OAL 4-29-2005 and filed 6-10-2005 (Register 2005, No. 23).

Ref.: Hanna § 32.05[3][c]; Herlick Handbook §§ 1.01[3][b], 6.04[5], 14.4.

§10166. Consultative Ratings Determinations.

(a) The Disability Evaluation Unit will prepare consultative rating determinations upon request of the appeals board, workers' compensation administrative law judges, settlement conference referees, arbitrators, workers' compensation judges pro tempore and information & assistance officers.

(b) Consultative rating determinations may be requested for the purpose of determining the ratable significance of factors, reviewing proposed compromise and release agreements for adequacy, determining commuted values, resolving occupational questions or any other matters within the expertise of the disability evaluators. Consultative Rating Determinations will not be admissible in judicial proceedings.

(c) The Disability Evaluation Unit may also prepare consultative rating determinations upon receipt of reasonable requests from employers, injured workers or their respective representatives. A request is not considered reasonable where an insurance carrier or self-insurer seeks a consultative rating determination for the purpose of terminating its liability or for negotiating a compromise and release settlement where the injured worker has no representative. Consultative rating determinations shall not to be used as a substitute for summary rating determinations.

(d) In all cases the person making a request for a consultative rating determination will provide the Disability Evaluation Unit with the occupation and age of the injured worker at the time of injury.

(e) No consultative rating determination will be provided on cases in which an application for adjudication of claim has been filed with the appeals board without prior written authorization of the Appeals Board, a workers' compensation administrative law judge, settlement conference referee, arbitrator, workers' compensation judge pro tempore, or information & assistance officer. In cases where an application has been filed, the disability evaluator may require that any request for consultative rating determination be accompanied by the appeals board file.

Note: Authority cited: Sections 133, 5307.3 and 5307.4, Labor Code. Reference: Sections 123.6, 123.7, 124, 5275, 5451, 5502, 5701 and 5703.5, Labor Code.

History: 1. New section filed 4-25-91; operative 4-25-91 (Register 91, No. 26). New section is exempt from review by OAL pursuant to Government Code section 11351.

2. Amendment of section filed 1-28-94; operative 1-28-94. Submitted to OAL for printing only pursuant to Government Code section 11351 (Register 94, No. 4).

3. Amendment of section heading and section filed 11-17-2008; operative 11-17-2008 pursuant to Government Code section 11343.4 (Register 2008, No. 47).

Ref.: Hanna §§ 32.01[3][d], [4], 32.05[1]–[6][b]; Herlick Handbook §§ 1.01[3][b], 6.04[4], [6], 14.4, 14.22.

§10166.1. Form (Request for Consultative Rating).

DWC-AD Form 104 (DEU)

[DWC-AD Form 104 (Rev. 11/2008) Not Reproduced]

NOTE: Form is available at no charge by downloading from the web at www.dir.ca.gov/dwc/forms.html or by requesting at 1-800-794-6900.

Note: Authority cited: Sections 133, 5307.3 and 5307.4, Labor Code. Reference: Sections 123.6, 123.7, 124, 5275, 5451, 5502, 5701 and 5703.5, Labor Code.

History: 1. New section filed 11-17-2008; operative 11-17-2008 pursuant to Government Code section 11343.4 (Register 2008, No. 47).

Ref.: Hanna §§ 32.01[3][d], [4], 32.05[1]–[6][b]; Herlick Handbook §§ 1.01[3][b], 14.4, 14.22.

§10167. Informal Ratings.

(a) An informal rating will be prepared by the Disability Evaluation Unit upon the request of the employee and/or his/her representative and the employer, or at the request of an Information and Assistance Officer providing the necessary information. Such requests shall be submitted on forms and in a manner prescribed by the administrative director. Informal ratings shall be issued only in those instances where an Application for Adjudication of Claim has not been filed with the appeals board. All medical reports pertaining to the case must be submitted with the request.

(b) The Disability Evaluation Unit will issue the informal rating, which will contain a statement that the informal rating is not: a) a finding, award, order or decision of the appeals board, and b) evidence as to the existence of the factors of disability.

(c) Where the informal rating indicates a life pension, or provision for future medical treatment appears indicated, the Disability Evaluation Unit will forward a copy of the rating to an Information and Assistance Officer for the purpose of obtaining a stipulated award, or other action as may be appropriate.

(d) Self-ratings prepared by the employer are not acceptable substitutes for informal ratings prepared by the Disability Evaluation Unit.

Note: Authority cited: Sections 133 and 5307.3, Labor Code. Reference: Section 4061, Labor Code.

History: 1. New section filed 12-27-96; operative 12-27-96. Submitted to OAL for printing only pursuant to Government Code section 11351 (Register 96, No. 52).

2. Amendment filed 11-17-2008; operative 11-17-2008 pursuant to Government Code section 11343.4 (Register 2008, No. 47).

Ref.: Hanna §§ 23.04, 31.10[2], 32.01[3][d], [4], 32.05[1]–[6][b]; Herlick Handbook §§ 1.01[3][b], 6.04[4], 14.4, 14.22.

§10168. Records, Destruction of. [Repealed]

Note: Authority cited: Sections 133, 135 and 5307.3, Labor Code. Reference: Sections 135 and 4061, Labor Code; and Section 14755, Government Code.

History: 1. New section filed 4-25-91; operative 4-25-91 (Register 91, No. 26). New section is exempt from review by OAL pursuant to Government Code section 11351.

2. Amendment filed 3-27-95; operative 3-27-95. Submitted to OAL for printing only pursuant to Government Code section 11351 (Register 95, No. 13).

3. Amendment of section and Note filed 12-27-96; operative 12-27-96. Submitted to OAL for printing only pursuant to Government Code section 11351 (Register 96, No. 52).

4. Repealer filed 11-17-2008; operative 11-17-2008 pursuant to Government Code section 11343.4 (Register 2008, No. 47).

§10169. Commutation Tables and Instructions.

Table 1 ("Present Value of Permanent Disability at 3% Interest") as issued in January 2001, Table 2 ("Present Value of Life Pension at 3% Interest for a Male") as issued in July 2001, Table 3 ("Present Value of Life Pension at 3% Interest for a Female") as issued in July 2001, and "Commutation Instructions" as issued in January 2001, are hereby incorporated by reference in their entirety as though they were set forth below. The tables and instructions are available from any office of the Division of Workers' Compensation and may be accessed and printed from the Division's homepage at www.dir.ca.gov.

Note: Authority cited: Sections 133, 5100, 5101, 5307.3 and 5307.4, Labor Code. Reference: Sections 5100 and 5101, Labor Code.

History: 1. New section filed 1-17-2001; operative 1-17-2001 pursuant to Government Code section 11343.4(c) (Register 2001, No. 3).

2. Change without regulatory effect amending section filed 7-18-2001 pursuant to section 100, title 1, California Code of Regulations (Register 2001, No. 29).

Ref.: Hanna §§ 9.03[4], 27.02[6]; Herlick Handbook §§ 1.01[3][b], 6.13[3].

§10169.1. Commutation of Life Pension and Permanent Disability Benefits.

(a) Determinations of the present value of a life pension under Labor Code Section 5101(b) shall be made in accordance with the Commutation Instructions contained in Section 10169, and shall be based on the actuarial data contained in Section 10169, Table 2 ("Present Value of Life Pension at 3% Interest for a Male") or Table 3 ("Present Value of Life Pension at 3% Interest for a Female").

(b) Determinations of the present value of permanent disability indemnity under Labor Code Section 5101(b) shall be made in accordance with the Commutation Instructions contained in Section 10169, and shall be based on the actuarial data contained in Section 10169, Table 1 ("Present Value of Permanent Disability at 3% Interest").

(c) The Administrative Director shall periodically revise Tables 2 and 3 of Section 10169 to incorporate revisions to the "U. S. Life Tables" and "Actuarial Tables Based On The U.S. Life Tables" issued by the United States government following each decennial census.

Note: Authority cited: Sections 133, 5100, 5101, and 5307.3, and 5307.4, Labor Code. Reference: Sections 5100, 5100.5, 5100.6, 5101, Labor Code.

History: 1. New section filed 1-17-2001; operative 1-17-2001 pursuant to Government Code section 11343.4(c) (Register 2001, No. 3).

Ref.: Hanna §§ 9.03[4], 27.02[6]; Herlick Handbook §§ 1.01[3][b], 6.13[2], [3].

SUBCHAPTER 1.7 [Repealed]

§10175. Definitions. [Repealed]

Note: Authority cited: Sections 133, 4612 and 5307.3, Labor Code. Reference: Section 4612, Labor Code.

History: 1. New subchapter 1.7 and section filed 8-31-93; operative 8-31-93. Submitted to OAL for printing only pursuant to Government Code section 11351 (Register 93, No. 36).

2. Change without regulatory effect repealing subchapter 1.7 (sections 10175-10181) and section filed 11-6-2019 pursuant to section 100, title 1, California Code of Regulations (Register 2019, No. 45).

§10176. Eligible Employers and Employees. [Repealed]

Note: Authority cited: Sections 133, 4612 and 5307.3, Labor Code. Reference: Section 4612, Labor Code.

History: 1. New section filed 8-31-93; operative 8-31-93. Submitted to OAL for printing only pursuant to Government Code section 11351 (Register 93, No. 36).

2. Change without regulatory effect repealing section filed 11-6-2019 pursuant to section 100, title 1, California Code of Regulations (Register 2019, No. 45).

§10177. Eligible Applicants. [Repealed]

Note: Authority cited: Sections 133, 4612 and 5307.3, Labor Code. Reference: Section 4612, Labor Code.

History: 1. New section filed 8-31-93; operative 8-31-93. Submitted to OAL for printing only pursuant to Government Code section 11351 (Register 93, No. 36).

2. Change without regulatory effect repealing section filed 11-6-2019 pursuant to section 100, title 1, California Code of Regulations (Register 2019, No. 45).

§10178. Pilot Project Proposal Requirements. [Repealed]

Note: Authority cited: Sections 133, 4612 and 5307.3, Labor Code. Reference: Section 4612, Labor Code.

History: 1. New section filed 8-31-93; operative 8-31-93. Submitted to OAL for printing only pursuant to Government Code section 11351 (Register 93, No. 36).

2. Change without regulatory effect repealing section filed 11-6-2019 pursuant to section 100, title 1, California Code of Regulations (Register 2019, No. 45).

§10179. Selection of Proposals; Priorities; Pilot Termination. [Repealed]

Note: Authority cited: Sections 133, 4612 and 5307.3, Labor Code. Reference: Section 4612, Labor Code.

History: 1. New section filed 8-31-93; operative 8-31-93. Submitted to OAL for printing only pursuant to Government Code section 11351 (Register 93, No. 36).

2. Amendment of section heading and subsection (c) filed 10-11-94; operative 10-11-94. Submitted to OAL for printing only pursuant to Government Code section 11351 (Register 94, No. 41).

3. Change without regulatory effect repealing section filed 11-6-2019 pursuant to section 100, title 1, California Code of Regulations (Register 2019, No. 45).

§10180. Employee Choice of Plans. [Repealed]

Note: Authority cited: Sections 133, 4612 and 5307.3, Labor Code. Reference: Section 4612, Labor Code.

History: 1. New section filed 8-31-93; operative 8-31-93. Submitted to OAL for printing only pursuant to Government Code section 11351 (Register 93, No. 36).

2. Change without regulatory effect repealing section filed 11-6-2019 pursuant to section 100, title 1, California Code of Regulations (Register 2019, No. 45).

§10181. Records, Claims Administration, Auditing, and Termination. [Repealed]

Note: Authority cited: Sections 133, 4612 and 5307.3, Labor Code. Reference: Sections 3700, 4612, 5300, 6409 and 6409.1, Labor Code.

History: 1. New section filed 8-31-93; operative 8-31-93. Submitted to OAL for printing only pursuant to Government Code section 11351 (Register 93, No. 36).

2. Change without regulatory effect repealing section filed 11-6-2019 pursuant to section 100, title 1, California Code of Regulations (Register 2019, No. 45).

SUBCHAPTER 1.8 COLLECTIVE BARGAINING AGREEMENTS UNDER LABOR CODE SECTIONS 3201.5 AND 3201.7

§10200. Definitions.

As used in this subchapter:

(a) "Employee" means an employee covered under either:

(1) A provision of a collective bargaining agreement recognized by the Administrative Director pursuant to Labor Code section 3201.5; or

(2) A labor-management agreement recognized by the Administrative Director pursuant to Labor Code section 3201.7.

(b) "Employer" means either:

(1) For the purpose of Labor Code section 3201.5, a private employer or group of employers actually engaged

in construction, construction maintenance, or activities limited to rock, sand, gravel, cement and asphalt operations, heavy-duty mechanics, surveying, and construction inspection in California. A public entity may be a member of a group of employers.

(2) For the purpose of Labor Code section 3201.7, a private employer, group of employers, or a city or county that is self-insured in compliance with Labor Code section 3700.

(c) "Labor-management agreement" under Labor Code section 3201.7 (or 3201.7 provision) means a provision, clause, addendum, or other section of a collective bargaining agreement that establishes or would establish any program permitted under Labor Code section 3201.7(a). Such a program shall be maintained solely for the purpose of complying with the requirements of Division 4 the Labor Code and shall be administered separately from any other employee benefit plan.

(d) "Provision of a collective bargaining agreement" under Labor Code section 3201.5 (or "3201.5 provision") means a provision, clause, addendum, or other section of a collective bargaining agreement that establishes or would establish any program permitted under Labor Code section 3201.5(a). Such a program shall be maintained solely for the purpose of complying with the requirements of Division 4 the Labor Code and shall be administered separately from any other employee benefit plan.

(e) "Union" means a bona fide labor organization that is the recognized or certified exclusive bargaining representative of the employees of an employer. A labor organization is bona fide under this regulation if:

(1) it actually represents employees in California as to wages, hours and working conditions,

(2) its officers have been elected by secret ballot or otherwise in a manner consistent with federal law, and

(3) it is free of domination or interference by any employer and has received no improper assistance or support from any employer.

Note: Authority cited: Sections 133, 3201.5 and 5307.3, Labor Code. Reference: Sections 3201.5 and 3201.7, Labor Code.

History: 1. New subchapter 1.8 and section filed 8-8-95; operative 8-8-95. Submitted to OAL for printing only pursuant to Government Code section 11351 (Register 95, No. 32).

2. Amendment of section and Note filed 4-22-2004 as an emergency; operative 4-22-2004 (Register 2004, No. 17). A Certificate of Compliance must be transmitted to OAL by 8-20-2004 or emergency language will be repealed by operation of law on the following day.

3. Certificate of Compliance as to 4-22-2004 order, including further amendment of section, transmitted to OAL 8-20-2004 and filed 10-4-2004 (Register 2004, No. 41).

Ref.: Herlick Handbook §§ 1.01[3][b], 3.4.

§10201. Procedure for Determining Eligibility Under Labor Code Section 3201.5.

(a) Every employer and union proposing to establish any program permitted by Labor Code section 3201.5 shall jointly request the Administrative Director to determine eligibility, as follows:

(1) Employers shall submit the following documents:

(A) Upon its original application and whenever it is renegotiated thereafter, a copy of the underlying collective bargaining agreement and the approximate number of employees who will be covered thereby. The collective bargaining agreement shall be complete, including side letters and all appendices and other documents referred to in the agreement that relate to the program permitted by Labor Code section 3201.5, including but not limited to trust agreements and agreements concerning providers. If the application is on behalf of a group of employers, the application shall clearly define the group and shall state whether all the members of the group are bound by the 3201.5 provision, or whether each member must individually agree to be bound.

(B) Upon its original application and annually thereafter, evidence of a valid and active license where that license is required by law as a condition of doing business in the state within the industries set forth in subdivision (a) of Section 3201.5.

(C) Upon its original application and annually thereafter, a statement signed under penalty of perjury, that no action has been taken by any administrative agency or court of the United States to invalidate the collective bargaining agreement.

(D) Upon its original application and annually thereafter, the name, address, and telephone number of the contact person of the employer.

(E) Upon its original application and annually thereafter, evidence that the employer is actually engaged in construction, construction maintenance, or activities limited to rock, sand, gravel, cement and asphalt operations, heavy-duty mechanics, surveying, or construction inspection in California, or has a plan for immediate engagement in one of those businesses.

(F) Upon its original application and annually thereafter, evidence that the employer:

(i) is developing or projecting an annual workers' compensation insurance premium, in California, of two hundred fifty thousand dollars ($250,000) or more, or has paid an annual workers' compensation insurance premium, in California, of two hundred fifty thousand dollars ($250,000) in at least one of the previous three years; or

(ii) is a group of employers engaged in a workers' compensation safety group complying with Sections 11656.6 and 11656.7 of the Insurance Code, and established pursuant to a joint labor management safety committee or committees, which develops or projects annual workers' compensation insurance premiums of two million dollars ($2,000,000) or more; or

(iii) is an employer or group of employers that is self-insured in compliance with Section 3700 that has projected annual workers' compensation costs that meet the requirements of, and that meet the other requirements of, paragraph (i) in the case of employers, or paragraph (ii) in the case of groups of employers; or

(iv) is an employer, who is properly signatory to a project agreement, and is covered by an owner or general contractor provided wrap-up insurance policy applicable to a single construction site that develops workers' compensation insurance premiums of two million dollars ($2,000,000) or more with respect to those employees covered by that wrap-up insurance policy.

Every member of a group of employers must maintain separately administered workers' compensation insurance or a self-insurance program distinct from all other types of insurance. Every member must maintain this insurance or self-insurance in one of the ways enumerated in Labor Code section 3700; but it is not necessary that all members maintain insurance or a self-insurance program in the same way. Every member must meet one of the minimum premium or cost requirements listed in paragraphs (i) through (iv) above.

(G) Upon its original application and annually thereafter a statement that it is able and willing to supply the data required by Labor Code section 3201.5(i).

(H) If the application is on behalf of a group of employers, evidence that:

(i) membership in the group is limited to employers that meet all the criteria of Labor Code section 3201.5 and these regulations;

(ii) the group shall, on behalf of its individual members, provide the data required by Labor Code section 3201.5(i);

(iii) the group shall maintain records of its membership satisfactory to the Administrative Director for the purpose of readily ascertaining the facts required by Section 10201(e)(3). Membership records shall include evidence of security for the payment of compensation for each member, including the insurance policy number, or a copy of the certificate of self-insurance issued pursuant to Labor Code section 3700. Membership records shall also include the approximate number of employees for each individual member of the group who is bound by the collective bargaining agreement. Copies of membership records shall be delivered to the Administrative Director on request.

(2) Unions shall submit the following documents:

(A) Upon its original application and annually thereafter, a copy of its most recent LM-2 or LM-3 filing with the United States Department of Labor, along with a statement, signed under penalty of perjury, that the document is a true and correct copy.

(B) Upon its original application and annually thereafter, the name, address, and telephone number of the contact person or persons of the collective bargaining representative or representatives.

(C) Upon its original application and annually thereafter evidence that the union is a bona fide labor organization in that:

(i) it actually represents employees engaged in construction, construction maintenance, or activities limited to rock, sand, gravel, cement and asphalt operations, heavy-duty mechanics, surveying, and construction inspection in California as to wages, hours and working conditions,

(ii) its officers have been elected by secret ballot or otherwise in a manner consistent with federal law, and

(iii) it is free of domination or interference of any employer and has received no improper assistance or support from any employer.

It will be presumed that a union is bona fide if for a period of five years it has actually entered into collective bargaining agreements with employers in California and has filed all appropriate reports with the United States Department of Labor in that period. If a union is not presumed to be bona fide, it shall present evidence satisfactory to the Administrative Director that it meets the criteria of a bona fide labor organization.

(3) Any person may submit documents to the Administrative Director that bear on the eligibility of an applicant. Copies of all such documents received shall be sent to the applicants for comment.

(b) [Reserved for regulation relating to confidentiality]

(c) Issuance of a Letter of Eligibility

Within 30 days after receiving an application, the Administrative Director shall notify the applicants that the application is complete or shall specify what further information is needed to complete the application. Within 30 days after the time an application is completed, the Administrative Director shall either (1) issue a letter of eligibility, or (2) deny eligibility. If eligibility is denied, the Administrative Director shall inform the parties of the reasons therefor. For good cause and upon written notice to the applicants, the Administrative Director may extend the periods of notification for an additional 30 days.

(d) Period of Eligibility

The letter of eligibility shall state the beginning date of eligibility, which shall be no earlier than 15 days before the parties submitted their request to the Administrative Director under this section. A letter of eligibility shall remain valid for the same period as the 3201.5 provision of the collective bargaining agreement, but no longer then three years from the date of issuance of the letter. Upon the effective date of this regulation, the Administrative Director shall re-issue letters of eligibility to parties which have already received them.

(e) Effect of a Letter of Eligibility

(1) A letter of eligibility is a determination by the Administrative Director that the parties meet the eligibility requirements of Labor Code section 3201.5. A letter of eligibility is not a determination by the Administrative Director that the collective bargaining agreement or any part of it is in compliance with Labor Code section 3201.5.

(2) A 3201.5 provision is valid and binding only if there was a letter of eligibility in effect at the time of injury.

(3) A letter of eligibility issued to a group of employers shall be valid as to an individual member of the group if all the following facts are established as of the time the provision is alleged to be in effect and at the time of injury:

(A) the group of employers possessed a current letter of eligibility;

(B) the individual employer was a member of the group;

(C) the individual employer had signed the 3201.5 provision;

(D) the individual employer was actually engaged in construction, construction maintenance, or activities limited to rock, sand, gravel, cement and asphalt operations, heavy-duty mechanics, surveying, or construction inspection in California and possesses a valid and active license as required by Labor Code section 3201.5(a); and

(E) the individual employer was is compliance with Labor Code section 3201.5(c).

(f) Renewal of Eligibility

(1) At least 30 days prior to the expiration of the letter of eligibility, the parties shall submit to the Administrative Director updated copies of the documents and other evidence required by subdivision (a) of this Section. However, if certain documents and other evidence are completely unchanged since the submission of the previous annual

report required by Section 10204, the party responsible for submitting the updates may instead submit a statement under penalty of perjury that there has been no change in the document or evidence since the previous annual report. The Administrative Director may nonetheless require any party to submit the actual documents or evidence.

(2) Within 30 days after receiving the information required under subdivision (f)(1), the Administrative Director shall either: (1) renew the letter of eligibility for the same period of time set forth in subdivision (d); or (2) deny eligibility. If eligibility is denied, the Administrative Director shall inform the parties of the reasons therefor.

(g) All insurers, self-insured employers, and third party administrators who adjust claims subject to a Section 3201.5 provision shall comply with the applicable provisions of Section 138.4 of the Labor Code and shall comply with the administrative regulations contained in Title 8, Cal. Code Regs., Division 1, Chapter 4.5:

(1) Subchapter 1: Article 1.1, commencing with Section 9700; Article 5, commencing with Section 9780; Article 6, commencing with Section 9796; Article 8, commencing with Section 9810; Article 8.5, commencing with Section 9880; Article 10, commencing with Section 9900;

(2) Subchapter 1.5: Article 1, commencing with Section 10100; Article 2, commencing with Section 10101; Article 3, commencing with Section 10105; Article 4, commencing with Section 10110; Article 5, commencing with Section 10111; Article 6, commencing with Section 10113; Article 7, commencing with Section 10115; Article 6, commencing with Section 10116; Article 7, commencing with Section 10122; and,

(3) Subchapter 1.6, commencing with Section 10150.

Note: Authority cited: Sections 133, 3201.5 and 5307.3, Labor Code. Reference: Section 3201.5, Labor Code.

History: 1. New section filed 8-8-95; operative 8-8-95. Submitted to OAL for printing only pursuant to Government Code section 11351 (Register 95, No. 32).

2. Amendment filed 4-22-2004 as an emergency; operative 4-22-2004 (Register 2004, No. 17). A Certificate of Compliance must be transmitted to OAL by 8-20-2004 or emergency language will be repealed by operation of law on the following day.

3. Certificate of Compliance as to 4-22-2004 order, including further amendment of section, transmitted to OAL 8-20-2004 and filed 10-4-2004 (Register 2004, No. 41).

Ref.: Hanna § 1.04[4]; Herlick Handbook §§ 1.01[3][b], 3.4.

§10202. Procedure for Recognizing Labor-Management Agreements Under Labor Code Section 3201.7.

(a) Any union in an industry not covered by Labor Code section 3201.5 who seeks to negotiate a 3201.7 provision with an employer shall file a petition with the Administrative Director, verified under penalty of perjury, on the "Petition for Permission to Negotiate a Section 3201.7 Labor-Management Agreement" form (DWC Form RGS-1), contained in Section 10202.1. A proof of service by mail declaration shall be attached to the petition indicating that the complete petition, including all attachments, was served on the employer, or group of employers.

(b) Within 10 days after receiving a petition, the Administrative Director shall notify the union that the petition is complete or shall specify what further information is needed to complete the petition. Within 30 days after the time the petition is completed, the Administrative Director shall either (1) issue to the union and employer, or group of employers, a letter of eligibility to negotiate a 3201.7 provision, or (2) deny the petition. If the petition is denied, the Administrative Director shall inform the union of the reasons therefor. For good cause and upon written notice to the union, the Administrative Director may extend the periods of notification for an additional 30 days.

(c) The letter of eligibility to negotiate shall remain valid for a period not to exceed one year from the date of issuance. Upon joint request by the union and the employer, or group of employers, an additional one year period to negotiate a 3201.7 agreement shall be granted.

(d) Upon receipt of the letter of eligibility to negotiate, the union and employer, or group of employers, may negotiate a 3201.7 provision. A negotiated and signed 3201.7 provision between a union and employer, or group of employers, will be recognized by the Department of Industrial Relations as valid and binding upon application by the parties to the Administrative Director.

(1) The employer, or group of employers, shall submit the following documents with the application:

(A) Upon its original application and whenever it is renegotiated thereafter, a copy of the 3201.7 provision, and the approximate number of employees who will be covered thereby. If the application is on behalf of a group of employers, the application shall clearly define the group and shall state whether all the members of the group are bound by the 3201.7 provision, or whether each member must individually agree to be bound.

(B) Upon its original application and annually thereafter, a statement signed under penalty of perjury, that no action has been taken by any administrative agency or court of the United States to invalidate the collective bargaining agreement.

(C) Upon its original application and annually thereafter, the name, address, and telephone number of the contact person of the employer, or group of employers.

(D) Upon its original application and annually thereafter, evidence of a valid and active license where that license is required by law as a condition of doing business in the state.

(E) Upon its original application and annually thereafter, evidence that the employer:

(i) is developing or projecting an annual workers' compensation insurance premium, in California, of fifty thousand dollars ($50,000) or more, and employing at least fifty (50) employees, or has paid an annual workers' compensation insurance premium, in California, of fifty thousand dollars ($50,000), and employing at least fifty (50) employees in at least one of the previous three years; or

(ii) is a group of employers engaged in a workers' compensation safety group complying with Sections 11656.6 and 11656.7 of the Insurance Code, and established pursuant to a joint labor management safety committee or committees, that develops or projects annual workers' compensation insurance premiums of five hundred thousand dollars ($500,000) or more; or

(iii) is an employer or group of employers, including cities and counties, that is self-insured in compliance with Labor Code section 3700 that has projected annual workers' compensation costs that meet the requirements of, and that meet the other requirements of, paragraph (i) in the case of employers, or paragraph (ii) in the case of groups of employers.

(F) Upon its original application and annually thereafter a statement that it is able and willing to supply the data required by Labor Code section 3201.7(h).

(G) If the application is on behalf of a group of employers, evidence that:

(i) membership in the group is limited to employers that meet all the criteria of Labor Code section 3201.7 and these regulations;

(ii) the group shall, on behalf of its individual members, provide the data required by Labor Code section 3201.7(h);

(iii) the group shall maintain records of its membership satisfactory to the Administrative Director for the purpose of readily ascertaining the facts required by subdivision (h) of the section. Membership records shall include evidence of security for the payment of compensation for each member, including the insurance policy number, or a copy of the certificate of self-insurance issued pursuant to Labor Code section 3700. Membership records shall also include the approximate number of employees for each individual member of the group who is bound by the collective bargaining agreement. Copies of membership records shall be delivered to the Administrative Director on request.

(2) Unions shall submit the following documents with the application:

(A) Upon its original application and annually thereafter, a copy of its most recent LM-2 or LM-3 filing with the United States Department of Labor, along with a statement, signed under penalty of perjury, that the document is a true and correct copy.

(B) Upon its original application and annually thereafter, the name, address, and telephone number of the contact person or persons of the collective bargaining representative or representatives.

(C) Upon its original application and annually thereafter evidence that the union is a bona fide labor organization in that:

(i) its officers have been elected by secret ballot or otherwise in a manner consistent with federal law, and

(ii) it is free of domination or interference of any employer and has received no improper assistance or support from any employer.

It will be presumed that a union is bona fide if for a period of five years it has actually entered into collective bargaining agreements with employers in California and has filed all appropriate reports with the United States Department of Labor in that period. If a union is not presumed to be bona fide, it shall present evidence satisfactory to the Administrative Director that it meets the criteria of a bona fide labor organization.

(e) Every member of a group of employers must maintain separately administered workers' compensation insurance or a self-insurance program distinct from all other types of insurance. Every member must maintain this insurance or self-insurance in one of the ways enumerated in Labor Code section 3700; but it is not necessary that all members maintain insurance or a self-insurance program in the same way. Every member must meet one of the minimum premium or cost requirements listed above in subdivision (d)(1)(E), paragraphs (i) through (iii).

(f) Any person may submit documents to the Administrative Director that bear on the application of the union and employer, or group of employers. Copies of all such documents received shall be sent to the union and employer, or group of employers, for comment.

(g) Within 30 days after receiving the application, the Administrative Director shall notify the union and employer, or group of employers, that the application is complete or shall specify what further information is needed to complete the application. Within 30 days after the time the application is completed, the Administrative Director shall either (1) issue to the union and employer, or group of employers, a letter recognizing the 3201.7 provision, or (2) deny the application. If the application is denied, the Administrative Director shall inform the union and employer, or group of employers, of the reasons therefor. For good cause and upon written notice to the union and employer, or group of employers, the Administrative Director may extend the periods of notification for an additional 30 days.

(h) The recognition of the Section 3201.7 provision is a determination by the Administrative Director that the parties meet the eligibility requirements of Labor Code section 3201.7. Recognition is not a determination by the Administrative Director that the 3201.7 agreement, or any part of it, is in compliance with Labor Code section 3201.7.

(1) A 3201.7 provision is valid and binding only if there was a complete application filed with the Administrative Director at the time of injury.

(2) A 3201.7 provision negotiated and signed by a group of employers shall be valid as to an individual member of the group if all the following facts are established as of the time the provision is alleged to be in effect and at the time of injury:

(A) the group of employers has a complete application filed with the Administrative Director;

(B) the individual employer was a member of the group;

(C) the individual employer had signed the 3201.7 provision;

(D) the individual employer was is compliance with Labor Code section 3201.7(c).

(i) All insurers, self-insured employers, and third party administrators who adjust claims subject to a Section 3201.7 provision shall comply with the applicable provisions of Section 138.4 of the Labor Code and the administrative regulations contained in Title 8, Cal. Code Regs., Division 1, Chapter 4.5:

(1) Subchapter 1: Article 1.1, commencing with Section 9700; Article 5, commencing with Section 9780; Article 6, commencing with Section 9796; Article 8, commencing with Section 9810; Article 8.5, commencing with Section 9880; Article 10, commencing with Section 9900;

(2) Subchapter 1.5: Article 1, commencing with Section 10100; Article 2, commencing with Section 10101; Article 3, commencing with Section 10105; Article 4,

commencing with Section 10110; Article 5, commencing with Section 10111; Article 6, commencing with Section 10113; Article 7, commencing with Section 10115; Article 6, commencing with Section 10116; Article 7, commencing with Section 10122; and,

(3) Subchapter 1.6, commencing with Section 10150.

Note: Authority cited: Sections 133 and 5307.3, Labor Code. Reference: Section 3201.7, Labor Code.

History: 1. New section filed 8-8-95; operative 8-8-95. Submitted to OAL for printing only pursuant to Government Code section 11351 (Register 95, No. 32).

2. Amendment of section heading, repealer and new section and amendment of Note filed 4-22-2004 as an emergency; operative 4-22-2004 (Register 2004, No. 17). A Certificate of Compliance must be transmitted to OAL by 8-20-2004 or emergency language will be repealed by operation of law on the following day.

3. Certificate of Compliance as to 4-22-2004 order, including further amendment of section, transmitted to OAL 8-20-2004 and filed 10-4-2004 (Register 2004, No. 41).

Ref.: Hanna §§ 1.04[4], 1.04A[1]; Herlick Handbook §§ 1.01[3][b], 3.4.

§10202.1. Petition for Permission to Negotiate a Section 3201.7 Labor-Management Agreement (DWC Form RGS-1).

[DWC Form RGS-1 (Rev. 4/2004) Not Reproduced]

NOTE: Form is available at no charge by downloading from the web at www.dir.ca.gov/dwc/forms.html or by requesting at 1-800-794-6900.

Note: Authority cited: Sections 133 and 5307.3, Labor Code. Reference: Section 3201.7, Labor Code.

History: 1. New section filed 4-22-2004 as an emergency; operative 4-22-2004 (Register 2004, No. 17). A Certificate of Compliance must be transmitted to OAL by 8-20-2004 or emergency language will be repealed by operation of law on the following day.

2. Certificate of Compliance as to 4-22-2004 order, including further amendment of section, transmitted to OAL 8-20-2004 and filed 10-4-2004 (Register 2004, No. 41).

Ref.: See Labor Code §3201.5; Hanna § 1.04A[1]; Herlick Handbook §§ 1.01[3][b], 14.4.

§10203. Reporting Data.

(a)(1) On or before March 31 of every year, every employer subject to either a 3201.5 or 3201.7 provision shall provide the information specified in subdivision (b) for the previous calendar year. For each claim with a date of injury on or after January 1, 2004, the information reported under subdivision (b)(8) through (16) in the first mandatory reporting year under subdivision (b)(8), shall also be updated annually thereafter for the following three calendar years.

(2) To provide the information required in subdivision (b), the employer shall either:

(A) Provide the information on a form prescribed by the administrative director, either DWC Form GV-1, as set forth in Section 10203.1, or DWC Form GV-2, as set forth in Section 10203.2; or

(B) Provide the administrative director with written authorization to collect the information from the appropriate claims administrator. If the administrative director is unable to obtain the information with the written authorization, the employer shall remain responsible for obtaining and submitting the information.

(3) Groups of employers shall report the information required by this section on behalf of its members. The information shall be reported as to every individual employer covered by the 3201.5 or 3201.7 provision. Groups shall also report aggregated figures for all employers in the group covered by the 3201.5 or 3201.7 provision.

(b) The report shall contain the following information:

(1) The name of the individual employer and the union.

(2) The principal business of the employer.

(3) The dates the 3201.5 or 3201.7 provision were in effect during the previous calendar year.

(4) The name of the insurer, if any, and the insurance policy number. If self-insured, the name and certificate number of the self-insured employer.

(5) The name, address and telephone number of any administrator, ombudsperson, mediator or arbitrator employed in an alternative dispute resolution system.

(6) Hours worked by covered employees, reported by trade or craft.

(7) Payroll in accordance with the rules of the Workers' Compensation Insurance Rating Bureau [WCIRB]. Payroll shall be reported by class code as set by the WCIRB.

(8) The number of claims filed in the previous calendar year pursuant to Labor Code section 5401. The claims shall be reported in the following categories:

A. The number of claims that were medical only. As to those claims, there shall also be a report on the total amount of paid costs and the total amount of incurred costs.

B. The number of claims that included a claim for indemnity. As to those claims, there shall also be a report on total amount of paid costs and total amount of incurred costs in each of the following categories: temporary disability, permanent disability, life pensions, death benefits, vocational rehabilitation, medical services, and medical-legal expenses.

(9) The number of claims filed pursuant to Labor Code section 5401 in the previous calendar year that were resolved and the number that remained unresolved on December 31 of the previous calendar year. These numbers together should equal the total number reported in subdivision (b)(8). For the purpose of this section, "resolved" means one in which ultimate liability has been determined, even though payments may be made beyond the reporting period.

(10) Of the claims that were filed and/or resolved in the previous calendar year, the number that were resolved with a denial of compensability.

(11) Of the claims that were filed and/or resolved in the previous calendar year, the number that were resolved at each of the following stages: before mediation, at or after mediation, at or after arbitration, at or after the appeals board, or at or after the court of appeals. If the 3201.5 or 3201.7 provision contains another dispute resolution procedure, whether instead of or in addition to arbitration or mediation, the report must identify the type of procedure, its stage in the overall alternate dispute resolution process,

and the same respective information regarding the resolution of claims.

(12) The title and case number of every application filed with the appeals board in the previous calendar year concerning a claim alleged by any party to fall within the 3201.5 or 3201.7 provision, regardless of whether the employee had the right to file such an application.

(13) The title and court number of every civil action, including petitions for writs and injunctions in any court, state or federal, filed in the previous calendar year, that concerned a claim alleged by any party to fall within the 3201.5 or 3201.7 provision.

(14) The number of injuries and illnesses reported on the United States Department of Labor OSHA Form No. 300 for those employees covered by the 3201.5 or 3201.7 provision. The same number multiplied by 200,000 and divided by hours worked (as reported in subdivision (b)(6)).

(15) The number of employees covered by the 3201.5 or 3201.7 provision who participated in vocational rehabilitation.

(16) If the 3201.5 or 3201.7 provision established a light-duty or return to work program, the number of employees who participated in that program.

(17) For employers covered by a 3201.7 provision, an employee survey that measures worker satisfaction with the 3201.7 alternative dispute resolution procedures. The survey shall be designed and administered by agreement between the employer and the union.

(c) In addition to the data above, the employer may include in its report any explanatory material, narrative account, or comment that the employer believes is necessary to understand the data.

(d) Notwithstanding this section, all employers shall be subject to the reporting requirements of the Workers' Compensation Information System, Title 8, Cal. Code Regs., Section 9700 et seq.

(e) The data obtained by the Administrative Director pursuant to Section 10203 shall be confidential and not subject to public disclosure under any law of this state. However, the Division of Workers' Compensation may create derivative works based on the collective bargaining agreements and data. Those derivative works shall not be confidential, but shall be public.

Note: Authority: Sections 133, 3201.5 and 5307.3, Labor Code. Reference: Sections 3201.5, 3201.7 and 3201.9, Labor Code.

History: 1. New section filed 2-14-96; operative 2-14-96. Submitted to OAL for printing only pursuant to Government Code section 11351 (Register 96, No. 7).

2. Amendment of subsections (a)(1), (b)3., (b)8., (b)9.-11. and (b)13.-15. filed 12-27-96; operative 12-27-96. Submitted to OAL for printing only pursuant to Government Code section 11351 (Register 96, No. 52).

3. Amendment of section and Note filed 4-22-2004 as an emergency; operative 4-22-2004 (Register 2004, No. 17). A Certificate of Compliance must be transmitted to OAL by 8-20-2004 or emergency language will be repealed by operation of law on the following day.

4. Certificate of Compliance as to 4-22-2004 order, including further amendment of section, transmitted to OAL 8-20-2004 and filed 10-4-2004 (Register 2004, No 41).

Ref.: Hanna § 1.04[4]; Herlick Handbook §§ 1.01[3][b], 3.4.

§10203.1. Aggregate Employer Annual Report (DWC Form GV-1).

STATE OF CALIFORNIA
Department of Industrial Relations
Division of Workers' Compensation
Administrative Director
Post Office Box 420603
San Francisco, CA 94142
Telephone: (415) 703-4600

Aggregate Employer Annual Report

Labor Code §§ 3201.5 and 3201.7; Title 8, California Code of Regulations § 10203

For the 12 month period ending December 31, 20_____.

The following information is being obtained by the Administrative Director pursuant to Labor Code §§ 3201.5 and 3201.7, and Title 8, California Code of Regulations Section 10203. This form shall be filed on or before March 31 of every year by every employer or group of employers participating in a "carve-out" program under Labor Code §§3201.5 or 3201.7. The information provided on this form shall be for the 12 month period ending December 31 of the previous calendar year. The information shall be confidential and not subject to public disclosure under any law of this state. However, the Division of Workers' Compensation may create derivative works based on collective bargaining agreements and data. Those derivative works shall not be confidential, but shall be public.

For groups of employers that have received an above-referenced letter of eligibility, information obtained from individual employers to provide the information required in this form shall be maintained by the administrator of the Section 3201.5 or 3201.7 program, or the contact person or persons identified in Title 8, California Code of Regulations § 10201(a)(1)(D) and (2)(B), or § 10202(d)(1)(C) and (2)(B). This information may be obtained using the form entitled "Individual Employer Reporting Data" (Contained in Title 8, California Code of Regulations §10203.2.) Such information shall be available for inspection by the Administrative Director upon reasonable written request.

Name of Program:

Statute Authorizing Program (circle one): 3201.5 – Construction 3201.7 – Other

1. List all employers with FEIN numbers (Federal Employers Identification Numbers) doing business under the Section 3201.5 or 3201.7 agreement. If you need more space, use separate pages.

Name:
FEIN:
Principal business of employer (please circle one or more):

3201.5: construction construction maintenance rock, sand, gravel, cement and asphalt operations heavy-duty mechanics surveying construction inspection
3201.7: education and health services financial activities government information leisure and hospitality manufacturing natural resources and mining professional and business services transportation and utilities wholesale and retail trade other (specify)

Name:
FEIN:
Principal business of employer (please circle one or more):

3201.5: construction construction maintenance rock, sand, gravel, cement and asphalt operations heavy-duty mechanics surveying construction inspection
3201.7: education and health services financial activities government information leisure and hospitality manufacturing natural resources and mining professional and business services transportation and utilities wholesale and retail trade other (specify)

Name:
FEIN:
Principal business of employer (please circle one or more):

3201.5: construction construction maintenance rock, sand, gravel, cement and asphalt operations heavy-duty mechanics surveying construction inspection
3201.7: education and health services financial activities government information leisure and hospitality manufacturing natural resources and mining professional and business services transportation and utilities wholesale and retail trade other (specify)

Name:
FEIN:
Principal business of employer (please circle one or more):

3201.5: construction construction maintenance rock, sand, gravel, cement and asphalt operations heavy-duty mechanics surveying construction inspection
3201.7: education and health services financial activities government information leisure and hospitality manufacturing natural resources and mining professional and business services transportation and utilities wholesale and retail trade other (specify)

Name:
FEIN:
Principal business of employer (please circle one or more):

3201.5: construction construction maintenance rock, sand, gravel, cement and asphalt operations heavy-duty mechanics surveying construction inspection
3201.7: education and health services financial activities government information leisure and hospitality manufacturing natural resources and mining professional and business services transportation and utilities wholesale and retail trade other (specify)

2. Name(s) of union(s) participating in the Section 3201.5 or 3201.7 agreement:

3. Dates that the Section 3201.5 or 3201.7 provision was in effect during the previous calendar year:
Beginning date: Ending date:

4. Name of insurer(s):

5. Insurance policy number(s):

5a. If an employer is legally self-insured under authority of the Department of Industrial Relations' Office of Self-Insurance Plans, list certificate number and name:

6. Name of administrator of ADR system:

7. Address of administrator:

8. Telephone number of administrator: ( )

9. Name of ombudsperson employed in an ADR system (if any).

10. Address of ombudsperson:

11. Telephone number of ombudsperson: ( )
(Note: If there is more than one ombudsperson, attach additional sheets with the required information).

12. Name of mediator employed in an ADR system (if any):

13. Address of mediator:

14. Telephone number of mediator: ( )
(Note: If there is more than one mediator, attach additional sheets with the required information).

15. Name of arbitrator employed in an ADR system (if any):

16. Address of arbitrator:

17. Telephone number of arbitrator: ( )
(Note: If there is more than one arbitrator, attach additional sheets with the required information).

18. Total person hours worked by covered employees, indicate by trade or craft:

Trade:	Person Hours:
Trade:	Person Hours:
Trade:	Person Hours:
Trade:	Person Hours:
Trade:	Person Hours:
Trade:	Person Hours:
Trade:	Person Hours:
Trade:	Person Hours:
Trade:	Person Hours:
Trade:	Person Hours:

(Note: If there are more trades represented, attach additional sheets with the required information on person hours worked.)

19. Attach payroll for the employer(s) in accordance with the rules of the Workers' Compensation Insurance Rating Bureau (WCIRB). Payroll shall be reported by class code as set by the WCIRB and provided in table format.

Questions 20 through 45 apply to claims filed in the previous calendar year pursuant to Labor Code §§ 5401 or 5402. For claims with a date of injury on or after January 1, 2003, the information reported shall be for the year in which the claim was filed, and the subsequent calendar years until the claim is resolved. However, information from no more than four calendar years (including the year the claim was filed) shall be reported on each claim.

20. Number of claims that were medical only:
21. Total amount of paid costs for medical only claims:
22. Total amount of incurred costs for medical only claims:
23. Number of claims that included a claim for indemnity:
24. Total amount of paid temporary disability for indemnity claims:
25. Total amount of incurred temporary disability for indemnity claims:
26. Total amount of paid permanent disability for indemnity claims:
27. Total amount of incurred permanent disability for indemnity claims:
28. Total amount of paid life pensions for indemnity claims:
29. Total amount of incurred life pensions for indemnity claims:
30. Total amount of paid death benefits for indemnity claims:
31. Total amount of incurred death benefits for indemnity claims:
32. Total amount of paid vocational rehabilitation for indemnity claims:
33. Total amount of incurred vocational rehabilitation for indemnity claims:
34. Total amount of paid medical services for indemnity claims:
35. Total amount of incurred medical services for indemnity claims:
36. Total amount of paid medical legal expenses for indemnity claims:
37. Total amount of incurred medical legal expenses for indemnity claims:
38. Number of claims that were resolved (resolved means one in which ultimate liability has been determined, even though payments may be made beyond the reporting period):
39. Number of claims that remained unresolved:

Note: The numbers in questions 38 and 39 added together should equal the summation of the number of medical only claims (question 20) and indemnity claims (question 23).

40. The number of claims that were resolved with a denial of compensability:
41. The number of claims that were resolved before mediation:
42. The number of claims that were resolved at or after mediation:
43. The number of claims that were resolved at or after arbitration.

Note: For employers, or group of employers, who utilize an alternative dispute resolution system that includes resolution procedures in addition to or in place of mediation and/or arbitration, please identify on an attachment each resolution procedure used and the number of claims that were resolved using that procedure.

44. The number of claims that were resolved at or after the Workers' Compensation Appeals Board (WCAB):
45. The number of claims that were resolved at or after the court of appeals:
46. Provide the title and number of every application filed with the WCAB during the previous calendar year concerning the claim alleged by any party to fall within the Section 3201.5 or 3201.7 provision, regardless of whether the employee had the right to file such a application (example in italics):

Title:	*Jane Doe vs. ABC Co*	Number:	*SFO 0123456*
Title:		Number:	
Title:		Number:	
Title:		Number:	
Title:		Number:	
Title:		Number:	
Title:		Number:	

Note: If there are more applications, attach additional sheets with the required information.

47. Provide the title and court number of every civil action, including petitions for writs and injunctions in any court, state or federal, filed in the previous calendar year, that concerned a claim alleged by any party to fall within the Section 3201.5 or 3201.7 provision (example in italics):

Title:	*Jane Doe vs. ABC Co*	Number:	*Alameda County No 3 76052*
Title:		Number:	
Title:		Number:	
Title:		Number:	
Title:		Number:	
Title:		Number:	
Title:		Number:	
Title:		Number:	
Title:		Number:	

Title: Number:

Note: If there are more civil actions, attach additional sheets with the required information.

48. The number of injuries and illnesses reported in the previous calendar year on the United States Department of Labor OSHA Form No. 300 for those employees covered by the Section 3201.5 or 3201.7 provision:

49. The number of employees covered by the Section 3201.5 or 3201.7 provision who participated in vocational rehabilitation:

50. The number of employees covered by the Section 3201.5 or 3201.7 provision who participated in a light duty program or modified return to work programs established under Section 3201.5 or 3201.7:

51. For an employer, or group of employers, who is covered by a 3201.7 provision, please provide an employee survey that measures worker satisfaction with the applicable 3201.7 alternative dispute resolution procedures. The survey shall be designed and administered by agreement between the employer and the union.

52. Please attach any explanatory material, narrative account or comment that you believe would enable the Division to understand your response(s).

Programs are encouraged to submit updated information covering prior calendar year claims reported to Division of Workers' Compensation.

DWC Form GV-1 (012004)

Note: Authority cited: Sections 133, and 5307.3, Labor Code. Reference: Sections 3201.5, 3201.7, and 3201.9, Labor Code.

History: 1. New section filed 4-22-2004 as an emergency; operative 4-22-2004 (Register 2004, No. 17). A Certificate of Compliance must be transmitted to OAL by 8-20-2004 or emergency language will be repealed by operation of law on the following day.

2. Certificate of Compliance as to 4-22-2004 order, including further amendment of section, transmitted to OAL 8-20-2004 and filed 10-4-2004 (Register 2004, No. 41).

Ref.: Hanna § 1.04[4]; Herlick Handbook §§ 1.01[3][b], 14.4.

§10203.2. Individual Employer Annual Report (DWC Form GV-2).

STATE OF CALIFORNIA
Department of Industrial Relations
Division of Workers' Compensation
Administrative Director
Post Office Box 420603
San Francisco, CA 94142
Telephone: (415) 703-4600

Individual Employer Annual Report

Labor Code §§ 3201.5 and 3201.7; Title 8, California Code of Regulations § 10203

For the 12 month period ending December 31, 20______.

The following information is being obtained by the Administrative Director pursuant to Labor Code §§ 3201.5 and 3201.7, and Title 8, California Code of Regulations Section 10203. An individual employer who is participating in a Section 3201.5 or 3201.7 program with a group of employers shall provide the information requested in this form to the administrator of the Section 3201.5 or 3201.7 program, or the contact person or persons identified in Title 8, California Code of Regulations § 10201(a)(1)(D) and (2)(B) or §10202(d)(1)(C) or (2)(B). The information provided to the program shall be confidential and not subject to public disclosure under any law of this state. However, the Division of Workers' Compensation may create derivative works based on collective bargaining agreements and data. Those derivative works shall not be confidential, but shall be public. The information provided by the employer shall be maintained by the administrator of the program and is available for inspection by the Administrative Director upon reasonable written request.

Name of Program:
Statute Authorizing Program (circle one): 3201.5 – Construction 3201.7 – Other

1. Employer Information.
Name:
FEIN:
Principal business of employer (please circle one or more):

3201.5: construction operations construction maintenance heavy-duty mechanics rock, sand, gravel, surveying cement and asphalt construction inspection

3201.7: education and health services financial activities government information leisure and hospitality manufacturing natural resources and mining professional and business services transportation and utilities wholesale and retail trade other (specify)

2. Name of union participating in the Section 3201.5 or 3201.7 agreement:

3. Dates that the Section 3201.5 or 3201.7 provision was in effect during the previous calendar year:
Beginning date: Ending date:

4. Name of insurer:

5. Insurance policy number:

5a. If an employer is legally self-insured under authority of the Department of Industrial Relations' Office of Self-Insurance Plans, list certificate number and name:

6. Attach payroll in accordance with the rules of the Workers' Compensation Insurance Rating Bureau (WCIRB). Payroll shall be reported by class code as set by the WCIRB and provided in table format.

7. Total person hours worked by covered employees, indicate by trade or craft:

Trade: Person Hours:

Trade: Person Hours:

Trade: Person Hours:

(Note: If there are more trades represented, attach additional sheets with the required information on person hours worked.)

Questions 8 through 27 apply to claims filed in the previous calendar year pursuant to Labor Code §§ 5401 or 5402. For claims with a date of injury on or after January 1, 2003, the information reported shall be for the year in which the claim was filed, and the subsequent calendar years until the claim is resolved. However, information from no more than four calendar years (including the year the claim was filed) shall be reported on each claim.

8. Number of claims that were medical only:

9. Total amount of paid costs for medical only claims:

10. Total amount of incurred costs for medical only claims:
11. Number of claims that included a claim for indemnity:
12. Total amount of paid temporary disability for indemnity claims:
13. Total amount of incurred temporary disability for indemnity claims:
14. Total amount of paid permanent disability for indemnity claims:
15. Total amount of incurred permanent disability for indemnity claims:
16. Total amount of paid life pensions for indemnity claims:
17. Total amount of incurred life pensions for indemnity claims:
18. Total amount of paid death benefits for indemnity claims:
19. Total amount of incurred death benefits for indemnity claims:
20. Total amount of paid vocational rehabilitation for indemnity claims:
21. Total amount of incurred vocational rehabilitation for indemnity claims:
22. Total amount of paid medical services for indemnity claims:
23. Total amount of incurred medical services for indemnity claims:
24. Total amount of paid medical legal expenses for indemnity claims:
25. Total amount of incurred medical legal expenses for indemnity claims:
26. Number of claims that were resolved (resolved means one in which ultimate liability has been determined, even though payments may be made beyond the reporting period):
27. Number of claims that remained unresolved:

Note: The numbers in questions 26 and 27 added together should equal the summation of the number of medical only claims (question 8) and indemnity claims (question 11).

28. The number of claims that were resolved with a denial of compensability:
29. The number of claims that were resolved before mediation:
30. The number of claims that were resolved at or after mediation:
31. The number of claims that were resolved at or after arbitration.

Note: For employers who utilize a alternative dispute resolution system that includes resolution procedures in addition to or in place of mediation and/or arbitration, please identify on an attachment each resolution procedure used and the number of claims that were resolved using that procedure.

32. The number of claims that were resolved at or after the Workers' Compensation Appeals Board (WCAB):
33. The number of claims that were resolved at or after the court of appeals:
34. Provide the title and number of every application filed with the WCAB during the previous calendar year concerning the claim alleged by any party to fall within the Section 3201.5 or 3201.7 provision, regardless of whether the employee had the right to file such a application (example in italics):

Title: *Jane Doe vs. ABC Co* Number: *SFO 0123456*
Title: Number:

Note: If there are more applications, attach additional sheets with the required information.

35. Provide the title and court number of every civil action, including petitions for writs and injunctions in any court, state or federal, filed in the previous calendar year, that concerned a claim alleged by any party to fall within the Section 3201.5 or 3201.7 provision (example in italics):

Title: *Jane Doe vs. ABC Co* Number: *Alameda County No 3 76052*
Title: Number:

Note: If there are more civil actions, attach additional sheets with the required information.

36. The number of injuries and illnesses reported in the previous calendar year on the United States Department of Labor OSHA Form No. 300 for those employees covered by the Section 3201.5 or 3201.7 provision:
37. The number of employees covered by the Section 3201.5 or 3201.7 provision who participated in vocational rehabilitation:
38. The number of employees covered by the Section 3201.5 or 3201.7 provision who participated in a light duty program or modified return to work programs established under Section 3201.5 or 3201.7:
39. For an employer who is covered by a 3201.7 provision, please provide an employee survey that measures worker satisfaction with the applicable 3201.7 alternative dispute resolution procedures. The survey shall be designed and administered by agreement between the employer and the union.
40. Please attach any explanatory material, narrative account or comment that you believe would enable the Division to understand your response(s).

Programs are encouraged to submit updated information covering prior calendar year claims reported to Division of Workers' Compensation.

DWC Form GV-2 (012004)

Note: Authority cited: Sections 133 and 5307.3, Labor Code. Reference: Sections 3201.5, 3201.7 and 3201.9, Labor Code.

History: 1. New section filed 4-22-2004 as an emergency; operative 4-22-2004 (Register 2004, No. 17). A Certificate of Compliance must be transmitted to OAL by 8-20-2004 or emergency language will be repealed by operation of law on the following day.

2. Certificate of Compliance as to 4-22-2004 order, including further amendment of section, transmitted to OAL 8-20-2004 and filed 10-4-2004 (Register 2004, No. 41).

Ref.: Hanna § 1.04[4]; Herlick Handbook §§ 1.01[3][b], 14.4.

§10204. Annual Reports.

(a) On or before March 31 of every year, the parties covered by the 3201.5 or 3201.7 provision shall submit updated copies of the documents and other evidence required by Section 10201 or Section 10202. However, if certain documents and other evidence are completely unchanged since the previous submission, the party responsible for submitting the annual update may instead submit a statement under penalty of perjury that there has been no change in the document or evidence since the previous submission. The Administrative Director may nonetheless require any party to submit the actual documents or evidence.

(b) If the parties have not submitted the updated documents required by this section, or if the employer has not timely submitted the data required by Section 10203 the Administrative Director may, after notice and an opportunity to respond, either: (1) revoke a letter of eligibility issued pursuant to Labor Code section 3201.5; (2) revoke the recognition given to the labor-management agreement negotiated pursuant to Labor Code section 3201.7; or (3) take such other steps as he or she deems necessary to secure the parties' compliance with reporting requirements.

Note: Authority cited: Sections 133, 3201.5 and 5307.3, Labor Code. Reference: Sections 3201.5, 3201.7 and 3201.9, Labor Code.

History: 1. New section filed 8-8-95; operative 8-8-95. Submitted to OAL for printing only pursuant to Government Code section 11351 (Register 95, No. 32).

2. Amendment of subsection (a) filed 2-14-96; operative 2-14-96. Submitted to OAL for printing only pursuant to Government Code section 11351 (Register 96, No. 7).

3. Amendment of section and Note filed 4-22-2004 as an emergency; operative 4-22-2004 (Register 2004, No. 17). A Certificate of Compliance must be transmitted to OAL by 8-20-2004 or emergency language will be repealed by operation of law on the following day.

4. Certificate of Compliance as to 4-22-2004 order transmitted to OAL 8-20-2004 and filed 10-4-2004 (Register 2004, No. 41).

Ref.: Hanna § 1.04[4]; Herlick Handbook §§ 1.01[3][b], 3.4.

SUBCHAPTER 1.8.1 ADMINISTRATIVE DIRECTOR — OTHER ADMINISTRATIVE PENALTIES [RENUMBERED]

ARTICLE 1 Administrative Penalties Pursuant to Labor Code Section 5814.6 [Renumbered]

History: 1. Change without regulatory effect renumbering former subchapter 1.8.1, article 1 (sections 10225-10225.2) to subchapter 1.5, article 5.5 (sections 10112.1-10112.3) filed 4-7-2008 pursuant to section 100, title 1, California Code of Regulations (Register 2008, No. 15).

SUBCHAPTER 1.8.5 ELECTRONIC ADJUDICATION MANAGEMENT SYSTEM RULES

ARTICLE 1 Definitions and General Provisions

§10205. Definitions.

(a) "Adjudication file" or "ADJ file" means a case file in which the jurisdiction of the Workers' Compensation Appeals Board has been invoked and which is maintained by the Division of Workers' Compensation in paper format, or electronic format, or both, including a temporary paper case file.

(b) "Administrative director" means the administrative director of the Division of Workers' Compensation or his or her designee.

(c) "Appeals board" means the commissioners and deputy commissioners of the Workers' Compensation Appeals Board acting en banc, in panels, or individually.

(d) "Applicant" means any person asserting a right to relief under the provisions of Labor Code section 5300.

(e) "Application for adjudication" or "application" means the initial pleading that asserts a right to relief under the provisions of Labor Code section 5300.

(f) "Central Registration Unit" is a unit within the Division of Workers' Compensation which maintains the website list of uniform names and addresses of claims administrators' offices and representatives' offices.

(g) "Claims administrator's office" means any office location that administers workers' compensation claims.

(h) "Cost" means any claim for reimbursement of expense or payment of service that is not allowable as a lien against compensation under Labor Code section 4903. "Costs" include, but are not limited to:

(1) expenses and fees under Labor Code section 5710;

(2) costs under Labor Code section 5811 other than interpreter services rendered during a medical treatment appointment;

(3) any amount payable as a medical-legal expense under Labor Code section 4620 et seq.; and

(4) any amount payable under Labor Code section 4600 that would not be subject to a lien against the employee's compensation, including but not limited to any amount payable directly to the injured employee for reasonable transportation, meal, and lodging expenses and for temporary disability indemnity for each day of lost wages.

(i) "Declaration of readiness to proceed" or "declaration of readiness" means a request for a proceeding before the district office.

(j) "Declaration of readiness to proceed to expedited hearing" means a request for a proceeding before the district office pursuant to Labor Code section 5502(b).

(k) "Defendant" means any person against whom a right to relief is claimed.

(*l*) "District office" means a trial level workers' compensation court.

(m) "Document" is a pleading, petition, medical report, record, declaration, exhibit, or another filing submitted by a party or lien claimant, including an electronically scanned version of a document that was filed in paper form. Each medical report or other record having a different author and/or a different date of service is a separate "document."

(n) "Document cover sheet" means Form 10232.1, which is placed on top of a document or set of documents filed at one time in a specific case.

(o) "Document separator sheet" means Form 10232.2, which is placed on top of each individual document, when one or more documents are being filed at the same time in the same case and placed on top of each individual attachment to each document being filed, when a document has one or more attachments.

(p) "Electronic Adjudication Management System" or "EAMS" means the computerized case management system used by the Division of Workers' Compensation to store and maintain adjudication files and to perform other case management functions.

(q) "Electronic filing" means electronic transmission of a document into EAMS in accordance with the provision of these regulations.

(r) "Electronic signature" means a signature electronically affixed by a workers' compensation administrative law judge or by the appeals board to any decision, findings, award, order or other document.

(s) "Fax" means a document that has been electronically served by a fax machine.

(t) To "file" a document means to either deliver a document or cause it to be delivered to the district office with venue or to the appeals board for the purpose of having it included in the adjudication file or to electronically file a document via EAMS in accordance with these regulations.

(u) "Hearing" means any trial, mandatory settlement conference, rating mandatory settlement conference, status conference, lien conference, or priority conference.

(v) "Initial lien" means any Labor Code section 4903(b) lien filed in a case on or after the effective date of these regulations by a lien claimant who has not previously filed a lien in the same case.

(w) "Lien claimant" means any person claiming payment under the provisions of Labor Code section 4903 or 4903.1.

(x) "Lien conference" means a proceeding, including a proceeding following an order of consolidation, held in accordance with section 10770.1 for the purpose of assisting the parties in resolving disputed lien claims or claims of costs filed as liens or, if the dispute cannot be resolved, to frame the issues and stipulations and to list witnesses and exhibits in preparation for a lien trial.

(y) "Mandatory settlement conference" means a proceeding to assist the parties in resolving their dispute or, if the dispute cannot be resolved, to frame the issues and stipulations and to list witnesses and exhibits in preparation for a trial.

(z) "Optical character recognition form" or "OCR form" means a paper form designed to be scanned so that its information is automatically extracted and stored in EAMS.

(aa) "Party" means: (1) a person claiming to be an injured employee or the dependent of a deceased employee; (2) a defendant; (3) an appellant from an independent medical review or independent bill review decision or an injured employee or provider seeking to enforce such a decision; (4) an interpreter filing a petition for costs in accordance with section 10451.3; or (5) a lien claimant where either (A) the underlying case of the injured employee or the dependent(s) of a deceased employee has been resolved or (B) the injured employee or the dependent(s) of a deceased employee chooses not to proceed with his, her, or their case.

(bb) "Petition" means any document filed containing a request for action other than an application for adjudication, an answer or a declaration of readiness to proceed.

(cc) "Priority conference" means a proceeding in which the applicant is represented by an attorney and the issues in dispute at the time of the proceeding include employment and/or injury arising out of and in the course of employment.

(dd) "Product delivery unit" means the unit within the Division of Workers' Compensation. The units are abbreviated as follows: Adjudication Unit "ADJ"; Disability Evaluation Unit "DEU"; Subsequent Injuries Benefits Trust Fund "SIF"; Uninsured Employers' Benefits Trust Fund "UEF"; Vocational Rehabilitation "VOC"; and Retraining and Return to Work Unit "RSU". For each product delivery unit there is an area in EAMS in which the case management information related to that product delivery unit is stored. That area is called the "product delivery case." "INT" is the integrated case, which is the umbrella for the individual product delivery cases for each unit residing in EAMS.

(ee) "Rating mandatory settlement conference" means a mandatory settlement conference conducted to facilitate the determination of the existence and extent of permanent disability through the use of informal ratings issued by the Disability Evaluation Unit, where the only unresolved issues are permanent disability and the need for future medical treatment.

(ff) "Representative's office" means any office location for a law firm, lawyer or representative of a party or lien claimant in a workers' compensation case.

(gg) "Regular hearing" means a trial.

(hh) "Section 4903(b) lien" means a lien claim filed in accordance with Labor Code section 4903(b) for medical treatment expenses incurred by or on behalf of the injured employee, as provided by Article 2 (commencing with Labor Code section 4600), including but not limited to expenses for interpreter services, copying and related services, and transportation services incurred in connection with medical treatment. It shall not include any amount payable directly to the injured employee.

(ii) To "serve" a document means to personally deliver a copy of the document, or to send it in a manner permitted by these rules and the rules of the appeals board, to a party, lien claimant, or attorney who is entitled to a copy of the document.

(jj) "Status conference" means a proceeding set for the purpose of ascertaining if there are genuine disputes requiring resolution, of providing assistance to the parties in resolving disputes, of narrowing the issues, and of facilitating preparation for trial if a trial is necessary.

(kk) "Submission" means the closing of the record to the receipt of further evidence or argument.

(*ll*) "Trial" means a proceeding set for the purpose of receiving evidence.

(mm) "Venue" means the district office, as established by Labor Code section 5501.5 or 5501.6, at which any proceedings will be conducted and from which any district office orders, decisions, or awards will be issued.

(nn) "Workers' compensation administrative law judge" as defined in Labor Code section 123.7 includes pro tempore judges appointed pursuant to California Code of Regulations, title 8, section 10350.

Note: Authority cited: Sections 111, 133, 138.2(b), 4903.05, 4903.06 and 5307.3, Labor Code; and Stats. 2011, c. 559, §17 (A.B. 1426). Reference: Sections 110, 4903, 4903.05, 4903.06, 4903.1, 5300, 5404.5, 5500.3, 5501.5, 5501.6, 5502(b) and 5502(c), Labor Code.

History: 1. New subchapter 1.8.5 (articles 1–8, sections 10205–10208.12) and article 1 (sections 10205–10205.2) and renumbering of former section 10210 to new section 10205, including amendment of section and Note, filed 12-10-2012 as a change without regulatory effect pursuant to section 100, title 1, California Code of Regulations by the Division of Workers' Compensation and as a file and print by the Workers' Compensation Appeals Board pursuant to Government Code section 11351 (Register 2012, No. 50).

2. New subsections (h), (q), (v) and (hh)-(hh)(3), subsection relettering, amendment of newly designated subsections (t) and (aa) and amendment of Note filed 12-31-2012 as an emergency; operative 1-1-2013 pursuant to Government Code section 11346.1(d) (Register 2013, No. 1). A Certificate of Compliance must be transmitted to OAL by 7-1-2013 or emergency language will be repealed by operation of law on the following day.

3. New subsections (h), (q), (v) and (hh)-(hh)(3), subsection relettering, amendment of newly designated subsections (t) and (aa) and amendment of Note refiled 6-26-2013 as an emergency; operative 7-1-2013 pursuant to Government Code section 11346.1(d) (Register 2013, No. 26). A Certificate of Compliance must be transmitted to OAL by 9-30-2013 or emergency language will be repealed by operation of law on the following day.

4. New subsections (h), (q), (v) and (hh)-(hh)(3), subsection relettering, amendment of newly designated subsections (t) and (aa) and amendment of Note refiled 9-30-2013 as an emergency; operative 10-1-2013 pursuant to Government Code section 11346.1(d) (Register 2013, No. 40). A Certificate of Compliance must be transmitted to OAL by 12-30-2013 or emergency language will be repealed by operation of law on the following day.

5. Certificate of Compliance as to 9-30-2013 order, including further amendment of subsections (h), (x), (y), (aa) and (hh), transmitted to OAL 11-8-2013 and filed 12-16-2013; amendments effective 12-16-2013 pursuant to Government Code section 11343.4(b)(3) (Register 2013, No. 51).

Ref.: Hanna §§ 1.11[5][a]–[e], 1.12[9][b], 1.13[1]–[7], 23.11[2], [2a], 23.12[2]–[3d], 23.16, 24.11[1][c], 25.06A, 25.08, 25.09, 26.01[3], 26.02, 26.04, 33.01[1][b], [2], [3][b]–[d], [4], 35.72[3]; Herlick Handbook §§ 1.01[3][b], 1.03[1], 1.04, 5.20, 10.03[2], [4], 10.04[1], 10.09[1], 14.5A, 16.23.

§10205.1. District Office Records Not Subject to Subpoena.

(a) The records, files and proceedings of the district office shall not be taken from its offices either on informal request or in response to a subpoena duces tecum or any order issued out of any other court or tribunal. The records, files and proceedings of the district office shall not be produced pursuant a subpoena issued under Labor Code section 130.

(b) Certified copies of portions of the records shall be delivered upon payment of fees as provided in California Code of Regulations, title 8, section 9990.

Note: Authority cited: Sections 111, 133, 138.2(b) and 5307.3, Labor Code; and Stats. 2011, c. 559, §17 (A.B. 1426). Reference: Sections 130, 138.7 and 5955, Labor Code.

History: 1. Renumbering of former section 10212 to new section 10205.1, including amendment of Note, filed 12-10-2012 as a change without regulatory effect pursuant to section 100, title 1, California Code of Regulations by the Division of Workers' Compensation and as a file and print by the Workers' Compensation Appeals Board pursuant to Government Code section 11351 (Register 2012, No. 50).

Ref.: Hanna §§ 1.11[5][a]–[e], 1.12[9][b], 1.13[1]–[7], 23.11[2], [2a], 23.12[2]–[3d], 23.16, 24.11[1][c], 25.06A, 25.08, 25.09, 26.01[3], 26.02, 26.04, 33.01[1][b], [2], [3][b]–[d], [4], 35.72[3]; Herlick Handbook §§ 1.01[3][b], 5.20, 14.5A, 16.23.

§10205.2. Compromise and Release Forms and Stipulations with Request for Award Forms.

The following optical character recognition forms shall be used to settle case by either a compromise and release or stipulation with request for award.

(a) DWC-CA form 10214(a) (Stipulations with request for award) revision dated 11/2008 is incorporated by reference;

(b) DWC-CA form 10214(b) (Stipulations with request for award, death case) dated 11/2008 is incorporated by reference;

(c) DWC-CA form 10214(c) (Compromise and release) revision dated 11/2008 is incorporated by reference;

(d) DWC-CA form 10214(d) (Compromise and release, dependency claim) revision dated 11/2008 is incorporated by reference;

(e) DWC-CA form 10214(e) (Compromise and release, third party settlement) revision dated 11/2008 is incorporated by reference.

Note: Authority cited: Sections 111, 133, 138.2(b) and 5307.3, Labor Code; and Stats. 2011, c. 559, §17 (A.B. 1426). Reference: Sections 5002, 5003, 5004 and 5005, Labor Code.

History: 1. Renumbering of former section 10214 to new section 10205.2, including amendment of Note, filed 12-10-2012 as a change without regulatory effect pursuant to section 100, title 1, California Code of Regulations by the Division of Workers' Compensation and as a file and print by the Workers' Compensation Appeals Board pursuant to Government Code section 11351 (Register 2012, No. 50).

Ref.: Hanna §§ 1.11[5][a]–[e], 1.12[9][b], 1.13[1]–[7], 23.11[2], [2a], 23.12[2]–[3d], 23.16, 24.11[1][c], 25.06A, 25.08, 25.09, 26.01[3], 26.02, 26.04, 33.01[1][b], [2], [3][b]–[d], [4], 35.72[3]; Herlick Handbook §§ 1.01[3][b], 5.20, 14.5A, 16.23.

ARTICLE 1.2
Electronic Filing

§10205.3. Case Names and Case Index.

An index of all cases filed with a district office shall be maintained in EAMS under the name of the person claimed to have been injured or the identification assigned to that person, whether or not that person is an applicant. Reference to the case shall be by the name of the injured person and the case number.

Note: Authority cited: Sections 111, 133, 138.2(b) and 5307.3, Labor Code; and Stats. 2011, c. 559, §17 (A.B. 1426). Reference: Section 126, Labor Code.

History: 1. New article 2 (sections 10205.3–10205.9) and renumbering of former section 10215 to new section 10205.3, including amendment of Note, filed 12-10-2012 as a change without regulatory effect pursuant to section 100, title 1, California Code of Regulations by the Division of Workers' Compensation and as a file and print by the Workers' Compensation Appeals Board pursuant to Government Code section 11351 (Register 2012, No. 50).

2. Renumbering of article 2 to article 1.2 filed 12-31-2012 as an emergency; operative 1-1-2013 pursuant to Government Code section 11346.1(d) (Register 2013, No. 1). A Certificate of Compliance must be transmitted to OAL by 7-1-2013 or emergency language will be repealed by operation of law on the following day.

3. Amendment renumbering article 2 to article 1.2 refiled 6-26-2013 as an emergency; operative 7-1-2013 pursuant to Government Code section 11346.1(d) (Register 2013, No. 26). A Certificate of Compliance must be transmitted to OAL by 9-30-2013 or emergency language will be repealed by operation of law on the following day.

4. Amendment renumbering article 2 to article 1.2 refiled 9-30-2013 as an emergency; operative 10-1-2013 pursuant to Government Code section 11346.1(d) (Register 2013, No. 40). A Certificate of Compliance must be transmitted to OAL by 12-30-2013 or emergency language will be repealed by operation of law on the following day.

5. Certificate of Compliance as to 9-30-2013 order transmitted to OAL 11-8-2013 and filed 12-16-2013 (Register 2013, No. 51).

Ref.: Hanna §§ 1.11[5][a]–[e], 1.12[9][b], 1.13[1]–[7], 23.11[2], [2a], 23.12[2]–[3d], 23.16, 24.11[1][c], 25.06A, 25.08, 25.09, 26.01[3], 26.02, 26.04, 33.01[1][b], [2], [3][b]–[d], [4], 35.72[3]; Herlick Handbook §§ 1.03[2], 5.20, 14.5A, 16.23.

§10205.4. Adjudication Files.

(a) All cases filed on and after the effective date of these regulations shall be maintained by the Division of Workers' Compensation in an electronic format in EAMS. All paper documents properly filed in such cases shall be scanned into the EAMS adjudication file and then destroyed no less than 30 business days after filing.

(b) All case opening documents shall be given a case number by the district office where no case number has been previously assigned for the injured worker for the alleged date of injury. The parties shall be notified of the case number by their preferred method of service.

(c) If a case number has been previously assigned by the Division of Workers' Compensation, a new case number will be assigned when a document is filed as follows: the prefix "ADJ" shall replace the previously assigned three letter prefix (i.e. "OAK") and precede the assigned case number.

(d) Except as provided in section 10208.7, the Division of Workers' Compensation shall maintain a paper adjudication file until it is converted to an electronic adjudication file. If, however, a paper adjudication file is maintained on or after the effective date of these regulations, an electronic adjudication file shall also be created and any documents filed thereafter shall be maintained electronically in EAMS, in accordance with subdivision (c).

(e) A paper adjudication file or a portion of a paper adjudication file may be converted to an electronic adjudication file by the Division of Workers' Compensation at any time. If a paper adjudication file is completely scanned into EAMS the Division of Workers' Compensation shall notify the parties to the case of the change in how the file is maintained; and the paper adjudication file may be destroyed no less than 30 business days after the issuance of the notification.

Note: Authority cited: Sections 111, 133, 138.2(b) and 5307.3, Labor Code; and Stats. 2011, c. 559, §17 (A.B. 1426). Reference: Section 126, Labor Code.

History: 1. Renumbering of former section 10216 to new section 10205.4, including amendment of subsection (d) and Note, filed 12-10-2012 as a change without regulatory effect pursuant to section 100, title 1, California Code of Regulations by the Division of Workers' Compensation and as a file and print by the Workers' Compensation Appeals Board pursuant to Government Code section 11351 (Register 2012, No. 50).

Ref.: Hanna §§ 1.11[5][a]–[e], 1.12[9][b], 1.13[1]–[7], 23.11[2], [2a], 23.12[2]–[3d], 23.16, 24.11[1][c], 25.06A, 25.08, 25.09, 26.01[3], 26.02, 26.04, 33.01[1][b], [2], [3][b]–[d], [4], 35.72[3]; Herlick Handbook §§ 1.01[3][b], 1.03[2], 5.20, 14.5A, 16.23.

§10205.5. Official Participant Record and Duty to Furnish Correct Address.

(a) The Division of Workers' Compensation shall maintain an official participant record for each adjudication file, which shall contain the names of all parties and lien claimants, and their attorneys or hearing representatives.

(b) In order to ensure case parties and documents are accurately associated to the correct electronic adjudication file, uniform names for claims administrators' offices and representatives' offices shall be used when filing documents in EAMS. The names will be assigned by the Division of Workers' Compensation.

(1) The Division of Workers' Compensation will maintain a list on its website (www.dwc.ca.gov/EAMS) of uniform names and mailing addresses and preferred method of service for the following entities: claims administrators' offices, and representatives' offices.

(2) Additions for new claims administrators' offices and representatives' offices and changes of name, location or address, telephone number, fax number, e-mail address or preferred method of service shall be registered by the entity requesting the change with the Central Registration Unit.

(A) The entity requesting the change must fax or e-mail a letter on letterhead with a signature from an authorized individual requesting the change to the Division of Workers' Compensation's Central Registration Unit within five business days of any change. The entity shall also advise all parties of any change of name, mailing address, or telephone number by furnishing the current information within five business days of any change.

(B) The fax number for the Central Registration Unit is: 1 (888) 822-9309. The e-mail address for the Central Registration Unit is: cru@dir.ca.gov.

(C) The new uniform name or address and preferred method of service will be posted by the Central Registration Unit within ten business days of receipt of the request.

(c) Except as required by subdivision (b), every party and every lien claimant having an interest in an active case pending before the district office or appeals board shall advise the district office and all parties of any change of mailing address and telephone numbers by furnishing the current information within five business days of any change

(d) Every lien claimant that has filed a lien in a case pending in a district office shall advise all parties within five business days of any change in the identity and/or telephone number of the person with authority to resolve the lien by furnishing the correct name and daytime telephone number of that person to the interested parties; and shall advise the Division of Workers' Compensation of any such change after a declaration of readiness is filed.

(e) Every party and lien claimant having an interest in an inactive case: (1) shall advise all other known parties, lien claimants, attorneys, and hearing representative within five business days of any change of address (which shall include any change of mailing address and telephone numbers) by furnishing the correct and current address and/or number; and (2) shall advise the Division of Workers' Compensation of any such change within five business days if there is an outstanding award of further medical treatment or if there is continuing jurisdiction pursuant to Labor Code sections 5410, 5803 and 5804.

Note: Authority cited: Sections 111, 133, 138.2(b) and 5307.3, Labor Code; and Stats. 2011, c. 559, §17 (A.B. 1426). Reference: Sections 126, 5316, 5410, 5504, 5803 and 5804, Labor Code.

History: 1. Renumbering of former section 10217 to new section 10205.5, including amendment of Note, filed 12-10-2012 as a change without regulatory effect pursuant to section 100, title 1, California Code of Regulations by the Division of Workers' Compensation and as a file and print by the Workers' Compensation Appeals Board pursuant to Government Code section 11351 (Register 2012, No. 50).

Ref.: Hanna §§ 1.11[5][a]–[e], 1.12[9][b], 1.13[1]–[7], 23.11[2], [2a], 23.12[2]–[3d], 23.16, 24.11[1][c], 25.06A, 25.08, 25.09, 26.01[3], 26.02, 26.04, 33.01[1][b], [2], [3][b]–[d], [4], 35.72[3]; Herlick Handbook §§ 1.01[3][b], 1.03[3], 5.20, 6.04[2], 14.5A, 16.23.

§10205.6. Designated Preferred Method of Service.

(a) Claims administrators' offices and representatives' offices may designate first class mail, electronic mail or fax as their preferred method of service for receiving documents from the district office and the appeals board. The designated method of service shall be the same for all active cases for that claims administrator's office or representative's office. A party, a lien claimant, or an attorney or other representative for a party or lien claimant who does not or cannot designate a preferred method of service shall be served by first class mail.

(b) A represented party, a lien claimant, or an attorney or other representative for a party or lien claimant may agree with any other represented party, lien claimant, or attorney or other representative for a party or lien claimant that any method of service may be utilized for receiving documents between the parties to the agreement. If such an agreement is made, service pursuant to the agreement shall constitute valid service. Absent such an agreement, service between these parties or entities shall be made by first class mail.

(c) If the service is being made by or on an unrepresented injured worker, unrepresented dependent or unrepresented uninsured employer, then the service shall be made by first class mail.

Note: Authority cited: Sections 111, 133, 138.2(b) and 5307.3, Labor Code; and Stats. 2011, c. 559, §17 (A.B. 1426). Reference: Section 126, Labor Code.

History: 1. Renumbering of former section 10218 to new section 10205.6, including amendment of Note, filed 12-10-2012 as a change without regulatory effect pursuant to section 100, title 1, California Code of Regulations by the Division of Workers' Compensation and as a file and print by the Workers' Compensation Appeals Board pursuant to Government Code section 11351 (Register 2012, No. 50).

Ref.: Hanna §§ 1.11[5][a]–[e], 1.12[9][b], 1.13[1]–[7], 23.11[2], [2a], 23.12[2]–[3d], 23.16, 24.11[1][c], 25.06A, 25.08, 25.09, 26.01[3], 26.02, 26.04, 33.01[1][b], [2], [3][b]–[d], [4], 35.72[3]; Herlick Handbook §§ 1.01[3][b], 1.03[4], 5.20, 6.04[2], [5], 14.5A, 16.23.

§10205.7. Failure to Comply with the Electronic Adjudication Management System Rules.

(a) If a document is not filed in compliance with the Administrative Director's rules, either because it does not comply with the procedural requirements or with the place of filing requirements, the Administrative Director may in his or her discretion take the following actions:

(1) Correct the defect and file the document; or

(2) Notify the filer that the document is not accepted for filing by service of a Notice of Document Discrepancy. The Notice shall state the discrepancy, the date of the attempted filing, and provide the filer with 15 business days from service to cure the discrepancy. If the document is corrected within 15 business days, or at a later date upon a showing of good cause, it shall be deemed filed on the original date the document was submitted.

(b) Notwithstanding the provisions of subdivision (a), the following documents shall not be filed with the district office or the appeals board, except as a non duplicative supporting exhibit or upon the order of a workers' compensation administrative law judge or the appeals board. Documents improperly submitted pursuant to this subdivision shall not be accepted for filing or deemed filed and shall not be acknowledged and may be discarded.

(1) letters to opposing parties or counsel;

(2) subpoenas;

(3) notices of taking deposition;

(4) medical appointment letters;

(5) proofs of service ordered pursuant to California Code of Regulations, title 8, section 10500;

(6) medical reports, except as required by section 10233;

(7) copies of any decision of any federal or state court opinion otherwise available.

(8) copies of any decision of the appeals board or a workers' compensation administrative law judge that is otherwise available.

(9) duplicate medical and medical-legal reports.

(10) no diagnostic imaging as defined in Labor Code section 139.3, subd. (b)(1), shall be transmitted to the district office or the appeals board unless it is ordered.

(c) No document shall be sent by electronic mail or by fax directly to the district office or the appeals board. If a document is sent by electronic mail or fax directly to the district office, it shall not be accepted for filing or deemed filed, shall not be acknowledged, and may be discarded unless otherwise ordered by the workers' compensation administrative law judge or the appeals board.

Note: Authority cited: Sections 111, 127, 133, 138.2(b) and 5307.3, Labor Code; and Stats. 2011, c. 559, §17 (A.B. 1426). Reference: Sections 126 and 139.3, Labor Code.

History: 1. Renumbering of former section 10222 to new section 10205.7, including amendment of section heading, subsection (a) and Note, filed 12-10-2012 as a change without regulatory effect pursuant to section 100, title 1, California Code of Regulations by the Division of Workers' Compensation and as a file and print by the Workers' Compensation Appeals Board pursuant to Government Code section 11351 (Register 2012, No. 50).

Ref.: Hanna §§ 1.11[5][a]–[e], 1.12[9][b], 1.13[1]–[7], 23.11[2], [2a], 23.12[2]–[3d], 23.16, 24.11[1][c], 25.06A, 25.08, 25.09, 26.01[3], 26.02, 26.04, 33.01[1][b], [2], [3][b]–[d], [4], 35.72[3]; Herlick Handbook §§ 1.01[3][b], 1.03[5], 5.20, 6.04[2], 14.5A, 16.23.

§10205.8. Corrective Measures for Misfiled or Misdirected Documents into the Case Management System.

(a) The Division of Workers' Compensation may perform document substitution on filed documents; repair scanned documents; and move documents to other adjudication files.

(b) A document substitution may occur where a technical problem of readability and/or legibility exists with a filed document. The filer may seek a substitution of the document by filing a petition to substitute. The proposed document for substitution must be appended to a petition to substitute. If the petition to substitute is granted, the proposed document for substitution will replace the document that was unreadable or illegible.

(c) A document repair may occur where a document scanned into an electronic adjudication file by the Division of Workers' Compensation fails to reflect the original paper document. The Division of Workers' Compensation may repair the document so that the scanned image accurately reflects the original paper document. The Division of Workers' Compensation may repair a document at any time or a party may request a document be repaired. EAMS will retain as viewable the original document for those who have access to the electronic file.

(d) A document may be moved when a document originally scanned by the Division of Workers' Compensation is filed into the wrong electronic file.

(e) Documents that are in the process of being substituted or repaired shall not be moved.

(f) The Division of Workers' Compensation will provide notice to all parties of moved, substituted, or repaired documents within 15 business days.

Note: Authority cited: Sections 111, 127, 133, 138.2(b) and 5307.3, Labor Code; and Stats. 2011, c. 559, §17 (A.B. 1426). Reference: Section 126, Labor Code.

History: 1. Renumbering of former section 10223 to new section 10205.8, including amendment of Note, filed 12-10-2012 as a change without regulatory effect pursuant to section 100, title 1, California Code of Regulations by the Division of Workers' Compensation and as a file and print by the Workers' Compensation Appeals Board pursuant to Government Code section 11351 (Register 2012, No. 50).

Ref.: Hanna §§ 1.11[5][a]–[e], 1.12[9][b], 1.13[1]–[7], 23.11[2], [2a], 23.12[2]–[3d], 23.16, 24.11[1][c], 25.06A, 25.08, 25.09, 26.01[3], 26.02, 26.04, 33.01[1][b], [2], [3][b]–[d], [4], 35.72[3]; Herlick Handbook §§ 1.01[3][b], 1.03[6], 5.20, 6.04[2], 14.5A, 16.23.

§10205.9. Extended System Unavailability.

(a) If, for any reason, there is a technical failure of EAMS for longer than 24 hours, the court administrator, in his or her discretion, may declare that EAMS is unavailable for an extended period of time.

(b) After issuing a declaration of extended system unavailability, the Administrative Director shall issue an order that includes, but is not limited to:

(1) requiring that the district office or the appeals board shall serve all documents by first class mail;

(2) providing that filed documents shall be maintained in temporary paper adjudication files;

(3) providing that the time for performing any action, whether by the parties or by the district office, shall be extended by a specified period or until EAMS is declared to be operational; or

(4) requiring or allowing any other actions or remedies, as deemed appropriate under the circumstances.

(c) The Administrative Director shall post the declaration of extended system unavailability on the website of the Division of Workers' Compensation, if the website remains operational, and shall post it at every district office and at the office of the appeals board.

(d) Any declaration of extended unavailability shall remain in effect until the Administrative Director issues a subsequent declaration that EAMS is operational.

(e) The Division of Workers' Compensation will maintain a list of any and all technical failures of EAMS that last longer than 24 hours on its website.

(f) EAMS shall be backed up daily pursuant to the State of California's information technology standards.

Note: Authority cited: Sections 111, 133, 138.2(b) and 5307.3, Labor Code; and Stats. 2011, c. 559, §17 (A.B. 1426). Reference: Sections 126 and 5700, Labor Code.

History: 1. Renumbering of former section 10225 to new section 10205.9, including amendment of section and Note, filed 12-10-2012 as a change without regulatory effect pursuant to section 100, title 1, California Code of Regulations by the Division of Workers' Compensation and as a file and print by the Workers' Compensation Appeals Board pursuant to Government Code section 11351 (Register 2012, No. 50).

Ref.: Hanna §§ 1.11[5][a]–[e], 1.12[9][b], 1.13[1]–[7], 23.11[2], [2a], 23.12[2]–[3d], 23.16, 24.11[1][c], 25.06A, 25.08, 25.09, 26.01[3], 26.02, 26.04, 33.01[1][b], [2], [3][b]–[d], [4], 35.72[3];

Herlick Handbook §§ 1.01[3][b], 1.03[7], 5.20, 6.04[2], 14.5A, 16.23.

ARTICLE 1.3
Filing of Documents by Parties or Lien Claimants

§10205.10. Manner of Filing Documents.

(a) Except as provided by section 10603, subd. (a), all documents shall be filed in paper form.

(b) All paper documents shall be scanned into the electronic adjudication file and then destroyed no less than 30 business days after filing, unless otherwise provided by these rules or ordered by a workers' compensation administrative law judge or the appeals board. A scanned document shall have the same legal effect as a document filed in paper form.

(c) Each of the following persons or entities shall file optical character recognition forms completed by using a computer or typewriter with the exception of OCR forms that are prepared at a hearing or that, for good cause, are filed at trial:

(1) any attorneys representing any party or any lien claimant;

(2) any insurance carrier or any representative of any insurance carrier (including any claims adjustor);

(3) any self-insured employer or any representative of a self-insured employer (including any claims adjustor);

(4) any third-party administrator or any representative of a third-party administrator (including any claims adjustor); and

(5) any lien claimant or any representative of any lien claimant, with the exception of: (A) a lien claimant (or a non-attorney representative of a lien claimant) asserting a living expenses lien under Labor Code section 4903(c); (B) a lien claimant (or a non-attorney representative of a lien claimant) asserting a burial expenses lien under Labor Code section 4903(d); or (C) a non-governmental lien claimant (or a non-attorney representative of a lien claimant) asserting a spousal or child support expenses lien under Labor Code section 4903(e).

(d) OCR forms will be posted in fillable format on the Division of Workers' Compensation website (http://www.dir.ca.gov/dwc/forms. html).

(e) All unrepresented employees, unrepresented dependents, unrepresented uninsured employers, or lien claimants listed in subdivision (c)(5)(A), (B) or (C) shall utilize optical character recognition forms, where such forms are required, but if they do not have ready access to a computer or typewriter, printed OCR forms will be available at the district offices and the information added to the form may be hand-printed in black ink.

(f) Whenever any party or lien claimant files any document utilizing an optical character recognition form, the party or lien claimant shall use the appropriate OCR form required by these rules.

(g) Except as set forth in subdivision (e), any OCR form that was not obtained from the Division of Workers' Compensation's website must function with EAMS in an equivalent manner as the Division's form.

Note: Authority cited: Sections 111, 133 and 5307.3, Labor Code; and Stats. 2011, c.559, §17 (A.B. 1426). Reference: Sections 126 and 4903, Labor Code.

History: 1. New article 3 (sections 10205.10–10205.14) and renumbering of former section 10228 to new section 10205.10, including amendment of Note, filed 12-10-2012 as a change without regulatory effect pursuant to section 100, title 1, California Code of Regulations by the Division of Workers' Compensation and as a file and print by the Workers' Compensation Appeals Board pursuant to Government Code section 11351 (Register 2012, No. 50).

2. Renumbering of article 3 to article 1.3 filed 12-31-2012 as an emergency; operative 1-1-2013 pursuant to Government Code section 11346.1(d) (Register 2013, No. 1). A Certificate of Compliance must be transmitted to OAL by 7-1-2013 or emergency language will be repealed by operation of law on the following day.

3. Editorial correction of History 1 (Register 2013, No. 3).

4. Amendment renumbering article 3 to article 1.3 refiled 6-26-2013 as an emergency; operative 7-1-2013 pursuant to Government Code section 11346.1(d) (Register 2013, No. 26). A Certificate of Compliance must be transmitted to OAL by 9-30-2013 or emergency language will be repealed by operation of law on the following day.

5. Amendment renumbering article 3 to article 1.3 refiled 9-30-2013 as an emergency; operative 10-1-2013 pursuant to Government Code section 11346.1(d) (Register 2013, No. 40). A Certificate of Compliance must be transmitted to OAL by 12-30-2013 or emergency language will be repealed by operation of law on the following day.

6. Certificate of Compliance as to 9-30-2013 order transmitted to OAL 11-8-2013 and filed 12-16-2013 (Register 2013, No. 51).

Ref.: Hanna §§ 1.11[5][a]–[e], 1.12[9][b], 1.13[1]–[7], 23.11[2], [2a], 23.12[2]–[3d], 23.16, 24.11[1][c], 25.06A, 25.08, 25.09, 26.01[3], 26.02, 26.04, 33.01[1][b], [2], [3][b]–[d], [4], 35.72[3]; Herlick Handbook §§ 1.01[3][b], 1.03[8], 1.04, 5.20, 6.04[2], 10.02[2], [6], 10.03[2], [6], 10.05, 14.5A, 14.15, 16.23.

§10205.11. Electronic Filing Exemption.

If a document is filed with EAMS as part of the electronic filing trial, that document does not need to be filed in compliance with regulation sections 10205.10 and 10205.12.

Note: Authority cited: Sections 111, 133 and 5307.3, Labor Code; and Stats. 2011, c. 559, §17 (A.B. 1426). Reference: Section 126, Labor Code.

History: 1. Renumbering of former section 10229 to new section 10205.11, including amendment of section and Note, filed 12-10-2012 as a change without regulatory effect pursuant to section 100, title 1, California Code of Regulations by the Division of Workers' Compensation and as a file and print by the Workers' Compensation Appeals Board pursuant to Government Code section 11351 (Register 2012, No. 50).

Ref.: Hanna §§ 1.11[5][a]–[e], 1.12[9][b], 1.13[1]–[7], 23.11[2], [2a], 23.12[2]–[3d], 23.16, 24.11[1][c], 25.06A, 25.08, 25.09, 26.01[3], 26.02, 26.04, 33.01[1][b], [2], [3][b]–[d], [4], 35.72[3]; Herlick Handbook §§ 1.01[3][b], 1.04, 5.20, 10.02[2], 14.5A, 16.23.

§10205.12. Form and Size Requirements for Filed Documents.

(a) All documents except the medical reports of treating physicians, secondary physicians, qualified or agreed medical evaluators and proposed exhibits, shall be filed in accordance with the following standards:

(1) Only one side of each paper shall be used;

(2) All documents shall be printed with black ink on white paper that is 8 1/2 x 11 inches and at least twelve pound weight. All margins shall be at least 1 inch and shall be without typed or handwritten text in any margin;

(3) The first page shall include a case caption that shall include the name of the injured worker or dependent claiming benefits, the name of the employer and the employer's insurer or indicating the employer is self-insured and a case number if one has been assigned by the district office. If a case number has been assigned the number shall be preceded by the abbreviation "ADJ";

(4) All non-form legal pleadings shall contain a heading above the case caption containing the name of the filing attorney and their state bar membership number and the attorney's law firm name and address;

(5) Except as otherwise provided in this section or section 10205.10, all OCR forms and documents shall be printed in Times New Roman, Times, Courier, Palatino, Century Schoolbook or similar serif font of at least 12 points in size;

(6) Except as otherwise provided in section 10205.10, all text added to the OCR forms shall be in capital letters.

(7) Response to the request on the OCR forms for social security numbers is optional, not mandatory.

(8) A list of body part codes is provided with the document cover sheet form and posted on the Division of Workers' Compensation website (http://www.dir.ca.gov/forms.html). The codes shall be used on OCR forms to describe the part of the body injured.

(9) A list of district office codes for place of venue is provided with the document cover sheet form and posted on the Division of Workers' Compensation website (http://www.dir.ca.gov/forms.html). The codes shall be used on OCR forms to describe the district office venue.

(10) No single document shall exceed 25 pages in length without the prior permission of the appeals board or the presiding workers' compensation administrative law judge of the district office with venue over the case;

(11) The text of a document shall be double spaced or one and one half spaces; however, captions, headings, headers, footnotes, footers and block quotations shall be single spaced.

(12) The documents shall be flat, without folds and without staples.

(13) OCR forms have bar codes at the top of the document. No other documents shall have bar codes on the top of the document.

(b) All documents shall be filed with document cover sheets and document separator sheets as follows:

(1) A completed document cover sheet shall be the first page of each individual document or set of documents filed at one time in the same case. The cover sheet provides space for information regarding 15 companion cases. Only the pages filled out need to be filed. A document separator sheet shall precede each document within a set of documents.

(2) If an individual document includes an attachment, a completed document separator sheet shall precede the attachment and if an individual document includes multiple attachments, a document separator sheet shall precede each individual attachment. A document separator sheet shall not be placed between a document and the proof of service for that document. Where one proof of service is used for multiple documents, a document separator sheet shall precede the proof of service.

(3) A list of document titles is provided with the document separator sheet form and posted on the Division of Workers' Compensation website (http://www.dir.ca.gov/forms.html). The document titles shall be used on document separator sheet to describe the attached document.

(4) The document separator sheet requires the filer to list the product delivery units, as defined in section 10205(dd), the date of the attached document, and the author of the attached document.

(5) This subdivision shall not apply to any unrepresented employees, unrepresented dependents or unrepresented uninsured employers who do not have ready access to document cover sheets and document separator sheets.

(c) Oversized documents shall be filed only at the time of trial in accordance with the provisions of section 10603.

(d) If an unrepresented worker, an unrepresented uninsured employer, or an unrepresented dependent does not have ready access to a computer or typewriter and compliance with subdivisions (a)(3) and (a)(5) is not feasible, a hand-printed document may be submitted. Any hand-printed document shall be legible and shall otherwise comply with subdivision (a), including the requirements of subdivision (a)(3) regarding margins and text in the margins.

Note: Authority cited: Sections 111, 133 and 5307.3, Labor Code; and Stats. 2011, c. 559, §17 (A.B. 1426). Reference: Section 126, Labor Code.

History: 1. Renumbering of former section 10232 to new section 10205.12, including amendment of subsections (a)(5)-(6) and (b)(4) and amendment of Note, filed 12-10-2012 as a change without regulatory effect pursuant to section 100, title 1, California Code of Regulations by the Division of Workers' Compensation and as a file and print by the Workers' Compensation Appeals Board pursuant to Government Code section 11351 (Register 2012, No. 50).

2. Amendment of subsection (b)(4) filed 12-31-2012 as an emergency; operative 1-1-2013 pursuant to Government Code section 11346.1(d) (Register 2013, No. 1). A Certificate of Compliance must be transmitted to OAL by 7-1-2013 or emergency language will be repealed by operation of law on the following day.

3. Amendment of subsection (b)(4) refiled 6-26-2013 as an emergency; operative 7-1-2013 pursuant to Government Code section 11346.1(d) (Register 2013, No. 26). A Certificate of Compliance must be transmitted to OAL by 9-30-2013 or emergency language will be repealed by operation of law on the following day.

4. Amendment of subsection (b)(4) refiled 9-30-2013 as an emergency; operative 10-1-2013 pursuant to Government Code section 11346.1(d) (Register 2013, No. 40). A Certificate of Compliance must be transmitted to OAL by 12-30-2013 or emergency language will be repealed by operation of law on the following day.

5. Certificate of Compliance as to 9-30-2013 order transmitted to OAL 11-8-2013 and filed 12-16-2013 (Register 2013, No. 51).

Ref.: Hanna §§ 1.11[5][a]–[e], 1.12[9][b], 1.13[1]–[7], 23.11[2], [2a], 23.12[2]–[3d], 23.16, 24.11[1][c], 25.06A, 25.08, 25.09, 26.01[3], 26.02, 26.04, 33.01[1][b], [2], [3][b]–[d], [4], 35.72[3]; Herlick Handbook §§ 1.01[3][b], 1.03[9], 1.04, 5.20, 6.04[2], [5], 14.5A, 16.23.

§10205.13. Document Cover Sheet Form.

DWC-CA form 10232.1 (Document cover sheet) revision dated 11/2017 is incorporated by reference.

Note: Authority cited: Sections 111, 133 and 5307.3, Labor Code; and Stats. 2011, c. 559, §17 (A.B. 1426). Reference: Section 126, Labor Code.

History: 1. Renumbering of former section 10232.1 to new section 10205.13, including amendment of Note, filed 12-10-2012 as a change without regulatory effect pursuant to section 100, title 1, California Code of Regulations by the Division of Workers' Compensation and as a file and print by the Workers' Compensation Appeals Board pursuant to Government Code section 11351 (Register 2012, No. 50).

2. Change without regulatory effect amending Form DWC-CA 10232.1 (incorporated by reference) and section filed 9-17-2014 pursuant to section 100, title 1, California Code of Regulations (Register 2014, No. 38).

3. Change without regulatory effect amending Form DWC-CA 10232.1 (incorporated by reference) and amending section filed 1-2-2018 pursuant to section 100, title 1, California Code of Regulations (Register 2018, No. 1).

Ref.: Hanna §§ 1.11[5][a]–[e], 1.12[9][b], 1.13[1]–[7], 23.11[2], [2a], 23.12[2]–[3d], 23.16, 24.11[1][c], 25.06A, 25.08, 25.09, 26.01[3], 26.02, 26.04, 33.01[1][b], [2], [3][b]–[d], [4], 35.72[3]; Herlick Handbook §§ 1.01[3][b], 5.20, 14.5A, 16.23.

§10205.14. Document Separator Sheet Form.

DWC-CA form 10232.2 (Document separator sheet) revision dated 11/2017 is incorporated by reference.

Note: Authority cited: Sections 111, 133 and 5307.3, Labor Code; and Stats. 2011, c. 559, §17 (A.B. 1426). Reference: Section 126, Labor Code.

History: 1. Renumbering of former section 10232.2 to new section 10205.14, including amendment of Note, filed 12-10-2012 as a change without regulatory effect pursuant to section 100, title 1, California Code of Regulations by the Division of Workers' Compensation and as a file and print by the Workers' Compensation Appeals Board pursuant to Government Code section 11351 (Register 2012, No. 50).

2. Change without regulatory effect amending section and DWC-CA form 10232.2 (incorporated by reference) filed 4-16-2014 pursuant to section 100, title 1, California Code of Regulations (Register 2014, No. 16).

3. Change without regulatory effect amending Form DWC-CA 10232.2 (incorporated by reference) and section filed 9-15-2014 pursuant to section 100, title 1, California Code of Regulations (Register 2014, No. 38).

4. Change without regulatory effect amending Form DWC-CA 10232.2 (incorporated by reference) and amending section filed 1-2-2018 pursuant to section 100, title 1, California Code of Regulations (Register 2018, No. 1).

Ref.: Hanna §§ 1.11[5][a]–[e], 1.12[9][b], 1.13[1]–[7], 23.11[2], [2a], 23.12[2]–[3d], 23.16, 24.11[1][c], 25.06A, 25.08, 25.09, 26.01[3], 26.02, 26.04, 33.01[1][b], [2], [3][b]–[d], [4], 35.72[3]; Herlick Handbook §§ 1.01[3][b], 5.20, 14.5A, 16.23.

ARTICLE 2
Electronic Filing System Rules

§10206. Electronic Document Filing; Electronic Adjudication Management System (EAMS) Reference Guide and Instructional Manual for E-Form Filers; Incorporation.

Electronic documents (E-forms) shall be filed upon a form approved by the appeals board. E-form filing shall follow the procedures set forth in the *Electronic Adjudication Management System (EAMS) Reference Guide and Instructional Manual for E-Form Filers (EAMS E-Form Filing Reference Guide)*, dated December 2013, which is incorporated by reference. It may be downloaded from the Division of Workers' Compensation through the Department of Industrial Relations' website at www.dir.ca.gov or may be obtained by writing to:

DIVISION OF WORKERS' COMPENSATION
ATTN: EAMS E-FORM FILING REFERENCE GUIDE
P.O. BOX 71010
OAKLAND, CA 94612

Note: Authority cited: Sections 111, 133, 138.2(b) and 5307.3, Labor Code; Stats. 2011, c. 559, §17 (A.B. 1426). Reference: Section 126, Labor Code.

History: 1. New article 2 (sections 10206–10206.2) and section filed 12-31-2012 as an emergency; operative 1-1-2013 pursuant to Government Code section 11346.1(d) (Register 2013, No. 1). A Certificate of Compliance must be transmitted to OAL by 7-1-2013 or emergency language will be repealed by operation of law on the following day.

2. New article 2 (sections 10206-10206.2) and section refiled 6-26-2013 as an emergency; operative 7-1-2013 pursuant to Government Code section 11346.1(d) (Register 2013, No. 26). A Certificate of Compliance must be transmitted to OAL by 9-30-2013 or emergency language will be repealed by operation of law on the following day.

3. New article 2 (sections 10206-10206.2) and section refiled 9-30-2013 as an emergency; operative 10-1-2013 pursuant to Government Code section 11346.1(d) (Register 2013, No. 40). A Certificate of Compliance must be transmitted to OAL by 12-30-2013 or emergency language will be repealed by operation of law on the following day.

4. Certificate of Compliance as to 9-30-2013 order, including amendment of section, transmitted to OAL 11-8-2013 and filed 12-16-2013; amendments effective 12-16-2013 pursuant to Government Code section 11343.4(b)(3) (Register 2013, No. 51).

Ref.: Herlick Handbook §§ 1.01[3][b], 1.04, 10.02[2], 10.03[3].

§10206.1. Electronic Document Filing; Electronic Adjudication Management System Business Rules for JET Filers; Incorporation.

JET filing shall follow the procedures set forth in the *Electronic Adjudication Management System JET File Business Rules and Technical Specifications*, Version Version 4.1, dated December 2013, which is incorporated by reference. This document may be downloaded from the Division of Workers' Compensation through the Department of Industrial Relations' website at www.dir.ca.gov or may be obtained by writing to:

DIVISION OF WORKERS' COMPENSATION
ATTN: EAMS JET FILING BUSINESS RULES
P.O. BOX 71010
OAKLAND, CA 94612

Note: Authority cited: Sections 111, 133, 138.2(b) and 5307.2, Labor Code. Reference: Section 126, Labor Code.

History: 1. New section filed 12-31-2012 as an emergency; operative 1-1-2013 pursuant to Government Code section 11346.1(d) (Register 2013, No. 1). A Certificate of Compliance must be transmitted to OAL by 7-1-2013 or emergency language will be repealed by operation of law on the following day.

2. New section refiled 6-26-2013 as an emergency; operative 7-1-2013 pursuant to Government Code section 11346.1(d) (Register 2013, No. 26). A Certificate of Compliance must be trans-

mitted to OAL by 9-30-2013 or emergency language will be repealed by operation of law on the following day.

3. New section refiled 9-30-2013 as an emergency; operative 10-1-2013 pursuant to Government Code section 11346.1(d) (Register 2013, No. 40). A Certificate of Compliance must be transmitted to OAL by 12-30-2013 or emergency language will be repealed by operation of law on the following day.

4. Certificate of Compliance as to 9-30-2013 order, including amendment of section, transmitted to OAL 11-8-2013 and filed 12-16-2013; amendments effective 12-16-2013 pursuant to Government Code section 11343.4(b)(3) (Register 2013, No. 51).

Editor's Note: It is the Publisher's belief that the amendment made by Register 2013, No. 51 of this section which reads "Version Version 4.1, dated December 2013," should be "Version 4.1, dated December 2013,".

Ref.: Herlick Handbook §§ 1.01[3][b], 1.04, 10.03[3].

§10206.2. Electronic Filing Exemption

All electronic documents must be filed in compliance with the Electronic Adjudication Management System regulations set forth in sections 10205, et seq., except that electronic documents do not need to be filed in compliance with sections 10205.10 and 10205.12. Documents submitted for filing by any unrepresented injured employee, any unrepresented dependent of an injured employee, or any unrepresented uninsured employer may be in paper form.

Note: Authority cited: Sections 111, 133 and 5307.3, Labor Code; Stats. 2011, c. 559, §17 (A.B. 1426). Reference: Section 126, Labor Code.

History: 1. New section filed 12-31-2012 as an emergency; operative 1-1-2013 pursuant to Government Code section 11346.1(d) (Register 2013, No. 1). A Certificate of Compliance must be transmitted to OAL by 7-1-2013 or emergency language will be repealed by operation of law on the following day.

2. New section refiled 6-26-2013 as an emergency; operative 7-1-2013 pursuant to Government Code section 11346.1(d) (Register 2013, No. 26). A Certificate of Compliance must be transmitted to OAL by 9-30-2013 or emergency language will be repealed by operation of law on the following day.

3. New section refiled 9-30-2013 as an emergency; operative 10-1-2013 pursuant to Government Code section 11346.1(d) (Register 2013, No. 40). A Certificate of Compliance must be transmitted to OAL by 12-30-2013 or emergency language will be repealed by operation of law on the following day.

4. Certificate of Compliance as to 9-30-2013 order transmitted to OAL 11-8-2013 and filed 12-16-2013 (Register 2013, No. 51).

Ref.: Herlick Handbook §§ 1.01[3][b], 1.04, 10.03[3].

ARTICLE 3
Manner of Filing of Electronic Documents

§10206.3. Time of Filing of Documents.

(a) An electronically transmitted document shall be deemed to have been received by EAMS when the electronic transmission of the document into EAMS is complete. A document received electronically after 5:00 pm of a court day (i.e., Monday through Friday, except designated State holidays) shall be deemed filed as of the next court day.

(b) When an e-form is filed electronically, the party filing the document shall verify completion of filing pursuant to the procedures set forth in the EAMS E-Form Filing Reference Guide. In the absence of following the procedures set forth in the EAMS E-Form Filing Reference Guide, there is no presumption that EAMS received the document.

(c) When a document is filed using jet filing, the party filing the document shall verify completion of filing pursuant to the EAMS JET File Business Rules and Technical Specifications, Version 4.1. In the absence of a confirmation of successful filing, there is no presumption that EAMS received the document.

Note: Authority cited: Sections 111, 133, 138.2(b) and 5307.3, Labor Code. Reference: Section 126, Labor Code.

History: 1. New article 3 (sections 10206.3–10206.5) and section filed 12-31-2012 as an emergency; operative 1-1-2013 pursuant to Government Code section 11346.1(d) (Register 2013, No. 1). A Certificate of Compliance must be transmitted to OAL by 7-1-2013 or emergency language will be repealed by operation of law on the following day.

2. New article 3 (sections 10206.3-10206.5) and section refiled 6-26-2013 as an emergency; operative 7-1-2013 pursuant to Government Code section 11346.1(d) (Register 2013, No. 26). A Certificate of Compliance must be transmitted to OAL by 9-30-2013 or emergency language will be repealed by operation of law on the following day.

3. New article 3 (sections 10206.3-10206.5) and section refiled 9-30-2013 as an emergency; operative 10-1-2013 pursuant to Government Code section 11346.1(d) (Register 2013, No. 40). A Certificate of Compliance must be transmitted to OAL by 12-30-2013 or emergency language will be repealed by operation of law on the following day.

4. Certificate of Compliance as to 9-30-2013 order, including amendment of subsections (b)-(c), transmitted to OAL 11-8-2013 and filed 12-16-2013; amendments effective 12-16-2013 pursuant to Government Code section 11343.4(b)(3) (Register 2013, No. 51).

Ref.: Herlick Handbook §§ 1.01[3][b], 1.04, 10.03[3], 14.15.

§10206.4. Uniform Assigned Names.

Uniform assigned names (UAN) shall be created and assigned for claims administrators, representatives and lien claimant organizations by the DWC Central Registration Unit. The Central Registration Unit shall maintain the website list of uniform names and addresses of claims administrators' offices, representatives' offices, and lien claimant organization.

Note: Authority cited: Sections 111, 133, 138.2(b) and 5307.3, Labor Code. Reference: Section 126, Labor Code.

History: 1. New section filed 12-31-2012 as an emergency; operative 1-1-2013 pursuant to Government Code section 11346.1(d) (Register 2013, No. 1). A Certificate of Compliance must be transmitted to OAL by 7-1-2013 or emergency language will be repealed by operation of law on the following day.

2. New section refiled 6-26-2013 as an emergency; operative 7-1-2013 pursuant to Government Code section 11346.1(d) (Register 2013, No. 26). A Certificate of Compliance must be transmitted to OAL by 9-30-2013 or emergency language will be repealed by operation of law on the following day.

3. New section refiled 9-30-2013 as an emergency; operative 10-1-2013 pursuant to Government Code section 11346.1(d) (Register 2013, No. 40). A Certificate of Compliance must be transmitted to OAL by 12-30-2013 or emergency language will be repealed by operation of law on the following day.

4. Certificate of Compliance as to 9-30-2013 order transmitted to OAL 11-8-2013 and filed 12-16-2013 (Register 2013, No. 51).

Ref.: Herlick Handbook §§ 1.01[3][b], 1.04, 10.03[3].

§10206.5. Form and Size Requirements for Electronic Filed Documents.

(a) Electronic document filing shall be filed in accordance with the following standards:

(1) All electronically filed documents shall be submitted by using the appropriate e-form or XML file.

(2) Any document that is required to accompany an electronic form shall be filed as an attachment to the electronic form and shall be submitted in one of the following four file formats: "PDF/A1-a (Portable Document Format)," "DOC (".doc" Microsoft Word document)," "XLS (".xls" Microsoft Excel worksheet sheet)," or "TIFF (".tif or .tiff" Tagged Image File Format)." Filing using the "PDF/A1-a" is preferred.

(3) With the exception of electronic forms and required attachments, no embedded data shall be allowed in electronically filed documents.

(4) The filing party shall take all reasonable steps to ensure that the filing does not contain computer code, including viruses that might be harmful to EAMS or to other users of EAMS. Any electronically submitted document that is determined to contain a virus or other potentially harmful computer code may not be processed and may be deleted.

(5) If it is necessary to attach a document to an e-form, the filing party shall verify the readability of the scanned document before submitting it to EAMS.

(b) Service of any document that has been filed electronically shall include a copy of the entire e-form, all attachments and EAMS cover sheet. The proof of service for any electronically filed document shall identify the serving office's EAMS administrator and provide that individual's contact information.

Note: Authority cited: Sections 111, 133 and 5307.3, Labor Code. Reference: Section 126, Labor Code.

History: 1. New section filed 12-31-2012 as an emergency; operative 1-1-2013 pursuant to Government Code section 11346.1(d) (Register 2013, No. 1). A Certificate of Compliance must be transmitted to OAL by 7-1-2013 or emergency language will be repealed by operation of law on the following day.

2. New section refiled 6-26-2013 as an emergency; operative 7-1-2013 pursuant to Government Code section 11346.1(d) (Register 2013, No. 26). A Certificate of Compliance must be transmitted to OAL by 9-30-2013 or emergency language will be repealed by operation of law on the following day.

3. New section refiled 9-30-2013 as an emergency; operative 10-1-2013 pursuant to Government Code section 11346.1(d) (Register 2013, No. 40). A Certificate of Compliance must be transmitted to OAL by 12-30-2013 or emergency language will be repealed by operation of law on the following day.

4. Certificate of Compliance as to 9-30-2013 order transmitted to OAL 11-8-2013 and filed 12-16-2013 (Register 2013, No. 51).

Ref.: Herlick Handbook §§ 1.01[3][b], 1.04, 10.03[3].

ARTICLE 4
DWC E-Forms, DWC Unstructured Forms, and DWC JET Forms

§10206.14. DWC E-Forms and DWC Unstructured Forms.

Authorized e-form filers shall use the e-forms from the external user home page. E-forms filing may be obtained from the DWC website at http://www.dir.ca.gov/dwc/forms.html#EAMSForms.

Note: Authority cited: Sections 111, 133 and 5307.3, Labor Code. Reference: Section 126, Labor Code.

History: 1. New article 4 (sections 10206.14–10206.15) and section filed 12-31-2012 as an emergency; operative 1-1-2013 pursuant to Government Code section 11346.1(d) (Register 2013, No. 1). A Certificate of Compliance must be transmitted to OAL by 7-1-2013 or emergency language will be repealed by operation of law on the following day.

2. New article 4 (sections 10206.14-10206.15) and section refiled 6-26-2013 as an emergency; operative 7-1-2013 pursuant to Government Code section 11346.1(d) (Register 2013, No. 26). A Certificate of Compliance must be transmitted to OAL by 9-30-2013 or emergency language will be repealed by operation of law on the following day.

3. New article 4 (sections 10206.14-10206.15) and section refiled 9-30-2013 as an emergency; operative 10-1-2013 pursuant to Government Code section 11346.1(d) (Register 2013, No. 40). A Certificate of Compliance must be transmitted to OAL by 12-30-2013 or emergency language will be repealed by operation of law on the following day.

4. Certificate of Compliance as to 9-30-2013 order transmitted to OAL 11-8-2013 and filed 12-16-2013 (Register 2013, No. 51).

Ref.: Herlick Handbook §§ 1.01[3][b], 1.04, 10.03[3].

§10206.15. DWC JET Forms.

Authorized JET filers shall file forms using the EAMS JET File Business Rules and Technical Specifications, Version 4.1. JET filing forms may be obtained from the DWC website at http://www.dir.ca.gov/dwc/forms.html.

Note: Authority cited: Sections 111, 133 and 5307.3, Labor Code. Reference: Section 126, Labor Code.

History: 1. New section filed 12-31-2012 as an emergency; operative 1-1-2013 pursuant to Government Code section 11346.1(d) (Register 2013, No. 1). A Certificate of Compliance must be transmitted to OAL by 7-1-2013 or emergency language will be repealed by operation of law on the following day.

2. New section refiled 6-26-2013 as an emergency; operative 7-1-2013 pursuant to Government Code section 11346.1(d) (Register 2013, No. 26). A Certificate of Compliance must be transmitted to OAL by 9-30-2013 or emergency language will be repealed by operation of law on the following day.

3. New section refiled 9-30-2013 as an emergency; operative 10-1-2013 pursuant to Government Code section 11346.1(d) (Register 2013, No. 40). A Certificate of Compliance must be transmitted to OAL by 12-30-2013 or emergency language will be repealed by operation of law on the following day.

4. Certificate of Compliance as to 9-30-2013 order, including amendment of section, transmitted to OAL 11-8-2013 and filed 12-16-2013; amendments effective 12-16-2013 pursuant to Government Code section 11343.4(b)(3) (Register 2013, No. 51).

Ref.: Herlick Handbook §§ 1.01[3][b], 1.04, 10.03[3].

ARTICLE 5
The Form of Minutes of Hearing and Electronically Filed Decisions, Findings, Awards, and Orders

§10206.20. Minutes of Hearing Form.

DWC-CA form 10245 (Minutes of Hearing form) revision dated 11/2008 is incorporated by reference.

Note: Authority cited: Sections 111, 133 and 5307.3, Labor Code; and Stats. 2011, c. 559, §17 (A.B. 1426). Reference: Sections 126, 5313, 5502(b) and 5502(c), Labor Code.

History: 1. New article 4 (section 10208.1) and renumbering of former section 10245 to new section 10208.1, including amendment of Note, filed 12-10-2012 as a change without regulatory effect pursuant to section 100, title 1, California Code of Regulations by the Division of Workers' Compensation and as a file and print by the Workers' Compensation Appeals Board pursuant to Government Code section 11351 (Register 2012, No. 50).

2. Renumbering of former article 4 to article 5 and renumbering of former section 10208.1 to new section 10206.20 filed 12-31-2012 as an emergency; operative 1-1-2013 pursuant to Government Code section 11346.1(d) (Register 2013, No. 1). A Certificate of Compliance must be transmitted to OAL by 7-1-2013 or emergency language will be repealed by operation of law on the following day.

3. Renumbering of former article 4 to article 5 and renumbering of former section 10208.1 to new section 10206.20 refiled 6-26-2013 as an emergency; operative 7-1-2013 pursuant to Government Code section 11346.1(d) (Register 2013, No. 26). A Certificate of Compliance must be transmitted to OAL by 9-30-2013 or emergency language will be repealed by operation of law on the following day.

4. Renumbering of former article 4 to article 5 and renumbering of former section 10208.1 to new section 10206.20 refiled 9-30-2013 as an emergency; operative 10-1-2013 pursuant to Government Code section 11346.1(d) (Register 2013, No. 40). A Certificate of Compliance must be transmitted to OAL by 12-30-2013 or emergency language will be repealed by operation of law on the following day.

5. Certificate of Compliance as to 9-30-2013 order transmitted to OAL 11-8-2013 and filed 12-16-2013 (Register 2013, No. 51).

Ref.: Hanna §§ 1.11[5][a]–[e], 1.12[9][b], 1.13[1]–[7], 23.11[2], [2a], 23.12[2]–[3d], 23.16, 24.11[1][c], 25.06A, 25.08, 25.09, 26.01[3], 26.02, 26.04, 33.01[1][b], [2], [3][b]–[d], [4], 35.72[3]; Herlick Handbook §§ 1.01[3][b], 5.20, 14.5A, 16.23.

ARTICLE 6
Initial Lien Filing and Lien Activation Fees

§10207. Initial Lien Filing Fees.

(a) Lien claims enumerated below shall be filed with the Workers' Compensation Appeals Board in writing or electronically upon a form approved by the Workers' Compensation Appeals Board. The lien shall be accompanied by a proof of service and any other documents required by the appeals board.

(1) Reasonable attorney's fees (Labor Code section 4903(a)).

(2) Living expense liens (Labor Code 4903(c)).

(3) Burial expense liens (Labor Code 4903(d)).

(4) Spousal and child support liens (Labor Code 4903(e)).

(5) Employment Development Department liens (Labor Code sections 4903, subdivisions (f), (g), and (h).

(6) Victims of Crime liens (Labor Code section 4903(i)).

(b) On or after January 1, 2013, any initial section 4903(b) lien or claim of costs filed as a lien shall be filed electronically using a form approved by the appeals board. The lien shall be accompanied by a proof of service and any other documents required by the appeals board.

(c) Every lien claimant, except those lien claimants listed in paragraph (1), which files an initial lien for medical costs pursuant to Labor Code section 4903(b), shall be responsible for payment of the initial lien filing fee required of providers by Labor Code section 4903.05 and as set forth in subdivision (d).

(1) The following lien claimants are exempted from the payment of the initial lien filing fee requirements under this section:

(A) A health care service plan licensed pursuant to section 1349 of the Health and Safety Code.

(B) A group disability insurer under a policy issued in this state pursuant to the provisions of Section 10270.5 of the Insurance Code.

(C) A self-insured employee welfare benefit plan, as defined in section 10121 of the Insurance Code issued in this state.

(D) A Taft-Hartley health and welfare fund.

(E) A publicly funded program providing medical benefits on a nonindustrial basis.

(2) The following lien claimants or parties are not required to pay the initial lien filing fee under this section as their liens are not liens for medical costs pursuant to Labor Code section 4903(b).

(A) Reasonable attorney's fees (Labor Code section 4903(a)).

(B) Living expense liens (Labor Code 4903(c)).

(C) Burial expense liens (Labor Code 4903(d)).

(D) Spousal and child support liens (Labor Code 4903(e)).

(E) Employment Development Department liens (Labor Code section 4903, subdivisions (f), (g), and (h)).

(F) Victims of Crime liens (Labor Code section 4903(i)).

(G) A defendant filing a Declaration of Readiness to Proceed on a lien claim.

(H) A party who is not a lien claimant.

(I) Companion case pursuant to subdivision (d) of this section.

(d) Except for liens that are exempt pursuant to Labor Code section 4903.06(b), prior to or at the filing of a section 4903(b) lien, the lien claimant shall submit a filing fee in the amount of one hundred fifty dollars ($150) to the Division of Workers' Compensation, using a form approved by the appeals board. The $150 fee is payment for the filing of a lien. A filing fee is required for each case in which the lien is filed; however, where one or more liens or one or more costs filed as a lien is filed in more than one case involving the same injured worker and same service or services by the same lien claimant, only one filing fee needs to be paid.

(1) The filing fee shall be collected by the Administrative Director and made electronically consistent with the following filing procedures:

(A) E-Forms filers shall pay the initial lien filing fee following the procedures set forth in the *EAMS E-Form Filing Reference Guide*.

(B) JET Filers shall pay the initial lien filing fee following the procedures set forth in the EAMS JET File Business Rules and Technical Specifications, Version 4.1.

(e) If the initial section 4903(b) lien filing fee has been previously paid, the lien claimant shall submit written documentation of confirmation of payment when filing the Declaration of Readiness to Proceed for a lien conference.

(f) When filing an initial lien, a lien claimant that claims that a filing fee is not required or that a lien filed under Labor Code section 4903(b) is exempt from the filing fee shall so indicate that status on the lien form.

(g) If no application exists for the employee at the time of the initial section 4903(b) lien filing, the lien claimant shall file any necessary application(s) and duty to investigate verification pursuant to section 10770.5. In such cases, the ADJ case number shall be assigned by the Workers' Compensation Appeals Board. The lien claimant will receive a Notice of Application assigning a case number. The lien claimant may thereafter file the initial lien claim or claim of cost filed as a lien accompanied with the filing fee required by Labor Code section 4903.05 or confirmation of payment.

(h) For an initial section 4903(b) lien that is not exempt pursuant to Labor Code section 4903.06(b) confirmation of payment shall be filed with the Declaration of Readiness to Proceed for a lien conference.

(i) The claims of two or more providers of goods or services shall not be merged into a single section 4903(b) lien.

(j) When a lien claimant files liens or claims of costs filed as a lien in more than one case at the same time, the filing fee or fees may be paid in a single transaction following the instructions set forth in the *EAMS E-Form Filing Reference Guide* or the EAMS JET File Business Rules and Technical Specifications, Version 4.1.

(k) A section 4903(b) lien or claims of costs filed as a lien submitted for filing on or after January 1, 2013 that does not comply with the requirements of this section shall be invalid, even if lodged with the Workers' Compensation Appeals Board, and shall not operate to preserve or toll any time limit for filing of the lien.

(*l*) Any section 4903(b) lien or claims of costs filed as a lien filed for goods or services that are not the proper subject of a lien may be dismissed upon request of a party by verified petition or on the appeals board's own motion. If the section 4903(b) lien or claim of costs filed as a lien is dismissed, the lien claimant will not be entitled to reimbursement of the filing fee.

(m) Unless exempt pursuant to Labor Code section 4903.06(b), no initial section 4903(b) lien or claim of costs filed as a lien shall be accepted for filing on or after the effective date of these regulations unless accompanied by full payment for the filing fee required by Labor Code section 4903.05. Until receipt of proper payment or confirmation of payment, the lien shall not be deemed to have been received or filed for any purpose.

(n) When the attorney for the employee or dependent or any assignee of the lien claimant files the initial section 4903(b) lien, that filing shall be deemed to have been made by an agent for the medical provider and payment of the filing fee required by Labor Code section 4903.05 shall be required of the filing party as if the lien had been filed directly by the lien claimant.

Note: Authority cited: Sections 111, 133, 4903.05 and 5307.3, Labor Code. Reference: Sections 126, 4903 and 4903.05, Labor Code; Section 1349, Health and Safety Code; and Sections 10121 and 10270.5, Insurance Code.

History: 1. New article 6 (sections 10207–10208) and section filed 12-31-2012 as an emergency; operative 1-1-2013 pursuant to Government Code section 11346.1(d) (Register 2013, No. 1). A Certificate of Compliance must be transmitted to OAL by 7-1-2013 or emergency language will be repealed by operation of law on the following day.

2. New article 6 (sections 10207-10208) and section refiled 6-26-2013 as an emergency; operative 7-1-2013 pursuant to Government Code section 11346.1(d) (Register 2013, No. 26). A Certificate of Compliance must be transmitted to OAL by 9-30-2013 or emergency language will be repealed by operation of law on the following day.

3. New article 6 (sections 102010-10208) and section refiled 9-30-2013 as an emergency; operative 10-1-2013 pursuant to Government Code section 11346.1(d) (Register 2013, No. 40). A Certificate of Compliance must be transmitted to OAL by 12-30-2013 or emergency language will be repealed by operation of law on the following day.

4. Certificate of Compliance as to 9-30-2013 order, including amendment of subsections (a), (b), (d), (d)(1)(B), (g)-(h), (j)-(k) and (n), transmitted to OAL 11-8-2013 and filed 12-16-2013; amendments effective 12-16-2013 pursuant to Government Code section 11343.4(b)(3) (Register 2013, No. 51).

Ref.: Herlick Handbook §§ 1.01[3][b], 10.03[4].

§10208. Lien Activation Fees.

(a) Any section 4903(b) lien filed prior to January 1, 2013, and any cost filed as a lien prior to January 1, 2013, shall be subject to a lien activation fee in the sum of one hundred dollars ($100.00), payable to the Division of Workers' Compensation. The $100 fee is payment for the activation of a lien. No lien claimant that is required to pay an activation fee shall file a declaration of readiness or participate in any lien conference including obtaining an order allowing its lien in whole or in part, without submitting written proof of prior timely payment of the fee, or without electronic proof of prior timely payment of the fee that is available to the judge and parties at the conference. "Prior timely payment" means payment of the activation fee (1) prior to the filing of a declaration of readiness for a lien claimant filing a declaration of readiness, or (2) prior to an appearance at a lien conference by a lien claimant of record that did not file the declaration of readiness.

(1) The following lien claimants are exempt from the payment of the lien activation fee requirements under this section:

(A) A health care service plan licensed pursuant to section 1349 of the Health and Safety Code.

(B) A group disability insurer under a policy issued in this state pursuant to the provisions of section 10270.5 of the Insurance Code.

(C) A self-insured employee welfare benefit plan, as defined in section 10121 of the Insurance Code issued in this state.

(D) A Taft-Hartley health and welfare fund.

(E) A publicly funded program providing medical benefits on a nonindustrial basis.

(2) The following lien claimants or parties are not required to pay the lien activation fee pursuant to Labor Code section 4903(b):

(A) Reasonable attorney's fees (Labor Code section 4903(a)).

(B) Living expense liens (Labor Code 4903(c)).

(C) Burial expense liens (Labor Code 4903(d)).

(D) Spousal and child support liens (Labor Code 4903(e)).

(E) Employment Development Department liens (Labor Code section 4903, subdivisions (f), (g), and (h)).

(F) Victims of Crime liens (Labor Code section 4903(i)).

(G) A defendant filing a Declaration of Readiness to Proceed on a lien claim.

(H) A party who is not a lien claimant.

(I) A lien claimant provides proof of having paid a filing fee as previously required by former section 4903.05, which required the filing of a payment fee in the amount of $100 when filing an initial medical costs or medical-legal expense lien pursuant to then Labor Code section 4903(b). (Chapter 639 of the Statutes of 2003), if the filing fee has not been reimbursed to the lien claimant.

(J) A companion case pursuant to subdivision (a) of this section.

(b) The lien activation fee shall be collected by the Administrative Director and made electronically consistent with the following filing procedures. All fees shall be deposited in the Workers' Compensation Administration Revolving Fund and applied for the purposes of that fund.

(1) E-Forms filers shall pay the lien activation fee following the procedures set forth in the *EAMS E-Form Filing Reference Guide*.

(2) JET filers shall pay the lien activation fee following the procedures set forth in the EAMS JET File Business Rules and Technical Specifications, Version 4.1.

(c) If the activation fee for a section 4903(b) lien filed prior to January 1, 2013 or the cost filed as a lien prior to January 1, 2013 has been previously paid, the lien claimant shall submit confirmation of payment with the Declaration of Readiness to Proceed for a lien conference.

(d) All lien claimants that are required to pay an activation fee pursuant to this article that did not file the Declaration of Readiness to Proceed for a lien conference and remain a lien claimant of record at the time of a lien conference or consolidated lien conference shall submit confirmation of payment of the lien activation fee at the lien conference.

Note: Authority cited: Sections 111, 133, 4903.06 and 5307.3, Labor Code. Reference: Sections 126, 4903 and 4903.06, Labor Code; Section 1349, Health and Safety Code; and Sections 10270.5 and 10121, Insurance Code.

History: 1. New section filed 12-31-2012 as an emergency; operative 1-1-2013 pursuant to Government Code section 11346.1(d) (Register 2013, No. 1). A Certificate of Compliance must be transmitted to OAL by 7-1-2013 or emergency language will be repealed by operation of law on the following day.

2. New section refiled 6-26-2013 as an emergency; operative 7-1-2013 pursuant to Government Code section 11346.1(d) (Register 2013, No. 26). A Certificate of Compliance must be transmitted to OAL by 9-30-2013 or emergency language will be repealed by operation of law on the following day.

3. New section refiled 9-30-2013 as an emergency; operative 10-1-2013 pursuant to Government Code section 11346.1(d) (Register 2013, No. 40). A Certificate of Compliance must be transmitted to OAL by 12-30-2013 or emergency language will be repealed by operation of law on the following day.

4. Certificate of Compliance as to 9-30-2013 order, including amendment of subsections (a) and (a)(2)(I)-(J), repealer of subsection (b), subsection relettering and amendment of newly designated subsections (b)(1)-(2), transmitted to OAL 11-8-2013 and filed 12-16-2013; amendments effective 12-16-2013 pursuant to Government Code section 11343.4(b)(3) (Register 2013, No. 51).

Ref.: Herlick Handbook §§ 1.01[3][b], 10.03[4].

§10208.1. Lien Fee Refunds.

(a) Lien filing and/or lien activation fees will be automatically refunded when any one of the following occurs:

(1) A lien filing or activation fee is paid properly but the lien or lien activation was not processed due to a system error. In this case, the filing or activation fee must be resubmitted in order for the lien or activation to be processed. However, the filing or activation date will be deemed to be the date on which the filing or activation fee was first properly paid.

(2) A lien activation fee is paid and it is confirmed by the fee payment system that such fee was paid previously for the same lien, or the lien is not available for activation.

(3) An improper amount is paid for a lien filing fee or activation fee. In this case, the filing or activation fee must be repaid in the proper amount in order for the lien filing or lien activation to be effective. The lien filing or activation date will be deemed to be the date that the filing or activation fee is properly paid.

(4) A lien filing fee is properly paid, but due to a procedural defect in the filing of the lien, the filing is not effective and the filer was not able to re-file and cure the defect with 15 days pursuant to California Code of Regulations, title 8, section 10222(a). The lien filing date will be deemed to be the date that the lien is properly filed.

(b) If for any reason a refund is not issued within ten (10) days under (a)(1) through (3), or within 25 days under (a)(4), the Lien Filing Fee Refund Request form set forth in subdivision (c) must be completed and submitted no later than thirty (30) days from the date of payment of the contested fee. Any required documentary proof must be filed with the request, or if specified by the Division, as a supplement to the request. A refund will only be provided upon a showing of good cause. Good cause for a refund includes, but is not limited to the following reasons:

(1) A fee was paid for a lien for which no filing or activation fee is required pursuant to sections 4903.05 or 4903.06 of the Labor Code.

(2) An activation fee was erroneously paid for a lien other than the lien for which payment was intended and the lien for which the activation fee was erroneously paid was filed by a lien claimant other than the lien claimant that paid the contested fee.

(3) An activation fee was erroneously paid for a lien other than the lien for which payment was intended and the lien for which the activation fee was erroneously paid was filed by the same lien claimant that paid the contested fee. In this case, a refund will be provided only if all of the following apply:

(A) The lien claimant did not file a declaration of readiness and was not a lien claimant of record at any lien conference with respect to the erroneously paid lien from January 1, 2013 up to the date of the filing of the request;

(B) The erroneously paid lien is not set for a lien conference on any date up to 30 days following the filing of the request; and

(C) Proof of payment for the correct lien is provided with the request for refund.

(4) An activation fee is paid that was paid previously for the same lien but the duplicate payment is not confirmed by the fee payment system and no refund was issued in accordance with (a) (2). Proof of the prior payment must be provided with the request.

(5) Based on a finding of good cause in accordance with these rules, a workers' compensation administrative law judge or the appeals board has determined that the lien claimant is entitled to a refund of the fee. A final order from a judge or the appeals board authorizing the refund must be provided with the request for refund.

(c) Lien claimants are required to use the Lien Fee Refund Request form (Version 1.0) obtained from the DWC website at https://www.dir.ca.gov/dwc/Liens/LienFeeRefundREQPayer.pdf

Note: Authority cited: Sections 111, 133, 4903.05, 4903.06 and 5307.3, Labor Code. Reference: Sections 126, 4903, 4903.05, 4903.06 and 4903.07, Labor Code.

History: 1. New article 4 (section 10208.1) and renumbering of former section 10245 to new section 10208.1, including amendment of Note, filed 12-10-2012 as a change without regulatory effect pursuant to section 100, title 1, California Code of Regulations by the Division of Workers' Compensation and as a file and print by the Workers' Compensation Appeals Board pursuant to Government Code section 11351 (Register 2012, No. 50).

2. Renumbering of former section 10208.1 to new section 10206.20 filed 12-31-2012 as an emergency; operative 1-1-2013 pursuant to Government Code section 11346.1(d) (Register 2013, No. 1). A Certificate of Compliance must be transmitted to OAL by 7-1-2013 or emergency language will be repealed by operation of law on the following day.

3. Renumbering of former section 10208.1 to new section 10206.20 refiled 6-26-2013 as an emergency; operative 7-1-2013 pursuant to Government Code section 11346.1(d) (Register 2013, No. 26). A Certificate of Compliance must be transmitted to OAL by 9-30-2013 or emergency language will be repealed by operation of law on the following day.

4. Renumbering of former section 10208.1 to new section 10206.20 refiled 9-30-2013 as an emergency; operative 10-1-2013 pursuant to Government Code section 11346.1(d) (Register 2013, No. 40). A Certificate of Compliance must be transmitted to OAL by 12-30-2013 or emergency language will be repealed by operation of law on the following day.

5. Certificate of Compliance as to 9-30-2013 order, including adoption of new section, transmitted to OAL 11-8-2013 and filed 12-16-2013; new section effective 12-16-2013 pursuant to Government Code section 11343.4(b)(3) (Register 2013, No. 51).

Ref.: Hanna § 30.20[1]; Herlick Handbook § 1.01[3][b].

ARTICLE 7
Declarations of Readiness to Proceed, Expedited Hearing and Pre-Trial Conference Statement Forms

§10208.2. Declaration of Readiness to Proceed Form.

DWC-CA form 10250.1 (Declaration of Readiness to Proceed form) revision dated 6/2011 is incorporated by reference.

Note: Authority cited: Sections 111, 133, 5502(a) and 5307.3, Labor Code; and Stats. 2011, c. 559, §17 (A.B. 1426). Reference: Sections 126 and 5502, Labor Code.

History: 1. New article 5 (sections 10208.2–10208.4) and renumbering of former section 10250.1 to new section 10208.2, including amendment of Note, filed 12-10-2012 as a change without regulatory effect pursuant to section 100, title 1, California Code of Regulations by the Division of Workers' Compensation and as a file and print by the Workers' Compensation Appeals Board pursuant to Government Code section 11351 (Register 2012, No. 50).

2. Renumbering of article 5 to article 7 filed 12-31-2012 as an emergency; operative 1-1-2013 pursuant to Government Code section 11346.1(d) (Register 2013, No. 1). A Certificate of Compliance must be transmitted to OAL by 7-1-2013 or emergency language will be repealed by operation of law on the following day.

3. Renumbering of article 5 to article 7 refiled 6-26-2013 as an emergency; operative 7-1-2013 pursuant to Government Code section 11346.1(d) (Register 2013, No. 26). A Certificate of Compliance must be transmitted to OAL by 9-30-2013 or emergency language will be repealed by operation of law on the following day.

4. Renumbering of article 5 to article 7 refiled 9-30-2013 as an emergency; operative 10-1-2013 pursuant to Government Code section 11346.1(d) (Register 2013, No. 40). A Certificate of Compliance must be transmitted to OAL by 12-30-2013 or emergency language will be repealed by operation of law on the following day.

5. Certificate of Compliance as to 9-30-2013 order transmitted to OAL 11-8-2013 and filed 12-16-2013 (Register 2013, No. 51).

Ref.: Hanna §§ 1.11[5][a]–[e], 1.12[9][b], 1.13[1]–[7], 23.11[2], [2a], 23.12[2]–[3d], 23.16, 24.11[1][c], 25.06A, 25.08, 25.09, 26.01[3], 26.02, 26.04, 33.01[1][b], [2], [3][b]–[d], [4], 35.72[3]; Herlick Handbook §§ 1.01[3][b], 5.20, 14.5A, 16.23.

§10208.3. Expedited Hearing Form.

DWC-CA form 10252.1 (Expedited Hearing form) revision dated 11/2008 is incorporated by reference.

Note: Authority cited: Sections 111, 133, 5502(b) and 5307.3, Labor Code; and Stats. 2011, c. 559, §17 (A.B. 1426). Reference: Sections 126 and 5502(b), Labor Code.

History: 1. Change without regulatory effect renumbering former section 10252.1 to new section 10208.3, including amendment of Note, filed 12-10-2012 pursuant to section 100, title 1, California Code of Regulations (Register 2012, No. 50).

Ref.: Hanna §§ 1.11[5][a]–[e], 1.12[9][b], 1.13[1]–[7], 23.11[2], [2a], 23.12[2]–[3d], 23.16, 24.11[1][c], 25.06A, 25.08, 25.09, 26.01[3], 26.02, 26.04, 33.01[1][b], [2], [3][b]–[d], [4], 35.72[3]; Herlick Handbook §§ 1.01[3][b], 5.20, 14.5A, 16.23.

§10208.4. Pre-Trial Conference Statement Form.

DWC-CA form 10253.1 (Pre-trial Conference Statement form) revision dated 9/2010 is incorporated by reference.

Note: Authority cited: Sections 111, 133, 5307.3 and 5502, Labor Code; and Stats. 2011, c. 559, §17 (A.B. 1426). Reference: Sections 126 and 5502, Labor Code.

History: 1. Renumbering of former section 10253.1 to new section 10208.4, including amendment of Note, filed 12-10-2012 as a change without regulatory effect pursuant to section 100, title 1, California Code of Regulations by the Division of Workers' Compensation and as a file and print by the Workers' Compensation Appeals Board pursuant to Government Code section 11351 (Register 2012, No. 50).

Ref.: Hanna §§ 1.11[5][a]–[e], 1.12[9][b], 1.13[1]–[7], 23.11[2], [2a], 23.12[2]–[3d], 23.16, 24.11[1][c], 25.06A, 25.08, 25.09, 26.01[3], 26.02, 26.04, 33.01[1][b], [2], [3][b]–[d], [4], 35.72[3]; Herlick Handbook §§ 1.01[3][b], 5.20, 14.5A, 16.23.

ARTICLE 8
Access to Records and Retention of Records

§10208.5. Access to and Viewing Adjudication Files.

(a) A party, a lien claimant, or an attorney or other representative for a party or lien claimant may access and view specific adjudication files in which the party, lien claimant, attorney, or representative is a case participant except as provided for in section 10208.6.

(b) Except as otherwise prohibited by law or sections 10208.6 and 10272, any person may inspect the contents of any electronic adjudication file at any district office, whether or not the district office has venue over the case.

(c) Except as otherwise prohibited by law or sections 10208.6 and 10272, any person may inspect the contents of any paper adjudication file at the district office or office of the appeals board where the file is located during regular office hours.

(d) The paper adjudication file and the records and documents contained therein may not be removed from the district office or the office of the appeals board for copying or for any other purpose.

(e) Copying operators must operate their equipment in the room assigned to them and any person copying a paper adjudication file must put papers back in the file in their original order and any person viewing or copying a file must return the file in the same order and condition in which it was received.

(f) A paper adjudication file shall not be sent from one office to another for inspection except for good cause by order of a workers' compensation administrative law judge or the appeals board and upon the payment of a fee required by California Code of Regulations, title 8, section 9990. At the request of a party to the case, or his or her attorney, a paper adjudication file that has been transferred to a record storage center for storage will be made available for inspection through the office from which the file was transferred. Paper adjudication files that have been transferred to a record storage center will be made available for inspection by any other person upon payment of the fee required by California Code of Regulations, title 8, section 9990.

Note: Authority cited: Sections 111, 133, 138.7 and 5307.3, Labor Code; and Stats. 2011, c. 559, §17 (A.B. 1426). Reference: Sections 126, 127 and 5502, Labor Code.

History: 1. New article 6 (sections 10208.5–10208.7) and renumbering of former section 10270 to new section 10208.5, including amendment of subsections (a)-(c) and Note, filed 12-10-2012 as a change without regulatory effect pursuant to section 100, title 1, California Code of Regulations by the Division of Workers' Compensation and as a file and print by the Workers' Compensation Appeals Board pursuant to Government Code section 11351 (Register 2012, No. 50).

2. Renumbering of article 6 to article 8 filed 12-31-2012 as an emergency; operative 1-1-2013 pursuant to Government Code section 11346.1(d) (Register 2013, No. 1). A Certificate of Compliance must be transmitted to OAL by 7-1-2013 or emergency language will be repealed by operation of law on the following day.

3. Renumbering of article 6 to article 8 refiled 6-26-2013 as an emergency; operative 7-1-2013 pursuant to Government Code section 11346.1(d) (Register 2013, No. 26). A Certificate of Compliance must be transmitted to OAL by 9-30-2013 or emergency language will be repealed by operation of law on the following day.

4. Renumbering of article 6 to article 8 refiled 9-30-2013 as an emergency; operative 10-1-2013 pursuant to Government Code section 11346.1(d) (Register 2013, No. 40). A Certificate of Compliance must be transmitted to OAL by 12-30-2013 or emergency language will be repealed by operation of law on the following day.

5. Certificate of Compliance as to 9-30-2013 order transmitted to OAL 11-8-2013 and filed 12-16-2013 (Register 2013, No. 51).

Ref.: Hanna §§ 1.11[5][a]–[e], 1.12[9][b], 1.13[1]–[7], 23.11[2], [2a], 23.12[2]–[3d], 23.16, 24.11[1][c], 25.06A, 25.08, 25.09, 26.01[3], 26.02, 26.04, 33.01[1][b], [2], [3][b]–[d], [4], 35.72[3]; Herlick Handbook §§ 1.01[3][b], 5.20, 14.5A, 16.23.

§10208.6. Prohibitions on Document Inspection.

The following documents shall not be made available for inspection by any person:

(a) Decisions, reports, opinions, orders, recommendations and other documents that are in the process of preparation, or, although fully prepared, have not yet been signed and filed.

(b) Ratings that have not yet been served.

(c) The working papers, personal notes, deliberation records, and other private notations made by a workers' compensation administrative law judge, commissioner, deputy commissioner or appeals board attorney or legal assistant in the course of hearing or deliberation relating to the case.

(d) Any legal memorandum or analysis prepared by a workers' compensation administrative law judge, commissioner, deputy commissioner, appeals board attorney or legal assistant to assist a workers' compensation administrative law judge, deputy commissioner or commissioner in his or her deliberations concerning a case.

Note: Authority cited: Sections 111, 133 and 5307.3, Labor Code; Section 6253.4, Government Code; and Stats. 2011, c. 559, §17 (A.B. 1426). Reference: Sections 126, 127 and 138.7, Labor Code.

History: 1. Renumbering of former section 10271 to new section 10208.6, including amendment of section and Note, filed 12-10-2012 as a change without regulatory effect pursuant to section 100, title 1, California Code of Regulations by the Division of Workers' Compensation and as a file and print by the Workers' Compensation Appeals Board pursuant to Government Code section 11351 (Register 2012, No. 50).

Ref.: Hanna §§ 1.11[5][a]–[e], 1.12[9][b], 1.13[1]–[7], 23.11[2], [2a], 23.12[2]–[3d], 23.16, 24.11[1][c], 25.06A, 25.08, 25.09, 26.01[3], 26.02, 26.04, 33.01[1][b], [2], [3][b]–[d], [4], 35.72[3]; Herlick Handbook §§ 1.01[3][b], 5.20, 14.5A, 16.23.

§10208.7. Retention, Return and Destruction of Records and Exhibits.

(a) The Division of Workers' Compensation shall retain the following records in an adjudication file after the filing of case opening documents (i.e., the initial application for adjudication of claim or, where an application has not previously been filed, either a stipulations with request for award or a compromise and release) for the time periods set forth in subdivisions (d) and (e):

(1) the application for adjudication of claim and any amended application;

(2) all settlement documents;

(3) all orders, decisions, or awards;

(4) all minutes of hearing;

(5) all minutes of hearing and summary of evidence;

(6) all medical-legal reports;

(7) all permanent and stationary medical reports of treating physicians;

(8) all rating instructions;

(9) all formal ratings, summary rating determinations, and consultative ratings; and

(10) any other documents as determined by the appeals board or the administrative director.

(b) After five years from the date of filing of the initial application, the Division of Workers' Compensation may eliminate from the adjudication file and destroy paper or electronic correspondence and other miscellaneous material or records, including non-permanent and stationary medical reports of treating physicians, not listed in subdivision (a), above with approval of the Secretary of State.

(c) At any time, with approval of the Secretary of State, the Division of Workers' Compensation may eliminate from the adjudication file and destroy any of the following paper or electronic documents:

(1) extra copies of pleadings, notices, findings, orders, decisions, awards and other documents; and

(2) any documents filed in violation of section 10205.7, subd. (b).

(d) Following a period of fifty (50) years after the filing of the application or other case opening document, the Division of Workers' Compensation may destroy the documents enumerated in subdivision (a) maintained in electronic form with approval of the Secretary of State.

(e) Following a period of twenty (20) years after the filing of the application or other case opening document, the Division of Workers' Compensation may destroy the documents enumerated in subdivision (a) maintained in paper form with approval of the Secretary of State.

(f) Any party filing an original document or other pieces of evidence pursuant to California Code of Regulations, title 8, section 10603, subd. (a), shall, at the time of filing, either (1) arrange for the return of the document or evidence, at the filing party's sole expense, at the conclusion of all proceedings and appeals thereof; or (2) be deemed by not making such arrangements, to have consented to destruction, without notice, of the document or other evidence at the conclusion of all proceedings and appeals thereof.

(g) Stenographic reporters' notes or electronic sound recording of testimony shall be retained for a period of six (6) years after the taking of them and thereafter may be destroyed or otherwise disposed of.

Note: Authority cited: Sections 111, 133 and 5307.3, Labor Code; and Stats. 2011, c. 559, §17 (A.B. 1426). Reference: Sections 126 and 135, Labor Code.

History: 1. Renumbering of former section 10273 to new section 10208.7, including amendment of subsections (a)(10) and (c)(2) and amendment of Note, filed 12-10-2012 as a change without regulatory effect pursuant to section 100, title 1, California Code of Regulations by the Division of Workers' Compensation and as a file and print by the Workers' Compensation Appeals Board pursuant to Government Code section 11351 (Register 2012, No. 50).

2. Amendment of subsections (a), (b), (c) and (d), new subsection (e) and subsection relettering filed 4-30-2015; operative 7-1-2015 (Register 2015, No. 18).

Ref.: Hanna §§ 1.11[5][a]–[e], 1.12[9][b], 1.13[1]–[7], 23.11[2], [2a], 23.12[2]–[3d], 23.16, 24.11[1][c], 25.06A, 25.08, 25.09, 26.01[3], 26.02, 26.04, 33.01[1][b], [2], [3][b]–[d], [4], 35.72[3]; Herlick Handbook §§ 1.01[3][b], 4.17[2], 5.20, 14.5A, 14.42, 16.23.

ARTICLE 9
Review of Administrative Orders Issued by the Administrative Director

§10208.8. Petition Appealing Order Granting or Denying Petition for Order Requiring Employee to Select Employer-Designated Physician.

(a) Upon receipt of a timely petition appealing a decision granting or denying a change of primary treating petition, pursuant to California Code of Regulations, title 8, section 9786, subd. (e)(2) or (e)(3), the matter shall be referred to a workers' compensation administrative law judge for hearing and determination of the issues raised. The petition shall be accompanied by a copy of the administrative director's order, a declaration of readiness, an application for adjudication if one has not been previously filed, and any other documents deemed relevant that have not been previously filed. A party aggrieved by the determination of the workers' compensation administrative law judge may seek relief therefrom within the same time and in the same manner specified for petitions for reconsideration.

(b) Any party aggrieved by an order issued by a workers' compensation administrative law judge pursuant to a referral under California Code of Regulations, title 8, section 9786, subd. (e)(4), of the rules of the administrative director may petition the appeals board for relief therefrom within twenty (20) days from the date of the issuance of the order in the same manner specified for petitions for reconsideration.

Note: Authority cited: Sections 111, 133 and 5307.3, Labor Code; and Stats. 2011, c. 559, §17 (A.B. 1426). Reference: Sections 126, 4600, 4603 and 4603.5, Labor Code.

History: 1. New article 7 (sections 10208.8–10208.11) and renumbering of former section 10290 to new section 10208.8, including amendment of Note, filed 12-10-2012 as a change without regulatory effect pursuant to section 100, title 1, California Code of Regulations by the Division of Workers' Compensation and as a file and print by the Workers' Compensation Appeals Board pursuant to Government Code section 11351 (Register 2012, No. 50).

2. Renumbering of article 7 to article 9 filed 12-31-2012 as an emergency; operative 1-1-2013 pursuant to Government Code section 11346.1(d) (Register 2013, No. 1). A Certificate of Compliance must be transmitted to OAL by 7-1-2013 or emergency

language will be repealed by operation of law on the following day.

3. Renumbering of article 7 to article 9 filed 12-31-2012 as an emergency; operative 1-1-2013 pursuant to Government Code section 11346.1(d) (Register 2013, No. 1). A Certificate of Compliance must be transmitted to OAL by 7-1-2013 or emergency language will be repealed by operation of law on the following day.

4. Renumbering of article 7 to article 9 refiled 6-26-2013 as an emergency; operative 7-1-2013 pursuant to Government Code section 11346.1(d) (Register 2013, No. 26). A Certificate of Compliance must be transmitted to OAL by 9-30-2013 or emergency language will be repealed by operation of law on the following day.

5. Renumbering of article 7 to article 9 refiled 9-30-2013 as an emergency; operative 10-1-2013 pursuant to Government Code section 11346.1(d) (Register 2013, No. 40). A Certificate of Compliance must be transmitted to OAL by 12-30-2013 or emergency language will be repealed by operation of law on the following day.

6. Certificate of Compliance as to 9-30-2013 order transmitted to OAL 11-8-2013 and filed 12-16-2013 (Register 2013, No. 51).

Ref.: Hanna §§ 1.11[5][a]–[e], 1.12[9][b], 1.13[1]–[7], 23.11[2], [2a], 23.12[2]–[3d], 23.16, 24.11[1][c], 25.06A, 25.08, 25.09, 26.01[3], 26.02, 26.04, 33.01[1][b], [2], [3][b]–[d], [4], 35.72[3]; Herlick Handbook §§ 1.01[3][b], 5.20, 14.5A, 16.23.

§10208.9. Petition Appealing Notice of Compensation Due.

(a) The petition appealing notice of compensation due shall be served on the injured worker or dependent and on the audit unit, concurrently with its filing.

(b) The petition appealing notice of compensation due shall specify the factual and legal basis for the petition and shall include the audit unit's file number. The petition appealing notice of compensation due shall be accompanied by a copy of the notice of compensation due, a declaration of readiness, an application for adjudication if one has not been previously filed, and any other documents deemed relevant.

(c) If an application for adjudication has not been previously filed, venue shall be designated and determined in accordance with Labor Code section 5501.5 and California Code of Regulations, title 8, section 10409. If an application for adjudication has been previously filed, the petition appealing notice of compensation due shall be filed at the district office having venue and the case number assigned to the application for adjudication shall be assigned to the petition.

(d) An appeal of notice of compensation due shall be set for a hearing before a workers' compensation administrative law judge within forty-five (45) days of filing unless the employee's claim is already before a workers' compensation administrative law judge on other substantive issues in which case the appeal may be considered with these other issues. The audit unit, insurer, self-insured employer or third party administrator and the injured worker shall receive notice of the hearing and copies of subsequent notices of orders issued in the case. Following the hearing, the workers' compensation administrative law judge shall issue findings of fact and an order affirming, modifying or rescinding the notice of compensation due, which complies with Labor Code section 5313.

(e) The copy of the appeal of notice of compensation due sent to the injured worker shall inform the injured worker of the right to consult an attorney. If the injured worker is represented by an attorney, the workers' compensation administrative law judge may determine the amount of attorney fees reasonably incurred in resisting the appeal of notice of compensation due and may assess reasonable attorney fees as a cost upon the employer filing the appeal of notice of compensation due in accordance with Labor Code section 129(c).

Note: Authority cited: Sections 111, 133 and 5307.3, Labor Code; and Stats. 2011, c. 559, §17 (A.B. 1426). Reference: Sections 126, 129, 129.5, 5300, 5313 and 5501.5, Labor Code.

History: 1. Renumbering of former section 10291 to new section 10208.9, including amendment of Note, filed 12-10-2012 as a change without regulatory effect pursuant to section 100, title 1, California Code of Regulations by the Division of Workers' Compensation and as a file and print by the Workers' Compensation Appeals Board pursuant to Government Code section 11351 (Register 2012, No. 50).

Ref.: Hanna §§ 1.11[5][a]–[e], 1.12[9][b], 1.13[1]–[7], 23.11[2], [2a], 23.12[2]–[3d], 23.16, 24.11[1][c], 25.06A, 25.08, 25.09, 26.01[3], 26.02, 26.04, 33.01[1][b], [2], [3][b]–[d], [4], 35.72[3]; Herlick Handbook §§ 1.01[3][b], 5.20, 14.5A, 16.23.

§10208.10. Petition Appealing Order of the Rehabilitation Unit.

(a) Appeals from decisions of the rehabilitation unit of the Division of Workers' Compensation shall be commenced as follows:

(1) if an application for adjudication is already on file, by filing and serving a declaration of readiness and a petition setting forth the reason for the appeal;

(2) if no application for adjudication is on file, by filing and serving an application for adjudication, a declaration of readiness, and a petition setting forth the reason for the appeal.

(b) The party appealing the rehabilitation unit decision and the party opposing the appeal shall file and serve any documents that the parties deem relevant that have not already been filed in the rehabilitation unit case file.

(c) If an application for adjudication has not been previously filed, venue shall be designated and determined in accordance with Labor Code section 5501.5 and California Code of Regulations, title 8, section 10409. If an application for adjudication has been previously filed, the petition appealing a decision of the rehabilitation unit shall be filed at the district office having venue and the case number assigned to the application for adjudication shall be assigned to the petition.

(d) A petition appealing a decision of the rehabilitation unit shall be filed within twenty (20) days from the date of the issuance of the rehabilitation unit decision.

Note: Authority cited: Sections 111, 133 and 5307.3, Labor Code; and Stats. 2011, c. 559, §17 (A.B. 1426). Reference: Sections 126, 5500 and 5501.5, Labor Code.

History: 1. Renumbering of former section 10293 to new section 10208.10, including amendment of Note, filed 12-10-2012 as a change without regulatory effect pursuant to section 100, title 1, California Code of Regulations by the Division of Workers' Compensation and as a file and print by the Workers' Compensation Appeals Board pursuant to Government Code section 11351 (Register 2012, No. 50).

Ref.: Hanna §§ 1.11[5][a]–[e], 1.12[9][b], 1.13[1]–[7], 23.11[2], [2a], 23.12[2]–[3d], 23.16, 24.11[1][c], 25.06A, 25.08, 25.09, 26.01[3], 26.02, 26.04, 33.01[1][b], [2], [3][b]–[d], [4], 35.72[3]; Herlick Handbook §§ 1.01[3][b], 5.20, 14.5A, 16.23.

§10208.11. Petition Appealing Determination Regarding Supplemental Job Displacement Benefits.

(a) Either party may appeal the determination and order of the administrative director issued under California Code of Regulations, title 8, section 10133.54 by filing a petition together with a declaration of readiness to proceed pursuant to section 10250 within twenty calendar days of the issuance of the decision or within twenty days after a request is deemed denied pursuant to California Code of Regulations, title 8, section 10133.54, subd. (f), except that the time for filing shall be extended in accordance with California Code of Regulations, title 8, sections 10507 and 10508. The petition shall set forth the specific factual and legal basis for the appeal.

(b) If an application for adjudication has been previously filed, the petition appealing the administrative director's notice shall be filed at the district office having venue and the case number assigned to the application for adjudication shall be assigned to the petition. If an application for adjudication has not been previously filed, an application shall be filed together with the petition, and venue shall be designated and determined in accordance with Labor Code section 5501.5 and California Code of Regulations, title 8, section 10409.

(c) A copy of the petition shall be concurrently served on the administrative director.

Note: Authority cited: Sections 111, 133 and 5307.3, Labor Code; and Stats. 2011, c. 559, §17 (A.B. 1426). Reference: Sections 126, 4658.5, 4658.6 and 4658.7, Labor Code.

History: 1. Change without regulatory effect renumbering former section 10294.5 to new section 10208.11, including amendment of Note, filed 12-10-2012 pursuant to section 100, title 1, California Code of Regulations (Register 2012, No. 50).

Ref.: Hanna §§ 1.11[5][a]–[e], 1.12[9][b], 1.13[1]–[7], 23.11[2], [2a], 23.12[2]–[3d], 23.16, 24.11[1][c], 25.06A, 25.08, 25.09, 26.01[3], 26.02, 26.04, 33.01[1][b], [2], [3][b]–[d], [4], 35.72[3]; Herlick Handbook §§ 1.01[3][b], 5.20, 14.5A, 16.23.

ARTICLE 10
Arbitration Submittal Form

§10208.12. Arbitration Submittal Form.

DWC-CA form 10297 (Arbitration Submittal form) revision dated 11/2008 is incorporated by reference.

Note: Authority cited: Sections 111, 133 and 5307.3, Labor Code; and Stats. 2011, c. 559, §17 (A.B. 1426). Reference: Section 126, Labor Code.

History: 1. New article 8 (section 10208.12) and renumbering of former section 10297 to new section 10208.12, including amendment of Note, filed 12-10-2012 as a change without regulatory effect pursuant to section 100, title 1, California Code of Regulations by the Division of Workers' Compensation and as a file and print by the Workers' Compensation Appeals Board pursuant to Government Code section 11351 (Register 2012, No. 50).

2. Renumbering of article 8 to article 10 filed 12-31-2012 as an emergency; operative 1-1-2013 pursuant to Government Code section 11346.1(d) (Register 2013, No. 1). A Certificate of Compliance must be transmitted to OAL by 7-1-2013 or emergency language will be repealed by operation of law on the following day.

3. Renumbering of article 8 to article 10 refiled 6-26-2013 as an emergency; operative 7-1-2013 pursuant to Government Code section 11346.1(d) (Register 2013, No. 26). A Certificate of Compliance must be transmitted to OAL by 9-30-2013 or emergency language will be repealed by operation of law on the following day.

4. Renumbering of article 8 to article 10 refiled 9-30-2013 as an emergency; operative 10-1-2013 pursuant to Government Code section 11346.1(d) (Register 2013, No. 40). A Certificate of Compliance must be transmitted to OAL by 12-30-2013 or emergency language will be repealed by operation of law on the following day.

5. Certificate of Compliance as to 9-30-2013 order transmitted to OAL 11-8-2013 and filed 12-16-2013 (Register 2013, No. 51).

Ref.: Hanna §§ 1.11[5][a]–[e], 1.12[9][b], 1.13[1]–[7], 23.11[2], [2a], 23.12[2]–[3d], 23.16, 24.11[1][c], 25.06A, 25.08, 25.09, 26.01[3], 26.02, 26.04, 33.01[1][b], [2], [3][b]–[d], [4], 35.72[3]; Herlick Handbook §§ 1.01[3][b], 5.20, 14.5A, 16.23.

SUBCHAPTER 1.9
RULES OF THE COURT ADMINISTRATOR [REPEALED]

History: 1. Relocation of subchapter 1.9 from preceding section 10250 to precede section 10210, new article 1 (sections 10210–10214) and new section filed 11-17-2008; operative 11-17-2008 pursuant to Government Code section 11343.4 (Register 2008, No. 47).

2. Renumbering of former section 10210 to new section 10205 filed 12-10-2012 as a change without regulatory effect pursuant to section 100, title 1, California Code of Regulations by the Division of Workers' Compensation and as a file and print by the Workers' Compensation Appeals Board pursuant to Government Code section 11351 (Register 2012, No. 50).

3. Repealer of subchapter 1.9 (articles 1–10, sections 10210–10297) filed 10-15-2014; operative 1-1-2015. Submitted to OAL for printing only pursuant to Government Code section 11351 (Register 2014, No. 42).

4. Editorial correction of History 3 (Register 2017, No. 8).

SUBCHAPTER 2
WORKERS' COMPENSATION APPEALS BOARD—RULES AND PRACTICE PROCEDURE

ARTICLE 1
General

§10300. Construction of Rules.

(a) The provisions of these rules are severable. If any provision of these rules, or the application thereof to any person or circumstances, is held invalid, that invalidity shall not affect other provisions or applications that can be given effect without the invalid provision or application.

(b) Article and section headings shall not be deemed to limit or modify the meaning or intent of the provisions of any rule hereof.

Note: Authority cited: Sections 133, 5307, 5309 and 5708, Labor Code. Reference: Section 5307, Labor Code.

History: 1. Repeal of chap. 4.5 (Industrial Accident Commission—Rules of Practice and Procedure) and new chap. 4.5 filed by Industrial Accident Commission 12-27-65; effective thirtieth day thereafter (Register 65, No. 25). For former chap. 4.5, see Registers 58, No. 14; 59, No. 21; 61, No. 9; 61, No. 12; 62, No. 7; 62, No. 21; 63, No. 2; 65, Nos. 5, 13 and 22.

2. Ratification and adoption by Workmen's Compensation Appeals Board, of regulations filed by Industrial Accident Commission on 12-27-65, filed 1-26-66 (Register 66, No. 3).

3. Repealer of subchapter 2 (articles 1-19, sections 10300-10957, not consecutive and Appendix) and new subchapter 2 (articles 1-20, sections 10300-10958, not consecutive) filed 6-1-81; designated effective 7-1-81 (Register 81, No. 23). For prior history, see Registers 79, No. 1; 78, No. 3; 77, No. 49; 76, No. 3; 75, No. 35; 75, No. 15; 75, No. 11; 74, No. 6; 73, No. 51; 73, No. 36; 73, No. 6; 68, No. 29; 66, No. 8; 66, No. 7; and 65, No. 25.

4. Amendment filed 12-23-93; operative 1-1-94. Submitted to OAL for printing only pursuant to Government Code section 11351 (Register 93, No. 52).

5. Designation of existing section as subsection (a), new subsection (b) and amendment of Note filed 9-23-2013; operative 10-23-2013. Submitted as a file and print by the Workers' Compensation Appeals Board pursuant to Government Code section 11351 (Register 2013, No. 39).

6. Repealer and new section filed 12-17-2019; operative 1-1-2020. Submitted to OAL for printing only pursuant to Government Code section 11351 (Register 2019, No. 51).

§10301. Definitions. [Renumbered]

Note: Authority cited. Sections 133, 5307, 5309 and 5708, Labor Code. Reference: Sections 20, 54, 110, 130, 131, 134, 3201.5 et seq., 4903 et seq., 5300, 5307, 5309, 5310, 5500, 5500.3, 5501, 5501.5, 5501.6, 5502, 5700, 5701 and 5808, Labor Code.

History: 1. Amendment of section and Note filed 12-19-2002; operative 1-1-2003. Submitted to OAL for printing only pursuant to Government Code section 11351 (Register 2002, No. 51).

2. Amendment of section and Note filed 11-17-2008; operative 11-17-2008. Submitted to OAL for printing only (Register 2008, No. 47).

3. Amendment of section and Note filed 9-23-2013; operative 10-23-2013. Submitted as a file and print by the Workers' Compensation Appeals Board pursuant to Government Code section 11351 (Register 2013, No. 39).

4. Renumbering of former section 10301 to section 10305 filed 12-17-2019; operative 1-1-2020. Submitted to OAL for printing only pursuant to Government Code section 11351 (Register 2019, No. 51).

§10302. Rulemaking Notices.

Notices required by Labor Code sections 5307 and 5307.4 shall be served by the Appeals Board by regular mail, fax, electronic mail or any similar technology on those who have filed a written request for notification with the Secretary of the Workers' Compensation Appeals Board.

Note: Authority cited: Sections 133, 5307, 5309 and 5708, Labor Code. Reference: Sections 5307, 5307.4 and 5309, Labor Code.

History: 1. Amendment of section heading, section and Note filed 11-17-2008; operative 11-17-2008. Submitted to OAL for printing only (Register 2008, No. 47).

2. Repealer and new section filed 12-17-2019; operative 1-1-2020. Submitted to OAL for printing only pursuant to Government Code section 11351 (Register 2019, No. 51).

Ref.: Hanna § 1.11[4].

§10304. Article and Section Headings. [Repealed]

Note: Authority cited: Sections 133, 5307, Labor Code. Reference: Sections 133, 5307, Labor Code.

History: 1. Repealer filed 12-17-2019; operative 1-1-2020. Submitted to OAL for printing only pursuant to Government Code section 11351 (Register 2019, No. 51).

§10305. Definitions.

As used in this subchapter:

(a) "Administrative Director" means the Administrative Director of the Division of Workers' Compensation or a designee.

(b) "Appeals Board" means the commissioners and deputy commissioners of the Workers' Compensation Appeals Board acting en banc, in panels or individually.

(c) "Appear" means to act on behalf of any party.

(d) "Applicant" or "injured employee" or "injured worker" or "dependent" means any person asserting a right to relief under the provisions of Labor Code section 5300.

(e) "Claims administrator" means an entity that reviews or adjusts workers' compensation claims on behalf of either (1) an insurer or (2) an employer that has secured a certificate of consent to self-insure from the Department of Industrial Relations, whether employed directly or as a third party.

(f) "Defendant" means any person against whom a right to relief is claimed.

(g) "Director" means the Director of Industrial Relations or a designee.

(h) "District office" means a location of a trial court of the Workers' Compensation Appeals Board and includes a permanently staffed satellite office.

(i) "Electronic Adjudication Management System" or "EAMS" means the computerized case management system used by the Division of Workers' Compensation to electronically store and maintain adjudication files and to perform other case management functions.

(j) "En Banc decision" means a decision of the Appeals Board as a whole, issued in order to achieve uniformity of decision or in a case presenting novel issues, that is binding on panels of the Appeals Board and workers' compensation judges as legal precedent under the principle of stare decisis.

(k) "Entity" means a corporation, limited liability company, limited partnership, general partnership, limited liability partnership, sole proprietorship or any other organizational structure.

(*l*) "Hearing" means any trial, mandatory settlement conference, status conference, lien conference, lien trial or priority conference at a district office, a remote location or before the Appeals Board.

(m) "Lien claimant" means any person or entity claiming payment under the provisions of Labor Code section 4903 et seq., including a claim of costs filed as a lien.

(n) "Non-attorney representative" means a person who is not licensed to practice law by the State of California who acts on behalf of a party in proceedings before the Workers' Compensation Appeals Board as allowed by Labor Code sections 5700 and 4907.

(o) "Party" means any person or entity joined in a case, including but not limited to:

(1) An applicant;

(2) A defendant; or

(3) A lien claimant.

(p) "Presiding workers' compensation judge" means the presiding workers' compensation judge of any district office and includes workers' compensation judges designated to perform the functions of a presiding workers' compensation judge.

(q) "Section 4903(b) lien" means a lien claim filed in accordance with Labor Code section 4903(b) for medical treatment expenses incurred by or on behalf of the injured employee, as provided by Article 2 (commencing with Labor Code section 4600), including but not limited to expenses for interpreter services, copying and related services and transportation services incurred in connection with medical treatment. It shall not include any amount payable directly to the injured employee.

(r) "Significant panel decision" means a decision of the Appeals Board that has been designated by all members of the Appeals Board as of significant interest and importance to the workers' compensation community. Although not binding precedent, significant panel decisions are intended to augment the body of binding appellate and en banc decisions by providing further guidance to the workers' compensation community.

(s) "Status conference" means a proceeding set for the purpose of ascertaining if there are genuine disputes requiring resolution, of providing assistance to the parties in resolving disputes, of narrowing the issues, and of facilitating preparation for trial if a trial is necessary.

(t) "Submission" means the closing of the record to the receipt of further evidence or argument.

(u) "Walk-through document" means a document that is presented to a workers' compensation judge for immediate action where no notice of hearing has issued.

(v) "Workers' Compensation Appeals Board" means the commissioners and deputy commissioners of the Appeals Board, presiding workers' compensation judges and workers' compensation judges.

(w) "Workers' compensation judge" means "workers' compensation administrative law judge" (formerly, "referee") and includes pro tempore judges appointed pursuant to section 10350.

Note: Authority cited: Sections 133, 5307, 5309 and 5708, Labor Code. Reference: Sections 20, 110(a), 5300, 5307, 5309, 5500, 5500.3, 5501, 5501.5, 5501.6, 5502, 5700 and 5701, Labor Code.

History: 1. Renumbering of former section 10301 to section 10305, including amendment of section and Note, filed 12-17-2019; operative 1-1-2020. Submitted to OAL for printing only pursuant to Government Code section 11351 (Register 2019, No. 51).

Ref.: Hanna §§ 23.14[2][d], 25.41[2], 26.01[1], [3][a], 26.04[2], 30.22[5][a], [6]; Herlick Handbook §§ 1.01, 14.30, 14.30A, 14.31.

§10306. Case Names. [Repealed]

Note: Authority cited: Sections 133 and 5307, Labor Code. Reference: Section 126, Labor Code.

History: 1. Amendment of section heading and section filed 12-19-2002; operative 1-1-2003. Submitted to OAL for printing only pursuant to Government Code section 11351 (Register 2002, No. 51).

2. Repealer filed 11-17-2008; operative 11-17-2008. Submitted to OAL for printing only (Register 2008, No. 47).

§10308. Official Address Record. [Repealed]

Note: Authority cited: Sections 133 and 5307, Labor Code. Reference: Section 126, Labor Code.

History: 1. Amendment filed 12-19-2002; operative 1-1-2003. Submitted to OAL for printing only pursuant to Government Code section 11351 (Register 2002, No. 51).

2. Repealer filed 11-17-2008; operative 11-17-2008. Submitted to OAL for printing only (Register 2008, No. 47).

ARTICLE 2
Powers, Duties and Responsibilities

§10320. Appeals Board Decisions and Orders.

The following orders, decisions and awards shall be issued only by a panel of the Appeals Board or the Appeals Board acting en banc:

(a) Any order, including a final, interim or interlocutory order, made more than 15 days after a petition for reconsideration is filed unless allowed by rule 10961.

(b) All orders dismissing, denying or granting petitions for reconsideration.

(c) All decisions after reconsideration that terminate proceedings on reconsideration, including, but not limited to, findings, orders, awards, orders approving or disapproving a Compromise and Release, orders allowing or disallowing a lien and orders for dismissal.

(d) All orders dismissing, denying or granting petitions for removal and all orders pertaining to removal.

(e) All orders in disciplinary proceedings pursuant to Labor Code section 4907.

(f) Decisions on remittitur.

(g) Orders disqualifying a workers' compensation judge under Labor Code section 5311.

Note: Authority cited: Sections 133 and 5307, Labor Code. Reference: Sections 115, 4907 and 5311, Labor Code.

History: 1. New article 2 heading and renumbering of former section 10340 to section 10320, including amendment of section and Note, filed 12-17-2019; operative 1-1-2020. Submitted to OAL for printing only pursuant to Government Code section 11351 (Register 2019, No. 51).

Ref.: Hanna §§ 1.11[6][b], 26.10[1]; Herlick Handbook §§ 1.01, 14.5.

§10322. Workers' Compensation Appeals Board Records Not Subject to Subpoena. [Repealed]

Note: Authority cited: Sections 133 and 5307, Labor Code. Reference: Sections 127 and 5811, Labor Code.

History: 1. Amendment filed 12-19-2002; operative 1-1-2003. Submitted to OAL for printing only pursuant to Government Code section 11351 (Register 2002, No. 51).

2. Repealer filed 12-17-2019; operative 1-1-2020. Submitted to OAL for printing only pursuant to Government Code section 11351 (Register 2019, No. 51).

Ref.: Herlick Handbook § 14.5.

§10324. Ex Parte Communications. [Renumbered]

Note: Authority cited: Sections 133, 5307, 5309 and 5708, Labor Code. Reference: Sections 5701, 5703.5, 5706, 5708 and 5906, Labor Code.

History: 1. Amendment filed 12-19-2002; operative 1-1-2003. Submitted to OAL for printing only pursuant to Government Code section 11351 (Register 2002, No. 51).

2. Amendment of section and Note filed 11-17-2008; operative 11-17-2008. Submitted to OAL for printing only (Register 2008, No. 47).

3. Renumbering of former section 10324 to section 10410 filed 12-17-2019; operative 1-1-2020. Submitted to OAL for printing only pursuant to Government Code section 11351 (Register 2019, No. 51).

Ref.: Herlick Handbook § 14.5.

§10325. En Banc and Significant Panel Decisions.

(a) En banc decisions of the Appeals Board are assigned by the chairperson on a majority vote of the commissioners and are binding on panels of the Appeals Board and workers' compensation judges as legal precedent under the principle of *stare decisis*.

(b) Significant panel decisions of the Appeals Board involve an issue of general interest to the workers' compensation community but are not binding precedent.

Note: Authority cited: Sections 133 and 5307, Labor Code. Reference: Section 115, Labor Code.

History: 1. Renumbering of former section 10341 to section 10325, including amendment of section heading and section, filed 12-17-2019; operative 1-1-2020. Submitted to OAL for printing only pursuant to Government Code section 11351 (Register 2019, No. 51).

Ref.: Hanna §§ 27.10[2][e], 28.35[1], 34.13[1]; Herlick Handbook §§ 1.01, 14.5, 14.34, 15.5.

§10330. Authority of Workers' Compensation Judges.

In any case that has been regularly assigned to a workers' compensation judge, the workers' compensation judge shall have full power, jurisdiction and authority to hear and determine all issues of fact and law presented and to issue any interim, interlocutory and final orders, findings, decisions and awards as may be necessary to the full adjudication of the case, including the fixing of the amount of the bond required in Labor Code section 3715. Orders, findings, decisions and awards issued by a workers' compensation judge shall be the orders, findings, decisions and awards of the Workers' Compensation Appeals Board unless reconsideration is granted.

Note: Authority cited: Sections 133, 5307, 5309 and 5708, Labor Code. Reference: Sections 3715, 5309 and 5310, Labor Code.

History: 1. Renumbering of former section 10348 to section 10330, including amendment of section and Note, filed 12-17-2019; operative 1-1-2020. Submitted to OAL for printing only pursuant to Government Code section 11351 (Register 2019, No. 51).

Ref.: Hanna §§ 1.11[3][c], [d], [6][a], 21.09[1], 26.03[1], 26.10[1]; Herlick Handbook §§ 13.4, 14.5.

§10338. Authority of Commissioners of the Appeals Board.

The following orders may be issued only by a commissioner:

(a) Approving undertakings on stays of proceedings on reconsideration and petitions for writ of review; and

(b) Directing exhumation or autopsy.

Note: Authority cited: Sections 133 and 5307, Labor Code. Reference: Sections 115, 5706, 5707 and 6002, Labor Code.

History: 1. Renumbering of former section 10342 to section 10338, including amendment of section heading, section and Note, filed 12-17-2019; operative 1-1-2020. Submitted to OAL for printing only pursuant to Government Code section 11351 (Register 2019, No. 51).

Ref.: Hanna §§ 1.11[3][c], [d], [6][b], 27.11[3][a]; Herlick Handbook § 14.5.

§10340. Appeals Board Decisions and Orders. [Renumbered]

Note: Authority cited: Sections 133 and 5307, Labor Code. Reference: Sections 115 and 5311, Labor Code.

History: 1. Amendment of subsections (b) and (d) filed 12-19-2002; operative 1-1-2003. Submitted to OAL for printing only pursuant to Government Code section 11351 (Register 2002, No. 51).

2. Repealer of article 2 heading and renumbering of former section 10340 to section 10320 filed 12-17-2019; operative 1-1-2020. Submitted to OAL for printing only pursuant to Government Code section 11351 (Register 2019, No. 51).

Ref.: Herlick Handbook § 14.5.

§10341. En Banc Decisions. [Renumbered]

Note: Authority cited: Sections 133 and 5307, Labor Code. Reference: Section 115, Labor Code.

History: 1. New section filed 12-19-2002; operative 1-1-2003. Submitted to OAL for printing only pursuant to Government Code section 11351 (Register 2002, No. 51).

2. Renumbering of former section 10341 to section 10325 filed 12-17-2019; operative 1-1-2020. Submitted to OAL for printing only pursuant to Government Code section 11351 (Register 2019, No. 51).

Ref.: Herlick Handbook § 14.5.

§10342. Appeals Board, Member Orders. [Renumbered]

Note: Authority cited: Sections 133 and 5307, Labor Code. Reference: Sections 115, 5706, 5707 and 6002, Labor Code.

History: 1. Amendment filed 12-23-93; operative 1-1-94. Submitted to OAL for printing only pursuant to Government Code section 11351 (Register 93, No. 52).

2. Renumbering of former section 10342 to section 10338 filed 12-17-2019; operative 1-1-2020. Submitted to OAL for printing only pursuant to Government Code section 11351 (Register 2019, No. 51).

Ref.: Herlick Handbook § 14.5.

§10344. Authority of Commissioners, Deputy Commissioners and Presiding Workers' Compensation Judges.

The following orders may be issued only by the Appeals Board, a commissioner, a deputy commissioner or a presiding workers' compensation judge:

(a) Orders issuing certified copies of orders, decisions or awards except that a certified copy may be issued by a presiding workers' compensation judge only if the time for seeking reconsideration and judicial review has expired, and no proceedings are pending on reconsideration or judicial review;

(b) Orders staying, quashing and recalling writs of execution and fixing and approving undertaking thereon;

(c) Orders directing entry of satisfaction of judgment; and

(d) Orders issuing, recalling, quashing, discharging and staying writs of attachment and fixing and approving undertakings thereon.

Note: Authority cited: Sections 133 and 5307, Labor Code. Reference: Sections 115, 5706, 5707 and 6002, Labor Code.

History: 1. Amendment of section heading, section and Note filed 12-17-2019; operative 1-1-2020. Submitted to OAL for printing only pursuant to Government Code section 11351 (Register 2019, No. 51).

Ref.: Hanna § 1.11[3][e]; Herlick Handbook § 14.5.

§10346. Authority of Presiding Workers' Compensation Judge to Assign or Transfer Cases.

(a) The presiding workers' compensation judge has full responsibility for the assignment of cases to the workers' compensation judges of each office and may utilize EAMS to assign cases.

(b) In the event of the death, extended absence, unavailability, retirement or disqualification of the workers' compensation judge, the presiding workers' compensation judge may reassign a case to another workers' compensation judge. Where testimony has been received, the new workers' compensation judge shall recommence the proceeding unless the parties agree to waive the requirements of Labor Code section 5700.

(c) To the extent practicable and fair, supplemental proceedings shall be assigned to the workers' compensation judge who heard the original proceedings.

(d) Any conflict that may arise between presiding workers' compensation judges of different district offices respecting assignment of a case, venue or priority of hearing where there is conflict in calendar settings will be resolved by a deputy commissioner of the Appeals Board.

(e) If a Compromise and Release or Stipulations with Request for Award have not been approved, disapproved or noticed for trial on the issue of adequacy and other disputed issues within 45 days after filing, the file shall be transferred to the presiding workers' compensation judge for review.

Note: Authority cited: Sections 133, 5307, 5309 and 5708, Labor Code. Reference: Sections 5309, 5310 and 5700, Labor Code.

History: 1. Amendment of section and Note filed 12-19-2002; operative 1-1-2003. Submitted to OAL for printing only pursuant to Government Code section 11351 (Register 2002, No. 51).

2. Amendment of section and Note filed 11-17-2008; operative 11-17-2008. Submitted to OAL for printing only (Register 2008, No. 47).

3. Amendment of section heading, section and Note filed 12-17-2019; operative 1-1-2020. Submitted to OAL for printing only pursuant to Government Code section 11351 (Register 2019, No. 51).

Ref.: Hanna §§ 1.11[3][e], 29.04[3][a]; Herlick Handbook §§ 11.05, 14.5, 14.31.

§10347. Assignment of Judges. [Repealed]

Note: Authority cited: Sections 133 and 5307, Labor Code. Reference: Sections 5309 and 5310, Labor Code.

History: 1. New section filed 12-19-2002; operative 1-1-2003. Submitted to OAL for printing only pursuant to Government Code section 11351 (Register 2002, No. 51). For prior history, see Register 96, No. 43.

2. Repealer filed 11-17-2008; operative 11-17-2008. Submitted to OAL for printing only (Register 2008, No. 47).

Ref.: Herlick Handbook § 14.5.

§10348. Authority of Workers' Compensation Judges. [Renumbered]

Note: Authority cited: Sections 133 and 5307, Labor Code. Reference: Sections 121, 134, 5309 and 5310, Labor Code.

History: 1. Amendment exempt from OAL review puruant to Government Code section 11351 filed 12-19-90; operative 1-1-91 (Register 91, No. 7).

2. Amendment of first paragraph filed 12-19-2002; operative 1-1-2003. Submitted to OAL for printing only pursuant to Government Code section 11351 (Register 2002, No. 51).

3. Renumbering of former section 10348 to section 10330 filed 12-17-2019; operative 1-1-2020. Submitted to OAL for printing only pursuant to Government Code section 11351 (Register 2019, No. 51).

Ref.: Herlick Handbook § 14.5.

§10349. Orders Equivalent to Notices of Intention. [Repealed]

Note: Authority cited: Sections 133 and 5307, Labor Code. Reference: Section !, Labor Code.

History: 1. New section filed 12-19-2002; operative 1-1-2003. Submitted to OAL for printing only pursuant to Government Code section 11351 (Register 2002, No. 51). For prior history, see Register 96, No. 43.

2. Repealer filed 12-17-2019; operative 1-1-2020. Submitted to OAL for printing only pursuant to Government Code section 11351 (Register 2019, No. 51).

Ref.: Hanna §§ 27.11[2], 23.14[1][c]; Herlick Handbook § 14.5.

§10350. Trials: Appointment and Authority of Pro Tempore Workers' Compensation Judges. [Repealed]

Note: Authority cited: Sections 133 and 5307, Labor Code. Reference: Sections 123.7, 5309 and 5310, Labor Code.

History: 1. New section filed 5-25-82; designated effective 7-1-82 (Register 82, No. 22).

2. Amendment of section heading, section and Note filed 12-19-2002; operative 1-1-2003. Submitted to OAL for printing only pursuant to Government Code section 11351 (Register 2002, No. 51).

3. Repealer filed 12-17-2019; operative 1-1-2020. Submitted to OAL for printing only pursuant to Government Code section 11351 (Register 2019, No. 51).

Ref.: Herlick Handbook § 14.5.

§10351. Conference Hearings: Appointment and Authority of Pro Tempore Workers' Compensation Judges. [Repealed]

Note: Authority cited: Sections 133 and 5307, Labor Code. Reference: Sections 123.7, 5309 and 5310, Labor Code.

History: 1. New section filed 5-25-82; designated effective 7-1-82 (Register 82, No. 22).

2. Amendment of section and Note filed 12-19-2002; operative 1-1-2003. Submitted to OAL for printing only pursuant to Government Code section 11351 (Register 2002, No. 51).

3. Repealer filed 12-17-2019; operative 1-1-2020. Submitted to OAL for printing only pursuant to Government Code section 11351 (Register 2019, No. 51).

Ref.: Herlick Handbook § 14.5.

§10352. Reconsideration of Pro Tempore Workers' Compensation Judge's Orders, Decisions or Awards. [Repealed]

Note: Authority cited: Sections 133 and 5307, Labor Code. Reference: Sections 121, 123.7, 5309, 5310 and 5900-5911, Labor Code.

History: 1. New section filed 5-25-82; designated effective 7-1-82 (Register 82, No. 22).

2. Editorial correction of NOTE filed 2-2-83 (Register 83, No. 6).

3. Repealer filed 12-17-2019; operative 1-1-2020. Submitted to OAL for printing only pursuant to Government Code section 11351 (Register 2019, No. 51).

Ref.: Herlick Handbook § 14.5.

§10353. Settlement Conference Authority. [Repealed]

Note: Authority cited: Sections 133, 5307 and 5502, Labor Code. Reference: Sections 5502 and 5502.5, Labor Code.

History: 1. New section exempt from OAL review pursuant to Government Code section 11351, filed 12-19-90; operative 1-1-91 (Register 91, No. 7).

2. Amendment of section heading and text filed 12-23-93; operative 1-1-94. Submitted to OAL for printing only pursuant to Government Code section 11351 (Register 93, No. 52).

3. Amendment of section and Note filed 12-19-2002; operative 1-1-2003. Submitted to OAL for printing only pursuant to Government Code section 11351 (Register 2002, No. 51).

4. Repealer filed 12-17-2019; operative 1-1-2020. Submitted to OAL for printing only pursuant to Government Code section 11351 (Register 2019, No. 51).

Ref.: Herlick Handbook § 14.5.

§10355. Appointment and Authority of Pro Tempore Workers' Compensation Judges.

A presiding workers' compensation judge may appoint a pro tempore workers' compensation judge to any conference hearing calendar including mandatory settlement conferences or status conferences.

(a) A pro tempore workers' compensation judge shall have the same power as a workers' compensation judge and shall be bound by the Rules of Practice and Procedure of the Workers' Compensation Appeals Board.

(b) Any order, decision or award filed by a pro tempore workers' compensation judge shall be subject to reconsideration or removal in the same manner as any order, decision, or award filed by a workers' compensation judge.

Note: Authority cited: Sections 133 and 5307, Labor Code. Reference: Sections 121, 123.7, 5309, 5310 and 5900-5911, Labor Code.

History: 1. New section filed 12-17-2019; operative 1-1-2020. Submitted to OAL for printing only pursuant to Government Code section 11351 (Register 2019, No. 51).

Ref.: Hanna § 1.11[3][f]; Herlick Handbook § 14.5.

§10360. Testimony of Judicial or Quasi-Judicial Officers.

(a) No judicial or quasi-judicial officer of the Workers' Compensation Appeals Board or of the Division of Workers' Compensation may be subpoenaed or ordered to testify regarding either:

(1) The reasons for or basis of any decision or ruling they have made; or

(2) Their opinion regarding any statements, conduct or events occurring in proceedings before them, except:

(A) The judicial or quasi-judicial officer may be ordered to testify where their testimony is necessary on an issue of disqualification under Labor Code section 5311 and Code of Civil Procedure section 641.

(B) The judicial or quasi-judicial officer may be ordered to testify where their testimony is necessary on an issue of an alleged ex parte communication.

(C) The judicial or quasi-judicial officer may be subpoenaed or ordered to testify as a percipient witness to statements, conduct or events that occurred in the proceedings before them, to the same extent as any other percipient witness.

(b) The testimony of a judicial or quasi-judicial officer shall be given only on the terms and conditions ordered by the presiding workers' compensation judge of the district office having venue, or by the Appeals Board, after the filing of a "Petition to Compel the Testimony of a Judicial or Quasi-Judicial Officer."

(1) The petition to compel shall set forth with specificity the facts (or alleged facts) and law that support the petition.

(2) The petition to compel shall be verified under penalty of perjury.

(3) The petition to compel shall be served on all other parties, on all lien claimants whose liens are presently pending in issue in the underlying claim to which the petition relates and on the Legal Unit of the Division of Workers' Compensation (DWC-Legal Unit), together with a proof of service.

(4) A petition to compel that does not meet all of the foregoing requirements may be summarily dismissed or denied.

(c) The other parties, lien claimants, and the DWC-Legal Unit shall have 15 days within which to file any objection to the petition to compel.

(d) The petition to compel shall be determined:

(1) By the presiding workers' compensation judge of the district office having venue; or

(2) By a deputy commissioner of the Appeals Board, if the petition to compel relates to the presiding workers' compensation judge of the district office having venue; or

(3) By the Appeals Board, if the petition to compel relates to a petition for reconsideration, removal or disqualification.

(e) The petition may be determined on the pleadings submitted or, in the discretion of the presiding workers' compensation judge, the deputy commissioner or the Appeals Board, the petition may be set for a hearing. In determining whether to grant the petition to compel, the presiding workers' compensation judge, the deputy commissioner or the Appeals Board may consider, among other things:

(1) Whether the testimony of the judicial or quasi-judicial officer is reasonably necessary, taking into consideration:

(A) Whether statements in the judicial or quasi-judicial officer's opinion on decision, report on reconsideration, removal or disqualification, or other similar statements are sufficient to resolve any allegation by a party; and

(B) If not, whether the judicial or quasi-judicial officer's factual statements may be fairly provided by an affidavit or declaration under penalty of perjury.

(2) Whether the testimony of the judicial or quasi-judicial officer under the "percipient witness" exception would be cumulative to the testimony of other percipient witnesses.

(f) For purposes of this rule, the term "judicial or quasi-judicial officer of the Workers' Compensation Appeals Board or of the Division of Workers' Compensation" shall include, but shall not be limited to:

(1) Any commissioner;

(2) Any deputy commissioner;

(3) Any presiding workers' compensation judge or workers' compensation judge;

(4) Any pro tempore workers' compensation judge;

(5) Any special master appointed by the Workers' Compensation Appeals Board;

(6) The Administrative Director and the Administrative Director's designee;

(7) Any workers' compensation consultant of the Retraining and Return to Work Unit; and

(8) Any arbitrator or mediator; and

(9) The Director of Industrial Relations and the Director of Industrial Relations' designee.

(g) For the purposes of this rule, the term "testify" shall include testimony in either oral or written form (e.g., affidavits, declarations or interrogatories) and shall include all testimony, whether given at a deposition or a hearing.

(h) This rule shall apply solely to testimony sought in connection with a matter within the jurisdiction of the Workers' Compensation Appeals Board, and it shall not apply to testimony sought pursuant to the authority of any other forum.

Note: Authority cited: Sections 133, 5307, 5309 and 5708, Labor Code. Reference: Sections 5300, 5301, 5309, 5311, 5700, 5701 and 5708, Labor Code; Section 641, Code of Civil Procedure; and Section 703.5, Evidence Code.

History: 1. Amendment of section and Note filed 12-19-2002; operative 1-1-2003. Submitted to OAL for printing only pursuant to Government Code section 11351 (Register 2002, No. 51).

2. Repealer of article 3 heading, renumbering of former section 10360 to section 10380 and renumbering of former section 10593 to section 10360, including amendment of section and Note, filed 12-17-2019; operative 1-1-2020. Submitted to OAL for printing only pursuant to Government Code section 11351 (Register 2019, No. 51).

Ref.: Hanna § 1.11[8]; Herlick Handbook § 14.5.

§10364. Parties Applicant. [Repealed]

Note: Authority cited: Sections 133 and 5307, Labor Code. Reference: Sections 5300, 5303, 5307.5, 5500 and 5503, Labor Code.

History: 1. New subsection (a) designator and new subsections (b) and (c) filed 10-21-96; operative 11-1-96. Submitted to OAL for printing only pursuant to Government Code section 11351 (Register 96, No. 43).

2. Amendment of subsection (a) filed 12-19-2002; operative 1-1-2003. Submitted to OAL for printing only pursuant to Government Code section 11351 (Register 2002, No. 51).

3. Repealer filed 12-17-2019; operative 1-1-2020. Submitted to OAL for printing only pursuant to Government Code section 11351 (Register 2019, No. 51).

Ref.: Herlick Handbook § 14.5.

§10368. Parties Defendant. [Repealed]

Note: Authority cited: Sections 133 and 5307, Labor Code. Reference: Sections 5300, 5303, 5307.5, 5500 and 5503, Labor Code.

History: 1. Repealer filed 10-21-96; operative 11-1-96. Submitted to OAL for printing only pursuant to Government Code section 11351 (Register 96, No. 43).

Ref.: Herlick Handbook § 14.5.

§10370. Extensions Of Time During Public Emergencies.

(a) Notwithstanding rule 10390 or any other rule in this title, in the event of a public emergency, including but not limited to an earthquake, fire or the destruction of or danger to a district office, the chief workers' compensation judge, the designee of the chief workers' compensation judge or the Appeals Board may:

(1) Extend by no more than 14 additional days the time to perform any act required or permitted under these rules, except for those acts subject to a statute of limitations or a jurisdictional time limitation, including but not limited to the filing of Petitions for Reconsideration or Removal, Petitions to Reopen, Applications for Adjudication of Claim or lien claim forms; or

(2) Authorize the presiding workers' compensation judge of a specific district office to extend by no more than 30 additional days the time to perform any act required or permitted under these rules, except for those acts subject to a statute of limitations or a jurisdictional time limitation, including but not limited to the filing of Petitions for

Reconsideration or Removal, Petitions to Reopen, Applications for Adjudication of Claim or lien claim forms; or

(3) Authorize any district office to accept for filing, including by fax, those documents required by statute or regulation to be filed in a district office that is closed due to a public emergency.

(b) Any order under (a)(1), (a)(2) or (a)(3) must specify the nature of the emergency and the district office or offices to which it applies. Any order under (a)(2) must also specify the length of the authorized extension and the reason for the extension.

(c) If made necessary by the nature or extent of the public emergency, the chief workers' compensation judge, the designee of the chief workers' compensation judge or the Appeals Board may extend or renew an order issued under (a)(1) or (a)(2) for no more than 30 days.

Note: Authority cited: Sections 133, 5307 and 5309, Labor Code. Reference: Sections 5301 and 5307, Labor Code.

History: 1. New section filed 12-17-2019; operative 1-1-2020. Submitted to OAL for printing only pursuant to Government Code section 11351 (Register 2019, No. 51).

Ref.: Hanna § 24.10; Herlick Handbook § 14.5.

§10372. Parties in Death Cases. [Repealed]

Note: Authority cited: Sections 133 and 5307, Labor Code. Reference: Sections 5300, 5303, 5307.5, 5500 and 5503, Labor Code.

History: 1. Repealer filed 10-21-96; operative 11-1-96. Submitted to OAL for printing only pursuant to Government Code section 11351 (Register 96, No. 43).

ARTICLE 3
Parties, Joinder and Consolidation

§10380. Necessary Parties.

Any applicant other than the injured employee shall join the injured employee as a party. In such instances the Application for Adjudication of Claim shall include the injured employee's address or, if not known, a statement of that fact.

Note: Authority cited: Sections 133 and 5307, Labor Code. Reference: Sections 126, 5307.5 and 5503, Labor Code.

History: 1. Amendment exempt from OAL review pursuant to Government Code section 11351, filed 12-19-90; operative 1-1-91 (Register 91, No. 7).

2. Amendment filed 12-19-2002; operative 1-1-2003. Submitted to OAL for printing only pursuant to Government Code section 11351 (Register 2002, No. 51).

3. New article 3 heading, repealer of former section 10380 and renumbering and amendment of former section 10360 to section 10380 filed 12-17-2019; operative 1-1-2020. Submitted to OAL for printing only pursuant to Government Code section 11351 (Register 2019, No. 51).

Ref.: Hanna § 26.01[2][a]; Herlick Handbook § 14.11.

§10382. Joinder of Parties.

The Appeals Board or a workers' compensation judge may order the joinder of additional parties not named in the Application for Adjudication of Claim, whose presence is necessary for the full adjudication of the case. A party shall not be joined until 10 days after service of either a petition for joinder by a party or a notice of intention to order joinder issued by a workers' compensation judge, unless the party to be joined waives its right to this notice period. The Workers' Compensation Appeals Board may designate the party or parties who are to make service.

(a) Any person in whom any right to relief is alleged to exist may appear, or be joined, as an applicant in any case or controversy before the Workers' Compensation Appeals Board.

(b) Any person against whom any right to relief is alleged to exist may be joined as a defendant.

(c) In death cases, all persons who may be dependents shall either join or be joined as applicants so that the entire liability of the employer or the insurer may be determined in one proceeding.

(d) If an objection is received within 10 days of service of a petition for joinder or a notice of intention to order joinder, the workers' compensation judge shall consider the objection before joining the party and, if requested in the objection, shall provide the objector the opportunity to be heard before ordering joinder.

Note: Authority cited: Sections 133 and 5307, Labor Code. Reference: Sections 5300, 5303, 5307.5, 5316, 5500 and 5503, Labor Code.

History: 1. New section filed 12-17-2019; operative 1-1-2020. Submitted to OAL for printing only pursuant to Government Code section 11351 (Register 2019, No. 51).

Ref.: Hanna §§ 1.11[3][d], 22.10, 23.14[2][f], 25.05[3], 25.10[7], 26.01[2][a], [b], 26.03[1]; Herlick Handbook § 14.11.

§10390. Proper Identification of Parties.

Any party that appears at a hearing or files a pleading, document or lien shall:

(a) Set forth the party's full legal name on the record of proceedings, pleading, document or lien;

(b) File a notice of representation if a party is represented and the attorney or non-attorney representative has not previously filed a notice of representation or an Application for Adjudication of Claim; and

(c) Identify the insurer and/or employer as the party or parties and not identify a third party administrator as a party. The third party administrator shall be included on the official address record and case caption if identified as such.

Note: Authority cited: Sections 133, 5307, 5309 and 5708, Labor Code. Reference: Sections 3755-3759, 4903.1(c), 5001, 5002, 5003, 5004, 5500, 5502, 5503, 5505, 5702 and 5709, Labor Code.

History: 1. New section filed 10-15-2014; operative 1-1-2015. Submitted to OAL for printing only pursuant to Government Code section 11351 (Register 2014, No. 42). For prior history, see Register 2008, No. 47.

2. Editorial correction of History 1 (Register 2017, No. 8).

3. Repealer of article 4 heading, repealer of former section 10390 and renumbering of former section 10550 to section 10390, including amendment of section heading and section, filed 12-17-2019; operative 1-1-2020. Submitted to OAL for printing only pursuant to Government Code section 11351 (Register 2019, No. 51).

Ref.: Hanna § 26.01[1].

§10391. Filing of Documentary Evidence. [Repealed]

Note: Authority cited: Sections 133, 5307, 5309 and 5708, Labor Code. Reference: Sections 126 and 5500.3, Labor Code.

History: 1. New section filed 10-15-2014; operative 1-1-2015. Submitted to OAL for printing only pursuant to Government Code section 11351 (Register 2014, No. 42). For prior history, see Register 2008, No. 47.

2. Editorial correction of History 1 (Register 2017, No. 8).

3. Repealer filed 12-17-2019; operative 1-1-2020. Submitted to OAL for printing only pursuant to Government Code section 11351 (Register 2019, No. 51).

§10392. Time of Filing Documents. [Repealed]

Note: Authority cited: Sections 133, 5307, 5309 and 5708, Labor Code. Reference: Sections 126 and 5500.3, Labor Code.

History: 1. New section filed 10-15-2014; operative 1-1-2015. Submitted to OAL for printing only pursuant to Government Code section 11351 (Register 2014, No. 42). For prior history, see Register 2008, No. 47.

2. Editorial correction of History 1 (Register 2017, No. 8).

3. Repealer filed 12-17-2019; operative 1-1-2020. Submitted to OAL for printing only pursuant to Government Code section 11351 (Register 2019, No. 51).

§10393. Filing of Medical Reports, Medical-Legal Reports, and Various Records. [Repealed]

Note: Authority cited: Sections 133, 5307, 5309 and 5708, Labor Code. Reference: Sections 126, 5316, 5500, 5501 and 5813, Labor Code.

History: 1. New section filed 10-15-2014; operative 1-1-2015. Submitted to OAL for printing only pursuant to Government Code section 11351 (Register 2014, No. 42).

2. Editorial correction of History 1 (Register 2017, No. 8).

3. Repealer filed 12-17-2019; operative 1-1-2020. Submitted to OAL for printing only pursuant to Government Code section 11351 (Register 2019, No. 51).

§10395. Improper Filing of Documents. [Repealed]

Note: Authority cited: Sections 133 and 5307, Labor Code. Reference: Section 126, Labor Code.

History: 1. New section filed 5-25-82; designated effective 7-1-82 (Register 82, No. 22).

2. Amendment filed 12-23-93; operative 1-1-94. Submitted to OAL for printing only pursuant to Government Code section 11351 (Register 93, No. 52).

3. New subsections (e)-(f), subsection relettering and amendment of last paragraph filed 12-19-2002; operative 1-1-2003. Submitted to OAL for printing only pursuant to Government Code section 11351 (Register 2002, No. 51).

4. Repealer filed 11-17-2008; operative 11-17-2008. Submitted to OAL for printing only (Register 2008, No. 47).

§10396. Consolidation of Cases.

(a) Consolidation of two or more related cases, involving either the same injured employee or multiple injured employees, rests in the sound discretion of the Workers' Compensation Appeals Board. In exercising that discretion, the Workers' Compensation Appeals Board shall take into consideration any relevant factors, including but not limited to the following:

(1) Whether there are common issues of fact or law;

(2) The complexity of the issues involved;

(3) The potential prejudice to any party, including but not limited to whether granting consolidation would significantly delay the trial of any of the cases involved;

(4) The avoidance of duplicate or inconsistent orders; and

(5) The efficient utilization of judicial resources.

Consolidation may be ordered for limited purposes or for all purposes.

(b) Consolidation may be ordered by the Workers' Compensation Appeals Board on its own motion, or may be ordered based upon a petition filed by one of the parties. A petition to consolidate shall:

(1) List all named parties in each case;

(2) Contain the adjudication case numbers of all the cases sought to be consolidated, with the lowest numbered case shown first;

(3) Be filed in each case sought to be consolidated; and

(4) Be served on all attorneys or non-attorney representatives of record and on all non-represented parties in each case sought to be consolidated.

(c) Any order regarding consolidation shall be filed in each case to which the order relates.

(d) If consolidation is ordered, the Workers' Compensation Appeals Board, in its discretion, may designate one case as the master file for exhibits and pleadings. If a master file is designated, any subsequent exhibits and pleadings filed by the parties during the period of consolidation shall be filed only in the master case. However, all pleadings and exhibit cover sheets filed shall include the caption and case number of the master file case, followed by the case numbers of all of the other consolidated cases.

(e) All relevant documentary evidence previously received in an individual case shall be deemed admitted in evidence in the consolidated proceedings and shall be deemed part of the record of each of the several consolidated cases.

(f) When cases are consolidated, joint minutes of hearing, summaries of evidence, opinions, decisions, orders, findings or awards may be used; however, copies shall be filed in the record of proceedings of each case.

Note: Authority cited: Sections 133, 5307, 5309 and 5708, Labor Code. Reference: Sections 5300, 5301, 5303 and 5708, Labor Code.

History: 1. Renumbering and amendment of former section 10589 to section 10396 filed 12-17-2019; operative 1-1-2020. Submitted to OAL for printing only pursuant to Government Code section 11351 (Register 2019, No. 51). For prior history of section 10396, see Register 208, No. 47.

Ref.: Hanna § 23.16; Herlick Handbook §§ 14.5, 14.17.

§10397. Restrictions on the Rejection for Filing of Documents Subject to a Statute of Limitations or a Jurisdictional Time Limitation. [Renumbered]

Note: Authority cited: Article XIV, Section 4, California Constitution; and Sections 133, 5307, 5309 and 5708, Labor Code. Reference: Sections 126, 5316, 5500, 5501 and 5813, Labor Code.

History: 1. New section filed 11-17-2008; operative 11-17-2008. Submitted to OAL for printing only (Register 2008, No. 47).

2. Amendment of subsection (b), redesignation of former subsections (d)–(f) as subsections (c)–(e), amendment of newly designated subsections (d) and (e) and amendment of Note filed 10-15-2014; operative 1-1-2015. Submitted to OAL for printing only pursuant to Government Code section 11351 (Register 2014, No. 42).

3. Editorial correction of History 2 (Register 2017, No. 8).

4. Renumbering of former section 10397 to section 10617 filed 12-17-2019; operative 1-1-2020. Submitted to OAL for printing only pursuant to Government Code section 11351 (Register 2019, No. 51).

§10398. Assignment of Consolidated Cases.

(a) Any request or petition to consolidate cases that are assigned to different workers' compensation judges in the same district office, or that have not been assigned but are venued at the same district office, shall be referred to the presiding workers' compensation judge of that office, whether the cases involve the same injured worker or multiple injured workers.

(b) Any request or petition to consolidate cases involving the same injured worker that are assigned to workers' compensation judges at different district offices, or that have not been assigned but are venued at different district offices, shall first be referred to the presiding workers' compensation judges of the district offices to which the cases are assigned. If the presiding workers' compensation judges are unable to agree on where the cases will be assigned for hearing, the conflict shall be resolved by the chief workers' compensation judge of the Division of Workers' Compensation or by their designee upon referral by one of the presiding workers' compensation judges.

(c) Any request or petition to consolidate cases involving multiple injured workers that are assigned to workers' compensation judges at different district offices, or that have not been assigned but are venued at different district offices, shall be referred to the chief workers' compensation judge or their designee.

(d) In resolving any request or petition to consolidate cases under subdivision (b) or (c), the chief workers' compensation judge or their designee shall set the request or petition for a conference regarding the place of hearing. At or after the conference, the chief workers' compensation judge or their designee shall determine the place of hearing and may determine the workers' compensation judge to whom the cases will be assigned, giving consideration to the factors set forth in rule 10396. In reaching any determination, the chief workers' compensation judge or their designee may assign a workers' compensation judge to hear any discovery motions and disputes in the action and to report their findings and recommendations to the chief workers' compensation judge or their designee.

(e) Any party aggrieved by the determination of the chief workers' compensation judge or their designee may request proceedings pursuant to Labor Code section 5310, except that an assignment to a particular workers' compensation judge shall be challenged only in accordance with the provisions of rules 10788 and 10960.

Note: Authority cited: Sections 133, 5307, 5309 and 5708, Labor Code. Reference: Sections 5300, 5301, 5303, 5310 and 5708, Labor Code.

History: 1. Renumbering of former section 10592 to section 10398, including amendment of section and Note, filed 12-17-2019; operative 1-1-2020. Submitted to OAL for printing only pursuant to Government Code section 11351 (Register 2019, No. 51).

Ref.: Hanna § 23.16; Herlick Handbook § 14.5.

ARTICLE 4
Conduct of Parties, Attorneys and Non-Attorney Representatives

§10400. Attorney Representatives.

(a) An attorney representative shall file and serve a notice of representation before filing a document or appearing on behalf of a party unless the information required to be included in the notice of representation is set forth on an opening document.

(b) The notice of representation or opening document shall comply with rule 10390 and shall include:

(1) The name of the represented party;

(2) The legal name and State Bar number of the attorney;

(3) The name-address, and telephone number of the law firm or other entity's agent for service of process;

(c) The name of the attorney representative and law firm or other entity shall be set forth on the record of proceedings at all appearances and on any pleading, document or lien prepared or filed by an attorney representative.

(d) Attorney representatives of lien claimants shall also comply with the requirements set forth in rule 10868.

Note: Authority cited: Sections 133, 5307, 5309 and 5708, Labor Code. Reference: Sections 3755-3759, 4903.1(c), 5001, 5002, 5003, 5004, 5500, 5502, 5503, 5505, 5702 and 5709, Labor Code.

History: 1. Repealer and new section exempt from OAL review pursuant to Government Code section 11351 filed 12-19-90; operative 1-1-91 (Register 91, No. 7).

2. Amendment of section filed 6-11-92 with Secretary of State by Workers' Compensation Appeals Board; operative 6-11-92. Submitted to OAL for printing only pursuant to Government Code section 11351 (Register 92, No. 24).

3. Amendment filed 12-23-93; operative 1-1-94. Submitted to OAL for printing only pursuant to Government Code section 11351 (Register 93, No. 52).

4. Editorial correction of article heading (Register 93, No. 53).

5. Amendment of section and Note filed 12-19-2002; operative 1-1-2003. Submitted to OAL for printing only pursuant to Government Code section 11351 (Register 2002, No. 51).

6. Amendment of section heading, section and Note filed 11-17-2008; operative 11-17-2008. Submitted to OAL for printing only (Register 2008, No. 47).

7. Amendment of article 5 heading filed 9-23-2013; operative 10-23-2013. Submitted as a file and print by the Workers' Compensation Appeals Board pursuant to Government Code section 11351 (Register 2013, No. 39).

8. Repealer of article 5 heading, new article 4 heading and repealer and new section filed 12-17-2019; operative 1-1-2020. Submitted to OAL for printing only pursuant to Government Code section 11351 (Register 2019, No. 51).

Ref.: Hanna § 20.01[1][a].

§10401. Non-Attorney Representatives.

(a) Except as prohibited by rule 10445, a non-attorney representative may act on behalf of a party in proceedings before the Workers' Compensation Appeals Board if the party has been informed that the non-attorney representative is not licensed to practice law by the State of California.

(b) A non-attorney representative shall be held to the same professional standards of conduct as an attorney.

(c) A non-attorney representative shall file and serve a notice of representation before filing a document or appearing on behalf of a party unless the information required to be included in the notice of representation is set forth on an opening document.

(1) If the non-attorney representative is appearing pursuant to an agreement between a law firm or other entity that provides non-attorney representatives and a party, the notice of representation shall include:

(A) The name of the represented party;

(B) The legal name, address, telephone number and form of the law firm or other entity;

(C) The name and address of the law firm or other entity's agent for service of process;

(D) The name of the person who entered into an agreement on behalf of the law firm or other entity with the party to provide non-attorney representatives; and

(E) The name of the non-attorney representative responsible for assuring that appearances are made on behalf of the party.

(2) If a non-attorney representative is appearing as an individual pursuant to an agreement between the non-attorney representative and a party, the notice of representation shall include the name of the represented party and the non-attorney representative's name, address and telephone number.

(d) The name of the non-attorney representative and any entity responsible for providing a party with the non-attorney representative shall be set forth on the record of proceedings at all appearances and on any pleading, document or lien prepared or filed by a non-attorney representative.

(e) If an attorney is responsible for supervising a non-attorney representative, the attorney shall be identified in all documents. The supervising attorney's specific written authorization must be included with all Compromise and Release agreements and Stipulations with Request for Award.

(f) A non-attorney representative whose name is not on the notice of representation must file a notice of appearance as provided in rule 10751 before appearing before the Workers' Compensation Appeals Board.

(g) Non-attorney representatives of lien claimants shall also comply with the requirements set forth in rule 10868.

Note: Authority cited: Sections 133, 5307 and 5700 Labor Code. Reference: Section 4907, Labor Code; and Section 6126, Business and Professions Code.

History: 1. Repealer and new section filed 12-17-2019; operative 1-1-2020. Submitted to OAL for printing only pursuant to Government Code section 11351 (Register 2019, No. 51).

Ref.: Hanna § 20.01[1][a].

§10402. Substitution or Dismissal of Attorneys and Non-Attorney Representatives.

(a) Substitution or dismissal of attorneys must be made in the manner provided by Code of Civil Procedure sections 284, 285 and 286.

(b) A non-attorney representative or entity providing non-attorney representatives pursuant to an agreement with a party shall continue to provide representation until the party consents to termination of representation or withdrawal is permitted by the Workers' Compensation Appeals Board.

(1) A party that consents to termination of representation shall serve and file a fully executed "Substitution of Non-attorney Representative" that includes the information required for a notice of representation filed pursuant to rules 10400 and 10401 or that identifies the party as self-represented and the name, address, telephone number and signature of the person authorized to consent to the substitution on behalf of the party.

(2) If a party does not consent to termination of representation, representation shall continue until the Appeals Board or the worker's compensation judge issues an order allowing withdrawal for good cause.

(c) Any changes in representation of lien claimants shall also comply with the requirements set forth in rule 10868.

Note: Authority cited: Sections 133 and 5307, Labor Code. Reference: Sections 4903 and 4906, Labor Code; and Sections 284, 285 and 286, Code of Civil Procedure.

History: 1. Amendment exempt from OAL review pursuant to Government Code section 11351 filed 12-19-90; operative 1-1-91 (Register 91, No. 7).

2. Repealer of second paragraph filed 12-19-2002; operative 1-1-2003. Submitted to OAL for printing only pursuant to Government Code section 11351 (Register 2002, No. 51).

3. Repealer of former section 10402 and renumbering of former section 10774 to section 10402, including amendment of section heading, section and Note, filed 12-17-2019; operative 1-1-2020. Submitted to OAL for printing only pursuant to Government Code section 11351 (Register 2019, No. 51).

Ref.: Hanna § 20.01[3].

§10403. Complaints Regarding Violations of Labor Code Section 4907.

(a) Any person may submit to the Secretary of the Appeals Board a written complaint that a non-attorney representative has violated the provisions of Labor Code section 4907. The complaint shall not be filed at any district office or in EAMS.

(b) The complaint shall be made under penalty of perjury and shall state in detail the acts and omissions of the non-attorney representative alleged to be in violation of the provisions of Labor Code section 4907, and shall identify relevant case numbers and documents.

(c) Upon receipt of a complaint, the Secretary shall review it for form and content.

(d) The non-attorney representative shall be served with notice of the complaint as part of any investigation by the Secretary and shall be provided with an opportunity to respond.

(e) Upon the conclusion of any investigation, the Secretary shall serve the complainant and the non-attorney representative with a written Notice of Determination.

(f) Nothing in this rule shall preclude the Appeals Board from initiating proceedings under Labor Code section 4907 in the absence of a complaint.

(g) Information gathered as part of any investigation under this rule and records of deliberation generated as part of any investigation under this rule shall be confidential and not subject to public disclosure under any law of this state pending the issuance of a Notice of Determination.

Note: Authority cited: Sections 4907 and 5307, Labor Code. Reference: Section 4907, Labor Code.

History: 1. New section filed 11-17-2008; operative 11-17-2008. Submitted to OAL for printing only (Register 2008, No. 47). For prior history, see Register 92, No. 24.

2. Repealer and new section filed 12-17-2019; operative 1-1-2020. Submitted to OAL for printing only pursuant to Government Code section 11351 (Register 2019, No. 51).

Ref.: Hanna § 20.01[2].

§10404. Suspension and Removal of a Non-Attorney Representative's Privilege to Appear Before the Workers' Compensation Appeals Board Under Labor Code Section 4907.

(a) Upon motion of the Appeals Board, a non-attorney representative may have the privilege to appear before the Workers' Compensation Appeals Board removed or suspended for good cause after a hearing.

(b) Good cause includes, but is not limited to, serious or repeated violations of these rules, failure to comply with rule 10400 or failure to pay a final order of sanctions, attorney's fees or costs issued under Labor Code section 5813 within 60 days.

(c) The Appeals Board shall designate a hearing officer to conduct the hearing and make initial rulings on all issues and objections. The hearing officer is subject to disqualification as provided in Labor Code section 5311 and rule 9721.12. A Petition for Disqualification of a Hearing Officer shall be filed with the Appeals Board as provided in rule 10960.

(d) The Appeals Board shall initiate proceedings by issuing a Notice of Proposed Action setting forth:

(1) the acts or omissions that constitute good cause for removal or suspension and any statutes and rules that the non-attorney representative is alleged to have violated;

(2) the intended action, whether removal or suspension, and the length of time of any proposed suspension;

(3) the date on which the hearing regarding suspension or removal of the non-attorney representative's privilege to appear will take place and the identity of the hearing officer; and

(4) the right to submit a written response to the Notice of Proposed Action within the time specified in the Notice of Proposed Action.

(e) The Appeals Board shall serve the non-attorney representative with the Notice of Proposed Action and copies of materials relied upon.

(f) Any pleadings, response, correspondence, requests and other documents shall be submitted in writing only to the Appeals Board and not filed at any district office or in EAMS.

(g) All hearings regarding the removal or suspension of a non-attorney representative's privilege to appear shall be held at the office of the Appeals Board, or at a District Office of the Workers' Compensation Appeals Board as designated by the Appeals Board.

(h) If the non-attorney representative does not testify on their own behalf, their testimony may be taken as if under cross-examination.

(i) After considering the evidence and any response submitted by the non-attorney representative, the hearing officer shall issue a recommended decision and findings of fact addressing all issues and objections and setting forth the recommended action to be taken. The recommended decision shall be submitted to the Appeals Board.

(j) The Appeals Board, acting en banc, may (1) adopt and incorporate the recommended decision of the hearing officer as its own in whole or in part; (2) review the record and increase or decrease the recommended action; or (3) take further or other action, including directing the conduct of a new hearing on one or more of the issues presented, as deemed just and appropriate. The Appeals Board shall serve the non-attorney representative and hearing officer with copies of its final decision as well as the hearing officer's recommended decision.

(k) Once the Appeals Board has served its final decision, any person may request a copy of all or a portion of the record, subject to any assertions of privilege, protective orders or provisions of law prohibiting disclosure. The complete record includes the pleadings, all notices and orders issued by the Appeals Board, any proposed decision by the hearing officer, the final decision, all exhibits whether admitted or rejected, the written evidence and any other papers in the case, except as provided by law.

(*l*) A non-attorney representative whose privilege to appear has been removed or suspended may petition the Appeals Board for reinstatement of the privilege after a period of not less than one year has elapsed from the date on which the decision of the Appeals Board took effect, or from the date of the denial of a similar petition.

Note: Authority cited: Sections 4907 and 5307, Labor Code. Reference: Sections 4907 and 5311, Labor Code.

History: 1. New section filed 12-23-93; operative 1-1-94. Submitted to OAL for printing only pursuant to Government Code section 11351 (Register 93, No. 52). For prior history, see Register 91, No. 7.

2. Amendment filed 12-19-2002; operative 1-1-2003. Submitted to OAL for printing only pursuant to Government Code section 11351 (Register 2002, No. 51).

3. Renumbering of former section 10404 to section 10470 and new section 10404 filed 12-17-2019; operative 1-1-2020. Submitted to OAL for printing only pursuant to Government Code section 11351 (Register 2019, No. 51).

Ref.: Hanna § 20.01[2].

§10405. Request for Findings of Fact. [Renumbered]

Note: Authority cited: Sections 133 and 5307, Labor Code. Reference: Sections 21164, 21166, 21537, 21538, 21540 and 21540.5, Government Code; and Sections 4800.5(d), 4801, 4804.2, 4807 and 4851, Labor Code.

History: 1. Amendment of section and Note filed 12-19-2002; operative 1-1-2003. Submitted to OAL for printing only pursuant to Government Code section 11351 (Register 2002, No. 51).

2. Renumbering of former section 10405 to section 10460 filed 12-17-2019; operative 1-1-2020. Submitted to OAL for printing only pursuant to Government Code section 11351 (Register 2019, No. 51).

§10406. Pre-Application and Miscellaneous Proceedings. [Repealed]

Note: Authority cited: Sections 133 and 5307, Labor Code. Reference: Sections 132a, 4553, 4751 and 5401, Labor Code.

History: 1. New section exempt from OAL review pursuant to Government Code section 11351 filed 12-19-90; operative 1-1-91 (Register 91, No. 7).

2. Amendment filed 12-23-93; operative 1-1-94. Submitted to OAL for printing only pursuant to Government Code section 11351 (Register 93, No. 52).

3. Repealer filed 12-19-2002; operative 1-1-2003. Submitted to OAL for printing only pursuant to Government Code section 11351 (Register 2002, No. 51).

§10407. Dismissal of Claim Form—Labor Code Section 5404.5. [Renumbered]

Note: Authority cited: Sections 133 and 5307, Labor Code. Reference: Section 5404.5, Labor Code.

History: 1. New section filed 12-23-93; operative 1-1-94. Submitted to OAL for printing only pursuant to Government Code section 11351 (Register 93, No. 52).

2. Renumbering of former section 10407 to new section 10583 filed 12-19-2002; operative 1-1-2003. Submitted to OAL for printing only pursuant to Government Code section 11351 (Register 2002, No. 51).

§10408. Application for Adjudication of Claim Form and Other Forms. [Renumbered]

Note: Authority: Sections 133, 5307, 5309 and 5708, Labor Code. Reference: Sections 3716, 4903.5, 5500, 5500.3, 5501.5 and 5502, Labor Code.

History: 1. Amendment filed 12-23-93; operative 1-1-94. Submitted to OAL for printing only pursuant to Government Code section 11351 (Register 93, No. 52).

2. Amendment filed 12-19-2002; operative 1-1-2003. Submitted to OAL for printing only pursuant to Government Code section 11351 (Register 2002, No. 51).

3. Amendment of section heading, section and Note filed 9-23-2013; operative 10-23-2013. Submitted as a file and print by the Workers' Compensation Appeals Board pursuant to Government Code section 11351 (Register 2013, No. 39).

4. Renumbering of former section 10408 to section 10500 filed 12-17-2019; operative 1-1-2020. Submitted to OAL for printing only pursuant to Government Code section 11351 (Register 2019, No. 51).

§10409. Venue. [Renumbered]

Note: Authority cited: Sections 133, 5307, 5309 and 5708, Labor Code. Reference: Sections 5500 and 5501.5, Labor Code.

History: 1. New section filed 11-17-2008; operative 11-17-2008. Submitted to OAL for printing only (Register 2008, No. 47).

2. Renumbering of former section 10409 to section 10480 filed 12-17-2019; operative 1-1-2020. Submitted to OAL for printing only pursuant to Government Code section 11351 (Register 2019, No. 51).

§10410. Ex Parte Communications.

(a) No document, including letters or other writings, shall be filed by a party with the Workers' Compensation Appeals Board unless service of a copy thereof is made on all parties together with the filing of a proof of service as provided for in rule 10625.

(b) When the Appeals Board or a workers' compensation judge receives an ex parte letter or other document from any party in a case pending before the Appeals Board or the workers' compensation judge, the Appeals Board or the workers' compensation judge shall serve copies of the letter or document on all other parties to the case with a cover letter explaining that the letter or document was received ex parte in violation of this rule.

(c) No party shall discuss with the Appeals Board or a workers' compensation judge the merits of any case pending before the Appeals Board or that workers' compensation judge without the presence of all necessary parties to the proceeding, except when submitting a walk-through document in accordance with rule 10789.

(d) All correspondence concerning the examination by and the reports of a physician appointed by a workers' compensation judge or the Appeals Board pursuant to Labor Code sections 5701, 5703.5, 5706 or 5906 shall be made, respectively, through the workers' compensation judge or the Appeals Board, and no party, attorney or non-attorney representative shall communicate with that physician regarding the merits of the case unless ordered to do so.

Note: Authority cited: Sections 133, 5307, 5309 and 5708, Labor Code. Reference: Sections 5701, 5703.5, 5706, 5708 and 5906, Labor Code.

History: 1. New section filed 12-19-2002; operative 1-1-2003. Submitted to OAL for printing only pursuant to Government Code section 11351 (Register 2002, No. 51).

2. Amendment of section heading, section and Note filed 11-17-2008; operative 11-17-2008. Submitted to OAL for printing only (Register 2008, No. 47).

3. Renumbering of former section 10410 to section 10488 and renumbering and amendment of former section 10324 to section 10410 filed 12-17-2019; operative 1-1-2020. Submitted to OAL for printing only pursuant to Government Code section 11351 (Register 2019, No. 51).

Ref.: Hanna §§ 23.01, 23.14[2][a]; Herlick Handbook § 14.5.

§10411. Petition for Change of Venue Under Labor Code Section 5501.6. [Renumbered]

Note: Authority cited: Sections 133, 5307, 5309 and 5708, Labor Code. Reference: Section 5501.6, Labor Code.

History: 1. New section filed 12-19-2002; operative 1-1-2003. Submitted to OAL for printing only pursuant to Government Code section 11351 (Register 2002, No. 51).

2. Amendment of section heading, section and Note filed 11-17-2008; operative 11-17-2008. Submitted to OAL for printing only (Register 2008, No. 47).

3. Renumbering of former section 10411 to section 10490 filed 12-17-2019; operative 1-1-2020. Submitted to OAL for printing only pursuant to Government Code section 11351 (Register 2019, No. 51).

§10412. Proceedings and Decisions After Venue Change. [Repealed]

Note: Authority cited: Sections 133, 5307, 5309 and 5708, Labor Code. Reference: Sections 126 and 5501.6, Labor Code.

History: 1. New section filed 12-19-2002; operative 1-1-2003. Submitted to OAL for printing only pursuant to Government Code section 11351 (Register 2002, No. 51). For prior history, see Register 93, No. 52.

2. Amendment of section heading, section and Note filed 11-17-2008; operative 11-17-2008. Submitted to OAL for printing only (Register 2008, No. 47).

3. Repealer filed 12-17-2019; operative 1-1-2020. Submitted to OAL for printing only pursuant to Government Code section 11351 (Register 2019, No. 51).

§10414. Declaration of Readiness to Proceed. [Renumbered]

Note: Authority cited: Sections 133, 5307, 5309 and 5708, Labor Code. Reference: Sections 4903.05, 4903.06, 5500.3, 5502 and 5813, Labor Code.

History: 1. New section filed 10-15-2014; operative 1-1-2015. Submitted to OAL for printing only pursuant to Government Code section 11351 (Register 2014, No. 42). For prior history, see Register 2008, No. 47.

2. Editorial correction of History 1 (Register 2017, No. 8).

3. Renumbering of former section 10414 to section 10742 filed 12-17-2019; operative 1-1-2020. Submitted to OAL for printing only pursuant to Government Code section 11351 (Register 2019, No. 51).

§10415. Declaration of Readiness to Proceed to Expedited Hearing. [Repealed]

Note: Authority cited: Sections 133 and 5307, Labor Code. Reference: Section 5502(b), Labor Code.

History: 1. New section filed 12-19-2002; operative 1-1-2003. Submitted to OAL for printing only pursuant to Government Code section 11351 (Register 2002, No. 51).

2. Repealer filed 11-17-2008; operative 11-17-2008. Submitted to OAL for printing only (Register 2008, No. 47).

§10416. Objection to Declaration of Readiness to Proceed. [Renumbered]

Note: Authority cited: Sections 133, 5307, 5309 and 5708, Labor Code. Reference: Sections 5500.3, 5502 and 5813, Labor Code.

History: 1. New section filed 10-15-2014; operative 1-1-2015. Submitted to OAL for printing only pursuant to Government Code section 11351 (Register 2014, No. 42). For prior history, see Register 2008, No. 47.

2. Editorial correction of History 1 (Register 2017, No. 8).

3. Renumbering of former section 10416 to section 10744 filed 12-17-2019; operative 1-1-2020. Submitted to OAL for printing only pursuant to Government Code section 11351 (Register 2019, No. 51).

§10417. Walk-Through Documents. [Renumbered]

Note: Authority cited: Sections 133 and 5307, Labor Code. Reference: Sections 4053, 4054, 5001, 5002, 5702 and 5710, Labor Code.

History: 1. New section filed 10-15-2014; operative 1-1-2015. Submitted to OAL for printing only pursuant to Government Code section 11351 (Register 2014, No. 42). For prior history, see Register 2002, No. 51.

2. Editorial correction of History 1 (Register 2017, No. 8).

3. Renumbering of former section 10417 to section 10789 filed 12-17-2019; operative 1-1-2020. Submitted to OAL for printing only pursuant to Government Code section 11351 (Register 2019, No. 51).

§10418. Letters of Appointment for Medical Examinations. [Renumbered]

Note: Authority cited: Sections 133 and 5307, Labor Code. Reference: Sections 5401 and 5703, Labor Code.

History: 1. Amendment exempt from OAL review pursuant to Government Code section 11351 filed 12-19-90; operative 1-1-91 (Register 91, No. 7).

2. Amendment filed 12-23-93; operative 1-1-94. Submitted to OAL for printing only pursuant to Government Code section 11351 (Register 93, No. 52).

3. Renumbering of former section 10418 to section 10430 filed 12-19-2002; operative 1-1-2003. Submitted to OAL for printing only pursuant to Government Code section 11351 (Register 2002, No. 51).

§10420. Setting the Case. [Renumbered]

Note: Authority cited: Sections 133 and 5307, Labor Code. Reference: Section 5310, Labor Code.

History: 1. Renumbering and amendment of former section 10417 to new section 10420 filed 12-19-2002; operative 1-1-2003. Submitted to OAL for printing only pursuant to Government Code section 11351 (Register 2002, No. 51).

2. Renumbering of former section 10420 to section 10745 filed 12-17-2019; operative 1-1-2020. Submitted to OAL for printing only pursuant to Government Code section 11351 (Register 2019, No. 51).

§10421. Sanctions.

(a) On its own motion or upon the filing of a petition pursuant to rule 10510, the Workers' Compensation Appeals Board may order payment of reasonable expenses, including attorney's fees and costs and, in addition, sanctions as provided in Labor Code section 5813. Before issuing such an order, the alleged offending party or attorney must be given notice and an opportunity to be heard. In no event shall the Workers' Compensation Appeals Board impose a monetary sanction pursuant to Labor Code section 5813 where the one subject to the sanction acted with reasonable justification or other circumstances make imposition of the sanction unjust.

(b) Bad faith actions or tactics that are frivolous or solely intended to cause unnecessary delay include actions or tactics that result from a willful failure to comply with a statutory or regulatory obligation, that result from a willful intent to disrupt or delay the proceedings of the Workers' Compensation Appeals Board, or that are done for an improper motive or are indisputably without merit. Violations subject to the provisions of Labor Code section 5813 shall include but are not limited to the following:

(1) Failure to appear or appearing late at a conference or trial where a reasonable excuse is not offered or the offending party has demonstrated a pattern of such conduct.

(2) Filing a pleading, petition or legal document unless there is some reasonable justification for filing the document.

(3) Failure to timely serve documents (including but not limited to medical reports and medical-legal reports) as required by the rules of the Workers' Compensation Appeals Board, or the Administrative Director, where the documents are within the party's possession or control, unless that failure resulted from mistake, inadvertence or excusable neglect.

(4) Failing to comply with the Workers' Compensation Appeals Board's Rules of Practice and Procedure, with the regulations of the Administrative Director, or with any award or order of the Workers' Compensation Appeals Board, including an order of discovery, which is not pending on reconsideration, removal or appellate review and which is not subject to a timely petition for reconsideration, removal or appellate review, unless that failure results from mistake, inadvertence, surprise or excusable neglect.

(5) Executing a declaration or verification to any petition, pleading or other document filed with the Workers' Compensation Appeals Board:

(A) That:

(i) Contains false or substantially false statements of fact;

(ii) Contains statements of fact that are substantially misleading;

(iii) Contains substantial misrepresentations of fact;

(iv) Contains statements of fact that are made without any reasonable basis or with reckless indifference as to their truth or falsity;

(v) Contains statements of fact that are literally true, but are intentionally presented in a manner reasonably calculated to deceive; and/or

(vi) Conceals or substantially conceals material facts; and

(B) Where a reasonable excuse is not offered or where the offending party has demonstrated a pattern of such conduct.

(6) Bringing a claim, conducting a defense or asserting a position:

(A) That is:

(i) Indisputably without merit;

(ii) Done solely or primarily for the purpose of harassing or maliciously injuring any person; and/or

(iii) Done solely or primarily for the purpose of causing unnecessary delay or a needless increase in the cost of litigation; and

(B) Where a reasonable excuse is not offered or where the offending party has demonstrated a pattern of such conduct.

(7) Presenting a claim or a defense, or raising an issue or argument, that is not warranted under existing law—unless it can be supported by a non-frivolous argument for an extension, modification or reversal of the existing law or for the establishment of new law—and where a reasonable excuse is not offered or where the offending party has demonstrated a pattern of such conduct. In determining whether a claim, defense, issue or argument is warranted under existing law, or if there is a reasonable excuse for it, consideration shall be given to:

(A) Whether there are reasonable ambiguities or conflicts in the existing statutory, regulatory or case law, taking into consideration the extent to which a litigant has researched the issues and found some support for its theories; and

(B) Whether the claim, defense, issue or argument is reasonably being asserted to preserve it for reconsideration or appellate review.

This subdivision is specifically intended not to have a "chilling effect" on a party's ability to raise and pursue legal arguments that reasonably can be regarded as not settled.

(8) Asserting a position that misstates or substantially misstates the law, and where a reasonable excuse is not offered or where the offending party has demonstrated a pattern of such conduct.

(9) Using any language or gesture at or in connection with any hearing, or using any language in any pleading or other document:

(A) Where the language or gesture:

(i) Is directed to the Workers' Compensation Appeals Board, to any of its officials or staff or to any party (or the attorney or non-attorney representative for a party); and

(ii) Is patently insulting, offensive, insolent, intemperate, foul, vulgar, obscene, abusive or disrespectful; or

(B) Where the language or gesture impugns the integrity of the Workers' Compensation Appeals Board or its commissioners, judges or staff.

Note: Authority cited: Sections 133, 5307, 5309 and 5708, Labor Code. Reference: Sections 4903.6(c), 5701, 5703.5, 5706, 5708, 5813 and 5906, Labor Code.

History: 1. Renumbering of former section 10561 to section 10421, including amendment of section and Note, filed 12-17-2019; operative 1-1-2020. Submitted to OAL for printing only pursuant to Government Code section 11351 (Register 2019, No. 51).

Ref.: Hanna § 23.15; Herlick Handbook §§ 13.4, 14.34, 14.42.

§10430. Vexatious Litigants.

(a) For purposes of this rule, "vexatious litigant" means:

(1) A party who, while acting in propria persona in proceedings before the Workers' Compensation Appeals Board, repeatedly relitigates, or attempts to relitigate, an issue of law or fact that has been finally determined against that party by the Workers' Compensation Appeals Board or by an appellate court;

(2) A party who, while acting in propria persona in proceedings before the Workers' Compensation Appeals Board, repeatedly files unmeritorious motions, pleadings or other papers, repeatedly conducts or attempts to conduct unnecessary discovery, or repeatedly engages in other tactics that are in bad faith, are frivolous or are solely intended to cause harassment or unnecessary delay; or

(3) A party who has previously been declared to be a vexatious litigant by any state or federal court of record in any action or proceeding based upon the same or substantially similar facts, transaction(s) or occurrence(s) that are the subject, in whole or in substantial part, of the party's workers' compensation case.

For purposes of this rule, the phrase "finally determined" shall mean:

(i) That all appeals have been exhausted or the time for seeking appellate review has expired; and

(ii) The time for reopening under Labor Code sections 5410 or 5803 and 5804 has passed or, although the time for reopening under those sections has not passed, there is no good faith and non-frivolous basis for reopening.

(b) Upon the petition of a party, or upon the motion of any workers' compensation judge or the Appeals Board, a presiding workers' compensation judge of any district office having venue or the Appeals Board may declare a party to be a vexatious litigant.

(c) No party shall be declared a vexatious litigant without being given notice and an opportunity to be heard. If a hearing is requested, the presiding workers' compensation judge or the Appeals Board, in their discretion, either may take and consider both oral and documentary evidence or may take and consider solely documentary evidence, including affidavits or other written declarations of fact made under penalty of perjury.

(d) If a party is declared to be a vexatious litigant, a presiding workers' compensation judge or the Appeals Board may enter a "prefiling order," i.e., an order which prohibits the vexatious litigant from filing, in propria persona, any Application for Adjudication of Claim, Declaration of Readiness to Proceed, petition or other request for action by the Workers' Compensation Appeals Board without first obtaining leave of the presiding workers' compensation judge of the district office where the request for action is proposed to be filed or, if the matter is pending before the Appeals Board on a petition for reconsideration, removal or disqualification, without first obtaining leave from the Appeals Board. For purposes of this rule, a "petition" shall include, but not be limited to, a petition to reopen under Labor Code sections 5410, 5803 and 5804, a petition to enforce a medical treatment award, a penalty petition or any other petition seeking to enforce or expand the vexatious litigant's previously determined rights.

(e) If a vexatious litigant proposes to file, in propria persona, any Application for Adjudication of Claim, Declaration of Readiness to Proceed, petition or other request for action by the Workers' Compensation Appeals Board, the request for action shall be conditionally filed. Thereafter, the presiding workers' compensation judge, or the Appeals Board if the petition is for reconsideration, removal or disqualification, shall deem the request for action to have been properly filed only if it appears that the request for action has not been filed in violation of subdivision (a). In determining whether the vexatious litigant's request for action has not been filed in violation of subdivision (a), the presiding workers' compensation judge, or the Appeals Board, shall consider the contents of the request for action and the Workers' Compensation Appeals Board's existing record of proceedings, as well as any other documentation that, in its discretion, the presiding workers' compensation judge or the Appeals Board asks to be submitted. Among the factors that the presiding workers' compensation judge or the Appeals Board may consider is whether there has been a significant change in circumstances (such as new or newly discovered evidence or a change in the law) that might materially affect an issue of fact or law that was previously finally determined against the vexatious litigant.

(f) If any in propria persona Application for Adjudication of Claim, Declaration of Readiness to proceed, petition or other request for action by the Workers' Compensation Appeals Board from a vexatious litigant subject to a prefiling order is inadvertently accepted for filing (other than conditional filing in accordance with subdivision (e) above), then any other party may file (and shall concurrently serve on the vexatious litigant and any other affected parties) a notice stating that the request for action is being submitted by a vexatious litigant subject to a prefiling order as set forth in subdivision (d). The filing of the notice shall automatically stay the request for action until it is determined, in accordance with subdivision (e), whether the request for action should be deemed to have been properly filed.

(g) A copy of any prefiling order issued by a presiding workers' compensation judge or by the Appeals Board shall be submitted to the Secretary of the Appeals Board, who shall maintain a record of vexatious litigants subject to those prefiling orders and who shall annually disseminate a list of those persons to all presiding workers' compensation judges.

Note: Authority cited: Sections 133, 5307, 5309 and 5708, Labor Code. Reference: Article XIV, section 4, California Constitution; Sections 5410, 5803 and 5804, Labor Code; and Sections 391, 391.2 and 391.7, Code of Civil Procedure.

History: 1. Renumbering and amendment of former section 10418 to new section 10430 filed 12-19-2002; operative 1-1-2003. Submitted to OAL for printing only pursuant to Government Code section 11351 (Register 2002, No. 51).

2. Repealer of former section 10430 and renumbering of former section 10782 to section 10430, including amendment of section and Note, filed 12-17-2019; operative 1-1-2020. Submitted to OAL for printing only pursuant to Government Code section 11351 (Register 2019, No. 51).

§10440. Contempt.

(a) A workers' compensation judge or a deputy commissioner may issue writs or summons, warrants of attachment, warrants of commitment and all necessary process in proceedings for direct and hybrid contempt as defined by Labor Code section 5309(c) in a like manner and to the same extent as courts of record.

(b) The Appeals Board may issue writs or summons, warrants of attachment, warrants of commitment and all necessary process in proceedings for direct, hybrid, or indirect contempt in a like manner and to the same extent as the courts of record.

Note: Authority cited: Sections 133, 134 and 5307, Labor Code. Reference: Sections 4550, 4551, 4552, 4553, 4553.1 and 5309(c), Labor Code; and Sections 1209-1222, Code of Civil Procedure.

History: 1. Amendment of section heading filed 12-19-2002; operative 1-1-2003. Submitted to OAL for printing only pursuant to Government Code section 11351 (Register 2002, No. 51).

2. Repealer and new section filed 12-17-2019; operative 1-1-2020. Submitted to OAL for printing only pursuant to Government Code section 11351 (Register 2019, No. 51).

Ref.: Hanna § 29.09[1].

§10445. Disbarred and Suspended Attorneys.

An attorney who has been disbarred or suspended by the Supreme Court for reasons other than nonpayment of State Bar fees, or who has been placed on involuntary inactive enrollment status by the State Bar or who has resigned while disciplinary action is pending shall be deemed unfit to appear as a non-attorney representative of any party before the Workers' Compensation Appeals Board during the time that the attorney is precluded from practicing law in this state.

Note: Authority cited: Sections 133, 5307, 5309 and 5708, Labor Code. Reference: Section 4907, Labor Code; and Section 6126, Business and Professions Code.

History: 1. Repealer of last paragraph filed 12-19-2002; operative 1-1-2003. Submitted to OAL for printing only pursuant to Government Code section 11351 (Register 2002, No. 51).

2. Repealer of former section 10445 and renumbering and amendment of former section 10779 to section 10445 filed 12-17-2019; operative 1-1-2020. Submitted to OAL for printing only pursuant to Government Code section 11351 (Register 2019, No. 51).

Ref.: Hanna § 20.01[1][b].

§10447. Pleadings—Discrimination. [Renumbered]

Note: Authority cited: Sections 133 and 5307, Labor Code. Reference: Section 132a, Labor Code.

History: 1. Editorial correction filed 2-2-83 (Register 83, No. 6).

2. Amendment of section heading and repealer of second paragraph filed 12-19-2002; operative 1-1-2003. Submitted to OAL for printing only pursuant to Government Code section 11351 (Register 2002, No. 51).

3. Renumbering of former section 10447 to section 10528 filed 12-17-2019; operative 1-1-2020. Submitted to OAL for printing only pursuant to Government Code section 11351 (Register 2019, No. 51).

ARTICLE 5
Applications and Answers

§10450. Invoking the Jurisdiction of the Workers' Compensation Appeals Board.

(a) Except as provided by rules 10990 and 10590, proceedings for the adjudication of rights and liabilities before the Workers' Compensation Appeals Board shall be initiated and jurisdiction of the Workers' Compensation Appeals Board invoked by the filing of an Application for Adjudication of Claim, a case opening Compromise and Release Agreement, a case opening Stipulations with Request for Award or a Request for Findings of Fact under rule 10460.

(b) Until an application or other case opening document has been filed, the Workers' Compensation Appeals Board may not conduct hearings, issue orders or authorize the commencement of formal, compelled discovery, including the use of subpoenas to obtain records or sworn testimony.

(c) The pre-application assignment of a non-adjudication EAMS case number by any ancillary unit of the Division of Workers' Compensation (e.g., the Disability Evaluation Unit, the Information and Assistance Office):

(1) Does not establish the jurisdiction of the Workers' Compensation Appeals Board and, therefore, does not permit it to conduct any hearings or to issue any orders;

(2) Does not toll the statute of limitations (except as provided in Labor Code section 5454 for submissions to the Information and Assistance Unit); and

(3) Does not authorize the commencement of formal, compelled discovery.

Nothing in this rule shall be construed to preclude any non-compelled pre-application medical evaluations or investigations.

Note: Authority cited: Sections 133, 5307, 5309 and 5708, Labor Code. Reference: Sections 126, 5300, 5301, 5316, 5454, 5500 and 5501, Labor Code.

History: 1. Amendment of section and Note filed 12-19-2002; operative 1-1-2003. Submitted to OAL for printing only pursuant to Government Code section 11351 (Register 2002, No. 51).

2. Amendment of section and Note filed 11-17-2008; operative 11-17-2008. Submitted to OAL for printing only (Register 2008, No. 47).

3. Amendment of section heading, section and Note filed 9-23-2013; operative 10-23-2013. Submitted as a file and print by the Workers' Compensation Appeals Board pursuant to Government Code section 11351 (Register 2013, No. 39).

4. New article 5 heading, renumbering of former section 10450 to section 10510 and new section 10450 filed 12-17-2019; operative 1-1-2020. Submitted to OAL for printing only pursuant to Government Code section 11351 (Register 2019, No. 51).

Ref.: Hanna § 25.05[1]; Herlick Handbook §§ 11.01, 11.05, 14.5, 14.11.

§10451.1. Determination of Medical-Legal Expense Disputes. [Repealed]

Note: Authority cited: Sections 133, 4622(e)(2), 4627, 5307, 5309 and 5708, Labor Code. Reference: Sections 139.5, 4603.3, 4603.6, 4620, 4621, 4622, 4903.05 and 4903.06, Labor Code; and Sections 9792.5.5(b)(2) and 9792.5.7(c)(5), title 8, California Code of Regulations.

History: 1. New section filed 9-23-2013; operative 10-23-2013. Submitted as a file and print by the Workers' Compensation Appeals Board pursuant to Government Code section 11351 (Register 2013, No. 39).

2. Repealer filed 12-17-2019; operative 1-1-2020. Submitted to OAL for printing only pursuant to Government Code section 11351 (Register 2019, No. 51).

Ref.: Herlick Handbook § 14.5.

§10451.2. Determination of Medical Treatment Disputes. [Repealed]

Note: Authority cited: Sections 133, 4606.2(f), 4604, 5304, 5307, 5309 and 5708, Labor Code. Reference: Sections 4061, 4601.5, 4062, 4600, 4603.2, 4603.3, 4604.5, 4610, 4610.5, 4610.6, 4616.3, 4616.4 and 4903(b), Labor Code.

History: 1. New section filed 9-23-2013; operative 10-23-2013. Submitted as a file and print by the Workers' Compensation Appeals Board pursuant to Government Code section 11351 (Register 2013, No. 39).

2. Repealer filed 12-17-2019; operative 1-1-2020. Submitted to OAL for printing only pursuant to Government Code section 11351 (Register 2019, No. 51).

Ref.: Herlick Handbook § 14.5.

§10451.3. Petition for Costs. [Renumbered]

Note: Authority cited: Sections 133, 5307, 5309 and 5708, Labor Code. Reference: Sections 4600, 4903 et seq., 5710, 5811 and 5813, Labor Code; and Section 10561, title 8, California Code of Regulations.

History: 1. New section filed 9-23-2013; operative 10-23-2013. Submitted as a file and print by the Workers' Compensation Appeals Board pursuant to Government Code section 11351 (Register 2013, No. 39).

2. Renumbering of former section 10451.3 to section 10545 filed 12-17-2019; operative 1-1-2020. Submitted to OAL for printing only pursuant to Government Code section 11351 (Register 2019, No. 51).

Ref.: Herlick Handbook § 14.5.

§10451.4. Petition to Enforce Independent Bill Review Determination. [Renumbered]

Note: Authority cited: Sections 133, 5307, 5309 and 5708, Labor Code. Reference: Sections 4603.6, 4622, 4903.05 and 4903.06, Labor Code.

History: 1. New section filed 9-23-2013; operative 10-23-2013. Submitted as a file and print by the Workers' Compensation Appeals Board pursuant to Government Code section 11351 (Register 2013, No. 39).

2. Renumbering of former section 10451.4 to section 10570 filed 12-17-2019; operative 1-1-2020. Submitted to OAL for printing only pursuant to Government Code section 11351 (Register 2019, No. 51).

Ref.: Herlick Handbook § 14.5.

§10452. Petition for Disqualification of Judge. [Renumbered]

Note: Authority cited: Section 5307, Labor Code. Reference: Sections 5310 and 5311, Labor Code.

History: 1. Renumbering of former section 10452 to section 10960 filed 12-17-2019; operative 1-1-2020. Submitted to OAL for printing only pursuant to Government Code section 11351 (Register 2019, No. 51).

Ref.: Herlick Handbook § 14.5.

§10453. Petition for Automatic Reassignment of Trial or Expedited Hearing to Another Workers' Compensation Judge. [Renumbered]

Note: Authority cited: Section 5307, Labor Code. Reference: Section 5310, Labor Code.

History: 1. Editorial correction filed 2-2-83 (Register 83, No. 6).

2. Amendment of section heading, section and Note filed 12-19-2002; operative 1-1-2003. Submitted to OAL for printing only pursuant to Government Code section 11351 (Register 2002, No. 51).

3. Renumbering of former section 10453 to section 10788 filed 12-17-2019; operative 1-1-2020. Submitted to OAL for printing only pursuant to Government Code section 11351 (Register 2019, No. 51).

Ref.: Herlick Handbook § 14.5.

§10454. Automatic Reassignment After Reversal. [Repealed]

Note: Authority cited: Sections 133 and 5307, Labor Code. Reference: Section 5310, Labor Code.

History: 1. Renumbering of former section 10454 to new section 10455 and new section 10454 filed 12-19-2002; operative 1-1-2003. Submitted to OAL for printing only pursuant to Government Code section 11351 (Register 2002, No. 51).

2. Repealer filed 12-17-2019; operative 1-1-2020. Submitted to OAL for printing only pursuant to Government Code section 11351 (Register 2019, No. 51).

Ref.: Herlick Handbook § 14.5.

§10455. Applications.

A separate Application for Adjudication of Claim shall be filed for each separate injury for which benefits are claimed. All applications shall conform to the following requirements:

(a) Only one application shall be filed for each injury. Duplicative applications are subject to summary dismissal.

(b) Upon filing an Application for Adjudication of Claim, the filing party shall concurrently serve a copy of the application and any accompanying documents on all other parties.

(c) When filing an amended application, the applicant shall indicate on the box set forth on the application form that it is an amended application.

(d) If the applicant is a minor or incompetent, the Application for Adjudication of Claim shall be accompanied by a Petition for Appointment of Guardian ad Litem and Trustee.

(e) An applicant is not required to disclose their social security number. If an applicant discloses their Social Security number on the application, the Social Security number will be used solely for identification and verification purposes in order to administer the workers' compensation system except with the consent of the applicant, or as permitted or required by statute, regulation or judicial order.

(f) Upon the filing of an initial application, the Workers' Compensation Appeals Board shall assign an adjudication case number and a venue. The case number and venue shall be indicated on a conformed copy of the application.

(1) If the party filing the application is unrepresented, the Workers' Compensation Appeals Board shall serve a conformed copy of the application on all parties and lien claimants on the proof of service to the application.

(2) If the party filing the application is represented, the Workers' Compensation Appeals Board shall serve a conformed copy of the application on the filing party or lien claimant. Upon receipt of the conformed copy of the application, the filing party shall forthwith serve a copy of the conformed application on all other parties and lien claimants.

Note: Authority cited: Sections 133, 5307, 5309 and 5708, Labor Code. Reference: Sections 126, 3208.2, 5307.5, 5316, 5500 and 5501, Labor Code.

History: 1. Renumbering of former section 10454 to new section 10455 filed 12-19-2002; operative 1-1-2003. Submitted to OAL for printing only pursuant to Government Code section 11351 (Register 2002, No. 51).

2. Renumbering of former section 10455 to section 10534 and new section 10455 filed 12-17-2019; operative 1-1-2020. Submitted to OAL for printing only pursuant to Government Code section 11351 (Register 2019, No. 51).

Ref.: Hanna §§ 23.14[1][b], 25.06[1]; Herlick Handbook §§ 14.5, 14.11, 14.13, 14.14.

§10458. Petition for New and Further Disability. [Renumbered]

Note: Authority cited: Sections 133 and 5307, Labor Code. Reference: Section 5803, Labor Code.

History: 1. Renumbering of former section 10458 to section 10534 filed 12-17-2019; operative 1-1-2020. Submitted to OAL for printing only pursuant to Government Code section 11351 (Register 2019, No. 51).

Ref.: Herlick Handbook § 14.5.

§10460. Request for Findings of Fact.

A request for findings of fact under Government Code sections 21164, 21166, 21537, 21538, 21540 or 21540.5 or under Labor Code sections 4800.5(d), 4801, 4804.2, 4807 or 4851 is a proceeding separate from a claim for workers' compensation benefits even though it arises out of the same incident, injury or exposure. The request for findings of fact shall be filed separately and a separate file folder and record of the proceeding will be maintained, but the request for findings of fact may be consolidated for hearing with a claim for workers' compensation benefits.

Note: Authority cited: Sections 133 and 5307, Labor Code. Reference: Sections 21164, 21166, 21537, 21538, 21540 and 21540.5, Government Code; Sections 4800.5(d), 4801, 4804.2, 4807 and 4851, Labor Code.

History: 1. Renumbering and amendment of former section 10405 to section 10460 filed 12-17-2019; operative 1-1-2020. Submitted to OAL for printing only pursuant to Government Code section 11351 (Register 2019, No. 51).

Ref.: Hanna § 33.02[2], [3][c], [4][c], [5][d]; Herlick Handbook §§ 14.5, 14.17.

§10462. Subsequent Injuries Benefits Trust Fund Application.

(a) All claims against the Subsequent Injuries Benefits Trust Fund shall be by an application in writing setting forth the date and nature of the industrial injury, together with all factors of disability alleged to have pre-existed the injury.

(b) All such applications shall be filed with the Workers' Compensation Appeals Board district office having venue or in EAMS, and a copy shall be served by mail on the Division of Workers' Compensation, Subsequent Injuries Benefits Trust Fund, in accordance with rules 10530 and 10540. Where joinder of the Subsequent Injuries Benefits Trust Fund has been ordered, the applicant shall forthwith file and serve an application as provided herein.

(c) After such an application is filed, any party who has previously filed medical reports shall serve copies on the Division of Workers' Compensation, Subsequent Injuries Benefits Trust Fund no later than 30 days prior to the mandatory settlement conference or other hearing, unless service is waived by the Division of Workers' Compensation, Subsequent Injuries Benefits Trust Fund.

Note: Authority cited: Sections 133, 5307, 5309 and 5708, Labor Code. Reference: Sections 4750, 4751, 4753, 4753.5 and 4754.5, Labor Code.

History: 1. Amendment filed 12-19-2002; operative 1-1-2003. Submitted to OAL for printing only pursuant to Government Code section 11351 (Register 2002, No. 51).

2. Repealer and new section filed 12-17-2019; operative 1-1-2020. Submitted to OAL for printing only pursuant to Government Code section 11351 (Register 2019, No. 51).

Ref.: Hanna §§ 23.14[2][p], 25.05[7], 31.20[4][b]; Herlick Handbook §§ 14.5, 14.17.

§10464. Contents of Petition to Terminate Liability. [Repealed]

Note: Authority cited: Sections 133 and 5307, Labor Code. Reference: Sections 4650 and 4651.1, Labor Code.

History: 1. Amendment filed 12-19-2002; operative 1-1-2003. Submitted to OAL for printing only pursuant to Government Code section 11351 (Register 2002, No. 51).

2. Repealer filed 12-17-2019; operative 1-1-2020. Submitted to OAL for printing only pursuant to Government Code section 11351 (Register 2019, No. 51).

Ref.: Herlick Handbook § 14.5.

§10465. Answers.

Any Answer to an Application for Adjudication of Claim shall be filed and served no later than the shorter of either: 10 days after service of a Declaration of Readiness to Proceed, or 90 days after service of the Application for Adjudication of Claim.

(a) The Answer used by the parties shall conform to a form prescribed and approved by the Appeals Board. Additional matters may be pleaded as deemed necessary by the answering party. A general denial is not an answer within this rule.

(b) The Answer shall be accompanied by a proof of service upon the opposing parties.

(c) Evidence upon matters and affirmative defenses not pleaded by Answer will be allowed only upon such terms and conditions as the Appeals Board or workers' compensation judge may impose in the exercise of sound discretion.

Note: Authority cited: Sections 133 and 5307, Labor Code. Reference: Sections 5500 and 5505, Labor Code.

History: 1. New section filed 12-17-2019; operative 1-1-2020. Submitted to OAL for printing only pursuant to Government Code section 11351 (Register 2019, No. 51).

Ref.: Hanna §§ 23.14[2][c], 25.23; Herlick Handbook §§ 14.5, 14.18.

§10466. Objections to Petition, Hearing, Interim Order. [Repealed]

Note: Authority cited: Sections 133 and 5307, Labor Code. Reference: Sections 4650 and 4651.1, Labor Code.

History: 1. Amendment of section and Note filed 12-19-2002; operative 1-1-2003. Submitted to OAL for printing only pursuant to Government Code section 11351 (Register 2002, No. 51).

2. Repealer filed 12-17-2019; operative 1-1-2020. Submitted to OAL for printing only pursuant to Government Code section 11351 (Register 2019, No. 51).

Ref.: Herlick Handbook § 14.5.

§10470. Labor Code Section 4906(h) Statement.

(a) The employee, insurer, employer and the attorneys for each party shall comply with Labor Code section 4906(h). Failure to file the statement required by Labor

Code section 4906(h) shall result in refusal to file that party's Application for Adjudication of Claim or Answer.

(b) If anyone subject to subdivision (a) of this rule is not available, cannot be located or is unwilling to sign, a declaration under penalty of perjury setting forth in specific detail the reasons and describing good faith efforts made to comply with this rule may be filed with the Application for Adjudication of Claim or Answer. If the presiding workers' compensation judge determines from the facts set forth in the declaration that good cause has been established, the presiding workers' compensation judge may accept the Application for Adjudication of Claim or Answer for filing. For the purpose of this rule, a Compromise and Release agreement or Stipulations with Request for Award shall not be treated as an Application for Adjudication of Claim.

Note: Authority cited: Sections 133 and 5307, Labor Code. Reference: Section 4906(h), Labor Code.

History: 1. New section filed 10-15-2014; operative 1-1-2015. Submitted to OAL for printing only pursuant to Government Code section 11351 (Register 2014, No. 42). For prior history, see Register 2002, No. 51.

2. Editorial correction of History 1 (Register 2017, No. 8).

3. Renumbering of former section 10470 to section 10530 and renumbering of former section 10404 to section 10470, including amendment of section heading, section and Note, filed 12-17-2019; operative 1-1-2020. Submitted to OAL for printing only pursuant to Government Code section 11351 (Register 2019, No. 51).

Ref.: Hanna §§ 25.06[3], 25.23; Herlick Handbook § 14.5.

ARTICLE 6
Venue

§10480. Venue.

When filing a case opening document, the filer shall designate venue and shall specify the basis for venue in accordance with Labor Code section 5501.5.

Note: Authority cited: Sections 133, 5307, 5309 and 5708, Labor Code. Reference: Sections 5500 and 5501.5, Labor Code.

History: 1. Amendment exempt from OAL review pursuant to Government Code section 11351 filed 12-19-90; operative 1-1-91 (Register 91, No. 7).

2. Amendment filed 12-23-93; operative 1-1-94. Submitted to OAL for printing only pursuant to Government Code section 11351 (Register 93, No. 52).

3. Amendment filed 12-19-2002; operative 1-1-2003. Submitted to OAL for printing only pursuant to Government Code section 11351 (Register 2002, No. 51).

4. New article 6 heading, repealer of former section 10480 and renumbering and amendment of former section 10409 to section 10480 filed 12-17-2019; operative 1-1-2020. Submitted to OAL for printing only pursuant to Government Code section 11351 (Register 2019, No. 51).

Ref.: Hanna § 25.06[1]; Herlick Handbook § 14.15.

§10482. Venue When Applicant is Employee of Division of Workers' Compensation.

When a Division of Workers' Compensation employee files an Application for Adjudication of Claim or other case opening document regardless of the venue designated by the employee, venue shall be determined as follows:

(a) The parties may agree on a venue, subject to the approval of the presiding workers' compensation judge of the agreed-upon venue.

(b) If the parties are unable to agree on a suitable venue, or for any other good cause shown, the presiding workers' compensation judge of the district office designated on the application or other case opening document shall consult with the Secretary or other deputy commissioner of the Appeals Board to determine the appropriate venue, with the secretary or other deputy commissioner issuing the appropriate venue order.

(c) The secretary or other deputy commissioner of the Appeals Board shall assign the case to a workers' compensation judge unfamiliar with the employee. When appropriate, a workers' compensation judge from a region other than the employee's region shall be assigned.

Note: Authority cited: Sections 133, 5307, 5309 and 5708, Labor Code. Reference: Sections 5500 and 5501.5, Labor Code.

History: 1. New section filed 12-17-2019; operative 1-1-2020. Submitted to OAL for printing only pursuant to Government Code section 11351 (Register 2019, No. 51).

Ref.: Hanna § 25.06[1]; Herlick Handbook § 14.15.

§10484. Procedural Requirement. [Repealed]

Note: Authority cited: Sections 133 and 5307, Labor Code. Reference: Sections 5500 and 5505, Labor Code.

History: 1. Amendment filed 12-23-93; operative 1-1-94. Submitted to OAL for printing only pursuant to Government Code section 11351 (Register 93, No. 52).

2. Amendment of second paragraph filed 12-19-2002; operative 1-1-2003. Submitted to OAL for printing only pursuant to Government Code section 11351 (Register 2002, No. 51).

3. Repealer filed 12-17-2019; operative 1-1-2020. Submitted to OAL for printing only pursuant to Government Code section 11351 (Register 2019, No. 51).

§10488. Objection to Venue Based on an Attorney's Principal Place of Business.

Pursuant to Labor Code section 5501.5(c), any employer or insurance carrier listed on an initial Application for Adjudication of Claim may file an objection to a venue selection, based on the employee's attorney's principal place of business under Labor Code section 5501.5(a)(3), within 30 days after notice of the adjudication case number and venue is received by the employer or insurance carrier. The objecting employer or insurance carrier shall state under penalty of perjury the date when the notice of the adjudication case number and venue was received. A timely objection shall result in venue being assigned in accordance with Labor Code section 5501.5(a)(1) or (a)(2).

Note: Authority cited: Sections 133, 5307, 5309 and 5708, Labor Code. Reference: Section 5501.5, Labor Code.

History: 1. Renumbering and amendment of former section 10410 to section 10488 filed 12-17-2019; operative 1-1-2020. Submitted to OAL for printing only pursuant to Government Code section 11351 (Register 2019, No. 51). For prior history of section 10488, see Register 93, No. 52.

Ref.: Hanna § 25.27; Herlick Handbook § 14.15.

§10490. Petition for Change of Venue for Good Cause.

A petition for change of venue pursuant to Labor Code section 5501.6 shall be filed at the district office or permanently staffed satellite office having venue. Any objection to a petition for a change of venue shall be filed within 10 days of the filing of the petition. The presiding workers' compensation judge of the district office having venue, or the workers' compensation judge of the permanently staffed satellite office having venue, shall grant or deny the petition for change of venue, or serve notice of a status conference concerning the petition, within 30 days of the filing of the petition.

Note: Authority cited: Sections 133, 5307, 5309 and 5708, Labor Code. Reference: Section 5501.6, Labor Code.

History: 1. Amendment of section heading and section filed 12-19-2002; operative 1-1-2003. Submitted to OAL for printing only pursuant to Government Code section 11351 (Register 2002, No. 51).

2. Renumbering of former section 10490 to section 10515 and renumbering of former section 10411 to section 10490, including amendment of section heading and section, filed 12-17-2019; operative 1-1-2020. Submitted to OAL for printing only pursuant to Government Code section 11351 (Register 2019, No. 51).

Ref.: Hanna § 25.27; Herlick Handbook § 14.15.

§10492. When Pleadings Deemed Amended. [Renumbered]

Note: Authority cited: Sections 133 and 5307, Labor Code. Reference: Section 5702, Labor Code.

History: 1. Renumbering of former section 10492 to section 10517 filed 12-17-2019; operative 1-1-2020. Submitted to OAL for printing only pursuant to Government Code section 11351 (Register 2019, No. 51).

§10496. Awards and Orders Without Hearing. [Repealed]

Note: Authority cited: Sections 133 and 5307, Labor Code. Reference: Section 5702, Labor Code.

History: 1. Repealer filed 12-17-2019; operative 1-1-2020. Submitted to OAL for printing only pursuant to Government Code section 11351 (Register 2019, No. 51).

§10497. Rejection of Stipulations. [Repealed]

Note: Authority cited: Sections 133 and 5307, Labor Code. Reference: Section 5702, Labor Code.

History: 1. Repealer filed 12-17-2019; operative 1-1-2020. Submitted to OAL for printing only pursuant to Government Code section 11351 (Register 2019, No. 51).

§10498. Special Requirements for Pleadings Filed or Served by Attorneys or by Non-Attorney Employees of an Attorney or Law Firm. [Renumbered]

Note: Authority: Sections 133, 5307, 5309 and 5708, Labor Code. Reference: Sections 5000, 5501, 5505 and 5900 et seq., Labor Code; Sections 10232(a)(4), 10450 and 10773, title 8, California Code of Regulations; and Rules 2.111(1) and 8.204(b)(10)(D), California Rules of Court.

History: 1. New section filed 9-23-2013; operative 10-23-2013. Submitted as a file and print by the Workers' Compensation Appeals Board pursuant to Government Code section 11351 (Register 2013, No. 39).

2. Renumbering of former section 10498 to section 10520 filed 12-17-2019; operative 1-1-2020. Submitted to OAL for printing only pursuant to Government Code section 11351 (Register 2019, No. 51).

ARTICLE 7
Petitions, Pleadings and Forms

§10500. Form Pleadings.

(a) No workers' compensation judge and no district office of the Workers' Compensation Appeals Board shall require the parties to use a form other than that prescribed and approved by the Appeals Board.

(b) Each of the following documents shall be on a form prescribed and approved by the Appeals Board:

(1) An Application for Adjudication of Claim for compensation benefits or death benefits;

(2) A lien;

(3) A Declaration of Readiness to Proceed;

(4) A Pre-Trial Conference Statement;

(5) Minutes of Hearing except Minutes of Hearing prepared by a court reporter;

(6) A Compromise and Release agreement;

(7) Stipulations with Request for Award;

(8) A petition to terminate liability for temporary disability indemnity;

(9) A special notice of lawsuit; and

(10) Any other form the Appeals Board, in its discretion, determines should be uniform and standardized.

(c) Any form prescribed and approved by the Appeals Board may be printed by the Division of Workers' Compensation for distribution at district offices of the Workers' Compensation Appeals Board. In addition, the Division of Workers' Compensation may create:

(1) Electronic versions of the prescribed and approved forms; and/or

(2) Optical character recognition versions of those forms, either in fillable format or otherwise, for posting on the Division of Workers' Compensation's Forms webpage.

(d) Any form for proceedings before the Workers' Compensation Appeals Board created by the Division of Workers' Compensation shall be presumed to have been prescribed and approved by the Appeals Board unless the Appeals Board issues an order or a formal written statement to the contrary.

Note: Authority cited: Sections 133, 5307, 5309 and 5708, Labor Code. Reference: Sections 3716, 4903.5, 5500, 5500.3, 5501.5 and 5502, Labor Code.

History: 1. Repealer and new section exempt from OAL review pursuant to Government Code section 11351 filed 12-19-90; operative 1-1-91 (Register 91, No. 7).

2. Amendment filed 12-16-92; operative 2-1-93 and exempt from OAL review pursuant to Government Code section 11351 (Register 92, No. 51).

3. Amendment of section and Note filed 12-23-93; operative 1-1-94. Submitted to OAL for printing only pursuant to Government Code section 11351 (Register 93, No. 52).

4. Amendment filed 12-19-2002; operative 1-1-2003. Submitted to OAL for printing only pursuant to Government Code section 11351 (Register 2002, No. 51).

5. Amendment of section heading, section and Note filed 11-17-2008; operative 11-17-2008. Submitted to OAL for printing only (Register 2008, No. 47).

6. Repealer of article 6 heading, new article 7 heading, repealer of former section 10500 and renumbering of former section 10408 to section 10500, including amendment of section heading and section, filed 12-17-2019; operative 1-1-2020. Submitted to OAL for printing only pursuant to Government Code section 11351 (Register 2019, No. 51).

Ref.: Hanna §§ 23.12[1], 25.05[1], 31.20[2]; Herlick Handbook §§ 14.5, 14.11.

§10501. Service in Death Cases. [Repealed]

Note: Authority cited: Sections 133 and 5307, Labor Code. Reference: Section 4706.5, Labor Code.

History: 1. Amendment of section heading and section filed 12-19-2002; operative 1-1-2003. Submitted to OAL for printing only pursuant to Government Code section 11351 (Register 2002, No. 51).

2. Repealer filed 12-17-2019; operative 1-1-2020. Submitted to OAL for printing only pursuant to Government Code section 11351 (Register 2019, No. 51).

Ref.: Herlick Handbook § 14.5.

§10505. Service by the Parties or Lien Claimants. [Repealed]

Note: Authority cited: Sections 133, 5307, 5309 and 5708, Labor Code. Reference: Section 5316, Labor Code.

History: 1. Amendment of section heading and text filed 12-23-93; operative 1-1-94. Submitted to OAL for printing pursuant to Government Code section 11351 (Register 93, No. 52).

2. Amendment filed 12-19-2002; operative 1-1-2003. Submitted to OAL for printing only pursuant to Government Code section 11351 (Register 2002, No. 51).

3. Amendment of section heading, section and Note filed 11-17-2008; operative 11-17-2008. Submitted to OAL for printing only (Register 2008, No. 47).

4. Repealer filed 12-17-2019; operative 1-1-2020. Submitted to OAL for printing only pursuant to Government Code section 11351 (Register 2019, No. 51).

Ref.: Herlick Handbook § 14.5.

§10506. Service: Mailbox. [Repealed]

Note: Authority cited: Sections 133 and 5307, Labor Code. Reference: Section 5316, Labor Code.

History: 1. New section filed 12-19-2002; operative 1-1-2003. Submitted to OAL for printing only pursuant to Government Code section 11351 (Register 2002, No. 51).

2. Repealer filed 12-17-2019; operative 1-1-2020. Submitted to OAL for printing only pursuant to Government Code section 11351 (Register 2019, No. 51).

Ref.: Herlick Handbook § 14.5.

§10507. Time Within Which to Act When a Document is Served by Mail, Fax, or E-Mail. [Renumbered]

Note: Authority cited: Sections 133, 5307, 5309 and 5708, Labor Code. Reference: Section 5316, Labor Code.

History: 1. Amendment of section heading and section filed 12-19-2002; operative 1-1-2003. Submitted to OAL for printing only pursuant to Government Code section 11351 (Register 2002, No. 51).

2. Amendment of section heading, section and Note filed 11-17-2008; operative 11-17-2008. Submitted to OAL for printing only (Register 2008, No. 47).

3. Renumbering of former section 10507 to section 10605 filed 12-17-2019; operative 1-1-2020. Submitted to OAL for printing only pursuant to Government Code section 11351 (Register 2019, No. 51).

Ref.: Herlick Handbook § 14.5.

§10508. Extension of Time for Weekends and Holidays. [Renumbered]

Note: Authority cited: Sections 133, 5307, 5309 and 5708, Labor Code. Reference: Section 5316, Labor Code; Sections 6700, 6701 and 6707, Government Code; and Sections 10, 12, 12a, 12b, 13 and 135, Code of Civil Procedure.

History: 1. New section filed 11-17-2008; operative 11-17-2008. Submitted to OAL for printing only (Register 2008, No. 47).

2. Renumbering of former section 10508 to section 10600 filed 12-17-2019; operative 1-1-2020. Submitted to OAL for printing only pursuant to Government Code section 11351 (Register 2019, No. 51).

Ref.: Herlick Handbook § 14.5.

§10510. Petitions and Answers to Petitions.

(a) After jurisdiction of the Workers' Compensation Appeals Board is invoked pursuant to rule 10450, a request for action by the Workers' Compensation Appeals Board, other than a rule 10500 form pleading, shall be made by petition. The caption of each petition shall contain the case title and adjudication case number and shall indicate the type of relief sought.

(b) All petitions and answers shall be filed in accordance with rule 10615 and served on all parties in accordance with rule 10625. A failure to concurrently file a proof of service with a petition or answer constitutes a valid ground for summarily dismissing or denying the petition or summarily rejecting the answer.

(c) An answer may be filed within 10 days after the service of a petition unless otherwise provided. The time limit for filing any shall be extended in accordance with rule 10605 unless otherwise provided.

(d) All petitions and answers shall be verified under penalty of perjury in the manner required for verified pleadings in courts of record. A failure to comply with the verification requirement constitutes a valid ground for summarily dismissing or denying a petition or summarily rejecting an answer.

(e) A document cover sheet and a document separator sheet shall be filed with each petition or answer. The appropriate title for the petition or answer shall be entered into the document title field of the document separator sheet.

(f) Any previously filed document shall not be attached to a petition or answer; any such document attached to a petition or answer may be discarded.

Note: Authority cited: Sections 133, 5307, 5309 and 5708, Labor Code. Reference: Sections 126 and 5905, Labor Code.

History: 1. Amendment filed 12-23-93; operative 1-1-94. Submitted to OAL for printing only pursuant to Government Code section 11351 (Register 93, No. 52).

2. Amendment of section heading, section and Note filed 11-17-2008; operative 11-17-2008. Submitted to OAL for printing only (Register 2008, No. 47).

3. Repealer of former section 10510 and renumbering of former section 10450 to section 10510, including amendment of section

heading and section, filed 12-17-2019; operative 1-1-2020. Submitted to OAL for printing only pursuant to Government Code section 11351 (Register 2019, No. 51).

Ref.: Hanna §§ 25.26, 27.02[5][a], 28.21[1], [2], 31.01, 31.10[2], [3], 31.11[1]; Herlick Handbook §§ 14.5, 14.19.

§10514. Proof of Service by Parties and Lien Claimants. [Repealed]

Note: Authority cited: Sections 133 and 5307, Labor Code. Reference: Section 5316, Labor Code.

History: 1. Amendment of section heading and text filed 12-23-93; operative 1-1-94. Submitted to OAL for printing only pursuant to Government Code section 11351 (Register 93, No. 52).
2. Amendment filed 12-19-2002; operative 1-1-2003. Submitted to OAL for printing only pursuant to Government Code section 11351 (Register 2002, No. 51).
3. Repealer filed 11-17-2008; operative 11-17-2008. Submitted to OAL for printing only (Register 2008, No. 47).

Ref.: Herlick Handbook § 14.5.

§10515. Demurrer, Judgment on the Pleadings and Summary Judgment Not Permitted.

Demurrers, petitions for judgment on the pleadings and petitions for summary judgment are not permitted.

Note: Authority cited: Sections 133 and 5307, Labor Code. Reference: Sections 5500 and 5708, Labor Code.

History: 1. Renumbering of former section 10490 to section 10515, including amendment of section heading and section, filed 12-17-2019; operative 1-1-2020. Submitted to OAL for printing only pursuant to Government Code section 11351 (Register 2019, No. 51).

Ref.: Hanna § 25.25; Herlick Handbook §§ 14.5, 14.43.

§10517. When Pleadings Deemed Amended.

Pleadings shall be deemed amended to conform to the stipulations and statement of issues agreed to by the parties on the record. Pleadings may be amended by the Workers' Compensation Appeals Board to conform to proof.

Note: Authority cited: Sections 133 and 5307, Labor Code. Reference: Section 5702, Labor Code.

History: 1. Renumbering and amendment of former section 10492 to section 10517 filed 12-17-2019; operative 1-1-2020. Submitted to OAL for printing only pursuant to Government Code section 11351 (Register 2019, No. 51).

Ref.: Hanna § 25.22[1]; Herlick Handbook §§ 14.5, 14.18.

§10520. Special Requirements for Pleadings Filed or Served by Representatives.

(a) Where a party is represented by an attorney, all pleadings filed with the Workers' Compensation Appeals Board or served on any party or other person shall include the name, State Bar number, law firm, if any, business address and business telephone number of the attorney.

(b) If a non-attorney employee of an attorney or law firm is executing the pleading being filed or served, the pleading shall include a heading containing the non-attorney's name and the name, State Bar number, law firm, if any, business address and business telephone number of the attorney primarily responsible for supervising the non-attorney.

(c) If a non-attorney representative who is not an employee of an attorney or law firm is executing the pleading being filed or served, the pleading shall include a heading containing the non-attorney representative's name followed by the words "Non-Attorney Representative," the name of the entity, if any, that employs the non-attorney representative, business address and business telephone number.

Note: Authority cited: Sections 133, 5307, 5309 and 5708, Labor Code. Reference: Sections 5000, 5501, 5505 and 5900 et seq., Labor Code; and Rules 2.111(1) and 8.204(b)(10)(D), California Rules of Court.

History: 1. Renumbering of former section 10498 to section 10520, including amendment of section heading, section and Note, filed 12-17-2019; operative 1-1-2020. Submitted to OAL for printing only pursuant to Government Code section 11351 (Register 2019, No. 51). For prior history of section 10520, see Register 2008, No. 47.

Ref.: Herlick Handbook §§ 14.5, 14.11.

§10525. Petition for Increased or Decreased Compensation — Serious and Willful Misconduct.

(a) Any claim(s) that an injury was caused by either the serious and willful misconduct of the employee or of the employer must be separately pleaded and must set out in sufficient detail the specific basis upon which a claim is founded. When a claim of serious and willful misconduct is based on more than one theory, the petition shall set forth each theory separately.

(b) Whenever a claim of serious and willful misconduct is predicated upon the violation of a particular safety order, the petition shall set forth the correct citation or reference and all of the particulars required by Labor Code section 4553.1.

Note: Authority cited: Sections 133 and 5307, Labor Code. Reference: Sections 4550, 4551, 4552, 4553 and 4553.1, Labor Code.

History: 1. New section filed 12-17-2019; operative 1-1-2020. Submitted to OAL for printing only pursuant to Government Code section 11351 (Register 2019, No. 51).

Ref.: Hanna §§ 25.05[4], 25.25; Herlick Handbook §§ 14.5, 14.16, 14.36.

§10528. Petition for Increased Compensation — Discrimination Under Labor Code Section 132a.

Any person seeking to initiate proceedings under Labor Code section 132a other than prosecution for misdemeanor must file a petition setting forth specifically and in detail the nature of each violation alleged, facts relied upon and the relief sought. Each alleged violation must be separately pleaded.

The Workers' Compensation Appeals Board may refer, or any worker may complain of, suspected violations of the criminal misdemeanor provisions of Labor Code section 132a to the Division of Labor Standards Enforcement or directly to the Office of the Public Prosecutor.

Note: Authority cited: Sections 133 and 5307, Labor Code. Reference: Section 132a, Labor Code.

History: 1. Renumbering of former section 10447 to section 10528, including amendment of section heading and section, filed

12-17-2019; operative 1-1-2020. Submitted to OAL for printing only pursuant to Government Code section 11351 (Register 2019, No. 51).

Ref.: Hanna §§ 10.11[4], 25.05[5]; Herlick Handbook §§ 14.5, 14.16, 14.37.

§10530. Emergency Petition for Stay.

(a) A party may present to the presiding workers' compensation judge of the district office having venue or the workers' compensation judge of the permanently staffed satellite office having venue a petition to stay an action by another party pending a hearing. Each district office will have a designee of the presiding workers' compensation judge available to assign petitions for stay from 8:00 a.m. to 11:00 a.m. and 1:00 p.m. to 4:00 p.m. on court days.

(b) A party who walks through a petition to stay an action shall provide notice by fax or e-mail to the opposing party or parties no later than 10:00 a.m. of the immediately preceding court day. This notice shall state with specificity the nature of the relief to be requested by the petition to stay and state the date, time and place that the petition to stay will be presented. A copy of the petition to stay shall be attached to the notice. If notice by fax or e-mail fails, or if an opposing party's fax number or e-mail address are unknown, notice shall be given in the manner best calculated to expeditiously provide the party or parties with notice including notice by phone or by overnight mail or delivery service. First-class mail shall not be utilized for notice of a petition to stay an action.

(c) A petition to stay an action shall be accompanied by a declaration regarding notice stating under penalty of perjury:

(1) The notice given, including the date, time, manner and name of the party informed;

(2) The relief sought; and

(3) Whether opposition is expected. In addition, if the petitioner was unable to give timely notice to the opposing party, the declaration under penalty of perjury shall state that the petitioner in good faith attempted to inform the opposing party but was unable to do so, and shall specify the efforts made to inform the opposing party.

(d) Upon the receipt of a proper petition to stay an action, the presiding workers' compensation judge shall, in their discretion, either:

(1) Deny the petition;

(2) Grant a temporary stay and set the petition for a hearing; or

(3) Set the petition for a hearing, without either denying the petition or granting a temporary stay.

Note: Authority cited: Sections 133 and 5307, Labor Code. Reference: Sections 4053, 4054, 4902, 5001, 5002, 5702 and 5710, Labor Code.

History: 1. Amendment exempt from OAL review pursuant to Government Code section 11351 filed 12-19-90; operative 1-1-91 (Register 91, No. 7).

2. Repealer of article 7 heading, renumbering of former section 10530 to section 10640 and renumbering and amendment of former section 10470 to section 10530 filed 12-17-2019; operative 1-1-2020. Submitted to OAL for printing only pursuant to Government Code section 11351 (Register 2019, No. 51).

Ref.: Hanna §§ 23.11[2a], 25.08[5]; Herlick Handbook §§ 14.5, 14.30B.

§10532. Notice to Appear or Produce. [Renumbered]

Note: Authority cited: Sections 133, 5307, Labor Code. Reference: Section 132, Labor Code.

History: 1. Renumbering of former section 10532 to section 10642 filed 12-17-2019; operative 1-1-2020. Submitted to OAL for printing only pursuant to Government Code section 11351 (Register 2019, No. 51).

Ref.: Herlick Handbook § 14.5.

§10534. Petition to Reopen.

Petitions invoking the continuing jurisdiction of the Workers' Compensation Appeals Board under Labor Code section 5803 shall set forth specifically and in detail the facts relied upon to establish good cause for reopening.

Note: Authority cited: Sections 133 and 5307, Labor Code. Reference: Section 5803, Labor Code.

History: 1. Amendment of section and Note filed 12-19-2002; operative 1-1-2003. Submitted to OAL for printing only pursuant to Government Code section 11351 (Register 2002, No. 51).

2. Renumbering of former section 10534 to section 10644 and renumbering of former section 10455 to section 10534 filed 12-17-2019; operative 1-1-2020. Submitted to OAL for printing only pursuant to Government Code section 11351 (Register 2019, No. 51).

Ref.: Herlick Handbook §§ 14.5, 14.9.

§10536. Petition for New and Further Disability.

The jurisdiction of the Workers' Compensation Appeals Board under Labor Code section 5410 shall be invoked by a petition setting forth specifically and in detail the facts relied upon to establish new and further disability.

If no prior Application for Adjudication of Claim has been filed, jurisdiction shall be invoked by the filing of an original Application for Adjudication of Claim.

Note: Authority cited: Sections 133 and 5307, Labor Code. Reference: Sections 5410 and 5803, Labor Code.

History: 1. Repealer and new section exempt from OAL review pursuant to Government Code section 11351 filed 12-19-90; operative 1-1-91 (Register 91, No. 7).

2. Amendment of section and Note filed 12-19-2002; operative 1-1-2003. Submitted to OAL for printing only pursuant to Government Code section 11351 (Register 2002, No. 51).

3. Renumbering of former section 10536 to section 10647 and renumbering and amendment of former section 10458 to section 10536 filed 12-17-2019; operative 1-1-2020. Submitted to OAL for printing only pursuant to Government Code section 11351 (Register 2019, No. 51).

Ref.: Hanna §§ 25.05[2], 31.05[5]; Herlick Handbook §§ 14.5, 14.19.

§10537. Subpoena for Medical Witness. [Renumbered]

Note: Authority cited: Sections 133, 5307, Labor Code. Reference: Section 132, Labor Code.

History: 1. Renumbering of former section 10537 to section 10650 filed 12-17-2019; operative 1-1-2020. Submitted to OAL for printing only pursuant to Government Code section 11351 (Register 2019, No. 51).

Ref.: Herlick Handbook § 14.5.

§10538. Subpoenas for Medical Information by Non-Physician Lien Claimants. [Renumbered]

Note: Authority cited: Sections 133, 4903.6(d), 5307, 5309 and 5708, Labor Code. Reference: Sections 130, 4903.6(d) and 5710(a), Labor Code; and Sections 56.05 and 56.10, Civil Code.

History: 1. New section filed 9-23-2013; operative 10-23-2013. Submitted as a file and print by the Workers' Compensation Appeals Board pursuant to Government Code section 11351 (Register 2013, No. 39).

2. Renumbering of former section 10538 to section 10655 filed 12-17-2019; operative 1-1-2020. Submitted to OAL for printing only pursuant to Government Code section 11351 (Register 2019, No. 51).

Ref.: Herlick Handbook § 14.5.

§10540. Petition to Terminate Liability for Continuing Temporary Disability.

(a) Any petition to terminate liability for temporary total disability indemnity awarded under a findings and award, decision or order of the Workers' Compensation Appeals Board shall include:

(1) A statement, in capital letters, that an order terminating liability for temporary total disability indemnity may issue unless objection thereto is served and filed on behalf of the employee within 14 days after service and filing of the petition, and

(2) All medical reports in the possession of the petitioner that have not previously been served and filed;

(b) If written objection to the petition to terminate is not served and filed within 14 days of the petition's service and filing, the Workers' Compensation Appeals Board may order temporary disability compensation terminated, in accordance with the facts as stated in the petition or in such other manner as may appear appropriate on the record. If the petition to terminate is not properly completed or executed in accordance with this rule, the Workers' Compensation Appeals Board may summarily deny or dismiss the petition.

(c) Written objection to the petition by the employee shall be served and filed within 14 days of service and filing of the petition, and shall state the facts in support of the employee's contention that the petition should be denied, and shall be accompanied by a Declaration of Readiness to Proceed to Expedited Hearing. All supporting medical reports shall be attached to the objection. The objection shall also show that service of the objection and the reports attached thereto has been made upon petitioner or counsel and a proof of service showing service of the objection upon petitioner.

(d) Upon the filing of a timely objection, where it appears that the employee is not or may not be working and is not or may not be receiving disability indemnity, the petition to terminate shall be set for expedited hearing not less than 10 nor more than 30 days from the date of the receipt of the objection.

(e) If complete disposition of the petition to terminate cannot be made at the hearing, the workers' compensation judge assigned thereto, based on the record, including the allegations of the petition, the objection thereto and the evidence (if any) at said hearing, shall forthwith issue an interim order directing whether temporary disability indemnity shall or shall not continue during the pendency of proceedings on the petition to terminate. Said interim order shall not be considered a final order, and will not preclude a complete adjudication of the petition to terminate or the issue of temporary disability or any other issue after full hearing of the issues.

Note: Authority cited: Sections 133 and 5307, Labor Code. Reference: Sections 4650 and 4651.1, Labor Code.

History: 1. New section filed 12-17-2019; operative 1-1-2020. Submitted to OAL for printing only pursuant to Government Code section 11351 (Register 2019, No. 51).

Ref.: Hanna §§ 7.02[1], 31.10[1]; Herlick Handbook §§ 14.5, 14.19.

§10541. Submission at Conference. [Renumbered]

Note: Authority cited: Sections 133, 5307, 5309 and 5708, Labor Code. Reference: Sections 5708 and 5709, Labor Code.

History: 1. Amendment filed 12-23-93; operative 1-1-94. Submitted to OAL for printing only pursuant to Government Code section 11351 (Register 93, No. 52).

2. Amendment of section heading, section and Note filed 12-19-2002; operative 1-1-2003. Submitted to OAL for printing only pursuant to Government Code section 11351 (Register 2002, No. 51).

3. Amendment of section and Note filed 11-17-2008; operative 11-17-2008. Submitted to OAL for printing only (Register 2008, No. 47).

4. Repealer of article 8 heading and renumbering of former section 10541 to section 10761 filed 12-17-2019; operative 1-1-2020. Submitted to OAL for printing only pursuant to Government Code section 11351 (Register 2019, No. 51).

Ref.: Herlick Handbook § 14.5.

§10544. Notice of Hearing. [Renumbered]

Note: Authority cited: Sections 133 and 5307, Labor Code. Reference: Section 5504, Labor Code.

History: 1. Amendment filed 12-23-93; operative 1-1-94. Submitted to OAL for printing only pursuant to Government Code section 11351 (Register 93, No. 52).

2. Amendment of section and Note filed 12-19-2002; operative 1-1-2003. Submitted to OAL for printing only pursuant to Government Code section 11351 (Register 2002, No. 51).

3. Renumbering of former section 10544 to section 10750 filed 12-17-2019; operative 1-1-2020. Submitted to OAL for printing only pursuant to Government Code section 11351 (Register 2019, No. 51).

Ref.: Herlick Handbook § 14.5.

§10545. Petition for Costs.

(a) A petition for costs is a petition seeking reimbursement of an expense or payment for service that is not allowable as a lien against compensation under Labor Code section 4903. A petition for costs may be filed only by:

(1) An employee or the dependent of a deceased employee;

(2) A defendant; or

(3) An interpreter for services other than those rendered at a medical treatment appointment or medical-legal examination.

(b) The caption of the petition shall identify it as a "Petition for Costs."

(c) A petition for costs filed by an employee or a dependent may include, but is not limited to, a claim for reimbursement of payment(s) previously made directly to a provider for medical-legal goods or services, subject to any applicable official fee schedule.

(d) A petition for costs filed by an interpreter shall contain, in addition to the general factual allegations of the petition:

(1) A statement of the name(s) of any interpreter(s) who performed the services;

(2) A statement that the services were actually performed; and

(3) Either:

(A) A statement of the certification number of the interpreter(s); or

(B) If not certified, a statement that specifies why a certified interpreter was not used and that sets forth the qualifications of the interpreter, including any qualifications for a non-certified interpreter established by the rules of the Administrative Director.

(e) A petition for costs shall not be filed or served until at least 60 days after a written demand for the costs has been served on the defendant or the person or entity from whom the costs are claimed. The petition shall append:

(1) A copy of the written demand, together with a copy of its proof of service; and

(2) A copy of the response, if any.

A petition that fails to comply with these provisions may be dismissed.

(f) A petition for costs submitted by any person or entity not listed in subdivision (a) shall be deemed dismissed by operation of law and shall not toll or extend any statute of limitations.

(g) The Workers' Compensation Appeals Board may, at any time, issue a notice of intention to allow or disallow the costs sought by the petition, in whole or in part. The notice of intention shall give the petitioner and any adverse party no less than 15 calendar days to file written objection showing good cause to the contrary. If no timely objection is filed, or if the objection on its face fails to show good cause, the Workers' Compensation Appeals Board, in its discretion, may:

(1) Issue an order regarding the petition for costs, consistent with the notice of intention; or

(2) Set the matter for hearing.

(h) If the filing of a petition for costs, or the failure to promptly make good faith payments on the costs sought by the petition, was the result of bad faith actions or tactics, the Workers' Compensation Appeals Board may impose monetary sanctions and allow reasonable attorney's fees and costs under Labor Code section 5813 and rule 10421. The amount of the attorney's fees, costs and sanctions payable shall be determined by the Workers' Compensation Appeals Board; however, for bad faith actions or tactics occurring on or after the effective date of this rule, the monetary sanctions shall not be less than $500.00.

Note: Authority cited: Sections 133, 5307, 5309 and 5708, Labor Code. Reference: Sections 4600, 4903 et seq., 5710, 5811 and 5813, Labor Code.

History: 1. Renumbering of former section 10451.3 to section 10545, including amendment of section and Note, filed 12-17-2019; operative 1-1-2020. Submitted to OAL for printing only pursuant to Government Code section 11351 (Register 2019, No. 51).

Ref.: Hanna § 23.13[3]; Herlick Handbook § 14.5.

§10547. Petition for Labor Code Section 5710 Attorney's Fees.

(a) A petition for attorney's fees pursuant to Labor Code section 5710 is a petition seeking attorney fees for representation of the applicant at a deposition allowable under Labor Code section 5710(b) as well as any other benefits listed under Labor Code section 5710(b)(1)-(5).

(b) The caption of the petition shall identify it as a "Petition for Attorney's Fees Pursuant to Labor Code Section 5710."

(c) A petition for attorney's fees pursuant to Labor Code section 5710 shall be verified upon oath in the manner required for verified pleadings in courts of record.

(d) A petition for attorney's fees pursuant to Labor Code section 5710 shall not be filed or served until at least 30 days after a written demand for the fees has been served on the defendant(s). The petition shall append:

(1) A copy of the written demand, together with a copy of the proof of service;

(2) A copy of the response, if any;

(3) A proof of service showing service on the injured worker and the defendant alleged to be liable for paying the fees; and

(e) Failure to comply with subdivisions (c) and (d)(1)-(3) of this rule shall constitute a valid ground for dismissing the petition.

(f) The petition shall contain the name of the attorney who attended the deposition along with the attorney's State Bar number.

Note: Authority cited: Sections 133, 5307, 5309 and 5708, Labor Code. Reference: Sections 4600, 4903 et seq., 5710, 5811 and 5813, Labor Code.

History: 1. New section filed 12-17-2019; operative 1-1-2020. Submitted to OAL for printing only pursuant to Government Code section 11351 (Register 2019, No. 51).

Ref.: Hanna § 25.41[2]; Herlick Handbook § 14.5.

§10548. Continuances. [Renumbered]

Note: Authority cited: Sections 133 and 5307, Labor Code. Reference: Article XIV, Section 4, California Constitution; and Sections 5502 and 5502.5, Labor Code.

History: 1. New section filed 10-15-2014; operative 1-1-2015. Submitted to OAL for printing only pursuant to Government Code section 11351 (Register 2014, No. 42). For prior history, see Register 2008, No. 47.

2. Editorial correction of History 1 (Register 2017, No. 8).

3. Renumbering of former section 10548 to section 10748 filed 12-17-2019; operative 1-1-2020. Submitted to OAL for printing only pursuant to Government Code section 11351 (Register 2019, No. 51).

Ref.: Herlick Handbook § 14.5.

§10549. Appearances in Settled Cases. [Renumbered]

Note: Authority cited: Sections 133 and 5307, Labor Code. Reference: Article XIV, Section 4, California Constitution; and Sections 5502 and 5502.5, Labor Code.

History: 1. New section filed 10-15-2014; operative 1-1-2015. Submitted to OAL for printing only pursuant to Government Code section 11351 (Register 2014, No. 42).

2. Editorial correction of History 1 (Register 2017, No. 8).

3. Renumbering of former section 10549 to section 10757 filed 12-17-2019; operative 1-1-2020. Submitted to OAL for printing only pursuant to Government Code section 11351 (Register 2019, No. 51).

Ref.: Herlick Handbook § 14.5.

§10550. Petition to Dismiss Inactive Cases.

(a) Unless a case is activated for hearing within one year after the filing of the Application for Adjudication of Claim or the entry of an order taking off calendar, the case may be dismissed after notice and opportunity to be heard. Such dismissals may be entered at the request of an interested party or upon the Workers' Compensation Appeals Board's own motion for lack of prosecution.

(b) At least 30 days before filing a petition to dismiss, the defendant seeking to dismiss the case shall send a letter to the applicant and, if represented, to the applicant's attorney or non-attorney representative, stating the defendant's intention to file a "Petition to Dismiss Inactive Case" 30 days after the date of that letter, unless the applicant or applicant's attorney or non-attorney representative objects in writing, demonstrating good cause for not dismissing the case.

(c) A petition to dismiss shall be filed with the district office having venue or in EAMS and the petition shall be served on all parties and all lien claimants pursuant to Rule 10625.

(d) A petition to dismiss shall be captioned "Petition to Dismiss Inactive Case [assigned ADJ number]."

(e) The following documents shall be filed with a petition to dismiss:

(1) A copy of the letter required by subdivision (a) of this rule; and

(2) Any reply to the letter required by subdivision (a) of this rule.

(f) A case may be dismissed after issuance of a 10-day notice of intention to dismiss and an opportunity to be heard, but not by an order with a clause rendering the order null and void if an objection showing good cause is filed.

Note: Authority cited: Sections 133 and 5307, Labor Code. Reference: Sections 5405 and 5406, Labor Code.

History: 1. New section filed 11-17-2008; operative 11-17-2008. Submitted to OAL for printing only (Register 2008, No. 47).

2. Renumbering of former section 10550 to section 10390 and renumbering of former section 10582 to section 10550, including amendment of section heading and section, filed 12-17-2019; operative 1-1-2020. Submitted to OAL for printing only pursuant to Government Code section 11351 (Register 2019, No. 51).

Ref.: Hanna §§ 23.11[5][c], 23.14[2][j], 31.14[5]; Herlick Handbook §§ 14.5, 14.8, 14.43.

§10552. Expedited Hearing Calendar. [Renumbered]

Note: Authority cited: Sections 133, 5307 and 5502, Labor Code. Reference: Section 5202, Labor Code.

History: 1. New section filed 10-15-2014; operative 1-1-2015. Submitted to OAL for printing only pursuant to Government Code section 11351 (Register 2014, No. 42).

2. Editorial correction of History 1 (Register 2017, No. 8).

3. Renumbering of former section 10552 to section 10782 filed 12-17-2019; operative 1-1-2020. Submitted to OAL for printing only pursuant to Government Code section 11351 (Register 2019, No. 51).

§10555. Petition for Credit.

(a) When a dispute arises as to a credit for any payments or overpayments of benefits pursuant to Labor Code section 4909, any petition for credit shall include:

(1) A description of the payments made by the employer;

(2) A description of the benefits against which the employer seeks a credit; and

(3) The amount of the claimed credit.

(b) When a dispute arises as to a credit for an employee's third party recovery pursuant to Labor Code section 3861, any petition for credit shall include:

(1) A copy of the settlement or judgment, if available; and

(2) An itemization of any credit applied to expenses and attorneys' fees pursuant to Labor Code sections 3856, 3858 and 3860.

(c) Where a copy of the settlement or judgment required under subdivision (b)(1) of this rule is not available, a workers' compensation judge may order its production for purposes of adjudicating a petition for credit under Labor Code section 3861.

Note: Authority cited: Sections 133 and 5307, Labor Code. Reference: Sections 3856, 3858, 3860, 3861 and 4909, Labor Code.

History: 1. New section filed 10-15-2014; operative 1-1-2015. Submitted to OAL for printing only pursuant to Government Code section 11351 (Register 2014, No. 42). For prior history, see Register 2008, No. 47.

2. Editorial correction of History 1 (Register 2017, No. 8).

3. Renumbering former section 10555 to section 10785 and new section 10555 filed 12-17-2019; operative 1-1-2020. Submitted to OAL for printing only pursuant to Government Code section 11351 (Register 2019, No. 51).

Ref.: Hanna § 7.04[9][a], [b].

ARTICLE 8
Petitions Related to Administrative Orders

§10560. Petitions Related to Orders Issued by the Division of Workers' Compensation Administrative Director or the Director of Industrial Relations.

(a) Where the Labor Code provides that the Workers' Compensation Appeals Board has jurisdiction over appeals from or enforcement of an order, any aggrieved party may appeal or seek to enforce an order issued by the Division of Workers' Compensation Administrative Director or the Director of Industrial Relations by filing a petition, and an Application for Adjudication of Claim if one has not already been filed.

(b) Any petition that fails to comply with any of the following requirements may be subject to summary dismissal:

(1) The petition must be timely filed with the Workers' Compensation Appeals Board within the timeframe set forth in the applicable statutes and rules.

(2) The petition shall be filed in accordance with rule 10615.

(3) The petition shall be served on all adverse parties, the employee and the Administrative Director or the Director as specified in the relevant rule.

(c) The petition shall set forth specifically and in full detail the factual and/or legal grounds upon which the petitioner considers the determination of the Administrative Director or the Director to be unjust or unlawful, and every issue to be considered. The petitioner shall be deemed to have finally waived all objections, irregularities and illegalities concerning the determination other than those set forth in the petition.

(d) The petition shall be adjudicated by a workers' compensation judge at the trial level of the Workers' Compensation Appeals Board utilizing the same procedures applicable to claims for ordinary benefits, including but not limited to the setting of a mandatory settlement conference and trial.

(e) Where a workers' compensation judge has issued a final decision, order or award, any aggrieved party may file a petition for reconsideration with the Workers' Compensation Appeals Board.

Note: Authority cited: Sections 133, 5307, 5309 and 5708, Labor Code. Reference: Sections 129, 4603, 4604, 5300, 5301 and 5302, Labor Code.

History: 1. Repealer and new section heading and section and amendment of Note filed 12-19-2002; operative 1-1-2003. Submitted to OAL for printing only pursuant to Government Code section 11351 (Register 2002, No. 51).

2. New article 8 heading and repealer and new section filed 12-17-2019; operative 1-1-2020. Submitted to OAL for printing only pursuant to Government Code section 11351 (Register 2019, No. 51).

Ref.: Hanna § 1.11[6][b]; Herlick Handbook § 15.1.

§10561. Sanctions. [Renumbered]

Note: Authority cited: Sections 133, 5307, 5309 and 5708, Labor Code. Reference: Sections 4903.6(c) and 5813, Labor Code.

History: 1. New section filed 12-23-93; operative 1-1-94. Submitted to OAL for printing only pursuant to Government Code section 11351 (Register 93, No. 52).

2. Amendment filed 12-19-2002; operative 1-1-2003. Submitted to OAL for printing only pursuant to Government Code section 11351 (Register 2002, No. 51).

3. Amendment of section and Note filed 11-17-2008; operative 11-17-2008. Submitted to OAL for printing only (Register 2008, No. 47).

4. Amendment of subsections (b)(3)-(4) filed 10-15-2014; operative 1-1-2015. Submitted to OAL for printing only pursuant to Government Code section 11351 (Register 2014, No. 42).

5. Editorial correction of History 4 (Register 2017, No. 8).

6. Renumbering of former section 10561 to section 10421 filed 12-17-2019; operative 1-1-2020. Submitted to OAL for printing only pursuant to Government Code section 11351 (Register 2019, No. 51).

§10561.5. Compliance with Rules of the Court Administrator. [Repealed]

Note: Authority cited: Sections 133, 5307(c) and 5500.3, Labor Code; and Stats. 2011, c. 559, §17 (A.B. 1426). Reference: Section 5813, Labor Code.

History: 1. Renumbering of former section 10211 to new section 10561.5, including amendment of Note, filed 12-10-2012 as a change without regulatory effect pursuant to section 100, title 1, California Code of Regulations by the Division of Workers' Compensation and as a file and print by the Workers' Compensation Appeals Board pursuant to Government Code section 11351 (Register 2012, No. 50).

2. Repealer filed 10-14-2014; operative 1-1-2015. Submitted to OAL for printing only pursuant to Government Code section 11351 (Register 2014, No. 42).

3. Editorial correction of History 2 (Register 2017, No. 8).

§10562. Failure to Appear. [Repealed]

Note: Authority cited: Sections 133 and 5307, Labor Code. Reference: Article XIV, Section 4, California Constitution; and Sections 5502(e) and 5708, Labor Code.

History: 1. Repealer and new section filed 12-23-93; operative 1-1-94. Submitted to OAL for printing only pursuant to Government Code section 11351 (Register 93, No. 52). For prior history, see Register 91, No. 7.

2. Amendment of section and Note filed 12-19-2002; operative 1-1-2003. Submitted to OAL for printing only pursuant to Government Code section 11351 (Register 2002, No. 51).

3. Repealer filed 12-17-2019; operative 1-1-2020. Submitted to OAL for printing only pursuant to Government Code section 11351 (Register 2019, No. 51).

§10563. Appearances Required of Parties to Case-in-Chief. [Repealed]

Note: Authority cited: Sections 133, 5307, 5309 and 5708, Labor Code. Reference: Sections 5502 and 5700, Labor Code.

History: 1. New section filed 10-15-2014; operative 1-1-2015. Submitted to OAL for printing only pursuant to Government Code section 11351 (Register 2014, No. 42). For prior history, see Register 2008, No. 47.

2. Editorial correction of History 1 (Register 2017, No. 8).

3. Repealer filed 12-17-2019; operative 1-1-2020. Submitted to OAL for printing only pursuant to Government Code section 11351 (Register 2019, No. 51).

§10563.1. Other Appearances Required. [Repealed]

Note: Authority cited: Sections 133, 5307, 5309 and 5708, Labor Code. Reference: Sections 5502 and 5700, Labor Code.

History: 1. New section filed 10-15-2014; operative 1-1-2015. Submitted to OAL for printing only pursuant to Government Code section 11351 (Register 2014, No. 42).

2. Editorial correction of History 1 (Register 2017, No. 8).

3. Repealer filed 12-17-2019; operative 1-1-2020. Submitted to OAL for printing only pursuant to Government Code section 11351 (Register 2019, No. 51).

§10564. Interpreters. [Renumbered]

Note: Authority cited: Sections 133 and 5307, Labor Code. Reference: Sections 4600, 4621, 5710 and 5811, Labor Code.

History: 1. Amendment of section and Note filed 12-23-93; operative 1-1-94. Submitted to OAL for printing only pursuant to Government Code section 11351 (Register 93, No. 52).

2. Amendment of section and Note filed 12-19-2002; operative 1-1-2003. Submitted to OAL for printing only pursuant to Government Code section 11351 (Register 2002, No. 51).

3. Renumbering of former section 10564 to section 10790 filed 12-17-2019; operative 1-1-2020. Submitted to OAL for printing only pursuant to Government Code section 11351 (Register 2019, No. 51).

§10565. Petition Appealing Denial of Return-to-Work Supplement.

(a) An injured worker may file a "Petition Appealing Denial of Return-to-Work Supplement" with the district office having venue or in EAMS.

(b) The petition shall be filed within 20 days of service of the decision denying the return-to-work supplement, in accordance with rule 10615 and rule 17309.

(c) The petition and any additional documents or pleadings related to the petition shall be served on the Department of Industrial Relations Return-to-Work Supplement Program in accordance with rule 10632.

(d) The petition shall be captioned "Petition Appealing Denial of Return-to-Work Supplement" and shall include the assigned ADJ number.

(e) The petition shall be based upon one or more of the grounds as prescribed for petitions for reconsideration in Labor Code section 5903.

(f) The Director may file an answer to the petition within 20 days of the date of service of the petition. A document cover sheet and a document separator sheet shall be filed with the answer, and "Return-to-Work Supplement Program Answer to Appeal" shall be entered into the document title field of the document separator sheet.

(g) The petition shall not be placed on calendar unless a Declaration of Readiness to Proceed is filed. The Declaration of Readiness to Proceed may not be filed until 30 days have elapsed from the service of the petition.

(h) If the Director of Industrial Relations acts under rule 17309 to amend, modify or rescind the decision being appealed, the resulting order by the Director shall be served on the parties within 15 days following the date the appeal was filed and shall be filed with the district office having venue or in EAMS.

Note: Authority cited: Sections 133, 139.48, 5307, 5309 and 5708, Labor Code. Reference: Section 5903, Labor Code.

History: 1. New section filed 12-17-2019; operative 1-1-2020. Submitted to OAL for printing only pursuant to Government Code section 11351 (Register 2019, No. 51).

Ref.: Hanna § 7.02[4][d][iii].

§10566. Minutes of Hearing and Summary of Evidence. [Repealed]

Note: Authority cited: Sections 133 and 5307, Labor Code. Reference: Section 5313, Labor Code.

History: 1. Amendment of subsection (d) filed 12-19-2002; operative 1-1-2003. Submitted to OAL for printing only pursuant to Government Code section 11351 (Register 2002, No. 51).

2. Repealer filed 12-17-2019; operative 1-1-2020. Submitted to OAL for printing only pursuant to Government Code section 11351 (Register 2019, No. 51).

§10567. Petition Appealing Independent Bill Review Determination.

(a) An aggrieved party may file a petition appealing an independent bill review (IBR) determination of the Administrative Director (AD). For purposes of this section, a "determination" includes a decision regarding the amount payable to the provider, if any, and/or a decision that a dispute is not subject to independent bill review.

(b) The petition shall comply with each of the following provisions:

(1) The petition shall be limited to raising one or more of the five grounds specified in Labor Code section 4603.6(f).

(2) The petition shall set forth specifically and in full detail the factual and/or legal grounds upon which the petitioner considers the IBR determination to be unjust or unlawful, and every issue to be considered by the Workers' Compensation Appeals Board. The petitioner shall be deemed to have finally waived all objections, irregularities, and illegalities concerning the IBR determination other than those set forth in the petition appealing.

(c) The petition shall be filed in accordance with rule 10615 no later than 20 days after service of the IBR determination.

(d) In addition to service as required by rule 10625, the petition and any additional documents or pleadings related to the petition shall be served on the IBR Unit in accordance with rule 10632.

(e) The petition shall be captioned "Petition Appealing Administrative Director's Independent Bill Review Determination" and shall include the assigned ADJ number and the IBR case number assigned by the Administrative director.

(f) The petition shall include a copy of the IBR determination and proof of service of that determination.

(g) Upon receiving notice of the petition, the IBR Unit may download the record of the independent bill review organization into EAMS, in whole or in part. The Workers' Compensation Appeals Board, in its discretion, may:

(1) Admit all or any part of the downloaded IBR record into evidence; and/or

(2) Permit the parties to offer in evidence documents that are duplicates of ones already existing in the downloaded IBR record.

(h) The petition shall not be placed on calendar unless a Declaration of Readiness to Proceed is filed and served on the Administrative Director, all adverse parties and the applicant.

(i) If the IBR determination is not affirmed by the workers' compensation judge or the Appeals Board, it shall be rescinded and the dispute returned to the Administrative Director with an order specifying the basis for the rescission, and an order to resubmit the dispute to IBR in accordance with Labor Code section 4603.6(g).

(j) If a final decision of the Workers' Compensation Appeals Board affirms the Administrative Director's IBR determination and results in the defendant being liable for any payment to the provider, the amount for which the defendant is liable shall be paid to the provider forthwith. If the defendant fails to pay forthwith, the provider need not file a lien claim and may file a petition to enforce under rule 10570.

Note: Authority cited: Sections 133, 5307, 5309 and 5708, Labor Code. Reference: Sections 4603.6, 5500, 5501, 5502, 5700 et seq., 5800 et seq. and 5900 et seq., Labor Code.

History: 1. Renumbering of former section 10957 to section 10567, including amendment of section heading, section and Note, filed 12-17-2019; operative 1-1-2020. Submitted to OAL for printing only pursuant to Government Code section 11351 (Register 2019, No. 51).

Ref.: Hanna § 5.02[2][e].

§10570. Petition to Enforce an Administrative Director Determination.

(a) An aggrieved party may file a "Petition to Enforce an Administrative Director Determination" after the Workers' Compensation Appeals Board has issued a final order affirming an IBR, IMR or other determination issued by the administrative director or after the time to appeal the determination to the Workers' Compensation Appeals Board has expired.

(b) The petition shall be captioned as a "Petition to Enforce an Administrative Director Determination" and shall include the assigned ADJ number and shall append a copy of the Administrative Director's determination.

(c) The petition shall be served on all parties in accordance with rule 10628.

(d) Within 15 days of the filing of the petition to enforce, the Workers' Compensation Appeals Board shall issue a notice of intention to grant or deny the petition, in whole or in part. The notice of intention shall give the petitioner and any adverse party no fewer than 15 calendar days to file written objection showing good cause to the contrary. If no timely written objection is filed, or if the written objection on its face fails to show good cause, the Workers' Compensation Appeals Board, in its discretion, may:

(1) Issue an order regarding the petition to enforce, consistent with the notice of intention; or

(2) Set the matter for hearing.

Note: Authority cited: Sections 133, 5307, 5309 and 5708, Labor Code. Reference: Sections 4603.6, 4622, 4903.05 and 4903.06, Labor Code.

History: 1. Renumbering of former section 10570 to section 10833 and renumbering of former section 10451.4 to section 10570, including amendment of section heading and section, filed 12-17-2019; operative 1-1-2020. Submitted to OAL for printing only pursuant to Government Code section 11351 (Register 2019, No. 51).

Ref.: Hanna § 5.02[2][e].

§10575. Petition Appealing Independent Medical Review Determination.

(a) An aggrieved party may file a petition appealing the Administrative Director's independent medical review (IMR) determination. For purposes of this rule, a "determination" includes a decision regarding medical necessity and/or a decision that a dispute is not eligible for independent medical review.

(b) The petition shall set forth specifically and in full detail the factual and/or legal grounds upon which the petitioner considers the IMR determination to be incorrect, and every issue to be considered by the Workers' Compensation Appeals Board. The petitioner shall be deemed to have finally waived all objections, irregularities and illegalities concerning the IMR determination other than those set forth in the petition. Any petition that fails to comply with any of the following requirements may be subject to summary dismissal.

(c) The petition shall be filed in accordance with rule 10615 no later than 30 days after service of the IMR determination.

(d) The petition and any additional documents or pleadings related to the petition shall be served on the IMR Unit in accordance with rule 10632.

(e) The petition shall be captioned "Petition Appealing Administrative Director's Independent Medical Review Determination" and shall include the assigned ADJ number and the IMR case number assigned by the Administrative Director.

(f) The petition shall include a copy of the IMR determination and proof of service of that determination.

(g) Upon receiving notice of the petition, the IMR Unit may download the record of the independent medical review organization into EAMS, in whole or in part. The Workers' Compensation Appeals Board, in its discretion, may:

(1) Admit all or any part of the downloaded IMR record into evidence; and/or

(2) Permit the parties to offer in evidence documents that are duplicates of ones already existing in the downloaded IMR record.

(h)(1) The petition shall not be placed on calendar unless a Declaration of Readiness to Proceed is filed.

(2) Notwithstanding the filing of a Declaration of Readiness to Proceed, a petition appealing an IMR determination shall be deferred if at the time of the determination the defendant is also disputing liability for the treatment for any reason besides medical necessity.

(i) If the IMR determination is rescinded by the workers' compensation judge or the Appeals Board, the medical treatment dispute shall be returned to the Administrative Director with an order specifying the basis for the rescission and an order to submit the dispute to IMR in accordance with Labor Code section 4610.6(i).

Note: Authority cited: Sections 133, 5307, 5309 and 5708, Labor Code. Reference: Sections 4610.6, 5500, 5501, 5502, 5700 et seq., 5800 et seq. and 5900 et seq., Labor Code.

History: 1. Renumbering of former section 10957.1 to section 10575, including amendment of section heading, section and Note, filed 12-17-2019; operative 1-1-2020. Submitted to OAL for printing only pursuant to Government Code section 11351 (Register 2019, No. 51).

Ref.: Hanna § 5.02[2][d].

§10578. Waiver of Summary of Evidence. [Repealed]

Note: Authority cited: Sections 133 and 5307, Labor Code. Reference: Section 5702, Labor Code.

History: 1. Amendment filed 12-19-2002; operative 1-1-2003. Submitted to OAL for printing only pursuant to Government Code section 11351 (Register 2002, No. 51).

2. Repealer filed 12-17-2019; operative 1-1-2020. Submitted to OAL for printing only pursuant to Government Code section 11351 (Register 2019, No. 51).

§10580. Petition Appealing Medical Provider Network Determination of the Administrative Director.

(a) Any aggrieved person or entity may file a petition appealing a determination of the Administrative Director to:

(1) Deny a medical provider network (MPN) application;

(2) Revoke or suspend an MPN plan;

(3) Place an MPN plan on probation;

(4) Deny a petition to revoke or suspend an MPN plan; or

(5) Impose administrative penalties relating to an MPN.

(b) The petition shall be filed only as follows:

(1) The petition shall be filed no later than 20 days after the date of service of the Administrative Director's determination. An untimely petition may be summarily dismissed.

(2) Notwithstanding any other provision of these rules or of Administrative Director rules 9767.8(i), 9767.13(f) and 9767.14(f), the petition shall be filed solely in paper form directly with the Office of the Commissioners of the Workers' Compensation Appeals Board.

(3) The petition shall not be submitted to any district office of the Workers' Compensation Appeals Board, including the San Francisco District Office, and it shall not be submitted electronically.

(4) A petition submitted in violation of this subdivision shall neither be accepted for filing nor deemed filed and shall not be acknowledged or returned to the submitting party.

(c) The caption of the petition shall identify it as a "Petition Appealing Administrative Director's Medical Provider Network Determination."

(d) The caption of the petition shall include:

(1) The name of the MPN or MPN applicant;

(2) The identity of the petitioner; and

(3) The case number assigned by the Administrative Director to the MPN determination.

(e) The petition shall include a copy of the Administrative Director's determination and proof of service of that determination.

(f) The petition shall comply with each of the following provisions:

(1) The petition may appeal the Administrative Director's determination upon one or more of the following grounds and no other:

(A) The determination was without or in excess of the Administrative Director's powers;

(B) The determination was procured by fraud;

(C) The evidence does not justify the determination;

(D) The petitioner has discovered new material evidence, which the petitioner could not, with reasonable diligence, have discovered and presented to the Administrative Director prior to the determination; and/or

(E) The Administrative Director's findings of fact do not support the determination.

(2) The petition shall set forth specifically and in full detail the factual and/or legal grounds upon which the petitioner considers the determination of the Administrative Director to be unjust or unlawful, and every issue to be considered by the Workers' Compensation Appeals Board. The petitioner shall be deemed to have finally waived all objections, irregularities and illegalities concerning the Administrative Director's determination other than those set forth in the petition appealing.

(3) The petition shall comply with the requirements of rules 10945(a) and (c), and 10972. It shall also comply with the provisions of rule 10940, including but not limited to the 25-page restriction.

(4) Any failure to comply with the provisions of this subdivision shall constitute valid ground for summarily dismissing or denying the petition.

(g) A copy of the petition shall be concurrently served on the Division of Workers' Compensation, Medical Provider Network Unit (MPN Unit).

(h) The petition shall be assigned to a panel of the Appeals Board in accordance with Labor Code section 115.

(i) Within 30 days after the filing of an answer or the lapse of the time allowed for filing one, the Appeals Board shall issue a notice for an evidentiary hearing regarding the petition. The evidentiary hearing shall be set for the purposes of specifying the issue(s) in dispute and any stipulations, taking testimony, and listing and identifying any documentary evidence offered. The proceedings shall be transcribed by a court reporter, which the Appeals Board in its discretion may order the petitioner to provide. The Appeals Board also may order the petitioner to pay the costs of the transcript(s) of the evidentiary hearing.

(j) In its discretion, the Appeals Board may provide that the evidentiary hearing shall be conducted by:

(1) One or more commissioners of the Appeals Board; or

(2) A workers' compensation judge appointed under Labor Code section 5309(b) for the sole purpose of holding hearings and ascertaining facts necessary to enable the Appeals Board to render a decision on the petition; a workers' compensation judge appointed for this purpose shall not render any factual determinations, but may make a recommendation regarding the credibility of any witness(es) presented.

The time, date, length and place of the evidentiary hearing shall be determined by the Appeals Board in its discretion.

(k) The assigned panel of the Appeals Board shall determine when the petition is submitted for decision. Within 60 days after submission, the panel shall render a decision on the petition unless, within that time, the panel orders that the time be extended so that it may further study the facts and relevant law.

(*l*) Where a timely request to the Administrative Director for a re-evaluation of an initial determination is filed in accordance with rules 9767.8(f), 9767.13(c), and 9767.14(c), the following procedures shall apply:

(1) If a request for re-evaluation is made to the Administrative Director prior to filing a petition with the Office of the Commissioners of the Appeals Board, the time for filing such a petition shall be tolled until the Administrative Director files and serves a decision and order regarding the request for re-evaluation.

(2) If a request for re-evaluation is made to the Administrative Director after a petition appealing the

Administrative Director's initial determination is filed with the Office of the Commissioners of the Appeals Board, the petitioner shall file a copy of the re-evaluation request with the Office of the Commissioners in accordance with subdivisions (b)(2) and (b)(3), together with a cover letter requesting that its petition be dismissed without prejudice. A copy of the cover letter and request for re-evaluation shall be concurrently served on the Division of Workers' Compensation MPN Unit.

Note: Authority cited: Sections 133, 5307, 5309 and 5708, Labor Code. Reference: Sections 4616 et seq., 5300(f), 5309 and 5900 et seq., Labor Code.

History: 1. Amendment filed 12-19-2002; operative 1-1-2003. Submitted to OAL for printing only pursuant to Government Code section 11351 (Register 2002, No. 51).

2. Renumbering of former section 10580 to section 10672 and renumbering and amendment of former section 10959 to section 10580 filed 12-17-2019; operative 1-1-2020. Submitted to OAL for printing only pursuant to Government Code section 11351 (Register 2019, No. 51).

Ref.: Hanna § 5.03[7].

§10582. Inactive Cases, Procedure, Subsequent Action. [Renumbered]

Note: Authority cited: Sections 133 and 5307, Labor Code. Reference: Section 5405 and 5406, Labor Code.

History: 1. Amendment exempt from OAL review pursuant to Government Code section 11351 filed 12-19-90; operative 1-1-91 (Register 91, No. 7).

2. Amendment of first paragraph filed 12-23-93; operative 1-1-94. Submitted to OAL for printing only pursuant to Government Code section 11351 (Register 93, No. 52).

3. Amendment of second and third paragraphs and amendment of Note filed 12-19-2002; operative 1-1-2003. Submitted to OAL for printing only pursuant to Government Code section 11351 (Register 2002, No. 51).

4. Renumbering of former section 10582 to section 10550 filed 12-17-2019; operative 1-1-2020. Submitted to OAL for printing only pursuant to Government Code section 11351 (Register 2019, No. 51).

§10582.5. Dismissal of Inactive Lien Claims for Lack of Prosecution. [Repealed]

Note: Authority cited: Sections 133, 5307, 5309 and 5708, Labor Code. Reference: Sections 4903, 4903.5, 4903.6 and 5404.5, Labor Code.

History: 1. New section filed 5-21-2012; operative 5-21-2012 pursuant to Government Code section 11343.4. Submitted to OAL for printing only pursuant to Government Code 11351 (Register 2012, No. 21).

2. Amendment of subsections (a)(1), (c)(2)(B)(i), (c)(2)(C), (d)(1), (d)(2) and (k) filed 9-23-2013; operative 10-23-2013. Submitted as a file and print by the Workers' Compensation Appeals Board pursuant to Government Code section 11351 (Register 2013, No. 39).

3. Repealer filed 12-17-2019; operative 1-1-2020. Submitted to OAL for printing only pursuant to Government Code section 11351 (Register 2019, No. 51).

§10583. Dismissal of Claim Form — Labor Code Section 5404.5. [Repealed]

Note: Authority cited: Sections 133 and 5307, Labor Code. Reference: Section 5404.5, Labor Code.

History: 1. Renumbering of former section 10407 to new section 10583 filed 12-19-2002; operative 1-1-2003. Submitted to OAL for printing only pursuant to Government Code section 11351 (Register 2002, No. 51).

2. Repealer filed 12-17-2019; operative 1-1-2020. Submitted to OAL for printing only pursuant to Government Code section 11351 (Register 2019, No. 51).

§10589. Consolidation of Cases. [Renumbered]

Note: Authority cited: Sections 133, 5307, 5309 and 5708, Labor Code. Reference: Sections 5300, 5301, 5303 and 5708, Labor Code.

History: 1. Renumbering of former section 10590 to new section 10589, including amendment of section and Note, filed 12-19-2002; operative 1-1-2003. Submitted to OAL for printing only pursuant to Government Code section 11351 (Register 2002, No. 51).

2. Amendment of section heading, section and Note filed 11-17-2008; operative 11-17-2008. Submitted to OAL for printing only (Register 2008, No. 47).

3. Renumbering of former section 10589 to section 10396 filed 12-17-2019; operative 1-1-2020. Submitted to OAL for printing only pursuant to Government Code section 11351 (Register 2019, No. 51).

§10590. Petition Appealing Audit Penalty Assessment — Labor Code Section 129.5(g).

(a) An insurer, self-insured employer or third-party administrator may appeal a civil penalty assessment issued pursuant to subdivision (g) of Labor Code section 129.5 by filing a petition only with the Office of the Commissioners of the Workers' Compensation Appeals Board in the same time and manner as a petition for reconsideration, except that a copy of the petition shall be served on the Administrative Director. The petition shall be accompanied by a completed document cover sheet.

(b) The Administrative Director may answer the petition in the same time and manner provided for the filing of an answer to a petition for reconsideration.

(c) After the filing of a petition appealing a civil penalty assessment issued pursuant to Labor Code section 129.5(g), an adjudication case will be created and an adjudication case number will be assigned. The adjudication case number will be served by the Appeals Board on the Administrative Director and on the parties and attorneys listed on the proof of service to the petition.

(d) Within 15 days after the Administrative Director receives a copy of petition appealing a civil penalty assessment issued pursuant to Labor Code section 129.5(g), the Administrative Director shall submit to the Appeals Board a certified copy of the complete record of proceedings created by the Administrative Director in accordance with Article 6 of the Administrative Director's rules (Cal. Code Regs., tit. 8, § 10113 et seq.) The certified copy of the record shall include, but shall not necessarily be limited to:

(1) The Order to Show Cause Re: Assessment of Civil Penalty and Notice of Hearing;

(2) The answer to the Order to Show Cause;

(3) Any amended complaint or supplemental Order to Show Cause that may have been issued, and any Amended Answer filed in response thereto;

(4) Any pre-hearing written statement filed by the claims administrator;

(5) Any pre-hearing Minutes and pre-hearing Orders;

(6) The Minutes of any Hearing, a transcript or summary of any oral testimony offered at the hearing, any documentary evidence or affidavits offered at the hearing; and

(7) The Administrative Director's written Determination and statement of the basis for the Determination. The original record of the proceedings conducted pursuant to Labor Code section 129.5(g) shall not be filed.

(e) The Appeals Board may scan the appeal, any answer and the photocopied record of the Administrative Director's proceedings into the adjudication file within EAMS. Upon scanning, the paper documents may be destroyed.

(f) The Appeals Board shall determine the appeal using the record created by the Administrative Director in accordance with Article 6 of the Administrative Director's rules (Cal. Code Regs., tit. 8, § 10113 et seq.). The Administrative Director's record shall be deemed part of the Workers' Compensation Appeals Board's record of proceedings.

Note: Authority cited: Sections 133, 5307, 5309 and 5708, Labor Code. Reference: Section 129.5(g), Labor Code.

History: 1. Renumbering and amendment of former section 10953 to section 10590 filed 12-17-2019; operative 1-1-2020. Submitted to OAL for printing only pursuant to Government Code section 11351 (Register 2019, No. 51). For prior history of section 10590, see Register 2008, No. 47.

Ref.: Hanna § 10.51[2][d]; Herlick Handbook § 15.4.

§10591. Consolidating Cases—Multiple Injured Workers. [Repealed]

Note: Authority cited: Sections 133 and 5307, Labor Code. Reference: Sections 5303, 5310 and 5708, Labor Code.

History: 1. New section filed 12-23-93; operative 1-1-94. Submitted to OAL for printing only pursuant to Government Code section 11351 (Register 93, No. 52).

2. Amendment of section heading, section and Note filed 12-19-2002; operative 1-1-2003. Submitted to OAL for printing only pursuant to Government Code section 11351 (Register 2002, No. 51).

3. Repealer filed 11-17-2008; operative 11-17-2008. Submitted to OAL for printing only (Register 2008, No. 47).

§10592. Assignment of Consolidated Cases. [Renumbered]

Note: Authority cited: Sections 133, 5307, 5309 and 5708, Labor Code. Reference: Sections 5300, 5301, 5303 and 5708, Labor Code.

History: 1. New section filed 10-15-2014; operative 1-1-2015. Submitted to OAL for printing only pursuant to Government Code section 11351 (Register 2014, No. 42). For prior history, see Register 2008, No. 47.

2. Editorial correction of History 1 (Register 2017, No. 8).

3. Renumbering of former section 10592 to section 10398 filed 12-17-2019; operative 1-1-2020. Submitted to OAL for printing only pursuant to Government Code section 11351 (Register 2019, No. 51).

§10593. Testimony of Judicial or Quasi-Judicial Officers. [Renumbered]

Note: Authority cited: Sections 133, 5307, 5309 and 5708, Labor Code. Reference: Sections 5300, 5301, 5309, 5700, 5701 and 5708, Labor Code; and Section 703.5, Evidence Code.

History: 1. New section filed 11-17-2008; operative 11-17-2008. Submitted to OAL for printing only (Register 2008, No. 47).

2. Amendment of section heading, repealer of subsection (f)(7), subsection renumbering, amendment of newly designated subsections (f)(7)-(8) and new subsection (f)(9) filed 10-15-2014; operative 1-1-2015. Submitted to OAL for printing only pursuant to Government Code section 11351 (Register 2014, No. 42).

3. Editorial correction of History 2 (Register 2017, No. 8).

4. Renumbering of former section 10593 to section 10360 filed 12-17-2019; operative 1-1-2020. Submitted to OAL for printing only pursuant to Government Code section 11351 (Register 2019, No. 51).

ARTICLE 9
Filing and Service of Documents

§10600. Time for Actions.

(a) The time in which any act provided by these rules is to be performed is computed by excluding the first day and including the last.

(b) Unless otherwise provided by law, if the last day for exercising or performing any right or duty to act or respond falls on a weekend, or on a holiday for which the offices of the Workers' Compensation Appeals Board are closed, the act or response may be performed or exercised upon the next business day.

Note: Authority cited: Sections 133, 5307, 5309 and 5708, Labor Code. Reference: Section 5316, Labor Code; Sections 6700, 6701 and 6707, Government Code; and Sections 10, 12, 12a, 12b, 13 and 135, Code of Civil Procedure.

History: 1. Amendment of section and Note filed 12-19-2002; operative 1-1-2003. Submitted to OAL for printing only pursuant to Government Code section 11351 (Register 2002, No. 51).

2. Amendment of article 9 heading, repealer of former section 10600 and renumbering of former section 10508 to section 10600, including amendment of section heading and section, filed 12-17-2019; operative 1-1-2020. Submitted to OAL for printing only pursuant to Government Code section 11351 (Register 2019, No. 51).

Ref.: Hanna §§ 30.20[1], 30.22[5][b].

§10601. Copies of Reports and Records. [Repealed]

Note: Authority cited: Sections 133 and 5307, Labor Code. Reference: Section 5502(e), Labor Code.

History: 1. Amendment of section heading, section and Note filed 12-19-2002; operative 1-1-2003. Submitted to OAL for printing only pursuant to Government Code section 11351 (Register 2002, No. 51).

2. Repealer filed 12-17-2019; operative 1-1-2020. Submitted to OAL for printing only pursuant to Government Code section 11351 (Register 2019, No. 51).

§10602. Formal Permanent Disability Rating Determinations. [Renumbered]

Note: Authority cited: Sections 133 and 5307, Labor Code. Reference: Sections 4660 and 5708, Labor Code.

History: 1. Amendment of section heading, section and Note filed 12-19-2002; operative 1-1-2003. Submitted to OAL for printing only pursuant to Government Code section 11351 (Register 2002, No. 51).

2. Renumbering of former section 10602 to section 10675 filed 12-17-2019; operative 1-1-2020. Submitted to OAL for printing only pursuant to Government Code section 11351 (Register 2019, No. 51).

§10603. Oversized Exhibits, Diagnostic Imaging, Physical Exhibits, and Exhibits on Media. [Renumbered]

Note: Authority cited: Sections 133, 5307, 5309 and 5708, Labor Code. Reference: Sections 5309, 5701, 5703, 5704 and 5708, Labor Code

History: 1. New section filed 11-17-2008; operative 11-17-2008. Submitted to OAL for printing only (Register 2008, No. 47).

2. Renumbering of former section 10603 to section 10677 filed 12-17-2019; operative 1-1-2020. Submitted to OAL for printing only pursuant to Government Code section 11351 (Register 2019, No. 51).

§10604. Certified Copies. [Repealed]

Note: Authority cited: Sections 133 and 5307, Labor Code. Reference: Sections 5703 and 5708, Labor Code.

History: 1. Amendment of section and Note filed 12-19-2002; operative 1-1-2003. Submitted to OAL for printing only pursuant to Government Code section 11351 (Register 2002, No. 51).

2. Repealer filed 12-17-2019; operative 1-1-2020. Submitted to OAL for printing only pursuant to Government Code section 11351 (Register 2019, No. 51).

§10605. Time Within Which to Act When a Document is Served by Mail, Fax or E-Mail.

(a) When any document is served by mail, fax, e-mail or any method other than personal service, the period of time for exercising or performing any right or duty to act or respond shall be extended by:

(1) Five calendar days from the date of service, if the place of address and the place of mailing of the party, attorney or other agent of record being served is within California;

(2) Ten calendar days from the date of service, if the place of address and the place of mailing of the party, attorney or other agent of record being served is outside of California but within the United States; and

(3) Twenty calendar days from the date of service, if the place of address and the place of mailing of the party, attorney or other agent of record being served is outside the United States.

(b) For purposes of this rule, "place of address and the place of mailing" means the street address or Post Office Box of the party, attorney or other agent of record being served, as reflected in the Official Address Record at the time of service, even if the method of service actually used was fax, e-mail or other agreed-upon method of service.

Note: Authority cited: Sections 133, 5307, 5309 and 5708, Labor Code. Reference: Section 5316, Labor Code.

History: 1. New section filed 12-19-2002; operative 1-1-2003. Submitted to OAL for printing only pursuant to Government Code section 11351 (Register 2002, No. 51).

2. Renumbering of former section 10605 to section 10680 and renumbering and amendment of former section 10507 to section 10605 filed 12-17-2019; operative 1-1-2020. Submitted to OAL for printing only pursuant to Government Code section 11351 (Register 2019, No. 51).

Ref.: Hanna §§ 23.14[3], 27.01[4], 28.20, 28.24; Herlick Handbook §§ 14.4, 15.4.

§10606. Physicians' Reports as Evidence. [Renumbered]

Note: Authority cited: Sections 133, 5307, 5309 and 5708, Labor Code. Reference: Sections 4061, 4603.2, 4603.3, 4603.6, 4610.5, 4610.6, 4616.3, 4616.4, 4628, 5703, 5708 and 5709, Labor Code.

History: 1. New subsections (i), (j) and (k) filed 5-25-82; designated effective 7-1-82 (Register 82, No. 22).

2. Editorial correction of subsection (h) filed 2-2-83 (Register 83, No. 6).

3. Amendment filed 12-23-93; operative 1-1-94. Submitted to OAL for printing only pursuant to Government Code section 11351 (Register 93, No. 52).

4. Amendment of section and Note filed 12-19-2002; operative 1-1-2003. Submitted to OAL for printing only pursuant to Government Code section 11351 (Register 2002, No. 51).

5. Amendment of section and Note filed 9-23-2013; operative 10-23-2013. Submitted as a file and print by the Workers' Compensation Appeals Board pursuant to Government Code section 11351 (Register 2013, No. 39).

6. Renumbering of former section 10606 to section 10682 filed 12-17-2019; operative 1-1-2020. Submitted to OAL for printing only pursuant to Government Code section 11351(Register 2019, No. 51).

§10606.5. Vocational Experts' Reports as Evidence. [Renumbered]

Note: Authority cited: Sections 133, 5307, 5309 and 5708, Labor Code. Reference: Sections 139.32, 4628, 5502(d)(3) and 5703(j), Labor Code.

History: 1. New section filed 9-23-2013; operative 10-23-2013. Submitted as a file and print by the Workers' Compensation Appeals Board pursuant to Government Code section 11351 (Register 2013, No. 39).

2. Renumbering of former section 10606.5 to section 10685 filed 12-17-2019; operative 1-1-2020. Submitted to OAL for printing only pursuant to Government Code section 11351 (Register 2019, No. 51).

§10607. Computer Printouts of Benefits Paid. [Repealed]

Note: Authority cited: Sections 133 and 5307, Labor Code. Reference: Sections 5502(e) and 5708, Labor Code.

History: 1. New section filed 12-19-2002; operative 1-1-2003. Submitted to OAL for printing only pursuant to Government Code section 11351 (Register 2002, No. 51).

2. Repealer filed 12-17-2019; operative 1-1-2020. Submitted to OAL for printing only pursuant to Government Code section 11351 (Register 2019, No. 51).

§10608. Service of Medical Reports, Medical-Legal Reports, and Other Medical Information. [Repealed]

Note: Authority cited: Sections 133, 4903.6(d), 5307, 5309 and 5708, Labor Code. Reference: Sections 4903.6(d), 5001, 5502, 5703 and 5708, Labor Code; and Sections 56.05 and 56.10, Civil Code.

History: 1. Repealer and new section filed 12-23-93; operative 1-1-94. Submitted to OAL for printing only pursuant to Government Code section 11351 (Register 93, No. 52).

2. Amendment of section heading, section and Note filed 12-19-2002; operative 1-1-2003. Submitted to OAL for printing only pursuant to Government Code section 11351 (Register 2002, No. 51).

3. Amendment of section heading, section and Note filed 11-17-2008; operative 11-17-2008. Submitted to OAL for printing only (Register 2008, No. 47).

4. Amendment of section heading, section and Note filed 9-23-2013; operative 10-23-2013. Submitted as a file and print by the Workers' Compensation Appeals Board pursuant to Government Code section 11351 (Register 2013, No. 39).

5. Repealer filed 12-17-2019; operative 1-1-2020. Submitted to OAL for printing only pursuant to Government Code section 11351 (Register 2019, No. 51).

§10608.5. Service by Parties and Lien Claimants of Reports and Records on Other Parties and Lien Claimants. [Repealed]

Note: Authority cited: Sections 133, 5307, 5309 and 5708, Labor Code. Reference: Art. XIV, § 4, Cal. Const.; Section 5307.9, Labor Code; and Section 250, Evidence Code.

History: 1. New section filed 9-23-2013; operative 10-23-2013. Submitted as a file and print by the Workers' Compensation Appeals Board pursuant to Government Code section 11351 (Register 2013, No. 39).

2. Repealer filed 12-17-2019; operative 1-1-2020. Submitted to OAL for printing only pursuant to Government Code section 11351 (Register 2019, No. 51).

§10609. Service on Lien Claimants. [Repealed]

Note: Authority cited: Sections 133 and 5307, Labor Code. Reference: Sections 4903.1, 5708 and 5709, Labor Code.

History: 1. Repealer filed 12-19-2002; operative 1-1-2003. Submitted to OAL for printing only pursuant to Government Code section 11351 (Register 2002, No. 51).

§10610. Filing and Service of Documents.

Unless a statute or rule provides for a different method for filing or service, a requirement to "file and serve" a document means that a copy of the document must be served on the attorney or non-attorney representative for each party separately represented, on each self-represented party and on any other person or entity when required by statute, rule or court order, and that the document and a proof of service of the document must be filed with the Workers' Compensation Appeals Board.

Note: Authority cited: Sections 133, 5307, 5309 and 5708, Labor Code. Reference: Section 5500.3, Labor Code.

History: 1. New section filed 12-17-2019; operative 1-1-2020. Submitted to OAL for printing only pursuant to Government Code section 11351 (Register 2019, No. 51). For prior history, see Register 2002, No. 51.

Ref.: Hanna §§ 23.14[2][b], 25.06[1].

§10615. Filing of Documents.

Except as otherwise provided by these rules or ordered by the Workers' Compensation Appeals Board, after the filing and processing of an initial Application for Adjudication of Claim or other case opening document, all documents required or permitted to be filed under the rules of the Workers' Compensation Appeals Board shall be filed only in EAMS or with the district office having venue.

(a) Except as provided by rule 10677(a), no "original" business records, medical records or other documentary evidence shall be filed with the Workers' Compensation Appeals Board. Only a photocopy or other reproduction of an original document shall be filed. All paper documents that are scanned into EAMS are destroyed after filing pursuant to rule 10205.10.

(b) A document is deemed filed on the date it is received, if received prior to 5:00 p.m. on a court day (i.e., Monday through Friday, except designated State holidays). An electronically transmitted document shall be deemed to have been received by EAMS when the electronic transmission of the document into EAMS is complete. A document received after 5:00 p.m. of a court day shall be deemed filed as of the next court day.

(c) When a paper document is filed by mail or by personal service, the Workers' Compensation Appeals Board shall affix on it an appropriate endorsement as evidence of receipt. The endorsement may be made by handwriting, hand-stamp, electronic date stamp or by other means. The endorsement shall serve as confirmation of successful filing unless the Administrative Director returns the document to the filer and notifies the filer, through the service of a Notice of Document Discrepancy, that the document has not been accepted for filing and the filer fails to correct the discrepancy within 15 days.

(d) When a document is filed electronically, confirmation of successful filing shall be made in the manner described by rule 10206.3.

Note: Authority cited: Sections 133, 5307, 5309 and 5708, Labor Code. Reference: Sections 126, 5500.3, 5501.5 and 5501.6, Labor Code.

History: 1. Repealer and new section filed 12-23-93; operative 1-1-94. Submitted to OAL for printing only pursuant to Government Code section 11351 (Register 93, No. 52).

2. Editorial correction of first sentence (Register 96, No. 5).

3. Amendment of section heading, repealer and new section and new Note filed 12-19-2002; operative 1-1-2003. Submitted to OAL for printing only pursuant to Government Code section 11351 (Register 2002, No. 51).

4. Repealer and new section filed 12-17-2019; operative 1-1-2020. Submitted to OAL for printing only pursuant to Government Code section 11351 (Register 2019, No. 51).

Ref.: Hanna §§ 23.12[2][a], [c], [h], 25.06A[2]; Herlick Handbook §§ 14.5, 14.11, 14.15, 15.3.

§10616. Employer-Maintained Medical Records. [Repealed]

Note: Authority cited: Sections 133, 5307, 5309 and 5708, Labor Code. Reference: Sections 4600, 5703 and 5708, Labor Code.

History: 1. Amendment of section and Note filed 12-19-2002; operative 1-1-2003. Submitted to OAL for printing only pursuant to Government Code section 11351 (Register 2002, No. 51).

2. Amendment of section heading, section and Note filed 11-17-2008; operative 11-17-2008. Submitted to OAL for printing only (Register 2008, No. 47).

3. Repealer filed 12-17-2019; operative 1-1-2020. Submitted to OAL for printing only pursuant to Government Code section 11351 (Register 2019, No. 51).

§10617. Restrictions on the Rejection for Filing of Documents Subject to a Statute of Limitations or a Jurisdictional Time Limitation.

(a) An Application for Adjudication of Claim, a petition for reconsideration, a petition to reopen or any other petition or other document that is subject to a statute of limitations or a jurisdictional time limitation shall not be rejected for filing solely on the basis that:

(1) The document is not filed in the proper office of the Workers' Compensation Appeals Board;

(2) The document has been submitted without the proper form, or it has been submitted with a form that is either incomplete or contains inaccurate information; or

(3) The document has not been submitted with the required document cover sheet and/or document separator sheet(s), or it has been submitted with a document cover sheet and/or document separator sheet(s) not containing all of the required information.

(b) A document that is subject to a statute of limitations or a jurisdictional time limitation may be rejected for filing if it does not contain a combination of information sufficient to establish the case or cases to which the document relates or, if it is a case opening document, sufficient information to open an adjudication file. If a document is rejected in accordance with this subdivision, the Administrative Director shall return the document to the filer and shall notify the filer, through the service of a Notice of Document Discrepancy, that the document has not been accepted for filing. The Notice of Document Discrepancy shall specify the nature of the discrepancy(ies) and the date of the attempted filing, and it shall state that the filer shall have 15 days from the service of the Notice within which to correct the discrepancy(ies) and resubmit the document for filing. If the document is corrected and resubmitted for filing within 15 days, or at a later date upon a showing of good cause, it shall be deemed filed as of the original date the document was submitted.

(c) Nothing in this rule shall preclude the discretionary or conditional acceptance for the filing of a document that is subject to a statute of limitations or a jurisdictional time limitation, even if it does not contain a combination of information sufficient to establish the case or cases to which the document relates or, if it is a case opening document, sufficient information to open an adjudication file.

(d) Where a document that is subject to a statute of limitations or a jurisdictional time limitation has been accepted for filing in accordance with this rule, but the document nevertheless cannot be processed by EAMS, the Administrative Director may serve a copy of the filed document on the filing party, together with a Notice of Document Discrepancy. The notice may specify the nature of the discrepancy(ies) and request that the party correct the discrepancy(ies) within 15 days after service of the Notice, however, a failure to timely correct the discrepancy(ies) shall not nullify the acceptance of the document for filing.

(e) Nothing in this rule shall be deemed to excuse non-compliance with any of other provisions of the rules of the Workers' Compensation Appeals Board or non-compliance with the rules of the Administrative Director. Any such non-compliance may still give rise to monetary sanctions, attorney's fees and costs under Labor Code section 5813 and rule 10421.

Note: Authority cited: Article XIV, Section 4, California Constitution; and Sections 133, 5307, 5309 and 5708, Labor Code. Reference: Sections 126, 5316, 5500, 5501 and 5813, Labor Code.

History: 1. Renumbering and amendment of former section 10397 to section 10617 filed 12-17-2019; operative 1-1-2020. Submitted to OAL for printing only pursuant to Government Code section 11351 (Register 2019, No. 51).

Ref.: Hanna § 23.12[2][b]; Herlick Handbook § 14.15.

§10618. X-Rays. [Renumbered]

Note: Authority cited: Sections 133 and 5307, Labor Code. Reference: Sections 4600 and 5708, Labor Code.

History: 1. Amendment of section heading, section and Note filed 12-19-2002; operative 1-1-2003. Submitted to OAL for printing only pursuant to Government Code section 11351 (Register 2002, No. 51).

2. Renumbering of former section 10618 to section 10660 filed 12-17-2019; operative 1-1-2020. Submitted to OAL for printing only pursuant to Government Code section 11351 (Register 2019, No. 51).

§10619. Subpoena of X-Rays. [Repealed]

Note: Authority cited: Sections 133, 5307, 5708 and 5709, Labor Code. Reference: Sections 4600, 5708 and 5709, Labor Code.

History: 1. Repealer filed 12-19-2002; operative 1-1-2003. Submitted to OAL for printing only pursuant to Government Code section 11351 (Register 2002, No. 51).

§10620. Filing Proposed Exhibits.

Any document that a party proposes to offer into evidence at a trial shall be filed with the Workers' Compensation Appeals Board at least 20 days prior to the trial unless otherwise ordered by the Workers' Compensation Appeals Board.

Note: Authority cited: Sections 133, 5307, 5309 and 5708, Labor Code. Reference: Sections 126, 5316, 5500, 5501 and 5813, Labor Code.

History: 1. New section filed 12-17-2019; operative 1-1-2020. Submitted to OAL for printing only pursuant to Government Code section 11351 (Register 2019, No. 51). For prior history, see Register 2002, No. 51.

Ref.: Hanna § 23.12[2][e].

§10622. Failure to Comply. [Repealed]

Note: Authority cited: Sections 133 and 5307, Labor Code. Reference: Sections 5703 and 5708, Labor Code.

History: 1. Amendment of section and Note filed 12-19-2002; operative 1-1-2003. Submitted to OAL for printing only pursuant to Government Code section 11351 (Register 2002, No. 51).

2. Amendment of section and Note filed 9-23-2013; operative 10-23-2013. Submitted as a file and print by the Workers' Compensation Appeals Board pursuant to Government Code section 11351 (Register 2013, No. 39).

3. Repealer filed 12-17-2019; operative 1-1-2020. Submitted to OAL for printing only pursuant to Government Code section 11351 (Register 2019, No. 51).

§10625. Service.

(a) Except as otherwise provided by these rules at 10300 et seq., service shall be made on the attorney or agent of record of each affected party unless that party is unrepresented, in which event service shall be made directly on the party.

(b) A document may be served using the following methods:

(1) Personal service;

(2) First class mail; or

(3) An alternative method that will effect service that is equivalent to or more expeditious than first class mail, limited to either:

(A) The use of express (overnight) or priority mail; or

(B) The use of a bona fide commercial delivery service or attorney service promising delivery within two business days, as shown on the service's invoice or receipt; or

(4) A party's preferred method of service if a method has been designated in accordance with rule 10205.6; or

(5) Another method if the serving and receiving parties have previously agreed to some other method of service.

(c) "Proof of service" means a dated and verified declaration identifying the document(s) served and the parties who were served, and stating that service has been made and the method by which it has been made. If the proof of service names attorneys for separately represented parties, it must also state which party or parties each of the attorneys served represents.

(d) Where a party receives notification that the service to one or more parties failed, the server shall promptly re-serve the document on the intended recipient(s) and execute a new proof of service.

Note: Authority cited: Sections 133, 5307, 5309 and 5708, Labor Code. Reference: Article XIV, Section 4, California Constitution; Sections 4906, 5307.9 and 5316, Labor Code; and Section 250, Evidence Code.

History: 1. New section filed 12-17-2019; operative 1-1-2020. Submitted to OAL for printing only pursuant to Government Code section 11351 (Register 2019, No. 51).

Ref.: Hanna §§ 23.14[2][a], 25.06[1]; Herlick Handbook § 14.11.

§10626. Examining and Copying Hospital and Physicians' Records. [Repealed]

Note: Authority cited: Sections 133, 5307, 5309 and 5708, Labor Code. Reference: Section 4600, Labor Code.

History: 1. Amendment filed 12-19-2002; operative 1-1-2003. Submitted to OAL for printing only pursuant to Government Code section 11351 (Register 2002, No. 51).

2. Amendment of section heading, section and Note filed 11-17-2008; operative 11-17-2008. Submitted to OAL for printing only (Register 2008, No. 47).

3. Repealer filed 12-17-2019; operative 1-1-2020. Submitted to OAL for printing only pursuant to Government Code section 11351 (Register 2019, No. 51).

§10628. Service by the Workers' Compensation Appeals Board.

(a) The Workers' Compensation Appeals Board shall serve the injured employee or any dependent(s) of a deceased employee, whether or not the employee or dependent is represented, and all parties of record with any final order, decision or award issued by it on a disputed issue after submission. The Workers' Compensation Appeals Board shall not designate a party, or their attorney or agent of record, to serve any final order, decision or award relating to a submitted issue.

(b) If the Workers' Compensation Appeals Board effects personal service of a document at a hearing or at a walk-through proceeding, the proof of personal service shall be made by endorsement on the document, setting forth legibly the name(s) of the person(s) served, the date of service and the fact of personal service. The endorsement shall bear the legibly printed name and signature of the person making the service.

(c) If the Workers' Compensation Appeals Board serves a document by mail, the proof of mail service shall be made by endorsement on the document, setting forth the fact of mail service on the persons or entities listed on the Official Address Record who have not designated e-mail or fax as their preferred method of service. The endorsement shall state the date of mail service and it shall bear the legibly printed name and the signature of the person making the service.

(d) If the Workers' Compensation Appeals Board electronically serves a document through EAMS on persons or entities listed on the official address record who have designated e-mail or fax as their preferred method of service, the proof of e-mail or fax service shall be made by endorsement on the document, setting forth the fact of e-mail or fax service on the persons or entities listed.

(e) Where a district office of the Workers' Compensation Appeals Board maintains mailboxes for outgoing documents and allows consenting parties, lien claimants and attorneys to obtain their documents from their mailboxes, documents so obtained shall be deemed to have been served on the party, lien claimant or attorney by mail on the date of service specified on the document.

Note: Authority cited: Sections 133, 5307, 5309 and 5708, Labor Code. Reference: Sections 5316 and 5504, Labor Code.

History: 1. New section filed 12-17-2019; operative 1-1-2020. Submitted to OAL for printing only pursuant to Government Code section 11351 (Register 2019, No. 51).

Ref.: Hanna § 23.14[1][a]; Herlick Handbook § 14.11.

§10629. Designated Service.

(a) The Workers' Compensation Appeals Board may, in its discretion, designate a party or their attorney or agent of record to serve any order that is not required to be served by the Workers' Compensation Appeals Board in accordance with rule 10628.

(b) When a party or their attorney or agent of record is designated to serve an order, the workers' compensation judge shall indicate which parties to serve.

(c) In addition to the service required by rule 10625, service shall also be made on the injured employee or any dependent of a deceased employee, whether or not the employee or dependent is represented.

(d) Within 10 days from the date on which designated service is ordered, the person designated to make service shall serve the document and shall file the proof of service.

Note: Authority cited: Sections 133, 5307, 5309 and 5708, Labor Code. Reference: Sections 5316 and 5504, Labor Code.

History: 1. New section filed 11-17-2008; operative 11-17-2008. Submitted to OAL for printing only (Register 2008, No. 47).

2. Repealer and new section filed 12-17-2019; operative 1-1-2020. Submitted to OAL for printing only pursuant to Government Code section 11351 (Register 2019, No. 51).

Ref.: Hanna § 23.14[1][a].

§10630. Return of Exhibits. [Repealed]

Note: Authority cited: Sections 133 and 5307, Labor Code. Reference: Section 126, Labor Code.

History: 1. Amendment of last paragraph filed 12-19-2002; operative 1-1-2003. Submitted to OAL for printing only pursuant to Government Code section 11351 (Register 2002, No. 51).

2. Repealer filed 11-17-2008; operative 11-17-2008. Submitted to OAL for printing only (Register 2008, No. 47).

§10631. Specific Finding of Fact — Labor Code Section 139.2(d)(2). [Renumbered]

Note: Authority cited: Sections 133 and 5307, Labor Code. Reference: Section 139.2(d)(2), Labor Code.

History: 1. New section filed 12-23-93; operative 1-1-94. Submitted to OAL for printing only pursuant to Government Code section 11351 (Register 93, No. 52).

2. Amendment of first paragraph filed 12-19-2002; operative 1-1-2003. Submitted to OAL for printing only pursuant to Government Code section 11351 (Register 2002, No. 51).

3. Renumbering of former section 10631 to section 10683 filed 12-17-2019; operative 1-1-2020. Submitted to OAL for printing only pursuant to Government Code section 11351 (Register 2019, No. 51).

§10632. Service on the Division of Workers' Compensation and the Director of Industrial Relations.

(a) When an Application for Adjudication of Claim, Stipulations with Request for Award or Compromise and Release is filed in a death case in which there is a bona fide issue as to partial or total dependency, the filing party shall serve copies of the documents on the Department of Industrial Relations. Death Without Dependents Unit.

(b) Service of all documents on the Subsequent Injuries Benefits Trust Fund shall be made on the Division of Workers' Compensation, Subsequent Injuries Benefits Trust Fund.

(c) Service of documents on the Uninsured Employers Benefits Trust Fund shall be made as follows:

(1) Service shall be made on the Division of Workers' Compensation. Uninsured Employers Benefits Trust Fund — Oakland if the employee's case is venued in one of the following District Offices: Bakersfield, Eureka, Fresno, Oakland, Oxnard, Redding, Riverside, Sacramento, Salinas, San Diego, San Francisco, San Jose, San Luis Obispo, Santa Ana, Santa Rosa, Stockton or Van Nuys.

(2) Service shall be made on the Division of Workers' Compensation, Uninsured Employers Benefits Trust Fund — Los Angeles if the employee's case is venued in one of the following District Offices: Anaheim, Los Angeles, Long Beach, Marina del Rey, Pomona or San Bernardino.

(d) Service of all documents on the Return-to-Work Supplement Program shall be made on the Director of Industrial Relations, Return-to-Work Supplement Program.

(e) Service of all documents on the Independent Bill Review Unit shall be made on the Division of Workers' Compensation, Independent Bill Review Unit.

(f) Service of all documents on the Independent Medical Review Unit shall be made on the Division of Workers' Compensation, Independent Medical Review Unit.

Note: Authority cited: Sections 133 and 5307, Labor Code. Reference: Sections 4706.5 and 5501.5, Labor Code.

History: 1. New section filed 12-23-93; operative 1-1-94. Submitted to OAL for printing only pursuant to Government Code section 11351 (Register 93, No. 52).

2. Amendment filed 12-19-2002; operative 1-1-2003. Submitted to OAL for printing only pursuant to Government Code section 11351 (Register 2002, No. 51).

3. Repealer and new section filed 12-17-2019; operative 1-1-2020. Submitted to OAL for printing only pursuant to Government Code section 11351 (Register 2019, No. 51).

Ref.: Hanna §§ 23.14[1][b], 25.06[1].

§10633. Proposed Rating — Labor Code Section 4065. [Repealed]

Note: Authority cited: Sections 133 and 5307, Labor Code. Reference: Section 4065, Labor Code.

History: 1. New section filed 12-23-93; operative 1-1-94. Submitted to OAL for printing only pursuant to Government Code section 11351 (Register 93, No. 52).

2. Amendment of first paragraph filed 12-19-2002; operative 1-1-2003. Submitted to OAL for printing only pursuant to Government Code section 11351 (Register 2002, No. 51).

3. Repealer filed 12-17-2019; operative 1-1-2020. Submitted to OAL for printing only pursuant to Government Code section 11351 (Register 2019, No. 51).

§10634. Labor Code Section 4628(k) Requests. [Repealed]

Note: Authority cited: Sections 133 and 5307, Labor Code. Reference: Section 4628(k), Labor Code.

History: 1. New section filed 12-23-93; operative 1-1-94. Submitted to OAL for printing only pursuant to Government Code section 11351 (Register 93, No. 52).

2. Repealer filed 12-17-2019; operative 1-1-2020. Submitted to OAL for printing only pursuant to Government Code section 11351 (Register 2019, No. 51).

§10635. Duty to Serve Documents.

(a) Where documents, including electronic media, are to be offered into evidence, copies shall be served on all adverse parties no later than the mandatory settlement conference, unless good cause is shown.

(b) If a party requests that a defendant provide a computer printout of benefits paid, the defendant shall provide the requesting party with a current computer printout of benefits paid within 20 days. The printout shall include the date and amount of each payment of temporary disability indemnity, permanent disability indemnity, the period covered by each payment, and the date, payee and amount of each payment for medical treatment. After receipt of a printout of benefits, another such request may not be made more frequently than once in a 120-day period unless there is a change in indemnity payments or a new dispute requiring updated payment periods.

(c) During the continuing jurisdiction of the Workers' Compensation Appeals Board, the parties have an ongoing duty to serve within 10 calendar days of receipt:

(1) Each other with any medical reports received; and

(2) A lien claimant who has requested service of medical reports with any medical reports received unless the lien claimant is not defined as a "physician" by Labor Code section 3209.3 and is not an entity described in Labor Code sections 4903.05(c)(7) and 4903.06(b); and

(3) Any written communication from a physician containing information listed in rule 10682 that is maintained in the employer's capacity as an employer. Records from an employee assistance program are not required to be filed or served unless ordered by the Workers' Compensation Appeals Board.

Note: Authority cited: Sections 133, 4903.6(d), 5307, 5309 and 5708, Labor Code. Reference: Sections 3209.3, 4600, 4903.05, 4903.06, 4903.6(d), 5001, 5502, 5502(e), 5703 and 5708, Labor Code.

History: 1. New section filed 12-17-2019; operative 1-1-2020. Submitted to OAL for printing only pursuant to Government Code section 11351 (Register 2019, No. 51). For prior history, see Register 91, No. 7.

Ref.: Hanna §§ 23.12[2][d], 25.06A[3], 30.20[3]; Herlick Handbook §§ 14.19, 14.20, 14.21, 14.24, 14.25, 17.27.

§10637. Service of Medical Reports, Medical-Legal Reports, and other Medical Information on a Non-Physician Lien Claimant.

The provisions of this rule shall apply to the service of medical reports, medical-legal reports, or other medical information on a non-physician lien claimant.

(a) If a party is requested by a non-physician lien claimant to serve a copy of any medical report, medical-legal report, or other medical information relating to the claim, the party receiving the request shall not serve a copy on the non-physician lien claimant unless ordered to do so by the Workers' Compensation Appeals Board.

(b) A non-physician lien claimant shall not subpoena any medical information. Any subpoena that, in whole or in part, requests medical information shall be deemed quashed in its entirety by operation of law.

(c) A non-physician lien claimant shall not seek to obtain any medical information using a waiver, release, or other authorization signed by the employee. Any such waiver, release, or other authorization shall be deemed invalid by operation of law.

(d) A non-physician lien claimant may petition the Workers' Compensation Appeals Board for an order directing a party or other lien claimant in possession or control of any medical report, medical-legal report, or other medical information to serve a copy of that report or information, or a particular portion thereof, on the non-physician lien claimant.

(e) For each document, or a portion thereof, containing medical information that is sought, the petition shall specify each of the following:

(1) The name of the issuing physician, medical organization (e.g., a group medical practice or hospital), or other entity and the date of the document containing medical information, if known, or if not known, sufficient information that the party from whom it is sought may reasonably be expected to identify it; and

(2) The specific reason(s) why the non-physician lien claimant believes that the document containing medical information, or a portion thereof, is or is reasonably likely to be relevant to its burden of proof on its lien claim or its petition for costs.

(f) When the petition is filed, a copy shall be concurrently served on the injured employee (or the dependent(s) of a deceased injured employee) and the defendant(s) or, if represented, their attorney or non-attorney of record. In addition, if the medical information is alleged to be in the possession or control of a non-party or another lien claimant, a copy of the petition shall be concurrently served on that non-party or other lien claimant or, if represented, its attorney or non-attorney of record.

(g) The caption of the petition shall identify it as a "Petition by Non-Physician Lien Claimant for Medical Information."

Note: Authority cited: Sections 133, 4903.6(d), 5307, 5309 and 5708, Labor Code. Reference: Sections 4903.6(d), 5001, 5502, 5703 and 5708, Labor Code; and Sections 56.05 and 56.10, Civil Code.

History: 1. New section filed 12-17-2019; operative 1-1-2020. Submitted to OAL for printing only pursuant to Government Code section 11351 (Register 2019, No. 51).

Ref.: Hanna §§ 23.12[2][g], 25.06A[6]; Herlick Handbook § 14.21.

ARTICLE 10
Subpoenas

§10640. Subpoenas.

The Workers' Compensation Appeals Board shall issue subpoenas and subpoenas duces tecum upon request in accordance with the provisions of Code of Civil Procedure sections 1985 and 1987.5 and Government Code section 68097.1. Subpoenas and subpoenas duces tecum shall be on forms prescribed and approved by the Workers' Compensation Appeals Board and shall contain an ADJ number.

Note: Authority cited: Sections 133 and 5307, Labor Code. Reference: Sections 130 and 5401, Labor Code; Sections 1985 and 1987.5, Code of Civil Procedure; and Section 68097.1, Government Code.

History: 1. New article 10 (sections 10640-10660) and renumbering and amendment of former section 10953 to section 10640 filed 12-17-2019; operative 1-1-2020. Submitted to OAL for printing only pursuant to Government Code section 11351 (Register 2019, No. 51). For prior history of article 10 (sections 10700-10727), see Register 2002, No. 51.

Ref.: Hanna §§ 25.10[2][a], 25.29[3][a], 25.43; Herlick Handbook § 14.43.

§10642. Notice to Appear or Produce.

A notice to appear or produce in accordance with Code of Civil Procedure section 1987 is permissible in proceedings before the Workers' Compensation Appeals Board.

Note: Authority cited: Sections 133 and 5307, Labor Code. Reference: Section 132, Labor Code; and Section 1987, Code of Civil Procedure.

History: 1. Renumbering of former section 10532 to section 10642, including amendment of Note, filed 12-17-2019; operative

1-1-2020. Submitted to OAL for printing only pursuant to Government Code section 11351 (Register 2019, No. 51).

Ref.: Hanna §§ 25.43, 26.05[3]; Herlick Handbook § 14.20.

§10644. Subpoenas of Electronic Records.

Where records or other documentary evidence have been recorded or reproduced using the methods described in section 1551 of the Evidence Code and the original records destroyed, the film, legible print thereof or electronic recording shall be produced in response to a subpoena duces tecum. A party offering a film or electronic recording in evidence may be required to provide legible prints thereof or reproductions from the electronic recording.

Note: Authority cited: Sections 133 and 5307, Labor Code. Reference: Section 130, Labor Code; and Section 1551, Evidence Code.

History: 1. Renumbering of former section 10534 to section 10644, including amendment of section heading, section and Note, filed 12-17-2019; operative 1-1-2020. Submitted to OAL for printing only pursuant to Government Code section 11351 (Register 2019, No. 51).

Ref.: Hanna § 25.44[1].

§10647. Witness Fees and Subpoenas.

Medical examiners appointed by the Workers' Compensation Appeals Board or agreed to by the parties when subpoenaed for cross-examination at the Workers' Compensation Appeals Board or deposition shall be paid by the party requiring the attendance of the witness in accordance with the rules of the Administrative Director.

Failure to serve the subpoena and tender the fee in advance based on the estimated time of the trial or deposition may be treated by the Workers' Compensation Appeals Board as a waiver of the right to examine the witness. Service and payment of the fee may be made by mail if the witness so agrees.

Note: Authority cited: Sections 133 and 5307, Labor Code. Reference: Sections 130, 131, 4621 and 5710, Labor Code; and Section 2034.430, 2034.440 and 2034.450, Code of Civil Procedure.

History: 1. Renumbering of former section 10536 to section 10647, including amendment of Note, filed 12-17-2019; operative 1-1-2020. Submitted to OAL for printing only pursuant to Government Code section 11351 (Register 2019, No. 51).

Ref.: Hanna §§ 23.13[2][b], 26.05[3].

§10650. Subpoena for Medical Witness.

A subpoena requiring the appearance of a medical witness before the Workers' Compensation Appeals Board must be served no fewer than 10 days before the time the witness is required to appear and testify.

Note: Authority cited: Sections 133 and 5307, Labor Code. Reference: Section 132, Labor Code.

History: 1. Renumbering and amendment of former section 10537 to section 10650 filed 12-17-2019; operative 1-1-2020. Submitted to OAL for printing only pursuant to Government Code section 11351 (Register 2019, No. 51).

Ref.: Hanna §§ 25.10[2][b], 25.43; Herlick Handbook § 14.43.

§10655. Subpoenas for Medical Information by Non-Physician Lien Claimants.

A lien claimant that is not either a "physician" as defined in Labor Code section 3209.3 or an entity described in Labor Code sections 4903.05(c)(7) and 4903.06(b) shall not issue any subpoena or subpoena duces tecum that seeks to obtain any medical information about an injured worker, but shall instead follow the procedure set forth in rule 10637.

Note: Authority cited: Sections 133, 4903.6(d), 5307, 5309 and 5708, Labor Code. Reference: Sections 130, 4903.6(d) and 5710(a), Labor Code; and Sections 56.05 and 56.10, Civil Code.

History: 1. Renumbering and amendment of former section 10538 to section 10655 filed 12-17-2019; operative 1-1-2020. Submitted to OAL for printing only pursuant to Government Code section 11351 (Register 2019, No. 51).

Ref.: Hanna § 25.43.

§10660. X-Rays.

Upon reasonable request of a party, X-rays in the possession of, or subject to the control of, an adverse party shall be made available for examination by the requesting party or persons designated by that party at a time or place convenient to the persons to make the examination.

Note: Authority cited: Sections 133 and 5307, Labor Code. Reference: Sections 4600 and 5708, Labor Code.

History: 1. Renumbering and amendment of former section 10618 to section 10660 filed 12-17-2019; operative 1-1-2020. Submitted to OAL for printing only pursuant to Government Code section 11351 (Register 2019, No. 51).

Ref.: Hanna §§ 25.07[6], 25.29[3][a], 25.43, 26.06[12][f]; Herlick Handbook § 14.21.

ARTICLE 11
Evidence

§10670. Documentary Evidence.

The filing of a document does not signify its receipt in evidence and, except for the documents listed in rule 10803, only those documents that have been received in evidence shall be included in the record of proceedings on the case.

(a) Certified copies of reports or records of any governmental agency, division or bureau shall be admissible in evidence in lieu of the original reports or records.

(b) The Workers' Compensation Appeals Board may decline to receive in evidence:

(1) Any document not listed on the Pre-Trial Conference Statement.

(2) Any document not served at or prior to the mandatory settlement conference, unless good cause is shown.

(3) Any document not filed 20 days prior to trial, unless otherwise ordered by a workers' compensation judge or good cause is shown.

(4) Any physician's report that does not comply with Labor Code section 4628 unless good cause has been shown for the failure to comply and, after notice of non-compliance, compliance takes place within a reasonable period of time or within a time prescribed by the workers' compensation judge.

(5) Any report that does not comply with the verification requirements of Labor Code section 5703(a)(2)or 5703(j)(2).

(c) Where a willful suppression of evidence is shown to exist, it shall be presumed that the evidence would be adverse, if produced.

(d) The remedies in this rule are cumulative to others authorized by law.

Note: Authority cited: Sections 133, 5307, 5309 and 5708, Labor Code. Reference: Sections 126, 4628, 5316, 5500, 5501, 5703, 5708 and 5813, Labor Code.

History: 1. New article 11 heading and new section filed 12-17-2019; operative 1-1-2020. Submitted to OAL for printing only pursuant to Government Code section 11351 (Register 2019, No. 51).

Ref.: Hanna §§ 22.08[4][e], 23.12[2][d], [g], 25.06A[3], 26.03[1], 26.06[9][c], [12][b][iii], [iv]; Herlick Handbook §§ 14.5, 14.24.

§10672. Evidence Taken Without Notice.

Transcripts or summaries of testimony taken without notice and copies of all reports and other matters added to the record, otherwise than during the course of an open hearing, shall be served upon the parties to the proceeding. Unless it is otherwise expressly provided, the parties shall be allowed 10 days after service of the testimony and reports within which to produce evidence in explanation or rebuttal or to request further proceedings before the case shall be deemed submitted for decision.

Note: Authority cited: Sections 133 and 5307, Labor Code. Reference: Section 5704, Labor Code.

History: 1. Renumbering of former section 10580 to section 10672 filed 12-17-2019; operative 1-1-2020. Submitted to OAL for printing only pursuant to Government Code section 11351 (Register 2019, No. 51).

Ref.: Hanna §§ 23.14[1][d], 26.06[11]; Herlick Handbook § 14.5.

§10675. Formal Permanent Disability Rating Determinations.

The Workers' Compensation Appeals Board may request the Disability Evaluation Unit to prepare a formal rating determination on a form prescribed for that purpose by the Administrative Director. The request may refer to an accompanying medical report or chart for the sole purpose of describing measurable physical elements of the condition that are clearly and exactly identifiable. In every instance the request shall describe the factors of disability in full.

The report of the Disability Evaluation Unit in response to the request shall constitute evidence only as to the percentage of the permanent disability based on the factors described, and the report shall not constitute evidence as to the existence of the permanent disability described.

The report of the Disability Evaluation Unit shall be filed and served on the parties and shall include or be accompanied by a notice that the case shall be submitted for decision 7 days after service unless written objection is made within that time.

Note: Authority cited: Sections 133 and 5307, Labor Code. Reference: Sections 4660 and 5708, Labor Code.

History: 1. Renumbering and amendment of former section 10602 to section 10675 filed 12-17-2019; operative 1-1-2020. Submitted to OAL for printing only pursuant to Government Code section 11351 (Register 2019, No. 51).

Ref.: Hanna §§ 23.14[1][a], 26.06[12][d], 32.02[7], 32.05[2], [6][a], [b], [c][i]; Herlick Handbook §§ 6.04, 14.5, 14.28, 14.29.

§10677. Oversized Exhibits, Diagnostic Imaging, Physical Exhibits and Exhibits on Media.

(a) The following exhibits shall be filed only at the time of trial:

(1) Oversized documents, other than medical reports, that are:

(A) Larger than 11 x 17 inches (e.g., maps, diagrams and schematic drawings); and

(B) Over 25 pages in length;

(2) Diagnostic imaging, including but not limited to any X-ray, computed axial tomography (CAT) scan, magnetic resonance imaging (MRI), nuclear medicine, positron emission tomography (PET) scan, mammography, ultrasound or other similar medical imaging that is stored on digital, film or other non-paper media;

(3) Original business or office records;

(4) Physical objects or other tangible things;

(5) Any CD-ROM, DVD or other digital media, including but not limited to:

(A) Digital photographs;

(B) Digital video recordings; and

(C) Digital audio recordings;

(6) Videotapes, audiotapes, films and other non-digital video and/or audio recordings or images; and

(7) Photographs printed on paper.

(b) Unless otherwise ordered by the Workers' Compensation Appeals Board, any exhibit listed in subdivision (a) that is offered into evidence (whether or not admitted into evidence) shall be retained by the filing party (or an agent of the filing party) until the later of either:

(1) Five years after the filing of the initial Application for Adjudication of Claim (or other case opening document); or

(2) At least six months after all appeals have been exhausted or the time for seeking appellate review has expired with respect to the decision on the issue(s) for which the exhibit was offered in evidence.

After expiration of the later of these two time periods, the party may destroy the exhibit, unless the Workers' Compensation Appeals Board has ordered that the exhibit be preserved for a longer period.

(c) Before and during the period of retention, the filing party shall:

(1) Maintain the exhibit under conditions that will protect it against loss, destruction or tampering, and that will preserve its quality and integrity as far as practicable;

(2) At the request of any other party to the action, promptly permit the party to inspect or view the exhibit; and

(3) At the request of any other party to the action, and if practicable, promptly furnish the party a copy of the exhibit or promptly permit the party to make a copy.

For purposes of subsection (c), the term "exhibit" shall include any item listed in subsection (a), whether or not the party in possession or control of that item intends to offer it in evidence.

(d) Any disputes regarding subdivision (c), including but not limited to issues of timing and costs, may be submitted for determination to the Workers' Compensation Appeals Board.

Note: Authority cited: Sections 133, 5307, 5309 and 5708, Labor Code. Reference: Sections 5309, 5701, 5703, 5704 and 5708, Labor Code.

History: 1. Renumbering and amendment of former section 10603 to section 10677 filed 12-17-2019; operative 1-1-2020. Submitted to OAL for printing only pursuant to Government Code section 11351 (Register 2019, No. 51).

Ref.: Hanna § 23.12[2][f]; Herlick Handbook §§ 14.5, 14.15.

§10680. Reproductions of Documents.

(a) It is presumed a filed photocopy is an accurate representation of the original document. If a party alleges that a filed photocopy is inaccurate or unreliable, the party alleging the document is inaccurate or unreliable shall state the basis for the objection. The filing party must establish that the document is an accurate representation of the original document.

(b) A nonerasable optical image reproduction provided that additions, deletions or changes to the original document are not permitted by the technology, a photostatic, microfilm, microcard, miniature photographic or other photographic copy or reproduction, or an enlargement thereof, of a writing is admissible as the writing itself if the copy or reproduction was made and preserved as a part of the records of a business (as defined by Evidence Code section 1270) in the regular course of that business. The introduction of the copy, reproduction or enlargement does not preclude admission of the original writing if it is still in existence. The Workers' Compensation Appeals Board may require the introduction of a hard copy printout of the document.

(c) A printed representation of images stored on a video or digital medium is presumed to be an accurate representation of the images it purports to represent. This presumption is a presumption affecting the burden of producing evidence. If a party to an action introduces evidence that a printed representation of images stored on a video or digital medium is inaccurate or unreliable, the party introducing the printed representation into evidence has the burden of proving by a preponderance of the evidence that the printed representation is an accurate representation of the existence and content of the images that it purports to represent.

Note: Authority cited: Sections 133 and 5307, Labor Code. Reference: Section 5708, Labor Code; and Section 1270, Evidence Code.

History: 1. Renumbering of former section 10605 to section 10680, including amendment of section and Note, filed 12-17-2019; operative 1-1-2020. Submitted to OAL for printing only pursuant to Government Code section 11351 (Register 2019, No. 51).

Ref.: Hanna §§ 23.12[2][h], 25.06A[7]; Herlick Handbook §§ 14.5, 14.27, 14.40.

§10682. Physicians' Reports as Evidence.

(a) The Workers' Compensation Appeals Board favors the production of medical evidence in the form of written reports. Direct examination of a medical witness will not be received at a trial except upon a showing of good cause. A continuance may be granted for rebuttal medical testimony subject to Labor Code section 5502.5.

(b) Medical reports should include where applicable:

(1) The date of the examination;

(2) The history of the injury;

(3) The patient's complaints;

(4) A listing of all information received in preparation of the report or relied upon for the formulation of the physician's opinion;

(5) The patient's medical history, including injuries and conditions, and residuals thereof, if any;

(6) Findings on examination;

(7) A diagnosis;

(8) Opinion as to the nature, extent and duration of disability and work limitations, if any;

(9) Cause of the disability;

(10) Treatment indicated, including past, continuing and future medical care;

(11) Opinion as to whether or not permanent disability has resulted from the injury and whether or not it is stationary. If stationary, a description of the disability with a complete evaluation;

(12) Apportionment of disability, if any;

(13) A determination of the percent of the total causation resulting from actual events of employment, if the injury is alleged to be a psychiatric injury;

(14) The reasons for the opinion; and

(15) The signature of the physician.

In death cases, the reports of non-examining physicians may be admitted into evidence in lieu of oral testimony.

(c) All medical-legal reports shall comply with the provisions of Labor Code section 4628. Except as otherwise provided by the Labor Code and the Rules of Practice and Procedure of the Workers' Compensation Appeals Board, failure to comply with the requirements of this rule will not make the report inadmissible but will be considered in weighing the evidence.

Note: Authority cited: Sections 133 and 5307, Labor Code. Reference: Sections 4628, 5502.5, 5703 and 5708, Labor Code.

History: 1. Renumbering of former section 10606 to section 10682, including amendment of section and Note, filed 12-17-2019; operative 1-1-2020. Submitted to OAL for printing only pursuant to Government Code section 11351 (Register 2019, No. 51).

Ref.: Hanna §§ 5.08[2][b], 22.08[3][a], [b], [d], [5][a], [6][b], 23.14[2][g], 25.04[1], 25.10[2][b], 26.06[5], [12][a], [b][ii], 32.06[4][a]; Herlick Handbook §§ 1.02, 14.5, 14.21, 14.23, 14.26, 14.38.

§10683. Specific Finding of Fact — Labor Code Section 139.2(d)(2).

Where a qualified medical evaluator's report has been considered and rejected pursuant to Labor Code section 139.2(d)(2), the workers' compensation judge or Appeals Board shall make and serve a specific finding on the qualified medical evaluator and the Division of Workers'

Compensation at the time of decision on the regular workers' compensation issues. The specific finding may be included in the decision.

If the Appeals Board, on reconsideration, affirms or sets aside the specific finding of fact filed by a workers' compensation judge, it shall advise the qualified medical evaluator and the Division of Workers' Compensation at the time of service of its decision on the petition for reconsideration. If the workers' compensation judge does not make a specific finding and the Appeals Board, on reconsideration, makes a specific finding of rejection pursuant to Labor Code section 139.2(d)(2), it shall serve its specific finding on the qualified medical evaluator and the Division of Workers' Compensation at the time it serves its decision after reconsideration.

Rejection of a qualified medical evaluator's report pursuant to Labor Code section 139.2(d)(2) shall occur where the qualified medical evaluator's report does not meet the minimum standards prescribed by the provisions of rule 10682 and the regulations of the Division of Workers' Compensation.

This rule shall apply to injuries on or after January 1, 1994.

Note: Authority cited: Sections 133 and 5307, Labor Code. Reference: Section 139.2(d)(2), Labor Code.

History: 1. Renumbering and amendment of former section 10631 to section 10683 filed 12-17-2019; operative 1-1-2020. Submitted to OAL for printing only pursuant to Government Code section 11351 (Register 2019, No. 51).

Ref.: Hanna § 1.12[2A][d]; Herlick Handbook §§ 1.02, 14.5.

§10685. Vocational Experts' Reports as Evidence.

(a) The Workers' Compensation Appeals Board favors the production of vocational expert evidence in the form of written reports. Direct examination of a vocational expert witness will not be received at a trial except upon a showing of good cause. Good cause shall not be found if the vocational expert witness has not issued a report and the party offering the witness fails to demonstrate that it exercised due diligence in attempting to obtain a report. A continuance may be granted for rebuttal testimony if a report that was not served sufficiently in advance of the close of discovery to permit rebuttal is admitted into evidence.

(b) A vocational expert's written report shall meet the following requirements:

(1) The report shall contain a declaration by the vocational expert signing the report stating: "I declare under penalty of perjury that the information contained in this report and its attachments, if any, is true and correct to the best of my knowledge, except as to information that I have indicated I received from others. As to that information, I declare under penalty of perjury that the information accurately describes the information provided to me and, except as noted herein, that I believe it to be true. I further declare under penalty of perjury that there has not been a violation of Labor Code section 139.32." The foregoing declaration shall be dated and signed by the vocational expert and shall indicate the county wherein it was signed.

(2) The report shall disclose the qualifications of the vocational expert signing the report, which may be satisfied by attaching a curriculum vitae.

(3) Except as provided in subdivision (b)(4), the body of the report shall contain a statement, above the declaration under penalty of perjury, that: "No person, other than the vocational expert signing the report, has participated in the non-clerical preparation of the report, including all of the following:

(i) Taking a history from the employee;

(ii) Reviewing and summarizing medical and/or non-medical records; and

(iii) Composing and drafting the conclusions of the report."

(4) Notwithstanding subdivision (b)(3), it is permissible for a person or persons, other than the vocational expert signing the report, to prepare an initial outline of the employee's history and/or to excerpt prior medical and non-medical records. If this is done, however, the vocational expert signing the report:

(A) Shall review the excerpts and the entire outline and shall make additional inquiries and examinations as are necessary and appropriate to identify and determine the relevant issues;

(B) Shall include in the statement required by subdivision (b)(3) that, as applicable, an initial outline of the employee's history and/or an excerpt of the employee's prior medical and non-medical records were prepared by another person or persons and that the vocational expert signing the report has reviewed any such excerpts and/or outline and has made any additional inquiries and examinations necessary and appropriate to identify and determine the relevant issues; and

(C) Shall comply with subdivision (b)(5), below.

(5) The report shall disclose the name(s) and qualifications of each person who performed any services in connection with the report, including diagnostic studies, other than its clerical preparation.

(c) The vocational expert's report should include, where applicable:

(1) The date(s) of any evaluation(s), interview(s) and test(s);

(2) The history of the injury;

(3) The employee's vocational history;

(4) The injured employee's complaints;

(5) A listing of all information reviewed in preparation of the report or relied upon for the formulation of the vocational expert's opinion;

(6) The injured employee's medical history, including injuries and conditions, and residuals thereof, if any;

(7) Findings and opinion on evaluation;

(8) The reasons for the opinion; and

(9) The signature of the vocational expert.

A failure to comply with the requirements of subdivision (c) will not make the report inadmissible but will be considered in weighing the evidence.

(d) Statements concerning any vocational expert's bill for services are admissible only if they comply with subdivision (b)(1).

Note: Authority cited: Sections 133, 5307, 5309 and 5708, Labor Code. Reference: Sections 139.32, 4628, 5502(d)(3) and 5703(j), Labor Code.

History: 1. Renumbering and amendment of former section 10606.5 to section 10685 filed 12-17-2019; operative 1-1-2020. Submitted to OAL for printing only pursuant to Government Code section 11351 (Register 2019, No. 51).

Ref.: Hanna § 22.08[7]; Herlick Handbook §§ 14.5, 14.27.

ARTICLE 12 Settlements

§10700. Approval of Settlements.

(a) When filing a Compromise and Release or a Stipulations with Request for Award, the filing party shall file all agreed medical evaluator reports, qualified medical evaluator reports, treating physician reports, and any other that are relevant to a determination of the adequacy of the Compromise and Release or Stipulations with Request for Award that have not been filed previously.

(b) The Workers' Compensation Appeals Board shall inquire into the adequacy of all Compromise and Release agreements and Stipulations with Request for Award, and may set the matter for hearing to take evidence when necessary to determine whether the agreement should be approved or disapproved, or issue findings and awards.

(c) Agreements that provide for the payment of less than the full amount of compensation due or to become due and undertake to release the employer from all future liability will be approved only where it appears that a reasonable doubt exists as to the rights of the parties or that approval is in the best interest of the parties.

Note: Authority cited: Sections 133 and 5307, Labor Code. Reference: Sections 4646, 5001, 5100.6, 5002 and 5702, Labor Code.

History: 1. Repealer of article 10 heading, new article 12 heading and new section filed 12-17-2019; operative 1-1-2020. Submitted to OAL for printing only pursuant to Government Code section 11351 (Register 2019, No. 51).

Ref.: Herlick Handbook §§ 11.01, 11.05, 11.06, 14.31.

§10702. Service of Settlements on Lien Claimants.

Where a lien claim is on file with the Workers' Compensation Appeals Board, and a Compromise and Release agreement or Stipulations with Request for Award is filed, a copy of the Compromise and Release agreement or Stipulations with Request for Award shall be served by the filing party on the lien claimant.

No lien claim shall be disallowed or reduced unless the lien claimant has been given notice and an opportunity to be heard.

Note: Authority cited: Sections 133 and 5307, Labor Code. Reference: Sections 4903, 4903.05, 4903.1, 4903.4, 4904, 4904.1, 4905 and 4906, Labor Code.

History: 1. Renumbering of former section 10886 to section 10702, including amendment of section heading, section and Note, filed 12-17-2019; operative 1-1-2020. Submitted to OAL for printing only pursuant to Government Code section 11351 (Register 2019, No. 51).

Ref.: Hanna §§ 23.14[2][m], 29.03[8], 29.04[3][b], [c], 30.21, 30.24[2][a]; Herlick Handbook § 11.09.

§10705. Procedures — Labor Code Section 3761.

Where the insurer has attached a declaration to the Compromise and Release agreement or Stipulations with Request for Award that it has complied with the provisions of Labor Code sections 3761(a) and 3761(b), the Workers' Compensation Appeals Board may approve the Compromise and Release or Stipulations with Request for Award without hearing or further proceedings.

Where a workers' compensation judge or the Appeals Board has approved a Compromise and Release or Stipulations with Request for Award and the insurer has failed to show proof of service pursuant to Labor Code section 3761(b), the workers' compensation judge or the Appeals Board, after giving notice and an opportunity to be heard to the insurer, shall award expenses as provided in Labor Code section 5813 upon request by the employer.

Any request for relief under Labor Code section 3761(b) or Labor Code section 3761(d) shall be made by the filing of a petition pursuant to rule 10510, together with a Declaration of Readiness to Proceed.

Note: Authority cited: Sections 133 and 5307, Labor Code. Reference: Section 3761, Labor Code.

History: 1. Renumbering and amendment of former section 10875 to section 10705 filed 12-17-2019; operative 1-1-2020. Submitted to OAL for printing only pursuant to Government Code section 11351 (Register 2019, No. 51).

Ref.: Hanna §§ 2.34, 29.04[7]; Herlick Handbook §§ 11.01, 11.05, 14.32.

§10740. Transcripts. [Renumbered]

Note: Authority cited: Sections 133, 5307, 5309 and 5708, Labor Code. Reference: Sections 5300, 5301, 5309, 5700, 5701 and 5708, Labor Code; and Section 703.5, Evidence Code.

History: 1. Amendment of first paragraph filed 12-19-2002; operative 1-1-2003. Submitted to OAL for printing only pursuant to Government Code section 11351 (Register 2002, No. 51).

2. Repealer of second paragraph and amendment of Note filed 10-15-2014; operative 1-1-2015. Submitted to OAL for printing only pursuant to Government Code section 11351 (Register 2014, No. 42).

3. Editorial correction of History 2 (Register 2017, No. 8).

4. Repealer of article 11 heading and renumbering of former section 10740 to section 10800 filed 12-17-2019; operative 1-1-2020. Submitted to OAL for printing only pursuant to Government Code section 11351 (Register 2019, No. 51).

ARTICLE 13 Hearings

§10742. Declaration of Readiness to Proceed.

(a) Except when a hearing is set on the Workers' Compensation Appeals Board's own motion, no matter shall be placed on calendar unless one of the parties has filed and served a Declaration of Readiness to Proceed in the form prescribed by the Appeals Board. The Declaration of Readiness to Proceed shall be served on all parties in accordance with rule 10610.

(b) A lien claimant shall not file a Declaration of Readiness to Proceed unless:

(1) The underlying case of the injured employee or the dependent(s) of a deceased employee has been resolved or

(2) The injured employee or the dependent(s) of a deceased employee choose(s) not to proceed with their case.

(c) All declarations of readiness to proceed shall state under penalty of perjury that the moving party has made a genuine, good faith effort to resolve the dispute before filing the Declaration of Readiness to Proceed, and shall state with specificity on the Declaration of Readiness to Proceed the efforts made to resolve those issues. Unless a status or priority conference is requested, the declarant shall also state under penalty of perjury that the moving party has completed discovery and is ready to proceed on the issues specified in the Declaration of Readiness to Proceed.

(d) If a party is represented by an attorney or non-attorney representative any Declaration of Readiness to Proceed filed on behalf of the party shall be executed by the attorney or non-attorney representative.

(e) If a Declaration of Readiness to Proceed is filed without complying with the provisions of this section, the Workers' Compensation Appeals Board may order the hearing off calendar and may impose sanctions and award attorney's fees and costs in accordance with Labor Code section 5813 and rule 10421.

Note: Authority cited: Sections 133, 5307, 5309 and 5708, Labor Code. Reference: Sections 4903.05, 4903.06, 5500.3, 5502 and 5813, Labor Code.

History: 1. New article 13 heading and renumbering and amendment of former section 10414 to section 10742 filed 12-17-2019; operative 1-1-2020. Submitted to OAL for printing only pursuant to Government Code section 11351 (Register 2019, No. 51).

Ref.: Hanna §§ 23.14[2][d], 25.05[1], 25.08[1]; Herlick Handbook §§ 14.7, 14.8, 14.11, 14.30.

§10744. Objection to Declaration of Readiness to Proceed.

(a) Any objection to a Declaration of Readiness to Proceed shall be filed and served within 10 calendar days after service of the declaration. The objection shall set forth, under penalty of perjury, the specific reason why the case should not be set or why the requested proceedings are inappropriate.

(b) A false declaration or certification filed under this rule by any party, petitioner, attorney or non-attorney representative may give rise to proceedings under Labor Code section 134 for contempt or Labor Code section 5813 for sanctions.

(c) If a party is represented by an attorney or non-attorney representative, any objection to the Declaration of Readiness to Proceed shall be executed by the attorney or non-attorney representative.

(d) If a party has received a copy of the Declaration of Readiness to Proceed and has not filed an objection under this rule, that party shall be deemed to have waived any and all objections to proceeding on the issues specified in the declaration, absent extraordinary circumstances.

Note: Authority cited: Sections 133, 5307, 5309 and 5708, Labor Code. Reference: Sections 134, 5500.3, 5502 and 5813, Labor Code.

History: 1. Renumbering of former section 10416 to section 10744, including amendment of section and Note, filed 12-17-2019; operative 1-1-2020. Submitted to OAL for printing only pursuant to Government Code section 11351 (Register 2019, No. 51).

Ref.: Hanna § 25.08[2]; Herlick Handbook §§ 14.8, 14.32.

§10745. Setting the Case.

The Workers' Compensation Appeals Board, upon the receipt of a Declaration of Readiness to Proceed, may, in its discretion, set the case for a type of proceeding other than that requested. The Workers' Compensation Appeals Board may, on its own motion, set any case for conference or trial.

Note: Authority cited: Sections 133 and 5307, Labor Code. Reference: Section 5310, Labor Code.

History: 1. Renumbering and amendment of former section 10420 to section 10745 filed 12-17-2019; operative 1-1-2020. Submitted to OAL for printing only pursuant to Government Code section 11351 (Register 2019, No. 51).

Ref.: Hanna §§ 25.08[1], 32.05[6][c][i]; Herlick Handbook § 14.30.

§10748. Continuances.

Requests for continuances are inconsistent with the requirement that workers' compensation proceedings be expeditious and are not favored. Continuances will be granted only upon a clear showing of good cause. Where possible, reassignment pursuant to rule 10346 shall be used to avoid continuances.

Note: Authority cited: Sections 133 and 5307, Labor Code. Reference: Article XIV, Section 4, California Constitution; and Sections 5502 and 5502.5, Labor Code.

History: 1. Renumbering and amendment of former section 10548 to section 10748 filed 12-17-2019; operative 1-1-2020. Submitted to OAL for printing only pursuant to Government Code section 11351 (Register 2019, No. 51).

Ref.: Hanna §§ 25.09[1], 26.02[3]; Herlick Handbook § 14.31.

§10750. Notice of Hearing.

The Workers' Compensation Appeals Board shall either serve or, under rule 10629, cause to be served notice on all parties and their attorneys or non-attorney representatives of record of the time and place of each hearing scheduled, whether or not the hearing affects all parties, as provided in rule 10610.

Notice of hearing shall be given at least 10 days before the date of hearing, except where:

(a) Notice is waived; or

(b) A different time is expressly agreed to by all parties and concurred in by the Workers' Compensation Appeals Board.

Note: Authority cited: Sections 133 and 5307, Labor Code. Reference: Section 5504, Labor Code.

History: 1. Amendment of section and Note filed 12-19-2002; operative 1-1-2003. Submitted to OAL for printing only pursuant to Government Code section 11351 (Register 2002, No. 51).

2. Amendment of section and Note filed 11-17-2008; operative 11-17-2008. Submitted to OAL for printing only (Register 2008, No. 47).

3. Amendment of subsection (a) filed 10-15-2014; operative 1-1-2015. Submitted to OAL for printing only pursuant to Government Code section 11351 (Register 2014, No. 42).

4. Editorial correction of History 3 (Register 2017, No. 8).

5. Repealer of article 12 heading, repealer of former section 10750 and renumbering and amendment of former section 10544 to section 10750 filed 12-17-2019; operative 1-1-2020. Submitted to OAL for printing only pursuant to Government Code section 11351 (Register 2019, No. 51).

Ref.: Hanna §§ 23.14[1][c], 24.11[1][b], 26.03[1], 26.04[1][b]; Herlick Handbook §§ 14.30, 14.31.

§10751. Appearances by Non-Attorney Representatives Not Identified on Notice of Representation.

(a) A non-attorney representative may appear on a party's behalf if identified on a notice of representation.

(b) A non-attorney representative who has not been identified on a notice of representation shall file a notice of appearance that includes the full legal name of the represented party and the name, address and telephone number of the attorney or non-attorney representative and associated entity, if any.

Note: Authority cited: Sections 133 and 5307, Labor Code. Reference: Sections 4903, 4903.6 and 4906, Labor Code

History: 1. New section filed 12-19-2002; operative 1-1-2003. Submitted to OAL for printing only pursuant to Government Code section 11351 (Register 2002, No. 51).

2. Amendment of section heading, section and Note filed 11-17-2008; operative 11-17-2008. Submitted to OAL for printing only (Register 2008, No. 47).

3. Amendment filed 10-15-2014; operative 1-1-2015. Submitted to OAL for printing only pursuant to Government Code section 11351 (Register 2014, No. 42).

4. Editorial correction of History 3 (Register 2017, No. 8).

5. Repealer of former section 10751 and new section filed 12-17-2019; operative 1-1-2020. Submitted to OAL for printing only pursuant to Government Code section 11351 (Register 2019, No. 51).

Ref.: Hanna § 20.01[1][a].

§10752. Appearances Required.

(a) Each applicant and defendant shall appear or have an attorney or non-attorney representative appear at all hearings pertaining to the case in chief. Neither a lien conference nor a lien trial is a hearing pertaining to the case in chief.

(b) Each required party shall have a person available with settlement authority at all hearings. This person need not be present if the party's attorney or non-attorney representative is present and can obtain immediate authority.

(c) A represented injured employee or dependent shall personally appear at any mandatory settlement conference. Failure to personally appear shall not be a basis for dismissal of the application.

(d) A lien claimant need not appear at any mandatory settlement conference or trial in the case in chief, but shall be immediately available by telephone with full settlement authority and shall notify defendant(s) of the telephone number at which the defendant(s) may reach the lien claimant. Failure to comply may give rise to monetary sanctions, attorney's fees and costs under Labor Code section 5813 and rule 10421.

(e) Any appearance required by this rule may be excused by the Workers' Compensation Appeals Board. Any appearance not required by this rule may be ordered by the Workers' Compensation Appeals Board.

Note: Authority cited: Sections 133, 5307, 5309 and 5708, Labor Code. Reference: Sections 5502 and 5700, Labor Code.

History: 1. New section filed 12-17-2019; operative 1-1-2020. Submitted to OAL for printing only pursuant to Government Code section 11351 (Register 2019, No. 51).

Ref.: Hanna §§ 26.01[3][a], 30.22[1], [5][a]; Herlick Handbook §§ 14.31, 14.34, 14.43.

§10753. Inspection of Files. [Repealed]

Note: Authority cited: Sections 133, 5307, 5309 and 5708, Labor Code. Reference: Section 126, Labor Code.

History: 1. Amendment of section and Note filed 12-19-2002; operative 1-1-2003. Submitted to OAL for printing only pursuant to Government Code section 11351 (Register 2002, No. 51).

2. Amendment of section and Note filed 11-17-2008; operative 11-17-2008. Submitted to OAL for printing only (Register 2008, No. 47).

3. Amendment filed 10-15-2014; operative 1-1-2015. Submitted to OAL for printing only pursuant to Government Code section 11351 (Register 2014, No. 42).

4. Editorial correction of History 3 (Register 2017, No. 8).

5. Repealer filed 12-17-2019; operative 1-1-2020. Submitted to OAL for printing only pursuant to Government Code section 11351 (Register 2019, No. 51).

§10754. Sealing Documents. [Renumbered]

Note: Authority cited: Sections 133, 5307, 5309 and 5708, Labor Code. Reference: Section 5708, Labor Code; Rule 2.551, California Rules of Court.

History: 1. Amendment filed 12-19-2002; operative 1-1-2003. Submitted to OAL for printing only pursuant to Government Code section 11351 (Register 2002, No. 51).

2. Amendment of section and Note filed 11-17-2008; operative 11-17-2008. Submitted to OAL for printing only (Register 2008, No. 47).

3. Amendment of section heading, repealer and new section and amendment of Note filed 10-15-2014; operative 1-1-2015. Submitted to OAL for printing only pursuant to Government Code section 11351 (Register 2014, No. 42).

4. Editorial correction of History 3 (Register 2017, No. 8).

5. Renumbering of former section 10754 to section 10813 filed 12-17-2019; operative 1-1-2020. Submitted to OAL for printing only pursuant to Government Code section 11351 (Register 2019, No. 51).

§10755. Failure to Appear at Mandatory Settlement Conference in Case in Chief.

(a) Where an applicant served with notice of a mandatory settlement conference fails to appear either in person or by attorney or non-attorney representative at the mandatory settlement conference, the workers' compensation judge may:

(1) Dismiss the application after issuing a 10-day notice of intention to dismiss, or

(2) Close discovery and set the case in chief for trial.

(b) Where a defendant served with notice of a mandatory settlement conference fails to appear either in person or by attorney or non-attorney representative at the mandatory settlement conference, the workers' compensation judge may:

(1) Close discovery and set the case for trial on all issues, or

(2) Set the case in chief for trial.

(c) Where a required party, after notice, fails to appear at a mandatory settlement conference in the case in chief and good cause is shown for failure to appear, the workers' compensation judge may take the case off calendar or may continue the case to a date certain.

(d) This rule shall not apply to lien conferences, which are governed by rule 10875.

Note: Authority cited: Sections 133 and 5307, Labor Code. Reference: Article XIV, Section 4, California Constitution; and Sections 5502(e) and 5708, Labor Code.

History: 1. Amendment of section and Note filed 11-17-2008; operative 11-17-2008. Submitted to OAL for printing only (Register 2008, No. 47).

2. Amendment filed 10-15-2014; operative 1-1-2015. Submitted to OAL for printing only pursuant to Government Code section 11351 (Register 2014, No. 42).

3. Editorial correction of History 2 (Register 2017, No. 8).

4. Renumbering of former section 10755 to section 10811 and new section 10755 filed 12-17-2019; operative 1-1-2020. Submitted to OAL for printing only pursuant to Government Code section 11351 (Register 2019, No. 51).

Ref.: Hanna § 26.04[2]; Herlick Handbook §§ 13.4, 14.43.

§10756. Failure to Appear at Trial in Case in Chief.

(a) Where an applicant served with notice of trial in the case in chief fails to appear either in person or by attorney or non-attorney representative at the trial, the workers' compensation judge may:

(1) Dismiss the application after issuing a 10-day notice of intention to dismiss, or

(2) Hear the evidence and, after service of the minutes of hearing and summary of evidence that shall include a 10-day notice of intention to submit, make such decision as is just and proper.

(b) Where a defendant served with notice of trial in the case in chief fails to appear either in person or by attorney or non-attorney representative at the trial, the workers' compensation judge may hear the evidence and, after service of the minutes of hearing and summary of evidence that shall include a 10-day notice of intention to submit, make such decision as is just and proper.

(c) Where a required party, after notice, fails to appear at a trial in the case in chief and good cause is shown for failure to appear, the workers' compensation judge may take the case off calendar or may continue the case to a date certain.

(d) This rule shall not apply to lien trials, which are governed by rule 10876.

Note: Authority cited: Sections 133 and 5307, Labor Code. Reference: Article XIV, Section 4, California Constitution; and Sections 5502(e) and 5708, Labor Code.

History: 1. New section filed 12-17-2019; operative 1-1-2020. Submitted to OAL for printing only pursuant to Government Code section 11351 (Register 2019, No. 51).

Ref.: Hanna § 26.01[3][a]; Herlick Handbook § 14.43.

§10757. Appearances in Settled Cases.

When the parties represent to the workers' compensation judge assigned to the case that a case has been settled, the case may be taken off calendar.

Note: Authority cited: Sections 133 and 5307, Labor Code. Reference: Article XIV, Section 4, California Constitution; and Sections 5502 and 5502.5, Labor Code.

History: 1. Renumbering and amendment of former section 10549 to section 10757 filed 12-17-2019; operative 1-1-2020. Submitted to OAL for printing only pursuant to Government Code section 11351 (Register 2019, No. 51).

Ref.: Hanna § 26.01[3][b].

§10758. Status Conferences.

At the discretion of the workers' compensation judge, any hearing except a trial may be re-designated as a status conference.

Note: Authority cited: Sections 133 and 5307, Labor Code. Reference: Article XIV, Section 4, California Constitution; and Sections 5502 and 5502.5, Labor Code.

History: 1. New section filed 12-17-2019; operative 1-1-2020. Submitted to OAL for printing only pursuant to Government Code section 11351 (Register 2019, No. 51). For prior history, see Register 2008, No. 47.

Ref.: Hanna §§ 25.09[2], 26.02[1].

§10759. Mandatory Settlement Conferences.

(a) In accordance with Labor Code section 5502, the workers' compensation judge shall have authority to inquire into the adequacy and completeness, including provision for lien claims, of Compromise and Release agreements or Stipulations with Request for Award or orders, and to issue orders approving Compromise and Release agreements or awards or orders based upon approved stipulations. The workers' compensation judge may temporarily adjourn a conference to a time certain to facilitate a specific resolution of the dispute(s) subject to Labor Code section 5502(d)(1).

Subject to the provisions of Labor Code section 5502.5 and rule 10744, upon a showing of good cause, the workers' compensation judge may continue a mandatory settlement conference to a date certain, may continue it to a status conference on a date certain, or may take the case off calendar. In such a case, the workers' compensation judge shall note the reasons for the continuance or order taking off calendar in the minutes. The minutes shall be served on all parties and their representatives.

(b) Absent resolution of the dispute(s), the parties shall file a joint Pre-Trial Conference Statement setting forth the issues and stipulations for trial, witnesses, and a list of exhibits. A defendant that has paid benefits shall have a current computer printout of benefits paid available for inspection at every mandatory settlement conference.

(1) Each exhibit listed must be clearly identified by author/provider, date, and title or type (e.g., "the July 1, 2008 medical report of John Doe, M.D. (3 pages)"). Each medical report, medical-legal report, medical record, or other paper or record having a different author/provider and/or a different date is a separate "document" and must be listed as a separate exhibit, with the exception that the following documents may be listed as a single exhibit,

unless otherwise ordered by the Workers' Compensation Appeals Board:

(A) Excerpted portions of physician, hospital or dispensary records, provided that the party offering the exhibit designates each excerpted portion by the title of the record or document, by the date or dates of treatment or other service(s) covered by the record or document, by the author or authors of the record or document, and by any available page number(s) (e.g., Bates-numbered pages of records or documents photocopied and numbered by a legal copy service). Only the relevant excerpts of physician, hospital or dispensary records shall be admitted in evidence;

(B) Excerpted portions of personnel records, wage records and statements, job descriptions, and other business records provided that the party offering the exhibit designates each excerpted portion by the title of the record or document, by the date or dates covered by the record or document, by the author or authors of the record or document, and by any available page number(s) (e.g., Bates-numbered pages of records or documents photocopied and numbered by a legal copy service). Only the relevant excerpts of personnel records, wage records and statements, job descriptions, and other business records shall be admitted in evidence; and

(C) Explanation of Benefits (EOB) letters.

(c) The workers' compensation judge may make orders and rulings regarding admission of evidence and discovery matters, including admission of offers of proof and stipulations of testimony where appropriate and necessary for resolution of the dispute(s) by the workers' compensation judge, and may submit and decide the dispute(s) on the record pursuant to the agreement of the parties.

(d) The joint Pre-Trial Conference Statement, the disposition, and any orders shall be filed by the workers' compensation judge in the record of the proceedings on a form prescribed and approved by the Appeals Board and shall be served on the parties.

Note: Authority cited: Sections 133, 5307 and 5502, Labor Code. Reference: Sections 5502 and 5502.5, Labor Code.

History: 1. New section filed 12-17-2019; operative 1-1-2020. Submitted to OAL for printing only pursuant to Government Code section 11351 (Register 2019, No. 51).

Ref.: Hanna § 26.04[2]; Herlick Handbook § 14.32.

§10760. Recording of Trial Level Proceedings. [Renumbered]

Note: Authority cited: Sections 133, 5307, 5309 and 5708, Labor Code. Reference: Rule 1.150, California Rules of Court.

History: 1. New section filed 10-15-2014; operative 1-1-2015. Submitted to OAL for printing only pursuant to Government Code section 11351 (Register 2014, No. 42).

2. Editorial correction of History 1 (Register 2017, No. 8).

3. Renumbering former section 10760 to section 10818 filed 12-17-2019; operative 1-1-2020. Submitted to OAL for printing only pursuant to Government Code section 11351 (Register 2019, No. 51).

§10761. Submission at Conference.

(a) A workers' compensation judge may receive evidence and submit an issue or issues for decision at a conference hearing if the parties agree.

(b) If documentary evidence is required to determine the issue or issues being submitted, the parties shall comply with the provisions of rule 10759 regarding the listing and filing of exhibits.

(c) After submission at a conference, the workers' compensation judge shall prepare minutes of hearing and a summary of evidence as set forth in rule 10787.

Note: Authority cited: Sections 133, 5307, 5309 and 5708, Labor Code. Reference: Sections 5708 and 5709, Labor Code.

History: 1. Renumbering and amendment of former section 10541 to section 10761 filed 12-17-2019; operative 1-1-2020. Submitted to OAL for printing only pursuant to Government Code section 11351 (Register 2019, No. 51).

Ref.: Hanna § 26.04[1][c].

§10762. Reporters' Notes. [Repealed]

Note: Authority cited: Section 133 and 5307, Labor Code. Reference: Section 14755, Government Code; and Section 5708, Labor Code.

History: 1. Amendment of first paragraph and Note filed 12-19-2002; operative 1-1-2003. Submitted to OAL for printing only pursuant to Government Code section 11351 (Register 2002, No. 51).

2. Repealer filed 11-17-2008; operative 11-17-2008. Submitted to OAL for printing only (Register 2008, No. 47).

§10770. Filing and Service of Lien Claims. [Repealed]

Note: Authority cited: Sections 133, 5307, 5309 and 5708, Labor Code. Reference: Sections 4903, 4903.05, 4903.06, 4903.8, 4903.1, 4903.4, 4903.5, 4903.6, 4904, 4603.2, 4603.3, 4603.6, 4610.5, 4610.6, 4616.3, 4616.4, 4622 and 5813, Labor Code; and Sections 9792.5, 9794, 9795.4, 10561 and 10770.5, title 8, California Code of Regulations.

History: 1. Amendment exempt from OAL review pursuant to Government Code section 11351 filed 12-19-90; operative 1-1-91 (Register 91, No. 7).

2. Amendment filed 12-23-93; operative 1-1-94. Submitted to OAL for printing only pursuant to Government Code section 11351 (Register 93, No. 52).

3. Amendment filed 12-19-2002; operative 1-1-2003. Submitted to OAL for printing only pursuant to Government Code section 11351 (Register 2002, No. 51).

4. Amendment of section and Note filed 11-17-2008; operative 11-17-2008. Submitted to OAL for printing only (Register 2008, No. 47).

5. Amendment of section heading, section and Note filed 5-21-2012; operative 5-21-2012 pursuant to Government Code section 11343.4. Submitted to OAL for printing only pursuant to Government Code 11351 (Register 2012, No. 21).

6. Amendment of section and Note filed 9-23-2013; operative 10-23-2013. Submitted as a file and print by the Workers' Compensation Appeals Board pursuant to Government Code section 11351 (Register 2013, No. 39).

7. Amendment of subsections (c)(2)-(3) filed 10-15-2014; operative 1-1-2015. Submitted to OAL for printing only pursuant to Government Code section 11351 (Register 2014, No. 42).

8. Editorial correction of History 8 (Register 2017, No. 8).

9. Amendment of subsections (a)(3)(A)-(B), repealer of subsection (c)(3), subsection renumbering, amendment of newly designated subsections (c)(5) and (c)(7) and subsections (d)(1), (d)(1)(C) and (*l*) and amendment of Note filed 2-24-2017; operative 3-26-2017 pursuant to Government Code section 11343.4(b)(3). Sub-

mitted as a file and print to OAL pursuant to Government Code section 11351 (Register 2017, No. 8).

10. Repealer of article 13 heading and renumbering of former section 10770.5 to section 10863 filed 12-17-2019; operative 1-1-2020. Submitted to OAL for printing only pursuant to Government Code section 11351 (Register 2019, No. 51).

§10770.1. Lien Conferences and Lien Trials. [Repealed]

Note: Authority cited: Sections 133, 5307, 5309 and 5708, Labor Code. Reference: Sections 4903, 4903.05, 4903.06, 4903.1, 4903.4, 4903.5, 4903.6, 4904, 5502 and 5502.5, Labor Code; Sections 351, 352, 451 and 452, Evidence Code; and Sections 10250, 10205.16, 10301(u), 10301(z), 10364(a), 10561, 10629 and 10770-10772, title 8, California Code of Regulations.

History: 1. New section filed 5-21-2012; operative 5-21-2012 pursuant to Government Code section 11343.4. Submitted to OAL for printing only pursuant to Government Code 11351 (Register 2012, No. 21).

2. Amendment of section and Note filed 9-23-2013; operative 10-23-2013. Submitted as a file and print by the Workers' Compensation Appeals Board pursuant to Government Code section 11351 (Register 2013, No. 39).

3. Amendment of subsections (a)(1), (c)(1)(A), (e) and (i) filed 10-15-2014; operative 1-1-2015. Submitted to OAL for printing only pursuant to Government Code section 11351 (Register 2014, No. 42).

4. Editorial correction of History 3 (Register 2017, No. 8).

5. Repealer filed 12-17-2019; operative 1-1-2020. Submitted to OAL for printing only pursuant to Government Code section 11351 (Register 2019, No. 51).

§10770.5. Verification to Filing of Lien Claim or Application by Lien Claimant. [Renumbered]

Note: Authority cited: Sections 133, 5307, 5309 and 5708, Labor Code. Reference: Sections 4903 and 4903.6, Labor Code.

History: 1. New section filed 11-17-2008; operative 11-17-2008. Submitted to OAL for printing only (Register 2008, No. 47).

2. Amendment filed 9-23-2013; operative 10-23-2013. Submitted as a file and print by the Workers' Compensation Appeals Board pursuant to Government Code section 11351 (Register 2013, No. 39).

3. Renumbering of former section 10770.5 to section 10863 filed 12-17-2019; operative 1-1-2020. Submitted to OAL for printing only pursuant to Government Code section 11351 (Register 2019, No. 51).

§10770.6. Verification to Filing of Declaration of Readiness By or on Behalf of Lien Claimant. [Renumbered]

Note: Authority cited: Sections 133, 5307, 5309 and 5708, Labor Code. Reference: Sections 4903 and 4903.6, Labor Code.

History: 1. New section filed 11-17-2008; operative 11-17-2008. Submitted to OAL for printing only (Register 2008, No. 47).

2. Amendment filed 9-23-2013; operative 10-23-2013. Submitted as a file and print by the Workers' Compensation Appeals Board pursuant to Government Code section 11351 (Register 2013, No. 39).

3. Renumbering of former section 10770.6 to section 10874 filed 12-17-2019; operative 1-1-2020. Submitted to OAL for printing only pursuant to Government Code section 11351 (Register 2019, No. 51).

§10770.7. Requirement for Liens Filed Before January 1, 2017. [Repealed]

Note: Authority cited: Sections 133, 5307 and 5708, Labor Code. Reference: Sections 4903 and 4903.05, and Labor Code; and Sections 9792.5, 9794, 9795.4, 10390 et seq., 10561, 10770 and 10770.5, title 8, California Code of Regulations.

History: 1. New section filed 2-24-2017; operative 3-26-2017 pursuant to Government Code section 11343.4(b)(3). Submitted as a file and print to OAL pursuant to Government Code section 11351 (Register 2017, No. 8).

2. Repealer filed 12-17-2019; operative 1-1-2020. Submitted to OAL for printing only pursuant to Government Code section 11351 (Register 2019, No. 51).

§10771. Medical–Legal Expense. [Repealed]

Note: Authority cited: Sections 133 and 5307, Labor Code. Reference: Sections 4903 and 4903.1, Labor Code.

History: 1. Amendment exempt from OAL review pursuant to Government Code section 11351 filed 12-19-90; operative 1-1-91 (Register 91, No. 7).

2. Amendment of section and Note filed 12-19-2002; operative 1-1-2003. Submitted to OAL for printing only pursuant to Government Code section 11351 (Register 2002, No. 51).

3. Repealer filed 11-17-2008; operative 11-17-2008. Submitted to OAL for printing only (Register 2008, No. 47).

§10772. Unemployment Compensation Disability Liens. [Repealed]

Note: Authority cited: Sections 133 and 5307, Labor Code. Reference: Sections 4903 and 4904, Labor Code.

History: 1. Amendment of last paragraph filed 12-19-2002; operative 1-1-2003. Submitted to OAL for printing only pursuant to Government Code section 11351 (Register 2002, No. 51).

2. Repealer filed 12-17-2019; operative 1-1-2020. Submitted to OAL for printing only pursuant to Government Code section 11351 (Register 2019, No. 51).

§10773. Law Firm Employees. [Repealed]

Note: Authority cited: Sections 133 and 5307, Labor Code. Reference: Section 4907, Labor Code.

History: 1. New section filed 12-19-2002; operative 1-1-2003. Submitted to OAL for printing only pursuant to Government Code section 11351 (Register 2002, No. 51). For prior history, see Register 96, No. 43.

2. Repealer filed 12-17-2019; operative 1-1-2020. Submitted to OAL for printing only pursuant to Government Code section 11351 (Register 2019, No. 51).

§10774. Substitution or Dismissal of Attorneys. [Renumbered]

Note: Authority cited: Sections 133, 5307, Labor Code. Reference: Sections 4903, 4906, Labor Code.

History: 1. Repealer of article 14 heading and renumbering of former section 10774 to section 10402 filed 12-17-2019; operative 1-1-2020. Submitted to OAL for printing only pursuant to Government Code section 11351 (Register 2019, No. 51).

§10774.5. Notices of Representation, Change of Representation, and Non-Representation for Lien Claimants. [Repealed]

Note: Authority: Sections 133, 5307, 5309 and 5708, Labor Code. Reference: Sections 4903(a), 4903.6(b), 4906, 4907, 5501, and 5700; Sections 284, 285 and 286, Code of Civil Procedure; and Sections 10774 and 10779, title 8, California Code of Regulations.

History: 1. New section filed 9-23-2013; operative 10-23-2013. Submitted as a file and print by the Workers' Compensation Appeals Board pursuant to Government Code section 11351 (Register 2013, No. 39).

2. Repealer filed 12-17-2019; operative 1-1-2020. Submitted to OAL for printing only pursuant to Government Code section 11351 (Register 2019, No. 51).

§10775. Reasonable Attorney's Fee. [Renumbered]

Note: Authority cited: Sections 133 and 5307, Labor Code. Reference: Sections 4903 and 4906, Labor Code.

History: 1. Amendment exempt from OAL review pursuant to Government Code section 11351 filed 12-19-90; operative 1-1-91 (Register 91, No. 7).

2. Amendment of first and penultimate paragraphs filed 12-19-2002; operative 1-1-2003. Submitted to OAL for printing only pursuant to Government Code section 11351 (Register 2002, No. 51).

3. Renumbering of former section 10775 to section 10844 filed 12-17-2019; operative 1-1-2020. Submitted to OAL for printing only pursuant to Government Code section 11351 (Register 2019, No. 51).

§10776. Approval of Attorney's Fee. [Renumbered]

Note: Authority cited: Sections 133 and 5307, Labor Code. Reference: Sections 4903 and 4906, Labor Code.

History: 1. Amendment of subsections (a)-(b) filed 12-19-2002; operative 1-1-2003. Submitted to OAL for printing only pursuant to Government Code section 11351 (Register 2002, No. 51).

2. Renumbering of former section 10776 to section 10840 filed 12-17-2019; operative 1-1-2020. Submitted to OAL for printing only pursuant to Government Code section 11351 (Register 2019, No. 51).

§10778. Request for Increase of Attorney's Fee. [Renumbered]

Note: Authority cited: Sections 133, 5307, Labor Code. Reference: Sections 4903, 4906, Labor Code.

History: 1. Renumbering of former section 10778 to section 10842 filed 12-17-2019; operative 1-1-2020. Submitted to OAL for printing only pursuant to Government Code section 11351 (Register 2019, No. 51).

§10779. Disbarred and Suspended Attorneys. [Renumbered]

Note: Authority cited: Sections 133, 5307, 5309 and 5708, Labor Code. Reference: Section 4907, Labor Code; and Section 6126, Business and Professions Code.

History: 1. Amendment of first paragraph filed 12-19-2002; operative 1-1-2003. Submitted to OAL for printing only pursuant to Government Code section 11351 (Register 2002, No. 51).

2. Amendment of section and Note filed 11-17-2008; operative 11-17-2008. Submitted to OAL for printing only (Register 2008, No. 47).

3. Renumbering of former section 10779 to section 10445 filed 12-17-2019; operative 1-1-2020. Submitted to OAL for printing only pursuant to Government Code section 11351 (Register 2019, No. 51).

§10780. Dismissal Orders. [Renumbered]

Note: Authority cited: Sections 133 and 5307, Labor Code.

History: 1. Repealer and new section filed 12-23-93; operative 1-1-94. Submitted to OAL for printing only pursuant to Government Code section 11351 (Register 93, No. 52).

2. Amendment of section and Note filed 12-19-2002; operative 1-1-2003. Submitted to OAL for printing only pursuant to Government Code section 11351 (Register 2002, No. 51).

3. Repealer of article 15 heading and renumbering of former section 10780 to section 10850 filed 12-17-2019; operative 1-1-2020. Submitted to OAL for printing only pursuant to Government Code section 11351 (Register 2019, No. 51).

§10782. Expedited Hearings.

(a) Where injury to any part or parts of the body is accepted as compensable by the employer, a party is entitled to an expedited hearing and decision upon the filing of an Application for Adjudication of Claim and a Declaration of Readiness to Proceed pursuant to rule 10625 establishing a bona fide, good faith dispute pursuant to Labor Code section 5502(b).

(b) An expedited hearing may be set upon request where injury to any part or parts of the body is accepted as compensable by the employer and the issues include medical treatment or temporary disability for a disputed body part or parts.

(c) A workers' compensation judge assigned to a case may re-designate the expedited hearing as a mandatory settlement conference, receive a Pre-Trial Conference Statement pursuant to Labor Code section 5502, close discovery and schedule the case for trial on the issues presented, if the workers' compensation judge determines that the case is not appropriate for expedited determination.

(d) Grounds for the re-designation of an expedited hearing include, but are not limited to, cases where the direct and cross-examination of the applicant will be prolonged, or where there are multiple witnesses who will offer extensive testimony.

(e) The parties are expected to submit for decision all matters properly in issue at a single trial and to produce all necessary evidence, including witnesses, documents, medical reports, payroll statements and all other matters considered essential in the proof of a party's claim or defense.

Note: Authority cited: Sections 133, 5307 and 5502, Labor Code. Reference: Section 5502, Labor Code.

History: 1. New section filed 11-17-2008; operative 11-17-2008. Submitted to OAL for printing only (Register 2008, No. 47).

2. Renumbering of former section 10782 to section 10430 and renumbering of former section 10552 to section 10782, including amendment of section heading and section, filed 12-17-2019; operative 1-1-2020. Submitted to OAL for printing only pursuant to Government Code section 11351 (Register 2019, No. 51).

Ref.: Hanna §§ 5.02[2][c], 5.07[3][a], 22.05[6][b][iii], [iv], 24.01[4], 24.11[1][c], 25.09[2], 25.20[4], 26.02[1]; Herlick Handbook § 14.8.

§10785. Priority Conferences.

(a) A priority conference shall be set upon the filing of a Declaration of Readiness to Proceed requesting a priority conference that shows that:

(1) The applicant is represented by an attorney and the issues in dispute include employment and/or injury arising out of and in the course of employment; or

(2) The applicant claims to have been employed by an illegally uninsured employer and the issues in dispute include employment and/or injury arising out of and in the course of employment.

(b) To the extent possible, all priority and status conferences in a case shall be conducted by the same workers' compensation judge. When discovery is complete, or when the workers' compensation judge determines that the parties have had sufficient time to complete reasonable discovery, the case shall be set for trial as expeditiously as possible.

Note: Authority cited: Sections 133, 5307 and 5502, Labor Code. Reference: Section 5502, Labor Code.

History: 1. New section filed 11-17-2008; operative 11-17-2008. Submitted to OAL for printing only (Register 2008, No. 47).

2. Repealer of former section 10785 and renumbering former section 10555 to section 10785, including amendment of section heading and section, filed 12-17-2019; operative 1-1-2020. Submitted to OAL for printing only pursuant to Government Code section 11351 (Register 2019, No. 51).

Ref.: Hanna §§ 24.11[1][c], 26.02[1]; Herlick Handbook § 14.30.

§10786. Determination of Medical-Legal Expense Dispute.

(a) Within 60 days of service of a medical-legal provider objection to a denial of all or a portion of the medical-legal provider's billing pursuant to Labor Code section 4622(c), the defendant shall file and serve a petition for determination of medical-legal expenses and a Declaration of Readiness to Proceed. Upon filing of a Declaration of Readiness to Proceed, the medical-legal provider shall be added to the official address record.

(b) If a defendant has failed to file and serve a petition for determination of medical-legal expenses and a Declaration of Readiness in compliance with subdivision (a), a medical-legal provider may file and serve a petition for reimbursement of medical-legal expenses and a Declaration of Readiness to Proceed. Upon filing of a petition for reimbursement of medical-legal expenses and a Declaration of Readiness to Proceed, the medical-legal provider shall be added to the official address record.

(c) Upon receipt of a Declaration of Readiness in accordance with the provisions of subdivisions (a) and (b) of this rule, the matter shall be set for either a status conference or a mandatory settlement conference, in the discretion of the workers' compensation judge.

(d) Notwithstanding any other provision of this rule, if there is a threshold issue relating to the case in chief that would entirely defeat the medical-legal expense claim that must be determined prior to adjudicating the medical-legal expense claim dispute, the Workers' Compensation Appeals Board may defer hearing and determining the medical-legal expense claim dispute until the underlying claim of the employee or dependent has been resolved or abandoned.

(e) A defendant shall be deemed to have waived all objections to a medical-legal provider's billing, other than compliance with Labor Code sections 4620 and 4621, if:

(1) The provider submitted a properly documented billing to the defendant and, within 60 days thereafter, the defendant failed to serve an explanation of review (EOR) that complies with Labor Code section 4603.3 and any applicable regulations adopted by the Administrative Director; or

(2) The defendant failed to make payment consistent with an explanation of review (EOR) that complies with Labor Code section 4603.3 and any applicable regulations adopted by the Administrative Director; or

(3) The provider submitted a timely and proper request for a second review to the defendant and, within 14 days thereafter, the defendant failed to serve a final written determination that complies with any applicable regulations adopted by the Administrative Director; or

(4) The defendant failed to make payment consistent with a final written determination that complies with any applicable regulations adopted by the Administrative Director.

(f) A defendant shall be deemed to have waived any objections to a medical-legal provider's billing, other than the amount payable pursuant to the fee schedule(s) in effect on the date the services were rendered and compliance with Labor Code sections 4620 and 4621, if the provider submitted a timely objection to the defendant's EOR regarding a dispute other than the amount payable and the defendant failed to file and serve a petition for determination of medical-legal expenses and a Declaration of Readiness as required by Labor Code section 4622 and subdivision (a) of this rule.

(g) A medical-legal provider's bill will be deemed satisfied, and neither the employee nor the employer shall be liable for any further payment, if the defendant issued a timely and proper EOR and made payment consistent with that EOR within 60 days after receipt of the provider's written billing and report and the provider failed to make a timely and proper request for second review in the form prescribed by the Rules of the Administrative Director within 90 days after service of the EOR.

(h) A medical-legal provider will be deemed to have waived any objection based on the amount payable under the fee schedule(s) in effect on the date the services were rendered if, within 14 days after receipt of the provider's request for second review, the defendant issued a timely and proper final written determination and made payment consistent with that determination and the provider failed to request IBR within 30 days after service of this second review determination.

(i) Bad Faith Actions or Tactics:

(1) If the Workers' Compensation Appeals Board determines that, as a result of bad faith actions or tactics, a defendant failed to comply with the requirements, timelines and procedures set forth in Labor Code sections 4622, 4603.3 and 4603.6 and the related Rules of the Administrative Director, the defendant shall be liable for the medical-legal provider's reasonable attorney's fees and costs and for sanctions under Labor Code section 5813 and rule 10421. The amount of the attorney's fees, costs and sanctions payable shall be determined by the Workers'

Compensation Appeals Board; however, for bad faith actions or tactics occurring on or after October 23, 2013, the monetary sanctions shall not be less than $500.00. These attorney's fees, costs and monetary sanctions shall be in addition to any penalties and interest that may be payable under Labor Code section 4622 or other applicable provisions of law, and in addition to any lien filing fee, lien activation fee or IBR fee that, by statute, the defendant might be obligated to reimburse to the medical-legal provider.

(2) If the Workers' Compensation Appeals Board determines that, as a result of bad faith actions or tactics, a medical-legal provider has improperly asserted that a defendant failed to comply with the requirements, timelines and procedures set forth in Labor Code sections 4622 and 4603.6 and the related Rules of the Administrative Director, the medical-legal provider shall be liable for the defendant's reasonable attorney's fees and costs and for sanctions under Labor Code section 5813 and rule 10421. The amount of the attorney's fees, costs and sanctions payable shall be determined by the Workers' Compensation Appeals Board; however, for bad faith actions or tactics occurring on or after October 23, 2013, the monetary sanctions shall not be less than $500.00.

Note: Authority cited: Sections 133, 4622, 4627 and 5307, Labor Code. Reference: Sections 4603.3, 4603.6, 4622 and 5813, Labor Code.

History: 1. New section filed 12-17-2019; operative 1-1-2020. Submitted to OAL for printing only pursuant to Government Code section 11351 (Register 2019, No. 51).

Ref.: Hanna §§ 5.08[2][c], 22.09[1].

§10787. Trials.

(a) The parties shall submit for decision all matters properly in issue at a single trial and produce at the trial all necessary evidence, including witnesses, documents, medical reports, payroll statements and all other matters considered essential in the proof of a party's claim or defense. However, a workers' compensation judge may order that the issues in a case be bifurcated and tried separately upon a showing of good cause.

(b) Unless already filed in EAMS, the parties shall have all proposed exhibits available at trial for review by and filing with the trial workers' compensation judge.

(c) Minutes of hearing and summary of evidence shall be prepared at the conclusion of each trial and filed in the record of proceedings. They shall include:

(1) The names of the commissioners, deputy commissioner or workers' compensation judge, reporter, the parties present, attorneys or other agents appearing therefor and witnesses sworn;

(2) The place and date of said trial;

(3) The admissions and stipulations, the issues and matters in controversy, a descriptive listing of all exhibits received for identification or in evidence (with the identity of the party offering the same);

(4) The disposition, and if the disposition is an order taking off calendar or a continuance, the reasons for the order which shall include the time and action, if any, required for submission;

(5) A summary of the evidence required by Labor Code section 5313 that shall include a fair and unbiased summary of the testimony given by each witness;

(6) If motion pictures are shown, a brief summary of their contents or a stipulation that parties waive a summary; and

(7) A fair statement of any offers of proof.

(d) Notwithstanding subdivision (c), the summary of evidence need not be filed upon issuance of a stipulated order, decision or award.

Note: Authority cited: Sections 133 and 5307, Labor Code. Reference: Sections 5708 and 5313, Labor Code.

History: 1. New section filed 12-17-2019; operative 1-1-2020. Submitted to OAL for printing only pursuant to Government Code section 11351 (Register 2019, No. 51).

Ref.: Hanna § 26.06[3]; Herlick Handbook §§ 14.31, 14.34.

§10788. Petition for Automatic Reassignment of Trial or Expedited Hearing to Another Workers' Compensation Judge.

A party shall be entitled to automatic reassignment of a trial or expedited hearing to another workers' compensation judge in accordance with the provisions of this rule. Consolidated cases are to be considered as one case within the meaning of this rule.

(a) An injured worker shall be entitled to one reassignment of a workers' compensation judge for trial or expedited hearing. The defendants shall be entitled to one reassignment of a workers' compensation judge for a trial or expedited hearing, which may be exercised by any of them. This rule is not applicable to conference hearings. In no event shall any motion or petition for reassignment be entertained after the swearing of the first witness at a trial or expedited hearing.

(b) If the parties are first notified of the identity of the workers' compensation judge assigned for trial at a mandatory settlement conference, at a status conference, at a lien conference, at a priority conference or upon reassignment at the time of trial, to exercise the right to automatic reassignment a party must make an oral motion immediately upon learning the name of the workers' compensation judge to whom the case has been assigned for trial. The motion shall be acted upon immediately by the presiding workers' compensation judge.

(c) If the parties are first notified of the identity of the workers' compensation judge assigned for trial or expedited hearing by a notice of trial served by mail, to exercise the right to automatic reassignment a party must file a petition requesting reassignment not more than 5 days after receipt of the notice of trial or expedited hearing. The presiding workers' compensation judge shall rule on any petition for automatic reassignment.

(d) If a petition for automatic reassignment is granted and results in a new trial date, a new notice of trial or expedited hearing shall be served. Unless required for the convenience of the Workers' Compensation Appeals Board, no continuance shall be granted by reason of a petition or motion under this rule. If a continuance is granted, another trial or expedited hearing shall be scheduled as early as possible.

(e) If a party files a petition or makes a motion for automatic reassignment and no other workers' compensation judge is available in the office, the assignment shall be made by a deputy commissioner of the Appeals Board.

Note: Authority cited: Section 5307, Labor Code. Reference: Section 5310, Labor Code.

History: 1. Renumbering and amendment of former section 10453 to section 10788 filed 12-17-2019; operative 1-1-2020. Submitted to OAL for printing only pursuant to Government Code section 11351 (Register 2019, No. 51).

Ref.: Hanna § 26.03[1A]; Herlick Handbook § 14.19.

§10789. Walk-Through Documents.

(a) The following documents may be submitted on a walk-through basis without a party filing a Declaration of Readiness to Proceed or the Workers' Compensation Appeals Board serving a notice of hearing:

(1) Compromise and Releases;

(2) Stipulations with Request for Award;

(3) Petitions for attorney's fees for representation of the applicant at a deposition;

(4) Petitions to compel attendance at a medical examination or deposition; and

(5) Petitions for Costs pursuant to rule 10545.

(b) The following procedures shall be followed for filing walk-through documents:

(1) A walk-through settlement document (i.e., a Compromise and Release or a Stipulations with Request for Award), and all supporting medical reports and other supporting documents not previously filed, shall be filed directly with the workers' compensation judge at the date and time of the walk-through. Permanent and stationary medical or medical-legal reports shall be indicated as such. In addition, each walk-through settlement document (i.e., a Compromise and Release or a Stipulations with Request for Award) shall be accompanied by a proof of service showing that the settlement document was served on all other parties to the settlement, on any defendant not executing the settlement who may be liable for the payment of additional compensation, and on all lien claimants whose liens have not been resolved. A case opening settlement document being submitted for a walk-through shall be submitted no later than noon (12:00 p.m.) of the court day before any action on the walk-through, and shall be designated as a walk-through document. All documents in support of the settlement document shall be submitted at the walk-through with the assigned workers' compensation judge.

(2) A walk-through petition (i.e., a petition for deposition attorney's fees, a petition for costs or a petition to compel attendance at a medical examination or deposition) and all other documents relating to the walk-through petition, including any supporting documentation shall be filed directly with the workers' compensation judge at the date and time of the walk-through. The party presenting the walk-through petition shall use the appropriate form, document cover sheet, and document separator sheet. In addition, at the date and time of the walk-through, the party filing the walk-through petition shall file a proof of service directly to the workers' compensation judge, as follows:

(A) For a petition for attorney's fees for representation of the applicant at a deposition, a proof of service showing service on the injured worker and the defendant alleged to be liable for paying the fees.

(B) For a petition to compel attendance at a medical examination or deposition, a proof of service showing service on the injured worker, the injured worker's attorney and all defendants.

(c) Each district office shall have a designee of the presiding workers' compensation judge available to assign walk-through cases from 8:00 a.m. to 11:00 a.m. and 1:00 p.m. to 4:00 p.m. on court days.

(d) When appearing for the walk-through proceeding, the party filing the walk-through document shall appear before the district office staff person designated by the presiding workers' compensation judge to assign the walk-through document to a workers' compensation judge. The filing party shall then appear before the assigned workers' compensation judge. If the assigned workers' compensation judge is unavailable for any reason, the filing party shall then proceed to the presiding workers' compensation judge for possible reassignment to another workers' compensation judge.

(e) A workers' compensation judge who is presented with a walk-through settlement document shall approve it, disapprove it, suspend action on it, or accept it for later review and action.

(f) A walk-through document may be acted on only by a workers' compensation judge at the district office that has venue. If an injured worker has existing cases at two or more district offices that have venue, a walk-through document may be filed at any office having venue over an existing case that is a subject of the walk-through document. An existing case is a case that has been filed and assigned a case number prior to the filing of the walk-through document.

(g) A walk-through document may be acted on by any workers' compensation judge except as follows:

(1) If a workers' compensation judge has taken testimony, any walk-through document in that case must be acted on by the judge who took testimony if that workers' compensation judge works at the district office to which the case is assigned, unless the presiding workers' compensation judge allows it to be acted on by another workers' compensation judge.

(2) If a workers' compensation judge has reviewed a document and declined to approve it, a walk-through document in that case must be acted on by the same workers' compensation judge, if that workers' compensation judge works at the district office to which the case is assigned, unless the presiding workers' compensation judge allows it to be acted on by another workers' compensation judge.

(h) A workers' compensation judge who is presented with a walk-through petition for attorney's fees, petition for costs or petition to compel attendance shall issue an order in compliance with rule 10832.

Note: Authority cited: Sections 133 and 5307, Labor Code. Reference: Sections 4053, 4054, 5001, 5002, 5702 and 5710, Labor Code.

History: 1. Renumbering and amendment of former section 10417 to section 10789 filed 12-17-2019; operative 1-1-2020. Submitted to OAL for printing only pursuant to Government Code section 11351 (Register 2019, No. 51).

Ref.: Hanna §§ 23.11[2], 23.14[2][m], 25.08[4]; Herlick Handbook §§ 14.8, 14.20, 14.21, 14.30A, 14.44.

§10790. Interpreters.

It shall be the responsibility of any party producing a witness requiring an interpreter to arrange for the presence of a qualified interpreter. Subject to the rules of the Administrative Director, the Workers' Compensation Appeals Board may in any case appoint an interpreter and fix the interpreter's compensation.

Note: Authority: Sections 130, 133, 5307 and 5708, Labor Code. Reference: Sections 4600, 4621, 5710 and 5811, Labor Code.

History: 1. Renumbering of former section 10564 to section 10790, including amendment of section and Note, filed 12-17-2019; operative 1-1-2020. Submitted to OAL for printing only pursuant to Government Code section 11351 (Register 2019, No. 51).

Ref.: Hanna §§ 26.05[3], 27.01[8][a].

ARTICLE 14
Record of Proceedings

§10800. Transcripts.

Testimony taken at hearings will not be transcribed except upon the written request of a party accompanied by the fee prescribed in the Rules of the Administrative Director, or unless ordered by a commissioner, a deputy commissioner or presiding workers' compensation judge. Any written request shall be served on all parties.

Note: Authority cited: Sections 133, 5307, 5309 and 5708, Labor Code. Reference: Sections 5300, 5301, 5309, 5700, 5701 and 5708, Labor Code; and Section 703.5, Evidence Code.

History: 1. New article 14 heading and renumbering and amendment of former section 10740 to section 10800 filed 12-17-2019; operative 1-1-2020. Submitted to OAL for printing only pursuant to Government Code section 11351 (Register 2019, No. 51).

Ref.: Hanna § 23.12[4].

§10803. Record of Proceedings Maintained in Adjudication File.

(a) The Workers' Compensation Appeals Board's adjudication file shall consist of:

(1) All documents filed by any party, attorney or other agent of record, and as provided in rule 10205.4; and

(2) The record of proceedings, which consists of: the pleadings, minutes of hearing, summaries of evidence, certified transcripts, proofs of service, admitted evidence, exhibits identified but not admitted as evidence, notices, petitions, briefs, findings, orders, decisions and awards, opinions on decision, reports and recommendations on petitions for reconsideration and/or removal, and the arbitrator's file, if any. Each of these documents is part of the record of proceedings, whether maintained in paper or electronic form. Documents that are in the adjudication file but have not been received or offered as evidence are not part of the record of proceedings.

(b) Upon approval of a Compromise and Release or Stipulations with Request for Award, all medical reports that have been filed as of the date of approval shall be deemed admitted in evidence and part of the record of proceedings.

Note: Authority cited: Sections 133, 5307, 5309 and 5708, Labor Code. Reference: Sections 126 and 5708, Labor Code.

History: 1. New section filed 12-17-2019; operative 1-1-2020. Submitted to OAL for printing only pursuant to Government Code section 11351 (Register 2019, No. 51).

Ref.: Hanna § 23.12[3]; Herlick Handbook § 14.5A.

§10807. Inspection of Workers' Compensation Appeals Board Records.

(a) The records and files of the Workers' Compensation Appeals Board shall not be taken from its offices on informal request, in response to a subpoena duces tecum, or in response to any order issued by any other court or tribunal.

(b) Except as precluded by Civil Code section 1798.24 or Government Code section 6254, certified copies of portions of the records desired by litigants shall be delivered upon payment of fees as provided in the Rules of the Administrative Director.

(c) Except as provided by rules 10208.6 and 10813, or as ordered by the presiding workers' compensation judge or the Appeals Board, the adjudication case files of the Workers' Compensation Appeals Board may be inspected in accordance with the provisions of rules 10208.5 and 10208.6.

Note: Authority cited: Sections 133, 5307, 5309 and 5708, Labor Code. Reference: Sections 126, 127, 5811 and 5955, Labor Code; Section 1798.24, Civil Code; and Section 6254, Government Code.

History: 1. New section filed 12-17-2019; operative 1-1-2020. Submitted to OAL for printing only pursuant to Government Code section 11351 (Register 2019, No. 51).

Ref.: Hanna § 23.12[3a].

§10811. Destruction of Records.

Except as otherwise provided by these rules, or as ordered by a workers' compensation judge or the Appeals Board, the adjudication case files of the Workers' Compensation Appeals Board shall be retained, returned, and destroyed in accordance with the provisions of rule 10208.7.

Note: Authority cited: Sections 133, 5307, 5309 and 5708, Labor Code. Reference: Section 135, Labor Code.

History: 1. Renumbering and amendment of former section 10755 to section 10811 filed 12-17-2019; operative 1-1-2020. Submitted to OAL for printing only pursuant to Government Code section 11351 (Register 2019, No. 51).

Ref.: Hanna § 23.12[3d].

§10813. Sealed Documents.

(a) The presiding workers' compensation judge or the Appeals Board may order sealed medical reports, medical records or other documents filed in a case containing references to or discussions of mental or emotional health of any person, sexual habits or practice, use of or addiction to alcohol or other drugs, or other matters of similar character. Sealed documents shall not be made available for public inspection except by order of the presiding workers' compensation judge or the Appeals Board upon a showing of good cause.

(b) A party requesting that documents be sealed shall file a petition to seal documents or portions thereof with either the district office having venue or with the Appeals Board, if the matter is pending there.

(1) Any petition to seal documents shall demonstrate good cause and shall be accompanied by a declaration containing facts sufficient to justify the sealing consistent with subdivision (c) of this rule.

(2) Documents that have not been filed prior to the petition to seal may be lodged with the Workers' Compensation Appeals Board concurrently with the filing of the petition to seal. A document shall be lodged in a sealed envelope with a coversheet that includes the ADJ number, a general description of the documents and a statement that "the documents are lodged pending the outcome of a petition to seal."

(3) If necessary to prevent disclosure, the petition, any opposition and any supporting documents must be filed in a public redacted version and lodged in a complete version conditionally under seal.

(4) If the presiding worker's compensation judge or the Appeals Board denies the petition to seal, the clerk shall return the lodged record to the submitting party and shall not place it in the adjudication file.

(5) Subsequently-filed documents shall not disclose material contained in a document previously sealed, conditionally sealed, or subject to a pending petition to seal.

(c) The presiding workers' compensation judge or the Appeals Board may order that a document be filed under seal or sealed only after expressly finding facts that establish:

(1) There exists an overriding public interest that overcomes the right of public access to the record;

(2) The overriding public interest supports sealing the record;

(3) A substantial probability exists that the overriding public interest will be prejudiced if the record is not sealed;

(4) The proposed sealing is narrowly tailored; and

(5) No less restrictive means exists to achieve the overriding public interest.

(d) Documents may be ordered sealed on the motion of the presiding workers' compensation judge or the Appeals Board if the injured employee is unrepresented or other good cause exists for sealing the documents. All parties shall be given notice and opportunity to be heard. After the issuance of a notice of intention to seal documents, the documents shall be lodged conditionally under seal pending the issuance of an order sealing the documents or an order finding no good cause to seal the documents.

(e)(1) An order sealing a document or documents shall be filed in the record of the proceedings. The order shall set forth the facts that support the findings and direct the sealing of only those documents and pages, or, if practicable, portions of those documents and pages containing the material that requires placement under seal.

(2) If the order directs that an entire document shall be sealed, and if the sealed document is contained in a paper adjudication file, the sealed document shall be placed in a sealed envelope, which shall be removed from the file before the file is made available for public inspection. If the sealed document is in an electronic adjudication file, the document shall be marked as sealed. No entirely sealed document in a paper file or an electronic file shall be available for public inspection.

(3) If the order directs that a portion or portions of a document be sealed, and if the partially sealed document is contained in a paper adjudication file, the partially sealed document shall be placed in a sealed envelope, however, a version of the document with the sealed portion redacted shall be made available for public inspection. If the sealed document is in an electronic adjudication file, a version of the document with the sealed portion redacted also shall be electronically maintained and shall be made available for public inspection.

(f) Sealed documents shall be made available for inspection by any party to the case or by their representative, subject to any reasonable conditions and limitations as the presiding workers' compensation judge or the Appeals Board may impose.

Note: Authority cited: Sections 133, 5307, 5309 and 5708, Labor Code. Reference: Section 5708, Labor Code; and Rule 2.551, California Rules of Court.

History: 1. Renumbering and amendment of former section 10754 to section 10813 filed 12-17-2019; operative 1-1-2020. Submitted to OAL for printing only pursuant to Government Code section 11351 (Register 2019, No. 51).

Ref.: Hanna § 23.12[3c]; Herlick Handbook § 14.5A.

§10818. Recording of Proceedings.

(a) For the purposes of this rule, "recording" means any photographing, recording, or broadcasting of trial level proceedings using video, film, audio, any digital media or other equipment.

(b) Except as provided in this rule, proceedings shall not be photographed, recorded, or broadcast. This rule does not prohibit the Division of Workers' Compensation (DWC) from photographing or videotaping sessions for judicial education or publications and is not intended to apply to closed-circuit television broadcasts solely within DWC or among DWC facilities if the broadcasts are controlled by DWC and DWC personnel.

(c) Recording shall be permitted only on written order by the assigned workers' compensation judge. The workers' compensation judge may permit, refuse or limit recording.

(1) Any person who wishes to record a proceeding shall make a written request to the assigned workers' compensation judge and shall serve the written request on all parties at least 10 business days before the proceeding commences unless good cause to shorten time is shown.

(2) The workers' compensation judge may hold a hearing on the request or rule on the request without a hearing.

(3) In ruling on the request, the workers' compensation judge shall consider the following factors:

(A) Importance of maintaining public trust and confidence in the workers' compensation system;

(B) Importance of promoting public access to the workers' compensation system;

(C) Parties' support of or opposition to the request;

(D) Nature of the case;

(E) Privacy rights of all participants in the proceeding, including witnesses;

(F) Effect on any minor who is a party, prospective witness, or other participant in the proceeding;

(G) Effect on any ongoing law enforcement activity in the case;

(H) Effect on any subsequent proceedings in the case;

(I) Effect of coverage on the willingness of witnesses to cooperate, including the risk that coverage will engender threats to the health or safety of any witness;

(J) Effect on excluded witnesses who would have access to the televised testimony of prior witnesses;

(K) Security and dignity of the trial level proceeding;

(L) Undue administrative or financial burden to DWC or participants;

(M) Interference with neighboring hearing rooms;

(N) Maintaining orderly conduct of the proceeding;

(O) Any other factor the workers' compensation judge deems relevant.

(4) The workers' compensation judge's ruling on the request to permit recording is not required to make findings or a statement of decision. The workers' compensation judge may condition the order permitting recording of the proceedings on the requestor's agreement to pay any increased costs incurred by DWC resulting from recording the proceeding (for example, for additional security). The requestor shall be responsible for ensuring that any person who records the trial level proceedings on their behalf know and follow the provisions of the order and this rule.

(5) The order permitting recordation may be modified or terminated on the workers' compensation judge's own motion or upon application to the workers' compensation judge without the necessity of a prior hearing or written findings. Notice of the application and any modification or termination ordered pursuant to the application shall be given to the parties and each person permitted by the previous order to record the proceeding.

(6) The workers' compensation judge shall not permit recording of the following:

(A) Proceedings held in chambers that are not transcribed by a hearing reporter;

(B) Proceedings closed to the public; and

(C) Conferences between an attorney and a client, witness, or aide, between attorneys, or between counsel and the workers' compensation judge at the bench, unless transcribed by a hearing reporter.

(7) The workers' compensation judge may require a demonstration that people and equipment comply with this rule. The workers' compensation judge may specify the placement of equipment to minimize disruption of the proceedings.

(8) The following rules shall apply to all recording:

(A) One video recording device and one still photographer shall be permitted.

(B) The equipment used shall not produce distracting sound or light. Signal lights or devices to show when equipment is operating shall not be visible.

(C) Microphones and wiring shall be unobtrusively located in places approved by the workers' compensation judge and shall be operated by one person.

(D) Operators shall not move equipment or enter or leave the courtroom while the proceeding is in session, or otherwise cause a distraction.

(E) Equipment or clothing shall not bear the insignia or marking of a media agency.

(9) If two or more people request recordation of a proceeding, they shall file a statement of agreed arrangements. If they are unable to agree, the workers' compensation judge may deny a request to record the proceeding.

(d) Any violation of this rule or an order made under this rule is an unlawful interference with the proceedings and may be the basis for an order terminating recording, a citation for contempt, or an order imposing monetary or other sanctions as provided by law.

(e) Notwithstanding (a) through (d), a workers' compensation judge may permit inconspicuous personal recording devices to be used by parties in a courtroom to make sound recordings as personal notes of the proceedings. A person proposing to use a recording device shall obtain advance permission from the workers' compensation judge before recording the proceeding. The recording shall not be used for any purpose other than as personal notes, and shall not constitute evidence as to any matter recorded. The right of any individual to use a personal recording device shall be suspended if, in the workers' compensation judge's sole discretion, it appears that:

(1) The continued recording of the proceedings will inhibit any party or witness from participation in the proceeding; or

(2) The recording is done in a manner that threatens to disrupt the proceeding.

(f) Only the stenographic recording provided by an Official Hearing Reporter shall be deemed the official recording of a proceeding.

Note: Authority cited: Sections 133, 5307, 5309 and 5708, Labor Code. Reference: Rule 1.150, California Rules of Court.

History: 1. Renumbering former section 10760 to section 10818, including amendment of section heading and section, filed 12-17-2019; operative 1-1-2020. Submitted to OAL for printing only pursuant to Government Code section 11351 (Register 2019, No. 51).

Ref.: Hanna § 26.02[4]; Herlick Handbook § 14.5.

§10820. When Certified Copies Will Issue.

(a) Certified copies of findings, awards and other final orders for the purpose of having judgment entered and execution issued by the clerk of a superior court shall be issued by the presiding workers' compensation judge only upon written request of the person seeking to have judgment entered and execution issued, or by their attorney or non-attorney representative, and upon payment of the fees prescribed by the Rules of the Administrative Director.

(b) Certified copies of such orders and awards against authorized insurance carriers, authorized self-insured employers, the State of California and all political subdivisions thereof shall be issued only upon receipt of a written request showing good cause therefor.

(c) Every request for a certified copy of any final order must state whether proceedings are pending on reconsideration or judicial review, whether a petition for reconsideration or a writ of review has been filed, and whether the decision, a certified copy of which is requested has become final.

(d) Nothing in these rules shall limit the power of the Workers' Compensation Appeals Board to issue a certified copy at any time upon its own motion without charge.

Note: Authority cited: Sections 133 and 5307, Labor Code. Reference: Sections 5806, 5807 and 5808, Labor Code.

History: 1. Amendment of section and Note filed 12-19-2002; operative 1-1-2003. Submitted to OAL for printing only pursuant to Government Code section 11351 (Register 2002, No. 51).

2. Repealer of article 16 heading and amendment of section filed 12-17-2019; operative 1-1-2020. Submitted to OAL for printing only pursuant to Government Code section 11351 (Register 2019, No. 51).

Ref.: Hanna § 27.10[3][a].

§10825. Withholding Certified Copies.

As an alternative to the issuance of an order staying execution, the Workers' Compensation Appeals Board may direct by order that no certified copy be issued. Such an order shall have the same effect as an order staying execution issued under similar circumstances.

(a) Before staying execution or issuing an order withholding issuance of a certified copy of an order, decision or award, the Workers' Compensation Appeals Board in its discretion may require the filing of a bond from an approved surety equivalent to twice the probable amount of liability in the case.

(b) The bond shall be filed in the record of the case.

Note: Authority cited: Sections 133 and 5307, Labor Code. Reference: Sections 130, 134, 5105, 5806, 5807, 5808, 5809, 6000, 6001 and 6002, Labor Code.

History: 1. Amendment of subsection (a) filed 12-17-2019; operative 1-1-2020. Submitted to OAL for printing only pursuant to Government Code section 11351 (Register 2019, No. 51).

§10828. Necessity for Bond. [Repealed]

Note: Authority cited: Sections 133 and 5307, Labor Code. Reference: Sections 5808, 5956, 6000, 6001 and 6002, Labor Code.

History: 1. Amendment of section and Note filed 12-19-2002; operative 1-1-2003. Submitted to OAL for printing only pursuant to Government Code section 11351 (Register 2002, No. 51).

2. Repealer filed 12-17-2019; operative 1-1-2020. Submitted to OAL for printing only pursuant to Government Code section 11351 (Register 2019, No. 51).

ARTICLE 15
Findings, Awards and Orders

§10832. Notices of Intention and Orders after Notices of Intention.

(a) The Workers' Compensation Appeals Board may issue a notice of intention for any proper purpose, including but not limited to:

(1) Allowing or disallowing a lien;

(2) Allowing or disallowing a petition for costs;

(3) Sanctioning a party;

(4) Submitting the matter on the record after a party fails to appear; or

(5) Dismissing an application.

(b) A Notice of Intention may be served by designated service in accordance with rule 10629.

(c) If an objection is filed within the time provided, the Workers' Compensation Appeals Board, in its discretion may:

(1) Sustain the objection;

(2) Issue an order consistent with the notice of intention together with an opinion on decision; or

(3) Set the matter for hearing.

(d) Any order issued after a notice of intention shall be served by the Workers' Compensation Appeals Board pursuant to rule 10628.

(e) An order with a clause rendering the order null and void if an objection is received is not a Notice of Intention and must be served by the Workers' Compensation Appeals Board.

Note: Authority cited: Sections 133 and 5307, Labor Code. Reference: Section 5307, Labor Code.

History: 1. New article 15 heading and new section filed 12-17-2019; operative 1-1-2020. Submitted to OAL for printing only pursuant to Government Code section 11351 (Register 2019, No. 51). For prior history, see Register 96, No. 43.

Ref.: Herlick Handbook § 14.43.

§10833. Minute Orders.

Interlocutory or interim orders, including but not limited to orders of dismissal of improper or unnecessary parties, may be entered upon the minutes of hearing and will become the order of the Workers' Compensation Appeal Board upon the filing thereof.

Note: Authority cited: Sections 133 and 5307, Labor Code. Reference: Section 5307.5, Labor Code.

History: 1. Renumbering and amendment of former section 10570 to section 10833 filed 12-17-2019; operative 1-1-2020. Submitted to OAL for printing only pursuant to Government Code section 11351 (Register 2019, No. 51).

Ref.: Herlick Handbook § 14.43.

§10835. Effect of Stipulations.

(a) Findings, awards and orders may be based upon stipulations of parties in open court or upon written stipulation signed by the parties.

(b) No finding shall be made contrary to a stipulation of the parties without giving the parties notice and an opportunity to be heard.

Note: Authority cited: Sections 133 and 5307, Labor Code. Reference: Section 5702, Labor Code.

History: 1. New section filed 12-17-2019; operative 1-1-2020. Submitted to OAL for printing only pursuant to Government Code section 11351 (Register 2019, No. 51).

Ref.: Hanna § 23.11[3]; Herlick Handbook §§ 14.38, 14.44.

§10840. Approval of Attorney's Fee by Workers' Compensation Appeals Board Required.

(a) No attorney or agent shall request, demand or accept any money from a worker or dependent of a worker for the purpose of representing the worker or dependent of a worker before the Workers' Compensation Appeals Board or in any appellate procedure related thereto until the fee has been approved or set by the Workers' Compensation Appeals Board or an appellate court.

(b) Any agreement between any attorney or agent and a worker or dependent of a worker for payment of a fee shall be submitted to the Workers' Compensation Appeals Board for approval within 10 days after the agreement is made.

Note: Authority cited: Sections 133 and 5307, Labor Code. Reference: Sections 4903 and 4906, Labor Code.

History: 1. Repealer and new section filed 12-16-92; operative 2-1-93 and exempt from OAL review pursuant to Government Code section 11351 (Register 92, No. 51).

2. Amendment of section heading and text filed 12-23-93; operative 1-1-94. Submitted to OAL for printing only pursuant to Government Code section 11351 (Register 93, No. 52).

3. Amendment of article heading, section heading, section and Note filed 11-17-2008; operative 11-17-2008. Submitted to OAL for printing only (Register 2008, No. 47).

4. Repealer of article 17 heading, repealer of former section 10840 and renumbering former section 10776 to section 10840, including amendment of section heading and section, filed 12-17-2019; operative 1-1-2020. Submitted to OAL for printing only pursuant to Government Code section 11351 (Register 2019, No. 51).

Ref.: Hanna §§ 20.02[1][a], [b], 25.01[4], 30.03[2].

§10842. Request for Increase of Attorney's Fee

All requests for an increase in attorney's fee shall be accompanied by proof of service on the applicant of written notice of the attorney's adverse interest and of the applicant's right to seek independent counsel. Failure to notify the applicant may constitute grounds for dismissal of the request for increase in fee.

Note: Authority cited: Sections 133 and 5307, Labor Code. Reference: Sections 4903 and 4906, Labor Code.

History: 1. New section filed 5-25-82; designated effective 7-1-82 (Register 82, No. 22).

2. Amendment of section heading and text filed 12-23-93; operative 1-1-94. Submitted to OAL for printing only pursuant to Government Code section 11351 (Register 93, No. 52).

3. Amendment of last paragraph filed 12-19-2002; operative 1-1-2003. Submitted to OAL for printing only pursuant to Government Code section 11351 (Register 2002, No. 51).

4. Amendment of section heading, section and Note filed 11-17-2008; operative 11-17-2008. Submitted to OAL for printing only (Register 2008, No. 47).

5. Renumbering of former section 10842 to section 10945 and renumbering and amendment of former section 10778 to section 10842 filed 12-17-2019; operative 1-1-2020. Submitted to OAL for printing only pursuant to Government Code section 11351 (Register 2019, No. 51).

Ref.: Hanna §§ 20.05, 23.14[2][n], 30.03[3].

§10843. Petitions for Removal and Answers. [Renumbered]

Note: Authority cited: Sections 133, 5307, 5309 and 5708, Labor Code. Reference: Section 5310, Labor Code.

History: 1. New section filed 12-23-93; operative 1-1-94. Submitted to OAL for printing only pursuant to Government Code section 11351 (Register 93, No. 52).

2. Amendment filed 12-12-2000; operative 1-1-2001. Submitted to OAL for printing only pursuant to Government Code section 11351 (Register 2000, No. 50).

5. Renumbering of former section 10842 to section 10945 and renumbering and amendment of former section 10778 to section 10842 filed 12-17-2019; operative 1-1-2020. Submitted to OAL for printing only pursuant to Government Code section 11351 (Register 2019, No. 51).

3. Amendment filed 12-19-2002; operative 1-1-2003. Submitted to OAL for printing only pursuant to Government Code section 11351 (Register 2002, No. 51).

4. Amendment of section heading, section and Note filed 11-17-2008; operative 11-17-2008. Submitted to OAL for printing only (Register 2008, No. 47).

5. Renumbering of former section 10843 to section 10955 filed 12-17-2019; operative 1-1-2020. Submitted to OAL for printing only pursuant to Government Code section 11351 (Register 2019, No. 51).

§10844. Reasonable Attorney's Fee.

In establishing a reasonable attorney's fee, the workers' compensation judge or arbitrator shall consider the:

(a) Responsibility assumed by the attorney;

(b) Care exercised in representing the applicant;

(c) Time involved; and

(d) Results obtained.

Note: Authority cited: Sections 133 and 5307, Labor Code. Reference: Sections 4903 and 4906, Labor Code.

History: 1. New section filed 11-17-2008; operative 11-17-2008. Submitted to OAL for printing only (Register 2008, No. 47).

2. Repealer of former section 10844 and renumbering and amendment of former section 10775 to section 10844 filed 12-17-2019; operative 1-1-2020. Submitted to OAL for printing only pursuant to Government Code section 11351 (Register 2019, No. 51).

Ref.: Hanna §§ 20.02[1][b], 20.03[1], [2], 29.04[3][e], 30.03[2]; Herlick Handbook § 11.09.

§10845. General Requirements for Petitions for Reconsideration, Removal, and Disqualification, and for Answers and Other Documents. [Repealed]

Note: Authority cited: Sections 133, 5307, 5309 and 5708, Labor Code. Reference: Sections 5310, 5311, 5900 and 5905, Labor Code.

History: 1. New section filed 11-17-2008; operative 11-17-2008. Submitted to OAL for printing only (Register 2008, No. 47).

2. Amendment of subsection (a) filed 9-23-2013; operative 10-23-2013. Submitted as a file and print by the Workers' Compensation Appeals Board pursuant to Government Code section 11351 (Register 2013, No. 39).

3. Amendment of subsection (a) filed 10-15-2014; operative 1-1-2015. Submitted to OAL for printing only pursuant to Government Code section 11351 (Register 2014, No. 42).

4. Editorial correction of History 3 (Register 2017, No. 8).

5. Repealer filed 12-17-2019; operative 1-1-2020. Submitted to OAL for printing only pursuant to Government Code section 11351 (Register 2019, No. 51).

§10846. Skeletal Petitions. [Renumbered]

Note: Authority cited: Sections 133, 5307, 5309 and 5708, Labor Code. Reference: Sections 5310, 5311, 5902, 5903 and 5904, Labor Code.

History: 1. Amendment of section and Note filed 11-17-2008; operative 11-17-2008. Submitted to OAL for printing only (Register 2008, No. 47).

2. Renumbering of former section 10846 to section 10972 filed 12-17-2019; operative 1-1-2020. Submitted to OAL for printing only pursuant to Government Code section 11351 (Register 2019, No. 51).

§10848. Supplemental Petitions. [Renumbered]

Note: Authority cited: Sections 133, 5307, 5309 and 5708, Labor Code. Reference: Sections 5310, 5311 and 5900, Labor Code.

History: 1. Repealer and new section filed 12-23-93; operative 1-1-94. Submitted to OAL for printing only pursuant to Government Code section 11351 (Register 93, No. 52).

2. Amendment of section and Note filed 11-17-2008; operative 11-17-2008. Submitted to OAL for printing only (Register 2008, No. 47).

3. Renumbering of former section 10848 to section 10964 filed 12-17-2019; operative 1-1-2020. Submitted to OAL for printing only pursuant to Government Code section 11351 (Register 2019, No. 51).

§10850. Order Dismissing Application.

(a) Orders of dismissal of Applications for Adjudication of Claim shall issue forthwith upon request by the employee unless there is good cause to not issue an order.

(b) All other orders of dismissal of Applications for Adjudication of Claim shall issue only after service of a notice of intention allowing at least 10 days for any adverse party to show good cause to the contrary, and not by an order with a clause rendering the order null and void if an objection showing good cause is filed.

Note: Authority cited: Sections 133 and 5307, Labor Code. Reference: Section 5307, Labor Code.

History: 1. Amendment of section and Note filed 12-19-2002; operative 1-1-2003. Submitted to OAL for printing only pursuant to Government Code section 11351 (Register 2002, No. 51).

2. Amendment of section and Note filed 11-17-2008; operative 11-17-2008. Submitted to OAL for printing only (Register 2008, No. 47).

3. Repealer of former section 10850 and renumbering of former section 10780 to section 10850, including amendment of section heading, section and Note, filed 12-17-2019; operative 1-1-2020. Submitted to OAL for printing only pursuant to Government Code section 11351 (Register 2019, No. 51).

Ref.: Hanna §§ 23.11[5][b], 23.14[1][c], 25.26, 31.04[4][b]; Herlick Handbook § 14.43.

§10852. Insufficiency of Evidence. [Repealed]

Note: Authority cited: Sections 133 and 5307, Labor Code. Reference: Sections 5902 and 5903, Labor Code.

History: 1. Amendment filed 12-19-2002; operative 1-1-2003. Submitted to OAL for printing only pursuant to Government Code section 11351 (Register 2002, No. 51).

2. Repealer filed 12-17-2019; operative 1-1-2020. Submitted to OAL for printing only pursuant to Government Code section 11351 (Register 2019, No. 51).

§10856. Allegations of Newly Discovered Evidence and Fraud. [Renumbered]

Note: Authority cited: Sections 133 and 5307, Labor Code. Reference: Sections 5902 and 5903, Labor Code.

History: 1. Amendment filed 12-19-2002; operative 1-1-2003. Submitted to OAL for printing only pursuant to Government Code section 11351 (Register 2002, No. 51).

2. Renumbering of former section 10856 to section 10974 filed 12-17-2019; operative 1-1-2020. Submitted to OAL for printing only pursuant to Government Code section 11351 (Register 2019, No. 51).

§10858. Correction of Errors. [Renumbered]

Note: Authority cited: Sections 133 and 5307, Labor Code. Reference: Section 5309, Labor Code.

History: 1. Renumbering of former section 10858 to section 10966 filed 12-17-2019; operative 1-1-2020. Submitted to OAL for printing only pursuant to Government Code section 11351 (Register 2019, No. 51).

§10859. Orders After Filing of Petition for Reconsideration. [Renumbered]

Note: Authority cited: Section 5307, Labor Code. Reference: Sections 5906, 5907 and 5908.5, Labor Code.

History: 1. Repealer and new section filed 12-16-92; operative 2-1-93 and exempt from OAL review pursuant to Government Code section 11351 (Register 92, No. 51).

2. Amendment filed 12-19-2002; operative 1-1-2003. Submitted to OAL for printing only pursuant to Government Code section 11351 (Register 2002, No. 51).

3. Renumbering of former section 10859 to section 10961 filed 12-17-2019; operative 1-1-2020. Submitted to OAL for printing only pursuant to Government Code section 11351 (Register 2019, No. 51).

§10860. Report of Workers' Compensation Judge. [Renumbered]

Note: Authority cited: Sections 133, 5307, 5309 and 5708, Labor Code. Reference: Sections 5900 and 5906, Labor Code.

History: 1. Amendment filed 12-23-93; operative 1-1-94. Submitted to OAL for printing only pursuant to Government Code section 11351 (Register 93, No. 52).

2. Amendment filed 12-19-2002; operative 1-1-2003. Submitted to OAL for printing only pursuant to Government Code section 11351 (Register 2002, No. 51).

3. Amendment of section and Note filed 11-17-2008; operative 11-17-2008. Submitted to OAL for printing only (Register 2008, No. 47).

4. Renumbering of former section 10860 to section 10962 filed 12-17-2019; operative 1-1-2020. Submitted to OAL for printing only pursuant to Government Code section 11351 (Register 2019, No. 51).

ARTICLE 16
Liens

§10862. Filing and Service of Lien Claims and Supporting Documents.

(a) A lien claim may be filed only if permitted by Labor Code section 4900 et seq. An otherwise permissible lien claim shall not be filed if doing so would violate the premature filing restrictions of Labor Code section 4903.6(a).

(b) A section 4903(b) lien shall only be filed electronically in accordance with section 4903.05 and not by any other method.

(c) All other lien claims may be filed utilizing an optical character recognition (OCR) lien claim form approved by the Appeals Board.

(d) The claims of two or more providers of goods or services shall not be merged into a single lien. An individual provider may claim more than one type of lien on a single lien form by marking the "Other Lien(s)" checkbox on the form and by specifying the nature and statutory basis for each lien in that checkbox's associated text box.

(e) The following documents shall be concurrently filed with each lien claim:

(1) A proof of service;

(2) The verification under penalty of perjury outlined in rule 10863, if required; and

(4) Any other declaration or form required by law to be concurrently filed with a lien claim, including but not limited to documents required by Labor Code sections 4903.05, 4903.06 and 4903.8.

(f) Nothing in this rule shall preclude a medical treatment lien claimant from filing a lien claim if there are other outstanding disputes, including but not limited to injury, employment, jurisdiction, or the statute of limitations.

(g) All original and amended lien claims, and all related documents, including a full statement or itemized voucher for any section 4903(b) lien and any document listed in rule 10862(e) shall be served on:

(1) The injured worker or, if deceased, the worker's dependent(s), unless:

(A) The worker or dependent(s) is represented by an attorney or other agent of record, in which event service may be made solely upon the attorney or agent of record; or

(B) The underlying case of the worker or dependent(s) has been resolved; or

(C) The worker or the dependent(s) chooses not to proceed with the case.

(2) Any employer(s) or insurance carrier(s) that are parties to the case and, if represented, their attorney(s) or other agent(s) of record.

(h) The service of a lien claim on a defendant, or the service of notice of any claim that would be allowable as a lien, shall not constitute the filing of a lien within the meaning of these rules unless allowed by statute.

(i) Where a lien has been served on a party, that party shall have no obligation to file that lien with the Workers' Compensation Appeals Board.

(j) When serving an amended lien claim, the lien claimant shall indicate in the box set forth on the lien form that it is an "amended" lien claim and shall provide the name, mailing address and telephone number of a person with authority to resolve the lien claim on behalf of the lien claimant.

(k) Any lien claim filed in violation of the provisions of this rule may be deemed not filed for any purpose, including tolling or extending the time for filing the lien claim, and may not be acknowledged or returned to the filer and may be destroyed at any time without notice.

Note: Authority cited: Sections 133, 5307 and 5708, Labor Code. Reference: Sections 4900 et seq., 4903, 4903.05, 4903.06, 4903.8, 4903.1, 4903.4, 4903.5, 4903.6, 4904, 4603.2, 4603.3, 4603.6, 4610.5, 4610.6, 4616.3, 4616.4, 4622 and 5813, Labor Code.

History: 1. Amendment of section and Note filed 12-19-2002; operative 1-1-2003. Submitted to OAL for printing only pursuant to Government Code section 11351 (Register 2002, No. 51).

2. New article 16 heading, renumbering of former section 10862 to section 10984 and new section 10862 filed 12-17-2019; operative 1-1-2020. Submitted to OAL for printing only pursuant to Government Code section 11351 (Register 2019, No. 51).

Ref.: Herlick Handbook § 14.34.

§10863. Verification of Compliance with Labor Code Section 4903.6 on Filing of Lien Claim or Application by Lien Claimant.

(a) Any section 4903(b) lien, any lien for medical-legal costs and any application related to any such lien shall have attached to it a verification under penalty of perjury which shall contain a statement specifying in detail the facts establishing that both of the following have occurred:

(1) Sixty days have elapsed since after the date of acceptance or rejection of liability for the claim, or the time provided for investigation of liability pursuant to Labor Code section 5402(b) has elapsed, whichever is earlier; and

(2) Either of the following:

(A) The time provided for payment of medical treatment bills pursuant to Labor Code section 4603.2 has expired and, if the employer objected to the amount of the bill, the reasonable fee has been determined pursuant to Labor Code section 4603.6, and, if authorization for the medical treatment has been disputed pursuant to Labor Code section 4610, the medical necessity of the medical treatment has been determined pursuant to Labor Code sections 4610.5 and 4610.6; or

(B) The time provided for payment of medical-legal expenses pursuant to Labor Code section 4622 has expired and, if the employer objected to the amount of the bill, the reasonable fee has been determined pursuant to Labor Code section 4603.6.

(b) The verification under penalty of perjury shall also contain a statement declaring that the lien is not being filed solely because of a dispute subject to the independent medical review and/or the independent bill review process.

(c) In addition, if an Application for Adjudication of Claim is also being filed, the verification under penalty of perjury shall contain:

(1) A statement specifying in detail the facts establishing that venue in the district office being designated is proper pursuant to Labor Code section 5501.5(a)(1) or Labor Code section 5501.5(a)(2); and

(2) A statement specifying in detail the facts establishing that the filing lien claimant has made a diligent search and has determined that no adjudication case number exists for the same injured worker and same date of injury at any district office. A diligent search shall include contacting the injured worker, contacting the employer or carrier, or inquiring at the district office with appropriate venue pursuant to Labor Code section 5501.5(a)(1) or Labor Code section 5501.5(a)(2).

(d) The verification shall be in the following form:

I declare under penalty of perjury under the laws of the State of California:

(1) That the time periods set forth in rule 10863(a) have elapsed;

(2) That the section 4903(b) lien, the lien for medical-legal costs, or the application is not being filed solely because of a dispute subject to the independent medical review and/or independent bill review process; and

(3) That, if an Application for Adjudication of Claim is being filed, that venue is proper as set forth in rule 10863(b) and that I have made a diligent search and have determined that no adjudication case number exists for the

same injured worker and the same date of injury. In determining that no adjudication case number exists for the same injured worker and the same date of injury, I have made a diligent search consisting of the following efforts (specify):

____

____

__________________________________ s/s

__________________________________ on

Failure to attach the verification or an incorrect verification may be a basis for sanctions.

(e) If the Appeals Board approves an e-form or optical character recognition (OCR) form for this declaration, lien claimants shall file the declaration using the adopted form.

Note: Authority cited: Sections 133, 5307, 5309 and 5708, Labor Code. Reference: Sections 4603.2, 4603.6, 4610.5, 4610.6, 4622, 4903, 4903.6, 5402 and 5501.5, Labor Code.

History: 1. Renumbering of former section 10770.5 to section 10863, including amendment of section heading, section and Note, filed 12-17-2019; operative 1-1-2020. Submitted to OAL for printing only pursuant to Government Code section 11351 (Register 2019, No. 51).

§10864. Authority of Workers' Compensation Judge After Decision After Reconsideration. [Renumbered]

Note: Authority cited: Sections 133 and 5307, Labor Code. Reference: Sections 5900, 5910 and 5911, Labor Code.

History: 1. Amendment filed 5-25-82; designated effective 7-1-82 (Register 82, No. 22).

2. Amendment filed 12-19-2002; operative 1-1-2003. Submitted to OAL for printing only pursuant to Government Code section 11351 (Register 2002, No. 51).

3. Renumbering of former section 10864 to section 10986 and new section 10862 filed 12-17-2019; operative 1-1-2020. Submitted to OAL for printing only pursuant to Government Code section 11351 (Register 2019, No. 51).

§10865. Reconsideration of Arbitration Decisions Made Pursuant To Labor Code Sections 3201.5 and 3201.7. [Renumbered]

Note: Authority cited: Sections 133, 5307, 5309 and 5708, Labor Code. Reference: Sections 3201.5 and 3201.7, Labor Code.

History: 1. New section filed 12-23-93; operative 1-1-94. Submitted to OAL for printing only pursuant to Government Code section 11351 (Register 93, No. 52).

2. Amendment of section heading, section and Note filed 12-19-2002; operative 1-1-2003. Submitted to OAL for printing only pursuant to Government Code section 11351 (Register 2002, No. 51).

3. Amendment of section heading, section and Note filed 11-17-2008; operative 11-17-2008. Submitted to OAL for printing only (Register 2008, No. 47).

4. Renumbering of former section 10865 to section 10990 filed 12-17-2019; operative 1-1-2020. Submitted to OAL for printing only pursuant to Government Code section 11351 (Register 2019, No. 51).

§10866. Reconsideration of Arbitrator's Decisions or Awards Made Pursuant to the Mandatory or Voluntary Arbitration Provisions of Labor Code Sections 5270 through 5275. [Renumbered]

Note: Authority cited: Sections 133, 5307, 5309 and 5708, Labor Code. Reference: Sections 5273, 5275, 5277(c) and 5900-5911, Labor Code.

History: 1. New section filed 12-23-93; operative 1-1-94. Submitted to OAL for printing only pursuant to Government Code section 11351 (Register 93, No. 52).

2. Amendment of section and Note filed 12-19-2002; operative 1-1-2003. Submitted to OAL for printing only pursuant to Government Code section 11351 (Register 2002, No. 51).

3. Amendment of section heading, section and Note filed 11-17-2008; operative 11-17-2008. Submitted to OAL for printing only (Register 2008, No. 47).

4. Renumbering of former section 10866 to section 10995 filed 12-17-2019; operative 1-1-2020. Submitted to OAL for printing only pursuant to Government Code section 11351 (Register 2019, No. 51).

§10867. Report of Arbitrator. [Repealed]

Note: Authority cited: Sections 133 and 5307, Labor Code. Reference: Sections 5275, 5277(c) and 5900-5911, Labor Code.

History: 1. New section filed 12-23-93; operative 1-1-94. Submitted to OAL for printing only pursuant to Government Code section 11351 (Register 93, No. 52).

2. Amendment of section and Note filed 12-19-2002; operative 1-1-2003. Submitted to OAL for printing only pursuant to Government Code section 11351 (Register 2002, No. 51).

3. Repealer filed 11-17-2008; operative 11-17-2008. Submitted to OAL for printing only (Register 2008, No. 47).

§10868. Notices of Representation for Lien Claimants.

(a) Whenever any lien claimant obtains representation after a lien has been filed, or changes such representation, the lien claimant shall, within 5 days, file and serve a notice of representation in accordance with rules 10390, 10400, 10401 and 10402. If a copy of the notice of representation is not in the record at the time of the hearing, the lien claimant's representative shall lodge a copy at the hearing and shall personally serve a copy on all parties appearing. Unless a representative signs an initial lien document on behalf of a lien claimant, a notice of representation is required.

(b) In addition to the requirements of rules 10390, 10400 and 10401, the notice shall:

(1) Include the caption, the case title (i.e., the name of the injured employee and the name of the defendant or primary defendant(s)) and the adjudication case number(s) to which the notice relates; and

(2) Set forth the full legal name, mailing address and telephone number of the lien claimant.

(c) The notice shall be verified by a declaration signed by the lien claimant and the lien claimant's representative under penalty of perjury stating:

(1) "I declare that the named initial or new representative has consented to represent the interests of the named lien claimant and that the named lien claimant has consented to this representation.";

(2) "This representation began on __________, ________, 20_____.

(A) "I am not aware of any other attorney or non-attorney who was previously representing the lien claimant."; or

(B) "I am aware that __________ [specify person or entity] was previously representing the lien claimant. This Notice of Representation supersedes any previous Notice of Representation. I hereby certify that I have notified the previous attorney or non-attorney representative in writing.";

(3) "By signing below, the representative affirms that they are not disqualified from appearing under Labor Code section 4907, WCAB rule 10445 (Cal. Code Regs., tit. 8, § 10445) or by any other rule, order or decision of the Workers' Compensation Appeals Board, the State Bar of California, or any court."

(d) Any violation of this rule may give rise to monetary sanctions, attorney's fees and costs under Labor Code section 5813 and rule 10421.

Note: Authority cited: Sections 133, 5307, 5309 and 5708, Labor Code. Reference: Sections 130, 4907 and 5710, Labor Code; Sections 284, 285 and 286, Code of Civil Procedure; and Sections 10390 and 10445, title 8, California Code of Regulations.

History: 1. New section filed 12-17-2019; operative 1-1-2020. Submitted to OAL for printing only pursuant to Government Code section 11351 (Register 2019, No. 51). For prior history, see Register 2002, No. 51.

§10869. Report of Settlement Conference Referee. [Repealed]

Note: Authority cited: Sections 133 and 5307, Labor Code. Reference: Sections 111, 5502 and 5307, Labor Code.

History: 1. New section filed 12-23-93; operative 1-1-94. Submitted to OAL for printing only pursuant to Government Code section 11351 (Register 93, No. 52).

2. Repealer filed 12-19-2002; operative 1-1-2003. Submitted to OAL for printing only pursuant to Government Code section 11351 (Register 2002, No. 51).

§10870. Approval of Compromise and Release. [Repealed]

Note: Authority cited: Sections 133 and 5307, Labor Code. Reference: Sections 4646, 5001, 5002 and 5100.6, Labor Code.

History: 1. Amendment of article 18 heading and amendment of section and Note filed 12-19-2002; operative 1-1-2003. Submitted to OAL for printing only pursuant to Government Code section 11351 (Register 2002, No. 51).

2. Repealer of article 18 heading and section filed 12-17-2019; operative 1-1-2020. Submitted to OAL for printing only pursuant to Government Code section 11351 (Register 2019, No. 51).

§10872. Notification of Resolution or Withdrawal of Lien Claims.

(a) Within seven days after a lien has been resolved or withdrawn, the lien claimant shall file and serve a notification of resolution or a withdrawal of the lien claim. For purposes of this rule, a lien is not resolved unless payment in accordance with an order or an informal agreement has been made and received.

(b) The lien claimant shall appear at any hearing that was noticed prior to the resolution or withdrawal of the lien unless excused by the Workers' Compensation Appeals Board. The lien claimant shall be excused from appearing at any subsequently noticed hearing.

(c) Any violation of this rule may give rise to monetary sanctions, attorney's fees and costs under Labor Code section 5813 and rule 10421.

Note: Authority cited: Sections 133, 5307, 5309 and 5708, Labor Code. Reference: Sections 4903, 4903.05, 4903.06, 4903.8, 4903.1, 4903.4, 4903.5, 4903.6, 4904, 4603.2, 4603.3, 4603.6, 4610.5, 4610.6, 4616.3, 4616.4, 4622 and 5813, Labor Code.

History: 1. New section filed 12-17-2019; operative 1-1-2020. Submitted to OAL for printing only pursuant to Government Code section 11351 (Register 2019, No. 51).

§10873. Lien Claimant Declarations of Readiness to Proceed.

(a) A lien conference shall be set when any party files a Declaration of Readiness to Proceed in accordance with rule 10742 on any issue(s) relating to lien claim other than in the case in chief, or by the Workers' Compensation Appeals Board on its own motion at any time.

(1) Based upon resources available and such other considerations as the Workers' Compensation Appeals Board in its discretion may deem appropriate, a lien conference may be set at any district office without the necessity of an order changing venue.

(2) Unless otherwise expressly stated in the notice of hearing, all unresolved lien claims and lien issues shall be heard at the lien conference, whether or not listed in any Declaration of Readiness to Proceed. An agreement to "pay, adjust or litigate" a lien claim, or its equivalent, or an award leaving a lien claim to be adjusted, is not a resolution of the lien claim or lien issue.

(3) Once a Declaration of Readiness to Proceed for a lien conference has been filed, it cannot be withdrawn. If the lien of a lien claimant that has filed a Declaration of Readiness to Proceed has been resolved, that lien claimant shall request that its lien be withdrawn in accordance with rule 10872.

(4) To the extent feasible, the date of the lien conference shall be no sooner than 60 days after the date the notice of hearing for it is served.

(b) When a party files and serves a Declaration of Readiness to Proceed on an issue relating to a lien claim other than in the case in chief, the party shall designate on the Declaration of Readiness to Proceed form that it is requesting a lien conference and shall not designate any other kind of conference. If a status conference or any other type of conference is requested or is set on the calendar, that status conference or other type of conference shall be deemed a lien conference and shall be governed by any and all rules applying to a lien conference.

(c) Nothing in this rule shall preclude the Workers' Compensation Appeals Board, in its discretion, from setting a type of hearing other than that requested in the Declaration of Readiness to Proceed.

(d) After a lien conference or lien trial has been ordered off calendar, no party or lien claimant shall file a new Declaration of Readiness to Proceed for at least 90 days. The Declaration of Readiness to Proceed shall designate that a lien conference is requested and shall state under penalty of perjury that there has been no hearing on the lien claim(s) or lien issue(s) within the preceding 90 days. Nothing in this subdivision shall preclude the Workers' Compensation Appeals Board from:

(1) Restoring the lien claim(s) or lien issue(s) to the lien conference or lien trial calendar on its own motion; or

(2) Restoring the lien claim(s) or lien issue(s) to the lien conference or lien trial calendar less than 90 days after the most recent hearing.

Note: Authority cited: Sections 133, 5307, 5309 and 5708, Labor Code. Reference: Sections 4903, 4903.05, 4903.06, 4903.1, 4903.4, 4903.5, 4903.6, 4904, 5502 and 5502.5, Labor Code.

History: 1. New section filed 12-17-2019; operative 1-1-2020. Submitted to OAL for printing only pursuant to Government Code section 11351 (Register 2019, No. 51).

§10874. Verification to Filing of Declaration of Readiness to Proceed by or on Behalf of Lien Claimant.

No Declaration of Readiness to Proceed shall be filed for a section 4903(b) lien, or for a lien claim for medical-legal costs, without an attached verification executed under penalty of perjury:

(a) Stating either that:

(1) The Declaration of Readiness to Proceed is not being filed because of a dispute solely subject to the independent medical review and/or independent bill review process; or

(2) A timely petition appealing the Administrative Director's determination regarding independent medical review and/or independent bill review has been filed; and

(b) Stating either that:

(1) The underlying case has been resolved; or

(2) At least six months have elapsed from the date of injury and the injured worker has chosen not to proceed with their case.

The declarant shall make a diligent search to determine that the injured worker has chosen not to proceed with their case and the verification shall specify the efforts made in conducting the diligent search. A diligent search shall include contacting the injured worker, contacting the employer or carrier, or inquiring at the district office with appropriate venue pursuant to Labor Code section 5501.5(a)(1) or Labor Code section 5501.5(a)(2).

The verification shall be in the following form:

I declare under penalty of perjury under the laws of the State of California that:

☐ The Declaration of Readiness to Proceed is not being filed because of a dispute subject to the independent medical review and/or independent bill review process; or

☐ A timely petition appealing the Administrative Director's determination regarding independent medical review and/or independent bill review has been filed (Check one box); and

☐ The underlying case has been resolved; or

☐ At least six months have elapsed from the date of injury and the injured worker has chosen not to proceed with their case (Check one box). In determining that the injured worker has chosen not to proceed with their case, I have made a diligent search consisting of the following efforts (specify):

____

____

____ s/s

____ on

____

Failure to attach the verification or an incorrect verification may be a basis for sanctions.

(c) If the Appeals Board approves an e-form or optical character recognition (OCR) form for this declaration, lien claimants shall file the declaration using the adopted form.

Note: Authority cited: Sections 133, 5307, 5309 and 5708, Labor Code. Reference: Sections 4903, 4903.6 and 5501.5, Labor Code.

History: 1. Repealer of former section 10874 and renumbering of former section 10770.6 to section 10874, including amendment of section heading, section and Note, filed 12-17-2019; operative 1-1-2020. Submitted to OAL for printing only pursuant to Government Code section 11351 (Register 2019, No. 51).

§10875. Lien Conferences.

(a) All defendants and lien claimants shall appear at all lien conferences, either in person or by attorney or non-attorney representative. Each defendant, lien claimant, attorney and non-attorney representative appearing at any lien conference:

(1) Shall have sufficient knowledge of the lien dispute(s) to inform the workers' compensation judge as to all relevant factual and/or legal issues in dispute;

(2) Shall have authority to enter into binding factual stipulations; and

(3) Shall either have full settlement authority or have full settlement authority immediately available by telephone.

(b) If a lien claimant fails to appear at a lien conference, the worker's compensation judge may issue a notice of intention to dismiss consistent with rule 10888, or defer the lien.

(c) If a defendant does not appear, or for any other reason any lien claim(s) or lien issue(s) cannot be fully resolved at the lien conference, the workers' compensation judge shall take one of the following actions:

(1) Set a lien trial and close discovery;

(2) Upon a showing of good cause, allow a continuance of the lien conference to another lien conference; or

(3) Upon a showing of good cause, order the lien conference off calendar.

Good cause shall not include the delayed or late appointment of an attorney or non-attorney representative by a defendant or lien claimant or the delayed receipt of the defendant's or lien claimant's file by that attorney or non-attorney representative.

The action taken shall apply to all unresolved lien claim(s) or lien issue(s).

(d) For any lien claim(s) or lien issue(s) not fully resolved at the lien conference by an order signed by a workers' compensation judge and set for trial, the defendant(s) and lien claimant(s) shall prepare, sign, and file with the workers' compensation judge a Pre-Trial Conference Statement, which shall include:

(1) All stipulations;

(2) The specific issues in dispute;

(3) All documentary evidence that might be offered at the lien trial; and

(4) All witnesses who might testify at the lien trial.

The right to present any issue, documentary evidence, or witness not listed in the Pre-Trial Conference Statement shall be deemed waived, absent a showing of good cause. Evidence not disclosed on the Pre-Trial Conference Statement or obtained thereafter shall not be admissible unless the proponent of the evidence can demonstrate that it was not available or could not have been discovered by the exercise of due diligence prior to the lien conference.

(e) Any violation of the provisions of this rule may give rise to monetary sanctions, attorney's fees and costs under Labor Code section 5813 and rule 10421.

Note: Authority cited: Sections 133, 5307, 5309 and 5708, Labor Code. Reference: Sections 4903, 4903.05, 4903.06, 4903.1, 4903.4, 4903.5, 4903.6, 4904, 5502 and 5502.5, Labor Code.

History: 1. New section filed 12-23-93; operative 1-1-94. Submitted to OAL for printing only pursuant to Government Code section 11351 (Register 93, No. 52).

2. Amendment of penultimate paragraph filed 12-19-2002; operative 1-1-2003. Submitted to OAL for printing only pursuant to Government Code section 11351 (Register 2002, No. 51).

3. Renumbering of former section 10875 to section 10705 and new section 10875 filed 12-17-2019; operative 1-1-2020. Submitted to OAL for printing only pursuant to Government Code section 11351 (Register 2019, No. 51).

§10876. Fees Required at Lien Conference.

(a) No lien claimant that is required to pay a lien filing or lien activation fee shall file a Declaration of Readiness to Proceed or participate in any lien conference, including obtaining an order allowing its lien in whole or in part, without submitting written proof of prior timely payment of the fee.

(b) At the lien conference, there shall be a rebuttable presumption that a lien claimant is required to pay a lien filing fee or activation fee.

(1) If a lien claimant asserts it is an entity listed in Labor Code sections 4903.05(c)(7) or 4903.06(b), it shall be prepared to file proof or submit a stipulation to that effect at the lien conference upon request by the workers' compensation judge. The workers' compensation judge, however, may formally or informally take judicial notice that the lien claimant is such an entity. This may include, but is not necessarily limited to, taking judicial notice of prior decisions of the Workers' Compensation Appeals Board and taking judicial notice based on the "common knowledge" or the "not reasonably subject to dispute" provisions of Evidence Code section 452(g) and (h).

(2) If a lien claimant asserts under Labor Code section 4903.06(a) that it already paid a filing fee as required by former Labor Code section 4903.05 as added by Chapter 639 of the Statutes of 2003, it shall submit written proof of such payment at the lien conference.

(c) The following requirements must be met to satisfy the lien claimant's burden of demonstrating prior timely payment:

(1) Proof of prior timely payment shall be in the form provided by the Rules of the Administrative Director or by a printout from the Public Information Search Tool of EAMS. An offer of proof or a stipulation that payment was made shall not be adequate.

(2) Proof of prior timely payment of a filing fee must establish that the fee was paid contemporaneously with the filing of the lien.

(3) Proof of prior timely payment of an activation fee must establish that the fee was paid before the scheduled starting time of the lien conference set forth in the notice of hearing, except that, if the lien claimant filed the Declaration of Readiness to Proceed, the proof shall establish that the activation fee was paid contemporaneously with the filing of the Declaration of Readiness to Proceed.

(d) If a lien claimant fails to submit proper written proof of prior timely payment, the Workers' Compensation Appeals Board may elect to conduct a search within the Electronic Adjudication Management System to confirm prior timely payment, but is not obligated to do so, and a failure to conduct such a search shall not be a proper basis for a petition for reconsideration, removal, or disqualification.

(e) If a lien claimant that is required to pay a lien filing or activation fee fails to provide proper written proof of prior timely payment, then:

(1) If the proof of prior timely payment of the activation fee is not submitted, the lien claim shall be dismissed with prejudice. This provision shall apply even if, but for the lien conference, the activation fee would not have been due until December 31, 2013.

(2) If the proof of prior timely payment of the filing fee is not submitted, the lien claim shall be deemed dismissed by operation of law as of the time of its filing, except that if the lien claimant filed a Declaration of Readiness to Proceed its lien shall be dismissed with prejudice; however, in neither case shall the dismissed lien toll, preserve, or extend any applicable statute of limitations.

(f) A lien claimant shall not avoid dismissal by attempting to pay the fee at or after the hearing.

Note: Authority cited: Sections 133, 5307, 5309 and 5708, Labor Code. Reference: Sections 4903, 4903.05, 4903.06, 4903.1, 4903.4, 4903.5, 4903.6, 4904, 5502 and 5502.5, Labor Code; and Sections 351, 352, 451 and 452, Evidence Code.

History: 1. New section filed 12-17-2019; operative 1-1-2020. Submitted to OAL for printing only pursuant to Government Code section 11351 (Register 2019, No. 51).

§10878. Submission at Lien Conferences.

(a) The workers' compensation judge may order that any unresolved lien claim(s) or lien issue(s) be submitted for decision solely on the exhibits listed in the Pre-Trial Conference Statement if no witnesses are listed in the Pre-Trial Conference Statement.

(b) If the disputed lien claim(s) or lien issue(s) are submitted for decision at the lien conference, the workers' compensation judge shall prepare minutes of hearing and a summary of evidence as set forth in rule 10787.

Note: Authority cited: Sections 133, 5307, 5309 and 5708, Labor Code. Reference: Sections 4903, 4903.05, 4903.06, 4903.1, 4903.4, 4903.5, 4903.6, 4904, 5502 and 5502.5, Labor Code; and Sections 351, 352, 451 and 452, Evidence Code.

History: 1. Amendment of section heading, section and Note filed 12-19-2002; operative 1-1-2003. Submitted to OAL for printing only pursuant to Government Code section 11351 (Register 2002, No. 51).

2. Repealer and new section filed 12-17-2019; operative 1-1-2020. Submitted to OAL for printing only pursuant to Government Code section 11351 (Register 2019, No. 51).

§10880. Lien Trials.

(a) All defendants and lien claimants shall appear at all lien trials, either in person or by attorney or non-attorney representative. Each defendant, lien claimant, attorney and non-attorney representative appearing at any lien trial:

(1) Shall have sufficient knowledge of the lien dispute(s) to inform the workers' compensation judge as to all relevant factual and/or legal issues in dispute;

(2) Shall have authority to enter into binding factual stipulations; and

(3) Shall either have full settlement authority or have full settlement authority immediately available by telephone.

(b) Where a lien claimant or defendant served with notice of a lien trial fails to appear either in person or by attorney or non-attorney representative, the workers' compensation judge may:

(1) Dismiss the lien claim after issuing a 10-day notice of intention to dismiss with or without prejudice, or

(2) Hear the evidence and, after service of the minutes of hearing and summary of evidence that shall include a 10-day notice of intention to submit, make such decision as is just and proper, or

(3) Defer the issue of the lien and submit the case on the remaining issues.

(c) If the workers' compensation judge defers a lien issue, upon the issuance of a decision on the remaining issues, the workers' compensation judge shall:

(1) Issue a 10-day notice of intention to order payment of the lien in full or in part, or

(2) Issue a 10-day notice of intention to disallow the lien, or

(3) Continue the lien issue to a lien conference.

(d) At the conclusion of a lien trial, the workers' compensation judge shall prepare minutes of hearing and a summary of evidence as set forth in rule 10787.

(e) Any violation of the provisions of this rule may give rise to monetary sanctions, attorney's fees and costs under Labor Code section 5813 and rule 10421.

Note: Authority cited: Sections 133 and 5307, Labor Code. Reference: Article XIV, Section 4, California Constitution; and Sections 5502(e) and 5708, Labor Code.

History: 1. New section filed 12-17-2019; operative 1-1-2020. Submitted to OAL for printing only pursuant to Government Code section 11351 (Register 2019, No. 51).

§10882. Action on Settlement Agreement. [Repealed]

Note: Authority cited: Sections 133 and 5307, Labor Code. Reference: Sections 5001, 5002 and 5702, Labor Code.

History: 1. Amendment of section heading, section and Note filed 12-19-2002; operative 1-1-2003. Submitted to OAL for printing only pursuant to Government Code section 11351 (Register 2002, No. 51).

2. Repealer filed 12-17-2019; operative 1-1-2020. Submitted to OAL for printing only pursuant to Government Code section 11351 (Register 2019, No. 51).

§10886. Service on Lien Claimants. [Renumbered]

Note: Authority cited: Sections 133 and 5307, Labor Code. Reference: Sections 4903, 4903.05, 4903.1, 4903.4, 4904, 4904.1, 4905 and 4906, Labor Code.

History: 1. Amendment exempt from OAL review pursuant to Government Code section 11351 filed 12-19-90; operative 1-1-91 (Register 91, No. 7).

2. Amendment filed 12-19-2002; operative 1-1-2003. Submitted to OAL for printing only pursuant to Government Code section 11351 (Register 2002, No. 51).

3. Amendment of section and Note filed 9-23-2013; operative 10-23-2013. Submitted as a file and print by the Workers' Compensation Appeals Board pursuant to Government Code section 11351 (Register 2013, No. 39).

4. Renumbering of former section 10886 to section 10702 filed 12-17-2019; operative 1-1-2020. Submitted to OAL for printing only pursuant to Government Code section 11351 (Register 2019, No. 51).

§10888. Dismissal of Lien Claims.

(a) The Appeals Board or a workers' compensation judge may order a lien dismissed for lack of prosecution, non-appearance by the lien claimant or failure to comply with the provisions of the Labor Code or these rules.

(b) A lien claim may be dismissed for lack of prosecution on a petition filed by a party or on the Appeals Board's or the workers' compensation judge's own motion if the lien claimant fails to file a Declaration of Readiness to Proceed within:

(1) 180 days after the underlying case of the injured employee or the dependent(s) of a deceased employee has been resolved or the injured employee or the dependent(s) of a deceased employee choose(s) not to proceed with the case; or

(2) 180 days after a lien conference or lien trial is ordered off calendar if the lien claim was at issue.

(c) A dismissal for failure to appear at a hearing shall only issue if the lien claimant was provided with notice of the lien conference or lien trial.

(d) A dismissal for failure to comply with the Labor Code or these rules shall only be issued if the lien claimant has failed to comply with a statute or rule that provides that a lien may be dismissed for non-compliance.

(e) Before issuing an Order dismissing a lien, the Workers' Compensation Appeals Board shall issue a Notice of Intention to Dismiss the lien claim consistent with rule 10832 that provides at least 10 days for the lien claimant to file and serve a response showing good cause why an Order dismissing the lien should not issue.

Note: Authority cited: Sections 133, 5307, 5309 and 5708, Labor Code. Reference: Sections 4903, 4903.05, 4903.06, 4903.1, 4903.4, 4903.5, 4903.6, 4904, 5502, 5502.5 and 5404.5, Labor Code.

History: 1. New section filed 12-19-2002; operative 1-1-2003. Submitted to OAL for printing only pursuant to Government Code section 11351 (Register 2002, No. 51).

2. Repealer and new section filed 12-17-2019; operative 1-1-2020. Submitted to OAL for printing only pursuant to Government Code section 11351 (Register 2019, No. 51).

§10890. Walk–Through Documents. [Repealed]

Note: Authority cited: Sections 133 and 5307, Labor Code. Reference: Sections 4053, 4054, 5001, 5002, 5702 and 5710, Labor Code.

History: 1. New section filed 12-19-2002; operative 1-1-2003. Submitted to OAL for printing only pursuant to Government Code section 11351 (Register 2002, No. 51).

2. Repealer filed 11-17-2008; operative 11-17-2008. Submitted to OAL for printing only (Register 2008, No. 47).

§10899. Unemployment Compensation Disability Liens.

When an unemployment compensation disability lien is filed by the Employment Development Department, there shall be a rebuttable presumption that the amounts stated therein have been paid to the injured worker by the Employment Development Department.

In any case involving a lien claim for unemployment compensation disability benefits or unemployment compensation benefits and extended duration benefits where it appears that further benefits may have been paid subsequent to the filing of the claim of lien, the workers' compensation judge shall notify the lien claimant when the case is ready for decision or for Order Approving Compromise and Release, and the lien claimant shall have five 5 days thereafter in which to file and serve an amended lien reflecting all payments made to and including the date of filing of the amended lien.

In cases where a Compromise and Release is filed and continuing unemployment compensation disability benefits or unemployment compensation benefits and extended duration benefits are being paid, the workers' compensation judge will ascertain the full amount of the lien claim as of the time of the approval of the Compromise and Release so that the allocation made under the authority of Labor Code section 4904 may be changed to reflect unemployment compensation disability or unemployment compensation and extended duration payments to the date of decision.

Note: Authority cited: Sections 133 and 5307, Labor Code. Reference: Sections 4903 and 4904, Labor Code.

History: 1. Renumbering and amendment of former section 10772 to section 10899 filed 12-17-2019; operative 1-1-2020. Submitted to OAL for printing only pursuant to Government Code section 11351 (Register 2019, No. 51).

Ref.: Herlick Handbook § 11.09.

ARTICLE 17
Arbitration

§10900. Mandatory Arbitration.

Unless the applicant is not represented by an attorney, any party may file an arbitration submittal form after a defendant denies liability for benefits because it disputes insurance coverage.

Any party may file an arbitration submittal form after a petition for contribution pursuant to Labor Code section 5500.5 has been filed.

Any party may file a petition objecting to arbitration submittal if the party asserts the issues in dispute are not subject to mandatory arbitration pursuant to Labor Code section 5275(a). Upon receipt of an arbitration submittal form or an objection to an arbitration submittal form, the presiding workers' compensation judge may set the matter for a status conference to determine if the issues in dispute are subject to mandatory arbitration.

Note: Authority cited: Sections 133, 5307, 5309 and 5708, Labor Code. Reference: Sections 5270, 5272, 5275, 5276, 5277 and 5500.5, Labor Code

History: 1. New article 17 heading and new section filed 12-17-2019; operative 1-1-2020. Submitted to OAL for printing only pursuant to Government Code section 11351 (Register 2019, No. 51).

Ref.: Hanna § 33.01[1][b]; Herlick Handbook § 14.32.

§10905. Voluntary Arbitration.

The parties agreeing to submit an issue or issues to voluntary arbitration shall jointly submit an arbitration submittal form outlining the issues they propose to submit to arbitration.

Unless there is an existing ADJ number, an Application for Adjudication of Claim shall be concurrently filed with an arbitration submittal form.

Upon receipt of an arbitration submittal form, the presiding workers' compensation judge may set the matter for a status conference to clarify the issues submitted to the arbitrator or to ensure compliance with Labor Code section 5270.

Note: Authority cited: Sections 133, 5307, 5309 and 5708, Labor Code. Reference: Sections 5270, 5271, 5272, 5273, 5275, 5276 and 5277, Labor Code.

History: 1. New section filed 12-17-2019; operative 1-1-2020. Submitted to OAL for printing only pursuant to Government Code section 11351 (Register 2019, No. 51).

Ref.: Hanna § 33.01[2][a], [b]; Herlick Handbook § 14.32.

§10910. Selection of Arbitrator.

(a) If the parties agree on an arbitrator, the parties shall file a proposed order appointing arbitrator concurrently with the arbitration submittal form. The presiding workers' compensation judge shall, within 10 days of receipt of the arbitration submittal form and proposed order, issue an Order Appointing Arbitrator or set the matter for a status conference.

(b) If the arbitration submittal form requests a panel pursuant to Labor Code section 5271, the presiding workers' compensation judge shall, within 10 days of receipt of the arbitration submittal form, serve on each of the parties an identical list of arbitrators selected at random pursuant to Labor Code 5271(b).

(1) Within 10 days of service of the list of arbitrators, any party may file a petition to disqualify an arbitrator for reasons set forth in section 170.1 of the Code of Civil Procedure. A timely petition for disqualification suspends the arbitrator selection process until the presiding workers' compensation judge acts on the petition. Together with any order issued regarding the petition for disqualification, the presiding workers' compensation judge shall set forth time limits for striking names.

(2) Within 15 days of service of the list of arbitrators, each party may strike two names from the list and serve notice of the names struck on all parties to the arbitration.

Failure to serve notice waives a party's right to participate in the arbitrator selection process.

(3) The presiding workers' compensation judge shall, within 30 days of receipt of the arbitration submittal form, issue an Order Appointing Arbitrator or set the matter for a status conference.

(c) Only the arbitrator named in the Order Appointing Arbitrator shall conduct the arbitration.

(d) An arbitrator shall not communicate with any party regarding the merits of the issues to be arbitrated until appointed as the named arbitrator in the Order Appointing Arbitrator.

Note: Authority cited: Sections 133, 5307, 5309 and 5708, Labor Code. Reference: Sections 5271, 5272, 5273, 5275, 5276 and 5277, Labor Code; and Section 170.1, Code of Civil Procedure.

History: 1. New section filed 12-17-2019; operative 1-1-2020. Submitted to OAL for printing only pursuant to Government Code section 11351 (Register 2019, No. 51).

Ref.: Hanna § 33.01[3][b]; Herlick Handbook § 14.32.

§10912. Disqualification of Arbitrator.

After service of a list of panel members pursuant to rule 10910, any party may, within 10 days, petition the presiding workers' compensation judge to remove any member from the panel pursuant to section 170.1 of the Code of Civil Procedure. If the presiding workers' compensation judge finds cause under section 170.1 of the Code of Civil Procedure, the presiding workers' compensation judge shall remove the member or members of the panel challenged and add to the original list the appropriate number of arbitrators at random to make a full panel and, within 10 days, serve the list on the parties.

If the presiding workers' compensation judge selects an arbitrator pursuant to rule 10910, the parties will have 10 days after service of the name of the arbitrator to petition to disqualify that arbitrator pursuant to section 170.1 of the Code of Civil Procedure. If the presiding workers' compensation judge finds cause, the presiding workers' compensation judge shall assign another arbitrator pursuant to Labor Code section 5271(d) and order the issue or issues in dispute submitted to that arbitrator.

Note: Authority cited: Sections 133, 5307, 5309 and 5708, Labor Code. Reference: Sections 5271, 5272, 5273, 5275, 5276 and 5277, Labor Code; and Section 170.1, Code of Civil Procedure.

History: 1. Renumbering of former section 10998 to section 10912, including amendment of section and Note, filed 12-17-2019; operative 1-1-2020. Submitted to OAL for printing only pursuant to Government Code section 11351 (Register 2019, No. 51).

Ref.: Hanna § 33.01[3][d]; Herlick Handbook § 14.32.

§10914. Record of Arbitration Proceeding.

(a) The arbitrator shall make and maintain the record of the arbitration proceeding and shall file the record with the Appeals Board when required by this rule or rule 10940.

(b) The parties shall provide the arbitrator with a copy of the Arbitration Submittal Form and the Order Appointing Arbitrator.

(c) The record of arbitration proceedings shall include the following:

(1) Order Appointing Arbitrator;

(2) Notices of appearance of the parties involved in the arbitration;

(3) Minutes of the arbitration proceedings, identifying those present, the date of the proceeding, the disposition and those served with the minutes or the identification of the party designated to serve the minutes;

(4) Pleadings, petitions, objections, briefs and responses filed by the parties with the arbitrator;

(5) Exhibits filed by the parties;

(6) Stipulations and issues entered into by the parties;

(7) Arbitrator's Summary of Evidence containing evidentiary rulings, a description of exhibits admitted into evidence, the identification of witnesses who testified and summary of witness testimony;

(8) Verbatim transcripts of witness testimony if witness testimony was taken under oath.

(9) Findings, orders, awards, decisions and opinions on decision made by the arbitrator; and

(10) Arbitrator's report on petition for reconsideration, removal or disqualification.

(d) The arbitrator shall file any finding, order or award together with the opinion on decision with the Appeals Board when it is served on the parties.

Note: Authority cited: Sections 133, 5307, 5309 and 5708, Labor Code. Reference: Sections 5271, 5272, 5273, 5275, 5276 and 5277, Labor Code.

History: 1. New section filed 12-17-2019; operative 1-1-2020. Submitted to OAL for printing only pursuant to Government Code section 11351 (Register 2019, No. 51).

Ref.: Hanna § 33.01[5]; Herlick Handbook § 14.32.

§10920. Arbitrator Fee and Cost Disputes.

Any dispute involving an arbitrator's fee or cost shall be resolved by the presiding workers' compensation judge of the district office having venue.

Any request to resolve a dispute about arbitrator fees or costs must be accompanied by any written agreement pertaining to arbitrator fees or costs and a statement that shall include the nature of the dispute and an itemization of the hours spent in actual arbitration hearing, in preparation for arbitration, and in preparation of the decision. The statement shall also include an itemization of the verifiable costs including use of facility, reporters and transcript preparation.

An arbitrator's fee shall not exceed a reasonable amount. In establishing a reasonable fee, the presiding workers' compensation judge shall consider:

(a) Responsibility assumed by the arbitrator;

(b) Experience of the arbitrator;

(c) Number and complexity of the issues being arbitrated;

(d) Time involved; and

(e) Expeditiousness and completeness of issue resolution.

The presiding workers' compensation judge of each district office shall maintain statistics on all arbitration fees awarded pursuant to Labor Code section 5273(c) including the amount and rationale for the award pursuant to (a) through (e) above.

Arbitration costs will be allowed in a reasonable amount pursuant to Labor Code section 5273(a).

Note: Authority: Sections 133, 5307, 5309 and 5708, Labor Code. Reference: Sections 5271, 5273, 5275, 5276 and 5277, Labor Code.

History: 1. Renumbering of former section 10999 to section 10920, including amendment of section and Note, filed 12-17-2019; operative 1-1-2020. Submitted to OAL for printing only pursuant to Government Code section 11351 (Register 2019, No. 51).

Ref.: Hanna § 33.01[6]; Herlick Handbook § 14.32.

ARTICLE 18
Reconsideration, Removal and Disqualification

§10940. Filing and Service of Petitions for Reconsideration, Removal, Disqualification and Answers.

(a) Petitions for reconsideration, removal, or disqualification and answers shall be filed in EAMS or with the district office having venue in accordance with Labor Code section 5501.5 unless otherwise provided. Petitions for reconsideration of decisions after reconsideration of the Appeals Board shall be filed with the office of the Appeals Board. Petitions filed in EAMS pursuant to this rule must comply with rules 10205.10-10205.14.

(b) No duplicate copies shall be filed with any district office or with the Appeals Board. No documents sent directly to the Appeals Board by fax or e-mail will be accepted for filing, unless otherwise ordered by the Appeals Board.

(c) Every petition and answer shall be verified upon oath in the manner required for verified pleadings in courts of record. A verification and a proof of service shall be attached to each petition and answer. Failure to file a proof of service shall constitute valid ground for dismissing the petition.

(d) A petition shall not exceed 25 pages and an answer shall not exceed 10 pages unless allowed by the Appeals Board. Any verification, proof of service, exhibit, document cover sheet or document separator sheet filed with the petition or answer shall not be counted in determining the page limitation. Upon its own motion or upon a showing of good cause, the Appeals Board may allow the filing of a petition or answer that exceeds the page limitations. A request to exceed the page limitations shall be made by a separate petition, made under penalty of perjury, that specifically sets forth reasons why the request should be granted.

(e) If the petition seeks removal or reconsideration of an arbitrator's decision or disqualification of an arbitrator, the petition and any answer shall be served on the arbitrator and all affected parties in accordance with rule 10610.

Note: Authority cited: Sections 133, 5307, 5309 and 5708, Labor Code. Reference: Sections 5501.5, 5900, 5902 and 5905, Labor Code.

History: 1. Amendment filed 6-28-83; designated effective 7-1-83 pursuant to Government Code Section 11346.2(d) (Register 83, No. 27).

2. Amendment of last paragraph filed 12-19-2002; operative 1-1-2003. Submitted to OAL for printing only pursuant to Government Code section 11351 (Register 2002, No. 51).

3. Repealer of article 19 heading, new article 18 heading and repealer and new section filed 12-17-2019; operative 1-1-2020. Submitted to OAL for printing only pursuant to Government Code section 11351 (Register 2019, No. 51).

Ref.: Hanna §§ 28.21[1], [2], 28.23, 28.26; Herlick Handbook §§ 14.32, 15.1, 15.3, 15.4.

§10942. Service. [Repealed]

Note: Authority cited: Sections 133 and 5307, Labor Code. Reference: Sections 4750, 4751, 4753, 4753.5 and 4754.5, Labor Code.

History: 1. Amendment filed 6-28-83; designated effective 7-1-83 pursuant to Government Code Section 11346.2(d) (Register 83, No. 27).

2. Amendment filed 12-19-2002; operative 1-1-2003. Submitted to OAL for printing only pursuant to Government Code section 11351 (Register 2002, No. 51).

3. Repealer filed 12-17-2019; operative 1-1-2020. Submitted to OAL for printing only pursuant to Government Code section 11351 (Register 2019, No. 51).

Ref.: Herlick Handbook §§ 15.1, 15.3.

§10944. Notice of Hearing. [Repealed]

Note: Authority cited. Sections 133 and 5307, Labor Code. Reference: Section 5502, Labor Code.

History: 1. Repealer filed 12-19-2002; operative 1-1-2003. Submitted to OAL for printing only pursuant to Government Code section 11351 (Register 2002, No. 51).

Ref.: Herlick Handbook §§ 15.1, 15.3.

§10945. Required Content of Petitions for Reconsideration, Removal, Disqualification and Answers.

(a) Every petition for reconsideration, removal or disqualification shall fairly state all of the material evidence relative to the point or points at issue. Each contention shall be separately stated and clearly set forth. A failure to fairly state all of the material evidence may be a basis for denying the petition.

(b) Every petition and answer shall support its evidentiary statements by specific references to the record.

(1) References to any stipulations, issues or testimony contained in any Minutes of Hearing, Summary of Evidence or hearing transcript shall specify:

(A) The date and time of the hearing; and

(B) If available, the page(s) and line number(s) of the Minutes, Summary, or transcript to which the evidentiary statement relates (e.g., "Summary of Evidence, 5/1/08 trial, 1:30pm session, at 6:11-6:15").

(2) References to any documentary evidence shall specify:

(A) The exhibit number or letter of the document;

(B) Where applicable, the author(s) of the document;

(C) Where applicable, the date(s) of the document; and

(D) The relevant page number(s) (e.g., "Exhibit M, Report of John A. Jones, M.D., 6/16/08 at p. 7.").

(3) References to any deposition transcript shall specify:

(A) The exhibit number or letter of the document;

(B) The name of the person deposed;

(C) The date of the deposition; and

(D) The relevant page number(s) and line(s) (e.g., "Exh. 3, 6/20/08 depo of William A. Smith, M.D., at 21:20-22:5]").

(c)(1) Copies of documents that have already been received in evidence or that have already been made part of the adjudication file shall not be attached or filed as exhibits to petitions for reconsideration, removal, or disqualification or answers. Documents attached in violation of this rule may be detached from the petition or answer and discarded.

(2) A document that is not part of the adjudication file shall not be attached to or filed with a petition for reconsideration or answer unless a ground for the petition for reconsideration is newly discovered evidence.

(3) A document shall not be attached to or filed with a petition for removal or disqualification or answer unless the document is not part of the adjudication file and is relevant to a petition for removal or disqualification.

Note: Authority cited: Sections 133, 5307, 5309 and 5708, Labor Code. Reference: Sections 126, 5310, 5311, 5900, 5902 and 5904, Labor Code.

History: 1. Renumbering of former section 10842 to section 10945, including amendment of section heading and section, filed 12-17-2019; operative 1-1-2020. Submitted to OAL for printing only pursuant to Government Code section 11351 (Register 2019, No. 51).

Ref.: Hanna §§ 28.21[1], 28.24; Herlick Handbook §§ 15.1, 15.3.

§10946. Medical Reports in Subsequent Injuries Benefits Trust Fund Cases. [Repealed]

Note: Authority cited: Sections 133, 5307, 5309 and 5708, Labor Code.

History: 1. Amendment filed 6-28-83; designated effective 7-1-83 pursuant to Government Code Section 11346.2(d) (Register 83, No. 27).

2. Amendment of section and Note filed 12-19-2002; operative 1-1-2003. Submitted to OAL for printing only pursuant to Government Code section 11351 (Register 2002, No. 51).

3. Amendment of section heading, section and Note filed 11-17-2008; operative 11-17-2008. Submitted to OAL for printing only (Register 2008, No. 47).

4. Repealer filed 12-17-2019; operative 1-1-2020. Submitted to OAL for printing only pursuant to Government Code section 11351 (Register 2019, No. 51).

Ref.: Herlick Handbook §§ 15.1, 15.3.

§10950. Petitions Appealing Orders Issued by the Administrative Director. [Repealed]

Note: Authority cited: Sections 133, 5307, 5309 and 5708, Labor Code. Reference: Sections 129, 4603, 4604, 5300, 5301 and 5302, Labor Code.

History: 1. Amendment of section and Note filed 12-19-2002; operative 1-1-2003. Submitted to OAL for printing only pursuant to Government Code section 11351 (Register 2002, No. 51).

2. Amendment of section heading, section and Note filed 11-17-2008; operative 11-17-2008. Submitted to OAL for printing only (Register 2008, No. 47).

3. Repealer of article 20 heading and section filed 12-17-2019; operative 1-1-2020. Submitted to OAL for printing only pursuant to Government Code section 11351 (Register 2019, No. 51).

Ref.: Herlick Handbook §§ 15.1, 15.3.

§10952. Appeal of Notice of Compensation Due. [Repealed]

Note: Authority cited: Sections 133 and 5307, Labor Code. Reference: Sections 129, 5300 and 5301, Labor Code.

History: 1. New section filed 6-11-92 with Secretary of State by Workers' Compensation Appeals Board; operative 6-11-92. Submitted to OAL for printing only pursuant to Government Code section 11351 (Register 92, No. 24).

2. Amendment filed 12-19-2002; operative 1-1-2003. Submitted to OAL for printing only pursuant to Government Code section 11351 (Register 2002, No. 51).

3. Repealer filed 11-17-2008; operative 11-17-2008. Submitted to OAL for printing only (Register 2008, No. 47).

Ref.: Herlick Handbook §§ 15.1, 15.3.

§10953. Petition Appealing Audit Penalty Assessment — Labor Code Section 129.5(g). [Renumbered]

Note: Authority cited: Sections 133, 5307, 5309 and 5708, Labor Code. Reference: Section 129.5(g), Labor Code.

History: 1. New section filed 12-19-2002; operative 1-1-2003. Submitted to OAL for printing only pursuant to Government Code section 11351 (Register 2002, No. 51).

2. Amendment of section and Note filed 11-17-2008; operative 11-17-2008. Submitted to OAL for printing only (Register 2008, No. 47).

3. Renumbering of former section 10953 to section 10590 filed 12-17-2019; operative 1-1-2020. Submitted to OAL for printing only pursuant to Government Code section 11351 (Register 2019, No. 51).

Ref.: Herlick Handbook §§ 15.1, 15.3.

§10955. Petitions for Removal and Answers.

(a) At any time within 20 days after the service of the order or decision, or of the occurrence of the action in issue, any party may petition for removal based upon one or more of the following grounds:

(1) The order, decision or action will result in significant prejudice.

(2) The order, decision or action will result in irreparable harm.

The petitioner must also demonstrate that reconsideration will not be an adequate remedy after the issuance of a final order, decision or award. Failure to file the petition to remove timely shall constitute valid ground for dismissing the petition for removal.

(b) The petition for removal and any answer shall be verified upon oath in the manner required for verified pleadings in courts of record.

(c) A copy of the petition for removal shall be served forthwith upon all parties by the petitioner. Any adverse party may file an answer within 10 days after service. No supplemental petitions, pleadings or responses shall be considered unless requested or approved by the Appeals Board.

(d) A workers' compensation judge may, within 15 days of the filing of the petition for removal, rescind the order or decision in issue, or take action to resolve the issue raised in the petition. If the workers' compensation judge so acts, or if the petitioner withdraws the petition at any time, the petition for removal will be deemed automatically dismissed, requiring no further action by the Appeals Board. The issuance of a new order or decision, or the occurrence of a new action, will recommence the time period for filing a petition for removal as described above.

(e) The filing of a petition for removal does not terminate the workers' compensation judge's authority to proceed in a case or require the workers' compensation judge to continue or cancel a previously scheduled hearing absent direction from the Appeals Board. After a petition for removal has been filed, the workers' compensation judge shall consult with the presiding workers' compensation judge prior to proceeding in the case or continuing or canceling a scheduled hearing.

Note: Authority cited: Sections 133, 5307, 5309 and 5708, Labor Code. Reference: Section 5310, Labor Code.

History: 1. Renumbering and amendment of former section 10843 to section 10955 filed 12-17-2019; operative 1-1-2020. Submitted to OAL for printing only pursuant to Government Code section 11351 (Register 2019, No. 51). For prior history, see Register 2008, No. 47.

Ref.: Hanna §§ 1.11[3][g], 26.03[4]; Herlick Handbook §§ 15.1, 15.3.

§10956. Rehabilitation Records. [Repealed]

Note: Authority cited: Sections 133 and 5307, Labor Code. Reference: Sections 139.5, 5708 and 5709, Labor Code.

History: 1. Repealer filed 12-19-2002; operative 1-1-2003. Submitted to OAL for printing only pursuant to Government Code section 11351 (Register 2002, No. 51).

Ref.: Herlick Handbook §§ 15.1, 15.3.

§10957. Petition Appealing Independent Bill Review Determination of the Administrative Director. [Renumbered]

Note: Authority: Sections 133, 5307, 5309 and 5708, Labor Code. Reference: Sections 4603.6, 5500, 5501, 5502, 5700 et seq., 5800 et seq. and 5900 et seq., Labor Code; and Sections 10250, 10409, 10507, 10508, 10842, 10845, 10846, 10852, 10856, 10859 and 10860, California Code of Regulations, title 8.

History: 1. New section filed 9-23-2013; operative 10-23-2013. Submitted as a file and print by the Workers' Compensation Appeals Board pursuant to Government Code section 11351 (Register 2013, No. 39). For prior history, see Register 2008, No. 47.

2. Renumbering of former section 10957 to section 10567 filed 12-17-2019; operative 1-1-2020. Submitted to OAL for printing only pursuant to Government Code section 11351 (Register 2019, No. 51).

Ref.: Herlick Handbook §§ 15.1, 15.3.

§10957.1. Petition Appealing Independent Medical Review Determination of the Administrative Director. [Renumbered]

Note: Authority: Sections 133, 5307, 5309 and 5708, Labor Code. Reference: Sections 4610.6, 5500, 5501, 5502, 5700 et seq., 5800 et seq. and 5900 et seq., Labor Code; and Sections 10250, 10409, 10507, 10508, 10842, 10845, 10846, 10852, 10856, 10859 and 10860, California Code of Regulations, title 8.

History: 1. New section filed 9-23-2013; operative 10-23-2013. Submitted as a file and print by the Workers' Compensation Appeals Board pursuant to Government Code section 11351 (Register 2013, No. 39).

2. Amendment of subsections (c) and (i) filed 10-15-2014; operative 1-1-2015. Submitted to OAL for printing only pursuant to Government Code section 11351 (Register 2014, No. 42).

3. Editorial correction of History 2 (Register 2017, No. 8).

4. Renumbering of former section 10957.1 to section 10575 filed 12-17-2019; operative 1-1-2020. Submitted to OAL for printing only pursuant to Government Code section 11351 (Register 2019, No. 51).

Ref.: Herlick Handbook §§ 15.1, 15.3.

§10958. Hearing and Burden of Proof. [Repealed]

Note: Authority cited: Sections 133 and 5307, Labor Code. Reference: Section 5708, Labor Code.

History: 1. Amendment of section and Note filed 12-19-2002; operative 1-1-2003. Submitted to OAL for printing only pursuant to Government Code section 11351 (Register 2002, No. 51).

2. Repealer filed 10-15-2014; operative 1-1-2015. Submitted to OAL for printing only pursuant to Government Code section 11351 (Register 2014, No. 42).

3. Editorial correction of History 2 (Register 2017, No. 8).

Ref.: Herlick Handbook §§ 15.1, 15.3.

§10959. Petition Appealing Medical Provider Network Determination of the Administrative Director. [Renumbered]

Note: Authority: Sections 133, 5307, 5309 and 5708, Labor Code. Reference: Sections 4616 et seq., 5300(f) and 5900 et seq., Labor Code.

History: 1. New section filed 9-23-2013; operative 10-23-2013. Submitted as a file and print by the Workers' Compensation Appeals Board pursuant to Government Code section 11351 (Register 2013, No. 39).

2. Renumbering of former section 10959 to section 10580 filed 12-17-2019; operative 1-1-2020. Submitted to OAL for printing only pursuant to Government Code section 11351 (Register 2019, No. 51).

Ref.: Herlick Handbook §§ 15.1, 15.3.

§10960. Petition for Disqualification of Workers' Compensation Judge.

Proceedings to disqualify a workers' compensation judge under Labor Code section 5311 shall be initiated by the filing of a petition for disqualification supported by an affidavit or declaration under penalty of perjury stating in detail facts establishing one or more of the grounds for disqualification specified in section 641 of the Code of Civil Procedure. The petition to disqualify a workers' compensation judge and any answer shall be verified upon oath in the manner required for verified pleadings in courts of record.

If the workers' compensation judge assigned to hear the matter and the grounds for disqualification are known, the petition for disqualification shall be filed not more than 10 days after service of notice of hearing or after grounds for disqualification are known.

A petition for disqualification shall be referred to and determined by a panel of three commissioners of the Appeals Board in the same manner as a petition for reconsideration.

Note: Authority cited: Section 5307, Labor Code. Reference: Section 641, Code of Civil Procedure; and Sections 5310 and 5311, Labor Code.

History: 1. Repealer of article 21 heading, renumbering of former section 10452 to section 10960, including amendment of section heading, section and Note, filed 12-17-2019; operative 1-1-2020. Submitted to OAL for printing only pursuant to Government Code section 11351 (Register 2019, No. 51).

Ref.: Hanna § 26.03[2]; Herlick Handbook §§ 14.19, 15.1, 15.3.

§10961. Actions by Workers' Compensation Judge After Petition for Reconsideration is Filed.

Within 15 days of the timely filing of a petition for reconsideration, a workers' compensation judge shall perform one of the following actions:

(a) Prepare a Report and Recommendation on Petition for Reconsideration in accordance with rule 10962;

(b) Rescind the entire order, decision or award and initiate further proceedings within 30 days; or

(c) Rescind the order, decision or award and issue an amended order, decision or award. The time for filing a petition for reconsideration pursuant to Labor Code section 5903 will run from the filing date of the amended order, decision or award.

After 15 days have elapsed from the filing of a petition for reconsideration, a workers' compensation judge shall not issue any order in the case until the Appeals Board has denied or dismissed the petition for reconsideration or issued a decision after reconsideration.

Note: Authority cited: Section 5307, Labor Code. Reference: Sections 5903, 5906, 5907 and 5908.5, Labor Code.

History: 1. Renumbering of former section 10859 to section 10961, including amendment of section heading, section and Note, filed 12-17-2019; operative 1-1-2020. Submitted to OAL for printing only pursuant to Government Code section 11351 (Register 2019, No. 51).

Ref.: Hanna §§ 26.10[1], 28.03[2], 28.25, 30.20[1]; Herlick Handbook §§ 15.1, 15.3, 15.4.

§10962. Report of Workers' Compensation Judge.

Petitions for reconsideration, petitions for removal and petitions for disqualification shall be referred to the workers' compensation judge from whose decisions or actions relief is sought. If the workers' compensation judge prepares a report, it shall contain:

(a) A statement of the contentions raised by the petition;

(b) A discussion of the support in the record for the findings of fact and the conclusions of law that serve as a basis for the decision or order as to each contention raised by the petition, or, in the case of a petition for disqualification, a specific response to the allegations and, if appropriate, a discussion of any failure by the petitioner to comply with the procedures set forth in rule 10960; and

(c) The action recommended on the petition.

The workers' compensation judge shall submit the report to the Appeals Board within 15 days after the petition is filed unless the Appeals Board grants an extension of time. The workers' compensation judge shall serve a copy of the report on the parties and any lien claimant, the validity of whose lien is specifically questioned by the petition, at the time the report is submitted to the Appeals Board.

If the workers' compensation judge assigned to the case is unavailable, the presiding workers' compensation judge shall prepare and serve the report.

Note: Authority cited: Sections 133, 5307, 5309 and 5708, Labor Code. Reference: Sections 5900 and 5906, Labor Code.

History: 1. Renumbering and amendment of former section 10860 to section 10962 filed 12-17-2019; operative 1-1-2020. Submitted to OAL for printing only pursuant to Government Code section 11351 (Register 2019, No. 51).

Ref.: Hanna §§ 26.03[4], 28.35[2]; Herlick Handbook §§ 15.1, 15.3.

§10964. Supplemental Petitions.

(a) When a petition for reconsideration, removal or disqualification has been timely filed, supplemental petitions or pleadings or responses other than the answer shall be considered only when specifically requested or approved by the Appeals Board.

(b) A party seeking to file a supplemental pleading shall file a petition setting forth good cause for the Appeals Board to approve the filing of a supplemental pleading and shall attach the proposed pleading.

(c) Supplemental petitions or pleadings or responses other than the answer shall neither be accepted nor deemed filed for any purpose except as provided by this rule.

Note: Authority cited: Sections 133, 5307, 5309 and 5708, Labor Code. Reference: Sections 5310, 5311 and 5900, Labor Code.

History: 1. Renumbering and amendment of former section 10848 to section 10964 filed 12-17-2019; operative 1-1-2020. Submitted to OAL for printing only pursuant to Government Code section 11351 (Register 2019, No. 51).

Ref.: Hanna § 28.21[3]; Herlick Handbook §§ 15.1, 15.3.

§10966. Correction of Errors.

Before a petition for reconsideration is filed, a workers' compensation judge may correct the decision for clerical, mathematical or procedural error or amend the decision for good cause under the authority and subject to the limitations set out in sections 5803 and 5804 of the Labor Code.

Note: Authority cited: Sections 133 and 5307, Labor Code. Reference: Sections 5309, 5803 and 5804, Labor Code.

History: 1. Renumbering of former section 10858 to section 10966, including amendment of Note, filed 12-17-2019; operative 1-1-2020. Submitted to OAL for printing only pursuant to Government Code section 11351 (Register 2019, No. 51).

Ref.: Hanna §§ 28.03[1][c], [2], 28.20; Herlick Handbook §§ 14.34, 15.1, 15.3.

§10972. Skeletal Petitions.

A petition for reconsideration, removal or disqualification may be denied or dismissed if it is unsupported by specific references to the record and to the principles of law involved.

Note: Authority cited: Sections 133, 5307, 5309 and 5708, Labor Code. Reference: Sections 126, 5310, 5311, 5900, 5902, 5903 and 5904, Labor Code.

History: 1. Renumbering of former section 10846 to section 10972, including amendment of Note, filed 12-17-2019; operative 1-1-2020. Submitted to OAL for printing only pursuant to Government Code section 11351 (Register 2019, No. 51).

Ref.: Hanna §§ 5.03[7], 28.21[1]; Herlick Handbook §§ 15.1, 15.3, 15.4.

§10974. Allegations of Newly Discovered Evidence and Fraud.

Where reconsideration is sought on the ground of newly discovered evidence that could not with reasonable diligence have been produced before submission of the case or on the ground that the decision had been procured by fraud, the petition must contain an offer of proof, specific and detailed, providing:

(a) The names of witnesses to be produced;

(b) A summary of the testimony to be elicited from the witnesses;

(c) A description of any documentary evidence to be offered;

(d) The effect that the evidence will have on the record and on the prior decision; and

(e) As to newly discovered evidence, a full and accurate statement of the reasons why the testimony or exhibits could not reasonably have been discovered or produced before submission of the case.

A petition for reconsideration sought upon these grounds may be denied if it fails to meet the requirements of this rule, or if it is based upon cumulative evidence.

Note: Authority cited: Sections 133 and 5307, Labor Code. Reference: Sections 5902 and 5903, Labor Code.

History: 1. Renumbering and amendment of former section 10856 to section 10974 filed 12-17-2019; operative 1-1-2020. Submitted to OAL for printing only pursuant to Government Code section 11351 (Register 2019, No. 51).

Ref.: Hanna §§ 26.04[2], 28.22[2], 28.32, 31.04[2][d]; Herlick Handbook §§ 15.1, 15.3, 15.4.

§10984. Hearing After Reconsideration Granted.

Where reconsideration has been granted and the case referred to a workers' compensation judge for proceedings on reconsideration, the workers' compensation judge shall, upon the conclusion thereof, prepare and serve upon the parties a summary of evidence received in the proceedings after reconsideration granted.

Unless otherwise instructed by the panel before which a case is pending, the workers' compensation judge to whom the case has been assigned for further proceedings may rule on requests for postponement and continuance of further hearing, join additional parties, dismiss unnecessary parties where such dismissal is not opposed by any other party to the case, make all interlocutory or procedural orders that are agreed to by all parties, issue subpoenas, rule on motions for discovery, rule on all evidentiary motions and objections and make all other rulings necessary to expedite and facilitate the trial and disposition of the case. The workers' compensation judge shall not order a medical examination, obtain a recommended disability evaluation, make an order taking the case off calendar nor make an order approving or disapproving Compromise and Release.

Note: Authority cited: Sections 133 and 5307, Labor Code. Reference: Sections 5309 and 5313, Labor Code.

History: 1. Renumbering and amendment of former section 10862 to section 10984 filed 12-17-2019; operative 1-1-2020. Submitted to OAL for printing only pursuant to Government Code section 11351 (Register 2019, No. 51).

Ref.: Hanna § 28.36[1], [2][a]; Herlick Handbook §§ 15.1, 15.3.

§10986. Authority of Workers' Compensation Judge After Decision After Reconsideration.

After a decision after reconsideration has become final, subsequent orders and decisions in a case shall be made by any trial level workers' compensation judge.

An order correcting a decision after reconsideration for clerical, mathematical or procedural error shall be made by the panel that made the decision or, if the composition of the Appeals Board has changed, by the successor panel.

Note: Authority cited: Sections 133 and 5307, Labor Code. Reference: Sections 5900, 5910 and 5911, Labor Code.

History: 1. Renumbering and amendment of former section 10864 to section 10986 filed 12-17-2019; operative 1-1-2020. Submitted to OAL for printing only pursuant to Government Code section 11351 (Register 2019, No. 51).

Ref.: Hanna §§ 28.03[2], 28.36[3]; Herlick Handbook §§ 15.1, 15.3.

§10990. Reconsideration of Arbitration Decisions Made Pursuant to Labor Code Sections 3201.5 and 3201.7.

(a) A petition for reconsideration from an arbitration decision made pursuant to Labor Code section 3201.5(a)(1) or section 3201.7(a)(1) (known as "carve-out" cases) shall be filed directly with the office of the Appeals Board within 20 days of the service of the final order, decision or award made and filed by the arbitrator or board of arbitrators. A copy of the petition for reconsideration shall be served on the arbitrator or arbitration board.

(b) Notwithstanding any other provision of these rules, a petition for reconsideration in a carve-out case shall be filed directly with the office of the Appeals Board, and not with any district office, including the San Francisco district office. Any petition for reconsideration in a carve-out case that is received by any district office shall neither be accepted for filing nor deemed filed for any purpose. If a carve-out petition for reconsideration is submitted to a district office in violation of this rule, the petition shall be returned to the petitioner with a letter referencing this rule, noting that the petition was improperly submitted to a district office and has been rejected, and indicating that the petition should be filed directly with the Appeals Board consistent with this rule.

(c) The petition for reconsideration in a carve-out case, which shall be submitted with a document cover sheet, shall also comply with each of the following requirements:

(1) It shall be captioned so as to identify it as a "Petition for Reconsideration from Arbitrator's Decision Under Labor Code section 3201.5 or 3201.7" and it shall include:

(A) The injured employee's first and last names;

(B) The name(s) of the defendant(s);

(C) The alternative dispute resolution (ADR) case number (i.e., the carve-out arbitration case number); and

(D) The Workers' Compensation Appeals Board adjudication case number, if previously assigned;

(2) It shall set forth the date on which the arbitrator or board of arbitrators served the arbitration decision. Proof of service of the arbitration decision on the parties shall be either by a verified statement of the arbitrator or the board of arbitrators indicating the date of service and listing the names and addresses of the persons served or by written acknowledgment of receipt by the parties at the time of the arbitration proceedings;

(3) It shall append, under a document separator sheet a copy of that portion of the collective bargaining agreement relating to the workers' compensation arbitration and reconsideration processes;

(4) It shall append, under a document separator sheet, a completed Application for Adjudication of Claim (but without any venue designation), which is required solely for the purpose of obtaining the information set forth therein (e.g., the injured employee's date(s) of injury and date of birth; the names and mailing addresses of the parties); therefore, it shall not be deemed an application for purposes of Labor Code section 4064(c); and

(5) It shall contain a proof of service of the petition, including service on the arbitrator or board of arbitrators.

(d) After the filing of the carve-out petition for reconsideration, an adjudication file will be created and an adjudication case number will be assigned, if there is no existing adjudication case number. Any new adjudication case number will be served by the Appeals Board on the parties and attorneys, and on the arbitrator or board of arbitrators, at the addresses listed in the proof of service to the petition.

(e) Following the Appeals Board's service of the adjudication case number (or, if there is an existing case, following the filing of the carve-out petition for reconsideration), and until the Appeals Board issues a decision disposing of all issues raised in the petition, all further documents shall be filed directly with the office of the Appeals Board, and not with any district office.

(f) Within 15 days after receiving the petition for reconsideration, the arbitrator or board of arbitrators shall perform one of the following actions:

(1) Rescind the entire order, decision or award and initiate further proceedings within 30 days; or

(2) Rescind the order, decision or award and issue an amended order, decision or award. The time for filing a petition for reconsideration pursuant to Labor Code section 5903 will run from the filing date of the amended order, decision or award; or

(3) Submit to the Appeals Board an electronic copy of the complete record of proceedings, including:

(A) The transcript of proceedings, if any;

(B) A summary of testimony if the proceedings were not transcribed;

(C) The documentary evidence submitted by each of the parties;

(D) An opinion that sets forth the rationale for the decision; and

(E) A report on the petition for reconsideration, consistent with the provisions of rule 10962. The original arbitration record shall not be filed.

(g) Upon receipt of the electronic copy of the complete record of proceedings, the Appeals Board may enter the petition for reconsideration, any answer and the record of the arbitration proceedings into the adjudication file within EAMS.

(h) The petition for reconsideration, any answer, and the arbitration record shall be deemed part of the Workers' Compensation Appeals Board's record of proceedings under rule 10803.

(i) After an arbitration decision has been made, the arbitrator or board of arbitrators shall maintain possession of the original record of the arbitration proceedings until the time for filing a petition for reconsideration has passed. Thereafter, one of the parties may be designated custodian of the arbitration record as provided for in the collective bargaining agreement.

Note: Authority cited: Sections 133, 5307, 5309 and 5708, Labor Code. Reference: Sections 3201.5, 3201.7 and 4064, Labor Code.

History: 1. Renumbering of former section 10865 to section 10990, including amendment of section and Note, filed 12-17-2019; operative 1-1-2020. Submitted to OAL for printing only pursuant to Government Code section 11351 (Register 2019, No. 51).

Ref.: Hanna §§ 25.06[1], 28.27, 33.01[7]; Herlick Handbook §§ 15.1, 15.3, 15.4.

§10995. Reconsideration of Arbitrator's Decisions or Awards Made Pursuant to the Mandatory or Voluntary Arbitration Provisions of Labor Code Sections 5270 through 5275.

(a) Any final order, decision or award filed by an arbitrator under the mandatory or voluntary arbitration provisions of Labor Code sections 5270 through 5275 shall be subject to the reconsideration process.

(b) A petition for reconsideration from any final order, decision or award filed by an arbitrator under the mandatory or voluntary arbitration provisions of Labor Code sections 5270 through 5275, and any answer, shall be filed in EAMS or with the district office having venue in accordance with Labor Code section 5501.5. No duplicate copies of petitions shall be filed with any other district office or with the Appeals Board.

(c) Within 15 days after receiving the petition for reconsideration, the arbitrator shall perform one of the following actions:

(1) Rescind the entire order, decision or award and initiate further proceedings within 30 days; or

(2) Rescind the order, decision or award and issue an amended order, decision or award. The time for filing a petition for reconsideration pursuant to Labor Code section 5903 will run from the filing date of the amended order, decision or award; or

(3) Prepare and serve a report on reconsideration as provided in rule 10962. Upon completion of the report on reconsideration, the arbitrator shall concurrently forward an electronic copy of the arbitrator's report and an electronic copy of the complete arbitration file directly to the presiding workers' compensation judge of the district office

having venue over the matter. Upon receipt of the arbitrator's report and the record of arbitration proceedings, the district office shall enter the report and the file into the EAMS adjudication file.

(d) The petition for reconsideration, any answer, and the arbitration record shall be deemed part of the Workers' Compensation Appeals Board's record of proceedings under rule 10803.

Note: Authority cited: Sections 133, 5307, 5309 and 5708, Labor Code. Reference: Sections 5270-5275, 5501.5 and 5900-5911, Labor Code.

History: 1. New section filed 10-15-2014; operative 1-1-2015. Submitted to OAL for printing only pursuant to Government Code section 11351 (Register 2014, No. 42). For prior history, see Register 2008, No. 47.

2. Editorial correction of History 1 (Register 2017, No. 8).

3. Repealer of article 22 heading, repealer of former section 10995 and renumbering of former section 10866 to section 10995, including amendment of section and Note, filed 12-17-2019; operative 1-1-2020. Submitted to OAL for printing only pursuant to Government Code section 11351 (Register 2019, No. 51).

Ref.: Hanna § 28.26; Herlick Handbook §§ 15.1, 15.3.

§10996. Voluntary Arbitration. [Repealed]

Note: Authority cited: Sections 133, 5307, 5309 and 5708, Labor Code. Reference: Sections 5270-5278, Labor Code.

History: 1. New section filed 10-15-2014; operative 1-1-2015. Submitted to OAL for printing only pursuant to Government Code section 11351 (Register 2014, No. 42). For prior history, see Register 2008, No. 47.

2. Editorial correction of History 1 (Register 2017, No. 8).

3. Repealer filed 12-17-2019; operative 1-1-2020. Submitted to OAL for printing only pursuant to Government Code section 11351 (Register 2019, No. 51).

§10997. Request for Arbitration. [Repealed]

Note: Authority cited: Sections 133 and 5307, Labor Code. Reference: Sections 5270 through 5277, Labor Code.

History: 1. New section filed 1-12-90; operative 1-12-90 (Register 90, No. 5). This section is exempt from review by OAL pursuant to Government Code section 11351.

2. Change without regulatory effect filed 1-26-90 (Register 90, No. 5).

3. Amendment exempt from OAL review pursuant to Government Code section 11351 filed 12-19-90; operative 1-1-91 (Register 91, No. 7).

4. Amendment filed 12-19-2002; operative 1-1-2003. Submitted to OAL for printing only pursuant to Government Code section 11351 (Register 2002, No. 51).

5. Repealer filed 12-17-2019; operative 1-1-2020. Submitted to OAL for printing only pursuant to Government Code section 11351 (Register 2019, No. 51).

§10998. Disqualification of Arbitrator. [Renumbered]

Note: Authority cited: Sections 133 and 5307, Labor Code. Reference: Section 5271(d), Labor Code.

History: 1. New section filed 1-12-90; operative 1-12-90 (Register 90, No. 5). This section is exempt from review by OAL pursuant to Government Code section 11351.

2. Change without regulatory effect filed 1-26-90 (Register 90, No. 5).

3. Amendment exempt from OAL review pursuant to Government Code section 11351 filed 12-19-90; operative 1-1-91 (Register 91, No. 7).

4. Amendment of first paragraph and Note filed 12-19-2002; operative 1-1-2003. Submitted to OAL for printing only pursuant to Government Code section 11351 (Register 2002, No. 51).

5. Renumbering of former section 10998 to section 10912 filed 12-17-2019; operative 1-1-2020. Submitted to OAL for printing only pursuant to Government Code section 11351 (Register 2019, No. 51).

§10999. Arbitrator Fee and Cost Disputes. [Renumbered]

Note: Authority cited: Sections 133 and 5307, Labor Code. Reference: Section 5273(c), Labor Code.

History: 1. New section filed 1-12-90; operative 1-12-90 (Register 90, No. 5). This section is exempt from review by OAL pursuant to Government Code section 11351.

2. Change without regulatory effect filed 1-26-90 (Register 90, No. 5).

3. Amendment exempt from OAL review pursuant to Government Code section 11351 filed 12-19-90; operative 1-1-91 (Register 91, No. 7).

4. Amendment of section and Note filed 12-19-2002; operative 1-1-2003. Submitted to OAL for printing only pursuant to Government Code section 11351 (Register 2002, No. 51).

5. Renumbering of former section 10999 to section 10920 filed 12-17-2019; operative 1-1-2020. Submitted to OAL for printing only pursuant to Government Code section 11351 (Register 2019, No. 51).

CHAPTER 7
DEPARTMENT OF INDUSTRIAL RELATIONS

SUBCHAPTER 1
OCCUPATIONAL INJURY OR ILLNESS REPORTS AND RECORDS

ARTICLE 1
Reporting of Occupational Injury or Illness

§14000. Definitions.

As used in this Article:

Computer input media. Techniques and means by which information or data can be entered into a computer system. Examples include magnetic tape, diskette, and telecommunications.

Division. The Division of Labor Statistics and Research of the Department of Industrial Relations.

Occupational illness. Any abnormal condition or disorder caused by exposure to environmental factors associated with employment, including acute and chronic illnesses or diseases which may be caused by inhalation, absorption, ingestion, or direct contact.

Self-insured employer. An employer who has secured from the Director of Industrial Relations a certificate of consent to self-insure against workers' compensation claims pursuant to Labor Code Section 3700.

Note: Authority cited: Section 6410, Labor Code. Reference: Sections 3700, 6409(b), 6410, Labor Code.

History: 1. New §§14000 to 14504, inclusive, filed 3-3-47; effective thirtieth day thereafter (Register 7).

2. Amendment filed 5-16-73; designated effective 7-1-73 (Register 73, No. 20).

3. Amendment filed 4-15-74; designated effective 6-1-74 (Register 74, No. 16).

4. Repealer and new section filed 2-8-80; designated effective 5-1-80 (Register 80, No. 6).

5. Amendment filed 3-18-87; effective thirtieth day thereafter (Register 87, No. 12).

6. Amendment 6-14-89; operative 7-14-89 (Register 89, No. 25).

7. Amendment of section and Note filed 1-14-93; operative 2-16-93 (Register 93, No. 3).

8. Amendment of chapter heading filed 9-21-2015; operative 10-1-2015 pursuant to Government Code section 11343.4(b)(3) (Register 2015, No. 39).

Ref.: Hanna §§ 22.08[2], 25.20[3].

§14001. Employer.

(a) Every employer shall file a complete report of every occupational injury or occupational illness to each employee which results in lost time beyond the date of such injury or illness or which requires medical treatment beyond first aid, as defined in Labor Code Section 5401(a). As used in this subdivision, "lost time" means absence from work for a full day or shift beyond the date of the injury or illness.

(b) In the event an employer has filed a report of injury or illness pursuant to subdivision 14001(a), and the employee subsequently dies as a result of the reported injury or illness, the employer shall file an amended report indicating such death, within five days after the employer is notified or learns of the death.

(c) The report(s) required by subdivisions 14001(a) and (b) shall be made on Form 5020, Rev. 6, Employer's Report of Occupational Injury or Illness, reproduced in accordance with Section 14005, or by use of computer input media, prescribed by the Division and compatible with the Division's computer equipment. However, reports may be submitted on Form 5020, Rev. 5 until June 30, 1993.

(d) In the case of a self-insured employer, the reports required by subdivision 14001(a) and (b) shall be filed directly with the Division within five days after the employer obtains knowledge of the injury, illness or death. In addition, the self-insured employer shall transmit the doctor's report filed in accordance with Section 14003 to the Division within five days of receipt.

(e) In the case of an insured employer, the report required by subdivisions 14001(a) and (b) shall be filed with the insurer within five days after such insured employer obtains knowledge of the injury, illness or death.

(f) To assure timely filing of the doctor's first report, the employer, upon request by the physician, shall immediately disclose the name and address of the employer's workers' compensation insurance provider.

Note: Authority cited: Section 6410, Labor Code. Reference: Sections 5401(a), 6409(a), 6409.1(a), Labor Code.

History: 1. New section filed 3-3-47; effective thirtieth day thereafter (Register 7).

2. Amendment filed 11-26-51; effective thirtieth day thereafter (Register 26, No. 5).

3. Repealer filed 5-16-73; designated effective 7-1-73 (Register 73, No. 20).

4. New section filed 2-8-80; designated effective 5-1-80 (Register 80, No. 6).

5. Amendment of subsection (b) filed 1-13-83; effective thirtieth day thereafter (Register 83, No. 3).

6. Amendment of subsections (b)–(d) filed 3-18-87; effective thirtieth day thereafter (Register 87, No. 12).

7. Amendment filed 6-14-89; operative 7-14-89 (Register 89, No. 25).

8. Editorial correction of printing error in subsections (a) and (b) (Register 90, No. 6).

9. Amendment of subsection (a), new subsection (b), subsection relettering, amendments of newly designated subsections (c)-(e), new subsection (f), and amendments of Note filed 1-14-93; operative 2-16-93 (Register 93, No. 3).

Ref.: Hanna §§ 22.08[2], 25.20[3].

§14002. Insurer.

(a) Immediately upon receipt, the insurer shall transmit to the Division the reports filed by the insured employer, as required by subdivisions 14001(a) and (b). The report(s) filed shall be on either Form 5020, Rev. 6, or the computer input media prescribed by the Division.

(b) In addition, the insurer shall transmit the doctor's report filed in accordance with Section 14003 to the Division within five days of receipt.

Note: Authority cited: Section 6410, Labor Code. Reference: Sections 6409(a), 6409.1(a), Labor Code.

History: 1. New section filed 5-16-73; designated effective 7-1-73 (Register 73, No. 20).

2. Amendment filed 4-15-74; designated effective 6-1-74 (Register 74, No. 16).

3. Repealer and new section filed 2-8-80; designated effective 5-1-80 (Register 80, No. 6).

4. Amendment of subsection (a) filed 3-18-87; effective thirtieth day thereafter (Register 87, No. 12).

5. Amendment filed 6-14-89; operative 7-14-89 (Register 89, No. 25).

6. Editorial correction of printing error in subsection (b) (Register 90, No. 6).

7. Amendment of subsection (a) filed 1-14-93; operative 2-16-93 (Register 93, No. 3).

Ref.: Hanna §§ 22.08[2], 25.20[3].

§14003. Physician.

(a) Every physician, as defined in Labor Code Section 3209.3, who attends an injured employee shall file, within five days after initial examination, a complete report of every occupational injury or occupational illness to such employee, with the employer's insurer, or with the employer, if self-insured. The injured or ill employee, if able to do so, shall complete a portion of such report describing how the injury or illness occurred. Unless the report is transmitted on computer input media, the physician shall file the original signed report with the insurer or self-insured employer.

(b) If treatment is for pesticide poisoning or for a condition suspected to be pesticide poisoning, the physician shall also file a complete report directly with the Division within five days after initial treatment. In no case shall treatment administered for pesticide poisoning or suspected pesticide poisoning be deemed to be first aid treatment.

(c) The reports required by this Section shall be made on Form 5021, Rev. 5, Doctor's First Report of Occupational Injury or Illness (sample forms may be secured from the Division), upon a form reproduced in accordance with Section 14007, or by use of computer input media prescribed by the Division and compatible with the Division's computer equipment. However, reports may be submitted on Revision 4 of Form 5021 for dates of service prior to October 1, 2015. Although ICD-10 coding is required on or after October 1, 2015, for a twelve-month period ending October 1, 2016, no medical treatment or medical-legal bill shall be denied based solely on an error in the level of specificity of the ICD-10 diagnosis code(s) used. Providers may use either version of the form until December 31, 2015. As of January 1, 2016, providers must use the 2015 version of the form.

(d) Physicians who use computerized data collection and reporting systems shall keep the injured worker's statement with the patient's medical records.

Note: Authority cited: Section 6410, Labor Code. Reference: Sections 6409(a), 6409.3, and 6410, Labor Code.

History: 1. New section filed 2-8-80; designated effective 5-1-80 (Register 80, No. 6).

2. Amendment of subsection (c) filed 1-13-83; effective thirtieth day thereafter (Register 83, No. 3).

3. Amendment filed 6-14-89; operative 7-14-89 (Register 89, No. 25).

4. Editorial correction of printing error in subsection (a) (Register 90, No. 6).

5. Amendment of subsections (a) and (c) filed 1-14-93; operative 2-16-93 (Register 93, No. 3).

6. Editorial correction of printing error in subsection (c) (Register 93, No. 44).

7. Amendment of subsection (c) filed 9-21-2015; operative 10-1-2015 pursuant to Government Code section 11343.4(b)(3) (Register 2015, No. 39).

Ref.: Hanna § 22.08[2]; Herlick Handbook § 4.08[2], [4].

§14004. Employer's Report of Occupational Injury or Illness, Form 5020, Rev. 7.

[DLSR Form 5020 (Rev. June 2002) Not Reproduced]

NOTE: Form is available at no charge by downloading from the web at www.dir.ca.gov/dwc/forms.html or by requesting at 1-800-794-6900.

Note: Authority cited: Sections 6409.1(a), 6410, and 6410.5, Labor Code. Reference: Sections 6409.1(a) and 6410, Labor Code.

History: 1. New section filed 2-8-80; designated effective 5-1-80 (Register 80, No. 6).

2. Amendment filed 1-13-83; effective thirtieth day thereafter (Register 83, No. 3).

3. Repealer and new section filed 3-18-7; effective thirtieth day thereafter (Register 87, No. 12).

4. Repealer and new section filed 1-14-93; operative 2-16-93 (Register 93, No. 3).

5. Amendment of section heading and new revision of Form 5020 filed 9-19-2002; operative 10-19-2002 (Register 2002, No. 38).

Ref.: Hanna § 25.20[3].

§14005. Reproduction of the Employer's Report.

(a) Insurers and self-insured employers shall reproduce Form 5020, Rev. 7, Employer's Report of Occupational Injury or Illness. In reproducing the form, all of the following conditions shall be met:

(1) The title of the reproduced form shall read: State of California Employer's Report of Occupational Injury or Illness. The size of type may be reduced to meet space requirements, but the words "Employer's Report of Occupational Injury or Illness" shall be in bold face type.

(2) The form shall prominently contain filing instructions and the following statements:

(A) "Any person who makes or causes to be made any knowingly false or fraudulent material statement or material representation for the purpose of obtaining or denying workers' compensation benefits or payments is guilty of a felony."

(B) "ATTENTION: This form contains information relating to employee health and must be used in a manner that protects the confidentiality of employees to the extent possible while the information is being used for occupational safety and health purposes." Reference: Section 14300.29(b)(6)-(10)

(C) Shaded boxes indicate confidential employee information as listed in CCR Title 8 14300.35(b)(2)(E)2.

(D) Confidential information may be disclosed to the employee, former employee, or their personal representative (8 CCR 14300.35), to others for the purpose of processing a workers' compensation or other insurance claim; and under certain circumstances to a public health or law enforcement agency or to a consultant hired by the employer (8 CCR 14300.30). 8 CCR 14300.40 requires provision upon request to certain state and federal workplace safety agencies.

(3) The notice block, coding column in the right hand margin, subheadings, spacing, numbering, arrangement, sequence and text of Questions 1 through 39 shall not be altered. However, self-insured employers may eliminate Questions 1A, 2A, 3A, and 37b from reproduced forms and utilize the space to collect other information.

Except as otherwise specified in this Section, any other modification to the content or layout of Form 5020, Rev. 7 may be made only with prior approval of a written request to:

DEPARTMENT OF INDUSTRIAL RELATIONS
CHIEF, DIVISION OF LABOR STATISTICS AND RESEARCH
P. O. BOX 420603
SAN FRANCISCO, CA 94142-0603

(4) Reproduced forms shall be printed on 81/2, by 11, paper stock.

(b) Insurers, self-insured employers or other persons reproducing Form 5020, Rev. 7 may rearrange the header block to permit imprinting the following:

(1) Name and address of the insurer, self-insured employer or claims administrator;

(2) Instructions for completing and filing the form;

(3) Coding lines or boxes for special use by the insurer, self-insured employer or claims administrator.

(c) The size of the header block may be altered to gain space for additional questions, which may be included at the bottom of the form, following Question 39, provided the proposed form has been reviewed and approved by the Division. The reverse of the form may be used for additional information or questions.

Note: Authority cited: Sections 6410 and 6410.5, Labor Code. Reference: Sections 5401.7, 6409.1(a) and 6410, Labor Code.

History: 1. New section filed 2-8-80; designated effective 5-1-80 (Register 80, No. 6).

2. Amendment of subsections (a) and (c) filed 1-13-83; effective thirtieth day thereafter (Register 83, No. 3).

3. Amendment filed 3-18-87; effective thirtieth day thereafter (Register 87, No. 12).

4. Amendment of subsection (a) filed 6-14-89; operative 7-14-89 (Register 89, No. 25).

5. Amendment of section and Note filed 1-14-93; operative 2-16-93 (Register 93, No. 3).

6. Amendment filed 9-19-2002; operative 10-19-2002 (Register 2002, No. 38).

Ref.: Hanna § 25.20[3].

§14006. Form 5021, Rev. 4, Doctor's First Report of Occupational Injury or Illness.

[DLSR Form 5021 (Rev. 1992) Not Reproduced]

NOTE: Form is available at no charge by downloading from the web at www.dir.ca.gov/dwc/forms.html or by requesting at 1-800-794-6900.

Note: Authority cited: Sections 6409(a), 6410, 6410.5, 6413.5, Labor Code; and Section 2950, Health and Safety Code. Reference: Sections 5401.7, 6410, Labor Code.

History: 1. New section filed 2-8-80; designated effective 5-1-80 (Register 80, No. 6).

2. Repealer and new section filed 6-14-89; operative 7-14-89 (Register 89, No. 25).

3. Repealer and new section filed 1-14-93; operative 2-16-93 (Register 93, No. 3).

Ref.: Hanna § 22.08[2]; Herlick Handbook § 4.08[2].

§ 14006.1. DIR Form 5021 (Rev. 5) 2015, Doctor's First Report of Occupational Injury or Illness.

[DLSR Form 5021 (Rev. 5) 2015 Not Reproduced]

NOTE: Form is available at no charge by downloading from the web at www.dir.ca.gov/dwc/forms.html or by requesting at 1-800-794-6900.

Note: Authority cited: Sections 6409(a), 6410, 6410.5 and 6413.5, Labor Code. Reference: Sections 5401.7 and 6410, Labor Code.

History: 1. New section filed 9-21-2015; operative 10-1-2015 pursuant to Government Code section 11343.4(b)(3) (Register 2015, No. 39).

§14007. Reproduction of the Doctor's Report.

(a) Insurers, self-insured employers, doctors, clinics, hospitals and other persons may reproduce Form 5021, Rev. 4 or 5, as appropriate (for dates of service prior to October 1, 2015, use Rev. 4; for dates of service on or after October 1, 2015, use Rev. 5), Doctor's First Report of Occupational Injury or Illness, if all of the following conditions are met:

(1) The title of the reproduced form shall read: Doctor's First Report of Occupational Injury or Illness State of California. The size of type may be reduced to meet space requirements, but the words "Doctor's First Report of Occupational Injury or Illness" shall be in bold face type.

(2) Filing instructions in the heading shall include the requirement for the physician to file a copy of the report directly with the Division of Labor Statistics and Research in the case of pesticide poisoning or suspected pesticide poisoning, and the statement "Failure to file a timely doctor's report may result in assessment of a civil penalty."

(3) The form shall prominently contain the following statement: "Any person who makes or causes to be made any knowingly false or fraudulent material statement or material representation for the purpose of obtaining or denying workers' compensation benefits or payments is guilty of a felony."

(4) Reproduced forms shall be printed on 8½″ x 11″ paper stock.

(5) The subheadings, arrangement, sequence and text of Questions 1 through 25, the coding column and the signature section shall not be altered, except that Question 1 may be eliminated on forms printed with the insurer's or self-insured employer's name at the top.

(b) Insurers, self-insured employers, doctors, clinics, hospitals and other persons reproducing Form 5021, may rearrange the heading to permit imprinting:

(1) The name and address of such insurer, self-insured employer, doctor, clinic, hospital or other persons;

(2) Coding lines or boxes for special use by the person reproducing the form;

(3) Instructions for forwarding the form and the number of copies required.

(c) Insurers, self-insured employers and other persons reproducing Form 5021, may use the back of the form for additional information, questions, or skeleton diagrams.

(d) Except as otherwise specified in subdivision 14007(b), any other modification to the content or layout of Form 5021 may be made only with prior approval of a written request to the Department of Industrial Relations, P.O. Box 420603, San Francisco, CA 94142-0603.

Note: Authority cited: Sections 6410 and 6410.5, Labor Code. Reference: Sections 5401.7 and 6410, Labor Code.

History: 1. New section filed 2-8-80; designated effective 5-1-80 (Register 80, No. 6).

2. Amendment of subsection (a) filed 1-13-83; effective thirtieth day thereafter (Register 83, No. 3).

3. Amendment filed 6-14-89; operative 7-14-89 (Register 89, No. 25).

4. Editorial correction of printing error in subsection (a)(2) (Register 90, No. 6).

5. Amendment of section and Note filed 1-14-93; operative 2-16-93 (Register 93, No. 3).

6. Amendment of subsections (a), (b), (c) and (d) filed 9-21-2015; operative 10-1-2015 pursuant to Government Code section 11343.4(b)(3) (Register 2015, No. 39).

Ref.: Hanna § 22.08[2]; Herlick Handbook § 4.08[2].

§14100. Insurer. [Repealed]

Note: Authority cited: Section 6410, Labor Code. Reference: Sections 6409(a), 6409.1(a), 6410, Labor Code.

History: 1. Amendment filed 5-16-73, designated effective 7-1-73 (Register 73, No. 20).

2. Amendment filed 4-15-74; designated effective 6-1-74 (Register 74, No. 16).

3. Repealer filed 2-8-80; designated effective 5-1-80 (Register 80, No. 6).

§14200. Physician or Surgeon. [Repealed]

Note: Authority cited: Section 6410, Labor Code. Reference: Sections 6409(a), 6409.1(a), 6410, Labor Code.

History: 1. Amendment filed 12-16-49 (Register 18, No. 7).

2. Amendment filed 12-4-51; effective thirtieth day thereafter (Register 26, No. 6).

3. Amendment of subsection (b) filed 4-15-74; designated effective 6-1-74 (Register 74, No. 16).

4. Repealer filed 2-8-80; designated effective 5-1-80 (Register 80, No. 6).

§14201. Form 5021, Rev. 1, Doctor's First Report of Occupational Injury or Illness. [Repealed]

Note: Authority cited: Section 6410, Labor Code. Reference: Sections 6409(a), 6409.1(a), 6410, Labor Code.

History: 1. Amendment filed 12-16-49 (Register 18, No. 7).

2. Amendment filed 4-15-74; designated effective 6-1-74 (Register 74, No. 16).

3. Repealer filed 2-8-80; designated effective 5-1-80 (Register 80, No. 6).

ARTICLE 2
Employer Records of Occupational Injury or Illness

§14300. Purpose.

The purpose of this rule (Article 2) is to require employers to record work-related fatalities, injuries and illnesses.

Note 1: Recording a work-related injury, illness, or fatality does not mean that the employer or employee was at fault, that a Cal/OSHA regulation has been violated, or that the employee is eligible for workers' compensation or other benefits.

Note 2: All employers covered by the California Occupational Safety and Health Act are covered by the provisions of Article 2. However, because of the partial exemptions provided by Sections 14300.1 and 14300.2, most employers do not have to keep OSHA injury and illness records unless they are asked in writing to do so by OSHA, the Bureau of Labor Statistics (BLS), or a state agency operating under the authority of OSHA or the BLS. For example, employers with 10 or fewer employees and establishments in certain industry classifications listed in Section 14300.2, Appendix A, are partially exempt from keeping Cal/OSHA injury and illness records.

Note: Authority cited: Section 6410, Labor Code. Reference: Section 6410, Labor Code.

History: 1. Repealer of former article 2 (sections 14300-14400), and new article 2 (sections 14300-14300.48) and section filed 1-15-2002; operative 1-15-2002 pursuant to Government Code section 11343.4 (Register 2002, No. 3). For prior history of article 2, see Register 83, No. 3.

§14300.1. Partial Exemption for Employers with 10 or Fewer Employees.

(a) Basic requirement.

(1) If your company had ten (10) or fewer employees at all times during the last calendar year, you do not need to keep Cal/OSHA injury and illness records unless OSHA or the BLS informs you in writing that you must keep records under the provisions of Section 14300.41 or Section 14300.42. However, all employers must continue to file reports of occupational injuries and illnesses with the Division of Labor Statistics and Research as required by Article 1 of this subchapter, and to immediately report to the Division of Occupational Safety and Health any workplace incident that results in serious injury or illness, or death, as required by Title 8 Section 342.

(2) If your company had more than ten (10) employees at any time during the last calendar year, you must keep Cal/OSHA injury and illness records unless your establishment is classified as a partially exempt industry under Section 14300.2.

(b) Implementation.

(1) Is the partial exemption for size based on the size of my entire company or on the size of an individual establishment?

The partial exemption for size is based on the number of employees in the entire company.

(2) How do I determine the size of my company to find out if I qualify for the partial exemption for size?

To determine if you are exempt because of size, you need to determine your company's peak employment during the last calendar year. If you had 10 or fewer employees at all times in the last calendar year, your company qualifies for the partial exemption for size.

Note: Authority cited: Section 6410, Labor Code. Reference: Section 6410, Labor Code.

History: 1. New section filed 1-15-2002; operative 1-15-2002 pursuant to Government Code section 11343.4 (Register 2002, No. 3).

§14300.2. Partial Exemption for Establishments in Certain Industries.

(a) Basic requirement.

(1) If you are an employer and your business establishment is classified in a specific industry group listed in Table 1 in Appendix A of this section, you do not need to keep Cal/OSHA injury and illness records required by Article 2 unless the government asks you to keep the records under Section 14300.41 or Section 14300.42. However, all employers must report to the Division of Occupational Safety and Health any workplace incident that results in a serious injury or illness, or death, as required at Title 8 Section 342.

(2) If one or more of your establishments are classified in a non-exempt industry, you must keep Cal/OSHA injury and illness records required by Article 2 for all such establishments except those partially exempted because of size under Section 14300.1.

(b) *Implementation.*

(1) *Is the partial industry classification exemption based on the industry classification of my entire company or on the classification of individual business establishments operated by my company?* The partial industry classification exemption applies to individual business establishments. If a company has several business establishments engaged in different classes of business activities, some of the company's establishments may be required to keep records, while others may be partially exempt.

(2) *How do I determine the correct NAICS code for my company or for individual establishments?* You can determine your NAICS code by using one of three methods, or you may contact your nearest OSHA office or State agency for help in determining your NAICS code:

(i) You can use the search feature at the U.S. Census Bureau NAICS main Web page: *http://www.census.gov/eos/www/naics/*. In the search box for the most recent NAICS, enter a keyword that describes your kind of business. A list of primary business activities containing that keyword and the corresponding NAICS codes will appear. Choose the one that most closely corresponds to your primary business activity, or refine your search to obtain other choices.

(ii) Rather than searching through a list of primary business activities, you may also view the most recent complete NAICS structure with codes and titles by clicking on the link for the most recent NAICS on the U.S. Census Bureau NAICS main Web page: *http://www.census.gov/eos/www/naics/*. Then click on the two-digit Sector code to see all the NAICS codes under that Sector. Then choose the six-digit code of your interest to see the corresponding definition, as well as cross-references and index items, when available.

(iii) If you know your old SIC code, you can also find the appropriate 2002 NAICS code by using the detailed conversion (concordance) between the 1987 SIC and 2002 NAICS available in Excel format for download at the "Concordances" link at the U.S. Census Bureau NAICS main Web page: *http://www.census.gov/eos/www/naics/*.

Appendix A to Section 14300.2

Employers are not required to keep Cal/OSHA injury and illness records for any establishment classified in the following North American Industry Classification System (NAICS) codes, unless they are asked in writing to do so by OSHA, the Bureau of Labor Statistics (BLS), or the Division of Occupational Safety and Health. All employers, including those partially exempted by reason of their size or industry classification, must report to the Division of Occupational Safety and Health any workplace incident that results in a serious injury or illness, or death, as required at Title 8 Section 342.

Table 1

NAICS Code	*Industry*
4412	Other Motor Vehicle Dealers.
4431	Electronics and Appliance Stores.
4461	Health and Personal Care Stores.
4471	Gasoline Stations.
4481	Clothing Stores.
4482	Shoe Stores.
4483	Jewelry, Luggage, and Leather Goods Stores.
4511	Sporting Goods, Hobby, and Musical Instrument Stores.
4512	Book, Periodical, and Music Stores.
4531	Florists.
4532	Office Supplies, Stationery, and Gift Stores.
4812	Nonscheduled Air Transportation.
4861	Pipeline Transportation of Crude Oil.
4862	Pipeline Transportation of Natural Gas.
4869	Other Pipeline Transportation.
4879	Scenic and Sightseeing Transportation, Other.
4885	Freight Transportation Arrangement.
5111	Newspaper, Periodical, Book, and Directory Publishers.
5112	Software Publishers.
5122	Sound Recording Industries.
5151	Radio and Television Broadcasting.
5331	Lessors of Nonfinancial Intangible Assets (except Copyrighted Works).
5411	Legal Services.
5412	Accounting, Tax Preparation, Bookkeeping, and Payroll Services.
5413	Architectural, Engineering, and Related Services.
5414	Specialized Design Services.
5415	Computer Systems Design and Related Services.
5416	Management, Scientific, and Technical Consulting Services.
5417	Scientific Research and Development Services.
5418	Advertising and Related Services.
5511	Management of Companies and Enterprises.
5611	Office Administrative Services.
5614	Business Support Services.
5615	Travel Arrangement and Reservation Services.
5616	Investigation and Security Services.
6111	Elementary and Secondary Schools.
6112	Junior Colleges.
6113	Colleges, Universities, and Professional Schools.
6114	Business Schools and Computer and Management Training.
6115	Technical and Trade Schools.
6116	Other Schools and Instruction.
6117	Educational Support Services.

NAICS Code	Industry
5172	Wireless Telecommunications Carriers (except Satellite).
5173	Telecommunications Resellers.
5179	Other Telecommunications.
5181	Internet Service Providers and Web Search Portals.
5182	Data Processing, Hosting, and Related Services.
5191	Other Information Services.
5211	Monetary Authorities-Central Bank.
5221	Depository Credit Intermediation.
5222	Nondepository Credit Intermediation.
5223	Activities Related to Credit Intermediation.
5231	Securities and Commodity Contracts Intermediation and Brokerage.
5232	Securities and Commodity Exchanges.
5239	Other Financial Investment Activities.
5241	Insurance Carriers.
5242	Agencies, Brokerages, and Other Insurance Related Activities.
5251	Insurance and Employee Benefit Funds.
5259	Other Investment Pools and Funds.
5312	Offices of Real Estate Agents and Brokers.
6211	Offices of Physicians.
6212	Offices of Dentists.
6213	Offices of Other Health Practitioners.
6214	Outpatient Care Centers.
6215	Medical and Diagnostic Laboratories.
6244	Child Day Care Services.
7114	Agents and Managers for Artists, Athletes, Entertainers, and Other Public Figures.
7115	Independent Artists, Writers, and Performers.
7213	Rooming and Boarding Houses.
7221	Full-Service Restaurants.
7222	Limited-Service Eating Places.
7224	Drinking Places (Alcoholic Beverages).
8112	Electronic and Precision Equipment Repair and Maintenance.
8114	Personal and Household Goods Repair and Maintenance.
8121	Personal Care Services.
8122	Death Care Services.
8131	Religious Organizations.
8132	Grantmaking and Giving Services.
8133	Social Advocacy Organizations.
8134	Civic and Social Organizations.
8139	Business, Professional, Labor, Political, and Similar Organizations.

NOTE: In California, establishments in NAICS Code 5121, Motion Picture and Video Industries are required to record. Federal law does not require these establishments to record. This is the only difference between the list of establishments shown in Table 1 above and the list shown in the equivalent federal rule at 29 CFR 1904.2.

Note: Authority cited: Section 6410, Labor Code. Reference: Section 6410, Labor Code.

History: 1. New section and Appendix A filed 1-15-2002; operative 1-15-2002 pursuant to Government Code section 11343.4 (Register 2002, No. 3).

2. Amendment of section and Appendix filed 8-20-2015; operative 1-1-2016 (Register 2015, No. 34).

§14300.3. Keeping Records for More than One Agency.

If you create records to comply with another government agency's injury and illness recordkeeping requirements, OSHA will consider those records as meeting OSHA's recordkeeping requirements if OSHA accepts the other agency's records under a memorandum of understanding with that agency, or if the other agency's records contain the same information as this article requires you to record. You may contact the nearest office of the Division of Occupational Safety and Health for help in determining whether your records meet the requirements of this article.

Note: Authority cited: Section 6410, Labor Code. Reference: Section 6410, Labor Code.

History: 1. New section filed 1-15-2002; operative 1-15-2002 pursuant to Government Code section 11343.4 (Register 2002, No. 3).

§14300.4. Recording Criteria.

(a) Basic requirement. Each employer required by this article to keep records of fatalities, injuries, and illnesses must record each fatality, injury and illness that:

(1) Is work-related; and

(2) Is a new case; and

(3) Meets one or more of the general recording criteria of Section 14300.7 or the application to specific cases of Section 14300.8 through Section 14300.12.

(b) Implementation.

What sections of this rule describe recording criteria for recording work-related injuries and illnesses?

The list below indicates which sections of the rule address each topic

(1) Determination of work-relatedness. See Section 14300.5;

(2) Determination of a new case. See Section 14300.6;

(3) General recording criteria. See Section 14300.7; and

(4) Additional criteria. (Needlestick and sharps injury cases, medical removal cases, hearing loss cases, tuberculosis cases, and musculoskeletal disorder cases.) See Section 14300.8 though Section 14300.12.

Note: Authority cited: Section 6410, Labor Code. Reference: Section 6410, Labor Code.

History: 1. New section filed 1-15-2002; operative 1-15-2002 pursuant to Government Code section 11343.4 (Register 2002, No. 3).

§14300.5. Determination of Work-Relatedness.

(a) Basic requirement. You must consider an injury or

illness to be work-related if an event or exposure in the work environment either caused or contributed to the resulting condition or significantly aggravated a pre-existing injury or illness. Work-relatedness is presumed for injuries and illnesses resulting from events or exposures occurring in the work environment, unless an exception in Section 14300.5(b)(2) specifically applies.

(b) Implementation.

(1) What is the "work environment"?

Work environment is defined as "the establishment and other locations where one or more employees are working or are present as a condition of their employment. The work environment includes not only physical locations, but also the equipment or materials used by the employee during the course of his or her work."

(2) Are there situations where an injury or illness occurs in the work environment and is not considered work-related?

Yes. An injury or illness occurring in the work environment that falls under one of the following exceptions is not work-related, and therefore is not recordable:

(A) At the time of the injury or illness, the employee was present in the work environment as a member of the general public rather than as an employee.

(B) The injury or illness involves signs or symptoms that surface at work but result solely from a non-work-related event or exposure that occurs outside the work environment.

(C) The injury or illness results solely from voluntary participation in a wellness program or in a medical, fitness, or recreational activity such as blood donation, physical examination, flu shot, exercise class, racquetball, or baseball.

(D) The injury or illness is solely the result of an employee eating, drinking, or preparing food or drink for personal consumption (whether bought on the employer's premises or brought in). For example, if the employee is injured by choking on a sandwich while in the employer's establishment, the case would not be considered work-related.

Note: If the employee is made ill by ingesting food contaminated by workplace contaminants (such as lead), or gets food poisoning from food supplied by the employer, the case would be considered work-related.

(E) The injury or illness is solely the result of an employee doing personal tasks (unrelated to their employment) at the establishment outside of the employee's assigned working hours.

(F) The injury or illness is solely the result of personal grooming, self-medication for a non-work-related condition, or is intentionally self-inflicted.

(G) The injury or illness is caused by a motor vehicle accident and occurs on a company parking lot or company access road while the employee is commuting to or from work.

(H) The illness is the common cold or flu (Note: contagious diseases such as tuberculosis, brucellosis, hepatitis A, or plague are considered work-related if the employee is infected at work).

(I) The illness is a mental illness. Mental illness will not be considered work-related unless the employee voluntarily provides the employer with an opinion from a physician or other licensed health care professional with appropriate training and experience (psychiatrist, psychologist, psychiatric nurse practitioner, etc.) stating that the employee has a mental illness that is work-related.

(3) How do I handle a case if it is not obvious whether the precipitating event or exposure occurred in the work environment or occurred away from work?

In these situations, you must evaluate the employee's work duties and environment to decide whether or not one or more events or exposures in the work environment either caused or contributed to the resulting condition or significantly aggravated a pre-existing condition.

(4) How do I know if an event or exposure in the work environment "significantly aggravated" a pre-existing injury or illness?

A pre-existing injury or illness has been significantly aggravated, for purposes of Cal/OSHA injury and illness recordkeeping required by this Article, when an event or exposure in the work environment results in any of the following:

(A) Death, provided that the pre-existing injury or illness would likely not have resulted in death but for the occupational event or exposure.

(B) Loss of consciousness, provided that the pre-existing injury or illness would likely not have resulted in loss of consciousness but for the occupational event or exposure.

(C) One or more days away from work, or days of restricted work, or days of job transfer that otherwise would not have occurred but for the occupational event or exposure.

(D) Medical treatment in a case where no medical treatment was needed for the injury or illness before the workplace event or exposure, or a change in medical treatment was necessitated by the workplace event or exposure.

(5) Which injuries and illnesses are considered pre-existing conditions?

An injury or illness is a pre-existing condition if it resulted solely from a non-work-related event or exposure that occurred outside the work environment.

(6) How do I decide whether an injury or illness is work-related if the employee is on travel status at the time the injury or illness occurs?

Injuries and illnesses that occur while an employee is on travel status are work-related if, at the time of the injury or illness, the employee was engaged in work activities "in the interest of the employer." Examples of such activities include travel to and from customer contacts, conducting job tasks, and entertaining or being entertained to transact, discuss, or promote business (work-related entertainment includes only entertainment activities being engaged in at the direction of the employer).

Injuries or illnesses that occur when the employee is on travel status do not have to be recorded if they meet one of the following exceptions:

EXCEPTION 1: When a traveling employee checks into a hotel, motel, or other temporary residence, he or she establishes a "home away from home." You must evaluate the employee's activities after he or she checks into the hotel, motel, or other temporary residence for their work-relatedness in the same manner as you evaluate the activities of a non-traveling employee. When the employee checks into the temporary residence, he or she is considered to have left the work environment. When the employee begins work each day, he or she re-enters the work environment. If the employee has established a "home away from home" and is reporting to a fixed worksite each day, you also do not consider injuries or illnesses work-related if they occur while the employee is commuting between the temporary residence and the job location.

EXCEPTION 2: Injuries or illnesses are not considered work-related if they occur while the employee is on a personal detour from a reasonably direct route of travel (e.g., has taken a side trip for personal reasons).

(7) How do I decide if a case is work-related when the employee is working at home?

Injuries and illnesses that occur while an employee is working at home, including work in a home office, will be considered work-related if the injury or illness occurs while the employee is performing work for pay or compensation in the home, and the injury or illness is directly related to the performance of work rather than to the general home environment or setting. For example, if an employee drops a box of work documents and injures his or her foot, the case is considered work-related. If an employee's fingernail is punctured by a needle from a sewing machine used to perform garment work at home, becomes infected and requires medical treatment, the injury is considered work-related. If an employee is injured because he or she trips on the family dog while rushing to answer a work phone call, the case is not considered work-related. If an employee working at home is electrocuted because of faulty home wiring, the injury is not considered work-related.

Note: Authority cited: Section 6410, Labor Code. Reference: Section 6410, Labor Code.

History: 1. New section filed 1-15-2002; operative 1-15-2002 pursuant to Government Code section 11343.4 (Register 2002, No. 3).

§14300.6. Determination of New Cases.

(a) Basic requirement. You must consider an injury or illness to be a "new case" if:

(1) The employee has not previously experienced a recorded injury or illness of the same type that affects the same part of the body, or

(2) The employee previously experienced a recorded injury or illness of the same type that affected the same part of the body but had recovered completely (all signs and symptoms had disappeared) from the previous injury or illness and an event or exposure in the work environment caused the signs or symptoms to reappear.

(b) Implementation.

(1) When an employee experiences the signs or symptoms of a chronic work-related illness, do I need to consider each recurrence of signs or symptoms to be a new case?

No. For occupational illnesses where the signs or symptoms may recur or continue in the absence of an exposure in the workplace, the case must only be recorded once. Examples may include occupational cancer, asbestosis, byssinosis and silicosis.

(2) When an employee experiences the signs or symptoms of an injury or illness as a result of an event or exposure in the workplace, such as an episode of occupational asthma, must I treat the episode as a new case?

Yes. Because the episode or recurrence was caused by an event or exposure in the workplace, the incident must be treated as a new case.

(3) May I rely on a physician or other licensed health care professional to determine whether a case is a new case or a recurrence of an old case?

You are not required to seek the advice of a physician or other licensed health care professional. However, if you do seek such advice, you must follow the physician or other licensed health care professional's recommendation about whether the case is a new case or a recurrence. If you receive recommendations from two or more physicians or other licensed health care professionals, you must make a decision as to which recommendation is the most authoritative (best documented, best reasoned, or most authoritative), and record the case based upon that recommendation.

Note: Authority cited: Section 6410, Labor Code. Reference: Section 6410, Labor Code.

History: 1. New section filed 1-15-2002; operative 1-15-2002 pursuant to Government Code section 11343.4 (Register 2002, No. 3).

§14300.7. General Recording Criteria.

(a) Basic requirement. You must consider an injury or illness to meet the general recording criteria, and therefore to be recordable, if it results in any of the following as detailed in subsections (b)(2) through (b)(6) of this section: death, days away from work, restricted work or transfer to another job, medical treatment beyond first aid, or loss of consciousness. You must also consider a case to meet the general recording criteria if it involves a significant injury or illness diagnosed by a physician or other licensed health care professional as detailed in subsection (b)(7) of this section, even if it does not result in death, days away from work, restricted work or job transfer, medical treatment beyond first aid, or loss of consciousness.

(b) Implementation.

(1) How do I decide if a case meets one or more of the general recording criteria?

A work-related injury or illness must be recorded if it results in one or more of the following:

(A) Death, See Section 14300.7(b)(2)

(B) Days away from work, See Section 14300.7(b)(3)

(C) Restricted work or transfer to another job, See Section 14300.7(b)(4)

(D) Medical treatment beyond first aid, See Section 14300.7(b)(5)

(E) Loss of consciousness, See Section 14300.7(b)(6)

(F) A significant injury or illness diagnosed by a physician or other licensed health care professional. See Section 14300.7(b)(7)

(2) How do I record a work-related injury or illness that results in a fatality?

You must record an injury or illness that results in a fatality, as defined in Section 14300.46 of this Article, by entering a mark on the Cal/OSHA Form 300 in the column labeled for cases resulting in death. You must also report any work-related fatality or serious injury or illness to the

Division of Occupational Safety and Health within eight (8) hours, as required by Title 8 Section 342.

(3) How do I record a work-related injury or illness that results in days away from work?

When an injury or illness involves one or more days away from work, you must record the injury or illness on the Cal/OSHA Form 300 with a mark in the space for cases involving days away and an entry of the number of calendar days away from work in the number of days column. If the employee is out for an extended period of time, you must enter an estimate of the days that the employee will be away, and update the day count when the actual number of days is known.

(A) Do I count the day on which the injury occurred or the illness began?

No. You begin counting days away on the day after the injury occurred or the illness began.

(B) How do I record an injury or illness when a physician or other licensed health care professional recommends that the worker stay at home but the employee comes to work anyway?

You must record these injuries and illnesses on the Cal/OSHA Form 300 using the check box for cases with days away from work and enter the number of calendar days away recommended by the physician or other licensed health care professional. If a physician or other licensed health care professional recommends days away, you should encourage your employee to follow that recommendation. However, the days away must be recorded whether the injured or ill employee follows the physician or licensed health care professional's recommendation or not. If you receive recommendations from two or more physicians or other licensed health care professionals, you may make a decision as to which recommendation is the most authoritative, and record the case based upon that recommendation.

(C) How do I handle a case when a physician or other licensed health care professional recommends that the worker return to work but the employee stays at home anyway?

In this situation, you must end the count of days away from work on the date the physician or other licensed health care professional recommends that the employee return to work.

(D) How do I count weekends, holidays, or other days the employee would not have worked anyway?

You must count the number of calendar days the employee was unable to work as a result of the injury or illness, regardless of whether or not the employee was scheduled to work on those day(s). Weekend days, holidays, vacation days or other days off are included in the total number of days recorded if the employee would not have been able to work on those days because of a work-related injury or illness.

(E) How do I record a case in which a worker is injured or becomes ill on a Friday and reports to work on a Monday, and was not scheduled to work on the weekend?

You need to record this case only if you receive information from a physician or other licensed health care professional indicating that the employee should not have worked, or should have performed only restricted work, during the weekend. If so, you must record the injury or illness as a case with days away from work or restricted work, and enter the day counts, as appropriate.

(F) How do I record a case in which a worker is injured or becomes ill on the day before scheduled time off such as a holiday, a planned vacation, or a temporary plant closing?

You need to record a case of this type only if you receive information from a physician or other licensed health care professional indicating that the employee should not have worked, or should have performed only restricted work, during the scheduled time off. If so, you must record the injury or illness as a case with days away from work or restricted work, and enter the day counts, as appropriate.

(G) Is there a limit to the number of days away from work I must count?

Yes. You may "cap" the total days away at 180 calendar days. You are not required to keep track of the number of calendar days away from work if the injury or illness resulted in more than 180 calendar days away from work and/or days of job transfer or restriction. In such a case, entering 180 in the total days away column will be considered adequate.

(H) May I stop counting days if an employee who is away from work because of an injury or illness retires or leaves my company?

Yes. If the employee leaves your company for some reason unrelated to the injury or illness, such as retirement, a plant closing, or to take another job, you may stop counting days away from work or days of restriction/job transfer. If the employee leaves your company because of the injury or illness, you must estimate the total number of days away or days of restriction/job transfer and enter the day count on the Cal/OSHA Form 300.

(I) If a case occurs in one year but results in days away during the next calendar year, do I record the case in both years?

No. You only record the injury or illness once. You must enter the number of calendar days away for the injury or illness on the Cal/OSHA Form 300 for the year in which the injury or illness occurred. If the employee is still away from work because of the injury or illness when you prepare the annual summary, estimate the total number of calendar days you expect the employee to be away from work, use this number to calculate the total for the annual summary, and then update the initial log entry later when the day count is known or reaches the 180-day cap.

(4) How do I record a work-related injury or illness that results in restricted work or job transfer?

When an injury or illness involves restricted work or job transfer but does not involve death or days away from work, you must record the injury or illness on the Cal/OSHA Form 300 by placing a mark in the space for job transfer or restriction and an entry of the number of restricted or transferred days in the restricted workdays column.

(A) How do I decide if the injury or illness resulted in restricted work?

Restricted work occurs when, as the result of a work-related injury or illness:

1. You keep the employee from performing one or more of the routine functions of his or her job, or from working the full workday that he or she would otherwise have been scheduled to work; or

2. A physician or other licensed health care professional recommends that the employee not perform one or more of the routine functions of his or her job, or not work the full workday that he or she would otherwise have been scheduled to work.

(B) What is meant by "routine functions"?

For recordkeeping purposes, an employee's routine functions are those work activities the employee regularly performs at least once per week.

(C) Do I have to record restricted work or job transfer if it applies only to the day on which the injury occurred or the illness began?

No. You do not have to record restricted work or job transfers if you, or the physician or other licensed health care professional, impose the restriction or transfer only for the day on which the injury occurred or the illness began.

(D) If you or a physician or other licensed health care professional recommends a work restriction, is the injury or illness automatically recordable as a "restricted work" case?

No. A recommended work restriction is recordable only if it affects one or more of the employee's routine job functions. To determine whether this is the case, you must evaluate the restriction in light of the routine functions of the injured or ill employee's job. If the restriction from you or the physician or other licensed health care professional keeps the employee from performing one or more of his or her routine job functions, or from working the full workday the injured or ill employee would otherwise have worked, the employee's work has been restricted and you must record the case.

(E) How do I record a case where the worker works only for a partial work shift because of a work-related injury or illness?

A partial day of work is recorded as a day of job transfer or restriction for recordkeeping purposes, except for the day on which the injury occurred or the illness began.

(F) If the injured or ill worker produces fewer goods or services than he or she would have produced prior to the injury or illness but otherwise performs all of the routine functions of his or her work, is the case considered a restricted work case?

No. The case is considered restricted work only if the worker does not perform all of the routine functions of his or her job or does not work the full shift that he or she would otherwise have worked.

(G) How do I handle vague restrictions from a physician or other licensed health care professional, such as that the employee engage only in "light duty" or "take it easy for a week"?

If you are not clear about the physician or other licensed health care professional's recommendation, you may ask that person whether the employee can do all of his or her routine job functions and work all of his or her normally assigned work shift. If the answer to both of these questions is "Yes," then the case does not involve a work restriction and does not have to be recorded as such. If the answer to one or both of these questions is "No," the case involves restricted work and must be recorded as a restricted work case. If you are unable to obtain this additional information from the physician or other licensed health care professional who recommended the restriction, record the injury or illness as a case involving restricted work.

(H) What do I do if a physician or other licensed health care professional recommends a job restriction meeting the definition in Section 14300.7(b)(4)(A), but the employee does all of his or her routine job functions anyway?

You must record the injury or illness on the Cal/OSHA Form 300 as a restricted work case. If a physician or other licensed health care professional recommends a job restriction, you should ensure that the employee complies with that restriction. If you receive recommendations from two or more physicians or other licensed health care professionals, you may make a decision as to which recommendation is the most authoritative, and record the case based upon that recommendation.

(I) How do I decide if an injury or illness involved a transfer to another job?

If you assign an injured or ill employee to a job other than his or her regular job for part of the day, the case involves transfer to another job.

Note: This does not include the day on which the injury or illness occurred.

(J) Are transfers to another job recorded in the same way as restricted work cases?

Yes. Both job transfer and restricted work cases are recorded in the same box on the Cal/OSHA Form 300. For example, if you assign, or a physician or other licensed health care professional recommends that you assign, an injured or ill worker to his or her routine job duties for part of the day and to another job for the rest of the day, the injury or illness involves a job transfer. You must record an injury or illness that involves a job transfer by placing a check in the box for job transfer.

(K) How do I count days of job transfer or restriction?

You count days of job transfer or restriction in the same way you count days away from work, using Sections 14300.7(b)(3)(A) to (H), above. The only difference is that, if you permanently assign the injured or ill employee to a job that has been modified or permanently changed in a manner that eliminates the routine functions the employee was restricted from performing, you may stop the day count when the modification or change is made permanent. You must count at least one day of restricted work or job transfer for such cases.

(5) How do I record an injury or illness that involves medical treatment beyond first aid?

If a work-related injury or illness results in medical treatment beyond first aid, you must record it on the Cal/OSHA Form 300. If the injury or illness did not involve death, one or more days away from work, one or more days of restricted work, or one or more days of job transfer, you enter a mark in the box for cases where the employee received medical treatment but remained at work and was not transferred or restricted.

(A) What is the definition of medical treatment?

"Medical treatment" means the management and care of a patient to combat disease or disorder. For the purposes of Article 2, medical treatment does not include:

1. Visits to a physician or other licensed health care professional solely for observation or counseling;

2. The conduct of diagnostic procedures, such as x-rays and blood tests, including the administration of

prescription medications used solely for diagnostic purposes (e.g., eye drops to dilate pupils); or

3. "First aid" as defined in subsection (b)(5)(B) of this section.

(B) What is "first aid"?

For the purposes of Article 2, "first aid" means the following:

1. Using a nonprescription medication at nonprescription strength (for medications available in both prescription and non-prescription form, a recommendation by a physician or other licensed health care professional to use a non-prescription medication at prescription strength is considered medical treatment for recordkeeping purposes);

2. Administering tetanus immunizations (other immunizations, such as Hepatitis B vaccine or rabies vaccine, are considered medical treatment);

3. Cleaning, flushing or soaking wounds on the surface of the skin;

4. Using wound coverings such as bandages, Band-AidsE, gauze pads, etc.; or using butterfly bandages or Steri-StripsE (other wound closing devices such as sutures, staples, etc. are considered medical treatment);

5. Using hot or cold therapy;

6. Using any non-rigid means of support, such as elastic bandages, wraps, non-rigid back belts, etc. (devices with rigid stays or other systems designed to immobilize parts of the body are considered medical treatment for recordkeeping purposes);

7. Using temporary immobilization devices while transporting an accident victim (e.g., splints, slings, neck collars, backboards, etc.);

8. Drilling of a fingernail or toenail to relieve pressure, or draining fluid from a blister;

9. Using eye patches;

10. Removing foreign bodies from the eye using only irrigation or a cotton swab;

11. Removing splinters or foreign material from areas other than the eye by irrigation, tweezers, cotton swabs or other simple means;

12. Using finger guards;

13. Using massages (physical therapy or chiropractic treatment are considered medical treatment for recordkeeping purposes); or

14. Drinking fluids for relief of heat stress.

(C) Are any other procedures included in first aid?

No. This is a complete list of all treatments considered first aid for purposes of Article 2.

(D) Does the professional status of the person providing the treatment have any effect on what is considered first aid or medical treatment?

No. The treatments listed in Section 14300.7(b)(5)(B) of this Article are considered to be first aid regardless of the professional status of the person providing the treatment. Even when these treatments are provided by a physician or other licensed health care professional, they are considered first aid for the purposes of Article 2. Similarly, treatment beyond first aid is considered to be medical treatment even when it is provided by someone other than a physician or other licensed health care professional.

(E) What if a physician or other licensed health care professional recommends medical treatment but the employee does not follow the recommendation?

If a physician or other licensed health care professional recommends medical treatment, you should encourage the injured or ill employee to follow that recommendation. However, you must record the case even if the injured or ill employee does not follow the physician or other licensed health care professional's recommendation.

(6) Is every work-related injury or illness case involving a loss of consciousness recordable?

Yes. You must record a work-related injury or illness if the worker becomes unconscious, regardless of the length of time the employee remains unconscious.

(7) What is a "significant" diagnosed injury or illness that is recordable under the general criteria even if it does not result in death, days away from work, restricted work or job transfer, medical treatment beyond first aid, or loss of consciousness?

Work-related cases involving cancer, chronic irreversible disease, a fractured or cracked bone, or a punctured eardrum must always be recorded under the general criteria at the time of diagnosis by a physician or other licensed health care professional.

Note to Section 14300.7: Most significant injuries and illnesses will result in one of the criteria listed in Section 14300.7(a): death, days away from work, restricted work or job transfer, medical treatment beyond first aid, or loss of consciousness. However, there are some significant injuries, such as a punctured eardrum or a fractured toe or rib, for which neither medical treatment nor work restrictions may be recommended. In addition, there are some significant progressive diseases, such as byssinosis, silicosis, and some types of cancer, for which medical treatment or work restrictions may not be recommended at the time of diagnosis but are likely to be recommended as the disease progresses. Cancer, chronic irreversible diseases, fractured or cracked bones, and punctured eardrums are generally considered significant injuries and illnesses, and must be recorded at the initial diagnosis even if medical treatment or work restrictions are not recommended, or are postponed, in a particular case.

Note: Authority cited: Section 6410, Labor Code. Reference: Section 6410, Labor Code.

History: 1. New section filed 1-15-2002; operative 1-15-2002 pursuant to Government Code section 11343.4 (Register 2002, No. 3).

§14300.8. Recording Criteria for Needlestick and Sharps Injuries.

(a) Basic requirement. You must record all work-related needlestick injuries and cuts from sharp objects that are contaminated with another person's blood or other potentially infectious material (as defined by Title 8, Section 5193). You must enter the case on the Cal/OSHA Form 300 as an injury. To protect the employee's privacy, you may not enter the employee's name on the Cal/OSHA Form 300 (see the requirements for privacy cases in Subsections 14300.29(b)(6) through 14300.29(b)(9)).

Note: The requirements of this section are not limited to health care and related establishments.

(b) Implementation.

(1) What does "other potentially infectious material" mean?

The term "other potentially infectious materials" is defined in the standard for Bloodborne Pathogens at Title 8 Section 5193(b) and includes the following materials:

(A) Human bodily fluids, tissues and organs, and

(B) Other materials infected with the HIV, hepatitis B virus (HBV) or hepatitis C virus (HCV) such as laboratory cultures or tissues from experimental animals.

(2) Does this mean that I must record all cuts, lacerations, punctures, and scratches?

No. You need to record cuts, lacerations, punctures, and scratches only if they are work-related and involve contamination with another person's blood or other potentially infectious material. If the cut, laceration, or scratch involves a clean object, or a contaminant other than blood or other potentially infectious material, you need to record the case only if it meets one or more of the recording criteria in Section 14300.7.

(3) If I record an injury and the employee is later diagnosed with an infectious bloodborne disease, do I need to update the Cal/OSHA Form 300?

Yes. You must update the classification of the case on the Cal/OSHA Form 300 if the case results in death, days away from work, restricted work, or job transfer. You must also update the description to identify the infectious disease and change the classification of the case from an injury to an illness.

(4) What if one of my employees is splashed or exposed to blood or other potentially infectious material without being cut or scratched? Do I need to record this incident?

You need to record such an incident on the Cal/OSHA Form 300 as an illness if:

(A) It results in the diagnosis of a bloodborne illness, such as HIV, hepatitis B, or hepatitis C; or

(B) It meets one or more of the recording criteria in Section 14300.7.

Note: Authority cited: Section 6410, Labor Code. Reference: Section 6410, Labor Code.

History: 1. New section filed 1-15-2002; operative 1-15-2002 pursuant to Government Code section 11343.4 (Register 2002, No. 3).

§14300.9. Recording Criteria for Cases Involving Medical Removal Under Cal/OSHA Standards.

(a) Basic requirement. If an employee is medically removed under the medical surveillance requirements of a Title 8 standard, you must record the case on the Cal/OSHA Form 300.

(b) Implementation.

(1) How do I classify medical removal cases on the Cal/OSHA Form 300?

You must enter each medical removal case on the Cal/OSHA Form 300 as either a case involving days away from work or a case involving restricted work activity, depending on how you decide to comply with the medical removal requirement. If the medical removal is the result of a chemical exposure, you must enter the case on the Cal/OSHA Form 300 by checking the "poisoning" column.

(2) Do all of Cal/OSHA's standards have medical removal provisions?

No. Some Title 8 standards, such as the standards covering bloodborne pathogens and noise, do not have medical removal provisions. Many Title 8 standards that cover specific chemical substances have medical removal provisions. These standards include, but are not limited to, lead, cadmium, methylene chloride, formaldehyde, and benzene.

(3) Do I have to record a case where I voluntarily removed the employee from exposure before the medical removal criteria in a Cal/OSHA standard are met?

No. If the case involves voluntary medical removal before the medical removal levels required by a Cal/OSHA standard, you do not need to record the case on the Cal/OSHA Form 300.

Note: Authority cited: Section 6410, Labor Code. Reference: Section 6410, Labor Code.

History: 1. New section filed 1-15-2002; operative 1-15-2002 pursuant to Government Code section 11343.4 (Register 2002, No. 3).

§14300.10. Recording Criteria for Cases Involving Occupational Hearing Loss.

(a) Basic requirement. If an employee's hearing test (audiogram) reveals that the employee has experienced a work-related Standard Threshold Shift (STS) in hearing in one or both ears, and the employee's total hearing level is 25 decibels (dB) or more above audiometric zero (averaged at 2000, 3000, and 4000 Hz) in the same ear(s) as the STS, you must record the case on the Cal/OSHA Form 300.

(b) Implementation.

(1) What is a Standard Threshold Shift? A Standard Threshold Shift, or STS, is defined in the occupational noise exposure standard at section 5097(d)(8) as a change in hearing threshold, relative to the baseline audiogram for that employee, of an average of 10 decibels (dB) or more at 2000, 3000, and 4000 hertz (Hz) in one or both ears.

(2) How do I evaluate the current audiogram to determine whether an employee has an STS and a 25-dB hearing level?

(i) STS. If the employee has never previously experienced a recordable hearing loss, you must compare the employee's current audiogram with that employee's baseline audiogram. If the employee has previously experienced a recordable hearing loss, you must compare the employee's current audiogram with the employee's revised baseline audiogram (the audiogram reflecting the employee's previous recordable hearing loss case).

(ii) 25-dB loss. Audiometric test results reflect the employee's overall hearing ability in comparison to audiometric zero. Therefore, using the employee's current audiogram, you must use the average hearing level at 2000, 3000, and 4000 Hz to determine whether or not the employee's total hearing level is 25 dB or more.

(3) May I adjust the current audiogram to reflect the effects of aging on hearing?

Yes. When you are determining whether an STS has occurred, you may age adjust the employee's current audiogram results by using Tables F as appropriate, in Appendix F of Title 8 General Industry Safety Orders, Article 105, section 5095 to 5100. You may not use an age adjustment when determining whether the employee's total hearing level is 25 dB or more above audiometric zero.

(4) Do I have to record the hearing loss if I am going to retest the employee's hearing?

No, if you retest the employee's hearing within 30 days of the first test, and the retest does not confirm the recordable STS, you are not required to record the hearing loss case on the Cal/OSHA 300 Log. If the retest confirms the recordable STS, you must record the hearing loss illness within seven (7) calendar days of the retest. If subsequent audiometric testing performed under the testing requirements of the noise standard at section 5097 indicates that an STS is not persistent, you may erase or line-out the recorded entry.

(5) Are there any special rules for determining whether a hearing loss case is work-related?

No. You must use the rules in section 14300.5 to determine if the hearing loss is work-related. If an event or exposure in the work environment either caused or contributed to the hearing loss, or significantly aggravated a pre-existing hearing loss, you must consider the case to be work related.

(6) If a physician or other licensed health care professional determines the hearing loss is not work-related, do I still need to record the case?

If a physician or other licensed health care professional determines that the hearing loss is not work-related or has not been significantly aggravated by occupational noise exposure, you are not required to consider the case work-related or to record the case on the Cal/OSHA Form 300.

(7) How do I complete the Form 300 for a hearing loss case?

When you enter a recordable hearing loss case on the Cal/OSHA Form 300, you must check the 300 Log column for hearing loss.

Note: Authority cited: Section 6410, Labor Code. Reference: Section 6410, Labor Code; and 29 Code of Federal Regulations Section 1904.10.

History: 1. New section filed 1-15-2002; operative 1-15-2002 pursuant to Government Code section 11343.4 (Register 2002, No. 3).

2. Repealer and new section filed 12-30-2002; operative 1-1-2003 pursuant to Government Code section 11343.4 (Register 2003, No. 1).

3. Amendment of subsections (a) and (a)(7) and amendment of Note filed 4-23-2004; operative 4-23-2004 pursuant to Government Code section 11343.4 (Register 2004, No. 17).

4. Change without regulatory effect amending subsections (a) and (b)(7) filed 8-22-2007 pursuant to section 100, title 1, California Code of Regulations (Register 2007, No. 34).

§14300.11. Recording Criteria for Work-Related Tuberculosis Cases.

(a) Basic requirement. If any of your employees has been occupationally exposed to anyone with a known case of active tuberculosis (TB), and that employee subsequently develops a tuberculosis infection, as evidenced by a positive skin test or diagnosis by a physician or other licensed health care professional, you must record the case on the Cal/OSHA Form 300 by checking the "respiratory condition" column.

(b) Implementation.

(1) Do I have to record, on the Cal/OSHA Form 300, a positive TB skin test result obtained at a pre-employment physical?

No. You do not have to record it because the employee was not occupationally exposed to a known case of active tuberculosis in your workplace.

(2) May I line-out or erase a recorded TB case if I obtain evidence that the case was not caused by occupational exposure?

Yes. You may line-out or erase the case from the Cal/OSHA Form 300 under the following circumstances:

(A) The worker is living in a household with a person who has been diagnosed with active TB;

(B) The Public Health Department has identified the worker as a contact of an individual with a case of active TB unrelated to the workplace; or

(C) A medical investigation shows that the employee's infection was caused by exposure to TB away from work, or proves that the case was not related to the workplace TB exposure.

Note: Authority cited: Section 6410, Labor Code. Reference: Section 6410, Labor Code.

History: 1. New section filed 1-15-2002; operative 1-15-2002 pursuant to Government Code section 11343.4 (Register 2002, No. 3).

§14300.12. Recording Criteria for Cases Involving Work-Related Musculoskeletal Disorders.

Record work-related injuries and illnesses involving muscles, nerves, tendons, ligaments, joints, cartilage and spinal discs in accordance with the requirements applicable to any injury or illness under Sections 14300.5, 14300.6, 14300.7, and 14300.29. For entry (M) on the Cal/OSHA Form 300, you must check either the entry for "injury" or for "all other illnesses."

Note: Authority cited: Section 6410, Labor Code. Reference: Section 6410, Labor Code; and 29 Code of Federal Regulations Section 1904.12.

History: 1. New section filed 1-15-2002; operative 1-15-2002 pursuant to Government Code section 11343.4 (Register 2002, No. 3).

2. Amendment of section and new Note filed 12-30-2002; operative 1-1-2003 pursuant to Government Code section 11343.4 (Register 2003, No. 1).

3. Amendment of section and Note filed 4-23-2004; operative 4-23-2004 pursuant to Government Code section 11343.4 (Register 2004, No. 17).

4. Change without regulatory effect amending section filed 8-22-2007 pursuant to section 100, title 1, California Code of Regulations (Register 2007, No. 34).

§14300.13–14300.28. [Reserved]

§14300.29. Forms.

(a) Basic requirement. You must use Cal/OSHA 300, 300A, and 301 forms, or equivalent forms, for recordable injuries and illnesses. The Cal/OSHA Form 300 is called the Log of Work-Related Injuries and Illnesses, the Cal/OSHA Form 300A is called the Summary of Work-Related Injuries and Illnesses, and the Cal/OSHA Form 301 is called the Injury and Illness Incident Report. Appendices A through C give samples of the Cal/OSHA forms. Appendices D through F provide elements for development of equivalent forms consistent with Section 14300.29(b)(4) requirements. Appendix G is a worksheet to assist in completing the Cal/OSHA Form 300A.

(b) Implementation.

(1) What do I need to do to complete the Cal/OSHA Form 300?

You must enter information about your establishment at the top of the Cal/OSHA Form 300 by entering a one or two line description for each recordable injury or illness, and summarizing this information on the Cal/OSHA Form 300A at the end of the year.

(2) What do I need to do to complete the Cal/OSHA Form 301 Incident Report?

You must complete a Cal/OSHA 301 Incident Report form, or an equivalent form, for each injury or illness required to be entered on the Cal/OSHA Form 300.

(3) How quickly must each injury or illness be recorded?

You must enter each recordable injury or illness on the Cal/OSHA Form 300 and Cal/OSHA Form 301 Incident Report within seven (7) calendar days of receiving information that a recordable injury or illness has occurred.

(4) What is an equivalent form?

An equivalent form is one that has the same information, is as readable and understandable to a person not familiar with it, and is completed using the same instructions as the Cal/OSHA form it replaces.

(5) May I keep my records on a computer?

Yes. If the computer can produce equivalent forms when they are needed, as described under Sections 14300.35 and 14300.40, you may keep your records using a computer system.

(6) Are there situations where I do not put the employee's name on the forms for privacy reasons?

Yes. If you have a "privacy concern case," as described in subsection (b)(7) of this section, you may not enter the employee's name on the Cal/OSHA Form 300. Instead, enter "privacy case" in the space normally used for the employee's name. This will protect the privacy of the injured or ill employee when another employee, a former employee, or an authorized employee representative is provided access to the Cal/OSHA Form 300 under Section 14300.35(b)(2). You must keep a separate, confidential list of the case numbers and employee names for your privacy concern cases so you can update the cases and provide the information to the government if asked to do so.

(7) How do I determine if an injury or illness is a privacy concern case?

You must consider the following injuries or illnesses to be privacy concern cases:

(A) An injury or illness to an intimate body part or the reproductive system;

(B) An injury or illness resulting from a sexual assault;

(C) Mental illnesses;

(D) HIV infection, hepatitis, or tuberculosis;

(E) Needlestick injuries and cuts from sharp objects that are contaminated with another person's blood or other potentially infectious material (see Section 14300.8 for definitions); and

(F) Other illnesses, if the employee independently and voluntarily requests that his or her name not be entered on the log.

(8) May I classify any other types of injuries and illnesses as privacy concern cases?

No. This is a complete list of all injuries and illnesses considered privacy concern cases for purposes of Article 2.

(9) If I have removed the employee's name, but still believe that the employee may be identified from the information on the forms, is there anything else that I can do to further protect the employee's privacy?

Yes. If you have a reasonable basis to believe that information describing the privacy concern case may be personally identifiable even though the employee's name has been omitted, you may use discretion in describing the injury or illness on both the Cal/OSHA forms 300 and 301. You must enter enough information to identify the cause of the incident and the general severity of the injury or illness, but you do not need to include details of an intimate or private nature. For example, a sexual assault case could be described as "injury from assault," or an injury to a reproductive organ could be described as "lower abdominal injury."

(10) What must I do to protect employee privacy if I wish to provide access to the Cal/OSHA forms 300 and 301 to persons other than government representatives, employees, former employees or authorized representatives?

If you decide to voluntarily disclose the forms to persons other than government representatives, employees, former employees or authorized representatives (as required by Sections 14300.35 and 14300.40), you must remove or hide the employees' names and other personally identifying information, except for the following cases. You may disclose the forms with personally identifying information only:

(A) to an auditor or consultant hired by the employer to evaluate the safety and health program;

(B) to the extent necessary for processing a claim for workers' compensation or other insurance benefits; or

(C) to a public health authority or law enforcement agency for uses and disclosures for which consent, an authorization, or opportunity to agree or object is not required under Department of Health and Human Services Standards for Privacy of Individually Identifiable Health Information, 45 CFR.164.512.

Note: Authority cited: Section 6410, Labor Code. Reference: Section 6410, Labor Code; and 29 Code of Federal Regulations Section 1904.29.

History: 1. New section filed 1-15-2002; operative 1-15-2002 pursuant to Government Code section 11343.4 (Register 2002, No. 3).

2. Amendment of subsection (b)(7)(F) filed 12-30-2002; operative 1-1-2003 pursuant to Government Code section 11343.4 (Register 2003, No. 1).

3. Amendment of subsections (a), (b)(1)-(3), (b)(6) and (b)(7)(F) and amendment of Note filed 4-23-2004; operative 4-23-2004 pursuant to Government Code section 11343.4 (Register 2004, No. 17).

4. Change without regulatory effect amending subsections (a), (b)(1)-(3) and (b)(6) filed 8-22-2007 pursuant to section 100, title 1, California Code of Regulations (Register 2007, No. 34).

§14300.30. Multiple Establishments.

(a) Basic requirement. You must keep a separate Cal/

OSHA Form 300 for each establishment that is expected to be in operation for one year or longer.

(b) Implementation.

(1) Do I need to keep injury and illness records for short-term establishments (i.e., establishments that will exist for less than a year)?

Yes. However, you do not have to keep a separate Cal/OSHA Form 300 for each such establishment. You may keep one Cal/OSHA Form 300 that covers all of your short-term establishments. You may also include the short-term establishments' recordable injuries and illnesses on a Cal/OSHA Form 300 that covers short-term establishments for individual company divisions or geographic regions.

(2) May I keep the records for all of my establishments at my headquarters location or at some other central location?

Yes. You may keep the records for an establishment at your headquarters or other central location if you:

(A) Transmit information about the injuries and illnesses from the establishment to the central location within seven (7) calendar days of receiving information that a recordable injury or illness has occurred.

Exception: If you have an establishment in SIC Code 781 and it is operated at a location that is remote from your central location, you must transmit the information to the central location within the lesser of 30 calendar days of learning of the injury or illness, or 7 calendar days of termination of operations at the remote location;

(B) Produce and send the records from the central location to the establishment within the time frames required by Section 14300.35 and Section 14300.40 when you are required to provide records to a government representative, employee, former employee or employee representative;

(C) Have the address and telephone number of the central location or headquarters where records are kept available at each worksite; and

(D) Have personnel available at the central location or headquarters where records are kept during normal business hours to transmit information from the records maintained there as required by Section 14300.35 and Section 14300.40.

(3) Some of my employees work at several different locations or do not work at any of my establishments at all. How do I record cases for these employees?

You must link each of your employees with one of your establishments, for recordkeeping purposes. You must record each injury and illness on the Cal/OSHA Form 300 of the injured or ill employee's establishment, or on a Cal/OSHA Form 300 that covers that employee's short-term establishment.

(4) How do I record an injury or illness when an employee of one of my establishments is injured or becomes ill while visiting or working at another of my establishments, or while working away from any of my establishments?

If the injury or illness occurs at one of your establishments, you must record the injury or illness on the Cal/OSHA Form 300 of the establishment at which the injury or illness occurred. If the employee is injured or becomes ill and is not at one of your establishments, you must record the case on the Cal/OSHA Form 300 for the establishment at which the employee normally works.

Note: Authority cited: Section 6410, Labor Code. Reference: Section 6410, Labor Code.

History: 1. New section filed 1-15-2002; operative 1-15-2002 pursuant to Government Code section 11343.4 (Register 2002, No. 3).

§14300.31. Covered Employees.

(a) Basic requirement. You must record on the Cal/OSHA Form 300 the recordable injuries and illnesses of all employees on your payroll, whether they are labor, executive, hourly, salary, part-time, seasonal, or migrant workers. You also must record the recordable injuries and illnesses that occur to employees who are not on your payroll if you supervise these employees on a day-to-day basis. If your establishment is organized as a sole proprietorship or partnership, the owner or partners are not considered employees for recordkeeping purposes.

(b) Implementation.

(1) If a self-employed person is injured or becomes ill while doing work at my establishment, do I need to record the injury or illness?

No. Self-employed individuals are not covered by the Cal/OSHA Act or this regulation.

(2) If I obtain employees from a temporary help service, employee leasing service, or personnel supply service, do I have to record an injury or illness occurring to one of those employees?

You must record these injuries and illnesses if you supervise these employees on a day-to-day basis.

(3) If an employee in my establishment is a contractor's employee, must I record an injury or illness occurring to that employee?

If the contractor's employee is under the day-to-day supervision of the contractor, the contractor is responsible for recording the injury or illness. If you supervise the contractor employee's work on a day-to-day basis, you must record the injury or illness.

(4) Must the personnel supply service, temporary help service, employee leasing service, or contractor also record the injuries or illnesses occurring to temporary, leased or contract employees that I supervise on a day-to-day basis?

No. You and the temporary help service, employee leasing service, personnel supply service, or contractor should coordinate your efforts to make sure that each injury and illness is recorded only once: either on your Cal/OSHA Form 300 (if you provide day-to-day supervision) or on the other employer's Cal/OSHA Form 300 (if that company provides day-to-day supervision).

Note: Authority cited: Section 6410, Labor Code. Reference: Section 6410, Labor Code.

History: 1. New section filed 1-15-2002; operative 1-15-2002 pursuant to Government Code section 11343.4 (Register 2002, No. 3).

§14300.32. Annual Summary.

(a) Basic requirement. At the end of each calendar year, you must:

(1) Review the Cal/OSHA Form 300 to verify that the entries are complete and accurate, and correct any deficiencies identified;

(2) Create an annual summary of injuries and illnesses recorded on the Cal/OSHA Form 300 using the Cal/OSHA Form 300A Annual Summary of Work-related Injuries and Illnesses;

(3) Certify the annual summary; and

(4) Post the annual summary.

(b) Implementation.

(1) How extensively do I have to review the Cal/OSHA Form 300 entries at the end of the year?

You must review the entries as extensively as necessary to make sure that they are complete and correct.

(2) How do I complete the annual summary?

You must:

(A) Total the columns on the Cal/OSHA Form 300 (if you had no recordable cases, enter zeros for each column total); and

(B) Enter the calendar year covered, the company's name, establishment name, establishment address, annual average number of employees covered by the Cal/OSHA Form 300, and the total hours worked by all employees covered by the Cal/OSHA Form 300.

(C) If you are using an equivalent form other than the Cal/OSHA 300A, as permitted under Section 14300.29(b)(4), the annual summary you use must also include the employee access and employer penalty statements found on the Cal/OSHA Form 300A.

(3) How do I certify the annual summary?

A company executive must certify that he or she has examined the Cal/OSHA Form 300 and that he or she reasonably believes, based on his or her knowledge of the process by which the information was recorded, that the annual summary is correct and complete.

(4) Who is considered a company executive?

The company executive who certifies the log must be one of the following persons:

(A) An owner of the company (this is required only if the company is a sole proprietorship or partnership);

(B) An officer of the corporation;

(C) The highest ranking company official working at the establishment; or

(D) The immediate supervisor of the highest ranking company official working at the establishment.

(5) How do I post the annual summary?

You must post a copy of the annual summary in each establishment in a conspicuous place or places where notices to employees are customarily posted. You must ensure that the posted annual summary is not altered, defaced or covered by other material.

(6) When do I have to post the annual summary?

You must post the annual summary no later than February 1 of the year following the year covered by the records and keep the posting in place until April 30.

(7) What must be done for employees who do not normally report at least weekly to a location where the annual summary is posted for the establishment at which they work? Employers are required to present or mail the annual summary to each employee who receives pay during the February through April posting period who does not normally report at least weekly to a location where the annual summary is posted for the establishment to which they are linked for recordkeeping purposes as described at Section 14300.30(b)(3).

(8) Do I have to post the annual summary at locations where I no longer have operations or employees?

For multi-establishment employers where operations have closed down in some establishments during the calendar year, it will not be necessary to post summaries for those establishments.

Note: Authority cited: Section 6410, Labor Code. Reference: Section 6410, Labor Code.

History: 1. New section filed 1-15-2002; operative 1-15-2002 pursuant to Government Code section 11343.4 (Register 2002, No. 3).

§14300.33. Retention and Updating.

(a) Basic requirement. You must save the Cal/OSHA Form 300, the privacy case list (if one exists), the Cal/OSHA Form 300A, and the Cal/OSHA Form 301 Incident Reports for five (5) years following the end of the calendar year that these records cover.

(b) Implementation.

(1) Do I have to update the Cal/OSHA 300 Form during the five-year storage period?

Yes. During the storage period, you must update your stored Cal/OSHA 300 forms to include newly discovered recordable injuries or illnesses and to show any changes that have occurred in the classification of previously recorded injuries and illnesses. If the description or outcome of a case changes, you must remove or line out the original entry and enter the new information.

(2) Do I have to update the Cal/OSHA 300A Annual Summary of Work-related Injuries and Illnesses?

No. You are not required to update the annual summary, but you may do so if you wish.

(3) Do I have to update the Cal/OSHA 301 Incident Reports?

No. You are not required to update the Cal/OSHA 301 Incident Reports, but you may do so if you wish.

Note: Authority cited: Section 6410, Labor Code. Reference: Section 6410, Labor Code.

History: 1. New section filed 1-15-2002; operative 1-15-2002 pursuant to Government Code section 11343.4 (Register 2002, No. 3).

§14300.34. Change in Establishment Ownership.

If your establishment changes ownership, you are responsible for recording and reporting work-related injuries and illnesses only for that period of the year during which you owned the establishment. You must transfer the records required by this article to the new owner. The new owner must save all records of the establishment kept by the prior owner, as required by Section 14300.33 of this Article, but need not update or correct the records of the prior owner.

Note: Authority cited: Section 6410, Labor Code. Reference: Section 6410, Labor Code.

History: 1. New section filed 1-15-2002; operative 1-15-2002 pursuant to Government Code section 11343.4 (Register 2002, No. 3).

§14300.35. Employee Involvement.

(a) Basic requirement. Your employees and their representatives must be involved in the recordkeeping system in several ways.

(1) You must inform each employee of how he or she is to report a work-related injury or illness to you.

(2) You must provide access to your injury and illness records for your employees and their representatives as described in paragraph (b)(2) of this section.

(b) Implementation.

(1) What must I do to make sure that employees report work-related injuries and illnesses to me?

(A) You must set up a way for employees to report work-related injuries and illnesses promptly and

(B) You must tell each employee how to report work-related injuries and illnesses to you.

(2) Do I have to give my employees and their representatives access to the injury and illness records required by this article?

Yes. Your employees, former employees, their personal representatives, and their authorized employee representatives have the right to access the injury and illness records required by this article, with some limitations, as discussed below.

(A) Who is an authorized employee representative?

An authorized employee representative is an authorized collective bargaining agent of employees.

(B) Who is a "personal representative" of an employee or former employee?

A personal representative is:

1. Any person that the employee or former employee designates as such, in writing; or

2. The legal representative of a deceased or legally incapacitated employee or former employee.

(C) If an employee or his or her representative asks for access to the Cal/OSHA Form 300 and annual summary when do I have to provide it?

When an employee, former employee, personal representative, or authorized employee representative asks for copies of your current or stored Cal/OSHA 300 forms or a current or stored annual summary for an establishment the employee or former employee has worked in, you must give the requester a copy of the relevant Cal/OSHA 300 forms and annual summaries by the end of the next business day.

Exception: If your establishment is in NAICS Code 5121, you must give the requester the information within seven (7) calendar days.

(D) May I remove the names of the employees or any other information from the Cal/OSHA Form 300 before I give copies to an employee, former employee, or employee representative?

No. You must leave the names on the Cal/OSHA Form 300. However, to protect the privacy of injured and ill employees, you may not record the employee's name on the Cal/OSHA Form 300 for certain "privacy concern cases," as specified in Sections 14300.29(b)(6) through 14300.29(b)(9).

(E) If an employee or representative asks for access to the Cal/OSHA 301 Incident Report, when do I have to provide it?

1. When an employee, former employee, or personal representative asks for a copy of the Cal/OSHA Form 301 Incident Report describing an injury or illness to that employee or former employee, you must give the requester a copy of the Cal/OSHA 301 Incident Report containing that information by the end of the next business day.

Exception: If your establishment is in NAICS Code 5121, you must give the requester the information within seven (7) calendar days.

2. When an authorized employee representative asks for copies of the Cal/OSHA 301 Incident Reports or equivalent forms for an establishment where the agent represents employees under a collective bargaining agreement, you must give copies of those forms to the authorized employee representative within seven (7) calendar days but with the following personally identifying information deleted:

1. Name;
2. Address;
3. Date of birth;
4. Date of hire;
5. Gender;
6. Name of physician;
7. Location where treatment was provided;
8. Whether the employee was treated in an emergency room; and
9. Whether the employee was hospitalized overnight as an in-patient.

(F) May I charge for the copies?

No. You may not charge for these copies the first time they are provided. However, if one of the designated persons asks for additional copies, you may assess a reasonable charge for retrieving and copying the records.

(c) With the exception of provisions to protect the privacy of employees in subsections (b)(2)(D) and (b)(2)(E) of this section and in subsections (b)(6) through (b)(10) in Section 14300.29, nothing in this section shall be deemed to preclude employees and employee representatives from collectively bargaining to obtain access to information relating to occupational injuries and illnesses in addition to the information made available under this section.

Note: Authority cited: Sections 150(b) and 6410, Labor Code. Reference: Section 6410, Labor Code.

History: 1. New section filed 1-15-2002; operative 1-15-2002 pursuant to Government Code section 11343.4 (Register 2002, No. 3).

2. Amendment of subsections (a)(1)-(2), (b)(1)(A), (b)(2)(C) and (b)(2)(E)1. filed 11-1-2018 as an emergency; operative 11-1-2018 (Register 2018, No. 44). A Certificate of Compliance must be transmitted to OAL by 4-30-2019 or emergency language will be repealed by operation of law on the following day.

3. Amendment of subsections (a)(1)-(2), (b)(1)(A), (b)(2)(C) and (b)(2)(E)1. refiled 4-25-2019 as an emergency; operative 5-1-2019 pursuant to Government Code section 11346.1(d) (Register 2019, No. 17). A Certificate of Compliance must be transmitted to OAL by 7-30-2019 or emergency language will be repealed by operation of law on the following day.

4. Amendment of subsections (a)(1)-(2), (b)(1)(A), (b)(2)(C) and (b)(2)(E)1. refiled 7-29-2019 as an emergency; operative 7-31-2019 pursuant to Government Code section 11346.1(d) (Register 2019, No. 31). A Certificate of Compliance must be transmitted to OAL by 10-29-2019 or emergency language will be repealed by operation of law on the following day.

5. Certificate of Compliance as to 7-29-2019 order, including amendment of Note, transmitted to OAL 10-29-2019 and filed 12-11-2019 (Register 2019, No. 50).

§14300.36. Prohibition Against Discrimination.

Section 11(c) of the Act and Sections 6310 and 6311 of the Labor Code prohibit you from discriminating against an employee for reporting a work-related fatality, injury, or illness. These provisions of the Labor Code also protect the employee who files a safety and health complaint, asks for access to records required by this article, or otherwise exercises any rights afforded by the Act or Sections 6310 and 6311 of the Labor Code.

Note: Authority cited: Sections 50.7 and 6410, Labor Code. Reference: Sections 50.7, 98.7, 6310, 6311 and 6410, Labor Code.

History: 1. New section filed 1-15-2002; operative 1-15-2002 pursuant to Government Code section 11343.4 (Register 2002, No. 3).

§14300.38. Variances from the Recordkeeping Rule.

(a) Basic requirement for private employers. If you are a private employer and wish to keep records in a different manner from the manner prescribed by the provisions of this article, you may submit a variance petition to the Assistant Secretary of Labor for Occupational Safety and Health (Assistant Secretary), U. S. Department of Labor, Washington, DC 20210. You can obtain a variance only if you can show that your alternative recordkeeping system:

(1) Collects the same information as this article requires,

(2) Meets the purposes of the Act; and

(3) Does not interfere with the administration of the Act.

(b) Implementation of the basic requirement for private employers.

(1) What do I need to include in my variance petition? You must include the following items in your petition:

(A) Your name and address;

(B) A list of the State(s) where the variance would be used;

(C) The address(es) of the establishment(s) involved;

(D) A description of why you are seeking a variance;

(E) A description of the different recordkeeping procedures you propose to use;

(F) A description of how your proposed procedures will collect the same information as would be collected by the provisions of this article and achieve the purpose of the Act; and

(G) A statement that you have informed your employees of the petition by giving them or their authorized representative a copy of the petition and by posting a statement summarizing the petition in the same way as notices are posted under Title 8 Section 340.

(2) How will the Assistant Secretary handle my variance petition?

The Assistant Secretary will take the following steps to process your variance petition.

(A) The Assistant Secretary will offer your employees and their authorized representatives an opportunity to submit written data, views, and arguments about your variance petition.

(B) The Assistant Secretary may allow the public to comment on your variance petition by publishing the petition in the Federal Register. If the petition is published, the notice will establish a public comment period and may include a schedule for a public meeting on the petition.

(C) After reviewing your variance petition and any comments from your employees and the public, the Assistant Secretary will decide whether or not your proposed recordkeeping procedures will meet the purposes of the Act, will not otherwise interfere with the Act, and will provide the same information as required by the provisions of this article provide. If your procedures meet these criteria, the Assistant Secretary may grant the variance subject to such conditions as he or she finds appropriate.

(D) If the Assistant Secretary grants your variance petition, OSHA will publish a notice in the Federal Register to announce the variance. The notice will include the practices the variance allows you to use, any conditions that apply, and the reasons for allowing the variance.

(3) If I apply for a variance, may I use my proposed recordkeeping procedures while the Assistant Secretary is processing the variance petition?

No. Alternative recordkeeping practices are only allowed after the variance is approved. You must comply with the provisions of this article while the Assistant Secretary is reviewing your variance petition.

(4) If I have already been cited by the Division of Occupational Safety and Health for not following the provisions of this article, will my variance petition have any effect on the citation and penalty?

No. In addition, the Assistant Secretary may elect not to review your variance petition if it includes an element for which you have been cited and the citation is still under review by a court, an Administrative Law Judge (ALJ), or the California Occupational Safety and Health Appeals Board.

(5) If I receive a variance, may the Assistant Secretary revoke the variance at a later date?

Yes. The Assistant Secretary may revoke your variance if he or she has good cause. The procedures revoking a variance will follow the same process as are used for reviewing variance petitions, as outlined in Section 14300.38(b)(2). Except in cases of willfulness or where necessary for public safety, the Assistant Secretary will:

(A) Notify you in writing of the facts or conduct that may warrant revocation of your variance; and

(B) Provide you, your employees, and authorized employee representatives with an opportunity to participate in the revocation procedures.

(c) Variances from the recordkeeping rule for public employers. A public agency employer wishing to keep records in a different manner from the manner prescribed in this article may write a letter to the Chief of the Division of Labor Statistics and Research stating his or her request. Such requests should include the information described in subsection (b)(1) of this section for private employer requests for variances from requirements of this article. The provisions of subsections (b)(2) through (b)(5) of this section will also apply to variance requests from public agency employers except that the determining authority will be the Chief of the Division of Labor Statistics and Research.

Note: Authority cited: Section 6410, Labor Code. Reference: Section 6410, Labor Code.

History: 1. New section filed 1-15-2002; operative 1-15-2002 pursuant to Government Code section 11343.4 (Register 2002, No. 3).

§14300.40. Providing Records to Government Representatives.

(a) Basic requirement. When an authorized government representative asks for the records you keep under the provisions of this article, you must provide within four (4) business hours, access to the original recordkeeping documents requested as well as, if requested, one set of copies free of charge.

Exception: If your establishment is in SIC Code 781, you must make a reasonable effort to comply as required by this section within 4 business hours of receiving the request. If it is not possible to comply with that deadline with reasonable effort, you must comply no later than by the end of the next business day.

(b) Implementation.

(1) What government representatives have the right to get copies of the records I keep as required by Article 2?

The government representatives authorized to receive the records are:

(A) A representative of the Chief of the Division of Occupational Safety and Health, or of the Director of the Department of Health Services;

(B) A representative of the Secretary of the U.S. Department of Labor conducting an inspection or investigation under the Act; and

(C) A representative of the Secretary of the U.S. Department of Health and Human Services (including the National Institute for Occupational Safety and Health—NIOSH) conducting an investigation under Section 20(b) of the Act;

(2) Do I have to produce the records within four (4) hours if my records are kept at a location in a different time zone?

Your response will be considered to be timely if you give the records to the government representative within four (4) business hours of the request. If you maintain the records at a location in a different time zone, you may use the business hours of the establishment at which the records are located when calculating the deadline.

Note: Authority cited: Section 6410, Labor Code. Reference: Section 6410, Labor Code.

History: 1. New section filed 1-15-2002; operative 1-15-2002 pursuant to Government Code section 11343.4 (Register 2002, No. 3).

§14300.41. Electronic Submission of Injury and Illness Records to OSHA.

(a) Basic requirement.

(1) Annual electronic submission of Cal/OSHA injury and illness records by establishments with 250 or more employees. If your establishment had 250 or more employees at any time during the previous calendar year, and this article requires your establishment to keep records, then you must electronically submit information from the Cal/OSHA Form 300A Summary of Work-Related Injuries and Illnesses that you keep under this part to OSHA or OSHA's designee. You must submit the information once a year, no later than the date listed in paragraph (c) of this section of the year after the calendar year covered by the forms.

(2) Annual electronic submission of Cal/OSHA Form 300A Summary of Work-Related Injuries and Illnesses by establishments with 20 or more employees but fewer than 250 employees in designated industries. If your establishment had 20 or more employees but fewer than 250 employees at any time during the previous calendar year, and your establishment is classified in an industry listed in Appendix H for Title 8 Sections 14300–14300.48, then you must electronically submit information from Cal/OSHA Form 300A Summary of Work-Related Injuries and Illnesses to OSHA or OSHA's designee. You must submit the information once a year, no later than the date listed in paragraph (c) of this section of the year after the calendar year covered by the form.

(3) Electronic submission of records upon notification. Upon notification, you must electronically submit the requested information from your Cal/OSHA injury and illness records to OSHA or OSHA's designee.

(4) Electronic submission of the Employer Identification Number (EIN). For each establishment that is subject to these reporting requirements, you must provide the EIN used by the establishment.

(b) Implementation.

(1) Does every employer have to routinely submit information from the Cal/OSHA injury and illness records to OSHA or its designee?

No, only two categories of employers must routinely submit information from their Cal/OSHA injury and illness records. First, if your establishment had 250 or more employees at any time during the previous calendar year, and this article requires your establishment to keep records, then you must submit the required Cal/OSHA Form 300A information to OSHA once a year. Second, if your establishment had 20 or more employees but fewer than 250 employees at any time during the previous calendar year, and your establishment is classified in an industry listed in Appendix H for Title 8 Sections 14300–14300.48, then you must submit the required Cal/OSHA Form 300A information to OSHA once a year. Employers in these two categories must submit the required information by the date listed in paragraph (c) of this section of the year after the calendar year covered by the form or forms (for example, 2018 for the 2017 forms). If you are not in either of these two categories, then you must submit information from the injury and illness records to OSHA only if OSHA notifies you to do so for an individual data collection.

(2) If I have to submit information under paragraph (a)(1) of this section, do I have to submit all of the information from the recordkeeping form?

Yes, you are required to submit all of the information from the Form 300A.

(3) Do part-time, seasonal, or temporary workers count as employees in the criteria for number of employees in paragraph (a) of this section?

Yes, each individual employed in the establishment at any time during the calendar year counts as one employee, including full-time, part-time, seasonal, and temporary workers.

(4) How will OSHA notify me that I must submit information from the injury and illness records as part of an individual data collection under paragraph (a)(3) of this section?

OSHA will notify you by mail if you will have to submit information as part of an individual data collection under paragraph (a)(3). OSHA will also announce individual data collections through publication in the Federal Register and the OSHA newsletter, and announcements on the OSHA Web site. If you are an employer who must routinely submit the information, then OSHA will not notify you about your routine submittal.

(5) Does this section affect the Division of Occupational Safety and Health's authority to inspect my workplace?

No. Nothing in this section affects the Division of Occupational Safety and Health's statutory authority to investigate conditions related to occupational safety and health.

(6) How often do I have to submit the information from the injury and illness records?

If you are required to submit information under paragraph (a)(1) or (2) of this section, then you must submit the information once a year, by the date listed in paragraph (c) of this section of the year after the calendar year covered by the form or forms. If you are submitting information because OSHA notified you to submit information as part of an individual data collection under paragraph (a)(3) of this section, then you must submit the information as often as specified in the notification.

(7) How do I submit the information?

You must submit the information electronically. OSHA will provide a secure Web site for the electronic submission of information. For individual data collections under paragraph (a)(3) of this section, OSHA will include the Web site's location in the notification for the data collection.

(8) Do I have to submit information if my establishment is partially exempt from keeping Cal/OSHA injury and illness records?

If you are partially exempt from keeping injury and illness records under §§ 14300.1 and/or 14300.2, then you do not have to routinely submit Article 2 information under paragraphs (a)(1) and (2) of this section. You will have to submit information under paragraph (a)(3) of this section if OSHA informs you in writing that it will collect injury and illness information from you. If you receive such a notification, then you must keep the Cal/OSHA injury and illness records required by Article 2 and submit information as directed.

(9) Do I have to submit information if I am located in a State Plan State?

Yes, the requirements apply to employers located in State Plan States.

(10) May an enterprise or corporate office electronically submit Cal/OSHA injury and illness records for its establishment(s)?

Yes, if your enterprise or corporate office had ownership of or control over one or more establishments required to submit information under paragraph (a)(1) or (2) of this section, then the enterprise or corporate office may collect and electronically submit the information for the establishment(s).

(c) Reporting dates.

(1) In 2018, establishments required to submit under paragraph (a)(1) or (2) of this section must submit the required information for 2017 according to the table in this paragraph (c)(1):

Submission year	*Establishments submitting under paragraph (a)(1) of this section must submit the required information from this form/these forms:*	*Establishments submitting under paragraph (a)(2) of this section must submit the required information from this form:*	Submission deadline
2018	300A	300A	December 31, 2018

(2) Beginning in 2019, establishments that are required to submit under paragraph (a)(1) or (2) of this section will have to submit all of the required information by March 2 of the year after the calendar year covered by the form or forms (for example, by March 2, 2019, for the forms covering 2018).

Note: Authority cited: Sections 150(b) and 6410, Labor Code. Reference: Section 6410, Labor Code.

History: 1. New section filed 1-15-2002; operative 1-15-2002 pursuant to Government Code section 11343.4 (Register 2002, No. 3).

2. Amendment of section heading and section filed 11-1-2018 as an emergency; operative 11-1-2018 (Register 2018, No. 44). A Certificate of Compliance must be transmitted to OAL by 4-30-2019 or emergency language will be repealed by operation of law on the following day.

3. Amendment of section heading and section refiled 4-25-2019 as an emergency; operative 5-1-2019 pursuant to Government Code section 11346.1(d) (Register 2019, No. 17). A Certificate of Compliance must be transmitted to OAL by 7-30-2019 or emergency language will be repealed by operation of law on the following day.

4. Amendment of section heading and section refiled 7-29-2019 as an emergency; operative 7-31-2019 pursuant to Government Code section 11346.1(d) (Register 2019, No. 31). A Certificate of Compliance must be transmitted to OAL by 10-29-2019 or emergency language will be repealed by operation of law on the following day.

5. Certificate of Compliance as to 7-29-2019 order, including new subsection (a)(4) and amendment of Note, transmitted to OAL 10-29-2019 and filed 12-11-2019 (Register 2019, No. 50).

§14300.42. Requests from the Bureau of Labor Statistics for Data.

(a) Basic requirement. If you receive a Survey of Occupational Injuries and Illnesses Form from the Bureau of Labor Statistics (BLS), or a BLS designee, you must promptly complete the form and return it following the instructions contained on the survey form.

(b) Implementation.

(1) Does every employer have to send data to the BLS?

No. Each year, the BLS sends injury and illness survey forms to randomly selected employers and uses the information to create the Nation's occupational injury and illness statistics. In any year, some employers will receive a BLS survey form and others will not. You do not have to send injury and illness data to the BLS unless you receive a survey form.

(2) If I get a survey form from the BLS, what do I have to do?

If you receive a Survey of Occupational Injuries and Illnesses Form from the Bureau of Labor Statistics (BLS), or a BLS designee, you must promptly complete the form and return it, following the instructions contained on the survey form.

(3) Do I have to respond to a BLS survey form if I am normally exempt from keeping injury and illness records as required by this article?

Yes. Even if you are exempt from keeping injury and illness records under one or more of the provisions of Section 14300.1 to Section 14300.3, the BLS may inform you in writing that it will be collecting injury and illness information from you in the coming year. If you receive such a letter, you must keep the injury and illness records required by this article and make a survey report for the year covered by the survey.

(4) Do I have to answer the BLS survey form if I am located in a State-Plan State?

Yes. All employers who receive a survey form must respond to the survey, even those in State-Plan States.

Note: Authority cited: Section 6410, Labor Code. Reference: Section 6410, Labor Code.

History: 1. New section filed 1-15-2002; operative 1-15-2002 pursuant to Government Code section 11343.4 (Register 2002, No. 3).

§14300.43. Annual Summary and Posting of the 2001 Data.

(a) Basic requirement. If you were required to keep Cal/OSHA Form 200 in 2001, you must post a 2001 annual summary from the Cal/OSHA Form 200 of occupational injuries and illnesses for each establishment.

(b) Implementation.

(1) What do I have to include in the annual summary?

(A) You must include a copy of the totals from the 2001 Cal/OSHA Form 200 Log and Summary and the following information from that form:

1. The calendar year covered;
2. Your company name;
3. The name and address of the establishment; and
4. The certification signature, title and date.

(B) If no injuries or illnesses occurred at your establishment in 2001, you must enter zeros on the totals line and post the 2001 annual summary.

(2) When am I required to summarize and post the 2001 information?

(A) You must complete the annual summary by February 1, 2002; and

(B) You must post a copy of the annual summary in each establishment in a conspicuous place or places where notices to employees are customarily posted. You must ensure that the annual summary is not altered, defaced or covered by other material.

(3) You must post the 2001 annual summary from February 1, 2002 to March 1, 2002.

Note: Authority cited: Section 6410, Labor Code. Reference: Section 6410, Labor Code.

History: 1. New section filed 1-15-2002; operative 1-15-2002 pursuant to Government Code section 11343.4 (Register 2002, No. 3).

§14300.44. Retention and Updating of Old Forms.

You must save your copies of the Cal/OSHA 200 forms and supplementary records for each occupational injury or illness for five years following the year to which they relate and continue to provide access to the data as though these forms were the Cal/OSHA 300 and 301 forms, as provided for in Section 14300.35 and Section 14300.40. You are not required to update your old Cal/OSHA 200 forms and supplementary records.

Note: Authority cited: Section 6410, Labor Code. Reference: Section 6410, Labor Code.

History: 1. New section filed 1-15-2002; operative 1-15-2002 pursuant to Government Code section 11343.4 (Register 2002, No. 3).

§14300.46. Definitions.

The Act. The Act means the federal Occupational Safety and Health Act of 1970 (29 U.S.C. 651 et seq.). The definitions contained in Section 3 of the Act (29 U.S.C. 652) and related interpretations apply to such terms when used in this article.

Authorized representative. See subsection 14300.35(b)(2)(A).

BLS. The Bureau of Labor Statistics in the U. S. Department of Labor.

Cal/OSHA. The California Occupational Safety and Health Program within the California Department of Industrial Relations.

Cal/OSHA Form 300 means the Cal/OSHA Form 300 Log of Work-Related Injuries and Illnesses (Rev. 7/2007)

Cal/OSHA Form 300A means the Cal/OSHA Form 300A Annual Summary of Work-Related Injuries and Illnesses (Rev. 7/2007)

Company. A public or private employer.

Covered employees. See Section 14300.31.

Equivalent form. See subsection 14300.29(b)(4).

Establishment. An establishment is a single physical location where business is conducted or where services or industrial operations are performed. For activities where employees do not work at a single physical location, such as construction; transportation; communications, electric, gas and sanitary services; and similar operations, the establishment is represented by main or branch offices, terminals, stations, etc. that either supervise such activities or are the base from which personnel carry out these activities.

(A) Can one business location include two or more establishments?

Normally, one business location has only one establishment. Under limited conditions, the employer may consider two or more separate establishments that share a single location to be separate establishments. An employer may divide one location into two or more establishments only when:

1. Each of the establishments represents a distinctly separate business;

2. Each establishment is engaged in a different economic activity;

3. No one industry description in the Standard Industrial Classification Manual (1987) applies to the joint activities of the establishments; and

4. Separate reports are routinely prepared for each establishment on the number of employees, their wages and salaries, sales or receipts, and other business information. For example, if an employer operates a construction company at the same location as a lumberyard, the employer may consider each business to be a separate establishment.

(B) Can an establishment include more than one physical location?

Yes, but only under certain conditions. An employer may combine two or more physical locations into a single establishment only when:

1. The employer operates the locations as a single business operation under common management;

2. The locations are all located in close proximity to each other; and

3. The employer keeps one set of business records for the locations, such as records on the number of employees, their wages and salaries, sales or receipts, and other kinds of business information. For example, one manufacturing establishment might include the main plant, a warehouse a few blocks away, and an administrative services building across the street.

(C) If an employee telecommutes from home, is his or her home considered a separate establishment?

No. For employees who telecommute from home, the employee's home is not an establishment and a separate Cal/OSHA Form 300 is not required. Employees who telecommute must be linked to one of your establishments under Section 14300.30(b)(3).

Fatality. Any occupational injury or illness which results in death, regardless of the time between injury and death, or the length of the illness.

First aid. See subsection 14300.7(b)(5)(B).

General recording criteria. See Section 14300.7.

Injury or illness. An injury or illness is an abnormal condition or disorder. Injuries include cases such as, but not limited to, a cut, fracture, sprain, or amputation. Illnesses include both acute and chronic illnesses, such as, but not limited to, a skin disease, respiratory disorder, or poisoning. (Note: Injuries and illnesses are recordable only if they are new, work-related cases that meet one or more of recording criteria provisions in this article.)

Job transfer. See subsection 14300.7(b)(4).

Medical treatment. See subsection 14300.7(b)(5)(A).

New case. See Section 14300.6.

OSHA. The Occupational Safety and Health Administration in the U.S. Department of Labor.

Personal representative. See subsection 14300.35(b)(2)(B).

Physician or other licensed health care professional. A physician or other licensed health care professional is an individual whose legally permitted scope of practice (i.e., license, registration, or certification) allows him or her to independently perform, or be delegated the responsibility to perform, the activities described by this regulation.

Pre-existing condition. See subsection 14300.5(b)(5).

Privacy concern case. See subsection 14300.29(b)(6).

Recordable. An injury or illness is "recordable" for the purposes of this article if it satisfies the conditions requiring recording found in subsection (a) of Section 14300.4.

Routine functions. See subsection 14300.7(b)(4)(B).

Restricted work. See subsection 14300.7(b)(4)(A).

Significant injury or illness. See subsection 14300.7(b)(7).

Work environment. See subsection 14300.5(b)(1).

You. "You" means an employer as defined by Sections 3300 and 3301 of the Labor Code.

Note: Authority cited: Section 6410, Labor Code. Reference: Section 6410, Labor Code.

History: 1. New section filed 1-15-2002; operative 1-15-2002 pursuant to Government Code section 11343.4 (Register 2002, No. 3).

2. Change without regulatory effect adding definitions of "Cal/OSHA Form 300" and "Cal/OSHA Form 300A," filed 8-22-2007 pursuant to section 100, title 1, California Code of Regulations (Register 2007, No. 34).

§14300.47. Recordkeeping Requirements for Employers Covered by the Federal Mine Safety and Health Act.

Employers whose employees' occupational injuries and illnesses are required to be recorded under the Federal Mine Safety and Health Act of 1977 are not required to comply with the recordkeeping requirements of this article to the extent that so complying would result in duplicating information, provided access to the records required by Code of Federal Regulations, Title 30, Chapter 1, Subchapter I, commencing with Section 50.20 is granted to authorized representatives of the official mine safety agency of the State.

Note: Authority cited: Section 6410, Labor Code. Reference: Section 6410, Labor Code.

History: 1. New section filed 1-15-2002; operative 1-15-2002 pursuant to Government Code section 11343.4 (Register 2002, No. 3).

§14300.48. Effective Date.

The provisions of this article take effect on January 1, 2002 or on the effective date of the regulation, whichever is later.

Note: Authority cited: Section 6410, Labor Code. Reference: Section 6410, Labor Code.

History: 1. New section and Appendices A-G filed 1-15-2002; operative 1-15-2002 pursuant to Government Code section 11343.4 (Register 2002, No. 3).

2. Amendment of appendices A, B, D and E and amendment of Notes for appendices D and E filed 4-23-2004; operative 4-23-2004 pursuant to Government Code section 11343.4 (Register 2004, No. 17).

3. Change without regulatory effect amending appendices A, B, D and E filed 8-22-2007 pursuant to section 100, title 1, California Code of Regulations (Register 2007, No. 34).

4. New Appendix H filed 11-1-2018 as an emergency; operative 11-1-2018 (Register 2018, No. 44). A Certificate of Compliance must be transmitted to OAL by 4-30-2019 or emergency language will be repealed by operation of law on the following day.

5. New Appendix H refiled 4-25-2019 as an emergency; operative 5-1-2019 pursuant to Government Code section 11346.1(d) (Register 2019, No. 17). A Certificate of Compliance must be transmitted to OAL by 7-30-2019 or emergency language will be repealed by operation of law on the following day.

6. Amendment of Appendix H refiled 7-29-2019 as an emergency; operative 7-31-2019 pursuant to Government Code section 11346.1(d) (Register 2019, No. 31). A Certificate of Compliance must be transmitted to OAL by 10-29-2019 or emergency language will be repealed by operation of law on the following day.

7. Certificate of Compliance as to 7-29-2019 order, including amendment of appendices B and E, transmitted to OAL 10-29-2019 and filed 12-11-2019 (Register 2019, No. 50).

Appendix A. Cal/OSHA Form 300 (Rev. 7/2007) Log of Work-Related Injuries and Illnesses

Editor's Note: For the text of Appendix A, please see Barclays *Official California Code of Regulations.*

Appendix B. Cal/OSHA Form 300A (Rev. 4/2019) Annual Summary of Work-Related Injuries and Illnesses

Editor's Note: For the text of Appendix B, please see Barclays *Official California Code of Regulations.*

Appendix C. Injury and Illness Incident Report

Editor's Note: For the text of Appendix C, please see Barclays *Official California Code of Regulations.*

Appendix D. Required Elements for the Cal/OSHA 300 Equivalent Form

I. California employers who are required to record work-related injuries and illnesses on the Cal/OSHA Form 300 may use an equivalent form that includes all of the following instructions and information.

Log of Work-Related Injuries and Illnesses

Instruction: You must record information about every work-related death and about every work-related injury or illness that involves loss of consciousness, restricted work activity or job transfer, days away from work, or medical treatment beyond first aid. You must also record significant work-related injuries and illnesses that are diagnosed by a physician or licensed health care professional. You must also record work-related injuries and illnesses that meet any of the specific recording criteria listed in 8 CCR 14300.8 through 14300.12. Feel free to use two lines for a single case if you need to. You must complete an Injury and Illness Incident Report (Cal/OSHA Form 301) or equivalent form for each injury or illness recorded on this form. If you're not sure whether a case is recordable, contact the nearest office of the Division of Occupational Safety and Health for assistance.

Establishment Name & Address

Identify the Person (A)-(C)

A. Case Number

B. Employee's Name

C. Job Title

Describe the Case (D)-(F):

D. Date of Injury or illness

E. Where the event occurred

F. Describe the injury or illness, part(s) of the body affected, and object/substance that directly injured or made the person ill

Classify the Case (G)-(M)

Using these four categories (G)-(J), indicate only the most serious result for each case:

G. "Death"

H. "Days away from work"

I. Remained at work as "Other recordable cases"

J. Remained at work with "Job transfer or restriction"

Enter the number of days the injured or ill worker was:

K. Number of days the injured or ill worker was "Away from work"

L. Number of days the injured or ill worker was "On job transfer or restrictions"

M. Indicate an injury or, one type of illness:

(1) Injury column

(2) Skin disorder column

(3) Respiratory condition column

(4) Poisoning column

(5) Occupational hearing loss

(6) All other illnesses column

Page Totals (for columns (G)-(M))

Instruction: Transfer these totals to the Summary page (Cal/OSHA Form 300A) before you post it.

Instructions for privacy concerns:

"ATTENTION: This form contains information relating to employee health and must be used in a manner that protects the confidentiality of employees to the extent possible while the information is being used for occupational safety and health purposes."

Note: Privacy Concern Cases: employers using forms equivalent to the Cal/OSHA 300 are required to follow the privacy concern disclosure restrictions specified in Section 14300.29(b)(6)-(10).

Note: Additional Criteria. Beginning January 1, 2002, employers are required to record the following as specific injury and illness conditions. These are:

1. Injury from a needle or other sharp object that is contaminated with blood or OPIM (Reference: Section 14300.8)

2. Cases of medical removal under the requirements of a Cal/OSHA standard. (Reference: Section 14300.9)

3. Tuberculosis infection as evidenced by a positive skin test or diagnosis by a physician (Reference: Section 14300.11)

Note: Authority cited: Section 6410, Labor Code. Reference: Section 6410, Labor Code; and 29 Code of Federal Regulations Section 1904.10.

Appendix E. Required Elements for the Cal/OSHA Form 300A, Annual Summary of Work-Related Injuries and Illnesses Equivalent Form.

A. Employers who are required to complete the Cal/OSHA Form 300A may use an equivalent form that provides all of the following information:

1. The number of cases:

(G) The total number of deaths

(H) The total number of cases with days away from work

(I) The total number of cases with job transfers or restriction

(J) The total number of other recordable cases

2. The number of days:

(K) The total number of days of job transfer or restriction

(L) The total number of days away from work

(M) Injury and Illness Types, the total numbers of:

1. Injuries
2. Skin disorders
3. Respiratory conditions
4. Poisonings
5. Hearing Loss
6. All other illnesses

3. Posting requirement statement: "Post this Annual Summary from February 1 to April 30 of the year following the year covered by the form."

4. Establishment information:

- The establishment name
- Street address
- City, State, Zip
- Industry description
- The North American Industrial Classification System, if known.

5. Employment information

- The annual average number of employees.
- The total hours worked by all employees last year.

(For assistance in calculating the annual average number of employees, and total hours worked, refer to Appendix G.)

6. Sign Here:

- Admonition: "Knowingly falsifying this statement may result in a fine."
- Certification statement: "I certify that I have examined this document and that to the best of my knowledge the entries are true, accurate, and complete."
- Space for the signature of the company executive, and title.

- Phone number of signatory.
- Date of the certification.

Note: Authority cited: Sections 150(b) and 6410, Labor Code. Reference: Section 6410, Labor Code.

Appendix F. Required Elements for the Cal/OSHA 301 Injury and Illness Incident Report Equivalent Form

I. An employer that is required to fill out a Cal/OSHA Form 301 may use an equivalent form that provides the following items of information:

A. Information about the employee:

1. Full name

2. Home street address, city, state and Zip code

3. Date of birth

4. Date hired

5. Employee gender

B. Information about the physician or other health care professional:

6. Name of the physician or other health care professional who treated the employee

7. Name and complete address of the facility where the employee received treatment (if applicable)

8. If the employee was treated in an emergency room (yes or no)

9. If the employee was hospitalized overnight as an in-patient (yes or no)

C. Information about the case:

10. The case number matching the Cal/OSHA Log 300 (or equivalent) entry

11. The date of the injury or illness

12. Time of employee began work AM/PM

13. Time of the event AM/PM; or indication that the time cannot be determined

14. Description of what the employee was doing just before the incident occurred

15. Description of what happened; how the injury/illness occurred

16. The specific injury/illness, part(s) of the body affected, and medical diagnosis if available

17. Identify the object or substance that directly harmed the employee

18. If the employee died, the date of death

D. The name of the person the form was completed by

E. The title of the person who completed the form

F. The phone number of the person who completed the form

Appendix G. Worksheet to Help You Fill Out the Annual Summary

Editor's Note: For the text of Appendix G, please see Barclays *Official California Code of Regulations*

Appendix H. Designated Industries for § 14300.41(a)(2) Annual Electronic Submission of Cal/OSHA Form 300A Summary of Work-Related Injuries and Illnesses by Establishments With 20 or More Employees but Fewer Than 250 Employees in Designated Industries

NAICS	*Industry*
11	Agriculture, forestry, fishing and hunting.
22	Utilities.
23	Construction.
31-33	Manufacturing.
42	Wholesale trade.
4413	Automotive parts, accessories, and tire stores.
4421	Furniture stores.
4422	Home furnishings stores.
4441	Building material and supplies dealers.
4442	Lawn and garden equipment and supplies stores.
4451	Grocery stores.
4452	Specialty food stores.
4521	Department stores.
4529	Other general merchandise stores.
4533	Used merchandise stores.
4542	Vending machine operators.
4543	Direct selling establishments.
4811	Scheduled air transportation.
4841	General freight trucking.
4842	Specialized freight trucking.

4851	Urban transit systems.
4852	Interurban and rural bus transportation.
4853	Taxi and limousine service.
4854	School and employee bus transportation.
4855	Charter bus industry.
4859	Other transit and ground passenger transportation.
4871	Scenic and sightseeing transportation, land.
4881	Support activities for air transportation.
4882	Support activities for rail transportation.
4883	Support activities for water transportation.
4884	Support activities for road transportation.
4889	Other support activities for transportation.
4911	Postal service.
4921	Couriers and express delivery services.
4922	Local messengers and local delivery.
4931	Warehousing and storage.
5152	Cable and other subscription programming.
5311	Lessors of real estate.
5321	Automotive equipment rental and leasing.
5322	Consumer goods rental.
5323	General rental centers.
5617	Services to buildings and dwellings.
5621	Waste collection.
5622	Waste treatment and disposal.
5629	Remediation and other waste management services.
6219	Other ambulatory health care services.
6221	General medical and surgical hospitals.
6222	Psychiatric and substance abuse hospitals.
6223	Specialty (except psychiatric and substance abuse) hospitals.
6231	Nursing care facilities.
6232	Residential mental retardation, mental health and substance abuse facilities.
6233	Community care facilities for the elderly.
6239	Other residential care facilities.
6242	Community food and housing, and emergency and other relief services.
6243	Vocational rehabilitation services.
7111	Performing arts companies.
7112	Spectator sports.
7121	Museums, historical sites, and similar institutions.
7131	Amusement parks and arcades.
7132	Gambling industries.
7211	Traveler accommodation.
7212	RV (recreational vehicle) parks and recreational camps.
7213	Rooming and boarding houses.
7223	Special food services.
8113	Commercial and industrial machinery and equipment (except automotive and electronic) repair and maintenance.
8123	Dry-cleaning and laundry services.

Note: Authority cited: Section 6410, Labor Code. Reference: Section 6410, Labor Code.

§14301. Log and Summary of Occupational Injuries and Illnesses. [Repealed]

Note: Authority cited: Section 6410, Labor Code. Reference: Section 6410, Labor Code.

History: 1. New sections (14301-14315) filed 5-22-75; designated effective 7-1-75 (Register 75, No. 21).

2. Amendment of subsection (b) filed 11-29-77; effective thirtieth day thereafter (Register 77, No. 49).

3. Amendment of subsections (a) and (b) filed 1-13-83; effective thirtieth day thereafter (Register 83, No. 3).

4. Repealer filed 1-15-2002; operative 1-15-2002 pursuant to Government Code section 11343.4 (Register 2002, No. 3).

§14303. Period Covered. [Repealed]

Note: Authority cited: Section 6410, Labor Code. Reference: Section 6410, Labor Code.

History: 1. Amendment filed 1-13-83; effective thirtieth day thereafter (Register 83, No. 3). For prior history, see Register 75, No. 21.

2. Repealer filed 1-15-2002; operative 1-15-2002 pursuant to Government Code section 11343.4 (Register 2002, No. 3).

§14304. Supplementary Record. [Repealed]

Note: Authority cited: Section 6410, Labor Code. Reference: Section 6410, Labor Code.

History: 1. Amendment filed 2-8-80; designated effective 5-1-80 (Register 80, No. 6). For prior history, see Register 75, No. 21.

2. Amendment of subsection (b)(1) filed 1-13-83; effective thirtieth day thereafter (Register 83, No. 3).

3. Amendment of subsection (b)(1) filed 3-18-87; effective thirtieth day thereafter (Register 87, No. 12).

4. Amendment of subsection (b)(1) filed 1-14-93; operative 2-16-93 (Register 93, No. 3).

5. Repealer filed 1-15-2002; operative 1-15-2002 pursuant to Government Code section 11343.4 (Register 2002, No. 3).

§14305. Annual Summary. [Repealed]

Note: Authority cited: Section 6410, Labor Code. Reference: Section 6410, Labor Code.

History: 1. Amendment of subsection (c) filed 5-6-76 as procedural and organizational; effective upon filing (Register 76, No. 19).

2. Amendment of subsection (a) and (c) filed 11-29-77; effective thirtieth day thereafter (Register 77, No. 49).

3. Amendment filed 1-13-83; effective thirtieth day thereafter (Register 83, No. 3).

4. Repealer filed 1-15-2002; operative 1-15-2002 pursuant to Government Code section 11343.4 (Register 2002, No. 3).

§14307. Retention of Records. [Repealed]

Note: Authority cited: Section 6410, Labor Code. Reference: Section 6410, Labor Code.

History: 1. Amendment filed 1-3-79; effective thirtieth day thereafter (Register 79, No. 1).

2. Amendment filed 1-13-83; effective thirtieth day thereafter (Register 83, No. 3).

3. Repealer filed 1-15-2002; operative 1-15-2002 pursuant to Government Code section 11343.4 (Register 2002, No. 3).

§14308. Access to Records. [Repealed]

Note: Authority cited: Section 6410, Labor Code. Reference: Section 6410, Labor Code.

History: 1. Amendment filed 10-5-78; effective thirtieth day thereafter (Register 78, No. 40).

2. Amendment filed 1-13-83; effective thirtieth day thereafter (Register 83, No. 3).

3. Repealer filed 1-15-2002; operative 1-15-2002 pursuant to Government Code section 11343.4 (Register 2002, No. 3).

§14309. Falsification, or Failure to Keep Records. [Repealed]

Note: Authority cited: Section 6410, Labor Code. Reference: Sections 6410, 6426 and 6431, Labor Code.

History: 1. Amendment of subsection (b) filed 1-13-83; effective thirtieth day thereafter (Register 83, No. 3).

2. Repealer filed 1-15-2002; operative 1-15-2002 pursuant to Government Code section 11343.4 (Register 2002, No. 3).

§14310. Change of Ownership. [Repealed]

Note: Authority cited: Section 6410, Labor Code. Reference: Section 6410, Labor Code.

History: 1. New Note filed 1-13-83; effective thirtieth day thereafter (Register 83, No. 3).

2. Repealer filed 1-15-2002; operative 1-15-2002 pursuant to Government Code section 11343.4 (Register 2002, No. 3).

§14311. Definitions. [Repealed]

Note: Authority cited: Section 6410, Labor Code. Reference: Section 6410, Labor Code.

History: 1. Amendment of subsection (e) filed 1-13-83; effective thirtieth day thereafter (Register 83, No. 3).

2. New subsection (f) filed 7-19-84; designated effective 8-1-84 pursuant to Government Code Section 11346.2(d) (Register 84, No. 29).

3. Repealer filed 1-15-2002; operative 1-15-2002 pursuant to Government Code section 11343.4 (Register 2002, No. 3).

§14312. Petitions for Recordkeeping Exceptions. [Repealed]

Note: Authority cited: Section 6410, Labor Code. Reference: Section 6410, Labor Code.

History: 1. Amendment filed 1-13-83; effective thirtieth day thereafter (Register 83, No. 3).

2. Repealer filed 1-15-2002; operative 1-15-2002 pursuant to Government Code section 11343.4 (Register 2002, No. 3).

§14313. Employees Not in Fixed Establishments. [Repealed]

Note: Authority cited: Section 6410, Labor Code. Reference: Section 6410, Labor Code.

History: 1. New Note filed 1-13-83; effective thirtieth day thereafter (Register 83, No. 3).

2. Repealer filed 1-15-2002; operative 1-15-2002 pursuant to Government Code section 11343.4 (Register 2002, No. 3).

§14314. Small Employers. [Repealed]

Note: Authority cited: Section 6410, Labor Code. Reference: Section 6410, Labor Code.

History: 1. Amendment filed 11-29-77; effective thirtieth day thereafter (Register 77, No. 49).

2. Amendment filed 2-8-80; designated effective 5-1-80 (Register 80, No. 6).

3. Amendment filed 1-13-83; effective thirtieth day thereafter (Register 83, No. 3).

4. Repealer filed 1-15-2002; operative 1-15-2002 pursuant to Government Code section 11343.4 (Register 2002, No. 3).

§14315. Employers Covered by the Federal Mine Safety and Health Act. [Repealed]

Note: Authority cited: Section 6410, Labor Code. Reference: Section 6410, Labor Code.

History: 1. Amendment filed 1-13-83; effective thirtieth day thereafter (Register 83, No. 3).

2. Repealer filed 1-15-2002; operative 1-15-2002 pursuant to Government Code section 11343.4 (Register 2002, No. 3).

§14316. Private Sector Establishments Classified in Standard Industrial Classification Codes (SIC) 52-89, (except 52-55, 57, 70, 75, 76, 781, 79 and 80), in Accordance with the 1972 Edition of the "Standard Industrial Classification Manual," Incorporating the 1977 Supplement, Published by the Office of Management and Budget, Executive Office of the President. [Repealed]

Note: Authority cited: Section 6410, Labor Code. Reference: Section 6410, Labor Code.

History: 1. New section filed 7-19-84; designated effective 8-1-84 pursuant to Government Code Section 11346.2(d) (Register 84, No. 29).

2. Repealer filed 1-15-2002; operative 1-15-2002 pursuant to Government Code section 11343.4 (Register 2002, No. 3).

§14400. Statistical Surveys. [Repealed]

Note: Authority cited: Sections 6410 and 6411, Labor Code. Reference: Section 6411, Labor Code.

History: 1. New section filed 5-22-75; designated effective 7-1-75 (Register 75, No. 21).

2. Amendment filed 11-29-77; effective thirtieth day thereafter (Register 77, No. 49).

3. New Note filed 1-13-83; effective thirtieth day thereafter (Register 83, No. 3).

4. Repealer filed 1-15-2002; operative 1-15-2002 pursuant to Government Code section 11343.4 (Register 2002, No. 3).

ARTICLE 3
Public Agency Records of Occupational Injury or Illness [Repealed]

History: 1. Repealer of Article 3 (Sections 14700-14710, not consecutive) filed 1-13-83; effective thirtieth day thereafter (Register 83, No. 3). For prior history, see Registers 79, No. 1 and 78, No. 40.

SUBCHAPTER 2
REPORTS OF INJURY TO BE FILED BY THE CALIFORNIA DEPARTMENT OF CORRECTIONS

ARTICLE 1
Prison Labor

§14900. Prison Labor.

Section 6413(a) of the Labor requires that, except for the injuries specifically exempted by the section itself, injury reports shall be filed for every injury to any state prisoner (inmate) resulting from any labor performed by the prisoner (inmate). No reports need be filed if "disability resulting from such injury does not last through the day or does not require medical service other than ordinary first aid treatment."

Note: Authority cited: Section 6413, Labor Code.

History: 1. New Group 2 (Sections 14900-14920, not consecutive) filed 9-23-74; designated effective 11-1-74 (Register 74, No. 39).

ARTICLE 2
Reports to Be Filed by Department of Corrections

§14901. Department of Corrections' Report of Injury (Form 5030).

The report shall be submitted in duplicate (Form 5030), to the Division of Labor Statistics and Research on a standard form (Form 5030) approved by the Department of Corrections and the Division of Labor Statistics and Research, Department of Industrial Relations. The following information shall be included on the standard form:

Name, address and phone number of correctional institution;

Name, inmate number, sex, and date of birth of injured inmate;

Date of incarceration;

Type of labor (work) when injured and extent of total experience at that type of labor, and extent of prison training and safety training in that type of labor;

Extent of supervision over work methods used:

Where did the injury occur;

What was the object or substance that directly injured inmate:

Nature of injury and part of body affected;

What was the primary correctable cause of this accident;

What arrangements could be made to eliminate hazard;

Name of physician;

Date of injury;

Was injured unable to work on any day after injury;

Actual or estimated date of injured's recovery;

Date of death if injured died.

§14902. Agreement Between Parties.

By agreement between the parties concerned Form 5030 may be modified as needs for pertinent information arise.

§14903. Color of Form 5030.

The copy of the form to be used for transmission to the Division of Labor Statistics and Research must be printed on light blue stock.

§14904. Time of Filing.

The report shall be filed within five days after the injury.

§14910. Physician or Surgeon (Report Form 5031).

(a) Every physician or surgeon who attends, within a Department of Corrections institution, any injured inmate shall file with the Division of Labor Statistics and Research a complete report of such injury unless disability resulting from such injury does not last through the day or does not require medical service other than ordinary first aid treatment.

(b) The report shall be submitted in duplicate to the Division of Labor Statistics and Research on a standard form (Form 5031) approved by the Department of Corrections and the Division of Labor Statistics and Research, Department of Industrial Relations. Pertinent data required will include a statement as to the cause of the injury and the nature and extent of injury.

§14911. Agreement Between Parties.

By agreement between the parties concerned Form 5031 may be modified as needs for pertinent information arise.

§14912. Color of Form 5031.

The copy of the form to be used for transmission to the Division of Labor Statistics and Research must be printed on light blue stock.

§14913. Time of Filing Form 5031.

The report shall be filed within five days after first treatment.

§14920. Effective Date.

The California Department of Corrections shall commence submitting said reports on all injuries occurring January 1, 1975, and thereafter.

CHAPTER 8
OFFICE OF THE DIRECTOR

SUBCHAPTER 2
ADMINISTRATION OF SELF-INSURANCE PLANS

ARTICLE 1
Definitions

§15200. Authority. [Repealed]

Note: Authority cited; Sections 54, 55, and 3702.10, Labor Code. Reference: Sections 54, 55 and 3702.10, Labor Code.

History: 1. New group 2 (sections 15200–15203, 15210–15213, 15220–15221, 15230, 15250–15253, 15300–15303, 15350–15352, 15360–15363, 15400–15403 and 15420–15423) filed 4-23-56; effective thirtieth day thereafter (Register 56, No. 8).

2. Repealer of group 2, and new group 2 (sections 15200–15203, 15210–15213, 15220, 15221, 15230, 15250–15252, 15300–15303, 15350–15352, 15360–15362, 15400–15405, 15420–15423) filed 6-17-66; effective thirtieth day thereafter (Register 66, No. 18). For prior amendments, see Registers 56, No. 19; 58, No. 7; 61, No. 7; 61, No. 10.

3. Amendment filed 6-1-72; effective thirtieth day thereafter (Register 72, No. 23).

4. Amendment of article heading, repealer of section, and amendment of Note filed 12-22-92; operative 1-21-93 (Register 93, No. 2).

§15201. Definitions.

The following definitions apply in Articles 1 through 13 of these regulations:

Actuarial Study. Also referred to as a 'study.' This is a complete actuarial study prepared by a qualified actuary presenting the full and complete results of the actuarial analysis and study performed by the actuary including, but not limited to, the requirements specified in section 15209 for private self-insurers or section 15481 for self-insured groups. The study will also serve as the basis for the completion of the actuarial summary and be attached to the actuarial summary.

Actuarial Summary. Also referred to as a 'summary.' This is a summary of the study prepared by the same qualified actuary that prepared the study. The summary is taken directly from the actuarial study, electronically filed with the Office of Self-Insurance Plans, and shall include the data specified in sections 15209 for private self-insurers or section 15481 for self-insured groups.

Adjusting Location. The office address designated in accordance with Section 15402 of these regulations where the named administrator of the self-insurer fulfills his/her function.

In the event that claims are administered at the home of a telecommuting adjuster, the location shall be considered as a separate adjusting location for reporting and audit purposes unless the telecommuting adjuster reports to a California location of the administrator no less than weekly.

Administrative Agency. The person or firm that performs the day-to-day claims administration functions of a workers' compensation self-insurance program. The administrative agency may be:

(1) An independent contractor possessing a certificate to administer and designated by a self-insurer to be the administrative agency for all or a portion of its claims; or

(2) A partnership or corporation possessing a master certificate to self-insure, which administers its own claims and the claims of other affiliate or subsidiary self-insurers issued affiliate or subsidiary certificates to self-insure under the same master certificate number;

(3) A joint powers authority possessing a master certificate to self-insure, which self administers in whole or part the claims of its affiliate public self-insurers issued affiliate certificates to self-insure under the same master certificate number of the joint powers authority; or

(4) The claims department of an insurance carrier admitted to transact workers' compensation insurance in California, which is exempt from the requirement to

possess a certificate to administer under Labor Code Section 3702.1(a).

Administrative Director. The Administrative Director of the Division of Workers' Compensation within the Department of Industrial Relations.

Administrator. A competent person pursuant to Section 15452 of these regulations, at an adjusting location, who is responsible for day-to-day management of an employer's self-insurance workers' compensation program. The responsibility includes but is not limited to, the making and reviewing of decisions relating to the furnishing of all workers' compensation benefits in accordance with law and the maintenance of the self-insurer's claim records.

Affiliate Certificate.

(1) A type of certificate to self-insure issued to a private self-insurer that has common ownership to another private self-insurer holding a master certificate to self-insure, but the affiliated certificate holder is not a subsidiary to the master certificate holder; or

(2) A type of certificate to self-insure issued to a public self-insurer that is a member of a joint powers authority for pooling of workers' compensation liabilities with the master certificate number issued to the joint powers authority.

(3) A type of certificate to self-insure issued to a private self-insurer that is a member of a group self-insurer for pooling of workers' compensation liabilities under the master certificate number issued to the group self-insurer.

Alternative Composite Deposit. A security deposit system pursuant to Labor Code Section 3701.8 whereby all eligible private self-insurers collectively secure, in whole or in part, aggregate self-insured worker's compensation liabilities through the Self-Insurer's Security Fund.

Audit. Any examination of self-insured workers' compensation claim files performed by or at the request of the Office of Self-Insurance Plans pursuant to Labor Code Section 3702.6.

Board of Trustees. In group self-insurance, the representative body in a group self-insurer selected by the group members to be responsible for managing the assets and directing the affairs of the group self-insurer corporation and assuring the group self-insurer, through the group members, is financially sound and able to meet the workers' compensation liabilities under the statutes and regulations applicable in California.

Cancellation of Surety Bond. An act whereby the surety gives written notice to the Chief, as beneficiary of the workers' compensation self-insurance surety bond, that the surety is terminating its contractual obligations under the named bond pursuant to Sections 996.320 and 996.330 of the California Code of Civil Procedure and the liability of the surety bond after the effective date of the cancellation is set forth in Section 996.360 of the California Code of Civil Procedure.

Certificate to Administer. A Certificate of Consent to Administer self-insured workers' compensation claims issued to an administrative agency, except exempt insurance carriers, pursuant to Labor Code Section 3702.1.

Certificate to Self-Insure. A Certificate of Consent to Self-Insure issued to an employer pursuant to Section 3700(b) of the Labor Code.

Chief. The Chief, Office of Self-Insurance Plans, in the Department of Industrial Relations.

Claim File. A case file containing all pertinent documents and matters relating to a specific work-injury claim. The claim file contents are specified in Section 15400 of these regulations.

Claim Log. A manual or electronic listing of workers' compensation claims maintained by the self-insurer or administrative agency for the self-insurer. The claim log for private self-insurers shall list each work injury claim by the calendar year in which the claim was reported to the employer or the claims administrator, whichever first occurred. The log for public self-insurers shall list each work injury claim by the fiscal year in which the claim was reported. The claim log contents are specified in Section 15400.1 of these regulations.

Closed Claim. A work-injury claim in which future provision of benefits cannot be reasonably expected to be due.

Compensation. Compensation as defined in Labor Code Section 3207, which includes every benefit or payment conferred by Division 4 of the Labor Code on an injured employee or the employee's dependents.

Contribution. The amount of payments required of each group member in order to fund the compensation and deposit obligations of the group self-insurer.

Director. The Director of the Department of Industrial Relations.

Exoneration of Surety Bond. The discharge of a surety from all past, present and future liability under its workers' compensation self-insurance surety bond by the execution of a "Release of Surety", Form A4-24 (Rev. 11/92) by the Chief.

First Aid. First Aid as defined in Labor Code Section 5401(a).

Group Administrator. The individual or business entity authorized to serve as the representative of a group self-insurer and its group members to execute the policies of the Board of Trustees of the group self-insurer and manage the activities of the group self-insurer corporation.

Group Member. A private employer issued an Affiliate Certificate as a member in a group self-insurance program that has, in turn, been issued a Certificate to Self-Insure as a group self-insurer.

Group Self-Insurer. A private, non-profit, mutual benefit corporation, a private, non-profit charitable corporation, a private, non-profit public benefit corporation, or a private, non-profit religious corporation created as set forth in Section 15470 of these regulations and pursuant to Part 3 of Division 2 of Title 1 of the California Corporation Code. Said corporation shall be established for the sole purpose of operating a group workers' compensation self-insurance program to pool the California workers' compensation liabilities of two or more private employers in the same homogeneous grouping pursuant to Section 15473. These regulations are not intended to deem a group self-insurer issued a Certificate of Consent to Self-Insure pursuant to Labor Code Section 3700, subdivision (b) to be an insurance company subject to regulations governing insurers contained in Title 10, California Code of Regulations, except as otherwise provided by statute and by Title 8, California Code of Regulations.

Indemnity Agreement and Power of Attorney. The written agreement executed by each group member or proposed group member of a group self-insurer pursuant to Section 15479 of these regulations.

Indemnity Claim. A work-injury case which has or may result in any of the following benefits:

(1) Temporary Disability or salary in lieu thereof, including benefits provided under Labor Code Sections 4800 and 4850

(2) Permanent Disability

(3) Life Pension

(4) Death Benefits

(5) Vocational Rehabilitation

(6) Supplemental Job Displacement Benefit Voucher

Industry. Employer classification as determined using the first three (3) digits of the North American Industry Classification System Code (NAICS Code), provided by the United States Department of Commerce, Bureau of Management and Budget.

Joint Powers Authority. A public entity created by agreement of two or more public agencies pursuant to Division 7, Chapter 5, Article 1, Sections 6500 et seq. of the California Government Code. These regulations apply only to Joint Powers Authorities who have among their purposes for existence, the forming of workers' compensation liability pooling arrangements.

Labor Code. The Labor Code of the State of California.

Manager. The Manager, Office of Self-Insurance Plans, in the Department of Industrial Relations. (Synonymous with Chief, above.)

Medical-Only Claim. A work-injury case which does not result in compensable lost time but results in medical treatment beyond first aid.

NOTE: Payment of medical examinations pursuant to Labor Code Section 4600 will be considered a medical payment.

Office of Self-Insurance Plans. The Department of Industrial Relations, Office of Self-Insurance Plans, that is responsible for the oversight and regulation of Workers' Compensation self-insurance programs under these regulations.

Open Claim. A work-injury case in which it appears that one or more future payments of workers' compensation benefits may be due.

Public Self-Insurer or Public Self-Insured Employer.

(1) Any county, city, school district, special purpose district, joint powers authority or other municipal corporation which has applied and received approval to be self-insured by the Office of Self-Insurance Plans.

(2) Any sub-agency of a public agency which is created by or pursuant to statute, ordinance, or other legislative act, including but not limited to planning commissions, library or park boards, commissions, and agencies which has applied and received approval to be self-insured by the Office of Self-Insurance Plans.

Qualified Actuary. A qualified actuary is any actuary that meets the minimum standards of experience, certification, licensure, insurance, and qualifications set forth in section 15209, subdivisions (a)(2) and (3), for private self-insurers or section 15481, subdivisions (a)(3) & (4), for self-insured groups.

Release of Surety Bond. Action of Chief of Self-Insurance Plans by which a surety is exonerated. A released surety bond does not constitute part of the security deposit of a self-insured entity.

Security Fund. The Self-Insurer's Security Fund as established by Labor Code section 3742.

Self-Insurer. An individual public or private sector employer or joint powers authority or private group of employers that has been issued and lawfully holds a valid Certificate to Self-Insure its workers' compensation liabilities pursuant to:

(1) The provisions of Section 29(a), Chapter 586, Laws of 1917 and amendments thereto; and/or

(2) Labor Code, Section 3700(b) for private sector employers or 3700(c) for public sector employers.

Special Audit. Any audit performed other than that in accordance with Labor Code Section 3702.6.

Subsidiary Certificate. A type of certificate to self-insure issued to a subsidiary of a self-insurer, where the self-insurer holds the master certificate to self-insure.

Termination of Surety Bond. See definition of "Cancellation of Surety Bond".

Work-Injury Claim. An injury that is reported or reportable to the Division of Labor Statistics and Research pursuant to Labor Code Sections 6409, 6409.1 and 6413.

Note: Authority cited: Sections 54, 55, 3701.8 and 3702.10, Labor Code. Reference: Sections 59, 129, 3700, 3701, 3701.5, 3701.8, 3702, 3702.3, 3702.5, 3702.6, 3702.10, 3703, 3705, 3740-3747 and 3850, Labor Code; Section 6500, Government Code; and Sections 995.430, 996.320 and 996.330, Code of Civil Procedure; and 5002, 5003, 5059, 5060, 5061 and 5080, Corporations Code.

History: 1. Repealer and new section filed 12-3-69; effective thirtieth day thereafter (Register 69, No. 49).

2. Repealer and new section filed 6-1-72; effective thirtieth day thereafter (Register 72, No. 23).

3. Repealer and new section filed 11-19-75; effective thirtieth day thereafter (Register 75, No. 47).

4. Amendment placing the defined terms in alphabetical order, removal of letter designators, amendment of existing terms, addition of terms "Administrative Director," "Affiliate Certificate," "Certificate to Administer," and "Joint Powers Authority" and addition of Note filed 12-22-92; operative 1-21-93 (Register 93, No. 2).

5. New definitions "Cancellation of Surety Bond," "Exoneration of Surety Bond," "Release of Surety Bond," and "Termination of Surety Bond" and amendment of Note filed 8-12-93; operative 9-13-93 (Register 93, No. 33).

6. Amendment filed 6-30-94; operative 6-30-94 (Register 94, No. 26).

7. Amendment of section and Note filed 5-30-2003 as an emergency; operative 5-30-2003 (Register 2003, No. 22). A Certificate of Compliance must be transmitted to OAL by 9-29-2003 or emergency language will be repealed by operation of law on the following day.

8. Certificate of Compliance as to 5-30-2003 order transmitted to OAL 9-29-2003 and filed 11-12-2003 (Register 2003, No. 46).

9. Amendment of subsections (a)(2) and (m) filed 2-9-2006; operative 3-11-2006 (Register 2006, No. 6).

10. Amendment of subsections (e)(3), (h)-(i), and (m); new subsection (p), subsection relettering, amendment of newly designated subsections (t), (v), (y)-(z) and (gg)(2) and amendment of

Note filed 3-2-2009; operative 3-2-2009 pursuant to Government Code section 11343.4 (Register 2009, No. 10).

11. New subsection (x)(6) filed 9-19-2011; operative 10-19-2011 (Register 2011, No. 38).

12. Amendment of subsections (i), (bb) and (ee) and new subsections (*ll*)-(pp)(2) filed 12-31-2012 as an emergency; operative 1-1-2013 pursuant to Government Code section 11346.1(d) (Register 2013, No. 1). A Certificate of Compliance must be transmitted to OAL by 7-1-2013 or emergency language will be repealed by operation of law on the following day.

13. Certificate of Compliance as to 1-1-2013 order, including additional nonsubstantive amendments, transmitted to OAL 7-1-2013 and filed 8-13-2013 (Register 2013, No. 33).

14. Amendment of definitions of "Adjusting Location," "Claim File," "Compensation," "Group Self-Insurer," "Indemnity Claim" and "Industry," new definitions of "Closed Claim" and "Office of Self-Insurance Plans" and repealer of definition of "Core Group" filed 12-14-2016; operative 1-1-2017 pursuant to Government Code section 11343.4(b)(3) (Register 2016, No. 51).

Ref.: Hanna §§ 1.19, 2.11; Herlick Handbook § 3.20.

§15202. Advisory Committee.

The Manager shall appoint an ad hoc committee to advise the Manager on proposed regulations relating to self-insurance.

Note: Authority cited: Sections 54, 55, 3702.10, Labor Code. Reference: Sections 54, 55, 59, 3702.10, 6160, Labor Code.

History: 1. Repealer and new section filed 6-1-72; effective thirtieth day thereafter (Register 72, No. 23).

2. Amendment of section and addition of Note filed 12-22-92; operative 1-21-93 (Register 93, No. 2).

ARTICLE 2
Certificate of Consent to Self-Insure

§15203. Applications and Required Forms.

(a) Application forms for individual Certificates of Consent to Self-Insure and other required self-insurance forms are available on the website of the Office of Self-Insurance Plans at http://dir.ca.gov/osip/. Every employer desiring to procure an initial, individual private or public certificate to self-insure its workers' compensation liabilities shall make application on:

(1) Form A-1 (1-2016) for private individual employer applicants seeking an individual Certificate to Self-Insure;

(2) Form A-2 (1-2016) for public employer applicants;

(3) Form A-3B (1-2016) for an interim self-insurer seeking a permanent Certificate to Self-Insure.

(b) A new application may be required when an existing, individual self-insurer reincorporates, merges, changes ownership, or adds a new or separate subsidiary or affiliate to its existing workers' compensation self-insurance program. In some cases, it may be possible to amend and transfer an existing certificate without a new application, which decision shall be made by the Chief.

(c) A complete application to self-insure by an individual, private employer (Form A-1 (1-2016)) shall include all attachments requested on the application form itself, and, as applicable, the following:

(1) A current, certified, independently audited financial statement complete with all schedules and notes for the past three (3) years. The application of a private sector subsidiary or affiliate does not require submission of a financial statement;

(2) An unaudited financial statement or published quarterly report, or a consolidated financial statement for the current year or portion thereof;

(3) A Guaranty of Workers' Compensation Liabilities (Form A-4 (1-2016)) for each self-insurer applicant executed by the parent employer, or majority owner, or partners;

(4) A Corporate Resolution (Form A-5 (1-2016)) authorizing the application to self-insure and empowering employees or officers of the applicant employer to sign the application form and any other necessary documents on behalf of the applicant employer and execute a Guaranty of Workers' Compensation Liabilities (Form A-4 (1-2016));

(5) Original Certificates of Status or other appropriate registration documents showing that the applicant employer is licensed or registered to do business in California;

(6) A certification that the applicant has implemented an effective injury and illness prevention program and contact name of the person responsible for overseeing the applicant's safety services pursuant to Section 15353 of these regulations; and

(7) Payment of any required application filing fee.

(d) A complete application to self-insure by a public employer (Form A-2 (1-2016)) shall include all attachments requested on the public sector application form and, as applicable, the following:

(1) A Guaranty of Workers' Compensation Liabilities (Form A-4 (1-2016)) for the predecessor agency due to a unification, merger, realignment of the boundaries of an existing self-insured public agency, or name change by the successor or surviving public agency;

(2) A Corporate Resolution (Form A-5 (1-2016)) authorizing the application to self-insure and empowering employees or officers of the applicant employer or joint powers authority to sign the application form and any other necessary documents on behalf of the applicant.

(3) Each public applicant shall indicate the proposed start up date of its self-insurance program as part of its application.

(e) A complete application to self-insure on a Form S-1 (1-2016) by a private group of employers shall include all information and documents as indicated in Section 15482 of these regulations.

(f) A complete application to self-insure on a Form S-2B (1-2016) by each member of a group self-insurer shall include all information as indicated in Section 15482.1 of these regulations.

(g) The Chief shall issue a Certificate of Consent to Self-Insure to an approved joint powers authority that pools the workers' compensation liabilities of its public agency members and the master certificate number shall be assigned to the joint powers authority. Each approved member of the joint powers authority shall be issued an affiliate certificate number under the certificate number issued to the joint powers authority.

(h) Upon receipt of a complete private individual employer application, the applicant will be notified within 21 days of the Director's decision to allow or deny self-insurance or to advise that the application is deficient.

A notice indicating that the application is deficient will include a list of items required to be included or completed.

(i) Upon receipt of a complete public entity application, the applicant will be notified within 21 days of approval or denial of application.

Note: Authority cited: Sections 54, 55, 59 and 3702.10, Labor Code. Reference: Sections 3700, 3700(b), 3701, 3702, 3702.5 and 6401.7(a), Labor Code.

History: 1. Repealer and new section filed 6-1-72; effective thirtieth day thereafter (Register 72, No. 23).

2. Amendment filed 11-19-75; effective thirtieth day thereafter (Register 75, No. 47).

3. Amendment filed 11-21-78; effective thirtieth day thereafter (Register 78, No. 47).

4. New article 2 heading, newly designated subsections (a) and (b)-(b)(1), new subsections (b)(2)-(g)(1), amendment of Note, and repealer of form filed 12-22-92; operative 1-21-93 (Register 93, No. 2).

5. Amendment filed 6-30-94; operative 6-30-94 (Register 94, No. 26).

6. Amendment of subsection (a)(4), new subsection (a)(5), amendment of Note 1 and amendment of subsections (g) and (h) filed 6-4-98; operative 7-4-98 (Register 98, No. 23).

7. Amendment of article heading, section heading, section and Note filed 3-2-2009; operative 3-2-2009 pursuant to Government Code section 11343.4 (Register 2009, No. 10).

8. Amendment of article heading and section filed 12-14-2016; operative 1-1-2017 pursuant to Government Code section 11343.4(b)(3) (Register 2016, No. 51).

9. Editorial correction of subsection (f) (Register 2019, No. 7).

Ref.: Hanna §§ 1.19, 2.11[1]; Herlick Handbook § 3.20.

§15203.1. Agreement of Assumption and Guarantee of Subsidiary's or Affiliate's Liabilities.

Each private subsidiary or affiliate applicant for a Certificate to Self Insure of an individual private self insurer shall provide an Agreement of Assumption and Guarantee of Liabilities executed by the holding company, ultimate parent corporation, controlling partners, owners, or other controlling entity in accordance with Section 15211.2 of these regulations. If the holding company, ultimate parent corporation, controlling partners, owners, or other controlling entity will not execute the Assumption and Guarantee agreement, the Director may:

(a) Require a deposit level of 200% of the master certificate holder's, subsidiary's or affiliate's estimated future liabilities for the payment of compensation, or higher, in lieu of the Agreement of Assumption and Guarantee of Liabilities; or

(b) Deny the application to self insure by the private applicant.

Note: Authority cited: Sections 54, 55 and 3702.10, Labor Code. Reference: Sections 59, 3550, 3700, 3701, 3701.5, 3702, 3702.10 and 3705, Labor Code.

History: 1. New section filed 11-21-78; effective thirtieth day thereafter (Register 78, No. 47).

2. Amendment of section heading and text filed 12-22-92; operative 1-21-93 (Register 93, No. 2).

3. Amendment filed 6-30-94; operative 6-30-94 (Register 94, No. 26).

4. Amendment filed 3-2-2009; operative 3-2-2009 pursuant to Government Code section 11343.4 (Register 2009, No. 10).

Ref.: Hanna §§ 1.19, 2.11; Herlick Handbook § 3.20.

§15203.2. Continuing Financial Capacity for Individual Private Self-Insurers.

(a) Each individual private self-insurer holding an active or revoked Certificate of Consent to Self-Insure shall submit annually via an online platform at http://www.dir.ca.gov/osip a copy of the employer's current, certified, independently audited financial statement complete with all notes and schedules. If the individual private self-insurer or former self-insurer did not prepare a current, certified, independently audited financial statement of its financial condition, or of a parent or holding company's financial condition if a Guaranty of Workers' Compensation Liabilities (Form A-4 (1-2016)) has been executed on its behalf by that parent or holding company pursuant to Section 15211.2 of these regulations, the self-insurer or former self-insurer shall advise the Chief in writing and submit a financial statement prepared by an independent certified public accountant. Failure to submit a qualifying financial statement pursuant to this section may result in an increased security deposit requirement pursuant to subsection (c) and/or revocation of the Certificate of Consent to Self-Insure for good cause pursuant to Labor Code Section 3702.

(b) Impairment of solvency of a current or former private individual self-insured employer, indicated by a marked reduction in financial strength, or the lack of an independently prepared, audited financial statement, is good cause for an increased security deposit pursuant to Section 15210.1 of these regulations and/or involuntary revocation of a Certificate of Consent to Self-Insure, an Affiliate Certificate, or a Subsidiary Certificate pursuant to Labor Code Section 3702.

(c) Each private employer applicant for a Certificate of Consent to Self-Insure shall meet the following minimum conditions: (1) three calendar years in business in a legally authorized business form (e.g. corporation, partnership, proprietorship, non-profit, etc.); (2) have three years of audited financial statements prepared by an independent certified public accountant; and (3) on the date of application to self-insure, have an acceptable credit rating, as specified in Section 15220(d)(2), for each of three full calendar years prior to the date of application as demonstrated pursuant to Section 15220.1, and directly post a security deposit as required by Section 15210(d).

Note: Authority cited: Sections 54, 55 and 3702.10, Labor Code. Reference: Sections 59, 3700, 3701, 3702 and 3702.10, Labor Code.

History: 1. New section filed 12-22-92; operative 1-21-93 (Register 93, No. 2).

2. Amendment of section and Note filed 6-30-94; operative 6-30-94 (Register 94, No. 26).

3. Amendment of section heading and section filed 3-2-2009; operative 3-2-2009 pursuant to Government Code section 11343.4 (Register 2009, No. 10).

4. Amendment of section heading and section filed 12-14-2016; operative 1-1-2017 pursuant to Government Code section 11343.4(b)(3) (Register 2016, No. 51).

5. Repealer and new subsection (d) filed 4-14-2017; operative 4-14-2017 pursuant to Government Code section 11343.4(b)(3) (Register 2017, No. 15).

6. Repealer of subsection (b) and subsection relettering filed 5-14-2020; operative 7-1-2020 (Register 2020, No. 20).

Ref.: Hanna §§ 1.19, 2.11; Herlick Handbook § 3.20.

§15203.3. Resolution To Authorize Self-Insurance for an Individual Private Employer.

(a) The Corporate Resolution to authorize self-insurance of workers' compensation (Form A-5 (1-2016)) required pursuant to Section 15203(c) of these regulations as part of the application for a certificate to self-insure by any individual private employer shall be adopted by the private employer's Board of Directors or the general partners of an applicant partnership or joint venture, or owner of an applicant sole proprietorship. The resolution to authorize self-insurance shall include the following:

(1) A statement identifying the applicant by corporate or other legal name, the state of registration, and the date that the resolution was adopted;

(2) Identification by title of appointed officers or other company employees authorized to sign the application, execute any and all documents required for the application, and do subsequent acts required to maintain self-insurance approval.

(b) If an individual private self-insurer reincorporates, merges, or changes its identity, a new resolution shall be submitted to the Chief within 30 days of the change. The resolution shall confirm and authorize the maintenance of the self-insurer's responsibility under the successor's identity. The Chief may extend the period of time to submit the resolution for good cause.

(c) The Chief shall provide a model Corporate Resolution (Form A-5 (1-2016)) as part of the application form and will provide a model resolution for a non-corporate entity upon request.

Note: Authority cited: Sections 54, 55 and 3702.10, Labor Code. Reference: Sections 59, 3700, 3701, 3702 and 3702.10, Labor Code.

History: 1. New section filed 11-21-78; effective thirtieth day thereafter (Register 78, No. 47).

2. Amendment filed 1-19-79; effective thirtieth day thereafter (Register 79, No. 3).

3. Amendment of section heading and text filed 12-22-92; operative 1-21-93 (Register 93, No. 2).

4. Amendment of section heading and text filed 6-30-94; operative 6-30-94 (Register 94, No. 26).

5. Amendment of section heading and section filed 3-2-2009; operative 3-2-2009 pursuant to Government Code section 11343.4 (Register 2009, No. 10).

6. Amendment of section heading and section filed 12-14-2016; operative 1-1-2017 pursuant to Government Code section 11343.4(b)(3) (Register 2016, No. 51).

Ref.: Hanna §§ 1.19, 2.11; Herlick Handbook § 3.20.

§15203.4. Resolution to Self Insure for Public Entities.

(a) The resolution of the governing body of a public entity or joint powers authority seeking approval for a Certificate of Consent to Self Insure shall be executed by the governing board and attached to the application form. The resolution shall be sealed with the seal of the adopting agency or the resolution's signatures shall be notarized.

(b) The officers of the joint powers authority which is the holder of the master Certificate to Self Insure may sign documents, including the Self Insurer's Annual Report, on behalf of the affiliated members of the JPA for self insurance purposes.

Note: Authority cited: Sections 54, 55 and 3702.10, Labor Code. Reference: Sections 59, 3700, 3702 and 3702.10, Labor Code.

History: 1. New section filed 12-22-92; operative 1-21-93 (Register 93, No. 2).

2. Amendment filed 3-2-2009; operative 3-2-2009 pursuant to Government Code section 11343.4 (Register 2009, No. 10).

Ref.: Hanna §§ 1.19, 2.11; Herlick Handbook § 3.20.

§15203.5. Agreement and Undertaking for Security Deposit.

(a) Each private individual employer applicant for self-insurance shall execute an Agreement and Undertaking For Security Deposit (Form A-6 (1-2016) as part of the application process.

(b) Each security deposit shall be posted in accordance with the provisions of the Agreement and Undertaking For Security Deposit (Form A-6 (1-2016).

(c) The form of such Agreement and Undertaking For Security Deposit (Form A-6 (1-2016) shall be supplied by the Chief as part of the application (Form A-1 (1-2016)) for an individual private employer).

(d) The Agreement and Undertaking for Security Deposit Form A-6 (1-2016), included as part of the application shall confirm the applicant employer's agreement to secure incurred liability for the payment of compensation as a condition to issuance of a Certificate of Consent to Self-Insure by posting a security deposit with the State of California to be held by the Department of Industrial Relations in trust for the applicant employer, with power to the Director of Industrial Relations to order the sale or use of said security deposit to pay any compensation that may become due and of which said employer may be in default.

Note: Authority cited: Sections 54, 55 and 3702.10, Labor Code. Reference: Sections 59, 3701, 3701.5 and 3702.10, Labor Code.

History: 1. New section filed 11-21-78; effective thirtieth day thereafter (Register 78, No. 47).

2. Renumbering and amendment of former section 15203.5 to section 15203.6 and renumbering and amendment of former section 15213 to section 15203.5 filed 12-22-92; operative 1-21-93 (Register 93, No. 2).

3. Amendment of subsection (c) and following Note filed 6-30-94; operative 6-30-94 (Register 94, No. 26).

4. Amendment filed 3-2-2009; operative 3-2-2009 pursuant to Government Code section 11343.4 (Register 2009, No. 10).

5. Amendment filed 12-14-2016; operative 1-1-2017 pursuant to Government Code section 11343.4(b)(3) (Register 2016, No. 51).

Ref.: Hanna §§ 1.19, 2.11; Herlick Handbook § 3.20.

§15203.6. Delayed Start-up of a Self-Insurance Program.

(a) The Certificate of Consent to Self-Insure for a public or individual private employer shall be initially valid for six months after the date of approval by the Director. If the self-insurer has not initiated its self-insurance program within the initial six month period, the approval of the certificate to self-insure shall be void and a new application shall be filed for approval.

(b) An individual private employer applicant that fails to initiate a self-insurance program within six months of notification of approval by the Director may be required to establish current good standing with the Secretary of State and to provide current financial information before issuance of a Certificate of Consent to Self-Insure.

Note: Authority cited: Sections 54, 55 and 3702.10, Labor Code. Reference: Sections 59, 3700 and 3702.10, Labor Code.

History: 1. Renumbering and amendment of former section 15203.5 to section 15203.6 filed 12-22-92; operative 1-21-93 (Register 93, No. 2).

2. Amendment filed 3-2-2009; operative 3-2-2009 pursuant to Government Code section 11343.4 (Register 2009, No. 10).

3. Amendment of section heading and subsection (b) filed 12-14-2016; operative 1-1-2017 pursuant to Government Code section 11343.4(b)(3) (Register 2016, No. 51).

Ref.: Hanna §§ 1.19, 2.11; Herlick Handbook § 3.20.

§15203.7. Documentation of Consent to Self-Insure and Notice to Employees of Self-Insured Status.

(a) The original Certificate of Consent to Self-Insure or a copy of the original Certificate of Consent to Self-Insure issued to each private individual self-insured employer or public self-insured employer shall be prominently displayed at the self-insurer's principal place of business in California.

(b) Notice to employees of workers' compensation coverage as required by Labor Code Section 3550 shall be accomplished by display of a copy of the self-insurer's Certificate of Consent to Self-Insure accompanied by a notice stating the name of the person(s) or administrative agency responsible for claims adjustment.

(c) If a self-insurer is required to provide evidence of its approved self-insured status to prove compliance with Labor Code Section 3700, the Chief shall provide a Certification of Self-Insurance upon request from the certificate holder. Whether or not an employer is self-insured can be determined electronically at the website of the Office of Self-Insurance Plans at http://dir.ca.gov/osip/. Beginning April 1, 2009, there is a ten dollar ($10) fee for signed certification of self-insured status requested by third parties.

Note: Authority cited: Sections 54, 55 and 3702.10, Labor Code. Reference: Sections 59, 3550, 3602, 3700, 3701, 3702 and 3702.10, Labor Code.

History: 1. Renumbering and amendment of former section 15203.7 to section 15203.8 and new section filed 12-22-92; operative 1-21-93 (Register 93, No. 2).

2. Amendment of section heading, section and Note filed 3-2-2009; operative 3-2-2009 pursuant to Government Code section 11343.4 (Register 2009, No. 10).

3. Amendment of section heading and subsection (c) filed 12-14-2016; operative 1-1-2017 pursuant to Government Code section 11343.4(b)(3) (Register 2016, No. 51).

Ref.: Hanna §§ 1.19, 2.11; Herlick Handbook § 3.20.

§15203.8. Change in Status.

(a) A public or individual private self insured employer shall notify the Manager in writing within 30 days of any of the following actions:

(1) Any amendment to the self insurer's articles, charter, or agreement of incorporation, association, or copartnership which changes its identity or business structure or ownership in a material manner from the status as it existed at the time of issuance of its Certificate of Consent to Self Insure; or

(2) If the self insurer proposes to cease doing business entirely, proposes to cease doing business in California, or proposes to dispose of, by sale or otherwise, the controlling interest of the business for which the Certificate of Consent to Self Insure was issued.

(b) If any self insurer desires to retain its self insured status following any amendment to the articles, charter, or agreement of incorporation, association, or copartnership which changes its identity or business structure or ownership, the self insurer shall provide to the Manager the following information:

(1) A written description of the change and of the date the event(s) occurred;

(2) Copies of Certificates of Status or other appropriate registration documents filed with the Secretary of State in which the self insurer is incorporated concerning the change of the self insurer's status; and

(3) Written notice indicating that the certificate holder will continue to provide an annual financial statement or that a financial statement will be issued by a parent corporation.

(c) If a self insured corporation reincorporates, merges, or changes its identity, a new resolution shall be submitted to the Manager in accordance with Section 15203.3 of these regulations.

Note: Authority cited: Sections 54, 55 and 3702.10, Labor Code. Reference: Sections 59, 3700, 3701, 3701.5, 3702, 3702.3, 3702.10 and 3703, Labor Code.

History: 1. New section filed 11-21-78; effective thirtieth day thereafter (Register 78, No. 47).

2. Renumbering and amendment of former section 15203.7 to section 15203.8 filed 12-22-92; operative 1-21-93 (Register 93, No. 2).

3. Amendment of subsection (a) filed 6-30-94; operative 6-30-94 (Register 94, No. 26).

4. Amendment filed 3-2-2009; operative 3-2-2009 pursuant to Government Code section 11343.4 (Register 2009, No. 10).

Ref.: Hanna §§ 1.19, 2.11; Herlick Handbook § 3.20.

§15203.9. Validity of Certificate of Consent to Self Insure.

(a) A Certificate of Consent to Self Insure shall be valid only to the individual private corporation, partnership, limited liability corporation, limited liability partnership, company, subsidiary, sole proprietorship, individual or affiliate public entity, or joint powers authority, to which the Certificate of Consent to Self Insure, Affiliate Certificate, Interim Certificate, or Subsidiary Certificate was issued. Each subsidiary or affiliate shall be issued its own Certificate of Consent to Self Insure.

(b) Except as provided in Labor Code Section 3701.7, the Manager may not issue a Certificate of Consent to Self Insure with an effective date earlier than the date the application and all other documents or information required by these regulations were submitted and deemed a complete application.

(c) Other than for an employer issued an Interim Certificate pursuant to Section 15205, once the self insurance program has been initiated by the employer, the Certificate of Consent to Self Insure shall be valid until revoked by order of the Director.

Note: Authority cited: Sections 54, 55 and 3702.10, Labor Code. Reference: Sections 59, 3700, 3701, 3701.5 and 3702.10, Labor Code.

History: 1. New section filed 12-22-92; operative 1-21-93 (Register 93, No. 2).

2. Amendment of subsection (a) filed 6-30-94; operative 6-30-94 (Register 94, No. 26).

3. Amendment of section heading, section and Note filed 3-2-2009; operative 3-2-2009 pursuant to Government Code section 11343.4 (Register 2009, No. 10).

Ref.: Hanna §§ 1.19, 2.11; Herlick Handbook § 3.20.

§15203.10. Reinstatement of a Certificate of Consent to Self-Insure.

(a) The Certificate of Consent to Self-Insure of an individual private or public self-insurer, that has had its self-insurance privilege terminated because of a legal change in business or corporate structure may be reinstated without lapse, providing the employer can re-qualify for self-insurance.

(b) To request reinstatement of a Certificate of Consent to Self-Insure without a lapse in self-insurance coverage, the applicant shall submit to the Chief a statement that the applicant assumes and guarantees all workers' compensation liabilities incurred during its prior period of self-insurance and will be responsible for any additional self-insured liabilities incurred after termination of its Certificate of Consent to Self-Insure. The Chief shall accept the statement of the employer's assumption of all past liabilities if signed by a corporate officer, attested to by the corporate secretary, and sealed with the corporate seal. If the statement is approved by the Chief, the applicant must submit within 90 days of the approval as part of the application a Guaranty of Workers' Compensation Liabilities fully executed pursuant to Section 15211.2 of these regulations. The Guaranty of Workers' Compensation Liabilities must be submitted before the Certificate to Self-Insure may be reinstated.

(c) A self-insured entity that has had its Certificate of Consent to Self-Insure voluntarily revoked, may request to become an active self-insurer again by making their request for re-activation of their Certificate of Consent to Self-Insure in writing to the Chief. The Chief may re-activate the Certificate of Consent to Self-Insure provided the former self-insurer is current in filing all required reports, and is otherwise in full compliance with their responsibilities related to self-insurance, or upon the entity becoming current in all filing and compliance responsibilities. No further application or documents shall be required provided all previously filed documents are currently accurate at the time of the request to reactivate their status as actively self-insuring their workers' compensation liabilities. A certificate that has been reactivated shall not cover any workers' compensation claims or liabilities that arise during the period between the date of prior revocation and the date the certificate is reactivated. All claims during the period between the two periods of self-insurance must have been covered by an insurance policy.

Note: Authority cited: Sections 54, 55 and 3702.10, Labor Code. Reference: Sections 59, 3700, 3701, 3702 and 3702.10, Labor Code.

History: 1. New section filed 12-22-92; operative 1-21-93 (Register 93, No. 2).

2. Amendment of section heading and section filed 3-2-2009; operative 3-2-2009 pursuant to Government Code section 11343.4 (Register 2009, No. 10).

3. Amendment of section heading and section filed 12-14-2016; operative 1-1-2017 pursuant to Government Code section 11343.4(b)(3) (Register 2016, No. 51).

Ref.: Hanna §§ 1.19, 2.11; Herlick Handbook § 3.20.

§15203.11. Continuing Financial Capacity for Public Self-Insurers.

(a) Each individual public self-insurer holding an active or revoked Certificate of Consent to Self-Insure shall submit annually a report on demographic data and a summary of the financial condition of its workers' compensation program on Form P-1 (1-2020) or in a similar format that includes the same data elements as Form P-1.

(1) This requirement applies only to individual public self-insurers that operate all or part of their program on a standalone basis pursuant to an active or revoked master Certificate of Consent to Self-Insure.

(2) A public self-insurer that operates part of its program on a standalone basis and provides coverage for other claims through membership in a joint powers authority, as described in subsection (b), shall limit the information specified in Part C, section 2, and Part D of Form P-1 to the part of its program operated on a standalone basis.

(b) Any joint powers authority that is solely responsible for the self-insurance claims of its public members and holds an active or revoked Certificate of Consent to Self-Insure shall submit annually a consolidated report on demographic data, types of coverage provided to its members, and a summary of the financial condition of its workers' compensation program on Form J-1 (1-2020) or in a similar format that includes the same data elements as Form J-1. The joint powers authority shall file with its Form J-1 report a current, certified, independently audited financial statement complete with all notes and schedules, if available.

(1) The demographic information specified in Part B of Form J-1 shall be limited to the active affiliate members of the joint powers authority.

(2) Each active affiliate member shall cooperate with the joint powers authority by ascertaining the Part B demographic information for its own agency and providing that information to the authority. Except as specified in

subsection (a), an affiliate member shall not be required to prepare or submit a separate Form P-1 report.

(c) The reports required by this section shall be submitted via an online platform at http://www.dir.ca.gov/osip on or before October 1 of each year and shall cover liabilities for the preceding July 1 - June 30 fiscal year.

(d) The financial information reported pursuant to this section shall be based on the *master* certificate holder's most recent certified, independently audited financial statement, if available. If no such statement is available or the most recent statement is over three years old, reported information shall be based on the *master* certificate holder's most recent financial statement by an independent Certified Public Accountant (CPA). If neither is available, the *master* certificate holder shall identify the source of information for its report, including the name of the document, source, date, and the name and contact information for the preparer or custodian.

(e) An Appendix of terms used in Public Self-Insurer Report Forms P-1, J-1, and AR-2 follows this section.

Note: Authority cited: Sections 54, 55 and 3702.10, Labor Code. Reference: Section 3702.2, Labor Code.

History: 1. New section and Appendix filed 5-14-2020; operative 7-1-2020 (Register 2020, No. 20).

APPENDIX

Terms used in Public Self-Insurer Report Forms P-1 and J-1 (§15203.11) and AR-2 (§15251(c))

The definitions in section 15201 of the Self-Insurance Plan regulations (Title 8, California Code of Regulations § 15201) apply to the terms used in these reporting forms. All terms shall be construed in a manner that is consistent with their usage in Division 4 (commencing with Section 3700) of the Labor Code and Chapters 1 (commencing with section 1), 4.5 (commencing with section 9700), and Subchapter 2 of Chapter 8 (commencing with section 15201) of Division 1 of Title 8 of the California Code of Regulations, including any definitive construction of a term by the Workers' Compensation Appeals Board or a court. However, if there is a conflict between a definition in section 15201 and a definition of the same terms found in another Title 8 regulation, the definition in section 15201 shall apply.

Terms that are not defined by statute or regulation should be understood as having the same meaning commonly understood and used by workers' compensation program administrators in the state of California. A good faith error or discrepancy in how reportable information is characterized for purposes of one of these reports shall not be treated as a reporting violation under Labor Code Sections 3702.3 or 3702.9.

The following additional guidance is provided for specific report terms.

Allocated Loss Adjustment Expense or **ALAE** means claim administration costs and expenses that are allocated to individual workers' compensation claims, including but not limited to medical cost containment expenses.

Catastrophic claim means a claim for workers' compensation based on a severe injury to the brain or spinal cord, loss of a limb, paralysis, severe burn or severe head injury, and includes any injury that would result in a conclusive presumption of total disability under Labor Code Section 4662(a).

Certificated employee has the same meaning used in the Education Code and refers to an employee in an academic, supervisory, or administrative position with a school or school district, community college or community college district, or state university who is required to hold a credential or similar certificate as a condition of employment.

Classified employee has the same meaning used in the Education Code and refers to an employee of a school or school district, community college or community college district, or state university who is not a certificated employee.

Diagnostics refers to medically-prescribed tests used to determine a diagnosis, the cause of symptoms, the nature or severity, or course of treatment for an illness or injury. It includes but is not limited to imaging and laboratory tests.

Full-Time Equivalent or **FTE** refers to the ratio of the total number of paid hours for all employees, whether full or part-time, divided by the number of hours in the employer's regular full-time work week. If the employer has a regular work week of 40 hours and 10 employees working a total of 200 hours during a regular work week, the full-time equivalent or FTE would be 5. (200 ÷ 40 = 5).

Industrial Disability Leave claims and benefits refers to salary-based payments made to public employees in lieu of workers' compensation temporary indemnity benefits pursuant to Education Code Section 45192, Education Code Section 89529.03, Government Code Section 19871, or equivalent statutes or employer policies governing compensated absences for job-related illnesses or injuries, insofar as those payments are categorized separately from other types of indemnity payments. For reporting purposes, Industrial Disability Leave claims and benefits *do not include* salary continuation benefits provided to Public Safety Employees pursuant to Articles 6 and 7 (commencing with Sections 4800 and 4850 respectively) of Chapter 2 of Part 2 of Division 4 of the Labor Code, even if designated Industrial Disability Leave by the employer. Those payments instead should be reported as Public Safety Employee claims and benefits.

Public Safety Employee means an employee of a fire department, police or sheriff's department, or other public protection or public safety agency who is entitled to receive salary continuation benefits in lieu of workers' compensation benefits pursuant to one or more statute within Articles 6 and 7 (commencing with Sections 4800 and 4850 respectively) of Chapter 2 of Part 2 of Division 4 of the Labor Code. For reporting purposes, employees of the California State University Police Department who are entitled to enhanced Industrial Disability Leave benefits pursuant to Labor Code Section 4816, shall be counted as "public safety employees," including for public safety employee payroll purposes, and their claims and benefits payments should be reported as public safety employee claims and benefits payments, even if designated by the employer as Industrial Disability Leave claims and benefits payments.

Surgery refers to payments made to surgeons, assistant surgeons, anesthesiologists, and other medical personnel for surgical services that are billed and paid for separately from facility costs. It does **not** include hospital and facility expenses.

Unallocated Loss Adjustment Expense or **ULAE** means claim administration costs and expenses that are not allocated to individual workers' compensation claims.

Volunteer means a person who provides volunteer services for the employer and includes persons for whom the employer has elected to provide workers' compensation coverage pursuant to Labor Code Section 3361.5, 3363.5, 3364, 3364.5, 3364.55, 3364.6, 3364.7, or equivalent statutes. The number of persons, if any, who are *neither* employees or volunteers, but for whom the employer is required to provide workers' compensation when participating in court-ordered community service, work for relief, or similar reasons should be estimated separately and entered on the line provided for that purpose in the Profile section (Part B) of the P-1 and J-1 forms.

Form AR-2 Addendum—Aggregate Claims Information
[Proposed Data Fields for Online Submission]

INJURY DATES

FY 19-20 FY 18-19 FY 17-18 FY 16-17 FY 15-16 Years prior to FY 15-16

Number of New Notices of Representation Received in FY

Total number of open claims in each category as of the end of the reporting period. (Individual claims that fit into more than one category should be included in the count for each category that applies.)

Indemnity Claims
Medical-Only Claims
Future Medical Claims
Public Safety Employee Benefit Claims
Industrial Disability Leave Claims
Industrial Disability Leave Claims
Fatality Claims

Aggregate amount of benefits paid for each disability category

Temporary Disability Benefits Paid ($ amount)

Number of Claims where TD benefits were provided

Public Safety Employee Benefits Paid ($ amount)

Number of Claims where Public Safety Employees received salary continuation benefits

Industrial Disability Leave Benefits Paid ($ amount)

Number of claims where Industrial Disability Leave benefits were provided

Permanent Disability Benefits Paid ($ paid in permanent total and permanent partial disability)

Number of Claims where PD benefits were paid

Supplemental Job Displacement Benefits Voucher paid ($ amount)

Number of Claims where SJDBV was issued

Death Benefits Benefits Paid, including burial costs ($ amount)

Number of Claims were death benefits were provided

Aggregate amount of Medical Costs paid for each category

Interpreters ($ amount)
Physician Visits ($ amount)
In-Patient Hospital ($ amount)
Out-Patient Hospital and Ambulatory Surgery Center ($ amount)
Diagnostics ($ amount)
DME supplies ($ amount)
Physical Therapy ($ amount)
Pharmaceutical ($ amount)
Surgery ($ amount)
In Home Support ($ amount)
Medical-Legal ($ amount)
All other Medical Costs not included above ($ amount)

Aggregate amount of Legal and Loss Adjustment Expenses for each category

Attorney Fees and Legal Costs ($ amount)
Photocopy Fees ($ amount)
Interpreter's Fees ($ amount)
Medical Cost Containment Fees—total ($ amount)
Bill Review, including IBR—total ($ amount)
Utilization Review ($ amount)
Independent Medical Review ($ amount)
Uncategorized Legal and Loss expenses or any other Legal and Loss Expenses not included above ($ amount)

Estimated Future Liabilities: (*Estimate of total incurred costs, less paid*) - OPEN CLAIMS ONLY

Temporary Disability ($ amount)
Permanent Disability ($ amount)
Public Safety Employee Benefits ($ amount)
Industrial Disability Leave Benefits ($ amount)
Supplemental Job Displacement Benefits Voucher ($ amount)
Death Benefits ($ amount)
Medical Costs ($ amount)

§15204. Application Filing Fee.

(a) Each private employer making application for an individual Certificate of Consent to Self-Insure shall, at the time of filing the application, pay a non-refundable filing fee of $500.

(b) Any subsequent filing of an application by an existing private individual self-insurer to add a new subsidiary or affiliate, or required due to merger, acquisition, or reincorporation shall be considered a new application and shall be subject to the payment of the fees set forth in subsection (a).

(c) No application filing fee shall be required from a public entity making application for a Certificate to Self-Insure.

Note: Authority cited: Sections 54, 55 and 3702.10, Labor Code. Reference: Sections 59, 3700, 3702.5 and 3702.10, Labor Code.

History: 1. New section filed 11-19-75; effective thirtieth day thereafter (Register 75, No. 47).

2. Amendment of section heading and text and adoption of Plates A-1 through C and Plate H filed 12-22-92; operative 1-21-93 (Register 93, No. 2).

3. Change without regulatory effect relocating Appendix Plates to section 15463 filed 9-14-93 pursuant to title 1, section 100, California Code of Regulations (Register 93, No. 38).

4. Designation of subsection (a) and new subsections (d)-(d)(4) filed 6-30-94; operative 6-30-94 (Register 94, No. 26).

5. Amendment of section heading and section filed 3-2-2009; operative 3-2-2009 pursuant to Government Code section 11343.4 (Register 2009, No. 10).

6. Amendment of subsection (a) and repealer of subsections (a)(1)-(3) filed 12-14-2016; operative 1-1-2017 pursuant to Government Code section 11343.4(b)(3) (Register 2016, No. 51).

Ref.: Hanna §§ 1.19, 2.11; Herlick Handbook § 3.20.

§15205. Interim Certificates.

(a) The Chief may issue an Interim Certificate of Consent to Self-Insure to a subsidiary or affiliate of an existing private individual self-insurer or an existing public agency self-insurer. The Interim Certificate of Consent to Self-Insure will be issued for a period not to exceed 180 days. A Certificate of Consent to Self-Insure to replace the Interim Certificate shall not be issued unless a completed application and accompanying documents required by Section 15203 and the application fee required by Section 15204 are submitted to the Chief within 180 days of the effective date of the Interim Certificate.

(b) To qualify for an Interim Certificate, the existing private individual self-insurer must demonstrate the following:

(1) Compliance with the requirements of Section 15203.2;

(2) The private self-insurer holding the Master Certificate of Consent to Self-Insure has furnished proof satisfactory to the Chief of financial responsibility and ability to guarantee the payment of any compensation due; and

(3) The subsidiary or affiliate being added to the self-insurance program does not represent more than 50% of the annual payroll of the existing self-insured as reported on the most recent Self-Insurers' Annual Report.

(c) A request for an Interim Certificate shall be made by the existing public agency or individual private self-insurer in writing to the Chief and provide the following information on each subsidiary or affiliate new to the self-insurance program:

(1) The full legal name, state of incorporation, and Federal Tax Identification Number;

(2) The requested effective date of the Interim Certificate;

(3) Documentation of the total annual payroll of the subsidiary or affiliate during the last 12 months and of the dates for which the payroll information represents or for the latest 12-month period for which payroll figures are available.

(4) A statement that the Master Certificate holder shall be financially responsible for payment of all workers' compensation claims arising out of the period of time its subsidiary or affiliate is granted an Interim Certificate.

Note: Authority cited: Sections 54, 55 and 3702.10, Labor Code. Reference: Sections 59, 3700, 3702.5 and 3702.10, Labor Code.

History: 1. New section filed 2-26-97; operative 3-28-97 (Register 97, No. 9).

2. Amendment of subsection (e) filed 6-4-98; operative 7-4-98 (Register 98, No. 23).

3. Amendment filed 3-2-2009; operative 3-2-2009 pursuant to Government Code section 11343.4 (Register 2009, No. 10).

4. Amendment of subsections (a), (b)(1)-(2) and (c) filed 12-14-2016; operative 1-1-2017 pursuant to Government Code section 11343.4(b)(3) (Register 2016, No. 51).

Ref.: Hanna §§ 1.19, 2.11[1], [2], [3]; Herlick Handbook § 3.20.

ARTICLE 3
Security Deposit Requirements

§15209. Actuarial Studies and Summaries.

(a) Current and former self-insurers, other than public self-insured employers, that are required to file a Self-Insurer's Annual Report, shall cause a qualified actuary to submit on their behalf to the Office of Self-Insurance Plans (OSIP) an actuarial study and summary not later than May 1 of each calendar year with a valuation date of December 31 of the immediately prior calendar year. The summary shall be prepared and submitted via an online platform provided by OSIP with a copy of the complete actuarial study attached.

(1) In the absence of an actuarial study or summary for any private self-insurer that fully satisfies the criteria of this section received by the deadline set forth above, the Chief shall establish a security deposit amount on behalf of the self-insurer as the Chief determines appropriate based on consideration of all financial and loss information available to the Chief at the time.

(2) The actuarial study and summary shall be prepared and submitted by an actuary meeting each of the following qualifications:

(A) The actuary must be independent with no common ownership or financial interest in the entity that is the subject of the actuarial study and summary, and

(B) Within the past ten (10) calendar years the actuary must have a minimum of five (5) years of experience making California workers' compensation actuarial projections, and

(C) The actuary must have a designation of Fellow of the Casualty Actuarial Society (FCAS), or be a member of the American Academy of Actuaries (MAAA), or be a member of the Society of Actuaries who is qualified to sign a statement of actuarial opinion on loss reserves.

(3) The qualified actuary or his/her employing actuarial firm shall maintain a minimum of $1,000,000 of professional liability and errors and omissions insurance coverage. Evidence of this coverage and limits must be submitted as a part of the actuarial study.

(4) Private self-insurers shall not be required to file an actuarial study or actuarial summary in years when their current year filed Self-Insurer's Annual Report reports either: (A) 10 or fewer open claims, or (B) less than $1,000,000 of total estimated future liabilities.

(b) The actuarial study shall identify the self-insurer's losses at the undiscounted 'expected level', also commonly referred to as the undiscounted 'actuarial central estimate,' including each of the following components: incurred but not reported (IBNR) liabilities, Allocated loss adjustment expense (ALAE), Unallocated loss adjusted expense (ULAE) and case reserves. The actuarial central estimate shall be reported at both the gross and net amounts of excess insurance values.

(c) The actuarial study shall identify the estimated future liabilities reported in the Private Self-Insurer Annual Report filed by the self-insurer's Third Party Administrator(s).

(d) The actuarial study and summary shall clearly identify any excess coverage by carrier, policy year and self-insured retentions, by year.

(e) The actuary shall declare in the study and the summary that the study and report may be used by the State of California and the Self-Insurers' Security Fund to set appropriate collateral and deposit amounts, and for any other regulatory purpose under these regulations.

(f) The actuarial study and summary shall specify that it is prepared for use by the Department of Industrial Relations, Office of Self-Insurance Plans and the Self-Insurers' Security Fund. The Office of Self-Insurance Plans and the Self-Insurers' Security Fund may share the study and report with consultants retained by the Department of Industrial Relations or the Self-Insurers' Security Fund for official purposes in accomplishing the purposes of these regulations.

(g) The actuarial study must include all of and only the self-insured employer's California self-insured liabilities for the master certificate holder and all affiliate or subsidiary certificate holders related to the master certificate.

(h) Failure by a self-insurer to submit a timely actuarial study and summary shall constitute good cause grounds for revocation of the self-insurer's self-insurance Certificate.

(i) The Chief may accept or reject any actuarial study or summary that does not fully satisfy the criteria of this section and require a second study and summary by another qualified actuary that does fully satisfy the criteria of this section be completed and submitted to OSIP at the self-insurer's expense.

Note: Authority cited: Sections 54, 55, 3701, 3701.8 and 3702.10, Labor Code. Reference: Sections 54, 55, 59, 3700, 3701, 3701.5, 3701.8, 3702, 3702.2, 3702.8, 3702.9 and 3702.10, Labor Code.

History: 1. New section filed 12-31-2012 as an emergency; operative 1-1-2013 pursuant to Government Code section 11346.1(d) (Register 2013, No. 1). A Certificate of Compliance must be transmitted to OAL by 7-1-2013 or emergency language will be repealed by operation of law on the following day.

2. Certificate of Compliance as to 1-1-2013 order, including nonsubstantive amendments, transmitted to OAL 7-1-2013 and filed 8-13-2013 (Register 2013, No. 33).

3. Amendment of subsections (b) and (i) filed 12-14-2016; operative 1-1-2017 pursuant to Government Code section 11343.4(b)(3) (Register 2016, No. 51).

§15210. Security Deposit.

(a) Public self-insurers are not required to post or maintain a security deposit with the Director for workers' compensation liabilities.

(b) Individual Private self-insurers shall post and maintain a security deposit, in accordance with the provisions of Labor Code Section 3701 and the requirements of Article 3 of this subchapter 2 and/or in accordance with Labor Code Section 3701.8 and Article 3.1 of this subchapter 2.

(c) The minimum required security deposit pursuant to Labor Code Section 3701 for existing, private self-insurers shall be equal to the self-insurer's losses at the undiscounted 'expected level' also commonly referred to as the undiscounted 'actuarial central estimate', including each of the following components: incurred but not reported (IBNR) liabilities, Allocated loss adjustment expense (ALAE), and Unallocated loss adjusted expense (ULAE), net of specific excess insurance coverage.

The required deposit may be increased at the Director's discretion as set forth in Article 3 of these regulations.

(d) New individual private self-insurers shall initially post a security deposit pursuant to Labor Code Section 3701 in an amount equal to the greater of the following:

(1) Sixty percent (60%) of the one (1) year average incurred liability calculated by averaging the prior three (3) years' incurred liability; or

(2) The statutory minimum required by Labor Code Section 3701(c); or

(3) A higher amount approved by the Director.

(e) Security deposit shall be posted in the form of:

(1) A surety bond executed on State issued bond and rider forms pursuant to Section 15212 of these regulations;

(2) An irrevocable letter of credit issued by a bank or savings institution or other financial institution pursuant to Section 15215 of these regulations;

(3) Approved securities in the form of government issued or corporate issued securities, meeting the requirements of Section 15213 of these regulations;

(4) Cash in trust deposited pursuant to requirements of Section 15214 of these regulations; or

(5) Any combination of one or more of the above four types of security deposit.

(f) Failure of an individual private self-insured employer to maintain the required amount of deposit or to post an acceptable form of deposit as set forth in this Article shall be good cause for assessment of civil penalties pursuant to Labor Code Section 3702.9(a) by the Chief and/or, in the Director's discretion, revocation of the Certificate to Self-Insure.

(g) Failure of an individual private self-insured employer to post and maintain the required amount of security deposit for a period of 60 days shall be good cause for the Chief to summarily revoke a Certificate of Consent to Self-Insure. The summary revocation of the Self-Insurer's Certificate of Consent will provide for a 15-day notice of termination, without a hearing.

(1) Notwithstanding subsection (g) above, the individual private self-insured employer may still request a hearing on the Chief's Revocation Order before the Director as provided in Article 11 of this subchapter 2.

(2) An individual private self-insurer requesting a hearing pursuant to subsection (g)(1) shall be required to provide proof of workers' compensation coverage under a policy from an admitted carrier for the period of time without security deposit or proof of compliance with the Chief's request to post security.

Note: Authority cited: Sections 54, 55, 3701.8 and 3702.10, Labor Code. Reference: Sections 59, 3700, 3701, 3701.5, 3701.8, 3702, 3702.3, 3702.6, 3702.10 and 3740-3745, Labor Code.

History: 1. Amendment of article heading, section heading and text and adoption of Note filed 12-22-92; operative 1-21-93 (Register 93, No. 2).

2. Change without regulatory effect amending subsection (f)(3) filed 8-27-98 pursuant to section 100, title 1, California Code of Regulations (Register 98, No. 35).

3. Change without regulatory effect amending subsections (c)(1) and (c)(3) filed 4-9-2003 pursuant to section 100, title 1, California Code of Regulations (Register 2003, No. 15).

4. Amendment of section and Note filed 5-30-2003 as an emergency; operative 5-30-2003 (Register 2003, No. 22). A Certificate of Compliance must be transmitted to OAL by 9-29-2003 or emergency language will be repealed by operation of law on the following day.

5. Certificate of Compliance as to 5-30-2003 order, including amendment of subsection (h)(1), transmitted to OAL 9-29-2003 and filed 11-12-2003 (Register 2003, No. 46).

6. Amendment filed 3-2-2009; operative 3-2-2009 pursuant to Government Code section 11343.4 (Register 2009, No. 10).

7. Amendment of subsection (c), repealer of subsections (c)(1)-(3) and amendment of subsections (g)-(h)(2) filed 12-31-2012 as an emergency; operative 1-1-2013 pursuant to Government Code section 11346.1(d) (Register 2013, No. 1). A Certificate of Compliance must be transmitted to OAL by 7-1-2013 or emergency language will be repealed by operation of law on the following day.

8. Certificate of Compliance as to 1-1-2013 order transmitted to OAL 7-1-2013 and filed 8-13-2013 (Register 2013, No. 33).

9. Amendment of subsection (d)(1), repealer of subsections (e)-(e)(2), subsection relettering and amendment of newly designated subsections (g)(1)-(2) filed 12-14-2016; operative 1-1-2017 pursuant to Government Code section 11343.4(b)(3) (Register 2016, No. 51).

Ref.: Hanna §§ 1.19, 2.11; Herlick Handbook § 3.20.

§15210.1. Adjustments in the Amount of Security Deposit.

(a) Pursuant to Labor Code Section 3701, the security deposit requirement of each individual private self-insured employer shall be reviewed by the Chief at least annually following receipt of the private Self-Insurer's Annual Report and Actuarial Study and Summary.

(b) The individual private self-insurer shall post any annual increase or decrease in security deposit required pursuant to Labor Code Section 3701 indicated in the annual actuarial study and summary as specified by these regulations or as determined by the Chief due to an audit, change in the self-insured employer's program or based on a change in required deposit made by the Chief under these regulations. This deposit posting is due no later than 30 days from the date the written notice of security deposit demand is made.

(c) No reduction or decrease in security deposit shall be made without prior written authorization of the Chief. The Chief shall review each individual private certificate holder's annual report and the certificate holder's file no less frequently than annually to determine the extent to which a decrease in deposit, if any, may be authorized.

(d) For good cause, the Chief may require the individual private self-insurer to post and maintain additional security deposit or adjust the required security deposit for a specific private self-insurer above the actuarially determined expected losses also commonly known as the actuarial central estimate, including incurred but not reported (IBNR) liabilities, Allocated loss adjustment expense (ALAE), and Unallocated loss adjustment expense (ULAE) as set forth in Labor Code Sections 3701, 3701.7, and 3701.8. Good cause includes, but is not limited to, understated future liability of claims on the Self-Insurer's Annual Report; the lack of, or an inadequate or unacceptable, actuarial study or summary; a pattern of understated liabilities in claim files audited in an audit; failure to report all claims; poor administration of claims or payment of benefits due injured workers found in the audit results of the Division of Workers' Compensation Audit Unit or audits by the Office of Self-Insurance Plans; lack of an effective safety and health program as indicated by final citations issued by the Division of Occupational Safety and Health showing repeat or willful violation of safety and health regulations; impairment of financial condition of the self-insurer as determined by the Chief; failure to provide and maintain current and complete parental Guaranty of Workers' Compensation Liabilities or board of director's resolutions; the result of evaluation of an application to self-insure; or to cover a period of unlawful self-insurance; or being required to post a security deposit in whole or part pursuant to Section 3701.8 of the Labor Code and Article 3.1 (commencing with Section 15220) of this subchapter 2.

(e) Whenever the Chief determines that a deposit increase is required, the Chief shall send written notice to the individual private self-insurer pursuant to Labor Code Section 3701(b) and (j). Notice of the amount of deposit due shall create a perfected security interest for the self-insurer's Security Fund.

(f) Any increase in the security deposit requirement for an individual private self-insurer following the Chief's determination that estimated future liabilities had been understated on the private employer's Self-Insurer's Annual Report, shall be reported to the Security Fund. The Security Fund shall be authorized to adjust the deposit assessment for the alternative composite deposit.

Note: Authority cited: Sections 54, 55, 3701.8 and 3702.10, Labor Code. Reference: Sections 59, 3700, 3701, 3701.5, 3701.7, 3701.8, 3702, 3702.3, 3702.6, 3702.10, 3740, 3741, 3742, 6319(f), 6401.7, Labor Code.

History: 1. New section filed 12-22-92; operative 1-21-93 (Register 93, No. 2).

2. Change without regulatory effect amending subsection (e) filed 8-27-98 pursuant to section 100, title 1, California Code of Regulations (Register 98, No. 35).

3. Amendment of section and Note filed 5-30-2003 as an emergency; operative 5-30-2003 (Register 2003, No. 22). A Certificate of Compliance must be transmitted to OAL by 9-29-2003 or emergency language will be repealed by operation of law on the following day.

4. Certificate of Compliance as to 5-30-2003 order transmitted to OAL 9-29-2003 and filed 11-12-2003 (Register 2003, No. 46).

5. Amendment filed 3-2-2009; operative 3-2-2009 pursuant to Government Code section 11343.4 (Register 2009, No. 10).

6. Amendment filed 12-31-2012 as an emergency; operative 1-1-2013 pursuant to Government Code section 11346.1(d) (Register 2013, No. 1). A Certificate of Compliance must be transmitted to OAL by 7-1-2013 or emergency language will be repealed by operation of law on the following day.

7. Certificate of Compliance as to 1-1-2013 order transmitted to OAL 7-1-2013 and filed 8-13-2013 (Register 2013, No. 33).

8. Amendment of subsections (a) and (d) filed 12-14-2016; operative 1-1-2017 pursuant to Government Code section 11343.4(b)(3) (Register 2016, No. 51).

Ref.: Hanna §§ 1.19, 2.11; Herlick Handbook § 3.20.

§15210.2. Deposit Adjustment Upon Revocation of Certificate to Self-Insure.

(a) As part of the revocation of a Certificate to Self-Insure pursuant to Sections 15422 and 15423 of these regulations, the Chief shall determine the need for a special revocation audit of the claims of any individual private self-insurer and the need for a deposit adjustment to secure future liabilities of the revoked private self-insurer pursuant to Labor Code Section 3701 and/or Section 3701.8.

(b) The amount of deposit required by the Chief on a revocation of a private self-insurer's certificate to self-insure may be at an amount above the minimum required by Labor Code Section 3701 and/or Section 3701.8. The Chief in his/her discretion shall adjust the amount of deposit down to secure the remaining workers' compensation liabilities for a revoked self-insurer as necessary over time as the liabilities of the remaining claims inventory are run off by the administrator.

Note: Authority cited: Sections 54, 55, 3701.8 and 3702.10, Labor Code. Reference: Sections 59, 129, 3700, 3701, 3701.5, 3701.8, 3702, 3702.3, 3702.6, 3702.8, 3740-3745, Labor Code.

History: 1. New section filed 12-22-92; operative 1-21-93 (Register 93, No. 2).

2. Amendment of section heading, section and Note filed 5-30-2003 as an emergency; operative 5-30-2003 (Register 2003, No. 22). A Certificate of Compliance must be transmitted to OAL by 9-29-2003 or emergency language will be repealed by operation of law on the following day.

3. Certificate of Compliance as to 5-30-2003 order transmitted to OAL 9-29-2003 and filed 11-12-2003 (Register 2003, No. 46).

4. Amendment of subsection (a) filed 3-2-2009; operative 3-2-2009 pursuant to Government Code section 11343.4 (Register 2009, No. 10).

5. Amendment of section heading and section filed 12-14-2016; operative 1-1-2017 pursuant to Government Code section 11343.4(b)(3) (Register 2016, No. 51).

Ref.: Hanna §§ 1.19, 2.11; Herlick Handbook § 3.20.

§15210.3. Insurance Coverage.

(a) Any public self insurer or individual private self insurer shall be permitted to insure any part of its liability to secure the payment of compensation pursuant to Labor Code Section 3700 with a standard workers' compensation insurance policy issued by a carrier. Full coverage of a self insurer's workers' compensation liability under a standard workers' compensation insurance policy shall be good cause for revocation of the certificate to self insure.

(b) All public self insurers and individual private self insurers shall provide the Manager with information on any standard workers' compensation insurance policies, specific excess workers' compensation insurance coverage, and any aggregate excess (stop loss) workers' compensation insurance coverage carried, as part of the Self Insurer's Annual Report or upon the request of the Manager. Evidence of any of these three types of insurance coverage shall also be provided to the Manager in the form of a Certificate of Insurance from the carrier, along with any changes, cancellations, revisions, or new policies.

(c) Upon the request of the Manager, any public self insurer or individual private self insurer shall provide a Certificate of Insurance or a copy of the workers' compensation insurance policy or policies maintained by the self insurer for any year or partial year in which claims have been reported.

(d) Specific excess workers' compensation insurance policies are not required to be purchased or maintained by any public self insurer or individual private self insurer.

(e) Any individual private self insurer who elects to purchase an aggregate workers' compensation excess policy shall not be given any credit by the Manager toward the security deposit to be posted due to aggregate excess insurance coverage.

Note: Authority cited: Sections 54, 55 and 3702.10, Labor Code. Reference: Sections 59, 129, 3700, 3701, 3701.5, 3702, 3740, 3743 and 3744, Labor Code.

History: 1. New section filed 12-22-92; operative 1-21-93 (Register 93, No. 2).

2. Amendment of subsections (c)-(e) filed 6-30-94; operative 6-30-94 (Register 94, No. 26).

3. Amendment filed 3-2-2009; operative 3-2-2009 pursuant to Government Code section 11343.4 (Register 2009, No. 10).

Ref.: Hanna §§ 1.19, 2.11; Herlick Handbook § 3.20.

§15211. Allocation of the Security Deposit for Private Individual Self-Insurers.

(a) The security deposit of each private individual self insurer shall apply to all subsidiaries and affiliates included under the Master Certificate of Consent to Self Insure issued to that self insurer during its respective period of self insurance, and no portion of the overall security deposit for that self insured plan may be limited to any specific affiliate or subsidiary under the Master Certificate. In the event that a subsidiary or affiliate certificate holder seeks to post a separate security covering its self insured liabilities only, a separate individual Certificate of Consent to Self Insure covering its period of self insurance shall be issued to that self insured employer and liabilities shall be transferred to a separate Certificate of Consent to Self Insure through an Order Amending and Transferring Liabilities.

(b) For purposes of these regulations, Section 189 of the California Corporations Code shall be used to define "subsidiary corporation" and "holding corporation."

(c) For purposes of these regulations, legal entities with common ownership are sufficient to qualify for a common security deposit and may be included as co-principals on the same surety bond, or as named entities on a letter of credit, or as co-trustors on securities or a cash deposit.

(d) The Manager may require certification or other proof of stock ownership of the self-insured subsidiary corporation or corporations before allowing a self insurer to be included in the deposit of another self insurer.

(e) If the private holding corporation loses its power to elect a majority of the directors of a subsidiary self-insured corporation or corporations, the holding corporation and subsidiary corporation or corporations shall notify the Manager within 30 days of the event.

Note: Authority cited: Sections 54, 55 and 3702.10, Labor Code. Reference: Sections 129, 3700, 3700(b), 3701, 3702, 3702.5, 3702.6, 3703, 3704, 3705 and 3740-3745, Labor Code; and Section 189, Corporations Code.

History: 1. Amendment filed 6-1-72; effective thirtieth day thereafter (Register 72, No. 23).

2. Amendment filed 11-19-75; effective thirtieth day thereafter (Register 75, No. 47).

3. Amendment filed 11-21-78; effective thirtieth day thereafter (Register 78, No. 47).

4. Editorial correction to remove duplicate history note (Register 78, No. 50).

5. Amendment filed 12-22-92; operative 1-21-93 (Register 93, No. 2).

6. Amendment of subsection (a) and new subsection (e) filed 6-30-94; operative 6-30-94 (Register 94, No. 26).

7. Editorial correction of History 6 (Register 96, No. 52).

8. Amendment of section heading and section filed 3-2-2009; operative 3-2-2009 pursuant to Government Code section 11343.4 (Register 2009, No. 10).

Ref.: Hanna §§ 1.19, 2.11; Herlick Handbook § 3.20.

§15211.1. Appeals to Increase in Security Deposit Due to Impaired Financial Condition of Self-Insurer.

(a) Where the Chief has required an increase in security deposit due to the impaired financial status of an individual private self-insurer and the self-insurer wishes to appeal the Chief's decision, upon receipt of the written appeal, the Chief shall order a detailed, third-party financial evaluation of the self-insurer in order to determine the employer's financial strength. The cost of the third party financial evaluation report shall be paid by the self-insurer.

(b) Upon receipt of the evaluation report, the appeal will be considered by the Chief, and if not resolved between the Chief and the self-insurer, addressed pursuant to Article 11 of these regulations and Labor Code Section 3701.5(g).

Note: Authority cited: Sections 54, 55 and 3702.10, Labor Code. Reference: Sections 3701 and 3701.5(g), Labor Code.

History: 1. New section filed 6-1-72; effective thirtieth day thereafter (Register 72, No. 23).

2. Repealer and new section filed 11-19-75; effective thirtieth day thereafter (Register 75, No. 47).

3. Repealer and new section filed 12-22-92; operative 1-21-93 (Register 93, No. 2).

4. Amendment of section and Note filed 3-2-2009; operative 3-2-2009 pursuant to Government Code section 11343.4 (Register 2009, No. 10).

5. Amendment of section heading and section filed 12-14-2016; operative 1-1-2017 pursuant to Government Code section 11343.4(b)(3) (Register 2016, No. 51).

Ref.: Hanna §§ 1.19, 2.11; Herlick Handbook § 3.20.

§15211.2. Guaranty of Workers' Compensation Liabilities.

(a) At the discretion of the Chief, the Workers' Compensation liabilities of a public, a private individual, subsidiary, or affiliate self-insurer may be assumed and guaranteed in whole or part by any other legal entity or person.

(b) The Guaranty of Workers' Compensation Liabilities shall be written upon a form provided by the Chief (Form A-4 (1-2016)). The form is contained in Plate D of the Appendix following Section 15463 of these regulations and is available on the website of the Office of Self-Insurance Plans at http://dir.ca.gov/osip/.

(c) Regardless of whether an individual private affiliate or subsidiary or the self-insurer's parent company's financial condition is relied upon to qualify the subsidiary or affiliate for self-insurance, the holding company, ultimate parent corporation, controlling partners, owner, or other controlling entity acceptable to the Chief shall execute a Guaranty of Workers' Compensation Liabilities on behalf of the affiliate or subsidiary. In the event that the holding company, ultimate parent corporation, controlling partners, owner, or other controlling entity declines to execute a Guaranty of Workers' Compensation Liabilities, the Chief may require an increase in the self-insurer's security deposit requirement pursuant to Section 15203.1 of these regulations.

(d) A corporate guarantor shall provide a Board of Directors resolution which authorizes the Guaranty of Workers' Compensation Liabilities of the affiliated or subsidiary company or public agency. The board resolution shall grant signature authority to the person or position title of the person signing the Guaranty of Workers' Compensation Liabilities.

NOTE 1: The assumption resolution may be worded in such a manner as to be applicable to only the specific applicants to self-insure or the assumption resolution may list all present subsidiaries or affiliates and authorize the addition of future, unnamed additions to the assumption resolution as an attachment without execution of a new resolution.

NOTE 2: The Chief shall provide an acceptable model resolution to any party upon request. The current model assumption resolutions are contained in Plate E of the Appendix following Section 15463 of these regulations.

(e) In the event that a public self-insurer or individual private self-insurer reincorporates, merges, or changes its identity, the surviving entity shall execute a new Guaranty of Workers' Compensation Liabilities and a new assumption resolution to cover the liabilities of the prior self-insurer as part of the reapplication process to continue self-insurance of workers' compensation liabilities.

(f) A foreign entity (i.e. outside the United States) may execute a parental Guaranty of Workers' Compensation Liabilities for a subsidiary or affiliate self-insurer provided such foreign entity:

(1) executes in the English language the Guaranty of Workers' Compensation Liabilities and the assumption resolution; and

(2) includes a statement in the Guaranty of Workers' Compensation Liabilities that, in the event of the Director's need to enforce the Guaranty of Workers' Compensation Liabilities executed by the foreign entity on behalf of a self-insured subsidiary or subsidiaries, the foreign entity will:

(A) become subject to the jurisdiction of California courts and administrative agencies; and

(B) become controlled by California law in the resolution of any dispute under the assumption and guarantee agreement.

(g) Execution of Guaranty of Workers' Compensation Liabilities shall not reduce the amount of security deposit required to be posted by any self-insurer as set forth in Sections 15210 and 15210.1.

(h) A Guaranty of Workers' Compensation Liabilities executed pursuant to this section may be terminated only upon the express written consent of both the Director and the Security Fund. Termination shall be effective upon the Guarantor's receipt of such express written consent. Termination shall not extinguish the Guarantor's continuing liability for any default of the guaranteed self-insurer in fully discharging all existing and potential Workers' Compensation liability on account of any injury suffered by any of the guaranteed self-insurer's employees prior to the date of termination.

Note: Authority cited: Sections 54, 55 and 3702.10, Labor Code. Reference: Sections 59, 129, 3700, 3701, 3701.5, 3702, 3702.5, 3702.6, 3702.10, 3703, 3705 and 3740-3744, Labor Code.

History: 1. New section filed 11-19-75; effective thirtieth day thereafter (Register 75, No. 47).

2. Amendment filed 11-21-78; effective thirtieth day thereafter (Register 78, No. 47).

3. Amendment filed 12-22-92; operative 1-21-93 (Register 93, No. 2).

4. Editorial correction of subsection (f)(2)(A) (Register 98, No. 8).

5. Change without regulatory effect amending subsection (b) filed 2-17-98 pursuant to section 100, title 1, California Code of Regulations (Register 98, No. 8).

6. Amendment of subsection (c) filed 6-25-98; operative 7-25-98 (Register 98, No. 26).

7. Amendment filed 3-2-2009; operative 3-2-2009 pursuant to Government Code section 11343.4 (Register 2009, No. 10).

8. Amendment of section heading and section filed 12-14-2016; operative 1-1-2017 pursuant to Government Code section 11343.4(b)(3) (Register 2016, No. 51).

Ref.: Hanna §§ 1.19, 2.11; Herlick Handbook § 3.20.

§15211.3. Agreement and Undertaking For Security Deposit.

(a) All security deposits shall be posted in accordance with the provisions of the Agreement and Undertaking, as required in Section 15203.5 of these regulations.

Note: Authority cited: Sections 54, 55 and 3702.10, Labor Code. Reference: Sections 59, 3701, 3701.5, 3702, 3702.6, 3702.10, 3703, 3705, 3740-3745, Labor Code.

History: 1. New section filed 12-22-92; operative 1-21-93 (Register 93, No. 2).

§15212. Surety Bonds.

(a) Surety bonds shall be accepted by the Manager only if written by an "admitted surety insurer" as defined by California Code of Civil Procedure, Chapter 2, Bonds and Undertaking, Section 995.120(a).

(b) A surety bond underwritten by an organization owned and/or controlled by the self insurer, who is also the principal on the surety bond, shall be rejected by the Manager unless the surety company is financially independent of its parent.

(c) The Manager shall make available, upon request of any self insurer, an appropriate quantity of surety bond forms (Form A4-20 (Rev. 11/92)), increase riders (Form A4-21b (Rev. 4/92)) decrease riders (Form A4-21a (Rev. 4/92)), name change riders (Form A4-22 (Rev. 4/92)), and special form change riders (Form A4-23 (Rev. 4/92)), and Release of Surety (Form A4-24 (11/92)), California Code of Regulations, Title 11, Chapter 2, Section 25, which are hereby incorporated by reference.

Note: The current surety bond forms and rider forms are contained in Plates F-1 through F-6 of the Appendix immediately following the last Article in these Subchapter 2 regulations.

(d) A surety bond accepted by the Manager as security deposit shall be continuous in form. Surety bonds shall be exonerated only by their terms and cancelled only according to the specific language in the bond form. Exoneration of a surety bond by the Manager shall only be done when the bond language includes a release provision and the self insurer has substituted another acceptable security deposit or combination of acceptable deposits that totals to the amount determined by the Director to be required as a security deposit.

Note: Bond forms previously accepted as security deposit have differing terms and conditions from the current surety bond forms and some of the prior bond forms may not include a release provision in the bond language. Such bonds cannot be exonerated by the Manager unless the prior bond form is changed to the current terms and conditions by means of reinstatement of the surety bond, if cancelled, and execution of a Special Form Change Rider.

(e) The surety company shall submit a Notice of Cancellation in writing to the Manager on any surety bond according to the terms of the bond. The surety shall give the Manager written notice at least (thirty) 30 days in advance of the effective date of cancellation of an existing surety bond. After receipt of the written cancellation notice and receipt of a replacement security deposit, as set forth in subsection (d) and (g), in the amount required by the Director, the Manager may issue a Release of Surety to the surety company for the cancelled bond.

(f) Surety bonds and all riders to the surety bonds shall be executed by the surety company's Attorney-In-Fact and the Attorney-In-Fact's appointment or power of attorney must accompany all copies of the bond or rider being submitted.

Note: The Attorney-In-Fact does not need to be a California Attorney-In-Fact.

(g) The self insurer shall substitute the deposit represented by the penal sum of the cancelled surety bond with another acceptable form of security deposit, in the full amount required by the Director, within thirty (30) days of the receipt of bond cancellation notice to the Manager.

Exceptions:

(1) A surety bond issued prior to the effective date of these regulations where the bond secures liabilities of a former self insurer.

(2) An active self insurer in the process of revocation on the effective date of this regulation of its self insurance authority and which has fully insured its workers' compensation liabilities with a standard workers' compensation policy from an admitted carrier prior to the effective date of this regulation.

(h) The surety company or its parent company shall have and maintain an acceptable credit rating as set forth below:

(1) Standard and Poors Insurer Financial Strength Rating of A or better rating, or

(2) A.M. Best Company, Financial Strength Rating of B+ or better rating.

(i) A surety bond shall be replaced by the self insurer in the event the surety is placed in conservatorship, or is seized, or declares insolvency, or the current credit rating is below the ratings required in subsection (h).

Note: Authority cited: Sections 54, 55 and 3702.10, Labor Code. Reference: Sections 3700, 3700(b), 3701, 3701.5, 3702.10, 3703, 3705 and 3740-3744, Labor Code; and Sections 995.120(a) and 995.430, Code of Civil Procedure.

History: 1. Repealer and new section filed 12-22-92; operative 1-21-93 (Register 93, No. 2).

2. Amendment filed 8-12-93; operative 9-13-93 (Register 93, No. 33).

3. New subsections (h)-(i) and amendment of Note filed 11-2-2001; operative 12-2-2001 (Register 2001, No. 44).

Ref.: See Labor Code §§59, 129, 3702, 3702.5, 3702.6.

§15213. Approved Securities.

(a) Approved securities shall be only those securities which meet the following:

(1) Securities are corporate or Federal, State or municipal government bonds or notes in book entry form, having a rating of AA or better by Standard and Poor's Rating Service or a rating of Aa or better by Moody's Investors Service Guide or a rating of AA or better by Fitch Investors Service Guide;

Exception 1. Securities issued by the State of California shall have a rating of B or better.

Exception 2. Securities in registered, physical form that meet all requirements of this section are acceptable until January 1, 1997 for posting by a self insurer. After that date, all securities shall be in book entry form.

(2) Securities shall be delivered in the name of the "Treasurer, State of California in trust for (insert the legal name of the self insurer)" or similar legible abbreviation to a custodian account designated by the State Treasurer.*

(3) Securities previously accepted and registered in the name of "Treasurer State of California" or "Treasurer of State of California in trust for [legal name of self insurer(s)] liabilities pursuant to Labor Code Sections 3700 and 3701" shall not have to be reregistered, but will be held until maturity or released by order of the Manager or Director.

(4) Mortgage backed securities shall not be acceptable and zero-coupon securities shall not be accepted.

(5) Securities issued by the self insurer or its subsidiaries, or its affiliated companies or parent companies, shall not be accepted for that particular self insurer's security deposit.

(b) Any private self insurer desiring to post or have released approved securities shall provide the Manager with a complete description of the security or securities, including the following:

(1) Whether the security is registered or book entry type;

(2) Complete name of security;

(3) Interest rate of security;

(4) Original issue date of security;

(5) Date of maturity of security;

(6) Par value of security;

(7) Current market value of security;

(8) Name of delivery agent and the telephone number of delivery agent who will actually deliver the security to the State on behalf of the self insured employer. [Note: This is usually a bank or brokerage firm.]; and

(9) The name and address where interest checks are to be sent for registered securities or a bank name and bank account number for wire transfer of interest payments for book entry securities.

(10) The self insurer's Federal Taxpayer Identification Number for interest payments on the securities.

(c) Approval by the Manager or Director, or other person authorized in writing by the Director, to the State Treasurer shall be required on all securities to be posted or released and the Manager shall transmit the approval order to the State Treasurer.

Note: The current model letter to request approval of securities is contained in Plate G of the Appendix following the last Article in these Subchapter 2 regulations.

(d) The Manager shall value approved securities at par value or market value, whichever is less, when computing the security deposit represented by the securities for any private self insurer. Each self insurer posting securities shall provide a statement of the current market value of the security or securities annually to the Manager on their Self Insurer's Annual Report as required by Section 15251(b)(6).

(e) No approved security shall be accepted for deposit at above its par value. Additional deposits of approved securities shall be required at any time when the market value of an approved security falls below its par value.

(f) The Manager may order called or matured securities to be redeemed by the State Treasurer and the resulting cash returned to or deposited in trust on behalf of the self-insured.

(g) Any self insurer with securities on deposit may request the release of the securities upon the posting of replacement security or upon the determination of the Manager that the securities represent surplus deposit above that required by Labor Code Section 3701 and these regulations.

*Note: The usual practice of the State Treasurer is to contact the delivery agent for the specific wire instructions for processing the securities transaction into or out of the State Treasurer's custodian account.

Note: Authority cited: Sections 54, 55 and 3702.10, Labor Code. Reference: Sections 59, 3700, 3701, 3701.5, 3702, 3702.6, 3702.10, 3703, 3705 and 3740-3745, Labor Code.

History: 1. Editorial correction to Form Nos. A4-30 and A4-31 (Register 74, No. 47).

2. Repealer and new section filed 12-22-92; operative 1-21-93 (Register 93, No. 2).

3. Amendment of subsections (a)(1) and (a)(2), repealer and new subsection (a)(3), and addition of footnote to subsection (a)(2) filed 12-23-96; operative 1-1-97 pursuant to Government Code section 11343.4(d) (Register 96, No. 52).

§15214. Cash in Trust.

(a) Cash shall be presented to the Manager in the form of a corporate check, cashier's check, certified check or money order and shall be made payable to "The Department of Industrial Relations In Trust For [the legal name of the self insurer]." A wire transfer of funds to a bank, or financial institution if approved in advance by the Manager may be used.

NOTE 1: Cash deposits shall be deposited by the Office of Self-Insurance Plans on the same day received or on the following business day with a bank or financial institution meeting the credit standards contained in Section 15215(e) into an interest bearing savings account or into a callable or brokered certificate of deposit not exceeding one year in duration with an automatic rollover upon maturity. A savings account or certificate of deposit shall be set up in such a manner to show the deposit is held in trust for the private self insurer by the Department of Industrial Relations, as the depositor, and the private self insurer has no ability to control any part of the savings account or certificate of deposit. The savings account, original certificate or other evidence of the deposit or account shall be held by the bank or financial institution who shall be the custodian of the deposit, pending written instruction from Self-Insurance Plans signed by the Manager to deliver documentary evidence of the deposit or account, to the Office of Self Insurance Plans.

NOTE 2: A private self insurer desiring to deposit cash to be held in trust as part of its security deposit should contact the Manager in advance of sending a cash deposit to the Office of Self-Insurance Plans. The private self insurer may advise the Manager in writing of any preference for a bank or financial institution into which the cash is to be deposited by the Department and length of the deposit term. However, the selection of the bank or financial institution and length of term of the deposit is at the discretion of the Manager.

(b) Certificates of deposit may be deposited with prior arrangements made with the Manager and subject to approval of the Manager as with any other registered securities pursuant to Section 15213 of these regulations.

(c) By order of the Manager, documentary evidence of the savings account or certificate of deposit shall be provided by the bank or financial institution to the Office of Self Insurance Plans. The savings account or certificate of deposit shall be released only upon written order of the Director and the Manager or other person designated by the Director.

(d) The Manager shall provide the private self insurer depositing cash with a written receipt for the deposit.

(e) The private self insurer may request and the Manager shall authorize the payment of any interest on the cash deposit to be sent to the self insurer from the bank or financial institution.

Note: Authority cited: Sections 54, 55 and 3702.10, Labor Code. Reference: Sections 59, 3700, 3701, 3701.5, 3702, 3702.6, 3702.10, 3703, 3705 and 3740-3745, Labor Code.

History: 1. New section filed 12-22-92; operative 1-21-93 (Register 93, No. 2).

2. Amendment filed 9-19-2011; operative 10-19-2011 (Register 2011, No. 38).

3. Editorial correction of Note 1 (Register 2011, No. 44).

§15215. Letters of Credit.

(a) An irrevocable standby letter of credit may be accepted by the Manager as all or part of the security deposit for a private self insurer. The Manager shall determine whether the letter of credit submitted is acceptable and if its language and format meets the requirements of this Section.

(b) Irrevocable letters of credit shall be issued by and payable at a branch in the continental United States, Alaska or Hawaii. The issuing bank or financial institution shall meet the requirements of this section and may be:

(1) A State of California chartered bank or savings institution; or

(2) A federally chartered bank or savings institution; or

(3) Any other foreign or domestic bank or savings institution; or

(4) A group (syndication) of domestic or foreign banks or savings institutions.

(5) A federally chartered or State of California chartered credit union

(c) The Manager shall provide a model letter of credit format and language that will meet the requirements for acceptance. The letter of credit shall include, but not be limited to, the following provisions:

(1) The letter of credit will be automatically extended without amendment for an additional one year from the expiry date or any subsequent expiry date unless, at least 45 days before the expiry date, the Manager is notified in writing by the bank or financial institution that the letter of credit will not be renewed;

(2) The letter of credit can be called if the self insurer fails to pay its workers' compensation liabilities; or the self insurer files bankruptcy; or the self insurer fails to renew or substitute acceptable security by ten days prior to the expiry date of the letter of credit; or any combination of these events;

(3) The letter of credit is not subject to any qualification or condition by the issuing or confirming bank or financial institution and is the bank or financial institution's individual obligation which is in no way contingent upon reimbursement;

(4) Payment of any amount under the letter of credit shall be made only by wire transfer in the name of "The Department of Industrial Relations In Trust For [the legal name of the self insurer]" to an account of the State Controller, State of California, at a designated bank;

(5) All letters of credit shall include a statement that if legal proceedings are initiated by any party with respect to the payment of any letter of credit, it is agreed that such proceedings shall be subject to the jurisdiction of California courts and administrative agencies and subject to California law; and

(6) Letters of credit shall be subject to the Uniform Customs and Practices for Documentary Credits, UCP600, 2007 Revision, ICC Publication No. 600, which is hereby incorporated by reference, and a reference to this publication shall be included within the text of the letter of credit.

(7) Discrepancy fees, if any, shall be payable by the self insurer.

NOTE: A model single bank letter of credit (Revised 7/94) is contained in Plate I of the Appendix following the last Article in these Subchapter 2 regulations.

(d) A syndicated letter of credit shall include all the language of the single bank or financial institution issued letter of credit and in addition:

(1) Authorize all demands for payment to be presented at a designated branch ("agent bank" or "agent") of one of the participating banks or financial institutions;

(2) Include a draft to be presented for payment of all or part of the credit available under the letter of credit;

(3) Permit any participating bank's or financial institution's portion of the total credit available to be drawn

upon if the participating bank's or financial institution's credit rating falls below the acceptable credit rating level specified in subsection (e) of this Section; and

(4) State that the obligations of the banks or financial institutions issuing a syndicated letter of credit are several and not joint, and neither the agent bank or financial institution or any other participating bank or financial institution shall be responsible for or otherwise liable for the failure of any other participating bank or financial institution to perform its obligations under the syndicated letter of credit. The failure of any participating bank or financial institution to perform its obligations under the syndicated letter of credit shall also not relieve any other participating bank or financial institution of its obligations under the syndicated letter of credit.

(e) The issuing bank(s) or financial institution(s) or the parent holding corporation of an unrated bank or financial institution issuing a letter of credit shall have at the time of issuance of the letter of credit an acceptable credit rating as set forth below:

(1) An "Aaa", "Aa", "A" long term certificate of deposit (CD) rating for the bank or financial institution in the current monthly edition of "Moody's Statistical Handbook" prepared by Moody's Investors Service, Inc., New York; or

(2) An "AAA", "AA" or "A" long term certificate of deposit (CD) rating for the bank or financial institution in the current quarterly edition or monthly supplement of "Financial Institutions Ratings" prepared by Standard & Poor's Corporation, New York; or

(3) An "AAA", "AA+" or "AA" credit quality rating for the issuing financial institution along with a CD/Debt Credit Limit Code above the dollar amount of the letter of credit as well as a Credit Limit Maturity Code of "a, b, c or d" in the current annual edition of "GFI Credit Ratings", or the latest monthly "GFI Bank Letter" supplement thereto; or

(4) If applicable, be backed by federally chartered instrumentalities of the United States operating under authority of the Farm Credit Act of 1971, as amended, or be a state or federally chartered credit union whose shares are insured by the National Credit Union Share Insurance Fund.

(f) A letter of credit issued by a bank or financial institution or syndication of banks or financial institutions that does not meet the credit rating set forth in subsection (e) at the time of issuance shall be accepted by the Manager with a confirming letter of credit issued by a bank or financial institution meeting the criteria of subsection (e). The confirming letter of credit shall state that the confirming bank or financial institution is primarily obligated to pay on demand the full amount of the letter of credit regardless of reimbursement from the bank or financial institution whose letter of credit is being confirmed.

NOTE: Advising letters of credit shall not be accepted in lieu of the confirmation requirement for the letter of credit bank with a unacceptable credit rating.

(g) If a bank or financial institution's rating subsequent to the issuance of the letter of credit falls below the acceptable rating level as set forth in subsection (e), the Manager shall, within 60 days of the publication of the lower credit rating, require the self insurer to:

(1) Replace the letter of credit with a new letter of credit issued by a bank or financial institution with an acceptable credit rating; or

(2) Confirm the letter of credit by a bank or financial institution with an acceptable rating.

Note: Authority cited: Sections 54, 55 and 3702.10, Labor Code. Reference: Sections 59, 3700, 3701, 3701.5, 3702, 3702.3, 3702.6, 3702.10, 3740, 3741 and 3742, Labor Code.

History: 1. New section filed 12-22-92; operative 1-21-93 (Register 93, No. 2).

2. New subsection (e)(3) and subsection redesignation, and amendment of subsections (e)(1) and (2) filed 3-24-94; operative 4-25-94 (Register 94, No. 12).

3. Amendment of subsection (c)(6) and (c)(7) Note filed 12-1-94; operative 1-2-95 (Register 94, No. 48).

4. Amendment filed 3-2-2009; operative 3-2-2009 pursuant to Government Code section 11343.4 (Register 2009, No. 10).

Ref.: Hanna §§ 1.19, 2.11; Herlick Handbook § 3.20.

§15216. Administration of Defaulted Self-Insurer's Claims.

(a) In the event the self-insurer fails to pay workers' compensation benefits due, the cost of administration and legal expenses of existing and new claims shall be made from the security deposit set aside for this purpose pursuant to Labor Code Section 3701.5.

(b) If claims have been administered from out of state, the Director may order all remaining and future claims to be administered from California or may turn them over to the Self-Insurer's Security Fund.

(c) If it is necessary for the Director to call or cash any security deposit, a trust shall be established by the Chief to receive the funds from the deposit, except in the following situations:

(1) Where the surety company elects, and the Director approves, handling of the claims directly by the provider of the surety bond; or

(2) Where the funds and responsibility for the claims are turned over to the Self-Insurer's Security Fund pursuant to Labor Code Section 3701.5, at which time the self-insurer, or its estate, forfeits all right, title and interest in the security deposit.

(d) In the event of a default, all security deposits, regardless of form that is posted by the self-insured employer, shall be the first in order to be called upon to pay benefits due. If any portion of the defaulting self-insurer's liabilities are secured in whole or part by an alternative composite deposit posted by the Security Fund, the alternative composite deposit shall be next in order to be called upon to pay benefits due. The Director may at his/her discretion call any portion of the entire security deposit posted at any time without waiting for the exhaustion of all funds in the prior level or call order contained in this subsection.

(e) The Chief shall advise the Self-Insurers' Security Fund of the receipt of any verified information indicating a self-insurer's failure to pay benefits due, the filing of bankruptcy, or inability to post and maintain required security deposit.

(f) The Director, at his/her discretion, may order the Security Fund to assume full liability for any self-insurer's insolvency or failure to pay benefits regardless of whether or not there is a shortfall in the deposit to pay benefits due.

(g) When responsibility for claims is turned over to the Self-Insurers' Security Fund pursuant to Labor Code section 3701.5, the Self-Insurers' Security Fund shall not be liable for the payment of penalties assessed for any act or omission on the part of any person or entity other than the Self-Insurers' Security Fund.

Note: Authority cited: Sections 54, 55, 3701.8 and 3702.10, Labor Code. Reference: Sections 59, 129, 3701, 3701.5, 3701.8, 3702, 3702.3, 3702.6, 3703, 3705 and 3740-3745, Labor Code.

History: 1. New section filed 12-22-92; operative 1-21-93 (Register 93, No. 2).

2. Amendment of section and Note filed 5-30-2003 as an emergency; operative 5-30-2003 (Register 2003, No. 22). A Certificate of Compliance must be transmitted to OAL by 9-29-2003 or emergency language will be repealed by operation of law on the following day.

3. Certificate of Compliance as to 5-30-2003 order transmitted to OAL 9-29-2003 and filed 11-12-2003 (Register 2003, No. 46).

4. Repealer of subsection (c), subsection relettering, amendment of newly designated subsections (c), (c)(2) and (e) and new subsection (g) filed 12-14-2016; operative 1-1-2017 pursuant to Government Code section 11343.4(b)(3) (Register 2016, No. 51).

Ref.: Herlick Handbook § 3.20.

ARTICLE 3.1
Alternative Composite Deposits

§15220. Participation in Alternative Composite Deposits.

(a) All private self-insured employers, active or revoked, shall be annually determined by the Chief to be either eligible or non-eligible for participation in the alternative composite deposit program. Participation shall be as a fully participating self-insured employer or as a partially participating self-insured employer as provided in subsection (c)(1).

(b) All non-eligible self-insurers shall be deemed "excluded". The following self-insured employers shall be excluded from the alternative composite deposit program:

(1) Any former private self-insured employer that possesses a revoked Certificate of Consent to Self-Insure and is no longer required to submit a Self-Insurer's Annual Report pursuant to Section 15251 of this subchapter 2 because all known claims costs have been reported and all known claims are closed.

(2) Any current or former private self-insured employer to the extent it has sold off all or any portion of its workers' compensation liabilities under a special excess workers compensation insurance policy to an admitted carrier and has continued to post security deposit to secure such sold off liabilities for 3 years from the policy issuance date.

(3) All private group self-insurers of workers' compensation liabilities as provided for in Article 13 of this subchapter 2.

(4) Any private self-insured employer to the extent that it transfers any or all of its existing self-insured workers' compensation liabilities to either: (A) a fully insured employer, such as in the merger, reorganization, sale or spin off of a division or subsidiary; or, (B) a carrier through a contractual sell off that is not a special excess workers' compensation insurance policy pursuant to Labor Code Section 3702.8(c) and (d).

(5) Any current or former private self-insured employer that has defaulted on the payment of its self-insured workers' compensation liabilities and whose liabilities have been turned over to the Security Fund by the Director.

(6) Any current or former private self-insured employer that has failed to post the full amount of security deposit required by Section 15210 for more than 60 consecutive days.

(7) Any former private self-insured employer that has posted a surety bond that contains no provision to release the carrier's liabilities under the surety bond.

(8) Any private self-insured employer that does not meet the minimum credit rating criteria for participation in the alternative composite deposit contained in subsection (d)(2).

(9) Any current or former private legally self-insured employer that is a member of a public sector healthcare joint powers authority pursuant to Government Code Section 6527.

(10) Any self-insured employer that has been specifically excluded by written request of the Security Fund. Notwithstanding other requirements of this section, the Security Fund may submit a written request to the Chief that any private self-insured employer otherwise excluded from participation in the alternative composite deposit program be included, and the Chief, upon such written request, may grant the request; the written request shall identify the private self-insured employer and shall state the reasons that such private self-insured employer should be included in the alternative composite deposit.

(c) All private self-insured employers determined by the Chief to be eligible shall be required to participate in the alternative composite deposit program.

(1) The Chief shall identify each eligible participant as one of the following:

(A) Fully participating employer, or

(B) Partially participating employer.

(d) To qualify as a fully participating private self-insured employer, the employer shall meet all the following requirements:

(1) The employer is not excluded by subsection (b) of this regulation;

(2) The employer possesses an acceptable credit rating on the date of the Security Fund's written alternative composite deposit proposal. An acceptable credit rating shall be any "A" or any "B" rating published by Moody's Investor Service, Standard & Poor's, Fitch Ratings, or equivalent.

In the event of multiple ratings for the same self-insured employer, the most recently published rating shall be utilized.

(e) The following self-insured employers shall qualify as partially participating members of the alternative composite deposit program:

(1) The employer is not excluded by subsection (b) of this regulation;

(2) The employer meets the qualifications of subsection (d) but has been identified as a partially participating self-insured employer by action of the Chief for cause.

Cause may include, but is not limited to, failure to provide a parental Guaranty of Workers' Compensation Liabilities; failure to file a complete and timely Self-Insurer's Annual Report; failure to file a complete and timely Actuarial Study and Summary; upon written request by the Self-Insurers Security Fund to make an employer partially instead of fully participating; failure to post the required security deposit by the required date; failure to report all claim liabilities or to estimate claims liabilities pursuant to Section 15300 of these regulations as determined in a routine audit or special audit; and/or, failure to post alternate deposit for new subsidiaries or affiliates of the self-insurer after the end of the cycle for the previous year's alternate composite deposit.

(f) Excluded self-insured employers shall not be eligible for any portion of their security deposit to be covered by the alternative composite deposit. The excluded private self-insurer shall continue to secure its workers' compensation liabilities as required in Article 3 and to pay assessments as provided in Article 4 of this subchapter 2.

(g) Any private self-insured employer that is eligible only as a partially participating member or is excluded to participate in the alternative composite deposit shall post the balance of the amount of required security deposit with the Director pursuant to Labor Code Section 3701 and Article 3 of this subchapter 2.

(h) For cause, the Chief may downgrade an eligible private self-insured employer from:

(1) fully participating employer to partially participating employer as provided in subsection (e)(2); or

(2) from partially participating employer to excluded.

Cause may include, but is not limited to, failure to submit the Self-Insurers' Annual Report and/or failure to estimate future claim liabilities on the Self-Insurers' Annual Report fully pursuant to Section 15300 as determined in an audit; failure to file a complete and timely Actuarial Study and Summary; upon written request by the Self-Insurers Security Fund to down grade an employer's status; inclusion of claim liabilities of subsidiaries or affiliates in their self-insurance program that have not been granted a Certificate to Self-Insure by the Director; failure to post a security deposit pursuant to Labor Code Section 3701 and these regulations; failure to meet the financial requirements for self-insurance pursuant to Section 15203.1; failure to submit a Guaranty of Workers' Compensation Liabilities pursuant to Section 15203.1; and/or, failure to pay any assessments, fees, and/or penalties pursuant to Labor Code Section 3702.9, this article, and/or Articles 4 or 9 of this subchapter 2.

Note: Authority cited: Sections 3701, 3701.8 and 3702.10, Labor Code. Reference: Sections 3701 and 3701.8, Labor Code; and Section 6527, Government Code.

History: 1. New article 3.1 (sections 15220-15220.8) and section filed 5-30-2003 as an emergency; operative 5-30-2003 (Register 2003, No. 22). A Certificate of Compliance must be transmitted to OAL by 9-29-2003 or emergency language will be repealed by operation of law on the following day. For prior history of sections 15220-15221, see Register 93, No. 2.

2. Certificate of Compliance as to 5-30-2003 order transmitted to OAL 9-29-2003 and filed 11-12-2003 (Register 2003, No. 46).

3. Amendment of subsections (b)(12) and (d)(3)(B) and amendment of Note filed 7-6-2004 as an emergency; operative 7-6-2004 (Register 2004, No. 28). A Certificate of Compliance must be transmitted to OAL by 11-3-2004 or emergency language will be repealed by operation of law on the following day.

4. Amendment of subsections (b)(12) and (d)(3)(B) and amendment of Note refiled 11-3-2004 as an emergency; operative 11-3-2004 (Register 2004, No. 45). A Certificate of Compliance must be transmitted to OAL by 3-3-2005 or emergency language will be repealed by operation of law on the following day.

5. Certificate of Compliance as to 11-3-2004 order transmitted to OAL 1-26-2005 and filed 3-8-2005 (Register 2005, No. 10).

6. Amendment filed 12-14-2016; operative 1-1-2017 pursuant to Government Code section 11343.4(b)(3) (Register 2016, No. 51).

§15220.1. Financial Information.

(a) In addition to the existing requirements to provide the current financial statement to the Manager contained in Section 15203.2 of these regulations, the Manager shall require financial information that includes designated general information and key financial items from such financial statement required by Section 15203.2, in a format approved by the Director pursuant to subsection (c)(3), from any private self insured employer that:

(1) does not have public financial statements (such as closely held or privately held employers) or has no published credit rating; and

(2) has a required security deposit equal to or greater than $2,000,000 or fails to meet the financial requirements to be self insured as contained in Section 15203.2.

(b) Financial information shall include the following designated general information and key financial items:

(1) General Information Items:

(A) Name of Employer

(B) Date of Last Annual Financial Statement

(2) Key Financial Information:

(A) Cash and Marketable Securities

(B) Inventory

(C) Total Current Assets

(D) Total Intangible Assets

(E) Total Assets

(F) Total Short Term Debt

(G) Total Current Liabilities

(H) Total Long Term Debt

(I) Long Term Pension Obligations

(J) Total Liabilities

(K) Total Shareholders' Equity

(L) Total Preferred Stock

(M) Retained Earnings

(N) Net Sales

(O) Cost of Goods Sold

(P) Selling, General & Administrative Expenses

(Q) Operating Profit/ (Loss)

(R) Earnings before Interest and Taxes

(S) Total Interest Expenses

(T) Rental Expense

(U) Net Income

(V) Depreciation & Amortization

(W) Extraordinary Items

(c) A private self insured employer that fails to file the financial information as determined by this section shall be ineligible to participate as a fully participating member in the current alternative composite deposit.

(1) The Manager shall utilize available financial information to assign a non-investment grade rating to any self insured employer that fails to submit financial information for eligibility as a partial participating member.

(2) The Manager shall be authorized to determine that a private self insurer that fails to submit financial information be ineligible for partial participation in the current alternative composite deposit program.

(3) After December 31, 2004, the financial information required by subsection (b) shall be submitted to the Manager electronically in a format provided by the Manager.

(d) Pursuant to Labor Code Section 3701.8(b)(5), the Manager may provide to the Security Fund any financial information needed to set the deposit assessments for self-insured employers participating in the alternative composite deposit program and to secure the composite deposit.

Note: Authority cited: Sections 3701.8 and 3702.10, Labor Code. Reference: Sections 3701.8 and 3702.10, Labor Code.

History: 1. New section filed 5-30-2003 as an emergency; operative 5-30-2003 (Register 2003, No. 22). A Certificate of Compliance must be transmitted to OAL by 9-29-2003 or emergency language will be repealed by operation of law on the following day.

2. Certificate of Compliance as to 5-30-2003 order, including amendment of subsection (a), subsection relettering and new subsection (d) — form A4-7, transmitted to OAL 9-29-2003 and filed 11-12-2003 (Register 2003, No. 46).

3. Amendment of section heading and subsections (a), (b) and (c)-(c)(2), new subsection (c)(3) and repealer and new subsection (d) filed 7-6-2004 as an emergency; operative 7-6-2004 (Register 2004, No. 28). A Certificate of Compliance must be transmitted to OAL by 11-3-2004 or emergency language will be repealed by operation of law on the following day.

4. Amendment of section heading and subsections (a), (a)(2) and (c)-(c)(2), new subsection (c)(3) and repealer and new subsection (d) refiled 11-3-2004 as an emergency; operative 11-3-2004 (Register 2004, No. 45). A Certificate of Compliance must be transmitted to OAL by 3-3-2005 or emergency language will be repealed by operation of law on the following day.

5. Certificate of Compliance as to 11-3-2004 order transmitted to OAL 1-26-2005 and filed 3-8-2005 (Register 2005, No. 10).

§15220.2. Listing of Security Deposit Amount Required.

(a) The Chief shall annually prepare a listing of the security deposit amount required to secure workers' compensation liabilities for each private self-insured employer pursuant to Labor Code Section 3701 and Article 3 of this subchapter 2. This listing of required security deposits shall be calculated pursuant to Sections 15210 and 15496 and/or other deposit adjustments as determined by the Chief for all private self-insured employers. This list shall be submitted to the Director annually.

(b) Any private self-insured employer that fails to file its required Self-Insurer's Annual Report and Actuarial Study and Summary by May 1 of each year shall be deemed by the Chief to have twice the liabilities indicated on the prior year's Actuarial Summary for the purpose of determining and recording the required security deposit in the above listing.

(c) The Chief shall provide the listing of required security deposits to the Security Fund by May 15 each year.

Note: Authority cited: Section 3701.8 and 3701.10, Labor Code. Reference: Sections 3701.8 and 3702.10, Labor Code.

History: 1. New section filed 5-30-2003 as an emergency; operative 5-30-2003 (Register 2003, No. 22). A Certificate of Compliance must be transmitted to OAL by 9-29-2003 or emergency language will be repealed by operation of law on the following day.

2. Certificate of Compliance as to 5-30-2003 order transmitted to OAL 9-29-2003 and filed 11-12-2003 (Register 2003, No. 46).

3. Amendment filed 12-14-2016; operative 1-1-2017 pursuant to Government Code section 11343.4(b)(3) (Register 2016, No. 51).

§15220.3. Alternative Composite Deposits.

(a) The Security Fund shall secure the aggregate security deposit amount required, in whole or part, for all eligible private self insured employers in the alternative composite deposit program, utilizing any one or combination of security instruments listed in Labor Code Section 3701 and/or Section 3701.8 and as provided for in subsection (b) of this section.

(b) These security instruments may include, but not be limited to, letters of credit, surety bonds, approved securities, and cash subject to the regulatory requirements for each contained in Article 3 (commencing with Section 15210) of this subchapter 2. It may also include, but not be limited to, insurance coverage, such as specific or aggregate excess policies, or special excess workers' compensation policies; or other financial instruments, such as commercial paper or reinsurance contracts; or the Security Fund's own secured or unsecured indebtedness; or financial guarantees, including the Security Fund's own guarantee backed by cash or securities.

(c) The Security Fund shall submit a written proposal as required in subsection (d) each year that the Security Fund proposes to replace individual security deposits with an aggregate composite deposit.

(d) Each formal written proposal for an alternative composite deposit to the Manager shall include:

(1) A complete description of the proposed composite deposit including what portions are cash and non-cash; any retentions, deductibles, or co-payments that are contemplated in each layer, if any; and any insurance or reinsurance being utilized as part of the proposal;

(2) A list of all proposed self insured employers to be covered; their amount of coverage; their applicable credit rating or equivalent credit rating as determined by Section 15220.1 of this subchapter 2; and the credit rating agency utilized to determine the credit rating;

(3) Specification of the call order, if any, of the instruments proposed to be posted as part of the alternative composite deposit.

(4) A proposed starting date for the proposed alternative composite deposit that is at least 30 days after the date of the official written proposal to the Manager.

(e) The Manager shall advise the Director of all written proposals submitted by the Security Fund for an alternative composite deposit and the details of the proposal.

(f) The Manager shall review and approve or reject the alternative composite deposit proposal in whole or part and shall advise the Security Fund of the decision within 30 days. If approved, the Security Fund shall have 30 days to post the alternative composite deposit instruments(s) with the Director, unless the Security Fund's approved proposal sets forth some other acceptable timetable for delivery of the instrument(s).

(g) The Manager shall not release security deposits posted by individual self insured employers pursuant to Labor Code Section 3701 until after the alternative composite deposit permitted by Labor Code Section 3701.8 is fully posted.

(h) The Security Fund may subsequently propose additions, extensions, replacements, substitutions, or other changes to the initial alternative composite deposit posted with the Manager, in whole or part, in the same manner as set forth in this section. Approval and posting of any changes in the alternative composite deposit shall comply with the provisions of this section.

(i) The Security Fund may provide its own guarantee for any portion of the alternative composite deposit in the form of a retention, a deductible, or its own guarantee, provided the guaranteed amount is secured by segregated cash or securities posted with the Director as set forth in Section 15220.8.

(j) At the time the Security Fund submits the written proposal each year as required by subsection (d), it shall list the self-insurers that it proposes to include in whole or in part in the composite deposit. Notwithstanding Section 15210.1(b) of these regulations, each self-insurer listed for inclusion shall have 60 days from the date of notification of the increase or until July 1 of that year, whichever is sooner, to post any indicated increase in security deposit, and that increase shall be either included in the composite deposit proposed by the Security Fund or separately posted, as required.

Note: Authority cited: Sections 3701.8 and 3702.10, Labor Code. Reference: Section 3701.8, Labor Code.

History: 1. New section filed 5-30-2003 as an emergency; operative 5-30-2003 (Register 2003, No. 22). A Certificate of Compliance must be transmitted to OAL by 9-29-2003 or emergency language will be repealed by operation of law on the following day.

2. Certificate of Compliance as to 5-30-2003 order transmitted to OAL 9-29-2003 and filed 11-12-2003 (Register 2003, No. 46).

3. Amendment of subsection (b) and new subsection (j) filed 7-6-2004 as an emergency; operative 7-6-2004 (Register 2004, No. 28). A Certificate of Compliance must be transmitted to OAL by 11-3-2004 or emergency language will be repealed by operation of law on the following day.

4. Amendment of subsection (b) and new subsection (j) refiled 11-3-2004 as an emergency; operative 11-3-2004 (Register 2004, No. 45). A Certificate of Compliance must be transmitted to OAL by 3-3-2005 or emergency language will be repealed by operation of law on the following day.

5. Certificate of Compliance as to 11-3-2004 order transmitted to OAL 1-26-2005 and filed 3-8-2005 (Register 2005, No. 10).

§15220.4. Deposit Assessments by the Security Fund for Participants of the Alternative Composite Deposit.

(a) The Security Fund shall collect an annual deposit assessment from all private self insurers participating in the alternative composite deposit as follows:

(1) A pro-rata cash contribution to build the net worth of the Security Fund to pay existing or future defaults on covered workers' compensation liabilities of eligible private self insured employers under an alternative composite deposit. This portion of the deposit assessment shall be called the Default Loss Fund Fee.

(2) A pro-rata cash contribution to pay the cost of any aggregate loss protection in excess of the level of liability provided through the Default Loss Fund. This portion of the deposit assessment shall be called the Excess Liability Protection Fee.

(3) A pro-rata cash contribution to fund security deposit shortfalls from existing private self insurer insolvencies and defaults formerly funded exclusively by the Security Fund's Insolvency Assessment pursuant to Labor Code Section 3745. This portion of the deposit assessment shall be called the Pre-Existing Deposit Shortfall Fee.

Exception: Private self insurers whose Certificate of Consent to Self Insure was revoked before January 1, 2003, shall remain subject to the assessments as provided by Labor Code Section 3745.

(b) Each private self insured employer participating in an alternative composite deposit with the Security Fund shall be required to annually pay the Security Fund deposit assessment.

(c) The Security Fund shall determine the pro-rata amount of the deposit assessment for each fully participating and partially participating private self insured employer based on all the following:

(1) Labor Code Section 3701.8(b) requirements;

(2) the cost of the security instruments permitted in Section 15220.2 including any cash holdings that will make up the Default Loss Fund and/or the Excess Liability Protection Fee portions of any alternative composite deposit proposed to the Director;

(3) the amount of the security deposit required by the Manager for each participating private self insured employer to secure its self insured workers' compensation liabilities;

(4) the participating private self insured employer's credit ratings or equivalent credit ratings as determined by Sections 15220, 15220.1, or Section 15220.3;

(5) an amount, if needed, for the pro-rata share of incurred but not fully reported liabilities aggregated across all private self insurers;

(6) an amount for the pro-rata share of pre-existing, unfunded defaulted liabilities of the Self Insurers' Security Fund to be collected for funding cash flow needs by the Pre-Existing Deposit Shortfall Fee;

(7) other measures of each private self insured employer's contribution to the cost of the alternative composite deposit proposed to the Director; and

(8) the amount, if any, of the security deposit required to be separately posted with the Director pursuant to Labor Code Section 3701 to secure that portion of the employer's self insured workers' compensation liabilities that is not secured in the alternative composite deposit.

(d) Where the participating self insurer has more than one credit rating from the credit rating agencies and the ratings are not in agreement, the most recently published credit rating shall be used to calculate the deposit assessment.

(e) Excluded private self insured employers shall be required to participate in the assessments. The Manager shall determine the amount of each deposit assessment due from private self insured employers excluded from participation in any alternative composite deposit and submit it to the Security Fund. The Security Fund shall collect the deposit assessments from excluded employers.

(f) The Security Fund may repay any indebtedness incurred as contemplated by Section 15220.3 from the annual deposit assessment. At the time the annual deposit assessment is determined, it may not be known whether any such indebtedness will be incurred, or the amount or repayment terms thereof. Accordingly, a portion of the annual deposit assessment may be contingent upon the actual incurrence of such indebtedness and delayed until the amount and repayment terms are known.

(g) If the Manager increases the security deposit requirement of a participating self-insured employer after the Security Fund has issued the annual assessment for the alternative composite deposit, the amount of the increase may be addressed through a supplemental assessment or by the posting of additional deposit separately as a partially participating self-insurer.

Note: Authority cited: Sections 3701, 3701.8, 3702.10 and 3745, Labor Code. Reference: Sections 3701, 3701.8, 3701.8(b), 3702.10 and 3745, Labor Code.

History: 1. New section filed 5-30-2003 as an emergency; operative 5-30-2003 (Register 2003, No. 22). A Certificate of Compliance must be transmitted to OAL by 9-29-2003 or emergency language will be repealed by operation of law on the following day.

2. Certificate of Compliance as to 5-30-2003 order, including amendment of Note, transmitted to OAL 9-29-2003 and filed 11-12-2003 (Register 2003, No. 46).

3. Amendment of subsection (c)(4), new subsections (d), (f) and (g) and subsection relettering filed 7-6-2004 as an emergency; operative 7-6-2004 (Register 2004, No. 28). A Certificate of Compliance must be transmitted to OAL by 11-3-2004 or emergency language will be repealed by operation of law on the following day.

4. Amendment of subsection (c)(4), new subsections (d), (f) and (g) and subsection relettering refiled 11-3-2004 as an emergency; operative 11-3-2004 (Register 2004, No. 45). A Certificate of Compliance must be transmitted to OAL by 3-3-2005 or emergency language will be repealed by operation of law on the following day.

5. Certificate of Compliance as to 11-3-2004 order transmitted to OAL 1-26-2005 and filed 3-8-2005 (Register 2005, No. 10).

§15220.5. Deposit Assessments; Failure to Pay; Assessment Liability.

(a) Each alternative composite deposit posted with the Director by the Security Fund shall be a binding agreement for all private self insured employers, fully participating and non-fully participating.

(b) Individual deposit assessment determinations, billings, and collection of these individual deposit assessments from participating private self insured employers shall be the responsibility of the Security Fund. The Security Fund shall advise the Manager in writing of any employer that fails to pay the assessment within the time period allocated by the Security Fund.

(c) The Manager shall assess a civil penalty pursuant to Labor Code Section 3701.8(d) against each private self insured employer who fails to pay the deposit assessment in the time allocated by the Security Fund. In addition to the civil penalty, the private self insured employer shall post a separate security deposit pursuant to Labor Code Section 3701 within 30 days of notice by the Manager.

(d) Failure by any participating private self insured employer to pay the deposit assessment in the time specified by the Security Fund, and/or failure to post and maintain the full amount of required security deposit pursuant to Labor Code Section 3701 for 60 days shall be good cause for the Manager to summarily revoke the private self insured employer's Certificate to Self Insure without a hearing as set forth in Section 15210.1.

(e) Any civil penalty assessed by the Manager pursuant to Labor Code Section 3701.8 shall not be discharged by the employer subsequently posting a security deposit. Any civil penalty or unpaid portion of the deposit assessment shall not be discharged by revocation of the employers' Certificate of Consent to Self Insure.

Note: Authority cited: Sections 3701.8 and 3702.10, Labor Code. Reference: Section 3701.8, Labor Code.

History: 1. New section filed 5-30-2003 as an emergency; operative 5-30-2003 (Register 2003, No. 22). A Certificate of Compliance must be transmitted to OAL by 9-29-2003 or emergency language will be repealed by operation of law on the following day.

2. Certificate of Compliance as to 5-30-2003 order transmitted to OAL 9-29-2003 and filed 11-12-2003 (Register 2003, No. 46).

§15220.6. New Self Insurers Fair Share Contribution Surcharge Fee.

(a) The Security Fund shall develop and track an annual historical schedule of cash contributions covering the initial ten years of the alternative security deposit program to build the net worth of the Default Loss Fund. A private self insured employer issued a Certificate to Self Insure after January 1, 2004, shall be surcharged a fair share contribution for the portion of the initial ten years that they did not contribute to the Default Loss Fund. This initial ten-year contribution for new self insurers shall be called the "New Self Insurer Fair Share Contribution Surcharge Fee" and shall be assessed and collected as a surcharge in addition to any other payment required of that new private self insurer into the Default Loss Fund. The Self Insurers Fair Share Contribution may be calculated as an average over a period of up to ten years.

(b) All funds collected from the New Self Insurer Fair Share Contribution Surcharge Fee shall be subject to the requirements of Section 15220.8.

Note: Authority cited: Sections 3701.8 and 3702.10, Labor Code. Reference: Section 3701.8, Labor Code.

History: 1. New section filed 5-30-2003 as an emergency; operative 5-30-2003 (Register 2003, No. 22). A Certificate of Compliance must be transmitted to OAL by 9-29-2003 or emergency language will be repealed by operation of law on the following day.

2. Certificate of Compliance as to 5-30-2003 order transmitted to OAL 9-29-2003 and filed 11-12-2003 (Register 2003, No. 46).

§15220.7. Appeals of Deposit Assessments and Appeals of Deposit Assessment Penalties.

(a) Any private self insured employer assessed a deposit assessment by the Security Fund may object or appeal the calculation or any other aspect of its deposit assessment to the Director as set forth in Article 11 (commencing with Section 15430). However, it shall be a condition precedent of such appeal that the full amount of the deposit assessment must first be paid to the Security Fund.

(b) Any private self insured employer assessed a civil penalty by the Manager for non-payment of the deposit assessment may appeal any civil penalties resulting from non-payment of the deposit assessment to the Director as set forth in Article 11 (commencing with Section 15430).

Note: Authority cited: Sections 3701.8 and 3702.10, Labor Code. Reference: Section 3701.8, Labor Code.

History: 1. New section filed 5-30-2003 as an emergency; operative 5-30-2003 (Register 2003, No. 22). A Certificate of Compliance must be transmitted to OAL by 9-29-2003 or emergency language will be repealed by operation of law on the following day.

2. Certificate of Compliance as to 5-30-2003 order transmitted to OAL 9-29-2003 and filed 11-12-2003 (Register 2003, No. 46).

§15220.8. Requirements for Use and Investment of Cash Generated from Deposit Assessments.

(a) The Security Fund shall provide the Director with a detailed accounting report of the monies collected for each deposit assessment within 90 days of the payment due date of the assessment.

(b) The accounting report shall include a summary of all funds collected, costs of each instrument posted as alternative composite deposit, all commissions and costs due or paid related to the alternative deposit system for that cycle, and any remaining excess funds.

(c) Following the purchase of any non-cash financial instruments to secure the liabilities of the alternative composite deposit, excess funds collected by the Security Fund in any deposit assessment and any additional funds subsequently collected shall be posted with the Director.

(d) All remaining cash collected from the assessments shall be deposited with the Director or as provided in subsection (f).

(e) All Security Fund cash deposits posted with the Director shall be held in the name of "Director of Industrial Relations in Trust for Self Insurers' Security Fund".

(f) The Director shall deposit and invest the Security Fund's cash in the Surplus Money Investment Fund pursuant to Labor Code Section 3702.5(b) and subject to the restrictions of use contained in Labor Code Section 3701.8, or the Director may permit the Security Fund to hire its own funds manager and invest the deposited cash on behalf of the Security Fund outside of the State Treasury subject to the following:

(1) As a condition precedent to the Security Fund managing such funds, the Security Fund shall adopt a cash investment policy outlining the types of investments in which such cash may be invested to preserve and protect the principal.

(2) The Security Fund shall insure that the Investment Fund manager submit a quarterly report to the Manager covering any of the Director's cash managed by the Security Fund.

(3) None of the Director's cash may be commingled with Security Fund cash, nor may any specific investments made with the Director's cash be commingled in the same instrument with Security Fund cash.

(4) Regardless of whether the Director or the Security Fund manages the cash posted, the funds shall remain in the name of the Director as set forth in subsection (e) of this section until such time as the Director may order any or all of the funds released to the Security Fund or refunded to the private self insured employers.

(g) Whenever the Director initially turns over the compensation liabilities of a private self insured employer to the Security Fund pursuant to Labor Code Section 3701.5 and such liabilities are covered in whole or part by the cash portion of an alternative composite deposit, the Director shall order the Manager to release enough cash to fund the payment of expected workers' compensation benefits for the remainder of the calendar year. If the amount released is inadequate, the Manager in consultation with the Security Fund shall advise the Director and request the Director to authorize the release of an additional amount to fund the payment of benefits and expenses for the period.

(h) The Security Fund shall annually notify the Manager and the Director in writing of the amount of funds that it will need to operate for the next calendar year for payment of benefits due, legal and administrative expenses, and other expenses of the Security Fund that will be funded from alternative composite deposits. The Manager shall be authorized to release the cash portion of the funds to the Self Insurers' Security Fund's possession.

Note: Authority cited: Sections 3701.8 and 3702.10, Labor Code. Reference: Section 3701.8, Labor Code.

History: 1. New section filed 5-30-2003 as an emergency; operative 5-30-2003 (Register 2003, No. 22). A Certificate of Compliance must be transmitted to OAL by 9-29-2003 or emergency language will be repealed by operation of law on the following day.

2. Certificate of Compliance as to 5-30-2003 order transmitted to OAL 9-29-2003 and filed 11-12-2003 (Register 2003, No. 46).

ARTICLE 4
Assessments

§15230. Private Sector License Fee Assessment.

(a) After July 1, 2001, an annual license fee shall be assessed by the Chief against each private self-insurer and paid by each private self-insurer on the following basis:

Number of Employees	*Single Adjusting Location**
0–2999	$4000
3000–6999	$6000
7000 and over	$8000

* An additional $300 per adjusting location for every location over 1.

The fees shall apply against the last full year Self-Insurer's Annual Report submitted. If two or more annual reports are prepared from separate records at the same address, they shall be counted as separate adjusting locations.

(b) If the above table fails to produce sufficient funds to meet the total anticipated costs for the administration of the self-insurance program by the Director, an additional charge per employee covered by each self-insurance plan shall be made to cover these costs.

(c) The Chief shall invoice each private self-insurer on or before December 1 of each year an assessment for the total cost of administration of the private Self-Insurance Plans program for the current fiscal year. Payment is due thirty (30) days after the date of the invoice.

(d) Each private self-insured certificate holder whose certificate is revoked after June 30, 2001 shall pay the full license fee assessment for the next five full calendar years after the date of revocation order or until it is no longer required to post a security deposit.

Note: Authority cited: Sections 54, 55, 3702.5 and 3702.10, Labor Code. Reference: Sections 59, 3700, 3702.5 and 3702.10, Labor Code.

History: 1. Repealer of article 4 (section 15230) and new article 4 (sections 15230-15233) filed 6-1-72; effective thirtieth day thereafter (Register 72, No. 23).

2. Amendment filed 1-21-92; operative 2-20-92 (Register 92, No. 13).

3. New subsection (e) filed 7-27-93; operative 8-26-93 (Register 93, No. 31).

4. Amendment of article heading filed 6-30-94; operative 6-30-94 (Register 94, No. 26).

5. Amendment of subsections (a), (c) and (e) filed 4-19-2001; operative 5-19-2001 (Register 2001, No. 16).

6. Amendment filed 3-2-2009; operative 3-2-2009 pursuant to Government Code section 11343.4 (Register 2009, No. 10).

7. Amendment filed 12-14-2016; operative 1-1-2017 pursuant to Government Code section 11343.4(b)(3) (Register 2016, No. 51).

Ref.: Hanna §§ 1.19, 2.11; Herlick Handbook § 3.20.

§15231. Public Sector License Fee.

A public sector self-insurer shall not be subject to the payment of the annual license fee assessment.

Note: Authority cited: Sections 54, 55 and 3702.10, Labor Code. Reference: Sections 59, 3700, 3702.5 and 3702.10, Labor Code.

History: 1. Amendment filed 11-19-75; effective thirtieth day thereafter (Register 75, No. 47).

2. Amendment filed 11-21-78; effective thirtieth day thereafter (Register 78, No. 47).

3. Amendment filed 1-21-92; operative 2-20-92 (Register 92, No. 13).

§15232. User Funding Assessment.

The Manager shall collect the user funding assessment from all self-insurers and the State of California as set forth in Sections 15600–15610 of these regulations.

Note: Authority cited: Sections 54, 55, 62.5 and 3702.10, Labor Code. Reference: Sections 59, 62.5, 3700, 3702.9 and 3702.10, Labor Code.

History: 1. Amendment filed 11-21-78; effective thirtieth day thereafter (Register 78, No. 47).

2. Amendment filed 1-21-92; operative 2-20-92 (Register 92, No. 13).

3. Editorial correction by official state publisher of section heading (Register 96, No. 36).

§15233. Fraud Investigation and Prosecution Assessment.

The Manager shall collect the state fraud investigation and prosecution surcharge from all self insurers and the State of California as set forth in Sections 15600-15610 of these regulations.

Note: Authority cited: Sections 54, 55, 62.5, 62.6 and 3702.10, Labor Code. Reference: Sections 59, 3700, 3702.5 and 3702.10, Labor Code.

History: 1. New section filed 6-30-94; operative 6-30-94 (Register 94, No. 26). For prior history, see Register 75, No. 47.

§15234. Cal/OSHA Targeted Inspection and Consultation Assessment.

The Manager shall collect the Cal/OSHA Targeted Inspection and Consultation Assessment from all affected self insurers as set forth in Sections 15600 and 15601.7 of these regulations.

Note: Authority cited: Sections 54, 55, 62.7, 62.9 and 3702.10, Labor Code. Reference: Sections 59, 62.7, 62.9, 3700, 3702.5 and 3702.10, Labor Code.

History: 1. New section filed 9-6-96; operative 10-6-96 (Register 96, No. 36).

ARTICLE 5
Self-Insurer's Annual Report

§15250. Required Deposit. [Repealed]

Note: Authority cited: Sections 54, 55 and 3702.10, Labor Code. Reference: Sections 55 and 3702.10, Labor Code.

History: 1. Repealer and new section filed 6-1-72; effective thirtieth day thereafter (Register 72, No. 23).

2. Amendment filed 11-19-75; effective thirtieth day thereafter (Register 75, No. 47).

3. Amendment filed 11-21-78; effective thirtieth day thereafter (Register 78, No. 47).

4. Amendment of article heading filed 10-16-92; operative 11-16-92 (Register 92, No. 42).

5. Repealer of section and amendment of Note filed 12-22-92; operative 1-21-93 (Register 93, No. 2).

6. Amendment of article heading filed 12-14-2016; operative 1-1-2017 pursuant to Government Code section 11343.4(b)(3) (Register 2016, No. 51).

§15250.1. Maintenance of Deposit. [Repealed]

Note: Authority cited: Sections 54, 55 and 3702.10, Labor Code. Reference: Sections 54, 55 and 3702.10, Labor Code.

History: 1. New section filed 6-1-72; effective thirtieth day thereafter (Register 72, No. 23).

2. Repealer of text and new Note filed 10-16-92; operative 11-16-92 (Register 92, No. 42).

§15251. Self-Insurer's Annual Report.

(a) Each self-insurer shall file a Self-Insurer's Annual Report every year as required by subsections (b) through (g) of this section and shall continue to file a Self-Insurer's Annual Report annually after revocation of the Certificate of Consent to Self-Insure until a final Self-Insurer's Annual Report has been filed showing all claims have been closed and there are no remaining claims with the expectation of future liabilities. Each year no later than sixty (60) days before the deadline for filing the Self-Insurer's Annual Report pursuant to subsection (b) or subsection (c) of this section, whichever applies, the Chief shall post the Annual Report form, along with instructions for completing the form and showing the years to be reported, on the website of the Office of Self-Insurance Plans at http://www.dir.ca.gov/osip. Each self-insurer shall file a Self-Insurer's Annual Report via an on-line platform provided by OSIP as follows:

(1) Form AR-1 (1-2016) for individual private and private group self-insurers;

(2) Form AR-2 (rev. 1-2020) for all public self-insurers, including those that are members of a Joint Powers Authority;

(b) For private self-insurers, individual or with a group, the report shall be filed on or before March 1 of each year and shall include the following information:

(1) General Information.

(A) Certificate to Self-Insure number, status of certificate, and period of report.

(B) Name and address of master certificate holder, state of incorporation, federal tax identification number, and first three (3) digits of North American Industry Classification System (NAICS).

(C) List of all subsidiaries or affiliate companies that are covered by the master certificate to self-insure, their state of incorporation, and their subsidiary/affiliate certificate number.

(D) Notification of any reincorporation, merger, change in name or identity or any additions to the self-insurance program by the master certificate holder or any subsidiary/affiliate company during the reporting period.

(E) Name and address of person to whom all correspondence related to self-insurance should be addressed.

(F) Employment and wages paid in that calendar year as reported to Employment Development Department on the employer's Form DE-9 Quarterly Report or other similar Employment Development form used to report employment and wages in that calendar year.

EXCEPTION: A Certificate to Self-Insure that is revoked for three full years is not required to submit this employment and wage information.

(2) Claims Liability and Administrator Information.

A Liabilities by Reporting Location report shall be submitted by each claims administrator administering claims for the said self-insurer and shall include:

(A) All claims reported on or before December 31 of each of the five (5) prior calendar years (January 1 through December 31), showing indemnity and medical payments grouped as incurred liability, paid to date and future liability.

(B) All open claims reported prior to the five (5) years shall also be reported as in subsection (b)(2)(A), but in a single line entry;

(C) For the reporting year of the annual report the total of indemnity and medical future liability, the total estimated future liability of claims, the total benefits paid, number of medical only cases reported, number of indemnity cases reported; number of fatality cases, number of claims for which the employer or administrator was notified of representation by an attorney or legal representative in the reporting year, and number of new applications for adjudication received for any claims that year.

(D) Total number of open indemnity cases in all years.

(E) Name, address and Certificate to Administer number of the self-insurer's claims administrator.

(F) Notification of any change in administrator during the period covered by the report and, if applicable, the name and address of the prior administrator.

(G) A certification by the qualified claims administrator that the report is true, correct and complete with respect to the workers' compensation liabilities incurred and paid, signed and dated with the name and address of the said administrator completing the Liabilities by Reporting Location page.

(3) Location of Claims Records Information. The name and address of any location other than the current administrator where self-insurance claims records are stored.

(4) Insurance Information. Name and policy number of any standard workers' compensation insurance policy, specific excess workers' compensation insurance policy, or aggregate worker's compensation insurance policy held by the self-insurer along with policy issue date and retention levels of liability of the policies.

(5) Open Indemnity Claims Information. A list of all open indemnity claims by reporting location by year, and alphabetically within each year. The list shall:

(A) Show the name of each claimant, date of injury, description of injury, amount of benefits paid-to-date in indemnity and medical payments and estimated future liability of claim for indemnity and medical benefits.

NOTE: Computer Loss Runs showing the information requested and organized as set forth in this subsection will be acceptable in lieu of the List of Open Indemnity Claims.

(B) Show any open claim reported to the carrier of a specific excess insurance policy, and for which the carrier has not denied in writing the claim liability in whole or part above the retention level of the policy. The list shall include the name of the claimant, claim number, date of injury, description of injury, carrier name and policy number, policy coverage period, retention level of policy and paid to date in indemnity or medical benefits, and the estimated future liability of the claim minus the total unpaid employer retention, which equals the total unpaid carrier liability. The list shall also indicate whether the claim has been reported to a carrier, if the claim has been accepted by the carrier, if the carrier has denied any part of the liability of the claim.

(6) Specific Excess Coverage Calculation. A calculation which includes a total of all unpaid carrier liability.

(7) Company Officer Certification Information. The name, title, address, phone number and signature of the company officer authorized to certify that the report is true, correct and complete and acknowledging the company's responsibility to post and maintain the required security deposit that is due as a result of this report.

(c) For all public self-insurers, whether or not a member of a joint powers authority, the report shall be filed by October 1 of each year to cover liabilities during the July 1-June 30 fiscal year and shall include:

(1) General Information.

(A) Name and address of master certificate holder (individual agency or joint powers authority as applicable), federal employer identification number, and type of public agency.

(B) Agency name and certificate numbers of all of the joint powers authority's members.

(C) A certification by the individual public agency or joint powers authority official that the report is true, correct and complete.

(D) Notification of any reincorporation, merger, change in name or identity or any additions to the self-insurance program by the master certificate holder or any subsidiary/affiliate company during the reporting period, and identification of any employees not included in the self-insurance program.

(E) Name, address, telephone number, and email address of person to whom all correspondence related to self-insurance should be addressed.

(F) Employment and wages paid in that fiscal year as reported to Employment Development Department on the employer's Form DE-9 Quarterly Report or other similar Employment Development form used to report employment and wages in that fiscal year.

EXCEPTION: A public employer whose Certificate of Consent to Self-Insure has been revoked is not required to submit employment and wage information.

(2) Liability Report and Administrator Information.

A Liabilities Report which shall include:

(A) All claims reported shall be on a fiscal year basis (starting July 1 and ending June 30 of the reporting years), with all claims reported on or before June 30 of each of the five prior fiscal years, showing indemnity and medical payments grouped as incurred liability, paid to date and future liability.

(B) All open claims reported prior to the five years shall also be reported as required in (b)(2)(A), but in a single line entry.

(C) Each Joint Powers Authorities (JPA) shall report the consolidated liabilities of all members of the JPA on one Liabilities Report.

(D) A Liabilities by Reporting Location Report shall be completed in full for each claims adjusting location in addition to the consolidated report totaling liabilities from all locations.

(E) For any Joint Powers Authority, one list of all open indemnity claims may be consolidated into a single listing for the entire JPA, as long as the individual JPA member is identified for each claim.

(3) Claims Information for each year shall meet the requirements of subsection (b), except that no deposit calculation page shall be submitted as required for private self-insurers pursuant to subsection (b)(7).

(4) Aggregate Claims Information. Specify for claims in the current fiscal year and in each of the past five fiscal years, and for claims reported prior to the five years in a single line entry, aggregate amounts for each of the indicated categories on Form AR-2, showing the number of claims, amount of disability benefits paid, amount of medical costs paid, legal and loss adjustment expenses paid, and estimated future liabilities. Figures must reflect amounts paid and number of claims, as specified on the Aggregate Claims Information portion of Form AR-2 during the reporting year, as of the end of the indicated fiscal year of the date of loss, for the life of the claim to date of the report.

(5) The claims information required by Form AR-2 may be submitted electronically or by hard copy that includes the same data elements required by Form AR-2. An Appendix of terms used in Public Self-Insurer Report Forms P-1, J-1, and AR-2 follows section 15203.11.

(d) The Chief may, for good cause, require any self-insurer to submit a Self-Insurer's Annual Report covering a six-month interim period, in addition to the annual report specified in subsection (b) and (c) of this section.

(1) For private self-insurers, such interim reports, when required, shall cover the period starting January 1 and ending June 30 of each year and shall be due on September 1 of each year.

(2) Public self-insurer's interim reports shall cover July 1 through December 31 and shall be due on March 1 of each year.

(e) The Chief shall assess the civil penalty set forth in Labor Code Section 3702.9(a) against any self-insurer for failure to file a complete and timely Self-Insurer's Annual Report. Continued failure to file an Annual Report sixty (60) days after assessment of civil penalties pursuant to Section 3702.9(a) shall be good cause for revocation of a certificate to self-insure.

(f) For good cause shown by the self-insurer or its administrative agency, the Chief may grant additional time to a self-insurer to file the report without penalty.

(g) Unless otherwise approved by the Chief, the consolidated liabilities report and reporting location reports (page 3 of the annual report) shall be signed by a competent person, as demonstrated pursuant to Section 15452(b) of these regulations, in the employment of the self-insurer or administrative agency for the self-insurance plan.

(h) The employer's certification on the Self-Insurer's report shall be signed by:

(1) an officer or employee of the self-insurer authorized to sign documents for self-insurance matters; or

(2) an authorized public self-insurer officer or employee; or

(3) an authorized officer or employee of the joint powers authority to which the public agency is a member; or

(4) an authorized officer or employee of the Self-Insurer's Security Fund where the Director has turned over responsibility for an insolvent private self-insurer's claim liability to the Fund pursuant to Labor Code Section 3701.5(c).

Note: Authority cited: Sections 54, 55 and 3702.10, Labor Code. Reference: Sections 59, 129, 3700, 3701.5, 3702.2, 3702.3, 3702.9 and 3702.10, Labor Code; and Sections 1063.1 and 1063.3, Insurance Code.

History: 1. Amendment filed 6-1-72; effective thirtieth day thereafter (Register 72, No. 23).

2. Amendment of section heading and text filed 10-16-92; operative 11-16-92 (Register 92, No. 42).

3. Amendment of subsections (a) and (b)(5)(B) and new subsection (b)(5)(B)1 filed 8-10-93; operative 8-10-93 (Register 93, No. 33).

4. Amendment of subsections (a)-(b), (b)(1)(F) Exception and (b)(5)(B) filed 6-30-94; operative 6-30-94 (Register 94, No. 26).

5. Change without regulatory effect amending subsections (b)(1)(F) and (c)(1)(F) filed 10-18-95 pursuant to section 100, title 1, California Code of Regulations (Register 95, No. 42).

6. Amendment filed 5-7-2001; operative 6-6-2001 (Register 2001, No. 19).

7. Change without regulatory effect amending subsection (a)(1) and form A4-40a (incorporated by reference) filed 8-1-2001 pursuant to section 100, title 1, California Code of Regulations (Register 2001, No. 31).

8. Change without regulatory effect amending subsection (b)(2)(A)(7.) filed 4-7-2003 pursuant to section 100, title 1, California Code of Regulations (Register 2003, No. 15).

9. Amendment of section and Note filed 3-2-2009; operative 3-2-2009 pursuant to Government Code section 11343.4 (Register 2009, No. 10).

10. Amendment of subsections (b)(1)(F) and (c)(1)(F) filed 9-19-2011; operative 10-19-2011 (Register 2011, No. 38).

11. Amendment of section heading and section filed 12-14-2016; operative 1-1-2017 pursuant to Government Code section 11343.4(b)(3) (Register 2016, No. 51).

12. Amendment of subsections (a)(2) and (c)(1)(E) and new subsections (c)(4)-(5) filed 5-14-2020; operative 7-1-2020 (Register 2020, No. 20).

Ref.: Hanna §§ 1.19, 2.11[1], [2], [3]; Herlick Handbook § 3.20.

§15252. Annual Report Form. [Repealed]

Note: Authority cited: Sections 54, 55 and 59, Labor Code. Reference: Sections 129, 3700, 3700(b), 3701, 3702, 3702.5, 3702.6, 3703, 3704 and 3705, Labor Code.

History: 1. Amendment filed 12-3-69; effective thirtieth day thereafter (Register 69, No. 49).

2. Repealer and new section filed 6-1-72; effective thirtieth day thereafter (Register 72, No. 23).

3. Amendment filed 11-19-75; effective thirtieth day thereafter (Register 75, No. 47).

4. Amendment filed 11-21-78; effective thirtieth day thereafter (Register 78, No. 47).

5. Repealer filed 10-16-92; operative 11-16-92 (Register 92, No. 42).

§15253. Late Annual Report Penalty. [Repealed]

Note: Authority cited: Sections 54, 55 and 3702.10, Labor Code. Reference: Sections 54, 55 and 3702.10, Labor Code.

History: 1. New section filed 6-1-72; effective thirtieth day thereafter (Register 72, No. 23).

2. Amendment filed 11-21-78; effective thirtieth day thereafter (Register 78, No. 47).

3. Repealer of text and amendment of Note filed 10-16-92; operative 11-16-92 (Register 92, No. 42).

4. Editorial correction restoring repealed section (Register 2016, No. 53).

ARTICLE 6
Estimating Work Injury Claims and Medical Reports

§15300. Estimating and Reporting Work Injury Claims.

(a) A list of open indemnity claims shall be submitted with each self insurer's annual report as required by Section 15251(b)(5)(A)-(B) and (c)(2)(A)-(B).

(b) The administrator shall set a realistic estimate of future liability for each indemnity claim listed on the self insurer's annual report based on computations which reflect the probable total future cost of compensation and medical benefits due or that can reasonably be expected to be due over the life of the claim. Each estimate listed on the self insurer's annual report shall be based on information in possession of the administrator at the-ending date of the period of time covered by the annual report. Estimated future liabilities listed on the annual report must represent the probable total future cost of compensation for the injury or disease based on information documented as in possession of the administrator at the ending date of the period of time covered by the annual report. In setting estimates of future liability, the administrator shall adhere to the following principles:

(1) Each estimate of future liability shall separately reflect an indemnity component and a medical component. The indemnity component shall include the estimated future cost of all temporary disability, permanent disability, death benefits including burial costs, supplemental job displacement benefit voucher and vocational rehabilitation including vendor costs. The medical component shall include the estimated future cost of all medical treatment, including costs of medical cost containment programs if those costs are allocated to the particular claim, and the estimated future cost of medical evaluations. On or after July 1, 2012 for public self insurers and on or after January 1, 2012 for private self insurers, the medical component shall not include the cost of medical cost containment programs incurred with respect to a particular claim or which can be allocated to a particular claim whether done by an outside vendor or by the self insurer. These costs shall be included as allocated loss adjustment expense amount. Any medical cost containment program costs that cannot be allocated to a particular claim shall be considered unallocated loss adjustment expenses.

NOTE: Medical cost containment program costs include but are not limited to:

(A) Bill audit expenses for any medical service rendered, such as hospital bills, nursing home bills, physician bills, chiropractic bills, medical equipment charges, pharmacy charges, physical therapy bills, and medical vendor bills;

(B) Hospital and other treatment utilization reviews including precertification/preadmission, and concurrent or retrospective reviews; and

(C) Access fees and other expenses incurred with respect to managed care organizations, such as, preferred provider networks/ organizations (PPOs), medical provider networks (MPNs), pharmacy benefit networks, and Health Care Organizations (HCOs).

Estimates of future liability shall include any increases in compensation in either the indemnity or medical component reasonably expected to be payable pursuant to Labor Code Sections 132a, 4553, and/or 5814.

(2) In estimating future permanent disability costs, where there are conflicting permanent disability ratings, the estimate shall be based on the higher rating unless there is sufficient evidence in the claim file to support a lower estimate.

(3) In estimating future medical costs where the injured worker's injury has not reached maximum medical improvement or permanent and stationary status, the estimate shall be based on projected costs for the total

anticipated period of treatment throughout the life of the claim.

(4) In estimating future medical costs where the injured worker's injury has reached maximum medical improvement or permanent and stationary status, the estimate shall be based on average annual costs over the past three years since the injury reached maximum medical improvement or permanent and stationary status, or a lesser period if three years have not passed since the injury reached maximum medical improvement or permanent and stationary status, projected over the life expectancy of the injured worker. Estimates shall include any additional costs such as medical procedures or surgeries that can reasonably be expected over the life of the claim.

(5) Estimates based on average past costs shall be increased to include any costs that can reasonably be expected to occur that are not included within the averages. Estimates based on average past costs may be reduced to account for any treatment not reasonably expected to occur in the future based on medical documentation in possession of the administrator.

(6) Estimates of future medical costs based on average past costs shall not be reduced based on undocumented anticipated reductions in frequency of treatment or to reflect the substitution of treatments with a lower cost than utilized by the injured worker that may be available but that the injured worker is not utilizing. Estimates based on average past costs may be reduced based on reductions in the approved medical fee schedule and based on utilization review, except that reductions in estimates based on utilization review may not be reduced if the reductions are reasonably disputed. Estimates of future liability may be reduced based on the expectation of a third party recovery only in instances where an Order allowing credit has been issued pursuant to Labor Code Section 3861.

(7) Estimates of lifetime medical care and life pension benefits shall be determined based on the injured worker's life expectancy according to the most recent U.S. Life Expectancy Tables as reported by the U.S. Department of Health and Human Services, Centers for Disease Control and Prevention. Note: the most recent life expectancy tables can be found at http://www.dir.ca.gov/SIP/pubandforms.htm.

(8) Estimates of permanent disability shall not be reduced based on apportionment unless the claim file includes documentation supporting apportionment.

(9) Estimates shall not be reduced to reflect present value of future benefits.

(c) All medical-only claims reported on the self insurer's annual report shall be estimated on the basis of computations which will develop the total future cost of medical benefits due or that can reasonably expected to be due based on information documented as in possession of the administrator at the ending date of the period of time covered by the annual report.

(d) Estimates of future liability shall not be decreased based on projected third party recoveries or projected reimbursements from aggregate excess insurance, nor shall reported paid costs be decreased based on third party recoveries or aggregate excess insurance reimbursements.

(e) The incurred liability estimate on known claims may be capped at the retention level of any specific excess workers' compensation insurance policy to the extent that each claim has not been denied in writing by the carrier. The self insurer's claims administrator shall list each claim covered by a specific excess insurance policy on Part VI-B of the Self Insurer's Annual Report. An adjustment to the total deposit required to be posted shall be made for claims covered by specific excess insurance policy on the annual report to the extent that they meet the requirements in Section 15251(b)(5)(B) of these regulations.

(f) Estimates of incurred liability, payments-made-to-date and estimated future liability of all compensation benefits shall be made immediately available at the time of audit if not already documented in the claim file, or when requested by the Manager.

(g) The administrator shall adjust the estimate immediately upon receipt of medical reports, orders of the Appeals Board, or other relevant information that affects the valuation of the claim. Each estimate shall be reviewed no less than annually. Estimates set by a prior administrator shall be reviewed by the current administrator before filing the Self Insurer's Annual Report.

Note: Authority cited: Sections 54, 55 and 3702.10, Labor Code. Reference: Sections 54, 55, 59, 129, 132a, 3700, 3702.3, 3702.6, 3702.10, 3703, 3740-3745, 3861, 4553 and 5814, Labor Code.

History: 1. Amendment filed 12-3-69; effective thirtieth day thereafter (Register 69, No. 49).

2. Amendment of article heading, section heading, section and new Note filed 8-10-93; operative 9-9-93 (Register 93, No. 33).

3. Repealer and new subsection (b), new subsections (b)(1)-(4), amendment of subsection (c), repealer and new subsection (d), new subsection (g) and amendment of Note filed 2-9-2006; operative 3-11-2006 (Register 2006, No. 6).

4. Amendment of subsections (a)-(b)(1), new subsections (b)(1)(A)-(C) and amendment of subsection (b)(7) filed 9-19-2011; operative 10-19-2011 (Register 2011, No. 38).

§15301. Revision of Estimates.

The Manager shall have authority to revise private sector self insurer's estimates when information from any relevant source in the Manager's possession indicates the estimates are inaccurate or inadequate. Deposit recalculations shall be made at the same time or after the self-insurer has been notified of the Manager's revisions and given an opportunity to object to the increases in deposit or revision to liability estimates.

Note: Authority cited: Sections 54, 55 and 3702.10, Labor Code. Reference: Sections 54, 55, 59, 129, 3700, 3701.5, 3702.3, 3702.6, 3702.10 and 3740-3745, Labor Code.

History: 1. Amendment of section and new Note filed 8-10-93; operative 9-9-93 (Register 93, No. 33).

§15302. Medical Reports.

The Manager, when deemed necessary for proper administration of self-insurance, may require a self-insurer to provide a true copy of any relevant medical report in the possession of the self-insurer, its agent, or representative.

Note: Authority cited: Sections 54, 55 and 3702.10, Labor Code. Reference: Sections 54, 55, 59, 129, 3700, 3701, 3701.5, 3702, 3702.3, 3702.6, 3702.10 and 3740-3745, Labor Code.

History: 1. Amendment filed 11-19-75; effective thirtieth day thereafter (Register 75, No. 47).

2. Amendment of section and new Note filed 8-10-93; operative 9-9-93 (Register 93, No. 33).

§15303. Medical, Surgical, Hospital Contract.

No contract for medical, surgical, or hospital services shall relieve the self-insurer from reporting the total future determined and estimated cost of said services in accordance with Section 15300 of these regulations. For purposes of this section, a valid and effective policy of workers' compensation insurance providing for full payment of medical, surgical, or hospital services shall not be construed as a contract for medical, surgical, or hospital services.

Note: Authority cited: Sections 54, 55 and 3702.10, Labor Code. Reference: Sections 54, 55, 59, 129, 3700, 3701, 3701.5, 3702.3, 3702.6, 3703 and 3740-3745, Labor Code.

History: 1. Amendment filed 11-19-75; effective thirtieth day thereafter (Register 75, No. 47).

2. Amendment of section and new Note filed 8-10-93; operative 9-9-93 (Register 93, No. 33).

ARTICLE 7

Injury and Illness Prevention Program

§15350. Validity of Certificate. [Repealed]

Note: Authority cited: Sections 54 and 55, Labor Code. Reference: Sections 3700, 3701, 3702, 3702.5, 3702.6, 3703, 3704 and 3705, Labor Code.

History: 1. Amendment filed 12-3-69; effective thirtieth day thereafter (Register 69, No. 49).

2. Amendment filed 11-19-75; effective thirtieth day thereafter (Register 75, No. 47).

3. Amendment of article heading, repealer of section, and adoption of Note filed 12-18-92; operative 1-19-93 (Register 92, No. 51).

§15350.1. Certificate. [Repealed]

Note: Authority cited: Sections 54 and 55, Labor Code. Reference: Sections 3700, 3700(b), 3701, 3702, 3702.5, 3702.6, 3703, 3704 and 3705, Labor Code.

History: 1. New section filed 11-21-78; effective thirtieth day thereafter (Register 78, No. 47).

2. Repealer of section and amendment of Note filed 12-18-92; operative 1-19-93 (Register 92, No. 51).

§15350.2. Notice to Employees. [Repealed]

Note: Authority cited: Sections 54 and 55, Labor Code. Reference: Sections 3700, 3700(b), 3701, 3702, 3702.5, 3702.6, 3703, 3704 and 3705, Labor Code.

History: 1. New section filed 11-21-78; effective thirtieth day thereafter (Register 78, No. 47).

2. Repealer of section and amendment of Note filed 12-18-92; operative 1-19-93 (Register 92, No. 51).

§15350.5. Non-Permitted Use. [Repealed]

Note: Authority cited: Sections 54 and 55, Labor Code. Reference: Sections 3700, 3700(b), 3701, 3702, 3702.5, 3702.6, 3703, 3704 and 3705, Labor Code.

History: 1. New section filed 11-21-78; effective thirtieth day thereafter (Register 78, No. 47).

2. Repealer of section and amendment of Note filed 12-18-92; operative 1-19-93 (Register 92, No. 51).

§15351. Extent of Coverage. [Repealed]

Note: Authority cited: Sections 54 and 55, Labor Code. Reference: Sections 3700, 3700(b), 3701, 3702, 3702.5, 3702.6, 3703, 3704 and 3705, Labor Code.

History: 1. Repealer and new section filed 6-1-72; effective thirtieth day thereafter (Register 72, No. 23).

2. Amendment filed 11-19-75; effective thirtieth day thereafter (Register 75, No. 47).

3. Repealer of section and adoption of Note filed 12-18-92; operative 1-19-93 (Register 92, No. 51).

§15352. Permitted Insurance. [Repealed]

Note: Authority cited: Sections 54 and 55, Labor Code. Reference: Sections 3700, 3700(b), 3701, 3702, 3702.5, 3702.6, 3703, 3704 and 3705, Labor Code.

History: 1. Repealer and new section filed 6-1-72; effective thirtieth day thereafter (Register 72, No. 23).

2. Amendment filed 11-19-75; effective thirtieth day thereafter (Register 75, No. 47).

3. Repealer of section and adoption of Note filed 12-18-92; operative 1-19-93 (Register 92, No. 51).

§15353. Injury and Illness Prevention Program.

(a) As part of the application process, an individual private sector applicant for a Certificate to Self-Insure shall certify they have implemented an effective Injury Illness Prevention Program as required by Labor Code section 6401.7 and provide the name, title and contact information for the person within their organization responsible for workplace safety.

NOTE: The pamphlet "A sample of an Injury and Illness Prevention Program" can be obtained from the Cal/OSHA Consultation Services.

Note: Authority cited: Sections 54, 55 and 3702.10, Labor Code. Reference: Sections 59, 3700, 3702, 3702.10, 6314.5, 6319 and 6401.7, Labor Code.

History: 1. New section filed 11-21-78; effective thirtieth day thereafter (Register 78, No. 47).

2. Amendment of section heading, section and Note filed 12-18-92; operative 1-19-93 (Register 92, No. 51).

3. Amendment of subsections (a)-(a)(1)(A) filed 3-2-2009; operative 3-2-2009 pursuant to Government Code section 11343.4 (Register 2009, No. 10).

4. Amendment filed 12-14-2016; operative 1-1-2017 pursuant to Government Code section 11343.4(b)(3) (Register 2016, No. 51).

5. Editorial correction implementing 12-14-2016 amendment (Register 2016, No. 53).

Ref.: Hanna §§ 1.19, 2.11; Herlick Handbook § 3.20.

§15354. Willful or Repeat Violation of Injury Prevention Program by a Self Insurer.

Any private employer self insurer identified to the Director by the Division of Occupational Safety and Health pursuant to Labor Code Section 6319(f) shall provide proof of abatement of the repeat or willful violation of Section 3203 of Title 8, California Code of Regulations to the Manager. Failure to abate shall be good cause to revoke the

Certificate to Self Insure issued to that self insurer after the opportunity for a hearing before the Director.

Note: Authority cited: Sections 54, 55 and 3702.10, Labor Code. Reference: Sections 54, 55, 59, 3700, 3702, 3702.10, 6314.5, 6319, 6401.7, Labor Code.

History: 1. New section filed 12-18-92; operative 1-19-93 (Register 92, No. 51).

ARTICLE 8
Transfer of Liabilities

§15360. Transfer of Claim Liabilities.

A current or former self insurer may transfer claim liabilities to a third party as set forth in subsections (a) through (e) of this section.

(a) Self-insured workers' compensation claim liabilities cannot be transferred to another entity without first applying for and receiving permission from the Director. Except as provided in Labor Code Section 3702.8(c), the claim liabilities being transferred shall be assumed and guaranteed with the standard Agreement of Assumption and Guarantee of Liabilities as provided for in Section 15211.2 of these regulations, with an assumption resolution executed by the Board of Directors if a corporation, by the general partners if a partnership, or by the owners if a sole proprietorship of the entity taking over the liabilities.

(1) The new holder of claim liabilities shall post the security deposit determined necessary by the Manager pursuant to Article 3 or Article 13 of these regulations, whichever is applicable.

(2) The Manager shall be provided with copies of the necessary documents involved in a sale or transfer of claim liabilities from a self-insurer to another party.

(3) All other duties of a self insured employer in Labor Code Section 3702.8(a) shall be complied with by the self insured employer.

(b) The Manager may authorize the contractual transfer of claim liabilities, other than through a special excess worker's compensation insurance policy, from a self-insurer to an admitted worker's compensation insurance carrier provided:

(1) A copy of the signed contract between the self-insurer and carrier is provided to the Manager;

(2) The self-insurer continues to post the amount of deposit required by the Manager pursuant to Article 3 of these regulations;

(3) The claims contractually transferred to the carrier are administered in California by an admitted carrier or by an administrative agency holding a Certificate to Administer;

(4) Self Insurer's Annual Reports are submitted by the self-insurer as required by these regulations until all claims are resolved; and

(5) All other duties of a self insurer in Labor Code Section 3702.8(a) are complied with by the self insured employer.

(c) Where a former self-insurer transfers liabilities to a carrier via a special excess workers' compensation insurance policy as provided in Labor Code Section 3702.8(c), but no carrier performance bond is posted, the self-insurer's security deposit shall be held for three years before release. Whether a performance bond is posted or not, the director shall not accept the special excess policy as meeting the requirements of Labor Code Section 3702.8(c)(3) unless the excess carrier or its parent company has an acceptable credit rating as set forth below:

(1) Standard and Poors Insurer Financial Strength Rating of A or better rating, or

(2) A.M. Best Company, Financial Strength Rating of B+ or better rating.

(d) Claim liabilities of a member public agency of a pooling workers' compensation joint powers authority may be transferred if:

(1) The joint powers authority agreement permits a member public agency to take their claim liabilities out of the joint powers authority pool if the public agency elects to do so;

(2) The public agency member elects to transfer its claim liability; and

(3) The claims are transferred to another workers' compensation joint authority, or to a self administered or administrative agency administered or carrier administered self insurance program.

(e) Private group self insurers and/or their group members or former group members shall not transfer their claim liabilities except as provided by Labor Code Section 3702.8(c) and subsection (c) of this section, or as provided by either subsection (f) or subsection (g) of this section.

(f) A current or former group member's claims may be transferred to another private self insured group if the Bylaws of the two groups permit the transfer, and if the transfer is approved by the Manager.

(g) A current or former group member's claims may be transferred entirely to the individual member under its individual Certificate of Consent to Self Insure if all of the following apply:

(1) If the Bylaws of the group self insurer permit the transfer;

(2) If a valid individual Certificate of Consent to Self Insure is issued to the former group member by the Director; and

(3) If the transfer is approved by the Manager.

Note: Authority cited: Sections 54, 55 and 3702.10, Labor Code. Reference: Sections 129, 3700, 3700(b), 3701, 3702, 3702.5, 3702.6, 3702.8, 3703, 3705 and 3740-3745, Labor Code.

History: 1. Amendment of article heading, repealer of section 15360, and renumbering and amendment of former section 15361.5 to section 15360 filed 10-27-93; operative 11-26-93 (Register 93, No. 44).

2. Amendment filed 6-30-94; operative 6-30-94 (Register 94, No. 26).

3. Amendment filed 3-2-2009; operative 3-2-2009 pursuant to Government Code section 11343.4 (Register 2009, No. 10).

Ref.: Hanna §§ 1.19, 2.11; Herlick Handbook § 3.20.

§15361. Cessation of Business, Etc. [Repealed]

Note: Authority cited: Sections 54, 55 and 3702.10, Labor Code. Reference: Sections 54, 55 and 3702.10, Labor Code.

History: 1. Amendment filed 6-1-72; effective thirtieth day thereafter (Register 72, No. 23).

2. Repealer filed 10-27-93; operative 11-26-93 (Register 93, No. 44).

§15361.5. Workers' Compensation Liabilities. [Renumbered]

Note: Authority cited: Sections 54, 55 and 3702.10, Labor Code. Reference: Sections 129, 3700, 3700(b), 3701, 3702, 3702.5, 3702.6, 3702.8, 3703, 3705 and 3740-3745, Labor Code.

History: 1. New section filed 11-21-78; effective thirtieth day thereafter (Register 78, No. 47).

2. Renumbering and amendment of former section 15361.5 to section 15360 filed 10-27-93; operative 11-26-93 (Register 93, No. 44).

§15362. Termination of Surety Bond. [Repealed]

Note: Authority cited: Sections 54, 55 and 3702.10, Labor Code. Reference: Sections 54, 55 and 3702.10, Labor Code.

History: 1. Amendment filed 11-21-78; effective thirtieth day thereafter (Register 78, No. 47).

2. Repealer filed 10-27-93; operative 11-26-93 (Register 93, No. 44).

ARTICLE 9
Recordkeeping and Audits

§15400. Claim File.

(a) Every self-insurer or its administrative agency shall keep a claim file of each indemnity and medical-only work-injury occurring on or after January 1, 1990, in accordance with Title 8, Section 10101 and Section 10101.1.

(b) For work injuries occurring prior to January 1, 1990, every self insurer shall keep a claim file including those claims which were denied. Said claim file shall contain, but not be limited to, a copy of:

(1) Employers Report of Occupational Injury or Illness, Form No. 5020;

(2) Every report made to the Administrative Director of the Division of Industrial Accidents; including but not limited to the letter of denial to the employee;

(3) Doctor's First Report of Occupational Injury or Illness, Form No. 5021;

(4) Every subsequent relevant medical report;

(5) All applicable orders of the Workers' Compensation Appeals Board and reports relating thereto;

(6) A record of payment of compensation benefits as compensation is defined in Section 3207 of the Labor Code, together with a record of the periods covered by disability payments, including a copy of DIA Form 500, Notice of Termination of Benefits;

(c) For injuries reported on or after January 1, 2006, each self administering self insurer and claims administrative agency shall maintain a claim file for each indemnity and medical-only claim, including denied claims, and shall ensure that each file is complete and current for each claim. Contents of claim files may be in hard copy, in electronic form, or some combination of hard copy and electronic form. Files maintained in hard copy shall be in chronological order with the most recently dated documents on top, or subdivided into sections such as medical reports, benefit notices, correspondence, claim notes, and vocational rehabilitation. In addition to the contents specified in Title 8, California Code of Regulations, Section 10101.1, each indemnity file shall contain itemized written documentation showing the basis for the calculation of estimated future liability and for each change in estimated future liability for the claim. Files or portions of files maintained in electronic form shall be easily retrievable.

Note: Authority cited: Sections 54, 55, 59 and 3702.10, Labor Code. Reference: Sections 59, 129, 3700, 3700(b), 3701, 3702, 3702.1, 3702.5, 3702.6, 3703, 3704 and 3705, Labor Code.

History: 1. Amendment filed 12-3-69; effective thirtieth day thereafter (Register 69, No. 49).

2. Amendment filed 11-19-75; effective thirtieth day thereafter (Register 75, No. 47).

3. New subsection (g) filed 11-21-78; effective thirtieth day thereafter (Register 78, No. 47).

4. Amendment filed 2-19-92; operative 3-20-92 (Register 92, No. 13).

5. Change without regulatory effect amending subsection (a) filed 11-3-96 pursuant to section 100, title 1, California Code of Regulations (Register 96, No. 46).

6. Repealer and new subsection (c) filed 2-9-2006; operative 3-11-2006 (Register 2006, No. 6).

1992 Note: The use of a "Reserve Worksheet" developed by the administrator to document initial estimates of incurred liability and subsequent adjustments to the estimate is recommended.

Ref.: Hanna § 2.11[2].

§15400.1. Claim Log.

(a) After January 1, 1993, every self-insurer or its administrative agency shall maintain:

(1) a manually prepared log of all work injury claims for each self-insurer at each adjusting location in accordance with Title 8, Section 10103 and 10103.1; or

(2) a computerized log of claims for each self-insurer at each adjusting location in accordance with Title 8, Section 10103 and 10103.1.

(b) The claim log shall be maintained at each of the self-insurer's or its administrative agency's claims adjusting locations. The claim log at each location shall be kept current and shall include all claims reported to the adjusting location.

(c) A claim log shall be found to be materially deficient if it fails to contain the elements of Title 8, Section 10103 and 10103.1; or fails to include all reported claims; or is not provided to the Manager or any subsequent administrator in readable form.

Note: Authority cited: Sections 54, 55 and 3702.10, Labor Code. Reference: Sections 59, 129, 3700, 3702.1 and 3702.10, Labor Code.

History: 1. New sections 15400.1, 15400.2, and 15400.3 filed 12-3-69; effective thirtieth day thereafter (Register 69, No. 49).

2. Amendment filed 2-19-92; operative 3-20-92 (Register 92, No. 13).

3. Change without regulatory effect amending subsections (a)(1)-(2) and (c) filed 10-18-95 pursuant to section 100, title 1, California Code of Regulations (Register 95, No. 42).

4. Change without regulatory effect amending subsections (a)(1)-(2) and (c) filed 1-9-98 pursuant to section 100, title 1, California Code of Regulations (Register 98, No. 2).

§15400.2. Maintenance of Records.

(a) All claim files shall be kept and maintained for a period of five years from the date of injury or from the date on which the last provision of compensation benefits occurred as defined in Labor Code Section 3207, whichever is later. Claim files with awards for future benefits shall not be destroyed, but two years after the date of the last provision of workers' compensation benefits as defined in Labor Code Section 3207, they may be converted to an inactive or closed status by the administrator, but only if there is no reasonable expectation that future benefits will be claimed or provided.

(b) Inactive and closed claim files may be microfilmed or electronically stored for storage. However, if the file is not microfilmed or electronically stored the original paper files shall be maintained for at least two years after the claim has been closed or become inactive. Such microfilmed or electronically stored files must be readily reproducible into legible paper form if requested by the Manager for an audit.

(c) All claim files and the claim logs shall be kept and maintained in California unless the Manager has given written approval to a self insurer or former self insurer to administer its workers' compensation self-insurance plan from a location outside of California.

(d) All claim files and claim logs, together with records of all compensation benefit payments, shall be readily available for inspection by the Manager or his representative.

Note: Authority cited: Sections 54, 55 and 3702.10, Labor Code. Reference: Sections 59, 129, 3700, 3702.1 and 3702.10, Labor Code.

History: 1. Amendment filed 2-19-92; operative 3-20-92 (Register 92, No. 13).

2. Amendment of subsection (a) filed 2-9-2006; operative 3-11-2006 (Register 2006, No. 6).

3. Amendment of subsection (b) filed 9-19-2011; operative 10-19-2011 (Register 2011, No. 38).

Ref.: Hanna § 2.11[2].

§15400.3. Maintenance of Records. [Repealed]

Note: Authority cited: Sections 54, 55 and 3702.10, Labor Code. Reference: Sections 55 and 3702.10, Labor Code.

History: 1. Repealer filed 2-19-92; operative 3-20-92 (Register 92, No. 13).

§15401. Self-Insurance Plan Administration. [Repealed]

Note: Authority cited: Sections 54, 55 and 3702.10, Labor Code. Reference: Sections 55 and 3702.10, Labor Code.

History: 1. Repealer filed 2-19-92; operative 3-20-92 (Register 92, No. 13).

§15401.1. Competence. [Repealed]

Note: Authority cited: Sections 54, 55 and 3702.10, Labor Code. Reference: Sections 55 and 3702.10, Labor Code.

History: 1. New section filed 6-1-72; effective thirtieth day thereafter (Register 72, No. 23).

2. Amendment filed 11-19-75; effective thirtieth day thereafter (Register 75, No. 47).

3. Repealer filed 2-19-92; operative 3-20-92 (Register 92, No. 13).

§15401.2. Competency at Adjusting Location. [Repealed]

Note: Authority cited: Sections 54, 55 and 3702.10, Labor Code. Reference: Sections 59 and 3702.10, Labor Code.

History: 1. New section filed 11-19-75; effective thirtieth day thereafter (Register 75, No. 47).

2. Repealer filed 2-19-92; operative 3-20-92 (Register 92, No. 13).

§15402. Notice of Change of Administrator and Location of Records.

(a) Each self-insurer or administrative agency shall annually report on the Self Insurer's Annual Report form to the Manager the name, title, and office address of the person or persons appointed to administer the employer's self-insurance plan and of the location or locations of records required to be kept and maintained pursuant to Section 15400 of these regulations.

(b) The new administrator shall report any changes of the administrative agency administering the employer's self-insurance plan, or any change of location or locations of records in writing to the Manager no later than the date of such change.

Note: Authority cited: Sections 54, 55 and 3702.10, Labor Code. Reference: Sections 59, 129, 3700, 3702.1 and 3702.10, Labor Code.

History: 1. Amendment filed 6-1-72; effective thirtieth day thereafter (Register 72, No. 23).

2. Amendment filed 11-19-75; effective thirtieth day thereafter (Register 75, No. 47).

3. Amendment filed 2-19-92; operative 3-20-92 (Register 92, No. 13).

1992 Note: Reporting required by subsection (b) may be done by submitting a "Report of Changes" on the appropriate Division of Workers' Compensation AE Form 101 or AE Form 102 (see Plate L-1 and L-2 of the Appendix).

§15402.1. Self Insurer's Interim Report.

(a) A self-insurer and its administrative agency shall jointly submit to the Manager a self-insurer's annual report, covering any interim period between regularly scheduled reporting periods whenever any of the following changes occur in the administration of the employer's self insurance plan:

(1) A change from an agency-administered plan to another agency-administered plan, (i.e. from one third party administrator to another third party administrator);

(2) A change from an agency-administered plan to a self-administered plan;

(3) A change from a self-administered plan to an agency-administered plan; or

(b) The interim Self Insurers Annual Report shall be made by the former administrator on the applicable form as required by Section 15251 of these regulations, showing the self-insurer's claims experience as of the date of the change of administrative agencies.

(c) The interim self insurer's annual report shall be due within thirty (30) days of the change of administrators. The self insurer shall provide a copy to the new administrator and three (3) copies to the Manager. The Manager may supply the new administrator with a copy of the interim report.

(d) The new administrator shall submit the year end self insurer's annual report for the self insurer which includes the total loss experience of all open and closed claims from all administrative agencies handling the self insurer's claims during the reporting period.

Note: Authority cited: Sections 54, 55 and 3702.10, Labor Code. Reference: Sections 59, 129, 3700, 3702.1, 3702.2 and 3702.10, Labor Code.

History: 1. New section filed 6-1-72; effective thirtieth day thereafter (Register 72, No. 23).

2. Amendment filed 11-19-75; effective thirtieth day thereafter (Register 75, No. 47).

3. Amendment filed 2-19-92; operative 3-20-92 (Register 92, No. 13).

4. Change without regulatory effect amending subsection (b) filed 12-24-96 pursuant to Government Code section 11343.4(d) (Register 96, No. 52).

5. Repealer of subsection (a)(4) filed 5-10-2001; operative 6-9-2001 (Register 2001, No. 19).

§15402.2. Report of Transfer of Records.

(a) After July 1, 1992, at the time of a change of administration of a self insurance plan, as set forth in Section 15402.1(a) of these regulations, the former administrative agency or previously self administering self insurer shall submit to the Manager and to the new administrative agency a written report containing the following:

(1) A list of all open and closed claims for the self insurer in the possession of the former administrative agency as of the date of the transfer; and

(2) A written description of the physical location of all claimed files, the required claim logs, and any computer data files of the self insurer's plan. Physical location shall include claim files sent to storage and where stored; files sent to the self insurer; and files sent to the new administrator.

(b) Except where specified in a contractual agreement between the self insurer and the former administrative agency, all claim files, claim logs and computerized data files shall be the property of the self insurer and shall be returned to the self insurer or delivered to the new administrator or administrative agency designated by the self insurer.

(c) Failure of an administrative agency or self insurer to provide a Report of Transfer of Records as set forth in this section may be good cause for revocation of a certificate to administer.

Note: Authority cited: Sections 54, 55 and 3702.10, Labor Code. Reference: Sections 59, 129, 3700, 3702, 3702.1, 3702.2, 3702.7 and 3702.10, Labor Code.

History: 1. New section filed 11-19-75; effective thirtieth day thereafter (Register 75, No. 47).

2. Amendment filed 2-19-92; operative 3-20-92 (Register 92, No. 13).

§15402.3. Notice of Change of Membership in a Joint Powers Authority or in a Private Group Self Insurer.

(a) The joint powers authority shall notify the Manager when a Public entity with an affiliate certificate to self insure changes its membership from the existing joint powers authority to

(1) another joint powers authority;

(2) a carrier insured plan or;

(3) an independent self insured plan.

(b) The group administrator of each private group self insurer shall notify the Manager when any group member holding an Affiliate Certificate changes its membership from the existing group self insurer to:

(1) another private group self insurer;

(2) a carrier insured plan; or

(3) an independent self insured plan.

(c) The Manager shall be notified no later than the date of such change.

Note: Authority cited: Sections 54, 55 and 3702.10, Labor Code. Reference: Sections 59, 3700, 3702.5 and 3702.10, Labor Code.

History: 1. New section filed 2-19-92; operative 3-20-92 (Register 92, No. 13).

2. Amendment of section heading, new subsections (b)-(b)(3) and subsection redesignation filed 6-30-94; operative 6-30-94 (Register 94, No. 26).

§15402.4. Transfer of Claim Files and Computerized Claim File Data Information.

(a) Upon change of an administrative agency, all open claims shall be transferred immediately to the new administrative agency, unless otherwise provided by agreement between the self insurer, former administrator and new administrator.

(b) All closed claim files in the possession of the former administrator shall be transferred to the new administrator within 30 days, unless otherwise provided by agreement between the self insurer, former administrator and new administrator.

(c) All computerized claim file data showing all historical claim information, including payments and reserve data as of the date of the transfer of the open claim files shall be provided by the former administrator on the date that all open claim files are transferred, unless otherwise provided for by written agreement between the self insurer, former administrator and the new administrator. In the event that an agreement precludes the transfer of electronic claim contents of claims being transferred to the new administrator, the former administrator will provide hard copies of any required contents to the new administrator at its own expense. The closing date of the transactions on the computerized data shall coincide with the date of the physical transfer of the claim files to the new administrator. In the event that computerized data pertaining to the specific administration is changed by the former administrator after the physical claims have been transferred and the data provided to the new administrator, the former administrator shall provide reported computerized information to the new administrator within 14 days of any such changes.

Note: Authority cited: Sections 54, 55 and 3702.10, Labor Code. Reference: Sections 59, 129, 3700, 3702.1 and 3702.10, Labor Code.

History: 1. New section filed 2-19-92; operative 3-20-92 (Register 92, No. 13).

2. Amendment of subsection (c) filed 2-9-2006; operative 3-11-2006 (Register 2006, No. 6).

§15403. Audits.

(a) Pursuant to Labor Code Sections 129 and 3702.6, the Manager may order an audit of any self insurer or individual claim file at such reasonable times as is deemed necessary. Such audits shall include, but not be limited to, an audit of the files and records required by Section 15400 of these regulations. Such files and records shall be made readily available by the self insured employer or its administrative agency.

(b) In the event of an audit, the Manager may require that claims administered at the home of a telecommuting adjuster be presented for audit at a California office location of the administrator, or at a California location of the self insured employer.

Note: Authority cited: Sections 54, 55 and 3702.10, Labor Code. Reference: Sections 59, 129, 3700, 3702 and 3702.6, Labor Code.

History: 1. Amendment filed 6-1-72; effective thirtieth day thereafter (Register 72, No. 23).

2. Amendment filed 2-19-92; operative 3-20-92 (Register 92, No. 13).

3. Amendment designating first paragraph as subsection (a) and new subsection (b) filed 2-9-2006; operative 3-11-2006 (Register 2006, No. 6).

Ref.: Hanna § 1.19.

§15403.1. Notice of Special Audit.

When in the discretion of the Manager, a special audit as defined in Section 15201 of these regulations is necessary, the Manager shall notify the self-insurer of the requirement in writing fourteen (14) calendar days prior to the special audit and give the reasons therefor.

Note: Authority cited: Sections 54, 55 and 3702.10, Labor Code. Reference: Sections 59, 129, 3702.6 and 3702.10, Labor Code.

History: 1. New section filed 6-1-72; effective thirtieth day thereafter (Register 72, No. 23).

2. Repealer and new section filed 11-19-75; effective thirtieth day thereafter (Register 75, No. 47).

3. Amendment filed 2-19-92; operative 3-20-92 (Register 92, No. 13).

§15403.2. Financial Information. [Repealed]

Note: Authority cited: Sections 54, 55 and 3702.10, Labor Code. Reference: Sections 59, 129, 3700, 3701 and 3702.10, Labor Code.

History: 1. New section filed 11-19-75; effective thirtieth day thereafter (Register 75, No. 47).

2. Amendment filed 11-21-78; effective thirtieth day thereafter (Register 78, No. 47).

3. Repealer filed 2-19-92; operative 3-20-92 (Register 92, No. 13).

§15404. Expense of Out-of-State Audit.

The audit of any self insurer, pursuant to Section 15403 of these regulations, at locations outside of the State of California, shall be at the expense of the self-insurer. The Manager shall bill the self insurer for the expense incurred in making such out-of-state audit.

Note: Authority cited: Sections 54, 55 and 3702.10, Labor Code. Reference: Sections 59, 129, 3702.6 and 3702.10, Labor Code.

History: 1. Amendment filed 2-19-92; operative 3-20-92 (Register 92, No. 13).

§15404.1. Expense of Revoked Certificate Audit.

A self-insurer whose certificate to self insure has been revoked shall pay any expenses incurred by the Director or his representative in conducting an audit pursuant to Section 15425 of these regulations. The Manager shall bill the self insurer for expenses incurred.

Note: Authority cited: Sections 54, 55 and 3702.10, Labor Code. Reference: Sections 59, 129, 3702.6 and 3702.10, Labor Code.

History: 1. New section filed 6-1-72; effective thirtieth day thereafter (Register 72, No. 23).

2. Amendment filed 2-19-92; operative 3-20-92 (Register 92, No. 13).

§15404.2. Expense of Special Audit.

A self-insurer shall pay the expenses incurred whenever a special audit as defined in Section 15201, of these regulations, is ordered by the Manager pursuant to Sections 15403, 15404 and 15404.1 of these regulations. The Manager shall bill the self insurer for expenses incurred.

Note: Authority cited: Sections 54, 55 and 3702.10, Labor Code. Reference: Sections 59, 129, 3702.6 and 3702.10, Labor Code.

History: 1. New section filed 11-19-75; effective thirtieth day thereafter (Register 75, No. 47).

2. Amendment filed 2-19-92; operative 3-20-92 (Register 92, No. 13).

3. Change without regulatory effect amending section filed 10-18-95 pursuant to section 100, title 1, California Code of Regulations (Register 95, No. 42).

§15405. Confidentiality.

(a) Financial information submitted to the Director or Chief to establish the solvency and worth of any self-insurer, applicant to be self-insured, third party administrator, or of a guarantor of a self-insurer or applicant to be self-insured shall be considered confidential in accordance with California Government Code Sections 6254 and 6255, and California Labor Code Section 3701.8(b)(5). Except as otherwise provided by law, such information shall not be disclosed to any other entity or person without an order from an appropriate court or administrative subpoena from an agency of the State, with the following exceptions:

(1) The Chief shall disclose any financial information to the Self-Insurers' Security Fund on any private self-insurer whose liabilities have been turned over to the Fund pursuant to Labor Code Section 3701.5, or that has filed bankruptcy, failed to pay its liabilities, or failed to post an increase in deposit due that would potentially put the Fund at risk for the self-insurer's liabilities.

(2) Pursuant to Labor Code Section 3701.8(b)(5) and Section 15220.1(d) of these regulations, the Chief may provide to the Self-Insurers' Security Fund any financial

information for any self-insurer needed to determine and set deposit assessments for self-insured employers.

(3) Notwithstanding this section, the Board of Trustees of any private group self-insurer currently or previously self-insured pursuant to Labor Code Section 3700(b) and sections 15470 through 15500 of these regulations shall upon written request provide a copy of the group's most recent certified, independently audited financial statement to any affiliate employer of the group. The Chief also may provide to the Self-Insurers' Security Fund financial information, including actuarial reports, of any group self-insurer, so that the Security Fund may determine the financial risk and stability of the group.

(b) Self-Insurers' Annual Reports filed with the Office of Self-Insurance Plans pursuant to Labor Code Section 3702.2 and Section 15251 of these regulations shall be considered confidential in accordance with Government Code Sections 6254 and 6255 and Labor Code Section 3701.8(b)(5). Except as otherwise provided by law, information from the annual reports showing the extent of liabilities of self-insured employers shall not be disclosed to any other entity or person without an order from an appropriate court or administrative subpoena from an agency of the State, with the following exceptions:

(1) The Chief shall provide copies of any Self-Insurer's Annual Reports and/or lists of open indemnity claims to the Self-Insurers' Security Fund for any private or group self-insurer whose liabilities have been turned over to the Fund pursuant to Labor Code Section 3701.5 or that has filed bankruptcy, failed to pay its liabilities, or failed to post an increase in deposit due that would potentially put the Fund at risk for the self-insurer's liabilities.

(2) Pursuant to Labor Code Section 3701.8(b)(5) and Section 15220.1(d) of these regulations, the Chief may provide to the Self-Insurers' Security Fund copies of any and all Self-Insurer's Annual Reports needed to determine and set deposit assessments for self-insured employers, except that lists of open indemnity claims shall not be provided to the Security Fund for the sole purpose of setting deposit assessments.

(3) For public self-insured employers and/or Joint Powers Authorities only, copies of and/or data from Self-Insurers' Annual Reports may be provided to parties pursuant to Labor Code Section 3702.2(c) and Government Code Section 6253 upon written request to the Chief, except that no information identifying injured workers or dependents or related to specific claims may be provided.

(c) Except as otherwise provided by law, information obtained from any audit regarding the nature, extent or financial liability of any self-insurer's workers' compensation claims, together with any and all specific information regarding any claims, shall not be disclosed to any other entity or person without an order from an appropriate court or administrative subpoena from an agency of the State, with the following exceptions:

(1) The Chief may provide copies of audit reports to the Self-Insurers' Security Fund for any private self-insurer whose liabilities have been turned over to the Fund pursuant to Labor Code Section 3742, et seq. or that has filed bankruptcy, failed to pay its liabilities, or failed to post an increase in deposit due that would potentially put the Fund at risk for the self-insurer's liabilities.

(2) The Chief may provide copies of any audit reports and/or Self-Insurer's Annual Reports to the Division of Workers' Compensation in conjunction with any requests for audit and/or investigation by the Division of Workers' Compensation or Office of Self-Insurance Plans.

(d) Except as otherwise provided by law, information obtained from actuarial reports shall not be disclosed to any other entity or person without an order from an appropriate court or administrative subpoena from an agency of the State, with the following exception: the Chief may provide copies of actuarial reports to the Self-Insurers' Security Fund.

Note: Authority cited: Sections 54, 55, 3701.8(b)(5), 3702.2 and 3702.10, Labor Code; and Sections 6253, 6254 and 6255, Government Code. Reference: Sections 59, 129, 3700, 3701.5, 3702.2, 3702.6, 3702.10, 3740, 3741, 3742, 3743, 3744, 3745 and 3746, Labor Code; and Sections 6253, 6254 and 6255, Government Code.

History: 1. Amendment filed 2-19-92; operative 3-20-92 (Register 92, No. 13).

2. Amendment of section and Note filed 3-2-2009; operative 3-2-2009 pursuant to Government Code section 11343.4 (Register 2009, No. 10).

3. Amendment of subsection (a)(3), new subsection (d) and amendment of Note filed 9-19-2011; operative 10-19-2011 (Register 2011, No. 38).

4. Amendment filed 12-14-2016; operative 1-1-2017 pursuant to Government Code section 11343.4(b)(3) (Register 2016, No. 51).

Ref.: Hanna §§ 1.19, 2.11; Herlick Handbook § 3.20.

§15406. Confidentiality. [Repealed]

Note: Authority cited: Sections 54, 55, and 3702, Labor Code. Reference: Sections 159, 3700, 3702.5 and 3702.10, Labor Code.

History: 1. New section filed 11-21-78; effective thirtieth day thereafter (Register 78, No. 47).

2. Repealer filed 2-19-92; operative 3-20-92 (Register 92, No. 13).

ARTICLE 10
Revocation of a Certificate to Self-Insure or Certificate to Administer and Continuing Jurisdiction

§15420. Compliance with Statutes and Regulatory Requirements.

Self-insured employers and their administrative agencies shall comply with applicable regulations governing the administration of self-insurance pursuant to Labor Code Sections 129, and 3700-3709.5, which are adopted in accordance with the provisions of the California Administrative Procedure Act (Government Code, Title 2, Division 3, Part 1, Chapters 3.5 [commencing with Section 11340]). Failure to comply with these statutes governing administration of self insurance or with these regulations may be good cause for revocation of a Certificate to Self Insure or Certificate to Administer or other action by the Director.

Note: Authority Cited: Sections 54, 55 and 3702.10, Labor Code. Reference: Sections 54, 55, 59, 129, 3700, 3701, 3701.5, 3702, 3702.3, 3702.5, 3702.6, 3702.10, 3703, 3705, 3740-3745, Labor Code.

History: 1. Repealer of Article 10 (§§ 15420–15423) and new Article 10 (§§ 15420–15427) filed 6-1-72; effective thirtieth day thereafter (Register 72, No. 23). For prior history, see Register 69, No. 49.

2. Amendment of article heading, section heading and section and new Note filed 11-24-93; operative 12-24-93 (Register 93, No. 48).

3. Amendment of article heading filed 12-14-2016; operative 1-1-2017 pursuant to Government Code section 11343.4(b)(3) (Register 2016, No. 51).

§15421. Safety Violations. [Repealed]

Note: Authority cited: Sections 55 and 3702.10, Labor Code. Reference: Sections 54, 55 and 3702.10, Labor Code.

History: 1. Repealer filed 11-24-93; operative 12-24-93 (Register 93, No. 48).

§15422. Voluntary Revocation.

Any self-insurer or administrative agency may voluntarily request that its Certificate to Self-Insure or Certificate to Administer be revoked at any time by informing the Chief in writing. The Director shall revoke the Certificate to Self-Insure or Certificate to Administer after the self-insurer or administrative agency has shown to the satisfaction of the Director that the self-insurer or administrative agency has established a program to discharge all liabilities and all responsibilities incurred by the self-insurer or administrator during the period the Certificate to Self-Insure or Certificate to Administer was in force.

Note: Authority Cited: Sections 54, 55 and 3702.10, Labor Code. Reference: Sections 54, 55, 59, 129, 3700, 3701, 3701.5, 3702, 3702.3, 3702.5, 3702.6, 3703, 3705, 3740-3745, Labor Code.

History: 1. Amendment of section and new Note filed 11-24-93; operative 12-24-93 (Register 93, No. 48).

2. Amendment filed 12-14-2016; operative 1-1-2017 pursuant to Government Code section 11343.4(b)(3) (Register 2016, No. 51).

Ref.: Hanna § 2.11[1], [2], [3].

§15423. Revocation.

Revocation for Cause. Proceedings to revoke a Certificate to Self Insure or Certificate to Administer for good cause as defined in Labor Code Section 3702 and in these regulations shall be after Notice of Intent and opportunity for a hearing in accordance with Article 11 of these Regulations. The Notice of Intention to Revoke a Certificate to Self Insure or Certificate to Administer shall include a clear description of cause for revocation.

Note: Authority cited: Sections 54, 55, 59, 129, 3700, 3700(b), 3701, 3701.5, 3702, 3702.5, 3702.6, 3703, 3705 and 3740-3745, Labor Code. Reference: Sections 129, 3700, 3700(b), 3701, 3702, 3702.5, 3702.6, 3703, 3705, Labor Code.

History: 1. Repealer and new section filed 11-21-78; effective thirtieth day thereafter (Register 78, No. 47).

2. Amendment of section heading and section and Note filed 11-24-93; operative 12-24-93 (Register 93, No. 48).

Ref.: Hanna § 2.11[3].

§15424. Revoked Certificate Report.

The Director shall require a former self-insurer whose certificate to self insure has been revoked to continue to submit self-insurer's annual reports pursuant to Section 15251 of these regulations, setting forth the status of all open work-injury claims until all claims are resolved.

Note: Authority cited: Sections 54, 55 and 3702.10, Labor Code. Reference: Sections 54, 55, 59, 129, 3700, 3701, 3701.5, 3702, 3702.3, 3702.6, 3702.10, 3703, 3705, 3740-3745, Labor Code.

History: 1. Amendment of section and new Note filed 11-24-93; operative 12-24-93 (Register 93, No. 48).

Ref.: Hanna § 2.11[3].

§15425. Revoked Certificate Audit.

Pursuant to Sections 15403 and 15427 of these regulations, the Manager shall continue to audit the work-injury cases of any former self-insurer whose certificate to self insure has been revoked.

Note: Authority cited: Sections 54, 55 and 3702.10, Labor Code. Reference: Sections 54, 55, 59, 129, 3700, 3701, 3701.5, 3702, 3702.3, 3702.6, 3702.10, 3703, 3705, 3740-3745, Labor Code.

History: 1. Amendment of section and new Note filed 11-24-93; operative 12-24-93 (Register 93, No. 48).

§15426. Release of Security Deposit.

(a) Upon any revocation of a private employer's certificate to self-insure, a new deposit level shall be determined by the Chief to be sufficient to secure all actual and potential liabilities. The former self-insurer shall continue to be responsible to increase the deposit at the written request of the Chief as required in Section 15210 of these regulations.

(b) Except as provided in Labor Code Section 3702.8(c), the deposit shall not be reduced below the required amount pursuant to Labor Code Section 3701.

(c) Upon issuance of an order of default pursuant to Labor Code section 3701.5, the self-insurer, or its estate, shall forfeit all right, title and interest in its security deposit and shall have no right to return of all or any portion of the security deposit from the Self-Insurers' Security Fund.

Note: Authority cited: Sections 54, 55 and 3702.10, Labor Code. Reference: Sections 54, 55, 59, 129, 3700, 3701, 3701.5, 3702, 3702.3, 3702.6, 3702.10, 3703, 3705, 3740-3745, Labor Code.

History: 1. Amendment of section heading and newly designated subsection (a), and new subsection (b) and Note filed 11-24-93; operative 12-24-93 (Register 93, No. 48).

2. Amendment filed 12-14-2016; operative 1-1-2017 pursuant to Government Code section 11343.4(b)(3) (Register 2016, No. 51).

§15427. Continuing Jurisdiction.

After revocation of a certificate to self insure, the Director's jurisdiction over work injuries sustained during the period of self-insurance shall continue until all liabilities and all responsibilities have been terminated in accordance with law.

Note: Authority cited: Sections 54, 55 and 3702.10, Labor Code. Reference: Sections 54, 55, 59, 129, 3700, 3701, 3701.5, 3702, 3702.3, 3702.6, 3702.10, 3703, 3705, 3740-3745, Labor Code.

History: 1. Amendment of section and new Note filed 11-24-93; operative 12-24-93 (Register 93, No. 48).

Ref.: Hanna § 2.11[3].

§15428. Administration of Claims After Revocation.

(a) A private sector self insurer whose certificate to self insure has been revoked shall continue to provide competent administration of workers' compensation claims incurred during the period of self insurance in accordance with Sections 15450-15463 of these regulations, and the claims shall be administered from within the State of California.

(b) If it is determined by the Manager that the claims are not being competently administered, the Manager shall arrange for the claims administration. The cost of administration shall be borne by the former self insurer.

Note: Authority cited: Sections 54, 55 and 3702.10, Labor Code. Reference: Sections 54, 55, 59, 129, 3700, 3701, 3701.5, 3702, 3702.3, 3702.6, 3702.10, 3703, 3705, 3740-3745, Labor Code.

History: 1. New section filed 11-24-93; operative 12-24-93 (Register 93, No. 48).

Ref.: Hanna § 2.11[3].

ARTICLE 11
Hearing and Appeal Procedures

§15430. Hearing.

The Director may initiate an investigation or hold a hearing to implement the law and regulations with respect to the following self insurance matters:

(a) Disputes specified in Labor Code section 3701.5(f) arising between or among a surety, the issuer of an agreement of assumption and guarantee of workers' compensation liabilities, the issuer of a letter of credit, any custodian of the security deposit, a self-insured employer, or the Self-Insurers' Security Fund;

(b) Disputes between any self-insurer and the Chief involving action by the Chief to involuntarily revoke an existing certificate for cause pursuant to Labor Code section 3702;

(c) Disputes involving action by the Chief to revoke or deny issuance of a certificate to administer pursuant to Labor Code sections 3702.1 and 3702.7;

(d) An appeal by a private sector self-insurer concerning the amount of the security deposit to be posted pursuant to Labor Code section 3701(b) or section 15210 of these regulations;

(e) An appeal by any self-insurer concerning any civil penalty assessment made pursuant to Labor Code section 3702.9;

(f) The appeal of an employer alleging its application for a certificate or by an administrator that its application for a certificate to administer has not been processed in a timely manner;

(g) To determine whether good cause exists to revoke any self-insurers' certificate for willful or repeat serious violations of occupational safety and health regulations as noted in Cal/OSHA citations issued by the Division of Occupational Safety and Health;

(h) An appeal by a private self insurer concerning the calculation, posting, or any other aspect of its deposit assessment after payment of the deposit assessment in the time provided to the Security Fund, and;

(i) An appeal by a private self insurer of any civil penalty assessed for failure to pay a deposit assessment to the Security Fund.

Note: Authority cited: Sections 54, 55, 3701.8 and 3702.10, Labor Code. Reference: Sections 59, 3700, 3701, 3701.5, 3701.8, 3702, 3702.1, 3702.5, 3702.6, 3702.7, 3702.9, 3705, and 3740-3747, Labor Code; and Sections 11181-11188 and 15378, Government Code.

History: 1. New article 11 (sections 15430-15437) filed 11-21-78; effective thirtieth day thereafter (Register 78, No. 47).

2. Amendment filed 12-17-90; operative 1-16-91 (Register 91, No. 6).

3. Change without regulatory effect amending subsection (d) filed 6-13-2000 pursuant to section 100, title 1, California Code of Regulations (Register 2000, No. 24).

4. Amendment of subsections (c) and (g), new subsections (h)-(i) and amendment of Note filed 5-30-2003 as an emergency; operative 5-30-2003 (Register 2003, No. 22). A Certificate of Compliance must be transmitted to OAL by 9-29-2003 or emergency language will be repealed by operation of law on the following day.

5. Certificate of Compliance as to 5-30-2003 order transmitted to OAL 9-29-2003 and filed 11-12-2003 (Register 2003, No. 46).

6. Amendment of subsections (a)–(c) filed 5-14-2020; operative 7-1-2020 (Register 2020, No. 20).

§15430.1. Definitions.

As used in article 11, the following definitions shall apply.

Aggrieved Party. Any person aggrieved as a result of failure to pass a Self Insurance Administrator examination pursuant to Labor Code section 3702.1(b) or the revocation of a certificate to administer pursuant to Labor Code sections 3702.1(a) or 3702.7 and as prescribed in article 12 of these regulations.

Appeals Board. A California Workers' Compensation Appeals Board.

Certificate. See section 15201 for definition.

Certificate to Administer. A Certificate of Consent to Administer issued to an administrative agency, except exempt insurance carrier, pursuant to section 3702.1 of the Labor Code.

Custodian of a Security Deposit. The Office of the State Treasurer for approved securities; the Manager of Self-Insurance Plans for surety bonds and letters of credit; a bank or financial institution for savings accounts and certificates of deposit.

Employer. Any private corporation or other private business entity or public agency as defined in Labor Code section 3300 that has or did have a Certificate of Consent to Self-Insure or any such private entity or public agency seeking a Certificate of Consent to Self Insure pursuant to Labor Code sections 3700 and 3701.

Letter of Credit, Maker of. Any financial institution providing an irrevocable letter of credit to a self-insured employer pursuant to Labor Code section 3701.

SISF. Self-Insurers' Security Fund (SISF), a nonprofit entity created pursuant to Labor Code section 3740 et seq.

Surety. Any corporation authorized to provide surety in the State of California and providing a surety bond to a self-insured employer pursuant to Labor Code section 3701.

Note: Authority cited: Sections 54, 55, and 3702.10, Labor Code. Reference: Sections 3300, 3700, 3701, 3701.5, 3702.1, 3702.7, 3740–3747, Labor Code; and Sections 11181–11188, Government Code.

History: 1. New section filed 12-17-90; operative 1-16-91 (Register 91, No. 6).

2. Amendment of definitions of "Aggrieved Party," "Appeals Board" and "Custodian of a Security Deposit" filed 9-19-2011; operative 10-19-2011 (Register 2011, No. 38).

§15431. Delegation of Authority.

(a) The Manager of Self-Insurance Plans is the authorized representative of the Director. The Manager is authorized to:

(1) Issue notice of intention to revoke a certificate and to deny a request for a certificate or a certificate to administer;

(2) Receive requests for a hearing by parties enumerated in Section 15430 of these regulations;

(3) Schedule hearings;

(4) Perform all administrative duties as required to conduct a hearing, including granting of extensions of time requested in writing upon a showing of good cause;

(5) Hear and determine an appeal by any party aggrieved by the result of the self-insurance administrator examination; and

(6) Hear and determine an appeal regarding the revocation of a certificate to administer prescribed in Article 12 of these regulations.

(b) In all other hearings and appeals the Director or hearing officer shall perform all functions necessary to conduct a hearing.

Note: Authority cited: Sections 54, 55, 3702.10, Labor Code. Reference: Sections 59, 3700, 3701, 3701.5, 3702, 3702.1, 3702.7, 3740–3747, Labor Code; and Sections 11181–11188, 15378, Government Code.

History: 1. Amendment filed 12-17-90; operative 1-16-91 (Register 91, No. 6).

Ref.: Hanna § 1.19.

§15431.1. Appeals and/or Requests for Hearings.

(a) Appeals and/or requests for hearing under this article, by an employer or aggrieved party, shall be in writing and shall include the following information:

(1) Name and address of the person making the appeal or requesting the hearing (i.e. the requesting party);

(2) The specific nature of the request (for example, "This request is to review action denying revoking a certificate to administer"; or "This request is to appeal the failure to pass the self-insurance administrator's examination");

(3) A statement of the requesting party's rationale, basis, evidence, facts, reasoning, arguments, documentation, or other supporting material which establishes and supports the position of the requesting party;

(4) A statement of whether the requesting party wishes a formal hearing or a written decision only on the matter; and

(5) When a formal hearing is requested, an additional statement estimating the number of witnesses, if any, to be called by the requesting party at the hearing and the amount of time the requesting party will require to present its case at the hearing.

(b) Requests for a hearing or appeal pursuant to Section 15430 of these regulations shall be mailed or delivered to: Chief, Self-Insurance Plans, 11050 Olson Drive, Suite 230, Rancho Cordova, CA 95670.

(c) An appeal or request for a hearing from an employer or aggrieved party must be served upon the Director in writing within twenty-one (21) calendar days after receipt of:

(1) Notice of intention to revoke or deny a certificate to self-insure;

(2) Notice of the default of a self-insured employer or surety;

(3) Notice of a failing score on the self-insurance administrator's examination;

(4) Notice of intent to revoke a certificate to administer; or

(5) The decision by the Chief not to renew or grant a certificate to administer.

(d) A hearing on a claim that Self-Insurance Plans has not timely processed an application as required by Government Code section 15378 may be requested at any time.

(e) An appeal or request for hearing shall be deemed timely received if the request is postmarked or delivered to the Director or the Chief by the end of business on the twenty second (22nd) calendar day, after receipt of the notice or decision being appealed, as set forth in subsection (c) of this section.

(f) The written appeal or hearing request shall be:

(1) Placed in the United States mail in a fully prepaid, postmarked and sealed envelope;

(2) Delivery to an overnight mail delivery service for delivery the following day; or

(3) Delivery by messenger or in person to the Office of Self-Insurance Plans.

Note: Authority cited: Sections 54, 55 and 3702.10, Labor Code. Reference: Sections 59, 3700, 3701, 3701.5, 3702, 3702.1, 3702.7, 3702.9, 3702.10 and 3740–3747, Labor Code; and Sections 11181–11188 and 15378, Government Code.

History: 1. New section filed 12-17-90; operative 1-16-91 (Register 91, No. 6).

2. Editorial correction of Note (Register 91, No. 46).

3. Change without regulatory effect amending subsection (b) filed 10-18-95 pursuant to section 100, title 1, California Code of Regulations (Register 95, No. 42).

4. Amendment of subsections (a)-(a)(1), (a)(3)-(4), (b), (c)(5) and (e) filed 12-14-2016; operative 1-1-2017 pursuant to Government Code section 11343.4(b)(3) (Register 2016, No. 51).

§15431.2. Complaints.

(a) Any self-insured employer, administrator, the Self-Insurers' Security Fund, or injured employee of a self-insured employer may file a complaint to the Manager in writing concerning the failure of any self-insured employer or administrator to provide timely payment of benefits due or to fund the payment of such benefits.

(b) The Manager shall review any complaints received and may investigate the complaint, determine what benefits may be due and order payment thereof, audit the claim records of the self-insurer or administrator, and take action to revoke the certificate or certificate to administer for cause.

(c) The Manager shall not seek to substitute his/her judgement for that of the Workers' Compensation Appeals Board on any adjudicated claim and may refuse to consider the complaint of any injured worker's entitlement to benefits or self-insurer where the matter involved in the complaint is awaiting the decision of the Appeals Board.

(d) Any written complaint shall include the following information:

(1) The basis of jurisdiction of the Director;

(2) The relief or action requested;

(3) The grounds for the requested relief or action;

(4) The facts involved in the complaint;

(5) A statement of whether or not the specific claim or claims is being adjudicated before the Workers' Compensation Appeals Board and the Appeal number of the claim before the Appeals Board; and

(6) The name of the parties known to the complainant against which any relief is sought or who have an interest in the proceeding. The complaint shall be served on these other persons who may have an interest in the proceedings by the person submitting the complaint.

Note: Authority cited: Sections 54, 55, 3702.10, Labor Code. Reference: Sections 59, 3700, 3701, 3701.5, 3702, 3702.1, 3702.7, 3702.9, 3702.10, 3740–3747, Labor Code; and Sections 11181–11188, 15378, Government Code.

History: 1. New section filed 12-17-90; operative 1-16-91 (Register 91, No. 6).

2. Editorial correction of printing error of NOTE (Register 91, No. 46).

§15432. Hearings; Special Requirements: Failure to Appear.

(a) Before seeking reconsideration by the Director an appeal shall be first made to the Manager in matters of:

(1) A failing score on any self-insurance administrator's examination; or

(2) The revocation of a certificate to administer or denial of a renewal of a certificate to administer.

(b) A written waiver of review by the Manager shall constitute satisfaction of section 15432(a) and allow immediate reconsideration by the Director in the matter.

(c) The SISF shall have thirty (30) days to contest a decision by the Director to require it to assume administration on behalf of a defaulting self-insured employer. The SISF shall not be required to bring a complaint action under section 15431.2 of these regulations within any specific time against a defaulting self-insurer, surety, custodian of securities or maker of a letter of credit after assuming the liabilities of responsible parties under Labor Code Sections 3743-3744. Nothing in this subsection shall be construed as to allow SISF to withhold or delay payments in any event.

(d) Failure to Appear.

(1) If after service of notice of hearing or continuance, a party fails to appear at the hearing either in person or by representative, the Director or the designated hearing officer may:

(A) Continue the proceeding; or

(B) After notice, dismiss the proceeding as a default and uphold the action appealed from, if the non-appearing party is the party requesting the hearing; or

(C) Receive evidence, including admissions, affidavit or declarations of the party, establish a prima facie case and render a decision.

(2) A party who has defaulted, and against whom a decision or determination is upheld, nevertheless has the right to make a showing by way of mitigation as to any remedy. The Director may consider documentary evidence or hold a hearing, and may decide to alter the remedy, both in the discretion of the Director.

Note: Authority cited: Sections 54, 55, 3702.10, Labor Code. Reference: Sections 59, 3700, 3701, 3701.5, 3702, 3702.1, 3702.5, 3702.6, 3702.7, 3702.9, 3702.10, 3705, 3740–3747, Labor Code; and Sections 11181–11188, 15378, Government Code.

History: 1. Amendment filed 12-17-90; operative 1-16-91 (Register 91, No. 6).

§15433. Hearing Officer: Appointment and Delegation of Authority.

(a) The appointed hearing officer shall have full power, jurisdiction and authority to:

(1) Hold a hearing and ascertain facts for the information of the Director;

(2) Hold a pre-hearing conference and/or to certify official acts;

(3) Regulate the course of the hearing;

(4) Join and dismiss parties in a complaint proceeding pursuant to Section 15431.2 of these regulations;

(5) Grant a withdrawal, disposition or amendment;

(6) Order a continuance or to extend the submittal date of the proceeding;

(7) Approve a stipulation voluntarily entered into by the parties;

(8) Administer oaths and affirmations;

(9) Rule on objections, privileges, defenses, and the receipt of relevant and material evidence;

(10) Request a party at any time to state his theory concerning any fact or issue in the proceeding;

(11) Hear and determine all issues of fact and law presented; and

(12) Issue interlocutory and final orders, findings and decisions as may be necessary for full adjudication of the matter.

(b) The hearing officer may issue subpoenas and subpoenas duces tecum in the name of the Director for the attendance of persons and the production of testimony, books, documents, or other things, to compel attendance of persons residing anywhere within the state, subject to the provisions of Government Code section 11185.

(c) For purposes of an appeal or hearing to be heard by the Manager, the Manager shall exercise the power of a designated hearing officer.

Note: Authority cited: Sections 54, 55, 3702.10, Labor Code. Reference: Sections 59, 3700, 3701, 3701.5, 3702, 3702.1, 3702.5, 3702.6, 3702.7, 3702.9, 3702.10, 3705, 3740–3747, Labor Code; Sections 11181–11188, 15378, Government Code; and Sections 1985–2031, 2033–2036, Code of Civil Procedure.

History: 1. Amendment filed 12-17-90; operative 1-16-91 (Register 91, No. 6).

§15434. Hearing Procedures.

(a) The affected employer, surety, any custodian of a surety deposit, maker of a letter of credit, the SISF, an aggrieved party, and any other affected parties or persons shall be notified of the time and place of the hearing by a notice issued by the Director, designated hearing officer or the Manager and such notice to be served on all parties.

(b) Notification shall be placed in the U.S. mail in a fully prepaid, postmarked and sealed envelope at least twenty-one (21) calendar days in advance of the hearing. Without good cause being shown and a written request for extended time to respond, the time to respond shall not be extended beyond the twenty-one (21) days by California Code of Civil Procedure Section 1013.

(c) The employer, surety, custodian of a security deposit, maker of a letter of credit, the SISF, an aggrieved party, and any other party, shall be given an opportunity to present evidence and/or written or oral arguments in support of its position.

(d) The hearing need not be conducted according to the technical rules of evidence. In the interest of expeditious and inexpensive adjudication, evidence by way of affidavit or declaration shall be allowed under the following conditions:

(1) At any time fifteen (15) days or more prior to the hearing date or continued hearing date, a party may mail or deliver to the opposing party or parties a copy of any affidavit or declaration which is proposed to be introduced in evidence, together with a notice as provided in subsection (2). Unless an opposing party, within ten (10) days after such mailing or deliver, mails or delivers to the proponent a request to cross-examine the affiant or declarant, his right to cross-examine such affiant or declarant is waived and the affidavit or declaration, if introduced into evidence, shall be given the same effect as if the affiant or declarant had testified orally. If an opportunity to cross-examine an affiant or declarant is not afforded after request therefor is made as herein provided, the affidavit or declaration may be introduced into evidence, but shall be given only the same effect as other hearsay evidence.

(2) The notice referred to in subsection (1) shall be substantially in the following form:

"The accompanying affidavit or declaration of (here insert name of affiant or declarant) will be introduced as evidence at the hearing in (here insert title and docket number of proceeding). (Here insert name) will not be called to testify orally and you will not be entitled to question him unless you notify (name of the proponent, representative, agent or attorney) at (here insert address) that you wish to cross-examine him. To be effective, your request must be mailed or delivered to (here insert name of proponent, representative, agent or attorney) on or before (here insert date ten (10) days after the date of mailing or delivering the affidavit or declaration to the opposing party)."

(e) All witnesses testifying before the hearing officer shall testify under oath, affirmation or penalty of perjury.

(f) Upon written request to the Director and for good cause shown, an aggrieved party may request the production of his or her own test and application records from Self-Insurance Plans. At the time of hearing or, upon written request to the Director and for good cause, an aggrieved party may request inspection of his/her own test records prior to the time of hearing.

(g) Discovery. The parties shall have the right to take depositions and to obtain discovery and to that end may exercise all of the same rights, remedies, and procedures, and shall be subject to all of the same duties, liabilities and obligations as provided in Part 4, Title 3, Chapter 3, of the Code of Civil Procedure, except that applications to the court or requests for relief from the court shall be considered as applications or requests of the hearing officer. All discovery shall be completed not less than fifteen (15) days prior to the date set for hearing, unless the Director, upon a showing of good cause, makes an order granting an extension of the time within which discovery must be completed. The hearing officer shall not have authority to impose monetary sanctions.

(h) Subpoena of Witnesses; Subpoena Duces Tecum. Subject to the provisions of Title 2, Division 3, Part 1, Chapter 2, of the Government Code and before the hearing has commenced, the Director shall issue a subpoena and subpoena duces tecum at the request of a party for attendance of a person or production of a document, object or thing determined to be reasonably relevant to the issues to be decided at the hearing.

After the hearing has commenced, the Director may issue a subpoena and subpoena duces tecum as follows:

(1) The subpoenaing party shall prepare the affidavit of good cause required by Section 1985 of the Code of Civil Procedure before a subpoena duces tecum will be issued.

(2) A subpoenaing party shall comply with Section 1985.3 of the Code of Civil Procedure. A person not a party to the matter, is not obliged to attend as a witness in any matter under this article at a place out of the county in which he resides, unless the distance is less than fifty (50) miles from his place of residence. A party or party-identified witness may be obliged to attend a deposition in like manner as in Code of Civil Procedure Section 2025.

(i) The hearing shall be recorded by audio recorder. Parties wishing a written transcript shall pay the cost of a transcription or may provide a certified reporter at the time of hearing. A copy of the recorded proceedings shall be provided to the Director if reconsideration is requested.

(j) The Director may appoint an interpreter and fix the interpreter's compensation in any matter where an interpreter is requested by the parties or determined to be needed by the Director or his/her designee. It shall be the responsibility of any party producing a witness requiring an interpreter to arrange for the presence of a qualified interpreter. Interpreter fees are to be paid by the party requesting the use of the interpreter. It shall be the responsibility of the party seeking to use an interpreter to show that the interpreter is proficient in the appropriate language and has sufficient knowledge relating to the terminology and procedures generally used in hearings before the Director to function satisfactorily. The Director may disqualify an interpreter due to conflict of interest, bias, prejudice, partiality or for disclosure of confidential or privileged information.

(k) A request for intervention may be allowed by the Director or designated hearing officer in like manner as in California Code of Civil Procedure Section 387.

(*l*) In the interests of the expeditious resolution of all disputes, the Director may allow time for settlement of disputes. The Director shall approve settlement of any dispute regarding a third-party administrator examination, a revocation of a third-party certificate or certificate of consent to self-insure. The Director, in his discretion, may approve resolution of disputes involving the Self-Insurers' Security Fund. Approval by the Director of disputes involving SISF is necessary only after a formal hearing on the merits has begun.

(m) An official address record shall be maintained by the Director or the designated hearing officer. Each party shall furnish one address and one telephone number, for itself or its representative, to which all communications by the Director and other parties shall be directed. If the address is a Post Office Box, a physical address shall also be provided for use when physical delivery other than by mail is intended. All communications by the Director or hearing officer, including all notices and decisions and determinations, shall be made to the addresses on the official address record. Service of anything required to be served shall be acceptable if mailed by registered or certified mail, with return receipt, if mailed to the official address. Legal service may also be made by personal delivery to the official address.

(n) No party or representative of a party shall communicate with a hearing officer on the merits of a matter except in the presence of the other parties or their representatives. No written communication shall be directed to a hearing officer or the Director unless it shows on the face of it or on an attached proof of service that the communication has been simultaneously served on other parties. No written communications in violation of this rule shall be received by the hearing officer or Director. The Director, after a hearing officer has been designated and while the hearing officer is continuing to act on the matter, shall not communicate with the hearing officer about the merits of the matter before the hearing officer.

(o) Foundation Evidence. Evidence of the genuineness of any document, and of the authenticity of records, shall be by affidavit or declaration only, unless good cause is shown by a party for the necessity for testimony in the presence of the hearing officer. At the discretion of the hearing officer, any other evidence of a foundational nature shall also be by declaration or affidavit, except where good cause is shown why it should be otherwise.

Note: Authority cited: Sections 54, 55, 3702.10, Labor Code. Reference: Sections 59, 3700, 3701, 3701.5, 3702, 3702.1, 3702.5, 3702.6, 3702.7, 3702.9, 3702.10, 3705, 3740–3747, Labor Code; Sections 11181–11188, 15378, Government Code; and Sections 1985–2031, 2033–2036, Code of Civil Procedure.

History: 1. Amendment filed 12-17-90; operative 1-16-91 (Register 91, No. 6).

§15435. Decision.

(a) The hearing officer shall conduct the hearing and provide a written recommendation to the Director and make available the entire record of the hearing. A matter is deemed submitted to the Director either at the close of the hearing, or, at the discretion of the hearing officer, upon the submission of any post-hearing briefs or arguments requested or allowed by the hearing officer.

(b) The decision of the Director shall reflect a summary of evidence, findings of fact and conclusions of law, together with citations to the controlling statutes applied in rendering the decision, and any determinations made by the Director.

(c) The decision shall be mailed within ninety (90) days of the date of submission, with copies to all parties of record. Issuance of a decision may be delayed to allow settlement, or as the interests of justice may require, in which case the Director shall give all parties of record written notice of such delay.

(d) The Director shall make determinations, as required, as to whether there was at the time of the notice of intention or at the time of the decision, good cause to revoke or deny a certificate or certificate to administer.

(e) If the Director determines that an appellant's application was not processed within the time limits which the Director has adopted in these regulations pursuant to Government Code section 15378, the decision shall include a refund of the fees paid by that appellant for that application.

(f) The decision of the Director shall be final, unless reconsideration pursuant to Section 15436 of these regulations is requested.

Note: Authority cited: Sections 54, 55, 3702.10, Labor Code. Reference: Sections 59, 3700, 3701, 3701.5, 3702, 3702.1, 3702.5, 3702.6, 3702.7, 3702.9, 3702.10, 3705, 3740–3747, Labor Code; Sections 11181–11188, 15378, Government Code; and Sections 1985–2031, 2033–2036, Code of Civil Procedure.

History: 1. Amendment filed 12-17-90; operative 1-16-91 (Register 91, No. 6).

§15436. Reconsideration.

(a) The Director has the discretion to reconsider and to take whatever action is appropriate and necessary to support and facilitate a decision or determination. The Director, in his/her discretion, may grant a stay of enforcement in any proceeding where reconsideration or appeal is initiated.

(b) The employer, surety, custodian of a security deposit, the SISF, or an aggrieved party, upon receipt of the decision, shall have ten (10) calendar days to request reconsideration of the decision by the Director. The request must be in writing and shall be limited to the grounds specified in Labor Code Section 5903.

(c) Upon receipt of a request for reconsideration, the Director may:

(1) Decline reconsideration;

(2) Grant reconsideration and issue an amended decision or determination after reconsideration based only upon the record and additional argument and evidence offered in the request for reconsideration and any response thereto; or,

(3) If the Director deems that, based upon the request for reconsideration and any response, further hearing is merited, grant reconsideration and hold further hearing pursuant to these regulations, and issue a decision or determination after reconsideration.

(d) A decision or determination of the Director, where reconsideration by the Director has been requested but not granted, becomes final upon service of the notice that reconsideration is declined. A decision or determination of the Director where reconsideration by the Director has been granted, becomes final upon service of the decision or determination after reconsideration.

(e) All requests for reconsideration by the Director shall be served on all other parties of record by the requesting party at the time of service on the Director. The Director shall not accept requests for reconsideration without a declaration of service attached indicating that all other parties to the matter, as reflected on the official address record, have been served with the request for reconsideration.

(f) If a party to a proceeding is adversely affected for the first time by the decision or determination after reconsideration, that party may then request further reconsideration of the original decision or determination after reconsideration.

Note: Authority cited: Sections 54, 55, 3702.10, Labor Code. Reference: Sections 59, 3700, 3701, 3701.5, 3702, 3702.1, 3702.5, 3702.6, 3702.7, 3702.9, 3702.10, 3705, 3740–3747, Labor Code; Sections 11181–11188, 15378, Government Code; and Sections 1985–2031, 2033–2036, Code of Civil Procedure.

History: 1. Amendment filed 12-17-90; operative 1-16-91 (Register 91, No. 6).

§15437. Appellate Review.

(a) Appeal from an adverse decision of the Director with regard to failure to pass the Self-Insurance Administrator examination or revocation of a Certificate to Administer, or with regard to the Office of Self Insurance Plans' timeliness of processing an application, shall be made to the Superior Court of California by writ as provided in the Code of Civil Procedure. A condition precedent to such appeal shall be exhaustion of all appeal requirements specified in this Article.

(b) Appeal from a decision or determination of the Director after hearing arising from a dispute between or among a surety, the issuer of an agreement of assumption and guarantee of workers' compensation liabilities, the issuer of a letter of credit, a custodian of a security deposit, an employer, or the SISF, concerning the posting, renewal, termination, exoneration, or return of all or any portion of the security deposit, or any liability arising out of the posting or failure to post security, or adequacy of the security or reasonableness of administrative costs, including legal fees, may be taken to the Superior Court, as provided in Labor Code Section 3701.5(g).

(c) Appeal from a determination of the Director after hearing in a proceeding under Labor Code Section 3702.8 involving private employers who have ceased to be self-insured employers may be taken to the Appeals Board. After January 1, 1991 such appeals shall be taken to the appropriate Superior Court by petition for writ of mandate.

(d) Appeal from a decision or determination of the Director after hearing which denies an application for a certificate or which revokes a certificate pursuant to Labor Code Section 3702(b), may be taken to the Appeals Board. It shall be a condition precedent to the filing of such an appeal that the appealing employer shall have first obtained workers' compensation insurance. A Certificate of Insurance showing the current existence of such insurance, issued by the insurer, shall be filed as part of the appeal.

(e) Appeal of any other determination of the Director may be taken to the Appeals Board.

(f) All appeals to the Appeals Board under this section shall be governed by Article 1 of Chapter 7 of Part 4 of Division 4 of the Labor Code, Reconsideration. Appeals shall be filed with the Appeals Board within twenty (20) days after service of the final decision or determination of the Director. Where service is by mail, the time to file shall be extended as provided in Code of Civil Procedure Section 1013.

Note: Authority cited: Sections 54, 55, 3702.10, Labor Code. Reference: Sections 59, 3700, 3701, 3701.5, 3702, 3702.1, 3702.5, 3702.6, 3702.7, 3702.8, 3702.9, 3702.10, 3705, 3740–3747, Labor Code; Sections 11181–11188, 15378, Government Code; and Sections 1985–2031, 2033–2036, Code of Civil Procedure.

History: 1. Renumbering and amendment of former section 15437 to section 15438 and new section 15437 filed 12-17-90; operative 1-16-91 (Register 91, No. 6). For prior history, see Register 78, No. 47.

§15438. Severability.

If any provision of these regulations or the application thereof to any party or circumstances is held invalid, such invalidity shall not affect other provisions or applications of these regulations which can be given effect without the invalid provision or applications, and to this end the provisions of the regulations are severable.

Note: Authority cited: Sections 54, 55, 3702.10, Labor Code. Reference: Sections 59, 3700, 3701, 3701.5, 3702, 3702.1, 3702.5, 3702.6, 3702.7, 3702.9, 3702.10, 3705, 3740–3747, Labor Code; Sections 11181–11188, 15378, Government Code; and Sections 1985–2031, 2033–2036, Code of Civil Procedure.

History: 1. Renumbering and amendment of former section 15437 to section 15438 filed 12-17-90; operative 1-16-91 (Register 91, No. 6).

2. Editorial correction of NOTE (Register 91, No. 46).

ARTICLE 12
Claims Administration

§15450. Certificate to Administer.

(a) A valid Certificate to Administer issued by the Manager shall be in the possession of each claims administrator, whether a person, firm, corporation, joint powers authority or self insured employer, to administer or adjust workers' compensation self insurance claims.

EXCEPTION 1: An insurer admitted to transact workers' compensation insurance in California is exempt from this requirement pursuant to Labor Code Section 3702.1(a);

NOTE: An insurance company subsidiary not admitted to transact workers' compensation insurance in California and engaged in the administration or adjustment of claims for a self insured employer is not exempt.

EXCEPTION 2: A private self insurer that administers its own claims and/or the claims of other private self insurers with common ownership or which are in the same Master Certificate file is exempt from this requirement.

EXCEPTION 3: A joint powers authority that holds a Master Certificate of Consent to Self Insure and administers its own claims; and/or the claims of other public self insurers which have an affiliate Certificate under the same Master Certificate file number held by the joint powers authority;

and/or the claims of a former member of the joint powers authority is exempt from this requirement.

EXCEPTION 4: A public self insurer that administers its own agency's claims is exempt from this requirement.

(b) Application for a Certificate to Administer shall be made on forms provided by Self-Insurance Plans (Form A4-50 (Rev. 4/91)). A complete application shall include the application form, and fees in accordance with Section 15454.

NOTE: The current application form is contained in Plate L of the Appendix following the last Article of these Group 2 regulations.

(1) The applicant will be notified in writing within 14 days of receipt if the application is deficient.

(2) A certificate to administer will be issued within 30 days of receipt of a complete application.

(c) The Certificate to Administer expires June 30 and reapplication must be made prior to June 1 for the subsequent renewal period. The applicant may request the Certificate to Administer to be issued for a period of 1, 2 or 3 years.

(d) Failure to comply with Articles 6 and 9 of these regulations or engaging in improper practices as described in Labor Code Section 3702(a) is good cause for revocation or non-renewal of the Certificate to Administer.

Note: Authority cited: Sections 54, 55, 59, and 3702.10, Labor Code. Reference: Sections 59, 3702 and 3702.1, Labor Code. Government Code Sections 15375, 15376.

History: 1. New article 12 (sections 15450–15463, not consecutive) filed 1-27-86; effective thirtieth day thereafter (Register 86, No. 5).

2. Amendment of article and section headings filed 2-19-92; operative 3-20-92 (Register 92, No. 13).

3. Amendment of subsections (a), (b)(2) and (d) filed 2-9-2006; operative 3-11-2006 (Register 2006, No. 6).

Ref.: Hanna § 2.11[3].

§15450.1. Third Party Claims Administration for New Private Self Insurers.

(a) Each private self insurer granted an initial, individual Certificate to Self Insure workers' compensation liabilities that has not been self insured or previously self insured for a total of three full years shall contract with a third party claims administrator for the first three (3) full calendar years of self insurance. The self insured employer's third party claims administrator shall hold a Certificate to Administer pursuant to Section 15450 of these regulations.

(b) Each private group self insurer granted its initial Certificate to Self Insure workers' compensation liabilities shall contract with a third party administrator for the first five (5) full calendar years of self insurance. The group self insurer's third party claims administrator shall hold a Certificate to Administer pursuant to Section 15450 of these regulations.

Note: Authority cited: Sections 54, 55, 59 and 3702.10, Labor Code. Reference: Sections 3700, 3701, 3701.5, 3702, 3702.1, 3702.2 and 3702.3, Labor Code.

History: 1. New section filed 6-30-94; operative 6-30-94 (Register 94, No. 26). For prior history, see Register 92, No. 13.

2. Amendment of subsections (a) and (b) and repealer of subsection (c) filed 2-9-2006; operative 3-11-2006 (Register 2006, No. 6).

Ref.: Hanna § 2.11[3].

§15452. Administrator Competence.

(a) Each self insurer or third party administrative agency shall conduct the administration of each self insurance program through the services of a competent person or persons located in California.

EXCEPTION 1: Upon a showing of good cause, the Manager may authorize administration from locations outside California by an administrator with staff who has demonstrated individual competence. The desire to consolidate claims from other states in one location or the desire to reduce expenses related to utilizing a third party administer are not good cause for out-of-state administration. The demonstration of individual competence of an out-of-state administrator is not in itself good cause for out-of-state administration.

EXCEPTION 2: The Manager shall not authorize claims administration outside of the State of California for any private group self insurer.

(b) Any person may demonstrate individual competence as an administrator for a self-administered self insurer or an agency administered self insurance program by successfully passing the written examination designed to test technical knowledge of workers' compensation law and claims administration. The Manager shall ensure that the test shall be administered at least twice a fiscal year (July 1 to June 30).

(c) Application for the administrator's examination shall be made on forms provided by the Manager (Form A4-100, Rev. 9/91). A complete application shall include the application form and fees in accordance with subsection (d) of this section. The applicant will be notified in writing within 14 days if the application is deficient. Confirmation of the test date will be sent two weeks before the scheduled test date.

(d) The fee to take the Self Insurance Administrator's examination shall be $150. The fee shall not be refundable after confirmation of entrance to the exam has been issued by the Office of Self Insurance Plans.

EXCEPTION 1: Upon a written showing of good cause, the Manager may authorize a refund of the application fee.

(e) Upon passing the written examination a Certificate of Achievement will be issued within eight weeks of the test date.

(f) Each adjusting location of a third party administrative agency or a self-administered self insurer shall have at least one person who has passed the self insurance administrator's examination. All workers' compensation self insurance claims at such reporting locations shall be administered and adjusted under the direct supervision of a person who has passed the self insurance administrator's examination. Supervision of claims decisions, setting of estimates of future liability of claims, and proper payment of benefits to injured workers shall be made or reviewed by a person who has passed the self insurance administrator's examination.

(g) Lack of competent administrators at any adjusting location shall be good cause for revocation of the certificate to administer for that location and may be grounds to revoke the certificate to self insure.

Note: Authority cited: Sections 54, 55, 59, and 3702.10, Labor Code. Reference: Sections 59, 3702, 3702.1 and 3702.10, Labor Code; and Sections 15375 and 15376, Government Code.

History: 1. Amendment filed 2-19-92; operative 3-20-92 (Register 92, No. 13).

2. New (a) Exception 2 and amendment of Note filed 6-30-94; operative 6-30-94 (Register 94, No. 26).

3. Amendment of subsections (a)-(f) filed 2-9-2006; operative 3-11-2006 (Register 2006, No. 6).

Ref.: Hanna § 2.11[3].

§15454. Certificate to Administer: Fees.

(a) The certificate fee shall be paid no later than June 1 in the year of application and shall be sufficient to cover the 1 to 3 year period of the application submitted, and shall accompany the application form. The fee is not prorated in the initial year of each application cycle and is not refundable for any portion of the current fiscal year.

(b) The minimum fee for each private certificate to administer the first adjusting location is $1,000 per year. There is an additional charge of $200 per year for each additional claims adjusting location.

(c) Public applicants are exempt from the payment of a fee for the Certificate to Administer provided all claims administered are for public self insurers. A public administrator for private sector self insurers shall pay the certificate fees due for a private Certificate to Administer.

Note: Authority cited: Sections 54, 55, 59, and 3702.10, Labor Code. Reference: Sections 59, 3702.1, 3702.5 and 3702.10, Labor Code.

History: 1. Amendment filed 2-19-92; operative 3-20-92 (Register 92, No. 13).

2. Amendment of subsection (b) filed 2-9-2006; operative 3-11-2006 (Register 2006, No. 6).

Ref.: Hanna § 2.11[3].

§15456. Exempt. [Repealed]

Note: Authority cited: Sections 54, 55 and 3702.10, Labor Code. Reference: Sections 59, 3702.1 and 3702.10, Labor Code.

History: 1. Repealer filed 2-19-92; operative 3-20-92 (Register 92, No. 13).

§15458. Claims Administration and Recordkeeping.

Workers' compensation claims and claim files shall be administered and maintained in accordance with the provisions of Articles 6 and 9 of these regulations.

Note: Authority cited: Sections 54, 55 and 3702.10, Labor Code. Reference: Sections 59, 129, 3700, 3701, 3702.1 and 3702.10, Labor Code.

History: 1. New section filed 1-27-86; effective thirtieth day thereafter (Register 86, No. 5).

2. Amendment filed 2-19-92; operative 3-20-92 (Register 92, No. 13).

Ref.: Hanna § 2.11[3].

§15459. Notification of Willful Failure to Pay Benefits.

The claims administrator shall notify the Manager in writing within three days of a self insured employer's willful failure to provide adequate funding for the timely payment of worker's compensation benefits in accordance with provision of the Labor Code.

Note: Authority cited: Sections 54, 55 and 3702.10, Labor Code. Reference: Sections 59, 129, 3700, 3701, 3702.1 and 3702.10, Labor Code.

History: 1. New section filed 1-27-86; effective thirtieth day thereafter (Register 86, No. 5).

2. Amendment filed 2-19-92; operative 3-20-92 (Register 92, No. 13).

Ref.: Hanna § 2.11[3].

§15461. Examination. [Repealed]

Note: Authority cited: Sections 54, 55 and 3702.10, Labor Code. Reference: Sections 59, 3702, 3702.1 and 3702.10, Labor Code.

History: 1. Repealer filed 2-19-92; operative 3-20-92 (Register 92, No. 13).

§15463. Revocation of Certificate.

(a) The Manager may issue a Notice of Intent to Revoke to any holder of a Certificate to Administer. The notice shall indicate the cause for the revocation action and advise the holder of the Certificate of the right to a hearing.

(b) The procedure for revocation of a Certificate of Consent to Administer shall be in accordance with Article 11 of these regulations.

Note: Authority cited: Sections 54, 55, 59 and 3702.10, Labor Code. Reference: Sections 59, 3702.1, 3702.7 and 3702.10, Labor Code.

History: 1. Amendment and new forms filed 2-19-92; operative 3-20-92 (Register 92, No. 13).

2. New Appendix plates D, E, F1-F6, G and I filed 12-22-92; operative 1-21-93 (Register 93, No. 2).

3. Amendment of Plate F-6 filed 8-12-93; operative 9-13-93 (Register 93, No. 33).

4. Change without regulatory effect relocating Appendix Plates A-1, A-2, B, C, and H from section 15204 to section 15463 filed 9-14-93 pursuant to title 1, section 100, California Code of Regulations (Register 93, No. 38).

5. Amendment of forms filed 6-30-94; operative 6-30-94 (Register 94, No. 26).

6. Amendment of Appendix Plate I filed 12-1-94; operative 1-2-95 (Register 94, No. 48).

7. Change without regulatory effect renumbering a portion of Form A4-3 (Agreement of Assumption and Guarantee of Workers' Compensation Liabilities) to new Form A4-6, including amendments, filed 2-17-98 pursuant to section 100, title 1, California Code of Regulations (Register 98, No. 8).

8. Amendment adding new form A4-5 filed 6-4-98; operative 7-4-98 (Register 98, No. 23).

9. Amendment filed 2-9-2006; operative 3-11-2006 (Register 2006, No. 6).

10. Amendment adding new forms A4-7, A4-40a and A4-40b filed 3-2-2009; operative 3-2-2009 pursuant to Government Code section 11343.4 (Register 2009, No. 10).

11. Amendment of Appendix repealing forms A4-1, A4-2, A4-3, A4-3G, A4-3M, A4-5, A4-6, A4-7, A4-8, A4-32, A4-40a, A4-40b and A4-GAU and adopting forms A-1, A-2, A-3B, A-4, A-5, A-6, S-1, S-2A, S-2B, S-4, S-5 and S-6 filed 12-14-2016; operative 1-1-2017 pursuant to Government Code section 11343.4(b)(3) (Register 2016, No. 51).

Publisher's Note: The following forms are available from:

STATE OF CALIFORNIA
DEPARTMENT OF INDUSTRIAL RELATIONS
OFFICE OF SELF-INSURANCE PLANS
11050 Olson Drive, Suite 230
Rancho Cordova, CA 95670
(916) 464-7000

Application for Certificate of Consent to Self Insure as a Private Employer Self Insurer
—Form A-1 (1-2016)

Application for Certificate of Consent to Self Insure as a Public Agency Employer Self Insurer
—Form A-2 (1-2016)

Application for Permanent Certificate of Consent to Self Insure for Interim Self Insurer
—Form A-3B (1-2016)

Office of Self-Insurance Plans Guaranty of Workers' Compensation Liabilities
—Form A-4 (1-2016)

Personal Agreement of Assumption & Guarantee of Workers' Compensation Liabilities
—Form A4-3A (2/91)

Model Resolution for Agreements of Parental Assumption and Guarantee
—Plate E

Model Partnership Agreement and Guarantee Resolution

Surety Bond
—Form No. A4-20 (4/92)

Surety Bond—Decrease Rider
—Form A4-21a (4/92)

Surety Bond—Increase Rider
—Form A4-21b (4/92)

Surety Bond—Name Change Rider
—Form A4-22 (4/92)

Surety Bond—Special Form Change Rider
—Form A4-23 (4/92)

Surety Bond—Release of Surety
—Form A4-24 (11/92)

Model Letter to Request Approval of Securities
—Plate G

Information Bulletin—Letter of Credit
—Plate "I" Revised (7/94)

Syndicated Letter of Credit

Certificate of Drawing

Amendment to Irrevocable Standby Letter of Credit
—(7/94)

Private Group Self-Insurer's Annual Report
—Form A4-40d (1/94)

Application for a Certificate of Consent to Administer Workers' Compensation Self Insurance Claims
—Form No. A4-50 (4/91)

Application for Self Insurance Administrator's Examination
—Form No. A4-100 (9/91)

Corporate Resolution Authorizing Application to the Director of Industrial Relations, State of California for a Certificate of Consent to Self Insure Workers' Compensation Liabilities
—Form A-5 (1-2016)

Agreement and Undertaking for Security Deposit
—Form A-6 (1-2016)

Workers' Compensation Self-Insured/Self-Administered Employer Report of Changes
—AE Form 101 (10-90)

Workers' Compensation Adjusting Agency/Third-Party Administrator Report of Changes
—AE Form 102 (10-90)

Group Resolution Authorizing Application to the Director of Industrial Relations, State of California for a Certificate of Self-Insure Workers' Compensation Liabilities
—Form GR-1 (Rev. 1/94)

Resolution of Agreement of Assumption and Guarantee of Workers' Compensation Liabilities for a Group Self Insurer
—Form GR-2 (Rev. 1/94)

Group Master Application for Certificate of Consent to Self Insure as a Group Self Insurer
—Form S-1 (1-2016)

Group Affiliate Member Interim Application
—Form S-2A (1-2016)

Application for Affiliate Certificate of Consent to Self Insure as a Member of a Group Self Insurer
—Form S-2B (1-2016)

Indemnity Agreement and Power of Attorney
—Form S-4 (1-2016)

Agreement of Assumption and Guarantee of Workers' Compensation Liabilities for Group and Affiliate Members
—Form S-5 (1-2016)

Agreement and Undertaking for Security Deposit
—Form S-6 (1-2016)

Ref.: Hanna §§ 1.19, 2.11[3]; Herlick Handbook § 3.20.

ARTICLE 13
Group Self-Insurance

§15470. General.

(a) In order to form and operate a group self insurer for private, for-profit employers, a mutual benefit corporation shall be formed pursuant to Part 3 (commencing with Section 7110) of Division 2 of Title 1 of the California Corporations Code. The mutual benefit corporation shall be the group self insurer and shall be formed for the sole purpose of operating a group workers' compensation self insurance fund to pool compensation liabilities of two or more for-profit private employers.

(b) In order to form and operate a group self insurer for private, non-profit employers, a non-profit corporation shall be formed pursuant to Division 2 of Title 1 of the Corporations Code. The non-profit corporation shall be a non-profit charitable corporation, a non-profit public benefit corporation, a non-profit mutual benefit corporation, or a non-profit religious or apostolic corporation, as is appropriate based on the nature and purpose of the non-profit employer. The non-profit corporation shall be the group self insurer and shall be formed for the sole purpose of operating a group workers' compensation self insurance fund to pool compensation liabilities of two or more non-profit private employers.

(c) The group self insurer will make application to the Manager for a Certificate of Consent to Self Insure as provided in Section 15482 of these regulations and, if granted approval by the Director, shall be the holder of the Certificate of Consent to Self Insure.

(d) Each initial proposed group member shall make application to the Manager for an Affiliate Certificate of Consent to Self Insure as one of the qualifying group applicants pursuant to Section 15482.1 of these regulations. Once a Certificate of Consent to Self Insure has been approved and issued, each subsequent proposed member shall make application to the Manager for an Affiliate Certificate of Consent to Self Insure pursuant to Section 15482.2 of these regulations. If granted by the Director, each approved member of a group self insurer shall be the holder of an Affiliate Certificate of Consent to Self Insure under the Certificate of Consent to Self Insure granted to the group self insurer.

(e) The group self insurer shall post and maintain a security deposit with the Manager as set forth in Sections 15210 and 15496 of these regulations to secure the expected workers' compensation liabilities of the group self insurer.

(f) The group self insurer shall file a Self Insurer's Annual Report as set forth in Article 5 of these regulations and shall estimate compensation liabilities as set forth in Article 6 of these regulations.

(g) The group self insurer shall not transfer liabilities to a third party except to a carrier meeting the requirements of Section 15360(c) under a special excess workers' compensation policy as provided by Labor Code Section 3702.8(c) and/or as provided by Article 8, Section 15360 of these regulations.

(h) The group self insurer shall fall under the continuing jurisdiction of the Director and any Certificates or Affiliate Certificates of Consent to Self Insure issued to a group self insurer or a group member may be revoked as set forth in Article 10 of these regulations.

(i) Hearing and appeal procedures set forth in Article 11 shall be applicable to self insurance matters set forth in Section 15430 involving group self insurers or group members.

(j) Each group self insurer shall comply with recordkeeping and audit requirements in Article 9 and the claims administration requirements of Article 12 of these regulations.

(k) Each private group self insurer shall be subject to assessments as set forth in Article 4 of these regulations.

(*l*) A group self insurer issued a Certificate of Consent to Self Insure pursuant to Labor Code Section 3700 and these regulations are not intended to deem such a group self insurer to be an insurance company and be subject to regulations governing insurers contained in Title 10, California Code of Regulations, except as otherwise provided by statute and by Title 8, California Code of Regulations.

Note: Authority cited: Sections 54, 55 and 3702.10, Labor Code. Reference: Sections 59, 3700, 3701, 3701.5, 3702, 3702.2, 3702.5 and 3702.10, Labor Code.

History: 1. New article 13 and section filed 6-30-94; operative 6-30-94 (Register 94, No. 26).

2. Amendment filed 3-2-2009; operative 3-2-2009 pursuant to Government Code section 11343.4 (Register 2009, No. 10).

3. Amendment of article heading filed 12-14-2016; operative 1-1-2017 pursuant to Government Code section 11343.4(b)(3) (Register 2016, No. 51).

Ref.: Hanna §§ 1.19, 2.11; Herlick Handbook § 3.20.

§15471. Initial Feasibility Study.

Included with each group self-insurer's initial application for a Certificate To Self-Insure required by Section 15482 of these regulations shall be a feasibility study report prepared by the prospective Group Administrator or an independent risk management individual or firm, consisting of the following:

(a) An analysis of the advantages and disadvantages of group self-insurance for the proposed group members as compared to the options of individual self-insurance or coverage under a policy issued by a carrier(s);

(b) Identification of all of the initial proposed group members and the combined total payroll for the proposed group self-insurer;

(c) A consolidated summary of the historical workers' compensation claims loss experience and the allocated loss expenses of the proposed group members for a minimum of the three most recent, full policy years, as well as the current policy year through the last completed quarter under the current policy at the time the application is submitted;

(d) A five (5) year pro forma financial statement including, but not limited to, an income statement, balance sheet, projected cash flows, and claims payout projections. The pro forma financial statement must include a detailed separation of assets, liabilities, retained earnings, taxes, and accrual and distribution of excess contributions. If any claims costs are discounted, the interest rate assumptions and payout patterns must be described and must be based on reasonable assumptions.

(e) A summary of the specific details of the group self-insurer's operating plan or the plan itself, including, but not limited to, descriptions of:

(1) The group self-insurer's legal and organizational structure;

(2) Method of governance;

(3) General management of the group self-insurer, including underwriting policies, insurance coverage, billing, commissions, fees, and all other expenses.

(4) Rating or contribution plans, or other means by which group funding during the first five years of operation will generated and the amounts to be generated by the methods proposed for each of the first 5 years of operation.

(f) The first 12 month budget of the group self-insurer;

(g) The names and credit ratings of any anticipated excess insurance coverage carriers, including estimated cost, levels of retention for specific excess insurance, aggregate excess insurance if obtained, and maximum liability levels of each excess policy;

(h) The company name and name of the person designated as the independent Group Administrator and the company name of the independent third party claims administrator chosen by the Board of Trustees;

(i) A description of safety and loss control services available from the group self-insurer to group members;

(j) A description of the underwriting requirements for member selection for the group self-insurer, including a description of any underwriting requirements or restrictions imposed by the specific excess insurance carrier;

(k) The name of the certified public accountant that will prepare annual financial reports for the group self-insurer;

(*l*) The name and professional actuarial designation of the actuary who will prepare actuarial reports for the group self-insurer, as well as an indication of how frequently actuarial reports will be completed;

(m) A statement indicating the means by which the group self-insurer will post the required security deposit; and

(n) A statement describing any fidelity insurance coverage and errors and omissions insurance coverage to be maintained by the group self-insurer, and/or by vendors with the group self-insurer named as beneficiary.

Note: Authority cited: Sections 54, 55 and 3702.10, Labor Code. Reference: Sections 3700, 3701 and 3702.1, Labor Code.

History: 1. New section filed 6-30-94; operative 6-30-94 (Register 94, No. 26).

2. Amendment filed 3-2-2009; operative 3-2-2009 pursuant to Government Code section 11343.4 (Register 2009, No. 10).

3. Repealer of subsection (d), subsection relettering and amendment of newly designated subsection (d) filed 12-14-2016; operative 1-1-2017 pursuant to Government Code section 11343.4(b)(3) (Register 2016, No. 51).

Ref.: Hanna §§ 1.19, 2.11; Herlick Handbook § 3.20.

§15472. Minimum Financial Requirements for a Group Self-Insurer.

(a) In addition to other requirements specified in this Article 13, no private group shall continue as a group self-insurer, unless it meets the funding and solvency requirements specified in section 15484(e) as demonstrated in independently audited financial statements meeting the requirements specified in section 15484(a) and (b) of this chapter. (Exception: A group self-insurer may continue if it is operating under a corrective action plan approved by the Chief.)

Note: Authority cited: Sections 54, 55 and 3702.10, Labor Code. Reference: Sections 3700, 3701, 3701.5, 3702, 3702.2 and 3702.10, Labor Code.

History: 1. New section filed 6-30-94; operative 6-30-94 (Register 94, No. 26).

2. Amendment of section heading and section filed 3-2-2009; operative 3-2-2009 pursuant to Government Code section 11343.4 (Register 2009, No. 10).

3. Amendment of section heading and section filed 12-14-2016; operative 1-1-2017 pursuant to Government Code section 11343.4(b)(3) (Register 2016, No. 51).

Ref.: Hanna §§ 1.19, 2.11; Herlick Handbook § 3.20.

§15473. Homogeneity of Group Members.

(a) Each private group self insurer shall demonstrate and maintain homogeneity of its group members by one of the following methods:

(1) Each group member shall share the same, predominant three-digit North American Industry Classification System (NAICS) Code; or

(2) Each group member shall share the same governing class code as established by the Workers' Compensation Insurance Rating Bureau (WCIRB) definition.

(b) In addition to the methods for demonstrating homogeneity indicated in subsections (a)(1) and (a)(2), applicants may demonstrate homogeneity for the purposes of eligibility for group self insurance if one of the following occurs:

(1) The group self insurer demonstrates to the Manager's satisfaction that the risk exposures of an affiliate group member or applicant affiliate group member are comparable to those contemplated in the feasibility study of the group self insurer.

(2) A group member shall be deemed as meeting homogeneity requirements if it is a wholly owned or majority owned subsidiary of a current group member that meets homogeneity requirements, its total payroll does not exceed the total payroll of that current member, and no more than 25% of the combined payroll of the existing member and the proposed group members' payroll fails to meet homogeneity requirements as set forth in subsection (a).

(3) The group self insurer demonstrates to the Manager's satisfaction that no less than 75% of payroll for each affiliate group self insurer or applicant affiliate group self insure is distributed among two shared industry-specific workers' compensation payroll classifications as established by the California Workers' Compensation Insurance Rating Bureau, and WCIRB insurance rates for those classifications are within 10% of each other.

(c) The Manager may require the group applicant or group self insurer to present additional information or documentation to verify that any or all group members or prospective group members meet the requirements of subsections (a) or (b).

(d) A group self insurer shall not modify its homogeneity underwriting requirements in any way unless it first obtains written approval from the Manager. In order to obtain approval from the Manager, the group self insurer must submit a written feasibility study and a draft of amended group self insurer's bylaws to the Manager no less than 30 days before the date of the change requested, addressing the following:

(1) The feasibility study must include:

(A) The reasons for the group self insurer's proposed modification of its homogeneity requirements;

(B) The proposed underwriting requirements for group self insurer membership;

(C) A demonstration that the risk exposures contemplated in the proposed modification are comparable, can reasonably be expected to develop comparable loss experience, and meet the requirements of subsections (a) or (b) of this section;

(D) A statement that the excess insurance carrier or carriers for the group self insurer approve of the modification;

(E) A statement by the Board of Trustees of the group self insurer in support of the modification;

(F) A plan for communication to all group members of the group self insurer describing the proposed modification of homogeneity requirements.

(2) The group self insurer's amended bylaws shall ensure that:

(A) No member of the group self insurer shall be penalized in any way for terminating membership in the group self insurer because of the change in homogeneity requirements;

(B) The modification to homogeneity requirements shall not disqualify any existing group member of the group self insurer that qualifies for membership before the modification of homogeneity requirements.

Note: Authority cited: Sections 54, 55 and 3702.10, Labor Code. Reference: Sections 3700 and 3702.10, Labor Code.

History: 1. New section filed 6-30-94; operative 6-30-94 (Register 94, No. 26).

2. Amendment filed 3-2-2009; operative 3-2-2009 pursuant to Government Code section 11343.4 (Register 2009, No. 10).

Ref.: Hanna §§ 1.19, 2.11; Herlick Handbook § 3.20.

§15474. Reporting Periods.

Regardless of the date that self insurance begins or the term of the program year of a group self insurer, the group self insurer shall file a Self Insurer's Annual Report by March 1 of each year as required by Section 15251. While the filing of the group self insurer's first Self Insurer's Annual Report may be for a period shorter than a year, the duration of the initial program year of the group self insurer, may be shorter or longer than twelve months.

Note: Authority cited: Sections 54, 55 and 3702.10, Labor Code. Reference: Sections 3700, 3702.1, 3702.2 and 3702.10, Labor Code.

History: 1. New section filed 6-30-94; operative 6-30-94 (Register 94, No 26).

2. Amendment filed 3-2-2009; operative 3-2-2009 pursuant to Government Code section 11343.4 (Register 2009, No. 10).

Ref.: Hanna §§ 1.19, 2.11; Herlick Handbook § 3.20.

§15475. Board of Trustees.

(a) Each group self insurer shall have a Board of Trustees that is responsible for all operations of the group self insurer.

(b) Each trustee on the Board of Trustees shall be elected by the group members or, if each group member has a seat on the Board of Trustees, the trustee may be appointed by the group members. At least two-thirds of the trustees shall be employees or officers of the group members. No service provider, director, officer, or employee of a service provider, or person with a direct or indirect management or financial interest in a service provider of the group self insurer shall serve as a voting member of the Board of Trustees of the group self insurer. The Group Administrator may be a non-voting member of the Board of Trustees but shall not vote on any matters before the Board. Service providers of the group self insurer include, but are not limited to, all service providers described in Section 15475.1 of these regulations.

(c) The duties of the Board of Trustees shall include the responsibility to approve or deny the request of any proposed member to join the group self insurer, subject to subsequent application and approval of the proposed group self insurer member by the Director of Industrial Relations.

(d) The Board of Trustees shall take all necessary precautions to protect the assets of the group self insurer, including all of the following:

(1) Designate a "Group Administrator" to administer the financial affairs and normal day-to-day operations of the group self insurer and ensure that there are no conflicts of interest or potential conflicts of interest involving the Board of Trustees, the Group Administrator, or any service providers utilized by the group self insurer, as provided by Section 15475.1;

The group administrator shall not be an owner, operator or employee of any member of the group self insurer or of the third party administrator handling the claims of the group self insurer.

(2) Obtain fidelity coverage in an amount determined by the Board of Trustees to be sufficient to ensure the integrity of affiliate group member or group funds handled by the Trustees and employees of the group self insurer, and obtain errors and omissions insurance coverage sufficient to protect its interests. Evidence of such bond shall be provided to the Chief upon request. The Group Administrator shall obtain and maintain fidelity insurance sufficient to cover funds handled for the group self insurer and errors and omissions insurance coverage sufficient to protect the group self insurer's and its members' interests.

(3) Contract with a third party claims administrator to work directly for the Board of Trustees to administer in California the workers' compensation claims of the group self insurer and require the third party claims administrator to carry fidelity insurance naming the group self insurer as beneficiary that is sufficient to protect the funds handled, and to carry errors and omissions insurance naming the group self insurer as beneficiary that is sufficient to protect against errors and omissions made in the claims handled.

(4) Manage disbursements for the payment of expenses of handling claims, administrative expenses, posting of security deposit, and other expenses necessary for operating the group self insurer;

(5) Appoint a financial institution and establish necessary accounts in California to handle the fiscal needs of the group self insurer and adopt a board resolution authorizing signature authority for each account;

(6) Immediately after the December 31 close of each reporting year, obtain an annual audit of the financial accounts and records of the each group self insurer by an independent, certified public accountant. The Group Administrator may not serve as the independent certified public accountant for the private group self insurer.

(7) Contract with an actuary that meets the requirements of Section 15481, subdivisions (a)(3) and (4) to conduct an annual actuarial review of the group self insurer's claims and produce a written actuarial study that projects ultimate liabilities of the group self insurer by program year at the undiscounted expected actuarial confidence level also commonly known as the undiscounted 'actuarial central estimate', inclusive of incurred but not reported (IBNR) liabilities, Allocated loss adjustment expense (ALAE), and unallocated loss adjustment expense (ULAE) to ensure that all claims and associated costs are recognized;

(8) Ensure that contributions are collected for each program year as required by Section 15484, subdivision (e).

(9) Ensure that funds collected from group members shall not be used for any purpose not directly related to the

payment of compensation liabilities of the group self insurer, posting of security deposit, payment of assessments and penalties as a group self insurer or the reasonable expenses of operation of the group self insurer. Excess moneys not needed for current operation of the group self insurer may be invested by the Board of Trustees, at its discretion, only as provided by Section 15475.3 of these regulations.

(10) Hold meetings no less frequently than annually to adopt a budget for the upcoming year, approve contribution rates, and review the investment portfolio for compliance with these regulations;

(11) Ensure that the Group Administrator immediately reports to the Chief, in writing, any information that indicates the private group self insurer is no longer in compliance with statutory or regulatory requirements of the workers' compensation self insurance program or of any instance wherein the group self insurer terminates an affiliate group self insurer's group membership for cause.

(e) If specifically authorized in the group self insurer's bylaws, the Board of Trustees may delegate specific functions to the Group Administrator of the private group self insurer, including, but not limited to:

(1) Contracting with one or more third party claims administrators for handling of claims;

(2) Calculating the annual contribution rates to or other means of cost sharing to be charged each group member;

(3) Investing funds subject to Section 15475.3 of these regulations and any restrictions adopted by the Board of Trustees in addition to those contained in subsection (d);

(4) Reviewing and accepting applications from prospective members to the group self insurer and advising the Board if the prospective members do not fully meet the underwriting criteria for group membership;

(5) Executing the Agreements of Assumption and Guarantee For Group Members and the Indemnity Agreement on behalf of the group self insurer;

(6) Establishing accounts in California financial institutions and accounting procedures for controlling funds and ensuring accurate financial reporting with the financial institutions selected by the Board of Trustees.

Note: Authority cited: Sections 54, 55 and 3702.10, Labor Code. Reference: Sections 3700, 3700.1, 3701, 3701.5, 3702.1, 3702.2 and 3702.10, Labor Code.

History: 1. New section filed 6-30-94; operative 6-30-94 (Register 94, No. 26).

2. Amendment filed 3-2-2009; operative 3-2-2009 pursuant to Government Code section 11343.4 (Register 2009, No. 10).

3. Amendment of subsections (d)(2), (d)(7)-(8) and (d)(11) filed 12-31-2012 as an emergency; operative 1-1-2013 pursuant to Government Code section 11346.1(d) (Register 2013, No. 1). A Certificate of Compliance must be transmitted to OAL by 7-1-2013 or emergency language will be repealed by operation of law on the following day.

4. Certificate of Compliance as to 1-1-2013 order, including additional nonsubstantive amendments to subsection (d)(8), transmitted to OAL 7-1-2013 and filed 8-13-2013 (Register 2013, No. 33).

Ref.: Hanna §§ 1.19, 2.11; Herlick Handbook § 3.20.

§15475.1. Separation Among Service Providers.

(a) No claims administrator or employee, officer, or director of a claims administrator shall be an employee, officer or director of, or have a direct or indirect management or financial interest in either the Group Administrator or an affiliate member of the private group self insurer, nor shall any owner or employee of the Group Administrator or affiliate member of the private group self insurer be an owner, employee, officer or director of, or have a direct or indirect management or financial interest in the claims administrator.

(b) No Group Administrator, claims administrator, or insurance broker or employee, officer, or director thereof, shall serve as the certified public accountant for any group self insurer for which it provides services as a Group Administrator, claims administrator or insurance broker, respectively, nor shall any owner or employee of an affiliate group member of group self insurer serve as the certified public accountant for the group self insurer.

(c) No insurance broker of a group self insurer, or employee, officer, or director of such insurance broker with a direct or indirect management or financial interest in the group self insurer's claims administrator shall be an employee, officer or director of, or have a direct or indirect management or financial interest in the Group Administrator of the same group self insurer unless the Group Administrator notifies the group self insurer in writing of its relationship, and in no event shall the group self insurer be required by the Group Administrator to utilize the Group Administrator as broker.

(d) No actuary of a private self insured group preparing a written actuarial report pursuant to Section 15475(d)(7) shall be an employee, officer or director of, or have a direct or indirect management or financial interest in the Group Administrator of the same private self insured group unless the Group Administrator notifies the group self insurer and the Manager in writing of its relationship; notwithstanding this subsection, the Manager at his or her discretion may require that a written actuarial report pursuant to Section 15475(d)(7) be prepared at the expense of the group self insurer by an independent actuary with no relationship to the group administrator.

(e) No claims bill reviewer of a group self insurer shall be an employee, officer, or director of, or have a direct or indirect management or financial interest in, the Group Administrator of the group self insurer unless the Group Administrator notifies the group self insurer and the Manager in writing of its relationship. In no event shall the group self insurer be required by the Group Administrator to utilize services of the claims bill reviewer in which the Group Administrator has a direct or indirect interest.

Note: Authority cited: Sections 54, 55 and 3702.10, Labor Code. Reference: Sections 3700, 3700.1, 3701, 3701.5, 3702.1, 3702.2 and 3702.10, Labor Code.

History: 1. New section filed 3-2-2009; operative 3-2-2009 pursuant to Government Code section 11343.4 (Register 2009, No. 10).

Ref.: Hanna §§ 1.19, 2.11; Herlick Handbook § 3.20.

§15475.2. Restriction on Use of Funds.

(a) The group self-insurer, its trustees, group members, Group Administrator, claims administrator, or other agents or vendors of the group self-insurer shall not utilize funds collected from group members or from other parties conducting business with the group self-insurer, and/or funds earned by the group self-insurer through investments for any purpose not directly related to the payment of claims, the payment of fees related to funding the group, including the posting of a security deposit, penalties, excess insurance premiums, or for any other reasonable obligations or costs of operation of the group self-insurer as determined and authorized by the Board, including the refunding of surplus funds authorized pursuant to Section 15477.

(b) The group self-insurer shall not lend any money to any trustee, core member or affiliate member of the private group self-insurer, or to the Group Administrator, the claims administrator, and/or any other agent, vendor, or service provider. The group self-insurer shall not lend or issue any debt instruments incur other encumbrances or obligations, or extend credit to any group member for the payment of contributions or assessments. Notwithstanding this section, the group self-insurer may:

(1) permit fixed installment plans not to exceed twelve (12) months to collect contributions for the payment of current group members;

(2) permit fixed installment plans approved by the Chief for the payment of special assessments to make up a funding insufficiency pursuant to Section 15477.

(c) Funds of the private group self-insurer shall not be commingled with the funds or assets of any group member or any other group self-insurer.

(d) Once surplus funds have been declared as excess funds and transferred to an escrow account pursuant to section 15477(a)(1), such surplus funds of the private group self-insurer shall not be commingled in the checking account(s) established for the payment of and administration of current liabilities of group member claims, assessments, and other expenses of the group self-insurer's operation.

Note: Authority cited: Sections 54, 55 and 3702.10, Labor Code. Reference: Sections 3700, 3701, 3701.5, 3702.1, 3702.2 and 3702.10, Labor Code.

History: 1. New section filed 3-2-2009; operative 3-2-2009 pursuant to Government Code section 11343.4 (Register 2009, No. 10).

2. Amendment of subsections (a), (b)(1)-(2) and (d) filed 12-14-2016; operative 1-1-2017 pursuant to Government Code section 11343.4(b)(3) (Register 2016, No. 51).

Ref.: Hanna §§ 1.19, 2.11; Herlick Handbook § 3.20.

§15475.3. Investment of Funds.

(a) Subject to the limitations set forth in Section 15475.2, the Board of Trustees of a group self-insurer may invest excess funds not immediately needed for the payment of the group insurer's liabilities in any of the following:

(1) United States Treasury Bills, Notes, and Bonds for which the full faith and credit of the United States are pledged for the payment of interest and principal.

(2) Federal agency or United States government-sponsored enterprise obligations, participations, or other instruments, including those issued by or fully guaranteed as to principal and interest by federal agencies or United States government sponsored enterprises.

(3) Certificates of Deposit that are FDIC or NCUA insured or collateralized by the issuing institution. Investments in eligible certificates of deposit, that are brokered into various FDIC and/or NCUA insured institutions, shall have a maximum maturity of no more than five (5) years, and shall not exceed fifty percent (50%) of the total portfolio as measured at the date of purchase.

(4) Money market accounts and savings accounts offered by financial institutions whose deposits are insured by a federal agency. Such deposit accounts in financial institutions shall be limited to offices or branches of the financial institutions located in the State of California. Should the amount deposited in any single account exceed the federally insured amount for any one account, the financial institution shall also meet the credit rating requirements as set forth in Section 15215(e).

(5) Bonds, notes, warrants, or other evidence of indebtedness of any local agency or State agency within the United States of America, including bonds payable solely out of the revenues from a revenue-producing property owned, controlled, or operated by the State or local agency, or by the department, board, agency, or authority of the State or local agency, provided the credit worthiness of the security meets the same requirements of securities posted with the Director as security deposit in Section 15213(a)(1).

(b) In addition to investments made pursuant to subsections (a)(1) through (a)(2) of this section, but only if invested through the services of a registered investment advisor, the Board of Trustees of a private group self-insurer may invest excess funds not immediately needed for the payment of group liabilities in any of the following:

(1) Prime Bankers' Acceptances of the 50 largest global banks.

(2) Commercial Paper rated A1/P1/F1 by a nationally recognized statistical rating organization. Investments in eligible commercial paper shall have a maximum maturity of 270 days or less, and shall not exceed 25% of the total portfolio as measured at the date of purchase.

(3) Medium-term notes, defined as all corporate and depository institution debt securities with a maximum remaining maturity of five years or less, issued by corporations organized and operating within the United States or by depository institutions licensed by the United States or any state and operating within the United States. Investments in eligible medium-term notes shall be rated "A" or better by a nationally recognized statistical rating organization, shall not exceed 30% of the total portfolio as measured at the date of purchase, and shall have a maximum remaining maturity not to exceed 10 years.

(4) Preferred stock issued by any solvent American institution registered as provided by the Securities and Exchange Act of 1934 (15 U.S.C. 78a-78kk); preferred stock shall not exceed 10% of the total portfolio as measured at the date of purchase.

(5) Bond Funds regulated by the Securities and Exchange Commission, and rated AA or better by a nationally recognized statistical rating organization.

(6) The maximum percentage of a self-insured group's portfolio that may be invested in equities securities is thirty percent (30%). In the event the investment in equity

securities exceeds 30% of the group self-insurer's portfolio, the group shall re-balance the portfolio in order to comply with this section.

(c) The Board of Trustees, whether through its registered investment advisor or not, shall not participate in "short selling" (a sale of a security not owned by the seller; a technique used to take advantage of an anticipated decline in price or to protect a profit), or "margin transactions" (purchase of a security on credit after a margin has been deposited).

(d) The Board of Trustees shall not invest in any of the following assets:

(1) Commodities or Futures Contracts;

(2) Investment in stock not listed on an exchange or sold to the public;

(3) Stock options;

(4) Limited partnerships.

(e) With the exception of United States Treasury Bills, Notes and Bonds, and United States government agency or government sponsored enterprise obligations, the maximum percentage of the group self-insurer's portfolio that may be invested in a single issuer or single mortgage-related security is 5%.

(f) The weighted average portfolio maturity may not exceed five years.

Note: Authority cited: Sections 54, 55 and 3702.10, Labor Code. Reference: Sections 3700, 3701, 3701.5, 3702.1, 3702.2 and 3702.10, Labor Code.

History: 1. New section filed 3-2-2009; operative 3-2-2009 pursuant to Government Code section 11343.4 (Register 2009, No. 10).

2. Amendment of subsection (a)(3) filed 12-14-2016; operative 1-1-2017 pursuant to Government Code section 11343.4(b)(3) (Register 2016, No. 51).

Ref.: Hanna §§ 1.19, 2.11; Herlick Handbook § 3.20.

§15476. Advanced Contribution Discounts.

The Board of Trustees of a group self-insurer using a contribution plan shall not authorize discounts to any member. Additionally, if any factors reflecting loss histories, such as experience modification calculations, are utilized to modify group self-insurer or individual member contributions, the contributions for the funding of the group self-insurer's program year[s] shall be no less than the funding required under Section 15484(e).

Note: Authority cited: Sections 54, 55 and 3702.10, Labor Code. Reference: Sections 3700, 3701 and 3702.10, Labor Code.

History: 1. New section filed 6-30-94; operative 6-30-94 (Register 94, No. 26).

2. Amendment of section heading and section filed 3-2-2009; operative 3-2-2009 pursuant to Government Code section 11343.4 (Register 2009, No. 10).

3. Amendment of section heading and section filed 12-14-2016; operative 1-1-2017 pursuant to Government Code section 11343.4(b)(3) (Register 2016, No. 51).

Ref.: Hanna §§ 1.19, 2.11; Herlick Handbook § 3.20.

§15477. Surplus or Insufficient Funding.

(a) The Board of Trustees of a group self insurer shall not declare that surplus contributions collected in excess of the amount necessary to fund all obligations for any given program year will be refunded to group members unless the group self insurer's most recent annual certified, independently audited financial statement indicates that the group self insurer's assets exceed its liabilities and unless the group self insurer's current actuarial report indicates a surplus of group funds for each program year as indicated in subsections (a)(1) and (a)(2) below.

(1) The group self insurer may transfer excess funds to an escrow account at any time, but shall not declare surplus fund amounts or distribute any surplus funds to group members for any given program year sooner than 23 months after the close of the program year without express written consent from the Chief. Any such disbursements made without written consent from the Chief, including any subsequent disbursements from the same program year or disbursements from a subsequent program year, shall only be from a program year that remains funded as required by Section 15484, subdivision (e). Approval from the Chief is not required as long as the group self insurer's current actuarial report and current financial statement support the determination of the surplus amount, and as long as claim funding for each program year meets or exceeds the funding required by Section 15484, subdivision (e).

(2) Notwithstanding subsection (a)(1) of this section, the group self insurer may request the Chief to allow that funds be released sooner than 23 months after the end of a program year and/or that the determination of a program year's surplus be based upon the actuarial study conducted with a confidence factor of less than the funding required by Section 15484, subdivision (e), and the Chief may allow such a release of surplus funds upon a showing of good cause by the group self insurer. The Chief may require that a special audit be conducted, an independent actuarial study be completed at the group self insurer's expense, and/or other documentation be submitted to support the request from the group self insurer. In no event shall surplus funds be distributed sooner than 23 months after the completion of a program year without express written consent of the Chief.

(3) No reduction in contribution rates for group members shall be authorized unless supported by an actuarial study less than one year old conducted pursuant to Section 15481 of these regulations.

(b) If at the end of any program year member funds collected and investment income associated with any program year are insufficient to completely fund all estimated future claim liabilities and expenses at the required confidence level for any program year, unfunded amounts by program year shall be immediately reported to the Chief, along with a proposed plan to achieve correction of the deficiency. Any plan to correct the deficiency shall be subject to approval by the Chief. The plan may include, but is not limited to, any or all of the following:

(1) Reallocation of surplus group self insurer funds collected in other program years that are unnecessary for the payment of claims or expenses for the program year collected;

(2) Reallocation of investment earnings associated with other program years that are not necessary for the payment of claims or expenses in the program year in which the earnings are associated;

(3) One or more special assessments of all group self insurer members participating in the program year or years in which the deficiency exists to make up the funding insufficiency;

(4) Re-evaluation of past group member contribution rates and the projected plan for future contributions from members to properly collect past rating shortfalls, and/or a revised current and future contribution rating plan for group members for any period of time necessary to correct past and present rate inequities.

(5) Prohibition of the addition of new members into the group; suspension of any distribution of over-collected contributions or assessments and any earnings on investments; or, the immediate collection of all assessments or any portion of such assessments until the group self insurer is deemed by the Chief to be adequately capitalized in accordance with this section;

(6) An examination and restructuring of the group self insurer's operations, contracts with vendors, and finances by an outside qualified professional acceptable to the Chief;

(7) Any other action the Chief may determine appropriate to promptly correct the group's funding deficiency.

(c) If the plan to achieve prompt correction of the funding deficiency for all claims is not approved by the Chief, the Chief may order the Board of Trustees of the group self insurer to show good cause before the Director why it should not be ordered by the Director to (1) immediately assess the group members for the full amount of the funding deficiency and/or (2) order that any surplus funds distributed to group members during the previous twelve calendar months from the date of discovery of the funding deficiency by the group self insurer be immediately returned to the group self insurer; and/or (3) why the Director should not order the appointment of a conservator or liquidator for the group self insurer.

(d) If the Director determines that actions specified in subsections (b) and (c) of this section will not achieve full funding of all claim liabilities for the group self insurer, the Director may in his or her discretion order that an outside conservator or liquidator, including the Self Insurer's Security Fund, be appointed at the expense of the group self insurer to manage the financial affairs of the group self insurer and to take whatever steps may be necessary in order to return a financially troubled group self insurer to full financial solvency or to liquidate the group's liabilities.

Note: Authority cited: Sections 54, 55 and 3702.10, Labor Code. Reference: Sections 3700, 3701, 3701.5 and 3702.10, Labor Code.

History: 1. New section filed 6-30-94; operative 6-30-94 (Register 94, No. 26).

2. Amendment of section heading and section filed 3-2-2009; operative 3-2-2009 pursuant to Government Code section 11343.4 (Register 2009, No. 10).

3. Amendment of subsections (a)(1)-(2), (b) and (b)(5)-(c) filed 12-31-2012 as an emergency; operative 1-1-2013 pursuant to Government Code section 11346.1(d) (Register 2013, No. 1). A Certificate of Compliance must be transmitted to OAL by 7-1-2013 or emergency language will be repealed by operation of law on the following day.

4. Certificate of Compliance as to 1-1-2013 order, including additional nonsubstantive amendments to subsections (a)(1)-(2), transmitted to OAL 7-1-2013 and filed 8-13-2013 (Register 2013, No. 33).

Ref.: Hanna §§ 1.19, 2.11; Herlick Handbook § 3.20.

§15478. Excess Insurance.

(a) Each group self insurer shall have and maintain in full force one or more specific excess workers' compensation insurance policies issued by an admitted casualty insurance carrier or carriers authorized to transact such business in the State of California by the California Department of Insurance. The specific excess policy shall not have a retention level above $500,000 nor an upper limit of less than twenty-five million dollars ($25,000,000) without express written consent of the Manager pursuant to subsection (b). The policy may not lapse, be canceled or otherwise terminated without prior written notice to the Manager and the group self insurer no later than 30 days prior to the date of cancellation or termination by the carrier. On the policy issuance date and on any subsequent renewal date of the policy, the excess carrier or its parent company shall have an adjusted policyholders' surplus of no less than twenty-five million dollars ($25,000,000) and an acceptable credit rating as set forth below:

(1) Standard and Poor's Insurer Financial Strength Rating of A or better rating, or

(2) A.M. Best Company, Financial Strength Rating of B+ or better rating.

If the group self insurer's specific excess carrier's credit rating falls below a B rating as rated by either rating agency specified in subsections (a)(1) or (a)(2), the group self insurer shall replace the policy or obtain new coverage for the remainder of the unused prior policy period and for future coverage through a specific excess carrier that meets the requirements of this section.

(b) Each private group self insurer seeking to maintain a specific excess policy with a retention level above $500,000 or an upper limit of less than twenty-five million dollars ($25,000,000) shall first demonstrate in writing to the satisfaction of the Manager through its audited financial statement(s) and a current written actuarial report or portion thereof specifically demonstrating that the group self insurer has the financial strength to assume a retention level above $500,000 per occurrence and/or an upper limit of the policy of less than twenty-five million dollars ($25,000,000). The Manager may consider the group self insurer's financial reports, actuarial reports, spread of risk, its level of contributions and/or assessments, current membership size, loss prevention program, any aggregate stop loss insurance policy in place, and/or other factors the requesting group wishes to have the Manager consider in making his or her determination on the request to grant the group self insurer permission to carry specific excess insurance above the $500,000 per occurrence level. The group self insurer shall maintain specific excess coverage with a minimum $500,000 self insurer's retention and an upper limit of the policy of no less than twenty-five million dollars ($25,000,000), unless written consent from the Manager for a higher retention level and/or upper limit of less than twenty-five million dollars ($25,000,000) is obtained. In no event shall the group self insurer's retention level be greater than $1,000,000 per occurrence.

(c) Any private group self insurer may have and maintain in full force an aggregate excess workers' compensation insurance policy. As set forth in Section 15210.3 of these regulations, no security deposit credit will be allowed for aggregate excess coverage.

(d) If the Director orders the Self Insurer's Security Fund to assume the liabilities of the group self insurer pursuant to Labor Code Section 3701.5, the specific excess carrier or aggregate excess carrier shall make all payments due directly to the Security Fund as would have been made by the excess carrier to the group self insurer after the retention level of the policy had been reached.

(e) The group self insurer or any affiliate member of the group self insurer shall not own or have controlling ownership in the specific excess carrier that issues the specific excess policy. Any known direct ownership in the specific excess carrier or carriers by any current or proposed service providers, including the Group Administrator, shall be disclosed in writing to the group's Board of Trustees along with the price quoted for the policy or policies. No group self insurer or member of a group self insurer shall function as a re-insurer of any specific excess insurance policy or policies issued to a group self insurer or renewed by a group self insurer.

Note: Authority cited: Sections 54, 55 and 3702.10, Labor Code. Reference: Sections 3700, 3701, 3701.5, 3702.10 and 3744, Labor Code.

History: 1. New section filed 6-30-94; operative 6-30-94 (Register 94, No. 26).

2. Amendment of section and Note filed 3-2-2009; operative 3-2-2009 pursuant to Government Code section 11343.4 (Register 2009, No. 10).

3. Amendment of subsection (b) filed 9-19-2011; operative 10-19-2011 (Register 2011, No. 38).

Ref.: Hanna §§ 1.19, 2.11; Herlick Handbook § 3.20.

§15479. Indemnity Agreement and Power of Attorney.

(a) Each member of a group self-insurer shall execute an Indemnity Agreement and Power of Attorney Form S-4 (1-2016).

(b) The Indemnity Agreement and Power of Attorney shall contain, in substance, the following provisions:

(1) An agreement under which each member of a group self-insurer agrees to assume and discharge, jointly and severally, any compensation liability under Labor Code Section 3700-3705 of any and all other employers that are parties to the group self-insurer indemnity agreement;

(2) The agreement provides that, in addition to the rights of the group self-insurer to enforce the indemnity agreement in the event of a failure of the group self-insurer to enforce such rights after reasonable notice to the group self-insurer, the Director of Industrial Relations independently shall have the right to enforce the indemnity agreement on behalf of the group self-insurer including the joint and several liability of group members for payment of all compensation liabilities under the indemnity agreement and the liability of group members for any unpaid contributions and assessments;

(3) Provisions requiring that the Board of Trustees of the group self-insurer designate and appoint a Group Administrator empowered to accept the service of process on behalf of the group members and authorized to act for and bind the group self-insurer and all group members in all transactions relating to or arising out of the operation of the group self-insurer;

(4) Provisions for the right of the Director of Industrial Relations to substitute an outside Conservator for the Group Administrator;

(5) A provision granting full power of attorney and signature authority to the Group Administrator of the group self-insurer to execute documents, enter contracts, accept service of process on behalf of the group self-insurer, and conduct the general business of the group self-insurer, and, that said signature of the Group Administrator shall bind each and every group member jointly and severally.

NOTE: A copy of S-4 (1-2016), Indemnity Agreement and Power of Attorney is available from the Chief and is available at http://www.dir.ca.gov/osip and is contained in the Appendix following Article 12 of Chapter 8, Subchapter 2.

Note: Authority cited: Sections 54, 55 and 3702.10, Labor Code. Reference: Sections 3700, 3701, 3701.5, 3702, 3702.1, 3702.2, 3702.3, 3702.5, 3702.7 and 3702.10, Labor Code.

History: 1. New section filed 6-30-94; operative 6-30-94 (Register 94, No. 26).

2. Amendment filed 3-2-2009; operative 3-2-2009 pursuant to Government Code section 11343.4 (Register 2009, No. 10).

3. Amendment of subsections (a) and (a)(5) filed 12-14-2016; operative 1-1-2017 pursuant to Government Code section 11343.4(b)(3) (Register 2016, No. 51).

Ref.: Hanna §§ 1.19, 2.11; Herlick Handbook § 3.20.

§15480. Termination of Membership in a Group Self-Insurer.

(a) No member of a group self-insurer may be involuntarily canceled or terminated from group membership by the group self-insurer unless at least 45 days advance written notice has been provided to the group member and to the Chief. Notice to a broker or other third party shall not be deemed as notice to the group member.

(b) In the case of cancellation or termination of coverage of a group member, whether voluntary or involuntary, the group self-insurer shall remain liable for all compensation liabilities of the group member resulting from any claim with a date of injury during the period of membership in the group self-insurer up to the effective date of the termination and revocation of the group member's Affiliate Certificate of Consent to Self-Insure, including the 45 day notice period in the event of involuntary termination. The group member shall remain responsible for all contributions and assessments for the period of membership in the private group self-insurer, including the 45 day notice period and/or any period during which the termination and revocation of the group member's Affiliate Certificate of Consent to Self-Insure was under appeal.

(c) Notwithstanding subsection (b), the following provisions apply in the case of the cancellation or termination of membership of a member in a group self-insured group, whether voluntary or involuntary:

(1) The group self-insurer shall not incur liability for any claim of a member incurred on or after the date a member obtains coverage through a standard workers' compensation policy issued by an admitted carrier.

(2) Liabilities of a group member may be transferred pursuant to Labor Code Section 3702.8 and/or Article 8, Section 15360 of these regulations.

(d) Notice to the Chief of involuntary cancellation or termination of a group member from a group self-insurer as set forth in subsection (a) shall be good cause for revocation of the Affiliate Certificate issued to the group member on the applicable effective date of the involuntary cancellation or termination date without issuance of further notice from the Chief.

(e) Any group member leaving a group self-insurer shall provide proof of workers' compensation coverage to the Chief and to the group self-insurer within 45 days after the notice of cancellation or termination. Notice to the Chief may be provided by the group self-insurer, the Group Administrator, or the group member. However, if the group member no longer has employees in California, the group member or group self-insurer shall notify the Chief and no proof of insurance need be provided. Unless the group member no longer has employees in California, the Chief shall notify the Labor Commissioner of any group member that voluntarily or involuntarily leaves a private group self-insurer and has failed to provide proof of coverage for workers' compensation liabilities in the form of a binder or certificate of insurance within 45 days after the notice of cancellation or termination.

(f) Any member of a group self-insurer may voluntarily withdraw from the group self-insurer at the end of a program year after obtaining alternate coverage and providing written notice to the Group Administrator of its intent to voluntarily end its participation in the group self-insurer. Notwithstanding this section, the group self-insurer's bylaws may require periods of membership longer than one year and, except as specified by Section 15473(d)(2), may specify penalties, loss of any return of surplus funds, or other sanctions for early termination of group membership.

(g) Any member of a group self-insurer that is involuntarily revoked by the group for non-payment of any member contribution or assessment must bring current all outstanding unpaid amounts in order to exercise their right to appeal the notice of intent to revoke.

Note: Authority cited: Sections 54, 55 and 3702.10, Labor Code. Reference: Sections 3700, 3701, 3701.5, 3702 and 3702.10, Labor Code.

History: 1. New section filed 6-30-94; operative 6-30-94 (Register 94, No. 26).

2. Amendment of section heading and section filed 3-2-2009; operative 3-2-2009 pursuant to Government Code section 11343.4 (Register 2009, No. 10).

3. Amendment of section heading and subsections (a)-(b) and (d)-(e) and new subsection (g) filed 12-14-2016; operative 1-1-2017 pursuant to Government Code section 11343.4(b)(3) (Register 2016, No. 51).

Ref.: Hanna §§ 1.19, 2.11; Herlick Handbook § 3.20.

§15481. Actuarial Studies and Summaries.

(a) The group administrator for current and former Self-Insured Groups that are required to file a Self-Insurer's Annual Report shall cause a qualified actuary to submit on the group's behalf to the Office of Self-Insurance Plans (OSIP) a complete actuarial study by program year of its historical loss development and actuarial summary not later than April 15 of each calendar year with a valuation date of December 31 of the immediately prior calendar year. The summary shall be prepared and submitted via an online platform provided by OSIP with a copy of the complete actuarial study attached.

(1) The analysis and results of the actuarial study shall be presented to the group self-insurer's Board of Trustees and made available, in a written or electronic form, to the Board of Trustees and to any present or former group member requesting a copy. The study shall be presented to the Group Administrator and the Board of Trustees not later than March 31 following the end of the group self-insurer's program year.

(2) In the absence of an actuarial study or summary for any Self-Insured Group that fully satisfies the criteria of this section received by the deadline set forth above, the Chief shall establish a security deposit amount on behalf of the group as the Chief determines appropriate based on consideration of all financial and loss information available to the Chief at the time.

(3) The actuarial study and summary shall be prepared and submitted by an actuary meeting each of the following qualifications:

(A) The actuary must be independent with no common ownership or financial interest in the entity that is the subject of the actuarial study and summary, and

(B) Within the past ten (10) calendar years the actuary must have a minimum of five (5) years of experience making California workers' compensation actuarial projections, and

(C) The actuary must have a designation of Fellow of the Casualty Actuarial Society (FCAS), or be a member of the American Academy of Actuaries (MAAA), or be a member of the Society of Actuaries who is qualified to sign a statement of actuarial opinion on loss reserves.

(4) The qualified actuary or his/her employing actuarial firm shall maintain a minimum of one million dollars ($1,000,000) of professional liability and errors and omissions insurance coverage. Evidence of this coverage and limits must be submitted as a part of the actuarial study.

(5) Group self-insurers shall not be required to file an actuarial study or actuarial summary in years when their current year filed Self-Insurer's Annual Report reports either: (A) ten (10) or fewer open claims, or (B) less than one million dollars ($1,000,000) of total estimated future liabilities.

(b) The actuarial study shall identify the group self-insurer's losses at the undiscounted 'expected level' also commonly known as the undiscounted 'actuarial central estimate' including each of the following components: incurred but not reported (IBNR) liabilities, Allocated loss adjustment expense (ALAE), Unallocated loss adjusted expense (ULAE) and case reserves. The expected losses shall be reported at both the gross and net amounts of excess insurance values. Included with the actuarial study shall be a separate page or pages with the following information for each program year reported on the Self-Insurer's Annual Report:

(1) The amount of ultimate losses projected at the expected actuarial confidence level, inclusive of incurred but not reported (IBNR) liabilities, Allocated loss adjust-

ment expense (ALAE), Unallocated loss adjusted expense (ULAE) in calculations for each of the program years covered by the annual report. The expected losses shall be reported at both the gross and net amounts of excess insurance values;

(2) The amount of contributions collected from affiliate group members for each of the program years covered by the annual report; and

(3) The amount of any surplus funds distributed to affiliate group members for the program years covered by the annual report.

(4) The Board of Trustees shall ensure that contribution rates for the initial funding of claims for each program year shall be based on the actuarial projection at the expected level, including each of the following components: incurred but not reported (IBNR) liabilities, Allocated loss adjustment expense (ALAE), Unallocated loss adjusted expense (ULAE) as provided by Section 15475(d)(8).

(c) The actuarial study shall identify the estimated future liabilities reported in the Private Self-Insurer Annual Report filed by the self-insurer's Third Party Administrator(s).

(d) The actuarial study and summary shall clearly identify any excess coverage by carrier, policy year and self-insured retentions, by year.

(e) The actuary shall declare in the study and the summary that the study and report may be used by the State of California and the Self-Insurers' Security Fund to set appropriate collateral and deposit amounts, and for any other regulatory purpose under these regulations.

(f) The actuarial study and summary shall specify that it is prepared for use by the Department of Industrial Relations, Office of Self-Insurance Plans and the Self-Insurers' Security Fund. The Office of Self-Insurance Plans and the Self-Insurers' Security Fund may share the study and report with consultants retained by the Department of Industrial Relations or the Self-Insurers' Security Fund for official purposes in accomplishing the purposes of these regulations.

(g) The actuarial study must include all of and only the group self-insurer's California self-insured liabilities for the master certificate holder and all affiliate or subsidiary certificate holders related to the master certificate.

(h) Failure by a group administrator to cause a timely actuarial study and summary to be submitted on the group's behalf shall constitute good cause grounds for revocation of the group self-insurer's self-insurance Certificate.

(i) The Chief may accept or reject any actuarial study or summary that does not fully satisfy the criteria of this section and require a second study and summary by another qualified actuary that does fully satisfy the criteria of this section to the Chief be completed and submitted to OSIP at the self-insurer's expense.

Note: Authority cited: Sections 54, 55 and 3702.10, Labor Code. Reference: Sections 3700, 3701, 3701.5 and 3702.10, Labor Code.

History: 1. New section filed 6-30-94; operative 6-30-94 (Register 94, No. 26).

2. Amendment of section heading and section filed 3-2-2009; operative 3-2-2009 pursuant to Government Code section 11343.4 (Register 2009, No. 10).

3. Amendment of subsection (c) filed 9-19-2011; operative 10-19-2011 (Register 2011, No. 38).

4. Amendment of section heading and repealer and new section filed 12-31-2012 as an emergency; operative 1-1-2013 pursuant to Government Code section 11346.1(d) (Register 2013, No. 1). A Certificate of Compliance must be transmitted to OAL by 7-1-2013 or emergency language will be repealed by operation of law on the following day.

5. Certificate of Compliance as to 1-1-2013 order, including nonsubstantive amendments, transmitted to OAL 7-1-2013 and filed 8-13-2013 (Register 2013, No. 33).

6. Amendment of subsections (a)-(a)(1), (a)(3) and (a)(4)-(5) filed 12-14-2016; operative 1-1-2017 pursuant to Government Code section 11343.4(b)(3) (Register 2016, No. 51).

Ref.: Hanna §§ 1.19, 2.11; Herlick Handbook § 3.20.

§15482. Private Group Application.

(a) Each private group of employers desiring to procure a private group Certificate of Consent to Self-Insure as provided in Section 15470 of these regulations shall submit to the Chief a complete Application For A Certificate Of Consent To Self-Insure By A Group Of Employers for the group and a complete Application For An Affiliate Certificate Of Consent To Self-Insure As A Member Of A Group Self-Insurer for each initial member of the group no less than 30 days before the requested effective date of self-insurance. Applications shall be made on:

(1) Form S-1 (1-2016) for a private group seeking a group Certificate of Consent to Self-Insure;

(2) Form S-2B (1-2016) for each member of a group seeking an Affiliate Certificate of Consent to Self-Insure. The Application for an Affiliate Certificate of Consent to Self-Insure shall be completed as provided in Section 15482.1 of these regulations.

(b) A complete application to self-insure for a private group of employers shall be submitted with complete applications for each initial proposed member of the group and shall include the attachments requested in the application form itself, and, as applicable, the following:

(1) A duly executed Resolution by the Board of Trustees of the group applicant authorizing execution of the application to become a group self-insurer and empowering the Group Administrator and other employees, officers, or Trustees of the group self-insurer applicant to sign the application form and other necessary documents on behalf of the group self-insurer applicant;

(2) A duly executed Resolution by the Board of Trustees of the group self-insurer applicant authorizing the execution of an Agreement of Assumption and Guarantee Of Workers' Compensation Liabilities on behalf of the proposed group members and any future members of the group self-insurer granted an Affiliate Certificate;

(3) An Agreement of Assumption and Guarantee of Workers' Compensation Liabilities For Group and Affiliate Members ((Form S-5 (1-2016)) executed by the applicant group self-insurer as required in Section 15483 of these regulations;

(4) An original Certificate of Status from the California Secretary of State or other appropriate registration documents showing that the group applicant is appropri-

ately registered to do business in California dated within 90 days of the date of receipt of the application by the Chief;

(5) A certification that the group has implemented an effective injury and illness prevention program and contact name of the person responsible for overseeing the group's safety services as specified in Section 15486.1 of these regulations;

(6) An original, duly executed Indemnity Agreement and Power of Attorney of Joint and Several Liability between the group self-insurer applicant and each proposed member pursuant to Section 15479 of these regulations.

(7) Payment of the required application fee(s) as required by Section 15491 of these regulations.

(8) A copy of the Initial Feasibility Study Report as required in Section 15471 of these regulations.

(9) A duly executed Agreement and Undertaking for Security Deposit as required by Section 15486.

Note: Authority cited: Sections 54, 55 and 3702.10, Labor Code. Reference: Sections 59, 3700, 3701, 3701.5, 3702, 3702.2, 3702.5 and 3702.10, Labor Code.

History: 1. New section filed 3-2-2009; operative 3-2-2009 pursuant to Government Code section 11343.4 (Register 2009, No. 10).

2. Amendment filed 12-14-2016; operative 1-1-2017 pursuant to Government Code section 11343.4(b)(3) (Register 2016, No. 51).

§15482.1. Private Group Member Application.

(a) A complete group member application to self-insure on Form S-2B (1-2016) by each member of a group self-insurer shall include all the attachments requested in the application form itself, and, as applicable, the following:

(1) The Board of Trustees, or the Group Administrator if authorized by the group bylaws, shall evaluate potential new members by reviewing their financial statements, tax returns, credit reports, or other appropriate documentation as specified in the bylaws of the group self-insurer;

(2) A duly executed Resolution authorizing completion of the application to become self-insured as a member of the group self-insurer;

(3) A duly executed Indemnity Agreement and Power of Attorney (Form S-4 (1-2016)), as required by Section 15479 of these regulations.

(b) A separate application shall be submitted for any new or separate subsidiary or affiliate of an affiliate group self-insurer in order for it to be considered for consent to self-insure.

(c) A new application may be required whenever an existing affiliate group self-insurer reincorporates, merges, or otherwise changes ownership.

Note: Authority cited: Sections 54, 55, 59 and 3702.10, Labor Code. Reference: Sections 3700, 3700(b), 3701, 3702, 3702.5 and 6401.7(a), Labor Code.

History: 1. New section filed 3-2-2009; operative 3-2-2009 pursuant to Government Code section 11343.4 (Register 2009, No. 10).

2. Amendment filed 12-14-2016; operative 1-1-2017 pursuant to Government Code section 11343.4(b)(3) (Register 2016, No. 51).

§15482.2. Interim Certificates to Group Members.

(a) The Chief may issue an Interim Certificate of Consent to Self-Insure to a new member of an existing private group self-insurer upon receipt of a qualifying Request for Interim Certificate and the filing fee as provided in Section 15491(a)(3). The Interim Certificate of Consent to Self-Insure will be issued for a period not to exceed 180 days. A Certificate of Consent to Self-Insure to replace the Interim Certificate shall not be issued unless a completed application and accompanying documents required by Section 15482.1 and the application fee required by Section 15491 are submitted to the Chief within 180 days of the effective date of the Interim Certificate.

(b) To qualify for issuance of an Interim Certificate to its group members, the existing private group self-insurer holding the Master Certificate of Consent to Self-Insure must be a group self-insurer in good standing, and shall not be prohibited from adding new members pursuant to Section 15477(b)(5).

(c) A Group Affiliate Members Interim Application (Form S-2A (1-2016)) on behalf of the new group member shall be submitted by the Group Administrator to the Chief. The request shall be in writing and shall include the following information regarding the proposed new group member:

(1) The proposed group member's full legal name, state of incorporation, and Federal Tax Identification Number;

(2) The requested effective date of the Interim Certificate;

(3) The annual payroll of the proposed group member during the last 12-months;

(4) The proposed member's three digit NAICS code or two digit SIC Code, experience modification, and a description of the type of business it conducts; and

(5) A signed statement from the Group Administrator certifying that the proposed group member meets the homogeneity and underwriting requirements of the group self-insurer and that the group self-insurer shall be financially responsible to pay all workers' compensation claims arising out of the period of time of the Interim Certificate.

(d) Upon receipt of a written request for an Interim Certificate from a private group self-insurer that meets the requirements of this section, the Chief shall issue the Interim Certificate within 14 days. If the request is incomplete or does not comply with this section, the Group Administrator for the group self-insurer will be notified within 14 days of receipt of the request.

(e) Before an Interim Certificate may be replaced with a Certificate of Consent to Self-Insure with no expiration date, the Interim Self-Insurer must submit within 180 days of the effective date of the Interim Certificate of Consent a complete and accurate Application Form as provided in Section 15482.1.

(f) Each group member issued an Interim Certificate of Consent to Self-Insure shall subject to the following provisions:

(1) If an Interim Certificate is revoked before the expiration date or allowed to expire without issuance of a permanent Affiliate Certificate of Consent to Self-Insure pursuant to subsection (e), the Interim Certificate holder

shall provide proof of workers' compensation insurance to the Chief and to the group self-insurer no later than 45 days after the date of revocation by the department. The group self-insurer shall remain liable for all compensation liabilities of the employer until the effective date of the insurance coverage, the expiration date of the Interim Certificate, or the 45th day any Notice of Intent to Revoke the Certificate issued by the Chief, whichever comes first. The employer shall remain liable for payment of contributions and assessments as required by the group self-insurer for the employer's period of coverage as a member of the group self-insurer.

(2) The Chief shall notify the Labor Commissioner if any employer granted membership in a private group self-insurer under an Interim Certificate of Consent to Self-Insure is subsequently denied an Affiliate Certificate of Consent to Self-Insure by the Chief and after 45 days from such denial has not produced proof of coverage for workers' compensation liabilities to the Chief in the form of a binder, certificate of insurance or policy.

Note: Authority cited: Sections 54, 55 and 3702.10, Labor Code. Reference: Sections 59, 3700, 3702.5 and 3702.10, Labor Code.

History: 1. New section filed 3-2-2009; operative 3-2-2009 pursuant to Government Code section 11343.4 (Register 2009, No. 10).

2. Amendment filed 12-14-2016; operative 1-1-2017 pursuant to Government Code section 11343.4(b)(3) (Register 2016, No. 51).

§15483. Agreement of Assumption and Guarantee of Group Member's Liabilities.

(a) Each group self-insurer shall provide an Agreement of Assumption and Guarantee of Liabilities of Workers' Compensation Liabilities For Group Members for each group member, executed by the group self-insurer or Group Administrator on its behalf if authorized in the group self-insurer's bylaws. If the group self-insurer does not execute an Agreement of Assumption and Guarantee of Liabilities of Workers' Compensation Liabilities For Group Members for any proposed group member, the Director shall deny the application to self-insure of the proposed group member, or, if an Interim Certificate of Consent to Self-Insure has been issued to a group member and the group self-insurer declines to execute an Agreement of Assumption and Guarantee of Liabilities of Workers' Compensation Liabilities For Group Members for that group member, it shall be cause for revocation of the Affiliate Certificate of Consent to Self-Insure of the group member.

(b) In addition, each group member that is a subsidiary or affiliate or is otherwise controlled or owned by another entity shall provide an Agreement of Assumption and Guarantee of Liabilities executed by the holding company, ultimate parent company, controlling general partners, owner, or owners having controlling ownership as required for subsidiaries and affiliates of individual private self insurers by Section 15211.2 of these regulations. If the holding company, ultimate parent company, controlling general partnership, or owner having controlling ownership of the group member declines to execute an Agreement of Assumption and Guarantee of Liabilities, the Director may deny the application of the proposed group member. If a group member is acquired by another entity while the group member is self-insured and that new holding company, ultimate parent company, controlling general partnership, or owner having controlling ownership declines to execute an Indemnity Agreement and Power of Attorney (Form S-4 (1-2016)), it shall be deemed cause for revocation of the group member's Affiliate Certificate of Consent to Self-Insure.

(c) The Agreement of Assumption and Guarantee of Liabilities For Group and Affiliate Members shall be written upon a form provided by the Chief (Form S-5 (1-2015)). The form is available on the website of the Office of Self-Insurance Plans at http://www.dir.ca.gov/osip.

Note: Authority cited: Sections 54, 55 and 3702.10, Labor Code. Reference: Sections 59, 3550, 3700, 3701, 3701.5, 3702, 3702.10 and 3705, Labor Code.

History: 1. New section filed 3-2-2009; operative 3-2-2009 pursuant to Government Code section 11343.4 (Register 2009, No. 10).

2. Amendment filed 12-14-2016; operative 1-1-2017 pursuant to Government Code section 11343.4(b)(3) (Register 2016, No. 51).

§15484. Continuing Financial Capacity of Group Self-Insurers.

(a) Each group self-insurer shall submit annually the group's un-audited financial statement to the Chief by March 1. The group self-insurer shall obtain a current certified, independently audited financial statement complete with all notes and schedules. The financial statement shall be prepared according to Generally Accepted Accounting Principles (GAAP) and shall be submitted to the Chief by July 1 following the end of the program year.

(b) The group self-insurer's financial statement for each year shall include exhibits indicating specific amounts collected as group member contributions and earned from investments, as well as specific amounts for the year reported for the following administrative costs:

(1) Fees and commissions paid to the Group Administrator

(2) Commissions paid to brokers

(3) Fees paid to the third party administrator

(4) Premium paid for excess insurance

(5) Premium paid for fidelity and errors and omissions coverage

(6) Fees paid for surety bonds, letters of credit, or any other security deposit related cost

(7) Fees paid to actuaries

(8) Fees paid to accountants

(9) Regulatory costs

(10) Taxes

(11) Other expenses

(c) Each group self-insurer shall ensure that group members maintain their suitability for group self-insurer membership as follows:

(1) Annually obtaining current financial statements showing that the members of the group self-insurer are financially suitable for continued membership in the group;

(2) For each group member, the group self-insurer may annually determine the group member's suitability for membership in the group self-insurer by review of a tax

return, credit report, or other appropriate documentation as specified in the bylaws of the group self-insurer.

(d) The Group Administrator shall submit to the Chief on request any financial documentation received pursuant to subsection (c), and shall advise the Chief of any group member not submitting its financial documentation to the group self-insurer.

(e) Each group self-insurer shall demonstrate sufficient income from annual member contributions and/or assessments to fund:

(1) One and one half (1.5) times the group self-insurer's most recent three-year average paid indemnity and medical claims expenses as reported on their current year filed Self-Insurer's Annual Report;

(2) The expected administrative and operating expenses needed to meet the group self-insurer's day to day financial obligations during the current calendar year;

(3) The continued posting of the required security deposit; and

(4) Any additional amount determined by the Chief, upon a showing of good cause, to ensure adequate funding of the group self-insurer.

(f) The Group Administrator shall immediately advise the Chief in writing if the group self-insurer does not meet the financial requirements set forth in Section 15472(a) of these regulations.

(g) A group self-insurer's solvency is presumed impaired if any of the following occurs:

(1) There is a marked reduction in financial strength as evidenced by the findings in the annual audit by the independent certified public accountant;

(2) The group self-insurer fails to submit a financial statement pursuant to subsection (a) of this section;

(3) The Group Administrator fails to submit documentation as provided by subsection (d) to substantiate that the group meets financial requirements as set forth in Section 15472(a);

(4) The contribution rates, rating plan, or contributions fail to generate sufficient funds to cover the requirements of subsection (e) of this Section.

(h) Demonstration of impaired solvency of the group self-insurer as described in subsection (g) of this section is good cause for increased security deposit or involuntary revocation of a Certificate of Consent to Self-Insure, Interim Certificate of Consent to Self-Insure, and/or Affiliate Certificate of Consent to Self-Insure.

(i) The Group Administrator shall, on or before March 1st of each year, file with the Office of Self-Insurance Plans the budget for the group's current year together with:

(1) The rates of contribution from members in effect for the current year,

(2) Any deviation from these rates,

(3) All actuarial reports and other documents supporting the rates of contribution,

(4) All minutes of board of trustees meetings or other evidence of board of trustees action where rates of contributions from members were discussed or approved.

(j) The Group Administrator shall file any changes in the rates of contribution from members with documents listed in subsection (i), (1) through (4) within 30 days of such change.

Note: Authority cited: Sections 54, 55 and 3702.10, Labor Code. Reference: Sections 59, 3700, 3701, 3702 and 3702.10, Labor Code.

History: 1. New section filed 3-2-2009; operative 3-2-2009 pursuant to Government Code section 11343.4 (Register 2009, No. 10).

2. Amendment of subsections (a), (e) and (g)(3), new subsections (i)-(j) filed 9-19-2011; operative 10-19-2011 (Register 2011, No. 38).

3. Amendment of subsections (a), (d), (e)(1) and (f) filed 12-31-2012 as an emergency; operative 1-1-2013 pursuant to Government Code section 11346.1(d) (Register 2013, No. 1). A Certificate of Compliance must be transmitted to OAL by 7-1-2013 or emergency language will be repealed by operation of law on the following day.

4. Certificate of Compliance as to 1-1-2013 order, including nonsubstantive amendments, transmitted to OAL 7-1-2013 and filed 8-13-2013 (Register 2013, No. 33).

5. Amendment of section heading and subsections (a), (c)(1)-(2), (f) and (g)(3) filed 12-14-2016; operative 1-1-2017 pursuant to Government Code section 11343.4(b)(3) (Register 2016, No. 51).

§15485. Resolution to Authorize Self Insurance for a Group Self Insurer or Group Member.

(a) The resolution to authorize self insurance of workers' compensation required as part of the application for a Certificate of Consent to Self Insure by any group member applicant shall be adopted by the board of directors of each corporation, the general partners of an applicant partnership or joint venture, the managing member of a limited liability corporation, the owner of an applicant sole proprietorship, or the Board of Trustees of an applicant group self insurer. The resolution to authorize self insurance shall include the following:

(1) A statement identifying the applicant by corporate or other legal name, the state of registration, and the date that the resolution was adopted;

(2) Identification by title of appointed officers or other authorized employees who have the authority to sign the application, execute any and all documents required for the application and do subsequent acts as required to maintain self insurance approval.

(b) A group self insurer resolution shall be executed by the group self insurer applicant's Board of Trustees and included as part of the application. A model group self insurer resolution, is available at http://sip.dir.ca.gov/.

(c) If a group member or group self insurer reincorporates, merges, or changes its identity, a new resolution shall be submitted to the Manager within 30 days to ratify the maintenance of the self insured's responsibility under the successor's identity. The Manager may extend the period of time for good cause. Good cause is determined within the sole discretion of the Manager.

Note: Authority cited: Sections 54, 55 and 3702.10, Labor Code. Reference: Sections 59, 3700, 3701, 3701.5, 3702, 3702.2, 3702.5 and 3702.10, Labor Code.

History: 1. New section filed 3-2-2009; operative 3-2-2009 pursuant to Government Code section 11343.4 (Register 2009, No. 10).

§15486. Agreement and Undertaking for Director to Utilize Security Deposit to Pay Benefits Due.

(a) Each group self-insurer applicant shall execute an Agreement and Undertaking For Security Deposit (Form S-6 (1-2016)) as part of the application process.

(b) All security deposits shall be posted in accordance with the provisions of the Agreement and Undertaking, and shall permit the Director of Industrial Relations to order the security deposit to be utilized to pay benefits due pursuant to Labor Code Section 3701.5.

Note: Authority cited: Sections 54, 55 and 3702.10, Labor Code. Reference: Sections 59, 3701, 3701.5 and 3702.10, Labor Code.

History: 1. New section filed 3-2-2009; operative 3-2-2009 pursuant to Government Code section 11343.4 (Register 2009, No. 10).

2. Amendment of subsection (a) filed 12-14-2016; operative 1-1-2017 pursuant to Government Code section 11343.4(b)(3) (Register 2016, No. 51).

§15486.1. Group Self-Insurer Injury and Illness Prevention Program.

(a) As part of the application process, a group self-insurer affiliate member applicant for a Certificate of Consent to Self-Insure shall certify they have implemented an effective Injury Illness Prevention Program as required by Labor Code section 6401.7 and provide the name, title and contact information for the person within their organization responsible for workplace safety.

(b) The Board of Trustees shall direct the Group Administrator to ensure ongoing risk control and safety support to group members. Ongoing risk control and safety support shall be under the general direction of a California Professional Engineer, a Certified Safety Professional, and/or a Certified Industrial Hygienist. The California Professional Engineer, Certified Safety Professional, or Certified Industrial Hygienist shall report the impact of safety and risk control activities to the Board of Trustees no less frequently than annually, and shall solicit continuing support and direction from the Board of Trustees.

Note: Authority cited: Sections 54, 55 and 3702.10, Labor Code. Reference: Sections 59, 3700, 3702, 3702.10, 6314.5, 6319 and 6401.7, Labor Code.

History: 1. New section filed 3-2-2009; operative 3-2-2009 pursuant to Government Code section 11343.4 (Register 2009, No. 10).

2. Amendment of section heading and section filed 12-14-2016; operative 1-1-2017 pursuant to Government Code section 11343.4(b)(3) (Register 2016, No. 51).

§15487. Delayed Start-Up of a Group Self-Insurer or Group Member Participation in Group Self-Insurance.

(a) The approval by the Director to grant a Certificate of Consent to Self-Insure to a group self-insurer and to any group member shall be initially valid for six (6) months after the date of approval by the Director. If the group self-insurer or any group member has not initiated its self-insurance program within the initial six month period, the approval to grant the Certificate of Consent to Self-Insure shall be void. If so, the group self-insurer or group member shall not be issued a Certificate of Consent to Self-Insure unless the applicant files a new application.

(b) Notwithstanding subsection (a), the Chief may extend the approval for a new group self-insurer or group member for an additional three (3) months upon a showing of good cause.

(c) If a group self-insurer applicant or group member applicant fails to initiate a self-insurance program within six (6) months of notification of approval by the Director, the Chief may require the applicant to provide updated loss information and may recalculate the required security deposit amount.

Note: Authority cited: Sections 54, 55 and 3702.10, Labor Code. Reference: Sections 59, 3700 and 3702.10, Labor Code.

History: 1. New section filed 3-2-2009; operative 3-2-2009 pursuant to Government Code section 11343.4 (Register 2009, No. 10).

2. Amendment of section heading and section filed 12-14-2016; operative 1-1-2017 pursuant to Government Code section 11343.4(b)(3) (Register 2016, No. 51).

§15488. Initial Issuance of the Certificate of Consent to Self Insure and Notice to Employees of Self Insured Status.

(a) No group self insurer applicant or affiliate group self insure applicant may commence self insurance until the applicant has posted the required security deposit with the Department of Industrial Relations through the Office of Self Insurance Plans and has submitted proof of specific excess insurance pursuant to Section 15478 of these regulations.

(b) The group member shall prominently display the original or a copy of the Certificate of Consent to Self Insure at the group member's place of business in California.

(c) Notice to employees of workers' compensation coverage as required by Labor Code Section 3550 shall be accomplished by display of a copy of the group member's Affiliate Certificate of Consent to Self Insure accompanied by a notice stating the name of the person(s) or administrative agency responsible for claims adjustment.

(d) If a private group self insurer or affiliate group member is required to provide evidence of its approved self insured status to prove compliance with Labor Code Section 3700, the Manager shall provide to the Group Administrator certification of self insurance to be distributed by the Group Administrator for this purpose One can determine whether an employer is self insured or not electronically at the website of the Office of Self Insurance Plans at http://sip.dir.ca.gov/. Beginning April 1, 2009, there is a ten dollar ($10) fee for signed certification of self insured status.

Note: Authority cited: Sections 54, 55 and 3702.10, Labor Code. Reference: Sections 59, 3700, 3701, 3702, 3702.10 and 3550, Labor Code.

History: 1. New section filed 3-2-2009; operative 3-2-2009 pursuant to Government Code section 11343.4 (Register 2009, No. 10).

§15489. Reporting Group Charter Amendments.

The Group Administrator and/or Board of Trustees of any group self insurer shall notify the Manager in writing and provide copies of any amendment, change, or update to the group self insurer's charter, Articles of Incorporation, or bylaws, including changes to the group self insurer's underwriting criteria, or group operating agreement. Notification shall be made within 30 days of the change.

Note: Authority cited: Sections 54, 55 and 3702.10, Labor Code. Reference: Sections 59, 3700, 3701, 3702, 3702.10 and 3550, Labor Code.

History: 1. New section filed 3-2-2009; operative 3-2-2009 pursuant to Government Code section 11343.4 (Register 2009, No. 10).

§15489.1. Change in Status.

(a) The group self insurer and/or group member shall notify the Manager in writing within 30 days of any of the following:

(1) Any amendment to an affiliate group member employer's charter, articles or agreement of incorporation, association, or co-partnership which changes its identity, business structure, or ownership in a material manner from the status as it existed at the time of issuance of its Certificate of Consent to Self Insure;

(2) If the group self insurer or any group member proposes to cease doing business entirely, proposes to cease doing business in California, or proposes to dispose of, by sale or otherwise, the controlling interest of the business for which the Certificate of Consent to Self Insure or Affiliate Certificate of Consent to Self Insure was issued.

(b) If any group self insurer or group member desires to retain its self insured status following any amendment to the articles, charter, or agreement of incorporation, association, or co-partnership which changes its identity or business structure or ownership, the group self insurer or Group Administrator shall provide to the Manager the following information:

(1) A written description of the event(s) and the date it occurred;

(2) Copies of Certificates of Status or other appropriate registration documents filed with the Secretary of State in which the self insurer is incorporated concerning the change of the self insurer's status; and

(3) Written notice indicating that the group self insurer and/or group member will continue to provide financial statements or other financial documentation pursuant to Section 15484;

(c) If a group self insurer or group member reincorporates, merges, or changes its identity, a new resolution shall be submitted to the Manager in accordance with Section 15485 of these regulations.

Note: Authority cited: Sections 54, 55 and 3702.10, Labor Code. Reference: Sections 59, 3700, 3701, 3701.5, 3702, 3702.3, 3702.10 and 3703, Labor Code.

History: 1. New section filed 3-2-2009; operative 3-2-2009 pursuant to Government Code section 11343.4 (Register 2009, No. 10).

§15490. Validity of Certificate to Group Self Insurer or Group Member.

(a) A Certificate of Consent to Self Insure shall be valid only to the private corporation, partnership, company, subsidiary, affiliate entity, limited liability corporation, group self insurer, or other group member to which the Certificate of Consent to Self Insure, Interim Certificate, or Affiliate Certificate of Consent to Self Insure was issued. No subsidiary or affiliate of an affiliate group self insurer shall be deemed self insured as a member of the group self insurer unless it has been issued an Interim Certificate of Consent to Self Insure pursuant to Section 15482.2 or has applied for and been approved for an Affiliate Certificate of Consent to Self Insure as a member of the group.

(b) Except as provided in Labor Code Section 3701.7, the Manager shall not issue a group member Interim or Affiliate Certificate of Consent to Self Insure with an effective date earlier than the date the approval of the group member by the Board of Directors of the group self insurer.

(c) Once the self insurance program of a group self insurer or a member of a group self insurer has been initiated after approval by the Director, the certificate issued shall be valid until revoked by order of the Director.

Note: Authority cited: Sections 54, 55 and 3702.10, Labor Code. Reference: Sections 59, 3701, 3701.5 and 3702.10, Labor Code.

History: 1. New section filed 3-2-2009; operative 3-2-2009 pursuant to Government Code section 11343.4 (Register 2009, No. 10).

§15490.1. Reinstatement of a Certificate or Affiliate Certificate of Consent to Self Insure.

(a) A group self insurer or group member that because of a legal change in business or corporate structure or in its legal name has had its self insurance privilege terminated may have its Certificate of Consent to Self Insure reinstated without lapse, provided that the group self insurer or group member can re-qualify for self insurance.

(b) To request reinstatement of a Certificate or of an Affiliate Certificate of Consent to Self Insure following a change in status by the group self insurer or a group member, the group self insurer or Group Administrator shall submit to the Manager a written statement describing the nature of the change. The Manager may request any documents necessary to verify the change in status which the group self insurer or Group Administrator shall provide. The group self insurer also shall provide to the Manager a statement signed by the Group Administrator that the group self insurer's Assumption and Guarantee of all workers' compensation liabilities will include any additional self insured liabilities incurred after a group member's change in status, or, if indicated, a new Assumption and Guarantee Agreement regarding the affected group member.

(c) Upon satisfactory compliance with subsection (b) the Manager may prepare and issue an order reflecting the change in status of the group self insurer and/or group members and reinstating its Certificate of Consent to Self Insure.

Note: Authority cited: Sections 54, 55 and 3702.10, Labor Code. Reference: Sections 59, 3700, 3701, 3702 and 3702.10, Labor Code.

History: 1. New section filed 3-2-2009; operative 3-2-2009 pursuant to Government Code section 11343.4 (Register 2009, No. 10).

§15491. Group Self-Insurer and Group Member Application Filing Fees.

(a) Each group self-insurer and/or group member making application for a Certificate of Consent to Self-Insure or requesting an Interim Certificate of Consent to Self-Insure shall pay a non-refundable filing fee at the time of filing the application or requesting the Interim Certificate on the following basis:

(1) A filing fee to accompany a new group self-insurer application shall be $1,000 for the group application;

(2) For each group member's application, the filing fee shall be $500;

(b) Any subsequent re-filing of an application by an existing group self-insurer or group member following a merger, acquisition, or reincorporation shall be considered a new group self-insurer or group member application and each such new filing shall be subject to a filing fee pursuant to subsections (a)(1) or (a)(2) of this section.

Note: Authority cited: Sections 54, 55 and 3702.10, Labor Code. Reference: Sections 59, 3700, 3702.5 and 3702.10, Labor Code.

History: 1. New section filed 3-2-2009; operative 3-2-2009 pursuant to Government Code section 11343.4 (Register 2009, No. 10).

2. Amendment of section heading and section filed 12-14-2016; operative 1-1-2017 pursuant to Government Code section 11343.4(b)(3) (Register 2016, No. 51).

§15496. Group Self-Insurer's Security Deposit.

(a) Each group self-insurer shall post and maintain a security deposit with the Director upon approval of its Certificate of Consent to Self-Insure. The security deposit amount shall be in accordance with the provisions of this section, and, once a Self-Insurer's Actuarial Study and Summary has been filed, no less than as determined pursuant to Labor Code Section 3701, calculated as the undiscounted expected actuarial confidence level including each of the following components: incurred but not reported (IBNR) liabilities, Allocated loss adjustment expense (ALAE), Unallocated loss adjusted expense (ULAE) net of specific excess insurance coverage.

The required deposit may be increased at the Director's discretion as set forth in Article 3 of these regulations.

(b) Upon approval of a Certificate of Consent to Self-Insure, the group self-insurer, in the manner provided in subsection (c), shall post an initial security deposit in an amount no less than the following:

(1) An amount equal to sixty percent (60%) of one year average incurred losses of the initial affiliate member(s). The average incurred losses shall be determined by taking the previous three years of incurred losses of the initial member(s), adding them together and dividing by three to determine the one year average incurred loss. The initial deposit shall be posted in four equal installments. The first installment shall be posted within thirty (30) days of the effective date of the certificate to self-insure, and each of the remaining installments shall be posted at ninety days intervals after the initial deposit;

(c) The group self-insurer's security deposit shall be posted in one of the following manners:

(1) A surety bond executed on State issued bond and rider forms pursuant to Section 15212 of these regulations;

(2) An irrevocable letter of credit issued by a bank, credit union, savings institution or other financial institution pursuant to Section 15215 of these regulations;

(3) Approved securities in the form of government issued or corporate issued securities, meeting the requirements of Section 15213 of these regulations;

(4) Cash in trust deposited pursuant to requirements of Section 15214 of these regulations; or

(5) Any combination of one or more of the foregoing methods.

(d) Failure to maintain the required amount of security deposit or to post an acceptable form of deposit as set forth in this Article shall be good cause for assessment of civil penalties pursuant to Labor Code Section 3702.9(a) and/or revocation of the Certificate of Consent to Self-Insure pursuant to Labor Code Section 3702, and Section 15423 of these regulations.

(e) A group self-insurer or group member requesting a hearing pursuant to Article 11 shall provide proof of workers' compensation coverage under a policy from an admitted carrier for the period of time without the required security deposit or deposit increase, or proof of compliance with the Chief's request to post security.

Note: Authority cited: Sections 54, 55, 3701.8 and 3702.10, Labor Code. Reference: Sections 59, 3700, 3701, 3701.5, 3701.8, 3702, 3702.3, 3702.6, 3702.10, 3740, 3741, 3742, 3743, 3744 and 3745, Labor Code.

History: 1. New section filed 3-2-2009; operative 3-2-2009 pursuant to Government Code section 11343.4 (Register 2009, No. 10).

2. Amendment of subsection (a), repealer of subsections (a)(1)-(3) and amendment of subsections (c) and (g) filed 12-31-2012 as an emergency; operative 1-1-2013 pursuant to Government Code section 11346.1(d) (Register 2013, No. 1). A Certificate of Compliance must be transmitted to OAL by 7-1-2013 or emergency language will be repealed by operation of law on the following day.

3. Certificate of Compliance as to 1-1-2013 order transmitted to OAL 7-1-2013 and filed 8-13-2013 (Register 2013, No. 33).

4. Amendment of section heading and section filed 12-14-2016; operative 1-1-2017 pursuant to Government Code section 11343.4(b)(3) (Register 2016, No. 51).

§15497. Adjustments in the Amount of a Group Self-Insurer's Security Deposit.

(a) Each group self-insurer's security deposit requirement pursuant to Labor Code Section 3701 shall be reviewed by the Chief at least annually following receipt of the private group's Self-Insurer's actuarial study and summary. If following the receipt of the group self-insurer's actuarial study and summary an increase in security deposit is required, the increase shall be calculated pursuant to Labor Code Section 3701 and Section 15496(a) of these regulations and shall be posted no later than thirty (30) days from the date the written notice of security deposit demand is made.

(b) In addition to any increase in the security deposit pursuant to subsection (a), the Chief may require the group self-insurer to post additional amounts pursuant to Section 15496 in the event that new affiliate members have been added to the group self-insurer but have not yet reported a full year of losses, in the event of audit increases pursuant to Section 15301, or in the event of a change in the deposit rate pursuant to Sections 15497 or 15497.1.

(c) No group self-insurer shall reduce its security deposit based on calculations pursuant to Section 15496(a) without prior written authorization from the Chief.

(d) For good cause, the Chief may require a group self-insurer to increase its security deposit at any time. Good cause includes, but is not limited to, impairment of financial condition of the self-insurer as determined by the Chief, increases in group membership, increases in losses as indicated in Self-Insurer's Annual Report, increases in losses as indicated in the actuarial study and summary or by audit over losses projected in actuarial reports, or failure of the group self-insurer to maintain total assets greater than its total liabilities.

(e) In the event that a security deposit increase is required and upon sending by the Chief to the group self-insurer a letter demanding the increase, a perfected security interest in the group self-insurer's and each affiliate group member's assets to the extent of any unsecured portion of the group self-insurer's incurred liabilities shall be created in favor of the Director pursuant to Labor Code Section 3701(k).

Note: Authority cited: Sections 54, 55, 3701.8 and 3702.10, Labor Code. Reference: Sections 59, 3700, 3701, 3701.5, 3701.7, 3701.8, 3702, 3702.3, 3702.6, 3702.10, 3740, 3741, 3742, 6319(f) and 6401.7, Labor Code.

History: 1. New section filed 3-2-2009; operative 3-2-2009 pursuant to Government Code section 11343.4 (Register 2009, No. 10).

2. Amendment filed 12-31-2012 as an emergency; operative 1-1-2013 pursuant to Government Code section 11346.1(d) (Register 2013, No. 1). A Certificate of Compliance must be transmitted to OAL by 7-1-2013 or emergency language will be repealed by operation of law on the following day.

3. Certificate of Compliance as to 1-1-2013 order transmitted to OAL 7-1-2013 and filed 8-13-2013 (Register 2013, No. 33).

4. Amendment of section heading and subsections (a) and (e) filed 12-14-2016; operative 1-1-2017 pursuant to Government Code section 11343.4(b)(3) (Register 2016, No. 51).

§15497.1. Security Deposit Adjustment upon Revocation of Group Self Insurer or Group Member Certificates.

(a) In the event of the revocation of a Certificate of Consent to Self Insure of a group self insurer or Affiliate Certificate of Consent to Self Insure of a group member, whether voluntarily or involuntarily, the Manager shall determine the need for a special revocation audit of the claims of the group self insurer and/or group member and the need for a deposit adjustment to secure future liabilities of the revoked group self insurer pursuant to Labor Code Section 3701 and Sections 15301 and 15497 of these regulations.

(b) The amount of security deposit and/or the deposit rate required by the Manager in conjunction with the revocation of the group self insurer's Certificate of Consent to Self Insure may be at an amount or rate above the minimum required by Labor Code Section 3701.

Note: Authority cited: Sections 54, 55, 3701.8 and 3702.10, Labor Code. Reference: Sections 59, 129, 3700, 3701, 3701.5, 3701.8, 3702, 3702.3, 3702.6, 3702.8 and 3744, Labor Code.

History: 1. New section filed 3-2-2009; operative 3-2-2009 pursuant to Government Code section 11343.4 (Register 2009, No. 10).

§15498. Insurance Coverage.

(a) Any group self insurer or group member shall be permitted to insure all or part of its liability to secure the payment of compensation pursuant to Labor Code Section 3700 by obtaining a standard workers' compensation insurance policy issued by an admitted carrier. Complete insurance coverage of a group member's workers' compensation liabilities under a standard workers' compensation insurance policy shall be good cause for revocation of the group member's Affiliate Certificate of Consent to Self Insure. Complete insurance coverage for all members of a group self insurer or a number of group members sufficient to reduce the size of the group self insurer to the extent that it no longer meets net worth and/or financial requirements to operate as a group self insurer shall be good cause for revocation of the group self insurer's Certificate of Consent to Self Insure.

(b) Each group self insurer shall provide the Manager with information regarding any standard workers' compensation insurance policies, specific excess workers' compensation insurance coverage, and/or any aggregate excess (stop loss) workers' compensation insurance coverage obtained for the group self insurer or any group.

(c) The Group Administrator of the group self insurer shall provide a Certificate of Insurance, a copy of the workers' compensation insurance policy or policies maintained by the group self insurer or its group members, including any binders or endorsements, and copies of insurer loss runs related to the group self insurer or any group member upon request of the Manager.

(d) A group self insurer that elects to purchase an aggregate excess policy shall not be given any credit or reductions in its security deposit requirement based on its aggregate excess coverage.

(e) A group self insurer or group member may sell off any or all of its workers' compensation liabilities through the purchase of a special excess workers' compensation insurance policy or policies pursuant to Labor Code Section 3702.8(c).

Note: Authority cited: Sections 54, 55 and 3702.10, Labor Code. Reference: Sections 59, 129, 3700, 3701, 3701.5, 3702, 3702.8, 3740, 3743 and 3744, Labor Code.

History: 1. New section filed 3-2-2009; operative 3-2-2009 pursuant to Government Code section 11343.4 (Register 2009, No. 10).

§15499. Allocation of the Security Deposit for a Group Self Insurer.

(a) The liabilities of each member of a group self insurer for its period of self insurance shall be included within the security deposit of the group self insurer.

(b) Each security deposit posted by a group self insurer, regardless of type of deposit, shall be applicable to the liabilities of all members of the group self insurer and shall be amended, if necessary, to include all new members added to the group self insurer.

(c) No portion of the overall security deposit for a group self insurer may be allocated or limited to any specific affiliate or subsidiary under the Master Certificate of the group self insurer.

Note: Authority cited: Sections 54, 55 and 3702.10, Labor Code. Reference: Sections 129, 3700, 3700(b), 3701, 3702, 3702.5, 3702.6, 3702.8, 3703, 3704, 3705 and 3744, Labor Code; and Section 189, Corporations Code.

History: 1. New section filed 3-2-2009; operative 3-2-2009 pursuant to Government Code section 11343.4 (Register 2009, No. 10).

§15499.5. Appeals of Increases in Security Deposits Based on Impaired Group Self Insurer Financial Condition.

(a) In the event the Manager has required an increase in security deposit based upon the impaired financial status of the group self insurer, and if the group self insurer seeks to appeal the Manager's decision, upon receipt of the written appeal the Manager shall order a detailed, independent third party financial and/or actuarial evaluation of the group self insurer by a group self insurance risk and/or actuarial consultant in order to evaluate the group self insurer's financial status. The cost of the third party financial evaluation report shall be paid by the group self insurer.

(b) Upon receipt of the evaluation report, the appeal will be considered by the Manager, and if not resolved between the Manager and the group self insurer, addressed pursuant to Labor Code Section 3701.5(g) and Article 11 of these regulations.

Note: Authority cited: Sections 54, 55 and 3702.10, Labor Code. Reference: Sections 3701 and 3701.5(g), Labor Code.

History: 1. New section filed 3-2-2009; operative 3-2-2009 pursuant to Government Code section 11343.4 (Register 2009, No. 10).

SUBCHAPTER 2.05 ENFORCEMENT OF WORKERS' COMPENSATION COVERAGE, PENALTY ASSESSMENT ORDERS, STOP ORDERS AND POSTING AND NOTICE REQUIREMENTS

ARTICLE 1 Delegation of Enforcement Authority

§15550. Delegation of Enforcement Authority.

The Director of Industrial Relations delegates concurrent authority to enforce Labor Code Sections 3700, 3710, 3710.1, 3710.2, 3711, 3712, 3713, 3714, 3718, 3722, 3723, 3725, 3726 and 3727 to the Division of Labor Standards Enforcement.

Note: Authority cited: Sections 55 and 3710, Labor Code. Reference: Sections 3700, 3710, 3710.1, 3710.2, 3711, 3712, 3713, 3714, 3718, 3722, 3723, 3725, 3726 and 3727, Labor Code.

History: 1. New Group 2.05 (Articles 1-15, Sections 15550-15596) filed 6-27-79; effective thirtieth day thereafter (Register 79, No. 26).

ARTICLE 2 Definitions

§15551. Direction to File Verified Statement.

"Direction to File Verified Statement" means the notice sent pursuant to Labor Code Section 3722 to employers found by the Workers' Compensation Appeals Board not to have secured the payment of compensation.

Note: Authority cited: Sections 55 and 3710, Labor Code. Reference: Sections 3700, 3710, 3710.1, 3710.2, 3711, 3712, 3713, 3714, 3718, 3722, 3723, 3725, 3726 and 3727, Labor Code.

§15552. Director.

"Director" means the Director of Industrial Relations or his designated agents or delegees.

Note: Authority cited: Sections 55 and 3710, Labor Code. Reference: Sections 3700, 3710, 3710.1, 3710.2, 3711, 3712, 3713, 3714, 3718, 3722, 3723, 3725, 3726 and 3727, Labor Code.

§15553. Division.

"Division" means Division of Labor Standards Enforcement unless otherwise specified.

Note: Authority cited: Sections 55 and 3710, Labor Code. Reference: Sections 3700, 3710, 3710.1, 3710.2, 3711, 3712, 3713, 3714, 3718, 3722, 3723, 3725, 3726 and 3727, Labor Code.

§15554. Findings.

"Findings" means Findings issued by the Division after a hearing on the objection to a Penalty Assessment Order or a Stop Order.

Note: Authority cited: Sections 55 and 3710, Labor Code. Reference: Sections 3700, 3710, 3710.1, 3710.2, 3711, 3712, 3713, 3714, 3718, 3722, 3723, 3725, 3726 and 3727, Labor Code.

§15555. Issue.

"Issue" means to issue and serve a Stop Order, a Penalty Assessment Order or a Notice on the employer.

Note: Authority cited: Sections 55 and 3710, Labor Code. Reference: Sections 3700, 3710, 3710.1, 3710.2, 3711, 3712, 3713, 3714, 3718, 3722, 3723, 3725, 3726 and 3727, Labor Code.

§15556. Notice of Findings on Penalty Assessment Order or Stop Order.

"Notice of Findings on Penalty Assessment Order or Stop Order" means the notice issued by the Division to an employer after a hearing on the objection to a Penalty Assessment Order or a Stop Order.

Note: Authority cited: Sections 55 and 3710, Labor Code. Reference: Sections 3700, 3710, 3710.1, 3710.2, 3711, 3712, 3713, 3714, 3718, 3722, 3723, 3725, 3726 and 3727, Labor Code.

§15557. Penalty Assessment Order.

"Penalty Assessment Order" means an order issued by the Division to an employer requiring the payment of penalties as set forth in Labor Code Sections 3710.1, 3711 or 3722.

Note: Authority cited: Sections 55 and 3710, Labor Code. Reference: Sections 3700, 3710, 3710.1, 3710.2, 3711, 3712, 3713, 3714, 3718, 3722, 3723, 3725, 3726 and 3727, Labor Code.

§15558. Special Judgment.

"Special Judgment" means the judgment entered by the clerk of the Superior Court pursuant to Labor Code Section 3726.

Note: Authority cited: Sections 55 and 3710, Labor Code. Reference: Sections 3700, 3710, 3710.1, 3710.2, 3711, 3712, 3713, 3714, 3718, 3722, 3723, 3725, 3726 and 3727, Labor Code.

§15559. Stop Order.

"Stop Order" means an order issued by the Director pursuant to Labor Code Section 3710.1 to an employer prohibiting the use of employees' labor until the employer secures the payment of compensation as required by Labor Code Section 3700.

Note: Authority cited: Sections 55 and 3710, Labor Code. Reference: Sections 3700, 3710, 3710.1, 3710.2, 3711, 3712, 3713, 3714, 3718, 3722, 3723, 3725, 3726 and 3727, Labor Code.

§15560. Uninsured Employer.

"Uninsured Employer" means any employer who has failed to secure the payment of compensation as required by Labor Code Section 3700.

Note: Authority cited: Sections 55 and 3710, Labor Code. Reference: Sections 3700, 3710, 3710.1, 3710.2, 3711, 3712, 3713, 3714, 3718, 3722, 3723, 3725, 3726 and 3727, Labor Code.

§15561. Verified Statement.

"Verified Statement" means a written form sent by the Workers' Compensation Appeals Board to an employer upon which such employer is directed to indicate (under penalty of perjury) the number of employees in his employ on the date of injury and submit this statement to the Division.

Note: Authority cited: Sections 55 and 3710, Labor Code. Reference: Sections 3700, 3710, 3710.1, 3710.2, 3711, 3712, 3713, 3714, 3718, 3722, 3723, 3725, 3726 and 3727, Labor Code.

§15562. Verified Petition.

"Verified Petition" means a written statement made and signed by an employer either (1) under oath taken before a notary public or other officer authorized to take affidavits and to administer oaths or (2) under a declaration stating in substance "I declare under penalty of perjury that the foregoing is true and correct" and further stating the date and place of execution. This petition is to be used by an employer who wishes to object to a Penalty Assessment Order and thereby request an administrative appeals.

Note: Authority cited: Sections 55 and 3710, Labor Code. Reference: Sections 3700, 3710, 3710.1, 3710.2, 3711, 3712, 3713, 3714, 3718, 3722, 3723, 3725, 3726 and 3727, Labor Code.

ARTICLE 3
Investigation of Employer's Workers' Compensation Status

§15563. Access to Places of Labor.

The Division, its deputies and agents shall have free access to information about workers' compensation coverage in all places of labor. The Division shall investigate any employer to determine whether he has secured the payment of workers' compensation as required by law.

Note: Authority cited: Sections 55 and 3710, Labor Code. Reference: Sections 3700, 3710, 3710.1, 3710.2, 3711, 3712, 3713, 3714, 3718, 3722, 3723, 3725, 3726 and 3727, Labor Code.

Ref.: Hanna § 10.20.

§15564. Inquiry Into Workers' Compensation Status.

The Division shall inquire of any employer the status of such employer's workers' compensation coverage pursuant to Section 3711 of the Labor Code.

Note: Authority cited: Sections 55 and 3710, Labor Code. Reference: Sections 3700, 3710, 3710.1, 3710.2, 3711, 3712, 3713, 3714, 3718, 3722, 3723, 3725, 3726 and 3727, Labor Code.

Ref.: Hanna § 10.20.

§15565. Posting Notice of Workers' Compensation Carrier.

Each employer is required to post a notice of his workers' compensation carrier at his headquarters or branch office together with the date of the expiration of his policy and the telephone number of the nearest office of the Labor Commissioner so that employees may call to report expiration of such coverage (as required by Labor Code Section 3713). Failure to post such notice is a misdemeanor.

Note: Authority cited: Sections 55 and 3710, Labor Code. Reference: Sections 3700, 3710, 3710.1, 3710.2, 3711, 3712, 3713, 3714, 3718, 3722, 3723, 3725, 3726 and 3727, Labor Code.

Ref.: Hanna § 10.26.

ARTICLE 4
Penalties

§15566. Assessment of Penalty.

Insured employers shall be assessed penalties for the failure or refusal to furnish information concerning the status of their workers' compensation coverage. Uninsured employers shall be assessed penalties for the failure to secure the payment of workers' compensation coverage for their employees.

Note: Authority cited: Sections 55 and 3710, Labor Code. Reference: Sections 3700, 3710, 3710.1, 3710.2, 3711, 3712, 3713, 3714, 3718, 3722, 3723, 3725, 3726 and 3727, Labor Code.

Ref.: Hanna § 10.22[1].

§15567. Penalty Assessment Orders.

Penalties shall be assessed by the issuance of Penalty Assessment Orders and shall be served as prescribed in these regulations.

Note: Authority cited: Sections 55 and 3710, Labor Code. Reference: Sections 3700, 3710, 3710.1, 3710.2, 3711, 3712, 3713, 3714, 3718, 3722, 3723, 3725, 3726 and 3727, Labor Code.

Ref.: Hanna § 10.22[1].

§15568. Types of Penalty Assessment Orders.

(a) Penalties in non-injury cases.

(1) A fifty ($50) dollar penalty shall be assessed against an insured employer who fails or refuses to make a

written response as to the status of his workers' compensation insurance when directed to do so by the Division.

(2) A one hundred ($100) dollar penalty shall be assessed an uninsured employer for each employee in his employ and not necessarily actually working at the time, a Stop Order is served upon him for failing to carry workers' compensation coverage on his employees.

(b) Penalties in Injury Cases.

(1) A one hundred ($100) dollar penalty per employee employed on the date of a claimed injury shall be assessed the employer where the Workers' Compensation Appeals Board finds (a) the employer was uninsured and (b) the injury was not compensable.

(2) A five hundred ($500) dollar penalty per employee employed on the date of injury shall be assessed an employer where the Workers' Compensation Appeals Board finds (a) the employer was uninsured and (b) the injury was compensable.

Note: Authority cited: Sections 55 and 3710, Labor Code. Reference: Sections 3700, 3710, 3710.1, 3710.2, 3711, 3712, 3713, 3714, 3718, 3722, 3723, 3725, 3726 and 3727, Labor Code.

Ref.: Hanna § 10.22[2].

§15569. Maximum Penalties.

The maximum penalties that may be assessed under Section 15568(a)(2) and Section 15568(b)(1) and (b)(2) shall not exceed ten thousand ($10,000) dollars.

Note: Authority cited: Sections 55 and 3710, Labor Code. Reference: Sections 3700, 3710, 3710.1, 3710.2, 3711, 3712, 3713, 3714, 3718, 3722, 3723, 3725, 3726 and 3727, Labor Code.

§15570. Number of Employees.

(a) Uninsured Employers in Non-Injury Cases. When issuing a one hundred ($100) dollar Penalty Assessment Order against an uninsured employer, the number of employees employed by such employer, and not necessarily those actually working at the time, in non-injury cases shall be ascertained by the Division at the time the Stop Order is served.

(b) Uninsured Employers in Injury Cases.

(1) After the issuance of a final decision of the Workers' Compensation Appeals Board, the Appeals Board shall mail to the uninsured employer and the Division a copy of the final decision and notice of the provisions of Labor Code Sections 3710.1 and 3722 which require such employer to pay penalties of one hundred ($100) dollars per employee and five hundred ($500) dollars per employee in non-compensable and compensable cases, respectively.

(2) In order to establish the number of employees, such employer shall submit to the Division within ten (10) days after service of the aforementioned documents by the Workers' Compensation Appeals Board, a verified statement of the number of employees in his employ on the date of injury.

(3) If such employer fails to submit to the Division a verified statement indicating the number of employees employed or if the Division disputes the accuracy of such verified statement, on the date of injury the Division shall issue a Penalty Assessment Order using such information regarding the number of such employees as the Division may have or otherwise obtain.

(4) Notice of the Penalty Assessment Order shall be mailed to the employer at his residence or usual place of business by registered or certified mail.

(5) The employer to whom the assessment is directed may file within twenty (20) days after receipt thereof a verified petition in writing, objecting to the assessment and setting forth the grounds for his objection.

(6) If such employer does not file a petition with the Division within said twenty (20) days, such assessment shall become conclusive and the amount thereof shall be due and payable from the employer so assessed to the Division for deposit in the State Treasury to the credit of the Uninsured Employers Fund.

Note: Authority cited: Sections 55 and 3710, Labor Code. Reference: Sections 3700, 3710, 3710.1, 3710.2, 3711, 3712, 3713, 3714, 3718, 3722, 3723, 3725, 3726 and 3727, Labor Code.

ARTICLE 5
Stop Order

§15571. When Issued.

Where an employer is found to be without workers' compensation insurance as required by law, the Division shall issue and serve a Stop Order on such employer (1) prohibiting his use of employee labor until he acquires coverage and (2) requiring him to pay lost wages to his employees affected by the work stoppage, not exceeding ten (10) days' pay, pending compliance by such employer.

Note: Authority cited: Sections 55 and 3710, Labor Code. Reference: Sections 3700, 3710, 3710.1, 3710.2, 3711, 3712, 3713, 3714, 3718, 3722, 3723, 3725, 3726 and 3727, Labor Code.

Ref.: Hanna § 10.21[1].

§15571.5. When Effective.

A Stop Order shall be effective immediately upon service and shall remain in effect during any appeal proceedings, unless and until the employer acquires workers' compensation coverage.

Note: Authority cited: Sections 55 and 3710, Labor Code. Reference: Sections 3700, 3710, 3710.1, 3710.2, 3711, 3712, 3713, 3714, 3718, 3722, 3723, 3725, 3726 and 3727, Labor Code.

Ref.: Hanna § 10.21[1].

§15572. Failure to Observe Stop Order Constitutes Misdemeanor.

Such Stop Order shall inform the employer that failure to observe same constitutes a misdemeanor, and if the employer if convicted thereof, the court is required to impose a mandatory jail sentence in the county jail of not less than ten (10) days and a fine of not less than three hundred ($300) dollars.

Note: Authority cited: Sections 55 and 3710, Labor Code. Reference: Sections 3700, 3710, 3710.1, 3710.2, 3711, 3712, 3713, 3714, 3718, 3722, 3723, 3725, 3726 and 3727, Labor Code.

Ref.: Hanna § 10.21[3].

§15573. Injunctive Relief.

Where an uninsured employer fails to comply with a Stop Order, the Division may seek injunctive relief from the courts.

Note: Authority cited: Sections 55 and 3710, Labor Code. Reference: Sections 3700, 3710, 3710.1, 3710.2, 3711, 3712, 3713, 3714, 3718, 3722, 3723, 3725, 3726 and 3727, Labor Code.

Ref.: Hanna § 10.21[3].

ARTICLE 6
Contents of Orders, of Direction to File Verified Statement and of Verified Statement

§15574. Stop Order.

The Stop Order issued and served on the uninsured employer pursuant to Labor Code Section 3710.1 shall contain the following information:

(a) The uninsured employer shall cease and desist the use of employee labor until he obtains the required workers' compensation coverage.

(b) Such employer shall be assessed a penalty of one hundred ($100) dollars per employee employed at the time the Stop Order is issued and served for failure to have obtained workers' compensation.

(c) The correct name and legal entity of the employer, the employer's address, the date, the time, the place of issuance, the signature and the name of the official who issues the Stop Order.

(d) The appeal procedure for objecting to a Stop Order.

Note: Authority cited: Sections 55 and 3710, Labor Code. Reference: Sections 3700, 3710, 3710.1, 3710.2, 3711, 3712, 3713, 3714, 3718, 3722, 3723, 3725, 3726 and 3727, Labor Code.

Ref.: Hanna § 10.21[1].

§15575. Penalty Assessment Orders.

(a) $50 Penalty Assessment Order. This order, issued pursuant to Labor Code Section 3711 shall contain the following information:

(1) The employer has failed to furnish a written statement to the Division stating the name of his workers' compensation insurance carrier.

(2) Failure to furnish such statement within ten (10) days constitutes prima facie evidence of the employer's neglect or failure to comply with the coverage requirements of the law.

(3) The employer, by virtue of the Order, is assessed a penalty of fifty ($50) dollars for such failure.

(4) The correct name and legal entity of the employer, the employer's address, the date, the place of issuance, the signature and the name of the official who issues the order.

(5) The appeal procedure for objecting to this penalty assessment order.

(6) The procedure used by the Division to obtain a judgment against the employer, should he fail to pay the assessment.

(b) $100 Non-Injury Penalty Assessment Order. The order, issued pursuant to Labor Code Section 3710.1 shall contain the following information:

(1) The employer has been found to be without the required workers' compensation insurance.

(2) The employer, by virtue of the Order, is assessed a penalty of one hundred ($100) dollars per employee employed at the time the Order is issued for failure to have workers' compensation coverage.

(3) The correct name and legal entity of the employer, the employer's address, the date, the time, the place of issuance, the signature and the name of the official who issued the Order.

(4) The appeal procedure for objecting to the Penalty Assessment Order.

(5) The procedure used by the Division to obtain a judgment against the employer, should he fail to pay the assessment.

(c) $100 Injury-related Penalty Assessment Order. The order, issued pursuant to Labor Code Section 3710.1 shall contain the following information:

(1) The Workers' Compensation Appeals Board has found the employer to be uninsured in a claimed injury and that such injury is noncompensable.

(2) The employer, by virtue of the Order, is assessed a penalty of one hundred ($100) dollars employee employed on the date of such claimed injury.

(3) The correct name and legal entity of the employer, the employer's address, the date, the place of issuance, the signature and the name of the official who issued the Order.

(4) The appeal procedure for objecting to the Order.

(5) The procedure used by the Division to obtain a judgment against the employer, should he fail to pay the assessment.

(d) $500 Injury-related Penalty Assessment Order. The Order issued pursuant to Labor Code Section 3722 shall contain the following information:

(1) The Workers' Compensation Appeals Board has found the employer to be uninsured and the claimed injury compensable.

(2) The employer, by virtue of the Order, is assessed a penalty of five hundred ($500) dollars per employee employed on the date of injury.

(3) The correct name and legal entity of the employer, the employer's address, the date, the place of issuance, the signature and the name of the official who issued the Order.

(4) The appeal procedure for objecting to the Order.

(5) The procedure used by the Division to obtain a judgment against the employer, should he fail to pay the assessment.

Note: Authority cited: Sections 55 and 3710, Labor Code. Reference: Sections 3700, 3710, 3710.1, 3710.2, 3711, 3712, 3713, 3714, 3718, 3722, 3723, 3725, 3726 and 3727, Labor Code.

Ref.: Hanna § 10.22[3].

§15576. Direction to File Verified Statement.

The statement, which shall be mailed to the employer by the Workers' Compensation Appeals Board simultaneously with the issuance and service of Findings of Fact, Findings and Order or Findings and Award, shall contain the following information:

(a) The Workers' Compensation Appeals Board has found the employer to be without the required workers' compensation coverage.

(b) The Division shall assess the employer a penalty of one hundred ($100) dollars or five hundred ($500) dollars per employee at the time of the injury pursuant to Labor Code Sections 3710.1 and 3722, respectively.

(c) The employer is requested to complete and submit to the Division within ten (10) days the verified statement on the reverse side of the Direction to File Verified Statement indicating the number of employees employed on the date of injury.

(d) The Division may dispute the accuracy of such verified statement.

(e) The Appeal procedure for objecting to the one hundred ($100) dollar injury-related Penalty Assessment Order (Labor Code Section 3710.1) and to the five hundred ($500) dollar injury-related Penalty Assessment Order (Labor Code Section 3722).

Note: Authority cited: Sections 55 and 3710, Labor Code. Reference: Sections 3700, 3710, 3710.1, 3710.2, 3711, 3712, 3713, 3714, 3718, 3722, 3723, 3725, 3726 and 3727, Labor Code.

§15577. Verified Statement.

The verified statement, which shall be mailed to the employer by the Workers' Compensation Appeals Board simultaneously with the issuance of Findings of Fact, Findings and Order or Findings and Award, shall be found on the reverse side of the Direction to File Verified Statement and shall contain the following information:

(a) That the employer must complete the verified statement and submit the requested information to the Division.

(b) The number of employees in the employer's employ on the date of injury.

(c) A certification under penalty of perjury by the employer that such number is true and correct.

(d) The employer's signature, address and the date and place of execution thereof.

ARTICLE 7
Service of Stop Order and Penalty Assessment Order

§15578. Service.

Any Stop Order or Penalty Assessment Order under the law and pursuant to these regulations issued to and served upon an employer may be served as follows:

(a) By delivering a copy of same to the employer if the employers is an individual;

(b) By delivering a copy of same to any general partner of the employer if the employer is a partnership;

(c) By delivering a copy of same to any person specified in Section 416.10 of the Code of Civil Procedure (specified corporate officers or designated agent) if the employer is a corporation;

(d) By any other manner authorized under the Code of Civil Procedure for the service of process in a civil action.

Note: Authority cited: Sections 55 and 3710, Labor Code. Reference: Sections 3700, 3710, 3710.1, 3710.2, 3711, 3712, 3713, 3714, 3718, 3722, 3723, 3725, 3726 and 3727, Labor Code.

ARTICLE 8
Review of Proceedings and Withdrawal Proceedings

§15579. Review of Proceedings to Correct Designation of Legal Entity or Clerical Error.

(a) During an appeal hearing, a hearing officer may establish the correct legal entity of the employer and may amend any necessary documents to reflect said true legal entity.

(b) The Division may correct a clerical error where such error has been made in an order, or decision until it becomes final to conform with the facts and the intended wording.

Note: Authority cited: Sections 55 and 3710, Labor Code. Reference: Sections 3700, 3710, 3710.1, 3710.2, 3711, 3712, 3713, 3714, 3718, 3722, 3723, 3725, 3726 and 3727, Labor Code.

§15580. Withdrawal of Orders.

The Division may withdraw a Stop Order or a Penalty Assessment Order:

(a) Where investigation indicates the employer had secured the payment of compensation as required by Section 3700 of the Labor Code at the time of service of such Orders; or

(b) Where an insured employer responded in writing within the prescribed time to a request to furnish the status of his workers' compensation coverage; or

(c) Where investigation indicates the employer had no employees.

Note: Authority cited: Sections 55 and 3710, Labor Code. Reference: Sections 3700, 3710, 3710.1, 3710.2, 3711, 3712, 3713, 3714, 3718, 3722, 3723, 3725, 3726 and 3727, Labor Code.

Ref.: Hanna §§ 10.21[4], 10.22[6].

ARTICLE 9
Appeal Procedures

§15581. Stop Order.

Where an employer objects to a Stop Order and desires a hearing thereon, such employer may make an oral or written request for a hearing. Upon receipt of such request, the Division shall set the matter for a hearing with five (5) days from the date of receipt thereof.

Note: Authority cited: Sections 55 and 3710, Labor Code. Reference: Sections 3700, 3710, 3710.1, 3710.2, 3711, 3712, 3713, 3714, 3718, 3722, 3723, 3725, 3726 and 3727, Labor Code.

§15582. Penalty Assessment Orders.

An employer may object to a Penalty Assessment Order within twenty (20) days after the service of the Order by filing a verified petition objecting to said Penalty Assessment Order and setting forth the ground(s) for such objections which are as set forth in Section 15584 of this Article. Upon the filing of such petition within the time prescribed, the Division shall set the matter for hearing within thirty (30) days thereafter.

Note: Authority cited: Sections 55 and 3710, Labor Code. Reference: Sections 3700, 3710, 3710.1, 3710.2, 3711, 3712, 3713, 3714, 3718, 3722, 3723, 3725, 3726 and 3727, Labor Code.

§15583. Grounds of Objection.

The grounds of objection are as follows:

(a) The Division acted without or in excess of its jurisdiction;

(b) The Stop Order, Penalty Assessment Orders, or Notice were not properly served;

(c) The correct legal entity is not set forth in the Order or Notice;

(d) The employer was legally insured for workers' compensation;

(e) No employment relationship exists between the workers and the person assessed or enjoined;

(f) The Division committed mistake, error or omission; or

(g) The Division acted arbitrarily, capriciously and in abuse of its discretion.

Note: Authority cited: Sections 55 and 3710, Labor Code. Reference: Sections 3700, 3710, 3710.1, 3710.2, 3711, 3712, 3713, 3714, 3718, 3722, 3723, 3725, 3726 and 3727, Labor Code.

§15584. Matters Not Grounds for Objection.

The following reasons which may be asserted are not sufficient or valid grounds for objection:

(a) Ignorance of the law;

(b) The employer's assertion that the workers' compensation insurance premiums are excessive; or

(c) The employer's mistaken belief that he had such insurance.

Note: Authority cited: Sections 55 and 3710, Labor Code. Reference: Sections 3700, 3710, 3710.1, 3710.2, 3711, 3712, 3713, 3714, 3718, 3722, 3723, 3725, 3726 and 3727, Labor Code.

ARTICLE 10
Hearing

§15585. Proceedings Under Oath.

All testimony adduced at the hearing shall taken under oath. The hearing officer shall administer such oath.

Note: Authority cited: Sections 55 and 3710, Labor Code. Reference: Sections 3700, 3710, 3710.1, 3710.2, 3711, 3712, 3713, 3714, 3718, 3722, 3723, 3725, 3726 and 3727, Labor Code.

§15586. Proceedings Shall Be Recorded.

Any proceedings heard before the Division shall be recorded.

Note: Authority cited: Sections 55 and 3710, Labor Code. Reference: Sections 3700, 3710, 3710.1, 3710.2, 3711, 3712, 3713, 3714, 3718, 3722, 3723, 3725, 3726 and 3727, Labor Code.

§15587. Conduct of Hearing.

Any Party to the hearing is entitled to be heard, to present evidence and to cross examine witnesses appearing at the hearing, but the Division is not bound by common law or statutory rules of evidence or procedure.

Note: Authority cited: Sections 55 and 3710, Labor Code. Reference: Sections 3700, 3710, 3710.1, 3710.2, 3711, 3712, 3713, 3714, 3718, 3722, 3723, 3725, 3726 and 3727, Labor Code.

§15588. Right to Subpoenas and Subpoenas Duces Tecum.

(a) Subpoenas.

Upon request of any party to a hearing on a Penalty Assessment Order or Stop Order, the Division may issue subpoenas for the attendance of witnesses before the Division at the time and place of hearing. Said subpoenas shall be served in the manner provided for serving subpoenas in civil actions. The Division shall not issue subpoenas in blank.

(b) Subpoenas Duces Tecum.

Upon the request of any party to a hearing on a Penalty Assessment Order or Stop Order, accompanied by a declaration of materiality thereof in the manner provided for in Section 1985 of the Code of Civil Procedure, the Division may issue subpoenas duces tecum requiring witnesses or parties to produce any books, documents or other materials under their control which they are bound by law to produce at the time and place of hearing. Subpoenas duces tecum served hereunder shall be served as provided therefor in civil actions.

Note: Authority cited: Sections 55 and 3710, Labor Code. Reference: Sections 3700, 3710, 3710.1, 3710.2, 3711, 3712, 3713, 3714, 3718, 3722, 3723, 3725, 3726 and 3727, Labor Code.

§15589. Custody of Papers Filed With the Division.

Books, documents and other material admitted into evidence may be withdrawn only on condition that an exact copy of any such books, documents or other materials sought to be removed, be offered in evidence in lieu thereof. In such event, there shall be made on the face of any such copy so admitted, a notation that the same is identical to the original withdrawn, and such notation shall be dated and signed by both the employer and the hearing officer.

Note: Authority cited: Sections 55 and 3710, Labor Code. Reference: Sections 3700, 3710, 3710.1, 3710.2, 3711, 3712, 3713, 3714, 3718, 3722, 3723, 3725, 3726 and 3727, Labor Code.

§15590. Decision of the Division.

(a) Stop Order. At the conclusion of a hearing on a Stop Order, the Division shall immediately affirm or dismiss said Stop Order. In addition, the Division shall issue and serve on any party to the hearing by registered or certified mail a written Notice of Findings and Findings within twenty-four (24) hours after the conclusion of such hearing.

(b) Penalty Assessment Order. The decision of the Division on any Penalty Assessment Order shall consist of Notice of Findings and written Findings which shall be served on any party to the hearing by registered or certified mail within fifteen (15) days after said hearing.

Note: Authority cited: Sections 55 and 3710, Labor Code. Reference: Sections 3700, 3710, 3710.1, 3710.2, 3711, 3712, 3713, 3714, 3718, 3722, 3723, 3725, 3726 and 3727, Labor Code.

Ref.: Hanna §§ 10.21[2], 10.22[4].

ARTICLE 11
Writ of Review

§15591. Employer's Right to Writ of Review.

An employer, upon receipt of Findings affirming or modifying any Penalty Assessment Order may file a Writ of Review from any such Findings to the appropriate superior court upon the execution by such employer of a bond to the State in double the amount so found due and ordered paid by such employer conditioned that such employer will pay any judgment and costs rendered against him for such assessment.

Note: Authority cited: Sections 55 and 3710, Labor Code. Reference: Sections 3700, 3710, 3710.1, 3710.2, 3711, 3712, 3713, 3714, 3718, 3722, 3723, 3725, 3726 and 3727, Labor Code.

Ref.: Hanna § 10.22[4].

ARTICLE 12
Special Judgment Procedure as to Penalty Assessment Orders

§15592. Procedures After Hearing or in the Absence of a Hearing.

(a) Where a hearing has been held and Notice of Findings and Findings have been issued and served on the uninsured employer, and after ten (10) days have expired since the issuance and service thereof, certified copies of the Penalty Assessment Order and the Findings shall be filed with the Judgment (Special) for the Uninsured Employers Fund with the clerk of the superior court who shall enter a judgment in favor of the Director of Industrial Relations as Administrator of the Uninsured Employers Fund, and against the uninsured employer in the amount shown on the Findings unless a Writ of Review has been filed within the said ten (10)-day period.

(b) Where a petition objecting to a Penalty Assessment Order has not been filed, a hearing has not been held and twenty (20) days have expired since the issuance and service of the Penalty Assessment Order, a certified copy of the Penalty Assessment Order may be filed with the Judgment (Special) for the Uninsured Employers Fund with the clerk of the superior court who shall enter a judgment in favor of the Director of Industrial Relations, as Administrator of the Uninsured Employers Fund, and against the uninsured employer in the amount shown on the assessment order.

(c) Upon the entry of a Special Judgment by the clerk of the superior court under Section 15592 (a) and (b) a Notice of Entry of Judgment (Special) for the Uninsured Employers Fund shall be filed and served upon the employer by regular first-class mail.

(d) After full payment has been made of a Judgment (Special) for the Uninsured Employers Fund, an Acknowledgment of Full Satisfaction of Judgment may be filed with the clerk of the superior court.

Note: Authority cited: Sections 55 and 3710, Labor Code. Reference: Sections 3700, 3710, 3710.1, 3710.2, 3711, 3712, 3713, 3714, 3718, 3722, 3723, 3725, 3726 and 3727, Labor Code.

§15593. Procedures Subsequent to Entry of Judgment.

After a Judgment (Special) has been entered and Notice of Entry of such Judgment has been mailed to the employer and he has failed or refused to pay such judgment, the Division may obtain a writ of execution thereon.

Note: Authority cited: Sections 55 and 3710, Labor Code. Reference: Sections 3700, 3710, 3710.1, 3710.2, 3711, 3712, 3713, 3714, 3718, 3722, 3723, 3725, 3726 and 3727, Labor Code.

ARTICLE 14
Penalty Liens

§15594. Recording of Penalty Lien.

Where the employer has failed to secure the payment of compensation, the Division shall file with the county recorder of any county in which such employer's property may be located, a certificate of the amount of penalty due from such employer and such amount shall be a lien in favor of the Division from the date of such filing against the real property and personal property of the employer within the county in which such certificate is filed in accordance with Labor Code Section 3727.

Note: Authority cited: Sections 55 and 3710, Labor Code. Reference: Sections 3700, 3710, 3710.1, 3710.2, 3711, 3712, 3713, 3714, 3718, 3722, 3723, 3725, 3726 and 3727, Labor Code.

Ref.: Hanna § 10.22[7].

§15595. Cancellation of Penalty Lien.

Upon Payment of the penalty assessment and upon the employer's request, the Division shall issue a certificate of cancellation of penalty assessment which may be recorded by the employer at his expense.

Note: Authority cited: Sections 55 and 3710, Labor Code. Reference: Sections 3700, 3710, 3710.1, 3710.2, 3711, 3712, 3713, 3714, 3718, 3722, 3723, 3725, 3726 and 3727, Labor Code.

Ref.: Hanna § 10.22[7].

ARTICLE 15
Notice of Right to Benefits

§15596. Notice of Employee's Right to Workers' Compensation Benefits.

(a) Employers shall notify, orally or in writing, every new employee, either at the time the employee is hired or by the end of his first pay period, of the employee's right to receive workers' compensation benefits should he be injured on the job at any time while in such employer's employ.

(b) Employers who need not give such notice are owners or occupants of residential dwellings whose employees perform duties which are incidental to the ownership, maintenance or use of the dwelling, including the care and supervision of children or whose duties are personal and not in the course of the trade, business, profession or occupation of such owner or occupant if such employees are employed for less than fifty-two (52) hours during a ninety (90)-day period and earn less than one hundred ($100) dollars.

Note: Authority cited: Sections 55 and 3710, Labor Code. Reference: Sections 3700, 3710, 3710.1, 3710.2, 3711, 3712, 3713, 3714, 3718, 3722, 3723, 3725, 3726 and 3727, Labor Code.

SUBCHAPTER 2.06 WORKERS' COMPENSATION—ADMINISTRATION REVOLVING FUND ASSESSMENT, UNINSURED EMPLOYERS BENEFITS TRUST FUND ASSESSMENT, SUBSEQUENT INJURIES BENEFITS TRUST FUND ASSESSMENTS, LABOR ENFORCEMENT AND COMPLIANCE FUND ASSESSMENT, OCCUPATIONAL SAFETY AND HEALTH FUND ASSESSMENT, AND FRAUD SURCHARGE

ARTICLE 1
Definitions

§15600. Definitions.

(a) Assessable Premium. The premium to which the assessment and/or surcharge is to be applied is the premium the insured is charged after all rating adjustments (experience rating, schedule rating, premium discounts, expense constants, etc.) except for adjustments resulting from the application of deductible plans, retrospective rating, or the return of policyholder dividends.

(b) Assessment. Includes those assessments levied upon insured and self-insured employers to establish and maintain the Workers' Compensation Administration Revolving Fund, the Uninsured Employers Benefits Trust Fund, the Labor Enforcement and Compliance Fund, the Occupational Safety and Health Fund, and the Subsequent Injuries Benefits Employers Trust Fund.

(c) Base Year. For purposes of calculating the self-insured employer assessment factors, that time period as provided by the Office of Self-Insurance Plans pursuant to section 15602. For public self-insured employers, the base year is a fiscal year basis. For private self-insured employers, the base year is a calendar year basis.

(d) Director. The Director of the Department of Industrial Relations.

(e) Expected total current year premium. Total direct workers' compensation premium of all insurers as reported to the Department of Insurance's designated licensed rating organization for the period of January 1 through June 30 of the year immediately preceding the assessment, and adjusted by the Department of Insurance's designated licensed rating organization, to a full year basis.

(f) Indemnity. The payments made by a self-insured employer directly to injured employees or their dependents as compensation pursuant to Labor Code divisions 4 and 4.5 including vocational rehabilitation maintenance and salary continuation payments pursuant to Labor Code sections 4800 and 4850. In reporting periods beginning July 1, 2013, and later, for the purpose of calculating self-insured employer assessments only, the indemnity amount attributable to payments made pursuant to Labor Code sections 4800 and 4850 will be calculated as if those payments had instead been made at the applicable temporary disability rate.

(g) Inception date. The inception date of a workers' compensation insurance policy is the normal anniversary rating date of a workers' compensation insurance policy as defined in the California Workers' Compensation Insurance Manual published by the Workers' Compensation Insurance Rating Bureau.

(h) Insured employer. Any employer, including any agency or division of the State of California, who secures workers' compensation insurance coverage under provisions of subdivision (a) of Labor Code section 3700.

(i) Insurer. Any person, including the State Compensation Insurance Fund, authorized to transact workers' compensation insurance in California.

(j) Insurance group. A group of insurers under the same management, direction, and control.

(k) Labor Enforcement and Compliance Fund. The Labor Enforcement and Compliance Fund established pursuant to the provisions of Labor Code section 62.5.

(*l*) Labor Enforcement and Compliance Fund Assessment. The user fee assessment levied upon insured and self-insured employers to establish and maintain the Labor Enforcement and Compliance Fund.

(m) Occupational Safety and Health Fund. The Occupational Safety and Health Fund established pursuant to the provisions of Labor Code section 62.5.

(n) Occupational Safety and Health Fund Assessment. The user fee assessment levied upon insured and self-insured employers to establish and maintain the Occupational Safety and Health Fund.

(o) Payroll. Remuneration subject to workers' compensation insurance premium for insured employers and that remuneration to employees of a self-insured employer which would be subject to premium charges if the employer were an insured employer.

(p) Revolving Fund. The Workers' Compensation Administration Revolving Fund established pursuant to the provisions of Labor Code section 62.5.

(q) Revolving Fund Assessment. The user fee assessment levied upon insured and self-insured employers to establish and maintain the Workers' Compensation Administration Revolving Fund.

(r) Self-insured employer. Any employer who is authorized by the Director to self-insure its workers' compensation liability under subdivisions (b) or (c) of Labor Code section 3700. A self-insured employer shall include the State of California.

(s) Subsequent Injuries Fund. The Subsequent Injuries Benefits Trust Fund established pursuant to the provisions of Labor Code section 62.5.

(t) Subsequent Injuries Fund Assessment. The user fee assessment levied upon insured and self-insured employers to establish and maintain the Subsequent Injuries Benefits Trust Fund.

(u) Surcharge. Surcharge means the "State Fraud Investigation and Prosecution Surcharge" assessed under authority of Labor Code Section 62.6.

(v) Uninsured Employers Fund. The Uninsured Employers Benefits Trust Fund established pursuant to the provisions of Labor Code section 62.5.

(w) Uninsured Employers Fund Assessment. The user fee assessment levied upon insured and self-insured employers to establish and maintain the Uninsured Employers Benefits Trust Fund.

Note: Authority cited: Sections 54, 55 and 62.5, Labor Code; and Section 1872.83, Insurance Code. Reference: Sections 51, 62.5, 62.6, 3700, 3701, 4800 and 4850, Labor Code; Section 1872.83, Insurance Code.

History: 1. New section filed 4-18-90 as an emergency; operative 4-18-90 (Register 90, No. 18). A Certificate of Compliance must be transmitted to OAL within 120 days or emergency language will be repealed by operation of law on 8-16-90.

2. Certificate of Compliance as to 4-18-90 order including amendment adding subsections (c) and (k) and renumbering existing subsections transmitted to OAL 8-14-90 and filed 9-13-90 (Register 90, No. 43).

3. Amendment of article heading, amendment of subsections (a), (b) and (g), new subsection (*l*), and amendment of Note filed 1-15-93 as an emergency; operative 1-15-93 (Register 93, No. 3). A Certificate of Compliance must be transmitted to OAL 5-17-93 or emergency language will be repealed by operation of law on the following day.

4. Certificate of Compliance as to 1-15-93 order including repealer of subsection (b), subsection relettering, and amendment of newly designated subsection (f) transmitted to OAL 5-10-93 and filed 6-16-93 (Register 93, No. 25).

5. Amendment of subchapter heading and subsection (b), new subsection (e) and subsection redesignation, amendment of subsections (f) and (*l*), new subsection (m) and amendment of Note filed 9-6-94 as an emergency; operative 9-6-94 (Register 94, No. 36). A Certificate of Compliance must be transmitted to OAL by 1-4-95 or emergency language will be repealed by operation of law on the following day.

6. Certificate of Compliance as to 9-6-94 order including amendment of subsection (a), new subsection (j), subsection relettering and amendment of subsection (k) transmitted to OAL 12-30-94 and filed 2-15-95 (Register 95, No. 7).

7. Amendment of subsection (a), new subsection (d), repealer of subsection (n), subsection relettering and amendment of Note filed 11-14-95 as an emergency; operative 12-1-95 (Register 95, No. 46). A Certificate of Compliance must be transmitted to OAL by 3-30-96 or emergency language will be repealed by operation of law on the following day.

8. Certificate of Compliance as to 11-14-95 order transmitted to OAL 3-29-96 and filed 5-8-96 (Register 96, No. 19).

9. New subsection (a), repealer of subsection (m), and subsection relettering filed 11-10-97; operative 11-10-97 pursuant to Government Code section 11343.4(d) (Register 97, No. 46).

10. Change without regulatory effect amending subchapter heading and subsections (a) and (b), repealing subsections (k) and (*l*), relettering subsections and amending Note filed 12-15-99 pursuant to section 100, title 1, California Code of Regulations (Register 99, No. 51).

11. Amendment of subchapter heading, amendment of subsections (a) and (b), new subsections (k) and (*l*), subsection relettering, and amendment of Note filed 1-14-2000 as an emergency; operative 1-14-2000 (Register 2000, No. 2). A Certificate of Compliance must be transmitted to OAL by 5-15-2000 or emergency language will be repealed by operation of law on the following day.

12. Certificate of Compliance as to 1-14-2000 order transmitted to OAL 5-9-2000 and filed 6-15-2000 (Register 2000, No. 24).

13. Amendment of subchapter heading and subsections (b), (c) and (k), new subsections (n), (o) and (q)-(s) and subsection relettering filed 12-18-2003; operative 12-18-2003. Submitted to OAL for printing only (Register 2003, No. 51).

14. Amendment of subchapter heading and subsection (b), new subsections (j)-(k) and subsection relettering filed 11-12-2008; operative 11-12-2008. Submitted to OAL for printing only (Register 2008, No. 46).

15. Amendment of subchapter heading and subsection (b), new subsections (j)-(k) and subsection relettering filed 11-19-2009; operative 11-19-2009. Submitted to OAL for printing only (Register 2009, No. 47).

16. Amendment of subsection (f) and Note filed 12-2-2013; operative 12-2-2013. Submitted to OAL for printing only pursuant to Labor Code section 62.5(f)(5) (Register 2013, No. 49).

17. Amendment of subchapter heading and subsection (a), new subsection (j), repealer of subsection (u), subsection relettering and amendment of newly designated subsection (r) filed 10-21-2015; operative 10-21-2015. Submitted to OAL for filing and printing only pursuant to Labor Code section 62.5(f)(5) (Register 2015, No. 43).

ARTICLE 2
Determination of Assessments and/or Surcharge

§15601. Determination of Revolving Fund, Subsequent Injuries Fund, Labor Enforcement and Compliance Fund, Occupational Safety and Health Fund, and Uninsured Employers Fund Total Assessment.

On or before November 1 of each year, the Director shall, in accordance with Labor Code Section 62.5:

(a) Determine the total amount of funds appropriated for the Division of Workers' Compensation;

(b) Determine the aggregate amount of the assessment for the Subsequent Injuries Fund;

(c) Determine the aggregate amount of the assessment for the Labor Enforcement and Compliance Fund;

(d) Determine the aggregate amount of the assessment for the Occupational Safety and Health Fund; and

(e) Determine the aggregate amount of the assessment for the Uninsured Employers Fund.

Note: Authority cited: Sections 54, 55 and 62.5, Labor Code. Reference: Section 62.5, Labor Code.

History: 1. New section filed 4-18-90 as an emergency; operative 4-18-90 (Register 90, No. 18). A Certificate of Compliance must be transmitted to OAL within 120 days or emergency language will be repealed by operation of law on 8-16-90.

2. Certificate of Compliance as to 4-18-90 order transmitted to OAL 8-14-90 and filed 9-13-90 (Register 90, No. 43).

3. New article 2 heading, amendment of section heading, amendment of subsection (a) and repealer of subsection (b) filed 1-15-93 as an emergency; operative 1-15-93 (Register 93, No. 3). A Certificate of Compliance must be transmitted to OAL 5-17-93 or emergency language will be repealed by operation of law on the following day.

4. Certificate of Compliance as to 1-15-93 order transmitted to OAL 5-10-93 and filed 6-16-93 (Register 93, No. 25).

5. Amendment of article heading, section and Note filed 9-6-94 as an emergency; operative 9-6-94 (Register 94, No. 36). A Certificate of Compliance must be transmitted to OAL by 1-4-95 or emergency language will be repealed by operation of law on the following day.

6. Certificate of Compliance as to 9-6-94 order including amendment of Note transmitted to OAL 12-30-94 and filed 2-15-95 (Register 95, No. 7).

7. Change without regulatory effect repealing section filed 12-15-99 pursuant to section 100, title 1, California Code of Regulations (Register 99, No. 51).

8. New section filed 1-14-2000 as an emergency; operative 1-14-2000 (Register 2000, No. 2). A Certificate of Compliance must be transmitted to OAL by 5-15-2000 or emergency language will be repealed by operation of law on the following day.

9. Certificate of Compliance as to 1-14-2000 order transmitted to OAL 5-9-2000 and filed 6-15-2000 (Register 2000, No. 24).

10. Amendment of section heading and section filed 12-18-2003; operative 12-18-2003. Submitted to OAL for printing only (Register 2003, No. 51).

11. Amendment of section heading and subsection (b), new subsection (c) and subsection relettering filed 11-12-2008; operative 11-12-2008. Submitted to OAL for printing only (Register 2008, No. 46).

12. Amendment of section heading, new subsection (c) and subsection relettering filed 11-19-2009; operative 11-19-2009. Submitted to OAL for printing only (Register 2009, No. 47).

§15601.5. Ascertainment of State Fraud Investigation and Prosecution Surcharge.

On or before September 1 of each year, the Director shall ascertain from the Fraud Assessment Commission the aggregate amount of the surcharge to be assessed.

The aggregate amount of the surcharge shall be allocated between insured and self-insured employers by applying the same proportional allocation and collection methodology as used to collect the Workers' Compensation Administration Revolving Fund Assessment.

Note: Authority cited: Sections 54 and 55, Labor Code. Reference: Section 62.6, Labor Code.

History: 1. New section filed 1-15-93 as an emergency; operative 1-15-93 (Register 93, No. 3). A Certificate of Compliance must be transmitted to OAL 5-17-93 or emergency language will be repealed by operation of law on the following day.

2. Certificate of Compliance as to 1-15-93 order transmitted to OAL 5-10-93 and filed 6-16-93 (Register 93, No. 25).

3. Amendment of Note filed 9-6-94 as an emergency; operative 9-6-94 (Register 94, No. 36). A Certificate of Compliance must be transmitted to OAL by 1-4-95 or emergency language will be repealed by operation of law on the following day.

4. Certificate of Compliance as to 9-6-94 order including amendment of Note transmitted to OAL 12-30-94 and filed 2-15-95 (Register 95, No. 7).

§15601.6. Determination of Targeted Inspection Assessment. [Repealed]

Note: Authority cited: Sections 54, 55, 62.5, 62.6 and 62.7, Labor Code. Reference: Section 62.7, Labor Code.

History: 1. New section filed 9-6-94 as an emergency; operative 9-6-94 (Register 94, No. 36). A Certificate of Compliance must be transmitted to OAL by 1-4-95 or emergency language will be; repealed by operation of law on the following day.

2. Certificate of Compliance as to 9-6-94 order including amendment of subsections (b)-(c) and repealer of subsection (d) transmitted to OAL 12-30-94 and filed 2-15-95 (Register 95, No. 7).

3. Repealer filed 11-14-95 as an emergency; operative 12-1-95 (Register 95, No. 46). A Certificate of Compliance must be transmitted to OAL by 3-30-96 or emergency language will be repealed by operation of law on the following day.

4. Certificate of Compliance as to 11-14-95 order transmitted to OAL 3-29-96 and filed 5-8-96 (Register 96, No. 19).

§15601.7. Determination of Self Insured Employers Subject to the Targeted Inspection Assessment.

On or before September 1 of each year, the Manager of Self-Insurance Plans shall identify for the Director each Private Self Insurer subject to the Targeted Inspection Assessment as determined below.

(a) The Targeted Inspection Assessment shall apply to each Self Insurer in each grouping set forth in subsection (b) that has a current 1-year average number of indemnity claims per 100 employees as calculated in subsection (e) below, that is equal to or in excess of 125 percent of the 3 year base figure determined for each grouping in subsection (d) of this section.

(b) The Manager shall categorize all private self insurers into groups for the purpose of calculating the Targeted Inspection Assessment. All private self insurers shall be categorized into groups by the first two digits of their North American Industry Classification System Code (NAICS Code) as reported on Page 1 of the Self Insurer's Annual Report for the reporting period immediately prior to the current budget year. For purposes of such categorization, each private group self insurer shall be considered as a single entity. The Manager may correct the NAICS Code reported for cause or where the Manager believes an error was made by the self insurer in designating their NAICS Code on the Annual Report. The Manager may also substitute the proper NAICS Code for the Standard Industrial Classification Code (SIC Code) if the SIC Code was reported rather than the NAICS Code.

(c) For each NAICS Code grouping set forth in subsection (a), the Manager shall calculate the historical average number of indemnity claims per 100 employees from the Consolidated Liabilities page of the full year Self Insurer's Annual Reports submitted by the members in each NAICS Code group for the 3 year reporting period immediately prior to the current 1-year period used to calculate the individual self insurer's indemnity claims per 100 employees.

(d) The Manager shall calculate a figure that will be 125 percent of each NAICS Code grouping's 3 year historical average number of indemnity claims per 100 employees.

(e) For each private self insurer, the Manager shall calculate an individual 1-year number of indemnity claims per 100 employees, using information reported by each self insurer on its last full year Self Insurer's Annual Report submitted for the reporting period immediately prior to the current budget year. In this calculation, the manager shall divide the total number of indemnity claims reported in the most recent claim year by the total number of California employees reported, with the result multiplied by 100. Any self insurer with less than 100 total employees shall be considered to have 100 employees for purposes of this calculation.

Note: Authority cited: Sections 54, 55, 62.7 and 62.9, Labor Code. Reference: Sections 62.7 and 62.9, Labor Code.

History: 1. New section filed 9-6-94 as an emergency; operative 9-6-94 (Register 94, No. 36). A Certificate of Compliance must be transmitted to OAL by 1-4-95 or emergency language will be repealed by operation of law on the following day.

2. Certificate of Compliance as to 9-6-94 order including amendment of first paragraph and subsections (a), (d), and (e), repealer of subsections (b)-(b)(3), and new subsection (b) transmitted to OAL 12-30-94 and filed 2-15-95 (Register 95, No. 7).

3. Amendment of section and Note filed 11-10-97; operative 11-10-97 pursuant to Government Code section 11343.4(d) (Register 97, No. 46).

4. Amendment of subsection (b) filed 12-18-2003; operative 12-18-2003. Submitted to OAL for printing only (Register 2003, No. 51).

5. Amendment of subsections (a)-(c) filed 3-2-2009; operative 3-2-2009 pursuant to Government Code section 11343.4 (Register 2009, No. 10).

§15601.8. Determination of Insured Employers' Payroll and Premium Data.

On or before September 1 of each year, the Director shall request that the Department of Insurance direct the designated licensed rating organization to provide the Director with a statement for each insurer authorized to transact workers' compensation insurance in the state of California showing the total payroll and premium generated by that insurer on policies subject to an experience modification of 1.25 or more for the most recent policy year available.

Note: Authority cited: Sections 54, 55 and 62.7, Labor Code. Reference: Section 62.7, Labor Code.

History: 1. New section filed 9-6-94 as an emergency; operative 9-6-94 (Register 94, No. 36). A Certificate of Compliance must be transmitted to OAL by 1-4-95 or emergency language will be repealed by operation of law on the following day.

2. Certificate of Compliance as to 9-6-94 order including amendment of section transmitted to OAL 12-30-94 and filed 2-15-95 (Register 95, No. 7).

§15602. Allocation of Revolving Fund Assessment, Subsequent Injuries Fund Assessment, Labor Enforcement and Compliance Fund Assessment, Occupational Safety and Health Fund Assessment, Uninsured Employers Fund Assessment, and/or Fraud Surcharge Among Insured and Self–Insured Employers.

(a) Not later than November 1 of each year, the Director shall determine the proportional payroll allocation factors to use to determine the total insured employer Revolving Fund Assessment, Subsequent Injuries Fund Assessment, Labor Enforcement and Compliance Fund Assessment, Occupational Safety and Health Fund Assessment, Uninsured Employers Fund Assessment, and Fraud Surcharge, and the total self-insured employer Revolving Fund Assessment, Subsequent Injuries Fund Assessment, Labor Enforcement and Compliance Fund Assessment, Occupational Safety and Health Fund Assessment, Uninsured Employers Fund Assessment, and Fraud Surcharge as follows:

(1) The aggregate payroll of all insured employers shall be determined from payroll information provided by the Department of Insurance's designated licensed rating organization for the most recent period available.

(2) The aggregate payroll of all self-insured employers shall be determined from payroll information provided by the Office of Self-Insurance Plans of the Department of Industrial Relations excluding payroll of insured employees of the State of California for the most recent base year available.

(3) The total payroll information shall then be determined by combining the most recent insured employer payroll with the most recent self-insured employer payroll.

(4) The insured employer proportional payroll allocation factor shall be determined by dividing the insured employer payroll by the total combined payroll.

(5) The self-insured employer proportional payroll allocation factor shall be determined by dividing the self-insured employer payroll by the total combined payroll. The self-insured employer payroll shall not include that portion of the State of California's payroll which was covered by a policy of insurance.

(b) The total insured employer Revolving Fund Assessment, Subsequent Injuries Fund Assessment, Labor Enforcement and Compliance Fund Assessment, Occupational Safety and Health Fund Assessment, Uninsured Employers Fund Assessment, and/or Fraud Surcharge shall be determined by multiplying each respective assessment and/or surcharge by the insured employer proportional payroll allocation factor.

(c) The total self-insured employer Revolving Fund Assessment, Subsequent Injuries Fund Assessment, Labor Enforcement and Compliance Fund Assessment, Occupational Safety and Health Fund Assessment, Uninsured Employers Fund Assessment, and/or Fraud Surcharge shall be determined by multiplying each respective assessment and/or surcharge by the self-insured employer proportional payroll allocation factor.

Note: Authority cited: Sections 54, 55, 62.5 and 62.6, Labor Code. Reference: Sections 62.5 and 62.6, Labor Code.

History: 1. New section filed 4-18-90 as an emergency; operative 4-18-90 (Register 90, No. 18). A Certificate of Compliance must be transmitted to OAL within 120 days or emergency language will be repealed by operation of law on 8-16-90.

2. Certificate of Compliance as to 4-18-90 order including amendment to subsection (a) transmitted to OAL 8-14-90 and filed 9-13-90 (Register 90, No. 43).

3. Amendment of section heading, section and Note filed 1-15-93 as an emergency; operative 1-15-93 (Register 93, No. 3). A Certificate of Compliance must be transmitted to OAL 5-17-93 or emergency language will be repealed by operation of law on the following day.

4. Certificate of Compliance as to 1-15-93 order including amendment of subsection (a)(2) transmitted to OAL 5-10-93 and filed 6-16-93 (Register 93, No. 25).

5. Amendment of subsections (a)(1) and (3) and Note filed 9-6-94 as an emergency; operative 9-6-94 (Register 94, No. 36). A Certificate of Compliance must be transmitted to OAL by 1-4-95 or emergency language will be repealed by operation of law on the following day.

6. Certificate of Compliance as to 9-6-94 order including amendment of section heading, subsections (a)-(a)(2), (b), (c) and Note transmitted to OAL 12-30-94 and filed 2-15-95 (Register 95, No. 7).

7. Change without regulatory effect amending section heading, section and Note filed 12-15-99 pursuant to section 100, title 1, California Code of Regulations (Register 99, No. 51).

8. Amendment of section heading, section and Note filed 1-14-2000 as an emergency; operative 1-14-2000 (Register 2000, No. 2). A Certificate of Compliance must be transmitted to OAL by 5-15-2000 or emergency language will be repealed by operation of law on the following day.

9. Certificate of Compliance as to 1-14-2000 order transmitted to OAL 5-9-2000 and filed 6-15-2000 (Register 2000, No. 24).

10. Amendment of section heading and section filed 12-18-2003; operative 12-18-2003. Submitted to OAL for printing only (Register 2003, No. 51).

11. Amendment of section heading and subsections (a), (b) and (c) filed 11-12-2008; operative 11-12-2008. Submitted to OAL for printing only (Register 2008, No. 46).

12. Amendment of section heading and subsections (a), (b) and (c) filed 11-19-2009; operative 11-19-2009. Submitted to OAL for printing only (Register 2009, No. 47).

§15603. Determination of Insured and Self–Insured Employer Revolving Fund Assessment, Subsequent Injuries Fund Assessment, Labor Enforcement and Compliance Fund Assessment, Occupational Safety and Health Fund Assessment, Uninsured Employers Fund Assessment, and Fraud Surcharge Factors.

(a) The insured employer Revolving Fund Assessment, Subsequent Injuries Fund Assessment, Labor Enforcement and Compliance Fund Assessment, Occupational Safety and Health Fund Assessment, Uninsured Employers Fund Assessment, and Fraud Surcharge factors shall be determined by dividing the total amount of each respective insured employer assessment and the total amount of the insured employer surcharge, as the case may be, by the expected total current year premium, as determined by the Department of Insurance's designated licensed rating organization.

(b) The self-insured employer Revolving Fund Assessment, Subsequent Injuries Fund Assessment, Labor Enforcement and Compliance Fund Assessment, Occupational Safety and Health Fund Assessment, Uninsured Employers Fund Assessment, and/or Fraud Surcharge factors shall be determined by dividing the total amount of each respective self-insured employer assessment or surcharge, as the case may be, by the total amount of workers' compensation indemnity paid under California law by all self-insured employers during the most recent base year available, as determined by the Office of Self-Insurance Plans.

Note: Authority cited: Sections 54, 55 and 62.5, Labor Code. Reference: Sections 62.5 and 62.6, Labor Code.

History: 1. New section filed 4-18-90 as an emergency; operative 4-18-90 (Register 90, No. 18). A Certificate of Compliance must be transmitted to OAL within 120 days or emergency language will be repealed by operation of law on 8-16-90.

2. Certificate of Compliance as to 4-18-90 order including amendment to subsection (b) transmitted to OAL 8-14-90 and filed 9-13-90 (Register 90, No. 43).

3. Amendment of section and Note filed 1-15-93 as an emergency; operative 1-15-93 (Register 93, No. 3). A Certificate of Compliance must be transmitted to OAL 5-17-93 or emergency language will be repealed by operation of law on the following day.

4. Certificate of Compliance as to 1-15-93 order including amendment of section (a)(2) transmitted to OAL 5-10-93 and filed 6-16-93 (Register 93, No. 25).

5. Amendment of section heading and text filed 9-6-94 as an emergency; operative 9-6-94 (Register 94, No. 36). A Certificate of Compliance must be transmitted to OAL by 1-4-95 or emergency language will be repealed by operation of law on the following day.

6. Certificate of Compliance as to 9-6-94 order transmitted to OAL 12-30-94 and filed 2-15-95 (Register 95, No. 7).

7. Amendment of subsection (a) filed 11-14-95 as an emergency; operative 12-1-95 (Register 95, No. 46). A Certificate of Compliance must be transmitted to OAL by 3-30-96 or emergency language will be repealed by operation of law on the following day.

8. Certificate of Compliance as to 11-14-95 order transmitted to OAL 3-29-96 and filed 5-8-96 (Register 96, No. 19).

9. Change without regulatory effect amending section heading, section and Note filed 12-15-99 pursuant to section 100, title 1, California Code of Regulations (Register 99, No. 51).

10. Amendment of section heading, section and Note filed 1-14-2000 as an emergency; operative 1-14-2000 (Register 2000, No. 2). A Certificate of Compliance must be transmitted to OAL by 5-15-2000 or emergency language will be repealed by operation of law on the following day.

11. Certificate of Compliance as to 1-14-2000 order transmitted to OAL 5-9-2000 and filed 6-15-2000 (Register 2000, No. 24).

12. Amendment of section heading and section filed 12-18-2003; operative 12-18-2003. Submitted to OAL for printing only (Register 2003, No. 51).

13. Amendment of section heading and section filed 11-12-2008; operative 11-12-2008. Submitted to OAL for printing only (Register 2008, No. 46).

14. Amendment of section heading and section filed 11-19-2009; operative 11-19-2009. Submitted to OAL for printing only (Register 2009, No. 47).

§15603.5. Determination of Targeted Inspection and Consultation Assessment Factors. [Repealed]

Note: Authority cited: Sections 54, 55 and 62.7, Labor Code. Reference: Section 62.7, Labor Code.

History: 1. New section filed 9-6-94 as an emergency; operative 9-6-94 (Register 94, No. 36). A Certificate of Compliance must be transmitted to OAL by 1-4-95 or emergency language will be repealed by operation of law on the following day.

2. Certificate of Compliance as to 9-6-94 order including amendment of section and Note transmitted to OAL 12-30-94 and filed 2-15-95 (Register 95, No. 7).

3. Repealer filed 11-14-95 as an emergency; operative 12-1-95 (Register 95, No. 46). A Certificate of Compliance must be transmitted to OAL by 3-30-96 or emergency language will be repealed by operation of law on the following day.

4. Certificate of Compliance as to 11-14-95 order transmitted to OAL 3-29-96 and filed 5-8-96 (Register 96, No. 19).

§15604. Surplus in Funding.

(a) In the event of an unexpended surplus in the Workers' Compensation Administration Revolving Fund balance for a fiscal year, the balance shall be carried forward and credited to the subsequent year's Revolving Fund assessment.

(b) In the event of an unexpended surplus in the Subsequent Injuries Fund balance for a fiscal year, the balance shall be carried forward and credited to the subsequent year's Subsequent Injuries Fund Assessment.

(c) In the event of an unexpended surplus in the Labor Enforcement and Compliance Fund balance for a fiscal year, the balance shall be carried forward and credited to the subsequent year's Labor Enforcement and Compliance Fund Assessment.

(d) In the event of an unexpended surplus in the Occupational Safety and Health Fund balance for a fiscal year, the balance shall be carried forward and credited to the subsequent year's Occupational Safety and Health Assessment.

(e) In the event of an unexpended surplus in the Uninsured Employers Fund balance for a fiscal year, the balance shall be carried forward and credited to the subsequent year's Uninsured Employers Fund Assessment.

Note: Authority cited: Sections 54, 55 and 62.5, Labor Code. Reference: Section 62.5, Labor Code.

History: 1. Renumbering of former section 15604 to section 15605 and new section 15604 filed 1-15-93 as an emergency; operative 1-15-93 (Register 93, No. 3). A Certificate of Compliance must be transmitted to OAL 5-17-93 or emergency language will be repealed by operation of law on the following day.

2. Certificate of Compliance as to 1-15-93 order transmitted to OAL 5-10-93 and filed 6-16-93 (Register 93, No. 25).

3. Change without regulatory effect repealing section filed 12-15-99 pursuant to section 100, title 1, California Code of Regulations (Register 99, No. 51).

4. New section filed 1-14-2000 as an emergency; operative 1-14-2000 (Register 2000, No. 2). A Certificate of Compliance must be transmitted to OAL by 5-15-2000 or emergency language will be repealed by operation of law on the following day.

5. Certificate of Compliance as to 1-14-2000 order transmitted to OAL 5-9-2000 and filed 6-15-2000 (Register 2000, No. 24).

6. Amendment filed 12-18-2003; operative 12-18-2003. Submitted to OAL for printing only (Register 2003, No. 51).

7. New subsection (c) and subsection relettering filed 11-12-2008; operative 11-12-2008. Submitted to OAL for printing only (Register 2008, No. 46).

8. New subsection (c) and subsection relettering filed 11-19-2009; operative 11-19-2009. Submitted to OAL for printing only (Register 2009, No. 47).

ARTICLE 3
Collection of Assessments and/or Surcharges

§15605. Collection of the Revolving Fund Assessment, Subsequent Injuries Fund Assessment, Labor Enforcement and Compliance Fund Assessment, Occupational Safety and Health Fund Assessment, Uninsured Employers Fund Assessment, and Fraud Surcharge from Self–Insured Employers.

(a) The Director designates the Manager of Self-Insurance Plans to collect the Revolving Fund Assessment, Subsequent Injuries Fund Assessment, Labor Enforcement and Compliance Fund Assessment, Occupational Safety and Health Fund Assessment, Uninsured Employers Fund Assessment, and/or Fraud Surcharge from self-insured employers on the Director's behalf.

(b) No later than December 1 of each year, the Manager of Self-Insurance Plans shall bill each self-insured employer for the amount of the individual self-insured employer's Revolving Fund Assessment, Subsequent Injuries Fund Assessment, Labor Enforcement and Compliance Fund Assessment, Occupational Safety and Health Fund Assessment, Uninsured Employers Fund Assessment, and/or Fraud Surcharge. The billing shall identify each assessment and/or surcharge separately and shall include the calculations utilized to determine each assessment factor. Each individual assessment and/or surcharge shall be determined by multiplying the self-insured employer assessment factor by the total amount of worker's compensation indemnity paid and reported by each self-insured employer on its Self-Insurer's Annual Report during the base year, as determined by the Office of Self-Insurance Plans. The Self-Insurer's Annual Report shall include all indemnity payments as defined in section 15600(f). For reporting periods beginning July 1, 2013, and later, the Self-Insurer's Annual Report shall include, as separate items, both: (1) the full amount of any vocational rehabilitation maintenance or salary continuation payments made pursuant to Labor Code sections 4800 and 4850, and (2) the amount that would have been paid for those benefits had they instead been paid at the applicable temporary disability rate. The latter amount will be used when calculating self-insured employers' assessments under this section.

(c) The amount of any assessment and/or surcharge shall be paid to the Office of Self-Insurance Plans within 30 days of the billing. Upon the request of any Joint Powers Authority, the Manager may agree to bill the Joint Powers Authority directly for the total amount of each assessment and/or surcharge owed by its public agency members.

(d) In the event the Manager collects funds in excess of the total self-insured employer assessment in the (1) Revolving Fund Assessment; (2) Subsequent Injuries Fund Assessment; (3) Labor Enforcement and Compliance Fund Assessment, (4) Occupational Safety and Health Fund Assessment; (5) Uninsured Employers Fund Assessment; and/or (6) Fraud Surcharge, such excess funds shall be paid over to the Director to be held in a trust account and credited to the next year's respective assessments and/or surcharge on self-insured employers.

(e) Should the Manager determine that any self-insured employer has understated or overstated its total payroll or indemnity paid on the self-insured employer's annual report, the Manager may issue a corrected billing.

(f) If an employer has paid the assessments and/or surcharge as an insured employer, and during the year of such assessments and/or surcharge is granted a certificate of consent to self-insure, the newly self-insured employer is not required to pay an additional assessments and/or surcharge as a self-insured employer for the current assessments and/or surcharge year. Such an employer shall submit to the Manager a copy of the assessments and/or surcharge billing paid as insured employer in lieu of payment as a self-insured employer.

(g) A self-insured employer that does not have a self-insurers' annual report on file with the Office of Self-Insurance Plans which covers the base year of the assessments and/or surcharge, and that did not pay the assessments and/or surcharge for the base year as an insured employer, shall pay the assessments and/or surcharge through the Office of Self-Insurance Plans.

(1) To enable the Manager to determine such self-insured employer's liability for the assessments and/or surcharge, each such self-insured employer shall file a report prescribed by the Manager, setting forth such self-insured employer's total annual payroll for the base year, and the total workers' compensation premium paid for each calendar quarter of the preceding year.

(2) The Manager shall bill the self-insured employer by applying the self-insured employer assessment factors to the last annual premium paid by the self-insured employer until the self-insured employer's experience as a self-insured employer exceeds two complete calendar years for private self-insured employers or two complete fiscal years for public self-insured employers.

(h) A self-insured employer that ceases to be self-insured and ceases to operate as a functioning employer with no legal requirement to secure the payment of compensation, but continues to have open workers' compensation claims arising from the period of self-insurance, shall continue to be liable for assessments and/or surcharge for a period of 3 calendar years following the termination, revocation, or surrender of the employer's certificate of consent to self-insure. The Manager shall bill the former self-insured employer in accordance with this Section.

Note: Authority cited: Sections 54, 55 and 62.5, Labor Code; and Section 1872.83, Insurance Code. Reference: Sections 62.5, 62.6, 4800 and 4850, Labor Code; and Section 1872.83, Insurance Code.

History: 1. New section filed 4-18-90 as an emergency; operative 4-18-90 (Register 90, No. 18). A Certificate of Compliance must be transmitted to OAL within 120 days or emergency language will be repealed by operation of law on 8-16-90.

2. Certificate of Compliance as to 4-18-90 order including amendment to subsections (b), (c) and (e) and adding subsection (f), (g) and (h) transmitted to OAL 8-14-90 and filed 9-13-90 (Register 90, No. 43).

3. Renumbering of former section 15605 to section 15606 and renumbering of former section 15604 to section 15605 and amendment of section heading, section, and Note filed 1-15-93 as an emergency; operative 1-15-93 (Register 93, No. 3). A Certificate of Compliance must be transmitted to OAL 5-17-93 or emergency language will be repealed by operation of law on the following day.

4. Editorial correction restoring inadvertently omitted article heading (Register 93, No. 25).

5. Certificate of Compliance as to 1-15-93 order including amendment of subsection (F) transmitted to OAL 5-10-93 and filed 6-16-93 (Register 93, No. 25).

6. Amendment of article heading, section heading, subsections (a), (e), (f) and (h) and Note filed 9-6-94 as an emergency; operative 9-6-94 (Register 94, No. 36). A Certificate of Compliance must be transmitted to OAL by 1-4-95 or emergency language will be repealed by operation of law on the following day.

7. Certificate of Compliance as to 9-6-94 order including amendment of subsections (a)-(c) transmitted to OAL 12-30-94 and filed 2-15-95 (Register 95, No. 7).

8. Amendment of subsection (f) filed 11-14-95 as an emergency; operative 12-1-95 (Register 95, No. 46). A Certificate of Compliance must be transmitted to OAL by 3-30-96 or emergency language will be repealed by operation of law on the following day.

9. Certificate of Compliance as to 11-14-95 order transmitted to OAL 3-29-96 and filed 5-8-96 (Register 96, No. 19).

10. Change without regulatory effect amending section heading, section and Note filed 12-15-99 pursuant to section 100, title 1, California Code of Regulations (Register 99, No. 51).

11. Amendment of section heading, section and Note filed 1-14-2000 as an emergency; operative 1-14-2000 (Register 2000, No. 2). A Certificate of Compliance must be transmitted to OAL by 5-15-2000 or emergency language will be repealed by operation of law on the following day.

12. Certificate of Compliance as to 1-14-2000 order transmitted to OAL 5-9-2000 and filed 6-15-2000 (Register 2000, No. 24).

13. Amendment of section heading and section filed 12-18-2003; operative 12-18-2003. Submitted to OAL for printing only (Register 2003, No. 51).

14. Amendment of section heading and subsections (a), (b) and (d) filed 11-12-2008; operative 11-12-2008. Submitted to OAL for printing only (Register 2008, No. 46).

15. Amendment of section heading and subsections (a), (b) and (d) filed 11-19-2009; operative 11-19-2009. Submitted to OAL for printing only (Register 2009, No. 47).

16. Amendment of subsection (b) and Note filed 12-2-2013; operative 12-2-2013. Submitted to OAL for printing only pursuant to Labor Code section 62.5(f)(5) (Register 2013, No. 49).

§15605.5. Collection of Targeted Inspection Assessment from Self-Insured Employers. [Repealed]

Note: Authority cited: Sections 54, 55 and 62.7, Labor Code. Reference: Section 62.7, Labor Code.

History: 1. New section filed 9-6-94 as an emergency; operative 9-6-94 (Register 94, No. 36). A Certificate of Compliance must be transmitted to OAL by 1-4-95 or emergency language will be repealed by operation of law on the following day.

2. Certificate of Compliance as to 9-6-94 order including amendment of section transmitted to OAL 12-30-94 and filed 2-15-95 (Register 95, No. 7).

3. Repealer filed 11-14-95 as an emergency; operative 12-1-95 (Register 95, No. 46). A Certificate of Compliance must be transmitted to OAL by 3-30-96 or emergency language will be repealed by operation of law on the following day.

4. Certificate of Compliance as to 11-14-95 order transmitted to OAL 3-29-96 and filed 5-8-96 (Register 96, No. 19).

§15606. Collection of Advances Against Insured Employers.

(a) Not later than December 1 of each year, the Director shall notify each workers' compensation insurer, of the amounts due from the insurer on behalf of its policyholders for, respectively, the Revolving Fund Assessment, Subsequent Injuries Fund Assessment, Uninsured Employers Fund Assessment, Labor Enforcement and Compliance Fund Assessment, Occupational Safety and Health Fund Assessment, and the Fraud Surcharge levied pursuant to the authority of Labor Code Sections 62.5 and 62.6 and these regulations. The notice shall include a bill that sets forth separately the total amounts of the assessments and the surcharge.

(b) The Insurer advances against the Revolving Fund Assessment, Subsequent Injuries Fund Assessment, Labor Enforcement and Compliance Fund Assessment, Occupational Safety and Health Fund Assessment, Uninsured Employers Fund Assessment, and Fraud Surcharge amounts shall be calculated by multiplying the insurer's California direct written workers' compensation premium as reported in the most recent year's financial statement on file with the Insurance Commissioner, multiplied by the ratio of the expected total current year premium to the total direct written workers' compensation premium of all insurers as reported in the latest year's annual financial statements on file with the Insurance Commissioner by the respective factors determined pursuant to subsection (a) of Section 15603 of these regulations.

(c) Where the amount of the assessments or surcharge owed is less than $5.00 the Director may elect not to bill the insurer therefor.

(d) Each insurer shall pay to the Director one half of the amounts billed under subsection (a) on behalf of its insured employers on or before the following January 1. Each insurer shall pay the balance of the assessments and surcharge to the Director on the following April 1.

(e) Upon agreement of the affected insurers, the Director may elect to consolidate in one billing the assessments and surcharge of all insured employers that are insured by insurers under the same management, direction and control.

(f) In the event the Director collects advances from insurers in excess of the total assessments and surcharge due from insured employers in the (1) Revolving Fund Assessment; (2) Subsequent Injuries Fund Assessment; (3) Labor Enforcement and Compliance Fund Assessment; (4) Occupational Safety and Health Fund Assessment; (5) Uninsured Employers Fund Assessment; and/or (6) Fraud

Surcharge, the excess funds shall be held by the Director in a trust account and credited to the subsequent year's total respective assessments and surcharge on insured employers.

(g) Commencing with the assessment payment due April 1, 1993, the insurer shall submit a summary report on a form provided by the Director, which includes the following information: (1) the total amount of assessments and surcharges billed insured employers by the insurer; (2) the respective factors used by the insurer in assessing and surcharging insured employers.

(h) The summary report due April 1, 1993 shall include the information specified in this subsection for all workers' compensation insurance policies with an inception date between August 1, 1990 and December 31, 1991. Commencing April 1, 1994, the summary report shall include the information specified in this subsection for all workers' compensation insurance policies with an inception date in the next preceding calendar years.

Note: Authority cited: Sections 54, 55 and 62.5, Labor Code; and Section 1872.83, Insurance Code. Reference: Sections 62.5 and 62.6, Labor Code; and Section 1872.83, Insurance Code.

History: 1. New section filed 4-18-90 as an emergency; operative 4-18-90 (Register 90, No. 18). A Certificate of Compliance must be transmitted to OAL within 120 days or emergency language will be repealed by operation of law on 8-16-90.

2. Certificate of Compliance as to 4-18-90 order including amendment to subsection (a), (d) and (e) transmitted to OAL 8-14-90 and filed 9-13-90 (Register 90, No. 43).

3. Renumbering of former section 15606 to 15607 and renumbering of former section 15605 to section 15606 and amendment of section and Note filed 1-15-93 as an emergency; operative 1-15-93 (Register 93, No. 3). A Certificate of Compliance must be transmitted to OAL 5-17-93 or emergency language will be repealed by operation of law on the following day.

4. Certificate of Compliance as to 1-15-93 order including amendment of subsection (a) and repealer of subsection (e)(3) transmitted to OAL 5-10-93 and filed 6-16-93 (Register 93, No. 25).

5. Amendment of subsections (a)-(d) and Note filed 9-6-94 as an emergency; operative 9-6-94 (Register 94, No. 36). A Certificate of Compliance must be transmitted to OAL by 1-4-95 or emergency language will be repealed by operation of law on the following day.

6. Certificate of Compliance as to 9-6-94 order including amendment of section heading, repealer of subsections (a)-(e) and new subsections (a)-(i) transmitted to OAL 12-30-94 and filed 2-15-95 (Register 95, No. 7).

7. Amendment of subsections (a)-(b), repealer of subsection (c), subsection relettering and amendment of Note filed 11-14-95 as an emergency; operative 12-1-95 (Register 95, No. 46). A Certificate of Compliance must be transmitted to OAL by 3-30-96 or emergency language will be repealed by operation of law on the following day.

8. Certificate of Compliance as to 11-14-95 order transmitted to OAL 3-29-96 and filed 5-8-96 (Register 96, No. 19).

9. Change without regulatory effect amending section and Note filed 12-15-99 pursuant to section 100, title 1, California Code of Regulations (Register 99, No. 51).

10. Amendment of section and Note filed 1-14-2000 as an emergency; operative 1-14-2000 (Register 2000, No. 2). A Certificate of Compliance must be transmitted to OAL by 5-15-2000 or emergency language will be repealed by operation of law on the following day.

11. Certificate of Compliance as to 1-14-2000 order transmitted to OAL 5-9-2000 and filed 6-15-2000 (Register 2000, No. 24).

12. Amendment of subsections (a), (b) and (f) filed 12-18-2003; operative 12-18-2003. Submitted to OAL for printing only (Register 2003, No. 51).

13. Amendment of section heading and subsections (a), (b) and (f) filed 11-12-2008; operative 11-12-2008. Submitted to OAL for printing only (Register 2008, No. 46).

14. Amendment of subsections (a), (b) and (f) filed 11-19-2009; operative 11-19-2009. Submitted to OAL for printing only (Register 2009, No. 47).

§15607. Collection of Revolving Fund Assessment, Subsequent Injuries Fund Assessment, Labor Enforcement and Compliance Fund Assessment, Occupational Safety and Health Fund Assessment, Uninsured Employers Fund Assessment, and Fraud Surcharge from Insured Employers.

(a) Every insurer shall collect the Revolving Fund Assessment, Subsequent Injuries Fund Assessment, Labor Enforcement and Compliance Fund Assessment, Occupational Safety and Health Fund Assessment, Uninsured Employers Fund Assessment, and Fraud Surcharge required by this article and Labor Code Sections 62.5 and 62.6, respectively, from each employer insured by it by applying a separate charge to all workers' compensation insurance policies issued by such insurer with an inception date in the year beginning January 1 after the determinations required by Sections 15601 and 15601.5 of these regulations. The amount of the assessment and surcharge shall be determined by multiplying the insured employer's estimated annual assessable premium by the assessment factors determined by the Director pursuant to subsection (a) of section 15603. The assessment factors in effect on the inception date of the policy shall be used to calculate the separate charges relative to that policy, including any additional or return premium.

(b) The respective amounts of the Revolving Fund Assessment, Subsequent Injuries Fund Assessment, Labor Enforcement and Compliance Fund Assessment, Occupational Safety and Health Fund Assessment, Uninsured Employers Fund Assessment, and Fraud surcharge shall each be rounded to the nearest whole dollar, and be respectively shown in the policy as "Workers' Compensation Administration Revolving Fund Assessment (amount)," "Subsequent Injuries Benefits Trust Fund Assessment (amount)," "Labor Enforcement and Compliance Fund Assessment (amount)," "Occupational Safety and Health Fund Assessment (amount)," "Uninsured Employers Benefits Trust Fund Assessment (amount)," and "State Fraud Surcharge (amount)".

(c) Commencing with policies effective on and after January 1, 1993, the insured employer's separate charges calculated under subsection (a) above shall be collected in full with the initial payment of assessable premium. If additional premium becomes due under the policy, the final amount of the separate charges shall be adjusted with the final premium bill for the policy. In the case of a retrospective rated policy, the respective assessment and/or surcharge should be applied to the policy premium at issuance, with recalculation at audit, and application of the factors to any retrospective adjustment premium.

(d) Notwithstanding the requirements of this Section, an insurer may elect not to bill an insured employer for the assessments and surcharge for the additional premium due under the policy if the amount of the additional assessments or surcharge does not exceed $10.00. In the event a return premium is due the employer, the insurer shall return a pro rata share of assessments and surcharge previously paid by the employer unless the assessments and surcharge overpayment does not exceed $10.00.

(e) A self-insurer whose certificate has been revoked during the base year or during the calendar year prior to the current assessments and/or surcharge billing by the Manager shall be exempt from payment of the assessments and/or surcharge as a self-insurer.

(f) If an employer has paid the assessments and/or surcharge as a self-insured employer, and during the year of such assessment and/or surcharge obtains a policy of workers' compensation insurance, the newly insured employer is not required to make assessments and/or surcharge payments as an insured employer for that year's assessments and/or surcharge. Such an employer shall submit to the insurer a copy of the assessments and/or surcharge billing paid as a self-insured employer, in lieu of payment as an insured employer.

Note: Authority cited: Sections 54, 55 and 62.5, Labor Code; and Section 1872.83, Insurance Code. Reference: Sections 62.5 and 62.6, Labor Code; and Section 1872.83, Insurance Code.

History: 1. New section filed 4-18-90 as an emergency; operative 4-18-90 (Register 90, No. 18). A Certificate of Compliance must be transmitted to OAL within 120 days or emergency language will be repealed by operation of law on 8-16-90.

2. Certificate of Compliance as to 4-18-90 order including amendment to subsections (a), (b), and (c) and adding subsection (d) transmitted to OAL 8-14-90 and filed 9-13-90 (Register 90, No. 43).

3. Renumbering of former section 15607 to 15608 and renumbering of former section 15606 to section 15607 and amendment of section heading, section, and Note filed 1-15-93 as an emergency; operative 1-15-93 (Register 93, No. 3). A Certificate of Compliance must be transmitted to OAL 5-17-93 or emergency language will be repealed by operation of law on the following day.

4. Certificate of Compliance as to 1-15-93 order including amendment of subsections (b) and (d) transmitted to OAL 5-10-93 and filed 6-16-93 (Register 93, No. 25).

5. Amendment of subsections (a), (b), (d) and Note filed 9-6-94 as an emergency; operative 9-6-94 (Register 94, No. 36). A Certificate of Compliance must be transmitted to OAL by 1-4-95 or emergency language will be repealed by operation of law on the following day.

6. Certificate of Compliance as to 9-6-94 order including amendment of section heading, subsections (a), (b), and (d), and Note transmitted to OAL 12-30-94 and filed 2-15-95 (Register 95, No. 7).

7. Amendment of subsections (a) and (d), and new subsections (e)-(f) filed 11-14-95 as an emergency; operative 12-1-95 (Register 95, No. 46). A Certificate of Compliance must be transmitted to OAL by 3-30-96 or emergency language will be repealed by operation of law on the following day.

8. Certificate of Compliance as to 11-14-95 order transmitted to OAL 3-29-96 and filed 5-8-96 (Register 96, No. 19).

9. Amendment of subsections (a), (c) and (d) filed 11-10-97; operative 11-10-97 pursuant to Government Code section 11343.4(d) (Register 97, No. 46).

10. Change without regulatory effect amending section heading, section and Note filed 12-15-99 pursuant to section 100, title 1, California Code of Regulations (Register 99, No. 51).

11. Amendment of section heading, section and Note filed 1-14-2000 as an emergency; operative 1-14-2000 (Register 2000, No. 2). A Certificate of Compliance must be transmitted to OAL by 5-15-2000 or emergency language will be repealed by operation of law on the following day.

12. Certificate of Compliance as to 1-14-2000 order transmitted to OAL 5-9-2000 and filed 6-15-2000 (Register 2000, No. 24).

13. Amendment of section heading and section filed 12-18-2003; operative 12-18-2003. Submitted to OAL for printing only (Register 2003, No. 51).

14. Amendment of section heading and subsections (a) and (b) filed 11-12-2008; operative 11-12-2008. Submitted to OAL for printing only (Register 2008, No. 46).

15. Amendment of section heading and subsections (a) and (b) filed 11-19-2009; operative 11-19-2009. Submitted to OAL for printing only (Register 2009, No. 47).

§15607.5. Collection of Targeted Inspection Assessment from Insured Employers. [Repealed]

Note: Authority cited: Sections 54, 55 and 62.7, Labor Code. Reference: Section 62.7, Labor Code.

History: 1. New section filed 9-6-94 as an emergency; operative 9-6-94 (Register 94, No. 36). A Certificate of Compliance must be transmitted to OAL by 1-4-95 or emergency language will be repealed by operation of law on the following day.

2. Certificate of Compliance as to 9-6-94 order including designation of subsections (a)-(e), amendment of subsections (b) and (d), and new subsections (f)-(g) transmitted to OAL 12-30-94 and filed 2-15-95 (Register 95, No. 7).

3. Repealer filed 11-14-95 as an emergency; operative 12-1-95 (Register 95, No. 46). A Certificate of Compliance must be transmitted to OAL by 3-30-96 or emergency language will be repealed by operation of law on the following day.

4. Certificate of Compliance as to 11-14-95 order transmitted to OAL 3-29-96 and filed 5-8-96 (Register 96, No. 19).

§15608. Assessment and/or Surcharge Collection in Excess of Insured Employer Assessment Advance.

If the summary report required by subsections (g) and (h) of Section 15606 of these regulations shows that the insurer has collected assessments and surcharges from employers in excess of the advances paid to the Director for policies incepting in the calendar year covered by the summary report, the insurer shall pay the excess amount to the Director upon submission of the summary report. The Director shall hold any excess amounts in a trust account and either credit the respective amounts to any deficiency in the current assessments and surcharge, or, if there is no deficiency, to the subsequent year's respective assessments and/or surcharges on insured employers.

Note: Authority cited: Sections 54, 55 and 62.5, Labor Code; and Section 1872.83, Insurance Code. Reference: Sections 62.5 and 62.6, Labor Code; and Section 1872.83, Insurance Code.

History: 1. New section filed 4-18-90 as an emergency; operative 4-18-90 (Register 90, No. 18). A Certificate of Compliance must be transmitted to OAL within 120 days or emergency language will be repealed by operation of law on 8-16-90.

2. Certificate of Compliance as to 4-18-90 order including amendment transmitted to OAL 8-14-90 and filed 9-13-90 (Register 90, No. 43).

3. Renumbering of former section 15608 to 15609 and renumbering of former section 15607 to section 15608 and amendment of section heading, section, and Note filed 1-15-93 as an emergency; operative 1-15-93 (Register 93, No. 3). A Certificate of Compliance must be transmitted to OAL 5-17-93 or emergency language will be repealed by operation of law on the following day.

4. Certificate of Compliance as to 1-15-93 order transmitted to OAL 5-10-93 and filed 6-16-93 (Register 93, No. 25).

5. Amendment of Note filed 9-6-94 as an emergency; operative 9-6-94 (Register 94, No. 36). A Certificate of Compliance must be transmitted to OAL by 1-4-95 or emergency language will be repealed by operation of law on the following day.

6. Certificate of Compliance as to 9-6-94 order including amendment of section transmitted to OAL 12-30-94 and filed 2-15-95 (Register 95, No. 7).

7. Amendment of section and Note filed 11-14-95 as an emergency; operative 12-1-95 (Register 95, No. 46). A Certificate of Compliance must be transmitted to OAL by 3-30-96 or emergency language will be repealed by operation of law on the following day.

8. Certificate of Compliance as to 11-14-95 order transmitted to OAL 3-29-96 and filed 5-8-96 (Register 96, No. 19).

9. Change without regulatory effect amending section heading, section and Note filed 12-15-99 pursuant to section 100, title 1, California Code of Regulations (Register 99, No. 51).

10. Amendment of section heading, section and Note filed 1-14-2000 as an emergency; operative 1-14-2000 (Register 2000, No. 2). A Certificate of Compliance must be transmitted to OAL by 5-15-2000 or emergency language will be repealed by operation of law on the following day.

11. Certificate of Compliance as to 1-14-2000 order transmitted to OAL 5-9-2000 and filed 6-15-2000 (Register 2000, No. 24).

12. Amendment filed 12-18-2003; operative 12-18-2003. Submitted to OAL for printing only (Register 2003, No. 51).

§15609. Credit for Undercollection.

(a) When an insurer demonstrates to the Director, within one year of the final audit conducted for premium adjustments for the policies with inception dates in the year subject to assessment, that the total assessments and/or surcharges, respectively, collected from its insured employers is less than the respective assessment and surcharge amounts advanced by the insurer under Section 15606 for that assessment year, the Director shall credit the amount of the difference against the subsequent year's respective advances due from the insurer on behalf of its insured employers.

(1) When an insurer demonstrates, to the satisfaction of the Director, within one year of the final audit conducted for premium adjustments for the policies with inception dates in the year subject to assessment, that it has accrued credit(s) for one or more assessments and/or surcharges in an amount that cannot be effectively utilized in a five year period to offset the specific assessment(s) and/or surcharge(s) on which the credit(s) accrued, the Director may, in his or her sole discretion, and to the extent that the Director finds that sufficient funds are available for this purpose without impairing the fiscal integrity of the programs funded by the respective assessment(s) and/or surcharge(s), refund the excess credit(s) in whole or in part. The Director may, in his or her sole discretion, structure the refund(s) over a period of from one to five years.

(2) When an insurance group, as defined in section 15600, subdivision (j), demonstrates good cause to the satisfaction of the Director, within one year of the final audit conducted for premium adjustments for the policies with inception dates in the year subject to assessment, that one or more members of the group has accrued excess credits in an amount cannot be effectively utilized in a five year period to offset the specific assessment(s) and/or surcharge(s) on which the credit(s) accrued, the Director may, in his or her sole discretion, allow the transfer of those excess credits from company to company within the group, for the specific assessment(s) and/or surcharge(s) on which the excess credit(s) accrued. The Director may, in his or her sole discretion, structure the transfer(s) over a period of from one to five years. Any credit transferred under this subdivision may only be used to offset the next year's assessment(s) and/or surcharge(s) after the credit is transferred.

(3) For purposes of subdivision (a)(2) above, "good cause" includes, but is not limited to, one or more individual insurers with excess credit, as defined in subdivision (a)(2), within the group withdrawing from the California market.

(b) No insurer shall receive any credit for any portion of an undercollection against advances paid by that insurer that is due to the insurer's failure to properly bill a policyholder for the appropriate assessments and/or surcharges applicable to the premium for that policyholder's policy.

Note: Authority cited: Sections 54, 55 and 62.5, Labor Code; and Section 1872.83, Insurance Code. Reference: Sections 62.5 and 62.6, Labor Code; and Section 1872.83, Insurance Code.

History: 1. New section filed 4-18-90 as an emergency; operative 4-18-90 (Register 90, No. 18). A Certificate of Compliance must be transmitted to OAL within 120 days or emergency language will be repealed by operation of law on 8-16-90.

2. Certificate of Compliance as to 4-18-90 order including amendment transmitted to OAL 8-14-90 and filed 9-13-90 (Register 90, No. 43).

3. Repealer of former section 15609 and renumbering and amendment of former section 15608 to section 15609 filed 1-15-93 as an emergency; operative 1-15-93 (Register 93, No. 3). A Certificate of Compliance must be transmitted to OAL 5-17-93 or emergency language will be repealed by operation of law on the following day.

4. Certificate of Compliance as to 1-15-93 order transmitted to OAL 5-10-93 and filed 6-16-93 (Register 93, No. 25).

5. Amendment of section and Note filed 9-6-94 as an emergency; operative 9-6-94 (Register 94, No. 36). A Certificate of Compliance must be transmitted to OAL by 1-4-95 or emergency language will be repealed by operation of law on the following day.

6. Certificate of Compliance as to 9-6-94 order including amendment of section transmitted to OAL 12-30-94 and filed 2-15-95 (Register 95, No. 7).

7. Amendment filed 5-8-96; operative 5-8-96 pursuant to Government Code section 11343.4(d) (Register 96, No. 19).

8. New subsection (a) designator and new subsection (b) filed 11-10-97; operative 11-10-97 pursuant to Government Code section 11343.4(d) (Register 97, No. 46).

9. Change without regulatory effect amending section and Note filed 12-15-99 pursuant to section 100, title 1, California Code of Regulations (Register 99, No. 51).

10. Amendment of section and Note filed 1-14-2000 as an emergency; operative 1-14-2000 (Register 2000, No. 2). A Certificate of Compliance must be transmitted to OAL by 5-15-2000 or emergency language will be repealed by operation of law on the following day.

11. Certificate of Compliance as to 1-14-2000 order transmitted to OAL 5-9-2000 and filed 6-15-2000 (Register 2000, No. 24).

12. New subsections (a)(1)-(3) filed 10-21-2015; operative 10-21-2015. Submitted to OAL for filing and printing only pursuant to Labor Code section 62.5(f)(5) (Register 2015, No. 43).

§15610. Collections of 1995 Interim Targeted Inspection Assessment. [Repealed]

Note: Authority cited: Sections 54, 55 and 62.7, Labor Code; and Section 1872.83, Insurance Code. Reference: Section 62.5, Labor Code; and Section 1872.83, Insurance Code.

History: 1. New section filed 4-18-90 as an emergency; operative 4-18-90 (Register 90, No. 18). A Certificate of Compliance must be transmitted to OAL within 120 days or emergency language will be repealed by operation of law on 8-16-90.

2. Certificate of Compliance as to 4-18-90 order transmitted to OAL 8-14-90 and filed 9-13-90 (Register 90, No. 43).

3. Repealer filed 1-15-93 as an emergency; operative 1-15-93 (Register 93, No. 3). A Certificate of Compliance must be transmitted to OAL 5-17-93 or emergency language will be repealed by operation of law on the following day.

4. Certificate of Compliance as to 1-15-93 order transmitted to OAL 5-10-93 and filed 6-16-93 (Register 93, No. 25).

5. New section filed 2-15-95; operative 3-17-95 (Register 95, No. 7).

6. Repealer filed 12-18-2003; operative 12-18-2003. Submitted to OAL for printing only (Register 2003, No. 51).

§15611. Collection of Interim Assessments.

(a) Notwithstanding the provisions of this subchapter, if the Director determines that there are insufficient funds to support the Workers' Compensation Administration Revolving Fund, the Subsequent Injuries Fund, the Labor Enforcement and Compliance Fund, the Occupational Safety and Health Fund, or the Uninsured Employers Fund for fiscal year 2003-2004, or any fiscal year thereafter, the Director may collect a single interim assessment for these respective funds, in an amount determined by the Director, to provide sufficient funding for these funds.

(b) Any assessment collected under this Section shall not reduce the amount to be collected in the subsequent year's assessments, except as provided by Section 15608 of these regulations.

(c) Any assessment collected under this Section shall be included on the next annual report required under Section 15606(g) of these regulations.

Note: Authority cited: Sections 54, 55 and 62.5, Labor Code. Reference: Section 62.5, Labor Code.

History: 1. New section filed 12-18-2003; operative 12-18-2003. Submitted to OAL for printing only (Register 2003, No. 51).

2. Amendment of subsection (a) filed 11-12-2008; operative 11-12-2008. Submitted to OAL for printing only (Register 2008, No. 46).

3. Amendment of subsection (a) filed 11-19-2009; operative 11-19-2009. Submitted to OAL for printing only (Register 2009, No. 47).

SUBCHAPTER 2.1 ILLEGALLY UNINSURED EMPLOYERS. DETERMINATIONS BY THE DIRECTOR: PRIMA FACIE ILLEGALLY UNINSURED, CORPORATE PARENT AND SUBSTANTIAL SHAREHOLDER; NOTICE; HEARINGS; APPEALS

ARTICLE 1 General

§15710. Definitions.

The following definitions are applicable to this group. Terms not defined here but used in the Labor Code shall have their meaning as so used. All references to the code or to code sections refer to the California Labor Code unless otherwise stated.

(a) Prima facie illegally uninsured. In addition to examples provided in the code, an employer against which there is any evidence from which, after considering any contradicting evidence except any testimony or statements by the employer or related persons, a reasonable person could conclude that the employer, as of the time of the injury, had not secured the payment of compensation as provided by code Section 3700.

(b) Prima facie a parent. A corporation against which there is any evidence from which, after considering any contradictory evidence except testimony or statements of shareholders, officers or beneficial owners of the parent or its subsidiary, a reasonable person could conclude that the corporation had been at the time of the injury or has been, at any subsequent time the parent of a corporation which, as of the time of the injury, had not secured the payment of compensation as provided by code Section 3700.

(c) Prima facie a substantial shareholder. A person against which there is any evidence from which, after considering any contradictory evidence except testimony or statements of that person or of related persons or other shareholders, a reasonable person could conclude that the person had been at the time of the injury or has been at any subsequent time a substantial shareholder in a corporation or the parent of a corporation, which corporation, as of the time of the injury, had not secured the payment of compensation as provided by code Section 3700.

(d) Prima facie case. A case for which there is any evidence from which, after considering any contradictory evidence, a reasonable person could conclude that the case were established as likely to be true.

(e) Director. The Director of Industrial Relations or his designated agents or delegates.

(f) Illegally uninsured. The status of having employees, one of whom was injured arising out of and in the course of the employee's employment at a time when the employer had not secured the payment of compensation as required by code Section 3800.

(g) Appeals board. The California Workers Compensation Appeals Board.

Note: Authority cited: Sections 54, 55, 59, 3702.10, 3710 and 3715, Labor Code. Reference: Sections 3715, 3717.2, 3720, 3720.1 and 3721, Labor Code.

History: 1. New section filed 6-19-89; operative 7-19-89 (Register 89, No. 27). For history of former Group 2.1 (Sections 15600-15670 and Sections 15700-15780, not consecutive), see Register 83, No. 31.

Ref.: Hanna § 10.24[2], [8][a].

§15711. Delegation of Authority.

The director delegates authority to the Chief of the Claims Bureau of the Uninsured Employers Fund to make the determinations under Labor Code Sections 3715(c), 3720(c), and 3720.1(a), to reconsider determinations made pursuant to code Sections 3715(c) and 3720.1(a), to file liens, to remove liens erroneously filed, to remove liens pursuant to code Section 3720(c), to collect funds on liens, refund funds erroneously collected, issue the notices pursuant to code Section 3715(d), and otherwise to administer the program relating to liens issued prior to the issuance of findings and awards of the appeals board, in appeals board cases involving illegally uninsured employers. The Chief of the Claims Bureau may, as he or she deems necessary, delegate all or any part of the authority granted herein to the area supervisors within the Claims Bureau.

History: 1. New section filed 6-19-89; operative 7-19-89 (Register 89, No. 27). For history of former Group 2.1 (Sections 15600-15670 and Sections 15700-15780, not consecutive), see Register 83, No. 31.

Ref.: Hanna § 10.24[2], [8][a].

ARTICLE 2
Determinations by Director

§15720. Determinations.

The director shall make all determinations under code Section 3715(c) of whether a person involved in a claim before the Appeals Board is prima facie illegally uninsured. The director may make determinations pursuant to code Section 3715(c) in any case in which the director, as administrator of the Uninsured Employers Fund, has been joined or otherwise made a party. In all cases where the employer or alleged employer is a corporation and where the director has not petitioned the appeals board to make a determination under code Section 3717.2 or, pending a determination in such cases, the director may make determinations pursuant to code Section 3720.1 of status of prima facie a parent or prima facie a substantial shareholder. The director shall record written reasons for his determinations. These reasons shall be included with the notice of determination.

Note: Authority cited: Sections 54, 55, 59, 3702.10, 3710 and 3715, Labor Code. Reference: Sections 3715, 3717.2, 3720, 3720.1 and 3721, Labor Code.

Ref.: Hanna § 10.24[2].

§15721. Negative Inferences.

If information or documentary proof has been requested by the director from the alleged uninsured employer, and the alleged uninsured employer has not supplied such information or documents, and if the information, documents or copies thereof can reasonably be assumed to be in the possession or control of the alleged uninsured employer, the director shall infer from the failure to comply with the request that the documents do not exist, or that the information or the contents of the documents establish that the alleged uninsured employer was illegally uninsured, or that there was substantial shareholder or parent status, whichever is applicable.

Note: Authority cited: Sections 54, 55, 59, 3702.10, 3710 and 3715, Labor Code. Reference: Sections 3715, 3717.2, 3720, 3720.1 and 3721, Labor Code.

History: 1. New section filed 6-19-89; operative 7-19-89 (Register 89, No. 27). For history of former Group 2.1 (Sections 15600-15670, not consecutive), see Register 83, No. 31.

Ref.: Hanna § 10.24[2], [8][a].

§15722. Reconsideration of Section 3715(c) Determinations; Finality.

Upon receipt of written protest or application for reconsideration from an aggrieved person, of a determination that an employer was prima facie illegally uninsured, the Chief of the Claims Bureau, Uninsured Employers Fund, on the director's behalf, shall informally reconsider the determination. The aggrieved person shall furnish a statement of reasons why the determination was in error, and any evidence in support of the position of the aggrieved person. The Chief of the Claims Bureau may uphold, rescind, or alter the original determination. The decision after reconsideration shall be mailed to the aggrieved person and to other persons to whom the original notice was sent, within five working days after receipt of the protest or application for reconsideration. A request for reconsideration under this section shall be a prerequisite to a filing of a petition with the appeals board pursuant to code Section 3715(d). For purposes of the time within which the petition must be filed with appeals board, the determination shall not be considered to be final until after the decision after reconsideration is mailed.

Note: Authority cited: Sections 54, 55, 59, 3702.10, 3710 and 3715, Labor Code. Reference: Sections 3715, 3717.2, 3720, 3720.1 and 3721, Labor Code.

History: 1. New section filed 6-19-89; operative 7-19-89 (Register 89, No. 27). For history of former Group 2.1 (Sections 15600-15670 and Sections 15700-15780, not consecutive), see Register 83, No. 31.

Ref.: Hanna § 10.24[3].

§15723. Reconsideration of Section 3720.1(a) Determinations; Finality.

Upon receipt of written protest or application for reconsideration from an aggrieved person of a determination that a person was prima facie a parent or a substantial shareholder, the Chief of the Claims Bureau, Uninsured Employers Fund, on the director's behalf, shall informally reconsider the determination. The aggrieved person shall furnish a statement of reasons why the determination was in error, and any evidence in support of the position of the aggrieved person. The Chief of the Claims Bureau may uphold, rescind, or alter the original determination. The decision after reconsideration shall be mailed to the aggrieved person, and to other persons to whom the original notice was sent, within five working days after receipt of the protest or application for reconsideration. A request for reconsideration under this section shall be a prerequisite to a filing of a request for a hearing pursuant to code Section 3720.1(b). A request for hearing filed prior to a protest or application for reconsideration shall be deemed a request for reconsideration. The time for filing a request for formal hearing shall not begin to run until the notice of decision after reconsideration is issued.

Note: Authority cited: Sections 54, 55, 59, 3702.10, 3710 and 3715, Labor Code. Reference: Sections 3715, 3717.2, 3720, 3720.1 and 3721, Labor Code.

History: 1. New section filed 6-19-89; operative 7-19-89 (Register 89, No. 27). For history of former Group 2.1 (Sections 15600-15670, not consecutive), see Register 83, No. 31.

Ref.: Hanna § 10.24[8][b].

ARTICLE 3
Hearings Under Code Section 3720.1

§15730. Administrative Hearing.

Upon the petition of an aggrieved person, if the petition is not treated as a request for informal reconsideration pursuant to Section 15723, the director shall hold a hearing to review prima facie substantial shareholder or parent status.

Note: Authority cited: Sections 54, 55, 59, 3702.10, 3710 and 3715, Labor Code. Reference: Sections 3715, 3717.2, 3720, 3720.1 and 3721, Labor Code.

History: 1. New section filed 6-19-89; operative 7-19-89 (Register 89, No. 27). For history of former Group 2.1 (Sections 15600-15670, not consecutive), see Register 83, No. 31.

Ref.: Hanna § 10.24[8][b].

§15731. Delegation of Authority.

The director delegates authority to the Chief Counsel of the Department of Industrial Relations to appoint hearing officers and to issue the notices for hearings held pursuant to code section 3720.1(b). The hearing officer appointed shall not have been involved in the representation of the director before the appeals board in that particular case.

Note: Authority cited: Sections 54, 55, 59, 3702.10, 3710 and 3715, Labor Code. Reference: Sections 3715, 3717.2, 3720, 3720.1 and 3721, Labor Code.

Ref.: Hanna § 10.24[8][b].

§15732. Conduct of Hearing.

(a) Hearing Officer. The hearing officer shall have full authority as the director would to make all decisions necessary for the proper conduct of the hearing and for the making of a decision thereon. Not limiting the foregoing, the hearing officer may administer oaths, take testimony, admit or exclude evidence, schedule the hearing, continue or adjourn the hearing, require a statement of contentions, issue a subpoena and subpoena duces tecum for the attendance of a person and the production of testimony, books, or documents, and to decide when the case is submitted for decision.

(b) Admissible Evidence. The California Evidence Code and the common law rules of evidence shall not apply in the hearing, and the hearing officer may admit, consider, and rely upon evidence which would not be admissible if such rules of evidence governed.

(c) Testimony under Oath. All witnesses testifying before the hearing officer shall testify under oath, affirmation or penalty of perjury.

(d) Transcripts. The hearing shall be recorded by audio tape recording. A party desiring a transcript must pay for the transcription or provide and pay for a court reporter. In either case, a copy of the transcript must be provided to the director.

(e) Witness fees. Costs of subpoenaing witnesses are to be borne by the party requesting the subpoena.

(f) Documents. If a person seeking to establish that the person is not a parent or substantial shareholder does not produce corporate documents which relate the ownership of the applicable corporation, and there is evidence that the person was a shareholder or owner of a beneficial interest in the corporation, the hearing officer may presume that the corporate documents not produced would contain evidence establishing the opposite of the contention asserted by the person not offering them.

History: 1. New section filed 6-19-89; operative 7-19-89 (Register 89, No. 27). For history of former Group 2.1 (Sections 15600–15670, not consecutive), see Register 83, No. 31.

Ref.: Hanna § 10.24[8][b].

SUBCHAPTER 2.1.1
UNINSURED EMPLOYERS FUND AND SUBSEQUENT INJURIES FUND BENEFITS TO ALIENS

ARTICLE 1
Limitations on Benefits

§15740. Limitations on Uninsured Employers Fund and Subsequent Injuries Fund Benefits for Aliens.

(a) All eligibility requirements contained herein shall be applied without regard to the race, creed, color, gender, religion, or national origin of the individual applying for the public benefit.

(b) Pursuant to Section 411 of the Personal Responsibility and Work Opportunity Reconciliation Act of 1996, (Pub. L. No. 104-193 (PRWORA)), (8 U.S.C. §1621), and notwithstanding any other provision of this division, aliens who are not qualified aliens, nonimmigrant aliens under the Immigration and Nationality Act (INA) (8 U.S.C. §1101 et seq.), or aliens paroled into the United States under Section 212(d)(5) of the INA (8 U.S.C. §1182(d)(5)), for less than one year, are not eligible to receive benefits, including death benefits as the dependent of a deceased employee, from the UEF or SIF as set forth in Labor Code Sections 3716, 3716.2 and 4750-4755.

(c) A qualified alien is an alien who, at the time he or she applies for, receives, or attempts to receive benefits from the UEF or SIF, including death benefits as the dependent of a deceased employee, is, under Section 431(b) of the PRWORA (8 U.S.C. §1641(b) and (c)), any of the following:

(1) An alien lawfully admitted for permanent residence under the INA (8 U.S.C. §1101 et seq.).

(2) An alien who is granted asylum under Section 208 of the INA (8 U.S.C. §1158).

(3) A refugee who is admitted to the United States under Section 207 of the INA (8 U.S.C. §1157).

(4) An alien who is paroled into the United States under Section 212(d)(5) of the INA (8 U.S.C. §1182(d)(5)) for a period of at least one year.

(5) An alien whose deportation is being withheld under Section 243(h) of the INA (8 U.S.C. §1253(h)) (as in effect immediately before the effective date of Section 307 of division C of Public Law 104-208) or Section 241(b)(2) of such Act (8 U.S.C. §1251(b)(3)) (as amended by Section 305(a) of division C of Public Law 104-208).

(6) An alien who is granted conditional entry pursuant to Section 203(a)(7) of the INA as in effect prior to April 1, 1980 (8 U.S.C. §1153(a)(7)) (See editorial note under 8 U.S.C. §1101, "Effective Date of 1980 Amendment").

(7) An alien who is a Cuban or Haitian entrant (as defined in Section 501(e) of the Refugee Education Assistance Act of 1980 (8 U.S.C. §1522 note)).

(8) An alien who, under Section 431(c)(1) of the PRWORA (8 U.S.C. §1641(c)(1), meets all of the conditions of subparagraphs (A), (B), (C), and (D) below:

(A) The alien has been battered or subjected to extreme cruelty in the United States by a spouse or a parent, or by a member of the spouse's or parent's family residing in the same household as the alien, and the spouse or parent of the alien consented to, or acquiesced in, such battery or cruelty. For purposes of this subsection, the term "battered or subjected to extreme cruelty" includes, but is not limited to being the victim of any act or threatened act of violence including any forceful detention, which results or threatens to result in physical or mental injury. Rape, molestation, incest (if the victim is a minor), or forced prostitution shall be considered acts of violence.

(B) There is a substantial connection between such battery or cruelty and the need for the benefits to be provided in the opinion of the UEF or SIF. For purposes of this subsection, the following circumstances demonstrate a substantial connection between the battery or cruelty and the need for the benefits to be provided:

(i) The benefits are needed to enable the alien to become self-sufficient following separation from the abuser.

(ii) The benefits are needed to enable the alien to escape the abuser and/or the community in which the abuser lives, or to ensure the safety of the alien from the abuser.

(iii) The benefits are needed due to a loss of financial support resulting from the alien's separation from the abuser.

(iv) The benefits are needed because the battery or cruelty, separation from the abuser, or work absences or lower job performance resulting from the battery or extreme cruelty or from legal proceedings relating thereto (including resulting child support, child custody, and divorce actions) cause the alien to lose his or her job or to earn less or to require the alien to leave his or her job for safety reasons.

(v) The benefits are needed because the alien requires medical attention or mental health counseling, or has become disabled, as a result of the battery or extreme cruelty.

(vi) The benefits are needed because the loss of a dwelling or source of income or fear of the abuser following separation from the abuser jeopardizes the alien's ability to care for his or her children (e.g., inability to house, feed, or clothe children or to put children into a day care for fear of being found by the abuser).

(vii) The benefits are needed to alleviate nutritional risk or need resulting from the abuse or following separation from the abuser.

(viii) The benefits are needed to provide medical care during a pregnancy resulting from the abuser's sexual assault or abuse of, or relationship with, the alien and/or to care for any resulting children.

(ix) Where medical coverage and/or health care services are needed to replace medical coverage or health care services the alien had when living with the abuser.

(C) The alien has been approved or has a petition pending which sets forth a prima facie case for:

(i) status as a spouse or child of a United States citizen pursuant to clause (ii), (iii), or (iv) of Section 204(a)(1)(A) of the INA (8 U.S.C. §1154(a)(1)(A)(ii), (iii) or (iv)),

(ii) classification pursuant to clause (ii) or (iii) of Section 204(a)(1)(B) of the INA (8 U.S.C. §1254(a)(1)(B)(ii) or (iii)),

(iii) cancellation of removal under 8 U.S.C. §1229b as in effect prior to April 1, 1997,

(iv) status as a spouse or child of a United States citizen pursuant to clause (i) of Section 204(a)(1)(A) of the INA (8 U.S.C. §1154(a)(1)(A)) or classification pursuant to clause (i) of Section 204(a)(1)(B) of the INA (8 U.S.C. §1154(a)(1)(B)(i)).

(v) cancellation of removal pursuant to Section 204A(b)(2) of the INA (8 U.S.C. §1229b(b)(2)).

(D) For the period for which benefits are sought, the individual responsible for the battery or cruelty does not reside in the same household or family eligibility unit as the individual subjected to the battery or cruelty.

(9) An alien who meets all of the conditions of subparagraphs (A), (B), (C), (D) and (E) below:

(A) The alien has a child who has been battered or subjected to extreme cruelty in the United States by a spouse or a parent of the alien (without the active participation of the alien in the battery or cruelty), or by a member of the spouse's or parent's family residing in the same household as the alien, and the spouse or parent consented or acquiesced to such battery or cruelty. For purposes of this subsection, the term "battered or subjected to extreme cruelty" includes, but is not limited to being the victim of any act or threatened act of violence including any forceful detention, which results or threatens to result in physical or mental injury. Rape, molestation, incest (if the victim is a minor), or forced prostitution shall be considered as acts of violence.

(B) The alien did not actively participate in such battery or cruelty.

(C) There is a substantial connection between such battery or cruelty and the need for the benefits to be provided-in the opinion of the UEF or SIF. For purposes of this subsection, the following circumstances demonstrate a substantial connection between the battery or cruelty and the need for the benefits to be provided:

(i) The benefits are needed to enable the alien's child to become self-sufficient following separation from the abuser.

(ii) The benefits are needed to enable the alien's child to escape the abuser and/or the community in which the abuser lives, or to ensure the safety of the alien's child from the abuser.

(iii) The benefits are needed due to a loss of financial support resulting from the alien's child's separation from the abuser.

(iv) The benefits are needed because the battery or cruelty, separation from the abuser, or work absences or lower job performance resulting from the battery or extreme cruelty or from legal proceedings relating thereto (including resulting child support, child custody, and divorce actions) cause the alien's child to lose his or her job or to earn less or to require the alien's child to leave his or her job for safety reasons.

(v) The benefits are needed because the alien's child requires medical attention or mental health counseling, or has become disabled, as a result of the battery or extreme cruelty.

(vi) The benefits are needed because the loss of a dwelling or source of income or fear of the abuser following separation from the abuser jeopardizes the alien's child's ability to care for his or her children (e.g., inability to house, feed, or clothe children or to put children into a day care for fear of being found by the abuser).

(vii) The benefits are needed to alleviate nutritional risk or need resulting from the abuse or following separation from the abuser.

(viii) The benefits are needed to provide medical care during a pregnancy resulting from the abuser's sexual assault or abuse of, or relationship with, the alien's child and/or to care for any resulting children.

(ix) Where medical coverage and/or health care services are needed to replace medical coverage or health care services the alien's child had when living with the abuser.

(D) The alien meets the requirements of subsection (c)(8)(C) above.

(E) For the period for which benefits are sought, the individual responsible for the battery or cruelty does not reside in the same household or family eligibility unit as the individual subjected to the battery or cruelty.

(10) An alien child who meets all of the conditions of subparagraphs (A), (B), and (C) below:

(A) The alien child resides in the same household as a parent who has been battered or subjected to extreme cruelty in the United States by that parent's spouse or by a member of the spouse's family residing in the same household as the parent and the spouse consented or acquiesced to such battery or cruelty. For purposes of this subsection, the term "battered or subjected to extreme cruelty" includes, but is not limited to being the victim of any act or threatened act of violence including any forceful detention, which results or threatens to result in physical or mental injury. Rape, molestation, incest (if the victim is a minor), or forced prostitution shall be considered acts of violence.

(B) There is a substantial connection between such battery or cruelty and the need for the benefits to be provided in the opinion of the UEF or SIF. For purposes of this subsection, the following circumstances demonstrate a substantial connection between the battery or cruelty and the need for the benefits to be provided:

(i) The benefits are needed to enable the alien child's parent to become self-sufficient following separation from the abuser.

(ii) The benefits are needed to enable the alien child's parent to escape the abuser and/or the community in which the abuser lives, or to ensure the safety of the alien child's parent from the abuser.

(iii) The benefits are needed due to a loss of financial support resulting from the alien child's parent's separation from the abuser.

(iv) The benefits are needed because the battery or cruelty, separation from the abuser, or work absences or lower job performance resulting from the battery or extreme cruelty or from legal proceedings relating thereto (including resulting child support, child custody, and divorce actions) cause the alien child's parent to lose his or her job or to earn less or to require the alien child's parent to leave his or her job for safety reasons.

(v) The benefits are needed because the alien child's parent requires medical attention or mental health counseling, or has become disabled, as a result of the battery or extreme cruelty.

(vi) The benefits are needed because the loss of a dwelling or source of income or fear of the abuser following separation from the abuser jeopardizes the alien child's parent's ability to care for his or her children (e.g., inability to house, feed, or clothe children or to put children into a day care for fear of being found by the abuser).

(vii) The benefits are needed to alleviate nutritional risk or need resulting from the abuse or following separation from the abuser.

(viii) The benefits are needed to provide medical care during a pregnancy resulting from the abuser's sexual assault or abuse of, or relationship with, the alien child's parent and/or to care for any resulting children.

(ix) Where medical coverage and/or health care services are needed to replace medical coverage or health care services the alien child's parent had when living with the abuser.

(c) The alien child meets the requirements of subsection (c)(8)(C) above.

(d) For purposes of this section, "nonimmigrant" is defined the same as in Section 101(a)(15) of the INA (8 U.S.C. §1101(a)(15)).

(e) For purposes of establishing eligibility for Uninsured Employers Fund (UEF) and Subsequent Injuries Fund (SIF) benefits, all of the following must be met:

(1) The applicant must declare himself or herself to be a citizen of the United States or a qualified alien under subsection (c), a nonimmigrant alien under subsection (d), or an alien paroled into the United States for less than one year under Section 212(d)(5) of the INA (8 U.S.C. §1182(d)(5)). The applicant shall declare that status through

use of the "Statement of Citizenship, Alienage, and Immigration Status for State Public Benefits," Form UEF-1.

(2) The applicant must present documents of a type acceptable to the Immigration and Naturalization Services (INS) which serve as reasonable evidence of the applicant's declared status.

(3) The applicant must complete and sign Form UEF-1.

(4) Where authorized by the INS, the documentation presented by an alien as reasonable evidence of the alien's declared immigration status must be submitted to the INS for verification through the Systematic Alien Verification for Entitlements (SAVE) system procedures as follows:

(A) Unless the primary SAVE system is unavailable for use, the primary SAVE system verification must be used to access the biographical/immigration status computer record contained in the Alien Status Verification Index maintained by the INS. Subject to subparagraph (B), this procedure must be used to verify the status of all aliens who claim to be qualified aliens and who present an INS-issued document that contains an alien registration or alien admission number.

(B) In any of the following cases, the secondary SAVE system verification procedure must be used to forward copies of original INS documents evidencing an alien's status as a qualified alien, as a nonimmigrant alien under the INA, or as an alien paroled into the United States under Section 212(d)(5) of the INA (8 U.S.C. §1182(d)(5)), for less than one year:

(i) The primary SAVE system is unavailable for verification.

(ii) A primary check of the Alien Status Verification Index instructs the Uninsured Employers Fund or Subsequent Injuries Fund to "institute secondary verification."

(iii) The document presented indicates immigration status but does not include an alien registration or alien admission number.

(iv) The Alien Status Verification Index record includes the alien registration or admission number on the document presented by the alien but does not match other information contained in the document.

(v) The document is suspected to be counterfeit or to have been altered.

(vi) The document includes an alien registration number in the A60 000 000 (not yet issued) or A80 000 000 (illegal border crossing) series.

(vii) The document is a fee receipt from INS for replacement of a lost, stolen, or unreadable INS document.

(viii) The document is one of the following: an INS Form I-181b notification letter issued in connection with an INS Form I-181 Memorandum of Creation of Record of Permanent Residence, an Arrival-Departure Record (INS Form I-94) or a foreign passport stamped "PROCESSED FOR I-551, TEMPORARY EVIDENCE OF LAWFUL PERMANENT RESIDENCE" that INS issued more than one year before the date of application for benefits from the UEF or SIF.

(5) Where verification through the SAVE system is not available, if the documents presented do not on their face reasonably appear to be genuine or to relate to the individual presenting them, the government entity that originally issued the document should be contacted for verification. With regard to naturalized citizens and derivative citizens presenting certificates of citizenship and aliens, the INS is the appropriate government entity to contact for verification. The UEF or SIF should request verification by the INS by filing INS Form G-845 with copies of the pertinent documents provided by the applicant with the local INS office. If the applicant has lost his her original documents, or presents expired documents or is unable to present any documentation evidencing his or her immigration status, the applicant should be referred to the local INS office to obtain documentation.

(6) If the INS advises that the applicant has citizenship status or immigration status which makes him or her a qualified alien under the PRWORA, the INS verification should be accepted. If the INS advises that it cannot verify that the applicant has citizenship status or an immigration status that makes him or her a qualified alien, benefits shall be denied and the applicant notified of his or her rights to appeal the denial of benefits.

(7) Provided that the alien has completed and signed Form UEF-1 under penalty of perjury, eligibility for UEF or SIF benefits shall not be delayed, denied, reduced or terminated while the status of the alien is verified.

(f) Pursuant to Section 432(d) of the PRWORA (8 U.S.C. §1642(d)), the UEF or SIF shall assure that a nonprofit charitable organization that provides federal, state, or local public benefits shall not be required to determine, verify, or otherwise require proof of eligibility of any applicant or beneficiary with respect to his or her immigration status or alienage.

(g) Pursuant to Section 434 of the PRWORA (8 U.S.C. §1644), where the UEF or SIF reasonably believes that an alien is unlawfully in the State based on the failure of the alien to provide reasonable evidence of the alien's declared status, after an opportunity to do so, said alien shall be reported to the Immigration and Naturalization Service.

(h) Nothing in this section shall be construed to withdraw eligibility for medical treatment required for an emergency medical condition under Section 411(b) of the PRWORA (8 U.S.C. §1621(b(1)).

(i) Any applicant who is denied benefits, or whose benefits are terminated, pursuant to subsections (b) and (e), may file a Request for Administrative Review of benefit determination with the UEF Manager within 20 days of service of the notice of denial or termination of benefits from the UEF or SIF. The Request for Administrative Review shall be verified under penalty of perjury with proof of service on all parties, and shall provide a statement of reasons, as well as any relevant evidence, explaining why the determination of the UEF or SIF was in error.

(j) Upon receipt of the Request for Administrative Review, the UEF Manager shall informally reconsider the determination and shall issue a decision granting or denying the request within 45 days. A Request for Administrative Review as provided in subsection (i) shall be a prerequisite to the filing of a petition before the Workers' Compensation Appeals Board pursuant to subsection (k).

(k) Any applicant aggrieved by a decision of the UEF Manager on a Request for Administrative Review of benefit determination may file, within 20 days of service of the decision, a petition for relief before the Workers' Compensation Appeals Board. The petition shall be filed at the appeals board office that is designated for applications for adjudication of claim pursuant to Labor Code Section 5501.5., and shall be assigned to a workers' compensation judge for hearing and determination of the issues raised. A party aggrieved by the determination of the workers' compensation judge may seek relief from the determination in the same manner as specified for petitions for reconsideration pursuant to Labor Code Section 5900.

Note: Authority cited: Sections 54, 55, 59, 3702.10, 3716, 3716.1, 3716.2 and 4751, Labor Code. Reference: Sections 1621, 1641 and 1642, Title 8, United States Code; and Sections 3716, 3716.1, 3716.2, 4750-4755 and 5501.5, Labor Code.

History: 1. New subchapter 2.1.1, article 1 (sections 15740-15741) and section filed 10-28-98; operative 11-27-98 (Register 98, No. 44).

Ref.: See Labor Code §§4751–4755; Hanna §§ 1.21, 2.13, 31.20[4][a]; Herlick Handbook §§ 2.3, 3.19, 6.16.

§15741. Statement of Citizenship, Alienage, and Immigration Status for State Public Benefits, Form UEF-1.

STATE OF CALIFORNIA
DEPARTMENT OF INDUSTRIAL RELATIONS
UNINSURED EMPLOYERS FUND-SUBSEQUENT INJURIES FUND

STATEMENT OF CITIZENSHIP, ALIENAGE, AND IMMIGRATION STATUS FOR STATE PUBLIC BENEFITS

Name of Applicant (the person seeking Uninsured Employers Fund or Subsequent Injuries Fund benefits)
Date

Name of Person Acting for Applicant, if any
Relationship to Applicant

STATE PUBLIC BENEFITS TO CITIZENS AND ALIENS

Citizens and nationals of the United States who meet all eligibility requirements may receive Uninsured Employers Fund or Subsequent Injuries Fund benefits and must fill out Sections A and D.

Aliens who meet all eligibility requirements may also receive Uninsured Employers Fund or Subsequent Injuries Fund benefits and must complete SECTIONS A, B, C and D of this form.

SECTION A: CITIZENSHIP/IMMIGRATION STATUS DECLARATION

1. Is the applicant a citizen or national of the United States?

Yes ☐ No ☐

If the answer to the above question is "Yes", where was he/she born?

__________ (State or Country)

2. To establish citizenship or nationality, please submit one of the documents on List A (attached to this form) which is legible and unaltered to establish proof.

IF YOU ARE A CITIZEN OR NATIONAL OF THE UNITED STATES, GO DIRECTLY TO SECTION D. IF YOU ARE AN ALIEN, PLEASE COMPLETE SECTION B, AND, IF NECESSARY, SECTION C.

SECTION B: ALIEN STATUS DECLARATION

IMPORTANT: Please indicate the applicant's alien status below, and submit documents evidencing such status. The alien status documents listed for each category are the most commonly used documents that the United States Immigration and Naturalization Service (INS) provides to aliens in those categories. You can provide other acceptable evidence of your alien status even if not listed below. Where authorized by the INS, the documents you provide will be submitted to the INS for verification through the Systematic Alien Verification for Entitlements ("SAVE") system. Should verification through the "SAVE" system be unavailable, the validity of the documents you provide may be verified directly with the issuing government agency.

1. An alien lawfully admitted for permanent residence under the Immigration and Naturalization Act (INA). (Evidence includes: ☐
   - INS Form I-551 (Alien Registration Receipt Card, commonly known as a "green card"); or
   - Unexpired Temporary I-551 stamp in foreign passport or on INS Form I-94.
2. An alien who is granted asylum under section 208 of the INA. (Evidence includes: ☐
   - INS Form I-94 annotated with stamp showing grant of asylum under section 208 of the INA;
   - INS Form I-688B (Employment Authorization Card) annotated "274a.12(a)(5)";
   - INS Form I-766 (Employment Authorization Document) annotated "A5";
   - Grant letter from the Asylum Office of INS; or

- Order of an immigration judge granting asylum.)

3. A refugee admitted to the United States under section 207 of the INA. ☐
(Evidence includes:
- INS Form I-94 annotated with stamp showing admission under section 207 of the INA;
- INS Form I-688B (Employment Authorization Card) annotated "274a.12(a)(3)";
- INS Form I-766 (Employment Authorization Document) annotated "A3"; or
- INS Form I-571 (Refugee Travel Document).

4. An alien paroled into the United States for at least one year under section 212(d)(5) of the INA. (Evidence includes: ☐
- INS Form I-94 with stamp showing admission for at least one year under section 212(d)(5) of the INA. (Applicant cannot aggregate periods of admission for less than one year to meet the one-year requirement.)

5. An alien whose deportation is being withheld under section 243(h) of the INA (as in effect immediately prior to September 30, 1996) or Section 241(b)(3) of such Act (as amended by section 305(a) of division C of Public Law 104-208). (Evidence includes: ☐
- INS Form I-688B (Employment Authorization Card) annotated "274a.12(a)(10)";
- INS Form I-766 (Employment Authorization Document) annotated "A10"; or
- Order from an immigration judge showing deportation withheld under section 243(h) of the INA as in effect prior to April 1, 1997, or removal withheld under section 241(b)(3) of the INA.)

6. An alien who is granted conditional entry under section 203(a)(7) of the INA as in effect prior to April 1, 1980. (Evidence includes: ☐
- INS Form I-94 with stamp showing admission under Section 203(a)(7) of the INA;
- INS Form I-688B (Employment Authorization Card) annotated "274a.12(a)(3)"; or
- INS Form I-766 (Employment Authorization Document) annotated "A3").

7. An alien who is a Cuban or Haitian entrant (as defined in section 501(e) of the Refugee Education Assistance Act of 1980). (Evidence includes: ☐
- INS Form I-551 (Alien Registration Receipt Card, commonly known as a "green card") with the code CU6, CU7, or CH6;
- Unexpired temporary I-551 stamp in foreign passport or on INS Form I-94 with the code CU6 or CU7; or
- INS Form I-94 with stamp showing parole as "Cuban/Haitian Entrant" under Section 212(d)(5) of the INA.)

8. An alien paroled into the United States for less than one year under section 212(d)(5) of the INA. (Evidence includes INS Form I-94 showing this status.) ☐

9. An alien not in categories 1 through 8 who has been admitted to the United States for a limited period of time (a non-immigrant). Non-immigrants are persons who have temporary status for a specific purpose. (Evidence includes INS Form I-94 showing this status.) ☐

SECTION C: DECLARATION FOR BATTERED ALIENS

IMPORTANT: Complete this section if the applicant, the applicant's child or the applicant child's parent has been battered or subjected to extreme cruelty in the United States.

1. Has the INS or the EOIR granted a petition or application filed by or on behalf of the applicant, the applicant's child, or the applicant's child's parent under the INA or found that a pending petition sets forth a prima facie case? Evidence includes one of the documents on List B (attached hereto) ☐
2. Has the applicant, the applicant's child, or the applicant child's parent been battered or subjected to extreme cruelty in the United States by a spouse or parent, or by a spouse's or parent's family member living in the same house (where the spouse or parent consented to, or acquiesced in the battery or cruelty)? ☐

SECTION D:

I DECLARE UNDER PENALTY OF PERJURY UNDER THE LAWS OF THE STATE OF CALIFORNIA THAT THE ANSWERS I HAVE GIVEN ARE TRUE AND CORRECT TO THE BEST OF MY KNOWLEDGE.

Applicant's Signature: ______________________________ Date: ____________________
Signature of Person
Acting for Applicant: ______________________________ Date: ____________________

LIST "A"

(For Applicants for Uninsured Employers Fund or Subsequent Injuries Fund benefits who are citizens or nationals of the United States.)

A. Primary Evidence

- A birth certificate showing birth in one of the 50 States, the District of Columbia, Puerto Rico (on or after January 13, 1941), Guam, the U.S. Virgin Islands (on or after January 17, 1917), American Samoa, Swain's Island or the Northern Mariana Islands, unless the person was born to foreign diplomats residing in the U.S.

Note: If the document shows that the individual was born in Puerto Rico, the U.S. Virgin Islands or the Northern Mariana Islands before these areas became part of the U.S., the individual may be a collectively naturalized citizen—(see Paragraph C below).

- United States passport (except limited passports, which are issued for periods of less than five years);
- Report of birth abroad of a U.S. citizen (FS-240) (issued by the Department of State to U.S. citizens);
- Certificate of birth (FS-545) (issued by a foreign service post) or Certification of Report of Birth (DS-1350) (issued by the Department of State), copies of which are available from the Department of State;
- Certificate of Naturalization (N-550 or N-570) (issued by INS through a Federal or State court, or through administrative naturalization after December 1990 to individuals who are individually naturalized; the N-570 is a replacement certificate issued when the N-550 has been lost or mutilated or the individual's name has been changed);
- Certificate of Citizenship (N-560 or N-561) (issued by the INS to individuals who derive U.S. citizenship through a parent; the N-561 is a replacement certificate issued when the N-560 has been lost or mutilated or the individual's name has been changed);
- United States Citizen Identification Card (I-197) (issued by the INS until April 7, 1983 to U.S. citizens living near the Canadian or Mexican border who needed it for frequent border crossings) (formerly Form I-179, last issued in February 1974);
- Northern Mariana Identification Card (issued by the INS to a collectively naturalized citizen of the U.S. who was born in the Northern Mariana Islands before November 3, 1986);
- Statement provided by a U.S. consular officer certifying that the individual is a U.S. citizen (this is given to an individual born outside the U.S. who derives citizenship through a parent but does not have an FS-240, FS-545 or DS-1350); or
- American Indian Card with a classification code "KIC" and a statement on the back (identifying U.S. citizen members of the Texas Band of Kickapoos living near the U.S./Mexican border).

B. Secondary Evidence

If the applicant cannot present one of the documents listed in A above, the following may be relied upon to establish U.S. citizenship or nationality:

- Religious record recorded in one of the 50 States, the District of Columbia, Puerto Rico (on or after January 13, 1941), Guam, the U.S. Virgin Islands (on or after January 17, 1917), American Samoa, Swain's Island or the Northern Mariana Islands (unless the person was born to foreign diplomats residing in such a jurisdiction) within three months after birth showing that the birth occurred in such jurisdiction and the date of birth or the individual's age at the time the record was made;
- Evidence of civil service employment by the U.S. government before June 1, 1976;
- Early school records (preferably from the first school) showing the date of admission to the school, the child's date and place of birth, and the name(s) and place(s) of birth of the parent(s);
- Census record showing name, U.S. citizenship or a U.S. place of birth, and date of birth or age of applicant;
- Adoption Finalization Papers showing the child's name and place of birth in one of the 50 States, the District of Columbia, Puerto Rico (on or after January 13, 1941), Guam, the U.S. Virgin Islands (on or after January 17, 1917), American Samoa, Swain's Island or the Northern Mariana Islands (unless the person was born to foreign diplomats residing in such a jurisdiction) or, where or adoption is not finalized and the State or other jurisdiction listed above in which the child was born will not release a birth certificate prior to final adoption, a statement from a state-approved adoption agency showing the child's name and place of birth in one of such jurisdictions (NOTE: the source of the information must be an original birth certificate and must be indicated in the statement); or
- Any other document that establishes a U.S. place of birth or in some way indicates U.S. citizenship (e.g., a contemporaneous hospital record of birth in that hospital in one of the 50 States, the District of Columbia, Puerto Rico (on or after January 13, 1941), Guam, the U.S. Virgin Islands (on or after January 17, 1917), American Samoa, Swain's Island or the Northern Mariana Islands (unless the person was born to foreign diplomats residing in such a jurisdiction).

C. Collective Naturalization

If the applicant cannot present one of the documents listed in A or B above, the following may be relied upon to establish U.S. citizenship for collectively naturalized individuals:

Puerto Rico:

- Evidence of birth in Puerto Rico on or after April 11, 1899 and the applicant's statement that he or she was residing in the U.S., a U.S. possession or Puerto Rico on January 13, 1941; or
- Evidence that the applicant was a Puerto Rican citizen and the applicant's statement that he or she was residing in Puerto Rico on March 1, 1917 and that he or she did not take an oath of allegiance to Spain.

U.S. Virgin Islands:

- Evidence of birth in the U.S. Virgin Islands, and the applicant's statement of residence in the U.S., a U.S. possession or the U.S. Virgin Islands on February 25, 1927;
- The applicant's statement indicating residence in the U.S. Virgin Islands as a Danish citizen on January 17, 1917 and residence in the U.S., a U.S. possession or the U.S. Virgin Islands on February 25, 1927, and that he or she did not make a declaration to maintain Danish citizenship; or
- Evidence of birth in the U.S. Virgin Islands and the applicant's statement indicating residence in the U.S., a U.S. possession or territory or the Canal Zone on June 28, 1932.

Northern Mariana Islands (NMI) (formerly part of the Trust Territory of the Pacific Islands (TTPI));

- Evidence of birth in the NMI, TTPI citizenship and residence in the NMI, the U.S., or a U.S. territory or possession on November 3, 1986 (NMI local time) and the applicant's statement that he or she did not owe allegiance to a foreign state on November 4, 1986 (NMI local time);
- Evidence of TTPI citizenship, continuous residence in the NMI since before November 3, 1981 (NMI local time), voter registration prior to January 1, 1975 and the applicant's statement that he or she did not owe allegiance to a foreign state on November 4, 1986 (NMI local time); or
- Evidence of continuous domicile in the NMI since before January 1, 1974 and the applicant's statement that he or she did not owe allegiance to a foreign state on November 4, 1986 (NMI local time). Note: If a person entered the NMI as a nonimmigrant and lived in the NMI since January 1, 1974, this does not constitute continuous domicile and the individual is not a U.S. citizen.

D. Derivative Citizenship

If the applicant cannot present one of the documents listed in A or B above, you should make a determination of derivative U.S. citizenship in the following situations:

Applicant born abroad to two U.S. citizen parents:

- Evidence of the U.S. citizenship of the parents and the relationship of the applicant to the parents, and evidence that at least one parent resided in the U.S. or an outlying possession prior to the applicant's birth.

Applicant born abroad to a U.S. citizen parent and a U.S. non-citizen national parent:

- Evidence that one parent is a U.S. citizen and that the other is a U.S. non-citizen national, evidence of the relationship of the applicant to the U.S. citizen parent, and evidence that the U.S. citizen parent resided in the U.S., a U.S. possession, American Samoa or Swain's Island for a period of at least one year prior to the applicant's birth.

Applicant born out of wedlock abroad to a U.S. citizen mother:

- Evidence of the U.S. citizenship of the mother, evidence of the relationship to the applicant and, for births on or before December 24, 1952, evidence that the mother resided in the U.S. prior to the applicant's birth or, for births after December 24, 1952, evidence that the mother had resided, prior to the child's birth, in the U.S. or a U.S. possession for a period of one year.

Applicant born in the Canal Zone or the Republic of Panama:

- A birth certificate showing birth in the Canal Zone on or after February 26, 1904 and before October 1, 1979 and evidence that one parent was a U.S. citizen at the time of the applicant's birth; or
- A birth certificate showing birth in the Republic of Panama on or after February 26, 1904 and before October 1, 1979 and evidence that at least one parent was a U.S. citizen and employed by the U.S. government or the Panama Railroad Company or its successor in title.

All other situations where an applicant claims to have a U.S. citizen parent and an alien parent, or claims to fall within one of the above categories but is unable to present the listed documentation:

- If the applicant is in the U.S., refer him or her to the local INS office for determination of U.S. citizenship;
- If the applicant is outside the U.S., refer him or her to the State Department for a U.S. citizenship determination.

E. Adoption of Foreign-Born Child by U.S. Citizen

- If the birth certificate shows a foreign place of birth and the applicant cannot be determined to be a naturalized citizen under any of the above criteria, obtain other evidence of U.S. citizenship;
- Since foreign-born adopted children do not automatically acquire U.S. citizenship by virtue of adoption by U.S. citizens, refer the applicant to the local INS district office for a determination of U.S. citizenship if the applicant provides no evidence of U.S. citizenship.

F. U.S. Citizenship by Marriage

A women acquired U.S. citizenship through marriage to a U.S. citizen before September 22, 1922. Ask for: Evidence of U.S. citizenship of the husband, and evidence showing the marriage occurred before September 22, 1922.

Note: If the husband was an alien at the time of the marriage, and became naturalized before September 22, 1922, the wife also acquired naturalized citizenship. If the marriage terminated, the wife maintained her U.S. citizenship if she was residing in the U.S. at that time and continued to reside in the U.S.

LIST "B"

(For Applicants for Uninsured Employers Fund or Subsequent Injuries Fund benefits who are citizens or nationals of the United States.)

A. Documentation Evidencing an Approved Petition or Application

- INS Form I-551 ("Resident Alien Card" or "Alien Registration Receipt Card" commonly known as a "green card") with one of the following INS class of admission ("COA") codes printed on the front of a white card or the back of a pink card; AR1, AR6, C20 through C29, CF1, CF2, CR1, CR2, CR6, CR7, CX1 through CX3, CX6 through CX8, F20 through F29, FX1 through FX3, FX6 through FX8, IF1, IF2, IR1 through IR4, IR6 through IR9, IW1, IW2, IW6, IW7, MR6, MR7, P21 through P23, or P26 through P28.

If an alien claiming approved status presents a code different than those enumerated, or if you cannot determine the class of admission from the I-551 stamp, you should file INS Form G-845, and the G-845 Supplement (mark item six on the Supplement) (attached hereto) along with a copy of the document(s) presented, with the local INS office in order to determine whether the applicant gained his or her status because he or she was the spouse, widow, or child of a U.S. citizen or the spouse, child, or unmarried son or daughter of an LPR (lawful permanent resident).

- INS Form I-551 with one of the following COA codes stamped on the lower left side of the back of a pink card: IB1 through IB3, IB6 through IB8, B11, B12, B16, B17, B20 through B29, B31 through B33, B36 through B38, BX1 through BX3, or BX6 through BX8.
- INS Form I-551 with COA code Z13.
- Unexpired Temporary I-551 stamp in foreign passport or on INS Form I-94 with one of the COA codes specified in the Subsections (1)-(3), above.
- INS Form I-797 indicating approval of an INS I-130 petition (only I-130 petitions describing the following relationships may be accepted: husbands or wives of U.S. citizens or LPRs, unmarried children under 21 years old of U.S. citizens or LPRs, or unmarried children 21 or older of LPRs), or approval of an I-360 petition (only I-360 approvals based on status as a widow/widower of a U.S. citizen or as a self-petitioning spouse or child of an abusive U.S. citizen or LPR may be accepted).
- A final order of an Immigration Judge or the Board of Immigration Appeals granting suspension of deportation under section 244(a)(3) of the INA as in effect prior to April 1, 1997, or cancellation of removal under section 240A(b)(2) of the INA.

B. Documentation Demonstrating that the Applicant has Established a Prima Facie Case

- INS Form I-797 indicating that the applicant has established a prima facie case; or
- An immigration court or Board of Immigration Appeals order indicating that the applicant has established a prima facie case for suspension of deportation under INA section 244(a)(3) as in effect prior to April 1, 1997, or cancellation of removal under section 240A(b)(2) of the INA.

C. Documentation Indicating that the Applicant has Filed a Petition or that a Petition has been Filed on the Applicant's Behalf, as Applicable, but with no Evidence of Approval of the Petition or Establishment of a Prima Facie Case

The benefit provider shall determine from the documentation when the petition was filed and take the actions set forth below:

- Applicants with petitions filed before June 7, 1997 should have an INS Form I-797 indicating filing of the I-360 petition by "self-petitioning spouse [or child] of abusive U.S.C. or LPR," a file-stamped copy of the petition, or another document demonstrating filing (including a cash register or computer-generated receipt indicating filing of Form I-360).
- Applicants with petitions filed after June 7, 1997 should have an INS Form I-797 indicating filing of the I-360 petition.

D. Documentation Indicating that the Applicant has filed a Petition or that a Petition was filed on His or Her Behalf, as Applicable

The following must indicate that the applicant is the widow/widower of a U.S. citizen, the husband or wife of a U.S. Citizen or LPR, the unmarried child under age 21 of a U.S. citizen or LPR, or the unmarried child age 21 or older of an LPR):

- For aliens on whose behalf a petition has been filed: INS Form I-797 indicating filing of an INS I-130 petition, a file-stamped copy of the petition, or another document demonstrating filing (including a cash register or computer-generated receipt indicating filing of Form I-130) (a sample copy of Form I-130 is attached to this Exhibit).

- For self-petitioning widows or widowers: a file-stamped copy of the INS I-360 petition, or another document demonstrating filing (including a cash register or computer-generated receipt indicating filing of Form I-360).

E. Documentation Indicating that the INS has Initiated Deportation or Removal Proceedings in which Relief may be Available

- an "Order to Show Cause";
- a "Notice to Appear"; or
- a "Notice of Hearing in Deportation Proceedings."

F. Minimal or no Documentation Regarding the Claimed Filing

If the applicant has some documentation, but it is insufficient to demonstrate filing, establishment of prima facie case or approval of a petition, you should fax the INS Request Form on your agency letterhead, as well as a copy of any document(s) provided by the applicant, to the INS Vermont Service Center in order to determine the applicant's status. If the applicant has no documentation, but is certain that a petition has been filed by his or her spouse or parent, you should fax the INS Request Form to the INS Vermont Service Center.

Note: Authority cited: Sections 54, 55, 59, 3702.10, 3716, 3716.1, 3716.2 and 4751, Labor Code. Reference: Sections 1621, 1641 and 1642, Title 8, United States Code; and Sections 3716, 3716.1, 3716.2 and 4750-4755, Labor Code.

History: 1. New section filed 10-28-98; operative 11-27-98 (Register 98, No. 44).

Ref.: See Labor Code §§4751–4755; Herlick Handbook § 6.16.

SUBCHAPTER 7 RETURN-TO-WORK SUPPLEMENT

ARTICLE 1

§17300. General, Scope and Application of Article.

(a) This article governs the return-to-work program established by Labor Code section 139.48. This program shall be called the Return-to-Work Supplement Program. The Return-to-Work Supplement Program is located at 1515 Clay Street, 17th Floor, Oakland, California, 94612.

(b) This program is intended to provide supplemental payments to workers whose permanent disability benefits are disproportionately low in comparison to their earnings loss. This program is based on findings of studies done by RAND concerning permanent disability and in particular the study entitled Identifying Permanently Disabled Workers with Disproportionate Earnings Losses for Supplemental Payments, RAND, February 2014. http://www.dir.ca.gov/chswc/Reports/2014/Earnings_ Losses_2014.pdf

Note: Authority cited: Sections 54, 55 and 139.48, Labor Code. Reference: Section 139.48, Labor Code.

History: 1. Amendment of subchapter heading and new subchapter 7, article 1 (sections 17300-17310) and section filed 4-6-2015; operative 4-6-2015 pursuant to Government Code section 11343.4(b)(3) (Register 2015, No. 15). For prior history of subchapter 7, see Register 2013, No. 12.

Ref.: Hanna § 7.02[4][d][iii]; Herlick Handbook § 5.20.

§17301. Definitions.

For the purpose of these rules:

(a) "Supplemental Job Displacement Benefit" means the benefit provided under Labor Code 4658.7.

(b) "Voucher" means a "Supplemental Job Displacement Nontransferable Voucher For Injuries Occurring on or After 1/1/13" (Form DWC-AD 10133.32) furnished by a claims administrator to an injured worker pursuant to section 10133.31.

Note: Authority cited: Sections 54, 55 and 139.48, Labor Code. Reference: Section 139.48 and 4658.7, Labor Code.

History: 1. New section filed 4-6-2015; operative 4-6-2015 pursuant to Government Code section 11343.4(b)(3) (Register 2015, No. 15).

Ref.: Hanna § 7.02[4][d][iii]; Herlick Handbook § 5.20.

§17302. Eligibility.

(a) To be eligible for the Return-to-Work Supplement, the individual must have received the Supplemental Job Displacement Benefit (SJDB) Voucher for an injury occurring on or after January 1, 2013.

(b) An individual who has received a Return-to-Work Supplement may not receive a second or subsequent Return-to Work-Supplement, except where the individual receives a Voucher for an injury which occurs subsequent to receipt of every previous Return to Work Supplement.

Note: Authority cited: Sections 54, 55 and 139.48, Labor Code. Reference: Section 139.48 and 4658.7, Labor Code.

History: 1. New section filed 4-6-2015; operative 4-6-2015 pursuant to Government Code section 11343.4(b)(3) (Register 2015, No. 15).

Ref.: Hanna § 7.02[4][d][iii]; Herlick Handbook § 5.20.

§17303. Notice.

Commencing 30 days after the effective date of these regulations, and continuing until the Administrative Director of the Division of Workers' Compensation amends Form DWC-AD 10133.32 to include notice of the Return-to-Work Supplement application process, all Vouchers issued shall be accompanied by a cover sheet, prepared by the claims administrator, containing the following notice: "Because you have received this Voucher and are unable to return to your usual employment you may be eligible for a Return-to-Work Supplement. You must apply within one year from the date this Voucher was served on you. You should make a copy of the Voucher which you will need to apply for the Return-to-Work Supplement. Details about the Return-to-Work supplement program are available from the Department of Industrial Relations on its web site, www.dir.ca.gov, or by calling 510-286-0787." The Director will arrange for publication on the Department web site of a notice targeted at eligible persons who received vouchers before the notice was included with the voucher.

Note: Authority cited: Sections 54, 55 and 139.48, Labor Code. Reference: Section 139.48 and 4658.7, Labor Code.

History: 1. New section filed 4-6-2015; operative 4-6-2015 pursuant to Government Code section 11343.4(b)(3) (Register 2015, No. 15).

Ref.: Hanna § 7.02[4][d][iii]; Herlick Handbook § 5.20.

§17304. Deadline for Application.

Note: *See Executive Order N-63-20 (2019 CA EO 63-20), issued in response to the COVID-19 pandemic, which extends certain deadlines related to applications for Return-to-Work Supplements.*

(a) An application for the Return-to-Work Supplement must be received by the Return-to-Work Supplement Program within one year from the date the Voucher (DWC-AD Form 10133.32 (SJDB) Rev: 10/1/15, or later version) was served on the individual.

(b) Notwithstanding subdivision (a) of this section, an application for the Return-to-Work Supplement from any individual who was issued a Voucher prior to December 1, 2015, for an injury occurring on or after January 1, 2013, must be received by the Return-to-Work Supplement Program no later than one year from the effective date of this subdivision.

Note: Authority cited: Sections 54, 55 and 139.48, Labor Code. Reference: Section 139.48, Labor Code.

History: 1. New section filed 4-6-2015; operative 4-6-2015 pursuant to Government Code section 11343.4(b)(3) (Register 2015, No. 15).

2. Amendment filed 3-14-2017; operative 3-20-2017 pursuant to Government Code section 11343.4(b)(3) (Register 2017, No. 11).

3. Governor Newsom issued Executive Order N-63-20 (2019 CA EO 63-20), dated May 7, 2020, which extended certain deadlines related to applications for Return-to-Work Supplements, due to the COVID-19 pandemic.

Ref.: Hanna § 7.02[4][d][iii]; Herlick Handbook § 5.20.

§17305. Method of Application.

An application must be submitted by electronic means through the Department of Industrial Relations web site. The Department will make access to this web site available at each Division of Workers' Compensation Information and Assistance Office location in the state.

Note: Authority cited: Sections 54, 55 and 139.48, Labor Code. Reference: Section 139.48, Labor Code.

History: 1. New section filed 4-6-2015; operative 4-6-2015 pursuant to Government Code section 11343.4(b)(3) (Register 2015, No. 15).

Ref.: Hanna § 7.02[4][d][iii]; Herlick Handbook § 5.20.

§17306. Application Contents.

The application shall be made on the electronic form on the Department of Industrial Relations web site and shall include a declaration under penalty of perjury that the information provided is true and correct. The application shall contain the individual's first name, last name and middle name, social security number or tax ID number, address, telephone number and email address, if available, and the ADJ number of any workers' compensation cases filed by the individual, and the individual shall submit a .pdf or .tiff of the Voucher as an attachment to the application. The individual shall indicate whether the individual is a California resident or a non-resident.

Note: Authority cited: Sections 54, 55 and 139.48, Labor Code. Reference: Section 139.48, Labor Code.

History: 1. New section filed 4-6-2015; operative 4-6-2015 pursuant to Government Code section 11343.4(b)(3) (Register 2015, No. 15).

Ref.: Hanna § 7.02[4][d][iii]; Herlick Handbook § 5.20.

§17307. Processing of Applications and Decision on Applications.

All completed and timely filed applications will be reviewed and a decision will be made on whether the individual is entitled to the supplement within 60 days of the receipt of the completed application. Applications satisfying the requirements of sections 17302, 17304, 17305 and 17306 will be approved. The individual will be notified by mail or, where available, email, of the decision. The decision is a final decision of the Director.

Note: Authority cited: Sections 54, 55 and 139.48, Labor Code. Reference: Section 139.48, Labor Code.

History: 1. New section filed 4-6-2015; operative 4-6-2015 pursuant to Government Code section 11343.4(b)(3) (Register 2015, No. 15).

Ref.: Hanna § 7.02[4][d][iii]; Herlick Handbook § 5.20.

§17308. Supplement Payment.

The Return-to-Work Supplement Program will provide a supplement of $5,000.00 to each eligible individual who submits a complete application by the deadline. The payment will be made within 25 days of the date the decision of the Director on the application and will be paid in one lump sum. Payment shall be made directly to the individual and is not assignable before payment. The amount of this supplement may be adjusted by the Director based on further studies conducted by the Director in accordance with Labor Code section 139.48.

Note: Authority cited: Sections 54, 55 and 139.48, Labor Code. Reference: Section 139.48, Labor Code.

History: 1. New section filed 4-6-2015; operative 4-6-2015 pursuant to Government Code section 11343.4(b)(3) (Register 2015, No. 15).

Ref.: Hanna § 7.02[4][d][iii]; Herlick Handbook § 5.20.

§17309. Appeal to the WCAB.

Note: *See Executive Order N-63-20 (2019 CA EO 63-20), issued in response to the COVID-19 pandemic, which extends certain deadlines related to Return-to-Work Supplement appeals.*

An individual dissatisfied with any final decision of the Director on his or her application for the Return-to-Work Supplement may, file an appeal at the Workers' Compensation Appeals Board (WCAB) District Office. The appeal must contain the name of the individual, the ADJ number of the case in which a voucher was provided, and a clear and concise statement of the facts constituting the basis for the appeal. A copy of the appeal shall be served on the

Return-to-Work Program located at 1515 Clay Street, 17th Floor, Oakland, California, 94612. Any appeal must be filed with the WCAB within 20 days of the service of the decision. After an appeal has been timely filed, the Return-to-Work Program may, within the period of fifteen (15) days following the date of filing of that appeal, amend or modify the decision or rescind the decision and take further action. Further action shall be initiated within 30 days from the order of rescission. The time for filing an appeal will run from the filing date of the new, amended or modified decision. Any such appeal will be subject to review at the trial level of the WCAB upon the same grounds as prescribed for petitions for reconsideration.

Note: Authority cited: Sections 54, 55 and 139.48, Labor Code. Reference: Section 139.48, Labor Code.

History: 1. New section filed 4-6-2015; operative 4-6-2015 pursuant to Government Code section 11343.4(b)(3) (Register 2015, No. 15).

2. Governor Newsom issued Executive Order N-63-20 (2019 CA EO 63-20), dated May 7, 2020, which extended certain deadlines related to Return-to-Work Supplement appeals, due to the COVID-19 pandemic.

Ref.: Hanna § 7.02[4][d][iii]; Herlick Handbook § 5.20.

§17310. False Claims.

An application for benefits from the Return-to-Work Supplement Program is a claim for benefits from the state.

The application shall contain the following notice:

"WARNING: any person who knowingly makes or uses a false record or statement material to the claim is liable for treble damages plus a civil penalty of not less than $5,500 and not more than $11,000 plus the cost of the action pursuant to the False Claims Act, Government Code sections 12650-12656."

This warning does not constitute a limitation on any penalties that may attach to any action in violation of the law.

Note: Authority cited: Sections 54, 55 and 139.48, Labor Code. Reference: Section 139.48, Labor Code; and Sections 12650, 12651, 12652, 12653, 12654, 12655 and 12656, Government Code.

History: 1. New section filed 4-6-2015; operative 4-6-2015 pursuant to Government Code section 11343.4(b)(3) (Register 2015, No. 15).

Ref.: Hanna § 7.02[4][d][iii]; Herlick Handbook § 5.20.

TITLE 10
INVESTMENTS

CHAPTER 5
INSURANCE COMMISSIONER

SUBCHAPTER 3
INSURERS

ARTICLE 20
Standards Applicable to Workers' Compensation Claims Adjusters and Medical Billing Entities and Certification of Those Standards by Insurers

§2592. Authority and Purpose.

These regulations are promulgated pursuant to authority granted to the Insurance Commissioner under the provisions of Section 11761 of the California Insurance Code. The purpose of these regulations is to set forth the minimum standards of training, experience, and skill that workers' compensation claims adjusters, including adjusters working for medical billing entities, must possess to perform their duties with regard to workers' compensation claims and to specify how insurers must meet and certify those standards to the Insurance Commissioner.

Note: Authority cited: Section 11761, Insurance Code. Reference: Section 11761, Insurance Code.

History: 1. New article 20 (sections 2592-2592.14) and section filed 1-23-2006; operative 2-22-2006 (Register 2006, No. 4).

Ref.: Hanna §§ 2.11[4], 2.37[1]–[7]; Herlick Handbook § 3.15.

§2592.01. Definitions.

As used in this article:

(a) "Certify" means a written statement made under penalty of perjury.

(b) "Claims adjuster" means a person who, on behalf of an insurer, including an employee or agent of an entity that is not an insurer, is responsible for determining the validity of a workers' compensation claim. The claims adjuster may also establish a case reserve, approve and process all workers' compensation benefits, may hire investigators, attorneys or other professionals and may negotiate settlements of claims. "Claims adjuster" also means a person who is responsible for the immediate supervision of a claims adjuster but does not mean an attorney representing the insurer or a person whose primary function is clerical. "Claims adjuster" also includes an experienced claims adjuster. "Claims adjuster" does not include the medical director or physicians utilized by an insurer for the utilization review process pursuant to Labor Code section 4610.

(c) "Classroom" means any space sufficiently designed so that the instructor and students can communicate with a high degree of privacy and relative freedom from outside interference. The instructor or the person or persons assisting the instructor may be physically present or may communicate with students by means of an electronic medium, including, but not limited to, audio, video, computer, or Internet.

(d) "Course" means any program of instruction taken or given to satisfy the requirements of Insurance Code Section 11761.

(e) "Curriculum" means a course of study that satisfies the requirements of Insurance Code Section 11761. The curriculum must provide sufficient content, including time allocated to each subject area, to enable claims adjusters, medical-only claims adjusters, and medical bill reviewers to meet minimum standards of training, experience, and skill to perform their duties with regard to workers' compensation claims.

(f) "Experienced claims adjuster" means a person who has had at least five (5) years within the past eight (8) years of on-the-job experience adjusting California workers' compensation claims or supervising claims adjusters handling California workers' compensation claims and is designated as an experienced claims adjuster by an insurer. A person who has successfully completed the written examination specified by Title 8, Section 15452 of the California Code of Regulations is also considered an experienced claims adjuster, provided that he or she has either (1) worked as a workers' compensation claims adjuster or supervised workers' compensation claims adjusters continuously since passing the examination and is designated as an experienced claims adjuster by an insurer or (2) passed the examination within the previous five (5) years and is designated as an experienced claims adjuster by an insurer. "Experienced claims adjuster" also includes a person who has already been trained and designated a claims adjuster and now meets the requirements of experience or examination completion noted above and is designated an experienced claims adjuster by an insurer.

(g) "Experienced medical-only claims adjuster" means a person who has had at least three (3) years within the past five (5) years of on-the-job experience adjusting California workers' compensation medical-only claims and is designated as an experienced medical-only claims adjuster by an insurer.

(h) "Experienced medical bill reviewer" means a person who has had at least three (3) years within the past five (5) years of on-the-job experience reviewing California workers' compensation medical bills and is designated as an experienced medical bill reviewer by a medical billing entity or by an insurer.

(i) "Instructor" means a person who conveys curriculum content to students on behalf of an insurer, a training entity, or a medical billing entity. An instructor shall have had at least five (5) years within the past eight (8) years of on-the-job experience adjusting California workers' compensation claims and have been designated as a claims adjuster by an insurer or be an individual who has had at least eight (8) years of experience in California workers' compensation within the past twelve (12) years. Persons knowledgeable about specific workers' compensation issues who are not instructors may train students under the direction of an instructor.

(j) "Insurer" means an insurance company admitted to transact workers' compensation insurance in California, the State Compensation Insurance Fund, an employer that has secured a certificate of consent to self-insure from the Department of Industrial Relations pursuant to Labor Code Section 3700(b) or (c), or a third party administrator that has secured a certificate of consent pursuant to Labor Code Section 3702.1.

(k) "Medical bill reviewer" means a person who is not a claims adjuster or medical-only claims adjuster and who only reviews or adjusts workers' compensation medical bills on behalf of an insurer, including employees or agents of the insurer or employees or agents of a medical billing entity. "Medical bill reviewer" also includes an experienced medical bill reviewer.

(*l*) "Medical billing entity" means a third party that reviews or adjusts workers' compensation medical bills for insurers.

(m) "Medical-only claims adjuster" means a person who, on behalf of an insurer, including an employee or agent of an entity that is not an insurer, is responsible for determining the validity of workers' compensation claims only involving medical workers' compensation benefits, as defined under Article 2 (commencing with Labor Code section 4600) of Chapter 2 of Part 2 of Division 4 of the Labor Code. The medical-only claims adjuster may also establish medical treatment reserves, approve and process medical benefits, and negotiate settlement of medical benefit claims. "Medical-only claims adjuster" also means a person who is responsible for the immediate supervision of a medical-only claims adjuster but does not mean an attorney representing the insurer or a person whose primary function is clerical. "Medical-only claims adjuster" also includes an experienced medical-only claims adjuster. "Medical-only claims adjuster" does not include the medical director or physicians utilized by an insurer for the utilization review process pursuant to Labor Code section 4610.

(n) "Post-designation training" means a course of study provided to trained or experienced workers' compensation claims adjusters and medical-only claims adjusters who have been designated by an insurer or provided to trained or experienced medical bill reviewers who have been designated by an insurer or medical billing entity. Post-designation training also includes seminars, workshops, or other informational meetings pertaining to California workers' compensation.

(o) "Student" or "trainee" means an individual taking a course that is required for that person in order to be a workers' compensation claims adjuster, medical-only claims adjuster, or medical bill reviewer.

(p) "Training" means to provide a course of instruction that includes the topics specified in Sections 2592.03 and 2592.04.

(q) "Training entity" means any person or organization that provides instructors or curriculum to an insurer or medical billing entity.

Note: Authority cited: Section 11761, Insurance Code. Reference: Section 11761, Insurance Code.

History: 1. New section filed 1-23-2006; operative 2-22-2006 (Register 2006, No. 4).

Ref.: Hanna §§ 2.11[4], 2.37[1]–[5]; Herlick Handbook § 3.15.

§2592.02. Training Required for Claims Adjusters and Medical-Only Claims Adjusters.

(a) Every insurer shall require all claims adjusters and medical-only claims adjusters who handle workers' compensation claims on the insurer's behalf, other than those who are defined in subdivisions (f) and (g) of Section 2592.01, to be trained pursuant to these subparagraphs:

(1) The insurer shall require at least 160 hours of training for claims adjusters, at least 120 hours of which shall be conducted in a classroom with an instructor. The insurer shall require at least 80 hours of training for medical-only claims adjusters, at least 50 hours of which shall be conducted in a classroom with an instructor. Any training not conducted in a classroom with an instructor may be done on the job under the supervision of an instructor or an experienced claims adjuster.

(2) A medical-only claims adjuster who has completed 80 hours of training pursuant to this section may be designated as a claims adjuster upon completion of 80 additional hours of workers' compensation claims training, 70 hours of which shall be in a classroom with an instructor, provided that such training is completed within six months of the claims adjuster beginning to adjust claims that include more than medical benefits.

(b) The training required by this section shall be completed within a twelve (12) consecutive month period, during which time a claims adjuster or medical-only claims adjuster trainee may adjust claims under the supervision of an instructor or experienced claims adjuster. No individual may adjust claims on behalf of one or more insurers for a combined total of more than twelve (12) months unless such individual has been trained pursuant to this article. However, if a claims adjuster or medical-only claims adjuster trainee requires leave from his or her employment because of illness, disability, military service, or leave required or permitted by state or federal law, and the leave has begun after the training has started, the training shall be completed within a period not to exceed 24 months after the commencement of the training.

(c) Any classes or courses taken within three (3) years before the effective date of these regulations that satisfy the curriculum requirement may be used to meet the hourly requirements upon verification by the student to the insurer of the type of course taken, the course of study, the date or dates taken, the person or organization providing the class or course, and the number of hours taken.

(d) Upon the effective date of these regulations, every insurer shall require a minimum of 30 hours of post-designation training every two (2) years for all claims adjusters and 20 hours of training every two (2) years for all medical-only claims adjusters.

(e) Post-designation training may include seminars, workshops, or other informational meetings pertaining to California workers' compensation and need not be in a classroom with an instructor. Such training shall be verified by the insurer with the type of course taken, the subject matter, the date or dates taken, the location of the training, the person or organization providing the training, and the number of hours taken.

(f) Failure of a claims adjuster or medical-only claims adjuster who has received a designation pursuant to subdivisions (a) or (b) of section 2592.05 to fulfill the requirements for post-designation training every two years pursuant to subdivisions (d) and (e) above shall result in that person being no longer considered a designated claims adjuster or medical-only claims adjuster. That person shall not be authorized to adjust claims until the requisite number of hours of post-designation training is completed.

(g) The insurer may provide the designation training directly or by sending its employees or its agents to be trained by a training entity for the entire designation curriculum. An insurer shall certify to the Insurance Commissioner that the course of instruction provided for training meets all the requirements set forth in this article and that all of the claims adjusters and medical-only claims adjusters who adjust claims on behalf of the insurer have actually attended the training for the required number of hours, in the manner provided for in sections 2592.07 and 2592.08.

(h) A claims adjuster or medical-only claims adjuster who has completed the training required by this section shall not be required to be re-trained and re-designated in order to adjust claims for a different insurer.

(i) An insurer may not authorize an individual to act in the capacity of claims adjuster or medical-only claims adjuster who has not been trained and designated pursuant to this article or who is not an experienced claims adjuster or an experienced medical-only claims adjuster and designated pursuant to this article, except that an individual who is undergoing training may adjust claims under the direct supervision of an instructor or experienced claims adjuster.

Note: Authority cited: Section 11761, Insurance Code. Reference: Section 11761, Insurance Code.

History: 1. New section filed 1-23-2006; operative 2-22-2006 (Register 2006, No. 4).

Ref.: Hanna § 2.37[2], [5]; Herlick Handbook § 3.15.

§2592.03. Curriculum.

(a) The course of study required by Section 2592.02 for claims adjusters shall include, but not be limited to, the following topics:

(1) Historical overview of the workers' compensation system.

(2) Organizational structure of the system.

(3) The workers' compensation insurance policy, its forms and endorsements, insurance principles of compensation.

(4) Concepts and terminology.

(5) Benefit provisions.

(6) Compensability.

(7) Notice requirements.

(8) Temporary disability.

(9) Permanent disability, including evaluation and rating.

(10) Death benefits.

(11) Return to work and vocational rehabilitation.

(12) Cumulative trauma.

(13) Serious and willful misconduct.

(14) Workers' Compensation Appeals Board procedures, forms, hearings, and penalties.

(15) Investigation.

(16) Fraud.

(17) Medical terminology.

(18) Knowledge and use of utilization guidelines (American College of Occupational and Environmental Medicine or other guidelines approved by the Administrative Director of the Division of Workers' Compensation.)

(19) Medical evidence.

(20) Medical dispute resolution (Qualified Medical Examiners, spinal surgery second opinions, predesignation of physicians, independent medical reviewers, utilization review.)

(21) Fee schedules.

(22) Liens.

(23) Apportionment.

(24) Subrogation.

(25) Reserving.

(26) Ethical issues.

(b) The course of study required for the training of medical-only claims adjusters shall include, at a minimum, all the topics specified in subdivision (a) above, with the exception of (8), (9), (10), (11), (13), and (23).

(c) The course of study required by Section 2592.02(d) for post-designation training shall include changes in the law that affect workers' compensation claims and any other topics relevant to the work of a claims adjuster or medical-only claims adjuster as specified in subdivision (a) above.

Note: Authority cited: Section 11761, Insurance Code. Reference: Section 11761, Insurance Code.

History: 1. New section filed 1-23-2006; operative 2-22-2006 (Register 2006, No. 4).

Ref.: Hanna § 2.37[2], [5]; Herlick Handbook § 3.15.

§2592.04. Training Required for Medical Bill Reviewers.

(a) Every insurer shall require all medical bill reviewers, other than those defined in section 2592.01(h), including employees and agents of medical billing entities used by the insurer, to be trained. The insurer shall require at least 40 hours of training for medical bill reviewers, at least 30 hours of which shall be conducted in a classroom by an instructor. No more than ten (10) hours of training may be done on the job.

(b) The training required by this section shall be completed within a twelve (12) month period, during which time a medical bill review trainee may review bills under the supervision of an instructor, experienced medical bill reviewer, or experienced claims adjuster. No individual may review medical bills on behalf of one or more insurers for a combined total of more than twelve (12) months unless the individual has been trained pursuant to this article.

(c) Any classes or courses taken within one (1) year before the effective date of these regulations that satisfy the curriculum requirement of subdivision (h) below may be used to meet the hourly requirements upon verification by the student to the insurer or medical billing entity of the type of course taken, the course of study, the date or dates taken, the person or organization providing the class or course, and the number of hours taken.

(d) Upon the effective date of these regulations, every insurer shall require a minimum of 16 hours every two (2) years of post-designation training for all medical bill reviewers and shall include in the post-designation training changes in the law affecting medical bill reviewers and topics as specified in subdivision (h) below.

(e) Failure of a medical bill reviewer designated pursuant to subdivisions (a) or (c) of section 2592.05 to fulfill the requirements for post-designation training every two years pursuant to subdivision (d) above shall result in that person being no longer considered a designated medical bill reviewer. That person shall not be authorized to review medical bills until the requisite number of hours of post-designation training is completed.

(f) The insurer may provide the designation training directly or by sending its employees or agents to be trained by a training entity for the entire designation curriculum. The insurer shall require all medical billing entities that review or adjust medical billings on its behalf to have the medical billing entities' employees or agents trained directly by the medical billing entity, the insurer, or by a training entity for the entire designation curriculum. The insurer shall certify, in the manner provided for in sections 2592.07 and 2592.09, that the course of instruction provided or that is provided by its medical billing entities meets all the requirements set forth in this article and that all medical bill reviewers of the insurer and its medical billing entities have actually attended the training for the required number of hours.

(g) A medical bill reviewer who has received a Designation as having completed the training required by this article shall not be required to be re-trained and re-designated in order to review medical bills for a different insurer.

(h) The curriculum for the training of medical bill reviewers shall include, but not be limited to, the following topics:

(1) The correct use of billing codes and detection of improper use of billing codes.

(2) All fee schedules applicable in California to workers' compensation medical care, including statutes and regulations authorizing the fee schedules.

(3) Workers' compensation benefit provisions.

(4) Fraud.

(5) Medical terminology.

(6) Utilization guidelines (American College of Occupational and Environmental Medicine or other guidelines approved by the Administrative Director of the Division of Workers' Compensation.)

(7) Medical evidence.

(8) Liens.

(9) Ethical issues.

(i) An insurer may not authorize an individual to act in the capacity of a medical bill reviewer who has not been trained pursuant to this article or who is not an experienced medical bill reviewer, except that an individual who is undergoing training may review medical bills under the direct supervision of an instructor, experienced medical bill reviewer or experienced claims adjuster.

Note: Authority cited: Section 11761, Insurance Code. Reference: Section 11761, Insurance Code.

History: 1. New section filed 1-23-2006; operative 2-22-2006 (Register 2006, No. 4).

Ref.: Hanna § 2.37[3], [5]; Herlick Handbook § 3.15.

§2592.05. Designation.

(a) A Designation shall be provided by the insurer to any person who successfully completes the claims adjuster, medical-only claims adjuster, or medical bill reviewer training required by sections 2592.02 and 2592.03 or section 2592.04, respectively. The Designation for a claims adjuster, medical-only claims adjuster or a medical bill reviewer shall be in the form specified in Section 2592.10 or 2592.11, respectively.

(b) An Experienced Claims Adjuster or Experienced Medical-Only Claims Adjuster Designation shall be provided by the insurer to a person as defined in Section 2592.01(f) or (g), respectively. The Experienced Claims Adjuster or Experienced Medical-Only Claims Adjuster Designation shall be in the form specified in Section 2592.12.

(c) An Experienced Medical Bill Reviewer Designation shall be provided by the insurer to a person as defined in Section 2592.01(h). The Experienced Medical Bill Reviewer Designation shall be in the form specified in Section 2592.13.

(d) An insurer shall provide to the claims adjuster, medical-only claims adjuster or medical bill reviewer a Post-Designation Training Form that states the course and hours taken for the post-designation training following the completion of the required training. The Post-Designation Training Form shall be on the form specified in Section 2592.14.

(e) A medical billing entity may provide medical bill reviewer and experienced medical bill reviewer Designations and Post-Designation Training Forms to its employees or agents that meet the requirements of this article so long as the insurer using the medical billing entity confirms that the medical billing entity has met all requirements of this article and obtains copies of all records required by this article.

Note: Authority cited: Section 11761, Insurance Code. Reference: Section 11761, Insurance Code.

History: 1. New section filed 1-23-2006; operative 2-22-2006 (Register 2006, No. 4).

Ref.: Hanna § 2.37[5], [24]; Herlick Handbook § 3.15.

§2592.06. Maintenance of Records.

(a) An insurer shall maintain copies of the Designation forms pertaining to trained and experienced claims adjusters, medical-only claims adjusters and medical bill reviewers in its employ or acting on its behalf, notwithstanding whether or not that person was designated by it or was employed or trained by or on behalf of another insurer or a medical billing entity, as long as the claims adjuster, medical-only claims adjuster, or medical bill reviewer is in its employ or acting on its behalf and thereafter for five (5) years.

(b) An insurer shall maintain copies of the Post-Designation Training Forms as long as the claims adjuster, medical-only claims adjuster, or medical bill reviewer is in its employ or acting on its behalf, notwithstanding whether or not that person received post-designation training by that insurer or was employed or trained by or on behalf of another insurer or medical billing entity, and thereafter for five (5) years.

(c) If a trained or experienced claims adjuster, medical-only claims adjuster, or medical bill reviewer is employed by or works on behalf of an insurer that did not designate him or her, the insurer that did designate the claims adjuster, medical-only claims adjuster, or medical bill reviewer shall send copies of the Designation Forms to the current insurer within 20 working days after a request for the Designation Forms has been received.

(d) All insurers shall maintain a record of all courses given or taken by claims adjusters, medical-only claims adjusters, or medical bill reviewers to comply with this article. The record shall include:

(1) The name and business address of all students, along with the beginning and ending date of the training of the student and a statement of whether or not the student has completed the training in all topic areas required to be covered.

(2) A complete description of the curriculum, including all topics covered with a detailed statement of how much time was spent training students in each topic, the name of the entity providing the instruction, and the name of the instructor or instructors and any persons who instructed under the direction of the instructor.

(e) All insurers shall maintain a record of all post-designation courses, seminars, workshops, or other training taken by claims adjusters, medical-only claims adjusters, and medical bill reviewers employed by or acting on their behalf. The record shall also include the dates of such training, the time spent in the training, and the topics covered.

(f) All records maintained pursuant to this article shall be made available to the Insurance Commissioner and to the Administrative Director of the Division of Workers' Compensation. Copies of all Designation Forms maintained pursuant to the article and issued to a claims adjuster, medical-only claims adjuster, or medical bill reviewer shall be provided by the insurer that issued the forms to that person within 20 working days of a request for copies of the forms from the claims adjuster, medical-only claims adjuster, or medical bill reviewer.

(g) Upon the request of a policyholder or an injured worker whose claim is being adjusted, the insurer shall provide to the requesting policyholder or injured worker a copy of the Designation Form of the claims adjuster, medical-only claims adjuster, or medical bill reviewer handling the claim demonstrating that person's qualifications in adjusting that claim.

Note: Authority cited: Section 11761, Insurance Code. Reference: Section 11761, Insurance Code.

History: 1. New section filed 1-23-2006; operative 2-22-2006 (Register 2006, No. 4).

Ref.: Hanna § 2.37[6]; Herlick Handbook § 3.15.

§2592.07. Certification and Submission of Documents.

(a) Each insurer shall submit to the commissioner annually by July 1 of each year a document certifying the following:

(1) the total number of persons adjusting claims on its behalf;

(2) the total number of claims adjusters and medical-only claims adjusters who are trained or experienced;

(3) the percentage of the claims adjusters and medical-only claims adjusters who are trained or experienced;

(4) all persons adjusting claims on behalf of the insurer are designated to do so or are in training; and

(5) the course of instruction provided for training of all claims adjusters and medical-only claims adjusters meets all requirements of this article and that all claims adjusters and medical-only claims adjusters have attended training for the required number of hours to be qualified to adjust workers' compensation claims.

The document, which shall be on the form specified in Section 2592.08, shall be signed under penalty of perjury by the person or executive officer responsible for the insurer's claims operations. The commissioner shall publish the information contained in this document on the Department of Insurance public website.

(b) Each insurer shall submit to the commissioner annually by July 1 of each year a document certifying the following:

(1) the total number of medical bill reviewers reviewing medical bills on its behalf;

(2) the total number of medical bill reviewers who are trained or experienced;

(3) the percentage of the medical bill reviewers who are trained or experienced medical bill reviewers;

(4) all persons reviewing medical bills on its behalf are designated to do so or are in training; and

(5) the course of instruction provided for training of all medical bill reviewers of the insurer and of medical billing entities used by the insurer meets all requirements set forth in this article and that all medical bill reviewers of the insurer and of medical billing entities used by the insurer have attended training for the required number of hours to be qualified to perform medical bill review.

The document, which shall be on the form specified in Section 2592.09, shall be signed under penalty of perjury by the person or executive officer responsible for the insurer's claims operations. The commissioner shall publish the information contained in this document on the Department of Insurance public website.

Note: Authority cited: Section 11761, Insurance Code. Reference: Section 11761, Insurance Code.

History: 1. New section filed 1-23-2006; operative 2-22-2006 (Register 2006, No. 4).

Ref.: Hanna § 2.37[2], [3], [7]; Herlick Handbook § 3.15.

§2592.08. Insurer Annual Certification Form—Claims Adjusters and Medical-Only Claims Adjusters.

ANNUAL CERTIFICATION OF CLAIMS ADJUSTERS AND MEDICAL-ONLY CLAIMS ADJUSTERS

To the Insurance Commissioner of the State of California Pursuant to California Insurance Code Section 11761 and California Code of Regulations, Title 10, Sections 2592.02 and 2592.07

As the person or officer responsible for the claims operation of:

____

(Name of Insurer)

☐ Insurance Company ☐ Self-Insured Employer ☐ Third-Party Administrator (Check One)

I hereby certify the following regarding California workers' compensation claims:

1. The total number of persons adjusting claims on this insurer's behalf is: ______.

2. The total number of experienced or trained claims adjusters and medical-only claims adjusters adjusting claims on the insurer's behalf is: ______.

3. The percentage of experienced or trained claims adjusters and medical-only claims adjusters adjusting claims on the insurer's behalf is: ______%

4. All persons adjusting claims on behalf of this insurer are designated to do so or are in training.

5. The course of instruction provided for training of all claims adjusters and medical-only claims adjusters meets all requirements set forth in Article 20 (commencing with section 2592) of Subchapter 3, Chapter 5, Title 10, California Code of Regulations, and that all claims adjusters and medical-only claims adjusters have attended training for the required number of hours to be qualified to adjust workers' compensation claims.

I certify under the penalty of perjury under the laws of the State of California that the foregoing is true and correct:

____

(Date and Place) (Signature)

Name of person certifying (print or type):

Title of person certifying:

Business address:

Note: Authority cited: Section 11761, Insurance Code. Reference: Section 11761, Insurance Code.

History: 1. New section filed 1-23-2006; operative 2-22-2006 (Register 2006, No. 4).

Ref.: Hanna § 2.37[2], [7]; Herlick Handbook § 3.15.

§2592.09. Insurer Annual Certification Form—Medical Bill Reviewers.

ANNUAL CERTIFICATION OF MEDICAL BILL REVIEWERS

To the Insurance Commissioner of the State of California Pursuant to California Insurance Code Section 11761 and California Code of Regulations, Title 10, Sections 2592.04 and 2592.07

As the person or officer responsible for the claims operation of:

____

(Name of Insurer)

☐ Insurance Company ☐ Self-Insured Employer ☐ Third-Party Administrator (Check One)

I hereby certify the following regarding California workers' compensation claims:

1. The total number of medical bill reviewers reviewing medical bills on this insurer's behalf is: ______.

2. The total number of experienced or trained medical bill reviewers reviewing medical bills on this insurer's behalf is: ______.

3. The percentage of experienced or trained medical bill reviewers reviewing medical bills on this insurer's behalf is: ______%

4. All persons reviewing medical bills on behalf of this insurer are designated to do so or are in training.

5. The course of instruction provided for training of all medical bill reviewers of this insurer and of medical billing entities used by this insurer meets all requirements set forth in Article 20 (commencing with section 2592) of Subchapter 3, Chapter 5, Title 10, California Code of Regulations, and that all medical bill reviewers of this insurer and of medical billing entities used by this insurer have attended training for the required number of hours to be qualified to perform medical bill review.

I certify under the penalty of perjury under the laws of the State of California that the foregoing is true and correct:

____

(Date and Place) (Signature)

Name of person certifying (print or type):

Title of person certifying:

Business address:

Note: Authority cited: Section 11761, Insurance Code. Reference: Section 11761, Insurance Code.

History: 1. New section filed 1-23-2006; operative 2-22-2006 (Register 2006, No. 4).

Ref.: Hanna § 2.37[3], [7]; Herlick Handbook § 3.15.

§2592.10. Designation—Claims Adjuster and Medical-Only Claims Adjuster.

CLAIMS ADJUSTER or MEDICAL-ONLY CLAIMS ADJUSTER DESIGNATION

This Designation is awarded to

____

(Adjuster's Name)

for: ☐ **Claims Adjuster** ☐ **Medical-Only Claims Adjuster**

(Check Only One)

as a result of successfully completing the required hours for workers' compensation training pursuant to California Insurance Code Section 11761 and California Code of Regulations, Title 10, Sections 2592.02 and 2592.03

Total Hours of Training Completed: ______

Designation Given By:

____

(Name of Insurance Company, Self-Insured Employer, or Third-Party Administrator)

______________ ______________

(Date) (Signature)

Name of person awarding designation (print or type):

Title of person awarding designation:

Business address:

Note: Authority cited: Section 11761, Insurance Code. Reference: Section 11761, Insurance Code.

History: 1. New section filed 1-23-2006; operative 2-22-2006 (Register 2006, No. 4).

Ref.: Hanna § 2.37[4]; Herlick Handbook § 3.15.

§2592.11. Designation—Medical Bill Reviewer.

MEDICAL BILL REVIEWER DESIGNATION

This Designation is awarded to

____

(Medical Bill Reviewer's Name)

for Medical Bill Reviewer Training

as a result of successfully completing the required hours for workers' compensation training pursuant to California Insurance Code Section 11761 and California Code of Regulations, Title 10, Section 2592.04

Total Hours of Training Completed: ______

Designation Given By:

____

(Name of Insurer or Medical Billing Entity)

______________ ______________

(Date) (Signature)

Name of person awarding designation (print or type):

Title of person awarding designation:

Business address:

Note: Authority cited: Section 11761, Insurance Code. Reference: Section 11761, Insurance Code.

History: 1. New section filed 1-23-2006; operative 2-22-2006 (Register 2006, No. 4).

Ref.: Hanna § 2.37[4]; Herlick Handbook § 3.15.

§2592.12. Designation—Experienced Claims Adjuster and Medical-Only Claims Adjuster.

EXPERIENCED CLAIMS ADJUSTER OR EXPERIENCED MEDICAL-ONLY CLAIMS ADJUSTER DESIGNATION

This Designation is awarded to

____

(Adjuster's Name)

for: ☐ Experienced Claims Adjuster

☐ Experienced Medical-Only Claims Adjuster

(Check Only One)

as a result of meeting the experience requirements for workers' compensation claims experience pursuant to California Insurance Code Section 11761 and California Code of Regulations, Title 10, Sections 2592.01 and 2592.05

Total Years of California Experience At Time of Designation: ________

and/or

Date Completed Examination Pursuant to Title 8, CCR Section 15452: ________

Designation Given By:

____

(Name of Insurance Company, Self-Insured Employer, or Third-Party Administrator)

____

(Date) (Signature)

Name of person awarding designation (print or type):

Title of person awarding designation:

Business address:

Note: Authority cited: Section 11761, Insurance Code. Reference: Section 11761, Insurance Code.

History: 1. New section filed 1-23-2006; operative 2-22-2006 (Register 2006, No. 4).

Ref.: Hanna § 2.37[4]; Herlick Handbook § 3.15.

§2592.13. Designation—Experienced Medical Bill Reviewer.

EXPERIENCED MEDICAL BILL REVIEWER DESIGNATION

This Designation is awarded to

____

(Medical Bill Reviewer's Name)

for Experienced Medical Bill Reviewer

as a result of meeting the requirements for workers' compensation medical bill reviewing experience pursuant to California Insurance Code Section 11761 and California Code of Regulations, Title 10, Sections 2592.01 and 2592.05

Total Years of California Experience At Time of Designation: ________

Designation Given By:

____

(Name of Insurer or Medical Billing Entity)

____

(Date) (Signature)

Name of person awarding designation (print or type):

Title of person awarding designation:

Business address:

Note: Authority cited: Section 11761, Insurance Code. Reference: Section 11761, Insurance Code.

History: 1. New section filed 1-23-2006; operative 2-22-2006 (Register 2006, No. 4).

Ref.: Hanna § 2.37[4]; Herlick Handbook § 3.15.

§2592.14. Post-Designation Training Form.

POST-DESIGNATION TRAINING FORM

____

(Adjuster's or Medical Bill Reviewer's Name)

☐ **Claims Adjuster**

☐ **Medical-Only Claims Adjuster**

☐ **Medical Bill Reviewer**

(Check Only One)

has successfully completed the post-designation workers' compensation training and hours noted below pursuant to California Insurance Code Section 11761 and California Code of Regulations, Title 10, Sections 2592.02, 2592.03, 2592.04, and 2592.05

Name and Topic of Post-Designation Training Taken:

____

Total Hours of Post-Designation Training Completed:

____

Date of Post-Designation Training: __________

Post-Designation Training Verified By:

____

(Name of Insurer or Medical Billing Entity)

____

(Date) (Signature)

Name of person awarding designation (print or type):

Title of person awarding designation:

Business address:

Note: Authority cited: Section 11761, Insurance Code. Reference: Section 11761, Insurance Code.

History: 1. New section filed 1-23-2006; operative 2-22-2006 (Register 2006, No. 4).

Ref.: Hanna § 2.37[5]; Herlick Handbook § 3.15.

ARTICLE 21
Workers' Compensation Rating Organization Internet Web Sites

§2593. Authority and Purpose.

The regulations set forth in this article are required to carry out the provisions of Section 11752.75 of Article 3 of Chapter 3 of Part 3 of Division 2 of the Insurance Code. The purpose of these regulations is to provide the standards required to allow a person to submit a query on a rating organization's Internet Web site for workers' compensation insurance coverage information concerning a specified employer on a specified date and to allow for employers to dispute with the rating organization or the employer's insurance company incorrect information displayed on the Internet Web site.

Note: Authority cited: Section 11752.75, Insurance Code. Reference: Section 11752.75, Insurance Code.

History: 1. New article 21 (sections 2593–2593.7) and section filed 2-10-2011; operative 3-12-2011 (Register 2011, No. 6).

§2593.1. Definitions.

For purposes of this Article:

(a) "Coverage Information" means the name of the employer, the employer's address or other identifying information, the date specified in the query for coverage information, and the name of the insurer on the date specified in the query for the coverage information.

(b) "Employer" means the person or entity that is a named insured on the workers' compensation insurance policy for which a query regarding coverage information is being made.

(c) "FEIN" means Federal employer identification number.

(d) "Insurer" means a California admitted workers' compensation insurance company that provided workers' compensation coverage to the specified employer on the specified date.

(e) "Policy" means a workers' compensation insurance policy issued by a California admitted workers' compensation insurance company.

(f) "Policy Information" means workers' compensation insurance policy data reported by a California admitted insurance company to a rating organization.

(g) "Query" means an inquiry on the rating organization's insurance coverage Internet Web site regarding workers' compensation coverage information for a specified employer on a specified date.

Note: Authority cited: Section 11752.75, Insurance Code. Reference: Section 11752.75, Insurance Code.

History: 1. New section filed 2-10-2011; operative 3-12-2011 (Register 2011, No. 6).

§2593.2. Employer Query Identifying Information.

A query shall allow for, but is not limited to, the following identifying information on an employer to inquire about the employer's coverage information on a specified date: Name of the employer; Name of the employer and a full or partial address of the employer, including, but not limited to, street name, city, and state; or FEIN.

Note: Authority cited: Section 11752.75, Insurance Code. Reference: Section 11752.75, Insurance Code.

History: 1. New section filed 2-10-2011; operative 3-12-2011 (Register 2011, No. 6).

§2593.3. Web Site Access Restrictions.

(a) A rating organization may establish protocols, rules, or other limitations and restrictions on its coverage Internet Web site to limit access to information concerning employer workers' compensation insurance coverage so as to allow for only queries for a specified employer on a specified date.

(b) The coverage Internet Web site shall prohibit the automated retrieval of information and shall give clear notice on the Internet Web site of this prohibition.

(c) The rating organization shall limit a person's use of the coverage Internet Web site to prevent unlimited or multiple queries of the information that could be used to determine policy inception or expiration dates or policy numbers or used for other purposes for which it was not intended by employing reasonable security or authentication measures to prevent multiple or automated retrieval of employer coverage information while not hindering the public's access to it. Such measures may include limiting the amount of time a person may use the Web site, limiting the number of queries in a single session, employing a challenge-response system, or any other criteria that meets generally accepted industry practices for limiting access to information on a Web site.

(d) The rating organization shall limit query results to identify as best as possible the specified employer being sought and to avoid query results that may list employers related by other criteria, such as employer safety groups or clients of labor contractors and professional employer organizations.

(1) When an employer is being queried for by using the employer's name, only employers with similar names or a portion of that name may be displayed as a result of the query.

(2) When an employer is being queried for by FEIN, only the employer associated with that FEIN may be displayed as a result of the query.

Note: Authority cited: Section 11752.75, Insurance Code. Reference: Section 11752.75, Insurance Code.

History: 1. New section filed 2-10-2011; operative 3-12-2011 (Register 2011, No. 6).

§2593.4. Disclaimers.

(a) The rating organization may provide disclaimers in its coverage Internet Web site regarding the limitations or deficiencies of the coverage information available on the Internet Web site or the policy information it collects from insurers.

(b) In addition to the disclaimers required pursuant to Insurance Code Section 11752.75, the rating organization shall also provide disclaimers regarding the following:

(1) The result of a query is not evidence or verification of workers' compensation insurance coverage, which should be obtained from or verified by the insurer directly.

(2) The results of a query should be confirmed both with the employer and the insurer before it is used for any purpose.

(3) Coverage information may not be available or complete for all employers due to limitations with the policy information, such as similar or duplicate employer names, multiple or alternate locations and addresses for employers, or more than one named insured employer on an insurance policy.

(4) The coverage Internet Web site may only provide coverage information for five years prior to the date of the query.

(5) If employer coverage information is not found on the coverage Internet Web site it may be due to the employer being self-insured, and inquiries concerning self-insured employers should be directed to the California Office of Self Insurance Plans.

Note: Authority cited: Section 11752.75, Insurance Code. Reference: Section 11752.75, Insurance Code.

History: 1. New section filed 2-10-2011; operative 3-12-2011 (Register 2011, No. 6).

§2593.5. Updating Coverage Information.

The rating organization shall post, update, or correct coverage information for an employer on its coverage Internet Web site in a timely manner following the submission of the policy information by insurers. The time to post, update, or correct the information on the web site shall not be more than thirty (30) days from the time the information is received from the insurer.

Note: Authority cited: Section 11752.75, Insurance Code. Reference: Section 11752.75, Insurance Code.

History: 1. New section filed 2-10-2011; operative 3-12-2011 (Register 2011, No. 6).

§2593.6. Disputes.

(a) An employer may dispute the accuracy of its coverage information displayed on a rating organization's Internet Web site by either contacting the insurer who provided the policy information for the coverage period or contacting the rating organization.

(b) If the insurer is contacted by an employer regarding the accuracy of its coverage information displayed on the rating organization's coverage Internet Web site, the insurer shall have thirty (30) days from the date it receives the employer's dispute to review and respond to the employer in writing and, if applicable, to provide corrected policy information to the rating organization. The response to the employer shall include the following:

(1) Whether or not the coverage information is accurate and, if applicable, any corrections that are being made.

(2) The name and contact information of the representative of the insurer who handled the dispute.

(c) The rating organization shall provide a toll-free telephone number and an email address that shall be conspicuously posted on its coverage Internet Web site for employers to contact the rating organization regarding the accuracy of coverage information displayed on the rating organization's coverage Internet Web site.

(d) If the rating organization is contacted by an employer regarding the accuracy of the coverage information displayed on its coverage Internet Web site, the rating organization shall have thirty (30) days from the date it receives the employer's dispute to confirm with the appropriate insurer that the coverage information displayed correctly reflects the policy information reported and respond to the employer in writing. The response to the employer shall include the following:

(1) Whether or not the coverage information correctly reflects the policy information reported and, if applicable, what is being corrected.

(2) The name and contact information of the representative of the insurer who handled the dispute.

(3) A notice that if the employer continues to believe the coverage information is inaccurate, that the employer should contact the insurer and its representative to determine if any further changes to the policy information are needed.

(e) Only the employer to whom the coverage information pertains may dispute with the insurer or the rating organization the accuracy of the coverage information displayed on the rating organization's coverage Internet Web site. The insurer or the rating organization may take reasonable steps to determine that the person disputing the accuracy of the information on the coverage Internet Web site is the employer, or a representative of the employer, for whom the information pertains.

(f) Only disputes regarding the accuracy of the policy information reported to the rating organization by the insurer and the coverage information displayed on the rating organization's Internet Web site shall be subject to this Article. Any disputes concerning the existence or extent of an insurance contract or the terms of either the contract or its insurance coverage shall not be subject to this Article.

Note: Authority cited: Section 11752.6 and 11752.75, Insurance Code. Reference: Section 11752.75, Insurance Code.

History: 1. New section filed 2-10-2011; operative 3-12-2011 (Register 2011, No. 6).

§2593.7. Statistics To Be Maintained by the Rating Organization.

The rating organization shall maintain statistics on usage, user complaints, and employer complaints or disputes to the rating organization or insurers concerning coverage information, along with any resulting correction of the policy or coverage information by the insurer or the rating organization for the coverage Internet Web site, to provide the necessary information to the insurance commissioner to monitor, evaluate, and report on whether the coverage Internet Web site is achieving its intended purpose.

Note: Authority cited: Section 11750.3, 11751.1 and 11752.75, Insurance Code. Reference: Section 11752.75, Insurance Code.

History: 1. New section filed 2-10-2011; operative 3-12-2011 (Register 2011, No. 6).

TITLE 16
PROFESSIONAL AND VOCATIONAL REGULATIONS

DIVISION 4
State Board of Chiropractic Examiners

(Originally Printed 12-5-46)

ARTICLE 2
Practice of Chiropractic

§310. Change of Name.

Any licensee who shall change his name according to the law, shall, within 10 days of such change, reregister his name with the Executive Officer of the board by submitting to the board office a written statement of the change and evidence of legal documentation.

Note: Authority cited: Sections 1000-4(b) and 1000-4(e), Business and Professions Code. Reference: Sections 1000-7 and 1000-10(b), Business and Professions Code.

History: 1. Amendment filed 1-4-77; effective thirtieth day thereafter (Register 77, No. 2).

2. Repealer and new section filed 7-30-87; operative 8-29-87 (Register 87, No. 32).

3. Change without regulatory effect amending section filed 10-5-2007 pursuant to section 100, title 1, California Code of Regulations (Register 2007, No. 40).

§310.1. Replacement License.

Any licensee shall be entitled to a replacement license if his original license is lost, stolen or mangled, or upon written request and legal documentation of name change. Each request for a replacement license must be accompanied by a nonrefundable fee of $25.00, and signed written statement as to the circumstances of loss of said license, or the return to the board office of the mangled license.

Note: Authority cited: Sections 1000-4(b) and 1000-4(e), Business and Professions Code. Reference: Sections 1000-7 and 1000-10(b), Business and Professions Code.

History: 1. Renumbering and amendment of former Section 310.1 to Section 310.2 and new Section 310.1 filed 7-30-87; operative 8-29-87 (Register 87, No. 32). For history of former Section 310.1, see Register 78, No. 50.

§310.2. Use of Title by Unlicensed Persons.

No person shall engage in the practice of chiropractic, as defined in Section 302, without holding a license, which is in an active status, issued by the Board.

Any person who advertises or promotes, in any manner, the words "doctor" or "chiropractor," the letters, prefixes or suffixes "Dr." or "D.C.," or any other word, title or letters indicating or implying that he or she is engaged in the practice of chiropractic, or who represents or holds himself or herself out as a doctor of chiropractic, without having, at the time of so doing, a valid, unrevoked, or unsurrendered license, is in violation of the Chiropractic Initiative Act.

Note: Authority cited: Section 1000-4(b), Business and Professions Code. Reference: Section 1000-15, Business and Professions Code.

History: 1. Renumbering and amendment of former Section 310.1 to Section 310.2 filed 7-30-87; operative 8-29-87 (Register 87, No. 32). For history of former Section 310.1, see Register 78, No. 50.

2. Editorial correction of Note (Register 2000, No. 2).

3. Amendment of section heading and section filed 7-20-2001; operative 8-19-2001 (Register 2001, No. 29).

§311. Advertisements.

Constructive educational publicity is encouraged, but the use by any licensee of advertising which contains misstatements, falsehoods, misrepresentations, distorted, sensational or fabulous statements, or which is intended or has a tendency to deceive the public or impose upon credulous or ignorant persons, constitutes grounds for the imposition of any of the following disciplinary penalties:

(a) Suspension of said licensee's right to practice in this State for a period not exceeding one (1) year.

(b) Placing said licensee upon probation.

(c) Taking such other action, excepting the revocation of said licensee's license, in relation to disciplining said licensee as the board in its discretion may deem proper.

§311.1. Chiropractic Specialties.

For purposes of the Department of Industrial Relations' Qualified Medical Evaluator Eligibility regulations (Division of Workers' Compensation, Title 8, California Code of Regulations, Section 12), the board recognizes only those specialty boards that are recognized by the American Chiropractic Association or the International Chiropractors Association.

Note: Authority cited: Section 1000-4(b), Business and Professions Code; and Chiropractic Initiative Act of California, Stats. 1923, p. 1xxxviii. Reference: Section 1000-4(b), Business and Professions Code; and Chiropractic Initiative Act of California, Stats. 1923, p. 1xxxviii.

History: 1. New section filed 3-16-2010; operative 4-15-2010 (Register 2010, No. 12).

§312. Illegal Practice.

Unlicensed individuals are not permitted to diagnose, analyze, or perform a chiropractic adjustment. An "unlicensed individual" is defined as any person, including a student or graduate of a chiropractic institution, who does not hold a valid California chiropractic license. An exemption is hereby created for student doctors participating in board approved preceptorship programs.

The permitted activities of unlicensed individuals are as follows:

(a) Unlicensed individuals may take the history of a patient. However, this activity is separate from the consultation which at all times must be conducted by the licensed doctor.

(b) Unlicensed individuals may conduct standard neurological, orthopedic, physical and chiropractic examinations, except they may not perform such examinations which require diagnostic or analytic interpretations nor may they render a conclusion either verbally or in writing regarding the patient's physical condition. As an example, unlicensed individuals may not perform evaluations of heart or lung soundings. Such individuals shall be at all times under the immediate and direct supervision of a licensed Doctor of Chiropractic.

"Immediate and direct supervision" means the licensed Doctor of Chiropractic shall be at all times on the premises where the examinations are being conducted. The licensed Doctor of Chiropractic shall be responsible for the verification of the recorded findings and will be solely responsible for rendering a conclusion based on the findings.

(c) Unlicensed individuals may administer physical therapy treatments as an adjunct to chiropractic adjustment, provided the physical therapy treatment is conducted under the adequate supervision of a licensed Doctor of Chiropractic. Adequate supervision shall include all of the following:

(1) The doctor shall be present in the same chiropractic facility with the unlicensed individual at least fifty percent of any work week or portion thereof the said individual is on duty unless this requirement has been waived by the board. The doctor shall be readily available to the said individual at all other times for advice, assistance and instruction.

(2) The doctor shall initially examine and prepare a written treatment program for a patient prior to the providing of physical therapy treatment by the unlicensed individual.

(3) The doctor shall provide periodic reevaluation of the treatment program and of the individual's performance in relation to the patient. "Periodic reevaluation" shall mean at least once every thirty days the patient is under active care.

(4) The doctor shall perform and record an evaluation of the patient and his or her response to treatment at the termination thereof.

(d) Unlicensed individuals may mark X-ray films administered by a Doctor of Chiropractic. "Marking X-rays" is defined as drawing and measuring between reference points and making angular and linear measurements. Unlicensed individuals are not permitted to make any diagnostic conclusions or chiropractic analytical listings, and the licensed doctor is responsible for any pathological entities covered or obstructed by the markings.

(e) Unlicensed individuals may not administer X-rays unless they hold a valid X-ray technician certificate from the Department of Health Services, or participate under the direct supervision of a licensed Doctor of Chiropractic in a training program approved by that department and set forth in Section 25668.1 of the California Health and Safety Code. This prohibition, set forth in Section 30403 of Title 17 of the California Administrative Code includes the following activities:

(1) Positioning of patient;

(2) Setting up of X-ray machines;

(3) Pushing a button;

(4) Developing of films. The Department of Health Services has determined that unlicensed individuals may develop X-ray film if that is their sole radiologic responsibility.

Unlicensed individuals who exceed the permitted scope of practice set forth in this regulation shall be in violation of Section 15 of the Chiropractic Act and shall be prohibited from applying for a California chiropractic license for such time as may be determined by the board. Student doctors participating in board approved preceptorship programs are not to be considered "unlicensed individuals" when working in said program.

Note: Authority cited: Section 4(b) of the Chiropractic Initiative Act of California (Stats. 1923, p. lxxxviii). Reference: Section 15 of the Chiropractic Initiative Act of California (Stats. 1923, p. lxxxviii) and Section 25668.1, California Health and Safety Code; Section 30403 of Title 17, California Administrative Code.

History: 1. Repealer and new section filed 7-16-79; effective thirtieth day thereafter (Register 79, No. 29).

2. Amendment filed 2-1-80; effective thirtieth day thereafter (Register 80, No. 5).

§312.1. Ownership of a Chiropractic Practice.

No unlicensed individual may own a chiropractic practice regardless of the form in which the practice is established (individual ownership, partnership, corporation, etc.). This does not preclude a layperson from owning the facilities in which the practice is conducted, and the equipment provided. It does prohibit a layperson from being in a position of making and/or influencing decisions relating to diagnosis, or treatment of patients which are matters requiring chiropractic licensure.

Note: Authority cited: Section 1000-4(b), Business and Professions Code. Reference: Sections 1000-7, 1000-10 and 1000-15, Business and Professions Code.

History: 1. New section filed 7-30-87; operative 8-29-87 (Register 87, No. 32).

§312.2. Ownership of Practice upon the Death or Incapacity of a Licensee.

In the event of the death of a chiropractic licensee, or the legal declaration of the mental incompetency of the licensee to practice, the unlicensed heirs or trustees of the chiropractor must dispose of the practice within six (6) months. At all times during that period the practice must be supervised by a licensed chiropractor. The board will consider a petition to extend this period if it is submitted within four (4) months after the death or the declaration of incompetence of the licensee, including identification of any extenuating circumstances that will prevent compliance.

Note: Authority cited: Section 1000-4(b), Business and Professions Code. Reference: Sections 1000-7, 1000-10 and 1000-15, Business and Professions Code.

History: 1. New section filed 7-30-87; operative 8-29-87 (Register 87, No. 32).

§313. Inducing Student to Practice Chiropractic.

No licensee of chiropractic in the State of California shall offer or cause to be offered to a student or prospective student of chiropractic any promise or inducement, either written or verbal, which may induce said student or prospective student to believe he or she, during the freshman, sophomore, junior or senior years, or within the time that he or she shall be a student in, and/or before graduation from chiropractic school or college, and/or before receiving a license from the board, may be legally employed in any chiropractic private office, or chiropractic school or college, to practice chiropractic, with or without compensation, and no student shall accept or rely upon any such promise or understanding except that junior or senior students only may, for professional instruction, be assigned to regular clinic practice, during regular clinic hours, in the clinic conducted upon the premises of a regularly incorporated chiropractic school or college, and then only when said clinic is in charge of a duly licensed chiropractor as clinic instructor. This section does not apply to students and doctors who participate in preceptorship programs sponsored by chiropractic institutions holding status with the Council on Chiropractic Education or seeking such status. Violation of this rule by any student shall be deemed to be also a violation of Section 312 hereof.

Note: Authority cited: Section 1000-4(b), Business and Professions Code. Reference: Sections 1000-10(b) and 1000-15, Business and Professions Code.

History: 1. Amendment filed 2-15-79; effective thirtieth day thereafter (Register 79, No. 7).

2. Amendment filed 7-30-87; operative 8-29-87 (Register 87, No. 32).

§314. Law Violators.

It shall be the duty of every licensee to notify the Executive Officer or his or her designee of any violation of the act, or of these rules and regulations, in order that the board may take appropriate disciplinary action.

Note: Authority cited: Sections 1000-4(b), Business and Professions Code (Chiropractic Initiative Act of California, Stats. 1923 p. 1xxxviii). Reference: Section 1000-4(b), Business and Professions Code (Chiropractic Initiative Act of California, Stats. 1923 p. 1xxxviii).

History: 1. Amendment of section and new Note filed 5-27-2010; operative 6-26-2010 (Register 2010, No. 22).

§315. Mental Illness.

(a) Administrative Adjudication. The proceedings under this regulation shall be conducted in accordance with Chapter 5 (commencing with Section 11500) of Part 1 of Division 3 of Title 2 of the Government Code, and the board shall have all the powers granted therein.

(b) Psychiatric Examinations. When reasonable cause exists that a person holding a license under this Act is mentally ill to the extent that it may affect his ability to conduct with safety to the public the practice authorized by such license, the board may order the license holder to be examined by one or more physicians specializing in psychiatry designated by the board. The report of such persons shall be made available to the license holder and may be received as direct evidence in a proceeding conducted pursuant to subsection (c) of this regulation.

(c) Probation, Suspension, etc., in Event of Mental Illness; Reinstatement. If a license holder has been found to be mentally ill by one or more physicians specializing in psychiatry designated by the board, the results of which indicates that such illness does effect his ability to conduct, with safety, the practice authorized by his license, the board may take action, in accordance with subdivision (a) of this regulation, by any one of the following methods:

(1) Placing him on probation.

(2) Suspending his right to practice for a period not exceeding one year.

(3) Revoking his license.

(4) Taking such other action in relation to his license as the board in its discretion deems proper.

The board shall not restore such license to good standing until it shall receive competent evidence, from one or more physicians specializing in psychiatry, designated by the board, of the absence or control of the condition which caused its action and until it is satisfied that with due regard to the public interest the licensee's right to practice may be safely reinstated.

Before reinstating such a person, the board may require the person to pass an oral or written examination, or both, to determine his present fitness to resume his practice.

(d) Conditions of Reinstatement. In setting aside action taken under subsection (c) of this regulation, the board may impose terms and conditions to be followed by the license holder after his license has been reinstated. The authority of the board to impose terms and conditions includes, but is not limited to, the following:

(1) Requiring the license holder to obtain additional professional training and to pass an examination upon the completion of the training. The examination may be written or oral, or both, and may be a practical or clinical examination, or both, at the option of the board.

(2) Requiring the license holder to submit to a complete diagnostic examination by one or more physicians appointed by the board. If the board requires the certificate holder to submit to such an examination, the board shall receive and consider any other report of a complete diagnostic examination given by one or more physicians of the license holder's choice.

(3) Setting any other requirement the board in its discretion deems proper.

History: 1. Amendment filed 8-19-77; effective thirtieth day thereafter (Register 77, No. 34).

§316. Responsibility for Conduct on Premises.

(a) Every licensee is responsible for the conduct of employees or other persons subject to his supervision in his place of practice, and shall insure that all such conduct in his place of practice conforms to the law and to the regulations herein.

(b) Where a chiropractic license is used in connection with any premises, structure or facility, no sexual acts or erotic behavior involving patients, patrons or customers, including, but not necessarily limited to, sexual stimulation, masturbation or prostitution, shall be permitted on said premises, structure or facility.

(c) The commission of any act of sexual abuse, sexual misconduct, or sexual relations by a licensee with a patient, client, customer or employee is unprofessional conduct and cause for disciplinary action. This conduct is substantially related to the qualifications, functions, or duties of a chiropractic license.

This section shall not apply to sexual contact between a licensed chiropractor and his or her spouse or person in an equivalent domestic relationship when that chiropractor provides professional treatment.

Note: Authority cited: Sections 1000-4, 1000-10 and 1057, Business and Professions Code. Reference: Sections 726 and 1000-10, Business and Professions Code.

History: 1. New section filed 7-13-71; effective thirtieth day thereafter (Register 71, No. 29).

2. New subsection (c) and amendment of Note filed 7-26-96; operative 8-25-96 (Register 96, No. 30).

§317. Unprofessional Conduct.

The board shall take action against any holder of a license who is guilty of unprofessional conduct which has been brought to its attention, or whose license has been procured by fraud or misrepresentation or issued by mistake.

Unprofessional conduct includes, but is not limited to, the following:

(a) Gross negligence;

(b) Repeated negligent acts;

(c) Incompetence;

(d) The administration of treatment or the use of diagnostic procedures which are clearly excessive as determined by the customary practice and standards of the local community of licensees;

(e) Any conduct which has endangered or is likely to endanger the health, welfare, or safety of the public;

(f) The administering to oneself, of any controlled substance, or the use of any dangerous drug or of alcoholic beverages to the extent or in a manner as to be dangerous or injurious to oneself, or to any other person or to the public, or to the extent that the use impairs the ability of the person to conduct with safety to the public the practice authorized by the license;

(g) Conviction of a crime which is substantially related to the qualifications, functions or duties of a chiropractor;

(h) Conviction of any offense, whether felony or misdemeanor, involving moral turpitude, dishonesty, physical violence or corruption. The board may inquire into the circumstances surrounding the commission of the crime in order to fix the degree of discipline or to determine if such conviction was of an offense involving moral turpitude, dishonesty, physical violence or corruption. A plea or verdict of guilty, or a plea of nolo contendere is deemed to be a conviction within the meaning of the board's disciplinary provisions, irrespective of a subsequent order under the provisions of Section 1203.4 of the Penal Code. The board may order a license to be suspended or revoked, or may decline to issue a license upon the entering of a conviction or judgement in a criminal matter.

(i) The conviction of more than one misdemeanor or any felony involving the use, consumption, or self-administration of any dangerous drug or alcoholic beverage, or any combination of those substances.

(j) The violation of any of the provisions of law regulating the dispensing or administration of narcotics, dangerous drugs, or controlled substances;

(k) The commission of any act involving moral turpitude, dishonesty, or corruption, whether the act is committed in the course of the individual's activities as a license holder, or otherwise;

(*l*) Knowingly making or signing any certificate or other document relating to the practice of chiropractic which falsely represents the existence or nonexistence of a state of facts;

(m) Violating or attempting to violate, directly or indirectly, or assisting in or abetting in the violation of, or conspiring to violate any provision or term of the Act or the regulations adopted by the board thereunder;

(n) Making or giving any false statement or information in connection with the application for issuance of a license;

(o) Impersonating an applicant or acting as a proxy for an applicant in any examination required by the board for the issuance of a license or certificate;

(p) The use of advertising relating to chiropractic which violates section 17500 of the Business and Professions Code;

(q) The participation in any act of fraud or misrepresentation;

(r) Except as may be required by law, the unauthorized disclosure of any information about a patient revealed or discovered during the course of examination or treatment;

(s) The employment or use of persons known as cappers or steerers to obtain business;

(t) The offering, delivering, receiving or accepting of any rebate, refund, commission, preference, patronage, dividend, discount or other consideration as compensation or inducement for referring patients to any person;

(u) Participation in information or referral bureaus which do not comply with section 317.1 of the regulations;

(v) Entering into an agreement to waive, abrogate, or rebate the deductible and/or co-payment amounts of any insurance policy by forgiving any or all of any patient's obligation for payment thereunder, when used as an advertising and/or marketing procedure, unless the insurer is notified in writing of the fact of such waiver, abrogation, rebate, or forgiveness in each such instance.

In all insurance billings where a waiver of a deductible or a co-payment is intended as an advertising and/or marketing procedure, the chiropractor's statement and insurance billing shall contain the following statement:

I/WE WAIVE CO-PAYMENT AND/OR DEDUCTIBLES. IT IS MY/OUR INTENTION TO DO THE FOLLOWING: (Indicate one choice below)

( ) BILL THE PATIENT $________ AFTER RECEIPT FROM YOU OF $________.

( ) WAIVE ANY FURTHER PAYMENT FROM THE PATIENT AFTER RECEIPT FROM YOU OF $________.

( ) IN CASES WHERE PREDETERMINATION OF INSURANCE BENEFITS IS NOT POSSIBLE, I/WE PROVIDE THE FOLLOWING WRITTEN EXPLANATION OF MY/OUR BILLING INTENTIONS:

____

____

____

(w) Not referring a patient to a physician and surgeon or other licensed health care provider who can provide the appropriate management of a patient's physical or mental condition, disease or injury within his or her scope of practice, if in the course of a diagnostic evaluation a chiropractor detects an abnormality that indicates that the patient has a physical or mental condition, disease, or injury that is not subject to appropriate management by chiropractic methods and techniques. This subsection shall not apply where the patient states that he or she is already under the care of such other physician and surgeon or other licensed health care provider who is providing the appropriate management for that physical or mental condition, disease, or injury within his or her scope of practice.

(x) The offer, advertisement, or substitution of a spinal manipulation for vaccination.

(y) [Reserved]

Note: Authority cited: Sections 1000-4(b) and 1000-10, Business and Professions Code (Chiropractic Initiative Act of California, Stats. 1923, p. lxxxviii). Reference: Sections 1000-4(b), and 1000-10, Business and Professions Code (Chiropractic Initiative Act of California, Stats. 1923, p. lxxxviii).

History: 1. New subsection (t) filed 12-12-78; effective thirtieth day thereafter (Register 78, No. 50). For prior history, see Register 77, No. 49.

2. Amendment of subsections (p) and (t) filed 7-30-87; operative 8-29-87 (Register 87, No. 32).

3. New subsection (u) filed 6-5-90; operative 7-5-90 (Register 90, No. 30).

4. Change without regulatory effect amending subsection (u) filed 8-13-90 pursuant to section 100, title 1, California Code of Regulations (Register 90, No. 43).

5. Amendment of subsection (u) filed 3-27-92; operative 4-27-92 (Register 92, No. 14).

6. Change without regulatory effect amending subsection (h) and Note filed 8-17-92 pursuant to title 1, section 100, California Code of Regulations (Register 92, No. 34).

7. New subsection (v) filed 4-16-93; operative 5-17-93 (Register 93, No. 16).

8. New subsections (w) and (x) and amendment of Note filed 6-21-93 as an emergency; operative 6-21-93 (Register 93, No. 26). A Certificate of Compliance must be transmitted to OAL 10-19-93 or emergency language will be repealed by operation of law on the following day.

9. New subsection (y) filed 9-27-93 as an emergency; operative 9-27-93 (Register 93, No. 40). A Certificate of Compliance must be transmitted to OAL by 1-25-94 or emergency language will be repealed by operation of law on the following day.

10. Repealed new subsections (w) and (x) and amendment of Note operative 6-21-93 by operation of law on 10-20-93 (Register 93, No. 46).

11. Reinstatement of new subsections (w) and (x) and amendment of Note, repealed 10-20-93, refiled 11-3-93 as an emergency; operative 11-8-93 (Register 93, No. 46). A Certificate of Compliance must be transmitted to OAL by 3-8-94 or emergency language will be repealed by operation of law on the following day.

12. Certificate of Compliance as to 11-3-93 order, including repeal of subsection (x), transmitted to OAL 11-10-93 and filed 12-23-93 (Register 93, No. 52).

13. Editorial correction of History 11 (Register 93, No. 52).

14. Certificate of Compliance as to 9-27-93 order transmitted to OAL 1-25-94; disapproved by OAL 3-9-94 and reinstatement of section as it existed prior to 9-27-93 emergency amendment operative 3-9-94 (Register 2004, No. 14).

15. Amendment of subsection (h) filed 7-29-96; operative 8-28-96 (Register 96, No. 31).

16. Amendment of subsections (f) and (h), new subsection (i) and subsection relettering filed 4-5-2000; operative 5-5-2000 (Register 2000, No. 14).

17. Amendment of subsection (h) filed 7-3-2003; operative 8-2-2003 (Register 2003, No. 27).

18. Editorial correction repealing subsection (z), adding History 14 and renumbering Histories (Register 2004, No. 14).

§317.1. Chiropractic Referral Services.

Chiropractic referral services shall conform to the following:

(1) A referral bureau shall be made up of at least five doctors, each of whom does not have fiduciary relationship one to the other, with one participating office representing no more than 20 percent of the bureau's available practitioners. The board will consider any extenuating circumstances which will prevent a service from complying with these requirements;

(2) An application shall be filed with the board office which has been approved by the board, and properly identifies the service, structure and members;

(a) A nonrefundable application fee of $25.00 shall be submitted with the referral service application.

(3) A telephone number shall be for a separate answering service;

(4) The answering service of the bureau shall refer the caller to the next doctor on the list on a rotating basis. The following are exceptions:

(a) A request for a specialist;

(b) Geographic considerations;

(c) Request for services in a language other than English.

(5) Records on each referral shall be kept and include the following:

(a) Date of referral;

(b) Name and address of patient;

(c) Name and address of doctor referred to.

(6) When a 24-hour emergency referral service is offered, a member of the group shall be available.

Note: Authority cited: Section 1000-4(b), Business and Professions Code. Reference: Section 651, Business and Professions Code.

History: 1. New section filed 7-30-87; operative 8-29-87 (Register 87, No. 32).

§317.5. Investigation and Enforcement Costs; Payment by Licentiate.

(a) In any order in resolution of a disciplinary proceeding before the Board of Chiropractic Examiners, the board may request the administrative law judge to direct a licentiate found to have committed a volition or violations of the Chiropractic Initiative Act to pay a sum not to exceed the reasonable costs of the investigation and enforcement of the case.

(b) A certified copy of the actual costs, or a good faith estimate of costs where actual costs are not available, signed by the board bringing the proceeding or its designated representative shall be prima facie evidence of reasonable costs of investigation and prosecution of the case. The costs shall include the amount of investigative and enforcement costs up to the date of the hearing, including, but not limited to, charges imposed by the Attorney General.

(c) The administrative law judge shall make a proposed finding of the amount of reasonable costs of investigation and prosecution of the case when requested pursuant to subdivision (a). The board may reduce or eliminate the cost award, or remand to the administrative law judge where the proposed decision fails to make a finding on costs requested pursuant to subdivision (a).

(d) Where an order for recovery of costs is made and timely payment is not made as directed in the board's decision, the board may enforce the order for repayment in any appropriate court. This right of enforcement shall be in addition to any other rights the board may have as to any licentiate to pay costs.

(e) In any action for recovery of costs, proof of the board's decision shall be conclusive proof of the validity of the order of payment and the terms for payment.

(f)(1) Except as provided in paragraph (2), the board shall not renew or reinstate any license of any licentiate who has failed to pay all of the costs ordered under this section.

(2) Notwithstanding paragraph (1), the board may, in its discretion, conditionally renew or reinstate for a maximum of one year the license of any licentiate who demonstrates financial hardship and who enters into a formal agreement with the board to reimburse the board within that one-year period for the unpaid costs.

(g) All costs recovered under this section shall be considered a reimbursement for costs incurred and shall be deposited in the fund of the board recovering the costs.

(h) Nothing in this section shall preclude the board from including the recovery of the costs of investigation and enforcement of a case in any stipulated settlement.

Note: Authority cited: Sections 1000-4(b) and 1000-10, Business and Professions Code. (Chiropractic Initiative Act of California, Stats. 1923, p. lxxxviii). Reference: Sections 1000-4(b) and 1000-10, Business and Professions Code. (Chiropractic Initiative Act of California, Stats. 1923, p. lxxxviii).

History: 1. New section filed 7-29-96; operative 8-28-96 (Register 96, No. 31).

§318. Chiropractic Patient Records/ Accountable Billings.

(a) Chiropractic Patient Records. Each licensed chiropractor is required to maintain all active and inactive chiropractic patient records for five years from the date of the doctor's last treatment of the patient unless state or federal laws require a longer period of retention. Active chiropractic records are all chiropractic records of patients treated within the last 12 months. Chiropractic patient records shall be classified as inactive when there has elapsed a period of more than 12 months since the date of the last patient treatment.

All chiropractic patient records shall be available to any representative of the Board upon presentation of patient's written consent or a valid legal order. Active chiropractic patient records shall be immediately available to any representative of the Board at the chiropractic office where the patient has been or is being treated. Inactive chiropractic patient records shall be available upon ten days notice to any representative of the Board. The location of said inactive records shall be reported immediately upon request.

Active and inactive chiropractic patient records must include all of the following:

(1) Patient's full name, date of birth, and social security number (if available);

(2) Patient gender, height and weight. An estimated height and weight is acceptable where the physical condition of the patient prevents actual measurement;

(3) Patient history, complaint, diagnosis/analysis, and treatment must be signed by the primary treating doctor. Thereafter, any treatment rendered by any other doctor must be signed or initialed by said doctor;

(4) Signature of patient;

(5) Date of each and every patient visit;

(6) All chiropractic X-rays, or evidence of the transfer of said X-rays;

(7) Signed written informed consent as specified in Section 319.1.

(b) Accountable Billings. Each licensed chiropractor is required to ensure accurate billing of his or her chiropractic services whether or not such chiropractor is an employee of any business entity, whether corporate or individual, and whether or not billing for such services is accomplished by an individual or business entity other than the licensee. In the event an error occurs which results in an overbilling, the licensee must promptly make reimbursement of the overbilling whether or not the licensee is in any way compensated for such reimbursement by his employer, agent or any other individual or business entity responsible for such error. Failure by the licensee, within 30 days after discovery or notification of an error which resulted in an overbilling, to make full reimbursement constitutes unprofessional conduct.

Note: Authority cited: Section 1000-4(b), Business and Professions Code (Chiropractic Initiative Act of California (Stats. 1923, p. 1xxxviii)). Reference: Section 1000-4(b), Business and Professions Code (Chiropractic Initiative Act of California (Stats. 1923, p. 1xxxviii)).

History: 1. New section filed 7-15-76; effective thirtieth day thereafter (Register 76, No. 29).

2. Renumbering of former Section 318 to Section 302(b) and new section filed 7-7-78; effective thirtieth day thereafter (Register 78, No. 27).

3. Amendment filed 2-5-80; effective thirtieth day thereafter (Register 80, No. 5).

4. Amendment of subsections (a) and (a)(6), new subsection (a)(7) and amendment of Note filed 3-8-2012; operative 4-7-2012 (Register 2012, No. 10).

§318.1. Standard of Care Regarding Manipulation Under Anesthesia (MUA).

(a) Manipulation Under Anesthesia (MUA) may only be performed in either:

(1) A hospital that is licensed by the California Department of Public Health Licensing and Certification Program; or

(2) An ambulatory surgery center that is licensed by the California Department of Public Health Licensing and Certification Program and that is either:

(A) Operating pursuant to section 1248.1 of the Health and Safety Code or

(B) Accredited by an agency approved by the Medical Board of California pursuant to Chapter 1.3 of Division 2 of the Health and Safety Code (commencing with section 1248).

(b) Notwithstanding subsection (a), above, MUA shall not be performed in a mobile van as defined in subdivision (h) of section 1248.1 of the Health and Safety Code.

(c) MUA may only be performed if the patient is administered anesthesia by a California licensed physician and surgeon or other health care provider authorized under California law to administer anesthesia.

(d) MUA may only be performed following an appropriate prior examination of the patient by a California licensed physician and surgeon.

(e) The chiropractor may not direct, instruct, interfere, or make any orders to the physician and surgeon or other health care provider who is administering and maintaining the anesthesia.

(f) MUA shall be performed by two licensed and competent chiropractors. The "primary chiropractor" shall formulate the chiropractic portion of the MUA treatment plan and shall be responsible for performing the chiropractic manipulation for that procedure. The "second chiropractor" shall insure that all movements are accomplished with patient care and safety as his or her primary focus and shall assist the "primary chiropractor" when necessary. The chiropractic portion of MUA is limited to techniques within the scope of practice of a chiropractor.

(g) For the purpose of this section, the primary chiropractor and the second chiropractor may not be involved in nor interfere with the physician and surgeon or other health care provider in the discharge of the patient following the MUA procedure.

(h) Failure by a chiropractor to follow the standard of care contained in this section when performing MUA shall constitute unprofessional conduct.

(i) "Manipulation Under Anesthesia" or "MUA" means the manipulation by a licensed chiropractor of a patient who is sedated by the administration of anesthesia by a physician and surgeon or other health care provider who is legally authorized to administer anesthesia.

Note: Authority cited: Sections 1000-4(b) and 1000-10, Business and Professions Code (Chiropractic Initiative Act of California, Stats. 1923 p. lxxxviii). Reference: Sections 1000-4(b), 1000-7 and 1000-10, Business and Professions Code (Chiropractic Initiative Act of California, Stats. 1923, p. lxxxviii).

History: 1. New section filed 2-16-2010; operative 3-18-2010 (Register 2010, No. 8).

Ref.: Hanna Ch. 5, § 5.02[3A].

§319. Free or Discount Services.

Licensees may advertise that they will perform certain designated routine professional services free or at a discount if such advertising claims are truthful. However, no charge shall be made for any other professional services rendered or commodities provided to a patient during any office visit in which free or discounted services are offered or provided unless, prior to the accrual of any charges, the patient shall have been informed of the cost of such additional services and/or commodities and shall have agreed to pay for them.

For the purposes of this section, no separate charge shall be made for the professional evaluation of diagnostic tests or procedures which are provided free or without cost, or at a discount, whether such professional evaluation is made at the time of the initial office visit or at any later time.

Note: Authority cited: Section 4(b), Chiropractic Initiative Act of California.

History: 1. New section filed 6-20-78; effective thirtieth day thereafter (Register 78, No. 25).

§319.1. Informed Consent.

(a) A licensed doctor of chiropractic shall verbally and in writing inform each patient of the material risks of proposed care. "Material" shall be defined as a procedure inherently involving known risk of serious bodily harm. The chiropractor shall obtain the patient's written informed consent prior to initiating clinical care. The signed written consent shall become part of the patient's record.

(b) A violation of this section constitutes unprofessional conduct and may subject the licensee to disciplinary action.

Note: Authority cited: Sections 1000-4(b) and 1000-10, Business and Professions Code (Chiropractic Initiative Act of California Stats. 1923 p. lxxxviii). Reference: Sections 1000-4(b) and 1000-10, Business and Professions Code (Chiropractic Initiative Act of California Stats. 1923 p. lxxxviii).

History: 1. New section filed 9-7-2011; operative 10-7-2011 (Register 2011, No. 36).

TABLES AND SCHEDULES

Revisions by Jay Shergill, Esq.*

SYNOPSIS

While every effort is made to ensure these materials are current, updated, complete and as widely applicable as possible, the reader is cautioned to obtain legal advice before relying upon these or any table, commentary, or other secondary resource. As these charts and tables cannot cover every factual scenario, it is recommended the reader confirm any calculations or values using the appropriate code sections.

PAGE

Tables and Schedules Dealing With Compensation

PART 1. Commutation

1. Commutation: Present Value of Permanent Disability 1339
2. Commutation: Present Value of Life Pension for a Male 1346
3. Commutation: Present Value of Life Pension for a Female 1348
4. Commutation: Instructions with Examples 1350

PART 2. Interest

5. Interest: Ten Percent Annually (One Lump Sum Due) 1360
6. Interest: Ten Percent Weekly (Successive Payments of $1/Week) 1363
7. Interest: Seven Percent Annually (One Lump Sum Duc) 1364

PART 3. Legislation

8. [Reserved] 1366

PART 4. Calendar Information

9. Number of Days Between Two Dates 1367

PART 5. The Schedules for Rating Permanent Disabilities

10. [Reserved] 1369
11. Guidelines for Work Capacity and Excerpts From the Schedule for Rating Permanent Disabilities, 4/1/97 to 12/31/04 1370

11A. 2005 Permanent Disability Revised Schedule (2005 PDRS) 1375

11B. Selected Pages of 1997 Permanent Disability Rating Schedule (1997 PDRS) 1464

PART 6. Medical-Legal Fee Schedule: Excerpts

12. Medical-Legal Fee Schedule 1478

PART 7. Death Benefits

13. Death Benefits Payable for Total and Partial Dependency 1479

PART 8. Indemnity and Earnings

14. Maximum and Minimum Indemnity and Earnings 1480

15. Percentage of Permanent Disability to Weeks of Indemnity 1484

16. Instructions for Applying New and Old Permanent Partial Disability Benefit Rates to Table 17 1485

PART 9. Permanent Disability: Weeks/Percents

17A. Permanent Partial Disability Indemnity for Injuries 2013, 2014 – 2021 1486

17B. Permanent Partial Disability Indemnity for Injuries 2006 – 2012 1487

17C. Permanent Partial Disability Indemnity for Injuries in 2005 1488

17D. Permanent Partial Disability Indemnity for Injuries 2003, 2004 1489

PART 10. Glossary

18. Glossary of Terms and Abbreviations Commonly Used in Workers' Compensation 1490

PART 11. Indemnity Calculations

19. Miscellaneous 1503

Jay Shergill has been practicing before the Workers Compensation Appeals Board since 2002. He is a certified specialist in workers' compensation and represents insurance companies, third party administrators, and self-insured employers as a defense attorney throughout California with Coleman Chavez & Associates.

Mr. Shergill is a published author in the field of robotics and 3D printing, builds robots in his spare time, and is the founder of PDRater.com, a collection of resources and calculators for workers' compensation professionals.

If you have any questions concerning these tables, you may call him at 916-787-2300 or email him at jshergill@cca-law.com.

Jay Shergill
Roseville, CA

PART 1. Commutation

TABLE 1
Commutation: Present Value of Permanent Disability

Use this table to commute, or calculate the determine the present value of, permanent disability benefits. The "Weeks" column refers to the number of weeks of permanent disability being commuted. The "PV" column contains the present value (PV) at $1 per week of the corresponding number of weeks of permanent disability. A fractional number of weeks of permanent disability may be commuted using interpolation. See Examples A, B and C under Commutation Procedures for an illustration of various types of commutations.

Weeks	PV	Weeks	PV	Weeks	PV	Weeks	PV
1	0.9989	29	28.7465	57	56.0575	85	82.9387
2	1.9977	30	29.7297	58	57.0252	86	83.8911
3	2.9955	31	30.7117	59	57.9918	87	84.8425
4	3.9932	32	31.6937	60	58.9583	88	85.7939
5	4.9898	33	32.6747	61	59.9238	89	86.7442
6	5.9864	34	33.6556	62	60.8893	90	87.6945
7	6.9819	35	34.6354	63	61.8537	91	88.6437
8	7.9774	36	35.6152	64	62.8181	92	89.5929
9	8.9717	37	36.5939	65	63.7814	93	90.5410
10	9.9661	38	37.5726	66	64.7447	94	91.4892
11	10.9593	39	38.5502	67	65.7069	95	92.4362
12	11.9525	40	39.5278	68	66.6691	96	93.3833
13	12.9446	41	40.5043	69	67.6302	97	94.3293
14	13.9367	42	41.4808	70	68.5914	98	95.2753
15	14.9277	43	42.4562	71	69.5514	99	96.2202
16	15.9187	44	43.4315	72	70.5114	100	97.1651
17	16.9085	45	44.4058	73	71.4704	101	98.1090
18	17.8984	46	45.3801	74	72.4293	102	99.0529
19	18.8871	47	46.3533	75	73.3872	103	99.9956
20	19.8759	48	47.3264	76	74.3450	104	100.9384
21	20.8635	49	48.2985	77	75.3018	105	101.8801
22	21.8511	50	49.2706	78	76.2586	106	102.8219
23	22.8376	51	50.2416	79	77.2143	107	103.7625
24	23.8241	52	51.2125	80	78.1700	108	104.7032
25	24.8095	53	52.1824	81	79.1246	109	105.6428
26	25.7948	54	53.1523	82	80.0792	110	106.5823
27	26.7791	55	54.1210	83	81.0327	111	107.5209
28	27.7634	56	55.0898	84	81.9862	112	108.4594

Title 8, Cal. Code of Reg., Section 10169 – Table 1

Weeks	PV	Weeks	PV	Weeks	PV	Weeks	PV
113	109.3968	155	148.3054	197	186.2992	239	223.3996
114	110.3343	156	149.2209	198	187.1931	240	224.2725
115	111.2707	157	150.1352	199	188.0860	241	225.1444
116	112.2071	158	151.0496	200	188.9789	242	226.0163
117	113.1424	159	151.9630	201	189.8707	243	226.8872
118	114.0778	160	152.8763	202	190.7626	244	227.7581
119	115.0121	161	153.7886	203	191.6535	245	228.6280
120	115.9463	162	154.7009	204	192.5443	246	229.4979
121	116.8796	163	155.6122	205	193.4342	247	230.3669
122	117.8128	164	156.5235	206	194.3240	248	231.2358
123	118.7449	165	157.4337	207	195.2129	249	232.1037
124	119.6771	166	158.3440	208	196.1017	250	232.9717
125	120.6082	167	159.2532	209	196.9896	251	233.8386
126	121.5393	168	160.1624	210	197.8774	252	234.7056
127	122.4694	169	161.0706	211	198.7642	253	235.5716
128	123.3994	170	161.9788	212	199.6511	254	236.4376
129	124.3284	171	162.8859	213	200.5369	255	237.3026
130	125.2574	172	163.7931	214	201.4227	256	238.1676
131	126.1854	173	164.6992	215	202.3075	257	239.0316
132	127.1133	174	165.6054	216	203.1924	258	239.8956
133	128.0402	175	166.5105	217	204.0762	259	240.7586
134	128.9671	176	167.4156	218	204.9600	260	241.6217
135	129.8930	177	168.3197	219	205.8428	261	242.4838
136	130.8188	178	169.2237	220	206.7257	262	243.3458
137	131.7436	179	170.1268	221	207.6075	263	244.2069
138	132.6684	180	171.0298	222	208.4893	264	245.0680
139	133.5922	181	171.9319	223	209.3701	265	245.9281
140	134.5159	182	172.8339	224	210.2510	266	246.7882
141	135.4386	183	173.7349	225	211.1308	267	247.6474
142	136.3613	184	174.6359	226	212.0106	268	248.5065
143	137.2830	185	175.5359	227	212.8894	269	249.3647
144	138.2047	186	176.4359	228	213.7683	270	250.2228
145	139.1253	187	177.3349	229	214.6461	271	251.0800
146	140.0459	188	178.2339	230	215.5239	272	251.9372
147	140.9655	189	179.1318	231	216.4008	273	252.7935
148	141.8851	190	180.0298	232	217.2776	274	253.6497
149	142.8036	191	180.9267	233	218.1535	275	254.5049
150	143.7221	192	181.8236	234	219.0293	276	255.3602
151	144.6396	193	182.7196	235	219.9042	277	256.2145
152	145.5571	194	183.6155	236	220.7790	278	257.0688
153	146.4736	195	184.5104	237	221.6529	279	257.9221
154	147.3900	196	185.4053	238	222.5268	280	258.7754

Weeks	PV	Weeks	PV	Weeks	PV	Weeks	PV
281	259.6278	323	295.0041	365	329.5486	407	363.2809
282	260.4801	324	295.8364	366	330.3613	408	364.0745
283	261.3315	325	296.6677	367	331.1732	409	364.8673
284	262.1829	326	297.4991	368	331.9850	410	365.6600
285	263.0333	327	298.3295	369	332.7959	411	366.4518
286	263.8837	328	299.1600	370	333.6068	412	367.2437
287	264.7332	329	299.9895	371	334.4168	413	368.0346
288	265.5827	330	300.8190	372	335.2268	414	368.8256
289	266.4312	331	301.6475	373	336.0358	415	369.6156
290	267.2797	332	302.4760	374	336.8449	416	370.4056
291	268.1272	333	303.3037	375	337.6530	417	371.1948
292	268.9747	334	304.1313	376	338.4612	418	371.9839
293	269.8213	335	304.9579	377	339.2684	419	372.7722
294	270.6679	336	305.7846	378	340.0757	420	373.5605
295	271.5135	337	306.6104	379	340.8820	421	374.3478
296	272.3591	338	307.4361	380	341.6883	422	375.1352
297	273.2038	339	308.2609	381	342.4937	423	375.9217
298	274.0485	340	309.0857	382	343.2991	424	376.7081
299	274.8922	341	309.9096	383	344.1036	425	377.4937
300	275.7359	342	310.7334	384	344.9081	426	378.2793
301	276.5786	343	311.5564	385	345.7117	427	379.0640
302	277.4214	344	312.3793	386	346.5153	428	379.8487
303	278.2632	345	313.2013	387	347.3180	429	380.6325
304	279.1050	346	314.0233	388	348.1207	430	381.4163
305	279.9458	347	314.8444	389	348.9224	431	382.1992
306	280.7866	348	315.6655	390	349.7242	432	382.9821
307	281.6265	349	316.4856	391	350.5250	433	383.7641
308	282.4664	350	317.3057	392	351.3259	434	384.5462
309	283.3054	351	318.1250	393	352.1259	435	385.3273
310	284.1443	352	318.9442	394	352.9258	436	386.1085
311	284.9823	353	319.7625	395	353.7249	437	386.8887
312	285.8203	354	320.5807	396	354.5239	438	387.6690
313	286.6573	355	321.3981	397	355.3220	439	388.4484
314	287.4944	356	322.2155	398	356.1202	440	389.2277
315	288.3305	357	323.0319	399	356.9174	441	390.0062
316	289.1665	358	323.8483	400	357.7147	442	390.7847
317	290.0017	359	324.6638	401	358.5110	443	391.5623
318	290.8368	360	325.4794	402	359.3073	444	392.3399
319	291.6710	361	326.2939	403	360.1028	445	393.1167
320	292.5052	362	327.1085	404	360.8982	446	393.8934
321	293.3385	363	327.9222	405	361.6927	447	394.6693
322	294.1718	364	328.7359	406	362.4873	448	395.4451

Title 8, Cal. Code of Reg., Section 10169 – Table 1

Tables & Schedules

Weeks	PV	Weeks	PV	Weeks	PV	Weeks	PV
449	396.2201	491	428.3848	533	459.7932	575	490.4632
450	396.9951	492	429.1415	534	460.5322	576	491.1847
451	397.7691	493	429.8974	535	461.2703	577	491.9055
452	398.5432	494	430.6533	536	462.0084	578	492.6263
453	399.3165	495	431.4084	537	462.7457	579	493.3462
454	400.0897	496	432.1634	538	463.4830	580	494.0662
455	400.8620	497	432.9176	539	464.2194	581	494.7853
456	401.6344	498	433.6718	540	464.9559	582	495.5044
457	402.4058	499	434.4251	541	465.6915	583	496.2228
458	403.1773	500	435.1784	542	466.4271	584	496.9411
459	403.9479	501	435.9309	543	467.1619	585	497.6586
460	404.7185	502	436.6834	544	467.8967	586	498.3761
461	405.4882	503	437.4350	545	468.6306	587	499.0928
462	406.2579	504	438.1866	546	469.3646	588	499.8095
463	407.0268	505	438.9374	547	470.0977	589	500.5254
464	407.7956	506	439.6882	548	470.8308	590	501.2413
465	408.5636	507	440.4381	549	471.5631	591	501.9563
466	409.3316	508	441.1880	550	472.2954	592	502.6714
467	410.0987	509	441.9371	551	473.0269	593	503.3857
468	410.8658	510	442.6862	552	473.7583	594	504.0999
469	411.6321	511	443.4344	553	474.4890	595	504.8134
470	412.3983	512	444.1826	554	475.2196	596	505.5268
471	413.1637	513	444.9300	555	475.9494	597	506.2395
472	413.9291	514	445.6774	556	476.6792	598	506.9521
473	414.6936	515	446.4239	557	477.4082	599	507.6640
474	415.4581	516	447.1704	558	478.1372	600	508.3758
475	416.2217	517	447.9161	559	478.8653	601	509.0868
476	416.9854	518	448.6618	560	479.5935	602	509.7979
477	417.7481	519	449.4067	561	480.3208	603	510.5081
478	418.5109	520	450.1515	562	481.0481	604	511.2183
479	419.2728	521	450.8955	563	481.7746	605	511.9278
480	420.0347	522	451.6395	564	482.5012	606	512.6372
481	420.7958	523	452.3827	565	483.2268	607	513.3458
482	421.5568	524	453.1258	566	483.9525	608	514.0544
483	422.3170	525	453.8681	567	484.6774	609	514.7622
484	423.0772	526	454.6104	568	485.4022	610	515.4701
485	423.8365	527	455.3519	569	486.1263	611	516.1771
486	424.5959	528	456.0934	570	486.8503	612	516.8841
487	425.3543	529	456.8340	571	487.5735	613	517.5903
488	426.1128	530	457.5747	572	488.2968	614	518.2965
489	426.8704	531	458.3145	573	489.0192	615	519.0019
490	427.6280	532	459.0543	574	489.7416	616	519.7074

Weeks	PV	Weeks	PV	Weeks	PV	Weeks	PV
617	520.4120	659	549.6566	701	578.2137	743	606.0993
618	521.1166	660	550.3447	702	578.8855	744	606.7553
619	521.8204	661	551.0320	703	579.5567	745	607.4107
620	522.5242	662	551.7192	704	580.2278	746	608.0660
621	523.2273	663	552.4057	705	580.8981	747	608.7206
622	523.9303	664	553.0922	706	581.5685	748	609.3752
623	524.6325	665	553.7779	707	582.2381	749	610.0290
624	525.3347	666	554.4636	708	582.9077	750	610.6829
625	526.0362	667	555.1486	709	583.5765	751	611.3360
626	526.7376	668	555.8335	710	584.2453	752	611.9891
627	527.4382	669	556.5177	711	584.9134	753	612.6415
628	528.1389	670	557.2018	712	585.5815	754	613.2938
629	528.8387	671	557.8852	713	586.2488	755	613.9455
630	529.5386	672	558.5686	714	586.9161	756	614.5971
631	530.2376	673	559.2512	715	587.5827	757	615.2480
632	530.9367	674	559.9339	716	588.2493	758	615.8989
633	531.6349	675	560.6157	717	588.9151	759	616.5490
634	532.3332	676	561.2975	718	589.5809	760	617.1992
635	533.0306	677	561.9786	719	590.2459	761	617.8486
636	533.7281	678	562.6597	720	590.9110	762	618.4980
637	534.4248	679	563.3400	721	591.5753	763	619.1467
638	535.1215	680	564.0203	722	592.2396	764	619.7954
639	535.8174	681	564.6998	723	592.9031	765	620.4434
640	536.5133	682	565.3793	724	593.5667	766	621.0913
641	537.2084	683	566.0581	725	594.2295	767	621.7385
642	537.9035	684	566.7368	726	594.8923	768	622.3857
643	538.5978	685	567.4148	727	595.5543	769	623.0322
644	539.2921	686	568.0928	728	596.2164	770	623.6787
645	539.9856	687	568.7701	729	596.8777	771	624.3245
646	540.6792	688	569.4473	730	597.5390	772	624.9702
647	541.3719	689	570.1237	731	598.1995	773	625.6152
648	542.0646	690	570.8002	732	598.8601	774	626.2602
649	542.7566	691	571.4759	733	599.5199	775	626.9045
650	543.4486	692	572.1516	734	600.1797	776	627.5488
651	544.1397	693	572.8265	735	600.8388	777	628.1924
652	544.8309	694	573.5014	736	601.4978	778	628.8359
653	545.5213	695	574.1756	737	602.1561	779	629.4788
654	546.2117	696	574.8497	738	602.8144	780	630.1216
655	546.9013	697	575.5231	739	603.4720	781	630.7637
656	547.5909	698	576.1965	740	604.1296	782	631.4058
657	548.2797	699	576.8692	741	604.7864	783	632.0472
658	548.9686	700	577.5418	742	605.4432	784	632.6886

Title 8, Cal. Code of Reg., Section 10169 – Table 1

Weeks	PV	Weeks	PV	Weeks	PV	Weeks	PV
785	633.3292	827	659.9189	869	685.8834	911	711.2375
786	633.9699	828	660.5445	870	686.4943	912	711.8340
787	634.6098	829	661.1694	871	687.1045	913	712.4298
788	635.2497	830	661.7943	872	687.7147	914	713.0256
789	635.8889	831	662.4184	873	688.3242	915	713.6208
790	636.5281	832	663.0426	874	688.9337	916	714.2160
791	637.1666	833	663.6661	875	689.5425	917	714.8105
792	637.8051	834	664.2895	876	690.1513	918	715.4050
793	638.4428	835	664.9123	877	690.7594	919	715.9988
794	639.0806	836	665.5350	878	691.3675	920	716.5926
795	639.7176	837	666.1571	879	691.9749	921	717.1857
796	640.3546	838	666.7791	880	692.5824	922	717.7789
797	640.9909	839	667.4005	881	693.1891	923	718.3713
798	641.6272	840	668.0218	882	693.7958	924	718.9638
799	642.2628	841	668.6425	883	694.4019	925	719.5556
800	642.8984	842	669.2631	884	695.0079	926	720.1474
801	643.5333	843	669.8831	885	695.6133	927	720.7386
802	644.1682	844	670.5030	886	696.2187	928	721.3297
803	644.8023	845	671.1222	887	696.8233	929	721.9202
804	645.4365	846	671.7415	888	697.4280	930	722.5106
805	646.0699	847	672.3600	889	698.0320	931	723.1004
806	646.7033	848	672.9786	890	698.6360	932	723.6902
807	647.3360	849	673.5964	891	699.2393	933	724.2793
808	647.9688	850	674.2142	892	699.8426	934	724.8685
809	648.6007	851	674.8314	893	700.4453	935	725.4569
810	649.2327	852	675.4485	894	701.0479	936	726.0454
811	649.8640	853	676.0650	895	701.6498	937	726.6332
812	650.4953	854	676.6814	896	702.2518	938	727.2210
813	651.1259	855	677.2971	897	702.8531	939	727.8081
814	651.7564	856	677.9129	898	703.4543	940	728.3952
815	652.3863	857	678.5279	899	704.0549	941	728.9817
816	653.0162	858	679.1430	900	704.6555	942	729.5681
817	653.6453	859	679.7573	901	705.2554	943	730.1539
818	654.2744	860	680.3717	902	705.8553	944	730.7397
819	654.9029	861	680.9853	903	706.4545	945	731.3249
820	655.5313	862	681.5990	904	707.0537	946	731.9100
821	656.1590	863	682.2119	905	707.6523	947	732.4945
822	656.7867	864	682.8249	906	708.2508	948	733.0789
823	657.4137	865	683.4371	907	708.8487	949	733.6628
824	658.0407	866	684.0494	908	709.4466	950	734.2466
825	658.6670	867	684.6610	909	710.0437	951	734.8297
826	659.2933	868	685.2725	910	710.6409	952	735.4129

Weeks	PV	Weeks	PV	Weeks	PV	Weeks	PV
953	735.9953	995	760.1711	1037	783.7785	1079	806.8308
954	736.5778	996	760.7399	1038	784.3339	1080	807.3731
955	737.1597	997	761.3081	1039	784.8887	1081	807.9149
956	737.7415	998	761.8762	1040	785.4435	1082	808.4566
957	738.3227	999	762.4437	1041	785.9976	1083	808.9977
958	738.9038	1000	763.0112	1042	786.5518	1084	809.5389
959	739.4843	1001	763.5781	1043	787.1053	1085	810.0794
960	740.0649	1002	764.1450	1044	787.6589	1086	810.6199
961	740.6447	1003	764.7112	1045	788.2118	1087	811.1598
962	741.2246	1004	765.2774	1046	788.7647	1088	811.6997
963	741.8038	1005	765.8430	1047	789.3170	1089	812.2390
964	742.3830	1006	766.4086	1048	789.8692	1090	812.7783
965	742.9615	1007	766.9735	1049	790.4209	1091	813.3170
966	743.5400	1008	767.5384	1050	790.9726	1092	813.8557
967	744.1179	1009	768.1027	1051	791.5236	1093	814.3938
968	744.6958	1010	768.6670	1052	792.0746	1094	814.9318
969	745.2731	1011	769.2307	1053	792.6250	1095	815.4693
970	745.8503	1012	769.7944	1054	793.1754	1096	816.0068
971	746.4269	1013	770.3574	1055	793.7252	1097	816.5436
972	747.0034	1014	770.9204	1056	794.2750	1098	817.0805
973	747.5794	1015	771.4828	1057	794.8242	1099	817.6167
974	748.1553	1016	772.0452	1058	795.3733	1100	818.1530
975	748.7306	1017	772.6069	1059	795.9219	1101	818.6886
976	749.3058	1018	773.1687	1060	796.4704	1102	819.2243
977	749.8805	1019	773.7298	1061	797.0183	1103	819.7593
978	750.4551	1020	774.2909	1062	797.5662	1104	820.2943
979	751.0291	1021	774.8514	1063	798.1135	1105	820.8288
980	751.6030	1022	775.4118	1064	798.6608	1106	821.3632
981	752.1764	1023	775.9717	1065	799.2075	1107	821.8970
982	752.7497	1024	776.5315	1066	799.7542	1108	822.4309
983	753.3224	1025	777.0907	1067	800.3003	1109	822.9641
984	753.8950	1026	777.6499	1068	800.8463	1110	823.4973
985	754.4671	1027	778.2085	1069	801.3918	1111	824.0299
986	755.0391	1028	778.7671	1070	801.9372	1112	824.5625
987	755.6105	1029	779.3250	1071	802.4820	1113	825.0945
988	756.1818	1030	779.8830	1072	803.0268	1114	825.6266
989	756.7526	1031	780.4403	1073	803.5711	1115	826.1580
990	757.3233	1032	780.9976	1074	804.1153	1116	826.6894
991	757.8934	1033	781.5543	1075	804.6589	1117	827.2202
992	758.4635	1034	782.1110	1076	805.2024	1118	827.7510
993	759.0329	1035	782.6670	1077	805.7454	1119	828.2812
994	759.6023	1036	783.2231	1078	806.2884	1120	828.8114

Title 8, Cal. Code of Reg., Section 10169 – Table 1

TABLE 2
Commutation: Present Value of Life Pension for a Male

TABLE 2 - PRESENT VALUE OF LIFE PENSION FOR A MALE

Use this table to commute, i.e. determine the present value (PV) of life pension benefits for a male. The "Age on DOC" column refers to the age of the injured employee as of the date of the commutation. The columns labeled "0, 1, 2, 3. . ." refer to the period of years between the DOC and the commencement of life pension, commonly referred to as the "deferral period". The number at the intersection of the row (representing age) and column (representing deferral period) contains the present value at $1 per week for that combination of age and deferral period. Fractional ages and commencement delays can be accommodated using interpolation. See Examples D, E, and F under Commutation Procedures. This table is based on the U.S. Decennial Life Tables for 1989-91.

Age on DOC	Number of years between date of commutation (DOC) and commencement of life pension														
	0	1	2	3	4	5	6	7	8	9	10	11	12	13	14
15	1401.79	1350.43	1300.62	1252.31	1205.48	1160.07	1116.06	1073.39	1032.04	991.95	953.10	915.45	878.96	843.60	809.32
16	1392.18	1340.83	1291.03	1242.75	1195.94	1150.56	1106.58	1063.94	1022.62	982.57	943.76	906.14	869.68	834.35	800.11
17	1382.60	1331.25	1281.46	1233.20	1186.41	1141.05	1097.09	1054.48	1013.18	973.16	934.37	896.77	860.34	825.04	790.83
18	1372.97	1321.63	1271.85	1223.59	1176.81	1131.47	1087.53	1044.94	1003.66	963.65	924.88	887.30	850.89	815.62	781.44
19	1363.21	1311.87	1262.09	1213.84	1167.08	1121.75	1077.82	1035.24	993.97	953.98	915.22	877.67	841.28	806.02	771.87
20	1353.22	1301.88	1252.11	1203.87	1157.11	1111.80	1067.88	1025.31	984.06	944.08	905.34	867.80	831.44	796.21	762.08
21	1343.02	1291.68	1241.91	1193.68	1146.93	1101.62	1057.71	1015.15	973.91	933.95	895.22	857.71	821.37	786.16	752.07
22	1332.57	1281.23	1231.47	1183.24	1136.50	1091.20	1047.29	1004.74	963.52	923.57	884.86	847.37	811.05	775.88	741.81
23	1321.88	1270.54	1220.78	1172.55	1125.81	1080.52	1036.62	994.08	952.87	912.94	874.25	836.78	800.49	765.35	731.31
24	1310.88	1259.54	1209.78	1161.56	1114.83	1069.53	1025.65	983.12	941.92	902.01	863.35	825.91	789.65	754.54	720.54
25	1299.58	1248.24	1198.48	1150.26	1103.53	1058.25	1014.37	971.86	930.68	890.80	852.16	814.75	778.52	743.44	709.49
26	1287.93	1236.59	1186.83	1138.62	1091.89	1046.62	1002.76	960.28	919.12	879.26	840.65	803.27	767.08	732.04	698.13
27	1275.93	1224.59	1174.84	1126.63	1079.92	1034.67	990.83	948.36	907.23	867.40	828.83	791.49	755.33	720.34	686.47
28	1263.61	1212.27	1162.53	1114.33	1067.63	1022.39	978.57	936.13	895.03	855.23	816.70	779.40	743.29	708.34	674.52
29	1250.98	1199.64	1149.91	1101.72	1055.04	1009.82	966.02	923.61	882.54	842.78	804.28	767.02	730.96	696.06	662.29
30	1238.06	1186.73	1137.00	1088.82	1042.16	996.96	953.19	910.80	869.77	830.04	791.58	754.37	718.35	683.50	649.78
31	1224.84	1173.51	1123.79	1075.63	1028.98	983.80	940.05	897.70	856.70	817.01	778.59	741.42	705.45	670.65	636.99
32	1211.32	1160.00	1110.28	1062.13	1015.50	970.34	926.62	884.30	843.33	803.68	765.31	728.18	692.25	657.51	623.92
33	1197.48	1146.16	1096.45	1048.31	1001.70	956.56	912.87	870.58	829.65	790.03	751.70	714.62	678.76	644.08	610.56
34	1183.31	1131.99	1082.29	1034.17	987.57	942.46	898.80	856.54	815.64	776.07	737.79	700.76	664.96	630.35	596.91
35	1168.82	1117.50	1067.81	1019.70	973.12	928.04	884.40	842.18	801.32	761.79	723.56	686.59	650.85	616.32	582.97
36	1153.99	1102.68	1052.99	1004.90	958.34	913.28	869.68	827.48	786.66	747.18	709.01	672.10	636.45	602.01	568.76
37	1138.83	1087.52	1037.85	989.77	943.23	898.19	854.62	812.46	771.68	732.25	694.14	657.32	621.75	587.41	554.28
38	1123.31	1072.01	1022.34	974.27	927.75	882.74	839.20	797.08	756.35	716.99	678.95	642.21	606.75	572.52	539.51
39	1107.41	1056.11	1006.45	958.40	911.90	866.91	823.40	781.33	740.67	701.38	663.42	626.78	591.43	557.33	524.46
40	1091.11	1039.80	990.16	942.12	895.64	850.69	807.23	765.21	724.62	685.41	647.56	611.03	575.80	541.84	509.13
41	1074.38	1023.09	973.45	925.43	878.98	834.07	790.66	748.72	708.20	669.09	631.35	594.94	559.86	526.06	493.53
42	1057.25	1005.95	956.33	908.33	861.92	817.06	773.72	731.85	691.43	652.43	614.81	578.55	543.63	510.01	477.69
43	1039.71	988.42	938.81	890.84	844.48	799.68	756.41	714.63	674.32	635.44	597.96	561.87	527.13	493.72	461.63
44	1021.80	970.52	920.93	873.00	826.69	781.95	738.77	697.09	656.90	618.16	580.84	544.93	510.40	477.22	445.37
45	1003.55	952.27	902.71	854.82	808.57	763.91	720.82	679.26	639.20	600.61	563.48	527.77	493.46	460.53	428.96
46	984.99	933.72	884.19	836.34	790.15	745.58	702.59	661.16	621.24	582.83	545.90	510.41	476.35	443.70	412.44
47	966.15	914.89	865.39	817.60	771.47	726.99	684.12	642.82	603.07	564.86	528.14	492.89	459.11	426.76	395.84
48	947.04	895.79	846.32	798.58	752.53	708.15	665.41	624.26	584.70	546.69	510.21	475.24	441.76	409.74	379.18
49	927.65	876.42	826.98	779.29	733.33	689.07	646.46	605.49	566.13	528.35	492.14	457.47	424.32	392.67	362.49
50	907.98	856.76	807.36	759.74	713.88	669.74	627.30	586.52	547.38	509.86	473.94	439.60	406.81	375.55	345.79

(Present Value of Life Pension for a Male - con't)

Age on DOC	Number of years between date of commutation (DOC) and commencement of life pension														
	0	1	2	3	4	5	6	7	8	9	10	11	12	13	14
51	888.05	836.85	787.49	739.96	694.21	650.21	607.94	567.37	528.48	491.25	455.65	421.67	389.27	358.43	329.12
52	867.93	816.75	767.44	719.99	674.36	630.53	588.45	548.12	509.50	472.58	437.33	403.73	371.74	341.35	312.52
53	847.65	796.48	747.24	699.88	654.38	610.71	568.85	528.78	490.46	453.88	419.00	385.80	354.26	324.34	296.02
54	827.23	776.08	726.89	679.64	634.29	590.81	549.19	509.39	471.40	435.17	400.70	367.93	336.86	307.45	279.65
55	806.69	755.57	706.45	659.31	614.12	570.85	529.49	489.99	452.34	416.50	382.45	350.15	319.57	290.69	263.46
56	786.06	734.96	685.91	638.90	593.89	550.85	509.76	470.59	433.31	397.88	364.28	332.47	302.42	274.09	247.46
57	765.34	714.27	665.31	618.44	573.62	530.84	490.05	451.22	414.33	379.34	346.21	314.92	285.42	257.69	231.69
58	744.61	693.57	644.71	597.99	553.39	510.86	470.39	431.93	395.45	360.92	328.30	297.54	268.63	241.53	216.22
59	723.94	672.93	624.17	577.61	533.23	490.98	450.84	412.76	376.72	342.67	310.57	280.39	252.11	225,68	201.09
60	703.35	652.39	603.73	557.34	513.18	471.22	431.42	393.75	358.16	324.61	293.07	263.50	235.89	210.18	186.35
61	682.82	631.89	583.34	537.12	493.20	451.55	412.12	374.87	339.75	306.74	275.80	246.89	219.98	195.04	172.00
62	662.31	611.41	562.97	516.94	473.29	431.96	392.91	356.11	321.50	289.07	258.77	230.57	204.43	180.28	158.08
63	641.80	590.95	542.64	496.81	453.43	412.44	373.81	337.48	303.44	271.64	242.03	214.59	189.24	165.94	144.61
64	621.35	570.55	522.37	476.75	433.66	393.03	354.84	319.05	285.61	254.48	225.63	198.98	174.48	152.05	131.62
65	600.97	550.22	502.17	456.78	413.99	373.76	336.06	300.84	268.05	237.66	209.59	183.78	160.15	138.64	119.15
66	580.64	529.94	482.04	436.88	394.43	354.64	317.47	282.87	250.80	221.18	193.94	169.01	146.30	125.73	107.22
67	560.33	509.68	461.93	417.05	374.98	335.68	299.10	265.18	233.86	205.06	178.70	154.69	132.94	113.36	95.86
68	540.05	489.46	441.90	397.33	355.68	316.92	280.98	247.80	217.28	189.35	163.91	140.87	120.12	101.58	85.14
69	519.90	469.38	422.03	377.80	336.63	298.46	263.21	230.79	201.13	174.10	149.63	127.59	107.89	90.43	75.09
70	499.97	449.53	402.42	358.56	317.90	280.36	245.83	214.23	185.45	159.38	135.90	114.92	96.32	79.98	65.75
71	480.35	430.00	383.14	339.69	299.57	262.68	228.91	198.16	170.30	145.22	122.80	102.92	85.46	70.26	57.13
72	461.09	410.84	364.25	321.23	281.68	245.47	212.49	182.61	155.72	131.68	110.37	91.64	75.34	61.27	49.23
73	442.23	392.08	345.77	303.19	264.22	228.72	196.56	167.61	141.74	118.80	98.64	81.09	65.95	53.00	42.05
74	423.71	373.67	327.66	285.54	247.17	212.42	181.14	153.17	128.38	106.60	87.63	71.27	57.27	45.44	35.56
75	405.48	355.54	309.84	268.21	230.50	196.56	166.21	139.31	115.67	95.09	77.33	62.15	49.30	38.58	29.75
76	387.49	337.68	292.31	251.22	214.22	181.15	151.83	126.07	103.64	84.28	67.73	53.73	42.05	32.42	24.61
77	369.79	320.10	275.10	234.59	198.37	166.26	138.05	113.49	92.29	74.17	58.84	46.05	35.51	26.95	20.12
78	352.36	302.83	258.23	218.36	183.02	151.97	124.93	101.60	81.65	64.77	50.69	39.08	29.67	22.15	16.25
79	335.28	285.90	241.76	202.63	168.25	138.32	112.48	80.39	71.72	56.12	43.27	32.85	24.52	17.99	12.97
80	318.61	269.42	225.82	187.50	154.14	125.35	100.74	79.92	62.54	48.22	36.60	27.33	20.05	14.46	10.24
81	302.57	253.60	210.57	173.11	140.78	113.13	89.75	70.23	54.16	41.11	30.69	22.52	16.23	11.50	8.00
82	287.28	238.54	196.10	159.48	128.16	101.68	79.56	61.35	46.57	34.76	25.51	18.39	13.03	9.06	6.19
83	272.73	224.21	182.33	146.53	116.25	90.97	70.14	53.24	39.75	29.16	21.03	14.89	10.36	7.07	4.74
84	258.66	210.35	169.04	134.11	104.94	80.92	61.42	45.85	33.64	24.26	17.18	11.95	8.16	5.47	3.59
85	244.80	196.73	156.08	122.13	94.17	71.48	53.36	39.16	28.23	20.00	13.91	9.50	6.36	4.17	2.68
86	231.26	183.47	143.57	110.70	84.03	62.73	46.03	33.18	23.50	16.35	11.16	7.48	4.91	3.15	1.98
87	218.27	170.80	131.70	99.97	74.63	54.76	39.48	27.96	19.45	13.28	8.89	5.84	3.75	2.35	1.44
88	205.91	158.77	120.52	89.97	66.01	47.59	33.71	23.45	16.01	10.72	7.04	4.52	2.84	1.73	1.03
89	194.15	147.37	110.02	80.72	58.20	41.22	28.68	19.58	13.11	8.60	5.53	3.47	2.12	1.26	0.73
90	183.01	136.62	100.24	72.27	51.19	35.61	24.32	16.28	10.69	6.86	4.31	2.63	1.57	0.91	0.51
91	172.58	126.63	91.29	64.67	44.99	30.72	20.57	13.50	8.67	5.44	3.33	1.98	1.15	0.64	0.35
92	163.03	117.54	83.25	57.92	39.55	26.48	17.38	11.16	7.00	4.28	2.55	1.47	0.83	0.44	0.23
93	154.41	109.37	76.09	51.95	34.79	22.83	14.66	9.20	5.63	3.35	1.94	1.08	0.58	0.30	0.15
94	146.60	101.99	69.64	46.63	30.60	19.65	12.33	7.54	4.49	2.60	1.45	0.78	0.40	0.20	0.09
95	139.36	95.15	63.72	41.81	26.85	16.85	10.31	6.14	3.55	1.99	1.07	0.55	0.27	0.12	0.05

TABLE 3 - PRESENT VALUE OF LIFE PENSION FOR A FEMALE

Use this table to commute, i.e. determine the present value (PV) of life pension benefits for a female. The "Age on DOC" column refers to the age of the injured employee as of the date of the commutation. The columns labeled "0, 1, 2. . . " refer to the period of years between the DOC and the commencement of life pension, commonly referred to as the "deferral period". The number at the intersection of the row (representing age) and column (representing deferral period) contains the present value at $1 per week for that combination of age and deferral period. Fractional ages and commencement delays can be accommodated using interpolation. See Examples D, E, and F under Commutation Procedures. This table is based on the U.S. Decennial Life Tables for 1989-91.

Age on DOC	Number of years between date of commutation (DOC) and commencement of life pension														
	0	1	2	3	4	5	6	7	8	9	10	11	12	13	14
15	1475.06	1423.69	1373.83	1325.44	1278.48	1232.92	1188.70	1145.80	1104.17	1063.77	1024.57	986.54	949.64	913.83	879.09
16	1466.91	1415.54	1365.68	1317.30	1270.35	1224.79	1180.59	1137.69	1096.07	1055.68	1016.49	978.47	941.57	905.78	871.05
17	1458.60	1407.23	1357.38	1309.00	1262.06	1216.50	1172.30	1129.41	1087.80	1047.42	1008.23	970.22	933.33	897.55	862.83
18	1450.11	1398.74	1348.89	1300.52	1253.57	1208.03	1163.83	1120.95	1079.33	1038.96	999.78	961.77	924.90	889.12	854.41
19	1441.41	1390.04	1340.19	1291.81	1244.88	1199.33	1155.14	1112.26	1070.65	1030.28	991.11	953.11	916.24	880.47	845.78
20	1432.45	1381.08	1331.24	1282.87	1235.93	1190.39	1146.20	1103.32	1061.72	1021.36	982.20	944.20	907.34	871.59	836.90
21	1423.26	1371.89	1322.04	1273.67	1226.74	1181.20	1137.02	1094.14	1052.55	1012.19	973.03	935.05	898.20	862.46	827.79
22	1413.81	1362.44	1312.59	1264.22	1217.29	1171.76	1127.58	1084.71	1043.12	1002.77	963.62	925.65	888.81	853.08	818.43
23	1404.09	1352.73	1302.88	1254.52	1207.59	1162.05	1117.88	1075.01	1033.43	993.09	953.95	915.99	879.17	843.45	808.82
24	1394.10	1342.73	1292.89	1244.52	1197.60	1152.07	1107.89	1065.04	1023.46	983.13	944.01	906.06	869.25	833.56	798.94
25	1383.82	1332.45	1282.60	1234.24	1187.32	1141.79	1097.63	1054.78	1013.21	972.89	933.78	895.85	859.06	823.38	788.78
26	1373.23	1321.86	1272.02	1223.66	1176.74	1131.22	1087.06	1044.22	1002.67	962.36	923.27	885.35	848.58	812.93	778.35
27	1362.34	1310.97	1261.13	1212.77	1165.86	1120.35	1076.20	1033.37	991.83	951.54	912.46	874.57	837.82	802.19	767.64
28	1351.13	1299.77	1249.93	1201.58	1154.67	1109.17	1065.03	1022.22	980.69	940.42	901.36	863.49	826.76	791.16	756.64
29	1339.64	1288.28	1238.44	1190.10	1143.20	1097.71	1053.58	1010.78	969.27	929.02	889.98	852.13	815.43	779.85	745.37
30	1327.86	1276.49	1226.66	1178.32	1131.43	1085.95	1041.83	999.05	957.56	917.32	878.31	840.48	803.81	768.27	733.82
31	1315.77	1264.41	1214.58	1166.25	1119.37	1073.90	1029.79	987.02	945.55	905.34	866.35	828.55	791.91	756.40	721.99
32	1303.38	1252.02	1202.20	1153.87	1107.00	1061.54	1017.45	974.70	933.24	893.05	854.09	816.32	779.71	744.24	709.88
33	1290.68	1239.32	1189.50	1141.18	1094.31	1048.86	1004.79	962.06	920.62	880.46	841.52	803.79	767.22	731.79	697.48
34	1277.65	1226.29	1176.47	1128.16	1081.30	1035.87	991.81	949.10	907.69	867.55	828.65	790.95	754.43	719.05	684.79
35	1264.28	1212.92	1163.11	1114.80	1067.96	1022.54	978.50	935.81	894.43	854.32	815.45	777.80	741.32	706.00	671.81
36	1250.57	1199.21	1149.41	1101.11	1054.28	1008.87	964.86	922.19	880.84	840.77	801.94	764.34	727.92	692.66	658.54
37	1236.51	1185.16	1135.36	1087.07	1040.25	994.87	950.87	908.24	866.92	826.89	788.11	750.56	714.21	679.02	644.97
38	1222.12	1170.76	1120.97	1072.69	1025.89	980.53	936.56	893.95	852.67	812.69	773.97	736.48	700.20	665.09	631.13
39	1207.37	1156.02	1106.24	1057.97	1011.19	965.84	921.90	879.33	838.10	798.17	759.51	722.09	685.88	650.87	617.01
40	1192.28	1140.93	1091.15	1042.90	996.13	950.82	906.91	864.38	823.20	783.33	744.73	707.40	671.28	636.36	602.61
41	1176.83	1125.48	1075.71	1027.48	980.73	935.45	891.58	849.10	807.97	768.17	729.65	692.40	656.38	621.57	587.95
42	1161.02	1109.68	1059.92	1011.70	964.99	919.74	875.91	833.49	792.43	752.69	714.27	677.11	641.20	606.51	573.02
43	1144.87	1093.54	1043.79	995.59	948.90	903.69	859.92	817.56	776.56	736.92	698.58	661.54	625.75	591.19	557.84
44	1128.37	1077.04	1027.31	979.13	932.48	887.31	843.60	801.30	760.39	720.84	682.61	645.68	610.02	575.61	542.41
45	1111.55	1060.22	1010.51	962.36	915.75	870.63	826.98	784.76	743.94	704.48	666.37	629.57	594.05	559.79	526.77
46	1094.42	1043.10	993.40	945.28	898.71	853.65	810.07	767.93	727.20	687.86	649.88	613.21	577.85	543.76	510.92
47	1076.99	1025.68	976.00	927.92	881.39	836.39	792.89	750.84	710.22	671.00	633.14	596.63	561.43	527.52	494.89
48	1059.29	1007.98	958.32	910.27	863.80	818.87	775.44	733.49	692.98	653.89	616.18	579.83	544.81	511.10	478.69
49	1041.29	989.99	940.36	892.35	845.93	801.07	757.73	715.88	675.50	636.54	598.99	562.81	527.99	494.51	462.32
50	1023.01	971.72	922.10	874.14	827.78	783.00	739.76	698.02	657.77	618.96	581.58	545.60	511.00	477.74	445.81

(Present Value of Life Pension for a Female - con't)

Age on DOC	Number of years between date of commutation (DOC) and commencement of life pension														
	0	1	2	3	4	5	6	7	8	9	10	11	12	13	14
51	1004.44	953.16	903.58	855.66	809.37	764.67	721.53	679.92	639.81	601.17	563.98	528.21	493.83	460.82	429.16
52	985.64	934.37	884.82	836.95	790.73	746.12	703.09	661.61	621.65	583.20	546.21	510.66	476.52	443.78	412.41
53	966.59	915.33	865.81	818.00	771.85	727.34	684.43	643.09	603.31	565.04	528.27	492.96	459.09	426.63	395.56
54	947.30	896.05	846.57	798.81	752.74	708.33	665.56	624.38	584.78	546.72	510.18	475.12	441.53	409.37	378.63
55	927.76	876.52	827.07	779.38	733.40	689.11	646.47	605.47	566.07	528.23	491.93	457.15	423.86	392.03	361.63
56	907.96	856.74	807.33	759.70	713.82	669.66	627.18	586.37	547.17	509.58	473.55	439.06	406.08	374.59	344.57
57	887.93	836.72	787.36	739.81	694.04	650.02	607.71	567.09	528.13	490.79	455.04	420.87	388.23	357.11	327.49
58	867.69	816.50	767.19	719.73	674.08	630.21	588.09	547.68	508.96	471.89	436.45	402.60	370.33	339.61	310.43
59	847.31	796.14	746.89	699.52	653.99	610.28	568.34	528.16	489.70	452.92	417.80	384.31	352.43	322.14	293.43
60	826.80	775.65	726.45	679.17	633.77	590.23	548.50	508.55	470.36	433.88	399.10	366.00	334.55	304.73	276.52
61	806.13	755.00	705.86	658.68	613.42	570.05	528.54	488.84	450.93	414.79	380.38	347.69	316.70	287.39	259.73
62	785.28	734.18	685.10	638.03	592.92	549.74	508.45	469.02	431.43	395.64	361.64	329.41	298.92	270.15	243.07
63	764.26	713.18	664.18	617.22	572.27	529.29	488.24	449.11	411.85	376.46	342.91	311.17	281.22	253.03	226.57
64	743.09	692.03	643.11	596.27	551.49	508.72	467.94	429.13	392.25	357.29	324.22	293.01	263.64	236.08	210.28
65	721.77	670.74	621.89	575.19	530.58	488.05	447.57	409.11	372.64	338.15	305.61	274.97	246.22	219.32	194.23
66	700.30	649.30	600.54	553.97	509.56	467.30	427.14	389.07	353.05	319.07	287.09	257.07	228.98	202.79	178.47
67	678.66	627.69	579.02	532.61	488.43	446.45	406.66	369.02	333.50	300.08	268.70	239.34	211.96	186.54	163.06
68	656.86	605.92	557.36	511.12	467.20	425.56	386.17	349.00	314.02	281.19	250.46	221.81	195.21	170.64	148.07
69	634.95	584.06	535.61	489.58	445.94	404.67	365.72	329.06	294.66	262.46	232.44	204.56	178.82	155.17	133.57
70	613.01	562.16	513.85	468.05	424.73	383.85	345.38	309.26	275.47	243.96	214.70	187.68	162.86	140.20	119.64
71	591.10	540.30	492.14	446.59	403.61	363.15	325.18	289.65	256.52	225.76	197.34	171.24	147.41	125.80	106.35
72	569.26	518.52	470.52	425.24	382.62	342.61	305.17	270.26	237.85	207.92	180.42	155.31	132.54	112.05	93.75
73	547.52	496.85	449.03	404.02	361.78	322.24	285.38	251.16	219.55	190.51	164.00	139.96	118.32	98.99	81.91
74	525.89	475.27	427.64	382.92	341.08	302.06	265.84	232.38	201.65	173.59	148.14	125.23	104.78	86.69	70.87
75	504.31	453.76	406.32	361.92	320.52	282.08	246.58	213.97	184.19	157.19	132.88	111.18	91.99	75.20	60.67
76	482.73	432.25	385.02	340.98	300.09	262.32	227.63	195.95	167.23	141.37	118.28	97.86	80.00	64.55	51.35
77	461.16	410.77	363.78	320.16	279.86	242.85	209.05	178.41	150.82	126.19	104.41	85.35	68.86	54.78	42.92
78	439.67	389.38	342.69	299.56	259.94	223.77	190.96	161.43	135.07	111.75	91.35	73.71	58.64	45.94	35.43
79	418.43	368.26	321.91	279.33	240.46	205.21	173.48	145.15	120.09	98.17	79.21	63.01	49.37	38.07	28.87
80	397.59	347.55	301.58	259.61	221.56	187.30	156.71	129.66	105.99	85.52	68.03	53.30	41.10	31.17	23.24
81	377.23	327.34	281.79	240.48	203.30	170.09	140.73	115.04	92.82	73.84	57.86	44.61	33.84	25.23	18.47
82	357.39	307.65	262.55	221.95	185.71	153.65	125.60	101.34	80.62	63.17	48.71	36.94	27.54	20.16	14.48
83	338.06	288.51	243.89	204.06	168.84	138.02	111.36	88.59	69.41	53.52	40.59	30.26	22.16	15.92	11.21
84	319.25	269.88	225.81	186.83	152.72	123.23	98.03	76.81	59.22	44.92	33.49	24.52	17.61	12.40	8.56
85	300.95	251.80	208.33	170.30	137.41	109.31	85.65	66.04	50.09	37.34	27.34	19.64	13.83	9.54	6.44
86	283.27	234.38	191.59	154.59	122.98	96.35	74.30	56.35	42.01	30.76	22.09	15.56	10.73	7.25	4.78
87	266.38	217.76	175.70	139.77	109.51	84.44	64.05	47.75	34.96	25.11	17.68	12.20	8.24	5.43	3.49
88	250.27	201.93	160.64	125.86	97.05	73.61	54.88	40.18	28.86	20.32	14.02	9.46	6.24	4.02	2.51
89	234.86	186.83	146.39	112.88	85.61	63.82	46.73	33.57	23.64	16.31	11.01	7.26	4.67	2.92	1.77
90	220.16	172.49	133.01	100.88	75.21	55.06	39.55	27.85	19.21	12.97	8.56	5.50	3.44	2.09	1.23
91	206.39	159.15	120.71	89.99	65.89	47.33	33.33	22.99	15.52	10.24	6.58	4.12	2.50	1.47	0.83
92	193.80	146.99	109.58	80.23	57.63	40.58	28.00	18.90	12.47	8,02	5.02	3.04	1.79	1.01	0.54
93	182.30	135.91	99.51	71.48	50.33	34.72	23.44	15.46	9.95	6.22	3.78	2.21	1.25	0.67	0.34
94	171.64	125.66	90.26	63.56	43.85	29.60	19.53	12.56	7.86	4.77	2.80	1.58	0.85	0.43	0.20
95	161.63	116.10	81.76	56.40	38.08	25.12	16.15	10.11	6.13	3.60	2.03	1.09	0.55	0.26	0.10

TABLE 4
Commutation: Instructions with Examples

COMMUTATION INSTRUCTIONS

The following examples illustrate various methods of commuting permanent disability and life pension benefits. Examples A, B and C apply to permanent disability and utilize Table 1, "Present Value of Fixed Annuity at 3% Interest". Examples D, E and F apply to life pension and utilize Tables 2 and 3 (for males and females respectively), "Present Value of Lifetime Annuity at 3% Interest..."

EXAMPLE A: COMMUTATION OF ALL REMAINING PD

In this example, all PD due for the period after the date of commutation is commuted.

Assumed facts for Example A:

Date of injury: 4/10/96
PD commencement date: 2/20/98
Date of commutation (DOC): 5/14/99

PD rating: 65%
Weekly PD rate: $164
Number of weeks of indemnity corresponding to 65% PD: 386.25

1) Determine weeks of PD remaining after date of commutation (DOC).

a)	#days from PD commencement through DOC inclusive...........	449
b)	Divide by 7 days/week..........	÷ 7
c)	#weeks from PD commencement through DOC..........	64.1429
d)	Total weeks of PD..........	386.2500
e)	Subtract weeks elapsed through DOC (from 1c)..........	− 64.1429
f)	Weeks of PD remaining after date of commutation..........	322.1071

2) Determine PV of weeks of PD remaining after DOC (1f).

a)	PV of #weeks just above 1f* (PV of 323 wks)..........	295.0041
b)	Subtract next lower PV from table* (PV of 322 wks)..........	−294.1718
c)	Difference of 2a and 2b..........	.8323
d)	Multiply by fractional portion of 1f..........	× .1071
e)	PV of fractional week..........	.0891
f)	Add 2b	+ 294.1718
g)	PV of weeks remaining after DOC..........	294.2609

* Values for 2a and 2b taken from PV column of Table 1.

(continued on next page)

(Example A continued)

3) Determine commuted value of all PD due for period after DOC.

a)	PV of weeks remaining after DOC (from 2g)	294.2609
b)	Multiply by PD rate	× 164
c)	Commuted value of all PD due for period after DOC	$48,258.79

Summary of Example A:

- On date of commutation (DOC), $48,258.79 would be due and payable. This is the commuted value of all remaining PD. If payment is made at a later date, interest at 10% per annum is due for the period from DOC to date of actual payment. For example, if the payment in this instance is made on 5/26/99, i.e. twelve days after the date of commutation, interest of $158.66 would be due calculated as follows: 48,258.79 X 12 X .1 ÷ 365*.

* The formula for calculation of interest is:
(Commuted value) X (#Days between DOC and payment date) X .1 ÷ 365

EXAMPLE B: COMMUTATION OF PD "OFF THE FAR END" TO PRODUCE A SPECIFIC LUMP SUM

In this example, sufficient monies are to be commuted off the far end of the PD award to produce a payment on the date of commutation of $11,500. All facts are identical to those used in Example A. The calculation of the number of weeks of PD remaining after DOC used in this example is illustrated in step 1 of Example A. The calculation of the PV of weeks remaining after DOC used in this example is illustrated in step 2 of Example A.

Assumed facts:

Date of injury: 4/10/96
PD commencement date: 2/20/98
Date of commutation (DOC): 5/14/99

PD rating: 65%
Weekly PD rate: $164
Number of weeks of indemnity corresponding to 65% PD: 386.25

Weeks of PD remaining after DOC (1f from Example A): 322.1071
PV of weeks remaining after DOC (2g from Example A): 294.2609

1) Determine PV (at $1/week) of amount to be commuted.

a)	Amount to be commuted	11,500
b)	Divide by weekly PD rate	÷ 164
c)	PV of amount to be commuted	70.1220

(continued on next page)

Tables & Schedules

(Example B continued)

2) Determine PV of weeks remaining after commutation off far end.

a)	PV of weeks remaining after DOC (2g from Ex. A)................	294.2609
b)	Subtract PV of amount to be commuted (1c from above).........	– 70.1220
c)	PV of weeks remaining after commutation off far end...............	224.1389

3) Determine number of weeks of PD remaining after commutation off far end.

a)	PV just above 2c* (corresponding to 240 wks PD).................	224.2725
b)	Subtract PV just below 2c* (corresp. to 239 wks PD)..............	– 223.3996
c)	Difference of 3a and 3b (PV of 240th week)...........................	.8729

*Values for 3a and 3b taken from PV column of Table 1.

d)	PV of weeks remaining after commut. off far end (2c)..............	224.1389
e)	Subtract 3b (PV of 239 weeks)..	– 223.3996
f)	Difference of 3d and 3e..	.7393
g)	Divide by 3c (PV of 240th week)..	÷ .8729
h)	Proportional amount of 240th week..	.8469
i)	Add to 239 weeks..	+ 239.0000
j)	#weeks PD remaining after commutation off far end................	239.8469

4) Determine amount of PD due after commutation off far end.

a)	#weeks PD remaining after commutation off far end (3j)...........	239.8469
b)	Multiply by PD rate..	× 164
c)	PD still owed for period after DOC..	$39,334.89

5) Determine number of weeks of PD eliminated from the far end.

a)	# weeks PD before commut. off far end (1f from Ex. A)..........	322.1071
b)	Subtract #weeks PD remaining after commut. (3j).....................	– 239.8469
c)	#weeks PD eliminated from far end...	82.2602

Summary of Example B:

- On date of commutation (DOC), $11,500 would be due and payable. If payment is made after the DOC, interest is due at 10% per annum. See Summary of Example A for interest calculation.
- Following the payment of $11,500, the claims administrator would still owe 239.8469 weeks of PD (3j) payable on a biweekly basis in the total amount of $39,334.89 (4c).
- The number of weeks of PD eliminated from the far end as a result of the commutation would be 82.2602 (5c).

(Continued on next page)

EXAMPLE C: COMMUTATION OF PD BY UNIFORM REDUCTION OF PAYMENTS

In this example, sufficient monies are commuted by uniform reduction of all future payments of PD to produce a payment on the date of commutation of $11,500. All facts from Example A apply here. The calculation of number of weeks of PD remaining after DOC used in this example is illustrated in step 1 of Example A. The calculation of PV of remaining weeks used in this example is illustrated in step 2 of Example A.

Assumed facts:

Date of injury: 4/10/96
PD commencement date: 2/20/98
Date of commutation (DOC): 5/14/99

PD rating: 65%
Weekly PD rate: $164
Number of weeks of indemnity corresponding to 65% PD: 386.25

Lump sum to be paid on DOC: $11,500
Number of weeks of PD remaining after DOC (1f from Example A): 322.1071
PV of weeks of PD remaining after DOC (2g from Ex. A): 294.2609

1) Determine amount of reduction required to produce lump sum

a)	Amount desired to be commuted	$11,500
b)	Divide by PV of remaining weeks (2g from Ex. A)	÷ 294.2609
c)	Amount of reduction after rounding to nearest whole cent	$39.08

2) Determine new PD rate after reduction

a)	Weekly PD rate	164.00
b)	Subtract amount of reduction (1c)	– 39.08
c)	New PD rate after reduction	$124.92

3) Determine amount of PD still owed for period after DOC

a)	#weeks of PD remaining after DOC (1f from Example A)	322.1071
b)	Multiply by new PD rate after reduction (2c)	× 124.92
c)	Amount of PD still owed for period after DOC	$40,237.62

Summary of Example C:

- On date of commutation (DOC), $11,500 would be due and payable. If payment is made after DOC, interest is due at 10% per annum. See Summary of Example A for interest calculation.
- As a result of the commutation, payments for the period following the DOC would be due at the reduced weekly rate of $124.92 (2c).
- Following the payment of $11,500, the balance of PD benefits owed would be 322.1071 weeks payable on a biweekly basis in the total amount of $40,237.62 (3c).

(Continued on next page)

EXAMPLE D - COMMUTATION OF ALL REMAINING LIFE PENSION AFTER LIFE PENSION HAS COMMENCED

In this example, the commutation occurs after the commencement of life pension. On the date of commutation, all life pension indemnity owed for the period thereafter is commuted.

Assumed facts for Example D:

Date of birth (DOB): 8/25/45
Date of injury: 4/10/87
Life pension commencement date: 3/21/98
Date of commutation: 5/14/99

Life pension rate: $33.92
Gender: male

1) Determine exact age on date of commutation.

a)	Number of days from DOB through DOC*............................	19620
b)	Divide by number of days per year....................................	÷ 365.24
c)	Exact age on date of commutation..	53.718

* Note that in determining exact age, the actual date of birth is not counted as the first day of the period. That is, an individual does not become one day old until the day after the DOB. This differs from the determination of the number of days for a period of benefits when the commencement date _is_ counted as the first day of the period. See, for example, step 1a of Example A.

2) Determine PV of life pension as of exact age on DOC

a)	PV for age in table below 1c* (age 53).............................	847.65
b)	PV for age in table above 1c (age 54)*.............................	− 827.23
c)	Difference of 2a and 2b...	20.42
d)	Multiply by fractional portion of age from 1c..........................	× .718
e)	Interpolation adjustment for 2d..	14.66
f)	PV for age in table below 1c* (from 2a above)........................	847.65
g)	Subtract 2e	− 14.66
h)	PV of life pension as of exact age on DOC..............................	832.99

* Value taken from column titled "Immed." in Table 2. [A note to our readers from LexisNexis Matthew Bender: "Immed." means the column in Table 2 labeled "0" years between DOC and the start of the life pension.]

3) Determine commuted value of all life pension indemnity due after DOC

a)	PV of life pension as of exact age on DOC (from 2h).............	832.99
b)	Multiply by life pension rate..	× 33.92
c)	Commuted value of all life pension due after DOC	$28,255.02

(Continued on next page)

(Example D continued)

Summary of Example D:

- On date of commutation, $28,255.02, the commuted value of all life pension indemnity for the period after DOC, would be due and payable(3c). No further life pension indemnity would be due. If payment was made after DOC, interest would be due at 10% per annum. See Summary of Example A for interest calculation.

EXAMPLE E - COMMUTATION OF ALL LIFE PENSION INDEMNITY PRIOR TO COMMENCEMENT OF LIFE PENSION

In this example, the commutation of all life pension is done prior to commencement of life pension while the injured worker is still receiving PD. Calculation of exact age at DOC used in this example is illustrated in step 1 of Example†D.

Assumed facts for Example E:

Date of birth: 8/25/45
Date of injury: 4/10/96
PD commencement: 11/15/97
Date of commutation (DOC): 5/14/99

Total weeks of PD: 525.50 (based on 81% PD rating)
Life pension rate: $65.42
Gender: female
Exact age on DOC (from 1c of Example D): 53.718

1) Determine number of years between date of commutation (DOC) and commencement of life pension.

a)	Total weeks of PD	525.5
b)	Multiply by 7 days per week	× 7
c)	Total days of PD	3678.5
d)	Subtract #days from PD commence through DOC inclusive	− 546.0
e)	Number of days from DOC to LP commencement	3132.5
f)	Divide by 365.24 days/year	÷ 365.24
g)	Period in years from DOC to start of LP*	8.577

* This is the period for which the commencement of LP is "deferred". It determines which columns are used in Tables 2 (for males) or 3 (for females). In this example, you would use columns entitled "Year 8" and "Year 9" in Table 3.

(Continued on next page)

Tables & Schedules

(Example E continued)

2) Determine PV of life pension for exact age at date of commutation (53.718 years from 1c of Example D) and for exact deferral period (8.577 years from†2g above).

a)	PV for age 53 deferred 8 years (from Table 3)	603.31
b)	Subtract PV for age 54 deferred 8 years (from Table 3)	584.78
c)	Difference of 2a and 2b	18.53
d)	Multiply by fractional portion of age at DOC	× .718
e)	Interpolation adjustment for age	13.30
f)	PV for age 53 deferred 8 years (from Table 3)	603.31
g)	Subtract PV for age 53 deferred 9 years (from Table 3)	– 565.04
h)	Difference of 2f and 2g	38.27
i)	Multiply by fractional portion of deferral period (from 1g)	× .577
j)	Interpolation adjustment for deferral period	22.08
k)	PV for age 53 deferred 8 years (from 2a)	603.31
l)	Subtract sum of 2e and 2j	– 35.38
m)	PV of life pension (for age 53.718 deferred 8.577 years)	567.93

3) Determine commuted value of all LP as of DOC

a)	PV of life pension (from 2m)	567.93
b)	Multiply by LP rate	× 65.42
c)	Commuted value of all life pension	$37,153.98

Summary of Example E:

- On date of commutation (DOC), $37,153.98, the commuted value of all life pension indemnity (3c), would be due and payable. No life pension would be due thereafter. (This amount would not include the commuted value of any future PD indemnity. If payment were made after DOC, interest would be due at 10% per annum. See Summary of Example A for interest calculation. To commute future PD, use the method illustrated in Example A.)

(Continued on next page)

EXAMPLE F - COMMUTATION OF PORTION OF REMAINING LIFE PENSION (LP) AFTER LP COMMENCEMENT BY UNIFORM REDUCTION OF LIFE PENSION PAYMENTS

In this example, the commutation of a portion of life pension is done after LP commencement. Sufficient monies are commuted through uniform reduction of payments from remaining life pension to produce an amount payable on the date of commutation of $11,500.

Assumed facts for Example F:

Date of birth (DOB): 8/25/45
Date of injury: 4/10/87
Life pension commencement date: 3/21/98
Date of commutation (DOC): 5/14/99

Life pension rate: $33.92
Gender: female
Lump sum to be paid on DOC: $11,500

1) Determine exact age on date of commutation.

a)	Number of days from DOB through DOC*	19620
b)	Divide by number of days per year	÷ 365.24
c)	Exact age on date of commutation	53.718

* Note that in determining exact age, the actual date of birth is not counted as the first day of the period. That is, an individual does not become one day old until the day after the DOB. This differs from the determination of the number of days for a period of benefits when the commencement date is counted as the first day of the period. See, for example, step 1a of Example A.

2) Determine PV of life pension as of exact age on DOC

a)	PV for age in table below 1c* (age 53)	966.59
b)	PV for age in table above 1c (age 54)*	– 947.30
c)	Difference of 2a and 2b	19.29
d)	Multiply by fractional portion of age from 1c	× .718
e)	Interpolation adjustment for 2d	13.85
f)	PV for age in table below 1c* (from 2a above)	966.59
g)	Subtract 2e	– 13.85
h)	PV of life pension as of exact age on DOC	952.74

* Value taken from column titled "Immed." in Table 3.

(Example F continued on next page)

Tables & Schedules

(Example F continued)

3) Calculate amount of reduction in LP rate necessary to produce desired lump sum.

a)	Amount to be commuted	$11,500
b)	Divide by PV of LP (2h from above)	÷ 952.74
c)	Amount of weekly reduction in LP (after rounding)	$12.07

4) Calculate LP rate after commutation.

a)	LP rate before commutation	$33.92
b)	Subtract weekly reduction in LP (from 3c above)	– $12.07
c)	LP rate after commutation	$21.85

Summary of Example F:

- On date of commutation, $11,500 would be due and payable. If payment were made after DOC, interest would be due at 10% per annum. See Summary of Example A for interest calculation.
- The life pension, when due, would be paid at the reduced rate of $21.85.

[Editor's Note: Several persons have asked for a method to commute a given percentage of remaining life pension. The following is a method contributed by James T. Stewart using the "Assumed facts for Example F," supra, however, instead of commuting $11,500 from the LP, assume instead 12% has been ordered commuted from the life pension for, e.g., attorney's fees. The example is the same through step 2). This method may be employed for any ongoing life pension or 100% PD award **providing it does not involve a Cost of Living Adjustment (COLA) based upon an increase in the State Average Weekly Wage (SAWW) per Table 14 for injuries on or after 1/1/2003. These claims need to be commuted per the methods outlined at the DEU website under "DEU forms," and then either *Commutation templates and instructions* or *Commutation request*:**

http://www.dir.ca.gov/dwc/DEU.html

3) Calculate amount of reduction in LP rate assuming 12% is commuted.

a) PV of LP from 2) h), supra, ... 952.74
b) Multiply by $33.92 LP rate before commutation .... × $33.92
c) Present value of all remaining LP (~, supra D) ... $32,316.94
d) Multiply by 12%, reduced to a decimal, 0.12 .... × 0.12
e) Commuted amount to paid to attorney $3,878.03

4) Recalculation of LP rate after commutation of 12% $33.92
a) Multiply LP by 12% .... × 0.12
b) Amount each future LP payment is reduced $4.07
c) Future payments of LP will bc made at $33.92 - 4.07 = $29.85
[An alternate way would be to multiply $33.92 by 0.88 = $29.85]

Tables & Schedules

PART 2. Interest

TABLE 5

Interest: Ten Percent Annually (One Lump Sum Due)

Labor Code §5800; Code of Civil Procedure §685.010

Days	Interest	Days	Interest	Days	Interest
1	0.000274	61	0.016712	121	0.033151
2	0.000548	62	0.016986	122	0.033425
3	0.000822	63	0.017260	123	0.033699
4	0.001096	64	0.017534	124	0.033973
5	0.001370	65	0.017808	125	0.034247
6	0.001644	66	0.018082	126	0.034521
7	0.001918	67	0.018356	127	0.034795
8	0.002192	68	0.018630	128	0.035068
9	0.002466	69	0.018904	129	0.035342
10	0.002740	**70**	0.019178	**130**	0.035616
11	0.003014	71	0.019452	131	0.035890
12	0.003288	72	0.019726	132	0.036164
13	0.003562	73	0.020000	133	0.036438
14	0.003836	74	0.020274	134	0.036712
15	0.004110	75	0.020548	135	0.036986
16	0.004384	76	0.020822	136	0.037260
17	0.004658	77	0.021096	137	0.037534
18	0.004932	78	0.021370	138	0.037808
19	0.005205	79	0.021644	139	0.038082
20	0.005479	**80**	0.021918	**140**	0.038356
21	0.005753	81	0.022192	141	0.038630
22	0.006027	82	0.022466	142	0.038904
23	0.006301	83	0.022740	143	0.039178
24	0.006575	84	0.023014	144	0.039452
25	0.006849	85	0.023288	145	0.039726
26	0.007123	86	0.023562	146	0.040000
27	0.007397	87	0.023836	147	0.040274
28	0.007671	88	0.024110	148	0.040548
29	0.007945	89	0.024384	149	0.040822
30	0.008219	**90**	0.024658	**150**	0.041096
31	0.008493	91	0.024932	151	0.041370
32	0.008767	92	0.025205	152	0.041644
33	0.009041	93	0.025479	153	0.041918
34	0.009315	94	0.025753	154	0.042192
35	0.009589	95	0.026027	155	0.042466
36	0.009863	96	0.026301	156	0.042740
37	0.010137	97	0.026575	157	0.043014
38	0.010411	98	0.026849	158	0.043288
39	0.010685	99	0.027123	159	0.043562
40	0.010959	**100**	0.027397	**160**	0.043836
41	0.011233	101	0.027671	161	0.044110
42	0.011507	102	0.027945	162	0.044384
43	0.011781	103	0.028219	163	0.044658
44	0.012055	104	0.028493	164	0.044932
45	0.012329	105	0.028767	165	0.045205
46	0.012603	106	0.029041	166	0.045479
47	0.012877	107	0.029315	167	0.045753
48	0.013151	108	0.029589	168	0.046027
49	0.013425	109	0.029863	169	0.046301
50	0.013699	**110**	0.030137	**170**	0.046575
51	0.013973	111	0.030411	171	0.046849
52	0.014247	112	0.030685	172	0.047123
53	0.014521	113	0.030959	173	0.047397
54	0.014795	114	0.031233	174	0.047671
55	0.015068	115	0.031507	175	0.047945
56	0.015342	116	0.031781	176	0.048219
57	0.015616	117	0.032055	177	0.048493
58	0.015890	118	0.032329	178	0.048767
59	0.016164	119	0.032603	179	0.049041
60	0.016438	**120**	0.032877	**180**	0.049315

Days	Interest	Days	Interest	Days	Interest
181	0.049589	243	0.066575	305	0.083562
182	0.049863	244	0.066849	306	0.083836
183	0.050137	245	0.067123	307	0.084110
184	0.050411	246	0.067397	308	0.084384
185	0.050685	247	0.067671	309	0.084658
186	0.050959	248	0.067945	**310**	0.084932
187	0.051233	249	0.068219	311	0.085205
188	0.051507	**250**	0.068493	312	0.085479
189	0.051781	251	0.068767	313	0.085753
190	0.052055	252	0.069041	314	0.086027
191	0.052329	253	0.069315	315	0.086301
192	0.052603	254	0.069589	316	0.086575
193	0.052877	255	0.069863	317	0.086849
194	0.053151	256	0.070137	318	0.087123
195	0.053425	257	0.070411	319	0.087397
196	0.053699	258	0.070685	**320**	0.087671
197	0.053973	259	0.070959	321	0.087945
198	0.054247	**260**	0.071233	322	0.088219
199	0.054521	261	0.071507	323	0.088493
200	0.054795	262	0.071781	324	0.088767
201	0.055068	263	0.072055	325	0.089041
202	0.055342	264	0.072329	326	0.089315
203	0.055616	265	0.072603	327	0.089589
204	0.055890	266	0.072877	328	0.089863
205	0.056164	267	0.073151	329	0.090137
206	0.056438	268	0.073425	**330**	0.090411
207	0.056712	269	0.073699	331	0.090685
208	0.056986	**270**	0.073973	332	0.090959
209	0.057260	271	0.074247	333	0.091233
210	0.057534	272	0.074521	334	0.091507
211	0.057808	273	0.074795	335	0.091781
212	0.058082	274	0.075068	336	0.092055
213	0.058356	275	0.075342	337	0.092329
214	0.058630	276	0.075616	338	0.092603
215	0.058904	277	0.075890	339	0.092877
216	0.059178	278	0.076164	**340**	0.093151
217	0.059452	279	0.076438	341	0.093425
218	0.059726	**280**	0.076712	342	0.093699
219	0.060000	281	0.076986	343	0.093973
220	0.060274	282	0.077260	344	0.094247
221	0.060548	283	0.077534	345	0.094521
222	0.060822	284	0.077808	346	0.094795
223	0.061096	285	0.078082	347	0.095068
224	0.061370	286	0.078356	348	0.095342
225	0.061644	287	0.078630	349	0.095616
226	0.061918	288	0.078904	**350**	0.095890
227	0.062192	289	0.079178	351	0.096164
228	0.062466	**290**	0.079452	352	0.096438
229	0.062740	291	0.079726	353	0.096712
230	0.063014	292	0.080000	354	0.096986
231	0.063288	293	0.080274	355	0.097260
232	0.063562	294	0.080548	356	0.097534
233	0.063836	295	0.080822	357	0.097808
234	0.064110	296	0.081096	358	0.098082
235	0.064384	297	0.081370	359	0.098356
236	0.064658	298	0.081644	**360**	0.098630
237	0.064932	299	0.081918	361	0.098904
238	0.065205	**300**	0.082192	362	0.099178
239	0.065479	301	0.082466	363	0.099452
240	0.065753	302	0.082740	364	0.099726
241	0.066027	303	0.083014	365	0.100000
242	0.066301	304	0.083288		

Example using Table 5:

Note: Per "Summary of Example A" in Table 4, Commutation Instructions, the formula for calculating annual interest on a lump sum due, the function of Table 5, is

$$\frac{(\text{Lump Sum Due} \times \text{\# of Days of Interest}) \times 0.1}{365}$$

Assume an award issued 23 days ago and the amount accrued, or due as of the date of the award is 64 weeks @ $140.00/week = $8,960.00. That amount will be owed, plus interest on the total amount due for 23 days, plus interest due on $140.00/week for 3 weeks 2 days. (Table 6 calculates this last period.)

Interest due on Accrued PD using the formula above is:
[$8,960.00 × 23 days × 0.1] ÷ 365 = **$56.46** [same as second step below]

Per Table 5, 23 days = 0.006301 which × $8,960.00 = interest due: **$56.46**

Summary of Accrued PD plus interest to date Award is paid:

1. Accrued PD indemnity, 64 wks @ $140.00 = ... $8,960.00
2. Plus Interest due on Accrued, 0.006301 × $8,960.00 = + 56.46
3. Total, Accrued PD plus Interest on Accrued PD = . . . $9,016.46

SUMMARY: TABLES 5 AND 6

Payments due on PD award in example, issued 23 days prior to payment:

Steps:

1. Accrued PD, 64 weeks @ $140/week = ... $8,960.00
2. Interest due on Accrued PD (See above, this page) = ... 56.46
3. 23 days of PD due after Award, calculated as follows:
   23 days ÷ 7 days/wk = 3.28571 which × $140/wk = . . 460.00
4. Interest on 3 wks 2 days @ $140/wk (from Table 6) = . . + 1.70
5. **Total amount due on the 23rd day after the award = . $9,478.16**

The decimal value in the third step above (3.28571) which calculates 23 days (3 weeks 2 days) of PD owed after the award, may also be obtained by adding to "3 weeks" the value for "2 days" from Table 19, 0.28571, for the total, 3.28571. (I prefer to divide 23 days by 7 days/week to get the decimal.)

To calculate interest owed on a lump sum beyond the one year shown in Table 5, e.g., 1 year and 56 days, use the following method:

1 year = 365 days . 0.100000
Plus 56 days +0.015342
1 year and 56 days . 0.115342 (Multiply this times the lump sum due.)

Try the formula at top of this page: 365 + 56 = 421 days. It's much easier!

TABLE 6

Interest: Ten Percent Weekly (Successive Payments of $1/Week)

Labor Code §5800; Code of Civil Procedure §685.020

Weeks	Interest Due	Weeks	Interest Due
1	0.0019	27	0.7250
2	0.0057	28	0.7786
3	0.0116	29	0.8343
4	0.0191	30	0.8917
5	0.0287	31	0.9513
6	0.0403	32	1.0125
7	0.0537	33	1.0759
8	0.0690	34	1.1411
9	0.0863	35	1.2083
10	0.1054	36	1.2773
11	0.1266	37	1.3483
12	0.1496	38	1.4211
13	0.1746	39	1.4958
14	0.2014	40	1.5726
15	0.2301	41	1.6513
16	0.2609	42	1.7317
17	0.2934	43	1.8143
18	0.3280	44	1.8986
19	0.3644	45	1.9850
20	0.4027	46	2.0731
21	0.4430	47	2.1633
22	0.4851	48	2.2553
23	0.5293	49	2.3493
24	0.5753	50	2.4451
25	0.6233	51	2.5430
26	0.6731	52	2.6427

Days	Interest Due	Days	Interest Due
1	0.0002739	4	0.001096
2	0.0005479	5	0.001370
3	0.0008218	6	0.001644

Add Interest Due for whole weeks and days together. Multiply the result by the weekly comp rate to determine the total interest due, e.g., following the example in Table 5:

23 days equals 3 weeks plus 2 days: Interest from Table 6, above:

	3 weeks	=	0.0116
	+ 2 days	=	+ 0.0005479
(Used in Table 5, step 4.)	Interest	=	0.0121479 × $140.00/week = **$1.70**

The amount shown seems trivial, however when payments are made many weeks after an award, e.g., after an appeal, several hundred dollars may be involved.

For instance, assume 60 weeks of Successive Payments at $140 are due since the award issued. PD due, 60 wks × $140 = $8,400, but how much interest is owed? Calculate the first 52 weeks of Successive Payments using Table 6, above. Then add interest owing on that lump sum *for the remaining time* (8 weeks in this example) from Table 5. Then add interest on the final 8 weeks for successive weekly payments due per Table 6 as follows:

1. Per Table 6, 52 successive weeks = 2.6427 and × $140 = .. **$369.98**
2. At the end of 1 year, 52 wks × $140 = **$7,280** is due. Interest on this amount is due for 8 wks × 7 days/wk = 56 days, and per, Table 5, interest on 56 days = 0.015342 and × **$7,280** = ... 111.69
3. 8 wks of payments from Table 6 above is 0.0690 and × $140 = + 9.66

Interest Due on 60 Successive Payments of $140/week = .. $491.33

TABLE 7
Interest: Seven Percent Annually (One Lump Sum Due)

Labor Code §4622

Days	Interest	Days	Interest	Days	Interest
1	0.000192	61	0.011699	121	0.023205
2	0.000384	62	0.011890	122	0.023397
3	0.000575	63	0.012082	123	0.023589
4	0.000767	64	0.012274	124	0.023781
5	0.000959	65	0.012466	125	0.023973
6	0.001151	66	0.012658	126	0.024164
7	0.001342	67	0.012849	127	0.024356
8	0.001534	68	0.013041	128	0.024548
9	0.001726	69	0.013233	129	0.024740
10	0.001918	70	0.013425	130	0.024932
11	0.002110	71	0.013616	131	0.025123
12	0.002301	72	0.013808	132	0.025315
13	0.002493	73	0.014000	133	0.025507
14	0.002685	74	0.014192	134	0.025699
15	0.002877	75	0.014384	135	0.025890
16	0.003068	76	0.014575	136	0.026082
17	0.003260	77	0.014767	137	0.026274
18	0.003452	78	0.014959	138	0.026466
19	0.003644	79	0.015151	139	0.026658
20	0.003836	80	0.015342	140	0.026849
21	0.004027	81	0.015534	141	0.027041
22	0.004219	82	0.015726	142	0.027233
23	0.004411	83	0.015918	143	0.027425
24	0.004603	84	0.016110	144	0.027616
25	0.004795	85	0.016301	145	0.027808
26	0.004986	86	0.016493	146	0.028000
27	0.005178	87	0.016685	147	0.028192
28	0.005370	88	0.016877	148	0.028384
29	0.005562	89	0.017068	149	0.028575
30	0.005753	90	0.017260	150	0.028767
31	0.005945	91	0.017452	151	0.028959
32	0.006137	92	0.017644	152	0.029151
33	0.006329	93	0.017836	153	0.029342
34	0.006521	94	0.018027	154	0.029534
35	0.006712	95	0.018219	155	0.029726
36	0.006904	96	0.018411	156	0.029918
37	0.007096	97	0.018603	157	0.030110
38	0.007288	98	0.018795	158	0.030301
39	0.007479	99	0.018986	159	0.030493
40	0.007671	100	0.019178	160	0.030685
41	0.007863	101	0.019370	161	0.030877
42	0.008055	102	0.019562	162	0.031068
43	0.008247	103	0.019753	163	0.031260
44	0.008438	104	0.019945	164	0.031452
45	0.008630	105	0.020137	165	0.031644
46	0.008822	106	0.020329	166	0.031836
47	0.009014	107	0.020521	167	0.032027
48	0.009205	108	0.020712	168	0.032219
49	0.009397	109	0.020904	169	0.032411
50	0.009589	110	0.021096	170	0.032603
51	0.009781	111	0.021288	171	0.032795
52	0.009973	112	0.021479	172	0.032986
53	0.010164	113	0.021671	173	0.033178
54	0.010356	114	0.021863	174	0.033370
55	0.010548	115	0.022055	175	0.033562
56	0.010740	116	0.022247	176	0.033753
57	0.010932	117	0.022438	177	0.033945
58	0.011123	118	0.022630	178	0.034137
59	0.011315	119	0.022822	179	0.034329
60	0.011507	120	0.023014	180	0.034521

Days	Interest	Days	Interest	Days	Interest
181	0.034712	243	0.046603	305	0.058493
182	0.034904	244	0.046795	306	0.058685
183	0.035096	245	0.046986	307	0.058877
184	0.035288	246	0.047178	308	0.059068
185	0.035479	247	0.047370	309	0.059260
186	0.035671	248	0.047562	310	0.059452
187	0.035863	249	0.047753	311	0.059644
188	0.036055	250	0.047945	312	0.059836
189	0.036247	251	0.048137	313	0.060027
190	0.036438	252	0.048329	314	0.060219
191	0.036630	253	0.048521	315	0.060411
192	0.036822	254	0.048712	316	0.060603
193	0.037014	255	0.048904	317	0.060795
194	0.037205	256	0.049096	318	0.060986
195	0.037397	257	0.049288	319	0.061178
196	0.037589	258	0.049479	320	0.061370
197	0.037781	259	0.049671	321	0.061562
198	0.037973	260	0.049863	322	0.061753
199	0.038164	261	0.050055	323	0.061945
200	0.038356	262	0.050247	324	0.062137
201	0.038548	263	0.050438	325	0.062329
202	0.038740	264	0.050630	326	0.062521
203	0.038932	265	0.050822	327	0.062712
204	0.039123	266	0.051014	328	0.062904
205	0.039315	267	0.051205	329	0.063096
206	0.039507	268	0.051397	330	0.063288
207	0.039699	269	0.051589	331	0.063479
208	0.039890	270	0.051781	332	0.063671
209	0.040082	271	0.051973	333	0.063863
210	0.040274	272	0.052164	334	0.064055
211	0.040466	273	0.052356	335	0.064247
212	0.040658	274	0.052548	336	0.064438
213	0.040849	275	0.052740	337	0.064630
214	0.041041	276	0.052932	338	0.064822
215	0.041233	277	0.053123	339	0.065014
216	0.041425	278	0.053315	340	0.065205
217	0.041616	279	0.053507	341	0.065397
218	0.041808	280	0.053699	342	0.065589
219	0.042000	281	0.053890	343	0.065781
220	0.042192	282	0.054082	344	0.065973
221	0.042384	283	0.054274	345	0.066164
222	0.042575	284	0.054466	346	0.066356
223	0.042767	285	0.054658	347	0.066548
224	0.042959	286	0.054849	348	0.066740
225	0.043151	287	0.055041	349	0.066932
226	0.043342	288	0.055233	350	0.067123
227	0.043534	289	0.055425	351	0.067315
228	0.043726	290	0.055616	352	0.067507
229	0.043918	291	0.055808	353	0.067699
230	0.044110	292	0.056000	354	0.067890
231	0.044301	293	0.056192	355	0.068082
232	0.044493	294	0.056384	356	0.068274
233	0.044685	295	0.056575	357	0.068466
234	0.044877	296	0.056767	358	0.068658
235	0.045068	297	0.056959	359	0.068849
236	0.045260	298	0.057151	360	0.069041
237	0.045452	299	0.057342	361	0.069233
238	0.045644	300	0.057534	362	0.069425
239	0.045836	301	0.057726	363	0.069616
240	0.046027	302	0.057918	364	0.069808
241	0.046219	303	0.058110	365	0.070000
242	0.046411	304	0.058301		

PART 3. Legislation

TABLE 8
[Reserved]

PART 4. Calendar Information

TABLE 9
Number of Days Between Two Dates

Date	Jan	Feb	Mar	Apr	May	Jun	Jul	Aug	Sep	Oct	Nov	Dec	Date
1	1	32	60	91	121	152	182	213	244	274	305	335	**1**
2	2	33	61	92	122	153	183	214	245	275	306	336	**2**
3	3	34	62	93	123	154	184	215	246	276	307	337	**3**
4	4	35	63	94	124	155	185	216	247	277	308	338	**4**
5	5	36	64	95	125	156	186	217	248	278	309	339	**5**
6	6	37	65	96	126	157	187	218	249	279	310	340	**6**
7	7	38	66	97	127	158	188	219	250	280	311	341	**7**
8	8	39	67	98	128	159	189	220	251	281	312	342	**8**
9	9	40	68	99	129	160	190	221	252	282	313	343	**9**
10	10	41	69	100	130	161	191	222	253	283	314	344	**10**
11	11	42	70	101	131	162	192	223	254	284	315	345	**11**
12	12	43	71	102	132	163	193	224	255	285	316	346	**12**
13	13	44	72	103	133	164	194	225	256	286	317	347	**13**
14	14	45	73	104	134	165	195	226	257	287	318	348	**14**
15	15	46	74	105	135	166	196	227	258	288	319	349	**15**
16	16	47	75	106	136	167	197	228	259	289	320	350	**16**
17	17	48	76	107	137	168	198	229	260	290	321	351	**17**
18	18	49	77	108	138	169	199	230	261	291	322	352	**18**
19	19	50	78	109	139	170	200	231	262	292	323	353	**19**
20	20	51	79	110	140	171	201	232	263	293	324	354	**20**
21	21	52	80	111	141	172	202	233	264	294	325	355	**21**
22	22	53	81	112	142	173	203	234	265	295	326	356	**22**
23	23	54	82	113	143	174	204	235	266	296	327	357	**23**
24	24	55	83	114	144	175	205	236	267	297	328	358	**24**
25	25	56	84	115	145	176	206	237	268	298	329	359	**25**
26	26	57	85	116	146	177	207	238	269	299	330	360	**26**
27	27	58	86	117	147	178	208	239	270	300	331	361	**27**
28	28	59	87	118	148	179	209	240	271	301	332	362	**28**
29	29	*	88	119	149	180	210	241	272	302	333	363	**29**
30	30		89	120	150	181	211	242	273	303	334	364	**30**
31	31		90		151		212	243		304		365	**31**

* On leap years, February has 29 days and the year, 366 days. Add 1 to every number after February 29th. The following are leap years. To determine leap years other than as listed, divide date by 4:

1924	1944	1964	1984	2004	2024	2044	2064
1928	1948	1968	1988	2008	2028	2048	2068
1932	1952	1972	1992	2012	2032	2052	2072
1936	1956	1976	1996	2016	2036	2056	2076
1940	1960	1980	2000	2020	2040	2060	2080

Date	Jan	Feb	Mar	Apr	May	Jun	Jul	Aug	Sep	Oct	Nov	Dec	Date
1	366	397	425	456	486	517	547	578	609	639	670	700	**1**
2	367	398	426	457	487	518	548	579	610	640	671	701	**2**
3	368	399	427	458	488	519	549	580	611	641	672	702	**3**
4	369	400	428	459	489	520	550	581	612	642	673	703	**4**
5	370	401	429	460	490	521	551	582	613	643	674	704	**5**
6	371	402	430	461	491	522	552	583	614	644	675	705	**6**
7	372	403	431	462	492	523	553	584	615	645	676	706	**7**
8	373	404	432	463	493	524	554	585	616	646	677	707	**8**
9	374	405	433	464	494	525	555	586	617	647	678	708	**9**
10	375	406	434	465	495	526	556	587	618	648	679	709	**10**
11	376	407	435	466	496	527	557	588	619	649	680	710	**11**
12	377	408	436	467	497	528	558	589	620	650	681	711	**12**
13	378	409	437	468	498	529	559	590	621	651	682	712	**13**
14	379	410	438	469	499	530	560	591	622	652	683	713	**14**
15	380	411	439	470	500	531	561	592	623	653	684	714	**15**
16	381	412	440	471	501	532	562	593	624	654	685	715	**16**
17	382	413	441	472	502	533	563	594	625	655	686	716	**17**
18	383	414	442	473	503	534	564	595	626	656	687	717	**18**
19	384	415	443	474	504	535	565	596	627	657	688	718	**19**
20	385	416	444	475	505	536	566	597	628	658	689	719	**20**
21	386	417	445	476	506	537	567	598	629	659	690	720	**21**
22	387	418	446	477	507	538	568	599	630	660	691	721	**22**
23	388	419	447	478	508	539	569	600	631	661	692	722	**23**
24	389	420	448	479	509	540	570	601	632	662	693	723	**24**
25	390	421	449	480	510	541	571	602	633	663	694	724	**25**
26	391	422	450	481	511	542	572	603	634	664	695	725	**26**
27	392	423	451	482	512	543	573	604	635	665	696	726	**27**
28	393	424	452	483	513	544	574	605	636	666	697	727	**28**
29	394	*	453	484	514	545	575	606	637	667	698	728	**29**
30	395		454	485	515	546	576	607	638	668	699	729	**30**
31	396		455		516		577	608		669		730	**31**

Example: Subtract first or earliest date from last date

Last day disabled: Oct.22. 1996 (see below. 1)* 660 + 1 = ... 661

First day disabled: Feb. 8. 1995 .... – 39

Number of days between two dates. ***not inclusive*** (see below. 2 & 3) 622

Since we are subtracting dates. add one to answer to make inclusive. 622 +1 = . **623**

* 1996 was a leap year: See prior page for other dates.

Additional notes:

1. Whenever leap year is involved. add one extra day to any period that includes February 29th.
2. The number of days given "between" two dates in this table is ***not inclusive***. Thus. you will always need to add one day if you are subtracting dates. For example. from January 1 to January 3 is three days. but if you subtract the two numbers you need to add one to make the result inclusive.
3. If you add three days to January 1. you need to subtract one day to make the result inclusive.
4. The two pages above apply for up to two years. If more years are involved. add 365 days/year.

PART 5. The Schedules for Rating Permanent Disabilities

TABLE 10

[Reserved]

TABLE 11
Guidelines for Work Capacity and Excerpts From the Schedule for Rating Permanent Disabilities, 4/1/97 to 12/31/04

Page numbers refer to the *Schedule* (See Table 8 for exceptions)

These apply to pulmonary, heart disease, abdominal weakness and spinal disabilities. Guidelines g) and h) may apply to lower extremity disabilities. (*)

a) **Disability Precluding Very Heavy Lifting** **10%**

contemplates the individual has lost approximately one-quarter of his pre-injury capacity for lifting.

[A statement "inability to lift 50 pounds" is not meaningful. The total lifting effort, including weight, distance, endurance, frequency, body position and similar factors should be considered with reference to the particular individual.]

b) **Disability Precluding Very Heavy Work** **15%**

contemplates the individual has lost approximately one-quarter of his pre-injury capacity for performing such activities as bending, stooping, lifting, pushing, pulling and climbing or other activities involving comparable physical effort.

c) **Disability Precluding Heavy Lifting** **20%**

contemplates the individual has lost approximately one-half of his pre-injury capacity for lifting.

[see statement regarding lifting under a) above.]

d) **Disability Precluding Heavy Lifting, Repeated Bending and Stooping** **25%**

contemplates the individual has lost approximately half of his pre-injury capacity for lifting, bending and stooping.

e) **Disability Precluding Heavy Work** **30%**

contemplates the individual has lost approximately half of his pre-injury capacity for performing such activities as bending, stooping, lifting, pushing, pulling, and climbing or other activities involving comparable physical effort.

f) **Disability Resulting in Limitation to Light Work** **50%**

contemplates the individual can do work in a standing or walking position, with a minimum of demands for physical effort.

g) **Disability Resulting in Limitation to Semi-Sedentary Work** **60%**

contemplates the individual can do work approximately one-half the time in a sitting position, and approximately one-half the time in a standing or walking position, with a minimum of demands for physical effort whether standing, walking or sitting.

h) **Disability Resulting in Limitation to Sedentary Work** **70%**

contemplates the individual can do work predominantly in a sitting position at a bench, desk or table with a minimum of demands for physical effort and with some degree of walking and standing being permitted.

(*) This amendment applies to injuries occurring on or after 1/1/73 to 12/31/04 (See Table 8).
This amendment applies to injuries occurring on or after 1/1/70 to 12/31/04 (See Table 8).

LOWER EXTREMITY GUIDELINES FOR INJURIES 4/1/97 TO 12/31/04 [1,2] (SEE TABLE 8)

WORK CAPACITY AS INDEX	STANDARD RATING
Disability Precluding Squatting and/or Kneeling .... contemplates loss of approximately 90–100% of worker's pre-injury capacity for squatting and/or kneeling.	5%
Disability Precluding Climbing .... contemplates loss of approximately 90–100% of worker's pre-injury capacity for climbing.	10%
Disability Precluding Walking Over Uneven Ground .... contemplates loss of approximately 90–100% of worker's pre-injury capacity for walking over rough terrain.	10%
Disability Precluding Very Heavy Lifting .... contemplates loss of approximately 90–100% of worker's pre-injury capacity for lifting.	10%
Disability Precluding Climbing, Walking Over Uneven Ground, Squatting, Kneeling, Crouching, Crawling, and Pivoting, or other activities involving comparable physical effort.	20%
Disability Precluding Prolonged Weight-Bearing .... contemplates ability to do work approximately 75% of time in standing and walking position, and requires sitting approximately 25% of time.	20%
Disability Precluding Heavy Lifting .... contemplates loss of approximately 50% of worker's pre-injury capacity for lifting.	20%
Disability Precluding Heavy Lifting, and Precluding Climbing, Walking Over Uneven Ground, Squatting, Kneeling, Crouching, Crawling, and Pivoting, or other activities involving comparable physical effort	30%
Disability Precluding Heavy Lifting, Prolonged Weight-Bearing, and Precluding Climbing, Walking Over Uneven Ground, Squatting, Kneeling, Crouching, Crawling, and Pivoting, or other activities involving comparable physical effort.	40%
Disability Resulting in Limitation of Weight-bearing to Half Time .... contemplates ability to do work approximately 50% of time in standing and walking position, and requires sitting approximately 50% of time.	40%
Disability Resulting in Limitation to Semi-Sedentary Work .... contemplates ability to do work approximately 50% of the time in a sitting position, and approximately 50% the time in a standing or walking position, with a minimum of demands for physical effort whether standing, walking or sitting.	60%
Disability Resulting in Limitation to Sedentary Work .... contemplates ability to do work predominantly in a sitting position at a bench, desk or table with a minimum of demands for physical effort and with some degree of walking and standing being permitted.	70%

---

1. Need for orthopedic appliances may be considered in conjunction with other elements comprising the disability.
2. When warranted by facts and evidence, additional factors may be considered resulting in a change in the disability rating.

Tables & Schedules

SPINE AND TORSO GUIDELINES FOR INJURIES 4/1/97 TO 12/31/04 [1,2] (SEE TABLE 8)

WORK CAPACITY OR SUBJECTIVE FACTOR AS INDEX [3,4,5] — **STANDARD RATING**

{Editorial Comment: Disability factors in these guidelines essentially duplicate the **Guidelines for Work Capacity** quoted on the first page of Table 11, except for additional entries as noted below.}

Disability Resulting from Constant Slight Pain **10%**
contemplates an individual with pain which can be tolerated, but causes some handicap in performance of activity. {Previously noted on page 13-B of Schedule}

Disability Precluding Repetitive Motions of Neck or Back **15%**
contemplates the individual has lost approximately 50% of pre-injury capacity for flexing, extending, bending, and rotating neck or back.

Disability Resulting from Constant Slight to Moderate Pain **30%**
{Previously noted on page 13-B of Schedule}

Disability Precluding Substantial Work **40%**
contemplates the individual has lost approximately 75% of pre-injury capacity for performing such activities as bending, stooping, lifting, pushing, pulling, and climbing or other activities involving comparable physical effort.

Disability Resulting from Constant Moderate Pain **50%**
contemplates an individual with pain which can be tolerated, but causes marked handicap in performance of activity. {Previously noted on page 13-B of Schedule}

---

1. Either or both indexes of disability may be used to describe a particular condition. The final rating is to be based on the index yielding the higher rating.
2. When warranted by facts and evidence, additional factors may be considered resulting in a change in the disability rating.
3. Guidelines using work capacity as an index apply to neck, back, pelvis, heart, pulmonary and abdominal disabilities.
4. Guidelines using subjective factors as index apply to neck, back, pelvis and abdominal disabilities. Subjective disability should be identified as prescribed in 8 CCR § 9727.
5. Objective factors of disability may be considered in conjunction with spine or torso pain.

Comparison of Disability Numbers for 4/1/97 vs. Prior Schedule[1]

Note: See Table 8 for possible application of Post-SB 899 PD Schedule

4/1/97 Schedule (D/A 4/1/97-12/31/04)		**Pre-4/1/97 Schedule** (D/A before 4/1/97)	
1.1	Paralysis	1.1	Paralysis
1.3	Epilepsy	1.3	Epilepsy
1.4	Psychiatric	1.4	Neurosis: Psychiatric Disability
1.5	Post-traumatic Head Synd.	1.5	Post-traumatic Head Syndrome
1.6	Vertigo	1.6	Vertigo
1.7	Headaches	1.7	Headaches
1.8	Cognitive Disability	1.8	Mental Deterioration
2.1	Sight-Cosmetic	2.141	Loss of Sight w. Marked Blemish
2.2 - 2.6	Vision	2.1- 2.8	Impairment of Visual Acuity
2.7	Lacrimation	2.61	Chronic Lacrimation (Tears)
3.1	Hearing Loss	3.1	Loss of Hearing
4.1	Cosmetic	4.1	Cosmetic Disfigurement
4.3 - 4.4	Skull	4.3 - 4.4	Skull Apertures
4.5	Jaw	4.5	Tooth, Mouth, & Jaw Injuries
4.7	Nose	4.7	Nose Injuries Affecting Function
5.2	Speech	5.2	Disabilities Affecting Speech
5.31	Smell	5.31	Loss of Sense of Smell
5.32	Taste	5.32	Loss of Sense of Taste
5.33	Smell, Taste	5.33	Loss of Sense of Taste & Smell
6.1	Skin - Preclude Outside Work		(Unscheduled)[2]
6.2	Skin - Preclude Wet Work		(Unscheduled)
7.1	Arm Amputation	7.1	Loss of Arm
7.3	Shoulder	7.3	Impairment, Function, Shoulder
7.5	Elbow	7.52	Impair, Elbow 70°- 100° Flexion
7.6	Forearm	7.54	Loss of Rotation of Forearm
7.7	Wrist	7.7	Impairment of Function, Wrist

Finger Amputations: T = Thumb; I = Index; M = Middle; R = Ring; & L = Little

8.11	Thumb Amputation	8.1	Thumb
8.12	Index Amputation	8.2	Index Finger
8.13	Middle Amputation	8.3	Middle Finger
8.14	Ring Amputation	8.4	Ring Finger
8.15	Little Amputation	8.5	Little Finger
8.2	Thumb + Index	9.1	Thumb & any one finger
	(Combine Disabilities)[3]	9.2	Index & any one finger
	(Combine Disabilities)	9.3	Middle & Ring or Little Finger
	(Combine Disabilities)	9.4	Ring and Little Fingers
8.3	T+I+M Amp	10.1	Thumb, Index, and Middle
	(Combine Disabilities)	10.2	Index, Middle, & Ring Fingers
	(Combine Disabilities)	10.3	Middle, Ring and Little Fingers
	(Combine Disabilities)	11.1	Thumb, Index, Middle & Ring
8.4	I+M+R+L Amp	11.2	Index, Middle, Ring & Little
8.5	All Fingers Amputation	12.1	Thumb and All Fingers

4/1/97 Schedule (D/A 4/1/97-12/31/04) **Pre-4/1/97 Schedule** (D/A < 4/1/97), contd.

Note: See Table 8 for possible application of Post-SB 899 PD Schedule

Finger Immobility: T = Thumb; I = Index; M = Middle; R = Ring; & L = Little

4/1/97 Schedule		Pre-4/1/97 Schedule	
9.11	Thumb Immobility	13.1	Thumb
9.12	Index Immobility	13.2	Index Finger
9.13	Middle Immobility	13.3	Middle Finger
9.14	Ring Immobility	13.4	Ring Finger
9.15	Little Immobility	13.5	Little Finger
9.2	T+I Immobility	14.1	Thumb & Index Finger
9.3	T+I+M Immobility	15.1	Thumb, Index & Middle
9.4	I+M+R+L Immobility	16.2	Index, Middle, Ring & Little
9.5	Immobility Thumb/Fingers	17.1	Thumb & All Fingers
10.5	Grip	16.8	Loss of Grasping Power
11.1	Pulmonary	6.1	Chronic . . . Pulmonary Tissues
11.3	Heart	6.3	Heart Disease
11.5	Rib Cage	6.5	Injuries to the Rib Cage
12.1	Spine	18.1	Neck, Spine or Pelvis
12.3	Spine - Paralysis	18.3	Spinal Cord . . . Paralysis
13.1	Abdomen - Hernia	19.1	Inoperable Hernia
13.2	Abdomen Organs	19.3	Loss/Impair Abdominal Organs
14.1	Leg Amputation	20.1	Amputations, Legs (or foot)
14.2	Toe Amputation	20.7	Amputations, toes
14.3	Leg Short	20.811	Shortening Lower Extremities
14.4	Hip	21.1-21.2	Motion, Hip/Other Dis., Hip
14.5	Knee, Thigh	21.3-21.4	Motion, Knee/Other Dis., Knee
14.531	Atrophy of Thigh Muscles	21.441	Thigh Atrophy
14.6	Ankle, Calf	21.5-21.6	Motion, Ankle/Other Dis., Ankle
14.631	Atrophy of Calf Muscles	21.641	Calf Atrophy
14.7	Toe Immobility	21.7	Impairment of Function, Toes
14.8	Post-thrombosis	21.8	Post Thrombophlebitic Disability

---

1. Entries for disability numbers such as "1.1" assume "1.1–" referring to the entire category beginning 1.1 et seq. An attempt has been made to keep the original wording of the disabilities, but some definitions have been shortened for the sake of brevity.

2. *Unscheduled* ratings are those which by definition are not contained within the Schedule. They rely on the judgment, experience and expertise of the disability evaluator.

3. *Combine Disabilities* refers to the calculation of a disability by combining data one has, such as the loss of an index finger with the loss of another finger, to reach a disability which represents the loss of the two fingers, even though the schedule does not specifically list the loss of those two fingers. Consult a rating manual for instructions. To combine disabilities generally, see the *4/1/97 Schedule*, pages 7-12 to 7-14.

TABLE 11A
2005 Permanent Disability Revised Schedule (2005 PDRS)

ARNOLD SCHWARZENEGGER
GOVERNOR OF CALIFORNIA

SCHEDULE FOR RATING PERMANENT DISABILITIES

UNDER THE PROVISIONS OF THE

LABOR CODE OF THE STATE OF CALIFORNIA

Compiled and Published by
STATE OF CALIFORNIA

LABOR AND WORKFORCE DEVELOPMENT AGENCY
DEPARTMENT OF INDUSTRIAL RELATIONS
DIVISION OF WORKERS' COMPENSATION

ANDREA LYNN HOCH
Administrative Director

January 2005

AUTHORITY

Labor Code section 4660, amended effective April 19, 2004, provides:

4660(a) In determining the percentages of permanent disability, account shall be taken of the nature of the physical injury or disfigurement, the occupation of the injured employee, and his or her age at the time of the injury, consideration being given to an employee's diminished future earning capacity.

(b)(1) For purposes of this section, the "nature of the physical injury or disfigurement" shall incorporate the descriptions and measurements of physical impairments and the corresponding percentages of impairments published in the American Medical Association (AMA) Guides to the Evaluation of Permanent Impairment (5th Edition).

(2) For purposes of this section, an employee's diminished future earning capacity shall be a numeric formula based on empirical data and findings that aggregate the average percentage of long-term loss of income resulting from each type of injury for similarly situated employees. The administrative director shall formulate the adjusted rating schedule based on empirical data and findings from the Evaluation of California's Permanent Disability Rating Schedule, Interim Report (December 2003), prepared by the RAND Institute for Civil Justice, and upon data from additional empirical studies.

(c) The Administrative Director shall amend the schedule for the determination of the percentage of permanent disability in accordance with this section at least once every five years. This schedule shall be available for public inspection and, without formal introduction in evidence, shall be prima facie evidence of the percentage of permanent disability to be attributed to each injury covered by the schedule.

(d) The schedule shall promote consistency, uniformity, and objectivity. The schedule and any amendment thereto or revision thereof shall apply prospectively and shall apply to and govern only those permanent disabilities that result from compensable injuries received or occurring on and after the effective date of the adoption of the schedule, amendment or revision, as the fact may be. For compensable claims arising before January 1, 2005, the schedule as revised pursuant to changes made in legislation enacted during the 2003-04 Regular and Extraordinary Sessions shall apply to the determination of permanent disabilities when there has been either no comprehensive medical-legal report or no report by a treating physician indicating the existence of permanent disability, or when the employer is not required to provide the notice required by Section 4061 to the injured worker.

(e) On or before January 1, 2005, the administrative director shall adopt regulations to implement the changes made to this section by the act that added this subdivision.

Pursuant to this authority, the Administrative Director has adopted this revised Schedule for Rating Permanent Disabilities.

TABLE OF CONTENTS

Section		Page
1	Introduction and Instructions	1-1
2	Impairment Number/Earning Capacity Adjustment	2-1
3	Occupations and Group Numbers	3-1
4	Occupational Variants	4-1
5	Occupational Adjustment	5-1
6	Age Adjustment	6-1
7	Examples	7-1
8	Combined Values Chart	8-1

SECTION 1 - INTRODUCTION AND INSTRUCTIONS

I. Introduction 1-2

II. Rating Procedures

A. Use of the AMA Guides 1-3

B. Calculation of Rating

1. Impairment Number 1-4
2. Impairment Standard 1-4
3. Adjustment for Diminished Future Earning Capacity 1-5
4. Occupational Grouping 1-8
5. Occupational Variant 1-9
6. Occupational Adjustment 1-9
7. Age Adjustment 1-9
8. Final Permanent Disability Rating 1-9
9. Rating Formula 1-9

C. Additional Rating Procedures

1. Formula for Combining Impairments and Disabilities 1-10
2. Adjusting AMA Impairments and Combining Ratings 1-11
3. Rating Impairment Based on Pain 1-12
4. Rating Psychiatric Impairment 1-12

SECTION 1 – INTRODUCTION AND INSTRUCTIONS

I. INTRODUCTION

This Schedule for Rating Permanent Disabilities (hereinafter referred to as the "Schedule") has been adopted by the Administrative Director pursuant to Labor Code section 4660. In accordance with this section, the schedule shall be amended at least once every five years.

The extent of permanent disability that results from an industrial injury can be assessed once an employee's condition becomes permanent and stationary. Permanent and stationary is defined as the point in time when the employee has reached maximal medical improvement (MMI), meaning his or her condition is well stabilized and unlikely to change substantially in the next year with or without medical treatment. (AMA Guides, p. 2.)

The calculation of a permanent disability rating is initially based on a evaluating physician's impairment rating, in accordance with the medical evaluation protocols and rating procedures set forth in the American Medical Association (AMA) *Guides to the Evaluation of Permanent Impairment, 5th Edition* (hereinafter referred to as the "AMA Guides"), which is hereby incorporated by reference.

Initial impairment ratings are consolidated by body part (see *Adjusting AMA Impairments and Combining Ratings* on page 1-11) and converted to a whole person impairment rating (hereinafter referred to as "impairment standard"). The impairment standard is then adjusted to account for diminished future earning capacity, occupation and age at the time of injury to obtain a final permanent disability rating.

A permanent disability rating can range from 0% to 100%. Zero percent signifies no reduction of earning capacity, while 100% represents permanent total disability. A rating between 0% and 100% represents permanent partial disability. Permanent total disability represents a level of disability at which an employee has sustained a total loss of earning capacity. Some impairments are conclusively presumed to be totally disabling. (Lab. Code, §4662.)

Each rating corresponds to a fixed number of weeks of compensation. Compensation is paid based on the number of weeks and the weekly compensation rate, in accordance with Labor Code section 4658.

II RATING PROCEDURES

A. Use of the AMA Guides

The AMA Guides are used by evaluating physicians to determine the extent of an individual's impairment. The AMA Guides use different scales to describe impairment for different parts and regions of the body. For example, finger impairment is measured using a finger scale that can range from 0% to 100%. Other commonly used scales in the AMA Guides are the hand, upper extremity, foot, lower extremity and whole person scales.

The scales that correspond to different body regions are equivalent to a percentage of the whole person scale; therefore these scales are converted to the whole person scale to determine the appropriate impairment rating. For example, an upper extremity impairment in the range of 0% to 100% is equivalent to a whole person impairment in the range of 0% to 60%. The upper extremity impairment is converted to a whole person impairment by multiplying by .6.

When combining two or more ratings to create a composite rating, the ratings must be expressed in the same scale. (See *Formula for combining impairments and disabilities* on page 1-10.)

The whole person impairment scale is referred to as WPI (whole person impairment). The upper and lower extremity scales are referred to as UE (upper extremity) and LE (lower extremity), respectively.

A final permanent disability rating is obtained only after the impairment rating obtained from an evaluating physician is adjusted for diminished future earning capacity, occupation and age at the time of injury.

B. Calculation of Rating

This schedule utilizes an impairment number and an impairment standard. The impairment standard is then modified to reflect diminished future earning capacity, the occupation and the age at the time of injury.

1. *Impairment Number*

The impairment number identifies the body part, organ system and/or nature of the injury and takes the form of "xx.xx.xx.xx". The first two digits correspond to the chapter number in the AMA Guides which address the body part/organ system. Subsequent pairs of digits further refine the identification of the impairment.

For example, soft tissue lesion of the neck rated under the range of motion (ROM) method would be represented as follows:

15.	01.	02.	02
Spine	Neck	ROM method	Soft tissue lesion

Under Section 2 of the Permanent Disability Rating Schedule, an appropriate impairment number can be found for most impairments.

2. *Impairment Standard*

After identification of the appropriate disability number(s), the next step is to calculate all relevant impairment standard(s) for the impairments being evaluated. An impairment standard is a whole person impairment rating under the AMA Guides, provided by the evaluating physician.

If an impairment based on an objective medical condition is not addressed by the AMA Guides, physicians should use clinical judgment, comparing measurable impairment resulting from the unlisted objective medical condition to measurable impairment resulting from similar objective medical conditions with similar impairment of function in performing activities of daily living. (AMA Guides, p. 11.)

A single injury can result in multiple impairments of several parts of the body. For example, an injury to the arm could result in limited elbow range of motion and shoulder instability. Multiple impairments must be combined in a prescribed manner to produce a final overall rating. (See, *Adjusting AMA Impairments and Combining Ratings* on page 1-11.)

It is not always appropriate to combine all impairment standards resulting from a single injury, since two or more impairments may have a duplicative effect on the function of the injured body part. The AMA Guides provide some direction on what impairments can be used in combination. Lacking such guidance, it is necessary for the evaluating physician to exercise his or her judgment in avoiding duplication.

The impairment standard is assumed to represent the degree of impairment for a theoretical average worker, i.e., a worker with average occupational demands on all parts of the body and at the average age of 39.

3. *Adjustment for Diminished Future Earning Capacity*

The adjustment for diminished future earning capacity (FEC) is applied to the impairment standard in accordance with procedures outlined in section 2 of the Schedule. An impairment must be expressed using the whole person impairment scale before applying the FEC adjustment.

The methodology and FEC Adjustment table is premised on a numerical formula based on empirical data and findings that aggregate the average percentage of long-term loss of income resulting from each type of injury for similarly situated employees. The empirical data was obtained from the interim report, "Evaluation of California's Permanent Disability Rating Schedule (December 2003), prepared by the RAND Institute for Justice. The result is that the injury categories are placed into different ranges (based on the ratio of standard ratings to proportional wage losses). Each of these ranges will generate a FEC adjustment between 10% and 40% for each injury category.

(a) Summary of Methodology:

1. RAND data was used to establish the ratio of average California standard ratings to proportional wage losses for each of 22 injury categories. (*Data for Adjusting Disability Ratings to Reflect Diminished Future Earnings and Capacity in Compliance with SB 899*, December 2004, RAND Institute for Civil Justice, Seabury, Reville, Neuhauser.) These ratios are listed in Table B.

2. The range of the ratios for all injury categories is .45 to 1.81. This numeric range was divided into eight evenly spaced ranges. (See the Range of Ratios columns in Table A.) Each injury category will fall within one of these eight ranges, based on its rating/wage loss ratio.

3. A series of FEC adjustment factors were established to correspond to the eight ranges described above. (See column 4 of Table A.) The smallest adjustment factor is 1.1000 which will result in a 10% increase when applied to the AMA whole person impairment rating. The largest is 1.4000 which will result in a 40% increase. The six intermediate adjustment factors are determined by dividing the difference between 1.1 and 1.4 into seven equal amounts.

4. The formula for calculating the maximum and minimum adjustment factors is **([1.81/a] x .1) +1** where a equals the minimum or maximum rating/loss ratio from Table B. AMA whole person impairment ratings for injury categories that correspond to a greater relative loss of earning capacity will receive a higher FEC adjustment. For example, a psychiatric impairment receives a higher FEC adjustment because RAND data shows that a relatively high wage loss corresponds to the average psychiatric standard permanent disability rating. A hand impairment would receive a lower FEC adjustment because RAND data shows a relatively low wage loss relative to the average psychiatric standard permanent disability rating.

The FEC rank and adjustment factors that correspond to relative earnings for the eight evenly-divided ranges are listed in Table A. The ratio of earnings to losses and the corresponding rank for each injury category are listed in Table B. To adjust an impairment standard for earning capacity, multiply it by the appropriate adjustment factor from Table A and round to the nearest whole number percentage. Alternatively, a table is provided at the end of Section 2 of the Schedule which provides the earning capacity adjustment for all impairment standards and FEC ranks.

Table A

Range of Ratios			
Low	**High**	**FEC Rank**	**Adjustment Factor**
1.647	1.810	One	1.100000
1.476	1.646	Two	1.142857
1.305	1.475	Three	1.185714
1.134	1.304	Four	1.228571
0.963	1.133	Five	1.271429
0.792	0.962	Six	1.314286
0.621	0.791	Seven	1.357143
0.450	0.620	Eight	1.400000

Table B

Part of the Body	Ratio of Rating over Losses	FEC Rank
Hand/fingers	1.810	One
Vision	1.810	One
Knee	1.570	Two
Other	1.530	Two
Ankle	1.520	Two
Elbow	1.510	Two
Loss of grasping power	1.280	Four
Wrist	1.210	Four
Toe(s)	1.110	Five
Spine Thoracic	1.100	Five
General lower extremity	1.100	Five
Spine Lumbar	1.080	Five
Spine Cervical	1.060	Five
Hip	1.030	Five
General upper extremity	1.000	Five
Heart disease	0.970	Five
General Abdominal	0.950	Six
PT head syndrome	0.930	Six
Lung disease	0.790	Seven
Shoulder	0.740	Seven
Hearing	0.610	Eight
Psychiatric	0.450	Eight

The FEC Rank for the "Other" category is based on average ratings and proportional earning losses for the following impairments:

Impaired rib cage
Cosmetic disfigurement
General chest impairment
Facial disfigurement or impairment
Impaired mouth or jaw
Speech impairment
Impaired nose
Impaired nervous system
Vertigo
Impaired smell
Paralysis
Mental Deterioration
Epilepsy
Skull aperture

4. *Occupational Grouping*

After the rating is adjusted for diminished future earning capacity, it is then modified to take into account the requirements of the specific occupation that the employee was engaged in when injured.

The Schedule divides the labor market into 45 numbered occupational groups. Each group is assigned a three-digit code called an occupational group number. The first digit of the code refers to the arduousness of the duties, ranking jobs from 1 to 5 in ascending order of physical arduousness; the second digit separates occupations into broad categories sharing common characteristics; the third digit differentiates between occupations within these groups. (See Occupational Group Chart in Section 3B of the Schedule for a breakdown of all occupational groups.)

To identify the appropriate occupational group number, look up the occupation in the list contained in Section 3A of the Schedule. Each job title is listed along with its corresponding group number. The appropriate occupation can generally be found listed under a scheduled or alternative job title. If the occupation cannot be found, an appropriate occupational group is determined by analogy to a listed occupation(s) based on a comparison of duties. (The table Occupational Group Characteristics in Section 3C of the Schedule provides a description of each occupational group to facilitate the determination of a group number.)

5. *Occupational Variant*

Section 4 of the Schedule contains tables that cross-reference impairment numbers and occupational group numbers to produce an "occupational variant," which is expressed as a letter. These tables are designed so that variant "F" represents average demands on the injured body part for the particular impairment being rated, with letters "E", "D" and "C" representing progressively lesser demands, and letters "G" through "J" reflecting progressively higher demands.

6. *Occupational Adjustment*

After the rating has been adjusted for diminished future earning capacity, the rating is adjusted next for occupation by reference to tables found in Section 5 of the Schedule. To use this section, find the earning capacity-adjusted rating in the column entitled "Rating" and then read across the table to the column headed with the appropriate occupational variant. The intersection of the row and column contains the occupation-adjusted rating.

7. *Age Adjustment*

Finally, the rating is adjusted to account for the worker's age on the date of injury. Section 6 of the Schedule contains tables for determining the age adjustment. To use this section, find the occupation-adjusted rating in the column entitled "Rating" and read across the table to the column with the injured worker's age on the date of injury.

8. *Final Permanent Disability Rating*

The number identified on the age adjustment table represents the final overall permanent disability rating percentage for a single impairment. (See Subdivisions C.1. and C.2. on pages 10 and 11 to combine multiple impairments and disabilities.)

9. *Rating Formula*

The final rating is generally expressed as a rating formula, as in the following example:

15.01.02.02 – 8 - [5]10 - 470H – 13 – 11%

Each component is described below:

15.01.02.02 – Impairment number for cervical spine, soft tissue lesion

8% – Impairment standard

10% – Rating after adjustment for earning capacity based on FEC rank 5

470 – Occupational group number for Furniture assembler, heavy

H – Occupational variant

13% – Rating after occupational adjustment

11% – Rating after adjustment for age of 30

C. Additional Rating Procedures

1. Formula for Combining Impairments and Disabilities

Impairments and disabilities are generally combined using the following formula where "a" and "b" are the decimal equivalents of the impairment or disability percentages:

a + b(1-a)

For example, the result of combining 15% and 25% would be calculated as follows:

.25 + .15(1-.25)

.25 + .15(.75)

.25 + .1125 = .3625 = 36%

Impairment ratings must be expressed in the same scale to be combined. For example, it would be inappropriate to combine 15% UE with 20% WPI. Likewise, one cannot combine an impairment rating with a disability rating.

Except as specified in the section below, when combining three or more ratings on the same scale into a single rating, combine the two largest ratings first, rounding the result to the nearest whole percent. Then combine that result with the next larger rating, and so on, until all ratings are combined. Each successive calculation result must be rounded before performing the next.

2. Adjusting AMA Impairments and Combining Ratings

As used here, the term "adjusting" refers to adjusting an AMA impairment rating for diminished future earning capacity, occupation and age.

Except as specified below, all impairments are converted to the whole person scale, adjusted, and then combined to determine a final overall disability rating.

Multiple impairments involving the hand or foot are combined using standard AMA Guides protocols. The resulting impairment is converted to whole person impairment and adjusted before being combined with other impairments of the same extremity.

Multiple impairments such as those involving a single part of an extremity, e.g. two impairments involving a shoulder such as shoulder instability and limited range of motion, are combined at the upper extremity level, then converted to whole person impairment and adjusted before being combined with other parts of the same extremity. Note that some impairments of the same body part may not be combined because of duplication.

Impairments with disability numbers in the 16.01 and 17.01 series are converted to whole person impairment and adjusted before being combined with any other impairment of the same extremity.

Impairments of an individual extremity are adjusted and combined at the whole person level with other impairments of the same extremity before being combined with impairments of other body parts. For example, an impairment of the left knee and ankle would be combined before further combination with an impairment of the opposing leg or the back.

The composite rating for an extremity (after adjustments) may not exceed the amputation value of the extremity adjusted for earning capacity, occupation and age. The occupational variant used to rate an entire extremity shall be the highest variant of the involved individual impairments.

3. *Rating Impairment Based on Pain*

Pursuant to Chapter 18 of the AMA Guides, a whole person impairment rating based on the body or organ rating system of the AMA Guides (Chapters 3 through 17) may be increased by 0% up to 3% WPI if the burden of the worker's condition has been increased by pain-related impairment in excess of the pain component already incorporated in the WPI rating in Chapters 3-17. (AMA Guides, p. 573.)

A physician may perform a formal pain-related impairment assessment if deemed necessary to justify the increase of an impairment rating based on the body or organ rating system. (See Section 18.3f of the AMA Guides starting on page 575.)

The maximum allowance for pain resulting from a single injury is 3% WPI regardless of the number of impairments resulting from that injury.

The addition of up to 3% for pain is to be made at the whole person level. For example, if an elbow impairment were to be increased by 3% for pain, the rating for the elbow would first be converted to the whole person scale, and then increased. The resultant rating would then be adjusted for diminished future earning capacity, occupation and age.

In the case of multiple impairments, the evaluating physician shall, when medically justifiable, attribute the pain in whole number increments to the appropriate impairments. The additional percentage added for pain will be applied to the respective impairments as described in the preceding paragraph.

4. *Rating Psychiatric Impairment*

Psychiatric impairment shall be evaluated by the physician using the Global Assessment of Function (GAF) scale shown below. The resultant GAF score shall then be converted to a whole person impairment rating using the GAF conversion table below.

(a) Instructions for Determining a GAF score:

STEP 1: Starting at the top level of the GAF scale, evaluate each range by asking "is either the individual's symptom severity OR level of functioning worse than what is indicated in the range description?"

STEP 2: Keep moving down the scale until the range that best matches the individual's symptom severity OR the level of functioning is reached, whichever is worse.

STEP 3: Look at the next lower range as a double-check against having stopped prematurely. This range should be too severe on both symptom severity and level of functioning. If it is, the appropriate range has been reached (continue with step 4). If not, go back to step 2 and continue moving down the scale.

STEP 4: To determine the specific GAF rating within the selected 10 point range, consider whether the individual is functioning at the higher or lower end of the 10 point range. For example, consider an individual who hears voices that do not influence his behavior (e.g., someone with long-standing Schizophrenia who accepts his hallucinations as part of his illness). If the voices occur relatively infrequently (once a week or less) a rating of 39 or 40 might be most appropriate. In contrast, if the individual hears voices almost continuously, a rating of 31 or 32 would be more appropriate.

(b) Global Assessment of Functioning (GAF) Scale

Consider psychological, social, and occupational functioning on a hypothetical continuum of mental health-illness. Do not include impairment in functioning due to physical (or environmental) limitations.

Code	
91 – 100	Superior functioning in a wide range of activities, life's problems never seem to get out of hand, is sought out by others because of his or her many positive qualities. No symptoms.
81 – 90	Absent or minimal symptoms (e.g., mild anxiety before an exam), good functioning in all areas, interested and involved in a wide range of activities, socially effective, generally satisfied with life, no more than everyday problems or concerns (e.g., an occasional argument with family members).
71 – 80	If symptoms are present, they are transient and expectable reactions to psychosocial stressors (e.g., difficulty concentrating after family argument); no more than slight impairment in social, occupational, or school functioning (e.g., temporarily falling behind in schoolwork).
61 – 70	Some mild symptoms (e.g., depressed mood and mild insomnia) OR some difficulty in social, occupational, or school functioning (e.g., occasional truancy, or theft within the household), but generally functioning pretty well, has some meaningful interpersonal relationships.
51 – 60	Moderate symptoms (e.g., flat affect and circumstantial speech, occasional panic attacks) OR moderate difficulty in social, occupational, or school functioning (e.g. few friends, conflicts with peers or co-workers).
41 – 50	Serious symptoms (e.g., suicidal ideation, severe obsessional rituals, frequent shoplifting) OR any serious impairment in social, occupational, or school functioning (e.g., no friends, unable to keep a job).

31 – 40 Some impairment in reality testing or communication (e.g., speech is at times illogical, obscure, or irrelevant) OR major impairment in several areas, such as work or school, family relations, judgment thinking, or mood (e.g., depressed man avoids friends, neglects family, and is unable to work; child frequently beats up younger children, is defiant at home and is failing at school).

21 – 30 Behavior is considerably influenced by delusions or hallucinations OR serious impairment in communication or judgment (e.g., sometimes incoherent, acts grossly inappropriately, suicidal preoccupation) OR inability to function in almost all areas (e.g., stays in bed all day; no job, home or friends).

11 – 20 Some danger of hurting self or others (e.g., suicide attempts without clear expectation of death; frequently violent; manic excitement) OR occasionally fails to maintain minimal personal hygiene (e.g., smears feces) OR gross impairment in communication (e.g., largely incoherent or mute).

1 – 10 Persistent danger of severely hurting self or others (e.g., recurrent violence) OR persistent inability to maintain minimal personal hygiene OR serious suicidal act with clear expectation of death.

0 Inadequate information.

(c) Converting the GAF Score to a Whole Person Impairment

Locate the GAF score in the table below and read across to determine the corresponding whole person impairment (WPI) rating.

GAF	WPI	GAF	WPI	GAF	WPI	GAF	WPI
1	90	34	63	67	5	100	0
2	89	35	61	68	3		
3	89	36	59	69	2		
4	88	37	57	70	0		
5	87	38	55	71	0		
6	87	39	53	72	0		
7	86	40	51	73	0		
8	85	41	48	74	0		
9	84	42	46	75	0		
10	84	43	44	76	0		
11	83	44	42	77	0		
12	82	45	40	78	0		
13	82	46	38	79	0		
14	81	47	36	80	0		
15	80	48	34	81	0		
16	80	49	32	82	0		
17	79	50	30	83	0		
18	78	51	29	84	0		
19	78	52	27	85	0		
20	77	53	26	86	0		
21	76	54	24	87	0		
22	76	55	23	88	0		
23	75	56	21	89	0		
24	74	57	20	90	0		
25	73	58	18	91	0		
26	73	59	17	92	0		
27	72	60	15	93	0		
28	71	61	14	94	0		
29	71	62	12	95	0		
30	70	63	11	96	0		
31	69	64	9	97	0		
32	67	65	8	98	0		
33	65	66	6	99	0		

SECTION 2 – IMPAIRMENT NUMBER/EARNING CAPACITY ADJUSTMENT

Category	Body Part/Function	Page
03	Cardiovascular System – Heart & Aorta	2-2
04	Cardiovascular System – Systemic & Pulmonary Arteries	2-2
05	Respiratory System	2-2
06	Digestive System	2-2
07	Urinary & Reproductive Systems	2-2
08	Skin	2-2
09	Hematopoietic System	2-2
10	Endocrine System	2-2
11	Ear, Nose & Throat	2-2
12	Visual System	2-2
13	Central & Peripheral Nervous System	2-2
14	Mental & Behavioral Disorders	2-3
15	Spine	2-3
16	Upper Extremities	2-4
17	Lower Extremities	2-4
18	Pain	2-5

Use this section to determine an impairment number and a future earning capacity (FEC) rank for each body part being evaluated. Then use the table at the end of this section to adjust the impairment standard for earning capacity. If the impairment is not addressed by the AMA Guides, choose the closest applicable impairment number, and replace the last pair of digits with the number 99. For example, a condition that was analogized to a spinal cord disorder affecting the respiratory system (impairment no. 13.10.01.00) would take the impairment number 13.10.01.99.

# Impairment	FEC Rank	Impairment
03 – CARDIOVASCULAR SYSTEM – HEART & AORTA		
03.01.00.00	5	Valvular Heart Disease
03.02.00.00	5	Coronary Heart Disease
03.03.00.00	5	Congenital Heart Disease
03.04.00.00	5	Cardiomyopathies
03.05.00.00	5	Pericardial Heart Disease
03.06.00.00	5	Arrhythmia
04 – CARDIOVASCULAR SYSTEM – SYSTEMIC & PULMONARY ARTERIES		
04.01.00.00	5	Hypertensive Cardiovascular Disease
04.02.00.00	5	Aortic Disease
04.03.01.00	5	Peripheral Vascular Disease, Upper Extremities
04.03.02.00	5	Peripheral Vascular Disease, Lower Extremities
04.04.00.00	7	Pulmonary Circulation Disease
05 – RESPIRATORY SYSTEM		
05.01.00.00	7	Asthma
05.02.00.00	7	Respiratory Disorders
05.03.00.00	7	Cancer
06 – DIGESTIVE SYSTEM		
06.01.00.00	6	Upper Digestive Tract
06.02.00.00	6	Colon, Rectum, Anus
06.03.00.00	6	Enterocutaneous Fistulas
06.04.00.00	6	Liver/Biliary Tract
06.05.00.00	6	Hernias
07 – URINARY & REPRODUCTIVE SYSTEMS		
07.01.00.00	2	Upper Urinary Tract
07.02.00.00	2	Urinary Diversion
07.03.00.00	2	Bladder
07.04.00.00	2	Urethra
07.05.00.00	2	Reproductive System

Impairment#	FEC Rank	Impairment
08 – SKIN		
08.01.00.00	2	Disfigurement
08.02.00.00	2	Scars & Skin Grafts
08.03.00.00	2	Contact Dermatitis
08.04.00.00	2	Latex Allergy
08.05.00.00	2	Skin Cancer
09 – HEMATOPOIETIC SYSTEM		
09.01.00.00	2	Hematopoietic Impairment
10 – ENDOCRINE SYSTEM		
10.01.00.00	2	Diabetes Mellitus
11 – EAR, NOSE & THROAT		
11.01.01.00	8	Ear – Hearing Impairment
11.01.02.00	8	Ear – Vestibular Disorder
11.02.01.00	2	Face/cosmetic
11.02.02.00	2	Face/eye/cosmetic
11.03.01.00	2	Nose/Throat/Related Structures – Respiration
11.03.02.00	2	Nose/Throat/Related Structures – Mastication & Deglutition
11.03.03.00	2	Nose/Throat/Related Structures – Olfaction & Taste
11.03.04.00	2	Nose/Throat/Related Structures – Voice & Speech
12 – VISUAL SYSTEM		
12.01.00.00	1	Visual Acuity
12.02.00.00	1	Visual Field
12.03.00.00	1	Visual System
13 – CENTRAL & PERIPHERAL NERVOUS SYSTEM		
13.01.00.00	6	Consciousness Disorder
13.02.00.00	2	Episodic Neurologic Disorder
13.03.00.00	6	Arousal Disorder
13.04.00.00	2	Cognitive Impairment

# Impairment	FEC Rank	Impairment
13.05.00.00	2	Language Disorder
13.06.00.00	8	Behavioral/Emotional Disorder
13.07.01.00	2	Cranial Nerve – Olfactory
13.07.02.00	1	Cranial Nerve – Optic
13.07.03.00	2	Cranial Nerve – Oculomotor, Trochlear & Abducens
13.07.04.00	2	Cranial Nerve – Trigeminal
13.07.05.00	2	Cranial Nerve – Facial
13.07.06.01	8	Cranial Nerve – Vestibulocochlear – Vertigo
13.07.06.02	8	Cranial Nerve – Vestibulocochlear – Tinnitus
13.07.07.00	2	Cranial Nerve – Glossopharyngeal & Valgus
13.07.08.00	2	Cranial Nerve – Spinal Accessory
13.07.09.00	2	Cranial Nerve – Hypoglossal
13.08.00.00	5	Station, Gait, Movement
13.09.00.00	5	Upper Extremities
13.10.01.00	7	Spinal Cord Disorder – Respiratory
13.10.02.00	2	Spinal Cord Disorder – Urinary
13.10.03.00	2	Spinal Cord Disorder – Anorectal
13.10.04.00	2	Spinal Cord Disorder – Sexual
13.11.01.01	5	Chronic Pain – Upper Extremities – Causalgia
13.11.01.02	5	Chronic Pain – Upper Extremities – Post-traumatic Neuralgia
13.11.01.03	5	Chronic Pain – Upper Extremities – Reflex Sympathetic Dystrophy
13.11.02.01	5	Chronic Pain – Lower Extremities – Causalgia
13.11.02.02	5	Chronic Pain – Lower Extremities – Post-traumatic Neuralgia
13.11.02.03	5	Chronic Pain – Lower Extremities – Reflex Sympathetic Dystrophy
13.12.01.01	5	Peripheral Nerve System – Spine – Sensory
13.12.01.02	5	Peripheral Nerve System – Spine – Motor
13.12.02.01	5	Peripheral Nerve System – Upper Extremity – Sensory
13.12.02.02	5	Peripheral Nerve System – Upper Extremity – Motor
13.12.03.01	5	Peripheral Nerve System – Lower Extremity – Sensory
13.12.03.02	5	Peripheral Nerve System – Lower Extremity – Motor

Impairment#	FEC Rank	Impairment
14 – MENTAL & BEHAVIORIAL DISORDERS		
14.01.00.00	8	Psychiatric – Mental and Behavioral
15 – SPINE		
15.01.01.00	5	Cervical – Diagnosis-related Estimate (DRE)
15.01.02.01	5	Cervical – Range of Motion (ROM) – Fracture
15.01.02.02	5	Cervical – Range of Motion – Soft Tissue Lesion
15.01.02.03	5	Cervical – Range of Motion – Spondylolysis, no operation
15.01.02.04	5	Cervical – Range of Motion – Stenosis, with operation
15.01.02.05	5	Cervical – Range of Motion – Nerve Root/Spinal Cord-Sensory
15.01.02.06	5	Cervical – Range of Motion – Nerve Root/Spinal Cord – Motor
15.02.01.00	5	Thoracic – Diagnosis-related Estimate
15.02.02.01	5	Thoracic – Range of Motion – Fracture
15.02.02.02	5	Thoracic – Range of Motion – Soft Tissue Lesion
15.02.02.03	5	Thoracic – Range of Motion – Spondylolysis, no operation
15.02.02.04	5	Thoracic – Range of Motion – Stenosis, with operation
15.02.02.05	5	Thoracic – Range of Motion – Nerve Root/Spinal Cord – Sensory
15.02.02.06	5	Thoracic – Range of Motion – Nerve Root/Spinal Cord – Motor
15.03.01.00	5	Lumbar – Diagnosis-related Estimate
15.03.02.01	5	Lumbar – Range of Motion – Fracture
15.03.02.02	5	Lumbar – Range of Motion – Soft Tissue Lesion
15.03.02.03	5	Lumbar – Range of Motion – Spondylolysis, no operation
15.03.02.04	5	Lumbar – Range of Motion – Stenosis, with operation
15.03.02.05	5	Lumbar – Range of Motion – Nerve Root/Spinal Cord – Sensory
15.03.02.06	5	Lumbar – Range of Motion – Nerve Root/Spinal Cord – Motor
15.04.01.00	5	Corticospinal Tract – One Upper Extremity
15.04.02.00	5	Corticospinal Tract – Two Upper Extremities
15.04.03.00	5	Corticospinal Tract – Station/Gait Disorder

# Impairment	FEC Rank	Impairment
15.04.04.00	2	Corticospinal Tract – Bladder Impairment
15.04.05.00	2	Corticospinal Tract – Anorectal Impairment
15.04.06.00	2	Corticospinal Tract – Sexual Impairment
15.04.07.00	7	Corticospinal Tract – Respiratory Impairment
15.05.01.00	5	Pelvic – Healed Fracture
15.05.02.00	5	Pelvic – Healed Fracture with Displacement
15.05.03.00	5	Pelvic – Healed Fracture with Deformity
16 – UPPER EXTREMITIES		
16.01.01.01	5	Arm – Amputation/Deltoid insertion proximally
16.01.01.02	5	Arm – Amputation/Bicipital insertion proximally
16.01.01.03	5	Arm – Amputation/Wrist proximally
16.01.01.04	5	Arm – Amputation/All fingers at MP joint proximally
16.01.02.01	5	Arm – Peripheral neuropathy – Brachial plexus
16.01.02.02	4	Arm – Peripheral neuropathy – Entrapment/compression – Carpal tunnel
16.01.02.03	5	Arm – Peripheral neuropathy – Entrapment/compression – Other
16.01.02.04	5	Arm – Peripheral neuropathy – CRPS I
16.01.02.05	5	Arm – Peripheral neuropathy – CRPS II
16.01.03.00	5	Arm – Peripheral vascular
16.01.04.00	4	Arm – Grip/pinch strength
16.01.05.00	5	Arm – Other
16.02.01.00	7	Shoulder – Range of motion
16.02.02.00	7	Shoulder – Other
16.03.01.00	2	Elbow/forearm – Range of motion
16.03.02.00	2	Elbow/forearm – Other
16.04.01.00	4	Wrist – Range of motion
16.04.02.00	4	Wrist – Other
16.05.01.00	1	Hand/multiple fingers – Range of motion
16.05.02.00	1	Hand/multiple fingers – Amputation
16.05.03.00	1	Hand/multiple fingers – Sensory
16.05.04.00	1	Hand/multiple fingers – Other
16.06.01.01	1	Thumb – Range of motion
16.06.01.02	1	Thumb – Amputation

Impairment#	FEC Rank	Impairment
16.06.01.03	1	Thumb – Sensory
16.06.01.04	1	Thumb – Other
16.06.02.01	1	Index – Range of motion
16.06.02.02	1	Index – Amputation
16.06.02.03	1	Index – Sensory
16.06.02.04	1	Index – Other
16.06.03.01	1	Middle – Range of motion
16.06.03.02	1	Middle – Amputation
16.06.03.03	1	Middle – Sensory
16.06.03.04	1	Middle – Other
16.06.04.01	1	Ring – Range of motion
16.06.04.02	1	Ring – Amputation
16.06.04.03	1	Ring – Sensory
16.06.04.04	1	Ring – Other
16.06.05.01	1	Little – Range of motion
16.06.05.02	1	Little – Amputation
16.06.05.03	1	Little – Sensory
16.06.05.04	1	Little – Other
17 – LOWER EXTREMITIES		
17.01.01.00	5	Leg – Limb Length
17.01.02.01	5	Leg – Amputation/Knee proximally
17.01.02.02	5	Leg – Amputation/MTP joint proximally
17.01.03.00	5	Leg – Skin Loss
17.01.04.00	5	Leg – Peripheral Nerve
17.01.05.00	5	Leg – Vascular
17.01.06.00	5	Leg – Causalgia/RSD
17.01.07.00	5	Leg – Gait Derangement
17.01.08.00	5	Leg – Other
17.02.10.00	5	Pelvis – Diagnosis-based estimate (DBE) – Fracture
17.03.01.00	5	Hip – Muscle Atrophy
17.03.02.00	5	Hip – Ankylosis
17.03.03.00	5	Hip – Arthritis
17.03.04.00	5	Hip – Range of Motion

# Impairment	FEC Rank	Impairment
17.03.05.00	5	Hip – Muscle Strength
17.03.06.00	5	Hip – Other
17.03.10.01	5	Hip – Diagnosis-based Estimate – Hip/Replacement
17.03.10.02	5	Hip – Diagnosis-based Estimate – Hip/Femoral Neck Fracture
17.03.10.03	5	Hip – Diagnosis-based Estimate – Hip/Arthroplasty
17.03.10.04	5	Hip – Diagnosis-based Estimate – Trochanteric bursitis
17.04.10.00	5	Femur – Diagnosis-based Estimate – Fracture
17.05.01.00	2	Knee – Muscle Atrophy
17.05.02.00	2	Knee – Ankylosis
17.05.03.00	2	Knee – Arthritis
17.05.04.00	2	Knee – Range of Motion
17.05.05.00	2	Knee – Muscle Strength
17.05.06.00	2	Knee – Other
17.05.10.01	2	Knee – Diagnosis-based Estimate – Subluxation/dislocation
17.05.10.02	2	Knee – Diagnosis-based Estimate – Fracture
17.05.10.03	2	Knee – Diagnosis-based Estimate – Patellectomy
17.05.10.04	2	Knee – Diagnosis-based Estimate – Menisectomy
17.05.10.05	2	Knee – Diagnosis-based Estimate – Cruciate/collateral Ligament
17.05.10.06	2	Knee – Diagnosis-based Estimate – Plateau Fracture
17.05.10.07	2	Knee – Diagnosis-based Estimate – Supra/Intercondylar Fracture
17.05.10.08	2	Knee – Diagnosis-based Estimate – Total Replacement
17.05.10.09	2	Knee – Diagnosis-based Estimate – Proximal Tibial osteotomy
17.06.10.00	5	Tibia/fibula – Diagnosis-based Estimate – fracture
17.07.01.00	2	Ankle – Muscle Atrophy
17.07.02.00	2	Ankle – Ankylosis
17.07.03.00	2	Ankle – Arthritis

Impairment#	FEC Rank	Impairment
17.07.04.00	2	Ankle – Range of Motion
17.07.05.00	2	Ankle – Muscle Strength
17.07.06.00	2	Ankle – Other
17.07.10.01	2	Ankle – Diagnosis-based Estimate – Ligament Instability
17.07.10.02	2	Ankle – Diagnosis-based Estimate – Fracture
17.08.01.00	2	Foot – Muscle Atrophy
17.08.02.00	2	Foot – Ankylosis
17.08.03.00	2	Foot – Arthritis
17.08.04.00	2	Foot – Range of Motion
17.08.05.00	2	Foot – Muscle Strength
17.08.06.00	2	Foot – Other
17.08.10.01	2	Foot – Diagnosis-based Estimate – Hind Foot Fracture
17.08.10.02	2	Foot – Diagnosis-based Estimate – Loss of Tibia
17.08.10.03	2	Foot – Diagnosis-based Estimate – Intra-articular Fracture
17.08.10.04	2	Foot – Diagnosis-based Estimate – Calvus
17.08.10.05	2	Foot – Diagnosis-based Estimate – Rocker Bottom
17.08.10.06	2	Foot – Diagnosis-based Estimate – Avascular Necrosis
17.08.10.07	2	Foot – Diagnosis-based Estimate – Metatarsal fracture
17.09.01.00	5	Toes – Muscle Atrophy
17.09.02.00	5	Toes – Ankylosis
17.09.03.00	5	Toes – Arthritis
17.09.04.00	5	Toes – Range of Motion
17.09.05.00	5	Toes – Muscle Strength
17.09.06.00	5	Toes – Amputation
17.09.07.00	5	Toes – Other
18 – PAIN		
18.00.00.00	Variable	Pain – use FEC rank for involved body part.

FUTURE EARNING CAPACITY (FEC) ADJUSTMENT TABLE

Directions: To adjust for earning capacity, look up the impairment standard in the top row (bolded numbers), and read down to the entry corresponding to the applicable future earning capacity rank

FEC	AMA Whole Person Impairment Standard																			
Rank	**1**	**2**	**3**	**4**	**5**	**6**	**7**	**8**	**9**	**10**	**11**	**12**	**13**	**14**	**15**	**16**	**17**	**18**	**19**	**20**
One	1	2	3	4	6	7	8	9	10	11	12	13	14	15	17	18	19	20	21	22
Two	1	2	3	5	6	7	8	9	10	11	13	14	15	16	17	18	19	21	22	23
Three	1	2	4	5	6	7	8	9	11	12	13	14	15	17	18	19	20	21	23	24
Four	1	2	4	5	6	7	9	10	11	12	14	15	16	17	18	20	21	22	23	25
Five	1	3	4	5	6	8	9	10	11	13	14	15	17	18	19	20	22	23	24	25
Six	1	3	4	5	7	8	9	11	12	13	14	16	17	18	20	21	22	24	25	26
Seven	1	3	4	5	7	8	10	11	12	14	15	16	18	19	20	22	23	24	26	27
Eight	1	3	4	6	7	8	10	11	13	14	15	17	18	20	21	22	24	25	27	28

FEC	AMA Whole Person Impairment Standard																			
Rank	**21**	**22**	**23**	**24**	**25**	**26**	**27**	**28**	**29**	**30**	**31**	**32**	**33**	**34**	**35**	**36**	**37**	**38**	**39**	**40**
One	23	24	25	26	28	29	30	31	32	33	34	35	36	37	39	40	41	42	43	44
Two	24	25	26	27	29	30	31	32	33	34	35	37	38	39	40	41	42	43	45	46
Three	25	26	27	28	30	31	32	33	34	36	37	38	39	40	42	43	44	45	46	47
Four	26	27	28	29	31	32	33	34	36	37	38	39	41	42	43	44	45	47	48	49
Five	27	28	29	31	32	33	34	36	37	38	39	41	42	43	45	46	47	48	50	51
Six	28	29	30	32	33	34	35	37	38	39	41	42	43	45	46	47	49	50	51	53
Seven	29	30	31	33	34	35	37	38	39	41	42	43	45	46	48	49	50	52	53	54
Eight	29	31	32	34	35	36	38	39	41	42	43	45	46	48	49	50	52	53	55	56

FEC	AMA Whole Person Impairment Standard																			
Rank	**41**	**42**	**43**	**44**	**45**	**46**	**47**	**48**	**49**	**50**	**51**	**52**	**53**	**54**	**55**	**56**	**57**	**58**	**59**	**60**
One	45	46	47	48	50	51	52	53	54	55	56	57	58	59	61	62	63	64	65	66
Two	47	48	49	50	51	53	54	55	56	57	58	59	61	62	63	64	65	66	67	69
Three	49	50	51	52	53	55	56	57	58	59	60	62	63	64	65	66	68	69	70	71
Four	50	52	53	54	55	57	58	59	60	61	63	64	65	66	68	69	70	71	72	74
Five	52	53	55	56	57	58	60	61	62	64	65	66	67	69	70	71	72	74	75	76
Six	54	55	57	58	59	60	62	63	64	66	67	68	70	71	72	74	75	76	78	79
Seven	56	57	58	60	61	62	64	65	67	68	69	71	72	73	75	76	77	79	80	81
Eight	57	59	60	62	63	64	66	67	69	70	71	73	74	76	77	78	80	81	83	84

FEC	AMA Whole Person Impairment Standard																			
Rank	**61**	**62**	**63**	**64**	**65**	**66**	**67**	**68**	**69**	**70**	**71**	**72**	**73**	**74**	**75**	**76**	**77**	**78**	**79**	**80**
One	67	68	69	70	72	73	74	75	76	77	78	79	80	81	83	84	85	86	87	88
Two	70	71	72	73	74	75	77	78	79	80	81	82	83	85	86	87	88	89	90	91
Three	72	74	75	76	77	78	79	81	82	83	84	85	87	88	89	90	91	92	94	95
Four	75	76	77	79	80	81	82	84	85	86	87	88	90	91	92	93	95	96	97	98
Five	78	79	80	81	83	84	85	86	88	89	90	92	93	94	95	97	98	99	100	100
Six	80	81	83	84	85	87	88	89	91	92	93	95	96	97	99	100	100	100	100	100
Seven	83	84	86	87	88	90	91	92	94	95	96	98	99	100	100	100	100	100	100	100
Eight	85	87	88	90	91	92	94	95	97	98	99	100	100	100	100	100	100	100	100	100

FEC	AMA Whole Person Impairment Standard																			
Rank	**81**	**82**	**83**	**84**	**85**	**86**	**87**	**88**	**89**	**90**	**91**	**92**	**93**	**94**	**95**	**96**	**97**	**98**	**99**	**100**
One	89	90	91	92	94	95	96	97	98	99	100	100	100	100	100	100	100	100	100	100
Two	93	94	95	96	97	98	99	100	100	100	100	100	100	100	100	100	100	100	100	100
Three	96	97	98	100	100	100	100	100	100	100	100	100	100	100	100	100	100	100	100	100
Four	100	100	100	100	100	100	100	100	100	100	100	100	100	100	100	100	100	100	100	100
Five	100	100	100	100	100	100	100	100	100	100	100	100	100	100	100	100	100	100	100	100
Six	100	100	100	100	100	100	100	100	100	100	100	100	100	100	100	100	100	100	100	100
Seven	100	100	100	100	100	100	100	100	100	100	100	100	100	100	100	100	100	100	100	100
Eight	100	100	100	100	100	100	100	100	100	100	100	100	100	100	100	100	100	100	100	100

SECTION 3 - OCCUPATIONS AND GROUP NUMBERS

Section 3 contains two parts. Part A contains an alphabetized list of occupations with their scheduled occupational group numbers. Find the occupation in the alphabetical list and record the associated group number. Note that some occupations may have more than one title and that all variations may not be listed. Also note that some titles may appear more than once, but pertain to different industries. Care should be taken to ensure that the industry designated also matches the occupation under consideration.

Part B contains an occupational group chart which illustrates the overall system for classifying occupations into groups. Part C contains a description and sample occupations of each group. This information may be useful if the occupation cannot be located in Part A. Simply determine the basic functions and activities of the occupation under consideration and relate it to a comparable scheduled occupation to determine the appropriate group number.

After establishing the occupation and group number, turn to Section 4 to determine the occupational variant.

PART A – LIST OF OCCUPATIONS AND GROUP NUMBERS

Group No.	Occupation	Industry
111	ABSTRACTOR	profess. & kin.
110	ACADEMIC DEAN	education
110	ACCOUNT EXECUTIVE	business ser.
111	ACCOUNT INFORMATION CLERK	utilities
111	ACCOUNTANT	profess. & kin.
111	ACCOUNTANT, PROPERTY	profess. & kin.
111	ACCOUNTING CLERK	clerical
590	ACROBAT	amuse. & rec.
210	ACTOR	amuse. & rec.
310	ACUPRESSURIST	medical ser.
211	ADDRESSING MACHINE OPERATOR	clerical
111	ADMINISTRATIVE ANALYST	any industry
211	ADMINISTRATIVE CLERK	clerical
212	ADMINISTRATOR, HEALTH CARE FACILITY	medical ser.
111	ADMISSIONS EVALUATOR	education
212	AIR ANALYST	profess. & kin.
481	AIR CONDITIONING INSTALLER SERV., WINDOW UNIT	construction
480	AIR HAMMER OPERATOR	construction
212	AIR TRAFFIC CONTROL SPECIALIST, TOWER	government ser.
380	AIRCRAFT BODY REPAIRER	air trans.
380	AIRCRAFT BONDED STRUCTURES REPAIRER	aircraft mfg.
460	AIRCRAFT SERVICE WORKER	air trans.
341	AIRCRAFT SERVICE ATTENDANT	air trans.
380	AIRFRAME AND POWER PLANT MECHANIC	aircraft mfg.
213	AIRLINE TRANSPORTATION AGENT	air trans.
213	AIRPLANE INSPECTOR	air trans.
250	AIRPLANE PILOT, COMMERCIAL	air trans.
322	AIRPLANE FLIGHT ATTENDANT	air trans.
380	ALARM SERVICE TECHNICIAN	business ser.
111	ALARM SIGNAL OPERATOR	any industry
560	AMBULANCE ATTENDANT	medical ser.
560	AMBULANCE DRIVER	medical ser.
340	AMUSEMENT PARK ATTENDANT	amuse. & rec.
210	AMUSEMENT PARK ENTERTAINER	amuse. & rec.
220	ANESTHESIOLOGIST	medical ser.
310	ANGIOGRAM TECHNOLOGIST	medical ser.
491	ANIMAL KEEPER	amuse. & rec.
390	ANIMAL TRAINER	amuse. & rec.
491	ANIMAL RIDE ATTENDANT	amuse. & rec.
210	ANNOUNCER	radio-tv broad.
460	ANODIZER	any industry
380	ANTENNA INSTALLER	any industry
380	ANTENNA INSTALLER, SATELLITE COMMUNICATIONS	any industry
110	APPEALS REFEREE	government ser.
111	APPOINTMENT CLERK	clerical
212	APPRAISER, ART	any industry
212	APPRAISER, BUSINESS EQPT.	any industry
213	APPRAISER, REAL ESTATE	real estate
330	ARBOR PRESS OPERATOR	any industry
370	ARC CUTTER	welding
212	ARCHITECT	profess. & kin.
111	ARCHIVIST	profess. & kin.
320	ARMATURE BANDER	any industry
350	ARMORED CAR DRIVER	business ser.
390	ARMORED CAR GUARD	business ser.
111	ART DIRECTOR	motion picture
221	ARTIFICIAL FLOWER MAKER	button & notion
220	ARTIFICIAL PLASTIC EYE MAKER	optical goods
480	ASPHALT RAKER	construction
351	ASPHALT SURFACE HEATER OPERATOR	construction
351	ASPHALT DISTRIBUTOR TENDER	construction
351	ASPHALT PAVING MACHINE OPERATOR	construction
120	ASSEMBLER	jewelry-silver.
221	ASSEMBLER	house. appl.
221	ASSEMBLER, ELECTRIC MOTOR	elec. equip.
370	ASSEMBLER, INTERNAL COMBUSTION ENGINE	engine-turbine
370	ASSEMBLER, MOTOR VEHICLE	auto. mfg.
221	ASSEMBLER, MUSICAL INSTRUMENTS	musical inst.

Group No.	Occupation	Industry
320	ASSEMBLER, OFFICE MACHINES	office machines
221	ASSEMBLER, PRODUCTION	any industry
120	ASSEMBLER, SEMICONDUCTOR	electron. comp.
221	ASSEMBLER, SMALL PRODUCTS	any industry
380	ASSEMBLER, SUBASSEMBLY	aircraft mfg.
380	ASSEMBLER-INSTALLER, GENERAL	aircraft mfg.
590	ATHLETE, PROFESSIONAL	amuse. & rec.
390	ATHLETIC TRAINER	amuse. & rec.
111	ATTENDANCE CLERK	education
111	AUCTION CLERK	retail trade
210	AUCTIONEER	retail trade
212	AUDIO OPERATOR	radio-tv broad.
221	AUDIO VIDEO REPAIRER	any industry
251	AUDIOVISUAL PRODUCTION SPECIALIST	profess. & kin.
111	AUDIT CLERK	clerical
111	AUDITOR	profess. & kin.
251	AUDITOR, FIELD	profess. & kin.
330	AUTOCLAVE OPERATOR	aircraft mfg.
370	AUTOMATED EQUIPMENT INSTALLER	machinery mfg.
370	AUTOMOBILE ASSEMBLER	auto. mfg.
340	AUTOMOBILE DETAILER	automotive ser.
111	AUTOMOBILE LOCATOR	retail trade
321	AUTOMOBILE UPHOLSTERER	automotive ser.
340	AUTOMOBILE WASHER & POLISHER	automotive ser.
460	AUTOMOBILE WRECKER	wholesale tr.
370	AUTOMOBILE ACCESSORIES INSTALLER	automotive ser.
370	AUTOMOBILE BODY REPAIRER	automotive ser.
214	AUTOMOBILE REPAIR SERVICE ESTIMATOR	automotive ser.
370	AUTOMOBILE SERVICE STATION MECHANIC	automotive ser.
321	AUTO PAINTER	any industry
380	AWNING MAKER	tex. prod., nec.
240	BABYSITTER	domestic ser.
460	BAGGAGE HANDLER	r.r. trans.
212	BAGGAGE SCREENER, AIRPO	air transport.
214	BAGGER	retail trade; groceries
490	BAILIFF	government ser.

Group No.	Occupation	Industry
322	BAKER	hotel & rest.
460	BAKER HELPER	bakery products
420	BAKER	bakery products
322	BAKERY SUPERVISOR	bakery products
330	BAND-SAWING MACHINE OPERATOR	fabrication, nec
230	BAND SAWMILL OPERATOR	saw. & plan.
211	BANK CLERK	financial
290	BARBER	personal ser.
330	BARREL ASSEMBLER	wood. container
460	BARREL FILLER	beverage
322	BARTENDER	hotel & rest.
221	BASKET MAKER	wood. container
230	BATCH STILL OPERATOR	chemical
321	BATTERY ASSEMBLER, DRY CELL	elec. equip.
321	BATTERY REPAIRER	any industry
290	BEAUTICIAN	personal ser.
230	BED LASTER	boot & shoe
491	BEEKEEPER	agriculture
360	BELLHOP	hotel & rest.
221	BENCH WORKER	optical goods
330	BENDING MACHINE OPERATOR	any industry
493	BICYCLE MESSENGER	business ser.
320	BICYCLE REPAIRER	any industry
480	BILLBOARD & SIGN ERECTOR	fabrication, nec
480	BILLBOARD ERECTOR HELPER	construction
112	BILLING CLERK	clerical
213	BILLPOSTER	business ser.
230	BINDERY WORKER	print. & pub.
212	BIOCHEMIST	profess. & kin.
110	BIOLOGY SPECIMEN TECHNICIAN	profess. & kin.
320	BIOMEDICAL EQUIPMENT TECHNICIAN	profess. & kin.
430	BLACKSMITH	forging
460	BLACKSMITH HELPER	forging
480	BLASTER	mining; construction
332	BLENDER	petrol. refin.
240	BLIND AIDE	personal ser.
330	BLISTER MACHINE OPERATOR	any industry
220	BLOCKER AND CUTTER, CONTACT LENS	optical goods

Group No.	Occupation	Industry
221	BLOCKER, HAND	hat & cap
230	BLUEPRINTING MACHINE OPERATOR	any industry
380	BOAT REPAIRER	ship-boat mfg.
380	BOAT RIGGER	retail trade
380	BOATBUILDER, WOOD	ship-boat mfg.
390	BODYGUARD	personal ser.
332	BOILER OPERATOR	any industry
332	BOILER TENDER	any industry
430	BOILERMAKER	struct. metal
460	BOILERMAKER HELPER	struct. metal
111	BONDING AGENT	business ser.
322	BONER, MEAT	meat products
221	BOOK REPAIRER	any industry
320	BOOKBINDER	print. & pub.
112	BOOKKEEPER	clerical
112	BOOKKEEPER, GENERAL LEDGER	clerical
351	BOOM CONVEYOR OPERATOR	any industry
330	BORING MACHINE OPERATOR	woodworking
230	BOTTLE PACKER	beverage
390	BOUNCER	amuse. & rec.
390	BOUNTY HUNTER	business ser.
221	BOW MAKER	any industry
493	BOWLER, PROFESSIONAL	amuse. and rec
331	BOWLING BALL MOLDER	toy-sport equip.
321	BOX MAKER, PAPERBOARD	any industry
321	BOX MAKER, WOOD	wood. container
230	BOX PRINTING MACHINE OPERATOR	any industry
230	BOX BLANK MACHINE OPERATOR	wood. container
460	BOX FOLDING MACHINE OPERATOR	paper goods
321	BOX SPRING MAKER	furniture
211	BRAILLE OPERATOR	print. & pub.
111	BRAILLE PROOFREADER	nonprofit org.
370	BRAKE REPAIRER	automotive ser.
330	BRAKE PRESS OPERATOR	any industry
330	BRAZING MACHINE OPERATOR	welding
330	BREAD WRAPPING MACHINE OPERATOR	any industry
332	BREWERY CELLAR WORKER	beverage
331	BRICK AND TILE MAKING MACHINE OPERATOR	brick & tile
481	BRICKLAYER	construction

Group No.	Occupation	Industry
481	BRICKLAYER APPRENTICE	construction
480	BRICKLAYER HELPER	construction
482	BRIDGE MAINTENANCE WORKER	construction
482	BRIDGE WORKER	construction
331	BRIQUETTE MACHINE OPERATOR	fabrication, nec
330	BROACHING MACHINE OPERATOR, PRODUCTION	machine shop
321	BROOM STITCHER	fabrication, nec
492	BUCKER	logging
111	BUDGET ANALYST	government ser.
321	BUFFER	any industry
230	BUFFING MACHINE TENDER, AUTOMATIC	any industry
480	BUILDING CLEANER, OUTSIDE	any industry
213	BUILDING INSPECTOR	government ser.
213	BUILDING INSPECTOR	insurance
380	BUILDING MAINTENANCE REPAIRER	any industry
351	BULLDOZER OPERATOR	any industry
380	BURGLAR ALARM INSTALLER/REPAIRER	business ser.
330	BURNING MACHINE OPERATOR	welding
250	BUS DRIVER	motor trans.
322	BUS PERSON	hotel & rest.
110	BUSINESS MANAGER	amuse. & rec.
111	BUSINESS REPRESENTATIVE, LABOR UNION	profess. & kin.
420	BUTCHER, ALL-ROUND	meat products
322	BUTCHER, MEAT	hotel & rest.
240	BUTLER	domestic ser.
460	BUTTERMAKER	dairy products
230	BUTTONHOLE AND BUTTON SEWING MACHINE OPERATOR	garment
320	CABINETMAKER	woodworking
320	CABLE ASSEMBLER AND SWAGER	aircraft mfg.
350	CABLE CAR OPERATOR	r.r. transportation
380	CABLE INSTALLER-REPAIRER	utilities
380	CABLE MAINTAINER	utilities
480	CABLE PULLER	construction
380	CABLE SPLICER	construction
481	CABLE TELEVISION INSTALLER	radio-tv broad.
380	CABLE TESTER	tel. & tel.
120	CAD DESIGNER	profess. & kindred

Group No.	Occupation	Industry
360	CADDIE	amuse. & rec.
322	CAFETERIA ATTENDANT	hotel & rest.
480	CAGER	mine & quarry
221	CAKE DECORATOR	bakery products
120	CALLIGRAPHER	profess. & kin.
360	CAMERA OPERATOR	motion picture
220	CAMERA REPAIRER	photo. appar.
390	CAMP COUNSELOR	amuse. & rec.
340	CAMPGROUND ATTENDANT	amuse. & rec.
230	CAN-FILLING AND CLOSING MACHINE TENDER	can. & preserv.
221	CANDLEMAKER	fabrication, nec
331	CANDY MAKER	sugar & conf.
221	CANER	furniture
230	CANNERY WORKER, HAND OR MACHINE	can. & preserv.
420	CANVAS REPAIRER	any industry
230	CAP-LINING MACHINE OPERATOR	any industry
320	CAPACITOR ASSEMBLER	elec. equip.
211	CARD DEALER	amusement and rec.
322	CAR HOP	hotel & rest.
460	CARBIDE POWDER PROCESSOR	machine shop
110	CARDIAC MONITOR TECHNICIAN	medical ser.
212	CARDIOPULMONARY TECHNOLOGIST	medical ser.
240	CARDROOM ATTENDANT	amuse. & rec.
360	CARGO AGENT	air trans.
380	CARPENTER	construction
380	CARPENTER APPRENTICE	construction
480	CARPENTER HELPER	construction
380	CARPENTER, ACOUSTICAL	construction
380	CARPENTER, MAINTENANCE	any industry
380	CARPENTER, RAILCAR	railroad equip.
481	CARPENTER, ROUGH	construction
380	CARPENTER, SHIP	ship-boat mfg.
480	CARPET CUTTER	retail trade
481	CARPET LAYER	retail trade
321	CARPET SEWER	carpet & rug
230	CARPET WEAVER	carpet & rug
480	CARPET LAYER HELPER	retail trade
120	CARTOGRAPHER	prof. & kindred
330	CARTON-FORMING MACHINE OPERATOR	any industry
460	CARTON-FORMING MACHINE TENDER	paper goods
120	CARTOONIST, MOTION PICTURES	motion picture
111	CASEWORKER	social ser.
320	CASH REGISTER SERVICER	any industry
111	CASHIER	clerical
214	CASHIER-CHECKER	retail trade
230	CASING MACHINE OPERATOR	meat products
330	CASTER	smelt. & refin.
331	CASTER	jewelry-silver.
320	CASTING REPAIRER	any industry
322	CATERER	personal ser.
491	CATTLE HERDER	agriculture
480	CAULKER	construction
330	CELLOPHANE BAG MACHINE OPERATOR	paper goods
481	CEMENT MASON	construction
480	CEMENT SPRAYER, NOZZLE	construction
480	CEMENT MASON HELPER	construction
480	CEMENTER, OILWELL	petrol. & gas
331	CENTER MACHINE OPERATOR	sugar & conf.
380	CENTRAL OFFICE REPAIRER	tel. & tel.
331	CENTRIFUGAL EXTRACTOR OPERATOR	any industry
230	CENTRIFUGE OPERATOR, PLASMA PROCESSING	medical ser.
230	CENTRIFUGE SEPARATOR OPERATOR	chemical
110	CEPHALOMETRIC ANALYST	medical ser.
331	CERAMIC COATER, MACHINE	any industry
460	CHAIN OFFBEARER	saw. & plan.
492	CHAIN SAW OPERATOR	logging
331	CHAR CONVEYOR TENDER	sugar & conf.
230	CHARGE PREPARATION TECHNICIAN	electron. comp.
492	CHASER	logging
250	CHAUFFEUR	any industry
111	CHECK CASHIER	business ser.
360	CHECKER	laundry & rel.
214	CHECKER, GROCERY	retail trade

Group No.	Occupation	Industry
360	CHECKER, UNLOADER	clerical
360	CHECKER, WAREHOUSE	retail trade
240	CHECKROOM ATTENDANT	any industry
322	CHEESE CUTTER	dairy products
322	CHEESEMAKER	dairy products
322	CHEF DE FROID	hotel & rest.
212	CHEMICAL ENGINEER	profess. & kin
212	CHEMICAL LABORATORY TECHNICIAN	profess. & kin
230	CHEMICAL PREPARER	chemical
212	CHEMIST	profess. & kin
240	CHILD MONITOR	domestic ser.
111	CHILD SUPPORT OFFICER	government ser.
340	CHILD-CARE ATTENDANT, HANDICAPPED	education
340	CHILDREN'S INSTITUTION ATTENDANT	any industry
341	CHIMNEY SWEEP	any industry
460	CHIPPER, ROUGH	any industry
311	CHIROPRACTOR	medical ser.
311	CHIROPRACTOR ASSISTANT	medical ser.
460	CHOCOLATE PRODUCTION MACHINE OPERATOR	sugar & conf.
560	CHOKE SETTER	logging
492	CHOPPER	logging
491	CHRISTMAS TREE FARM WORKER	forestry
320	CHUCKING LATHE OPERATOR	machine shop
330	CIRCULAR SAWYER, STONE	stonework
212	CIVIL ENGINEER	profess. & kin.
251	CLAIM ADJUSTER, FIELD	insurance; business ser.
111	CLAIM ADJUSTER, INSIDE	insurance
111	CLAIMS CLERK	insurance
221	CLAY MODELER	any industry
340	CLEANER, COMMERCIAL OR INSTITUTIONAL	any industry
340	CLEANER, EQUIPMENT	any industry
340	CLEANER, HOSPITAL	medical ser.
340	CLEANER, LABORATORY EQUIPMENT	any industry
341	CLEANER, WINDOW	any industry
210	CLERGY MEMBER	profess. & kin.
111	CLERK, ADVERTISING SPACE	print. & pub.
111	CLERK, ANIMAL HOSPITAL	medical ser.
112	CLERK, BILLING	clerical
111	CLERK, COLLECTION	clerical
111	CLERK, CONTRACT, AUTOMOBILE	retail trade
111	CLERK, COURT	government ser.
111	CLERK, CREDIT	clerical
111	CLERK, ELECTION	government ser.
214	CLERK, FILE	clerical
211	CLERK, GENERAL	clerical
211	CLERK, INVENTORY CONTROL	clerical
214	CLERK, SALES	retail trade
360	CLERK, SHIPPING	clerical
112	CLERK, STATISTICAL	clerical
111	CLERK, WIRE TRANSFER	financial
112	CLERK-TYPIST	clerical
110	CLINICAL PSYCHOLOGIST	profess. & kin.
330	CLOTH PRINTER	any industry
221	CLOTH TESTER, QUALITY	textile
390	COACH, PROFESSIONAL ATHLETES	amuse. & rec.
331	COATER OPERATOR	any industry
331	COATING MACHINE OPERATOR	paper & pulp
320	COBBLER	boot & shoe
322	COFFEEMAKER	hotel & rest.
230	COFFEE ROASTER	food prep., nec
230	COIL WINDER	elec. equip.
221	COIL WINDER, REPAIR	any industry
214	COIN COUNTER AND WRAPPER	clerical
251	COIN MACHINE COLLECTOR	business ser.
370	COIN MACHINE SERVICE REPAIRER	svc. ind. mach.
111	COLLECTION CLERK	clerical
251	COLLECTOR, OUTSIDE	clerical
230	COLOR PRINTER OPERATOR	photofinishing
111	COLUMNIST/COMMENTATOR	print. & pub.
111	COMMUNITY ORGANIZATION WORKER	social serv.
250	COMMUNITY SERVICE OFFICER, PATROL	social serv.
240	COMPANION	domestic ser.
221	COMPOSITOR, TYPESETTER	print. & pub.
230	COMPOUNDER	petrol. refin.
360	COMPRESSED GAS PLANT WORKER	chemical

Group No.	Occupation	Industry
332	COMPRESSOR OPERATOR	any industry
112	COMPUTER KEYBOARD OPERATOR	clerical
230	COMPUTER OPERATOR, MAINFRAME	clerical
111	COMPUTER PROCESSING SCHEDULER	clerical
112	COMPUTER PROGRAMMER	profess. & kin.
320	COMPUTER REPAIRER	office machines
111	COMPUTER SECURITY SPECIALIST	profess. & kin.
320	COMPUTER SET-UP PERSON	business serv.
111	COMPUTER SUPPORT ANALYST	profess. & kin.
351	CONCRETE PAVING MACHINE OPERATOR	construction
480	CONCRETE STONE FINISHER	concrete prod.
480	CONCRETE VIBRATOR OPERATOR	construction
340	CONDUCTOR, ALL RAILS	r.r. trans.
213	CONDUCTOR, PASSENGER CAR	r.r. trans.
370	CONSTRUCTION EQUIPMENT MECHANIC	construction
110	CONSULTANT, EDUCATION	education
230	CONTACT LENS MOLDER	optical goods
330	CONTOUR BAND SAW OPERATOR, VERTICAL	machine shop
213	CONTRACTOR	construction
120	CONTROLS DESIGNER	profess. & kin.
360	CONVEYOR FEEDER-OFFBEARER	any industry
360	CONVEYOR TENDER	any industry
370	CONVEYOR MAINTENANCE MECHANIC	any industry
360	CONVEYOR SYSTEM OPERATOR	any industry
322	COOK	domestic ser.
322	COOK	any industry
322	COOK ASSISTANT	hotel & rest.
322	COOK, CHIEF	hotel & rest.
322	COOK, FAST FOOD	hotel & rest.
322	COOK, PASTRY	hotel & rest.
322	COOK, SPECIALTY	hotel & rest.
110	COORDINATOR, SKILL-TRAINING PROGRAM	government ser.
111	COPY READER	print. & pub.
111	COPY WRITER	profess. & kin.
112	COPYIST	any industry
480	CORE DRILL OPERATOR	any industry

Group No.	Occupation	Industry
330	COREMAKER	paper goods
331	COREMAKER, FLOOR	foundry
490	CORRECTION OFFICER	government ser.
290	COSMETOLOGIST	personal ser.
110	COUNSELOR	profess. & kin.
390	COUNSELOR, CAMP	amuse. & rec.
322	COUNTER ATTENDANT, CAFETERIA	hotel & rest.
250	COURIER	any industry
111	COURT CLERK	government ser.
112	COURT REPORTER	clerical
491	COWPUNCHER	agriculture
360	CRANE FOLLOWER	any industry
360	CRANE HOOKER	any industry
351	CRANE OPERATOR	any industry
360	CRATE MAKER	any industry
111	CREDIT AUTHORIZER	clerical
111	CREDIT CLERK	clerical
111	CREDIT COUNSELOR	profess. & kin.
460	CREMATOR	personal ser.
111	CREW SCHEDULER	air trans.
230	CRIMPING MACHINE OPERATOR	any industry
330	CROSSBAND LAYER	millwork-plywood
460	CRUSHER OPERATOR	concrete prod.
112	CRYPTOGRAPHIC MACHINE OPERATOR	clerical
330	CRYSTAL GROWER	comm. equip.
330	CRYSTAL SLICER	electron. comp.
212	CURATOR	museums
211	CURRENCY COUNTER	financial
340	CUSTODIAN	any industry
360	CUSTODIAN, ATHLETIC EQUIPMENT	amuse. & rec.
211	CUSTODIAN, PROPERTY	government ser.
211	CUSTOMER SERVICE CLERK	retail trade
213	CUSTOMER SERVICE REPRESENTATIVE	utilities
112	CUSTOMER SERVICE REPRESENTATIVE – INSIDE	utilities
212	CUSTOMS BROKER	financial
330	CUT-OFF SAW OPERATOR	woodworking
330	CUT-OFF SAW OPERATOR, METAL	machine shop
230	CUTTER	photofinishing
330	CUTTER OPERATOR	any industry

Group No.	Occupation	Industry
230	CUTTER, MACHINE	any industry
230	CUTTING MACHINE OPERATOR, AUTOMATED	aircraft mfg.
460	CUTTING MACHINE OPERATOR	textile
330	CUTTING MACHINE TENDER	any industry
460	CYLINDER FILLER	chemical
460	CYLINDER PRESS FEEDER	print. & pub.
120	CYTOTECHNOLOGIST	medical ser.
460	DAIRY PROCESSING EQUIPMENT OPERATOR	dairy products
590	DANCER	amuse. & rec.
111	DATA BASE ADMINISTRATOR	profess. & kin.
380	DATA COMMUNICATIONS INSTALLER	any industry
112	DATA ENTRY CLERK	clerical
221	DECAL APPLIER	any industry
491	DECKHAND	water trans., fishing & hunt.
331	DECONTAMINATOR, RADIOACTIVE MATERIAL	any industry
221	DECORATOR	bakery products
380	DECORATOR, SPECIAL EVENT	any industry
480	DECORATOR, STREET AND BUILDING	any industry
322	DELI CUTTER-SLICER	retail trade
250	DELIVERER, CAR RENTAL	automotive ser.
250	DELIVERER, FLORAL ARRANGEMENTS	retail trade
213	DELIVERER, NON-DRIVING	clerical
250	DELIVERER, PIZZA	retail trade
212	DEMONSTRATOR	retail trade
212	DENTAL ASSISTANT	medical ser.
220	DENTAL HYGIENIST	medical ser.
220	DENTAL LABORATORY TECHNICIAN	protective dev.
220	DENTIST	medical ser.
490	DEPUTY, COURT	government ser.
480	DERRICK WORKER, WELL SERVICE	petrol. & gas
230	DESIGN PRINTER, BALLOON	rubber goods
490	DETECTIVE	government ser.
390	DETECTIVE, STORE	retail trade
212	DIALYSIS TECHNICIAN	medical ser.
330	DIE CASTING MACHINE OPERATOR	foundry
330	DIE CUTTER	any industry
120	DIE DESIGNER	machine shop
320	DIE MAKER	machine shop
320	DIE SINKER	machine shop
322	DIETARY AIDE, HOSPITAL SERVICES	medical ser.
212	DIETITIAN, CLINICAL	profess. & kin.
322	DINING ROOM ATTENDANT	hotel & rest.
351	DINKEY OPERATOR	any industry
221	DIPPER	jewelry-silver.
331	DIPPER	any industry
110	DIRECTOR, FUNDRAISING	nonprofit org.
110	DIRECTOR, MOTION PICTURE	motion picture
212	DIRECTOR, RECREATION CENTER	social ser.
110	DIRECTOR, REGULATORY AGENCY	government ser.
110	DIRECTOR, RESEARCH AND DEVELOPMENT	any industry
110	DIRECTOR, SERVICE	retail trade
210	DIRECTOR, SOCIAL	hotel & rest.
112	DIRECTORY ASSISTANCE OPERATOR	tel. & tel.
322	DISHWASHER, HAND OR MACHINE	hotel & rest.
111	DISPATCHER, MOTOR VEHICLE	clerical
380	DISPLAY MAKER	fabrication, nec
330	DISPLAY SCREEN FABRICATOR	electron. comp.
360	DISPLAYER, MERCHANDISE	retail trade
460	DISTILLERY WORKER, GENERAL	beverage
221	DISTRESSER	furniture
480	DITCH DIGGER	construction
492	DIVER	any industry
230	DIVIDING MACHINE OPERATOR	bakery products
111	DOCUMENT PREPARER, MICROFILMING	business ser.
491	DOG CATCHER	government ser.
491	DOG GROOMER	personal ser.
251	DOG LICENSER	nonprofit org.
560	DOLLY PUSHER	radio-tv broad.
390	DOUBLE	motion picture
460	DOUGH BRAKE MACHINE OPERATOR	bakery products
322	DOUGH MOLDER, HAND	bakery products
322	DOUGHNUT MAKER	bakery products
330	DOWEL MACHINE OPERATOR	woodworking
120	DRAFTER, ARCHITECTURAL	profess. & kin.

Group No.	Occupation	Industry
120	DRAFTER, ASSISTANT	profess. & kin.
120	DRAFTER, CIVIL	profess. & kin.
120	DRAFTER, ELECTRICAL	profess. & kin.
120	DRAFTER, ELECTROMECHANISMS DESIGN	profess. & kin.
120	DRAFTER, LANDSCAPE	profess. & kin.
120	DRAFTER, MECHANICAL	profess. & kin.
351	DRAGLINE OPERATOR	any industry
380	DRAPERY HANGER	retail trade
110	DRAWINGS CHECKER, ENGINEERING	profess. & kin.
221	DRESSMAKER	any industry
230	DRIER OPERATOR	food prep., nec
331	DRIER OPERATOR	chemical
330	DRILL PRESS OPERATOR	machine shop
330	DRILL PRESS OPERATOR, NUMERICAL CONTROL	machine shop
321	DRILLER, HAND	any industry
240	DRIVE-IN THEATER ATTENDANT	amuse. & rec.
251	DRIVER'S LICENSE EXAMINER	government ser.
350	DRIVER, NEWSPAPER DELIVERY	wholesale tr.
430	DROPHAMMER OPERATOR	aircraft mfg.
430	DRUM STRAIGHTENER	any industry
340	DRY CLEANER	laundry & rel.
331	DRY-PRESS OPERATOR	brick & tile
380	DRY WALL APPLICATOR	construction
481	DUCT INSTALLER	construction
330	DYNAMITE PACKING MACHINE OPERATOR	chemical
212	ECHOCARDIOGRAPH TECHNICIAN	medical ser.
110	EDITOR, MANAGING, NEWSPAPER	print. & pub.
111	EDITOR, NEWSPAPER	print. & pub.
111	EDITOR, PUBLICATIONS	print. & pub.
112	EDITORIAL WRITER	print. & pub.
221	EGG CANDLER	any industry
380	ELECTRIC METER INSTALLER	utilities
221	ELECTRIC MOTOR ASSEMBLER	elec. equip.
320	ELECTRIC MOTOR CONTROL UNIT ASSEMBLER	elec. equip.
320	ELECTRIC SIGN ASSEMBLER	fabrication, nec
212	ELECTRICAL ENGINEER	profess. & kin.
212	ELECTRICAL TECHNICIAN	profess. & kin.
221	ELECTRICAL APPLIANCE REPAIRER, SMALL	any industry
370	ELECTRICAL APPLIANCE SERVICER	any industry
460	ELECTRICAL APPLIANCE UNCRATER	any industry
221	ELECTRICAL INSTRUMENT REPAIRER	any industry
380	ELECTRICIAN	construction
380	ELECTRICIAN	ship-boat mfg.
380	ELECTRICIAN APPRENTICE	construction
380	ELECTRICIAN HELPER	any industry
370	ELECTRICIAN, AUTOMOTIVE	automotive ser.
380	ELECTRICIAN, MAINTENANCE	any industry
380	ELECTRICIAN, POWERHOUSE	utilities
460	ELECTROLESS PLATER, PRINTED CIRCUIT BOARD PANELS	electron. comp.
290	ELECTROLOGIST	personal ser.
220	ELECTROMECHANICAL TECHNICIAN	inst. & app.
320	ELECTROMEDICAL EQUIPMENT REPAIRER	any industry
212	ELECTROMYOGRAPHIC TECHNICIAN	medical ser.
221	ELECTRONIC COMPONENT PROCESSOR	electron. comp.
221	ELECTRONICS ASSEMBLER	comm. equip.
212	ELECTRONICS TECHNICIAN	profess. & kin.
221	ELECTRONICS TESTER	comm. equip.
212	ELECTRONICS DESIGN ENGINEER	profess. & kin.
351	ELEVATING GRADER OPERATOR	construction
482	ELEVATOR CONSTRUCTOR	construction
380	ELEVATOR EXAMINER AND ADJUSTER	any industry
460	ELEVATOR OPERATOR, FREIGHT	any industry
380	ELEVATOR REPAIRER	any industry
111	ELIGIBILITY WORKER	government ser.
420	EMBALMER	personal ser.
331	EMBOSSER	any industry
230	EMBOSSING PRESS OPERATOR	print. & pub.
460	EMERGENCY MEDICAL TECHNICIAN	medical ser.
111	EMPLOYEE RELATIONS SPECIALIST	profess. & kin.
111	EMPLOYMENT INTERVIEWER	profess. & kin.
320	ENGINE LATHE OPERATOR	machine shop
213	ENGINEER, AERONAUTICAL TEST	aircraft mfg.
111	ENGINEER, AERONAUTICAL DESIGN	aircraft mfg.

Group No.	Occupation	Industry
212	ENGINEER, AGRICULTURAL	profess. & kin.
212	ENGINEER, AUTOMOTIVE	auto. mfg.
111	ENGINEER, BIOMEDICAL	profess. & kin.
212	ENGINEER, CHEMICAL	profess. & kin.
212	ENGINEER, CIVIL	profess. & kin.
111	ENGINEER, ELECTRO-OPTICAL	profess. & kin.
212	ENGINEER, ELECTRONICS DESIGN	profess. & kin.
212	ENGINEER, FACTORY LAY-OUT	profess. & kin.
213	ENGINEER, FIELD SERVICE	profess. & kin.
212	ENGINEER, MECHANICAL	profess. & kin.
111	ENGINEER, NUCLEAR	profess. & kin.
111	ENGINEER, PACKAGING	profess. & kin.
111	ENGINEER, POWER DISTRIBUTION	utilities
111	ENGINEER, PRODUCT SAFETY	profess. & kin.
212	ENGINEER, RAILROAD	profess. & kin.
213	ENGINEER, SOILS	profess. & kin.
320	ENGRAVER, HAND, HARD METALS	engraving
120	ENGRAVER, HAND, SOFT METALS	engraving; jewelry
230	ENGRAVER, MACHINE	engraving
213	ENVIRONMENTAL ANALYST	profess. & kin.
111	EQUAL OPPORTUNITY REPRESENTATIVE	government ser.
340	EQUIPMENT CLEANER	any industry
370	EQUIPMENT INSTALLER, VEHICLES	any industry
111	ESCROW OFFICER	profess. & kin
111	ESTATE PLANNER	insurance
213	ESTIMATOR/CRUISER	forestry
221	ETCHED CIRCUIT PROCESSOR	electron. comp.
221	ETCHER	engraving
320	ETCHER, HAND	print. & pub.
370	EVAPORATIVE COOLER INSTALLER	any industry
111	EXAMINER	government ser.
390	EXERCISE PHYSIOLOGIST	medical ser.
491	EXERCISER, HORSE	amuse. & rec.
380	EXHIBIT BUILDER	museums
111	EXPEDITER	clerical
360	EXPEDITER, MATERIAL	clerical
380	EXPERIMENTAL AIRCRAFT MECHANIC	aircraft mfg.
213	EXTERMINATOR	business ser.
480	EXTERMINATOR, TERMITE	business ser.
213	EXTRA, ACTOR	amuse. & rec.; motion picture
330	EXTRUDER OPERATOR	rubber goods
220	EYEGLASS LENS CUTTER	optical goods
230	FABRIC STRETCHER	furniture
320	FABRICATING MACHINE OPERATOR, METAL	any industry
221	FABRICATOR, FOAM RUBBER	any industry
330	FABRICATOR/ASSEMBLER, METAL PRODUCTS	any industry
210	FACULTY MEMBER, COLLEGE OR UNIVERSITY	education
492	FALLER	logging
492	FALLER, TIMBER	logging
491	FARM LABORER, GENERAL	agriculture
351	FARM MACHINE OPERATOR	agriculture
491	FARMER, GENERAL	agriculture
491	FARMWORKER, FRUIT	agriculture
491	FARMWORKER, VEGETABLE	agriculture
120	FASHION ARTIST	retail trade
251	FASHION COORDINATOR	retail trade
212	FASHION DESIGNER	profess. & kin.
322	FAST FOODS WORKER	hotel & rest.
460	FEEDER	print. & pub.
331	FELTING MACHINE OPERATOR	tex. prod., nec
481	FENCE ERECTOR	construction
330	FIBERGLASS LAMINATOR	ship-boat mfg.;vehicles nec.
330	FIBERGLASS MACHINE OPERATOR	glass products
213	FIELD ENGINEER	radio-tv broad.
214	FILE CLERK	clerical
221	FILLER	tex. prod., nec
230	FILM DEVELOPER	motion picture
230	FILM OR VIDEOTAPE EDITOR	motion picture
230	FILM PRINTER	motion picture
214	FILM OR TAPE LIBRARIAN	clerical
331	FILTER OPERATOR	any industry
460	FILTER PRESS OPERATOR	any industry
320	FINAL ASSEMBLER	office machines
110	FINANCIAL PLANNER	profess. & kin.
110	FINANCIAL AIDS OFFICER	education
120	FINGERNAIL FORMER	personal ser.

Group No.	Occupation	Industry
490	FIRE FIGHTER	any industry
490	FIRE LOOKOUT	forestry
490	FIRE RANGER	forestry
320	FIRE EXTINGUISHER REPAIRER	any industry
490	FIRE INSPECTOR	government serv.
332	FIRER, HIGH PRESSURE	any industry
320	FIRESETTER	elec. equip.
360	FIREWORKS DISPLAY SPECIALIST	any industry
490	FISH AND GAME WARDEN	government ser.
322	FISH CLEANER	can. & preserv.
491	FISH FARMER	fishing & hunt.
491	FISH HATCHERY LABORER	fishing & hunt.
492	FISHER, DIVING	fishing & hunt.
491	FISHER, LINE	fishing & hunt.
491	FISHER, NET	fishing & hunt.
481	FITTER	construction, pipe lines
430	FITTER, METAL	any industry
320	FIXTURE REPAIRER-FABRICATOR	any industry
213	FLAGGER, TRAFFIC CONTROL	construction
230	FLATWORK FINISHER	laundry & rel.
322	FLIGHT ATTENDANT	air trans.
212	FLIGHT ENGINEER	air trans.
211	FLIGHT INFORMATION EXPEDITER	air trans.
380	FLOOR LAYER	construction
480	FLOOR FINISHER HELPER	construction
221	FLORIST	retail trade
460	FLOUR BLENDER	grain-feed mills
230	FOLDER SEAMER, AUTOMATIC	any industry
230	FOLDING MACHINE OPERATOR	print. & pub.
330	FOLDING MACHINE OPERATOR	paper goods
330	FOLDING MACHINE OPERATOR	textile
322	FOOD ASSEMBLER, KITCHEN	hotel & rest.
492	FOREST WORKER	forestry
490	FOREST FIRE FIGHTER	forestry
213	FORESTER	profess. & kin.
491	FORESTER AIDE	forestry
460	FORGE HELPER	forging
430	FORGING PRESS OPERATOR	forging
351	FORKLIFT OPERATOR	any industry
481	FORM BUILDER	construction
480	FORM STRIPPER	construction

Group No.	Occupation	Industry
480	FORM TAMPER	construction
480	FORM TAMPER OPERATOR	construction
320	FORMER, HAND	any industry
331	FORMING MACHINE OPERATOR	glass mfg.
111	FORMS ANALYST	profess. & kin.
331	FOURDRINIER MACHINE OPERATOR	paper & pulp
470	FRAME REPAIRER	furniture
370	FRAME STRAIGHTENER	motor-bicycles
230	FREEZER OPERATOR	dairy products
491	FRUIT PICKER	agriculture
360	FRUIT BUYING INSPECTOR	can. & preserv.
331	FRUIT GRADER OPERATOR	agriculture
332	FUEL ATTENDANT, PLANT	any industry
480	FUMIGATOR	business ser.
212	FUND RAISER	nonprofit org.
340	FUNERAL ATTENDANT	personal ser.
560	FUNERAL CAR CHAUFFEUR	personal ser.
212	FUNERAL DIRECTOR	personal ser.
341	FURNACE CLEANER	any industry
380	FURNACE INSTALLER AND REPAIRER, HOT AIR	any industry; utilities
321	FURNITURE ASSEMBLER	furniture
470	FURNITURE ASSEMBLER/HEAVY	woodworking
360	FURNITURE CRATER	any industry
221	FURNITURE FINISHER	woodworking
560	FURNITURE MOVER	motor trans.
321	FURNITURE UPHOLSTERER	any industry
221	FURRIER	fur goods
370	GARAGE SERVICER, TRANSPORTATION EQUIPMENT	any industry
560	GARBAGE COLLECTOR, MANUAL	motor trans.
491	GARDENER	domestic ser.
221	GARMENT CUTTER, HAND	any industry
321	GARMENT CUTTER, MACHINE	any industry
332	GAS COMPRESSOR OPERATOR	any industry
332	GAS ENGINE OPERATOR	any industry
320	GAS METER ADJUSTER	utilities
212	GATE AGENT	air trans.
213	GEOLOGIST	profess. & kin.
221	GIFT WRAPPER	retail trade
221	GILDER, METAL LEAF	any industry
230	GINNER	agriculture

Group No.	Occupation	Industry
221	GLASS BLOWER, HAND	glass mfg
420	GLASS CUTTER	any industry
221	GLASS FINISHER	glass products
370	GLASS INSTALLER	automotive ser.
370	GLASS INSTALLER	woodworking
321	GLASS POLISHER	glass mfg.
380	GLAZIER	construction
330	GLUER	woodworking
251	GOLF COURSE RANGER	amuse. & rec.
390	GOLF INSTRUCTOR	amuse. & rec.
493	GOLFER, PROFESSIONAL	amuse. & rec.
340	GOLF RANGE ATTENDANT	amuse. & rec.
360	GRAINER, MACHINE	any industry
110	GRANT COORDINATOR	profess. & kin.
230	GRANULATOR OPERATOR	sugar & conf.
120	GRAPHIC DESIGNER	profess. & kin.
480	GRAVE DIGGER	real estate
340	GREASER	any industry
460	GREEN CHAIN OFFBEARER	millwork-plywood
331	GRINDER OPERATOR	grain-feed mills
320	GRINDER OPERATOR, PRECISION	machine shop
330	GRINDER SET-UP OPERATOR, CENTERLESS	machine shop
330	GRINDER, BENCH	any industry
321	GRINDER, DISK, BELT OR WHEEL	any industry
330	GRINDER, TOOL	any industry
460	GRINDER-CHIPPER, ROUGH	any industry
330	GRINDING MACHINE TENDER	machine shop
482	GRIP	amuse. & rec.
482	GRIP, PROPERTY HANDLER	motion picture
482	GRIP, STAGE CONSTRUCTION	motion picture
214	GROCERY CHECKER	retail trade
230	GROMMET MACHINE OPERATOR	any industry
491	GROOM	any industry
491	GROUNDSKEEPER	any industry
490	GROUP SUPERVISOR	government ser.
490	GUARD, CORRECTIONAL FACILITY	government ser.
240	GUARD, SCHOOL-CROSSING	government ser.
590	GUIDE, ALPINE	personal ser.
213	GUIDE, ESTABLISHMENT	any industry
491	GUIDE, HUNTING AND FISHING	amuse. & rec.
220	GUNSMITH	any industry

Group No.	Occupation	Industry
290	HAIR STYLIST	personal ser.
211	HAND LABELER	any industry
380	HANDYPERSON	any industry
110	HARBOR MASTER	government ser.
380	HARDWOOD FLOOR LAYER	construction
320	HARNESS MAKER	leather prod.
230	HAT AND CAP SEWER	hat & cap
110	HAZARDOUS WASTE MANAGEMENT SPECIALIST	government ser.
110	HEARING OFFICER	government ser.
112	HEARING REPORTER	clerical
330	HEAT TREATER	heat treating
430	HEATER	forging
380	HEATING AND AIR CONDITIONING INSTALLER-SERVICER	construction
230	HEMMER, AUTOMATIC	tex. prod., nec
420	HIDE PULLER	meat products
480	HOD CARRIER	construction
351	HOISTING ENGINEER	any industry
111	HOLTER SCANNING TECHNICIAN	medical ser.
340	HOME ATTENDANT	personal ser.
491	HORSESHOER	agriculture
213	HORTICULTURIST	profess. & kin.
111	HOSPITAL ADMITTING CLERK	medical ser.
240	HOST/HOSTESS	any industry
211	HOTEL CLERK	hotel & rest.
470	HOUSEHOLD APPLIANCE INSTALLER	any industry
340	HOUSEKEEPER, DOMESTIC	domestic ser.; hotel & rest.
332	HYDROELECTRIC STATION OPERATOR	utilities
331	ICE CREAM MAKER	dairy products
460	ICE CUTTER	food prep., nec
120	ILLUSTRATOR	profess. & kin.
110	IMPORT-EXPORT AGENT	any industry
111	INDUSTRIAL ENGINEER	profess. & kin.
213	INDUSTRIAL HYGIENIST	profess. & kin.
111	INFORMATION CLERK	clerical
111	INFORMATION AND REFERRAL AIDE	government ser.
230	INJECTION WAX MOLDER	foundry; jewelry-silver.

Group No.	Occupation	Industry
230	INJECTION MOLDING MACHINE TENDER	plastic prod.
330	INKER	print. & pub.
460	INMATE, LABORER	any industry
120	INSPECTOR	jewelry-silver.
221	INSPECTOR	plastic prod.
221	INSPECTOR	pharmaceut.
213	INSPECTOR, AGRICULTURAL COMMODITIES	government ser.
213	INSPECTOR, AIR CARRIER	government ser.
213	INSPECTOR, AIRPLANE	air trans.
221	INSPECTOR, CANNED FOOD RECONDITIONING	can. & preserv.
320	INSPECTOR, EDDY CURRENT	steel & rel.
221	INSPECTOR, ELECTRONICS	comm. equip.
221	INSPECTOR, FABRIC	any industry
251	INSPECTOR, FOOD AND DRUG	government ser.
321	INSPECTOR, FURNITURE	furniture
221	INSPECTOR, GARMENT	any industry
221	INSPECTOR, GLASS	any industry
251	INSPECTOR, HEALTH CARE FACILITIES	government ser.
120	INSPECTOR, JEWEL	clock & watch
213	INSPECTOR, METAL FABRICATING	any industry
221	INSPECTOR, METAL FINISH	any industry
221	INSPECTOR, PRINTED CIRCUIT BOARDS	electron. comp.
251	INSPECTOR, QUALITY ASSURANCE	government ser.
251	INSPECTOR, TRANSPORTATION	motor trans.
213	INSPECTOR, WEIGH STATION	government ser.
493	INSTRUCTOR, AEROBICS	amuse. & rec.
251	INSTRUCTOR, DRIVING	education
390	INSTRUCTOR, PHYSICAL EDUCATION	education
390	INSTRUCTOR, SPORTS	amuse. & rec.
214	INSTRUCTOR, VOCATIONAL TRAINING	education
320	INSTRUMENT REPAIRER	any industry
220	INSTRUMENT MAKER AND REPAIRER	any industry
380	INSULATION WORKER	construction
221	INTEGRATED CIRCUIT FABRICATOR	electron. comp.

Group No.	Occupation	Industry
120	INTEGRATED CIRCUIT LAYOUT DESIGNER	profess. & kin.
214	INTERIOR DESIGNER	profess. & kin.
220	INTERNIST	medical ser.
210	INTERPRETER	profess. & kin.
212	INTERPRETER, DEAF	profess. & kin.
111	INTERVIEWER, EMPLOYMENT	profess. & kin.
212	INTERVIEWER/SURVEY WORKER	clerical
360	INVENTORY CLERK	clerical
251	INVESTIGATOR	government ser.
111	INVESTIGATOR, CREDIT FRAUD	retail trade
251	INVESTIGATOR, INSIDE/OUTSIDE	business ser.
490	INVESTIGATOR, VICE	government ser.
110	INVESTMENT ANALYST	financial
111	INVOICE CONTROL CLERK	clerical
491	IRRIGATOR, GRAVITY FLOW	agriculture
491	IRRIGATOR, SPRINKLING SYSTEM	agriculture
480	JACKHAMMER OPERATOR	mine & quarry
490	JAILER	government ser.
340	JANITOR	any industry
120	JEWELER	jewelry-silver.
320	JIG MAKER	machine shop
330	JIG-BORING MACHINE OPERATOR, NUMERICAL CONTROL	machine shop
330	JIGSAW OPERATOR	woodworking
212	JOB ANALYST	profess. & kin.
110	JOB DEVELOPMENT SPECIALIST	profess. & kin.
320	JOB SETTER, HONING	machine shop
590	JOCKEY	amuse. & rec.
380	JOINER	ship-boat mfg.
330	JOINTER OPERATOR	woodworking
110	JUDGE	government ser.
221	KEY CUTTER	any industry
230	KICK PRESS OPERATOR	any industry
230	KILN OPERATOR	woodworking
360	KILN WORKER	pottery & porc.
322	KITCHEN HELPER	hotel & rest.
230	KNITTING MACHINE OPERATOR, HOSIERY	knitting
330	KNITTING MACHINE OPERATOR	knitting
492	KNOT BUMPER	logging

Group No.	Occupation	Industry
212	LABORATORY ASSISTANT, BLOOD AND PLASMA	medical ser.
340	LABORATORY EQUIPMENT CLEANER	any industry
220	LABORATORY TESTER	any industry
460	LABORER	meat products
460	LABORER	pharmaceut.
460	LABORER, CHEMICAL PROCESSING	chemical
480	LABORER, CONCRETE PAVING	construction
480	LABORER, CONCRETE MIXING PLANT	construction
480	LABORER, CONSTRUCTION	construction
491	LABORER, FARM	agriculture
360	LABORER, GENERAL	plastic prod.
460	LABORER, GENERAL	machine shop
460	LABORER, GENERAL	nonfer. metal
460	LABORER, GENERAL	steel & rel.
460	LABORER, MILL	woodworking
460	LABORER, PETROLEUM REFINERY	petrol. refin.
480	LABORER, ROAD	construction
460	LABORER, SHIPYARD	ship-boat mfg.
480	LABORER, WRECKING & SALVAGING	construction
460	LABORER, YARD	paper & pulp
331	LACQUERER	plastic prod.
330	LAMINATING MACHINE FEEDER	wood prod., nec.
330	LAMINATING MACHINE OPERATOR	furniture
430	LAMINATING PRESS OPERATOR	plastic prod.
330	LAMINATOR	ship-boat mfg.;vehicles nec.
213	LAND SURVEYOR	profess. & kin.
491	LANDSCAPE GARDENER	agriculture
370	LASER TECHNICIAN/REPAIRER	electron. comp.
230	LASER BEAM MACHINE OPERATOR	welding
230	LASER BEAM TRIM OPERATOR	electron. comp.
330	LATHE OPERATOR, NUMERICAL CONTROL	machine shop
330	LATHE OPERATOR, SWING-TYPE	woodworking
330	LATHE OPERATOR, WOOD-TURNING	woodworking
460	LATHE SPOTTER	millwork-plywood
330	LATHE TENDER	machine shop
380	LATHER, METAL OR WOOD	construction
340	LAUNDERER, HAND	laundry & rel.
491	LAWN SERVICE WORKER	agriculture
110	LAWYER	profess. & kin.
320	LAY-OUT MAKER	sheet metal; any industry
120	LAY-OUT TECHNICIAN	optical goods
491	LEAD PONY RIDER, RACETRACK	amuse. & rec.
221	LEATHER CUTTER	leather prod.
230	LEATHER GARMENT PRESSER	laundry & rel.
320	LEATHER WORKER	leather prod.
110	LEGISLATIVE ASSISTANT	government ser.
220	LENS EXAMINER	optical goods
230	LENS HARDENER	optical goods
320	LENS MOUNTER, OPTICAL	optical goods
220	LENS POLISHER, HAND	optical goods
220	LENS FABRICATING MACHINE TENDER	optical goods
214	LIBRARIAN	library
212	LIBRARIAN, CATALOG	library
214	LIBRARY ASSISTANT	library
211	LICENSE CLERK	government ser.
590	LIFEGUARD	amuse. & rec.
250	LIGHT RAIL CAR OPERATOR	r.r. trans.
341	LIGHT FIXTURE SERVICER	any industry
482	LINE INSTALLER-REPAIRER	tel. & tel.; utilities
341	LINE SERVICE ATTENDANT	air trans.
213	LINE WALKER	petrol. & gas
360	LINEN ROOM CLERK	hotel & rest.
110	LITERARY AGENT	business ser.
491	LIVESTOCK YARD ATTENDANT	any industry
460	LOADER/UNLOADER	any industry
110	LOAN OFFICER	financial
212	LOCATION MANAGER	motion picture
120	LOCK ASSEMBLER	cutlery-hrdwr.
221	LOCKSMITH	any industry
250	LOCOMOTIVE ENGINEER	r.r. trans.
213	LOG SCALER	logging
491	LOG SORTER	logging
492	LOGGER, ALL-ROUND	logging
351	LOGGING TRACTOR OPERATOR	forestry
370	LOOM FIXER	narrow fabrics
340	LUBRICATION SERVICER	automotive ser.

Group No.	Occupation	Industry
320	LUGGAGE REPAIRER	any industry
221	LUMBER GRADER	woodworking
460	LUMBER HANDLER/STACKER	woodworking
360	LUMBER SORTER	woodworking
350	LUNCH TRUCK DRIVER	hotel & rest.
370	MACHINE ASSEMBLER/BUILDER	machinery mfg.
360	MACHINE FEEDER	any industry
460	MACHINE FEEDER, RAW STOCK	tex. prod., nec
330	MACHINE MOLDER	foundry
230	MACHINE OPERATOR, ROOFING MATERIALS	build. mat., nec
320	MACHINE SET-UP OPERATOR	machine shop
221	MACHINE TESTER	office machines
320	MACHINIST	machine shop
320	MACHINIST, AUTOMOTIVE	automotive ser.
370	MACHINIST, BENCH	machinery mfg.
112	MAGNETIC TAPE COMPOSER OPERATOR	print. & pub.
211	MAIL CLERK	clerical
230	MAILING MACHINE OPERATOR	print. & pub.
370	MAINTENANCE MACHINIST	machine shop
470	MAINTENANCE MECHANIC	any industry
380	MAINTENANCE REPAIRER, BUILDING	any industry
470	MAINTENANCE REPAIRER, INDUS. MACHINES & PLANTS	any industry
480	MAINTENANCE WORKER, MUNICIPAL	government ser.
311	MAKE-UP ARTIST, BODY	amuse. & rec.
110	MANAGEMENT ANALYST	profess. & kin.
212	MANAGEMENT TRAINEE	any industry
212	MANAGER, ADVERTISING AGENCY	business ser.
212	MANAGER, APARTMENT HOUSE	real estate
213	MANAGER, AUTOMOBILE SERVICE STATION	retail trade
110	MANAGER, BENEFITS	profess. & kin.
110	MANAGER, BUS TRANSPORTATION	motor trans.
212	MANAGER, CONVENTION	hotel & rest.
212	MANAGER, CUSTOMER SERVICES	business ser.
213	MANAGER, DAIRY FARM	agriculture
110	MANAGER, DATA PROCESSING	profess. & kin.
110	MANAGER, DEPARTMENT	any industry
212	MANAGER, FAST FOOD SERVICES	retail trade
110	MANAGER, HOTEL OR MOTEL	hotel & rest.
212	MANAGER, HOTEL RECREATIONAL FACILITIES	amuse. & rec.
212	MANAGER, LABOR RELATIONS	profess. & kin.
212	MANAGER, MOBILE HOME PARK	real estate
213	MANAGER, NURSERY	agriculture
111	MANAGER, OFFICE	any industry
212	MANAGER, PARTS	retail trade
111	MANAGER, PERSONNEL	profess. & kin.
213	MANAGER, PROPERTY	real estate
212	MANAGER, QUALITY CONTROL	profess. & kin.
212	MANAGER, RETAIL STORE	retail trade
212	MANAGER, STAGE	amuse. & rec.
212	MANAGER, THEATER	amuse. & rec.
110	MANAGER, TRAFFIC	air trans.; any industry
212	MANAGER, VEHICLE LEASING AND RENTAL	automotive ser.
212	MANAGER, WAREHOUSE	any industry
120	MANICURIST	personal ser.
330	MARBLE POLISHER, MACHINE	stonework
481	MARBLE SETTER	construction
480	MARBLE SETTER HELPER	construction
211	MARKER	retail trade
111	MARKET RESEARCH ANALYST	profess. & kin.
221	MASKER, PARTS	any industry
311	MASSEUR/MASSEUSE	personal ser.
212	MASTER CONTROL OPERATOR	radio-tv broad.
221	MAT CUTTER, PICTURE FRAMES	wood prod., nec
360	MATERIAL EXPEDITER	clerical
460	MATERIAL STACKER	any industry
321	MATTRESS MAKER	furniture
322	MEAT CARVER, DISPLAY	hotel & rest.
322	MEAT CLERK	retail trade
322	MEAT CUTTER	retail trade
331	MEAT GRINDER	meat products
380	MECHANIC, AIRCRAFT	aircraft mfg.
370	MECHANIC, AUTOMOBILE	automotive ser.
470	MECHANIC, DIESEL	any industry
370	MECHANIC, FRONT-END	automotive ser.
481	MECHANIC, POWERHOUSE	utilities

Group No.	Occupation	Industry
380	MECHANIC, RADAR	any industry
370	MECHANIC, RADIATOR	automotive ser.
481	MECHANIC, REFRIGERATION	svc. ind. mach.
370	MECHANIC, ROCKET ENGINE COMPONENT	aircraft mfg.
470	MECHANIC, SAFE AND VAULT	business ser.
370	MECHANIC, SMALL ENGINE	any industry
370	MECHANIC, TRACTOR	automotive ser.
370	MECHANIC, TRANSMISSION	automotive ser.
370	MECHANIC, TUNE-UP	automotive ser.
214	MEDIA SPECIALIST, SCHOOL LIBRARY	library
212	MEDICAL ASSISTANT, OFFICE	medical ser.
220	MEDICAL LABORATORY TECHNOLOGIST	medical ser.
470	MEDICAL EQUIPMENT REPAIRER	protective dev.
212	MEDICAL LABORATORY TECHNICIAN	medical ser.
211	MEDICAL RECORD CLERK	medical ser.
321	MELTER	jewelry-silver.
340	MENTAL RETARDATION AIDE, INSTITUTION	medical ser.
213	MESSENGER, NON-DRIVING	clerical
430	METAL FABRICATOR	any industry
321	METAL GRINDER AND FINISHER	any industry
321	METAL SPRAYER, PRODUCTION	any industry
331	METAL CLEANER, IMMERSION	any industry
230	METALLIZATION EQUIPMENT TENDER, SEMICONDUCTORS	comm. equip.
212	METALLURGICAL TESTER	profess. & kin.
213	METER READER	utilities
320	METER REPAIRER	any industry
220	MICROELECTRONICS TECHNICIAN	electron. comp.
230	MICROFILM PROCESSOR	business ser.
212	MICROPHONE BOOM OPERATOR	motion picture
491	MILKER, MACHINE	agriculture
331	MILL OPERATOR	any industry
320	MILLING MACHINE OPERATOR, NUMERICAL CONTROL	machine shop
481	MILLWRIGHT	any industry
480	MILLWRIGHT HELPER	any industry
213	MINE INSPECTOR	mine & quarry

Group No.	Occupation	Industry
560	MINER	mine & quarry
560	MINER HELPER	mine & quarry
221	MINIATURE SET CONSTRUCTOR	motion picture
460	MIXER	paint & varnish
460	MIXER, CLAY	brick & tile
480	MIXER, CONCRETE	construction
460	MIXER, DOUGH	bakery products
460	MIXER, FLOUR	bakery products
480	MIXER, MORTAR	construction
221	MIXER, PAINT (HAND)	any industry
460	MIXER, PAINT (MACHINE)	any industry
331	MIXER, SAND (MACHINE)	foundry
331	MIXING MACHINE OPERATOR	food prep., nec
460	MIXING MACHINE OPERATOR	any industry
380	MOBILE HOME ASSEMBLER	mfd. bldgs.
212	MOBILE HOME PARK MANAGER	real estate
240	MODEL	garment
221	MODEL MAKER	any industry
240	MODEL, ARTISTS'	any industry
213	MODEL, PHOTOGRAPHERS'	any industry
321	MOLD REPAIRER	any industry
221	MOLD AND MODEL MAKER, PLASTER	concrete prod.
330	MOLDER	aircraft mfg.
420	MOLDER, HAND	brick & tile
320	MOLDER, PATTERN	foundry
230	MOLDING MACHINE TENDER, COMPRESSION	plastic prod.
340	MORGUE ATTENDANT	medical ser.
230	MOTION PICTURE PROJECTIONIST	amuse. & rec.
351	MOTOR-GRADER OPERATOR	construction
351	MOTORBOAT OPERATOR	any industry
370	MOTORCYCLE ASSEMBLER	motor-bicycles
250	MOTORCYCLE DRIVER, DELIVERY	retail trade
490	MOTORCYCLE POLICE OFFICER	government ser.
370	MOTORCYCLE REPAIRER	automotive ser.
120	MOUNTER, HAND	photofinishing
310	MRI TECHNOLOGIST	medical ser.
370	MUFFLER INSTALLER	automotive ser.
460	MUNITIONS HANDLER	ordnance
212	MUSEUM ATTENDANT & GUIDE	museums
380	MUSEUM PREPARATOR	museums

Group No.	Occupation	Industry
220	MUSICIAN, INSTRUMENTAL	amuse. & rec.
330	NAILING MACHINE OPERATOR	any industry
111	NAVIGATOR	air trans.
360	NEWS GATHERING TECHNICIAN	radio-tv broad.
210	NEWSCASTER	radio-tv broad.
330	NIBBLER OPERATOR	any industry
111	NIGHT AUDITOR	hotel & rest.
460	NITROGLYCERIN DISTRIBUTOR	chemical
310	NUCLEAR MEDICINE TECHNOLOGIST	medical ser.
330	NUMERICAL CONTROL MACHINE OPERATOR	machine shop
340	NURSE AIDE	medical ser.
220	NURSE ANESTHETIST	medical ser.
212	NURSE CASE MANAGER	medical ser.
311	NURSE, GENERAL DUTY	medical ser.
311	NURSE, LICENSED VOCATIONAL	medical ser.
311	NURSE, PRIVATE DUTY	medical ser.
212	NURSE, SCHOOL	medical ser.
311	NURSE-MIDWIFE	medical ser.
460	NUT ROASTER	can. & preserv.
212	OCCUPATIONAL ANALYST	profess. & kin.
311	OCCUPATIONAL THERAPIST	medical ser.
340	OCCUPATIONAL THERAPY AIDE	medical ser.
213	OCCUPATIONAL SAFETY AND HEALTH INSPECTOR	government ser.
211	OFFICE CLERK, GENERAL	clerical
320	OFFICE MACHINE SERVICER	any industry
330	OFFSET PRESS HELPER	print. & pub.
230	OFFSET DUPLICATING MACHINE OPERATOR	clerical
230	OFFSET PRESS OPERATOR	print. & pub.
480	OIL WELL DRILLER	petrol. & gas
340	OILER	any industry
332	OPERATING ENGINEER	any industry
332	OPERATING ENGINEER, REFRIGERATION	any industry
111	OPTICAL ENGINEER	profess. & kin.
220	OPTICIAN, DISPENSING	optical goods
220	OPTICIAN, LENS GRINDER	optical goods
220	OPTOMETRIST	medical ser.
491	ORCHARD SPRAYER, HAND	agriculture
360	ORDER CHECKER	clerical
111	ORDER CLERK	clerical
214	ORDER CLERK	clerical
214	ORDER FILLER, CATALOG SALES	retail trade
460	ORDERLY	medical ser.
481	ORNAMENTAL IRON WORKER	construction
120	ORTHODONTIC TECHNICIAN	protective dev.
320	ORTHOTICS TECHNICIAN	protective dev.
310	ORTHOTIST	medical ser.
331	OVEN TENDER	bakery products
351	OVERHEAD CRANE OPERATOR	any industry
331	OXIDIZED FINISH PLATER	any industry
221	OXIDIZER	jewelry-silver.
330	PACKAGE SEALER, MACHINE	any industry
330	PACKAGER, MACHINE	any industry
360	PACKER, AGRICULTURAL PRODUCE	agriculture
360	PACKER, HAND	any industry
380	PAINTER	construction
480	PAINTER HELPER	construction
221	PAINTER, AIRBRUSH	any industry
482	PAINTER, BRIDGE, STRUCTURAL STEEL	construction
321	PAINTER, BRUSH	any industry
120	PAINTER, HAND, DECORATIVE	any industry
380	PAINTER, SIGN	any industry
321	PAINTER, SPRAY GUN	any industry
321	PAINTER, TOUCH-UP	any industry
350	PAINTER, TRAFFIC LINE	construction
380	PAINTER, TRANSPORTATION EQUIPMENT	aircraft mfg.
230	PALLETIZER OPERATOR, AUTOMATIC	any industry
230	PAPER CUTTER, MACHINE	beverage
460	PAPER-BALING MACHINE TENDER	any industry
331	PAPER-MAKING MACHINE OPERATOR	paper & pulp
460	PAPERCUTTING MACHINE OPERATOR	print. & pub.
380	PAPERHANGER	construction
321	PARACHUTE RIGGER	air trans.
211	PARALEGAL	profess. & kin.
490	PARAMEDIC	medical ser.

Group No.	Occupation	Industry
211	PARIMUTUEL TICKET SELLER	amuse. & rec.
490	PARK RANGER	government ser.
250	PARKING ENFORCEMENT OFFICER	government ser.
240	PARKING LOT ATTENDANT, BOOTH	automotive serv.
214	PARKING LOT ATTENDANT	automotive ser.
490	PAROLE OFFICER	profess. & kin.
214	PARTS CLERK	clerical
214	PARTS ORDER AND STOCK CLERK	clerical
460	PASTEURIZER	dairy products
250	PATROL OFFICER, VOLUNTEER	government serv.
230	PATTERN-PUNCHING MACHINE OPERATOR	tex. prod., nec
320	PATTERNMAKER, ALL-AROUND	foundry
320	PATTERNMAKER, METAL	foundry
320	PATTERNMAKER, WOOD	foundry
221	PEELER, HAND	can. & preserv.
230	PEELER, MACHINE	can. & preserv.
320	PERCUSSION INSTRUMENT REPAIRER	any industry
310	PERFUSIONIST	medical ser.
390	PERSONAL TRAINER	amuse. & rec.
111	PERSONNEL RECORDS CLERK	clerical
111	PERSONNEL RECRUITER	profess. & kin.
220	PHARMACIST	medical ser.
220	PHLEBOTOMIST	medical ser.
211	PHOTOCOPYING MACHINE OPERATOR	clerical
221	PHOTOENGRAVER	print. & pub.
221	PHOTOFINISHING LABORATORY WORKER	photofinishing
213	PHOTOGRAPHER	amuse. & rec.
212	PHOTOGRAPHER, STILL	profess. & kin.
221	PHOTOGRAPHIC PLATE MAKER	electron. comp.
213	PHOTOJOURNALIST	print. & pub.
230	PHOTOTYPESETTER OPERATOR	print. & pub.
310	PHYSIATRIST	medical ser.
311	PHYSICAL THERAPIST	medical ser.
340	PHYSICAL THERAPY AIDE	medical ser.
212	PHYSICIAN ASSISTANT	medical ser.
220	PHYSICIAN, GENERAL PRACTITIONER	medical ser.
320	PIANO TECHNICIAN	any industry
221	PIANO TUNER	any industry
491	PICKER, FRUIT	agriculture
330	PICKING MACHINE OPERATOR	any industry
221	PICTURE FRAMER	retail trade
351	PILE-DRIVER OPERATOR	construction
370	PINSETTER ADJUSTER, AUTOMATIC	toy-sport equip.
380	PINSETTER MECHANIC, AUTOMATIC	any industry
380	PIPE COVERER AND INSULATOR	ship-boat mfg.
481	PIPE FITTER	construction
480	PIPE LAYER	construction
481	PIPE FITTER HELPER	construction
480	PIPE LAYER HELPER	construction
380	PIPE ORGAN TUNER AND REPAIRER	any industry
480	PIPELINER	pipe lines
214	PIT BOSS/FLOOR PERSON	amusement & rec.
330	PLANER OPERATOR	woodworking
430	PLANER OPERATOR, METAL CASTINGS	machine shop
212	PLANT ENGINEER	profess. & kin.
321	PLASTER MAKER	nonmet. min.
320	PLASTER MOLDER	foundry
420	PLASTER DIE MAKER	pottery & porc.
380	PLASTERER	construction
480	PLASTERER HELPER	construction
230	PLATEN PRESS FEEDER	print. & pub.
230	PLATEN PRESS OPERATOR	print. & pub.
330	PLATER	electroplating
460	PLATER, ELECTROLESS, PRINTED CIRCUIT BOARDS	electron. comp.
460	PLATER, HOT DIP	galvanizing
460	PLATER, PRINTED CIRCUIT BOARD PANELS	electron. comp.
221	PLATER, SEMICONDUCTOR WAFERS & COMPONENTS	electron. comp.
230	PLEATING MACHINE OPERATOR	any industry
481	PLUMBER	construction
481	PLUMBER APPRENTICE	construction
481	PLUMBER HELPER	construction
370	PNEUMATIC TOOL REPAIRER	any industry
380	PNEUMATIC TUBE REPAIRER	any industry
220	PODIATRIST	medical ser.
251	POLICE ARTIST	government ser.

Group No.	Occupation	Industry
490	POLICE CAPTAIN	government ser.
111	POLICE CLERK	government ser.
490	POLICE OFFICER	government ser.
490	POLICE OFFICER, STATE HIGHWAY	government ser.
120	POLISHER, EYEGLASS FRAMES	optical goods
321	POLISHER/BUFFER	any industry
330	POLISHING MACHINE OPERATOR	any industry
212	POLYGRAPH EXAMINER	profess. & kin.
360	PORTER	air trans.
360	PORTER, BAGGAGE	hotel & rest.
330	POTTERY MACHINE OPERATOR	pottery & porc.
322	POULTRY DRESSER	agriculture
430	POWER BRAKE OPERATOR	any industry
230	POWER BARKER OPERATOR	paper & pulp
332	POWER PLANT OPERATOR	utilities
330	POWER PRESS TENDER	any industry
332	POWER REACTOR OPERATOR	utilities
351	POWER SHOVEL OPERATOR	any industry
481	POWERHOUSE MECHANIC	utilities
370	PRECISION ASSEMBLER & REPAIRER	aircraft mfg.
320	PRECISION ASSEMBLER, BENCH	aircraft mfg.
110	PRESIDENT	any industry
230	PRESS OPERATOR	laundry & rel.
330	PRESS OPERATOR, CYLINDER	print. and pub.
430	PRESS OPERATOR, HEAVY DUTY	any industry
331	PRESS OPERATOR, MEAT	meat products
230	PRESS OPERATOR, OFFSET	print. & pub.
330	PRESS OPERATOR, ROTOGRAVURE	print. & pub.
321	PRESSER, ALL-AROUND	laundry & rel.
221	PRESSER, HAND	any industry
321	PRESSER, MACHINE	any industry
230	PRINT DEVELOPER, AUTOMATIC	photofinishing
221	PRINTED CIRCUIT BOARD ASSEMBLER, HAND	comm. equip.
120	PRINTED CIRCUIT DESIGNER	profess. & kin.
320	PRINTER, JOB	print. & pub.
390	PROBATION OFFICER	profess. & kin.
251	PROCESS SERVER	business ser.
360	PRODUCE CLERK, RETAIL	retail trade
212	PRODUCER	radio-tv broad.
212	PROMPTER	amuse. & rec.
211	PROOFREADER	print. & pub.
111	PROOFREADER, PRODUCTION	print. & pub.
380	PROP MAKER	amuse. & rec.
320	PROSTHETICS TECHNICIAN	protective dev.
310	PROSTHETIST	medical ser.
311	PSYCHIATRIC TECHNICIAN	medical ser.
340	PSYCHIATRIC WARD ATTENDANT	medical ser.
110	PSYCHOLOGIST, CLINICAL	profess. & kin.
110	PSYCHOLOGIST, COUNSELING	profess. & kin.
110	PUBLIC HEALTH SERVICE OFFICER	government ser.
380	PUBLIC ADDRESS SETTER-UP & SERVICER	any industry
111	PUBLIC RELATIONS REPRESENTATIVE	profess. & kin.
212	PULMONARY FUNCTION TECHNICIAN	medical ser.
470	PUMP INSTALLER	any industry
370	PUMP SERVICER	any industry
330	PUMP MACHINE OPERATOR	any industry
332	PUMP STATION OPERATOR, WATERWORKS	waterworks
330	PUNCH PRESS OPERATOR	any industry
430	PUNCH PRESS OPERATOR, AUTOMATIC	any industry
251	PURCHASING AGENT	profess. & kin.
111	PURSER	water trans.
321	PUTTY GLAZER, POTTERY	any industry
221	QUALITY ASSURANCE MONITOR	auto. mfg.
212	QUALITY CONTROL TECHNICIAN	profess. & kin.
480	QUARRY WORKER	mine & quarry
120	QUICK SKETCH ARTIST	amuse. & rec.
221	RACKET STRINGER	toy-sport equip.
330	RADIAL ARM SAW OPERATOR	woodworking
320	RADIAL DRILL PRESS SETUP	machine shop
310	RADIATION THERAPY TECHNOLOGIST	medical ser.
212	RADIOGRAPHER, INDUSTRIAL	any industry
310	RADIOLOGIC TECHNOLOGIST	medical ser.
380	RADIOLOGICAL EQUIPMENT SPECIALIST	inst. & app.
212	RADIOTELEPHONE OPERATOR	any industry
481	RAILROAD CAR BUILDER	railroad equip.
481	RAILWAY CAR REPAIRER	railroad equip.

Group No.	Occupation	Industry
460	RAMP ATTENDANT	air trans.
111	RATER	insurance
251	REAL ESTATE AGENT	profess. & kin.
321	REAMER, HAND	machine shop
330	REAMING MACHINE TENDER	nonfer. metal
111	RECEPTIONIST	clerical
212	RECORDING ENGINEER	radio-tv broad.
360	RECORDING STUDIO SET-UP WORKER	recording
230	RECORDIST	motion picture
214	RECREATION AIDE	social ser.
310	RECREATIONAL THERAPIST	medical ser.
111	RECRUITER, PERSONNEL	profess. & kin.
111	REGISTRATION CLERK	government ser.
212	REHABILITATION CENTER MANAGER	government ser.
481	REINFORCING IRON WORKER	construction
221	REPAIRER	furniture
220	REPAIRER, ART OBJECTS	any industry
320	REPAIRER, OFFICE MACHINES	any industry
320	REPAIRER, SALVAGED PARTS	any industry
320	REPAIRER, SMALL APPLIANCE	house. appl.
320	REPAIRER, WIND INSTRUMENT	any industry
220	REPAIRER/ADJUSTER	office machines
251	REPORTER	print. & pub.
110	REPORTS ANALYST	profess. & kin.
213	REPOSSESSOR	clerical
460	RESAW OPERATOR	woodworking
111	RESEARCHER	profess. & kin.
111	RESERVATION CLERK	clerical
111	RESERVATIONS AGENT	air trans.
311	RESPIRATORY THERAPIST	medical ser.
340	RESPIRATORY THERAPY AIDE	medical ser.
240	REST ROOM ATTENDANT	any industry
380	RESTORATION TECHNICIAN	museums
214	RETAIL CLERK	retail trade
111	REVIEWER, FINAL APPLICATION	insurance
330	REWINDER OPERATOR	paper goods
230	RICE GRADER	grain-feed mills
240	RIDE OPERATOR	amuse. & rec.
482	RIGGER	ship-boat mfg.
482	RIGGER, HIGH	amuse. & rec.

Group No.	Occupation	Industry
481	RIGGER/SLINGER	any industry
330	RIPSAW OPERATOR	woodworking
230	RIVET AND BOLT MAKER	any industry
330	RIVETER, HYDRAULIC	any industry
481	RIVETER, PNEUMATIC	any industry
330	RIVETING MACHINE OPERATOR, AUTOMATIC	aircraft mfg.
330	RIVETING MACHINE OPERATOR	any industry
351	ROAD ROLLER OPERATOR	construction
330	ROBOTIC MACHINE OPERATOR	aircraft mfg.
470	ROBOTICS SERVICE TECHNICIAN	machinery mfg.
351	ROCK DRILL OPERATOR	construction
560	ROLL TENDER/SETTER	print. & pub.
330	ROLLER MACHINE OPERATOR	metal prod., nec
230	ROLLING MILL ATTENDANT	steel & rel.
380	ROOFER	construction
480	ROOFER HELPER	construction
322	ROOM SERVICE CLERK	hotel & rest.
480	ROTARY DRILLER	petrol. & gas
480	ROTARY DRILLER HELPER	petrol. & gas
230	ROUGHER, BAR MILL	steel & rel.
480	ROUGHNECK	petrol. & gas
480	ROUSTABOUT	petrol. & gas
211	ROUTER	clerical
330	ROUTER OPERATOR	any industry
330	ROUTER OPERATOR	woodworking
460	RUBBER CUTTER	rubber goods
230	RUBBER MILL OPERATOR	plastic-synth.
340	RUG CLEANER, HAND OR MACHINE	laundry & rel.
321	RUG REPAIRER	laundry & rel.
420	SADDLE MAKER	leather prod.
212	SAFETY ENGINEER	profess. & kin.
212	SAFETY MANAGER	profess. & kin.
380	SAIL MAKER	ship-boat mfg.
322	SALAD MAKER	water trans.
212	SALES AGENT, INSURANCE	insurance
214	SALES CLERK	retail trade
251	SALES REP, FARM, GARDEN EQPT. & SUPPLIES	wholesale tr.
212	SALES REP, ADVERTISING	print. & pub.
251	SALES REP, COMPUTERS AND EDP SYSTEMS	wholesale tr.

Group No.	Occupation	Industry
212	SALES REP, DATA PROCESSING SERVICES	business ser.
251	SALES REP, DOOR-TO-DOOR	retail trade
212	SALES REP, FINANCIAL SERVICES	financial
251	SALES REP, LIVESTOCK	wholesale tr.
251	SALES REP, OFFICE MACHINES	retail trade
251	SALES REP, RECREATION, SPORTING GOODS	wholesale tr.
251	SALES REP, SECURITY SYSTEMS	business ser.
212	SALES REP, UPHOLSTERY, FURNITURE REPAIR	retail trade
251	SALES REP, WOMEN'S AND GIRLS' APPAREL	wholesale tr.
251	SALESPERSON, AUTOMOBILES	retail trade
214	SALESPERSON, GENERAL MERCHANDISE	retail trade
214	SALESPERSON, PARTS	retail trade
214	SALESPERSON, SHOES	retail trade
430	SALVAGE CUTTER	welding
480	SANDBLASTER	any industry
330	SANDER, MACHINE	woodworking
322	SANDWICH MAKER	hotel & rest.
331	SAUSAGE MAKER	meat products
331	SAUSAGE STUFFER	meat products
321	SAW BLADE FILER	any industry
360	SAWMILL WORKER	saw. & plan.
330	SAWYER	plastic prod.; plastic-synth.
230	SAWYER, CIRCULAR HEAD	saw. & plan.
230	SAWYER, CORK SLABS	wood prod., nec
330	SAWYER, TRIMMER	saw. & plan.
111	SCHEDULER	clerical
212	SCHOOL PRINCIPAL	education
111	SCOREBOARD OPERATOR	amuse. & rec.
251	SCOUT, PROFESSIONAL SPORTS	amuse. & rec.
460	SCRAP HANDLER	any industry
320	SCREEN MAKER, PHOTOGRAPHIC PROCESS	any industry
221	SCREEN MAKER, WALLPAPER	paper goods
330	SCREW MACHINE OPERATOR, MULTIPLE SPINDLE	machine shop
330	SCROLL MACHINE OPERATOR	struct. metal

Group No.	Occupation	Industry
321	SCULPTOR	stonework
112	SECRETARY	clerical
112	SECRETARY, LEGAL	clerical
112	SECRETARY, MEDICAL	medical ser.
112	SECRETARY, SOCIAL	clerical
212	SECURITY GUARD, GATE	any industry
213	SECURITY GUARD, PLANT	any industry
390	SECURITY OFFICER	any industry
230	SEED PELLETER	agriculture
212	SEISMOLOGIST	profess. & kin.
330	SEMICONDUCTOR PROCESSOR	electron. comp.
380	SEPTIC TANK INSTALLER	construction
480	SEPTIC TANK SERVICER	construction
214	SERVICE MANAGER	automotive ser.
213	SERVICE REPRESENTATIVE	utilities
340	SERVICE STATION ATTENDANT	automotive ser.
213	SET DESIGNER	motion picture
320	SETTER, AUTOMATIC SPINNING LATHE	any industry
360	SET-UP PERSON, TRADE SHOW	retail trade
480	SEWAGE DISPOSAL WORKER	sanitary ser.
221	SEWER, HAND	any industry
480	SEWER LINE REPAIRER	sanitary ser.
341	SEWER PIPE CLEANER	business ser.
230	SEWING MACHINE OPERATOR	tex. prod., nec
370	SEWING MACHINE REPAIRER	any industry
330	SHAPER OPERATOR	woodworking
330	SHAPING MACHINE OPERATOR	machine shop
430	SHEAR OPERATOR	any industry
370	SHEETMETAL MECHANIC	any industry
320	SHEETMETAL FABRICATING MACHINE OPERATOR	any industry
491	SHELLFISH GROWER	fishing & hunt.
490	SHERIFF, DEPUTY	government ser.
481	SHIPFITTER	ship-boat mfg.
480	SHIPFITTER HELPER	ship-boat mfg.
360	SHIPPING AND RECEIVING CLERK	clerical
214	SHIPPING CHECKER	clerical
380	SHIPWRIGHT	ship-boat mfg.
221	SHOE REPAIRER	personal ser.
214	SHOP ESTIMATOR	automotive ser.
210	SHOW HOST/HOSTESS	radio-tv broad.

Group No.	Occupation	Industry
250	SHUTTLE BUS DRIVER	any industry
380	SIDER	construction
341	SIGN POSTER	any industry
120	SIGN WRITER, HAND	any industry
221	SILK SCREEN ETCHER	engraving
221	SILK SCREEN PRINTER	any industry
221	SILK SCREEN FRAME ASSEMBLER	any industry
220	SILVERSMITH	jewelry-silver.
210	SINGER	amuse. & rec.
493	SKI INSTRUCTOR	amuse. & rec.
240	SKI LIFT OPERATOR	amuse. & rec.
590	SKI PATROLLER	amuse. & rec.
221	SKI REPAIRER, PRODUCTION	toy-sport equip.
420	SKINNER	meat products
480	SKIP TENDER	mine & quarry
111	SKIP TRACER	clerical
460	SLASHER TENDER	textile
230	SLICING MACHINE OPERATOR	bakery products
460	SLITTING MACHINE OPERATOR HELPER	any industry
331	SLURRY BLENDER	cement
370	SMOG TECHNICIAN	automotive ser.
590	SMOKE JUMPER	forestry
351	SNOWPLOW OPERATOR	government ser.
230	SOAP MAKER	soap & rel.
111	SOCIAL WORKER	social ser.
111	SOFTWARE ENGINEER	profess. & kin.
213	SOIL CONSERVATIONIST	profess. & kin.
481	SOLAR ENERGY SYSTEM INSTALLER	any industry
470	SOLAR FABRICATION TECHNICIAN	machine shop
120	SOLDERER	jewelry-silver.
111	SORTER	clerical
221	SORTER, AGRICULTURAL PRODUCE	agriculture
221	SORTER, REMNANT	textile
214	SORTER-PRICER	nonprofit org.
212	SOUND MIXER	motion picture
212	SOUND EFFECTS TECHNICIAN	radio-tv broad.
322	SOUS CHEF	hotel & rest.
490	SPECIAL AGENT	government ser.
390	SPECIAL POLICEMAN	any industry
212	SPEECH PATHOLOGIST	profess. & kin.
331	SPINNER	sugar & conf.

Group No.	Occupation	Industry
430	SPINNER, HYDRAULIC	any industry
330	SPINNING LATHE OPERATOR	any industry
221	SPORTS EQUIPMENT REPAIRER	any industry
221	SPOT CLEANER	laundry & rel.
111	SPOTTER, PHOTOGRAPHIC	photofinishing
330	SPRAY PAINTING MACHINE OPERATOR	any industry
460	SPREADER MACHINE, CLOTH	textile
491	STABLE ATTENDANT	any industry
230	STAMPING PRESS OPERATOR	any industry
390	STAND-IN	motion picture
330	STAPLING MACHINE OPERATOR	any industry
380	STATION INSTALLER AND REPAIRER	tel. & tel.
332	STATIONARY ENGINEER	any industry
111	STATISTICIAN, APPLIED	profess. & kin.
340	STEAM CLEANER	automotive ser.
482	STEEL ERECTOR	construction
380	STEEL PLATE CAULKER	any industry
482	STEEPLE JACK	construction
112	STENOCAPTIONER	radio-tv broad.
112	STENOGRAPHER	clerical
112	STENOTYPE OPERATOR	clerical
330	STEREOTYPE CASTER & MOLDER	print. & pub.
230	STERILIZER	medical ser.
351	STEVEDORE	water trans.
230	STILL TENDER	any industry
230	STITCHER, STANDARD MACHINE	boot & shoe
230	STITCHER, WIRE, SADDLE AND SIDE	print. & pub.
214	STOCK CLERK	clerical
360	STOCK CLERK	clerical
360	STOCK CLERK	retail trade
214	STOCK CLERK, AUTOMOTIVE EQPT.	clerical
321	STONE CARVER	stonework
480	STONE DRILLER	stonework
220	STONE SETTER	jewelry-silver.
480	STONE SPLITTER OPERATOR	stonework
321	STONECUTTER, HAND	stonework
330	STONECUTTER, MACHINE	stonework
380	STONEMASON	construction
120	STONER	jewelry-silver.
470	STOVE REFINISHER	any industry
321	STRAIGHTENER, HAND	any industry

Group No.	Occupation	Industry
330	STRAIGHTENING PRESS OPERATOR	any industry
330	STRANDING MACHINE OPERATOR	elec. equip.
460	STRAPPING MACHINE OPERATOR	wood. container
340	STREET CLEANER/SWEEPER, MANUAL	government ser.
380	STREET LIGHT SERVICER	utilities
351	STREET SWEEPER OPERATOR	government ser.
111	STRESS ANALYST	aircraft mfg.
212	STRESS TEST TECHNICIAN	medical ser.
230	STRETCHING MACHINE TENDER, FRAME	leather mfg.
221	STRIPER & LETTERER, HAND, MOTORCYCLES	any industry
331	STRIPPER-ETCHER, PRINTED CIRCUIT BOARDS	electron. comp.
482	STRUCTURAL STEEL WORKER	construction
482	STRUCTURAL STEEL WORKER HELPER	construction
380	STUCCO MASON	construction
590	STUNT PERFORMER	amuse. & rec.
320	SUBASSEMBLER	machinery mfg.
332	SUBSTATION OPERATOR	utilities
250	SUBWAY CAR OPERATOR	r.r. trans.
332	SUPERCALENDER OPERATOR	paper & pulp
212	SUPERINTENDENT, BUILDING	any industry
213	SUPERINTENDENT, CONSTRUCTION	construction
212	SUPERINTENDENT, PLANT PROTECTION	any industry
360	SUPPLY CLERK	clerical
220	SURGEON	medical ser.
230	SURGICAL DRESSING MAKER, MACHINE	protective dev.
212	SURGICAL TECHNICIAN	medical ser.
213	SURVEYOR	surveying/cartographic
360	SURVEYOR HELPER	any industry
340	SWIMMING POOL SERVICER	any industry
111	SWITCHBOARD OPERATOR, POLICE DISTRICT	government ser.
331	SYRUP MAKER	beverage
111	SYSTEMS ANALYST	profess. & kin.
111	SYSTEMS PROGRAMMER	profess. & kin.

Group No.	Occupation	Industry
230	TACKING MACHINE OPERATOR	any industry
221	TAILOR, ALTERATION	garment
221	TAILOR, CUSTOM	garment
460	TANK CLEANER	any industry
380	TAPER	construction
120	TAPER, PRINTED CIRCUIT LAYOUT	electron. comp.
330	TAPPING MACHINE TENDER	nut & bolt
111	TAX CLERK	clerical
111	TAX PREPARER	business ser.
250	TAXI DRIVER	motor trans.
311	TAXIDERMIST	profess. & kin.
214	TEACHER AIDE	education
212	TEACHER, ADULT EDUCATION	education
214	TEACHER, ELEMENTARY SCHOOL	education
214	TEACHER, INDUSTRIAL ARTS	education
214	TEACHER, LEARNING DISABLED	education
214	TEACHER, MUSIC	education
390	TEACHER, PHYSICAL EDUCATION	education
214	TEACHER, PHYSICALLY IMPAIRED	education
214	TEACHER, PRESCHOOL/KINDERGARTEN	education
212	TEACHER, SECONDARY SCHOOL	education
214	TEACHER, VOCATIONAL TRAINING	education
120	TECHNICAL ILLUSTRATOR	profess. & kin.
112	TELEGRAPH OPERATOR	clerical
112	TELEPHONE OPERATOR	clerical
112	TELEPHONE ANSWERING SERVICE OPERATOR	business ser.
350	TELEPHONE DIRECTORY DELIVERER	business ser.
111	TELEVISION CONSOLE MONITOR	radio-tv broad.
380	TELEVISION RECEIVER/ANTENNA INSTALLER	any industry
470	TELEVISION TECHNICIAN	radio-tv broad.
320	TELEVISION AND RADIO REPAIRER	any industry
211	TELLER	financial
214	TELLER, VAULT	financial
320	TEMPLATE MAKER	any industry
380	TERRAZZO INSTALLER	construction
480	TERRAZZO INSTALLER HELPER	construction
220	TEST TECH, SEMICONDUCTOR PROCESSING EQUIPMENT	electron. comp.
320	TESTER, NONDESTRUCTIVE	profess. & kin.

Group No.	Occupation	Industry
212	TESTING MACHINE OPERATOR, METAL	profess. & kin.
370	THERMAL CUTTER, HAND	welding
330	THERMAL CUTTING-MACHINE OPERATOR	welding
320	THERMOSTAT REPAIRER	inst. & app.
221	THREAD CUTTER, HAND OR MACHINE	any industry
330	THREADING MACHINE OPERATOR	machine shop
321	THROWER	pottery & porc.
212	TICKET AGENT	any industry
213	TICKET INSPECTOR, TRANSPORTATION	r.r. transportation
230	TICKET PRINTER	any industry
240	TICKET TAKER	amuse. & rec.
330	TILE MAKER	brick & tile
380	TILE SETTER	construction
480	TILE SETTER HELPER	construction
330	TIMBER-SIZER OPERATOR	saw. & plan.
212	TIME AND MOTION STUDY ANALYST	profess. & kin.
321	TIRE BUILDER, AUTOMOBILE	rubber tire
460	TIRE CHANGER	automotive ser.
460	TIRE MOLDER	rubber tire
321	TIRE RECAPPER	automotive ser.
460	TIRE REPAIRER	automotive ser.
420	TIRE TRIMMER, HAND	rubber tire
211	TITLE SEARCHER	real estate
211	TOLL COLLECTOR	government ser.
220	TOOL DESIGNER	profess. & kin.
330	TOOL DRESSER	any industry
320	TOOL MAKER	machine shop
320	TOOL MAKER, BENCH	machine shop
120	TOOL PROGRAMMER, NUMERICAL CONTROL	electron. comp.
360	TOOL AND EQUIPMENT RENTAL CLERK	business ser.
360	TOOL CRIB ATTENDANT	clerical
430	TORCH STRAIGHTENER AND HEATER	any industry
221	TOUCH-UP PAINTER, HAND	any industry
482	TOWER ERECTOR	construction

Group No.	Occupation	Industry
212	TOXICOLOGIST	pharmaceut.
221	TOY ASSEMBLER	toy-sport equip.
351	TRACTOR OPERATOR	any industry
351	TRACTOR CRANE OPERATOR	any industry
111	TRAFFIC CLERK	business ser.
212	TRAFFIC ENGINEER	government ser.
490	TRAFFIC OFFICER	government ser.
111	TRAIN DISPATCHER	r.r. trans.
112	TRANSCRIBING MACHINE OPERATOR	clerical
370	TRANSFORMER ASSEMBLER	elec. equip.
111	TRANSLATOR, DOCUMENTS	profess. & kin.
492	TREE CUTTER	agriculture
491	TREE PRUNER, LOW LEVEL/BUCKET	agriculture
482	TREE SURGEON	agriculture
482	TREE TRIMMER	tel. & tel.
230	TRIMMER, MACHINE	garment
322	TRIMMER, MEAT	meat products
221	TROPHY ASSEMBLER	jewelry-silver.
350	TRUCK DRIVER	any industry
350	TRUCK DRIVER, CONCRETE MIXING	construction
350	TRUCK DRIVER, DUMP TRUCK	any industry
350	TRUCK DRIVER, GARBAGE	motor trans.
350	TRUCK DRIVER, LOGS	logging
351	TRUCK DRIVER, ROAD OILING	construction
350	TRUCK DRIVER, SALES ROUTE	retail trade
350	TRUCK DRIVER, TANK TRUCK	petrol. refin.
350	TRUCK DRIVER, TOW TRUCK	automotive ser.
350	TRUCK DRIVER, TRACTOR-TRAILER	any industry
460	TRUCK LOADER	any industry
460	TRUCK DRIVER HELPER	any industry
380	TRUSS BUILDER, CONSTRUCTION	construction
320	TUBE ASSEMBLER, CATHODE RAY	electron. comp.
221	TUBE BENDER, HAND	any industry
341	TUBE CLEANER	any industry
330	TUBULAR FURNITURE MAKER	any industry
111	TUMOR REGISTRAR	medical ser.
332	TURBINE ATTENDANT	utilities
332	TURBINE OPERATOR	utilities
330	TURRET LATHE OPERATOR	machine shop
212	TUTOR	education
221	TYPESETTER/COMPOSITOR	print. & pub.

Group No.	Occupation	Industry
230	TYPESETTING MACHINE TENDER	print. & pub.
112	TYPIST	clerical
212	ULTRASOUND TECHNOLOGIST	medical ser.
214	UMPIRE	amuse. & rec.
110	UNDERWRITER, MORTGAGE LOAN	financial
321	UPHOLSTERY REPAIRER	furniture
110	URBAN PLANNER	profess. & kin.
370	USED CAR RENOVATOR	retail trade
240	USHER	amuse. & rec.
330	UTILITY OPERATOR	saw. & plan.
320	VACUUM CLEANER REPAIRER	any industry
351	VACUUM CLEANER OPERATOR, INDUSTRIAL	any industry
250	VALET, PARKING	automotive serv.
330	VARIETY SAW OPERATOR	woodworking
112	VARITYPE OPERATOR	clerical
214	VAULT CASHIER	business ser.
213	VENDOR	amuse. & rec.
340	VENETIAN BLIND CLEANER AND REPAIRER	any industry
311	VETERINARIAN	medical ser.
311	VETERINARIAN, LABORATORY ANIMAL CARE	medical ser.
311	VETERINARY TECHNICIAN	medical ser.
212	VIDEOTAPE OPERATOR, STUDIO	radio-tv broad.
110	VOCATIONAL REHABILITATION CONSULTANT	government ser.
212	VOICE PATHOLOGIST	profess. & kin.
221	WAFER FAB OPERATOR	electron. comp.
322	WAITER/WAITRESS	hotel & rest.
480	WALLPAPER REMOVER, STEAM	construction
360	WAREHOUSE WORKER	any industry
331	WASHER, MACHINE	any industry
340	WASHER, MACHINE	laundry & rel.
460	WASHING MACHINE LOADER AND PULLER	laundry & rel.
460	WASTE DISPOSAL ATTENDANT, RADIOACTIVE	any industry
332	WASTE TREATMENT OPERATOR	chemical
332	WASTEWATER TREATMENT PLANT OPERATOR	sanitary ser.
220	WATCH REPAIRER	clock & watch
380	WATER METER INSTALLER	waterworks
332	WATER PUMP TENDER	any industry
460	WATER SOFTENER SERVICER AND INSTALLER	business ser.
332	WATER TREATMENT PLANT OPERATOR	waterworks
481	WAYSMAN	ship-boat mfg.
230	WEAVER, TEXTILE	nonmet. min.
330	WEB PRESS OPERATOR HELPER, OFFSET	print. & pub.
330	WEB PRESS OPERATOR	print. & pub.
360	WEIGHER, PRODUCTION	any industry
214	WEIGHER, SHIPPING AND RECEIVING	clerical
240	WEIGHT REDUCTION SPECIALIST	personal services
460	WELDER HELPER	welding
430	WELDER, ARC	welding
370	WELDER, COMBINATION	welding
370	WELDER, GAS	welding
370	WELDER, GUN	welding
370	WELDER, PRODUCTION LINE	welding
430	WELDER, TACK	welding
380	WELDER-FITTER	welding
330	WELDING MACHINE OPERATOR, ARC	welding
480	WELL DIGGER	construction
480	WELL PULLER	petrol. & gas
480	WELL DRILL OPERATOR	construction
480	WELL DRILL OPERATOR HELPER	construction
320	WHEEL LACER AND TRUER	motor-bicycles
482	WIND GENERATING ELECTRIC POWER INSTALLER	construction
482	WIND TURBINE TECHNICIAN	construction; utilities
330	WINDER	paper goods
460	WINDER OPERATOR, FLOOR COVERINGS	fabrication
230	WINDER, MAGNETIC TAPE	recording
330	WINDER, YARN	tex. prod., nec
330	WINDING-MACHINE OPERATOR, CLOTH	textile
341	WINDOW CLEANER	any industry

Group No.	Occupation	Industry	Group No.	Occupation	Industry
380	WINDOW REPAIRER	any industry			
213	WINE MAKER	beverage			
240	WINE STEWARD/STEWARDESS	hotel & rest.			
332	WINERY WORKER	beverage			
221	WIRE HARNESS ASSEMBLER	elec. equip.			
330	WIRE DRAWING MACHINE TENDER	nonfer. metal			
230	WIRE WRAPPING MACHINE OPERATOR	electron. comp.			
330	WOOD-CARVING MACHINE OPERATOR	woodworking			
321	WOOL AND PELT GRADER	meat products			
112	WORD PROCESSING MACHINE OPERATOR	clerical			
330	WRAPPING MACHINE OPERATOR	any industry			
480	WRECKER, CONSTRUCTION	construction			
112	WRITER, PROSE, FICTION AND NONFICTION	profess. & kin.			
112	WRITER, TECHNICAL PUBLICATIONS	profess. & kin.			
212	XRAY OPERATOR, INDUSTRIAL	any industry			
310	XRAY TECHNOLOGIST	medical ser.			
460	YARD ATTENDANT, BUILDING MATERIALS	retail trade			
351	YARDER OPERATOR, FIXED/PORTABLE	logging			

PART B - OCCUPATIONAL GROUP CHART

OCCUPATION DESIGNATOR		STRENGTH DESIGNATOR				
		1 Very Light	2 Light	3 Medium	4 Heavy	5 Very Heavy
1	Professional, Technical, Clerical	110, 111, 112 Case worker Auditor Editor	210, 211, 212, 213, 214 Adm. clerk Bank clerk Clerk, general	310, 311 Physical therapist Chiropractor Psych. tech.		
2	Hand Intensive	120 Drafter, civil Cartoonist Assemb/semi-cond.	220, 221 Dentist Microelect. tech. Surgeon	320, 321, 322 Die maker Meter repair Precision assem.	420 Butcher Saddle maker Hide puller	
3	Machine Operators, Tenders		230 Coil winder Cutter, machine Palletizer oper.	330, 331, 332 Bend. mach. Oper. Cut-off sawyer Laminating mach.	430 Boiler maker . Metal fabricator Welder-arc	
4	Cleaners, Attendants		240 Child monitor Restroom attend. Ticket taker	340, 341 Auto washer Janitor Nurse's aide		
5	Drivers		250, 251 Coin-mach. collector Bus driver	350, 351 Truckdriver/ Tractor-trailer Truckdriver/ dump		
6	Laborers, Material Handlers			360 Warehouse worker Crate maker Material expediter	460 Baker's helper Material stacker Ramp attendant	560 Ambul. Attendant Furniture mover Miner
7	Mechanics, Installers, Repairers, Servicers			370 Mechanic-tractor Precision assemb. Welder, gas	470 Mechanic-diesel Furn. assemb/heavy TV tech.	

	OCCUPATION DESIGNATOR	1 Very Light	2 Light	3 Medium	4 Heavy	5 Very Heavy
8	Construction Workers			380 Electrician Carpenter-Const Handy person	480, 481, 482 Bricklayer Carpenter/ Rough Millwright	
9	Miscellaneous		290 Beautician Barber Cosmetologist	390 Security officer Counselor, camp	490, 491, 492, 493 Farm laborer Gardener Log sorter	590 Athlete Jockey Dancer

PART C – OCCUPATIONAL GROUP CHARACTERISTICS

Group 110

Professional Occupations

Some use of keyboards but less than 112 or 112; greater standing and walking demands than 112 and 120.

Typical occupations: Lawyer, Loan Officer, Urban Planner

Spine	C
Shoulder	C
Elbow	D
Wrist	D
Finger motion.	F
Grip	D
Leg	D
Psych	J

Group 111

Professional and Clerical Occupations

Substantial use of keyboards; greater demands for standing and walking than 112 and 120.

Typical occupations: Accountant, Claims Clerk, Reservations Agent

Spine	C
Shoulder	D
Elbow	F
Wrist	G
Finger motion	G
Grip	E
Leg	D
Psych	I

Group 112

Mostly Clerical Occupations

Highest demand for use of keyboard; prolonged sitting.

Typical occupations: Billing Clerk, Computer Keyboard Operator, Secretary

Spine	D
Shoulder	D
Elbow	G
Wrist	H
Finger motion	I
Grip	E
Leg	C
Psych	I

Group 120

Most Technical Occupations

Precision work requiring skill and dexterity; use of hand tools; more sitting than 110 and 111.

Typical occupations: Electrical drafter, Illustrator, Jeweler

Spine	D
Shoulder	E
Elbow	G
Wrist	H
Finger motion	H
Grip	F
Leg	C
Psych	I

Group 210

Mostly Professional Occupations

Extensive speech and hearing; standing and sitting; may require driving to business locations; other physical demands at the lower end of the light category.

Typical occupations: Actor, Announcer. Clergy member

Spine	D
Shoulder	C
Elbow	D
Wrist	D
Finger motion	E
Grip	C
Leg	E
Psych	I

Group 211

Description	Body part	Variant
Mostly Clerical Occupations	Spine	D
	Shoulder	D
Emphasis on frequent fingering, handling, and possibly some keyboard work; spine and leg demands similar to 210.	Elbow	F
	Wrist	G
	Finger motion	G
	Grip	E
	Leg	E
Typical occupations: Bank clerk, Inventory clerk, License clerk	Psych	H

Group 212

Description	Body part	Variant
Mostly Professional and Medical Occupations	Spine	E
	Shoulder	E
	Elbow	E
Work predominantly performed indoors, but may require driving to locations of business; less use of hands than 211; slightly higher demands on spine than 210 & 211.	Wrist	F
	Finger motion	F
	Grip	E
	Leg	E
	Psych	J
Typical occupations: Chemist, Dialysis Technician, Secondary School Teacher		

Group 213

Description	Body part	Variant
Mostly Professional Occupations	Spine	F
	Shoulder	E
Work performed indoors and outdoors; occasional climbing and uneven ground required, therefore spine and legs have slightly higher variants for this strength level.	Elbow	E
	Wrist	E
	Finger motion	F
	Grip	E
	Leg	F
	Psych	I
Typical occupations: Airplane Inspector, Meter Reader, Property Manager		

Group 214

Description	Body part	Variant
Clerical (physically active) Occupations; Educators, & Retail Sales Occupations	Spine	F
	Shoulder	F
	Elbow	F
	Wrist	G
Very high demand for speech, hearing and vision; high demand for fingering and handling; spine and leg demands at highest level for 200 series.	Finger motion	G
	Grip	F
	Leg	F
	Psych	I
Typical occupations: Auto Shop Estimator, Elementary School Teacher, Retail Sales Clerk		

Group 220

Description	Body part	Variant
Fine precision Occupations in medical, electronic and optical industries	Spine	E
	Shoulder	F
	Elbow	G
	Wrist	H
Very high demands for vision; high demands for hand activity – use of hand tools; highest variants in this strength category for fingering and arm Disabilities.	Finger motion	H
	Grip	F
	Leg	E
	Psych	J
Typical occupations: Dental Hygienist, Instrument Maker & Repairer, Surgeon		

Group 221

Light Assembly Occupations, Food Preparation Occupations

Vision important; repetitive fingering and use of hand tools; similar to 220 for all parts of body except for wrist and finger motion which is one variant lower.

Typical occupations: Assembler, small products Inspector, electronics Produce Sorter

Spine	E
Shoulder	F
Elbow	G
Wrist	G
Finger motion	G
Grip	F
Leg	E
Psych	F

Group 230

Machine Operator and Tenders

Average demands for this strength level on spine and legs; hand activities are most significant.

Typical occupations: Bottle Packer, Circular Saw Operator' Offset Press Operator

Spine	E
Shoulder	F
Elbow	F
Wrist	F
Finger motion	G
Grip	G
Leg	E
Psych	F

Group 240

Mostly Attendants (providing services)

Minimal hand activities; low on arm activities; average for 200 series on spine and legs.

Typical occupations: Host/Hostess, Parking Lot Attendant, booth, Weight Reduction Specialist

Spine	E
Shoulder	D
Elbow	E
Wrist	E
Finger motion	E
Grip	D
Leg	E
Psych	G

Group 250

Public Transportation Drivers & Light Delivery Drivers

Operates light automotive equipment over public thoroughfares; vision, hearing and other head disabilities important; highest variants for spine and leg activities in 200 series (along with 213 & 214); grip demands similar to 251.

Typical occupations: Parking Enforcement Officer, Subway Car Operator, Taxi Driver

Spine	F
Shoulder	F
Elbow	G
Wrist	F
Finger motion	F
Grip	F
Leg	F
Psych	H

Group 251

Outside Sales, Inspectors, & Business Agents (performing extensive driving to reach business locations)

Work requires extensive driving of light automotive equipment over public thoroughfares to reach business locations; vision, hearing and other head disabilities important; average demand for spine and leg activities for this strength level; arms are one variant lower that 250.

Spine	E
Shoulder	D
Elbow	F
Wrist	E
Finger motion	F
Grip	F
Leg	E
Psych	I

Typical occupations: Food & Drug Inspector, Real Estate Agent. Sales, Rep. sporting goods

Group 290

Personal Attendants

Vision important; cosmetic appearance important; arms variants at high end for 200 series.

Typical occupations: Hair Stylist

Spine	E
Shoulder	G
Elbow	G
Wrist	H
Finger motion	G
Grip	F
Leg	E
Psych	H

Group 310

Medical Occupations

Low end of 300 series for most parts of body; head disabilities, including speech, hearing, PTHS are highest in 300 series.

Typical occupations: Acupressurist, MRI Technologist, X-ray Technologist

Spine	F
Shoulder	F
Elbow	F
Wrist	F
Finger motion	F
Grip	F
Leg	F
Psych	I

Group 311

Mostly Medical Occupations

Medical treatments performed result in higher spine demands; head disabilities are at the highest levels.

Typical occupations: Masseur/Masseuse Nurse – LVN, Psychiatric Technician

Spine	G
Shoulder	F
Elbow	G
Wrist	G
Finger motion	G
Grip	F
Leg	F
Psych	J

Group 320

Assemblers

Precision work requiring use of hand tools; highest arm variants for the 320 series; lower end variants for 300 series for spine & leg (same as 321 & 322); highest head variants in 320 series.

Typical occupations: Machinist, Office Machine Servicer, Television & Radio Repairer

Spine	F
Shoulder	F
Elbow	H
Wrist	I
Finger motion	H
Grip	H
Leg	F
Psych	H

Group 321

Assemblers

Use of hand tools required; precision requirements less than 320 – arm variants slightly lower; same demand on spine and legs as 320 & 322.

Typical occupations: Furniture

Spine	F
Shoulder	F
Elbow	G
Wrist	H
Finger motion	G
Grip	G
Leg	F
Psych	F

Assembler, Garment Cutter, machine Painter, spray gun

Group 322

Description	Part	Variant
Food Preparation and Service Occupations	Spine	F
	Shoulder	F
Least precise work in 320 series – arm variants the lowest; spine & legs same as 320 & 321	Elbow	G
	Wrist	G
	Finger motion	G
	Grip	G
Typical occupations: Airline Flight Attendant, Cook, Waiter/Waitress	Leg	F
	Psych	G

Group 330

Description	Part	Variant
Press Operators, Sawyers, etc.	Spine	F
	Shoulder	F
Most demanding on arms of machine operations series (330s); spine and legs at lower end for 300 series, & same as 331 & 322.	Elbow	G
	Wrist	F
	Finger motion	G
	Grip	G
Typical occupations: Blister Machine Operator, Power Press Tender, Tubular Furniture Maker	Leg	F
	Psych	F

Group 331

Description	Part	Variant
Machine Tending & Processing	Spine	F
	Shoulder	F
Observation and control of machinery; occasional stooping required; mechanical adjustments performed; variants similar to 332.	Elbow	F
	Wrist	F
	Finger motion	F
	Grip	F
Typical occupations: Coating Machine Op, Mixing Machine Op, food prep; Washer, machine	Leg	F
	Psych	F

Group 332

Description	Part	Variant
Observation of Large Stationary Equipment	Spine	F
	Shoulder	F
Work performed in a plant or other large facility, some mechanical adjustments of machinery performed lowest variants for 300 series for most parts of body.	Elbow	F
	Wrist	E
	Finger motion	F
	Grip	F
Typical occupations: Brewery Cellar Worker, Power Reactor Operator, Stationary Engineer	Leg	F
	Psych	G

Group 340

Description	Part	Variant
Mostly Cleaners	Spine	G
	Shoulder	F
Work involves cleaning equipment and/or buildings; operation of cleaning devices, some lifting , some climbing, lowest variants for head disabilities of 300 series; lower end of 300 series for arms; highest demands are for spine & leg activities	Elbow	G
	Wrist	F
	Finger motion	F
	Grip	F
	Leg	G
	Psych	D
Typical occupations: Auto Washer & Polisher, Janitor, Nurse Aide		

Group 341

Description	Body part	Variant
Cleaners (working at high levels)	Spine	G
	Shoulder	G
Work generally performed at high levels – higher end of 300 series for spine & legs; average demands on arms.	Elbow	G
	Wrist	F
	Finger motion	F
	Grip	F
	Leg	G
Typical occupations: Aircraft Service Attendant, Sign Poster, Window Cleaner	Psych	D

Group 350

Description	Body part	Variant
Truck Drivers	Spine	G
	Shoulder	F
Operate heavy vehicle over public thoroughfares; may do some loading of materials, may tie down loads, may hook up hoses, etc., and performs related duties; head disabilities highest in 300 series.	Elbow	H
	Wrist	F
	Finger motion	G
	Grip	G
	Leg	G
	Psych	H
Typical occupations: Armored Car Driver, Lunch Truck Driver, Truck Driver		

Group 351

Description	Body part	Variant
Heavy Equipment Operators	Spine	G
	Shoulder	G
Operates heavy construction equipment at work sites; arm demands at lower end of 300 series; spine & leg demands at higher end of 300 series.	Elbow	H
	Wrist	G
	Finger motion	G
	Grip	G
	Leg	G
	Psych	G
Typical occupations: Crane Operator, Forklift Operator, Snowplow Operator		

Group 360

Description	Body part	Variant
Porters, Packers	Spine	G
	Shoulder	G
Significant lifting and carrying required; significant walking required; may occasionally climb at low levels; variants are "G" for most parts of body; head disabilities are mostly "F"or lower.	Elbow	G
	Wrist	F
	Finger motion	F
	Grip	G
	Leg	G
	Psych	E
Typical occupations: Clerk, Shipping; Conveyor Tender; Warehouse worker		

Group 370

Description	Body part	Variant
Mechanical Assembly, Installation, Repairers	Spine	G
	Shoulder	G
	Elbow	I
Mechanical work on automobiles, machinery and other equipment, requiring a combination of some skill and significant physical effort; highest variants in 300 series for arm	Wrist	J
	Finger motion	H
	Grip	H
	Leg	G
	Psych	H

and head disabilities

Typical occupations: Automobile Accessories Installer; Mechanic, automobile; Welder, Combination

Group 380

Skilled Construction Work

Work requires construction of buildings or large structure; strenuous demands on arms, legs & spine result in highest variants in 300 series; significant climbing required.

Typical occupations: Burglar Alarm, Carpenter Electrician

Spine	H
Shoulder	H
Elbow	I
Wrist	J
Finger motion	H
Grip	H
Leg	I
Psych	H

Group 390

Security Officers, Coaches

Inside and outside work requiring significant walking, some uneven ground, and climbing –leg demands are most significant aspect of duties; work may be high risk but not necessarily highly physical; demands for arms & spine are at middle of 300 series.

Typical occupations: Bodyguard, Instructor, Physical education, Security Officer

Spine	G
Shoulder	G
Elbow	G
Wrist	G
Finger motion	G
Grip	G
Leg	H
Psych	H

Group 420

Meat Processing +

Heavy demands placed on arms; spine demand similar to most in 400 series; leg demands lowest in 400 series.

Typical occupations: Baker, Butcher, Glass Cutter

Spine	H
Shoulder	G
Elbow	H
Wrist	I
Finger motion	G
Grip	H
Leg	G
Psych	F

Group 430

Machine-assisted Metal Shaping

Heavy demands on spine & legs in lifting & carrying; work performed at ground level; requires use of heavy hand tools or force with arms.

Typical occupations: Boilermaker, Power Brake Operator, Shear Operator

Spine	H
Shoulder	H
Elbow	I
Wrist	H
Finger motion	H
Grip	H
Leg	H
Psych	G

Group 460

Material Handlers & Machine Loaders & Unloaders

Strenuous demands on spine & legs for lifting and carrying heavy objects; lowest demand for specialized arm activities in 400 series.

Typical occupations: Baggage Handler, Chain Offbearer, Laborer,

Spine	H
Shoulder	G
Elbow	G
Wrist	G
Finger motion	F
Grip	G
Leg	H
Psych	E

Group 470

Description	Body part	Rating
Installers & Repairers	Spine	H
	Shoulder	H
Strenuous demands on all parts of body – variants are at the higher end of the 400 series.	Elbow	I
	Wrist	J
	Finger motion	H
	Grip	H
Typical occupations: Household Appliance Installer, Maintenance Mechanic, Television Technician	Leg	H
	Psych	H

Group 480

Description	Body part	Rating
Construction Helpers, Oil Field Workers & Some Skilled Construction Workers	Spine	I
	Shoulder	H
	Elbow	H
	Wrist	G
Heavy laboring work at construction sites or other work sites; very strenuous use of spine for lifting and exerting force; heavy demands on arms (similar to 492); leg requirements lower than for 481 & 492.	Finger motion	G
	Grip	G
	Leg	H
	Psych	E
Typical occupations: Carpenter Helper; Laborer, construction; Roughneck		

Group 481

Description	Body part	Rating
Skilled Construction Workers	Spine	I
	Shoulder	H
Work requires construction of buildings or large structures; skilled work performed at various levels, with significant demands for climbing, but lower demands on legs than 482; strenuous use of arms (same as 470).	Elbow	I
	Wrist	J
	Finger motion	H
	Grip	H
	Leg	I
	Psych	H
Typical occupations: Cable Television Installer, Millwright, Pipe Fitter		

Group 482

Description	Body part	Rating
Skilled Construction Workers	Spine	J
	Shoulder	I
Construction and maintenance work performed at high and dangerous levels – balance required; demands on spine & legs similar to 590; very strenuous use of arms.	Elbow	J
	Wrist	J
	Finger motion	I
	Grip	J
	Leg	J
	Psych	I
Typical occupations: Bridge Maintenance Worker, Grip (movie industry), Tree Trimmer		

Group 490

Description	Body part	Rating
Mostly Sworn Officers – Police & Fire (legal presumptions apply)	Spine	I
	Shoulder	I
	Elbow	I
Workers called upon to perform demanding activities in unpredictable and dangerous circumstances;	Wrist	H
	Finger motion	H
	Grip	I

significant demands on all parts of body.

Leg	I
Psych	J

Typical occupations: Fire Fighter, Paramedic.Police Officer

Group 491

Agricultural & Livestock Workers

Work requires tending the land and/or caring for animals; physical demands & variants similar to 460 but slightly lower in mental demands.

Spine	H
Shoulder	G
Elbow	G
Wrist	G
Finger motion	F
Grip	G
Leg	H
Psych	D

Typical occupations: Dog Catcher; Farmer, General; Gardener

Group 492

Logging & Fishing Occupations

Very physical work performed outside; high demand on spine & legs for balancing, working on rugged terrain, and climbing; arm and other variants similar to 560.

Spine	I
Shoulder	H
Elbow	H
Wrist	H
Finger motion	G
Grip	H
Leg	I
Psych	E

Typical occupations: Bucker, Logger, all-round

Group 493

Mostly Professional Athletes

Substantial athletic performance required but less arduous than Group 590

Spine	H
Shoulder	H
Elbow	H
Wrist	H
Finger motion	G
Grip	H
Leg	I
Psych	H

Typical occupations: Bowler, professional, Ski instructor, Aerobic instructor

Group 560

Mostly Material Handlers

Requires lifting of large and/or very heavy objects or exerting very significant force – very strenuous demands placed on spine & legs.

Spine	J
Shoulder	H
Elbow	H
Wrist	H
Finger motion	G
Grip	H
Leg	I
Psych	D

Typical occupations: Ambulance Attendant; Furniture Mover; Garbage Collector, manual

Group 590

Mostly Professional Athletes

Peak athletic performance requiring whole body strength with specialized training and skills; highest variants for all parts of the body.

Spine	J
Shoulder	J
Elbow	J
Wrist	J
Finger motion	I
Grip	J
Leg	J
Psych	I

Typical occupations: Athlete, professional; Stunt Performer

SECTION 4 - OCCUPATIONAL VARIANTS

Use this section to determine the occupational variant for the particular impairment and occupation under consideration.

Locate the row on which the impairment number appears*, and the column headed by the group number. Record the letter appearing at the intersection of the row and column. This letter is the "Occupational Variant" which is represented by a letter between "C" and "J" inclusive.

After establishing the occupational variant, turn to Section 5, page 5-1 to adjust the rating for occupation.

*All impairment numbers contain eight numbers in the form XX.XX.XX.XX. Ranges of impairment numbers with the same variants are represented in two ways. As an example, numbers beginning with 03.01-, 03.02- and 03.03- are represented as 03.01--03.03. And all impairment numbers beginning with 13.11.01- are shown as 13.11.01.XX.

		110	111	112	120	210	211	212	213	214	220	221	230	240	250	251	290	310	311	320	321	322	330
03.01 -- 03.06	CARDIO-HEART	G	F	E	E	F	F	G	G	G	G	E	E	F	G	G	F	G	H	F	F	F	F
04.01.00.00	HYPERTENSION	G	F	E	E	F	F	G	G	G	G	E	E	F	G	G	F	G	H	F	F	F	F
04.02.00.00	AORTIC DISEASE	G	F	E	E	F	F	G	G	G	G	E	E	F	G	G	F	G	H	F	F	F	F
04.03.01.00	PERIPH - UE	E	G	H	H	E	G	F	E	G	H	G	G	E	F	F	G	F	G	H	G	G	G
04.03.02.00	PERIPH - LE	D	D	D	D	E	E	E	F	F	E	E	E	E	F	E	E	F	F	F	F	F	F
04.04.00.00	PULM CIRC	F	E	D	D	H	E	F	F	F	E	E	E	E	F	F	F	F	G	F	F	F	F
05.01 -- 05.03	RESPIRATORY	F	E	D	D	H	E	F	F	F	E	E	E	E	F	F	F	F	G	F	F	F	F
06.01.00.00	UPPER DIGEST	F	F	F	F	F	F	F	F	F	F	F	F	F	F	F	F	F	F	F	F	F	F
06.02.00.00	COLON, RECTUM	F	F	F	F	F	F	F	H	F	F	F	F	G	G	G	F	F	F	F	F	F	F
06.03.00.00	FISTULAS	F	F	F	F	F	F	F	F	F	F	F	F	F	F	F	F	F	F	F	F	F	F
06.04.00.00	LIVER	F	F	F	F	F	F	F	F	F	F	F	F	F	F	F	F	F	F	F	F	F	F
06.05.00.00	HERNIA	C	C	C	C	C	D	E	F	F	D	D	E	E	F	E	D	F	G	F	F	F	F
07.01 -- 07.04	URINARY	F	F	F	F	F	F	F	H	F	F	F	F	G	G	G	F	F	F	F	F	F	F
07.05.00.00	REPRODUCTIVE	F	F	F	F	F	F	F	F	F	F	F	F	F	F	F	F	F	F	F	F	F	F
08.01 -- 08.02	SKIN-SCARS	I	I	I	H	J	I	I	H	J	J	G	E	J	H	J	J	I	J	E	E	H	E
08.03 -- 08.04	DERMATITIS	F	F	F	F	F	F	F	F	F	G	F	F	F	F	F	H	F	G	G	F	H	F
08.05.00.00	SKIN CANCER	F	F	F	F	F	F	F	H	F	F	F	F	G	G	G	F	F	F	F	F	F	F
09.01.00.00	HEMATOPOIETIC	F	F	F	F	F	F	F	F	F	F	F	F	F	F	F	F	F	F	F	F	F	F
10.01.00.00	DIABETES	F	F	F	F	F	F	F	F	F	F	F	F	F	F	F	F	F	F	F	F	F	F
11.01.01.00	EAR-HEARING	J	H	I	F	J	H	I	H	J	H	D	E	H	H	J	I	J	J	E	D	H	E
11.01.02.00	VESTIBULAR	D	D	D	D	E	D	E	H	F	F	F	F	E	G	F	E	F	F	F	F	F	F
11.02.01.00	FACE-COSMETIC	I	I	I	H	J	I	I	H	J	J	G	E	J	H	J	J	I	J	E	E	H	E
11.02.02.00	FACE-EYE	I	I	J	J	J	I	I	I	J	J	H	G	G	I	I	J	I	J	I	H	H	G
11.03.01.00	NOSE - SMELL	F	F	F	F	F	F	F	F	F	F	F	F	F	F	F	G	F	F	F	F	H	F
11.03.02.00	MASTICATION	I	H	H	F	J	H	I	H	J	I	F	F	G	G	I	H	H	I	F	F	G	F
11.03.03.00	TASTE-SMELL	F	F	F	F	F	F	F	F	F	F	F	F	F	F	F	G	F	F	F	F	H	F
11.03.04.00	VOICE-SPEECH	J	I	I	F	J	I	I	H	J	I	D	D	H	H	J	I	I	I	D	C	G	D
12.01 -- 12.03	VISION	H	I	J	J	I	I	I	I	I	J	H	G	F	I	H	I	I	I	I	H	G	G

		331	332	340	341	350	351	360	370	380	390	420	430	460	470	480	481	482	490	491	492	493	560	590
03.01 – 03.06	CARDIO-HEART	F	F	G	G	H	G	G	G	H	H	H	H	H	H	H	H	I	I	H	H	I	H	J
04.01.00.00	HYPERTENSION	F	F	G	G	H	G	G	G	H	H	H	H	H	H	H	H	I	I	H	H	I	H	J
04.02.00.00	AORTIC DISEASE	F	F	G	G	H	G	G	G	H	H	H	H	H	H	H	H	I	I	H	H	I	H	J
04.03.01.00	PERIPH - UE	F	F	F	F	G	G	G	H	H	G	H	H	G	H	G	H	J	I	G	H	I	H	J
04.03.02.00	PERIPH - LE	F	F	G	G	G	G	G	G	I	H	G	H	H	H	H	I	J	I	H	I	I	I	J
04.04.00.00	PULM CIRC	F	F	G	G	G	G	G	G	H	H	G	H	G	H	H	H	I	I	G	H	I	H	J
05.01 – 05.03	RESPIRATORY	F	F	G	G	G	G	G	G	H	H	G	H	G	H	H	H	I	I	G	H	I	H	J
06.01.00.00	UPPER DIGEST	F	F	F	F	F	F	F	F	F	F	F	F	F	F	F	F	F	F	F	F	F	F	F
06.02.00.00	COLON, RECTUM	F	F	F	H	G	G	F	F	H	G	F	F	F	F	H	H	H	H	H	H	H	G	H
06.03.00.00	FISTULAS	F	F	F	F	F	F	F	F	F	F	F	F	F	F	F	F	F	F	F	F	F	F	F
06.04.00.00	LIVER	F	F	F	F	F	F	F	F	F	F	F	F	F	F	F	F	F	F	F	F	F	F	F
06.05.00.00	HERNIA	F	F	G	G	G	F	G	G	H	G	H	H	H	H	H	H	J	H	H	H	H	I	J
07.01 – 07.04	URINARY	F	F	F	H	G	G	F	F	H	G	F	F	F	F	H	H	H	H	H	H	H	G	H
07.05.00.00	REPRODUCTIVE	F	F	F	F	F	F	F	F	F	F	F	F	F	F	F	F	F	F	F	F	F	F	F
08.01 – 08.02	SKIN-SCARS	E	E	G	E	G	E	F	F	F	H	E	E	F	F	E	F	E	J	E	E	I	E	I
08.03 – 08.04	DERMATITIS	G	F	G	G	F	F	F	G	G	F	H	F	F	G	F	G	F	F	F	F	F	F	F
08.05.00.00	SKIN CANCER	F	F	F	H	G	G	F	F	H	G	F	F	F	F	H	H	H	H	H	H	H	G	H
09.01.00.00	HEMATOPOIETIC	F	F	F	F	F	F	F	F	F	F	F	F	F	F	F	F	F	F	F	F	F	F	F
10.01.00.00	DIABETES	F	F	F	F	F	F	F	F	F	F	F	F	F	F	F	F	F	F	F	F	F	F	F
11.01.01.00	EAR-HEARING	E	G	F	E	H	G	G	G	G	H	D	F	F	G	F	G	H	I	F	F	I	F	I
11.01.02.00	VESTIBULAR	F	F	F	I	G	G	F	H	J	G	F	G	F	H	G	J	J	I	F	H	I	H	J
11.02.01.00	FACE-COSMETIC	E	E	G	E	G	E	F	F	F	H	E	E	F	F	E	F	E	J	E	E	I	E	I
11.02.02.00	FACE - EYE	F	G	F	F	I	H	F	H	H	H	G	G	F	H	F	H	I	J	F	G	I	F	I
11.03.01.00	NOSE - SMELL	F	F	F	F	H	F	F	F	G	H	F	G	F	F	F	G	I	J	F	G	F	F	J
11.03.02.00	MASTICATION	F	F	F	F	G	F	F	F	F	G	F	F	F	F	F	F	G	H	F	G	F	F	G
11.03.03.00	TASTE-SMELL	F	F	F	F	F	F	F	F	F	G	F	F	F	F	F	F	F	G	F	F	F	F	F
11.03.04.00	VOICE-SPEECH	D	F	G	F	H	F	G	F	G	H	C	D	F	F	F	G	G	I	F	G	H	F	H
12.01 – 12.03	VISION	F	G	F	F	I	H	F	H	H	G	G	G	F	H	F	H	I	I	F	G	I	F	I

		110	111	112	120	210	211	212	213	214	220	221	230	240	250	251	290	310	311	320	321	322	330
13.01.00.00	CONSCIOUSNESS	I	H	H	H	H	H	H	I	H	H	G	F	G	H	H	G	H	H	H	F	G	F
13.02.00.00	EPISODIC NEURO	H	G	I	I	H	G	H	I	H	I	H	F	F	J	I	H	I	I	I	G	H	H
13.03.00.00	AROUSAL	I	H	H	H	H	H	H	I	H	H	G	F	G	H	H	G	H	H	H	F	G	F
13.04.00.00	COGNITIVE IMP	I	H	H	H	H	H	H	I	H	H	G	F	G	H	H	G	H	H	H	F	G	F
13.05.00.00	LANGUAGE DISOR	J	I	I	F	J	I	I	H	J	I	D	D	H	H	J	I	I	I	D	C	G	D
13.06.00.00	BEHAV-EMOT	J	I	I	H	I	H	J	I	I	J	F	F	G	H	I	H	I	J	H	F	G	F
13.07.01.00	CRANIAL-OLFACTORY	F	F	F	F	F	F	F	F	F	F	F	F	F	F	F	G	F	F	F	F	H	F
13.07.02.00	CRANIAL-OPTIC	H	I	J	J	I	I	I	I	I	J	H	G	F	I	H	I	I	I	I	H	G	G
13.07.03.00	CRANIAL-OCULO	H	I	J	J	I	I	I	I	I	J	H	G	F	I	H	I	I	I	I	H	G	G
13.07.04.00	CRANIAL-TRIGEM	I	H	H	F	J	H	I	H	J	I	F	F	G	G	I	H	H	I	F	F	G	F
13.07.05.00	CRANIAL-FACIAL	I	I	I	H	J	I	I	H	J	J	G	E	J	H	J	J	I	J	E	E	H	E
13.07.06.01	CRANIAL-VERTIGO	D	D	D	D	E	D	E	H	F	F	F	F	E	G	F	E	F	F	F	F	F	F
13.07.06.02	CRANIAL-TINNITUS	J	H	I	F	J	H	I	H	J	H	D	E	H	H	J	I	J	J	E	D	H	E
13.07.07.00	CRANIAL-GLOSSO	F	F	F	F	F	F	F	F	F	F	F	F	F	F	F	F	F	F	F	F	F	F
13.07.08.00	CRANIAL-SPINAL ACC	This impairment can affect swallowing and speech, head turning and shoulder motion. Use variant from 11.03.04.00, 15.01.XX.XX, or 16.02.01.00 as appropriate.																					
13.07.09.00	CRANIAL-HYPOGLOS	J	I	I	F	J	I	I	H	J	I	D	D	H	H	J	I	I	I	D	C	G	D
13.08.00.00	STATION GAIT	D	D	C	C	E	E	E	F	F	E	E	E	E	F	E	E	F	F	F	F	F	F
13.09.00.00	UPPER EXTREM	E	G	H	H	E	G	F	E	G	H	G	G	E	F	F	G	F	G	H	G	G	G
13.10.01.00	SPINAL-RESPIR	F	E	D	D	H	E	F	F	F	E	E	E	E	F	F	F	F	G	F	F	F	F
13.10.02.00	SPINAL-URINARY	F	F	F	F	F	F	F	H	F	F	F	F	G	G	G	F	F	F	F	F	F	F
13.10.03.00	SPINAL-ANORECT	F	F	F	F	F	F	F	H	F	F	F	F	G	G	G	F	F	F	F	F	F	F
13.10.04.00	SPINAL-SEXUAL	F	F	F	F	F	F	F	F	F	F	F	F	F	F	F	F	F	F	F	F	F	F
13.11.01.XX	PAIN-UE	E	G	H	H	E	G	F	E	G	H	G	G	E	F	F	G	F	G	H	G	G	G
13.11.02.XX	PAIN-LE	D	D	C	C	E	E	E	F	F	E	E	E	E	F	E	E	F	F	F	F	F	F
13.12.01.XX	PERIPH-SPINE	C	C	D	D	D	D	E	F	F	E	E	E	E	F	E	E	F	G	F	F	F	F
13.12.02.XX	PERIPH-UE	E	G	H	H	E	G	F	E	G	H	G	G	E	F	F	G	F	G	H	G	G	G
13.12.03.XX	PERIPH-LE	D	D	C	C	E	E	E	F	F	E	E	E	E	F	E	E	F	F	F	F	F	F
14.01.00.00	PSYCHIACTRIC	J	I	I	H	I	H	J	I	I	J	F	F	G	H	I	H	I	J	H	F	G	F

		331	332	340	341	350	351	360	370	380	390	420	430	460	470	480	481	482	490	491	492	493	560	590
13.01.00.00	CONSCIOUSNESS	F	F	D	H	H	G	E	H	I	G	F	H	E	H	F	I	J	I	D	G	G	E	J
13.02.00.00	EPISODIC NEURO	G	G	F	I	J	J	F	I	J	G	G	I	G	I	H	J	J	J	G	H	G	H	J
13.03.00.00	AROUSAL	F	F	D	H	H	G	E	H	I	G	F	H	E	H	F	I	J	I	D	G	G	E	J
13.04.00.00	COGNITIVE IMP	F	F	D	H	H	G	E	H	I	G	F	H	E	H	F	I	J	I	D	G	G	E	J
13.05.00.00	LANGUAGE DISOR	D	F	G	F	H	F	G	F	G	H	C	D	F	F	F	G	G	I	F	G	H	F	H
13.06.00.00	BEHAV-EMOT	F	G	D	D	H	G	E	H	H	H	F	G	E	H	E	H	I	J	D	E	H	D	I
13.07.01.00	CRANIAL-OLFACTORY	F	F	F	F	F	F	F	F	F	G	F	F	F	F	F	F	F	G	F	F	F	F	F
13.07.02.00	CRANIAL-OPTIC	F	G	F	F	I	H	F	H	H	G	G	G	F	H	F	H	I	I	F	G	I	F	I
13.07.03.00	CRANIAL-OCULO	F	G	F	F	I	H	F	H	H	G	G	G	F	H	F	H	I	I	F	G	I	F	I
13.07.04.00	CRANIAL-TRIGEM	F	F	F	F	G	F	F	F	F	G	F	F	F	F	F	F	G	H	F	G	G	F	G
13.07.05.00	CRANIAL-FACIAL	E	E	G	E	G	E	F	F	F	H	E	E	F	F	E	F	E	J	E	E	H	E	I
13.07.06.01	CRANIAL-VERTIGO	F	F	F	I	G	G	F	H	J	G	F	G	F	H	G	J	J	I	F	H	I	H	J
13.07.06.02	CRANIAL-TINNITUS	E	G	F	E	H	G	G	G	G	H	D	F	F	G	F	G	H	I	F	F	I	F	I
13.07.07.00	CRANIAL-GLOSSO	F	F	F	F	F	F	F	F	F	F	F	F	F	F	F	F	F	F	F	F	F	F	F
13.07.08.00	CRANIAL-SPINAL ACC	This impairment can affect swallowing and speech, head turning and shoulder motion. Use variant from 11.03.04.00, 15.01.XX.XX, or 16.02.01.00 as appropriate.																						
13.07.09.00	CRANIAL-HYPOGLOS	D	F	G	F	H	F	G	F	G	H	C	D	F	F	F	G	G	I	F	G	H	F	H
13.08.00.00	STATION GAIT	F	F	G	G	G	G	G	G	I	H	G	H	H	H	H	I	J	I	H	I	I	I	J
13.09.00.00	UPPER EXTREM	F	F	F	F	G	G	G	H	H	G	H	H	G	H	G	H	J	I	G	H	H	H	J
13.10.01.00	SPINAL-RESPIR	F	F	G	G	G	G	G	G	H	H	G	H	G	H	H	H	I	I	G	H	I	H	J
13.10.02.00	SPINAL-URINARY	F	F	F	H	G	G	F	F	H	G	F	F	F	F	H	H	H	H	H	H	H	G	H
13.10.03.00	SPINAL-ANORECT	F	F	F	H	G	G	F	F	H	G	F	F	F	F	H	H	H	H	H	H	H	G	H
13.10.04.00	SPINAL-SEXUAL	F	F	F	F	F	F	F	F	F	F	F	F	F	F	F	F	F	F	F	F	F	F	F
13.11.01.XX	PAIN-UE	F	F	F	F	G	G	G	H	H	G	H	H	G	H	G	H	J	I	G	H	H	H	J
13.11.02.XX	PAIN-LE	F	F	G	G	G	G	G	G	I	H	G	H	H	H	H	I	J	I	H	I	I	I	J
13.12.01.XX	PERIPH-SPINE	F	F	G	G	G	G	G	G	H	G	H	H	H	H	I	I	J	I	H	I	H	J	J
13.12.02.XX	PERIPH-UE	F	F	F	F	G	G	G	H	H	G	H	H	G	H	G	H	J	I	G	H	H	H	J
13.12.03.XX	PERIPH-LE	F	F	G	G	G	G	G	G	I	H	G	H	H	H	H	I	J	I	H	I	I	I	J
14.01.00.00	PSYCHIACTRIC	F	G	D	D	H	G	E	H	H	H	F	G	E	H	E	H	I	J	D	E	H	D	I

		110	111	112	120	210	211	212	213	214	220	221	230	240	250	251	290	310	311	320	321	322	330
15.01 -- 15.03	SPINE-DRE-ROM	C	C	D	D	D	D	E	F	F	E	E	E	E	F	E	E	F	G	F	F	F	F
15.04.01.00	CORTIC-ONE UE	E	G	H	H	E	G	F	E	G	H	G	G	E	F	F	G	F	G	H	G	G	G
15.04.02.00	CORTIC-TWO UE	E	G	H	H	E	G	F	E	G	H	G	G	E	F	F	G	F	G	H	G	G	G
15.04.03.00	CORTIC-GAIT	D	D	C	C	E	E	E	F	F	E	E	E	E	F	E	E	F	F	F	F	F	F
15.04.04.00	CORTIC-BLADDER	F	F	F	F	F	F	F	H	F	F	F	F	G	G	G	F	F	F	F	F	F	F
15.04.05.00	CORTIC-ANOREC	F	F	F	F	F	F	F	H	F	F	F	F	G	G	G	F	F	F	F	F	F	F
15.04.06.00	CORTIC-SEXUAL	F	F	F	F	F	F	F	F	F	F	F	F	F	F	F	F	F	F	F	F	F	F
15.04.07.00	CORTIC-RESPIR	F	E	D	D	H	E	F	F	F	E	E	E	E	F	F	F	F	G	F	F	F	F
15.05.XX.XX	PELVIC	C	C	D	D	D	D	E	F	F	E	E	E	E	F	E	E	F	G	F	F	F	F
16.01.01.XX	ARM-AMPUT	E	G	H	H	E	G	F	E	G	H	G	G	E	F	F	G	F	G	H	G	G	G
16.01.02.01	BRACHIAL PLEX	E	G	H	H	E	G	F	E	G	H	G	G	E	F	F	G	F	G	H	G	G	G
16.01.02.02	CARPAL TUNNEL	D	G	H	H	D	G	F	E	G	H	G	F	E	F	E	H	F	G	I	H	G	F
16.01.02.03	ENTRAP-OTHER	E	G	H	H	E	G	F	E	G	H	G	G	E	F	F	G	F	G	H	G	G	G
16.01.02.04	CRPS I	E	G	H	H	E	G	F	E	G	H	G	G	E	F	F	G	F	G	H	G	G	G
16.01.02.05	CRPS II	E	G	H	H	E	G	F	E	G	H	G	G	E	F	F	G	F	G	H	G	G	G
16.01.03.00	PERIPH VASC	E	G	H	H	E	G	F	E	G	H	G	G	E	F	F	G	F	G	H	G	G	G
16.01.04.00	ARM-GRIP/PINCH	D	E	E	F	C	E	E	E	F	F	F	G	D	F	F	F	F	F	H	G	G	G
16.01.05.00	ARM-OTHER	E	G	H	H	E	G	F	E	G	H	G	G	E	F	F	G	F	G	H	G	G	G
16.02.01.00	SHOULER-ROM	C	D	D	E	C	D	E	E	F	F	F	F	D	F	D	G	F	F	F	F	F	F
16.02.02.00	SHOULDER-OTHER	E	G	H	H	E	G	F	E	G	H	G	G	E	F	F	G	F	G	H	G	G	G
16.03.01.00	ELBOW-ROM	D	F	G	G	D	F	E	E	F	G	G	F	E	G	F	G	F	G	H	G	G	G
16.03.02.00	ELBOW-OTHER	E	G	H	H	E	G	F	E	G	H	G	G	E	F	F	G	F	G	H	G	G	G
16.04.01.00	WRIST-ROM	D	G	H	H	D	G	F	E	G	H	G	F	E	F	E	H	F	G	I	H	G	F
16.04.02.00	WRIST-OTHER	E	G	H	H	E	G	F	E	G	H	G	G	E	F	F	G	F	G	H	G	G	G
16.05.XX.XX	HAND	F	G	I	H	E	G	F	F	G	H	G	G	E	F	F	G	F	G	H	G	G	G
16.06.01.XX	THUMB	F	G	G	H	E	G	F	F	G	H	H	G	E	F	F	H	F	G	H	G	G	G
16.06.02.XX	INDEX	F	H	I	I	E	H	G	F	H	I	H	G	E	F	F	H	G	H	I	H	H	G
16.06.03.XX	MIDDLE	F	H	I	I	E	H	G	F	H	I	H	G	E	F	F	H	G	H	I	H	H	G
16.06.04.XX	RING	F	G	I	G	E	G	F	F	G	G	G	F	E	F	F	F	F	G	H	G	G	F
16.06.05.XX	LITTLE	F	G	I	G	E	G	F	F	G	G	G	F	E	F	F	F	F	G	H	G	G	F

		331	332	340	341	350	351	360	370	380	390	420	430	460	470	480	481	482	490	491	492	493	560	590
15.01 – 15.03	SPINE-DRE-ROM	F	F	G	G	G	G	G	G	H	G	H	H	H	H	I	I	J	I	H	I	H	J	J
15.04.01.00	CORTIC-ONE UE	F	F	F	F	G	G	G	H	H	G	H	H	G	H	G	H	J	I	G	H	H	H	J
15.04.02.00	CORTIC-TWO UE	F	F	F	F	G	G	G	H	H	G	H	H	G	H	G	H	J	I	G	H	H	H	J
15.04.03.00	CORTIC-GAIT	F	F	G	G	G	G	G	G	I	H	G	H	H	H	H	I	J	I	H	I	I	I	J
15.04.04.00	CORTIC-BLADDER	F	F	F	H	G	G	F	F	H	G	F	F	F	F	H	H	H	H	H	H	H	G	H
15.04.05.00	CORTIC-ANOREC	F	F	F	H	G	G	F	F	H	G	F	F	F	F	H	H	H	H	H	H	H	G	H
15.04.06.00	CORTIC-SEXUAL	F	F	F	F	F	F	F	F	F	F	F	F	F	F	F	F	F	F	F	F	F	F	F
15.04.07.00	CORTIC-RESPIR	F	F	G	G	G	G	G	G	H	H	G	H	G	H	H	H	I	I	G	H	I	H	J
15.05.XX.XX	PELVIC	F	F	G	G	G	G	G	G	H	G	H	H	H	H	I	I	J	I	H	I	H	J	J
16.01.01.XX	ARM-AMPUT	F	F	F	F	G	G	G	H	H	G	H	H	G	H	G	H	J	I	G	H	H	H	J
16.01.02.01	BRACHIAL PLEX	F	F	F	F	G	G	G	H	H	G	H	H	G	H	G	H	J	I	G	H	H	H	J
16.01.02.02	CARPAL TUNNEL	F	E	F	F	F	G	F	J	J	G	I	H	G	J	G	J	J	H	G	H	H	H	J
16.01.02.03	ENTRAP-OTHER	F	F	F	F	G	G	G	H	H	G	H	H	G	H	G	H	J	I	G	H	H	H	J
16.01.02.04	CRPS I	F	F	F	F	G	G	G	H	H	G	H	H	G	H	G	H	J	I	G	H	H	H	J
16.01.02.05	CRPS II	F	F	F	F	G	G	G	H	H	G	H	H	G	H	G	H	J	I	G	H	H	H	J
16.01.03.00	PERIPH VASC	F	F	F	F	G	G	G	H	H	G	H	H	G	H	G	H	J	I	G	H	H	H	J
16.01.04.00	ARM-GRIP/PINCH	F	F	F	F	G	G	G	H	H	G	H	H	G	H	G	H	J	I	G	H	H	H	J
16.01.05.00	ARM-OTHER	F	F	F	F	G	G	G	H	H	G	H	H	G	H	G	H	J	I	G	H	H	H	J
16.02.01.00	SHOULER-ROM	F	F	F	G	F	G	G	G	H	G	G	H	G	H	H	H	I	I	G	H	H	H	J
16.02.02.00	SHOULDER-OTHER	F	F	F	F	G	G	G	H	H	G	H	H	G	H	G	H	J	I	G	H	H	H	J
16.03.01.00	ELBOW-ROM	F	F	G	G	H	H	G	I	I	G	H	I	G	I	H	I	J	I	G	H	H	H	J
16.03.02.00	ELBOW-OTHER	F	F	F	F	G	G	G	H	H	G	H	H	G	H	G	H	J	I	G	H	H	H	J
16.04.01.00	WRIST-ROM	F	E	F	F	F	G	F	J	J	G	I	H	G	J	G	J	J	H	G	H	H	H	J
16.04.02.00	WRIST-OTHER	F	F	F	F	G	G	G	H	H	G	H	H	G	H	G	H	J	I	G	H	H	H	J
16.05.XX.XX	HAND	F	F	F	F	G	G	F	H	H	G	G	H	F	H	G	H	I	H	F	G	G	G	I
16.06.01.XX	THUMB	F	F	F	F	G	G	F	H	H	G	H	H	G	H	G	H	I	H	G	H	G	H	I
16.06.02.XX	INDEX	F	F	F	F	G	G	F	I	I	G	G	H	F	I	G	I	I	H	F	G	G	G	I
16.06.03.XX	MIDDLE	F	F	F	F	G	G	F	I	I	G	G	H	F	I	G	I	I	H	F	G	G	G	I
16.06.04.XX	RING	F	F	F	F	F	F	F	H	H	G	G	H	F	H	G	H	H	H	F	G	G	G	I
16.06.05.XX	LITTLE	F	F	F	F	F	F	F	H	H	G	G	H	F	H	G	H	H	H	F	G	G	G	I

		110	111	112	120	210	211	212	213	214	220	221	230	240	250	251	290	310	311	320	321	322	330
17.01.01.00	LEG-LENGTH	C	C	C	C	D	D	D	E	D	D	D	D	D	D	D	D	D	E	E	E	E	E
17.01.02.XX	LEG-AMPUT	D	D	C	C	E	E	E	F	F	E	E	E	E	F	E	E	F	F	F	F	F	F
17.01.03.00	LEG-SKIN LOSS	D	D	D	D	E	E	E	F	F	E	E	E	E	F	E	E	F	F	F	F	F	F
17.01.04.00	LEG-PERIPH NRV	D	D	C	C	E	E	E	F	F	E	E	E	E	F	E	E	F	F	F	F	F	F
17.01.05.00	LEG-VASCULAR	D	D	D	D	E	E	E	F	F	E	E	E	E	F	E	E	F	F	F	F	F	F
17.01.06.00	LEG-CAUSALGIA	D	D	C	C	E	E	E	F	F	E	E	E	E	F	E	E	F	F	F	F	F	F
17.01.07.00	LEG-GAIT	D	D	C	C	E	E	E	F	F	E	E	E	E	F	E	E	F	F	F	F	F	F
17.01.08.00	LEG-OTHER	D	D	C	C	E	E	E	F	F	E	E	E	E	F	E	E	F	F	F	F	F	F
17.02.10.00	PELVIS-FX	D	D	C	C	E	E	E	F	F	E	E	E	E	F	E	E	F	F	F	F	F	F
17.03.XX.XX	HIP	D	D	C	C	E	E	E	F	F	E	E	E	E	F	E	E	F	F	F	F	F	F
17.04.10.00	FEMUR-FX	D	D	C	C	E	E	E	F	F	E	E	E	E	F	E	E	F	F	F	F	F	F
17.05.XX.XX	KNEE	D	D	C	C	E	E	E	F	F	E	E	E	E	F	E	E	F	F	F	F	F	F
17.06.10.00	TIBIA-FX	D	D	C	C	E	E	E	F	F	E	E	E	E	F	E	E	F	F	F	F	F	F
17.07.XX.XX	ANKLE	D	D	C	C	E	E	E	F	F	E	E	E	E	F	E	E	F	F	F	F	F	F
17.08.01.00	FOOT-ATROPHY	D	D	C	C	E	E	E	F	F	E	E	E	E	F	E	E	F	F	F	F	F	F
17.08.02.00	FOOT-ANKYLOSIS	C	C	C	C	D	D	D	E	D	D	D	D	D	D	D	D	D	E	E	E	E	E
17.08.03.00	FOOT-ARTHRITIS	D	D	C	C	E	E	E	F	F	E	E	E	E	F	E	E	F	F	F	F	F	F
17.08.04.00	FOOT-ROM	C	C	C	C	D	D	D	E	D	D	D	D	D	D	D	D	D	E	E	E	E	E
17.08.05.00	FOOT-STRENGTH	D	D	C	C	E	E	E	F	F	E	E	E	E	F	E	E	F	F	F	F	F	F
17.08.06.00	FOOT-OTHER	D	D	C	C	E	E	E	F	F	E	E	E	E	F	E	E	F	F	F	F	F	F
17.08.10.XX	FOOT-DBE	D	D	C	C	E	E	E	F	F	E	E	E	E	F	E	E	F	F	F	F	F	F
17.09.01.00	TOE-ATROPHY	C	C	C	C	D	D	D	E	D	D	D	D	D	D	D	D	D	E	E	E	E	E
17.09.02.00	TOE-ANKYLOSIS	C	C	C	C	D	D	D	E	D	D	D	D	D	D	D	D	D	E	E	E	E	E
17.09.03.00	TOE-ARTHRITIS	C	C	C	C	D	D	D	E	D	D	D	D	D	D	D	D	D	E	E	E	E	E
17.09.04.00	TOE-ROM	C	C	C	C	D	D	D	E	D	D	D	D	D	D	D	D	D	E	E	E	E	E
17.09.05.00	TOE-STRENGTH	D	D	C	C	E	E	E	F	F	E	E	E	E	F	E	E	F	F	F	F	F	F
17.09.06.00	TOE-AMPUTATION	D	D	C	C	E	E	E	F	F	E	E	E	E	F	E	E	F	F	F	F	F	F
17.09.07.00	TOE-OTHER	D	D	C	C	E	E	E	F	F	E	E	E	E	F	E	E	F	F	F	F	F	F

		331	332	340	341	350	351	360	370	380	390	420	430	460	470	480	481	482	490	491	492	493	560	590
17.01.01.00	LEG-LENGTH	E	F	E	G	E	E	E	F	G	F	F	F	F	F	G	G	H	G	F	G	I	G	H
17.01.02.00	LEG-AMPUT	F	F	G	G	G	G	G	G	I	H	G	H	H	H	H	I	J	I	H	I	I	I	J
17.01.03.00	LEG-SKIN LOSS	F	F	G	G	G	G	G	G	I	H	G	H	H	H	H	I	J	I	H	I	I	I	J
17.01.04.00	LEG-PERIPH NRV	F	F	G	G	G	G	G	G	I	H	G	H	H	H	H	I	J	I	H	I	I	I	J
17.01.05.00	LEG-VASCULAR	F	F	G	G	G	G	G	G	I	H	G	H	H	H	H	I	J	I	H	I	I	I	J
17.01.06.00	LEG-CAUSALGIA	F	F	G	G	G	G	G	G	I	H	G	H	H	H	H	I	J	I	H	I	I	I	J
17.01.07.00	LEG-GAIT	F	F	G	G	G	G	G	G	I	H	G	H	H	H	H	I	J	I	H	I	I	I	J
17.01.08.00	LEG-OTHER	F	F	G	G	G	G	G	G	I	H	G	H	H	H	H	I	J	I	H	I	I	I	J
17.02.10.00	PELVIS-FX	F	F	G	G	G	G	G	G	I	H	G	H	H	H	H	I	J	I	H	I	I	I	J
17.03.XX.XX	HIP	F	F	G	G	G	G	G	G	I	H	G	H	H	H	H	I	J	I	H	I	I	I	J
17.04.10.00	FEMUR-FX	F	F	G	G	G	G	G	G	I	H	G	H	H	H	H	I	J	I	H	I	I	I	J
17.05.XX.XX	KNEE	F	F	G	G	G	G	G	G	I	H	G	H	H	H	H	I	J	I	H	I	I	I	J
17.06.10.00	TIBIA-FX	F	F	G	G	G	G	G	G	I	H	G	H	H	H	H	I	J	I	H	I	I	I	J
17.07.XX.XX	ANKLE	F	F	G	G	G	G	G	G	I	H	G	H	H	H	H	I	J	I	H	I	I	I	J
17.08.01.00	FOOT-ATROPHY	F	F	G	G	G	G	G	G	I	H	G	H	H	H	H	I	J	I	H	I	I	I	J
17.08.02.00	FOOT-ANKYLOSIS	E	F	E	G	E	E	E	F	G	F	F	F	F	F	G	G	H	G	F	G	I	G	H
17.08.03.00	FOOT-ARTHRITIS	F	F	G	G	G	G	G	G	I	H	G	H	H	H	H	I	J	I	H	I	I	I	J
17.08.04.00	FOOT-ROM	E	F	E	G	E	E	E	F	G	F	F	F	F	F	G	G	H	G	F	G	I	G	H
17.08.05.00	FOOT-STRENGTH	F	F	G	G	G	G	G	G	I	H	G	H	H	H	H	I	J	I	H	I	I	I	J
17.08.06.00	FOOT-OTHER	F	F	G	G	G	G	G	G	I	H	G	H	H	H	H	I	J	I	H	I	I	I	J
17.08.10.XX	FOOT-DBE	F	F	G	G	G	G	G	G	I	H	G	H	H	H	H	I	J	I	H	I	I	I	J
17.09.01.00	TOE-ATROPHY	E	F	E	G	E	E	E	F	G	F	F	F	F	F	G	G	H	G	F	G	H	G	H
17.09.02.00	TOE-ANKYLOSIS	E	F	E	G	E	E	E	F	G	F	F	F	F	F	G	G	H	G	F	G	H	G	H
17.09.03.00	TOE-ARTHRITIS	E	F	E	G	E	E	E	F	G	F	F	F	F	F	G	G	H	G	F	G	H	G	H
17.09.04.00	TOE-ROM	E	F	E	G	E	E	E	F	G	F	F	F	F	F	G	G	H	G	F	G	H	G	H
17.09.05.00	TOE-STRENGTH	F	F	G	G	G	G	G	G	I	H	G	H	H	H	H	I	J	I	H	I	H	I	J
17.09.06.00	TOE-AMPUTATION	F	F	G	G	G	G	G	G	I	H	G	H	H	H	H	I	J	I	H	I	H	I	J
17.09.07.00	TOE-OTHER	F	F	G	G	G	G	G	G	I	H	G	H	H	H	H	I	J	I	H	I	H	I	J

SECTION 5 - OCCUPATIONAL ADJUSTMENT

Use this table to adjust the rating for occupation.

Locate the row on which the rating (after adjustment for diminished future earning capacity) appears and the column headed by the occupation variant (obtained from the Occupational Variant Table in Section 4). Record the number appearing at the intersection of this row and column. This is the rating after adjustment for occupation.

After adjusting the rating for occupation, turn to Section 6, page 6-1 to adjust for age.

OCCUPATIONAL ADJUSTMENT TABLE

Standard Rating Percent	C	D	E	F	G	H	I	J	Standard Rating Percent	C	D	E	F	G	H	I	J
0	0	0	0	0	0	0	0	0									
1	1	1	1	1	2	2	2	2	**26**	19	22	24	26	29	31	34	37
2	1	2	2	2	3	3	4	4	**27**	20	23	25	27	30	33	35	38
3	2	2	3	3	4	5	5	6	**28**	21	24	26	28	31	34	36	39
4	3	3	4	4	5	6	7	8	**29**	22	24	27	29	32	35	37	40
5	3	4	4	5	6	7	8	9	**30**	23	25	28	30	33	36	38	41
6	4	5	5	6	7	8	9	11	**31**	24	26	29	31	34	37	40	43
7	5	5	6	7	8	10	11	12	**32**	25	27	30	32	35	38	41	44
8	6	6	7	8	9	11	12	14	**33**	25	28	30	33	36	39	42	45
9	6	7	8	9	11	12	14	15	**34**	26	29	31	34	37	40	43	46
10	7	8	9	10	12	13	15	16	**35**	27	30	32	35	38	41	44	47
11	7	9	10	11	13	14	16	18	**36**	28	31	33	36	39	42	45	48
12	8	10	11	12	14	16	17	19	**37**	29	32	34	37	40	43	46	49
13	9	10	12	13	15	17	18	20	**38**	30	32	35	38	41	44	47	50
14	10	11	13	14	16	18	20	22	**39**	31	33	36	39	42	45	48	51
15	11	12	14	15	17	19	21	23	**40**	32	34	37	40	43	46	49	52
16	11	13	14	16	18	20	22	24	**41**	33	35	38	41	44	47	50	54
17	12	14	15	17	19	21	23	26	**42**	34	36	39	42	45	48	51	55
18	13	15	16	18	20	22	24	27	**43**	35	37	40	43	46	49	52	56
19	14	15	17	19	21	24	26	28	**44**	36	38	41	44	47	50	53	57
20	15	16	18	20	22	25	27	29	**45**	36	39	42	45	48	51	54	58
21	16	17	19	21	23	26	28	31	**46**	37	40	43	46	49	52	55	59
22	16	18	20	22	24	27	29	32	**47**	38	41	44	47	50	53	56	60
23	17	19	21	23	26	28	31	33	**48**	39	42	45	48	51	54	57	61
24	18	20	22	24	27	29	32	34	**49**	40	43	46	49	52	55	58	62
25	18	21	23	25	28	30	33	36	**50**	41	44	47	50	53	56	59	62

OCCUPATIONAL ADJUSTMENT TABLE

Standard Rating Percent	C	D	E	F	G	H	I	J	Standard Rating Percent	C	D	E	F	G	H	I	J
51	42	45	48	51	54	57	60	64	**76**	68	70	73	76	78	80	82	84
52	43	46	49	52	55	58	61	65	**77**	69	71	74	77	79	81	83	85
53	44	47	50	53	56	59	62	65	**78**	70	72	75	78	80	82	84	86
54	45	48	51	54	57	60	63	66	**79**	71	74	76	79	81	83	84	86
55	46	49	52	55	58	61	64	67	**80**	72	75	77	80	82	83	85	87
56	47	50	53	56	59	62	65	68	**81**	73	76	78	81	83	84	86	88
57	48	51	54	57	60	63	66	69	**82**	74	77	79	82	84	85	87	88
58	49	52	55	58	61	64	67	70	**83**	76	78	81	83	84	86	87	89
59	50	53	56	59	62	65	68	71	**84**	77	79	82	84	85	87	88	90
60	51	54	57	60	63	66	69	72	**85**	78	81	83	85	86	88	89	90
61	52	55	58	61	64	67	69	72	**86**	79	82	84	86	87	89	90	91
62	53	56	59	62	65	68	70	73	**87**	81	83	85	87	88	89	90	92
63	54	57	60	63	66	69	71	74	**88**	82	84	86	88	89	90	91	92
64	55	58	61	64	67	69	72	75	**89**	84	85	87	89	90	91	92	93
65	56	59	62	65	68	70	73	76	**90**	85	87	88	90	91	92	93	94
66	57	60	63	66	69	71	74	77	**91**	86	88	89	91	92	93	93	94
67	58	61	64	67	70	72	75	77	**92**	88	89	91	92	93	93	94	95
68	59	62	65	68	71	73	76	78	**93**	89	91	92	93	94	94	95	96
69	60	63	66	69	71	74	76	79	**94**	91	92	93	94	95	95	96	96
70	61	64	67	70	72	75	77	80	**95**	93	93	94	95	96	96	97	97
71	62	65	68	71	73	76	78	80	**96**	94	94	95	96	96	97	98	98
72	63	66	69	72	74	77	79	81	**97**	95	96	96	97	97	98	98	98
73	65	67	70	73	75	77	79	82	**98**	97	97	98	98	98	98	98	99
74	66	68	71	74	76	78	80	83	**99**	98	99	99	99	99	99	100	100
75	67	69	72	75	77	79	81	83	**100**	100	100	100	100	100	100	100	100

SECTION 6 - AGE ADJUSTMENT

Use this table to modify the rating for age.

Locate the row on which the rating (already adjusted for earning capacity and occupation) appears, and the column headed by the age at time of injury. Record the number appearing at the intersection of the row and column. This is the rating adjusted for earning capacity, occupation and age.

Rating	AGE AT TIME OF INJURY									
	21 and under	22 - 26	27 - 31	32 - 36	37 - 41	42 - 46	47 - 51	52 - 56	57 - 61	62 and over
1	1	1	1	1	1	1	1	1	1	1
2	2	2	2	2	2	2	2	3	3	3
3	2	2	3	3	3	3	3	4	4	4
4	3	3	3	4	4	4	5	5	5	6
5	4	4	4	5	5	5	6	6	6	7
6	5	5	5	6	6	6	7	7	8	8
7	5	6	6	7	7	8	8	9	9	10
8	6	6	7	7	8	9	9	10	10	11
9	7	7	8	8	9	10	10	11	12	12
10	8	8	9	9	10	11	11	12	13	13
11	8	9	10	10	11	12	13	13	14	15
12	9	10	10	11	12	13	14	15	15	16
13	10	11	11	12	13	14	15	16	16	17
14	11	11	12	13	14	15	16	17	18	19
15	12	12	13	14	15	16	17	18	19	20
16	12	13	14	15	16	17	18	19	20	21
17	13	14	15	16	17	18	19	20	21	22
18	14	15	16	17	18	19	20	21	23	24
19	15	16	17	18	19	20	22	23	24	25
20	16	17	18	19	20	21	23	24	25	26
21	17	18	19	20	21	22	24	25	26	27
22	17	18	20	21	22	23	25	26	28	29
23	18	19	20	22	23	24	26	27	29	30
24	19	20	21	23	24	25	27	28	30	31
25	20	21	22	24	25	27	28	29	31	32

	AGE AT TIME OF INJURY									
Rating	**21 and under**	**22 - 26**	**27 - 31**	**32 - 36**	**37 - 41**	**42 - 46**	**47 - 51**	**52 - 56**	**57 - 61**	**62 and over**
26	21	22	23	25	26	28	29	31	32	33
27	22	23	24	26	27	29	30	32	33	35
28	23	24	25	27	28	30	31	33	34	36
29	24	25	26	28	29	31	32	34	36	37
30	24	25	27	28	30	32	33	35	37	38
31	25	26	28	30	31	33	35	36	38	39
32	26	27	29	31	32	34	36	37	39	40
33	27	28	30	32	33	35	37	38	40	42
34	28	29	31	33	34	36	38	39	41	43
35	29	30	32	34	35	37	39	41	42	44
36	30	31	33	35	36	38	40	42	43	45
37	31	32	34	36	37	39	41	43	44	46
38	32	33	35	37	38	40	42	44	46	47
39	33	34	36	38	39	41	43	45	47	48
40	34	35	37	39	40	42	44	46	48	50
41	35	36	38	40	41	43	45	47	49	51
42	36	37	39	41	42	44	46	48	50	52
43	36	37	39	41	43	45	47	49	51	53
44	37	38	40	42	44	46	48	50	52	54
45	38	39	41	43	45	47	49	51	53	55
46	39	40	42	44	46	48	50	52	54	56
47	40	41	43	45	47	49	51	53	55	57
48	41	42	44	46	48	50	52	54	56	58
49	42	43	45	47	49	51	53	55	57	59
50	43	44	46	48	50	52	54	56	58	60

Rating	AGE AT TIME OF INJURY									
	21 and under	22 - 26	27 - 31	32 - 36	37 - 41	42 - 46	47 - 51	52 - 56	57 - 61	62 and over
51	44	45	47	49	51	53	55	57	59	61
52	45	46	48	50	52	54	56	58	60	62
53	46	47	49	51	53	55	57	59	61	63
54	47	48	50	52	54	56	58	60	62	64
55	48	49	51	53	55	57	59	61	63	65
56	49	50	52	54	56	58	60	62	64	66
57	50	51	53	55	57	59	61	63	65	67
58	51	53	55	57	58	60	62	64	66	68
59	52	54	56	58	59	61	63	65	67	69
60	53	55	57	59	60	62	64	66	68	70
61	54	56	58	60	61	63	65	67	69	71
62	55	57	59	61	62	64	66	68	69	71
63	57	58	60	62	63	65	67	69	70	72
64	58	59	61	63	64	66	68	70	71	73
65	59	60	62	64	65	67	69	71	72	74
66	60	61	63	65	66	68	70	72	73	75
67	61	62	64	66	67	69	70	72	74	76
68	62	63	65	67	68	70	71	73	75	77
69	63	64	66	68	69	71	72	74	76	78
70	64	65	67	69	70	72	73	75	76	78
71	65	66	68	70	71	73	74	76	77	79
72	66	67	69	71	72	74	75	77	78	80
73	68	69	70	72	73	75	76	78	79	81
74	69	70	71	73	74	76	77	79	80	82
75	70	71	72	74	75	77	78	80	81	83

Rating	AGE AT TIME OF INJURY									
	21 and under	22 - 26	27 - 31	32 - 36	37 - 41	42 - 46	47 - 51	52 - 56	57 - 61	62 and over
76	71	72	73	75	76	78	79	80	82	83
77	72	73	74	76	77	79	80	81	82	84
78	73	74	75	77	78	80	81	82	83	85
79	74	75	76	78	79	81	82	83	84	86
80	76	77	78	79	80	81	82	84	85	86
81	77	78	79	80	81	82	83	85	86	87
82	78	79	80	81	82	83	84	86	87	88
83	79	80	81	82	83	84	85	86	87	89
84	80	81	82	83	84	85	86	87	88	89
85	81	82	83	84	85	86	87	88	89	90
86	83	83	84	85	86	87	88	89	90	91
87	84	85	85	86	87	88	89	90	91	92
88	85	86	86	87	88	89	90	91	91	92
89	86	87	87	88	89	90	91	91	92	93
90	88	88	89	89	90	91	91	92	93	93
91	89	89	90	90	91	92	92	93	94	94
92	90	90	91	92	92	93	93	94	94	95
93	91	92	92	93	93	94	94	95	95	96
94	92	93	93	94	94	95	95	95	96	96
95	94	94	94	95	95	96	96	96	97	97
96	95	95	95	96	96	96	97	97	97	98
97	96	96	97	97	97	97	97	98	98	98
98	97	98	98	98	98	98	98	98	99	99
99	99	99	99	99	99	99	99	99	99	99
100	100	100	100	100	100	100	100	100	100	100

SECTION 7 – EXAMPLES

The examples in this section illustrate all the basic components of disability rating including converting AMA scales, adjusting for diminished future earning capacity, occupation and age.

Example A – Multiple impairments within a single extremity

A 30-year-old stevedore injures his right arm resulting in the following impairment ratings:

Limited motion of index finger = 50% Digit impairment
Limited motion of ring finger = 80% Digit impairment
Limited motion of shoulder = 20% Upper extremity (UE)
Shoulder instability = 12% UE

1. Follow AMA protocols[1] for combining individual finger impairments into one overall hand impairment. The hand impairment for this example is 18%.

2. Convert hand impairment[2] to whole person scale.

   18% Hand impairment × .9 = 16% UE

   16 % UE × .6 = 10% Whole person impairment (WPI)

3. Combine[3] shoulder impairments.

   20% UE C 12% UE = 30% UE

4. Convert overall shoulder impairment to whole person scale

   30% UE × .6 = 18% WPI

5. Apply earning capacity, occupation and age adjustments[4] to hand and shoulder ratings:

   Hand: 16.05.01.00 – 10 – [1]11 – 351G – 13 – 11 PD

   Shoulder: 16.02.02.00 – 18 – [7]24 – 351G – 27 – 24 PD

6. Combine adjusted ratings for hand and shoulder to obtain final disability.

   24% PD C 11% PD = 32% PD

   The final overall PD rating for this example is 32%.

Example B – Applying the single extremity maximum

A 30-year-old stevedore sustains an injury to his left leg resulting in the following impairment ratings:

Amputation of left leg below knee = 80% LE
Limited motion of left knee = 35% LE
Pain in stump is substantially aggravated by performing ADL's = 3% add-on[5]

---

1 See Chapter 16 of the AMA Guides, 5th edition for protocols.
2 See AMA Guides, 5th edition, pages 438-439, for upper extremity conversion factors.
3 The symbol used to represent the operation of combining is "C". Use the Combined Values Chart on page 8-2 of the Schedule to combine ratings.
4 Rating adjustments and formulas are explained in Section 1 of this Schedule.
5 See Section 1 of PDRS for information regarding add-on's for pain.

1. Convert individual impairments[6] to the whole person scale.

Left leg amputation: 80% LE × .4 = 32% WPI
Left knee motion: 35% LE × .4 = 14% WPI

2. Apply 3% add-on for pain.

32% WPI + 3% WPI = 35% WPI

3. Apply earning capacity, occupation and age adjustments[7] to each whole person impairment.

L leg amp.: 17.01.02.02 – 35 – [5]45 – 351G – 48 – 44 PD
L knee motion: 17.05.04.00 – 14 – [2]16 – 351G–18 – 16 PD

4. Combine[8] the adjusted impairments for the left leg.

44% PD C 16% PD = 53% PD

5. Calculate the maximum value for a single leg adjusted for earning capacity, age and occupation. The maximum rating for a leg before adjustments is 40%.

17.01.02.01 – 40 – [5]51 – 351G – 54 – 50 PD

[6] See AMA Guides, 5th edition, page 527, for lower extremity conversion factors.
[7] Rating adjustments and formulas are explained in Section 1 of this Schedule.
[8] The symbol used to represent the operation of combining is "C". Use the Combined Values Chart on page 8-2 of the Schedule to combine ratings.

6. Compare the results of step 4 and 5 above. Choose the lower as the final value. The correct disability rating for the left leg is 50% PD.

Example C – Multiple impairments to different regions of body

A 30-year-old stevedore sustains injuries to his right arm, low back and legs resulting in the following impairment ratings.

Herniated lumbar disk (DRE Category 3) = 10% WPI

Limited motion of right index finger = 50% Digit impairment
Limited motion of right ring finger = 80% Digit impairment
Limited motion of right shoulder = 20% Upper extremity (UE)
Right shoulder instability = 12% UE

Amputation of left leg two inches below knee = 80% LE
Limited motion of left knee = 35% LE
Pain in stump is substantially aggravated by performing ADL's = 3% add-on[9]

Limited motion of right knee = 8% LE

1. Calculate disability rating for the back by adjusting the back impairment rating for earning capacity, occupation and age.

15.03.01.00 – 10 – [5]13 – 351G – 15 – 13 PD

[9] See Section 1 of PDRS for information regarding add-on's for pain.

2. Calculate disability rating for right arm in accordance with Example A above. The overall disability rating for the arm is 39% PD after adjustment for earning capacity, occupation and age.

3. Calculate the disability rating for the left leg in accordance with Example B above. The overall disability rating for the left leg is 61% PD after adjustment for earning capacity, occupation and age.

4. Calculate disability rating for the right leg as follows:

   a. Convert the lower extremity impairment rating for the right knee to whole person impairment.

      8% LE × .4 = 3% WPI

   b. Adjust the right knee impairment rating for earning capacity, occupation and age.

      17.05.04.00 – 3 – [2]4 – 351G – 5 – 4 PD

5. Combine the ratings for the right arm, back, and each leg in the order from the largest to the smallest. The final overall PD rating for this example is 71%.

   50% PD (left leg) C 32% PD (right arm) = 66% PD
   66% PD C 13% PD (back) = 70% PD
   70% PD C 4% PD (right leg) = 71% PD

SECTION 8 - COMBINED VALUES CHART

Use this chart to combine two or more impairments, or two or more disabilities. When combining groups of three or more values, always combine the larger two first, and then successively combine the result with the next smaller until all values are combined.

COMBINED VALUES CHART

DIRECTIONS: To combine any two values, locate the larger value on the left side of the chart, and the smaller value at the bottom of the chart. The intersection of that row and column contains the combined value.

	1	2	3	4	5	6	7	8	9	10	11	12	13	14	15	16	17	18	19	20	21	22	23	24	25	26	27	28	29	30	31	32	33	34	35	36	37	38	39	40	41	42	43	44	45	46	47	48	49	50
1	2																																																	
2	3	4																																																
3	4	5	6																																															
4	5	6	7	8																																														
5	6	7	8	9	10																																													
6	7	8	9	10	11	12																																												
7	8	9	10	11	12	13	14																																											
8	9	10	11	12	13	14	14	15																																										
9	10	11	12	13	14	14	15	16	17																																									
10	11	12	13	14	15	15	16	17	18	19																																								
11	12	13	14	15	15	16	17	18	19	20	21																																							
12	13	14	15	16	16	17	18	19	20	21	22	23																																						
13	14	15	16	16	17	18	19	20	21	22	23	23	24																																					
14	15	16	17	17	18	19	20	21	22	23	23	24	25	26																																				
15	16	17	18	18	19	20	21	22	23	24	24	25	26	27	28																																			
16	17	18	19	19	20	21	22	23	24	24	25	26	27	28	29	29																																		
17	18	19	19	20	21	22	23	24	24	25	26	27	28	29	29	30	31																																	
18	19	20	20	21	22	23	24	25	25	26	27	28	29	29	30	31	32	33																																
19	20	21	21	22	23	24	25	25	26	27	28	29	30	30	31	32	33	34	34																															
20	21	22	22	23	24	25	26	26	27	28	29	30	30	31	32	33	34	34	35	36																														
21	22	23	23	24	25	26	27	27	28	29	30	30	31	32	33	34	34	35	36	37	38																													
22	23	24	24	25	26	27	27	28	29	30	31	31	32	33	34	34	35	36	37	38	38	39																												
23	24	25	25	26	27	28	28	29	30	31	31	32	33	34	35	35	36	37	38	38	39	40	41																											
24	25	26	26	27	28	29	29	30	31	32	32	33	34	35	35	36	37	38	38	39	40	41	41	42																										
25	26	27	27	28	29	30	30	31	32	33	33	34	35	36	36	37	38	39	39	40	41	42	42	43	44																									
26	27	27	28	29	30	30	31	32	33	33	34	35	36	36	37	38	39	39	40	41	42	42	43	44	45	45																								
27	28	28	29	30	31	31	32	33	34	34	35	36	36	37	38	39	39	40	41	42	42	43	44	45	45	46	47																							
28	29	29	30	31	32	32	33	34	34	35	36	37	37	38	39	40	40	41	42	42	43	44	45	45	46	47	47	48																						
29	30	30	31	32	33	33	34	35	35	36	37	38	38	39	40	40	41	42	42	43	44	45	45	46	47	47	48	49	50																					
30	31	31	32	33	34	34	35	36	36	37	38	38	39	40	41	41	42	43	43	44	45	45	46	47	48	48	49	50	50	51																				
31	32	32	33	34	34	35	36	37	37	38	39	39	40	41	41	42	43	43	44	45	45	46	47	48	48	49	50	50	51	52	52																			
32	33	33	34	35	35	36	37	37	38	39	39	40	41	42	42	43	44	44	45	46	46	47	48	48	49	50	50	51	52	52	53	54																		
33	34	34	35	36	36	37	38	38	39	40	40	41	42	42	43	44	44	45	46	46	47	48	48	49	50	50	51	52	52	53	54	54	55																	
34	35	35	36	37	37	38	39	39	40	41	41	42	43	43	44	45	45	46	47	47	48	49	49	50	51	51	52	52	53	54	54	55	56	56																
35	36	36	37	38	38	39	40	40	41	42	42	43	43	44	45	45	46	47	47	48	49	49	50	51	51	52	53	53	54	55	55	56	56	57	58															
36	37	37	38	39	39	40	40	41	42	42	43	44	44	45	46	46	47	48	48	49	49	50	51	51	52	53	53	54	55	55	56	56	57	58	58	59														
37	38	38	39	40	40	41	41	42	43	43	44	45	45	46	46	47	48	48	49	50	50	51	51	52	53	53	54	55	55	56	57	57	58	58	59	60	60													
38	39	39	40	40	41	42	42	43	44	44	45	45	46	47	47	48	49	49	50	50	51	52	52	53	54	54	55	55	56	57	57	58	58	59	60	60	61	62												
39	40	40	41	41	42	43	43	44	44	45	46	46	47	48	48	49	49	50	51	51	52	52	53	54	54	55	55	56	57	57	58	59	59	60	60	61	62	62	63											
40	41	41	42	42	43	44	44	45	45	46	47	47	48	48	49	50	50	51	51	52	53	53	54	54	55	56	56	57	57	58	59	59	60	60	61	62	62	63	63	64										
41	42	42	43	43	44	45	45	46	46	47	47	48	49	49	50	50	51	52	52	53	53	54	55	55	56	56	57	58	58	59	59	60	60	61	62	62	63	63	64	65	65									
42	43	43	44	44	45	45	46	47	47	48	48	49	50	50	51	51	52	52	53	54	54	55	55	56	57	57	58	58	59	59	60	61	61	62	62	63	63	64	65	65	66	66								
43	44	44	45	45	46	46	47	48	48	49	49	50	50	51	52	52	53	53	54	54	55	56	56	57	57	58	58	59	60	60	61	61	62	62	63	64	64	65	65	66	66	67	68							
44	45	45	46	46	47	47	48	48	49	50	50	51	51	52	52	53	54	54	55	55	56	56	57	57	58	59	59	60	60	61	61	62	62	63	64	64	65	65	66	66	67	68	68	69						
45	46	46	47	47	48	48	49	49	50	51	51	52	52	53	53	54	54	55	55	56	57	57	58	58	59	59	60	60	61	62	62	63	63	64	64	65	65	66	66	67	68	68	69	69	70					
46	47	47	48	48	49	49	50	50	51	51	52	52	53	54	54	55	55	56	56	57	57	58	58	59	60	60	61	61	62	62	63	63	64	64	65	65	66	67	67	68	68	69	69	70	70	71				
47	48	48	49	49	50	50	51	51	52	52	53	53	54	54	55	55	56	57	57	58	58	59	59	60	60	61	61	62	62	63	63	64	64	65	66	66	67	67	68	68	69	69	70	70	71	71	72			
48	49	49	50	50	51	51	52	52	53	53	54	54	55	55	56	56	57	57	58	58	59	59	60	60	61	62	62	63	63	64	64	65	65	66	66	67	67	68	68	69	69	70	70	71	71	72	72	73		
49	50	50	51	51	52	52	53	53	54	54	55	55	56	56	57	57	58	58	59	59	60	60	61	61	62	62	63	63	64	64	65	65	66	66	67	67	68	68	69	69	70	70	71	71	72	72	73	73	74	
50	51	51	52	52	53	53	54	54	55	55	56	56	57	57	58	58	59	59	60	60	61	61	62	62	63	63	64	64	65	65	66	66	67	67	68	68	69	69	70	70	71	71	72	72	73	73	74	74	75	75

COMBINED VALUES CHART (CON'T)

	1	2	3	4	5	6	7	8	9	10	11	12	13	14	15	16	17	18	19	20	21	22	23	24	25	26	27	28	29	30	31	32	33	34	35	36	37	38	39	40	41	42	43	44	45	46	47	48	49	50
51	51	52	52	53	53	54	54	55	55	56	56	57	57	58	58	59	59	60	60	61	61	62	62	63	63	64	64	65	65	66	66	67	67	68	68	69	69	70	70	71	71	72	72	73	73	74	74	75	75	76
52	52	53	53	54	54	55	55	56	56	57	57	58	58	59	59	60	60	61	61	62	62	63	63	64	64	64	65	65	66	66	67	67	68	68	69	69	70	70	71	71	72	72	73	73	74	74	75	75	76	76
53	53	54	54	55	55	56	56	57	57	58	58	59	59	60	60	61	61	61	62	62	63	63	64	64	65	65	66	66	67	67	68	68	69	69	69	70	70	71	71	72	72	73	73	74	74	75	75	76	76	77
54	54	55	55	56	56	57	57	58	58	59	59	60	60	60	61	61	62	62	63	63	64	64	65	65	66	66	66	67	67	68	68	69	69	70	70	71	71	71	72	72	73	73	74	74	75	75	76	76	77	77
55	55	56	56	57	57	58	58	59	59	60	60	60	61	61	62	62	63	63	64	64	64	65	65	66	66	67	67	68	68	69	69	69	70	70	71	71	72	72	73	73	73	74	74	75	75	76	76	77	77	78
56	56	57	57	58	58	59	59	60	60	60	61	61	62	62	63	63	63	64	64	65	65	66	66	67	67	67	68	68	69	69	70	70	71	71	71	72	72	73	73	74	74	74	75	75	76	76	77	77	78	78
57	57	58	58	59	59	60	60	60	61	61	62	62	63	63	63	64	64	65	65	66	66	66	67	67	68	68	69	69	69	70	70	71	71	72	72	72	73	73	74	74	75	75	75	76	76	77	77	78	78	79
58	58	59	59	60	60	61	61	61	62	62	63	63	63	64	64	65	65	66	66	66	67	67	68	68	69	69	69	70	70	71	71	71	72	72	73	73	74	74	74	75	75	76	76	76	77	77	78	78	79	79
59	59	60	60	61	61	61	62	62	63	63	64	64	64	65	65	66	66	66	67	67	68	68	68	69	69	70	70	70	71	71	72	72	73	73	73	74	74	75	75	75	76	76	77	77	77	78	78	79	79	80
60	60	61	61	62	62	62	63	63	64	64	64	65	65	66	66	66	67	67	68	68	68	69	69	70	70	70	71	71	72	72	72	73	73	74	74	74	75	75	76	76	76	77	77	78	78	78	79	79	80	80
61	61	62	62	63	63	63	64	64	65	65	65	66	66	66	67	67	68	68	68	69	69	70	70	70	71	71	72	72	72	73	73	73	74	74	75	75	75	76	76	77	77	77	78	78	79	79	79	80	80	81
62	62	63	63	64	64	64	65	65	65	66	66	67	67	67	68	68	68	69	69	70	70	70	71	71	72	72	72	73	73	73	74	74	75	75	75	76	76	76	77	77	78	78	78	79	79	79	80	80	81	81
63	63	64	64	64	65	65	66	66	66	67	67	67	68	68	69	69	69	70	70	70	71	71	72	72	72	73	73	73	74	74	74	75	75	76	76	76	77	77	77	78	78	79	79	79	80	80	80	81	81	82
64	64	65	65	65	66	66	67	67	67	68	68	68	69	69	69	70	70	70	71	71	72	72	72	73	73	73	74	74	74	75	75	76	76	76	77	77	77	78	78	78	79	79	79	80	80	81	81	81	82	82
65	65	66	66	66	67	67	67	68	68	69	69	69	70	70	70	71	71	71	72	72	72	73	73	73	74	74	74	75	75	76	76	76	77	77	77	78	78	78	79	79	79	80	80	80	81	81	81	82	82	83
66	66	67	67	67	68	68	68	69	69	69	70	70	70	71	71	71	72	72	72	73	73	73	74	74	75	75	75	76	76	76	77	77	77	78	78	78	79	79	79	80	80	80	81	81	81	82	82	82	83	83
67	67	68	68	68	69	69	69	70	70	70	71	71	71	72	72	72	73	73	73	74	74	74	75	75	75	76	76	76	77	77	77	78	78	78	79	79	79	80	80	80	81	81	81	82	82	82	83	83	83	84
68	68	69	69	69	70	70	70	71	71	71	72	72	72	72	73	73	73	74	74	74	75	75	75	76	76	76	77	77	77	78	78	78	79	79	79	80	80	80	80	81	81	81	82	82	82	83	83	83	84	84
69	69	70	70	70	71	71	71	71	72	72	72	73	73	73	74	74	74	75	75	75	76	76	76	76	77	77	77	78	78	78	79	79	79	80	80	80	80	81	81	81	82	82	82	83	83	83	84	84	84	85
70	70	71	71	71	72	72	72	72	73	73	73	74	74	74	75	75	75	75	76	76	76	77	77	77	78	78	78	78	79	79	79	80	80	80	81	81	81	81	82	82	82	83	83	83	84	84	84	84	85	85
71	71	72	72	72	72	73	73	73	74	74	74	74	75	75	75	76	76	76	77	77	77	77	78	78	78	79	79	79	79	80	80	80	81	81	81	81	82	82	82	83	83	83	83	84	84	84	85	85	85	86
72	72	73	73	73	73	74	74	74	75	75	75	75	76	76	76	76	77	77	77	78	78	78	78	79	79	79	80	80	80	80	81	81	81	82	82	82	82	83	83	83	83	84	84	84	85	85	85	85	86	86
73	73	74	74	74	74	75	75	75	75	76	76	76	77	77	77	77	78	78	78	78	79	79	79	79	80	80	80	81	81	81	81	82	82	82	82	83	83	83	84	84	84	84	85	85	85	85	86	86	86	87
74	74	75	75	75	75	76	76	76	76	77	77	77	77	78	78	78	78	79	79	79	79	80	80	80	81	81	81	81	82	82	82	82	83	83	83	83	84	84	84	84	85	85	85	85	86	86	86	86	87	87
75	75	76	76	76	76	77	77	77	77	78	78	78	78	79	79	79	79	80	80	80	80	81	81	81	81	82	82	82	82	83	83	83	83	84	84	84	84	85	85	85	85	86	86	86	86	87	87	87	87	88
76	76	76	77	77	77	77	78	78	78	78	79	79	79	79	80	80	80	80	81	81	81	81	82	82	82	82	82	83	83	83	83	84	84	84	84	85	85	85	85	86	86	86	86	87	87	87	87	88	88	88
77	77	77	78	78	78	78	79	79	79	79	80	80	80	80	80	81	81	81	81	82	82	82	82	83	83	83	83	83	84	84	84	84	85	85	85	85	86	86	86	86	86	87	87	87	87	88	88	88	88	89
78	78	78	79	79	79	79	80	80	80	80	80	81	81	81	81	82	82	82	82	82	83	83	83	83	84	84	84	84	84	85	85	85	85	85	86	86	86	86	87	87	87	87	87	88	88	88	88	89	89	89
79	79	79	80	80	80	80	80	81	81	81	81	82	82	82	82	82	83	83	83	83	83	84	84	84	84	84	85	85	85	85	86	86	86	86	86	87	87	87	87	87	88	88	88	88	88	89	89	89	89	90
80	80	80	81	81	81	81	81	82	82	82	82	82	83	83	83	83	83	84	84	84	84	84	85	85	85	85	85	86	86	86	86	86	87	87	87	87	87	88	88	88	88	88	89	89	89	89	89	90	90	90
81	81	81	82	82	82	82	82	83	83	83	83	83	83	84	84	84	84	84	85	85	85	85	85	86	86	86	86	86	87	87	87	87	87	87	88	88	88	88	88	89	89	89	89	89	90	90	90	90	90	91
82	82	82	83	83	83	83	83	83	84	84	84	84	84	85	85	85	85	85	85	86	86	86	86	86	87	87	87	87	87	87	88	88	88	88	88	88	89	89	89	89	89	90	90	90	90	90	90	91	91	91
83	83	83	84	84	84	84	84	84	85	85	85	85	85	85	86	86	86	86	86	86	87	87	87	87	87	87	88	88	88	88	88	88	89	89	89	89	89	89	90	90	90	90	90	90	91	91	91	91	91	92
84	84	84	84	85	85	85	85	85	85	86	86	86	86	86	86	87	87	87	87	87	87	88	88	88	88	88	88	88	89	89	89	89	89	89	90	90	90	90	90	90	91	91	91	91	91	91	92	92	92	92
85	85	85	85	86	86	86	86	86	86	87	87	87	87	87	87	87	88	88	88	88	88	88	88	89	89	89	89	89	89	90	90	90	90	90	90	90	91	91	91	91	91	91	91	92	92	92	92	92	92	93
86	86	86	86	87	87	87	87	87	87	87	88	88	88	88	88	88	88	89	89	89	89	89	89	89	90	90	90	90	90	90	90	90	91	91	91	91	91	91	91	92	92	92	92	92	92	92	93	93	93	93
87	87	87	87	88	88	88	88	88	88	88	88	89	89	89	89	89	89	89	89	90	90	90	90	90	90	90	91	91	91	91	91	91	91	91	92	92	92	92	92	92	92	92	93	93	93	93	93	93	93	94
88	88	88	88	88	89	89	89	89	89	89	89	89	90	90	90	90	90	90	90	90	91	91	91	91	91	91	91	91	91	92	92	92	92	92	92	92	92	93	93	93	93	93	93	93	93	94	94	94	94	94
89	89	89	89	89	90	90	90	90	90	90	90	90	90	91	91	91	91	91	91	91	91	91	92	92	92	92	92	92	92	92	92	93	93	93	93	93	93	93	93	93	94	94	94	94	94	94	94	94	94	95
90	90	90	90	90	91	91	91	91	91	91	91	91	91	91	92	92	92	92	92	92	92	92	92	92	93	93	93	93	93	93	93	93	93	93	94	94	94	94	94	94	94	94	94	94	95	95	95	95	95	95
91	91	91	91	91	91	92	92	92	92	92	92	92	92	92	92	92	93	93	93	93	93	93	93	93	93	93	93	94	94	94	94	94	94	94	94	94	94	94	95	95	95	95	95	95	95	95	95	95	95	96
92	92	92	92	92	92	92	93	93	93	93	93	93	93	93	93	93	93	93	94	94	94	94	94	94	94	94	94	94	94	94	94	95	95	95	95	95	95	95	95	95	95	95	95	96	96	96	96	96	96	96
93	93	93	93	93	93	93	93	94	94	94	94	94	94	94	94	94	94	94	94	94	94	95	95	95	95	95	95	95	95	95	95	95	95	95	95	96	96	96	96	96	96	96	96	96	96	96	96	96	96	97
94	94	94	94	94	94	94	94	94	95	95	95	95	95	95	95	95	95	95	95	95	95	95	95	95	96	96	96	96	96	96	96	96	96	96	96	96	96	96	96	96	96	97	97	97	97	97	97	97	97	97
95	95	95	95	95	95	95	95	95	95	96	96	96	96	96	96	96	96	96	96	96	96	96	96	96	96	96	96	96	96	97	97	97	97	97	97	97	97	97	97	97	97	97	97	97	97	97	97	97	97	98
96	96	96	96	96	96	96	96	96	96	96	96	96	97	97	97	97	97	97	97	97	97	97	97	97	97	97	97	97	97	97	97	97	97	97	97	97	97	98	98	98	98	98	98	98	98	98	98	98	98	98
97	97	97	97	97	97	97	97	97	97	97	97	97	97	97	97	97	98	98	98	98	98	98	98	98	98	98	98	98	98	98	98	98	98	98	98	98	98	98	98	98	98	98	98	98	98	98	98	98	98	99
98	98	98	98	98	98	98	98	98	98	98	98	98	98	98	98	98	98	98	98	98	98	98	98	98	99	99	99	99	99	99	99	99	99	99	99	99	99	99	99	99	99	99	99	99	99	99	99	99	99	99
99	99	99	99	99	99	99	99	99	99	99	99	99	99	99	99	99	99	99	99	99	99	99	99	99	99	99	99	99	99	99	99	99	99	99	99	99	99	99	99	99	99	99	99	99	99	99	99	99	99	100

COMBINED VALUES CHART (CON'T)

	51	52	53	54	55	56	57	58	59	60	61	62	63	64	65	66	67	68	69	70	71	72	73	74	75	76	77	78	79	80	81	82	83	84	85	86	87	88	89	90	91	92	93	94	95	96	97	98	99
51	76																																																
52	76	77																																															
53	77	77	78																																														
54	77	78	78	79																																													
55	78	78	79	79	80																																												
56	78	79	79	80	80	81																																											
57	79	79	80	80	81	81	82																																										
58	79	80	80	81	81	82	82	82																																									
59	80	80	81	81	82	82	82	83	83																																								
60	80	81	81	82	82	82	83	83	84	84																																							
61	81	81	82	82	82	83	83	84	84	84	85																																						
62	81	82	82	83	83	83	84	84	84	85	85	86																																					
63	82	82	83	83	83	84	84	84	85	85	86	86	86																																				
64	82	83	83	83	84	84	85	85	85	86	86	86	87	87																																			
65	83	83	84	84	84	85	85	85	86	86	86	87	87	87	88																																		
66	83	84	84	84	85	85	85	86	86	86	87	87	87	88	88	88																																	
67	84	84	84	85	85	85	86	86	86	87	87	87	88	88	88	89	89																																
68	84	85	85	85	86	86	86	87	87	87	88	88	88	88	89	89	89	90																															
69	85	85	85	86	86	86	87	87	87	88	88	88	89	89	89	89	90	90	90																														
70	85	86	86	86	87	87	87	87	88	88	88	89	89	89	90	90	90	90	91	91																													
71	86	86	86	87	87	87	88	88	88	88	89	89	89	90	90	90	90	91	91	91	92																												
72	86	87	87	87	87	88	88	88	89	89	89	89	90	90	90	90	91	91	91	92	92	92																											
73	87	87	87	88	88	88	88	89	89	89	89	90	90	90	91	91	91	91	92	92	92	92	93																										
74	87	88	88	88	88	89	89	89	89	90	90	90	90	91	91	91	91	92	92	92	92	93	93	93																									
75	88	88	88	89	89	89	89	90	90	90	90	91	91	91	91	92	92	92	92	93	93	93	93	94	94																								
76	88	88	89	89	89	89	90	90	90	90	91	91	91	91	92	92	92	92	93	93	93	93	94	94	94	94																							
77	89	89	89	89	90	90	90	90	91	91	91	91	91	92	92	92	92	93	93	93	93	94	94	94	94	94	95																						
78	89	89	90	90	90	90	91	91	91	91	91	92	92	92	92	93	93	93	93	93	94	94	94	94	95	95	95	95																					
79	90	90	90	90	91	91	91	91	91	92	92	92	92	92	93	93	93	93	93	94	94	94	94	95	95	95	95	95	96																				
80	90	90	91	91	91	91	91	92	92	92	92	92	93	93	93	93	93	94	94	94	94	94	95	95	95	95	95	96	96	96																			
81	91	91	91	91	91	92	92	92	92	92	93	93	93	93	93	94	94	94	94	94	94	95	95	95	95	95	96	96	96	96	96																		
82	91	91	92	92	92	92	92	92	93	93	93	93	93	94	94	94	94	94	94	95	95	95	95	95	96	96	96	96	96	96	97	97																	
83	92	92	92	92	92	93	93	93	93	93	93	94	94	94	94	94	94	95	95	95	95	95	95	96	96	96	96	96	96	97	97	97	97																
84	92	92	92	93	93	93	93	93	93	94	94	94	94	94	94	95	95	95	95	95	95	96	96	96	96	96	96	96	97	97	97	97	97	97															
85	93	93	93	93	93	93	94	94	94	94	94	94	94	95	95	95	95	95	95	96	96	96	96	95	96	96	97	97	97	97	97	97	97	98	98														
86	93	93	93	94	94	94	94	94	94	94	95	95	95	95	95	95	95	96	96	96	96	96	96	96	97	97	97	97	97	97	97	97	98	98	98	98													
87	94	94	94	94	94	94	94	95	95	95	95	95	95	95	95	96	96	96	96	96	96	96	96	97	97	97	97	97	97	97	98	98	98	98	98	98	98												
88	94	94	94	94	95	95	95	95	95	95	95	95	96	96	96	96	96	96	96	96	97	97	97	97	97	97	97	97	97	98	98	98	98	98	98	98	98	99											
89	95	95	95	95	95	95	95	95	95	96	96	96	96	96	96	96	96	96	97	97	97	97	97	97	97	97	97	98	98	98	98	98	98	98	98	98	99	99	99										
90	95	95	95	95	96	96	96	96	96	96	96	96	96	96	97	97	97	97	97	97	97	97	97	97	98	98	98	98	98	98	98	98	98	98	99	99	99	99	99	99									
91	96	96	96	96	96	96	96	96	96	96	96	97	97	97	97	97	97	97	97	97	97	97	98	98	98	98	98	98	98	98	98	98	98	99	99	99	99	99	99	99	99								
92	96	96	96	96	96	96	97	97	97	97	97	97	97	97	97	97	97	97	98	98	98	98	98	98	98	98	98	98	98	98	98	99	99	99	99	99	99	99	99	99	99	99							
93	97	97	97	97	97	97	97	97	97	97	97	97	97	97	98	98	98	98	98	98	98	98	98	98	98	98	98	98	99	99	99	99	99	99	99	99	99	99	99	99	99	99	100						
94	97	97	97	97	97	97	97	97	98	98	98	98	98	98	98	98	98	98	98	98	98	98	98	98	99	99	99	99	99	99	99	99	99	99	99	99	99	99	99	99	99	100	100	100					
95	98	98	98	98	98	98	98	98	98	98	98	98	98	98	98	98	98	98	98	99	99	99	99	99	99	99	99	99	99	99	99	99	99	99	99	99	99	99	99	100	100	100	100	100	100				
96	98	98	98	98	98	98	98	98	98	98	98	98	99	99	99	99	99	99	99	99	99	99	99	99	99	99	99	99	99	99	99	99	99	99	99	99	99	100	100	100	100	100	100	100	100	100			
97	99	99	99	99	99	99	99	99	99	99	99	99	99	99	99	99	99	99	99	99	99	99	99	99	99	99	99	99	99	99	99	99	99	100	100	100	100	100	100	100	100	100	100	100	100	100	100		
98	99	99	99	99	99	99	99	99	99	99	99	99	99	99	99	99	99	99	99	99	99	99	99	99	100	100	100	100	100	100	100	100	100	100	100	100	100	100	100	100	100	100	100	100	100	100	100	100	
99	100	100	100	100	100	100	100	100	100	100	100	100	100	100	100	100	100	100	100	100	100	100	100	100	100	100	100	100	100	100	100	100	100	100	100	100	100	100	100	100	100	100	100	100	100	100	100	100	100

8-4

Tables & Schedules

TABLE 11B
SELECTED PAGES OF 1997 PERMANENT DISABILITY RATING SCHEDULE (1997 PDRS)

WARNING: Table 11B contains only selected tables from the 1997 Permanent Disability Rating Schedule. To view the complete 1997 PDRS, go to the DWC website at http://www.dir.ca.gov/dwc/PDR1997.pdf. These selected tables, referenced by the pagination convention used within the 1997 PDRS itself, are as follows:

Chart		Start	End
Occupational Variant Table	____________	4-2	4-5
Occupational Adjustment	____________	5-2	5-3
Age Adjustment	____________	6-2	6-5
Multiple Disabilities Table	____________	7-15	7-16

PETE WILSON
GOVERNOR OF CALIFORNIA

SCHEDULE FOR RATING PERMANENT DISABILITIES

UNDER PROVISIONS OF THE

LABOR CODE OF THE STATE OF CALIFORNIA

Compiled and Published by
STATE OF CALIFORNIA

DEPARTMENT OF INDUSTRIAL RELATIONS
DIVISION OF WORKERS' COMPENSATION

CASEY L. YOUNG
Administrative Director

April 1997

OCCUPATIONAL VARIANT TABLE

		110	111	112	120	210	211	212	213	214	220	221	230	240	250	251	290	310	311	320	321	322	330
1.1	PARALYSIS	D	F	G	G	E	F	E	F	F	G	G	F	E	F	E	G	F	G	H	G	G	G
1.3	EPILEPSY	H	G	I	I	H	G	H	I	H	I	H	F	F	J	I	H	I	I	I	G	H	H
1.4	PSYCHIATRIC	J	I	I	H	I	H	J	I	I	J	F	F	G	H	I	H	I	J	H	F	G	F
1.5	PST-TRAUM HEAD	I	H	H	H	H	H	H	I	H	H	G	F	G	H	H	G	H	H	H	F	G	F
1.6	VERTIGO	D	D	D	D	E	D	E	H	F	F	F	F	E	G	F	E	F	F	F	F	F	F
1.7	HEADACHES	I	H	H	H	H	H	H	I	H	H	G	F	G	H	H	G	H	H	H	F	G	F
1.8	COGNITIVE DIS	I	H	H	H	H	H	H	I	H	H	G	F	G	H	H	G	H	H	H	F	G	F
2.1--	SIGHT-COSMETIC	I	I	J	J	J	I	I	I	J	J	H	G	G	I	I	J	I	J	I	H	H	G
2.2-2.6	VISION	H	I	J	J	I	I	I	I	I	J	H	G	F	I	H	I	I	I	I	H	G	G
2.7	LACRIMATION	I	I	J	J	J	I	I	I	J	J	H	G	G	I	I	J	I	J	I	H	H	G
3.1	HEARING LOSS	J	H	I	F	J	H	I	H	J	H	D	E	H	H	J	I	J	J	E	D	H	E
4.1	COSMETIC	I	I	I	H	J	I	I	H	J	J	G	E	J	H	J	J	I	J	E	E	H	E
4.3-4.4	SKULL	C	C	C	C	D	C	C	F	C	C	D	F	D	F	D	C	C	D	F	F	F	F
4.5	JAW	I	H	H	F	J	H	I	H	J	I	F	F	G	G	I	H	H	I	F	F	G	F
4.7	NOSE	H	H	H	F	J	H	H	H	H	G	F	F	F	F	F	H	F	F	F	F	F	F
5.2	SPEECH	J	I	I	F	J	I	I	H	J	I	D	D	H	H	J	I	I	I	D	C	G	D
5.31	SMELL	F	F	F	F	F	F	F	F	F	F	F	F	F	F	F	G	F	F	F	F	H	F
5.32	TASTE	F	F	F	F	F	F	F	F	F	F	F	F	F	F	F	F	F	F	F	F	F	F
5.33	SMELL, TASTE	F	F	F	F	F	F	F	F	F	F	F	F	F	F	F	G	F	F	F	F	H	F
6.1	SKIN - OUTSIDE	F	F	F	F	F	F	F	H	F	F	F	F	G	G	G	F	F	F	F	F	F	F
6.2	SKIN - WET WK	F	F	F	F	F	F	F	F	F	G	F	F	F	F	F	H	F	G	G	F	H	F
7.1	ARM AMP	E	G	H	H	E	G	F	E	G	H	G	G	E	F	F	G	F	G	H	G	G	G
7.3	SHOULDER	C	D	D	E	C	D	E	E	F	F	F	F	D	F	D	G	F	F	F	F	F	F
7.5	ELBOW	D	F	G	G	D	F	E	E	F	G	G	F	E	G	F	G	F	G	H	G	G	G
7.6	FOREARM	D	G	H	H	D	G	F	E	G	H	G	F	E	F	E	H	F	G	I	H	G	F
7.7	WRIST	D	G	H	H	D	G	F	E	G	H	G	F	E	F	E	H	F	G	I	H	G	F
8.11	THUMB AMP	F	G	G	H	E	G	F	F	G	H	H	G	E	F	F	H	F	G	H	G	G	G
8.12	INDEX AMP	F	H	I	I	E	H	G	F	H	I	H	G	E	F	F	H	G	H	I	H	H	G
8.13	MIDDLE AMP	F	H	I	I	E	H	G	F	H	I	H	G	E	F	F	H	G	H	I	H	H	G
8.14	RING AMP	F	G	I	G	E	G	F	F	G	G	G	F	E	F	F	F	F	G	H	G	G	F
8.15	LITTLE AMP	F	G	I	G	E	G	F	F	G	G	G	F	E	F	F	F	F	G	H	G	G	F

OCCUPATIONAL VARIANT TABLE

		331	332	340	341	350	351	360	370	380	390	420	430	460	470	480	481	482	490	491	492	560	590
1.1	PARALYSIS	F	F	G	H	G	G	G	I	J	H	H	H	H	I	H	J	J	I	H	I	I	J
1.3	EPILEPSY	G	G	F	I	J	J	F	I	J	G	G	I	G	I	H	J	J	J	G	H	H	J
1.4	PSYCHIATRIC	F	G	D	D	H	G	E	H	H	H	F	G	E	H	E	H	I	J	D	E	D	I
1.5	PST-TRAUM HEAD	F	F	D	H	H	G	E	H	I	G	F	H	E	H	F	I	J	I	D	G	E	J
1.6	VERTIGO	F	F	F	I	G	G	F	H	J	G	F	G	F	H	G	J	J	I	F	H	H	J
1.7	HEADACHES	F	F	D	H	H	G	E	H	I	G	F	H	E	H	F	I	J	I	D	G	E	J
1.8	COGNITIVE DIS	F	F	D	H	H	G	E	H	I	G	F	H	E	H	F	I	J	I	D	G	E	J
2.1--	SIGHT-COSMETIC	F	G	F	F	I	H	F	H	H	H	G	G	F	H	F	H	I	J	F	G	F	I
2.2-2.6	VISION	F	G	F	F	I	H	F	H	H	G	G	G	F	H	F	H	I	I	F	G	F	I
2.7	LACRIMATION	F	G	F	F	I	H	F	H	H	H	G	G	F	H	F	H	I	J	F	G	F	I
3.1	HEARING LOSS	E	G	F	E	H	G	G	G	G	H	D	F	F	G	F	G	H	I	F	F	F	I
4.1	COSMETIC	E	E	G	E	G	E	F	F	F	H	E	E	F	F	E	F	E	J	E	E	E	I
4.3-4.4	SKULL	F	D	F	H	F	F	F	F	I	G	F	I	F	F	H	I	J	J	F	I	G	J
4.5	JAW	F	F	F	F	G	F	F	F	F	G	F	F	F	F	F	F	G	H	F	G	F	G
4.7	NOSE	F	F	F	F	H	F	F	F	G	H	F	G	F	F	F	G	I	J	F	G	F	J
5.2	SPEECH	D	F	G	F	H	F	G	F	G	H	C	D	F	F	F	G	G	I	F	G	F	H
5.31	SMELL	F	F	F	F	F	F	F	F	F	G	F	F	F	F	F	F	F	G	F	F	F	F
5.32	TASTE	F	F	F	F	F	F	F	F	F	F	F	F	F	F	F	F	F	F	F	F	F	F
5.33	SMELL, TASTE	F	F	F	F	F	F	F	F	F	G	F	F	F	F	F	F	F	G	F	F	F	F
6.1	SKIN - OUTSIDE	F	F	F	H	G	G	F	F	H	G	F	F	F	F	H	H	H	H	H	H	G	H
6.2	SKIN - WET WK	G	F	G	G	F	F	F	G	G	F	H	F	F	G	F	G	F	F	F	F	F	F
7.1	ARM AMP	F	F	F	F	G	G	G	H	H	G	H	H	G	H	G	H	J	I	G	H	H	J
7.3	SHOULDER	F	F	F	G	F	G	G	G	H	G	G	H	G	H	H	H	I	I	G	H	H	J
7.5	ELBOW	F	F	G	G	H	H	G	I	I	G	H	I	G	I	H	I	J	I	G	H	H	J
7.6	FOREARM	F	E	F	F	F	G	F	J	J	G	I	H	G	J	G	J	J	H	G	H	H	J
7.7	WRIST	F	E	F	F	F	G	F	J	J	G	I	H	G	J	G	J	J	H	G	H	H	J
8.11	THUMB AMP	F	F	F	F	G	G	F	H	H	G	H	H	G	H	G	H	I	H	G	H	H	I
8.12	INDEX AMP	F	F	F	F	G	G	F	I	I	G	G	H	F	I	G	I	I	H	F	G	G	I
8.13	MIDDLE AMP	F	F	F	F	G	G	F	I	I	G	G	H	F	I	G	I	I	H	F	G	G	I
8.14	RING AMP	F	F	F	F	F	F	F	H	H	G	G	H	F	H	G	H	H	H	F	G	G	I
8.15	LITTLE AMP	F	F	F	F	F	F	F	H	H	G	G	H	F	H	G	H	H	H	F	G	G	I

OCCUPATIONAL VARIANT TABLE

		110	111	112	120	210	211	212	213	214	220	221	230	240	250	251	290	310	311	320	321	322	330
8.2	T+I AMP	F	H	I	I	E	H	G	F	H	I	H	G	E	G	F	H	G	H	I	H	H	G
8.3	T+I+M AMP	F	H	I	I	E	H	G	F	H	I	H	G	E	G	F	H	G	H	I	H	H	G
8.4	I+M+R+L AMP	F	G	I	H	E	G	F	F	G	H	G	G	E	F	F	G	F	G	H	G	G	G
8.5	ALL FGRS AMP	F	G	I	H	E	G	F	F	G	H	G	G	E	F	F	G	F	G	H	G	G	G
9.11	THUMB IMMOB	F	G	G	H	E	G	F	F	G	H	H	G	E	F	F	H	F	G	H	G	G	G
9.12	INDEX IMMOB	F	H	I	I	E	H	G	F	H	I	H	G	E	F	F	H	G	H	I	H	H	G
9.13	MIDDLE IMMOB	F	H	I	I	E	H	G	F	H	I	H	G	E	F	F	H	G	H	I	H	H	G
9.14	RING IMMOB	F	G	I	G	E	G	F	F	G	G	G	F	E	F	F	F	F	G	H	G	G	F
9.15	LITTLE IMMOB	F	G	I	G	E	G	F	F	G	G	G	F	E	F	F	F	F	G	H	G	G	F
9.2	T+I IMMOB	F	H	I	I	E	H	G	F	H	I	H	G	E	G	F	H	G	H	I	H	H	G
9.3	T+I+M IMMOB	F	H	I	I	E	H	G	F	H	I	H	G	E	G	F	H	G	H	I	H	H	G
9.4	I+M+R+L IMMOB	F	G	I	H	E	G	F	F	G	H	G	G	E	F	F	G	F	G	H	G	G	G
9.5	ALL FGRS IMMOB	F	G	I	H	E	G	F	F	G	H	G	G	E	F	F	G	F	G	H	G	G	G
10.5	GRIP	D	E	E	F	C	E	E	E	F	F	F	G	D	F	F	F	F	F	H	G	G	G
11.1	PULMONARY	F	E	D	D	H	E	F	F	F	E	E	E	E	F	F	F	F	G	F	F	F	F
11.3	HEART	G	F	E	E	F	F	G	G	G	G	E	E	F	G	G	F	G	H	F	F	F	F
11.5	RIB	F	E	D	D	H	E	F	F	F	E	E	E	E	F	F	F	F	G	F	F	F	F
12.1	SPINE	C	C	D	D	D	D	E	F	F	E	E	E	E	F	E	E	F	G	F	F	F	F
12.3	SPINE - PARALYSIS	100	100	100	100	100	100	100	100	100	100	100	100	100	100	100	100	100	100	100	100	100	100
13.1	ABDOM - HERNIA	C	C	C	C	C	D	E	F	F	D	D	E	E	F	E	D	F	G	F	F	F	F
13.2	ABDOM ORGANS	F	F	F	F	F	F	F	F	F	F	F	F	F	F	F	F	F	F	F	F	F	F
14.1	LEG AMP	D	D	C	C	E	E	E	F	F	E	E	E	E	F	E	E	F	F	F	F	F	F
14.2	TOE AMP	D	D	C	C	E	E	E	F	F	E	E	E	E	F	E	E	F	F	F	F	F	F
14.3	LEG SHORT	C	C	C	C	D	D	D	E	D	D	D	D	D	D	D	D	D	E	E	E	E	E
14.4	HIP	D	D	C	C	E	E	E	F	F	E	E	E	E	F	E	E	F	F	F	F	F	F
14.5	KNEE, THIGH	D	D	C	C	E	E	E	F	F	E	E	E	E	F	E	E	F	F	F	F	F	F
14.6	ANKLE, CALF	D	D	C	C	E	E	E	F	F	E	E	E	E	F	E	E	F	F	F	F	F	F
14.7	TOE IMMOB	C	C	C	C	D	D	D	E	D	D	D	D	D	D	D	D	D	E	E	E	E	E
14.8	POST-THROM	D	D	D	D	E	E	E	F	F	E	E	E	E	F	E	E	F	F	F	F	F	F

OCCUPATIONAL VARIANT TABLE

		331	332	340	341	350	351	360	370	380	390	420	430	460	470	480	481	482	490	491	492	560	590
8.2	T+I AMP	F	F	F	F	G	G	F	I	I	G	G	H	F	I	G	I	J	H	F	H	H	I
8.3	T+I+M AMP	F	F	F	F	G	G	F	I	I	G	G	H	F	I	G	I	J	H	F	H	H	I
8.4	I+M+R+L AMP	F	F	F	F	G	G	F	H	H	G	G	H	F	H	G	H	I	H	F	G	G	I
8.5	ALL FGRS AMP	F	F	F	F	G	G	F	H	H	G	G	H	F	H	G	H	I	H	F	G	G	I
9.11	THUMB IMMOB	F	F	F	F	G	G	F	H	H	G	H	H	G	H	G	H	I	H	G	H	H	I
9.12	INDEX IMMOB	F	F	F	F	G	G	F	I	I	G	G	H	F	I	G	I	I	H	F	G	G	I
9.13	MIDDLE IMMOB	F	F	F	F	G	G	F	I	I	G	G	H	F	I	G	I	I	H	F	G	G	I
9.14	RING IMMOB	F	F	F	F	F	F	F	H	H	G	G	H	F	H	G	H	H	H	F	G	G	I
9.15	LITTLE IMMOB	F	F	F	F	F	F	F	H	H	G	G	H	F	H	G	H	H	H	F	G	G	I
9.2	T+I IMMOB	F	F	F	F	G	G	F	I	I	G	G	H	F	I	G	I	J	H	F	H	H	I
9.3	T+I+M IMMOB	F	F	F	F	G	G	F	I	I	G	G	H	F	I	G	I	J	H	F	H	H	I
9.4	I+M+R+L IMMOB	F	F	F	F	G	G	F	H	H	G	G	H	F	H	G	H	I	H	F	G	G	I
9.5	ALL FGRS IMMOB	F	F	F	F	G	G	F	H	H	G	G	H	F	H	G	H	I	H	F	G	G	I
10.5	GRIP	F	F	F	F	G	G	G	H	H	G	H	H	G	H	G	H	J	I	G	H	H	J
11.1	PULMONARY	F	F	G	G	G	G	G	G	H	H	G	H	G	H	H	H	I	I	G	H	H	J
11.3	HEART	F	F	G	G	H	G	G	G	H	H	H	H	H	H	H	H	I	I	H	H	H	J
11.5	RIB	F	F	G	G	G	G	G	G	H	H	G	H	G	H	H	H	I	I	G	H	H	J
12.1	SPINE	F	F	G	G	G	G	G	G	H	G	H	H	H	H	I	I	J	I	H	I	J	J
12.3	SPINE - PARALYSIS	100	100	100	100	100	100	100	100	100	100	100	100	100	100	100	100	100	100	100	100	100	100
13.1	ABDOM - HERNIA	F	F	G	G	G	F	G	G	H	G	H	H	H	H	H	H	J	H	H	H	I	J
13.2	ABDOM ORGANS	F	F	F	F	F	F	F	F	F	F	F	F	F	F		F	F	F	F	F	F	F
14.1	LEG AMP	F	F	G	G	G	G	G	G	I	H	G	H	H	H	H	I	J	I	H	I	I	J
14.2	TOE AMP	F	F	G	G	G	G	G	G	I	H	G	H	H	H	H	I	J	I	H	I	I	J
14.3	LEG SHORT	E	F	E	G	E	E	E	F	G	F	F	F	F	F	G	G	H	G	F	G	G	H
14.4	HIP	F	F	G	G	G	G	G	G	I	H	G	H	H	H	H	I	J	I	H	I	I	J
14.5	KNEE, THIGH	F	F	G	G	G	G	G	G	I	H	G	H	H	H	H	I	J	I	H	I	I	J
14.6	ANKLE, CALF	F	F	G	G	G	G	G	G	I	H	G	H	H	H	H	I	J	I	H	I	I	J
14.7	TOE IMMOB	E	F	E	G	E	E	E	F	G	F	F	F	F	F	G	G	H	G	F	G	G	H
14.8	POST-THROM	F	F	G	G	G	G	G	G	I	H	G	H	H	H	H	I	J	I	H	I	I	J

OCCUPATIONAL ADJUSTMENT TABLE

Standard Rating Percent	C	D	E	F	G	H	I	J
0	0	0	0	0	0	0	0	0
1	1	1	1	1	2	2	2	2
2	1	2	2	2	3	3	4	4
3	2	2	3	3	4	5	5	6
4	3	3	4	4	5	6	7	8
5	3	4	4	5	6	7	8	9
6	4	5	5	6	7	8	9	11
7	5	5	6	7	8	10	11	12
8	6	6	7	8	9	11	12	14
9	6	7	8	9	11	12	14	15
10	7	8	9	10	12	13	15	16
11	7	9	10	11	13	14	16	18
12	8	10	11	12	14	16	17	19
13	9	10	12	13	15	17	18	20
14	10	11	13	14	16	18	20	22
15	11	12	14	15	17	19	21	23
16	11	13	14	16	18	20	22	24
17	12	14	15	17	19	21	23	26
18	13	15	16	18	20	22	24	27
19	14	15	17	19	21	24	26	28
20	15	16	18	20	22	25	27	29
21	16	17	19	21	23	26	28	31
22	16	18	20	22	24	27	29	32
23	17	19	21	23	26	28	31	33
24	18	20	22	24	27	29	32	34
25	18	21	23	25	28	30	33	36

Standard Rating Percent	C	D	E	F	G	H	I	J
26	19	22	24	26	29	31	34	37
27	20	23	25	27	30	33	35	38
28	21	24	26	28	31	34	36	39
29	22	24	27	29	32	35	37	40
30	23	25	28	30	33	36	38	41
31	24	26	29	31	34	37	40	43
32	25	27	30	32	35	38	41	44
33	25	28	30	33	36	39	42	45
34	26	29	31	34	37	40	43	46
35	27	30	32	35	38	41	44	47
36	28	31	33	36	39	42	45	48
37	29	32	34	37	40	43	46	49
38	30	32	35	38	41	44	47	50
39	31	33	36	39	42	45	48	51
40	32	34	37	40	43	46	49	52
41	33	35	38	41	44	47	50	54
42	34	36	39	42	45	48	51	55
43	35	37	40	43	46	49	52	56
44	36	38	41	44	47	50	53	57
45	36	39	42	45	48	51	54	58
46	37	40	43	46	49	52	55	59
47	38	41	44	47	50	53	56	60
48	39	42	45	48	51	54	57	61
49	40	43	46	49	52	55	58	62
50	41	44	47	50	53	56	59	62

OCCUPATIONAL ADJUSTMENT TABLE

Standard Rating Percent	C	D	E	F	G	H	I	J	Standard Rating Percent	C	D	E	F	G	H	I	J
51	42	45	48	51	54	57	60	64	**76**	68	70	73	76	78	80	82	84
52	43	46	49	52	55	58	61	65	**77**	69	71	74	77	79	81	83	85
53	44	47	50	53	56	59	62	65	**78**	70	72	75	78	80	82	84	86
54	45	48	51	54	57	60	63	66	**79**	71	74	76	79	81	83	84	86
55	46	49	52	55	58	61	64	67	**80**	72	75	77	80	82	83	85	87
56	47	50	53	56	59	62	65	68	**81**	73	76	78	81	83	84	86	88
57	48	51	54	57	60	63	66	69	**82**	74	77	79	82	84	85	87	88
58	49	52	55	58	61	64	67	70	**83**	76	78	81	83	84	86	87	89
59	50	53	56	59	62	65	68	71	**84**	77	79	82	84	85	87	88	90
60	51	54	57	60	63	66	69	72	**85**	78	81	83	85	86	88	89	90
61	52	55	58	61	64	67	69	72	**86**	79	82	84	86	87	89	90	91
62	53	56	59	62	65	68	70	73	**87**	81	83	85	87	88	89	90	92
63	54	57	60	63	66	69	71	74	**88**	82	84	86	88	89	90	91	92
64	55	58	61	64	67	69	72	75	**89**	84	85	87	89	90	91	92	93
65	56	59	62	65	68	70	73	76	**90**	85	87	88	90	91	92	93	94
66	57	60	63	66	69	71	74	77	**91**	86	88	89	91	92	93	93	94
67	58	61	64	67	70	72	75	77	**92**	88	89	91	92	93	93	94	95
68	59	62	65	68	71	73	76	78	**93**	89	91	92	93	94	94	95	96
69	60	63	66	69	71	74	76	79	**94**	91	92	93	94	95	95	96	96
70	61	64	67	70	72	75	77	80	**95**	93	93	94	95	96	96	97	97
71	62	65	68	71	73	76	78	80	**96**	94	94	95	96	96	97	98	98
72	63	66	69	72	74	77	79	81	**97**	95	96	96	97	97	98	98	98
73	65	67	70	73	75	77	79	82	**98**	97	97	98	98	98	98	98	99
74	66	68	71	74	76	78	80	83	**99**	98	99	99	99	99	99	100	100
75	67	69	72	75	77	79	81	83	**100**	100	100	100	100	100	100	100	100

AGE ADJUSTMENT TABLE

Rating	AGE AT TIME OF INJURY									
	21 and under	22 - 26	27 - 31	32 - 36	37 - 41	42 - 46	47 - 51	52 - 56	57 - 61	62 and over
1	1	1	1	1	1	1	1	1	1	1
2	2	2	2	2	2	2	2	3	3	3
3	2	2	3	3	3	3	3	4	4	4
4	3	3	3	4	4	4	5	5	5	6
5	4	4	4	5	5	5	6	6	6	7
6	5	5	5	6	6	6	7	7	8	8
7	5	6	6	7	7	8	8	9	9	10
8	6	6	7	7	8	9	9	10	10	11
9	7	7	8	8	9	10	10	11	12	12
10	8	8	9	9	10	11	11	12	13	13
11	8	9	10	10	11	12	13	13	14	15
12	9	10	10	11	12	13	14	15	15	16
13	10	11	11	12	13	14	15	16	16	17
14	11	11	12	13	14	15	16	17	18	19
15	12	12	13	14	15	16	17	18	19	20
16	12	13	14	15	16	17	18	19	20	21
17	13	14	15	16	17	18	19	20	21	22
18	14	15	16	17	18	19	20	21	23	24
19	15	16	17	18	19	20	22	23	24	25
20	16	17	18	19	20	21	23	24	25	26
21	17	18	19	20	21	22	24	25	26	27
22	17	18	20	21	22	23	25	26	28	29
23	18	19	20	22	23	24	26	27	29	30
24	19	20	21	23	24	25	27	28	30	31
25	20	21	22	24	25	27	28	29	31	32

AGE ADJUSTMENT TABLE

	AGE AT TIME OF INJURY									
Rating	**21 and under**	**22 - 26**	**27 - 31**	**32 - 36**	**37 - 41**	**42 - 46**	**47 - 51**	**52 - 56**	**57 - 61**	**62 and over**
26	21	22	23	25	26	28	29	31	32	33
27	22	23	24	26	27	29	30	32	33	35
28	23	24	25	27	28	30	31	33	34	36
29	24	25	26	28	29	31	32	34	36	37
30	24	25	27	28	30	32	33	35	37	38
31	25	26	28	30	31	33	35	36	38	39
32	26	27	29	31	32	34	36	37	39	40
33	27	28	30	32	33	35	37	38	40	42
34	28	29	31	33	34	36	38	39	41	43
35	29	30	32	34	35	37	39	41	42	44
36	30	31	33	35	36	38	40	42	43	45
37	31	32	34	36	37	39	41	43	44	46
38	32	33	35	37	38	40	42	44	46	47
39	33	34	36	38	39	41	43	45	47	48
40	34	35	37	39	40	42	44	46	48	50
41	35	36	38	40	41	43	45	47	49	51
42	36	37	39	41	42	44	46	48	50	52
43	36	37	39	41	43	45	47	49	51	53
44	37	38	40	42	44	46	48	50	52	54
45	38	39	41	43	45	47	49	51	53	55
46	39	40	42	44	46	48	50	52	54	56
47	40	41	43	45	47	49	51	53	55	57
48	41	42	44	46	48	50	52	54	56	58
49	42	43	45	47	49	51	53	55	57	59
50	43	44	46	48	50	52	54	56	58	60

AGE ADJUSTMENT TABLE

	AGE AT TIME OF INJURY									
Rating	**21 and under**	**22 - 26**	**27 - 31**	**32 - 36**	**37 - 41**	**42 - 46**	**47 - 51**	**52 - 56**	**57 - 61**	**62 and over**
51	44	45	47	49	51	53	55	57	59	61
52	45	46	48	50	52	54	56	58	60	62
53	46	47	49	51	53	55	57	59	61	63
54	47	48	50	52	54	56	58	60	62	64
55	48	49	51	53	55	57	59	61	63	65
56	49	50	52	54	56	58	60	62	64	66
57	50	51	53	55	57	59	61	63	65	67
58	51	53	55	57	58	60	62	64	66	68
59	52	54	56	58	59	61	63	65	67	69
60	53	55	57	59	60	62	64	66	68	70
61	54	56	58	60	61	63	65	67	69	71
62	55	57	59	61	62	64	66	68	69	71
63	57	58	60	62	63	65	67	69	70	72
64	58	59	61	63	64	66	68	70	71	73
65	59	60	62	64	65	67	69	71	72	74
66	60	61	63	65	66	68	70	72	73	75
67	61	62	64	66	67	69	70	72	74	76
68	62	63	65	67	68	70	71	73	75	77
69	63	64	66	68	69	71	72	74	76	78
70	64	65	67	69	70	72	73	75	76	78
71	65	66	68	70	71	73	74	76	77	79
72	66	67	69	71	72	74	75	77	78	80
73	68	69	70	72	73	75	76	78	79	81
74	69	70	71	73	74	76	77	79	80	82
75	70	71	72	74	75	77	78	80	81	83

AGE ADJUSTMENT TABLE

	AGE AT TIME OF INJURY									
Rating	21 and under	22 - 26	27 - 31	32 - 36	37 - 41	42 - 46	47 - 51	52 - 56	57 - 61	62 and over
76	71	72	73	75	76	78	79	80	82	83
77	72	73	74	76	77	79	80	81	82	84
78	73	74	75	77	78	80	81	82	83	85
79	74	75	76	78	79	81	82	83	84	86
80	76	77	78	79	80	81	82	84	85	86
81	77	78	79	80	81	82	83	85	86	87
82	78	79	80	81	82	83	84	86	87	88
83	79	80	81	82	83	84	85	86	87	89
84	80	81	82	83	84	85	86	87	88	89
85	81	82	83	84	85	86	87	88	89	90
86	83	83	84	85	86	87	88	89	90	91
87	84	85	85	86	87	88	89	90	91	92
88	85	86	86	87	88	89	90	91	91	92
89	86	87	87	88	89	90	91	91	92	93
90	88	88	89	89	90	91	91	92	93	93
91	89	89	90	90	91	92	92	93	94	94
92	90	90	91	92	92	93	93	94	94	95
93	91	92	92	93	93	94	94	95	95	96
94	92	93	93	94	94	95	95	95	96	96
95	94	94	94	95	95	96	96	96	97	97
96	95	95	95	96	96	96	97	97	97	98
97	96	96	97	97	97	97	97	98	98	98
98	97	98	98	98	98	98	98	98	99	99
99	99	99	99	99	99	99	99	99	99	99
100	100	100	100	100	100	100	100	100	100	100

MULTIPLE DISABILITIES TABLE

	10	15	20	25	30	35	40	45	50	55	60	65	70	75	80	85	90	95
6	16	21	25	30	35	40	44	49	54	58	63	68	72	77	82	87	91	96
7	17	22	26	31	36	40	45	50	54	59	64	68	73	77	82	87	91	96
8	18	23	27	32	36	41	46	50	55	59	64	69	73	78	82	87	92	96
9	19	24	28	33	37	42	46	51	55	60	65	69	74	78	83	87	92	96
10	20	25	29	33	38	43	47	52	56	61	65	70	74	79	83	88	92	97
11		25	30	34	39	43	48	52	57	61	66	70	74	79	83	88	92	97
12		26	31	35	40	44	48	53	57	62	66	70	75	79	84	88	92	97
13		27	32	36	40	45	49	53	58	62	67	71	75	80	84	88	93	97
14		28	33	37	41	46	50	54	58	63	67	71	76	80	84	89	93	97
15		29	34	38	42	46	51	55	59	63	68	72	76	80	85	89	93	97
16			34	39	43	47	51	55	60	64	68	72	76	81	85	89	93	97
17			35	39	44	48	52	56	60	64	69	73	77	81	85	89	93	98
18			36	40	44	49	53	57	61	65	69	73	77	81	85	90	94	98
19			37	41	45	49	53	57	61	65	70	74	78	82	86	90	94	98
20			38	42	46	50	54	58	62	66	70	74	78	82	86	90	94	98
21				43	47	51	55	59	63	67	71	74	78	82	86	90	94	98
22				44	48	52	55	59	63	67	71	75	79	83	87	91	94	98
23				45	48	52	56	60	64	68	72	75	79	83	87	91	95	98
24				45	49	53	57	61	64	68	72	76	80	83	87	91	95	99
25				46	50	54	58	61	65	69	73	76	80	84	88	91	95	99
26					51	55	58	62	66	69	73	77	80	84	88	92	95	99
27					52	55	59	63	66	70	74	77	81	84	88	92	95	99
28					52	56	60	63	67	70	74	78	81	85	88	92	96	99
29					53	57	60	64	67	71	75	78	82	85	89	92	96	99
30					54	58	61	65	68	72	75	79	82	86	89	93	96	100
31						58	62	65	69	72	76	79	82	86	89	93	96	100
32						59	62	66	69	73	76	79	83	86	90	93	96	100
33						60	63	66	70	73	77	80	83	87	90	93	97	100
34						61	64	67	70	74	77	80	84	87	90	94	97	100
35						61	65	68	71	74	78	81	84	87	91	94	97	100

Directions:

Locate the column headed by the larger rating, and the row commencing with the smaller rating.

The combined disability rating is located at the intersection of this row and column.

(continued on next page)

MULTIPLE DISABILITIES TABLE (Cont.)

	40	45	50	55	60	65	70	75	80	85	90	95
36	65	68	72	75	78	81	84	88	91	94	97	100
37	66	69	72	75	79	82	85	88	91	94	97	100
38	67	70	73	76	79	82	85	88	91	95	98	100
39	67	70	73	76	80	83	86	89	92	95	98	100
40	68	71	74	77	80	83	86	89	92	95	98	100
41		72	75	78	81	83	86	89	92	95	98	100
42		72	75	78	81	84	87	90	93	96	98	100
43		73	76	79	82	84	87	90	93	96	99	100
44		74	76	79	82	85	88	90	93	96	99	100
45		74	77	80	83	85	88	91	94	96	99	100
46			78	80	83	86	88	91	94	97	99	100
47			78	81	84	86	89	91	94	97	99	100
48			79	81	84	87	89	92	94	97	100	100
49			79	82	85	87	90	92	95	97	100	100
50			80	83	85	88	90	93	95	98	100	100
51				83	86	88	90	93	95	98	100	100
52				84	86	88	91	93	96	98	100	100
53				84	87	89	91	94	96	98	100	100
54				85	87	89	92	94	96	99	100	100
55				85	88	90	92	94	97	99	100	100
56					88	90	92	95	97	99	100	100
57					89	91	93	95	97	99	100	100
58					89	91	93	95	97	100	100	100
59					90	92	94	96	98	100	100	100
60					90	92	94	96	98	100	100	100
61						92	94	96	98	100	100	100
62						93	95	97	99	100	100	100
63						93	95	97	99	100	100	100
64						94	96	97	99	100	100	100
65						94	96	98	100	100	100	100
66							96	98	100	100	100	100
67							97	98	100	100	100	100
68							97	99	100	100	100	100
69							98	99	100	100	100	100
70							98	100	100	100	100	100

PART 6. Medical-Legal Fee Schedule: Excerpts

TABLE 12
Medical-Legal Fee Schedule, adopted 8/3/93:

[8 Cal. Code Reg. §9795]

Evaluation Type and Code:	Description:	Amount Presumed Reasonable
FOLLOW-UP EVAL **ML101**: RV 5	Within 9 mos. paid @ lesser of U&C or $62.50/¼ hr =	**$250.00/hr**
BASIC EVAL **ML102**: RV 50	All evaluations, other than Supplemental, Complex or Extraordinary	**$625.00**
COMPLEX EVAL **ML103**: RV 75	**INCLUDES THREE OR MORE OF THE FOLLOWING:** 1) 2 or more hours physician face-to-face with patient; 2) 2 or more hours of record review by the physician; 3) 2 or more hours of medical research by physician; 4) 4 or more hours on 2 of 3 above complexity factors; 5) 6 or more hours on any combination of 3 factors; 6) Addressing the issue of medical causation; 7) Addressing the issue of apportionment, old or new Schedule; 8) Monitoring after toxic chemical, mineral or biologic exposure; 9) Psychiatric/Psychological evaluation is primary focus of eval; 10) Denial/Mod of treatment after UR, L.C. §4610	**$937.50**
Extraordinary [1, 4] **Eval** **ML104**: RV 5	Eval requires: 4 or more ML-103 factors; prior injuries to same body part; complex medical issues + 3 of 6 factors & 3 hrs spent; & AME after QMEs; verification of time spent; contents of report true per L.C. § 4628(j): Lesser of U&C or $62.50/¼hr or	**$250/hr**
Med-Legal **Testimony** [1, 4] **ML105**: RV 5	1 hour minimum for depo & including reasonable preparation & travel time: Lesser of U&C or $62.50/¼hr or	**$250/hr**
Supplemental **Med-Legal Eval** [1, 4] **ML106**, RV 5	Not for review of information previously available or for tests ordered at initial eval: Lesser of U&C or $62.50/¼hr or .	**$250/hr**

Circumstances Allowing Modification: Per Exam or Per Hour [2]

Evaluation Type:	Modifier -93	Modifier -94	Modifier -93 & -94
With →	**Interpreter** [3]	**AME** [4]	**Interpreter & AME** [4]
Multiplier →	**× 1.1**	**× 1.25**	**× 1.35**
Follow-up	(Not applicable)[4]	$312.50/hr	($312.50/hr) [4]
Basic ($625.00) [4]	$687.50	$781.25	$843.75
Complex (937.50) [4]	$1,031.25	$1,171.88	$1,265.63
Extraordinary	(Not applicable)[4]	$312.50/hr	($312.50/hr) [4]

[1] Comprehensive Medical-Legal Evaluation Involving Extraordinary Circumstances; Medical-Legal Testimony, or Supplemental Medical-Legal Evaluations, 8 Cal. Code Reg. §9795, ML104/105/106.

[2] Modifier -92: Evaluation by Primary Treating Physician, before 7/1/06; after 7/1/06 for info only; Follow-up = $160.00/hr before 7/1/06, and after, $250.00/hr; Basic = $500.00; Complex = $750.00; Modifiers -95, -96 and -97 are to identify only & do not affect values.

[3] Or other circumstances which significantly increase the time necessary to conduct the examination.

[4] Modifier -93 is **only applicable to ML 102 or ML 103** while -94 applies to an evaluation or testimony by an AME at $250.00/hr × 1.25 = $312.50/hr. (Use of an interpreter's may take longer, i.e., more hours, but there is no additional fee, just more hours at $312.50/hour.)

PART 7. Death Benefits

TABLE 13
Death Benefits Payable for Total and Partial Dependency

Any accrued and unpaid compensation shall be paid to the dependents, or, if there are no dependents, to the personal representative of the deceased employee or heirs or other persons entitled thereto, without administration. Labor Code § 4700.

Death benefits are payable in installments in the same manner and amounts as temporary disability indemnity per Labor Code § 4702(b).

Death Benefit Maximum

Dependents		Death From Injury On or After				
Total	**Partial**	**1/1/84**	**1/1/91**	**7/1/94**	**7/1/96**	**1/1/06**
1	0	$70,000	$95,000	$115,000	$125,000	$250,000
0	1+	4x annual support, up to $70,000	4x annual support, up to $95,000	4x annual support, up to $115,000	4x annual support, up to $125,000	8x annual support, up to $250,000
1	1+	$70,000 + 4x annual support, up to $95,000	$95,000 + 4x annual support, up to $115,000	$115,000 + 4x annual support, up to $125,000	$125,000 + 4x annual support, up to $145,000	$250,000 + 4x annual support, up to $290,000
2	0+	$95,000	$115,000	$135,000	$145,000	$290,000
3+	0+	$95,000	$115,000	$150,000	$160,000	$320,000

Maximum Burial Expense Benefit: Labor Code § 4701(a) 2013

Date of Injury	Maximum Monetary Benefit
Prior to 1/1/1991	$2,000.00
1/1/1991 to 12/31/2012	$5,000.00
1/1/2013 on	$10,000.00

It is important to note Labor Code § 4702(a)(6)(B) was struck down as unconstitutional in Six Flags, Inc. v. Workers' Comp. Appeals Bd., 145 Cal. App. 4th 91. In the case of an industrial death without dependents, Labor Code § 4706.5(a) dictates the sum equal to the amount due a surviving spouse with no dependent minor children to the Department of Industrial Relations.

PART 8. Indemnity and Earnings

TABLE 14

Maximum and Minimum Indemnity and Earnings

Temporary Total Disability

Date of Injury	Earnings, Average Weekly (From – To)	Rate Paid/Week
7-1-96	$ 0.00 - $ 126.00	Actual earnings
to	126.01 - $ 189.00	$126.00
12-31-02	189.01 - $ 735.00 × 2/3 = up to	$490.00
2003	$ 0.00 - $ 189.00	$126.00
	189.01 - $ 903.00 × 2/3 = up to	$602.00
2004	$ 0.00 - $ 189.00	$126.00
	189.01 - $ 1,092.00 × 2/3 = up to	$728.00
2005	$ 0.00 - $ 189.00	$126.00
	189.01 - $ 1,260.00 × 2/3 = up to	$840.00
2006	No change from 2005 because the SAWW did not increase in 2005	*
2007	$ 0.00 - $ 189.00 + 4.9593 % = $ **198.37** & × 2/3 =	$132.25 *
	198.38 - $ 1,260.00 + 4.9593 % = $ **1,322.49** & × 2/3 =	$881.66 *
2008	$ 0.00 - $ 198.37 + 3.9318 % = $ **206.17** & × 2/3 =	$137.45 *
	206.18 - $ 1,322.49 + 3.9318 % = $ **1,374.49** & × 2/3 =	$916.33 *
2009	$ 0.00 - $ 206.17 + 4.5484 % = $ **215.55** & × 2/3 =	$143.70 *
	215.56 - $ 1,374.49 + 4.5484 % = $ **1,437.01** & × 2/3 =	$958.01 *
2010	$ 0.00 - $ 215.55 + 2.9941 % = $ **222.00** & × 2/3 =	$148.00 *
	222.01 - $ 1,437.01 + 2.9941 % = $ **1,480.04** & × 2/3 =	$986.69 *
2011	No change from 2010 because the SAWW did not increase in 2010	
2012	$ 0.00 - $ 222.00 + 2.4135 % = $ **227.35** & × 2/3 =	$151.57 *
	227.36 - $ 1,480.04 + 2.4135 % = $ **1,515.75** & × 2/3 =	$1,010.50 *
2013	$ 0.00 - $ 227.35 + 5.5633 % = $ **240.00** & × 2/3 =	$160.00 *
	240.01 - $ 1,515.75 + 5.5633 % = $ **1,600.08** & × 2/3 =	$1,066.72 *
2014	$ 0.00 - $ 240.00 + 0.7429 % = $ **241.78** & × 2/3 =	$161.19 *
	241.79 - $ 1,600.08 + 0.7429 % = $ **1,611.96** & × 2/3 =	$1,074.64 *
2015	$ 0.00 - $ 241.78 + 2.6657 % = $ **248.22** & × 2/3 =	$165.49 *
	248.23 - $ 1,611.96 + 2.6657 % = $ **1,654.94** & × 2/3 =	$1,103.29 *
2016	$ 0.00 - $ 248.22 + 2.2789 % = $ **253.88** & × 2/3 =	$169.26 *
	253.89 - $ 1,654.94 + 2.2789 % = $ **1,692.65** & × 2/3 =	$1,128.43 *
2017	$ 0.00 - $ 253.88 + 3.9119 % = $ **263.81** & × 2/3 =	$175.88 *
	263.82 - $ 1,692.65 + 3.9119 % = $ **1,758.86** & × 2/3 =	$1,172.57 *
2018	$ 0.00 - $ 263.81 + 3.6419 % = $ **273.42** & × 2/3 =	$182.29 *
	273.43 - $ 1,758.86 + 3.6419 % = $ **1,822.91** & × 2/3 =	$1,215.27 *
2019	$ 0.00 - $ 273.42 + 2.9712 % = $ **281.54** & × 2/3 =	$187.71 *
	281.55 - $ 1,822.91 + 2.9712 % = $ **1,877.07** & × 2/3 =	$1,251.38 *
2020	$ 0.00 - $ 281.54 + 3.8401 % = $ **292.36** & × 2/3 =	$194.91 *
	292.37 - $ 1,877.07 + 3.8401 % = $ **1,949.15** & × 2/3 =	$1,299.43 *
2021	$ 0.00 - $ 292.36 + 4.3774 % = $ **305.16** & × 2/3 =	$203.44 *
	305.17 - $ 1,949.15 + 4.3774 % = $ **2,034.47** & × 2/3 =	$1,356.31 *

Temporary total disability maximum and minimums pursuant to Labor Code § 4453(a).

*TD SAWW increases apply to the maximum/minimum *rates*, not to the amount paid.

TTD paid 2 or more yrs after injury: Check for a possible rate increase or 104 weeks under L.C. §§ 4661.5, 4656(c)(1), (2). Supplemental job displacement vouchers may apply for injuries on or after 1/1/2004, L.C. §§ 4658.5, 4658.6 and generally Tit. 8 CCR §§ 10133.50 – 10133.60.

Permanent Partial Disability (PD): Minimum and Maximum Rates

Date of Injury		Min – Max PD Rate	Labor Code Section
1/1/91 – 6/30/94	1:0 to 24:3	$70 – $140	L.C. §4453(b)(2)
	25:0 to 99:3	$70 – $148	L.C. §4453(b)(4)
7/1/94 – 6/30/95	1:0 to 14:3	$70 – $140	L.C. §4453(b)(2)
	15:0 to 24:3	$70 – $148	L.C. §4453(b)(3)
	25:0 to 69:3	$70 – $158	L.C. §4453(b)(5)
	70:0 to 99:3	$70 – $168	L.C. §4453(b)(6)
7/1/95 – 6/30/96	1:0 to 14:3	$70 – $140	L.C. §4453(b)(2)
	15:0 to 24:3	$70 – $154	L.C. §4453(b)(3)
	25:0 to 69:3	$70 – $164	L.C. §4453(b)(5)
	70:0 to 99:3	$70 – $198	L.C. §4453(b)(6)
7/1/96 – 12/31/02	1:0 to 14:3	$70 – $140	L.C. §4453(b)(2)
	15:0 to 24:3	$70 – $160	L.C. §4453(b)(3)
	25:0 to 69:3	$70 – $170	L.C. §4453(b)(5)
	70:0 to 99:3	$70 – $230	L.C. §4453(b)(6)
2003	1:0 to 69:3	$100 – $185	L.C. §4453(b)(6)
	70:0 to 99:3	$100 – $230	L.C. §4453(b)(7)
2004	1:0 to 69:3	$105 – $200	L.C. §4453(b)(6)
	70:0 to 99:3	$105 – $250	L.C. §4453(b)(7)
2005*	1:0 to 69:3	$105 – $220	L.C. §4453(b)(6)
	70:0 to 99:3	$105 – $270	L.C. §4453(b)(7)
2006 – 2012*	1:0 to 69:3	$130 – $230	L.C. §4453(b)(6)
	70:0 to 99:3	$130 – $270	L.C. §4453(b)(7)
2013	1:0 to 54:3	$160 – $230	L.C. §4453(b)(8)
	55:0 to 69:3	$160 – $270	L.C. §4453(b)(8)
	70:0 to 99:3	$160 – $290	L.C. §4453(b)(8)
2014 – 2021	1:0 to 99:3	$160 – $290	L.C. §4453(b)(9)

* Labor Code § 4658(d) provides for a 15% increase or decrease in the permanent disability rate, depending upon whether the employer has more than 50 employees and whether the employer offered a modified or alternative work position within 60 days of the injured worker reaching a permanent and stationary status.

NOTE: Prior to the 1997 permanent disability rating schedule, permanent partial disability was expressed using quarter-percentage increments. Rather than writing out a decimal, percentages were written in a notation which using a colon and a number from 0 to 3 (0 indicating a full percentage point, 1 indicating a quarter percentage point, 2 indicating a half percentage point, and 3 indicating a three-quarter percentage point). For consistency's sake, the same convention is used above.

Tables & Schedules

Life Pension (LP): Minimum and Maximum Rates

For permanent partial disability rates from 70:0% to 99:3% the injured worker would be due a weekly life pension payment after the exhaustion of the permanent disability indemnity. Labor Code § 4659.

The formula for computing a life pension rate, as per Labor Code § 4659(a). The minimum life pension rate is calculated using the minimum permanent disability rate pursuant to Labor Code § 4453. The maximum life pension rate is calculated using an average weekly wage defined by Labor Code § 4659(a). The formula for calculating the life pension rate per Labor Code § 4659(a) is as follows:

Life Pension Rate = (PD% - 60) x 0.015 x AWW

Effective Dates			**AWW:** Min/Max per week			PD 70:0 to 99:3 **Paid:** Min/Max per week		
07-01-94	to	06-30-95	$105.00	to	$157.69	$15.75	to	$94.02
07-01-95	to	06-30-96	$105.00	to	$207.69	$15.75	to	$123.84
07-01-96	to	12-31-02	$105.00	to	$257.69	$15.75	to	$153.65
01-01-03	to	12-31-03 *	$150.00	to	$257.69	$22.50	to	$153.65
01-01-04	to	12-31-04 *	$157.00	to	$257.69	$23.55	to	$153.65
01-01-05	to	12-31-05 *	$157.00	to	$257.69	$23.55	to	$153.65
01-01-06	on	*	$195.00	to	$515.38	$29.25	to	$307.30

EXAMPLE: Let's consider a 77% permanent disability award for an injured worker with a date of injury of 12/20/2002. Their life pension rate would be computed as follows: (77 – 60) x 0.015 x $257.69 = $65.71 / week

* For injuries on or after 1/1/2003, beginning on 1/1/2004, a Cost of Living Adjustment (COLA) is to be made to the ***Life Pension*** or ***Permanent Total Disability*** <u>***rate paid each year***</u> based on an increase, if any, in the state average weekly wage (SAWW) compared to the prior year, L.C. § 4659(c). If there is no increase, then rate from prior year continues in following year.

The Supreme Court of California decision in **Baker vs WCAB (X.S.) 39 CWCR 169, 76 Cal. Comp. Cases 701, Sup. Tc. #S179194** instructs that the life pensions for dates of injury on or after 1/1/2003 are to be increased by the COLA starting the year after the commencement of the life pension benefits. Thus, although the starting life pension rate can be determined in advance once the final permanent disability percentage is known, the following year's life pension rate for dates of injury on or after 1/1/2003 cannot be determined in advance.

Calculations on the following page list annual increases and give annual multiplication factors.

Additional Information to Aid in Using Table 14

The 1st page of Table 14 gives maximum wages and temporary disability indemnity payment rates. Increases in the State Average Weekly Wage (SAWW) here ***apply only to the maximum and minimum wages***, not to the indemnity payment *rates* paid.

The 2nd page of Table 14 first covers permanent partial disability indemnity minimum and maximum rates. This latter part has a Cost of Living Adjustment (COLA) based on the annual change in SAWW. These increases apply to payments made, as noted.

SAWW data is based on the year ending March 31 per U.S. Department of Labor. Readers may call (202) 693-3039 or write Division of Fiscal & Actuarial Services, Room C-4514, 200 Constitution Ave., NW, Washington D.C. 20210.

Calculations of Change in State Average Weekly Wage by Year

Year	DWCNewsline	SAWW	Current ÷ Prior		=	Increase (If any)	
2004	18-03 (12/22/03)	$790.50	$790.50 ÷	$794.95	=	0.994402	(No increase)
2005	64-04 (12/15/04)	$806.11	$806.11 ÷	$790.50	=	1.019747	
2006	80-05 (12/20/05)	$838.42	$838.42 ÷	$806.11	=	1.040081	
2007	54-06 (10/10/06)	$880.00	$880.00 ÷	$838.42	=	1.049593	
2008	66-07 (10/03/07)	$914.60	$914.60 ÷	$880.00	=	1.039318	
2009	66-08 (10/31/08)	$956.20	$956.20 ÷	$914.60	=	1.045484	
2010	52-09 (10/07/09)	$984.83	$984.83 ÷	$956.20	=	1.029941	
2011	56-10 (10/14/10)	$979.90	$979.90 ÷	$984.83	=	0.994994	(No increase)
2012	24-11 (06/16/11)	$1,003.55	$1,003.55 ÷	$979.90	=	1.024135	
2013	28-12 (06/14/12)	$1,059.38	$1,059.38 ÷	$1,003.55	=	1.055633	
2014	35-13 (06/05/13)	$1,067.25	$1,067.25 ÷	$1,059.38	=	1.007429	
2015	2014-50 (06/09/14)	$1,095.70	$1,095.70 ÷	$1,067.25	=	1.026657	
2016	2015-57 (06/25/15)	$1,120.67	$1,120.67 ÷	$1,095.70	=	1.022789	
2017	2016-65 (06/14/16)	$1,164.51	$1,164.51 ÷	$1,120.67	=	1.039119	
2018	2017-46 (06/20/17)	$1,206.92	$1,206.92 ÷	$1,164.51	=	1.036419	
2019	2018-45 (06/26/18)	$1,242.78	$1,242.78 ÷	$1,206.92	=	1.029712	
2020	2019-73 (09/12/19)	$1,325.00	$1,325.00 ÷	$1,276.00	=	1.038401	
2021	2020-95 (11/02/20)	$1,383.00	$1,383.00 ÷	$1,325.00	=	1.043774	

The Supreme Court of California decision in **Baker vs WCAB (X.S.) 39 CWCR 169, 76 Cal. Comp. Cases 701, Sup. Tc. #S179194** instructs that the life pensions for dates of injury on or after 1/1/2003 are to be increased by the COLA starting the year after the start of life pension benefits.

EXAMPLE: Let's consider a 100% permanent total disability award for an injured worker with a date of injury in 2010 with an average weekly wage of $900.00/week who became permanent and stationary in 2015. The temporary disability rate is 2/3 of that, or $600.00/week. The permanent total disability rate would be paid out as follows:

Year Starting	Rate		Multiplier		Weekly Rate
1/1/2010	$600.00	*	None first year	=	$600.00
1/1/2011	$600.00	*	No increase	=	$600.00
1/1/2012	$600.00	*	1.024135	=	$614.48
1/1/2013	$614.48	*	1.055633	=	$648.67
1/1/2014	$648.67	*	1.007429	=	$653.49
1/1/2015	$653.49	*	1.026657	=	$670.91
1/1/2016	$670.91	*	1.022789	=	$686.19
1/1/2017	$686.19	*	1.039119	=	$713.04
1/1/2018	$713.04	*	1.036419	=	$739.01
1/1/2019	$739.01	*	1.029712	=	$760.96
1/1/2020	$760.96	*	1.038401	=	$790.19
1/1/2021	$790.19	*	1.043774	=	$824.78

Tables & Schedules

TABLE 15
Percentage of Permanent Disability to Weeks of Indemnity

The permanent disability rating schedule which became effective for **injuries occurring April 1, 1972 to December 31, 1991** provided for an increase in indemnity as the percent of disability increased as follows:

Percentage Range of Permanent Disability Rating	Number of Weeks For Each 1% Within the Range
Under 10	3
10 - 19.75	4
20 - 29.75	5
30 - 49.75	6
50 - 69.75	7
70 - 99.75	8

The cumulative effect of the formula precludes the use of a straight-line method of calculating the number of weeks of benefits. Therefore, to determine the number of weeks of indemnity for a permanent disability rating, we must either refer to a chart or use one of the following equations. ("R" is the permanent disability rating.)

If "R" is Between	Then total Number of Weeks is
1% - 9.75%	3 R
10% - 19.75%	4(R - 9.75) + 29.25
20% - 29.75%	5(R - 19.75) + 69.25
30% - 49.75%	6(R - 29.75) + 119.25
50% - 69.75%	7(R - 49.75) + 239.25
70% - 99.75%	8(R - 69.75) + 379.25

% of PD	Injuries 1/1/92 to 12/31/02
1% - 9.75%	3 R
10% - 19.75%	4(R - 9.75) + 29.25
20% - 24.75%	5(R - 19.75) + 69.25
25% - 29.75%	6(R - 24.75) + 94.25
30% - 49.75%	7(R - 29.75) + 124.25
50% - 69.75%	8(R - 49.75) + 264.25
70% - 99.75%	9(R - 69.75) + 424.25

% of PD	1/1/03 to 12/31/03	1/1/04 to 12/31/04	%PD 01/01/05 to ? See Table 8	
1 - 9.75	3R (3 × Rating)	4R (4 × Rating)	0.25-9.75	3R (3 × Rating)
10 - 19.75	4(R - 9.75) + 29.25	5(R - 9.75) + 39	10-14.75	4(R- 9.75)+ 29.25
20 - 24.75	5(R - 19.75) + 69.25	5(R - 19.75) + 89	15-24.75	5(R- 19.75)+ 74.25
25 - 29.75	6(R - 24.74) + 94.25	6(R - 24.75) + 114	25-29.75	6(R- 24.75)+ 99.25
30 - 49.75	7(R - 29.75) + 124.25	7(R - 29.75) + 144	30-49.75	7(R- 29.75)+129.25
50 - 69.75	8(R - 49.75) + 264.25	8(R - 49.75) + 284	50-69.75	8(R- 49.75)+269.25
70 - 99.75	9(R - 69.75) + 424.25	9(R - 69.75) + 444	70-99.75	16(R-69.75)+429.25

Example: Injury of 12-20-03. Calculate the number of weeks of P.D. for **37%**:
7(**37** - 29.75) + 124.25 = 7(7.25) + 124.25 = 50.75 + 124.25 = 175.00 weeks

TABLE 16
Instructions for Applying New and Old Permanent Partial Disability Benefit Rates to Table 17

1. Match the date of injury to the appropriate column in Table 17. Weeks of indemnity paid do not increase for injuries on or after 1992. However, the maximum permanent partial disability rates vary as the percentage of disability increases. The minimum paid is $70/week for all injuries on or after 1/1/84.

2. If the injury occurred in 1983, the maximum is $130/week and the minimum is $50/week. To calculate the amount owed for a given percent of permanent disability, multiply the number of weeks in the second column from the left (next to the % of P.D.) by the applicable weekly P.D. rate.

3. If the date of injury is from 1/1/77 to 12/31/82, the maximum is $70/week and the minimum, $30/week. From 4/1/72 to 12/31/76 the maximum was also $70/week, but the minimum was $20/week. To calculate the amount owed for a given percent of permanent disability, multiply the number of weeks in the second column from the left (next to the percent of P.D.) by the weekly P.D. rate. The minimum P.D. rate is $70/week for injuries on or after 1/1/84.

4. Note: Whenever the P.D. rate is less than $70 (1983 and prior) and the percent of disability is 29½ or less, compare with pre–1972 rates which were 4 weeks for each percent of P.D., but with a maximum of $52.50. The higher benefit applies.

5. Permanent disability rates are subject to the maximum/minimum values in effect on the date of injury. The following are three different methods for calculating the permanent partial disability rate from an average weekly wage, e.g. of $125 per week:
   (1) Multiply by 2 & divide by 3: Earnings of $125.00 × 2 ÷ 3 = **$83.33;**
   (2) Multiply by 0.66667: Earnings of $125.00 × 0.66667 = **$83.33;** or
   (3) Divide by 1.5. Earnings of $125.00 ÷ 1.5 = **$83.33** (The first method is most common.)

Summary: Permanent Partial Disability (PD) and Minimum / Maximum Rates

Date of Injury:	Min	Max	Weekly Rates
04/01/72 to 12/31/76	$20	$ 70	(Table 17 is for injuries on or after 1984.
01/01/77 to 12/31/82	$30	$ 70	Steps 2, 3 & 4 above calculate PD for
01/01/83 to 12/31/83	$50	$130	dates of injury back to 04/01/72 from the
01/01/84 to 12/31/90	$70	$140	1st # of weeks column in Table 17.)

Subsequent Minimum / Maximum weekly values depending on the Percent of PD:

Date of Injury:	Min	Max 1:0–14:3	Max 15:0–24:3	Max 25:0–69:3	Max 70:0–99:3
01/01/91 to 06/30/94	$70	$140	$140	$148	$148
07/01/94 to 06/30/95	$70	$140	$148	$158	$168
07/01/95 to 06/30/96	$70	$140	$154	$164	$198
07/01/96 to 12/31/02	$70	$140	$160	$170	$230

Date of Injury:	Min	Max 1:0–69:3	Max 70:0–99:3	
01/01/03 to 12/31/03	$100	$185	$230	Plus Life Pension
01/01/04 to 12/31/04	$105	$200	$250	See Table 14, page 2
01/01/05 to 12/31/05	$105	$220	$270	"
01/01/06 to 12/31/06	$130	$230	$270	"

PART 9. Permanent Disability: Weeks/Percents

TABLE 17A

Permanent Partial Disability Indemnity for Injuries 2013, 2014 – 2021

2014 – 2019 Permanent Disability Rates

%	Weeks	Indemnity	%	Weeks	Indemnity	%	Weeks	Indemnity	%	Weeks	Indemnity
1	3.00	870.00	**26**	106.75	30,957.50	**51**	279.25	80,982.50	**76**	529.25	153,482.50
2	6.00	1,740.00	**27**	112.75	32,697.50	**52**	287.25	83,302.50	**77**	545.25	158,122.50
3	9.00	2,610.00	**28**	118.75	34,437.50	**53**	295.25	85,622.50	**78**	561.25	162,762.50
4	12.00	3,480.00	**29**	124.75	36,177.50	**54**	303.25	87,942.50	**79**	577.25	167,402.50
5	15.00	4,350.00	**30**	131.00	37,990.00	**55**	311.25	90,262.50	**80**	593.25	172,042.50
6	18.00	5,220.00	**31**	138.00	40,020.00	**56**	319.25	92,582.50	**81**	609.25	176,682.50
7	21.00	6,090.00	**32**	145.00	42,050.00	**57**	327.25	94,902.50	**82**	625.25	181,322.50
8	24.00	6,960.00	**33**	152.00	44,080.00	**58**	335.25	97,222.50	**83**	641.25	185,962.50
9	27.00	7,830.00	**34**	159.00	46,110.00	**59**	343.25	99,542.50	**84**	657.25	190,602.50
10	30.25	8,772.50	**35**	166.00	48,140.00	**60**	351.25	101,862.50	**85**	673.25	195,242.50
11	34.25	9,932.50	**36**	173.00	50,170.00	**61**	359.25	104,182.50	**86**	689.25	199,882.50
12	38.25	11,092.50	**37**	180.00	52,200.00	**62**	367.25	106,502.50	**87**	705.25	204,522.50
13	42.25	12,252.50	**38**	187.00	54,230.00	**63**	375.25	108,822.50	**88**	721.25	209,162.50
14	46.25	13,412.50	**39**	194.00	56,260.00	**64**	383.25	111,142.50	**89**	737.25	213,802.50
15	50.50	14,645.00	**40**	201.00	58,290.00	**65**	391.25	113,462.50	**90**	753.25	218,442.50
16	55.50	16,095.00	**41**	208.00	60,320.00	**66**	399.25	115,782.50	**91**	769.25	223,082.50
17	60.50	17,545.00	**42**	215.00	62,350.00	**67**	407.25	118,102.50	**92**	785.25	227,722.50
18	65.50	18,995.00	**43**	222.00	64,380.00	**68**	415.25	120,422.50	**93**	801.25	232,362.50
19	70.50	20,445.00	**44**	229.00	66,410.00	**69**	423.25	122,742.50	**94**	817.25	237,002.50
20	75.50	21,895.00	**45**	236.00	68,440.00	**70**	433.25	125,642.50	**95**	833.25	241,642.50
21	80.50	23,345.00	**46**	243.00	70,470.00	**71**	449.25	130,282.50	**96**	849.25	246,282.50
22	85.50	24,795.00	**47**	250.00	72,500.00	**72**	465.25	134,922.50	**97**	865.25	250,922.50
23	90.50	26,245.00	**48**	257.00	74,530.00	**73**	481.25	139,562.50	**98**	881.25	255,562.50
24	95.50	27,695.00	**49**	264.00	76,560.00	**74**	497.25	144,202.50	**99**	897.25	260,202.50
25	100.75	29,217.50	**50**	271.25	78,662.50	**75**	513.25	148,842.50			

2013 Permanent Disability Rates

%	Weeks	Indemnity	%	Weeks	Indemnity	%	Weeks	Indemnity	%	Weeks	Indemnity
1	3.00	690.00	**26**	106.75	24,552.50	**51**	279.25	64,227.50	**76**	529.25	153,482.50
2	6.00	1,380.00	**27**	112.75	25,932.50	**52**	287.25	66,067.50	**77**	545.25	158,122.50
3	9.00	2,070.00	**28**	118.75	27,312.50	**53**	295.25	67,907.50	**78**	561.25	162,762.50
4	12.00	2,760.00	**29**	124.75	28,692.50	**54**	303.25	69,747.50	**79**	577.25	167,402.50
5	15.00	3,450.00	**30**	131.00	30,130.00	**55**	311.25	84,037.50	**80**	593.25	172,042.50
6	18.00	4,140.00	**31**	138.00	31,740.00	**56**	319.25	86,197.50	**81**	609.25	176,682.50
7	21.00	4,830.00	**32**	145.00	33,350.00	**57**	327.25	88,357.50	**82**	625.25	181,322.50
8	24.00	5,520.00	**33**	152.00	34,960.00	**58**	335.25	90,517.50	**83**	641.25	185,962.50
9	27.00	6,210.00	**34**	159.00	36,570.00	**59**	343.25	92,677.50	**84**	657.25	190,602.50
10	30.25	6,957.50	**35**	166.00	38,180.00	**60**	351.25	94,837.50	**85**	673.25	195,242.50
11	34.25	7,877.50	**36**	173.00	39,790.00	**61**	359.25	96,997.50	**86**	689.25	199,882.50
12	38.25	8,797.50	**37**	180.00	41,400.00	**62**	367.25	99,157.50	**87**	705.25	204,522.50
13	42.25	9,717.50	**38**	187.00	43,010.00	**63**	375.25	101,317.50	**88**	721.25	209,162.50
14	46.25	10,637.50	**39**	194.00	44,620.00	**64**	383.25	103,477.50	**89**	737.25	213,802.50
15	50.50	11,615.00	**40**	201.00	46,230.00	**65**	391.25	105,637.50	**90**	753.25	218,442.50
16	55.50	12,765.00	**41**	208.00	47,840.00	**66**	399.25	107,797.50	**91**	769.25	223,082.50
17	60.50	13,915.00	**42**	215.00	49,450.00	**67**	407.25	109,957.50	**92**	785.25	227,722.50
18	65.50	15,065.00	**43**	222.00	51,060.00	**68**	415.25	112,117.50	**93**	801.25	232,362.50
19	70.50	16,215.00	**44**	229.00	52,670.00	**69**	423.25	114,277.50	**94**	817.25	237,002.50
20	75.50	17,365.00	**45**	236.00	54,280.00	**70**	433.25	125,642.50	**95**	833.25	241,642.50
21	80.50	18,515.00	**46**	243.00	55,890.00	**71**	449.25	130,282.50	**96**	849.25	246,282.50
22	85.50	19,665.00	**47**	250.00	57,500.00	**72**	465.25	134,922.50	**97**	865.25	250,922.50
23	90.50	20,815.00	**48**	257.00	59,110.00	**73**	481.25	139,562.50	**98**	881.25	255,562.50
24	95.50	21,965.00	**49**	264.00	60,720.00	**74**	497.25	144,202.50	**99**	897.25	260,202.50
25	100.75	23,172.50	**50**	271.25	62,387.50	**75**	513.25	148,842.50			

These charts are based upon L.C. §§ 4453, 4658 and the maximum weekly rates for permanent disability.

TABLE 17B
Permanent Partial Disability Indemnity for Injuries 2006 – 2012

%	Weeks	Indemnity	-15%	+15%	%	Weeks	Indemnity	-15%	+15%
1	3.00	690.00	586.50	690.00	51	279.25	64,227.50	54,593.38	73,565.91
2	6.00	1,380.00	1,173.00	1,380.00	52	287.25	66,067.50	56,157.38	75,681.91
3	9.00	2,070.00	1,759.50	2,084.79	53	295.25	67,907.50	57,721.38	77,797.91
4	12.00	2,760.00	2,346.00	2,878.29	54	303.25	69,747.50	59,285.38	79,913.91
5	15.00	3,450.00	2,932.50	3,671.79	55	311.25	71,587.50	60,849.38	82,029.91
6	18.00	4,140.00	3,519.00	4,465.29	56	319.25	73,427.50	62,413.38	84,145.91
7	21.00	4,830.00	4,105.50	5,258.79	57	327.25	75,267.50	63,977.38	86,261.91
8	24.00	5,520.00	4,692.00	6,052.29	58	335.25	77,107.50	65,541.38	88,377.91
9	27.00	6,210.00	5,278.50	6,845.79	59	343.25	78,947.50	67,105.38	90,493.91
10	30.25	6,957.50	5,913.88	7,705.41	60	351.25	80,787.50	68,669.38	92,609.91
11	34.25	7,877.50	6,695.88	8,763.41	61	359.25	82,627.50	70,233.38	94,725.91
12	38.25	8,797.50	7,477.88	9,821.41	62	367.25	84,467.50	71,797.38	96,841.91
13	42.25	9,717.50	8,259.88	10,879.41	63	375.25	86,307.50	73,361.38	98,957.91
14	46.25	10,637.50	9,041.88	11,937.41	64	383.25	88,147.50	74,925.38	101,073.91
15	50.50	11,615.00	9,872.75	13,061.54	65	391.25	89,987.50	76,489.38	103,189.91
16	55.50	12,765.00	10,850.25	14,384.04	66	399.25	91,827.50	78,053.38	105,305.91
17	60.50	13,915.00	11,827.75	15,706.54	67	407.25	93,667.50	79,617.38	107,421.91
18	65.50	15,065.00	12,805.25	17,029.04	68	415.25	95,507.50	81,181.38	109,537.91
19	70.50	16,215.00	13,782.75	18,351.54	69	423.25	97,347.50	82,745.38	111,653.91
20	75.50	17,365.00	14,760.25	19,674.04	70	433.25	116,977.50	99,430.88	134,176.98
21	80.50	18,515.00	15,737.75	20,996.54	71	449.25	121,297.50	103,102.88	139,144.98
22	85.50	19,665.00	16,715.25	22,319.04	72	465.25	125,617.50	106,774.88	144,112.98
23	90.50	20,815.00	17,692.75	23,641.54	73	481.25	129,937.50	110,446.88	149,080.98
24	95.50	21,965.00	18,670.25	24,964.04	74	497.25	134,257.50	114,118.88	154,048.98
25	100.75	23,172.50	19,696.63	26,352.66	75	513.25	138,577.50	117,790.88	159,016.98
26	106.75	24,552.50	20,869.63	27,939.66	76	529.25	142,897.50	121,462.88	163,984.98
27	112.75	25,932.50	22,042.63	29,526.66	77	545.25	147,217.50	125,134.88	168,952.98
28	118.75	27,312.50	23,215.63	31,113.66	78	561.25	151,537.50	128,806.88	173,920.98
29	124.75	28,692.50	24,388.63	32,700.66	79	577.25	155,857.50	132,478.88	178,888.98
30	131.00	30,130.00	25,610.50	34,353.79	80	593.25	160,177.50	136,150.88	183,856.98
31	138.00	31,740.00	26,979.00	36,205.29	81	609.25	164,497.50	139,822.88	188,824.98
32	145.00	33,350.00	28,347.50	38,056.79	82	625.25	168,817.50	143,494.88	193,792.98
33	152.00	34,960.00	29,716.00	39,908.29	83	641.25	173,137.50	147,166.88	198,760.98
34	159.00	36,570.00	31,084.50	41,759.79	84	657.25	177,457.50	150,838.88	203,728.98
35	166.00	38,180.00	32,453.00	43,611.29	85	673.25	181,777.50	154,510.88	208,696.98
36	173.00	39,790.00	33,821.50	45,462.79	86	689.25	186,097.50	158,182.88	213,664.98
37	180.00	41,400.00	35,190.00	47,314.29	87	705.25	190,417.50	161,854.88	218,632.98
38	187.00	43,010.00	36,558.50	49,165.79	88	721.25	194,737.50	165,526.88	223,600.98
39	194.00	44,620.00	37,927.00	51,017.29	89	737.25	199,057.50	169,198.88	228,568.98
40	201.00	46,230.00	39,295.50	52,868.79	90	753.25	203,377.50	172,870.88	233,536.98
41	208.00	47,840.00	40,664.00	54,720.29	91	769.25	207,697.50	176,542.88	238,504.98
42	215.00	49,450.00	42,032.50	56,571.79	92	785.25	212,017.50	180,214.88	243,472.98
43	222.00	51,060.00	43,401.00	58,423.29	93	801.25	216,337.50	183,886.88	248,440.98
44	229.00	52,670.00	44,769.50	60,274.79	94	817.25	220,657.50	187,558.88	253,408.98
45	236.00	54,280.00	46,138.00	62,126.29	95	833.25	224,977.50	191,230.88	258,376.98
46	243.00	55,890.00	47,506.50	63,977.79	96	849.25	229,297.50	194,902.88	263,344.98
47	250.00	57,500.00	48,875.00	65,829.29	97	865.25	233,617.50	198,574.88	268,312.98
48	257.00	59,110.00	50,243.50	67,680.79	98	881.25	237,937.50	202,246.88	273,280.98
49	264.00	60,720.00	51,612.00	69,532.29	99	897.25	242,257.50	205,918.88	278,248.98
50	271.25	62,387.50	53,029.38	71,449.91					

This chart is based upon L.C. §§ 4453, 4658 and the maximum weekly rates for permanent disability. Any L.C. § 4658(d) decreases are applied immediately and any increases are applied after the 60th day. Reprinted with permission by license from Jay Shergill,

TABLE 17C
Permanent Partial Disability Indemnity for Injuries in 2005

%	Weeks	Indemnity	-15%	+15%	%	Weeks	Indemnity	-15%	+15%
1	3.00	660.00	561.00	660.00	51	279.25	61,435.00	52,219.75	70,367.39
2	6.00	1,320.00	1,122.00	1,320.00	52	287.25	63,195.00	53,715.75	72,391.39
3	9.00	1,980.00	1,683.00	1,994.14	53	295.25	64,955.00	55,211.75	74,415.39
4	12.00	2,640.00	2,244.00	2,753.14	54	303.25	66,715.00	56,707.75	76,439.39
5	15.00	3,300.00	2,805.00	3,512.14	55	311.25	68,475.00	58,203.75	78,463.39
6	18.00	3,960.00	3,366.00	4,271.14	56	319.25	70,235.00	59,699.75	80,487.39
7	21.00	4,620.00	3,927.00	5,030.14	57	327.25	71,995.00	61,195.75	82,511.39
8	24.00	5,280.00	4,488.00	5,789.14	58	335.25	73,755.00	62,691.75	84,535.39
9	27.00	5,940.00	5,049.00	6,548.14	59	343.25	75,515.00	64,187.75	86,559.39
10	30.25	6,655.00	5,656.75	7,370.39	60	351.25	77,275.00	65,683.75	88,583.39
11	34.25	7,535.00	6,404.75	8,382.39	61	359.25	79,035.00	67,179.75	90,607.39
12	38.25	8,415.00	7,152.75	9,394.39	62	367.25	80,795.00	68,675.75	92,631.39
13	42.25	9,295.00	7,900.75	10,406.39	63	375.25	82,555.00	70,171.75	94,655.39
14	46.25	10,175.00	8,648.75	11,418.39	64	383.25	84,315.00	71,667.75	96,679.39
15	50.50	11,110.00	9,443.50	12,493.64	65	391.25	86,075.00	73,163.75	98,703.39
16	55.50	12,210.00	10,378.50	13,758.64	66	399.25	87,835.00	74,659.75	100,727.39
17	60.50	13,310.00	11,313.50	15,023.64	67	407.25	89,595.00	76,155.75	102,751.39
18	65.50	14,410.00	12,248.50	16,288.64	68	415.25	91,355.00	77,651.75	104,775.39
19	70.50	15,510.00	13,183.50	17,553.64	69	423.25	93,115.00	79,147.75	106,799.39
20	75.50	16,610.00	14,118.50	18,818.64	70	433.25	116,977.50	99,430.88	134,176.98
21	80.50	17,710.00	15,053.50	20,083.64	71	449.25	121,297.50	103,102.88	139,144.98
22	85.50	18,810.00	15,988.50	21,348.64	72	465.25	125,617.50	106,774.88	144,112.98
23	90.50	19,910.00	16,923.50	22,613.64	73	481.25	129,937.50	110,446.88	149,080.98
24	95.50	21,010.00	17,858.50	23,878.64	74	497.25	134,257.50	114,118.88	154,048.98
25	100.75	22,165.00	18,840.25	25,206.89	75	513.25	138,577.50	117,790.88	159,016.98
26	106.75	23,485.00	19,962.25	26,724.89	76	529.25	142,897.50	121,462.88	163,984.98
27	112.75	24,805.00	21,084.25	28,242.89	77	545.25	147,217.50	125,134.88	168,952.98
28	118.75	26,125.00	22,206.25	29,760.89	78	561.25	151,537.50	128,806.88	173,920.98
29	124.75	27,445.00	23,328.25	31,278.89	79	577.25	155,857.50	132,478.88	178,888.98
30	131.00	28,820.00	24,497.00	32,860.14	80	593.25	160,177.50	136,150.88	183,856.98
31	138.00	30,360.00	25,806.00	34,631.14	81	609.25	164,497.50	139,822.88	188,824.98
32	145.00	31,900.00	27,115.00	36,402.14	82	625.25	168,817.50	143,494.88	193,792.98
33	152.00	33,440.00	28,424.00	38,173.14	83	641.25	173,137.50	147,166.88	198,760.98
34	159.00	34,980.00	29,733.00	39,944.14	84	657.25	177,457.50	150,838.88	203,728.98
35	166.00	36,520.00	31,042.00	41,715.14	85	673.25	181,777.50	154,510.88	208,696.98
36	173.00	38,060.00	32,351.00	43,486.14	86	689.25	186,097.50	158,182.88	213,664.98
37	180.00	39,600.00	33,660.00	45,257.14	87	705.25	190,417.50	161,854.88	218,632.98
38	187.00	41,140.00	34,969.00	47,028.14	88	721.25	194,737.50	165,526.88	223,600.98
39	194.00	42,680.00	36,278.00	48,799.14	89	737.25	199,057.50	169,198.88	228,568.98
40	201.00	44,220.00	37,587.00	50,570.14	90	753.25	203,377.50	172,870.88	233,536.98
41	208.00	45,760.00	38,896.00	52,341.14	91	769.25	207,697.50	176,542.88	238,504.98
42	215.00	47,300.00	40,205.00	54,112.14	92	785.25	212,017.50	180,214.88	243,472.98
43	222.00	48,840.00	41,514.00	55,883.14	93	801.25	216,337.50	183,886.88	248,440.98
44	229.00	50,380.00	42,823.00	57,654.14	94	817.25	220,657.50	187,558.88	253,408.98
45	236.00	51,920.00	44,132.00	59,425.14	95	833.25	224,977.50	191,230.88	258,376.98
46	243.00	53,460.00	45,441.00	61,196.14	96	849.25	229,297.50	194,902.88	263,344.98
47	250.00	55,000.00	46,750.00	62,967.14	97	865.25	233,617.50	198,574.88	268,312.98
48	257.00	56,540.00	48,059.00	64,738.14	98	881.25	237,937.50	202,246.88	273,280.98
49	264.00	58,080.00	49,368.00	66,509.14	99	897.25	242,257.50	205,918.88	278,248.98
50	271.25	59,675.00	50,723.75	68,343.39					

This chart is based upon L.C. §§ 4453, 4658 and the maximum weekly rates for permanent disability. Any L.C. § 4658(d) decreases are applied immediately and any increases are applied after the 60th day. Reprinted with permission by license from Jay Shergill,

TABLE 17D
Permanent Partial Disability Indemnity for Injuries 2003, 2004

2004 Permanent Disability Rates

%	Weeks	Indemnity	%	Weeks	Indemnity	%	Weeks	Indemnity	%	Weeks	Indemnity
1	4.00	800.00	26	121.50	24,300.00	51	294.00	58,800.00	76	500.25	125,062.50
2	8.00	1,600.00	27	127.50	25,500.00	52	302.00	60,400.00	77	509.25	127,312.50
3	12.00	2,400.00	28	133.50	26,700.00	53	310.00	62,000.00	78	518.25	129,562.50
4	16.00	3,200.00	29	139.50	27,900.00	54	318.00	63,600.00	79	527.25	131,812.50
5	20.00	4,000.00	30	145.75	29,150.00	55	326.00	65,200.00	80	536.25	134,062.50
6	24.00	4,800.00	31	152.75	30,550.00	56	334.00	66,800.00	81	545.25	136,312.50
7	28.00	5,600.00	32	159.75	31,950.00	57	342.00	68,400.00	82	554.25	138,562.50
8	32.00	6,400.00	33	166.75	33,350.00	58	350.00	70,000.00	83	563.25	140,812.50
9	36.00	7,200.00	34	173.75	34,750.00	59	358.00	71,600.00	84	572.25	143,062.50
10	40.25	8,050.00	35	180.75	36,150.00	60	366.00	73,200.00	85	581.25	145,312.50
11	45.25	9,050.00	36	187.75	37,550.00	61	374.00	74,800.00	86	590.25	147,562.50
12	50.25	10,050.00	37	194.75	38,950.00	62	382.00	76,400.00	87	599.25	149,812.50
13	55.25	11,050.00	38	201.75	40,350.00	63	390.00	78,000.00	88	608.25	152,062.50
14	60.25	12,050.00	39	208.75	41,750.00	64	398.00	79,600.00	89	617.25	154,312.50
15	65.25	13,050.00	40	215.75	43,150.00	65	406.00	81,200.00	90	626.25	156,562.50
16	70.25	14,050.00	41	222.75	44,550.00	66	414.00	82,800.00	91	635.25	158,812.50
17	75.25	15,050.00	42	229.75	45,950.00	67	422.00	84,400.00	92	644.25	161,062.50
18	80.25	16,050.00	43	236.75	47,350.00	68	430.00	86,000.00	93	653.25	163,312.50
19	85.25	17,050.00	44	243.75	48,750.00	69	438.00	87,600.00	94	662.25	165,562.50
20	90.25	18,050.00	45	250.75	50,150.00	70	446.25	111,562.50	95	671.25	167,812.50
21	95.25	19,050.00	46	257.75	51,550.00	71	455.25	113,812.50	96	680.25	170,062.50
22	100.25	20,050.00	47	264.75	52,950.00	72	464.25	116,062.50	97	689.25	172,312.50
23	105.25	21,050.00	48	271.75	54,350.00	73	473.25	118,312.50	98	698.25	174,562.50
24	110.25	22,050.00	49	278.75	55,750.00	74	482.25	120,562.50	99	707.25	176,812.50
25	115.50	23,100.00	50	286.00	57,200.00	75	491.25	122,812.50			

2003 Permanent Disability Rates

%	Weeks	Indemnity	%	Weeks	Indemnity	%	Weeks	Indemnity	%	Weeks	Indemnity
1	3.00	555.00	26	101.75	18,823.75	51	274.25	50,736.25	76	480.50	110,515.00
2	6.00	1,110.00	27	107.75	19,933.75	52	282.25	52,216.25	77	489.50	112,585.00
3	9.00	1,665.00	28	113.75	21,043.75	53	290.25	53,696.25	78	498.50	114,655.00
4	12.00	2,220.00	29	119.75	22,153.75	54	298.25	55,176.25	79	507.50	116,725.00
5	15.00	2,775.00	30	126.00	23,310.00	55	306.25	56,656.25	80	516.50	118,795.00
6	18.00	3,330.00	31	133.00	24,605.00	56	314.25	58,136.25	81	525.50	120,865.00
7	21.00	3,885.00	32	140.00	25,900.00	57	322.25	59,616.25	82	534.50	122,935.00
8	24.00	4,440.00	33	147.00	27,195.00	58	330.25	61,096.25	83	543.50	125,005.00
9	27.00	4,995.00	34	154.00	28,490.00	59	338.25	62,576.25	84	552.50	127,075.00
10	30.25	5,596.25	35	161.00	29,785.00	60	346.25	64,056.25	85	561.50	129,145.00
11	34.25	6,336.25	36	168.00	31,080.00	61	354.25	65,536.25	86	570.50	131,215.00
12	38.25	7,076.25	37	175.00	32,375.00	62	362.25	67,016.25	87	579.50	133,285.00
13	42.25	7,816.25	38	182.00	33,670.00	63	370.25	68,496.25	88	588.50	135,355.00
14	46.25	8,556.25	39	189.00	34,965.00	64	378.25	69,976.25	89	597.50	137,425.00
15	50.25	9,296.25	40	196.00	36,260.00	65	386.25	71,456.25	90	606.50	139,495.00
16	54.25	10,036.25	41	203.00	37,555.00	66	394.25	72,936.25	91	615.50	141,565.00
17	58.25	10,776.25	42	210.00	38,850.00	67	402.25	74,416.25	92	624.50	143,635.00
18	62.25	11,516.25	43	217.00	40,145.00	68	410.25	75,896.25	93	633.50	145,705.00
19	66.25	12,256.25	44	224.00	41,440.00	69	418.25	77,376.25	94	642.50	147,775.00
20	70.50	13,042.50	45	231.00	42,735.00	70	426.50	98,095.00	95	651.50	149,845.00
21	75.50	13,967.50	46	238.00	44,030.00	71	435.50	100,165.00	96	660.50	151,915.00
22	80.50	14,892.50	47	245.00	45,325.00	72	444.50	102,235.00	97	669.50	153,985.00
23	85.50	15,817.50	48	252.00	46,620.00	73	453.50	104,305.00	98	678.50	156,055.00
24	90.50	16,742.50	49	259.00	47,915.00	74	462.50	106,375.00	99	687.50	158,125.00
25	95.75	17,713.75	50	266.25	49,256.25	75	471.50	108,445.00			

These charts are based upon L.C. §§ 4453, 4658 and the maximum weekly rates for permanent disability.

Tables & Schedules

PART 10. Glossary

TABLE 18
Glossary of Terms and Abbreviations Commonly Used in Workers' Compensation

(Adapted from the *Workers' Compensation Index*, by Richard L. Montarbo & James T. Stewart,)

AA, A/A or EEA . . . . Applicant's Attorney or Employee's Attorney

AC . . . . Appeals Council (SSA)

ACA . . . . Affordable Care Act (see PPACA)

ACOEM . . . . American College of Occupational & Environmental Medicine

A.D. . . . . Administrative Director

A.D. Dec. . . . . Administrative Director's Decisions reported in CWCR

Ad Litem . . . . Usually as in "guardian ad litem," a person appointed as a guardian of a minor or adult person incompetent to manage their own affairs for the purpose of the litigation of a claim

ADA . . . . Americans with Disabilities Act (Federal)

ADJ (EAMS) . . . . "A district office adjudication case."

ADJ PJ (EAMS) . . . . "The presiding judge (PJ) in the district office."

Adjourn (hearing) (EAMS) . . . . When a hearing is ended and another must be scheduled later

Adjudicate . . . . The deciding of case by a WCALJ (aka, "WCJ" or "judge") who issues an "Opinion" or "Findings and Award" (F&A)

ADL . . . . Activities of Daily Living, *AMA Guides,* p27, and PDRS

ADR . . . . Alternative Dispute Resolution, Lab. Code, § 3201.7, "carve out"

ALJ . . . . Administrative Law Judge, now usually "WCALJ" is a Workers' Compensation Administrative Law Judge or WCJ

AMA Findings . . . . Findings of Dr. re, e.g., limitation of ADL's

AMA Guides . . . . *American Medical Association Guides to the Evaluation of Permanent Impairment* © (5th Ed.), p27, Lab. Code, § 4660(b)(1)

AME . . . . Agreed Medical Examiner, Examination, or Evaluator

AME Dance . . . . Requirement parties must attempt to agree to an AME when employee is represented, Lab. Code, §§ 4061(c), 4062.2 o/a 1/1/05

Answer . . . . A formal response by the party, usually the employer or representative, opposing the party who filed an Application

AOE/COE . . . . Arising Out Of Employment and Occurring in the Course Of Employment

Ap, AP or App . . . . Application for Adjudication of Claim, usually filed by the employee or his or her representative; usually spoken, with the full word, "application" used in written form

Appeals (EAMS) . . . . "A request by a case participant to change a case decision."

Appeals Board . . . . WCAB, i.e., local offices & "The WCAB" in San Francisco

Applicant . . . . Party, usually the employee, who files an Application

Apportionment	The process of removing from a PD award portions not owed by a defendant because the disability or impairment either pre-existed or would have existed regardless of injury; Lab. Code, §§ 4663, 4664; the Sup. Ct. of Calif. has resolved some questions, **<u>Brodie, Welcher, et al. v. WCAB</u> 72 Cal. Comp. Cases 565**
APQME	Agreed Panel QME; Cal. Code Regs., tit. 8, §§ 1(d), 31.7–38
ASOP	Agreed Second Opinion Physician, Lab. Code, § 4062(b)
Authority	A published opinion by a District Court of Appeal or the Supreme Court of California or WCAB en banc opinion
Award	Award by WCAB, as in "Findings and Award," or F & A
AWW or AWE	Average Weekly Wage or Earnings
Baby Splitters	Quote of the Month from an article by York McGavin, 34 CWCR 339; refers to AMEs who "split the baby" and give each side part of what they like and part they don't like to generate repeat business, rather than deciding based upon their own best judgment and appearing to favor one "side."
Baseball Arbitration	Ratings proposed by each party contesting other's QME, Lab. Code, §§ 4065, 5502(d)(3), repealed 2002
BKA	Below Knee Amputation
Board	Workers' Compensation Appeals Board
Body Part	Hands and feet are considered one body part for combining impairment ratings under *AMA Guides* and PDRS
BRBS	Benefits Review Board Service–Longshore Reporter; (LexisNexis) (800) 223-1940
Brigham	Christopher Brigham; one of the authors of the "AMA Guides," supra and a frequent lecturer regarding them
BUE or BUEX	Bilateral Upper Extremities; UE or UEX, Upper Extremities
Bureau	Rehabilitation Bureau, now Rehabilitation Unit
C and R or C&R	Compromise and Release, a final settlement in Comp
CA or C/A	Claims Administrator
CAAA	California Applicants' Attorneys Association
Cal. Code Regs., tit. 8	Title 8 of the California Code of Regulations
Cal. Comp. Cases	California Compensation Cases (LexisNexis) (800) 223-1940
Cal. Wrk. Comp. P.D. LEXIS	Noteworthy Panel Decisions available on lexis.com and Lexis Advance (800) 223-1940; proper cite is, e.g., "2009 **Cal. Wrk. Comp. P.D. LEXIS** 118"; see also NPD
Cancel (hearing) (EAMS)	Cancellation of a scheduled hearing; previously called "OTOC"
Carve Out	Collective bargaining agreement in certain industries, e.g., construction, Lab. Code, § 3201.5, using alternative dispute resolution with WCAB having appellate jurisdiction
CCC	*California Compensation Cases* (LexisNexis) (800) 223-1940
CE or C/E	Claims Examiner (same as "CA," supra)
CEB	Continuing Education of the Bar's book, 4th ed., *California Workers' Compensation Practice*, a.k.a., "The CEB Book"; see http://ceb.com/
CFRA	California Family Rights Act, e.g., Gov. Code, §§ 12945.1, 12945.2
Chapter Shop	Obtaining an impairment rating using analogous methods in AMA Guides
CHSWC	Commission on Health and Safety & Workers' Compensation; commonly spoken as "Cheese-Whiz"
CIC	Case in Chief; the part of a trial where the party with the burden of proof presents its evidence

CIGA	California Insurance Guarantee Association
Client (EAMS)	Used to identify the primary client on AP; essentially the EE
CME	Comprehensive Medical Examiner/Examination
CMS	Centers for Medicare & Medicaid Services of the U.S. Dept. of Health and Human Services; Cal. Code Regs., tit. 8, § 9789.10(b)
COBRA	Group health coverage offered some employees under Federal law after employment terminates
COE	Course Of Employment, see "AOE/COE," above
COLA	Cost of Living Adjustment (See Table 14)
Commutation	Reducing a sum of money due at a certain rate, for a period of time, to its present value
Comp	Workers' Compensation, Gov. Code, § 24
Companion Case (EAMS)	Cases sharing a common factor, e.g., the EE, D/A where there are multiple EEs hurt the same way, same ER, CC or lien claimant
Complete (hearing) (EAMS)	Recording details of a hearing, e.g., attendees, date/time of hearing, notes about disposition and orders relating to the case(s)
Consolidate	The process of bringing together for a hearing separate claims to avoid delay and duplication of effort
Continue (hearing) (EAMS)	A hearing postponed prior to the date of the hearing and then rescheduled for another date
Contribution	A process where defendant #1 seeks to recover from #2 for payments made by the #1 which are alleged owed by #2; e.g., Lab. Code, § 5500.5(e)
CPT	Current Procedural Terminology; a 5 digit code for billing medical procedures; Cal. Code Regs., tit. 8, § 9789.10(d)
CRPS	Complex Regional Pain Syndrome
CSIMS	California Society of Industrial Medicine and Surgery
CT	Cumulative Trauma, Lab. Code, § 5500.5
CT Scan or CAT Scan	Computerized Axial Tomography; combines separate X-Rays to produce detailed pictures, especially of bones {See "MRI"}
CWCE	*California Workers' Compensation Educator* {Formerly, "Enquirer." No longer published?}
CWCI	California Workers' Compensation Institute
CWCLP	*California Workers' Compensation Law & Practice,* by Richard L. Newman, Daniel A. Dobrin, Alexander Wong & Sheldon C. St. Clair by James Publishing, Inc.; 3505 Cadillac Ave., Suite H; Costa Mesa, CA 92626; 800-440-4780
CWDP	*California Workers' Damages Practice,* 2nd ed., http://ceb.com/
CWCR	*California Workers' Compensation Reporter*; P.O. Box 520; Berkeley, CA 94701: A monthly magazine. Add 72 to the # before "CWCR" in a cite for the year of the issue and usually the decision. For a sample copy, call (510) 843-1381
Cytokine testing	Testing of DNA for cytokines released when exposed to toxic substances each with their own "signature," including chronic pain; see URL: http://www.cytokineinstitute.com/
D/A, DA or DOI	Date of Accident or Injury (D.A. is District Attorney)
DA, D/C or DefAtty	Defense Attorney or Counsel (D.C. = Dr. of Chiropractic)
DBA	Defense Base Act, 42 U.S.C.S. §§ 1651–1654
DCA	District Court of Appeal

Decertified	Calif. Supreme Court decertifies a Court of Appeal opinion and orders the Reporter of Decisions not to publish the case in the Official Reports (aka depublication); such cases are not citeable; compare "not published"
Δ or Def	Greek letter "Delta," not spoken, meaning "Defendant," i.e., either an employer, adjusting agent or representative
Demand	An offer to settle made by employee; a counter offer by the defendant is called an "Offer"
Depo	Deposition; a statement under oath recorded by court reporter
DES	Disability Evaluation Specialist
DEU	Disability Evaluation Unit; Cal. Code Regs., tit. 8, § 10150
D&I	Deny and Incorporate; relates to when the WCAB denies a petition for reconsideration and incorporates the WCJ's Report and Recommendation on Petition for Reconsideration in their decision, without offering any further analysis or discussion of the issues
DI, D/I or DOI	Date of Injury
Dicta	Comments made by a court in a decision concerning something not then being decided or not part of the holding in the case; it is not binding on other courts
DIR	Division of Industrial Relations
Disability	Effect of an impairment on ability to meet occupational requirements, measured against future earning capacity loss
DME	Durable Medical Equipment
Doctor shopping	Seeking a favorable medical opinion from a different doctor
DR, DRP or DOR	Declaration of Readiness to Proceed
DRE	Diagnosis Related Estimate from "AMA Guides" for e.g., describing spine impairment as opposed to "ROM" which utilizes Range Of Motion
DSM-5®	Diagnostic and Statistical Manual of Mental Disorders Fifth Edition (DSM-5®), published by the American Psychiatric Association
DWC	Division of Workers' Compensation
DWC Seminar	Division of Workers' Compensation annual seminars, material on line at http://www.dir.ca.gov/dwc/dwc_home_page.htm
DWC-1	Claim Form
DWCNewsline	http://www.dir.ca.gov/dwc/dwc_newsline.html
DWDU	Death Without Dependents Unit
DX or Dx	Diagnosis
E and O or E&O	Errors and Omissions insurance coverage, e.g., by an insurance agent, claims person or attorney
EAMS	Electronic Adjudication Management System (paperless) which the DWC "launched" 8/25/08 at all WCAB offices, statewide; pronunciation of acronym rhymes with "Screams"; terms used in EAMS here shown as "(EAMS)"; see generally, http://www.dir.ca.gov/dwc/EAMS/EAMS.htm
EBM	Evidence Based Medicine, Lab. Code, § 5307.27
EDD	Employment Development Dept. pays State Disability or SDI
EDEX	DWC's Electronic Data Exchange system http://www.dir.ca.gov/dwc/edex.html
E-Discovery	Discovery of records and information stored electronically, Code Civ. Proc., § 2017.710 et seq.
EE or ee	Employee and/or representative, written only
EEOC	Equal Employment Opportunity Commission (Federal)

Tables & Schedules

e-forms (EAMS) . . . . Forms submitted to the WCAB electronically as opposed to hard copy which has to be scanned

Employer, ER or Def . . . . Employer, insurance carrier, self-insurance administrator and/or representative

Employer (EAMS) . . . . Per EAMS glossary, "Used to describe any group that needs to be registered in EAMS that is an entity of more than one person."

en banc or in bank . . . . A decision made by all of the members of a court or, e.g., the WCAB Commissioners (binding on WCJs, Cal. Code Regs., tit. 8, § 10341)

EOP or EOB . . . . Explanation Of Payment or Benefit (i.e., describing &/or summarizing)

ER, ERA . . . . Employer, Employer's Attorney

ERISA . . . . Federal law governing retirement plans

Esq. . . . . Esquire (English title) now indicating a person is a practicing and licensed attorney

Estoppel . . . . A legal "stopping" of a party from making an argument

et al. . . . . Latin for "et allia" meaning "and others"

et seq. . . . . Latin for "et sequens" meaning "and the following"

ex parte . . . . Latin "for one party"; e.g., all "parties" are supposed to appear at the same time before a judge with no private conversations with the judge regarding an issue remaining to be decided; also, a letter sent to an AME with no copy to other "parties" at the same time; Cal. Code Regs., tit. 8, § 10334; Lab. Code, § 4062.2(f), (g)

F and A, F&A . . . . Findings and Award, a decision by the WCAB

FA&O . . . . Findings Award and Order

Far End . . . . Commutation off the far end of the Award, i.e., calculated from the end of a series of payments back towards present

FCA . . . . Full Compliance Audit, Lab. Code, §§ 129, 129.5, Cal. Code Regs., tit. 8, § 10107.1

FCE . . . . Functional Capacity Evaluation, *AMA Guides* and PDRS

FEC . . . . Future Earning Capacity, *AMA Guides* and PDRS

FEHA . . . . Fair Employment Housing Act (State anti-discrimination)

FEHC . . . . Fair Employment Housing Commission

FEIN . . . . Federal Employer Identification Number (for, e.g., WCIRB)

FME . . . . Formal Medical Evaluation

FMLA . . . . Family Medical Leave Act (Federal, 1993); see CFRA (California)

Foust . . . . *California Lien Claims in Workers' Compensation Cases* by Pamela W. Foust; James Publishing, Inc.; 3505 Cadillac Ave., Suite H; Costa Mesa, CA 92626; (800) 440-4780

GAF . . . . Global Assessment of Function, from *AMA Guides*

Ghost Statutes . . . . See "Ghost Statutes," p95, *Rehab Index,* 10th Ed. {out of print}

GINA . . . . Genetic Information Nondiscrimination Act of 2008

GL § . . . . Rehab Unit Administrative Guidelines; GL § 8-50-01 ¶ 7 cites them as "A.G. § "

Going and Coming . . . . General rule that injuries during a normal commute to or from work are not industrial, with many exceptions

Greens . . . . Employee's Permanent Disability Questionnaire, DEU-100, injuries on or after 1-1-91

Guardian ad litem . . . . Guardian appointed only for the case being litigated

Guides . . . . *AMA Guides to the Evaluation of Permanent Impairment,* 5th Edition

Hanna . . . . *California Law of Employee Injuries and Workers' Compensation,* Revised 2nd Ed. (LexisNexis) (800) 223-1940

HCO . . . . Health Care Organization, e.g., as in Lab. Code, § 4600.5

Hearing (EAMS) . . . . "This is a meeting before a hearing official."

Hearing official (EAMS) . . . . "A judge or rehabilitation consultant."

Herlick . . . . *California Workers' Compensation Handbook* (LexisNexis) (800) 223-1940

HHC . . . . Home Health Care

HIPAA . . . . Health Insurance Portability and Accountability Act of 1996 (HIPAA, Title II); deals with privacy of medical records

Home (EAMS) . . . . "A link in EAMS that will take you back to the home page."

I & A Officer . . . . Information and Assistance Officer

IAC . . . . Industrial Accident Commission, predecessor of the WCAB; a cite to it indicates a case before the Cal. Comp. Cases began in 1936

IBR . . . . Independent Bill Review

IBRO . . . . Independent Bill Review Organization

IC . . . . Insurance Carrier

ICD-9 . . . . International Statistical Classification of Diseases and Related Health Problems, 9th Ed. for coding of a medical diagnosis

ICD-10 . . . . International Statistical Classification of Diseases and Related Health Problems, 10th Ed. for coding of a medical diagnosis

IDL . . . . Industrial Disability Leave (State employees)

IEA . . . . Insurance Educational Association; 100 California St., #100; San Francisco, CA 94111

IJ or IW . . . . Injured person or worker, also commonly referred to as "ee" or "applicant" though technically a defendant may file an "AP"

IMC . . . . Industrial Medical Council, changed to DWC Medical Unit

IME . . . . Independent or Impartial Medical Examiner, used in tort claims, not a doctor chosen by one of the parties in "comp"

Impairment . . . . Loss of use or damage to a body part or function as measured against activities of daily living; results in disability

IMR . . . . Independent Medical Review; compare UR-IMR with MPN-IMR

IMRO . . . . Independent Medical Review Organization (see Maximus)

In Pro Per . . . . An individual acting as his or her own attorney, Latin for "in propria persona"

INS, INSA . . . . Insurance Co. or "Defendant" + A = their attorney

Insider (EAMS) . . . . A DWC newsletter about EAMS: http://www.dir.ca.gov/dwc/EAMS/EAMS_Insider/EAMS_Insider.htm

IPA . . . . Independent Practice Association

Joinder . . . . Adding parties after filing an AP, Cal. Code Regs., tit. 8, §§ 10360–10380

Jones Act . . . . 46 U.S.C.S. §§ 30104, 30105 providing protection for merchant seaman

Judge . . . . Since 1993, Lab. Code, § 27, has changed from Workers' Comp "Judge," (WCJ) to "Referee," (WCR), then to "Workers' Compensation Administrative Law Judge," WCALJ, but still usually called a "WCJ"

LAF . . . . Lien Activation Fee

Larson . . . . Larson's *Workers' Compensation Law*; (LexisNexis) (800) 223-1940

Lawyer's Guide . . . . *The Lawyer's Guide to the AMA Guides and California Workers' Compensation* by Robert G. Rassp, (LexisNexis) (800) 223-1940

L.C. . . . . Labor Code of California, as cited in *Workers' Compensation Laws of California* which contains the Labor Code and most other laws relating to Workers' Comp in CA. Often called, "The Labor Code Book," {CWCLP § 22:224}; it contains *much* more. (LexisNexis) (800) 223-1940

LDW . . . . Last Day Worked

Legacy system (EAMS) . . . . "The current system of record, like DEU's system or the WCAB online system."

LEX . . . . Lower Extremity (UEX, upper extremity)

Lexis or LexisNexis® . . . . Legal and Professional Publisher; Lexis is also the Official California Court Reporter for appellate cases; see http://www.lexisnexis.com

LHWCA or L & H . . . . Longshore and Harbor Workers' Compensation Act

Linked case (EAMS) . . . . Cases with some relationship with each other are "linked." These cases need to be designated as "master" or "non-master" cases

LTD . . . . Long Term Disability

MAA . . . . Medical Access Assistants

Master Case (EAMS) . . . . . . "… Actions taken on cases linked to the master case are noted on the master case rather than the linked case."

Maximus . . . . Maximum Federal Services, Inc., the IMRO

MCLE . . . . Mandatory Continuing Legal Education

MCSS . . . . Multiple Chemical Sensitivity Syndrome

MDT . . . . Multiple Disability Table, 4/97 PDRS §§ 7-15, 7-16; sometimes mistakenly used for the 1/05 PDRS "Combined Values Chart"

Medical Foods . . . . Specific foods prescribed to help cure or relieve the effects of an industrial injury; not mentioned in any case reported on the www.lexis.com web site, but a search on the DIR web site www.dir.ca.gov yielded 20 "hits" for "medical foods"

Med–Legal . . . . Medical–Legal examination or expense, at request of a party; employee's is owed by def. Lab. Code, §§ 4620 et seq.

Mediator . . . . A person hired by parties to assist in reaching agreements; differs from an "Arbitrator" who is more similar to a judge

DWC – Medical Unit P.O. Box 71010 Oakland, CA 94612	**Street Address:** 1515 Clay Street, 18th floor Oakland, CA 94612

Phone: 510-286-3700 or 800-794-6900

Medical Unit, URL . . . . http://www.dir.ca.gov/dwc/MedicalUnit/imchp.html

MMD . . . . Medical Marijuana Dispensary

MMI . . . . Maximum Medical Improvement, Cal. Code Regs., tit. 8, § 10152

MPN . . . . Medical Provider Network, Lab. Code, § 4616

MPN-IMR . . . . Medical Provider Network-Independent Medical Review, relating to medical treatment disputes regarding second and third opinions of the MPN's primary treating physician's recommended medical treatment in the MPN system must be resolved using the process set forth in Lab. Code, §§ 4616.3, 4616.4

MRI . . . . Magnetic Resonance Imaging, especially useful in showing soft tissue structures better than X-Ray or CAT Scans

MSA . . . . Medicare Set-Aside (also "Set aside") Trust

MSC . . . . Mandatory Settlement Conference, Lab. Code, § 5502(e)

MS-DRGs . . . . Medicare Severity Diagnostic Related Groups, Lab. Code, § 5307.1(m)

MSP Guidebook . . . . *The Complete Guide to Medicare Secondary Payer Compliance,* Jennifer C. Jordan, Editor-in-Chief (LexisNexis) (800) 223-1940

MTUS . . . . Medical Treatment Utilization Schedule

Mx . . . . Medical Treatment

Navigation (EAMS) . . . . "Navigation supplies related links to other screens as found on the current EAMS screen. EAMS offers both top level and left-handed navigation."

NCM . . . . Nurse Case Manager

New and Further . . . . Petition to Reopen for New and Further Disability

NIT . . . . Notice of Intention To: Usually a WCJ's advice to parties something is about to be done, e.g., dismiss a lien or party

NOPE . . . . Notice of Potential Eligibility for vocational rehabilitation, Cal. Code Regs., tit. 8, § 9813 & return to work notices

Not Published . . . . Court of Appeal decision not certified for publication (aka unpublished) may not be cited or relied upon in the reviewing court; compare "decertified"

Notice comments (EAMS) . . . . . . Comments on notices sent out to participants by EAMS

NPD . . . . Noteworthy Panel Decisions; LexisNexis editorial consultants deem a panel decision noteworthy because it does one or more of the following:
(1) Establishes a new rule of law, applies an existing rule to a set of facts significantly different from those stated in other decisions, or modifies, or criticizes with reasons given, an existing rule;
(2) Resolves or creates an apparent conflict in the law;
(3) Involves a legal issue of continuing public interest;
(4) Makes a significant contribution to legal literature by reviewing either the development of workers' compensation law or the legislative, regulatory, or judicial history of a constitution, statute, regulation, or other written law; and/or
(5) Makes a contribution to the body of law available to attorneys, claims personnel, judges, the Board, and others seeking to understand the workers' compensation law of California

Numbers of Codes/Rules commonly spoken with a general topic intended: . . . . .

132a . . . . Lab. Code, § 132a, Discrimination {Note "a" is not in "( )'s}
1013 . . . . Code Civ. Proc., § 1013, Time for service by mail, usually 5 days
1877.3 . . . . . . Ins. Code, § 1877.3, Duty to report fraud
3202 . . . . Lab. Code, § 3202, Liberal construction by courts
3600 . . . . Lab. Code, § 3600(a), 10 Reasons to deny a claim
4061, 4062 . . . . Lab. Code, §§ 4061, 4062, notice of PD, disputes & AME or QME
4600 . . . . Lab. Code, § 4600, Medical treatment
4601 . . . . Lab. Code, § 4601, Employee requests new doctor or consult
4650(d) . . . . . . Lab. Code, § 4650(d), Self imposed 10% penalty
4660(d) . . . . . . Lab. Code, § 4660(d), Old or New PD Schedule?
4661.5 . . . . . . Lab. Code, § 4661.5, after 2 years TD rate paid may increase
4663, 4664 . . . . Lab. Code, §§ 4663, 4664, Apportionment
4800/4850 . . . . . Lab. Code, § 4800 or 4850, 1 year leave with pay
4906(g) . . . . . . Lab. Code, § 4906(g), Statement re unlawful dr. referrals
5020 . . . . Lab. Code, § 5020, Employer's Report of Injury
5021 . . . . Lab. Code, § 5021, Dr.'s 1st Report of Occ. Injury
5500.5 . . . . . . Lab. Code, § 5500.5, Cumulative Trauma
5813 . . . . Lab. Code, § 5813, Sanctions for bad-faith actions
5814 . . . . Lab. Code, § 5814, penalty, unreasonable delay
9785 . . . . Cal. Code Regs., tit. 8, § 9785, Dr.'s duty to report to adjuster

OACR . . . . Order Approving C&R

Tables & Schedules

O'Brien	*California Workers' Compensation Claims and Benefits,* 11th Ed., with 2007 Supplement by FS&K Publishing®; 23801 Calabasas Rd, Suite 2025; Calabasas, CA 91302-1547
Occupational Group	Numbered groups of occupations from the *Schedule for Evaluation of Permanent Disability*, two-digit numbers for injuries up to 3-31-97 and three-digit o/a 4-1-97
OCR (EAMS)	Optical Character Recognition; paper forms more easily scanned
ODG	*Official Disability Guidelines* published by the Work Loss Data Institute; approved in many states, similar to ACOEM guidelines
OII	*Occupational Injuries and Illnesses* (LexisNexis Matthew Bender) (800) 223-1940
Old PD Schedule	The 4/1/97 Schedule for evaluating Permanent Disability effective 4/1/97 to 12/31/04, with exceptions, Lab. Code, § 4660(d); there were earlier PD schedules, now almost never seen
OMFS	Official Medical Fee Schedule; Cal. Code Regs., tit. 8, § 9789.10 et seq.
OSHA	Occupational Safety and Health Act
OTOC	Order Taking Off Calendar; PPM § 1.55
π	Greek letter, pi, sometimes written as "TT." Written only, not spoken. It is used for "plaintiff" in tort claims. In workers' comp it means "applicant," "claimant" or "employee."
P&A	Points and Authorities; legal brief supporting a position
PA	Physician's Assistant
Panel QME	Panel of 3 QMEs assigned by Medical Unit at request of a party; if represented by an attorney, D/A o/a 1/1/05, Lab. Code, § 4062.2; if unrepresented, injury o/a 4/19/04, Lab. Code, § 4062.1
Participant (EAMS)	A person or employer, registered in EAMS, which may be linked to a case becoming a "case participant"
PBM	Pharmacy Benefit Manager
PBN	Pharmacy Benefit Network noted in Lab. Code, § 4600.2(a)
PD or PPD	Permanent Disability or Permanent Partial Disability
PDA	Permanent Disability Advance
PDR	Permanent Disability Rating
PDRS	Permanent Disability Rating Schedule; see "Schedule," *infra*
Peer Review	Treating Dr. and U.R. Dr. review of treatment proposed
PEO	Professional Employer Organizations (aka staff leasing companies)
PERS	Public Employees' Retirement System
Person (EAMS)	Per EAMS glossary, "The term used for any single person that needs to be listed in EAMS in order to act as a party in a case. Single-owner businesses will be listed as 'employers'."
Petition	A pleading or prayer for relief, e.g., a Petition for a Writ of Review or for an Award
Pill Mills	Pain clinics
P&P	DWC/WCAB Policy and Procedural Manual (see also PPM)
PPACA	Patient Protection and Affordable Care Act
PPET	Policy, Program Evaluation and Training Unit
PPM	DWC/WCAB Policy and Procedure Manual (see also P&P)
PPO	Preferred Provider Organization (Medical)
PQME or 3PQME	Panel QME or 3 Panel QME; see "Panel QME," supra
PR-2	PTP Progress Report, Cal. Code Regs., tit. 8, § 9785.2

PR-3	PTP P&S Report, 4/97 PD Schedule, Cal. Code Regs., tit. 8, § 9785.3
PR-4	PTP P&S Report, 1/05 PD Schedule, Cal. Code Regs., tit. 8, § 9785.4
Pre-Designation	Selection of a physician before injury; Lab. Code, § 4600(d)
Prima Facie	The bare minimum elements of a claim, which, if not refuted, will allow a party to prevail
Primary (EAMS)	Usage depends on context, e.g., "Primary client" refers to the injured worker in EAMS
PRN	A doctor's release of patient to return "as needed"
Pro Bono	Usually legal services rendered free of charge to the indigent
Pro Per	A person is "in pro per," when acting as their own attorney
P&S	Permanent and Stationary, Cal. Code Regs., tit. 8, § 9785(a)(8); maximum medical improvement, Cal. Code Regs., tit. 8, § 10152
PSI	Permissibly Self-Insured
PTP	Primary Treating Physician, Cal. Code Regs., tit. 8, § 9785
PTSD	Post Traumatic Stress Disorder
QIW	Qualified Injured Worker (i.e., unable to RTW @ U&C)
QME	Qualified Medical Evaluator, Examiner or Examination
QRR	Qualified Rehabilitation Representative (Vendor)
Quash	To nullify or set aside, e.g., a subpoena or notice to produce
RAND Study	Evaluation of California's Permanent Disability Rating Schedule, Interim Report (12/03), prepared by the RAND Institute for Civil Justice, Lab. Code, § 4660(a)(2)
Rassp & Herlick	*California Workers' Compensation Law*, Seventh Edition, by Robert G. Rassp & Standford D. Herlick (LexisNexis) (800) 223-1940
Rating	A calculation of the percentage of permanent disability
RB	Rehabilitation Bureau, now called the Rehabilitation Unit
Recon	Petition for Reconsideration, the first level of appeal of a workers' compensation case
Referee or WCR	Workers' Comp Referee, see "Judge," or "WCJ," Lab. Code, § 27
Rehab Index	Previously, *Vocational Rehabilitation in California: A General Index & Desk Reference*; 10th Ed. {Now out of print}
Rehab or Voc Rehab	Vocational rehabilitation, not "medical rehab" or treatment following an injury, Lab. Code, § 139.5; includes all services reasonably necessary to return an injured employee to work for injuries from 1975 to 12/31/03. Thereafter, Supplemental Job Displacement Voucher, Lab. Code, § 4658.5 (1/04)
Removal	Petition requesting Application be "removed" to main WCAB in San Francisco; Cal. Code Regs., tit. 8, § 10843
Reschedule hearing (EAMS)	Setting a new date for a hearing before the original has "occurred."
Retro	Retroactive benefits claimed, e.g., "retro TD"
Rev. Den.	Review Denied; relates to a Petition for Review to the Calif. Supreme Court denied by the Court
RFA	Request for Authorization (of medical treatment); Cal. Code Regs., tit. 8, § 9792.6(o)
ROM	Range of Motion, e.g., ankle, shoulder, etc.
RTW, RRTW	Return to Work, Release to Return to Work

RTWF . . . . Return to Work Fund; Lab. Code, § 139.48 provides an annual fund of $120,000,000.00 from which eligible injured workers may receive money that compensates them in cases where there is a disproportional difference between their permanent disability ratings and their loss of future earning capacity

RU . . . . Rehabilitation Unit, formerly the Rehabilitation Bureau

Rules . . . . Rules and Regulations of the Administrative Director, Title 8 of the California Code of Regulations, usually abbreviated, CCR; in speech, "Rules" or "Regs"

RX or Rx . . . . Prescription; Rx is used more by doctors

S & W . . . . Serious and Willful misconduct of employee or employer

SAWE . . . . Statutory Average Weekly Earnings

SAWW . . . . State Average Weekly Wage in, e.g., Lab. Code, § 4659(c)

SB 863 . . . . Senate Bill 863, approved 9/18/12; sea change in the law

SB 899 . . . . Senate Bill 899, approved 4/19/04; massive w/c reform

Schedule . . . . *Schedule for Evaluation of Permanent Disability*. "Old" Schedule is used for injuries before 4/1/97, & the "4/97" Schedule for injuries 4/1/97 to 12/31/04; the 1/1/05 Schedule may apply before 1/1/05, per Lab. Code, § 4660(d)

Schedule (hearing) (EAMS) . . . . "The first time a hearing is scheduled."

SCIF . . . . State Compensation Insurance Fund, pronounced "skiff"

SDT . . . . Subpoena Duces Tecum; request for, e.g., medical records

§ or §§ . . . . Section or sections, e.g., Lab. Code, §§ 4600-4601

Self-Procured . . . . Medical treatment of employee which has not been authorized by the employer/claims adjuster

SGE . . . . Suitable Gainful Employment

SIF . . . . Subsequent Injuries Fund, renamed, "Subsequent Injuries Benefit Trust Fund," Lab. Code, §§ 4751–4755

SII, or SIP . . . . Self Imposed Increase or Penalty, Lab. Code, § 4650(d)

SIU . . . . Special Investigation Unit, insurance carriers writing comp required to maintain a fraud unit, Ins. Code, § 1875.24 (9/04)

SJDB . . . . Supplemental Job Displacement Benefits

SJDV . . . . Supplemental Job Displacement Voucher, Lab. Code, § 4658.5 (1/04)

SOC . . . . *Sullivan on Comp,* by Michael Sullivan & Assoc.; phone 310.337.5580 or SullivanOnComp@mikeslaw.com

SOL or S.O.L. . . . . Statute of Limitations or "bleep" Out of Luck, depending on context

SOP . . . . Second Opinion Physician, Lab. Code, § 4062(b)

SPD . . . . Significant Panel Decision (by "the" WCAB in San Francisco); compare NPD

Split . . . . Difference between 2 PD ratings; not always "split" 50-50

SSA . . . . Social Security Administration

SSD, SSDI . . . . Social Security Disability Indemnity

SSI . . . . Supplemental Security Income (Social Security welfare benefit payable to disabled and poor persons)

SSN . . . . Social Security Number

SSPG . . . . *Social Security Practice Guide*, by National Organization of Social Security Claimants' Representatives (LexisNexis) (800) 223-1940

SSSO . . . . Spinal Surgery Second Opinion (repealed)

St. Clair, now CWCLP . . . . . . *California Workers' Compensation Law & Practice*, by Richard L. Newman, Daniel A. Dobrin, Alexander Wong & Sheldon C. St. Clair 10/09 by James Publishing, Inc.; 3505 Cadillac Ave., Suite H; Costa Mesa, CA 92626; (800) 440-4780

Standard Rating . . . . A level of PD before adjusting for age and occupation

State Disability . . . . Disability insurance through the Employment Development Department (EDD)

Status (employer) (EAMS) . . . . "Shows whether the employer has cases that are active in EAMS."

Status (person) (EAMS) . . . . "Shows whether the person has a case or cases that are active in EAMS. A person's status stays active until death. After that the status is closed."

Statute . . . . Statute of Limitations

Stip or Stips . . . . Stipulations with Request for Award, signed by the parties. Following approval by the WCAB, "and Award" is added to the heading of the document

Stips & Issues . . . . Pretrial Conference Statement noting agreements as well as issues in dispute, proposed ratings, listing exhibits & disclosing witnesses, Lab. Code, § 5502(e)(3)

STP . . . . Secondary Treating Physician

Strikes . . . . Represented EE, injury o/a 1/1/05, Lab. Code, § 4062.2 (c), each "side" strikes 1 of 3 doctors & Dr. left is the "Panel or PQME"

Sub Rosa . . . . Private investigation, usually a video of employee's activities

Subrogation . . . . CA's claim for payment from 3rd party which is alleged to have caused injury; Lab. Code, §§ 3850–3864; Ins. Code, § 11662

Summary Rating . . . . Cal. Code Regs., tit. 8, §§ 10160–10165; one of several ratings done by DEU

SWAG . . . . Scientific Wild-Assed Guess {See Lab. Code, § 4663 & EBM}

SX . . . . Symptoms

Take Nothing . . . . "… used to indicate a finding of no entitlement to any benefits at all …." Editorial in Title Records, Inc. vs WCAB (Shahbazian) 25 CWCR 205, 206

TBI . . . . Traumatic Brain Injury

TD, TTD or TDI . . . . Temporary Total Disability Indemnity

TKR . . . . Total Knee Replacement

Tort . . . . A civil claim, e.g., for negligent operation of a motor vehicle causing a personal injury

TP . . . . Treating physician

TPA . . . . Third Party Administrator (of a self-insured employer)

TPD . . . . Temporary Partial Disability Indemnity

TX . . . . Treatment, i.e., Medical Treatment (see also "Mx")

U and C . . . . Usual and Customary employment

UEF, now UEBTF . . . . Uninsured Employers Fund, renamed, "Uninsured Employers Benefit Trust Fund" {Commonly, just "UEF"}

UEX . . . . Upper Extremities; BUE, bilateral upper extremities

UI . . . . Unemployment Insurance

UIAB . . . . Unemployment Insurance Appeals Board

UR . . . . Utilization Review, Lab. Code, § 5307.27, Cal. Code Regs., tit. 8, §§ 9792.6-9791.11

UR-IMR	Utilization Review-Independent Medical Review, for all other medical treatment disputes other than those related to MPNs and for injuries after January 1, 2013 and for medical treatment requests and UR decisions after July 1, 2013 , see Lab. Code, § 4610.5 for the SB 863 IMR process
USL&H	U.S. Longshore and Harbor Workers' Compensation Act
VA	Veteran's Administration
Voucher	Supplemental Job Displacement Voucher, Lab. Code, § 4658.5 (1/04)
VR	Vocational Rehabilitation or "Rehab"
VRMA	Vocational Rehabilitation Maintenance Allowance
VRTD	Vocational Rehabilitation Temporary Total Disability
Walk-Through	Documents "walked through" a local WCAB office for approval, per Cal. Code Regs., tit. 8 § 10280 as opposed to mailing them
W/C, W.C. or WC	Workers' Compensation or "Work Comp"
WCAB	Workers' Compensation Appeals Board
WCC	WorkCompCentral.com
WCCP	Workers' Comp Claims Professional
WCIRB	Workers' Compensation Insurance Rating Bureau
WCJ or WCALJ	Workers' Compensation Judge, changed to "workers' compensation administrative law judge" (Lab. Code, § 27), but "WCJ" or "Judge" is used almost exclusively
WCMSA	Workers' Compensation Medicare Set-Aside
WCR	Workers' Compensation Referee; see WCALJ, supra
WHCA	War Hazards Compensation Act, 42 U.S.C.S. §§ 1701–1717
Window Period	Injuries occurring from 1990 through 1993
Work Comp Index	Previously titled, *Workers' Compensation in California: A General Index & Desk Reference*; 9th Edition
WP, WPI	Whole Person, Whole Person Impairment
Writ	Petition for Writ of Review, the 2nd level of appeal to a Dist. Court of Appeal following a lost petition for Recon
Zombie Liens	A lien filed a long time after litigation has apparently ended; see the Legal Briefs Newsletter for August 2012 by McDermott & Clawson, LLP, re new provisions in Cal. Code Regs., tit. 8, § 10582.5

PART 11. Indemnity Calculations

TABLE 19
Miscellaneous

To obtain a TD, PD or VRMA rate: Earnings × 2 ÷ 3 = or,
Earnings ÷ 1.5 = (subject to earnings maximum/minimums)

If you have the rate and want to calculate the earnings it was derived from, reverse the process:

Earnings × 3 ÷ 2 = or, Earnings × 1.5 =

If your calculator has a date key, remember to make answers *inclusive*, or running from one date, to ***& including*** another date:

When *subtracting* dates, ***add 1 to*** answer
When *adding* dates, ***1 from*** answer

Rounding %'s of PD

Rounding for injuries on/after 4/1/97 is to the nearest whole percent, per the *Schedule for Rating Permanent Disabilities*, April 1997. Quarter %'s are given in Table 17 C through 12-31-02 due to requests for continuity in the tables & for compromises.

Days as a part of a week

Days	Part of a week
1	0.14286
2	0.28571
3	0.42857
4	0.57143
5	0.71429
6	0.85714

Temporary Partial Disability (TPD) or "Wage Loss," Lab. Code, §§ 4654, 4657

Assume D/A 8-15-04, payment to be made 8-30-04 & earnings of $1,500.00/wk. The employee was returned to work for ½ days only from 8/17/04 to 8/30/04 and is paid $750.00/week. How is "TPD" calculated? (Were payment > 2 yrs, see Lab. Code, § 4661.5)

$1,092.00	. . .	Maximum allowable earnings for TD, injuries 1-1-04 to 12-31-04
– 750.00	. . .	Less wages earned upon return to work
$ 342.00	. . .	= "Wage Loss"/week and × 2/3 = $228.00/wk TPD due

Concurrent employment: Lab. Code, § 4453(c)(2), "Where the employee is working for two or more employers at or about the time of the injury …" average weekly wage (AWW) is total earnings from both, but not greater than at the hourly rate where injured. Thus, if employer #1 pays $10/hr, but employer #2 pays $12/hr and injury occurs with employer #2, total earnings are used. However, if injury occurs with employer #1, hours worked at employer #2 are multiplied by the rate at employer #1. Assume 20 hrs/wk worked at each employer: $10/hr × 20 hrs = $200 (#1) and $12/hr × 20 hrs/wk = $240/wk (#2). Thus, an injury at employer #2 produces an AWW of $440/wk, but only $400/wk if injury is at employer #1.

SB 899: To decrease or increase PD by 15%, multiply PD **RATE** by 0.85 or 1.15.

UNITED STATES CODE

SYNOPSIS

TITLE 5
GOVERNMENT ORGANIZATION AND EMPLOYEES

PART III
EMPLOYEES

SUBPART A
GENERAL PROVISIONS

CHAPTER 21
DEFINITIONS

§2105. Employee.

SUBPART G
INSURANCE AND ANNUITIES

CHAPTER 81
COMPENSATION FOR WORK INJURIES

SUBCHAPTER II
EMPLOYEES OF NONAPPROPRIATED FUND INSTRUMENTALITIES

§8171. Compensation for work injuries; generally.
§8172. Employees not citizens or residents of the United States.
§8173. Liability under this subchapter exclusive.

TITLE 26
INTERNAL REVENUE CODE

SUBTITLE A
INCOME TAXES

CHAPTER 1
NORMAL TAXES AND SURTAXES

SUBCHAPTER B
COMPUTATION OF TAXABLE INCOME

PART III
ITEMS SPECIFICALLY EXCLUDED FROM GROSS INCOME

§101. Certain death benefits.
§104. Compensation for injuries or sickness.

SUBTITLE F
PROCEDURE AND ADMINISTRATION

CHAPTER 64
COLLECTION

SUBCHAPTER C
LIEN FOR TAXES

PART II
LIENS

§6323. Validity and priority against certain persons.

SUBCHAPTER D
SEIZURE OF PROPERTY FOR COLLECTION OF TAXES

PART II
LEVY

§6334. Property exempt from levy.

TITLE 28
JUDICIARY AND JUDICIAL PROCEDURE

PART IV
JURISDICTION AND VENUE

CHAPTER 83
COURTS OF APPEALS

§1291. Final decisions of district courts.

CHAPTER 85
DISTRICT COURTS; JURISDICTION

§1333. Admiralty, maritime and prize cases.
§1346. United States as defendant.

CHAPTER 87
DISTRICT COURTS; VENUE

§1402. United States as defendant.

PART VI
PARTICULAR PROCEEDINGS

CHAPTER 161
UNITED STATES AS PARTY GENERALLY

§2401. Time for commencing action against United States.

U.S.C.

§2402. Jury trial in actions against United States.
§2412. Costs and fees.

CHAPTER 171
TORT CLAIMS PROCEDURE

§2671. Definitions.
§2672. Administrative adjustment of claims.
§2674. Liability of United States.
§2675. Disposition by federal agency as prerequisite; evidence.
§2676. Judgment as bar.
§2677. Compromise.
§2678. Attorney fees; penalty.
§2679. Exclusiveness of remedy.
§2680. Exceptions.

TITLE 33
NAVIGATION AND NAVIGABLE WATERS

CHAPTER 18
LONGSHORE AND HARBOR WORKERS' COMPENSATION

§901. Short title.
§902. Definitions.
§903. Coverage.
§904. Liability for compensation.
§905. Exclusiveness of liability.
§906. Compensation.
§907. Medical services and supplies.
§908. Compensation for disability.
§909. Compensation for death.
§910. Determination of pay.
§911. Guardian for minor or incompetent.
§912. Notice of injury or death.
§913. Filing of claims.
§914. Payment of compensation.
§915. Invalid agreements.
§916. Assignment and exemption from claims of creditors.
§917. Lien against compensation.
§918. Collection of defaulted payments; special fund.
§919. Procedure in respect of claims.
§920. Presumptions.
§921. Review of compensation orders.
§921a. Appearance of attorneys for Secretary, deputy commissioner, or Board.
§922. Modification of awards.
§923. Procedure before deputy commissioner or Board.
§924. Witnesses.
§925. Witness fees.
§926. Costs in proceedings brought without reasonable grounds.
§927. Powers of deputy commissioners or Board.
§928. Fees for services.
§929. Record of injury or death.
§930. Reports to Secretary.
§931. Penalty for misrepresentation.
§932. Security for compensation.
§933. Compensation for injuries where third persons are liable.
§934. Compensation notice.
§935. Substitution of carrier for employer.
§936. Insurance policies.
§937. Certificate of compliance with chapter.
§938. Penalties.
§939. Administration by Secretary.
§940. Deputy commissioners.
§941. Safety rules and regulations.
§942. Annual report.
§944. Special fund.
§948. Laws inapplicable.
§948a. Discrimination against employees who bring proceedings; penalties; deposit of payments in special fund; civil actions; entitlement to restoration of employment and compensation, qualifications requirement; liability of employer for penalties and payments; insurance policy exemption from liability.
§949. Effect of unconstitutionality.
§950. Separability.

TITLE 40
PUBLIC BUILDINGS, PROPERTY, AND WORKS

SUBTITLE II
PUBLIC BUILDINGS AND WORKS

PART A
GENERAL

CHAPTER 31
GENERAL

SUBCHAPTER VI
MISCELLANEOUS

§3172. Extension of state workers' compensation laws to buildings, works, and property of the Federal Government.

TITLE 42
THE PUBLIC HEALTH AND WELFARE

CHAPTER 11
COMPENSATION FOR DISABILITY OR DEATH TO PERSONS EMPLOYED AT MILITARY, AIR, AND NAVAL BASES OUTSIDE THE UNITED STATES

§1651. Compensation authorized.
§1652. Computation of benefits; application to aliens and nonnationals.
§1653. Compensation districts; judicial proceedings.
§1654. Persons excluded from benefits.
§1655. Requirement for Department of Defense to adopt an acquisition strategy for Defense Base Act insurance.

CHAPTER 12
COMPENSATION FOR INJURY, DEATH, OR DETENTION OF EMPLOYEES OF CONTRACTORS WITH THE UNITED STATES OUTSIDE THE UNITED STATES

SUBCHAPTER I
COMPENSATION, REIMBURSEMENT, ETC., BY SECRETARY OF LABOR

§1701. Compensation for injury or death resulting from war-risk hazard.

§1702. Application of Longshore and Harbor Workers' Compensation Act.
§1703. "Contractor with the United States" defined.
§1704. Reimbursement.
§1705. Receipt of workmen's compensation benefits.
§1706. Administration.

SUBCHAPTER II
MISCELLANEOUS PROVISIONS

§1711. Definitions.
§1712. Disqualification from benefits.
§1713. Fraud; penalties.
§1714. Legal services.
§1715. Finality of Secretary's decisions.
§1716. Presumption of death or detention.
§1717. Assignment of benefits; execution, levy, etc., against benefits.

TITLE 43
PUBLIC LANDS

CHAPTER 29
SUBMERGED LANDS

SUBCHAPTER III
OUTER CONTINENTAL SHELF LANDS

§1331. Definitions.
§1333. Laws and regulations governing lands.

TITLE 45
RAILROADS

CHAPTER 2
LIABILITY FOR INJURIES TO EMPLOYEES

§51. Liability of common carriers by railroad, in interstate or foreign commerce, for injuries to employees from negligence; employee defined.
§52. Carriers in Territories or other possessions of United States.
§53. Contributory negligence; diminution of damages.
§54. Assumption of risks of employment.
§54a. Regulation, standard, or requirement under chapter 201 of title 49, United States Code, deemed to be statute under sections 3 and 4.
§55. Contract, rule, regulation, or device exempting from liability; set-off.
§56. Actions; limitation; concurrent jurisdiction of courts.
§57. Who included in term "common carrier."
§58. Duty or liability of common carriers and rights of employees under other acts not impaired.
§59. Survival of right of action of person injured.
§60. Penalty for suppression of voluntary information incident to accidents; separability.

TITLE 46
SHIPPING

SUBTITLE III
MARITIME LIABILITY

CHAPTER 301
GENERAL LIABILITY PROVISIONS

§30101. Extension of jurisdiction to cases of damage or injury on land.
§30104. Personal injury to or death of seamen.
§30105. Restriction on recovery by non-citizens and non-resident aliens for incidents in waters of other countries.
§30106. Time limit on bringing maritime action for personal injury or death.

CHAPTER 303
DEATH ON THE HIGH SEAS

§30301. Short title.
§30302. Cause of action.
§30303. Amount and apportionment of recovery.
§30304. Contributory negligence.
§30305. Death of plaintiff in pending action.
§30306. Foreign cause of action.
§30307. Commercial aviation accidents.
§30308. Nonapplication.

CHAPTER 309
SUITS IN ADMIRALTY AGAINST THE UNITED STATES

§30901. Short title.
§30902. Definition.
§30903. Waiver of immunity.
§30904. Exclusive remedy.
§30905. Period for bringing action.
§30906. Venue.
§30907. Procedure for hearing and determination.
§30908. Exemption from arrest or seizure.
§30909. Security.
§30910. Exoneration and limitation.
§30911. Costs and interest.
§30912. Arbitration, compromise, or settlement.
§30913. Payment of judgment or settlement.

CHAPTER 311
SUITS INVOLVING PUBLIC VESSELS

§31101. Short title.
§31102. Waiver of immunity.
§31103. Applicable procedure.
§31104. Venue.
§31105. Security when counterclaim filed.
§31106. Exoneration and limitation.
§31107. Interest.
§31108. Arbitration, compromise, or settlement.
§31109. Payment of judgment or settlement.
§31110. Subpoenas to officers or members of crew.
§31111. Claims by nationals of foreign countries.
§31112. Lien not recognized or created.

SELECTED PROVISIONS Of The UNITED STATES CODE

TITLE 5 GOVERNMENT ORGANIZATION AND EMPLOYEES

PART III EMPLOYEES

SUBPART A GENERAL PROVISIONS

CHAPTER 21 DEFINITIONS

§2105. Employee.

[Subsections (a) and (b) Not Reproduced]

(c) An employee paid from nonappropriated funds of the Army and Air Force Exchange Service, Navy Ships Stores Program, Navy exchanges, Marine Corps exchanges, Coast Guard exchanges, and other instrumentalities of the United States under the jurisdiction of the armed forces conducted for the comfort, pleasure, contentment, and mental and physical improvement of personnel of the armed forces is deemed not an employee for the purpose of—

(1) laws administered by the Office of Personnel Management, except—

(A) section 7204 [5 U.S.C. § 7204];

(B) as otherwise specifically provided in this title;

(C) the Fair Labor Standards Act of 1938 [29 U.S.C. §§ 201 et seq.];

(D) for the purpose of entering into an interchange agreement to provide for the noncompetitive movement of employees between such instrumentalities and the competitive service; or

(E) subchapter V of chapter 63 [5 U.S.C. §§ 6381 et seq.], which shall be applied so as to construe references to benefit programs to refer to applicable programs for employees paid from nonappropriated funds; or

(2) subchapter I of chapter 81 [5 U.S.C. §§ 8101 et seq.], chapter 84 (except to the extent specifically provided therein) [5 U.S.C. §§ 8401 et seq.], and section 7902 of this title [5 U.S.C. § 7902].

This subsection does not affect the status of these nonappropriated fund activities as Federal instrumentalities.

[Subsections (d)–(f) Not Reproduced]

(Sept. 6, 1966, P.L. 89-554, §1, 80 Stat. 409; Aug. 13, 1968, P.L. 90-486, §4, 82 Stat. 757; Aug. 12, 1970, P.L. 91-375, §6(c)(4), 84 Stat. 775; Aug. 19, 1972, P.L. 92-392, §2, 86 Stat. 573; Oct. 13, 1978, P.L. 95-454, Title VII, §703(c)(1), Title IX, §906(a)(2), 92 Stat. 1217, 1224; Aug. 14, 1979, P.L. 96-54, §2(a)(5), 93 Stat. 381; June 6, 1986, P.L. 99-335, Title II, §207(a), 100 Stat. 594; Nov. 10, 1986, P.L. 99-638, §2(b)(1), 100 Stat 3536; Nov. 5, 1990, P.L. 101-508, Title II, Subtitle C, §7202(b), 104 Stat. 1388-335; Feb. 5, 1993, P.L. 103-3, Title II, §201(b), 107 Stat. 23; Oct. 29, 1994, P.L. 103-424, §7, 108 Stat. 4364; Sept. 23, 1996, P.L. 104-201, Div A, Title III, Subtitle F, §370(b), 110 Stat. 2499; Nov. 18, 1997, P.L. 105-85, Div B, Title XXVIII, Subtitle E, §2871(c)(2), 111 Stat. 2015; Dec. 26, 2013, P.L. 113-66, Div A, Title VI, Subtitle E, §642, 127 Stat. 787.)

SUBPART G INSURANCE AND ANNUITIES

CHAPTER 81 COMPENSATION FOR WORK INJURIES

SUBCHAPTER II EMPLOYEES OF NONAPPROPRIATED FUND INSTRUMENTALITIES

§8171. Compensation for work injuries; generally.

(a) The Longshore and Harbor Workers' Compensation Act (33 U.S.C. 901 et seq.) applies with respect to disability or death resulting from injury, as defined by section 2(2) of such Act (33 U.S.C. 902(2)), occurring to an employee of a nonappropriated fund instrumentality described by section 2105(c) of this title [5 U.S.C. § 2105(c)], or to a volunteer providing such an instrumentality with services accepted under section 1588 of title 10, who is—

(1) a United States citizen or a permanent resident of the United States or a territory or possession of the United States employed outside the continental United States; or

(2) employed inside the continental United States.

However, that part of section 3(a) of such Act (33 U.S.C. 903(a)) which follows the second comma does not apply to such an employee.

(b) For the purpose of this subchapter [5 U.S.C. §§ 8171 et seq.], the term "employer" in section 2(4) of the Longshore and Harbor Workers' Compensation Act (33 U.S.C. 902(4)) includes the nonappropriated fund instrumentalities described by section 2105(c) of this title [5 U.S.C. § 2105(c)].

(c) The Secretary of Labor may—

(1) extend compensation districts established under section 39(b) of the Longshore and Harbor Workers' Compensation Act (33 U.S.C. 939(b)), or establish new districts to include the areas outside the continental United States; and

(2) assign to each district one or more deputy commissioners as the Secretary considers advisable.

(d) Judicial proceedings under sections 18 and 21 of the Longshore and Harbor Workers' Compensation Act (33 U.S.C. 918 and 921) with respect to an injury or death occurring outside the continental United States shall be instituted in the district court within the territorial jurisdiction of which is located the office of the deputy commissioner having jurisdiction with respect to the injury or death. (Sept. 6, 1966, P.L. 89-554, §1, 80 Stat. 555; Oct. 5, 1994, P.L. 103-337, Div A, Title X, Subtitle G, §§1061(c), 1070(d)(8)(A), 108 Stat. 2847, 2858; Feb. 10, 1996, P.L. 104-106, Div A, Title XV, §1505(b)(1), 110 Stat. 514.)

§8172. Employees not citizens or residents of the United States.

In case of disability or death resulting from injury, as defined by section 2(2) of the Longshore and Harbor Workers' Compensation Act (33 U.S.C. 902(2)), occurring to an employee of a nonappropriated fund instrumentality described by section 2105(c) of this title [5 U.S.C. § 2105(c)] who is—

(1) not a citizen or permanent resident of the United States or a territory or possession of the United States; and

(2) employed outside the continental United States;

compensation shall be provided in accordance with regulations prescribed by the Secretary of the military department concerned and approved by the Secretary of Defense or regulations prescribed by the Secretary of Transportation, as the case may be. (Sept. 6, 1966, P.L. 89-554, §1, 80 Stat. 556; July 5, 1994, P.L. 103-272, §4(b)(3), 108 Stat. 1361; Oct. 5, 1994, P.L. 103-337, Div A, Title X, Subtitle G, §1070(d)(8)(B), 108 Stat. 2859; Feb. 10, 1996, P.L. 104-106, Div A, Title XV, §1505(b)(2), 110 Stat. 514.)

§8173. Liability under this subchapter exclusive.

The liability of the United States or of a nonappropriated fund instrumentality described by section 2105(c) of this title [5 U.S.C. § 2105(c)], with respect to the disability or death resulting from injury, as defined by section 2(2) of the Longshore and Harbor Workers' Compensation Act (33 U.S.C. 902(2)), of an employee referred to by sections 8171 and 8172 of this title [5 U.S.C. §§ 8171 and 8172], shall be determined as provided by this subchapter [5 U.S.C. §§ 8171 et seq.]. This liability is exclusive and instead of all other liability of the United States or the instrumentality to the employee, his legal representative, spouse, dependents, next of kin, and any other person otherwise entitled to recover damages from the United States or the instrumentality because of the disability or death in a direct judicial proceeding, in a civil action, or in admiralty, or by an administrative or judicial proceeding under a workmen's compensation statute or under a Federal tort liability statute. (Sept. 6, 1966, P.L. 89-554, §1, 80 Stat. 556; Oct. 5, 1994, P.L. 103-337, Div A, Title X, Subtitle G, §1070(d)(8)(B), 108 Stat. 2859; Feb. 10, 1996, P.L. 104-106, Div A, Title XV, §1505(b)(2), 110 Stat. 514.)

TITLE 26
INTERNAL REVENUE CODE

SUBTITLE A
INCOME TAXES

CHAPTER 1
NORMAL TAXES AND SURTAXES

SUBCHAPTER B
COMPUTATION OF TAXABLE INCOME

PART III
ITEMS SPECIFICALLY EXCLUDED FROM GROSS INCOME

§101. Certain death benefits.

[Subsection (a) Not Reproduced]

(b) **[Repealed August 20, 1996]** Employees' death benefits.—

(1) General rule. Gross income does not include amounts received (whether in a single sum or otherwise) by the beneficiaries or the estate of an employee, if such amounts are paid by or on behalf of an employer and are paid by reason of the death of an employee.

(2) Special rules for paragraph (1)—

A. $5,000 limitation. The aggregate amounts excludable under paragraph (1) with respect to the death of any employee shall not exceed $5,000.

[Subsections (b)(2)B.–(h) Not Reproduced]

(i) Certain employee death benefits payable by reason of death of certain terrorist victims or astronauts.

(1) In general. Gross income does not include amounts (whether in a single sum or otherwise) paid by an employer by reason of the death of an employee who is a specified terrorist victim (as defined in section 692(d)(4) [26 U.S.C. § 692(d)(4)]).

(2) Limitation.

(A) In general. Subject to such rules as the Secretary may prescribe, paragraph (1) shall not apply to amounts which would have been payable after death if the individual had died other than as a specified terrorist victim (as so defined).

(B) Exception. Subparagraph (A) shall not apply to incidental death benefits paid from a plan described in section 401(a) [26 U.S.C. § 401(a)] and exempt from tax under section 501(a) [26 U.S.C. § 501(a)].

(3) Treatment of self-employed individuals. For purposes of paragraph (1), the term "employee" includes a self-employed individual (as defined in section 401(c)(1) [26 U.S.C. § 401(c)(1)]).

(4) Relief with respect to astronauts. The provisions of this subsection shall apply to any astronaut whose death occurs in the line of duty.

(j) Treatment of certain employer-owned life insurance contracts.

(1) General rule. In the case of an employer-owned life insurance contract, the amount excluded from gross income of an applicable policyholder by reason of paragraph (1) of subsection (a) shall not exceed an amount equal to the sum of the premiums and other amounts paid by the policyholder for the contract.

(2) Exceptions. In the case of an employer-owned life insurance contract with respect to which the notice and consent requirements of paragraph (4) are met, paragraph (1) shall not apply to any of the following:

(A) Exceptions based on insured's status. Any amount received by reason of the death of an insured who, with respect to an applicable policyholder—

(i) was an employee at any time during the 12-month period before the insured's death, or

(ii) is, at the time the contract is issued—

(I) a director,

(II) a highly compensated employee within the meaning of section 414(q) [26 U.S.C. § 414(q)] (without regard to paragraph (1)(B)(ii) thereof), or

(III) a highly compensated individual within the meaning of section 105(h)(5) [26 U.S.C. § 105(h)(5)], except that "35 percent" shall be substituted for "25 percent" in subparagraph (C) thereof.

(B) Exception for amounts paid to insured's heirs. Any amount received by reason of the death of an insured to the extent—

(i) the amount is paid to a member of the family (within the meaning of section 267(c)(4) [26 U.S.C. § 267(c)(4)]) of the insured, any individual who is the designated beneficiary of the insured under the contract (other than the applicable policyholder), a trust established for the benefit of any such member of the family or designated beneficiary, or the estate of the insured, or

(ii) the amount is used to purchase an equity (or capital or profits) interest in the applicable policyholder from any person described in clause (i).

(3) Employer-owned life insurance contract.

(A) In general. For purposes of this subsection, the term "employer-owned life insurance contract" means a life insurance contract which—

U.S.C.

(i) is owned by a person engaged in a trade or business and under which such person (or a related person described in subparagraph (B)(ii)) is directly or indirectly a beneficiary under the contract, and

(ii) covers the life of an insured who is an employee with respect to the trade or business of the applicable policyholder on the date the contract is issued.

For purposes of the preceding sentence, if coverage for each insured under a master contract is treated as a separate contract for purposes of sections 817(h), 7702, and 7702A [26 U.S.C. §§ 817(h), 7702, and 7702A], coverage for each such insured shall be treated as a separate contract.

(B) Applicable policyholder. For purposes of this subsection—

(i) In general. The term "applicable policyholder" means, with respect to any employer-owned life insurance contract, the person described in subparagraph (A)(i) which owns the contract.

(ii) Related persons. The term "applicable policyholder" includes any person which—

(I) bears a relationship to the person described in clause (i) which is specified in section 267(b) or 707(b)(1) [26 U.S.C. § 267(b) or 707(b)(1)], or

(II) is engaged in trades or businesses with such person which are under common control (within the meaning of subsection (a) or (b) of section 52 [26 U.S.C. § 52]).

(4) Notice and consent requirements. The notice and consent requirements of this paragraph are met if, before the issuance of the contract, the employee—

(A) is notified in writing that the applicable policyholder intends to insure the employee's life and the maximum face amount for which the employee could be insured at the time the contract was issued,

(B) provides written consent to being insured under the contract and that such coverage may continue after the insured terminates employment, and

(C) is informed in writing that an applicable policyholder will be a beneficiary of any proceeds payable upon the death of the employee.

(5) Definitions. For purposes of this subsection—

(A) Employee. The term "employee" includes an officer, director, and highly compensated employee (within the meaning of section 414(q) [26 U.S.C. § 414(q)]).

(B) Insured. The term "insured" means, with respect to an employer-owned life insurance contract, an individual covered by the contract who is a United States citizen or resident. In the case of a contract covering the joint lives of 2 individuals, references to an insured include both of the individuals. (Aug. 16, 1954, ch 736, 68A Stat. 26; Sept. 2, 1958, P.L. 85-866, Title I, §23(d), 72 Stat. 1622; Oct. 10, 1962, P.L. 87-792, §7(c), 76 Stat. 829; March 8, 1966, P.L. 89-365, §1(c), 80 Stat. 32; Dec. 30, 1969, P.L. 91-172, Title I, §101(j)(l), 83 Stat. 526; Sept. 2, 1974, P.L. 93-406, Title II, §§2005(c)(15), 2007(b)(3), 88 Stat. 992, 994; Oct. 4, 1976, P.L. 94-455, Title XIX, §§1901(a)(16), 1906(b)(13)(A), 90 Stat. 1765, 1834; Sept. 3, 1982, P.L. 97-248, Title II, §§239, 266(a), (b), 96 Stat. 514, 547, 550; July 18, 1984, P.L. 98-369, Div A, Title II, §221(b)(2), Title IV, §421(b)(2), Title VII, §713(e), 98 Stat. 772, 794, 958; Oct. 22, 1986, P.L. 99-514, Title X, §1001(a)-(c), 100 Stat. 2387; Aug. 20, 1996, P.L. 104-188, Title I, §1402(a), (b)(1), 110 Stat. 1789; Aug. 21, 1996, P.L. 104-191, Title III, §331(a), 110 Stat. 2067; Aug. 5, 1997, P.L. 105-34, Title X, §1084(b)(2), Title XV, §1528(a), 111 Stat. 952, 1074; Jan. 23, 2002, P.L. 107-134, Title I, §102(a), 115 Stat. 2429; Nov. 11, 2003, P.L. 108-121, Title I, §110(b)(1), (2), 117 Stat. 1342; Aug. 17, 2006, P.L. 109-280, Title VIII, Subtitle F, §863(a), (c)(1), 120 Stat. 1021, 1024; Jan. 2, 2013, P.L. 112-239, Div A, Title X, Subtitle H, §1086(b)(3)(B), 126 Stat. 1968; Dec. 22, 2017, P.L. 115-97, Title I, Subtitle C, Part VI, Subpart B, §13522(a), (b), 131 Stat. 2151, 2152.)

2006 Note: Act Aug. 17, 2006, P.L. 109-280, Title VIII, Subtitle F, § 863(d), 120 Stat. 1024, provides: "The amendments made by this section [adding 26 U.S.C. § 101(j)] shall apply to life insurance contracts issued after the date of the enactment of this Act, except for a contract issued after such date pursuant to an exchange described in section 1035 of the Internal Revenue Code of 1986 [26 U.S.C. § 1035] for a contract issued on or prior to that date. For purposes of the preceding sentence, any material increase in the death benefit or other material change shall cause the contract to be treated as a new contract except that, in the case of a master contract (within the meaning of section 264(f)(4)(E) of such Code [26 U.S.C. § 264(f)(4)(E)]), the addition of covered lives shall be treated as a new contract only with respect to such additional covered lives.".

2003 Note: The amendments made by Pub. L. 108–121 shall apply to amounts paid after December 31, 2002, with respect to deaths occurring after such date. Pub. L. 108–121, Title I, §110(b)(3), 117 Stat. 1342.

2002 Note: Application of Jan. 23, 2001 amendment; waiver of limitations. Act Jan. 23, 2002, P.L. 107-134, Title I, Subtitle A, §102(b), 115 Stat. 2429, provides:

(1) Effective date. The amendment made by this section [adding subsec. (i) of this section] shall apply to taxable years ending before, on, or after September 11, 2001.

(2) Waiver of limitations. If refund or credit of any overpayment of tax resulting from the amendments made by this section [adding subsec. (i) of this section] is prevented at any time before the close of the 1-year period beginning on the date of the enactment of this Act by the operation of any law or rule of law (including res judicata), such refund or credit may nevertheless be made or allowed if claim therefor is filed before the close of such period.

1996 Note: The repeal of subsection (b) made by §1402(a) of Pub. L. 104-188 applies with respect to decedents dying after August 20, 1996. Pub. L. 104-188 §1402(c).

The Publisher has retained the language of repealed subsection (b), above, for use in cases in which the decedent died prior to August 20, 1996.

§104. Compensation for injuries or sickness.

(a) In general. Except in the case of amounts attributable to (and not in excess of) deductions allowed under section 213 [26 U.S.C. § 213] (relating to medical, etc., expenses) for any prior taxable year, gross income does not include—

(1) amounts received under workmen's compensation acts as compensation for personal injuries or sickness;

(2) the amount of any damages (other than punitive damages) received (whether by suit or agreement and whether as lump sums or as periodic payments) on account of personal physical injuries or physical sickness;

(3) amounts received through accident or health insurance (or through an arrangement having the effect of accident or health insurance) for personal injuries or sickness (other than amounts received by an employee, to the extent such amounts (A) are attributable to contribu-

tions by the employer which were not includible in the gross income of the employee, or (B) are paid by the employer);

(4) amounts received as a pension, annuity, or similar allowance for personal injuries or sickness resulting from active service in the armed forces of any country or in the Coast and Geodetic Survey or the Public Health Service, or as a disability annuity payable under the provisions of section 808 of the Foreign Service Act of 1980 [22 U.S.C. § 4048];

(5) amounts received by an individual as disability income attributable to injuries incurred as a direct result of a terroristic or military action (as defined in section 692(c)(2)) [26 U.S.C. § 692(c)(2)]; and

(6) amounts received pursuant to–

(A) section 1201 of the Omnibus Crime Control and Safe Streets Act of 1968 (42 U.S.C. 3796); or

(B) a program established under the laws of any State which provides monetary compensation for surviving dependents of a public safety officer who has died as the direct and proximate result of a personal injury sustained in the line of duty,

except that subparagraph (B) shall not apply to any amounts that would have been payable if death of the public safety officer had occurred other than as the direct and proximate result of a personal injury sustained in the line of duty.

For purposes of paragraph (3), in the case of an individual who is, or has been, an employee within the meaning of section 401(c)(1) [26 U.S.C. § 401(c)(1)] (relating to self-employed individuals), contributions made on behalf of such individual while he was such an employee to a trust described in section 401(a) [26 U.S.C. § 401(a)] which is exempt from tax under section 501(a) [26 U.S.C. § 501(a)], or under a plan described in section 403(a) [26 U.S.C. § 403(a)], shall, to the extent allowed as deductions under section 404 [26 U.S.C. § 404], be treated as contributions by the employer which were not includible in the gross income of the employee. For purposes of paragraph (2), emotional distress shall not be treated as a physical injury or physical sickness. The preceding sentence shall not apply to an amount of damages not in excess of the amount paid for medical care (described in subparagraph (A) or (B) of section 213(d)(1) [26 U.S.C. § 213(d)(1)]) attributable to emotional distress.

(b) Termination of application of subsection (a)(4) in certain cases.

(1) In general. Subsection (a)(4) shall not apply in the case of any individual who is not described in paragraph (2).

(2) Individuals to whom subsection (a)(4) continues to apply. An individual is described in this paragraph if—

(A) on or before September 24, 1975, he was entitled to receive any amount described in subsection (a)(4),

(B) on September 24, 1975, he was a member of any organization (or reserve component thereof) referred to in subsection (a)(4) or under a binding written commitment to become such a member,

(C) he receives an amount described in subsection (a)(4) by reason of a combat-related injury, or

(D) on application therefor, he would be entitled to receive disability compensation from the Department of Veterans Affairs.

(3) Special rules for combat-related injuries. For purposes of this subsection, the term "combat-related injury" means personal injury or sickness—

(A) which is incurred—

(i) as a direct result of armed conflict,

(ii) while engaged in extrahazardous service, or

(iii) under conditions simulating war; or

(B) which is caused by an instrumentality of war. In the case of an individual who is not described in subparagraph (A) or (B) of paragraph (2), except as provided in paragraph (4), the only amounts taken into account under subsection (a)(4) shall be the amounts which he receives by reason of a combat-related injury.

(4) Amount excluded to be not less than veterans' disability compensation. In the case of any individual described in paragraph (2), the amounts excludable under subsection (a)(4) for any period with respect to any individual shall not be less than the maximum amount which such individual, on application therefor, would be entitled to receive as disability compensation from the Veterans' Administration.

(c) Application of prior law in certain cases. The phrase "(other than punitive damages)" shall not apply to punitive damages awarded in a civil action—

(1) which is a wrongful death action, and

(2) with respect to which applicable State law (as in effect on September 13, 1995 and without regard to any modification after such date) provides, or has been construed to provide by a court of competent jurisdiction pursuant to a decision issued on or before September 13, 1995, that only punitive damages may be awarded in such an action.

This subsection shall cease to apply to any civil action filed on or after the first date on which the applicable State law ceases to provide (or is no longer construed to provide) the treatment described in paragraph (2).

(d) Cross references.

(1) For exclusion from employee's gross income of employer contributions to accident and health plans, see section 106 [26 U.S.C. § 106].

(2) For exclusion of part of disability retirement pay from the application of subsection (a)(4) of this section, see section 1403 of title 10, United States Code (relating to career compensation laws). (Aug. 16, 1954, ch 736, 68A Stat. 30; Sept. 8, 1960, P.L. 86-723, §51, 74 Stat. 847; Oct. 10, 1962, P.L. 87-792, §7(d), 76 Stat. 829; Oct. 4, 1976, P.L. 94-455, Title V, §§505(b), (e)(1), Title XIX, §1901(a)(18), 90 Stat. 1567, 1568, 1766; Oct. 17, 1980, P.L. 96-465, Title II, §2206(e)(1), 94 Stat. 2162; Jan. 14, 1983, P.L. 97-473, Title I, §101(a), 96 Stat. 2605; Dec. 19, 1989, P.L. 101-239, Title VII, §7641(a), 103 Stat. 2379; Aug. 20, 1996, P.L. 104-188, Title I, §1605(a)-(c), 110 Stat. 1838; Aug. 21, 1996, P.L. 104-191, Title III, §311(b), 110 Stat. 2053; Jan. 23, 2002, P.L. 107-134, Title I, §113(a), 115 Stat. 2435; May 22, 2015, P.L. 114-14, §2, 129 Stat. 198; Mar. 23, 2018, P.L. 115-141, Div U, Title IV, §401(a)(2)(A), 132 Stat. 1184.)

2002 Note: The amendments made by this section shall apply to taxable years ending on or after September 11, 2001. Pub. L. 107-134 §113(c).

1996 Notes: The amendments to subsections (a) [closing paragraph], (a)(2), (c), and (d) made by Pub. L. 104-188 §1605 apply to amounts received after August 20, 1996, in taxable years ending after this date; except, the amendments made by Pub. L. 104-188 §1605 shall not apply to any amount received under a written binding agreement, court decree, or mediation award in effect on (or issued on or before) September 13, 1995. Pub. L. 104-188 §1605(d).

The amendment to subsection (a)(3) by Pub. L. 104-191 §311(b) applies to taxable years beginning after December 31, 1996. Pub. L. 104-191 §311(c).

SUBTITLE F PROCEDURE AND ADMINISTRATION

CHAPTER 64 COLLECTION

SUBCHAPTER C LIEN FOR TAXES

PART II LIENS

§6323. Validity and priority against certain persons.

[Subsection (a) Not Reproduced]

(b) Protection for certain interests even though notice filed. Even though notice of a lien imposed by section 6321 has been filed, such lien shall not be valid—

[Subsections (b)(1)–(7) Not Reproduced]

(8) Attorneys' liens. With respect to a judgment or other amount in settlement of a claim or of a cause of action, as against an attorney who, under local law, holds a lien upon or a contract enforcible against such judgment or amount, to the extent of his reasonable compensation for obtaining such judgment or procuring such settlement, except that this paragraph shall not apply to any judgment or amount in settlement of a claim or of a cause of action against the United States to the extent that the United States offsets such judgment or amount against any liability of the taxpayer to the United States.

[Subsections (b)(9)–(j) Not Reproduced]

(Aug. 16, 1954, ch 736, 68A Stat. 779; Feb. 26, 1964, P.L. 88-272, Title II, §236(a), (c)(1), 78 Stat. 127, 128; July 5, 1966, P.L. 89-493, §17(a), 80 Stat. 266; Nov. 2, 1966, P.L. 89-719, Title I, §101(a), 80 Stat. 1125; Oct. 4, 1976, P.L. 94-455, Title XII, §1202(h)(2), Title XIX, §1906(b)(13)(A), Title XX, §2008(c), 90 Stat. 1688, 1834, 1892; Nov. 6, 1978, P.L. 95-600, Title VII, §702(q)(1), (2), 92 Stat. 2937, 2938; Oct. 22, 1986, P.L. 99-514, Title XV, §1569(a), 100 Stat. 2764; Nov. 10, 1988, P.L. 100-647, Title I, §1015(s)(1), 102 Stat. 3573; Nov. 5, 1990, P.L. 101-508, Title XI, §§11317(b), 11704(a)(26), 104 Stat. 1388-458, 1388-519; July 30, 1996, P.L. 104-168, Title V, §501(a), 110 Stat. 1460; July 22, 1998, P.L. 105-206, Title I, §1102(d)(1)(A), Title III, §3435(a), (b), 112 Stat. 704, 760, 761; Dec. 22, 2017, P.L. 115-97, Title I, Subtitle A, Part I, §11002(d)(1)(HH), 131 Stat. 2060.)

SUBCHAPTER D SEIZURE OF PROPERTY FOR COLLECTION OF TAXES

PART II LEVY

§6334. Property exempt from levy.

(a) Enumeration. There shall be exempt from levy—

[Subsections (a)(1)–(6) Not Reproduced]

(7) Workmen's compensation. Any amount payable to an individual as workmen's compensation (including any portion thereof payable with respect to dependents) under a workmen's compensation law of the United States, any State, the District of Columbia, or the Commonwealth of Puerto Rico.

[Subsections (a)(8)–(g) Not Reproduced]

(Aug. 16, 1954, ch 736, 68A Stat. 784; Aug. 28, 1958, P.L. 85-840, Title IV, §406, 72 Stat. 1047; June 21, 1965, P.L. 89-44, Title VIII, §812(a), 79 Stat. 170; Nov. 2, 1966, P.L. 89-719, Title I, §104(c), 80 Stat. 1137; Dec. 30, 1969, P.L. 91-172, Title IX, §945(a), 83 Stat. 729; Oct. 4, 1976, P.L. 94-455, Title XII, §1209(a)-(c), Title XIX, §1906(b)(13)(A), 90 Stat. 1709, 1710, 1834; Sept. 3, 1982, P.L. 97-248, Title III, §347(a), 96 Stat. 638; July 18, 1984, P.L. 98-369, Div B, Title VI, §2661(o)(5), 98 Stat. 1159; Oct. 22, 1986, P.L. 99-514, Title XV, §1565(a), 100 Stat. 2763; Nov. 10, 1988, P.L. 100-647, Title I, §1015(o), Title VI, §6236(c), 102 Stat. 3572, 3738; Aug. 6, 1991, P.L. 102-83, §5(c)(2), 105 Stat. 406; July 30, 1996, P.L. 104-168, Title V, §502(a)-(c), 110 Stat. 1461; Aug. 22, 1996, P.L. 104-193, Title I, §110(*l*)(3) [110(*l*)(6)], 110 Stat. 2173; Aug. 5, 1997, P.L. 105-33, Title V, §5514(a)(2), (3), 111 Stat. 620; Aug. 5, 1997, P.L. 105-34, Title III, §312(d)(1), Title X, §1025(a), 111 Stat. 839, 924; July 22, 1998, P.L. 105-206, Title III, §§3431(a)-(c), 3445(a), (b), 112 Stat. 758, 762, 763; Dec. 22, 2017,P.L. 115-97, Title I, Subtitle A, Part I, §11002(d)(1)(II), Part V, §11041(d), 131 Stat. 2060, 2084; March 23, 2018, P.L. 115-141, Div U, Title IV, §401(a)(283), 132 Stat. 1198.)

TITLE 28
JUDICIARY AND JUDICIAL PROCEDURE

PART IV
JURISDICTION AND VENUE

CHAPTER 83
COURTS OF APPEALS

§1291. Final decisions of district courts.

The courts of appeals (other than the United States Court of Appeals for the Federal Circuit) shall have jurisdiction of appeals from all final decisions of the district courts of the United States, the United States District Court for the District of the Canal Zone, the District Court of Guam, and the District Court of the Virgin Islands, except where a direct review may be had in the Supreme Court. The jurisdiction of the United States Court of Appeals for the Federal Circuit shall be limited to the jurisdiction described in sections 1292(c) and (d) and 1295 of this title [28 U.S.C. §§ 1292(c) and (d) and 1295]. (June 25, 1948, ch 646, 62 Stat. 929; Oct. 31, 1951, ch 655, §48, 65 Stat. 726; July 7, 1958, P.L. 85-508, §12(e), 72 Stat. 348; April 2, 1982, P.L. 97-164, Title I, Part A, §124, 96 Stat. 36.)

CHAPTER 85
DISTRICT COURTS; JURISDICTION

§1333. Admiralty, maritime and prize cases.

The district courts shall have original jurisdiction, exclusive of the courts of the States, of:

(1) Any civil case of admiralty or maritime jurisdiction, saving to suitors in all cases all other remedies to which they are otherwise entitled.

(2) Any prize brought into the United States and all proceedings for the condemnation of property taken as prize. (June 25, 1948, ch 646, 62 Stat. 931; May 24, 1949, ch 139, §79, 63 Stat. 101.)

§1346. United States as defendant.

[Subsection (a) Not Reproduced]

(b)(1) Subject to the provisions of chapter 171 of this title [28 U.S.C. §§ 2671 et seq.], the district courts, together with the United States District Court for the District of the Canal Zone and the District Court of the Virgin Islands, shall have exclusive jurisdiction of civil actions on claims against the United States, for money damages, accruing on and after January 1, 1945, for injury or loss of property, or personal injury or death caused by the negligent or wrongful act or omission of any employee of the Government while acting within the scope of his office or employment, under circumstances where the United States, if a private person, would be liable to the claimant in accordance with the law of the place where the act or omission occurred.

(2) No person convicted of a felony who is incarcerated while awaiting sentencing or while serving a sentence may bring a civil action against the United States or an agency, officer, or employee of the Government, for mental or emotional injury suffered while in custody without a prior showing of physical injury or the commission of a sexual act (as defined in section 2246 of title 18).

(c) The jurisdiction conferred by this section includes jurisdiction of any set-off, counterclaim, or other claim or demand whatever on the part of the United States against any plaintiff commencing an action under this section.

[Subsections (d)–(g) Not Reproduced]

(June 25, 1948, ch 646, 62 Stat. 933; April 25, 1949, ch 92, §2(a), 63 Stat. 62; May 24, 1949, ch 139, §80(a), (b), 63 Stat. 101; Oct. 31, 1951, ch 655, §50(b), 65 Stat. 727; July 30, 1954, ch 648, §1, 68 Stat. 589; July 7, 1958, P.L. 85-508, §12(e), 72 Stat. 348; Aug. 30, 1964, P.L. 88-519, 78 Stat. 699; Nov. 2, 1966, P.L. 89-719, Title II, §202(a), 80 Stat. 1148; July 23, 1970, P.L. 91-350, §1(a), 84 Stat. 449; Oct. 25, 1972, P.L. 92-562, §1, 86 Stat. 1176; Oct. 4, 1976, P.L. 94-455, Title XII, §1204(c)(1), Title XIII, 1306(b)(7), 90 Stat. 1697, 1719; Nov. 1, 1978, P.L. 95-563, §14(a), 92 Stat. 2389; April 2, 1982, P.L. 97-164, Title I, Part A, §129, 96 Stat. 39; Sept. 3, 1982, P.L. 97-248, Title IV, §402(c)(17), 96 Stat. 669; April 26, 1996, P.L. 104-134, Title I [Title VIII, §806], 110 Stat. 1321-75; May 2, 1996, P.L. 104-140, §1(a), 110 Stat. 1327; Oct. 26, 1996, P.L. 104-331, §3(b)(1), 110 Stat. 4069; Jan. 4, 2011, P.L. 111-350, §5(g)(6), 124 Stat. 3848; Mar. 7, 2013, P.L. 113-4, Title XI, §1101(b), 127 Stat. 134.)

CHAPTER 87
DISTRICT COURTS; VENUE

§1402. United States as defendant.

[Subsection (a) Not Reproduced]

(b) Any civil action on a tort claim against the United States under subsection (b) of section 1346 of this title [28 U.S.C. § 1346] may be prosecuted only in the judicial district where the plaintiff resides or wherein the act or omission complained of occurred.

[Subsections (c) and (d) Not Reproduced]

(June 25, 1948, ch 646, 62 Stat. 937; Sept. 2, 1958, P.L. 85-920, 72 Stat. 1770; Nov. 2, 1966, P.L. 89-719, Title II, §202(b), 80 Stat. 1149; Oct. 25, 1972, P.L. 92-562, §2, 86 Stat. 1176; April 2, 1982, P.L. 97-164, Title I, Part A, §131, 96 Stat. 39.)

PART VI PARTICULAR PROCEEDINGS

CHAPTER 161 UNITED STATES AS PARTY GENERALLY

§2401. Time for commencing action against United States.

[Subsection (a) Not Reproduced]

(b) A tort claim against the United States shall be forever barred unless it is presented in writing to the appropriate Federal agency within two years after such claim accrues or unless action is begun within six months after the date of mailing, by certified or registered mail, of notice of final denial of the claim by the agency to which it was presented. (June 25, 1948, ch 646, 62 Stat. 971; April 25, 1949, ch 92, §1, 63 Stat. 62; Sept. 8, 1959, P.L. 86-238, §1(3), 73 Stat. 472; July 18, 1966, P.L. 89-506, §7, 80 Stat. 307; Nov. 1, 1978, P.L. 95-563, §14(b), 92 Stat. 2389.)

§2402. Jury trial in actions against United States.

Subject to chapter 179 of this title [28 U.S.C. §§ 3901 et seq.], any action against the United States under section 1346 [28 U.S.C. § 1346] shall be tried by the court without a jury, except that any action against the United States under section 1346(a)(1) [28 U.S.C. § 1346(a)(1)] shall, at the request of either party to such action, be tried by the court with a jury. (June 25, 1948, ch 646, 62 Stat. 971; July 30, 1954, ch. 648, §2(a), 68 Stat. 589; Oct. 26, 1996, P.L. 104-331, §3(b)(3), 110 Stat. 4069.)

§2412. Costs and fees.

(a)(1) Except as otherwise specifically provided by statute, a judgment for costs, as enumerated in section 1920 of this title [28 U.S.C. § 1920], but not including the fees and expenses of attorneys, may be awarded to the prevailing party in any civil action brought by or against the United States or any agency or any official of the United States acting in his or her official capacity in any court having jurisdiction of such action. A judgment for costs when taxed against the United States shall, in an amount established by statute, court rule, or order, be limited to reimbursing in whole or in part the prevailing party for the costs incurred by such party in the litigation.

(2) A judgment for costs, when awarded in favor of the United States in an action brought by the United States, may include an amount equal to the filing fee prescribed under section 1914(a) of this title [28 U.S.C. § 1914(a)]. The preceding sentence shall not be construed as requiring the United States to pay any filing fee.

(b) Unless expressly prohibited by statute, a court may award reasonable fees and expenses of attorneys, in addition to the costs which may be awarded pursuant to subsection (a), to the prevailing party in any civil action brought by or against the United States or any agency or any official of the United States acting in his or her official capacity in any court having jurisdiction of such action. The United States shall be liable for such fees and expenses to the same extent that any other party would be liable under the common law or under the terms of any statute which specifically provides for such an award.

(c)(1) Any judgment against the United States or any agency and any official of the United States acting in his or her official capacity for costs pursuant to subsection (a) shall be paid as provided in sections 2414 and 2517 of this title [28 U.S.C. §§ 2414 and 2517] and shall be in addition to any relief provided in the judgment.

(2) Any judgment against the United States or any agency and any official of the United States acting in his or her official capacity for fees and expenses of attorneys pursuant to subsection (b) shall be paid as provided in sections 2414 and 2517 of this title [28 U.S.C. §§ 2414 and 2517], except that if the basis for the award is a finding that the United States acted in bad faith, then the award shall be paid by any agency found to have acted in bad faith and shall be in addition to any relief provided in the judgment.

(d)(1)(A) Except as otherwise specifically provided by statute, a court shall award to a prevailing party other than the United States fees and other expenses, in addition to any costs awarded pursuant to subsection (a), incurred by that party in any civil action (other than cases sounding in tort), including proceedings for judicial review of agency action, brought by or against the United States in any court having jurisdiction of that action, unless the court finds that the position of the United States was substantially justified or that special circumstances make an award unjust.

(B) A party seeking an award of fees and other expenses shall, within thirty days of final judgment in the action, submit to the court an application for fees and other expenses which shows that the party is a prevailing party and is eligible to receive an award under this subsection, and the amount sought, including an itemized statement from any attorney or expert witness representing or appearing in behalf of the party stating the actual time expended and the rate at which fees and other expenses were computed. The party shall also allege that the position of the United States was not substantially justified. Whether or not the position of the United States was substantially justified shall be determined on the basis of the record (including the record with respect to the action or failure to act by the agency upon which the civil action is based) which is made in the civil action for which fees and other expenses are sought.

(C) The court, in its discretion, may reduce the amount to be awarded pursuant to this subsection, or deny an award, to the extent that the prevailing party during the course of the proceedings engaged in conduct which unduly and unreasonably protracted the final resolution of the matter in controversy.

(D) If, in a civil action brought by the United States or a proceeding for judicial review of an adversary adjudication described in section 504(a)(4) of title 5, the demand by the United States is substantially in excess of the judgment finally obtained by the United States and is unreasonable when compared with such judgment, under the facts and circumstances of the case, the court shall award to the party the fees and other expenses related to defending against the excessive demand, unless the party has committed a willful violation of law or otherwise acted in bad faith, or special circumstances make an award unjust. Fees and expenses awarded under this subparagraph shall be paid only as a consequence of appropriations provided in advance.

(2) For the purposes of this subsection—

(A) "fees and other expenses" includes the reasonable expenses of expert witnesses, the reasonable cost of any study, analysis, engineering report, test, or project which is found by the court to be necessary for the preparation of the party's case, and reasonable attorney fees (The amount of fees awarded under this subsection shall be based upon prevailing market rates for the kind and quality of the services furnished, except that (i) no expert witness shall be compensated at a rate in excess of the highest rate of compensation for expert witnesses paid by the United States; and (ii) attorney fees shall not be awarded in excess of $125 per hour unless the court determines that an increase in the cost of living or a special factor, such as the limited availability of qualified attorneys for the proceedings involved, justifies a higher fee.);

(B) "party" means (i) an individual whose net worth did not exceed $2,000,000 at the time the civil action was filed, or (ii) any owner of an unincorporated business, or any partnership, corporation, association, unit of local government, or organization, the net worth of which did not exceed $7,000,000 at the time the civil action was filed, and which had not more than 500 employees at the time the civil action was filed; except that an organization described in section 501(c)(3) of the Internal Revenue Code of 1954 [1986] (26 U.S.C. 501(c)(3)) exempt from taxation under section 501(a) of such Code, or a cooperative association as defined in section 15(a) of the Agricultural Marketing Act (12 U.S.C. 1141j(a)), may be a party regardless of the net worth of such organization or cooperative association or for purposes of subsection (d)(1)(D), a small entity as defined in section 601 of title 5;

(C) "United States" includes any agency and any official of the United States acting in his or her official capacity;

(D) "position of the United States" means, in addition to the position taken by the United States in the civil action, the action or failure to act by the agency upon which the civil action is based; except that fees and expenses may not be awarded to a party for any portion of the litigation in which the party has unreasonably protracted the proceedings;

(E) "civil action brought by or against the United States" includes an appeal by a party, other than the United States, from a decision of a contracting officer rendered pursuant to a disputes clause in a contract with the Government or pursuant to chapter 71 of title 41 [41 U.S.C. §§ 7101 et seq.];

(F) "court" includes the United States Claims Court [United States Court of Federal Claims] and the United States Court of Appeals for Veterans Claims;

(G) "final judgment" means a judgment that is final and not appealable, and includes an order of settlement;

(H) "prevailing party", in the case of eminent domain proceedings, means a party who obtains a final judgment (other than by settlement), exclusive of interest, the amount of which is at least as close to the highest valuation of the property involved that is attested to at trial on behalf of the property owner as it is to the highest valuation of the property involved that is attested to at trial on behalf of the Government; and

(I) "demand" means the express demand of the United States which led to the adversary adjudication, but shall not include a recitation of the maximum statutory penalty (i) in the complaint, or (ii) elsewhere when accompanied by an express demand for a lesser amount.

(3) In awarding fees and other expenses under this subsection to a prevailing party in any action for judicial review of an adversary adjudication, as defined in subsection (b)(1)(C) of section 504 of title 5 [5 U.S.C. § 504(b)(1)(C)], or an adversary adjudication subject to chapter 71 of title 41 [41 U.S.C. §§ 7101 et seq.], the court shall include in that award fees and other expenses to the same extent authorized in subsection (a) of such section, unless the court finds that during such adversary adjudication the position of the United States was substantially justified, or that special circumstances make an award unjust.

(4) Fees and other expenses awarded under this subsection to a party shall be paid by any agency over which the party prevails from any funds made available to the agency by appropriation or otherwise.

(5)(A) Not later than March 31 of the first fiscal year beginning after the date of enactment of the John D. Dingell, Jr. Conservation, Management, and Recreation Act [enacted March 12, 2019], and every fiscal year thereafter, the Chairman of the Administrative Conference of the United States shall submit to Congress and make publicly available online a report on the amount of fees and other expenses awarded during the preceding fiscal year pursuant to this subsection.

(B) Each report under subparagraph (A) shall describe the number, nature, and amount of the awards, the claims involved in the controversy, and any other relevant information that may aid Congress in evaluating the scope and impact of such awards.

(C)(i) Each report under subparagraph (A) shall account for all payments of fees and other expenses awarded under this subsection that are made pursuant to a settlement agreement, regardless of whether the settlement agreement is sealed or otherwise subject to a nondisclosure provision.

(ii) The disclosure of fees and other expenses required under clause (i) shall not affect any other information that is subject to a nondisclosure provision in a settlement agreement.

(D) The Chairman of the Administrative Conference of the United States shall include and clearly identify in each annual report under subparagraph (A), for each case in which an award of fees and other expenses is included in the report—

(i) any amounts paid under section 1304 of title 31 for a judgment in the case;

(ii) the amount of the award of fees and other expenses; and

(iii) the statute under which the plaintiff filed suit.

(6) As soon as practicable, and in any event not later than the date on which the first report under paragraph (5)(A) is required to be submitted, the Chairman of the Administrative Conference of the United States shall create and maintain online a searchable database containing, with respect to each award of fees and other expenses under this subsection made on or after the date of enactment of the John D. Dingell, Jr. Conservation, Management, and Recreation Act [enacted March 12, 2019], the following information:

(A) The case name and number, hyperlinked to the case, if available.

(B) The name of the agency involved in the case.

(C) The name of each party to whom the award was made as such party is identified in the order or other court document making the award.

(D) A description of the claims in the case.

(E) The amount of the award.

(F) The basis for the finding that the position of the agency concerned was not substantially justified.

(7) The online searchable database described in paragraph (6) may not reveal any information the disclosure of which is prohibited by law or a court order.

(8) The head of each agency (including the Attorney General of the United States) shall provide to the Chairman of the Administrative Conference of the United States in a timely manner all information requested by the Chairman to comply with the requirements of paragraphs (5), (6), and (7).

(e) The provisions of this section shall not apply to any costs, fees, and other expenses in connection with any proceeding to which section 7430 of the Internal Revenue Code of 1954 [1986] [26 U.S.C. § 7430] applies (determined without regard to subsections (b) and (f) of such section [26 U.S.C. § 7430(b), (f)]). Nothing in the preceding sentence shall prevent the awarding under subsection (a) of this section, of costs enumerated in section 1920 of this title [28 U.S.C. § 1920] (as in effect on October 1, 1981).

(f) If the United States appeals an award of costs or fees and other expenses made against the United States under this section and the award is affirmed in whole or in part, interest shall be paid on the amount of the award as affirmed. Such interest shall be computed at the rate determined under section 1961(a) of this title [28 U.S.C. § 1961(a)], and shall run from the date of the award through the day before the date of the mandate of affirmance. (June 25, 1948, ch 646, 62 Stat. 973; July 18, 1966, P.L. 89-507, §1, 80 Stat. 308; Oct. 21, 1980, P.L. 96-481, Title II, §204(a), (c), 94 Stat. 2327, 2329; Sept. 3, 1982, P.L. 97-248, Title II, Subtitle G, §292(c), 96 Stat. 574; Aug. 5, 1985, P.L. 99-80, §§2, 6, 99 Stat. 184, 186; Oct. 29, 1992, P.L. 102-572, Title III, §301(a), Title V, §§502(b), 506(a), 106 Stat. 4511, 4512, 4513; Dec. 21, 1995, P.L. 104-66, Title I, Subtitle I, §1091(b), 109 Stat. 722; March 29, 1996, P.L. 104-121, Title II, Subtitle C, §232, 110 Stat. 863; Nov. 11, 1998, P.L. 105-368, Title V, Subtitle B, §512(b)(1)(B), 112 Stat. 3342; Jan. 4, 2011, P.L. 111-350, §5(g)(9), 124 Stat. 3848; March 12, 2019, P.L. 116-9, Title IV, Subtitle C, §4201(a)(2), (3), 133 Stat. 763, 764.)

2002 Note: Act Dec. 6, 2002, Pub. L. 107-330, §403, 116 Stat. 2833, provides: "The authority of the United States Court of Appeals for Veterans Claims to award reasonable fees and expenses of attorneys under section 2412(d) of title 28, United States Code, shall include authority to award fees and expenses, in an amount determined appropriate by the United States Court of Appeals for Veterans Claims, of individuals admitted to practice before the Court as non-attorney practitioners under subsection (b) or (c) of Rule 46 of the Rules of Practice and Procedure of the United States Court of Appeals for Veterans Claims."

CHAPTER 171
TORT CLAIMS PROCEDURE

§2671. Definitions.

As used in this chapter [28 U.S.C. §§ 2671 et seq.] and sections 1346(b) and 2401(b) of this title [28 U.S.C. §§ 1346(b) and 2401(b)], the term "Federal agency" includes the executive departments, the judicial and legislative branches, the military departments, independent establishments of the United States, and corporations primarily acting as instrumentalities or agencies of the United States, but does not include any contractor with the United States.

"Employee of the government" includes (1) officers or employees of any federal agency, members of the military or naval forces of the United States, members of the National Guard while engaged in training or duty under section 115, 316, 502, 503, 504, or 505 of title 32 [32 U.S.C. § 115, 316, 502, 503, 504, or 505], and persons acting on behalf of a federal agency in an official capacity, temporarily or permanently in the service of the United States, whether with or without compensation, and (2) any officer or employee of a Federal public defender organization, except when such officer or employee performs professional services in the course of providing representation under section 3006A of title 18 [18 U.S.C. § 3006A].

"Acting within the scope of his office or employment", in the case of a member of the military or naval forces of the United States or a member of the National Guard as defined in section 101(3) of title 32 [32 U.S.C. § 101(3)], means acting in line of duty. (June 25, 1948, ch 646, 62 Stat. 982; May 24, 1949, ch 139, §124, 63 Stat. 106; July 18, 1966, P.L. 89-506, §8, 80 Stat. 307; Dec. 29, 1981, P.L. 97-124, §1, 95 Stat. 1666; Nov. 18, 1988, P.L. 100-694, §3, 102 Stat. 4564; Oct. 30, 2000, P.L. 106-398, §1, 114 Stat. 1654; Nov. 13, 2000, P.L. 106-518, Title IV, §401, 114 Stat. 2421.)

§2672. Administrative adjustment of claims.

The head of each Federal agency or his designee, in accordance with regulations prescribed by the Attorney General, may consider, ascertain, adjust, determine, compromise, and settle any claim for money damages against the United States for injury or loss of property or personal injury or death caused by the negligent or wrongful act or omission of any employee of the agency while acting within the scope of his office or employment, under circumstances where the United States, if a private person, would be liable to the claimant in accordance with the law of the place where the act or omission occurred: Provided, That any award, compromise, or settlement in excess of $25,000 shall be effected only with the prior written approval of the Attorney General or his designee. Notwithstanding the proviso contained in the preceding sentence, any award, compromise, or settlement may be effected without the prior written approval of the Attorney General or his or her designee, to the extent that the Attorney General delegates to the head of the agency the authority to make such award, compromise, or settlement. Such delegations may not exceed the authority delegated by the Attorney General to the United States attorneys to settle claims for money damages against the United States. Each Federal agency may use arbitration, or other alternative means of dispute resolution under the provisions of subchapter IV of chapter 5 of title 5 [5 U.S.C. §§ 571 et seq.], to settle any tort claim against the United States, to the extent of the agency's authority to award, compromise, or settle such claim without the prior written approval of the Attorney General or his or her designee.

Subject to the provisions of this title relating to civil actions on tort claims against the United States, any such award, compromise, settlement, or determination shall be final and conclusive on all officers of the Government, except when procured by means of fraud.

Any award, compromise, or settlement in an amount of $2,500 or less made pursuant to this section shall be paid by the head of the Federal agency concerned out of appropriations available to that agency. Payment of any award, compromise, or settlement in an amount in excess of $2,500 made pursuant to this section or made by the Attorney General in any amount pursuant to section 2677 of this title [28 U.S.C. § 2677] shall be paid in a manner similar to judgments and compromises in like causes and appropriations or funds available for the payment of such judgments and compromises are hereby made available for the payment of awards, compromises, or settlements under this chapter [28 U.S.C. §§ 2671 et seq.].

The acceptance by the claimant of any such award, compromise, or settlement shall be final and conclusive on the claimant, and shall constitute a complete release of any claim against the United States and against the employee of the government whose act or omission gave rise to the claim, by reason of the same subject matter. (June 25, 1948, ch 646, 62 Stat. 983; April 25, 1949, ch 92, §2(b), 63 Stat. 62; May 24, 1949, ch 139, §125, 63 Stat. 106; Sept. 23, 1950, ch 1010, §9, 64 Stat. 987; Sept. 8, 1959, P.L. 86-238, §1(1), 73 Stat. 471; July 18, 1966, P.L. 89-506, §§1, 9(a), 80 Stat. 306, 308; Nov. 15, 1990, P.L. 101-552, §8(a), 104 Stat. 2746.)

§2674. Liability of United States.

The United States shall be liable, respecting the provisions of this title relating to tort claims, in the same manner and to the same extent as a private individual under like circumstances, but shall not be liable for interest prior to judgment or for punitive damages.

If, however, in any case wherein death was caused, the law of the place where the act or omission complained of occurred provides, or has been construed to provide, for damages only punitive in nature, the United States shall be liable for actual or compensatory damages, measured by the pecuniary injuries resulting from such death to the persons respectively, for whose benefit the action was brought, in lieu thereof.

With respect to any claim under this chapter [28 U.S.C. §§ 2671 et seq.], the United States shall be entitled to assert any defense based upon judicial or legislative immunity which otherwise would have been available to the employee of the United States whose act or omission gave rise to the claim, as well as any other defenses to which the United States is entitled.

With respect to any claim to which this section applies, the Tennessee Valley Authority shall be entitled to assert any defense which otherwise would have been available to the employee based upon judicial or legislative immunity, which otherwise would have been available to the employee of the Tennessee Valley Authority whose act or omission gave rise to the claim as well as any other defenses to which the Tennessee Valley Authority is entitled under this chapter [28 U.S.C. §§ 2671 et seq.]. (June 25, 1948, ch 646, 62 Stat. 983; Nov. 18, 1988, P.L. 100-694, §§4, 9(c), 102 Stat. 4564, 4567.)

§2675. Disposition by federal agency as prerequisite; evidence.

(a) An action shall not be instituted upon a claim against the United States for money damages for injury or loss of property or personal injury or death caused by the negligent or wrongful act or omission of any employee of the Government while acting within the scope of his office or employment, unless the claimant shall have first presented the claim to the appropriate Federal agency and his claim shall have been finally denied by the agency in writing and sent by certified or registered mail. The failure of an agency to make final disposition of a claim within six months after it is filed shall, at the option of the claimant any time thereafter, be deemed a final denial of the claim for purposes of this section. The provisions of this subsection shall not apply to such claims as may be asserted under the Federal Rules of Civil Procedure by third party complaint, cross-claim, or counterclaim.

(b) Action under this section shall not be instituted for any sum in excess of the amount of the claim presented to the federal agency, except where the increased amount is based upon newly discovered evidence not reasonably discoverable at the time of presenting the claim to the federal agency, or upon allegation and proof of intervening facts, relating to the amount of the claim.

(c) Disposition of any claim by the Attorney General or other head of a federal agency shall not be competent evidence of liability or amount of damages. (June 25, 1948, ch 646, 62 Stat. 983; May 24, 1949, ch 139, §126, 63 Stat. 107; July 18, 1966, P.L. 89-506, §2, 80 Stat. 306.)

§2676. Judgment as bar.

The judgment in an action under section 1346(b) of this title [28 U.S.C. § 1346(b)] shall constitute a complete bar to any action by the claimant, by reason of the same subject matter, against the employee of the government whose act or omission gave rise to the claim. (June 25, 1948, ch 646, 62 Stat. 984.)

§2677. Compromise.

The Attorney General or his designee may arbitrate, compromise, or settle any claim cognizable under section 1346(b) of this title [28 U.S.C. § 1346(b)], after the commencement of an action thereon. (June 25, 1948, ch

646, 62 Stat. 984; July 18, 1966, P.L. 89-506, §3, 80 Stat. 307.)

§2678. Attorney fees; penalty.

No attorney shall charge, demand, receive, or collect for services rendered, fees in excess of 25 per centum of any judgment rendered pursuant to section 1346(b) of this title [28 U.S.C. § 1346(b)] or any settlement made pursuant to section 2677 of this title [28 U.S.C. § 2677], or in excess of 20 per centum of any award, compromise, or settlement made pursuant to section 2672 of this title [28 U.S.C. § 2672].

Any attorney who charges, demands, receives, or collects for services rendered in connection with such claim any amount in excess of that allowed under this section, if recovery be had, shall be fined not more than $2,000 or imprisoned not more than one year, or both. (June 25, 1948, ch 646, 62 Stat. 984; July 18, 1966, P.L. 89-506, §4, 80 Stat. 307.)

§2679. Exclusiveness of remedy.

(a) The authority of any federal agency to sue and be sued in its own name shall not be construed to authorize suits against such federal agency on claims which are cognizable under section 1346(b) of this title [28 U.S.C. § 1346(b)], and the remedies provided by this title in such cases shall be exclusive.

(b)(1) The remedy against the United States provided by sections 1346(b) and 2672 of this title [28 U.S.C. §§ 1346(b) and 2672] for injury or loss of property, or personal injury or death arising or resulting from the negligent or wrongful act or omission of any employee of the Government while acting within the scope of his office or employment is exclusive of any other civil action or proceeding for money damages by reason of the same subject matter against the employee whose act or omission gave rise to the claim or against the estate of such employee. Any other civil action or proceeding for money damages arising out of or relating to the same subject matter against the employee or the employee's estate is precluded without regard to when the act or omission occurred.

(2) Paragraph (1) does not extend or apply to a civil action against an employee of the Government—

(A) which is brought for a violation of the Constitution of the United States, or

(B) which is brought for a violation of a statute of the United States under which such action against an individual is otherwise authorized.

(c) The Attorney General shall defend any civil action or proceeding brought in any court against any employee of the Government or his estate for any such damage or injury. The employee against whom such civil action or proceeding is brought shall deliver within such time after date of service or knowledge of service as determined by the Attorney General, all process served upon him or an attested true copy thereof to his immediate superior or to whomever was designated by the head of his department to receive such papers and such person shall promptly furnish copies of the pleadings and process therein to the United States attorney for the district embracing the place wherein the proceeding is brought, to the Attorney General, and to the head of his employing Federal agency.

(d)(1) Upon certification by the Attorney General that the defendant employee was acting within the scope of his office or employment at the time of the incident out of which the claim arose, any civil action or proceeding commenced upon such claim in a United States district court shall be deemed an action against the United States under the provisions of this title and all references thereto, and the United States shall be substituted as the party defendant.

(2) Upon certification by the Attorney General that the defendant employee was acting within the scope of his office or employment at the time of the incident out of which the claim arose, any civil action or proceeding commenced upon such claim in a State court shall be removed without bond at any time before trial by the Attorney General to the district court of the United States for the district and division embracing the place in which the action or proceeding is pending. Such action or proceeding shall be deemed to be an action or proceeding brought against the United States under the provisions of this title and all references thereto, and the United States shall be substituted as the party defendant. This certification of the Attorney General shall conclusively establish scope of office or employment for purposes of removal.

(3) In the event that the Attorney General has refused to certify scope of office or employment under this section, the employee may at any time before trial petition the court to find and certify that the employee was acting within the scope of his office or employment. Upon such certification by the court, such action or proceeding shall be deemed to be an action or proceeding brought against the United States under the provisions of this title and all references thereto, and the United States shall be substituted as the party defendant. A copy of the petition shall be served upon the United States in accordance with the provisions of Rule 4(d)(4) of the Federal Rules of Civil Procedure. In the event the petition is filed in a civil action or proceeding pending in a State court, the action or proceeding may be removed without bond by the Attorney General to the district court of the United States for the district and division embracing the place in which it is pending. If, in considering the petition, the district court determines that the employee was not acting within the scope of his office or employment, the action or proceeding shall be remanded to the State court.

(4) Upon certification, any action or proceeding subject to paragraph (1), (2), or (3) shall proceed in the same manner as any action against the United States filed pursuant to section 1346(b) of this title [28 U.S.C. § 1346(b)] and shall be subject to the limitations and exceptions applicable to those actions.

(5) Whenever an action or proceeding in which the United States is substituted as the party defendant under this subsection is dismissed for failure first to present a claim pursuant to section 2675(a) of this title [28 U.S.C. § 2675(a)], such a claim shall be deemed to be timely presented under section 2401(b) of this title [28 U.S.C. § 2401(b)] if—

(A) the claim would have been timely had it been filed on the date the underlying civil action was commenced, and

(B) the claim is presented to the appropriate Federal agency within 60 days after dismissal of the civil action.

(e) The Attorney General may compromise or settle any claim asserted in such civil action or proceeding in the manner provided in section 2677 [28 U.S.C. § 2677], and with the same effect. (June 25, 1948, ch 646, 62 Stat. 984; Sept. 21, 1961, P.L. 87-258, §1, 75 Stat. 539; July 18, 1966, P.L. 89-506, §5(a), 80 Stat. 307; Nov. 18, 1988, P.L. 100-694, §§5, 6, 102 Stat. 4564.)

§2680. Exceptions.

The provisions of this chapter [28 U.S.C. §§2671 et seq.] and section 1346(b) of this title [28 U.S.C. §1346(b)] shall not apply to—

(a) Any claim based upon an act or omission of an employee of the Government, exercising due care, in the execution of a statute or regulation, whether or not such statute or regulation be valid, or based upon the exercise or performance or the failure to exercise or perform a discretionary function or duty on the part of a federal agency or an employee of the Government, whether or not the discretion involved be abused.

[Subsections (b) and (c) Not Reproduced]

(d) Any claim for which a remedy is provided by chapter 309 or 311 of title 46 [46 U.S.C. §§30901 et seq. or 31101 et seq.] relating to claims or suits in admiralty against the United States.

[Subsections (e)–(g) Not Reproduced]

(h) Any claim arising out of assault, battery, false imprisonment, false arrest, malicious prosecution, abuse of process, libel, slander, misrepresentation, deceit, or interference with contract rights: *Provided,* That, with regard to acts or omissions of investigative or law enforcement officers of the United States Government, the provisions of this chapter [28 U.S.C. §§2671 et seq.] and section 1346(b) of this title [28 U.S.C. §1346(b)] shall apply to any claim arising, on or after the date of the enactment of this proviso [enacted March 16, 1974], out of assault, battery, false imprisonment, false arrest, abuse of process, or malicious prosecution. For the purpose of this subsection, "investigative or law enforcement officer" means any officer of the United States who is empowered by law to execute searches, to seize evidence, or to make arrests for violations of Federal law.

[Subsection (i) Not Reproduced]

(j) Any claim arising out of the combatant activities of the military or naval forces, or the Coast Guard, during time of war.

(k) Any claim arising in a foreign country.

(*l*) Any claim arising from the activities of the Tennessee Valley Authority.

(m) Any claim arising from the activities of the Panama Canal Company.

(n) Any claim arising from the activities of a Federal land bank, a Federal intermediate credit bank, or a bank for cooperatives. (June 25, 1948, ch 646, §1, 62 Stat. 984; July 16, 1949, ch 340, 63 Stat. 444; Sept. 26, 1950, ch 1049, §§2(a)(2), 13(5), 64 Stat. 1038, 1043; Aug. 18, 1959, P.L. 86-168, Title II, §202(b), 73 Stat. 389; March 16, 1974, P.L. 93-253, §2, 88 Stat. 50; April 25, 2000, P.L. 106-185, §3(a), 114 Stat. 211; Oct. 6, 2006, P.L. 109-304, §17(f)(4), 120 Stat. 1708.)

TITLE 33
NAVIGATION AND NAVIGABLE WATERS

CHAPTER 18
LONGSHORE AND HARBOR WORKERS' COMPENSATION

§901. Short title.

This chapter may be cited as "Longshore and Harbor Workers' Compensation Act." (March 4, 1927, ch 509, §1, 44 Stat. 1424; Sept. 28, 1984, P.L. 98-426, §27(d)(1), 98 Stat. 1654.)

§902. Definitions.

When used in this chapter—

(1) The term "person" means individual, partnership, corporation, or association.

(2) The term "injury" means accidental injury or death arising out of and in the course of employment, and such occupational disease or infection as arises naturally out of such employment or as naturally or unavoidably results from such accidental injury, and includes an injury caused by the willful act of a third person directed against an employee because of his employment.

(3) The term "employee" means any person engaged in maritime employment, including any longshoreman or other person engaged in longshoring operations, and any harbor-worker including a ship repairman, shipbuilder, and ship-breaker, but such term does not include—

(A) individuals employed exclusively to perform office clerical, secretarial, security, or data processing work;

(B) individuals employed by a club, camp, recreational operation, restaurant, museum, or retail outlet;

(C) individuals employed by a marina and who are not engaged in construction, replacement, or expansion of such marina (except for routine maintenance);

(D) individuals who (i) are employed by suppliers, transporters, or vendors, (ii) are temporarily doing business on the premises of an employer described in paragraph (4), and (iii) are not engaged in work normally performed by employees of that employer under this chapter;

(E) aquaculture workers;

(F) individuals employed to build any recreational vessel under sixty-five feet in length, or individuals employed to repair any recreational vessel, or to dismantle any part of a recreational vessel in connection with the repair of such vessel;

(G) a master or member of a crew of any vessel; or

(H) any person engaged by a master to load or unload or repair any small vessel under eighteen tons net;

if individuals described in clauses (A) through (F) are subject to coverage under a State workers' compensation law.

(4) The term "employer" means an employer any of whose employees are employed in maritime employment, in whole or in part, upon the navigable waters of the United States (including any adjoining pier, wharf, dry dock, terminal, building way, marine railway, or other adjoining area customarily used by an employer in loading, unloading, repairing, or building a vessel).

(5) The term "carrier" means any person or fund authorized under section 932 of this title to insure under this chapter and includes self-insurers.

(6) The term "Secretary" means the Secretary of Labor.

(7) The term "deputy commissioner" means the deputy commissioner having jurisdiction in respect of an injury or death.

(8) The term "State" includes a Territory and the District of Columbia.

(9) The term "United States" when used in a geographical sense means the several States and Territories and the District of Columbia, including the territorial waters thereof.

(10) "Disability" means incapacity because of injury to earn the wages which the employee was receiving at the time of injury in the same or any other employment; but such term shall mean permanent impairment, determined (to the extent covered thereby) under the guides to the evaluation of permanent impairment promulgated and modified from time to time by the American Medical Association, in the case of an individual whose claim is described in section 910(d)(2) of this title.

(11) "Death" as a basis for a right to compensation means only death resulting from an injury.

(12) "Compensation" means the money allowance payable to an employee or to his dependents as provided for in this chapter, and includes funeral benefits provided therein.

(13) The term "wages" means the money rate at which the service rendered by an employee is compensated by an employer under the contract of hiring in force at the time of the injury, including the reasonable value of any advantage which is received from the employer and included for purposes of any withholding of tax under subtitle C of title 26 (relating to employment taxes). The term wages does not include fringe benefits, including (but not limited to) employer payments for or contributions to a retirement, pension, health and welfare, life insurance, training, social security or other employee or dependent benefit plan for the employee's or dependent's benefit, or any other employee's dependent entitlement.

(14) "Child" shall include a posthumous child, a child legally adopted prior to the injury of the employee, a child in relation to whom the deceased employee stood in loco parentis for at least one year prior to the time of injury, and a stepchild or acknowledged illegitimate child dependent upon the deceased, but does not include married children unless wholly dependent on him. "Grandchild" means a child as above defined of a child as above defined. "Brother" and "sister" includes stepbrothers and stepsisters, half brothers and half sisters, and brothers and sisters by adoption, but does not include married brothers nor married sisters unless wholly dependent on the employee. "Child", "grandchild", "brother", and "sister" include only a person who is under eighteen years of age, or who, though eighteen years of age or over, is (1) wholly dependent upon the employee and incapable of self-support by reason of mental or physical disability, or (2) a student as defined in paragraph (19) [(18)] of this section.

(15) The term "parent" includes step-parents and parents by adoption, parents-in-law, and any person who for more than three years prior to the death of the deceased employee stood in the place of a parent to him, if dependent on the injured employee.

(16) The terms "widow or widower" includes only the decedent's wife or husband living with or dependent for support upon him or her at the time of his or her death; or living apart for justifiable cause or by reason of his or her desertion at such time.

(17) The terms "adoption" or "adopted" mean legal adoption prior to the time of the injury.

(18) The term "student" means a person regularly pursuing a full-time course of study or training at an institution which is—

(A) a school or college or university operated or directly supported by the United States, or by any State or local government or political subdivision thereof,

(B) a school or college or university which has been accredited by a State or by a State recognized or nationally recognized accrediting agency or body,

(C) a school or college or university not so accredited but whose credits are accepted, on transfer, by not less than three institutions which are so accredited, for credit on the same basis as if transferred from an institution so accredited, or

(D) an additional type of educational or training institution as defined by the Secretary,

but not after he reaches the age of twenty-three or has completed four years of education beyond the high school level, except that, where his twenty-third birthday occurs during a semester or other enrollment period, he shall continue to be considered a student until the end of such semester or other enrollment period. A child shall not be deemed to have ceased to be a student during any interim between school years if the interim does not exceed five months and if he shows to the satisfaction of the Secretary that he has a bona fide intention of continuing to pursue a full-time course of education or training during the semester or other enrollment period immediately following the interim or during periods of reasonable duration during which, in the judgment of the Secretary, he is prevented by factors beyond his control from pursuing his education. A child shall not be deemed to be a student under this chapter during a period of service in the Armed Forces of the United States.

(19) The term "national average weekly wage" means the national average weekly earnings of production or nonsupervisory workers on private nonagricultural payrolls.

(20) The term "Board" shall mean the Benefits Review Board.

(21) Unless the context requires otherwise, the term "vessel" means any vessel upon which or in connection with which any person entitled to benefits under this chapter suffers injury or death arising out of or in the course of his employment, and said vessel's owner, owner pro hac vice, agent, operator, charter or bare boat charterer, master, officer, or crew member.

(22) The singular includes the plural and the masculine includes the feminine and neuter. (March 4, 1927, ch 509, §2, 44 Stat. 1424; June 25, 1938, ch 685, §1, 52 Stat. 1164; Oct. 27, 1972, P.L. 92-576, §§2(a)(b) 3, 5(b), 15(c), 18(b), 20(c), 86 Stat. 1251, 1262; Sept. 28, 1984, P.L. 98-426, §§2, 5(a)(2), 27(a)(1), 98 Stat. 1639, 1641, 1654; Feb. 17, 2009, P.L. 111-5, Div A, Title VIII, §803, 123 Stat. 187.)

§903. Coverage.

(a) Disability or death; injuries occurring upon navigable waters of United States. Except as otherwise provided in this section, compensation shall be payable under this chapter in respect of disability or death of an employee, but only if the disability or death results from an injury occurring upon the navigable waters of the United States (including any adjoining pier, wharf, dry dock, terminal, building way, marine railway, or other adjoining area customarily used by an employer in loading, unloading, repairing, dismantling, or building a vessel).

(b) Governmental officers and employees. No compensation shall be payable in respect of the disability or death of an officer or employee of the United States, or any agency thereof, or of any State or foreign government, or any subdivision thereof.

(c) Intoxication; willful intention to kill. No compensation shall be payable if the injury was occasioned solely by the intoxication of the employee or by the willful intention of the employee to injure or kill himself or another.

(d) Small vessels.

(1) No compensation shall be payable to an employee employed at a facility of an employer if, as certified by the Secretary, the facility is engaged in the business of building, repairing, or dismantling exclusively small vessels (as defined in paragraph (3) of this subsection), unless the injury occurs while upon the navigable waters of the United States or while upon any adjoining pier, wharf, dock, facility over land for launching vessels, or facility over land for hauling, lifting, or drydocking vessels.

(2) Notwithstanding paragraph (1), compensation shall be payable to an employee—

(A) who is employed at a facility which is used in the business of building, repairing, or dismantling small vessels if such facility receives Federal maritime subsidies; or

(B) if the employee is not subject to coverage under a State workers' compensation law.

(3) For purposes of this subsection, a small vessel means—

(A) a commercial barge which is under 900 lightship displacement tons; or

(B) a commercial tugboat, towboat, crew boat, supply boat, fishing vessel, or other work vessel which is under 1,600 tons gross as measured under section 14502 of title 46, or an alternate tonnage measured under section 14302 of that title as prescribed by the Secretary under section 14104 of that title.

(e) Credit for benefits paid under other laws. Notwithstanding any other provision of law, any amounts paid to an employee for the same injury, disability, or death for which benefits are claimed under this chapter pursuant to any other workers' compensation law or section 30104 of title 46 shall be credited against any liability imposed by this chapter. (March 4, 1927, ch 509. §3, 44 Stat. 1426; Oct. 27, 1972, P.L. 92-576, §§2(c), 21, 86 Stat. 1251, 1265; Sept. 28, 1984, P.L. 98-426, §3, 98 stat. 1640; Oct. 19, 1996, P.L. 104-324, Title VII, §703, 110 Stat. 3933.)

§904. Liability for compensation.

(a) Every employer shall be liable for and shall secure the payment to his employees of the compensation payable under sections 907, 908, and 909 of this title. In the case of an employer who is a subcontractor, only if such subcontractor fails to secure the payment of compensation shall the contractor be liable for and be required to secure the payment of compensation. A subcontractor shall not be deemed to have failed to secure the payment of compensation if the contractor has provided insurance for such compensation for the benefit of the subcontractor.

(b) Compensation shall be payable irrespective of fault as a cause for the injury. (March 4, 1927, ch 509, §4, 44 Stat. 1426; Sept. 28, 1984, P.L. 98-426, §4(a), 98 Stat. 1641.)

§905. Exclusiveness of liability.

(a) Employer liability; failure of employer to secure payment of compensation. The liability of an employer prescribed in section 904 of this title shall be exclusive and in place of all other liability of such employer to the employee, his legal representative, husband or wife, parents, dependents, next of kin, and anyone otherwise entitled to recover damages from such employer at law or in admiralty on account of such injury or death, except that if an employer fails to secure payment of compensation as required by this chapter, an injured employee, or his legal representative in case death results from the injury, may elect to claim compensation under the chapter, or to maintain an action at law or in admiralty for damages on account of such injury or death. In such action the defendant may not plead as a defense that the injury was caused by the negligence of a fellow servant, or that the employee assumed the risk of his employment, or that the injury was due to the contributory negligence of the employee. For purposes of this subsection, a contractor shall be deemed the employer of a subcontractor's employees only if the subcontractor fails to secure the payment of compensation as required by section 904 of this title.

(b) Negligence of vessel. In the event of injury to a person covered under this chapter caused by the negligence of a vessel, then such person, or anyone otherwise entitled to recover damages by reason thereof, may bring an action against such vessel as a third party in accordance with the provisions of section 933 of this title, and the employer shall not be liable to the vessel for such damages directly or indirectly and any agreements or warranties to the contrary shall be void. If such person was employed by the vessel to provide stevedoring services, no such action shall be permitted if the injury was caused by the negligence of persons engaged in providing stevedoring services to the vessel. If such person was employed to provide shipbuilding, repairing, or breaking services and such person's employer was the owner, owner pro hac vice, agent, operator, or charterer of the vessel, no such action shall be permitted, in whole or in part or directly or indirectly, against the injured person's employer (in any capacity, including as the vessel's owner, owner pro hac vice, agent, operator, or charterer) or against the employees of the employer. The liability of the vessel under this subsection shall not be based upon the warranty of seaworthiness or a breach thereof at the time the injury occurred. The remedy provided in this subsection shall be exclusive of all other remedies against the vessel except remedies available under this chapter.

(c) Outer Continental Shelf. In the event that the negligence of a vessel causes injury to a person entitled to receive benefits under this chapter by virtue of section 1333 of title 43, then such person, or anyone otherwise entitled to recover damages by reason thereof, may bring an action against such vessel in accordance with the provisions of subsection (b) of this section. Nothing contained in subsection (b) of this section shall preclude the enforcement according to its terms of any reciprocal indemnity provision whereby the employer of a person entitled to receive benefits under this chapter by virtue of section 1333 of title 43 and the vessel agree to defend and indemnify the other for cost of defense and loss or liability for damages arising out of or resulting from death or bodily injury to their employees. (March 4, 1927, ch 509, §5, 44 Stat. 1426; Oct. 27, 1972, P.L. 92-576, §18(a), 86 Stat. 1263; Sept. 28, 1984, P.L. 98-426, §§4(b), 5(a)(1), (b), 98 Stat. 1641.)

§906. Compensation.

(a) Time for commencement. No compensation shall be allowed for the first three days of the disability, except the benefits provided for in section 907 of this title: Provided, however, That in case the injury results in disability of more than fourteen days the compensation shall be allowed from the date of the disability.

(b) Maximum rate of compensation.

(1) Compensation for disability or death (other than compensation for death required by this chapter to be paid in a lump sum) shall not exceed an amount equal to 200 per centum of the applicable national average weekly wage, as determined by the Secretary under paragraph (3).

(2) Compensation for total disability shall not be less than 50 per centum of the applicable national average weekly wage determined by the Secretary under paragraph (3), except that if the employee's average weekly wages as computed under section 910 of this title are less than 50 per centum of such national average weekly wage, he shall receive his average weekly wages as compensation for total disability.

(3) As soon as practicable after June 30 of each year, and in any event prior to October 1 of such year, the Secretary shall determine the national average weekly wage for the three consecutive calendar quarters ending June 30. Such determination shall be the applicable national average weekly wage for the period beginning with October 1 of that year and ending with September 30 of the next year. The initial determination under this paragraph shall be made as soon as practicable after October 27, 1972.

(c) Applicability of determinations. Determinations under subsection (b)(3) of this section with respect to a period shall apply to employees or survivors currently receiving compensation for permanent total disability or death benefits during such period, as well as those newly awarded compensation during such period. (March 4, 1927, ch 509, §6, 44 Stat. 1426; June 24, 1948, ch 623, §1, 62 Stat. 602; July 26, 1956, ch 735, §1, 70 Stat. 654; July 14, 1961, P.L. 87-87, §1, 75 Stat. 203; Oct. 27, 1972, P.L. 92-576, §§4, 5(a), 86 Stat. 1252; Sept. 28, 1984, P.L. 98-426, §6, 98 Stat. 1641.)

§907. Medical services and supplies.

(a) General requirement. The employer shall furnish such medical, surgical, and other attendance or treatment, nurse and hospital service, medicine, crutches, and apparatus, for such period as the nature of the injury or the process of recovery may require.

(b) Physician selection; administrative supervision; change of physicians and hospitals. The employee shall have the right to choose an attending physician authorized by the Secretary to provide medical care under this chapter as hereinafter provided. If, due to the nature of the injury, the employee is unable to select his physician and the nature of the injury requires immediate medical treatment and care, the employer shall select a physician for him. The Secretary shall actively supervise the medical care rendered to injured employees, shall require periodic reports as to the medical care being rendered to injured employees, shall have authority to determine the necessity, character, and sufficiency of any medical aid furnished or to be furnished, and may, on his own initiative or at the request of the employer, order a change of physicians or hospitals when in his judgment such change is desirable or necessary in the interest of the employee or where the charges exceed those prevailing within the community for the same or similar services or exceed the provider's customary charges. Change of physicians at the request of employees shall be permitted in accordance with regulations of the Secretary.

(c) Physicians and health care providers not authorized to render medical care or provide medical services.

(1)(A) The Secretary shall annually prepare a list of physicians and health care providers in each compensation district who are not authorized to render medical care or provide medical services under this chapter. The names of physicians and health care providers contained on the list required under this subparagraph shall be made available to employees and employers in each compensation district through posting and in such other forms as the Secretary may prescribe.

(B) Physicians and health care providers shall be included on the list of those not authorized to provide medical care and medical services pursuant to subparagraph (A) when the Secretary determines under this section, in accordance with the procedures provided in subsection (j) of this section, that such physician or health care provider—

(i) has knowingly and willfully made, or caused to be made, any false statement or misrepresentation of a material fact for use in a claim for compensation or claim for reimbursement of medical expenses under this chapter;

(ii) has knowingly and willfully submitted, or caused to be submitted, a bill or request for payment under this chapter containing a charge which the Secretary finds to be substantially in excess of the charge for the service, appliance, or supply prevailing within the community or in excess of the provider's customary charges, unless the Secretary finds there is good cause for the bill or request containing the charge;

(iii) has knowingly and willfully furnished a service, appliance, or supply which is determined by the Secretary to be substantially in excess of the need of the recipient thereof or to be of a quality which substantially fails to meet professionally recognized standards;

(iv) has been convicted under any criminal statute (without regard to pending appeal thereof) for fraudulent activities in connection with any Federal or State program for which payments are made to physicians or providers of similar services, appliances, or supplies; or

(v) has otherwise been excluded from participation in such program.

(C) Medical services provided by physicians or health care providers who are named on the list published by the Secretary pursuant to subparagraph (A) of this section shall not be reimbursable under this chapter; except that the Secretary shall direct the reimbursement of medical claims for services rendered by such physicians or health care providers in cases where the services were rendered in an emergency.

(D) A determination under subparagraph (B) shall remain in effect for a period of not less than three years and until the Secretary finds and gives notice to the public that there is reasonable assurance that the basis for the determination will not reoccur.

(E) A provider of a service, appliance, or supply shall provide to the Secretary such information and certification as the Secretary may require to assure that this subsection is enforced.

(2) Whenever the employer or carrier acquires knowledge of the employee's injury, through written notice or otherwise as prescribed by the chapter, the employer or carrier shall forthwith authorize medical treatment and care from a physician selected by an employee pursuant to subsection (b) of this section. An employee may not select a physician who is on the list required by paragraph (1) of this subsection. An employee may not change physicians after his initial choice unless the employer, carrier, or deputy commissioner has given prior consent for such change. Such consent shall be given in cases where an employee's initial choice was not of a specialist whose services are necessary for and appropriate to the proper care and treatment of the compensable injury or disease. In all other cases, consent may be given upon a showing of good cause for change.

(d) Request of treatment or services prerequisite to recovery of expenses; formal report of injury and treatment; suspension of compensation for refusal of treatment or examination; justification.

(1) An employee shall not be entitled to recover any amount expended by him for medical or other treatment or services unless—

(A) the employer shall have refused or neglected a request to furnish such services and the employee has complied with subsections (b) and (c) of this section and the applicable regulations; or

(B) the nature of the injury required such treatment and services and the employer or his superintendent or foreman having knowledge of such injury shall have neglected to provide or authorize same.

(2) No claim for medical or surgical treatment shall be valid and enforceable against such employer unless, within ten days following the first treatment, the physician giving such treatment furnishes to the employer and the deputy commissioner a report of such injury or treatment, on a form prescribed by the Secretary. The Secretary may excuse the failure to furnish such report within the ten-day period whenever he finds it to be in the interest of justice to do so.

(3) The Secretary may, upon application by a party in interest, make an award for the reasonable value of such medical or surgical treatment so obtained by the employee.

(4) If at any time the employee unreasonably refuses to submit to medical or surgical treatment, or to an examination by a physician selected by the employer, the Secretary or administrative law judge may, by order, suspend the payment of further compensation during such time as such refusal continues, and no compensation shall be paid at any time during the period of such suspension, unless the circumstances justified the refusal.

(e) Physical examination; medical questions; report of physical impairment; review or reexamination; costs. In the event that medical questions are raised in any case, the Secretary shall have the power to cause the employee to be examined by a physician employed or selected by the Secretary and to obtain from such physician a report containing his estimate of the employee's physical impairment and such other information as may be appropriate. Any party who is dissatisfied with such report may request a review or reexamination of the employee by one or more different physicians employed or selected by the Secretary. The Secretary shall order such review or reexamination unless he finds that it is clearly unwarranted. Such review or reexamination shall be completed within two weeks from the date ordered unless the Secretary finds that because of extraordinary circumstances a longer period is required. The Secretary shall have the power in his discretion to charge the cost of examination or review under this subsection to the employer, if he is a self-insurer, or to the insurance company which is carrying the risk, in appropriate cases, or to the special fund in section 944 of this title.

(f) Place of examination; exclusion of physicians other than examining physician of Secretary; good cause for conclusions of other physicians respecting impairment; examination by employer's physician; suspension of proceedings and compensation for refusal of examination. An employee shall submit to a physical examination under subsection (e) of this section at such place as the Secretary may require. The place, or places, shall be designated by the Secretary and shall be reasonably convenient for the employee. No physician selected by the employer, carrier, or employee shall be present at or participate in any manner in such examination, nor shall conclusions of such physicians as to the nature or extent of impairment or the cause of impairment be available to the examining physician unless otherwise ordered, for good cause, by the Secretary. Such employer or carrier shall, upon request, be entitled to have the employee examined immediately thereafter and upon the same premises by a qualified physician or physicians in the presence of such physician as the employee may select, if any. Proceedings shall be suspended and no compensation shall be payable for any period during which the employee may refuse to submit to examination.

(g) Fees and charges for examinations, treatment, or service; limitation; regulations. All fees and other charges for medical examinations, treatment, or service shall be limited to such charges as prevail in the community for such treatment, and shall be subject to regulation by the Secretary. The Secretary shall issue regulations limiting the nature and extent of medical expenses chargeable against the employer without authorization by the employer or the Secretary.

(h) Third party liability. The liability of an employer for medical treatment as herein provided shall not be affected by the fact that his employee was injured through the fault or negligence of a third party not in the same employ, or that suit has been brought against such third party. The employer shall, however, have a cause of action against such third party to recover any amounts paid by him for such medical treatment in like manner as provided in section 933(b) of this title.

(i) Physicians' ineligibility for subsection (e) physical examinations and reviews because of workmen's compensation claim employment or fee acceptance or participation. Unless the parties to the claim agree, the Secretary shall not employ or select any physician for the purpose of making examinations or reviews under subsection (e) of this section who, during such employment, or during the period of two years prior to such employment, has been employed by, or accepted or participated in any fee relating to a workmen's compensation claim from any insurance carrier or any self-insurer.

(j) Procedure; judicial review.

(1) The Secretary shall have the authority to make rules and regulations and to establish procedures, not inconsistent with the provisions of this chapter, which are necessary or appropriate to carry out the provisions of subsection (c) of this section, including the nature and extent of the proof and evidence necessary for actions under this section and the methods of taking and furnishing such proof and evidence.

(2) Any decision to take action with respect to a physician or health care provider under this section shall be based on specific findings of fact by the Secretary. The Secretary shall provide notice of these findings and an opportunity for a hearing pursuant to section 556 of title 5 for a provider who would be affected by a decision under this section. A request for a hearing must be filed with the Secretary within thirty days after notice of the findings is

received by the provider making such request. If a hearing is held, the Secretary shall, on the basis of evidence adduced at the hearing, affirm, modify, or reverse the findings of fact and proposed action under this section.

(3) For the purpose of any hearing, investigation, or other proceeding authorized or directed under this section, the provisions of section [sections] 49 and 50 of title 15 (relating to the attendance of witnesses and the production of books, papers, and documents) shall apply to the jurisdiction, powers, and duties of the Secretary or any officer designated by him.

(4) Any physician or health care provider, after any final decision of the Secretary made after a hearing to which he was a party, irrespective of the amount in controversy, may obtain a review of such decision by a civil action commenced within sixty days after the mailing to him of notice of such decision, but the pendency of such review shall not operate as a stay upon the effect of such decision. Such action shall be brought in the court of appeals of the United States for the judicial circuit in which the plaintiff resides or has his principal place of business, or the Court of Appeals for the District of Columbia. As part of his answer, the Secretary shall file a certified copy of the transcript of the record of the hearing, including all evidence submitted in connection therewith. The findings of fact of the Secretary, if based on substantial evidence in the record as a whole, shall be conclusive.

(k) Refusal of treatment on religious grounds.

(1) Nothing in this chapter prevents an employee whose injury or disability has been established under this chapter from relying in good faith on treatment by prayer or spiritual means alone, in accordance with the tenets and practice of a recognized church or religious denomination, by an accredited practitioner of such recognized church or religious denomination, and on nursing services rendered in accordance with such tenets and practice, without suffering loss or diminution of the compensation or benefits under this chapter. Nothing in this subsection shall be construed to except an employee from all physical examinations required by this chapter.

(2) If an employee refuses to submit to medical or surgical services solely because, in adherence to the tenets and practice of a recognized church or religious denomination, the employee relies upon prayer or spiritual means alone for healing, such employee shall not be considered to have unreasonably refused medical or surgical treatment under subsection (d) of this section. (March 4, 1927, ch 509, §7, 44 Stat. 1427; May 26, 1934, ch 354, §1, 48 Stat. 806; June 25, 1938, ch 685, §§2, 3, 52 Stat. 1165; Sept. 13, 1960, P.L. 86-757, 74 Stat. 900; Oct. 27, 1972, P.L. 92-576 §6, 86 Stat. 1254; Sept. 28, 1984, P.L. 98-426, §7, 98 Stat. 1642.)

§908. Compensation for disability.

Compensation for disability shall be paid to the employee as follows:

(a) Permanent total disability: In case of total disability adjudged to be permanent 66⅔ per centum of the average weekly wages shall be paid to the employee during the continuance of such total disability. Loss of both hands, or both arms, or both feet, or both legs, or both eyes, or of any two thereof shall, in the absence of conclusive proof to the contrary, constitute permanent total disability. In all other cases permanent total disability shall be determined in accordance with the facts.

(b) Temporary total disability: In case of disability total in character but temporary in quality 66⅔ per centum of the average weekly wages shall be paid to the employee during the continuance thereof.

(c) Permanent partial disability: In case of disability partial in character but permanent in quality the compensation shall be 66⅔ per centum of the average weekly wages, which shall be in addition to compensation for temporary total disability or temporary partial disability paid in accordance with subsection (b) or subsection (e) of this section, respectively, and shall be paid to the employee, as follows:

(1) Arm lost, three hundred and twelve weeks' compensation.

(2) Leg lost, two hundred and eighty-eight weeks' compensation.

(3) Hand lost, two hundred and forty-four weeks' compensation.

(4) Foot lost, two hundred and five weeks' compensation.

(5) Eye lost, one hundred and sixty weeks' compensation.

(6) Thumb lost, seventy-five weeks' compensation.

(7) First finger lost, forty-six weeks' compensation.

(8) Great toe lost, thirty-eight weeks' compensation.

(9) Second finger lost, thirty weeks' compensation.

(10) Third finger lost, twenty-five weeks' compensation.

(11) Toe other than great toe lost, sixteen weeks' compensation.

(12) Fourth finger lost, fifteen weeks' compensation.

(13) Loss of hearing:

(A) Compensation for loss of hearing in one ear, fifty-two weeks.

(B) Compensation for loss of hearing in both ears, two-hundred weeks.

(C) An audiogram shall be presumptive evidence of the amount of hearing loss sustained as of the date thereof, only if (i) such audiogram was administered by a licensed or certified audiologist or a physician who is certified in otolaryngology, (ii) such audiogram, with the report thereon, was provided to the employee at the time it was administered, and (iii) no contrary audiogram made at that time is produced.

(D) The time for filing a notice of injury, under section 912 of this title, or a claim for compensation, under section 913 of this title, shall not begin to run in connection with any claim for loss of hearing under this section, until the employee has received an audiogram, with the accompanying report thereon, which indicates that the employee has suffered a loss of hearing.

(E) Determinations of loss of hearing shall be made in accordance with the guides for the evaluation of permanent impairment as promulgated and modified from time to time by the American Medical Association.

(14) Phalanges: Compensation for loss of more than one phalange of a digit shall be the same as for loss of the entire digit. Compensation for loss of the first phalange

shall be one-half of the compensation for loss of the entire digit.

(15) Amputated arm or leg: Compensation for an arm or a leg, if amputated at or above the elbow or the knee, shall be the same as for a loss of the arm or leg; but, if amputated between the elbow and the wrist or the knee and the ankle, shall be the same as for loss of a hand or foot.

(16) Binocular vision or per centum of vision: Compensation for loss of binocular vision or for 80 per centum or more of the vision of an eye shall be the same as for loss of the eye.

(17) Two or more digits: Compensation for loss of two or more digits, or one or more phalanges of two or more digits, of a hand or foot may be proportioned to the loss of use of the hand or foot occasioned thereby, but shall not exceed the compensation for loss of a hand or foot.

(18) Total loss of use: Compensation for permanent total loss of use of a member shall be the same as for loss of the member.

(19) Partial loss or partial loss of use: Compensation for permanent partial loss or loss of use of a member may be for proportionate loss or loss of use of the member.

(20) Disfigurement: Proper and equitable compensation not to exceed $7,500 shall be awarded for serious disfigurement of the face, head, or neck or of other normally exposed areas likely to handicap the employee in securing or maintaining employment.

(21) Other cases: In all other cases in the class of disability, the compensation shall be 66⅔ per centum of the difference between the average weekly wages of the employee and the employee's wage-earning capacity thereafter in the same employment or otherwise, payable during the continuance of partial disability.

(22) In any case in which there shall be a loss of, or loss of use of, more than one member or parts of more than one member set forth in paragraphs (1) to (19) of this subsection, not amounting to permanent total disability, the award of compensation shall be for the loss of, or loss of use of, each such member or part thereof, which awards shall run consecutively, except that where the injury affects only two or more digits of the same hand or foot, paragraph (17) of this subsection shall apply.

(23) Notwithstanding paragraphs (1) through (22), with respect to a claim for permanent partial disability for which the average weekly wages are determined under section 910(d)(2) of this title, the compensation shall be 66⅔ per centum of such average weekly wages multiplied by the percentage of permanent impairment, as determined under the guides referred to in section 902(10) of this title, payable during the continuance of such impairment.

(d)(1) If an employee who is receiving compensation for permanent partial disability pursuant to subsection (c)(1)–(20) of this section dies from causes other than the injury, the total amount of the award unpaid at the time of death shall be payable to or for the benefit of his survivors, as follows:

(A) if the employee is survived only by a widow or widower, such unpaid amount of the award shall be payable to such widow or widower,

(B) if the employee is survived only by a child or children, such unpaid amount of the award shall be paid to such child or children in equal shares,

(C) if the employee is survived by a widow or widower and a child or children, such unpaid amount of the award shall be payable to such survivors in equal shares,

(D) if there be no widow or widower and no surviving child or children, such unpaid amount of the award shall be paid to the survivors specified in section 909(d) (other than a wife, husband, or child); and the amount to be paid each such survivor shall be determined by multiplying such unpaid amount of the award by the appropriate percentage specified in section 909(d) of this title, but if the aggregate amount to which all such survivors are entitled, as so determined, is less than such unpaid amount of the award, the excess amount shall be divided among such survivors pro rata according to the amount otherwise payable to each under this subparagraph.

(2) Notwithstanding any other limitation in section 909 of this title, the total amount of any award for permanent partial disability pursuant to subsection (c)(1)–(20) of this section unpaid at time of death shall be payable in full in the appropriate distribution.

(3) An award for disability may be made after the death of the injured employee. Except where compensation is payable under subsection (c)(21) of this section if there be no survivors as prescribed in this section, then the compensation payable under this subsection shall be paid to the special fund established under section 944(a) of this title.

(e) Temporary partial disability: In case of temporary partial disability resulting in decrease of earning capacity the compensation shall be two-thirds of the difference between the injured employee's average weekly wages before the injury and his wage-earning capacity after the injury in the same or another employment, to be paid during the continuance of such disability, but shall not be paid for a period exceeding five years.

(f) Injury increasing disability:

(1) In any case in which an employee having an existing permanent partial disability suffers injury, the employer shall provide compensation for such disability as is found to be attributable to that injury based upon the average weekly wages of the employee at the time of the injury. If following an injury falling within the provisions of subsection (c)(1)–(20) of this section, the employee is totally and permanently disabled, and the disability is found not to be due solely to that injury, the employer shall provide compensation for the applicable prescribed period of weeks provided for in that section for the subsequent injury, or for one hundred and four weeks, whichever is the greater, except that, in the case of an injury falling within the provisions of subsection (c)(13) of this section, the employer shall provide compensation for the lesser of such periods. In all other cases of total permanent disability or of death, found not to be due solely to that injury, of an employee having an existing permanent partial disability, the employer shall provide in addition to compensation under subsections (b) and (e) of this section, compensation payments or death benefits for one hundred and four weeks only. If following an injury falling within the provisions of subsection (c)(1)–(20) of this section, the employee has a permanent partial disability and the disability is found not to be due solely to that injury, and such disability is materially and substantially greater than that which would have resulted from the subsequent injury alone, the em-

U.S.C.

ployer shall provide compensation for the applicable period of weeks provided for in that section for the subsequent injury, or for one hundred and four weeks, whichever is the greater, except that, in the case of an injury falling within the provisions of subsection (c)(13) of this section, the employer shall provide compensation for the lesser of such periods.

In all other cases in which the employee has a permanent partial disability, found not to be due solely to that injury, and such disability is materially and substantially greater than that which would have resulted from the subsequent injury alone, the employer shall provide in addition to compensation under subsections (b) and (e) of this section, compensation for one hundred and four weeks only.

(2)(A) After cessation of the payments for the period of weeks provided for herein, the employee or his survivor entitled to benefits shall be paid the remainder of the compensation that would be due out of the special fund established in section 944 of this title, except that the special fund shall not assume responsibility with respect to such benefits (and such payments shall not be subject to cessation) in the case of any employer who fails to comply with section 932(a) of this title [33 U.S.C. § 932(a)].

(B) After cessation of payments for the period of weeks provided for in this subsection, the employer or carrier responsible for payment of compensation shall remain a party to the claim, retain access to all records relating to the claim, and in all other respects retain all rights granted under this chapter prior to cessation of such payments.

(3) Any request, filed after September 28, 1984, for apportionment of liability to the special fund established under section 944 of this title for the payment of compensation benefits, and a statement of the grounds therefore, shall be presented to the deputy commissioner prior to the consideration of the claim by the deputy commissioner. Failure to present such request prior to such consideration shall be an absolute defense to the special fund's liability for the payment of any benefits in connection with such claim, unless the employer could not have reasonably anticipated the liability of the special fund prior to the issuance of a compensation order.

(g) Maintenance for employees undergoing vocational rehabilitation: An employee who as a result of injury is or may be expected to be totally or partially incapacitated for a remunerative occupation and who, under the direction of the Secretary as provided by section 939(c) of this title, is being rendered fit to engage in a remunerative occupation, shall receive additional compensation necessary for his maintenance, but such additional compensation shall not exceed $25 a week. The expense shall be paid out of the special fund established in section 944 of this title.

(h) The wage-earning capacity of an injured employee in cases of partial disability under subsection (c)(21) of this section or under subsection (e) of this section shall be determined by his actual earnings if such actual earnings fairly and reasonably represent his wage-earning capacity: Provided, however, That if the employee has no actual earnings or his actual earnings do not fairly and reasonably represent his wage-earning capacity, the deputy commissioner may, in the interest of justice, fix such wage-earning capacity as shall be reasonable, having due regard to the nature of his injury, the degree of physical impairment, his usual employment, and any other factors or circumstances in the case which may affect his capacity to earn wages in his disabled condition, including the effect of disability as it may naturally extend into the future.

(i)(1) Whenever the parties to any claim for compensation under this chapter, including survivors benefits, agree to a settlement, the deputy commissioner or administrative law judge shall approve the settlement within thirty days unless it is found to be inadequate or procured by duress. Such settlement may include future medical benefits if the parties so agree. No liability of any employer, carrier, or both for medical, disability, or death benefits shall be discharged unless the application for settlement is approved by the deputy commissioner or administrative law judge. If the parties to the settlement are represented by counsel, then agreements shall be deemed approved unless specifically disapproved within thirty days after submission for approval.

(2) If the deputy commissioner disapproves an application for settlement under paragraph (1), the deputy commissioner shall issue a written statement within thirty days containing the reasons for disapproval. Any party to the settlement may request a hearing before an administrative law judge in the manner prescribed by this chapter. Following such hearing, the administrative law judge shall enter an order approving or rejecting the settlement.

(3) A settlement approved under this section shall discharge the liability of the employer or carrier, or both. Settlements may be agreed upon at any stage of the proceeding including after entry of a final compensation order.

(4) The special fund shall not be liable for reimbursement of any sums paid or payable to an employee or any beneficiary under such settlement, or otherwise voluntarily paid prior to such settlement by the employer or carrier, or both.

(j)(1) The employer may inform a disabled employee of his obligation to report to the employer not less than semiannually any earnings from employment or self-employment, on such forms as the Secretary shall specify in regulations.

(2) An employee who—

(A) fails to report the employee's earnings under paragraph (1) when requested, or

(B) knowingly and willfully omits or understates any part of such earnings, and who is determined by the deputy commissioner to have violated clause (A) or (B) of this paragraph, forfeits his right to compensation with respect to any period during which the employee was required to file such report.

(3) Compensation forfeited under this subsection, if already paid, shall be recovered by a deduction from the compensation payable to the employee in any amount and on such schedule as determined by the deputy commissioner. (March 4, 1927, ch 509, §8, 44 Stat. 1427; May 26, 1934, ch 354, §§2, 3, 48 Stat. 806; June 25, 1938, ch 685, §§4, 5, 52 Stat. 1165; June 24, 1948, ch 623, §2, 62 Stat. 602; July 26, 1956, ch 735, §§2, 3, 70 Stat. 655; Oct. 27, 1972, P.L. 92-576, §§5(c), 7, 9, 20(a), 86 Stat. 1253, 1255, 1257, 1264; Sept. 28, 1984, P.L. 98-426, §§8, 27(a)(2), 98 Stat. 1644, 1654.)

§909. Compensation for death.

If the injury causes death, the compensation therefore shall be known as a death benefit and shall be payable in the amount and to or for the benefit of the persons following:

(a) Reasonable funeral expenses not exceeding $3,000.

(b) If there be a widow or widower and no child of the deceased, to such widow or widower 50 per centum of the average wages of the deceased, during widowhood, or dependent widowerhood, with two years' compensation in one sum upon remarriage; and if there be a surviving child or children of the deceased, the additional amount of 16⅔ per centum of such wages for each such child; in case of the death or remarriage of such widow or widower, if there be one surviving child of the deceased employee, such child shall have his compensation increased to 50 per centum of such wages, and if there be more than one surviving child of the deceased employee, to such children, in equal parts, 50 per centum of such wages increased by 16⅔ per centum of such wages for each child in excess of one: Provided, That the total amount payable shall in no case exceed 66⅔ per centum of such wages. The deputy commissioner having jurisdiction over the claim may, in his discretion, require the appointment of a guardian for the purpose of receiving the compensation of a minor child. In the absence of such a requirement the appointment of a guardian for such purposes shall not be necessary.

(c) If there be one surviving child of the deceased, but no widow or widower, then for the support of such child 50 per centum of the wages of the deceased; and if there be more than one surviving child of the deceased, but no widow or dependent husband, then for the support of such children, in equal parts 50 per centum of such wages increased by 16⅔ per centum of such wages for each child in excess of one: Provided, That the total amount payable shall in no case exceed 66⅔ per centum of such wages.

(d) If there be no surviving wife or husband or child, or if the amount payable to a surviving wife or husband and to children shall be less in the aggregate than 66⅔ per centum of the average wages of the deceased; then for the support of grandchildren or brothers and sisters, if dependent upon the deceased at the time of the injury, and any other persons who satisfy the definition of the term "dependent" in section 152 of title 26, but are not otherwise eligible under this section, 20 per centum of such wages for the support of each such person during such dependency and for the support of each parent, or grandparent, of the deceased if dependent upon him at the time of the injury, 25 per centum of such wages during such dependency. But in no case shall the aggregate amount payable under this subsection exceed the difference between 66⅔ per centum of such wages and the amount payable as hereinbefore provided to widow or widower and for the support of surviving child or children.

(e) In computing death benefits, the average weekly wages of the deceased shall not be less than the national average weekly wage as prescribed in section 906(b) of this title, but—

(1) the total weekly benefits shall not exceed the lesser of the average weekly wages of the deceased or the benefit which the deceased employee would have been eligible to receive under section 906(b)(1) of this title; and

(2) in the case of a claim based on death due to an occupational disease for which the time of injury (as determined under section 910(i) of this title) occurs after the employee has retired, the total weekly benefits shall not exceed one fifty-second part of the employee's average annual earnings during the 52-week period preceding retirement.

(f) All questions of dependency shall be determined as of the time of the injury.

(g) Aliens: Compensation under this chapter to aliens not residents (or about to become nonresidents) of the United States or Canada shall be the same in amount as provided for residents, except that dependents in any foreign country shall be limited to surviving wife and child or children, or if there be no surviving wife or child or children, to surviving father or mother whom the employee has supported, either wholly or in part, for the period of one year prior to the date of the injury, and except that the Secretary may, at his option or upon the application of the insurance carrier shall, commute all future installments of compensation to be paid to such aliens by paying or causing to be paid to them one-half of the commuted amount of such future installments of compensation as determined by the Secretary. (March 4, 1927, ch 509, §9, 44 Stat. 1429; June 25, 1938, ch 685, §6, 52 Stat. 1166; June 24, 1948, ch 623, §3, 62 Stat. 602; July 26, 1956, ch 735, §4, 70 Stat. 655; July 14, 1961, P.L. 87-87, §2, 75 Stat. 203; Oct. 27, 1972, P.L. 92-576, §5(d), 10, 20(c)(2), 86 Stat. 1253, 1257, 1265; Sept. 28, 1984, P.L. 98-426, §9, 98 Stat. 1647.)

§910. Determination of pay.

Except as otherwise provided in this chapter, the average weekly wage of the injured employee at the time of the injury shall be taken as the basis upon which to compute compensation and shall be determined as follows:

(a) If the injured employee shall have worked in the employment in which he was working at the time of the injury, whether for the same or another employer, during substantially the whole of the year immediately preceding his injury, his average annual earnings shall consist of three hundred times the average daily wage or salary for a six-day worker and two hundred and sixty times the average daily wage or salary for a five-day worker, which he shall have earned in such employment during the days when so employed.

(b) If the injured employee shall not have worked in such employment during substantially the whole of such year, his average annual earnings, if a six-day worker, shall consist of three hundred times the average daily wage or salary, and, if a five-day worker, two hundred and sixty times the average daily wage or salary, which an employee of the same class working substantially the whole of such immediately preceding year in the same or in similar employment in the same or a neighboring place shall have earned in such employment during the days when so employed.

(c) If either of the foregoing methods of arriving at the average annual earnings of the injured employee cannot reasonably and fairly be applied, such average annual earnings shall be such sum as, having regard to the previous earnings of the injured employee in the employment in which he was working at the time of the injury, and of other employees of the same or most similar class working in the same or most similar employment in the same or neighboring locality, or other employment of such employee, including the reasonable value of the services of the employee if engaged in self-employment, shall reasonably represent the annual earning capacity of the injured employee.

(d)(1) The average weekly wages of an employee shall be one fifty-second part of his average annual earnings.

(2) Notwithstanding paragraph (1), with respect to any claim based on a death or disability due to an occupational disease for which the time of injury (as determined under subsection (i) of this section) occurs—

(A) within the first year after the employee has retired, the average weekly wages shall be one fifty-second part of his average annual earnings during the 52-week period preceding retirement; or

(B) more than one year after the employee has retired, the average weekly wage shall be deemed to be the national average weekly wage (as determined by the Secretary pursuant to section 906(b) of this title) applicable at the time of the injury.

(e) If it be established that the injured employee was a minor when injured, and that under normal conditions his wages should be expected to increase during the period of disability the fact may be considered in arriving at his average weekly wages.

(f) Effective October 1 of each year, the compensation or death benefits payable for permanent total disability or death arising out of injuries subject to this chapter shall be increased by the lesser of—

(1) a percentage equal to the percentage (if any) by which the applicable national weekly wage for the period beginning on such October 1, as determined under section 906(b) of this title, exceeds the applicable national average weekly wage, as so determined, for the period beginning with the preceding October 1; or

(2) 5 per centum.

(g) The weekly compensation after adjustment under subsection (f) of this section shall be fixed at the nearest dollar. No adjustment of less than $1 shall be made, but in no event shall compensation or death benefits be reduced.

(h)(1) Not later than ninety days after October 27, 1972, the compensation to which an employee or his survivor is entitled due to total permanent disability or death which commenced or occurred prior to October 27, 1972, shall be adjusted. The amount of such adjustment shall be determined in accordance with regulations of the Secretary by designating as the employee's average weekly wage the applicable national average weekly wage determined under section 906(b) of this title and (A) computing the compensation to which such employee or survivor would be entitled if the disabling injury or death had occurred on the day following October 27, 1972, and (B) subtracting therefrom the compensation to which such employee or survivor was entitled on October 27, 1972; except that no such employee or survivor shall receive total compensation amounting to less than that to which he was entitled on October 27, 1972. Notwithstanding the foregoing sentence, where such an employee or his survivor was awarded compensation as the result of death or permanent total disability at less than the maximum rate that was provided in this chapter at the time of the injury which resulted in the death or disability, then his average weekly wage shall be determined by increasing his average weekly wage at the time of such injury by the percentage which the applicable national average weekly wage has increased between the year in which the injury occurred and the first day of the first month following October 27, 1972. Where such injury occurred prior to 1947, the Secretary shall determine, on the basis of such economic data as he deems relevant, the amount by which the employee's average weekly wage shall be increased for the pre-1947 period.

(2) Fifty per centum of any additional compensation or death benefit paid as a result of the adjustment required by paragraphs (1) and (3) of this subsection shall be paid out of the special fund established under section 944 of this title, and 50 per centum shall be paid from appropriations.

(3) For the purposes of subsections (f) and (g) of this section an injury which resulted in permanent total disability or death which occurred prior to October 27, 1972, shall be considered to have occurred on the day following such date.

(i) For purposes of this section with respect to a claim for compensation for death or disability due to an occupational disease which does not immediately result in death or disability, the time of injury shall be deemed to be the date on which the employee or claimant becomes aware, or in the exercise of reasonable diligence or by reason of medical advice should have been aware, of the relationship between the employment, the disease, and the death or disability. (March 4, 1927, ch 509, §10, 44 Stat. 1431; June 24, 1948, ch 623, §4, 62 Stat. 603; Oct. 27, 1972, P.L. 92-576, §11, 86 Stat. 1258; Sept. 28, 1984, P.L. 98-426, §10, 98 Stat. 1647.)

§911. Guardian for minor or incompetent.

The deputy commissioner may require the appointment by a court of competent jurisdiction, for any person who is mentally incompetent or a minor, of a guardian or other representative to receive compensation payable to such person under this chapter and to exercise the powers granted to or to perform the duties required of such person under this chapter. (March 4, 1927, ch 509, §11, 44 Stat. 1431.)

§912. Notice of injury or death.

(a) Time limitation. Notice of an injury or death in respect of which compensation is payable under this chapter shall be given within thirty days after the date of such injury or death, or thirty days after the employee or beneficiary is aware, or in the exercise of reasonable diligence or by reason of medical advice should have been aware, of a relationship between the injury or death and the employment, except that in the case of an occupational disease which does not immediately result in a disability or death, such notice shall be given within one year after the employee or claimant becomes aware, or in the exercise of reasonable diligence or by reason of medical advice should have been aware, of the relationship between the employment, the disease, and the death or disability. Notice shall be given (1) to the deputy commissioner in the compensation district in which the injury or death occurred, and (2) to the employer.

(b) Form and content. Such notice shall be in writing, shall contain the name and address of the employee and a statement of the time, place, nature, and cause of the injury or death, and shall be signed by the employee or by some person on his behalf, or in case of death, by any person claiming to be entitled to compensation for such death or by a person on his behalf.

(c) Delivery requirements. Notice shall be given to the deputy commissioner by delivering it to him or sending it by mail addressed to his office, and to the employer by delivering it to him or by sending it by mail addressed to him at his last known place of business. If the employer is a partnership, such notice may be given to any partner, or if a corporation, such notice may be given to any agent or officer thereof upon whom legal process may be served or who is in charge of the business in the place where the injury occurred. Each employer shall designate those agents or other responsible officials to receive such notice, except that the employer shall designate as its representatives individuals among first line supervisors, local plant management, and personnel office officials. Such designations shall be made in accordance with regulations prescribed by the Secretary and the employer shall notify his employees and the Secretary of such designation in a manner prescribed by the Secretary in regulations.

(d) Failure to give notice. Failure to give such notice shall not bar any claim under this chapter (1) if the employer (or his agent or agents or other responsible official or officials designated by the employer pursuant to subsection (c) of this section) or the carrier had knowledge of the injury or death, (2) the deputy commissioner determines that the employer or carrier has not been prejudiced by failure to give such notice, or (3) if the deputy commissioner excuses such failure on the ground that (i) notice, while not given to a responsible official designated by the employer pursuant to subsection (c) of this section, was given to an official of the employer or the employer's insurance carrier, and that the employer or carrier was not prejudiced due to the failure to provide notice to a responsible official designated by the employer pursuant to subsection (c) of this section, or (ii) for some satisfactory reason such notice could not be given; nor unless objection to such failure is raised before the deputy commissioner at the first hearing of a claim for compensation in respect of such injury or death. (March 4, 1927, ch 509, §12, 44 Stat. 1431; Oct. 27, 1972, P.L. 92-576, §12(a), 86 Stat. 1259; Sept. 28, 1984, P.L. 98-426, §11, 98 Stat. 1648.)

§913. Filing of claims.

(a) Time to file. Except as otherwise provided in this section, the right to compensation for disability or death under this chapter shall be barred unless a claim therefore is filed within one year after the injury or death. If payment of compensation has been made without an award on account of such injury or death, a claim may be filed within one year after the date of the last payment. Such claim shall be filed with the deputy commissioner in the compensation district in which such injury or death occurred. The time for filing a claim shall not begin to run until the employee or beneficiary is aware, or by the exercise of reasonable diligence should have been aware, of the relationship between the injury or death and the employment.

(b) Failure to file.

(1) Notwithstanding the provisions of subsection (a) of this section failure to file a claim within the period prescribed in such subsection shall not be a bar to such right unless objection to such failure is made at the first hearing of such claim in which all parties in interest are given reasonable notice and opportunity to be heard.

(2) Notwithstanding the provisions of subsection (a) of this section, a claim for compensation for death or disability due to an occupational disease which does not immediately result in such death or disability shall be timely if filed within two years after the employee or claimant becomes aware, or in the exercise of reasonable diligence or by reason of medical advice should have been aware, of the relationship between the employment, the disease, and the death or disability, or within one year of the date of the last payment of compensation, whichever is later.

(c) Effect on incompetents and minors. If a person who is entitled to compensation under this chapter is mentally incompetent or a minor, the provisions of subsection (a) of this section shall not be applicable so long as such person has no guardian or other authorized representative, but shall be applicable in the case of a person who is mentally incompetent or a minor from the date of appointment of such guardian or other representative, or in the case of a minor, if no guardian is appointed before he becomes of age, from the date he becomes of age.

(d) Tolling provision. Where recovery is denied to any person, in a suit brought at law or in admiralty to recover damages in respect of injury or death, on the ground that such person was an employee and that the defendant was an employer within the meaning of this chapter and that such employer had secured compensation to such employee under this chapter, the limitation of time prescribed in subsection (a) of this section shall begin to run only from the date of termination of such suit. (March 4, 1927, ch 509, §13, 44 Stat. 1432; Oct. 27, 1972, P.L. 92-576, §12(b), 86 Stat. 1259; Sept. 28, 1984, P.L. 98-426, §12, 98 Stat. 1649.)

§914. Payment of compensation.

(a) Manner of payment. Compensation under this chapter shall be paid periodically, promptly, and directly to the person entitled thereto, without an award, except where liability to pay compensation is controverted by the employer.

(b) Period of installment payments. The first installment of compensation shall become due on the fourteenth day after the employer has been notified pursuant to section 912 of this title, or the employer has knowledge of the injury or death, on which date all compensation then due shall be paid. Thereafter compensation shall be paid in installments, semimonthly, except where the deputy commissioner determines that payment in installments should be made monthly or at some other period.

(c) Notification of commencement or suspension of payment. Upon making the first payment, and upon suspension of payment for any cause, the employer shall immediately notify the deputy commissioner, in accordance with a form prescribed by the Secretary, that payment of compensation has begun or has been suspended, as the case may be.

(d) Right to compensation controverted. If the employer controverts the right to compensation he shall file with the deputy commissioner on or before the fourteenth day after he has knowledge of the alleged injury or death, a notice, in accordance with a form prescribed by the Secretary stating that the right to compensation is controverted, the name of the claimant, the name of the employer, the date of the alleged injury or death, and the grounds upon which the right to compensation is controverted.

(e) Additional compensation for overdue installment payments payable without award. If any installment of compensation payable without an award is not paid within fourteen days after it becomes due, as provided in subsection (b) of this section, there shall be added to such unpaid installment an amount equal to 10 per centum thereof, which shall be paid at the same time as, but in addition to, such installment, unless notice is filed under subsection (d) of this section, or unless such nonpayment is excused by the deputy commissioner after a showing by the employer that owing to conditions over which he had no control such installment could not be paid within the period prescribed for the payment.

(f) Additional compensation for overdue installment payments payable under terms of award. If any compensation, payable under the terms of an award, is not paid within ten days after it becomes due, there shall be added to such unpaid compensation an amount equal to 20 per centum thereof, which shall be paid at the same time as, but in addition to, such compensation, unless review of the compensation order making such award is had as provided in section 921 of this title and an order staying payment has been issued by the Board or court.

(g) Notice of payment; penalty. Within sixteen days after final payment of compensation has been made, the employer shall send to the deputy commissioner a notice, in accordance with a form prescribed by the Secretary, stating that such final payment has been made, the total amount of compensation paid, the name of the employee and of any other person to whom compensation has been paid, the date of the injury or death, and the date to which compensation has been paid. If the employer fails to so notify the deputy commissioner within such time the Secretary shall assess against such employer a civil penalty in the amount of $100.

(h) Investigations, examinations, and hearings for controverted, stopped, or suspended payments. The deputy commissioner (1) may upon his own initiative at any time in a case in which payments are being made without an award, and (2) shall in any case where right to compensation is controverted, or where payments of compensation have been stopped or suspended, upon receipt of notice from any person entitled to compensation, or from the employer, that the right to compensation is controverted, or that payments of compensation have been stopped or suspended, make such investigations, cause such medical examinations to be made, or hold such hearings, and take such further action as he considers will properly protect the rights of all parties.

(i) Deposit by employer. Whenever the deputy commissioner deems it advisable he may require any employer to make a deposit with the Treasurer of the United States to secure the prompt and convenient payment of such compensation, and payments therefrom upon any awards shall be made upon order of the deputy commissioner.

(j) Reimbursement for advance payments. If the employer has made advance payments of compensation, he shall be entitled to be reimbursed out of any unpaid installment or installments of compensation due.

(k) Receipt for payment. An injured employee, or in case of death his dependents or personal representative, shall give receipts for payment of compensation to the employer paying the same and such employer shall produce the same for inspection by the deputy commissioner, whenever required. (March 4, 1927, ch 509, §14, 44 Stat. 1432; May 26, 1934, ch 354, §4, 48 Stat. 807; June 25, 1938, ch 685, §7, 52 Stat. 1167; June 24, 1948, ch 623, §5, 62 Stat. 603; July 26, 1956, ch 735, §5, 70 Stat. 655; July 14, 1961, P.L. 87-87, §3, 75 Stat. 203; Oct. 27, 1972, P.L. 92-576, §§5(e), 15(d), 86 Stat. 1254, 1262; Sept. 28, 1984, P.L. 98-426, §13, 98 Stat. 1649.)

§915. Invalid agreements.

(a) No agreement by an employee to pay any portion of premium paid by his employer to a carrier or to contribute to a benefit fund or department maintained by such employer for the purpose of providing compensation or medical services and supplies as required by this chapter shall be valid, and any employer who makes a deduction for such purpose from the pay of any employee entitled to the benefits of this chapter shall be guilty of a misdemeanor, and upon conviction thereof shall be punished by a fine of not more than $1,000.

(b) No agreement by an employee to waive his right to compensation under this chapter shall be valid. (March 4, 1927, ch 509, §15, 44 Stat. 1434.)

§916. Assignment and exemption from claims of creditors.

No assignment, release, or commutation of compensation or benefits due or payable under this chapter, except as provided by this chapter, shall be valid, and such compensation and benefits shall be exempt from all claims of creditors and from levy, execution, and attachment or other remedy for recovery or collection of a debt, which exemption may not be waived. (March 4, 1927, ch 509, §16, 44 Stat. 1434.)

§917. Lien against compensation.

Where a trust fund which complies with section 186(c) of title 29 established pursuant to a collective-bargaining agreement in effect between an employer and an employee covered under this chapter has paid disability benefits to an employee which the employee is legally obligated to repay by reason of his entitlement to compensation under this chapter or under a settlement, the Secretary shall authorize a lien on such compensation in favor of the trust fund for the amount of such payments. (March 4, 1927, ch 509, §17, 44 Stat. 1434; June 25, 1938, ch 685, §8, 52 Stat. 1167; Oct. 27, 1972, P.L. 92-576, §20(b), 86 Stat. 1264; Sept. 28, 1984, P.L. 98-426, §14, 98 Stat. 1649.)

§918. Collection of defaulted payments; special fund.

(a) In case of default by the employer in the payment of compensation due under any award of compensation for a period of thirty days after the compensation is due and payable, the person to whom such compensation is payable may, within one year after such default, make application to the deputy commissioner making the compensation order or [for] a supplementary order declaring the amount of the default. After investigation, notice, and hearing, as provided in section 919 of this title, the deputy commissioner shall make a supplementary order, declaring the amount of the default, which shall be filed in the same manner as the compensation order. In case the payment in default is an installment of the award, the deputy commissioner may, in his discretion, declare the whole of the award as the amount in default. The applicant may file a certified copy of such supplementary order with the clerk of the Federal district court for the judicial district in which the employer has his principal place of business or maintains an office, or for the judicial district in which the injury occurred. In case such principal place of business or office or place where the injury occurred is in the District of Columbia, a copy of such supplementary order may be filed with the clerk of the United States District Court for the District of Columbia. Such supplementary order of the deputy commissioner shall be final, and the court shall, upon the filing of the copy, enter judgment for the amount declared in default by the supplementary order if such supplementary order is in accordance with law. Review of the judgment so entered may be had as in civil suits for damages at common law. Final proceedings to execute the judgment may be had by writ of execution in the form used by the court in suits at common law in actions of assumpsit. No fee shall be required for filing the supplementary order nor for entry of judgment thereon, and the applicant shall not be liable for costs in a proceeding for review of the judgment unless the court shall otherwise direct. The court shall modify such judgment to conform to any later compensation order upon presentation of a certified copy thereof to the court.

(b) In cases where judgment cannot be satisfied by reason of the employer's insolvency or other circumstances precluding payment, the Secretary of Labor may, in his discretion and to the extent he shall determine advisable after consideration of current commitments payable from the special fund established in section 944 of this title, make payment from such fund upon any award made under this chapter, and in addition, provide any necessary medical, surgical, and other treatment required by section 907 of this title in any case of disability where there has been a default in furnishing medical treatment by reason of the insolvency of the employer. Such an employer shall be liable for payment into such fund of the amounts paid therefrom by the Secretary of Labor under this subsection; and for the purpose of enforcing this liability, the Secretary of Labor for the benefit of the fund shall be subrogated to all the rights of the person receiving such payment or benefits as against the employer and may by a proceeding in the name of the Secretary of Labor under this section or under subsection (c) of section 921 of this title, or both, seek to recover the amount of the default or so much thereof as in the judgment of the Secretary is possible, or the Secretary may settle and compromise any such claim. (March 4, 1927, ch 509, §18, 44 Stat. 1434; July 26, 1956, ch 735, §6, 70 Stat. 655; Sept. 28, 1984, P.L. 98-426, §27(b), 98 Stat. 1654.)

§919. Procedure in respect of claims.

(a) Filing of claim. Subject to the provisions of section 913 of this title a claim for compensation may be filed with the deputy commissioner in accordance with regulations prescribed by the Secretary at any time after the first seven days of disability following any injury, or at any time after death, and the deputy commissioner shall have full power and authority to hear and determine all questions in respect of such claim.

(b) Notice of claim. Within ten days after such claim is filed the deputy commissioner, in accordance with regulations prescribed by the Secretary, shall notify the employer and any other person (other than the claimant), whom the deputy commissioner considers an interested party, that a claim has been filed. Such notice may be served personally upon the employer or other person, or sent to such employer or person by registered mail.

(c) Investigations; order for hearing; notice; rejection or award. The deputy commissioner shall make or cause to be made such investigations as he considers necessary in respect of the claim, and upon application of any interested party shall order a hearing thereon. If a hearing on such claim is ordered the deputy commissioner shall give the claimant and other interested parties at least ten days' notice of such hearing, served personally upon the claimant and other interested parties or sent to such claimant and other interested parties by registered mail or by certified mail, and shall within twenty days after such hearing is had, by order, reject the claim or make an award in respect of the claim. If no hearing is ordered within twenty days after notice is given as provided in subsection (b) of this section, the deputy commissioner shall, by order, reject the claim or make an award in respect of the claim.

(d) Provisions governing conduct of hearing; administrative law judges. Notwithstanding any other provisions of this chapter, any hearing held under this chapter shall be conducted in accordance with the provisions of section 554 of title 5. Any such hearing shall be conducted by a [an] administrative law judge qualified under section 3105 of that title. All powers, duties, and responsibilities vested by this chapter, on October 27, 1972, in the deputy commissioners with respect to such hearings shall be vested in such administrative law judges.

(e) Filing and mailing of order rejecting claim or making award. The order rejecting the claim or making the award (referred to in this chapter as a compensation order) shall be filed in the office of the deputy commissioner, and a copy thereof shall be sent by registered mail or by certified mail to the claimant and to the employer at the last known address of each.

(f) Awards after death of employee. An award of compensation for disability may be made after the death of an injured employee.

(g) Transfer of case. At any time after a claim has been filed with him, the deputy commissioner may, with the approval of the Secretary, transfer such case to any other deputy commissioner for the purpose of making investiga-

U.S.C.

tion, taking testimony, making physical examinations or taking such other necessary action therein as may be directed.

(h) Physical examination of injured employee. An injured employee claiming or entitled to compensation shall submit to such physical examination by a medical officer of the United States or by a duly qualified physician designated or approved by the Secretary as the deputy commissioner may require. The place or places shall be reasonably convenient for the employee. Such physician or physicians as the employee, employer, or carrier may select and pay for may participate in an examination if the employee, employer, or carrier so requests. Proceedings shall be suspended and no compensation be payable for any period during which the employee may refuse to submit to examination. (March 4, 1927, ch 509, §19, 44 Stat. 1435; June 25, 1938, ch 685, §9, 52 Stat. 1167; June 11, 1960, P.L. 86-507, §1(30), (31), 74 Stat. 202; Oct. 27, 1972, P.L. 92-576, §14, 86 Stat. 1261; March 27, 1978, P.L. 95-251, §2(a)(10), 92 Stat. 183.)

§920. Presumptions.

In any proceeding for the enforcement of a claim for compensation under this chapter it shall be presumed, in the absence of substantial evidence to the contrary—

(a) That the claim comes within the provisions of this chapter.

(b) That sufficient notice of such claim has been given.

(c) That the injury was not occasioned solely by the intoxication of the injured employee.

(d) That the injury was not occasioned by the willful intention of the injured employee to injure or kill himself or another. (March 4, 1927, ch 509, §20, 44 Stat. 1436.)

§921. Review of compensation orders.

(a) Effectiveness and finality of orders. A compensation order shall become effective when filed in the office of the deputy commissioner as provided in section 919 of this title, and, unless proceedings for the suspension or setting aside of such order are instituted as provided in subsection (b) of this section, shall become final at the expiration of the thirtieth day thereafter.

(b) Benefits Review Board; establishment; members; chairman; quorum; voting; questions reviewable; record; conclusiveness of findings; stay of payments; remand.

(1) There is hereby established a Benefits Review Board which shall be composed of five members appointed by the Secretary from among individuals who are especially qualified to serve on such Board. The Secretary shall designate one of the members of the Board to serve as chairman. The Chairman shall have the authority, as delegated by the Secretary, to exercise all administrative functions necessary to operate the Board.

(2) For the purpose of carrying out its functions under this chapter, three members of the Board shall constitute a quorum and official action can be taken only on the affirmative vote of at least three members.

(3) The Board shall be authorized to hear and determine appeals raising a substantial question of law or fact taken by any party in interest from decisions with respect to claims of employees under this chapter and the extensions thereof. The Board's orders shall be based upon the hearing record. The findings of fact in the decision under review by the Board shall be conclusive if supported by substantial evidence in the record considered as a whole. The payment of the amounts required by an award shall not be stayed pending final decision in any such proceeding unless ordered by the Board. No stay shall be issued unless irreparable injury would otherwise ensue to the employer or carrier.

(4) The Board may, on its own motion or at the request of the Secretary, remand a case to the administrative law judge for further appropriate action. The consent of the parties in interest shall not be a prerequisite to a remand by the Board.

(5) Notwithstanding paragraphs (1) through (4), upon application of the Chairman of the Board, the Secretary may designate up to four Department of Labor administrative law judges to serve on the Board temporarily, for not more than one year. The Board is authorized to delegate to panels of three members any or all of the powers which the Board may exercise. Each such panel shall have no more than one temporary member. Two members shall constitute a quorum of a panel. Official adjudicative action may be taken only on the affirmative vote of at least two members of a panel. Any party aggrieved by a decision of a panel of the Board may, within thirty days after the date of entry of the decision, petition the entire permanent Board for review of the panel's decision. Upon affirmative vote of the majority of the permanent members of the Board, the petition shall be granted. The Board shall amend its Rules of Practice to conform with this paragraph. Temporary members, while serving as members of the Board, shall be compensated at the same rate of compensation as regular members.

(c) Court of appeals; jurisdiction; persons entitled to review; petition; record; determination and enforcement; service of process; stay of payments. Any person adversely affected or aggrieved by a final order of the Board may obtain a review of that order in the United States court of appeals for the circuit in which the injury occurred, by filing in such court within sixty days following the issuance of such Board order a written petition praying that the order be modified or set aside. A copy of such petition shall be forthwith transmitted by the clerk of the court, to the Board, and to the other parties, and thereupon the Board shall file in the court the record in the proceedings as provided in section 2112 of title 28. Upon such filing, the court shall have jurisdiction of the proceeding and shall have the power to give a decree affirming, modifying, or setting aside, in whole or in part, the order of the Board and enforcing same to the extent that such order is affirmed or modified. The orders, writs, and processes of the court in such proceedings may run, be served, and be returnable anywhere in the United States. The payment of the amounts required by an award shall not be stayed pending final decision in any such proceeding unless ordered by the court. No stay shall be issued unless irreparable injury would otherwise ensue to the employer or carrier. The order of the court allowing any stay shall contain a specific finding, based upon evidence submitted to the court and identified by reference thereto, that irreparable damage would result to the employer, and specifying the nature of the damage.

(d) District court; jurisdiction; enforcement of orders; application of beneficiaries of awards or deputy commissioner; process for compliance with orders. If any employer or his officers or agents fails to comply with a compensation order making an award, that has become final, any beneficiary of such award or the deputy commissioner making the order, may apply for the enforcement of the order to the Federal district court for the judicial district in which the injury occurred (or to the United States District Court for the District of Columbia if the injury occurred in the District). If the court determines that the order was made and served in accordance with law, and that such employer or his officers or agents have failed to comply therewith, the court shall enforce obedience to the order by writ of injunction or by other proper process, mandatory or otherwise, to enjoin upon such person and his officers and agents compliance with the order.

(e) Institution of proceedings for suspension, setting aside, or enforcement of compensation orders. Proceedings for suspending, setting aside, or enforcing a compensation order, whether rejecting a claim or making an award, shall not be instituted otherwise than as provided in this section and section 918 of this title. (March 4, 1927, ch 509, §21, 44 Stat. 1436; Oct. 27, 1972, P.L. 92-576, §15(a), (b), 86 Stat. 1261, 1262; March 27, 1978, P.L. 95-251, §2(a)(10), 92 Stat. 183; Sept. 28, 1984, P.L. 98-426, §15, 98 Stat. 1649.)

2004 Note: Act Dec. 8, 2004, P.L. 108-447, Div F, Title I, 118 Stat. 3121, provides: "No funds made available by this Act [Div F of Act Dec. 8, 2004, P.L. 108-447; for full classification, consult U.S.C. Tables volumes] may be used by the Solicitor of Labor to participate in a review in any United States court of appeals of any decision made by the Benefits Review Board under section 21 of the Longshore and Harbor Workers' Compensation Act (33 U.S.C. 921) where such participation is precluded by the decision of the United States Supreme Court in Director, Office of Workers' Compensation Programs v. Newport News Shipbuilding, 115 S. Ct. 1278 [131 L. Ed. 2d 160] (1995), notwithstanding any provisions to the contrary contained in Rule 15 of the Federal Rules of Appellate Procedure: *Provided further*, That no funds made available by this Act may be used by the Secretary of Labor to review a decision under the Longshore and Harbor Workers' Compensation Act (33 U.S.C. 901 et seq.) that has been appealed and that has been pending before the Benefits Review Board for more than 12 months: *Provided further*, That any such decision pending a review by the Benefits Review Board for more than 1 year shall be considered affirmed by the Benefits Review Board on the 1-year anniversary of the filing of the appeal, and shall be considered the final order of the Board for purposes of obtaining a review in the United States courts of appeals: *Provided further*, That these provisions shall not be applicable to the review or appeal of any decision issued under the Black Lung Benefits Act (30 U.S.C. 901 et seq.)."

Similar provisions were contained in Acts April 26, 1996, P.L. 104-134, Title I, 110 Stat. 1321-218, as amended May 2, 1996, P.L. 104-140, §1(a), 110 Stat. 1327; Sept. 30, 1996, P.L. 104-208, Div A, Title I, §101(e) [Title I], 110 Stat. 3009-241; Nov. 13, 1997, P.L. 105-78, Title I, 111 Stat. 1475; Oct. 21, 1998, P.L. 105-277, Div A, §101(f) [Title I], 112 Stat. 2681-345; Nov. 29, 1999, P.L. 106-113, Div B, §1000(a)(4), 113 Stat. 1535 (enacting into law Title I of H.R. 3424 (113 Stat. 1501A-224), as introduced on Nov. 17, 1999); Dec. 21, 2000, P.L. 106-554, §1(a)(1), 114 Stat. 2763 (enacting into law Title I of H.R. 5656 (114 Stat. 2763A-10), as introduced on Dec. 14, 2000); Jan. 10, 2002, P.L. 107-116, Title I, 115 Stat. 2185; Feb. 20, 2003, P.L. 108-7, Div G, Title I, 117 Stat. 306; Jan. 23, 2004, P.L. 108-199, Div E, Title I, 118 Stat. 234.

§921a. Appearance of attorneys for Secretary, deputy commissioner, or Board.

Attorneys appointed by the Secretary shall represent the Secretary, the deputy commissioner, or the Board in any court proceedings under section 921 of this title or other provisions of this chapter except for proceedings in the Supreme Court of the United States. (May 4, 1928, ch 502, 45 Stat. 490; Oct. 27, 1972, P.L. 92-576, §16, 86 Stat. 1262.)

§922. Modification of awards.

Upon his own initiative, or upon the application of any party in interest (including an employer or carrier which has been granted relief under section 908(f) of this title), on the ground of a change in conditions or because of a mistake in a determination of fact by the deputy commissioner, the deputy commissioner may, at any time prior to one year after the date of the last payment of compensation, whether or not a compensation order has been issued, or at any time prior to one year after the rejection of a claim, review a compensation case (including a case under which payments are made pursuant to section 944(i) of this title) in accordance with the procedure prescribed in respect of claims in section 919 of this title, and in accordance with such section issue a new compensation order which may terminate, continue, reinstate, increase, or decrease such compensation, or award compensation. Such new order shall not affect any compensation previously paid, except that an award increasing the compensation rate may be made effective from the date of the injury, and if any part of the compensation due or to become due is unpaid, an award decreasing the compensation rate may be made effective from the date of the injury, and any payment made prior thereto in excess of such decreased rate shall be deducted from any unpaid compensation, in such manner and by such method as may be determined by the deputy commissioner with the approval of the Secretary. This section does not authorize the modification of settlements. (March 4, 1927, ch 509, §22, 44 Stat. 1437; May 26, 1934, ch 354, §5, 48 Stat. 807; June 25, 1938, ch 685, §10, 52 Stat. 1167; Sept. 28, 1984, P.L. 98-426, §§16, 27(a)(2), 98 Stat. 1650, 1654.)

§923. Procedure before deputy commissioner or Board.

(a) In making an investigation or inquiry or conducting a hearing the deputy commissioner or Board shall not be bound by common law or statutory rules of evidence or by technical or formal rules of procedure, except as provided by this chapter; but may make such investigation or inquiry or conduct such hearing in such manner as to best ascertain the rights of the parties. Declarations of a deceased employee concerning the injury in respect of which the investigation or inquiry is being made or the hearing conducted shall be received in evidence and shall, if corroborated by other evidence, be sufficient to establish the injury.

(b) Hearings before a deputy commissioner or Board shall be open to the public and shall be stenographically reported, and the deputy commissioners or Board, subject to the approval of the Secretary, are authorized to contract for the reporting of such hearings. The Secretary shall by regulation provide for the preparation of a record of the hearings and other proceedings before the deputy commissioners or Board. (March 4, 1927, ch 509, §23, 44 Stat. 1437; Oct. 27, 1972, P.L. 92-576, §15(e), 86 Stat. 1262; Sept. 28, 1984, P.L. 98-426, §27(a)(2), 98 Stat. 1654.)

§924. Witnesses.

No person shall be required to attend as a witness in any proceeding before a deputy commissioner at a place outside of the State of his residence and more than one hundred miles from his place of residence, unless his lawful mileage and fee for one day's attendance shall be first paid or tendered to him; but the testimony of any witness may be taken by deposition or interrogatories according to the rules of practice of the Federal district court for the judicial district in which the case is pending (or of the United States District Court for the District of Columbia if the case is pending in the District). (March 4, 1927, ch 509, §24, 44 Stat. 1437.)

§925. Witness fees.

Witnesses summoned in a proceeding before a deputy commissioner or whose depositions are taken shall receive the same fees and mileage as witnesses in courts of the United States. (March 4, 1927, ch 509, §25, 44 Stat. 1437.)

§926. Costs in proceedings brought without reasonable grounds.

If the court having jurisdiction of proceedings in respect of any claim or compensation order determines that the proceedings in respect of such claim or order have been instituted or continued without reasonable ground, the costs of such proceedings shall be assessed against the party who has so instituted or continued such proceedings. (March 4, 1927, ch 509, §26, 44 Stat. 1438.)

§927. Powers of deputy commissioners or Board.

(a) The deputy commissioner or Board shall have power to preserve and enforce order during any such proceedings; to issue subpoenas for, to administer oaths to, and to compel the attendance and testimony of witnesses, or the production of books, papers, documents, and other evidence, or the taking of depositions before any designated individual competent to administer oaths; to examine witnesses; and to do all things conformable to law which may be necessary to enable him effectively [effectively] to discharge the duties of his office.

(b) If any person in proceedings before a deputy commissioner or Board disobeys or resists any lawful order or process, or misbehaves during a hearing or so near the place thereof as to obstruct the same, or neglects to produce, after having been ordered to do so, any pertinent book, paper, or document, or refuses to appear after having been subpoenaed, or upon appearing refuses to take the oath as a witness, or after having taken the oath refuses to be examined according to law, the deputy commissioner or Board shall certify the facts to the district court having jurisdiction in the place in which he is sitting (or to the United States District Court for the District of Columbia if he is sitting in such District) which shall thereupon in a summary manner hear the evidence as to the acts complained of, and if the evidence so warrants, punish such person in the same manner and to the same extent as for a contempt committed before the court, or commit such person upon the same conditions as if the doing of the forbidden act had occurred with reference to the process of or in the presence of the court. (March 4, 1927, ch 509, §27, 44 Stat. 1438; Oct. 27, 1972, P.L. 92-576, §15(e), 86 Stat. 1262.)

§928. Fees for services.

(a) Attorney's fee; successful prosecution of claim. If the employer or carrier declines to pay any compensation on or before the thirtieth day after receiving written notice of a claim for compensation having been filed from the deputy commissioner, on the ground that there is no liability for compensation within the provisions of this chapter, and the person seeking benefits shall thereafter have utilized the services of an attorney at law in the successful prosecution of his claim, there shall be awarded, in addition to the award of compensation, in a compensation order, a reasonable attorney's fee against the employer or carrier in an amount approved by the deputy commissioner, Board, or court, as the case may be, which shall be paid directly by the employer or carrier to the attorney for the claimant in a lump sum after the compensation order becomes final.

(b) Attorney's fee; successful prosecution for additional compensation; independent medical evaluation of disability controversy; restriction of other assessments. If the employer or carrier pays or tenders payment of compensation without an award pursuant to section 914(a) and (b) of this title, and thereafter a controversy develops over the amount of additional compensation, if any, to which the employee may be entitled, the deputy commissioner or Board shall set the matter for an informal conference and following such conference the deputy commissioner or Board shall recommend in writing a disposition of the controversy. If the employer or carrier refuse to accept such written recommendation, within fourteen days after its receipt by them, they shall pay or tender to the employee in writing the additional compensation, if any, to which they believe the employee is entitled. If the employee refuses to accept such payment or tender of compensation, and thereafter utilizes the services of an attorney at law, and if the compensation thereafter awarded is greater than the amount paid or tendered by the employer or carrier, a reasonable attorney's fee based solely upon the difference between the amount awarded and the amount tendered or paid shall be awarded in addition to the amount of compensation. The foregoing sentence shall not apply if the controversy relates to degree or length of disability, and if the employer or carrier offers to submit the case for evaluation by physicians employed or selected by the Secretary, as authorized in section 907(e) of this title and offers to tender an amount of compensation based upon the degree or length of disability found by the independent medical report at such time as an evaluation of disability can be made. If the claimant is successful in review proceedings before the Board or court in any such case an award may be made in favor of the claimant and against the employer or carrier for a reasonable attorney's fee for claimant's counsel in accord with the above provisions. In all other cases any claim for legal services shall not be assessed against the employer or carrier.

(c) Approval; payment; lien. In all cases fees for attorneys representing the claimant shall be approved in the manner herein provided. If any proceedings are had before the Board or any court for review of any action, award, order, or decision, the Board or court may approve an attorney's fee for the work done before it by the attorney for the claimant. An approved attorney's fee, in cases in which the obligation to pay the fee is upon the claimant, may be made a lien upon the compensation due under an award; and the deputy commissioner, Board, or court shall fix in the award approving the fee, such lien and manner of payment.

(d) Costs; witnesses' fees and mileage; prohibition against diminution of compensation to claimant. In cases where an attorney's fee is awarded against an employer or carrier there may be further assessed against such employer or carrier as costs, fees and mileage for necessary witnesses attending the hearing at the instance of claimant. Both the necessity for the witness and the reasonableness of the fees of expert witnesses must be approved by the hearing officer, the Board, or the court, as the case may be. The amounts awarded against an employer or carrier as attorney's fees, costs, fees and mileage for witnesses shall not in any respect affect or diminish the compensation payable under this chapter.

(e) Unapproved fees; solicitation; penalty. A person who receives a fee, gratuity, or other consideration on account of services rendered as a representative of a claimant, unless the consideration is approved by the deputy commissioner, administrative law judge, Board, or court, or who makes it a business to solicit employment for a lawyer, or for himself, with respect to a claim or award for compensation under this chapter, shall, upon conviction thereof, for each offense be punished by a fine of not more than $1,000 or be imprisoned for not more than one year, or both. (March 24, 1927, ch 509, §28, 44 Stat. 1438; Oct. 27, 1972, P.L. 92-576, §13, 86 Stat. 1259; Sept. 28, 1984, P.L. 98-426, §17, 98 Stat. 1650.)

§929. Record of injury or death.

Every employer shall keep a record in respect of any injury to an employee. Such record shall contain such information of disease, other disability, or death in respect of such injury as the Secretary may by regulation require, and shall be available to inspection by the Secretary or by any State authority at such times and under such conditions as the Secretary may by regulation prescribe. (March 4, 1927, ch 509, §29, 44 Stat. 1438; Sept. 28, 1984, P.L. 98-426, §27(a)(2), 98 Stat. 1654.)

§930. Reports to Secretary.

(a) Time for sending; contents; copy to deputy commissioner. Within ten days from the date of any injury, which causes loss of one or more shifts of work, or death or from the date that the employer has knowledge of a disease or infection in respect of such injury, the employer shall send to the Secretary a report setting forth (1) the name, address, and business of the employer; (2) the name, address, and occupation of the employee; (3) the cause and nature of the injury or death; (4) the year, month, day, and hour when and the particular locality where the injury or death occurred; and (5) such other information as the Secretary may require. A copy of such report shall be sent at the same time to the deputy commissioner in the compensation district in which the injury occurred. Notwithstanding the requirements of this subsection, each employer shall keep a record of each and every injury regardless of whether such injury results in the loss of one or more shifts of work.

(b) Additional reports. Additional reports in respect of such injury and of the condition of such employee shall be sent by the employer to the Secretary and to such deputy commissioner at such times and in such manner as the Secretary may prescribe.

(c) Use as evidence. Any report provided for in subsection (a) or (b) of this section shall not be evidence of any fact stated in such report in any proceeding in respect of such injury or death on account of which the report is made.

(d) Compliance by mailing. The mailing of any such report and copy in a stamped envelope, within the time prescribed in subsections (a) or (b) of this section, to the Secretary and deputy commissioner, respectively, shall be a compliance with this section.

(e) Penalty for failure or refusal to send report. Any employer, insurance carrier, or self-insured employer who knowingly and willfully fails or refuses to send any report required by this section or knowingly or willfully makes a false statement or misrepresentation in any such report shall be subject to a civil penalty not to exceed $10,000 for each such failure, refusal, false statement, or misrepresentation.

(f) Tolling provision. Where the employer or the carrier has been given notice, or the employer (or his agent in charge of the business in the place where the injury occurred) or the carrier has knowledge, of any injury or death of an employee and fails, neglects, or refuses to file report thereof as required by the provisions of subsection (a) of this section, the limitations in subsection (a) of section 913 of this title shall not begin to run against the claim of the injured employee or his dependents entitled to compensation, or in favor of either the employer or the carrier, until such report shall have been furnished as required by the provisions of subsection (a) of this section. (March 4, 1927, ch 509, §30, 44 Stat. 1439; June 25, 1938, ch 685, §11, 52 Stat. 1167; Sept. 28, 1984, P.L. 98-426, §§18, 27(a)(2), 98 Stat. 1650, 1654.)

§931. Penalty for misrepresentation.

(a) Felony; fine; imprisonment.

(1) Any claimant or representative of a claimant who knowingly and willfully makes a false statement or representation for the purpose of obtaining a benefit or payment under this chapter shall be guilty of a felony, and on conviction thereof shall be punished by a fine not to exceed $10,000, by imprisonment not to exceed five years, or by both.

(2) The United States attorney for the district in which the injury is alleged to have occurred shall make every reasonable effort to promptly investigate each complaint made under this subsection.

(b) List of persons disqualified from representing claimants.

(1) No representation fee of a claimant's representative shall be approved by the deputy commissioner, an administrative law judge, the Board, or a court pursuant to section 928 of this title, if the claimant's representative is on the list of individuals who are disqualified from representing claimants under this chapter maintained by the Secretary pursuant to paragraph (2) of this subsection.

(2)(A) The Secretary shall annually prepare a list of those individuals in each compensation district who have represented claimants for a fee in cases under this chapter and who are not authorized to represent claimants. The names of individuals contained on the list required under this subparagraph shall be made available to employees and employers in each compensation district through posting and in such other forms as the Secretary may prescribe.

(B) Individuals shall be included on the list of those not authorized to represent claimants under this chapter if the Secretary determines under this section, in accordance with the procedure provided in subsection (j) of section 907 of this title, that such individual—

(i) has been convicted (without regard to pending appeal) of any crime in connection with the representation of a claimant under this chapter or any workers' compensation statute;

(ii) has engaged in fraud in connection with the presentation of a claim under this or any workers' compensation statute, including, but not limited to, knowingly making false representations, concealing or attempting to conceal material facts with respect to a claim, or soliciting or otherwise procuring false testimony;

(iii) has been prohibited from representing claimants before any other workers' compensation agency for reasons of professional misconduct which are similar in nature to those which would be grounds for disqualification under this paragraph; or

(iv) has accepted fees for representing claimants under this chapter which were not approved, or which were in excess of the amount approved pursuant to section 928 of this title.

(C) Notwithstanding subparagraph (B), no individual who is on the list required to be maintained by the Secretary pursuant to this section shall be prohibited from presenting his or her own claim or from representing without fee, a claimant who is a spouse, mother, father, sister, brother, or child of such individual.

(D) A determination under subparagraph (A) shall remain in effect for a period of not less than three years and until the Secretary finds and gives notice to the public that there is reasonable assurance that the basis for the determination will not reoccur.

(3) No employee shall be liable to pay a representation fee to any representative whose fee has been disallowed by reason of the operation of this paragraph.

(4) The Secretary shall issue such rules and regulations as are necessary to carry out this section.

(c) False statements or representation to reduce, deny, or terminate benefits. A person including, but not limited to, an employer, his duly authorized agent, or an employee of an insurance carrier who knowingly and willfully makes a false statement or representation for the purpose of reducing, denying, or terminating benefits to an injured employee, or his dependents pursuant to section 909 of this title if the injury results in death, shall be punished by a fine not to exceed $10,000, by imprisonment not to exceed five years, or by both. (March 4, 1927, ch 509, §31, 44 Stat. 1439; Sept. 28, 1984, P.L. 98-426, §19, 98 Stat. 1650.)

§932. Security for compensation.

(a) Every employer shall secure the payment of compensation under this chapter—

(1) By insuring and keeping insured the payment of such compensation with any stock company or mutual company or association, or with any other person or fund, while such person or fund is authorized (A) under the laws of the United States or of any State, to insure workmen's compensation, and (B) by the Secretary, to insure payment of compensation under this chapter; or

(2) By furnishing satisfactory proof to the Secretary of his financial ability to pay such compensation and receiving an authorization from the Secretary to pay such compensation directly. The Secretary may, as a condition to such authorization, require such employer to deposit in a depository designated by the Secretary either an indemnity bond or securities (at the option of the employer) of a kind and in an amount determined by the Secretary, based on the employer's financial condition, the employer's previous record of payments, and other relevant factors, and subject to such conditions as the Secretary may prescribe, which shall include authorization to the Secretary in case of default to sell any such securities sufficient to pay compensation awards or to bring suit upon such bonds, to procure prompt payment of compensation under this chapter. Any employer securing compensation in accordance with the provisions of this paragraph shall be known as a self-insurer.

(b) In granting authorization to any carrier to insure payment of compensation under this chapter, the Secretary may take into consideration the recommendation of any State authority having supervision over carriers or over workmen's compensation, and may authorize any carrier to insure the payment of compensation under this chapter in a limited territory. Any marine protection and indemnity mutual insurance corporation or association, authorized to write insurance against liability for loss or damage from personal injury and death, and for other losses and damages, incidental to or in respect of the ownership, operation, or chartering of vessels on a mutual assessment plan, shall be deemed a qualified carrier to insure compensation under this chapter. The Secretary may suspend or revoke any such authorization for good cause shown after a hearing at which the carrier shall be entitled to be heard in person or by counsel and to present evidence. No suspension or revocation shall affect the liability of any carrier already incurred. (March 4, 1927, ch 509, §32, 44 Stat. 1439; Sept. 28, 1984, P.L. 98-426, §§20, 27(a)(2), 98 Stat. 1652, 1654.)

§933. Compensation for injuries where third persons are liable.

(a) Election of remedies. If on account of a disability or death for which compensation is payable under this chapter, the person entitled to such compensation determines that some person other than the employer or a person or persons in his employ is liable in damages, he need not elect whether to receive such compensation or to recover damages against such third person.

(b) Acceptance of compensation operating as assignment. Acceptance of compensation under an award in a compensation order filed by the deputy commissioner, an administrative law judge, or the Board shall operate as an assignment to the employer of all rights of the person entitled to compensation to recover damages against such third person unless such person shall commence an action against such third person within six months after such acceptance. If the employer fails to commence an action against such third person within ninety days after the cause of action is assigned under this section, the right to bring such action shall revert to the person entitled to compensation. For the purpose of this subsection, the term "award" with respect to a compensation order means a formal order issued by the deputy commissioner, an administrative law judge, or Board.

(c) Payment into section 944 fund operating as assignment. The payment of such compensation into the fund established in section 944 of this title shall operate as an assignment to the employer of all right of the legal representative of the deceased (hereinafter referred to as "representative") to recover damages against such third person.

(d) Institution of proceedings or compromise by assignee. Such employer on account of such assignment may either institute proceedings for the recovery of such damages or may compromise with such third person either without or after instituting such proceeding.

(e) Recoveries by assignee. Any amount recovered by such employer on account of such assignment, whether or not as the result of a compromise, shall be distributed as follows:

(1) The employer shall retain an amount equal to—

(A) the expenses incurred by him in respect to such proceedings or compromise (including a reasonable attorney's fee as determined by the deputy commissioner or Board);

(B) the cost of all benefits actually furnished by him to the employee under section 907 of this title;

(C) all amounts paid as compensation;

(D) the present value of all amounts thereafter payable as compensation, such present value to be computed in accordance with a schedule prepared by the Secretary, and the present value of the cost of all benefits thereafter to be furnished under section 907 of this title, to be estimated by the deputy commissioner, and the amounts so computed and estimated to be retained by the employer as a trust fund to pay such compensation and the cost of such benefits as they become due, and to pay any sum finally remaining in excess thereof to the person entitled to compensation or to the representative; and

(2) The employer shall pay any excess to the person entitled to compensation or to the representative.

(f) Institution of proceedings by person entitled to compensation. If the person entitled to compensation institutes proceedings within the period prescribed in subsection (b) of this section the employer shall be required to pay as compensation under this chapter, a sum equal to the excess of the amount which the Secretary determines is payable on account of such injury or death over the net amount recovered against such third person. Such net amount shall be equal to the actual amount recovered less the expenses reasonably incurred by such person in respect to such proceedings (including reasonable attorneys' fees).

(g) Compromise obtained by person entitled to compensation.

(1) If the person entitled to compensation (or the person's representative) enters into a settlement with a third person referred to in subsection (a) of this section for an amount less than the compensation to which the person (or the person's representative) would be entitled under this chapter, the employer shall be liable for compensation as determined under subsection (f) of this section only if written approval of the settlement is obtained from the employer and the employer's carrier, before the settlement is executed, and by the person entitled to compensation (or the person's representative). The approval shall be made on a form provided by the Secretary and shall be filed in the office of the deputy commissioner within thirty days after the settlement is entered into.

(2) If no written approval of the settlement is obtained and filed as required by paragraph (1), or if the employee fails to notify the employer of any settlement obtained from or judgment rendered against a third person, all rights to compensation and medical benefits under this chapter shall be terminated, regardless of whether the employer or the employer's insurer has made payments or acknowledged entitlement to benefits under this chapter.

(3) Any payments by the special fund established under section 944 of this title shall be a lien upon the proceeds of any settlement obtained from or judgment rendered against a third person referred to under subsection (a) of this section. Notwithstanding any other provision of law, such lien shall be enforceable against such proceeds, regardless of whether the Secretary on behalf of the special fund has agreed to or has received actual notice of the settlement or judgment.

(4) Any payments by a trust fund described in section 917 of this title shall be a lien upon the proceeds of any settlement obtained from or judgment recorded against a third person referred to under subsection (a) of this section. Such lien shall have priority over a lien under paragraph (3) of this subsection.

(h) Subrogation. Where the employer is insured and the insurance carrier has assumed the payment of the compensation, the insurance carrier shall be subrogated to all the rights of the employer under this section.

(i) Right to compensation as exclusive remedy. The right to compensation or benefits under this chapter shall be the exclusive remedy to an employee when he is injured, or to his eligible survivors or legal representatives if he is killed, by the negligence or wrong of any other person or persons in the same employ: Provided, That this provision shall not affect the liability of a person other than an officer or employee of the employer. (March 4, 1927, ch 509, §33, 44 Stat. 1440; June 25, 1938, ch 685, §§12, 13, 52 Stat. 1168; Aug. 18, 1959, P.L. 86-171, 73 Stat. 391; Oct. 27, 1972, P.L. 92-576, §15(f)-(h), 86 Stat. 1262; Sept. 28, 1984, P.L. 98-426, §21, 98 Stat. 1652.)

§934. Compensation notice.

Every employer who has secured compensation under the provisions of this chapter shall keep posted in a conspicuous place or places in and about his place or places of business typewritten or printed notices, in accordance with a form prescribed by the Secretary, stating that such employer has secured the payment of compensation in accordance with the provisions of this chapter. Such notices shall contain the name and address of the carrier, if any, with whom the employer has secured payment of compensation and the date of the expiration of the policy. (March 4, 1927, ch 509, §34, 44 Stat. 1441; Sept. 28, 1984, P.L. 98-426, §27(a)(2), 98 Stat. 1654.)

§935. Substitution of carrier for employer.

In any case where the employer is not a self-insurer, in order that the liability for compensation imposed by this chapter may be most effectively discharged by the employer, and in order that the administration of this chapter in respect of such liability may be facilitated, the Secretary shall by regulation provide for the discharge, by the carrier for such employer, of such obligations and duties of the employer in respect to such liability, imposed by this chapter upon the employer, as it considers proper in order to effectuate the provisions of this chapter. For such purposes (1) notice to or knowledge of an employer of the occurrence of the injury shall be notice to or knowledge of the carrier, (2) jurisdiction of the employer by a deputy commissioner, the Board, or the Secretary, or any court under this chapter shall be jurisdiction of the carrier, and (3) any requirement by a deputy commissioner, the Board, or the Secretary, or any court under any compensation order, finding, or decision shall be binding upon the carrier in the same manner and to the same extent as upon the employer. (March 4, 1927, ch 509, §35, 44 Stat. 1441; Oct. 27, 1972, P.L. 92-576, §15(i), 86 Stat. 1262; Sept. 28, 1984, P.L. 98-426, §27(a)(2), 98 Stat. 1654.)

§936. Insurance policies.

(a) Every policy or contract of insurance issued under authority of this chapter shall contain (1) a provision to carry out the provisions of section 935 of this title, and (2) a provision that insolvency or bankruptcy of the employer and/or discharge therein shall not relieve the carrier from payment of compensation for disability or death sustained by an employee during the life of such policy or contract.

(b) No contract or policy of insurance issued by a carrier under this chapter shall be canceled prior to the date specified in such contract or policy for its expiration until at least thirty days have elapsed after a notice of cancellation has been sent to the deputy commissioner and to the employer in accordance with the provisions of subsection (c) of section 912 of this title. (March 4, 1927, ch 509, §36, 44 Stat. 1441.)

§937. Certificate of compliance with chapter.

No stevedoring firm shall be employed in any compensation district by a vessel or by hull owners until it presents to such vessel or hull owners a certificate issued by a deputy commissioner assigned to such district that it has complied with the provisions of this chapter requiring the securing of compensation to its employees. Any person violating the provisions of this section shall be punished by a fine of not more than $1,000, or by imprisonment for not more than one year, or by both such fine and imprisonment. (March 4, 1927, ch 509, §37, 44 Stat. 1442.)

§938. Penalties.

(a) Failure to secure payment of compensation. Any employer required to secure the payment of compensation under this chapter who fails to secure such compensation shall be guilty of a misdemeanor and, upon conviction thereof, shall be punished by a fine of not more than $10,000, or by imprisonment for not more than one year, or by both such fine and imprisonment; and in any case where such employer is a corporation, the president, secretary, and treasurer thereof shall be also severally liable to such fine or imprisonment as herein provided for the failure of such corporation to secure the payment of compensation; and such president, secretary, and treasurer shall be severally personally liable, jointly with such corporation, for any compensation or other benefit which may accrue under the said chapter in respect to any injury which may occur to any employee of such corporation while it shall so fail to secure the payment of compensation as required by section 932 of this title.

(b) Avoiding payment of compensation. Any employer who knowingly transfers, sells, encumbers, assigns, or in any manner disposes of, conceals, secretes, or destroys any property belonging to such employer, after one of his employees has been injured within the purview of this chapter, and with intent to avoid the payment of compensation under this chapter to such employee or his dependents, shall be guilty of a misdemeanor and, upon conviction thereof, shall be punished by a fine of not more than $10,000, or by imprisonment for not more than one year, or by both such fine and imprisonment; and in any case where such employer is a corporation, the president, secretary, and treasurer thereof shall be also severally liable to such penalty of imprisonment as well as jointly liable with such corporation for such fine.

(c) Effect on other liability of employer. This section shall not affect any other liability of the employer under this chapter. (March 4, 1927, ch 509, §38, 44 Stat. 1442; June 25, 1938, ch 685, §14, 52 Stat. 1168; Sept. 28, 1984, P.L. 98-426, §22, 98 Stat. 1653.)

§939. Administration by Secretary.

(a) Prescribing rules and regulations; appointing and fixing compensation of employees; making expenditures. Except as otherwise specifically provided, the Secretary shall administer the provisions of this chapter, and for such purpose the Secretary is authorized (1) to make such rules and regulations; (2) to appoint and fix the compensation of such temporary technical assistants and medical advisers, and, subject to the provisions of the civil service laws, to appoint, and, in accordance with chapter 51 and subchapter III of chapter 53 of title 5, to fix the compensation of such deputy commissioners (except deputy commissioners appointed under subsection (a) of section 940 of this title) and other officers and employees; and (3) to make such expenditures (including expenditures for personal services and rent at the seat of government and elsewhere, for law books, books of reference, periodicals, and for printing and binding) as may be necessary in the administration of this chapter. All expenditures of the Secretary in the administration of this chapter shall be allowed and paid as provided in section 945 of this title upon the presentation of itemized vouchers therefor approved by the Secretary.

(b) Establishing compensation districts. The Secretary shall establish compensation districts, to include the high seas and the areas within the United States to which this chapter applies, and shall assign to each such district one or more deputy commissioners, as the Secretary deems advisable. Judicial proceedings under sections 918 and 921 of this title in respect of any injury or death occurring on the high seas shall be instituted in the district court within whose territorial jurisdiction is located the office of the deputy commissioner having jurisdiction in respect of such injury or death (or in the United States District Court for the District of Columbia if such office is located in such District).

(c) Furnishing information and assistance; directing vocational rehabilitation.

(1) The Secretary shall, upon request, provide persons covered by this chapter with information and assistance relating to the chapter's coverage and compensation and the procedures for obtaining such compensation and including assistance in processing a claim. The Secretary may, upon request, provide persons covered by this chapter with legal assistance in processing a claim. The Secretary shall also provide employees receiving compensation information on medical, manpower, and vocational rehabilitation services and assist such employees in obtaining the best such services available.

(2) The Secretary shall direct the vocational rehabilitation of permanently disabled employees and shall arrange with the appropriate public or private agencies in States or Territories, possessions, or the District of Columbia for such rehabilitation. The Secretary may in his discretion furnish such prosthetic appliances or other apparatus made necessary by an injury upon which an award has been made under this chapter to render a disabled employee fit to engage in a remunerative occupation. Where necessary rehabilitation services are not available otherwise, the Secretary of Labor may, in his discretion, use the fund provided for in section 944 of this title in such amounts as may be necessary to procure such services, including necessary prosthetic appliance or other apparatus. This fund shall also be available in such amounts as may be authorized in annual appropriations for the Department of Labor for the costs of administering this subsection. (March 4, 1927, ch 509, §39, 44 Stat. 1442; July 26, 1956, ch 735, §7, 70 Stat. 656; Oct. 27, 1972, P.L. 92-576, §17, 86 Stat. 1262; Sept. 28, 1984, P.L. 98-426, §27(a)(2), (c), 98 Stat. 1654.)

§940. Deputy commissioners.

(a) Appointment; use of personnel and facilities of boards, commissions, or other agencies; expenses and salaries. The Secretary may appoint as deputy commissioners any member of any board, commission, or other agency of a State to act as deputy commissioner for any compensation district or part thereof in such State, and may make arrangements with such board, commission, or other agency for the use of the personnel and facilities thereof in the administration of this chapter. The Secretary may make such arrangements as may be deemed advisable by him for the payment of expenses of such board, commission, or other agency, incurred in the administration of this chapter pursuant to this section, and for the payment of salaries to such board, commission, or other agency, or the members thereof, and may pay any amounts agreed upon to the proper officers of the State, upon vouchers approved by the Secretary.

(b) Appointment in Territories and District of Columbia; compensation. In any Territory of the United States or in the District of Columbia a person holding an office under the United States may be appointed deputy commissioner and for services rendered as deputy commissioner may be paid compensation, in addition to that he is receiving from the United States, in an amount fixed by the Secretary in accordance with chapter 51 and subchapter III of chapter 53 of title 5.

(c) Transfers to other districts; temporary details. Deputy commissioners (except deputy commissioners appointed under subsection (a) of this section) may be transferred from one compensation district to another and may be temporarily detailed from one compensation district for service in another in the discretion of the Secretary.

(d) Maintaining offices. Each deputy commissioner shall maintain and keep open during reasonable business hours an office, at a place designated by the Secretary, for the transaction of business under this chapter, at which office he shall keep his official records and papers. Such office shall be furnished and equipped by the Secretary, who shall also furnish the deputy commissioner with all necessary clerical and other assistants, records, books, blanks, and supplies. Wherever practicable such office shall be located in a building owned or leased by the United States; otherwise the Secretary shall rent suitable quarters.

(e) Records and papers. If any deputy commissioner is removed from office, or for any reason ceases to act as such deputy commissioner, all of his official records and papers and office equipment shall be transferred to his successor in office or, if there be no successor, then to the Secretary or to a deputy commissioner designated by the Secretary.

(f) Conflict of interest. Neither a deputy commissioner or Board member nor any business associate of a deputy commissioner or Board member shall appear as attorney in any proceeding under this chapter, and no deputy commissioner or Board member shall act in any such case in which he is interested, or when he is employed by any party in interest or related to any party in interest by consanguinity or affinity within the third degree, as determined by the common law. (March 4, 1927, ch 509, §40, 44 Stat. 1443; Oct. 27, 1972, P.L. 92-576, §15(j), 86 Stat. 1262; Sept. 28, 1984, P.L. 98-426, §27(a)(2), 98 Stat. 1654.)

§941. Safety rules and regulations.

(a) Safe place of employment; installation of safety devices and safeguards. Every employer shall furnish and maintain employment and places of employment which shall be reasonably safe for his employees in all employments covered by this chapter and shall install, furnish, maintain, and use such devices and safeguards with particular reference to equipment used by and working conditions established by such employers as the Secretary may determine by regulation or order to be reasonably necessary to protect the life, health, and safety of such employees, and to render safe such employment and places of employment, and to prevent injury to his employees. However, the Secretary may not make determinations by regulation or order under this section as to matters within the scope of title 52 of the Revised Statutes and Acts supplementary or amendatory thereto, the Act of June 15, 1917 (ch. 30, 40 Stat. 220), as amended, or section 1333(e) of title 43.

(b) Studies and investigations by Secretary. The Secretary, in enforcing and administering the provisions of this section, is authorized in addition to such other powers and duties as are conferred upon him—

(1) to make studies and investigations with respect to safety provisions and the causes and prevention of injuries in employments covered by this chapter, and in making such studies and investigations to cooperate with any agency of the United States or with any State agency engaged in similar work;

(2) to utilize the services of any agency of the United States or any State agency engaged in similar work (with the consent of such agency) in connection with the administration of this section;

(3) to promote uniformity in safety standards in employments covered by this chapter through cooperative action with any agency of the United States or with any State agency engaged in similar work;

(4) to provide for the establishment and supervision of programs for the education and training of employers and employees in the recognition, avoidance, and prevention of unsafe working conditions in employments covered by this chapter, and to consult with and advise employers as to the best means of preventing injuries;

(5) to hold such hearings, issue such orders, and make such decisions, based upon findings of fact, as are deemed to be necessary to enforce the provisions of this section, and for such purposes the Secretary and the district courts shall have the authority and jurisdiction provided by section 39 of title 41, and the Secretary shall be represented in any court proceedings as provided in section 921a of this title.

(c) Inspection of places and practices of employment. The Secretary or his authorized representative may inspect such places of employment, question such employees, and investigate such conditions, practices, or matters in connection with employment subject to this chapter, as he may deem appropriate to determine whether any person has violated any provision of this section, or any rule or regulation issued thereunder, or which may aid in the enforcement of the provisions of this section. No employer or other person shall refuse to admit the Secretary or his authorized representatives to any such place or shall refuse to permit any such inspection.

(d) Requests for advice; variations from safety rules and regulations. Any employer may request the advice of the Secretary or his authorized representative, in complying with the requirements of any rule or regulation adopted to carry out the provisions of this section. In case of practical difficulties or unnecessary hardships, the Secretary in his discretion may grant variations from any such rule or regulation, or particular provisions thereof, and permit the use of other or different devices if he finds that the purpose of the rule or regulation will be observed by the variation and the safety of employees will be equally secured thereby. Any person affected by such rule or regulation, or his agent, may request the Secretary to grant such variation, stating in writing the grounds on which his request is based. Any authorization by the Secretary of a variation shall be in writing, shall describe the conditions under which the variation shall be permitted, and shall be published as provided in section 552 of title 5. A properly indexed record of all variations shall be kept in the office of the Secretary and open to public inspection.

(e) Jurisdiction to restrain violations. The United States district courts, [together with the District Court for the Territory of Alaska], shall have jurisdiction for cause shown, in any action brought by the Secretary, represented as provided in 921a of this title, to restrain violations of this section or of any rule, regulation, or order of the Secretary adopted to carry out the provisions of this section.

(f) Violations and penalties. Any employer who, willfully, violates or fails or refuses to comply with the provisions of subsection (a) of this section, or with any lawful rule, regulation, or order adopted to carry out the provisions of this section, and any employer or other person who willfully interferes with, hinders, or delays the Secretary or his authorized representative in carrying out his duties under subsection (c) of this section by refusing to admit the Secretary or his authorized representative to any place, or to permit the inspection or examination of any employment or place of employment, or who willfully hinders or delays the Secretary or his authorized representative in the performance of his duties in the enforcement of this section, shall be guilty of an offense, and, upon conviction thereof, shall be punished for each offense by a fine of not less than $100 nor more than $3,000; and in any case where such employer is a corporation, the officer who willfully permits any such violation to occur shall be guilty of an offense, and, upon conviction thereof, shall be punished also for each offense by a fine of not less than $100 nor more than $3,000. The liability hereunder shall not affect any other liability of the employer under this chapter.

(g) Inapplicability to certain employments.

(1) The provisions of this section shall not apply in the case of any employment relating to the operations for the exploration, production, or transportation by pipeline of mineral resources upon the navigable waters of the United States, nor under the authority of the Act of August 7, 1953 (ch. 345, 67 Stat. 462) [43 U.S.C. §§ 1331 et seq.], nor in the case of any employment in connection with lands (except filled in, made or reclaimed lands) beneath the navigable waters as defined in the Act of May 22, 1953 (ch. 65, 67 Stat. 29) [43 U.S.C. §§ 1301 et seq.] nor in the case of any employment for which compensation in case of disability or death is provided for employees under the authority of the Act of May 17, 1928 (ch. 612, 45 Stat. 600), as amended, nor under the authority of the Act of August 16, 1941 (ch. 357, 55 Stat. 622), as amended [42 U.S.C. §§ 1651 et seq.].

(2) The provisions of this section, with the exception of paragraph (1) of subsection (b) of this section, shall not be applied under the authority of subchapter I of chapter 81 of title 5. (March 4, 1927, ch 509, §41, 44 Stat. 1444; Aug.

23, 1958, P.L. 85-742, §1, 72 Stat. 835; Dec. 21, 1982, P.L. 97-375, Title I, §110(b), 96 Stat. 1820.)

§942. Annual report.

The Secretary shall make to Congress at the end of each fiscal year, a report of the administration of this chapter for the preceding fiscal year, including a detailed statement of receipts of and expenditures from the fund established in section 944 of this title, together with such recommendations as the Secretary deems advisable. Such report shall include the annual report required under section 936(b) of title 30 and shall be identified as the Annual Report of the Office of Workers' Compensation Programs. (March 4, 1927, ch 509, §42, as added Sept. 28, 1984, P.L. 98-426, §23, 98 Stat. 1653; Dec. 21, 1995, P.L. 104-66, Title I, Subtitle J, §1102(b)(1), 109 Stat. 722.)

§944. Special fund.

(a) Establishment; administration; custody, trust. There is established in the Treasury of the United States a special fund. Such fund shall be administered by the Secretary. The Treasurer of the United States shall be the custodian of such fund, and all moneys and securities in such fund shall be held in trust by such Treasurer and shall not be money or property of the United States.

(b) Disbursements; bond of custodian. The Treasurer is authorized to disburse moneys from such fund only upon order of the Secretary. He shall be required to give bond in an amount to be fixed and with securities to be approved by the Secretary of the Treasury and the Comptroller General of the United States conditioned upon the faithful performance of his duty as custodian of such fund.

(c) Payments into fund. Payments into such fund shall be made as follows:

(1) Whenever the Secretary determines that there is no person entitled under this chapter to compensation for the death of an employee which would otherwise be compensable under this chapter, the appropriate employer shall pay $5,000 as compensation for the death of such an employee.

(2) At the beginning of each calendar year the Secretary shall estimate the probable expenses of the fund during that calendar year and the amount of payments required (and the schedule therefor) to maintain adequate reserves in the fund. Each carrier and self-insurer shall make payments into the fund on a prorated assessment by the Secretary determined by—

(A) computing the ratio (expressed as a percent) of (i) the carrier's or self-insured's workers' compensation payments under this chapter during the preceding calendar year, to (ii) the total of such payments by all carriers and self-insureds under this chapter during such year;

(B) computing the ratio (expressed as a percent) of (i) the payments under section 908(f) of this title during the preceding calendar year which are attributable to the carrier or self-insured, to (ii) the total of such payments during such year attributable to all carriers and self-insureds;

(C) dividing the sum of the percentages computed under subparagraphs (A) and (B) for the carrier or self-insured by two; and

(D) multiplying the percent computed under subparagraph (C) by such probable expenses of the fund (as determined under the first sentence of this paragraph).

(3) All amounts collected as fines and penalties under the provisions of this chapter shall be paid into such fund.

(d) Investigations; records, availability; recordkeeping; provisions of sections 49 and 50 of title 15 applicable to Secretary.

(1) For the purpose of making rules, regulations, and determinations under this section under and for providing enforcement thereof, the Secretary may investigate and gather appropriate data from each carrier and self-insurer. For that purpose, the Secretary may enter and inspect such places and records (and make such transcriptions thereof), question such employees, and investigate such facts, conditions, practices, or matters as he may deem necessary or appropriate.

(2) Each carrier and self-insurer shall make, keep, and preserve such records, and make such reports and provide such additional information, as prescribed by regulation or order of the Secretary, as the Secretary deems necessary or appropriate to carry out his responsibilities under this section.

(3) For the purpose of any hearing or investigation related to determinations or the enforcement of the provisions of this section, the provisions of sections 49 and 50 of title 15 (relating to the attendance of witnesses and the production of books, papers, and documents) are hereby made applicable to the jurisdiction, powers, and duties of the Secretary of Labor.

(e) Depositories; investments. The Treasurer of the United States shall deposit any moneys paid into such fund into such depository banks as the Secretary may designate and may invest any portion of the funds which, in the opinion of the Secretary, is not needed for current requirements, in bonds or notes of the United States or of any Federal land bank.

(f) Limitation of liability. Neither the United States nor the Secretary shall be liable in respect of payments authorized under section 908 of this title in an amount greater than the money or property deposited in or belonging to such fund.

(g) Audit by Comptroller General; finality of payment determinations; credits of disbursing officers. The Comptroller General of the United States shall audit the account for such fund, but the action of the Secretary in making payments from such fund shall be final and not subject to review, and the Comptroller General is authorized and directed to allow credit in the accounts of any disbursing officer of the Secretary for payments made from such fund authorized by the Secretary.

(h) Civil actions for civil penalties and unpaid assessments. All civil penalties and unpaid assessments provided for in this chapter shall be collected by civil suit brought by the Secretary.

(i) Proceeds available for certain payments. The proceeds of this fund shall be available for payments:

(1) Pursuant to sections [section] 910 of this title with respect to certain initial and subsequent annual adjustments in compensation for total permanent disability or death.

(2) Under section 908(f) and (g), under section 918(b), and under section 939(c) of this title.

(3) To repay the sums deposited in the fund pursuant to subsection (d) of this section.

U.S.C.

(4) To defray the expense of making examinations as provided in section 907(e) of this title.

(j) Audit to Congress. The fund shall be audited annually and the results of such audit shall be included in the annual report required by section 942 of this title.

(k) [Redesignated] (March 4, 1927, ch 509, §44, 44 Stat. 1444; July 26, 1956, ch 735, §8, 70 Stat. 656; Oct. 27, 1972, P.L. 92-576, §8, 86 Stat. 1256; Sept. 28, 1984, P.L. 98-426, §24, 27(a)(2) in part, 98 Stat. 1653, 1654.)

§948. Laws inapplicable.

Nothing in sections 4283, 4284, 4285, 4286, or 4289 of the Revised Statutes, as amended [46 U.S.C. §§ 30501, 30502, 30505, 30506, 30507, 30508, 30510, or 30511], nor in section 18 of the Act entitled "An act to remove certain burdens on the American merchant marine and encourage the American foreign carrying trade, and for other purposes," approved June 26, 1884, as amended [46 U.S.C. § 30505], shall be held to limit the amount for which recovery may be had (1) in any suit at law or in admiralty where an employer has failed to secure compensation as required by this chapter, or (2) in any proceeding for compensation, any addition to compensation, or any civil penalty. (March 4, 1927, ch 509, §48, 44 Stat. 1446.)

§948a. Discrimination against employees who bring proceedings; penalties; deposit of payments in special fund; civil actions; entitlement to restoration of employment and compensation, qualifications requirement; liability of employer for penalties and payments; insurance policy exemption from liability.

It shall be unlawful for any employer or his duly authorized agent to discharge or in any other manner discriminate against an employee as to his employment because such employee has claimed or attempted to claim compensation from such employer, or because he has testified or is about to testify in a proceeding under this chapter. The discharge or refusal to employ a person who has been adjudicated to have filed a fraudulent claim for compensation is not a violation of this section. Any employer who violates this section shall be liable to a penalty of not less than $1,000 or more than $5,000, as may be determined by the deputy commissioner. All such penalties shall be paid to the deputy commissioner for deposit in the special fund as described in section 944 of this title, and if not paid may be recovered in a civil action brought in the appropriate United States district court. Any employee so discriminated against shall be restored to his employment and shall be compensated by his employer for any loss of wages arising out of such discrimination: Provided, That if such employee shall cease to be qualified to perform the duties of his employment, he shall not be entitled to such restoration and compensation. The employer alone and not his carrier shall be liable for such penalties and payments. Any provision in an insurance policy undertaking to relieve the employer from the liability for such penalties and payments shall be void. (March 4, 1927, ch 509, §49, as added Oct. 27, 1972, P.L. 92-576, §19, 86 Stat. 1263; Sept. 28, 1984, P.L. 98-426, §26, 98 Stat. 1654.)

§949. Effect of unconstitutionality.

If any part of this chapter is adjudged unconstitutional by the courts, and such adjudication has the effect of invalidating any payment of compensation under this chapter, the period intervening between the time the injury was sustained and the time of such adjudication shall not be computed as a part of the time prescribed by law for the commencement of any action against the employer in respect of such injury; but the amount of any compensation paid under this chapter on account of such injury shall be deducted from the amount of damages awarded in such action in respect of such injury. (March 4, 1927, ch 509, §50 [49], 44 Stat. 1446; Oct. 27, 1972, P.L. 92-576, §19, 86 Stat. 1263.)

§950. Separability.

If any provision of this chapter is declared unconstitutional or the applicability thereof to any person or circumstances is held invalid, the validity of the remainder of the chapter and the applicability of such provision to other persons and circumstances shall not be affected thereby. (March 4, 1927, ch 509, §51 [50], 44 Stat. 1446; Oct. 27, 1972, P.L. 92-576, §19, 86 Stat. 1263.)

TITLE 40
PUBLIC BUILDINGS, PROPERTY, AND WORKS

SUBTITLE II
PUBLIC BUILDINGS AND WORKS

PART A
GENERAL

CHAPTER 31
GENERAL

SUBCHAPTER VI
MISCELLANEOUS

§3172. Extension of state workers' compensation laws to buildings, works, and property of the Federal Government.

(a) Authorization of Extension. The state authority charged with enforcing and requiring compliance with the state workers' compensation laws and with the orders, decisions, and awards of the authority may apply the laws to all land and premises in the State which the Federal Government owns or holds by deed or act of cession, and to all projects, buildings, constructions, improvements, and property in the State and belonging to the Government, in the same way and to the same extent as if the premises were under the exclusive jurisdiction of the State in which the land, premises, projects, buildings, constructions, improvements, or property are located.

(b) Limitation on Relinquishing Jurisdiction. The Government under this section does not relinquish its jurisdiction for any other purpose.

(c) Nonapplication. This section does not modify or amend subchapter I of chapter 81 of title 5. (Aug. 21, 2002, P.L. 107-217, § 1, 116 Stat. 1154.)

U.S.C.

TITLE 42
THE PUBLIC HEALTH AND WELFARE

CHAPTER 11
COMPENSATION FOR DISABILITY OR DEATH TO PERSONS EMPLOYED AT MILITARY, AIR, AND NAVAL BASES OUTSIDE THE UNITED STATES

§1651. Compensation authorized.

(a) Places of employment. Except as herein modified, the provisions of the Longshore and Harbor Workers' Compensation Act, approved March 4, 1927 (44 Stat. 1424), as amended [33 U.S.C. 901 et seq.], shall apply in respect to the injury or death of any employee engaged in any employment—

(1) at any military, air, or naval base acquired after January 1, 1940, by the United States from any foreign government; or

(2) upon any lands occupied or used by the United States for military or naval purposes in any Territory or possession outside the continental United States (including the United States Naval Operating Base, Guantanamo Bay, Cuba; and the Canal Zone); or

(3) upon any public work in any Territory or possession outside the continental United States (including the United States Naval Operating Base, Guantanamo Bay, Cuba; and the Canal Zone), if such employee is engaged in employment at such place under the contract of a contractor (or any subcontractor or subordinate subcontractor with respect to the contract of such contractor) with the United States; but nothing in this paragraph shall be construed to apply to any employee of such a contractor or subcontractor who is engaged exclusively in furnishing materials or supplies under his contract;

(4) under a contract entered into with the United States or any executive department, independent establishment, or agency thereof (including any corporate instrumentality of the United States), or any subcontract, or subordinate contract with respect to such contract, where such contract is to be performed outside the continental United States and at places not within the areas described in subparagraphs (1)–(3) of this subdivision, for the purpose of engaging in public work, and every such contract shall contain provisions requiring that the contractor (and subcontractor or subordinate contractor with respect to such contract) (1) shall, before commencing performance of such contract, provide for securing to or on behalf of employees engaged in such public work under such contract the payment of compensation and other benefits under the provisions of this chapter, and (2) shall maintain in full force and effect during the term of such contract, subcontract, or subordinate contract, or while employees are engaged in work performed thereunder, the said security for the payment of such compensation and benefits, but nothing in this paragraph shall be construed to apply to any employee of such contractor or subcontractor who is engaged exclusively in furnishing materials or supplies under his contract;

(5) under a contract approved and financed by the United States or any executive department, independent establishment, or agency thereof (including any corporate instrumentality of the United States), or any subcontract or subordinate contract with respect to such contract, where such contract is to be performed outside the continental United States, under the Mutual Security Act of 1954, as amended (other than title II of chapter II thereof unless the Secretary of Labor, upon the recommendation of the head of any department or other agency of the United States, determines a contract financed under a successor provision of any successor Act should be covered by this section), and not otherwise within the coverage of this section, and every such contract shall contain provisions requiring that the contractor (and subcontractor or subordinate contractor with respect to such contract) (A) shall, before commencing performance of such contract, provide for securing to or on behalf of employees engaged in work under such contract the payment of compensation and other benefits under the provisions of this Act [42 U.S.C. §§ 1651 et seq.], and (B) shall maintain in full force and effect during the term of such contract, subcontract, or subordinate contract, or while employees are engaged in work performed thereunder, the said security for the payment of such compensation and benefits, but nothing in this paragraph shall be construed to apply to any employee of such contractor or subcontractor who is engaged exclusively in furnishing materials or supplies under his contract;

(6) outside the continental United States by an American employer providing welfare or similar services for the benefit of the Armed Forces pursuant to appropriate authorization by the Secretary of Defense,

irrespective of the place where the injury or death occurs, and shall include any injury or death occurring to any such employee during transportation to or from his place of employment, where the employer or the United States provides the transportation or the cost thereof.

(b) Definitions. As used in this section—

(1) the term "public work" means any fixed improvement or any project, whether or not fixed, involving construction, alteration, removal or repair for the public use

U.S.C.

of the United States or its allies, including but not limited to projects or operations under service contracts and projects in connection with the national defense or with war activities, dredging, harbor improvements, dams, roadways, and housing, as well as preparatory and ancillary work in connection therewith at the site or on the project;

(2) the term "allies" means any nation with which the United States is engaged in a common military effort or with which the United States has entered into a common defensive military alliance;

(3) the term "war activities" includes activities directly relating to military operations;

(4) the term "continental United States" means the States and the District of Columbia.

(c) Liability as exclusive. The liability of an employer, contractor (or any subcontractor or subordinate subcontractor with respect to the contract of such contractor) under this chapter shall be exclusive and in place of all other liability of such employer, contractor, subcontractor, or subordinate contractor to his employees (and their dependents) coming within the purview of this chapter, under the workmen's compensation law of any State, Territory, or other jurisdiction, irrespective of the place where the contract of hire of any such employee may have been made or entered into.

(d) "Contractor" defined. As used in this section, the term "contractor" means any individual, partnership, corporation, or association, and includes any trustee, receiver, assignee, successor, or personal representative thereof, and the rights, obligations, liability, and duties of the employer under such Longshore and Harbor Workers' Compensation Act shall be applicable to such contractor.

(e) Contracts within section; waiver of application of section. The liability under this chapter of a contractor, subcontractor, or subordinate contractor engaged in public work under subparagraphs (3) and (4), subdivision (a) of this section, and the conditions set forth therein, shall become applicable to contracts and subcontracts heretofore entered into but not completed at August 16, 1941, and the liability under this chapter of a contractor, subcontractor, or subordinate contractor engaged in performance of contracts, subcontracts, or subordinate contracts specified in subparagraph (5), subdivision (a) of this section, and the conditions set forth therein, shall hereafter be applicable to the remaining terms of such contracts, subcontracts, and subordinate contracts entered into prior to but not completed on the date of enactment of any successor Act to the Mutual Security Act of 1954, as amended, and contracting officers of the United States are authorized to make such modifications and amendments of existing contracts as may be necessary to bring such contracts into conformity with the provisions of this chapter. No right shall arise in any employee or his dependent under subparagraphs (3) and (4) of, subdivision (a) of this section, prior to two months after the approval of this chapter. Upon the recommendation of the head of any department or other agency of the United States, the Secretary of Labor, in the exercise of his discretion, may waive the application of this section with respect to any contract, subcontract, contract, or subordinate contract, work location under such contracts, or classification of employees. Upon recommendation of any employer referred to in paragraph (6) of subsection (a) of this section, the Secretary of Labor may waive the application of this section to any employee or class of employees of such employer, or to any place of employment of such an employee or class of employees.

(f) Liability to prisoners of war and protected persons. The liability under this chapter of a contractor, subcontractor, or subordinate contractor engaged in public work under paragraphs (1), (2), (3), and (4) of, subsection (a) of this section or in any work under paragraph (5) of subsection (a) of this section does not apply with respect to any person who is a prisoner of war or a protected person under the Geneva Conventions of 1949 and who is detained or utilized by the United States. (Aug. 16, 1941, ch 357, §1, 55 Stat. 622; Dec. 2, 1942, ch 668, Title III, §301, 56 Stat. 1035; June 30, 1953, ch 176, §4, 67 Stat. 135; June 30, 1958, P.L. 85-477, Subch V, §502(a), 72 Stat. 272; Sug. 8, 1958, P.L. 85-608, Title II, §201, 72 Stat. 537; June 25, 1959, P.L. 86-70, §40, 73 Stat. 150; July 24, 1959, P.L. 86-108, Subch VII, §701(a), 73 Stat. 257; Sept. 4, 1961, P.L. 87-195, Part IV, §701, 75 Stat. 463.)

§1652. Computation of benefits; application to aliens and nonnationals.

(a) The minimum limit on weekly compensation for disability, established by section 906(b) of title 33, and the minimum limit on the average weekly wages on which death benefits are to be computed, established by section 909(e) of title 33, shall not apply in computing compensation and death benefits under this chapter.

(b) Compensation for permanent total or permanent partial disability under section 908(c)(21) of title 33, or for death under this chapter to aliens and nonnationals of the United States not residents of the United States or Canada shall be in the same amount as provided for residents, except that dependents in any foreign country shall be limited to surviving wife and child or children, or if there be no surviving wife or child or children, to surviving father or mother whom the employee has supported, either wholly or in part, for the period of one year immediately prior to the date of the injury, and except that the Secretary of Labor may, at his option or upon the application of the insurance carrier shall, commute all future installments of compensation to be paid to such aliens or nonnationals of the United States by paying or causing to be paid to them one-half of the commuted amount of such future installments of compensation as determined by the Secretary. (Aug. 16, 1941, ch. 357, §2, 55 Stat. 623; 1946 Reorg. Plan No. 2, §3, eff. July 16, 1946, 11 F.R. 7873, 60 Stat. 1095; 1950 Reorg. Plan No. 19, §1, eff. May 24, 1950, 15 F.R. 3178, 64 Stat. 1271; Sept. 28, 1984, P.L. 98-426, §27(d)(2), 98 Stat. 1654.)

§1653. Compensation districts; judicial proceedings.

(a) The Secretary of Labor is authorized to extend compensation districts established under the Longshore and Harbor Workers' Compensation Act, approved March 4, 1927 (44 Stat. 1424) [33 U.S.C. 901 et seq.], or to establish new compensation districts, to include any area to which this chapter applies; and to assign to each such district one or more deputy commissioners, as the Secretary may deem necessary.

(b) Judicial proceedings provided under sections 18 and 21 of the Longshore and Harbor Workers' Compensation Act [33 U.S.C. 918, 921] in respect to a compensation order made pursuant to this chapter shall be instituted in the United States district court of the judicial district wherein is located the office of the deputy commissioner whose compensation order is involved if his office is located in a judicial district, and if not so located, such judicial proceedings shall be instituted in the judicial district nearest the base at which the injury or death occurs. (Aug. 16, 1941, ch. 357, §3, 55 Stat. 623; 1946 Reorg. Plan No. 2, §3, eff. July 16, 1946, 11 F.R. 7873, 60 Stat. 1095; 1950 Reorg. Plan No. 19, §1, eff. May 24, 1950, 15 F.R. 3178, 64 Stat. 1271; Sept. 28, 1984, P.L. 98-426, §27(d)(2), 98 Stat. 1654.)

§1654. Persons excluded from benefits.

This chapter shall not apply in respect to the injury or death of (1) an employee subject to the provisions of subchapter I of chapter 81 of title 5; (2) an employee engaged in agriculture, domestic service, or any employment that is casual and not in the usual course of the trade, business, or profession of the employer; and (3) a master or member of a crew of any vessel. (Aug. 16, 1941, ch 357, §4, 55 Stat. 623.)

§1655. Requirement for Department of Defense to adopt an acquisition strategy for Defense Base Act insurance.

(a) In general. The Secretary of Defense shall adopt an acquisition strategy for insurance required by the Defense Base Act (42 U.S.C. 1651 et seq.) which minimizes the cost of such insurance to the Department of Defense and to defense contractors subject to such Act.

(b) Criteria. The Secretary shall ensure that the acquisition strategy adopted pursuant to subsection (a) addresses the following criteria:

(1) Minimize overhead costs associated with obtaining such insurance, such as direct or indirect costs for contract management and contract administration.

(2) Minimize costs for coverage of such insurance consistent with realistic assumptions regarding the likelihood of incurred claims by contractors of the Department.

(3) Provide for a correlation of premiums paid in relation to claims incurred that is modeled on best practices in government and industry for similar kinds of insurance.

(4) Provide for a low level of risk to the Department.

(5) Provide for a competitive marketplace for insurance required by the Defense Base Act to the maximum extent practicable.

(c) Options. In adopting the acquisition strategy pursuant to subsection (a), the Secretary shall consider such options (including entering into a single Defense Base Act insurance contract) as the Secretary deems to best satisfy the criteria identified under subsection (b).

(d) Report.

(1) Not later than 270 days after the date of enactment of this Act [enacted Oct. 14, 2008], the Secretary shall submit to the Committees on Armed Services of the Senate and the House of Representatives, the Committee on Homeland Security and Governmental Affairs of the Senate, and the Committee on Oversight and Government Reform of the House of Representatives a report on the acquisition strategy adopted pursuant to subsection (a).

(2) The report shall include a discussion of each of the options considered pursuant to subsection (c) and the extent to which each option addresses the criteria identified under subsection (b), and shall include a plan to implement within 18 months after the date of enactment of this Act the acquisition strategy adopted by the Secretary.

(e) Review of acquisition strategy. As considered appropriate by the Secretary, but not less often than once every 3 years, the Secretary shall review and, as necessary, update the acquisition strategy adopted pursuant to subsection (a) to ensure that it best addresses the criteria identified under subsection (b). (Oct. 14, 2008, P.L. 110-417, [Div A,] Title VIII, Subtitle E, § 843, 122 Stat. 4540.)

CHAPTER 12
COMPENSATION FOR INJURY, DEATH, OR DETENTION OF EMPLOYEES OF CONTRACTORS WITH THE UNITED STATES OUTSIDE THE UNITED STATES

SUBCHAPTER I
COMPENSATION, REIMBURSEMENT, ETC., BY SECRETARY OF LABOR

§1701. Compensation for injury or death resulting from war-risk hazard.

(a) Persons covered. In case of injury or death resulting from injury—

(1) to any person employed by a contractor with the United States, if such person is an employee specified in chapter 11 of this title, and no compensation is payable with respect to such injury or death under such chapter; or

(2) to any person engaged by the United States under a contract for his personal services outside the continental United States; or

(3) to any person employed outside the continental United States as a civilian employee paid from nonappropriated funds administered by the Army and Air Force Exchange Service, Army and Air Force Motion Picture Service, Navy Ship's Store Ashore, Navy exchanges, Marine Corps exchanges, officers' and noncommissioned officers' open messes, enlisted men's clubs, service clubs, special service activities, or any other instrumentality of the United States under the jurisdiction of the Department of Defense and conducted for the mental, physical, and morale improvement of personnel of the Department of Defense and their dependents; or

(4) to any person who is an employee specified in section 1651(a)(5) of this title, if no compensation is payable with respect to such injury or death under chapter 11 of this title or to any person engaged under a contract for his personal services outside the United States approved and financed by the United States under the Mutual Security Act of 1954, as amended (other than title II of chapter II thereof unless the Secretary of Labor, upon the recommendation of the head of any department or other agency of the United States Government, determines a contract financed under a successor provision of any successor Act should be covered by this section): Provided, That in cases where the United States is not a formal party to contracts approved and financed under the Mutual Security Act of 1954, as amended, the Secretary, upon the recommendation of the head of any department or agency of the United States, may, in the exercise of his discretion, waive the application of the provisions of this subparagraph with respect to any such contracts, subcontracts, or subordinate contracts, work location under such contracts, subcontracts, or subordinate contracts, or classification of employees; or

(5) to any person employed or otherwise engaged for personal services outside the continental United States by an American employer providing welfare or similar services for the benefit of the Armed Forces pursuant to appropriate authorization by the Secretary of Defense,

and such injury proximately results from a war-risk hazard, whether or not such person then actually was engaged in the course of his employment, the provisions of subchapter I of chapter 81 of title 5, as amended, and as modified by this chapter, shall apply with respect thereto in the same manner and to the same extent as if the person so employed were a civil employee of the United States and were injured while in the performance of his duty, and any compensation found to be due shall be paid from the compensation fund established pursuant to section 8147 of title 5. This subsection shall not be construed to include any person who would otherwise come within the purview of subchapter I of chapter 81 of title 5.

(b) Missing persons considered as totally disabled.

(1) Any person specified in subsection (a) of this section who—

(A) is found to be missing from his place of employment, whether or not such person then actually was engaged in the course of his employment, under circumstances supporting an inference that his absence is due to the belligerent action of a hostile force or person, or

(B) is known to have been taken by a hostile force or person as a prisoner, hostage, or otherwise, or

(C) is not returned to his home or to the place where he was employed by reason of the failure of the United States or its contractor to furnish transportation,

until such time as he is returned to his home, to the place of his employment, or is able to be returned to the jurisdiction of the United States, shall, under such regulations as the Secretary of Labor may prescribe, be regarded solely for the purposes of this subsection as totally disabled, and the same benefits as are provided for such disability under this title [42 U.S.C. §§ 1701 et seq.] shall be credited to his account and be payable to him for the period of such absence or until his death is in fact established or can be legally presumed to have occurred: Provided, That if such person has dependents residing in the United States or its Territories or possessions (including the United States Naval Operating Base, Guantanamo Bay, Cuba, the Canal Zone), the Secretary during the period of such absence may disburse a part of such compensation, accruing for such total disability, to such dependents, which shall be equal to the monthly benefits otherwise payable for death under this title [42 U.S.C. §§ 1701 et seq.], and the balance of such compensation for total disability shall accrue and be payable to such person upon his return from such absence. Any payment made pursuant to this subsection shall not in any case be included in computing the maximum aggregate or total compensation payable for disability or death, as provided in section 102(a) [42 U.S.C. § 1702(a)]: Provided further, That no such payment to such person or his dependent, on account of such absence, shall be made during any period such person or dependent, respectively, has received, or may be entitled to receive, any other payment from the United States, either directly or indirectly, because of such absence, unless such person or dependent refunds or renounces such other benefit or payment for the period claimed.

Benefits found to be due under this subsection shall be paid from the compensation fund established pursuant to section 35 of such Act of September 7, 1916 [5 U.S.C. § 8147], as amended: Provided, That the determination of dependents, dependency, and amounts of payments to dependents shall be made in the manner specified in such Act: Provided further, That claim for such detention benefits shall be filed in accordance with and subject to the limitation provisions of such Act, as modified by section 106(c) of this Act [42 U.S.C. § 1706(c)]: And provided further, That except in cases of fraud or willful misrepresentation, the Secretary may waive recovery of money erroneously paid under this subdivision whenever it finds that such recovery would be impracticable or would cause hardship to the beneficiary affected: And provided further, That where such person is found to be missing from his place of employment, whether or not such person then actually was engaged in the course of his employment, under circumstances supporting an inference that his absence is due to the belligerent action of a hostile force or person or is known to have been taken by a hostile force or person as a prisoner, hostage, or otherwise, the amount of benefits to be credited to the account of such person under this subsection, and for the purposes of this subsection only, shall be 100 per centum of the average weekly wages of such person, except that in computing such benefits such average weekly wages (a) shall not exceed the average weekly wages paid to civilian employees of the United States in the same or most similar occupation in the area nearest to the place of employment where such person was last employed, and (b) shall not exceed the average weekly wages of such absent person at the time such absence began; and 70 per centum of such average weekly wage so determined shall be disbursed to the dependent or dependents of such person, irrespective of the limitations of section 9 of the Longshoremen's and Harbor Workers' Compensation Act [33 U.S.C. § 909], but should there be more than one such dependent, the distribution of such 70 per centum shall be proportionate to the percentages allowed for dependents by section 9 of such Longshoremen's and Harbor Workers' Compensation Act [33 U.S.C. § 909], and if such manner of disbursement in any case would result in injustice or excessive allowance for a dependent, the Secretary of Labor may, in its discretion, modify such percentage or apportionment to meet the requirements of the case; and in such cases benefits for detention shall accrue from January 1, 1942, unless the beginning of absence occurred upon a later date in which event benefits shall accrue from such later date, and for the period of such absence shall be 100 per centum of the average weekly wages, determined as herein provided: And provided further, That compensation for disability under this title [42 U.S.C. §§ 1701 et seq.] (except under allowance for scheduled losses of members or functions of the body, within the purview of section 102(a) [42 U.S.C. § 1702(a)]) shall not be paid in any case in respect to any period of time during which benefits for detention may accrue under this title [42 U.S.C. §§ 1701 et seq.] in the same case, and should a person entitled to benefits for detention also be entitled to workmen's compensation or similar benefits under any other law, agreement or plan (except allowances for scheduled losses of members or functions of the body), where such other benefits are paid or to be paid directly or indirectly by the United States, the amount thereof accruing as to the period of absence shall be taken into account and the benefits credited to the account of the detained person reduced accordingly: And provided further, That where through mistake of fact, absence of proof of death, or error through lack of adequate information or otherwise, payments as for detention have in any case been erroneously made or credited, any resulting overpayment of detention benefits (the recovery of which is not waived as otherwise provided for in this section) shall be recouped by the Commission [Secretary of Labor] in such manner as it shall determine from any unpaid accruals to the account of the detained person, and if such accruals are insufficient for such purpose, then from any allowance of compensation for injury or death in the same case (whether under this title [42 U.S.C. §§ 1701 et seq.] or under any other law, agreement, or plan if the United States pays, or is obligated to pay, such benefits, directly or indirectly), but only to the extent of the amount of such compensation benefits payable for the particular period of such overpayment, and in cases of erroneous payments of compensation for injury or death, made through mistake of fact, whether under this title [42 U.S.C. §§ 1701 et seq.] or under any other law, agreement, or plan (if the United States is obligated to pay such compensation, directly or indirectly), the Secretary is authorized to recoup from any unpaid benefits for detention, the amount of any overpayment thus arising; and any amounts recovered under this section shall be covered into such compensation fund, and for the foregoing purposes the Secretary shall have a right of lien, intervention, and recovery in any claim or proceeding for compensation.

(2) Upon application by such person, or someone on his behalf, the Secretary may, under such regulations as it may prescribe, furnish transportation or the cost thereof (including reimbursement) to any such person from the point where his release from custody by a hostile force or person is effected, to his home, the place of his employment, or other place within the jurisdiction of the United States; but no transportation, or the cost thereof, shall be furnished under this paragraph where such person is furnished such transportation, or the cost thereof, under any agreement with his employer or under any other provision of law.

(3) In the case of death of any such person, if his death occurred away from his home, the body of such person shall, in the discretion of the Secretary, and if so desired by his next of kin, near relative, or legal representative, be embalmed and transported in a hermetically sealed casket or other appropriate container to the home of such person or to such other place as may be designated by such next of kin, near relative, or legal representative. No expense shall be incurred under this paragraph by the Secretary in any case where death takes place after repatriation, unless such death proximately results from a war-risk hazard.

(4) Such benefits for detention, transportation expenses of repatriated persons, and expenses of embalming,

providing sealed or other appropriate container, and transportation of the body, and attendants (if required), as approved by the Secretary, shall be paid out of the compensation fund established under section 8147 of title 5.

(c) Persons not citizens or residents of United States. Compensation for permanent total or permanent partial disability or for death payable under this section to persons who are not citizens of the United States and who are not residents of the United States or Canada, shall be in the same amount as provided for residents; except that dependents in any foreign country shall be limited to surviving wife or husband and child or children, or if there be no surviving wife or husband or child or children, to surviving father or mother whom such person has supported, either wholly or in part, for the period of one year immediately prior to the date of the injury; and except that the Secretary, at his option, may commute all future installments of compensation to be paid to such persons by paying to them one-half of the commuted amount of such future installments of compensation as determined by the Secretary.

(d) Persons excepted from coverage. The provisions of this section shall not apply in the case of any person (1) whose residence is at or in the vicinity of the place of his employment, and (2) who is not living there solely by virtue of the exigencies of his employment, unless his injury or death resulting from injury occurs or his detention begins while in the course of his employment, or (3) who is a prisoner of war or a protected person under the Geneva Conventions of 1949 and who is detained or utilized by the United States. (Dec. 2, 1942, ch. 668, title I, §101, 56 Stat. 1028; Dec. 23, 1943, ch. 380, title I, 57 Stat. 626; Aug. 7, 1946, ch. 805, §1, 60 Stat. 899; June 30, 1953, ch. 176, §§2, 3, 67 Stat. 135; June 30, 1958, P.L. 85-477, ch. V, §502(g), 72 Stat. 273; Aug. 8, 1958, P.L. 85-608, title I, §§101, 104, title IV, Sec. 401, 72 Stat. 536, 537, 539; June 25, 1959, P.L. 86-70, §42(a), 73 Stat. 151; Sept. 4, 1961, P.L. 87-195, pt. IV, §702, 75 Stat. 463; Sept. 28, 1984, P.L. 98-426, §27(d)(2), 98 Stat. 1654.)

§1702. Application of Longshore and Harbor Workers' Compensation Act.

(a) In the administration of the provisions of subchapter I of chapter 81 of title 5 with respect to cases coming within the purview of section 1701 of this title, the scale of compensation benefits and the provisions for determining the amount of compensation and the payment thereof as provided in sections 908 and 909 of title 33, so far as the provisions of said sections can be applied under the terms and conditions set forth therein shall be payable in lieu of the benefits, except medical benefits, provided under subchapter I of chapter 81 of title 5: Provided, That the total compensation payable under this subchapter for injury or death shall in no event exceed the limitations upon compensation as fixed in section 914(m) of title 33 as such section may from time to time be amended except that the total compensation shall not be less than that provided for in the original enactment of this chapter.

(b) For the purpose of computing compensation with respect to cases coming within the purview of section 1701 of this title, the provisions of sections 906 and 910 of title 33 shall be applicable: Provided, That the minimum limit on weekly compensation for disability, established by section 906(b) of title 33, and the minimum limit on the average weekly wages on which death benefits are to be computed, established by section 909(e) of title 33, shall not apply in computing compensation under this subchapter. (Dec. 2, 1942, ch. 668, title I, §102, 56 Stat. 1031; July 3, 1948, ch. 826, §4(c), 62 Stat. 1242; Aug. 8, 1958, P.L. 85-608, title I, §102, 72 Stat. 536; Sept. 28, 1984, P.L. 98-426, §27(d)(2), 98 Stat. 1654.)

§1703. "Contractor with the United States" defined.

As used in this subchapter, the term "contractor with the United States" includes any subcontractor or subordinate subcontractor with respect to the contract of such contractor. (Dec. 2, 1942, ch 668, Title I, §103, 56 Stat. 1031.)

§1704. Reimbursement.

(a) Payments reimbursable; filing claim for reimbursement; regulations for payment of direct benefits. Where any employer or his insurance carrier or compensation fund pays or is required to pay benefits—

(1) to any person or fund on account of injury or death of any person coming within the purview of this subchapter or chapter 11 of this title, if such injury or death arose from a war-risk hazard, which are payable under any workmen's compensation law of the United States or of any State, Territory, or possession of the United States, or other jurisdiction; or

(2) to any person by reason of any agreement outstanding on December 2, 1942 made in accordance with a contract between the United States and any contractor therewith to pay benefits with respect to the death of any employee of such contractor occurring under circumstances not entitling such person to benefits under any workmen's compensation law or to pay benefits with respect to the failure of the United States or its contractor to furnish transportation upon the completion of the employment of any employee of such contractor to his home or to the place where he was employed; or

(3) to any person by reason of an agreement approved or authorized by the United States under which a contractor with the United States has agreed to pay workmen's compensation benefits or benefits in the nature of workmen's compensation benefits to an injured employee or his dependents on account of detention by a hostile force or person or on account of injury or death arising from a war-risk hazard;

such employer, carrier, or fund shall be entitled to be reimbursed for all benefits so paid or payable, including funeral and burial expenses, medical, hospital, or other similar costs for treatment and care; and reasonable and necessary claims expense in connection therewith. Claim for such reimbursement shall be filed with the Secretary under regulations promulgated by him, and such claims, or such part thereof as may be allowed by the Secretary, shall be paid from the compensation fund established under section 8147 of title 5. The Secretary may, under such regulations as he shall prescribe, pay such benefits, as they accrue and in lieu of reimbursement, directly to any person entitled thereto, and the insolvency of such employer, insurance carrier, or compensation fund shall not affect the right of the beneficiaries of such benefits to receive the compensation directly from the said compensation fund established under section 8147 of title 5. The Secretary may also, under such regulations as he shall prescribe, use any private facilities, or such Government facilities as may be available, for the treatment or care of any person entitled thereto.

(b) Charging of premiums as prohibiting reimbursement. No reimbursement shall be made under this subchapter in any case in which the Secretary finds that the benefits paid or payable were on account of injury, detention, or death which arose from a war- risk hazard for which a premium (which included an additional charge or loading for such hazard) was charged.

(c) Injury or death occurring within any State. The provisions of this section shall not apply with respect to benefits on account of any injury or death occurring within any State. (Dec. 2, 1942, ch 668, Title I, §104, 56 Stat. 1031; Aug. 8, 1958, P.L. 85-608, Title I, §104, 72 Stat. 537; June 25, 1959, P.L. 86-70, §42(b), 73 Stat. 151.)

§1705. Receipt of workmen's compensation benefits.

(a) Receipt of benefits under other provisions. No benefits shall be paid or furnished under the provisions of this subchapter for injury or death to any person who recovers or receives workmen's compensation benefits for the same injury or death under any other law of the United States, or under the law of any State, Territory, possession, foreign country, or other jurisdiction, or benefits in the nature of workmen's compensation benefits payable under an agreement approved or authorized by the United States pursuant to which a contractor with the United States has undertaken to provide such benefits.

(b) Lien and right of recovery against compensation payable under other provisions. The Secretary shall have a lien and a right of recovery, to the extent of any payments made under this subchapter on account of injury or death, against any compensation payable under any other workmen's compensation law on account of the same injury or death; and any amounts recovered under this subsection shall be covered into the fund established under section 8147 of title 5.

(c) Receipt of wages as credit against payment under this subchapter; intervention by Secretary in proceeding to recover wages, etc. Where any person specified in section 1701(a) of this title, or the dependent, beneficiary, or allottee of such person, receives or claims wages, payments in lieu of wages, insurance benefits for disability or loss of life (other than workmen's compensation benefits), and the cost of such wages, payments, or benefits is provided in whole or in part by the United States, the amount of such wages, payments, or benefits shall be credited, in such manner as the Secretary shall determine, against any payments to which any such person is entitled under this subchapter.

Where any person specified in section 1701(a) of this title, or the dependent, beneficiary, or allottee of such person, receives or claims wages, payments in lieu of wages, insurance benefits for disability or loss of life (other than workmen's compensation benefits), and the cost of such wages, payments, or benefits is provided in whole or in part by the United States, the amount of such wages, payments, or benefits shall be credited, in such manner as the Secretary shall determine, against any payments to which any such person is entitled under this subchapter. Where any person specified in section 1701(a) of this title, or any dependent, beneficiary, or allottee of such person, or the legal representative or estate of any such entities, after having obtained benefits under this subchapter, seeks through any proceeding, claim, or otherwise, brought or maintained against the employer, the United States, or other person, to recover wages, payments in lieu of wages, or any sum claimed as for services rendered, or for failure to furnish transportation, or for liquidated or unliquidated damages under the employment contract, or any other benefit, and the right in respect thereto is alleged to have accrued during or as to any period of time in respect of which payments under this subchapter in such case have been made, and in like cases where a recovery is made or allowed, the Secretary shall have the right of intervention and a lien and right of recovery to the extent of any payments paid and payable under this subchapter in such case, provided the cost of such wages, payments in lieu of wages, or other such right, may be directly or indirectly paid by the United States; and any amounts recovered under this subsection shall be covered into the fund established under section 8147 of title 5.

(d) Entitlement to benefits by national of a foreign government under foreign laws. Where a national of a foreign government is entitled to benefits on account of injury or death resulting from a war-risk hazard, under the laws of his native country or any other foreign country, the benefits of this subchapter shall not apply.

(e) Receipt of benefits for prior accident or disease. If at the time a person sustains an injury coming within the purview of this subchapter said person is receiving workmen's compensation benefits on account of a prior accident or disease, said person shall not be entitled to any benefits under this subchapter during the period covered by such workmen's compensation benefits unless the injury from a war-risk hazard increases his disability, and then only to the extent such disability has been so increased. (Dec. 2, 1942, ch 668, Title I, §105, 56 Stat. 1032; Dec. 23, 1943, ch 380, Title I, 57 Stat. 627.)

§1706. Administration.

(a) Rules and regulations. The provisions of this subchapter shall be administered by the Secretary of Labor, and the Secretary is authorized to make rules and regulations for the administration thereof and to contract with insurance carriers for the use of the service facilities of such carriers for the purpose of facilitating administration.

(b) Agreements and working arrangements with other agencies, etc. In administering the provisions of this subchapter the Secretary may enter into agreements or cooperative working arrangements with other agencies of the United States or of any State (including the District of Columbia, Hawaii, Alaska, Puerto Rico, and the Virgin Islands) or political subdivision thereof, and with other public agencies and private persons, agencies, or institutions, within and outside the United States, to utilize their services and facilities and to compensate them for such use. The Secretary may delegate to any officer or employee, or to any agency, of the United States or of any State, or of any political subdivision thereof, or Territory or possession of the United States, such of his powers and duties as he finds necessary for carrying out the purposes of this subchapter.

(c) Waiver of notice of injury and filing of claims. The Secretary, in his discretion, may waive the limitation provisions of subchapter I of chapter 81 of title 5 with respect to notice of injury and filing of claims under this subchapter, whenever the Secretary shall find that, because of circumstances beyond the control of an injured person or his beneficiary, compliance with such provisions could not have been accomplished within the time therein specified. (Dec. 2, 1942, ch 668, Title I, §106, 56 Stat. 1033.)

SUBCHAPTER II MISCELLANEOUS PROVISIONS

§1711. Definitions.

When used in this chapter—

(a) The term "Secretary" means the Secretary of Labor.

(b) The term "war-risk hazard" means any hazard arising during a war in which the United States is engaged; during an armed conflict in which the United States is engaged, whether or not war has been declared; or during a war or armed conflict between military forces of any origin, occurring within any country in which a person covered by this chapter is serving; from—

(1) the discharge of any missile (including liquids and gas) or the use of any weapon, explosive, or other noxious thing by a hostile force or person or in combating an attack or an imagined attack by a hostile force or person; or

(2) action of a hostile force or person, including rebellion or insurrection against the United States or any of its Allies; or

(3) the discharge or explosion of munitions intended for use in connection with a war or armed conflict with a hostile force or person as defined herein (except with respect to employees of a manufacturer, processor, or transporter of munitions during the manufacture, processing, or transporting thereof, or while stored on the premises of the manufacturer, processor, or transporter); or

(4) the collision of vessels in convoy or the operation of vessels or aircraft without running lights or without other customary peacetime aids to navigation; or

(5) the operation of vessels or aircraft in a zone of hostilities or engaged in war activities.

(c) The term "hostile force or person" means any nation, any subject of a foreign nation, or any other person serving a foreign nation (1) engaged in a war against the United States or any of its allies, (2) engaged in armed conflict, whether or not war has been declared, against the United States or any of its allies, or (3) engaged in a war or armed conflict between military forces of any origin in any country in which a person covered by this chapter is serving.

(d) The term "allies" means any nation with which the United States is engaged in a common military effort or with which the United States has entered into a common defensive military alliance.

(e) The term "war activities" includes activities directly relating to military operations.

(f) The term "continental United States" means the States and the District of Columbia. (Dec. 2, 1942, ch 668, Title II, §201, 56 Stat. 1033; June 30, 1953, ch 176, §1, 67 Stat. 134; June 30, 1954, ch 431, §1, 68 Stat. 336; June 30, 1955, ch 257, §1, 69 Stat. 241; July 9, 1956, c. 537, §1, 70 Stat. 519; June 29, 1957, P.L. 85-70, 71 Stat. 242; Aug. 8, 1958, P.L. 85-608, Title I, §§103, 104, 72 Stat. 536, 537; June 25, 1959, P.L. 86-70, §42(c), 73 Stat. 151.)

§1712. Disqualification from benefits.

No person convicted in a court of competent jurisdiction of any subversive act against the United States or any of its Allies, committed after the declaration by the President on May 27, 1941, of the national emergency, shall be entitled to compensation or other benefits under subchapter I of this chapter, nor shall any compensation be payable with respect to his death or detention under said subchapter, and upon indictment or the filing of an information charging the commission of any such subversive act, all such compensation or other benefits shall be suspended and remain suspended until acquittal or withdrawal of such charge, but upon conviction thereof or upon death occurring prior to a final disposition thereof, all such payments and all benefits under said subchapter shall be forfeited and terminated. If the charge is withdrawn, or there is an acquittal, all such compensation withheld shall be paid to the person or persons entitled thereto. (Dec. 2, 1942, ch 668, Title II, §202, 56 Stat. 1034.)

§1713. Fraud; penalties.

Whoever, for the purpose of causing an increase in any payment authorized to be made under this chapter, or for the purpose of causing any payment to be made where no payment is authorized hereunder, shall knowingly make or cause to be made, or aid or abet in the making of any false statement or representation of a material fact in any application for any payment under subchapter I of this chapter, or knowingly make or cause to be made, or aid or abet in the making of any false statement, representation, affidavit, or document in connection with such an application, or claim, shall be guilty of a misdemeanor and upon conviction thereof shall be fined not more than $1,000 or imprisoned for not more than one year, or both. (Dec. 2, 1942, ch 668, Title II, §203, 56 Stat. 1034.)

§1714. Legal services.

No claim for legal services or for any other services rendered in respect of a claim or award for compensation under subchapter I of this chapter to or on account of any person shall be valid unless approved by the Secretary; and any claim so approved shall, in the manner and to the extent fixed by the said Secretary, be paid out of the compensation payable to the claimant; and any person who receives any fee, other consideration, or any gratuity on account of services so rendered, unless such consideration or gratuity is so approved, or who solicits employment for another person or for himself in respect of any claim or award for compensation under said subchapter shall be guilty of a misdemeanor and upon conviction thereof shall, for each offense, be fined not more than $1,000 or imprisoned not more than one year, or both. (Dec. 2, 1942, ch 668, Title II, §204, 56 Stat. 1034.)

§1715. Finality of Secretary's decisions.

The action of the Secretary in allowing or denying any payment under subchapter I of this chapter shall be final and conclusive on all questions of law and fact and not subject to review by any other official of the United States or by any court by mandamus or otherwise, and the Comptroller General is authorized and directed to allow credit in the accounts of any certifying or disbursing officer for payments in accordance with such action. (Dec. 2, 1942, ch 668, Title II, §205, 56 Stat. 1034.)

§1716. Presumption of death or detention.

A determination that an individual is dead or a determination that he has been detained by a hostile force or person may be made on the basis of evidence that he has disappeared under circumstances such as to make such death or detention appear probable. (Dec. 2, 1942, ch 668, Title II, §206, 56 Stat. 1034; Aug. 8, 1958, P.L. 85-608, Title I, §104, 72 Stat. 537.)

§1717. Assignment of benefits; execution, levy, etc., against benefits.

The right of any person to any benefit under subchapter I of this chapter shall not be transferable or assignable at law or in equity except to the United States, and none of the moneys paid or payable (except money paid hereunder as reimbursement for funeral expenses or as reimbursement with respect to payments of workmen's compensation or in the nature of workmen's compensation benefits), or rights existing under said subchapter, shall be subject to execution, levy, attachment, garnishment, or other legal process or to the operation of any bankruptcy or insolvency law. (Dec. 2, 1942, ch 668, Title II, §207, 56 Stat. 1035.)

TITLE 43
PUBLIC LANDS

CHAPTER 29
SUBMERGED LANDS

SUBCHAPTER III
OUTER CONTINENTAL SHELF LANDS

§1331. Definitions.

When used in this suchapter—

(a) The term "outer Continental Shelf" means all submerged lands lying seaward and outside of the area of lands beneath navigable waters as defined in section 1301 [See note, below] of this title, and of which the subsoil and seabed appertain to the United States and are subject to its jurisdiction and control;

[Subsections (b)–(q) Not Reproduced]

(Aug. 7, 1953, ch 345, §2, 67 Stat. 462; Sept. 18, 1978, P.L. 95-372, Title II, §201, 92 Stat. 632.)

2011 Note: Construction of "qualified Outer Continental Shelf revenues". Act Dec. 23, 2011, P.L. 112-74, Div E, Title I, 125 Stat. 994, 995, provides: "For fiscal year 2012 and each fiscal year thereafter, the term 'qualified Outer Continental Shelf revenues', as defined in section 102(9)(A) of the Gulf of Mexico Energy Security Act, division C of Public Law 109-432, shall include only the portion or rental revenues that would have been collected by the Secretary at the rental rates in effect before August 5, 1993."

Note: Section 1301 provides the following definition of the term "lands beneath navigable waters":

(1) all lands within the boundaries of each of the respective States which are covered by nontidal waters that were navigable under the laws of the United States at the time such State became a member of the Union, or acquired sovereignty over such lands and waters thereafter, up to the ordinary high water mark as heretofore or hereafter modified by accretion, erosion, and reliction;

(2) all lands permanently or periodically covered by tidal waters up to but not above the line of mean high tide and seaward to a line three geographical miles distance from the cost line of each such State and to the boundary line of each such State where in any case such boundary as it existed seaward (or into the Gulf of Mexico) beyond three geographical miles, and

(3) all filled in, made, or reclaimed lands which formerly were lands beneath navigable waters, as hereinabove defined.

§1333. Laws and regulations governing lands.

[Subsection (a) Not Reproduced]

(b) Longshore and Harbor Workers' Compensation Act applicable; definitions. With respect to disability or death of an employee resulting from any injury occurring as the result of operations, conducted on the outer Continental Shelf for the purpose of exploring for, developing, removing, or transporting by pipeline the natural resources, or involving rights to the natural resources, of the subsoil and seabed of the outer Continental Shelf, compensation shall be payable under the provisions of the Longshoremen's and Harbor Workers' Compensation Act. For the purposes of the extension of the provisions of the Longshoremen's and Harbor Workers' Compensation Act under this section—

(1) the term "employee" does not include a master or member of a crew of any vessel, or an officer or employee of the United States or any agency thereof or of any State or foreign government, or of any political subdivision thereof;

(2) the term "employer" means an employer any of whose employees are employed in such operations; and

(3) the term "United States" when used in a geographical sense includes the outer Continental Shelf and artificial islands and fixed structures thereon.

[Subsections (c)–(f) Not Reproduced]

(Aug. 7, 1953, ch 345, §4, 67 Stat. 462; Jan. 3, 1975, P.L. 93-627, §19(f), 88 Stat. 2146; Sept. 18, 1978, P.L. 95-372, Title II, §203, 92 Stat. 635.)

TITLE 45
RAILROADS

CHAPTER 2
LIABILITY FOR INJURIES TO EMPLOYEES

§51. Liability of common carriers by railroad, in interstate or foreign commerce, for injuries to employees from negligence; employee defined.

Every common carrier by railroad while engaging in commerce between any of the several States or Territories, or between any of the States and Territories, or between the District of Columbia or any of the States or Territories and any foreign nation or nations, shall be liable in damages to any person suffering injury while he is employed by such carrier in such commerce, or, in case of the death of such employee, to his or her personal representative for the benefit of the surviving widow or husband and children of such employee; and, if none, then of such employee's parents; and, if none, then of the next of kin dependent upon such employee, for such injury or death resulting in whole or in part from the negligence of any of the officers, agents, or employees of such carrier, or by reason of any defect or insufficiency, due to its negligence, in its cars, engines, appliances, machinery, track, roadbed, works, boats, wharves, or other equipment.

Any employee of a carrier, any part of whose duties as such employee shall be the furtherance of interstate or foreign commerce; or shall, in any way directly or closely and substantially, affect such commerce as above set forth shall, for the purpose of this Act [45 U.S. Code 51-60], be considered as being employed by such carrier in such commerce and shall be considered as entitled to the benefits of this Act and of an Act entitled "An Act relating to the liability of common carriers by railroad to their employees in certain cases" (approved April 22, 1908), as the same has been or may hereafter be amended. (Apr. 22, 1908, ch 149, §1, 35 Stat. 65; Aug. 11, 1939, ch 685, §1, 53 Stat. 1404.)

§52. Carriers in Territories or other possessions of United States.

Every common carrier by railroad in the Territories, the District of Columbia, the Panama Canal Zone, or other possessions of the United States shall be liable in damages to any person suffering injury while he is employed by such carrier in any of said jurisdictions, or, in case of the death of such employee, to his or her personal representative, for the benefit of the surviving widow or husband and children of such employee; and, if none, then of such employee's parents; and, if none, then of the next of kin dependent upon such employee, for such injury or death resulting in whole or in part from the negligence of any of the officers, agents, or employees of such carrier, or by reason of any defect or insufficiency, due to its negligence, in its cars, engines, appliances, machinery, track, roadbed, works, boats, wharves, or other equipment. (Apr. 22, 1908, ch 149, §2, 35 Stat. 65.)

§53. Contributory negligence; diminution of damages.

In all actions hereafter brought against any such common carrier by railroad under or by virtue of any of the provisions of this act [45 U.S.C. §§ 51 et seq.] to recover damages for personal injuries to an employee, or where such injuries have resulted in his death, the fact that the employee may have been guilty of contributory negligence shall not bar a recovery, but the damages shall be diminished by the jury in proportion to the amount of negligence attributable to such employee: Provided, That no such employee who may be injured or killed shall be held to have been guilty of contributory negligence in any case where the violation by such common carrier of any statute enacted for the safety of employees contributed to the injury or death of such employee. (Apr. 22, 1908, ch 149, §3, 35 Stat. 66.)

§54. Assumption of risks of employment.

In any action brought against any common carrier under or by virtue of any of the provisions of this Act [45 U.S.C. §§ 51 et seq.] to recover damages for injuries to, or the death of, any of its employees, such employee shall not be held to have assumed the risks of his employment in any case where such injury or death resulted in whole or in part from the negligence of any of the officers, agents, or employees of such carrier; and no employee shall be held to have assumed the risks of his employment in any case where the violation by such common carrier of any statute enacted for the safety of employees contributed to the injury or death of such employee. (Apr. 22, 1908, ch 149, §4, 35 Stat. 66; Aug. 11, 1939, ch 685, §1, 53 Stat. 1404.)

§54a. Regulation, standard, or requirement under chapter 201 of title 49, United States Code, deemed to be statute under sections 3 and 4.

A regulation, standard, or requirement in force, or prescribed by the Secretary of Transportation under chapter 201 of title 49, United States Code [49 U.S.C. §§ 20101 et seq.], or by a State agency that is participating in investigative and surveillance activities under section 20105 of title 49, is deemed to be a statute under sections 3 and 4 of

U.S.C.

this Act [45 U.S.C. §§ 53, 54]. (April 22, 1908, c. 149, §4A, as added July 5, 1994, P.L. 103-272, §4(i), 108 Stat. 1365.)

§55. Contract, rule, regulation, or device exempting from liability; set-off.

Any contract, rule, regulation, or device whatsoever, the purpose or intent of which shall be to enable any common carrier to exempt itself from any liability created by this chapter [45 U.S.C. §§ 51 et seq.], shall to that extent be void: Provided, That in any action brought against any such common carrier under or by virtue of any of the provisions of this chapter [45 U.S.C. §§ 51 et seq.], such common carrier may set off therein any sum it has contributed or paid to any insurance, relief benefit, or indemnity that may have been paid to the injured employee or the person entitled thereto on account of the injury or death for which said action was brought. (Apr. 22, 1908, ch 149, §5, 35 Stat. 66.)

§56. Actions; limitation; concurrent jurisdiction of courts.

No action shall be maintained under this chapter [45 U.S.C. §§ 51 et seq.] unless commenced within three years from the day the cause of action accrued.

Under this chapter [45 U.S.C. §§ 51 et seq.] an action may be brought in a district court of the United States, in the district of the residence of the defendant, or in which the cause of action arose, or in which the defendant shall be doing business at the time of commencing such action. The jurisdiction of the courts of the United States under this chapter [45 U.S.C. §§ 51 et seq.] shall be concurrent with that of the courts of the several States. (Apr. 22, 1908, ch 149, §6, 35 Stat. 66; Apr. 5, 1910, ch 143, §1, 36 Stat. 291; Aug. 11, 1939, ch 685, §2, 53 Stat. 1404; June 25, 1948, ch 646, §18, 62 Stat. 989.)

§57. Who included in term "common carrier."

The term "common carrier" as used in this chapter [45 U.S.C. §§ 51 et seq.] shall include the receiver or receivers or other persons or corporations charged with the duty of the management and operation of the business of a common carrier. (Apr. 22, 1908, ch 149, §7, 35 Stat. 66.)

§58. Duty or liability of common carriers and rights of employees under other acts not impaired.

Nothing in this chapter [45 U.S.C. §§ 51 et seq.] shall be held to limit the duty or liability of common carriers or to impair the rights of their employees under any other Act or Acts of Congress. (Apr. 22, 1908, ch 149, §8 in part, 35 Stat. 66.)

§59. Survival of right of action of person injured.

Any right of action given by this chapter [45 U.S.C. §§ 51 et seq.] to a person suffering injury shall survive to his or her personal representative, for the benefit of the surviving widow or husband and children of such employee, and, if none, then of such employee's parents; and, if none, then of the next of kin dependent upon such employee, but in such cases there shall be only one recovery for the same injury. (Apr. 22, 1908, ch 149, §9, as added Apr. 5, 1910, ch 143, §2, 36 Stat. 291.)

§60. Penalty for suppression of voluntary information incident to accidents; separability.

Any contract, rule, regulation, or device whatsoever, the purpose, intent, or effect of which shall be to prevent employees of any common carrier from furnishing voluntarily information to a person in interest as to the facts incident to the injury or death of any employee, shall be void, and whoever, by threat, intimidation, order, rule, contract, regulation, or device whatsoever, shall attempt to prevent any person from furnishing voluntarily such information to a person in interest, or whoever discharges or otherwise disciplines or attempts to discipline any employee for furnishing voluntarily such information to a person in interest, shall, upon conviction thereof, be punished by a fine of not more than $1,000 or imprisoned for not more than one year, or by both such fine and imprisonment, for each offense: Provided, That nothing herein contained shall be construed to void any contract, rule, or regulation with respect to any information contained in the files of the carrier, or other privileged or confidential reports.

If any provision of this Act [45 U.S.C. §§ 51 et seq.] is declared unconstitutional or the applicability thereof to any person or circumstances is held invalid, the validity of the remainder of the Act [45 U.S.C. §§ 51 et seq.] and the applicability of such provision to other persons and circumstances shall not be affected thereby. (Apr. 22, 1908, ch 149, §10, as added Aug. 11, 1939, ch 685, §3, 53 Stat. 1404.)

TITLE 46
SHIPPING

SUBTITLE III
MARITIME LIABILITY

CHAPTER 301
GENERAL LIABILITY PROVISIONS

§30101. Extension of jurisdiction to cases of damage or injury on land.

(a) In general. The admiralty and maritime jurisdiction of the United States extends to and includes cases of injury or damage, to person or property, caused by a vessel on navigable waters, even though the injury or damage is done or consummated on land.

(b) Procedure. A civil action in a case under subsection (a) may be brought in rem or in personam according to the principles of law and the rules of practice applicable in cases where the injury or damage has been done and consummated on navigable waters.

(c) Actions against United States.

(1) Exclusive remedy. In a civil action against the United States for injury or damage done or consummated on land by a vessel on navigable waters, chapter 309 or 311 of this title [46 U.S.C. §§30901 et seq. or 31101 et seq.], as appropriate, provides the exclusive remedy.

(2) Administrative claim. A civil action described in paragraph (1) may not be brought until the expiration of the 6-month period after the claim has been presented in writing to the agency owning or operating the vessel causing the injury or damage. (Oct. 6, 2006, P.L. 109-304, §6(c), 120 Stat. 1509.)

§30104. Personal injury to or death of seamen.

A seaman injured in the course of employment or, if the seaman dies from the injury, the personal representative of the seaman may elect to bring a civil action at law, with the right of trial by jury, against the employer. Laws of the United States regulating recovery for personal injury to, or death of, a railway employee apply to an action under this section. (Oct. 6, 2006, P.L. 109-304, §6(c), 120 Stat. 1510; Jan. 8, 2008, P.L. 110-181, Div C, Title XXXV, Subtitle C, §3521(a), 122 Stat. 596.)

2008 Note: Act Jan. 8, 2008, P.L. 110-181, Div C, Title XXXV, Subtitle C, §3521(b), 122 Stat. 596, provides: "The amendment made by subsection (a) [amending this section] shall be effective as if included in the enactment of Public Law 109-304 [enacted Oct. 6, 2006].".

§30105. Restriction on recovery by non-citizens and non-resident aliens for incidents in waters of other countries.

(a) Definition. In this section, the term "continental shelf" has the meaning given that term in article I of the 1958 Convention on the Continental Shelf.

(b) Restriction. Except as provided in subsection (c), a civil action for maintenance and cure or for damages for personal injury or death may not be brought under a maritime law of the United States if—

(1) the individual suffering the injury or death was not a citizen or permanent resident alien of the United States at the time of the incident giving rise to the action;

(2) the incident occurred in the territorial waters or waters overlaying the continental shelf of a country other than the United States; and

(3) the individual suffering the injury or death was employed at the time of the incident by a person engaged in the exploration, development, or production of offshore mineral or energy resources, including drilling, mapping, surveying, diving, pipelaying, maintaining, repairing, constructing, or transporting supplies, equipment, or personnel, but not including transporting those resources by a vessel constructed or adapted primarily to carry oil in bulk in the cargo spaces.

(c) Nonapplication. Subsection (b) does not apply if the individual bringing the action establishes that a remedy is not available under the laws of—

(1) the country asserting jurisdiction over the area in which the incident occurred; or

(2) the country in which the individual suffering the injury or death maintained citizenship or residency at the time of the incident. (Oct. 6, 2006, P.L. 109-304, §6(c), 120 Stat. 1510.)

§30106. Time limit on bringing maritime action for personal injury or death.

Except as otherwise provided by law, a civil action for damages for personal injury or death arising out of a maritime tort must be brought within 3 years after the cause of action arose. (Oct. 6, 2006, P.L. 109-304, §6(c), 120 Stat. 1511.)

CHAPTER 303
DEATH ON THE HIGH SEAS

§30301. Short title.

This chapter [46 U.S.C. §§30301 et seq.] may be cited as the "Death on the High Seas Act". (Oct. 6, 2006, P.L. 109-304, §6(c), 120 Stat. 1511.)

U.S.C.

§30302. Cause of action.

When the death of an individual is caused by wrongful act, neglect, or default occurring on the high seas beyond 3 nautical miles from the shore of the United States, the personal representative of the decedent may bring a civil action in admiralty against the person or vessel responsible. The action shall be for the exclusive benefit of the decedent's spouse, parent, child, or dependent relative. (Oct. 6, 2006, P.L. 109-304, §6(c), 120 Stat. 1511.)

§30303. Amount and apportionment of recovery.

The recovery in an action under this chapter [46 U.S.C. §§30301 et seq.] shall be a fair compensation for the pecuniary loss sustained by the individuals for whose benefit the action is brought. The court shall apportion the recovery among those individuals in proportion to the loss each has sustained. (Oct. 6, 2006, P.L. 109-304, §6(c), 120 Stat. 1511.)

§30304. Contributory negligence.

In an action under this chapter [46 U.S.C. §§30301 et seq.], contributory negligence of the decedent is not a bar to recovery. The court shall consider the degree of negligence of the decedent and reduce the recovery accordingly. (Oct. 6, 2006, P.L. 109-304, §6(c), 120 Stat. 1511.)

§30305. Death of plaintiff in pending action.

If a civil action in admiralty is pending in a court of the United States to recover for personal injury caused by wrongful act, neglect, or default described in section 30302 of this title [46 U.S.C. §30302], and the individual dies during the action as a result of the wrongful act, neglect, or default, the personal representative of the decedent may be substituted as the plaintiff and the action may proceed under this chapter [46 U.S.C. §§30301 et seq.] for the recovery authorized by this chapter [46 U.S.C. §§30301 et seq.]. (Oct. 6, 2006, P.L. 109-304, §6(c), 120 Stat. 1511.)

§30306. Foreign cause of action.

When a cause of action exists under the law of a foreign country for death by wrongful act, neglect, or default on the high seas, a civil action in admiralty may be brought in a court of the United States based on the foreign cause of action, without abatement of the amount for which recovery is authorized. (Oct. 6, 2006, P.L. 109-304, §6(c), 120 Stat. 1511.)

§30307. Commercial aviation accidents.

(a) Definition. In this section, the term "nonpecuniary damages" means damages for loss of care, comfort, and companionship.

(b) Beyond 12 nautical miles. In an action under this chapter [46 U.S.C. §§30301 et seq.], if the death resulted from a commercial aviation accident occurring on the high seas beyond 12 nautical miles from the shore of the United States, additional compensation is recoverable for nonpecuniary damages, but punitive damages are not recoverable.

(c) Within 12 nautical miles. This chapter [46 U.S.C. §§30301 et seq.] does not apply if the death resulted from a commercial aviation accident occurring on the high seas 12 nautical miles or less from the shore of the United States. (Oct. 6, 2006, P.L. 109-304, §6(c), 120 Stat. 1512.)

§30308. Nonapplication.

(a) State law. This chapter [46 U.S.C. §§30301 et seq.] does not affect the law of a State regulating the right to recover for death.

(b) Internal waters. This chapter [46 U.S.C. §§30301 et seq.] does not apply to the Great Lakes or waters within the territorial limits of a State. (Oct. 6, 2006, P.L. 109-304, §6(c), 120 Stat. 1512.)

CHAPTER 309
SUITS IN ADMIRALTY AGAINST THE UNITED STATES

§30901. Short title.

This chapter [46 U.S.C. §§30901 et seq.] may be cited as the "Suits in Admiralty Act". (Oct. 6, 2006, P.L. 109-304, §6(c), 120 Stat. 1517.)

§30902. Definition.

In this chapter [46 U.S.C. §§30901 et seq.], the term "federally-owned corporation" means a corporation in which the United States owns all the outstanding capital stock. (Oct. 6, 2006, P.L. 109-304, §6(c), 120 Stat. 1517.)

§30903. Waiver of immunity.

(a) In general. In a case in which, if a vessel were privately owned or operated, or if cargo were privately owned or possessed, or if a private person or property were involved, a civil action in admiralty could be maintained, a civil action in admiralty in personam may be brought against the United States or a federally-owned corporation. In a civil action in admiralty brought by the United States or a federally-owned corporation, an admiralty claim in personam may be filed or a setoff claimed against the United States or corporation.

(b) Non-jury. A claim against the United States or a federally-owned corporation under this section shall be tried without a jury. (Oct. 6, 2006, P.L. 109-304, §6(c), 120 Stat. 1518.)

§30904. Exclusive remedy.

If a remedy is provided by this chapter [46 U.S.C. §§30901 et seq.], it shall be exclusive of any other action arising out of the same subject matter against the officer, employee, or agent of the United States or the federally-owned corporation whose act or omission gave rise to the claim. (Oct. 6, 2006, P.L. 109-304, §6(c), 120 Stat. 1518.)

§30905. Period for bringing action.

A civil action under this chapter [46 U.S.C. §§30901 et seq.] must be brought within 2 years after the cause of action arose. (Oct. 6, 2006, P.L. 109-304, §6(c), 120 Stat. 1518.)

§30906. Venue.

(a) In general. A civil action under this chapter [46 U.S.C. §§30901 et seq.] shall be brought in the district court of the United States for the district in which—

(1) any plaintiff resides or has its principal place of business; or

(2) the vessel or cargo is found.

(b) Transfer. On a motion by a party, the court may transfer the action to any other district court of the United States. (Oct. 6, 2006, P.L. 109-304, §6(c), 120 Stat. 1518.)

§30907. Procedure for hearing and determination.

(a) In general. A civil action under this chapter [46 U.S.C. §§30901 et seq.] shall proceed and be heard and determined according to the principles of law and the rules of practice applicable in like cases between private parties.

(b) In rem.

(1) Requirements. The action may proceed according to the principles of an action in rem if—

(A) the plaintiff elects in the complaint; and

(B) it appears that an action in rem could have been maintained had the vessel or cargo been privately owned and possessed.

(2) Effect on relief in personam. An election under paragraph (1) does not prevent the plaintiff from seeking relief in personam in the same action. (Oct. 6, 2006, P.L. 109-304, §6(c), 120 Stat. 1518.)

§30908. Exemption from arrest or seizure.

The following are not subject to arrest or seizure by judicial process in the United States:

(1) A vessel owned by, possessed by, or operated by or for the United States or a federally-owned corporation.

(2) Cargo owned or possessed by the United States or a federally-owned corporation. (Oct. 6, 2006, P.L. 109-304, §6(c), 120 Stat. 1518.)

§30909. Security.

Neither the United States nor a federally-owned corporation may be required to give a bond or admiralty stipulation in a civil action under this chapter [46 U.S.C. §§30901 et seq.]. (Oct. 6, 2006, P.L. 109-304, §6(c), 120 Stat. 1519.)

§30910. Exoneration and limitation.

The United States is entitled to the exemptions from and limitations of liability provided by law to an owner, charterer, operator, or agent of a vessel. (Oct. 6, 2006, P.L. 109-304, §6(c), 120 Stat. 1519.)

§30911. Costs and interest.

(a) In general. A judgment against the United States or a federally-owned corporation under this chapter [46 U.S.C. §§30901 et seq.] may include costs and interest at the rate of 4 percent per year until satisfied. Interest shall run as ordered by the court, except that interest is not allowable for the period before the action is filed.

(b) Contract providing for interest. Notwithstanding subsection (a), if the claim is based on a contract providing for interest, interest may be awarded at the rate and for the period provided in the contract. (Oct. 6, 2006, P.L. 109-304, §6(c), 120 Stat. 1519.)

§30912. Arbitration, compromise, or settlement.

The Secretary of a department of the United States Government, or the board of trustees of a federally-owned corporation, may arbitrate, compromise, or settle a claim under this chapter [46 U.S.C. §§30901 et seq.]. (Oct. 6, 2006, P.L. 109-304, §6(c), 120 Stat. 1519.)

§30913. Payment of judgment or settlement.

(a) In general. The proper accounting officer of the United States shall pay a final judgment, arbitration award, or settlement under this chapter [46 U.S.C. §§30901 et seq.] on presentation of an authenticated copy.

(b) Source of payment. Payment shall be made from an appropriation or fund available specifically for the purpose. If no appropriation or fund is specifically available, there is hereby appropriated, out of money in the Treasury not otherwise appropriated, an amount sufficient to pay the judgment, award, or settlement. (Oct. 6, 2006, P.L. 109-304, §6(c), 120 Stat. 1519.)

CHAPTER 311
SUITS INVOLVING PUBLIC VESSELS

§31101. Short title.

This chapter [46 U.S.C. §§31101 et seq.] may be cited as the "Public Vessels Act". (Oct. 6, 2006, P.L. 109-304, §6(c), 120 Stat. 1521.)

§31102. Waiver of immunity.

(a) In general. A civil action in personam in admiralty may be brought, or an impleader filed, against the United States for—

(1) damages caused by a public vessel of the United States; or

(2) compensation for towage and salvage services, including contract salvage, rendered to a public vessel of the United States.

(b) Counterclaim or setoff. If the United States brings a civil action in admiralty for damages caused by a privately owned vessel, the owner of the vessel, or the successor in interest, may file a counterclaim in personam, or claim a setoff, against the United States for damages arising out of the same subject matter. (Oct. 6, 2006, P.L. 109-304, §6(c), 120 Stat. 1521.)

§31103. Applicable procedure.

A civil action under this chapter [46 U.S.C. §§31101 et seq.] is subject to the provisions of chapter 309 of this title [46 U.S.C. §§30901 et seq.] except to the extent inconsistent with this chapter [46 U.S.C. §§31101 et seq.]. (Oct. 6, 2006, P.L. 109-304, §6(c), 120 Stat. 1521.)

§31104. Venue.

(a) In general. A civil action under this chapter [46 U.S.C. §§31101 et seq.] shall be brought in the district court of the United States for the district in which the vessel or cargo is found within the United States.

(b) Vessel or cargo outside territorial waters. If the vessel or cargo is outside the territorial waters of the United States—

(1) the action shall be brought in the district court of the United States for any district in which any plaintiff resides or has an office for the transaction of business; or

(2) if no plaintiff resides or has an office for the transaction of business in the United States, the action may be brought in the district court of the United States for any district. (Oct. 6, 2006, P.L. 109-304, §6(c), 120 Stat. 1521.)

§31105. Security when counterclaim filed.

If a counterclaim is filed for a cause of action for which the original action is filed under this chapter [46 U.S.C. §§31101 et seq.], the respondent to the counterclaim shall give security in the usual amount and form to respond to the counterclaim, unless the court for cause shown orders otherwise. The proceedings in the original action shall be stayed until the security is given. (Oct. 6, 2006, P.L. 109-304, §6(c), 120 Stat. 1522.)

§31106. Exoneration and limitation.

The United States is entitled to the exemptions from and limitations of liability provided by law to an owner, charterer, operator, or agent of a vessel. (Oct. 6, 2006, P.L. 109-304, §6(c), 120 Stat. 1522.)

§31107. Interest.

A judgment in a civil action under this chapter [46 U.S.C. §§31101 et seq.] may not include interest for the period before the judgment is issued unless the claim is based on a contract providing for interest. (Oct. 6, 2006, P.L. 109-304, §6(c), 120 Stat. 1522.)

§31108. Arbitration, compromise, or settlement.

The Attorney General may arbitrate, compromise, or settle a claim under this chapter [46 U.S.C. §§31101 et seq.] if a civil action based on the claim has been commenced. (Oct. 6, 2006, P.L. 109-304, §6(c), 120 Stat. 1522.)

§31109. Payment of judgment or settlement.

The proper accounting officer of the United States shall pay a final judgment, arbitration award, or settlement under this chapter [46 U.S.C. §§31101 et seq.] on presentation of an authenticated copy. Payment shall be made from any money in the Treasury appropriated for the purpose. (Oct. 6, 2006, P.L. 109-304, §6(c), 120 Stat. 1522.)

§31110. Subpoenas to officers or members of crew.

An officer or member of the crew of a public vessel may not be subpoenaed in a civil action under this chapter [46 U.S.C. §§31101 et seq.] without the consent of—

(1) the Secretary of the department or the head of the independent establishment having control of the vessel at the time the cause of action arose; or

(2) the master or commanding officer of the vessel at the time the subpoena is issued. (Oct. 6, 2006, P.L. 109-304, §6(c), 120 Stat. 1522.)

§31111. Claims by nationals of foreign countries.

A national of a foreign country may not maintain a civil action under this chapter [46 U.S.C. §§31101 et seq.] unless it appears to the satisfaction of the court in which the action is brought that the government of that country, in similar circumstances, allows nationals of the United States to sue in its courts. (Oct. 6, 2006, P.L. 109-304, §6(c), 120 Stat. 1522.)

§31112. Lien not recognized or created.

This chapter [46 U.S.C. §§31101 et seq.] shall not be construed as recognizing the existence of or as creating a lien against a public vessel of the United States. (Oct. 6, 2006, P.L. 109-304, §6(c), 120 Stat. 1522.)

INDEX

★

ABBREVIATIONS

NOTE: Entries previously cited to Calif. Administrative Code are now cited to Calif. Code of Regulations (CCR).

B&P	Business and Professions Code
CA Const	California Constitution
2 CCR	California Code of Regulations (Title 2)
8 CCR	California Code of Regulations (Title 8)
10 CCR	California Code of Regulations (Title 10)
16 CCR	California Code of Regulations (Title 16)
CCP	California Code of Civil Procedure
CC	Civil Code
Ed	Education Code
Ev	Evidence Code
Gov	Government Code
Har&N	Harbors and Navigation Code
H&S	Health and Safety Code
Ins	Insurance Code
Lab	Labor Code
Mil&Vet	Military and Veterans Code
Pen	Penal Code
Table	Tables and Schedules
UI	Unemployment Insurance Code
USC	United States Code
Veh	Vehicle Code
W&I	Welfare and Institutions Code

How To Use This Index

This Index is arranged according to Code sections, rather than page numbers. To locate an individual Code section, first find your material in the Index. Then refer to the Table of Abbreviations, above, to identify the individual Code. Under each Code in this book, sections are arranged in numerical order.

For example, "Lab §3600" under "Suicide" means Section 3600 of the Labor Code. Find the Labor Code tab on the back cover of this book and follow it to the Labor Code. Then find Section 3600 within the Labor Code.

Some Code sections, such as the Civil Code and Government Code, do not have tabs. They can generally be found in the Miscellaneous Provisions section.

INDEX

A

ABANDONED SPOUSES
Husband and wife privileges waived in proceedings for . . . Ev §972

ABATEMENT
Substitution of insurer . . . Lab §3758

ABBREVIATIONS
Table of . . . Table 18

ABORTION PROTESTS
Commercial or property insurance
 Cancellation or nonrenewal of policies
  Hate crime or anti-reproductive-rights crime generating losses, factoring in decisions . . . Ins §676.10

ABSENTEES
Witnesses . . . Ev §240

ACCRUAL OF CAUSE OF ACTION
Appeals Board (WCAB) . . . Lab §5901
Occupational Safety and Health Appeals Board . . . Lab §6615

ACQUIRED IMMUNE DEFICIENCY SYNDROME (AIDS) (See HUMAN IMMUNODEFICIENCY VIRUS (HIV))

ACQUISITIONS AND MERGERS
Employing units, unemployment compensation and disability benefits . . . UI §3254.5

ACRONYMS
Table of . . . Table 18

ACTUARIAL ANALYSIS
Group self-insurance . . . 8 CCR §15481
Self-insurance
 Definitions . . . 8 CCR §15201
 Submission of actuarial study and summary to office . . . 8 CCR §15209

ACUPUNCTURISTS
Chosen by injured worker . . . Lab §4600.3
Defined . . . Lab §3209.3
Determination of disability by . . . Lab §3209.3
Educational materials for treating physicians . . . Lab §4602.8
Employer-provided treatment
 Lien of provider
  Fraud against workers' compensation system, medical billing, insurance, Medicare or Medi-Cal, stay of provider lien . . . Lab §4615
Employer-provided treatment by . . . Lab §4600
Knox-Keene Health Care Service Plan Act . . . Lab §4600.5

ACUPUNCTURISTS—Cont.
Medical treatment
 Utilization schedule
  Acupuncture medical treatment guidelines . . . 8 CCR §9792.24.1
Personal acupuncturist, designation . . . 8 CCR §9783.1
Physicians, not considered to be . . . Lab §3209.9
 Personal acupuncturist, designation . . . 8 CCR §9783.1
Provision of care by . . . Lab §4600.5
Qualified medical evaluators (QMEs)
 QME competency examination for acupuncturists
  Defined . . . 8 CCR §1
 Referrals . . . 8 CCR §32
Services and supplies provided by . . . Lab §3209.5
Surgeons, not considered to be . . . Lab §3209.9

ADJUDICATION OF CLAIMS
Appeals Board (WCAB), by (See APPEALS BOARD (WCAB))
Applications for adjudication
 Defendant's answer to . . . Lab §5505
 Definition of applicants . . . Lab §5503
 Dismissal without hearing . . . Lab §5507
 Filing . . . Lab §5501
 Pleadings, required . . . Lab §5500
 Procedures following filing . . . Lab §5501
 Where to file . . . Lab §5501.5
Court administrator rules
 Electronic adjudication management system . . . 8 CCR §§10205 to 10208.12 (See ELECTRONIC ADJUDICATION MANAGEMENT SYSTEM (EAMS))
 Generally (See COURT ADMINISTRATOR RULES)
Filing
 Applications for adjudication . . . Lab §5501
 Notice exceptions for injured workers filing for . . . 8 CCR §9884
 Procedures . . . Lab §5501.5
Medical examination, following completion of . . . Lab §4063
Notice exceptions for injured workers filing for . . . 8 CCR §9884

ADMINISTRATION
Claims (See CLAIMS PROCEDURES)
Industrial Relations Department (See INDUSTRIAL RELATIONS DEPARTMENT)
Longshore and Harbor Workers' Compensation Act
 Carrier substituted for employer . . . 33 USC §935
 Secretary of Labor, administration by . . . 33 USC §939
Self-insurance (See SELF-INSURANCE)
Workers' Compensation Division (See WORKERS' COMPENSATION DIVISION)

ADMINISTRATION REVOLVING FUND
Advances against insured employers
Collection . . . 8 CCR §15606
Excess collections . . . 8 CCR §15608
Undercollection . . . 8 CCR §15609
Allocation among insured and self-insured employers . . . 8 CCR §15602
Assessments
Allocation among insured and self-insured employers . . . 8 CCR §15602
Collection . . . 8 CCR §15606
Insured employers, from . . . 8 CCR §15607
Interim assessments . . . 8 CCR §15611
Self-insured employers . . . 8 CCR §15605
Cal-OSHA targeted inspection and consultation assessment
Generally . . . Lab §62.7
Determining self-insurers subject to . . . 8 CCR §15601.7
Collection of surcharge
Advances against insured employers (See subhead: Advances against insured employers)
Excess collections . . . 8 CCR §15608
Insured employers, from . . . 8 CCR §15607, Lab §62.5
Interim assessments . . . 8 CCR §15611
Self-insured employers, from . . . 8 CCR §15605, Lab §62.5
Under collection . . . 8 CCR §15609
Creation of Fund . . . Lab §62.5
Definitions pertinent to . . . 8 CCR §15600
Determination of assessment . . . 8 CCR §§15601, 15603
Fraud surcharge
Allocation of assessment amongst insured and self-insured employers . . . 8 CCR §15602
Collection
Insured employers, from . . . 8 CCR §15607
Self-insured employers, from . . . 8 CCR §15605
Determination of amount . . . 8 CCR §15601.5
Determination of insured and self-insured employer surcharge factors . . . 8 CCR §15603
Notice of amount of assessment . . . 8 CCR §15606
Self-insurers
Collection of assessment from . . . 8 CCR §15605
Determination of insured and self-insured employer surcharge factors . . . 8 CCR §15603
Notice of amount of assessment . . . 8 CCR §15606
Payroll determinations of insured employers . . . 8 CCR §15601.8, Lab §62.5
Premium data of insured employers . . . 8 CCR §15601.8, Lab §62.5
Refund of excess credits . . . 8 CCR §15609
Self-insurers
Generally . . . 8 CCR §15233
Collection of surcharge from . . . 8 CCR §15605, Lab §62.5
Determination of surcharge factors . . . 8 CCR §15603
Surplus in funding . . . 8 CCR §15604

ADMINISTRATIVE LAW
Adoption, amendment, or repeal of regulations
Judicial notice of . . . Ev §451

ADMINISTRATIVE LAW JUDGES (ALJS)
Electronic adjudication management system
Definition of workers' compensation administrative law judge . . . 8 CCR §10205
Workers' compensation judges (WCJs) (See JUDGES (WCJS))

ADMINISTRATIVE PENALTIES (See PENALTIES AND FINES)

ADMIRALTY AND MARITIME JURISDICTION
Damages caused by public vessels or for towage or salvage services, suits against United States for (See SHIPPING)
District courts . . . 28 USC §1333
Judicial notice of Admiralty Court Rules . . . Ev §451
Land, damages or injury on
Extension of jurisdiction . . . 46 USC §30101
Libel in rem or in personam (See SHIPPING)
Shipping (See SHIPPING)
State Compensation Insurance Fund ability to insure under maritime law . . . Ins §11779
United States vessels or cargo, suits by or against (See SHIPPING)

ADMISSIBILITY OF EVIDENCE
Administrative assistance of Workers' Compensation Division, effect of . . . Lab §5455
Admissibility of accounts . . . Ev §§1270 to 1272
Appeals Board (WCAB) hearings . . . Lab §5703
Business records, copies and affidavits . . . Ev §1562
Employer's report of occupational injury or illness . . . Lab §6412
Occupational disease or injury reports . . . Lab §6412
Occupational Safety and Health Division investigations . . . Lab §6315.5
Sexual conduct, injuries arising from . . . Lab §3208.4
Support obligations, proceedings related to . . . Ev §1567

ADVERTISING
Generally . . . 8 CCR §9823
Advising employers, penalties for advertising qualifications for . . . Ins §703.5
Appeals Board (WCAB) qualifications . . . 8 CCR §9825
Attorneys
Exclusions . . . 8 CCR §9821
Legal terms for services provided, use of . . . 8 CCR §9828
Name required in advertisement for workers' compensation legal services . . . B&P §5499.30
Unlicensed . . . 8 CCR §9826
Chiropractors . . . 16 CCR §311
Free or discount services . . . 16 CCR §319
Compliance orders . . . 8 CCR §9835
Covered entities . . . 8 CCR §9821
Cumulative remedies . . . 8 CCR §9836
Definitions
Pertinent terms . . . 8 CCR §9820
Truth in Advertising Act, definition of advertiser for purposes of . . . Lab §5434
Exclusions from coverage . . . 8 CCR §9821
Filing (See FILING)
Fraudulent or misleading advertising
Deceptive advertising . . . 8 CCR §9771.66

ADVERTISING—Cont.
Fraudulent or misleading advertising—Cont.
False or misleading, prohibition of . . . Lab §§139.43, 139.45
QMEs
Complaints, filing . . . 8 CCR §155
Definitions pertinent to . . . 8 CCR §150
Determination of violation . . . 8 CCR §157
Documents, filing . . . 8 CCR §151
Intent and purpose of . . . 8 CCR §152
Penalties and fines . . . 8 CCR §158
Permissible advertising content . . . 8 CCR §154
Prohibition of false or misleading . . . 8 CCR §153
Review of copy . . . 8 CCR §156
Severability of articles . . . 8 CCR §159
Regulations, promulgation of . . . Lab §139.45
Health care organizations (HCOs) (See HEALTH CARE ORGANIATIONS (HCOS))
Hearings . . . 8 CCR §9837
Identification as Nonattorney representative or advisor . . . 8 CCR §9824
Information
Order to provide . . . 8 CCR §9834
Required from referral panelists . . . 8 CCR §9829
Supplied to referral panelists . . . 8 CCR §9830
Investigations . . . 8 CCR §9833
Legal terms for services provided, use of . . . 8 CCR §9828
Medical goods or services, unlicensed . . . 8 CCR §9827
Medical terms for services provided, use of . . . 8 CCR §9828
Penalties and fines
QMEs, fraudulent or misleading advertising . . . 8 CCR §158
Qualifications to advise employers . . . Ins §703.5
Physicians, exclusions for . . . 8 CCR §9821
Records and recordkeeping
Access to records . . . 8 CCR §9832
Maintenance of records . . . 8 CCR §9832
Production of records on demand . . . 8 CCR §9834
Referral services
Information required from panelists . . . 8 CCR §9829
Information supplied to panelists . . . 8 CCR §9830
Registration statements . . . 8 CCR §9831
Remedies for violations . . . 8 CCR §9836
Severability of portions of article . . . 8 CCR §9822
State compensation insurance fund
Disclaimer as to status as branch of state . . . Ins §11771.5
Truth in Advertising Act (See TRUTH IN ADVERTISING ACT)
Violations
Compliance orders . . . 8 CCR §9835
Hearings . . . 8 CCR §9837
Remedies . . . 8 CCR §9836
Workers' Compensation Truth in Advertising Act (See TRUTH IN ADVERTISING ACT)

AERIAL PASSENGER TRAMWAYS
Passenger tramways generally . . . Lab §§7340 to 7357 (See PASSENGER TRAMWAYS)

AFFIDAVITS
Business records as evidence . . . Ev §§1561, 1562

AFFIDAVITS—Cont.
Judge's (WCJ's) affidavit as to pending cases
Form for . . . 8 CCR §9714.5
Submission of . . . 8 CCR §9714
Police officer's personnel record
Good cause for discovery of . . . Ev §1043

AFFILIATES
Group self-insurance
Certificates to self-insure
Reinstatement . . . 8 CCR §15490.1
Self-insurance
Agreement of assumption and guarantee of liability for certificate of . . . 8 CCR §15203.1
Certificates
Definition of affiliate certificate . . . 8 CCR §15201
Interim certificates . . . 8 CCR §15205
Security deposits . . . 8 CCR §15211

AFFIRMATIVE DEFENSES
Generally . . . Lab §3600

AGED PERSONS
Medical assistance
In-home supportive services for aged, blind and disabled
Direct payments to provider or recipients, workers' compensation, unemployment compensation, etcobligations . . . W&I §§12302.2, 12302.5
Unlawful employment practices
Health benefit reductions or elimination upon medicare eligibility not prohibited . . . Gov §12940

AGENTS
Payment of claim directly to . . . Lab §4902

AGREED MEDICAL EVALUATORS (AMES)
Extension of time to complete medical evaluation . . . 8 CCR §38
Guidelines for evaluation and reporting
Compliance by AME . . . 8 CCR §35.5
Information provided to evaluator . . . Lab §4062.3
Party agreement . . . Lab §4602.2
Written communications with AME . . . Lab §4602.3

AGRICULTURE
COVID-19
Infection prevention best practices
Dissemination among agricultural employees . . . Lab §6725
Elevators, escalators, chair lifts and other conveyances
Certified competent conveyance mechanics
Agricultural production, processing and handling facilities, exemptions from requirement of certified competent conveyance mechanic . . . Lab §7311.25
Farm labor vehicle (See FARM LABOR VEHICLE)
Pesticide regulation in compliance with Food and Agriculture Code . . . Lab §6399.1

AIDS (See HUMAN IMMUNODEFICIENCY VIRUS (HIV))

AIR FORCE SERVICE (See MILITARY SERVICE)

Index

ALCOHOL
App-based drivers and services
Driving under the influence
ero tolerance policies . . . B&P §7460
Intoxication defense . . . Lab §3600

ALIENS
Immigrant workers generally (See IMMIGRANT WORKERS)

ALIMONY (See SUPPORT OBLIGATIONS)

ALJS (ADMINISTRATIVE LAW JUDGES)
Workers' compensation judges (WCJs) (See JUDGES (WCJS))

ALTERNATIVE COMMUTE PROGRAMS
Participants' eligibility for coverage . . . Lab §3600.8

ALTERNATIVE DISPUTE RESOLUTION
Collective bargaining agreements, AD provisions in . . . Lab §3201.7
Construction industry . . . Lab §3201.5
Workers' compensation insurance rates . . . Ins §11741
Jockeys, licensed . . . Lab §3201.81
Insurance
Disclosure to employer as to choice of law and venue when dispute resolution to be used . . . Ins §11658.5
Mediators
Testimony of judicial or quasi-judicial officers . . . 8 CCR §10360
Medical treatment
Utilization review
Standards for review, 2013 and forward . . . 8 CCR §9792.10.1
Standards for review, pre-2013 . . . 8 CCR §9792.10
Supplemental job displacement benefits
Dispute resolution . . . 8 CCR §10133.54
Request for dispute resolution before administrative director . . . 8 CCR §10133.55

AMBULANCE SERVICES
Official medical fee schedule . . . 8 CCR §9789.70

AMBULATORY SURGICAL CENTERS
Official medical fee schedule
Outpatient departments and ambulatory surgical centers (See OFFICIAL MEDICAL FEE SCHEDULE)

AME (See AGREED MEDICAL EVALUATORS (AMES))

AMERICAN COLLEGE OF OCCUPATIONAL AND ENVIRONMENTAL MEDICINE
Occupational Medicine Practice Guidelines . . . Lab §4600

AMERICAN MEDICAL ASSOCIATION
Guides to the Evaluation of Permanent Impairment . . . Lab §§4660, 4660.1
Physician's Current Procedural Terminology (CPT) . . . 8 CCR §§9789.10, 9789.30, 9789.31

AMERICANS WITH DISABILITIES ACT COMPLIANCE
Employment discrimination . . . Gov §§12926, 12940

AMPUTATIONS
Temporary disability
Aggregate disability payments
Single injury . . . Lab §4656

ANKLE DISABILITY
Guidelines for evaluation . . . 8 CCR §46.1
Medical treatment
Utilization schedule
Ankle disorders . . . 8 CCR §9792.23.7

ANNUAL AVERAGE EARNINGS
Defined . . . Lab §4451
Military service (See MILITARY SERVICE)

ANSWER
Appeals Board (WCAB) (See APPEALS BOARD (WCAB))
Defendant's answer . . . Lab §5505

ANTI-FEATHERBEDDING LAW OF 1964 (See RAILROADS)

ANTINEOPLASTIC DRUGS
Occupational safety and health
Adoption of occupational safety and health standard for handling antineoplastic drugs in health care facilities . . . Lab §144.8

ANTI-REPRODUCTIVE RIGHTS CRIMES
Commercial or property insurance
Cancellation or nonrenewal of policies
Hate crime or anti-reproductive-rights crime generating losses, factoring in decisions . . . Ins §676.10

APP-BASED DRIVERS AND SERVICES . . . B&P §§7448 to 7467
Antidiscrimination and public safety . . . B&P §§7456 to 7462
Benefits
Healthcare subsidy . . . B&P §7454
Loss and liability protection . . . B&P §7455
Criminal background checks of drivers . . . B&P §7458
Definitions . . . B&P §7463
Discrimination
Prohibited . . . B&P §7456
Driving under the influence
ero tolerance policies . . . B&P §7460
Earnings guarantee . . . B&P §7453
Healthcare subsidy . . . B&P §7454
Hours of work
Rest requirements for drivers . . . B&P §7461
Impersonating app-based driver . . . B&P §7462
Income reporting system . . . B&P §7464.5
Independence of app-based drivers . . . B&P §§7451 to 7452.5
Contract and termination of provisions between driver and company . . . B&P §7452
Independent contractor worker classification
Protection of classification . . . B&P §§7451, 7452.5

APP-BASED DRIVERS AND SERVICES—Cont.
Independent contractor worker classification
Protection of classification . . . B&P §§7451, 7452.5
Insurance
Loss and liability protection . . . B&P §7455
Investigations of emergencies, exigent circumstances and critical incidents
Law enforcement information requests
Mechanism for requests, company to provide . . . B&P §7460.5
Legislative amendment to provisions . . . B&P §7465
Legislative findings and intent . . . B&P §7449
Protect app-based drivers and services act
Short title of provisions . . . B&P §7448
Purpose of provisions . . . B&P §7450
Rest requirements . . . B&P §7461
Rulemaking to implement and administer provisions . . . B&P §7466
Safety training of drivers . . . B&P §7459
Severability of provisions . . . B&P §7467
Sexual harassment
Prevention . . . B&P §7457
Short title of provisions . . . B&P §7448
Uniform work standards
Preemption of local requirements by state . . . B&P §7464
Zero tolerance policies . . . B&P §7460

APPEALS
Compensation due, notice of . . . 8 CCR §10115
Crane safety, revocation of license to certify . . . Lab §7377
Disability benefits (See DISABILITY BENEFITS)
District courts, jurisdiction over appeals from . . . 28 USC §1291
Electronic adjudication management system (EAMS)
Review of orders issued by administrative director . . . 8 CCR §§10208.8 to 10208.11
Independent bill review (IBR) . . . Lab §4603.6
Petition to appeal determination . . . 8 CCR §10567
Independent medical review
Binding nature of review . . . Lab §4610.6
Petition appealing determination . . . 8 CCR §10575
Judicial review of (See JUDICIAL REVIEW)
Labor Standards Enforcement Division hearings (See LABOR STANDARDS ENFORCEMENT DIVISION)
Longshore and Harbor Workers' Compensation Act Benefits Review Board . . . 33 USC §921
Medical provider networks
Petition to appeal determination . . . 8 CCR §10580
Occupational Safety and Health Appeals Board (See OCCUPATIONAL SAFETY AND HEALTH APPEALS BOARD)
Occupational Safety and Health Division permits, denial or revocation of . . . Lab §6506
Occupational safety and health standards, temporary variances from
Decisions on . . . Lab §6457
Time limits on . . . Lab §6455
Penalty assessment orders, notice of
Generally . . . 8 CCR §15582
Conference following appeal . . . 8 CCR §10115.2
Contents of appeal . . . 8 CCR §10115.1

APPEALS—Cont.
Penalty assessment orders, notice of—Cont.
Filing appeal . . . 8 CCR §10115.1
Findings on appeal, issuance of . . . 8 CCR §10115.2
Labor Standards Enforcement Division . . . 8 CCR §15582
Payment following appeal . . . 8 CCR §10115.2
Petition appealing audit penalty assessment . . . 8 CCR §10590
Petition for writ of mandate . . . 8 CCR §10115.2
Primary treating physician, appeal of grant or denial of petition to change . . . 8 CCR §9787
Public disability accommodations
Request for accommodations
Appeal of decision . . . 8 CCR §9708.6
Public Employees' Retirement System (See PUBLIC EMPLOYEES' RETIREMENT SYSTEM)
Qualified medical evaluators (QMEs)
Evaluations
Additional evaluation ordered on appeal . . . 8 CCR §32.6
Rating organizations
Decision, action, or omission of rating organization . . . Ins §11753.1
Noncompliance ruling against rating organization by Commissioner . . . Ins §11754.5
Reconsideration and judicial review . . . Lab §§5900 to 5956
Return to work programs
Supplement program
Appeals of decision . . . 8 CCR §17309
Denial of return-to-work supplement, petition appealing . . . 8 CCR §10565
Revocation of license, permit, or certification
Crane safety, revocation of license to certify . . . Lab §7377
Occupational Safety and Health Division permits, denial or revocation of . . . Lab §6506
Self-insurance (See SELF-INSURANCE)
Stop orders . . . 8 CCR §15581
Vocational rehabilitation, decisions and orders regarding (See VOCATIONAL REHABILITATION)
Voluntary disability benefit plan denials . . . UI §3264
Workers' Compensation Appeals Board (WCAB) (See APPEALS BOARD (WCAB))

APPEALS BOARD (WCAB)
Accrual of cause of action . . . Lab §5901
Administrative director determination
Petition to enforce . . . 8 CCR §10570
Advertising qualification before . . . 8 CCR §9825
Amendment of pleadings . . . 8 CCR §10517
Answers to pleadings
Demurrer . . . 8 CCR §10515
Filing and service of petitions and answers to petitions . . . 8 CCR §§10465, 10510
Procedural requirements . . . 8 CCR §10465
Reconsideration, removal or disqualification, answers to petitions . . . 8 CCR §10940
Contents of petitions and answers . . . 8 CCR §10945
Service and proof of service . . . 8 CCR §10940
Size, format, etc of petitions, etc . . . 8 CCR §10940

Index

APPEALS BOARD (WCAB)—Cont.
Answers to pleadings—Cont.
Reconsideration, removal or disqualification, answers to petitions —Cont.
Supplemental petitions or responses . . . 8 CCR §10964
Verification of petition for disqualification . . . 8 CCR §10940
Appearance before board
Removal of privilege to appear . . . Lab §4907
Applications for adjudication of claims
Contents . . . Lab §4906
Dismissal of application
Order dismissing . . . 8 CCR §10850
Initiation of proceedings . . . 8 CCR §10450
Labor Code 4906(h) statements . . . 8 CCR §10470
Minors as applicants . . . 8 CCR §10455
Procedure . . . 8 CCR §10455
Separate application for each injury . . . 8 CCR §10455
Appointment of
Chairperson . . . Lab §113
Members . . . Lab §112
Apportionment
Occupational diseases or cumulative injury, employer liability
Proceedings with appeals board to determine apportionment or right of contribution . . . Lab §5500.5
Arbitration (See ARBITRATION)
Assignment of cases . . . 8 CCR §10346
Consolidated cases . . . 8 CCR §10398
Attachment, authority to order writs of . . . Lab §5600
Attorney discipline
Barring of disbarred, suspended, etc attorneys from representing parties before board . . . 8 CCR §10445
Attorneys
Attorney representatives generally . . . 8 CCR §10400
Pleadings
Filing by attorneys or other representatives, special requirements . . . 8 CCR§10520
Substitution or dismissal of attorneys and non-attorney representatives . . . 8 CCR §10402
Attorneys' fees
Approval by board . . . 8 CCR §10840
Deposition of employee requested by employer
Petition for attorney fees . . . 8 CCR §10547
Attorney's fees for hearings before . . . 8 CCR §10421
Autopsy, authority to order . . . Lab §§5706, 5707
Awards by (See AWARD)
Bad faith actions or tactics . . . Lab §5813
Cases
Assignment or transfer . . . 8 CCR §10346
Setting . . . 8 CCR §10745
Certified copies of awards
Filing . . . Lab §5806
Judgment roll, as . . . Lab §5807
Certified copies of decisions
Filing . . . Lab §5806
Judgment roll, as . . . Lab §5807
Certified copies of orders
Filing . . . Lab §5806

APPEALS BOARD (WCAB)—Cont.
Certified copies of orders—Cont.
Issuance . . . 8 CCR §10820
Judgment roll, as . . . Lab §5807
Withholding . . . 8 CCR §10825
Certified copies of reports
Documentary evidence, admissibility . . . 8 CCR §10670
Chairperson, appointment of . . . Lab §113
Collateral estoppel on subsequent criminal proceedings (See COLLATERAL ESTOPPEL)
Commissioners
Testimony of judicial or quasi-judicial officers . . . 8 CCR §10360
Compensation due, appeal of notice of . . . 8 CCR §10115
Composition of . . . Lab §112
Compromise and release (See SETTLEMENT, COMPROMISE AND RELEASE)
Conference hearings
Priority conferences . . . 8 CCR §10785
Submissions at conference . . . 8 CCR §10761
Consolidated cases
Assignment . . . 8 CCR §10398
Criteria for consolidation . . . 8 CCR §10396
Contempt
Proceedings . . . 8 CCR §10440, Lab §134
Subpoena, refusal to obey . . . Lab §132
Continuing jurisdiction . . . Lab §5803
Contribution
Occupational diseases or cumulative injury, employer liability
Proceedings with appeals board to determine apportionment or right of contribution . . . Lab §5500.5
Costs
Petition for costs . . . 8 CCR §10545
Court administrator rules
Petition appealing orders of administrative director or director of industrial relations . . . 8 CCR §10560
Court costs
Generally . . . Lab §5811
Hearings . . . 8 CCR §10421
Credit for payments, overpayments, etc
Petition for credit . . . 8 CCR §10555
Decisions
Generally . . . Lab §§115, 5313
Acting on . . . Lab §5315
Altered decision, effect of . . . Lab §5805
Appeals Board, only issuable by . . . 8 CCR §10320
Certified copy
Filing . . . Lab §5806
Judgment roll, as . . . Lab §5807
Collateral estoppel effect, lack of . . . Lab §5816
En banc decisions . . . 8 CCR §10325
Errors, correcting . . . 8 CCR §10966
Judicial review (See JUDICIAL REVIEW)
Method of service of . . . Lab §5316
Public official, service of . . . Lab §5317
Reconsideration (See RECONSIDERATION)
Service by board of orders, decisions, awards, etc . . . 8 CCR §10628
Statement of determination of issues . . . Lab §5815
Stay of execution of (See subhead: Stay of execution of decision during judicial review)

APPEALS BOARD (WCAB)—Cont.
Decisions—Cont.
Suspension of decision by filing petition for reconsideration . . . Lab §5910
Thirty-day period for . . . Lab §§5313, 5800.5
Time limits for acting on judge's (WCJ's) decision . . . Lab §5315
Declaration of readiness to proceed
Forms required . . . 8 CCR §10500
Hearings not set until declaration filed . . . 8 CCR §10742
Objections to declaration . . . 8 CCR §10744
Definitions . . . 8 CCR §10305
Demurrer . . . 8 CCR §10515
Deposition of witnesses
Generally . . . Lab §5710
Employee, deposition requested by employer
Attorney fees, petition . . . 8 CCR §10547
Deputy commissioners
Testimony of judicial or quasi-judicial officers . . . 8 CCR §10360
Designated service . . . 8 CCR §10629
Discovery
Application
Filing as prerequisite to discovery . . . 8 CCR §10450
Dismissal orders
Application, order dismissing . . . 8 CCR §10850
Disqualification
Petition for disqualification . . . 8 CCR §10940
Contents . . . 8 CCR §10945
Report of WCJ on petitions . . . 8 CCR §10962
Service and proof of service . . . 8 CCR §10940
Size, format, etc of petitions, etc . . . 8 CCR §10940
Skeletal petitions unsupported by reference to record or law, denial or dismissal . . . 8 CCR §10972
Supplemental petitions or responses . . . 8 CCR §10964
Verification . . . 8 CCR §10940
Testimony of judicial or quasi-judicial officers . . . 8 CCR §10360
Documents
Filing and service of documents . . . 8 CCR §10610
Electronic adjudication management system
Definition of appeals board . . . 8 CCR §10205
Email, service by
Time within which to act . . . 8 CCR §10605
En banc decisions . . . 8 CCR §10325
Evidence before
Documentary evidence . . . 8 CCR §10670
Exhibits . . . 8 CCR §10677
Filing and listing
Proposed exhibits . . . 8 CCR §10620
Ex parte communications . . . 8 CCR §10410
Testimony of judicial or quasi-judicial officers . . . 8 CCR §10360
Expedited hearing
Reassignment to another judge
Petition . . . 8 CCR §10788
Extensions of time
Holidays . . . 8 CCR §10600

APPEALS BOARD (WCAB)—Cont.
Extensions of time—Cont.
Public emergencies . . . 8 CCR §10370
Weekends . . . 8 CCR §10600
Failure to secure payment, filing with Board due to employer's . . . Lab §3715
Fax service
Time within which to act . . . 8 CCR §10605
Fees (See FEES)
Filing of documents with attorneys or representatives
Filing and service of documents generally . . . 8 CCR §10610
Filing of documents with board
Answers to petitions . . . 8 CCR §§10510, 104645
Certified copies of awards . . . Lab §5806
Certified copies of decisions . . . Lab §5806
Certified copies of orders . . . Lab §5806
Decisions, certified copy of . . . Lab §5806
Electronic documents
Time to file documents . . . 8 CCR §10615
Evidence
Documentary evidence . . . 8 CCR §10670
Exhibits
Proposed exhibits. . . 8 CCR §10620
Judicial review
Time limits on filing for . . . Lab §5950
Undertaking on stay order . . . Lab §6002
Ongoing duty to serve . . . 8 CCR §10635
Petitions and answers to petitions . . . 8 CCR §10510
Place of filing
Documents subsequent to initial documents . . . 8 CCR §10615
Rejections of documents for filing
Statute of limitations or jurisdictional time limitation implicated, restrictions on rejection . . . 8 CCR §10617
Suspension of order by filing petition for reconsideration . . . Lab §5910
Time limits on filing for judicial review . . . Lab §5950
Time to file documents . . . 8 CCR §10615
Undertaking as to stay of execution of decision during judicial review, filing . . . Lab §6002
Findings
Certified copy of . . . Lab §5807
Collateral estoppel and subsequent criminal proceedings . . . Lab §§5006, 5413, 5816
Judicial review, findings of fact not subject to . . . Lab §5953
Modifying . . . Lab §5315
Reconsideration of (See RECONSIDERATION)
Request for findings of fact . . . 8 CCR §10460
Setting aside . . . Lab §5315
Thirty-day period for . . . Lab §5313
Fraud, petition for reconsideration presenting evidence of . . . 8 CCR §10974
Frivolous pleadings
Sanctions . . . 8 CCR §10421
Vexatious litigants . . . 8 CCR §10430
Hearings (See HEARINGS)
Inactive cases
Dismissal of inactive cases
Lien claims . . . 8 CCR §10888

APPEALS BOARD (WCAB)—Cont.
Inactive cases—Cont.
Dismissal of inactive cases —Cont.
Petition to dismiss . . . 8 CCR §10550
Independent bill review determination
Appeal of determination . . . 8 CCR §10567
Petition to enforce administrative director determination . . . 8 CCR §10570
Independent medical review
Petition appealing determination . . . 8 CCR §10575
Intention, notice of
Objections . . . 8 CCR §10832
Orders issued after notice of intention . . . 8 CCR §10832
Permitted purposes . . . 8 CCR §10832
Service . . . 8 CCR §10832
Interim orders
Entry as minute orders . . . 8 CCR §10833
Interlocutory orders
Entry as minute orders . . . 8 CCR §10833
Joinder of actions . . . Lab §5303
Joinder of parties . . . 8 CCR §10382
Judges (WCJs)
Appointment of . . . Lab §5310
Board power over WCJ . . . Lab §5309
Reconsideration of decisions, findings, orders, and awards
Authority following decision after reconsideration . . . 8 CCR §10986
Report of judge . . . 8 CCR §10962
Removal . . . Lab §5310
Testimony of judicial or quasi-judicial officers . . . 8 CCR §10360
Time limit for Appeals Board to act on decision of . . . Lab §5315
Judgment on the pleadings . . . 8 CCR §10515
Judgment roll, what constitutes . . . Lab §5807
Judicial review (See JUDICIAL REVIEW)
Jurisdiction (See JURISDICTION)
Labor Code, references in Workers' compensation division of . . . Lab §3205.5
Liens and lien claimants (See LIENS)
Longshore and Harbor Workers' Compensation Act . . . Lab §128
Mailbox maintained in district office
Service
Receipt of documents from mailbox as service . . . 8 CCR §10628
Mail service . . . CCP §1013
Time within which to act . . . 8 CCR §10605
Masters
Testimony of judicial or quasi-judicial officers . . . 8 CCR §10360
Mediators
Testimony of judicial or quasi-judicial officers . . . 8 CCR §10360
Medical examinations (See MEDICAL EXAMINATIONS)
Medical-legal expenses
Procedures for determination of disputes . . . 8 CCR §10786
Promulgation of rules and regulations regarding . . . Lab §4627

APPEALS BOARD (WCAB)—Cont.
Medical provider networks
Petition to appeal determination . . . 8 CCR §10580
Medical records
Certified copies of reports
Documentary evidence, admissibility . . . 8 CCR §10670
Employer records as evidence
Service, ongoing duty . . . 8 CCR §10635
Physicians' reports (See subhead: Physicians' reports)
Medi-Cal, reimbursement of . . . W&I §14101.7
Medical reports (See MEDICAL REPORTS)
Medical treatment
Jurisdiction over medical treatment . . . Lab §5304
Misconduct
Employer's willful misconduct . . . Lab §4553
Reduction in compensation due to employee's willful misconduct . . . Lab §4552
New and further disability, petition to establish . . . 8 CCR §10536
Non-attorney representatives . . . 8 CCR §10401
Complaints for violations jeopardizing right to appear . . . 8 CCR §10403
Substitution or dismissal of attorneys and non-attorney representatives . . . 8 CCR §10402
Suspension and removal of privilege to appear before WCAB . . 8 CCR §10404
Notice (See NOTICE)
Oaths, administration of . . . Lab §130
Orders
Administrative director determination, petition to enforce . . . 8 CCR §10570
Appeal and review of (See subhead: Appeal and review of decisions and orders of)
Certified copies (See subhead: Certified copies of orders)
Commissioner, issuable by . . . 8 CCR §§10338, 10344
Deputy Commissioner, issuable by . . . 8 CCR §10344
Designated service . . . 8 CCR §10629
Dismissal of application . . . 8 CCR §10850
Intention, notice of
Orders issued after notice of intention . . . 8 CCR §10832
Judicial review (See JUDICIAL REVIEW)
Minute orders . . . 8 CCR §10833
Modifying . . . Lab §5315
Only issuable by Appeals Board . . . 8 CCR §§10320, 10344
Presiding judge, issuable by . . . 8 CCR §10344
Qualified medical evaluators (QMEs), loss of reappointment for failure to comply with Board order or ruling by . . . 8 CCR §56
Reconsideration of (See RECONSIDERATION)
Service by board of orders, decisions, awards, etc . . . 8 CCR §10628
Setting aside . . . Lab §5315
Statement of determination of issues . . . Lab §5815
Suspension of order by filing petition for reconsideration . . . Lab §5910
Termination of liability, interim order on . . . 8 CCR §10540

APPEALS BOARD (WCAB)—Cont.
Orders—Cont.
 Vexatious litigants
  Prefiling orders . . . 8 CCR §10430
Out-of-state injuries of resident, jurisdiction over . . . Lab §5305
Parties to cases under
 Appearance of parties or representatives . . . 8 CCR §19752
 Attendance permitted . . . Lab §5700
 Ex parte communications . . . 8 CCR §10410
 Identification . . . 8 CCR §10390
 Joinder of parties . . . 8 CCR §10382
 Necessary parties . . . 8 CCR §10380
 Non-attorney representatives . . . 8 CCR §10401
  Complaints for violations jeopardizing right to appear . . . 8 CCR §10403
  Substitution or dismissal . . . 8 CCR §10402
  Suspension and removal of privilege to appear before WCAB . . . 8 CCR §10404
 Service by . . . 8 CCR §10625
 Vexatious litigants . . . 8 CCR §10430
Payment of benefits, determination of . . . Lab §5801
Penalties and fines
 Appeals of penalty assessments (See APPEALS)
 Hearings, ordered at . . . 8 CCR §10421
Permanent disability rating determinations
 Formal determinations . . . 8 CCR §10675
Petitions
 Administrative director determination, petition to enforce . . . 8 CCR §10570
 Costs . . . 8 CCR §10545
 Credit for payments, overpayments, etc
  Petition for credit . . . 8 CCR §10555
 Disqualification of judge . . . 8 CCR §10960
 Filing petitions and answers to petitions . . . 8 CCR §10510
 New and further disability
  Petition to establish . . . 8 CCR §10536
 Reassignment of trial or expedited hearing to another judge . . . 8 CCR §10788
 Reconsideration, for (See RECONSIDERATION)
 Removal petitions . . . 8 CCR §10955
 Reopening of case . . . 8 CCR §10534
 Stay of action pending hearing
  Emergency petition . . . 8 CCR §10530
 Termination of liability, for (See subhead: Termination of liability, petition for)
 Testimony of judicial or quasi-judicial officers, compelling . . . 8 CCR §10360
Physicians' reports
 Evidence, as . . . 8 CCR §10682
 Failure to provide examining physician's curriculum vitae . . . 8 CCR §10670
 Ongoing duty to serve . . . 8 CCR §10635
 Qualified medical evaluator's (QME's) report (See QUALIFIED MEDICAL EVALUATORS (QMES))
 Service of copies of documents, electronic media, etc, offered into evidence . . . 8 CCR §10635
  Lien claimants who are not physicians, service on . . . 8 CCR §10637
Pleadings
 Amendment . . . 8 CCR §10517
 Answers (See subhead: Answers to pleadings)

APPEALS BOARD (WCAB)—Cont.
Pleadings—Cont.
 Applications for adjudication of claims
  Contents . . . Lab §4906
  Dismissal of application, order . . . 8 CCR §10850
  Incompetents as applicants . . . 8 CCR §10455
  Initiation of proceedings . . . 8 CCR §10450
  Labor Code 4906(h) statements . . . 8 CCR §10470
  Minors as applicants . . . 8 CCR §10455
  Procedure . . . 8 CCR §10455
  Separate application for each injury . . . 8 CCR §10455
 Attorneys or other representatives filing
  Special requirements . . . 8 CCR§10520
 Case opening documents
  Initiation of proceedings . . . 8 CCR §10450
 Declarations of readiness to proceed
  Hearings not set until declaration filed . . . 8 CCR §10742
  Objections to declaration . . . 8 CCR §10744
 Declarative statements . . . Lab §4906
 Demurrer . . . 8 CCR §10515
 Discovery
  Filing application as prerequisite . . . 8 CCR §10450
 Discrimination against injured employees, allegations . . . 8 CCR §10528
 Findings of fact, request for . . . 8 CCR §10460
 Form for application . . . 8 CCR §10500
 Frivolous pleadings
  Sanctions . . . 8 CCR §10421
 Judgment on the pleadings . . . 8 CCR §10515
 Judicial review of Appeals Board (WCAB) decisions, service of pleadings upon . . . Lab §5954
 Jurisdiction
  Filing application as prerequisite to invocation of jurisdiction . . . 8 CCR §10450
 Petitions, filing (See subhead: Petitions)
 Serious and willful misconduct (See SERIOUS AND WILLFUL MISCONDUCT)
 Service . . . 8 CCR §10500
 Setting the case . . . 8 CCR §10745
 Stay of action of other party pending hearing
  Emergency petition . . . 8 CCR §10530
 Vexatious litigants
  Prefiling orders . . . 8 CCR §10430
 Walk-through documents . . . 8 CCR §10789
Powers of . . . Lab §§111, 133, 5307.5
Presumptions regarding decisions of . . . Lab §5302
Pretrial conference statements
 Forms required . . . 8 CCR §10500
Primary treating physician, appeal of grant or denial of petition to change . . . 8 CCR §9787
Priority conferences . . . 8 CCR §10785
Public Employees' Retirement System (See PUBLIC EMPLOYEES' RETIREMENT SYSTEM)
Public employment (See PUBLIC EMPLOYMENT)
Qualified medical evaluator's (QME's) report (See QUALIFIED MEDICAL EVALUATORS (QMES))
Quasi-judicial officers
 Testimony of judicial or quasi-judicial officers . . . 8 CCR §10360

Index

APPEALS BOARD (WCAB)—Cont.
Reassignment
  Petition for automatic reassignment . . . 8 CCR §10788
Reconsideration of decisions, findings, orders, and awards (See RECONSIDERATION)
Record of proceedings . . . 8 CCR §10803
  Adjudication file . . . 8 CCR §10803
    Destruction of records . . . 8 CCR §10811
  Destruction of records . . . 8 CCR §10811, Lab §135
  Inspection of . . . 8 CCR §10807
  Sealed documents . . . 8 CCR §10813
  Trial level proceedings, recording . . . 8 CCR §10818
Records and recordkeeping
  Certified copies of reports
    Documentary evidence, admissibility . . . 8 CCR §10670
  Destruction of records . . . 8 CCR §10811, Lab §135
  Employer records as evidence
    Service, ongoing duty . . . 8 CCR §10635
  Evidence (See EVIDENCE)
  Exhibits generally . . . 8 CCR §10677
  Ex parte communications . . . 8 CCR §10410
  Filing documents (See subhead: Filing of documents with)
  Proceedings, record of (See subhead: Record of proceedings)
  Public Employees' Retirement System disability retirement reviews . . . Gov §21169
  Subpoena of electronic records . . . 8 CCR §10644
  X-rays (See X-RAYS)
Reductions in compensation due to injured worker's misconduct . . . Lab §4552
Regulations, right to change . . . Lab §5307
Removal
  Board's authority to remove itself . . . Lab §5310
  Judge's removal by Board . . . Lab §5310
  Petition for removal . . . 8 CCR §10940
    Contents . . . 8 CCR §10945
    Grounds . . . 8 CCR §10955
    Service and proof of service . . . 8 CCR §10940
    Size, format, etc of petitions, etc . . . 8 CCR §10940
    Skeletal petitions unsupported by reference to record or law, denial or dismissal . . . 8 CCR §10972
    Supplemental petitions or responses . . . 8 CCR §10964
  Report of WCJ on removal . . . 8 CCR §10962
Reopening of case, petition for . . . 8 CCR §10534
Reports
  Certified copies
    Documentary evidence, admissibility . . . 8 CCR §10670
  Evidence (See EVIDENCE)
  Judge's (WCJ's) report on petition for reconsideration . . . 8 CCR §10962
  Medical reports (See MEDICAL REPORTS)
  Physicians' reports (See subhead: Physicians' reports)
  Qualified medical evaluator's (QME's) report (See QUALIFIED MEDICAL EVALUATORS (QMES))

APPEALS BOARD (WCAB)—Cont.
Representation, notice of
  Attorney representatives . . . 8 CCR §10400
  Lien claimants . . . 8 CCR §10868
  Non-attorney representatives . . . 8 CCR §10401
Rights (See RIGHTS)
Rulemaking procedures . . . 8 CCR §10300
Sanctions . . . 8 CCR §10421
Satisfaction of judgment in fact . . . Lab §5809
Seal, use of . . . Lab §116
Self-employed persons, insurance controversies involving . . . Lab §5308
Serious and willful misconduct (See SERIOUS AND WILLFUL MISCONDUCT)
Service (See SERVICE)
Settlement conferences (See SETTLEMENT, COMPROMISE AND RELEASE)
Statement of determination in orders, decisions, and awards . . . Lab §5815
Statutes of limitation
  Filing of documents with board, rejection
    Restrictions on rejection when statute of limitations or jurisdictional time limitation implicated . . . 8 CCR §10617
Stay of action of other party pending hearing
  Petitions
    Emergency petition . . . 8 CCR §10530
Stay of execution of decision during judicial review
  Generally . . . Lab §5956
  Automatic stay . . . Lab §5956
  Limitations on authority of reviewing court to issue . . . Lab §6000
  Reconsideration, during . . . Lab §5808
  Undertaking
    Filing . . . Lab §6002
    Requirements . . . Lab §6001
Stipulations (See STIPULATIONS)
Subpoenas (See SUBPOENAS)
Subsequent injuries benefits trust fund (See SUBSEQUENT INJURIES BENEFITS TRUST FUND)
Summary judgment . . . 8 CCR §10515
Suspension of order, decision, or award by filing petition for reconsideration . . . Lab §5910
Temporary disability
  Petition to terminate liability for indemnity
    Forms required . . . 8 CCR §10500
Termination of liability, petition for
  Generally . . . 8 CCR §10462
  Temporary total disability, petition to terminate liability . . . 8 CCR §10540
    Hearings . . . 8 CCR §10540
    Interim orders . . . 8 CCR §10540
    Objections to petition . . . 8 CCR §10540
Terms used for . . . Lab §110
Time
  Extensions of time
    Holidays 8 CCR §10600
    Public emergencies . . . 8 CCR §10370
    Weekends . . . 8 CCR §10600
  Hearings . . . Lab §5502
  Judge (WCJ), time limits for Appeals Board to act on decision of . . . Lab §5315
  Judicial review, filing for . . . Lab §5950

APPEALS BOARD (WCAB)—Cont.
Transcripts
Generally . . . Lab §5704
Requests for . . . 8 CCR §10800
Taking of . . . 8 CCR §10800
Transfer of cases . . . 8 CCR §10346
Treating physician's report
Ongoing duty to serve . . . 8 CCR §10635
Trial . . . 8 CCR §10787
Uniformity of procedures, forms, and settings . . . Lab §5500.3
Venue
Designation in case opening document . . . 8 CCR §10480
Division of workers' compensation employee filing application . . . 8 CCR §10482
Objection to venue
Attorney's place of business as basis for objection . . . 8 CCR §10488
Petition for change . . . 8 CCR §10490, Lab §5501.6
Vexatious litigants . . . 8 CCR §10430
Vocational experts
Evidentiary effect of reports of vocational experts . . . 8 CCR §10685
Vocational rehabilitation
Appeal and review of decisions and orders of Appeals Board regarding (See subhead: Appeal and review of decisions and orders of)
Walk-through documents . . . 8 CCR §10789
Witnesses
Cross-examination (See subhead: Cross-examination before)
Deposition of
Generally . . . Lab §5710
Direct examination of . . . Lab §5701
Fees and mileage for . . . 8 CCR §10647, Lab §131
Medical witnesses . . . 8 CCR §10650
Subpoenas . . . 8 CCR §10647
Medical witnesses . . . 8 CCR §10650

APPORTIONMENT OF LIABILITY . . . Lab §§4663, 4664
Cumulative injury
Employer liability
Proceedings with appeals board to determine apportionment or right of contribution . . . Lab §5500.5
Longshore and Harbor Workers' Compensation Act . . . 33 USC §908
Occupational diseases
Employer liability
Proceedings with appeals board to determine apportionment or right of contribution . . . Lab §5500.5
Permanent disability . . . 8 CCR §§10162, 10163

ARBITRATION
Appeals Board (WCAB)
Public employment controversies before
Power of Appeals Board as arbitrator . . . Lab §6146
Submission of controversies . . . Lab §6145
Reconsideration from arbitration decision
Procedures . . . 8 CCR §§10990, 10995

ARBITRATION—Cont.
Appeals Board (WCAB)—Cont.
Settlement conferences prior to hearings, arbitration at . . . Lab §5502
Arbitrators
Disqualification of arbitrator . . . 8 CCR §10912
Fees and costs, disputes over . . . 8 CCR §10920
Selection of arbitrator . . . 8 CCR §10910, Lab §5271
Attorney, representation by . . . Lab §5270
Award
Generally . . . Lab §5277
Service of . . . Lab §5277
Baseball arbitration . . . Lab §5502
Costs, payment of . . . Lab §5273
Date, time, and place of proceedings . . . Lab §5276
Disqualification of arbitrator . . . 8 CCR §10912
Drugs, medical treatment utilization schedule (MTUS)
Formulary
Dispute resolution . . . 8 CCR §9792.27.17
Duties of arbitrator . . . Lab §5272
Electronic adjudication management system (EAMS)
Submittal form . . . 8 CCR §10208.12
Eligible arbitrators, list of . . . Lab §5270.5
Fees and costs, disputes over . . . 8 CCR §10920
Findings . . . Lab §5277
Insurance
Disclosure to employer as to choice of law and venue when dispute resolution to be used . . . Ins §11658.5
Interpreters
Qualifications of interpreter . . . 8 CCR §9795.1.5
Directories of qualified interpreters . . . 8 CCR §9795.5
Limits on powers of arbitrator . . . Lab §5272
Mandatory arbitration . . . 8 CCR §10900
Objections to arbitration . . . 8 CCR §10900
Powers of arbitrator . . . Lab §5272
Public employment controversies before Appeals Board (WCAB)
Power of Appeals Board as arbitrator . . . Lab §6146
Submission of controversies . . . Lab §6145
Record of arbitration proceeding . . . 8 CCR §10914
Selection of arbitrator . . . 8 CCR §10910, Lab §5271
Service of findings and award . . . Lab §5277
Settlements . . . Lab §5278
Shipping
Public vessels, damages caused by or towage and salvage rendered to . . . 46 USC §31108
United States vessels or cargo, suits in admiralty involving
Arbitration of claims . . . 46 USC §30912
Payment of settlement or judgment . . . 46 USC §30913
Types of disputes suitable for arbitration . . . Lab §5275
Mandatory arbitration . . . 8 CCR §10900
Voluntary arbitration . . . 8 CCR §10905
United States, tort claims against . . . 28 USC §2677
Voluntary arbitration . . . 8 CCR §10905

ARISING OUT OF EMPLOYMENT/COURSE OF EMPLOYMENT
Generally . . . Lab §3600
California State University Police Department, injuries incurred by . . . Lab §4817

Index

ARISING OUT OF EMPLOYMENT/COURSE OF EMPLOYMENT—Cont.
Condition of compensation liability, as . . . Lab §3600
COVID-19, compensation for injury or death . . . Lab §3212.86
Firefighters, peace officers, health workers, etc . . . Lab §3212.87
Testing positive, outbreak at place of employment . . . Lab §3212.88
Highway Patrol, injuries incurred by . . . Lab §4801
Justice Department employees, injuries incurred by . . . Lab §4801
Military service
Injury suffered in line of duty (See MILITARY SERVICE)
San Francisco Port Commission employees, injuries incurred by . . . Lab §4801
Seamen, injury in course of employment
Actions . . . 46 USC §30104
Non-citizens or non-resident aliens, restrictions on recovery for incidents in foreign waters . . . 46 USC §30105
University of California
Fire department employees, injuries incurred by . . . Lab §4804.2
Law enforcement officers, injuries incurred by . . . Lab §4807

ARMED FORCES (See MILITARY SERVICE)

ASBESTOS
Adjustment of claims . . . Lab §4409
Advances, payment as . . . Lab §4407
Asbestos Workers' Account, creation of . . . Lab §5406.5
Attorneys for . . . Lab §4415
Claims procedures . . . Lab §4403
Collection proceedings, time limits on . . . Lab §5406.5
Contract for corrective work as condition for inspection . . . Lab §6509.5
Death benefits . . . Lab §4407.3
Definitions pertinent to . . . Lab §§4402, 6501.7, 6501.8
Effective date of provisions . . . Lab §4418
Establishment of . . . Lab §4403
Friable . . . Lab §6325.5
Inspection, contract for corrective work as condition for . . . Lab §6509.5
Investigations . . . Lab §4409
Judges (WCJs), appointment of . . . Lab §4409.5
Jurisdiction of claims . . . Lab §6436
Liens . . . Lab §§4414, 4416
Lump-sum payments . . . Lab §4407.5
Payment of benefits . . . Lab §4407
Permit requirements for asbestos-related work
Generally . . . Lab §6501.5
Contract for corrective work as condition for inspection . . . Lab §6509.5
Definitions . . . Lab §§6501.7, 6501.8
Determining presence of asbestos . . . Lab §6501.9
Penalties for failure to determine presence of asbestos . . . Lab §6505.5
Safety conferences . . . Lab §6503.5
Personnel assisting asbestos workers
Information and assistance officers . . . Lab §4410
Judges (WCJs), appointment of . . . Lab §4409.5

ASBESTOS—Cont.
Personnel assisting asbestos workers—Cont.
Support staff for examining claims of . . . Lab §4409.5
Presence of asbestos
Failure to determine . . . Lab §6505.5
Persons who may determine . . . Lab §6501.9
Procedures for seeking payment . . . Lab §4408
Prohibition of entry into workplace . . . Lab §6325.5
Recovery of amounts from responsible employer . . . Lab §4412
Registration of asbestos-related work (See subhead: Permit requirements for asbestos-related work)
Requirements for receipt of benefits . . . Lab §4406
Responsible employer, identification of
Generally . . . Lab §4405
Claims made against employer . . . Lab §4411
Lien procedures . . . Lab §4414
Scope of provisions on . . . Lab §4404
State policy on asbestosis . . . Lab §4401
Statutes of limitation . . . Lab §4413
Temporary remedy prior to establishing identity of responsible employer . . . Lab §4405
Termination of benefits . . . Lab §4411
Third party suits . . . Lab §4417
Uninsured Employers Fund . . . Lab §4412
Workers' Compensation Division information and Assistance program . . . 8 CCR §9928.1

ASSASSINATION
Death benefits
Public officials, assassinated (See DEATH BENEFITS)

ASSAULT
Invasion of privacy
Assault with intent to capture visual image or sound recording . . . CC §1708.8

ASSESSMENTS
Penalty assessment orders (See PENALTY ASSESSMENT ORDERS)
Self-insurers (See SELF-INSURANCE)

ASSIGNMENT OF BENEFITS
Death benefits . . . Lab §4704
Foreign employment by contractors with U.Sworking outside U.S . . . 42 USC §1717

ASSIGNMENT OF CLAIMS
Generally . . . Lab §4900
Labor Standards Enforcement Division . . . Lab §96
Longshore and Harbor Workers' Compensation Act . . . 33 USC §916

ASSIGNMENT OF LIENS . . . Lab §4903.8

ASTHMA
Medical treatment
Utilization schedule
Occupational/work-related asthma medical treatment guideline . . . 8 CCR §9792.23.11

ATASCADERO STATE HOSPITAL
Heart disease suffered by security officers of . . . Lab §3212.2

ATHLETES
Professional sports
Occupational disease or cumulative injury
Out-of-state hires, exemption . . . Lab §3600.5

ATTACHMENT AND GARNISHMENT
Appeals Board (WCAB) authority to order writs of . . . Lab §5600
Discharge of . . . Lab §5602
Employer's property attached for failure to secure payment . . . Lab §3706.5
Foreign employment by contractors with U.Sworking outside U.S . . . 42 USC §1717
Issuance of . . . Lab §5602
Preference in levy of . . . Lab §5603
Procedures . . . Lab §5601

ATTENDING PHYSICIANS (See CONSULTING OR ATTENDING PHYSICIANS)

ATTORNEY GENERAL
Public Employees' Retirement System
Representation of retirement system before Appeals Board . . . Gov §20130
Third party recovery, contract for . . . Gov §20253
State teachers' retirement system, subrogation of claims under . . . Ed §24501
United States, tort claims against
Compromise, settlement, or arbitration of . . . 28 USC §2677
Defense of suits . . . 28 USC §2679

ATTORNEYS
Advertising (See ADVERTISING)
Appeals board (WCAB)
Attorney representatives generally . . . 8 CCR §10400
Pleadings
Filing by attorneys or other representatives, special requirements . . . 8 CCR §10520
Arbitration, representation in . . . Lab §5270
Asbestos Workers' Account . . . Lab §4414
Conduct, judicial notice of . . . Ev §450
Corrections, Department of inmates, attorney referral for . . . Lab §3371
Depositions
Subpoenas
Issuance by attorney of record . . . CCP §2020.210
Disbarred
Appeals board
Barring of disbarred, suspended, etc attorneys from representing parties before board . . . 8 CCR §10445
Disciplinary action
Discovery
Attorney work product . . . CCP §2018.070
Dismissal . . . 8 CCR §10402
Filing of documents with attorneys or representatives
Filing and service of documents generally . . . 8 CCR §10610
Financial interests in entities providing services
Conflicts of interest . . . Lab §139.32
Lien claimants obtaining representation
Notice of representation, change of representation or non-representation . . . 8 CCR §10868

ATTORNEYS—Cont.
Longshore and Harbor Workers' Compensation Act representatives . . . 33 USC §921a
Payment of claim directly to . . . Lab §4902
Privilege of representation, removal of . . . Lab §4907
Professional misconduct, discipline
Financial interests in entities providing services
Conflicts of interest . . . Lab §139.32
Referral services
Privileged communications
Crime, using service to enable . . . Ev §968
Definitions . . . Ev §965
Description of privilege . . . Ev §966
Fraud, using service to enable . . . Ev §968
Lawyer referral service-client privilege . . . Ev §§965 to 968
Mandatory claim of privilege by service . . . Ev §967
Prevention of criminal act likely to result in death or bodily harm, disclosure . . . Ev §968
Waiver of attorney referral service-client privilege . . . Ev §912
Who may claim privilege . . . Ev §966
Rules of Professional Conduct
Judicial notice . . . Ev §451
Service on
Appeals board cases . . . 8 CCR §10625
Filing of documents with attorneys or representatives
Filing and service of documents generally . . . 8 CCR §10610
Subsequent injuries
Assignment of legal representation . . . Lab §4755
Representation of state in cases of . . . Lab §4753.5
Substitutions . . . 8 CCR §10402
Suspended
Appeals board
Barring of disbarred, suspended, etc attorneys from representing parties before board . . . 8 CCR §10445
Vocational rehabilitation
State hospitals
Vocational rehabilitation work assignments for patients, attorney referral for patients . . . Lab §3371.1
Workers' Compensation Division, counsel for
Appointment of . . . Lab §117
Duties of . . . Lab §119
Work product doctrine
Discovery
Attorney work product generally . . . CCP §§2018.010 to 2018.080

ATTORNEYS' FEES
Appeals board (WCAB)
Deposition of employee requested by employer
Petition for attorney fees . . . 8 CCR §10547
Appeals Board (WCAB) hearings . . . 8 CCR §10421
Approval . . . 8 CCR §10840
Bad faith actions or tactics . . . Lab §5813
Disclosure statement
Required use of . . . 8 CCR §10135
Sample form . . . 8 CCR §10134
Service of . . . 8 CCR §10135.1

Index

ATTORNEYS' FEES—Cont.
Failure to secure payment . . . Lab §4555
Foreign employment by contractors with U.Sworking outside U.S . . . 42 USC §1714
Increase
  Request for increase . . . 8 CCR §10842
Insurance frauds prevention act
  Actions brought under act . . . Ins §1871.7
Labor code private attorneys general
  Actions by aggrieved employee . . . Lab §2699
Lien claimants . . . 26 USC §6323, Lab §4903.2
  Filing lien . . . Lab §4903.6
Longshore and Harbor Workers' Compensation Act . . . 33 USC §928
Occupational Safety and Health Appeals Board, award by . . . Lab §149.5
Payment of benefits, unreasonable delay in payment or refusal to pay . . . Lab §5814.5
Reasonable attorney fees . . . 8 CCR §10844
Reduction in workers' compensation, suits seeking . . . Lab §5410.1
Subrogation . . . Lab §3856
Termination of benefits, denial of petition for . . . Lab §4607
Termination or decrease in disability, denial of petition alleging . . . Lab §4651.3
United States as party
  Generally . . . 28 USC §2412
  Tort claims . . . 28 USC §2678

AUDIO MEDIA
Appeals board (WCAB)
  Exhibits generally . . . 8 CCR §10677

AUDIT
Claims administration
  Generally . . . 8 CCR §10105
  Civil penalty assessment and claims administration audit (See PENALTIES AND FINES)
  Complaint tracking . . . 8 CCR §10106.1
  Discretionary nature of audit . . . 8 CCR §§10105, 10106
  Files and logs . . . 8 CCR §10105
  Full compliance audit penalty schedules . . . 8 CCR §10111.2
  Investigations triggered by . . . 8 CCR §§10106, 10106.5
  Nonrandom audits . . . 8 CCR §10106
  Notice of audit . . . 8 CCR §10107
    Post-2002 audits . . . 8 CCR §10107.1
  Post-2002 audits
    Notice . . . 8 CCR §10107.1
  Procedures for audit . . . 8 CCR §§10107, 10108
    Post-2002 audits . . . 8 CCR §10107.1
  Production of files and logs for audit . . . 8 CCR §10107
    Post-2002 audits . . . 8 CCR §10107.1
  Random audits . . . 8 CCR §10106
  Routine audit subject selection . . . 8 CCR §10106.1
  Selection of files and logs for audit . . . 8 CCR §10107
    Post-2002 audits . . . 8 CCR §10107.1
  Targeted audits
    Penalty schedule . . . 8 CCR §10111.2

AUDIT—Cont.
Claims administration—Cont.
  Targeted audits—Cont.
    Subject selection . . . 8 CCR §10106.1
  Violation of audit procedures . . . 8 CCR §10108
Confidentiality of individually identifiable information . . . 8 CCR §9703, Lab §138.7
Employers
  Insurers, audit by . . . Ins §11760.1
Group self-insurance
  Financial statements
    Duties of group self-insurer . . . 8 CCR §15484
Insurance
  Roofing contractors
    Payroll audit by issuers of workers' compensation insurance . . . Ins §11665
Payroll audits
  Insurers, audit by . . . Ins §11760.1
Penalty schedules . . . 8 CCR §10111.2
Qualified medical evaluators (QMEs)
  Definition of audit . . . 8 CCR §1
Self-insurance
  Generally . . . 8 CCR §15403, Lab §3702.6
  Confidentiality . . . 8 CCR §15405
  Definition of audit . . . 8 CCR §15201
  Expenses
    Out-of-state audit . . . 8 CCR §15404
    Revoked certificate audit . . . 8 CCR §15404.1
    Special audit . . . 8 CCR §15404.2
  Out-of-state audit . . . 8 CCR §15404
  Revoked certificate audit
    Generally . . . 8 CCR §15425
    Expenses of . . . 8 CCR §15404.1
  Special audit
    Expenses of . . . 8 CCR §15404.2
    Notice of . . . 8 CCR §15403.1
Self-Insurers' Security Fund . . . Lab §3746
Workers' Compensation Division . . . Lab §129

AUTOMATED PEOPLE MOVERS . . . Lab §§7300 to 7324.2
Generally (See ELEVATORS, ESCALATORS, CHAIR LIFTS AND OTHER CONVEYANCES)

AUTOMOBILE LIABILITY INSURANCE
Fraud
  Motor vehicle insurance fraud reporting . . . Ins §1874.1
Nonrenewal notices . . . Ins §678
  Electronic transmission of written notice . . . Ins §678
Required provisions . . . Ins §11580.1
Uninsured motorist provisions, reimbursement under . . . Ins §11580.2

AUTOMOBILES GENERALLY (See MOTOR VEHICLES)

AUTOPSY
Appeals Board (WCAB) authority to order . . . Lab §§5706, 5707

AUXILIARY OFFICERS
Reserve or auxiliary officers (See POLICE)

AVERAGE EARNINGS
Annual earnings
  Defined . . . Lab §4451
  Military service (See MILITARY SERVICE)
California National Guard, organized militia, or unorganized militia . . . Mil&Vet §341
Definitions
  Annual average earnings . . . Lab §4451
  Permanent disability . . . Lab §4452.5
Firefighters . . . Lab §§4458, 4458.5
Law enforcement officers . . . Lab §§4458.2, 4458.5
Longshore and Harbor Workers' Compensation Act . . . 33 USC §§906, 910
Military
  Average weekly earnings of persons employed on overseas bases . . . 42 USC §1652
  Average yearly earnings of persons in military service (See MILITARY SERVICE)
Minimum and maximum limits . . . Lab §4452
Partnership agreements, workers under . . . Lab §4457
Permanent disability
  Average weekly earnings . . . Lab §4659
  Definition of permanent total and permanent partial disability . . . Lab §4452.5
Previous disability . . . Lab §4459
Termination of firefighter's or police officer's active service, injury following . . . Lab §4458.5
Unemployment work relief program participants . . . Lab §4456
Weekly earnings
  Annual earnings computed from . . . Lab §4451
  Board and lodging . . . Lab §4454
  Children under 18 . . . Lab §4455
  Computing . . . Lab §4453
  Firefighters . . . Lab §§4458, 4458.5
  Law enforcement officers . . . Lab §§4458.2, 4458.5
  Longshore and Harbor Workers' Compensation Act . . . 33 USC §§906, 910
  Military bases outside U.S., persons employed on . . . 42 USC §1652
  Military bases overseas, service on . . . 42 USC §1652
  Overtime . . . Lab §4454
  Partnership agreements, workers under . . . Lab §4457
  Permanent disability . . . Lab §4659
  Previous disability . . . Lab §4459
  Termination of firefighter's or police officer's active service, injury following . . . Lab §4458.5

AVERAGE WEEKLY WAGE . . . Lab §4453
Generally (See AVERAGE EARNINGS)

AVIATION ACCIDENTS
Death on the high seas
  Commercial aviation accidents
    Applicability of provisions . . . 46 USC §30307

AWARD
Appeals Board (WCAB)
  Certified copy of award
    Filing . . . Lab §5806
    Judgment roll, as . . . Lab §5807
  Determination of . . . Lab §5801

AWARD—Cont.
Appeals Board (WCAB)—Cont.
  Five year limitations period on alteration of . . . Lab §5804
  Judicial review (See JUDICIAL REVIEW)
  Modifying award . . . Lab §5315
  Reconsideration of (See RECONSIDERATION)
  Service by board of orders, decisions, awards, etc . . . 8 CCR §10628
  Setting aside award . . . Lab §5315
  Statement of determination of issues . . . Lab §5815
  Suspension of award by filing petition for reconsideration . . . Lab §5910
  Time period for making award . . . Lab §5313
Arbitration (See ARBITRATION)
Attorneys' fees (See ATTORNEYS' FEES)
Child support judgment, workers' compensation award applied to . . . CCP §704.160
Compromise and release, entry of award following . . . Lab §5002
Court costs (See COURT COSTS)
Death on the high seas
  Amount of recovery . . . 46 USC §30303
  Apportionment of recovery . . . 46 USC §30303
Denial of petition to reduce . . . Lab §4555.5
Electronic adjudication management system (EAMS)
  Request for awards
    Forms . . . 8 CCR §10205.2
  Retention, return and destruction of records . . . 8 CCR §10208.7
Emergency awards for crime victims (See CRIME VICTIMS)
Liens
  Based on workers' compensation award . . . CCP §697.330
  Payment of lien not affecting payment of balance of award . . . Lab §4904.1
Longshore and Harbor Workers' Compensation Act
  Generally . . . 33 USC §911
  Judicial review of award . . . 33 USC §921
  Minors . . . 33 USC §911
  Modification of awards under . . . 33 USC §922
Minors
  Child support judgment, workers' compensation award applied to . . . CCP §704.160
  Longshore and Harbor Workers' Compensation Act . . . 33 USC §911
Nominal disability indemnity, award of . . . Lab §5802
Occupational Safety and Health Appeals Board award of attorneys' fees and court costs . . . Lab §149.5
Reconsideration of (See RECONSIDERATION)
Service
  Appeals Board (WCAB)
    Service by board of orders, decisions, awards, etc . . . 8 CCR §10628
Statutes of limitation on alteration of . . . Lab §5804
Stipulations
  Effect of stipulations . . . 8 CCR §10835
Support judgment, workers' compensation award applied to . . . CCP §704.160
Suspension of
  Appeals Board (WCAB) order, decision, or award suspended by filing petition for reconsideration . . . Lab §5910

AWARD—Cont.
Suspension of—Cont.
Occupational Safety and Health Appeals Board decision suspended by filing for reconsideration . . . Lab §6625

B

BACK INJURIES
Health care workers
Patient protection and health care worker back and musculoskeletal injury prevention . . . Lab §6403.5
Medical treatment
Utilization schedule
Cervical and thoracic spine disorders . . . 8 CCR §9792.23.1
Low back disorders . . . 8 CCR §9792.23.5

BACK TO WORK PROGRAMS (See RETURN TO WORK PROGRAMS)

BAD FAITH
Appeals Board (WCAB)
Medical-legal expenses
Procedures for determination of disputes . . . 8 CCR §10786
Appeals Board (WCAB) sanctions for . . . Lab §5813

BANKRUPTCY
Insurance
Employer insolvency or bankruptcy, effect on insurer liability of . . . Ins §11655
Judicial notice of general orders and forms in . . . Ev §451
Self-insurance
Defaulting insurers, claims against . . . 8 CCR §15216
Priority of debts of . . . Lab §3705
Security deposits used to administer claims of defaulting insurers . . . 8 CCR §15216
Self-insurers' Security Fund (See SELF-INSURERS' SECURITY FUND)

BATTERY OR CRUELTY
Aliens, uninsured employers fund and subsequent injuries fund benefits for . . . 8 CCR §15740

BELTS
Building and construction industry safe workplace requirements
Generally . . . Lab §7108
Steel framed buildings . . . Lab §§7253, 7265

BENEFITS
Acupuncture services
Lien of provider
Fraud against workers' compensation system, medical billing, insurance, Medicare or Medi-Cal, stay of provider lien . . . Lab §4615
Assignment
Death benefits . . . Lab §4704
Foreign employment by contractors with U.Sworking outside U.S . . . 42 USC §1717
Death (See DEATH BENEFITS)
Disability (See DISABILITY BENEFITS)

BENEFITS—Cont.
Early return to work program
False or fraudulent statements in connection with . . . Ins §1871.4
Family care leave, paid
Benefits in accord with provisions . . . UI §3304
Lifeguards
Leave of absence in lieu of disability payments . . . Lab §4850
Longshore and Harbor Workers' Compensation Act . . . 33 USC §905
Medical care
Fees and expenses
Fraud against workers' compensation system, medical billing, insurance, Medicare or Medi-Cal, stay of provider lien . . . Lab §4615
Lien of provider
Fraud against workers' compensation system, medical billing, insurance, Medicare or Medi-Cal, stay of provider lien . . . Lab §4615
Medicines and medical supplies
Fraud against workers' compensation system, medical billing, insurance, Medicare or Medi-Cal, stay of provider lien . . . Lab §4615
Personal physician, employee's right to use
Fraud against workers' compensation system, medical billing, insurance, Medicare or Medi-Cal, stay of provider lien . . . Lab §4615
Prosthetic and orthotic devices
Fraud against workers' compensation system, medical billing, insurance, Medicare or Medi-Cal, stay of provider lien . . . Lab §4615
Medical-legal expenses
Lien of provider
Fraud against workers' compensation system, medical billing, insurance, Medicare or Medi-Cal, stay of provider lien . . . Lab §4615
Notice of (See NOTICE)
Orthotic devices
Lien of provider
Fraud against workers' compensation system, medical billing, insurance, Medicare or Medi-Cal, stay of provider lien . . . Lab §4615
Overpayment of
Disability benefits (See DISABILITY BENEFITS)
Unemployment compensation benefits, liability for overpayment of . . . UI §1375.3
Payment of (See PAYMENT OF BENEFITS)
Prosthetic and orthotic devices
Lien of provider
Fraud against workers' compensation system, medical billing, insurance, Medicare or Medi-Cal, stay of provider lien . . . Lab §4615
Supplemental job displacement benefits . . . 8 CCR §§10133.31 to 10133.60, Lab §§4658.5, 4658.6 (See SUPPLEMENTAL JOB DISPLACEMENT BENEFITS)
2013, injuries occurring in or after . . . Lab §4658.7
Termination (See TERMINATION OF BENEFITS)
Unemployment compensation (See UNEMPLOYMENT COMPENSATION)
Utilization review
Employer duties . . . Lab §4610

BENEFITS REVIEW BOARD
Longshore and Harbor Workers' Compensation Act (See LONGSHORE AND HARBOR WORKERS' COMPENSATION ACT)

BIGAMY
Spousal testimony in bigamy proceedings
Admissibility of . . . Ev §972

BILLING COMPANIES
Competence standards for medical bill reviewers
Certification . . . 10 CCR §2592.09
Designation for successful completion of training . . . 10 CCR §§2592.05, 2592.11
Documentation maintained by insurer . . . 10 CCR §2592.07
Experienced medical bill reviewer, designation . . . 10 CCR §2592.13
Post-designation training . . . 10 CCR §2592.14
Training . . . 10 CCR §2592.04
Fraud
Medical billing and provider fraud
Reporting protocol . . . Lab §3823
Medical claims, release of information for . . . CC §56.10

BILLING FOR MEDICAL TREATMENT
Billing and payment rules (October 2011) . . . 8 CCR §§9792.5.0 to 9792.5.15 (See MEDICAL TREATMENT)

BILL REVIEW
Independent bill review (See INDEPENDENT BILL REVIEW (IBR))

BIOLOGICAL WEAPONS
Law enforcement officers
Compensability of injuries from exposure to biochemical substances . . . Lab §3212.85

BLIND PERSONS
Medical assistance
In-home supportive services for aged, blind and disabled
Direct payments to provider or recipients, workers' compensation, unemployment compensation, etcobligations . . . W&I §§12302.2, 12302.5

BLOODBORNE DISEASES
Health care workers injured as result of preventive care for . . . Lab §3208.05
HIV-related diseases, time limitations for claims for injury or death due to . . . Lab §5406.6
Needle safety standards, Occupational Safety and Health Board responsibilities regarding . . . Lab §144.7

BOILERS (See TANKS AND BOILERS)

BONDS
Health care organizations (HCOs) . . . 8 CCR §9771.73
Insurer's bond
Award (See AWARD)
Deposits (See DEPOSITS)
Filings (See FILING)
Self-insurer's security deposit, surety bonds accepted for . . . 8 CCR §15212

BONDS—Cont.
Shipping
Public vessels, damages caused by or towage and salvage rendered to
Counterclaims, security on . . . 46 USC §31105
United States vessels or cargo, suits in admiralty involving
Security not to be required of US or federally owned corporation . . . 46 USC §30909
State Compensation Insurance Fund president . . . Ins §11786
Workers' compensation bond fund . . . Ins §§1063.70 to 1063.77

BONUSES
Health care organization (HCO) grants or bonuses in aid of solicitation of employers . . . 8 CCR §9771.61

BOOKS AND RECORDS (See RECORDS AND RECORDKEEPING)

BRACING REGULATIONS
Swimming pool excavations . . . Lab §6705.5

BRAIN INJURIES
Medical treatment
Utilization schedule
Traumatic brain injury guideline . . . 8 CCR §9792.24.5
Presumption of total disability for brain injuries leading to mental incapacity . . . Lab §4662

BREATHING APPARATUS
Occupational Safety and Health Division testing . . . Lab §6331

BUILDING AND CONSTRUCTION INDUSTRY
Aerial passenger tramways
Passenger tramways generally . . . Lab §§7340 to 7357 (See PASSENGER TRAMWAYS)
Alternative dispute resolution systems through collective bargaining agreements . . . Lab §3201.5
Asbestos (See ASBESTOS)
Belts, safety
Generally . . . Lab §7108
Steel framed buildings . . . Lab §§7253, 7265
Citations on multiemployer worksites . . . Lab §6400
Concrete buildings, protective flooring in . . . Lab §7102
Construction elevators (See CONSTRUCTION ELEVATORS)
Contractors, grounds for disciplinary proceedings against . . . B&P §7110
Contracts (See CONSTRUCTION CONTRACTS)
Cranes (See CRANES)
Definition of building
Construction elevator provisions, for purposes of . . . Lab §7200
Flooring and wall requirements, for purposes of . . . Lab §7100
Sections of buildings as buildings
Flooring and walls . . . Lab §7106
Steel framed buildings . . . Lab §7264
Steel framed buildings, for purposes of . . . Lab §7250

BUILDING AND CONSTRUCTION INDUSTRY—Cont.
Definition of building—Cont.
Window cleaning safety devices, for purposes of . . . Lab §7325
Demolition
Occupational Safety and Health Division permit requirements . . . Lab §6500
Salvaging of materials during . . . Lab §6401.5
Disciplinary proceedings, grounds for
Contractors, against . . . B&P §7110
Structural pest control operators, against . . . B&P §8636
Elevators, escalators, chair lifts and other conveyances (See ELEVATORS, ESCALATORS, CHAIR LIFTS AND OTHER CONVEYANCES)
Enforcement
Citations on multiemployer worksites . . . Lab §6400
Elevator requirements, penalty enforcement and appeals . . . Lab §7321.5
Floor and wall requirements . . . Lab §7110
Scaffolding requirements . . . Lab §7158
Steel framed building requirements . . . Lab §7267
Window cleaning safety device requirements . . . Lab §7332
Excavations
Bids for local government projects involving . . . Lab §6707
Swimming pool excavations . . . Lab §6705.5
Trench excavations (See TRENCH EXCAVATIONS)
Flooring, protective
Generally . . . Lab §7101
Concrete buildings . . . Lab §7102
Planked floors . . . Lab §7107
Replanking . . . Lab §7105
Scaffolding . . . Lab §7153
Steel framed buildings (See STEEL FRAMED BUILDINGS)
Supportive intermediate beams . . . Lab §7104
Wooden flooring . . . Lab §7103
Working without . . . Lab §7109
High voltage, misdemeanors associated with . . . Pen §385
Housing permits . . . H&S §17922.5
Lead-related construction work . . . Lab §§6716, 6717
Nets, safety
Requirements . . . Lab §7108
Working without . . . Lab §7109
Occupational Safety and Health Division
Elevators, escalators, chair lifts and other conveyances (See ELEVATORS, ESCALATORS, CHAIR LIFTS AND OTHER CONVEYANCES)
Floor and wall requirements, enforcement of . . . Lab §7110
Permit requirements . . . Lab §6500
Scaffolding requirements
Enforcement of . . . Lab §7158
Powers of Division . . . Lab §7157
Standards, enforcement . . . Lab §142
Steel framed building requirements, enforcement of . . . Lab §7267
Window cleaning safety device requirements
Enforcement of . . . Lab §7332
Powers regarding . . . Lab §7331
Passenger tramways . . . Lab §§7340 to 7357 (See PASSENGER TRAMWAYS)

BUILDING AND CONSTRUCTION INDUSTRY—Cont.
Penalties and fines
Construction elevator requirements, violations of . . . Lab §7205
Cranes (See CRANES)
Elevators, escalators, chair lifts and other conveyances (See ELEVATORS, ESCALATORS, CHAIR LIFTS AND OTHER CONVEYANCES)
Scaffolding violations . . . Lab §§7155, 7156
Steel framed buildings . . . Lab §7266
Window cleaning safety devices (See WINDOW CLEANING SAFETY DEVICES)
Planked floors . . . Lab §7107
Private attorneys general act, labor code
Applicability of act
Work in construction industry done under collective bargaining agreement . . . Lab §2699.6
Public works contracts (See PUBLIC WORKS CONTRACTS)
Safety belts
Generally . . . Lab §7108
Steel framed buildings . . . Lab §§7253, 7265
Scaffolding (See SCAFFOLDING)
Sections of buildings as buildings
Flooring and walls . . . Lab §7106
Steel framed buildings . . . Lab §7264
Staging as part of scaffolding . . . Lab §7150
Standards
Adoption of . . . Lab §142.4
Approval of . . . Lab §142.3
Steel framed buildings (See STEEL FRAMED BUILDINGS)
Structural pest control operators, grounds for disciplinary proceedings against . . . B&P §8636
Supportive intermediate beams . . . Lab §7104
Swimming pool excavations . . . Lab §6705.5
Trench excavations (See TRENCH EXCAVATIONS)
Unsafe or unhealthy worksites, prohibition on construction of . . . Lab §6405
Valley Fever awareness training . . . Lab §6709
Window cleaning safety devices (See WINDOW CLEANING SAFETY DEVICES)
Wooden flooring, protective . . . Lab §7103

BURDEN OF PROOF
Appeals Board (WCAB) hearings . . . Lab §5705
Confidential communication, claim for . . . Ev §917
Defined . . . Ev §115
Degree of proof required in proceedings . . . Ev §115
Failure to secure payment of benefits . . . Lab §3708
Negligence of employer in failure to secure payment of compensation . . . Lab §3708
Preponderance of evidence
Requisite degree of proof required except where higher degree of proof otherwise required by law . . . Ev §115
Preponderance of the evidence standard
Worker's compensation division of Labor Code . . . Lab §3202.5

BURIAL EXPENSES
Generally . . . Lab §4701
Economic Opportunity Program enrollees . . . Lab §4214

BURIAL EXPENSES—Cont.
Employer liability for . . . Lab §4701
Maximum benefits, table of . . . Table 13
Survivors, lack of . . . Lab §4706

BURNS
Temporary disability
Aggregate disability payments
Single injury . . . Lab §4656

BUSINESS RECORDS
Evidence (See EVIDENCE)

C

CALENDAR
Number of days between 2 dates . . . Table 9

CALIFORNIA CADET CORPS
Benefit rights . . . Mil&Vet §520

CALIFORNIA CONSTITUTION . . . CA Const Art XIV

CALIFORNIA EMERGENCY SERVICES ACT (See EMERGENCY AND DISASTER SERVICES)

CALIFORNIA FAMILY RIGHTS ACT (CFRA)
Family care leave, paid
Concurrent leave with FMLA and CFRA . . . UI §3303.1

CALIFORNIA HIGHWAY PATROL (See HIGHWAY PATROL)

CALIFORNIA INSURANCE GUARANTEE ASSOCIATION (CIGA)
Generally . . . Ins §1063
Authority of . . . Ins §1063.2
Board of governors
Open meetings . . . Ins §1063.17
Covered claims
Defined . . . Ins §1063.1
Denial of nonworker's compensation claims
Challenge of denial . . . Ins §1063.18
Exceptions to . . . Ins §1063.2
Submission, when permitted . . . Ins §1063.18
Definitions pertinent to . . . Ins §1063.1
Duties of . . . Ins §1063.2
Overpayments
Recovery . . . Ins §1063.2
Penalties for late payments for services
Not covered claim . . . Ins §1063.1
Premiums
Charges against member insurers
Collection . . . Ins §1063.45
Collection and allocation of payments from member insurers . . . Ins §1063.5
Net direct written premiums
Defined . . . Ins §1036.1
Surcharges on . . . Ins §§1063.14, 1063.135
Reinsurance agreements or transfer of liabilities . . . Ins §1063.2
Statutes of limitation . . . Ins §1063.15

CALIFORNIA INSURANCE GUARANTEE ASSOCIATION (CIGA)—Cont.
Unpaid reimbursements owed by employer under workers' compensation policy
Recovery by association . . . Ins §1063.2
Workers' compensation bond fund . . . Ins §§1063.70 to 1063.77
Assessment of member insurers . . . Ins §1063.74
Bonds used to pay claims against insolvent insurers . . . Ins §1063.70
Collateral
Defined . . . Ins §1063.71
Use . . . Ins §1063.76
Creation . . . Ins §1063.72
Definitions . . . Ins §1063.71
Lien on collateral . . . Ins §1063.76
Resolution to request issuance of bonds . . . Ins §1063.73
Security and marketability of bonds
Contracts to improve . . . Ins §1063.77
Terms and conditions of bonds . . . Ins §1063.75
Workers' compensation insurance
Deposits by workers' compensation insurers
Insolvency of member found . . . Ins §11698.3

CALIFORNIA NATIONAL GUARD (See MILITARY SERVICE)

CALIFORNIA REFINERY AND CHEMICAL PLANT WORKER SAFETY ACT (See REFINERIES AND CHEMICAL PLANTS)

CALIFORNIA STATE UNIVERSITY
First disability payment, timing of . . . Lab §4650.5
Industrial disability leave for employees of
Administrative rules and regulations, adoption of . . . Ed §89529.10
Amount of leave . . . Ed §89529.03
Commencement of leave . . . Ed §89529.08
Continuation of other benefits . . . Ed §89529.04
Cooperation of injured worker, payments contingent on . . . Ed §89529.09
Coordination with temporary disability . . . Ed §89529.05
Deductions from payments . . . Ed §89529.03
Definitions pertinent to . . . Ed §89529.02
Effective date of provisions regarding . . . Ed §89529.11
Eligible employees . . . Ed §89529
Entitlement to . . . Ed §89529.03
Medical certification, payments contingent on . . . Ed §89529.09
Memorandum of Understanding as controlling document for . . . Ed §89529.01
Payments, computation of . . . Ed §89529.03
Vocational rehabilitation
Payments contingent on . . . Ed §89529.09
Public employee provisions, inapplicability of . . . Ed §89529.06
Police department
Collective bargaining agreement for enhanced industrial disability leave . . . Lab §4816
Course of employment, injuries occurring during . . . Lab §4817

CALIFORNIA STATE UNIVERSITY—Cont.
Police department—Cont.
One year, disability continuing beyond . . . Lab §4819
Permanent disability . . . Lab §4819
Salary payments, temporary disability payments concurrent with . . . Lab §4820
Temporary disability (See subhead: Temporary disability)
Safety violations, fines and penalties for . . . Lab §6434
Temporary disability
Continuation after expiration of industrial disability leave . . . Ed §89529.07
Coordination of industrial disability leave with . . . Ed §89529.05
Police Department
Collective bargaining agreement . . . Lab §4816
One year, disability continuing beyond . . . Lab §4819
Relationship of disability to duty, determining . . . Lab §4817
Salary payments, prohibition of disability payments concurrent with . . . Lab §4820
Vocational rehabilitation
Cooperation of injured worker, industrial disability leave payments contingent on . . . Ed §89529.09
Public employee provisions, inapplicability of . . . Ed §89529.06

CAL-OSHA TARGETED INSPECTION AND CONSULTATION FUND
Generally . . . Lab §62.7
Definitions . . . 8 CCR §15600
Loans from fund . . . Lab §62.8
Self-insurers' assessment
Generally . . . 8 CCR §15234
Determination of self-insurers subject to . . . 8 CCR §15601.7
Transfers from fund . . . Lab §62.5

CAPPERS
Insurance Frauds Prevention Act, use prohibited under . . . Ins §1871.7

CARDIAC DISEASE (See HEART DISEASE)

CARE GIVERS
Family care leave, paid . . . UI §§3300 to 3306 (See FAMILY CARE LEAVE, PAID)
Medical records release to . . . CC §56.1007

CARGO (See SHIPPING)

CARS (See MOTOR VEHICLES)

CARVE-OUT PROGRAM (See PRIVATIATION OF WORKERS' COMPENSATION)

CASH IN TRUST
Self-insurer's security deposit, as . . . 8 CCR §15214

CASH REVOLVING FUND
Subsequent injuries . . . Lab §4755
Uninsured employers benefits trust fund payments . . . Lab §3728

CASUAL EMPLOYEES
Election to cover . . . Lab §4153

CERTIFICATION
Appeals Board (WCAB)
Awards, certified copies of
Filing . . . Lab §5806
Judgment roll, as . . . Lab §5807
Decisions, certified copies of
Filing . . . Lab §5806
Judgment roll, as . . . Lab §5807
Orders, certified copies of (See APPEALS BOARD (WCAB))
Reports, certified copies
Documentary evidence, admissibility . . . 8 CCR §10670
Consulting or attending physicians (See CONSULTING OR ATTENDING PHYSICIANS)
Court interpreters . . . Gov §68562
Crane safety (See CRANES)
Health care organizations (HCOs) (See HEALTH CARE ORGANIZATIONS (HCOS))
Insurance
Licensure, certificate of insurance or self-insurance required for
Generally . . . B&P §7125
Cancellation of policy, reporting requirements for . . . B&P §7125
Exceptions and exemptions . . . B&P §7125
Longshore and Harbor Workers' Compensation Act . . . 33 USC §937
Penalty for violation of provisions . . . B&P §7126
Recertification of exemption . . . B&P §7125.5
Reinstatement of license retroactive to effective date of certificate . . . B&P §7125.1
Renewal of license . . . B&P §7125.5
Suspension of license for failure to maintain insurance . . . B&P §7125.2
Self-insurance
Certificate of consent to self-insure (See SELF-INSURANCE)
Certificate to administer claims (See SELF-INSURANCE)
Lien cancellation following payment of compensation, certificate of . . . Lab §3721
Mining and tunneling testers and safety representatives (See MINING AND TUNNELING)
Qualified medical evaluators (QMEs) (See QUALIFIED MEDICAL EVALUATORS (QMES))
Revocation (See REVOCATION OF LICENSE, PERMIT, OR CERTIFICATION)
Self-insurance
Certificate of consent to self-insure (See SELF-INSURANCE)
Certificate to administer claims (See SELF-INSURANCE)
Licensure, certificate of insurance or self-insurance required for (See subhead: Insurance)
Suspension of (See SUSPENSION OF LICENSE, PERMIT, OR CERTIFICATION)

CHAIR LIFTS . . . Lab §§7300 to 7324.2
Generally (See ELEVATORS, ESCALATORS, CHAIR LIFTS AND OTHER CONVEYANCES)

CHANGE IN BENEFITS
Notice of . . . 8 CCR §9812

CHANGE IN ORGANIZATION
Self-insurance and
Certification and change in status . . . 8 CCR §15203.8
Membership, notice of change in . . . 8 CCR §15402.3

CHARGES (See FEES)

CHARITIES
Sexual harassment of volunteer workers . . . Gov §12940

CHARTS (See SCHEDULES, CHARTS, AND TABLES)

CHEERLEADERS
Employment relationship
Classification of cheerleaders for professional sports teams as employees . . . Lab §2754

CHEMICAL PLANTS (See REFINERIES AND CHEMICAL PLANTS)

CHEMICAL WEAPONS
Law enforcement officers
Compensability of injuries from exposure to biochemical substances . . . Lab §3212.85

CHILDREN GENERALLY (See MINORS)

CHILD SUPPORT
Award applied to support judgment . . . CCP §704.160
Workers' Compensation Notification Project . . . Lab §138.5

CHIROPRACTORS
Advertising . . . 16 CCR §311
Free or discount services . . . 16 CCR §319
Anesthesia
Manipulation under anesthesia (MUA)
Standard of care . . . 16 CCR §318.1
Cap on visits . . . Lab §4604.5
Change of name . . . 16 CCR §310
Change of physician
Employee request . . . Lab §§4601, 4603
Chosen by injured worker . . . Lab §4600.3
Conduct of premises
Responsibility of chiropractor . . . 16 CCR §316
Death
Ownership of chiropractic practice
Death or incapacity of licensee . . . 16 CCR §312.2
Discipline
Fraud investigations
Forwarding information to disciplinary body . . . Ins §1872.84
Investigations and enforcement
Costs, responsibility . . . 16 CCR §317.5
Discount services . . . 16 CCR §319
Employees of chiropractor
Responsibility for actions of employees . . . 16 CCR §316
Employer-provided treatment . . . Lab §4600
Fraud against workers' compensation system, medical billing, insurance, Medicare or Medi-Cal, stay of provider lien . . . Lab §4615

CHIROPRACTORS—Cont.
Employer-provided treatment —Cont.
Lien of provider
Fraud against workers' compensation system, medical billing, insurance, Medicare or Medi-Cal, stay of provider lien . . . Lab §4615
Exception to cap on visits . . . Lab §4604.5
Fraud investigations . . . Ins §1872.95
Authorized governmental agency
Defined to include licensing agency under chiropractic initiative act . . . Ins §1877.2
Forwarding information concerning chiropractors to disciplinary body . . . Ins §1872.84
Free services . . . 16 CCR §319
Health care organization (HCO) referrals to . . . 8 CCR §9773.1
Illegal practice . . . 16 CCR §§310.2, 312
Informed consent
Material risks of proposed care, informing patient . . . 16 CCR §319.1
Knox-Keene Health Care Service Plan Act . . . Lab §4600.5
Medical treatment generally (See MEDICAL TREATMENT)
Mental illness of license holder . . . 16 CCR §315
Network, disclosure of provider's participation in . . . Lab §4609
Notice of violations
Licensees to notify executive officer . . . 16 CCR §314
Ownership of chiropractic practice . . . 16 CCR §312.1
Death or incapacity of licensee . . . 16 CCR §312.2
Patient records
Responsibility as to patient records . . . 16 CCR §318
Personal chiropractor, designation . . . 8 CCR §9783.1
Physicians
Classifying chiropractors as physicians . . Lab §3209.3
Holding out of chiropractor as physician not permitted by classification . . . Lab §3209.6
Educational materials for treating physicians . . . Lab §4602.8
Personal chiropractor, designation . . . 8 CCR §9783.1
Practice of chiropractic . . . 16 CCR §§310 to 319
Provision of care by . . . Lab §4600.5
Qualified medical evaluators (QMEs)
Certification . . . 8 CCR §14, Lab §139.2
Eligibility . . . 8 CCR §11
Referral services . . . 16 CCR §317.1
Regulation of . . . Lab §4600.5
Replacement license . . . 16 CCR §310.1
Services and supplies provided by . . . Lab §3209.5
Specialization . . . 16 CCR §311.1
Student practice
Inducing student practice . . . 16 CCR §313
Suspension from participation, procedure . . . 8 CCR §§9788.1 to 9788.6
Unauthorized practice . . . 16 CCR §§310.2, 312
Unprofessional conduct . . . 16 CCR §317
Utilization review
Cap on visits . . . Lab §4604.5

CHIROPRACTORS—Cont.
Utilization review—Cont.
Health care organization, chiropractic care under . . . Lab §4600.5

CHOICE OF PHYSICIAN (See PHYSICIANS)

CHRONIC PAIN
Medical treatment
Utilization schedule
Chronic pain guidelines . . . 8 CCR §9792.24.2

CIGA (See CALIFORNIA INSURANCE GUARANTEE ASSOCIATION (CIGA))

CIGARETTES
Electronic cigarettes
Smoking in the workplace, prohibitions
Applicability to electronic cigarettes . . . Lab §6404.5
Mining and tunneling . . . Lab §§7970, 7978

CITATIONS
Indemnification of employees for losses or expenditures incurred in performance of duties
Violation of obligation by employer . . . Lab §2802
Occupational Safety and Health Division (See OCCUPATIONAL SAFETY AND HEALTH DIVISION)
Sick days, paid
Enforcement . . . Lab §248.5

CITY GOVERNMENTS GENERALLY (See LOCAL GOVERNMENTS AND AGENCIES)

CIVIL ACTIONS
Client employer-labor contractor responsibilities
Retaliation for filing action prohibited . . . Lab §2810.3
Conditions of employer liability . . . Lab §3600
Death on the high seas . . . 46 USC §30302
Foreign cause of action . . . 46 USC §30306
State law causes of actions, effect of provisions . . . 46 USC §30308
Insurance Frauds Prevention Act . . . Ins §1871.7
Labor code private attorneys general
Actions brought by private aggrieved employee . . . Lab §2699
Cure of violation . . . Lab §§2699.3, 2699.5
Investigations by agencies . . . Lab §§2699.3, 2699.5
Notice . . . Lab §§2699.3, 2699.5
Settlements . . . Lab §§2699.3, 2699.5
Labor contractor-client employer responsibilities
Retaliation for filing action prohibited . . . Lab §2810.3
Seamen, injury in course of employment . . . 46 USC §30104
Non-citizens or non-resident aliens, restrictions on recovery for incidents in foreign waters . . . 46 USC §30105
Shipping
Public vessels, damages caused by or towage and salvage rendered to . . . 46 USC §§31101 to 31112 (See SHIPPING)

CIVIL ACTIONS—Cont.
Shipping—Cont.
United States vessels or cargo, suits in admiralty involving . . . 46 USC §§30901 to 30913 (See SHIPPING)
Sick days, paid
Enforcement . . . Lab §248.5
Third parties (See THIRD PARTIES)

CIVIL DISCOVERY ACT
Short title . . . CCP §2016.010

CIVIL PENALTIES (See PENALTIES AND FINES)

CIVIL RIGHTS
Prisoners (See PRISONERS)

CIVIL SERVICE
Judicial notice of regulations by state personnel board . . . Ev §451

CLAIM FILES
Audits . . . 8 CCR §10105
Contents
Injuries before 1/1/1994 . . . 8 CCR §10101
Injuries on or after 1/1/1994 . . . 8 CCR §10101.1
Investigations (See INVESTIGATIONS)
Retention of . . . 8 CCR §10102
Self-insurers
Recordkeeping requirements . . . 8 CCR §15400
Transfer of claim files . . . 8 CCR §15402.4

CLAIM FORMS
Generally . . . 8 CCR §10136
Definitions pertinent to . . . 8 CCR §10136
Mandatory form . . . 8 CCR §10138
Notice of potential eligibility for benefits . . . 8 CCR §§10138, 10139
Obligations of employer, effect on . . . 8 CCR §10137
Penalty notice on . . . Ins §1871.2, Lab §5401.7
Processing, employer responsibility for . . . 8 CCR §10140
Provision of . . . 8 CCR §10140, Lab §5401
Reproduced claim forms utilized for pharmacy benefits . . . Lab §4608
Statements on . . . Lab §5401.7

CLAIM LOG
Audits . . . 8 CCR §10105
Contents and maintenance for injuries
After or on 1/1/1994 . . . 8 CCR §10103.1
Before 1/1/1994 . . . 8 CCR §10103
Post-2002 . . . 8 CCR §10103.2
Investigations (See INVESTIGATIONS)
Self-insurers' recordkeeping requirements . . . 8 CCR §15400.1

CLAIMS ADJUSTERS
Certification of claims adjusters . . . 10 CCR §2592.08
Compensation offered to . . . Lab §3219
Competence standards . . . 10 CCR §§2592 to 2592.14
Authority to promulgate regulations . . . 10 CCR §2592
Certification of claims adjusters . . . 10 CCR §2592.08
Definitions . . . 10 CCR §2592.01

CLAIMS ADJUSTERS—Cont.
Competence standards —Cont.
Documentation maintained by insurer . . . 10 CCR §2592.07
Experience
Designation for experienced claims adjusters or medical-only claims adjusters . . . 10 CCR §2592.12
Medical bill reviewers
Certification . . . 10 CCR §2592.09
Designation for successful completion of training . . . 10 CCR §§2592.05, 2592.11
Documentation maintained by insurer . . . 10 CCR §2592.07
Experienced medical bill reviewer, designation . . . 10 CCR §2592.13
Post-designation training . . . 10 CCR §2592.14
Training . . . 10 CCR §2592.04
Purpose of provisions . . . 10 CCR §2592
Training . . . 10 CCR §2592.02
Curriculum . . . 10 CCR §2592.03
Designation for successful completion . . . 10 CCR §§2592.05, 2592.10
Medical bill reviewers . . . 10 CCR §2592.04
Post-designation training . . . 10 CCR §2592.14
Recordkeeping by insurers . . . 10 CCR §2592.06
Documentation maintained by insurer . . . 10 CCR §2592.07
Experience standards . . . 10 CCR §§2592 to 2592.14, Ins §11761
Designation for experienced claims adjusters or medical-only claims adjusters
Form . . . 10 CCR §2592.12
Medical-only claims adjusters
Certification of claims adjusters . . 10 CCR §2592.08
Experience standards
Designation for experienced claims adjusters or medical-only claims adjusters . . . 10 CCR §2592.12
Training standards
Curriculum . . . 10 CCR §2592.03
Designation for successful completion of training . . . 10 CCR §§2592.05, 2592.10
Detailed . . . 10 CCR §2592.02
Skill standards . . . 10 CCR §§2592 to 2592.14, Ins §11761
Subsequent injuries
Assignment of claims adjustment services in subsequent injuries cases . . . Lab §4755
Training standards . . . 10 CCR §§2592 to 2592.14, Ins §11761
Curriculum . . . 10 CCR §2592.03
Designation for successful completion of training . . . 10 CCR §2592.05
Form . . . 10 CCR §2592.10
Detailed . . . 10 CCR §2592.02
Medical bill reviewers . . . 10 CCR §2592.04
Post-designation training
Form . . . 10 CCR §2592.14
Recordkeeping by insurers . . . 10 CCR §2592.06

CLAIMS PROCEDURES
Adjudication (See ADJUDICATION OF CLAIMS)

CLAIMS PROCEDURES—Cont.
Adjustment of claims related to economic opportunity program enrollees (See ECONOMIC OPPORTUNITY PROGRAMS)
Administration of claims
Audits (See AUDIT)
Civil penalty assessment and claims administration audit (See PENALTIES AND FINES)
Files (See CLAIM FILES)
Good faith, duty of . . . 8 CCR §10109
Inventory, annual report of . . . 8 CCR §10104
Investigations
Claim logs and files (See INVESTIGATIONS)
Log (See CLAIM LOG)
Penalties and fines
Administrative penalties (See PENALTIES AND FINES)
Civil penalty assessment and claims administration audit (See PENALTIES AND FINES)
Workers' Compensation Division, assistance from (See WORKERS' COMPENSATION DIVISION)
Administrative assistance of Workers' Compensation Division (See WORKERS' COMPENSATION DIVISION)
Answer . . . Lab §5505
Appeals Board (WCAB), before (See APPEALS BOARD (WCAB))
Applications for adjudication of claims (See ADJUDICATION OF CLAIMS)
Asbestos Workers' Account . . . Lab §4403
Assignment of claims (See ASSIGNMENT OF CLAIMS)
Certification of claims by Labor Standards Enforcement Division . . . Lab §96.5
Collection proceedings, time limits on (See COLLECTION PROCEEDINGS)
Death of employer, employee's rights against estate following . . . Lab §5306
Debts, effect of . . . Lab §4901
Defendants
Answer . . . Lab §5505
Defined . . . Lab §5503
Failure to appear or answer . . . Lab §5506
Denial of claim
Date . . . 8 CCR §10142
Time lost, injuries involving
Medical treatment outside of system, rulemaking to provide for notice of employee option to pursue . . . Lab §138.4
Disability benefits (See DISABILITY BENEFITS)
Discharge of claims, payment of compensation as . . . Lab §3603
Dismissal of application without hearing . . . Lab §5507
Dismissal of claim
Inactive for more than 180 days . . . Lab §5404.5
Economic opportunity program enrollees, adjustment of claims related to (See ECONOMIC OPPORTUNITY PROGRAMS)
Files, administration of (See CLAIM FILES)
Filing application for benefits (See FILING)
Foreign employment by contractors with U.Sworking outside U.S . . . 42 USC §1706
Good faith, duty of . . . 8 CCR §10109

Index

CLAIMS PROCEDURES—Cont.
Inactive claims, dismissal of . . . 8 CCR §10141
Inventory, annual report of . . . 8 CCR §10104
Investigations
Claim logs and files (See INVESTIGATIONS)
Liens (See LIENS)
Log (See CLAIM LOG)
Longshore and Harbor Workers' Compensation Act (See LONGSHORE AND HARBOR WORKERS' COMPENSATION ACT)
Medical care
Payment for services
Time to request payment . . . Lab §4603.2
Medical-legal expenses
Request for payment
Time for request . . . Lab §4625
Payment of claims (See PAYMENT OF BENEFITS)
Penalties and fines
Administrative penalties (See PENALTIES AND FINES)
Personal physician, right to use
Lien of provider
Fraud against workers' compensation system, medical billing, insurance, Medicare or Medi-Cal, stay of provider lien . . . Lab §4615
Physicians and other health care providers
Lien of provider
Fraud against workers' compensation system, medical billing, insurance, Medicare or Medi-Cal, stay of provider lien . . . Lab §4615
Suspension of physician, practitioner or provider from participation in system for cause . . . Lab §139.21
Procedure for provider suspension . . . 8 CCR §§9788.1 to 9788.6
Pleadings, required . . . Lab §5500
Reimbursements . . . Lab §4903.1
Report of inventory, annual . . . 8 CCR §10104
Representation, removal of privilege of . . . Lab §4907
Self-insurance (See SELF-INSURANCE)
Time limits
Affirmative defense, time limits as . . . Lab §5409
Aggravation of preexisting disease . . . Lab §5410
Collection proceedings (See COLLECTION PROCEEDINGS)
Dismissal of claims inactive for more than 180 days . . . Lab §5404.5
Further claims barred by timely filing . . . Lab §5404
Notice of injury . . . Lab §5400
Untimely claims, barring of . . . Lab §5404
Time lost, injuries involving
Denial of claim
Medical treatment outside of system, rulemaking to provide for notice of employee option to pursue . . . Lab §138.4
Uniformity of procedures, forms, and settings . . . Lab §5500.3
Untimely claims, barring of . . . Lab §5404
Venue, petition for change of . . . Lab §5501.6

CLASSIFICATION
Mines (See MINING AND TUNNELING)
Rating insurance premiums . . . Ins §§11734, 11738
Rating organizations (See RATING ORGANIATIONS)
Tunnels (See MINING AND TUNNELING)

CLASSIFICATION—Cont.
Uninsured employers benefits trust fund, responsibility to designate job classifications of payees . . . Lab §3716.5
Worker classification . . . Lab §§2775 to 2785 (See WORKER CLASSIFICATION)

CLASSIFIED SERVICE EMPLOYEES
Industrial accident or illness leave for school district employees . . . Ed §45192

CLEAR AND CONVINCING EVIDENCE
Requirement for burden of proof . . . Ev §115

CLINICAL SOCIAL WORKERS
Medical information disclosures
Threat to health or safety, release of information to alleviate . . . CC §56.10
Treatment of injuries by . . . Lab §3209.8

COBRA
Continuation coverage under, employer obligations regarding . . . Lab §2800.2

COERCION
Privileged matter disclosed . . . Ev §919

COLLATERAL
Insurance policy deductibles, collateral or security for . . . Ins §11736.5
Receivables, collateral or security for recognition of . . . Ins §11736.5

COLLATERAL ESTOPPEL
Appeals Board (WCAB) findings and subsequent criminal proceedings
Compromise and release . . . Lab §5006
Findings and awards . . . Lab §5816
Limitations on claims procedures . . . Lab §5413
Compromise and release, and subsequent criminal proceedings . . . Lab §5006

COLLECTION PROCEEDINGS
Time limits on
Generally . . . Lab §§5405, 5406
Asbestosis . . . Lab §5406.5
Dependent death benefits
Limitations period for commencement of proceedings to collect dependency death benefits . . . Lab §5406.7
Employer misconduct, cases involving . . . Lab §5407
HIV-related diseases, limitations on action regarding . . . Lab §5406.6

COLLECTIVE BARGAINING AGREEMENTS
Alternative dispute resolution provisions in agreements . . . Lab §3201.7
Construction industry . . . Lab §3201.5
Workers' compensation insurance rates . . . Ins §11741
Jockeys, licensed . . . Lab §3201.81
Annual report . . . 8 CCR §10204
California State University Police Department . . . Lab §4816
Definitions pertinent to . . . 8 CCR §10200

COLLECTIVE BARGAINING AGREEMENTS—Cont.
Eligibility
Determining . . . 8 CCR §10201
Letter of
Effect . . . 8 CCR §10201
Labor Standards Enforcement Division . . . Lab §96
Petition for permission to negotiate . . . 8 CCR §10202.1
Recognizing
Procedures . . . 8 CCR §10202
Reporting requirements . . . 8 CCR §§10203, 10204
Aggregate employer annual report . . . 8 CCR §10203.1
Contents of reports . . . Lab §3201.9
Individual employer annual report . . . 8 CCR §10203.2
Validity of . . . Lab §3201.5

COMBINED DISABILITIES
Cumulative injury (See CUMULATIVE INJURY)
Subsequent injuries, due to (See SUBSEQUENT INJURIES)
Work capacity guidelines . . . Table 11

COMMERCE
Foreign commerce using railroads . . . 45 USC §51
Interstate commerce
Railroads . . . 45 USC §51
Workers' compensation division of Labor Code, inapplicability of . . . Lab §3203

COMMERCIAL DRIVERS
Independent contractors
Motor carrier employer amnesty program for carriers performing drayage services . . . Lab §2750.8

COMMERCIAL INSURANCE
Cancellation or nonrenewal of policy . . . Ins §§676.2, 676.6, 677
Foster home activities
Discrimination against insuring foster home activities . . . Ins §676.7
Prohibited basis for cancellation or nonrenewal . . . Ins §676.75
Hate crime or anti-reproductive-rights crime generating losses, factoring in decisions . . . Ins §676.10
Length of term . . . Ins §676.5
Notice of . . . Ins §§676.6, 677, 677.2, 678
Electronic transmission of written notice . . . Ins §678
Discriminatory practices, victims of domestic violence . . . Ins §676.9

COMMISSIONERS
Insurance (See INSURANCE COMMISSIONER)
Longshore and Harbor Workers' Compensation Act deputy commissioners
Deputy commissioners (See LONGSHORE AND HARBOR WORKERS' COMPENSATION ACT)

COMMISSION ON HEALTH AND SAFETY WORKERS' COMPENSATION (See HEALTH AND SAFETY WORKERS' COMPENSATION COMMISSION)

COMMISSIONS
Financial interests in entities providing services
Conflicts of interest . . . Lab §139.32

COMMON CARRIER
Defined . . . 45 USC §57
Railroads (See RAILROADS)

COMMUNICATION (See INFORMATION SYSTEMS)

COMMUNITY COLLEGES
Districts (See SCHOOL DISTRICTS)

COMMUTATION
Female pension, present value of . . . Table 3
Instructions and examples for commutation . . . Table 4
Lump-sum payments, commutation to . . . Lab §5100
Male pension, present value of . . . Table 2
Permanent disability, instructions and tables for commutation . . . 8 CCR §§10169, 10169.1, Table 1

COMMUTING
Alternative commute program participants . . . Lab §3600.8

COMPARATIVE NEGLIGENCE
Death on the high seas
Contributory negligence not bar to recovery . . . 46 USC §30304

COMPENSATION, SALARY, AND WAGES
Claims adjuster, offered to . . . Lab §3219
Continuation of salary during periods of temporary disability . . . 8 CCR §9814
Determinations as to compensation
Financial interests in entities providing services . . . Lab §139.32
Insurance Code, defined for purposes of . . . Ins §11630
Labor Code, defined for Workers' compensation division of . . . Lab §3207
Notice of compensation due (See NOTICE)
Referral of clients or patients, for (See REFERRALS AND REFERRAL SERVICES)

COMPLEX LITIGATION
Depositions
Time limits for witness examination
Exception for complex cases . . . CCP §2025.290

COMPLIANCE ORDERS
Advertising violations . . . 8 CCR §9835
Rating organizations
Noncompliance, order of compliance upon . . . Ins §11754.2
Penalties and fines for failing to comply with final order . . . Ins §11756
Self-insurers . . . Lab §3702.9

COMPOUNDED DRUG PRODUCTS
Pharmaceutical fee schedule . . . Lab §5307.1

COMPREHENSIVE MEDICAL-LEGAL EVALUATIONS (See MEDICAL-LEGAL EXPENSES)

COMPROMISE AND RELEASE
Settlement, compromise and release (See SETTLEMENT, COMPROMISE AND RELEASE)

COMPROMISE AND RELEASE FORMS
Electronic adjudication management system (EAMS) . . . 8 CCR §10205.2

COMPUTATION OF WORKERS' COMPENSATION
Average earnings (See AVERAGE EARNINGS)
Both partial and total temporary disability . . . Lab §4655
Both temporary and permanent disability . . . Lab §4661
Children under 16, injuries to illegally employed . . . Lab §4557
Court costs following denial of petition to reduce award . . . Lab §4555.5
Death benefits . . . Lab §4702
Definitions pertinent to schedules of compensation . . . Lab §4558
Denial of petition to reduce award . . . Lab §4555.5
Disability benefits (See DISABILITY BENEFITS)
Failure to secure payment
  Attorneys' fees . . . Lab §4555
  Increase in amount of compensation due to . . . Lab §4554
Longshore and Harbor Workers' Compensation Act
  Amount of compensation (See LONGSHORE AND HARBOR WORKERS' COMPENSATION ACT)
Lump-sum payments, determining amount of . . . Lab §5101
Maximum amounts, punitive increases not affected by . . . Lab §4556
Misconduct affecting (See MISCONDUCT)
Permanent disability
  Generally . . . Lab §4658
  Average weekly earnings . . . Lab §4659
  15 percent bump up or bump down . . . Lab §4658
  Percentage of . . . Lab §4660
    2013, injuries occurring in or after . . . Lab §4660.1
  Schedules . . . Lab §§4658, 4660
    2013, injuries occurring in or after . . . Lab §4660.1
  Temporary and permanent disabilities combined . . . Lab §4661
Serious and willful misconduct (See SERIOUS AND WILLFUL MISCONDUCT)
Subsequent injuries . . . Lab §4754
Temporary disability
  Partial . . . Lab §§4654, 4657
  Permanent and temporary disabilities combined . . . Lab §4661
  Total
    Amount of compensation for . . . Lab §4653
    Payment made two or more years after injury . . . Lab §4661.5

COMPUTERS
Evidence, computer printouts as . . . Ev §1552
Self-insurers' computerized claim file data, transfer of . . . 8 CCR §15402.4

CONCRETE BUILDINGS
Protective flooring in . . . Lab §7102

CONFIDENTIALITY
Independent medical review
  Organizations providing review
    Quality assurance mechanisms . . . Lab §139.5
Individually identifiable information held by Workers' Compensation Division . . . 8 CCR §9703, Lab §138.7
Liens
  Confidentiality of medical information . . . Lab §4903.6
Medical records and information
  Definitions pertinent to medical information disclosure . . . CC §56.05
  Diagnosis, confidentiality of . . . Lab §3762
  Employer's right to information, limitations on . . . Lab §3762
  Exceptions to disclosure rule . . . CC §56.30
  Health care providers
    Regulatory authority to insure confidentiality in payment processing . . . Lab §4603.4
  HIV status, disclosure of . . . CC §56.31
Occupational Safety and Health Division inspections, information obtained in . . . Lab §6322
Public disability accommodations
  Request for accommodations . . . 8 CCR §9708.3
Reports on occupational disease or injury . . . Lab §6412
Self-insurers' financial information . . . 8 CCR §15405
Trade secrets, protection from disclosure of . . . Lab §6396
Workers' Compensation Insurance Fraud Reporting Act, information acquired under . . . Ins §1877.3

CONFLICT OF LAWS
Judicial notice of foreign law . . . Ev §452

CONFLICTS OF INTEREST
Depositions
  Officer conducting proceedings . . . CCP §2025.320
Drugs, medical treatment utilization schedule (MTUS)
  Pharmacy and therapeutics committee . . . 8 CCR §9792.27.20
    Disclosure form . . . 8 CCR §9792.27.21
Financial interests in entities providing services . . . Lab §139.32
Group self-insurance
  Service providers, conflicts of interest among . . . 8 CCR §15475.1
Health care organizations (HCOs) . . . 8 CCR §9771.71
Independent medical examiners (IMES)
  Financial interest, referral to person with whom physician has . . . Lab §§139.3, 139.31
Independent medical review
  IMR's conflicts . . . 8 CCR §9768.2
  Independence of organizations . . . Lab §139.5
Judges (WCJs)
  Disclosures of conflicts of interest . . . 8 CCR §9721.11
    Manner of disclosure . . . 8 CCR §9721.14
  Disqualification
    Grounds . . . 8 CCR §9721.12
  Ethical requirements for judges generally . . . 8 CCR §§9720.1 to 9723 (See ETHICAL REQUIREMENTS)
  Financial interests in educational programs . . . 8 CCR §9721.31

CONFLICTS OF INTEREST—Cont.
Qualified medical evaluators (QMEs)
Evaluators' conflicts of interest . . . 8 CCR §41.5
Disclosure and objection/waiver form . . . 8 CCR §123
Gifts to medical evaluators . . . 8 CCR §41.7
Procedures after notice and waiver of conflict . . . 8 CCR §41.6
Faculty disclosure of interest form . . . 8 CCR §119
Financial interest, referral to person with whom physician has . . . Lab §§139.3, 139.31
Panel
Replacement requests . . . 8 CCR §31.5
Specified financial interests
Affecting assignment to panels . . . 8 CCR §29
Attachment to certain forms . . . 8 CCR §124
Defined . . . 8 CCR §1
State compensation insurance fund
Board of directors . . . Ins §11770
Lobbying restrictions for former officers or directors . . . Ins §11785.5

CONGRESS OF THE UNITED STATES
Judicial notice of acts by . . . Ev §§451, 452

CONSERVATOR OR GUARDIAN
Longshore and Harbor Workers' Compensation Act, awards under . . . 33 USC §911
Medical information, authorization for release of . . . CC §56.10
Pre-employment physical of minor ward, disclosure of information from . . . CC §56.10
Rights of injured minors or incompetents . . . Lab §5408

CONSOLIDATION OF ACTIONS
Appeals board (WCAB)
Assignment of consolidated cases . . . 8 CCR §10398
Criteria for consolidation . . . 8 CCR §10396
Failure of employer to secure payment of compensation . . . Lab §3708.5
Subrogation . . . Lab §3853

CONSTITUTIONAL LAW
Judicial notice of constitutional provisions . . . Ev §§451, 452

CONSTRUCTION CONTRACTS
Certificate of insurance required for permit . . . Lab §3800
Disciplinary proceedings against contractors, grounds for . . . B&P §7110
Labor law compliance
Funding in contract to be sufficient for contractor to comply with labor laws . . . Lab §2810

CONSTRUCTION ELEVATORS
Building defined for purposes of . . . Lab §7200
Defined . . . Lab §7200
Inspection of . . . Lab §7204
Penalties for violation of requirements for . . . Lab §7205
Signal system for
Employee charged with providing signals . . . Lab §7202
Establishment and implementation of . . . Lab §7201

CONSTRUCTION ELEVATORS—Cont.
Signal system for—Cont.
Regulation of signals . . . Lab §7203

CONSTRUCTION INDUSTRY (See BUILDING AND CONSTRUCTION INDUSTRY)

CONSTRUCTIVE INVASION OF PRIVACY . . . CC §1708.8

CONSULTING OR ATTENDING PHYSICIANS
Certification of
Criterion for . . . 8 CCR §9799
Notice of competence . . . 8 CCR §9802
Procedure for . . . 8 CCR §9796
Requested by injured worker . . . Lab §4602
Employee's expense, hired at . . . Lab §4605
Qualified medical evaluators (QMEs) as consultants
Determinations by QMES as to report of consulting or attending physician . . . Lab §4605

CONSULTING SERVICES
Safe workplace (See SAFE WORKPLACE)

CONTEMPT
Appeals Board (WCAB)
Contempt proceedings . . . 8 CCR §10440, Lab §134
Subpoenas, refusal to obey . . . Lab §132
Prisoners incarcerated for, employment of . . . Pen §4017.5
Privileged information, nondisclosure . . . Ev §914

CONTINENTAL SHELF LANDS
Defined . . . 43 USC §1331
Longshore and Harbor Workers' Compensation Act, applicability of . . . 43 USC §1333

CONTINUANCES
Clear showing of good cause . . . 8 CCR §10748

CONTINUING EDUCATION
Elevators, escalators dumbwaiters, and other conveyances, safety
Certifications requiring . . . Lab §7311.3
Qualified medical evaluators (QMEs)
Course evaluation form . . . 8 CCR §117
Definition of continuing education program . . . 8 CCR §1
Faculty disclosure of interest form . . . 8 CCR §119
Providers
Application for accreditation or re-accreditation as education provider, form . . . 8 CCR §118
Reappointment . . . 8 CCR §55

CONTRACTORS' STATE LICENSE BOARD
Notice of Occupational Safety and Health Division penalty . . . Lab §6652

CONTRACTS AND CONTRACTORS
App-based drivers and services
Independence of app-based drivers
Contract and termination of provisions between driver and company . . . B&P §7452
Construction contracts (See CONSTRUCTION CONTRACTS)

CONTRACTS AND CONTRACTORS—Cont.
Disciplinary proceedings against contractors, grounds for . . . B&P §7110
Misclassification as independent contractor
Advising employers to misclassify, liability . . . Lab §2753
Willful misclassification . . . Lab §226.8
Employment contracts defined . . . Lab §2750
Health care organizations (HCOs) (See HEALTH CARE ORGANIATIONS (HCOS))
Independent contractors (See INDEPENDENT CONTRACTORS)
Independent medical review (See INDEPENDENT MEDICAL REVIEW)
Insurance
Certificates of coverage . . . B&P §7125
Stop order prohibiting use of employee labor for failure to secure workers' compensation coverage . . . B&P §7127
Failure to maintain . . . B&P §7125.2
False certificate of insurance coverage . . . B&P §7125.4
License maintained by maintaining certificate . . . B&P §7125.3
Labor contractors
Premium payments . . . Lab §3302
Labor law compliance
Funding in contract to be sufficient for contractor to comply with labor laws . . . Lab §2810
Medical provider networks
Independent medical reviews
Contracts for reviews . . . Lab §4616.4
Misclassification as independent contractor
Advising employers to misclassify
Liability . . . Lab §2753
Willful misclassification . . . Lab §226.8
Occupational safety and health
Investigation reports
Transmittal to contractors' state license board . . . Lab §6313.5
Refinery and chemical plant hazards, warning employees of contractors about . . . Lab §7862
Roofing contractors
Certificate of workers' compensation insurance or self-insurance
Removal of C-39 roofing classification from license for failure to provide certificate to registrar . . . B&P §7125
Insurer for workers' compensation coverage to perform payroll audit . . . Ins §11665
Unlicensed contractors in violation of security for payment requirement
Criminal enforcement . . . B&P §7126
U.Scontractors working outside U.S (See FOREIGN EMPLOYMENT)

CONTRIBUTIONS
Cumulative injury
Employer liability
Proceedings with appeals board to determine apportionment or right of contribution . . . Lab §5500.5
Disability benefits
State employees . . . UI §2783

CONTRIBUTIONS—Cont.
Disability benefits—Cont.
Unemployment Compensation Disability Fund, to (See UNEMPLOYMENT COMPENSATION DISABILITY FUND)
Voluntary disability benefit plans, to
Generally . . . UI §3252
Trust fund, employee contributions treated as . . . UI §3261
Insurance, employee contributions to . . . Lab §3751
Longshore and Harbor Workers' Compensation Act . . . 33 USC §915
Occupational disease
Employer liability
Proceedings with appeals board to determine apportionment or right of contribution . . . Lab §5500.5
Temporarily incapacitated county firefighters, contributions from . . . Gov §32338
Unemployment compensation
Definition of contribution for purposes of . . . UI §144
Disability benefits (See DISABILITY BENEFITS)
Rates and percentages . . . UI §984
Unemployment Compensation Disability Fund, to (See UNEMPLOYMENT COMPENSATION DISABILITY FUND)
Voluntary disability benefit plans, to
Generally . . . UI §3252
Trust fund, employee contributions treated as . . . UI §3261

CONTRIBUTORY NEGLIGENCE
Action to recover personal injury damages . . . Lab §2801
Death on the high seas
Not bar to recovery . . . 46 USC §30304
Failure of employer to secure payment of compensation . . . Lab §3708
Railroads . . . 45 USC §53

CONVERSION/CONTINUATION COVERAGE
Health care coverage (See HEALTH CARE COVERAGE)

CONVICTS (See PRISONERS)

COPIES OF FORMS (See REPRODUCTION OF FORMS)

CORONARY DISEASE (See HEART DISEASE)

CORONAVIRUS (See COVID-19)

CORONERS AND MEDICAL EXAMINERS
Medical records, disclosure of to coroners . . . CC §56.10

CORPORATE LIABILITY
Uninsured Employers Fund, to . . . Lab §3717

CORPORATIONS
Depositions
Notice of deposition
Description of matters on which examination requested . . . CCP §2025.230

CORRECTIONS AND REHABILITATION DEPARTMENT
Inmates (See PRISONERS)

CORRECTIONS AND REHABILITATION DEPARTMENT—Cont.
Juvenile Court
Volunteers (See VOLUNTEERS)
Wards of (See MINORS)
Labor programs, contracts for . . . CA Const Art XIV §5
Officers and guards
Death benefit scholarships for dependents of . . . Lab §4709
Early intervention program for . . . Lab §3214
Heart disease . . . Lab §§3212.2, 3212.10
Occupational safety and health issues . . . Lab §6304.2
Pneumonia, tuberculosis and meningitis as compensable injuries . . . Lab §3212.10
Public Employees' Retirement System, state and local safety members of (See PUBLIC EMPLOYEES' RETIREMENT SYSTEM)
Tuberculosis . . . Lab §3212.6
Safe workplace issues
Applicability of provisions . . . Lab §6304.5
Evidence Code, applicability of . . . Lab §6304.5
Industry safety committee, establishment of . . . Lab §6304.3
Inmates as employees . . . Lab §§6304.2, 6304.4
Labor Statistics and Research, Division of . . . Lab §6413.2
Officers as employees . . . Lab §6304.2
Report of injury to inmate . . . Lab §6413

COSMETICS
Hazardous substances contained in cosmetics or disinfectants
Manufacturer or importer duties . . . Lab §6390.2

COSTS
Appeals board (WCAB)
Petition for costs . . . 8 CCR §10545
Arbitration . . . Lab §5273
Court costs (See COURT COSTS)
Insurance, failure to secure payment
Investigation costs, responsibility for . . . Lab §3700.5
Insurance frauds prevention act
Actions brought under act . . . Ins §1871.7
Rating organization investigations . . . Ins §11752.2
Shipping
United States vessels or cargo, suits in admiralty involving
Inclusion in judgment against US . . . 46 USC §30911

COUNSEL (See ATTORNEYS)

COUNTERCLAIMS
Shipping
Public vessels, damages caused by or towage and salvage rendered to
Security on counterclaims . . . 46 USC §31105

COUNTY EMPLOYEES
Definitions pertinent to . . . Gov §31000.8
Extraterritorial application of privileges and immunities of local agent . . . Gov §53023

COUNTY EMPLOYEES—Cont.
Firefighters
Contributions from temporarily incapacitated members . . . Gov §32338
Performing duty not under direction of employer . . . Gov §50926
Insurance, provision of . . . Gov §54462
Peace officers
Defined . . . Gov §50920
Performing duty not under direction of employer . . . Gov §50921
Prisoners of county facilities (See PRISONERS)
Reserve account for . . . Gov §25263
Retirement systems
Board of retirement members, benefits for . . . Gov §31520.4
Subrogation . . . Gov §31820
Self-insured counties . . . Gov §31000.8
Subrogation . . . Gov §31820

COUNTY SUPERINTENDENT OF SCHOOLS
Insurance taken out by
Coverage, extent of . . . Ed §1297
Payment of cost of . . . Ed §1297
State Compensation Insurance Fund, with . . . Ed §1252

COURSE OF EMPLOYMENT (See ARISING OUT OF EMPLOYMENT/COURSE OF EMPLOYMENT)

COURSE OF TRADE, BUSINESS, PROFESSION, OR OCCUPATION
Election to cover employees not in . . . Lab §4153
Employment relations under Labor Code . . . Lab §3355

COURT ADMINISTRATOR RULES
Electronic adjudication management system (EAMS) . . . 8 CCR §§10205 to 10208.12 (See ELECTRONIC ADJUDICATION MANAGEMENT SYSTEM (EAMS))
Filings
Electronic adjudication management system (EAMS) generally . . . 8 CCR §§10205 to 10208.12 (See ELECTRONIC ADJUDICATION MANAGEMENT SYSTEM (EAMS))

COURT COSTS
Appeals Board (WCAB)
Generally . . . Lab §5811
Hearings . . . 8 CCR §10421
Bad faith actions or tactics . . . Lab §5813
Denial of petition to reduce award, following . . . Lab §4555.5
Longshore and Harbor Workers' Compensation Act . . . 33 USC §926
Occupational Safety and Health Appeals Board, award by . . . Lab §149.5
Subrogation . . . Lab §3856
United States as party . . . 28 USC §2412

COURT INTERPRETERS (See INTERPRETERS)

COURT OF CLAIMS
Judicial notice of rules of . . . Ev §451

COURT REPORTERS
Depositions, transcripts and other recordings of
Transcript of deposition . . . CCP §2025.510
Notice of availability for reading, correcting and signing . . . CCP §2025.520
Workers' Compensation Division
Reporter employed by . . . Lab §123.3

COURT REVIEW (See JUDICIAL REVIEW)

COVER PAGE FOR MEDICAL PROVIDER NETWORK APPLICATION FORM . . . 8 CCR §9767.4

COVER PAGE FOR MEDICAL PROVIDER NETWORK REAPPROVAL PLAN FORM . . . 8 CCR §9767.4

COVID-19
Agricultural employees
Infection prevention best practices
Dissemination among agricultural employees . . . Lab §6725
Compensation for injury or death from COVID-19 . . . Lab §3212.86
Firefighters . . . Lab §3212.87
Health care occupations . . . Lab §3212.87
Peace officers . . . Lab §3212.87
Testing positive, outbreak at place of employment . . . Lab §3212.88
Health and safety workers' compensation commission
Study of impact on workers' compensation system . . . Lab §77.8
Occupational safety and health division
No-entry/no-use orders
Imminent hazard, authority to issue order . . . Lab §6325
Serious violations by employers
Provisions applicable during pandemic . . . Lab §6432
Qualified medical evaluators (QMES)
Electronic service
Emergency regulation . . . 8 CCR §36.7
Evaluation procedures
Emergency regulation . . . 8 CCR §46.2
Reporting requirements
Exposure, employer notice requirements . . . Lab §6409.6
Safe workplace
Exposure, employer notice requirements . . . Lab §6409.6
No-entry/no-use orders
Imminent hazard, authority to issue order . . . Lab §6325
Sick days, paid
Covered workers, supplemental paid sick leave . . . Lab §248.1
Food sector workers, supplemental paid sick leave . . . Lab §248

C&R (COMPROMISE AND RELEASE) AGREEMENTS
Settlement, compromise and release generally (See SETTLEMENT, COMPROMISE AND RELEASE)

CRANES
Boomstops for crawler and wheel cranes . . . Lab §6704

CRANES—Cont.
Certification of crane safety
Appeal of revocation of license to certify . . . Lab §7377
Fees for license to certify . . . Lab §7380
Fraudulent certification . . . Lab §7378
Penalties for certification without license . . . Lab §7379
Suspension or revocation of license to certify . . . Lab §7376
Crawler cranes, boomstops for . . . Lab §6704
Death resulting from violation of safety standards . . . Lab §7381
Fees for examination and licensing of crane certifiers . . . Lab §7380
License to certify crane safety
Appeal of revocation of license to certify . . . Lab §7377
Fees . . . Lab §7380
Penalties for certification without license . . . Lab §7379
Suspension or revocation of license to certify . . . Lab §7376
Tower crane permits (See TOWER CRANES)
Penalties and fines
Fraudulent certification . . . Lab §7378
License, certification without . . . Lab §7379
Safety standard violations . . . Lab §7381
Serious violations . . . Lab §7381
Presence of safety representative for installing, dismantling, or jumping cranes . . . Lab §7382
Revocation of license, permit, or certification (See REVOCATION OF LICENSE, PERMIT, OR CERTIFICATION)
Suspensions
License to certify . . . Lab §7376
Tower crane permits . . . Lab §7374
Tower cranes (See TOWER CRANES)
Wheel cranes, boomstops for . . . Lab §6704

CREDIT
State Compensation Insurance Fund . . . Ins §§11776, 11777
Third party recovery by injured worker credited to employer liability . . . Lab §3861
Voluntary disability benefit plans . . . UI §3266

CREDITS AGAINST TAX
Vocational rehabilitation . . . W&I §19005.5

CRIME VICTIMS
Eligibility for workers' compensation, notice of . . . Lab §3553
Human trafficking victim-caseworker privilege
Waiver . . . Ev §912
Invasion of privacy . . . CC §1708.8
Notice regarding eligibility for worker's compensation . . . Lab §3553
Physical or mental trauma, inability to testify due to . . . Ev §240

CRIMINAL ACTS LEADING TO INJURY
Conditions of employer liability for compensation . . . Lab §3600

CRIMINAL ACTS LEADING TO INJURY—Cont.
Employer crime against employee
Payments by workers' compensation carrier to employee
Restitution for crime not offset by payments received . . . Lab §3602

CRIMINAL HISTORY INFORMATION RECORDS
App-based drivers and services
Background checks of drivers . . . B&P §7458
Evidence
Microphotographed files, records, photographs, etc., in custody of criminal justice agency
Reproductions, admissibility in evidence . . . Ev §1550.1
Genetic characteristics, disclosure of test results for . . . CC §56.17

CRIMINAL LAW
App-based drivers and services
Impersonating app-based driver . . . B&P §7462
Appeals Board (WCAB) findings, no collateral estoppel as result of (See COLLATERAL ESTOPPEL)
Asbestos-related complaints . . . Lab §6436
Attorney referral service-client privilege
Use of service to perpetrate fraud or crime . . . Ev §968
Claims adjuster, compensation offered to . . . Lab §3219
Collateral estoppel as result of Appeals Board (WCAB) findings (See COLLATERAL ESTOPPEL)
Compromise and release, no collateral estoppel as result of . . . Lab §5006
Contractors
Insurance
False certificate of insurance coverage . . . B&P §7125.4
Unlicensed contractors in violation of security for payment requirement
Criminal enforcement . . . B&P §7126
Financial interests in entities providing services
Conflicts of interest . . . Lab §139.32
Fraud
False or fraudulent claims, making . . . Pen §550
Internet posting of convicted violators . . . Ins §1871.9
Solicitation or referral for purposes of . . . Pen §549
High voltage, misdemeanors associated with . . . Pen §385
Judicial notice of federal rules . . . Ev §451
Prisoners (See PRISONERS)
Referral of clients or patients, compensation received for . . . Lab §3215
Safe workplace
Emergency closing of areas for public health or safety menace
Directing employee to remain in or enter close areas . . . Lab §6311.5
Search warrants
Grounds for issuance . . . Pen §1524
Statute of limitations
Discovery of offense . . . Pen §803
Steam boilers causing death, imprisonment for . . . Lab §7771
Victims of crime (See CRIME VICTIMS)

CRIMINAL REHABILITATION
Juvenile Court volunteers
Regional youth facility
Wards committed to facility . . . Lab §3364.7
Traffic offenders . . . Lab §3364.6
Wards . . . Lab §3364.55
Licenses available under Labor Code for rehabilitated criminals . . . Lab §26

CRIMINAL TRIALS
Genetic characteristics, disclosure of test results for . . . CC §56.17
Judicial notice of federal rules . . . Ev §451

CROSS-EXAMINATION
Appeals Board, before (See APPEALS BOARD (WCAB))

CRUELTY OR BATTERY
Aliens, uninsured employers fund and subsequent injuries fund benefits for . . . 8 CCR §15740

CUMULATIVE INJURY
Generally . . . Lab §3208.1
Compromise and release . . Lab §5005
Date of . . . Lab §5412
Employer liability . . . Lab §5500.5
Professional sports
Out-of-state hires, exemption . . . Lab §3600.5

CUMULATIVE REMEDIES
Advertising violations . . . 8 CCR §9836

CUSTOMS COURT
Judicial notice of rules of . . . Ev §451

D

DAMAGES
Conditions of employer liability . . . Lab §3600
Defined . . . Lab §3209
Depositions
Subpoenas
Disobedience of subpoena . . . CCP §2020.240
Evidence of amount payable as benefit as measure of . . . CC §3333.1
Failure to secure payment of benefits, action based on
Attachment of property for . . . Lab §3707
Consolidation of actions . . . Lab §3708.5
Defenses . . . Lab §3708
Exceptions . . . Lab §3706.5
Grounds for action . . . Lab §3706
Judgments . . . Lab §3709
Negligence, presumption of . . . Lab §3708
Relief from obligation to pay more compensation following close of case . . . Lab §3709.5
Service of complaint . . . Lab §3708.5
Invasion of privacy . . . CC §1708.8
Public vessels or cargo, caused by (See SHIPPING)
Railroad awards and contributory negligence . . . 45 USC §53
Shipping (See SHIPPING)

DANGEROUS DRUGS OR DEVICES
Pharmaceutical fee schedule . . . Lab §5307.1

Index

DAY PROGRAMS
Employment discrimination or harassment
Action for harassment or discrimination by employees of nonprofit sheltered workshops, day programs or rehabilitation facilities . . . Gov §12926.05

DEATH
Benefits (See DEATH BENEFITS)
Crane safety, death resulting from violation of . . . Lab §7381
Employee (See DEATH OF EMPLOYEE)
Employer's death, employee's rights against estate following . . . Lab §5306
Employer's records of occupational injury or illness
Criteria for recording
General recording criteria . . . 8 CCR §14300.7
Definition of fatality . . . 8 CCR §14300.46
High seas, death on . . . 46 USC §§30301 to 30308 (See DEATH ON THE HIGH SEAS)
Shipping
Death on the high seas . . . 46 USC §§30301 to 30308
Steam boilers causing . . . Lab §7771
Witnesses unavailable due to . . . Ev §240

DEATH BENEFITS
Generally . . . Lab §4700
Asbestos workers . . . Lab §4407.3
Assassinated public officials (See subhead: Public officials, assassinated)
Assignment . . . Lab §4704
Burial expenses (See BURIAL EXPENSES)
Compromise and release . . . Lab §5004
Computation . . . Lab §4702
COVID-19, compensation for injury or death . . . Lab §3212.86
Firefighters, peace officers, health workers, etc . . . Lab §3212.87
Testing positive, outbreak at place of employment . . . Lab §3212.88
Dependents . . . Lab §§3501 to 3503
Generally . . . Lab §4701
Children . . . Lab §4703.5
Death of . . . Lab §4706
Limitations period for commencement of proceedings to collect dependency death benefits . . . Lab §5406.7
Longshore and Harbor Workers' Compensation Act . . . 33 USC §909
No surviving dependents . . . Lab §4706.5
Police officers, computation of benefit . . . Lab §4706.5
Notice to . . . 8 CCR §9812
Rights of . . . Lab §4703
Safety members, minor children of . . . Lab §4703.6
Table of benefits payable for total and partial dependency . . . Table 13
Economic Opportunity Program enrollees . . . Lab §§4212, 4214
Employer liability . . . Lab §§4700, 4701
Firefighters
Generally . . . Lab §4856
Continued health benefits to surviving spouse and dependents . . . Lab §4856

DEATH BENEFITS—Cont.
Firefighters—Cont.
Scholarships for dependents of . . . Lab §4709
Foreign employment
Contractors with U.Sworking outside U.S . . . 42 USC §1701
Military bases outside U.S., employees of . . . 42 USC §1651
Funeral expenses (See BURIAL EXPENSES)
HIV-related diseases, time limitations for benefits for health care workers for death from . . . Lab §5406.6
Industrial Relations Department, payment to . . . Lab §4706.5
Installment payments . . . Lab §4702
Interest on payments . . . Lab §5800
Longshore and Harbor Workers' Compensation Act . . . 33 USC §909
Military bases overseas, service on . . . 42 USC §1651
Notice of death
DIA Form 510 for . . . 8 CCR §9910
Reproduction of DIA Form 510 . . . 8 CCR §9914
Payment of
Generally . . . Lab §4701
Installment payments . . . Lab §4702
No surviving dependents . . . Lab §4706.5
Public officials, assassinated . . . Lab §4725
Table of benefits payable for total and partial dependency . . . Table 13
Police officers
Generally . . . Lab §4856
Continued health benefits to surviving spouse and dependents . . . Lab §4856
Scholarships for dependents . . . Lab §4709
Public Employees' Retirement System (See PUBLIC EMPLOYEES' RETIREMENT SYSTEM)
Public officials, assassinated
Assassin's ineligibility for benefits . . . Lab §4727
Definitions . . . Lab §4720
Election of type of special death benefits . . . Lab §4723
Filing claims for . . . Lab §4724
Joint adoption of rules for . . . Lab §4726
Persons entitled to special death benefits . . . Lab §4722
Scholarships for dependents of . . . Lab §4728
Special death benefits for . . . Lab §4721
State Compensation Insurance Fund, disbursement of benefits by . . . Lab §4725
Scholarships
Police officers, correctional officers, and firefighters, dependents of . . . Lab §4709
Public officials, dependents of . . . Lab §4728
Sheriffs
Special officer of sheriff, Orange county
Scholarships for dependents . . . Lab §4709
Subrogation and . . . Lab §3851
Survivors' rights (See SURVIVORS' RIGHTS)
Table of benefits payable for total and partial dependency . . . Table 13
Trustees . . . Lab §4705

DEATH OF EMPLOYEE
Notice of
DIA Form 510 for . . . 8 CCR §9910

DEATH OF EMPLOYEE—Cont.
Notice of—Cont.
Employer duties . . . 8 CCR §9900
Incomplete or deficient notice . . . 8 CCR §9905
Reproduction of DIA Form 510 . . . 8 CCR §9914
Service of notice to administrative director . . . 8 CCR §9918
Penalties and fines for violations leading to . . . Lab §6425
Reporting requirements . . . Lab §6409.1
School district payments to surviving spouse of murdered employee . . . Ed §44017
Serious violations
Rebuttable presumption of serious violation . . . Lab §6432
Service
Dependency at issue
Division of workers' compensation and director of industrial relations, service on . . . 8 CCR §10632
Third party causing injury or death
Personal relationship not inferred due to certain beliefs of third party . . . Lab §3600

DEATH OF EMPLOYER
Employee's rights against estate following . . . Lab §5306

DEATH ON THE HIGH SEAS . . . 46 USC §§30301 to 30308
Action . . . 46 USC §30302
Foreign cause of action . . . 46 USC §30306
State law causes of actions, effect of provisions . . . 46 USC §30308
Amount of recovery . . . 46 USC §30303
Apportionment of recovery . . . 46 USC §30303
Commercial aviation accidents
Applicability of provisions . . . 46 USC §30307
Comparative negligence
Contributory negligence not bar to recovery . . . 46 USC §30304
Contributory negligence not bar to recovery . . . 46 USC §30304
Foreign cause of action . . . 46 USC §30306
Internal waters
Applicability of provisions . . . 46 USC §30308
Parties
Substitution of personal representative upon death of plaintiff while action pending . . . 46 USC §30305
Plaintiff dying while action pending
Substitution of personal representative upon death of plaintiff while action pending . . . 46 USC §30305
Short title of provisions . . . 46 USC §30301

DEBTS
Claims, effect on . . . Lab §§4901, 4908
Priority of . . . Lab §3705

DECISIONS
Appeals Board (WCAB) (See APPEALS BOARD (WCAB))
Contractors with U.Sworking outside U.S., finality of decisions of Secretary of Labor regarding . . . 42 USC §1715
Electronic adjudication management system (EAMS)
Inspection of documents
Prohibitions . . . 8 CCR §10208.6

DECISIONS—Cont.
Electronic adjudication management system (EAMS)—Cont.
Retention, return and destruction of records . . . 8 CCR §10208.7
Judges (WCJs)
Authority following decision after reconsideration . . . 8 CCR §10986
Procedures for submitting case to . . . 8 CCR §9715
Reconsideration
Authority following decision after . . . 8 CCR §10986
Timing of . . . Lab §§5313, 5800.5
Judicial review of (See JUDICIAL REVIEW)
Labor Standards Enforcement Division
Hearing following decision . . . 8 CCR §15590
Issuance of decisions . . . 8 CCR §§15555, 15571
Occupational Safety and Health Appeals Board (See OCCUPATIONAL SAFETY AND HEALTH APPEALS BOARD)
Occupational Safety and Health Standards Board (See OCCUPATIONAL SAFETY AND HEALTH STANDARDS BOARD)
Penalty assessment orders, decision following appeal hearing . . . 8 CCR §15590
Rating organization decision, action, or omission, appeal of . . . Ins §11753.1
Reconsideration of (See RECONSIDERATION)
Self-insurance, decisions of hearing officer regarding . . . 8 CCR §15435
Service
Appeals Board (WCAB)
Service by board of orders, decisions, awards, etc . . . 8 CCR §10628
Stop orders, decision following appeal hearing . . . 8 CCR §15590
Suspension of
Appeals Board (WCAB) order, decision, or award suspended by filing petition for reconsideration . . . Lab §5910
Occupational Safety and Health Appeals Board decision suspended by filing for reconsideration . . . Lab §6625

DECLARATION OF READINESS TO PROCEED (DOR)
Appeals board (WCAB)
Forms required . . . 8 CCR §10500
Hearings not set until declaration filed . . . 8 CCR §10742
Objections to declaration . . . 8 CCR §10744
Attorneys' fees
Unrepresented employee when DOR filed
Employer liability for employee fees in connection with DOR . . . Lab §4064
Defined
Electronic adjudication management system . . . 8 CCR §10205
Electronic adjudication management system
Definition of DOR . . . 8 CCR §10205
Expedited hearing calendar . . . 8 CCR §10208.3
Electronic adjudication management system (EAMS)
Form . . . 8 CCR §10208.2

Index

DECLARATION OF READINESS TO PROCEED (DOR)—Cont.
Form
Appeals board (WCAB)
Requirement of form . . . 8 CCR §10500
Liens
Claimant declaraion . . . 8 CCR §10873
Verification . . . 8 CCR §10874
Medical examination, following completion of
Payment of benefits or filing declaration . . . Lab §4063
Time for hearing after filing DOR . . . Lab §5502

DEDUCTIBLES
Insurance policy deductibles, collateral or security for . . . Ins §11736.5

DEDUCTIONS
California State University personnel on industrial disability leave . . . Ed §89529.03
Longshore and Harbor Workers' Compensation Act . . . 33 USC §915
School district employees on extended leave, salary deductions for . . . Ed §44983
Voluntary disability benefit plans . . . UI §§3256, 3260
Excess deductions . . . UI §3260.5
Increased deductions . . . UI §3260.5

DEFENDANTS
Claims procedures (See CLAIMS PROCEDURES)
Death benefits suits, joinder of Public Employees' Retirement System as defendant in . . . Lab §4708
United States as defendant (See FEDERAL GOVERNMENT AND LAW)

DEFENSES
Affirmative defenses, generally . . . Lab §3600
Appeals Board (WCAB) hearings . . . Lab §5705
Burden of proof for affirmative defenses . . . Lab §5705
Civil service hiring violations . . . Lab §3604
Contributory negligence . . . Lab §§2801, 3708
Failure of employer to secure payment of compensation . . . Lab §3708
Invasion of privacy . . . CC §1708.8
Statutes of limitation as . . . Lab §5409

DEFERRED COMPENSATION PLANS
Employer-managed . . . Lab §2809

DEFINITIONS
ACOEM practice guidelines
Medical treatment utilization schedule . . . 8 CCR §9792.20
Utilization review standards . . . 8 CCR §9792.6
Action
Civil discovery act . . . CCP §2016.020
Activities of daily living
Family care leave, paid . . . UI §3302.2
Acupuncturists . . . Lab §3209.3
Billing and payment rules, medical treatment . . . 8 CCR §9792.5.0
ADJ file
Electronic adjudication management system (EAMS) . . . 8 CCR §10205

DEFINITIONS—Cont.
Adjudication file
Electronic adjudication management system (EAMS) . . . 8 CCR §10205
Adjusted conversion factor
Official medical fee schedule, outpatient departments and ambulatory surgical centers . . . 8 CCR §9789.30
Adjusting location
Unreasonable delay in or refusal to make payment, administrative penalties and fines . . . 8 CCR §10112.1
Administer
Drugs, medical treatment utilization schedule (MTUS)
Formulary . . . 8 CCR §9792.27.1
Fee schedule maximums . . . Lab §5307.1
Administration Revolving Fund definitions . . . 8 CCR §15600
Administrative director
Electronic adjudication management system (EAMS) . . . 8 CCR §10205
Unreasonable delay in or refusal to make payment, administrative penalties and fines . . . 8 CCR §10112.1
Advertising
Pertinent terms . . . 8 CCR §9820
Truth in Advertising Act, definition of advertiser for purposes of . . . Lab §5434
Agency
Labor and workforce agency . . . Lab §18.5
Aggrieved employee
Labor code private attorneys general . . . Lab §2699
Agricultural employees
COVID-19, infection prevention best practices communications . . . Lab §6725
Alternative work
Disability . . . Lab §4658.1
Return to work programs . . . 8 CCR §10116.9
Ambulatory payment classifications (APC)
Official medical fee schedule, outpatient departments and ambulatory surgical centers . . . 8 CCR §9789.30
Ambulatory surgical center (ASC)
Official medical fee schedule, outpatient departments and ambulatory surgical centers . . . 8 CCR §9789.30
Ambulatory surgical center payment system
Official medical fee schedule, outpatient departments and ambulatory surgical centers . . . 8 CCR §9789.30
American College of Occupational and Environmental Medicine Practice Guidelines
Independent medical review . . . 8 CCR §9768.1
Ancillary services
Medical provider networks . . . 8 CCR §9767.1
Annual utilization report of specialty clinics
Official medical fee schedule, outpatient departments and ambulatory surgical centers . . . 8 CCR §9789.30
Antineoplastic drugs
Occupational safety and health, standards for handling . . . Lab §144.8

DEFINITIONS—Cont.
APC payment rate
Official medical fee schedule, outpatient departments and ambulatory surgical centers . . . 8 CCR §9789.30
APC relative weight
Official medical fee schedule, outpatient departments and ambulatory surgical centers . . . 8 CCR §9789.30
App-based drivers
App-based drivers and services . . . B&P §7463
Appeals Board (WCAB) defined as Workers' Compensation Appeals Board for purposes of Labor Code . . . Lab §3205.5
Appeals Board (WCAB), definitions pertinent to . . . 8 CCR §10305
Applicable minimum wage
App-based drivers and services . . . B&P §7453
Piece-rate basis of compensation . . . Lab §226.2
Applicants
Electronic adjudication management system (EAMS) . . . 8 CCR §10205
Applicants for benefits . . . Lab §5503
Application for adjudication
Electronic adjudication management system (EAMS) . . . 8 CCR §10205
Applications
Electronic adjudication management system (EAMS) . . . 8 CCR §10205
Appraisal of guidelines for research evaluation II (AGREE II) instrument
Medical treatment utilization schedule, medical evidence evaluation . . . 8 CCR §9792.25
Appropriate specialty
Independent medical review . . . 8 CCR §9768.1
Approved training facility
Return to work programs . . . 8 CCR §10116.9
Asbestos definitions . . . Lab §§4402, 6501.7, 6501.8
ASCE 21
Elevators, escalators, dumbwaiters, and other conveyances, safety . . . Lab §7300.1
ASME A17.1
Elevators, escalators, dumbwaiters, and other conveyances, safety . . . Lab §7300.1
ASME A17.3
Elevators, escalators, dumbwaiters, and other conveyances, safety . . . Lab §7300.1
ASME A18.1
Elevators, escalators, dumbwaiters, and other conveyances, safety . . . Lab §7300.1
Assassinated public officials, death benefits for . . . Lab §4720
Assignee
Billing and payment rules, medical treatment . . . 8 CCR §9792.5.0
Authorization
Utilization review standards . . . 8 CCR §§9792.6, 9792.6.1
Workers' compensation division, document copy and electronic transaction fees . . . 8 CCR §9980
Authorization through prospective review
Drugs, medical treatment utilization schedule (MTUS)
Formulary . . . 8 CCR §9792.27.1

DEFINITIONS—Cont.
Authorized governmental agency
Workers' compensation insurance fraud reporting act . . . Ins §§1877.1, 1877.2
Authorized representative
Employer's records of occupational injury or illness . . . 8 CCR §14300.46
Automated people mover
Elevators, escalators, dumbwaiters, and other conveyances, safety . . . Lab §7300.1
Auxiliary aids
Public disability accommodations . . . 8 CCR §9708.1
Average ACA contribution
App-based drivers and services . . . B&P §7463
Average earnings
Annual . . . Lab §4451
Permanent disability . . . Lab §4452.5
Average monthly Covered California premiums
App-based drivers and services . . . B&P §7463
Average weekly earnings
App-based drivers and services, loss and liability protection . . . B&P §7455
Bank
California insurance guarantee association (CIGA), workers' compensation bond fund . . . Ins §1063.71
Basic value
Official medical fee schedule, physician services . . . 8 CCR §9789.10
Beneficiary . . . Lab §4609
Benefit notices . . . 8 CCR §9811
Bias
Medical treatment utilization schedule, medical evidence evaluation . . . 8 CCR §9792.25
Billing agents
Billing and payment rules, medical treatment . . . 8 CCR §9792.5.0
Biochemical substance . . . Lab §3212.85
Biologic plausibility
Medical treatment utilization schedule, medical evidence evaluation . . . 8 CCR §9792.25
Blinding
Medical treatment utilization schedule, medical evidence evaluation . . . 8 CCR §9792.25
BLS
Employer's records of occupational injury or illness . . . 8 CCR §14300.46
Boilers and tanks (See TANKS AND BOILERS)
Bonds
California insurance guarantee association (CIGA), workers' compensation bond fund . . . Ins §1063.71
Borello
Worker classification . . . Lab §2775
Braille
Public disability accommodations . . . 8 CCR §9708.1
Brand name drugs
Drugs, medical treatment utilization schedule (MTUS)
Formulary . . . 8 CCR §9792.27.1
Buildings (See BUILDING AND CONSTRUCTION INDUSTRY)
Burden of producing evidence . . . Ev §110
Burden of proof . . . Ev §115
Business . . . Ev §1270

DEFINITIONS—Cont.
Business records as evidence . . . Ev §1560
California-based teams
Cheerleaders, employment classification . . . Lab §2754
Professional athletes, workers' compensation coverage . . . Lab §3600.5
California Insurance Guarantee Association (CIGA), definitions pertinent to . . . Ins §1063.1
California State University, industrial disability leave for employees of . . . Ed §89529.02
Cal/OSHA
Employer's records of occupational injury or illness . . . 8 CCR §14300.46
Cal/OSHA form 300
Employer's records of occupational injury or illness . . . 8 CCR §14300.46
Cal/OSHA form 300A
Employer's records of occupational injury or illness . . . 8 CCR §14300.46
Care provider
Family care leave, paid . . . UI §3302
Care recipient
Family care leave, paid . . . UI §3302
Case-control study
Medical treatment utilization schedule, medical evidence evaluation . . . 8 CCR §9792.25
Case reports
Medical treatment utilization schedule, medical evidence evaluation . . . 8 CCR §9792.25
Case-series
Medical treatment utilization schedule, medical evidence evaluation . . . 8 CCR §9792.25
Central registration unit
Electronic adjudication management system (EAMS) . . . 8 CCR §10205
Certified competent conveyance mechanic
Elevators, escalators, dumbwaiters, and other conveyances, safety . . . Lab §7300.1
Certified qualified conveyance company
Elevators, escalators, dumbwaiters, and other conveyances, safety . . . Lab §7300.1
Charter party carrier of passengers (TCP)
App-based drivers and services . . . B&P §7463
Cheerleaders
Employment classification . . . Lab §2754
Chemical plants, process safety management for . . . Lab §7853
Child
Family care leave, paid . . . UI §3302
Special death benefit . . . Gov §21541
Chronic pain
Medical treatment utilization schedule . . . 8 CCR §9792.20
CIGA
California insurance guarantee association (CIGA), workers' compensation bond fund . . . Ins §1063.71
Claim file
Unreasonable delay in or refusal to make payment, administrative penalties and fines . . . 8 CCR §10112.1
Claim forms . . . 8 CCR §10136
Claims
Medical-legal expenses, comprehensive medical-legal evaluations . . . 8 CCR §9793

DEFINITIONS—Cont.
Claims—Cont.
Unreasonable delay in or refusal to make payment, administrative penalties and fines . . . 8 CCR §10112.1
Claims adjusters and medical billing entities, competence standards . . . 10 CCR §2592.01
Claims administrator . . . 8 CCR §9785
Benefit notices . . . 8 CCR §9811
Billing and payment rules, medical treatment . . . 8 CCR §9792.5.0
Claim forms . . . 8 CCR §10136
Medical-legal expenses, comprehensive medical-legal evaluations . . . 8 CCR §9793
Medical treatment utilization schedule . . . 8 CCR §9792.20
Physicians, choice . . . 8 CCR §9780
Return to work programs . . . 8 CCR §10116.9
Unreasonable delay in or refusal to make payment, administrative penalties and fines . . . 8 CCR §10112.1
Utilization review standards . . . 8 CCR §§9792.6, 9792.6.1
Workers' compensation division, document copy and electronic transaction fees . . . 8 CCR §9980
Claims administrator's office
Electronic adjudication management system (EAMS) . . . 8 CCR §10205
Client
Attorney referral service-client privilege . . . Ev §965
Discovery, attorney work product . . . CCP §2018.010
Client employers
Client employer-labor contractor responsibilities . . . Lab §2810.3
CMS
Official medical fee schedule, outpatient departments and ambulatory surgical centers . . . 8 CCR §9789.30
Official medical fee schedule, physician services . . . 8 CCR §9789.10
Cohort study
Medical treatment utilization schedule, medical evidence evaluation . . . 8 CCR §9792.25
Collateral
California insurance guarantee association (CIGA), workers' compensation bond fund . . . Ins §1063.71
Collective bargaining agreement definitions . . . 8 CCR §10200
Combination drugs
Drugs, medical treatment utilization schedule (MTUS)
Formulary . . . 8 CCR §9792.27.1
Commercial driver
Independent contractors, motor carrier employer amnesty program . . . Lab §2750.8
Common carrier . . . 45 USC §57
Company
Employer's records of occupational injury or illness . . . 8 CCR §14300.46
Compensable workers' compensation claim
Workers' compensation insurers' deposits . . . Ins §11690
Compensation
Insurance Code, defined for purposes of . . . Ins §11630

DEFINITIONS—Cont.
Compensation—Cont.
Unreasonable delay in or refusal to make payment, administrative penalties and fines . . . 8 CCR §10112.1
Workers' compensation division of Labor Code, defined for purposes of . . . Lab §3207
Compensation order
Unreasonable delay in or refusal to make payment, administrative penalties and fines . . . 8 CCR §10112.1
Compounded drug products
Fee schedule maximums . . . Lab §5307.1
Compounded drugs
Drugs, medical treatment utilization schedule (MTUS)
Formulary . . . 8 CCR §9792.27.1
Comprehensive medical-legal evaluation
Medical-legal expenses, comprehensive medical-legal evaluations . . . 8 CCR §9793
Computer-aided realtime translation (CART)
Public disability accommodations . . . 8 CCR §9708.1
Concealment of allocation
Medical treatment utilization schedule, medical evidence evaluation . . . 8 CCR §9792.25
Concurrent medical treatment authorization
Unreasonable delay in or refusal to make payment, administrative penalties and fines . . . 8 CCR §10112.1
Concurrent review
Utilization review standards . . . 8 CCR §§9792.6, 9792.6.1
Confidential communication between client and lawyer referral service
Attorney referral service-client privilege . . . Ev §965
Confounding variable
Medical treatment utilization schedule, medical evidence evaluation . . . 8 CCR §9792.25
Construction code (See BUILDING AND CONSTRUCTION INDUSTRY)
Construction elevators . . . Lab §7200
Construction of Labor Code, definitions governing . . . Lab §3350
Contested claims
Medical-legal expenses, comprehensive medical-legal evaluations . . . 8 CCR §9793
Continuing medical treatment
Primary treating physician, reporting duties . . . 8 CCR §9785
Contracting agent . . . Lab §4609
Contractors with U.Sworking outside U.S . . . 42 USC §§1703, 1711
Contracts of employment . . . Lab §2750
Conversion factor
Official medical fee schedule, physician services . . . 8 CCR §9789.10
Conveyance
Elevators, escalators, dumbwaiters, and other conveyances, safety . . . Lab §7300.1
Conveyance inspector
Elevators, escalators, dumbwaiters, and other conveyances, safety . . . Lab §7300.1
Copy and related services
Workers' compensation division, document copy and electronic transaction fees . . . 8 CCR §9980

DEFINITIONS—Cont.
Cost
Electronic adjudication management system (EAMS) . . . 8 CCR §10205
Cost to charge ratio for ASC
Official medical fee schedule, outpatient departments and ambulatory surgical centers . . . 8 CCR §9789.30
Cost to charge ratio for hospital outpatient department
Official medical fee schedule, outpatient departments and ambulatory surgical centers . . . 8 CCR §9789.30
County employees . . . Gov §31000.8
Course of treatment
Utilization review standards . . . 8 CCR §§9792.6, 9792.6.1
Court
Civil discovery act . . . CCP §2016.020
Coverage information
Rating organizations, queries on website to organization on coverage information for employers . . . 10 CCR §2593.1
Covered active duty
Family care leave, paid . . . UI §3302.1
Covered California
App-based drivers and services . . . B&P §7463
Covered claims
California insurance guarantee association (CIGA), workers' compensation bond fund . . . Ins §1063.71
Covered employees
Employer's records of occupational injury or illness . . . 8 CCR §14300.46
Medical provider networks . . . 8 CCR §9767.1
Covered worker
COVID-19 supplemental paid sick leave for covered workers . . . Lab §248.1
COVID-19
Compensation for injury or death . . . Lab §3212.86
Firefighters, peace officers, health workers, etc . . . Lab §3212.87
Outbreak at place of employment, positive test . . . Lab §3212.88
Exposure, employer notice requirements . . . Lab §6409.6
COVID-19 food sector supplemental paid sick leave . . . Lab §248
COVID-19 supplemental paid sick leave
Covered workers . . . Lab §248.1
CPT
Official medical fee schedule, physician services . . . 8 CCR §9789.10
Crime victims (See CRIME VICTIMS)
Cross-sectional study
Medical treatment utilization schedule, medical evidence evaluation . . . 8 CCR §9792.25
Cure
Labor code private attorneys general . . . Lab §2699
Custodian of records
Workers' compensation division, document copy and electronic transaction fees . . . 8 CCR §9980
Customers
App-based drivers and services . . . B&P §7463
Damages . . . Lab §3209

DEFINITIONS—Cont.
Dangerous devices
Fee schedule maximums . . . Lab §5307.1
Dangerous drugs
Fee schedule maximums . . . Lab §5307.1
Data aggregators
Worker classification, exceptions involving data aggregators . . . Lab §2782
Date of knowledge of injury
Benefit notices . . . 8 CCR §9811
Date of knowledge of injury and disability
Benefit notices . . . 8 CCR §9811
Death benefits for assassinated public officials . . . Lab §4720
Declaration of readiness to proceed
Electronic adjudication management system (EAMS) . . . 8 CCR §10205
Declaration of readiness to proceed to expedited hearing
Electronic adjudication management system (EAMS) . . . 8 CCR §10205
Defendants
Electronic adjudication management system (EAMS) . . . 8 CCR §10205
Defendants in claims procedures . . . Lab §5503
Delay
Utilization review standards . . . 8 CCR §9792.6.1
Delinquency proceeding
Workers' compensation insurers' deposits . . . Ins §11690
Delivery network company (DNC)
App-based drivers and services . . . B&P §7463
Delivery network company courier (DNC courier)
App-based drivers and services . . . B&P §7463
Delivery service(s)
App-based drivers and services . . . B&P §7463
Denial
Utilization review standards . . . 8 CCR §9792.6.1
Dependents
Benefit notices . . . 8 CCR §9811
Determination and order
Unreasonable delay in or refusal to make payment, administrative penalties and fines . . . 8 CCR §10112.1
Diagnostic tests
Medical treatment utilization schedule, medical evidence evaluation . . . 8 CCR §9792.25
Direct financial interest
Drugs, medical treatment utilization schedule (MTUS)
Pharmacy and therapeutics committee, conflicts of interest . . . 8 CCR §9792.27.20
Disability . . . UI §2626
Public disability accommodations . . . 8 CCR §9708.1
Disability accommodation
Public disability accommodations . . . 8 CCR §9708.1
Disability accommodation request
Public disability accommodations . . . 8 CCR §9708.1
Disability benefit period
Family care leave, paid . . . UI §3302.1
Disability benefits (See DISABILITY BENEFITS)
Disability coordinator
Public disability accommodations . . . 8 CCR §9708.1
Disabled . . . UI §2626

DEFINITIONS—Cont.
Disease incidence
Medical treatment utilization schedule, medical evidence evaluation . . . 8 CCR §9792.25
Disease prevalence
Medical treatment utilization schedule, medical evidence evaluation . . . 8 CCR §9792.25
Dispense
Drugs, medical treatment utilization schedule (MTUS)
Formulary . . . 8 CCR §9792.27.1
Dispensed
Fee schedule maximums . . . Lab §5307.1
Disputed medical fact
Medical-legal expenses, comprehensive medical-legal evaluations . . . 8 CCR §9793
Disputed medical treatment
Independent medical review, review of utilization review decision . . . Lab §4610.5
Utilization review standards . . . 8 CCR §9792.6.1
Dispute liability
Utilization review standards . . . 8 CCR §§9792.6, 9792.6.1
District office
Electronic adjudication management system (EAMS) . . . 8 CCR §10205
Division
Elevators, escalators, dumbwaiters, and other conveyances, safety . . . Lab §7300.1
Medical provider networks . . . 8 CCR §9767.1
Public disability accommodations . . . 8 CCR §9708.1
Document
Civil discovery act . . . CCP §2016.020
Electronic adjudication management system (EAMS) . . . 8 CCR §10205
Document cover sheet
Electronic adjudication management system (EAMS) . . . 8 CCR §10205
Documented paid costs
Fee schedule maximums . . . Lab §5307.1
Document separator sheet
Electronic adjudication management system (EAMS) . . . 8 CCR §10205
Domestic partner
Family care leave, paid . . . UI §3302
Dormant elevator, dumbwaiter, or escalator
Elevators, escalators, dumbwaiters, and other conveyances, safety . . . Lab §7300.1
Duration
Benefit notices . . . 8 CCR §9811
Duty day
Professional athletes, workers' compensation coverage . . . Lab §3600.5
Dynamex
Worker classification . . . Lab §2775
EAMS
Electronic adjudication management system (EAMS) . . . 8 CCR §10205
Earnings period
App-based drivers and services . . . B&P §7453
Economic opportunity programs (See ECONOMIC OPPORTUNITY PROGRAMS)
Economic profiling
Medical provider networks . . . 8 CCR §9767.1

DEFINITIONS—Cont.
Electronic
Civil discovery act . . . CCP §2016.020
Electronic adjudication management system (EAMS) . . . 8 CCR §10205
Electronically stored information
Civil discovery act . . . CCP §2016.020
Electronic filing
Electronic adjudication management system (EAMS) . . . 8 CCR §10205
Electronic signatures
Electronic adjudication management system (EAMS) . . . 8 CCR §10205
Elevators . . . Lab §7300.1
Eligible motor carriers
Independent contractors, motor carrier employer amnesty program . . . Lab §2750.8
Emergency and disaster services workers (See EMERGENCY AND DISASTER SERVICES WORKERS)
Emergency health care services
Medical provider networks . . . 8 CCR §9767.1
Physicians, choice . . . 8 CCR §9780
Utilization review standards . . . 8 CCR §§9792.6, 9792.6.1
Employee in the construction industry
Private-attorneys general act, labor code, applicability . . . Lab §2699.6
Employees
Generally . . . Lab §3351
Benefit notices . . . 8 CCR §9811
Claim forms . . . 8 CCR §10136
County employees . . . Gov §31000.8
Occupational safety and health, retaliation or discrimination against employee for exercising rights . . . Lab §6310
Safe workplace . . . Lab §§6304.1, 6304.2
Sick days, paid . . . Lab §245.5
Subrogation, employer and employee defined for purposes of . . . Lab §3850
Unreasonable delay in or refusal to make payment, administrative penalties and fines . . . 8 CCR §10112.1
Employee's or claimant's remedies
Benefit notices . . . 8 CCR §9811
Employer-provided or employer-required educational program or training
Employers, indemnification of employees by . . . Lab §2802.1
Employers
Generally . . . Lab §3300
Benefit notices . . . 8 CCR §9811
Direct patient care providers, PPE stockpiles . . . Lab §6403.3
Independent medical review, review of utilization review decision . . . Lab §4610.5
Medical provider networks . . . 8 CCR §9767.1, Lab §4616.5
Occupational safety and health, retaliation or discrimination against employee for exercising rights . . . Lab §6310
Prima facie illegally uninsured employer, parent, or substantial shareholder . . . 8 CCR §15710
Rating organizations, queries on website to organization on coverage information for employers . . . 10 CCR §2593.1

DEFINITIONS—Cont.
Employers—Cont.
Return to work programs . . . 8 CCR §10116.9
Safe workplace . . . Lab §6304
Sick days, paid . . . Lab §245.5
Subrogation, employer and employee defined for purposes of . . . Lab §3850
Substantial shareholders and parents . . . 8 CCR §15710, Lab §3717
Uninsured employers . . . 8 CCR §15560
Unreasonable delay in or refusal to make payment, administrative penalties and fines . . . 8 CCR §10112.1
Employment
Safe workplace . . . Lab §6303
Employment contracts . . . Lab §2750
Employment discrimination . . . Gov §12926
Enclosed space
Smoking in workplaces, OSHA standards . . . Lab §6404.5
Engaged miles
App-based drivers and services . . . B&P §7463
Engaged time
App-based drivers and services . . . B&P §7463
Entity that provides ancillary services
Medical provider networks . . . Lab §4616.5
Entity that provides physician network services
Medical provider networks . . . 8 CCR §9767.1, Lab §4616.5
Equivalent form
Employer's records of occupational injury or illness . . . 8 CCR §14300.46
Escalator
Elevators, escalators, dumbwaiters, and other conveyances, safety . . . Lab §7300.1
Essential functions
Return to work programs . . . 8 CCR §10116.9
Establishment
Employer's records of occupational injury or illness . . . 8 CCR §14300.46
Ethical requirements for judges (WCJs) . . . 8 CCR §9720.2
Evidence . . . Ev §140
Evidence-based medicine (EBM)
Medical treatment utilization schedule . . . 8 CCR §9792.20
Evidence, business records as . . . Ev §1560
Executive medical director
Drugs, medical treatment utilization schedule (MTUS)
Formulary . . . 8 CCR §9792.27.1
Exempt drugs
Drugs, medical treatment utilization schedule (MTUS)
Formulary . . . 8 CCR §9792.27.1
Existing installation
Elevators, escalators, dumbwaiters, and other conveyances, safety . . . Lab §7300.1
Expedited review
Drugs, medical treatment utilization schedule (MTUS)
Formulary . . . 8 CCR §9792.27.1
Utilization review standards . . . 8 CCR §§9792.6, 9792.6.1

DEFINITIONS—Cont.
Expert . . . Ev §240
Expert opinion
Medical treatment utilization schedule, medical evidence evaluation . . . 8 CCR §9792.25
Expert reviewer
Utilization review standards . . . 8 CCR §§9792.6, 9792.6.1
Explanation of review
Medical-legal expenses, comprehensive medical-legal evaluations . . . 8 CCR §9793
Extrahazardous mines and tunnels . . . Lab §7977
Facility
Physicians, choice . . . 8 CCR §9780
Facility only services
Official medical fee schedule, outpatient departments and ambulatory surgical centers . . . 8 CCR §9789.30
Family care leave
Family care leave, paid . . . UI §3302
Family member
Family care leave, paid . . . UI §3302
Sick days, paid . . . Lab §245.5
Fatality
Employer's records of occupational injury or illness . . . 8 CCR §14300.46
Fax
Electronic adjudication management system (EAMS) . . . 8 CCR §10205
FDA
Drugs, medical treatment utilization schedule (MTUS)
Formulary . . . 8 CCR §9792.27.1
FDA-approved drugs
Drugs, medical treatment utilization schedule (MTUS)
Formulary . . . 8 CCR §9792.27.1
FEIN
Rating organizations, queries on website to organization on coverage information for employers . . . 10 CCR §2593.1
File
Electronic adjudication management system (EAMS) . . . 8 CCR §10205
Financial interest in another entity
Conflicts of interest among entities providing services . . . Lab §139.32
Firefighter . . . Lab §3211.5
Firefighting member . . . Lab §3211.5
First aid
Employer's records of occupational injury or illness . . . 8 CCR §14300.46
Physicians, choice . . . 8 CCR §9780
Follow-up medical-legal evaluation
Medical-legal expenses, comprehensive medical-legal evaluations . . . 8 CCR §9793
Food sector worker
COVID-19 food sector supplemental paid sick leave . . . Lab §248
For a commercial purpose
Invasion of privacy . . . CC §1708.8
Fraud
Workers' Compensation Insurance Fraud Reporting Act . . . Ins §1877.1

DEFINITIONS—Cont.
Full maintenance service contract
Elevators, escalators, dumbwaiters, and other conveyances, safety . . . Lab §7300.1
Functional improvement
Medical treatment utilization schedule . . . 8 CCR §9792.20
Furnished
Return to work programs . . . 8 CCR §10116.9
Future medical treatment
Primary treating physician, reporting duties . . . 8 CCR §9785
General business practice
Unreasonable delay in or refusal to make payment, administrative penalties and fines . . . 8 CCR §10112.1
General recording criteria
Employer's records of occupational injury or illness . . . 8 CCR §14300.46
Generic drugs
Drugs, medical treatment utilization schedule (MTUS)
Formulary . . . 8 CCR §9792.27.1
Geocoding
Medical provider networks . . . 8 CCR §9767.1
Glossary of . . . Table 18
Good cause
Qualified medical evaluators (QMES), panel selection in different specialty . . . 8 CCR §31.7
Grandchild
Family care leave, paid . . . UI §3302
Grandparent
Family care leave, paid . . . UI §3302
Group disability insurance policy
Medical provider networks . . . 8 CCR §9767.1
Group insurance coverage . . . Ins §42
Group self-insurance . . . 8 CCR §15201
Guidance documents
COVID-19, infection prevention best practices communications . . . Lab §6725
Hazard evaluation system and information service
Occupational safety and health, toxic materials information repository . . . Lab §147.2
HCPCS
Official medical fee schedule, outpatient departments and ambulatory surgical centers . . . 8 CCR §9789.30
HCPCS level 1 codes
Official medical fee schedule, outpatient departments and ambulatory surgical centers . . . 8 CCR §9789.30
Health care employers
Personal protective equipment (PPE) inventory, duties of employer . . . Lab §6403.1
Health care facility
Billing and payment rules, medical treatment . . . 8 CCR §9792.5.0
Health care organizations (HCOs) . . . 8 CCR §§9770, 9771.60
Medical provider networks . . . 8 CCR §9767.1
Health care providers
Billing and payment rules, medical treatment . . . 8 CCR §9792.5.0

DEFINITIONS—Cont.
Health care providers—Cont.
Sick days, paid . . . Lab §245.5
Utilization review standards . . . 8 CCR §§9792.6, 9792.6.1
Health care service plan
Medical provider networks . . . 8 CCR §9767.1
Health care shortage
Medical provider networks . . . 8 CCR §9767.1
Health care workers . . . Lab §5406.6
Patient protection and health care worker back and musculoskeletal injury prevention . . . Lab §6403.5
Personal protective equipment (PPE) inventory, duties of employer . . . Lab §6403.1
Health facility
Official medical fee schedule, outpatient departments and ambulatory surgical centers . . . 8 CCR §9789.30
Hearings
Electronic adjudication management system (EAMS) . . . 8 CCR §10205
HESIS
Occupational safety and health, toxic materials information repository . . . Lab §147.2
Hiring entity
COVID-19 food sector supplemental paid sick leave . . . Lab §248
COVID-19 supplemental paid sick leave for covered workers . . . Lab §248.1
Holder of privilege
Attorney referral service-client privilege . . . Ev §965
Psychotherapist-patient privilege . . . Ev §1013
Hospital outpatient department
Official medical fee schedule, outpatient departments and ambulatory surgical centers . . . 8 CCR §9789.30
Hospital outpatient department services
Official medical fee schedule, outpatient departments and ambulatory surgical centers . . . 8 CCR §9789.30
Hospital outpatient prospective payment system (HOPPS)
Official medical fee schedule, outpatient departments and ambulatory surgical centers . . . 8 CCR §9789.30
Illness or injury
Employer's records of occupational injury or illness . . . 8 CCR §14300.46
Immediate family members
Drugs, medical treatment utilization schedule (MTUS)
Pharmacy and therapeutics committee, conflicts of interest . . . 8 CCR §9792.27.20
Immediately
Utilization review standards . . . 8 CCR §§9792.6, 9792.6.1
Inception cohort study
Medical treatment utilization schedule, medical evidence evaluation . . . 8 CCR §9792.25
Indemnity
Unreasonable delay in or refusal to make payment, administrative penalties and fines . . . 8 CCR §10112.1
Independent contractors . . . Lab §3353

DEFINITIONS—Cont.
Independent medical examiners (IMEs) . . . Lab §28
Independent medical reviewer . . . 8 CCR §9768.1
Index test
Medical treatment utilization schedule, medical evidence evaluation . . . 8 CCR §9792.25
Indirect financial interest
Drugs, medical treatment utilization schedule (MTUS)
Pharmacy and therapeutics committee, conflicts of interest . . . 8 CCR §9792.27.20
Individual
Worker classification, exception for contract for professional services . . . Lab §2778
Individually identifiable information . . . Lab §138.7
Industrial accident or illness . . . Gov §20046
Industrial relations department
Director . . . 8 CCR §15552, Lab §20
Head of department . . . Lab §53
Infectious period
COVID-19 exposure, employer notice requirements . . . Lab §6409.6
Information systems, definitions pertinent to Workers' Compensation Division . . . 8 CCR §9701
Initial liens
Electronic adjudication management system (EAMS) . . . 8 CCR §10205
Injury (See INJURY)
In-person examinations
Independent medical review . . . 8 CCR §9768.1
Insolvent insurer
California insurance guarantee association (CIGA), workers' compensation bond fund . . . Ins §1063.71
Insolvent self-insurers
Self-insurers' security fund, reimbursement . . . Lab §3744
Insurance (See INSURANCE)
Insurance premium rating . . . Ins §11730
Insurer
Claims adjusters standards, workers' compensation claims adjusters . . . Ins §11761
Insurance Code, as used by . . . Ins §11631
Labor Code, as used by . . . Lab §3211
Medical provider networks . . . 8 CCR §9767.1
Rating organizations, queries on website to organization on coverage information for employers . . . 10 CCR §2593.1
Return to work programs . . . 8 CCR §10116.9
Unreasonable delay in or refusal to make payment, administrative penalties and fines . . . 8 CCR §10112.1
Intention to treat
Medical treatment utilization schedule, medical evidence evaluation . . . 8 CCR §9792.25
Interested party
Conflicts of interest among entities providing services . . . Lab §139.32
Interpreters . . . 8 CCR §9795.1
Investigations
Unreasonable delay in or refusal to make payment, administrative penalties and fines . . . 8 CCR §10112.1
IWC wage orders
COVID-19 food sector supplemental paid sick leave . . . Lab §248

DEFINITIONS—Cont.
Job transfer
Employer's records of occupational injury or illness . . . 8 CCR §14300.46
Joint powers authority
Unreasonable delay in or refusal to make payment, administrative penalties and fines . . . 8 CCR §10112.1
Judges (WCJs)
Labor Code, definition of WCJs under . . . Lab §27
Pertinent terms . . . 8 CCR §§9712, 9720.2
Judicial or quasi-judicial officers
Testimony of judicial or quasi-judicial officers . . . 8 CCR §10360
Knowingly
Unreasonable delay in or refusal to make payment, administrative penalties and fines . . . 8 CCR §10112.1
Labor
Client employer-labor contractor responsibilities . . . Lab §2810.3
Labor commissioner . . . Lab §21
Labor contractors
Client employer-labor contractor responsibilities . . . Lab §2810.3
Labor-related share
Official medical fee schedule, outpatient departments and ambulatory surgical centers . . . 8 CCR §9789.30
Labor Standards Enforcement Division (See LABOR STANDARDS ENFORCEMENT DIVISION)
Lien claimants
Electronic adjudication management system (EAMS) . . . 8 CCR §10205
Lien conferences
Electronic adjudication management system (EAMS) . . . 8 CCR §10205
Lift teams
Patient protection and health care worker back and musculoskeletal injury prevention . . . Lab §6403.5
Local government
App-based drivers and services . . . B&P §7463
Longshore and Harbor Workers' Compensation Act definitions . . . 33 USC §902
Low risk of bias
Medical treatment utilization schedule, medical evidence evaluation . . . 8 CCR §9792.25
Mandatory settlement conference
Electronic adjudication management system (EAMS) . . . 8 CCR §10205
Market basket inflation factor
Official medical fee schedule, outpatient departments and ambulatory surgical centers . . . 8 CCR §9789.30
Material alteration
Elevators, escalators, dumbwaiters, and other conveyances, safety . . . Lab §7300.1
Material familial affiliation
Independent medical review . . . 8 CCR §9768.1, Lab §139.5
Material financial affiliation
Independent medical review . . . 8 CCR §9768.1, Lab §139.5

DEFINITIONS—Cont.
Material modification
Utilization review standards . . . 8 CCR §§9792.6, 9792.6.1
Material professional affiliation
Independent medical review . . . 8 CCR §9768.1, Lab §139.5
"May" defined as permissive . . . Lab §15
Medical billing entity
Claims adjusters standards, workers' compensation claims adjusters . . . Ins §11761
Medical determination
Primary treating physician, reporting duties . . . 8 CCR §9785
Medical director . . . Lab §29
Utilization review standards . . . 8 CCR §§9792.6, 9792.6.1
Medical emergency
Independent medical review . . . 8 CCR §9768.1
Medical issue
Benefit notices . . . 8 CCR §9811
Medical-legal expenses
Comprehensive medical-legal evaluations . . . 8 CCR §9793
Pertinent terms . . . Lab §4620
Medical-legal testimony
Medical-legal expenses, comprehensive medical-legal evaluations . . . 8 CCR §9793
Medically necessary
Independent medical review, review of utilization review decision . . . Lab §4610.5
Medical necessity
Independent medical review, review of utilization review decision . . . Lab §4610.5
Medical provider network contact (MPN contact)
Independent medical review . . . 8 CCR §9768.1
Medical provider network geographic service area
Medical provider networks . . . 8 CCR §9767.1
Medical provider network identification numbers
Medical provider networks . . . 8 CCR §9767.1
Medical provider network medical access assistants
Medical provider networks . . . 8 CCR §9767.1
Medical provider network plan . . . 8 CCR §9767.1
Medical provider networks . . . 8 CCR §9767.1
Medical record and information disclosure . . . CC §56.05
Medical research
Medical-legal expenses, comprehensive medical-legal evaluations . . . 8 CCR §9793
Medical services
Utilization review standards . . . 8 CCR §§9792.6, 9792.6.1
Medical treatment (See MEDICAL TREATMENT)
Medical treatment guidelines
Medical treatment utilization schedule . . . 8 CCR §9792.20
Medical treatment utilization schedule
Utilization review standards . . . 8 CCR §§9792.6, 9792.6.1
Medicare rate
Official medical fee schedule, physician services . . . 8 CCR §9789.10
Member insurer
California insurance guarantee association (CIGA), workers' compensation bond fund . . . Ins §1063.71

DEFINITIONS—Cont.
Member of a fire department . . . Lab §§3211.5, 3212.85
Meta-analysis
Medical treatment utilization schedule, medical evidence evaluation . . . 8 CCR §9792.25
Military member
Family care leave, paid . . . UI §3302
Military service
Bases outside U.S., military service at . . . 42 USC §1651
Minimum wage
Worker classification, exceptions involving data aggregators . . . Lab §2782
Mining and tunneling . . . Lab §§7951, 7977
Modification
Utilization review standards . . . 8 CCR §9792.6.1
Modified work
Disability . . . Lab §4658.1
Return to work programs . . . 8 CCR §10116.9
Modifying units
Official medical fee schedule, physician services . . . 8 CCR §9789.10
Motor carriers
Independent contractors, motor carrier employer amnesty program . . . Lab §2750.8
Moving sidewalk
Elevators, escalators, dumbwaiters, and other conveyances, safety . . . Lab §7300.1
Moving walk
Elevators, escalators, dumbwaiters, and other conveyances, safety . . . Lab §7300.1
MPN applicant
Medical provider networks . . . 8 CCR §9767.1
MPN contact
Independent medical review . . . 8 CCR §9768.1
Medical provider networks . . . 8 CCR §9767.1
MTUS drug formulary
Drugs, medical treatment utilization schedule (MTUS) . . . 8 CCR §9792.27.1
MTUS drug list
Drugs, medical treatment utilization schedule (MTUS) . . . 8 CCR §9792.27.1
Nationally recognized
Medical treatment utilization schedule . . . 8 CCR §9792.20
Nature of physical injury or disfigurement
Permanent disability percentage . . . Lab §§4660, 4660.1
Net earnings
App-based drivers and services . . . B&P §7453
Net earnings floor
App-based drivers and services . . . B&P §7453
Network companies
App-based drivers and services . . . B&P §7463
New case
Employer's records of occupational injury or illness . . . 8 CCR §14300.46
NIOSH
Occupational safety and health, standards for handling . . . Lab §144.8
Non-exempt drug
Drugs, medical treatment utilization schedule (MTUS)
Formulary . . . 8 CCR §9792.27.1

DEFINITIONS—Cont.
Nonprescription drugs
Drugs, medical treatment utilization schedule (MTUS)
Formulary . . . 8 CCR §9792.27.1
Nontransferable vouchers
Return to work programs . . . 8 CCR §10116.9
Notice of assessment
Unreasonable delay in or refusal to make payment, administrative penalties and fines . . . 8 CCR §10112.1
Notice of potential exposure
COVID-19 exposure, employer notice requirements . . . Lab §6409.6
Notices
Return to work programs . . . 8 CCR §10116.9
Occupational medicine
Medical provider networks . . . 8 CCR §9767.1
Occupational safety and health (See SAFE WORKPLACE)
Occurrence
Occupational safety and health, time to issue citation or notice . . . Lab §6317
OCR forms
Electronic adjudication management system (EAMS) . . . 8 CCR §10205
ODG
Medical treatment utilization schedule . . . 8 CCR §9792.20
Offer of modified or alternative work
Return to work programs . . . 8 CCR §10116.9
Official medical fee schedule
Inpatient hospital fee schedule . . . 8 CCR §9789.21
Physician services . . . 8 CCR §9789.10
Official medical fee schedule 2003
Physician services . . . 8 CCR §9789.10
Off-label use
Drugs, medical treatment utilization schedule (MTUS)
Formulary . . . 8 CCR §9792.27.1
Offshore lands . . . 43 USC §1331
OFMS
Official medical fee schedule, physician services . . . 8 CCR §9789.10
OFMS 2003
Official medical fee schedule, physician services . . . 8 CCR §9789.10
OMFS RBRVS
Official medical fee schedule, outpatient departments and ambulatory surgical centers . . . 8 CCR §9789.30
Online
App-based drivers and services, loss and liability protection . . . B&P §7455
Optical character recognition form
Electronic adjudication management system (EAMS) . . . 8 CCR §10205
OSHA
Employer's records of occupational injury or illness . . . 8 CCR §14300.46
OTC monograph
Drugs, medical treatment utilization schedule (MTUS)
Formulary . . . 8 CCR §9792.27.1

DEFINITIONS—Cont.
Other benefits
Disability benefits eligibility . . . UI §2629
Other nonproductive time
Piece-rate basis of compensation . . . Lab §226.2
Other services
Official medical fee schedule, outpatient departments and ambulatory surgical centers . . . 8 CCR §9789.30
Outbreak
Compensation for injury or death
Outbreak at place of employment, positive test . . . Lab §3212.88
Outer continental shelf lands . . . 43 USC §1331
Outlier threshold
Official medical fee schedule, outpatient departments and ambulatory surgical centers . . . 8 CCR §9789.30
Owner-operated business
Smoking in workplaces, OSHA standards . . . Lab §6404.5
Paid sick days
Sick days, paid . . . Lab §245.5
Panel
Independent medical review . . . 8 CCR §9768.1
Parent
Family care leave, paid . . . UI §3302
Parental leave
School district employees . . . Ed §44977.5
Parent-in-law
Family care leave, paid . . . UI §3302
Participating payees
App-based drivers and services, income reporting system . . . B&P §7464.5
Parties
Electronic adjudication management system (EAMS) . . . 8 CCR §10205
Return to work programs . . . 8 CCR §10116.9
Passenger tramway . . . Lab §7340
Passenger vehicles
App-based drivers and services . . . B&P §7463
Patient
Psychotherapist-patient privilege . . . Ev §1011
Payor . . . Lab §4609
Payor summary . . . Lab §4609
Peace officer . . . Gov §50920
Peer reviewed
Medical treatment utilization schedule . . . 8 CCR §9792.20
Penalty assessment orders
Generally . . . 8 CCR §15557
Special judgments . . . 8 CCR §15558
Penalty award
Unreasonable delay in or refusal to make payment, administrative penalties and fines . . . 8 CCR §10112.1
Percentage reduction calculation
Official medical fee schedule, physician services . . . 8 CCR §9789.10
Perioperative fill
Drugs, medical treatment utilization schedule (MTUS)
Formulary . . . 8 CCR §9792.27.1

DEFINITIONS—Cont.
Permanent and stationary
Return to work programs . . . 8 CCR §10116.9
Permanent and stationary status
Benefit notices . . . 8 CCR §9811
Primary treating physician, reporting duties . . . 8 CCR §9785
Permanent partial disability . . . Lab §4452.5
Permanent partial disability award
Return to work programs . . . 8 CCR §10116.9
Permanent total disability . . . Lab §4452.5
Permit . . . Lab §7340
Elevators, escalators, dumbwaiters, and other conveyances, safety . . . Lab §7300.1
Person . . . Lab §§18, 3210
Labor code private attorneys general . . . Lab §2699
Person acting on behalf of employer
Occupational safety and health, retaliation or discrimination against employee for exercising rights . . . Lab §6310
Personal physician
Physicians, choice . . . 8 CCR §9780
Personal protective equipment
Direct patient care providers, PPE stockpiles . . . Lab §6403.3
Personal representative
Employer's records of occupational injury or illness . . . 8 CCR §14300.46
Petition appealing determination and order
Unreasonable delay in or refusal to make payment, administrative penalties and fines . . . 8 CCR §10112.1
Petitions
Electronic adjudication management system (EAMS) . . . 8 CCR §10205
Pharmaceutical company
Confidentiality of medical information . . . CC §56.05
Pharmaceutical entities
Drugs, medical treatment utilization schedule (MTUS)
Pharmacy and therapeutics committee, conflicts of interest . . . 8 CCR §9792.27.20
Pharmacy goods
Fee schedule maximums . . . Lab §5307.1
Financial interest, referral to person with whom physician has . . . Lab §139.3
Physical invasion of privacy . . . CC §1708.8
Physician or other licensed health care professional
Employer's records of occupational injury or illness . . . 8 CCR §14300.46
Physicians
Generally . . . Lab §3209.3
Billing and payment rules, medical treatment . . . 8 CCR §9792.5.0
Choice of . . . 8 CCR §9780
Drugs, medical treatment utilization schedule (MTUS)
Formulary . . . 8 CCR §9792.27.1
Primary treating physician . . . 8 CCR §9785
Secondary physician . . . 8 CCR §9785
Physician service
Official medical fee schedule, physician services . . . 8 CCR §9789.10

DEFINITIONS—Cont.
Place of employment
COVID-19, compensation for injury or death . . . Lab §3212.86
Smoking in workplaces, OSHA standards . . . Lab §6404.5
Place of employment for safe workplace purposes . . . Lab §6303
Police (See POLICE)
Policy
Rating organizations, queries on website to organization on coverage information for employers . . . 10 CCR §2593.1
Policy information
Rating organizations, queries on website to organization on coverage information for employers . . . 10 CCR §2593.1
Port
Independent contractors, motor carrier employer amnesty program . . . Lab §2750.8
Post-marketing surveillance
Medical treatment utilization schedule, medical evidence evaluation . . . 8 CCR §9792.25
PPE
Personal protective equipment (PPE) inventory, duties of employer . . . Lab §6403.1
Pre-existing condition
Employer's records of occupational injury or illness . . . 8 CCR §14300.46
Premiums
Rating insurance premiums . . . Ins §11730
Prescription drugs
Drugs, medical treatment utilization schedule (MTUS)
Formulary . . . 8 CCR §9792.27.1
Price adjustment
Official medical fee schedule, outpatient departments and ambulatory surgical centers . . . 8 CCR §9789.30
Prima facie illegally uninsured employer, parent, or substantial shareholder . . . 8 CCR §15710
Primary care physician
Physicians, choice . . . 8 CCR §9780
Primary treating physician
Medical-legal expenses, comprehensive medical-legal evaluations . . . 8 CCR §9793
Medical provider networks . . . 8 CCR §9767.1
Priority conference
Electronic adjudication management system (EAMS) . . . 8 CCR §10205
Privacy concern case
Employer's records of occupational injury or illness . . . 8 CCR §14300.46
Private, personal, and familial activities
Invasion of privacy . . . CC §1708.8
Private smokers' lounge
Smoking in workplaces, OSHA standards . . . Lab §6404.5
Privileged information and communications
Psychotherapist-patient privilege . . . Ev §§1010 to 1013
Probation
Medical provider networks . . . 8 CCR §9767.1

DEFINITIONS—Cont.
Process safety management for refineries and chemical plants . . . Lab §7853
Product delivery unit
Electronic adjudication management system (EAMS) . . . 8 CCR §10205
Professional athletes
Workers' compensation, coverage . . . Lab §3600.5
Professional services
Worker classification, exception for contract for professional services . . . Lab §2778
Professional sports teams
Cheerleaders, employment classification . . . Lab §2754
Prognosis
Medical treatment utilization schedule, medical evidence evaluation . . . 8 CCR §9792.25
Program
Independent contractors, motor carrier employer amnesty program . . . Lab §2750.8
Proof of service
Unreasonable delay in or refusal to make payment, administrative penalties and fines . . . 8 CCR §10112.1
Property and casualty insurer
Actuarial opinion statements . . . Ins §923.6
Prospective medical treatment authorization
Unreasonable delay in or refusal to make payment, administrative penalties and fines . . . 8 CCR §10112.1
Prospective review
Drugs, medical treatment utilization schedule (MTUS)
Formulary . . . 8 CCR §9792.27.1
Utilization review standards . . . 8 CCR §§9792.6, 9792.6.1
Provider . . . Lab §4609
Medical provider networks . . . 8 CCR §9767.1
Psychologists . . . Lab §3209.3
Billing and payment rules, medical treatment . . . 8 CCR §9792.5.0
Psychotherapist
Confidentiality of medical information . . . CC §56.104
Evidence code . . . Ev §1010
Psychotherapist-patient privilege . . . Ev §1010
PT committee
Drugs, medical treatment utilization schedule (MTUS)
Formulary . . . 8 CCR §9792.27.1
Public Employees' Retirement System
Industrial death or disability . . . Gov §20046
Public officials, assassinated, death benefits for . . . Lab §4720
Qualified medical evaluators (QMEs) . . . 8 CCR §1, Lab §28
Time guidelines . . . 8 CCR §49
Qualifying exigency
Family care leave, paid . . . UI §3302.2
Qualifying health plans
App-based drivers and services . . . B&P §7463
Qualifying individual
COVID-19 exposure, employer notice requirements . . . Lab §6409.6

DEFINITIONS—Cont.
Query
Rating organizations, queries on website to organization on coverage information for employers . . . 10 CCR §2593.1
Railroads (See RAILROADS)
Randomized trial
Medical treatment utilization schedule, medical evidence evaluation . . . 8 CCR §9792.25
Rating insurance premiums . . . Ins §11730
Rating mandatory settlement conference
Electronic adjudication management system (EAMS) . . . 8 CCR §10205
Rating organizations . . . Ins §11750.1
Reasonable costs
Business records, costs of production . . . Ev §1563
Reasonable geographic area
Physicians, choice . . . 8 CCR §9780
Receipt
Return to work programs . . . 8 CCR §10116.9
Receiver
Workers' compensation insurers' deposits . . . Ins §11690
Recommended determination and order
Unreasonable delay in or refusal to make payment, administrative penalties and fines . . . 8 CCR §10112.1
Recordable
Employer's records of occupational injury or illness . . . 8 CCR §14300.46
Recording
Trial level proceedings, recording . . . 8 CCR §10818
Recording device
Black box or recording device, search warrants . . . Pen §1524
Reference standard
Medical treatment utilization schedule, medical evidence evaluation . . . 8 CCR §9792.25
Refineries, process safety management for . . . Lab §7853
Regional area listing
Medical provider networks . . . 8 CCR §9767.1
Regular hearing
Electronic adjudication management system (EAMS) . . . 8 CCR §10205
Regular work
Disability . . . Lab §4658.1
Return to work programs . . . 8 CCR §10116.9
Relative value scale adjustment factor
Official medical fee schedule . . . Lab §5307.1
Released from care
Primary treating physician, reporting duties . . . 8 CCR §9785
Relevant medical records
Independent medical review . . . 8 CCR §9768.1
Repair
Elevators, escalators, dumbwaiters, and other conveyances, safety . . . Lab §7300.1
Reportable payment transactions
App-based drivers and services, income reporting system . . . B&P §7464.5
Reports and documents required by administrative director
Medical-legal expenses, comprehensive medical-legal evaluations . . . 8 CCR §9793

DEFINITIONS—Cont.
Representative's office
Electronic adjudication management system (EAMS) . . . 8 CCR §10205
Request for authorization
Utilization review standards . . . 8 CCR §§9792.6, 9792.6.1
Requestor
Public disability accommodations . . . 8 CCR §9708.1
Residence
Independent medical review . . . 8 CCR §9768.1
Medical provider networks . . . 8 CCR §9767.1
Restricted work
Employer's records of occupational injury or illness . . . 8 CCR §14300.46
Retail or wholesale tobacco shops
Smoking in workplaces, OSHA standards . . . Lab §6404.5
Retrospective medical treatment authorization
Unreasonable delay in or refusal to make payment, administrative penalties and fines . . . 8 CCR §10112.1
Retrospective review
Utilization review standards . . . 8 CCR §§9792.6, 9792.6.1
Return to work programs . . . 8 CCR §10116.9
Reviewer
Utilization review standards . . . 8 CCR §§9792.6, 9792.6.1
Revocation
Medical provider networks . . . 8 CCR §9767.1
Rideshare service(s)
App-based drivers and services . . . B&P §7463
Risk of bias
Medical treatment utilization schedule, medical evidence evaluation . . . 8 CCR §9792.25
Routine functions
Employer's records of occupational injury or illness . . . 8 CCR §14300.46
RVU
Official medical fee schedule, physician services . . . 8 CCR §9789.10
Safe patient handling policy
Patient protection and health care worker back and musculoskeletal injury prevention . . . Lab §6403.5
Safe workplace (See SAFE WORKPLACE)
Salary continuation
Benefit notices . . . 8 CCR §9811
Unreasonable delay in or refusal to make payment, administrative penalties and fines . . . 8 CCR §10112.1
Scaffolding . . . Lab §7150
Schedules of compensation . . . Lab §4558
Scientifically based
Medical treatment utilization schedule . . . 8 CCR §9792.20
Seasonal work
Return to work programs . . . 8 CCR §10116.9
Seasons
Professional athletes, workers' compensation coverage . . . Lab §3600.5
Second opinion
Medical provider networks . . . 8 CCR §9767.1

DEFINITIONS—Cont.
Secretary
Labor and workforce development agency . . . Lab §19.5
Section 4903(b) liens
Electronic adjudication management system (EAMS) . . . 8 CCR §10205
Section defined for purposes of Labor Code . . . Lab §10
Selective outcome reporting
Medical treatment utilization schedule, medical evidence evaluation . . . 8 CCR §9792.25
Self-insurance (See SELF-INSURANCE)
Serious bodily injury
Black box or recording device, search warrants . . . Pen §1524
Serious health condition
Family care leave, paid . . . UI §3302
Serious physical harm
Occupational safety and health . . . Lab §6432
Serve
Electronic adjudication management system (EAMS) . . . 8 CCR §10205
Unreasonable delay in or refusal to make payment, administrative penalties and fines . . . 8 CCR §10112.1
Services
Conflicts of interest among entities providing services . . . Lab §139.32
Worker classification, corporations performing contract to provide services for single-engagement event . . . Lab §2779
Set of records
Workers' compensation division, document copy and electronic transaction fees . . . 8 CCR §9980
"Shall" defined as mandatory . . . Lab §15
Sheriff . . . Lab §25
Siblings
Family care leave, paid . . . UI §3302
Signature or subscription . . . Lab §17
Significant injury or illness
Employer's records of occupational injury or illness 8 CCR §14300.46
Single-engagement event
Worker classification, corporations performing contract to provide services for single-engagement event . . . Lab §2779
Small-business third party administrator
Voluntary disability benefit plans . . . UI §3254.1
Smoking
Smoking in workplaces, OSHA standards . . . Lab §6404.5
Special bond assessment
California insurance guarantee association (CIGA), workers' compensation bond fund . . . Ins §1063.71
Special fill
Drugs, medical treatment utilization schedule (MTUS)
Formulary . . . 8 CCR §9792.27.1
Specific place of employment
Compensation for injury or death
Outbreak at place of employment, positive test . . . Lab §3212.88
Spouse
Family care leave, paid . . . UI §3302

DEFINITIONS—Cont.
Spouse—Cont.
Registered domestic partner
Inclusion in definition of spouse . . . Lab §12.2
Special death benefit . . . Gov §21541
Standards board
Elevators, escalators, dumbwaiters, and other conveyances, safety . . . Lab §7300.1
Statewide disability coordinator
Public disability accommodations . . . 8 CCR §9708.1
Status conference
Electronic adjudication management system (EAMS) . . . 8 CCR §10205
Steel framed buildings . . . Lab §7250
Stipulated orders
Unreasonable delay in or refusal to make payment, administrative penalties and fines . . . 8 CCR §10112.1
Stop orders . . . 8 CCR §15559
Strength of evidence
Medical treatment utilization schedule . . . 8 CCR §9792.20
Submerged lands . . . 43 USC §1331
Submission
Electronic adjudication management system (EAMS) . . . 8 CCR §10205
Subrogation, employer and employee defined for purposes of . . . Lab §3850
Subsequent injuries benefits trust fund definitions . . . 8 CCR §15600
Substantial financial conflict of interest
Drugs, medical treatment utilization schedule (MTUS)
Pharmacy and therapeutics committee, conflicts of interest . . . 8 CCR §9792.27.20
Substantial number of non-English-speaking applicants
Paid family day care leave . . . UI §3308
Substantial shareholders and parents . . . 8 CCR §15710, Lab §3717
Supplemental job displacement benefits . . . 8 CCR §10116.9
Return to work programs . . . 8 CCR §10116.9
Return to work supplement . . . 8 CCR §17301
Unreasonable delay in or refusal to make payment, administrative penalties and fines . . . 8 CCR §10112.1
Supplemental medical-legal evaluation
Medical-legal expenses, comprehensive medical-legal evaluations . . . 8 CCR §9793
Suspension
Medical provider networks . . . 8 CCR §9767.1
Suspension from participation
Provider suspension procedure . . . 8 CCR §9788.1
Systematic review
Medical treatment utilization schedule, medical evidence evaluation . . . 8 CCR §9792.25
Taft-Hartley health and welfare fund
Medical provider networks . . . 8 CCR §9767.1
Tanks and boilers (See TANKS AND BOILERS)
Temporarily dormant elevator, dumbwaiter, or escalator
Elevators, escalators, dumbwaiters, and other conveyances, safety . . . Lab §7300.1
Temporary disability payments
Benefit notices . . . 8 CCR §9811

Index

DEFINITIONS—Cont.
Temporary permit
Elevators, escalators, dumbwaiters, and other conveyances, safety . . . Lab §7300.1
Termination
Medical provider networks . . . 8 CCR §9767.1
Test
Compensation for injury or death
Outbreak at place of employment, positive test . . . Lab §3212.88
COVID-19, compensation for injury or death
Firefighters, peace officers, health workers, etc . . . Lab §3212.87
Testify
Testimony of judicial or quasi-judicial officers . . . 8 CCR §10360
Testing
Compensation for injury or death
Outbreak at place of employment, positive test . . . Lab §3212.88
COVID-19, compensation for injury or death
Firefighters, peace officers, health workers, etc . . . Lab §3212.87
Therapeutic equivalent
Drugs, medical treatment utilization schedule (MTUS)
Formulary . . . 8 CCR §9792.27.1
Third opinion
Medical provider networks . . . 8 CCR §9767.1
Third-party administrator
Unreasonable delay in or refusal to make payment, administrative penalties and fines . . . 8 CCR §10112.1
Third party settlement organizations
App-based drivers and services, income reporting system . . . B&P §7464.5
Time value
Official medical fee schedule, physician services . . . 8 CCR §9789.10
Tobacco product
Smoking in workplaces, OSHA standards . . . Lab §6404.5
Tort claims against United States . . . 28 USC §2671
Total gross charges
Official medical fee schedule, outpatient departments and ambulatory surgical centers . . . 8 CCR §9789.30
Total operating costs
Official medical fee schedule, outpatient departments and ambulatory surgical centers . . . 8 CCR §9789.30
Tower cranes . . . Lab §7371
Trade secret
Petroleum refinery turnaround, occupational safety and health . . . Lab §7873
Transportation network company (TNC)
App-based drivers and services . . . B&P §7463
Transportation network company driver (TNC driver)
App-based drivers and services . . . B&P §7463
Treating physician
Medical provider networks . . . 8 CCR §9767.1
Treatment benefits
Medical treatment utilization schedule, medical evidence evaluation . . . 8 CCR §9792.25

DEFINITIONS—Cont.
Treatment harms
Medical treatment utilization schedule, medical evidence evaluation . . . 8 CCR §9792.25
Trial
Electronic adjudication management system (EAMS) . . . 8 CCR §10205
Turnaround
Petroleum refineries, occupational safety and health . . . Lab §7872
Twelve-month period
Family care leave, paid . . . UI §3302
Unavailable as a witness . . . Ev §240
Unemployment compensation (See UNEMPLOYMENT COMPENSATION)
Unemployment Compensation Disability Fund (See UNEMPLOYMENT COMPENSATION DISABILITY FUND)
Uninsured employers benefits trust fund (See UNINSURED EMPLOYERS BENEFITS TRUST FUND)
Uninsured employers benefits trust fund definitions . . . 8 CCR §15600
Unlisted drugs
Drugs, medical treatment utilization schedule (MTUS)
Formulary . . . 8 CCR §9792.27.1
Usual course of business
Client employer-labor contractor responsibilities . . . Lab §2810.3
Utilization review . . . Lab §4610
Utilization review decision
Independent medical review, review of utilization review decision . . . Lab §4610.5
Utilization review standards . . . 8 CCR §9792.6.1
Utilization review files
Unreasonable delay in or refusal to make payment, administrative penalties and fines . . . 8 CCR §10112.1
Utilization review plan
Utilization review standards . . . 8 CCR §§9792.6, 9792.6.1
Utilization review process
Utilization review standards . . . 8 CCR §§9792.6, 9792.6.1
Valid claim
Family care leave, paid . . . UI §3302
Verified statement
Generally . . . 8 CCR §15561
Direction to file . . . 8 CCR §15551
Vexatious litigants . . . 8 CCR §10430
Violation of Labor Code . . . Lab §22
Vocational & return to work counselor (VRTWC)
Return to work programs . . . 8 CCR §10116.9
Volatile flammable liquids . . . Lab §7800
Voluntary plans
Voluntary disability benefit plans . . . UI §3254.1
Voucher
Return to work supplement . . . 8 CCR §17301
Wage index
Official medical fee schedule, outpatient departments and ambulatory surgical centers . . . 8 CCR §9789.30
Wages
Client employer-labor contractor responsibilities . . . Lab §2810.3

DEFINITIONS—Cont.
Warehouse
Labor law compliance, funding in contract to be sufficient for contractor to comply with labor laws . . . Lab §2810
Weekly benefit amount
Family care leave, paid . . . UI §3301
Window cleaning safety devices . . . Lab §7325
Withdrawal
Medical provider networks . . . 8 CCR §9767.1
Work environment
Employer's records of occupational injury or illness . . . 8 CCR §14300.46
Worker
Client employer-labor contractor responsibilities . . . Lab §2810.3
Workers' compensation administrative law judge
Electronic adjudication management system (EAMS) . . . 8 CCR §10205
Workers' compensation appeals board
Unreasonable delay in or refusal to make payment, administrative penalties and fines . . . 8 CCR §10112.1
Workers' Compensation Division
Administrative director . . . Lab §§110, 3206
Pertinent terms . . . Lab §110
Workers' compensation division of Labor Code
Definitions of chapter governing . . . Lab §3204
Division defined . . . Lab §3205
Workers' Compensation Insurance Fraud Reporting Act . . . Ins §1877.1
Workers' compensation multiplier
Official medical fee schedule, outpatient departments and ambulatory surgical centers . . . 8 CCR §9789.30
Workplace
Medical provider networks . . . 8 CCR §9767.1
Work restrictions
Return to work programs . . . 8 CCR §10116.9
Worksite
COVID-19 exposure, employer notice requirements . . . Lab §6409.6
Wrap-up insurance policy
Loss reporting . . . Ins §11751.82
Writing . . . Lab §8
Civil discovery act . . . CCP §2016.020
Evidence code . . . Ev §250
Written
Utilization review standards . . . 8 CCR §§9792.6, 9792.6.1
You
Employer's records of occupational injury or illness . . . 8 CCR §14300.46

DELIVERY SERVICES
App-based drivers and services . . . B&P §§7448 to 7467 (See APP-BASED DRIVERS AND SERVICES)

DEMOLITION
Occupational Safety and Health Division permit requirements . . . Lab §6500
Salvaging materials during . . . Lab §6401.5

DENTISTS
Confidentiality of records . . . CC §56.101

DENTISTS—Cont.
Malpractice
Insurance, remedial underwriting . . . Ins §676.3
Peer review underwriting of malpractice insurance . . . Ins §676.3
Suspension of providers for cause . . . Lab §139.21
Procedure for provider suspension . . . 8 CCR §§9788.1 to 9788.6

DEPARTMENT OF FINANCE (STATE)
State Compensation Insurance Fund, master agreement with . . . Lab §§6111, 6112

DEPARTMENT OF HEALTH SERVICES (STATE)
Safe workplace, role in promoting . . . Lab §6307.1

DEPARTMENT OF INDUSTRIAL RELATIONS (See INDUSTRIAL RELATIONS DEPARTMENT)

DEPARTMENT OF JUSTICE (See JUSTICE DEPARTMENT)

DEPENDENT ADULTS
Discovery
Elder abuse and dependent adult civil protection act . . . CCP §§2017.310, 2017.320

DEPENDENTS
Aliens, uninsured employers fund and subsequent injuries fund benefits for . . . 8 CCR §15740
Children, death benefits . . . Lab §4703.5
Death benefits (See DEATH BENEFITS)
Factual determination of dependency . . . Lab §3502
Incapacitated adults as . . . Lab §3501
Longshore and Harbor Workers' Compensation Act . . . 33 USC §909
Minor children
Death benefits for . . . Lab §4703.6
Jurisdictional hearings
Testimonial privileges, inapplicability . . . Ev §972
Presumed to be dependents . . . Lab §3501
Presumptions . . . Lab §3501
Qualifications for dependency . . . Lab §3503
Spouses as . . . Lab §3501

DEPOSITIONS
Answer
Audiotaping depositions, procedure for
Changing answers, time for . . . CCP §2025.530
Transcript of deposition
Changing answers, time for . . . CCP §2025.520
Appeals Board (WCAB)
Generally . . . Lab §5710
Employee, deposition requested by employer
Attorney fees, petition . . . 8 CCR §10547
Attendance
Failure of party giving notice to attend
Sanctions . . . CCP §2025.430
Subpoena not served, causing failure to attend
Sanctions . . . CCP §2025.440
Attorneys of record
Subpoenas
Issuance . . . CCP §2020.210

Index

DEPOSITIONS—Cont.
Business records, production of
Methods of discovery
Nonparty discovery . . . CCP §2020.010
Notice of deposition . . . CCP §2025.220
Subpoenas
Attendance and testimony also commanded, requirements of subpoena . . . CCP §2020.510
Business records produced for copying . . . CCP §§2020.410 to 2020.440
Clerk of court
Subpoenas
Issuance . . . CCP §2020.210
Complex cases
Time limits for witness examination
Exception for complex cases . . . CCP §2025.290
Conduct of deposition . . . CCP §§2025.310 to 2025.340
Cross-examination of deponent . . . CCP §2025.330
Examination of deponent . . . CCP §2025.330
Oath of deponent . . . CCP §2025.330
Officer conducting proceedings . . . CCP §2025.320
Recording, audio or video . . . CCP §2025.340
Stenographic taking of testimony and objections . . . CCP §2025.330
Telephonic or other remote electronic means . . . CCP §2025.310
Written questions propounded to deponent . . . CCP §2025.330
Cross-examination of deponent . . . CCP §2025.330
Deposition officers . . . CCP §2025.320
Transcript of deposition
Certification by deposition officer . . . CCP §2025.540
Duration of deposition . . . CCP §2025.290
Mesothelioma or silicosis of deponent . . . CCP §2025.295
Electronic oral depositions
Remote electronic means of taking depositions
Telephonic or other remote electronic means . . . CCP §2025.310
Employer and employee
Time limits for witness examination
Exceptions for cases arising out of employment relationship . . . CCP §2025.290
Employment records pertaining to an employee
Subpoenas
Service to include copy of proof of service of notice to employee or employee's release . . . CCP §2020.510
Evidence
Use of depositions as evidence . . . CCP §2025.620
Examination of deponent . . . CCP §2025.330
Time limits
Witness examination . . . CCP §2025.290
Expert witnesses
Time limits for witness examination . . . CCP §2025.290
Workers' compensation cases, fees . . . CCP §2034.430
Fees
Witness fees and mileage . . . CCP §2020.230
Foreign states or nations
Taking depositions in foreign countries . . . CCP §2027.010

DEPOSITIONS—Cont.
Foreign states or nations—Cont.
Taking out-of-state depositions . . . CCP §2026.010
Interpreters
Employer responsibility to pay for interpreter services at deposition . . . Lab §5710
Qualifications of interpreter . . . 8 CCR §9795.1.5
Directories of qualified interpreters . . . 8 CCR §9795.5
Methods of discovery . . . CCP §2019.010
Nonparty discovery . . . CCP §2020.010
Motion to compel
Answer to question or production of document . . . CCP §2025.480
Notice of deposition, motion to compel compliance . . . CCP §2025.450
Production of documents . . . CCP §2025.480
Nonparty discovery
Methods of discovery . . . CCP §2020.010
Subpoenas . . . CCP §2020.020
Notice of deposition . . . CCP §§2025.210 to 2025.295
Consumer records
Service of notice on consumer . . . CCP §2025.240
Contents . . . CCP §2025.220
Corporations and other non-natural person deponents
Description of matters on which examination requested . . . CCP §2025.230
Method for notice . . . CCP §2025.210
Noncompliance with notice
Sanctions . . . CCP §2025.450
Parties appearing
Notice to all parties appearing . . . CCP §2025.240
Place for taking deposition . . . CCP §2025.250
Mote distant location, motion and ruling . . . CCP §2025.260
Scheduling deposition, interval between notice or subpoena . . . CCP §2025.270
Service, effect . . . CCP §2025.280
Subpoena service with notice . . . CCP §2025.240
When deposition subpoena required . . . CCP §2025.280
Time limit for or duration of deposition
Mesothelioma or silicosis of deponent . . . CCP §2025.295
Unlawful detainer actions
Time for taking deposition . . . CCP §2025.270
Oath of deponent . . . CCP §2025.330
Objections
Errors and irregularities ad deposition . . . CCP §2025.460
Privileged and protected information
Waiver absent objection . . . CCP §2025.460
Service of written objection . . . CCP §2025.410
Occupational Safety and Health Appeals Board . . . Lab §6613
Officer conducting proceedings
Subpoenas
Business records produced for copying . . . CCP §§2020.420, 2020.430
Oral depositions
Inside California . . . CCP §§2025.010 to 2025.620
Conduct of depositions . . . CCP §§2025.310 to 2025.340

DEPOSITIONS—Cont.
Oral depositions—Cont.
Inside California —Cont.
Notice . . . CCP §§2025.210 to 2025.290
Objections, sanctions, protective orders, etc . . . CCP §§2025.410 to 2025.480
Post-deposition procedures . . . CCP §§2025.610, 2025.620
Transcript or recording . . . CCP §§2025.510 to 2025.570
Methods of discovery . . . CCP §2019.010
Nonparty discovery . . . CCP §2020.010
Outside California . . . CCP §2026.010
Place of depositions . . . CCP §2025.250
More distant location, motion and ruling . . . CCP §2025.260
Post-deposition procedures . . . CCP §2025.610
Evidence, use of deposition as . . . CCP §2025.620
Subsequent depositions . . . CCP §2025.610
Privileged and protected information
Waiver absent objection . . . CCP §2025.460
Production, motion to compel
Subpoenas
Attendance and testimony also commanded, requirements of subpoena . . . CCP §2020.510
Production of business records
Methods of discovery
Nonparty discovery . . . CCP §2020.010
Notice of deposition . . . CCP §2025.220
Subpoenas
Business records produced for copying . . . CCP §§2020.410 to 2020.440
Protective orders
Motion for protective order . . . CCP §2025.420
Recording, audio or video
Availability of recording for review, notice of . . . CCP §2025.530
Copies
Furnishing . . . CCP §2025.570
Party access to recording . . . CCP §2025.560
Retention by operator . . . CCP §2025.560
Rough draft transcript
Use prohibited . . . CCP §2025.540
Scheduling deposition
Interval between notice or subpoena . . . CCP §2025.270
Service
Subpoenas . . . CCP §2020.220
Stenographic record of deposition
Testimony and objections . . . CCP §2025.330
Timely payment for services . . . CCP §2025.510
Transcript of deposition
Official record, stenographic testimony as . . . CCP §2025.510
Retaining stenographic notes . . . CCP §2025.510
Stipulations
Suspension of taking deposition . . . CCP §2025.470
Subpoenas (See DEPOSITION SUBPOENAS)
Subsequent depositions, taking of . . . CCP §2025.610
Suspension of deposition for failure to answer or produce material . . . CCP §2025.470
Telephone oral depositions
Conduct of depositions . . . CCP §2025.310

DEPOSITIONS—Cont.
Territories
Oral depositions outside California . . . CCP §2026.010
Time limits
Scheduling deposition
Interval between notice or subpoena . . . CCP §2025.270
Witness examination . . . CCP §2025.290
Transcript . . . CCP §2025.510
Certification by deposition officer . . . CCP §2025.540
Changing answers, time for . . . CCP §2025.520
Copies
Furnishing . . . CCP §2025.570
Notice of availability for reading, correcting and signing . . . CCP §2025.520
Recording
Availability of recording for review, notice of . . . CCP §2025.530
Retention by attorney . . . CCP §2025.550
Rough draft transcript
Use prohibited . . . CCP §2025.540
Transmittal to attorney . . . CCP §2025.550
Trial, use of depositions at . . . CCP §2025.620
Video or audio depositions
Availability of recording for review, notice of . . . CCP §2025.530
Copies
Furnishing . . . CCP §2025.570
Party access to recording . . . CCP §2025.560
Procedure . . . CCP §2025.340
Retention by operator . . . CCP §2025.560
Witness fees . . . CCP §2020.230
Written questions
Propounding written question to deponent at oral deposition . . . CCP §2025.330
Written questions, depositions by
Methods of discovery . . . CCP §2019.010
Nonparty discovery . . . CCP §2020.010

DEPOSITION SUBPOENAS . . . CCP §§2020.210 to 2020.240
Attendance and testimony commanded . . . CCP §2020.310
Business records production also requested, requirements of subpoena . . . CCP §2020.510
Attorney of record
Issuance . . . CCP §2020.210
Business records produced for copying . . . CCP §§2020.410 to 2020.440
Affidavit . . . CCP §2020.430
Attendance and testimony also commanded, requirements of subpoena . . . CCP §2020.510
Consumer records . . . CCP §2020.410
Contents . . . CCP §2020.410
Custody of records . . . CCP §2020.430
Delivery to officer . . . CCP §2020.430
Description of records . . . CCP §2020.410
Notice of deposition . . . CCP §2025.220
Officer for deposition . . . CCP §2020.420
Providing copies to specified parties . . . CCP §2020.440

DEPOSITION SUBPOENAS—Cont.
Clerk of court
Issuance . . . CCP §2020.210
Contempt for disobedience of . . . CCP §2020.240
Damages for disobedience . . . CCP §2020.240
Electronically stored information (ESI)
Notice
Contents of deposition notice . . . CCP §2025.220
Service, effect . . . CCP §2025.280
Forfeiture for disobedience . . . CCP §2020.240
Issuance . . . CCP §2020.210
Nonparty discovery . . . CCP §§2020.020, 2020.030
Notice of deposition served with subpoena . . . CCP §2025.240
When deposition subpoena required . . . CCP §2025.280
Scheduling deposition, interval between notice or subpoena . . . CCP §2025.270
Service of deposition subpoena . . . CCP §2020.220
Service of process
Failure to serve causing deponent to fail to attend
Sanctions . . . CCP §2025.440
Witness fees and mileage . . . CCP §2020.230

DEPOSITS
Self-insurers
Security deposits (See SELF-INSURANCE)
State Compensation Insurance Fund excess money . . . Ins §11800
Unabsorbed premium deposits, payment of . . . Ins §11757

DIAGNOSIS-RELATED GROUP (DRG) WEIGHT
Fee schedules for medical treatment . . . 8 CCR §9790.1
Table of DRG weights and revised weights . . . 8 CCR §9792.1 Appx B

DIGITAL MEDIA
Appeals board (WCAB)
Exhibits generally . . . 8 CCR §10677
Evidence, printed representation as . . . Ev §1553
Invasion of privacy to acquire video or sound recordings . . . CC §1708.8

DIPSOMANIA
Conditions of employer liability for compensation . . . Lab §3600

DIRECTION TO FILE VERIFIED STATEMENT
Contents . . . 8 CCR §15576
Defined . . . 8 CCR §15551

DIRECT PATIENT CARE PROVIDERS
Health care workers generallly (See HEALTH CARE WORKERS)
Personal protective equipment (PPE)
Stockpile of PPE, employer duties . . . Lab §6403.3

DISABILITY
Alternative work
Defined . . . Lab §4658.1
Combined disabilities
Cumulative injury (See CUMULATIVE INJURY)
Subsequent injuries, due to (See SUBSEQUENT INJURIES)

DISABILITY—Cont.
Combined disabilities—Cont.
Work capacity guidelines . . . Table 11
Cumulative injury (See CUMULATIVE INJURY)
Death of employee
Third party causing injury or death
Personal relationship not inferred due to certain beliefs of third party . . . Lab §3600
Decrease in or termination of (See subhead: Petition alleging termination or decrease in disability)
Defined . . . UI §2626
Description of
Evaluation of (See subhead: Evaluation of)
Measurement, method of (See subhead: Measurement, method of)
Evaluation of
Measurement of disability (See subhead: Measurement, method of)
Time guidelines for QMEs . . . 8 CCR §§49 to 49.9 (See QUALIFIED MEDICAL EVALUATORS (QMES))
Further disability, petition to establish . . . 8 CCR §10536
Injury, disability suffered after employee leaves work due to . . . Lab §4652
Measurement, method of
Evaluation of disability (See subhead: Evaluation of)
Guidelines for . . . 8 CCR §9725
Psychiatric disability . . . 8 CCR §9726
Subjective disability . . . 8 CCR §9727
Medical assistance
In-home supportive services for aged, blind and disabled
Direct payments to provider or recipients, workers' compensation, unemployment compensation, etcobligations . . . W&I §§12302.2, 12302.5
Medical examination, disability caused or aggravated by refusal or failure to submit to . . . Lab §4056
Military service
Disability equality act . . . Mil&Vet §§345, 346
Modified work
Defined . . . Lab §4658.1
Multiple disabilities
Cumulative injury (See CUMULATIVE INJURY)
Subsequent injuries, due to (See SUBSEQUENT INJURIES)
Work capacity guidelines . . . Table 11
New disability, petition to establish . . . 8 CCR §10536
Partial
Permanent (See PERMANENT PARTIAL DISABILITY)
Temporary (See TEMPORARY PARTIAL DISABILITY)
Payment of benefits (See PAYMENT OF BENEFITS)
Permanent (See PERMANENT DISABILITY)
Permanent partial (See PERMANENT PARTIAL DISABILITY)
Permanent total (See PERMANENT TOTAL DISABILITY)
Petition alleging termination or decrease in disability
Denial of . . . Lab §4651.3
Limitations on . . . Lab §4651.2
Presumptions following . . . Lab §4651.1
Previous (See PREVIOUS DISABILITY)

DISABILITY—Cont.
Public disability accommodations . . . 8 CCR §§9708.1 to 9708.6
Public employees retirement system
Disability retirement (See PUBLIC EMPLOYEES' RETIREMENT SYSTEM)
Regular work
Defined . . . Lab §4658.1
Specific disabilities, work capacity guidelines for . . . Table 11
Subjective disability, identification and degree of . . . 8 CCR §9727
Subsequent injuries, due to (See SUBSEQUENT INJURIES)
Temporary (See TEMPORARY DISABILITY)
Temporary partial (See TEMPORARY PARTIAL DISABILITY)
Temporary total (See TEMPORARY TOTAL DISABILITY)
Termination or decrease in (See subhead: Petition alleging termination or decrease in disability)
Time limits for performing evaluations of . . . Lab §4051
Completion of examination . . . Lab §4062.5
Qualified medical evaluators (QMEs), time guidelines . . . 8 CCR §§49 to 49.9 (See QUALIFIED MEDICAL EVALUATORS (QMES))
Total
Permanent (See PERMANENT TOTAL DISABILITY)
Temporary (See TEMPORARY TOTAL DISABILITY)
Work capacity guidelines . . . Table 11

DISABILITY BENEFITS
Administrative review
Voluntary plans, denial of claims under . . . UI §§3264, 3265
Appeals
Voluntary plan denial of benefits . . . UI §3264
California National Guard, organized militia, or unorganized militia
Injured in service of state . . . Mil&Vet §340.1
Transfers under mutual aid or interagency agreements . . . Mil&Vet §340.2
California State University personnel on industrial disability leave (See CALIFORNIA STATE UNIVERSITY)
Claims procedures
Confidentiality of medical records . . . Lab §3762
Medical records, confidentiality of . . . Lab §3762
Confidentiality of medical records . . . Lab §3762
Contributions
Disability Fund, to (See UNEMPLOYMENT COMPENSATION DISABILITY FUND)
State employees . . . UI §2783
Voluntary disability benefit plans, to . . . UI §3252
Generally . . . UI §3252
Trust fund, employee contributions treated as . . . UI §3261
Definitions . . . UI §140.5
Disabled or disability . . . UI §2626
Industrially disabled persons . . . UI §2776
Designations for . . . UI §140.5
Disqualification from receiving
Industrially disabled persons, effect of actions prior to disability . . . UI §2778

DISABILITY BENEFITS—Cont.
Eligibility
Disabled or disability defined for purposes of eligibility . . . UI §2626
Disqualification (See subhead: Disqualification from receiving)
Other benefits
Eligibility for disability benefits while receiving other benefits . . . UI §2629
State employees . . . UI §2781
Family temporary disability insurance benefits
Liens for benefits paid against workers' compensation benefits . . . Lab §4903
Amount, determination . . . Lab §4904
Foreign employment
Contractors with U.Sworking outside U.S . . . 42 USC §1701
Military bases outside U.S., employees of . . . 42 USC §1651
Fund (See UNEMPLOYMENT COMPENSATION DISABILITY FUND)
Gross income, what constitutes . . . 26 USC §104
Industrially disabled persons
Actions prior to disability, effect of . . . UI §2778
California State University personnel (See CALIFORNIA STATE UNIVERSITY)
Definitions pertinent to . . . UI §2776
Quarters of base period, determining . . . UI §2777
Rights of . . . UI §§2775 to 2778
Liens and overpayment
Filing lien claim or application for adjudication . . . Lab §4903.6
Satisfaction of overpayment claim by payment of lien claim . . . UI §2741
Longshore and Harbor Workers' Compensation Act . . . 33 USC §908
Medical information, release to insurer . . . CC §§56.10 to 56.16
Medical records, access to . . . CC §56.10
Medical records, confidentiality of . . . Lab §3762
Military bases overseas, service on . . . 42 USC §1651
Military service
California National Guard, organized militia, or unorganized militia
Injured in service of state . . . Mil&Vet §340.1
Transfers under mutual aid or interagency agreements . . . Mil&Vet §340.2
Overpayments
Liens (See subhead: Liens and overpayment)
Payment of (See PAYMENT OF BENEFITS)
Public Employees' Retirement System (See PUBLIC EMPLOYEES' RETIREMENT SYSTEM)
Recordkeeping requirements
State employees . . . UI §2783
Reporting requirements
State employees . . . UI §2783
Rights
Industrially disabled persons . . . UI §2775
Simultaneous Disability Fund and voluntary plan benefits . . . UI §3253
State employees
Contributions . . . UI §2783
Eligibility . . . UI §2781

Index

DISABILITY BENEFITS—Cont.
State employees—Cont.
Information and reporting requirements regarding . . . UI §2783
Limitations . . . UI §2782
Payment of benefits to . . . UI §2783
Public Employees' Retirement System (See PUBLIC EMPLOYEES' RETIREMENT SYSTEM)
Recordkeeping requirements . . . UI §2783
Teachers (See STATE TEACHERS' RETIREMENT SYSTEM)
Teachers (See STATE TEACHERS' RETIREMENT SYSTEM)
Unemployment compensation benefits
Contributions (See subhead: Contributions)
Overpayments (See subhead: Overpayments)
Unemployment Compensation Disability Fund (See UNEMPLOYMENT COMPENSATION DISABILITY FUND)
Voluntary plans (See VOLUNTARY DISABILITY BENEFIT PLANS)
Worker contributions
State employees . . . UI §2783
Unemployment compensation disability fund, contributions to
Designations . . . UI §144
State employees . . . UI §2783
Voluntary disability benefit plans, to
Generally . . . UI §3252
Trust fund, employee contributions treated as . . . UI §3261

DISABILITY FUND (See UNEMPLOYMENT COMPENSATION DISABILITY FUND)

DISASTER SERVICES (See EMERGENCY AND DISASTER SERVICES)

DISCHARGE OF ATTACHMENT
Procedures for . . . Lab §5602

DISCHARGE OF CLAIMS
Payment of compensation as . . . Lab §3603

DISCIPLINARY PROCEEDINGS
Contractors, against . . . B&P §7110
Qualified medical evaluators (QMEs), against (See QUALIFIED MEDICAL EVALUATORS (QMES))
Structural pest control operators, against . . . B&P §8636

DISCLOSURES
Arbitrator, disclosure of settlement arrangements to . . . Lab §5278
Attorneys' fees disclosure statements (See ATTORNEYS' FEES)
Financial interests in entities providing services . . . Lab §139.32
Genetic characteristics, test results for . . . CC §56.17
Health care organizations (HCOs) (See HEALTH CARE ORGANIATIONS (HCOS))
Health care provider's disclosure of participation in network . . . Lab §4609
HIV status, confidentiality of . . . CC §56.31
Independent medical review
Organizations providing review
Financial disclosures . . . Lab §139.5

DISCLOSURES—Cont.
Medical examinations
Unrepresented injured workers . . . Lab §4062.1
Medical provider networks
Contracting agent disclosures . . . Lab §4616
Economic profiling
Policies, public access to . . . Lab §4616.1
Truth in Advertising Act . . . Lab §5433
Waiver of privilege . . . Ev §919

DISCOVERY
Abuse of discovery process, sanctions for (See DISCOVERY ABUSES, SANCTIONS FOR)
Actions
Defined . . . CCP §2016.020
Appeals board (WCAB)
Application
Filing as prerequisite to discovery . . . 8 CCR §10450
Attorney work product . . . CCP §§2018.010 to 2018.080
Breach of attorney-client relationship . . . CCP §2018.080
Clients
Defined . . . CCP §2018.010
Construction of provisions to restate existing law . . . CCP §2018.040
Crime or fraud, participation by attorney
No protection of work product . . . CCP §2018.050
Disciplinary proceedings of state bar . . . CCP §2018.070
In camera hearings . . . CCP §2018.060
Inspection demands
Electronically stored information, responses to inspection demands . . . CCP §2031.285
Policy of state . . . CCP §2018.020
When discoverable . . . CCP §2018.030
Civil discovery act
Short title of provisions . . . CCP §2016.010
Contact information of those likely to have discoverable information
Initial disclosures . . . CCP §2016.090
Courts
Defined . . . CCP §2016.020
Criminal cases
Law enforcement personnel records . . . Ev §§915, 1043
Official information acquired in confidence . . . Ev §§915, 1043
Trade secret privilege . . . Ev §915
Cut off of discovery . . . Lab §5502
Definitions . . . CCP §2016.020
Dependent adults
Elder abuse and dependent adult civil protection act . . . CCP §§2017.310, 2017.320
Depositions
Generally (See DEPOSITIONS)
Methods of discovery . . . CCP §2019.010
Documents and records
Definition of document . . . CCP §2016.020
Initial disclosures . . . CCP §2016.090
Elder abuse and dependent adult civil protection act . . . CCP §§2017.310, 2017.320

DISCOVERY—Cont.
Electronically stored information
Civil discovery act, applicability to ESI . . . CCP §2019.040
Defined . . . CCP §2016.020
Deposition subpoenas . . . CCP §§2020.020, 2020.220
Attendance and testimony commanded along with production of business records . . . CCP §2020.510
Business records, production for copying . . . CCP §2020.410
Inspection demands . . . CCP §§2031.010 to 2031.320
Sanctions for failure to provide
Good faith operation of electronic information system preventing provision of ESI . . . CCP §§2017.020, 2023.030
Scope of discovery . . . CCP §2017.010
Electronically stored information (ESI)
Compelling discovery, motion . . . CCP §2025.480
Deposition subpoenas
Contents of deposition notice . . . CCP §2025.220
Effect of service of notice . . . CCP §2025.280
Failure to comply with deposition notice . . . CCP §2025.450
Outside California, discovery in foreign jurisdictions . . . CCP §2026.010
Foreign nations . . . CCP §2027.010
Protective orders . . . CCP §2025.420
Undue burden or expense to produce
Objections to production . . . CCP §2025.460
Expert witnesses, discovery of
Simultaneous exchanges of information
Methods of discovery . . . CCP §2019.010
Extent of discovery
Limitation . . . CCP §2019.030
Failure to confer
Sanctions . . . CCP §§2023.010, 2023.020
Frequency of discovery
Limitation . . . CCP §2019.030
Informal discovery conference . . . CCP §2016.080
Initial disclosures . . . CCP §2016.090
Inspection
Demands (See INSPECTION DEMANDS)
Methods of discovery . . . CCP §2019.010
Insurance coverage, discovery of . . . CCP §2017.210
Initial disclosures . . . CCP §2016.090
Interrogatories
Methods of discovery . . . CCP §2019.010
Law enforcement personnel records . . . Ev §915
Medical examinations
Information provided to evaluator . . . Lab §4062.3
Meet and confer
Declaration
Contents . . . CCP §2016.040
Failure to reach informal resolution
Informal discovery conference at request of party or on court's own motion . . . CCP §2016.080
Mental examinations, discovery procedure for
Methods of discovery . . . CCP §2019.010

DISCOVERY—Cont.
Methods of . . . CCP §2019.010
Nonparty discovery . . . CCP §2020.010
Trade secrets . . . CCP §2019.210
Misuse of discovery, acts constituting
Sanctions . . . CCP §§2023.010, 2023.030
Motions
Service, methods . . . CCP §2016.050
Nonparty discovery . . . CCP §§2020.010 to 2020.510
Physical examinations, discovery procedure for
Methods of discovery . . . CCP §2019.010
Privileges
Inspection demands
Electronically stored information, responses to inspection demands . . . CCP §2031.285
Protective orders
Attorney work product
Disciplinary action by state bar . . . CCP §2018.070
Elder abuse and dependent adult civil protection act . . . CCP §2017.320
Electronically stored information (ESI) . . . CCP §2025.420
Unsuccessfully making or opposing motion for protective order . . . CCP §2017.020
Qualified medical evaluators (QMEs)
Information provided to . . . 8 CCR §35
Requests for admissions
Methods of discovery . . . CCP §2019.010
Sanctions
Abuse of discovery procedure . . . CCP §2023.010
Amounts . . . CCP §2023.050
Failure to confer . . . CCP §§2023.010, 2023.020
Grounds for imposition . . . CCP §2023.050
Inspection demands
Electronically stored information . . . CCP §§2031.060, 2031.320
Misuse of discovery process . . . CCP §§2023.010, 2023.030
Process for imposition . . . CCP §2023.050
Protective orders
Unsuccessfully making or opposing motion for protective order . . . CCP §2017.020
Request for sanctions . . . CCP §2023.040
Sexual conduct of plaintiff
Unsuccessfully making or opposing motions . . . CCP §2017.220
Scope of discovery . . . CCP §§2017.010 to 2017.320
Elder abuse and dependent adult civil protection act
Confidential settlements . . . CCP §2017.310
Protective order to protect certain information . . . CCP §2017.320
Insurance information . . . CCP §2017.210
Limiting scope . . . CCP §2017.020
Protective orders
Elder abuse and dependent adult civil protection act . . . CCP §2017.320
Limiting scope of discovery . . . CCP §2017.020
Sexual conduct of plaintiff in certain actions . . . CCP §2017.220
Standard scope . . . CCP §2017.010
Sequence of discovery . . . CCP §2019.020
Trade secrets . . . CCP §2019.210

DISCOVERY—Cont.
Service
Methods of service . . . CCP §2016.050
Sexual conduct
Injuries arising from . . . Lab §3208.4
Plaintiff's sexual conduct . . . CCP §2017.220
Stipulations
Modification of discovery procedures . . . CCP §2016.030
Time limitations on
Saturday, Sunday or holiday, deadline falling on . . . CCP §2016.060
Timing of discovery . . . CCP §2019.020
Trade secrets
Discovery for misappropriation of
Method and sequence . . . CCP §2019.210
Privilege to refuse disclosure . . . Ev §915
Work product doctrine
Attorney work product generally . . . CCP §§2018.010 to 2018.080
Writings
Defined . . . CCP §2016.020

DISCOVERY ABUSES, SANCTIONS FOR . . . CCP §2023.010
Attendance at deposition
Failure of party giving notice to attend . . . CCP §2025.430
Subpoena not served, causing failure to attend . . . CCP §2025.440
Electronically stored information (ESI)
Sanctions for failure to provide
Good faith operation of electronic information system preventing provision of ESI, defense to sanctions . . . CCP §§2025.410, 2025.450
Motion to compel answer or production
Unsuccessfully making or opposing . . . CCP §2025.480
Notice of deposition
Failure to comply . . . CCP §2025.450
Objections
Unsuccessfully making or opposing objection . . . CCP §2025.410
Electronically stored information (ESI), good faith operation of electronic information system as defense to sanctions . . . CCP §2025.410
Protective orders
Unsuccessfully making or opposing motion for protective order
Depositions . . . CCP §2025.420

DISCRETION OF COURT
Judicial notice . . . Ev §452

DISCRIMINATION
Affirmative relief
Defined . . . Gov §12926
Age
Defined . . . Gov §12926
App-based drivers and services
Antidiscrimination and public safety . . . B&P §§7456 to 7462

DISCRIMINATION—Cont.
Applicants and witnesses, prohibition of discrimination against . . . Lab §132a
Death of employee
Third party causing injury or death
Personal relationship not inferred due to certain beliefs of third party . . . Lab §3600
Definitions . . . Gov §12926
Employees
Defined . . . Gov §12926
Employers
Defined . . . Gov §12926
Employer's records of occupational injury or illness
Reporters of injuries or illnesses, protection from discrimination . . . 8 CCR §14300.36
Employment agencies
Defined . . . Gov §12926
Employment discrimination (See EMPLOYMENT DISCRIMINATION)
Essential functions
Defined . . . Gov §12926
Gender
Defined . . . Gov §12926
Employment discrimination . . . Gov §12940
Genetic information
Defined . . . Gov §12926
Employment discrimination . . . Gov §12940
Health care providers
Certification requirements
Nondiscrimination . . . Lab §4600.6
Insurance premium rates (See RATING)
Labor organizations
Defined . . . Gov §12926
Longshore and Harbor Workers' Compensation Act requirements . . . 33 USC §948a
Medical condition
Defined . . . Gov §12926
Mental disability
Defined . . . Gov §12926
National origin discrimination
Defined . . . Gov §12926
Occupational Safety and Health Division, prohibition by . . . Lab §§6310, 6312
Physical disability
Defined . . . Gov §12926
Pleadings alleging discrimination against injured employee . . . 8 CCR §10528
Prospective relief
Defined . . . Gov §12926
Protective hairstyles
Defined . . . Gov §12926
Race
Defined . . . Gov §12926
Reasonable accommodation
Defined . . . Gov §12926
Religion
Accommodations . . . Gov §12940
Definitions . . . Gov §12926
Sex
Definitions . . . Gov §12926
Sexual orientation
Defined . . . Gov §12926
Supervisor
Defined . . . Gov §12926

DISCRIMINATION—Cont.
Undue hardship
Defined . . . Gov §12926
Veteran or military status
Defined . . . Gov §12926

DISEASE
Medical information disclosure
Prevention of disease outbreaks . . . CC §56.10
Occupational disease (See OCCUPATIONAL DISEASE)

DISINFECTANTS
Hazardous substances contained in cosmetics or disinfectants
Manufacturer or importer duties . . . Lab §6390.2

DISMISSAL OF CLAIM
Inactive for more than 180 days . . . Lab §5404.5
Lack of prosecution
Dismissal of inactive cases
Petition to dismiss . . . 8 CCR §10550
Lien claims . . . 8 CCR §10888
Lien claims . . . 8 CCR §10888
Order dismissing application . . . 8 CCR §10850

DISPUTE RESOLUTION
Arbitration (See ARBITRATION)
Drugs, medical treatment utilization schedule (MTUS)
Formulary . . . 8 CCR §9792.27.17
Health care organization (HCO) procedures . . . 8 CCR §9775
Vocational rehabilitation (See VOCATIONAL REHABILITATION)
Workers' Compensation Division information and Assistance program, mediation by . . . 8 CCR §9775

DISTRICT COURT
Jurisdiction of
Admiralty jurisdiction . . . 28 USC §1333
Maritime jurisdiction . . . 28 USC §1333
Prizes brought into U.Sand property taken as prize . . . 28 USC §1333
United States as defendant . . . 28 USC §1346
Jurisdiction over appeals from . . . 28 USC §1291
Venue, United States as defendant . . . 28 USC §1402

DIVIDENDS
Insurance policyholders, payments to
Filing requirements . . . Ins §11739
Rating organizations . . . Ins §11757
Restrictions . . . Ins §11739
State Compensation Insurance Fund . . . Ins §§11776, 11777

DIVISION OF INDUSTRIAL ACCIDENTS (See INDUSTRIAL ACCIDENTS DIVISION)

DIVISION OF LABOR STANDARDS ENFORCEMENT (See LABOR STANDARDS ENFORCEMENT DIVISION)

DIVISION OF LABOR STATISTICS AND RESEARCH (See LABOR STATISTICS AND RESEARCH DIVISION)

DIVISION OF OCCUPATIONAL SAFETY AND HEALTH (See OCCUPATIONAL SAFETY AND HEALTH DIVISION)

DIVISION OF WORKERS' COMPENSATION (See WORKERS' COMPENSATION DIVISION)

DOCKS (See SHIPPING)

DOCUMENTARY EVIDENCE
Appeals board (WCAB)
Conference, submission at . . . 8 CCR §10761
Definitions . . . Ev §250
Service of copies of documents, electronic media, etc, offered into evidence . . . 8 CCR §10635
Lien claimants who are not physicians, service on . . . 8 CCR §10637
Writing
Defined . . . Ev §250

DOCUMENTATION (See RECORDS AND RECORDKEEPING)

DOCUMENT COVER SHEET FORM
Electronic adjudication management system (EAMS) . . . 8 CCR §10205.13

DOCUMENT SEPARATOR SHEET FORMS
Electronic adjudication management system (EAMS) . . . 8 CCR §10205.14

DOMESTIC PARTNERS
Family care leave, paid
Definition of domestic partner . . . UI §3302
Medical records disclosures to . . . CC §56.1007
Privileged communications . . . Ev §980
Spouse defined to include registered domestic partner . . . Lab §12.2

DOMESTIC SERVICE (See HOUSEHOLD EMPLOYEES)

DOMESTIC TERRORISM
Nurse case manager support to obtain medically necessary treatment . . . Lab §4600.05

DOMESTIC VIOLENCE
Aliens, uninsured employers fund and subsequent injuries fund benefits for . . . 8 CCR §15740
Insurance, refusal to cover victims . . . Ins §676.9
Sick days, paid
Privacy of health and domestic relations information . . . Lab §249

DOMESTIC WORK EMPLOYEES
Occupational safety and health division
Discrimination against injured workers filing complaints
Applicability to certain domestic work employees . . . Lab §6310
Safe workplace
Unsafe conditions
Refusal of employee to work due to unsafe conditions . . . Lab §6311

DOR (See DECLARATION OF READINESS TO PROCEED (DOR))

DRAYAGE SERVICES
Commercial drivers
Independent contractor, misclassification
Motor carrier employer amnesty program for carriers performing drayage services . . . Lab §2750.8

DRG (DIAGNOSIS-RELATED GROUP) WEIGHT
Fee schedules for medical treatment . . . 8 CCR §9790.1
Table of DRG weights and revised weights . . . 8 CCR §9792.1 Appx B

DRINKING WATER
Requirement to provide . . . Lab §2441

DRIVERS
App-based drivers and services . . . B&P §§7448 to 7467 (See APP-BASED DRIVERS AND SERVICES)

DRIVING UNDER THE INFLUENCE
App-based drivers and services
ero tolerance policies . . . B&P §7460

DRUG ABUSE
App-based drivers and services
Driving under the influence
Zero tolerance policies . . . B&P §7460
Conditions of employer liability for compensation . . . Lab §3600

DRUG FORMULARY
Medical treatment utilization review, schedules
Drug formulary using evidence-based medicine . . . Lab §5307.27
Quarterly updates . . . Lab §5307.29
Review of medical necessity, procedures . . . Lab §§4610.5, 4610.6
Stakeholders, consultation regarding establishment of formulary . . . Lab §5307.28
Medical treatment utilization schedule (MTUS) (See DRUGS, MEDICAL TREATMENT UTILIZATION SCHEDULE (MTUS))

DRUGS, MEDICAL TREATMENT UTILIZATION SCHEDULE (MTUS) . . . 8 CCR §§9792.27.1 to 9792.27.23
Formulary
Access to drugs not listed as exempt drug on list . . . 8 CCR §9792.27.6
Brand name drugs . . . 8 CCR §9792.27.7
Compounded drugs . . . 8 CCR §9792.27.9
Definitions . . . 8 CCR §9792.27.1
Dispensing
Physician-dispensed drugs . . . 8 CCR §9792.27.8
Dispute resolution . . . 8 CCR §9792.27.17
Generic drugs . . . 8 CCR §9792.27.7
Health and safety regulations
Treatment through formulary subject to health and safety regulations . . . 8 CCR §9792.27.14
Off-label use . . . 8 CCR §9792.27.5
Pharmacy benefits managers . . . 8 CCR §9792.27.4
Pharmacy networks . . . 8 CCR §9792.27.4
Scope of coverage . . . 8 CCR §9792.27.2

DRUGS, MEDICAL TREATMENT UTILIZATION SCHEDULE (MTUS) —Cont.
List
Access to drugs not listed as exempt drug on list . . . 8 CCR §9792.27.6
Exempt drugs . . . 8 CCR §9792.27.10
Link to contents of drug list . . . 8 CCR §9792.27.15
National drug codes
Publication for use with list . . . 8 CCR §9792.27.16
Non-exempt drugs . . . 8 CCR §9792.27.10
Perioperative fill . . . 8 CCR §9792.27.13
Prospective review . . . 8 CCR §9792.27.10
Waiver . . . 8 CCR §9792.27.11
Scope of coverage . . . 8 CCR §9792.27.2
Special fill . . . 8 CCR §9792.27.12
Unique pharmaceutical identifiers
Publication for use with list . . . 8 CCR §9792.27.16
Unlisted drugs . . . 8 CCR §9792.27.10
Updates . . . 8 CCR §9792.27.23
Pharmacy and therapeutics committee
Application for appointment . . . 8 CCR §9792.27.18
Form . . . 8 CCR §9792.27.19
Composition . . . 8 CCR §9792.27.18
Conflicts of interest . . . 8 CCR §9792.27.20
Disclosure form . . . 8 CCR §9792.27.21
Creation by administrative director . . . 8 CCR §9792.27.18
Duties . . . 8 CCR §9792.27.18
Meetings . . . 8 CCR §9792.27.22
Purpose . . . 8 CCR §9792.27.18
Updates to drug list . . . 8 CCR §9792.27.23

DUMBWAITER SAFETY . . . Lab §§7300 to 7324.2
Generally (See ELEVATORS, ESCALATORS, CHAIR LIFTS AND OTHER CONVEYANCES)

DURABLE MEDICAL EQUIPMENT
Official medical fee schedule . . . 8 CCR §9789.60

E

EARNINGS
Average (See AVERAGE EARNINGS)
Evaluations of future earnings capacity
Financial interests in entities providing services . . . Lab §139.32
Minimum/maximum . . . Table 14

EARTHQUAKE PREDICTION EVALUATION COUNCIL
Responsibilities and immunities . . . Gov §8657

ECONOMIC OPPORTUNITY PROGRAMS
Adjustment of claims
Federal benefits, effect of . . . Lab §4226
Medical benefits provided by federal government
Effect of . . . Lab §4227
Reimbursement, in form of . . . Lab §4228
Right to recover federal benefits . . . Lab §4229
Application of legislation . . . Lab §§4201, 4209
Burial expenses . . . Lab §4214
Death of enrollee . . . Lab §§4212, 4214

ECONOMIC OPPORTUNITY PROGRAMS—Cont.
Definitions
Economic opportunity program . . . Lab §4202
Enrollees . . . Lab §4203
Participating agency . . . Lab §4205
Sponsoring agency . . . Lab §4204
Enrollees defined . . . Lab §4203
Exclusive remedy provision . . . Lab §4208
Federal statute, benefits and medical treatment provided under
Effect of . . . Lab §4226
Medical benefits
Effect of . . . Lab §4227
Reimbursement, in form of . . . Lab §4228
Right to recover federal benefits . . . Lab §4229
Injury of enrollee . . . Lab §4212
Limitations on workers' compensation under . . . Lab §4211
Medical treatment or reimbursement provided by federal government . . . Lab §§4227, 4228
Participating agency defined . . . Lab §4205
Permanent disability . . . Lab §4213
Preemption of state law . . . Lab §4229
Purpose of legislation . . . Lab §4201
Requirements for workers' compensation awards under . . . Lab §4207
Rights
Recovery of federal benefits . . . Lab §4229
Workers' compensation benefits . . . Lab §4206
Sponsoring agency defined . . . Lab §4204

EDUCATION
California State University (See CALIFORNIA STATE UNIVERSITY)
Claims adjusters
Training standards . . . Ins §11761
County superintendent of schools (See COUNTY SUPERINTENDENT OF SCHOOLS)
Death benefit scholarships
Police officers, correctional officers, and firefighters, dependents of . . . Lab §4709
Public officials, dependents of . . . Lab §4728
Health care organization (HCO) patient education programs . . . 8 CCR §9776.1
Judges (WCJs)
Continuing education of . . . Lab §5311.5
Financial interests in educational programs, with . . . 8 CCR §9721.31
Occupational Safety and Health Division programs (See OCCUPATIONAL SAFETY AND HEALTH DIVISION)
Qualified medical evaluators (QMEs), continuing education requirements for . . . 8 CCR §55
Safety violations, fines and penalties for . . . Lab §6434
Safe workplace programs
Education and research programs (See OCCUPATIONAL SAFETY AND HEALTH DIVISION)
School districts (See SCHOOL DISTRICTS)
State teachers' retirement system (See STATE TEACHERS' RETIREMENT SYSTEM)
Supplemental job displacement benefits
Eligibility . . . Lab §4658.5
2013, injuries occurring in or after . . . Lab §4658.7

EDUCATION—Cont.
Supplemental job displacement benefits—Cont.
Modified or alternative work not accepted, employer not liable for benefits . . . Lab §4658.6
Voucher for education related retraining or skill enhancement . . . Lab §§4658.5, 4658.7
University of California (See UNIVERSITY OF CALIFORNIA)

EDUCATIONAL ORGANIZATIONS
Commercial or property insurance
Cancellation or nonrenewal of policies
Hate crime or anti-reproductive crime generating losses, factor in decision . . . Ins §676.10

ELBOW INJURIES
Medical treatment
Utilization schedule
Elbow disorders . . . 8 CCR §9792.23.3

ELECTION OF COMPENSATION LIABILITY
Generally . . . Lab §4150
Casual employees . . . Lab §4153
Course of trade, business, profession, or occupation, persons not in . . . Lab §4153
Deemed acceptance of employer election by employee . . . Lab §4154
Effective date of Labor Code division on . . . Lab §4156
Independent contractors selling periodicals and newspapers . . . Lab §4157
Joint election by employer and employee . . . Lab §4150
Methods of . . . Lab §4151
Nonemployees . . . Lab §4150
Persons included in statement of acceptance . . . Lab §4153
Public agencies
Presumption of election by state institutions . . . Lab §4155
Voluntary offering of benefits to public employees . . . Lab §6110
Statement of election . . . Lab §4152
Time period covered by . . . Lab §4152
Waiver of election by worker . . . Lab §4154

ELECTRONIC ADJUDICATION MANAGEMENT SYSTEM (EAMS) . . . 8 CCR §§10205 to 10208.12
Address information . . . 8 CCR §10205.5
ADJ files
Defined . . . 8 CCR §10205
Adjudication files . . . 8 CCR §10205.4
Access to files . . . 8 CCR §10208.5
Defined . . . 8 CCR §10205
Retention, return and destruction of records . . . 8 CCR §10208.7
Administrative director
Defined . . . 8 CCR §10205
Appeals
Review of orders issued by administrative director . . . 8 CCR §§10208.8 to 10208.11
Appeals board
Defined . . . 8 CCR §10205
Application for adjudication
Applicants
Defined . . . 8 CCR §10205

Index

ELECTRONIC ADJUDICATION MANAGEMENT SYSTEM (EAMS) —Cont.
Application for adjudication—Cont.
Defined . . . 8 CCR §10205
Retention, return and destruction of records . . . 8 CCR §10208.7
Arbitration
Submittal form . . . 8 CCR §10208.12
Awards
Request for awards
Forms . . . 8 CCR §10205.2
Retention, return and destruction of records . . . 8 CCR §10208.7
Case names and index . . . 8 CCR §10205.3
Central registration unit
Defined . . . 8 CCR §10205
Claims administrators
Office
Definition of claims administrator's office . . . 8 CCR §10205
Uniform assigned names (UAN)
Creation and assignment . . . 8 CCR §10206.4
Compensation
Notice of compensation due
Review of orders issued by administrative director . . . 8 CCR §10208.9
Conferences
Pretrial conference statement form . . . 8 CCR §10208.4
Costs
Defined . . . 8 CCR §10205
Decisions
Inspection of documents
Prohibitions . . . 8 CCR §10208.6
Retention, return and destruction of records . . . 8 CCR §10208.7
Declaration of readiness to proceed
Defined . . . 8 CCR §10205
Expedited hearing calendar
Declaration of readiness to proceed to expedited hearing defined . . . 8 CCR §10205
Form . . . 8 CCR §10208.3
Form . . . 8 CCR §10208.2
Defendants
Defined . . . 8 CCR §10205
Definitions . . . 8 CCR §10205
District office
Defined . . . 8 CCR §10205
Document cover sheet
Defined . . . 8 CCR §10205
Form . . . 8 CCR §10205.13
Documents
Definitions . . . 8 CCR §10205
Inspection of documents
Prohibitions . . . 8 CCR §10208.6
Retention, return and destruction of records . . . 8 CCR §10208.7
Document separator sheets
Defined . . . 8 CCR §10205
Form . . . 8 CCR §10205.14
Electronic filing system rules . . . 8 CCR §§10206 to 10206.2
Definition of electronic filing . . . 8 CCR §10205

ELECTRONIC ADJUDICATION MANAGEMENT SYSTEM (EAMS) —Cont.
Electronic filing system rules —Cont.
E-forms, filing . . . 8 CCR §10206
Exemptions from electronic filing . . . 8 CCR §10206.2
JET filing procedures . . . 8 CCR §10206.1
Reference guide and instructional manual . . . 8 CCR §10206
Electronic signatures
Defined . . . 8 CCR §10205
Evidence
Summary of evidence
Retention, return and destruction of records . . . 8 CCR §10208.7
Exhibits
Retention, return and destruction . . . 8 CCR §10208.7
Expedited hearings
Declaration of readiness to proceed to expedited hearing
Defined . . . 8 CCR §10205
Form . . . 8 CCR §10208.3
Extended unavailability . . . 8 CCR §10205.9
Fax
Defined . . . 8 CCR §10205
Filings
Defined . . . 8 CCR §10205
Definition of file . . . 8 CCR §10205
Electronic filing system rules . . . 8 CCR §§10206 to 10206.2
Form requirements for electronic documents . . . 8 CCR §10206.5
Manner of filing electronic documents . . . 8 CCR §§10206.3 to 10206.5
Optical character recognition (OCR) forms
Defined . . . 8 CCR §10205
Party or lien claimant document filings
Document cover sheet form . . . 8 CCR §10205.13
Document separator sheet form . . . 8 CCR §10205.14
Electronic filing exemption . . . 8 CCR §10205.11
Form of filed documents . . . 8 CCR §10205.12
Manner of filing . . . 8 CCR §10205.10
Size of filed documents . . . 8 CCR §10205.12
Retention, return and destruction of records . . . 8 CCR §10208.7
Size requirements for electronic documents . . . 8 CCR §10206.5
Time for filing documents . . . 8 CCR §10206.3
Forms
JET filers, authorized forms . . . 8 CCR §10206.15
Requirements for electronic documents . . . 8 CCR §10206.5
Use of e-forms and unstructured forms . . . 8 CCR §10206.14
Hearings
Defined . . . 8 CCR §10205
Expedited hearings
Form . . . 8 CCR §10208.3
Minutes of hearing
Form . . . 8 CCR §10206.20

ELECTRONIC ADJUDICATION MANAGEMENT SYSTEM (EAMS) —Cont.
Hearings—Cont.
Minutes of hearing—Cont.
Retention, return and destruction of records . . . 8 CCR §10208.7
Regular hearing
Defined . . . 8 CCR §10205
Inspection of documents
Prohibitions . . . 8 CCR §10208.6
Liens
Activation fees . . . 8 CCR §10208
Claimants
Definition of lien claimant . . . 8 CCR §10205
Conference
Definition of lien conference . . . 8 CCR §10205
Definitions . . . 8 CCR §10205
Filing fees
Initial lien filing fee . . . 8 CCR §10207
Refunds . . . 8 CCR §10208.1
Initial liens
Defined . . . 8 CCR §10205
Refund of fees . . . 8 CCR §10208.1
Section 4903(b) liens
Defined . . . 8 CCR §10205
Uniform assigned names (UAN)
Creation and assignment for lien claimant organizations . . . 8 CCR §10206.4
Mandatory arbitration
Submittal form . . . 8 CCR §10208.12
Mandatory settlement conference
Defined . . . 8 CCR §10205
Rating mandatory settlement conference
Defined . . . 8 CCR §10205
Manner of filing electronic documents . . . 8 CCR §§10206.3 to 10206.5
Form and size requirements . . . 8 CCR §10206.5
Time for filing . . . 8 CCR §10206.3
Uniform assigned names (UAN) . . . 8 CCR §10206.4
Minutes
Hearing minutes
Form . . . 8 CCR §10206.20
Retention, return and destruction of records . . . 8 CCR §10208.7
Misfiled or misdirected documents
Corrective measures . . . 8 CCR §10205.8
Noncompliance with rules . . . 8 CCR §10205.7
Notice of compensation due
Review of orders issued by administrative director . . . 8 CCR §10208.9
OCR forms
Defined . . . 8 CCR §10205
Official participant records . . . 8 CCR §10205.5
Opinions
Inspection of documents
Prohibitions . . . 8 CCR §10208.6
Optical character recognition forms
Defined . . . 8 CCR §10205
Orders
Inspection of documents
Prohibitions . . . 8 CCR §10208.6
Retention, return and destruction of records . . . 8 CCR §10208.7

ELECTRONIC ADJUDICATION MANAGEMENT SYSTEM (EAMS) —Cont.
Orders—Cont.
Review of orders issued by administrative director . . . 8 CCR §§10208.8 to 10208.11
Parties
Defined . . . 8 CCR §10205
Permanent disability
Filing . . . 8 CCR §10151
Petitions
Defined . . . 8 CCR §10205
Physicians
Selection by employee of employer-designated physician, order
Review of orders issued by administrative director . . . 8 CCR §10208.8
Pretrial conference statements
Form . . . 8 CCR §10208.4
Priority conferences
Defined . . . 8 CCR §10205
Product delivery units
Defined . . . 8 CCR §10205
Rating mandatory settlement conference
Defined . . . 8 CCR §10205
Ratings
Inspection of documents
Prohibitions . . . 8 CCR §10208.6
Retention, return and destruction of records . . . 8 CCR §10208.7
Readiness to proceed
Declaration of readiness to proceed
Defined . . . 8 CCR §10205
Expedited hearing calendar . . . 8 CCR §10208.3
Form . . . 8 CCR §10208.2
Records
District office records
Subpoenas and informal requests not effective to obtain records . . . 8 CCR §10205.1
Retention, return and destruction . . . 8 CCR §10208.7
Rehabilitation unit orders
Review of orders issued by administrative director . . . 8 CCR §10208.10
Reports
Inspection of documents
Prohibitions . . . 8 CCR §10208.6
Retention, return and destruction of records . . . 8 CCR §10208.7
Representative's office
Defined . . . 8 CCR §10205
Return to work programs . . . 8 CCR §10116.1
Converting paper files to electronic . . . 8 CCR §10116.6
Electronic filing exemption . . . 8 CCR §10116.2
Injury or findings required to file . . . 8 CCR §10116.8
Misfiled or misdirected documents . . . 8 CCR §10116.7
Technical problems with filing . . . 8 CCR §10116.5
Review of orders issued by administrative director . . . 8 CCR §§10208.8 to 10208.11
Service
Definition of serve . . . 8 CCR §10205
Preferences as to, designation . . . 8 CCR §10205.6

Index

ELECTRONIC ADJUDICATION MANAGEMENT SYSTEM (EAMS) —Cont.
Settlements
Compromise and release forms . . . 8 CCR §10205.2
Mandatory settlement conferences
Defined . . . 8 CCR §10205
Rating mandatory settlement conferences
Defined . . . 8 CCR §10205
Retention, return and destruction of records . . . 8 CCR §10208.7
Signatures
Electronic signatures
Defined . . . 8 CCR §10205
Size requirements for electronic documents . . . 8 CCR §10206.5
Status conference
Defined . . . 8 CCR §10205
Submission
Defined . . . 8 CCR §10205
Summary of evidence
Retention, return and destruction of records . . . 8 CCR §10208.7
Supplemental job displacement benefits . . . 8 CCR §10116.1
Converting paper files to electronic . . . 8 CCR §10116.6
Electronic filing exemption . . . 8 CCR §10116.2
Injury or findings required to file . . . 8 CCR §10116.8
Misfiled or misdirected documents . . . 8 CCR §10116.7
Review of orders issued administrative director . . . 8 CCR §10208.11
Technical problems with filing . . . 8 CCR §10116.5
Time for filing documents . . . 8 CCR §10206.3
Trial
Defined . . . 8 CCR §10205
Uniform assigned names (UAN)
Creation and assignment . . . 8 CCR §10206.4
Venue
Defined . . . 8 CCR §10205
Voluntary arbitration
Submittal form . . . 8 CCR §10208.12
Workers' compensation administrative law judge
Defined . . . 8 CCR §10205
Legal memoranda, analysis, etc
Inspection of documents, prohibitions . . . 8 CCR §10208.6
Working papers, notes, etc
Inspection of documents, prohibitions . . . 8 CCR §10208.6

ELECTRONICALLY STORED INFORMATION (ESI)
Deposition subpoenas
Notice
Contents of deposition notice . . . CCP §2025.220
Service, effect . . . CCP §2025.280
Discovery
Compelling discovery, motion . . . CCP §2025.480
Deposition subpoenas
Failure to comply with deposition notice . . . CCP §2025.450

ELECTRONICALLY STORED INFORMATION (ESI)—Cont.
Discovery—Cont.
Outside California, discovery in foreign jurisdictions . . . CCP §2026.010
Foreign nations . . . CCP §2027.010
Protective orders . . . CCP §2025.420
Undue burden or expense to produce
Objections to production . . . CCP §2025.460

ELECTRONIC BILLING
Medical treatment
Payment for services
Time for payments . . . Lab §4603.4

ELECTRONIC CIGARETTES
Smoking in the workplace, prohibitions
Applicability to electronic cigarettes . . . Lab §6404.5

ELECTRONIC DEPOSITIONS
Remote electronic means of taking oral depositions . . . CCP §2025.310

ELECTRONIC DISCOVERY ACT . . . CCP §2016.020
Inspection demands . . . CCP §§2031.010 to 2031.320

ELECTRONIC HEALTH RECORD SYSTEM . . . CC §56.101

ELECTRONIC MAIL
Email generally (See EMAIL)

ELECTRONIC MEDICAL BILLING AND PAYMENT
Guides for medical billing and payment . . . 8 CCR §9792.5.1
Conformity to guide . . . 8 CCR §9792.5.3

ELECTRONIC SERVICE OF PROCESS . . . CCP §1013
Qualified medical evaluators (QMES)
Emergency regulation, COVID-19 . . . 8 CCR §36.7

ELECTRONIC TRANSACTIONS
Workers' Compensation Division fees for . . . 8 CCR §9990

ELEVATORS, ESCALATORS, CHAIR LIFTS AND OTHER CONVEYANCES
Building code standards
Compliance . . . Lab §7324
Certified competent conveyance mechanics . . . Lab §7311.2
Agricultural production, processing and handling facilities
Exemptions from requirement of certified competent conveyance mechanic . . . Lab §7311.25
Duration of certificate . . . Lab §7311.3
Experience requirement . . . Lab §7311.5
Fees for certifications . . . Lab §7311.4
Renewal of certificate . . . Lab §7311.3
Certified qualified conveyance companies . . . Lab §7311.1
Defined . . . Lab §7300.1
Duration of certificate . . . Lab §7311.3

ELEVATORS, ESCALATORS, CHAIR LIFTS AND OTHER CONVEYANCES—Cont.
Certified qualified conveyance companies —Cont.
Experience requirement . . . Lab §7311.5
Fees for certifications . . . Lab §7311.4
Renewal of certificate . . . Lab §7311.3
Construction elevators (See CONSTRUCTION ELEVATORS)
Construction of elevators, etc
Certified competent conveyance mechanics . . . Lab §7311.2
Certified qualified conveyance companies
Required . . . Lab §7311.1
Permits . . . Lab §7301.1
Penalty for proceeding without permit . . . Lab §§7302.1, 7302.2
Coverage of provisions . . . Lab §7300.2
Exclusions from coverage . . . Lab §§7300.3, 7300.4
Dangerous operation . . . Lab §7321
Enforcement . . . Lab §7321.5
Definitions . . . Lab §7300.1
Effective date for applicability . . . Lab §7324.2
Emergency certified competent conveyance mechanics
Certification
Rules . . . Lab §7301.5
Emergency regulations . . . Lab §7301.5
Exclusions from coverage . . . Lab §§7300.3, 7300.4
Exempt elevators . . . Lab §7317
Fees for inspections
Collection of . . . Lab §7314
Disposition of . . . Lab §7316
Payment of . . . Lab §7315
Reporting requirements . . . Lab §7316
Setting . . . Lab §7314
Suspension of fees . . . Lab §7314
Fire regulations . . . Lab §7301.5
Fire standards
Compliance . . . Lab §7324
Inspections and inspectors
Generally . . . Lab §§7309, 7310
Annual inspection of conveyances . . . Lab §7304
Disposition of fees . . . Lab §7316
Duration of certificate . . . Lab §7311.3
Fees for certifications . . . Lab §7311.4
Fees for inspections (See subhead: Fees for inspections)
Payment of inspection fee . . . Lab §7315
Qualifications of inspectors . . . Lab §§7309.1, 7311
Qualified conveyance inspectors of municipality, issuance of permit based on certificate of . . . Lab §7310
Renewal of certificate . . . Lab §7311.3
Requirements for inspection reports . . . Lab §7313
Requirements for inspectors . . . Lab §7311
Installation of elevators, etc
Certified competent conveyance mechanics . . . Lab §7311.2
Certified qualified conveyance companies
Required . . . Lab §7311.1
Permits . . . Lab §7301.1
Penalty for proceeding without permit . . . Lab §§7302.1, 7302.2
Liability of owners, operators, etc., of conveyances
Chapter provisions not to reduce . . . Lab §7324.1

ELEVATORS, ESCALATORS, CHAIR LIFTS AND OTHER CONVEYANCES—Cont.
Material alterations
Certified competent conveyance mechanics . . . Lab §7311.2
Agricultural production, processing and handling facilities, exemptions from requirement of certified competent conveyance mechanic . . . Lab §7311.25
Certified qualified conveyance companies
Required . . . Lab §7311.1
Permits . . . Lab §7301.1
Penalty for proceeding without permit . . . Lab §§7302.1, 7302.2
Occupational Safety and Health Appeals Board, appeal of penalty to . . . Lab §7321.5
Occupational Safety and Health Division
Authority over safety orders . . . Lab §7318
Orders of, challenging . . . Lab §7306
Penalty enforcement and appeals . . . Lab §7321.5
Power over unsafe elevators . . . Lab §7305
Procedures . . . Lab §7307
Orders
Disregarding or defacing . . . Lab §7322
Hearing on order prohibiting use of elevator . . . Lab §7322
Occupational Safety and Health Division orders, challenging . . . Lab §7306
Penalties and fines
Appeals . . . Lab §7321.5
Dangerous operation . . . Lab §7321
Enforcement . . . Lab §7321.5
Orders prohibiting use
Disregarding or defacing . . . Lab §7322
Permits
Construction, installation or material alteration, requirement of permit . . . Lab §§7302.1, 7302.2
Failure to post . . . Lab §7320
Operation without . . . Lab §§7302, 7320
Repairs or alterations
Operation while awaiting repair . . . Lab §7307
Seat for operator, failure to provide . . . Lab §7319
Unsafe operator, operation of . . . Lab §7321
Permits
Construction, installation or material alteration, requirement of permit . . . Lab §7301.1
Penalty for proceeding without permit . . . Lab §§7302.1, 7302.2
Failure to post . . . Lab §7320
Fees . . . Lab §7315
Issuance of . . . Lab §7304
Operation without . . . Lab §§7302, 7303
Misdemeanors . . . Lab §7302
Qualified conveyance inspectors of municipality, issuance based on certificate of . . . Lab §7310
Remedies for dangerous operation without . . . Lab §7303
Requirements . . . Lab §7301
Revocation of . . . Lab §7312
Temporary . . . Lab §7308
Withholding of . . . Lab §7307
Purpose of provisions . . . Lab §7300

Index

ELEVATORS, ESCALATORS, CHAIR LIFTS AND OTHER CONVEYANCES—Cont.
Remedies for dangerous operation without permit . . . Lab §7303
Repairs or alterations
Certified competent conveyance mechanics . . . Lab §7311.2
Agricultural production, processing and handling facilities, exemptions from requirement of certified competent conveyance mechanic . . . Lab §7311.25
Certified qualified conveyance companies
Required . . . Lab §7311.1
Operation while awaiting repair . . . Lab §7307
Reporting requirements
Inspection fee funds . . . Lab §7316
Inspection reports . . . Lab §7313
Retroactive application of provisions . . . Lab §7324.2
Seat for operator . . . Lab §7319
Standards for safety
Rulemaking . . . Lab §7323
Temporarily dormant elevators, dumbwaiters and escalators
Precautions . . . Lab §7300.1

EMAIL
Appeals board (WCAB)
Service by email
Time within which to act . . . 8 CCR §10605
Evidence
Writings, classification of email as . . . Ev §250
Privileged communications
Presumption of confidentiality of communication . . . Ev §917
Writings
Classification of email as . . . Ev §250

EMERGENCY AND DISASTER SERVICES
Appeals Board (WCAB)
Time
Extensions of time, public emergencies . . . 8 CCR §10370
Certification of accredited disaster councils . . . Gov §8612
COVID-19
Sick leave, paid
Supplemental paid sick leave for covered workers . . . Lab §248.1
Disclosure of medical information during disaster . . . CC §56.10
Earthquake Prediction Evaluation Council . . . Gov §8657
Emergency services
Office of emergency services . . . Gov §8585.5
Immunity
Earthquake Prediction Evaluation Council . . . Gov §8657
Public employees . . . Gov §8656
Liability
Earthquake Prediction Evaluation Council . . . Gov §8657
Immunity . . . Gov §8656
Physicians . . . Gov §8659
Privileges . . . Gov §8656
States other than California rendering aid . . . Gov §8660

EMERGENCY AND DISASTER SERVICES—Cont.
Liability—Cont.
Veterinarians . . . Gov §8659
Volunteers, damages suffered by . . . Gov §8657
Local disaster councils, authority to create . . . Gov §8610
Medical records, disclosure to disaster relief organizations . . . CC §56.10
Office of emergency services
Fire and rescue service coordinators
Post-traumatic stress injury, coverage . . . Lab §3212.15
Review of emergency plans submitted to office . . . Gov §8610
Physician's liability in state of emergency . . . Gov §8659
Privilege . . . Gov §8656
States other than California rendering aid . . . Gov §8660
Workers (See EMERGENCY AND DISASTER SERVICES WORKERS)

EMERGENCY AND DISASTER SERVICES WORKERS
Accredited disaster council . . . Lab §3211.91
Appropriated money, compensation limited to . . . Lab §4352
COVID-19
Sick leave, paid
Supplemental paid sick leave for covered workers . . . Lab §248.1
Definitions
Accredited disaster council . . . Lab §3211.91
Disaster council . . . Lab §3211.9
Disaster services . . . Lab §3211.93
Disaster service workers . . . Lab §3211.92
Eligibility for benefits . . . Lab §3600.6
Employees, not considered to be . . . Lab §3352.94
Exceptions to included activities or functions . . . Lab §3211.93a
Exclusive remedy provisions . . . Lab §4351
Maximum benefits . . . Lab §4353
Permanent disability . . . Lab §4354
Reduction in state benefits for federal benefits received . . . Lab §4355
Reserve fund . . . Lab §4352
State compensation insurance fund
Appropriated money, compensation limited to
Liability of fund when appropriated money insufficient . . . Lab §4352
Volunteers
Emergency services office, administration of provisions . . . Lab §4350
Liability for damages suffered by . . . Gov §8657
State agencies . . . Gov §8574.3
Workers deemed disaster service workers . . . Gov §8609

EMERGENCY AWARDS
Crime victims (See CRIME VICTIMS)

EMERGENCY CLOSING OF AREAS
Safe workplace
Emergency closing of areas for public health or safety menace
Directing employee to remain in or enter closed area, criminal offense . . . Lab §6311.5

EMERGENCY MEDICAL TREATMENT
COVID-19
Compensation for injury or death from COVID-19 . . . Lab §3212.87
Employer's duty to provide despite injured worker choice of physician . . . 8 CCR §9780.1

EMERGENCY PLANS
Mining and tunneling . . . Lab §7957
Refineries and chemical plants . . . Lab §7868

EMERGENCY PRECAUTIONS FOR MINES AND TUNNELS
Rescues (See MINING AND TUNNELING)

EMERGENCY REGULATIONS
Generally . . . Lab §142.4
Elevators . . . Lab §7301.5

EMOTIONAL DISTRESS
Genetic characteristics, disclosure of test results for . . . CC §56.17
Witnesses, unavailability caused by . . . Ev §240

EMPLOYEE RETIREMENT INCOME SECURITY ACT (ERISA)
Employee welfare benefit plans under ERISA
Medical claims, release of information for . . . CC §56.10
Health care coverage . . . Lab §2803.4

EMPLOYEES
Benefits, notice of right to . . . 8 CCR §15596
County (See COUNTY EMPLOYEES)
Coverage by workers' compensation division of Labor Code, effect of . . . Lab §3369
Covered persons . . . Lab §3351.5
Client employer-labor contractor responsibilities . . . Lab §2810.3
Crime victims, notice requirements for . . . Lab §3553
Death of (See DEATH OF EMPLOYEE)
Death of employer, employee's rights against estate following . . . Lab §5306
Defined (See DEFINITIONS)
Depositions
Time limits for witness examination
Exceptions for cases arising out of employment relationship . . . CCP §2025.290
Disaster services workers not considered to be . . . Lab §3352.94
Election of compensation liability with employer . . . Lab §4150
Excluded persons . . . Lab §3352
Firefighters as (See FIREFIGHTERS)
Fish and game wardens . . . Lab §3363
Hazardous substances, duties of employers regarding . . . Lab §6398
Household workers (See HOUSEHOLD EMPLOYEES)
Immigration status irrelevant to enforcement of employment law . . . Lab §1171.5
Indemnification
Performance of duties, loss sustained in . . . Lab §2802
Want of care by employer, against . . . Lab §2800

EMPLOYEES—Cont.
Information provided to
Information systems generally (See INFORMATION SYSTEMS)
Newly hired employees
Notice by employer to new hire concerning pay, allowances, payday, contact information, etc . . . Lab §2810.5
Insurance Frauds Prevention Act, civil actions brought under . . . Ins §1871.7
Law enforcement officers as (See POLICE)
Legislative provision for general welfare of . . . CA Const Art XIV §1
Liability for workers' compensation for another employee . . . Lab §3601
Liens against employer, priority of . . . Ins §1871.7
Minimum wages, legislative provision for . . . CA Const Art XIV §1
Misconduct
Injured workers, misconduct by (See MISCONDUCT)
MSDSs, access to . . . Lab §§6398, 6399
Newly hired employees
Notice by employer to new hire concerning pay, allowances, payday, contact information, etc . . . Lab §2810.5
Partners for a particular piece of work . . . Lab §3360
Payments made by . . . Lab §3751
Personal liability . . . Lab §3601
Physicians as independent contractor
Rebuttable presumption . . . Lab §2750.6
Presumption of employee status (See PRESUMPTIONS)
Rating organization personnel
Examination of . . . Ins §11752.1
Liability, exemption from . . . Ins §11759
Safe workplace issues (See SAFE WORKPLACE)
Serious and willful misconduct (See SERIOUS AND WILLFUL MISCONDUCT)
Services rendered leading to presumption regarding status . . . Lab §3357
Student work experience, community, or vocational education programs . . . Lab §3368
Survivor's rights following death of . . . Lab §2803
Watchmen not considered to be . . . Lab §3358

EMPLOYEE'S DISABILITY QUESTIONNAIRE FORM . . . 8 CCR §10161

EMPLOYEE WELFARE BENEFIT PLANS
Medical claims, release of information for . . . CC §56.10

EMPLOYERS
Advertising qualifications for advising employers, penalties for . . . Ins §703.5
Apportionment proceedings with appeals board
Liability of employer for occupational disease or cumulative injury
Instituting contribution or apportionment proceedings with board . . . Lab §5500.5
Asbestos workers
Responsible employer, identification . . . Lab §4405
Claims made against employer . . . Lab §4411
Lien procedures . . . Lab §4414
Audit by insurer . . . Ins §11760.1

Index

EMPLOYERS—Cont.
Client employer-labor contractor responsibilities . . . Lab §2810.3
Contribution proceedings with appeals board
Liability of employer for occupational disease or cumulative injury
Instituting contribution or apportionment proceedings with board . . . Lab §5500.5
Conversion coverage obligations
Availability of coverage . . . Lab §2800.3
COBRA . . . Lab §2800.2
Deferred compensation plans, employer-managed . . . Lab §2809
Defined (See DEFINITIONS)
Depositions
Time limits for witness examination
Exceptions for cases arising out of employment relationship . . . CCP §2025.290
Direct patient care providers
Personal protective equipment (PPE) stockpile, employer duties . . . Lab §6403.3
Direct recovery of compensation from . . . Lab §3753
Election of compensation liability by (See ELECTION OF COMPENSATION LIABILITY)
Employment referral services
Premium payments . . . Lab §3302
Failure to cooperate with insurer's payroll audit . . . Ins §11760.1
Firefighters not acting under immediate direction of
Local firefighters . . . Lab §3600.4
State firefighters . . . Lab §3600.1
Former private self-insured employers, obligations of . . . Lab §3702.8
Hazardous substances, duties towards employees regarding . . . Lab §6398
Health care organizations (HCOs) soliciting
Advertising (See HEALTH CARE ORGANIATIONS (HCOS))
Health care workers
Personal protective equipment (PPE) inventory
Duties of employer . . . Lab §6403.1
Indemnification of employees by
Performance of duties, loss sustained in . . . Lab §2802
Training required by employer
Patient care employees . . . Lab §2802.1
Want of care by employer, against . . . Lab §2800
Injury
Liability for . . . Lab §5500.5
Reporting requirements (See EMPLOYER'S REPORT OF OCCUPATIONAL INJURY OR ILLNESS)
Insurance (See INSURANCE)
Labor contractor-client employer responsibilities . . . Lab §2810.3
Labor contractors
Premium payments . . . Lab §3302
Law enforcement officers not acting under immediate direction of . . . Lab §3600.2
Liability
Asbestos workers
Responsible employer, identification of . . . Lab §§4405, 4411, 4414

EMPLOYERS—Cont.
Liability—Cont.
Conditions of compensation for . . . Lab §3600
Death benefits . . . Lab §§4700, 4701
Election of (See ELECTION OF COMPENSATION LIABILITY)
Household employees, injury or occupational disease of . . . Lab §5500.6
Injury . . . Lab §5500.5
Joinder of insurer, relief from liability on . . . Lab §3759
Medical evaluation costs . . . Lab §4064
Medical-legal expenses . . . Lab §4622
Occupational disease . . . Lab §5500.5
Payment of benefits . . . Lab §4550
Personal . . . Lab §3602
Substitution of insurer, relief from liability on . . . Lab §3757
Third party recovery by injured worker credited to employer liability . . . Lab §3861
Uninsured Employers Fund, to . . . Lab §3717
Longshore and Harbor Workers' Compensation Act, liability under . . . 33 USC §904
Medical examinations
Failure or refusal to submit to examination on order of employer . . . Lab §4053
Ordered by employer . . . Lab §4050
Medical information, use and disclosure by employers . . . CC §§56.10, 56.20, 56.21
Misconduct by (See MISCONDUCT)
MSDSs, duties towards employees regarding . . . Lab §§6398, 6399
Musical instruments, safeguard of . . . Lab §2800.1
Newly hired employees
Notice by employer to new hire concerning pay, allowances, payday, contact information, etc . . . Lab §2810.5
Obligations of
Contracting for labor
Funding to be sufficient for contractor to comply with labor laws . . . Lab §2810
Conversion coverage
Availability . . . Lab §§2800.3, 2807
Notification . . . Lab §2800.2
Deferred compensation plans . . . Lab §2809
Discontinuation of coverage . . . Lab §2806
ERISA requirements for health benefits . . . Lab §2803.4
Former private self-insured employers . . . Lab §3702.8
Indemnification of employees . . . Lab §§2800, 2802
Medicaid or Medi-Cal covered employees, towards . . . Lab §2803.4
Minors, health care coverage of . . . Lab §2803.5
Musical instruments, safeguard of . . . Lab §2800.1
Newly hired employees
Notice by employer to new hire concerning pay, allowances, payday, contact information, etc . . . Lab §2810.5
Survivor's rights . . . Lab §2803
Occupational disease or injury, reporting requirements regarding (See EMPLOYER'S REPORT OF OCCUPATIONAL INJURY OR ILLNESS)

EMPLOYERS—Cont.
Out-of-state, insurance certificate for . . . Lab §3600.5
Payroll audits
Audit by insurer . . . Ins §11760.1
Penalty assessments
Uninsured employers . . . Lab §3722
Personal liability . . . Lab §3602
Premium, right to information and documents regarding . . . Lab §3762
Qualified medical evaluators (QMEs)
Definition of employers . . . 8 CCR §1
Rating organizations
Classification assignment, notice of change in . . . Ins §11752.6
Release of policy information to . . . Ins §11752.6
Records
Audit by insurer
Access to records to be afforded by employer . . . Ins §11760.1
Relief from obligation to pay further compensation following judgment . . . Lab §3709.5
Rights of
Premium, right to information and documents regarding . . . Lab §3762
Subrogation of insurer to employer rights . . . Ins §11662
Writ of review following findings, employer's right to . . . 8 CCR §15591
Safe workplace issues (See SAFE WORKPLACE)
Self-insured (See SELF-INSURANCE)
Serious and willful misconduct (See SERIOUS AND WILLFUL MISCONDUCT)
Smoking in the workplace, responsibilities regarding . . . Lab §6404.5
Sponsors not considered to be . . . Lab §3301
State Compensation Insurance Fund (See STATE COMPENSATION INSURANCE FUND)
Subrogation of insurer to employer rights . . . Ins §11662
Temporary employment agencies
Premium payments . . . Lab §3302

EMPLOYER'S RECORDS OF OCCUPATIONAL INJURY OR ILLNESS . . . 8 CCR §§14300 to 14300.48
Access to records
Providing to government representatives . . . 8 CCR §14300.40
Authorized representative
Defined . . . 8 CCR §14300.46
BLS
Defined . . . 8 CCR §14300.46
Requests for data . . . 8 CCR §14300.42
Cal/OSHA
Defined . . . 8 CCR §14300.46
Cal/OSHA form 300
Defined . . . 8 CCR §14300.46
Cal/OSHA form 300A
Defined . . . 8 CCR §14300.46
Certain businesses
Partial exemption . . . 8 CCR §14300.2
Changes in ownership . . . 8 CCR §14300.34
Company
Defined . . . 8 CCR §14300.46
Covered employees . . . 8 CCR §14300.31
Defined . . . 8 CCR §14300.46

EMPLOYER'S RECORDS OF OCCUPATIONAL INJURY OR ILLNESS—Cont.
Criteria for recording . . . 8 CCR §14300.4
General recording criteria . . . 8 CCR §14300.7
Hearing loss . . . 8 CCR §14300.10
Medical removal . . . 8 CCR §14300.9
Musculoskeletal disorders . . . 8 CCR §14300.12
Needlestick injuries . . . 8 CCR §14300.8
New cases . . . 8 CCR §14300.6
Occupational hearing loss . . . 8 CCR §14300.10
Sharps injuries . . . 8 CCR §14300.8
Tuberculosis . . . 8 CCR §14300.11
Work relatedness . . . 8 CCR §14300.5
Days away from work
Criteria for recording
General recording criteria . . . 8 CCR §14300.7
Death
Criteria for recording
General recording criteria . . . 8 CCR §14300.7
Definition of fatality . . . 8 CCR §14300.46
Definitions . . . 8 CCR §14300.46
Discrimination
Reporters of injuries or illnesses, protection from discrimination . . . 8 CCR §14300.36
Educating employees to participate in system . . . 8 CCR §14300.35
Effective date of provisions . . . 8 CCR §14300.48
Electronic submission of injury or illness records to OSHA . . . 8 CCR §14300.41
Designated industries . . . 8 CCR §14300.48 Appx H
Employees covered by provisions . . . 8 CCR §14300.31
Equivalent form
Defined . . . 8 CCR §14300.46
Required elements . . . 8 CCR §§14300.48 Appx D to 14300.48 Appx F
Establishment
Defined . . . 8 CCR §14300.46
Exemptions
Certain businesses
Partial exemption . . . 8 CCR §14300.2
10 or fewer employed
Partial exemption . . . 8 CCR §14300.1
Fatality
Criteria for recording
General recording criteria . . . 8 CCR §14300.7
Defined . . . 8 CCR §14300.46
First aid
Defined . . . 8 CCR §14300.46
Forms . . . 8 CCR §14300.29
Equivalent form
Defined . . . 8 CCR §14300.46
Required elements . . . 8 CCR §§14300.48 Appx D to 14300.48 Appx F
Old forms . . . 8 CCR §14300.44
Retention and updating . . . 8 CCR §14300.33
Old forms . . . 8 CCR §14300.44
Review and correction . . . 8 CCR §14300.32
Separate form for each establishment . . . 8 CCR §14300.30
Short term establishments . . . 8 CCR §14300.30
General recording data
Defined . . . 8 CCR §14300.46
Government representatives
Access to records . . . 8 CCR §14300.40

Index

EMPLOYER'S RECORDS OF OCCUPATIONAL INJURY OR ILLNESS—Cont.
Hearing loss . . . 8 CCR §14300.10
Illness
Defined . . . 8 CCR §14300.46
Incident report
Injury and illness incident report . . . 8 CCR §14300.48 Appx C
Injury
Defined . . . 8 CCR §14300.46
Involvement of employees . . . 8 CCR §14300.35
Job transfer
Criteria for recording
General recording criteria . . . 8 CCR §14300.7
Defined . . . 8 CCR §14300.46
Labor statistics, bureau of
Definition of BLS . . . 8 CCR §14300.46
Requests for data . . . 8 CCR §14300.42
Log of work-related injuries and illnesses . . . 8 CCR §14300.48 Appx A
Loss of consciousness
Criteria for recording
General recording criteria . . . 8 CCR §14300.7
Medical removals . . . 8 CCR §14300.9
Medical treatment
Criteria for recording
General recording criteria . . . 8 CCR §14300.7
Defined . . . 8 CCR §14300.46
Mine safety and health act (federal)
Employees covered by act . . . 8 CCR §14300.47
Multiple agencies, recordkeeping for
Memorandum of understanding for OSHA to accept records compiled for another agency . . . 8 CCR §14300.3
Multiple establishments
Separate form for each establishment . . . 8 CCR §14300.30
Musculoskeletal disorders . . . 8 CCR §14300.12
Needlestick injuries . . . 8 CCR §14300.8
New cases
Defined . . . 8 CCR §14300.46
Determination of whether case is a new case . . . 8 CCR §14300.6
Occupational hearing loss . . . 8 CCR §14300.10
OSHA
Defined . . . 8 CCR §14300.46
Ownership changes . . . 8 CCR §14300.34
Personal representative
Defined . . . 8 CCR §14300.46
Physician or other licensed health care professional
Defined . . . 8 CCR §14300.46
Pre-existing condition
Defined . . . 8 CCR §14300.46
Privacy concern case
Defined . . . 8 CCR §14300.46
Purpose of rule . . . 8 CCR §14300
Recordable
Defined . . . 8 CCR §14300.46
Report
Injury and illness incident report . . . 8 CCR §14300.48 Appx C
Restricted work
Criteria for recording
General recording criteria . . . 8 CCR §14300.7

EMPLOYER'S RECORDS OF OCCUPATIONAL INJURY OR ILLNESS—Cont.
Restricted work—Cont.
Defined . . . 8 CCR §14300.46
Retaliatory discrimination
Reporters of injury or illness, protection from discrimination . . . 8 CCR §14300.36
Retention of forms . . . 8 CCR §14300.33
Old forms . . . 8 CCR §14300.44
Routine functions
Defined . . . 8 CCR §14300.46
Sharps injuries . . . 8 CCR §14300.8
Short term establishments
Forms . . . 8 CCR §14300.30
Significant illness or injury
Defined . . . 8 CCR §14300.46
Significant work
Defined . . . 8 CCR §14300.46
Summary of recorded entries . . . 8 CCR §14300.32
Annual summary . . . 8 CCR §14300.48 Appx B
2001 data . . . 8 CCR §14300.43
Worksheet to help fill out summary . . . 8 CCR §14300.48 Appx G
Survey
Annual OSHA injury and illness survey . . . 8 CCR §14300.41
10 or fewer employed
Partial exemption . . . 8 CCR §14300.1
Transfer to another job
Criteria for recording
General recording criteria . . . 8 CCR §14300.7
Definition of job transfer . . . 8 CCR §14300.46
Tuberculosis . . . 8 CCR §14300.11
2001 data
Posting . . . 8 CCR §14300.43
Updating of forms . . . 8 CCR §14300.33
Old forms . . . 8 CCR §14300.44
Variances . . . 8 CCR §14300.38
Work environment
Defined . . . 8 CCR §14300.46
Work relatedness . . . 8 CCR §14300.5
Worksheet to help fill out summary . . . 8 CCR §14300.48 Appx G
You
Defined . . . 8 CCR §14300.46

EMPLOYER'S REPORT OF OCCUPATIONAL INJURY OR ILLNESS
Admissibility . . . Lab §6412
Reproduction of . . . 8 CCR §14005
Responsibilities of employer regarding . . . 8 CCR §14001, Lab §6409.1
Sample copy of Form 5020 . . . 8 CCR §14004

EMPLOYMENT
Defined (See DEFINITIONS)
Prisoners (See PRISONERS)
Public (See PUBLIC EMPLOYMENT)
Termination of (See TERMINATION OF EMPLOYMENT)

EMPLOYMENT AGENCIES, TEMPORARY
Client employer-labor contractor responsibilities . . . Lab §2810.3

EMPLOYMENT AGENCIES, TEMPORARY—Cont.
Discrimination
Definition of employment agency . . . Gov §12926
Labor law compliance
Funding in contract to be sufficient for contractor to comply with labor laws . . . Lab §2810
Premium payments . . . Lab §3302

EMPLOYMENT CONTRACTS
Defined . . . Lab §2750

EMPLOYMENT DEVELOPMENT DEPARTMENT
Client employer-labor contractor responsibilities
Rulemaking to enforce provisions . . . Lab §2810.3
Director
Voluntary disability benefit plans (See VOLUNTARY DISABILITY BENEFIT PLANS)
Labor contractor-client employer responsibilities
Rulemaking to enforce provisions . . . Lab §2810.3

EMPLOYMENT DISCRIMINATION . . . Gov §12940
Client employer-labor contractor responsibilities
Retaliation for reporting violations . . . Lab §2810.3
Day programs
Action for harassment or discrimination by employees of nonprofit sheltered workshops, day programs or rehabilitation facilities . . . Gov §12926.05
Definitions . . . Gov §12926
Employment agencies
Defined . . . Gov §12926
Labor contractor-client employer responsibilities
Retaliation for reporting violations . . . Lab §2810.3
Medical condition as including genetic characteristics . . . Gov §12926
Rehabilitation facilities
Action for harassment or discrimination by employees of nonprofit sheltered workshops, day programs or rehabilitation facilities . . . Gov §12926.05
Religious entities, limitation on exemptions . . . Gov §12926.2
Sheltered workshops
Action for harassment or discrimination by employees of nonprofit sheltered workshops, day programs or rehabilitation facilities . . . Gov §12926.05
Sick days, paid
Discrimination or retaliation for using sick days . . . Lab §246.5

EMPLOYMENT REFERRAL SERVICES (See REFERRALS AND REFERRAL SERVICES)

EMPLOYMENT RELATIONSHIP
Cheerleaders for professional sports teams classified as employees . . . Lab §2754
Contracts of employment defined . . . Lab §2750
Course of trade, business, profession, or occupation . . . Lab §3355
Definition of employment (See DEFINITIONS)
Disability benefits (See DISABILITY BENEFITS)
Physicians as independent contractors
Rebuttable presumption . . . Lab §2750.6

EMPLOYMENT RELATIONSHIP—Cont.
Scope of Division of . . . Lab §2700
Services rendered leading to presumption regarding . . . Lab §3357
Trade, business, profession, or occupation . . . Lab §3356
Workers, rebuttable presumption of employee status of . . . Lab §2750.5

EN BANC DECISIONS . . . 8 CCR §10325

ENFORCEMENT
Building and construction industry requirements (See BUILDING AND CONSTRUCTION INDUSTRY)
Fair Labor Standards Act (FLSA) . . . Lab §50.6
Industrial Relations Department (See INDUSTRIAL RELATIONS DEPARTMENT)
Labor Standards Enforcement Division (See LABOR STANDARDS ENFORCEMENT DIVISION)
Nonjudicial foreclosure in enforcement of judgment against uninsured employer . . . Lab §3716.3
Occupational Safety and Health Division, by (See OCCUPATIONAL SAFETY AND HEALTH DIVISION)
Occupational Safety and Health Standards Board . . . Lab §§50.7, 144
Subrogation
Judgment lien by employer against third party, enforcement of . . . Lab §3862
State Teachers' Retirement System . . . Ed §24502
Third party, enforcement of judgment lien by employer against . . . Lab §3862
Uninsured employer, enforcement of judgment against . . . Lab §3716.3
Workers' Compensation Division, by . . . Lab §124

ENGLISH LANGUAGE
Judicial notice of English language . . . Ev §451

ENTERTAINMENT INDUSTRY
Occupational Safety and Health Division permit requirements . . . Lab §6500

ERGONOMICS
Legislative concern over repetitive motion injuries . . . Lab §6719
Occupational Safety and Health Standards Board to adopt standard for . . . Lab §6357

ERISA (EMPLOYEE RETIREMENT INCOME SECURITY ACT)
Health care coverage . . . Lab §2803.4

ESCALATOR SAFETY . . . Lab §§7300 to 7324.2
Generally (See ELEVATORS, ESCALATORS, CHAIR LIFTS AND OTHER CONVEYANCES)

ESCAPE CHAMBERS AND ROUTES FROM MINES AND TUNNELS
Rescues (See MINING AND TUNNELING)

ESTIMATED WORK INJURY CLAIMS
Reporting requirements for self-insurers . . . 8 CCR §§15300, 15301, 15303

ESTOPPEL (See COLLATERAL ESTOPPEL)

Index

ETHICAL REQUIREMENTS
Advisory committee on ethics
Composition and duties of . . . 8 CCR §9722
Investigations of ethical lapses by . . . 8 CCR §9722.1
Health care organization (HCO) grants or bonuses in aid of solicitation of employers . . . 8 CCR §9771.61
Interpreters
Standards for interpreters . . . Lab §5811
Judges (WCJs) . . . 8 CCR §§9720.1 to 9723
Administrative Director of Workers' Compensation Division
Investigations of ethical lapses by . . . 8 CCR §9722.1
Request for opinion of . . . 8 CCR §9723
Advisory Committee on ethics . . . 8 CCR §9722
Authority regarding . . . 8 CCR §9720.1
Code of conduct for . . . 8 CCR §9721.1, Lab §123.6
Definitions pertinent to . . . 8 CCR §9720.2
Disclosures of conflicts of interest . . . 8 CCR §9721.11
Manner of disclosure . . . 8 CCR §9721.14
Disqualification
Factors not considered grounds for disqualification . . . 8 CCR §9721.13
Grounds . . . 8 CCR §9721.12
Educational programs, financial interests in . . . 8 CCR §9721.31
Gifts . . . 8 CCR §9721.2
Honoraria . . . 8 CCR §9721.2
Investigations of ethical lapses
Commencing . . . 8 CCR §9722.1
Entities investigating . . . 8 CCR §9722.2
Other investigations, article not affecting . . . 8 CCR §9723
Investments
Restrictions on investments . . . 8 CCR §9721.21
Previously earned compensation . . . 8 CCR §9721.33
Reporting ethical violations, duty . . . 8 CCR §9721.32
Rights and obligations, article not affecting . . . 8 CCR §9723
Travel . . . 8 CCR §9721.2
Medical examinations by QMEs . . . 8 CCR §41
Workers' Compensation advisory committee on ethics
Composition and duties of . . . 8 CCR §9722
Investigations of ethical lapses by . . . 8 CCR §9722.1

EVALUATIONS (See TESTS, EXAMINATIONS, AND EVALUATIONS)

EVIDENCE
Admissibility
Generally (See ADMISSIBILITY OF EVIDENCE)
Hearing, admissibility at . . . Lab §5703
Appeals board (WCAB)
Evidence before
Documentary evidence . . . 8 CCR §10670
Benefits paid
Computer printout of benefits paid
Service of copies of documents, electronic media, etc, offered into evidence . . . 8 CCR §10635

EVIDENCE—Cont.
Best and secondary evidence
Microphotographed files, records, photographs, etc., in custody of criminal justice agency
Reproductions, admissibility . . . Ev §1550.1
Business records
Generally . . . Ev §1550
Admissibility of copies and affidavits . . . Ev §1562
Affidavit accompanying . . . Ev §§1561, 1562
Applicable proceedings . . . Ev §1566
Copies . . . Ev §§1560, 1562
Definitions pertinent to . . . Ev §1560
Fees and costs of witnesses and custodians involved in production . . . Ev §1563
Hearsay rule . . . Ev §§1270 to 1272
Production of . . . Ev §1560
Subpoena of
Custodian as witness of service of . . . Ev §1565
Transmittal of copies . . . Ev §1560
Support obligations, proceedings related to . . . Ev §1567
Witnesses and custodians (See WITNESSES)
Certified copies of reports
Documentary evidence, admissibility . . . 8 CCR §10670
Computer printouts . . . Ev §1552
Benefits paid
Service of copies of documents, electronic media, etc, offered into evidence . . . 8 CCR §10635
Degree of proof required . . . Ev §115
Depositions
Use of deposition as evidence . . . CCP §2025.620
Destroyed written evidence . . . Ev §1551
Digital medium, printed representation of . . . Ev §1553
Documentary evidence
Appeals board (WCAB)
Conference, submission at . . . 8 CCR §10761
Definitions . . . Ev §250
Service of copies of documents, electronic media, etc, offered into evidence . . . 8 CCR §10635
Lien claimants who are not physicians, service on . . . 8 CCR §10637
Writing
Defined . . . Ev §250
Electronic adjudication management system (EAMS)
Summary of evidence
Retention, return and destruction of records . . . 8 CCR §10208.7
Employer records
Service, ongoing duty . . . 8 CCR §10635
Filing of documents
Effect as evidence
Receipt in evidence of filing required . . . 8 CCR §10670
Formal permanent disability rating determinations as . . . 8 CCR §10158
Fraud, petition for reconsideration presenting evidence of . . . 8 CCR §10974
Injury . . . Lab §3600
Laying foundation
Privileged matter, claim of . . . Ev §914
Lost written evidence . . . Ev §1551
Medical reports (See MEDICAL REPORTS)

EVIDENCE—Cont.
Medical treatment utilization schedule
Evidence-based medicine (EBM) as basis . . . 8 CCR §9792.21
Definition of evidence-based medicine (EBM) . . . 8 CCR §9792.20
Evaluation of medical evidence, definitions . . . 8 CCR §9792.25
Evaluation of medical evidence, medical evidence evaluation advisory commission . . 8 CCR §9792.26
Evaluation of medical evidence, methodology . . . 8 CCR §9792.25.1
Microphotographed files, records, photographs, etc., in custody of criminal justice agency
Reproductions, admissibility . . . Ev §1550.1
New evidence, petition for reconsideration presenting . . . 8 CCR §10974
Notice, taken without . . . 8 CCR §10672
Permanent disability rating determinations
Formal determinations . . . 8 CCR §10675
Physicians' reports as evidence . . . 8 CCR §10682
Ongoing duty to serve . . . 8 CCR §10635
Service of copies of documents, electronic media, etc, offered into evidence . . . 8 CCR §10635
Lien claimants who are not physicians, service on . . . 8 CCR §10637
Preponderance of the evidence standard
Conditions of employer liability for compensation . . . Lab §3600
Worker's compensation division of Labor Code . . . Lab §3202.5
Qualified medical evaluator's (QME's) report . . . 8 CCR §10683
Records
Appeals board (WCAB)
Exhibits generally . . . 8 CCR §10677
Rejection of QME's report . . . 8 CCR §10683
Reports
Qualified medical evaluator's (QME's) report . . . 8 CCR §10683
Specified additional evidence . . . Lab §5703
Reproduction of documents . . . 8 CCR §10680
Service, proof of . . . CCP §1013
Specified additional evidence allowed . . . Lab §5703
Stipulations . . . Lab §5702
Subrogation action by employer alone, evidence of amount paid in cases of . . . Lab §3854
Summary
Preparation at conclusion of trial . . . 8 CCR §10787
Waiver of summary of evidence . . . 8 CCR §10787
Unavailability of witness due to trauma, expert testimony establishing . . . Ev §240
Video medium, printed representation of . . . Ev §1553
Vocational experts
Evidentiary effect of reports of vocational experts . . . 8 CCR §10685
Waiver of summary . . . 8 CCR §10787
Witnesses (See WITNESSES)
Written evidence
Business records (See subhead: Business records)
Computer information, printed representation of . . . Ev §1552

EVIDENCE—Cont.
Written evidence—Cont.
Destroyed . . . Ev §1551
Lost . . . Ev §1551
Video or digital medium, printed representation of . . . Ev §1553
X-rays (See X-RAYS)

EXAMINATIONS (See TESTS, EXAMINATIONS, AND EVALUATIONS)

EXCAVATIONS
Bids for local government projects involving . . . Lab §6707
Swimming pool excavations . . . Lab §6705.5
Trench excavations (See TRENCH EXCAVATIONS)

EXCLUSIVE REMEDY . . . Lab §3601
Disaster service workers . . . Lab §4351
Economic Opportunity Programs . . . Lab §4208
Exceptions . . . Lab §3602
Longshore and Harbor Workers' Compensation Act . . . 33 USC §905
Nonappropriated fund instrumentalities, non-citizen non-resident employees of . . . 5 USC §8172
United States, tort claims against . . . 28 USC §2679

EXECUTORS AND ADMINISTRATORS
Medical information
Release by . . . CC §§56.11, 56.21
Release to . . . CC §56.1007

EXHAUST PURIFIER DEVICES
Internal combustion engines . . . Lab §6702

EXHIBITS
Appeals board (WCAB) . . . 8 CCR §10677
Filing and listing of exhibits
Proposed exhibits . . . 8 CCR §10620
Electronic adjudication management system (EAMS)
Court administrator rules
Retention, return and destruction . . . 8 CCR §10208.7

EXPEDITED HEARINGS . . . Lab §5502
Electronic adjudication management system (EAMS)
Declaration of readiness to proceed to expedited hearing
Defined . . . 8 CCR §10205
Filing request for
Form for request . . . 8 CCR §10208.3
Setting hearing . . . 8 CCR §10782

EXPERIENCE RATING
Availability of information on . . . Ins §11752.7
Required provisions of plan . . . Ins §11736
Revision of . . . Ins §11751.9
Uniform plan, adherence to . . . Ins §11734

EXPERT AND OPINION EVIDENCE
Appeals board (WCAB)
Vocational experts
Evidentiary effect of reports of vocational experts . . . 8 CCR §10685

EXPERT AND OPINION EVIDENCE—Cont.
Deposition of listed expert witness
  Time limits for witness examination . . . CCP §2025.290
Discovery
  Simultaneous information exchange, discovery by
    Methods of discovery . . . CCP §2019.010
Lists of expert witnesses
  Discovery by simultaneous information exchange
    Methods of discovery . . . CCP §2019.010
Simultaneous information exchange about expert witnesses, discovery by means of
  Deposition of expert witness
    Workers' compensation cases, fees . . . CCP §2034.430
  Methods of discovery . . . CCP §2019.010
Vocational experts
  Fee schedule
    Establishment by administrative director . . . Lab §5307.7
  Reports
    Admissibility . . . 8 CCR §10685, Lab §5703

EXPLOSIVES
Generally . . . Lab §6710
Mining and tunneling (See MINING AND TUNNELING)
Snow avalanche blasting . . . Lab §6711

EXTENDED LEAVE FOR SCHOOL DISTRICT EMPLOYEES
Generally . . . Ed §44977
Salary deductions . . . Ed §44983

EXTRAHAZARDOUS MINES AND TUNNELS (See MINING AND TUNNELING)

EYES
Medical treatment
  Utilization schedule . . . 8 CCR §9792.23.9
Presumption of total disability due to loss of . . . Lab §4662
Temporary disability
  Aggregate disability payments
    Single injury . . . Lab §4656

F

FAIR EMPLOYMENT AND HOUSING
Definitions . . . Gov §§12925 to 12926.2
Employees, personal liability for harassment . . . Gov §12940
Genetic characteristic, testing for as unlawful employment practice . . . Gov §12940

FAIR LABOR STANDARDS ACT (FLSA)
Department of Industrial Relations responsibility for enforcement of . . . Lab §50.6
Nonappropriated fund instrumentalities, employees of . . . 5 USC §2105

FALSE IMPRISONMENT
Invasion of privacy
  False imprisonment with intent to capture visual image or sound recording . . . CC §1708.8

FAMILY CARE LEAVE, PAID
Activities of daily living
  Defined . . . UI §3302.2
Application for benefits . . . UI §3308
Benefits in accord with provisions . . . UI §3304
Care provider
  Defined . . . UI §3302
Care recipient
  Defined . . . UI §3302
  Examination to determine eligibility of care provider . . . UI §3306
  Same recipient
    Disability benefit period for same recipient . . . UI §3302.1
Child
  Defined . . . UI §3302
Claims
  Time to file . . . UI §3301
Covered active duty
  Defined . . . UI §3302.1
  Qualifying exigency . . . UI §3307
    Defined . . . UI §3302.2
    Information in support of request for leave due to qualifying exigency . . . UI §3307
Definitions . . . UI §3302
Disability benefit period
  Defined . . . UI §3302.1
Domestic partner
  Defined . . . UI §3302
Double dipping
  Restrictions on eligibility . . . UI §3303.1
Eligibility . . . UI §3303
  Evidence . . . UI §3306
  Restrictions . . . UI §3303.1
False certifications as to medical condition, penalty . . . UI §3305
Family care leave
  Defined . . . UI §3302
Family medical leave act (FMLA)
  Concurrent leave with FMLA and CFRA . . . UI §3303.1
Family member
  Defined . . . UI §3302
Grandchild
  Defined . . . UI §3302
Grandparents
  Defined . . . UI §3302
Legislative findings . . . UI §3300
Maximum payable . . . UI §3301
Military
  Covered active duty
    Defined . . . UI §3302.1
    Information in support of request for leave due to qualifying exigency . . . UI §3307
    Qualifying exigency . . . UI §§3302.2, 3307
  Military members
    Defined . . . UI §3302
Parent
  Defined . . . UI §3302
Parent-in-law
  Defined . . . UI §3302
Pregnancy
  Disability benefit period . . . UI §3302.1

FAMILY CARE LEAVE, PAID—Cont.
Purpose of provisions . . . UI §3301
Qualifying exigency
Defined . . . UI §3302.2
Information in support of request for leave due to qualifying exigency . . . UI §3307
Serious health condition
Defined . . . UI §3302
Evidence of existence . . . UI §3306
Siblings
Defined . . . UI §3302
Spouse
Defined . . . UI §3302
Twelve-month period
Defined . . . UI §3302
Vacation leave
Conditioning eligibility on using 2 weeks . . . UI §3303.1
Valid claim
Defined . . . UI §3302
Weekly benefit amount . . . UI §3301

FAMILY MEDICAL LEAVE ACT (FMLA)
Family care leave, paid
Concurrent leave with FMLA and CFRA . . . UI §3303.1

FAMILY MEMBERS
Aliens, uninsured employers fund and subsequent injuries fund benefits for . . . 8 CCR §15740
State Compensation Insurance Fund policies . . . Ins §11843

FAMILY RIGHTS ACT
Family care leave, paid
Concurrent leave with FMLA and CFRA . . . UI §3303.1

FAMILY THERAPISTS
Treatment of injuries by . . . Lab §3209.8

FARM LABOR CONTRACTS
Labor law compliance
Funding in contract to be sufficient for contractor to comply with labor laws . . . Lab §2810

FARM LABOR VEHICLE
Transportation of passengers in unsafe vehicle . . . Veh §31403
Unsafe condition
Notice of . . . Veh §31402
Operation following notice of . . . Veh §31402
Transportation of passengers in unsafe vehicle . . . Veh §31403

FAX
Electronic adjudication management system (EAMS)
Definition of fax . . . 8 CCR §10205
Evidence
Writings, classification of fax transmissions as . . . Ev §250
Privileged communications
Presumption of confidentiality of communication . . . Ev §917

FAX—Cont.
Service by fax . . . CCP §1013
Appeals Board (WCAB)
Time within which to act . . . 8 CCR §10605
Writings
Classification of fax transmissions as . . . Ev §250

FEATHERBEDDING PROHIBITIONS (See RAILROADS)

FEDERAL GOVERNMENT AND LAW
ADA
Physical disability . . . Gov §§12926, 12926.1
Buildings, works, etc., of federal government
Applicability of state workers' compensation laws to . . . 40 USC §3172
Civil procedure, judicial notice of federal rules of . . . Ev §451
Criminal procedure, judicial notice of rules of . . . Ev §451
Economic opportunity program enrollees, medical treatment and benefits available to (See ECONOMIC OPPORTUNITY PROGRAMS)
Emergency and disaster services workers
Reduction in state benefits for federal benefits received . . . Lab §4355
ERISA, health care coverage under . . . Lab §2803.4
Judicial notice of federal laws . . . Ev §§451, 452
Longshore and Harbor Workers' Compensation Act (See LONGSHORE AND HARBOR WORKERS' COMPENSATION ACT)
Nonappropriated fund instrumentalities, employees of (See NONAPPROPRIATED FUND INSTRUMENTALITIES)
Shipping
United States vessels or cargo, suits in admiralty involving . . . 46 USC §§30901 to 30913 (See SHIPPING)
Shipping suits involving U.Svessels or cargo (See SHIPPING)
State Compensation Insurance Fund claims (See STATE COMPENSATION INSURANCE FUND)
Stevedores, federal in lieu of state benefits for . . . Har&N §6869
Targeted jobs tax credit for vocational rehabilitation . . . W&I §19005.5
Taxcs
Exclusions from gross income . . . 26 USC §§101, 104
Levy . . . 26 USC §6334
Liens . . . 26 USC §6323
Territories and possessions of United States, common carriers by railroad in . . . 45 USC §52
Tort claims (See TORT CLAIMS AGAINST UNITED STATES)
United States as defendant
Tort claims (See TORT CLAIMS AGAINST UNITED STATES)
Venue . . . 28 USC §1402
United States as party
Attorneys' fees
Generally . . . 28 USC §2412
Tort claims . . . 28 USC §2678
Court costs . . . 28 USC §2412

Index

FEDERAL GOVERNMENT AND LAW—Cont.
United States as party—Cont.
Defendant, US as
Jurisdiction . . . 28 USC §1346
Jury trials . . . 28 USC §2402
Shipping (See SHIPPING)
Time for commencing action against . . . 28 USC §2401

FEE-FOR-SERVICE ARRANGEMENTS
Health care organizations (HCOs) . . . 8 CCR §9771.75

FEES
Appeals Board (WCAB)
Hearing transcripts . . . 8 CCR §10800
Interpreters . . . Lab §5811
Limitations . . . Lab §5811
Witnesses . . . Lab §131
Arbitration fees and costs, disputes over . . . 8 CCR §10920
Boilers (See TANKS AND BOILERS)
Comprehensive medical-legal evaluation expense fees, reasonableness . . . 8 CCR §9795
Copy and related services fees
Establishing schedule . . . Lab §5307.9
Crane certifiers, examination and licensing of . . . Lab §7380
Elevators, escalators, chair lifts and other conveyances (See ELEVATORS, ESCALATORS, CHAIR LIFTS AND OTHER CONVEYANCES)
Group self-insurance
Certificates to self-insure
Application for certificate to self-insure . . . 8 CCR §15491
Health care organizations (HCOs) (See HEALTH CARE ORGANIATIONS (HCOS))
Home health care services
Services not covered by Medicare or official medical fee schedule . . . Lab §5307.8
Independent medical review
Reviewers, fees for . . . 8 CCR §9768.15
Interpreter services (See INTERPRETERS)
Liens
Activation fees . . . Lab §4903.06
Reimbursement . . . Lab §4903.07
Filing fees . . . Lab §4903.05
Reimbursement . . . Lab §4903.07
Medical-legal expenses (See MEDICAL-LEGAL EXPENSES)
Medical services contracts obtained via false statements . . . Lab §3219
Medical treatment, fee schedule for (See MEDICAL TREATMENT)
Occupational Safety and Health Division permits . . . Lab §6507
Official medical fee schedule . . . Lab §5307.1
Qualified medical evaluators (QMEs) (See QUALIFIED MEDICAL EVALUATORS (QMES))
Rating organizations
Licensing fees . . . Ins §§11751, 11751.25
Public hearings . . . Ins §11751.55
Reasonableness of medical-legal evaluation expense fees . . . 8 CCR §9795

FEES—Cont.
Refineries and chemical plants . . . Lab §7870
Schedules, charts, and tables of (See SCHEDULES, CHARTS, AND TABLES)
Self-insurance
Certificate to administer claims . . . 8 CCR §15454
Certificate to self-insure, filing application for . . . 8 CCR §15204
Private sector license fee assessment . . . 8 CCR §15230
Public sector license fee assessment . . . 8 CCR §15231
Tanks (See TANKS AND BOILERS)
Vocational expert fee schedule
Establishment by administrative director . . . Lab §5307.7
Vocational rehabilitation, fee schedule for . . . Lab §139.5
Witnesses (See WITNESSES)
Workers' Compensation Division (See WORKERS' COMPENSATION DIVISION)

FIDELITY BONDS
Health care organizations (HCOs) . . . 8 CCR §9771.73

FIELD SANITATION
Occupational Safety and Health Division requirements . . . Lab §6712

FILES
Claim files (See CLAIM FILES)

FILING
Adjudication of claims (See ADJUDICATION OF CLAIMS)
Advertising
Health care organizations (HCOs) . . . 8 CCR §9771.65
Industrial Medical Council rules
Documents, filing . . . 8 CCR §151
Appeal of notice of penalty assessment order . . . 8 CCR §10115.1
Appeals Board (WCAB) (See APPEALS BOARD (WCAB))
Assassinated public officials, death benefit claims for . . . Lab §4724
Claims for benefits
Assassinated public officials, death benefit claims for . . . Lab §4724
Procedures . . . Lab §5501
Time limits . . . Lab §5404
Compromise and release, filing form for . . . Lab §5002
Direction to file verified statement
Contents . . . 8 CCR §15576
Defined . . . 8 CCR §15551
Discrimination against injured workers filing complaints with Occupational Safety and Health Division . . . Lab §6310
Dividend payments to insurance policyholders . . . Ins §11739
Electronic adjudication management system (EAMS)
Definition of filing . . . 8 CCR §10205
File
Definition of file . . . 8 CCR §10205
Optical character recognition (OCR) forms
Defined . . . 8 CCR §10205

FILING—Cont.
Electronic adjudication management system (EAMS)—Cont.
Retention, return and destruction of records . . . 8 CCR §10208.7
Health care organization (HCO) advertising and disclosure forms . . . 8 CCR §9771.65
Insurance
Dividend payments to insurance policyholders . . . Ins §11739
Rate information and plans . . . Ins §11735
Self-insurance filing failures, penalties and fines for
Late filing . . . Lab §3702.5
Reporting requirements, failure to meet . . . 8 CCR §15251, Lab §3702.3
Judicial review (See JUDICIAL REVIEW)
Labor Standards Enforcement Division (See LABOR STANDARDS ENFORCEMENT DIVISION)
Longshore and Harbor Workers' Compensation Act claims . . . 33 USC §913
Material safety data sheet (MSDS)
Industrial Relations Department, copy sent to . . . Lab §6394
Trade secrets, protection from disclosure of . . . Lab §6394
Occupational Safety and Health Appeals Board
Suspension of decision by filing for reconsideration . . . Lab §6625
Writ of mandate . . . Lab §§6627, 6631
Occupational Safety and Health Division, discrimination against injured workers filing complaints with . . . Lab §6310
Penalties and fines for failure to file
Self-insurance
Late filing . . . Lab §3702.5
Reporting requirements, failure to meet . . . 8 CCR §15251, Lab §3702.3
Penalty assessment orders, appeal of notice of . . . 8 CCR §10115.1
Permanent disability
Electronic adjudication management system (EAMS) . . . 8 CCR §10151
Electronic filing exemption . . . 8 CCR §10151.1
Misfiled or misdirected documents . . . 8 CCR §10150.4
Requirements . . . 8 CCR §10151
Retention of files . . . 8 CCR §10150.3
Technical problems . . . 8 CCR §10150.2
Prisoners, report of injury to
Department of Corrections Report of Injury Form 5030, time of filing . . . 8 CCR §14904
Physician or surgeon report, Form 5031, time of filing . . . 8 CCR §14913
Return to work programs . . . 8 CCR §10116.1
Converting paper files to electronic . . . 8 CCR §10116.6
Electronic filing exemption . . . 8 CCR §10116.2
Incomplete filings . . . 8 CCR §10116.3
Injury or findings required to file . . . 8 CCR §10116.8
Misfiled or misdirected documents . . . 8 CCR §10116.7
Retention of files . . . 8 CCR §10116.6
Technical problems with filing . . . 8 CCR §10116.5

FILING—Cont.
Safe workplace complaints, discrimination against injured workers filing . . . Lab §6310
Self-insurance filing failures, penalties and fines for
Late filing . . . Lab §3702.5
Reporting requirements, failure to meet . . . 8 CCR §15251, Lab §3702.3
Supplemental job displacement benefits . . . 8 CCR §10116.1
Converting paper files to electronic . . . 8 CCR §10116.6
Electronic filing exemption . . . 8 CCR §10116.2
Incomplete filings . . . 8 CCR §10116.3
Injury or findings required to file . . . 8 CCR §10116.8
Misfiled or misdirected documents . . . 8 CCR §10116.7
Retention of files . . . 8 CCR §10116.6
Technical problems with filing . . . 8 CCR §10116.5
Suspension of order by filing petition for reconsideration
Appeals Board (WCAB) . . . Lab §5910
Occupational Safety and Health Appeals Board . . . Lab §6625
Uninsured Employers Fund
Procedures for cases involving . . . Lab §3714
Weekend or holiday filing rule . . . Lab §3730
Verified statement, direction to file
Contents . . . 8 CCR §15576
Defined . . . 8 CCR §15551

FILM INDUSTRY
Occupational Safety and Health Division permit requirements . . . Lab §6500

FINANCE DEPARTMENT (STATE)
State Compensation Insurance Fund, master agreement with . . . Lab §§6111, 6112

FINANCE INDUSTRY
Employer's records of occupational injury or illness
Partial exemption from requirements . . . 8 CCR §14300.2

FINANCIAL STATEMENTS
Self-insurers required to submit . . . 8 CCR §15203.2

FINDINGS
Appeals Board (WCAB) (See APPEALS BOARD (WCAB))
Arbitration . . . Lab §5277
Industrial Relations Department reporting requirements as to clinical and research findings . . . Lab §50.8
Insurer bound by findings against employer . . . Ins §11654
Labor Standards Enforcement Division (See LABOR STANDARDS ENFORCEMENT DIVISION)
Occupational Safety and Health Appeals Board . . . Lab §6608
Penalty assessment orders
Appeal of notice of penalty assessment, notice of findings on . . . 8 CCR §10115.2
Notice of findings on . . . 8 CCR §15556
Writ of review following findings confirming or modifying, employer's right to . . . 8 CCR §15591
Qualified medical evaluators (QMEs)
Summary form for QME . . . 8 CCR §111
Reconsideration of (See RECONSIDERATION)

FINDINGS—Cont.
Stipulations
Effect of stipulations . . . 8 CCR §10835
Stop order, notice of findings on . . . 8 CCR §15554
Treating physician
Bias, finding of . . . Lab §4068

FINES (See PENALTIES AND FINES)

FIRE
Mining and tunneling (See MINING AND TUNNELING)
Volatile flammable liquids (See VOLATILE FLAMMABLE LIQUIDS)

FIRE AND RESCUE SERVICE COORDINATORS
Cancer, presumption as to arising out of and in course of employment . . . Lab §3212.1

FIREFIGHTERS
Advanced disability pension payments . . . Lab §4850.3
Grounds for denying payment . . . Lab §4850.4
Average weekly earnings . . . Lab §§4458, 4458.5
Cancer . . . Lab §3212.1
County employees
Contributions from temporarily incapacitated members . . . Gov §32338
Performing duty not under direction of employer . . . Gov §50926
COVID-19
Compensation for injury or death from COVID-19 . . . Lab §3212.87
Death benefits
Generally . . . Lab §4856
Continued health benefits to surviving spouse and dependents . . . Lab §4856
Scholarships for dependents of deceased firefighters . . . Lab §4709
Defined . . . Lab §3211.5
Employee status
Persons engaged in suppressing fires . . . Lab §3365
Technical assistants . . . Lab §3367
Volunteer firefighters . . . Lab §§3361, 3365
Employer's immediate direction, not acting under
Local firefighters . . . Lab §3600.4
State firefighters . . . Lab §3600.1
Entitlement to benefits . . . Lab §4850.7
Firefighting vehicles
Exposure to carcinogenic materials by mechanics who repair and clean vehicles
Study and report . . . Lab §77.7
Garment manufacturing hazards, report of . . . Lab §6409.5
Heart disease . . . Lab §§3212, 3212.4
Hepatitis . . . Lab §3212.8
Hernias . . . Lab §§3212, 3212.4
Justice Department employees (See JUSTICE DEPARTMENT)
Juvenile wards of court engaged in fire suppression work, age limits on . . . W&I §883
Medical treatment . . . Lab §4852
Meningitis . . . Lab §3212.9
Methicillan-resistant Staphylococcus aureus (MRSA)
Presumption that disease arose out of and in course of employment . . . Lab §3212.8

FIREFIGHTERS—Cont.
Occupationally-related accident, called to scene of . . . Lab §6409.2
Occupational safety and health
Penalties and fines
Refunds . . . Lab §6434.5
Personal protective clothing and equipment
Standards, evaluating and upgrading . . . Lab §147.2
One year, disability continuing beyond . . . Lab §4853
Paid leave of absence . . . Lab §4850
Performing duty not under direction of employer . . . Gov §50926
Permanent disability
Advanced disability pension payments . . . Lab §4850.3
Grounds for denying . . . Lab §4850.4
One year, disability continuing beyond . . . Lab §4853
Personal protective clothing and equipment
Occupational safety and health
Standards for clothing and equipment, evaluating and upgrading . . . Lab §147.2
Persons engaged in suppressing fires . . . Lab §3365
Pneumonia
Generally . . . Lab §3212
University of California fire department . . . Lab §3212.4
Post-traumatic stress injury
Coverage . . . Lab §3212.15
Presumptions
Cancer
William Dallas Jones cancer presumption act of 2010 . . . Lab §3212.1
Prisoners engaged in fire suppression work (See PRISONERS)
Public Employees' Retirement System, state and local safety members of (See PUBLIC EMPLOYEES' RETIREMENT SYSTEM)
Request to make disability determinations . . . Lab §4851
Reserve or auxiliary officers as county employees . . . Lab §4855
Salary payments, temporary disability payments concurrent with . . . Lab §4854
San Luis Obispo firefighters, probation and sheriff's office employees, benefits for . . . Lab §4850.5
Technical assistants . . . Lab §3367
Temporary disability
Advanced payments . . . Lab §4850
Determinations, request to make . . . Lab §4850
Medical, surgical, and hospital benefits, effect on . . . Lab §4852
Paid leave of absence in lieu of TD . . . Lab §4850
Salary payments, prohibition on disability benefits concurrent with . . . Lab §4854
San Luis Obispo personnel . . . Lab §4850.5
Termination of active service, injury following . . . Lab §4458.5
Tuberculosis . . . Lab §3212.6
University of California fire department (See UNIVERSITY OF CALIFORNIA)
Volunteer firefighters . . . Lab §§3212.1, 3361, 3365

FIRE REGULATIONS
Elevators . . . Lab §7301.5

FIRST AID
Employer's duty to provide despite injured worker choice of physician
Predesignation of personal physician . . . 8 CCR §9780.1
Occupational Safety and Health Standards Board requirements, compliance with . . . Lab §2440
Pesticide poisoning treatment not regarded as first aid . . . Lab §6409.3
Requirements as to availability of adequate treatment . . . Lab §6708

FISH AND GAME WARDENS
Employee status . . . Lab §3363

FISH AND WILDLIFE DEPARTMENT
Law enforcement officers employed by department
Paid leave of absence . . . Lab §4800

FLEXIBLE SPENDING ACCOUNTS
Notice to employee of deadlines, employer duties . . . Lab §2810.7

FLOORING (See BUILDING AND CONSTRUCTION INDUSTRY)

FLSA (See FAIR LABOR STANDARDS ACT (FLSA))

FOOD AND AGRICULTURE CODE
Pesticide regulation in compliance with . . . Lab §6399.1

FOOD SECTOR WORKERS
COVID-19
Sick leave for food sector workers
Supplemental paid sick leave for food sector workers . . . Lab §248

FOOT AND ANKLE DISABILITY
Guidelines for evaluation . . . 8 CCR §46.1
Medical treatment
Utilization schedule
Foot disorders . . . 8 CCR §9792.23.7

FOREARM DISORDERS
Medical treatment
Utilization schedule . . . 8 CCR §9792.23.4

FORECLOSURE
Enforcement of nonjudicial foreclosure judgment against uninsured employer . . . Lab §3716.3

FOREIGN COMMERCE
Railroads . . . 45 USC §51

FOREIGN COUNTRIES
Depositions
Taking depositions in foreign countries . . . CCP §2027.010
Military areas, employees in . . . 5 USC §§2105, 8171 to 8173
Organization of foreign nations, judicial notice of . . . Ev §452

FOREIGN EMPLOYMENT
Contractors with U.Sworking outside U.S
Administration of claims . . . 42 USC §1706

FOREIGN EMPLOYMENT—Cont.
Contractors with U.Sworking outside U.S—Cont.
Assignment of benefits . . . 42 USC §1717
Attachment and garnishment . . . 42 USC §1717
Attorneys' fees . . . 42 USC §1714
Death benefits . . . 42 USC §1701
Definitions pertinent to . . . 42 USC §§1703, 1711
Disqualification from benefits . . . 42 USC §§1705, 1712
Fraud . . . 42 USC §1713
Legal services, claims for . . . 42 USC §1714
Levy . . . 42 USC §1717
Liens on inappropriately disbursed funds . . . 42 USC §1705
Longshore and Harbor Workers' Compensation Act, applicability of . . . 42 USC §1702
Missing persons as totally disabled . . . 42 USC §1701
Penalties and fines . . . 42 USC §1713
Presumption of death or detention . . . 42 USC §1716
Receipt of workers' compensation benefits from another source . . . 42 USC §1705
Reimbursements . . . 42 USC §1704
Secretary of Labor
Administration by . . . 42 USC §1706
Finality of decisions of . . . 42 USC §1715
Subversive acts, persons committing . . . 42 USC §1712
War-risk hazard, compensation for injury or death resulting from . . . 42 USC §1701
Death benefits
Bases outside U.S., employment on . . . 42 USC §1651
Contractors with U.Sworking outside U.S . . . 42 USC §1701
Disability benefits
Contractors with U.Sworking outside U.S . . . 42 USC §1701
Military bases outside U.S., employees of . . . 42 USC §1651
Longshore and Harbor Workers' Compensation Act (See LONGSHORE AND HARBOR WORKERS' COMPENSATION ACT)
Military bases outside U.S., service on (See MILITARY SERVICE)
War-risk hazard, compensation for injury or death resulting from
Contractors with U.Sworking outside U.S . . . 42 USC §1701
Military bases overseas, employees of . . . 42 USC §1651

FOREIGN LANGUAGE
Family care leave, paid
Application for benefits . . . UI §3308
Workers' compensation division
Notices and forms, availability in various languages . . . Lab §124

FORENSIC PATHOLOGISTS
Medical records
Disclosure of medical records to coroners, medical examiners or forensic pathologists . . . CC §56.10

FORESTRY AND FIRE PROTECTION DEPARTMENT
Occupational safety and health
Penalties and fines
Refunds . . . Lab §6434.5

FORMS
Alienage, citizenship, and immigration status, uninsured employers fund and subsequent injuries fund benefits (Form UEF-1) . . . 8 CCR §15741
Attorneys' fees, disclosure statement regarding . . . 8 CCR §10134
Citizenship, alienage, and immigration status, uninsured employers fund and subsequent injuries fund benefits . . . 8 CCR §15741
Claim forms (See CLAIM FORMS)
Claim log (See CLAIM LOG)
Claims adjusters
Certification of claims adjusters . . . 10 CCR §2592.08
Experience standards
Designation for experienced claims adjusters or medical-only claims adjusters . . . 10 CCR §2592.12
Medical-only claims adjusters
Certification of claims adjusters . . . 10 CCR §2592.08
Training standards
Designation for successful completion of training . . . 10 CCR §2592.10
Post-designation training . . . 10 CCR §2592.14
Death of employee, DIA Form 510 for notice of . . . 8 CCR §9910
Doctor's first report of occupational disease or injury (Form 5021) . . . 8 CCR §14006
Electronic adjudication management system (EAMS)
Arbitration
Submittal form . . . 8 CCR §10208.12
Declaration of readiness to proceed . . . 8 CCR §10208.2
Expedited hearings . . . 8 CCR §10208.3
Filings by party or lien claimant
Document cover sheet form . . . 8 CCR §10205.13
Document separator sheet form . . . 8 CCR §10205.14
Minutes of hearings . . . 8 CCR §10206.20
Pretrial conference statements . . . 8 CCR §10208.4
Settlement and stipulation forms . . . 8 CCR §10205.2
Employer's records of occupational injury or illness . . . 8 CCR §14300.29
Equivalent form
Defined . . . 8 CCR §14300.46
Required elements . . . 8 CCR §§14300.48 Appx D to 14300.48 Appx F
Old forms . . . 8 CCR §14300.44
Retention and updating . . . 8 CCR §14300.33
Old forms . . . 8 CCR §14300.44
Review and correction . . . 8 CCR §14300.32
Separate form for each establishment . . . 8 CCR §14300.30
Short term establishments . . . 8 CCR §14300.30
Employer's Report of Occupational Injury or Illness, Form 5020 (See EMPLOYER'S REPORT OF OCCUPATIONAL INJURY OR ILLNESS)

FORMS—Cont.
Expedited hearing, filing request for
Electronic adjudication management system (EAMS) . . . 8 CCR §10208.3
Health care organizations (HCOs)
Application for authorization as . . . 8 CCR §9771.62
Enrollment Form 1194 . . . 8 CCR §9779.4
Individual information sheet for person completing authorization form . . . 8 CCR §9771.63
Immigration, alienage, and citizenship status, uninsured employers fund and subsequent injuries fund benefits . . . 8 CCR §15741
Independent medical review
Independent medical reviewer
Contract applications . . . 8 CCR §9768.5
Request for review
Application form . . . 8 CCR §9768.10
Judges (WCJs)
Affidavit as to pending cases . . . 8 CCR §9714.5
Medical bill reviewers
Certification . . . 10 CCR §2592.09
Designation for successful completion of training . . . 10 CCR §2592.11
Experienced medical bill reviewer, designation . . . 10 CCR §2592.13
Post-designation training . . . 10 CCR §2592.14
Medical provider networks
Complaint forms . . . 8 CCR §9767.16.5
Cover page for application . . . 8 CCR §9767.4
Cover page for reapproval plan . . . 8 CCR §9767.4
Modification of plan
Notice of modification . . . 8 CCR §9767.8
Suspension or revocation
Petition for suspension or revocation of MPN . . . 8 CCR §9767.17
Medical treatment
Billing and payment rules (October 2011)
Standardized forms . . . 8 CCR §9792.5.2
Occupational injury or illness
Doctor's first report (Form 5021) . . . 8 CCR §14006
Employer's Report, Form 5020 . . . 8 CCR §14004
Prison inmates
Report of injury to (See PRISONERS)
Permanent and stationary report, form of treating physician's . . . 8 CCR §§9785.3, 9785.4
Services beginning October 1, 2015 . . . 8 CCR §9785.4.1
Permanent disability
Apportionment of disability
Referral . . . 8 CCR §10163
Consultative rating determinations
Request form . . . 8 CCR §10166.1
Notice of options following rating determination . . . 8 CCR §10165.5
Summary rating determinations
Questionnaire . . . 8 CCR §10161
Reproduction of forms . . . 8 CCR §10161.1
Request for . . . 8 CCR §10161
Petition for change of primary treating physician . . . 8 CCR §9786.1
Physicians
Acupuncturists
Change of treating physician to personal chiropractor or acupuncturist, notice form . . . 8 CCR §9783.1

FORMS—Cont.
Physicians—Cont.
Chiropractors
Change of treating physician to personal chiropractor or acupuncturist, notice form . . . 8 CCR §9783.1
Predesignation of personal physician . . . 8 CCR §9783
Prisoners
Report of injury to
Department of corrections report of injury form (See PRISONERS)
Progress report, form of treating physician's . . . 8 CCR §9785.2
Qualified Medical Evaluator (See QUALIFIED MEDICAL EVALUATORS (QMES))
Reproduction of (See REPRODUCTION OF FORMS)
Response to petition for change of primary treating physician . . . 8 CCR §9786.1
Return to work programs
Offer of work
Notice . . . 8 CCR §10118
Subsequent injuries fund and uninsured employers fund benefits, Form UEF-1 statement of citizenship, alienage, and immigration status . . . 8 CCR §15741
Supplemental job displacement benefits
Dispute resolution
Request for dispute resolution before administrative director . . . 8 CCR §10133.55
Notice
Offer of modified or alternative work . . . 8 CCR §§10133.35, 10133.53
Vouchers for training, nontransferable . . . 8 CCR §10133.57
Injuries occurring from 2013 forward . . . 8 CCR §10133.32
Treating physician
Petition for change of primary treating physician . . . 8 CCR §9786.1
Progress report, form of . . . 8 CCR §9785.2
Response to petition for change of primary treating physician . . . 8 CCR §9786.1
Uninsured employers fund and subsequent injuries fund benefits, Form UEF-1 statement of citizenship, alienage, and immigration status . . . 8 CCR §15741

FOSTER HOMES
Commercial insurance
Cancellation or nonrenewal of policy
Prohibited basis for cancellation or nonrenewal . . . Ins §676.75
Discrimination against insuring foster home activities . . . Ins §676.7

FRAUD
Administration revolving fund fraud investigation and prosecution assessment (See ADMINISTRATION REVOLVING FUND)
Advertising
Fraudulent or misleading advertising (See ADVERTISING)
App-based drivers and services
Impersonating app-based driver . . . B&P §7462

FRAUD—Cont.
Appeals Board (WCAB) petition for reconsideration presenting evidence of . . . 8 CCR §10974
Attorneys, participation in fraud
Discovery of attorney work product
Not protected . . . CCP §2018.050
Chiropractors
Fraud investigations . . . Ins §1872.95
Authorized governmental agency, defined to include licensing agency under chiropractic initiative act . . . Ins §1877.2
Forwarding information concerning chiropractors to disciplinary body . . . Ins §1872.84
Definitions
Workers' Compensation Insurance Fraud Reporting Act . . . Ins §1877.1
Disability benefits (See DISABILITY BENEFITS)
Foreign employment by contractors with U.Sworking outside U.S . . . 42 USC §1713
Health care organizations (HCOs)
Advertising, deceptive . . . 8 CCR §9771.66
Name changes, deceptive . . . 8 CCR §9771.68
Insurance
Generally . . . Ins §1871
Criminal law
False or fraudulent claims, making . . . Ins §1871.9, Pen §550
Solicitation or referral for purposes of . . . Pen §549
False or fraudulent claims, making . . . Pen §550
Internet posting of convicted violators . . . Ins §1871.9
Insurance Frauds Prevention Act (See INSURANCE FRAUDS PREVENTION ACT)
Internet posting of convicted violators of provisions . . . Ins §1871.9
Legislative intent . . . Ins §1871
Motor vehicle insurance fraud reporting . . . Ins §1874.1
Premiums, payroll misrepresented to lower
Insurer's acceptance of false payroll information . . . Ins §757
Penalties and fines . . . Ins §756
Rating organizations, false or misleading information provided by . . . Ins §11755
Reduced rate, misrepresentation to obtain . . . Ins §§11760, 11880
Internet posting of convicted violators . . . Ins §1871.9
Reporting investigation information to disciplinary bodies . . . Ins §1872.84
Solicitation or referral for purposes of insurance fraud . . . Pen §549
Workers' Compensation Insurance Fraud Reporting Act (See WORKERS' COMPENSATION INSURANCE FRAUD REPORTING ACT)
Longshore and Harbor Workers' Compensation Act . . . 33 USC §931
Medical billing and provider fraud
Reporting protocol . . . Lab §3823
Medi-Cal, Medicare, Medicaid or workers' compensation system
Suspension of physician, practitioner or provider from participation in workers' compensation system for cause . . . Lab §139.21
Procedure for provider suspension . . . 8 CCR §§9788.1 to 9788.6

FRAUD—Cont.
Medical services contracts obtained via false statements . . . Lab §3219
Occupational Safety and Health Division violations . . . Lab §§6317.5, 6426
Penalties and fines
Generally . . . Lab §3820
Insurance Frauds Prevention Act (See INSURANCE FRAUDS PREVENTION ACT)
Petitions before WCAB alleging fraud . . . 8 CCR §10974
Premium, misrepresentation of payroll to lower
Insurer's acceptance of false payroll information . . . Ins §757
Penalties and fines . . . Ins §756
Privileged communications
Attorney referral service-client privilege
Use of service to perpetrate fraud or crime . . . Ev §968
Punishment for referral or solicitation for purposes of insurance fraud . . . Pen §549
Rating organizations, false or misleading information provided by . . . Ins §11755
Reconsideration based on fraud . . . 8 CCR §10974, Lab §§5903, 5908
Referral or solicitation for purposes of insurance fraud . . . Pen §549
Self-insurance fraud investigation and prosecution assessment . . . 8 CCR §15233
Solicitation or referral for purposes of insurance fraud . . . Pen §549
State Compensation Insurance Fund, misrepresentation to obtain reduced rate from . . . Ins §11880
Internet posting of convicted violators . . . Ins §1871.9
Surcharge for state fraud investigations by Department of Industrial Relations . . . Lab §62.6
Warning notices
Annual fraud warning notices . . . Lab §3822
Workers' Compensation Fraud Account . . . Lab §3820
Workers' Compensation Insurance Fraud Reporting Act (See WORKERS' COMPENSATION INSURANCE FRAUD REPORTING ACT)

FRIENDS
Medical records
Disclosures to friends . . . CC §56.1007

FRIVOLOUS PLEADINGS
Appeals board (WCAB)
Sanctions . . . 8 CCR §10421
Vexatious litigants . . . 8 CCR §10430

FUNERAL EXPENSES (See BURIAL EXPENSES)

G

GARMENT LABOR CONTRACTS
Labor law compliance
Funding in contract to be sufficient for contractor to comply with labor laws . . . Lab §2810

GARMENT MANUFACTURING HAZARDS
Reporting requirements . . . Lab §6409.5

GARNISHMENT (See ATTACHMENT AND GARNISHMENT)

GAS
Mine and tunnel precautions (See MINING AND TUNNELING)
Volatile flammable liquid, as (See VOLATILE FLAMMABLE LIQUIDS)

GASOLINE
Vapor emissions test procedures for vehicles transporting . . . Lab §6718

GAS PIPELINES
Presumptions regarding . . . Lab §6700

GASSY MINES AND TUNNELS (See MINING AND TUNNELING)

GENDER CHANGES IN CODE SECTIONS (See WORKMEN'S COMPENSATION CHANGED TO WORKERS' COMPENSATION)

GENDER HARASSMENT
Employment discrimination . . . Gov §12940

GENDER IDENTITY OR GENDER EXPRESSION
Commercial or property insurance
Cancellation or nonrenewal of policies
Hate crime or anti-reproductive-rights crime generating losses, factoring in decisions . . . Ins §676.10
Definition of gender . . . Gov §12926
Employment discrimination . . . Gov §12940

GENERIC DRUGS . . . Lab §4600.1
Drugs, medical treatment utilization schedule (MTUS)
Formulary . . . 8 CCR §9792.27.7

GENETIC INFORMATION
Defined . . . Gov §12926
Employment discrimination . . . Gov §12940
Test results, unauthorized disclosures . . . CC §56.17

GIFTS
Judges (WCJs) . . . 8 CCR §9721.2
Qualified medical evaluators (QMEs)
Gifts to evaluators . . . 8 CCR §41.7

GLASS
Laminated safety glass requirements for railroads (See RAILROADS)
Window cleaning (See WINDOW CLEANING SAFETY DEVICES)

GLOSSARY
Commonly used terms and abbreviations . . . Table 18

GOOD FAITH
Appeals Board (WCAB) sanctions for bad faith actions . . . Lab §5813
Claims administration and procedures . . . 8 CCR §10109
Mental injuries, compensability of good faith personnel actions causing . . . Lab §3208.3
Occupational Safety and Health Division citations . . . Lab §6319.5
Workers' Compensation Insurance Fraud Reporting Act, immunity for good faith actions under . . . Ins §1877.5

GOOD FAITH PERSONNEL ACTIONS
Compensability of mental injuries . . . Lab §3208.3

GRANTS
Application for, review of . . . Lab §78
Health care organization (HCO) grants or bonuses in aid of solicitation of employers . . . 8 CCR §9771.61

GRIEVANCE PROCEDURES (See DISPUTE RESOLUTION)

GROIN DISORDERS
Medical treatment
Utilization schedule
Hip and groin guidelines . . . 8 CCR §9792.23.10

GROSS INCOME EXCLUSIONS
Federal law . . . 26 USC §§101, 104

GROUP INSURANCE POLICIES
Definition of group coverage . . . Ins §42
Self-insurance (See GROUP SELF-INSURANCE)

GROUP SELF-INSURANCE . . . 8 CCR §15470
Actuarial analysis . . . 8 CCR §15481
Advance contribution discounts, prohibition on . . . 8 CCR §15476
Application for certificate to self-insure . . . 8 CCR §15482
Fees . . . 8 CCR §15491
Member applications . . . 8 CCR §15482.1
Assumption and guarantee agreements . . . 8 CCR §15483
Board of trustees for . . . 8 CCR §15475
Definition of board of trustees . . . 8 CCR §15201
Budgets
Filed with office . . . 8 CCR §15484
Certificates to self-insure
Application for certificate to self-insure . . . 8 CCR §15482
Fees . . . 8 CCR §15491
Member applications . . . 8 CCR §15482.1
Delayed start-up . . . 8 CCR §15487
Issuance . . . 8 CCR §15488
Reinstatement . . . 8 CCR §15490.1
Revocation
Security deposit, amount adjustment . . . 8 CCR §15497.1
Scope of certificate . . . 8 CCR §15490
Change in status of group or members . . . 8 CCR §15489.1
Charter of group
Amendments
Reporting . . . 8 CCR §15489
Conflicts of interest among service providers . . . 8 CCR §15475.1
Contribution
Defined . . . 8 CCR §15201
Definitions pertinent to . . . 8 CCR §15201
Delayed start-up . . . 8 CCR §15487
Excess insurance . . . 8 CCR §15478
Feasibility study requirements . . . 8 CCR §15471
Financial requirements
Budgets
Filed with office . . . 8 CCR §15484

GROUP SELF-INSURANCE—Cont.
Financial requirements—Cont.
Insufficient funding . . . 8 CCR §15477
Minimum financial requirements . . . 8 CCR §15472
Security deposit
Increase in light of impaired financial condition . . . 8 CCR §15499.5
Statements, annual submission . . . 8 CCR §15484
Surplus funding . . . 8 CCR §15477
Funds collected from group members
Investment of excess funds . . . 8 CCR §15475.3
Restrictions on use . . . 8 CCR §15475.2
Group members
Defined . . . 8 CCR §15201
Homogeneity of group members . . . 8 CCR §15473
Indemnity agreements . . . 8 CCR §15479
Defined . . . 8 CCR §15201
Insufficient funding . . . 8 CCR §15477
Insuring to secure payment of compensation . . . 8 CCR §15498
Interim certificates of consent to self-insure
Members of groups . . . 8 CCR §15482.2
Losses
Actuarial studies and summaries . . . 8 CCR §15481
Minimum financial requirements . . . 8 CCR §15472
Notice to employees of self-insured status . . . 8 CCR §15488
Power of attorney . . . 8 CCR §15479
Defined . . . 8 CCR §15201
Preventive care
Injury and illness prevention program . . . 8 CCR §15486.1
Private group application for certificate to self-insure . . . 8 CCR §15482
Fees . . . 8 CCR §15491
Interim certificates to group members . . . 8 CCR §15482.2
Member application . . . 8 CCR §15482.1
Reporting requirements . . . 8 CCR §15474
Resolution to authorize . . . 8 CCR §15485
Security deposit
Actuarial analysis . . . 8 CCR §15481
Agreement and undertaking for security deposit . . . 8 CCR §15486
Allocation of deposit . . . 8 CCR §15499
Amount
Adjustment . . . 8 CCR §§15497, 15497.1
Increase in light of impaired financial condition . . . 8 CCR §15499.5
Maintaining and posting . . . 8 CCR §15496
Surplus funding . . . 8 CCR §15477
Termination of membership in . . 8 CCR §15480

GUARDIAN OR CONSERVATOR
Longshore and Harbor Workers' Compensation Act, awards under . . . 33 USC §911
Medical treatment of ward
Information, release of medical information . . . CC §56.10
Pre-employment physical, disclosure of information from . . . CC §56.10
Rights of injured minors or incompetents . . . Lab §5408

Index

H

HAND INJURIES
Medical treatment
Utilization schedule
Hand disorders . . . 8 CCR §9792.23.4
Presumption of total disability due to loss or loss of use of . . . Lab §4662

HARASSMENT
Employees
Personal liability for harassment . . . Gov §12940
Employer liability for harassment by nonemployees . . . Gov §12940
Sheltered workshops, day programs or rehabilitation facilities
Action for harassment or discrimination by employees of nonprofit sheltered workshops, day programs or rehabilitation facilities . . . Gov §12926.05

HARBOR POLICE
San Francisco (See SAN FRANCISCO PORT COMMISSION)

HARBOR WORKERS (See LONGSHORE AND HARBOR WORKERS' COMPENSATION ACT)

HATE CRIMES
Commercial or property insurance
Cancellation or nonrenewal of policies
Hate crime or anti-reproductive-rights crime generating losses, factoring in decisions . . . Ins §676.10

HAZARD ANALYSIS
Refineries and chemical plants . . . Lab §7859

HAZARDOUS INDUSTRIES
Inspection and investigation of high-hazard industries . . . Lab §6314.1

HAZARDOUS SUBSTANCES
Cosmetics
Hazardous substances contained in cosmetics or disinfectants
Manufacturer or importer duties . . . Lab §6390.2
Disinfectants
Hazardous substances contained in cosmetics or disinfectants
Manufacturer or importer duties . . . Lab §6390.2
Effective date of provisions . . . Lab §6399.2
Employer duties towards employees . . . Lab §6398
Cleaning products, printable information
Availability to employees . . . Lab §6398.5
Food and Agricultural Code, compliance with . . . Lab §6399.1
Labeling requirements . . . Lab §6390.5
List of hazardous substances, compilation . . . Lab §6380
Material safety data sheets (MSDSs) for (See MATERIAL SAFETY DATA SHEET (MSDS))

HAZARDOUS SUBSTANCES—Cont.
Removal, standards for . . . Lab §142.7

HCOS (See HEALTH CARE ORGANIATIONS (HCOS))

HEALTH AND HUMAN SERVICES DEPARTMENT
Employer's records of occupational injury or illness
Providing access to government representatives . . . 8 CCR §14300.40

HEALTH AND SAFETY WORKERS' COMPENSATION COMMISSION
COVID-19
Study of impact on workers' compensation system . . . Lab §77.8
Duties and powers of . . . Lab §77
Firefighting vehicles
Exposure to carcinogenic materials by mechanics who repair and clean vehicles
Study and report . . . Lab §77.7
Grant applications, review of . . . Lab §78
Medical treatment utilization standards
Survey and review of standards of care . . . Lab §77.5
Organization and composition of . . . Lab §75
Personnel of . . . Lab §76

HEALTH CARE ASSISTANCE
Eligibility for, establishing . . . W&I §14011

HEALTH CARE COVERAGE
App-based drivers and services
Healthcare subsidy . . . B&P §7454
Children . . . Lab §2803.5
COBRA . . . Lab §2800.2
Conversion/continuation coverage
Generally . . . Lab §2800.3
COBRA . . . Lab §2800.2
Notice of availability . . . Lab §2807
Discontinuation of coverage . . . Lab §2806
ERISA . . . Lab §2803.4
Medicaid . . . Lab §2803.4
Medi-Cal benefits . . . Lab §2803.4
Waiver of benefits . . . Lab §2804

HEALTH CARE ORGANIZATIONS (HCOS)
Administrative expenses, reimbursement for . . . 8 CCR §9779.5
Advertising
Bonuses or grants in aid of . . . 8 CCR §9771.61
Contracts with solicitor firms . . . 8 CCR §9771.72
Deceptive . . . 8 CCR §9771.66
Disclosure requirements . . . 8 CCR §9771.65
Forms, filing . . . 8 CCR §9771.65
Organizational assurances prior to . . . 8 CCR §9771.64
Application for authorization as . . . 8 CCR §9771.62
Application for certification as . . . 8 CCR §9771
Alternatives to application for certification . . . 8 CCR §9771
Updating applications . . . 8 CCR §9771.1
Bonds . . . 8 CCR §9771.74
Bonuses or grants in aid of solicitation of employers . . . 8 CCR §9771.61

HEALTH CARE ORGANIZATIONS (HCOS)—Cont.
Books and records
  Fees for copies of documents . . . 8 CCR §9779.8
  Financial statements . . . 8 CCR §9771.81
  Maintenance . . . 8 CCR §9771.82
  Removal from state, prohibition of . . . 8 CCR §9771.78
  Requirements regarding . . . 8 CCR §9771.82
  Retention . . . 8 CCR §9771.83
Certification . . . Lab §4600.5
  Alternatives to application for certification . . . 8 CCR §9771
  Application for . . . 8 CCR §9771
    Updating applications . . . 8 CCR §9771.1
  Procedures . . . 8 CCR §9779
  Recertification . . . 8 CCR §9779
  Suspension or revocation of . . . 8 CCR §9779.2
Chiropractors, referrals to . . . 8 CCR §9773.1
Conflicts of interest, disclosure of . . . 8 CCR §9771.71
Contracts
  Generally . . . 8 CCR §9771.69
  Conflicts of interest, disclosure of . . . 8 CCR §9771.71
  Employer obligations . . . 8 CCR §9779.3
  Providers, with . . . 8 CCR §9771.70
  Solicitor firms, with . . . 8 CCR §9771.72
Correction of deficiencies, report of . . . 8 CCR §9771.77
Deceptive advertising . . . 8 CCR §9771.66
Deceptive name changes . . . 8 CCR §9771.68
Definitions pertinent to . . . 8 CCR §§9770, 9771.60
Disclosure requirements
  Conflicts of interest, disclosure of . . . 8 CCR §9771.71
  Filing disclosure forms . . . 8 CCR §9771.65
  Form for . . . 8 CCR §9771.67
  Provider's disclosure of network participation . . . Lab §4609
Dispute resolution procedures . . . 8 CCR §9775
Education programs . . . 8 CCR §9777
Enrollment
  Generally . . . 8 CCR §9779.3
  Form 1194 . . . 8 CCR §9779.4
  Minimum enrollment periods for choice . . . 8 CCR §9779.45
  Notice to employees . . . 8 CCR §9777
Evaluation reports . . . 8 CCR §9778
Fee-for-service arrangements . . . 8 CCR §9771.75
Fees
  Copies of documents . . . 8 CCR §9779.8
  Late payments . . . Lab §4603.2
  Reimbursement of costs and expenses . . . 8 CCR §9779.5
Fidelity bonds . . . 8 CCR §9771.74
Filing advertising and disclosure forms . . . 8 CCR §9771.65
Financial statements . . . 8 CCR §9771.81
Fiscal soundness, demonstration of . . . 8 CCR §9771.73
Forms (See FORMS)
Fraud
  Advertising, deceptive . . . 8 CCR §9771.66
  Name changes, deceptive . . . 8 CCR §9771.68
Grants or bonuses in aid of solicitation of employers . . . 8 CCR §9771.61

HEALTH CARE ORGANIZATIONS (HCOS)—Cont.
Grievance procedures . . . 8 CCR §9775
Hearing on suspension or revocation of certification . . . 8 CCR §9779.2
Individual information sheet for person completing authorization form . . . 8 CCR §9771.63
Inspections, onsite medical survey procedures for (See subhead: Medical surveys)
Insurance . . . 8 CCR §9771.73
Investigation of violations . . . 8 CCR §9779.2
Medical surveys
  Generally . . . 8 CCR §9771.76
  Books and records (See subhead: Books and records)
  Correction of deficiencies, report of . . . 8 CCR §9771.77
  Duties of HCO regarding . . . 8 CCR §9779.1
  Evaluation reports . . . 8 CCR §9778
  Financial statements . . . 8 CCR §9771.81
  Investigation of violations . . . 8 CCR §9779.2
  Procedures . . . 8 CCR §9771.76
  Regular and additional or nonroutine examinations . . . 8 CCR §§9771.79, 9771.80
  Reimbursement of costs and expenses . . . 8 CCR §9779.5
  Reporting requirements . . . 8 CCR §9779.1
  Unannounced . . . 8 CCR §§9771.79, 9771.80
Medical treatment
  Payment for services (See MEDICAL TREATMENT)
  Standards and requirements for . . . 8 CCR §9773
Minimum enrollment periods for choice . . . 8 CCR §9779.45
Name changes, deceptive . . . 8 CCR §9771.68
Notice
  Deficiencies . . . 8 CCR §9779.1
  Enrollment, patient notification of . . . 8 CCR §9777
  Proceedings against HCO, provision of information about . . . 8 CCR §9771.2
Onsite medical survey procedures (See subhead: Medical surveys)
Patient assistance, notification, and education . . . 8 CCR §9777
Payment for services (See MEDICAL TREATMENT)
Provider's disclosure of network participation . . . Lab §4609
Quality of care programs . . . 8 CCR §9774
Records and recordkeeping (See subhead: Books and records)
Regulations, applicability of . . . 8 CCR §9771.6
Reporting requirements
  Correction of deficiencies . . . 8 CCR §9771.77
  Evaluation reports . . . 8 CCR §9778
  Financial statements . . . 8 CCR §9771.81
  Medical surveys . . . 8 CCR §9779.1
Return to work programs . . . 8 CCR §9776.1
Revocation of certification . . . 8 CCR §9779.2
Safe workplace requirements . . . 8 CCR §9776
Solicitation of employers (See subhead: Advertising)
Standards and requirements
  Generally . . . 8 CCR §9772
  Certification . . . 8 CCR §9779
  Chiropractors, referrals to . . . 8 CCR §9773.1
  Dispute resolution/grievance procedures . . . 8 CCR §9775

HEALTH CARE ORGANIZATIONS (HCOS)—Cont.
Standards and requirements—Cont.
Evaluation reports . . . 8 CCR §9778
Medical treatment . . . 8 CCR §9773
Patient assistance, notification, and education . . . 8 CCR §9777
Quality of care programs . . . 8 CCR §9774
Return to work programs . . . 8 CCR §9776.1
Safe workplace . . . 8 CCR §9776
Surveys (See subhead: Medical surveys)
Suspension of certification . . . 8 CCR §9779.2
Violations of regulations regarding . . . 8 CCR §9779.2
Workers' Compensation Division Administrative director, certification by (See subhead: Certification)

HEALTH CARE PROVIDERS
Advertising by unlicensed providers . . . 8 CCR §9827
Certification of health care organizations . . . Lab §4600.5
Certification requirements . . . Lab §§4600.5, 4600.6
Chiropractors (See CHIROPRACTORS)
Choice of provider by injured worker . . . Lab §4600.3
Confidentiality
Regulatory authority to insure confidentiality in payment processing . . . Lab §4603.4
Contract between provider and contracting agent
Effect on rights and obligations of provider . . . Lab §4611
COVID-19
Sick leave, paid
Supplemental paid sick leave for covered workers . . . Lab §248.1
Disclosure of provider's participation in network . . . Lab §4609
False statements, contracts obtained via . . . Lab §3219
HCOs, contracts with . . . 8 CCR §9771.70
Health care organizations (HCOs) certified by Workers' Compensation Division administrative director (See HEALTH CARE ORGANIZATIONS (HCOS))
Knox-Keene Health Care Service Plan Act . . . Lab §4600.5
Managed Care Fund . . . Lab §4600.7
Medical records
Disclosure . . . CC §§56.10 to 56.16
Network, disclosure of provider's participation in . . . Lab §4609
Nonoccupational health care plan, minimum enrollment periods for choice under . . . 8 CCR §9779.45
Notice of eligible providers to injured workers . . . Lab §4600.3
Notice requirements . . . Lab §4603.5
Occupational Safety and Health Standards Board requirements, compliance with . . . Lab §2440
Payment for services . . . Lab §§4614, 4614.1
Processing
Regulatory authority for payment processing . . . Lab §4603.4
Physicians (See PHYSICIANS)
Preventive care, injuries resulting from . . . Lab §3208.05
Reimbursement
Licensing of entities seeking to reimburse . . . Lab §4600.35
Request for one-time change of physician by injured workers . . . Lab §4601

HEALTH CARE PROVIDERS—Cont.
Rules and procedures required for certification . . . Lab §4600.6
Self-insured employers, payment by . . . Lab §4614.1
Standards for contracts . . . Lab §4600.3
Violence against community health care workers, employers to keep record of . . . Lab §6332

HEALTH CARE SERVICE PLANS
Genetic tests results, disclosure of . . . CC §56.17
Medical provider networks . . . 8 CCR §§9767.1 to 9767.16, Lab §§4616 to 4616.7 (See MEDICAL PROVIDER NETWORKS)
Medical records
Confidentiality . . . CC §§56.10 to 56.16
Steps to protect confidential medical information . . . CC §56.107

HEALTH CARE WORKERS
Indemnification, applicability to employer-required training for patient care employment . . . Lab §2802.1
Patient protection and health care worker back and musculoskeletal injury prevention . . . Lab §6403.5
Personal protective equipment (PPE)
Direct patient care providers
Stockpile of PPE, employer duties . . . Lab §6403.3
Inventory
Employer duties . . . Lab §6403.1

HEALTH INSURANCE
Medical records, confidentiality . . . CC §§56.10 to 56.16

HEALTH MAINTENANCE ORGANIZATIONS
Confidentiality of medical records . . . CC §§56.10 to 56.16

HEALTH SERVICES DEPARTMENT (STATE)
Employer's records of occupational injury or illness
Providing access to government representatives . . . 8 CCR §14300.40
Safe workplace, role in promoting . . . Lab §6307.1

HEALTHY WORKPLACES, HEALTHY FAMILIES ACT OF 2014
Citation of provisions . . . Lab §245
Sick days, paid . . . Lab §§245 to 249 (See SICK DAYS, PAID)

HEARINGS
Adjournment . . . Lab §5700
Advertising violations . . . 8 CCR §9837
Appearances
Failure to appear at trial in case in chief . . . 8 CCR §10756
Non-attorney representatives . . . 8 CCR §10751
Required appearances . . . 8 CCR §10752
Settled cases . . . 8 CCR §10757
Application for (See ADJUDICATION OF CLAIMS)
Attorneys' fees and costs . . . 8 CCR §10421
Autopsy, authority to order . . . Lab §§5706, 5707
Burden of proof . . . Lab §5705
Claims administration audit, civil penalty assessment following . . . 8 CCR §10114
Designation of hearing officer . . . 8 CCR §10113.3

HEARINGS—Cont.
Claims administration audit, civil penalty assessment following —Cont.
Evidence . . . 8 CCR §10113.4
Prehearing conference and order . . . 8 CCR §10113.5
Conference hearings
Priority conferences . . . 8 CCR §10785
Status conference . . . 8 CCR §10758
Submissions at conference . . . 8 CCR §10761
Consolidated cases
Assignment . . . 8 CCR §10398
Continuances . . . Lab §5502.5
Clear showing of good cause . . . 8 CCR §10748
Court costs . . . 8 CCR §10421
Defenses . . . Lab §5705
Deposition of witnesses . . . Lab §5710
Dismissal of application without . . . Lab §5507
Electronic adjudication management system (EAMS)
Definitions . . . 8 CCR §10205
Expedited hearings
Form . . . 8 CCR §10208.3
Minutes of hearing
Form . . . 8 CCR §10206.20
Retention, return and destruction of records . . . 8 CCR §10208.7
Elevator, order prohibiting use of . . . Lab §7322
Evidence (See EVIDENCE)
Expedited hearings . . . Lab §5502
Electronic adjudication management system (EAMS)
Filing request for expedited hearing . . . 8 CCR §10208.3
Form for request . . . 8 CCR §10208.3
Setting hearing . . . 8 CCR §10782
Failure to appear at . . . 8 CCR §10756
Sanctions . . . 8 CCR §10421
Health care organization (HCO) certification, suspension or revocation of . . . 8 CCR §9779.2
Inactive cases
Dismissal of inactive cases
Lien claims . . . 8 CCR §10888
Petition to dismiss . . . 8 CCR §10550
Informality of proceedings . . . Lab §5709
Interpreter services . . . 8 CCR §10790
Qualifications of interpreter . . . 8 CCR §9795.1.5
Directories of qualified interpreters . . . 8 CCR §9795.5
Judges (WCJs), before (See JUDGES (WCJS))
Judicial review of Appeals Board (WCAB) decisions, right to appear at . . . Lab §5953
Labor Standards Enforcement Division, appeal hearings (See LABOR STANDARDS ENFORCEMENT DIVISION)
Longshore and Harbor Workers' Compensation Act . . . 33 USC §923
Mandatory settlement conference . . . 8 CCR §10759, Lab §5502
Minutes
Forms required . . . 8 CCR §10500
Interlocutory or interim orders entered as minute orders . . . 8 CCR §10833
Preparation at conclusion of trial . . . 8 CCR §10787
Non-attorney representatives
Appearances . . . 8 CCR §10751

HEARINGS—Cont.
Notice . . . 8 CCR §10750
Occupational Safety and Health Appeals Board (See OCCUPATIONAL SAFETY AND HEALTH APPEALS BOARD)
Occupational Safety and Health Division . . . Lab §6308.5
Occupational Safety and Health Standards Board
Procedures . . . Lab §143.2
Variances, applying for . . . Lab §§143, 146
Parties
Appearance of parties or representatives . . . 8 CCR §10752
Attendance permitted . . . Lab §5700
Penalties and fines ordered at . . . 8 CCR §10421
Priority conferences . . . 8 CCR §10785, Lab §5502
Public Employees' Retirement System disability retirement . . . Gov §21166
Rehearing petition . . . Gov §21167
Public hearings
Insurance (See INSURANCE)
Regulations, changes to . . . Lab §5307.4
Qualified medical evaluator (QME)
Disciplinary proceedings against . . . 8 CCR §61
Examination of injured worker by . . . Lab §5703.5
Reconsideration, petition for (See RECONSIDERATION)
Recording
Trial level proceedings . . . 8 CCR §10818
Rules used to conduct . . . Lab §5708
Sanctions . . . 8 CCR §10421
Self-insurers (See SELF-INSURANCE)
Service of notice . . . Lab §5504
Settlement conferences . . . Lab §5502
Failure to appear . . . 8 CCR §10755
Specified additional evidence allowed . . . Lab §5703
Status conference . . . 8 CCR §10758
Stipulations . . . Lab §5702
Testimony
Authority to take . . . Lab §5701
Transcripts (See APPEALS BOARD (WCAB))
Witnesses (See APPEALS BOARD (WCAB))
Time limits . . . Lab §5502
Transcripts of
Appeals board (See APPEALS BOARD (WCAB))
Trial . . . 8 CCR §10787
Failure to appear at trial in case in chief . . . 8 CCR §10756
Lien trials . . . 8 CCR §§10875, 10880
Uninsured employers benefits trust fund cases (See UNINSURED EMPLOYERS BENEFITS TRUST FUND)
Witnesses
Appeals board (See APPEALS BOARD (WCAB))

HEARSAY
Business records . . . Ev §§1270 to 1272
Unavailable as witness
Defined . . . Ev §240

HEART DISEASE
Atascadero State Hospital, security officers employed by . . . Lab §3212.2
Corrections, Department of . . . Lab §3212.2
Firefighters . . . Lab §§3212, 3212.4
Highway patrol . . . Lab §§3212.3, 3212.5
Law enforcement officers (See POLICE)

HEART DISEASE—Cont.
Method of evaluating
Cardiac disability . . . 8 CCR §45
Pulmonary disability . . . 8 CCR §44
Time taken to complete evaluation
Cardiovascular evaluations . . . 8 CCR §49.4
University of California fire department . . . Lab §3212.4
Youth Authority, Department of . . . Lab §3212.2

HEAT-RELATED ILLNESS AND INJURY
Occupational safety and health
Indoor workers
Standard to minimize illness and injury . . . Lab §6720
Outdoor work, heat illness prevention standards
Maria Isabel Vasquez Jimenez heat illness standard . . . Lab §6721

HEPATITIS
Occupational disease suffered by law enforcement and firefighters . . . Lab §3212.8
Temporary disability
Aggregate disability payments
Single injury . . . Lab §4656

HERNIAS
Firefighters . . . Lab §3212
Law enforcement officers and firefighters . . . Lab §3212.4
Police officers . . . Lab §3212

HIGHER EDUCATION
California State University (See CALIFORNIA STATE UNIVERSITY)
University of California (See UNIVERSITY OF CALIFORNIA)

HIGH HAZARDOUS INDUSTRIES
Inspection and investigation of . . . Lab §6314.1

HIGH VELOCITY EYE INJURIES
Temporary disability
Aggregate disability payments
Single injury . . . Lab §4656

HIGH VOLTAGE
Misdemeanors associated with . . . Pen §385

HIGHWAY PATROL
Back injury when required to wear duty belt . . . Lab §3213.2
Course of duty, injury occurring in . . . Lab §4801
Heart disease or pneumonia suffered by . . . Lab §§3212.3, 3212.5
Medical treatment . . . Lab §4802
One year, disability continuing beyond . . . Lab §4803
Paid leave of absence . . . Lab §4800.5
Permanent disability . . . Lab §4803
Salary payments, temporary disability payments concurrent with . . . Lab §4804
Temporary disability
Duty, disability occurring in course of . . . Lab §4801
Entitlement to medical, surgical, and hospital benefits . . . Lab §4802
One year, disability continuing beyond . . . Lab §4803
Paid leave of absence . . . Lab §4800.5

HIGHWAY PATROL—Cont.
Temporary disability—Cont.
Salary payments concurrent with, prohibition of . . . Lab §4804

HIP DISORDERS
Medical treatment
Utilization schedule
Hip and groin guidelines . . . 8 CCR §9792.23.10

HIRING ENTITIES
Sick leave, paid
Supplemental paid sick leave
Covered workers . . . Lab §248.1
Food sector workers . . . Lab §248

HOLIDAYS
Appeals board (WCAB)
Extensions of time . . . 8 CCR §10600
Discovery, effect on time limits for . . . CCP §2016.060

HOME HEALTH CARE
COVID-19
Compensation for injury or death from COVID-19 . . . Lab §3212.87
Fee schedule
Services not covered by Medicare or official medical fee schedule . . . Lab §5307.8
Medical treatment
Employer-provided medical treatment
Conditions where home health care services provided as medical treatment . . . Lab §4600
Payment for treatment
Request for payment . . . Lab §4603.2

HOMICIDE
Death benefits
Public officials, assassinated (See DEATH BENEFITS)
School district payments to surviving spouse of murdered employee . . . Ed §44017

HONORARIA
Judges (WCJs) . . . 8 CCR §9721.2, Lab §123.6

HOSPITAL RECORDS
Confidentiality of medical information . . . CC §§56.10 to 56.21
Patient's general condition, release of information regarding . . . CC §56.10

HOSPITALS
Direct patient care providers
Personal protective equipment (PPE) stockpile
Employer duties . . . Lab §6403.3
Occupational safety and health
Antineoplastic drugs
Adoption of occupational safety and health standard for handling antineoplastic drugs in health care facilities . . . Lab §144.8
Violence prevention plan . . . Lab §6401.8
Official medical fee schedule (See OFFICIAL MEDICAL FEE SCHEDULE)

HOSPITAL TREATMENT (See MEDICAL TREATMENT)

HOT WORK PERMITS
Chemical plants and refineries . . . Lab §7865

HOUSEHOLD EMPLOYEES
Employer liability for injury or occupational disease of . . . Lab §5500.6
Exclusion from Labor Code coverage . . . Lab §3354
Personal liability insurance for
  Generally . . . Ins §11590
  Exceptions to applicability of Section 11590 . . . Ins §11591
  Premiums . . . Ins §11593
  Rating of carriers . . . Ins §11592
Ratings organization provisions not applicable to . . . Ins §11590

HOUSING
Building permits . . . H&S §17922.5

HUMAN IMMUNODEFICIENCY VIRUS (HIV)
Disclosure of HIV status . . . CC §56.31
Temporary disability
  Aggregate disability payments
    Single injury . . . Lab §4656
Time limitations for claims for injury or death . . . Lab §5406.6

HUMAN RESOURCES DEPARTMENT
State Compensation Insurance Fund, master agreement with . . . Ins §11871

HUMAN TRAFFICKING
Victim-caseworker privileged . . . Ev §912

HUSBAND AND WIFE
Abandonment proceedings . . . Ev §972
Juvenile delinquency proceedings . . . Ev §972
Medical information, authorization for release of . . . CC §56.11
Mental illness, testifying as to . . . Ev §972
Privilege (See MARITAL PRIVILEGE)
Spouse defined to include registered domestic partner . . . Lab §12.2

I

IBR
Independent bill review (See INDEPENDENT BILL REVIEW (IBR))

IDENTITY THEFT
Individually identifiable information held by Workers' Compensation Division
  Protection of individually identifiable information . . . 8 CCR §9703

ILLEGALLY EMPLOYED MINORS
Increase in workers' compensation to injured children under age 16 . . . Lab §4557
Insurance for . . . Ins §11661.5

ILLEGALLY UNINSURED EMPLOYERS (See UNINSURED EMPLOYERS BENEFITS TRUST FUND)

ILLNESS (See OCCUPATIONAL DISEASE)

IMES (See INDEPENDENT MEDICAL EXAMINERS (IMES))

IMMIGRANT WORKERS
Arising out of employment/course of employment
  Seamen, injury in course of employment
    Non-citizens or nonresident aliens, restrictions on recovery for incidents in foreign waters . . . 46 USC §30105
Employees
  Defined to include aliens . . . Lab §3351
Employment law enforcement
  Immigration status irrelevant to enforcement . . . Lab §1171.5
Longshore and Harbor Workers' Compensation Act
  Computation of benefits
    Aliens and nonnationals . . . 42 USC §1652
  Death
    Compensation of aliens . . . 33 USC §909
Military bases overseas, service on
  Computation of benefits
    Aliens and nonnationals . . . 42 USC §1652
Nonappropriated fund instrumentalities, non-citizen nonresident employees
  Regulations under which compensation paid . . . 5 USC §8172
Subsequent injury payments
  Compensation not affected by immigration of citizenship status . . . Lab §4756
Uninsured employers benefits trust fund
  Immigration or citizenship status
    Compensation not affected by immigration or citizenship status . . . Lab §3733
Uninsured employers fund and subsequent injuries fund benefits
  Immigration or alien status, effect on eligibility . . . 8 CCR §15740
  Statement of citizenship, alienage and immigration status for state public benefits
    Form UEF-1 . . . 8 CCR §15741

IMMUNITY
Emergency and disaster services
  Earthquake Prediction Evaluation Council . . . Gov §8657
  Public employees . . . Gov §8656
Local agents . . . Gov §53023
Workers' Compensation Insurance Fraud Reporting Act, good faith actions under . . . Ins §1877.5

IMMUNOLOGIC DISABILITY
Method of evaluating . . . 8 CCR §47

IMPRISONMENT (See PRISONERS)

INCAPACITY
Appeals Board (WCAB)
  Incompetents,application by . . . 8 CCR §10455
Dependents, incapacitated adults presumed to be . . . Lab §3501
Guardian or conservator, appointment of . . . Lab §5408
Longshore and Harbor Workers' Compensation Act, awards under . . . 33 USC §911
Presumption of total disability for brain injuries leading to mental incapacity . . . Lab §4662

INCARCERATION (See PRISONERS)

INCOME TAX
App-based drivers and services
Income reporting system . . . B&P §7464.5
Exclusions from gross income
Federal law . . . 26 USC §§101, 104

INCOMPETENTS (See INCAPACITY)

INDEMNITY
Application of permanent partial disability rates to permanent disability indemnity table . . . Table 16
Employees, indemnification of
Performance of duties, loss sustained in . . . Lab §2802
Want of care by employer, against . . . Lab §2800
Group self-insurance . . . 8 CCR §15479
Definition of indemnity agreement . . . 8 CCR §15201
Insurance against increase in . . . Ins §11661.6
Minimum/maximum indemnity and earnings . . . Table 14
Nominal disability indemnity, award of . . . Lab §5802
Percentage of permanent disability to weeks of indemnity . . . Table 15
Permanent disability indemnity table
Injuries occurring from 2006 through 2012 . . . Table 17B
Injuries occurring from 2013 to 2019 . . . Table 17A
Injuries occurring in 2003 through 2004 . . . Table 17D
Injuries occurring in 2005 . . . Table 17C
Subsequent statutory changes in amount, benefits payable not affected by . . . Lab §4453.5

INDEPENDENT BILL REVIEW (IBR)
Administrative director determination
Petition to enforce . . . 8 CCR §10570
Appeals . . . Lab §4603.6
Petition to appeal determination . . . 8 CCR §10567
Billing and payment rules (October 2011)
Second review and independent bill review . . . 8 CCR §§9792.5.4 to 9792.5.15
Cost of review . . . Lab §4603.6
Form for request . . . Lab §4603.6
Medical-legal expenses, contesting by employer . . . Lab §4622
Provider dispute of amount paid for medical treatment
Second review, dispute continuing
Request for independent bill review . . . Lab §4603.2
Request of independent bill review . . . Lab §4603.6
Explanation of review to include information on requesting IBR . . . Lab §4603.3
Reviewer's duties . . . Lab §4603.6
Time for request . . . Lab §4603.6

INDEPENDENT CONTRACTORS
App-based drivers and services generally . . . B&P §§7448 to 7467 (See APP-BASED DRIVERS AND SERVICES)
Cheerleaders for professional sports teams classified as employees . . . Lab §2754
Defined . . . Lab §3353
Election of compensation liability by vendors of newspapers and periodicals . . . Lab §4157
Misclassification as independent contractor
Advising employers to misclassify
Liability . . . Lab §2753

INDEPENDENT CONTRACTORS—Cont.
Misclassification as independent contractor—Cont.
Motor carrier employer amnesty program for carriers performing drayage services . . . Lab §2750.8
Willful misclassification . . . Lab §226.8
Newspaper and periodical vendors, election of compensation liability by . . . Lab §4157
Physicians as independent contractors
Presumptions . . . Lab §2750.6
Proof of status
Generally . . . Lab §2750.5
Worker classification
App-based drivers and services generally . . . B&P §§7448 to 7467 (See APP-BASED DRIVERS AND SERVICES)
Generally . . . Lab §§2775 to 2785 (See WORKER CLASSIFICATION)

INDEPENDENT MEDICAL EXAMINERS (IMES)
Appointment . . . Lab §139.2
Financial interest, referral to person with whom physician has . . . Lab §§139.3, 139.31
Labor Code definition . . . Lab §28
Qualified medical evaluators (QMEs) (See QUALIFIED MEDICAL EVALUATORS (QMES))
Referrals . . . Lab §§139.3, 139.31

INDEPENDENT MEDICAL REVIEW . . . 8 CCR §§9768.1 to 9768.17, Lab §4616.4
Adoption of determinations . . . 8 CCR §9768.16
American College of Occupational and Environmental Medicine Practice Guidelines
Defined . . . 8 CCR §9768.1
Appeals
Binding nature of review . . Lab §4610.6
Petition appealing determination . . . 8 CCR §10575
Application form . . . 8 CCR §9768.10
Appropriate specialty
Defined . . . 8 CCR §9768.1
Binding nature of review . . . Lab §4610.6
Charges
Payment by employer or insurer . . . 8 CCR §9768.15
Conflicts of interest . . . 8 CCR §9768.2
Independence of organizations . . . Lab §139.5
Consultants
Organizations providing review as consultant . . . Lab §139.5
Contracts
Independent medical reviewers, contract to serve as
Action on application . . . 8 CCR §9768.6
Applications . . . 8 CCR §9768.4
Form of application . . . 8 CCR §9768.5
Independent medical reviews, contract for . . . Lab §4616.4
Organizations providing review
Contracts with administrative director . . . Lab §139.5
Cost of review
Employer responsibility . . . Lab §4610.6
Decision
Appeals
Petition appealing determination . . . 8 CCR §10575
Binding nature of review . . . Lab §4610.6

INDEPENDENT MEDICAL REVIEW—Cont.
Decision—Cont.
Prompt implementation by employer . . . Lab §4610.6
Definitions . . . 8 CCR §9768.1
Delay of process
Employer causing delay . . . Lab §4610.5
Destruction of records . . . 8 CCR §9768.13
Expedited review
Circumstances requiring . . . Lab §4610.5
Fees for reviewers . . . 8 CCR §9768.15
Imminent and serious threat to employee health
Expedited review
Circumstances requiring . . . Lab §4610.5
Independence of organizations . . . Lab §139.5
Independent medical reviewer
Conflicts of interest . . . 8 CCR §9768.2
Contract applications . . . 8 CCR §9768.4
Action on application . . . 8 CCR §9768.6
Form . . . 8 CCR §9768.5
Defined . . . 8 CCR §9768.1
Fees and charges . . . 8 CCR §9768.15
Qualifications . . . 8 CCR §9768.3
Removal of physicians from list . . . 8 CCR §9768.8
Voluntary inactive status . . . 8 CCR §9768.7
In-person examinations
Defined . . . 8 CCR §9768.1
Procedure for review . . . 8 CCR §9768.11
Material familial affiliation
Defined . . . 8 CCR §9768.1
Material financial affiliation
Defined . . . 8 CCR §9768.1
Material professional affiliation
Defined . . . 8 CCR §9768.1
Medical emergency
Defined . . . 8 CCR §9768.1
Medical provider network contact (MPN contact)
Defined . . . 8 CCR §9768.1
Medical provider networks . . . 8 CCR §§9768.1 to 9768.17
Objection to diagnosis or treatment recommendation
Resolution through medical review process . . . Lab §4062
Out of network treatment . . . 8 CCR §9768.17
Medical treatment utilization schedule
Out-of-schedule treatment
Medical evidence search sequence . . . 8 CCR §9792.21.1
Medication prescribed pursuant to drug formulary
Utilization review, review of decision
Applicability of review provisions . . . Lab §4610.5
Objection to medical evaluation decision
Resolution by independent medical review process . . . Lab §4062
Organizations providing review
Binding nature of review . . . Lab §4610.6
Conflicts of interest . . . Lab §139.5
Contracts with administrative director . . . Lab §139.5
Cost of review
Employer responsibility . . . Lab §4610.6
Decision
Communication . . . Lab §4610.6
Time to make and present . . . Lab §4610.6

INDEPENDENT MEDICAL REVIEW—Cont.
Organizations providing review—Cont.
Disclosures
Financial and other disclosures . . . Lab §139.5
Medical director . . . Lab §139.5
Medical necessity
Determination . . . Lab §4610.6
Medications prescribed pursuant to drug formulary, procedures . . . Lab §4610.6
Physicians
Conflicts of interest . . . Lab §139.5
Qualifications for reviewing physicians . . . Lab §139.5
Prompt review . . . Lab §4610.6
Quality assurance mechanisms . . . Lab §139.5
Requirements as to independence . . . Lab §139.5
Scope of review . . . Lab §4610.6
Out of network treatment . . . 8 CCR §9768.17
Panel
Defined . . . 8 CCR §9768.1
Relevant medical records
Defined . . . 8 CCR §9768.1
Record review procedure . . . 8 CCR §9768.11
Removal of physicians from reviewer list . . . 8 CCR §9768.8
Reports
Contents of reports . . . 8 CCR §9768.12
Retention of records . . . 8 CCR §9768.14
Request for review
Form for application . . . 8 CCR §9768.10
Procedure . . . 8 CCR §9768.9
Utilization review decision, review . . . Lab §4610.5
Residence
Defined . . . 8 CCR §9768.1
Scope . . . Lab §4064
State function . . . Lab §139.5
Utilization review, review of decision . . . Lab §4610.5
Appeal from determination . . . 8 CCR §9792.10.7
Application . . . 8 CCR §9792.10.2
Assignment for review . . . 8 CCR §9792.10.4
Costs of review . . . 8 CCR §9792.10.8
Implementing determination . . . 8 CCR §9792.10.7
Initial review of application . . . 8 CCR §9792.10.3
Medical records to be provided . . . 8 CCR §9792.10.5
Medication prescribed pursuant to drug formulary
Applicability of review provisions . . . Lab §4610.5
Notice to parties of assignment for review . . . 8 CCR §9792.10.4
Publishing of determinations . . . 8 CCR §9792.10.9
Standards for review . . . 8 CCR §9792.10.6
Timeline for review . . . 8 CCR §9792.10.6
Voluntary inactive status of reviewer . . . 8 CCR §9768.7

INDEPENDENT MEDICAL REVIEW APPLICATION FORM . . . 8 CCR §9768.10

INDUSTRIAL ACCIDENT OR ILLNESS
California State University personnel (See CALIFORNIA STATE UNIVERSITY)
Disability benefits for industrially disabled persons (See DISABILITY BENEFITS)
Public Employees' Retirement System (See PUBLIC EMPLOYEES' RETIREMENT SYSTEM)

Index

INDUSTRIAL ACCIDENT OR ILLNESS—Cont.
School district personnel . . . Ed §§44984, 45192

INDUSTRIAL ACCIDENTS DIVISION
Appeals Board (WCAB) (See APPEALS BOARD (WCAB))
Terms referring to . . . Ins §20.5

INDUSTRIAL RELATIONS DEPARTMENT
Generally . . . Lab §50
Administration
  Department, of . . . Lab §55
  Labor Code, of . . . Lab §60
  Occupational Safety and Health Administration (OSHA) standards . . . Lab §50.7
Appeals Board (WCAB) (See APPEALS BOARD (WCAB))
Cal-OSHA Targeted Inspection and Consultation Fund (See CAL-OSHA TARGETED INSPECTION AND CONSULTATION FUND)
Chiefs of divisions . . . Lab §57
Death benefits paid to . . . Lab §4706.5
  Death cases, dependency at issue
    Service on division of workers' compensation and director of industrial relations . . . 8 CCR §10632
Director
  Appeals
    Petition appealing orders of administrative director or director of industrial relations . . . 8 CCR §10560
  Appointment of . . . Lab §51
  Comments by . . . Lab §50.9
  Crane safety, appeal of revocation of license to certify . . . Lab §7377
  Defined
    Generally . . . 8 CCR §15552
    Head of department . . . Lab §53
    Labor Code, defined for . . . Lab §20
  Duties of . . . Lab §54
  Enforcement authority, delegation of . . . 8 CCR §15550
  Head of department defined as . . . Lab §53
  Illegally uninsured employers (See UNINSURED EMPLOYERS BENEFITS TRUST FUND)
  Labor Code, defined for . . . Lab §§19, 20
  Order for payment of compensation . . . Lab §3702.9
  Payment of benefits penalties payable by employer to . . . Lab §5814.1
  Regulations, authorization to adopt, amend, and repeal . . . Lab §3702.10
  Self-insurers with revoked certificates to self-insure, continuing jurisdiction over . . . 8 CCR §15427
  Stop orders issued by (See STOP ORDERS)
  Testimony of judicial or quasi-judicial officers . . . 8 CCR §10360
  Trade secrets, protection from disclosure of . . . Lab §6396
  Uninsured employers benefits trust fund
    Determinations of director . . . 8 CCR §15711
    Hearings held by director . . . 8 CCR §15731
    Powers of director . . . Lab §3710
Divisions
  Chiefs of . . . Lab §57

INDUSTRIAL RELATIONS DEPARTMENT—Cont.
Divisions—Cont.
  Enumeration of . . . Lab §56
Enforcement
  Generally . . . Lab §59
  Fair Labor Standards Act (FLSA) . . . Lab §50.6
  Labor Code . . . Lab §60
  Labor Standards Enforcement Division, by (See LABOR STANDARDS ENFORCEMENT DIVISION)
  Occupational Safety and Health Administration (OSHA) standards . . . Lab §50.7
Expenditures . . . Lab §62
Fair Labor Standards Act (FLSA), responsibility to enforce . . . Lab §50.6
Functions of . . . Lab §50.5
Government Code, applicability of . . . Lab §52
Health and Safety Workers' Compensation Commission (See HEALTH AND SAFETY WORKERS' COMPENSATION COMMISSION)
Industrial Accidents Division (See INDUSTRIAL ACCIDENTS DIVISION)
Labor Standards Enforcement Division (See LABOR STANDARDS ENFORCEMENT DIVISION)
Legal services for . . . Lab §54.5
Medical research programs (See subhead: Occupational disease research programs)
MSDS sent to . . . Lab §6394
Occupational disease
  Programs for occupational health and medicine (See subhead: Occupational disease research programs)
  Reporting requirements as to clinical and research findings . . . Lab §50.8
Occupational disease research programs
  Departmental responsibility for developing . . . Lab §50.8
  Grant applications, review of . . . Lab §78
  Reporting requirements as to clinical and research findings . . . Lab §50.8
Occupational Safety and Health Appeals Board (See OCCUPATIONAL SAFETY AND HEALTH APPEALS BOARD)
Occupational Safety and Health Division (See OCCUPATIONAL SAFETY AND HEALTH DIVISION)
Occupational Safety and Health Standards Board (See OCCUPATIONAL SAFETY AND HEALTH STANDARDS BOARD)
Organization of
  Administration . . . Lab §55
  Chiefs of divisions . . . Lab §§56, 57.1
  Departmental divisions . . . Lab §56
Property of, title to . . . Lab §58
Reporting requirements as to clinical and research findings . . . Lab §50.8
Research programs (See subhead: Occupational disease research programs)
Self-Insurance Plans, Office of
  Advisory Committee to Manager . . . 8 CCR §15202
  Delegation of authority by manager . . . 8 CCR §§15431, 15433
  Hearings on disputes between self-insurer and chief . . . 8 CCR §15430
  Manager . . . 8 CCR §15201
State Compensation Insurance Fund (See STATE COMPENSATION INSURANCE FUND)

INDUSTRIAL RELATIONS DEPARTMENT—Cont.
Trade secrets, protection from disclosure of . . . Lab §6396
Uninsured employers benefits trust fund
Director of department
Determinations by director . . . 8 CCR §15711
Hearings held by director . . . 8 CCR §15731
Powers . . . Lab §3710
Unpaid wages
Collection and disbursement of . . . Lab §96.7
Unpaid Wage Fund . . . Lab §96.6
Workers' Compensation Division (See WORKERS' COMPENSATION DIVISION)

INDUSTRIAL RELATIONS UNPAID WAGE FUND
Creation and purpose of . . . Lab §96.6

INFORMATION SYSTEMS
Advertising (See ADVERTISING)
Employee information
Exceptions to requirements regarding . . . 8 CCR §9884
New employees, written notice to . . . 8 CCR §9880
Posting notices . . . 8 CCR §9881
Contents of poster . . . 8 CCR §9881.1
Publication upon approval . . . 8 CCR §9883
Spanish translations, availability of . . . 8 CCR §9883
Written notice to new employees . . . 8 CCR §9880
Longshore and Harbor Workers' Compensation Act . . . 33 USC §939
Mining and tunneling communications
Communication systems . . . Lab §7963
Notices (See NOTICE)
Railroad accident, suppression of information regarding . . . 45 USC §60
Records (See RECORDS AND RECORDKEEPING)
Refineries and chemical plants, process safety management of . . . Lab §§7858, 7859
Reporting requirements (See REPORTING REQUIREMENTS)
Toxic materials . . . Lab §147.2
Voluntary disability benefit plans
Availability of information . . . UI §3267
Obligation to furnish information . . . UI §3268
Workers' compensation division
Advisory Committee for WCIS . . . 8 CCR §9704
Authority to implement . . . 8 CCR §9700
Claim information required to be reported . . . 8 CCR §§9702, 9778
Confidentiality . . . 8 CCR §9703
Definitions . . . 8 CCR §9701
Development of information systems by . . . Lab §§138.6, 139.6
Electronic data reporting . . . 8 CCR §§9702, 9778
Employee information requirements (See subhead: Employee information)
Information and Assistance Program (See WORKERS' COMPENSATION DIVISION)

INFORMED CONSENT
Chiropractors
Material risks of proposed care, informing patient . . . 16 CCR §319.1
Spouse called as adverse witness . . . Ev §971

IN-HOME SUPPORTIVE SERVICES FOR AGED, BLIND AND DISABLED
COVID-19
Compensation for injury or death from COVID-19 . . . Lab §3212.87
Direct payments to provider or recipients, workers' compensation, unemployment compensation, etcobligations . . . W&I §12302.2
Agents for recipient-employers to comply with employer obligations . . . W&I §12302.5
Providers
Sick leave
Paid sick leave work group for in-home supportive services providers . . . Lab §246
Sick leave for providers of in-home supportive services
Eligibility for paid sick leave . . . Lab §245.5

INITIAL PHYSICAL AGGRESSOR
Conditions of employer liability for compensation . . . Lab §3600

INJUNCTIONS
Elevators, escalators dumbwaiters, and other conveyances, safety
Dangerous operation . . . Lab §7321.5
Permits, operation without . . . Lab §7303
Occupational Safety and Health Division
Generally . . . Lab §6323
Stop orders, failure to observe . . . 8 CCR §15573
Temporary restraining orders (See TEMPORARY RESTRAINING ORDERS)

INJURY
Biological weapons
Law enforcement officers
Exposure to biochemical substances . . . Lab §3212.85
Cardiac disease (See HEART DISEASE)
Chemical weapons
Law enforcement officers
Exposure to biochemical substances . . . Lab §3212.85
Combined . . . Lab §3208.2
Conditions of employer liability for compensation . . . Lab §3600
Coronary disease (See HEART DISEASE)
Correctional inmates, injury to . . . Lab §6413
COVID-19, compensation for injury or death . . . Lab §3212.86
Firefighters, peace officers, health workers, etc . . . Lab §3212.87
Testing positive, outbreak at place of employment . . . Lab §3212.88
Crime, caused by . . . Lab §3600
Cumulative (See CUMULATIVE INJURY)
Date of . . . 8 CCR §§10100, 10100.1, Lab §§3600, 5411, 5412
Post-2002 audit, applicable definitions . . . 8 CCR §10100.2
Defined
Generally . . . Lab §3208
COVID-19, compensation for injury or death . . . Lab §3212.86
Firefighters, peace officers, health workers, etc . . . Lab §3212.87

Index

INJURY—Cont.
Defined—Cont.
COVID-19, compensation for injury or death —Cont.
Testing positive, outbreak at place of employment . . . Lab §3212.88
Employer's records of occupational injury or illness . . . 8 CCR §14300.46
On or after 1/1/1994 . . . 8 CCR §10100.1
Post-2002 audit
Applicable definitions . . . 8 CCR §10100.2
Prior to 1/1/1994 . . . 8 CCR §10100
Workers' compensation, law enforcement officers . . . Lab §§3212.12, 3212.85
Disability suffered after injured worker leaves work due to . . . Lab §4652
Economic Opportunity Program enrollees . . . Lab §4212
Employers
Liability of . . . Lab §5500.5
Reporting requirements (See EMPLOYER'S REPORT OF OCCUPATIONAL INJURY OR ILLNESS)
Evidence of . . . Lab §3600
Forms
Occupational injury or illness
Doctor's first report (Form 5021) . . . 8 CCR §14006
Employer's report, Form 5020 . . . 8 CCR §14004
Prisoners, report of injury (See PRISONERS)
Hand injuries
Presumption of total disability due to loss or loss of use of . . . Lab §4662
Health care workers, injuries sustained from preventive care . . . Lab §3208.05
Heart disease (See HEART DISEASE)
Hernias suffered by law enforcement officers and firefighters . . . Lab §§3212, 3212.4
Household employees . . . Lab §5500.6
Industrial accident or illness (See INDUSTRIAL ACCIDENT OR ILLNESS)
Knowledge of employer about injury
Insurer, imputed to . . . Ins §11652
Notice, equivalent to . . . Lab §5402
Layoff and . . . Lab §3600
Lyme disease
Law enforcement officers . . . Lab §3212.12
Mental (See PSYCHIATRIC INJURIES)
Minors, injured (See MINORS)
Neck injuries
Work capacity guidelines . . . Table 11
Ninety-day presumption . . . Lab §5402
Notice of
Conditions of employer liability . . . Lab §3600
Defective notice . . . Lab §5403
Failure to give . . . Lab §5403
Knowledge of employer about injury equivalent to . . . Lab §5402
Ninety-day presumption . . . Lab §5402
Time limits on . . . Lab §5400
Pneumonia (See PNEUMONIA)
Prevention programs
Injury prevention programs (See SAFE WORKPLACE)
Psychiatric (See PSYCHIATRIC INJURIES)

INJURY—Cont.
Records
Employer recordkeeping . . . 8 CCR §§14300 to 14300.48 (See EMPLOYER'S RECORDS OF OCCUPATIONAL INJURY OR ILLNESS)
Reporting requirements
Occupational disease or injury (See REPORTING REQUIREMENTS)
Safe workplace
Injury prevention programs (See SAFE WORKPLACE)
Second injury (See SUBSEQUENT INJURIES)
Self-inflicted . . . Lab §3600
Sexual conduct, arising from . . . Lab §3208.4
Specific . . . Lab §3208.1
Subsequent injuries (See SUBSEQUENT INJURIES)
Termination of employment and . . . Lab §3600
Third party causing injury or death
Personal relationship not inferred due to certain beliefs of third party . . . Lab §3600
Time
Date of injury . . . 8 CCR §§10100, 10100.1
Post-2002 audit, applicable definitions . . . 8 CCR §10100.2
Loss of, injuries involving . . . Lab §138.4
Treating physicians, reports of . . . Lab §6409
Treatment of (See MEDICAL TREATMENT)
Tuberculosis (See TUBERCULOSIS)

INMATES (See PRISONERS)

INSANITY
Presumption of total disability for brain injuries leading to mental incapacity . . . Lab §4662

INSOLVENCY (See BANKRUPTCY)

INSPECTION DEMANDS . . . CCP §§2031.010 to 2031.510
Attorney work product claimed
Electronically stored information . . . CCP §2031.285
Contents of demand . . . CCP §2031.030
Defendants
Making demand at any time . . . CCP §2031.020
Electronically stored information
Definition of electronically stored information . . . CCP §2016.020
Format and content of demand . . . CCP §2031.030
Objections . . . CCP §2031.240
Privilege log
Objections to inspection demand . . . CCP §2031.240
Protective orders and sanctions . . . CCP §2031.060
Response . . . CCP §§2031.210 to 2031.320
Right to discovery . . . CCP §2031.010
Service of demand . . . CCP §2031.040
Supplemental inspection demands . . . CCP §2031.050
Time for making demand . . . CCP §2031.020
Format of demand . . . CCP §2031.030
Identification by set and number . . . CCP §2031.030
Methods of discovery . . . CCP §§2019.010, 2031.010
Numbering demands . . . CCP §2031.030
Plaintiffs
When plaintiff may make demand . . . CCP §2031.020

INSPECTION DEMANDS—Cont.
Privilege claimed
Electronically stored information . . . CCP §2031.285
Protective orders and sanctions . . . CCP §2031.060
Response . . . CCP §§2031.210 to 2031.320
Timely response not filed . . . CCP §2031.300
Right to discovery by . . . CCP §2031.010
Sanctions
Protective orders
Unsuccessfully making or opposing motion for protective order . . . CCP §2031.060
Service of demand . . . CCP §2031.040
Supplemental inspection demands . . . CCP §2031.050

INSPECTIONS
Appeals board (WCAB)
Record of proceedings
Inspection of . . . 8 CCR §10807
Asbestos contract for corrective work as condition for . . . Lab §6509.5
Boilers (See TANKS AND BOILERS)
Cal-OSHA Targeted Inspection and Consultation Fund (See CAL-OSHA TARGETED INSPECTION AND CONSULTATION FUND)
Construction elevators . . . Lab §7204
Demands (See INSPECTION DEMANDS)
Electronic adjudication management system (EAMS)
Documents, inspection
Prohibitions on inspection of certain documents . . . 8 CCR §10208.6
Elevators . . . Lab §§7309, 7310
Annual inspection of conveyances . . . Lab §7304
Disposition of fees . . . Lab §7316
Duration of certificate . . . Lab §7311.3
Fees for certifications . . . Lab §7311.4
Fees for inspections . . . Lab §7314
Collection of . . . Lab §7314
Payment . . . Lab §7315
Suspension of fees . . . Lab §7314
Qualifications of inspectors . . . Lab §§7309.1, 7311
Qualified conveyance inspectors of municipality, issuance of permit based on certificate of . . . Lab §7310
Renewal of certificate . . . Lab §7311.3
Reports . . . Lab §7313
Health care organizations (HCOs)
Medical surveys (See HEALTH CARE ORGANIATIONS (HCOS))
Mines (See MINING AND TUNNELING)
Occupational Safety and Health Division (See OCCUPATIONAL SAFETY AND HEALTH DIVISION)
Refineries and chemical plants . . . Lab §7864
Tanks (See TANKS AND BOILERS)
Tower cranes (See TOWER CRANES)
Tunneling (See MINING AND TUNNELING)

INSTALLMENT PAYMENTS
Death benefits . . . Lab §4702

INSURANCE
Actuarial opinion statement
Submission of statement of actuarial opinion by property and casualty insurers . . . Ins §923.6

INSURANCE—Cont.
App-based drivers and services
Loss and liability protection . . . B&P §7455
Arbitration
Disclosure to employer as to choice of law and venue when dispute resolution to be used . . . Ins §11658.5
Associations or organizations of employers (See GROUP INSURANCE POLICIES)
Attachment of employer's property for failure to secure payment . . . Lab §3707
Audit of employer payroll by insurer . . . Ins §11760.1
Automobile liability insurance (See AUTOMOBILE LIABILITY INSURANCE)
Bankruptcy (See BANKRUPTCY)
Certification requirements (See CERTIFICATION)
Children, illegally employed . . . Ins §11661.5
Classes of . . . Ins §100
COBRA continuation coverage . . . Lab §2800.2
Commissioner (See INSURANCE COMMISSIONER)
Compensation defined for purposes of . . . Ins §11630
Compromise and release, insurer's declaration attached to . . . 8 CCR §10705, Lab §3761
Contractors
Certificate of workers' compensation insurance . . . B&P §7125
False certificates . . . B&P §7125.4
License maintained by maintaining certificate . . . B&P §7125.3
Renewal or recertification . . . B&P §7125.5
Stop order prohibiting use of employee labor for failure to secure workers' compensation coverage . . . B&P §7127
Reports . . . B&P §7125
Self-insured employers
Certification of self-insurance . . . B&P §7125
False certificates . . . B&P §7125.4
License maintained by maintaining certificate . . . B&P §7125.3
Renewal or recertification . . . B&P §7125.5
Conversion coverage
Availability of . . . Lab §2800.3
COBRA . . . Lab §2800.2
County employees . . . Gov §54462
County superintendent of schools, taken out by (See COUNTY SUPERINTENDENT OF SCHOOLS)
Crimes against insured property and insurers
False or fraudulent claims, making . . . Pen §550
Internet posting of convicted violators . . . Ins §1871.9
Solicitation or referral for purposes of insurance fraud . . . Pen §549
Deductible on policy, collateral or security for . . . Ins §11736.5
Definitions
Common carrier liability insurance . . . Ins §110
Compensation . . . Ins §11630
Fraud
Workers' Compensation Insurance Fraud Reporting Act . . . Ins §1877.1
Group coverage . . . Ins §42
Insurer (See DEFINITIONS)
Rating organizations, definitions pertinent to . . . Ins §11750.1

INSURANCE—Cont.
Definitions—Cont.
Security . . . Lab §3700.1
Self-insurance (See SELF-INSURANCE)
Workers' compensation insurance . . . Ins §109
Deposits by workers' compensation insurers . . . Ins §§11690 to 11703
Accounting for funds received . . . Ins §11698.1
Adjustments on annual basis . . . Ins §11693
Certificates of authority
Prerequisite of deposit . . . Ins §11692
Revocation for noncompliance with provisions . . . Ins §11701
Computation of amounts to be deposited . . . Ins §11694
Conditions for use of proceeds . . . Ins §11698.02
Control of deposit by commissioner
Authority upon . . . Ins §11698.01
Events triggering . . . Ins §11698
Insurance guarantee association member insurers found insolvent . . . Ins §11698.3
Definitions . . . Ins §11690
Exceptions to coverage . . . Ins §11702
Fees . . . Ins §11691.1
Late filing fee . . . Ins §11692.5
Insurance guarantee association member insurers
Insolvency found . . . Ins §11698.3
List of authorized insurers and reinsurers . . . Ins §11691.3
Occupational safety and health loss control consultation services
Providing by insurer . . . Ins §11703
Possession of deposit by commissioner
Authority upon . . . Ins §11698.01
Events triggering . . . Ins §11698
Insurance guarantee association member insurers found insolvent . . . Ins §11698.3
Proceeds
Conditions for use . . . Ins §11698.02
Satisfaction of claims by commissioner payment from deposit . . . Ins §11697
Reinsurance and assumption agreement between commissioner and insurers . . . Ins §11698.01
Contents . . . Ins §11698.2
Impairment of solvency of insurer, disqualification from entering agreement . . . Ins §11698.22
Reimbursements . . . Ins §11698.21
Repayment to insurer . . . Ins §11699
Reports . . . Ins §11694.5
Requirements . . . Ins §11691
Satisfaction of claims by commissioner payment from deposit . . . Ins §11697
Unpaid claims
Proceeds used to pay unpaid claims . . . Ins §11696
Satisfaction by commissioner payment from deposit . . . Ins §11697
Use of deposit . . . Ins §§11691.2, 11700
Valuation of securities
Software, use of . . . Ins §11693
Voluntary cessation of business in state
Fixing deposit to cover beneficiaries . . . Ins §11695

INSURANCE—Cont.
Deposits by workers' compensation insurers —Cont.
Withdrawal
Circumstances . . . Ins §11691.2
Disability (See DISABILITY BENEFITS)
Discovery of insurance coverage
Scope of discovery . . . CCP §2017.210
Discriminatory rates
Insurance premiums (See RATING)
Dispute resolution
Disclosure to employer as to choice of law and venue when dispute resolution to be used . . . Ins §11658.5
Dividend payments (See DIVIDENDS)
Effect . . . Lab §3753
Employee contributions and payments . . . Lab §3751
Employer
Bankruptcy or insolvency, effect on liability of insurer of . . . Ins §11655
Findings against, insurer bound by . . . Ins §11654
General employers . . . Ins §11663
Jurisdiction of . . . Ins §11653
Knowledge of injury imputed to insurer . . . Ins §11652
Lien priority against . . . Ins §11656
Organizations or associations of employers (See GROUP INSURANCE POLICIES)
Personal liability . . . Lab §3602
Rating organizations
Internet sites to assist persons in determining whether employer is insured . . . 10 CCR §§2593 to 2593.7, Ins §11752.75
Serious and willful misconduct of, no insurance against liability for . . . Ins §11661
Special employers . . . Ins §11663
Subrogation of insurer to rights of . . . Ins §11662
Employer's records of occupational injury or illness
Partial exemption from requirements . . . 8 CCR §14300.2
Experience rating (See EXPERIENCE RATING)
Failure to secure payment
Generally . . . Lab §3700.5
Amount of compensation recoverable, increase in . . . Lab §4554
Appeals Board (WCAB), proceedings before . . . Lab §3714
Attachment of employer's property for . . . Lab §3707
Attorneys' fees . . . Lab §4555
Court proceedings . . . Lab §3712
Criminal penalties . . . Lab §3700.5
Damages, action for (See DAMAGES)
Defenses . . . Lab §3708
Employee remedies . . . Lab §3715
Exceptions to penalty for . . . Lab §3706.5
Fraudulent failure to secure payment
Legislative intent . . . Ins §1871
Internet posting of convicted violators . . . Ins §1871.9
Judgments (See JUDGMENTS)
Negligence, presumption of . . . Lab §3708
Penalties and fines
Generally . . . Lab §3700.5

INSURANCE—Cont.
Failure to secure payment—Cont.
Penalties and fines—Cont.
Internet posting of convicted violators . . . Ins §1871.9
Penalty assessment order (See PENALTY ASSESSMENT ORDERS)
Uninsured employers . . . Lab §3722
Search warrants
Grounds for issuance . . . Pen §1524
Stop orders (See STOP ORDERS)
Subsequent convictions, penalties . . . Lab §3700.5
Third party liability . . . Lab §3732
Uninsured employers benefits trust fund (See UNINSURED EMPLOYERS BENEFITS TRUST FUND)
Filings (See FILING)
Findings against employer, insurer bound by . . . Ins §11654
Fraud
Generally (See FRAUD)
Workers' compensation insurance fraud reporting act (See WORKERS' COMPENSATION INSURANCE FRAUD REPORTING ACT)
General employers . . . Ins §11663
Group policies (See GROUP INSURANCE POLICIES)
Group self-insurance
Insuring to secure payment of compensation . . . 8 CCR §15498
Health care organizations (HCOs) . . . 8 CCR §9771.73
Health care providers
Contract between provider and contracting agent
Effect on rights and obligations of provider . . . Lab §4611
Household employees (See HOUSEHOLD EMPLOYEES)
Insurer (See INSURER)
Joinder of insurer, employer relief from liability on . . . Lab §3759
Joint powers agreement between public agencies . . . Gov §6516
Jurisdiction of insurer and employer . . . Ins §11653
Knowledge of injury by employer imputed to insurer . . . Ins §11652
Liability
Person entitled to compensation, liability not affected by insurance or other benefits held by . . . Lab §3752
Liability insurance (See LIABILITY INSURANCE)
Licensure, certificate of insurance required for (See CERTIFICATION)
Lien priority . . . Ins §§1871.7, 11656
Local governments and agencies . . . Gov §54462
Longshore and Harbor Workers' Compensation Act, liability under (See LONGSHORE AND HARBOR WORKERS' COMPENSATION ACT)
Loss
Corrections or revision reported by insurer to rating organization . . . Ins §11751.8
Premium and loss history report, insurer providing . . . Ins §11663.5
Rating organizations, losses and expenses reported by . . . Ins §11759.1

INSURANCE—Cont.
Loss—Cont.
State Compensation Insurance Fund annual accounting requirements . . . Ins §11776
Wrap-up insurance policies
Reporting workers' compensation losses and payroll information . . . Ins §11751.82
Loss control consultation services, maintenance of by insurers . . . Ins §11703
Medical information, release of . . . CC §56.150
Medical provider networks . . . 8 CCR §§9767.1 to 9767.16, Lab §§4616 to 4616.7 (See MEDICAL PROVIDER NETWORKS)
Medical treatment
Employer-provided medical treatment
Nonoccupational injury insurance coverage, applicability of insurance code provisions . . . Lab §4600
Military service
Bases outside U.S., employment on
Acquisition strategy for insurance required under provisions . . . 42 USC §1655
Misconduct of employer, no insurance against liability for . . . Ins §11661
Motor vehicle policies
Automobile liability insurance (See AUTOMOBILE LIABILITY INSURANCE)
Nonrenewal notices . . . Ins §§678, 11664
Electronic transmission of written notice . . . Ins §678
Notice
Facts to disprove claims, employer notice to insurer of . . . Lab §3761
Indemnity claims, insurer notice to employer of . . . Lab §3761
Injury report to insurer . . . Lab §3760
Insurance Frauds Prevention Act
Claim forms, penalty notice on . . . Ins §1871.2, Lab §5401.7
Temporary disability benefits, notice to injured workers on fraudulent receipt of . . . Ins §1871.8
Liability of insurer . . . Lab §3756
Nonrenewal of policy . . . Ins §11664
Posting notice of carrier . . . 8 CCR §15565
Rating laws, notice to policyholder about . . . Ins §11752.8
Rating organizations (See RATING ORGANIZATIONS)
Reserve amounts . . . Lab §3761
Occupational safety and health
Loss control consultation services, provision of . . . Ins §11703, Lab §6354.5
Organizations or associations of employers (See GROUP INSURANCE POLICIES)
Out-of-state employers . . . Lab §3600.5
Penalties and fines
Failure to secure payment . . . Lab §3700.5
Internet posting of convicted violators . . . Ins §1871.9
Penalty assessment order (See PENALTY ASSESSMENT ORDERS)
Insurance Frauds Prevention Act (See INSURANCE FRAUDS PREVENTION ACT)

INSURANCE—Cont.
Penalties and fines—Cont.
Premium, misrepresentation of payroll to lower . . . Ins §756
Reduced rate from State Compensation Insurance Fund, misrepresentation to obtain . . . Ins §11880
Internet posting of convicted violators . . . Ins §1871.9
Policies, cancellation or rescission
Fraud . . . Ins §676
Grounds . . . Ins §§676, 676.2
Malpractice insurance, peer review underwriting . . . Ins §676.3
Posting notice of carrier . . . 8 CCR §15565
Premiums (See PREMIUMS)
Presumptions
Compliance . . . Ins §11650
Rates presumed to create monopoly . . . Ins §11732
Proof of insurance . . . Lab §3711
Property insurance
Actuarial opinion statement
Submission of statement of actuarial opinion by property and casualty insurers . . . Ins §923.6
Cancellation or nonrenewal of policies
Hate crime or anti-reproductive-rights crime generating losses, factoring in decisions . . . Ins §676.10
Notice of cancellation . . . Ins §677.4
Public agencies
Joint powers agreement between . . . Gov §6516
Public employment . . . Lab §6130
Public hearings
Rating organizations . . . Ins §11751.55
Public works contracts, certificate of insurance requirements . . . Lab §1861
Rating (See RATING)
Rating organizations (See RATING ORGANIZATIONS)
Receivables, collateral or security for recognition of . . . Ins §11736.5
Referral or solicitation for purposes of insurance fraud . . . Pen §549
Reinsurance (See REINSURANCE)
Reporting requirements
Cancellation
Conditions requiring report by insurer of cancellation . . . B&P §7125
Deposits by workers' compensation insurers . . . Ins §11694.5
Injury report to insurer . . . Lab §3760
Loss corrections or revisions reported by insurer . . . Ins §11751.8
Losses and expenses of rating organization . . . Ins §11759.1
Occupational disease or injury, insurer reporting requirements regarding . . . 8 CCR §14002
State Compensation Insurance Fund (See STATE COMPENSATION INSURANCE FUND)
Statistical reporting
Rating organizations, by . . . Ins §11751.5
Wrap up insurance policies
Workers' compensation losses and payroll information . . . Ins §11751.82
Reserve requirements
Generally . . . Ins §923.5

INSURANCE—Cont.
Reserve requirements—Cont.
Employer notice of reserve amounts to insurer . . . Lab §3761
Security for establishment of . . . Ins §11736.5
Retaliatory discrimination . . . Lab §132a
Revocation of license, permit, or certification
Self-insurance (See SELF-INSURANCE)
Rights and privileges (See RIGHTS)
Roofing contractors
Certificate of workers' compensation insurance or self-insurance
Removal of C-39 roofing classification from license for failure to provide certificate to registrar . . . B&P §7125
Payroll audit by issuers of workers' compensation insurance . . . Ins §11665
School districts (See COUNTY SUPERINTENDENT OF SCHOOLS)
Security provisions (See SECURITY FOR PAYMENT)
Self-employed persons, jurisdiction over insurance controversies involving . . . Lab §5308
Self-insurance (See SELF-INSURANCE)
Serious and willful misconduct of, no insurance against liability for . . . Ins §11661
Solicitation or referral for purposes of insurance fraud . . . Pen §549
Special employers . . . Ins §11663
State Compensation Insurance Fund (See STATE COMPENSATION INSURANCE FUND)
Statement of insurer's liability . . . Ins §11651
Statistical reporting requirement
Rating organizations . . . Ins §11751.5
Subrogation of insurer to rights of employer . . . Ins §11662
Substitution of insurer (See INSURER)
Taxation of (See TAXATION)
Termination of coverage
Group self-insurance membership, termination of . . . 8 CCR §15480
Voluntary plan termination, employee eligibility for Unemployment Compensation Disability Fund benefits on . . . UI §3263
Voluntary disability benefit plans, insurers' substituted liability for . . . UI §3259

INSURANCE COMMISSIONER
Examination of rating organizations by . . . Ins §11752
Rate disapproved by . . . Ins §11737
State Compensation Insurance Fund, examination of . . . Ins §738
Statistical reporting by rating organizations . . . Ins §11751.5

INSURANCE COMPANIES
Discriminatory practices
Domestic violence victims . . . Ins §676.9

INSURANCE FRAUDS PREVENTION ACT
Generally . . . Ins §1871
Access to records for inspection . . . Ins §1871.1
Carrier actions . . . Ins §1871.7
Civil actions under, bringing . . . Ins §1871.7

INSURANCE FRAUDS PREVENTION ACT—Cont.
Claim forms, penalty notice on . . . Ins §1871.2, Lab §5401.7
Employee actions . . . Ins §1871.7
Fraud division
  Generally . . . Ins §1872.95
  Reconsideration, referral to District Attorney or division . . . Lab §5908
Injured worker, notice on fraudulent receipt of temporary disability benefits to . . . Ins §1871.8
Investigations
  Access to records for . . . Ins §1871.1
  Fraud divisions . . . Ins §1872.95
  Workers' Compensation Insurance Fraud Reporting Act . . . Ins §1877.3
Notice
  Claim forms, penalty notice on . . . Ins §1871.2, Lab §5401.7
  Temporary disability benefits, notice to injured workers on fraudulent receipt of . . . Ins §1871.8
Oral statements, false or fraudulent . . . Ins §1871.4
Penal Code Section 781 applicable to prosecutions under . . . Ins §1871.6
Penalties and fines
  Generally . . . Ins §1871.7
  Amounts of . . . Ins §1871.7
  Claim forms, notice on . . . Ins §1871.2, Lab §5401.7
  Ineligibility to receive or retain compensation . . . Ins §1871.5
  Intent of . . . Ins §1871.7
  Temporary disability benefits, notice to injured workers on fraudulent receipt of . . . Ins §1871.8
  Written or oral statements, false or fraudulent . . . Ins §1871.4
Private right of action . . . Ins §1871.7
Procurement, employment of persons for purposes of . . . Ins §1871.7
Records, access to . . . Ins §1871.1
Temporary disability benefits, notice to injured workers on fraudulent receipt of . . . Ins §1871.8
Workers' Compensation Insurance Fraud Reporting Act (See WORKERS' COMPENSATION INSURANCE FRAUD REPORTING ACT)
Written statements, false or fraudulent . . . Ins §1871.4

INSURER
Bankruptcy
  Employer's bankruptcy or insolvency, effect on liability of insurer . . . Ins §11655
Defined . . . Ins §11631
Deposits by workers' compensation insurers . . . Ins §§11690 to 11703
Facts to disprove claims, employer notice to insurer of . . . Lab §3761
Findings against employer, bound by . . . Ins §11654
Indemnity claims, insurer notice to employer of . . . Lab §3761
Injury and illness prevention programs
  Review and report on IIPP's of insureds . . . Lab §6401.7
Injury report to insurer . . . Lab §3760
Joinder of . . . Lab §3759
Jurisdiction of . . . Ins §11653

INSURER—Cont.
Knowledge of employer about injury imputed to insurer . . . Ins §11652
Liability, notice of . . . Lab §3756
Lien priority against employer . . . Ins §11656
Loss corrections or revisions reported by . . . Ins §11751.8
Occupational safety and health loss control consultation services, provision of . . . Lab §6354.5
Rate supervision . . . Ins §11732
  Compliance criteria . . . Ins §11733
  Uniform experience rating plan . . . Ins §11734
Rating organization member, as . . . Ins §11751.4
Reserve amounts, notice from employer of . . . Lab §3761
Statement of liability of . . . Ins §11651
Subrogation to rights of employer . . . Ins §11662
Substitution of
  Generally . . . Lab §3755
  Abatement of proceedings on, lack of . . . Lab §3758
  Employer relief from liability . . . Lab §3757

INTEREST
Death benefits or workers' compensation payments . . . Lab §5800
Medical treatment, employer payment for . . . Lab §4603.2
7 percent annually for lump-sum payments . . . Table 7
Shipping
  Public vessels, damages caused by or towage and salvage rendered to
    Judgments, when to include interest . . . 46 USC §31107
  United States vessels or cargo, suits in admiralty involving
    Inclusion of interest in judgment against US . . . 46 USC §30911
Successive payments, ten percent weekly interest for . . . Table 6
10 percent
  Annually for lump-sum payments . . . Table 5
  Weekly for successive payments . . . Table 6

INTERNAL COMBUSTION ENGINES
Exceptions to rules for internal use of . . . Lab §6703
Exhaust purifier devices . . . Lab §6702
Structures, used within . . . Lab §§6701, 6703

INTERNET
Fraud
  Insurance
    Posting of convicted violators of provisions on internet . . . Ins §1871.9
Medical provider networks
  Contact information for network posted on internet . . . Lab §4616
Rating organizations
  Queries on website to organization on coverage information for employers . . . 10 CCR §§2593 to 2593.7, Ins §11752.75
Workers' compensation insurance
  Rate comparison guide online . . . Ins §11742
  Rating organizations
    Internet sites to assist persons in determining whether employer is insured . . . 10 CCR §§2593 to 2593.7, Ins §11752.75

INTERPRETERS
Administrative hearing interpreters, certification
List of certified interpreters, maintenance and publication . . . Gov §11435.30
Arbitration
Qualifications of interpreter . . . 8 CCR §9795.1.5
Directories of qualified interpreters . . . 8 CCR §9795.5
Certification of court interpreters . . . Gov §68562
Administrative hearing interpreters, certification
List of certified interpreters, maintenance and publication . . . Gov §11435.30
Medical examination interpreters, certification
List of certified interpreters, maintenance and publication . . . Gov §11435.35
Definitions . . . 8 CCR §9795.1
Depositions
Employer responsibility to pay for interpreter services at deposition . . . Lab §5710
Qualifications of interpreter . . . 8 CCR §9795.1.5
Directories of qualified interpreters . . . 8 CCR §9795.5
Directories . . . 8 CCR §9795.5
Fees for services
Procedures for charging and paying . . . 8 CCR §9795.3
Reasonable, actual, and necessary requirement . . . Lab §5811
Time of payment . . . 8 CCR §9795.4
Financial interests in entities providing services . . . Lab §139.32
Findings and awards
Fees for interpreters . . . Lab §5811
Hearings
Qualifications of interpreter . . . 8 CCR §9795.1.5
Directories of qualified interpreters . . . 8 CCR §9795.5
Witnesses requiring interpreter
Party's duty as to presence of qualified interpreter . . . 8 CCR §10790
Identity and credentials of individuals providing interpreter services
Rulemaking to establish criteria . . . Lab §5811
Medical examination interpreters, certification
List of certified interpreters, maintenance and publication . . . Gov §11435.35
Medical examinations, at . . . Lab §4600
Medical legal examinations
Qualification of interpreters at medical treatment appointments or medical legal exams . . . 8 CCR §9795.1.6
Directories of qualified interpreters . . . 8 CCR §9795.5
Medical-legal expenses
Interpreter expenses . . . Lab §4620
Directories of qualified interpreters . . . 8 CCR §9795.5
Qualifications of interpreters . . . 8 CCR §9795.1.6
Medical treatment
Appointments
Directories of qualified interpreters . . . 8 CCR §9795.5

INTERPRETERS—Cont.
Medical treatment—Cont.
Appointments —Cont.
Qualification of interpreters at medical treatment appointments or medical legal exams . . . 8 CCR §9795.1.6
Employer-provided medical treatment
Entitlement of employee to services of qualified interpreter . . . Lab §4600
Notice of right to . . . 8 CCR §9795.2
Payment of fees and expenses . . . 8 CCR §9795.4
Witnesses requiring interpreters
Standards for interpreters . . . Lab §5811

INTERROGATORIES
Methods of discovery . . . CCP §2019.010

INTERSTATE AID
Emergency, during state of . . . Gov §8660

INTERSTATE COMMERCE
Railroads . . . 45 USC §51
Workers' compensation division of Labor Code, inapplicability of . . . Lab §3203

INTOXICATION
App-based drivers and services
Driving under the influence
Zero tolerance policies . . . B&P §7460
Conditions of employer liability for compensation . . . Lab §3600

INVASION OF PRIVACY
Visual images and sound recordings . . . CC §1708.8

INVESTIGATIONS
Advertising . . . 8 CCR §9833
Asbestos . . . Lab §4409
Audits of claim logs and files, triggered by . . . 8 CCR §§10106, 10106.5
Claim logs and files
Audit, investigations triggered by . . . 8 CCR §§10106, 10106.5
Civil penalty investigations . . . 8 CCR §10106.5
Complaints and information, triggered by . . . 8 CCR §10106
Duty to conduct . . . 8 CCR §10109
Court administrator
Ethical violations by judges . . . 8 CCR §9722.2
Fraud division (See INSURANCE FRAUDS PREVENTION ACT)
Fraud investigation and prosecution assessment (See ADMINISTRATION REVOLVING FUND)
Health care organization (HCO) violations . . . 8 CCR §9779.2
High hazardous industries . . . Lab §6314.1
Insurance, failure to secure payment
Investigation costs, responsibility for . . . Lab §3700.5
Search warrants
Grounds for issuance . . . Pen §1524
Insurance Frauds Prevention Act (See INSURANCE FRAUDS PREVENTION ACT)
Judges (WCJs) (See JUDGES (WCJS))

INVESTIGATIONS—Cont.
Labor Standards Enforcement Division . . . 8 CCR §15563
Longshore and Harbor Workers' Compensation Act . . . 33 USC §923
Medical treatment
Utilization review standards
Employer violations . . . Lab §2750.11
Investigation of utilization review process . . . 8 CCR §9792.11
Mining and tunneling operations, specified gas readings from . . . Lab §7961
Occupational Safety and Health Division (See OCCUPATIONAL SAFETY AND HEALTH DIVISION)
Public employees' retirement system
Insurance companies
Request for information from companies in relation to investigations . . . Ins §1877.35
Rating organizations
Generally . . . Ins §§11751.2, 11752
Costs of investigation, payment for . . . Ins §11752.2
License, examination for purposes of issuing . . . Ins §11751.2
Records, examination of . . . Ins §11752.1
Reports accepted in lieu of investigation . . . Ins §11752
Refinery and chemical plant incidents . . . Lab §7867
Uninsured Employers Fund investigations . . . Lab §3716.1
Workers' Compensation Division administrative director, by . . . 8 CCR §§9722.2, 9723
Workers' Compensation Ethics Advisory Committee, by . . . 8 CCR §9722.1
Workers' Compensation Insurance Fraud Reporting Act . . . Ins §1877.3

J

JAIL
Guards (See CORRECTIONS AND REHABILITATION DEPARTMENT)
Inmates (See PRISONERS)

JANITORIAL LABOR CONTRACTS
Labor law compliance
Funding in contract to be sufficient for contractor to comply with labor laws . . . Lab §2810

JOCKEYS
Collective bargaining agreements
Alternative dispute resolution . . . Lab §3201.81

JOINDER OF ACTIONS
Appeals Board (WCAB) . . . Lab §5303
Death benefits suits, joinder of Public Employees' Retirement System as defendant in . . . Lab §4708
Subrogation . . . Lab §3855
Uninsured employer, substantial shareholders and parents joining against . . . Lab §§3717.1, 3718

JOINDER OF INSURERS
Employer relief from liability on . . . Lab §3759

JOINDER OF PARTIES
Appeals Board (WCAB) cases . . . 8 CCR §10382

JOINT POWERS
Public agencies, agreements between . . . Gov §6516
Self-insurance
Public entity or joint powers authority (See SELF-INSURANCE)

JUDGES (WCJS)
Generally . . . Lab §123.5
Administrative regulations, effective date of . . . 8 CCR §9711
Affidavit as to pending cases
Form . . . 8 CCR §9714.5
Submission . . . 8 CCR §9714
Appeals Board (WCAB) and (See APPEALS BOARD (WCAB))
Appointment of . . . Lab §5310
Asbestos workers . . . Lab §4409.5
Assignment of cases . . . 8 CCR §10346
Authority of . . . 8 CCR §§9710, 9720.1, 10330
Certified workers' compensation specialists as pro tempore judges . . . Lab §123.7
Contempt . . . 8 CCR §10440
Continuing education requirements . . . Lab §5311.5
Court administrator rules
Workers' compensation administrative law judges generally (See COURT ADMINISTRATOR RULES)
Decisions by (See DECISIONS)
Definitions
Labor Code, definition of WCJs under . . . Lab §27
Pertinent terms . . . 8 CCR §§9712, 9720.2
Designations for . . . 8 CCR §10302
Disqualification of judge
Factors not considered grounds for disqualification . . . 8 CCR §9721.13
Grounds . . . 8 CCR §9721.12
Petition . . . 8 CCR §10960
Education
Continuing education requirements . . . Lab §5311.5
Financial interests in educational programs, judges with . . . 8 CCR §9721.31
Electronic adjudication management system (EAMS)
Definition of workers' compensation administrative law judge . . . 8 CCR §10205
Ethical conduct (See ETHICAL REQUIREMENTS)
Forms
Affidavit as to pending cases . . . 8 CCR §9714.5
Gifts . . . 8 CCR §9721.2
Hearings before
Generally . . . 8 CCR §9715
Honoraria . . . 8 CCR §9721.2, Lab §123.6
Investigations of
Administrative director, by . . . 8 CCR §9722.2
Commencing . . . 8 CCR §9722.1
Court administrator . . . 8 CCR §9722.2
Leave pending . . . 8 CCR §9723
Unsustained complaints, documentation of . . . 8 CCR §9723
Labor Code, defined under . . . Lab §27
Objections to specific judges . . . Lab §5311
Orders of presiding judge . . . 8 CCR §10344
Pending causes, receipt of salary affected by
Affidavit
Form for . . . 8 CCR §9714.5

Index

JUDGES (WCJS)—Cont.
Pending causes, receipt of salary affected by—Cont.
Affidavit —Cont.
Submission of . . . 8 CCR §9714
Requirements regarding . . . 8 CCR §9713, Lab §123.5
Powers of . . . Lab §5307.5
Procedural rights, specific provisions not affecting . . . 8 CCR §9723
Pro tempore judges
Generally . . . Lab §123.7
Trials
Appointment and authority of pro tempore workers' compensation judges . . . 8 CCR §10355
Reassignment of trial or expedited hearing to another judge, petition for . . . 8 CCR §10788
Receipt of salary . . . 8 CCR §§9713 to 9714.5, Lab §123.5
Reconsideration
Authority following decision after . . . 8 CCR §10986
Report on petition . . . 8 CCR §10962
Removal by Board . . . Lab §5310
Reporters providing stenographic or clerical assistance as directed by . . . Lab §123.3
Reporting ethical violations, duty . . . 8 CCR §9721.32
Rights of
Ethics requirements not affecting rights and obligations of . . . 8 CCR §9723
Procedural rights, specific provisions not affecting . . . 8 CCR §9723
Settlement conference authority
Mandatory settlement conferences . . . 8 CCR §10759
Swearing in of . . . Lab §5312
Testimony of judicial or quasi-judicial officers . . . 8 CCR §10360
Transfer of cases . . . 8 CCR §10346
Travel expenses . . . 8 CCR §9721.2, Lab §123.6
Trials
Partially tried case
Completion by same trial judge . . . Lab §5700
Pro tempore judges
Appointment and authority of pro tempore workers' compensation judges . . . 8 CCR §10355
Workers' compensation division
Administrative director (See WORKERS' COMPENSATION DIVISION)

JUDGMENT LIENS
Third party, enforcement of judgment lien by employer against . . . Lab §3862
Workers' compensation award, based on . . . CCP §697.330

JUDGMENT ROLL
Appeals Board (WCAB) findings and order, decision, and award, certified copy of . . . Lab §5807

JUDGMENTS
Failure to secure payment
Damages, action by injured worker for . . . Lab §3709
Enforcement by nonjudicial foreclosure . . . Lab §3716.3

JUDGMENTS—Cont.
Failure to secure payment—Cont.
Motor carriers, transmittal of judgment against . . . Lab §3716.4
Labor commissioner enforcement of judgments . . . Lab §96.8
Money judgments
Discovery
Civil discovery act, effect on enforcement of money judgments . . . CCP §2016.070
Enforcement of
Civil discovery act, effect on enforcement of money judgments . . . CCP §2016.070
Penalty assessment orders
Special judgments (See PENALTY ASSESSMENT ORDERS)
Port drayage motor carriers
Judgments against carriers
Unsatisfied court judgments, posting . . . Lab §2810.4
Satisfaction in fact . . . Lab §5809
Shipping
Public vessels, damages caused by or towage and salvage rendered to
Interest, when judgments may include . . . 46 USC §31107
Payment . . . 46 USC §31109
United States vessels or cargo, suits in admiralty involving
Costs, inclusion in judgments against US . . . 46 USC §30911
Interest, inclusion in judgments against US . . . 46 USC §30911
Payment of judgments . . . 46 USC §30913
Support judgment, application of workers' compensation award to . . . CCP §704.160

JUDICIAL COUNCIL
Court interpreters, certification of . . . Gov §68562

JUDICIAL NOTICE
Statutes . . . Ev §§451 to 452

JUDICIAL PROCEEDINGS
Military bases outside U.S., employment on . . . 42 USC §1653

JUDICIAL REVIEW
Appeals Board (WCAB) decisions, orders, findings, and awards
Generally . . . Lab §5810
Code of Civil Procedure, governed by . . . Lab §5954
Exclusive jurisdiction of state Supreme Court and appellate courts . . . Lab §5955
Extent of review . . . Lab §5952
Filing of undertaking on stay order . . . Lab §6002
Findings of fact not reviewable . . . Lab §5953
Hearing, right to appear at . . . Lab §5953
Limitations on issuance of stay order . . . Lab §6000
Record of Appeals Board, writ based on . . . Lab §5951
Service of pleadings . . . Lab §5954
Stay of decision during judicial review (See APPEALS BOARD (WCAB))

JUDICIAL REVIEW—Cont.
Appeals Board (WCAB) decisions, orders, findings, and awards—Cont.
Time limits on filing for review . . . Lab §5950
Undertaking on stay order . . . Lab §§6001, 6002
Writ of review . . . Lab §5950
Filing
Appeals Board (WCAB) decisions, orders, findings, and awards
Time limits on filing for review . . . Lab §5950
Undertaking on stay order . . . Lab §6002
Occupational Safety and Health Appeals Board decisions, filing for writ of mandate on . . . Lab §§6627, 6631
Longshore and Harbor Workers' Compensation Act awards . . . 33 USC §921
Occupational Safety and Health Appeals Board decisions
Generally . . . Lab §148.6
Finality of appeals board's findings of fact . . . Lab §6630
Jurisdiction . . . Lab §6632
Postponement of operation of decision . . . Lab §6633
Procedures for superior court review . . . Lab §6628
Scope of superior court review . . . Lab §6629
Writ of mandate, filing for . . . Lab §§6627, 6631
Self-insurance hearing officer, decision of . . . 8 CCR §15437

JURISDICTION
Admiralty jurisdiction (See ADMIRALTY AND MARITIME JURISDICTION)
Appeals Board (WCAB)
Generally . . . Lab §5301
Application
Filing as prerequisite to invocation of jurisdiction . . . 8 CCR §10450
Continuing . . . Lab §5803
Filing of documents with, rejection
Restrictions on rejection when statute of limitations or jurisdictional time limitation implicated . . . 8 CCR §10617
Judicial review of Appeals Board decisions . . . Lab §5955
Medical treatment . . . Lab §5304
Medical treatment, disputes over . . . Lab §4604
Out-of-state injuries of resident . . . Lab §5305
Proceedings handled by . . . Lab §5300
Public Employees' Retirement System
Disability retirement jurisdiction . . . Gov §§21166, 21171
Special death benefits jurisdiction . . . Gov §§21537, 21540.5
Self-employed persons, insurance controversies involving . . . Lab §5308
Asbestos-related complaints . . . Lab §6436
District courts (See DISTRICT COURT)
Maritime jurisdiction (See ADMIRALTY AND MARITIME JURISDICTION)
Occupational Safety and Health Appeals Board decisions, judicial review of . . . Lab §6632
Prizes brought into U.Sand property taken as prize . . . 28 USC §1333
Public Employees' Retirement System Appeals Board (WCAB) jurisdiction
Disability retirement . . . Gov §§21166, 21171

JURISDICTION—Cont.
Public Employees' Retirement System Appeals Board (WCAB) jurisdiction—Cont.
Special death benefits . . . Gov §§21537, 21540.5
Railroads . . . 45 USC §56
Safe workplace issues
Generally . . . Lab §6303.5
Self-insurers with revoked certificates to self-insure, continuing jurisdiction over . . . 8 CCR §15427
State Supreme Court and courts of appeal, exclusive jurisdiction over judicial review of Appeals Board decisions . . . Lab §5955
Workers' Compensation Division
Generally . . . Lab §133
Information and Assistance program . . . 8 CCR §9927

JURY TRIALS
Jury instructions
Privileges, evidentiary, invocation of . . . Ev §913
United States as defendant . . . 28 USC §2401

JUSTICE DEPARTMENT
Course of duty, injury occurring in . . . Lab §4801
Medical treatment . . . Lab §4802
One year, disability continuing beyond . . . Lab §4803
Paid leave of absence . . . Lab §4800
Permanent disability . . . Lab §4803
Salary payments, temporary disability payments concurrent with . . . Lab §4804
Temporary disability
Duty, disability occurring in course of . . . Lab §4801
Eligibility for medical, surgical, and hospital benefits . . . Lab §4802
One year, disability continuing beyond . . . Lab §4803
Paid leave of absence . . . Lab §4800
Tuberculosis suffered by employees of . . . Lab §3212.7

JUVENILE COURT
Volunteers
Regional youth facility
Wards committed to facility . . . Lab §3364.7
Traffic offenders . . . Lab §3364.6
Wards . . . Lab §3364.55
Wards of juvenile court (See MINORS)

JUVENILES (See MINORS)

K

KILL BUTTONS
Mining and tunneling equipment . . . Lab §7975

KNEE INJURIES
Medical treatment
Utilization schedule
Knee disorders . . . 8 CCR §9792.23.6

KNOX-KEENE HEALTH CARE SERVICE PLAN ACT
Provisions of . . . Lab §4600.5

L

LABELING
Hazardous substances . . . Lab §6390.5

Index

LABOR AND WORKFORCE DEVELOPMENT AGENCY
Definitions . . . Lab §18.5
Secretary . . . Lab §19.5
Industrial relations department
Composition of agency . . . Lab §50
Occupational safety and health
Insurance loss control services coordinator . . . Lab §6354.7
Secretary of labor and workforce development
Defined . . . Lab §19.5

LABORATORY SERVICES
Official medical fee schedule . . . 8 CCR §9789.50

LABOR CODE CONSTRUCTION
County, city included in . . . Lab §14
Department defined as Department of Industrial Relations . . . Lab §19
Director defined as Director of Industrial Relations . . . Lab §20
Gender, use of . . . Lab §§12, 12.1
General provisions governing . . . Lab §5
Headings, intent not affected by . . . Lab §6
Independent medical examiner equivalent to qualified medical evaluator (QME) . . . Lab §28
Invalid provisions, effect of . . . Lab §24
Judges (WCJs) defined . . . Lab §27
Labor Commissioner defined . . . Lab §21
Mailing requirements . . . Lab §8
Man to be exchanged for person in Code amendment process . . . Lab §12.1
Mark and acknowledgment of mark . . . Lab §17
Marshall included in use of Sheriff . . . Lab §25
"May" defined as permissive . . . Lab §15
Medical director defined for purposes of . . . Lab §29
New and existing provisions . . . Lab §2
Oath, affirmation included in . . . Lab §16
Penalties and fines under . . . Lab §23
Person
Defined . . . Lab §18
Use of man to be exchanged for . . . Lab §12.1
Powers granted by . . . Lab §7
Qualified medical evaluator (QME), independent medical examiner equivalent to . . . Lab §28
References to . . . Lab §9
Rehabilitated criminals, availability of licenses for . . . Lab §26
Section defined for purposes of . . . Lab §10
"Shall" defined as mandatory . . . Lab §15
Sheriff defined for purposes of . . . Lab §25
Signature or subscription defined for purposes of . . . Lab §17
Singulars and plurals, use of . . . Lab §13
Tenses . . . Lab §11
Title of . . . Lab §1
Violation defined for purposes of . . . Lab §22
Workers' compensation division of Labor Code
Administrative director defined as Workers' Compensation Division director . . . Lab §3206
Appeals Board (WCAB) defined as Workers' Compensation Appeals Board for purposes of . . . Lab §3205.5
Compensation defined for purposes of . . . Lab §3207

LABOR CODE CONSTRUCTION—Cont.
Workers' compensation division of Labor Code—Cont.
Construction, definitions governing . . . Lab §3350
Definitions of chapter governing . . . Lab §3204
Division defined for purposes of . . . Lab §3205
Employee coverage by, effect of . . . Lab §3369
Insurer defined for purposes of . . . Lab §3211
Interstate commerce, inapplicability to . . . Lab §3203
Liberal construction of . . . Lab §3202
Person defined for purposes of . . . Lab §3210
Preponderance of the evidence standard . . . Lab §3202.5
Purpose of . . . Lab §3201
Writing defined for purposes of . . . Lab §8

LABOR CODE PRIVATE ATTORNEYS GENERAL . . . Lab §§2698 to 2699.6
Actions brought by private aggrieved employee . . . Lab §2699
Cure of violation . . . Lab §§2699.3, 2699.5
Investigations by agencies . . . Lab §§2699.3, 2699.5
Notice . . . Lab §§2699.3, 2699.5
Settlements
Review . . . Lab §§2699.3, 2699.5
Applicability of act
Construction industry, work done under collective bargaining agreement . . . Lab §2699.6
Citation . . . Lab §2698

LABOR COMMISSIONER
Client employer-labor contractor responsibilities
Rulemaking to enforce provisions . . . Lab §2810.3
Defined . . . Lab §21
Judgments, enforcement
Labor commissioner enforcement of judgments . . . Lab §96.8
Labor contractor-client employer responsibilities
Rulemaking to enforce provisions . . . Lab §2810.3
Sick days, paid
Enforcement . . . Lab §248.5

LABOR CONTRACTORS
Client employer-labor contractor responsibilities . . . Lab §2810.3
Premium payments . . . Lab §3302

LABOR ENFORCEMENT AND COMPLIANCE FUND . . . Lab §62.5
Advances against insured employers
Collection . . . 8 CCR §15606
Assessment . . . 8 CCR §15600
Allocation . . . 8 CCR §15602
Collection of assessment . . . 8 CCR §§15605, 15607
Determining aggregate assessment . . . 8 CCR §15601
Determining assessment . . . 8 CCR §15603
Interim assessments
Collection . . . 8 CCR §15611
Defined . . . 8 CCR §15600
Surplus . . . 8 CCR §15604

LABOR-MANAGEMENT AGREEMENTS
Collective bargaining agreements (See COLLECTIVE BARGAINING AGREEMENTS)

LABOR SECRETARY
Employer's records of occupational injury or illness
    Providing access to government representatives . . . 8 CCR §14300.40
Foreign employees of contractors with U.Sworking outside U.S
    Administration . . . 42 USC §1706
    Finality of decisions . . . 42 USC §1715
Longshore and Harbor Workers' Compensation Act
    Secretary of Labor (See LONGSHORE AND HARBOR WORKERS' COMPENSATION ACT)

LABOR STANDARDS ENFORCEMENT DIVISION
Appeal hearings and procedures
    Conduct of hearing . . . 8 CCR §15587
    Custody of papers filed with Division . . . 8 CCR §15589
    Decision at conclusion of . . . 8 CCR §15590
    Designation of legal entity, correction of . . . 8 CCR §15579
    Errors, correction of . . . 8 CCR §15579
    Invalid grounds for . . . 8 CCR §15584
    Oath, proceedings under . . . 8 CCR §15585
    Penalty assessment orders . . . 8 CCR §15582
    Record of proceedings . . . 8 CCR §15586
    Stop orders . . . 8 CCR §15581
    Subpoenas and subpoenas duces tecum . . . 8 CCR §15587
    Valid grounds for . . . 8 CCR §15583
    Withdrawal of orders . . . 8 CCR §15580
    Writ of review following findings, employer's right to . . . 8 CCR §15591
Assignment of claims by . . . Lab §96
Certification of claims by . . . Lab §96.5
Collective bargaining agreements . . . Lab §96.3
Custody of papers filed with . . . 8 CCR §15589
Decisions
    Hearing, following . . . 8 CCR §15590
    Issuance of . . . 8 CCR §§15555, 15571
Definitions
    Direction to file verified statement . . . 8 CCR §15551
    Division . . . 8 CCR §15553
    Enforcement, pertinent to (See subhead: Enforcement by)
    Findings issued by division . . . 8 CCR §15554
    Uninsured employers . . . 8 CCR §15560
Direction to file verified statement
    Contents . . . 8 CCR §15576
    Defined . . . 8 CCR §15551
Employee complaints
    Port drayage motor carriers
        Illegal acts of carriers, posting . . . Lab §2810.4
Enforcement by
    Generally . . . Lab §61
    Access to workplaces for purposes of . . . 8 CCR §15563
    Appeal hearings (See subhead: Appeal hearings and procedures)
    Definitions pertinent to
        Generally . . . 8 CCR §§15551 to 15562
        Direction to file verified statement . . . 8 CCR §15551
        Director . . . 8 CCR §15552

LABOR STANDARDS ENFORCEMENT DIVISION—Cont.
Enforcement by—Cont.
    Definitions pertinent to—Cont.
        Division . . . 8 CCR §15553
        Findings . . . 8 CCR §15554
        Issue . . . 8 CCR §15555
        Notice of findings on penalty assessment order or stop order . . . 8 CCR §15556
        Penalty assessment order . . . 8 CCR §15557
        Special judgment . . . 8 CCR §15558
        Stop order . . . 8 CCR §15559
        Uninsured employer . . . 8 CCR §15560
        Verified petition . . . 8 CCR §15561
        Verified statement . . . 8 CCR §15561
    Delegation of authority to Division . . . 8 CCR §15550
    Direction to file verified statement
        Contents . . . 8 CCR §15576
        Defined . . . 8 CCR §15551
    Inquiry into insurance coverage . . . 8 CCR §15564
    Investigations . . . 8 CCR §15563
    Payment for workers' compensation coverage . . . Lab §90.3
    Penalty assessment orders (See PENALTY ASSESSMENT ORDERS)
    Penalty liens
        Cancellation of . . . 8 CCR §15595
        Recording of . . . 8 CCR §15594
    Stop orders (See STOP ORDERS)
    Uninsured employers defined for purposes of . . . 8 CCR §15560
    Verified petition . . . 8 CCR §15562
    Verified statement (See VERIFIED STATEMENT)
Filing
    Custody of papers filed with Division . . . 8 CCR §15589
    Direction to file verified statement
        Contents . . . 8 CCR §15576
        Defined . . . 8 CCR §15551
Findings issued by
    Generally . . . 8 CCR §§15555, 15571
    Definition of findings . . . 8 CCR §15554
    Notice of findings on penalty assessment order or stop order . . . 8 CCR §15554
    Writ of review following . . . 8 CCR §15591
Hearings on appeal (See subhead: Appeal hearings and procedures)
Investigations . . . 8 CCR §15563
Issuance of orders, decisions, findings, and notices . . . 8 CCR §§15555, 15571
Judgments, enforcement
    Labor commissioner enforcement of judgments . . . Lab §96.8
Minimum labor standards, enforcement . . . Lab §90.5
Payment for workers compensation coverage
    Enforcement . . . Lab §90.3
Penalty assessment orders (See PENALTY ASSESSMENT ORDERS)
Penalty liens
    Cancellation of . . . 8 CCR §15595
    Recording of . . . 8 CCR §15594
Stop orders (See STOP ORDERS)

LABOR STANDARDS ENFORCEMENT DIVISION—Cont.
Uninsured employer identification . . . Lab §90.3
Unpaid Wage Fund . . . Lab §96.6
Verified petition . . . 8 CCR §15562
Verified statement (See VERIFIED STATEMENT)
Wage claims
Report to finance department on wage claims . . . Lab §96.1

LABOR STATISTICS AND RESEARCH DIVISION
Correctional Department and . . . Lab §6413.2
Occupational disease or injury, reporting requirements regarding (See REPORTING REQUIREMENTS)

LABOR STATISTICS, BUREAU OF
Employer's records of occupational injury or illness
Definition of BLS . . . 8 CCR §14300.46
Requests for data . . . 8 CCR §14300.42

LAMINATED SAFETY GLASS
Railroad safety requirements (See RAILROADS)

LAYOFFS
Injury, date of . . . Lab §3600

LEAD POISONING
Occupational safety and health division
Investigations and inspections
Complaints charging serious violation, lead poisoning report as . . . Lab §147.3
Occupational safety and health standards board
Rulemaking to revise lead standards for general industry safety orders and construction safety orders . . . Lab §6717.5

LEAD-RELATED CONSTRUCTION WORK
Occupational Safety and Health Division requirements . . . Lab §§6716, 6717
Occupational safety and health standards board
Rulemaking to revise lead standards for general industry safety orders and construction safety orders . . . Lab §6717.5

LEASES
Financial interests in entities providing services
Conflicts of interest
Exceptions . . . Lab §139.32

LEASING OF EMPLOYEES
Self-insurance
Certificate of consent to self-insure
Restrictions on issuance . . . Lab §3701.9
Rulemaking on obligations of self-insurers . . . Lab §3702.10

LEAVE OF ABSENCE
Paid leave (See PAID LEAVE OF ABSENCE)

LEGAL SERVICES
Advertisement for workers' compensation legal services, attorney's name required in . . . B&P §5499.30
Attorneys' fees (See ATTORNEYS' FEES)
Foreign employment by contractors with U.Sworking outside U.S . . . 42 USC §1714

LEGAL SERVICES—Cont.
Industrial Relations, legal services for Department of . . . Lab §54.5

LEGISLATURE AND LEGISLATORS
Judicial notice of acts by . . . Ev §§451, 452

LETTERS OF CREDIT
Self-insurer's security deposit, as . . . 8 CCR §15215

LEVY
Attachment, preference in levy of . . . Lab §5603
Federal government tax law . . . 26 USC §6334
Foreign employment by contractors with U.Sworking outside U.S . . . 42 USC §1717

LIABILITY INSURANCE
Child care providers . . . Ins §676.1
Common carrier liability insurance
Railroads (See RAILROADS)
Coverage limitations . . . Ins §11580.2
Discriminatory practices, domestic violence victims . . . Ins §676.9
Household employees (See HOUSEHOLD EMPLOYEES)
Limitations . . . Ins §11580.2
Motor vehicles (See AUTOMOBILE LIABILITY INSURANCE)
Personal liability insurance for household employees (See HOUSEHOLD EMPLOYEES)
Types of insurance included in . . . Ins §108
Uninsured employers benefits trust fund (See UNINSURED EMPLOYERS BENEFITS TRUST FUND)
Workers' compensation insurers, liability insurers as . . . Ins §108.1

LIBEL IN REM OR IN PERSONAM
Suits in admiralty (See SHIPPING)

LIBERAL CONSTRUCTION
Safety in employment (Division 5), liberal construction in favor of injured worker . . . Lab §3202
Workers' compensation (Division 4), liberal construction in favor of injured worker . . . Lab §3202

LICENSED PROFESSIONAL CLINICAL COUNSELORS
Privileged communications with patients . . . Ev §§1010 to 1016

LICENSES AND PERMITS
Asbestos
Permit requirements for asbestos-related work (See ASBESTOS)
Building permits for housing . . . H&S §17922.5
Business license applications . . . B&P §16545
Chemical plants and refineries, hot work permits for . . . Lab §7865
Construction permit, certificate of insurance required for . . . Lab §3800
Contractors' State License Board, notice of Occupational Safety and Health Division penalty to . . . Lab §6652
Cranes (See CRANES)
Elevators, escalators, chair lifts and other conveyances
Permits (See ELEVATORS, ESCALATORS, CHAIR LIFTS AND OTHER CONVEYANCES)

LICENSES AND PERMITS—Cont.
Hot work, permits for . . . Lab §7865
Housing, building permits for . . . H&S §17922.5
Insurance (See CERTIFICATION)
Mining (See MINING AND TUNNELING)
Occupational Safety and Health Appeals Board denial or revocation of . . . Lab §6506
Occupational Safety and Health Division permit requirements
  Permit requirements (See OCCUPATIONAL SAFETY AND HEALTH DIVISION)
Rating organization license (See RATING ORGANIATIONS)
Refineries and chemical plants, hot work permits for . . . Lab §7865
Rehabilitated criminals, Labor Code licenses available for . . . Lab §26
Revocation (See REVOCATION OF LICENSE, PERMIT, OR CERTIFICATION)
Self-insurance
  Certificate of insurance or self-insurance required for licensure (See CERTIFICATION)
  Private sector license fee assessment . . . 8 CCR §15230
  Public sector license fee assessment . . . 8 CCR §15231
Suspension of (See SUSPENSION OF LICENSE, PERMIT, OR CERTIFICATION)
Tower crane
  Permits (See TOWER CRANES)
Treating physician's bias reported to appropriate licensing body . . . Lab §4068
Tunneling (See MINING AND TUNNELING)

LIENS
Generally . . . Lab §4903
Activation fees . . . Lab §4903.06
  Reimbursement . . . Lab §4903.07
Adjustment of . . . Lab §4904
Appeals Board (WCAB)
  Claimants
    Ex parte communications . . . 8 CCR §10410
    Identification of parties . . . 8 CCR §10390
  Compensation, claims on
    Verification of compliance with filing requirements . . . 8 CCR §10863
  Compromise and release agreements . . . 8 CCR §10702
  Conferences
    Fees required at lien conferences . . . 8 CCR §10876
    Lien conferences . . . 8 CCR §10875
    Submission at lien conferences . . . 8 CCR §10878
  Declaration of readiness
    Claimant declaration . . . 8 CCR §10873
    Verification . . . 8 CCR §10874
  Form for liens . . . 8 CCR §10500
  Representation of lien claimants
    Notice of representation, change of representation or nonrepresentation . . . 8 CCR §10868
  Trials
    Lien trials . . . 8 CCR §§10875, 10880

LIENS—Cont.
Appeals Board (WCAB)—Cont.
  Unemployment compensation disability liens . . . 8 CCR §10899
  Unrepresented lien claimants
    Notice of nonrepresentation . . . 8 CCR §10868
  Unrequested liens
    Award for unrequested lien . . . Lab §4905
  Verification
    Declaration of readiness by or on behalf of lien claimants . . . 8 CCR §10874
  Vexatious litigants . . . 8 CCR §10430
Appearances
  Lien claimants . . . 8 CCR §10752
Asbestos Workers' Account . . . Lab §§4414, 4416
Assignment of lien . . . Lab §4903.8
Attorneys' fees . . . 26 USC §6323, Lab §4903.2
  Filing lien . . . Lab §4903.6
Award
  Lien based on . . . CCP §697.330
  Payment of lien not affecting payment of balance of award . . . Lab §4904.1
California insurance guarantee association (CIGA)
  Workers' compensation bond fund
    Collateral, lien on . . . Ins §1063.76
Certificate of cancellation of lien following payment of compensation . . . Lab §3721
Claims
  Contents . . . Lab §4903.05
  Electronic filing . . . Lab §4903.05
  Written claims
    Required . . . Lab §4903.05
Compromise and release agreements
  Service of . . . 8 CCR §10702
Confidentiality of medical information . . . Lab §4903.6
Deemed requested . . . Lab §4905
Disability benefit overpayments (See DISABILITY BENEFITS)
Disallowance of . . . Lab §4904
Dismissal of lien claims . . . 8 CCR §10888
Duplicate payments . . . Lab §3865
Electronic adjudication management system (EAMS)
  Activation fees . . . 8 CCR §10208
    Refunds . . . 8 CCR §10208.1
  Definitions . . . 8 CCR §10205
  Filing fees
    Initial lien filing fee . . . 8 CCR §10207
    Refunds . . . 8 CCR §10208.1
  Refund of fees . . . 8 CCR §10208.1
  Uniform assigned names (UAN), creation and assignment for claims administrators, representatives and lien claimant organizations . . . 8 CCR §10206.4
Electronic filing of claims . . . Lab §4903.05
Employee liens against employers . . . Ins §1871.7
Expenses
  Disputes over liens for . . . Lab §4903.4
  Injured employee, expenses incurred by or on behalf of . . . Lab §4903
    Deemed requested, exception for expenses . . . Lab §4905
    Requirements before filing lien claim or application for adjudication . . . Lab §4903.6

LIENS—Cont.
Family temporary disability insurance benefits
Liens for benefits paid against workers' compensation benefits . . . Lab §4903
Amount, determination . . . Lab §4904
Federal tax liens . . . 26 USC §6323
Filing and service of lien claims and supporting documents . . . 8 CCR §10862
Resolution or withdrawal of claims
Notification . . . 8 CCR §10872
Filing fees . . . Lab §4903.05
Reimbursement . . . Lab §4903.07
Foreign employment by contractors with U.Sworking outside U.S . . . 42 USC §1705
Inactive cases
Dismissal of inactive lien claims . . . 8 CCR §10888
Insurer liens against employer . . . Ins §11656
Judgment liens
Employer against third party . . . Lab §3862
Workers' compensation award, based on . . . CCP §697.330
Lien activation fees . . . Lab §4903.06
Reimbursement . . . Lab §4903.07
Limitation period for filing lien claim . . . Lab §4903.5
Longshore and Harbor Workers' Compensation Act . . . 33 USC §917
Medical reports, medical-legal reports, other medical information
Service on non-physician lien claimants . . . 8 CCR §10637
Multiple assignment of lien . . . Lab §4903.8
Payment of lien
Not affecting payment of balance of award . . . Lab §4903.6
Person to whom paid . . . Lab §4903.8
Payment of lien not affecting payment of balance of award . . . Lab §4904.1
Penalty liens
Cancellation of . . . 8 CCR §15595
Recording . . . 8 CCR §15594
Priority of
Asbestos Workers' Account . . . Lab §4416
Employee liens against employer . . . Ins §1871.7
Insurer liens against employer . . . Ins §11656
Reimbursements, determining . . . Lab §4903.1
Filing or activation fee reimbursements . . . Lab §4903.07
Grounds for denying . . . Lab §4903.1
Resolution of claims
Notification of resolution or withdrawal of claims . . . 8 CCR §10872
Service
Filing and service of lien claims and supporting documents . . . 8 CCR §10862
Medical reports, medical-legal reports, other medical information
Service on non-physician lien claimants . . . 8 CCR §10637
Resolution or withdrawal of lien claims
Notification . . . 8 CCR §10872
Statutes of limitation
Limitation period for filing lien claim . . . Lab §4903.5

LIENS—Cont.
Subpoenas
Medical information
Non-physician claimants, subpoena for medical information . . . 8 CCR §10655
Subsequent compensation paid by employer, for . . . Lab §3857
Tax liens, federal . . . 26 USC §6323
Unemployment compensation . . . 8 CCR §10899, Lab §4904
Unrepresented lien claimants
Notice of nonrepresentation . . . 8 CCR §10868
Unrequested liens
Appeals board authority to award for unrequested lien . . . Lab §4905
Withdrawal of claims
Notification of resolution or withdrawal of claims . . . 8 CCR §10872
Written claims
Required . . . Lab §4903.05

LIFEGUARDS
Disability payments
Leave of absence in lieu of disability payments . . . Lab §4850
Skin cancer . . . Lab §3212.11

LIFE PENSIONS
Female pension, present value of . . . Table 3
Indemnity and earnings, minimum/maximum . . . Table 14
Instructions and examples for commutation . . . Table 4
Instructions and tables for commutation . . . 8 CCR §§10169, 10169.1
Male pension, present value of . . . Table 2
Permanent disability . . . Lab §4659
Instructions and tables for commutation . . . 8 CCR §10169.1
Partial disability
70 percent to less than 100 percent disability . . . Lab §4659
Present value, table for . . . Table 1
Present value
Female pension . . . Table 3
Male pension . . . Table 2

LIMITED POLICIES
Insurance (See INSURANCE)

LITIGATION EXPENSES (See ATTORNEYS' FEES; COURT COSTS)

LOANS
Financial interests in entities providing services
Conflicts of interest
Exceptions . . . Lab §139.32

LOCAL GOVERNMENTS AND AGENCIES
County employees (See COUNTY EMPLOYEES)
Emergency and disaster councils, authority to create . . . Gov §8610
Extraterritorial application of privileges and immunities of local agent . . . Gov §53023
Firefighters (See FIREFIGHTERS)
Insurance, provision of . . . Gov §54462
Law enforcement officers (See POLICE)

LOCAL GOVERNMENTS AND AGENCIES—Cont.
Public Employees' Retirement System
State or local safety members (See PUBLIC EMPLOYEES' RETIREMENT SYSTEM)

LOCOMOTIVES
Laminated safety glass requirements (See RAILROADS)

LONGSHORE AND HARBOR WORKERS' COMPENSATION ACT
Administration
Carrier substituted for employer . . . 33 USC §935
Secretary of Labor, by . . . 33 USC §939
Aliens . . . 33 USC §909, 42 USC §1652
Amount of compensation
Average weekly earnings, based on . . . 33 USC §§906, 910
Death benefits . . . 33 USC §909
Disability benefits . . . 33 USC §908
Appeals Board (WCAB) . . . Lab §128
Appeal to Benefits Review Board . . . 33 USC §921
Apportionment of liability . . . 33 USC §908
Assignment of claims . . . 33 USC §916
Attorneys' fees . . . 33 USC §928
Attorneys for Board, Deputy Commissioner, or Secretary . . . 33 USC §921a
Audit of fund . . . 33 USC §942
Average weekly earnings, compensation based on . . . 33 USC §§906, 910
Award under (See AWARD)
Benefits Review Board
Designations of . . . 33 USC §902
Establishment of . . . 33 USC §921
Powers of . . . 33 USC §927
Benefits under . . . 33 USC §906
Certificates of compliance . . . 33 USC §937
Civilian employees or volunteers at military installations, compensation for injury or death of . . . 5 USC §§2105, 8171 to 8173
Claims procedures
Generally . . . 33 USC §919
Disability benefits . . . 33 USC §908
Failure to file claims . . . 33 USC §913
Filing claims . . . 33 USC §913
Collection of defaulted payments . . . 33 USC §918
Compensation districts . . . 33 USC §939, 42 USC §1653
Constitutional issues . . . 33 USC §949
Contributions . . . 33 USC §915
Court costs . . . 33 USC §926
Coverage . . . 33 USC §903
Creditors' claims . . . 33 USC §916
Death benefits . . . 33 USC §909
Deductions . . . 33 USC §915
Defaulted payments, collection of . . . 33 USC §918
Definitions pertinent to . . . 33 USC §902
Dependents . . . 33 USC §909
Deputy commissioners
Generally . . . 33 USC §940
Appearance of attorneys for . . . 33 USC §921a
Appointment of . . . 33 USC §940
Defined . . . 33 USC §902
Duties of . . . 33 USC §940
Powers of . . . 33 USC §927
Procedure before . . . 33 USC §923

LONGSHORE AND HARBOR WORKERS' COMPENSATION ACT—Cont.
Designation of Code chapter as . . . 33 USC §901
Determination of compensation under . . . 33 USC §§906, 910
Disability benefits . . . 33 USC §908
Discrimination . . . 33 USC §948a
Exclusive remedies . . . 33 USC §905
Exemptions . . . 33 USC §903
Failure to file claims . . . 33 USC §913
Filing claims . . . 33 USC §913
First three days of disability, no benefits for . . . 33 USC §906
Foreign employment
Contractors with U.Sworking outside U.S . . . 42 USC §1702
Military bases, service on
Alien nonresidents . . . 42 USC §1652
Compensation districts . . . 42 USC §1653
Fraud and misrepresentation . . . 33 USC §931
Guardians for minors and incompetents . . . 33 USC §911
Hearings . . . 33 USC §923
Immigrant workers . . . 33 USC §909, 42 USC §1652
Foreign employment
Military bases, service on by alien nonresidents . . . 42 USC §1652
Inapplicable law . . . 33 USC §948
Information, provision of . . . 33 USC §939
Insurance
Administration by carrier for employer . . . 33 USC §935
Certificates . . . 33 USC §937
Duty to obtain . . . 33 USC §932
Failure to obtain . . . 33 USC §938
Policies . . . 33 USC §936
Invalid agreements . . . 33 USC §915
Investigations . . . 33 USC §923
Judicial review . . . 33 USC §921
Liability of employers under . . . 33 USC §904
Liens . . . 33 USC §917
Medical reports . . . 33 USC §907
Medical treatment . . . 33 USC §907
Military bases outside U.S., service on
Alien nonresidents . . . 42 USC §1652
Compensation districts . . . 42 USC §1653
Modification of awards under . . . 33 USC §922
Negligence . . . 33 USC §905
Nonappropriated fund instrumentalities, employees of
Coverage . . . 5 USC §8171
Exclusive liability . . . 5 USC §8173
Non-citizen nonresident employees . . . 5 USC §8172
Notice
Compensation . . . 33 USC §934
Injury or death . . . 33 USC §§908, 912
Offshore lands, applicability to . . . 43 USC §1333
Outer continental shelf lands, applicability to . . . 43 USC §1333
Payment of benefits
Generally . . . 33 USC §914
Defaulted payments, collection of . . . 33 USC §918
Special fund, payment out of . . . 33 USC §918
Penalties and fines
Failure to secure payment of compensation . . . 33 USC §938

Index

LONGSHORE AND HARBOR WORKERS' COMPENSATION ACT—Cont.
Penalties and fines—Cont.
Fraud and misrepresentation . . . 33 USC §931
Safe workplace requirements . . . 33 USC §941
Permanent disability . . . 33 USC §908
Physicians . . . 33 USC §907
Premium payments, contributions to . . . 33 USC §915
Presumptions . . . 33 USC §920
Recordkeeping requirements . . . 33 USC §929
Reporting requirements
Annual report . . . 33 USC §942
Injury and death . . . 33 USC §930
Medical reports . . . 33 USC §907
Review of compensation orders . . . 33 USC §921
Safe workplace requirements . . . 33 USC §941
Secretary of Labor
Administration by . . . 33 USC §939
Attorneys representing . . . 33 USC §921a
Designation of . . . 33 USC §902
Reports to . . . 33 USC §§930, 942
Security . . . 33 USC §932
Self-employed persons . . . 33 USC §908
Settlements . . . 33 USC §908
Severability of provisions . . . 33 USC §950
Special fund, payment of benefits out of . . . 33 USC §§918, 944
Spouses . . . 33 USC §909
Submerged lands, applicability to . . . 43 USC §1333
Subsequent injuries . . . 33 USC §908
Temporary disability . . . 33 USC §908
Third party liability . . . 33 USC §933
Time limits
Filing claims . . . 33 USC §913
Payment of benefits . . . 33 USC §914
Unconstitutionality . . . 33 USC §949
Vocational rehabilitation . . . 33 USC §§908, 939
Waiver of rights to compensation . . . 33 USC §915
Witnesses . . . 33 USC §§924, 925

LOS ANGELES
State Compensation Insurance Fund's authority to acquire property in . . . Ins §11781.5

LOSS CONTROL CONSULTATION SERVICES
Insurers required to provide . . . Lab §6354.5
Workers' compensation insurers required to provide . . . Ins §11703

LOW BACK PAIN
Medical treatment
Utilization schedule
Low back disorders . . . 8 CCR §9792.23.5

LUMP-SUM PAYMENTS
Amount, determining . . . Lab §5101
Asbestos workers . . . Lab §4407.5
Certificate for . . . Lab §5105
Commutation to . . . Lab §5100
Interest
7 percent annually . . . Table 7
10 percent annually . . . Table 5
Method of payment . . . Lab §5102
Receipt for . . . Lab §5105

LUMP-SUM PAYMENTS—Cont.
Subsequent injuries adding to permanent partial disability . . . Lab §5100.5
Trustees
Deposited lump sum, payments from . . . Lab §5103
Preference in appointment of . . . Lab §5104
Uninsured employer's future payments, present worth of . . . Lab §5106
Vocational rehabilitation benefits . . . Lab §5100.6

LUNG DISEASE
Chronic lung disease
Temporary disability
Aggregate disability payments
Single injury . . . Lab §4656
Medical treatment
Utilization schedule
Occupational interstitial lung disease guideline . . . 8 CCR §9792.23.12

LYME DISEASE
Law enforcement officers
Compensable injuries . . . Lab §3212.12

M

MAILBOXES
Appeals Board (WCAB)
Mailbox maintained in district office
Receipt of documents from mailbox as service . . . 8 CCR §10628

MAIL SERVICE
Appeals Board (WCAB) cases
Time within which to act . . . 8 CCR §10605
Requirements for service by mail, express mail, overnight, and facsimile . . . CCP §1013

MANAGED CARE FUND
Establishment of . . . Lab §4600.7

MARITAL PRIVILEGE . . . Ev §980
Adverse party, spouse called as witness by . . . Ev §971
Domestic partners . . . Ev §980
Exception to privilege
Grounds . . . Ev §972
Medical information, authorization for release of . . . CC §56.11
Party claiming . . . Ev §§912, 918
Waiver of privilege . . . Ev §§912, 973

MARITIME JURISDICTION (See ADMIRALTY AND MARITIME JURISDICTION)

MARRIAGE AND FAMILY THERAPISTS
Medical information disclosures
Settlement or compromise of malpractice case . . . CC §56.105
Threat to health or safety, release of information to alleviate . . . CC §56.10
Privileged communications with patients . . . Ev §§1010 to 1016
Treatment of injuries by therapists . . . Lab §3209.8

MATERIAL SAFETY DATA SHEET (MSDS)
Generally . . . Lab §6390

MATERIAL SAFETY DATA SHEET (MSDS)—Cont.
Cosmetics
Hazardous substances contained in cosmetics or disinfectants
Manufacturer or importer duties . . . Lab §6390.2
Direct purchasers, provided to . . . Lab §6397
Disinfectants
Hazardous substances contained in cosmetics or disinfectants
Manufacturer or importer duties . . . Lab §6390.2
Employer duties towards employees . . . Lab §§6398, 6399
Cleaning products, printable information
Availability to employees . . . Lab §6398.5
Entire product mixture, required for . . . Lab §6395
Federal MSDS as proof of compliance with state requirements . . . Lab §6392
Industrial Relations Department, copy sent to . . . Lab §6394
Information provided on . . . Lab §6391
Preparation and provision of . . . Lab §6390
Relief from obligation of providing . . . Lab §6393
Trade secrets, protection from disclosure of . . . Lab §§6394, 6396

MATERNITY LEAVE
School districts
Salary deductions during absence . . . Ed §44977.5

MEAL BREAKS
Wages, hours, and working conditions
Piece-rate basis of compensation . . . Lab §226.2

MEDICAID
Fraud
Suspension of physician, practitioner or provider from participation in workers' compensation system for cause . . . Lab §139.21
Procedure for provider suspension . . . 8 CCR §§9788.1 to 9788.6
Health care benefits under ERISA . . . Lab §2803.4

MEDI-CAL
Fraud
Suspension of physician, practitioner or provider from participation in workers' compensation system for cause . . . Lab §139.21
Procedure for provider suspension . . . 8 CCR §§9788.1 to 9788.6
Health care benefits under ERISA . . . Lab §2803.4
Reimbursement by Appeals Board (WCAB) . . . W&I §14101.7

MEDICAL ASSISTANCE
Eligibility for, establishing . . . W&I §14011
In-home supportive services for aged, blind and disabled
Direct payments to provider or recipients, workers' compensation, unemployment compensation, etcobligations . . . W&I §12302.2
Agents for recipient-employers to comply with employer obligations . . . W&I §12302.5

MEDICAL BILLING
Billing and payment rules (October 2011) . . . 8 CCR §§9792.5.0 to 9792.5.15
Definitions . . . 8 CCR §9792.5.0
Electronic medical billing and payment
Guides for medical billing and payment . . . 8 CCR §9792.5.1
Forms
Standardized forms . . . 8 CCR §9792.5.2
Guides for medical billing and payment . . . 8 CCR §9792.5.1
Conformity to guide . . . 8 CCR §9792.5.3
Independent bill review . . . 8 CCR §§9792.5.4 to 9792.5.15
Appeals of determination . . . 8 CCR §10567
Second review and independent bill review . . . 8 CCR §§9792.5.4 to 9792.5.15
Appeal of determination . . . 8 CCR §§9792.5.15, 10567
Application of relevant authority to determine review . . . 8 CCR §9792.5.13
Consolidation of independent review requests . . . 8 CCR §9792.5.12
Definitions . . . 8 CCR §9792.5.4
Determination of independent review . . . 8 CCR §§9792.5.14, 9792.5.15
Document filing for independent review . . . 8 CCR §9792.5.10
Form for provider request for second review . . . 8 CCR §9792.5.6
Form for request for independent review . . . 8 CCR §9792.5.8
Implementation of determination . . . 8 CCR §9792.5.15
Request for independent review . . . 8 CCR §§9792.5.7, 9792.5.8
Request for second review . . . 8 CCR §§9792.5.5, 9792.5.6
Screening request for independent review for eligibility . . . 8 CCR §9792.5.9
Separation of independent review requests . . . 8 CCR §9792.5.12
Withdrawal of request for independent review . . . 8 CCR §9792.5.11
Competence standards for medical bill reviewers
Certification . . . 10 CCR §2592.09
Designation for successful completion of training . . . 10 CCR §§2592.05, 2592.11
Documentation maintained by insurer . . . 10 CCR §2592.07
Experienced medical bill reviewer, designation . . . 10 CCR §2592.13
Post-designation training . . . 10 CCR §2592.14
Training . . . 10 CCR §2592.04
Fraud
Medical billing and provider fraud
Reporting protocol . . . Lab §3823

MEDICAL CANNABIS/MARIJUANA
Occupational safety and health
Armed robbery risk
Advisory committee to study . . . Lab §147.6
Combustion risk
Advisory committee to study . . . Lab §147.6

Index

MEDICAL CANNABIS/MARIJUANA—Cont.
Occupational safety and health—Cont.
Evaluation of need for industry-specific regulations . . . Lab §§147.5, 147.6
Repetitive strain injury risk
Advisory committee to study . . . Lab §147.6
Second-hand marijuana smoke by employees
Advisory committee to study . . . Lab §147.6

MEDICAL CERTIFICATION
Disability benefits, for (See DISABILITY BENEFITS)

MEDICAL COLLABORATION
Psychologists, treatment by . . . Lab §3209.3

MEDICAL COVERAGE
COBRA (See HEALTH CARE COVERAGE)

MEDICAL DIRECTOR
Appointment . . . Lab §122
Labor Code definition . . . Lab §29

MEDICAL EVALUATIONS
Medical examinations generally (See MEDICAL EXAMINATIONS)

MEDICAL EXAMINATIONS
Generally . . . Lab §§4050, 4060, 4062.1, 4062.2
Agreed medical evaluators (AMEs) (See AGREED MEDICAL EVALUATORS (AMES))
Ankle disability
Guidelines for evaluation . . . 8 CCR §46.1
Appeals Board (WCAB)
Failure or refusal to submit to examination on order of . . . Lab §4054
Hearing, examination of injured worker ordered at . . . Lab §5703.5
Ordered by . . . Lab §4050
Qualified medical examiner, Board authority to order examination by . . . Lab §5703.5
Testimony and direct examination, Board authority to take . . . Lab §5701
Attorney representing employee . . . Lab §4062.2
Cardiovascular evaluations
Method of measuring disability . . . 8 CCR §45
Time taken to complete evaluation . . . 8 CCR §49.4
Communications with evaluators . . . Lab §4062.3
Compensability, determining . . . Lab §4060
Comprehensive medical evaluation to resolve injury dispute
Attorney representing employee . . . Lab §4062.2
Costs, employer liability for . . . Lab §4064
Discovery procedure, physical examinations
Methods of discovery . . . CCP §2019.010
Effective date of Article on . . . Lab §4067.5
Employer
Failure or refusal to submit to examination on order of . . . Lab §4053
Ordered by . . . Lab §4050
Ethical requirements . . . 8 CCR §41
Evaluator
Agreed medical evaluator . . . Lab §4602.2
Ex parte communications with evaluators . . . Lab §4062.3
Expenses related to . . . Lab §4600
Failure to submit to (See subhead: Refusal or failure to submit to)

MEDICAL EXAMINATIONS—Cont.
Foot and ankle disability
Guidelines for evaluation . . . 8 CCR §46.1
Immunologic disability, method of measuring . . . 8 CCR §47
Independent medical examiners (IMEs) (See INDEPENDENT MEDICAL EXAMINERS (IMES))
Information provided to evaluator . . . Lab §4062.3
Interpreter, provision of . . . Lab §4600
Neuromusculoskeletal evaluations
Method of measuring disability . . . 8 CCR §46
Objection to medical determination . . . Lab §4062
Medical evaluation
Attorney representing employee . . . Lab §4062.2
Unrepresented employees . . . Lab §4062.1
Occupational Safety and Health Standards Board . . . Lab §142.3
Permanent disability, determining . . . Lab §4061
Medical evaluation
Attorney representing employee . . . Lab §4062.2
Unrepresented employees . . . Lab §4062.1
Personal physician of injured worker
Presence of . . . Lab §4052
Treating physician, opinion of . . . Lab §4061.5
Physician conducting
Agreed medical evaluators (AMEs) (See AGREED MEDICAL EVALUATORS (AMES))
Choice of . . . Lab §4050
Independent medical examiners (IMEs) (See INDEPENDENT MEDICAL EXAMINERS (IMES))
Personal physician of injured worker
Presence of . . . Lab §4052
Treating physician, opinion of . . . Lab §4061.5
Qualified medical evaluators (QMEs) (See QUALIFIED MEDICAL EVALUATORS (QMES))
Report by . . . Lab §4055
Treating physician (See TREATING PHYSICIAN)
Place of . . . Lab §4051
Psychiatric evaluations
Method of measuring disability . . . 8 CCR §43
Public Employees' Retirement System, disability retirement under . . . Gov §§21155, 21192
Pulmonary evaluations
Method of measuring disability . . . 8 CCR §44
Time taken to complete . . . 8 CCR §49.6
Qualified medical evaluators (QMEs) (See QUALIFIED MEDICAL EVALUATORS (QMES))
Records, subpoena of . . . Lab §4055.2
Refusal or failure to submit to
Appeals Board (WCAB) order . . . Lab §4054
Disability caused or aggravated by . . . Lab §4056
Employer's order . . . Lab §4053
Longshore and Harbor Workers' Compensation Act . . . 33 USC §907
Report by physician conducting . . . Lab §4055
Subsequent examinations . . . Lab §4067
Time of
Generally . . . Lab §4051
Completion of examination, timely . . . Lab §4062.5
Failure to complete timely medical evaluation . . . Lab §4062.5

MEDICAL EXAMINATIONS—Cont.
Time of—Cont.
Qualified medical evaluators (QMEs), time guidelines . . . 8 CCR §§49 to 49.9 (See QUALIFIED MEDICAL EVALUATORS (QMES))
Treating physician (See TREATING PHYSICIAN)
Unrepresented injured workers . . . Lab §§4060, 4062.1
Unrepresented workers examined by QMEs (See QUALIFIED MEDICAL EVALUATORS (QMES))

MEDICAL GOODS OR SERVICES
Advertising by unlicensed medical provider . . . 8 CCR §9827

MEDICAL-LEGAL EXPENSES
Appeals board (WCAB)
Procedures for determination of disputes . . . 8 CCR §10786
Comprehensive medical-legal evaluations
Generally . . . Lab §§4060, 4062.1, 4062.2
Definitions pertinent to . . . 8 CCR §9793
Interpreters
Directories of qualified interpreters . . . 8 CCR §9795.5
Qualifications of interpreters . . . 8 CCR §9795.1.6
Medical evaluation
Attorney representing employee . . . Lab §4062.2
Unrepresented employees . . . Lab §4062.1
Procedures after CME . . . Lab §4061
Reasonableness of fees . . . 8 CCR §9795
Reimbursement of expenses . . . 8 CCR §9794
Contesting by employer
Explanation of review to contest . . . Lab §4622
Independent bill review . . . Lab §4622
Definitions
Comprehensive medical-legal evaluations . . . 8 CCR §9793
Pertinent terms . . . Lab §4620
Diagnostic tests, fee schedule for . . . Lab §4626
Disputes, determination
Appeals board (WCAB)
Procedures for determination of disputes . . . 8 CCR §10786
Employer liability for . . . Lab §4622
Fee schedule
Adoption of . . . Lab §5307.6
Diagnostic tests . . . Lab §4626
Physician fees . . . Table 12
Reasonableness of charges . . . 8 CCR §9795, Lab §§4625, 4906
Table of fees . . . Table 12
Interpreter expenses . . . Lab §4620
Liens and lien claimants before Appeals Board (WCAB) . . . 8 CCR §10899
Penalties and fines for failure to pay . . . Lab §4622
Physicians
Fee schedules . . . Table 12
Responsibilities of physician signing report . . . Lab §4628
Prompt payment requirement . . . Lab §4625
Reasonableness of charges . . . 8 CCR §9795, Lab §§4625, 4906

MEDICAL-LEGAL EXPENSES—Cont.
Reimbursement . . . 8 CCR §9794, Lab §4621
Request for payment
Time for request . . . Lab §4625
Rules and regulations, promulgation of . . . Lab §4627

MEDICAL MALPRACTICE
Malpractice insurance
Health care facilities, changes in rate or conditions of coverage . . . Ins §676.4
Peer review underwriting . . . Ins §676.3
Patient records
Release to accompany settlement demand . . . CC §56.105

MEDICAL PROVIDER NETWORKS . . . 8 CCR §§9767.1 to 9767.16, Lab §§4616 to 4616.7
Access assistants
Provision of medical access assistants by MPN . . . Lab §4616
Access standards . . . 8 CCR §9767.5
Additional examinations
Preclusion . . . Lab §4616.6
Administrative director
Regulatory and enforcement authority . . . Lab §4616
Administrative penalties . . . 8 CCR §9767.19
Ancillary services
Defined . . . 8 CCR §9767.1
Appeal of determination
Petition . . . 8 CCR §10580
Applications . . . 8 CCR §9767.3
Cover page . . . 8 CCR §9767.4
Denial . . . 8 CCR §9767.13
Re-evaluation . . . 8 CCR §9767.13
Review . . . 8 CCR §9767.2
Complaints . . . 8 CCR §9767.16
Forms . . . 8 CCR §9767.16.5
Contact information for network
Internet, posting . . . Lab §4616
Continuity of care policy . . . 8 CCR §9767.10
Filing and approval . . . Lab §4616.2
Revisions . . . Lab §4616.2
Covered employees
Defined . . . 8 CCR §9767.1
Cover page for application . . . 8 CCR §9767.4
Cover page for reapproval plans . . . 8 CCR §9767.4
Current regulations, compliance
Modification of plan made under emergency regulations . . . 8 CCR §9767.15
Definitions . . . 8 CCR §9767.1
Disclosures
Contracting agent disclosures . . . Lab §4616
Economic profiling
Filing of profiling policies . . . Lab §4616.1
Dispute as to diagnosis or treatment . . . Lab §4616.3
Division
Defined . . . 8 CCR §9767.1
Economic profiling
Defined . . . 8 CCR §9767.1
Filing of profiling policies . . . 8 CCR §9767.11, Lab §4616.1
Emergency health care services
Defined . . . 8 CCR §9767.1

MEDICAL PROVIDER NETWORKS—Cont.
Emergency health care services—Cont.
Hospitals
Access standards for plans . . . 8 CCR §9767.5
Employers
Defined . . . 8 CCR §9767.1, Lab §4616.5
Enforcement of provisions
Administrative penalties . . . 8 CCR §9767.19
Entity that provides ancillary services
Defined . . . Lab §4616.5
Reimbursement contract more than 20% below official fee schedule
Written disclosure when contract specifies reimbursement . . . Lab §5307.12
Entity that provides physician network services
Defined . . . 8 CCR §9767.1, Lab §4616.5
Reimbursement contract more than 20% below official fee schedule
Written disclosure when contract specifies reimbursement . . . Lab §5307.12
Establishment . . . Lab §4616
Forms
Cover page for application . . . 8 CCR §9767.4
Cover page for reapproval plans . . . 8 CCR §9767.4
Modification of plan
Notice of modification . . . 8 CCR §9767.8
Geocoding
Defined . . . 8 CCR §9767.1
Group disability insurance policies
Conditions for approval . . . Lab §4616.7
Defined . . . 8 CCR §9767.1
Health care organizations (HCOs)
Conditions for approval . . . Lab §4616.7
Defined . . . 8 CCR §9767.1
Health care service plans
Conditions for approval . . . Lab §4616.7
Defined . . . 8 CCR §9767.1
Health care shortage
Defined . . . 8 CCR §9767.1
Hospitals
Access standards for plans . . . 8 CCR §9767.5
Identification numbers
Assignment of MPN identification numbers . . . 8 CCR §9767.2
Definition of medical provider network identification numbers . . . 8 CCR §9767.1
Independent medical reviews
Contract . . . Lab §4616.4
Generally . . . 8 CCR §§9768.1 to 9768.17 (See INDEPENDENT MEDICAL REVIEW)
Objection to diagnosis or treatment recommendation
Resolution through medical review process . . . Lab §4062
Out of network treatment . . . 8 CCR §9768.17
Initial medical evaluation
Employer duty upon notice of injury . . . Lab §4616.3
Insurers
Defined . . . 8 CCR §9767.1
Medical access assistance . . . 8 CCR §9767.5
Provision by MPN . . . Lab §4616
Medical provider network geographic service area
Defined . . . 8 CCR §9767.1
Medical provider network identification numbers
Defined . . . 8 CCR §9767.1

MEDICAL PROVIDER NETWORKS—Cont.
Medical provider network medical access assistants
Defined . . . 8 CCR §9767.1
Requirements . . . 8 CCR §9767.5
Modification of plan . . . 8 CCR §9767.8
Current regulations, compliance . . . 8 CCR §9767.15
MPN applicants
Defined . . . 8 CCR §9767.1
MPN contact
Defined . . . 8 CCR §9767.1
Notice of random review . . . 8 CCR §9767.18
Notice to employees
Coverage notice . . . 8 CCR §9767.12
End of coverage notice . . . 8 CCR §9767.12
New hires
Implementation notice . . . 8 CCR §9767.12
Pre-implementation notice to employees . . . 8 CCR §9767.12
Objections to medical determination
Resolution . . . Lab §4602
Occupational medicine
Defined . . . 8 CCR §9767.1
Providers of occupational health services and specialists
Access standards for plans . . . 8 CCR §9767.5
Out of network treatment
Access standards . . . 8 CCR §9767.5
Independent medical reviews
Disagreement with network treatment . . . 8 CCR §9768.17
Obtaining treatment . . . 8 CCR §9767.7
Physician primarily engaged in treatment of nonoccupational injuries
Goals for membership in network . . . Lab §4616
Physicians
Acknowledgment affirmatively electing to be member of MPN . . Lab §4616
Change of physician within network . . . 8 CCR §9767.6
Goals for membership in network . . . Lab §4616
Approval of plans . . . Lab §4616.7
Independent medical reviews
Contracts for reviews . . . Lab §4616.4
Predesignation of personal physician
Relationship between predesignation and MPN's . . . 8 CCR §9780.1
Roster of participating providers
Posting on internet . . . Lab §4616
Treatment within network . . . 8 CCR §9767.6
Plans
Contents . . . 8 CCR §9767.3
Definition of medical provider network plan . . . 8 CCR §9767.1
Modification of plan . . . 8 CCR §9767.8
Reapproval plans
Cover page . . . 8 CCR §9767.4
Current regulations, compliance . . . 8 CCR §9767.15
Denial . . . 8 CCR §9767.13
Review . . . 8 CCR §9767.2
Requirements . . . 8 CCR §9767.3, Lab §4616
Suspension, revocation or probation . . . 8 CCR §9767.14

MEDICAL PROVIDER NETWORKS—Cont.
Predesignation of personal physician
Relationship between predesignation and MPN's . . . 8 CCR §9780.1
Primary treating physicians
Access standards for plans . . . 8 CCR §9767.5
Defined . . . 8 CCR §9767.1
Probation
Defined . . . 8 CCR §9767.1
Plans . . . 8 CCR §9767.14
Providers
Defined . . . 8 CCR §9767.1
Quality of care and performance of medical personnel . . . Lab §4616
Random review of MPN . . . 8 CCR §9767.18
Reapproval plans
Cover page . . . 8 CCR §9767.4
Current regulations, compliance . . . 8 CCR §9767.15
Denial . . . 8 CCR §9767.13
Review . . . 8 CCR §9767.2
Regional area listing
Defined . . . 8 CCR §9767.1
Reports
Additional reports
Preclusion . . . Lab §4616.6
Residence
Defined . . . 8 CCR §9767.1
Review of MPN
Random review . . . 8 CCR §9767.18
Revocation
Defined . . . 8 CCR §9767.1
Petition for suspension or revocation of MPN . . . 8 CCR §9767.17
Form . . . 8 CCR §9767.17.5
Plans . . . 8 CCR §9767.14
Revocation of plan . . . 8 CCR §9767.14
Roster of participating providers
Posting on internet . . . Lab §4616
Rural areas
Access standards for plans . . . 8 CCR §9767.5
Second opinions . . . 8 CCR §9767.7
Defined . . . 8 CCR §9767.1
Suspension
Defined . . . 8 CCR §9767.1
Petition for suspension or revocation of MPN . . . 8 CCR §9767.17
Form . . . 8 CCR §9767.17.5
Plans . . . 8 CCR §9767.14
Suspension of plan . . . 8 CCR §9767.14
Taft-Hartley health and welfare fund
Conditions for approval . . . Lab §4616.7
Defined . . . 8 CCR §9767.1
Terminated providers
Continuity of care policy . . . 8 CCR §9767.10
Completion of treatment . . . Lab §4616.2
Termination
Defined . . . 8 CCR §9767.1
Third opinions . . . 8 CCR §9767.7
Defined . . . 8 CCR §9767.1
Transfer of ongoing care into network . . . 8 CCR §9767.9
Treating physicians
Defined . . . 8 CCR §9767.1
Second opinions from other physician within network . . . 8 CCR §9767.7

MEDICAL PROVIDER NETWORKS—Cont.
Treating physicians—Cont.
Selection by employee . . . Lab §4616.3
Third opinions from other physician within network . . . 8 CCR §9767.7
Withdrawal
Defined . . . 8 CCR §9767.1
Workplace
Defined . . . 8 CCR §9767.1

MEDICAL RECORDS
Appeals board (WCAB)
Certified copies of reports
Documentary evidence, admissibility . . . 8 CCR §10670
Employer records as evidence
Service, ongoing duty . . . 8 CCR §10635
Physicians' reports
Generally (See APPEALS BOARD (WCAB))
Qualified medical evaluator's report (See QUALIFIED MEDICAL EVALUATORS (QMES))
Caregivers, disclosures to . . . CC §56.1007
Confidentiality . . . CC §§56.10 to 56.21
Authorization for release of information . . . CC §§56.11 to 56.16
Confidential communications request
Written or electronic requests . . . CC §56.107
Definitions pertinent to medical information disclosure . . . CC §56.05
Diagnosis, confidentiality of . . . Lab §3762
Disclosure, when permitted or required . . . CC §56.10
Electronic health record system . . . CC §56.101
Employers receiving medical information . . . CC §§56.20, 56.21
Employer's right to information, limitations on . . . Lab §3762
Exceptions to disclosure rule . . . CC §56.30
Health care service plans
Steps to protect confidential medical information . . . CC §56.107
HIV status, disclosure of . . . CC §56.31
Coroners, disclosure of medical records to . . . CC §56.10
Disasters, disclosure of medical records to disaster relief organizations . . . CC §56.10
Domestic partners, disclosures to . . . CC §56.1007
Electronic health record system . . . CC §56.101
Family members, disclosures to . . . CC §56.1007
Forensic pathologists
Disclosure of medical records to coroners, medical examiners or forensic pathologists . . . CC §56.10
Friends, disclosures to . . . CC §56.1007
Genetic characteristics, disclosure of test results for . . . CC §56.17
Independent medical review
Access for purposes of review . . . Lab §4610.5
Medical malpractice
Authorization to accompany settlement demand . . . CC §56.105
Minors
Disclosure of mental health records
Removal from physical custody of parent or guardian, protection of mental health records from release . . . CC §56.106

MEDICAL RECORDS—Cont.
Minors—Cont.
Release in furtherance of coordination of health care services and medical treatment . . . CC §56.103
Personal representatives, disclosures to . . . CC §56.1007
Utilization review
Independent medical review
Medical records to be provided . . . 8 CCR §9792.10.5

MEDICAL REPORTS
Appeals board (WCAB), before
Failure to comply with requirements regarding
Inferences . . . 8 CCR §10670
Failure to provide examining physician's curriculum vitae . . . 8 CCR §10670
Permanent disability rating determinations
Formal determinations . . . 8 CCR §10675
Physicians' reports as evidence . . . 8 CCR §10682
Qualified medical evaluator's (QME's) report (See QUALIFIED MEDICAL EVALUATORS (QMES))
Service of copies of documents, electronic media, etc, offered into evidence . . . 8 CCR §10635
Lien claimants who are not physicians, service on . . . 8 CCR §10637
Subsequent Injuries Fund . . . 8 CCR §10462
X-rays (See X-RAYS)
Evidence
Service of documents . . . 8 CCR §10635
Lien claimants who are not physicians, service on . . . 8 CCR §10637
Independent medical examiners (IMEs), by (See INDEPENDENT MEDICAL EXAMINERS (IMES))
Longshore and Harbor Workers' Compensation Act . . . 33 USC §907
Permanent and stationary report, form of treating physician's . . . 8 CCR §§9785.3, 9785.4
Services beginning October 1, 2015 . . . 8 CCR §9785.4.1
Qualified medical evaluator's (QME's) report (See QUALIFIED MEDICAL EVALUATORS (QMES))
Self-insurers' submission of . . . 8 CCR §15302
Treating physician's progress report, form of . . . 8 CCR §9785.2

MEDICAL RESEARCH
Industrial relations department
Occupational disease research programs
Development of programs . . . Lab §50.8
Grant applications, review . . . Lab §78
Reporting requirements . . . Lab §50.8
Safe workplace programs
Education and research programs (See OCCUPATIONAL SAFETY AND HEALTH DIVISION)

MEDICAL SURVEY PROCEDURES
Health care organizations (HCOs) (See HEALTH CARE ORGANIATIONS (HCOS))

MEDICAL TREATMENT
Access of injured workers to medical treatment
Study of access . . . Lab §5307.2

MEDICAL TREATMENT—Cont.
Appeals board (WCAB)
Jurisdiction over disputes . . . Lab §4604
Authorized persons providing treatment . . . Lab §§3209.3 to 3209.6
Billing and payment rules (October 2011) . . . 8 CCR §§9792.5.0 to 9792.5.15
Definitions . . . 8 CCR §9792.5.0
Electronic medical billing and payment
Guides for medical billing and payment . . . 8 CCR §9792.5.1
Forms
Standardized forms . . . 8 CCR §9792.5.2
Guides for medical billing and payment . . . 8 CCR §9792.5.1
Conformity to guide . . . 8 CCR §9792.5.3
Independent bill review . . . 8 CCR §§9792.5.4 to 9792.5.15
Appeals of determination . . . 8 CCR §10567
Second review and independent bill review . . . 8 CCR §§9792.5.4 to 9792.5.15
Appeal of determination . . . 8 CCR §§9792.5.15, 10567
Application of relevant authority to determine review . . . 8 CCR §9792.5.13
Consolidation of independent review requests . . . 8 CCR §9792.5.12
Definitions . . . 8 CCR §9792.5.4
Determination of independent review . . . 8 CCR §§9792.5.14, 9792.5.15
Document filing for independent review . . . 8 CCR §9792.5.10
Form for provider request for second review . . . 8 CCR §9792.5.6
Form for request for independent review . . . 8 CCR §9792.5.8
Implementation of determination . . . 8 CCR §9792.5.15
Request for independent review . . . 8 CCR §§9792.5.7, 9792.5.8
Request for second review . . . 8 CCR §§9792.5.5, 9792.5.6
Screening request for independent review for eligibility . . . 8 CCR §9792.5.9
Separation of independent review requests . . . 8 CCR §9792.5.12
Withdrawal of request for independent review . . . 8 CCR §9792.5.11
Caps on visits
Exceptions to cap on visits . . . Lab §4604.5
Chiropractors
Cap on visits . . . Lab §4604.5
General provisions concerning chiropractors (See CHIROPRACTORS)
Health care organization, chiropractic care under . . . Lab §4600.5
Choice of health care provider by injured worker . . . Lab §4600.3
Claim filed
Duty of employer upon filing as to providing medical treatment . . . Lab §5402
Contested charges . . . 8 CCR §9792.5, Lab §4603.2
Cosignature of treating physician required for nurse practitioner or physician's assistant . . . Lab §3209.10

MEDICAL TREATMENT—Cont.
Definitions pertinent to
Generally . . . 8 CCR §9792.5
Billing and payment rules (October 2011), second review and independent bill review . . . 8 CCR §9792.5.4
Fee schedule . . . 8 CCR §9790.1
Medical treatment utilization schedule . . . 8 CCR §9792.20
Payment for services . . . 8 CCR §9792.5
Diagnosis-related group (DRG) weight
Generally . . . 8 CCR §9790.1
Table of weights and revised weights . . . 8 CCR §9792.1 Appx B
Disputes regarding medical treatment
Appeals board (WCAB)
Jurisdiction over disputes . . . Lab §4604
Documentation of bills for . . . 8 CCR §9792.5
Domestic terrorism
Nurse case manager support to obtain medically necessary treatment . . . Lab §4600.05
Drugs, medical treatment utilization schedule (MTUS) . . . 8 CCR §§9792.27.1 to 9792.27.23 (See DRUGS, MEDICAL TREATMENT UTILIZATION SCHEDULE (MTUS))
Economic Opportunity Program enrollees, medical treatment and reimbursement provided by federal government to . . . Lab §§4227, 4228
Educational materials for treating physicians . . . Lab §4602.8
Electronic medical billing and payment
Guides for medical billing and payment . . . 8 CCR §9792.5.1
Conformity to guide . . . 8 CCR §9792.5.3
Emergency treatment
Employer's duty to provide despite injured worker choice of physician . . . 8 CCR §9780.1
Utilization review
Applicability . . . Lab §4610
Employer-employee agreements as to . . . Lab §3209.7
Employer-provided . . . Lab §4600
Fraud against workers' compensation system, medical billing, insurance, Medicare or Medi-Cal, stay of provider lien . . . Lab §4615
Evidence-based guidelines
Occupational Medicine Practice Guidelines . . . Lab §4600
Utilization guidelines . . . Lab §4604.5
Exceptions to cap on visits . . . Lab §4604.5
Extent of medical treatment
Utilization schedules
Presumptive correctness of schedule as to scope and extent of medical treatment . . . Lab §4604.5
Fee schedule
Alternative payments to providers
Study and report . . . Lab §127.1
Authority to make rules and regulations governing . . . 8 CCR §9790
Composite factors appendix for inpatient services . . . 8 CCR §9792.1 Appx A
Contents of . . . 8 CCR §9791.1
Contracting out of services . . . Lab §5307.11

MEDICAL TREATMENT—Cont.
Fee schedule—Cont.
Copies, obtaining . . . 8 CCR §9791.1
Definitions pertinent to . . . 8 CCR §9790.1
Determination of fee . . . 8 CCR §9792
Diagnosis-related group (DRG) weight
Generally . . . 8 CCR §9790.1
Table of DRG weights . . . 8 CCR §9792.1 Appx B
Home health care
Services not covered by Medicare or official medical fee schedule . . . Lab §5307.8
Inpatient services, payment for . . . 8 CCR §9792.1
Medical treatment to which injured worker is entitled, payment for . . . 8 CCR §9792.5
Official medical fee schedule . . . 8 CCR §§9789.10 to 9789.111, Lab §5307.1
Pharmaceutical fee schedule covered under official medical fee schedule . . . 8 CCR §9789.40, Lab §5307.1
Resource-based relative value scale for physician and nonphysician practitioner services
Adoption and review of schedule based on model . . . Lab §5307.1
Services covered by . . . 8 CCR §9791
Setting . . . Lab §5307.11
Financial interests in entities providing services . . . Lab §139.32
Firefighters . . . Lab §4852
First aid (See FIRST AID)
Fraud
Medical billing and provider fraud
Reporting protocol . . . Lab §3823
Generic drugs . . . Lab §4600.1
Health care organizations (HCOs)
Payment for services (See subhead: Payment for services)
Standards and requirements . . . 8 CCR §9773
Health care providers
Reimbursement
Licensing of entities seeking to reimburse . . . Lab §4600.35
Highway Patrol . . . Lab §4802
Hospitals
Official medical fee schedule generally . . . 8 CCR §§9789.10 to 9789.111
Independent bill review . . . 8 CCR §§9792.5.4 to 9792.5.15
Administrative director determinations
Petition to enforce . . . 8 CCR §10570
Interpreters
Qualification of interpreters at medical treatment appointments or medical legal exams . . . 8 CCR §9795.1.6
Directories of qualified interpreters . . . 8 CCR §9795.5
Jurisdiction of Appeals Board (WCAB) over disputes regarding . . . Lab §4604
Justice Department employees . . . Lab §4802
Late payment, penalties and fines for . . . Lab §4603.2
Longshore and Harbor Workers' Compensation Act . . . 33 USC §907
Marriage and family therapists . . . Lab §3209.8

Index

MEDICAL TREATMENT—Cont.
Medical provider networks . . . 8 CCR §§9767.1 to 9767.16, Lab §§4616 to 4616.7 (See MEDICAL PROVIDER NETWORKS)
Medicine
  Continuing availability for injured employees . . . Lab §4600.2
  Generic drugs . . . Lab §4600.1
  Pharmaceutical fee schedule covered under official medical fee schedule . . . 8 CCR §9789.40, Lab §5307.1
Modifying authorized treatment
  Employer prohibited from rescinding or modifying authorization for treatment already provided . . . Lab §4610.3
Nonoccupational health care plan, minimum enrollment periods for choice under . . . 8 CCR §9779.45
Notice requirements . . . Lab §4603.5
Occupational therapists
  Cap on visits . . . Lab §4604.5
Official medical fee schedule . . . 8 CCR §§9789.10 to 9789.111, Lab §5307.1
Payment for services
  Generally . . . 8 CCR §9792.5
  Adjustment of payment, itemization, etc
    Explanation of review . . . Lab §§4603.3, 4603.4
  Billing and payment rules (October 2011) . . . 8 CCR §§9792.5.0 to 9792.5.15
  Contested charges . . . 8 CCR §9792.5, Lab §4603.2
  Definitions pertinent to . . . 8 CCR §9792.5
  Denial of payment, itemization, etc
    Explanation of review . . . Lab §§4603.3, 4603.4
  Documentation of charges . . . 8 CCR §9792.5
  Electronic billing
    Time for payments . . . Lab §4603.4
  Employer, by . . . Lab §4603.2
  Explanation of review . . . Lab §§4603.3, 4603.4
    Employer contesting medical-legal expenses, use of explanation of review to contest . . . Lab §4622
  Health care organizations (HCOs), treatment provided by
    Generally . . . Lab §4603.2
    Self-insured employers, payments from . . . Lab §4614.1
    Time requirements as to payment . . . Lab §4614
  Independent bill review (See INDEPENDENT BILL REVIEW (IBR))
  Interest on delayed payments . . . Lab §4603.2
  Itemization review
    Explanation of review . . . Lab §§4603.3, 4603.4
    Financial interests in entities providing services . . . Lab §139.32
    Request for payment to itemize services . . . Lab §4603.2
  Objection by employer to employee physician based on nonmembership in medical provider network
    Scope of employer liability for payment . . . Lab §4603.2
  Penalties and fines for unreasonable delay in payment or refusal to pay . . . Lab §5814
    Administrative penalties . . . 8 CCR §§10112.1 to 10112.3, Lab §5814.6

MEDICAL TREATMENT—Cont.
Payment for services—Cont.
  Penalties and fines for unreasonable delay in payment or refusal to pay —Cont.
    Attorneys' fees . . . Lab §5814.5
    Employer's penalty paid to Industrial Relations Director . . . Lab §5814.1
    Ten percent increase . . . Lab §5814
    Utilization review, delays to complete not counted towards unreasonable delay . . . Lab §4610.1
  Prescription, copy . . . Lab §4603.2
  Processing payments
    Regulatory authority . . . Lab §4603.4
  Provider dispute of amount paid
    Independent bill review (See INDEPENDENT BILL REVIEW (IBR))
    Second review request . . . Lab §4603.2
  Reimbursement of health care providers
    Licensing of entities seeking to reimburse . . . Lab §4600.35
  Self-insured employer payments to health care organizations (HCOs) . . . Lab §4614.1
  Time to request payment . . . Lab §4603.2
Personal physician
  Conditions for treatment of employee . . . Lab §4600
  Objection by employer
    Medical provider network, physician not member . . . Lab §4603.2
Pesticide poisoning treatment not regarded as first aid . . . Lab §6409.3
Physical therapists
  Cap on visits . . . Lab §4604.5
Physicians
  Suspension of physician, practitioner or provider from participation in system for cause . . . Lab §139.21
    Procedure for provider suspension . . 8 CCR §§9788.1 to 9788.6
Police . . . Lab §4852
Records of . . . 8 CCR §9792.5
Request for authorization for medical treatment
  Form . . . 8 CCR §9785.5
Rescinding authorized treatment
  Employer prohibited from rescinding or modifying authorization for treatment already provided . . . Lab §4610.3
San Francisco Port Commission employees . . . Lab §4802
Scope of medical treatment
  Utilization schedules
    Presumptive correctness of schedule as to scope and extent of medical treatment . . . Lab §4604.5
Self-insurance
  Ninety-day limitations not applicable to . . . Lab §4606
  Payment of treatment costs by . . . Lab §4614.1
Social workers, by . . . Lab §3209.8
Supplies
  Continuing availability of medical supplies for injured employees . . . Lab §4600.2
Transfers
  Choice of physicians (See PHYSICIANS)

MEDICAL TREATMENT—Cont.
Uninsured Employers Fund, provided out of . . . Lab §4903.3
University of California
  Fire department employees . . . Lab §4804.3
  Law enforcement officers . . . Lab §4808
Utilization review
  Availability of services during working hours . . . Lab §4600.4
  Chiropractors
    Cap on visits . . . Lab §4604.5
    Health care organization, chiropractic care under . . . Lab §4600.5
  Criteria . . . Lab §4610
  Definitions . . . Lab §4610
    From 2013 forward . . . 8 CCR §9792.6.1
    Prior to 2013 . . . 8 CCR §9792.6
  Emergency treatment
    Applicability . . . Lab §4610
  Exceptions to cap on visits . . . Lab §4604.5
  Financial interests in entities providing services . . . Lab §139.32
  Guidelines for medical treatment . . . Lab §4604.5
  Incomplete or insufficient information causing denial or delay of medical service
    Specifying information needed . . . Lab §4610
  Independent medical review
    Appeal from determination . . . 8 CCR §9792.10.7
    Application . . . 8 CCR §9792.10.2
    Assignment for review . . . 8 CCR §9792.10.4
    Costs of review . . . 8 CCR §9792.10.8
    Implementing determination . . . 8 CCR §9792.10.7
    Initial review of application . . . 8 CCR §9792.10.3
    Medical records to be provided . . . 8 CCR §9792.10.5
    Notice to parties of assignment for review . . . 8 CCR §9792.10.4
    Publishing of determinations . . . 8 CCR §9792.10.9
    Standards for review . . . 8 CCR §9792.10.6
    Timeline for review . . . 8 CCR §9792.10.6
  Investigation of utilization review process . . . 8 CCR §9792.11
    Employer violations . . . Lab §2750.11
  Notice of permanent disability indemnity
    Applicability to utilization review . . . Lab §4601
  Occupational therapists
    Cap on visits . . . Lab §4604.5
  Physical therapists
    Cap on visits . . . Lab §4604.5
  Process to be established . . . Lab §4610
  Provider utilization data
    Publication on website for physicians treating 10 or more patients . . . Lab §138.8
  Request for authorization . . . Lab §4610
    Form . . . 8 CCR §9785.5
  Retrospective utilization review
    Emergency treatment . . . Lab §4610
  Review of review decision . . . Lab §4610.5
    Independent medical review generally (See INDEPENDENT MEDICAL REVIEW)

MEDICAL TREATMENT—Cont.
Utilization review—Cont.
  Schedules for medical treatment utilization . . . Lab §4604.5
    Adoption . . . Lab §5307.27
    Drug formulary using evidence-based medicine . . . Lab §§5307.27 to 5307.29
  Scope . . . Lab §4064
  Standards for review . . . 8 CCR §§9792.6 to 9792.15
    Adjustment factors for penalties . . . 8 CCR §9792.13
    Administrative procedure for imposing penalty . . . 8 CCR §9792.15
    Applicability . . . 8 CCR §9792.7
    Dispute resolution, 2013 and forward . . . 8 CCR §9792.10.1
    Dispute resolution, pre-2013 . . . 8 CCR §9792.10
    Investigation of employer violations . . . Lab §2750.11
    Liability for penalty assessments . . . 8 CCR §9792.14
    Medically-based criteria . . . 8 CCR §9792.8
    Notice, 2013 and forward . . . 8 CCR §9792.9.1
    Notice, pre-2013 . . . 8 CCR §9792.9
    Penalties . . . 8 CCR §§9792.12 to 9792.15
    Procedures, 2013 and forward . . . 8 CCR §9792.9.1
    Procedures, pre-2013 . . . 8 CCR §9792.9
    Schedule of penalties . . . 8 CCR §9792.12
    Timeframe, 2013 and forward . . . 8 CCR §9792.9.1
    Timeframe, pre-2013 . . . 8 CCR §9792.9
  Standards of care
    Health and safety workers' compensation commission, survey and review of standards of care . . . Lab §77.5
  Unreasonable delay in provision of medical treatment
    Time waiting for review not counted towards unreasonable delay . . . Lab §4610.1
Utilization schedule . . . 8 CCR §§9792.20 to 9792.26
  Acupuncture medical treatment guidelines . . . 8 CCR §9792.24.1
  Adoption of schedule or guidelines . . . 8 CCR §§9792.21 to 9792.24.4
  Ankle disorders . . . 8 CCR §9792.23.7
  Asthma
    Occupational/work-related asthma medical treatment guideline . . . 8 CCR §9792.23.11
  Back disorders
    Cervical and thoracic spine disorders . . . 8 CCR §9792.23.1
    Low back disorders . . . 8 CCR §9792.23.5
  Cervical and thoracic spine disorders . . . 8 CCR §9792.23.1
  Chronic pain guidelines . . . 8 CCR §9792.24.2
  Clinical topics
    Adoption of schedule . . . 8 CCR §9792.23
    Special topics in need of further supplementation . . . 8 CCR §9792.24
  Definitions . . . 8 CCR §9792.20
  Drugs, medical treatment utilization schedule (MTUS) . . . 8 CCR §§9792.27.1 to 9792.27.23 (See DRUGS, MEDICAL TREATMENT UTILIZATION SCHEDULE (MTUS))

Index

MEDICAL TREATMENT—Cont.
Utilization schedule —Cont.
Elbow disorders . . . 8 CCR §9792.23.3
Evidence-based medicine (EBM) as basis . . . 8 CCR §9792.21
Definition of evidence-based medicine (EBM) . . . 8 CCR §9792.20
Evaluation of medical evidence, definitions . . . 8 CCR §9792.25
Evaluation of medical evidence, medical evidence evaluation advisory commission . . . 8 CCR §9792.26
Evaluation of medical evidence, methodology . . . 8 CCR §9792.25.1
Eyes . . . 8 CCR §9792.23.9
Foot disorders . . . 8 CCR §9792.23.7
Forearm disorders . . . 8 CCR §9792.23.4
General approach
Adoption of schedule . . . 8 CCR §9792.22
Groin disorder guidelines . . . 8 CCR §9792.23.10
Hand disorders . . . 8 CCR §9792.23.4
Hip disorder guidelines . . . 8 CCR §9792.23.10
Knee disorders . . . 8 CCR §9792.23.6
Low back complaints . . . 8 CCR §9792.23.5
Lung disease
Occupational interstitial lung disease guideline . . . 8 CCR §9792.23.12
Medical evidence search sequence . . . 8 CCR §9792.21.1
Neck complaints
Cervical and thoracic spine disorders . . . 8 CCR §9792.23.1
Opioids guidelines . . . 8 CCR §9792.24.4
Out-of-schedule treatment
Criteria . . . 8 CCR §9792.21
Medical evidence search sequence . . . 8 CCR §9792.21.1
Postsurgical rehabilitation guidelines . . . 8 CCR §9792.24.3
Presumption of correctness
Medical evidence search sequence when presumption challenged . . . 8 CCR §9792.21.1
Out-of-schedule treatments . . . 8 CCR §9792.21
Shoulder disorders . . . 8 CCR §9792.23.2
Special topics in need of further supplementation . . 8 CCR §9792.24
Stress-related conditions . . . 8 CCR §9792.23.8
Traumatic brain injury guideline . . . 8 CCR §9792.24.5
Wrist disorders . . . 8 CCR §9792.23.4

MEDICARE
Aged persons
Unlawful employment practices
Health benefit reductions or elimination upon medicare eligibility not prohibited . . . Gov §12940
Fraud
Suspension of physician, practitioner or provider from participation in workers' compensation system for cause . . . Lab §139.21
Procedure for provider suspension . . . 8 CCR §§9788.1 to 9788.6

MEDICARE—Cont.
Official medical fee schedule
Changes in medicare
Time to adjust rules in light of . . . 8 CCR §§9789.36, 9789.110

MEDICINE
Compounded drug products
Pharmaceutical fee schedule . . . Lab §5307.1
Continuing availability of medicine and medical supplies for injured employees . . . Lab §4600.2
Dangerous drugs or devices
Pharmaceutical fee schedule . . . Lab §5307.1
Generic drugs . . . Lab §4600.1
Pharmaceutical fee schedule
Covered under official medical fee schedule . . . 8 CCR §9789.40, Lab §5307.1
Pharmacy goods
Pharmaceutical fee schedule . . . Lab §5307.1

MENINGITIS
Occupational disease suffered by law enforcement and firefighters . . . Lab §§3212.9, 3212.10

MENTAL EXAMINATIONS
Discovery procedure
Methods of discovery . . . CCP §2019.010

MENTAL ILLNESS OR COMPETENCY
Chiropractors
Mental illness of license holder . . . 16 CCR §315
Confidentiality of records . . . CC §§56.10 to 56.21
Husband and wife privileges, waiver of . . . Ev §972
Medical treatment
Utilization schedule
Workplace mental health . . . 8 CCR §9792.23.8
Minors, mental health information disclosures
Release for purposes of coordinating health care services and medical treatment . . . CC §56.103
Removal from physical custody
Protection of mental health records from release . . . CC §56.106
Qualified medical evaluators (QMEs)
Comprehensive medical-legal evaluations
Psyche, injury to . . . 8 CCR §§36.5, 120
Evaluations for psychiatric disability
Method of evaluation . . . 8 CCR §43
Time guidelines . . . 8 CCR §49.8
Records
Declaration regarding protection of mental health record, form . . . 8 CCR §121
Definition of mental health records . . . 8 CCR §1
Witness unavailable because of mental disability . . . Ev §240

MENTAL INJURIES (See PSYCHIATRIC INJURIES)

MERCHANT SEAMEN (See SHIPPING)

MERGERS AND ACQUISITIONS
Employing units, unemployment compensation and disability benefits . . . UI §3254.5

METHICILLAN-RESISTANT STAPHYLOCOCCUS AUREUS (MRSA)
Firefighters and law enforcement officers
Presumption that disease arose out of and in course of employment . . . Lab §3212.8

MILEAGE
Witnesses
Fees and mileage for (See WITNESSES)

MILITARY SERVICE
Average weekly earnings of persons employed on bases outside U.S., compensation based on . . . 42 USC §1652
Average yearly earnings, determining
California Cadet Corps . . . Mil&Vet §520
California National Guard, organized militia, or unorganized militia . . . Mil&Vet §341
State guard . . . Mil&Vet §562
Bases outside U.S., employment on
Alien nonresidents . . . 42 USC §1652
Authorized workers' compensation for . . . 42 USC §1651
Average weekly earnings, compensation based on . . . 42 USC §1652
Compensation districts, establishment of . . . 42 USC §1653
Death benefits . . . 42 USC §1651
Definitions pertinent to . . . 42 USC §1651
Disability benefits . . . 42 USC §1651
Excluded persons . . . 42 USC §1654
Exclusive remedy . . . 42 USC §1651
Insurance
Acquisition strategy for insurance required under provisions . . . 42 USC §1655
Judicial proceedings . . . 42 USC §1653
Longshore and Harbor Workers' Compensation Act
Alien nonresidents . . . 42 USC §1652
Compensation districts . . . 42 USC §1653
Cadet Corps . . . Mil&Vet §520
Civilian employees or volunteers, compensation for injury or death of . . . 5 USC §§2105, 8171 to 8173
Definitions
Bases outside U.S., military service at . . . 42 USC §1651
Disability benefits
Disability equality act . . . Mil&Vet §§345, 346
National Guard, organized militia, or unorganized militia
Injured in service of state . . . Mil&Vet §340.1
Transfers under mutual aid or interagency agreements . . . Mil&Vet §340.2
Overseas military bases, service on . . . 42 USC §1651
Employment discrimination
Unlawful employment practices . . . Gov §12940
Veteran or military status defined . . . Gov §12926
Family care leave, paid
Covered active duty
Defined . . . UI §3302.1
Information in support of request for leave due to qualifying exigency . . . UI §3307
Qualifying exigency . . . UI §§3302.2, 3307
Fires, persons engaged in suppressing . . . Lab §3365

MILITARY SERVICE—Cont.
Immigrant workers
Bases outside U.S., employment on
Alien nonresidents . . . 42 USC §1652
Injury suffered in line of duty
Cadet Corps . . . Mil&Vet §520
National Guard, organized militia, or unorganized militia
Determination of benefits . . . Mil&Vet §341
Right to benefits following . . . Mil&Vet §340
State guard . . . Mil&Vet §562
National Guard, organized militia, or unorganized militia
Average yearly earnings, determining . . . Mil&Vet §341
Determination of benefits . . . Mil&Vet §341
Disability benefits
Injured in service of state . . . Mil&Vet §340.1
Transfers under mutual aid or interagency agreements . . . Mil&Vet §340.2
Disability equality act . . . Mil&Vet §§345, 346
Injury suffered in line of duty
Determination of benefits . . . Mil&Vet §341
Right to benefits following . . . Mil&Vet §340
Jurisdiction of Appeals Board (WCAB) . . . Mil&Vet §342
Workers' compensation benefits . . . Mil&Vet §340
Right to benefits
California Cadet Corps . . . Mil&Vet §520
National Guard, organized militia, or unorganized militia members' right to benefits following injury suffered in line of duty . . . Mil&Vet §340
State guard . . . Mil&Vet §562
State guard
Compensation for injury or death in line of duty . . . Mil&Vet §562
Unlawful employment practices
Veteran preferences not affected by sex discrimination provisions . . . Gov §12940

MINE SAFETY AND HEALTH ACT (FEDERAL)
Employer's records of occupational injury or illness
Employees covered by act . . . 8 CCR §14300.47

MINIMUM WAGE REQUIREMENTS
Legislative provision for . . . CA Const Art XIV §1
Piece-rate basis of compensation . . . Lab §226.2

MINING AND TUNNELING
Access shafts, fireproof . . . Lab §7964
Additional personnel, facilities, and services, obtaining . . . Lab §7954
Air composition of extrahazardous mines and tunnels . . . Lab §7979
Air flow and air samples, employer obligation to record . . . Lab §7982
Alarm systems . . . Lab §7985
Classification of mines and tunnels
Generally . . . Lab §7955
Posting classification . . . Lab §7956
Reclassification . . . Lab §7955
Testing based on . . . Lab §7966
Communication systems
Generally . . . Lab §7963
Definitions pertinent to . . . Lab §§7951, 7977

Index

MINING AND TUNNELING—Cont.
Electrical lighting and power plans, review of . . . Lab §7969
Emergencies (See subhead: Rescues)
Equipment requirements for gassy and extrahazardous mines and tunnels . . . Lab §§7975, 7980
Escape chambers and routes (See subhead: Rescues)
Explosives, use of
  Licensing requirements (See subhead: Licenses and permits)
  Limitations on . . . Lab §7990
Extrahazardous mines and tunnels
  Air composition of . . . Lab §7979
  Defined . . . Lab §7977
  Equipment in . . . Lab §7980
  Escape chambers and routes . . . Lab §7981
  Main fan lines . . . Lab §7983
  Mechanical excavation to test for gas and vapors in . . . Lab §7984
  Open flames in . . . Lab §7978
  Permissible gas or vapor levels . . . Lab §7985
  Records of air flow and air samples . . . Lab §7982
  Smoking in . . . Lab §7978
  Testing for gas and vapors
    Devices used for . . . Lab §7985
    Mechanical excavation, by . . . Lab §7984
Fire
  Access shafts, fireproof . . . Lab §7964
  Extinguishers for gassy tunnels and mines . . . Lab §7976
  Ignition
    Procedures upon . . . Lab §7971
    Sources of . . . Lab §7970
  Open flames . . . Lab §7978
  Smoking prohibitions . . . Lab §§7970, 7978
  Welding and cutting . . . Lab §7978
Gassy mines and tunnels
  Electrical plan, review of . . . Lab §7969
  Fire in
    Extinguishers . . . Lab §7976
    Procedures for handling . . . Lab §7970
  Ignition sources, prohibition of . . . Lab §7970
  Kill buttons for electrical equipment . . . Lab §7975
  Notice
    Special orders following inspection, posting . . . Lab §7973
    Specified gas levels . . . Lab §7967
  Operational procedures . . . Lab §7965
  Probe holes . . . Lab §7966
  Removal of workers at specified gas levels . . . Lab §7972
  Shutdown orders for testing . . . Lab §7968
  Smoking prohibitions . . . Lab §7970
  Specified gas levels
    Notice of . . . Lab §7967
    Removal of workers at . . . Lab §7972
  Tests for gas . . . Lab §7966
  Ventilation . . . Lab §7974
General orders, review and update of . . . Lab §7997
Inspections and investigations
  Generally . . . Lab §7953
  Employee notice following . . . Lab §7973
  Safety engineers unit established for . . . Lab §7952

MINING AND TUNNELING—Cont.
Inspections and investigations—Cont.
  Specified gas readings . . . Lab §7961
  Testing for gas or vapors (See subhead: Testing for gas or vapors)
Kill buttons . . . Lab §7975
Licenses and permits
  Explosives, use of
    Generally . . . Lab §7991
  Safety equipment, approval required for . . . Lab §7996
  Underground activities, permit requirements for . . . Lab §6500
Main fan lines . . . Lab §7983
Mechanical excavation to test for gas or vapors . . . Lab §7984
Notice requirements
  Employee notice following inspection . . . Lab §7973
  Occupational Safety and Health Division notice of specified gas levels . . . Lab §7957
  Operation or construction, notice required prior to . . . Lab §7955
  Specified gas readings . . . Lab §7967
Occupational Safety and Health Division
  Authority of . . . Lab §7964.5
  Notice of specified gas readings . . . Lab §7957
  Safety engineers unit . . . Lab §7952
Permissible gas or vapor levels . . . Lab §7985
Permits (See subhead: Licenses and permits)
Posting requirements . . . Lab §§7956, 7973
Preconstruction and preoperation requirements . . . Lab §7955
Probe holes . . . Lab §7966
Reclassification of mines and tunnels . . . Lab §7955
Recordkeeping requirements
  Air flow and air samples . . . Lab §7982
Removal of workers at specified gas readings . . . Lab §7972
Rescues
  Access shafts, fireproof . . . Lab §7964
  Emergency rescue plans . . . Lab §7957
  Equipment for . . . Lab §7981
  Extrahazardous mines and tunnels, escape chambers and routes for . . . Lab §7981
  Trained rescue crews . . . Lab §§7958, 7959
Safety engineers unit established for . . . Lab §7952
Safety equipment, approval required for . . . Lab §7996
Safety representatives
  Generally . . . Lab §7962
Shutdown orders for testing . . . Lab §7968
Smoking prohibitions . . . Lab §§7970, 7978
Specified gas readings
  Investigations . . . Lab §7961
  Notification requirements . . . Lab §7967
  Removal of workers following . . . Lab §7972
Testing for gas or vapors
  Generally . . . Lab §7960
  Classification, based on . . . Lab §7966
  Devices for . . . Lab §7985
  Mechanical excavation, using . . . Lab §7984
  Permissible gas or vapor levels . . . Lab §7985
  Shutdown orders for . . . Lab §7968
Tom Carrell Memorial Tunnel and Mine Safety Act . . . Lab §7950

MINING AND TUNNELING—Cont.
Ventilation in gassy and extrahazardous tunnels . . . Lab §§7974, 7983
Welding and cutting . . . Lab §7978

MINORS
Aliens, uninsured employers fund and subsequent injuries fund benefits for . . . 8 CCR §15740
Appeals Board (WCAB)
  Applications by minors . . . 8 CCR §10455
Awards to
  Child support judgment, workers' compensation award applied to . . . CCP §704.160
  Longshore and Harbor Workers' Compensation Act . . 33 USC §911
Child care providers
  Insurance coverage . . . Ins §676.1
Death benefits for dependent children . . . Lab §4703.5
Dependents
  Death benefits for . . . Lab §4703.5
  Minor children presumed to be . . . Lab §3501
Employment
  Pre-employment physical, disclosure of information from . . . CC §56.10
Employment discrimination against mothers of newborns . . . Gov §12940
Health care coverage . . . Lab §2803.5
Illegally employed
  Increase in workers' compensation to injured children under age 16 . . . Lab §4557
  Insurance for . . . Ins §11661.5
Injured minors
  Appeals Board (WCAB)
    Applications by minors . . . 8 CCR §10455
  Average weekly earnings of injured children under age 18 . . . Lab §4455
  Guardian or conservator . . . Lab §5408
  Illegally employed (See subhead: Illegally employed)
  Increase in compensation to illegally employed children under age 16 . . . Lab §4557
  Payment of compensation to . . . Lab §3605
Juvenile Court
  Volunteers
    Regional youth facility, wards committed to . . . Lab §3364.7
    Traffic offenders . . . Lab §3364.6
    Wards . . . Lab §3364.55
  Wards of (See subhead: Wards of juvenile court)
Longshore and Harbor Workers' Compensation Act, awards under . . . 33 USC §911
Medical information
  Mental health records, disclosure
    Removal from physical custody of parent or guardian, protection of mental health records from release . . . CC §56.106
  Release for purposes of coordinating health care services and medical treatment . . . CC §56.103
Pre-employment physical, disclosure of information from . . . CC §56.10
Support payments for (See CHILD SUPPORT)
Wards of juvenile court
  Benefits, right to . . . W&I §219
  Juvenile homes, ranches, or camps, committed to . . . W&I §883

MINORS—Cont.
Wards of juvenile court—Cont.
  Rehabilitative work, engaged in . . . W&I §219
Youth Authority Department employees (See CORRECTIONS AND REHABILITATION DEPARTMENT)

MINUTES OF HEARING FORM
Electronic adjudication management system (EAMS) . . 8 CCR §10206.20

MISCLASSIFICATION AS INDEPENDENT CONTRACTOR
Advising employers to misclassify
  Liability . . . Lab §2753
Drayage services, drivers performing
  Motor carrier employer amnesty program for carriers performing drayage services . . . Lab §2750.8
Employee *versus* **independent contractor . . . Lab §§2775 to 2785**
  App-based drivers and services generally . . . B&P §§7448 to 7467 (See APP-BASED DRIVERS AND SERVICES)
  Applicability of exceptions to classification preference . . . Lab §2785
  Business-to-business contracting relationship
    Exception to classification preference . . . Lab §2776
  Construction industry, contractor and individual performing work pursuant to subcontract
    Exception to classification preference . . . Lab §2781
  Data aggregators and individuals providing feedback
    Exception to classification preference . . . Lab §2782
  Declaratory of existing law, classification preference as . . . Lab §2785
  General standard . . . Lab §2775
  Injunction to enforce provisions . . . Lab §2786
  Motor clubs, relationship with individual performing services pursuant to contract between club and third party . . . Lab §2784
  Professional services, contract for
    Exception to classification preference . . . Lab §2778
  Referral agency and service provider, relationship between
    Exception to classification preference . . . Lab §2777
  Severability of provisions . . . Lab §2787
  Single-engagement event
    Sole proprietor or business entity performing contract to provide services for single-engagement event . . . Lab §2779
  Sound recordings or musical compositions, creation, marketing, promoting, etc
    Exception to classification preference . . . Lab §2780
  Specific occupations excepted from classification preference . . . Lab §2783
Willful misclassification . . . Lab §226.8

MISCONDUCT
Appeals Board determination of misconduct by applicant leading to reduction in compensation . . . Lab §4552

Index

MISCONDUCT—Cont.
Employers, by
Collection proceedings, time limits on . . . Lab §5407
Compensation amounts increased by . . . Lab §4553
Failure to secure payment, willful . . . Lab §4554
Insurance against employer misconduct, lack of . . . Ins §11661
Pleadings before Appeals Board alleging serious and willful misconduct . . . 8 CCR §10525
Injured workers, by
Conditions of compensation liability, affecting . . . Lab §3600
Reduction in compensation due to misconduct by
Generally . . . Lab §4551
Appeals Board (WCAB), reduction by . . . Lab §4552
Time limits on reduction of compensation proceedings . . . Lab §5407.5
Judges (WCJs)' duty to report ethical violations . . . 8 CCR §9721.32
Serious and willful misconduct (See SERIOUS AND WILLFUL MISCONDUCT)

MISREPRESENTATION (See FRAUD)

MISSING PERSONS
Foreign employment
Contractors with U.Sworking outside U.S
Missing persons as totally disabled . . . 42 USC §1701
Witnesses . . . Ev §240

MONOPOLY
Insurance rates presumed to create . . . Ins §11732
Rates presumed to create . . . Ins §11732

MOTION PICTURE INDUSTRY
Occupational Safety and Health Division permit requirements . . . Lab §6500

MOTOR CARRIERS
Independent contractors
Motor carrier employer amnesty program for carriers performing drayage services . . . Lab §2750.8
Port drayage motor carriers
Employment complaints against carrier
Illegal action found, posting . . . Lab §2810.4
Joint and several liability
Customers of carrier jointly liable after posting of information concerning unsatisfied judgments, tax liability or labor law illegalities . . . Lab §2810.4
Judgments against carriers
Unsatisfied court judgments, posting . . . Lab §2810.4
Tax assessments or liens
Unsatisfied obligations, posting . . . Lab §2810.4

MOTOR VEHICLES
App-based drivers and services . . . B&P §§7448 to 7467 (See APP-BASED DRIVERS AND SERVICES)
Automobile liability insurance (See AUTOMOBILE LIABILITY INSURANCE)

MOTOR VEHICLES—Cont.
Black box or recording device
Search warrant when it would be evidence of felony or misdemeanor causing serious bodily injury . . . Pen §1524
California Highway Patrol (See HIGHWAY PATROL)
Farm labor vehicle (See FARM LABOR VEHICLE)
Highway Patrol (See HIGHWAY PATROL)
Insurance policies
Automobile liability insurance (See AUTOMOBILE LIABILITY INSURANCE)
Internal combustion engines (See INTERNAL COMBUSTION ENGINES)
Judgments against carriers, transmittal of . . . Lab §3716.4
Liability insurance (See AUTOMOBILE LIABILITY INSURANCE)
Passengers
Farm labor vehicles in unsafe condition . . . Veh §31403
Public employment
Transportation by privately owned vehicles . . . 2 CCR §599.631
Stop orders issued to carriers . . . Lab §3710.3
Vapor emissions of vehicles transporting gasoline, test procedures for . . . Lab §6718

MOVING SIDEWALKS . . . Lab §§7300 to 7324.2
Generally (See ELEVATORS, ESCALATORS, CHAIR LIFTS AND OTHER CONVEYANCES)

MPN . . . 8 CCR §§9767.1 to 9767.16, Lab §§4616 to 4616.7 (See MEDICAL PROVIDER NETWORKS)

MRSA
Firefighters and law enforcement officers
Presumption that disease arose out of and in course of employment . . . Lab §3212.8

MSDS (See MATERIAL SAFETY DATA SHEET (MSDS))

MULTIPLE DISABILITIES
Cumulative injury (See CUMULATIVE INJURY)
Subsequent injuries, due to (See SUBSEQUENT INJURIES)
Work capacity guidelines . . . Table 11

MULTIPLE EMPLOYERS
Voluntary disability benefit plans . . . UI §3255

MUNICIPAL FIREFIGHTERS (See FIREFIGHTERS)

MUNICIPAL GOVERNMENTS GENERALLY (See LOCAL GOVERNMENTS AND AGENCIES)

MUNICIPAL POLICE (See POLICE)

MURDER
Death benefits
Public officials, assassinated (See DEATH BENEFITS)
School district payments to surviving spouse of murdered employee . . . Ed §44017

MUSICAL INSTRUMENTS
Employer obligation to safeguard . . . Lab §2800.1

N

NATIONAL GUARD
Military service (See MILITARY SERVICE)

NATIONAL ORIGIN DISCRIMINATION
Defined . . . Gov §12926

NATURAL GAS
Volatile flammable liquid, as (See VOLATILE FLAMMABLE LIQUIDS)

NAVAL SERVICE (See MILITARY SERVICE)

NAVIGATION AND NAVIGABLE WATERS
Admiralty and maritime jurisdiction (See ADMIRALTY AND MARITIME JURISDICTION)
Longshore and Harbor Workers' Compensation Act (See LONGSHORE AND HARBOR WORKERS' COMPENSATION ACT)
Shipping (See SHIPPING)

NECK INJURIES
Medical treatment
  Utilization schedule
    Cervical and thoracic spine disorders . . . 8 CCR §9792.23.1
Work capacity guidelines . . . Table 11

NEEDLE SAFETY STANDARDS
Occupational Safety and Health Board responsibilities . . . Lab §144.7

NEGLIGENCE
Chiropractors
  Unprofessional conduct . . . 16 CCR §317
Contributory (See CONTRIBUTORY NEGLIGENCE)
Employer's negligence in failure to secure payment of compensation . . . Lab §3708
Longshore and Harbor Workers' Compensation Act . . . 33 USC §905
Railroads (See RAILROADS)

NETS (See SAFETY NETS)

NETWORK COMPANIES
App-based drivers and services . . . B&P §§7448 to 7467 (See APP-BASED DRIVERS AND SERVICES)

NEUROMUSCULOSKELETAL EVALUATIONS
Method of measuring disability . . . 8 CCR §46
Time taken to complete . . . 8 CCR §49.2

NEWLY HIRED EMPLOYEES
Notice from employer to new hire concerning pay, allowances, payday, contact information, etc . . . Lab §2810.5

NEWSPAPERS AND PERIODICALS
Election of compensation liability by independent contractors selling . . . Lab §4157

NO-ENTRY/NO-USE ORDERS
Occupational Safety and Health Division (See OCCUPATIONAL SAFETY AND HEALTH DIVISION)

NOMINAL DISABILITY INDEMNITY
Appeals Board (WCAB) award of . . . Lab §5802

NONADMISSIBLE EVIDENCE
Sexual conduct, injuries arising from . . . Lab §3208.4

NONAPPROPRIATED FUND INSTRUMENTALITIES
Exemptions for employees of . . . 5 USC §2105
Longshore and Harbor Workers' Compensation Act (See LONGSHORE AND HARBOR WORKERS' COMPENSATION ACT)

NOT-FOR-PROFIT ORGANIZATIONS
Volunteers, employee status . . . Lab §3363.6

NOTICE
Administration revolving fund assessment, amount of . . . 8 CCR §15606
Appeals Board (WCAB)
  Compensation due, review of notice of . . . 8 CCR §10110
  Evidence taken at hearing without notice . . . 8 CCR §10672
  Hearings . . . 8 CCR §10750
  Rulemaking procedures . . . 8 CCR §§10300, 10302
  Special notice of lawsuit
    Forms required . . . 8 CCR §10500
  Subpoena notice to appear or produce . . . 8 CCR §10642
Audits of claim logs and files . . . 8 CCR §10107
  Post-2002 audits . . . 8 CCR §10107.1
Benefit notices
  Generally . . . 8 CCR §9810
  Changed benefit rate, payment amount or schedule . . . 8 CCR §9812
  Corrected notices . . . 8 CCR §9815
  Definitions pertinent to . . . 8 CCR §9811
  Delay in determining liability . . . 8 CCR §9812
  Denial of liability . . . 8 CCR §9812
  Dependent notices in death cases . . . 8 CCR §9812
  Electronic notice . . . 8 CCR §9810
  Modified or alternative work, offers of . . . 8 CCR §9813.1
  Permanent disability . . . 8 CCR §9812
  Resumed benefit payment . . . 8 CCR §9812
  Salary continuation . . . 8 CCR §9814
  Supplemental job displacement benefits . . . 8 CCR §9813.1
  Temporary disability . . . 8 CCR §9812
  Termination of benefits . . . 8 CCR §9812
Claim logs and files, audit of . . . 8 CCR §10107
  Post-2002 audits . . . 8 CCR §10107.1
Compensation due notice
  Generally . . . 8 CCR §10110
  Appeal of . . . 8 CCR §10115
  Intent to issue, notice of . . . 8 CCR §10110
  Review by Appeals Board (WCAB) . . . 8 CCR §10110
Corrections to . . . 8 CCR §9815
COVID-19
  Exposure, employer notice requirements . . . Lab §6409.6
Crime victims
  Worker's compensation eligibility . . . Lab §3553
Death of employee (See DEATH OF EMPLOYEE)

Index

NOTICE—Cont.
Deferred compensation plans, employer-managed . . . Lab §2809
Disability benefits (See DISABILITY BENEFITS)
Electronic adjudication management system (EAMS)
  Notice of compensation due
    Review of orders issued by administrative director . . . 8 CCR §10208.9
Farm labor vehicle, unsafe condition of . . . Veh §31402
Fraud surcharge, amount . . . 8 CCR §15606
Fraud warning notices
  Annual fraud warning notices . . . Lab §3822
Group self-insurance
  Change in status of group or members . . . 8 CCR §15489.1
  Charter of group
    Amendments, reporting . . . 8 CCR §15489
  Employees notified of self-insured status . . . 8 CCR §15488
Health care continuation coverage, availability of . . . Lab §2807
Health care organizations (HCOs) (See HEALTH CARE ORGANIATIONS (HCOS))
Health care providers, eligibility of . . . Lab §§4600.3, 4603.5
Inactive claims, dismissal of . . . 8 CCR §10141
Information systems
  Employee information (See INFORMATION SYSTEMS)
Injury (See INJURY)
Insurance (See INSURANCE)
Insurance Frauds Prevention Act
  Claim forms, penalty notice on . . . Ins §1871.2, Lab §5401.7
  Temporary disability benefits, notice to injured workers on fraudulent receipt of . . . Ins §1871.8
Interpreter services, right to . . . 8 CCR §9795.2
Knowledge of employer about injury equivalent to . . . Lab §5402
Lien claimants
  Representation, change of representation or nonrepresentation . . . 8 CCR §10868
Longshore and Harbor Workers' Compensation Act
  Compensation . . . 33 USC §934
  Injury or death . . . 33 USC §§908, 912
Medical provider networks
  Notice to employees
    Coverage notice . . . 8 CCR §9767.12
    End of coverage notice . . . 8 CCR §9767.12
    New hires . . . 8 CCR §9767.12
    Pre-implementation notice to employees . . . 8 CCR §9767.12
Medical treatment . . . Lab §4603.5
Mining and tunneling requirements (See MINING AND TUNNELING)
New employees, written notice to . . . 8 CCR §9880
Newly hired employees
  Employer notice to new hire concerning pay, allowances, payday, contact information, etc . . . Lab §2810.5
Ninety-day presumption . . . Lab §5402
Occupational Safety and Health Division (See OCCUPATIONAL SAFETY AND HEALTH DIVISION)

NOTICE—Cont.
Occupational Safety and Health Standards Board public meetings . . . Lab §142.1
Penalty assessment order
  Appeal of notice (See APPEALS)
  Findings on . . . 8 CCR §15554
Permanent disability . . . Lab §4601
  Benefits and payments . . . 8 CCR §9812
  Rating determination, notice of options following . . . 8 CCR §10165.5
Permanent partial disability
  Supplemental job displacement benefits
    Alternative work, offer of modified or alternative work . . . 8 CCR §§10133.34, 10133.35, 10133.53
Personal physician of injured worker
  Name and address, notice to employer of . . . Lab §4603.2
Physicians
  Acupuncturists
    Change of treating physician to personal chiropractor or acupuncturist, form for notice . . . 8 CCR §9783.1
  Chiropractors
    Change of treating physician to personal chiropractor or acupuncturist, form for notice . . . 8 CCR §9783.1
  Choice of
    Request for change of physician by injured worker . . . 8 CCR §9781
    Right of injured worker to choose . . . 8 CCR §9782
  Consulting physician, notice of competency of . . . 8 CCR §9802
  Predesignation of personal physician
    Right to predesignate, notice of . . . 8 CCR §9782
Posting (See POSTING REQUIREMENTS)
Potential eligibility, notice of . . . Lab §5401
Prisoners, vocational rehabilitation services for . . . Pen §5069
Publication of notices . . . 8 CCR §9883
Public employees, availability of vocational rehabilitation for . . . Lab §6201
Qualified medical evaluators (QMEs) (See QUALIFIED MEDICAL EVALUATORS (QMES))
Rating organizations (See RATING ORGANIZATIONS)
Return to work programs
  Offer of work . . . 8 CCR §9813.2
    Form . . . 8 CCR §10118
Right to benefits
  Employee notice requirements . . . 8 CCR §15596
  Employer notification requirements . . . Lab §4603.5
  Injured workers, notice to . . . Lab §138.3
Salary continuation . . . 8 CCR §9814
Self-insurance (See SELF-INSURANCE)
Service by mail . . . CCP §1013
Spanish, availability of notice in . . . 8 CCR §9883
Stop order, notice of findings on . . . 8 CCR §15554
Temporary disability benefits and payments . . . 8 CCR §9812
Treating physician's bias reported to appropriate licensing body . . . Lab §4068

NOTICE—Cont.
Truth in Advertising Act requirements . . . Lab §5432
Vocational rehabilitation (See VOCATIONAL REHABILITATION)
Workers' Compensation Division (See WORKERS' COMPENSATION DIVISION)
Written notice to new employees . . . Lab §3551

NOTICE OF MEDICAL PROVIDER NETWORK PLAN MODIFICATION FORM . . . 8 CCR §9767.8

NOTICE OF OFFER OF MODIFIED OR ALTERNATIVE WORK FORM . . . 8 CCR §§10133.34, 10133.35, 10133.53

NOTICE OF OFFER OF REGULAR WORK . . . 8 CCR §10118

NURSES
COVID-19
Compensation for injury or death from COVID-19 . . . Lab §3212.87
Medical information disclosures
Threat to health or safety, release of information to alleviate . . . CC §56.10
Occupational safety and health
Antineoplastic drugs
Adoption of occupational safety and health standard for handling antineoplastic drugs in health care facilities . . . Lab §144.8
Psychotherapists, status of registered nurses as . . . Ev §1010

O

OATHS
Affirmation included in references to . . . Lab §16
Appeals Board (WCAB) . . . Lab §130
Depositions
Oath of deponent . . . CCP §2025.330
Judge (WCJ), swearing in of . . . Lab §5312
Occupational Safety and Health Appeals Board hearing officer . . . Lab §6607
State Compensation Insurance Fund president . . . Ins §11786

OCCUPATIONAL DISEASE
Asthma
Medical treatment
Utilization schedule
Occupational/work-related asthma medical treatment guideline . . . 8 CCR §9792.23.11
Bloodborne diseases
Health care workers injured as result of preventive care for . . . Lab §3208.05
HIV-related diseases, time limitations for claims for injury or death due to . . . Lab §5406.6
Needle safety standards, Occupational Safety and Health Board responsibilities regarding . . . Lab §144.7
Compromise and release . . . Lab §5005
Date of . . . Lab §5412
Employer liability . . . Lab §5500.5
Forms (See FORMS)

OCCUPATIONAL DISEASE—Cont.
Hepatitis suffered by law enforcement and firefighters . . . Lab §3212.8
Household employees . . . Lab §5500.6
Industrial accident or illness (See INDUSTRIAL ACCIDENT OR ILLNESS)
Industrial Relations Department (See INDUSTRIAL RELATIONS DEPARTMENT)
Meningitis suffered by law enforcement and firefighters . . . Lab §§3212.9, 3212.10
Methicillan-resistant Staphylococcus aureus (MRSA)
Presumption that disease arose out of and in course of employment . . . Lab §3212.8
Pneumonia (See PNEUMONIA)
Records
Employer recordkeeping . . . 8 CCR §§14300 to 14300.48 (See EMPLOYER'S RECORDS OF OCCUPATIONAL INJURY OR ILLNESS)
Generally (See RECORDS AND RECORDKEEPING)
Reporting requirements
Occupational disease or injury (See REPORTING REQUIREMENTS)
Research programs
Grant applications
Review . . . Lab §78
Industrial relations department
Duties at to programs . . . Lab §50.8
Reporting requirements . . . Lab §50.8
Treating physicians, reports of . . . Lab §6409
Tuberculosis
Corrections Department employees . . . Lab §3212.10
Justice Department employees . . . Lab §3212.7
Police officers, firefighters, and correctional officers . . . Lab §3212.6

OCCUPATIONAL INJURY (See INJURY)

OCCUPATIONAL SAFETY AND HEALTH (See SAFE WORKPLACE)

OCCUPATIONAL SAFETY AND HEALTH ADMINISTRATION (OSHA)
Cal-OSHA targeted inspection and consultation fund (See CAL-OSHA TARGETED INSPECTION AND CONSULTATION FUND)
Department of Industrial Relations responsibility for administration and enforcement of standards . . . Lab §50.7

OCCUPATIONAL SAFETY AND HEALTH APPEALS BOARD
Generally . . . Lab §148
Accrual of cause of action . . . Lab §6615
Attorneys' fees, award of . . . Lab §149.5
Award of attorneys' fees and court costs . . . Lab §149.5
Chairperson
Deputy, authorization of . . . Lab §149
Designation of . . . Lab §148
Composition of . . . Lab §148
Court costs, award of . . . Lab §149.5
Decisions
Generally . . . Lab §6608
Action on . . . Lab §6609
Alteration of decision, effect of . . . Lab §6622

Index

OCCUPATIONAL SAFETY AND HEALTH APPEALS BOARD—Cont.
Decisions—Cont.
Informality of proceedings not affecting validity of . . . Lab §6612
Judicial review (See JUDICIAL REVIEW)
Reconsideration of (See RECONSIDERATION)
Service of . . . Lab §6610
Suspension of decision by filing for reconsideration . . . Lab §6625
Depositions, use of . . . Lab §6613
Elevator penalties, appeals of . . . Lab §7321.5
Failure of employer to appear at appeal . . . Lab §6611
Filing
Suspension of decision by filing for reconsideration . . . Lab §6625
Writ of mandate . . . Lab §§6627, 6631
Finality of decisions made by . . . Lab §148.5
Findings . . . Lab §6608
Hearing officer
Duties of . . . Lab §6604
Oath, required to take . . . Lab §6607
Objections to . . . Lab §6606
Powers of . . . Lab §6605
Hearing on reconsideration
Decision based on record without further hearing . . . Lab §6621
Notice of . . . Lab §6620
Hearings generally . . . Lab §148.7
Informality of proceedings not affecting validity of decision . . . Lab §6612
Judicial review (See JUDICIAL REVIEW)
Permits, denial or revocation of . . . Lab §6506
Personnel . . . Lab §148.2
Procedures for appeal . . . Lab §§6602, 6603
Reconsideration (See RECONSIDERATION)
Rules of practice and procedure . . . Lab §§6602, 6603
Service
Notice, order, or decision . . . Lab §6610
Reconsideration, petition for . . . Lab §6619
Suspension of decision by filing for reconsideration . . . Lab §6625
Term of office of members . . . Lab §148.1
Time limits
Citations and penalties . . . Lab §§6600, 6601
Reconsideration . . . Lab §§6614, 6626
Special orders or action orders . . . Lab §§6600.5, 6601.5
Waiver of objections not set forth in reconsideration petition . . . Lab §6618
Writing, orders and decisions required to be in . . . Lab §148.4
Writ of mandate, filing . . . Lab §§6627, 6631

OCCUPATIONAL SAFETY AND HEALTH DIVISION
Abatement requirements
Affirming or modifying . . . Lab §6319.5
Appeals board, reconsideration of order or decision
Serious, repeat serious or willful serious violations, abatement not stayed or suspended by reconsideration . . . Lab §6625
Failure to effect abatement . . . Lab §6320

OCCUPATIONAL SAFETY AND HEALTH DIVISION—Cont.
Agricultural employees
COVID-19, infection prevention best practices communications
Dissemination among agricultural employees . . . Lab §6725
Annual report to legislature . . . Lab §6330
Appeal of denial or revocation of permit . . . Lab §6506
Asbestos, friable . . . Lab §6325.5
Boilers (See TANKS AND BOILERS)
Boomstops for crawler and wheel cranes . . . Lab §6704
Bracing regulations for unsafe swimming pool excavations . . . Lab §6705.5
Breathing apparatus, testing . . . Lab §6331
Building and construction industry (See BUILDING AND CONSTRUCTION INDUSTRY)
Bureau of Investigations . . . Lab §§6315, 6315.3
Citations
Abatement requirements, affirming or modifying . . . Lab §6319.5
Appeals (See OCCUPATIONAL SAFETY AND HEALTH APPEALS BOARD)
Fraud . . . Lab §6317.5
Good faith compliance efforts . . . Lab §6319.5
Issuance of . . . Lab §6319
Posting . . . Lab §6318
Time for issuance . . . Lab §6317
Consulting services . . . Lab §6354
Crawler cranes, boomstops for . . . Lab §6704
Discrimination against injured workers filing complaints . . . Lab §§6310, 6312
Duties and powers of . . . Lab §§60.5, 6307
Education and research programs
Generally . . . Lab §6350
Breathing apparatus, testing . . . Lab §6331
Consulting services . . . Lab §6354
Continuing research . . . Lab §6353
Information on safety and health, preparation and distribution of . . . Lab §6351
Occupational safety and health education fund . . . Lab §6354.7
Safety training . . . Lab §6352
Worker safety bilingual investigative support, enforcement, and training account . . . Lab §6356
Elevators, escalators, chair lifts and other conveyances (See ELEVATORS, ESCALATORS, CHAIR LIFTS AND OTHER CONVEYANCES)
Employer's records of occupational injury or illness
Providing access to government representatives . . . 8 CCR §14300.40
Enforcement powers
Generally . . . Lab §6308
Building and construction industry requirements (See BUILDING AND CONSTRUCTION INDUSTRY)
Employers violating regulations, steps taken against . . . Lab §6317
Equipment, prohibition of use of (See subhead: No-entry/no-use orders)
Excavations
Bids for local government projects involving . . . Lab §6707

OCCUPATIONAL SAFETY AND HEALTH DIVISION—Cont.
Excavations—Cont.
Swimming pool excavations . . . Lab §6705.5
Trench excavations (See TRENCH EXCAVATIONS)
Explosives
Generally . . . Lab §6710
Mining and tunneling (See MINING AND TUNNELING)
Snow avalanche blasting . . . Lab §6711
Failure of Division to act, injured worker's action upon . . Lab §6327.5
Field sanitation requirements . . . Lab §6712
Fraud . . . Lab §§6317.5, 6426
Friable asbestos . . . Lab §6325.5
Garment manufacturing hazards . . . Lab §6409.5
Gas pipelines . . . Lab §6700
Good faith compliance efforts . . . Lab §6319.5
Health Services, role of State Department of . . . Lab §6307.1
Hearings . . . Lab §6308.5
High hazardous industries . . . Lab §6314.1
Informational notices . . . Lab §6328
Information on safety and health, preparation and distribution of . . . Lab §6351
Injunctions
Generally . . . Lab §6323
Tanks and boilers constituting a serious menace . . . Lab §7961
Injury or illness reports
Improve tracking of workplace injuries and illnesses, federal administrative rules
Electronic submission of data, rulemaking and implementation to be monitored . . . Lab §6410.2
Strong reporting standards
Legislative intent . . . Lab §6410.1
Internal combustion engines (See INTERNAL COMBUSTION ENGINES)
Investigations and inspections
Access to place of employment for purposes of . . . Lab §6314
Admissibility of evidence . . . Lab §6315.5
Advance warning of . . . Lab §6321
Boilers (See TANKS AND BOILERS)
Bureau of Investigations . . . Lab §§6315, 6315.3
Cases eligible for . . . Lab §6313
Confidentiality of information obtained in . . . Lab §6322
Elevators, escalators, chair lifts and other conveyances (See ELEVATORS, ESCALATORS, CHAIR LIFTS AND OTHER CONVEYANCES)
High hazardous industries . . . Lab §6314.1
Lead poisoning reports
Complaints charging serious violation, report as . . . Lab §147.3
Mining (See MINING AND TUNNELING)
Procedures . . . Lab §6309
Refineries and chemical plants . . . Lab §§7864, 7867
Reinspections . . . Lab §6320
Reporting requirements . . . Lab §6313.5
Scope of inspection . . . Lab §6314.5
Tanks (See TANKS AND BOILERS)
Tower cranes (See TOWER CRANES)

OCCUPATIONAL SAFETY AND HEALTH DIVISION—Cont.
Investigations and inspections—Cont.
Transmittal of reports . . Lab §6313.5
Tunneling (See MINING AND TUNNELING)
Lead poisoning reports
Complaints charging serious violation, report as . . . Lab §147.3
Lead-related construction work . . . Lab §§6716, 6717
Mining and tunneling (See MINING AND TUNNELING)
No-entry/no-use orders . . . Lab §6325
Contesting . . . Lab §6327
Friable asbestos, workplaces containing . . . Lab §6325.5
Violation of no-entry/no-use orders . . . Lab §6326
Notice
Appeals (See OCCUPATIONAL SAFETY AND HEALTH APPEALS BOARD)
Contractors' State License Board, notice of penalty to . . . Lab §6652
Informational notices . . . Lab §6328
No violation, notice of . . . Lab §6317.7
Posting requirements (See subhead: Posting requirements)
Violation, notice of
Generally . . . Lab §6317
Fraud . . . Lab §6317.5
Occupational Safety and Health Standards Board, duties regarding . . . Lab §§144.5, 147.1
Orders
Generally . . . Lab §6308
Appeals of (See OCCUPATIONAL SAFETY AND HEALTH APPEALS BOARD)
Elevator orders, challenging . . . Lab §7306
Issuance of . . . Lab §6319
No-entry/no-use orders (See subhead: No-entry/no-use orders)
Reinspections following . . . Lab §6320
Penalties and fines
Generally . . . Lab §§6317, 6423
Advance warning of investigations . . . Lab §6321
Appeals of (See OCCUPATIONAL SAFETY AND HEALTH APPEALS BOARD)
Asbestos, failure to determine presence of . . . Lab §6505.5
Building and construction industry (See BUILDING AND CONSTRUCTION INDUSTRY)
Civil penalties distinguished from other penalties . . . Lab §6433
Construction elevator requirements, violations of . . . Lab §7205
Contractors' State License Board, notice to . . . Lab §6652
Cranes (See CRANES)
Death or serious injury, violations causing . . . Lab §6425
Educational entities, civil and administrative penalties on . . . Lab §6434
Failure to correct violations . . . Lab §6430
Fraud . . . Lab §§6317.5, 6426
Injury prevention program, failure to establish . . . Lab §6428
Misdemeanors . . . Lab §6423

OCCUPATIONAL SAFETY AND HEALTH DIVISION—Cont.
Penalties and fines—Cont.
New employees, civil penalties assessed against . . . Lab §6319.3
No-entry/no-use orders, violation of . . . Lab §6326
Non-serious violations . . . Lab §6427
Notice requirements, violation of . . . Lab §6431
Payment into state treasury . . . Lab §6329
Permit violations . . . Lab §§6435, 6509
Posting requirements, violation of . . . Lab §6431
Recordkeeping requirements, violation of . . . Lab §6431
Refunds . . . Lab §6434.5
Repetitious violations . . . Lab §6429
Reporting requirements . . . Lab §6413.5
Scaffolding violations . . . Lab §§7155, 7156
Serious violations . . . Lab §6428
Setting . . . Lab §6319
Steel framed buildings . . . Lab §7266
Time limit on action to collect . . . Lab §6651
Unpaid civil penalties . . . Lab §6650
Willful violations . . . Lab §6429
Permit requirements
Generally . . . Lab §6500
Appeal of denial or revocation of permit . . . Lab §6506
Asbestos-related work (See ASBESTOS)
Boilers (See TANKS AND BOILERS)
Building and construction industry . . . Lab §6500
Crane safety, license to certify (See CRANES)
Dangerous employment or places of employment . . . Lab §6500
Demolitions . . . Lab §6500
Denial of permit . . . Lab §6506
Elevators, escalators, chair lifts and other conveyances (See ELEVATORS, ESCALATORS, CHAIR LIFTS AND OTHER CONVEYANCES)
Entertainment industry . . . Lab §6500
Exempt entities . . . Lab §6508
Fees . . . Lab §6507
Information required from employer . . . Lab §6501
Issuance of . . . Lab §6502
Mining
Licenses and permits (See MINING AND TUNNELING)
Mining and tunneling
Licenses and permits (See MINING AND TUNNELING)
Penalties and fines for violations of . . . Lab §§6435, 6509
Posting of permits by employers . . . Lab §6504
Public Utilities Commission exemption . . . Lab §6508
Registration, no exemption from . . . Lab §6508.5
Revocation of . . . Lab §§6505, 6506
Safety conferences . . . Lab §§6503, 6503.5
Tanks (See TANKS AND BOILERS)
Temporary restraining order for violations of . . . Lab §6510
Tower cranes (See TOWER CRANES)
Trench excavations . . . Lab §6706
Underground activities . . . Lab §6500

OCCUPATIONAL SAFETY AND HEALTH DIVISION—Cont.
Posting requirements
Generally . . . Lab §6410
Penalty for violation of . . . Lab §6431
Permits . . . Lab §6504
Recordkeeping requirements
Generally . . . Lab §6410
Information provided to employees . . . Lab §6408
Penalties for violation of . . . Lab §6431
Registration, no exemption from . . . Lab §6508.5
Reporting occupational disease or injury (See REPORTING REQUIREMENTS)
Scaffolding requirements
Enforcement of . . . Lab §7158
Powers of Division regarding . . . Lab §7157
Serious physical harm
Defined . . . Lab §6432
Shoring regulations for unsafe swimming pool excavations . . . Lab §6705.5
Sloping regulations for unsafe swimming pool excavations . . . Lab §6705.5
Snow avalanche blasting . . . Lab §6711
Swimming pool excavations . . . Lab §6705.5
Tanks (See TANKS AND BOILERS)
Temporary restraining orders (See TEMPORARY RESTRAINING ORDERS)
Trench excavations (See TRENCH EXCAVATIONS)
Tunneling (See MINING AND TUNNELING)
Tunneling and mining safety engineers unit . . . Lab §7952
Variances (See OCCUPATIONAL SAFETY AND HEALTH STANDARDS BOARD)
Violations by employers
Citations (See subhead: Citations)
Fraud . . . Lab §6317.5
Notice of no violation . . . Lab §6317.7
Notice of violation
Generally . . . Lab §6317
Fraud . . . Lab §6317.5
Penalties and fines (See subhead: Penalties and fines)
Procedures for handling . . . Lab §6317
Serious violations
Investigations . . . Lab §6432
Rebuttable presumptions . . . Lab §6432
Substantial probability of death or serious physical harm . . . Lab §6432
Wheel cranes, boomstops for . . . Lab §6704
Window cleaning safety device requirements
Enforcement of . . . Lab §7332
Powers regarding . . . Lab §7331

OCCUPATIONAL SAFETY AND HEALTH FUND
Assessments
Allocation . . . 8 CCR §15602
Collection
Advanced collection, insured employers . . . 8 CCR §15606
Insured employers . . . 8 CCR §15607
Interim assessments . . . 8 CCR §15611
Self-insurers . . . 8 CCR §15605
Determination of assessment . . . 8 CCR §§15601, 15603
Creation . . . Lab §62.5

OCCUPATIONAL SAFETY AND HEALTH FUND—Cont.
Definitions . . . 8 CCR §15600
Surplus . . . 8 CCR §15604
Transfers from other funds . . . Lab §62.5
Use of funds
Purposes for which used . . . Lab §62.5

OCCUPATIONAL SAFETY AND HEALTH STANDARDS BOARD
Generally . . . Lab §140
Adoption of standards . . . Lab §142.4
Appeals of temporary variances
Decisions on . . . Lab §6457
Time limits on . . . Lab §6455
Building standards . . . Lab §142.3
Chemical plants and refineries, standards for (See REFINERIES AND CHEMICAL PLANTS)
Compensation of members of . . . Lab §141
Composition of . . . Lab §140
Decisions
Judicial review of . . . Lab §148.6
Majority of board, by . . . Lab §148.9
Temporary variances . . . Lab §6457
Deputy, chairperson designating . . . Lab §149
Elevators, adoption of fire and emergency standards for . . . Lab §7301.5
Emergency regulations
Generally . . . Lab §142.4
Elevators . . . Lab §7301.5
Enforcement of standards . . . Lab §§50.7, 142, 144
Ergonomics standard, adoption of . . . Lab §6357
Evaluation of variances and standards from other sources . . . Lab §147
Federal standards . . . Lab §§142.3, 147.1
First aid standards . . . Lab §2440
Garment manufacturing hazards . . . Lab §6409.5
Gasoline, test procedures for vapor emissions of vehicles transporting . . . Lab §6718
Hazardous substance removal . . . Lab §142.7
Hearings
Procedural rules for . . . Lab §143.2
Variances, requests for . . . Lab §§143, 146
HESIS
Definition of hazard evaluation system and information service (HESIS) . . . Lab §147.2
Manufacturers, formulators, distributors, etc of toxic substances used in workplaces
Customer names and information, providing to HESIS . . . Lab §147.2
Judicial review of decisions . . . Lab §148.6
Lead-related construction work . . . Lab §6717
Rulemaking to revise lead standards for general industry safety orders and construction safety orders . . . Lab §6717.5
Majority of board, decisions by . . . Lab §148.9
Medical examinations . . . Lab §142.3
Medical marijuana facilities
Evaluation of need for industry-specific regulations . . . Lab §147.5
Medical services standards . . . Lab §2440
Needle safety . . . Lab §144.7
Notice of public meetings . . . Lab §142.1

OCCUPATIONAL SAFETY AND HEALTH STANDARDS BOARD—Cont.
Occupational Safety and Health Division, duties of . . . Lab §§144.5, 147.1
OSHA standards, administration and enforcement of . . . Lab §50.7
Personnel . . . Lab §145
Powers of . . . Lab §§145.1, 148.8
Process safety management standards for refineries and chemical plants (See REFINERIES AND CHEMICAL PLANTS)
Proposed standards . . . Lab §147.1
Public meetings
Generally . . . Lab §142.1
Notice of . . . Lab §142.1
Proposals made at . . . Lab §142.2
Refineries and chemical plants, standards for (See REFINERIES AND CHEMICAL PLANTS)
Temporary variances
Generally . . . Lab §6450
Appeals of
Decisions on . . . Lab §6457
Time limits on . . . Lab §6455
Application process . . . Lab §6450
Binding nature of . . . Lab §6456
Decisions on . . . Lab §6457
Information required for application . . . Lab §6451
New techniques, testing . . . Lab §6452
Rules and regulations for . . . Lab §6454
Terms of office for members of . . . Lab §§140, 141
Toxic materials
Information repository on . . . Lab §147.2
Manufacturers, formulators, distributors, etc of toxic substances
Customer names and information, providing to HESIS . . . Lab §147.2
Standards . . . Lab §144.6
Vapor emissions of vehicles transporting gasoline, test procedures for . . . Lab §6718
Variances
Evaluation of variances from other sources . . . Lab §147
Hearings on requests for . . . Lab §143.1
Permanent variances, applying for . . . Lab §§143, 146
Temporary (See subhead: Temporary variances)
Voting requirements and procedures . . . Lab §142.3
Warnings to employees . . . Lab §142.3

OCCUPATIONAL THERAPISTS
Cap on visits . . . Lab §4604.5

OFF-DUTY ACTIVITY
Conditions of employer liability for compensation . . . Lab §3600

OFFICE OF SELF-INSURANCE PLANS
Industrial Relations Department (See INDUSTRIAL RELATIONS DEPARTMENT)

OFFICIAL MEDICAL FEE SCHEDULE . . . 8 CCR §§9789.10 to 9789.111, Lab §5307.1
Ambulance services . . . 8 CCR §9789.70
Anesthesia . . . 8 CCR §§9789.18.1 to 9789.18.12
Claims modifiers . . . 8 CCR §9789.18.11

OFFICIAL MEDICAL FEE SCHEDULE—Cont.
Anesthesia —Cont.
Concurrent medically directed anesthesia procedures . . . 8 CCR §9789.18.4
Base unit reduction . . . 8 CCR §9789.18.9
Medical and surgical services performed in addition to anesthesia . . . 8 CCR §9789.18.7
Medically directed rate . . . 8 CCR §9789.18.3
Concurrent medically directed anesthesia procedures . . . 8 CCR §§9789.18.4, 9789.18.9
Medically supervised rate . . . 8 CCR §9789.18.5
Monitored anesthesia care . . . 8 CCR §9789.18.10
Multiple anesthesia procedures . . . 8 CCR §9789.18.6
Payment
General payment rule . . . 8 CCR §9789.18.1
Personally performed rate . . . 8 CCR §9789.18.2
Same physician performing anesthesia and medical/surgical services . . . 8 CCR §9789.18.12
Table listing services rendered in 2019 and beyond . . . 8 CCR §9789.19.1
Time and time unit calculations . . . 8 CCR §9789.18.8
CFR provisions incorporated by reference . . . 8 CCR §9789.38
Durable medical equipment . . . 8 CCR §9789.60
Effective date of provisions . . . 8 CCR §9789.111
High cost outlier
Election
Form . . . 8 CCR §9789.37
Hospitals
Cost to charge ratios, specific outliers and composite factors
Incorporation by reference . . . 8 CCR §9789.23
Inpatient hospital fee schedule . . . 8 CCR §9789.20
Definitions . . . 8 CCR §9789.21
Diagnostic related groups . . . 8 CCR §9789.24
Discharge date, federal regulations, federal register notices and payment impact file by discharge date . . . 8 CCR §9789.25
Federal regulations, federal register notices and payment impact file by discharge date . . . 8 CCR §9789.25
Geometric mean length of stay . . . 8 CCR §9789.24
Payment impact file by discharge date . . . 8 CCR §9789.25
Payment of hospital services . . . 8 CCR §9789.22
Relative weights . . . 8 CCR §9789.24
Outpatient departments and ambulatory surgical centers
Applicability of fee schedule . . . 8 CCR §9789.32
CFR provisions incorporated by reference . . . 8 CCR §9789.38
Definitions . . . 8 CCR §9789.30
Federal regulations and federal register notices by date of service . . . 8 CCR §9789.39
High cost outlier election form . . . 8 CCR §9789.37
Maximum reasonable fee . . . 8 CCR §9789.33
Standards . . . 8 CCR §9789.31

OFFICIAL MEDICAL FEE SCHEDULE—Cont.
Hospitals—Cont.
Outpatient departments and ambulatory surgical centers—Cont.
Table of wage index and conversion factors for localities . . . 8 CCR §§9789.34, 9789.35
Laboratory services . . . 8 CCR §9789.50
Medicare changes
Time to adjust rules in light of . . . 8 CCR §§9789.36, 9789.110
Miscellaneous equipment and supplies . . . 8 CCR §9789.60
Non-physician practitioners (NPP)
Anesthetist services, qualified non-physician . . . 8 CCR §9789.15.3
Diagnostic cardiovascular procedures, multiple procedure payment reduction . . . 8 CCR §9789.15.6
Incident to services . . . 8 CCR §9789.15.2
Multiple procedure payment reduction, diagnostic cardiovascular procedures . . . 8 CCR §9789.15.6
Multiple procedure payment reduction, ophthalmology procedures . . . 8 CCR §9789.15.5
Multiple procedure payment reduction, physical medicine/chiropractic/acupuncture . . . 8 CCR §9789.15.4
Ophthalmology procedures, multiple procedure payment reduction . . . 8 CCR §9789.15.5
Payment methodology . . . 8 CCR §9789.15.1
Physical medicine/chiropractic/acupuncture, multiple procedure payment reduction . . . 8 CCR §9789.15.4
Orthotics . . . 8 CCR §9789.60
Outpatient departments and ambulatory surgical centers
Applicability of fee schedule . . . 8 CCR §9789.32
CFR provisions incorporated by reference . . . 8 CCR §9789.38
Definitions . . . 8 CCR §9789.30
Federal regulations and federal register notices by date of service . . . 8 CCR §9789.39
High cost outlier election form . . . 8 CCR §9789.37
Maximum reasonable fee . . . 8 CCR §9789.33
Standards . . . 8 CCR §9789.31
Table of wage index and conversion factors for localities . . . 8 CCR §§9789.34, 9789.35
Pathology and laboratory services . . . 8 CCR §9789.50
Pharmacy fees . . . 8 CCR §9789.40
Physician services
Anesthesia . . . 8 CCR §§9789.18.1 to 9789.18.12
Biologicals administered by physician . . . 8 CCR §9789.13.2
Blood products administered by physician . . . 8 CCR §9789.13.2
Bonus payments
Shortage areas, health professional services . . . 8 CCR §9789.12.6
Conversion factors . . . 8 CCR §9789.12.5
Date of services . . . 8 CCR §9789.11
Definitions . . . 8 CCR §9789.10
Drugs administered by physician . . . 8 CCR §9789.13.2
Drugs dispensed by physicians . . . 8 CCR §9789.13.3
Fee schedule
2014 and beyond . . . 8 CCR §9789.12.1

OFFICIAL MEDICAL FEE SCHEDULE—Cont.
Physician services—Cont.
Maximum reasonable fee calculations
Anesthesia excluded . . . 8 CCR §9789.12.2
Conversion factors . . . 8 CCR §9789.12.5
Relative value file/relative value units (RVUs), use in determining . . . 8 CCR §9789.12.7
Non-physician practitioners (NPP)
Anesthetist services, qualified non-physician . . . 8 CCR §9789.15.3
Diagnostic cardiovascular procedures, multiple procedure payment reduction . . . 8 CCR §9789.15.6
Incident to services . . . 8 CCR §9789.15.2
Multiple procedure payment reduction, diagnostic cardiovascular procedures . . . 8 CCR §9789.15.6
Multiple procedure payment reduction, ophthalmology procedures . . . 8 CCR §9789.15.5
Multiple procedure payment reduction, physical medicine/chiropractic/acupuncture . . . 8 CCR §9789.15.4
Ophthalmology procedures, multiple procedure payment reduction . . . 8 CCR §9789.15.5
Payment methodology . . . 8 CCR §9789.15.1
Physical medicine/chiropractic/acupuncture, multiple procedure payment reduction . . . 8 CCR §9789.15.4
Physician-administered drugs, biologicals, vaccines or blood products . . . 8 CCR §9789.13.2
Physician-dispensed drugs . . . 8 CCR §9789.13.3
Professional component (PC)/Technical component (TC) indicators
Adoption for workers' compensation . . . 8 CCR §9789.12.9
Radiology consultations . . . 8 CCR §9789.17.2
Radiology diagnostic imaging
Film used, additional payment reductions . . . 8 CCR §9789.17.3
Multiple procedures . . . 8 CCR §9789.17.1
Reports, chart notes, etc
Reimbursement . . . 8 CCR §9789.14
Shortage areas, health professional services
Bonus payments . . . 8 CCR §9789.12.6
Mental health services, bonus payments . . . 8 CCR §9789.12.6
Status codes
California-specific codes . . . 8 CCR §9789.12.14
California-specific modifier appended to CPT or California-specific codes . . . 8 CCR §9789.12.15
C, I, N and R . . . 8 CCR §9789.12.3
Consultation services coding . . . 8 CCR §9789.12.12
Correct coding initiative . . . 8 CCR §9789.12.13
Enumeration and description of codes for workers' compensation . . . 8 CCR §9789.12.8
Established patient coding . . . 8 CCR §9789.12.11
Evaluation and management . . . 8 CCR §9789.12.11
New patient coding . . . 8 CCR §9789.12.11

OFFICIAL MEDICAL FEE SCHEDULE—Cont.
Physician services—Cont.
Status codes—Cont.
Reference for current procedural terminology, 4th edition . . . 8 CCR §9789.12.10
Unlisted procedures, reimbursement . . . 8 CCR §9789.12.4
Visit codes used for consultation services . . . 8 CCR §9789.12.12
Supplies . . . 8 CCR §9789.13.1
Surgery . . . 8 CCR §§9789.16.1 to 9789.16.8
Table listing services rendered in 2014 and beyond . . . 8 CCR §9789.19
Unlisted procedures
Reimbursement . . . 8 CCR §9789.12.4
Vaccines administered by physician . . . 8 CCR §9789.13.2
Prosthetics . . . 8 CCR §9789.60
Radiology consultations . . . 8 CCR §9789.17.2
Radiology diagnostic imaging
Film used, additional payment reductions . . . 8 CCR §9789.17.3
Multiple procedures . . . 8 CCR §9789.17.1
Reports, chart notes, etc
Reimbursement . . . 8 CCR §9789.14
Resource-based relative value scale for physician and nonphysician practitioner services
Adoption and review of schedule based on model . . . Lab §5307.1
Surgery . . . 8 CCR §§9789.16.1 to 9789.16.8
Assistants-at-surgery . . . 8 CCR §9789.16.7
Bilateral surgery . . . 8 CCR §9789.16.6
Co-surgeons . . . 8 CCR §9789.16.7
Endoscopy payments . . . 8 CCR §9789.16.5
Global fee . . . 8 CCR §9789.16.1
Billing requirements . . . 8 CCR §9789.16.2
E&M code during global period . . . 8 CCR §9789.16.4
Miscellaneous rules . . . 8 CCR §9789.16.3
Primary treating physician's progress report (PR-2) during global period . . . 8 CCR §9789.16.4
Multiple surgeries . . . 8 CCR §9789.16.5
Team surgeons . . . 8 CCR §9789.16.7
Table of wage index and conversion factors for localities . . . 8 CCR §§9789.34, 9789.35

OFFSHORE LANDS
Defined . . . 43 USC §1331
Longshore and Harbor Workers' Compensation Act, applicability of . . . 43 USC §1333

OFMS (See OFFICIAL MEDICAL FEE SCHEDULE)

OIL REFINERIES (See REFINERIES AND CHEMICAL PLANTS)

OMFS (See OFFICIAL MEDICAL FEE SCHEDULE)

ONSITE MEDICAL SURVEY PROCEDURES
Health care organizations (HCOs)
Medical surveys (See HEALTH CARE ORGANIATIONS (HCOS))

OPEN EXCAVATIONS
Bids for local government projects involving . . . Lab §6707

OPIOIDS
Medical treatment
  Utilization schedule
    Opioids guidelines . . . 8 CCR §9792.24.4

OPTOMETRISTS
Physicians, not regarded as . . . Lab §3209.4

ORDERS
Appeals Board (WCAB) (See APPEALS BOARD (WCAB))
Compliance (See COMPLIANCE ORDERS)
Electronic adjudication management system (EAMS)
  Inspection of documents
    Prohibitions . . . 8 CCR §10208.6
  Retention, return and destruction of records . . . 8 CCR §10208.7
  Review of orders issued by administrative director . . . 8 CCR §§10208.8 to 10208.11
Elevators
  Hearing on order prohibiting use of . . . Lab §7322
  Occupational Safety and Health Division orders, challenging . . . Lab §7306
Information, order to provide . . . 8 CCR §9834
Judges (WCJs)
  Presiding workers' compensation judges . . . 8 CCR §10344
Labor Standards Enforcement Division, issued by . . . 8 CCR §§15555, 15571
No-entry/no-use orders (See OCCUPATIONAL SAFETY AND HEALTH DIVISION)
Occupational Safety and Health Division (See OCCUPATIONAL SAFETY AND HEALTH DIVISION)
Payment of compensation . . . Lab §3702.9
Penalty assessment orders (See PENALTY ASSESSMENT ORDERS)
Rating organizations, orders of compliance upon . . . Ins §11754.2
Reconsideration of (See RECONSIDERATION)
Service
  Appeals Board (WCAB)
    Service by board of orders, decisions, awards, etc . . . 8 CCR §10628
Stipulations
  Effect of stipulations . . . 8 CCR §10835
Stop orders (See STOP ORDERS)
Suspension of
  Appeals Board (WCAB) order, decision, or award suspended by filing petition for reconsideration . . . Lab §5910
  Occupational Safety and Health Appeals Board decision suspended by filing for reconsideration . . . Lab §6625

ORGANIZATIONAL CHANGE (See CHANGE IN ORGANIZATION)

ORGANIZED MILITIA
Military service (See MILITARY SERVICE)

ORTHOTICS
Official medical fee schedule . . . 8 CCR §9789.60

OSHA (See OCCUPATIONAL SAFETY AND HEALTH ADMINISTRATION (OSHA))

OSTEOPATHS
Services and supplies provided by . . . Lab §3209.5

OUTER CONTINENTAL SHELF LANDS
Defined . . . 43 USC §1331
Longshore and Harbor Workers' Compensation Act, applicability of . . . 43 USC §1333

OUT-OF-STATE ISSUES
California National Guard, organized militia, or unorganized militia transferred under mutual aid or interagency agreements . . . Mil&Vet §340.2
Employer, insurance certificate for out-of-state . . . Lab §3600.5
Health care organization (HCO) books and records, prohibition on removal out of state . . . 8 CCR §9771.78
Nonappropriated fund instrumentalities, non-citizen nonresident employees of . . . 5 USC §8172
Resident, out-of-state injury of
  Generally . . . Lab §3600.5
  Appeals Board (WCAB) jurisdiction over . . . Lab §5305
Self-insurance audit, expenses for out-of-state . . . 8 CCR §15404
State Compensation Insurance Fund coverage for workers temporarily absent from California . . . Ins §11780.5

OUTPATIENT SURGERY FACILITIES
Medical care
  Outpatient fee schedule covered under official medical fee schedule . . . 8 CCR §§9789.30 to 9789.39, Lab §5307.1
Payments for treatments . . . 8 CCR §9792.5, Lab §4603.2

OVERPAYMENTS OF BENEFITS
Disability benefits (See DISABILITY BENEFITS)
Unemployment compensation benefits, liability for overpayment of . . . UI §1375.3

OVERPAYMENTS OF INSURANCE
California insurance guarantee association (CIGA)
  Recovery of overpayments . . . Ins §1063.2
Self-insured employers, returned to . . . Lab §3701.3

OWNERSHIP CHANGES (See CHANGE IN ORGANIZATION)

P

PAGA
Private attorneys general act, labor code . . . Lab §§2698 to 2699.6

PAID-IN CAPITAL REQUIREMENTS
Insurance (See INSURANCE)

PAID LEAVE OF ABSENCE
Highway Patrol . . . Lab §4800.5
Justice Department employees . . . Lab §4800

PAID LEAVE OF ABSENCE—Cont.
Lifeguards . . . Lab §4850
Police and firefighters . . . Lab §4850
San Francisco Port Commission employees . . . Lab §4800
School district employees (See SCHOOL DISTRICTS)
University of California
Fire department employees . . . Lab §4804.1
Law enforcement officers . . . Lab §4806

PAID SICK DAYS . . . Lab §§245 to 249 (See SICK DAYS, PAID)

PANELS
Qualified medical evaluators (QMEs) (See QUALIFIED MEDICAL EVALUATORS (QMES))
Referral panelists
Information required from . . . 8 CCR §9829
Information supplied to . . . 8 CCR §9830

PARALYSIS
Presumption of total disability . . . Lab §4662

PARENTAL LEAVE
School districts
Salary deductions during absence . . . Ed §44977.5

PARENT AND CHILD
Pre-employment physical, disclosure of information from . . . CC §56.10

PARENT COMPANIES
Uninsured employers, actions against
Substantial shareholders and parents (See UNINSURED EMPLOYERS BENEFITS TRUST FUND)

PARKS AND RECREATION DISTRICTS
Volunteers, employee status . . . Lab §3361.5

PARTIAL DISABILITY
Permanent (See PERMANENT PARTIAL DISABILITY)
Temporary (See TEMPORARY PARTIAL DISABILITY)

PARTIES
Appeals Board cases (See APPEALS BOARD (WCAB))
Death on the high seas
Substitution of personal representative upon death of plaintiff while action pending . . . 46 USC §30305
Electronic adjudication management system (EAMS)
Definition of party . . . 8 CCR §10205
Joinder of parties in Appeals Board (WCAB) cases . . . 8 CCR §10382
Service
Appeals Board (WCAB)
Reports and records, service on other parties or representatives . . . 8 CCR §10625
Third parties (See THIRD PARTIES)

PARTIES TO ACTIONS
Disclosure, claiming privilege of . . . Ev §§911 to 916

PARTNERSHIP AGREEMENTS
Average weekly earnings of workers under . . . Lab §4457

PASSENGER CARRIERS
App-based drivers and services generally . . . B&P §§7448 to 7467 (See APP-BASED DRIVERS AND SERVICES)

PASSENGER TRAMWAYS
Certification
Construction and repair plans . . . Lab §7353
Permit, required . . . Lab §7354
Definitions . . . Lab §7340
Fees for inspections
Collection . . . Lab §7350
Disposition . . . Lab §7352
Failure to pay . . . Lab §7350
Payment . . . Lab §7351
Setting . . . Lab §7350
Injury reports . . . Lab §7356
Inspections and inspectors . . . Lab §7344
Disposition of fees . . . Lab §7352
Payment of fees . . . Lab §7351
Ski lifts . . . Lab §7354.5
Temporary permits . . . Lab §7349
Occupational safety and health division
Authority . . . Lab §7355
Orders, challenging . . . Lab §7346
Procedures of . . . Lab §7347
Unsafe tramways, powers over . . . Lab §7345
Operators, qualifications of . . . Lab §7357
Permits
Certification required . . . Lab §7354
Defined . . . Lab §7340
Issuance of . . . Lab §7344
Operation without . . . Lab §§7342, 7343
Requirements . . . Lab §7341
Remedies for dangerous operation of . . . Lab §7343
Reports of tramway injuries . . . Lab §7356
Temporary permits . . . Lab §7348
Inspections and . . . Lab §7349
Payment of fees . . . Lab §7351

PATERNITY LEAVE
School districts
Salary deductions during absence . . . Ed §44977.5

PATHOLOGY AND LABORATORY SERVICES
Official medical fee schedule . . . 8 CCR §9789.50

PAYMENT OF BENEFITS
Appeals Board (WCAB) determination of . . . Lab §5801
Asbestos workers . . . Lab §4407
Attorney or agent, direct payment of claim to . . . Lab §4902
Children, injured . . . Lab §3605
Commencement of . . . Lab §4063
Damages
Failure to secure payment of benefits, action based on (See DAMAGES)
Death benefits (See DEATH BENEFITS)
Director's order for . . . Lab §3702.9
Disability benefits
15 percent bump up or bump down
Permanent disability payments . . . Lab §4658
First payment . . . Lab §4650.5
Methods of payment . . . Lab §4651

PAYMENT OF BENEFITS—Cont.
Disability benefits—Cont.
Petition alleging decrease or termination of disability, presumptions following . . . Lab §4651.1
Return to work
Positions for employees relieving employer of obligation to make indemnity payment . . . Lab §4650
State employees, to . . . UI §2783
Timing of payment . . . Lab §§4650, 4650.5
Discharge of claims, as . . . Lab §3603
Employer liability for . . . Lab §4550
Failure to secure payment
Insurance (See INSURANCE)
Judgments regarding (See JUDGMENTS)
Penalties and fines (See subhead: Penalties and fines for unreasonable delay in payment or refusal to pay)
Failure to secure payment, action based on (See DAMAGES)
15 percent bump up or bump down
Permanent disability payments . . . Lab §4658
Health care organizations (HCOs), treatment by
Payment for services (See MEDICAL TREATMENT)
Indemnity amount, benefits payable not affected by subsequent statutory changes in . . . Lab §4453.5
Installment payments of death benefits . . . Lab §4702
Interest on payments . . . Lab §5800
Judgment, credited against . . . Lab §3709
Lien payment not affecting payment of balance of award . . . Lab §4904.1
Liens against compensation payable . . . Lab §4903
Filing lien claim or application for adjudication . . . Lab §4903.6
Longshore and Harbor Workers' Compensation Act (See LONGSHORE AND HARBOR WORKERS' COMPENSATION ACT)
Lump-sum payments (See LUMP-SUM PAYMENTS)
Medical examination, following completion of . . . Lab §4063
Medical treatment
Payment for services
Billing and payment rules (October 2011) . . . 8 CCR §§9792.5.0 to 9792.5.15 (See MEDICAL TREATMENT)
Generally (See MEDICAL TREATMENT)
Notice
Benefit notices (See NOTICE)
Penalties and fines for unreasonable delay in payment or refusal to pay
Generally . . . Lab §5814
Administrative penalties . . . 8 CCR §§10112.1 to 10112.3, Lab §5814.6
Administrative procedure for imposing penalty . . . 8 CCR §10112.3
Definitions . . . 8 CCR §10112.1
Schedule of penalties . . . 8 CCR §10112.2
Attorneys' fees . . . Lab §5814.5
California insurance guarantee association (CIGA)
Covered claims under CIGA do not include penalties or fines for late payments . . . Ins §1063.1

PAYMENT OF BENEFITS—Cont.
Penalties and fines for unreasonable delay in payment or refusal to pay—Cont.
Employer's penalty paid to Industrial Relations Director . . . Lab §5814.1
Ten percent increase . . . Lab §5814
Utilization review
Delays to complete review not counted towards unreasonable delay . . . Lab §4610.1
Public employment (See PUBLIC EMPLOYMENT)
Recovery, effect on . . . Lab §3754
Refusal to pay (See subhead: Penalties and fines for unreasonable delay in payment or refusal to pay)
Self-insurance
Generally . . . Lab §3701.5
Notice of willful failure to pay . . . 8 CCR §15459
Settlement of claim, prior to . . . Lab §4909
State Compensation Insurance Fund, by . . . Lab §4909.1
Subsequent injuries . . . Lab §4754
Successive payments at ten percent weekly interest . . . Table 6
Timing of payment
Disability benefits . . . Lab §§4650, 4650.5
Health care organizations (HCOs), treatment provided by . . . Lab §4614
Longshore and Harbor Workers' Compensation Act . . . 33 USC §914
Unreasonable delay in (See subhead: Penalties and fines for unreasonable delay in payment or refusal to pay)

PAYROLL
Premium, misrepresentation of payroll to lower
Audit of payroll by insurer
Failure of employer to cooperate, liability for triple premiums . . . Ins §11760.1
Insurer's acceptance of false payroll information . . . Ins §757
Penalties and fines . . . Ins §756

PEACE OFFICERS (See POLICE)

PENALTIES AND FINES
Administrative penalties
Full compliance audit penalty schedules . . . 8 CCR §10111.2
Injuries on or after 1/1/1990 and before 1/1/1994 . . . 8 CCR §10111
Injuries on or after 1/1/1994 . . . 8 CCR §10111.1
Liability for assessments . . . 8 CCR §10112
Medical provider networks
Enforcement of provisions . . . 8 CCR §9767.19
Medical treatment
Unreasonable delay in payment or refusal to pay . . . 8 CCR §§10112.1 to 10112.3, Lab §5814.6
Utilization review . . . 8 CCR §§9792.12, 9792.15
Target audit penalty schedule . . . 8 CCR §10111.2
Advertising
QMEs, fraudulent or misleading advertising . . . 8 CCR §158
Qualifications to advise employers . . . Ins §703.5
App-based drivers and services
Impersonating app-based driver . . . B&P §7462
Appeal of notice of penalty assessment (See APPEALS)

PENALTIES AND FINES—Cont.
Appeals Board (WCAB)
Hearings, ordered at . . . 8 CCR §10421
Penalty assessment appeals (See APPEALS)
Audits of claim logs and files . . . 8 CCR §10106.5
Bad faith actions or tactics . . . Lab §5813
Boilers (See TANKS AND BOILERS)
Building and construction industry (See BUILDING AND CONSTRUCTION INDUSTRY)
Civil penalty assessment and claims administration audit
Affidavits . . . 8 CCR §10114.2
Complaint
Amended complaint . . . 8 CCR §10113.2
Determinations . . . 8 CCR §10114.4
Evidence . . . 8 CCR §§10113.4, 10114.1
Hearing and determination regarding . . . 8 CCR §10114
Designation of hearing officer . . . 8 CCR §10113.3
Evidence . . . 8 CCR §10113.4
Prehearing conference and order . . . 8 CCR §10113.5
Investigations . . . 8 CCR §10106.5
Notice of . . . 8 CCR §10113
Oaths . . . 8 CCR §10114.3
Order to show cause . . . 8 CCR §10113
Answer . . . 8 CCR §10113.1
Supplemental order to show cause before submission of case . . . 8 CCR §10113.2
Prehearing conference and order . . . 8 CCR §10113.5
Subpoenas . . . 8 CCR §10113.6
Witnesses
Affidavits . . . 8 CCR §10114.2
Examination . . . 8 CCR §10114.1
Oaths . . . 8 CCR §10114.3
Written statement and supporting evidence . . . 8 CCR §10113.4
Claims administration
Administrative penalties (See subhead: Administrative penalties)
Civil penalty assessments (See subhead: Civil penalty assessment and claims administration audit)
Construction elevator requirements, violations of . . . Lab §7205
COVID-19, compensation for injury or death
Testing positive, outbreak at place of employment
Failure to report positive tests . . . Lab §3212.88
False or misleading information . . . Lab §3212.88
Cranes (See CRANES)
Death or serious injury, violations leading to . . . Lab §6425
Deposition officer, civil penalties for discovery violations by . . . CCP §2025.320
Discovery
Sanctions
Amounts . . . CCP §2023.050
Elevators, escalators, chair lifts and other conveyances (See ELEVATORS, ESCALATORS, CHAIR LIFTS AND OTHER CONVEYANCES)
Family care leave, paid
False certifications as to medical condition . . . UI §3305
Filing failures (See FILING)

PENALTIES AND FINES—Cont.
Foreign employment by contractors with U.Sworking outside U.S . . . 42 USC §1713
Fraud
Generally . . . Lab §3820
Insurance Frauds Prevention Act (See INSURANCE FRAUDS PREVENTION ACT)
Genetic characteristics, disclosure of test results for . . . CC §56.17
Health care workers
Personal protective equipment (PPE) inventory
Employer duties . . . Lab §6403.1
High voltage, misdemeanors associated with . . . Pen §385
Independent medical review
Delay of process
Employer causing delay . . . Lab §4610.5
Enforcement of provisions . . . Lab §4610.6
Information systems
Workers' compensation division
Violation of data reporting requirements . . . Lab §138.6
Insurance (See INSURANCE)
Insurance Frauds Prevention Act (See INSURANCE FRAUDS PREVENTION ACT)
Invasion of privacy . . . CC §1708.8
Labor code private attorneys general
Actions by aggrieved employee . . . Lab §2699
Labor Code, under . . . Lab §23
Labor Standards Enforcement Division
Penalty assessment orders (See PENALTY ASSESSMENT ORDERS)
Penalty liens
Cancellation of . . . 8 CCR §15595
Recording of . . . 8 CCR §15594
Licensure, certificate of insurance required for . . . B&P §7126
Longshore and Harbor Workers' Compensation Act (See LONGSHORE AND HARBOR WORKERS' COMPENSATION ACT)
Medical-legal expenses, failure to pay . . . Lab §4622
Medical provider networks
Administrative penalties
Enforcement of provisions . . . 8 CCR §9767.19
Medical treatment
Late payment for . . . Lab §4603.2
Payment for services
Penalties and fines for unreasonable delay in payment or refusal to pay . . . 8 CCR §§10112.1 to 10112.3, Lab §§5814, 5814.6
Utilization review
Adjustment factors . . . 8 CCR §9792.13
Administrative procedure for imposing penalty . . . 8 CCR §9792.15
Failure to establish process . . . Lab §4610
Liability for penalties assessed . . . 8 CCR §9792.14
Schedule of penalties . . . 8 CCR §9792.12
Misclassification as independent contractor
Advising employers to misclassify
Joint and several liability with employer . . . Lab §2753
Willful misclassification . . . Lab §226.8

PENALTIES AND FINES—Cont.
Occupational safety and health
Reports and records
Employer responsibilities . . . Lab §6409.1
Occupational Safety and Health Division (See OCCUPATIONAL SAFETY AND HEALTH DIVISION)
Orders, appeal
Penalty assessment orders, notice of (See APPEALS)
Payment of benefits (See PAYMENT OF BENEFITS)
Premium, misrepresentation of payroll to lower . . . Ins §756
Privacy, invasion . . . CC §1708.8
Railroad safety (See RAILROADS)
Rating organizations
Final order, noncompliance with . . . Ins §11756
Suspension or revocation of license of . . . Ins §§11754.2 to 11754.4
Referral of clients or patients, compensation received for . . . Lab §3218
Revocation of license, permit, or certification (See REVOCATION OF LICENSE, PERMIT, OR CERTIFICATION)
Scaffolding violations . . . Lab §§7155, 7156
Self-insurance (See SELF-INSURANCE)
Sick days, paid
Enforcement
Administrative penalties . . . Lab §248.5
Posting notice of rights under of provisions
Willful violation of posting requirements . . . Lab §247
Smoking in the workplace, prohibition
Enforcement of provisions . . . Lab §6404.5
State Compensation Insurance Fund, misrepresentation to obtain reduced rate from . . . Ins §11880
Internet posting of convicted violators . . . Ins §1871.9
Steam boilers
Death, imprisonment for causing . . . Lab §7771
Undue quantity of steam endangering human life . . . Lab §7770
Steel framed building violations . . . Lab §7266
Stop orders, failure to observe . . . Lab §3710.2
Suspension
Attorneys . . . 8 CCR §10445
License, permit, or certification (See SUSPENSION OF LICENSE, PERMIT, OR CERTIFICATION)
Qualified medical evaluators (QMEs) . . . Lab §139.2
Tanks (See TANKS AND BOILERS)
Truth in Advertising Act . . . Lab §5434
Uninsured employers
Generally . . . Lab §3700.5
Internet posting of convicted violators . . . Ins §1871.9
Penalty assessment orders (See PENALTY ASSESSMENT ORDERS)
United States, tort claims against . . . 28 USC §2678
Window cleaning safety devices (See WINDOW CLEANING SAFETY DEVICES)
Workers' Compensation Division . . . Lab §129.5
Appealing audit penalty assessment . . . 8 CCR §10590

PENALTY ASSESSMENT ORDERS
Appeal hearings and procedures (See APPEALS)

PENALTY ASSESSMENT ORDERS—Cont.
Certificate of . . . Lab §3727
Contents . . . 8 CCR §15575
Contest of . . . Lab §3725
Decision following appeal hearing . . . 8 CCR §15590
Definitions
Order defined . . . 8 CCR §15557
Special judgments . . . 8 CCR §15558
Entry of judgment, special judgment procedures following . . . 8 CCR §15593
Findings (See FINDINGS)
Injury cases . . . 8 CCR §15568
Issuance of . . . 8 CCR §15567, Lab §3722
Liens on failure to observe terms of
Cancellation of . . . 8 CCR §15595
Recording of . . . 8 CCR §15594
Maximum penalty amounts . . . 8 CCR §15569
Non-injury cases . . . 8 CCR §15568
Notice
Appeals (See APPEALS)
Findings on . . . 8 CCR §15556
Number of employees
Determining . . . 8 CCR §15570
Penalty amount assessed based on . . . 8 CCR §15568
Personal service of . . . Lab §3731
Reasons for issuing . . . 8 CCR §15566
Service (See SERVICE)
Special judgments
Generally . . . Lab §3726
Defined . . . 8 CCR §15558
Entry of judgment, special judgment procedures following . . . 8 CCR §15593
Hearing, special judgment procedures following . . . 8 CCR §15592
No hearing, special judgment procedures in cases of . . . 8 CCR §15592
Types of . . . 8 CCR §15568
Uncontested . . . Lab §3726
Withdrawal . . . 8 CCR §15580, Lab §3727.1
Writ of review following findings confirming or modifying, employer's right to . . . 8 CCR §15591

PENALTY LIENS
Cancellation of . . . 8 CCR §15595
Recording . . . 8 CCR §15594

PENDING ACTIONS
Judges' (WCJs') salaries and (See JUDGES (WCJS))

PENSION PLANS (See RETIREMENT AND PENSION PLANS)

PEOPLE MOVERS . . . Lab §§7300 to 7324.2

PERIODICALS AND NEWSPAPERS
Election of compensation liability by independent contractors selling . . . Lab §4157

PERMANENT DISABILITY
Accumulation of disability awards . . . Lab §4664
American Medical Association's Guides to the Evaluation of Permanent Impairment . . . Lab §§4660, 4660.1
Apportionment of disability . . . 8 CCR §10162, Lab §4663
Referral form . . . 8 CCR §10163

PERMANENT DISABILITY—Cont.
Average earnings
  Defined for purposes of . . . Lab §4452.5
  Weekly . . . Lab §4659
Both temporary and permanent disability . . . Lab §4661
Calculating rate . . . Table 19
California State University Police Department . . . Lab §4819
Causation
  Apportionment of disability
    Use of causation to apportion . . . Lab §4663
  Liability for percentage caused by injury . . . Lab §4664
Comprehensive medical examination (See MEDICAL-LEGAL EXPENSES)
Computation of benefit (See COMPUTATION OF WORKERS' COMPENSATION)
Consultative rating determinations . . . 8 CCR §10166
  Request form . . . 8 CCR §10166.1
Criteria for permanence . . . 8 CCR §10152
Determinations as to permanent disability
  Financial interests in entities providing services . . . Lab §139.32
Disability evaluation unit . . . 8 CCR §10150
  File retention . . . 8 CCR §10150.3
  Signatures . . . 8 CCR §10150.1
  Summary rating determinations . . . 8 CCR §10160
Disaster service workers . . . Lab §4354
Economic Opportunity Program enrollees . . . Lab §4213
Evaluation
  Reports as evidence at Appeals Board hearings . . . 8 CCR §10675
  Supplemental reports . . . Lab §4601
15 percent bump up or bump down . . . Lab §4658
Filing
  Electronic adjudication management system (EAMS) . . . 8 CCR §10151
  Electronic filing exemption . . . 8 CCR §10151.1
  Misfiled or misdirected documents . . . 8 CCR §10150.4
  Requirements . . . 8 CCR §10151
  Retention of files . . . 8 CCR §10150.3
  Technical problems . . . 8 CCR §10150.2
Financial interests in entities providing services . . . Lab §139.32
Firefighters
  Advanced payments . . . Lab §4850.3
  One year, disability continuing for more than . . . Lab §4853
Formal rating determinations . . . 8 CCR §§10156, 10158
Forms (See FORMS)
Highway patrol . . . Lab §4803
Informal rating determinations . . . 8 CCR §10167
Justice Department employees . . . Lab §4803
Longshore and Harbor Workers' Compensation Act awards . . . 33 USC §908
Medical examination to determine . . . Lab §4061
  Attorney representing employee . . . Lab §4062.2
  Unrepresented employee . . . Lab §4062.1
Misfiled or misdirected documents . . . 8 CCR §10150.4
Nature of physical injury or disfigurement
  Percentage of disability, determining . . . Lab §4660
    2013, injuries occurring in or after . . . Lab §4660.1

PERMANENT DISABILITY—Cont.
Notice
  Benefits and payments . . . 8 CCR §9812
  Rating determination, options following . . . 8 CCR §10165.5
Partial (See PERMANENT PARTIAL DISABILITY)
Payment of benefits generally (See PAYMENT OF BENEFITS)
Percentage of disability
  Determining . . . Lab §4660
    2013, injuries occurring in or after . . . Lab §4660.1
  Liability for percentage caused by injury . . . Lab §4664
  Weeks of indemnity, compared to . . . Table 15
Police
  Advanced payments . . . Lab §4850.3
  One year, disability continuing for more than . . . Lab §4853
Presumption of total disability . . . Lab §4662
Ratings
  Agreement on, lack of . . . Lab §4061
  American Medical Association's Guides to the Evaluation of Permanent Impairment . . . Lab §§4660, 4660.1
  Calculating . . . Table 19
  Consultative rating determinations . . . 8 CCR §10166
    Request form . . . 8 CCR §10166.1
  Determining . . . 8 CCR §§10150 to 10167
    Formal permanent disability rating determinations . . . 8 CCR §10675
  Evidence, formal determinations as . . . 8 CCR §10158
  Formal determinations . . . 8 CCR §§10156, 10158
  Informal rating determinations . . . 8 CCR §10167
  Notice of options following determination . . . 8 CCR §10165.5
  Percentage of permanent disability to weeks of indemnity . . . Table 15
  Schedule . . . 8 CCR §9805
    1997 schedule . . . Table 11B
    2005 schedule . . . Table 11A
    Evaluation and revision . . . 8 CCR §9805.1
  Sleep disorders, sexual dysfunction and psychiatric disorders
    Impairment ratings . . . Lab §4660.1
  Summary determinations (See subhead: Summary rating determinations)
San Francisco Port Commission employees . . . Lab §4803
Schedules, charts, and tables (See SCHEDULES, CHARTS, AND TABLES)
Subjective factors defined . . . 8 CCR §9727
Summary rating determinations
  Apportionment of disability . . . 8 CCR §10162
    Referral form . . . 8 CCR §10163
  Comprehensive medical examination (See MEDICAL-LEGAL EXPENSES)
  Deadline for issuing determination . . . 8 CCR §10159
  Primary treating physician's report for unrepresented injured workers . . 8 CCR §10160.1
  Procedures for obtaining . . . 8 CCR §10160

Index

PERMANENT DISABILITY—Cont.
Summary rating determinations—Cont.
Questionnaire . . . 8 CCR §10161
Reconsideration requests for unrepresented injured workers . . . 8 CCR §10164
Represented injured workers . . . 8 CCR §10160.5
Reproduction of forms . . . 8 CCR §10161.1
Request for . . . 8 CCR §10161
Service of . . . 8 CCR §10165
Unrepresented workers
Comprehensive medical evaluation . . . 8 CCR §10160
Reconsideration of report . . . 8 CCR §10164
Treating physician, report of . . . 8 CCR §10160.1
Total (See PERMANENT TOTAL DISABILITY)
University of California
Fire department employees . . . Lab §4804.4
Law enforcement officers . . . Lab §4809
Unrepresented workers, summary rating determination reports on
Comprehensive medical evaluation . . . 8 CCR §10160
Reconsideration of report . . . 8 CCR §10164
Treating physician, report of . . . 8 CCR §10160.1
When permanence is considered achieved . . . 8 CCR §10152
Work capacity guidelines . . . Table 11

PERMANENT PARTIAL DISABILITY
Application of permanent partial disability rates to permanent disability indemnity table . . . Table 16
Average earnings, defined for purposes of . . . Lab §4452.5
Indemnity and earnings, minimum/maximum . . . Table 14
Life pensions
Generally (See LIFE PENSIONS)
70 percent to less than 100 percent disability . . . Lab §4659
Longshore and Harbor Workers' Compensation Act . . . 33 USC §908
Lump-sum payments . . . Lab §5100.5
Subsequent injuries adding to . . . Lab §4751
Supplemental job displacement benefits . . . 8 CCR §§10133.31 to 10133.60
Alternative work
Offer of modified or alternative work, notice . . . 8 CCR §§10133.34, 10133.35, 10133.53
Approved training facilities
Criteria for state approval . . . 8 CCR §10133.58
Dispute resolution . . . 8 CCR §10133.54
Request for dispute resolution before administrative director, form . . . 8 CCR §10133.55
Eligibility . . . 8 CCR §10133.56, Lab §4658.5
2013, injuries occurring in or after . . . Lab §4658.7
Modified or alternative work not accepted, employer not liable for benefits . . . Lab §4658.6
Modified work
Offer of modified or alternative work, notice . . . 8 CCR §§10133.34, 10133.35, 10133.53
Nontransferable training vouchers
Termination of administrator liability for benefit . . . 8 CCR §10133.60

PERMANENT PARTIAL DISABILITY—Cont.
Supplemental job displacement benefits —Cont.
Notice
Offer of modified or alternative work . . . 8 CCR §§10133.34, 10133.35, 10133.53
Offer of modified or alternative work
Notice . . . 8 CCR §§10133.34, 10133.35, 10133.53
Termination of administrator liability for benefit . . . 8 CCR §10133.60
Vocational & return to work counselor (VRTWC)
List . . . 8 CCR §10133.59
Vouchers for training, nontransferable
Eligibility . . . 8 CCR §10133.56
Form . . . 8 CCR §10133.57
Injuries occurring from 2013 forward, form . . . 8 CCR §10133.32

PERMANENT TOTAL DISABILITY
Average earnings, defined for purposes of . . . Lab §4452.5
Life pensions (See LIFE PENSIONS)
Longshore and Harbor Workers' Compensation Act . . . 33 USC §908
Presumptions . . . Lab §4662

PERMITS (See LICENSES AND PERMITS)

PERSONAL INCOME TAX
Exclusions from gross income
Federal law . . . 26 USC §§101, 104

PERSONAL INJURIES
Husband and wife privileges, waiver of . . . Ev §972

PERSONAL LIABILITY
Employees . . . Lab §3601
Employers . . . Lab §3602
Household employees, personal liability insurance for (See HOUSEHOLD EMPLOYEES)

PERSONAL PHYSICIANS (See PHYSICIANS)

PERSONAL PROTECTIVE EQUIPMENT (PPE)
Direct patient care providers
Stockpile of PPE, employer duties . . . Lab §6403.3
Health care workers
Inventory
Employer duties . . . Lab §6403.1

PERSONAL RESPONSIBILITY AND WORK OPPORTUNITY RECONCILIATION ACT (PRWORA)
Uninsured employers fund and subsequent injuries fund benefits for aliens . . . 8 CCR §15740

PESTICIDES
Handling (See HAARDOUS SUBSTANCES)
Occupational disease or injury, physician reporting requirements regarding . . . 8 CCR §14003
Treatment for pesticide poisoning not regarded as first aid . . . Lab §6409.3

PETITIONS
Appeals Board (WCAB) (See APPEALS BOARD (WCAB))
Disability, termination or decrease in (See DISABILITY)

PETITIONS—Cont.
Electronic adjudication management system (EAMS)
Definition of petition . . . 8 CCR §10205
Filing petitions and answers to petitions . . . 8 CCR §10510

PETROLEUM
Refiners and distributors
Refinery and Chemical Plant Worker Safety Act . . . Lab §§7850 to 7873
Volatile flammable liquid, as (See VOLATILE FLAMMABLE LIQUIDS)

PHARMACEUTICAL FEE SCHEDULE
Compounded drug products . . . Lab §5307.1
Covered under official medical fee schedule . . . Lab §5307.1
Official medical fee schedule . . . 8 CCR §9789.40

PHARMACISTS
Medical records
Confidentiality to be maintained . . . CC §56.101
Waiver of confidentiality not to be required by companies . . . CC §56.05
Occupational safety and health
Antineoplastic drugs
Adoption of occupational safety and health standard for handling antineoplastic drugs in health care facilities . . . Lab §144.8

PHARMACY BENEFITS
Reproduced claim form utilized for . . . Lab §4608

PHARMACY BENEFITS MANAGERS
Drugs, medical treatment utilization schedule (MTUS)
Formulary . . . 8 CCR §9792.27.4

PHARMACY GOODS
Pharmaceutical fee schedule . . . Lab §5307.1

PHARMACY NETWORKS
Drugs, medical treatment utilization schedule (MTUS)
Formulary . . . 8 CCR §9792.27.4

PHOTOCOPIED FORMS (See REPRODUCTION OF FORMS)

PHOTOGRAPHS
Appeals board (WCAB)
Exhibits generally . . . 8 CCR §10677
Evidence, use as
Microphotographed files, records, photographs, etc., in custody of criminal justice agency . . . Ev §1550.1
Writing, classified as . . . Ev §250

PHYSICAL EXAMINATIONS (See MEDICAL EXAMINATIONS)

PHYSICAL THERAPISTS
Cap on visits . . . Lab §4604.5
Medical treatment generally (See MEDICAL TREATMENT)

PHYSICIAN CONTRACT APPLICATION FORMS . . . 8 CCR §9768.5

PHYSICIANS
Acupuncturists
Change of treating physician to personal chiropractor or acupuncturist, form for notice . . . 8 CCR §9783.1
Not regarded as physicians . . . Lab §3209.9
Advertising, exclusion of physicians from coverage by article regarding . . . 8 CCR §9821
Appeals Board (WCAB)
Primary treating physician, appeal of grant or denial of petition to change . . . 8 CCR §9787
Reports of physicians (See APPEALS BOARD (WCAB))
Attending (See CONSULTING OR ATTENDING PHYSICIANS)
Certification of consulting or attending physicians, injured worker request for . . . Lab §4602
Chiropractors
Change of treating physician to personal chiropractor or acupuncturist, form for notice . . . 8 CCR §9783.1
Classifying chiropractors as physicians . . . Lab §3209.3
Holding out of chiropractor as physician not permitted by classification . . . Lab §3209.6
Choice of
Acupuncturists
Change of treating physician to personal chiropractor or acupuncturist, form for notice . . . 8 CCR §9783.1
Chiropractors
Change of treating physician to personal chiropractor or acupuncturist, form for notice . . . 8 CCR §9783.1
Definitions pertinent to . . . 8 CCR §9780
Duties regarding
Reporting responsibilities of primary treating physician . . . 8 CCR §9785
First aid and emergency treatment, duty of employer to provide . . . 8 CCR §9780.1
Longshore and Harbor Workers' Compensation Act . . . 33 USC §907
Notice to injured worker of rights regarding . . . 8 CCR §9782
Personal physician, injured worker selection of . . . 8 CCR §9780.1
Primary treating physician
Appeal of grant or denial of petition to change . . . 8 CCR §9787
Form of petition for change of primary treating physician . . . 8 CCR §9786.1
Petition for change of primary treating physician . . . 8 CCR §9786
Reporting responsibilities of primary treating physician . . . 8 CCR §9785
Response to petition for change of primary treating physicianform of . . . 8 CCR §9786.1
Request for change of physician by injured worker . . . 8 CCR §9781
Confidentiality of medical information . . . CC §§56.10 to 56.21
Consulting (See CONSULTING OR ATTENDING PHYSICIANS)

PHYSICIANS—Cont.
Cosignature of treating physician required . . . Lab §3209.10
Defined
  Generally . . . Lab §3209.3
  Choice of physician, terms pertinent to . . . 8 CCR §9780
Drugs, medical treatment utilization schedule (MTUS)
  Formulary
    Physician-dispensed drugs . . . 8 CCR §9792.27.8
Educational materials for treating physicians . . . Lab §4602.8
Electronic adjudication management system (EAMS)
  Selection by employee of employer-designated physician, order
    Review of orders issued by administrative director . . . 8 CCR §10208.8
Emergency, liability during state of . . . Gov §8659
Employer request for change of . . . Lab §4603
Fee schedule
  Official medical fee schedule . . . Lab §5307.1
    Date of physician services . . . 8 CCR §9789.11
    Definitions . . . 8 CCR §9789.10
Financial interests in entities providing services
  Conflicts of interest . . . Lab §139.32
Independent contractor status
  Presumption . . . Lab §2750.6
Independent medical review
  Organizations providing review
    Conflicts of interest . . . Lab §139.5
    Qualifications for reviewing physicians . . . Lab §139.5
Longshore and Harbor Workers' Compensation Act . . . 33 USC §907
Medical examinations (See MEDICAL EXAMINATIONS)
Medical-legal expenses
  Fee schedules . . . Table 12
  Report, responsibilities of physician signing . . . Lab §4628
Medical provider networks . . . 8 CCR §§9767.1 to 9767.16, Lab §§4616 to 4616.7 (See MEDICAL PROVIDER NETWORKS)
Medical treatment
  Payment for services
    Provider dispute of amount paid . . . Lab §4603.2
  Personal physician
    Conditions for treatment of employee . . . Lab §4600
Network, disclosure of provider's participation in . . . Lab §4609
Occupational disease or injury
  Reporting requirements regarding (See REPORTING REQUIREMENTS)
Occupational safety and health
  Antineoplastic drugs
    Adoption of occupational safety and health standard for handling antineoplastic drugs in health care facilities . . . Lab §144.8
Official medical fee schedule, physician services . . . Lab §5307.1
  Anesthesia . . . 8 CCR §§9789.18.1 to 9789.18.12

PHYSICIANS—Cont.
Official medical fee schedule, physician services —Cont.
  Biologicals administered by physician . . . 8 CCR §9789.13.2
  Blood products administered by physician . . . 8 CCR §9789.13.2
  Bonus payments
    Shortage areas, health professional services . . . 8 CCR §9789.12.6
  Conversion factors . . . 8 CCR §9789.12.5
  Date of services . . . 8 CCR §9789.11
  Definitions . . . 8 CCR §9789.10
  Drugs administered by physician . . . 8 CCR §9789.13.2
  Drugs dispensed by physicians . . . 8 CCR §9789.13.3
  Fee schedule
    2014 and beyond . . . 8 CCR §9789.12.1
  Maximum reasonable fee calculations
    Anesthesia excluded . . . 8 CCR §9789.12.2
    Conversion factors . . . 8 CCR §9789.12.5
    Relative value file/relative value units (RVUs), use in determining . . . 8 CCR §9789.12.7
  Non-physician practitioners (NPP)
    Anesthetist services, qualified non-physician . . . 8 CCR §9789.15.3
    Diagnostic cardiovascular procedures, multiple procedure payment reduction . . . 8 CCR §9789.15.6
    Incident to services . . . 8 CCR §9789.15.2
    Multiple procedure payment reduction, diagnostic cardiovascular procedures . . . 8 CCR §9789.15.6
    Multiple procedure payment reduction, ophthalmology procedures . . . 8 CCR §9789.15.5
    Multiple procedure payment reduction, physical medicine/chiropractic/acupuncture . . . 8 CCR §9789.15.4
    Ophthalmology procedures, multiple procedure payment reduction . . . 8 CCR §9789.15.5
    Payment methodology . . . 8 CCR §9789.15.1
    Physical medicine/chiropractic/acupuncture, multiple procedure payment reduction . . . 8 CCR §9789.15.4
Optometrists not regarded as . . . Lab §3209.4
Peer review proceedings
  Disclosure of medical information to committees . . . CC §56.10
  Malpractice insurance, remedial underwriting practices . . . Ins §676.3
Personal physician of injured worker
  Choice of physician . . . 8 CCR §9780.1
  Conditions for treatment of employee . . . Lab §4600
  Consulting or attending physicians hired at injured worker's expense . . . Lab §4605
  Medical examinations
    Presence at . . . Lab §4052
    Treating physician, opinion of . . . Lab §4061.5
  Notice
    Name and address, notice to employer of . . . Lab §4603.2
  Objection by employer
    Medical provider network, physician not member . . . Lab §4603.2

PHYSICIANS—Cont.
Personal physician of injured worker—Cont.
One-time change of . . . Lab §4601
Treating physician, opinion of . . . Lab §4061.5
Pharmaceutical fee schedule
Physician-dispensed pharmacy goods, dangerous drugs or devices, etc . . . Lab §5307.1
Predesignation of personal physician
Conditions for treatment by predesignated physician . . . 8 CCR §9780.1
Definitions . . . 8 CCR §9780
First aid and emergency treatment, duty of employer to provide . . . 8 CCR §9780.1
Form . . . 8 CCR §9783
Medical provider networks
Relationship between predesignation and MPN's . . . 8 CCR §9780.1
Notice of right to predesignate . . . 8 CCR §9782
Privilege, physician-patient . . . Ev §996
Procuring patients, prohibition on employment of persons for purposes of . . . Ins §1871.7
Qualified medical evaluators (QMEs) (See QUALIFIED MEDICAL EVALUATORS (QMES))
Referrals
Generally (See REFERRALS AND REFERRAL SERVICES)
Limitations on referrals . . . Lab §§139.3, 139.31
Medical treatment by employer
Medically appropriate referrals, right to . . . Lab §4600
Reports
Appeals Board (WCAB) evidence, as (See APPEALS BOARD (WCAB))
Occupational disease or injury (See REPORTING REQUIREMENTS)
Prisoners
Report of injury to prisoner (See PRISONERS)
Specialist QMEs (See QUALIFIED MEDICAL EVALUATORS (QMES))
Suspension of physician, practitioner or provider from participation in system for cause . . . Lab §139.21
Procedure for suspension of providers . . . 8 CCR §§9788.1 to 9788.6
Determination and order of suspension, amendment . . . 8 CCR §9788.5
Hearings, conduct . . . 8 CCR §9788.3
Hearings, request . . . 8 CCR §9788.2
Notice of suspension . . . 8 CCR §§9788.1, 9788.4
Order of suspension, amendment . . . 8 CCR §9788.5
Service of process . . . 8 CCR §9788.6
Time, computation . . . 8 CCR §9788.6
Treating physician (See TREATING PHYSICIAN)

PIERS (See SHIPPING)

PLACE OF EMPLOYMENT
COVID-19, compensation for injury or death
Testing positive, outbreak at place of employment . . . Lab §3212.88
Safety issues (See SAFE WORKPLACE)

PLANKING AND PLANKED FLOORS
Generally . . . Lab §7107

PLANKING AND PLANKED FLOORS—Cont.
Replanking . . . Lab §7105
Steel framed buildings (See STEEL FRAMED BUILDINGS)

PLEADINGS
Appeals Board (WCAB) (See APPEALS BOARD (WCAB))
Judicial review of Appeals Board (WCAB) decisions, service of pleadings upon . . . Lab §5954
Required . . . Lab §5500

PNEUMONIA
Firefighters . . . Lab §§3212, 3212.4
Law enforcement officers (See POLICE)
University of California fire department . . . Lab §3212.4

POLICE
Advanced disability pension payments . . . Lab §4850.3
Grounds for denying payment . . . Lab §4850.4
App-based drivers and services
Investigations of emergencies, exigent circumstances and critical incidents
Law enforcement information requests, company to provide mechanism . . . B&P §7460.5
Assistance in active law enforcement, persons engaged in . . . Lab §3366
Auxiliary officers (See subhead: Reserve or auxiliary officers)
Average weekly earnings . . . Lab §4458.2
Back injury when required to wear duty belt . . . Lab §3213.2
California State University
Police department (See CALIFORNIA STATE UNIVERSITY)
Cancer . . . Lab §3212.1
Citizen complaints
Discovery or disclosure . . . Ev §§915, 1043
City government (See POLICE)
County employees
Defined . . . Gov §50920
Peace officer performing duty not under direction of employer . . . Gov §50921
COVID-19
Compensation for injury or death from COVID-19 . . . Lab §3212.87
Death benefits
Generally . . . Lab §4856
Computation where no dependents . . . Lab §4702
Continued health benefits to surviving spouse and dependents . . . Lab §4856
Scholarships for dependents of police officers . . . Lab §4709
Defined
County employees . . . Gov §50920
Police . . . Gov §50920
Sheriff . . . Lab §25
Discipline and disciplinary proceedings
Discovery or disclosure of records . . . Ev §§915, 1043
Employee status
Active officers . . . Lab §3362
Assistance in active law enforcement, persons engaged in . . . Lab §3366

POLICE—Cont.
Employee status—Cont.
Reserve or auxiliary officers . . . Lab §3362.5
Sheriff's reserve volunteers . . . Lab §3364
Technical assistants . . . Lab §3367
Employer's immediate direction, not acting under . . . Lab §3600.2
Harbor police, San Francisco (See SAN FRANCISCO PORT COMMISSION)
Heart disease
Generally . . . Lab §§3212, 3212.5
Highway Patrol . . . Lab §3212.3
University of California Law enforcement officers . . . Lab §3213
Hepatitis . . . Lab §3212.8
Hernias . . . Lab §3212
Highway Patrol (See HIGHWAY PATROL)
Justice Department peace officers (See JUSTICE DEPARTMENT)
Local peace officers (See POLICE)
Medical treatment . . . Lab §4852
Meningitis . . . Lab §§3212.9, 3212.10
Methicillan-resistant Staphylococcus aureus (MRSA)
Presumption that disease arose out of and in course of employment . . . Lab §3212.8
Occupationally-related accident, called to scene of . . . Lab §6409.2
Occupational safety and health
Penalties and fines
Refunds . . . Lab §6434.5
Off-duty . . . Lab §3600.3
One year, disability continuing beyond . . . Lab §4853
Paid leave of absence . . . Lab §4850
Peace officer
Performing duty not under direction of employer . . . Gov §50921
Permanent disability
Advanced disability pension payments . . . Lab §4850.3
Grounds for denying . . . Lab §4850.4
One year, disability continuing beyond . . . Lab §4853
Personnel records
Discovery or disclosure . . . Ev §915
Pneumonia
Generally . . . Lab §§3212, 3212.5
Correction Department employees . . . Lab §3212.10
Highway Patrol . . . Lab §3212.3
University of California Law enforcement officers . . . Lab §3213
Post-traumatic stress injury
Coverage . . . Lab §3212.15
Presumptions
Cancer
William Dallas Jones cancer presumption act of 2010 . . . Lab §3212.1
Public Employees' Retirement System, state and local safety members of (See PUBLIC EMPLOYEES' RETIREMENT SYSTEM)
Request to make disability determinations . . . Lab §4851
Reserve or auxiliary officers
Employee status . . . Lab §§3362.5, 3364
Public safety officers as county employees . . . Lab §4855

POLICE—Cont.
Reserve or auxiliary officers—Cont.
Sheriff's reserve volunteers, employee status of . . . Lab §3364
Salary payments, temporary disability payments concurrent with . . . Lab §4854
San Francisco harbor police (See SAN FRANCISCO PORT COMMISSION)
San Luis Obispo firefighters, probation and sheriff's office employees, benefits for . . . Lab §4850.5
Sheriff's reserve volunteers . . . Lab §3364
Technical assistants . . . Lab §3367
Temporary disability
Advanced payments . . . Lab §4850
Determinations, request to make . . . Lab §4850
Medical, surgical, and hospital benefits, effect on . . . Lab §4852
Paid leave of absence in lieu of TD . . . Lab §4850
Salary payments, prohibition on disability benefits concurrent with . . . Lab §4854
San Luis Obispo personnel . . . Lab §4850.5
Termination of active service, injury following . . . Lab §4458.5
Tuberculosis . . . Lab §§3212.6, 3212.10
University of California (See UNIVERSITY OF CALIFORNIA)

PORT DISTRICTS
San Francisco Port Commission (See SAN FRANCISCO PORT COMMISSION)
Shipping (See SHIPPING)
Stevedores (See STEVEDORES)

PORT DRAYAGE MOTOR CARRIERS
Employment complaints against carrier
Illegal action found, posting . . . Lab §2810.4
Joint and several liability
Unsatisfied judgments or tax liability or labor law complaints
Customers of carrier jointly liable after posting of information . . . Lab §2810.4
Judgments against carriers
Unsatisfied court judgments, posting . . . Lab §2810.4
Tax assessments or liens
Unsatisfied obligations, posting . . . Lab §2810.4

POSSESSIONS AND TERRITORIES OF UNITED STATES
Railroads . . . 45 USC §51

POSTING REQUIREMENTS
Generally . . . Lab §3550
Employee notices . . . 8 CCR §9881
Contents of poster . . . 8 CCR §9881.1
Insurance carrier, requirement to post notice of . . . 8 CCR §15565
Medical provider networks
Initial medical evaluation
Consequences of failure to post information about MPN procedures . . . Lab §4616.3
Mines and tunnels . . . Lab §§7956, 7973
Occupational Safety and Health Division (See OCCUPATIONAL SAFETY AND HEALTH DIVISION)
Sick days, paid
Posting notice of rights under of provisions . . . Lab §247

POSTING REQUIREMENTS—Cont.
Workers' Compensation Division notices . . . 8 CCR §9881
Contents of poster . . . 8 CCR §9881.1

POSTOPERATIVE REHABILITATION
Guidelines . . . 8 CCR §9792.24.3

POST-TRAUMATIC STRESS INJURY
Fire and rescue service coordinators
Coverage . . . Lab §3212.15
Firefighters
Coverage . . . Lab §3212.15
Police
Coverage . . . Lab §3212.15

POWER OF ATTORNEY
Group self-insurance . . . 8 CCR §15479
Definition of power of attorney . . . 8 CCR §15201

PREEMPTION OF LOCAL REGULATION
App-based drivers and services
Uniform work standards
State preemption of local requirements . . . B&P §7464

PREEMPTION OF STATE LAW
Economic opportunity program enrollees . . . Lab §4229

PREEXISTING CONDITIONS
Aggravation of
Time limits on claim for . . . Lab §5410
Permanent disability
Apportionment of disability
Disclosure of previous disabilities and impairments . . . Lab §4663

PREMIUMS
California Insurance Guarantee Association (CIGA) . . . Ins §1063.5
Surcharges on premiums . . . Ins §§1063.14, 1063.135
Definitions
Rating insurance premiums . . . Ins §11730
Employer right to information and documents regarding . . . Lab §3762
Group self-insurance, advance contribution discount prohibitions for . . . 8 CCR §15476
Household employees, personal liability insurance for . . . Ins §11593
Longshore and Harbor Workers' Compensation Act, invalid agreements under . . . 33 USC §915
Payroll misrepresented to lower
Audit of employer payroll by insurer
Failure of employer to cooperate, liability of employer for triple premiums . . . Ins §11760.1
Insurer's acceptance of false payroll information . . . Ins §757
Penalties and fines . . . Ins §756
Public employment . . . Lab §6131
Rating (See RATING)
Report on premiums and loss history, insurer providing . . . Ins §11663.5

PREMIUMS—Cont.
Triple premiums
Payroll audit, failure of employer to cooperate . . . Ins §11760.1
Unabsorbed premium deposits, payment of . . . Ins §11757

PREPAID CARDS
Payment of benefits
Disability benefits
Methods of payment . . . Lab §4651

PREPONDERANCE OF THE EVIDENCE STANDARD
Burden of proof generally required . . . Ev §115
Conditions of employer liability for compensation . . . Lab §3600
Workers' compensation division of Labor Code . . . Lab §3202.5

PRESCRIPTIONS
Access of injured workers to medical treatment or prescription drugs
Study of access . . . Lab §5307.2
Compounded drug products
Pharmaceutical fee schedule . . . Lab §5307.1
Continuing availability of medicine and medical supplies for injured employees . . . Lab §4600.2
Dangerous drugs or devices
Pharmaceutical fee schedule . . . Lab §5307.1
Generic drug substitutions . . . Lab §4600.1
Medical treatment
Payment for services
Copy of prescription, conditions governing need for submission . . . Lab §4603.2
Medical treatment utilization review, schedules
Drug formulary using evidence-based medicine . . . Lab §5307.27
Quarterly updates . . . Lab §5307.29
Stakeholders, consultation regarding establishment of formulary . . . Lab §5307.28
Pharmaceutical fee schedule
Covered under official medical fee schedule . . . 8 CCR §9789.40, Lab §5307.1
Pharmacy goods
Pharmaceutical fee schedule . . . Lab §5307.1

PRESUMPTIONS
Appeals Board (WCAB) decisions . . . Lab §5302
Award, lawfulness of . . . Lab §5302
Cancer presumption for firefighters and police officers . . . Lab §3212.1
Compensability . . . Lab §5402
Continuing medical treatment, requirement for . . . Lab §4651.1
Contractors with U.Sworking outside U.S., presumption of death or detention of . . . 42 USC §1716
Dependent status . . . Lab §3501
Election of compensation liability by state institutions, presumption of . . . Lab §4155
Employee status
Physicians as independent contractors . . . Lab §2750.6
Services rendered . . . Lab §3357
Workers . . . Lab §2750.5

Index

PRESUMPTIONS—Cont.
Foreign employment by contractors working outside U.S., presumption of death or detention . . . 42 USC §1716
Gas pipelines . . . Lab §6700
Heart problems AOE . . . Lab §3212
Hepatitis AOE . . . Lab §3212.8
Hernia AOE . . . Lab §3212
Insurance
  Policy provision requirements, compliance with . . . Ins §11650
  Rates presumed to create monopoly . . . Ins §11732
Longshore and Harbor Workers' Compensation Act . . . 33 USC §920
Medical treatment
  Scope or extent of medical treatment
    Utilization schedules, presumptive correctness as to . . . Lab §4604.5
Meningitis AOE . . . Lab §§3212.9, 3212.10
Methicillan-resistant Staphylococcus aureus (MRSA)
  Firefighters and law enforcement officers
    Presumption that disease arose out of and in course of employment . . . Lab §3212.8
Monopoly, insurance rates presumed to create . . . Ins §11732
Negligence of employer presumed in failure to secure payment of benefits . . . Lab §3708
Ninety-day presumption . . . Lab §5402
Petition alleging decrease or termination of disability, presumptions following . . . Lab §4651.1
Pneumonia AOE . . . Lab §3212
Privileges, evidentiary . . . Ev §§913, 917
Safety regulations, reasonableness of . . . Lab §6315.5
Total permanent disability, conditions presuming . . . Lab §4662

PREVENTIVE CARE
Group self-insurance
  Injury and illness prevention program . . . 8 CCR §15486.1
Health care workers injured as result of . . . Lab §3208.05
Injury prevention programs (See SAFE WORKPLACE)
Self-insurance programs
  Requirement to provide . . . 8 CCR §15353
  Willful or repeated violations of . . . 8 CCR §15354

PREVIOUS DISABILITY
Average weekly earnings, computing . . . Lab §4459
Permanent disability
  Apportionment of disability
    Disclosure of previous disabilities and impairments . . . Lab §4663
Preexisting condition, aggravation of
  Time limits on claim for . . . Lab §5410
Preexisting conditions (See PREEXISTING CONDITIONS)
Subsequent injuries (See SUBSEQUENT INJURIES)

PRIMARY TREATING PHYSICIAN (See TREATING PHYSICIAN)

PRIORITY ISSUES
Liens (See LIENS)

PRISONERS
Attorney referral for . . . Lab §3371

PRISONERS—Cont.
Contempt, persons imprisoned for . . . Pen §4017.5
County industrial farms, fire suppression work by inmates of . . . Pen §4125.1
County jails, employment of prisoners in
  Generally . . . Pen §4017
  Contempt, persons imprisoned for . . . Pen §4017.5
  Firefighting, employed in . . . Pen §4017
Employment of
  Contempt, persons imprisoned for . . . Pen §4017.5
  County jails, prisoners in (See subhead: County jails, employment of prisoners in)
  Firefighting . . . Pen §4017
  Labor programs, contracts for . . . CA Const Art XIV §5
  Road camps, at . . . Pen §4125.1
Entitlement to workers' compensation benefits . . . Lab §3370
Firefighting, employed in
  Contracting for fire suppression work . . . Pen §4125.1
  County jails, employment of prisoners in . . . Pen §4017
  Juvenile wards of court engaged in fire suppression work, age limits on . . . W&I §883
Forms (See subhead: Report of injury to)
Juvenile Court
  Volunteers
    Regional youth facility, wards committed to . . . Lab §3364.7
    Traffic offenders . . . Lab §3364.6
    Wards . . . Lab §3364.55
  Wards of juvenile court (See MINORS)
Labor programs, contracts for . . . CA Const Art XIV §5
Notice to inmate of rehabilitation services . . . Pen §5069
Occupational disease or injury reports (See REPORTING REQUIREMENTS)
Public Employees' Retirement System appointed state member's death caused by . . . Gov §21540
Report of injury to
  Generally . . . Lab §6413
  Department of Corrections Report of Injury Form 5030
    Color of . . . 8 CCR §14903
    Modification by agreement . . . 8 CCR §14902
    Submission of . . . 8 CCR §14901
    Time of filing . . . 8 CCR §14904
  Effective date of requirements regarding . . . 8 CCR §14920
  Labor, injury resulting from . . . 8 CCR §14900
  Physician or surgeon report, Form 5031
    Color of . . . 8 CCR §14912
    Modification by agreement . . . 8 CCR §14911
    Submission of . . . 8 CCR §14910
    Time of filing . . . 8 CCR §14913
Road camps, employment at . . . Pen §4125.1
Safe workplace issues . . . Lab §§6304.2, 6304.4
Vocational rehabilitation for . . . Pen §5069

PRISON GUARDS (See CORRECTIONS AND REHABILITATION DEPARTMENT)

PRISON SENTENCES
Steam boilers causing death, imprisonment for . . . Lab §7771

PRIVACY
Employer's records of occupational injury or illness
Privacy concern case
Defined . . . 8 CCR §14300.46
Genetic test results, unauthorized disclosures
Generally . . . CC §56.17
Individually identifiable information held by Workers' Compensation Division . . . 8 CCR §9703
Medical information . . . CC §§56.10 to 56.21
Sick days, paid
Privacy of health and domestic relations information . . . Lab §249

PRIVATE ATTORNEYS GENERAL, LABOR CODE . . . Lab §§2698 to 2699.6

PRIVATE RIGHT OF ACTION
Insurance Frauds Prevention Act . . . Ins §1871.7

PRIVATIZATION OF WORKERS' COMPENSATION
Collective bargaining agreements, programs established by . . . 8 CCR §§10200 to 10204, Lab §§3201.5, 3201.7
Construction industry . . . Lab §3201.5
Workers' compensation insurance rates . . . Ins §11741
Jockeys, licensed . . . Lab §3201.81
Petition for permission to negotiate . . . 8 CCR §10202.1
Recognizing
Procedures . . . 8 CCR §10202
Eligibility procedure . . . 8 CCR §10201
Letter of eligibility, effect of . . . 8 CCR §10201
Reporting requirements . . . 8 CCR §§10203, 10204
Aggregate employer annual report . . . 8 CCR §10203.1
Individual employer annual report . . . 8 CCR §10203.2

PRIVILEGE AGAINST SELF-INCRIMINATION
Presumptions and inferences from exercise . . . Ev §913

PRIVILEGED INFORMATION AND COMMUNICATIONS
Attorney-client privilege
Breach of duty
Discovery of attorney work product . . . CCP §2018.080
Definitions
Holder of privilege . . . Ev §953
Waiver of . . . Ev §912
Attorney referral service-client privilege . . . Ev §§965 to 968
Clients
Defined . . . Ev §965
Confidential communication between client and lawyer referral service
Defined . . . Ev §965
Crimes
Use of service to perpetrate fraud or crime . . . Ev §968
Definitions . . . Ev §965
Description of privilege . . . Ev §966
Fraud
Use of service to perpetrate fraud or crime . . . Ev §968

PRIVILEGED INFORMATION AND COMMUNICATIONS—Cont.
Attorney referral service-client privilege —Cont.
Holder of the privilege
Defined . . . Ev §965
Lawyer-referral service
Defined . . . Ev §965
Waiver of attorney referral service-client privilege . . . Ev §912
Who may claim . . . Ev §966
When service must claim privilege . . . Ev §967
Burden of proof, confidentiality of communication . . . Ev §917
Comment on exercise of privilege . . . Ev §913
Contempt, failure to comply with disclosure order . . . Ev §914
Determination of claim . . . Ev §§914 to 920
Disallowance of claim, who may assert error . . . Ev §918
Disclosure
Consent of . . . Ev §912
Forced disclosure . . . Ev §919
Judges' chambers, disclosure in . . . Ev §915
Discovery
Inspection demands
Electronically stored information, responses to inspection demands . . . CCP §2031.285
Domestic partners . . . Ev §980
Domestic violence counselor-victim privilege
Waiver of privilege . . . Ev §912
Emergency and disaster services . . . Gov §8656
Forced disclosure of privileged information . . . Ev §919
Human trafficking victim-caseworker privilege
Waiver . . . Ev §912
Husband and wife (See MARITAL PRIVILEGE)
Inspection demands
Electronically stored information, responses to inspection demands . . . CCP §2031.285
Joint holders . . . Ev §912
Local agents . . . Gov §53023
Marital privilege (See MARITAL PRIVILEGE)
Medical information . . . CC §§56.10 to 56.21
Minor and mental health counselor . . . Ev §1010
Official information acquired in confidence . . . Ev §§915, 1043
Parties claiming privilege . . . Ev §§911 to 916
Physician-patient privilege . . . Ev §996
Waiver of . . . Ev §912
Preliminary determination of privilege . . . Ev §914
Presumptions
Confidentiality of communication . . . Ev §917
Exercise of privilege . . . Ev §913
Prior hearing, exercise of privilege in . . . Ev §913
Psychotherapist-patient privilege . . . Ev §§1010 to 1016
Definitions . . . Ev §§1010 to 1016
Release of information to prevent harm to victims or potential victims . . . CC §56.10
Waiver of . . . Ev §912
Search warrants . . . Ev §915
Sexual assault counselor-victim privilege
Waiver of . . . Ev §912
Spouses . . . Ev §§918, 971 to 973
Sua sponte exclusion of information . . . Ev §916
Trade secrets . . . Ev §915

PRIVILEGED INFORMATION AND COMMUNICATIONS—Cont.
Waiver of privilege . . . Ev §§912, 919
Workers' Compensation Insurance Fraud Reporting Act, information acquired under . . . Ins §1877.3

PRIVILEGE NOT TO TESTIFY
Spouses . . . Ev §§918, 971 to 973

PRIZES BROUGHT INTO U.SAND PROPERTY TAKEN AS PRIZE
Jurisdiction of district courts . . . 28 USC §1333

PROBATION
Qualified medical evaluators (QMEs) . . . 8 CCR §62

PROBE HOLES
Mining and tunneling requirements . . . Lab §7966

PROCESS SAFETY MANAGEMENT (See REFINERIES AND CHEMICAL PLANTS)

PROFESSIONAL CLINICAL COUNSELORS
Treatment of injuries by . . . Lab §3209.8

PROFESSIONAL EMPLOYER ORGANIZATIONS
Self-insurance
Certificate of consent to self-insure
Restrictions on issuance . . . Lab §3701.9
Rulemaking on obligations of self-insurers . . . Lab §3702.10

PROFESSIONAL LIABILITY INSURANCE
Remedial underwriting practices . . . Ins §676.3

PROFESSIONAL SERVICES
Worker classification
Contracts for performance of professional services
Exception to classification preference . . . Lab §2778

PROFESSIONAL SPORTS
Athletes
Occupational disease or cumulative injury
Out-of-state hires, exemption . . . Lab §3600.5
Cheerleaders for professional sports teams
Employment relationship
Classification of cheerleaders for professional sports teams as employees . . . Lab §2754

PROOF
Burden of (See BURDEN OF PROOF)
Evidence (See EVIDENCE)
Independent contractor status
Generally . . . Lab §2750.5

PROPERTY INSURANCE
Actuarial opinion statement
Submission of statement of actuarial opinion by property and casualty insurers . . . Ins §923.6
Cancellation or nonrenewal of policies
Hate crime or anti-reproductive-rights crime generating losses, factoring in decisions . . . Ins §676.10
Notice of cancellation . . . Ins §677.4
Nonrenewal
Notice of nonrenewal for residential property insurance . . . Ins §678

PROSECUTORS
Public employees' retirement system
Death benefits
Special death benefit, when and to whom payable . . . Gov §21540.5

PROSTHETICS
Official medical fee schedule . . . 8 CCR §9789.60

PROTECT APP-BASED DRIVERS AND SERVICES ACT
Generally . . . B&P §§7448 to 7467 (See APP-BASED DRIVERS AND SERVICES)
Short title of provisions . . . B&P §7448

PROTECTIVE FLOORING
Building and construction industry
Flooring, protective (See BUILDING AND CONSTRUCTION INDUSTRY)

PROTECTIVE ORDERS
Discovery
Inspection demands
Electronically stored information . . . CCP §2031.060
Unsuccessfully making or opposing motion for protective order . . . CCP §2017.020

PRO TEMPORE JUDGES (See JUDGES (WCJS))

PRWORA (PERSONAL RESPONSIBILITY AND WORK OPPORTUNITY RECONCILIATION ACT)
Uninsured employers fund and subsequent injuries fund benefits for aliens . . . 8 CCR §15740

PSYCHIATRIC INJURIES
Compensability . . . Lab §3208.3
Description of psychiatric disability . . . 8 CCR §9726
Good faith personnel actions . . . Lab §3208.3
Impairment ratings . . . Lab §4660.1
Marriage and family therapists and social workers, treatment by . . . Lab §3209.8
Method of measuring psychiatric disability . . . 8 CCR §§43, 9726
Presumption of total disability for brain injuries leading to mental incapacity . . . Lab §4662
Psychologists, treatment by
Definition of psychologist . . . Lab §3209.3
Medical collaboration . . . Lab §3209.3
Work capacity guidelines . . . Table 11

PSYCHIATRISTS
Medical information disclosures
Threat to health or safety, release of information to alleviate . . . CC §56.10

PSYCHOLOGISTS
Confidentiality of patient information . . . CC §56.104
Defined . . . Lab §3209.3
Educational materials for treating physicians . . . Lab §4602.8
Medical collaboration . . . Lab §3209.3
Medical information disclosures
Threat to health or safety, release of information to alleviate . . . CC §56.10

PSYCHOLOGISTS—Cont.
Qualified medical evaluators (QMEs), standards for appointment or reappointment as . . . Lab §139.2

PSYCHOTHERAPISTS
Defined . . . Ev §1010
Medical information disclosures
Threat to health or safety, release of information to alleviate . . . CC §56.10

PTP
Right to select personal physician (See PHYSICIANS)

PUBLIC AGENCIES
Election of compensation liability
Presumption of election by state institutions . . . Lab §4155
Voluntary offering of benefits to public employees . . . Lab §6110
Election of compensation liability, presumption of . . . Lab §4155
Emergency and disaster services (See EMERGENCY AND DISASTER SERVICES)
Insurance
Joint powers agreement between agencies . . . Gov §6516
Joint powers agreement . . . Gov §6516
Payment of benefits dependent on agreement with claimant . . . Lab §6147
Self-insurance
Public entity or joint powers authority (See SELF-INSURANCE)
State Compensation Insurance Fund annual agreements . . . Ins §11872
Tort claims against United States
Administrative adjustment of claims . . . 28 USC §2672
Exclusiveness of remedy . . . 28 USC §2679
Prerequisite, denial by public agency as . . . 28 USC §2675
Uniform rate agreement with State Compensation Insurance Fund . . . Lab §6112
Volunteers, employee status . . . Lab §3363.5

PUBLIC DEFENDERS
Public employees' retirement system
Death benefits
Special death benefit, when and to whom payable . . . Gov §21540.5

PUBLIC DISABILITY ACCOMMODATIONS . . . 8 CCR §§9708.1 to 9708.6
Definitions . . . 8 CCR §9708.1
Request for accommodations
Appeal of decision . . . 8 CCR §9708.6
Case-by-case consideration . . . 8 CCR §9708.5
Confidentiality . . . 8 CCR §9708.3
Decision-making . . . 8 CCR §9708.5
Division hearings . . . 8 CCR §9708.4
Process . . . 8 CCR §9708.2

PUBLIC EMPLOYEES' RETIREMENT SYSTEM
Accounts
Reinstatement
Crediting of account . . . Gov §§21200, 21201

PUBLIC EMPLOYEES' RETIREMENT SYSTEM—Cont.
Appeals Board (WCAB)
Disability retirement determinations
Application for writ of review . . . Gov §21168
Continuing jurisdiction . . . Gov §21171
Denial or grant of petition for rehearing . . . Gov §21168
Evidence on writ of review . . . Gov §21169
Grounds for petition for rehearing . . . Gov §21167
Industrial nature of disability, subsequent determination of . . . Gov §21174
Jurisdiction . . . Gov §§21166, 21171
Record of Appeals Board, certification of . . . Gov §21169
Scope of review . . . Gov §21170
Jurisdiction
Disability retirement determinations . . . Gov §§21166, 21171
Special death benefits . . . Gov §§21537, 21540.5
Representation of retirement system before Appeals Board by State Compensation Insurance Fund . . . Gov §20130
Scope of review . . . Gov §21170
Special death benefits jurisdiction . . . Gov §§21537, 21540.5
Writ of review, certification of record on . . . Gov §21169
Attorney General
Representation of retirement system before Appeals Board by . . . Gov §20130
Third party recovery, contract for . . . Gov §20253
Contribution
Reinstatement
Rate of contribution . . . Gov §§21200, 21201
Death benefits
Election to receive regular death benefit in lieu of special death benefit . . . Gov §21542
Industrial death . . . Gov §20046
Joinder of Public Employees' Retirement System as defendant . . . Lab §4708
Limitations on . . . Lab §4707
Monthly allowance in lieu of basic death benefit
Firefighters' survivors . . . Gov §21547.7
State bargaining unit members subject to memoranda of understanding . . . Gov §21547
Preretirement death benefits
Lump sum payments . . . Gov §21543
Special death benefit, amount . . . Gov §21541
Special death benefit, when and to whom payable . . . Gov §§21537, 21537.5, 21540.5
Stopping special benefit payments . . . Gov §21543
State or local safety members, special death benefit for (See subhead: State or local safety members)
Surviving spouse benefits . . . Gov §21551
Allowance for spouses of certain members . . . Gov §21548
Violence, special death benefit for death caused by . . . Gov §21540.5
Disability benefits
Generally . . . Gov §§21150 to 21175

Index

PUBLIC EMPLOYEES' RETIREMENT SYSTEM—Cont.
Disability benefits—Cont.
Comp time availability . . . Gov §21163
Determination of disability . . . Gov §20130
Industrial disability . . . Gov §20046
Mandatory disability retirement . . . Gov §21151
Retirement on disability (See subhead: Disability retirement)
Sick leave availability . . . Gov §21163
Disability retirement
Appeals (See subhead: Appeals Board (WCAB))
Application for . . . Gov §§21153, 21154
Hearings . . . Gov §21166
Incapacity of member to perform duties
Board retiring member for disability . . . Gov §21156
Industrial disability, determination of . . . Gov §§21166, 21174
Local safety members . . . Gov §§21164, 21192, 21413
Medical examination . . . Gov §§21155, 21156, 21192
Minimum age, recipient under . . . Gov §21192
Rehearing petition . . . Gov §21167
Denial . . . Gov §21168
Reimbursement of expenses related to medical examination for . . . Gov §21155
Reinstatement . . . Gov §21191
Application for . . . Gov §21192
Cancellation of retirement allowance . . . Gov §21201
Procedure . . . Gov §21197
Requirements . . . Gov §21195
Retroactive payments for state safety members . . . Gov §21416
Advanced disability payments, deduction from retroactive payments . . . Gov §21419
Scope of review . . . Gov §21170
State safety members . . . Gov §21416
Subsequent determination that disability is industrial . . . Gov §§21166, 21174
Substituting disability retirement for discipline of employee . . . Gov §21156
Writ of review . . . Gov §21169
Employed retirees
Reinstatement
Unlawfully employed retirees . . . Gov §21202
Industrial accident or illness
Definition of industrial . . . Gov §20046
Determination of industrial disability . . . Gov §21166
Special death benefit, determination of industrial nature of death for purposes of . . . Gov §21544
State or local safety member special death benefits . . . Gov §21537
Subsequent determinations . . . Gov §21174
Insurance companies
Request for information from companies in relation to investigations . . . Ins §1877.35
Investigations
Insurance companies
Request for information from companies in relation to investigations . . . Ins §1877.35

PUBLIC EMPLOYEES' RETIREMENT SYSTEM—Cont.
Involuntary termination of employment
Reinstatement . . . Gov §21198
Jurisdiction of Appeals Board (WCAB)
Disability retirement determinations . . . Gov §§21166, 21171
Special death benefits . . . Gov §§21537, 21540.5
Medical examination for disability retirement . . . Gov §§21155, 21192
Partial retirement
Reinstatement from partial retirement . . . Gov §21194
Police and firefighters
Advanced disability pension payments for . . . Lab §4850.3
Entitlement of firefighters to benefits . . . Lab §4850.7
Reinstatement . . . Gov §21190
Board or commission appointment . . . Gov §21203
Cancellation of retirement allowance . . . Gov §21200
Disability retirement . . . Gov §21201
Contribution rate . . . Gov §21200
Disability retirement . . . Gov §21201
Crediting of account . . . Gov §21200
Disability retirement . . . Gov §21201
Disability retirement . . . Gov §21191
Application . . . Gov §21192
Cancellation of retirement allowance . . . Gov §21201
Contribution rate . . . Gov §21201
Crediting of account . . . Gov §21201
Procedure . . . Gov §21197
Requirements . . . Gov §21195
Governor's appointment of person to position . . . Gov §21199
Involuntary termination of employment, reinstatement after . . . Gov §21198
Partial retirement, reinstatement from . . . Gov §21194
Procedure . . . Gov §21196
Specially qualified employees . . . Gov §21203
Unlawfully employed retirees . . . Gov §21202
Representation of retirement system before Appeals Board by State Compensation Insurance Fund . . . Gov §20130
Request to make disability determinations . . . Lab §4851
State Compensation Insurance Fund
Designations for . . . Gov §20251
Representation of retirement system before Appeals Board by . . . Gov §20130
Third party recovery, contract for . . . Gov §20253
State or local safety members
Disability retirement
Local safety members . . . Gov §§21164, 21192
State safety members . . . Gov §21416
Police and firefighters
Advanced disability pension payments for . . . Lab §4850.3
Entitlement of firefighters to benefits . . . Lab §4850.7
Special death benefits
Generally . . . Gov §21537
Accrual of . . . Gov §21542
Appeals Board (WCAB) jurisdiction . . . Gov §§21537, 21540.5

PUBLIC EMPLOYEES' RETIREMENT SYSTEM—Cont.
State or local safety members—Cont.
Special death benefits—Cont.
Appointed members . . . Gov §§21538, 21540
Conduct of prison inmate, death arising from . . . Gov §21540
Election to receive regular death benefit in lieu of . . . Gov §21542
Industrial accident or illness, death due to . . . Gov §21537
Industrial nature of death . . . Gov §21544
Violence, death caused by . . . Gov §21540.5
Subrogation
Application of recovered amounts . . . Gov §20254
Contracts with State Compensation Insurance Fund or Attorney General for third party recovery . . . Gov §20253
Limitations on . . . Gov §20250
Right of . . . Gov §20250
Statutes of limitation . . . Gov §20255
Third parties, recovery from . . . Gov §§20252, 20253
Violence, special death benefit for death caused by . . . Gov §21540.5
Workers' compensation benefits, effect of receipt of . . . Gov §21257

PUBLIC EMPLOYMENT
Generally . . . Lab §6100
Agreement of claimant
Insurer payment dependent on . . . Lab §6148
Negotiation of . . . Lab §6149
Public agency payment dependent on . . . Lab §6147
Appeals Board (WCAB)
Arbitration
Power of Appeals Board as arbitrator . . . Lab §6146
Submission of controversies for . . . Lab §6145
Controversies, right to try and determine . . . Lab §6144
Powers of . . . Lab §6143
Arbitration by Appeals Board (WCAB)
Power of Appeals Board as arbitrator . . . Lab §6146
Submission of controversies . . . Lab §6145
Collective bargaining agreements
Alternative dispute resolution provisions in agreements
Applicability to state of California . . . Lab §3201.7
County employees (See COUNTY EMPLOYEES)
Disability benefits
Public Employees' Retirement System (See PUBLIC EMPLOYEES' RETIREMENT SYSTEM)
State employees (See DISABILITY BENEFITS)
Education (See EDUCATION)
Emergency and disaster services (See EMERGENCY AND DISASTER SERVICES)
Entitlement to benefits . . . Lab §6140
Exceptions applicable to . . . Lab §6142
Federal government employees of nonappropriated fund instrumentalities
Exemptions for . . . 5 USC §2105

PUBLIC EMPLOYMENT—Cont.
Federal government employees of nonappropriated fund instrumentalities—Cont.
Longshore and Harbor Workers' Compensation Act (See LONGSHORE AND HARBOR WORKERS' COMPENSATION ACT)
Firefighters (See FIREFIGHTERS)
First disability payment, timing of . . . Lab §4650.5
Insurance from insurers other than State Compensation Insurance Fund . . . Lab §6130
Law enforcement officers (See POLICE)
Limitations applicable to . . . Lab §6141
Motor vehicles
Transportation by privately owned vehicles . . . 2 CCR §599.631
Nonappropriated fund instrumentalities, federal government employees of
Exemptions for . . . 5 USC §2105
Longshore and Harbor Workers' Compensation Act (See LONGSHORE AND HARBOR WORKERS' COMPENSATION ACT)
Payment of benefits
Insurer, by . . . Lab §6148
Negotiation of agreement regarding . . . Lab §6149
Public agency, by . . . Lab §6147
Premiums, payment of . . . Lab §6131
Procedures applicable to . . . Lab §6141
Retirement systems
Public Employees' Retirement System (See PUBLIC EMPLOYEES' RETIREMENT SYSTEM)
State teachers' retirement system (See STATE TEACHERS' RETIREMENT SYSTEM)
State Compensation Insurance Fund coverage (See STATE COMPENSATION INSURANCE FUND)
Unlawful employment defense . . . Lab §3604
Vocational rehabilitation
Generally . . . Lab §6200
Additional benefit not affecting other compensation, regarded as . . . Lab §6207
California State University personnel, inapplicability of provisions to . . . Ed §89529.06
Cooperation of injured worker with plan . . . Lab §6204
Extent of services . . . Lab §6206
Initiation of plan for . . . Lab §6202
Notice of availability . . . Lab §6201
State approval of plan . . . Lab §6205
Subsistence allowance . . . Lab §6203
Voluntary nature of plan . . . Lab §6208
Voluntary offering of benefits to . . . Lab §6110

PUBLIC HEARINGS
Insurance
Rating organizations . . . Ins §11751.55
Regulations, changes to . . . Lab §5307.4

PUBLIC MEETINGS
California insurance guarantee association (CIGA)
Board of governors . . . Ins §1063.17
Occupational Safety and Health Standards Board (See OCCUPATIONAL SAFETY AND HEALTH STANDARDS BOARD)

PUBLIC OFFICIALS
Appeals Board (WCAB) decision, service of . . . Lab §5317
Assassinated
Death benefits
Public officials, assassinated (See DEATH BENEFITS)
Confidential information
Privilege not to disclose official information . . . Ev §§915, 1043
Psychotherapists, employees functioning as . . . Ev §1010

PUBLIC SAFETY OFFICIALS
Firefighters (See FIREFIGHTERS)
Law enforcement (See POLICE)
Public Employees' Retirement System, state and local safety members of (See PUBLIC EMPLOYEES' RETIREMENT SYSTEM)

PUBLIC SOCIAL SERVICES
Medical assistance
Eligibility for . . . W&I §14011
In-home supportive services for aged, blind and disabled
Direct payments to provider or recipients, workers' compensation, unemployment compensation, etcobligations . . . W&I §§12302.2, 12302.5
Reimbursement of Medi-Cal by Appeals Board (WCAB) . . . W&I §14101.7
Treatment of injuries by social workers . . . Lab §3209.8

PUBLIC UTILITIES COMMISSION (PUC)
Judgments against motor carriers, transmittal of . . . Lab §3716.4
Occupational Safety and Health Division permit exemption . . . Lab §6508
Railroad safety (See RAILROADS)
Stop orders issued to motor carriers, transmittal of . . . Lab §3710.3

PUBLIC VESSELS ACT
Shipping
Public vessels, damages caused by or towage and salvage rendered to . . . 46 USC §§31101 to 31112 (See SHIPPING)

PUBLIC WORKS CONTRACTS
Certificate of insurance requirements . . . Lab §1861
Excavations, bids for local government projects involving . . . Lab §6707
Wage regulations
Recordkeeping . . . Lab §1776
Workers' compensation clause requirements . . . Lab §1860

PUC (See PUBLIC UTILITIES COMMISSION (PUC))

PULMONARY EVALUATIONS
Method of measuring disability . . . 8 CCR §44
Time taken to complete . . . 8 CCR §49.6

PULMONARY FIBROSIS
Temporary disability
Aggregate disability payments
Single injury . . . Lab §4656

Q

QME (See QUALIFIED MEDICAL EVALUATORS (QMES))

QUALIFIED MEDICAL EVALUATORS (QMES)
Accreditation
Defined . . . 8 CCR §1
ACOEM
Defined . . . 8 CCR §1
Acupuncture
QME competency examination for acupuncturists
Defined . . . 8 CCR §1
Referrals . . . 8 CCR §32
Advertising
Fraudulent or misleading advertising
Complaints, filing . . . 8 CCR §155
Definitions pertinent to . . . 8 CCR §150
Determination of violation . . . 8 CCR §157
Documents, filing . . . 8 CCR §151
False or misleading, prohibition of . . . 8 CCR §153
Intent and purpose of . . . 8 CCR §152
Penalties and fines . . . 8 CCR §158
Permissible advertising content . . . 8 CCR §154
Review of copy . . . 8 CCR §156
Severability of articles . . . 8 CCR §159
Agreed panel QME
Defined . . . 8 CCR §1
AMA guides
Defined . . . 8 CCR §1
AME
Defined . . . 8 CCR §1
Ankle disability
Evaluations
Method of evaluation . . . 8 CCR §46.1
Appeals Board (WCAB)
Evaluations
Additional evaluation ordered on appeal . . . 8 CCR §32.6
Examination of injured worker ordered at hearing . . . Lab §5703.5
Rejection of report by . . . 8 CCR §10683
Applications for appointment as . . . 8 CCR §10
Forms . . . 8 CCR §100
Reappointment, application for . . . 8 CCR §50
Forms . . . 8 CCR §104
Specified financial interest attachment . . . 8 CCR §124
Specified financial interest attachment . . . 8 CCR §124
Time period for consideration of . . . 8 CCR §20
Appointment . . . 8 CCR §10, Lab §139.2
Application for appointment (See subhead: Applications for appointment as)
Cancellation of appointment . . . 8 CCR §34
Denial of appointment or reappointment
Disciplinary procedure . . . 8 CCR §63
Initial appointment
Eligibility . . . 8 CCR §11
Notice of appointment . . . 8 CCR §34
Forms . . . 8 CCR §110
Reappointment (See subhead: Reappointment)

QUALIFIED MEDICAL EVALUATORS (QMES)—Cont.
Appointment —Cont.
Retired or teaching physicians . . . 8 CCR §15
Scheduling appointment with panel QME . . . 8 CCR §31.3
Audit
Defined . . . 8 CCR §1
Cancellation of appointment . . . 8 CCR §34
Cardiac disability
Evaluations
Method of evaluation . . . 8 CCR §45
Time guidelines for cardiovascular evaluation . . . 8 CCR §49.4
Certification
Chiropractors . . . 8 CCR §14
Loss of QME status for performing without QME certification . . . 8 CCR §57
QME status . . . 8 CCR §19
Change of office locations . . . 8 CCR §26
Chiropractors
Certification . . . 8 CCR §14
Eligibility . . . 8 CCR §11
Claims administrators
Defined . . . 8 CCR §1
Communications with evaluators . . . Lab §4062.3
Compliance with appropriate evaluation procedures . . . 8 CCR §35.5
Comprehensive medical-legal evaluations
Defined . . . 8 CCR §1
Electronic service
Emergency regulation, COVID-19 . . . 8 CCR §36.7
Reports . . . 8 CCR §36
Psyche, injury to . . . 8 CCR §§36.5, 120
Service, declaration . . . 8 CCR §122
Request for factual correction . . . 8 CCR §37
Defined . . . 8 CCR §1
Consultants
Consulting or attending physicians hired at employee expense
Determinations by QMES as to report of consulting or attending physician . . . Lab §4605
Restrictions on using . . . 8 CCR §32
Continuing education . . . 8 CCR §55
Course evaluation form . . . 8 CCR §117
Faculty disclosure of interest form . . . 8 CCR §119
Program
Defined . . . 8 CCR §1
Providers
Application for accreditation or re-accreditation as education provider, form . . . 8 CCR §118
Course
Defined . . . 8 CCR §1
Evaluation form . . . 8 CCR §117
Credit hours
Defined . . . 8 CCR §1
Definitions . . . 8 CCR §1
Evaluation
Time guidelines . . . 8 CCR §49
Fraudulent or misleading advertising . . . 8 CCR §150
DEU
Defined . . . 8 CCR §1

QUALIFIED MEDICAL EVALUATORS (QMES)—Cont.
Direct medical treatment
Defined . . . 8 CCR §1
Disability evaluation reports
Writing course . . . 8 CCR §11.5
Eligibility for initial appointment . . . 8 CCR §11
Disciplinary proceedings
Denial of appointment or reappointment
Procedure for denial . . . 8 CCR §63
Hearings . . . 8 CCR §61
Probation . . . 8 CCR §62
Reasons for . . . 8 CCR §60
Sanctions . . . 8 CCR §65
Disclosures to injured workers . . . 8 CCR §40
Discontinuance of evaluation
Disclosures to injured workers . . . 8 CCR §40
Distance learning
Defined . . . 8 CCR §1
Education providers
Application for accreditation or re-accreditation as education provider
Form . . . 8 CCR §118
Defined . . . 8 CCR §1
Faculty disclosure of interest form . . . 8 CCR §119
Electronic service
Emergency regulation, COVID-19 . . . 8 CCR §36.7
Eligibility requirements . . . 8 CCR §11
Fees
Determination of . . . 8 CCR §16
Employers
Defined . . . 8 CCR §1
Ethical requirements . . . 8 CCR §41
Evaluations
Additional evaluation ordered on appeal . . . 8 CCR §32.6
Ankle disability
Method of evaluation . . . 8 CCR §46.1
Cardiac disability
Method of evaluation . . . 8 CCR §45
Time guidelines for cardiovascular evaluation . . . 8 CCR §49.4
Conflicts of interest of evaluators . . . 8 CCR §41.5
Gifts to medical evaluators . . . 8 CCR §41.7
Procedures after notice and waiver of conflict . . . 8 CCR §41.6
Disclosures to injured workers . . . 8 CCR §40
Foot disability
Method of evaluation . . . 8 CCR §46.1
Guidelines for evaluation and reporting
Compliance by QME . . . 8 CCR §35.5
Immunologic disability
Method of evaluation . . . 8 CCR §47
Neuromusculoskeletal disability
Method of evaluation . . . 8 CCR §46
Time guidelines . . . 8 CCR §49.2
Procedures for evaluation . . . 8 CCR §§40 to 47
Professional standards for evaluators . . . 8 CCR §41
Psychiatric disability
Method of evaluation . . . 8 CCR §43
Time guidelines for psychiatric evaluation . . . 8 CCR §49.8
Pulmonary disability
Method of evaluation . . . 8 CCR §44

QUALIFIED MEDICAL EVALUATORS (QMES)—Cont.
Evaluations—Cont.
Pulmonary disability—Cont.
Time guidelines for cardiovascular evaluation . . . 8 CCR §49.6
Record review and injured worker electronic interview summary reports
Emergency regulation, COVID-19 . . . 8 CCR §46.2
Rescheduling appointments
Emergency regulation, COVID-19 . . . 8 CCR §46.2
Telehealth
Emergency regulation, COVID-19 . . . 8 CCR §46.2
Time guidelines . . . 8 CCR §§49 to 49.9
Definitions . . . 8 CCR §49
Evaluators defined . . . 8 CCR §1
Ex parte communications with evaluators . . . 8 CCR §35, Lab §4062.3
Extension of time to complete medical evaluation . . . 8 CCR §38
Denial
Notice form . . . 8 CCR §113
Request for extension
Forms . . . 8 CCR §112
Face to face time
Defined . . . 8 CCR §49
Failure to assign panel in timely fashion . . . Lab §139.2
Fees
Determination of . . . 8 CCR §16
Due dates . . . 8 CCR §18
Fee assessment form . . . 8 CCR §103
Specified financial interest attachment . . . 8 CCR §124
Fee assessment notice form . . . 8 CCR §10.2
Schedules . . . 8 CCR §17
Financial interests
Assignments to panels
Specified financial interests affecting . . . 8 CCR §29
Conflicts of interest by evaluators . . . 8 CCR §41.5
Disclosure and objection/waiver form . . . 8 CCR §123
Gifts to medical evaluators . . . 8 CCR §41.7
Procedures after notice and waiver of conflict . . . 8 CCR §41.6
Referral to person with whom physician has . . . Lab §§139.3, 139.31
Findings
Summary form for QME . . . 8 CCR §111
Follow-up comprehensive medical-legal evaluation
Defined . . . 8 CCR §1
Reports . . . 8 CCR §36
Foot disability
Evaluations
Method of evaluation . . . 8 CCR §46.1
Forms
Application for appointment . . . 8 CCR §100
Specified financial interest attachment . . . 8 CCR §124
Appointment notification form . . . 8 CCR §110

QUALIFIED MEDICAL EVALUATORS (QMES)—Cont.
Forms—Cont.
Conflicts of interest of QME/AME
Disclosure and objection/waiver form . . . 8 CCR §123
Course evaluation form . . . 8 CCR §117
Education providers
Application for accreditation or re-accreditation as education provider . . . 8 CCR §118
Extension request form . . . 8 CCR §112
Faculty disclosure of interest form . . . 8 CCR §119
Fee assessments . . . 8 CCR §103
Notice form . . . 8 CCR §10.2
Specified financial interest attachment . . . 8 CCR §124
Findings summary form for QME . . . 8 CCR §111
Late QME report, notice
Extension not requested form . . . 8 CCR §116
Medical-legal reports, service
Declaration . . . 8 CCR §122
Mental health records
Declaration regarding protection of mental health record . . . 8 CCR §121
Panel request
Unrepresented . . . 8 CCR §105
Panel selection form . . . 8 CCR §107
Psyche, injury
Voluntary directive for alternative service of medical-legal report . . . 8 CCR §120
QME competency examinations, application for . . . 8 CCR §102
Reappointment application . . . 8 CCR §104
Specified financial interest attachment . . . 8 CCR §124
Request for panel . . . 8 CCR §106
Selection of panel instruction form . . . 8 CCR §108
Specified financial interests
Attachment to certain forms . . . 8 CCR §124
Time extension denial notice form . . . 8 CCR §113
Unavailability, notice of QME . . . 8 CCR §109
Future medical care
Defined . . . 8 CCR §1
Geographic limits
Failure to assign panel in timely fashion
Right to obtain evaluation from QME within reasonable geographic area . . . Lab §139.2
Gifts to evaluators . . . 8 CCR §41.7
Immunologic disability
Evaluation
Method of evaluating . . . 8 CCR §47
Independent medical examiners (IMEs) (See INDEPENDENT MEDICAL EXAMINERS (IMES))
Information provided to . . . 8 CCR §35
Labor Code definition . . . Lab §28
Late reports
Notice
Extension not requested, form . . . 8 CCR §116
Locations for evaluation
Change of office locations . . . 8 CCR §26
Geographic limits
Choice of QME restricted to reasonable geographic area . . . Lab §139.2

QUALIFIED MEDICAL EVALUATORS (QMES)—Cont.
Locations for evaluation—Cont.
 Number limited . . . Lab §139.2
 Office locations . . . 8 CCR §26
Medical director
 Defined . . . 8 CCR §1
Medical examinations by (See MEDICAL EXAMINATIONS)
Medical reports
 Evidence, treated as . . . 8 CCR §10683
 Rejection of . . . 8 CCR §§54, 10683
Medical treatment utilization schedule (MTUS)
 Defined . . . 8 CCR §1
Mental health
 Comprehensive medical-legal evaluations
  Psyche, injury to . . . 8 CCR §§36.5, 120
 Evaluations
  Psychiatric disability, method of evaluation . . . 8 CCR §43
  Psychiatric disability, time guidelines . . . 8 CCR §49.8
 Records
  Declaration regarding protection of mental health record, form . . . 8 CCR §121
  Defined . . . 8 CCR §1
Neuromusculoskeletal disability
 Evaluations
  Method of evaluation . . . 8 CCR §46
  Time guidelines . . . 8 CCR §49.2
Notice
 Appointment . . . 8 CCR §34
  Form for appointment notification . . . 8 CCR §110
 Fee assessment notice form . . . 8 CCR §10.2
 Unavailability
  Form . . . 8 CCR §109
Objection to report
 Attachment of written objection to request for panel . . . 8 CCR §30
Offices
 Change of location . . . 8 CCR §26
 Locations . . . 8 CCR §26
Order or ruling, loss of reappointment for failure to comply with Board . . . 8 CCR §56
Panel
 Appointment . . . Lab §139.2
  Scheduling appointment with panel QME . . . 8 CCR §31.3
 Financial interests affecting panel assignments . . . 8 CCR §29
 Replacement requests . . . 8 CCR §31.5
 Request . . . 8 CCR §30
  Represented, form . . . 8 CCR §106
  Unrepresented, form . . . 8 CCR §105
 Unavailability for service on . . . 8 CCR §33
 Unrepresented employees
  Medical evaluation . . . Lab §4062.1
  Preference in assigning panels . . . Lab §139.2
Panel QME
 Defined . . . 8 CCR §1
 Replacement requests . . . 8 CCR §31.5
 Scheduling appointment with panel QME . . . 8 CCR §31.3

QUALIFIED MEDICAL EVALUATORS (QMES)—Cont.
Panel selection . . . 8 CCR §31, Lab §139.2
 Disputes
  Represented cases . . . 8 CCR §31.1
 Financial interests affecting panel assignments . . . 8 CCR §29
 Form for panel selection . . . 8 CCR §107
 Instruction form . . . 8 CCR §108
 Requests . . . 8 CCR §30
  Represented, form . . . 8 CCR §106
  Unrepresented, form . . . 8 CCR §105
 Specialists . . . 8 CCR §30.5
  Additional panel in different specialty . . . 8 CCR §31.7
Physicians
 Eligibility . . . 8 CCR §11
 Office
  Definition of physician's office . . . 8 CCR §1
 Retired or teaching . . . 8 CCR §15
 Specialists (See subhead: Specialists)
 Specialty of . . . 8 CCR §13
Probation . . . 8 CCR §62
Procedures for evaluation . . . 8 CCR §§40 to 47
Psychologists
 Eligibility . . . 8 CCR §11
Pulmonary disability
 Evaluations
  Method of evaluation . . . 8 CCR §44
  Time guidelines for cardiovascular evaluation 8 CCR §49.6
QME competency examination . . . 8 CCR §1
 Application for examination
  Forms . . . 8 CCR §102
 Eligibility for initial appointment . . . 8 CCR §11
Qualifications . . . 8 CCR §§10, 11, Lab §139.2
Reappointment . . . Lab §139.2
 Application for . . . 8 CCR §50
  Forms . . . 8 CCR §104
  Specified financial interest attachment . . . 8 CCR §124
 Certification, loss of QME status for performing without QME . . . 8 CCR §57
 Continuing education . . . 8 CCR §55
 Denial of appointment or reappointment
  Disciplinary procedure . . . 8 CCR §63
 Order or ruling, loss of reappointment for failure to comply with Board . . . 8 CCR §56
 Rejection of evaluations by Appeals Board . . . 8 CCR §54
 Time frame, failure to comply with . . . 8 CCR §51
 Unavailability notification . . . 8 CCR §52
Records
 Destruction of . . . 8 CCR §39
 Retention of . . . 8 CCR §39.5
Referrals . . . 8 CCR §9926, Lab §§139.3, 139.31
Rejection of evaluations by Appeals Board . . . 8 CCR §§54, 10683
Replacement requests . . . 8 CCR §31.5
Request for factual correction . . . 8 CCR §37
 Defined . . . 8 CCR §1
Retired physicians . . . 8 CCR §15
Sanctions . . . 8 CCR §65

QUALIFIED MEDICAL EVALUATORS (QMES)—Cont.
Scheduling appointment with panel QME . . . 8 CCR §31.3
Significant financial interest or affiliation held by faculty
  Defined . . . 8 CCR §1
Specialists
  Consulting
    Restrictions . . . 8 CCR §32
  Designation of . . . 8 CCR §30.5
  Panel selection
    Additional panel in different specialty . . . 8 CCR §31.7
  Physician's specialty . . . 8 CCR §13
  Recognition of specialty boards . . . 8 CCR §12
Specified financial interests
  Attachment to certain forms . . . 8 CCR §124
  Defined . . . 8 CCR §§1, 29
Standards governing evaluations by . . . Lab §139.2
Supplemental medical-legal evaluations
  Defined . . . 8 CCR §1
  Reports . . . 8 CCR §36
Suspension of . . . Lab §139.2
Teaching physicians . . . 8 CCR §15
Termination of . . . Lab §139.2
Time
  Amount of time taken to complete evaluation . . . 8 CCR §49.9
  Application for QME status, time period for processing . . . 8 CCR §20
  Extension of time to complete medical evaluation . . . 8 CCR §38
    Denial notice form . . . 8 CCR §113
    Request forms . . . 8 CCR §112
  Failure to complete timely medical evaluation . . . Lab §4062.5
  Guidelines for evaluations . . . 8 CCR §§49 to 49.9
  Medical examinations (See MEDICAL EXAMINATIONS)
  Reappointment time frame, failure to comply with . . . 8 CCR §51
Treating physicians
  Defined . . . 8 CCR §1
Unavailability . . . 8 CCR §33
  Notice
    Form . . . 8 CCR §109
  Reappointment
    Unavailability notification . . . 8 CCR §52
Unrepresented workers examined by
  Generally . . . Lab §4062.1
  Comprehensive evaluations
    Reports . . . 8 CCR §36
  Definition of unrepresented employees . . . 8 CCR §1
  Information provided to QME . . . 8 CCR §35
  Panel requests . . . 8 CCR §30
    Form . . . 8 CCR §105
  Scheduling appointment with panel QME . . . 8 CCR §31.3
  Supplemental reports from QME, request . . . Lab §4061
Workers' Compensation Division Information and Assistance Program, referrals by . . . 8 CCR §9926

QUALITY OF CARE PROGRAMS
Health care organization (HCO) standards and requirements . . . 8 CCR §9773

R

RAILROADS
Common carriers, liability of
  Definition of common carrier . . . 45 USC §57
  Duty or obligation under other law . . . 45 USC §58
  Interstate or foreign commerce . . . 45 USC §51
  Territories and possessions of U.S . . . 45 USC §52
Contributory negligence . . . 45 USC §53
Damages, diminution of . . . 45 USC §53
Definitions
  Common carrier . . . 45 USC §57
Exemption from liability by contract, rule, regulation, or device . . . 45 USC §55
Foreign commerce . . . 45 USC §51
Information regarding accident, suppression of . . . 45 USC §60
Interstate commerce . . . 45 USC §51
Jurisdiction . . . 45 USC §56
Negligence
  Contributory . . . 45 USC §53
  Interstate and foreign commerce carriers, liability of . . . 45 USC §51
  Territories and possessions of U.S., common carriers in . . . 45 USC §52
Penalties and fines
  Suppression of information regarding accident . . . 45 USC §60
Risks, assumption of . . . 45 USC §54
Safety investigations and surveillance
  Regulations deemed statutes . . . 45 USC §54a
Severability of provisions . . . 45 USC §60
Statutes of limitation . . . 45 USC §56
Survivors' rights . . . 45 USC §59
Territories and possessions of U.S . . . 45 USC §52
Violations
  Penalties and fines for (See subhead: Penalties and fines)

RAPE AND OTHER SEX OFFENSES
Sick days, paid
  Privacy of health and domestic relations information . . . Lab §249

RATING
Disapproval of rates . . . Ins §11737
Discriminatory rates on insurance premiums (See subhead: Insurance premiums)
Electronic adjudication management system (EAMS)
  Inspection of documents
    Prohibitions . . . 8 CCR §10208.6
  Retention, return and destruction of records . . . 8 CCR §10208.7
Experience rating (See EXPERIENCE RATING)
Filing rate information with commissioner . . . Ins §11735
Increase of rates
  Approval in light of legislative enactment . . . Ins §11737
Insurance premiums
  Applicability of provisions . . . Ins §11731

RATING—Cont.
Insurance premiums—Cont.
Classification
Factors not allowed to be considered in . . . Ins §11738
Rating organizations assisting with . . . Ins §11734
Collateral or security requirements . . . Ins §11736.5
Compliance with provisions, determining . . . Ins §11733
Definitions applicable to . . . Ins §11730
Disapproval of rate by Commissioner . . . Ins §11737
Discriminatory rates
Determining discrimination . . . Ins §11732.5
Dividend payments and . . . Ins §11739
Factors not allowed in rate classification . . . Ins §11738
Effective dates . . . Ins §11740
Experience rating (See EXPERIENCE RATING)
Filing of rate information and plans . . . Ins §11735
Household employees, personal liability insurance for . . . Ins §11592
Insurance company rating (See INSURANCE)
Limitations on rates . . . Ins §11732
Misrepresentation to obtain reduced rate . . . Ins §11760
Internet posting of convicted violators . . . Ins §1871.9
Monopoly presumption . . . Ins §11732
Reduced rate, misrepresentation to obtain . . . Ins §11760
Internet posting of convicted violators . . . Ins §1871.9
State Compensation Insurance Fund
Employers and employees, same rates for . . . Ins §11844
Establishment of rates . . . Ins §11820
Factors considered in setting rates . . . Ins §11821
Percentage basis of rates . . . Ins §11822
Reduced rate, willful misrepresentation to obtain . . . Ins §§1871.9, 11880
Supplementary rate information . . . Ins §11740
Workers' compensation insurance online rate comparison guide . . . Ins §11742
Permanent disability (See PERMANENT DISABILITY)
Privatized workers' compensation coverage . . . Ins §11741
Rates and rating organizations
Regulation of rates . . . Ins §11732
Taxicab industry underreporting of exposure
Report on . . . Ins §11759.2
Regulation of rates
Criteria . . . Ins §11733
Temporary disability rate, calculating . . . Table 19
Uniform loss experience rating plan . . . Ins §11734
Workers' compensation insurance online rate comparison guide . . . Ins §11742

RATING ORGANIZATIONS
Generally . . . Ins §11750
Appeals
Decision, action, or omission of rating organization . . . Ins §11753.1

RATING ORGANIZATIONS—Cont.
Appeals—Cont.
Noncompliance ruling against rating organization by Commissioner . . . Ins §11754.5
Authority of . . . Ins §11753.3
Changes to rating organization rubrics, notice of . . . Ins §11753
Classification
Assistance with . . . Ins §11734
Change in assignment
Effective date of . . . Ins §11753.2
Notice to employer of . . . Ins §§11752.9, 11753.1
Compliance orders
Noncompliance, order of compliance upon . . . Ins §11754.2
Penalties and fines for failing to comply with final order . . . Ins §11756
Cost of examination, payment for . . . Ins §11752.2
Definitions pertinent to . . . Ins §11750.1
Denial of license . . . Ins §11754.4
Dividends, payment of . . . Ins §11757
Employees (See subhead: Personnel)
Employer
Classification assignment, notice of change in . . . Ins §11752.6
Insurance for workers' compensation, information as to
Internet sites to assist persons in determining whether employer is insured . . . 10 CCR §§2593 to 2593.7, Ins §11752.75
Release of policy information to . . . Ins §11752.6
Examination of
Generally . . . Ins §11752
Cost of . . . Ins §11752.2
Personnel and records . . . Ins §11752.1
Refusal to allow . . . Ins §11756
Substitutes for . . . Ins §11752
Exemptions
Household employees . . . Ins §11758.1
Liability . . . Ins §11759
Licensing requirements . . . Ins §11753.3
Experience rating (See EXPERIENCE RATING)
False or misleading information provided by . . . Ins §11755
Fees
License, filing for . . . Ins §§11751, 11751.25
Public hearings . . . Ins §11751.55
Filing requirements
Advisory organizations . . . Ins §11753
Applications . . . Ins §11751
Governmental agency access to policy information . . . Ins §11752.5
Hearings . . . Ins §11750
Household employees, exemptions for . . . Ins §11758.1
Insurer as member . . . Ins §11751.4
Internet
Insurance of employer for workers' compensation, information as to
Internet site to assist persons investigating whether employer covered . . . Lab §3600
Investigations (See INVESTIGATIONS)
Liability, exemption from . . . Ins §11759

Index

RATING ORGANIZATIONS—Cont.
Licensing
Denial of application for . . . Ins §11751.2
Duration of license . . . Ins §11751.2
Fees . . . Ins §§11751.1, 11751.25
Filing for . . . Ins §11751
Investigations . . . Ins §11751.2
Requirements . . . Ins §11751.1
Loss corrections or revisions reported by insurer . . . Ins §11751.8
Losses and expenses, annual report of . . . Ins §11759.1
Managing committee, public members of . . . Ins §11751.35
Noncompliance
Final order, penalties and fines for noncompliance with . . . Ins §11756
Notice regarding . . . Ins §11754
Order of compliance upon . . . Ins §11754.2
Suspension or revocation of license as result of (See subhead: Suspension or revocation of license)
Willful or uncorrected . . . Ins §11754.1
Notice
Changes to rating organization rubrics . . . Ins §11753
Classification assignment, notice to employer of change in . . . Ins §§11752.9, 11753.1
Policyholder notice of rating laws . . . Ins §11752.8
Penalties and fines
Final order, noncompliance with . . . Ins §11756
Suspension or revocation of license (See subhead: Suspension or revocation of license)
Personnel
Examination of . . . Ins §11752.1
Liability, exemption from . . . Ins §11759
Policyholder, notice of rating laws to . . . Ins §11752.8
Policy information, availability of
Employers . . . Ins §11752.6
Governmental agencies . . . Ins §11752.5
Public hearings . . . Ins §11751.55
Public members . . . Ins §11751.35
Public members of managing committee . . . Ins §11751.3
Purpose of . . . Ins §§11750, 11750.3
Queries on website to organization on coverage information for employers . . . 10 CCR §§2593 to 2593.7
Accuracy of information
Dispute resolution . . . 10 CCR §2593.6
Correcting information . . . 10 CCR §2593.5
Definitions . . . 10 CCR §2593.1
Disclaimers . . . 10 CCR §2593.4
Dispute resolution . . . 10 CCR §2593.6
Identification of employer . . . 10 CCR §2593.2
Purpose of provisions . . . 10 CCR §2593
Restrictions on website . . . 10 CCR §2593.3
Statistics and metrics maintained by organization . . . 10 CCR §2593.7
Statutory authority . . . 10 CCR §2593, Ins §11752.75
Updating information . . . 10 CCR §2593.5
Records
Employer access to . . . Ins §11752.6
Examination of . . . Ins §11752.1
Experience rating information, availability of . . . Ins §11752.7
Governmental agency access to . . . Ins §11752.5
Reporting requirements
Losses and expenses . . . Ins §11759.1

RATING ORGANIZATIONS—Cont.
Reporting requirements—Cont.
Statistical reporting . . . Ins §11751.5
Revocation of license (See subhead: Suspension or revocation of license)
Rules and requirements . . . Ins §11751.3
Savings, payment of . . . Ins §11757
Scope of Article on . . . Ins §11750.2
Statistics
Agent of organization, information provided by . . . Ins §11751.7
Assistance provided by organization regarding . . . Ins §11734
Reporting to Commissioner . . . Ins §11751.5
Suspension or revocation of license
Grounds for . . . Ins §11754.2
Procedures . . . Ins §11754.4
Time limits, noncompliance within . . . Ins §11754.3
Unabsorbed premium deposits, payment of . . . Ins §11757
Unfair practices . . . Ins §11753
Violations of state laws . . . Ins §11758
Workers' compensation insurance fraud reporting act
Licensed rating organization
Defined . . . Ins §1877.1
Release of information to governmental agency . . . Ins §1877.3
Wrap-up policies
Reporting workers' compensation losses and payroll information to rating organization . . . Ins §11751.82

REAL ESTATE INDUSTRY
Employer's records of occupational injury or illness
Partial exemption from requirements . . . 8 CCR §14300.2

REASONABLE ACCOMMODATION
Failure to make . . . Gov §12940

REBATES
Financial interests in entities providing services
Conflicts of interest . . . Lab §139.32

RECEIVABLES
Collateral or security for recognition of . . . Ins §11736.5

RECONSIDERATION
Appeals Board (WCAB) decisions, findings, orders, and awards
Generally . . . Lab §§115, 5803.5
Accrual of cause of action . . . Lab §5901
Administrative director
Petition appealing orders of administrative director or director of industrial relations . . . 8 CCR §10560
Arbitration decisions, from (See ARBITRATION)
Contents of petition . . . 8 CCR §10945
Decision, order, award, or finding following appeal for reconsideration
Acting on . . . Lab §5315
Effect of . . . Lab §5908
Hearing, decision without . . . Lab §5907
Modifying . . . Lab §5315
Procedures for making . . . Lab §5908.5

RECONSIDERATION—Cont.
Appeals Board (WCAB) decisions, findings, orders, and awards—Cont.
Decision, order, award, or finding following appeal for reconsideration—Cont.
Setting aside . . . Lab §5315
Time limits for acting on judge's (WCJ's) decision . . . Lab §5315
Denial of petition for . . . Lab §5909
Errors, correcting . . . 8 CCR §10966
Filing and service of petition . . . 8 CCR §10940
Contents . . . 8 CCR §10945
Filing petition for . . . Lab §5910
Service and proof of service . . . 8 CCR §10940
Size, format, etc of petitions, etc . . . 8 CCR §10940
Skeletal petitions unsupported by reference to record or law, denial or dismissal . . . 8 CCR §10972
Supplemental petitions or responses . . . 8 CCR §10964
Fraud
Petitions alleging fraud . . . 8 CCR §10974
Reconsideration based on . . . Lab §5903
Grounds for . . . Lab §5903
Hearing
Grant of petition for reconsideration, hearing following . . . 8 CCR §10984
Notice of . . . Lab §5906
Order, decision, or award made without . . . Lab §5907
Judges (WCJs)
Authority following decision after reconsideration . . . 8 CCR §10986
Report of judge . . . 8 CCR §10962
Time limit for Appeals Board to act on decision of . . . Lab §5315
New evidence, petitions alleging . . . 8 CCR §10974
Order, decision, or award following . . . 8 CCR §10961, Lab §§5315, 5907, 5908
Petition for . . . Lab §5900
Prevention of, construction of Article not leading to . . . Lab §5911
Proof of service of petition . . . 8 CCR §10940
Removal process, petition for . . . 8 CCR §10955
Requirements for petitions . . . Lab §5902
Service of petition for . . . Lab §5905
Service of petition, proof of
Reconsideration, removal or disqualification petitions . . . 8 CCR §10940
Skeletal petitions with insufficient grounds for . . . 8 CCR §10972
Supplemental petitions . . . 8 CCR §10964
Time limits for Appeals Board to act on decision . . . Lab §5315
Waiver of irregularities by petition . . . Lab §5904
Arbitration
Reconsideration from arbitration decision
Procedures . . . 8 CCR §§10990, 10995
Fraud
Petitions alleging fraud before WCAB . . . 8 CCR §10974
Reconsideration based on . . . Lab §5903

RECONSIDERATION—Cont.
Fraud—Cont.
Referral to District Attorney or fraud division . . . Lab §5908
Judges (WCJs)
Authority following decision after reconsideration . . . 8 CCR §10986
Report on petition for reconsideration . . . 8 CCR §10962
Time limits for acting on judge's (WCJ's) decision . . . Lab §5315
Occupational Safety and Health Appeals Board
Accrual of cause of action . . . Lab §6615
Alteration of decision, effect of . . . Lab §6622
Decision based on record without further hearing . . . Lab §6621
Denial of . . . Lab §6624
Grounds for . . . Lab §6617
Hearing on reconsideration
Decision based on record without further hearing . . . Lab §6621
Notice of . . . Lab §6620
Information required in petition . . . Lab §6616
Notice of hearing . . . Lab §6620
Petition for . . . Lab §6614
Power of Appeals Board to reconsider . . . Lab §6620
Procedures for making altered decision on . . . Lab §6623
Service of petition . . . Lab §6619
Suspension of decision by filing for . . . Lab §6625
Time limits . . . Lab §§6614, 6626
Waiver of objections not set forth in petition . . . Lab §6618
Self-insurance, reconsideration of decision of hearing officer regarding
Appeals prior to . . . 8 CCR §15432
Procedures for obtaining . . . 8 CCR §15436
Summary rating determinations for unrepresented injured workers . . . 8 CCR §10164
Uninsured Employers Fund determinations
Parent or substantial shareholders . . . 8 CCR §15723
Prima facie illegally uninsured employers . . . 8 CCR §15722

RECORDS AND RECORDKEEPING
Advertising (See ADVERTISING)
Appeals Board (WCAB) (See APPEALS BOARD (WCAB))
Arbitration
Record of arbitration proceeding . . . 8 CCR §10914
Business records as evidence (See EVIDENCE)
Chiropractors
Patient records
Responsibility as to patient records . . . 16 CCR §318
Claims adjusters
Training standards
Recordkeeping by insurers . . . 10 CCR §2592.06
Copy and document reproduction
Financial interests in entities providing services . . . Lab §139.32
Disability benefits
State employees . . . UI §2783

RECORDS AND RECORDKEEPING—Cont.
Electronic adjudication management system (EAMS)
District office records
Subpoenas and informal requests not effective to obtain records . . . 8 CCR §10205.1
Official participant records . . . 8 CCR §10205.5
Retention, return and destruction of records . . . 8 CCR §10208.7
Employers
Audit by insurer
Access to records to be afforded by employer . . . Ins §11760.1
Employer's records of occupational injury or illness generally . . . 8 CCR §§14300 to 14300.48 (See EMPLOYER'S RECORDS OF OCCUPATIONAL INJURY OR ILLNESS)
Evidence
Microphotographed files, records, photographs, etc., in custody of criminal justice agency
Reproductions, admissibility . . . Ev §1550.1
Health care organizations (HCOs)
Books and records (See HEALTH CARE ORGANIATIONS (HCOS))
Insurance Frauds Prevention Act, access to records under . . . Ins §1871.1
Judicial notice of court records . . . Ev §452
Labor Standards Enforcement Division hearings . . . 8 CCR §15586
Longshore and Harbor Workers' Compensation Act . . . 33 USC §929
Medical examination records, subpoena of . . . Lab §4055.2
Medical treatment, proper documentation of bills for . . . 8 CCR §9792.5
Mining and tunneling
Air flow and air samples in . . . Lab §7982
Occupational injuries and illnesses
Generally . . . Lab §6410
Employer records . . . 8 CCR §§14300 to 14300.48 (See EMPLOYER'S RECORDS OF OCCUPATIONAL INJURY OR ILLNESS)
Occupational Safety and Health Division (See OCCUPATIONAL SAFETY AND HEALTH DIVISION)
Official information acquired in confidence . . . Ev §§915, 1043
Payroll audits by insurer
Access to records to be afforded by employer . . . Ins §11760.1
Penalty assessment order appeals hearings . . . 8 CCR §15586
Penalty liens . . . 8 CCR §15594
Premium information and documents, employer right to . . . Lab §3762
Public Employees' Retirement System disability retirement determinations . . . Gov §21169
Public works
Wage regulations . . . Lab §1776
Qualified medical evaluators (QMEs)
Destruction of records . . . 8 CCR §39
Retention of records . . . 8 CCR §39.5
Rating organization records (See RATING ORGANIZATIONS)
Self-insurance (See SELF-INSURANCE)

RECORDS AND RECORDKEEPING—Cont.
Sick days, paid
Recordkeeping by employers . . . Lab §247.5
Stop order appeals hearings . . . 8 CCR §15586
Subpoenas
Electronic records . . . 8 CCR §10644
Workers' Compensation Division
Fees for copies of records and transcripts . . . 8 CCR §9990
Recordkeeping requirements . . . Lab §126

RECREATIONAL ACTIVITY
Conditions of employer liability for compensation . . . Lab §3600

RECREATION AND PARK DISTRICTS
Volunteers, employee status . . . Lab §3361.5

REDUCTIONS IN WORKERS' COMPENSATION
Attorneys' fees . . . Lab §5410.1
Misconduct of injured worker, due to . . . Lab §4552
Subsequent injuries . . . Lab §4753
Time limits on proceedings for reduction due to employee misconduct . . . Lab §5407.5

REEMPLOYMENT AND REINSTATEMENT
Public Employees' Retirement System disability retirement, application for reinstatement following . . . Gov §21192

REFEREES (See JUDGES (WCJS))

REFERRALS AND REFERRAL SERVICES
Apportionment of permanent disability . . . 8 CCR §§10162, 10163
Chiropractors . . . 16 CCR §317.1
Compensation for referral of clients or patients
Criminal nature of . . . Lab §3215
Exceptions to prohibition on . . . Lab §3217
Penalties and fines . . . Lab §3218
Financial interests in entities providing services
Conflicts of interest . . . Lab §139.32
Independent medical examiners (IMES) . . . Lab §§139.3, 139.31
Insurance fraud, referral or solicitation for purposes of . . . Pen §549
Medical treatment by employer
Medically appropriate referrals, right to . . . Lab §4600
Panelists
Information required from . . . 8 CCR §9829
Information supplied to . . . 8 CCR §9830
Premium payments . . . Lab §3302
Qualified medical evaluators (QMES) . . . 8 CCR §9926, Lab §139.3
Vocational rehabilitation
Education or training programs, referrals to . . . Lab §139.5
Work evaluation facilities, referral to . . . Lab §139.5

REFINERIES AND CHEMICAL PLANTS
Changes, procedures for management of . . . Lab §7866
Contractors, employees of . . . Lab §7862
Emergency action plans . . . Lab §7868
Fees . . . Lab §7870

REFINERIES AND CHEMICAL PLANTS—Cont.
Hazard analysis . . . Lab §7859
Hot work, permits for . . . Lab §7865
Information about safety issues . . . Lab §§7858, 7859
Inspections . . . Lab §7864
Investigation of incidents . . . Lab §7867
Operating procedures, written . . . Lab §7860
Permits for hot work . . . Lab §7865
Prescribed items, standards to include . . . Lab §7857
Prestartup safety review for new and modified facilities . . . Lab §7863
Process safety management
Defined . . . Lab §7853
Federal standards, adoption of . . . Lab §7856
Purpose of . . . Lab §7855
Purpose of regulation of . . . Lab §§7851, 7852
Refinery and Chemical Plant Worker Safety Act of 1990 . . . Lab §§7850 to 7873
Testing procedures . . . Lab §7864
Title of Act regulating . . . Lab §7850
Training requirements . . . Lab §7861
Turnarounds, occupational safety and health
Definition of turnaround . . . Lab §7872
Scheduling . . . Lab §7872
Trade secret, turnaround information as . . . Lab §7873
When required . . . Lab §7872

REFUNDS
Voluntary disability benefit plans . . . UI §3266

REGISTRATION
Advertising, registration statements . . . 8 CCR §9831
Asbestos-related work
Permit requirements for asbestos-related work (See ASBESTOS)
Occupational Safety and Health Division registration, no exemption from . . . Lab §6508.5

REHABILITATION
Criminal
Juvenile Court volunteers
Regional youth facility, wards committed to . . . Lab §3364.7
Traffic offenders . . . Lab §3364.6
Wards . . . Lab §3364.55
Licenses available under Labor Code for rehabilitated criminals . . . Lab §26
Employment discrimination or harassment
Action for harassment or discrimination by employees of nonprofit sheltered workshops, day programs or rehabilitation facilities . . . Gov §12926.05
Medical treatment
Utilization schedule
Postsurgical rehabilitation guidelines . . . 8 CCR §9792.24.3
Vocational (See VOCATIONAL REHABILITATION)

REHABILITATION MAINTENANCE ALLOWANCE . . . Lab §139.5

REIMBURSEMENTS
Claims procedures . . . Lab §4903.1
Disability benefits (See DISABILITY BENEFITS)

REIMBURSEMENTS—Cont.
Economic Opportunity Program enrollees, medical treatment and reimbursement provided by federal government to . . . Lab §§4227, 4228
Foreign employment by contractors with U.Sworking outside U.S . . . 42 USC §1704
Health care organizations (HCOs) . . . 8 CCR §9779.5
Longshore and Harbor Workers' Compensation Act . . . 33 USC §907
Medical-legal expenses . . . 8 CCR §9794, Lab §4621
Medi-Cal reimbursements by Appeals Board (WCAB) . . . W&I §14101.7
Public Employees' Retirement System, disability retirement under . . . Gov §21155
State Compensation Insurance Fund reimbursement for public employment expenditures . . . Lab §6114
Subrogation
Employer's claim for reimbursement on release or settlement . . . Lab §3860
Third parties . . . Lab §3864
Subsequent injuries . . . Lab §4754
Uninsured motorist provisions, reimbursement under . . . Ins §11580.2

REINSTATEMENT AND REEMPLOYMENT
Public Employees' Retirement System disability retirement, application for reinstatement following . . . Gov §21192

REINSURANCE
Deposits by workers' compensation insurers . . . Ins §§11690 to 11703

RELEASE FROM LIABILITY
Medical records, release of . . . CC §§56.10 to 56.21

RELEASES
Compromise and (See SETTLEMENT, COMPROMISE AND RELEASE)
Subrogation
Releases or settlements (See SUBROGATION)
Subsequent injuries . . . Lab §4754
Waiver and release (See WAIVERS)

RELIEF (See REMEDIES AND RELIEF)

RELIGIOUS BELIEF
Death of employee
Third party causing injury or death
Personal relationship not inferred due to certain beliefs of third party . . . Lab §3600
Discrimination . . . Gov §12926
Accommodation . . . Gov §12940

RELIGIOUS CORPORATIONS, NONPROFIT
Commercial or property insurance
Cancellation or nonrenewal of policies
Hate crime or anti-reproductive crime generating losses, factor in decision . . . Ins §676.10
Employment discrimination
Limitation on exceptions . . . Gov §12926.2

REMEDIES AND RELIEF
Advertising violations . . . 8 CCR §9836

REMEDIES AND RELIEF—Cont.
Cumulative remedies for advertising violations . . . 8 CCR §9836
Elevators, dangerous operation of . . . Lab §7303
Exclusive remedy (See EXCLUSIVE REMEDY)
Failure to secure payment of workers' compensation . . . Lab §3715
Injunctive relief (See INJUNCTIONS)
Temporary restraining orders (See TEMPORARY RESTRAINING ORDERS)

REMOVAL
Appeals board
Authority to remove itself . . . Lab §5310
Board's authority to remove itself . . . Lab §5310
Judge's removal by Board . . . Lab §5310
Petition for removal . . . 8 CCR §10940
Contents . . . 8 CCR §10945
Grounds . . . 8 CCR §10955
Service and proof of service . . . 8 CCR §10940
Size, format, etc of petitions, etc . . . 8 CCR §10940
Skeletal petitions unsupported by reference to record or law, denial or dismissal . . . 8 CCR §10972
Supplemental petitions or responses . . . 8 CCR §10964
Report of WCJ on removal . . . 8 CCR §10962
Federal court, removal of tort claims to . . . 28 USC §2679
Judge's removal by Board . . . Lab §5310
Report of WCJ on removal . . . 8 CCR §10962

REOPENING OF CASE . . . Lab §§5803 to 5805
Petitions to reopen . . . 8 CCR §10534

REPORTERS
Workers' Compensation Division
Reporter employed by administrative director . . . Lab §123.3

REPORTING REQUIREMENTS
Appeals Board (WCAB) (See APPEALS BOARD (WCAB))
Collective bargaining agreements . . . 8 CCR §§10203, 10204
Aggregate employer annual report . . . 8 CCR §10203.1
Contents of reports . . . Lab §3201.9
Individual employer annual report . . . 8 CCR §10203.2
Correctional inmates, injury to . . . Lab §6413
COVID-19 exposures
Employer notice requirements . . . Lab §6409.6
Death of employee, occupational disease or injury resulting in . . . Lab §§6409.1, 6409.2
Deferred compensation plans, employer-managed . . . Lab §2809
Department of Industrial Relations clinical and research findings . . . Lab §50.8
Disability benefits
State employees . . . UI §2783
Elevator safety
Inspection fee funds . . . Lab §7316
Inspection reports . . . Lab §7313

REPORTING REQUIREMENTS—Cont.
Garment manufacturing hazards . . . Lab §6409.5
Group self-insurance . . . 8 CCR §15474
Health care organizations (HCOs) (See HEALTH CARE ORGANIATIONS (HCOS))
Independent medical review
Contents of reports . . . 8 CCR §9768.12
Retention of records . . . 8 CCR §9768.14
Insurance (See INSURANCE)
Insurers
Injury and illness prevention programs
Review and report on IIPP's of insureds . . . Lab §6401.7
Inventory for adjusting locations, annual report of . . . 8 CCR §10104
Longshore and Harbor Workers' Compensation Act (See LONGSHORE AND HARBOR WORKERS' COMPENSATION ACT)
Medical examinations . . . Lab §4055
Medical reports (See MEDICAL REPORTS)
Occupational disease or injury
Generally . . . Lab §6409.1
Admissibility as evidence . . . Lab §6412
Annual report to legislature . . . Lab §6330
Bureau of investigations . . . Lab §6315.3
Confidentiality . . . Lab §6412
Correctional inmates . . . Lab §6413
COVID-19 exposures
Employer notice requirements . . . Lab §6409.6
Death of employee, resulting in . . . Lab §§6409.1, 6409.2
Definitions pertinent to . . . 8 CCR §14000
Employer responsibilities (See EMPLOYER'S REPORT OF OCCUPATIONAL INJURY OR ILLNESS)
Firefighters called to accident scene . . . Lab §6409.2
Form 5020, Employer's Report of Occupational Injury or Illness . . . 8 CCR §14004
Forms, completion of . . . Lab §§6409.1, 6411
Garment manufacturing hazards . . . Lab §6409.5
Improve tracking of workplace injuries and illnesses, federal administrative rules
Electronic submission of data, rulemaking and implementation to be monitored . . . Lab §6410.2
Insurer responsibilities . . . 8 CCR §14002
Investigations . . . Lab §§6313.5, 6315.3
Law enforcement officers called to accident scene . . . Lab §6409.2
Penalties and fines for violations . . . Lab §6413.5
Physician responsibilities . . . 8 CCR §14003
Generally . . . 8 CCR §14002
Form 14006, Doctor's First Report . . . 8 CCR §14006
Prison inmates, report of injury (See PRISONERS)
Reproduction of Doctor's First Report . . . 8 CCR §14007
Treating physician's reporting duties . . . 8 CCR §9785
Prison inmates
Report of injury to (See PRISONERS)
Reproduction
Doctor's First Report . . . 8 CCR §14007

REPORTING REQUIREMENTS—Cont.
Occupational disease or injury—Cont.
Reproduction—Cont.
Employer's Report . . . 8 CCR §14005
Requirements for reports and records . . . Lab §6410
Statement accompanying report . . . Lab §6410.5
Strong reporting standards
Legislative intent . . . Lab §6410.1
Treating physicians . . . Lab §6409
Occupational Safety and Health Division
Annual report to legislature . . . Lab §6330
Bureau of Investigations . . . Lab §6315.3
Physicians' reports
Appeals Board (WCAB) evidence, as (See APPEALS BOARD (WCAB))
Occupational disease or injury (See subhead: Occupational disease or injury)
Prisoners
Report of injury to prisoner (See PRISONERS)
Prison inmates
Report of injury to prisoner (See PRISONERS)
Rating organizations
Losses and expenses . . . Ins §11759.1
Statistical reporting . . . Ins §11751.5
Self-insurance (See SELF-INSURANCE)
Self-Insurers' Security Fund . . . Lab §3746
State Compensation Insurance Fund (See STATE COMPENSATION INSURANCE FUND)
Vocational rehabilitation (See VOCATIONAL REHABILITATION)
Workers' Compensation Division, electronic claim information requirements for . . . 8 CCR §§9702, 9778
Workers' compensation information system . . . Lab §138.6
Confidentiality of individually identifiable information . . . Lab §138.7

REPRESENTATION
Attorneys, by (See ATTORNEYS)
Lien claimants obtaining representation
Notice of representation, change of representation or nonrepresentation . . . 8 CCR §10868
Unrepresented workers (See UNREPRESENTED WORKERS)

REPRODUCTION OF FORMS
Death of employee, notice of (DIA Form 510) . . . 8 CCR §9914
Employer's Report of Occupational Injury or Illness (Form 5020) . . . 8 CCR §14005
Occupational disease or injury reports
Doctor's First Report . . . 8 CCR §14007
Employer's Report . . . 8 CCR §14005
Permanent disability summary rating determinations . . . 8 CCR §10161.1
Pharmacy benefits, claim form utilized for . . . Lab §4608

REQUEST FOR ADMISSION
Methods of discovery . . . CCP §2019.010

REQUEST FOR CONSULTATIVE RATING (RCR) FORM . . . 8 CCR §10166.1

REQUEST FOR DISPUTE RESOLUTION BEFORE ADMINISTRATIVE DIRECTOR FORM . . . 8 CCR §10133.55

REQUEST FOR RECONSIDERATION OF SUMMARY RATING . . . 8 CCR §10164

REQUEST FOR SUMMARY DETERMINATION OF PRIMARY TREATING PHYSICIAN'S REPORT . . . 8 CCR §10161

REQUEST FOR SUMMARY DETERMINATION OF QUALIFIED MEDICAL EVALUATOR'S REPORT . . . 8 CCR §10161

RESCUE PLANS
Mining and tunneling (See MINING AND TUNNELING)

RESEARCH
Individually identifiable information held by Workers' Compensation Division
Protection of individually identifiable information . . . 8 CCR §9703
Industrial relations department
Occupational disease research programs
Duties of department as to programs . . . Lab §50.8
Grant applications, review . . . Lab §78
Reporting requirements . . . Lab §50.8
Labor Statistics and Research Division (See LABOR STATISTICS AND RESEARCH DIVISION)
Medical information disclosed for purposes of . . . CC §56.10
Safe workplace programs
Education and research programs (See OCCUPATIONAL SAFETY AND HEALTH DIVISION)

RESERVE
Disaster service workers' reserve fund . . . Lab §4352
Insurance (See INSURANCE)
Military reserve, benefit rights of . . . Mil&Vet §520
Police officers (See POLICE)

RESIDENCY REQUIREMENTS
Nonappropriated fund instrumentalities, non-citizen nonresident employees of . . . 5 USC §8172
Out-of-state issues (See OUT-OF-STATE ISSUES)

RESOURCE-BASED RELATIVE VALUE SCALE
Official medical fee schedule
Resource-based relative value scale for physician and nonphysician practitioner services
Adoption and review of schedule based on model . . . Lab §5307.1

REST BREAKS
App-based drivers and services
Rest requirements . . . B&P §7461
Wages, hours, and working conditions
Piece-rate basis of compensation . . . Lab §226.2

RESTITUTION
Crime by employer against employee
Payments by workers' compensation carrier to employee
Restitution for crime not offset by payments received . . . Lab §3602
Insurance
Crimes against insured property and insurers
False or fraudulent claims, making . . . Pen §550

RESTITUTION—Cont.
Insurance—Cont.
Referral or solicitation for purposes of insurance fraud . . . Pen §549
Self-insurance
Director's order for compliance, restitution, and civil penalty . . . Lab §3702.9

RESUMPTION OF BENEFIT PAYMENTS
Notice of . . . 8 CCR §9812

RETAIL INDUSTRY
Employer's records of occupational injury or illness
Partial exemption from requirements . . . 8 CCR §14300.2

RETALIATORY DISCRIMINATION
COVID-19 exposures
Disclosures of positive test or quarantine, etc, order
Prohibition of employer retaliation . . . Lab §6409.6
Employer's records of occupational injury or illness
Reporters of injury or illness, protection from discrimination . . . 8 CCR §14300.36
Occupational Safety and Health Division
Filing complaint with division, instituting proceedings, committee participation, etc
Prohibition of retaliation, discrimination, etc . . . Lab §6310
Unlawful employment practices . . . Gov §12940
Workers' Compensation Division, prohibition by . . . Lab §132a

RETIREMENT AND PENSION PLANS
County employees
Board of retirement members, benefits for . . . Gov §31520.4
Subrogation . . . Gov §31820
Deferred compensation plans, employer-managed . . . Lab §2809
Life pensions (See LIFE PENSIONS)
Public Employees' Retirement System (See PUBLIC EMPLOYEES' RETIREMENT SYSTEM)
State teachers' retirement system (See STATE TEACHERS' RETIREMENT SYSTEM)

RETRAINING
Supplemental job displacement benefits generally . . . 8 CCR §§10133.31 to 10133.60 (See SUPPLEMENTAL JOB DISPLACEMENT BENEFITS)

RETURN TO WORK PROGRAMS . . . 8 CCR §§10116 to 10118
Adjustment of permanent disability payments . . . 8 CCR §10117
Definitions . . . 8 CCR §10116.9
Disability benefits, payment
Positions for employees relieving employer of obligation to make indemnity payment . . . Lab §4650
Education of employers
Program established . . . Lab §139.47
Electronic adjudication management system (EAMS) . . . 8 CCR §10116.1
Converting paper files to electronic . . . 8 CCR §10116.6

RETURN TO WORK PROGRAMS—Cont.
Electronic adjudication management system (EAMS)—Cont.
Electronic filing exemption . . . 8 CCR §10116.2
Injury or findings required to file . . . 8 CCR §10116.8
Misfiled or misdirected documents . . . 8 CCR §10116.7
Technical problems with filing . . . 8 CCR §10116.5
Established . . . Lab §139.48
False or fraudulent statements in connection with . . . Ins §1871.4
Filing requirements . . . 8 CCR §10116.1
Converting paper files to electronic . . . 8 CCR §10116.6
Electronic filing exemption . . . 8 CCR §10116.2
Incomplete filings . . . 8 CCR §10116.3
Injury or findings required to file . . . 8 CCR §10116.8
Misfiled or misdirected documents . . . 8 CCR §10116.7
Retention of files . . . 8 CCR §10116.6
Technical problems with filing . . . 8 CCR §10116.5
Forms
Offer of work
Notice . . . 8 CCR §10118
Funding . . . Lab §139.48
Health care organizations (HCOs) . . . 8 CCR §9776.1
Jurisdiction
Injury or findings required to file . . . 8 CCR §10116.8
Misfiled or misdirected documents . . . 8 CCR §10116.7
Offer of work . . . 8 CCR §10117
Notice . . . 8 CCR §9813.2
Form . . . 8 CCR §10118
Purpose . . . Lab §139.48
Regulations to implement . . . Lab §139.48
Reporting requirements . . . 8 CCR §10116.1
Injury or findings required to file . . . 8 CCR §10116.8
Treating physician
Return to work & voucher report . . . 8 CCR §9785
Study of program . . . Lab §139.49
Supplement program . . . 8 CCR §§17300 to 17310
Amount of payment . . . 8 CCR §17308
Appeals of decision . . . 8 CCR §17309
Denial of return-to-work supplement, petition appealing . . . 8 CCR §10565
Applications for supplement
Contents . . . 8 CCR §17306
Deadline . . . 8 CCR §17304
Decisions . . . 8 CCR §17307
Electronic submission . . . 8 CCR §17305
False claims warning . . . 8 CCR §17310
Processing . . . 8 CCR §17307
Definitions . . . 8 CCR §17301
Eligibility for supplement . . . 8 CCR §17302
False claims warning . . . 8 CCR §17310
Nonassignability of payment . . . 8 CCR §17308
Notice of program . . . 8 CCR §17303
Purpose of program . . . 8 CCR §17300
Scope of provisions . . . 8 CCR §17300
Supplemental job displacement benefits
Defined . . . 8 CCR §17301
Time for payment . . . 8 CCR §17308
Vouchers
Defined . . . 8 CCR §17301

REVOCATION OF LICENSE, PERMIT, OR CERTIFICATION
Appeals
Crane safety, revocation of license to certify . . . Lab §7377
Occupational Safety and Health Division permits, denial or revocation of . . . Lab §6506
Cranes
License to certify crane safety, revocation of
Appeal of revocation . . . Lab §7377
Reasons for revocation . . . Lab §7376
Tower crane permits, suspension or revocation of . . . Lab §7374
Elevator permits, revocation of . . . Lab §7312
Health care organizations (HCOs), revocation of certification of . . . 8 CCR §9779.2
Insurance
Self-insurance (See SELF-INSURANCE)
Occupational Safety and Health Division permits . . . Lab §§6505, 6506
Rating organizations
Suspension or revocation of license of . . . Ins §§11754.2 to 11754.4
Self-insurance
Certificate to administer claims . . . 8 CCR §15463
Certificate to self-insure (See SELF-INSURANCE)
Tower crane permits, suspension or revocation of . . . Lab §7374

RIDESHARING
App-based drivers and services . . . B&P §§7448 to 7467 (See APP-BASED DRIVERS AND SERVICES)

RIGHTS
Appeals Board (WCAB)
Judicial review of Appeals Board (WCAB) decisions, right to appear at . . . Lab §5953
Public employment controversies, right to try and determine . . . Lab §6144
Regulations, right to change . . . Lab §5307
California Cadet Corps benefit rights . . . Mil&Vet §520
Death of employer, employee's rights against estate following . . . Lab §5306
Dependents and death benefits . . . Lab §4703
Disability benefits (See DISABILITY BENEFITS)
Economic opportunity programs
Recovery of federal benefits . . . Lab §4229
Workers' compensation benefits . . . Lab §4206
Employers (See EMPLOYERS)
Incapacitated workers . . . Lab §5408
Insurance
Generally . . . Lab §3750
Private right of action under Insurance Frauds Prevention Act . . . Ins §1871.7
Subrogation of insurer to rights of employer . . . Ins §11662
Interpreter, notice of right to . . . 8 CCR §9795.2
Judges (WCJs)
Ethics requirements not affecting rights and obligations of . . . 8 CCR §9723
Procedural rights, specific provisions not affecting . . . 8 CCR §9723
Judicial review of Appeals Board (WCAB) decisions, right to appear at . . . Lab §5953

RIGHTS—Cont.
Longshore and Harbor Workers' Compensation Act, waiver of rights under . . . 33 USC §915
Military service (See MILITARY SERVICE)
Minors . . . Lab §5408
Notice of right to benefits (See NOTICE)
Physicians, choice of . . . 8 CCR §9782
Prisoners, civil rights of (See PRISONERS)
Shipping suits, right of action in (See SHIPPING)
State Compensation Insurance Fund right to recover from third parties . . . Lab §6115
Subrogation (See SUBROGATION)
Survivors (See SURVIVORS' RIGHTS)
Workers' Compensation Division administrative director
Procedural rights, specific provisions not affecting . . . 8 CCR §9723

RIVER PORT DISTRICTS
Federal benefits in lieu of state benefits for stevedores . . . Har&N §6869

ROAD CAMPS
Prisoners employed in . . . Pen §4125.1

ROOFING CONTRACTORS
Certificate of workers' compensation insurance or self-insurance
Removal of C-39 roofing classification from license for failure to provide certificate to registrar . . . B&P §7125
Insurer for workers' compensation coverage to perform payroll audit . . . Ins §11665

RUNNERS
Insurance Frauds Prevention Act, use prohibited under . . . Ins §1871.7

S

SAFETY BELTS
Building and construction industry safe workplace requirements
Generally . . . Lab §7108
Steel framed buildings . . . Lab §§7253, 7265

SAFETY NETS
Requirements regarding . . . Lab §7108
Steel framed buildings . . . Lab §7265
Working without . . . Lab §7109

SAFETY OFFICIALS
Firefighters (See FIREFIGHTERS)
Law enforcement (See POLICE)
Pail leave of absence . . . Lab §4850
Public Employees' Retirement System, state and local safety members of (See PUBLIC EMPLOYEES' RETIREMENT SYSTEM)

SAFE WORKPLACE
Aerial passenger tramways
Passenger tramways generally . . Lab §§7340 to 7357 (See PASSENGER TRAMWAYS)
Antineoplastic drugs
Adoption of occupational safety and health standard for handling antineoplastic drugs in health care facilities . . . Lab §144.8

SAFE WORKPLACE—Cont.
Bilingual investigative support, enforcement, and training account . . . Lab §6356
Bloodborne diseases
Health care workers injured as result of preventive care for . . . Lab §3208.05
HIV-related diseases, time limitations for claims for injury or death due to . . . Lab §5406.6
Needle safety standards, Occupational Safety and Health Board responsibilities regarding . . . Lab §144.7
Boilers (See TANKS AND BOILERS)
Building safety
Aerial passenger tramways
Passenger tramways generally . . . Lab §§7340 to 7357 (See PASSENGER TRAMWAYS)
Generally (See BUILDING AND CONSTRUCTION INDUSTRY)
Passenger tramways . . . Lab §§7340 to 7357 (See PASSENGER TRAMWAYS)
California Occupational Safety and Health Act . . . Lab §6300
Cal-OSHA targeted inspection and consultation fund (See CAL-OSHA TARGETED INSPECTION AND CONSULTATION FUND)
Cancer
Antineoplastic drugs
Adoption of occupational safety and health standard for handling antineoplastic drugs in health care facilities . . . Lab §144.8
Chemical plants (See REFINERIES AND CHEMICAL PLANTS)
Citations on multiemployer worksites . . . Lab §6400
Cleaning products
Printable information to be made available to employees . . . Lab §6398.5
Client employer-labor contractor responsibilities . . . Lab §2810.3
Construction and interpretation . . . Lab §6301
Construction elevators (See CONSTRUCTION ELEVATORS)
Construction industry (See BUILDING AND CONSTRUCTION INDUSTRY)
Consulting services
Employer immunity from prosecution based on request for or acceptance of . . . Lab §6355
Insurers required to provide . . . Lab §6354.5
Occupational Safety and Health Division, provided by . . . Lab §6354
Corrections department (See CORRECTIONS AND REHABILITATION DEPARTMENT)
COVID-19
Exposure, employer notice requirements . . . Lab §6409.6
Cranes (See CRANES)
Definitions
Employees . . . Lab §§6304.1, 6304.2
Employers . . . Lab §6304
Employment . . . Lab §6303
Health . . . Lab §6306
Pertinent terms . . . Lab §6302
Place of employment . . . Lab §6303
Reporting requirements for occupational disease or injury . . . 8 CCR §14000

SAFE WORKPLACE—Cont.
Definitions—Cont.
Safe . . . Lab §6306
Safeguard . . . Lab §6306
Safety . . . Lab §6306
Safety devices . . . Lab §6306
Serious violations defined . . . Lab §6432
Direct patient care providers
Personal protective equipment (PPE) stockpile
Employer duties . . . Lab §6403.3
Discrimination against employees filing complaints . . . Lab §§6310, 6312
Education and research programs (See OCCUPATIONAL SAFETY AND HEALTH DIVISION)
Elevators, escalators, chair lifts and other conveyances (See ELEVATORS, ESCALATORS, CHAIR LIFTS AND OTHER CONVEYANCES)
Emergency closing of areas for public health or safety menace
Directing employee to remain in or enter closed area
Criminal offense . . . Lab §6311.5
Employees
Defined . . . Lab §§6304.1, 6304.2
Information provided to . . . Lab §6408
Interference with or failure to provide safe and healthful equipment and practices . . . Lab §6406
Regulations, obligation to comply with . . . Lab §6407
Employer defined . . . Lab §6304
Employer responsibilities
Generally . . . Lab §6403
Citations on multiemployer worksites . . . Lab §6400
Construction of unsafe or unhealthy worksites, prohibition on . . . Lab §6405
Information provided to employees . . . Lab §6408
Injury prevention program, requirement to establish . . . Lab §6401.7
Interference with or failure to provide safe and healthful equipment and practices . . . Lab §6406
Patient protection and health care worker back and musculoskeletal injury prevention . . . Lab §6403.5
Place of employment that is safe and healthy, requirement to provide . . . Lab §§6400, 6404
Practices and procedures that are safe and healthy, requirement to provide . . . Lab §6401
Regulations, obligation to comply with . . . Lab §6407
Reporting requirements, occupational disease or injury . . . Lab §6409.1
Smoking in the workplace . . . Lab §6404.5
Unsafe conditions, prohibition on allowing employees to work under . . . Lab §6402
Employment defined . . . Lab §6303
Farm labor vehicles (See FARM LABOR VEHICLE)
Firefighters
Personal protective clothing and equipment
Standards for clothing and equipment, evaluating and upgrading . . . Lab §147.2
Flooring (See BUILDING AND CONSTRUCTION INDUSTRY)
Garment manufacturing hazards, report of . . . Lab §6409.5

SAFE WORKPLACE—Cont.
Glass
Laminated safety glass requirements for railroads (See RAILROADS)
Window cleaning (See WINDOW CLEANING SAFETY DEVICES)
Hazardous industries, inspection and investigation of . . . Lab §6314.1
Hazardous substances (See HAARDOUS SUBSTANCES)
Health care organization (HCO) standards and requirements . . . 8 CCR §9776
Patient protection and health care worker back and musculoskeletal injury prevention
Safe patient handling . . . Lab §6403.5
Health care workers
Personal protective equipment (PPE) inventory
Employer duties . . . Lab §6403.1
Heat-related illness and injury
Indoor workers
Standard to minimize illness and injury . . . Lab §6720
Outdoor work, heat illness prevention standards
Maria Isabel Vasquez Jimenez heat illness standard . . . Lab §6721
HIV-related diseases, time limitations for filing claims for . . . Lab §5406.6
Hospitals
Violence prevention plan . . . Lab §6401.8
Injury prevention programs
Employers required to establish . . . Lab §6401.7
Failure to provide, penalty for . . . Lab §6428
Operative programs, criteria for . . . Lab §6428.5
Training provided by . . . Lab §6401.7
Interference with or failure to provide safe and healthful equipment and practices . . . Lab §6406
Jurisdiction
Generally . . . Lab §6303.5
Labor contractor-client employer responsibilities . . . Lab §2810.3
Laminated safety glass requirements for railroads (See RAILROADS)
Longshore and Harbor Workers' Compensation Act requirements . . . 33 USC §941
Medical cannabis/marijuana facilities
Armed robbery risk
Advisory committee to study . . . Lab §147.6
Combustion risk
Advisory committee to study . . . Lab §147.6
Evaluation of need for industry-specific regulations . . . Lab §§147.5, 147.6
Repetitive strain injury risk
Advisory committee to study . . . Lab §147.6
Second-hand marijuana smoke by employees
Advisory committee to study . . . Lab §147.6
Mining (See MINING AND TUNNELING)
No-entry/no-use orders
Contesting . . . Lab §6327
Division authority to issue . . . Lab §6325
Friable asbestos, workplaces containing . . . Lab §6325.5
Violation of no-entry/no-use orders . . . Lab §6326

SAFE WORKPLACE—Cont.
Occupational safety and health division
Orders
Passenger tramway orders, challenging . . . Lab §7346
Temporary restraining orders
Passenger tramways, dangerous operation of . . . Lab §7343
Passenger tramways . . . Lab §§7340 to 7357 (See PASSENGER TRAMWAYS)
Patient protection and health care worker back and musculoskeletal injury prevention
Employer duties . . . Lab §6403.5
Place of employment
Access for investigation of . . . Lab §6314
Construction of unsafe or unhealthy worksites, prohibition on . . . Lab §6405
Defined . . . Lab §6303
Employers required to provide safe and healthy workplace . . . Lab §§6400, 6404
Friable asbestos, containing . . . Lab §6325.5
No-entry/no-use orders (See OCCUPATIONAL SAFETY AND HEALTH DIVISION)
Unsafe, prohibition on . . . Lab §6404
Powers of Occupational Safety and Health Division regarding . . . Lab §6307
Powers of other governing bodies not limited by provisions regarding . . . Lab §6316
Railroads (See RAILROADS)
Refineries
Generally (See REFINERIES AND CHEMICAL PLANTS)
Refinery and Chemical Plant Worker Safety Act of 1990 . . . Lab §§7850 to 7873
Refusal of employee to work due to threats to . . . Lab §6311
Reporting requirements
Occupational disease or injury (See REPORTING REQUIREMENTS)
Research and education programs
Education and research programs (See OCCUPATIONAL SAFETY AND HEALTH DIVISION)
Salvaging during demolition, prohibition of . . . Lab §6401.5
Scaffolding (See SCAFFOLDING)
Ships and vessels (See SHIPPING)
Smoking in the workplace . . . Lab §6404.5
Staging as part of scaffolding . . . Lab §7150
Tanks (See TANKS AND BOILERS)
Temporary restraining orders . . . Lab §§6324, 6510
Training programs . . . Lab §6352
Tunneling (See MINING AND TUNNELING)
Unsafe conditions
Emergency closing of areas for public health or safety menace
Directing employee to remain in or enter closed area, criminal offense . . . Lab §6311.5
Employer responsibility to prohibit employees from working under . . . Lab §6402
Place of employment, unsafe . . . Lab §6404
Refusal of employee to work due to . . . Lab §6311
Volatile flammable liquids (See VOLATILE FLAMMABLE LIQUIDS)
Window cleaning safety devices (See WINDOW CLEANING SAFETY DEVICES)

SAFE WORKPLACE—Cont.
Workers' occupational safety and health education fund . . . Lab §6354.7

SALVAGE
Demolition, during . . . Lab §6401.5
Suits against United States for salvage services (See SHIPPING)

SAN FRANCISCO PORT COMMISSION
Course of duty, injury occurring in . . . Lab §4801
Medical treatment . . . Lab §4802
One year, disability continuing beyond . . . Lab §4803
Paid leave of absence . . . Lab §4800
Permanent disability . . . Lab §4803
Salary payments, temporary disability payments concurrent with . . . Lab §4804
Temporary disability
  Disability occurring in course of duty . . . Lab §4801
  Entitlement to medical, surgical, and hospital benefits . . . Lab §4802
  One year, disability continuing beyond . . . Lab §4803
  Paid leave of absence . . . Lab §4800
  Salary payments concurrent with, prohibition of . . . Lab §4804

SAN LUIS OBISPO
Firefighters, probation and sheriff's office employees, benefits for . . . Lab §4850.5

SATURDAYS
Appeals board (WCAB)
  Extensions of time . . . 8 CCR §10600
Discovery, effect on time limits for . . . CCP §2016.060

SAVE (SYSTEMATIC ALIEN VERIFICATION FOR ENTITLEMENTS) SYSTEM
Uninsured employers fund and subsequent injuries fund benefits for aliens . . . 8 CCR §15740

SCAFFOLDING
Defined . . . Lab §7150
Floors of . . . Lab §7153
Lean-to scaffolds . . . Lab §7154.1
Occupational Safety and Health Division
  Enforcement by . . . Lab §7158
  Powers of . . . Lab §7157
Penalty for violation of standards . . . Lab §§7155, 7156
Platforms . . . Lab §7153
Safety lines for . . . Lab §7152
Staging included as part of . . . Lab §7150
Suspended scaffolding . . . Lab §7151

SCHEDULES, CHARTS, AND TABLES
Administrative penalties
  Full compliance audit penalty schedules . . . 8 CCR §10111.2
  Injuries on or after 1/1/1990 and before 1/1/1994 . . . 8 CCR §10111
  Injuries on or after 1/1/1994 . . . 8 CCR §10111.1
  Target audit penalty schedule . . . 8 CCR §10111.2
Audits of claim logs and files, selection of files for . . . 8 CCR §10107
  Post-2002 audits . . . 8 CCR §10107.1
Burial expenses, maximum benefits . . . Table 13

SCHEDULES, CHARTS, AND TABLES—Cont.
Claim file selection for audit . . . 8 CCR §10107
  Post-2002 audits . . . 8 CCR §10107.1
Commutation
  Instructions and examples for commutation . . . Table 4
Composite factors appendix for inpatient services . . . 8 CCR §9792.1 Appx A
Comprehensive medical-legal evaluations, fees . . . 8 CCR §9795
Copy and related services fees
  Establishing schedule . . . Lab §5307.9
Death benefits payable for total and partial dependency . . . Table 13
Diagnosis-related group (DRG) weight ratios
  Generally . . . 8 CCR §9790.1
  Table of weights and revised weights . . . 8 CCR §9792.1 Appx B
Earnings, minimum/maximum indemnity and . . . Table 14
Fee schedules for medical treatment
  Composite factors appendix for inpatient services . . . 8 CCR §9792.1 Appx A
  Comprehensive medical-legal evaluations . . . 8 CCR §9795
  Determination of fee . . . 8 CCR §9792
  Diagnosis-related group (DRG) weight ratios
    Generally . . . 8 CCR §9790.1
    Table of DRG weights and revised weights . . . 8 CCR §9792.1 Appx B
  Medical-legal fee schedule . . . Table 12
Female pension, present value . . . Table 3
Fidelity bonds for health care organizations (HCOs) . . . 8 CCR §9771.73
Forms (See FORMS)
Glossary
  Commonly used terms and abbreviations . . . Table 18
Health care organizations (HCOs), coverage schedule for fidelity bonds . . . 8 CCR §9771.74
Home health care fee schedule
  Services not covered by Medicare or official medical fee schedule . . . Lab §5307.8
Insurance
  Self-insurance, private sector license fee assessments . . . 8 CCR §15230
Interest
  7 percent annually, 1 lump sum . . . Table 7
  Ten percent annually, lump-sum payments . . . Table 5
  Ten percent weekly, successive payments . . . Table 6
Life pensions (See LIFE PENSIONS)
Male pension, present value . . . Table 2
Medical-legal fee schedule . . . Table 12
Number of days between two dates . . . Table 9
Old schedule and new schedule disability numbers, comparison of . . . Table 11
Permanent disability
  Application of permanent partial disability rates to permanent disability indemnity table . . . Table 16
  Calculating rate . . . Table 19
  Commutation
    Present value of permanent disability . . . Table 1
  Computation of . . . Lab §4658

SCHEDULES, CHARTS, AND TABLES—Cont.
Permanent disability—Cont.
Indemnity table
Injuries occurring from 2006 through 2012 . . . Table 17B
Injuries occurring from 2013 to 2019 . . . Table 17A
Injuries occurring in 2003 through 2004 . . . Table 17D
Injuries occurring in 2005 . . . Table 17C
Minimum/maximum indemnity and earnings . . . Table 14
Percentage of permanent disability to weeks of indemnity . . . Table 15
Rating schedule for . . . 8 CCR §9805
1997 schedule . . . Table 11B
2005 schedule . . . Table 11A
Evaluation and revision . . . 8 CCR §9805.1
Work capacity guidelines . . . Table 11
Pharmaceutical fee schedule
Pharmaceutical fee schedule covered under official medical fee schedule . . . 8 CCR §9789.40, Lab §5307.1
Self-insurance, private sector license fee assessments . . . 8 CCR §15230
Temporary disability
Calculating rates . . . Table 19
Minimum/maximum benefits for temporary total disability . . . Table 14
Utilization schedule
Medical treatment utilization schedule . . . 8 CCR §§9792.20 to 9792.26 (See MEDICAL TREATMENT)
Vocational expert fee schedule
Establishment by administrative director . . . Lab §5307.7
Vocational rehabilitation
Calculating VRMA rate . . . Table 19
Work capacity guidelines . . . Table 11

SCHOLARSHIPS
Death benefits for dependents
Police officers, correctional officers, and firefighters . . . Lab §4709
Public officials . . . Lab §4728

SCHOOL DISTRICTS
Classified service employees, industrial accident or illness leave for . . . Ed §45192
County superintendent of schools (See COUNTY SUPERINTENDENT OF SCHOOLS)
Extended leave, employees on
Generally . . . Ed §44977
Salary deductions . . . Ed §44983
Industrial accident or illness leave . . . Ed §§44984, 45192
Loaned equipment, liability related to . . . Ed §32350
Maternity or paternity leave
Salary deductions during absence . . . Ed §44977.5
Murdered employees, payments to surviving spouses of . . . Ed §44017
Paid leave
Classified service employees, industrial accident or illness leave for . . . Ed §45192

SCHOOL DISTRICTS—Cont.
Paid leave—Cont.
Extended leave, employees on
Generally . . . Ed §44977
Salary deductions . . . Ed §44983
Industrial accident or illness leave . . . Ed §§44984, 45192
Maternity or paternity leave
Salary deductions during absence . . . Ed §44977.5
Temporary disability, restrictions for employees on . . . Ed §44043
Safety violations, fines and penalties for . . . Lab §6434
Salary restrictions for employees on temporary disability . . . Ed §44043
State teachers' retirement system (See STATE TEACHERS' RETIREMENT SYSTEM)
Student work experience, community, or vocational education programs . . . Lab §3368
Temporary disability benefits . . . Ed §44043
Volunteers . . . Lab §3364.5

SEALING OF DOCUMENTS
Appeals board (WCAB)
Record of proceedings
Sealed documents . . . 8 CCR §10813

SEAMEN (See SHIPPING)

SEARCH WARRANTS
Business records
Criminal cases, custody of business that is nonparty and was not scene of crime
Compliance with warrant . . . Ev §1560
Grounds for issuance . . . Pen §1524

SECOND INJURIES (See SUBSEQUENT INJURIES)

SECRETARY OF LABOR
Foreign employees of contractors with U.Sworking outside U.S
Administration . . . 42 USC §1706
Finality of decisions . . . 42 USC §1715
Longshore and Harbor Workers' Compensation Act (See LONGSHORE AND HARBOR WORKERS' COMPENSATION ACT)

SECRETARY OF STATE
Judicial notice of regulations filed with . . . Ev §451

SECURITIES
State Compensation Insurance Fund
Custodian, State Treasurer as . . . Ins §11788
Delivery of securities to State Treasurer . . . Ins §11790

SECURITY FOR PAYMENT
Group self-insurance
Security deposit
Agreement and undertaking for security deposit . . . 8 CCR §15486
Allocation of deposit . . . 8 CCR §15499
Amount, adjustment . . . 8 CCR §§15497, 15497.1

SECURITY FOR PAYMENT—Cont.
Group self-insurance—Cont.
Security deposit—Cont.
Increase in light of impaired financial condition . . . 8 CCR §15499.5
Maintaining and posting . . . 8 CCR §15496
Insurance
Attachment of employer's property for failure to secure payment . . . Lab §3707
Debts, priority of . . . Lab §3705
Definitions pertinent to . . . Lab §3700.1
Deposits by workers' compensation insurers . . . Ins §§11690 to 11703
Employer's means of securing payment . . . Lab §3700
Failure to secure payment (See INSURANCE)
Fraudulent failure to secure payment
Legislative intent . . . Ins §1871
Illegal uninsurance, conditions required following period of . . . Lab §3701.7
Insurance policy deductibles, collateral or security for . . . Ins §11736.5
Penalty for failure to secure payment . . . Lab §3700.5
Internet posting of convicted violators . . . Ins §1871.9
Purpose of . . . Lab §3712
Receivables, collateral or security for recognition of . . . Ins §11736.5
Self-insurers (See SELF-INSURANCE)
Targeting employers for enforcement . . . Lab §90.3
Longshore and Harbor Workers' Compensation Act . . . 33 USC §932
Self-insurers (See SELF-INSURANCE)
Voluntary disability benefit plans . . . UI §3258

SECURITY GUARD CONTRACTS
Labor law compliance
Funding in contract to be sufficient for contractor to comply with labor laws . . . Lab §2810

SECURITY OFFICERS
Atascadero State Hospital security officers, heart disease suffered by . . . Lab §3212.2

SELF-EMPLOYED PERSONS
Appeals Board (WCAB) jurisdiction over insurance controversies involving . . . Lab §5308
Longshore and Harbor Workers' Compensation Act . . . 33 USC §908
State Compensation Insurance Fund policies . . . Ins §11846

SELF-INFLICTED INJURIES
Conditions of employer liability for compensation . . . Lab §3600

SELF-INSURANCE
Actuarial study
Defined . . . 8 CCR §15201
Submission to office . . . 8 CCR §15209
Actuarial summary
Defined . . . 8 CCR §15201
Submission to office . . . 8 CCR §15209
Adjusting location
Defined . . . 8 CCR §15201

SELF-INSURANCE—Cont.
Administration procedures
Certificate to administer claims (See subhead: Certificate to administer claims)
Claims administration (See subhead: Claims procedures)
Costs of . . . Lab §3702.5
Independence of . . . Lab §3703
Administration revolving fund (See ADMINISTRATION REVOLVING FUND)
Administrative agency
Defined . . . 8 CCR §15201
Administrative director
Defined . . . 8 CCR §15201
Administrators
Defined . . . 8 CCR §15201
Advisory Committee to Manager, Office of Self-Insurance Plans . . . 8 CCR §15202
Affiliates
Agreement of assumption and guarantee of liability . . . 8 CCR §15203.1
Certificate
Definition of affiliate certificate . . . 8 CCR §15201
Interim certificates . . . 8 CCR §15205
Security deposits . . . 8 CCR §15211
Agreement of assumption and guarantee of liability
Generally . . . 8 CCR §15211.2
Affiliates . . . 8 CCR §15203.1
Security deposits . . . 8 CCR §15211.3
Subsidiaries . . . 8 CCR §15203.1
Alternative composite deposit
Accounting for deposit assessment funds . . . 8 CCR §15220.8
Amounts required, listing . . . 8 CCR §15220.2
Appeals, deposit assessments and penalties . . . 8 CCR §15220.7
Defaulting self-insurer, payment of claims from . . . 8 CCR §15216
Defined . . . 8 CCR §15201
Deposit assessments
Accounting for funds generated by assessment . . . 8 CCR §15220.8
Appeal of assessments and penalties . . . 8 CCR §15220.7
Liability for failure to pay . . . 8 CCR §15220.5
Security fund assessing . . . 8 CCR §15220.4
Exclusions from program . . . 8 CCR §15220
Fair share contribution surcharge fee, new self-insurers . . . 8 CCR §15220.6
Financial information . . . 8 CCR §15220.1
Partial participation . . . 8 CCR §15220
Participation in deposits . . . 8 CCR §15220
Security fund securing deposits . . . 8 CCR §15220.3
Appeals
Hearings, for . . . 8 CCR §§15430, 15431.1
Judicial review . . . 8 CCR §15437
Reconsideration, prior to . . . 8 CCR §15432
Assessments
Cal-OSHA targeted inspection and consultation assessment
Generally . . . 8 CCR §15234

SELF-INSURANCE—Cont.
Assessments—Cont.
Cal-OSHA targeted inspection and consultation assessment —Cont.
Determining self-insurers subject to . . . 8 CCR §15601.7
Fraud investigation and prosecution (See ADMINISTRATION REVOLVING FUND)
Private sector license fees . . . 8 CCR §15230
Public sector license fees . . . 8 CCR §15231
Self-Insurers' Security Fund . . . Lab §3745
User funding . . . 8 CCR §15232
Assumption, agreement of (See subhead: Agreement of assumption and guarantee of liability)
Audit of records (See AUDIT)
Authorization of
Individual private employer applicants . . . 8 CCR §15203.3
Public entities . . . 8 CCR §15203.4
Bankruptcy (See BANKRUPTCY)
Board of trustees
Defined . . . 8 CCR §15201
Generally (See GROUP SELF-INSURANCE)
Cal-OSHA targeted inspection and consultation assessment
Generally . . . 8 CCR §15234
Determining self-insurers subject to . . . 8 CCR §15601.7
Cancellation of surety bond
Defined . . . 8 CCR §15201
Certificate of consent to self-insure
Generally . . . Lab §3702
Agreement of assumption and guarantee of liability . . . 8 CCR §15203.1
Application for . . . 8 CCR §15203
Change in status of self-insurer . . . 8 CCR §15203.8
Definition of certificate to self-insure . . . 8 CCR §15201
Delayed startups . . . 8 CCR §15203.6
Fee for application . . . 8 CCR §15204
Fine in lieu of revocation . . . Lab §3702.7
Group self-insurance (See GROUP SELF-INSURANCE)
Interim certificates . . . 8 CCR §15205
Issuance of certificate . . . 8 CCR §15203.7
Licensure, required for (See CERTIFICATION)
Preventive programs, requirement to provide . . . 8 CCR §15353
Reinstatement . . . 8 CCR §15203.10
Resolution to authorize self-insurance (See subhead: Resolution to authorize self-insurance)
Restrictions on issuance . . . Lab §3701.9
Revocation of (See subhead: Revocation of certificate to self-insure)
Scope of certificate . . . 8 CCR §15203.9
Security deposit required for . . . 8 CCR §15203.5
Third-party administration . . . Lab §3702.1
Time certificate is valid . . . 8 CCR §15203.6
Validity of certificate . . . 8 CCR §15203.9
Certificate to administer claims . . . 8 CCR §15450
Definition of certificate to administer . . . 8 CCR §15201
Fees for . . . 8 CCR §15454

SELF-INSURANCE—Cont.
Certificate to administer claims —Cont.
Revocation of . . . 8 CCR §15463
Certificate to self-insure
Consent, certificate (See Subhead: Certificate of consent to self-insure)
Defined . . . 8 CCR §15201
Change in organization
Certification and change in status . . . 8 CCR §15203.8
Membership, notice of change in . . . 8 CCR §15402.3
Chief
Defined . . . 8 CCR §15201
Claim files
Defined . . . 8 CCR §15201
Recordkeeping requirements . . . 8 CCR §15400
Transfer of claim files . . . 8 CCR §15402.4
Claim liabilities, transfer of
Generally . . . 8 CCR §15360
Agreement of assumption and guarantee of liability upon (See subhead: Agreement of assumption and guarantee of liability)
Claim log
Defined . . . 8 CCR §15201
Claims procedures
Certificate to administer claims (See subhead: Certificate to administer claims)
Competence of administrator . . . 8 CCR §15452
Compliance with laws and regulations . . . 8 CCR §15458
Records and recordkeeping . . . 8 CCR §15458
Revocation of certificate, following . . . 8 CCR §15428
Third-party claims administration . . . 8 CCR §15450.1
Willful failure to pay benefits, notice of . . . 8 CCR §15459
Collective securing of payment of aggregate incurred liabilities . . . Lab §3701.8
Compensation
Defined . . . 8 CCR §15201
Complaints, hearings on . . . 8 CCR §§15430, 15431.2
Compliance requirements . . . 8 CCR §15420
Confidentiality of financial information . . . 8 CCR §15405
Contractors
Certification of self-insurance . . . B&P §7125
Renewal or recertification . . . B&P §7125.5
False certificates . . . B&P §7125.4
License maintained by maintaining certificate . . . B&P §7125.3
Contribution
Defined . . . 8 CCR §15201
Group self-insurance generally (See GROUP SELF-INSURANCE)
Core group members
Defined . . . 8 CCR §15201
Group self-insurance generally (See GROUP SELF-INSURANCE)
Counties, self-insured . . . Gov §31000.8
Coverage by standard insurance policies . . . 8 CCR §15210.3
Covered claims
Defined . . . Ins §1063.1

SELF-INSURANCE—Cont.
Debts, priority of . . . Lab §3705
Decisions of hearing officer regarding . . . 8 CCR §15435
Definitions pertinent to
    Hearings . . . 8 CCR §15430.1
    Public entity or joint powers authority . . . 8 CCR §15201
    Self-insurer's security fund . . . Lab §3741
Director defined
    Defined . . . 8 CCR §15201
Director's order for compliance, restitution, and civil penalty . . . Lab §3702.9
Estimated work injury claims, reporting requirements for (See subhead: Reporting requirements)
Excess coverage policies
    Covered claims . . . Ins §1063.1
Excess policies required by formerly self-insured employers . . . Lab §3702.8
Exoneration of surety bond
    Defined . . . 8 CCR §15201
Fees (See FEES)
Filing failures
    Late filing . . . Lab §3702.5
    Reporting requirements, failure to meet . . . 8 CCR §15251, Lab §3702.3
Financial requirements
    Confidentiality of financial information . . . 8 CCR §15405
    Group self-insurance (See GROUP SELF-INSURANCE)
    Public self-insurers, continuing financial capacity . . . 8 CCR §15203.11
    Security deposit increase due to impaired financial condition of self-insurer . . . 8 CCR §15211.1
    Submission of financial statements . . . 8 CCR §15203.2
First aid
    Defined . . . 8 CCR §15201
Former private self-insured employers, obligations of . . . Lab §3702.8
Fraud investigation and prosecution assessment (See ADMINISTRATION REVOLVING FUND)
Group administrator
    Defined . . . 8 CCR §15201
Group members
    Defined . . . 8 CCR §15201
Group self-insurance (See GROUP SELF-INSURANCE)
Guarantee of liability (See subhead: Agreement of assumption and guarantee of liability)
Hearings . . . 8 CCR §15430
    Appeals for . . . 8 CCR §§15430, 15431.1
    Appointment of hearing officer . . . 8 CCR §15433
    Complaints . . . 8 CCR §§15430, 15431.2
    Decision of hearing officer . . . 8 CCR §15435
    Definitions pertinent to . . . 8 CCR §15430.1
    Delegation of authority by manager . . . 8 CCR §§15431, 15433
    Disputes between self-insurer and chief . . . 8 CCR §15430
    Judicial review of decision . . . 8 CCR §15437
    Notice . . . 8 CCR §15434
    Procedures . . . 8 CCR §15434

SELF-INSURANCE—Cont.
Hearings —Cont.
    Reasons for . . . 8 CCR §15430
    Reconsideration of decision of hearing officer
        Appeals prior to . . . 8 CCR §15432
        Procedures for obtaining . . . 8 CCR §15436
    Requests for . . . 8 CCR §15431.1
    Severability of provisions regarding . . . 8 CCR §15438
Illegal uninsurance, conditions required following period of . . . Lab §3701.7
Indemnity agreement
    Defined . . . 8 CCR §15201
    Group self-insurance generally (See GROUP SELF-INSURANCE)
Indemnity claim
    Defined . . . 8 CCR §15201
Industrial Relations Department, Office of Self-Insurance Plans (See INDUSTRIAL RELATIONS DEPARTMENT)
Industry
    Defined . . . 8 CCR §15201
Insolvency (See BANKRUPTCY)
Insolvent self-insurer defined . . . Lab §3744
Interim certificates . . . 8 CCR §15205
Joint powers authority (See subhead: Public entity or joint powers authority)
Judicial review of decision of hearing officer . . . 8 CCR §15437
Labor code
    Defined . . . 8 CCR §15201
Liability
    Guarantee of (See subhead: Agreement of assumption and guarantee of liability)
    Insurance coverage limitations . . . Ins §11580.2
Licensing
    Certificate of insurance or self-insurance required for licensure (See CERTIFICATION)
    Private sector license fee assessment . . . 8 CCR §15230
    Public sector license fee assessment . . . 8 CCR §15231
Manager
    Defined . . . 8 CCR §15201
Medical-only claims
    Defined . . . 8 CCR §15201
Medical reports, submission of . . . 8 CCR §15302
Medical treatment
    Ninety-day limitation not applicable for . . . Lab §4606
    Payment for . . . Lab §4614.1
Membership, notice of change in . . . 8 CCR §15402.3
Notice
    Change of membership . . . 8 CCR §15402.3
    Employee notice of status . . . 8 CCR §15203.7
    Hearings . . . 8 CCR §15434
    Records location and administration, changes in . . . 8 CCR §15402
    Revocation
        Certificate to administer claims . . . 8 CCR §15463
        Certificate to self-insure . . . 8 CCR §15423
    Willful failure to pay benefits . . . 8 CCR §15459

SELF-INSURANCE—Cont.
Office of Self-Insurance Plans, Department of Industrial Relations (See INDUSTRIAL RELATIONS DEPARTMENT)
Open claims
  Defined . . . 8 CCR §15201
Overpayments returned to self-insured employers . . . Lab §3701.3
Payment of benefits
  Generally . . . Lab §3701.5
  Notice of willful failure to pay . . . 8 CCR §15459
Penalties and fines
  Certificate of consent to self-insure, fine in lieu of revocation . . . Lab §3702.7
  Director's order for . . . Lab §3702.9
  Late filing . . . Lab §3702.5
  Reporting requirements, failure to meet . . . 8 CCR §15251, Lab §3702.3
Power of attorney
  Defined . . . 8 CCR §15201
  Group self-insurance generally (See GROUP SELF-INSURANCE)
Preventive programs
  Requirement to provide . . . 8 CCR §15353
  Willful or repeated violations of . . . 8 CCR §15354
Public entity or joint powers authority
  Definitions . . . 8 CCR §15201
  Examination of public self-insured program . . . Lab §3702.4
  Notice of change of membership . . . 8 CCR §15402.3
  Reporting requirements
    Annual report . . . Lab §3702.2
    Examination of public self-insured program, report . . . Lab §3702.4
  Resolution to self-insure for . . . 8 CCR §15203.4
  Security deposit . . . 8 CCR §15210
Reconsideration of decision of hearing officer
  Appeals prior to . . . 8 CCR §15432
  Procedures for obtaining . . . 8 CCR §15436
Records and recordkeeping
  Administrator . . . 8 CCR §15402
  Audits of (See AUDIT)
  Claim files
    Requirement to keep . . . 8 CCR §15400
    Transfer of records . . . 8 CCR §15402.4
  Claim logs . . . 8 CCR §15400.1
  Claims procedures . . . 8 CCR §15458
  Interim reports on changes in . . . 8 CCR §15402.1
  Location of . . . 8 CCR §15402
  Maintenance and retention of records . . . 8 CCR §15400.2
  Notice of changes as to administration or location . . . 8 CCR §15402
  Transfer of records
    Claim files . . . 8 CCR §15402.4
    Report of . . . 8 CCR §15402.2
Release of surety bonds
  Defined . . . 8 CCR §15201
Reporting requirements
  Additional time to submit report for good cause . . . 8 CCR §15251
  Annual report . . . 8 CCR §15251, Lab §3702.2
  Estimated work injury claims
    Generally . . . 8 CCR §15300

SELF-INSURANCE—Cont.
Reporting requirements—Cont.
  Estimated work injury claims—Cont.
    Contracts for medical services not affecting requirements . . . 8 CCR §15303
    Revision of estimates . . . 8 CCR §15301
  Failure to submit reports . . . 8 CCR §15251, Lab §3702.3
  Financial statements . . . 8 CCR §15203.2
  Group self-insurance . . . 8 CCR §15474
  Interim reports . . . 8 CCR §15402.1
  Medical reports . . . 8 CCR §15302
  Penalties for failure to file or timely file . . . 8 CCR §15251, Lab §3702.3
  Public entity or joint powers authority
    Continuing financial capacity of public self-insurers . . . 8 CCR §15203.11
    Examination of public self-insured program, report . . . Lab §3702.4
  Recordkeeping changes
    Interim report . . . 8 CCR §15402.1
    Transfer of records . . . 8 CCR §15402.2
  Revoked self-insurers . . . 8 CCR §15424
  Self-Insurers' Security Fund . . . Lab §3746
Resolution to authorize self-insurance
  Individual private employer applicants . . . 8 CCR §15203.3
  Public entities . . . 8 CCR §15203.4
Revocation of certificate to administer claims . . . 8 CCR §15463
Revocation of certificate to self-insure
  Audit
    Generally . . . 8 CCR §15425
    Expense of . . . 8 CCR §15404.1
  Claims procedures following . . . 8 CCR §15428
  Continuing jurisdiction following . . . 8 CCR §15427
  Fine in lieu of revocation . . . Lab §3702.7
  Good cause, for . . . Lab §§3702, 3702.7
  Insurance coverage, extent of . . . 8 CCR §15210.3
  Noncompliance, due to . . . 8 CCR §15420
  Notice of intent to revoke . . . 8 CCR §15423
  Preventive programs, willful or repeated violations of . . . 8 CCR §15354
  Proceedings . . . 8 CCR §15423
  Reporting requirements of revoked self-insurers . . . 8 CCR §15424
  Security deposit
    Adjustment of . . . 8 CCR §15210.2
    Failure to post and maintain deposit . . . 8 CCR §15210
    Release of . . . 8 CCR §15426
  Voluntary revocation . . . 8 CCR §15422
Rulemaking on obligations of self-insurers . . . Lab §3702.10
Security deposits
  Generally . . . 8 CCR §15210, Lab §3701
  Actuarial studies and summaries
    Defined . . . 8 CCR §15201
    Submission to office . . . 8 CCR §15209
  Affiliates . . . 8 CCR §15211
  Agreement and undertaking for . . . 8 CCR §15203.5
  Agreement of assumption and guarantee of liability . . . 8 CCR §15211.3

Index

SELF-INSURANCE—Cont.
Security deposits—Cont.
Alternative composite deposit
Accounting for deposit assessment funds . . . 8 CCR §15220.8
Amounts required, listing . . . 8 CCR §15220.2
Appeals, deposit assessments and penalties . . . 8 CCR §15220.7
Defaulting self-insurer, payment of claims from . . . 8 CCR §15216
Defined . . . 8 CCR §15201
Deposit assessments . . . 8 CCR §§15220.4, 15220.5, 15220.7, 15220.8
Exclusions from program . . . 8 CCR §15220
Fair share contribution surcharge fee, new self-insurers . . . 8 CCR §15220.6
Financial information . . . 8 CCR §15220.1
Partial participation . . . 8 CCR §15220
Participation in deposits . . . 8 CCR §15220
Security fund securing deposits . . . 8 CCR §15220.3
Amount
Adjustments . . . 8 CCR §§15210.1, 15210.2
Determining . . . 8 CCR §15210
Approved securities . . . 8 CCR §15213
Cash . . . 8 CCR §15214
Defaulting insurers, claims against . . . 8 CCR §15216
Group self-insurance (See GROUP SELF-INSURANCE)
Increase due to impaired financial condition of self-insurer . . . 8 CCR §15211.1
Letters of credit . . . 8 CCR §15215
Revocation of certificate to self-insure
Adjustment of amount following . . . 8 CCR §15210.2
Failure to post and maintain deposit . . . 8 CCR §15210
Release of deposit following . . . 8 CCR §15426
Subsidiaries . . . 8 CCR §15211
Surety Bonds . . . 8 CCR §15212
Security fund
Defined . . . 8 CCR §15201
Self-insurer
Defined . . . 8 CCR §15201
Study
Defined . . . 8 CCR §15201
Submission of actuarial studies and summaries to office . . . 8 CCR §15209
Subsidiaries
Agreement of assumption and guarantee of liability . . . 8 CCR §15203.1
Certificates
Definition of subsidiary certificate . . . 8 CCR §15201
Interim certificates . . . 8 CCR §15205
Security deposits . . . 8 CCR §15211
Summary
Defined . . . 8 CCR §15201
Submission of actuarial studies and summaries to office . . . 8 CCR §15209
Termination of surety bond
Defined . . . 8 CCR §15201

SELF-INSURANCE—Cont.
Third-party claims administration . . . 8 CCR §15450.1
Transfer of claim liabilities
Generally . . . 8 CCR §15360
Agreement of assumption and guarantee of liability upon (See subhead: Agreement of assumption and guarantee of liability)
Transfer of records
Claim files . . . 8 CCR §15402.4
Report of . . . 8 CCR §15402.2
User funding assessment . . . 8 CCR §15232

SELF-INSURERS' SECURITY FUND
Administration and organization of . . . Lab §3742
Annual report . . . Lab §3746
Assessment of members . . . Lab §3745
Assets, maintaining . . . Lab §3745
Assumption of obligations of insolvent self-insurer . . . Lab §3743
Audit . . . Lab §3746
Collective securing of payment of aggregate incurred liabilities . . . Lab §3701.8
Definitions pertinent to . . . Lab §3741
Insolvent self-insurers
Reimbursement of fund . . . Lab §3744
Nonprofit Mutual Benefit Corporation, established as . . . Lab §3742
Obligations of
Generally . . . Lab §3742
Insolvent self-insurers, assumption of obligations of . . . Lab §3743
Reimbursement, obtaining . . . Lab §3743
Purpose of . . . Lab §3740
Reporting requirements . . . Ins §1063.3, Lab §3746
Rights of . . . Lab §3744
Young-La Follette Self-Insurers' Security Act, referred to as . . . Lab §3747

SENIOR CITIZENS
Dependent adults
Discovery
Elder abuse and dependent adult civil protection act . . . CCP §§2017.310, 2017.320
Elder abuse
Discovery
Elder abuse and dependent adult civil protection act . . . CCP §§2017.310, 2017.320

SERIOUS AND WILLFUL MISCONDUCT
Allegations of serious and willful misconduct . . . 8 CCR §10525
Appeals Board determination of misconduct by applicant leading to reduction in compensation by . . . Lab §4552
Burden of proof . . . Lab §5705
Decrease in compensation . . . Lab §4551
Defenses, generally . . . Lab §3600
Employee misconduct leading to reduction of compensation . . . Lab §4551
Employer misconduct leading to increase of compensation . . . Lab §4553
Findings by Appeals Board (WCAB), criteria for safety order violation . . . Lab §4553.1
Increase of compensation . . . Lab §4553

SERIOUS AND WILLFUL MISCONDUCT—Cont.
Insurance coverage for serious and willful violations . . . Ins §11661
Longshore injuries . . . 33 USC §920
Maximum amounts, punitive increases not affected by . . . Lab §4556
Minors, affecting recovery by . . . Lab §4551
Other employees, liability to . . . Lab §3601
Pleadings alleging serious and willful misconduct . . . 8 CCR §10525
Reduction of compensation . . . Lab §4551
Responsibility of employers and employees . . . Lab §§6400 to 6413.5
Time limitations
  Employee . . . Lab §5407.5
  Employer . . . Lab §5407

SERVICE
Appeals Board (WCAB)
  Attorney, service on . . . 8 CCR §10625
  Death cases
    Dependency at issue, service on division of workers' compensation and director of industrial relations . . . 8 CCR §10632
  Decisions, method of service of . . . Lab §5316
  Designated service . . . 8 CCR §10629
  Documents, service of . . . 8 CCR §10410
  Email, service by
    Time within which to act . . . 8 CCR §10605
  Fax service
    Time within which to act . . . 8 CCR §10605
  Hearing, service of notice of . . . Lab §§5504, 5906
  Judicial review of Appeals Board (WCAB) decisions, service of pleadings upon . . . Lab §5954
  Lien claimants (See subhead: Lien claimants)
  Mail . . . CCP §1013
    Time within which to act . . . 8 CCR §10605
  Mailbox maintained in district office
    Receipt of documents from mailbox as service . . . 8 CCR §10628
  Medical and medical-legal reports
    Lien claimants who are not physicians, service on . . . 8 CCR §10637
    Service of copies of documents, electronic media, etc, offered into evidence . . . 8 CCR §10635
  Methods of service . . . 8 CCR §10625
  Nondependent death cases . . . 8 CCR §10632
  Parties, service by . . . 8 CCR §10625
    Reports and records, service on other parties or representatives . . . 8 CCR §10625
  Physicians' reports
    Lien claimants who are not physicians, service on . . . 8 CCR §10637
    Ongoing duty to serve . . . 8 CCR §10635
    Service of copies of documents, electronic media, etc, offered into evidence . . . 8 CCR §10635
  Proof of service
    Reconsideration, removal or disqualification petitions . . . 8 CCR §10940
  Public official, service of decision on . . . Lab §5317
  Reconsideration, removal or disqualification petitions
    Proof of service . . . 8 CCR §10940

SERVICE—Cont.
Appeals Board (WCAB)—Cont.
  Reconsideration, service of petition for . . . Lab §5905
    Service by board of orders, decisions, awards, etc . . . 8 CCR §10628
    Subsequent Injuries Fund documents . . . 8 CCR §10632
Arbitration findings and award . . . Lab §5277
Attorneys
  Service on attorney or agent of record . . . 8 CCR §10625
    Documents, filing and service generally . . . 8 CCR §10610
Attorneys' fees disclosure statements . . . 8 CCR §10135.1
Death cases
  Dependency at issue
    Division of workers' compensation and director of industrial relations, service on . . . 8 CCR §10632
Depositions
  Subpoenas
    Service of deposition subpoena . . . CCP §2020.220
Designated service . . . 8 CCR §10629
Discovery
  Methods of service . . . CCP §2016.050
Electronic adjudication management system (EAMS)
  Preferences as to, designation . . . 8 CCR §10205.6
  Serve
    Defined . . . 8 CCR §10205
Electronic service . . . CCP §1013
Evidence
  Documentary evidence
    Lien claimants who are not physicians, service on . . . 8 CCR §10637
    Service of copies of documents, electronic media, etc, offered into evidence . . . 8 CCR §10635
Express mail, service by . . . CCP §1013
Facsimile, service by . . . CCP §1013
  Appeals Board (WCAB)
    Time within which to act . . . 8 CCR §10605
Failure to secure payment of benefits, action based on . . . Lab §3708.5
Five-day mail service in California, requirements for . . . CCP §1013
Inspection demands
  Service of demand . . . CCP §2031.040
Lien claimants
  Assignment of liens . . . Lab §4903.8
  Compromise and Release, service on claimants of . . . 8 CCR §10702
  Filing and service of lien claims and supporting documents . . . 8 CCR §10862
  Resolution or withdrawal of lien claims
    Notification . . . 8 CCR §10872
Mail, service by . . . CCP §1013
  Appeals Board (WCAB)
    Time within which to act . . . 8 CCR §10605
Medical examinations
  Information provided to evaluator
    Opposing party, service upon . . . Lab §4062.3

SERVICE—Cont.
Medical reports
Service of documents . . . 8 CCR §10635
Lien claimants who are not physicians, service on . . . 8 CCR §10637
Methods of service . . . 8 CCR §10625
Nondependent death cases
Division of workers' compensation and director of industrial relations, service on . . . 8 CCR §10632
Occupational Safety and Health Appeals Board
Notice, order, or decision . . . Lab §6610
Reconsideration, petition for . . . Lab §6619
Overnight mail, service by . . . CCP §1013
Parties, by . . . 8 CCR §10625, CCP §1013
Penalty assessment orders
Generally . . . 8 CCR §15567, Lab §3722
Means of service . . . 8 CCR §15578
Personal service of . . . Lab §3731
Proof of . . . CCP §1013
Qualified medical evaluators (QMES)
Comprehensive medical-legal evaluations
Reports . . . 8 CCR §36
Stop orders
Generally . . . 8 CCR §15578
Personal service of . . . Lab §3731
Subrogation rules of copies of service of complaint on third party . . . Lab §3853
Subsequent Injuries Fund documents . . . 8 CCR §10632
Summary permanent disability rating determination . . . 8 CCR §10165
Supplemental job displacement benefits
Offer of modified or alternative work
Injuries occurring in 2013 and beyond . . . 8 CCR §10133.34
Suspension of physician, practitioner or provider from participation in system for cause
Procedure for suspension of providers . . . 8 CCR §9788.6
Third-party actions, copies of service of complaint in . . . Lab §3853

SERVICE INDUSTRY
Employer's records of occupational injury or illness
Partial exemption from requirements . . . 8 CCR §14300.2

SETTLEMENT, COMPROMISE AND RELEASE
Appeals board (WCAB)
Agreements
Forms required . . . 8 CCR §10500
Appearance in settled case . . . 8 CCR §10757
Approval of settlements . . . 8 CCR §10700
Authority and duties of Appeals Board regarding agreements of . . . 8 CCR §10700
Hearings, settlement conferences pursuant to . . . Lab §5502
Mandatory settlement conferences . . . 8 CCR §10759
Appearances
Required appearances . . . 8 CCR §10752
Approval of settlements . . . 8 CCR §10700
Arbitrator, disclosure to . . . Lab §5278
Authority and duties of Appeals Board regarding agreements of . . . 8 CCR §10700

SETTLEMENT, COMPROMISE AND RELEASE—Cont.
Collateral estoppel on subsequent criminal proceedings . . . Lab §5006
Cumulative injury . . . Lab §5005
Death benefits . . . Lab §5004
Electronic adjudication management system (EAMS)
Forms . . . 8 CCR §10205.2
Mandatory settlement conferences
Defined . . . 8 CCR §10205
Rating mandatory settlement conferences
Defined . . . 8 CCR §10205
Retention, return and destruction of records . . . 8 CCR §10208.7
Entry of award following . . . Lab §5002
Failure to appear at settlement conferences . . . 8 CCR §10755
Filing form for . . . Lab §5002
Forms for compromise and release
Electronic adjudication management system (EAMS) . . . 8 CCR §10205.2
Information required for . . . Lab §§5003, 5004
Insurer's declaration attached to . . . 8 CCR §10705, Lab §3761
Judges (WCJs), authority of
Mandatory settlement conferences . . . 8 CCR §10759
Labor code private attorneys general
Actions brought by private aggrieved employee
Review of settlements . . . Lab §§2699.3, 2699.5
Lien claimants, service on . . . 8 CCR §10702
Limitations . . . Lab §5000
Longshore and Harbor Workers' Compensation Act . . . 33 USC §908
Occupational disease . . . Lab §5005
Payment of benefits prior to . . . Lab §4909
Shipping
Public vessels, damages caused by or towage and salvage rendered to . . . 46 USC §31108
Payment . . . 46 USC §31109
United States vessels or cargo, suits in admiralty involving
Settlement of claims . . . 46 USC §30912
Subrogation
Releases or settlements (See SUBROGATION)
Subsequent injuries, compromises regarding . . . Lab §4754.5
Uninsured Employers Fund suits against employers, compromise or prosecution of . . . Lab §3719
United States, tort claims against . . . 28 USC §2677
Validity of . . . Lab §5001

SEX-SPECIFIC TERMINOLOGY IN CODE SECTIONS (See WORKMEN'S COMPENSATION CHANGED TO WORKERS' COMPENSATION)

SEXUAL CONDUCT
Discovery
Sexual conduct of plaintiff . . . CCP §2017.220
Injuries arising from . . . Lab §3208.4

SEXUAL DYSFUNCTION
Impairment ratings . . . Lab §4660.1

SEXUAL HARASSMENT
App-based drivers and services
Prevention of sexual harassment . . . B&P §7457

SEXUAL HARASSMENT—Cont.
Discovery
Sexual conduct of plaintiff . . . CCP §2017.220
Employer liability for harassment by nonemployees . . . Gov §12940
Employment practices . . . Gov §12940

SHARES AND SHAREHOLDERS
Uninsured employers, actions against
Substantial shareholders and parents (See UNINSURED EMPLOYERS BENEFITS TRUST FUND)

SHELTERED WORKSHOPS
Employment discrimination or harassment
Action for harassment or discrimination by employees of nonprofit sheltered workshops, day programs or rehabilitation facilities . . . Gov §12926.05

SHERIFFS
Death benefits
Special officer of sheriff, Orange county
Continued health benefits to surviving spouse and dependents . . . Lab §4856
Scholarships for dependents . . . Lab §4709

SHIPPING
Admiralty jurisdiction (See ADMIRALTY AND MARITIME JURISDICTION)
Death on high seas . . . 46 USC §§30301 to 30308 (See DEATH ON THE HIGH SEAS)
District courts, admiralty and maritime jurisdiction of . . . 28 USC §1333
Immigrant workers
Seamen, injury in course of employment
Non-citizens or nonresident aliens, restrictions on recovery for incidents in foreign waters . . . 46 USC §30105
Land, damage or injury on caused by vessel
Jurisdiction . . . 46 USC §30101
Longshore and Harbor Workers' Compensation Act (See LONGSHORE AND HARBOR WORKERS' COMPENSATION ACT)
Maritime jurisdiction (See ADMIRALTY AND MARITIME JURISDICTION)
Public vessels, damages caused by or towage and salvage rendered to . . . 46 USC §§31101 to 31112
Arbitration of claims . . . 46 USC §31108
Counterclaims
Security . . . 46 USC §31105
Exoneration
Availability to US . . . 46 USC §31106
Foreign nationals
Reciprocity to determine eligibility to bring action . . . 46 USC §31111
Interest
Judgments, when to include interest . . . 46 USC §31107
Judgments
Interest, when judgments may include . . . 46 USC §31107
Payment of judgment . . . 46 USC §31109
Liens against vessels not created by provisions . . . 46 USC §31112

SHIPPING—Cont.
Public vessels, damages caused by or towage and salvage rendered to —Cont.
Limitations of liability
Availability to US . . . 46 USC §31106
Payment of judgment . . . 46 USC §31109
Provisions applicable . . . 46 USC §31103
Settlement of claims . . . 46 USC §31108
Payment . . . 46 USC §31109
Short title of provisions . . . 46 USC §31101
Subpoenas to officers or crew . . . 46 USC §31110
Venue . . . 46 USC §31104
Waiver of immunity . . . 46 USC §31102
Seamen
Death on the high seas . . . 46 USC §§30301 to 30308 (See DEATH ON THE HIGH SEAS)
Injury in course of employment
Actions . . . 46 USC §30104
Non-citizens or non-resident aliens, restrictions on recovery for incidents in foreign waters . . . 46 USC §30105
State Compensation Insurance Fund ability to insure under maritime law . . . Ins §11779
United States vessels or cargo, suits in admiralty involving . . . 46 USC §§30901 to 30913
Admiralty stipulation not to be required of US or federally owned corporation . . . 46 USC §30909
Arbitration of claims . . . 46 USC §30912
Arrest of vessels or cargos of US or federally owned corporation . . . 46 USC §30908
Bonds not to be required of US or federally owned corporation . . . 46 USC §30909
Civil actions
Procedure . . . 46 USC §30907
Costs
Inclusion in judgment against US . . . 46 USC §30911
Exclusive remedies . . . 46 USC §30904
Exoneration
Availability to US . . . 46 USC §30910
Federally owned corporation
Defined . . . 46 USC §30902
In rem proceedings
Conditions for proceeding in rem . . . 46 USC §30907
Interest on claims
Inclusion in judgment against US . . . 46 USC §30911
Judgments
Costs, inclusion in judgments against US . . . 46 USC §30911
Interest, inclusion in judgments against US . . . 46 USC §30911
Payment . . . 46 USC §30913
Limitations of liability
Availability to US . . . 46 USC §30910
Settlement of claims . . . 46 USC §30912
Payment . . . 46 USC §30913
Short title . . . 46 USC §30901
Statutes of limitation . . . 46 USC §30905
Venue . . . 46 USC §30906
Waiver of immunity . . . 46 USC §30903
Wrongful act, death on high seas by . . . 46 USC §§30301 to 30308 (See DEATH ON THE HIGH SEAS)

SHORING REGULATIONS
Swimming pool excavations . . . Lab §6705.5

SHOULDER INJURIES
Medical treatment
Utilization schedule
Shoulder disorders . . . 8 CCR §9792.23.2

SICK DAYS, PAID . . . Lab §§245 to 249
Accrual . . . Lab §246
Back pay
Enforcement . . . Lab §248.5
Citations
Enforcement . . . Lab §248.5
Civil actions
Enforcement . . . Lab §248.5
Conditions on using days . . . Lab §246.5
COVID-19
Covered workers, supplemental paid sick leave . . . Lab §248.1
Food sector workers, supplemental paid sick leave . . . Lab §248
Definitions . . . Lab §245.5
Discrimination or retaliation for using sick days . . . Lab §246.5
Enforcement . . . Lab §248.5
Entitlement to paid sick days . . . Lab §246
Existing paid sick days programs
Effect of provisions . . . Lab §246
In-home supportive services providers
Paid sick leave work group for in-home supportive services providers . . . Lab §246
Lending by employer in advance of accrual . . . Lab §246
Minimum nature of provisions . . . Lab §249
Notice by employee as to need for sick time . . . Lab §246
Notice by employer to employee of balance available . . . Lab §246
Posting notice of rights under of provisions . . . Lab §247
Privacy of health and domestic relations information . . . Lab §249
Purposes justifying paid sick leave . . . Lab §246.5
Rate of pay . . . Lab §246
Recordkeeping by employers . . . Lab §247.5
Reinstatement
Enforcement . . . Lab §248.5
Short title . . . Lab §245
Statutory construction
Additional nature of provisions . . . Lab §245
Independent nature of provisions . . . Lab §245

SICK LEAVE
Paid sick days . . . Lab §§245 to 249

SIGHT
Presumption of total disability due to loss of . . . Lab §4662

SIGNAL SYSTEMS
Construction elevators, for (See CONSTRUCTION ELEVATORS)

SIGNATURES
Definition of signature or subscription . . . Lab §17
Electronic adjudication management system (EAMS)
Electronic signatures
Defined . . . 8 CCR §10205

SIGNATURES—Cont.
Medical information, authorization for release of . . . CC §§56.10, 56.11
Medical treatment
Cosignature of treating physician required for nurse practitioner or physician's assistant . . . Lab §3209.10
Permanent disability
Disability evaluation unit . . . 8 CCR §10150.1

SKIING AND SKI RESORTS
Lifts
Passenger tramways, safety on . . . Lab §§7340 to 7357 (See PASSENGER TRAMWAYS)

SLEEP DISORDERS
Impairment ratings . . . Lab §4660.1

SLOPING REGULATIONS
Swimming pool excavations . . . Lab §6705.5

SMOKING
Electronic cigarettes
Smoking in the workplace, prohibitions
Applicability to electronic cigarettes . . . Lab §6404.5
Employer responsibility for regulating workplace smoking . . . Lab §6404.5
Mining and tunneling . . . Lab §§7970, 7978
Owner-operated businesses
Smoking in workplace, prohibition
Applicability to owner-operated businesses . . . Lab §6404.5

SNOW AVALANCHE BLASTING
Occupational Safety and Health Division requirements . . . Lab §6711

SOCIAL ACTIVITY
Conditions of employer liability for compensation . . . Lab §3600

SOCIAL SERVICES (See PUBLIC SOCIAL SERVICES)

SOCIAL WORKERS
Medical information disclosures
Threat to health or safety, release of information to alleviate . . . CC §56.10
Privileged communications with patients . . . Ev §§1010 to 1016
Psychologists and psychotherapists
Psychiatric social workers as psychologist . . . Ev §1010
Treatment of injuries by . . . Lab §3209.8

SOLICITATION AND REFERRAL
Advertising (See ADVERTISING)
Insurance fraud, for purposes of . . . Pen §549
Referral services (See REFERRALS AND REFERRAL SERVICES)

SOVEREIGN IMMUNITY
Shipping
Public vessels, damages caused by or towage and salvage rendered to
Waiver of immunity . . . 46 USC §31102

SOVEREIGN IMMUNITY—Cont.
Shipping—Cont.
United States vessels or cargo, suits in admiralty involving
Waiver of immunity . . . 46 USC §30903

SPECIALISTS
Qualified medical evaluators (QMEs) (See QUALIFIED MEDICAL EVALUATORS (QMES))

SPINAL SURGERY
Medical treatment generally (See MEDICAL TREATMENT)
Objections to medical determination
Medical evaluation
Unrepresented employees . . . Lab §4062.1

SPOUSES
Aliens, uninsured employers fund and subsequent injuries fund benefits for . . . 8 CCR §15740
Defined to include registered domestic partner . . . Lab §12.2
Dependents, presumed to be . . . Lab §3501
Longshore and Harbor Workers' Compensation Act . . . 33 USC §909
Privileged communications . . . Ev §980
School district payments to surviving spouse of murdered employee . . . Ed §44017
Support obligations (See SUPPORT OBLIGATIONS)

STAIRWAY CHAIR LIFTS . . . Lab §§7300 to 7324.2

STALKING
Invasion of privacy . . . CC §1708.8

STANDARDS
Building and construction industry (See BUILDING AND CONSTRUCTION INDUSTRY)
Chiropractors
Anesthesia
Manipulation under anesthesia (MUA), standard of care . . . 16 CCR §318.1
Evaluation of standards from other sources . . . Lab §147
Hazardous substances removal . . . Lab §142.7
Health care organizations (HCOs) (See HEALTH CARE ORGANIATIONS (HCOS))
Occupational Safety and Health Standards Board (See OCCUPATIONAL SAFETY AND HEALTH STANDARDS BOARD)
Preponderance of the evidence standard
Conditions of employer liability for compensation . . . Lab §3600
Workers' compensation division of Labor Code . . . Lab §3202.5
Qualified medical evaluators (QMEs), standards governing evaluations by . . . Lab §139.2

STATE AGENCIES (See PUBLIC AGENCIES)

STATE COMPENSATION INSURANCE FUND . . . Ins §11770
Ability to transact workers' compensation insurance . . . Ins §11778
Federal law, ability to insure under . . . Ins §11779
Maritime law, ability to insure under . . . Ins §11779

STATE COMPENSATION INSURANCE FUND—Cont.
Ability to transact workers' compensation insurance —Cont.
State law, ability to insure under . . . Ins §11780
Temporary absence from California . . . Ins §11780.5
Account or fund in State Treasury, establishment of . . . Ins §11800.1
Advertising
Disclaimer as to status as branch of state . . . Ins §11771.5
Annual accounting requirements . . . Ins §11776
Annual report to Legislature . . . Ins §11805
Assassinated public officials, payment of death benefits for . . . Lab §4725
Assets of fund
Sale of assets and liabilities of fund . . . Ins §§11885 to 11886.2
Board of directors . . . Ins §11770
Alternative names for . . . Ins §11881
Limited liability . . . Ins §11772
Lobbying restrictions for former directors . . . Ins §11785.5
Officers of fund . . . Ins §11785
Lobbying restrictions for former officers . . . Ins §11785.5
Powers of . . . Ins §11781, Lab §57.5
President of fund
Authority over . . . Ins §11785
Delegation of authority to . . . Ins §11787
Sale of assets and liabilities of fund
Participation by directors . . . Ins §11885.3
Business name . . . Ins §11782
Casual employees, policies for . . . Ins §11846
Competitiveness . . . Ins §11775
Contracts, terms of . . . Ins §11840
County superintendent of schools . . . Ed §1252
Credits . . . Ins §§11776, 11777
Death benefits for assassinated public officials, payment of . . . Lab §4725
Deposit of excess money . . . Ins §11800
Dividends . . . Ins §§11776, 11777
Emergency and disaster services workers (See EMERGENCY AND DISASTER SERVICES WORKERS)
Employers
Estimates of wage values . . . Ins §11845
Policies for . . . Ins §11843
Public (See subhead: Public employers, coverage of)
Same compensation and rates for employers and employees . . . Ins §11844
Examination by Commissioner . . . Ins §738
Excess assets
Account or fund in State Treasury, establishment of . . . Ins §11800.1
Deposit of excess money . . . Ins §11800
Dividends and credits . . . Ins §11776
Investment of excess money . . . Ins §11797
Expenditures made by, exemptions for . . . Ins §11793
Family members, policies for . . . Ins §11843
Federal claims
Funds acquired for held in separate account . . . Ins §11802
Paid from separate account . . . Ins §11803

STATE COMPENSATION INSURANCE FUND—Cont.
Federal claims—Cont.
Prohibition on use of certain assets to satisfy . . . Ins §11801
Separate account
Funds acquired for . . . Ins §11802
Paid from . . . Ins §11803
Federal law, ability to insure under . . . Ins §11779
Investment of excess money . . . Ins §11797
Joint use of office space, facilities, and supplies, charges for . . . Ins §11804
Liabilities and assets of fund
Sale of assets and liabilities of fund . . . Ins §§11885 to 11886.2
Limited liability
Directors and personnel . . . Ins §11772
State . . . Ins §11771
Lobbying restrictions for former directors or officers . . . Ins §11785.5
Los Angeles, authority to acquire property in . . . Ins §11781.5
Loss, annual accounting of . . . Ins §11776
Maritime law, ability to insure under . . . Ins §11779
Misrepresentation to obtain reduced rate from . . . Ins §11880
Internet posting of convicted violators . . . Ins §1871.9
Organization . . . Ins §11770
Payment of benefits by . . . Lab §4909.1
Penalties and fines for misrepresentation to obtain reduced rate from . . . Ins §11880
Internet posting of convicted violators . . . Ins §1871.9
Policies for employees . . . Ins §11843
Policies, terms of . . . Ins §11840
Powers
Board of Directors . . . Ins §11781
Fund . . . Ins §11783
President of fund . . . Ins §11784
President of fund
Appointment of . . . Ins §11785
Board's authority as to . . . Ins §11785
Bond and oath of . . . Ins §11786
Delegation of authority by board of directors to . . . Ins §11787
Powers of . . . Ins §11784
Public Employees' Retirement System (See PUBLIC EMPLOYEES' RETIREMENT SYSTEM)
Public employers, coverage of
Generally . . . Ins §11870
Authorization of Fund to make expenditures . . . Lab §6113
Controller's warrant, State Treasurer's payment of . . . Ins §11874
Finance, master agreement with Department of . . . Lab §§6111, 6112
Human resources department, master agreement . . . Ins §11871
Laws applicable to public employment . . . Ins §11873
Premiums . . . Ins §11870
Reimbursement of Fund for expenditures made . . . Lab §6114

STATE COMPENSATION INSURANCE FUND—Cont.
Public employers, coverage of—Cont.
State agencies, annual agreements with . . . Ins §11872
Third parties, right of Fund to recover from . . . Lab §6115
Uniform rate agreement with public agencies . . . Lab §6112
Public enterprise fund, organized as . . . Ins §11773
Public officials, payment of death benefits for assassinated . . . Lab §4725
Rating
Insurance premiums
Employers and employees, same rates for . . . Ins §11844
Establishment of rates . . . Ins §11820
Factors considered in setting rates . . . Ins §11821
Percentage basis of rates . . . Ins §11822
Reduced rate, willful misrepresentation to obtain . . . Ins §§1871.9, 11880
Reporting requirements
Accounting requirements, annual . . . Ins §11776
Legislature, annual report to . . . Ins §11805
Sale of assets and liabilities of fund . . . Ins §§11885 to 11886.2
Advisers, engaging
Applicability of certain provisions . . . Ins §11885.9
Process . . . Ins §11886
Qualifications . . . Ins §11886
Approvals of certain officers not required . . . Ins §11885.5
Deposit of proceeds of sale . . . Ins §11885.7
Directors
Participation by directors . . . Ins §11885.3
Finance director
Authority as to sale . . . Ins §11885
Deposit of proceeds of sale . . . Ins §11885.7
Reporting to joint legislative budget committee . . . Ins §11886.2
Goals of sale . . . Ins §11885
Same compensation and rates for employers and employees . . . Ins §11844
Securities of fund
Custodian, State Treasurer as . . . Ins §11788
Delivery of securities to State Treasurer . . . Ins §11790
Self-employed persons, policies for . . . Ins §11846
Special ledger account by State Controller . . . Ins §11800.2
State law, ability to insure under . . . Ins §11780
State teachers' retirement system, subrogation of claims under . . . Ed §24501
Subsequent injuries . . . Lab §4755
Surrender of policy, limitations on . . . Ins §11841
Temporary coverage . . . Ins §11841
Use of fund assets . . . Ins §11774

STATE GOVERNMENT EMPLOYMENT (See PUBLIC EMPLOYMENT)

STATE HOSPITALS
Vocational rehabilitation work assignments for patients
  Coverage . . . Lab §3370.1
    Attorney referral for patients . . . Lab §3371.1

STATE INDUSTRIAL ACCIDENT COMMISSION (See INDUSTRIAL ACCIDENTS DIVISION)

STATE MILITARY RESERVE
Benefit rights . . . Mil&Vet §520

STATE MILITIA
Military service (See MILITARY SERVICE)

STATE OFFICERS AND EMPLOYEES
Compensation and benefits
  Generally . . . Gov §19820

STATE TEACHERS' RETIREMENT SYSTEM
Subrogation
  Application of recovered amounts . . . Ed §24504
  Compromising claims . . . Ed §24503
  Contract for recovery of funds . . . Ed §24501
  Enforcement actions . . . Ed §24502
  Right of . . . Ed §24500
  Statutes of limitation . . . Ed §24505

STATISTICS
Rating organizations (See RATING ORGANIATIONS)

STATUTES OF LIMITATION . . . Lab §§5400 to 5410
Affirmative defense, as . . . Lab §5409
Appeals board (WCAB)
  Filing of documents with, rejection
    Restrictions on rejection when statute of limitations or jurisdictional time limitation implicated . . . 8 CCR §10617
Asbestos Workers Account . . . Lab §4413
Award, five year limitations period on alteration of . . . Lab §5804
California Insurance Guarantee Association . . . Ins §1063.15
Collection proceedings, time limits . . . Lab §§5405, 5406
  Asbestosis . . . Lab §5406.5
  Dependent death benefits
    Limitations period for commencement of proceedings to collect dependency death benefits . . . Lab §5406.7
  Employer misconduct, cases involving . . . Lab §5407
  HIV-related diseases, limitations on action regarding . . . Lab §5406.6
Criminal offenses
  Discovery of offense . . . Pen §803
Denial of claim, date of . . . 8 CCR §10142
Liens
  Limitation period for filing lien claim . . . Lab §4903.5
Occupational safety and health division
  Citations
    Time for issuance . . . Lab §6317
Public Employees' Retirement System subrogation . . . Gov §20255
Railroads . . . 45 USC §56
Shipping
  United States vessels or cargo, suits in admiralty involving . . . 46 USC §30905

STATUTES OF LIMITATION—Cont.
State teachers' retirement system, subrogation of claims under . . . Ed §24505
Tolling period and date of denial of claim . . . 8 CCR §10142
Workers' Compensation Division Information and Assistance Program, submissions to . . . Lab §5454

STAY OF EXECUTION
Appeals Board (WCAB) decision (See APPEALS BOARD (WCAB))

STEAM BOILERS
Death, imprisonment for causing . . . Lab §7771
Undue quantity of steam endangering human life . . . Lab §7770

STEEL FRAMED BUILDINGS
Applicable buildings . . . Lab §7251
Belts, safety . . . Lab §§7253, 7265
Column openings, covering . . . Lab §7257
Decking (See subhead: Flooring)
Definition of building . . . Lab §7250
Derricks, decking of . . . Lab §7252
Enforcement by Occupational Safety and Health Division . . . Lab §7267
Flooring
  Column openings, covering . . . Lab §7257
  Derricks, decking of . . . Lab §7252
  Extension of planks . . . Lab §7256
  Metal decking instead of wood planking . . . Lab §7258
  Removal of planks
    Instruction of workers prior to . . . Lab §7260
    Protection while removing planking . . . Lab §7262
    Temporary planking, removal of . . . Lab §7261
  Replacement of floor planks . . . Lab §7259
  Temporary floors (See subhead: Temporary floors)
  Working floors, decking of . . . Lab §7252
Nets, safety . . . Lab §7265
Penalties for violations regarding . . . Lab §7266
Safety belts . . . Lab §7253
Section of building as building . . . Lab §7264
Stability of frame, maintaining . . . Lab §7263
Temporary floors
  Construction of . . . Lab §7254
  Displacement protections . . . Lab §7255
  Protection during removal of . . . Lab §7262
  Removal of planking . . . Lab §7261
  Requirements, basic . . . Lab §7253
Working floors, decking of . . . Lab §7252

STEERERS
Insurance Frauds Prevention Act, use prohibited under . . . Ins §1871.7

STEVEDORES
Federal benefits in lieu of state benefits for . . . Har&N §6869
Longshore and Harbor Workers' Compensation Act (See LONGSHORE AND HARBOR WORKERS' COMPENSATION ACT)
Workers' compensation benefits for . . . Har&N §6276

Index

STIPULATIONS
Appeals Board (WCAB)
Forms required . . . 8 CCR §10500
Hearings . . . Lab §5702
Effect of stipulations . . . 8 CCR §10835

STIPULATIONS WITH REQUEST FOR AWARD FORMS
Compromise and release
Electronic adjudication management system (EAMS) . . . 8 CCR §10205.2
Electronic adjudication management system (EAMS) . . . 8 CCR §10205.2

STOCK OWNERSHIP
Financial interests in entities providing services
Conflicts of interest
Exceptions . . . Lab §139.32

STOP ORDERS
Appeal hearings and procedures . . . 8 CCR §15581
Contents . . . 8 CCR §15574
Decision following appeal hearing . . . 8 CCR §15590
Defined . . . 8 CCR §15559
Effective dates . . . 8 CCR §15571.5
Failure to observe
Injunctive relief for . . . 8 CCR §15573
Misdemeanor, as . . . 8 CCR §15572
Penalties and fines . . . Lab §3710.2
Injunctive relief against employers failing to observe . . . 8 CCR §15573
Insurance
Contractor failing to secure workers' compensation insurance
Barring use of employee labor . . . B&P §7127
Issuance of . . . 8 CCR §§15555, 15571, Lab §3710.1
Misdemeanor, failure to observe stop order as . . . 8 CCR §15572
Motor carriers, issued to . . . Lab §3710.3
Notice of findings on . . . 8 CCR §15556
Penalties and fines for failure to observe . . . Lab §3710.2
Personal service of . . . Lab §3731
Service
Generally . . . 8 CCR §15578
Personal service . . . Lab §3731
Withdrawal of . . . 8 CCR §15580, Lab §3727.1

STRESS
Medical treatment
Utilization schedule
Stress-related conditions . . . 8 CCR §9792.23.8

STRUCTURAL PEST CONTROL OPERATORS
Disciplinary proceedings against, grounds for . . . B&P §8636

STRUCTURAL STEEL FRAMED BUILDINGS (See STEEL FRAMED BUILDINGS)

SUBJECTIVE DISABILITY
Identification and degree of . . . 8 CCR §9727

SUBMERGED LANDS
Defined . . . 43 USC §1331

SUBMERGED LANDS—Cont.
Longshore and Harbor Workers' Compensation Act, applicability of . . . 43 USC §1333

SUBPOENAS
Appeals Board (WCAB)
Generally . . . Lab §132
Electronic records . . . 8 CCR §10534
Fees for witnesses . . . 8 CCR §10647
Issuance of . . . 8 CCR §10640
Medical witnesses . . . 8 CCR §10650
Notice to appear or produce . . . 8 CCR §10642
Business records as evidence
Custodian as witness of service of subpoena . . . Ev §1565
Transmittal of copies . . . Ev §1560
Labor Standards Enforcement Division hearings . . . 8 CCR §15588
Liens
Medical information
Non-physician claimants, subpoena for medical information . . . 8 CCR §10655
Medical records . . . Lab §4055.2
Penalties and fines
Civil penalty assessment and claims administration audit . . . 8 CCR §10113.6
Penalty assessment order appeals hearings . . . 8 CCR §15588
Records and recordkeeping
Electronic records, subpoena . . . 8 CCR §10644
Medical examinations, records . . . Lab §4055.2
Shipping
Public vessels, damages caused by or towage and salvage rendered to
Officers or crew, subpoena . . . 46 USC §31110
Stop order appeals hearings . . . 8 CCR §15588

SUBROGATION
Amount paid, evidence of . . . Lab §3854
Attorneys' fees . . . Lab §3856
Consolidation of actions . . . Lab §3853
County employees . . . Gov §31820
Court costs . . . Lab §3856
Death of employee, effect of . . . Lab §3851
Definition of employer and employee for purposes of . . . Lab §3850
Duplicate payments, liens against . . . Lab §3865
Effect of claim for compensation on third party actions . . . Lab §3852
Employer alone, action by . . . Lab §3854
Enforcement
Judgment lien by employer against third party, enforcement of . . . Lab §3862
State Teachers' Retirement System . . . Ed §24502
Evidence of amount paid . . . Lab §3854
Insurer's subrogation to employer rights . . . Ins §11662
Joinder of actions . . . Lab §3855
Judgment lien by employer against third party, enforcement of . . . Lab §3862
Liens for subsequent compensation paid by employer . . . Lab §3857
Public Employees' Retirement System (See PUBLIC EMPLOYEES' RETIREMENT SYSTEM)

SUBROGATION—Cont.
Recovery by injured worker credited to employer liability . . . Lab §3861
Reimbursement
Employer's claim for reimbursement on release or settlement . . . Lab §3860
Third parties . . . Lab §3864
Releases or settlements
Employer's claim for reimbursement . . . Lab §3860
Employer's release from further compensation . . . Lab §3858
Expenses related to . . . Lab §3860
Third party claims . . . Lab §3859
Validity of . . . Lab §§3859, 3860
Rights regarding
Employer rights, subrogation of insurer to . . . Ins §11662
Public Employees' Retirement System, right of subrogation under . . . Gov §20250
State Teachers' Retirement System . . . Ed §24500
Service of complaint on third party, copies of . . . Lab §3853
State teachers' retirement system (See STATE TEACHERS' RETIREMENT SYSTEM)

SUBSEQUENT INJURIES
Attorneys
Assignment of legal representation . . . Lab §4755
State, representation in cases of . . . Lab §4753.5
Cash revolving fund . . . Lab §4755
Claims adjustment services
Assignment in subsequent injuries cases . . . Lab §4755
Compromises regarding . . . Lab §4754.5
Computation of compensation for . . . Lab §4754
Cumulative injury (See CUMULATIVE INJURY)
Immigrant workers
Compensation not affected by immigration or citizenship status . . . Lab §4756
Form UEF-1 for . . . 8 CCR §15741
Limitations on . . . 8 CCR §15740
Longshore and Harbor Workers' Compensation Act . . . 33 USC §908
Lump-sum payments . . . Lab §5100.5
Payment of benefits . . . Lab §4754
Permanent partial disability, additions to . . . Lab §4751
Reduction of additional compensation for . . . Lab §4753
Reimbursements . . . Lab §4754
Releases . . . Lab §4754.5
Special additional compensation for . . . Lab §4754
State Compensation Insurance Fund . . . Lab §4755
Work capacity guidelines for combined or multiple disabilities . . . Table 11

SUBSEQUENT INJURIES BENEFITS TRUST FUND
Allocation among insured and self-insured employers . . . 8 CCR §15602
Applications to . . . 8 CCR §10462
Assessment
Allocation among insured and self-insured employers . . . 8 CCR §15602
Collection
Advanced collection, insured employers . . . 8 CCR §15606

SUBSEQUENT INJURIES BENEFITS TRUST FUND—Cont.
Assessment—Cont.
Collection—Cont.
Insured employers . . . 8 CCR §15607
Interim assessments . . . 8 CCR §15611
Determination of assessment . . . 8 CCR §§15601, 15603
Self-insured employers, from . . . 8 CCR §15605
Created . . . Lab §62.5
Definitions pertinent to . . . 8 CCR §15600
Medical reports . . . 8 CCR §10462
Purpose . . . Lab §62.5
Service of documents directed to . . . 8 CCR §10632
Surcharges to provide funds . . . Lab §62.5
Collection
Excess collections . . . 8 CCR §15608
Insured employers, from . . . 8 CCR §15607
Interim assessments . . . 8 CCR §15611
Self-insured employers, from . . . 8 CCR §15605
Determination of assessment or surcharge . . . 8 CCR §15603
Surplus in funding . . . 8 CCR §15604

SUBSEQUENT INJURIES FUND
Change of name to subsequent injuries benefits trust fund . . . Lab §62.5
Generally (See SUBSEQUENT INJURIES BENEFITS TRUST FUND)

SUBSIDIARIES
Self-insurance
Agreement of assumption and guarantee of liability for certificate of . . . 8 CCR §15203.1
Certificates
Definition of subsidiary certificate . . . 8 CCR §15201
Interim certificates . . . 8 CCR §15205
Security deposits . . . 8 CCR §15211

SUBSISTENCE ALLOWANCE
Vocational rehabilitation for public employees . . . Lab §6203

SUBSTANCE ABUSE
App-based drivers and services
Driving under the influence
ero tolerance policies . . . B&P §7460
Conditions of employer liability for compensation . . . Lab §3600
Disability benefits (See DISABILITY BENEFITS)

SUBVERSIVE ACTS
Foreign employment by contractors with U.Sworking outside U.S . . . 42 USC §1712

SUCCESSIVE PAYMENTS
Ten percent weekly interest . . . Table 6

SUICIDE
Conditions of employer liability for compensation . . . Lab §3600

SUITS IN ADMIRALTY ACT
United States vessels or cargo, suits in admiralty involving . . . 46 USC §§30901 to 30913 (See SHIPPING)

SUMMARY JUDGMENT
Appeals board (WCAB) . . . 8 CCR §10515

SUMMARY RATING DETERMINATIONS
Permanent disability (See PERMANENT DISABILITY)

SUNDAYS
Appeals board (WCAB)
Extensions of time . . . 8 CCR §10600
Discovery, effect on time limits for . . . CCP §2016.060

SUPPLEMENTAL JOB DISPLACEMENT BENEFITS . . . 8 CCR §§10133.31 to 10133.60
Alternative work
Offer of modified or alternative work
Failure to accept, employer not liable for benefits . . . Lab §4658.6
Notice . . . 8 CCR §§9813.1, 10133.34, 10133.35, 10133.53
Approved training facilities
Criteria for state approval . . . 8 CCR §10133.58
Definitions . . . 8 CCR §10116.9
Description of employee job duties form
Sending form to physician prior to medical evaluation . . . 8 CCR §10133.33
Dispute resolution . . . 8 CCR §10133.54
Request for dispute resolution before administrative director
Form . . . 8 CCR §10133.55
Electronic adjudication management system (EAMS) . . . 8 CCR §10116.1
Converting paper files to electronic . . . 8 CCR §10116.6
Electronic filing exemption . . . 8 CCR §10116.2
Injury or findings required to file . . . 8 CCR §10116.8
Misfiled or misdirected documents . . . 8 CCR §10116.7
Review of orders issued administrative director . . . 8 CCR §10208.11
Technical problems with filing . . . 8 CCR §10116.5
Eligibility . . . 8 CCR §10133.56, Lab §4658.5
2013, injuries occurring in or after . . . Lab §4658.7
Filing requirements . . . 8 CCR §10116.1
Converting paper files to electronic . . . 8 CCR §10116.6
Electronic filing exemption . . . 8 CCR §10116.2
Incomplete filings . . . 8 CCR §10116.3
Injury or findings required to file . . . 8 CCR §10116.8
Misfiled or misdirected documents . . . 8 CCR §10116.7
Retention of files . . . 8 CCR §10116.6
Technical problems with filing . . . 8 CCR §10116.5
Jurisdiction
Injury or findings required to file . . . 8 CCR §10116.8
Misfiled or misdirected documents . . . 8 CCR §10116.7
Modified work
Offer of modified or alternative work
Failure to accept, employer not liable for benefits . . . Lab §4658.6
Notice . . . 8 CCR §§9813.1, 10133.34, 10133.35, 10133.53
Notice . . . 8 CCR §9813.1
Offer of modified or alternative work . . . 8 CCR §9813.1
Form . . . 8 CCR §§10133.35, 10133.53

SUPPLEMENTAL JOB DISPLACEMENT BENEFITS—Cont.
Offer of modified or alternative work
Injuries occurring from 2004 to 2012 . . . 8 CCR §10133.53
Injuries occurring in 2013 and beyond . . . 8 CCR §10133.34
Form . . . 8 CCR §10133.35
Notice . . . 8 CCR §9813.1
Form . . . 8 CCR §§10133.35, 10133.53
Reporting requirements . . . 8 CCR §10116.1
Injury or findings required to file . . . 8 CCR §10116.8
Return-to-work report
Physician's return-to-work & voucher report . . . 8 CCR §10133.36
Termination of administrator liability for benefit . . . 8 CCR §10133.60
Vocational & return to work counselor (VRTWC)
List . . . 8 CCR §10133.59
Vouchers for training, nontransferable . . . Lab §§4658.5 to 4658.7
Eligibility . . . 8 CCR §10133.56
Form
Injuries occurring from 2004 to 2012 . . . 8 CCR §10133.57
Termination of administrator liability for benefit . . . 8 CCR §10133.60
Vouchers, injuries occurring from 2013 forward
Form . . . 8 CCR §10133.32
Issuance . . . 8 CCR §10133.31
Physician's return-to-work & voucher report . . . 8 CCR §10133.36

SUPPLEMENTAL JOB DISPLACEMENT NONTRANSFERABLE TRAINING VOUCHER FORM . . . 8 CCR §10133.57
Injuries occurring from 2013 forward . . . 8 CCR §10133.32

SUPPORT OBLIGATIONS
Admissibility of evidence . . . Ev §1567
Child support (See CHILD SUPPORT)
Workers' compensation award applied to support judgment . . . CCP §704.160

SURGEONS
Acupuncturists not regarded as . . . Lab §3209.9

SURGICAL TREATMENT
Medical treatment generally (See MEDICAL TREATMENT)
Official medical fee schedule . . . 8 CCR §§9789.16.1 to 9789.16.8 (See OFFICIAL MEDICAL FEE SCHEDULE)

SURVEYS
Employer's records of occupational injury or illness
Annual OSHA injury and illness survey . . . 8 CCR §14300.41
Health care organizations (HCOs)
Medical surveys (See HEALTH CARE ORGANIATIONS (HCOS))

SURVIVORS' RIGHTS
Generally . . . Lab §2803
Death benefits (See DEATH BENEFITS)

SURVIVORS' RIGHTS—Cont.
Railroads . . . 45 USC §59
School district payments to surviving spouse of murdered employee . . . Ed §44017

SUSPENDED SCAFFOLDING
Requirements for . . . Lab §7151

SUSPENSION OF DECISION, ORDER, OR AWARD
Appeals Board (WCAB) order, decision, or award suspended by filing petition for reconsideration . . . Lab §5910
Occupational Safety and Health Appeals Board decision suspended by filing for reconsideration . . . Lab §6625

SUSPENSION OF LICENSE, PERMIT, OR CERTIFICATION
Cranes
License to certify crane safety . . . Lab §7376
Tower crane permits . . . Lab §7374
Health care organization (HCO) certification . . . 8 CCR §9779.2
Insurance license suspended for failure to maintain insurance . . . B&P §7125.2
Rating organizations
Suspension or revocation of license . . . Ins §§11754.2 to 11754.4
Tower crane permits . . . Lab §7374

SWEARING IN (See OATHS)

SWIMMING POOL EXCAVATIONS
Shoring, bracing, and sloping regulations . . . Lab §6705.5

SYSTEMATIC ALIEN VERIFICATION FOR ENTITLEMENTS (SAVE) SYSTEM
Uninsured employers fund and subsequent injuries fund benefits for aliens . . . 8 CCR §15740

T

TABLES (See SCHEDULES, CHARTS, AND TABLES)

TANKS AND BOILERS
Penalties and fines
Steam boilers
Death, imprisonment for causing . . . Lab §7771
Undue quantity of steam endangering human life . . . Lab §7770
Steam boilers (See STEAM BOILERS)

TARGETED JOBS TAX CREDIT
Vocational rehabilitation . . . W&I §19005.5

TAXATION
Credit against tax for vocational rehabilitation . . . W&I §19005.5
Exclusions from gross income
Federal law . . . 26 USC §§101, 104
Federal taxes (See FEDERAL GOVERNMENT AND LAW)
Gross income, items excluded from
Federal law . . . 26 USC §§101, 104
Personal income tax, items excluded from gross income for purposes of
Federal law . . . 26 USC §§101, 104

TAXATION—Cont.
Port drayage motor carriers
Tax assessments or liens
Unsatisfied obligations, posting . . . Lab §2810.4
Targeted jobs tax credit for vocational rehabilitation . . . W&I §19005.5

TAXICABS
Workers' compensation insurance rates
Underreporting of exposure, report on . . . Ins §11759.2

TD (See TEMPORARY DISABILITY)

TEACHERS (See STATE TEACHERS' RETIREMENT SYSTEM)

TELEHEALTH
Qualified medical evaluators (QMES)
Evaluations using telehealth
Emergency regulation, COVID-19 . . . 8 CCR §46.2

TELEPHONES
Depositions
Remote electronic means of taking oral depositions . . . CCP §2025.310

TELEVISION INDUSTRY
Occupational Safety and Health Division permit requirements . . . Lab §6500

TEMP AGENCIES
Labor law compliance
Funding in contract to be sufficient for contractor to comply with labor laws . . . Lab §2810
Newly hired employees
Notice by employer to new hire concerning pay, allowances, payday, contact information, etc . . . Lab §2810.5
Premium payments . . . Lab §3302
Self-insurance
Certificate of consent to self-insure
Restrictions on issuance . . . Lab §3701.9
Rulemaking on obligations of self-insurers . . . Lab §3702.10

TEMPORARY DISABILITY
Aggregate disability payments
Single injury . . . Lab §4656
Alternative work
Defined . . . Lab §4658.1
Appeals board (WCAB)
Petition to terminate liability for indemnity
Forms required . . . 8 CCR §10500
Both temporary and permanent disability . . . Lab §4661
Both total and partial temporary disability . . . Lab §4655
California State University personnel (See CALIFORNIA STATE UNIVERSITY)
Computation (See COMPUTATION OF WORKERS' COMPENSATION)
Family care leave, paid . . . UI §§3300 to 3306 (See FAMILY CARE LEAVE, PAID)
Firefighters (See FIREFIGHTERS)

TEMPORARY DISABILITY—Cont.
Fraudulent receipt, notice of penalties and prosecution for . . . Ins §1871.8
Highway patrol (See HIGHWAY PATROL)
Justice Department employees (See JUSTICE DEPARTMENT)
Longshore and Harbor Workers' Compensation Act . . . 33 USC §908
Maximum period for . . . Lab §4656
Modified work
  Defined . . . Lab §4658.1
Notices as to benefits and payments . . . 8 CCR §9812
Partial (See TEMPORARY PARTIAL DISABILITY)
Payment, notice of . . . 8 CCR §9812
Police (See POLICE)
Rates, calculating . . . Table 19
Regular work
  Defined . . . Lab §4658.1
Salary continuation, notice of . . . 8 CCR §9814
San Francisco Port Commission employees (See SAN FRANCISCO PORT COMMISSION)
Schedules, charts, tables, and forms
  Calculating rates . . . Table 19
  Minimum/maximum benefits for temporary total disability . . . Table 14
School district employees . . . Ed §44043
Total (See TEMPORARY TOTAL DISABILITY)
University of California
  Fire department employees (See UNIVERSITY OF CALIFORNIA)
  Law enforcement officers (See UNIVERSITY OF CALIFORNIA)

TEMPORARY EMPLOYMENT AGENCIES
Labor law compliance
  Funding in contract to be sufficient for contractor to comply with labor laws . . . Lab §2810
Premium payments . . . Lab §3302

TEMPORARY PARTIAL DISABILITY
Amount of benefit . . . Lab §4654
Longshore and Harbor Workers' Compensation Act . . . 33 USC §908
Lost wages . . . Lab §4657, Table 19
Rate, calculating . . . Table 19

TEMPORARY RESTRAINING ORDERS
Occupational Safety and Health Division
  Generally . . . Lab §6324
  Elevators, dangerous operation without permit . . . Lab §7303
  Permit requirements . . . Lab §6510

TEMPORARY TOTAL DISABILITY
Amount of benefit . . . Lab §4653
Longshore and Harbor Workers' Compensation Act . . . 33 USC §908
Minimum/maximum benefits . . . Table 14
Termination of liability, petition for . . . 8 CCR §10540
Two or more years after injury, payment made following . . . Lab §4661.5

TEMPORARY VARIANCES
Occupational safety and health standards, from (See OCCUPATIONAL SAFETY AND HEALTH STANDARDS BOARD)

TERMINATION OF BENEFITS
Asbestos workers . . . Lab §4411
Denial of termination petition . . . Lab §4607
Notice regarding . . . 8 CCR §9812

TERMINATION OF DISABILITY
Petition alleging termination or decrease in disability
  Denial . . . Lab §4651.3
  Limitations . . . Lab §4651.2
  Presumptions . . . Lab §4651.1

TERMINATION OF EMPLOYMENT
Firefighters and law enforcement officers injured following termination of active service . . . Lab §4458.5
Injury, date of . . . Lab §3600
Qualified medical evaluators (QMEs) . . . Lab §139.2

TERMINATION OF INSURANCE
Group self-insurance membership, termination of . . . 8 CCR §15480
Voluntary plan termination, employee eligibility for Unemployment Compensation Disability Fund benefits on . . . UI §3263

TERMINATION OF LIABILITY
Petition for (See APPEALS BOARD (WCAB))

TERRITORIES AND POSSESSIONS OF UNITED STATES
Railroads . . . 45 USC §51

TERRORISM
Domestic terrorism
  Nurse case manager support to obtain medically necessary treatment . . . Lab §4600.05

TESTS, EXAMINATIONS, AND EVALUATIONS
Agreed medical evaluators (AMEs) (See AGREED MEDICAL EVALUATORS (AMES))
Breathing apparatus, Occupational Safety and Health Division testing of . . . Lab §6331
Chemical plants, testing procedures for . . . Lab §7864
Comprehensive medical-legal evaluations (See MEDICAL-LEGAL EXPENSES)
Diagnostic tests, fee schedule for . . . Lab §4626
Disability evaluations (See DISABILITY)
Gasoline, vapor emissions test procedures for vehicles transporting . . . Lab §6718
Health care organization (HCO) medical surveys
  Evaluation reports . . . 8 CCR §9778
  Regular and additional or nonroutine examinations . . . 8 CCR §§9771.79, 9771.80
Independent medical examiners (IMEs) (See INDEPENDENT MEDICAL EXAMINERS (IMES))
Medical examinations (See MEDICAL EXAMINATIONS)
Mine and tunnel precautions
  Testing for gas or vapors (See MINING AND TUNNELING)
Occupational Safety and Health Standards Board evaluation of variances and standards from other sources . . . Lab §147
Physicals (See MEDICAL EXAMINATIONS)
Qualified medical evaluators (See QUALIFIED MEDICAL EVALUATORS (QMES))

TESTS, EXAMINATIONS, AND EVALUATIONS—Cont.
Rating organizations
Examination (See RATING ORGANIATIONS)
Refineries, testing procedures for . . . Lab §7864

THEATERS
Occupational Safety and Health Division permit requirements . . . Lab §6500

THIRD PARTIES
Asbestos workers . . . Lab §4417
Longshore and Harbor Workers' Compensation Act, liability under . . . 33 USC §933
Public Employees' Retirement System subrogation . . . Gov §§20252, 20253
Self-insured claims administration . . . 8 CCR §15450.1
Service of complaint, copies of . . . Lab §3853
State Compensation Insurance Fund recovery of public employment expenditures from . . . Lab §6115
Subrogation (See SUBROGATION)
Uninsured Employers Fund payments and third party liability . . . Lab §3732

TIME
Appeals Board (WCAB) (See APPEALS BOARD (WCAB))
Arbitration proceedings . . . Lab §5276
Claims procedures (See CLAIMS PROCEDURES)
Collection proceedings (See COLLECTION PROCEEDINGS)
Cumulative injury, date of . . . Lab §5412
Days between two dates, number of . . . Table 9
Denial of claim, date of . . . 8 CCR §10142
Disability benefits (See DISABILITY BENEFITS)
Disability evaluations, time limits for performing evaluations of . . . Lab §4051
Completion of examination . . . Lab §4062.5
Qualified medical evaluators (QMEs), time guidelines . . . 8 CCR §§49 to 49.9 (See QUALIFIED MEDICAL EVALUATORS (QMES))
Discovery
Saturday, Sunday or holiday, deadline falling on . . . CCP §2016.060
Election of compensation liability, time period covered by statement of . . . Lab §4152
Hazardous substances provisions, effective date of . . . Lab §6399.2
HIV-related diseases, time limits on claims for . . . Lab §5406.6
Injury
Date of . . . Lab §§5411, 5412
Loss of time, involving . . . Lab §138.4
Interpreter services, payment for . . . 8 CCR §9795.4
Longshore and Harbor Workers' Compensation Act
Filing claims under . . . 33 USC §913
Payment of benefits . . . 33 USC §914
Medical examinations (See MEDICAL EXAMINATIONS)
Occupational disease, date of . . . Lab §5412
Occupational Safety and Health Appeals Board (See OCCUPATIONAL SAFETY AND HEALTH APPEALS BOARD)

TIME—Cont.
Occupational Safety and Health Division penalties, time limits on action to collect . . . Lab §6651
Occupational safety and health standards, time limits on appeals of temporary variances from . . . Lab §6455
Payment of benefits (See PAYMENT OF BENEFITS)
Prison inmates' occupational disease or injury, reporting . . . 8 CCR §§14904, 14913
Qualified medical evaluators (QMEs) (See QUALIFIED MEDICAL EVALUATORS (QMES))
Rating organization license, duration of . . . Ins §11751.2
Self-insurance certificate, validity of . . . 8 CCR §15203.6
Statutes of limitation (See STATUTES OF LIMITATION)
Stop order, effective date of . . . 8 CCR §15571.5
United States as defendant, time for commencing action against . . . 28 USC §2401

TISSUE BANKS
Disclosures of patient information to . . . CC §56.10

TOLLING PERIOD
Denial of claim, date of . . . 8 CCR §10142

TOM CARRELL MEMORIAL TUNNEL AND MINE SAFETY ACT
Designation of Code provisions as . . . Lab §7950

TORT CLAIMS AGAINST UNITED STATES
Administrative adjustment of claims . . . 28 USC §2672
Arbitration of claim . . . 28 USC §2677
Attorney general
Compromise, settlement, or arbitration by . . . 28 USC §2677
Defense of suits by . . . 28 USC §2679
Attorneys' fees . . . 28 USC §2678
Compromise . . . 28 USC §2677
Definitions pertinent to . . . 28 USC §2671
Exclusiveness of remedy . . . 28 USC §2679
Joint powers agreement between public agencies . . . Gov §6516
Judgments in action by district court as bar to . . . 28 USC §2676
Liability of United States . . . 28 USC §2674
Penalties and fines . . . 28 USC §2678
Prerequisite, denial by public agency as . . . 28 USC §2675
Public agencies (See PUBLIC AGENCIES)
Settlement of claim . . . 28 USC §2677

TOTAL DISABILITY
Permanent (See PERMANENT TOTAL DISABILITY)
Temporary (See TEMPORARY TOTAL DISABILITY)

TOWAGE SERVICES
Suits against United States for (See SHIPPING)

TOWER CRANES
Definitions . . . Lab §7371
Inspections and inspectors
Employment of inspectors . . . Lab §7372
Establishment of program . . . Lab §7372
Priority of inspections . . . Lab §7370
Permits
Issuance of . . . Lab §7373
Requirements . . . Lab §7373
Suspension or revocation of . . . Lab §7374

TOWER CRANES—Cont.
Permits—Cont.
Validity of . . . Lab §7373
Presence of safety representative for installing, dismantling, or jumping cranes . . . Lab §7382

TOXIC MATERIALS
Information repository on . . . Lab §147.2
Standards . . . Lab §144.6

TPD
Temporary partial disability (See TEMPORARY PARTIAL DISABILITY)

TRADE, BUSINESS, PROFESSION, OR OCCUPATION
Employment relations under Labor Code . . . Lab §3356

TRADE SECRETS
Discovery actions concerning
Method and sequence of discovery . . . CCP §2019.210
Petroleum refinery turnarounds, occupational safety and health
When refinery turnaround information considered trade secret . . . Lab §7873
Privilege to refuse disclosure . . . Ev §915
Protection from disclosure of . . . Lab §6396

TRAINEES WITH MILITARY SERVICE
Disability benefits for (See DISABILITY BENEFITS)

TRAINING
Injury prevention programs . . . Lab §6401.7
Mine and tunnel rescues . . . Lab §7958
Refinery and chemical plant safety and health hazard training . . . Lab §7861
Safety training programs . . . Lab §6352

TRAMWAYS
Passenger tramways . . . Lab §§7340 to 7357 (See PASSENGER TRAMWAYS)

TRANSCRIPTS
Appeals Board (WCAB) (See APPEALS BOARD (WCAB))
Workers' Compensation Division fees for copies of records and transcripts . . . 8 CCR §9990

TRANSPORTATION
Financial interests in entities providing services . . . Lab §139.32
Motor vehicles (See MOTOR VEHICLES)

TRANSPORTATION NETWORK COMPANIES (TNC)
App-based drivers and services . . . B&P §§7448 to 7467 (See APP-BASED DRIVERS AND SERVICES)

TRAUMA
Brain injuries
Medical treatment utilization schedule
Traumatic brain injury guideline . . . 8 CCR §9792.24.5
Witnesses, unavailability due to physical or emotional trauma . . . Ev §240

TRAVEL EXPENSES
Judges (WCJs) . . . 8 CCR §9721.2

TREATING PHYSICIAN
Bias, finding of . . . Lab §4068
Choice of physician (See PHYSICIANS)
Cosignature of treating physician required . . . Lab §3209.10
Dispute resolution . . . 8 CCR §9785
Educational materials for treating physicians
Preparation by administrative director . . . Lab §4062.8
Findings
Bias . . . Lab §4068
Injury, report of . . . Lab §6409
Medical provider networks . . . 8 CCR §§9767.1 to 9767.16, Lab §§4616 to 4616.7 (See MEDICAL PROVIDER NETWORKS)
Medical treatment utilization schedule
Out-of-schedule treatment
Medical evidence search sequence . . . 8 CCR §9792.21.1
New treating physician
Designation . . . 8 CCR §9785
Occupational disease, report of . . . Lab §6409
Opinion of, value and weight given to . . . Lab §4061.5
Payment for medical treatment provided by . . . Lab §4603.2
Permanent and stationary report, form of treating physician's . . . 8 CCR §§9785.3, 9785.4
Services beginning October 1, 2015 . . . 8 CCR §9785.4.1
Petition for change of primary treating physician
Appeal of grant or denial of petition to change . . . 8 CCR §9787
Form . . . 8 CCR §9786.1
Procedure . . . 8 CCR §9786
Response to petition, form of . . . 8 CCR §9786.1
Progress report, form of treating physician's . . . 8 CCR §9785.2
Reporting duties of primary treating physician . . . 8 CCR §9785
Return to work & voucher report . . . 8 CCR §9785
Summary permanent disability rating determination report for unrepresented injured worker . . . 8 CCR §10160.1
Utilization review, mandatory availability of services during business hours for . . . Lab §4600.4

TREATMENT FOR MEDICAL CONDITIONS (See MEDICAL TREATMENT)

TRENCH EXCAVATIONS
Bids for local government projects involving . . . Lab §6707
Permits per project, number allowed for . . . Lab §6706
Restrictions on contracts involving . . . Lab §6705

TRIAL . . . 8 CCR §10787
Failure to appear at trial in case in chief . . . 8 CCR §10756
Lien trials . . . 8 CCR §§10875, 10880

TRUSTEES
Death benefits . . . Lab §4705
Group self-insurance, board of trustees for . . . 8 CCR §15475
Definition of board of trustees . . . 8 CCR §15201

TRUSTEES—Cont.
Lump-sum payments
Deposited lump sum, payments from . . . Lab §5103
Preference in appointment of trustee . . . Lab §5104

TRUST FUNDS
Voluntary disability benefit plan employee contributions treated as . . . UI §3261

TRUTH IN ADVERTISING ACT
Definition of advertiser . . . Lab §5434
Disclosure requirements . . . Lab §5433
Notice requirements . . . Lab §5432
Penalties and fines . . . Lab §5434
Purpose of Act . . . Lab §5431
Title of Act . . . Lab §5430

TUBERCULOSIS
Corrections Department employees . . . Lab §3212.10
Employer's records of occupational injury or illness . . . 8 CCR §14300.11
Justice Department employees . . . Lab §3212.7
Police officers, firefighters, and correctional officers . . . Lab §3212.6

TUNNELING (See MINING AND TUNNELING)

U

UNDERGROUND ECONOMY, JOINT ENFORCEMENT STRIKE FORCE
Public works
Payroll records
Access of strike force to records upon request . . . Lab §1776

UNEMPLOYMENT COMPENSATION
Benefits
Availability for employment . . . UI §1255.5
Definitions
Benefits . . . UI §§128, 140.5
Unemployment compensation disability benefits . . . UI §140.5
Disability (See subhead: Disability benefits)
Handicapped and disabled persons
Workers' compensation benefits, effect . . . UI §1255.5
Interim cash payments leading to ineligibility for . . . UI §1255.5
Overpayments
Disability benefits (See DISABILITY BENEFITS)
Liability for . . . UI §1375.3
Contributions
Defined . . . UI §144
Disability benefits (See DISABILITY BENEFITS)
Rates and percentages . . . UI §984
Definitions
Benefits . . . UI §§128, 140.5
Contributions . . . UI §144
Unemployment compensation disability benefits . . . UI §140.5
Unemployment Compensation Disability Fund (See UNEMPLOYMENT COMPENSATION DISABILITY FUND)

UNEMPLOYMENT COMPENSATION—Cont.
Disability benefits
Contributions (See DISABILITY BENEFITS)
Overpayments (See DISABILITY BENEFITS)
Disability fund (See UNEMPLOYMENT COMPENSATION DISABILITY FUND)
Employing unit
Merger, acquisition, or change of organization . . . UI §3254.5
Family care leave, paid . . . UI §§3300 to 3306 (See FAMILY CARE LEAVE, PAID)
Joint powers agreement between public agencies . . . Gov §6516
Liens on . . . 8 CCR §10899, Lab §4904
Overpayments, liability for . . . UI §1375.3
Paid family care leave . . . UI §§3300 to 3305 (See FAMILY CARE LEAVE, PAID)
Public agencies, joint powers agreement between . . . Gov §6516
Rates for contributions . . . UI §984
Small-business-third-party administrator (SBTPA) . . . UI §3254.1

UNEMPLOYMENT COMPENSATION DISABILITY FUND
Contributions to
Designations for . . . UI §144
State employees . . . UI §2783
Definitions
Contributions to Fund . . . UI §144
Termination of voluntary plan, employee eligibility for Disability Fund benefits on . . . UI §3263
Voluntary plan benefits simultaneous with benefits from . . . UI §3253

UNEMPLOYMENT WORK RELIEF PROGRAMS
Average earnings of participants, computing . . . Lab §4456

UNIFORM BUSINESS RECORDS AS EVIDENCE ACT . . . Ev §§1270 to 1272

UNINSURED EMPLOYER IDENTIFICATION . . . Lab §90.3

UNINSURED EMPLOYERS BENEFITS TRUST FUND
Action for failure of employer to secure payment, copy of . . . Lab §3708
Administrative expenses
Reimbursement . . . Lab §§3716, 3716.1
Allocation among insured and self-insured employers . . . 8 CCR §15602
Asbestos workers, recovery of benefits paid to . . . Lab §4412
Assessments
Allocation among insured and self-insured employers . . . 8 CCR §15602
Collection
Advanced collection, insured employers . . . 8 CCR §15606
Insured employers, from . . . 8 CCR §15607
Interim assessments . . . 8 CCR §15611
Self-insured employers, from . . . 8 CCR §15605

Index

UNINSURED EMPLOYERS BENEFITS TRUST FUND—Cont.
Assessments—Cont.
Determination of assessment . . . 8 CCR §§15601, 15603
Cash revolving fund . . . Lab §3728
Certificate of cancellation of lien on payment . . . Lab §3721
Certificate that employer is uninsured . . . Lab §3720
Corporate liability to . . . Lab §3717
Created . . . Lab §62.5
Definitions pertinent to . . . 8 CCR §15600
Prima facie illegally uninsured employer, parent, or substantial shareholder . . . 8 CCR §15710
Substantial shareholders and parents . . . 8 CCR §15710, Lab §3717
Uninsured employer defined . . . 8 CCR §15560
Delegation of authority
Determinations, authority to make . . . 8 CCR §15711
Hearings, authority to hold . . . 8 CCR §15731
Determinations
Generally . . . 8 CCR §15720
Finality
Prima facie illegally uninsured employers, determinations regarding . . . 8 CCR §15722
Prima facie parent or substantial shareholders, determinations regarding . . . 8 CCR §15723
Negative inferences . . . 8 CCR §15721
Prima facie illegally uninsured employer status . . . 8 CCR §15723, Lab §3715
Prima facie parent or substantial shareholder status . . . Lab §3720.1
Reconsideration of
Prima facie illegally uninsured employers . . . 8 CCR §15722
Prima facie parent or substantial shareholders, determinations regarding . . . 8 CCR §15723
Director of Industrial Relations Department
Delegation of authority by
Determinations, authority to make . . . 8 CCR §15711
Hearings, authority to hold . . . 8 CCR §15731
Powers of . . . Lab §3710
Enforcement of judgment against uninsured employer . . . Lab §3716.3
Filing
Procedures for cases involving Fund . . . Lab §3714
Weekend or holiday filing rule . . . Lab §3730
Hearings
Generally . . . 8 CCR §15730
Conduct of hearing . . . 8 CCR §15732
Delegation of authority regarding . . . 8 CCR §15731
Procedures . . . Lab §3714
Representation at . . . Lab §3716.1
Immigration or citizenship status
Aliens, benefits for
Form UEF-1 for . . . 8 CCR §15741
Compensation not affected by immigration or citizenship status . . . Lab §3733
Limitations on benefits . . . 8 CCR §15740
Industrial Relations Director (See subhead: Director of Industrial Relations Department)
Investigations . . . Lab §3716.1

UNINSURED EMPLOYERS BENEFITS TRUST FUND—Cont.
Job classifications of payees, responsibility to designate . . . Lab §3716.5
Liability to . . . Lab §3717
Lien, certificate of cancellation of . . . Lab §3721
Lump-sum payment based on present worth of uninsured employer's future payments . . . Lab §5106
Medical treatment provided from . . . Lab §4903.3
Parent companies (See subhead: Substantial shareholders and parents)
Payments made by . . . Lab §§3716, 3716.2, 3732
Prima facie illegally uninsured employers
Defined . . . 8 CCR §15710
Determination of status . . . Lab §3715
Finality of determinations regarding . . . 8 CCR §15722
Reconsideration of determinations regarding . . . 8 CCR §15722
Prima facie parent or substantial shareholder
Defined . . . 8 CCR §15710
Determination of status . . . Lab §3720.1
Finality of determinations regarding . . . 8 CCR §15723
Reconsideration of determinations regarding . . . 8 CCR §15723
Proceedings . . . Lab §§3712, 3714, 3715
Purpose . . . Lab §§62.5, 3716
Reconsideration of determinations
Prima facie illegally uninsured employers . . . 8 CCR §15722
Prima facie parent or substantial shareholders, determinations regarding . . . 8 CCR §15723
Relief from obligation to pay further compensation following judgment . . . Lab §3709.5
Representation before . . . Lab §3716.1
Security conditions required following period of uninsurance . . . Lab §3701.7
Self-insurance conditions required following period of uninsurance . . . Lab §3701.7
Stop orders (See STOP ORDERS)
Substantial shareholders and parents
Board of Appeals determination of status . . . Lab §3717.2
Definitions pertinent to . . . 8 CCR §15710, Lab §3717
Joinder of action against uninsured employer . . . Lab §§3717.1, 3718
Prima facie parent or substantial shareholder (See subhead: Prima facie parent or substantial shareholder)
Suits against employers, compromise or prosecution of . . . Lab §3719
Surcharges to provide funds . . . Lab §62.5
Collection
Excess collections . . . 8 CCR §15608
Insured employers, from . . . 8 CCR §15607
Interim assessments . . . 8 CCR §15611
Self-insured employers, from . . . 8 CCR §15605
Determination of assessment or surcharge . . . 8 CCR §15603
Surplus in funding . . . 8 CCR §15604
Third party liability . . . Lab §3732

UNINSURED EMPLOYERS BENEFITS TRUST FUND—Cont.
Weekend or holiday filing rule . . . Lab §3730

UNINSURED EMPLOYERS FUND
Generally (See UNINSURED EMPLOYERS BENEFITS TRUST FUND)
Name changed to uninsured employers benefits trust fund . . . Lab §62.5

UNINSURED MOTORIST PROVISIONS
Reimbursement under . . . Ins §11580.2

UNIONS
Collective bargaining agreements (See COLLECTIVE BARGAINING AGREEMENTS)

UNITED STATES (See FEDERAL GOVERNMENT AND LAW)

UNIVERSITY OF CALIFORNIA
Fire department employees
  Arising out of employment/course of employment requirements . . . Lab §4804.2
  Heart disease, pneumonia, and hernias suffered by . . . Lab §3212.4
  Medical treatment . . . Lab §4804.3
  One year, disability continuing beyond . . . Lab §4804.4
  Paid leave of absence . . . Lab §4804.1
  Permanent disability . . . Lab §4804.4
  Salary payments, temporary disability payments concurrent with . . . Lab §4804.5
  Temporary disability
    Duty, occurring in course of . . . Lab §4804.2
    Eligibility for medical, surgical, and hospital benefits . . . Lab §4804.3
    One year, disability continuing beyond . . . Lab §4804.4
    Paid leave of absence . . . Lab §4804.1
    Salary payments, prohibition on benefits concurrent with . . . Lab §4804.5
First disability payment, timing of . . . Lab §4650.5
Law enforcement officers
  Arising out of employment/course of employment requirements . . . Lab §4807
  Back injury when required to wear duty belt . . . Lab §3213.2
  Heart disease and pneumonia suffered by . . . Lab §3213
  Medical treatment . . . Lab §4808
  One year, disability continuing beyond . . . Lab §4809
  Paid leave of absence . . . Lab §4806
  Permanent disability . . . Lab §4809
  Salary payments, temporary disability payments concurrent with . . . Lab §4810
  Temporary disability
    Duty, relationship of disability to . . . Lab §4807
    Eligibility for medical, surgical, and hospital benefits . . . Lab §4808
    One year, disability continuing beyond . . . Lab §4809
    Paid leave of absence for . . . Lab §4806

UNIVERSITY OF CALIFORNIA—Cont.
Law enforcement officers—Cont.
  Temporary disability—Cont.
    Salary payments, prohibition on benefits concurrent with . . . Lab §4810
Permanent disability
  Fire department employees . . . Lab §4804.4
  Law enforcement officers . . . Lab §4809
Safety violations, fines and penalties for . . . Lab §6434
Temporary disability
  Fire department employees (See subhead: Fire department employees)
  Law enforcement officers (See subhead: Law enforcement officers)

UNORGANIZED MILITIA
Military service (See MILITARY SERVICE)

UNPAID WAGES
Collection and disbursement of . . . Lab §96.7
Unpaid Wage Fund . . . Lab §96.6

UNREPRESENTED LIEN CLAIMANTS
Notice of nonrepresentation . . . 8 CCR §10868

UNREPRESENTED WORKERS
Electronic adjudication management system (EAMS)
  Electronic filing system rules
    Exemptions from electronic filing . . . 8 CCR §10206.2
Qualified medical evaluators (QMEs), examined by (See QUALIFIED MEDICAL EVALUATORS (QMES))
Summary permanent disability rating determination report
  Comprehensive medical evaluation . . . 8 CCR §10160
  Reconsideration of report . . . 8 CCR §10164
  Treating physician, report of . . . 8 CCR §10160.1

UNSAFE CONDITIONS (See SAFE WORKPLACE)

USER FUNDING ASSESSMENT
Self-insurers . . . 8 CCR §15232

UTILIZATION REVIEW
Medical treatment (See MEDICAL TREATMENT)

UTILIZATION SCHEDULE
Drugs, medical treatment utilization schedule (MTUS) . . . 8 CCR §§9792.27.1 to 9792.27.23 (See DRUGS, MEDICAL TREATMENT UTILIATION SCHEDULE (MTUS))
Medical treatment utilization schedule . . . 8 CCR §§9792.20 to 9792.26 (See MEDICAL TREATMENT)

V

VALLEY FEVER
Building and construction industry
    Training for Valley Fever awareness . . . Lab §6709

VAPOR EMISSIONS
Gasoline, vapor emissions test procedures for vehicles transporting . . . Lab §6718

VAPOR EMISSIONS—Cont.
Mining and tunneling
Testing for gas or vapors (See MINING AND TUNNELING)

VARIANCES
Employer's records of occupational injury or illness . . . 8 CCR §14300.38
Occupational safety and health standards, from (See OCCUPATIONAL SAFETY AND HEALTH STANDARDS BOARD)

VEHICLES (See MOTOR VEHICLES)

VENUE
Adjudication of claims
Applications for adjudication
Where to file . . . Lab §5501.5
Appeals board (WCAB)
Designation in case opening document . . . 8 CCR §10480
Division of workers' compensation employee filing application . . . 8 CCR §10482
Objection to venue
Attorney's place of business as basis for objection . . . 8 CCR §10488
Petition for change . . . 8 CCR §10490, Lab §5501.6
Electronic adjudication management system (EAMS)
Definition of venue . . . 8 CCR §10205
Insurance
Arbitration or dispute resolution
Disclosure to employer as to choice of law and venue when dispute resolution to be used . . . Ins §11658.5
Petition for change of . . . Lab §5501.6
Shipping
Public vessels, damages caused by or towage and salvage rendered to . . . 46 USC §31104
United States vessels or cargo, suits in admiralty involving . . . 46 USC §30906
United States as defendant . . . 28 USC §1402

VERIFIED STATEMENT
Contents
Direction to file verified statement . . . 8 CCR §15576
Verified statement . . . 8 CCR §15577
Definitions
Direction to file verified statement . . . 8 CCR §15551
Verified statement . . . 8 CCR §15561
Direction to file
Contents . . . 8 CCR §15576
Defined . . . 8 CCR §15551

VESSELS (See SHIPPING)

VETERANS (See MILITARY SERVICE)

VETERINARIANS
Emergency, liability during state of . . . Gov §8659

VICTIMS OF CRIME (See CRIME VICTIMS)

VIDEO
Appeals board (WCAB)
Exhibits generally . . . 8 CCR §10677

VIDEO—Cont.
Evidence, printed representation of video medium as . . . Ev §1553
Invasion of privacy . . . CC §1708.8

VIOLENCE
Crime victims (See CRIME VICTIMS)
Domestically abused aliens, uninsured employers fund and subsequent injuries fund benefits for . . . 8 CCR §15740
Health care workers, employers to keep record of violence against community . . . Lab §6332
Hospitals
Violence prevention plan . . . Lab §6401.8
Public Employees' Retirement System special death benefits . . . Gov §21540.5
Workplace violence
Nurse case manager support to obtain medically necessary treatment . . . Lab §4600.05

VISION
Presumption of total disability due to loss of . . . Lab §4662

VOC (VICTIMS OF CRIME) (See CRIME VICTIMS)

VOCATIONAL EXPERTS
Fee schedule
Establishment by administrative director . . . Lab §5307.7
Reports
Evidence, admissibility . . . 8 CCR §10685, Lab §5703

VOCATIONAL REHABILITATION
California State University personnel
Cooperation of injured worker, industrial disability leave payments contingent on . . . Ed §89529.09
Public employee provisions, inapplicability of . . . Ed §89529.06
Customary work, definition for retrained employee . . . UI §2626
Fee schedule . . . Lab §139.5
Forms (See FORMS)
Longshore and Harbor Workers' Compensation Act . . . 33 USC §§908, 939
Lump-sum payments . . . Lab §5100.6
Maintenance allowance (See VOCATIONAL REHABILITATION MAINTENANCE ALLOWANCE (VRMA))
Notices
Public employees, availability of rehabilitation for . . . Lab §6201
Prisoners, for . . . Pen §5069
Public employment (See PUBLIC EMPLOYMENT)
Return to work programs
False or fraudulent statements in connection with . . . Ins §1871.4
Schedules, charts, and tables pertinent to (See SCHEDULES, CHARTS, AND TABLES)
State hospitals
Vocational rehabilitation work assignments for patients
Attorney referral for patients . . . Lab §3371.1
Coverage . . . Lab §3370.1

VOCATIONAL REHABILITATION—Cont.
Tax credits, eligibility for . . . W&I §19005.5
Unit
Establishment of vocational rehabilitation unit . . . Lab §139.5
VRMA (See VOCATIONAL REHABILITATION MAINTENANCE ALLOWANCE (VRMA))

VOCATIONAL REHABILITATION MAINTENANCE ALLOWANCE (VRMA)
Computation of . . . Table 19
Longshore and Harbor Workers' Compensation Act . . . 33 USC §908

VOLATILE FLAMMABLE LIQUIDS
Defined . . . Lab §7800
Extinguishment of flames, provision of means of . . . Lab §7803

VOLUNTARY DISABILITY BENEFIT PLANS . . . UI §3251
Administrative costs, obligation to determine . . . UI §3269
Amendment of . . . UI §3271
Appeal of benefit denials . . . UI §3264
Applicability of specified articles to . . . UI §3272
Approval
Obtaining . . . UI §3254
Selection of risks, effective date for . . . UI §3270
Withdrawal of . . . UI §3262
Contributions . . . UI §3252
Generally . . . UI §3252
Trust fund, employee contributions treated as . . . UI §3261
Coverage under . . . UI §§3257, 3263
Credits . . . UI §3266
Deductions for . . . UI §§3256, 3260
Excess deductions . . . UI §3260.5
Increased deductions . . . UI §3260.5
Director of Employment Development Department
Administrative costs, obligation to determine . . . UI §3269
Determination of credits and refunds . . . UI §3265
Failure to pay, intercession in . . . UI §3265
Information, obligation to furnish . . . UI §3268
Disability Fund benefits available on termination of plan or coverage . . . UI §3263
Establishment of . . . UI §3257
Excess deductions . . . UI §3260.5
Failure to pay benefits . . . UI §3265
Increased deductions . . . UI §3260.5
Information
Availability of . . . UI §3267
Obligation to furnish . . . UI §3268
Insurer, substituted liability of . . . UI §3259
Merger or acquisition by other employing unit . . . UI §3254.5
Multiple employers . . . UI §3255
Refunds . . . UI §3266
Selection of risks, effective date for . . . UI §3270
Simultaneous Disability Fund and voluntary plan benefits . . . UI §3253
Small business third party administrator clients and employees
Single voluntary plan . . . UI §3254.1

VOLUNTARY DISABILITY BENEFIT PLANS—Cont.
Surety requirements . . . UI §3258
Termination of plan . . . UI §3263
Trust fund, employee contributions treated as . . . UI §3261
Withdrawal of approval . . . UI §3262

VOLUNTEERS
Emergency and disaster services
Disaster service workers employed by state agencies . . . Gov §8609
Liability for damages suffered by volunteers . . . Gov §8657
State agencies . . . Gov §8574.3
Firefighters . . . Lab §3361
Post-traumatic stress injury, coverage . . . Lab §3212.15
Juvenile Court
Regional youth facility, wards committed to . . . Lab §3364.7
Traffic offenders . . . Lab §3364.6
Wards . . . Lab §3364.55
Law enforcement officers . . . Lab §3364
Not-for-profit organizations . . . Lab §3363.6
Public agencies . . . Lab §3363.5
Recreation and park districts . . . Lab §3361.5
School districts . . . Lab §3364.5
Sexual harassment protection . . . Gov §12940
Sheriff's reserve . . . Lab §3364

VRMA (See VOCATIONAL REHABILITATION MAINTENANCE ALLOWANCE (VRMA))

W

WAGES, HOURS, AND WORKING CONDITIONS
App-based drivers and services
Earnings guarantee . . . B&P §7453
Hours of work
Rest requirements for drivers . . . B&P §7461
Claims
Labor standards enforcement division
Report to finance department on wage claims . . . Lab §96.1
Flexible spending accounts
Notice to employee of deadlines, employer duties . . . Lab §2810.7
Immigration status irrelevant to enforcement of employment law . . . Lab §1171.5
Labor contractor-client employer responsibilities . . . Lab §2810.3
Piece-rate basis of compensation . . . Lab §226.2
Sick days
Paid sick days . . . Lab §§245 to 249
Smoking in workplaces, OSHA standards . . . Lab §6404.5

WAIVERS
Appeals Board (WCAB) decision, irregularities waived by petition for reconsideration of . . . Lab §5904
Client employer-labor contractor responsibilities
Void and unenforceable nature of waivers . . . Lab §2810.3

Index

WAIVERS—Cont.
Election of compensation liability waived by worker . . . Lab §4154
Health care benefits . . . Lab §2804
Labor contractor-client employer responsibilities
Void and unenforceable nature of waivers . . . Lab §2810.3
Longshore and Harbor Workers' Compensation Act, waiver of rights under . . . 33 USC §915
Occupational Safety and Health Appeals Board decision, waiver of objections not set forth in petition for reconsideration of . . . Lab §6618

WALK-THROUGH DOCUMENTS . . . 8 CCR §10789

WARDS OF JUVENILE COURT (See MINORS)

WAREHOUSE CONTRACTORS
Labor law compliance
Funding in contract to be sufficient for contractor to comply with labor laws . . . Lab §2810

WAR-RISK HAZARD
Contractors with U.Sworking outside U.S . . . 42 USC §1701
Military bases overseas, employees of . . . 42 USC §1651

WATCHMEN
Employees, not considered to be . . . Lab §3358

WCAB (See APPEALS BOARD (WCAB))

WCJS (See JUDGES (WCJS))

WEEKLY AVERAGE EARNINGS (See AVERAGE EARNINGS)

WELFARE (See PUBLIC SOCIAL SERVICES)

WHARVES
Shipping generally (See SHIPPING)

WHEEL CRANES
Boomstops for . . . Lab §6704

WHISTLEBLOWER PROTECTION
Medical billing and provider fraud
Reports, protection of persons making . . . Lab §3823

WIDOWS AND WIDOWERS (See SPOUSES)

WILLFUL MISCONDUCT (See SERIOUS AND WILLFUL MISCONDUCT)

WILLIAM DALLAS JONES CANCER PRESUMPTION ACT OF 2010 . . . Lab §3212.1

WINDOW CLEANING SAFETY DEVICES
Alternative fixtures, approval of . . . Lab §7327
Building defined for purposes of . . . Lab §7325
Frame fixtures . . . Lab §7326
Occupational Safety and Health Division
Enforcement by . . . Lab §7332
Powers of . . . Lab §7331
Penalties and fines
Employers directing or permitting labor on windows without devices . . . Lab §7328

WINDOW CLEANING SAFETY DEVICES—Cont.
Penalties and fines—Cont.
Failure to provide safety devices . . . Lab §7330
Installation and maintenance of fixtures, failure to ensure . . . Lab §7329
Sill fixtures . . . Lab §7326

WITNESSES
Absence of . . . Ev §240
Adverse parties or witnesses
Spouse called as witness by . . . Ev §971
Adverse witnesses, examination of . . . Ev §776
Appeals Board (WCAB) hearings (See APPEALS BOARD (WCAB))
Business records, witnesses and custodians involved in production of
Applicable proceedings . . . Ev §1566
Custodian as witness of party serving first subpoena . . . Ev §1565
Fees and mileage for . . . Ev §1563
Personal attendance by . . . Ev §1564
Cross-examination
Depositions
Cross-examination of deponent . . . CCP §2025.330
Death
Unavailability because of . . . Ev §240
Exclusion from courtroom . . . Ev §777
Fees and mileage for
Appeals Board (WCAB) hearings . . . 8 CCR §10647, Lab §131
Business records, production of . . . Ev §1563
Depositions . . . CCP §2020.230
Longshore and Harbor Workers' Compensation Act . . . 33 USC §926
Subpoenas and fees . . . 8 CCR §10647
Illness
Unavailability because of . . . Ev §240
Impeachment and credibility
Privileges, evidentiary, inferences from exercise . . . Ev §913
Longshore and Harbor Workers' Compensation Act . . . 33 USC §§924, 925
Retaliatory discrimination against . . . Lab §132a
Trauma from crime, unavailable because of . . . Ev §240
Unavailability
Defined . . . Ev §240
Physical or mental trauma . . . Ev §240

WORK CAPACITY GUIDELINES
Table of . . . Table 11

WORKER CLASSIFICATION . . . Lab §§2775 to 2785
App-based drivers and services generally . . . B&P §§7448 to 7467 (See APP-BASED DRIVERS AND SERVICES)
Applicability of exceptions to classification preference . . . Lab §2785
Business-to-business contracting relationship
Exception to classification preference . . . Lab §2776
Construction industry, contractor and individual performing work pursuant to subcontract
Exception to classification preference . . . Lab §2781

WORKER CLASSIFICATION—Cont.
Data aggregators and individuals providing feedback
Exception to classification preference . . . Lab §2782
Employee *versus* **independent contractor . . . Lab §2775**
Declaratory of existing law, classification preference as . . . Lab §2785
Injunction to enforce provisions . . . Lab §2786
Motor clubs, relationship with individual performing services pursuant to contract between club and third party . . . Lab §2784
Professional services, contract for
Exception to classification preference . . . Lab §2778
Referral agency and service provider, relationship between
Exception to classification preference . . . Lab §2777
Severability of provisions . . . Lab §2787
Single-engagement event
Sole proprietor or business entity performing contract to provide services for single-engagement event . . . Lab §2779
Sound recordings or musical compositions, creation, marketing, promoting, etc
Exception to classification preference . . . Lab §2780
Specific occupations excepted from classification preference . . . Lab §2783

WORKERS' COMPENSATION ADMINISTRATION REVOLVING FUND (See ADMINISTRATION REVOLVING FUND)

WORKERS' COMPENSATION APPEALS BOARD (See APPEALS BOARD (WCAB))

WORKERS' COMPENSATION BOND FUND . . . Ins §§1063.70 to 1063.77 (See CALIFORNIA INSURANCE GUARANTEE ASSOCIATION (CIGA))

WORKERS' COMPENSATION DIVISION
Administration . . . Lab §124
Administrative assistance provided by
Generally . . . Lab §5450
Effect of . . . Lab §5455
Information and Assistance Program (See subhead: Information and Assistance Program)
Administrative director
Advertising, fraudulent or misleading
Review of copy . . . Lab §139.4
Appointment . . . Lab §138.1
Authority . . . Lab §127
Copy and related services fees
Establishing schedule . . . Lab §5307.9
Death benefits for assassinated public officials, provisions for . . . Lab §4726
Death of employee, service of notice of . . . 8 CCR §9918
Definitions pertinent to . . . Lab §110
Deputy, appointment of . . . Lab §138
Health Care Organization (HCO) certification by (See HEALTH CARE ORGANIATIONS (HCOS))
Home health care fee schedule
Services not covered by Medicare or official medical fee schedule . . . Lab §5307.8
Judges (WCJs)
Appointment of . . . Lab §5310

WORKERS' COMPENSATION DIVISION—Cont.
Administrative director—Cont.
Judges (WCJs) —Cont.
Investigations of . . . 8 CCR §9722.2
Request for opinion of Administrative Director . . . 8 CCR §9723
Labor Code, references in Workers' compensation division of . . . Lab §3206
Medical-legal expenses, adoption of fee schedules for . . . Lab §5307.6
Medical-legal expenses, promulgation of rules and regulations regarding . . . Lab §4627
Medical treatment, adoption of fee schedules for . . . Lab §5307.1
Official medical fee schedule . . . 8 CCR §§9789.10 to 9789.111
Official medical fee schedule
Resource-based relative value scale for physician and nonphysician practitioner services, adoption and review of schedule based on model . . . Lab §5307.1
Outpatient fee schedule covered under official medical fee schedule . . . 8 CCR §§9789.30 to 9789.39, Lab §5307.1
Qualified medical evaluators
Powers and duties as to . . . Lab §139.2
Regulations, right to change . . . Lab §5307.3
Reporters employed by . . . Lab §123.3
Return to work programs
Implementation of program . . . Lab §139.48
Study of program . . . Lab §139.49
Rights and obligations
Regulations, right to change . . . Lab §5307.3
Specific provisions, not affected by . . . 8 CCR §9723
Salary . . . Lab §138.1
Treating physician
Educational materials for treating physicians, preparation by director . . . Lab §4062.8
Vocational expert fee schedule
Establishment by administrative director . . . Lab §5307.7
Vocational rehabilitation unit
Establishment by director . . . Lab §139.5
Administrative offices . . . Lab §138.2
Administrative personnel . . . Lab §123
Appeals Board (See APPEALS BOARD (WCAB))
Appointments
Administrative director . . . Lab §138.1
Attorney as counsel . . . Lab §117
Deputies . . . Lab §138
Secretaries . . . Lab §120
Attorney as counsel
Appointment of . . . Lab §117
Duties of . . . Lab §119
Audits . . . Lab §129
Blank forms . . . Lab §125
Child Support Notification Project . . . Lab §138.5
Confidentiality of individually identifiable information . . . 8 CCR §9703, Lab §138.7
Copies
Fees
Document copy and electronic transaction fees . . . 8 CCR §§9980 to 9991

WORKERS' COMPENSATION DIVISION—Cont.
Death cases
Dependency at issue
Service on division of workers' compensation and director of industrial relations . . . 8 CCR §10632
Definitions
Administrative director . . . Lab §§110, 3206
Pertinent terms . . . Lab §110
Deputies
Appointment of . . . Lab §138
Validity of acts by . . . Lab §121
Discrimination, prohibition of . . . Lab §132a
Document copy and electronic transaction fees . . . 8 CCR §§9980 to 9991
Advance payment of fees . . . 8 CCR §9991
Allowable services . . . 8 CCR §9982
Bills for copy services . . . 8 CCR §9981
Case file inspections
Division fees . . . 8 CCR §9990
Certifications
Division fees . . . 8 CCR §9990
Copies
Division fees . . . 8 CCR §9990
Definitions . . . 8 CCR §9980
Electronic transactions
Division fees . . . 8 CCR §9990
Schedule of reasonable maximum fees . . . 8 CCR §9983
Transcripts
Division fees for transcripts . . . 8 CCR §9990
Electronic transactions
Fees
Document copy and electronic transaction fees . . . 8 CCR §§9980 to 9991
Employee information requirements (See INFORMATION SYSTEMS)
Enforcement responsibilities . . . Lab §124
Fees
Document copy and electronic transaction fees . . . 8 CCR §§9980 to 9991
Information and Assistance Program . . . 8 CCR §9929
Limitations on . . . Lab §5811
Forms . . . Lab §124
Blank forms . . . Lab §125
Headquarters of . . . Lab §138.2
Individually identifiable information, confidentiality of . . . 8 CCR §9703, Lab §138.7
Information and Assistance Program
Appointment of officers . . . 8 CCR §9923
Asbestos workers . . . 8 CCR §9928.1
Disputes, mediation of . . . 8 CCR §9928
Duties of officers . . . Lab §5451
Effective dates . . . 8 CCR §9921
Fees and costs . . . 8 CCR §9929
Jurisdiction . . . 8 CCR §9927
Mediation of disputes . . . 8 CCR §9928
Purpose and intent . . . 8 CCR §9922
Qualified medical evaluators (QMEs), referrals to . . . 8 CCR §9926
Recommendations of . . . 8 CCR §9928, Lab §5453
Scope of duties . . . 8 CCR §9924

WORKERS' COMPENSATION DIVISION—Cont.
Information and Assistance Program—Cont.
Statutes of limitation on submissions to . . . Lab §5454
Use of Division facilities by . . . 8 CCR §9925
Information systems
Employee information (See INFORMATION SYSTEMS)
Workers' compensation division (See INFORMATION SYSTEMS)
Judges (WCJs), powers over (See subhead: Administrative director)
Jurisdiction
Generally . . . Lab §133
Information and Assistance Program . . . 8 CCR §9927
Medical fee schedule
Alternative payments to providers, study and report . . . Lab §127.1
Notice
Adjudication of claims, employees filing for . . . 8 CCR §9884
Child support . . . Lab §138.5
Injured workers, right to benefits of . . . Lab §138.3
New employees . . . 8 CCR §9880
Posting . . . 8 CCR §9881
Contents of poster . . . 8 CCR §9881.1
Publication of . . . 8 CCR §9883
Public meetings . . . Lab §138.2
Spanish, in . . . 8 CCR §9883
Official reporters . . . Lab §123.3
Penalties and fines . . . Lab §129.5
Appealing audit penalty assessment . . . 8 CCR §10590
Powers of . . . Lab §133
Provider utilization data
Publication on website for physicians treating 10 or more patients . . . Lab §138.8
Public disability accommodations
Request for accommodations
Division hearings . . . 8 CCR §9708.4
Public meetings, notice of . . . Lab §138.2
Records and recordkeeping
Fees for copies of records and transcripts . . . 8 CCR §9990
Requirements . . . Lab §126
Secretaries, appointment of . . . Lab §120
Supplemental job displacement benefits . . . 8 CCR §§10133.31 to 10133.60
Eligibility . . . Lab §4658.5
2013, injuries occurring in or after . . . Lab §4658.7
Modified or alternative work not accepted, employer not liable for benefits . . . Lab §4658.6
Time, injuries involving loss of . . . Lab §138.4
Transcripts, fees for . . . 8 CCR §9990
Vocational rehabilitation unit . . . Lab §139.5

WORKERS' COMPENSATION DIVISION OF LABOR CODE (See LABOR CODE CONSTRUCTION)

WORKERS' COMPENSATION ETHICS ADVISORY COMMITTEE
Composition and duties of . . . 8 CCR §9722

WORKERS' COMPENSATION ETHICS ADVISORY COMMITTEE—Cont.
Investigations by . . . 8 CCR §9722.1

WORKERS' COMPENSATION FRAUD ACCOUNT
Penalties paid to . . . Lab §3820

WORKERS' COMPENSATION INSURANCE FRAUD REPORTING ACT
Generally . . . Ins §1877
Authorized governmental agency
    Defined . . . Ins §§1877.1, 1877.2
    Insurer's or rating organization's release of requested information to . . . Ins §1877.3
Confidentiality of acquired information . . . Ins §1877.4
Definitions pertinent to . . . Ins §1877.1
Immunity for good faith actions under . . . Ins §1877.5
Licensed rating organization
    Defined . . . Ins §1877.1
    Release of information to governmental agency . . . Ins §1877.3
Privileged status of acquired information . . . Ins §1877.4
Release by insurer or rating organization of requested information . . . Ins §1877.3

WORKERS' COMPENSATION JUDGES (See JUDGES (WCJS))

WORKERS' COMPENSATION MANAGED CARE FUND
Establishment of . . . Lab §4600.7

WORKERS' COMPENSATION REFEREES (See JUDGES (WCJS))

WORKERS' COMPENSATION SYSTEM
Legislative provision for . . . CA Const Art XIV §4

WORKERS' COMPENSATION TRUTH IN ADVERTISING ACT (See TRUTH IN ADVERTISING ACT)

WORK EXPERIENCE AND WORK STUDY PROGRAMS
Students, for (See SCHOOL DISTRICTS)

WORKMEN'S COMPENSATION CHANGED TO WORKERS' COMPENSATION
Government Code . . . Gov §24
Insurance Code . . . Ins §46
Labor Code . . . Lab §3200

WORK PRODUCT DOCTRINE
Discovery
    Attorney work product generally . . . CCP §§2018.010 to 2018.080
        Electronically stored information, responses to inspection demands . . . CCP §2031.285

WRIST INJURIES
Medical treatment
    Utilization schedule
        Wrist disorders . . . 8 CCR §9792.23.4

WRITINGS
Definition of writing . . . Ev §250
Evidence
    Microphotographed files, records, photographs, etc., in custody of criminal justice agency
        Reproductions, admissibility . . . Ev §1550.1
Medical records, authorization for release of . . . CC §§56.10, 56.11

WRIT OF REVIEW
Petitions . . . Lab §5950

WRONGFUL DEATH
High seas, death on . . . 46 USC §§30301 to 30308 (See DEATH ON THE HIGH SEAS)

X

X-RAYS
Medical-legal expense . . . Lab §4626
Transmittal upon request for examination . . . 8 CCR §10660

Y

YEARLY AVERAGE EARNINGS
Defined . . . Lab §4451
Military service (See MILITARY SERVICE)

YOUNG-LA FOLLETTE SELF-INSURERS' SECURITY ACT
Self-Insurers' Security Fund established by . . . Lab §3747

YOUTH AUTHORITY
Employees of department of (See CORRECTIONS AND REHABILITATION DEPARTMENT)
Juvenile Court
    Volunteers (See VOLUNTEERS)
    Wards of (See MINORS)
Juvenile offenders (See MINORS)